35th Edition

ULRICH'S™

INTERNATIONAL PERIODICALS DIRECTORY

1997

Ulrich's International Periodicals Directory
is compiled by
R.R. Bowker
Serials Bibliography Department

Leigh C. Yuster-Freeman, Vice President, Database Production
Andrew Grabois, Managing Director, Bibliographies

Editorial
Judith Salk, Publisher and Editorial Director
Edvika Popilskis, Managing Editor
Ewa Kowalska, Dawn Lombardy, Senior Editors
Henry Wessells, Senior Associate Editor
Egill Halldorsson, Christopher King, Zhaoxia Lian, Associate Editors
Françoise Guineé, Diane Shpiz, Assistant Editors
Mary Crouthers, O'Sheila Delgado, Editorial Assistants

Thomas J. Anerine, Thomas Berry, Terence Carlson, Maria Christopher, Michael Dalelio
Karl Dusza, Katherine Eaton, Dolores Felezzola, Qingye Guo, Eileen Healey, Michael Helme,
Evelyn Irvine, Bronislaw Jan Kowalski, Margareta Leon, Karen Lombardy, Stefan Miarka,
Olga Neville, Eline van de Poel-Becker, and Alina Warda, Contributing Editors

Production
Doreen Gravesande, Production Director
Myriam Nunez, Managing Editor
Frank McDermott, Senior Editor

Editorial Systems Group
Gary Aiello, Director, Bibliographical and Advertising Systems
Nana Rizinashvili, and Robert Michniewicz, Senior Systems Analysts

Computer Operations Group
Nick Wikowski, Director, Network/Computer Operations
Jack Murphy, Supervisor

Reed Technology and Information Services
Donna Brinkmann, Donna Colahan, Account Managers

35th Edition

ULRICH'S™

INTERNATIONAL PERIODICALS DIRECTORY

1997

including
Irregular Serials & Annuals

Volume 5

Indexes
U.S. Newspapers and
Newspaper Index

THE BOWKER INTERNATIONAL SERIALS DATABASE

R.R. BOWKER
New Providence, New Jersey

Published by R.R. Bowker
121 Chanlon Rd., New Providence, NJ 07974

Peter E. Simon, Vice President and Publisher

Ulrich's Hotline (U.S. only): 1-800-346-6049
Editorial (Canada only, call collect): 1-908-665-2875
Serials Fax (overseas users): 908-771-7725
Serials E-mail: ulrich's@reedref.com

International Standard Book Number 0-8352-3806-7
(5 Volume set)
International Standard Book Number 0-8352-3807-5
(Volume 1)
International Standard Book Number 0-8352-3808-3
(Volume 2)
International Standard Book Number 0-8352-3809-1
(Volume 3)
International Standard Book Number 0-8352-3810-5
(Volume 4)
International Standard Book Number 0-8352-3811-3
(Volume 5)
International Standard Serial Number 0000-0175

Library of Congress Catalog Card Number 32-16320

Printed and bound in the United States of America

Contents

BOWKER/ULRICH'S SERIALS LIBRARIANSHIP
    AWARD WINNERS vi

PREFACE vii

USER'S GUIDE ix

INTERNATIONAL STANDARD SERIAL NUMBER (ISSN) xvii

ABBREVIATIONS

    General Abbreviations and Special Symbols xx
    Money Symbols xx
    Country of Publication Codes xxi
    Document Suppliers xxiv
    Micropublishers and Distributors xxv
    Reprint Services xxx
    Wire Services xxxi
    Abstracting and Indexing Services xxxii

SUBJECT GUIDE TO ABSTRACTING AND INDEXING xlv

SUBJECTS xlvi

VOLUME 1

CLASSIFIED LIST OF SERIALS/SUBJECTS A to D 1

VOLUME 2

CLASSIFIED LIST OF SERIALS/SUBJECTS E to L 2203

VOLUME 3

CLASSIFIED LIST OF SERIALS/SUBJECTS M to Z 4335

VOLUME 4

CROSS-INDEX TO SUBJECTS 7023

CESSATIONS 7055

ISSN INDEX 7283

TITLE INDEX 8713

TITLE CHANGE INDEX 9325

VOLUME 5

REFEREED 9347

SERIALS AVAILABLE ON CD-ROM 9571

PRODUCER LISTING/SERIALS ON CD-ROM 9621

SERIALS AVAILABLE ONLINE 9625

VENDOR LISTING/SERIALS ONLINE 9775

INDEX TO PUBLICATIONS OF INTERNATIONAL ORGANIZATIONS 9811

    International Organizations 9811
    International Congress Proceedings 9323
    European Communities 9327
    United Nations 9329

CONTROLLED CIRCULATION SERIALS 9337

U.S. NEWSPAPERS

USER'S GUIDE li

ABBREVIATIONS liv

DAILY NEWSPAPERS — US 9955

WEEKLY NEWSPAPERS — US 10057

TITLE INDEX 10311

DAILY NEWSPAPER INDEX 10387

WEEKLY NEWSPAPER INDEX 10405

GEOGRAPHIC INDEX 10463

CESSATIONS 10531

Bowker/Ulrich's Serials Librarianship Award

Presented by the Serials Section
Association for Library Collections and Technical Services (ALCTS)
Division of the American Library Association (ALA)

Sponsored by R.R. Bowker

This annual award is given in recognition of distinguished and ongoing contributions to serials librarianship. Qualified individuals demonstrate leadership in serials-related activities through their participation in professional associations, groups, and/or library education programs; make significant contributions to serials literature; and, in general, strive to enhance our comprehension of the serials world.

AWARD RECIPIENTS

1985	Marcia Tuttle
1986	Ruth C. Carter
1987	James P. Danky
1988	Marjorie E. Bloss
1989	John E. Merriman
1990	Jean S. Cook
1991	Deana L. Astle/Charles A. Hamaker
1992	Linda K. Bartley
1993	Ann L. Okerson
1994	Tina Feick
1995	Peter Gellatly
1996	Jean L. Hirons

Preface

Now in its 35th edition, **Ulrich's International Periodicals Directory** upholds its reputation for excellence in the provision of serials information. In the 64 years since it was first published, **Ulrich's** has established itself as the premier serials reference source in the world, providing serials users with essential bibliographic and access information.

Beginning with the last edition, the publication date of **Ulrich's** moved from August to November. Publication in November has allowed us to provide thousands of updated prices for 1997. Most publishers establish prices for the upcoming year between May and September. Prices set and received by us later than mid-September did not get updated for this print edition. However, data are entered as received, so price changes and all other information received after mid-September will appear in subsequent quarterly CD-ROM versions of **Ulrich's PLUS**™ and monthly online versions (available through Knight-Ridder Information, Inc./DIALOG file number 480; OVID Technologies/file name: ULRI; and LEXIS®-NEXIS®/library: BUSREF, file name: ULRICHS).

As libraries, institutions, and researchers evaluate new opportunities and technologies that enable them to access individual articles on demand rather than to acquire serials in their entirety, our coverage of document delivery services has expanded to include CISTI (Canada Institute for Scientific and Technical Information, National Research Council of Canada) and Library KNAW (Library of the Royal Netherlands Academy of Arts and Sciences). We now identify 14 different document delivery services from which the full text of articles from serials listed in **Ulrich's** may be obtained (see pg. xxiv). For a brief explanation of and contact information for these useful services, please refer to the section entitled "Document Suppliers" in the User's Guide of **Ulrich's**, pg.xiv of the prefatory material of Volumes 1-4. (The Faxon Company, Inc., while no longer listed herein as a document delivery supplier, still provides its Faxon Finder® table of contents and current citation alerting services. For article delivery, Faxon has formed alliances with some of the document suppliers listed in **Ulrich's** to provide document delivery for Faxon Finder subscribers.)

Further access to serials in **Ulrich's** is facilitated through the inclusion of nearly 250,000 indicators denoting coverage by some 800 abstracting and indexing services; 12,000 notations of reprint availability; 18,000 e-mail addresses; and 10,000 URLs (Uniform Resource Locators on the World Wide Web). The number of URLs includes publisher sites as well as sites for individual journals.

Serials, whether in print or in an electronic medium, are as important as ever as primary sources of current information and topical news in all fields of endeavor. Though the printed serial is by no means on the wane, the proliferation of serials in electronic formats, whether online or on CD-ROM continues unabated, especially with dramatically increased use of the Internet as a publishing medium. This edition of **Ulrich's** includes 6,661 serials available exclusively online or in addition to hard copy, and 2,240 serials available on CD-ROM. These serials are indicated by a notation and a bullet (●) in the main entry.

Ulrich's now includes for the first time 12,000 Rights & Permissions contact names, along with telephone contact information, if provided. Users anticipating forthcoming serial launches will find 121 titles announced for publication in 1997.

The 35th edition of **Ulrich's** contains information on over 165,000 serials published throughout the world, arranged under 969 subject headings. More than 112,000 entries have been updated to reflect the most current information available and nearly 6,000 serials have been added this year, some of which have since ceased or suspended publication. Included in this edition is cessation or suspension information which has been recorded in our database during the past three years for 9,983 titles. The ceased or suspended titles are preceded by a dagger (†) in the TITLE INDEX for instant identification. Users can identify newer serials, over 3,700 of which are known to have begun publication since January 1, 1994, by looking for an upside-down solid triangle (▼) in both the CLASSIFIED LIST OF SERIALS and the TITLE INDEX. This symbol is also used to highlight forthcoming publications. In addition, more than 12,600 refereed serials notations; nearly 66,000 brief descriptions; almost 41,500 LC Classification Numbers; over 19,670 CODEN; and 4,584 vendor file names or numbers for 6,661 serials available in an online format appear in this edition.

Included in **Ulrich's** are serials which are currently available, issued more frequently than once a year and usually published at regular intervals, as well as publications issued annually or less frequently than once a year, or irregularly. Due to the vast number of serials, we have established certain criteria for inclusion, while maintaining our aim of maximum title coverage that will satisfy the widest range of use. We include all publications that meet the definition of a serial except administrative publications of governmental agencies below state level that can be easily found elsewhere, membership directories, comic books, and puzzle and game books.

This edition of **Ulrich's** is arranged within five volumes, as follows: the first three volumes comprise the CLASSIFIED LIST OF SERIALS; the fourth volume contains the CROSS-INDEX TO SUBJECTS, CESSATIONS INDEX, ISSN INDEX, TITLE INDEX, and TITLE CHANGE INDEX. The fifth volume comprises the remaining indexes: REFEREED SERIALS, SERIALS AVAILABLE ON CD-ROM, PRODUCER LISTING/SERIALS ON CD-ROM, SERIALS AVAILABLE ONLINE, VENDOR LISTING/ SERIALS ONLINE, INDEX TO INTERNATIONAL ORGANIZATIONS, and CONTROLLED CIR-CULATION SERIALS, as well as the NEWSPAPERS section listing general-interest daily and weekly newspapers published in the United States.

International data inquiries are mailed annually to nearly 80,000 publishers to secure accurate and up-to-date information on current titles, new titles, title changes, and cessations. Updating of the database occurs daily using information received from publishers throughout the year and from serials research conducted in our editorial department. All post office returns are researched, and entries from publishers whose addresses cannot be verified are suspended from the file. Information about title changes, cessations, and new titles not received by the deadline for this edition will appear in **Ulrich's Update**, in the **Ulrich's Online** file as noted above, on **Ulrich's PLUS**™ CD-ROM, and on **Ulrich's Microfiche**.

Your purchase and use of **Ulrich's** is complemented by some additional services. **Ulrich's Update**, provided free of charge, twice a year in March and July, is a supplemental service to the annual directory. The **Ulrich's Hotline** is a toll-free number that subscribers can call to get help in solving particular serials research problems and questions. Canadian users are asked to call a special number collect, and our overseas users are asked to use a designated fax number. (Please see page iv for our mailing address, telephone/fax numbers, and e-mail address.) Finally, **The Cornerstone**, a quarterly newsletter which includes not only valuable information about serials and **Ulrich's** but also contains news about other Bowker titles and pertinent topics, is sent free of charge to subscribers of **Ulrich's**.

As we continue to research, plan, and implement enhancements to the **Ulrich's** database and our database maintenance system, we consider feedback from our users to be essential. Please contact us to let us know your thoughts. We want **Ulrich's** and its family of products to provide all necessary reference information quickly and effectively. Comments and suggestions are encouraged in order to help keep our directory of the highest quality. There is a wide variety of communication modes for you to select. You may write to us, send us a fax, call us on the telephone, or send us an e-mail. Also, be sure to visit the Reed Reference Publishing Home Page on the World Wide Web. Look for a Home Page for **Ulrich's** in the future. Please refer to page iv for all contact information.

My sincere gratitude is extended to the entire staff of **Ulrich's** for their unflagging dedication and diligent work in updating and maintaining the serials database in preparation of the 35th edition of **Ulrich's**. Appreciation is also extended to all vendors and service suppliers for working with us to produce this directory. Finally, I would like to thank the various information specialists, serialists, national libraries, and serials publishers throughout the world who have aided us in updating **Ulrich's**. We consider their participation and interest in the dissemination of accurate and comprehensive serials information to be of tremendous value to **Ulrich's** and its users.

Judith Salk
Publisher and Editorial Director

This directory offers two primary access methods for locating periodicals: by subject in the CLASSIFIED LIST OF SERIALS (Volumes 1-3), and alphabetically in the TITLE INDEX (Volume 4). Ceased serials are listed in a separate CESSATIONS section (Volume 4) and are also accessible by means of the TITLE INDEX. Other indexes provide listings of selected periodicals in specific categories. These indexes, in Volume 5 unless otherwise noted, are REFEREED SERIALS, CONTROLLED CIRCULATION SERIALS, SERIALS AVAILABLE ON CD-ROM, PRODUCER LISTING/SERIALS ON CD-ROM, SERIALS AVAILABLE ONLINE, VENDOR LISTING/SERIALS ONLINE, PUBLICATIONS OF INTERNATIONAL ORGANIZATIONS, ISSN INDEX (Volume 4), and TITLE CHANGE INDEX (Volume 4). See the User's Guide in Volume 5 for a content description and use instructions for the U.S. NEWSPAPERS section.

In addition, separate subheadings for "Abstracting, Bibliographies and Statistics" under major subject headings provide convenient access to these types of publications. Page references for these subheadings are given in the "Subject Guide to Abstracting and Indexing" on p. xlv. This listing provides an overview of subjects for which abstracting and indexing publications have been identified.

The "User's Guide" is separated into three divisions for ease of use: (I) Section Descriptions (II) Full Entry Content Description, and (III) Cataloging Rules for Main Entry Title.

Section Descriptions

CLASSIFIED LIST OF SERIALS

This is the main section of the book, containing bibliographic information for currently published serials classified by subject. Entries are arranged alphabetically by title within each subject heading. Subject cross-references in the text direct the user to the location of subheadings.

Volume 1 contains subjects A-D, from "Abstracting and Indexing" through "Drug Abuse and Alcoholism." Volume 2 contains subjects E-L, "Earth Sciences" through "Lumber and Wood." Volume 3 contains subjects M-Z, from "Machine Theory" through "Zoology."

A complete listing of the "Subjects" used in the CLASSIFIED LIST OF SERIALS appears on p. xlvi. To aid international users, this list is translated into four languages. For additional guidance on the subject classification scheme, the user should also consult the CROSS-INDEX TO SUBJECTS on p. 7023, which contains additional key word references.

Each serial is listed with full bibliographic information only once. If a serial covers several subjects, title cross-references appear under the related headings, directing the user to the heading where the full entry is listed.

New serials beginning publication in the past three years, as well as titles announced for publication in the coming year are highlighted by a ▼ in front of the title.

The "Cataloging Rules for Main Entry Title" section of this "User's Guide" explains the title cataloging rules followed in compiling **Ulrich's**.

CROSS-INDEX TO SUBJECTS

This index lists alphabetically all main subject headings in the **Ulrich's** Subject Heading File, as well as keyword references that direct users to main or subheadings where publications on those topics are likely to be found. The number following each subject term directs users to the page on which the subject begins within the CLASSIFIED LIST OF SERIALS.

A keyword may refer the user to more than one subject category. In this case, the subject references are listed in alphabetical order and are not necessarily listed in hierarchical order.

Main subject headings appear uppercased, e.g. AGRICULTURE. Subheadings contain the main subject term in uppercase and the specific subheading term in mixed case, e.g. AGRICULTURE—Agricultural Economics. The keywords, except for acronyms, are displayed entirely in mixed case.

CESSATIONS

In this section, entries for serials for which cessation was noted in the past three years are listed alphabetically by title. The cessation entry includes: title, Dewey Decimal

Classification number, former frequency of publication, publisher name and address, country-of-publication code, and, if available, other information such as ISSN, CODEN, LC number, subtitle, corporate author, year of first issue and year ceased. Titles which were originally planned as continuing series but which have closed are included in the CESSATIONS section although back issues may still be available.

If a title has "ceased" because a new title is being used, there will not be an entry in the CESSATIONS section. Instead, the entry is maintained in the CLASSIFIED LIST OF SERIALS under the new title, with a **"Formerly"** or **"Former titles"** indication.

ISSN INDEX

The ISSN INDEX lists serials in order by ISSN number. It includes all serials contained in the Bowker International Serials Database, whether current, ceased, or inactive, to which an ISSN has been assigned in our file. A dagger symbol (†) indicates that the title is ceased. If an ISSN appears twice, it usually indicates that the serial has split into two or more parts. Titles that have changed and for which new ISSNs have been assigned will show cross-references from one ISSN to the new ISSN. If no new ISSN has been assigned, the cross-reference is from ISSN to new title. Entries for inactive titles do not appear in the book.

Italicized type indicates the page number where a complete entry can be found for active titles. Titles for which cessation was noted in the last three years have a page reference to the listing in the CESSATIONS INDEX. If no page reference appears for a ceased title, it means that the cessation was noted more than three years ago and is not listed in this edition. ISSNs of inactive titles likewise do not have page references and are not listed in this book.

A full description of the ISSN and its use is provided on p. xviii.

TITLE INDEX

The TITLE INDEX is the second major access point for serials. To locate a serial by its title, the user should be familiar with title cataloging rules as described in the "Cataloging Rules for Main Entry Titles" paragraphs of this "User's Guide."

The TITLE INDEX lists all current and ceased serials included in this directory. **Boldface** type indicates the page number where the complete entry will be found; page numbers in roman type refer to related subject categories.

For serials with identical titles published within a country, the city of publication is added in parentheses, and sometimes the year of first publication is given to further distinguish the titles.

If a serial title consists of or contains an acronym, a cross-reference is provided from the full name to the acronym form of the title.

Cross-references are provided from former titles and variant titles, and from the alternate language titles of multi-language publications. Recent title changes are noted, with a reference to the current title. The TITLE INDEX also lists the country code for all serials, along with the ISSN, if known.

The ▼ used in the "Classified List of Serials" to indicate new serials also appears in this index, preceding the title. A (†) appears preceding the title if the publication has ceased.

TITLE CHANGE INDEX

The TITLE CHANGE INDEX lists former titles alphabetically with references to new titles. Page numbers indicate where bibliographic entries are listed in the CLASSIFIED LIST OF SERIALS. This index cumulates all title changes recorded in the **Ulrich's** database since the publication of the previous, or 34th, edition.

REFEREED SERIALS

This section is an alphabetical listing by title of all serials known to be refereed, or peer reviewed. It includes the publisher name, address, and telephone number, if known. The italicized number at the end of each entry is the page number where the full entry appears in the CLASSIFIED LIST OF SERIALS.

Omission of a title from this index does not mean that the journal is not peer-reviewed; nor does **Ulrich's** make any attempt to rate or judge the relative value of an individual journal's peer review process.

SERIALS AVAILABLE ON CD-ROM

This section is an alphabetical listing of all serials known to be available on CD-ROM, either in addition to hardcopy, or on CD-ROM only. It includes the publisher name, address, telephone and fax numbers, if known. It also includes the name of CD-ROM producers, when known. The italicized number at the end of each entry is the page number where the full entry appears in the CLASSIFIED LIST OF SERIALS.

PRODUCER LISTING/SERIALS ON CD-ROM

This section is an alphabetical listing of identified producers of serials on CD-ROM. Entries include the producer address, telephone and fax numbers, and an alphabetical listing of all serial titles known to be available. If known, the serial on CD-ROM product name is listed in parentheses after the serial title. All serials listed in this index also have full bibliographic entries in the CLASSIFIED LIST OF SERIALS. Consult the TITLE INDEX or the

SERIALS AVAILABLE ON CD-ROM listing for page numbers.

SERIALS AVAILABLE ONLINE

This section is an alphabetical listing of all serials known to be available online, either in addition to hardcopy, or online only. Entries include publisher name, address, telephone and fax numbers, plus names of online vendors and file names or numbers if known. Certain electronic journals may not have a physical mailing address listed. The number in parentheses at the end of each entry is the page number where the full entry appears in the CLASSIFIED LIST OF SERIALS.

VENDOR LISTING/SERIALS ONLINE

This section is an alphabetical listing of identified vendors of online periodicals. Entries include addresses, telephone and fax numbers for the vendor, and an alphabetical listing of all titles known to be available with file names or numbers, if known. All serials listed in this index also have full bibliographic entries in the CLASSIFIED LIST OF SERIALS. Consult the TITLE INDEX or the SERIALS AVAILABLE ONLINE listing for page numbers.

INDEX TO PUBLICATIONS OF INTERNATIONAL ORGANIZATIONS

Complexity of corporate author structure, as well as title page variations in multilingual texts, compound the problems in cataloging publications of international organizations. This special index is provided so that the user may have one reference point for these titles. This index consists of four sections:

International Organizations
International Congress Proceedings
European Communities
United Nations

The index contains all current titles listed in the Bowker International Serials Database. The user must consult the CLASSIFIED LIST OF SERIALS for the full bibliographic information pertaining to these titles. Page references are provided.

CONTROLLED CIRCULATION SERIALS

This section is an alphabetical listing of all serials identified as having controlled circulations. It includes the publisher name and address, telephone and fax numbers, and circulation figure, if known. The italicized number at the end of each entry is a reference to the page on which the full entry appears in the CLASSIFIED LIST OF SERIALS.

Full Entry Content Description

Basic Information
The following elements are mandatory for listing and appear in all entries: main entry title, frequency of publication, publisher address, country code, and Dewey Decimal Classification number.

Certain electronic journals may not have a physical mailing address; the URL and/or E-mail address provide a means of contacting the publication.

Dewey Decimal Classification Number
The Dewey Decimal number is printed at the top left of each entry. More than one Dewey number may have been assigned if a serial covers several subjects.

LC Classification Number
The Library of Congress classification number, if known, appears directly below the Dewey Decimal number. Shelf numbers are not included.

Country Code
The Country Code is printed at the top right of each entry following the Dewey Decimal number. A complete list of country codes used will be found on p. xxii.

ISSN
The ISSN for the main entry title is printed immediately following the country code. Not all publications have been assigned an ISSN, and lack of a number does not render a publication ineligible for listing.

CODEN
The CODEN designation, if known, s printed directly below the country code and ISSN. The CODEN is an alphanumeric code, applied uniquely to a specific publication. Devised by the American Society for Testing and Materials, it is used primarily for scientific and technical titles. New CODEN are assigned by Chemical Abstracts Service.

Title Information
The main title is printed in **boldface** and upper case as the first item in the entry. Titles are catalogued according to rules described below in the "Cataloging Rules for Main Entry Title" section. For multi-language publications, the parallel language title is also printed in upper case, immediately following the main entry title, and is separated from it by a slash.

A ▼ printed before the title indicates that the title began publishing within the past three years. This symbol also appears before titles announced for publication in the coming year.

An asterisk (*) printed after the title indicates that the information in the entry was not verified by the publisher for this edition.

The subtitle is printed in lower case after the title.

Variant titles or translated edition titles are given within the entry and are labeled as such.

Former titles are given at the end of the entry, along with publication dates if known. If a former title also had an ISSN, the ISSN is listed in parentheses after the former title. Many entries contain extensive former title information, providing a history of changes which may be useful for bibliographic record-keeping.

The Key Title, which is assigned at the time of ISSN assignment by the responsible center of the International Serials Data System, is given only if it is different from the main entry title.

Year First Published

The year first published is given if provided by the publisher. If information is lacking, a volume number and specific year may be provided to indicate the approximate age of the publication.

Frequency

The frequency of publication is given in abbreviated form, such as "a." for annual, "irreg." for irregular, "m." for monthly, "3/yr." for three times per year. All abbreviations used are listed in the "General Abbreviations" on p. xx.

Price

Unless otherwise indicated, the price given is the annual price for an individual subscription in the currency of the

---

SAMPLE ENTRY

(1) 930.198 490.996   **(2)** US   **(3)** ISSN 1055-7644
(4) DZ991   **(5)** CODEN: JAAPL9
(6) JOURNAL OF ANTARCTIC ARCHAEOLOGY AND PROTOLINGUISTICS; communications and research.   **(8)** (Supplement avail.)   **(9)** (Text in English, French, Polynesian languages)   **(10)** 1927.   **(11)** 2/yr.   **(12)** $39 to individuals; institutions $99 (includes supplement) (effective 1996); newsstand price: $20   **(13)** (Societe d'Archaeologie et de Linguistique Pacifiques—Society of Pacific Archaeology and Linguistics)   **(14)** W.A. Translations (Subsidiary of: Temporary Culture),   **(15)** Box 43072, Upper Montclair, NJ 07043-7072.   **(16)** TEL 908-665-2869.   **(17)** FAX 508-555-0010.   **(18)** TELEX 123458.   **(19)** E-mail: antarchaeol@miskaton.edu; URL: http://www.miskaton.edu/.   **(20)** (Subscr. to: Department of Archaeology and Proto-Linguistics, 7 Old College Walk, Arkham, MA 01901-1011. TEL 508-555-0110. FAX 508-555-4112;   **(21)** Dist. in Europe by: Editions d'Erlette, Ch. de Kerangat, 56120 Plumelec, France. TEL 33-76-63-94. FAX 33-76-205).   **(22)** (Co-sponsor: Miskatonic University, Department of Archaeology and Proto-Linguistics)   **(23)** Eds. A.H. Whateley, J.M. Snyrnat;   **(24)** Pub. M.J. Smith.   **(25)** R&P contact: J.M. Snyrnat. TEL 508-555-0011.   **(26)** adv.: B&W page $400; trim 8 1/8 x 10;   **(27)** adv. contact: Arthur Dunwich;   **(28)** bk.rev.; abstr.; bibl.; illus.; index;   **(29)** circ. 500 (paid); 500 (controlled).   **(30)** (also avail. in microform from SWZ, UMI; also avail. on diskette; back issues avail.; reprint service avail. from SWZ, UMI).
(31) Indexed: Abstr. Anthropol., Br.Archaeol.Abstr.   **(32)** (1991–), Onoma (1986–), Ref.Zh.
(33) Document type: academic/scholarly publication.
(34) ● Also available online.   **(35)** Vendor(s): UTOPIA (Miskatonic).
(36) Also available on CD-ROM.   **(37)** Producer(s): TEMPCULT (Miskatonic).
(38) —BLDSC (9999.000000); CIS   **(39) CCC.**
(40) Supersedes (in 1986): Miskatonic Annals of Antarctic Archaeology and Extraterrestrial Linguistics
(41) (ISSN 0055-1298).
(42) Description: Publishes archaeological field research on prehistoric civilizations in the Pacific Islands and Antarctica, with relevant contributions discussing worldwide linguistic evidence of contacts among civilizations.
(43) *Refereed Serial*

KEY

(1) Dewey Decimal Classification
(2) Country Code
(3) ISSN
(4) LC Classification
(5) CODEN
(6) Main Entry Title
(7) Subtitle
(8) Bibliographic Note
(9) Language
(10) First Published
(11) Frequency
(12) Price
(13) Corporate Author
(14) Publishing Company
(15) Address
(16) Telephone
(17) Fax
(18) Telex
(19) E-mail; URL
(20) Subscription Address, Tel & Fax
(21) Distributor Address, Tel & Fax
(22) Co-sponsor
(23) Editor
(24) Publisher
(25) Rights & Permissions Contact, Telephone
(26) Advertising Rate
(27) Advertising Contact
(28) Special Features
(29) Circulation
(30) Format
(31) Indexed
(32) Years of Coverage
(33) Document Type
(34) Online Availability
(35) Online Vendor/File Name
(36) CD-ROM Availability
(37) CD-ROM Producer(s)
(38) Document Suppliers
(39) Copyright Clearance Center Registration Notation
(40) Title Changes
(41) Former ISSN
(42) Brief Description
(43) Refereed

country of origin. The price in U.S. dollars may also be given in parentheses if it is provided by the publisher. No attempt is made to convert foreign currency to U.S. dollars. Separate postage information is not given, since postal rates vary widely.

Publishing Company Information

Many serials are editorially controlled by a sponsoring organization or corporate author and published by a commercial publisher. In these instances, the commercial publishing company's name and address are given, and the name of the corporate author is given in parentheses immediately preceding. In other instances, either a sponsoring organization or a commercial publishing company has sole responsibility, and only one name is given. We avoid listing printers as publishing companies, preferring the name and address of someone with editorial responsibility. For the same reason, we avoid listing distributors as publishing companies.

If no publishing company name is given, it is assumed that the publishing company name is the same as the title.

Telephone, Fax, Telex Numbers, E-mail, and Web Site Addresses

Telephone, fax, telex numbers and e-mail as well as web site addresses (URLs) are given when provided by the publisher. U.S. and Canadian numbers are given in standard North American format. Toll-free numbers within U.S. and Canada are also included, when available. Numbers in other countries are provided in the same format as supplied by the publisher, resulting in some inconsistencies (e.g. sometimes with a country and/or city code, sometimes without). Users are advised to consult an international operator before placing calls.

Subscription or Distribution Address

A second address is given only if the address for ordering subscriptions is different from the publishing company's address. Distributors are listed only if we have been informed that a particular organization is the exclusive distributor. Additional subscription and/or distribution offices of international publishers are listed, if known. Telephone and fax numbers for subscription and/or distribution offices appear if provided by the publisher.

Editor

Only one or two names are given when known, preceded by the notation "Ed." or "Eds." Advanced degrees and titles are omitted, except for medical, military and religious titles; absence of a title does not mean that the editor has none. The abbreviation "Ed.Bd." indicates editorship by three or more persons.

Publisher

Only one or two names are given when known, preceded by the notation "Pub." or "Pubs." Advanced degrees and titles are omitted, except for medical, military and religious titles; absence of a title does not mean that the publisher has none.

If the publisher is also the editor, and no publishing company name is available, the person's name is given with the notation "Ed. & Pub."

Rights and Permissions Contact

A name is given when supplied, preceded by the notation "R&P contact". The telephone number information follows, when known and different from the main number.

Advertising Rates and Contact

When provided by the publisher, the name of the advertising contact, as well as full-page advertising rates and trim size are indicated. Most dimensions are listed in millimeters, except for U.S. publications, the dimensions of which are usually in inches.

Special Features

A listing of special features may include such items as book or other types of reviews, advertising (usually meaning commercial, not classified advertising), charts, illustrations, bibliography section, article abstracts, and an annual index to the periodical's contents.

Reprint Services

If a serial is known to be available from a reprint service, a code referring to the service appears in the entry. More than one code may be listed. For a list of reprint services and a translation of the codes, please refer to p. xxx.

Circulation

All circulation figures used are approximate. Circulation is given only if provided by the publisher. The notation "controlled" indicates that the publication is available only to the qualified persons, usually members of a particular trade or profession.

Format

Formats other than standard magazine format are noted in parentheses. Other formats may be looseleaf, duplicated (mimeographed), tabloid. If a publication is available in microform, a notation is made which includes a three-letter code for the vendor, if known. A list of names, addresses, telephone and fax numbers of micropublishers begins on p. xxvi.

Abstracting and Indexing

The notation **"Indexed:"** precedes a list of abbreviations for all abstracting and indexing services known to cover the serial on a regular basis. Years of coverage immediately follow each abstracting and indexing service code, if known. The complete names of the abstracting and indexing services are listed with their abbreviations on p. xxxii. All currently published abstracting and indexing services are also listed as entries in the CLASSIFIED LIST OF SERIALS.

Document Type

Notations are included to indicate type of publication, e.g. trade publication, newsletter, or abstracting/indexing. The words "**Document type:**" appear in boldface, followed by the document type description, in entries where this information is known. More than one document type may be listed for a single publication, if applicable.

Online Availability and CD-ROM Availability

If a serial is known to be available in a full-text online format and/or on CD-ROM, a bullet symbol (●) precedes the information. Online and CD-ROM availability are noted whether they exist in addition to hardcopy or in one or both formats exclusively. Online vendors and CD-ROM producers are also listed, if known.

For a listing of serials available online, consult the SERIALS AVAILABLE ONLINE index on p. 9625. Complete names and addresses of vendors, with a listing of serials known to be available through them, are in a separate index, VENDOR LISTING/SERIALS ONLINE on p. 9775.

For a listing of serials available on CD-ROM, consult the SERIALS AVAILABLE ON CD-ROM index on p. 9571. Complete names and addresses of producers, with a list of CD-ROMs known to be available through them, are in a separate index, PRODUCER LISTING/SERIALS ON CD-ROM on p. 9621.

Document Suppliers

The **Ulrich's** database and the individual databases of the following document suppliers were matched on the presence of ISSNs. When a match was successful, the appropriate document supplier code was noted. Not all serials titles in general, or in these individual databases, have ISSNs. Therefore, the absence of one or any document supplier code in an **Ulrich's** listing does not necessarily mean the title is unavailable from one or any of these suppliers.

ADONIS™

The notation, ADONIS, appearing in a serial entry indicates the availability of that serial for document delivery through ADONIS's service, by permission from the copyright owner. Such permission is subject to change without notice.

For further information, contact: ADONIS B.V., Spuistraat 112D, 1012VA Amsterdam, The Netherlands; tel: 31-20-6262629, fax: 31-20-6261437; ADONIS USA, 238 Main St., Cambridge, MA 02142, USA; tel: 800-944-6415; fax: 617-876-7022; URL: http://adonis.blacksci.co.uk/.

British Library Document Supply Centre

The notation, BLDSC, appearing in a serial entry indicates the availability of that serial for document delivery from the British Library Document Supply Centre, by permission from the copyright owner. The BLDSC shelfmark number, a unique identifier of each serial, is preceded by an em-dash (—) which is followed by the notation "BLDSC (0000.000000)." The format of the shelfmark is four digits, a decimal point, then six digits.

For further information about BLDSC's services, contact: Customer Services, BLDSC, Boston Spa, Wetherby, LS23 7BQ, UK; tel: 44-1937-546060; fax: 44-1937-546333; e-mail: dsc-customer-services@bl.uk.

Chemical Abstracts Service

The notation, CASDDS, appearing in a serial entry indicates the availability of that serial for document delivery through Chemical Abstracts Service Document Detective Service.

For further information, contact CAS Client Services, Document Detective Service, 2540 Olentangy River Rd., P.O. Box 3012, Columbus, OH 43210-0012, USA; tel: 800-631-1884, 614-447-3870; fax: 614-447-3648; e-mail: dds@cas.org; URL: http://www.cas.org/Support/dds.html.

CISTI

The notation, CISTI, appearing in a serial entry indicates the availability of that serial for document delivery from the Canada Institute for Scientific and Technical Information, by permission from the copyright owner. Such permission is subject to change without notice.

For further information, contact: Client Assistant, Document Delivery, CISTI, National Research Council Canada, Ottawa K1A 0S2, Canada; tel: 800-668-1222 (Canada & US) or 613-993-9251; fax: 613-993-7619; e-mail: cisti.docdel@nrc.ca.

Congressional Information Service, Inc.

The notation, CIS, appearing in a serial entry indicates the availability of that serial for document delivery through CIS Documents on Demand Service, by permission from the copyright owner. Such permission is subject to change without notice.

For further information, contact Congressional Information Service, Inc., 4520 East-West Hwy., Ste. 800, Bethesda, MD 20814-3389, USA; tel: 301-654-1550, 800-227-2477; fax: 301-654-4033; e-mail: EAINET@US.NET; URL: http://www.cispubs.com.

EMDOCS

The notation, EMDOCS, appearing in a serial entry indicates the availability of that serial for document delivery through EMDOCS: The EMBASE Document Delivery Service, by permission from the copyright owner. Such permission is subject to change without notice.

For further information, contact EMDOCS, 469 Union Avenue, Westbury, NY 11590, USA; tel: 800-282-2720 or 516-997-0796; fax: 516-997-0890; e-mail: dds@work4u.artx.com.

Engineering Information Inc.

The notation, Ei, appearing in a serial entry indicates the availability of that serial for document delivery through EiDDS, the Ei Document Delivery Service, by permission from the copyright owner. Such permission is subject to change without notice.

For further information, contact EiDDS, One Castle Point Terrace, Hoboken, NJ 07030-5996, USA; tel: 800-221-1044 (USA & Canada), 201-216-8500; fax: 201-216-8532; e-mail: dds@ei.org; URL: http://www.ei.org.

The Genuine Article

The notation, Genuine Article, appearing in a serial entry indicates the availability of that serial for document delivery through The Institute for Scientific Information's Genuine Article, by permission from the copyright owner. Such permission is subject to change without notice.

For further information, contact The Genuine Article, 3501 Market Street, Philadelphia, PA 19104, USA; tel: 215-386-4399; fax: 215-386-4343; e-mail: tga@isinet.com.

Haworth Document Delivery Service

The notation, Haworth, appearing in a serial entry indicates the availability of that serial for document delivery through The Haworth Press's Document Delivery Service. This service is available for all Haworth journals. As the copyright holder, there will be no permission fee, but other fees are applicable.

For further information, contact Haworth Document Delivery Service, 10 Alice Street, Binghamton, NY 13904-1580, USA; tel: 800-HAWORTH; fax: 800-895-0582; e-mail: getinfo@haworth.com.

Library KNAW

The notation, KNAW, appearing in a serial entry indicates the availability of that serial for document delivery through the Library KNAW (Library of the Royal Netherlands Academy of Arts and Sciences). Document delivery can take place according to three main delivery procedures: regular (4 day service), urgent mail and urgent fax (both 24-hour services). These services are available for all Library KNAW journals. Fees are applicable.

For further information, contact Library KNAW, Information and Loans Department, P.O. Box 41950, 1009 DD Amsterdam, The Netherlands; tel: 31-20-6685511; fax: 31-20-6685079; e-mail: info@library.knaw.nl; URL: http://www.library.knaw.nl.

Petroleum Abstracts - Document Delivery Service (PADDS)

The notation, PADDS, appearing in a serial entry indicates the availability of that serial for document delivery through PADDS document delivery service, by permission from the copyright owner. Such permission is subject to change without notice.

For further information, contact Petroleum Abstracts - Document Delivery Service, University of Tulsa, McFarlin Library, 2933 E. 6th Street, Tulsa, OK 74104-3123, USA; tel: 800-247-8678; fax: 918-631-3823; e-mail: PADDS@TUred.pa.utulsa.edu.

SWETS

The notation, SWETS, appearing in a serial entry indicates the availability of that serial's table of contents in SwetScan, and document delivery through Swets, by permission from the copyright owner. Such permission is subject to change without notice.

For further information, contact Swets & Zeitlinger BV, Heereweg 347B, P.O. Box 830 2160 SZ Lisse, The Netherlands; tel: 31-252-435111; fax: 31-252-415888; telex: 41325; e-mail: infoho@swets.nl; URL: http://www.swets.nl.

UMI

The notation, UMI, appearing in a serial entry indicates the availability of that serial for document delivery through UMI InfoStore service, by permission from the copyright owner. Such permission is subject to change without notice.

For further information, contact UMI InfoStore, 500 Sansome Street, Ste. 400, San Francisco, CA 94111-3219, USA; tel: 800-248-0360 (US & Canada), 415-433-5500; fax: 415-433-0100; e-mail: orders@infostore.com.

The UnCover Company

The notation, UnCover, appearing in a serial entry indicates that the material is indexed in the UnCover database. Copies of articles are available through Uncover's document delivery service if the copyright owner has granted permission. Such permission is subject to change without notice.

For further information, contact the UnCover Co., 3801 E. Florida Ave., Ste. 200, Denver, CO 80210, USA; tel: 300-787-7979 (outside US & Canada: 303-758-3030); fax: 303-758-5946; e-mail: uncover@carl.org; URL: http://www.carl.org/uncover.

Copyright Clearance Center, Inc.

The Copyright Clearance Center, Inc. (CCC) is a not-for-profit collective licensing organization. The CCC grants permissions to institutions and individuals to photocopy works of its registered publishers upon payment of publisher set royalties. The CCC does not supply copies of registered works directly to anyone.

The boldfaced **CCC** notation appears in the entries of titles for which the CCC has been authorized by the publisher to grant photocopy permissions through its Transactional Reporting Service (TRS). Additional titles may be available for certain publishers who have authorized the CCC to grant photocopy permissions on any of their works. The same inclusive country-wide coverage is available for publishers in the following countries: Canada, the Commonwealth of Independent States, Germany, New Zealand, Norway, and Spain. To register with the CCC, please contact TRS Customer Service, 222 Rosewood Dr., Danvers, MA 01923, USA; tel: 508-750-8400; fax: 508-750-4470; URL: http://www.copyright.com/

Brief Description

A brief description of the contents and editorial focus of the publication may be provided, preceded by the word **"Description:"** at the end of the entry. These descriptions were submitted by the publisher or were written by editorial staff after examination of sample copies or publisher catalogs.

Refereed Serial

The manuscript peer review and evaluation system is utilized to protect, maintain and raise the quality of scholarly material published in serials. If a serial is known to be refereed or juried, the notation *"Refereed Serial"* appears in italics at the end of the entry. This information is generally provided by the serial publisher.

Newspaper-Specific Data Elements

Ownership

The name of the owner(s) of a newspaper is listed, usually accompanied by the owner(s) address, and telephone and fax numbers. The owner address may differ from the newspaper location address. Owner information is preceded by the notation "Owner(s):."

Wire Services

If a newspaper is known to use one or more news or photo wire services, abbreviations or names of the services used are listed in the entry. Such information is preceded by the words "Wire Service(s):." Abbreviations for wire services used are listed on page xxxi of this volume.

Pages Per Issue; Columns Per Page

When known, the number of pages per issue (pp./issue:) and/or columns per page (cols./p.:) is/are noted.

Cataloging Rules for Main Entry Title

The majority of titles in the Bowker International Serials Database were cataloged according to *Anglo-American Cataloging Rules* prior to 1978, the date of the new edition of *Anglo-American Cataloging Rules*. The new *AACR II* reflects a trend toward the Key Title concept of cataloging

as used by the International Serials Data System (ISDS) and published in its *International Standard Bibliographic Description for Serials* (1974).

Because recataloging a database the size of Bowker's was not feasible, our cataloging rules were modified but not radically changed. Cross-references are provided in the TITLE INDEX from variant forms of title, such as Key Title, to aid users searching by other methods.

Whenever possible, main entry title cataloging is done from a sample of the title page of the most recent issue, according to the following rules:

Articles at the beginning of titles are omitted, or are bypassed in filing.

Serials with distinctive titles are usually entered under title. For example:

Annual Bulletin of Historical Literature
Business Week
Milton Studies

If a title consists only of a generic term followed by the name of the issuing body, or if the name of the issuing body clarifies the content of the publication, entry is under the name of the issuing body. For example:

Newsletter of the American Theological Library Association

is entered as

American Theological Library Association. Newsletter

Economic Performance and Prospects, issued by the Private Development Corporation of the Philippines

is entered as

Private Development Corporation of the Philippines. Economic Performance and Prospects

A title which consists of a subject modified generic term followed by the name of the issuing body is considered nondistinctive and is entered under the name of the issuing body. For example:

Annual Meeting Scientific Proceedings of the American Animal Hospital Association

is entered as

American Animal Hospital Association. Annual Meeting Scientific Proceedings

Government publications with nondistinctive titles are entered under the name of the government jurisdiction of the issuing body, although distinctive titles of government organizations may be entered directly under title. For example:

Great Britain. Economic and Social Research Council. Annual Report

but

Statistical Abstract of Iceland

Titles which begin with the initials of the issuing body are entered under the initials. Cross-references from the full name are provided in the TITLE INDEX.

If a geographic name is part of the name of the issuing body, entry will be under the common form of the name of the body. For example:

University of the West Indies. Vice-Chancellor's Report

not

West Indies. University. Vice-Chancellor's Report

Note, however, that government publications retain similar cataloging as government jurisdiction.

Canada. Statistics Canada. Field Crop Reporting Series

Multilingual titles are entered under the first title given on the title page, or the first title reported by the publisher if the title page is not available. Titles in other languages are entered directly after the main entry title. Cross-references are provided in the TITLE INDEX for each language title.

FILING RULES

Due to the restrictions imposed by computer filing of titles, the following special filing rules should be noted.

Articles and prepositions within titles are alphabetized as words:

Journal of the West

precedes

Journal of Theological Studies

Hyphenated words are treated as separate words:

Pre-Text

precedes

Preaching

However, words indicating compass points (northeast, southwest, etc.) are filed as one word regardless of how printed:

Southeast Asia Builder
South-East Asia Stamp Catalogue
Southeast Dragster
South East Magazine

Titles entered under corporate author or government jurisdiction are sequenced before distinctive titles that begin with the same words:

British Columbia. Ministry of Energy, Mines and
    Petroleum Resources. Mineral Market Update

precedes

British Columbia Catholic

Acronyms and initials are treated as such and are listed at the beginning of each letter of the alphabet. Exceptions are the abbreviations of U.N. (United Nations), U.S. (United States), Gt. Britain (Great Britain), and St. (Saint), which are filed as words:

U R A M Newsletter
United Mutual Fund Sector
U.S. Environmental Protection Agency. Clean Water
    Report to Congress

Titles in excess of 36 characters which are identical may not sort sequentially. The editors suggest that users scan the entire sequence of identical titles to locate specific entries.

Diacritical marks have been omitted. The German and Scandinavian umlaut has been replaced by the letter "e" following the vowels a, e, o, and u. In Danish, Norwegian and Swedish, the letter å is sequenced as "aa" and the letter ø as "oe."

International Standard Serial Number (ISSN)

1. What is the ISSN?

An internationally accepted, concise, unique, and unambiguous code for the identification of serial publications. One ISSN represents one serial title.

The ISSN consists of seven numbers with an eighth check digit calculated according to Modulus 11 and used to verify the number in computer processing. A hyphen is printed after the fourth digit, as a visual aid, and the acronym, ISSN, precedes the number.

2. How did the ISSN evolve as an international system?

The International Organization for Standardization Technical Committee 46 (ISO/TC 46) is the agency responsible for the development of the ISSN as an international standard. The organization responsible for the administration and coordination of ISSN assignments worldwide is the ISSN International Centre in Paris, which is supported by the French government and UNESCO.

ISSNs are assigned by over 50 national centers worldwide. The National Serials Data Program (NSDP) is the U.S. national center. The centers form a network which is coordinated by the ISSN International Centre located in Paris.

The implementation of the ISSN system started with the numbering of 70,000 titles in the serials database of R.R. Bowker (*Ulrich's International Periodicals Directory* and *Irregular Serials and Annuals*). The next serials database numbering was the *New Serials Titles 1950-70* cumulation listing 220,000 titles, cumulated, converted to magnetic tape, and published by R.R. Bowker in collaboration with the Serials Record Division of the Library of Congress. These two databases were used as the starting base for the implementation of the ISSN.

3. What types of publications are assigned ISSNs?

For assignment of an ISSN, a serial is defined as a publication in print or non-print form, issued in successive parts, usually having numerical or chronological designations, and intended to be continued indefinitely.

4. How is the ISSN used?

The ISSN is employed as a component of bar codes and as a tool for the communication of basic information about a serial title and for such processes as ordering, billing, inventory control, abstracting, and indexing. In library processes, the ISSN is used in operations such acquisitions, claiming, binding, accessioning, shelving, cooperative cataloguing, circulation, interlibrary loans, and retrieval of requests.

5. May a publication have an International Standard Book Number (ISBN) and an ISSN?

Yes! Monographic series (separate works issued indefinitely under a common title, generally in a uniform format with numeric designations) and annuals or titles planned to be issued indefinitely under the same title may be defined as serials. The ISSN is assigned to the serial title, while an ISBN is assigned to each individual title or monograph in the series.

A new ISBN is assigned to each volume or edition by the publisher, while the ISSN, which is assigned by the ISSN International Centre or national ISSN centers, remains the same for each issue. Both numbers should be printed on the copyright page or other appropriate page of each volume, with their acronyms or words preceding each number for immediate identification. With the availability of both an ISSN and ISBN, the problem of defining the overlap of serials and monographs has been resolved.

SAMPLE TITLE

Advances in the Biosciences
ISSN 0065-3446
Vol. 1 Proceedings: Berlin. Schering Symposium of Endocrinology, Berlin. Ed. by Gerhard Raspe. 1969. 40.00 (ISBN 0-08-013395-9). Pergamon.

Vol. 2 Proceedings. Schering Symposium on Biodynamics & Mechanisms of Action of Steroid Hormones, Berlin. Ed. by Gerhard Raspe. 1969. 41.25 (ISBN 0-08-006942-8). Pergamon.

Vol. 3 Proceedings. Schering Workshop on Steroid Metabolism "in Vitro Versus in Vivo," Berlin. Ed. by Gerhard Raspe. 1969. 41.25 (ISBN 0-08-017544-9). Pergamon.

Vol. 4 Proceedings. Schering Symposium on Mechanisms Involved in Conception. Berlin. Ed. by Gerhard Raspe. 1970. text ed. 41.25 (ISBN 0-08-017546-5). Pergamon.

Vol. 25 Development of Responsiveness to Steroid Hormones. Alvin M. Kaye & Myra Kaye et al. LC 79-42938. 1980. 66.00 (ISBN 0-08-024949-X). Pergamon.

6. Where should the ISSN appear on the serial?

In a prominent position on or in each issue of the serial, such as the front cover, back cover, masthead, title, or copyright pages. The international standard recommendation is that the ISSN of a periodical be printed, whenever possible, in the upper right corner of the front cover.

Promotional and descriptive materials about the serial should include the ISSN.

7. When a title changes, is a new ISSN assigned?

In most instances, a new ISSN is assigned when a title changes. However, the determination is made by the ISSN International Centre or the appropriate national ISSN centers. Publishers should report all the title changes to their respective centers.

8. How does a publisher apply for an ISSN?

The publisher should contact the appropriate national ISSN center or the ISSN International Centre. Centers require bibliographic evidence of a serial, including a copy of the title page and cover. There is no charge to publishers for the assignment of ISSNs.

For full information, publishers should contact the national library or bibliographic center in the country where they are publishing. The address of the ISSN International Centre is:

ISSN International Centre
20, rue Bachaumont
75002 Paris
France
Tel: +33 (1) 44 88 22 20
Fax: +33 (1) 40 26 32 43
Telex: 219847F
E-mail: issnic@issn.org
URL: http://www.issn.org

The address for the U.S. national ISSN center is:

National Serials Data Program (NSDP)
Library of Congress
Washington, DC 20540-4160
Tel: 202-707-6452
Fax: 202-707-6333
E-mail: ISSN@loc.gov
URL: http://lcweb.loc.gov/issn/

9. What is SISAC?

SISAC stands for the Serials Industry Systems Advisory Committee. SISAC is an industry group formed to develop voluntary standardized formats for electronically transmitting serials business transaction information. SISAC provides a forum where serial (particularly journal) publishers, library system vendors, and librarians can discuss mutual concerns regarding the electronic transmission of serial information and develop cooperative solutions, in the form of standardized formats, to efficiently address these concerns. *(Reprinted with permission from SISAC.)*

10. What is the SISAC Symbol (SICI) and its relationship to the ISSN?

The Serial Item and Contribution Identifier (SICI) is a serial identification code which follows the ISSN and is a string of letters and/or numbers which uniquely identify a particular issue of a serial. Encoded in the SICI are chronological and enumeration data which identify serials by date and volume/issue numbers. According to SISAC, "the ANSI* standard extends the code down to the article level by adding location number and necessary title information, plus a record validation character. Code 128 is the bar code symbology selected by SISAC for displaying this number string in scannable form. When displayed in the Code 128 symbology, the SICI is called the SISAC symbol." The SICI is the ANSI standard; the SISAC symbol is the bar code. *(Reprinted with permission from SISAC.)*

*ANSI American National Standards Institute. Organization that coordinates the voluntary standards system in the United States. U.S. member of the International Standards Organization (ISO).

Abbreviations

General Abbreviations and Special Symbols

a.	annual		N.S.	New Series
abstr.	abstracts		no.	number
adv.	advertising		pat.	patents
approx.	approximately		play rev.	play reviews (theater reviews)
avail.	available		pp./issue	pages per issue
bi-m.	bimonthly (every two months)		Prof.	Professor
bi-w.	biweekly (every two weeks)		Pub., Pubs.	Publisher, Publishers
bibl.	bibliographies		q.	quarterly
bk.rev.	book reviews		R&P	Rights & Permissions
CCC	Copyright Clearance Center		rec.rev.	record reviews
c/o	care of		s-a.	semiannually (twice annually)
circ.	circulation		s-m.	semimonthly (twice monthly)
cols./p.	columns per page		s-w.	semiweekly (twice weekly)
cum.index	cumulative index		stat.	statistics
Cy.	county		subscr.	subscription
d.	daily		tele.rev.	television reviews
dance rev.	dance reviews		3/m.	3 times a month
Dir.	Director		3/yr.	3 times a year
dist.	distributed		tr.lit.	trade literature (manufacturers' catalogues, reader response cards)
Ed., Eds.	Editor, Editors			
Ed.Bd.	Editorial Board		tr.mk.	trade marks
film rev.	film reviews		URL	Uniform Resource Locator
fortn.	fortnightly (every two weeks)		video rev.	video reviews
ISSN	International Standard Serial Number		vol.	volume
illus.	illustrations		w.	weekly
irreg.	irregular		*	not updated / unverified
m.	monthly		●	online and / or CD-ROM availability
mkt.	market prices		▼	new serial
music rev.	music reviews		†	ceased

SYMBOL	UNIT	COUNTRY
Af.	afghani	Afghanistan
Arg.$	peso	Argentina
Aus.$	dollar	Australia
B.	baht	Thailand
B.$	dollar	Belize, Bermuda, Brunei Darussalam
BEF	franc	Belgium
Bl.	balboa	Panama
Bol.$	peso	Bolivia
Br.	birr	Ethiopia
Bs.	bolivar	Venezuela
BTN	bonus do tesouro nacional	Brazil
BTNF	bonus do tesouro nacional fiscal	Brazil
C.$	cordoba; dollar; peso	Nicaragua, Cayman Islands, Cuba
Can.$	dollar	Canada
CFPF	franc	New Caledonia
Ch.$	peso	Chile
Col.	colon	Costa Rica, El Salvador
Col.$	peso	Colombia
Cr.$	cruzerio	Brazil
Cz.$	cruzado	Brazil
D.	dalasi	Gambia
DH., Dh.	dirham	Morocco, United Arab Emirates
DKK	krone	Denmark
DM.	mark	Germany
din.	dinar	Algeria, Jordan, Kuwait, Libya, Tunisia, Yugoslavia
$	dollar; peso	various
Dr.	drachma	Greece
E.	emalageni	Swaziland
EAs.	shilling	East Africa, Somalia, Tanzania, Uganda
EC$.	dollar	Dominica, Grenada, St. Lucia, Eastern Caribbean
ECU	European currency unit	European Communities/European Union
EEK	kroon	Estonia
Esc.	escudo	Angola, Cape Verde, Mozambique, Portugal
F.	franc	Djibouti, France, Guadeloupe, Mali, Martinique, Monaco, Rwanda
F$	dollar	Fiji
FIM	markka	Finland
fl.	guilder; florin	Netherlands, Netherlands Antilles, Surinam
FMG.	franc	Malagasy Republic
Fmk.	mark; markka	Finland
Fr.	franc	Belgium, Liechtenstein, Luxembourg, Switzerland
Fr.CFA	franc	African Financial Community, Benin, Burkina Faso, Burundi, Cameroon, Central African Republic, Chad, Congo, Gabon, Ivory Coast, Niger, Reunion, Senegal, Togo
Ft.	forint	Hungary
g.	guarani	Paraguay
Gde.	gourde	Haiti
GS.	franc	Guinea
G.$	dollar	Guyana
HK$	dollar	Hong Kong
HRK	kuna	Croatia
£	pound	Ireland
ID.	dinar	Iran, Iraq
RI.	riyal	Iran
S	shekel	Israel
SK	krona	Iceland
J.$	dollar	Jamaica
Jam.$	dollar	Jamaica

SYMBOL	UNIT	COUNTRY
K.	kina; kwacha; kyat	Malawi, Papua New Guinea, Union of Myanmar (Burma), Zambia
Kc.	koruna	Czech Republic
Kcs.	koruny	Czechoslovakia
kip	kip	Laos
Kr.	krona; krone	Scandinavian countries
KShs.	shilling	Kenya
L.	lempira; lira	Honduras, Italy
Le.	leone	Sierra Leone
lek	lek	Albania
lei	lei	Rumania
Lit.	lira italiana	Italy
Ls.	lats	Latvia
Lt.	litas	Lithuania
lv.	lev	Bulgaria
M.$	dollar; ringgit	Malaysia
Mex.$	peso	Mexico
MKD	denar	Macedonia
$m.n.	moneda nacional	various
mt.	metical	Mozambique
N$	new Uruguay peso	Uruguay
NC.	cedi	Ghana
NOK	krone	Norway
NT.$	dollar	Republic of China (Taiwan)
N.Z.$	dollar	New Zealand
ORI.	riyal	Oman
P.	pula; pataca; peso	Botswana, Macao, Philippines, various
PG.	peso	Guinea-Bissau
QRI.	riyal	Qatar
£	pound	Ireland, Gt. Britain, Malta
£C	pound	Cyprus
£E	pound	Egypt
£L	pound; dinar	Lebanon
£N	pound; naira	Nigeria
£S	pound	Syria
ptas.	peseta	Spain
Q.	quetzal	Guatemala
R.	rand	South Africa, Lesotho, Namibia
RD.$	peso	Dominican Republic
Rps.	rupiah	Indonesia
Rs.	riel; rial; rupee	Cambodia, India, Iran, Mauritius, Nepal, Pakistan, Seychelles, Sri Lanka
Rub.	ruble	Commonwealth of Independent States
S/	sucre; sole	Ecuador, Peru
S.	schilling	Austria
S.$	dollar	Singapore, Western Samoa
SEK	krona	Sweden
SFr.	franc	Liechtenstein, Switzerland
SI$	dollar	Solomon Islands
SK.	koruna	Slovakia
SL.	pound	Sudan
SLT	talar	Slovenia
SRI.	riyal	Saudia Arabia
$T.	dollar	Tonga
TK.	taka	Bangladesh
TL.	pound; lira	Turkey
T.T.$	dollar	Trinidad and Tobago
tugrik	tugrik	Mongolia
UM	ouguiya	Mauritania
Urg.$	peso	Uruguay
vatu	vatu	Vanuatu
VN.$	dollar	Vietnam
Won	won (hwan)	Korea
Y	yuan	People's Republic of China
Yen	yen	Japan
YRI.	rial	Yemen
Z	zaire	Zaire
Z.$	dollar	Zimbabwe
Zl.	zloty	Poland

Country of Publication Codes

This list of countries and their codes has been taken from the list used by the Library of Congress in the MARC II format, 1992. The list used here is not the complete list of the MARC II format and is limited to countries and territories with publications listed in **Ulrich's**. The states of the United States, provinces and territories of Canada, and divisions of the United Kingdom are not listed separately.

The codes are mnemonic in most cases. Special codes not in the MARC format are used for publications of two international organizations: EI for European Communities and UN for United Nations and related organizations; and KR for Ukraine.

Country Code Sequence

AA	- ALBANIA	GH	- GHANA	PG	- GUINEA-BISSAU
AE	- ALGERIA	GI	- GIBRALTAR	PH	- PHILIPPINES
AF	- AFGHANISTAN	GL	- GREENLAND	PK	- PAKISTAN
AG	- ARGENTINA	GM	- GAMBIA	PL	- POLAND
AI	- ARMENIA	GO	- GABON	PN	- PANAMA
AJ	- AZERBAIJAN	GP	- GUADELOUPE	PO	- PORTUGAL
AN	- ANDORRA	GR	- GREECE	PP	- PAPUA NEW GUINEA
AO	- ANGOLA	GS	- GEORGIA	PR	- PUERTO RICO
AQ	- ANTIGUA	GT	- GUATEMALA	PY	- PARAGUAY
AS	- AMERICAN SAMOA	GU	- GUAM	QA	- QATAR
AT	- AUSTRALIA	GV	- GUINEA	RE	- REUNION
AU	- AUSTRIA	GW	- GERMANY	RH	- ZIMBABWE
AY	- ANTARCTICA	GY	- GUYANA	RM	- RUMANIA
BA	- BAHRAIN	HK	- HONG KONG	RU	- RUSSIA
BB	- BARBADOS	HO	- HONDURAS	RW	- RWANDA
BD	- BURUNDI	HT	- HAITI	SA	- SOUTH AFRICA
BE	- BELGIUM	HU	- HUNGARY	SE	- SEYCHELLES
BF	- BAHAMAS	IC	- ICELAND	SF	- SAO TOME E PRINCIPE
BG	- BANGLADESH	IE	- IRELAND	SG	- SENEGAL
BH	- BELIZE	II	- INDIA	SI	- SINGAPORE
BL	- BRAZIL	IO	- INDONESIA	SJ	- SUDAN
BM	- BERMUDA	IQ	- IRAQ	SL	- SIERRA LEONE
BN	- BOSNIA HERCEGOVINA	IR	- IRAN	SM	- SAN MARINO
BO	- BOLIVIA	IS	- ISRAEL	SO	- SOMALIA
BP	- SOLOMON ISLANDS	IT	- ITALY	SP	- SPAIN
BR	- UNION OF MYANMAR (FORMERLY BURMA)	IV	- IVORY COAST	SQ	- SWAZILAND
		JA	- JAPAN	SR	- SURINAM
BS	- BOTSWANA	JM	- JAMAICA	SU	- SAUDI ARABIA
BT	- BHUTAN	JO	- JORDAN	SW	- SWEDEN
BU	- BULGARIA	KE	- KENYA	SX	- NAMIBIA (FORMERLY SOUTH-WEST AFRICA)
BW	- BELARUS	KG	- KYRGYZSTAN		
BX	- BRUNEI DARUSSALAM	KN	- KOREA, NORTH	SY	- SYRIA
CB	- CAMBODIA	KO	- KOREA, SOUTH	SZ	- SWITZERLAND
CC	- CHINA, PEOPLE'S REPUBLIC OF	KR	- UKRAINE	TA	- TAJIKISTAN
CD	- CHAD	KU	- KUWAIT	TC	- TURKS AND CAICOS ISLANDS
CE	- SRI LANKA	KZ	- KAZAKHSTAN	TG	- TOGO
CF	- CONGO (BRAZZAVILLE)	LB	- LIBERIA	TH	- THAILAND
CH	- CHINA, REPUBLIC OF	LE	- LEBANON	TI	- TUNISIA
CI	- CROATIA	LH	- LIECHTENSTEIN	TK	- TURKMENISTAN
CJ	- CAYMAN ISLANDS	LI	- LITHUANIA	TO	- TONGA
CK	- COLOMBIA	LO	- LESOTHO	TR	- TRINIDAD & TOBAGO
CL	- CHILE	LS	- LAOS	TS	- UNITED ARAB EMIRATES
CM	- CAMEROON	LU	- LUXEMBOURG	TU	- TURKEY
CN	- CANADA	LV	- LATVIA	TV	- TUVALU
CQ	- COMOROS	LY	- LIBYA	TZ	- TANZANIA
CR	- COSTA RICA	MC	- MONACO	UA	- EGYPT (ARAB REPUBLIC OF EGYPT)
CS	- CZECHOSLOVAKIA	MF	- MAURITIUS	UG	- UGANDA
CU	- CUBA	MG	- MADAGASCAR	UI	- UNITED KINGDOM MISC. ISLANDS
CV	- CAPE VERDE	MH	- MACAO	UK	- UNITED KINGDOM
CX	- CENTRAL AFRICAN REPUBLIC	MJ	- MONTSERRAT	UN	- UNITED NATIONS
CY	- CYPRUS	MK	- OMAN	US	- UNITED STATES
DK	- DENMARK	ML	- MALI	UV	- BURKINA FASO
DM	- BENIN	MM	- MALTA	UY	- URUGUAY
DQ	- DOMINICA	MP	- MONGOLIA	UZ	- UZBEKISTAN
DR	- DOMINICAN REPUBLIC	MQ	- MARTINIQUE	VB	- BRITISH VIRGIN ISLANDS
EA	- ERITREA	MR	- MOROCCO	VC	- VATICAN CITY
EC	- ECUADOR	MU	- MAURITANIA	VE	- VENEZUELA
EG	- EQUATORIAL GUINEA	MV	- MOLDOVA	VI	- U.S. VIRGIN ISLANDS
EI	- EUROPEAN COMMUNITIES/ EUROPEAN UNION	MW	- MALAWI	VN	- VIETNAM
		MX	- MEXICO	WS	- WESTERN SAMOA
ER	- ESTONIA	MY	- MALAYSIA	XC	- MALDIVE ISLANDS
ES	- EL SALVADOR	MZ	- MOZAMBIQUE	XE	- MARSHALL ISLANDS
ET	- ETHIOPIA	NA	- NETHERLANDS ANTILLES	XI	- SAINT KITTS-NEVIS
FA	- FAEROE ISLANDS	NE	- NETHERLANDS	XK	- SAINT LUCIA
FG	- FRENCH GUIANA	NG	- NIGER	XM	- SAINT VINCENT
FI	- FINLAND	NL	- NEW CALEDONIA	XN	- MACEDONIA
FJ	- FIJI	NN	- VANUATU (NEW HEBRIDES)	XO	- SLOVAKIA
FK	- FALKLAND ISLANDS	NO	- NORWAY	XR	- CZECH REPUBLIC
FM	- FEDERATED STATES OF MICRONESIA	NP	- NEPAL	XV	- SLOVENIA
FP	- FRENCH POLYNESIA	NQ	- NICARAGUA	YE	- YEMEN, REPUBLIC OF
FR	- FRANCE	NR	- NIGERIA	YU	- YUGOSLAVIA
FT	- DJIBOUTI	NU	- NAURU	ZA	- ZAMBIA
GB	- KIRIBATI	NX	- NORFOLK ISLAND	ZR	- ZAIRE
GD	- GRENADA	NZ	- NEW ZEALAND		
GE	- GERMANY, EAST	PE	- PERU		

Country Sequence

AFGHANISTAN - AF
ALBANIA - AA
ALGERIA - AE
AMERICAN SAMOA - AS
ANDORRA - AN
ANGOLA - AO
ANTARCTICA - AY
ANTIGUA - AQ
ARGENTINA - AG
ARMENIA - AI
AUSTRALIA - AT
AUSTRIA - AU
AZERBAIJAN - AJ
BAHAMAS - BF
BAHRAIN - BA
BANGLADESH - BG
BARBADOS - BB
BELARUS - BW
BELGIUM - BE
BELIZE - BH
BENIN - DM
BERMUDA - BM
BHUTAN - BT
BOLIVIA - BO
BOSNIA HERCEGOVINA - BN
BOTSWANA - BS
BRAZIL - BL
BRITISH VIRGIN ISLANDS - VB
BRUNEI DARUSSALAM - BX
BULGARIA - BU
BURKINA FASO - UV
BURUNDI - BD
CAMBODIA - CB
CAMEROON - CM
CANADA - CN
CAPE VERDE - CV
CAYMAN ISLANDS - CJ
CENTRAL AFRICAN REPUBLIC - CX
CHAD - CD
CHILE - CL
CHINA, REPUBLIC OF - CC
CHINA, PEOPLE'S REPUBLIC OF - CH
COLOMBIA - CK
COMOROS - CQ
CONGO (BRAZZAVILLE) - CF
COSTA RICA - CR
CROATIA - CI
CUBA - CU
CYPRUS - CY
CZECH REPUBLIC - XR
CZECHOSLOVAKIA - CS
DENMARK - DK
DJIBOUTI - FT
DOMINICA - DQ
DOMINICAN REPUBLIC - DR
ECUADOR - EC
EGYPT (ARAB REPUBLIC OF EGYPT) - UA
EL SALVADOR - ES
EQUATORIAL GUINEA - EG
ERITREA - EA
ESTONIA - ER
ETHIOPIA - ET
EUROPEAN COMMUNITIES/
    EUROPEAN UNION - EI
FAEROE ISLANDS - FA
FALKLAND ISLANDS - FK
FEDERATED STATES OF MICRONESIA - FM
FIJI - FJ
FINLAND - FI
FRANCE - FR
FRENCH GUIANA - FG
FRENCH POLYNESIA - FP
GABON - GO
GAMBIA - GM

GEORGIA - GS
GERMANY - GW
GERMANY, EAST - GE
GHANA - GH
GIBRALTAR - GI
GREECE - GR
GREENLAND - GL
GRENADA - GD
GUADELOUPE - GP
GUAM - GU
GUATEMALA - GT
GUINEA - GV
GUINEA-BISSAU - PG
GUYANA - GY
HAITI - HT
HONDURAS - HO
HONG KONG - HK
HUNGARY - HU
ICELAND - IC
INDIA - II
INDONESIA - IO
IRAN - IR
IRAQ - IQ
IRELAND - IE
ISRAEL - IS
ITALY - IT
IVORY COAST - IV
JAMAICA - JM
JAPAN - JA
JORDAN - JO
KAZAKHSTAN - KZ
KENYA - KE
KIRIBATI - GB
KOREA, NORTH - KN
KOREA, SOUTH - KO
KUWAIT - KU
KYRGYZSTAN - KG
LAOS - LS
LATVIA - LV
LEBANON - LE
LESOTHO - LO
LIBERIA - LB
LIBYA - LY
LIECHTENSTEIN - LH
LITHUANIA - LI
LUXEMBOURG - LU
MACAO - MH
MACEDONIA - XN
MADAGASCAR - MG
MALAWI - MW
MALAYSIA - MY
MALDIVE ISLANDS - XC
MALI - ML
MALTA - MM
MARSHALL ISLANDS - XE
MARTINIQUE - MQ
MAURITANIA - MU
MAURITIUS - MF
MEXICO - MX
MOLDOVA - MV
MONACO - MC
MONGOLIA - MP
MONTSERRAT - MJ
MOROCCO - MR
MOZAMBIQUE - MZ
NAMIBIA (FORMERLY SOUTH-WEST AFRICA)- SX
NAURU - NU
NEPAL - NP
NETHERLANDS - NE
NETHERLANDS ANTILLES - NA
NEW CALEDONIA - NL
NEW ZEALAND - NZ
NICARAGUA - NQ
NIGER - NG

NIGERIA - NR
NORFOLK ISLAND - NX
NORWAY - NO
OMAN - MK
PAKISTAN - PK
PANAMA - PN
PAPUA NEW GUINEA - PP
PARAGUAY - PY
PERU - PE
PHILIPPINES - PH
POLAND - PL
PORTUGAL - PO
PUERTO RICO - PR
QATAR - QA
REUNION - RE
RUMANIA - RM
RUSSIA - RU
RWANDA - RW
SAINT KITTS-NEVIS - XI
SAINT LUCIA - XK
SAINT VINCENT - XM
SAN MARINO - SM
SAO TOME E PRINCIPE - SF
SAUDI ARABIA - SU
SENEGAL - SG
SEYCHELLES - SE
SIERRA LEONE - SL
SINGAPORE - SI
SLOVAKIA - XO
SLOVENIA - XV
SOLOMON ISLANDS - BP
SOMALIA - SO
SOUTH AFRICA - SA
SPAIN - SP
SRI LANKA - CE
SUDAN - SJ
SURINAM - SR
SWAZILAND - SQ
SWEDEN - SW
SWITZERLAND - SZ
SYRIA - SY
TAJIKISTAN - TA
TANZANIA - TZ
THAILAND - TH
TOGO - TG
TONGA - TO
TRINIDAD & TOBAGO - TR
TUNISIA - TI
TURKEY - TU
TURKMENISTAN - TE
TURKS AND CAICOS ISLANDS - TC
TUVALU - TV
U.S. VIRGIN ISLANDS - VI
U.S.S.R. - UR
UGANDA - UG
UKRAINE - KR
UNION OF MYANMAR (FORMERLY BURMA) - BR
UNITED ARAB EMIRATES - TS
UNITED STATES - US
UNITED NATIONS - UN
UNITED KINGDOM - UK
UNITED KINGDOM MISC. ISLANDS - UI
URUGUAY - UY
UZBEKISTAN - UZ
VANUATU (NEW HEBRIDES) - NN
VATICAN CITY - VC
VENEZUELA - VE
VIETNAM - VN
WESTERN SAMOA - WS
YEMEN, REPUBLIC OF - YE
YUGOSLAVIA - YU
ZAIRE - ZR
ZAMBIA - ZA
ZIMBABWE - RH

Document Suppliers

ADONIS

ADONIS B.V. (main office)
Spuistraat 112D
1012 VA Amsterdam
The Netherlands
Tel: 31-20-6262629
Fax: 31-20-6261437

ADONIS USA
238 Main St.
Cambridge, MA 02142
USA
Tel: 800-944-6415
Fax: 617-876-7022
URL: http://adonis.blacksci.co.uk/

BLDSC

British Library Document Supply Centre
Customer Services
Boston Spa, Wetherby
W. Yorkshire LS23 7BQ
England
Tel: 44-1937-546060
Fax: 44-1937-546333
E-mail: dsc-customer-services@bl.uk

CASDDS

CAS Client Services
Document Detective Service
2540 Olentangy River Rd.
P.O. Box 3012
Columbus, OH 43210-0012
USA
Tel: 800-631-1884; 614-447-3870
Fax: 614-447-3648
E-mail: dds@cas.org
URL: http://www.cas.org./Support/
dds.html

CIS

Congressional Information Service, Inc.
CIS Documents on Demand
4520 East-West Hwy., Ste. 800
Bethesda, MD 20814-3389
USA
Tel: 301-654-1550, 800-227-2477
Fax: 301-654-4033
E-mail: EAINET@US.NET
URL: http://www.cispubs.com

CISTI

Canada Institute for Scientific and Technical Information
Document Delivery, CISTI
National Research Council Canada
Ottawa K1A 0S2
Canada
Tel: 800-668-1222 (Canada & US), or
613-993-9251
Fax: 613-993-7619
E-mail: cisti.docdel@nrc.ca

Ei

Engineering Information Inc.
Ei Document Delivery Service
One Castle Point Terrace
Hoboken, NJ 07030-5996
USA
Tel: 800-221-1044 (USA & Canada),
201-216-8500
Fax: 201-216-8532
E-mail: dds@ei.org.
URL: http://www.ei.org

EMDOCS

EMDOCS: The EMBASE Document Delivery Service
469 Union Ave.
Westbury, NY 11590
USA
Tel: 800-282-2720, 516-997-0796
Fax: 516-997-0890
E-mail: dds@work4u.artx.com

Genuine Article

The Institute for Scientific Information
The Genuine Article
3501 Market St.
Philadelphia, PA 19104
USA
Tel: 215-386-4399
Fax: 215-386-4343
E-mail: tga@isinet.com

Haworth

Haworth Press
Haworth Document Delivery Service
10 Alice St.
Binghamton, NY 13904-1580
USA
Tel: 800-HAWORTH
Fax: 800-895-0582
E-mail: getinfo@haworth.com

KNAW

Library KNAW
Library of the Royal Netherlands Academy of
Arts and Sciences
Information and Loans Department
P.O. Box 41950
1009 DD Amsterdam
The Netherlands
Tel: 31-20-6685511
Fax: 31-20-6685079
E-mail: info@library.knaw.nl
URL: http://www.library.knaw.nl

PADDS

**Petroleum Abstracts -
Document Delivery Service**
University of Tulsa, McFarlin Library
2933 E. 6th St.
Tulsa, OK 74104-3123
USA
Tel: 800-247-8678
Fax: 918-631-3823
E-mail: PADDS@TUred.pa.utulsa.edu

UMI

UMI InfoStore
500 Sansome St., Ste. 400
San Francisco, CA 94111-3219
USA
Tel: 800-248-0360 (USA & Canada)
415-433-5500
Fax: 415-433-0100
E-mail: orders@infostore.com

SWETS

Swets & Zeitlinger bv
Heereweg 347B
P.O. Box 830
2160 SZ Lisse
The Netherlands
Tel: 31-252-435111
Fax: 31-252-415888
Telex: 41325
E-mail: infoho@swets.nl
URL: http://www.swets.nl

UnCover

The UnCover Co.
3801 E. Florida Ave. Ste. 200
Denver, CO 80210
USA
Tel: 800-787-7979,
(outside US & Canada: 303-758-3030)
Fax: 303-758-5946
E-mail: uncover@carl.org
URL: http://www.carl.org/uncover

Micropublishers and Distributors

ACR   **A.C.R.P.P.**
(Association pour la Conservation et la
Reproduction Photographique de la Presse)
B.P. 21
77313 Marne-La-Vallee Cedex 2
France
Tel: 33-1-60-17-68-10; **Fax:** 33-1-60-17-68-05

ADL   **Advanced Library Systems, Inc.**
100 Brickstone Sq.
P.O. Box 246
Andover, MA 01810-0005
USA
Tel: 508-470-0610; **Fax:** 508-475-2672

AFS   **Fertility and Sterility**
(no longer producer)
2140 11 Ave. S., Ste. 200
Birmingham, AL 35205-2800
USA
Tel: 205-933-8494; **Fax:** 205-930-9904

AGU   **American Geophysical Union**
2000 Florida Ave., N.W.
Washington, DC 20009
USA
Tel: 202-462-6900; **Fax:** 202-328-0566

AIP   **American Institute of Physics**
500 Sunnyside Blvd.
Woodbury, NY 11797-2999
USA
Tel: 516-576-2270; **Fax:** 516-349-9704

AIR   **Aircraft Technical Publishers**
101 S. Hill Dr.
Brisbane, CA 94005
USA
Tel: 415-468-1705; **Fax:** 415-468-1596

AJP   **American Jewish Periodical Center**
Hebrew Union College - Jewish Institute
of Religion
3101 Clifton Ave.
Cincinnati, OH 45220
USA
Tel: 513-221-1875; **Fax:** 513-221-0519

ALP   **Alpha Com**
Sportallee 6
22335 Hamburg
Germany
Tel: 49-40-51302-123; **Fax:** 49-40-51302111

AMP   **Adam Matthew Publications**
8 Oxford St.
Marlborough, Wiltshire SN8 1AP
England
Tel: 44-1672-511921; **Fax:** 44-1672-511663

AMS   **AMS Press, Inc.**
(no longer producer)
56 E. 13th St.
New York, NY 10003
USA
Tel: 212-777-4700; **Fax:** 212-995-5413

ATL   **American Theological Library
Association, Preservation Board**
820 Church St., Ste. 300
Evanston, IL 60201
USA
Tel: 847-847-7788; **Fax:** 847-847-8513

BHP   **Brookhaven Press**
P.O. Box 2287
La Crosse, WI 54602-2287
USA
Tel: 608-781-0850; **Fax:** 608-781-3883

BIO   **BIOSIS**
2100 Arch St.
Philadelphia, PA 19103-1399
USA
Tel: 215-587-4800, 800-523-4806
Fax: 215-587-2041

BKR   **Bowker A&I Publishing**
(See: CIS)

BLC   **Bloch & Company**
P.O. Box 18058
Cleveland, OH 44118
USA
Tel: 216-371-0979

BLH   **Bell & Howell**
(Micropublishing now operated by UMI)

BLI   **Balch Institute**
Research Library
18 S. 7th St.
Philadelphia, PA 19106
USA
Tel: 215-925-8090; **Fax:** 215-925-8195
E-mail: balchlib@hslc.org

BNB   **British Library National Bibliographic Service**
Boston Spa, Wetherby
W. Yorkshire LS23 7BQ
England
Tel: 44-1937-546585; **Fax:** 44-1937-546586

BNQ   **Bibliotheque Nationale du Quebec
Section de la Reproduction**
125, rue Sherbrooke Ouest
Montreal, PQ H2X 1X4
Canada
Tel: 514-873-1100; **Fax:** 514-873-9932

BWC   **Butterworth & Co., Ltd.**
88 Kingsway
London WC2B 6AB
England
Tel: 44-171-4056900; **Fax:** 44-171-4051332

CDS   **Current Digest of the Past-Soviet Press**
3857 N. High St.
Columbus, OH 43214
USA
Tel: 614-292-4234; **Fax:** 614-267-6310

CHL   **Chadwyck-Healey Ltd.**
The Quorum, Barnwell Rd.
Cambridge CB5 8SW
England
Tel: 44-1223-215512; **Fax:** 44-1223-515514
E-mail: mail@chadwyck.co.uk

Chadwyck-Healey Inc.
1101 King St.
Alexandria, VA 22314-2944
USA
Tel: 703-683-4890; **Fax:** 703-683-7589
E-mail: mktg@chadwyck.com

CIS   **Congressional Information Service, Inc.**
4520 East-West Hwy., Ste. 800
Bethesda, MD 20814-3389
USA
Tel: 301-654-1550, 800-638-8380
Fax: 301-654-4033

CLA   **Canadian Library Association**
(no longer producer)
Microfilm Department
200 Elgin St., Ste. 602
Ottawa, ON K2P 1L5
Canada
Tel: 613-232-9625; **Fax:** 613-563-9895

CLS   **CLASS**
(Cooperative Library Agency for
Systems & Services)
1415 Koll Circle, Ste. 101
San Jose, CA 95112-4698
USA
Tel: 510-444-1011; **Fax:** 510-453-5379

CMC   **Computer Microfilm Corp.**
3655 Wheeler Ave.
Alexandria, VA 22304
USA
Tel: 703-461-4400; **Fax:** 703-461-0042

CML   **Commonwealth Microfilm Products**
202 Amber St.
Markham, ON L3R 3J8
Canada
Tel: 905-415-9498; **Fax:** 905-415-9616

EDR   **Eric Document Reproduction Service**
(See: CMC)

EEE   **Institute of Electrical and Electronics
Engineers Inc.**
345 E. 47th St.
New York, NY 10017
USA
Tel: 212-705-7900; **Fax:** 212-705-7682

EMP   **Emmett Publishing, Ltd.**
W. House 21, West St.
Haslemere, Surrey GU27 2AB
England
Tel: 44-1428-654443; **Fax:** 44-1428-661582

FCM   **Fairchild Books & Visuals**
7 W. 34th St.
New York, NY 10001
USA
Tel: 212-630-3880; **Fax:** 212-630-3868

GCS   **Preston Publications**
6600 W. Touhy Ave.
P.O. Box 48312
Niles, IL 60714
USA
Tel: 847-647-2900; **Fax:** 847-647-1155

GMC   **General Microfilm Co.**
(acquired by OMNISYS Corp.)

HPL   **Harvester Press Microfilm Publications Ltd.**
(Now wholly owned and operated
by Primary Source Media)

IAM   **SIAM Publications**
3600 University City Science Center
Philadelphia, PA 19104-2688
USA
Tel: 215-382-9800; **Fax:** 215-386-7999

ICS   **Editions I.C.S.**
23 Ave. Villemain
75014 Paris
France
Tel: 33-1-45392244; **Fax:** 33-1-45434680

IDC   **IDC Microform Publishers bv**
P.O. Box 11205
2301 EE Leiden
The Netherlands
Tel: 31-71-5142700; **Fax:** 31-71-5131721

IFA   **International Federation of Film
Archives (FIAF)**
6 Nottingham St.
London W1M 3RB
England
Tel: 44-171-2240991; **Fax:** 44-171-2241203

ILO   **ILO Publications**
49 Sheridan Ave.
Albany, NY 12210
USA
Tel: 518-436-9686; **Fax:** 518-436-7433

IMI   **Irish Microforms, Ltd.**
Unit 56
Sandyford Industrial Estate
Dublin 18
Ireland
Tel: 353-1-2893626; **Fax:** 353-1-2954270

IPC   **Institute of Paper Science & Technology, Inc.**
500 Tenth St. N.W.
Atlanta, GA 30318
USA
Tel: 404-894-5700; **Fax:** 404-894-4778

IRE **International Research and Evaluation**
21098 IRE-Control Center
Eagan, MN 55121-0098
USA
Tel: 612-888-9635; **Fax:** 612-888-9124

ISI **Institute for Scientific Information**
3501 Market St.
Philadelphia, PA 19104
USA
Tel: 215-386-0100
Fax: 215-386-6362, 215-386-2911

JOH **Johnson Reprint Microeditions**
(Out of business)

JSC **J.S. Canner & Co.**
(Ceased operations)
10 Charles St.
Needham Heights, MA 02194
USA
Tel: 617-449-9103; **Fax:** 617-449-1767

KHS **Kansas State Historical Society**
Microfilm Publications
6425 S.W. Sixth Ave.
Topeka, KS 66615-1099
USA
Tel: 913-272-8681; **Fax:** 913-272-8682

KTO **Kraus Microform**
(Micropublishing now operated by
Norman Ross Publishing, Inc.)

LCP **The Library of Congress**
Photoduplication Service
Washington, DC 20540-5230
USA
Tel: 202-707-5640; **Fax:** 202-707-1771

LIB **Library Microfilms**
1115 E. Arques Ave.
Sunnyvale, CA 94086
USA
Tel: 408-736-7444; **Fax:** 408-736-4397

LOP **Lomond Publications**
P.O. Box 88
Mt. Airy, MD 21771
USA
Tel: 301-829-1496, 800-443-6299

MCA **Microfilming Corporation of America**
(Acquired by UMI;
operation phased out)

MCE **Microcard Editions**
(See: CIS)

MEL **Metropolitan Library Service Agency**
(MELSA)
570 Asbury St., Ste. 201
St. Paul, MN 55104-1849
USA
Tel: 612-645-5731; **Fax:** 612-649-3169

MIM **Elsevier Science Ltd.**
The Blvd., Langford Ln.
Kidlington, Oxford OX5 1GB
England
Tel: 44-1865-843000; **Fax:** 44-1865-843010

MIS **Moody's Investors Service**
Sales Department
99 Church St.
New York, NY 10007
USA
Tel: 212-553-0300; **Fax:** 212-553-4700

MML **Micromedia Limited**
20 Victoria St.
Toronto, ON M5C 2N8
Canada
Tel: 416-362-5211, 800-387-2689
Fax: 416-362-6161
E-mail: info@mmltd.com

MMP **McLaren Micropublishing Ltd.**
P.O. Box 972, Sta. F
Toronto, ON M4Y 2N9
Canada
Tel: 416-960-4801; **Fax:** 416-964-3745

MUE **University Music Editions**
Div. of High Density Systems, Inc.
P.O. Box 192, Ft. George Sta.
New York, NY 10040
USA
Tel: 212-569-5340, 5393; **Fax:** 212-569-1269

NBI **Newsbank, Inc.**
58 Pine St.
New Canaan, CT 06840
USA
Tel: 203-966-1100, 800-762-8182
Fax: 203-966-6254

NRP **Norman Ross Publishing, Inc.**
330 W. 58th St., Ste. 214
New York, NY 10019
USA
Tel: 212-765-8200, 800-648-8850
Fax: 212-765-2393
E-mail: nross@igc.apc.org

NTI **National Technical Information Service**
5285 Port Royal Rd.
Springfield, VA 22161
USA
Tel: 703-487-4600; **Fax:** 703-321-8547

NYL **New York Law Publishing Co.**
345 Park Ave., S.
New York, NY 10010
USA
Tel: 212-779-9200; **Fax:** 212-481-8110

NYT **New York Times Information Bank**
(Operation phased out)
229 W. 43rd St.
New York, NY 10036
USA
Tel: 212-481-8110

OEC Organization for Economic Cooperation &
Development, Publications & Information
Center
2001 L St., N.W., Ste. 650
Washington, DC 20036-4910
USA
Tel: 202-785-6323; **Fax:** 202-785-0350

OMN OMNISYS Corp.
32 Wexford St.
Needham Heights, MA 02194
USA
Tel: 617-444-4123; **Fax:** 617-444-5590

OMP Oxford Microform Publication Ltd.
(Acquired by UMI)

PMC Princeton Microfilm Corp.
P.O. Box 2073
Princeton, NJ 08543
USA
Tel: 609-452-2066, 800-257-9502
Fax: 609-275-6201

PSL The Pretoria State Library
P.O. Box 397
Pretoria 0001
Republic of South Africa
Tel: 27-12-218931; **Fax:** 27-12-3255984

RPI Primary Source Media
12 Lunar Dr.
Woodbridge, CT 06525
USA
Tel: 203-397-2600, 800-444-0799
Fax: 203-397-3893

RRI Fred B. Rothman & Co.
10368 W. Centennial Rd.
Littleton, CO 80127
USA
Tel: 303-979-5657, 800-457-1986
Fax: 303-978-1457

SAL South African Library
P.O. Box 469
Capetown 8000
Republic of South Africa
Tel: 27-21-246320; **Fax:** 27-21-244848

SAS Society for Applied Spectroscopy
201-B Broadway St.
Frederick, MD 21701
USA
Tel: 301-694-8122; **Fax:** 301-694-6860

SOC Societe Canadienne du Microfilm Inc. -
Canadian Microfilming Co. Ltd.
464 rue Saint-Jean
Montreal, PQ H2Y 2S1
Canada
Tel: 514-288-5404; **Fax:** 514-843-4690

SWZ Swets & Zeitlinger bv
Backsets Department
P.O. Box 810
2160 SZ Lisse
The Netherlands
Tel: 31-252-435111; **Fax:** 31-252-415888
URL: http://www.swets.nl

TMI Tennessee Microfilms
P.O. Box 23075
Nashville, TN 37202
USA
Tel: 615-242-3632

UMI University Microfilms International
(A Bell & Howell Company)
300 N. Zeeb Rd.
Ann Arbor, MI 48103
USA
Tel: 313-761-4700, 800-521-0600
Fax: 313-761-1203

UPD Updata Publications, Inc.
1736 Westwood Blvd.
Los Angeles, CA 90024
USA
Tel: 310-474-5900; **Fax:** 310-474-4095

VCI VCH Publishers, Inc.
303 N.W. 12th Ave.
Deerfield Beach, FL 33442-1788
USA
Tel: 305-428-5566
Fax: 305-428-8201, 800-367-8247

VFN Voltaire Foundation Ltd.
99 Banbury Rd.
Oxford OX2 6JX
England
Tel: 44-1865-284600; **Fax:** 44-1865-284610

WDS Dawson Microfiche
(Distributor only)
Cannon House
Parkfarm Rd.
Folkestone, Kent CT19 5EE
England
Tel: 44-1303-850101; **Fax:** 44-1303-850440

WMP World Microfilm Publications Ltd
Microworld House, 2-6 Foscote Mews
London W9 2HH
England
Tel: 44-171-2662202; **Fax:** 44-171-2662314

WSH William S. Hein & Co., Inc.
Hein Bldg., 1285 Main St.
Buffalo, NY 14209-1987
USA
Tel: 716-882-2600, 800-828-7571
Fax: 716-883-8100

WWS Williams & Wilkins
351 W. Camden St.
Baltimore, MD 21201
USA
Tel: 410-528-8555, 800-633-6423
Fax: 410-528-8596

Reprint Services

CIS Congressional Information Service, Inc.
4520 East-West Hwy., Ste. 800
Bethesda, MD 20814-3389
USA
Tel: 301-654-1550, 800-638-8380
Fax: 301-657-3203

CMC Computer Microfilm Corp.
3655 Wheeler Ave.
Alexandria, VA 22304
USA
Tel: 703-461-4400
Fax: 703-461-0042

HAW The Haworth Press
10 Alice St.
Binghamton, NY 13904
USA
Tel: 607-722-5857
Fax: 607-722-1424

IRC International Reprint Corp.
968 Admiral Callaghan Ln., #268
Vallejo, CA 94590
USA
Tel: 707-746-8740
Fax: 707-746-8762
E-mail: reprints@intlreprints.com

ISI Institute for Scientific Information
3501 Market St.
Philadelphia, PA 19104
USA
Tel: 215-386-0100
Fax: 215-386-6362, 215-386-2911

JOH Johnson Reprint Microeditions
(out of business)

KTO Kraus Microform
(reprint service acquired by
Periodicals Service Co., PSC)

NRP Norman Ross Publishing, Inc.
330 W. 58th St., Ste. 214
New York, NY 10019
USA
Tel: 212-765-8200, 800-648-8850
Fax: 212-765-2393
E-mail: nross@igc.apc.org

NTI National Technical Information Service
5285 Port Royal Rd.
Springfield, VA 22161
USA
Tel: 703-487-4600
Fax: 703-321-8547

PSC Periodicals Service Co.
11 Main St.
Germantown, NY 12526
USA
Tel: 518-537-4700
Fax: 518-537-5899

RPI Primary Source Media
12 Lunar Dr.
Woodbridge, CT 06525
USA
Tel: 203-397-2600, 800-444-0799
Fax: 203-397-3893

RRI Fred B. Rothman & Co.
10368 W. Centennial Rd.
Littleton, CO 80127
USA
Tel: 303-979-5657, 800-457-1986
Fax: 303-978-1457

SCH Schmidt Periodicals GmbH
Dettendorf
D 83075 Bad Feilnbach
Germany
Tel: 49-8064221
Fax: 49-8064557

SWZ Swets & Zeitlinger bv
Backsets Department
P.O. Box 810
2160 SZ Lisse
The Netherlands
Tel: 31-252-43511
Fax: 31-252-415888
Telex: 41325
URL: http://www.swets.nl

UMI University Microfilms International
(A Bell & Howell Company)
300 N. Zeeb Rd.
Ann Arbor, MI 48103
USA
Tel: 313-761-4700, 800-521-0600
Fax: 313-761-1203

WDS Dawson Microfiche
Cannon House
Parkfarm Rd.
Folkestone, Kent CT19 5EE
England
Tel: 44-1303-85010
Fax: 44-1303-850440

WSH William S. Hein & Co., Inc.
Hein Bldg., 1285 Main St.
Buffalo, NY 14209-1987
USA
Tel: 716-882-2600, 800-828-7571
Fax: 716-883-8100

AAP	Australian Associated Press Information Services
AFP	Agence France-Press
ANP	Algemeen Nederlands Persbureau (Netherlands Press Agency)
AP	Associated Press (USA)
APP	Associated Press of Pakistan
BNS	Baltic News Service
CanP	Canadian Press
EFE	Agencia EFE (Spain)
KR	Knight-Ridder Financial News
LAT-WP	Los Angeles Times-Washington Post News Service
NPA	New Zealand Associated Press
NYT	New York Times News Service
PAP	Polska Agencja Prasowa (Polish Press Agency)
PPI	Pakistan Press International
RN	Reuters News Agency
SAPA	South African Press Association
SHNA	Scripps-Howard Newspaper Alliance - Scripps-Howard News Service
TASS	Telegrafnoe Agentstvo Suverennykh Stran (Telegraphic Agency of the Sovereign Countries)
UK News	United Kingdom News
UPI	United Press International

Abstracting and Indexing Services

This list contains the full names of all abstracting and indexing services whose abbreviations are used in entries in the CLASSIFIED LIST OF SERIALS. For all currently published abstracting and indexing services, entries containing full bibliographic information will be found in the CLASSIFIED LIST OF SERIALS. Consult the TITLE INDEX for page numbers. (Bibliographic information on titles for which cessations were noted more than three years ago are not listed in this book. To view information on such titles, one must refer to **Ulrich's PLUS**™ or **Ulrich's Online** services.)

A

A.A.P.P.Abstr. — Amino Acids, Peptides & Proteins Abstracts (Now: Cambridge Scientific Biochemistry Abstracts, Part 3: Amino Acids, Peptides & Proteins) (Ceased)

AAR — Accounting Articles

ABC — Abstracts in BioCommerce

A.B.C.Pol.Sci. — ABC Pol Sci; A Bibliography of Contents: Political Science and Government

ABI Inform. — A B I - INFORM

ABTICS — Abstracts and Book Title Index Card Services (Ceased)

A.D.& D. — Alcohol, Drugs and Driving: Abstracts and Reviews (Now: Alcohol, Drugs and Driving)

AESIS — A E S I S Quarterly (Australian Earth Sciences Information System)

A.I.Abstr. — Artificial Intelligence Abstracts (United States) (Ceased)

A.I.C.P. — Anthropological Index to Current Periodicals in the Library of the Museum of Mankind Library

A.I.D.Res.Dev. Abstr. — A.I.D. Research & Development Abstracts (Agency for International Development)

AIDS Abstr. — AIDS Abstracts

AIM — Abridged Index Medicus

A.I.P.P. — Annual Index to Poetry in Periodicals (Now: Roth's American Poetry Annual) (Ceased)

AIT Reports — A I T Reports and Publications on Renewable Energy Resources. Abstracts (Asian Institute of Technology) (Now: A I T Reports and Publications on Energy. Abstracts)

ALISA — A L I S A (Australian Library and Information Science Abstracts)

API Abstr. — A P I Abstracts: Literature (American Petroleum Institute) (Now: Technical Literature Abstracts)

API Catal. — A P I Abstracts: Catalysts & Catalysis (Now: Technical Literature Abstracts: Catalysts - Zeolites)

API Hlth.& Environ. — A P I Abstracts: Health & Environment (Now: Technical Literature Abstracts: Health & Environment)

API Oil. — A P I Abstracts: Oilfield Chemicals (Now: Technical Literature and Abstracts: Oilfield Chemicals)

API Pet.Ref. — A P I Abstracts: Petroleum Refining and Petrochemicals (Now: Technical Literature Abstracts: Petroleum Refining and Petrochemicals)

API Pet.Subst. — A P I Abstracts: Petroleum Substitutes (Now: Technical Literature Abstracts: Petroleum Substitutes)

API Transport. — A P I Abstracts: Transportation and Storage (Now: Technical Literature Abstracts: Transportation and Storage)

A.S.& T.Ind. — Applied Science & Technology Index

ASCA — Automatic Subject Citation Alert (Now: Research Alert (Philadelphia))

ASEAN Manage. Abstr. — A S E A N Management Abstracts (Association of South East Asian Nations)

ASSIA — A S S I A: Applied Social Sciences Index & Abstracts

ASTIS — A S T I S Bibliography (Arctic Science & Technology Information System)

Abr.R.G. — Abridged Readers' Guide to Periodical Literature

Abstr.Anthropol. — Abstracts in Anthropology

Abstr.Bk.Rev. Curr.Leg.Per. — Abstracts of Book Reviews in Current Legal Periodicals (Ceased)

Abstr.Bulg.Sci.Med.Lit. Abstracts of Bulgarian Scientific Medical Literature

Abstr.Bull.Inst.Pap.Chem. Institute of Paper Chemistry. Abstract Bulletin (Now: Institute of Paper Science and Technology. Abstract Bulletin)

Abstr.Crim.& Pen. Abstracts on Criminology and Penology (Now: Criminology, Penology & Police Science Abstracts)

Abstr.Engl.Stud. Abstracts of English Studies (Ceased)

Abstr.Folk.Stud. Abstracts of Folklore Studies (Ceased)

Abstr.Health Care Manage.Stud. Abstracts of Health Care Management Studies (Ceased)

Abstr.Hosp.Manage.Stud. Abstracts of Hospital Management Studies (Now: Abstracts of Health Care Management Studies) (Ceased)

Abstr.Hum.Comp.Inter. Abstracts in Human-Computer Interaction

Abstr.Hyg. Abstracts on Hygiene and Communicable Diseases

Abstr.Inter.Med. Abstracts in Internal Medicine (Now: Abstracts in Medicine and Key Word Index) (Ceased)

Abstr.J.Earthq.Eng. Abstract Journal in Earthquake Engineering

Abstr.Mil.Bibl. Abstracts of Military Bibliography

Abstr.Musl.Rel. European Muslims and Christian- Muslim Relations. Abstracts. (Ceased)

Abstr.N.Amer.Geol. Abstracts of North American Geology (Ceased)

Abstr.Pop.Cult. Abstracts of Popular Culture (Ceased)

Abstr.Rural Dev.Trop. Abstracts on Rural Development in the Tropics (Ceased)

Abstr.Soc.Geront. Abstracts in Social Gerontology: Current Literature on Aging

Abstr.Soc.Work. Abstracts for Social Workers (Now: Social Work Abstracts)

Abstr.Trop.Agri. Abstracts on Tropical Agriculture

Acad.Ind. Academic Index

Access Access: the Supplementary Index to Periodicals

Account.& Data Proc.Abstr. Accounting & Data Processing Abstracts (Now: Accounting & Finance Abstracts) (Also see: Anbar)

Account.Ind. Accountant's Index (Now: Accounting and Tax Index)

Acid Pre.Dig. Acid Precipitation Digest (Ceased)

Acid Rain Abstr. Acid Rain Abstracts (Now: Environment Abstracts)

Acid Rain Ind. Acid Rain Annual Index (Now: Environment Abstracts Annual)

Acoust.Abstr. Acoustics Abstracts

Adol.Ment.Hlth.Abstr. Adolescent Mental Health Abstracts (Ceased)

Agri.Eng.Abstr. Agricultural Engineering Abstracts

Agri.Ind. Agricultural Index (Now: Biological & Agricultural Index)

Agrindex Agrindex

Agroforest.Abstr. Agroforestry Abstracts

Air Un.Lib.Ind. Air University Library Index to Military Periodicals

Alloys Ind. Alloys Index

Alt.Press Ind. Alternative Press Index

Amer.Bibl.Slavic & E.Ear.Stud. American Bibliography of Slavic and East European Studies

Amer.Hist.& Life America: History & Life

Amer.Hum.Ind. American Humanities Index

Amer.Stat.Ind. American Statistics Index

Anal.Abstr. Analytical Abstracts

Anbar Anbar Management Services Abstracts (Now: Operations & Production Management Abstracts; Marketing & Distribution Abstracts; Personnel & Training Abstracts) (Also see: Account.& Data Proc.Abstr.; also see: Computer Abstr.; also see: Top Manage.Abstr.)

Anim.Behav.Abstr. Animal Behavior Abstracts

Anim.Breed.Abstr. Animal Breeding Abstracts

Anthropol.Lit. Anthropological Literature

Ap.Ind. Apple Index

Apic.Abstr. Apicultural Abstracts

Appl.Ecol.Abstr. Applied Ecology Abstracts (Now: Ecology Abstracts)

Appl.Mech.Rev. Applied Mechanics Reviews

Aqua.Sci.& Fish.Abstr. Aquatic Sciences & Fisheries Abstracts (Parts 1, 2)

Aquacult.Abstr. A S F A Aquaculture Abstracts

Archit.Per.Ind. Architectural Periodicals Index (Now: Architectural Publications Index)

Arct.Bibl. Arctic Bibliography (Ceased)

Art & Archaeol.Tech.Abstr. Art and Archaeology Technical Abstracts

Art Ind. Art Index

Art.Hosp.& Tour. Articles in Hospitality and Tourism

Art.Int.Abstr. Artificial Intelligence Abstracts (England) (Ceased)

Artbibl. Artbibliographies Current Titles

Artbibl.Mod. Artbibliographies Modern

Arts & Hum.Cit.Ind. Arts & Humanities Citation Index

Ash.G.Bot.Per. Asher's Guide to Botanical Periodicals (Now: Guide to Botanical Periodicals) (Ceased)

Asian-Pac.Econ.Lit. Asian-Pacific Economic Literature

Astron.& Astrophys.Abstr. Astronomy and Astrophysics Abstracts

Aus.Educ.Ind. Australian Education Index

Aus.Leg.Mon.Dig. Australian Legal Monthly Digest

Aus.P.A.I.S. — Australian Public Affairs Information Service (Now: APAIS: Australian Public Affairs Information Service)

Aus.Rd.Ind. — Australian Road Index (Ceased)

Aus.Sci.Ind. — Australian Science Index (Ceased)

Aus.Speleo Abstr. — Australian Speleo Abstracts

Avery Ind. Archit.Per. — Avery Index to Architectural Periodicals

B

B.C.I.R.A. — B.C.I.R.A. Abstracts of International Foundry Literature (British Cast Iron Research Association) (Now: B C I R A Abstracts on International Literature on Metal Castings Production)

BIM — Bibliography and Index of Micropaleontology

BMT — B M T Abstracts (British Maritime Technology)

BNI — B N I (British Newspaper Index)

B.P.I. — Business Periodicals Index

BPIA — Business Publications Index and Abstracts (Ceased)

B.R.I. — BioResearch Index (Now: Biological Abstracts - R R M (Reports, Reviews, Meetings))

BSL Biol. — Abstracts of Bulgarian Scientific Literature. Biology (Ceased)

BSL Econ. — Abstracts of Bulgarian Scientific Literature. Economics and Law (Ceased)

BSL Geo. — Abstracts of Bulgarian Scientific Literature. Geosciences (Ceased)

BSL Indus. — Abstracts of Bulgarian Scientific Literature. Industry, Building and Transport

BSL Math. — Abstracts of Bulgarian Scientific Literature. Mathematical and Physical Sciences (Ceased)

Bangladesh Agr. Sci.Abstr. — Bangladesh Agricultural Sciences Abstracts

Bank.Lit.Ind. — Banking Literature Index

Behav.Abstr. — Behavioural Abstracts (Ceased)

Behav.Med. Abstr. — Behavioral Medicine Abstracts (Now: Annals of Behavioral Medicine)

Ber.Biochem. Biol. — Berichte Biochemie und Biologie (Ceased)

Bibl Agri. — Bibliography of Agriculture

Bibl.& Ind.Geol. — Bibliography & Index of Geology (see: GeoRef)

Bibl.Cart. — Bibliographia Cartographica

Bibl.Dev.Med.& Child Neur. — Bibliography of Developmental Medicine & Child Neurology. Books and Articles Received (Ceased)

Bibl.Engl.Lang. & Lit. — Bibliography of English Language and Literature (Now: Annual Bibliography of English Language and Literature)

Bibl.Ind. — Bibliographic Index

Bibl.Ling. — Linguistic Bibliography/Bibliographie Linguistique

Bibl.Repro. — Bibliography of Reproduction (Now: Human Reproduction Update)

Bibliogr.Bras. Odontol. — Bibliografia Brasileira de Odontologia

Bio-Contr.News & Info. — Bio-Control News and Information

Biodet.Abstr. — Biodeterioration Abstracts

Bioeng.Abstr. — Bioengineering Abstracts

Biog.Ind. — Biography Index

Biol.Abstr. — Biological Abstracts

Biol.& Agr.Ind. — Biological & Agricultural Index

Biol.Dig. — Biology Digest

Biostat. — Biostatistica

Biotech.Abstr. — Biotechnology Research Abstracts (Now: Agricultural & Environmental Biotechnology Abstracts; Medical & Pharmaceutical Biotechnology Abstracts)

Biwk.Pap.Rad. Chem.& Photochem. — Biweekly List of Papers on Radiation Chemistry and Photochemistry (Ceased)

Bk.Rev.Dig. — Book Review Digest

Bk.Rev.Ind. — Book Review Index

Bk.Rev.Mo. — Book Reviews of the Month (Ceased)

Br.Archaeol. Abstr. — British Archaeological Abstracts (Now: British Archaeological Bibliography)

Br.Ceram.Abstr. — British Ceramic Abstracts (Now: World Ceramics Abstracts)

Br.Educ.Ind. — British Education Index

Br.Geol.Lit. — British Geological Literature

Br.Hum.Ind. — British Humanities Index

Br.Rail.Bd. — British Railways Board. Monthly Review of Technical Literature (Ceased)

Br.Tech.Ind. — British Technology Index (Now: Current Technology Index)

Build.Manage. Abstr. — Building Management Abstracts (Now: Construction Information File - C I F)

Bull.Anal.Ent. Med.Vet. — Bulletin Analytique d'Entomologie Medicale et Veterinaire (Ceased)

Bull.Signal. — Bulletin Signaletique (Now: P A S C A L Explore, P A S C A L Folio, P A S C A L Thema) (Programme Applique a la Selection et la Compilation Automatique de la Literature)

Bull.Thermodyn. & Thermochem. — Bulletin of Thermodynamics & Thermochemistry (Now: Bulletin of Chemical Thermodynamics) (Ceased)

Bus.Comput.Ind. — Business Computer Index

Bus.Educ.Ind. — Business Education Index

Bus.Ind. — Business Index

C

CAD CAM Abstr. — C A D - C A M Abstracts (Ceased)

CALL — C A L L (Current Awareness—Library Literature)

C.C.I.Ob.Gyn. — Combined Cumulative Index to Obstetrics and Gynecology

C.C.I.P.	Combined Cumulative Index to Pediatrics
C.C.L.P.	Contents of Current Legal Periodicals (Now: Legal Contents) (Ceased)
C.C.M.J.	Contents of Contemporary Mathematical Journals (Now: Current Mathematical Publications)
CCR	Current Christian Abstracts (Now: Current Thoughts & Trends)
CERDIC	Universite de Strasbourg. Centre de Recherche et de Documentation des Institutions Chretiennes. Bulletin du CERDIC (Ceased)
CHNI	Consumer Health & Nutrition Index
C.I.J.E.	Current Index to Journals in Education
CINAHL (also C.I.N.L.)	Cumulative Index to Nursing and Allied Health Literature
CIRF Abstr.	C I R F Abstracts (Now: T&D Abstracts) (Ceased)
C.I.S. Abstr.	C I S Abstracts (Centre International d'Information de Securite et Hygiene du Travail) (Now: Safety and Health at Work)
C.I.S. Ind.	C I S Index to Publications of the United States Congress (Congressional Information Service)
CJPI	Criminal Justice Periodical Index
C.L.I.	Current Law Index
CLOA	Current Literature on Aging (Now: Abstracts in Social Gerontology: Current Literature on Aging)
CLOSS	Current Literature on Science of Science
CMI	Canadian Magazine Index (Now: Canadian Index)
C.P.I.	Current Physics Index
C.R.E.J.	Contents of Recent Economics Journals
C.R.I.Abstr.	C R I Abstracts (Cement Research Institute of India)
C.R.I.Curr. Cont.	C R I Current Contents
CS Ind.	Canadian Statistics Index (Now: Directory of Statistics in Canada
CWHM	Current Work in the History of Medicine
Cadscan	Cadscan
Cal.Per.Ind.	California Periodicals Index
Cal.Tiss.Abstr.	Calcified Tissue Abstracts (Now: Calcium and Calcified Tissue Abstracts)
Can.B.P.I.	Canadian Business Periodicals Index (Now: Canadian Index)
Can.Educ.Ind.	Canadian Education Index
Can.Lit.Ind.	Canadian Literature Index (Ceased)
Can.Per.Ind.	Canadian Periodical Index
Can.Rev.Comp. Lit.	Canadian Review of Comparative Literature (Abstracting discontinued)
Can.Wom.Per. Ind.	Canadian Women's Periodicals Index (Ceased)
Canadiana	Canadiana
Canon Law Abstr.	Canon Law Abstracts
Cath.Ind.	Catholic Periodical & Literature Index
Ceram.Abstr.	Ceramic Abstracts
Chem.Abstr.	Chemical Abstracts
Chem.Cit.Ind.	Chemistry Citation Index
Chem.Eng.Abstr.	Chemical Engineering Abstracts (Now: Process and Chemical Engineering
Chem.Infd.	Chemischer Informationsdienst (Now: ChemInform)
Chem.Titles	Chemical Titles
Chemorec.Abstr.	Chemoreception Abstracts
Chicago Psychoanal. Lit.Ind.	Chicago Psychoanalytic Literature Index (Ceased)
Chic.Per.Ind.	Chicano Periodical Index (Now: Chicano Index)
Child.Auth.& Illus.	Children's Authors and Illustrators
Child.Bk.Rev.Ind.	Children's Book Review Index
Child Devel.Abstr.	Child Development Abstracts and Bibliography
Child.Lit.Abstr.	Children's Literature Abstracts
Chr.Per.Ind.	Christian Periodical Index
Coll.Stud.Pers. Abstr.	College Student Personnel Abstracts (Now: Higher Education Abstracts)
Commun.Abstr.	Communication Abstracts
Community Ment.Health Rev.	Community Mental Health Review (Now: Journal of Prevention and Intervention in the Community)
Compumath	Compumath Citation Index
Comput.Abstr.	Computer Abstracts (Also see: Anbar)
Comput.& Info. Sys.	Computer and Information Systems Abstracts Journal
Comput.Bus.	Computer Business (Ceased)
Comput.Cont.	Computer Contents (Ceased)
Comput.Dtbs.	Computer Database
Comput.Ind.	Computer Index
Comput.Indus.Up.	Computer Industry Update (Ceased)
Comput.Lit.Ind.	Computer Literature Index
Comput.Rev.	Computing Reviews
Concr.Abstr.	Concrete Abstracts
Consum.Ind.	Consumers Index
Cont.Pg.Educ.	Contents Pages in Education
Cont.Pg.Manage.	Contents Pages in Management
Copper Abstr.	Copper Abstracts (Now: International Copper Information Bulletin) (Ceased)
Corros.Abstr.	Corrosion Abstracts
Cott.& Trop.Fibr. Abstr.	Cotton and Tropical Fibres Abstracts (Now: Cotton and Tropical Fibres)
Crim.Just.Abstr.	Criminal Justice Abstracts
Crime Delinq. Abstr.	Crime and Delinquency Abstracts (Ceased)
Crop Physiol. Abstr.	Crop Physiology Abstracts
Curr.Adv. Biochem.	Current Advances in Biochemistry (Now: Current Advances in Protein Biochemistry)

Curr.Adv.Cancer. Res. Current Advances in Cancer Research

Curr.Adv.Cell & Devel.Biol. Current Advances in Cell and Developmental Biology

Curr.Adv.Clin. Chem. Current Advances in Clinical Chemistry

Curr.Adv.Ecol. Sci. Current Advances in Ecological Sciences (Now: Current Advances in Ecological and Environmental Sciences)

Curr.Adv. Genetics & Molec.Biol. Current Advances in Genetics and Molecular Biology

Curr.Adv. Neurosci. Current Advances in Neuroscience

Curr.Adv.Physiol. Current Advances in Physiology (Now: Current Advances in Endocrinology & Metabolism)

Curr.Adv.Plant Sci. Current Advances in Plant Science

Curr.Aus.N.Z.Leg. Lit.Ind. Current Australian and New Zealand Legal Literature Index (Ceased)

Curr.Biotech. Abstr. Current Biotechnology Abstracts (Now: Current Biotechnology)

Curr.Bk.Rev.Cit. Current Book Review Citations (Ceased)

Curr.Chem.React. Current Chemical Reactions

Curr.Cont. Current Contents
consists of:
Current Contents: Agriculture, Biology & Environmental Sciences
Current Contents: Arts & Humanities
Current Contents: Clinical Medicine
Current Contents: Engineering, Computing & Technology
Current Contents: Health Services Administration (Ceased)
Current Contents: Life Sciences
Current Contents: Physical, Chemical & Earth Sciences
Current Contents: Social & Behavioral Sciences

Curr.Cont.Africa Current Contents Africa (Ceased)

Curr.Cont.M.E. Current Contents of Periodicals on the Middle East

Curr.Dig.Sov. Press Current Digest of the Soviet Press (Now: Current Digest of the Post-Soviet Press)

Curr.Ind.Stat. Current Index to Statistics

Curr.Leather Lit. Current Leather Literature (Now: Leather Science Abstracts)

Curr.Lit.Fam. Plan. Current Literature in Family Planning (Ceased)

Curr.Pack.Abstr. Current Packaging Abstracts (Ceased)

Curr.Ref. Fish Res. Current References in Fish Research

Curr.Tit.Dent. Current Titles in Dentistry

Curr.Tit. Electrochem. Current Titles in Electrochemistry

Curr.Tit.Ocean Current Titles in Ocean, Coastal, Lake & Waterway Sciences (Ceased)

Cyb.Abstr. Cybernetics Abstracts

D

DAAI Design and Applied Arts Index

DM&T Defense Markets and Technology (Now: Aerospace Defense Markets and Technology) (Ceased)

DNP Digest of Neurology & Psychiatry

DSH Abstr. DSH Abstracts (Deafness, Speech and Hearing) (Ceased)

Dairy Sci.Abstr. Dairy Science Abstracts

Data Process.Dig. Data Processing Digest

Deep Sea Res.& Oceanogr.Abstr. Deep Sea Research & Oceanographic Abstracts (Now: Oceanographic Literature Review)

Dent.Abstr. Dental Abstracts

Dent.Ind. Index to Dental Literature

Diab.Cont. Diabetes Contents

Diab.Lit.Ind. Diabetes Literature Index (Ceased)

Diar.Dis.Res. Journal of Diarrhoeal Diseases Research

Doc.Geogr. Documentatio Geographica (Now: Dokumentation zur Raumentwicklung) (Ceased)

Documentatie-blad Documentatieblad: The Abstracts Journal of the African Studies Centre Leiden (Now: African Studies Abstracts)

Dok.Arbeitsmed. Dokumentation Arbeitsmedizin (Now: Arbeitsmedizin)

Dok.Raum. Dokumentation zur Raumentwicklung (Ceased)

Dok.Str. Dokumentation Strasse

E

E & P Hlth. Exploration and Production Health, Safety and Environment

EC Ind. EC Index (European Communities)

E.I. E I (Excerpta Indonesica)

ELLIS E L L I S (European Legal Literature Information Service)

ERIC Eric Clearinghouse (See: C.I.J.E.)

Ecol.Abstr. Ecological Abstracts

Ecol.Zoo.& Plant Sci.Abstr. Essential Ecology, Zoology & Plant Science Abstracts

Econ.Abstr. Economic Abstracts (Now: Key to Economic Science) (Ceased)

Educ.Admin. Abstr. Educational Administration Abstracts

Educ.Ind. Education Index

Educ.Tech.Abstr. Educational Technology Abstracts

Ekist.Ind. Ekistic Index of Periodicals

Electroanal.Abstr. Electroanalytical Abstracts (Ceased)

Electron.& Communic. Abstr.J. Electronics and Communications Abstracts Journal

Endocrin.Ind. Endocrinology Index (Ceased)

Energy Abstr. Energy Abstracts

Energy Ind. Energy Index (Now: Energy Information Abstracts Annual)

Energy Info.Abstr. Energy Information Abstracts

Energy Res.Abstr. Energy Research Abstracts

Energy Rev. Energy Review (Santa Barbara) (Ceased)

Eng.Ind. Engineering Index (Now: Engineering Index Monthly)

Eng.Mat.Abstr. Engineered Materials Abstracts

Entomol.Abstr. Entomology Abstracts

Environ.Abstr. Environment Abstracts

Environ.Ind. Environment Index (Now: Environment Abstracts Annual)

Environ.Per.Bibl. Environmental Periodicals Bibliography

Ergon.Abstr. Ergonomics Abstracts

Euro.LJI European Legal Journals Index

Except.Child Educ.Abstr. Exceptional Child Education Abstracts (Now: Exceptional Child Education Resources)

Excerp.Bot. Excerpta Botanica (Sections A, B)

ExtraMED ExtraMED

Excerp.Med. Excerpta Medica

F

F.A.C.T. Fuel Abstracts and Current Titles (Now: Fuel and Energy Abstracts)

FAMLI F A M L I (Family Medicine Literature Index) (Ceased)

F.R. Fanatic Reader

Fababean Abstr. Faba Bean Abstracts (Ceased)

Farm & Garden Ind. Farm & Garden Index (Ceased)

Fed Print Fed in Print

Fert.Abstr. Fertilizer Abstracts (Ceased)

Field Crop Abstr. Field Crop Abstracts

Film Lit.Ind. Film Literature Index

Fish.Abstr. Essential Fisheries Abstracts

Fluidex Fluidex
consists of:
Civil Engineering Hydraulics Abstracts (Now: Fluid Abstracts: Civil Engineering)
Current Fluid Engineering Titles (Ceased)
Fluid Flow Measurement Abstracts (Now: Fluid Abstracts: Process Engineering)
Fluid Power Abstracts (Now: Fluid Abstracts: Process Engineering)
Fluid Sealing Abstracts (Now: Fluid Abstracts: Process Engineering)
Industrial Aerodynamics Abstracts (Now: Fluid Abstracts: Civil Engineering)
Industrial Jetting Report (Ceased)
Offshore Engineering Abstracts (Now: Fluid Abstracts: Civil Engineering)
Pipelines Abstracts (Now: Fluid Abstracts: Process Engineering)
Pumps & Other Fluids Machinery Abstracts (Now: Fluid Abstracts: Process Engineering)
Pumps and Turbines (Ceased)
River and Flood Control Abstracts (Ceased)
Solid-Liquid Flow Abstracts (Now: Fluid Abstracts: Process Engineering)
Tribos-Tribology Abstracts (Now: Tribology & Corrosion Abstracts) (Ceased)
World Ports and Harbours Abstracts (Now: Fluid Abstracts: Civil Engineering)
World Ports and Harbours News (Ceased)

Food Sci.& Tech. Abstr. Food Science and Technology Abstracts

Foreign Leg.Per. Index to Foreign Legal Periodicals

Forest.Abstr. Forestry Abstracts

Forest.& Wildfire Abstr. Essential Forestry & Wildfire Abstracts

Forest Prod. Abstr. Forest Products Abstracts

Foul.Prev.Res. Dig. Fouling Prevention Research Digest (Now: H T F S Digest (Heat Transfer & Fluid Flow Service))

Fuel & Energy Abstr. Fuel & Energy Abstracts

Fut.Abstr. Future - Abstracts

Fut.Surv. Future Survey

G

G.Indian Per.Lit. Guide to Indian Periodical Literature

G.Perf.Arts. Guide to the Performing Arts (Ceased)

G.Soc.Sci.& Rel. Per.Lit. Guide to Social Sciences and Religion in Periodical Literature

Gard.Lit. Garden Literature

Gas Abstr. Gas Abstracts

Gas Process.& Ppl. Gas Processing and Pipelining

Gastroenterol. Abstr.& Cit. Gastroenterology Abstracts & Citations (Ceased)

Gdlns. Guidelines

Gen.Phys.Adv. Abstr. General Physics Advance Abstracts

Gen.Sci.Ind. General Science Index

Geneal.Per.Ind. Genealogical Periodical Annual Index

Genet.Abstr. Genetics Abstracts

Geo.Abstr.H.G. (also Geo.Abstr.) Geographical Abstracts: Human Geography

Geo.Abstr.P.G. (also Geo.Abstr.) Geographical Abstracts: Physical Geography

Geol.Abstr. Geological Abstracts

Geophys.Abstr. Geophysical Abstracts (Ceased)

GeoRef Bibliography and Index of Geology (Also known as GeoRef)

Geosci.Doc. Geoscience Documentation

Geotech.Abstr. Geotechnical Abstracts

Ger.J.Psych. German Journal of Psychology (Now: European Psychologist) (Abstracting discontinued)

Graph.Arts Abstr. Graphic Arts Abstracts (Now: G A T F World)

Graph.Arts Lit. Abstr. Graphic Arts Literature Abstracts (Now: Institute of Paper Science and Technology. Graphic Arts Bulletin)

H

HMA Healthcare Marketing Abstracts

HR Rep. Human Rights Internet Reporter

HRIS H R I S Abstracts (Now: T R I S Electronic Bibliographic Data Base (Transportation Research Information Services))

Helminthol.Abstr. Helminthological Abstracts. Series A (Now: Helminthological Abstracts)
Helminthological Abstracts. Series B (Now: Nematological Abstracts)

Herb.Abstr. Herbage Abstracts (Now: Grasslands and Forage Abstracts)

High.Educ.Abstr. Higher Education Abstracts

High.Educ.Curr. Aware.Bull. Higher Education Current Awareness Bulletin (Ceased)

Hisp.Amer.Per. Ind. Hispanic American Periodicals Index

Hist.Abstr. Historical Abstracts (Parts A, B)

Hlth.Ind. Health Index

Hort.Abstr. Horticultural Abstracts

Hosp.Abstr. Hospital Abstracts (Now: Health Service Abstracts)

Hosp.Abstr.Serv. Hospital Abstracts Service (Ceased)

Hosp.Lit.Ind. Hospital Literature Index

Hospit.Ind. Hospitality Index

Hum.Ind. Humanities Index

Human Resour. Abstr. Human Resources Abstracts

Hung.Build.Bull. Hungarian Building Bulletin (Ceased)

Hung.Lib.& Info. Sci.Abstr. Hungarian Library and Information Science Abstracts

Hwy.Res.Abstr. Highway Research Abstracts (Now: Transportation Research Abstracts) (Ceased)

I

IBM PC Ind. IBM PC Index (Personal Computer)

IBR Internationale Bibliographie der Rezensionen Wissenschaftlicher Literatur/International Bibliography of Book Reviews of Scholarly Literature

IBZ Internationale Bibliographie der Zeitschriftenliteratur aus allen Gebieten des Wissens/International Bibliography of Periodicals from all Fields of Knowledge

I.C.U.I.S.Abstr. I C U I S Abstracts Service (Institute on the Church in Urban Industrial Society) (Now: I C U I S Justice Ministries) (Ceased)

IDA International Development Abstracts

IIS Index to International Statistics

IJCS Index to Journals in Communication Studies

IMFL Inventory of Marriage and Family Literature (Now: Family Studies Database)

I.M.M.Abstr. I M M Abstracts (Institute of Mining & Metallurgy) (Now: I M M Abstracts and Index)

I.N.E.P. Index to New England Periodicals

INIS Atomind. I N I S Atomindex (International Nuclear Information System)

INSPEC INSPEC (The Institution of Electrical Engineers):
Computers & Control Abstracts (Alternative title: INSPEC, Section C. Represents: Science Abstracts. Section C)
Current Papers in Computers & Control
Current Papers in Electrical & Electronics Engineering
Current Papers in Physics
Electrical & Electronics Abstracts (Alternative title: INSPEC, Section B. Represents: Science Abstracts. Section B.)
Key Abstracts - Advanced Materials
Key Abstracts - Antennas & Propagation
Key Abstracts - Artificial Intelligence
Key Abstracts - Business Automation
Key Abstracts - Computer Communication and Storage
Key Abstracts - Computing in Electronics & Power
Key Abstracts - Electronic Circuits
Key Abstracts - Electronic Instrumentation
Key Abstracts - Factory Automation
Key Abstracts - High-Temperature Superconductors
Key Abstracts - Human-Computer Interaction
Key Abstracts - Machine Vision
Key Abstracts - Measurements in Physics
Key Abstracts - Microelectronics & Printed Circuits
Key Abstracts - Microwave Technology
Key Abstracts - Neural Networks
Key Abstracts - Optoelectronics
Key Abstracts - Power Systems & Applications
Key Abstracts - Rotobics & Control
Key Abstracts - Semiconductor Devices
Key Abstracts - Software Engineering
Key Abstracts - Telecommunications
Physics Abstracts (Alternative title: INSPEC, Section A. Represents: Science Abstracts. Section A)

I.P.A. International Pharmaceutical Abstracts

ISMEC	I S M E C Bulletin (Information Service in Mechanical Engineering) (Now: Mechanical Engineering Abstracts)
Ind.Agri.Am.Lat. Caribe	Indice Agricole de America Latina y el Caribe (Ceased)
Ind.Amer.Per. Verse	Index of American Periodical Verse
Ind.Artic.Jew. Stud.	Index of Articles on Jewish Studies
Ind.Bk.Rev.Hum.	Index to Book Reviews in the Humanities (Ceased)
Ind.Bus.Rep.	Index to Business Reports
Ind.Can.L.P.L.	Index to Canadian Legal Periodical Literature
Ind.Chem.	Index Chemicus
Ind.Child.Mag.	Subject Index to Children's Magazines (Now: Children's Magazine Guide)
Ind.Curr.Urb. Doc.	Index to Current Urban Documents
Ind.Free.Per.	Index to Free Periodicals (Ceased)
Ind.Heb.Per.	Index to Hebrew Periodicals
Ind.How To Do It	Index to How to Do It Information
Ind.Hyg.Dig.	Industrial Hygiene Digest
Ind.India	Index India
Ind.Islam.	Index Islamicus
Ind.Jew.Per.	Index to Jewish Periodicals
Ind.Lit.Amer. Indian	Index to Literature on the American Indian (Ceased)
Ind.Lit.Dent.	Indice de la Literatura Dental Periodica en Castellano
Ind.Little Mag.	Index to Little Magazines (Ceased)
Ind.Med.	Index Medicus
Ind.Med.Esp.	Indice Medico Espanol
Ind.N.Z.Per.	Index to New Zealand Periodicals (Now: Index New Zealand)
Ind.Per.Art.Relat. Law	Index to Periodical Articles Related to Law
Ind.Per.Blacks	Index to Periodical Articles by and about Blacks (Now: Index to Black Periodicals)
Ind.Per.Lit.	Index to Indian Periodical Literature (Ceased)
Ind.Per.Negroes	Index to Periodical Articles by & about Negroes (Now: Index to Black Periodicals)
Ind.Phil.Per.	Index to Philippine Periodicals
Ind.Rheum.	Annual Index of Rheumatology (Ceased)
Ind.S.A.Per.	Index to South African Periodicals
Ind.Sci.Rev.	Index to Scientific Reviews
Ind.Sel.Per.	Index to Selected Periodicals (Now: Index to Black Periodicals)
Ind.SST.	Indice Espanol de Ciencia y Tecnologia
Ind.U.S.Gov.Per.	Index to U.S. Government Periodicals (Now: U S Government Periodicals Index)
Ind.Vet.	Index Veterinarius
Indian Lib.Sci. Abstr.	Indian Library Science Abstracts
Indian Psychol. Abstr.	Indian Psychological Abstracts (Now: Indian Psychological Abstracts and Reviews)
Indian Sci.Abstr.	Indian Science Abstracts
Indian Sci.Ind.	Indian Science Index (Ceased)
Info.Media & Tech.	Information Media and Technology (Now: Information Management & Technology)
Inform.Sci.Abstr.	Information Science Abstracts
Inpharma	InPharma
Int.Abstr.Biol.Sci.	International Abstracts of Biological Sciences (Now: Current Awareness in Biological Sciences)
Int.Abstr.Oper. Res.	International Abstracts in Operations Research
Int.Aerosp.Abstr.	International Aerospace Abstracts
Int.Bibl.Soc.Sci.	International Bibliography of the Social Sciences: Anthropology, Political Science, Economics, Sociology (Ceased)
Int.Build.Serv. Abstr.	International Building Services Abstracts
Int.G.Class.Stud.	International Guide to Classical Studies (Ceased)
Int.Ind.Film Per.	International Index to Film Periodicals
Int.Lab.Doc.	International Labor Documentation
Int.Nurs.Ind.	International Nursing Index
Int.Packag.Abstr.	International Packaging Abstracts
Int.Polit.Sci.Abstr.	International Political Science Abstracts
Int.Sci.Rev.	International Science Review Series (Ceased)
Int.Z.Bibelwiss.	Internationale Zeitschriftenschau fuer Bibelwissenschaft und Grenzgebiete
InterActions Bibl.	InterActions Bibliography
Intl.Bibl.S.S.Econ.	International Bibliography of the Social Sciences: Economics
Intl.Bibl.S.S.Pol. Sci.	International Bibliography of the Social Sciences: Political Science
Intl.Bibl.S.S. Soc.Cult.Anthro.	International Bibliography of the Social Sciences: Anthropology
Intl.Civil Eng. Abstr.	International Civil Engineering Abstracts
Intl.Ind.TV.	International Index to Television Periodicals
Intl.Mgmt.Info.	International Management Information Business Digest (Ceased)
Intl.Polym.Sci.& Tech.	International Polymer Science and Technology
Iron & Steel Indus.Pr.	Iron and Steel Industry Profiles (Ceased)
Irr.& Drain.Abstr.	Irrigation & Drainage Abstracts

J

JAMA	JAMA: The Journal of the American Medical Association
JCT	Japan Computer Technology and Applications Abstracts (Ceased)

JTA — Japanese Technical Abstracts (Now: Japan Technology Series) (Ceased)

J.Cont. Quant.Meth. — Journal Contents in Quantitative Methods

J.Curr.Laser Abstr. — Journal of Current Laser Abstracts

J.of Abstr.Int. Educ. — Journal of Abstracts in International Education

J.of Econ.Abstr. (also: J.of Econ. Lit.) — Journal of Economic Abstracts (Now: Journal of Economic Literature)

J.of Ferroc. — Journal of Ferrocement

Jap.Per.Ind. — Japanese Periodicals Index (Humanities and Social Sciences Section; Medical Sciences and Pharmacology (Ceased); Science and Technology)

Jun.High Mag. Abstr. — Junior High Magazine Abstracts

K

Key to Econ.Sci. — Key to Economic Science (Ceased)

Key Word Ind. Wildl.Res. — Key Word Index of Wildlife Research

Kidney — Kidney (New York, 1992)

L

LAMP — L A M P (Literature Analysis of Microcomputer Publications)

LCR — Literary Criticism Register

LHTN — Library Hi Tech News

L.I.I. — Life Insurance Index (Ceased)

LISA — L I S A: Library & Information Science Abstracts

LJI — Legal Journals Index

L.R.I. — Legal Resource Index (Now: LegalTrac)

Lab.Haz.Bull. — Laboratory Hazards Bulletin

Landwirt. Zentralbl. — Landwirtschaftliches Zentralblatt (Now: Agroselekt) (Ceased)

Lang.& Lang. Behav.Abstr. — Language and Language Behaviour Abstracts (Now: Linguistics and Language Behavior Abstracts)

Lang.Teach.& Ling.Abstr. — Language Teaching and Linguistics Abstracts (Now: Language Teaching)

Law Ofc.Info.Svc. — Law Office Information Service

Lead Abstr. — Lead Abstracts (Now: Leadscan)

Left Ind. — Left Index

Leg.Cont. — Legal Contents (Ceased)

Leg.Info.Manage. Ind. — Legal Information Management Index

Leg.Per. — Index to Legal Periodicals

Lib.Lit. — Library Literature

Lib.Sci.Abstr. — Library Science Abstracts (Now: L I S A: Library & Information Science Abstracts)

Ling.Abstr. — Linguistics Abstracts

Lit.Automat. — Literature on Automation (Now: Excerpta Automatica)

Lod.Restr.& Tour.Ind. — Lodging, Restaurant & Tourism Index

M

MEDOC — Medoc: Index to U.S. Government Publications in the Medical and Health Sciences (Ceased)

MEDSOC — Medical Socioeconomic Research Sources (Ceased)

MELSA — MELSA Messenger (Metropolitan Library Service) (Ceased)

M.L.A. — M L A Abstracts of Articles in Scholarly Journals (Ceased)

M.M.R.I. — Multi-Media Reviews Index (Now: Media Review Digest)

Mag.Ind. — Magazine Index

Maize Abstr. — Maize Abstracts

Manage.Abstr. — Management Abstracts (India) (Now: Indian Management)

Manage.Cont. — Management Contents

Mar.Aff.Bibl. — Marine Affairs Bibliography

Mar.Sci.Cont.Tab. — Marine Science Contents Tables

Mark.Res.Abstr. — Market Research Abstracts

Mass Spectr.Bull. — Mass Spectrometry Bulletin

Mat.Sci.Cit.Ind. — Materials Science Citation Index

Math.R. — Mathematical Reviews

Med.Abstr. — Medical Abstract Service (Ceased)

Med.& Surg. Dermat. — Medical & Surgical Dermatology

Med.Care Rev. — Medical Care Review

Media Rev.Dig. — Media Review Digest

Ment.Retard. Abstr. — Mental Retardation Abstracts (Now: Developmental Disabilities Abstracts) (Ceased)

Met.Abstr. — Metallurgical Abstracts (Now: Metals Abstracts)

Met.Abstr.Ind. — Metals Abstracts Index

Met.Finish.Abstr. — Metal Finishing Abstracts (Now: Surface Treatment Technology Abstracts)

Meteor.& Geoastrophys. Abstr. — Meteorological & Geoastrophysical Abstracts

Meth.Per.Ind. — Methodist Periodical Index (Now: United Methodist Periodical Index) (Ceased)

Mgmt.& Market. Abstr. — Management & Marketing Abstracts

Mich.Mag.Ind. — Michigan Magazine Index (Ceased)

Microbiol.Abstr. — Microbiological Abstracts (Sections A, B, C)

Microcomp.Ind. — Microcomputer Index

Microcomp. Indus.Up. — Microcomputer Industry Update (Ceased)

Mid.East: Abstr. & Ind. — Middle East: Abstracts and Index

Mineral.Abstr. — Mineralogical Abstracts

Mkt.Inform. Guide — Marketing Information Guide (Ceased)

Mult.Ed.Abstr.	Multicultural Education Abstracts
Multi.Scler.Abstr.	Multiple Sclerosis Indicative Abstracts (Ceased)
Music Artic.Guide	Music Article Guide
Music Ind.	Music Index
Mycol.Abstr.	Abstracts of Mycology

N

NAA	N A A (Nordic Archaeological Abstracts)
NBA	Notiziario Bibliografico di Audiologia ORL e Foniatria
NRN	Nutrition Research Newsletter
Neurosci.Abstr.	Neurosciences Abstracts (Now: CSA Neurosciences Abstracts)
Neurosci.Cit.Ind.	Neuroscience Citation Index
New Per.Ind.	New Periodicals Index (Ceased)
New Test.Abstr.	New Testament Abstracts
Noise Pollut. Publ.Abstr.	Noise Pollution Publications Abstracts (Ceased)
Nonfer.Met.Alert	Nonferrous Metals Alert
Nucl.Sci.Abstr.	Nuclear Science Abstracts (Now INIS Atomindex)
Numis.Lit.	Numismatic Literature
Nurs.Abstr.	Nursing Abstracts
Nurs.Res.Abstr.	Nursing Research Abstracts
Nutr.Abstr.	Nutrition Abstracts & Reviews (Now: Nutrition Abstracts and Reviews Series A: Human and Experimental; Nutrition Abstracts and Reviews Series B: Livestock Feeds and Feeding)

O

Ocean.Abstr.	Oceanic Abstracts
Ocean.Abstr.Bibl.	Oceanographic Abstracts and Bibliography (Now: Oceanographic Literature Review)
Ocean.Ind.	Oceanic Index (Now: Oceanic Abstracts)
Off.Tech.	Offshore Technology
Old Test.Abstr.	Old Testament Abstracts
Oncol.Abstr.	Oncology Abstracts (Ceased)
Oper.Res. Manage.Sci.	Operations Research - Management Science
Ophthal.Lit.	Ophthalmic Literature
Oral Res.Abstr.	Oral Research Abstracts (Ceased)
Ornam.Hort.	Ornamental Horticulture
Ornithol.Abstr.	Essential Ornithological Abstracts

P

P.A.I.S.	P A I S Bulletin (Public Affairs Information Service) (Now: P A I S International in Print)
P.A.I.S.For. Lang.Ind.	Public Affairs Information Service Foreign Language Index (Now: P A I S International in Print)

PC Abstr.	P C Abstracts (Personal Computing) (Ceased)
PCC Alert	Polymers, Ceramics, Composites Alert
PCR2	P C R2 (Personal Computer Review - Squared)
PHRA	Poverty & Human Resources Abstracts (Now: Human Resources Abstracts)
P.I.R.A.	P.I.R.A. Marketing Abstracts (Packaging Industry Research Association) (Now: Management and Marketing Abstracts)
P.L.E.S.A.	Quarterly Index to Periodical Literature, Eastern and Southern Africa
P.L.I.I.	Property & Liability Insurance Index (Ceased)
P.M.I.	Photography Magazine Index (Ceased)
PMR	Popular Magazine Review (Now: Magazine Article Summaries)
P.N.I.	Pharmaceutical News Index
PROMT	Predicasts Overview of Markets and Technologies
PSI	Philanthropic Studies Index
Packag.Sci.Tech.	Packaging Science and Technology Abstracts
Paper.& Bd.Abstr.	Paper and Board Abstracts (Now: Paperbase Abstracts)
Past.Care & Couns.Abstr.	Pastoral Care & Counseling Abstracts (Now: Abstracts of Research in Pastoral Care and Counseling)
Peace Res.Abstr.	Peace Research Abstracts Journal
Per.Islam.	Periodica Islamica
Perf.Arts Biog. Master Ind.	Performing Arts Biography Master Index
Periodex	Periodex (Now: Point de Repere)
Pers.Lit.	Personnel Literature
Pers.Manage. Abstr.	Personnel Management Abstracts
Petrol.Abstr.	Petroleum Abstracts
Petrol.Energy B.N.I.	Petroleum - Energy Business News Index
Phil.Ind.	Philosopher's Index
Philip.Abstr.	Philippine Abstracts (Now: Philippine Science & Technology Abstracts)
Photo.Abstr.	Photographic Abstracts (Now: Imaging Abstracts)
Photo.Ind.	Photography Index
Phys.Ber.	Physikalische Berichte (Now: Physics Briefs - Physikalsche Berichte) (Ceased)
Phys.Ed.Ind.	Physical Education Index
Pig News & Info.	Pig News and Information
Pinpointer	Pinpointer (Ceased)
Plant Breed. Abstr.	Plant Breeding Abstracts
Plant Grow.Reg. Abstr.	Plant Growth Regulator Abstracts
Plast.Abstr.	Plastics Abstracts (Ceased)

Pol.Tech.Abstr. Polish Technical Abstracts (Now: Polish Technical and Economic Abstracts) (Ceased)

Polit.Sci.Abstr. Political Science Abstracts

Pollut.Abstr. Pollution Abstracts

Pop.Mus.Per.Ind. Popular Music Periodicals Index (Ceased)

Pop.Per.Ind. Popular Periodical Index

Popul.Ind. Population Index

Potato Abstr. Potato Abstracts

Poult.Abstr. Poultry Abstracts

Print.Abstr. Printing Abstracts

Protozool.Abstr. Protozoological Abstracts

Psychoanal. Abstr. Psychoanalysis Abstracts (Now: Psychoanalytic Abstracts)

Psychol.Abstr. Psychological Abstracts

Psychol.R.G. Psychological Reader's Guide (Ceased)

Psycho-pharmacol. Abstr. Psychopharmacology Abstracts (Ceased)

Psycscan Psycscan: Applied Psychology

Psycscan C.P. Psycscan: Clinical Psychology

Psycscan D.P. Psycscan: Developmental Psychology

Pt.de Rep. Point de Repere (Formed by the merger of Periodex and RADAR)

Pub.Admin.Abstr. Public Administration Abstracts and Index of Articles (Now: Documentation in Public Administration)

Q

Q.Abstr. Quality Abstracts (Ceased)

Qual.Contr. Appl.Stat. Quality Control and Applied Statistics

R

RADAR Repertoire Analytique d'Articles des Revues du Quebec (Now: Point de Repere)

RAPRA R A P R A Abstracts (Rubber and Plastics Research Association of Great Britain)

R.G. Readers' Guide to Periodical Literature

R.G.Abstr. Readers' Guide Abstracts

RICS R I C S Abstracts and Reviews (Now: R I C S Library Information Service Abstracts and Reviews) (Royal Institute of Chartered Surveyors)

RILA R I L A (Repertoire International de la Litterature d'Art) (Now: BHA (Bibliography of the History of Art))

RILM R I L M Abstracts of Music Literature (Repertoire International de la Litterature Musicale)

Reac. Reactions (Now: Reactions Weekly)

Ref.Pt.Food Indus.Abstr. Reference Point: Food Industry Abstracts

Ref.Sour. Reference Sources (Ceased)

Ref.Zh. Referativnyi Zhurnal

Refug.Abstr. Refugee Abstracts (Now: Refugee Survey Quarterly)

Rehabil.Lit. Rehabilitation Literature (Ceased)

Rel.& Theol. Abstr. Religious & Theological Abstracts

Rel.Ind.One Religion Index One: Periodicals

Rel.Ind.Two Religion Index Two: Multi-Author Works

Rel.Per. Index to Religious Periodical Literature (Now: Religion Index One: Periodicals)

Repindex Repindex

Res.Educ. Research in Education (Now: Resources in Education)

Res.High.Educ. Abstr. Research into Higher Education Abstracts

Resour.Ctr.Ind. Resource Center Index

Rev.Appl. Entomol. Review of Applied Entomology. Series A (Now: Review of Agricultural Entomology) Review of Applied Entomology. Series B (Now: Review of Medical and Veterinary Entomology)

Rev.Appl.Mycol. Review of Applied Mycology (Now: Review of Plant Pathology)

Rev.Med.& Vet.Mycol. Review of Medical and Veterinary Mycology

Rev.Plant Path. Review of Plant Pathology

Rheol.Abstr. Rheology Abstracts

Rice Abstr. Rice Abstracts

Risk Abstr. Risk Abstracts

Robomat. Robomatix Reporter (Now: Robotics Abstracts) (Ceased)

Rural Devel. Abstr. Rural Development Abstracts

Rural Ext.Educ.& Tr.Abstr. Rural Extension, Education and Training Abstracts (Ceased)

Rural Recreat. Tour.Abstr. Rural Recreation and Tourism Abstracts (Now: Leisure, Recreation and Tourism Abstracts)

S

SASA State Academies of Science Abstracts

S.A.Waterabstr. S.A. Waterabstracts (South Africa) (Ceased)

SCIMP S C I M P (Selective Cooperative Index of Management Periodicals) (Ceased)

SOMA School Organization & Management Abstracts

SOPODA Social Planning, Policy and Development Abstracts

SRI Statistical Reference Index

SSCI Social Sciences Citation Index

Saf.Sci.Abstr. Safety Science Abstracts Journal (Now: Health and Safety Science Abstracts)

Sage Fam.Stud. Abstr. Sage Family Studies Abstracts

Sage Pub.Admin. Abstr. Sage Public Administration Abstracts

Sage Race Rel.Abstr. — Sage Race Relations Abstracts

Sage Urb.Stud. Abstr. — Sage Urban Studies Abstracts

Sci.Cit.Ind. — Science Citation Index

Sci.Res.Abstr. — Science Research Abstracts (Now: Solid State and Superconductivity Abstracts)

Search — Search (Devon)

Seed Abstr. — Seed Abstracts

Sel.J.Water. — Selected Journals on Water (Ceased)

Sel. Water Res. Abstr. — Selected Water Resources Abstracts

Sh.& Vib.Dig. — Shock and Vibration Digest

Small Anim. Abstr. — Small Animal Abstracts (Now: Small Animals)

So.Pac.Per.Ind. — South Pacific Periodicals Index

Soc.Sci.Ind. — Social Sciences Index

Soc.Work Res.& Abstr. — Social Work Research & Abstracts (Now: Social Work Abstracts)

Sociol.Abstr. — Sociological Abstracts

Sociol.Educ. Abstr. — Sociology of Education Abstracts

Soft.Abstr.Eng. — Software Abstracts for Engineers

Soils & Fert. — Soils & Fertilizers

Solid St.Abstr. — Solid State Abstracts (Now: Solid State and Superconductivity Abstracts)

Sorghum & Millets Abstr. — Sorghum and Millets Abstracts (Now: Sorghum and Millets)

South.Bap.Per. Ind. — Southern Baptist Periodical Index (Ceased)

Soyabean Abstr. — Soyabean Abstracts

Sp.Ed.Needs Abstr. — Special Education Needs Abstracts

Speleol.Abstr. — Speleological Abstracts

Sport Fish.Abstr. — Sport Fishery Abstracts (Now: Fisheries Review)

Sports Per.Ind. — Sports Periodicals Index (Ceased)

Sportsearch — Sportsearch

Sri Lanka Sci. Ind. — Sri Lanka Science Index

Stat.Theor.Meth. Abstr. — Statistical Theory and Method Abstracts

Steels Alert — Steels Alert

Stud.Wom.Abstr. — Studies on Women Abstracts

Sugar Ind.Abstr. — Sugar Industry Abstracts

T

T.C.E.A. — Theoretical Chemical Engineering Abstracts (Now: Theoretical Chemical Engineering)

TOM — T O M (Text on Microfilm)

Tech.Educ.Abstr. — Technical Education Abstracts (Now: Technical Education & Training Abstracts)

Tel.Abstr. — Telecommunications Abstracts (Ceased)

Tel.Alert — Telecommunications Alert

Telegen — Telegen Reporter (Now: Telegen Abstracts) (Ceased)

Text.Tech.Dig. — Textile Technology Digest

Therm.Abstr. — Thermal Abstracts (Now: International Building Services Abstracts)

Tob.Abstr. — Tobacco Abstracts

Top Manage. Abstr. — Top Management Abstracts (Also see Anbar)

Tox.Abstr. — Toxicology Abstracts

Tr.& Dev.Alert — Training and Development Alert

Tr.& Indus.Ind. — Trade & Industry Index

Trans.Res.Abstr. — Transportation Research Abstracts (Ceased)

Triticale Abstr. — Triticale Abstracts (Now: Wheat, Barley and Triticale Abstracts)

Trop.Abstr. — Tropical Abstracts (Now: Abstracts or Tropical Agriculture)

Trop.Dis.Bull. — Tropical Diseases Bulletin

Trop.Oil Seeds Abstr. — Tropical Oil Seeds Abstracts (Now: Tropical Oil Seeds)

U

Urb.Aff.Abstr. — Urban Affairs Abstracts

V

Va.Hist.Abstr. — Virginia Historical Abstracts (Ceased)

Vert.File Ind. — Vertical File Index

Vet.Bull. — Veterinary Bulletin

Viol.& Abuse Abstr. — Violence & Abuse Abstracts

Virol.Abstr. — Virology Abstracts (Now: Virology and AIDS Abstracts)

Vis.Ind. — Vision Index (Ceased)

VITIS — Vitis - Viticulture and Enology Abstracts

W

W.R.C.Inf. — W.R.C. Information (Water Research Centre) (Now: Aqualine Abstracts)

Water Pollut. Abstr. — Water Pollution Abstracts (Now: Aqualine Abstracts)

Water Resour. Abstr. — Water Resources Abstracts (Now: Hydro-Abstracts)

Weed Abstr. — Weed Abstracts

Wild Life Rev. — Wildlife Review (Ceased)

Wild.Rev. — Wildlife Review (Fort Collins)

Wildlife & Conserv.Biol. Abstr. — Essential Wildlife & Conservation Biology Abstracts

Wom.Stud.Abstr. — Women Studies Abstracts

Work Rel.Abstr. — Work Related Abstracts

World Agri.Econ. & Rural Sociol. Abstr. — World Agricultural Economics & Rural Sociology Abstracts

World Alum. Abstr. — World Aluminum Abstracts

World Bank. Abstr. — World Banking Abstracts

World Bibl.Soc. Sec. — World Bibliography of Social Security

World Fish.Abstr. — World Fisheries Abstracts (Ceased)

World Surf.Coat. — World Surface Coatings Abstracts

World Text.Abstr. — World Textile Abstracts

Y

Yrbk.Assoc.Educ. & Rehab.Blind — Association for Education and Rehabilitation of the Blind and Visually Impaired. Yearbook (Ceased)

Z

Zent.Math. — Zentralblatt fuer Mathematik und ihre Grenzgebiete

Zincscan — Zincscan

Zoo.Rec. — Zoological Record

Subject Guide to Abstracting and Indexing

The 135 subject headings listed below are major subjects which contain a sub-category headed "Abstracting, Bibliographies, Statistics." This sub-category, which follows the major subject headings in the CLASSIFIED LIST OF SERIALS, identifies publications which abstract and/or index publications in the relevant subject. Bibliographies and statistical publications pertaining to the subject are also included in this sub-category. This guide will enable users to quickly locate subject areas of interest for which abstracting and indexing publications have been identified and to build profiles by combination of relevant subject areas. Page numbers refer to the first page on which the sub-category appears.

SUBJECT CATEGORY	PAGE
Advertising and Public Relations	47
Aeronautics and Space Flight	82
Agriculture	165
Alternative Medicine	293
Animal Welfare	298
Anthropology	327
Archaeology	380
Architecture	407
Art	462
Arts and Handicrafts	471
Astronomy	488
Beauty Culture	494
Beverages	514
Biography	563
Biology	615
Birth Control	828
Building and Construction	880
Business and Economics	973
Ceramics, Glass and Pottery	1661
Chemistry	1697
Children and Youth	1782
Civil Defense	1817
Classical Studies	1827
Cleaning and Dyeing	1830
Clothing Trade	1837
College and Alumni	1894
Communications	1921
Computers	2000
Conservation	2148
Consumer Education and Protection	2156
Criminology and Law Enforcement	2179
Dance	2192
Drug Abuse and Alcoholism	2202
Earth Sciences	2217
Education	2385
Electronics	2535
Energy	2561
Engineering	2624
Environmental Studies	2827
Ethnic Interests	2917
Fire Prevention	2924
Fish and Fisheries	2946
Folklore	2958
Food and Food Industries	2995
Forests and Forestry	3030
Funerals	3041
Gardening and Horticulture	3069

SUBJECT CATEGORY	PAGE
Genealogy and Heraldry	3107
Geography	3279
Gerontology and Geriatrics	3298
Handicapped	3308
Heating, Plumbing and Refrigeration	3334
History	3364
Hobbies	3519
Home Economics	3528
Homosexuality	3539
Hospitals	3557
Hotels and Restaurants	3574
Housing and Urban Planning	3599
How-to and Do-it-Yourself	3604
Humanities: Comprehensive Works	3631
Instruments	3638
Insurance	3670
Interior Design and Decoration	3683
Jewelry, Clocks and Watches	3699
Journalism	3714
Labor Unions	3732
Law	3873
Leather and Fur Industries	3962
Leisure and Recreation	3968
Library and Information Sciences	4036
Linguistics	4127
Literary and Political Reviews	4175
Literature	4291
Machinery	4348
Mathematics	4405
Matrimony	4415
Medical Sciences	4547
Meetings and Congresses	4938
Metallurgy	4980
Meteorology	4989
Metrology and Standardization	5011
Military	5054
Mines and Mining Industry	5082
Motion Pictures	5116
Museums and Art Galleries	5136
Music	5207
Numismatics	5228
Nutrition and Dietetics	5243
Occupational Health and Safety	5260
Occupations and Careers	5275

SUBJECT CATEGORY	PAGE
Oriental Studies	5296
Packaging	5305
Paints and Protective Coatings	5311
Paleontology	5319
Paper and Pulp	5328
Parapsychology and Occultism	5334
Patents, Trademarks and Copyrights	5346
Petroleum and Gas	5381
Pets	5396
Pharmacy and Pharmacology	5449
Philately	5465
Philosophy	5507
Photography	5523
Physical Fitness and Hygiene	5538
Physics	5577
Plastics	5628
Political Science	5720
Population Studies	5734
Printing	5820
Psychology	5888
Public Administration	5929
Public Health and Safety	5981
Publishing and Book Trade	6012
Real Estate	6039
Religions and Theology	6106
Rubber	6220
Sciences: Comprehensive Works	6299
Shoes and Boots	6309
Social Sciences: Comprehensive Works	6355
Social Services and Welfare	6400
Sociology	6440
Sound Recording and Reproduction	6448
Sports and Games	6493
Technology: Comprehensive Works	6671
Textile Industries and Fabrics	6690
Theater	6708
Tobacco	6712
Transportation	6735
Travel and Tourism	6928
Veterinary Science	6961
Water Resources	6982
Women's Health	6986
Women's Interests	7014
Women's Studies	7022

Subjects

ENGLISH	FRENCH	GERMAN	SPANISH
Abstracting and Indexing Services	Services d'Analyse et d'Indexage	Referate- und Indexdienste	Servicios de Extractos e Indices
Advertising and Public Relations	Publicité et Relations Publiques	Reklamewesen und Public Relations	Publicidad y Relaciones Públicas
Aeronautics and Space Flight	Aéronautique et Astronautique	Luft- und Raumfahrt	Aeronáutica y Vuelo Espacial
Computer Applications	Applications des Ordinateurs	Computer Anwendung	Aplicaciones de los Ordenadores
Agriculture	Agriculture	Landwirtschaft	Agricultura
Agricultural Economics	Agriculture Économique	Agrarökonomie	Economía Agrícola
Agricultural Equipment	Outillage Agricole	Landwirtschaftsgeräte	Aparatos Agrícolas
Computer Applications	Applications des Ordinateurs	Computer Anwendung	Aplicaciones de los Ordenadores
Crop Production and Soil	Récolte et Terre	Ernte und Acker	Producción de Cosecha, Tierra
Dairying and Dairy Products	Production Laitière	Milchwirtschaft	Lechería y Productos Lácteos
Feed, Flour and Grain	Pature, Farine et Grain	Futter, Mehl und Getreide	Forraje, Granos y Harina
Poultry and Livestock	Élevage	Geflügel- und Viehwirtschaft	Ganadería
Alternative Medicine	Médecine Alternative	Alternative Heilkunde	Medicina Alternativa
Animal Welfare	Protection des Animaux	Tierschutz	Bienestar Animal
Anthropology	Anthropologie	Anthropologie	Antropología
Antiques	Antiquités	Antiquitäten	Antigüedades
Archaeology	Archeologie	Archaeologie	Arqueología
Computer Applications	Applications des Ordinateurs	Computer Anwendung	Aplicaciones de los Ordenadores
Architecture	Architecture	Architektur	Arquitectura
Computer Applications	Applications des Ordinateurs	Computer Anwendung	Aplicaciones de los Ordenadores
Art	Art	Kunst	Arte
Computer Applications	Applications des Ordinateurs	Computer Anwendung	Aplicaciones de los Ordenadores
Arts and Handicrafts	Arts et Métiers	Kunst und Handwerk	Artes y Obras de Mano
Astrology	Astrologie	Astrologie	Astrología
Astronomy	Astronomie	Astronomie	Astronomía
Computer Applications	Applications des Ordinateurs	Computer Anwendung	Aplicaciones de los Ordenadores
Beauty Culture	Soins de Beauté	Schönheitspflege	Belleza Personal
Perfumes and Cosmetics	Parfums et Cosmétiques	Kosmetik und Parfüme	Perfumes y Cosméticos
Beverages	Boissons	Getränke	Bebidas
Bibliographies	Bibliographies	Bibliographien	Bibliografías
Biography	Biographie	Biographie	Biografía
Biology	Biologie	Biologie	Biología
Bioengineering	Biogénie	Bioingenieurwesen	Bio-ingeniería
Biological Chemistry	Chimie Biologique	Biochemie	Química Biológica
Biophysics	Biophysique	Biophysik	Biofísica
Biotechnology	Biotechnologie	Biotechnologie	Biotecnología
Botany	Botanique	Botanik	Botánica
Computer Applications	Applications des Ordinatures	Computer Anwendung	Aplicaciones de los Ordenadores
Cytology and Histology	Cytologie et Histologie	Zytologie und Histologie	Citología e Histología
Entomology	Entomologie	Entomologie	Entomología
Genetics	Génétique	Genetik	Genética
Microbiology	Microbiologie	Mikrobiologie	Microbiología
Microscopy	Microscopie	Mikroskopie	Microscopia
Ornithology	Ornithologie	Ornithologie	Ornitología
Physiology	Physiologie	Physiologie	Fisiología
Zoology	Zoologie	Zoologie	Zoología
Birth Control	Limitation des Naissances	Geburtenregelung	Reglamentación del Nacimiento
Building and Construction	Bâtiment et Construction	Bauwesen	Edificios y Construcción
Carpentry and Woodwork	Charpenterie et Menuiserie	Zimmerhandwerk und Holzbau	Carpintería y Ebanistería
Hardware	Quincaillerie	Metallbaustoffe	Ferretería
Business and Economics	Affaires et Économie	Wirtschaft und Handel	Negocios y Economía
Accounting	Comptabilité	Rechnungswesen	Contabilidad
Banking and Finance	Banque et Finance	Bank- und Finanzwesen	Bancos y Finanzas
Banking and Finance-Computer Applications	Banque et Finance-Applications des Ordinateurs	Bank- und Finanzwesen-Computer Anwendung	Bancos y Finanzas-Aplicaciones de los Ordenadores
Chamber of Commerce Publications	Publications des Chambres de Commerce	Veröffentlichungen von Handelskammern	Publicaciones de las Cámaras de Comercio
Computer Applications	Applications des Ordinateurs	Computer Anwendung	Aplicaciones de los Ordenadores
Cooperatives	Coopératives	Genossenschaften	Cooperativos
Domestic Commerce	Commerce Interieur	Binnenhandel	Comercio Interior
Economic Situation and Conditions	Situations et Conditions Économiques	Wirtschaftliche Situation und Verhältnisse	Situaciones y Condiciones Económicas
Economic Systems and Theories, Economic History	Systèmes et Théories Économiques, Histoire Économique	Ökonomische Systeme und Theorien, Wirtschaftsgeschichte	Sistemas y Teorías Económicos, Historia Económica
International Commerce	Commerce International	Aussenhandel	Comercio Internacional
International Development and Assistance	Développement et Assistance Internationaux	Internationale Entwicklungshilfe	Desarrollo y Asistencia Internacionales
Investments	Investissements	Investitionen	Inversiones
Labor and Industrial Relations	Travail et Relations Industrielles	Arbeits und Industrielle Beziehungen	Trabajo y Relaciones Industriales
Macroeconomics	Macroéconomique	Makroökonomie	Macroeconomía
Management	Gestion	Betriebsführung	Gerencia
Marketing and Purchasing	Cours et Achats	Marketing und Kauf	Compra y Venta
Office Equipment and Services	Matériel et Entretien de Bureaux	Büroeinrichtung und Service	Equipo y Servicios de Oficinas
Personnel Management	Direction de Personnel	Personal Führung	Dirección de Empleados
Production of Goods and Services	Production	Produktion	Producción
Public Finance, Taxation	Finance Publique, Impots	Staatsfinanzen, Steuerwesen	Finanza Publica, Impuestos
Small Business	Petites et Moyennes Affaires	Kleinbetrieb	Negocios Pequeños
Trade and Industrial Directories	Directoires de Commerce et d'Industrie	Firmenverzeichnisse	Directorios de Comercio e Industria

Ceramics, Glass and Pottery	Céramique, Verrerie et Poterie	Keramik, Glas und Töpferei	Cerámica, Vidrio y Porcelana
Chemistry	Chimie	Chemie	Química
Analytical Chemistry	Chimie Analytique	Analytische Chemie	Química Analítica
Computer Applications	Applications des Ordinateurs	Computer Anwendung	Aplicaciones de los Ordenadores
Crystallography	Cristallographie	Kristallographie	Cristalografía
Electrochemistry	Électrochimie	Elektrochemie	Electroquímica
Inorganic Chemistry	Chimie Inorganique	Anorganische Chemie	Química Inorganica
Organic Chemistry	Chimie Organique	Organische Chemie	Química Orgánica
Physical Chemistry	Chimie Physique	Physikalische Chemie	Fisicoquímica
Children and Youth	Enfance et Adolescence	Kinder und Jugend	Niños y Jóvenes
About	Au Sujet de	Über	Acerca
For	Pour	Für	Para
Civil Defense	Défense Civile	Ziviler Bevölkerungsschutz	Defensa Civil
Classical Studies	Études Classiques	Klassische Studien	Estudios Clásicos
Cleaning and Dyeing	Nettoyage et Teinturerie	Reinigen und Färben	Limpieza y Tintura
Clothing Trade	Vêtement	Bekleidungsgewerbe	Industria de Vestidos
Fashions	Mode	Moden	Modas
Clubs	Clubs	Klubs	Clubes
College and Alumni	Université et Diplomés	Universitäten und Hochschulabsolventen	Universidades y Exalumnos
Communications	Communications	Nachrichtentechnik	Comunicaciones
Computer Applications	Applications des Ordinateurs	Computer Anwendung	Aplicaciones de los Ordenadores
Postal Affairs	Postes	Postwesen	Correo
Radio	Radio	Rundfunk	Radio
Telephone and Telegraph	Téléphone et Télégraphe	Telephon und Telegraph	Teléfono y Telégrafo
Television and Cable	Télévision	Fernsehen und Bildfrequenzkanal	Television y Cable
Video	Vidéo	Video	Video
Computers	Ordinateurs	Computer	Ordenadores
Artificial Intelligence	Intelligence Artificielle	Künstliche Intelligenz	Inteligencia Artificial
Automation	Automation	Automatisierung	Automación
Calculating Machines	Calculateurs	Rechenmaschine	Calculadores
Circuits	Circuits	Schaltungen	Circuitos
Computer Architecture	Architecture de la Machine	Computer Architektur	Arquitectura de los Ordenadores
Computer-Assisted Instruction	Enseignement Assisté par Ordinateur	Computerunterstützter Unterricht	Instrucción con la Ayuda de Ordenador
Computer Engineering	Technique d'Ordinateur	Computerentwicklung	Ingeniería de Ordenador
Computer Games	Jeux d'Ordinateurs	Computer Spiele	Juegos de Ordenadores
Computer Graphics	Conception Assistée par Ordinateur	Computergraphik	Diseño con la Ayuda de Ordenador
Computer Industry	Industrie d'Ordinateur	Computerbetrieb	Industria de los Ordenadores
Computer Industry Directories	Annuaire de l'Industrie Ordinateur	Computerbetriebverzeichnisse	Directorios de la Industria de los Ordenadores
Computer Industry, Vocational Guidance	Industrie d'Ordinateur, Orientation Professionnelle	Computerbetrieb Berufsberatung	Industria de los Ordenadores, Gobierno Práctico
Computer Music	Musique d'Ordinateur	Computer Musik	Música de Ordenadores
Computer Networks	Reseaux d'Ordinateurs	Rechnernetz	Red para Transmisión de Datos
Computer Programming	Programme Machine	Computerprogrammierung	Programación de Ordenadores
Computer Sales	Ventes des Ordinateurs	Computervertrieb	Ventas de Ordenadores
Computer Security	Protection des Ordinateurs	Computersicherheit	Protección de los Ordenadores
Computer Simulation	Simulation des Ordinateurs	Computersimulation	Simulación por Ordenador
Computer Systems	Systèmes des Ordinateurs	Computersystemen	Sistemas de los Ordenadores
Cybernetics	Cybernetiques	Kybernetik	Cibernética
Data Base Management	Gestion de Base de Données	Datenbankverwaltung	Datos de Comunicación
Data Communications, Data Transmission Systems	Données de Communication	Datenübertragung, Datenübertragungssystem	Gestión de Banco de Datos
Electronic Data Processing	Traitement de l'Information Électronique	Elektronische Datenverarbeitung	Proceso de Datos Electrónicos
Hardware	Materiel	Hardware	Equipo Físico
Information Science, Information Theory	Théorie de l'Information	Informationstheorie	Ciencia, Teoría de la Información
Machine Theory	Théorie de Machine	Maschinetheorie	Teoría de la Maquina
Microcomputers	Micro-Ordinateurs	Mikrocomputer	Microordenadores
Minicomputers	Mini-Ordinateurs	Minicomputer	Miniordenadores
Personal Computers	Ordinateurs Privés	Persönlichecomputer	Ordenadores Personales
Robotics	Robotique	Robotersysteme	Robótica
Software	Logiciel	Software	Soporte Lógico
Theory of Computing	Théorie de Traitement	Computertheorie	Theoría de Cálculo
Word Processing	Traitement de Textes	Textverarbeitung	Tratamiento de Textos
Conservation	Conservation	Landschaftsschutz	Conservación
Consumer Education and Protection	Protection de Consommateur	Verbraucherswirtschaftsschutz	Protección del Consumidor
Criminology and Law Enforcement	Criminologie et Police	Kriminologie und Strafvollzug	Criminología y Acción Policial
Computer Applications	Applications des Ordinateurs	Computer Anwendung	Aplicaciones de los Ordenadores
Security	Securité	Sicherheit	Seguridad
Dance	Danse	Tanz	Baile
Drug Abuse and Alcoholism	Toxicomanie et Alcoolisme	Rauschgiftsucht und Alkoholismus	Drogadismo y Alcoholismo
Earth Sciences	Sciences Géologiques	Wissenschaften der Erde	Ciencias Geológicas
Computer Applications	Applications des Ordinateurs	Computer Anwendung	Aplicaciones de los Ordenadores
Geology	Géologie	Geologie	Geología
Geophysics	Géophysique	Geophysik	Geofísica
Hydrology	Hydrologie	Hydrologie	Hidrología
Oceanography	Océanographie	Ozeanographie	Oceanografía
Education	Éducation	Bildungswesen	Educación
Adult Education	Enseignement des Adultes	Erwachsenenbildung	Enseñanza de Adultos
Computer Applications	Applications des Ordinateurs	Computer Anwendung	Aplicaciones de los Ordenadores
Guides to Schools and Colleges	Guides d'Écoles et Colleges	Führer zur Schulen und Universitäten	Guías de Escuelas y Colegios
Higher Education	Enseignement Supérieur	Hochschulwesen	Enseñanza Superior
International Education Programs	Programmes d'Éducation Internationale	Internazionale Erziehungsprogramme	Programas de Enseñanza Internacional
School Organization and Administration	Organisation et Administration de l'École	Organisation und Verwaltung von dem Schule	Administración y Dirección de la Escuela
Special Education and Rehabilitation	Enseignement Special et Réhabilitation	Fachunterricht und Rehabilitierung	Enseñanza Especial y Rehabilitación
Teaching Methods and Curriculum	Méthodes Pédagogiques et Programmes Scolaires	Lehrmethoden und Lehrplan	Métodos de Enseñanza y Planes de Estudios

Electronics	Électronique	Elektronik	Electrónicos
Computer Applications	Applications des Ordinateurs	Computer Anwendung	Aplicaciones de los Ordenadores
Encyclopedias and General Almanacs	Encyclopédies et Almanachs Générales	Enzyklopädien und Allgemeine Nachschlagewerke	Enciclopedias y Almanaques Generales
Energy	Énergie	Energie	Energía
Computer Applications	Applications des Ordinateurs	Computer Anwendung	Aplicaciones de los Ordenadores
Electrical Energy	Énergie Électrique	Elektrizitätsenergie	Energía Eléctrica
Geothermal Energy	Énergie Géothermique	Thermalenergie	Energía Geotérmica
Hydroelectrical Energy	Énergie Hydraulique	Hydroelektroenergie	Energía Hidroeléctrica
Nuclear Energy	Énergie Nucléaire	Kernenergie	Energía Nuclear
Solar Energy	Énergie Solaire	Sonnenenergie	Energía Solar
Wind Energy	Énergie à Vent	Windenergie	Energía de Viento
Engineering	Génie	Ingenieurwesen	Ingeniería
Chemical Engineering	Génie Chimique	Chemieingenieurwesen	Ingeniería Química
Civil Engineering	Génie Civil	Bauingenieurwesen	Ingeniería Civil
Computer Applications	Applications des Ordinateurs	Computer Anwendung	Aplicaciones de los Ordenadores
Electrical Engineering	Génie Électrique	Elektrotechnik	Ingeniería Eléctrica
Engineering Mechanics and Materials	Méchanique de Génie et Materiels	Ingenieurwesen Mechanik und Materialien	Mecanica de Ingeniería y Materiales
Hydraulic Engineering	Génie Hydraulique	Wasserbau	Ingeniería Hidráulica
Industrial Engineering	Génie Industriel	Industrieingenieurwesen	Ingeniería Industrial
Mechanical Engineering	Génie Mécanique	Maschinenbau	Ingeniería Mecánica
Environmental Studies	Science de l'Environnement	Umweltschutz	Ciencias Ecológias
Computer Applications	Applications des Ordinateurs	Computer Anwendung	Aplicaciones de los Ordenadores
Pollution	Pollution	Umweltverschmutzung	Contaminación
Toxicology and Environmental Safety	Toxicologie et Sécurité de l'Environnement	Toxokologie und Umweltsicherheit	Toxicología y Seguridad Ambiental
Waste Management	Gestion de Déchets	Abfallwirtschaft	Manejo de la Basura
Ethnic Interests	Publications de l'Orientation Ethnique	Allgemeine Völkerkunde	Publicaciones de Temas Etnicos
Fire Prevention	Précaution contre l'Incendie	Brandbekämpfung	Prevención del Fuego
Fish and Fisheries	Poisson et Pêche	Fische und Fischerei	Pesca y Pesquerías
Folklore	Folklore	Volkskunde	Folklore
Food and Food Industries	Alimentation et Industries Alimentaires	Nahrungsmittel und Lebensmittel-industrie	Alimentos e Industrias Alimenticias
Bakers and Confectioners	Boulangerie et Confiserie	Bäcker- und Konditorgewerbe	Panaderías y Dulcerías
Grocery Trade	Épicerie	Kolonialwarenhandel	Abacerías
Forest and Forestry	Forêts et Exploitation Forestiére	Forstwesen und Waldwirtschaft	Bosques y Selvicultura
Lumber and Wood	Bois	Holz	Maderas
Funerals	Funérailles	Beerdigungen	Funerales
Gardening and Horticulture	Jardinage et Horticulture	Gartenpflege und Gartenbau	Jardinería y Horticultura
Florist Trade	Commerce des Fleurs	Blumenhandel	Floristas
Genealogy and Heraldry	Généalogie et Science Héraldique	Genealogie und Wappenkunde	Genealogía y Heráldica
Computer Applications	Applications des Ordinateurs	Computer Anwendung	Aplicaciones de los Ordenadores
General Interest Periodicals (Subdivided by country)	Publications d'Intérêt Général (Selon pays)	Allgemeine Zeitschriften (nach Land)	Periódicos de Interés General (por país)
Geography	Géographie	Geographie	Geografía
Computer Applications	Applications de Ordinateurs	Computer Anwendung	Aplicaciones de los Ordenadores
Gerontology and Geriatrics	Gérontologie	Gerontologie	Gerontología y Geriátrica
Giftware and Toys	Cadeaux et Jouets	Geschenkartikel und Spielwaren	Regalos y Juguetes
Handicapped	Handicapés	Behinderung	Desventajados
Computer Applications	Applications des Ordinateurs	Computer Anwendung	Aplicaciones de los Ordenadores
Hearing Impaired	Sourds	Schwerhörigkeit	Debilitado del Oído
Physically Impaired	Handicapés Physique	Körperbehinderung	Debilitado Físicamente
Visually Impaired	Aveugles	Blindheit	Debilitado Visualmente
Heating, Plumbing, and Refrigeration	Chauffage, Plomberie et Réfrigeration	Heizung, Kühlung und Installation	Calefacción, Plomería y Refrigeración
History	Histoire	Geschichte	Historia
Computer Applications	Applications des Ordinateurs	Computer Anwendung	Aplicaciones de los Ordenadores
History of Africa	Histoire de l'Afrique	Geschichte-Afrika	Historia de Africa
History of Asia	Histoire de l'Asie	Geschichte-Asien	Historia de Asia
History of Australasia and Other Areas	Histoire de l'Australasie et Autre Pays	Geschichte-Australasien und Andere Gebieten	Historia de Australasia y Otras Areas
History of Europe	Histoire de l'Europe	Geschichte-Europa	Historia de la Europa
History of North and South America	Histoire de l'Amérique du Nord et du Sud	Geschichte-Nord- und Südamerika	Historia de la América del Norte y de la del Sur
History of Near East	Histoire du Proche-Orient	Geschichte-Nahe Osten	Historia del Cercano Oriente
Hobbies	Passe-Temps	Hobbies	Pasatiempos
Home Economics	Enseignement Ménager	Hauswirtschaft	Economía Doméstica
Homosexuality	Homosexualisme	Homosexualität	Homosexualismo
Hospitals	Hôpitaux	Krankenhäuser	Hospitales
Computer Applications	Applications des Ordinateurs	Computer Anwendung	Aplicaciones de los Ordenadores
Hotels and Restaurants	Hôtels et Restaurants	Hotels und Restaurants	Hoteles y Restaurantes
Computer Applications	Applications des Ordinateurs	Computer Anwendung	Aplicaciones de los Ordenadores
Housing and Urban Planning	Logement et Urbanisme	Wohnungswesen und Stadtplanung	Viviendas y Urbanismo
Computer Applications	Applications des Ordinateurs	Computer Anwendung	Aplicaciones de los Ordenadores
How-To and Do-It-Yourself	Bricolage	Selbstanfertigung	Cómo Hacerlo y Hágalo Si Mismo
Humanities: Comprehensive Works	Humanités: Oeuvres Compréhensives	Klassische Philologie	Humanidades: Obras Comprensivas
Computer Applications	Applications des Ordinateurs	Computer Anwendung	Aplicaciones de los Ordenadores
Instruments	Instruments	Instrumente	Instrumentos
Insurance	Assurances	Versicherungswesen	Seguros
Computer Applications	Applications des Ordinateurs	Computer Anwendung	Aplicaciones de los Ordenadores
Interior Design and Decoration	Agencements Intérieurs et Décoration	Innenarchitektur und Innenausstattung	Diseño del Interior y Ornamentación
Furniture and House Furnishings	Meubles et Articles pour la Maison	Möbel und Wohnungseinrichtung	Muebles y Articulos para el Hogar
Jewelry, Clocks and Watches	Bijouterie et Horlogerie	Schmuck und Uhren	Joyería y Relojería
Journalism	Journalisme	Journalismus	Periodismo

Labor Unions	Syndicalisme	Gewerkschaften	Sindicatos
Law	Droit	Rechtswissenschaft	Derecho
Civil Law	Droit Civil	Zivilrecht	Derecho Civil
Computer Applications	Applications des Ordinateurs	Computer Anwendung	Aplicaciones de los Ordenadores
Constitutional Law	Droit Constitutionel	Verfassungsrecht	Derecho Constitucional
Corporate Law	Droit Commercial	Handelsrecht	Derecho Corporativo
Criminal Law	Droit Pénal	Strafrecht	Derecho Criminal
Estate Planning	Succession	Mobiliarvermögensrecht	Planificación de los Bienes
Family and Matrimonial Law	Droit Familial et Matrimonial	Ehegesetz und Familienrecht	Derecho Familial y Matrimonial
International Law	Droit International	Völkerrecht	Derecho Internacional
Judicial Systems	Système Judiciaire	Gerichtswesen	Sistemas Judiciales
Legal Aid	Assistance Judiciaire	Rechtshilfe	Ayuda Legal
Maritime Law	Droit Maritime	Seerecht	Derecho Marítimo
Military Law	Droit Militaire	Kriegsrecht	Derecho Militar
Leather and Fur Industries	Maroquinerie et Pelleterie	Leder und Pelz	Pieles y Cuero
Leisure and Recreation	Loisirs et Récréation	Freizeit und Unterhaltung	Ocio y Recreo
Library and Information Science	Bibliothéconomie et Informatique	Bibliothek- und Informationswissenschaft	Bibliotecología y Ciencia de la Información
Computer Applications	Applications des Ordinateurs	Computer Anwendung	Aplicaciones de los Ordenadores
Linguistics	Lingistique	Sprachwissenschaft	Lingüística
Computer Applications	Applications des Ordinateurs	Computer Anwendung	Aplicaciones de los Ordenadores
Literary and Political Reviews	Revues Littéraires et Politiques	Literarische und Politische Zeitschriften	Revistas Literarias y Políticas
Literature	Littérature	Literatur	Literatura
Adventure and Romance	Aventure et Romance	Abenteuer und Romantik	Aventura y Romance
Mystery and Detective	Mystère et Policier	Geheimnis und Detektivroman	Misterio y Detective
Poetry	Poésie	Poesie	Poesía
Science Fiction, Fantasy, Horror	Science-Fiction, Oeuvres Fantaisiste, Oeuvre d'Epouvante	Zukunftsroman, Phantasiegebilde, Grausen	Ciencie Ficción, Fantasía, Horror
Machinery	Machines	Maschinenwesen	Maquinaria
Computer Applications	Applications des Ordinateurs	Computer Anwendung	Aplicaciones de los Ordenadores
Mathematics	Mathématiques	Mathematik	Matemática
Computer Applications	Applications des Ordinateurs	Computer Anwendung	Aplicaciones de los Ordenadores
Matrimony	Mariage	Ehestand	Matrimonio
Computer Applications	Applications des Ordinateurs	Computer Anwendung	Aplicaciones de los Ordenadores
Medical Sciences	Sciences Médicales	Medizinische Wissenschaften	Ciencias Médicas
Allergology and Immunology	Allergologie et Immunologie	Allergie und Immunologie	Alergología e Imunología
Anaesthesiology	Anesthésiologie	Anaesthesiology	Anestesiología
Cardiovascular Diseases	Maladies Cardiovasculaires	Kreislauferkrankungen	Enfermedades Cardiovasculares
Chiropractic, Homeopathy, Osteopathy	Chiropraxie, Homéopathie, Ostéopathie	Chiropraktik, Homöopathie, Osteopathie	Quiropráctica, Homeopatía, Osteopatía
Communicable Diseases	Maladies Contagieuses	Infektiöse Krankheiten	Enfermedades Contagiosas
Computer Applications	Applications des Ordinateurs	Computer Anwendung	Aplicaciones de los Ordenadores
Dentistry	Dentisterie	Zahnmedizin	Dentistería
Dermatology and Venereology	Dermatologie et Maladies Vénériennes	Dermatologie und Geschlechtskrankheiten	Dermatología y Venereología
Endocrinology	Endocrinologie	Endokrinologie	Endocrinología
Experimental Medicine Laboratory Technique	Médecine Expérimentale, Techniques de Laboratoire	Versuchsmedizin, Laboratoriumstechnik	Medicina Experimental, Técnicas del Laboratorio
Forensic Sciences	Médecine Légale	Gerichtliche Medizin	Ciencias Forenses
Gastroenterology	Gastroentérologie	Gastroenterologie	Gastroenterología
Hematology	Hématologie	Hämatologie	Hematología
Hypnosis	Hypnose	Hypnose	Hipnotismo
Internal Medicine	Médecine Interne	Innere Medizin	Medicina Interna
Nurses and Nursing	Personnel et Soins Infirmiers	Krankenpflege	Enfermeros y Enfermería
Obstetrics and Gynecology	Obstétrique et Gynécologie	Gynäkologie und Geburtshilfe	Obstetricia y Ginecología
Oncology	Cancer	Onkologie	Oncología
Ophthalmology and Optometry	Ophtalmologie et Optométrie	Opthalmologie und Optometrie	Oftalmología y Optometría
Orthopedics and Traumatology	Orthopédie et Traumatologie	Orthopädie und Traumatologie	Ortopedia y Traumatología
Otorhinolaryngology	Otorhinolaryngologie	Otorhinolaryngologie	Otorrinolaringología
Pediatrics	Pédiatrie	Pädiatrie	Pediatría
Physical Medicine and Rehabilitation	Médecine Physique et Réhabilitation	Physikalische Heilkunde und Rehabilitation	Medicina Física y Rehabilitación
Psychiatry and Neurology	Psychiatrie et Neurologie	Psychiatrie und Neurologie	Psiquiatría y Neurología
Radiology and Nuclear Medicine	Radiologie et Médecine Nucléaire	Radiologie und Nuklearmedizin	Radiología y Medicina Nuclear
Respiratory Diseases	Maladies Respiratoires	Atmungskrankheiten	Enfermedades Respiratorias
Rheumatology	Rhumatologie	Rheumatologie	Reumatología
Sports Medicine	Médecine du Sport	Sportmedizin	Medicina de Deportes
Surgery	Chirurgie	Chirurgie	Cirugía
Urology and Nephrology	Urologie et Néphrologie	Urologie und Nephrologie	Urología y Nefrología
Meetings and Congresses	Réunions et Congrès	Tagungen und Kongresse	Conferencias y Congresos
Men's Health	Santé de l'Homme	Gesundheit von Männern	Salud Masculina
Men's Interests	Publications d'Intérêt Masculin	Männer Interessen	Intereses Masculinos
Men's Studies	Études de l'Homme	Männerstudien	Estudios de los Hombres
Metallurgy	Métallurgie	Metallurgie	Metalurgia
Computer Applications	Applications des Ordinateurs	Computer Anwendung	Aplicaciones de los Ordenadores
Welding	Soudure	Schweissen	Soldadura
Meteorology	Météorologie	Meteorologie	Meteorología
Computer Applications	Applications des Ordinateurs	Computer Anwendung	Aplicaciones de los Ordenadores
Metrology and Standardization	Métrologie et Standardisation	Mass- und Gewichtskunde, Normung	Metrología y Normalización
Computer Applications	Applications des Ordinateurs	Computer Anwendung	Aplicaciones de los Ordenadores
Military	Militaires	Militärwesen	Militares
Mines and Mining Industry	Mines et Resources Minières	Bergwesen und Bergbauindustrie	Mines y Minerales
Computer Applications	Applications des Ordinateurs	Computer Anwendung	Aplicaciones de los Ordenadores
Motion Pictures	Cinéma	Film und Kino	Películas
Museums and Art Galleries	Musées et Galleries	Museen und Kunstgalerien	Museos y Galerías del Arte
Music	Musique	Musik	Música
Computer Applications	Applications des Ordinateurs	Computer Anwendung	Aplicaciones de los Ordenadores
Needlework	Travaux d'Aiguille	Näherei	Bordado
New Age	Nouvelle Ere	New Age	Nueva Epoca
Numismatics	Numismatique	Numismatik	Numismática
Nutrition and Dietetics	Nutrition et Diététique	Ernährung und Diätetik	Nutrición y Dietética
Occupational Health and Safety	Médecine du Travail et Prévention	Berufsgesundheitspflege und Sicherheit	Sanidad y Seguridad de Oficio
Occupations and Careers	Occupations et Carrières	Berufe	Empleos y Ocupaciones
Oriental Studies	Études Orientales	Orientalistik	Estudios Orientales

Packaging	Emballage	Verpackung	Empaque
Computer Applications	Applications des Ordinateurs	Computer Anwendung	Aplicaciones de los Ordenadores
Paints and Protective Coatings	Couleurs et Peintures	Farben und Beläge	Pinturas y Revestimientos Protectores
Paleontology	Paléontologie	Paleontologie	Paleontología
Computer Applications	Applications des Ordinateurs	Computer Anwendung	Aplicaciones de los Ordenadores
Paper and Pulp	Papier et Pulpe	Papier und Papierstoff	Papel y Pasta
Parapsychology and Occultism	Parapsychologie et Occultisme	Parapsychologie und Okkultismus	Parapsicología y Ocultismo
Patents, Trademarks and Copyrights	Brevets, Marques de Fabrique et Droits d'Auteur	Patente, Schutzmarken und Urheberrechte	Patentes, Marcas de Fabrica y Derechos de Autor
Petroleum and Gas	Pétrole et Gas Naturel	Petroleum und Gas	Petróleo y Gas Natural
Computer Applications	Applications des Ordinateurs	Computer Anwendung	Aplicaciones de los Ordenadores
Pets	Animaux Familiers	Haustiere	Animales Domésticos
Pharmacy and Pharmacology	Pharmacie et Pharmacologie	Pharmazie und Pharmakologie	Farmacia y Farmacología
Computer Applications	Applications des Ordinateurs	Computer Anwendung	Aplicaciones de los Ordenadores
Philately	Philatélie	Briefmarkenkunde	Filatelia
Philosophy	Philosophie	Philosophie	Filosofía
Photography	Photographie	Photographie	Fotografía
Computer Applications	Applications des Ordinateurs	Computer Anwendung	Aplicaciones de los Ordenadores
Physical Fitness and Hygiene	Santé Physique et Hygiène	Gesundheitszustand und Hygiene	Salud Física e Higiene
Physics	Physique	Physik	Física
Computer Applications	Applications des Ordinateurs	Computer Anwendung	Aplicaciones de los Ordenadores
Electricity	Électricité	Élektrizität	Electricidad
Heat	Chaleur	Wärme	Calor
Mechanics	Mécanique	Mechanik	Mecánica
Nuclear Physics	Physique Nucléaire	Kernphysik	Física Nuclear
Optics	Optique	Optik	Optica
Sound	Son	Schall	Sonido
Plastics	Plastiques	Kunststoffe	Plásticos
Computer Applications	Applications des Ordinateurs	Computer Anwendung	Aplicaciones de los Ordenadores
Political Science	Sciences Politiques	Politische Wissenschafte	Ciencias Políticas
Civil Rights	Droits Civiques	Bürgerrechte	Derechos Civiles
International Relations	Relations Internationales	Internationale Beziehungen	Relaciones Internacionales
Population Studies	Démographie	Bevölkerungswissenschaft	Demografía
Printing	Imprimerie	Druck	Imprenta
Computer Applications	Applications des Ordinateurs	Computer Anwendung	Aplicaciones de los Ordenadores
Psychology	Psychologie	Psychologie	Psicología
Public Administration	Administration Publique	Öffentliche Verwaltung	Administración Pública
Computer Applications	Applications des Ordinateurs	Computer Anwendung	Aplicaciones de los Ordenadores
Municipal Government	Gouvernement Municipal	Kommunalverwaltung	Gobierno Municipal
Public Health and Safety	Santé Publique et Prévention	Öffentliche Gesundheitspflege	Salud Pública y Seguridad
Publishing and Book Trade	Édition et Commerce du Livre	Verlagswesen und Buchhandel	Editoriales y Libreria
Computer Applications	Applications des Ordinateurs	Computer Anwendung	Aplicaciones de los Ordenadores
Real Estate	Immobilièrs	Grundbesitz und Immobilien	Bienes Raíces
Computer Applications	Applications des Ordinateurs	Computer Anwendung	Aplicaciones de los Ordenadores
Religions and Theology	Religions et Théologie	Religion and Theologie	Religión y Teología
Buddhist	Bouddhisme	Buddhist	Budista
Eastern Orthodox	Églises Orthodoxes	Orthodox	Ortodoxo Oriental
Hindu	Hindou	Hindu	Hindú
Islamic	Islamique	Islamische	Islámico
Judaic	Judaïque	Jüdäistische	Judaico
Protestant	Protestant	Evangelische	Protestante
Roman Catholic	Catholique Romain	Römisch-katholische	Católico Romano
Other Denominations and Sects	Autres Sectes	Andere Bekenntnisse und Sekte	Otras Denominaciones y Sectas
Rubber	Caoutchouc	Gummi	Caucho
Computer Applications	Applications des Ordinateurs	Computer Anwendung	Aplicaciones de los Ordenadores
Sciences: Comprehensive Works	Sciences: Oeuvres Compréhensives	Wissenschaften: Umfassende Werke	Ciencias: Obras Comprensivas
Computer Applications	Applications des Ordinateurs	Computer Anwendung	Aplicaciones de los Ordenadores
Shoes and Boots	Chaussures et Bottes	Schuhe und Stiefel	Zapatos y Botas
Singles' Interests and Lifestyles	Intérêts et Style de Vie Célibataire	Ledigenstandinteressen	Intereses y Estilos de Vivir de los Solteros
Social Sciences: Comprehensive Works	Sciences Sociales: Oeuvres Compréhensives	Sozialwissenschaften: Umfassende Werke	Ciencias Sociales: Obras Comprensivas
Social Service and Welfare	Service Social et Protection Sociale	Sozialpflege und Fürsorge	Asistencia Social y Bienestar
Sociology	Sociologie	Soziologie	Sociología
Computer Applications	Applications des Ordinateurs	Computer Anwendung	Aplicaciones de los Ordenadores
Sound Recording and Reproduction	Enregistrement et Reproduction du Son	Tonaufnahme und Tonwiedergabe	Grabaciones y Reproducciones Sonoras
Computer Applications	Applications des Ordinateurs	Computer Anwendung	Aplicaciones de los Ordenadores
Sports and Games	Sports et Jeux	Sport und Spiele	Deportes y Juegos
Ball Games	Jeux de Balle	Ballspiele	Juegos de Pelota
Bicycles and Motorcycles	Bicyclettes et Motocyclettes	Fahrräder und Motorräder	Bicicletas y Motocicletas
Boats and Boating	Bateaux et Canotage	Boote und Bootfahren	Botes y Bartelaje
Horses and Horsemanship	Equitation	Pferde und Reitsport	Caballos y Equitación
Outdoor Life	Vie en Plein Air	Im Freien	Vida de Campo
Statistics	Statistique	Statistik	Estadísticas
Technology: Comprehensive Works	Technologie: Oeuvres Compréhensives	Technologie: Umfassende Werke	Tecnología: Obras Comprensivas
Textile Industries and Fabrics	Textiles	Textil	Textiles y Telas
Computer Applications	Applications des Ordinateurs	Computer Anwendung	Aplicaciones de los Ordenadores
Theater	Théâtre	Theater	Teatro
Tobacco	Tabac	Tabak	Tabaco
Transportation	Transports	Transport	Transportación
Air Transport	Transport Aérien	Luftverkehr	Transporte Aéreo
Automobiles	Automobiles	Kraftfahrzeugen	Automóviles
Computer Applications	Applications des Ordinateurs	Computer Anwendung	Aplicaciones de los Ordenadores
Railroads	Chemins de Fer	Eisenbahnen	Ferrocarriles
Roads and Traffic	Routes et Circulation	Strassen und Strassenverkehr	Caminos y Tráfico
Ships and Shipping	Navires et Transport Maritimes	Schiffe und Schiffahrt	Barcos y Embarques
Trucks and Trucking	Transports Routiers	Lastkraftwagen	Camiones
Travel and Tourism	Voyages et Tourisme	Reisen und Tourismus	Viaje y Turismo
Airline Inflight and Hotel Inroom	Revues de Vol de Lignes Aériennes et de Chambres d'Hôtels	Fluggesellschaft und Hotel Veröffentlichungen	Aerolínea en-Vuelo y Hotel en-Cuarto
Veterinary Sciences	Science Vétérinaire	Tierheilkunde	Veterinaria
Computer Applications	Applications des Ordinateurs	Computer Anwendung	Aplicaciones de los Ordenadores
Water Resources	Ressources de l'Eau	Wasserwirtschaft	Recursos de Aqua
Computer Applications	Applications des Ordinateurs	Computer Anwendung	Aplicaciones de los Ordenadores
Women's Health	Santé de la Femme	Gesundheit von Frauen	Salud Feminina
Women's Interests	Publications d'Intérêt Féminin	Fraueninteresse	Intereses Femininas
Women's Studies	Études de la Femme	Frauenstudien	Estudios de las Mujeres

Refereed Serials

A A C N CLINICAL ISSUES.
Lippincott - Raven Publishers 227 E. Washington Sq., Philadelphia, PA 19106. TEL 215-238-4200. *4416*

A A C N NURSING SCAN IN CRITICAL CARE.
Nursecom Inc., 1211 Locust St., Philadelphia, PA 19107. TEL 215-545-7222. FAX 215-545-8107. *4547*

A A M A EXECUTIVE.
American Academy of Medical Administrators, 30555 Southfield Rd., Ste. 150, Southfield, MI 48076. TEL 810-540-4310. FAX 810-645-0590. *4416*

A A P G BULLETIN.
American Association of Petroleum Geologists, Box 979, Tulsa, OK 74101. TEL 918-584-2555. FAX 918-584-0469. *5348*

A A P G STUDIES IN GEOLOGY SERIES.
American Association of Petroleum Geologists, Box 979, Tulsa, OK 74101. TEL 918-584-2555. *5348*

A A P P O JOURNAL.
Health Care Communications, Inc., 1 Bridge Plaza, Fort Lee, NJ 07024. TEL 201-947-5545. FAX 201-947-8406. *890*

A A S HISTORY SERIES.
Univelt, Inc., Box 28130, San Diego, CA 92198-0198. TEL 619-746-4005. FAX 619-746-3139. *50*

A A T T NEWSLETTER.
American Association of Teachers of Turkic Languages, Near Eastern Studies Department, NES 110 Jones Hall, Princeton University, Princeton, NJ 08544-1008. TEL 609-285-1435. FAX 609-258-1242. *2449*

A A V S O BULLETIN: PREDICTED DATES OF MAXIMA AND MINIMA OF LONG PERIOD VARIABLE STARS.
American Association of Variable Star Observers, 25 Birch St., Cambridge, MA 02138. TEL 617-354-0484. *473*

A A V S O REPORTS AND MONOGRAPHS.
American Association of Variable Star Observers, 25 Birch St., Cambridge, MA 02138. TEL 617-354-0484. *474*

A - B: AUTO - BIOGRAPHY STUDIES.
University of Kansas, Joyce & Elizabeth Hall Center for the Humanities, Lawrence, KS 66045-2967. *554*

A B N F JOURNAL.
Tucker Publications, Inc., Box 580, Lisle, IL 60532. TEL 708-969-3809. FAX 708-969-3895. *4708*

A C C CURRENT JOURNAL REVIEW.
Elsevier Science Inc., Box 945, New York, NY 10159-0945. TEL 212-633-3730. FAX 212-633-3680. *4547*

A C M MONOGRAPH SERIES.
Academic Press, Inc., 525 B St., Ste. 1900, San Diego, CA 92101-4495. TEL 619-231-0926. FAX 619-699-6715. *1981*

A C O G CLINICAL REVIEW.
Elsevier Science Inc., Box 945, New York, NY 10159-0945. TEL 212-633-3730. FAX 212-633-3680. *4548*

A C S SYMPOSIUM SERIES.
American Chemical Society, 1155 16th St. N.W., Washington, DC 20036. TEL 800-227-5558. FAX 202-872-4615. *1662*

A D M.
Asociacion Dental Mexicana, A.C., Ezequiel Montes No. 92, Col. Revolucion, Delegacion Cuauhtemoc, Mexico, D.F. 06030, Mexico. TEL 52-5-29400095. FAX 52-5-2945143. *4633*

A E J M C NEWS.
Association for Education in Journalism and Mass Communications, 1621 College St., University of South Carolina, Columbia, SC 29208-0251. TEL 803-777-2005. *3699*

A.F.F.H.O. NEWSLETTER.
Australasian Federation of Family History Organisations, 6-48 May St., Bayswater, W.A. 6053, Australia. FAX 61-2-2714311. *3072*

A F I P ATLAS OF RADIOLOGIC-PATHOLOGIC CORRELATION.
Armed Forces Institute of Pathology, 6825 16th St., N.W., Washington, DC 20306-6000. *4416*

A G A R D REPORTS.
U.S. National Aeronautics and Space Administration, National Technology Transfer Center, c/o Wheeling Jesuit University, 316 Washignton Ave., Wheeling, WV 26003. TEL 304-243-2440. FAX 304-243-4390. *51*

A G S O JOURNAL OF AUSTRALIAN GEOLOGY AND GEOPHYSICS.
Australian Geolcgical Survey Organisation, G.P.O. Box 378, Canberra, A.C.T. 2601, Australia. TEL 61-6-2499519. FAX 61-6-2499982. *2222*

A H A F JOURNAL.
American Handwriting Analysis Foundation, Box 6210, San Jose, CA 95150. TEL 804-979-2848. *2309*

A I A A JOURNAL.
American Institute of Aeronautics and Astronautics, Inc., 370 L'Enfant Promenade, S.W., Washington, DC 20024. TEL 202-646-7400. *51*

A I APPLICATIONS.
University of Idaho, Box 3066, Moscow, ID 83843. TEL 208-885-7033. FAX 208-885-6226. *2832*

A I C C M BULLETIN.
Australian Institute for the Conservation of Cultural Material, Inc., P.O. Box 1638, Canberra, A.C.T. 2601, Australia. TEL 06-243-4531. FAX 06-243-4531. *408*

A.I.CH.E. EQUIPMENT TESTING PROCEDURES.
American Institute of Chemical Engineers, 345 E. 47th St., New York, NY 10017. TEL 212-705-7657. FAX 212-705-8400. *2631*

A.I.CH.E. JOURNAL.
American Institute of Chemical Engineers, 345 E. 47th St., New York, NY 10017. TEL 212-705-7563. FAX 212-752-3294. *2631*

A I CH E M I MODULAR INSTRUCTION. SERIES A: PROCESS CONTROL.
American Institute of Chemical Engineers, 345 E. 47th St., New York, NY 100.7. TEL 212-705-7657. FAX 212-705-8400. *2631*

A I CH E M I MODULAR INSTRUCTION. SERIES C: TRANSPORT.
American Institute of Chemical Engineers, 345 E. 47th St., New York, NY 10017. TEL 212-705-7657. FAX 212-752-3294. *2631*

A I CH E M I MODULAR INSTRUCTION. SERIES D: THERMODYNAMICS.
American Institute of Chemical Engineers, 345 E. 47th St., New York, NY 10017. TEL 212-705-7657. FAX 212-752-3294. *2631*

A I CH E M I MODULAR INSTRUCTION. SERIES E: KINETICS.
American Institute of Chemical Engineers, 345 E. 47th St., New York, NY 10017. TEL 212-705-7657. FAX 212-752-3294. *2631*

A I CH E M I MODULAR INSTRUCTION. SERIES F: MATERIAL AND ENERGY BALANCES.
American Institute of Chemical Engineers, 345 E. 47th St., New York, NY 10017. TEL 212-705-7657. FAX 212-752-3294. *2631*

A I CH E M I MODULAR INSTRUCTION. SERIES G: DESIGN OF EQUIPMENT.
American Institute of Chemical Engineers, 345 E. 47th St., New York, NY 10017. TEL 212-705-7657. FAX 212-752-3294. *2631*

A I CH E SYMPOSIUM SERIES.
American Institute of Chemical Engineers, 345 E. 47th St., New York, NY 10017. TEL 212-705-7657. FAX 212-752-3294. *2632*

A I D VERBRAUCHERDIENST.
Auswertungs- und Informationsdienst fuer Ernaehrung, Landwirtschaft und Forsten e.V., Konstantinstr. 124, 53179 Bonn, Germany. TEL 49-228-84990. FAX 49-228-9526952. *5228*

A I M INTERNATIONAL.
Africa Inland Mission International, Box 178, Pearl River, NY 10965. TEL 914-735-4014. FAX 914-735-1814. *6041*

A J N R.
American Society of Neuroradiology, 2210 Midwest Rd., Ste. 207, Oak Brook, IL 60521. TEL 708-574-0220. FAX 708-574-0661. *4872*

A J R.
American Roentgen Ray Society, Attn.: Leigh Myzk, 1891 Preston White Dr., VA 22091. TEL 703-648-8992. FAX 703-264-8863. *4872*

A J S REVIEW.
Yeshiva University Press - Ktav Publishing House, Inc., 900 Jefferson St., No. 6249, Hoboken, NJ 07030-7205. TEL 201-963-9524. FAX 201-963-0102. *2859*

A L A N REVIEW.
National Council of Teachers of English, Assembly on Literature for Adolescents, Office of the Dean, College of Education & Human Development, Box 6960, Radford University, VA 24142. TEL 703-831-5439. FAX 703-831-6053. *2477*

A L T - J. ASSOCIATION FOR LEARNING TECHNOLOGY JOURNAL.
University of Wales Press, 6 Gwennyth St., Cathays, Cardiff CF2 4YD, Wales. TEL 44-1222-231919. FAX 44-1222-230908. *2403*

A M A T Y C REVIEW.
American Mathematical Association of Two-Year Colleges, c/o Joseph Browne, Ed., Onondaga Community College, Syracuse, NY 13215. TEL 315-469-2649. *2418*

A M E CHURCH REVIEW.
African Methodist Episcopal Church, 500 Eighth Ave. S., Nashville, TN 37203. TEL 615-256-7020. FAX 615-256-7092. *6131*

A M I A NEWSLETTER.
Association of Moving Image Archivists, c/o National Center for Film and Video Preservation, American Film Institute, 2021 N. Western Ave., Los Angeles, CA 90027. TEL 213-856-7637. FAX 213-467-4578. *3969*

A M S STUDIES IN ANTHROPOLOGY.
A M S Press, Inc., 56 E. 13th St., New York, NY 10003. TEL 212-777-4700. FAX 212-995-5413. *299*

A N N A JOURNAL.
Jannetti Publications, Inc., East Holly Ave., Box 56, Pitman, NJ 08071-0056. TEL 609-256-2300. FAX 609-589-7463. *4708*

A N Q: A QUARTERLY JOURNAL OF SHORT ARTICLES, NOTES AND REVIEWS.
Heldref Publications, 1319 Eighteenth St., N.W., Washington, DC 20036-1802. TEL 202-296-6267. FAX 202-296-5149. *4176*

A N R E D ALERT.
Anorexia Nervosa & Related Eating Disorders, Inc., Box 5102, Eugene, OR 97405. TEL 541-344-1144. *5821*

A N Z A NEWS.
Down-Under Publications, 3 W. 8th Ave., Vancouver, BC V5Y 1M8, Canada. TEL 604-876-7128. *3110*

A O A C INTERNATIONAL JOURNAL.
A O A C International, 481 N. Frederick Ave., Ste. 500, Gaithersburg, MD 20877-2417. TEL 703-522-3032. FAX 703-522-5468. *1712*

A O J T NEWS.
Association of Orthodox Jewish Teachers, 1577 Coney Island Ave., Brooklyn, NY 11230. TEL 718-258-3585. FAX 718-258-3586. *2309*

A P M I S.
Munksgaard International Publishers Ltd., 35 Noerre Soegade, P.O. Box 2148, DK-1016 Copenhagen K, Denmark. TEL 45-33-127030. FAX 45-33-129387. *563*

A R A NEWSLETTER.
A R A Publications (Tempe), c/o Aleksandra Gruzinska, Ed., Foreign Languages Department, Arizona State University, Tempe, AZ 85287-0202. TEL 602-965-6281. FAX 602-965-0135. *2418*

A R I E L.
University of Calgary, Department of English, SS 1152, 2500 University Dr. N.W., Calgary, AB T2N 1N4, Canada. TEL 403-220-4657. FAX 403-289-1123. *4176*

A R S C JOURNAL.
Association for Recorded Sound Collections, Inc., Box 543, Annapolis, MD 21404-0543. TEL 410-757-0488. FAX 410-379-0175. *6443*

A S A E TRANSACTIONS.
American Society of Agricultural Engineers, 2950 Niles Rd., St. Joseph, MI 49085-9659. TEL 616-429-0300. FAX 616-429-3852. *84*

A S A E TRANSACTIONS. FOOD & PROCESS ENGINEERING.
American Society of Agricultural Engineers, 2950 Niles Rd., St. Joseph, MI 49085-9659. TEL 616-429-0300. FAX 616-429-3852. *2958*

A S A E TRANSACTIONS. INFORMATION AND ELECTRICAL TECHNOLOGIES - EMERGING TECHNOLOGIES.
American Society of Agricultural Engineers, 2950 Niles Rd., St. Joseph, MI 49084-9659. TEL 616-429-0300. FAX 616-429-3852. *2681*

A S A E TRANSACTIONS. POWER & MACHINERY.
American Society of Agricultural Engineers, 2950 Niles Rd., St. Joseph, MI 49085-9659. TEL 616-429-0300. FAX 616-429-3852. *202*

A S A E TRANSACTIONS. SOIL & WATER.
American Society of Agricultural Engineers, 2950 Niles Rd., St. Joseph, MI 49085-9659. TEL 616-429-0300. FAX 616-429-3852. *208*

A S A E TRANSACTIONS. STRUCTURES & ENVIRONMENT.
American Society of Agricultural Engineers, 2950 Niles Rd., St. Joseph, MI 49085-9659. TEL 616-429-0300. FAX 616-429-3852. *2652*

A S D NEWSLETTER.
Association for the Study of Dreams, Box 1600, Vienna, VA 22183. TEL 703-242-8888. FAX 510-527-7929. *5822*

A S H E - E R I C HIGHER EDUCATION REPORT SERIES.
A S H E - E R I C Higher Education Reports, George Washington University, One Dupont Circle, Ste. 630, Washington, DC 20036. TEL 202-296-2597. FAX 202-452-1844. *2418*

A S H R A E JOURNAL.
American Society of Heating, Refrigerating and Air-Conditioning Engineers, Inc., 1791 Tullie Circle, N.E., Atlanta, GA 30329. TEL 404-636-8400. FAX 404-321-5478. *3325*

A T E A JOURNAL.
American Technical Education Association, Inc., North Dakota State College of Science, Wahpeton, ND 58076. TEL 701-671-2240. FAX 701-671-2260. *2309*

A T I P.
Association Technique de l'Industrie Papetiere, 154 bd. Haussmann, 75008 Paris, France. FAX 33-1-45-63-53-09. *5320*

A T P ENERGIA Y MOVIMIENTO.
Obsidiana Editores, S.A., Czda. de Tlalpan 2365, Col. Ciudad Jardin, 04370 Mexico DF, Mexico. TEL 6899133. *4896*

A.U.M.L.A.
Australian Universities Language and Literature Association (AULLA), University of Canterbury, Dept. of French, Private Bag 4800, Christchurch, New Zealand. TEL 64-3-3667001. FAX 64-3-3642999. *4047*

A X I S.
Whurr Publishers Ltd., 19b Compton Terrace, London N1 2UN, England. TEL 44-171-359-5979. FAX 44-171-226-5290. *1981*

AARDRIJKSKUNDE.
Vereniging Leraars Aardrijkskunde, Instituut voor Sociale en Economische Geografie, 42 de Croylaan, 3001 Leuven-Heverlee, Belgium. TEL 32-16-322441. *3246*

AARHUS UNIVERSITET. PSYKOLOGISK SKRIFTSERIE.
Aarhus Universitet, Psykologisk Institut, DK-8000 Aarhus C, Denmark. TEL 45-89-42-49-00. FAX 45-89-42-49-01. *5822*

ABDOMINAL IMAGING.
Springer-Verlag, Medical Journals, 175 Fifth Ave., New York, NY 10010. TEL 212-460-1500. FAX 212-473-6272. *4689*

ABERDEEN LETTERS IN ECOLOGY.
University of Aberdeen, Department of Agriculture, MacRobert Bldg., 581 King St., Aberdeen AB24 5UA, Scotland. TEL 44-1224-480480. FAX 44-1224-273731. *564*

ABERTAY HISTORICAL SOCIETY. SERIES OF MONOGRAPHS.
Abertay Historical Society, Archive & Record Centre, Publications Secretary, 21 City Sq., Dundee DD1 3BY, Scotland. TEL 44-1382-434494. FAX 44-1382-434666. *3390*

ABHIGYAN.
Foundation for Organisational Research and Education, Adhitam Kendra, B-18, Qutab Institutional Area, New Delhi 110 016, India. TEL 91-11-6863396. FAX 91-11-6856294. *6312*

ABORIGINAL HISTORY.
Aboriginal History Inc., G.P.O. Box 2837, Canberra, A.C.T. 2601, Australia. FAX 61-6-2394324. *3387*

ABRAHAM LINCOLN ASSOCIATION. JOURNAL.
University of Illinois Press, 1325 S. Oak St., Champaign, IL 61820. TEL 217-333-0950. FAX 217-244-8082. *3335*

ABSTRACTS IN ANTHROPOLOGY.
Baywood Publishing Co., Inc., 26 Austin Ave., Box 337, Amityville, NY 11701. TEL 516-691-1270. FAX 516-691-1770. *327*

ACADEMIA CHILENA DE LA HISTORIA. BOLETIN.
Academia Chilena de la Historia, Clasificador 245, Correo Central, Santiago, Chile. TEL 6399323. *3457*

ACADEMIA COLOMBIANA. BOLETIN.
Academia Colombiana de la Lengua, Carrera 3-A, Numero 17-34, Bogota, Colombia. TEL 3343152 ext. 7. *4048*

ACADEMIA ECONOMIC PAPERS.
Academia Sinica, Institute of Economics, Nankang, Taipei, Taiwan 11529, Republic of China. TEL 02-782-2791. FAX 02-785-3946. *891*

ACADEMIC EMERGENCY MEDICINE.
Hanley & Belfus, Inc., 210 S. 13th St., Philadelphia, PA 19107. TEL 215-546-7293. FAX 215-790-9330. *4779*

ACADEMIC MEDICINE.
Association of American Medical Colleges, 2450 N St., Washington, DC 20037-1126. TEL 202-828-0416. FAX 202-828-1123. *4417*

ACADEMIC PRESS GEOLOGY SERIES.
Academic Press, Inc., 525 B St., Ste. 1900, San Diego, CA 92101-4495. TEL 619-231-0926. FAX 619-699-6715. *2222*

ACADEMIC PRESS SERIES IN COGNITION AND PERCEPTION.
Academic Press, Inc., 525 B St., Ste. 1900, San Diego, CA 92101-4495. TEL 619-231-0926. FAX 619-699-6715. *5822*

ACADEMIC PSYCHIATRY.
American Psychiatric Press, Inc., Journals Division, 1400 K St., N.W., Ste. 1101, Washington, DC 20005. TEL 202-682-6240. FAX 202-789-6341. *4821*

ACADEMIE DE DROIT INTERNATIONAL DE LA HAYE. RECUEIL DES COURS.
Kluwer Academic Publishers, Postbus 17, 3300 AA Dordrecht, Netherlands. TEL 31-78-6392392. FAX 31-78-6392254. *3921*

ACADEMIE DES SCIENCES. COMPTES RENDUS. SERIE 3: SCIENCES DE LA VIE.
John Libbey Eurotext, 127 av.de la Republique, 92120 Montrouge Cedex, France. TEL 1-46-73-06-60. FAX 1-40-84-09-99. *564*

ACADEMIE ET SOCIETE LORRAINES DE SCIENCES. BULLETIN.
Academie et Societe Lorraines des Sciences, Biologie Vegetales, B.P. 239, 54506 Vandoeuvre Cedex, France. TEL 83-91-22-53. FAX 83-91-22-53. *6222*

ACADEMIE INTERNATIONALE D'HISTOIRE DES SCIENCES. COLLECTION DES TRAVAUX.
E.J. Brill, P.O. Box 9000, 2300 PA Leiden, Netherlands. TEL 31-71-5353500. FAX 31-71-5317532. *6222*

ACADEMIE POLONAISE DES SCIENCES. CENTRE D'ARCHEOLOGIE MEDITERRANEENNE. ETUDES ET TRAVAUX.
Polska Akademia Nauk, Zaklad Archeologii Srodziemnomorskiej, Palac Kultury i Nauki, p. 2105, 00-901 Warsaw, Poland. TEL 48-22-248593. FAX 48-22-6207651. *336*

ACADEMIE POLONAISE DES SCIENCES. CENTRE D'ARCHEOLOGIE MEDITERRANEENE. TRAVAUX.
Polska Akademia Nauk, Zaklad Archeologii Srodziemnomorskiej, Palac Kultury i Nauki, p. 2105, 00-901 Warsaw, Poland. TEL 48-22-248593. FAX 48-22-6207651. *336*

ACADEMY FOR EVANGELISM IN THEOLOGICAL EDUCATION. JOURNAL.
Academy for Evangelism in Theological Education, c/o Richard S. Armstrong, Ed., Princeton Theological Seminary, Box 821, Princeton, NJ 08542. TEL 609-924-2997. FAX 609-924-2973. *6042*

ACADEMY OF MARKETING SCIENCE. JOURNAL.
Sage Publications, Inc., 2455 Teller Rd., Thousand Oaks, CA 91320. TEL 805-499-0721. FAX 805-499-0871. *1452*

ACADEMY OF REHABILITATIVE AUDIOLOGY. JOURNAL.
Academy of Rehabilitative Audiology, c/o Robert J. Dunlop, Ph.D., JARA Circ. Mgr., Audiology Section (126A), VA Medical Center, Temple, TX 76504. *4793*

ACAROLOGIA.
61 rue de Buffon, 75231 Paris Cedex 05, France. FAX 33-1-40-79-35-76. *795*

ACCADEMIA NAZIONALE DEI LINCEI. ATTI. RENDICONTI LINCEI. MATEMATICA E APPLICAZIONI.
Accademia Nazionale dei Lincei, Via della Lungara 10, 00165 Rome, Italy. TEL 39-6-6838831. *4349*

ACCADEMIA NAZIONALE DEI LINCEI. ATTI. RENDICONTI LINCEI. SCIENZE FISICHE E NATURALI.
Accademia Nazionale dei Lincei, Via della Lungara 10, 00165 Rome, Italy. TEL 39-6-6838831. *6223*

ACCELERATORS AND STORAGE RINGS SERIES.
Harwood Academic Publishers, c/o International Publishers Distributor, 820 Town Center Dr., Langhorne, PA 19047. TEL 215-750-2642. FAX 215-750-6343. *5592*

ACCIDENT ANALYSIS & PREVENTION.
Elsevier Science Ltd., Pergamon, P.O. Box 800, Kidlington, Oxford OX5 1DX, England. TEL 44-1865-843000. FAX 44-1865-843010. *5953*

ACCOMMODATOR.
Motels Ontario, 347 Pido Rd., Unit 2, R.R. 6, Peterborough, ON K9J 6X7, Canada. TEL 705-745-4982. FAX 705-745-4983. *3558*

ACCOUNTABILITY IN RESEARCH.
Gordon & Breach Science Publishers, c/o International Publishers Distributor, P.O. Box 3054, Langhorne, PA 19047-3054. TEL 215-750-2642. FAX 215-750-6343. *6223*

ACCOUNTANCY S A.
South African Institute of Chartered Accountants, P.O. Box 59875, Kengray 2100, South Africa. TEL 27-11-622-6655. FAX 27-11-622-3321. *1037*

ACCOUNTING EDUCATION.
Chapman & Hall, Journals Department 2-6 Boundary Row, London SE1 8HN, England. TEL 44-171-8650066. FAX 44-171-8659623. *1038*

ACCOUNTING EDUCATION.
J A I Press Inc., 55 Old Post Rd., No. 2, Box 1678, Greenwich, CT 06336-1678. TEL 203-661-7602. FAX 203-661-0792. *1038*

ACCOUNTING HISTORIANS JOURNAL.
Academy of Accounting Historians, c/o William D. Samson, Culverhouse School of Accountancy, University of Alabama, Tuscaloosa, AL 35487. TEL 205-348-2903. *1039*

ACCOUNTING, MANAGEMENT AND INFORMATION TECHNOLOGIES.
Elsevier Science Ltd., Pergamon, P.O. Box 800, Kidlington, Oxford OX5 1DX, England. TEL 44-1865-843000. FAX 44-1865-843010. *1039*

ACCOUNTING, ORGANIZATIONS AND SOCIETY.
Elsevier Science Ltd., Pergamon, P.O. Box 800, Kidlington, Oxford OX5 1DX, England. TEL 44-1865-843000. FAX 44-1865-843010. *1039*

ACCOUNTS OF CHEMICAL RESEARCH.
American Chemical Society, 1155 16th St., N.W., Washington, DC 20036. TEL 202-872-4363. FAX 614-447-3671. *1662*

ACCREDITED PROFESSIONAL PROGRAMS OF COLLEGES AND SCHOOLS OF PHARMACY.
American Council on Pharmaceutical Education, 311 W. Superior St., Chicago, IL 60610. TEL 312-664-3575. FAX 312-664-4652. *5396*

DE ACHTTIENDE EEUW. DOCUMENTATIEBLAD WERKGROEP 18E EEUW.
Werkgroep 18e Eeuw, Institute for the History of Science, Nieuwe Gracht 187, 3512 LM Utrecht, Netherlands. TEL 31-30-2538283. FAX 31-30-2536313. *3390*

ACOUSTICAL IMAGING.
Plenum Publishing Corp., 233 Spring St., New York, NY 10013-1578. TEL 212-620-8000. FAX 212-463-0742. *5613*

ACOUSTICAL SOCIETY OF AMERICA. JOURNAL.
American Institute of Physics, One Physics Ellipse, College Park, MD 20740-3843. TEL 301-209-3100. *5613*

ACOUSTICAL SOCIETY OF JAPAN. JOURNAL.
Acoustical Society of Japan, Ikeda Bldg., 7-7, Yoyogi 2-chome, Shibuya-ku, Tokyo 151, Japan. TEL 81-3-3379-1200. FAX 81-3-3379-1456. *5613*

ACOUSTICS LETTERS.
Parjon Information Services, P.O. Box 144, Haywards Heath, Sussex RH16 2YX, England. *5613*

ACQUISITIONS LIBRARIAN.
Haworth Press, Inc., 10 Alice St., Binghamton, NY 13904. TEL 607-722-5857. FAX 607-722-1424. *3970*

ACTA ACADEMICA.
Acta Academica, c/o UOVS-Sasol-Bibliotheek, Posbus 301, 9300 Bloemfontein, South Africa. TEL 27-51-4012351. FAX 27-51-482879. *3605*

ACTA ACUSTICA.
Editions de Physique, B.P. 112, 7, Av. du Hoggar, Zone Industrielle de Courtaboeuf, 91944 Les Ulis Cedex, France. TEL 69-07-36-83. FAX 69-28-84-91. *5613*

ACTA AGRICULTURAE SCANDINAVICA. SECTION A, ANIMAL SCIENCE.
Scandinavian University Press, P.O. Box 2959 Toeyen, N-0608 Oslo, Norway. TEL 47-22-57-54-00. FAX 47-22-57-53-53. *262*

ACTA AGRICULTURAE SCANDINAVICA. SECTION B, SOIL AND PLANT SCIENCE.
Scandinavian University Press, P.O. Box 2959 Toeyen, N-0608 Oslo, Norway. TEL 47-22-57-53-53. FAX 47-22-57-53-53. *203*

ACTA AMAZONICA.
Instituto Nacional de Pesquisas da Amazonia, Alameda Cosme Ferreira 1756 P.O. Box 478, 69083-000 Manaus, Amazonas, Brazil. TEL 55-92-6423220. FAX 55-92-643-3030. *6223*

ACTA ANAESTHESIOLOGICA SCANDINAVICA.
Munksgaard International Publishers Ltd., Noerre Soegade, P.O. Box 2148, DK-1016 Copenhagen K, Denmark. TEL 45-33-127030. FAX 45-33-129387. *4588*

ACTA ANATOMICA.
S. Karger AG, Allschwilerstr. 10, P.O. Box, CH-4009 Basel, Switzerland. TEL 061-3061111. FAX 061-3061234. *4418*

ACTA APPLICANDAE MATHEMATICAE.
Kluwer Academic Publishers, Postbus 17, 3300 AA Dordrecht, Netherlands. TEL 31-78-6392392. FAX 31-78-6392254. *4350*

ACTA ARACHNOLOGICA.
Arachnological Society of Japan, Biological Laboratory, Otemon-Gakuin University, 2-1-15 Nishiai, Ibaraki, Osaka 567, Japan. FAX 0726-43-5427. *795*

ACTA ARCHAEOLOGICA.
Munksgaard International Publishers Ltd., 35 Noerre Soegade, P.O. Box 2148, DK-1016 Copenhagen K, Denmark. TEL 45-33-127030. FAX 45-33-129387. *337*

ACTA ARITHMETICA.
Polska Akademia Nauk, Instytut Matematyczny, Dzial Wydawnictw, Ul. Sniadeckich 8, P.O. Box 137, 00-950 Warsaw, Poland. TEL 48-22-6282471. FAX 48-22-6293997. *4350*

ACTA ASTRONAUTICA.
Elsevier Science Ltd., Pergamon, P.O. Box 800, Kidlington, Oxford OX5 1DX, England. TEL 44-1865-843000. FAX 44-1865-843010. *51*

ACTA ASTRONOMICA.
Copernicus Foundation for Polish Astronomy, Al. Ujazdowskie 4, 00-478 Warsaw, Poland. TEL 48-2-6295346. FAX 48-2-6294967. *474*

ACTA BALTICO - SLAVICA.
Polska Akademia Nauk, Instytut Slawistyki, Al. Ujazdowskie 18 m.16 00-478 Warsaw, Poland. TEL 48-22-6250054. FAX 48-22-6290075. *3391*

ACTA BIOLOGICA PARANAENSE.
Universidade Federal do Parana, Setor de Ciencias Biologicas, Cx. Postal 19020, 81531-990 Curitiba Farana, Brazil. TEL 55-41-3663144 ext. 165. FAX 55-41-2662042. *565*

ACTA BIOLOGICA VENEZUELICA.
Universidad Central de Venezuela, Instituto de Zoologia Tropical, Facultad de Ciencias, Apdo. 47058, Caracas 1041-A, Venezuela. FAX 58-2-6052136. *565*

ACTA BIOTHEORETICA
Kluwer Academic Publishers, Postbus 17, 3300 AA Dordrecht, Netherlands. TEL 31-78-6392392. FAX 31-78-6392254. *565*

ACTA BOTANICA BARCINONENSIA.
Universitat de Barcelona, Facultat de Biologia, Avda. Diagonal, 615, 08028 Barcelona, Spain. TEL 34-3-4021472. FAX 34-3-4112842. *666*

ACTA BOTANICA INDICA.
Society for the Advancement of Botany, Department of Botany, Meerut College, Meerut 250006, India. *667*

ACTA BOTANICA MALACITANA.
Universidad de Malaga, Facultad de Ciencias, Apdo. 59, 29080 Malaga, Spain. TEL 34-52-131944. FAX 34-52-131944. *667*

ACTA BOTANICA NEERLANDICA.
Blackwell Science Ltd., Osney Mead, Oxford OX2 OEL, England. TEL 44-1865-206206. FAX 44-1865-721205. *667*

ACTA CHEMICA SCANDINAVICA.
Munksgaard International Publishers Ltd., 35 Noerre Soegade, P.O. Box 2148, DK-1016 Copenhagen K, Denmark. TEL 45-33-127030. FAX 45-33-129387. *1747*

ACTA CHIMICA SLOVENICA.
Slovensko Kemijsko Drustvo, Hajdrihova 19, 61115 Ljubljana, Slovenia. TEL 386-61-176-0200. FAX 386-61-125-9244. *1662*

ACTA CIENTIFICA VENEZOLANA.
Asociacion Venezolana para el Avance de la Ciencia, Av. Neveri, Colinas de Bello Monte, Apdo. 47286, Caracas, Venezuela. TEL 752-1002. FAX 751-1420. *6223*

ACTA CLASSICA.
Classical Association of South Africa, P.O. Box 392, Pretoria 0001, South Africa. TEL 27-12-429-6501. FAX 27-12-429-3221. *1817*

ACTA CRIMINOLOGICA.
Unisa Press, Periodicals, P.O. Box 392, Pretoria 0001, South Africa. TEL 27-12-4293111. FAX 27-12-4293221. *2157*

ACTA CRYSTALLOGRAPHICA. SECTION A: FOUNDATIONS OF CRYSTALLOGRAPHY.
Munksgaard International Publishers Ltd., 35 Noerre Soegade, P.O. Box 2148, DK-1016 Copenhagen K, Denmark. TEL 45-33-127030. FAX 45-33-129387. *1725*

ACTA CRYSTALLOGRAPHICA. SECTION B: STRUCTURAL SCIENCE.
Munksgaard International Publishers Ltd., 35 Noerre Soegade, P.O. Box 2148, DK-1016 Copenhagen K, Denmark. TEL 45-33-127030. FAX 45-33-129387. *1725*

ACTA CRYSTALLOGRAPHICA. SECTION C: CRYSTAL STRUCTURE COMMUNICATIONS.
Munksgaard International Publishers Ltd., 35 Noerre Soegade, P.O. Box 2148, DK-1016 Copenhagen K, Denmark. TEL 45-33-127030. FAX 45-33-129387. *1725*

ACTA CRYSTALLOGRAPHICA. SECTION D: BIOLOGICAL CRYSTALLOGRAPHY.
Munksgaard International Publishers Ltd., 35 Noerre Soegade, P.O. Box 2148, DK-1016 Copenhagen K, Denmark. TEL 45-33-127030. FAX 45-33-129387. *1725*

ACTA CYTOLOGICA.
Science Printers and Publishers, Inc., 8342 Olive Blvd., St. Louis, MO 63132. TEL 314-991-4440. FAX 314-991-4654. *710*

ACTA ENTOMOLOGICA CHILENA.
Universidad Metropolitana de Ciencias de la Educacion, Instituto de Entomologia, Casilla 147, Santiago, Chile. FAX 56-2-2392067. *720*

ACTA GEOLOGICA HISPANICA.
Universidad de Barcelona, Biblioteca Facultat de Geologia, Marti Franques s-n, 08028 Barcelona, Spain. TEL 34-3-4021420. FAX 34-3-4021421. *2222*

ACTA HAEMATOLOGICA.
S. Karger AG, Allschwilerstr. 10, P.O. Box, CH-4009 Basel, Switzerland. TEL 061-3061111. FAX 061-3061234. *4697*

ACTA HISTOCHEMICA ET CYTOCHEMICA.
Japan Society of Histochemistry and Cytochemistry, c/o Nakanishi Printing Co., Shimotachiuri-Ogawa, Kamikyo-ku, Kyoto 602, Japan. TEL 075-415-3661. FAX 075-415-3662. *710*

ACTA HYDROBIOLOGICA.
Polska Akademia Nauk, Zaklad Biologii Wod im. Karola Starmacha, Ul. Slawkowska 17, 31-016 Krakow, Poland. TEL 48-12-215082. FAX 48-12-222115. *565*

ACTA ICHTHYOLOGICA ET PISCATORIA.
Akademia Rolnicza w Szczecinie, Dzial Wydawnictw, Ul. Doktora Judyma 22, 71-460 Szczecin, Poland. TEL 48-91-541639. FAX 48-91-541642. *2924*

ACTA IRANICA.
E.J. Brill, P.O. Box 9000, 2300 PA Leiden, Netherlands. TEL 31-71-5353500. FAX 31-71-5317532. *3494*

ACTA MATERIALIA.
Elsevier Science Ltd., Pergamon, P.O. Box 800, Kidlington, Oxford OX5 1DX, England. TEL 44-1865-843000. FAX 44-1865-843010. *4948*

ACTA MATHEMATICA HUNGARICA.
Kluwer Academic Publishers, Postbus 17, 3300 AA Dordrecht, Netherlands. TEL 31-78-6392392. FAX 31-78-6392254. *4350*

ACTA MATHEMATICA SCIENTIA.
Baltzer Science Publishers B.V., Asterweg 1A, 1031 HL Amsterdam, Netherlands. TEL 31-20-6370061. FAX 31-20-6323651. *4350*

ACTA MATHEMATICA SINICA, NEW SERIES.
Science Press, Marketing and Sales Department, 16 Donghuangchenggen North St., Beijing 100717, People's Republic of China. TEL 4010624. FAX 4019810. *4350*

ACTA MATHEMATICAE APPLICATAE SINICA.
Science Press, Marketing and Sales Department, 16 Donghuangchenggen North St., Beijing 100717, People's Republic of China. *4350*

ACTA MECHANICA SINICA.
Science Press, Marketing and Sales Department, 16 Donghuangchenggen North St., Beijing 100717, People's Republic of China. TEL 4010642. FAX 4012180. *5586*

ACTA MEDICA BALTICA.
Pabst Science Publishers, Am Eichengrund 28, 49525 Lengerich, Germany. TEL 49-5484-308. FAX 49-5484-550. *4418*

ACTA MEDICA BULGARICA.
Tsentar Informatsiia po Meditsina, 1, Sv. Georgi Sofiiski St., 1431 Sofia, Bulgaria. TEL 395-2-522342. FAX 359-2-522393. *4419*

ACTA MEDICA IRANICA.
Tehran University of Medical Sciences, Faculty of Medicine, Poursina St., Tehran 14174, Iran. TEL 98-21-6112743. FAX 98-21-6404377. *4419*

ACTA MEDICA KINKI UNIVERSITY.
Kinki University Medical Association, 2-377, Ohno-Higashi, Osaka-Sayama, Osaka 589, Japan. TEL 0723-66-0221. FAX 0723-67-8810. *4419*

ACTA MEDICA NAGASAKIENSIA.
Nagasaki Daigaku, Igakubu, 12-4 Sakamoto-machi, Nagasaki-shi, Nagasaki-ken 852, Japan. TEL 81-958-49-7353. FAX 81-958-49-7357. *4419*

ACTA METEOROLOGICA SINICA.
China Meteorological Press, 46 Baishiqiao Rd., West Suburb, Beijing 100081, People's Republic of China. TEL 86-10-217-2277. FAX 81-10-217-5925. *4990*

ACTA NEUROLOGICA SCANDINAVICA.
Munksgaard International Publishers Ltd., 35 Noerre Soegade, P.O. Box 1248, DK-1016 Copenhagen K, Denmark. TEL 45-33-127030. FAX 45-33-129387. *4821*

ACTA NEUROLOGICA SCANDINAVICA. SUPPLEMENTUM.
Munksgaard International Publishers Ltd., 35 Noerre Soegade, P.O. Box 2148, DK-1016 Copenhagen K, Denmark. TEL 45-33-127030. FAX 45-33-129387. *4821*

ACTA NEUROPSYCHIATRICA.
Misset P.O. Box 1110, 3600 BC Maarssen, Netherlands. TEL 31-346-558222. FAX 31-346-554287. *4821*

ACTA OBSTETRICA ET GYNECOLOGICA SCANDINAVICA.
Munksgaard International Publishers Ltd., 35 Noerre Soegade, P.O. Box 2148, DK-1016 Copenhagen K, Denmark. TEL 45-33-127030. FAX 45-33-129387. *4730*

ACTA OCEANOLOGICA SINICA.
China Ocean Press, International Cooperation Department, Haimao Dalou, 1 Fuxingmenwai Dajie, Beijing 100860, People's Republic of China. TEL 8032211. FAX 8033515. *2290*

ACTA ORIENTALIA.
Munksgaard International Publishers Ltd., 35 Noerre Soegade, P.O Box 2148, DK-1016 Copenhagen K, Denmark. TEL 45-33-127030. FAX 45-33-129387. *5277*

ACTA ORTHOPAEDICA SCANDINAVICA.
Scandinavian University Press, P.O. Box 2959-Toeyen, N-0608 Oslo, Norway. TEL 47-22-57-54-00. FAX 47-22-57-53-53. *4779*

ACTA PAEDIATRICA SINICA.
Chinese Taipei Pediatric Association, No. 11, Ching-Tao West Road, 4F-4, Taipei, Taiwan 10022, Republic of China. TEL 886-2-331-4917. FAX 886-2-314-2184. *4801*

ACTA PALAEOBOTANICA.
Polska Akademia Nauk, Instytut Botaniki im. W. Szafera, Ul. Lubicz 46, 31-512 Krakow, Poland. TEL 48-12-215144. FAX 48-12-219790. *667*

ACTA PALAEONTOLOGICA POLONICA.
Polska Akademia Nauk, Instytut Paleobiologii, Al. Zwirki i Wigury 93, 02-089 Warsaw. FAX 48-22-221652. *5312*

ACTA PARASITOLOGICA.
Polska Akademia Nauk, Instytut Parazytologii Witolda Stefanskiego, Ul. Pasteura 3, 00-937 Warsaw, Poland. TEL 48-22-222562. *752*

ACTA PHARMACEUTICA TURCICA.
ETAM A.S. Matbaa Tesisleri, 26470 Eskisehir, Turkey. TEL 90-222-2360051. *5396*

ACTA PHYSICA POLONICA. SERIES B: ELEMENTARY PARTICLE PHYSICS, NUCLEAR PHYSICS, STATISTICAL PHYSICS, THEORY OF RELATIVITY, FIELD THEORY.
Uniwersytet Jagiellonski, Instytut Fizyki, Reymonta 4, 30-059 Krakow, Poland. TEL 48-12-336377. *5539*

ACTA PHYSIOLOGIAE PLANTARUM.
Agencja Wydawnicza ARIES, Ul. Zorzy 22, 40-639 Warsaw, Poland. TEL 48-22-153162. FAX 48-22-153162. *667*

ACTA PHYSIOLOGICA SCANDINAVICA.
Blackwell Science Ltd., Osney Mead, Oxford OX2 OEL, England. TEL 44-1865-206206. FAX 44-1865-721205. *783*

ACTA POLONIAE PHARMACEUTICA.
Polskie Towarzystwo Farmaceutyczne, Ul. Dluga 16, 00-238 Warsaw, Poland. TEL 48-22-310241. FAX 48-22-310243. *5396*

ACTA PSIQUIATRICA Y PSICOLOGICA DE AMERICA LATINA.
Fundacion Acta Fondo para la Salud Mental, Malabia 2274 13 A, 1425 Buenos Aires, Argentina. TEL 541-832-3286. FAX 541-856-7108. *4821*

ACTA PSYCHIATRICA SCANDINAVICA.
Munksgaard International Publishers Ltd., 35 Noerre Soegade, P.O. Box 2148, DK-1016 Copenhagen K. TEL 45-33-127030. FAX 45-33-129387. *4822*

ACTA PSYCHOLOGICA.
North-Holland P.O. Box 211, 1000 AE Amsterdam, Netherlands. TEL 31-20-4853911. FAX 31-20-4853598. *5822*

ACTA RADIOLOGICA.
Munksgaard International Publishers Ltd., 35 Noerre Soegade, P.O. Box 2148, DK-1016 Copenhagen K, Denmark. TEL 45-33-127030. FAX 45-33-129387. *4872*

ACTA REPRODUCTIVA TURCICA.
Hacettepe University, Department of Gynecology and Obstetrics, Ankara, Turkey. *4730*

ACTA SEISMOLOGICA SINICA.
Seismological Society of China, c/o Institute of Geophysics, State Seismological Bureau, No. 5, Minzuxueyuan Nanlu, Haidian District, Beijing 100081, People's Republic of China. TEL 86-10-8417744. FAX 86-10-8415372. *2269*

ACTA STEREOLOGICA.
Institute of Histology and Embryology, Medical Faculty, Korytkova 2, 61105 Ljubljana, Slovenia. TEL 386-61-441121. FAX 386-61-1401294. *566*

ACTA TECHNICA C S A V.
Ceska Akademie Ved, Ustav pro Elektrotechniku, Dolejskova 5, 182 00 Prague 8, Czech Republic. TEL 42-2-6883422. FAX 42-2-6883422. *2588*

ACTA THERIOLOGICA.
Polska Akademia Nauk, Zaklad Badania Ssakow, Ul. Gen. Waszkiewicza 1, 17-230 Bialowieza, Poland. TEL 48-835-12289. FAX 48-835-12289. *795*

ACTA TROPICA.
Elsevier Science B.V., P.O. Box 211, 1000 AE Amsterdam, Netherlands. TEL 31-20-4853911. FAX 31-20-4853598. *4615*

ACTA UNIVERSITATIS PALACKIANAE OLOMUCENSIS. FACULTATIS MEDICAE.
Universita Palackeho, Olomouc, Lekarska Fakulta, Hnevotinska 3, 775 15 Olomouc, Czech Republic. TEL 42-68-5412551. FAX 42-68-541-3541. *4420*

ACTA VETERINARIA BRNO.
Vysoka Skola Veterinarni, Brno, Palackiho 1-3, 612 42 Brno, Czech Republic. TEL 42-5-41321107. FAX 42-5-4121151. *6939*

ACTA ZOOLOGICA.
Elsevier Science Ltd., Pergamon, P.O. Box 800, Kidlington, Oxford OX5 1DX, England. TEL 44-1865-843000. FAX 44-1865-843010. *795*

ACTA ZOOLOGICA CRACOVIENSIA.
Polska Akademia Nauk, Instytut Systematyki i Ewolucji Zwierzat, Ul. Slawkowska 17, 31-016 Krakow, Poland. TEL 48-12-221891. FAX 48-12-224294. *796*

ACTIVE AND PASSIVE ELECTRONIC COMPONENTS.
Gordon & Breach Science Publishers, c/o International Publishers Distributor, P.O. Box 3054, Langhorne, PA 19047-3054. TEL 215-750-2642. FAX 215-750-6343. *2682*

ACTIVE LEARNING.
Computers in Teaching Initiative Support Service, University of Oxford, 13 Banbury Rd., Oxford OX2 6NN, England. TEL 44-1865-273273. FAX 44-1865-273275. *2403*

THE ACTIVIST.
Amnesty International, Canadian Section (English Speaking), 214 Montreal Rd., Ste 401, Vanier, ON K1L 1A4, Canada. TEL 613-744-7667. FAX 613-746-2411. *5724*

ACTIVITIES, ADAPTATION & AGING.
Haworth Press, Inc., 10 Alice St., Binghamton, NY 13904. TEL 607-722-5857. FAX 607-722-1424. *3282*

ACTIVNEWS.
Activ Foundation Inc., P.O. Box 446, Jolimont, W.A. 6014, Australia. TEL 61-9-3870555. FAX 61-9-3870599. *6359*

ACTUALIDAD TABAQUERA.
Tabapress, S.A., Barquillo 7, 28004 Madrid, Spain. TEL 34-1-5229399. FAX 34-1-5325562. *6708*

ACTUARIAL DIGEST.
Actuarial Digest Publishing Company, Box 1127, Ponte Vedra Beach, FL 32004-1127. TEL 904-273-1245. *3639*

ACUPUNCTURE AND ELECTRO-THERAPEUTICS RESEARCH.
Cognizant Communication Corporation, 3 Hartsdale Rd., Elmsford, NY 10523-3701. TEL 914-592-7720. FAX 914-592-8981. *288*

ACUTE CORONARY CARE.
Kluwer Academic Publishers, Postbus 17, 3300 AA Dordrecht, Netherlands. TEL 31-78-6392392. FAX 31-78-6392254. *4594*

ADAPTED PHYSICAL ACTIVITY QUARTERLY.
Human Kinetics Publishers, Inc., Box 5076, Champaign, IL 61825-5076. TEL 217-351-5076. FAX 217-351-2674. *2465*

ADAPTIVE BEHAVIOR.
M I T Press, 55 Hayward St., Cambridge, MA 02142. TEL 617-253-2889. FAX 617-258-6779. *2004*

ADAY.
Mindanao State University, Mamitua Saber Research Center, P.O. Box 5594, Iligan City 9200, Philippines. *4177*

ADDICTION.
Carfax Publishing Co., P.O. Box 25, Abingdon, Oxon. OX14 3UE, England. TEL 44-1235-401000. FAX 44-1235-401550. *2192*

ADDICTIVE BEHAVIORS.
Elsevier Science Ltd., Pergamon, P.O. Box 800, Kidlington, Oxford OX5 1DX, England. TEL 44-1865-843000. FAX 44-1865-843010. *2193*

ADELAIDE LAW REVIEW.
Adelaide Law Review Association, c/o Department of Law, University of Adelaide, Adelaide, S.A. 5005, Australia. TEL 61-8-303-4440. FAX 61-8-303-4344. *3736*

ADHESION.
Elsevier Science Ltd., Books Division, P.O. Box 800, Kidlington, Oxford OX5 1DX, England. TEL 44-1865-843000. FAX 44-1865-843010. *5617*

ADICCIONES.
Socidrogalcohol, C Rambla 15, 2a 3a, 07003 Palma de Mallorca, Spain. TEL 34-71-727434. FAX 34-71-718073. *2193*

ADIRONDACK JOURNAL OF ENVIRONMENTAL STUDIES.
Chimera Press, AJES, SSHE Division, Paul Smith's College, Paul Smiths, NY 12970. TEL 518-327-6377. FAX 518-327-6369. *2774*

ADMINISTRATION AND POLICY IN MENTAL HEALTH.
Human Sciences Press, Inc. 233 Spring St., New York, NY 10013-1578. TEL 212-620-8000. FAX 212-463-0742. *4420*

ADMINISTRATION IN SOCIAL WORK.
Haworth Press, Inc., 10 Alice St., Binghamton, NY 13904. TEL 607-722-5857. FAX 607-722-1424. *6359*

ADMINISTRATIVE RADIOLOGY.
Glendale Publishing Corp., 1305 Glenoaks Blvd., Glendale, CA 91201. TEL 818-500-1872. *4872*

ADMINISTRATIVE SCIENCE QUARTERLY.
Cornell University, Johnson Graduate School of Management, 20 Thornwood Dr., Ste. 100, Ithaca, NY 14850-1265. TEL 607-254-7143. FAX 607-254-7100. *5890*

ADMINISTRATIVE SCIENCES ASSOCIATION OF CANADA. PROCEEDINGS, ANNUAL CONFERENCE.
A S A C Publications, c/o Irene Lepine, Dept. of Administrative Sciences, Universite du Quebec a Montreal, P.O. Box 6192, Sta. Centreville, Montreal, PQ H3C 4R2, Canada. TEL 514-987-3697. FAX 514-987-3343. *1404*

ADOBE MAGAZINE.
Adobe Systems, 411 First Ave., S., Seattle, WA 98104. TEL 206-622-5500. FAX 206-343-3273. *2107*

ADOLESCENT MEDICINE (PHILADELPHIA).
Hanley & Belfus, Inc., 210 S. 13th St., Philadelphia, PA 19107. TEL 215-546-7293. FAX 215-790-9330. *4801*

ADOLESCENT PSYCHIATRY.
University of Chicago Press, Journals Division, 5720 S. Woodlawn Ave., Chicago, IL 60637. TEL 773-753-3347. FAX 773-753-0811. *4822*

ADORERIAN.
Nihon Adora Shinri Gakkai, 5-12-15-301 Nishinakajima, Yodogawa-ku, Osaka 532, Japan. TEL 06-306-4699. FAX 06-306-0160. *5822*

ADSORPTION.
Kluwer Academic Publishers, Postbus 17, 3300 AA Dordrecht, Netherlands. TEL 31-78-6392392. FAX 31-78-6392254. *2632*

ADSORPTION SCIENCE AND TECHNOLOGY.
Multi-Science Publishing Co. Ltd., 107 High St., Brentwood, Essex CM14 4RX, England. TEL 44-1277-224632. FAX 44-1277-223453. *2632*

ADULT EDUCATION QUARTERLY.
American Association for Adult and Continuing Education, 1200 19th St., N.W., Ste. 300, Washington, DC 20036. TEL 202-429-5131. *2395*

ADULT RESIDENTIAL CARE JOURNAL.
John M. McCoin, Ed. & Pub., 4913 W. Colonial Way, Lawrence, KS 66049. TEL 913-842-1386. *6360*

ADVANCE - TITAN.
Advance - Titan, 800 Algoma Blvd., Oshkosh, WI 54901. TEL 414-424-3047. FAX 414-424-0866. *1855*

ADVANCED CARDIAC LIFE SUPPORT.
American Health Consultants, Inc., 3525 Piedmont Rd. N.E., Bldg. 6, Ste. 400, Atlanta, GA 30305. TEL 800-688-2421. FAX 800-284-3291. *4594*

ADVANCED CEMENT BASED MATERIALS.
Elsevier Science Inc., Box 945, New York, NY 10159-0945. TEL 212-533-3730. FAX 212-533-3630. *2632*

ADVANCED COMPOSITE MATERIALS.
V S P, P.O. Box 346, 3700 AH Zeist, Netherlands. TEL 31-30-6925790. FAX 31-30-6932081. *2723*

ADVANCED COMPOSITES LETTERS.
Woodhead Publishing Ltd., Abington Hall, Abington, Cambridge CB1 6AH, England. TEL 44-1223-891358. FAX 44-1223 893694. *5617*

ADVANCED DRUG DELIVERY REVIEWS.
Elsevier Science B.V., P.O. Box 211, 1000 AE Amsterdam, Netherlands. TEL 31-20-4853911. FAX 31-20-4853598. *5397*

ADVANCED LABANOTATION.
Harwood Academic Publishers, c/o International Publishers Distributor, P.O. Box 3054, Langhorne, PA 19047-3054. TEL 215-750-2642. FAX 215-750-6343. *2185*

ADVANCED MATERIALS FOR OPTICS AND ELECTRONICS.
John Wiley & Sons Ltd., Journals, Baffins Ln., Chichester, W. Sussex PO19 1UD, England. TEL 44-1243-779777. FAX 44-1243-843232. *1728*

ADVANCED PERFORMANCE MATERIALS.
Kluwer Academic Publishers, Postbus 17, 3300 AA Dordrecht, Netherlands. TEL 31-78-6392392. FAX 31-78-6392254. *2724*

ADVANCED POWDER TECHNOLOGY.
V S P, P.O. Box 346, 3700 AH Zeist, Netherlands. TEL 31-30-6925790. FAX 31-30-6932081. *2632*

ADVANCED ROBOTICS.
V S P, P.O. Box 346, 3700 AH Zeist, Netherlands. TEL 31-30-6925790. FAX 31-30-6932081. *2104*

ADVANCED SERIES IN MANAGEMENT.
Elsevier Science B.V., Books Division, P.O. Box 211, 1000 AE Amsterdam, Netherlands. TEL 31-20-4853911. FAX 31-20-4853705. *1404*

ADVANCED STUDIES IN CONTEMPORARY MATHEMATICS.
Gordon & Breach Science Publishers, c/o International Publishers Distributor, P.O. Box 3054, Langhorne, PA 19047-3054. TEL 215-750-2642. FAX 215-750-6343. *4351*

ADVANCED STUDIES IN THEORETICAL AND APPLIED ECONOMETRICS.
Kluwer Academic Publishers, Postbus 17, 3300 AA Dordrecht, Netherlands. TEL 31-78-6392392. FAX 31-78-6392254. *1247*

ADVANCED TEXTBOOKS IN ECONOMICS.
Elsevier Science B.V., Books Division, P.O. Box 211, 1000 AE Amsterdam, Netherlands. TEL 31-20-4853911. FAX 31-20-4853705. *1247*

ADVANCES IN AGRICULTURAL BIOTECHNOLOGY.
Kluwer Academic Publishers, Postbus 17, 3300 AA Dordrecht, Netherlands. TEL 31-78-6392392. FAX 31-78-6392254. *656*

ADVANCES IN AGRICULTURAL SCIENCES.
Akademia Rolnicza w Szczecinie, Dzial Wydawnictw, Ul. Doktora Judyma 22, 71-460 Szczecin, Poland. TEL 48-91-541639. FAX 48-91-541642. *85*

ADVANCES IN AGRONOMY.
Academic Press, Inc., 525 B St., Ste. 1900, San Diego, CA 92101-4495. TEL 619-231-0926. FAX 619-699-6715. *85*

ADVANCES IN ANATOMIC PATHOLOGY.
Lippincott - Raven Publishers 227 E. Washington Sq., Philadelphia, PA 19106. TEL 215-238-4200. *4420*

ADVANCES IN ANATOMY, EMBRYOLOGY AND CELL BIOLOGY.
Springer-Verlag, 175 Fifth Ave., New York, NY 10010. TEL 212-460-1500. FAX 212-473-6272. *566*

ADVANCES IN APPLIED MATHEMATICS.
Academic Press, Inc., Journal Division, 525 B St., Ste. 1900, San Diego, CA 92101-4495. TEL 619-230-1840. FAX 619-699-6800. *4351*

ADVANCES IN APPLIED MECHANICS.
Academic Press, Inc., 525 B St., Ste. 1900, San Diego, CA 92101-4495. TEL 619-231-0926. FAX 619-699-6715. *5587*

ADVANCES IN APPLIED MICROBIOLOGY.
Academic Press, Inc., 525 B St., Ste. 1900, San Diego, CA 92101-4495. TEL 619-231-0926. FAX 619-699-6715. *752*

ADVANCES IN APPLIED PROBABILITY.
Applied Probability Trust, School of Mathematics, University of Sheffield, Sheffield S3 7RH, England. TEL 44-114-282-4269. FAX 44-114-272-9782. *4351*

ADVANCES IN APPLIED SOCIAL PSYCHOLOGY.
Lawrence Erlbaum Associates, Inc., 10 Industrial Dr., Mahwah, NJ 07430-2262. TEL 201-236-9500. FAX 201-236-0072. *5822*

ADVANCES IN ATMOSPHERIC SCIENCES.
China Ocean Press, International Cooperation Department, Haimao Dalou, 1 Fuxingmenwai Dajie, Beijing 100860, People's Republic of China. TEL 8032211. FAX 8033515. *4990*

ADVANCES IN AUDIOLOGY.
S. Karger AG, Allschwilerstr. 10, P.O. Box, CH-4009 Basel, Switzerland. TEL 061-3061111. FAX 061-3061234. *4794*

ADVANCES IN BEHAVIORAL BIOLOGY.
Plenum Publishing Corp., 233 Spring St., New York, NY 10013-1578. TEL 212-620-8000. FAX 212-463-0742. *5822*

ADVANCES IN BIOCHEMICAL PSYCHOPHARMACOLOGY.
Lippincott - Raven Publishers 227 E. Washington Sq., Philadelphia, PA 19106. TEL 215-238-4200. FAX 215-238-4235. *5397*

ADVANCES IN BIOENGINEERING.
American Society of Mechanical Engineers, 22 Law Dr., Fairfield, NJ 07007-2300. *625*

ADVANCES IN BIOLOGICAL PSYCHIATRY.
S. Karger AG, Allschwilerstr. 10, P.O. Box, CH-4009 Basel, Switzerland. TEL 061-3061111. FAX 061-3061234. *4822*

ADVANCES IN BIOMATERIALS.
Elsevier Science B.V., Books Division, P.O. Box 211, 1000 AE Amsterdam, Netherlands. TEL 31-20-4853911. FAX 31-20-4853705. *628*

ADVANCES IN BIOPHYSICS.
Elsevier Science Ireland Ltd., P.O. Box 85, Limerick, Ireland. TEL 353-61-471944. FAX 353-61-472144. *651*

ADVANCES IN BOTANICAL RESEARCH.
Academic Press, Inc., 525 B St., Ste. 1900, San Diego, CA 92101-4495. TEL 619-231-0926. FAX 619-699-6715. *668*

ADVANCES IN C A D FOR V L S I.
Elsevier Science B.V., Books Division, P.O. Box 211, 1000 AE Amsterdam, Netherlands. TEL 31-20-4853911. FAX 31-20-4853705. *2025*

ADVANCES IN CANCER RESEARCH.
Academic Press, Inc., 525 B St., Ste. 1900, San Diego, CA 92101-4495. TEL 619-231-0926. FAX 619-699-6715. *4747*

ADVANCES IN CARBOHYDRATE CHEMISTRY AND BIOCHEMISTRY.
Academic Press, Inc., 525 B St., Ste. 1900, San Diego, CA 92101-4495. TEL 619-231-0926. FAX 619-699-6715. *1734*

ADVANCES IN CARDIOLOGY.
S. Karger AG, Allschwilerstr. 10, P.O. Box, CH-4009 Basel, Switzerland. TEL 061-3061111. FAX 061-3061234. *4594*

ADVANCES IN CARDIOVASCULAR PHYSICS.
S. Karger AG, Allschwilerstr. 10, P.O. Box, CH-4009 Basel, Switzerland. TEL 061-3061111. FAX 061-3061234. *4594*

ADVANCES IN CATALYSIS.
Academic Press, Inc., 525 B St., Ste. 1900, San Diego, CA 92101-4495. TEL 619-231-0926. FAX 619-699-6715. *1747*

ADVANCES IN CELL CULTURE.
Academic Press, Inc., 525 B St., Ste. 1900, San Diego, CA 92101-4495. TEL 619-231-0926. FAX 619-699-6715. *710*

ADVANCES IN CELLULAR AND MOLECULAR BIOLOGY OF PLANTS.
Kluwer Academic Publishers, Postbus 17, 3300 AA Dordrecht, Netherlands. TEL 31-78-6392392. FAX 31-78-6392254. *710*

ADVANCES IN CEMENT RESEARCH.
Thomas Telford Services Ltd., Thomas Telford House, 1 Heron Quay, London E14 4JD, England. TEL 44-171-987-6999. FAX 44-171-538-9620. *830*

ADVANCES IN CHEMICAL ENGINEERING.
Academic Press, Inc., 525 B St., Ste. 1900, San Diego, CA 92101-4495. TEL 619-231-0923. FAX 619-699-6715. *2632*

ADVANCES IN CHEMICAL PHYSICS.
John Wiley & Sons, Inc., 605 Third Ave., New York, NY 10158-0012. TEL 212-850-6000. FAX 212-850-6099. *5540*

ADVANCES IN CHEMISTRY SERIES.
American Chemical Society, 1155 16th St., N.W., Washington, DC 20036. TEL 800-227-5558. FAX 202-872-4615. *1663*

ADVANCES IN CHILD DEVELOPMENT AND BEHAVIOR.
Academic Press, Inc., 525 B St., Ste. 1900, San Diego, CA 92101-4495. TEL 619-231-0926. FAX 619-699-6715. *5823*

ADVANCES IN CHROMATOGRAPHY.
Marcel Dekker, Inc., 270 Madison Ave., New York, NY 10016. TEL 212-696-9000. FAX 212-685-4540. *1712*

ADVANCES IN CLINICAL CHEMISTRY.
Academic Press, Inc., 525 B St., Ste. 1900, San Diego, CA 92101-4495. TEL 619-231-0926. FAX 619-699-6715. *628*

ADVANCES IN CLINICAL CHILD PSYCHOLOGY.
Plenum Publishing Corp., 233 Spring St., New York, NY 10013-1578. TEL 212-620-8000. FAX 212-463-0742. *5823*

ADVANCES IN CLINICAL PHARMACOLOGY.
Lippincott - Raven Publishers 227 E. Washington Sq., Philadelphia, PA 19106. TEL 215-238-4200. FAX 215-238-4235. *5397*

ADVANCES IN COLLOID AND INTERFACE SCIENCE.
Elsevier Science B.V., P.O. Box 211, 1000 AE Amsterdam, Netherlands. TEL 31-20-4853911. FAX 31-20-4853598. *1748*

ADVANCES IN COMPUTATIONAL ECONOMICS.
Kluwer Academic Publishers, Postbus 17, 3300 AA Dordrecht, Netherlands. TEL 31-78-6392392. FAX 31-78-6392254. *1152*

ADVANCES IN COMPUTATIONAL MATHEMATICS.
Baltzer Science Publishers B.V., Asterweg 1A, 1031 HL Amsterdam, Netherlands. TEL 31-20-6370061. FAX 31-20-6323651. *4407*

ADVANCES IN COMPUTERS.
Academic Press, Inc., 525 B St., Ste. 1900, San Diego, CA 92101-4495. TEL 619-231-0926. FAX 619-699-6715. *1981*

ADVANCES IN CONSUMER RESEARCH.
Association for Consumer Research, Brigham Young University, Graduate School of Management, 632 TNRB, Provo, UT 84602. TEL 801-378-2080. FAX 801-378-5984. *1452*

ADVANCES IN CONTRACEPTION.
Kluwer Academic Publishers, Postbus 17, 3300 AA Dordrecht, Netherlands. TEL 31-78-6392392. FAX 31-78-6392254. *826*

ADVANCES IN CONTRACEPTIVE DELIVERY SYSTEMS.
Reproductive Health Center, 78 Surfsong Rd., Kiawah Island, SC 29455. TEL 803-768-5556. FAX 803-769-6494. *826*

ADVANCES IN CRYOGENIC ENGINEERING.
Plenum Publishing Corp., 233 Spring St., New York, NY 10013-1578. TEL 212-620-8000. FAX 212-463-0742. *5583*

ADVANCES IN DESCRIPTIVE PSYCHOLOGY.
Jessica Kingsley Publishers, 116 Pentonville Rd., London N1 9JB, England. TEL 071-278-0433. FAX 071-837-2917. *5823*

ADVANCES IN DESERT AND ARID LAND TECHNOLOGY AND DEVELOPMENT SERIES.
Harwood Academic Publishers, c/o International Publishers Distributor, P.O. Box 3054, Langhorne, PA 19047-3054. TEL 215-750-2642. FAX 215-750-6343. *3246*

ADVANCES IN DEVELOPMENTAL AND BEHAVIORAL PEDIATRICS.
Jessica Kingsley Publishers, 116 Pentonville Rd., London N1 9JB, England. TEL 071-833-2307. FAX 071-837-2917. *4802*

ADVANCES IN DEVELOPMENTAL PSYCHOLOGY.
Lawrence Erlbaum Associates, Inc., 10 Industrial Dr., Mahwah, NJ 07430-2262. TEL 201-236-9500. FAX 201-236-0072. *5823*

ADVANCES IN DIFFERENTIAL EQUATIONS.
Khayyam Publishing Company, Inc., Box 429, Athens, OH 45701. TEL 614-592-6136. FAX 614-592-1252. *4351*

ADVANCES IN DRUG RESEARCH.
Academic Press, Inc., 525 B St., Ste. 1900, San Diego, CA 92101-4495. TEL 619-231-0926. FAX 619-699-6715. *5397*

ADVANCES IN ECHO-CONTRAST.
Kluwer Academic Publishers, Postbus 17, 3300 AA Dordrecht, Netherlands. TEL 31-78-6392392. FAX 31-78-6392254. *4629*

ADVANCES IN ECOLOGICAL RESEARCH.
Academic Press, Inc., 525 B St., Ste. 1900, San Diego, CA 92101-4495. TEL 619-231-0926. FAX 619-699-6715. *2774*

ADVANCES IN ECONOMIC BOTANY.
New York Botanical Garden, Scientific Publications Department, Bronx, NY 10458-5126. TEL 718-817-8721. FAX 718-817-8842. *668*

ADVANCES IN EICOSANOID RESEARCH.
Kluwer Academic Publishers, Postbus 17, 3300 AA Dordrecht, Netherlands. TEL 31-78-6392392. FAX 31-78-6392254. *629*

ADVANCES IN ELECTROMAGNETIC FIELDS IN LIVING SYSTEMS.
Plenum Publishing Corp., 233 Spring St., New York, NY 10013-1578. TEL 212-620-8000. FAX 212-463-0742. *625*

ADVANCES IN ENGINEERING.
Swets & Zeitlinger b.v., P.O. Box 825, 2160 SZ Lisse, Netherlands. TEL 31-252-435111. FAX 31-252-415888. *2588*

ADVANCES IN ENGINEERING.
Society of Automotive Engineers, 400 Commonwealth Dr., Warrendale, PA 15096-0001. TEL 412-776-4841. FAX 412-776-3036. *6767*

ADVANCES IN ENGINEERING SOFTWARE.
Elsevier Science Ltd., P.O. Box 800, Kidlington, Oxford OX5 1DX, England. TEL 44-1865-843000. FAX 44-1865-843010. *2677*

ADVANCES IN ENVIRONMENTAL PSYCHOLOGY.
Lawrence Erlbaum Associates, Inc., 10 Industrial Dr., Mahwah, NJ 07430-2262. TEL 201-236-9500. FAX 201-236-0072. *5823*

ADVANCES IN ENVIRONMENTAL SCIENCE AND ENGINEERING.
Gordon & Breach Science Publishers, c/o International Publishers Distributor, P.O. Box 3054, Langhorne, PA 19047-3054. TEL 215-750-2642. FAX 215-750-6343. *2774*

ADVANCES IN ENVIRONMENTAL SCIENCE AND TECHNOLOGY.
Krieger Publishing Co., Box 9542, Melbourne, FL 32902. TEL 407-724-9542. FAX 407-951-3671. *2774*

ADVANCES IN ENZYME REGULATION.
Elsevier Science Ltd., Pergamon, P.O. Box 800, Kidlington, Oxford OX5 1DX, England. TEL 44-1865-843000. FAX 44-1865-843010. *4420*

ADVANCES IN ENZYMOLOGY AND RELATED AREAS OF MOLECULAR BIOLOGY.
John Wiley & Sons, Inc. 605 Third Ave., New York, NY 10158-0012. TEL 212-850-6800. *629*

ADVANCES IN EPILEPTOLOGY.
Lippincott - Raven Publishers 227 E. Washington Sq., Phialdelphia, PA 19106. TEL 215-238-4200. FAX 215-238-4235. *4822*

ADVANCES IN EXPERIMENTAL MEDICINE AND BIOLOGY.
Plenum Publishing Corp., 233 Spring St., New York, NY 10013-1578. TEL 212-620-8000. FAX 212-463-0742. *566*

ADVANCES IN EXPLORATION GEOPHYSICS.
Elsevier Science B.V., Books Division, P.O. Box 211, 1000 AE Amsterdam, Netherlands. TEL 31-20-4853911. FAX 31-20-4853705. *2270*

ADVANCES IN FINANCE, INVESTMENT AND BANKING.
Elsevier Science B.V., Books Division, P.O. Box 211, 1000 AE Amsterdam, Netherlands. TEL 31-20-4853911. FAX 31-20-4853705. *1318*

ADVANCES IN GENETICS.
Academic Press, Inc., 525 B St., Ste. 1900, San Diego, CA 92101-4495. TEL 619-231-0926. FAX 619-699-6715. *737*

ADVANCES IN GEOPHYSICS.
Academic Press, Inc., 525 B St., Ste. 1900, San Diego, CA 92101-4495. TEL 619-231-0926. FAX 619-699-6715. *2270*

ADVANCES IN HEALTH ECONOMICS AND HEALTH SERVICES RESEARCH.
J A I Press Inc., 55 Old Post Rd., No. 2, Box 1678, Greenwich, CT 06836-1678. TEL 203-661-7602. *5524*

ADVANCES IN HEALTH EDUCATION: CURRENT RESEARCH.
A M S Press, Inc., 56 E. 13th St., New York, NY 10003. TEL 212-777-4700. FAX 212-995-5413. *2478*

ADVANCES IN HEALTH SCIENCES EDUCATION.
Kluwer Academic Publishers, Postbus 17, 3300 AA Dordrecht, Netherlands. TEL 31-78-6392392. FAX 31-78-6392254. *4420*

ADVANCES IN HEAT TRANSFER.
Academic Press, Inc., 525 B St., Ste. 1900, San Diego, CA 92101-4495. TEL 619-231-0926. FAX 619-699-6715. *5583*

ADVANCES IN HETEROCYCLIC CHEMISTRY.
Academic Press, Inc., 525 B St., Ste. 1900, San Diego, CA 92101-4495. TEL 619-231-0926. FAX 619-699-6715. *1734*

ADVANCES IN HORTICULTURAL SCIENCE.
Universita degli Studi di Firenze, Dipartimento di Ortoflorofrutticoltura, Via Donizetti 6, 50144 Florence, Italy. TEL 055-333462. FAX 055-331497. *3042*

ADVANCES IN HUMAN - COMPUTER INTERACTION.
Ablex Publishing Corporation, 355 Chestnut St., Norwood, NJ 07648. TEL 201-767-8455. FAX 201-767-6717. *2011*

ADVANCES IN HUMAN FACTORS - ERGONOMICS.
Elsevier Science B.V., Books Division, P.O. Box 211, 1000 AE Amsterdam, Netherlands. TEL 31-20-4853911. FAX 31-20-4853705. *5823*

ADVANCES IN HUMAN GENETICS.
Plenum Publishing Corp., 233 Spring St., New York, NY 10013-1578. TEL 212-620-8000. FAX 212-463-0742. *737*

ADVANCES IN HUMAN PSYCHOPHARMACOLOGY.
Jessica Kingsley Publishers, 116 Pentonville Rd., London N1 9JB, England. TEL 071-833-2307. FAX 071-837-2917. *5397*

ADVANCES IN IMAGING AND ELECTRON PHYSICS.
Academic Press, Inc., 525 B St., Ste. 1900, San Diego, CA 92101-4495. TEL 619-231-0926. FAX 619-699-6715. *2682*

ADVANCES IN INCLUSION SCIENCE.
Kluwer Academic Publishers, Postbus 17, 3300 AA Dordrecht, Netherlands. TEL 31-78-6392392. FAX 31-78-6392254. *1734*

ADVANCES IN INDUSTRIAL ENGINEERING.
Elsevier Science B.V., Books Division, P.O. Box 211, 1000 AE Amsterdam, Netherlands. TEL 31-20-4853911. FAX 31-20-4853705. *2746*

ADVANCES IN INFANCY RESEARCH.
Ablex Publishing Corporation, 355 Chestnut St., Norwood, NJ 07648. TEL 201-767-8455. FAX 201-767-6717. *4802*

ADVANCES IN INFLAMMATION RESEARCH.
Lippincott - Raven Publishers 227 E. Washington Sq., Philadelphia, PA 19106. TEL 215-238-4200. FAX 215-238-4235. *4420*

ADVANCES IN INORGANIC BIOCHEMISTRY.
Elsevier Science B.V., Books Division, P.O. Box 211, 1000 AE Amsterdam, Netherlands. TEL 31-20-4853911. FAX 31-20-4853705. *1730*

ADVANCES IN INORGANIC CHEMISTRY.
Academic Press, Inc., 525 B St., Ste. 1900, San Diego, CA 92101-4495. TEL 619-231-0926. FAX 619-699-6715. *1730*

ADVANCES IN INSECT PHYSIOLOGY.
Academic Press, Inc., 525 B St., Ste. 1900, San Diego, CA 92101-4495. TEL 619-231-0926. FAX 619-699-6715. *720*

ADVANCES IN INSTRUCTIONAL PSYCHOLOGY.
Lawrence Erlbaum Associates, Inc., 10 Industrial Dr., Mahwah, NJ 07430-2262. TEL 201-236-9500. FAX 201-236-0072. *5823*

ADVANCES IN INSTRUMENTATION AND CONTROL.
Instrument Society of America, 67 Alexander Dr., Box 12277, Research Triangle Park, NC 27709. TEL 919-549-8411. FAX 919-549-8288. *3633*

ADVANCES IN LEARNING AND BEHAVIORAL DISABILITIES.
J A I Press Inc., 55 Old Post Rd., No. 2, Box 1678, Greenwich, CT 06836-1678. TEL 203-661-7602. FAX 203-661-0792. *2455*

ADVANCES IN LIPID RESEARCH.
Academic Press, Inc., 525 B St. Ste. 1900, San Diego, CA 92101-4495. TEL 619-231-0926. FAX 619-699-6715. *629*

ADVANCES IN M R I - CONTRAST.
Kluwer Academic Publishers, Postbus 17, 3300 AA Dordrecht, Netherlands. TEL 31-78-6392392. FAX 31-78-6392254. *4873*

ADVANCES IN MAGNETIC AND OPTICAL RESONANCE.
Academic Press, Inc., 525 B St., Ste. 1900, San Diego, CA 92101-4495. TEL 619-231-0926. FAX 619-699-6715. *5540*

ADVANCES IN MAGNETIC RESONANCE IMAGING.
Ablex Publishing Corporation, 355 Chestnut St., Norwood, NJ 07648. TEL 201-767-8455. FAX 201-767-6717. *2025*

ADVANCES IN MARINE BIOLOGY.
Academic Press, Inc., 525 B St., Ste. 1900, San Diego, CA 92101-4495. TEL 619-231-0926. FAX 619-699-6715. *566*

ADVANCES IN MATHEMATICS.
Academic Press, Inc., Journal Division, 525 B St., Ste. 1900, San Diego, CA 92101-4495. TEL 619-230-1840. FAX 619-699-6800. *4351*

ADVANCES IN MEDICAL SOCIAL SCIENCE.
Gordon & Breach Science Publishers, c/o International Publishers Distributor, P.O. Box 3054, Langhorne, PA 19047-3054. TEL 215-750-2542. FAX 215-750-6343. *6312*

ADVANCES IN METABOLISM.
Academic Press, Inc., 525 B St., Ste. 1900, San Diego, CA 92101-4495. TEL 619-231-0926. FAX 619-699-6715. *6565*

ADVANCES IN MICROBIAL ECOLOGY.
Plenum Publishing Corp., 233 Spring St., New York, NY 10013-1578. TEL 212-620-8000. FAX 212-463-0742. *752*

ADVANCES IN MICROBIAL PHYSIOLOGY.
Academic Press, Inc., 525 B St., Ste. 1900, San Diego, CA 92101-4495. TEL 619-231-0926. FAX 619-699-6715. *752*

ADVANCES IN MICROWAVES.
Academic Press, Inc., 525 B St., Ste. 1900, San Diego, CA 92101-4495. TEL 619-231-0926. FAX 619-699-6715. *2582*

ADVANCES IN MINING SCIENCE AND TECHNOLOGY.
Elsevier Science B.V., Books Division, P.O. Box 211, 1000 AE Amsterdam, Netherlands. TEL 31-20-4853911. FAX 31-20-4853705. *5056*

ADVANCES IN MODELLING & ANALYSIS. A: GENERAL MATHEMATICAL & COMPUTER TOOLS.
A M S E Press, 16 av. de Grange Blanche, 69160 Tassin-la-Demi-Lune, France. TEL 78-34-36-04. FAX 78-34-54-17. *4407*

ADVANCES IN MOLTEN SALT CHEMISTRY.
Elsevier Science B.V., Books Division, P.O. Box 211, 1000 AE Amsterdam, Netherlands. TEL 31-20-4853911. FAX 31-20-4853705. *1730*

ADVANCES IN MOTOR DEVELOPMENT RESEARCH.
A M S Press, Inc., 56 E 13th St., New York, NY 10003. TEL 212-777-4700. FAX 212-995-5413. *5524*

ADVANCES IN NATURAL AND TECHNOLOGICAL HAZARDS RESEARCH.
Kluwer Academic Publishers, Postbus 17, 3300 AA Dordrecht, Netherlands. TEL 31-78-6392392. FAX 31-78-6392254. *5953*

ADVANCES IN NEURAL AND BEHAVIORAL DEVELOPMENT.
Ablex Publishing Corporation, 355 Chestnut St., Norwood, NJ 07648. TEL 201-767-8455. FAX 201-767-6717. *5823*

ADVANCES IN NEUROCHEMISTRY.
Plenum Publishing Corp., 233 Spring St., New York, NY 10013-1578. TEL 212-620-8000. FAX 212-463-0742. *629*

ADVANCES IN NEUROIMMUNOLOGY.
Elsevier Science Ltd., Pergamon, P.O. Box 800, Kidlington, Oxford OX5 1DX, England. TEL 44-1865-843000. FAX 44-1865-843010. *4577*

ADVANCES IN NEUROLOGY.
Lippincott - Raven Publishers 227 E. Washington Sq., Philadelphia, PA 19106. TEL 215-238-4200. FAX 215-238-4235. *4822*

ADVANCES IN NEUROPSYCHIATRY AND PSYCHOPHARMACOLOGY.
Lippincott - Raven Publishers 227 E. Washington Sq., Philadelphia, PA 19106. TEL 215-238-4200. FAX 215-238-4235. *4822*

ADVANCES IN NEUROSCIENCE.
Lippincott - Raven Publishers 227 E. Washington Sq., Philadelphia, PA 19106. TEL 215-238-4200. FAX 215-238-4235. *4822*

ADVANCES IN NUCLEAR PHYSICS.
Plenum Publishing Corp., 233 Spring St., New York, NY 10013-1578. TEL 212-620-8000. FAX 212-463-0742. *5592*

ADVANCES IN NUCLEAR SCIENCE AND TECHNOLOGY.
Plenum Publishing Corp., 233 Spring St., New York, NY 10013-1578. TEL 212-620-8047. *5593*

ADVANCES IN NURSING SCIENCE.
Aspen Publishers, Inc., 200 Orchard Ridge Dr., Gaithersburg, MD 20878. TEL 301-417-7500. FAX 301-417-7550. *4709*

ADVANCES IN NUTRITIONAL RESEARCH.
Plenum Publishing Corp., 233 Spring St., New York, NY 10013-1578. TEL 212-620-8000. FAX 212-463-0742. *5228*

ADVANCES IN OPHTHALMIC PLASTIC & RECONSTRUCTIVE SURGERY.
c/o McGraw Hill, Monterey Ave., Blue Ridge Summit, PA 17294. *4766*

ADVANCES IN OPTO-ELECTRONICS.
Kluwer Academic Publishers, Postbus 17, 3300 AA Dordrecht, Netherlands. TEL 31-78-6392392. FAX 31-78-6392254. *2507*

ADVANCES IN ORGANOMETALLIC CHEMISTRY.
Academic Press, Inc., 525 B St., Ste. 1900, San Diego, CA 92101-4495. TEL 619-231-0926. FAX 619-699-6715. *1734*

ADVANCES IN ORTHOPAEDIC SURGERY.
Lippincott - Raven Publishers 227 E. Washington Sq., Philadelphia, PA 19106. TEL 215-238-4200. *4780*

ADVANCES IN OTO-RHINO-LARYNGOLOGY.
S. Karger AG, Allschwilerstr. 10, P.O. Box, CH-4009 Basel, Switzerland. TEL 061-3061111. FAX 061-3061234. *4794*

ADVANCES IN PAIN RESEARCH AND THERAPY.
Lippincott - Raven Publishers 227 E. Washington Sq., Philadelphia, PA 19106. TEL 215-238-4200. FAX 215-238-4235. *4822*

ADVANCES IN PARALLEL COMPUTING.
Elsevier Science B.V., Books Division, P.O. Box 211, 1000 AE Amsterdam, Netherlands. TEL 31-20-4853911. FAX 31-20-4853705. *2035*

ADVANCES IN PARASITOLOGY.
Academic Press, Inc., 525 B St., Ste. 1900, San Diego, CA 92101-4495. TEL 619-231-0926. FAX 619-699-6715. *796*

ADVANCES IN PERSONALITY ASSESSMENT.
Lawrence Erlbaum Associates, Inc., 10 Industrial Dr., Mahwah, NJ 07430-2262. TEL 201-236-9500. FAX 201-236-0072. *5823*

ADVANCES IN PETROLEUM GEOCHEMISTRY.
Academic Press, Inc., 525 B St., Ste. 1900, San Diego, CA 92101-4495. TEL 619-231-6616. FAX 619-699-6715. *5348*

ADVANCES IN PHARMACEUTICAL SCIENCES.
Academic Press, Inc., 525 B St., Ste. 1900, San Diego, CA 92101-4495. TEL 619-231-0926. FAX 619-699-6715. *5397*

ADVANCES IN PHARMACOLOGY.
Academic Press, Inc., 525 B St., Ste. 1900, San Diego, CA 92101-4495. TEL 619-231-0926. FAX 619-699-6715. *5397*

ADVANCES IN PHOTOCHEMISTRY.
John Wiley & Sons, Inc., 605 Third Ave., New York, NY 10158-0012. TEL 212-850-6645. *1748*

ADVANCES IN PHOTOSYNTHESIS.
Kluwer Academic Publishers, Postbus 17, 3300 AA Dordrecht, Netherlands. TEL 31-78-6392392. FAX 31-78-6392254. *668*

ADVANCES IN PHYSICAL ORGANIC CHEMISTRY.
Academic Press, Inc., 525 B St., Ste. 1900, San Diego, CA 92101-4495. TEL 619-231-0926. FAX 619-699-6715. *1748*

ADVANCES IN PHYSICS.
Taylor & Francis Ltd., 1 Gunpowder Sq., London EC4A 3DE, England. TEL 44-171-583-0490. FAX 44-171-583-0585. *5540*

ADVANCES IN PLANT PATHOLOGY.
Academic Press, Inc., 525 B St., Ste. 1900, San Diego, CA 92101-4495. TEL 305-345-2000. FAX 619-699-6715. *668*

ADVANCES IN POLYMER TECHNOLOGY.
John Wiley & Sons, Inc., Journals, 605 Third Ave., New York, NY 10158-0012. TEL 212-850-6645. FAX 212-850-6021. *5618*

ADVANCES IN POROUS MEDIA.
Elsevier Science B.V., Books Division, P.O. Box 211, 1000 AE Amsterdam, Netherlands. TEL 31-20-4853911. FAX 31-20-4853705. *2203*

ADVANCES IN PRIMATOLOGY.
Plenum Publishing Corp., 233 Spring St., New York, NY 10013-1578. TEL 212-620-8000. FAX 212-463-0742. *796*

ADVANCES IN PROSTAGLANDIN, THROMBOXANE, AND LEUKOTRIENE RESEARCH.
Lippincott - Raven Publishers 227 E. Washington Sq., Philadelphia, PA 19106. TEL 215-238-4200. FAX 215-238-4235. *5397*

ADVANCES IN PROTEIN CHEMISTRY.
Academic Press, Inc., 525 B St., Ste. 1900, San Diego, CA 92101-4495. TEL 619-231-0926. FAX 619-699-6715. *629*

ADVANCES IN PSYCHOLOGY.
Elsevier Science B.V., Books Division, P.O. Box 211, 1000 AE Amsterdam, Netherlands. TEL 31-20-4853911. FAX 31-20-4853705. *5823*

ADVANCES IN PSYCHOSOMATIC MEDICINE.
S. Karger AG, Allschwilerstr. 10, P.O. Box, CH-4009 Basel, Switzerland. TEL 061-3061111. FAX 061-3061234. *4823*

ADVANCES IN QUANTUM CHEMISTRY.
Academic Press, Inc., 525 B St., Ste. 1900, San Diego, CA 92101-4495. TEL 619-231-0926. FAX 619-699-6715. *1663*

ADVANCES IN RADIATION BIOLOGY.
Academic Press, Inc., 525 B St., Ste. 1900, San Diego, CA 92101-4495. TEL 619-231-0926. FAX 619-699-6715. *651*

ADVANCES IN REGULATION OF CELL GROWTH SERIES.
Lippincott - Raven Publishers 227 E. Washington Sq., Philadelphia, PA 19106. TEL 215-238-4200. FAX 215-238-4235. *566*

ADVANCES IN REPRODUCTIVE HEALTH CARE.
Kluwer Academic Publishers, Postbus 17, 3300 AA Dordrecht, Netherlands. TEL 31-78-6392392. FAX 31-78-6392254. *4731*

ADVANCES IN RISK ANALYSIS.
Plenum Publishing Corp., 233 Spring St., New York, NY 10013-1578. TEL 212-620-8000. FAX 212-463-0742. *5981*

ADVANCES IN SCHOOL PSYCHOLOGY.
Lawrence Erlbaum Associates, Inc., 10 Industrial Dr., Mahwah, NJ 07430-2262. TEL 201-236-9500. FAX 201-236-0072. *5824*

ADVANCES IN SECOND MESSENGER AND PHOSPHOPROTEIN RESEARCH.
Lippincott - Raven Publishers 227 E. Washington Sq., Philadelphia, PA 19106. TEL 215-238-4200. FAX 215-238-4235. *629*

ADVANCES IN SMALL ANIMAL MEDICINE AND SURGERY.
W.B. Saunders Co. Curtis Center, 3rd Fl., Independence Sq. W., Philadelphia, PA 19106-3399. TEL 215-238-7800. FAX 215-238-6445. *6939*

ADVANCES IN SOFTWARE ENGINEERING.
J A I Press Inc., 55 Old Post Rd., No. 2, Box 1678, Greenwich, CT 06836-1678. TEL 203-661-7602. *2107*

ADVANCES IN SOFTWARE SCIENCE AND TECHNOLOGY.
Academic Press, Inc., 525 B St., Ste. 1900, San Diego, CA 92101-4495. TEL 619-231-6616. FAX 619-699-6715. *2107*

ADVANCES IN SOLAR ENERGY: AN ANNUAL REVIEW OF RESEARCH AND DEVELOPMENT.
Plenum Publishing Corp., 233 Spring St., New York, NY 10013-1578. TEL 212-620-8000. FAX 212-463-0742. *2585*

ADVANCES IN SOLID STATE TECHNOLOGY.
Kluwer Academic Publishers, Postbus 17, 3300 AA Dordrecht, Netherlands. TEL 31-78-6392392. FAX 31-78-6392254. *5540*

ADVANCES IN SPACE RESEARCH.
Elsevier Science Ltd., Pergamon, P.O. Box 800, Kidlington, Oxford OX5 1DX, England. TEL 44-1865-843000. FAX 44-1865-843010. *52*

ADVANCES IN SPATIAL REASONING.
Ablex Publishing Corporation, 355 Chestnut St., Norwood, NJ 07648. TEL 201-767-8455. FAX 201-676-6717. *2004*

ADVANCES IN SUBSTANCE ABUSE: BEHAVIORAL AND BIOLOGICAL RESEARCH.
Jessica Kingsley Publishers, 116 Pentonville Rd., London N1 9JB, England. TEL 071-833-2307. FAX 071-837-2917. *2193*

ADVANCES IN SUICIDOLOGY.
E.J. Brill, P.O. Box 9000, 2300 PA Leiden, Netherlands. TEL 31-71-5353500. FAX 31-71-5317532. *4823*

ADVANCES IN THE MECHANICS AND PHYSICS OF SURFACES SERIES.
Harwood Academic Publishers, c/o International Publishers Distributor, P.O. Box 3054, Langhorne, PA 19047-3054. TEL 215-750-2642. FAX 215-750-6343. *5587*

ADVANCES IN THE PSYCHOLOGY OF HUMAN INTELLIGENCE.
Lawrence Erlbaum Associates, Inc., 10 Industrial Dr., Mahwah, NJ 07430-2262. TEL 201-236-9500. FAX 201-236-0072. *5824*

ADVANCES IN THE STUDY OF AGGRESSION.
Academic Press, Inc., 525 B St., Ste. 1900, San Diego, CA 92101-4495. TEL 619-231-6616. FAX 619-699-6715. *5824*

ADVANCES IN THE STUDY OF BEHAVIOR.
Academic Press, Inc., 525 B St., Ste. 1900, San Diego, CA 92101-4495. TEL 619-231-0926. FAX 619-699-6715. *5824*

ADVANCES IN THE STUDY OF COMMUNICATION AND AFFECT.
Plenum Publishing Corp., 233 Spring St., New York, NY 10013-1578. TEL 212-620-8000. FAX 212-463-0742. *5824*

ADVANCES IN THERAPY.
Health Communications Inc., 20 Highland Ave., Metuchen, NJ 08840. TEL 908-548-9130. FAX 908-548-8555. *5397*

ADVANCES IN TRANSPORT PROCESSES.
Elsevier Science B.V., P.O. Box 211, 1000 AE
Amsterdam, Netherlands. TEL 31-20-4853911.
FAX 31-20-4853598. *2632*

**ADVANCES IN UNDERWATER TECHNOLOGY, OCEAN
SCIENCE AND OFFSHORE ENGINEERING.**
Kluwer Academic Publishers, Postbus 17, 3300 AA
Dordrecht, Netherlands. TEL 31-78-6392392.
FAX 31-78-6392254. *2290*

**ADVANCES IN URETHANE SCIENCE AND
TECHNOLOGY.**
Technomic Publishing Co., Inc., 851 New Holland
Ave., Box 3535, Lancaster, PA 17604. TEL 717-
291-5609. FAX 717-295-4538. *1734*

ADVANCES IN VEGETATION SCIENCE.
Kluwer Academic Publishers, Postbus 17, 3300 AA
Dordrecht, Netherlands. TEL 31-78-6392392.
FAX 31-78-6392254. *668*

ADVANCES IN VETERINARY DERMATOLOGY.
Elsevier Science Ltd., Books Division, P.O. Box 800,
Kidlington, Oxford OX5 1DX, England. TEL 44-1865-
843000. FAX 44-1865-843010. *6939*

**ADVANCES IN VETERINARY SCIENCE AND
COMPARATIVE MEDICINE.**
Academic Press, Inc., 525 B St., Ste. 1900, San
Diego, CA 92101-4495. TEL 619-231-0926.
FAX 619-699-6715. *6940*

ADVANCES IN VIRAL ONCOLOGY.
Lippincott - Raven Publishers 227 E. Washington
Sq., Philadelphia, PA 19106. TEL 215-238-4200.
FAX 215-238-4235. *4747*

ADVANCES IN VIRUS RESEARCH.
Academic Press, Inc., 525 B St., Ste. 1900, San
Diego, CA 92101-4495. TEL 619-231-0926.
FAX 619-699-6715. *752*

ADVANCES IN WATER RESOURCES.
Elsevier Science Ltd., P.O. Box 800, Kidlington,
Oxford OX5 1DX, England. TEL 44-1865-843000.
FAX 44-1865-843010. *6962*

ADVANCES IN WORLD AQUACULTURE.
World Aquaculture Society, 143 J M Parker
Coliseum, Louisiana State University, Baton Rouge,
LA 70803. TEL 504-388-3137. FAX 504-388-
3493. *2290*

ADVANCES IN WOUND CARE.
Springhouse Corporation 1111 Bethlehem Pike, Box
908, Springhouse, PA 19477. TEL 215-646-8700.
4658

ADVANCES IN X-RAY ANALYSIS.
Plenum Publishing Corp., 233 Spring St., New York,
NY 10013-1578. TEL 212-620-8000. FAX 212-
463-0742. *4948*

ADVENTURE WEST.
Adventure Media, Inc., Box 3210, Incline Village, NV
89450-3210. TEL 702-832-3700. FAX 702-832-
3775. *6865*

ADVERSE DRUG REACTION BULLETIN.
Chapman & Hall, Journals Department 2-6
Boundary Row, London SE1 8HN, England. TEL 44-
171-8650066. FAX 44-171-5229623. *5397*

ADVERTISING LAW ANTHOLOGY.
International Library Law Book Publishers, Inc.,
4301 N. Fairfax Dr., Ste. 875, Arlington, VA
22203. TEL 703-528-1000. FAX 703-528-6060.
3736

ADVOCATE (BETHESDA).
Autism Society of America, 7910 Woodmont Ave.,
Ste. 650, Bethesda, MD 20814-3015. TEL 301-
657-0881. FAX 301-657-0869. *2465*

THE ADVOCATE (BOISE).
Idaho State Bar, 525 Jefferson St., Box 895, Boise,
ID 83701. TEL 208-334-4500. FAX 208-334-
4515. *3736*

AEROBIOLOGIA.
Elsevier Science Ireland Ltd., P.O. Box 85, Limerick,
Ireland. TEL 353-61-4714944. FAX 353-61-
472144. *566*

AERONAUTICAL MANUFACTURING TECHNOLOGY.
Beijing Hangkong Gongyi Yanjiusuo, P.O. Box 863,
Beijing 100024, People's Republic of China.
TEL 5761731. FAX 5762306. *52*

AERONAUTICAL SATELLITE NEWS.
Inmarsat, 99 City Rd., London EC1Y 1AX, England.
TEL 0171-723-1449. FAX 0171-728-1344. *52*

AEROSOL SCIENCE AND TECHNOLOGY.
Elsevier Science Inc., Box 945, New York, NY
10159-0945. TEL 212-633-3730. FAX 212-633-
3680. *1663*

AESTHETIC PLASTIC SURGERY.
Springer-Verlag, Medical Journals, 175 Fifth Ave.,
New York, NY 10010. TEL 212-460-1500.
FAX 212-473-6272. *4902*

AESTHETIC SURGERY QUARTERLY.
Mosby - Year Book. Inc. 11830 Westline Industrial
Dr., St. Louis, MO 63146-3318. TEL 314-872-
8370. FAX 314-432-1380. *4902*

AETHIOPICA.
Harrassowitz Verlag, Taunusstr. 14, 65183
Wiesbaden, Germany. TEL 49-611-530555.
FAX 49-611-530559. *3368*

AFGHANISTAN STUDIES JOURNAL.
Center for Afghanistan Studies, University of
Nebraska at Omaha, Omaha, NE 68182-0006.
TEL 402-554-2901. FAX 402-554-3242. *3377*

AFINIDAD.
Instituto Quimico de Sarria, Asociacion de Quimicos,
Via Augusta 390, 08017 Barcelona, Spain. TEL 34-
3-2804276. FAX 34-3-2804276. *1663*

AFRICA.
Istituto Italo-Africano, Via Ulisse Aldrovandi 16,
00197 Rome, Italy. TEL 39-6-3221297. FAX 39-6-
3225348. *3369*

AFRICA (EDINBURGH).
Edinburgh University Press, 22 George Sq.,
Edinburgh EH8 9LF, Scotland. TEL 44-131-650-
6207. FAX 44-131-662-0053. *3369*

AFRICA MEDIA REVIEW.
African Council for Communication Education, P.O.
Box 47495, Nairobi, Kenya. TEL 254-2-227043.
FAX 254-2-216135. *1895*

AFRICA TODAY.
Lynne Rienner Publishers, 1800 30th St., Ste. 314,
Boulder, CO 80301. TEL 303-444-6684. FAX 303-
444-0824. *5631*

AFRICAN ARCHAEOLOGICAL REVIEW.
Plenum Publishing Corp., 233 Spring St., New York,
NY 10013-1578. TEL 212-620-8000. FAX 212-
463-0742. *338*

AFRICAN CROP SCIENCE JOURNAL.
African Crop Science Society, Faculty of Agriculture
and Forestry, Makerere University, P.O. Box 7062,
Kampala, Uganda. TEL 256-041-540464.
FAX 256-041-543382. *208*

AFRICAN DEVELOPMENT REVIEW.
African Development Bank, B.P. 1387, Abidjan 01,
Ivory Coast. *1301*

AFRICAN JOURNAL OF ECOLOGY.
Blackwell Science Ltd., Osney Mead, Oxford OX2
0EL, England. TEL 44-1865-206206. FAX 44-
1865-206219. *2119*

AFRICAN JOURNAL OF HEALTH SCIENCES.
African Forum for Health Sciences, P.O. Box 54840,
Nairobi, Kenya. TEL 254-2-722541. FAX 254-2-
720030. *2421*

**AFRICAN JOURNAL OF LIBRARY, ARCHIVES AND
INFORMATION SCIENCE.**
Archlib & Information Services Ltd., P.O. Box
20492, Ibadan, Oyo State, Nigeria. *3971*

**AFRICAN JOURNAL OF MEDICINE & MEDICAL
SCIENCES.**
Spectrum Books Ltd., College of Medicine, University
College Hospital, Ibadan, Oyo State, Nigeria.
TEL 234-02-2410088. *4421*

AFRICAN LIVESTOCK RESEARCH.
International Livestock Centre for Africa, P.O. Box
5689, Addis Ababa, Ethiopia. *262*

AFRICAN VIOLET MAGAZINE.
African Violet Society of America, Inc., 2375 North,
Beaumont, TX 77702-1722. TEL 409-839-4725.
FAX 409-839-4329. *3042*

AFRICAN WOMAN.
Akina Mama wa Afrika, 4 Wild Ct., London WC2B
5AL, England. TEL 44-171-405-0678. FAX 44-
171-831-3947. *6987*

AFRICAN YEARBOOK OF INTERNATIONAL LAW.
Martinus Nijhoff Publishers, Human Rights and
International Law Postbus 163, 3300 AD
Dordrecht, Netherlands. TEL 31 78-334911.
FAX 31-78-334254. *3521*

AFRICHE.
Società delle Missioni Africane, Via Borghero 4,
16148 Genova, Italy. TEL 39-10-3733657.
FAX 39-10-3733664. *3370*

**AFRO-AMERICANS IN NEW YORK LIFE AND
HISTORY.**
Afro-American Historical Association of the Niagara
Frontier, Buffalo State College, Box 63, Buffalo, NY
14222. TEL 716-878-4078. *2861*

AFRO-HISPANIC REVIEW.
University of Missouri at Columbia, Romance
Languages Department, c/o Dr. Edward Muller,
143, Arts & Sciences, Columbia, MO 65211.
TEL 314-882-2030. FAX 314-382-3404. *2861*

AGAIN.
Conciliar Press, 10090 A Hwy. 9, Box 76, Ben
Lomond, CA 95005-0076. TEL 408-336-5118.
FAX 408-336-8882. *6112*

AGAINST THE GRAIN.
Katina & Bruce Strauch, Ed. & Pub., Citadel Sta.,
Charleston, SC 29409. TEL 803-723-3536.
FAX 803-723-3536. *3971*

AGE.
American Aging Association, 2129 Providence Ave.,
Chester, PA 19013. TEL 610-874-7550. FAX 610-
876-7715. *3282*

AGGIORNAMENTI DI TERAPIA OFTALMOLOGICA.
Farmigea S.p.A., Via Carmignani, 2, 56127 Pisa,
Italy. TEL 39-50-544000. FAX 39-50-544304.
4766

AGGRESSION AND VIOLENT BEHAVIOR.
Elsevier Science Ltd., Pergamon, P.O. Box 800,
Kidlington, Oxford OX5 1DX, England. TEL 44-1865-
843000. FAX 44-1865-843010. *5824*

AGGRESSIVE BEHAVIOR
John Wiley & Sons, Inc. Journals, 605 Third Ave.,
New York, NY 10158. TEL 212-850-6645.
FAX 212-850-6021. *5824*

AGING (NEW YORK).
Lippincott - Raven Publishers 227 E. Washington
Sq., Philadelphia, PA 19106. TEL 215-238-4200.
FAX 215-238-4235. *5282*

AGING & MENTAL HEALTH.
Carfax Publishing Co., P.O. Box 25, Abingdon, Oxon
OX14 3UE, England. TEL 44-1235-401000.
FAX 44-1235-401550 *3282*

AGING ARKANSAS.
Arkansas Aging Foundation, Inc., 706 S. Pulaski St.,
Little Rock, AR 72201. TEL 501-376-6083.
FAX 501-376-6084. *3282*

AGREKON (ENGLISH EDITION).
Landbou-Ekonomie Vereniging van Suid-Afrika,
Posbus 12986, Hatfield 0028, South Africa.
TEL 27-12-4203248. FAX 27-12-3422713. *185*

AGRI DERGISI.
Turk Algoloji Dernegin i, Istanbul Tip Fakultesi, Agri
Merkezi, Capa Klinikler, 34390 Istanbul, Turkey.
TEL 90-212-6350135. FAX 90-212-6310541.
4823

AGRI-PRACTICE.
Veterinary Practice Publishing Co., 7 Ashley Ave. S.,
Santa Barbara, CA 93103-9589. TEL 805-965-
1028. FAX 805-965-3722. *6940*

AGRIBUSINESS (NEW YORK).
John Wiley & Sons, Inc., Journals, 605 Third Ave., New York, NY 10158-6012. TEL 212-850-6645. FAX 212-850-6021. *185*

AGRICULTURAL AND BIOLOGICAL RESEARCH.
Young Environmentalist Association, 64 Khurshed Bagh, Lucknow 226 004, India. TEL 91-522-226091. *89*

AGRICULTURAL AND FOOD SCIENCE IN FINLAND.
Agricultural Research Centre of Finland, Editorial Office, 31600 Jokioinen, Finland. FAX 358-16-418-83-39. *89*

AGRICULTURAL AND FOREST METEOROLOGY.
Elsevier Science B.V., P.O. Box 211, 1000 AE Amsterdam, Netherlands. TEL 31-20-4853911. FAX 31-20-4853598. *4990*

AGRICULTURAL ECONOMICS.
Elsevier Science B.V., P.O. Box 211, 1000 AE Amsterdam, Netherlands. TEL 31-20-4853911. FAX 31-20-4853598. *186*

AGRICULTURAL ENGINEER.
Institution of Agricultural Engineers, West End Rd., Silsoe, Beds. MK45 4DU, England. TEL 44-1525-861096. FAX 44-1525-861660. *89*

AGRICULTURAL ENGINEERING AUSTRALIA.
Society for Engineering in Agriculture, Institution of Engineers, 11 National Circuit, Barton, A.C.T. 2600, Australia. TEL 61-6-270-6555. FAX 61-6-273-1488. *89*

AGRICULTURAL ENGINEERING JOURNAL.
Asian Association for Agricultural Engineering, c/o Division of Agricultural and Food Engineering, Asian Institute of Technology, G.P.O. Box 2754, Bangkok 10501, Thailand. TEL 66-2-524-5478. FAX 66-2-524-6200. *89*

AGRICULTURAL FINANCE REVIEW.
Cornell University, Department of Agricultural Economics, 155 Warren Hall, Ithaca, NY 14853-7801. TEL 607-255-4534. FAX 607-255-9984. *186*

AGRICULTURAL FINANCIAL STATISTICS.
Statistics Canada, Ottawa, ON K1A 0T6, Canada. TEL 613-951-7277. FAX 613-951-1584. *166*

AGRICULTURAL HISTORY.
University of California Press, Journals Division, 2120 Berkeley Way, No. 5812, Berkeley, CA 94720-5812. TEL 510-643-7154. FAX 510-642-9917. *89*

AGRICULTURAL SYSTEMS.
Elsevier Science Ltd., P.O. Box 800, Kidlington, Oxford OX5 1DX, England. TEL 44-1865-843000. FAX 44-1865-843010. *91*

AGRICULTURAL WATER MANAGEMENT.
Elsevier Science B.V., P.O. Box 211, 1000 AE Amsterdam, Netherlands. TEL 31-20-4853911. FAX 31-20-4853598. *209*

AGRICULTURE, ECOSYSTEMS AND ENVIRONMENT.
Elsevier Science B.V., P.O. Box 211, 1000 AE Amsterdam, Netherlands. TEL 31-20-4853911. FAX 31-20-4853598. *92*

AGRICULTURE ET DEVELOPPEMENT.
C I R A D - C A, B.P. 5035, 34032 Montpellier Cedex, France. TEL 67-61-59-18. FAX 67-61-59-21. *92*

AGRO AMBIENTE.
Iacico s.r.l., Via A. Poliziano 80, 00184 Rome, Italy. TEL 39-6-4873183. FAX 39-6-4873144. *92*

AGRO FOOD INDUSTRY HI-TECH.
Teknoscienze s.r.l., Via Aurelio Saffi 23, 20123 Milan, Italy. TEL 39-2-4818118. FAX 39-2-4818070. *93*

AGRO SUR.
Universidad Austral de Chile, Facultad de Ciencias Agrarias, Casilla 567, Valdivia, Chile. TEL 56-63-221660. FAX 56-63-221460. *93*

AGROBOREALIS.
University of Alaska at Fairbanks, Agricultural and Forestry Experiment Station, Fairbanks, AK 99775. TEL 907-474-7653. *93*

AGROCHIMICA.
Gruppo Agrochimica, Via S. Michele degli Scalzi 2, 56124 Pisa, Italy. TEL 39-50-571557. FAX 39-50-598614. *93*

AGROCIENCIA.
Colegio de Postgraduados, Instituto de Estudios, Investigaciones y Servicio Agripefor Chapingo S.C., Cerro del Vigilante 166, Col. Romero de Terrenos, 04310 Mexico DF, Mexico. TEL 915-5-541304. *93*

AGROFORESTRY SYSTEMS.
Kluwer Academic Publishers, Postbus 17, 3300 AA Dordrecht, Netherlands. TEL 31-78-6392392. FAX 31-78-6392254. *93*

AGRONOMIE.
Editions Scientifiques et Medicales Elsevier, 141 rue de Javel, 75747 Paris, France. TEL 33-1-45589022. FAX 33-1-45589421. *210*

AICHI MEDICAL UNIVERSITY ASSOCIATION. JOURNAL.
Aichi Medical University Association, 21, Yazakokarimata, Nagakutecho, Aichi-gun, Aichi-ken 480-11, Japan. TEL 81-561-62-3311. FAX 81-561-62-3348. *4422*

AIDA PARKER NEWSLETTER.
Aida Parker Newsletter Pty. Ltd., P.O. Box 91059, Auckland Park 2006, Johannesburg, South Africa. TEL 27-11-726-6856. FAX 27-11-726-5537. *5631*

AIDS ALERT.
American Health Consultants, Inc., 3525 Piedmont Rd., N.E., Bldg. 6, Ste. 400, Atlanta, GA 30305. FAX 800-284-3291. *4615*

AIDS & BEHAVIOR.
Plenum Publishing Corp., 233 Spring St., New York, NY 10013-1578. TEL 212-620-8000. FAX 212-463-0742. *4577*

AIDS & PUBLIC POLICY JOURNAL.
University Publishing Group, Inc., 107 E. Church St., Frederick, MD 21701. *4615*

AIDS CARE.
Carfax Publishing Co., P.O. Box 25, Abingdon, Oxon. OX14 3UE, England. TEL 44-1235-401000. FAX 44-1235-401550. *4616*

AIDS EDUCATION AND PREVENTION.
Guilford Publications, Inc., 72 Spring St., 4th Fl., New York, NY 10012. TEL 212-431-9800. FAX 212-966-6708. *4616*

AIDS INFORMATION EXCHANGE.
U.S. Conference of Mayors, Office of Public Affairs, 1620 Eye St., N.W., Washington, DC 20006. TEL 202-293-7330. FAX 202-293-2352. *4616*

AIDS PATIENT CARE AND S T DS.
Mary Ann Liebert, Inc. Publishers, 2 Madison Ave., Larchmont, NY 10538. TEL 914-834-3100. FAX 914-834-3688. *4616*

AIDS PREVENTION AND MENTAL HEALTH.
Plenum Publishing Corp., 233 Spring St., New York, NY 10013-1578. TEL 212-620-8000. FAX 212-463-0742. *4616*

AIDS RESEARCH AND HUMAN RETROVIRUSES.
Mary Ann Liebert, Inc. Publishers, 2 Madison Ave., Larchmont, NY 10358. TEL 914-834-3100. FAX 914-384-3688. *4617*

AINM.
Ulster Place-Name Society, Department of Celtic, Queen's University of Belfast, Belfast BT7 1NN, N. Ireland. TEL 245133. *4050*

AIR FORCE JOURNAL OF LOGISTICS.
U.S. Air Force, Logistics Management Agency, Gunter Annex, Maxwell A.F.B., AL 36114-3236. TEL 205-416-4087. FAX 205-596-4638. *5020*

AIR MEDICAL JOURNAL.
Mosby - Year Book, Inc. 11830 Westline Industrial Dr., St. Louis, MO 63146-3318. TEL 314-872-8370. FAX 314-432-1380. *4422*

AIR POWER HISTORY.
Air Force Historical Foundation, 170 Luke Ave., Ste. 400, Bolling AFB, DC 20332-5113. TEL 202-767-5088. FAX 202-767-5527. *55*

AIR QUALITY MONOGRAPHS.
Elsevier Science B.V., Books Division, P.O. Box 211, 1000 AE Amsterdam, Netherlands. TEL 31-20-4853911. FAX 31-20-4853705. *2833*

AIR TRAFFIC CONTROL QUARTERLY.
John Wiley & Sons, Inc., Journals, 605 Third Ave., New York, NY 10158-0012. TEL 212-850-6645. FAX 212-850-6021. *6749*

AIRPOWER JOURNAL.
U.S. Air Force, Air University, 401 Chennault Circle, Maxwell Air Force Base, AL 36112-6428. TEL 334-953-5322. FAX 334-953-6739. *5020*

AKADEMIA ROLNICZA W SZCZECINIE. INFORMATORY.
Akademia Rolnicza w Szczecinie, Dzial Wydawnictw, Ul. Doktora Judyma 22, 71-460 Szczecin, Poland. TEL 48-91-541639. FAX 48-91-541642. *95*

AKADEMIA ROLNICZA W SZCZECINIE. ROZPRAWY.
Akademia Rolnicza w Szczecinie, Dzial Wydawnictw, Ul. Doktora Judyma 22, 71-460 Szczecin, Poland. TEL 48-91-54169. FAX 48-91-541642. *95*

AKADEMIA ROLNICZA W SZCZECINIE. ZESZYTY NAUKOWE. NAUKI SPOLECZNE I EKONOMICZNE.
Akademia Rolnicza w Szczecinie, Dzial Wydawnictw, Ul. Doktora Judyma 22, 71-460 Szczecin, Poland. TEL 48-91-541639. FAX 48-91-541642. *6313*

AKADEMIA ROLNICZA W SZCZECINIE. ZESZYTY NAUKOWE. ROLNICTWO.
Akademia Rolnicza w Szczecinie, Dzial Wydawnictw, Ul. Doktora Judyma 22, 71-460 Szczecin, Poland. TEL 48-91-541639. FAX 48-91-541642. *210*

AKADEMIA ROLNICZA W SZCZECINIE. ZESZYTY NAUKOWE. RYBACTWO MORSKIE I TECHNOLOGIA ZYWNOSCI.
Akademia Rolnicza w Szczecinie, Dzial Wydawnictw, Ul. Doktora Judyma 22, 71-460 Szczecin, Poland. TEL 48-91-541639. FAX 48-91-541642. *2924*

AKADEMIA ROLNICZA W SZCZECINIE. ZESZYTY NAUKOWE. ZOOTECHNIKA.
Akademia Rolnicza w Szczecinie, Dzial Wydawnictw, Ul. Doktora Judyma 22, 71-460 Szczecin, Poland. TEL 48-91-541639. FAX 48-91-541642. *262*

AKITA IGAKU.
Akita Daigaku, Igakubu, 1-1, Hondo 1-chome, Akita-shi, Akita-ken 010, Japan. FAX 81-188-33-1740. *4422*

AL RAFIDAYN - JAHRBUCH ZU GESCHICHTE UND KULTUR DES MODERNEN IRAQ.
Ergon-Verlag, Grombuehlstr. 7, 97080 Wuerzburg, Germany. TEL 0931-280084. FAX 0931-282872. *3494*

ALABAMA COUNSELING ASSOCIATION. JOURNAL.
Alabama Counseling Association, c/o Dr. Ervin L. Wood, Sta. 36, UWA, Livingston, AL 35470. TEL 205-652-9661. FAX 205-652-4065. *5262*

ALABAMA GENEALOGICAL SOCIETY MAGAZINE.
Alabama Genealogical Society, Samford University, Box 2296, 800 Lakeshore Dr., Birmingham, AL 35229. *3073*

ALABAMA GEOLOGICAL SOCIETY. GUIDEBOOK FOR THE ANNUAL FIELD TRIP.
Alabama Geological Society, Box 6184, Tuscaloosa, AL 35486. TEL 205-349-2852. *2223*

ALABAMA REVIEW.
University of Alabama Press, Box 870380, Tuscaloosa, AL 35487-0380. TEL 205-348-5180. FAX 205-348-9201. *3457*

ALALUZ.
University of California, Riverside, Department of Spanish and Portuguese, Riverside, CA 92502. TEL 909-788-9009. FAX 909-787-9422. *4178*

ALASKA. DIVISION OF GEOLOGICAL AND GEOPHYSICAL SURVEYS. GEOLOGIC - PROFESSIONAL REPORT.
Department of Natural Resources, Division of Geological and Geophysical Surveys, 794 University Ave., Ste.200, Fairbanks, AK 99709-3645. TEL 907-474-7147. FAX 907-479-4779. *2223*

ALASKA. DIVISION OF GEOLOGICAL AND GEOPHYSICAL SURVEYS. INFORMATION CIRCULAR.
Department of Natural Resources, Division of Geological and Geophysical Surveys, 794 University Ave. Ste. 200, Fairbanks, AK 99709-3645. TEL 907-474-7147. FAX 907-479-4779. *2223*

ALASKA. DIVISION OF GEOLOGICAL AND GEOPHYSICAL SURVEYS. REPORT OF INVESTIGATIONS.
Department of Natural Resources, Division of Geological and Geophysical Surveys, 794 University Ave., Ste. 200, Fairbanks, AK 99709-3645. TEL 907-474-7147. FAX 907-479-4779. *2223*

ALASKA. DIVISION OF GEOLOGICAL AND GEOPHYSICAL SURVEYS. SPECIAL REPORT.
Department of Natural Resources, Division of Geological and Geophysical Surveys, 794 University Ave. Ste. 200, Fairbanks, AK 99709-3645. TEL 907-474-7147. FAX 907-479-4779. *2223*

ALASKA FISHERY RESEARCH BULLETIN.
Department of Fish and Game, Commercial Fisheries Management and Development Division, Box 25526, Juneau, AK 99802-5526. TEL 907-465-4210. FAX 907-465-2604. *2925*

ALASKA MEDICINE.
Alaska State Medical Association, American Society for Circumpolar Health, 4107 Laurel St., Anchorage, AK 99508. TEL 907-562-2662. FAX 907-561-2063. *4422*

ALBANY LAW REVIEW.
Albany Law School, 80 New Scotland Ave., Albany, NY 12208. TEL 518-445-2372. FAX 518-472-5857. *3738*

ALBATROZ.
Association Albatroz, BP 404, 75969 Paris Cedex 20, France. *4178*

ALBERTA LAW REVIEW.
University of Alberta, Faculty of Law, Edmonton, AB T6G 2H5, Canada. TEL 403-492-5559. FAX 403-492-4924. *3738*

ALCES.
Bookstore, Lakehead University, 855 Oliver Rd., Thunder Bay, ON P7B 5E1, Canada. TEL 807-343-8528. FAX 807-346-7796. *796*

ALCOHOL (NEW YORK).
Elsevier Science Inc., Box 945, New York, NY 10159-0945. TEL 212-633-3730. FAX 212-633-3680. *2193*

ALCOHOL & ALCOHOLISM.
Oxford University Press, Oxford Journals, Walton St., Oxford OX2 6DP, England. TEL 01865-267907. FAX 01865-267773. *2193*

ALCOHOL HEALTH & RESEARCH WORLD.
U.S. National Institute on Alcohol Abuse and Alcoholism, 6000 Executive Blvd., Bethesda, MD 20892-7003. TEL 301-443-3860. FAX 301-480-1726. *2194*

ALCOHOLISM: CLINICAL AND EXPERIMENTAL RESEARCH.
Williams & Wilkins, 351 W. Camden St., Baltimore, MD 21201. TEL 410-528-4000. FAX 410-528-4312. *2194*

ALCOHOLISM TREATMENT QUARTERLY.
Haworth Press, Inc., 10 Alice St., Binghamton, NY 13904. TEL 607-722-5857. FAX 607-722-1424. *2194*

ALERT DIVER.
Divers Alert Network, Box 3823, Duke University Medical Center, Durham, NC 27710. TEL 919-684-2948. FAX 919-490-6630. *6449*

ALEXANDRIA JOURNAL OF AGRICULTURAL RESEARCH.
University of Alexandria, Faculty of Agriculture, Alexandria, Egypt. FAX 20-3-5972780. *96*

ALEXANDRIA SCIENCE EXCHANGE.
Prof. Dr. A.M. Balba Group for Soil and Water Research, College of Agriculture, University of Alexandria, El-Shatby, Alexandria 21545. TEL 03-5975405. FAX 03-5954684. *6225*

ALEXANDRIE.
Polska Akademia Nauk, Zaklad Archeologii Srodziemnomorskiej, Palac Kultury i Nauki, p. 2105, 00-901 Warsaw, Poland. TEL 48-22-248593. FAX 48-22-6207651. *338*

ALGEBRA AND LOGIC.
Plenum Publishing Corp., Consultants Bureau, 233 Spring St., New York, NY 10013-1578. TEL 212-620-8468. FAX 212-463-0742. *4352*

ALGEBRA, LOGIC AND APPLICATIONS.
Gordon & Breach Science Publishers, c/o International Publishers Distributor, P.O. Box 3054, Langhorne, PA 19047-3054. TEL 215-750-2642. FAX 215-750-6343. *4352*

ALGONQUIAN CONFERENCE. PAPERS.
Algonquian Conference, Department of Linguistics, University of Manitoba, Winnipeg, MB R3T 2N2, Canada. TEL 204-474-9596. *299*

ALGORITHMICA.
Springer-Verlag, Science Journals, 175 Fifth Ave., New York, NY 10010. TEL 212-460-1500. FAX 212-473-6272. *1982*

ALIMENTARY PHARMACOLOGY AND THERAPEUTICS.
Blackwell Science Ltd., Osney Mead, Oxford OX2 OEL, England. TEL 44-1865-206206. FAX 44-1865-206219. *4689*

ALISO.
Rancho Santa Ana Botanic Garden, 1500 N. College Ave., Claremont, CA 91711. TEL 909-625-8767. FAX 909-626-7670. *669*

THE ALKALOIDS.
Academic Press, Inc., 525 B St., Ste. 1900, San Diego, CA 92101-4495. TEL 619-231-0926. FAX 619-699-6715. *1734*

ALLEGRO.
Associated Musicians of Greater New York, AFM, Local 802, 322 W. 48th St., 5th Fl., New York, NY 10036. TEL 212-245-4802. FAX 212-245-6255. *3717*

ALLELOPATHY JOURNAL.
International Allelopathy Foundation, E-2, Married Flats, CCS Haryana Agricultural University, Hisar 125 004, India. TEL 91-1662-78083. *669*

ALLERGOLOGICUM; TRANSACTIONS OF THE COLLEGIUM INTERNATIONALE.
S. Karger AG, Allschwilerstr. 10, P.O. Box, CH-4009 Basel, Switzerland. TEL 061-3061111. FAX 061-3061234. *4577*

ALLERGOLOGY INTERNATIONAL.
Blackwell Science Pty Ltd, P.O. Box 378, Carlton South, Vic. 3053, Australia. TEL 61-3-93470300. FAX 61-3-93493016. *4577*

ALLERGY.
Munksgaard International Publishers Ltd., 35 Noerre Soegade, P.O. Box 2148, DK-1016 Copenhagen K, Denmark. TEL 45-33-127030. FAX 45-33-129387. *4577*

ALLERTONIA.
National Tropical Botanical Garden, Box 340, Lawai, Kauai, HI 96765. TEL 808-332-7324. FAX 808-332-9765. *669*

ALLIONIA.
Universita degli Studi di Torino, Dipartimento di Biologia Vegetale, Viale P.A. Mattioli 25, 10125 Turin, Italy. TEL 39-11-6699884. FAX 39-11-655839. *669*

ALLURE.
Target s.r.l. Via Bondi 23, 2, 40138 Bologna, Italy. TEL 39-51-342426. FAX 39-51-345554. *494*

ALPE ADRIA MICROBIOLOGY JOURNAL.
Biomedia s.r.l., Via C. Farini 70, 21059 Milan, Italy. TEL 39-2-69001316. FAX 39-2-69001311. *752*

ALTBABYLONISCHE BRIEFE IM UMSCHRIFT UND UEBERSETZUNG.
E.J. Brill, P.O. Box 9000, 2300 PA Leiden, Netherlands. TEL 31-71-5353500. FAX 31-71-5317532. *5277*

ALTERNATE ROUTES.
c/o Department of Sociology-Anthropology, Carleton University, Ottawa, ON K1S 5B5, Canada. TEL 613-788-7400. FAX 613-788-4062. *6313*

ALTERNATIVE HEALTH PRACTITIONER.
Springer Publishing Company, 536 Broadway, New York, NY 10012-3955 TEL 212-431-4370. FAX 212-941-7842. *239*

ALTERNATIVE THERAPIES IN HEALTH AND MEDICINE.
American Association of Critical Care Nurses, 101 Columbia, Aliso Viejo, CA 92656. TEL 714-362-2000. *289*

ALTERNATIVES (BOULDER).
Lynne Rienner Publishers, 1800 30th St., Ste. 314, Boulder, CO 80301-1032. TEL 303-444-6684. FAX 303-444-0824. *5740*

ALTERNATIVES JOURNAL.
University of Waterloo, Faculty of Environmental Studies, Waterloo, ON N2L 3G1, Canada. TEL 519-885-1221 ext. 6783. FAX 519-746-0292. *2775*

ALTERNATIVES TO LABORATORY ANIMALS: A T L A.
Fund for the Replacement of Animals in Medical Experiments, Russell & Burch House, 96-98 N. Sherwood St., Nottingham NG1 4EE, England. TEL 44-115-958-4740. FAX 44-115-950-3570. *4676*

ALUMNUS - THE CITY COLLEGE OF NEW YORK.
City College of New York, Alumni Association, Box 177, New York, NY 10027. TEL 212-234-3000. FAX 212-368-6576. *1956*

ALYTES.
International Society for the Study and Conservation of Amphibians, c/o Laboratoire des Reptiles et Amphibians, Museum National d'Histoire Naturelle, 25 rue Cuvier, 75005 Paris, France. *797*

ALZHEIMER DISEASE AND ASSOCIATED DISORDERS.
Lippincott - Raven Publishers 227 E. Washington Sq., Philadelphia, PA 19106. TEL 215-238-4200. *4823*

AM ERKER.
Verlag Am Erker, Dahlweg 64, 48153 Muenster, Germany. TEL 49-251-799580. FAX 49-251-799580. *4179*

AMATEUR GOLF.
Fore Golf Publications Ltd., 129A High St., Dovercourt, Harwich, Essex CO12 3AX, England. TEL 01255-507526. FAX 01255-508483. *6496*

AMATEUR MUSICIAN.
Canadian Amateur Musicians (CAMMAC), 1751 Richardson, Ste. 2509, Montreal, Que. H3K 1G6, Canada. TEL 514-932-3755. FAX 514-932-9811. *5138*

AMBIO.
Royal Swedish Academy of Sciences, P.O. Box 50005, S-104 05 Stockholm Sweden. TEL 46-8-673-95-51. FAX 46-8-166251. *2775*

AMBIX.
Black Bear Press Ltd., Kings Hedges Rd., Cambridge CB4 2PQ, England. *1664*

AMBULATORY SURGERY.
Butterworth - Heinemann, Part of the Reed Elsevier group, Linacre House, Jordan Hill, Oxford OX2 8DP, England. TEL 44-1865 310366. FAX 44-1865-310898. *4902*

AMERASIA JOURNAL.
University of California at Los Angeles, Asian American Studies Center, 3230 Campbell Hall, Los Angeles, CA 90095-1546. TEL 310-825-2968. FAX 310-206-9844. *5404*

AMERICAN ACADEMY OF CHILD AND ADOLESCENT PSYCHIATRY. JOURNAL.
Williams & Wilkins, 351 W. Camden St., Baltimore, MD 21201. TEL 410-528-4000. FAX 410-528-4312. *4823*

AMERICAN ACADEMY OF DERMATOLOGY. JOURNAL.
Mosby - Year Book, Inc. 11830 Westline Industrial Dr., St. Louis, MO 63146-3318. TEL 314-872-8370. FAX 314-432-1380. *4658*

AMERICAN ACADEMY OF NURSE PRACTITIONERS. JOURNAL.
Slack, Inc., 6900 Grove Rd., Thorofare, NJ 08086-9447. TEL 609-848-1000. FAX 609-853-5991. *4709*

AMERICAN ACADEMY OF ORTHOPAEDIC SURGEONS. JOURNAL.
American Academy of Orthopaedic Surgeons, 6300 N. River Rd., Rosemont, IL 60018. TEL 847-384-4130. FAX 847-823-8033. *4780*

AMERICAN ACADEMY OF PHYSICIAN ASSISTANTS. JOURNAL.
Medical Economics Publishing Co., Inc., 5 Paragon Dr., Montvale, NJ 07645. TEL 201-358-7200. FAX 201-573-1045. *4423*

AMERICAN ACADEMY OF PSYCHOANALYSIS. JOURNAL.
Guilford Publications, Inc., 72 Spring St., 4th Fl., New York, NY 10012. TEL 212-431-9800. FAX 212-966-6708. *5824*

AMERICAN ANIMAL HOSPITAL ASSOCIATION. JOURNAL.
American Animal Hospital Association, Box 150899, Denver, CO 80215-0899. TEL 303-986-2800. FAX 303-986-1700. *6940*

AMERICAN ANNALS OF THE DEAF.
Convention of American Instructors of the Deaf, KDES, PAS-6, 800 Florida Ave., N.E., Washington, DC 20002. TEL 202-651-5340. FAX 202-651-5708. *3310*

AMERICAN ANTHROPOLOGIST.
American Anthropological Association, 4350 N. Fairfax Dr., Ste. 640, Arlington, VA 22203-1621. TEL 703-528-1902. *300*

AMERICAN ANTHROPOLOGIST. SPECIAL PUBLICATION.
American Anthropological Association, 4350 N. Fairfax Dr., Ste. 640, Arlington, VA 22203-1621. TEL 703-538-1902. *300*

AMERICAN ANTIQUITY.
Society for American Archaeology, 900 Second St., N.W., No. 12, Washington, DC 20002-3557. TEL 202-789-8200. FAX 202-789-0284. *338*

AMERICAN ART.
Smithsonian Institution, National Museum of American Art, 601 Indiana Ave., Ste. 200, Washington, DC 20004. TEL 202-357-1812. *409*

AMERICAN ASSOCIATION FOR CANCER RESEARCH. PROCEEDINGS OF THE ANNUAL MEETING.
American Association for Cancer Research, Public Ledger Bldg., 150 S. Independence Mall West, Ste. 816, Philadelphia, PA 19106. TEL 215-440-9300. FAX 215-440-9354. *4747*

AMERICAN ASSOCIATION FOR MEDICAL TRANSCRIPTION. JOURNAL.
American Association for Medical Transcription, Box 576187, Modesto, CA 95357. TEL 209-551-0883. FAX 209-551-9317. *4423*

AMERICAN ASSOCIATION OF OCCUPATIONAL HEALTH NURSES JOURNAL.
Slack, Inc., 6900 Grove Rd., Thorofare, NJ 08086-9447. TEL 609-848-1000. FAX 609-853-5991. *4709*

AMERICAN ASSOCIATION OF PETROLEUM GEOLOGISTS. MEMOIR.
American Association of Petroleum Geologists, Box 979, Tulsa, OK 74101. TEL 918-584-2555. *2224*

AMERICAN ASSOCIATION OF STRATIGRAPHIC PALYNOLOGISTS. CONTRIBUTIONS SERIES.
American Association of Stratigraphic Palynologists Foundation, c/o Vaughn M. Bryant, Jr., Palynology Laboratory, Anthropology Bldg., Texas A & M University, College Station, TX 77843-4352. TEL 409-845-5242. FAX 409-845-4070. *5312*

AMERICAN ASSOCIATION OF STRATIGRAPHIC PALYNOLOGISTS. NEWSLETTER.
American Association of Stratigraphic Palynologists Foundation, Inc., c/o Vaughn M. Bryant, Jr., Palynology Laboratory, Texas A & M Univ., College Station, TX 77843-4352. TEL 409-845-5242. FAX 409-845-4070. *2224*

AMERICAN ASSOCIATION OF VARIABLE STAR OBSERVERS. JOURNAL.
American Association of Variable Star Observers, 25 Birch St., Cambridge, MA 02138. TEL 617-354-0484. *474*

AMERICAN BENEDICTINE REVIEW.
American Benedictine Review, Inc., Assumption Abbey, Box A, Richardton, ND 58652. TEL 701-974-3315. FAX 701-974-3317. *6167*

THE AMERICAN BIOLOGY TEACHER.
National Association of Biology Teachers, Inc., 11250 Roger Bacon Dr., Ste. 19, Reston, VA 22090. TEL 703-471-1134. *567*

AMERICAN BOARD OF FAMILY PRACTICE. JOURNAL.
American Board of Family Practice, 2228 Young Dr., Lexington, KY 40505. TEL 606-269-5626. FAX 606-266-9699. *4423*

AMERICAN BOTTOM ARCHAEOLOGY.
University of Illinois Press, 1325 S. Oak St., Champaign, IL 61820. TEL 217-333-0950. FAX 217-244-8082. *338*

AMERICAN BUSINESS LAW JOURNAL.
Academy of Legal Studies in Business, c/o Daniel J. Herron, Dept. of Finance, 120 Upham Hall, Miami University, Oxford, OH 45056. TEL 513-529-2945. FAX 513-529-6992. *3893*

AMERICAN BUSINESS REVIEW.
University of New Haven, School of Business, West Haven, CT 06516. *892*

AMERICAN CATHOLIC HISTORICAL SOCIETY OF PHILADELPHIA. RECORDS.
American Catholic Historical Society of Philadelphia, Box 84, Philadelphia, PA 19105-0084. TEL 215-925-5752. *6167*

AMERICAN CERAMIC SOCIETY. JOURNAL.
American Ceramic Society, 735 Ceramic Pl., Westerville, OH 43081. TEL 614-890-4700. FAX 614-899-6109. *1651*

AMERICAN CHIROPRACTIC ASSOCIATION. JOURNAL.
American Chiropractic Association, Inc., 8229 Maryland Ave., St. Louis, MO 63105. TEL 314-862-7800. FAX 314-721-5171. *4611*

AMERICAN COLLEGE OF CARDIOLOGY. JOURNAL.
Elsevier Science Inc., Box 945, New York, NY 10159-0945. TEL 212-633-3730. FAX 212-633-3680. *4594*

AMERICAN COLLEGE OF DENTISTS. JOURNAL.
American College of Dentists, 839 Quince Orchard Blvd., Gaithersburg, MD 20878. TEL 301-977-3223. FAX 301-977-3330. *4634*

AMERICAN COLLEGE OF LABORATORY ANIMAL MEDICINE SERIES.
Academic Press, Inc., 525 B St., Ste. 1900, San Diego, CA 92101-4495. TEL 619-231-6616. FAX 619-699-6715. *4676*

AMERICAN COLLEGE OF NUTRITION. JOURNAL.
American College of Nutrition, c/o Hospital for Joint Deseases, 301 E. 17th St., New York, NY 10003. TEL 718-283-7906. FAX 718-283-7005. *5228*

AMERICAN COLLEGE OF SURGEONS. JOURNAL.
American College of Surgeons, Publishing Department, 54 E. Erie St., Chicago, IL 60611-2798. TEL 312-787-9282. FAX 312-440-7026. *4902*

AMERICAN COLLEGE OF TOXICOLOGY. JOURNAL.
Lippincott - Raven Publishers 227 E. Washington Sq., Philadelphia, PA 19106. TEL 215-238-4200. *2842*

AMERICAN DENTAL ASSOCIATION. JOURNAL.
American Dental Association, 211 E. Chicago Ave., Chicago, IL 60611. TEL 312-440-2500. FAX 312-440-3538. *4634*

AMERICAN DIALECT SOCIETY. PUBLICATIONS.
University of Alabama Press, Box 870380, Tuscaloosa, AL 35487-0380. TEL 205-348-5180. FAX 205-348-9201. *4051*

AMERICAN DIETETIC ASSOCIATION. JOURNAL.
American Dietetic Association, 216 W. Jackson Blvd., Ste. 800, Chicago, IL 60606-6995. TEL 312-899-0040. FAX 312-899-1757. *5228*

AMERICAN ECONOMIST.
Omicron Delta Epsilon Fraternity, c/o Michael Szenberg, Ed., Graduate School of Business, Dept. of Economics, Pace University, New York, NY 10038. TEL 212-346-1921. FAX 212-346-1573. *1173*

AMERICAN EDUCATIONAL RESEARCH JOURNAL.
American Educational Research Association, 1230 17th St., N.W., Washington, DC 20036-3078. TEL 202-223-9485. FAX 202-775-1824. *2311*

AMERICAN FAMILY PHYSICIAN.
American Academy of Family Physicians, 8880 Ward Pkwy., Kansas City, MO 64114. TEL 816-333-9700. FAX 816-333-0303. *4423*

AMERICAN FAMILY THERAPY ACADEMY NEWSLETTER.
American Family Therapy Academy, Inc., 2020 Pennsylvania Ave., N.W., Ste. 273, Washington, DC 20006. TEL 202-994-2776. FAX 202-994-2775. *5824*

AMERICAN FERN JOURNAL.
American Fern Society, Inc., c/o Dr. David B. Lellinger, 326 West St., N.W., Vienna, VA 22180-4151. *669*

AMERICAN FISHERIES SOCIETY. TRANSACTIONS.
American Fisheries Society, 5410 Grosvenor Ln., Ste. 110, Bethesda, MD 20814-2199. TEL 301-897-8616. FAX 301-897-8096. *2925*

AMERICAN FOREIGN POLICY LIBRARY.
Harvard University Press, 79 Garden St., Cambridge, MA 02138. TEL 617-495-2600. FAX 617-495-5898. *5740*

AMERICAN FRIENDS OF LAFAYETTE. GAZETTE.
American Friends of Lafayette, Skillman Library, Lafayette College, Easton, PA 18042-1797. TEL 610-250-5161. FAX 610-252-0370. *3458*

AMERICAN GENEALOGIST.
David L. Greene, Ed. & Pub., Box 398, Demorest, GA 30535-0398. TEL 706-865-6440. *3073*

AMERICAN GEOPHYSICAL UNION. GEOPHYSICAL MONOGRAPHS BOOK SERIES.
American Geophysical Union, 2000 Florida Ave., N.W., Washington, DC 20009. TEL 202-462-6900. *2270*

AMERICAN GERIATRICS SOCIETY. JOURNAL.
Williams & Wilkins, 351 W. Camden St., Baltimore, MD 21201. TEL 410-528-4000. FAX 410-528-4312. *3283*

AMERICAN GROUP PSYCHOTHERAPY MONOGRAPH SERIES.
International Universities Press, Inc., 59 Boston Post Rd., Box 1524, Madison, CT 06443-1524. TEL 203-245-4000. *5824*

AMERICAN HARP JOURNAL.
American Harp Society, Inc., c/o Jane Weidensawl, Ed., 1274 Academy Ln., Teaneck, NJ 07666. TEL 201-836-8909. *5138*

AMERICAN HAWKWATCHER.
Wildlife Information Center, Inc., Box 198, Slatington, PA 18080-0198. TEL 610-760-8889. *771*

AMERICAN HEART ASSOCIATION. SUPPLEMENTS.
American Heart Association, 7272 Greenville Ave., Dallas, TX 75231-4596. TEL 214-706-1310. FAX 214-691-2704. *4595*

AMERICAN HEART JOURNAL.
Mosby - Year Book, Inc. 11830 Westline Industrial Dr., St. Louis, MO 63146-3318. TEL 314-872-8370. FAX 314-432-1380. *4595*

AMERICAN HISTORICAL REVIEW.
American Historical Association, 400 A St., S.E., Washington, DC 20003-3889. TEL 202-544-2422. FAX 202-544-8307. *3336*

AMERICAN IMAGO.
Johns Hopkins University Press, Journals Publishing Division, 2715 N. Charles St., Baltimore, MD 21218. TEL 410-516-6980. FAX 410-516-6968. *4824*

AMERICAN INDIAN ART MAGAZINE.
American Indian Art, Inc., 7314 E. Osborn Dr., Scottsdale, AZ 85251. TEL 602-994-5445. *410*

AMERICAN INDIAN CULTURE AND RESEARCH JOURNAL.
University of California at Los Angeles, American Indian Studies Center, Box 951548, Campbell Hall, Los Angeles, CA 90095-1548. TEL 310-825-7315. FAX 310-206-7060. *2862*

AMERICAN INDIAN REPORT.
Falmouth Institute, Inc., 3918 Prosperity Ave., Ste. 302, Fairfax, VA 22031-3333. TEL 703-641-9100. FAX 703-641-1558. *2863*

AMERICAN INDUSTRIAL HYGIENE ASSOCIATION JOURNAL.
American Industrial Hygiene Association, 2700 Prosperity Ave., Ste. 250, Fairfax, VA 22031-4307. TEL 703-849-8888. FAX 703-207-3561. *5244*

AMERICAN INSTITUTE FOR CONSERVATION OF HISTORIC & ARTISTIC WORKS. JOURNAL.
American Institute for Conservation of Historic and Artistic Works, 1717 K St., N.W., Ste. 301, Washington, DC 20006. TEL 202-452-9545. FAX 202-452-9328. *410*

AMERICAN JOURNAL OF ACUPUNCTURE.
1840 41st Ave., Ste. 102, Box 610, Capitola, CA 95010. TEL 408-475-1700. FAX 408-475-1439. *289*

AMERICAN JOURNAL OF ALTERNATIVE AGRICULTURE.
Henry A. Wallace Institute for Alternative Agriculture, Inc., 9200 Edmonston Rd., Ste. 117, Greenbelt, MD 20770-1551. TEL 301-441-8777. FAX 301-220-0164. *97*

AMERICAN JOURNAL OF ALZHEIMER'S DISEASE.
Prime National Publishing Corp., 470 Boston Post Rd., Weston, MA 02193. TEL 617-899-2702. FAX 617-899-4900. *4824*

AMERICAN JOURNAL OF ANCIENT HISTORY.
Robinson Hall, Harvard University, Cambridge, MA 02138. TEL 617-495-2545. FAX 617-496-3425. *3336*

AMERICAN JOURNAL OF ART THERAPY.
Vermont College of Norwich University, Montpelier, VT 05602. TEL 802-828-8540. FAX 802-828-8855. *2465*

AMERICAN JOURNAL OF ASTHMA & ALLERGY FOR PEDIATRICIANS.
Slack, Inc., 6900 Grove Rd., Thorofare, NJ 08086-9447. TEL 609-848-1000. FAX 609-853-5991. *4578*

AMERICAN JOURNAL OF BOTANY.
Botanical Society of America, Inc. (Columbus), Business Office, 1735 Neil Ave., Columbus, OH 43210. TEL 614-292-3519. *669*

AMERICAN JOURNAL OF CARDIAC IMAGING.
W.B. Saunders Co. Curtis Center, 3rd Fl., Independence Sq. W., Philadelphia, PA 19106-3399. TEL 215-238-7800. FAX 215-238-6445. *4595*

AMERICAN JOURNAL OF CARDIOLOGY.
Excerpta Medica, Inc. 105 Raider Blvd., Belle Mead, NJ 08502. TEL 908-874-8550. FAX 908-874-8419. *4595*

AMERICAN JOURNAL OF CARDIOVASCULAR PATHOLOGY.
Field & Wood Medical Periodicals, Inc., Box 975, Blue Bell, PA 19422. TEL 610-828-4010. FAX 215-482-0225. *4595*

AMERICAN JOURNAL OF CLINICAL NUTRITION.
American Society for Clinical Nutrition, Inc., 9650 Rockville Pike, Rm. 2310, Bethesda, MD 20814-3998. TEL 301-530-7026. FAX 301-530-7001. *5229*

AMERICAN JOURNAL OF CLINICAL ONCOLOGY.
Lippincott - Raven Publishers 227 E. Washington Sq., Philadelphia, PA 19106. TEL 215-238-4200. FAX 215-238-4235. *4748*

AMERICAN JOURNAL OF CLINICAL PATHOLOGY.
Lippincott - Raven Publishers, 227 E. Washington Sq., Philadelphia, PA 19106. TEL 215-238-4200. *4424*

AMERICAN JOURNAL OF CLINICAL RESEARCH.
Brookwood Medical Publications, Orchard House, Brookwood, Surrey GU34 0AT, England. TEL 44-1483-797975. FAX 44-1483-797915. *4676*

AMERICAN JOURNAL OF COMMUNITY PSYCHOLOGY.
Plenum Publishing Corp., 233 Spring St., New York, NY 10013-1578. TEL 212-620-8000. FAX 212-463-0742. *6404*

AMERICAN JOURNAL OF CONTACT DERMATITIS.
W.B. Saunders Co. Curtis Center, 3rd Fl., Independence Sq. W., Philadelphia, PA 19106-3399. TEL 215-238-7800. FAX 215-238-6445. *4658*

AMERICAN JOURNAL OF CRITICAL CARE.
American Association of Critical Care Nurses, 101 Columbia, Aliso Viejo, CA 92656. TEL 714-362-2000. FAX 714-362-2020. *4709*

AMERICAN JOURNAL OF DANCE THERAPY.
Human Sciences Press, Inc. 233 Spring St., New York, NY 10013-1578. TEL 212-620-8000. FAX 212-463-0742. *2185*

AMERICAN JOURNAL OF DERMATOPATHOLOGY.
Lippincott - Raven Publishers 227 E. Washington Sq., Philadelphia, PA 19106. TEL 215-238-4200. *4424*

AMERICAN JOURNAL OF DISTANCE EDUCATION.
Pennsylvania State University, College of Education, 403 S. Allen St., Ste. 206, University Park, PA 16801-5202. TEL 814-863-3764. FAX 814-865-5878. *2396*

AMERICAN JOURNAL OF DRUG AND ALCOHOL ABUSE.
Marcel Dekker Journals, 270 Madison Ave., New York, NY 10016. TEL 212-696-9000. FAX 212-685-4540. *2194*

AMERICAN JOURNAL OF EDUCATION.
University of Chicago Press, Journals Division, Box 37005, Chicago, IL 60637. TEL 773-753-3347. FAX 773-753-0811. *2311*

AMERICAN JOURNAL OF ELECTRONEURODIAGNOSTIC TECHNOLOGY.
American Society of Electroneurodiagnostic Technologists, Inc., Executive Office, 204 W. Seventh, Carroll, IA 51401. TEL 712-792-2978. FAX 712-792-6962. *4824*

AMERICAN JOURNAL OF EMERGENCY MEDICINE.
W.B. Saunders Co. Curtis Center, 3rd Fl., Independence Sq. W., Philadelphia, PA 19106-3399. TEL 215-238-7800. FAX 215-238-6445. *4780*

AMERICAN JOURNAL OF ENOLOGY AND VITICULTURE.
American Society for Enology and Viticulture, Box 1855, Davis, CA 95617. TEL 916-753-3142. FAX 916-753-3318. *499*

AMERICAN JOURNAL OF EPIDEMIOLOGY.
Johns Hopkins University School of Hygiene and Public Health, Candler Bldg., Ste. 840, 111 Market Place, Baltimore, MD 21202-6709. TEL 410-223-1600. FAX 410-223-1620. *4424*

AMERICAN JOURNAL OF FAMILY LAW.
John Wiley & Sons, Inc., Journals, 605 Third Ave., New York, NY 10158. TEL 212-850-6645. FAX 212-850-6021. *3917*

AMERICAN JOURNAL OF FORENSIC MEDICINE AND PATHOLOGY.
Lippincott - Raven Publishers 227 E. Washington Sq., Philadelphia, PA 19106. TEL 215-238-4200. *4685*

AMERICAN JOURNAL OF FORENSIC PSYCHIATRY.
American College of Forensic Psychiatry, Box 5870, Balboa Island, CA 92662. *4685*

AMERICAN JOURNAL OF FORENSIC PSYCHOLOGY.
American College of Forensic Psychology, Box 5870, Balboa Island, CA 92662. *5825*

AMERICAN JOURNAL OF GASTROENTEROLOGY.
Williams & Wilkins, 351 W. Camden St., Baltimore, MD 21201. TEL 410-528-4000. FAX 410-528-4312. *4689*

AMERICAN JOURNAL OF GERIATRIC CARDIOLOGY.
LeJacq Communications Inc., 777 W. Putnam Ave., Greenwich, CT 06830-6014. TEL 203-531-0450. FAX 203-531-0533. *4595*

AMERICAN JOURNAL OF GERIATRIC PSYCHIATRY.
American Psychiatric Press, Inc., Journals Division, 1400 K St., N.W., Ste. 1101, Washington, DC 20005. TEL 202-682-6240. FAX 202-682-6341. *3283*

AMERICAN JOURNAL OF GERMANIC LINGUISTICS AND LITERATURES.
Society for Germanic Philology c/o Robert B. Howell, Sec.-Treas., Dept. of German, 818 Van Hise Hall, University of Wisconsin, 1220 Linden Dr., Madison, WI 53706. TEL 608-262-2192. FAX 608-262-7949. *4051*

AMERICAN JOURNAL OF HEALTH BEHAVIOR.
P N G Publications, Box 4593, Star City, WV 26504-4593. TEL 304-293-4699. FAX 304-293-4693. *5524*

AMERICAN JOURNAL OF HEALTH PROMOTION.
Mosby - Year Book, Inc. 11830 Westline Industrial Dr., St. Louis, MO 63146-3318. TEL 314-872-8370. FAX 314-432-1380. *5954*

AMERICAN JOURNAL OF HEALTH - SYSTEM PHARMACY.
American Society of Health - System Pharmacists, 7272 Wisconsin Ave., Bethesda, MD 20814. TEL 301-657-3000. FAX 301-657-1258. *5398*

AMERICAN JOURNAL OF HEMATOLOGY.
John Wiley & Sons, Inc., Journals, 605 Third Ave., New York, NY 10158. TEL 212-850-6645. FAX 212-850-6021. *4697*

THE AMERICAN JOURNAL OF HOSPICE & PALLIATIVE CARE.
Prime National Publishing Corp., 470 Boston Post Rd., Weston, MA 02193. TEL 617-899-2702. *3283*

AMERICAN JOURNAL OF HUMAN BIOLOGY.
John Wiley & Sons, Inc., Journals, 605 Third Ave., New York, NY 10158. TEL 212-850-6645. FAX 212-850-6021. *567*

AMERICAN JOURNAL OF HUMAN GENETICS.
University of Chicago Press, Journals Division, Box 37005, Chicago, IL 60637. TEL 773-753-3347. FAX 773-753-0811. *737*

AMERICAN JOURNAL OF HYPERTENSION.
Elsevier Science Inc., Box 945, New York, NY 10159-0945. TEL 212-633-3730. FAX 212-633-3680. *4595*

AMERICAN JOURNAL OF INDUSTRIAL MEDICINE.
John Wiley & Sons, Inc., Journals, 605 Third Ave., New York, NY 10158. TEL 212-850-6645. FAX 212-850-6021. *5244*

AMERICAN JOURNAL OF INFECTION CONTROL.
Mosby - Year Book, Inc. 11830 Westline Industrial Dr., St. Louis, MO 63146-3318. TEL 314-872-8370. FAX 314-432-1380-3318. *4617*

AMERICAN JOURNAL OF ISLAMIC SOCIAL SCIENCES.
Association of Muslim Social Scientists, 555 Grove St., Box 669, Herndon, VA 22070. TEL 703-471-1133. FAX 703-471-3922. *6116*

AMERICAN JOURNAL OF KIDNEY DISEASES.
W.B. Saunders Co. Curtis Center, 3rd Fl., Independence Sq. W., Philadelphia, PA 19106-3399. TEL 215-238-7800. FAX 215-238-6445. *4924*

AMERICAN JOURNAL OF KNEE SURGERY.
Slack, Inc., 6900 Grove Rd., Thorofare, NJ 08086-9447. TEL 609-848-1000. FAX 609-853-5991. *4903*

AMERICAN JOURNAL OF LAW & MEDICINE.
American Society of Law, Medicine & Ethics, 765 Commonwealth Ave., Ste. 1634, Boston, MA 02215. TEL 617-262-4990. FAX 617-437-7596. *3740*

AMERICAN JOURNAL OF MATHEMATICAL AND MANAGEMENT SCIENCES.
American Sciences Press, Inc., 20 Cross Rd., Syracuse, NY 13224-2144. *4352*

AMERICAN JOURNAL OF MEDICAL GENETICS.
John Wiley & Sons, Inc., Journals, 605 Third Ave., New York, NY 10158. TEL 212-850-6645. FAX 212-850-6021. *737*

AMERICAN JOURNAL OF MEDICAL QUALITY.
Williams & Wilkins, 351 W. Camden St., Baltimore, MD 21201. TEL 410-528-4000. FAX 410-528-4312. *1405*

THE AMERICAN JOURNAL OF MEDICINE.
Excerpta Medica, Inc. 105 Raider Blvd., Belle Mead, NJ 08502. TEL 908-874-8550. FAX 908-874-8419. *4424*

AMERICAN JOURNAL OF NEPHROLOGY.
S. Karger AG, Allschwilerstr. 10, P.O. Box, CH-4009 Basel, Switzerland. TEL 061-3061111. FAX 061-3061234. *4924*

AMERICAN JOURNAL OF NONINVASIVE CARDIOLOGY.
S. Karger AG, Allschwilerstr. 10, P.O. Box, CH-4009 Basel, Switzerland. TEL 061-3061111. FAX 061-3061234. *4595*

AMERICAN JOURNAL OF NURSING.
American Journal of Nursing Co., 555 W. 57th St., New York, NY 10019. TEL 212-582-8820. FAX 212-586-5462. *4709*

AMERICAN JOURNAL OF OBSTETRICS AND GYNECOLOGY.
Mosby - Year Book, Inc. 11830 Westline Industrial Dr., St. Louis, MO 63146-3318. TEL 314-872-8370. FAX 314-432-1380. *4731*

AMERICAN JOURNAL OF OCCUPATIONAL THERAPY.
American Occupational Therapy Association, Inc., Box 31220, Bethesda, MD 20824-1220. TEL 301-652-2682. FAX 301-652-7711. *5244*

AMERICAN JOURNAL OF OPHTHALMOLOGY.
Ophthalmic Publishing Co., 77 W. Wacker Dr., Ste. 660, Chicago, IL 60601-1632. TEL 312-629-1690. FAX 312-629-1744. *4766*

AMERICAN JOURNAL OF ORTHODONTICS AND DENTOFACIAL ORTHOPEDICS.
Mosby - Year Book, Inc. 11830 Westline Industrial Dr., St. Louis, MO 63146-3318. TEL 314-872-8370. FAX 314-432-1380. *4634*

THE AMERICAN JOURNAL OF ORTHOPEDICS.
Quadrant HealthCom, 105 Raider Blvd., Belle Mead, NJ 08502-1510. TEL 908-874-0707. FAX 908-874-5611. *4780*

AMERICAN JOURNAL OF ORTHOPSYCHIATRY.
American Orthopsychiatric Association, Inc., 330 Seventh Ave., 18th Fl., New York, NY 10001. TEL 212-564-5930. FAX 212-564-6180. *5825*

AMERICAN JOURNAL OF OTOLARYNGOLOGY.
W.B. Saunders Co. Curtis Center, 3rd Fl., Independence Sq. W., Philadelphia, PA 19106-3399. TEL 215-238-7800. FAX 215-238-6445. *4794*

AMERICAN JOURNAL OF PASTORAL COUNSELING.
Haworth Press, Inc., 10 Alice St., Binghamton, NY 13904. TEL 607-722-5857. FAX 607-722-1424. *6043*

AMERICAN JOURNAL OF PATHOLOGY.
American Society for Investigative Pathology, 9650 Rockville Pike, Bethesda, MD 20814. TEL 301-571-0107. FAX 301-571-0108. *4424*

AMERICAN JOURNAL OF PERINATOLOGY.
Thieme, 381 Park Ave. S., Ste. 1501, New York, NY 10016. TEL 212-683-5088. FAX 212-779-9020. *4731*

AMERICAN JOURNAL OF PHARMACEUTICAL EDUCATION.
American Association of Colleges of Pharmacy, 1426 Prince St., Alexandria, VA 22314-2815. TEL 703-739-2330. *5398*

AMERICAN JOURNAL OF PHARMACY.
Philadelphia College of Pharmacy and Science, 600 S. 43rd St., Philadelphia, PA 19104-4495. TEL 215-596-8800. *5398*

AMERICAN JOURNAL OF PHYSICAL ANTHROPOLOGY.
John Wiley & Sons, Inc., Journals, 605 Third Ave., New York, NY 10158. TEL 212-850-6645. FAX 212-850-6021. *300*

AMERICAN JOURNAL OF PHYSICAL MEDICINE AND REHABILITATION.
Williams & Wilkins, 351 W. Camden St., Baltimore, MD 21201. TEL 410-528-4000. FAX 410-528-4312. *4815*

AMERICAN JOURNAL OF PHYSICS.
American Association of Physics Teachers, One Physics Ellipse, College Park, MD 20740-3845. TEL 301-209-3333. FAX 301-209-0845. *5541*

AMERICAN JOURNAL OF PHYSIOLOGY.
American Physiological Society, 9650 Rockville Pike, Bethesda, MD 20814. TEL 301-530-7164. FAX 301-571-3813. *784*

AMERICAN JOURNAL OF PHYSIOLOGY: CELL PHYSIOLOGY.
American Physiological Society, 9650 Rockville Pike, Bethesda, MD 20814. TEL 301-530-7164. FAX 301-571-8313. *784*

AMERICAN JOURNAL OF PHYSIOLOGY: ENDOCRINOLOGY AND METABOLISM.
American Physiological Society, 9650 Rockville Pike, Bethesda, MD 20814. TEL 301-530-7071. FAX 301-571-8313. *784*

AMERICAN JOURNAL OF PHYSIOLOGY: GASTROINTESTINAL AND LIVER PHYSIOLOGY.
American Physiological Society, 9650 Rockville Pike, Bethesda, MD 20814. TEL 301-530-7164. FAX 301-571-8313. *784*

AMERICAN JOURNAL OF PHYSIOLOGY: HEART AND CIRCULATORY PHYSIOLOGY.
American Physiological Society, 9650 Rockville Pike, Bethesda, MD 20814. TEL 301-530-7164. FAX 301-571-8313. *4595*

AMERICAN JOURNAL OF PHYSIOLOGY: LUNG CELLULAR AND MOLECULAR PHYSIOLOGY.
American Physiological Society, 9650 Rockville Pike, Bethesda, MD 20814. TEL 301-530-7164. FAX 301-571-8313. *784*

AMERICAN JOURNAL OF PHYSIOLOGY: REGULATORY, INTEGRATIVE AND COMPARATIVE PHYSIOLOGY.
American Physiological Society, 9650 Rockville Pike, Bethesda, MD 20814. TEL 301-530-7164. FAX 301-571-3813. *784*

AMERICAN JOURNAL OF PHYSIOLOGY: RENAL, FLUID AND ELECTROLYTE PHYSIOLOGY.
American Physiological Society, 9650 Rockville Pike, Bethesda, MD 20814. TEL 301-530-7164. FAX 301-571-3813. *784*

AMERICAN JOURNAL OF PREVENTIVE MEDICINE.
Oxford University Press, Journals, 2001 Evans Rd., Cary, NC 27513. TEL 919-677-0977. FAX 919-677-1714. *4425*

AMERICAN JOURNAL OF PRIMATOLOGY.
John Wiley & Sons, Inc., Journals, 605 Third Ave., New York, NY 10108. TEL 212-850-6645. FAX 212-850-6021. *568*

AMERICAN JOURNAL OF PSYCHIATRY.
American Psychiatric Association, 1400 K St., N.W., Washington, DC 20005. TEL 202-682-6020. FAX 202-682-6016. *4824*

AMERICAN JOURNAL OF PSYCHOANALYSIS.
Human Sciences Press, Inc. 233 Spring St., New York, NY 10013. TEL 212-620-8000. FAX 212-463-0742. *5825*

AMERICAN JOURNAL OF PSYCHOLOGY.
University of Illinois Press, 1325 S. Oak St., Champaign, IL 61820. TEL 217-333-0950. FAX 217-244-8082. *5825*

AMERICAN JOURNAL OF PSYCHOTHERAPY.
Association for the Advancement of Psychotherapy, Belfer Education Center, 1300 Morris Park Ave., Rm. 402, Bronx, NY 10461-1602. TEL 718-430-3503. FAX 718-430-8907. *4824*

AMERICAN JOURNAL OF PUBLIC HEALTH.
American Public Health Association, 1015 15th St., N.W., Washington, DC 20005. TEL 202-789-5600. *5954*

AMERICAN JOURNAL OF REPRODUCTIVE IMMUNOLOGY.
Munksgaard International Publishers Ltd., P.O. Box 2148, DK-1016 Copenhagen K, Denmark. TEL 45-33-127030. FAX 45-33-129387. *4578*

AMERICAN JOURNAL OF RESPIRATORY AND CRITICAL CARE MEDICINE.
American Lung Association, 1740 Broadway, New York, NY 10019-4374. TEL 212-315-8700. *4886*

AMERICAN JOURNAL OF SCIENCE.
American Journal of Science, Box 6666, Yale Sta., New Haven, CT 06511-8130. TEL 203-432-3131. FAX 203-432-5668. *2204*

AMERICAN JOURNAL OF SOCIOLOGY.
University of Chicago Press, Journals Division, Box 37005, Chicago, IL 60637. TEL 773-753-3347. FAX 773-753-0811. *6404*

AMERICAN JOURNAL OF SPORTS MEDICINE.
American Orthopaedic Society for Sports Medicine, 230 Calvary St., Waltham, MA 02154. TEL 617-736-0707. FAX 617-736-0607. *4897*

AMERICAN JOURNAL OF SURGERY.
Excerpta Medica, Inc. 105 Raider Blvd., Belle Mead, NJ 08502. TEL 908-874-8550. FAX 908-874-8419. *4903*

AMERICAN JOURNAL OF SURGICAL PATHOLOGY.
Lippincott - Raven Publishers 227 E. Washington Sq., Philadelphia, PA 19106. TEL 215-238-4200. *4425*

AMERICAN JOURNAL OF THE MEDICAL SCIENCES.
Lippincott - Raven Publishers 227 E. Washington Sq., Philadelphia, PA 19106. TEL 215-238-4200. *4425*

AMERICAN JOURNAL OF THERAPEUTICS.
Chapman & Hall, Journals Department 2-6 Boundary Row, London SE1 8HN, England. TEL 44-171-8560066. FAX 44-171-5229623. *4425*

AMERICAN JOURNAL OF THERAPY.
McMahon Publishing Co., 83 Peaceable St., West Redding, CT 06896. TEL 203-544-9343. *4425*

AMERICAN JOURNAL OF VETERINARY RESEARCH.
American Veterinary Medical Association, 1931 N. Meacham Rd., Ste. 100, Schaumburg, IL 60173-4360. TEL 847-925-8070. FAX 847-925-1329. *6940*

AMERICAN JOURNALISM.
American Journalism Historians Association, Univ. of Georgia, Grady College of Journalism, Athens, GA 30602. TEL 706-542-5033. FAX 706-542-4785. *3700*

AMERICAN LEATHER CHEMISTS ASSOCIATION. JOURNAL.
American Leather Chemists Association, Campus Sta., Box 210014, Cincinnati, OH 45221. TEL 513-556-1197. *3959*

AMERICAN LITERATURE.
Duke University Press, Box 90660, Durham, NC 27708-0660. TEL 919-687-3600. FAX 919-688-4574. *4179*

AMERICAN MALACOLOGICAL BULLETIN.
American Malacological Union, Inc., c/o Dr. Ronald Toll, Biology Department, Wesleyan College, Macon, GA 31297. TEL 912-474-7057. FAX 912-477-7572. *797*

AMERICAN MATHEMATICAL SOCIETY. ABSTRACTS OF PAPERS PRESENTED.
American Mathematical Society, Box 6248, Providence, RI 02940-6248. TEL 401-455-4000. *4405*

AMERICAN MATHEMATICAL SOCIETY. BULLETIN. NEW SERIES.
American Mathematical Society, Box 6248, Providence, RI 02940-6248. TEL 401-455-4000. *4353*

AMERICAN MATHEMATICAL SOCIETY. C B M S REGIONAL CONFERENCE SERIES IN MATHEMATICS.
American Mathematical Society, Box 6248, Providence, RI 02940-6248. TEL 401-455-4000. *4353*

AMERICAN MATHEMATICAL SOCIETY. COLLOQUIUM PUBLICATIONS.
American Mathematical Society, Box 6248, Providence, RI 02940-6248. TEL 401-455-4000. *4353*

AMERICAN MATHEMATICAL SOCIETY. JOURNAL.
American Mathematical Society, Box 6248, Providence, RI 02940-6248. TEL 401-455-4000. *4353*

AMERICAN MATHEMATICAL SOCIETY. MEMOIRS.
American Mathematical Society, Box 6248, Providence, RI 02940-6248. TEL 401-455-4000. *4353*

AMERICAN MATHEMATICAL SOCIETY. NOTICES.
American Mathematical Society, Box 6248, Providence, RI 02940-6248. TEL 401-455-4000. *4353*

AMERICAN MATHEMATICAL SOCIETY. PROCEEDINGS.
American Mathematical Society, Box 6248, Providence, RI 02940-6248. TEL 401-455-4000. *4353*

AMERICAN MATHEMATICAL SOCIETY. PROCEEDINGS OF SYMPOSIA IN APPLIED MATHEMATICS.
American Mathematical Society, Box 6248, Providence, RI 02940-6248. TEL 401-455-4000. *4353*

AMERICAN MATHEMATICAL SOCIETY. PROCEEDINGS OF SYMPOSIA IN PURE MATHEMATICS.
American Mathematical Society, Box 6248, Providence, RI 02940-6248. TEL 401-455-4000. *4353*

AMERICAN MATHEMATICAL SOCIETY. TRANSACTIONS.
American Mathematical Society, Box 6248, Providence, RI 02940-6248. TEL 401-455-4000. *4353*

AMERICAN MEDICAL INFORMATICS ASSOCIATION. JOURNAL.
Hanley & Belfus, Inc., 210 S. 13th St., Philadelphia, PA 19107. TEL 215-546-7293. FAX 215-790-9330. *4629*

AMERICAN MEDICAL WOMEN'S ASSOCIATION. JOURNAL.
American Medical Women's Association, Inc., 801 N. Fairfax St., Ste. 400, Alexandria, VA 22314. TEL 212-387-3864. FAX 212-387-3897. *4425*

AMERICAN METEOROLOGICAL SOCIETY. BULLETIN.
American Meteorological Society, 45 Beacon St., Boston, MA 02108-3693. TEL 617-227-2425. FAX 618-742-8718. *4990*

AMERICAN METEOROLOGICAL SOCIETY. HISTORICAL MONOGRAPH SERIES.
American Meteorological Society, 45 Beacon St., Boston, MA 02108-3693. TEL 617-227-2425. FAX 617-742-8718. *4990*

AMERICAN METEOROLOGICAL SOCIETY. METEOROLOGICAL MONOGRAPHS.
American Meteorological Society, 45 Beacon St., Boston, MA 02108-3693. TEL 617-227-2425. FAX 617-742-8718. *4990*

AMERICAN MIDLAND NATURALIST.
University of Notre Dame, Department of Biological Sciences, Box 369, Notre Dame, IN 46556. TEL 219-631-7481. *6225*

AMERICAN MINERALOGIST.
Mineralogical Society of America, 1015 Eighteenth St., N.W., Washington, DC 20036-5203. TEL 202-775-4344. FAX 202-775-0018. *5056*

AMERICAN MOSQUITO CONTROL ASSOCIATION. JOURNAL.
American Mosquito Control Association, Box 5416, Lake Charles, LA 70606. TEL 318-474-2723. FAX 318-478-9434. *720*

AMERICAN MUSEUM NOVITATES.
American Museum of Natural History, Central Park W. at 79th St., New York, NY 10024-5192. TEL 212-769-5545. FAX 212-769-5009. *797*

AMERICAN MUSEUM OF NATURAL HISTORY. ANTHROPOLOGICAL PAPERS.
American Museum of Natural History, Central Park W. at 79th St., New York, NY 10024-5192. TEL 212-769-5545. FAX 212-769-5009. *300*

AMERICAN MUSIC.
University of Illinois Press, 1325 S. Oak St., Champaign, IL 61820. TEL 217-333-0950. FAX 217-244-8082. *5138*

THE AMERICAN NATURALIST.
University of Chicago Press, Journals Division, Box 37005, Chicago, IL 60637. TEL 773-753-3347. FAX 773-753-0811. *568*

AMERICAN NUCLEAR SOCIETY TRANSACTIONS.
American Nuclear Society, 555 N. Kensington Ave., La Grange Park, IL 60525. TEL 708-352-6611. FAX 708-352-0499. *2573*

AMERICAN OIL CHEMISTS' SOCIETY. JOURNAL.
A O C S Press, 1608 Broadmoor Dr., Box 3489, Champaign, IL 61821-0489. TEL 217-359-2344. FAX 217-351-8091. *1735*

AMERICAN OPTOMETRIC ASSOCIATION. JOURNAL.
American Optometric Association, 243 N. Lindbergh Blvd., St. Louis, MO 63141. TEL 314-991-4100. FAX 314-991-4101. *4766*

AMERICAN ORTHOPTIC JOURNAL.
University of Wisconsin Press, Journal Division, 114 N. Murray St., Madison, WI 53715. TEL 608-262-4952. FAX 608-262-7560. *4766*

AMERICAN PERIODICALS.
University of North Texas Press, Journals Division, Box 5096, Denton, TX 76203-5096. TEL 817-565-2134. FAX 317-369-8770. *4179*

AMERICAN PHARMACEUTICAL ASSOCIATION. JOURNAL.
American Pharmaceutical Association, 2215 Constitution Ave., N.W., Washington, DC 20037. TEL 202-628-4410. *5398*

AMERICAN PODIATRIC MEDICAL ASSOCIATION. JOURNAL.
American Podiatric Medical Association, 9312 Old Georgetown Rd., Bethesda, MD 20814-1698. TEL 301-571-9200. FAX 301-530-2752. *4780*

AMERICAN POLITICAL SCIENCE REVIEW.
American Political Science Association, 1527 New Hampshire Ave., N.W., Washington, DC 20036. TEL 202-483-2512. FAX 202-483-2657. *5633*

AMERICAN POTATO JOURNAL.
Potato Association of America, 157 Park St., Ste. 23, Bangor, ME 04401. TEL 207-942-9732. FAX 207-942-9733. *210*

AMERICAN PROFESSIONAL CONSTRUCTOR.
American Institute of Constructors, 466 94th Ave., N., St. Petersburg, FL 33702-2522. TEL 813-578-0317. FAX 813-578-9932. *831*

THE AMERICAN PROSPECT.
New Prospect, Inc., Box 383080, Cambridge, MA 02238-3080. TEL 617-547-2950. FAX 617-547-3896. *5633*

AMERICAN PSYCHIATRIC NURSES ASSOCIATION. JOURNAL.
Mosby - Year Book, Inc. 11830 Westline Industrial Dr., St. Louis, MO 63146-3318. TEL 314-872-8370. FAX 314-872-9154. *4709*

AMERICAN PSYCHOANALYTIC ASSOCIATION. JOURNAL.
International Universities Press, Inc., 59 Boston Post Rd., Box 1524, Madison, CT 06443-1524. TEL 203-245-4000. FAX 203-245-0775. *5825*

AMERICAN PSYCHOANALYTIC ASSOCIATION. JOURNAL. MONOGRAPH.
International Universities Press Inc., 59 Boston Post Rd., Box 1524, Madison, CT 06443-1524. TEL 203-245-4000. *5325*

AMERICAN PSYCHOANALYTIC ASSOCIATION. WORKSHOP SERIES.
International Universities Press Inc., 59 Boston Post Rd., Box 1524, Madison, CT 06443-1524. TEL 203-245-4000. *5325*

AMERICAN PSYCHOLOGIST.
American Psychological Association, 750 First St., N.E., Washington, DC 20002-4242. TEL 202 336-5600. FAX 202-336-5568. *5825*

AMERICAN PSYCHOPATHOLOGICAL ASSOCIATION SERIES.
Lippincott - Raven Publishers 227 E. Washington sq , Philadelphia, PA 19106. TEL 215-238-4200. FAX 215-238-4235. *4824*

AMERICAN READING FORUM. YEARBOOK.
American Reading Forum, c/o Dept. of Elementary Education, Utah State University, Logan, UT 84322-2805. TEL 801-797-0399. FAX 801-797-0372. *2312*

AMERICAN REVIEW.
Japanese Association for American Studies, University of Tokyo, Center for American Studies, 8-1, 3-chome, Komaba, Meguro ku, Tokyo 153, Japan. TEL 03-5454-6 63. *3458*

AMERICAN ROMANIAN ACADEMY OF ARTS AND SCIENCES. JOURNAL.
A R A Publications, Department of French and Italian, University of California Sproul Hall, Davis, CA 95616. TEL 916-758-7720. *2419*

AMERICAN SECONDARY EDUCATION.
c/o John K. Bailey, Ed., Rm. 101 Kates Center, Ashland University, Ashland, OH 44805. TEL 419-289-5273. FAX 419-289-5037. *2312*

AMERICAN SOCIETY FOR INFORMATION SCIENCE. JOURNAL.
John Wiley & Sons, Inc., Journals, 605 Third Ave., New York, NY 10158. TEL 2 2-850-6645. FAX 212-850-6021. *3972*

AMERICAN SOCIETY FOR MASS SPECTROMETRY. JOURNAL.
Esevier Science Inc., Box 945, New York, NY 10159-0945. TEL 212-633-3730. FAX 212-633-3680. *5601*

AMERICAN SOCIETY FOR TESTING AND MATERIALS. DATA SERIES PUBLICATIONS.
American Society for Testing and Materials, 100 Barr Harbor Dr., W. Conshohocken, PA 19428-2959. TEL 610-832-9500. FAX 610-832-9555. *2724*

AMERICAN SOCIETY FOR TESTING AND MATERIALS. FIVE-YEAR INDEX TO A S T M TECHNICAL PAPERS AND REPORTS.
American Society for Testing and Materials, 100 Barr Harbor Dr., W. Conshohecken, PA 19428-2959. TEL 610-832-9500. FAX 610-832-9555. *2724*

AMERICAN SOCIETY FOR TESTING AND MATERIALS. SPECIAL TECHNICAL PUBLICATIONS.
American Society for Testing and Materials, 100 Barr Harbor Dr., W. Conshohocken, PA 19428-2959. TEL 610-832-9500. FAX 610-832-9555. *2724*

AMERICAN SOCIETY OF BREWING CHEMISTS. JOURNAL.
American Society of Brewing Chemists, 3340 Pilot Knob Rd., St. Paul, MN 55121-2097. TEL 612-454-7250. FAX 612-454-0766. *499*

AMERICAN SOCIETY OF ECHOCARDIOGRAPHY. JOURNAL.
Mosby - Year Book, Inc. 11830 Westline Industrial Dr., St. Louis, MO 63146-3318. TEL 314-872-8370. FAX 314-432-1380. *4596*

AMERICAN SOCIETY OF FARM MANAGERS AND RURAL APPRAISERS. JOURNAL.
American Society of Farm Managers and Rural Appraisers, 950 S. Cherry St., Ste. 508, Denver, CO 80222. TEL 303-758-3513. FAX 303-758-0190. *97*

AMERICAN SOCIETY OF HYPERTENSION. SYMPOSIUM SERIES.
Lippincott - Raven Publishers 227 E. Washington Sq., Philadelphia, PA 19106. TEL 215-238-4200. FAX 215-238-4235. *4596*

AMERICAN SOCIETY OF MAMMALOGISTS. SPECIAL PUBLICATIONS.
American Society of Mammalogists, c/o Dr. H. Duane Smith, Sec.-Treas., Monte L. Bean Life Science Museum, Brigham Young University, Provo, UT 84602. TEL 801-378-2492. *797*

AMERICAN SOCIETY OF NEPHROLOGY. JOURNAL.
Williams & Wilkins, 351 W. Camden St., Baltimore, MD 21201. TEL 410-528-4000. FAX 410-528-4312. *4925*

AMERICAN SOCIOLOGIST.
Transaction Publishers, Transaction Periodicals Consortium, Department 3092, Rutgers University, New Brunswick, NJ 08903. TEL 908-445-2280. FAX 908-445-3138. *6405*

AMERICAN SPEECH.
University of Alabama Press, Box 870380, Tuscaloosa, AL 35487-0380. TEL 205-348-5180. FAX 205-348-9201. *4051*

AMERICAN STRING TEACHER.
American String Teachers Association, 400 S. Land Ave., Ste. 1, Pittsburgh, PA 15208-2902. TEL 412-243-2834. FAX 412-243-9211. *5139*

AMERICAN STUDIES.
University of Kansas at Lawrence, American Studies Department, 2120 Wescoe Hall, Lawrence, KS 66045-2117. TEL 913-864-4878. FAX 913-864-5742. *6314*

AMERICAN SURGEON.
Waverly Press, Inc. 351 W. Camden St., Baltimore, MD 21201. TEL 410-528-4000. FAX 410-528-4412. *4903*

AMERICAN TAXATION ASSOCIATION. JOURNAL.
American Accounting Association, Paul F. Gerhardt Bldg., 5717 Bessie Dr., Sarasota, FL 34233. TEL 941-921-7747. FAX 941-923-4093. *1534*

AMERICAN UNIVERSITY STUDIES. SERIES 8. PSYCHOLOGY.
Peter Lang Publishing, Inc., 275 Seventh Ave., 28th Fl., New York, NY 10001. TEL 212-647-7700. FAX 212-647-7707. *5825*

AMERICAN VETERINARY MEDICAL ASSOCIATION. JOURNAL.
American Veterinary Medical Association, 1931 N. Meacham Rd., Ste. 100, Schaumburg, IL 60173-4360. TEL 847-925-8070. FAX 847-925-1329. *6940*

AMERICAN WATER WORKS ASSOCIATION. JOURNAL.
American Water Works Association, 6666 W. Quincy Ave., Denver, CO 80235. TEL 303-794-7711. FAX 303-794-7310. *6962*

AMERICAN ZOOLOGIST.
Society for Integrative and Comparative Biology, P.O. Box 809278, Chicago, IL 60680-9278. TEL 312-527-6697. FAX 312-245-1085. *797*

THE AMERICAS.
Academy of American Franciscan History, 1712 Euclid Ave., Berkeley, CA 94709-1208. TEL 510-843-4803. *3458*

AMETHYST REVIEW.
23 Riverside Ave., Truro, N.S. B2N 4G2, Canada. TEL 902-895-1345. *4300*

AMPHIBIA REPTILIA.
E.J. Brill, P.O. Box 9000, 2300 PA Leiden, Netherlands. TEL 31-71-5353500. FAX 31-71-5317532. *797*

AMSTERDAM MONOGRAPHS IN AMERICAN STUDIES.
Editions Rodopi B.V., Keizersgracht 302-304, 1016 EX Amsterdam, Netherlands. TEL 31-20-6227507. FAX 31-20-6380948. *3607*

AMTSBLATT DES LANDKREISES HOF.
Landratsamt Hof, Schaumbergstr. 14, 95032 Hof, Germany. TEL 49-9281-57-0. FAX 49-9281-58340. *5891*

AMYLOID.
Parthenon Publishing Group, Casterton Hall, Carnforth, Lancs. LA6 2LA, England. TEL 44-152-427-2084. FAX 44-152-427-1587. *4892*

ANAEROBE.
Academic Press Ltd. 24-28 Oval Rd., London NW1 7DX, England. TEL 44-171-482-2893. FAX 44-171-267-0362. *752*

ANAIS BRASILEIROS DE DERMATOLOGIA.
Sociedade Brasileira de Dermatologia, Caixa Postal 389, 20001-970 Rio de Janeiro, Brazil. TEL 55-21-2536747. FAX 55-21-2536747. *4658*

ANALECTA HUSSERLIANA.
Kluwer Academic Publishers, Postbus 17, 3300 AA Dordrecht, Netherlands. TEL 31-78-6392392. FAX 31-78-6392254. *5467*

ANALES GALDOSIANOS.
International Association of Galdos Scholars, Queen's University, Department of Spanish & Italian, Kingston, ON K7L 3N6, Canada. TEL 613-545-2112. FAX 613-545-6496. *4181*

ANALGESIA.
Cognizant Communication Corporation, 3 Hartsdale Rd., Elmsford, NY 10523-3701. TEL 914-592-7720. FAX 914-592-8981. *4589*

ANALOG INTEGRATED CIRCUITS AND SIGNAL PROCESSING.
Kluwer Academic Publishers Boston, Box 358, Accord Sta., Hingham, MA 02018-0358. TEL 617-871-6600. FAX 617-871-6528. *2077*

ANALUSIS.
Editions Scientifiques et Medicales Elsevier, 141 rue de Javel, 75747 Paris, France. TEL 33-1-45589022. FAX 33-1-45589421. *1712*

ANALYSE.
Nederlandse Vereniging van BioMedische Laboratoriummedewerkers, Wilhelminapark 52, 3581 NM Utrecht, Netherlands. TEL 31-30-2522881. FAX 31-30-2541814. *4676*

THE ANALYST.
The Royal Society of Chemistry, Thomas Graham House, Science Park, Milton Rd., Cambridge CB4 4WF, England. TEL 44-1223-420066. FAX 44-1223-423429. *1712*

ANALYTICA CHIMICA ACTA.
Elsevier Science B.V., P.O. Box 211, 1000 AE Amsterdam, Netherlands. TEL 31-20-4853911. FAX 31-20-4853598. *1713*

ANALYTICAL & ENUMERATIVE BIBLIOGRAPHY.
Bibliographical Society of Northern Illinois, c/o Department of English, Northern Illinois University, DeKalb, IL 60115. TEL 815-753-6634. FAX 815-753-0606. *516*

ANALYTICAL AND QUANTITATIVE CYTOLOGY AND HISTOLOGY.
Science Printers and Publishers, Inc., 8342 Olive Blvd., St. Louis, MO 63132. TEL 314-991-4440. FAX 314-991-4654. *711*

ANALYTICAL BIOCHEMISTRY.
Academic Press, Inc., Journal Division, 525 B. St., Ste. 1900, San Diego, CA 92101-4495. TEL 619-230-1840. FAX 619-699-6800. *629*

ANALYTICAL CELLULAR PATHOLOGY.
I O S Press, Van Diemenstraat 94, 1013 CN Amsterdam, Netherlands. TEL 31-20-6382189. FAX 31-20-6203419. *711*

ANALYTICAL CHEMISTRY SYMPOSIA SERIES.
Elsevier Science B.V., Books Division, P.O. Box 211, 1000 AE Amsterdam, Netherlands. TEL 31-20-4853911. FAX 31-20-4853705. *1713*

ANALYTICAL COMMUNICATIONS.
The Royal Society of Chemistry, Thomas Graham House, Science Park, Milton Rd., Cambridge CB4 4WF, England. TEL 44-1223-420066. FAX 44-1223-423429. *1713*

ANALYTICAL LETTERS.
Marcel Dekker Journals, 270 Madison Ave., New York, NY 10016. TEL 212-696-9000. FAX 212-685-4540. *1713*

ANALYTICAL PROFILES OF DRUG SUBSTANCES.
Academic Press, Inc., 525 B St., Ste. 1900, San Diego, CA 92101-4495. TEL 619-231-0926. FAX 609-699-6715. *5398*

ANALYTICAL SPECTROSCOPY LIBRARY.
Elsevier Science B.V., Books Division, P.O. Box 211, 1000 AE Amsterdam, Netherlands. TEL 31-20-4853911. FAX 31-20-4853705. *1714*

ANALYTISCHE PSYCHOLOGIE.
S. Karger AG, Allschwilerstr. 10, P.O. Box, CH-4009 Basel, Switzerland. TEL 061-3061111. FAX 061-3061234. *5826*

ANANDA BICHITRA.
Dainik Bangla Bhaban, 1 Rajuk Avenue, Dhaka 100, Bangladesh. TEL 880-2-955-2086. FAX 880-2-955-2940. *3114*

ANARCHIST STUDIES.
White Horse Press, 10 High St., Knapwell, Cambridge CB3 8NR, England. TEL 44-1954-267527. FAX 44-1954-267527. *5633*

THE ANATOMICAL RECORD.
John Wiley & Sons, Inc., Journals, 605 Third Ave., New York, NY 10158. TEL 212-850-6645. FAX 212-850-6021. *568*

ANATOMICAL SOCIETY OF INDIA. JOURNAL.
Anatomical Society of India, Department of Anatomy, M.L.B. Medical College, Jhansi 284128 (U.P.), India. TEL 0517-442032. *568*

ANCESTORING.
Augusta Genealogical Society, Inc., Box 3743, Augusta, GA 30914-3743. TEL 706-738-2241. *3073*

ANCIENT CIVILIZATIONS FROM SCYTHIA TO SIBERIA.
E.J. Brill, P.O. Box 9000, 2300 PA Leiden, Netherlands. TEL 31-71-5353500. FAX 31-71-5317532. *3377*

ANCIENT HISTORY.
Macquarie Ancient History Association, School of History, Philosophy and Politics, North Ryde, N.S.W. 2109, Australia. TEL 61-2-8508852. FAX 61-2-8508892. *3336*

ANCIENT MESOAMERICA.
Cambridge University Press, Edinburgh Bldg., Shaftesbury Rd., Cambridge CB2 2RU, England. TEL 44-1223-312393. FAX 44-1223-315052. *3459*

ANCIENT T L.
Laboratoire de Physique Copusculaire, 63177 Aubiere Cedex, France. TEL 73-40-72-89. FAX 73-26-45-98. *339*

ANCIENT WORLD.
Ares Publishers, Inc., 7406 N. Sheridan Rd., Chicago, IL 60626-2012. TEL 312-743-1405. FAX 312-743-0657. *3336*

ANDEAN PAST.
Cornell University, Latin American Studies Program, Ithaca, NY 14853. TEL 607-255-2245. FAX 607-255-8919. *339*

ANDREWS UNIVERSITY SEMINARY STUDIES.
Andrews University Press, Berrien Springs, MI 49104. TEL 616-471-6023. FAX 616-471-6202. *6043*

ANESTESIA EN MEXICO.
Obsidiana Editores, S.A., Czda. de Tlalpan 2365, Col. Ciudad Jardin, 04370 Mexico DF, Mexico. TEL 6899133. *4589*

ANESTHESIA AND ANALGESIA.
Williams & Wilkins, 351 W. Camden St., Baltimore, MD 21201. TEL 410-528-4000. FAX 410-528-4312. *4590*

ANESTHESIA PROGRESS.
Elsevier Science Inc., Box 945, New York, NY 10159-0945. TEL 212-633-3730. FAX 212-633-3680. *4634*

ANESTHESIOLOGY.
Lippincott - Raven Publishers 227 E. Washington Sq., Philadelphia, PA 19106. TEL 215-238-4200. *4590*

ANGELAKI.
44 Abbey Rd., Oxford OX2 0AE, England. TEL 44-1865-793891. *5467*

ANGIOLOGY.
Westminster Publications, Inc., 708 Glen Cove Ave., Glen Head, NY 11545. TEL 516-759-0025. FAX 516-759-5524. *4596*

ANGLICAN THEOLOGICAL REVIEW.
Anglican Theological Review, Inc., 600 Haven St., Evanston, IL 60201. TEL 708-864-6024. FAX 708-328-9624. *6043*

ANGLO-CATALAN SOCIETY. OCCASIONAL PUBLICATIONS.
Anglo-Catalan Society, c/o Dr. Alan Yates, Ed., Department of Hispanic Studies, University of Sheffield, Sheffield S10 2VJ, England. TEL 44-114-2824402. FAX 44-114-2824402. *3392*

ANGLO-NORMAN TEXT SOCIETY. OCCASIONAL PUBLICATIONS SERIES.
Anglo-Norman Text Society, Birkbeck College, London WC1E 7HX, England. *3392*

ANGOLITE.
Louisiana State Penitentiary, Angola, LA 70712. TEL 504-655-4411. *2157*

ANGORA GOAT & MOHAIR JOURNAL.
S.A. Mohair Grower's Association, P.O. Box 50, Jansenville 6265, South Africa. TEL 27-24-4932-140. *263*

ANIMAL BIOTECHNOLOGY.
Marcel Dekker Journals, 270 Madison Ave., New York, NY 10016. TEL 212-696-9000. FAX 212-685-4540. *656*

ANIMAL FEED SCIENCE AND TECHNOLOGY.
Elsevier Science B.V., P.O. Box 211, 1000 AE Amsterdam, Netherlands. TEL 31-20-4853911. FAX 31-20-4853598. *256*

ANIMAL FEEDING AND NUTRITION.
Academic Press, Inc., 525 B St., Ste. 1900, San Diego, CA 92101-4495. TEL 619-231-6616. FAX 619-699-6715. *6941*

ANIMAL GENETICS.
Blackwell Science Ltd., Osney Mead, Oxford OX2 0EL, England. TEL 44-1865-206206. FAX 44-1865-721205. *737*

ANIMAL KEEPERS' FORUM.
American Association of Zoo Keepers, Inc., 635 S.W. Gage Blvd., Topeka, KS 66606-2066. TEL 913-273-1980. FAX 913-273-1980. *797*

ANIMAL LEARNING & BEHAVIOR.
Psychonomic Society, Inc., 1710 Fortview Rd., Austin, TX 78704. TEL 512-462-2442. *5826*

ANIMAL PRODUCTION IN AUSTRALIA.
A.S.A.P. Publications, Animal Science Department, University of New England, Armidale, N.S.W. 2351, Australia. TEL 61-67-733773. FAX 61-67-733773. *264*

ANIMAL REPRODUCTION SCIENCE.
Elsevier Science B.V., P.O. Box 211, 1000 AE Amsterdam, Netherlands. TEL 31-20-4853911. FAX 31-20-4353598. *264*

ANIMAL SCIENCE.
Durrant Periodicals, Winton Lea, Pencaitland, E. Lothian EH34 5AY, Scotland. TEL 01875-340354. FAX 01875-340354. *264*

ANIMALS' AGENDA.
Animal Rights Network, Inc., Box 25881, Baltimore, MD 21224. TEL 410-675-4566. FAX 410-675-0066. *295*

ANIMALS' VOICE.
Ontario S P C A, 16640 Yonge St., Newmarket, ON L3Y 4V8, Canada. TEL 905-898-7122. FAX 905-853-8643. *295*

ANIMATION JOURNAL.
A J Press, 2011 Kingsboro Circle, Tustim, CA 92680-6733. TEL 714-544-6255. FAX 714-997-6700. *5093*

ANIMATRIX.
University of California at Los Angeles, Department of Film and Television, 405 Hilgard Ave., Los Angeles, CA 90024. TEL 310-825-5829. FAX 310-825-3383. *5093*

ANKA.
13 rue Santeuil, 75231 Paris Cedex 05, France. TEL 45-35-31-15 FAX 44-08-89-79. *4181*

ANNALES ACADEMIAE SCIENTIARUM FENNICAE. SERIES A, III: GEOLOGICA-GEOGRAPHICA.
Suomalainer Tiedeakatemia, Mariankatu 5, FIN-00170 Helsinki, Finland. *2224*

ANNALES ACADEMIAE SCIENTIARUM FENNICAE MATHEMATICA.
Suomalainer Tiedeakatemia, Mariankatu 5, FIN-00170 Helsinki, Finland. *4353*

ANNALES DE BIOCHIMIE CLINIQUE DU QUEBEC.
Marc Letellier, Ed. & Pub., c/o Marc Letellier, Ed., Dept. de Biochimie Clinique, C H U S, Sherbrooke, PQ J1H 5N4, Canada. TEL 819-563-5555. FAX 819-820-6425. *4677*

ANNALES DE BIOLOGIE CLINIQUE.
Editions Scientifiques et Medicales Elsevier, 141 rue de Javel, 75747 Paris, France. TEL 33-1-45589068 FAX 33-1-45589421. *568*

ANNALES DE DROIT DE LOUVAIN.
Bruylant, 67 rue de la Regence, 1000 Brussels, Belgium. TEL 32-2-5129845. FAX 32-2-5117202. *3922*

ANNALES DE MEDECINE VETERINAIRE.
Imprimerie Bietlot, 20 Bd. de Colonster, B42, B-4000 Sart Tilman, Liege, Belgium. TEL 32-41-664020. FAX 32-41-662935. *6941*

ANNALES DE READAPTATION ET DE MEDECINE PHYSIQUE.
Editions Scientifiques et Medicales Elsevier, 141 rue de Javel, 75747 Paris, France. TEL 33-1-45589026. FAX 33-1-45589421. *4815*

ANNALES DE ZOOTECHNIE.
Editions Scientifiques et Medicales Elsevier, 141 rue de Javel, 75747 Paris, France. TEL 33-1-45589022. FAX 33-1-45589421. *798*

ANNALES DES SCIENCES FORESTIERES.
Editions Scientifiques et Medicales Elsevier, 141 rue de Javel, 75747 Paris, France. TEL 33-1-45589022. FAX 33-1-45589421. *3010*

ANNALES DES TELECOMMUNICATIONS.
Presses Polytechniques et Universitaires Romandes, EPFL - Ecublens, CH-1015 Lausanne, Switzerland. TEL 021-6934140. FAX 021-6934027. *1855*

ANNALES FRANCAISES D'ANESTHESIE ET DE REANIMATION.
Editions Scientifiques et Medicales Elsevier, 141 rue de Javel, 75747 Paris, France. TEL 33-1-45589026. FAX 33-1-45589421. *4590*

ANNALES GEOPHYSICAE.
Springer-Verlag, Heidelberger Patz 3, 14197 Berlin, Germany. TEL 49 30-8207-0. FAX 49-30-8214091. *2270*

ANNALES POLONICI MATHEMATICI.
Polska Akademia Nauk, Instytut Matematyczny, Dzial Wydawnictw, Ul. Sniadeckich 8, P.O. Box 137, 00-950 Warsaw, Poland *4354*

ANNALI DI MICROBIOLOGIA ED ENZIMOLOGIA.
Universita degli Studi di Milano Dipartimento di Scienze e Tecnologie Alimentar e Microbiologiche, Via G. Celoria 2, 20133 Milan, Italy. TEL 39-2-23573444. FAX 39-2-70630829. *753*

ANNALS OF AIR AND SPACE LAW.
McGill University, Centre for Research of Air and Space Law, 3661 Peel St., Montreal, PQ H3A 1X1, Canada. TEL 514-398-5095. FAX 514-398-8197. *56*

ANNALS OF ALLERGY, ASTHMA. & IMMUNOLOGY.
American College of Allergy, Asthma, & Immunology, 85 W. Algonquin Rd., Ste. 550, Arlington Heights, IL 60005-4425. TEL 703-821-5461. *4578*

ANNALS OF BEHAVIORAL SCIENCE AND MEDICAL EDUCATION.
Association for the Behavioral Sciences & Medical Education, 3900 E. Camelback Rd., Ste. 200, Phoenix, AZ 85018. TEL 602-912-5317. FAX 602-957-4828. *2478*

ANNALS OF BIOMEDICAL ENGINEERING.
Blackwell Science Inc., 238 Main St., Cambridge, MA 02142. TEL 617-876-7022. FAX 617-492-5263. *4426*

ANNALS OF CHILD DEVELOPMENT.
Jessica Kingsley Publishers, 1 6 Pentonville Rd., London N1 9JB, England. TEL 071-833-2307. FAX 071-837-2917. *5826*

ANNALS OF CLINICAL BIOCHEMISTRY.
Royal Society of Medicine Press Ltd., 1 Wimpole St., London W1M 8AE, England. TEL 0171-290-2900. FAX 0171-290-2929. *629*

ANNALS OF CLINICAL PSYCHIATRY.
Plenum Publishing Corp., 233 Spring St., New York, NY 10013-1578. TEL 212-620-8000. FAX 212-463-0742. *4825*

ANNALS OF COMBINATORICS.
Springer-Verlag, Heidelberger Platz 3, 14197 Berlin, Germany. TEL 49-30-82787358. FAX 49-30-82797448. *4354*

ANNALS OF DISCRETE MATHEMATICS.
Elsevier Science B.V., Books Division, P.O. Box 211, 1000 AE Amsterdam, Netherlands. TEL 31-20-4853911. FAX 31-20-4853705. *4354*

ANNALS OF DYSLEXIA.
Orton Dyslexia Society, 8600 LaSalle Rd., Ste. 382, Baltimore, MD 21286-2044. TEL 410-296-0232. *2465*

ANNALS OF EMERGENCY MEDICINE.
Mosby - Year Book, Inc. 11830 Westline Industrial Dr., St. Louis, MO 63146-3318. TEL 314-872-8370. FAX 314-432-1380. *4780*

ANNALS OF EPIDEMIOLOGY.
E sevier Science Inc., Box 945, New York, NY 10159-0945. TEL 212-633-3730. FAX 212-633-3680. *5954*

ANNALS OF EXPERIMENTAL AND CLINICAL MEDICINE.
Graffham Press Ltd., 6 York Pl., Edinburgh EH1 3EP, Scotland. TEL 0131-555-7887. FAX 0131-556-1129. *4677*

ANNALS OF GLOBAL ANALYSIS AND GEOMETRY.
Kluwer Academic Publishers, Postbus 17, 3300 AA
Dordrecht, Netherlands. TEL 31-78-6392392.
FAX 31-78-6392254. *4354*

ANNALS OF HUMAN BIOLOGY.
Taylor & Francis Ltd., 1 Gunpowder Sq., London
EC4A 3DE, England. TEL 44-171-583-0490.
FAX 44-171-583-0585. *569*

ANNALS OF INTERNAL MEDICINE.
American College of Physicians, Independence Mall
W., Sixth St. at Race, Philadelphia, PA 19106-
1572. TEL 215-351-2400. FAX 215-351-2644.
4705

ANNALS OF MEDICAL SCIENCES.
Cukurova Universitesi, Tip Fakultesi, Yayin ve
Dokumentasyon Kurulu, Balcali, 01330 Adana,
Turkey. TEL 90-322-3386060. *4427*

ANNALS OF MEDICINE.
Blackwell Science Ltd., Osney Mead, Oxford OX2
0EL, England. TEL 44-1865-206206. FAX 44-
1865-721205. *4677*

ANNALS OF NEUROLOGY.
Little, Brown and Company, Medical Journals, 34
Beacon St., Boston, MA 02108. TEL 617-859-
5500. FAX 617-859-0629. *4825*

ANNALS OF NUCLEAR ENERGY.
Elsevier Science Ltd., Pergamon, P.O. Box 800,
Kidlington, Oxford OX5 1DX, England. TEL 44-1865-
843000. FAX 44-1865-843010. *2573*

ANNALS OF NUMERICAL MATHEMATICS.
Baltzer Science Publishers B.V., Asterweg 1A, 1031
HL Amsterdam, Netherlands. TEL 31-20-6370061.
FAX 31-20-6323651. *4354*

ANNALS OF NUTRITION AND METABOLISM.
S. Karger AG, Allschwilerstr. 10, P.O. Box, CH-4009
Basel, Switzerland. TEL 061-3061111. FAX 061-
3061234. *5229*

ANNALS OF OCCUPATIONAL HYGIENE.
Elsevier Science Ltd., Pergamon, P.O. Box 800,
Kidlington, Oxford OX5 1DX, England. TEL 44-1865-
843000. FAX 44-1865-843010. *5245*

ANNALS OF ONCOLOGY.
Kluwer Academic Publishers, Postbus 17, 3300 AA
Dordrecht, Netherlands. TEL 31-78-6392392.
FAX 31-78-6392254. *4748*

ANNALS OF OPHTHALMOLOGY.
American Society of Contemporary Ophthalmology,
4711 Golf Rd., Ste. 408, Skokie, IL 60076-1242.
TEL 847-568-1500. FAX 847-568-1527. *4766*

**ANNALS OF OTOLOGY, RHINOLOGY AND
LARYNGOLOGY.**
Annals Publishing Co., 4507 Laclede Ave., St. Louis,
MO 63108. TEL 314-367-4987. FAX 314-367-
4988. *4795*

THE ANNALS OF PHARMACOTHERAPY.
Harvey Whitney Books Company, Box 42696,
Cincinnati, OH 45242. TEL 513-793-3555.
FAX 513-793-3600. *5398*

ANNALS OF PHYSICS.
Academic Press, Inc., Journal Division, 525 B St.,
Ste. 1900, San Diego, CA 92101-4495. TEL 619-
230-1840. FAX 619-699-6800. *5542*

ANNALS OF PLASTIC SURGERY.
Little, Brown and Company, Medical Journals, 34
Beacon St., Boston, MA 02108. TEL 617-859-
5500. FAX 617-267-3507. *4903*

ANNALS OF PROBABILITY.
Institute of Mathematical Statistics, Business Office,
3401 Investment Blvd., Ste. 7, Hayward, CA
94545-3819. TEL 510-783-8141. FAX 510-783-
4131. *4354*

ANNALS OF PURE AND APPLIED LOGIC.
North-Holland P.O. Box 211, 1000 AE Amsterdam,
Netherlands. TEL 31-20-4853911. FAX 31-20-
4853598. *4354*

ANNALS OF SAUDI MEDICINE.
King Faisal Specialist Hospital and Research Centre,
P.O. Box 3354, Riyadh 11211, Saudi Arabia.
TEL 966-1-4647272. FAX 966-1-4427237. *4427*

ANNALS OF SOFTWARE ENGINEERING.
Baltzer Science Publishers B.V., Asterweg 1A, 1031
HL Amsterdam, Netherlands. TEL 31-20-6370061.
FAX 31-20-6323651. *2107*

ANNALS OF SURGERY.
Lippincott - Raven Publishers 227 E. Washington
Sq., Philadelphia, PA 19106. TEL 215-238-4200.
4903

ANNALS OF SURGICAL ONCOLOGY.
Lippincott - Raven Publishers 227 E. Washington
Sq., Philadelphia, PA 19106. TEL 215-238-4200.
4903

ANNALS OF THE RHEUMATIC DISEASES.
B M J Publishing Group, B.M.A. House, Tavistock
Sq., London WC1H 9JR, England. TEL 44-171-383-
6270. FAX 44-171-383-6402. *4892*

ANNALS OF THEORETICAL PSYCHOLOGY.
Plenum Publishing Corp., 233 Spring St., New York,
NY 10013-1578. TEL 212-670-8000. FAX 212-
463-0742. *5826*

ANNALS OF THORACIC SURGERY.
Elsevier Science Inc., Box 945, New York, NY
10159-0945. TEL 212-633-3730. FAX 212-633-
3680. *4904*

ANNALS OF TOURISM RESEARCH.
Elsevier Science Ltd., Pergamon, P.O. Box 800,
Kidlington, Oxford OX5 1DX, England. TEL 44-1865-
843000. FAX 44-1865-843010. *6866*

ANNALS OF TROPICAL PAEDIATRICS.
Carfax Publishing Co., P.O. Box 25, Abingdon, Oxon.
OX14 3UE, England. TEL 44-1235-401000.
FAX 44-1235-401550. *4802*

ANNALS OF TROPICAL RESEARCH.
Visayas State College of Agriculture, Baybay, Leyte
6521-A, Philippines. TEL 415-2617. *97*

**ANNUAL ALLERTON CONFERENCE ON
COMMUNICATION, CONTROL AND COMPUTING.**
University of Illinois at Urbana-Champaign,
Coordinated Science Laboratory, Urbana, IL 61801.
TEL 217-333-0282. FAX 217-244-1653. *2683*

**ANNUAL BIBLIOGRAPHY OF THE HISTORY OF THE
PRINTED BOOK AND LIBRARY.**
Kluwer Academic Publishers, Postbus 17, 3300 AA
Dordrecht, Netherlands. TEL 31-78-6392392.
FAX 31-78-6392254. *5820*

ANNUAL EDITIONS: AGING.
Dushkin Publishing Group, Sluice Dock, Guilford, CT
06437-9989. TEL 203-453-4351. FAX 203-453-
6000. *3284*

ANNUAL EDITIONS: AMERICAN GOVERNMENT.
Dushkin Publishing Group, Sluice Dock, Guilford, CT
06437-9989. TEL 203-453-4351. FAX 203-453-
6000. *5634*

ANNUAL EDITIONS: AMERICAN HISTORY.
Dushkin Publishing Group, Sluice Dock, Guilford, CT
06437-9989. TEL 203-453-4351. FAX 203-453-
6000. *3459*

ANNUAL EDITIONS: ANTHROPOLOGY.
Dushkin Publishing Group, Sluice Dock, Guilford, CT
06437-9989. TEL 203-453-4351. FAX 203-453-
6000. *300*

ANNUAL EDITIONS: BUSINESS ETHICS.
Dushkin Publishing Group, Sluice Dock, Guilford, CT
06437-9989. TEL 203-453-4351. FAX 203-543-
6000. *893*

ANNUAL EDITIONS: CANADIAN POLITICS.
Dushkin Publishing Group, Sluice Dock, Guilford, CT
06437-9989. TEL 203-453-4351. FAX 203-453-
6000. *5634*

ANNUAL EDITIONS: COMPARATIVE POLITICS.
Dushkin Publishing Group, Sluice Dock, Guilford, CT
06437-9989. TEL 203-453-4351. FAX 203-453-
6000. *5634*

ANNUAL EDITIONS: CRIMINAL JUSTICE.
Dushkin Publishing Group, Sluice Dock, Guilford, CT
06437-9989. TEL 203-453-4351. FAX 203-453-
6000. *2157*

ANNUAL EDITIONS: DEVELOPING THIRD WORLD.
Dushkin Publishing Group, Sluice Dock, Guilford, CT
06437-9989. TEL 203-453-4351. FAX 203-453-
6000. *3247*

**ANNUAL EDITIONS: EARLY CHILDHOOD
EDUCATION.**
Dushkin Publishing Group, Sluice Dock, Guilford, CT
06437-9989. TEL 203-453-4351. FAX 203-453-
6000. *2312*

ANNUAL EDITIONS: ECONOMICS.
Dushkin Publishing Group, Sluice Dock, Guilford, CT
06437-9989. TEL 203-453-4351. FAX 203-453-
6000. *893*

**ANNUAL EDITIONS: EDUCATING EXCEPTIONAL
CHILDREN.**
Dushkin Publishing Group, Sluice Dock, Guilford, CT
06437-9989. TEL 203-453-4351. FAX 203-453-
6000. *2465*

ANNUAL EDITIONS: EDUCATION.
Dushkin Publishing Group, Sluice Dock, Guilford, CT
06437-9989. TEL 203-453-4351. FAX 203-453-
6000. *2312*

ANNUAL EDITIONS: EDUCATIONAL PSYCHOLOGY.
Dushkin Publishing Group, Sluice Dock, Guilford, CT
06437-9989. TEL 203-453-4351. FAX 203-453-
6000. *5826*

ANNUAL EDITIONS: ENVIRONMENT.
Dushkin Publishing Group, Sluice Dock, Guilford, CT
06437-9989. TEL 203-453-4351. FAX 203-453-
6000. *2776*

ANNUAL EDITIONS: GEOGRAPHY.
Dushkin Publishing Group, Sluice Dock, Guilford, CT
06437-9989. TEL 203-453-4351. FAX 203-453-
6000. *3247*

ANNUAL EDITIONS: GLOBAL ISSUES.
Dushkin Publishing Group, Sluice Dock, Guilford, CT
06437-9989. TEL 203-453-4351. FAX 203-453-
6000. *3247*

ANNUAL EDITIONS: HEALTH.
Dushkin Publishing Group, Sluice Dock, Guilford, CT
06437-9989. TEL 203-453-4351. FAX 203-453-
6000. *5524*

ANNUAL EDITIONS: HUMAN DEVELOPMENT.
Dushkin Publishing Group, Sluice Dock, Guilford, CT
06437-9989. TEL 203-453-4351. FAX 203-453-
6000. *785*

ANNUAL EDITIONS: HUMAN RESOURCES.
Dushkin Publishing Group, Sluice Dock, Guilford, CT
06437-9989. TEL 203-453-4351. FAX 203-453-
6000. *6405*

ANNUAL EDITIONS: HUMAN SEXUALITY.
Dushkin Publishing Group, Sluice Dock, Guilford, CT
06437-9989. TEL 203-453-4351. FAX 203-453-
6000. *569*

ANNUAL EDITIONS: INTERNATIONAL BUSINESS.
Dushkin Publishing Group, Sluice Dock, Guilford, CT
06437-9989. TEL 203-453-4351. FAX 203-453-
6000. *1264*

ANNUAL EDITIONS: MACROECONOMICS.
Dushkin Publishing Group, Sluice Dock, Guilford, CT
06437-9989. TEL 203-453-4351. FAX 203-453-
6000. *1400*

ANNUAL EDITIONS: MANAGEMENT.
Dushkin Publishing Group, Sluice Dock, Guilford, CT
06437-9989. TEL 203-453-4351. FAX 203-453-
6000. *1405*

ANNUAL EDITIONS: MARKETING.
Dushkin Publishing Group, Sluice Dock, Guilford, CT
06437-9989. TEL 203-453-4351. FAX 203-453-
6000. *1453*

ANNUAL EDITIONS: MARRIAGE AND FAMILY.
Dushkin Publishing Group, Sluice Dock, Guilford, CT
06437-9989. TEL 203-453-4351. FAX 203-453-
6000. *4412*

ANNUAL EDITIONS: MICROECONOMICS.
Dushkin Publishing Group, Sluice Dock, Guilford, CT
06437-9989. TEL 203-453-4351. FAX 203-453-
6000. *1248*

ANNUAL EDITIONS: MONEY AND BANKING.
Dushkin Publishing Group, Sluice Dock, Guilford, CT
06437-9989. TEL 203-453-4351. FAX 203-453-
6000. *1059*

ANNUAL EDITIONS: NUTRITION.
Dushkin Publishing Group, Sluice Dock, Guilford, CT
06437-9989. TEL 203-453-4351. FAX 203-453-
6000. *5229*

**ANNUAL EDITIONS: PERSONAL GROWTH AND
BEHAVIOR.**
Dushkin Publishing Group, Sluice Dock, Guilford, CT
06437-9989. TEL 203-453-4351. FAX 203-453-
6000. *5826*

ANNUAL EDITIONS: PSYCHOLOGY.
Dushkin Publishing Group, Sluice Dock, Guilford, CT
06437-9989. TEL 203-453-4351. FAX 203-453-
6000. *5826*

ANNUAL EDITIONS: PUBLIC ADMINISTRATION.
Dushkin Publishing Group, Sluice Dock, Guilford, CT
06437-9989. TEL 203-453-4351. FAX 203-453-
6000. *5891*

ANNUAL EDITIONS: RACE & ETHNIC RELATIONS.
Dushkin Publishing Group, Sluice Dock, Guilford, CT
06437-9989. TEL 203-453-4351. FAX 203-453-
6000. *6405*

ANNUAL EDITIONS: SOCIAL PROBLEMS.
Dushkin Publishing Group, Sluice Dock, Guilford, CT
06437-9989. TEL 203-453-4351. FAX 203-453-
6000. *6361*

ANNUAL EDITIONS: SOCIOLOGY.
Dushkin Publishing Group, Sluice Dock, Guilford, CT
06437-9989. TEL 203-453-4351. FAX 203-453-
6000. *6405*

ANNUAL EDITIONS: STATE & LOCAL GOVERNMENT.
Dushkin Publishing Group, Sluice Dock, Guilford, CT
06437-9989. TEL 203-453-4351. FAX 203-453-
6000. *5892*

ANNUAL EDITIONS: URBAN SOCIETY.
Dushkin Publishing Group, Sluice Dock, Guilford, CT
06437-9989. TEL 203-453-4351. FAX 203-453-
6000. *6405*

ANNUAL EDITIONS: VIOLENCE AND TERRORISM.
Dushkin Publishing Group, Sluice Dock, Guilford, CT
06437-9989. TEL 203-453-4351. FAX 203-453-
6000. *2157*

ANNUAL EDITIONS: WESTERN CIVILIZATION.
Dushkin Publishing Group, Sluice Dock, Guilford, CT
06437-9989. TEL 203-453-4351. FAX 203-453-
6000. *3337*

ANNUAL EDITIONS: WORLD HISTORY.
Dushkin Publishing Group, Sluice Dock, Guilford, CT
06437-9989. TEL 203-453-4351. FAX 203-453-
6000. *3337*

ANNUAL EDITIONS: WORLD POLITICS.
Dushkin Publishing Group, Sluice Dock, Guilford, CT
06437-9989. TEL 203-453-4351. FAX 203-453-
6000. *5741*

ANNUAL OF ARMENIAN LINGUISTICS.
c/o John A.C. Greppin, Ed., Cleveland State
University, Cleveland, OH 44115. TEL 216-687-
3967. FAX 216-687-9214. *4052*

**ANNUAL PROGRESS IN CHILD PSYCHIATRY AND
CHILD DEVELOPMENT.**
Brunner-Mazel Publishing Co., 19 Union Sq. W.,
New York, NY 10003. TEL 212-924-3344.
FAX 212-242-6339. *4825*

ANNUAL REPORTS IN MEDICINAL CHEMISTRY.
Academic Press, Inc., 525 B St., Ste. 1900, San
Diego, CA 92101-4495. TEL 619-231-0926.
FAX 619-699-6715. *5399*

ANNUAL REPORTS IN ORGANIC SYNTHESIS.
Academic Press, Inc., 525 B St., Ste. 1900, San
Diego, CA 92101-4495. TEL 619-231-0926.
FAX 619-699-6715. *1748*

ANNUAL REPORTS ON N M R SPECTROSCOPY.
Academic Press, Inc., 525 B St., Ste. 1900, San
Diego, CA 92101-4495. TEL 619-231-0926.
FAX 619-699-6715. *5601*

ANNUAL REVIEW IN AUTOMATIC PROGRAMMING.
Elsevier Science Ltd., Pergamon, P.O. Box 800,
Kidlington, Oxford OX5 1DX, England. TEL 44-1865-
843000. FAX 44-1865-843010. *2042*

**ANNUAL REVIEW OF BIOPHYSICS AND
BIOMOLECULAR STRUCTURE.**
Annual Reviews Inc., 4139 El Camino Way, Box
10139, Palo Alto, CA 94303-0139. TEL 415-493-
4400. FAX 415-424-0910. *651*

ANNUAL REVIEW OF FISH DISEASES.
Elsevier Science Ltd., Pergamon, P.O. Box 800,
Kidlington, Oxford OX5 1DX, England. TEL 44-1865-
843000. FAX 44-1865-843010. *798*

**ANNUAL REVIEW OF INFORMATION SCIENCE AND
TECHNOLOGY.**
Information Today, Inc., 143 Old Marlton Pike,
Medford, NJ 08055. TEL 609-654-6266. FAX 609-
654-4309. *3973*

ANNUAL REVIEW OF WOMEN IN WORLD RELIGIONS.
State University of New York Press, State University
Plaza, Albany NY 12246. TEL 518-472-5000.
FAX 518-472-5033. *7014*

ANNUAL SIMULATION SYMPOSIUM. PROCEEDINGS.
Society for Computer Simulation, Box 17900, San
Diego, CA 92177. TEL 619-277-3888. FAX 619-
277-3930. *2051*

ANTARCTIC.
New Zealand Antarctic Society, Box 404,
Christchurch, New Zealand. TEL 64-3-3650344.
FAX 64-3-3654255. *3247*

ANTARCTIC SCIENCE.
Blackwell Science Ltd., Osney Mead, Oxford OX2
OEL, England. TEL 44-1865-206206. FAX 44-
1865-721205. *569*

ANTHROPOLOGIAI KOZLEMENYEK.
Magyar Biologiai Tarsasag, c/o Eotvos Lorand
University, Dept. Anthropology, Puskin u. 3, 1088
Budapest, Hungary. TEL 36-1-2667857. *301*

ANTHROPOLOGICA.
Wilfrid Laurier University Press, 75 University Ave.
W., Waterloo, ON N2L 3C5, Canada. TEL 519-884-
0710. FAX 519-725-1399. *301*

ANTHROPOLOGICAL FORUM.
University of Western Australia, Department of
Anthropology, Nedlands, W.A. 6009, Australia.
TEL 61-9-380-2851. FAX 61-9-380-1062. *301*

ANTHROPOLOGICAL LINGUISTICS.
Indiana University, Anthropology Department,
Student Services Bldg. Rm. 130, Bloomington, IN
47405. TEL 812-355-4123. FAX 812-855-7529.
4052

ANTHROPOLOGY AND ARCHEOLOGY OF EURASIA.
M.E. Sharpe, Inc., 80 Business Park Dr., Armonk,
NY 10504. TEL 914-273-1800. FAX 914-273-
2106. *302*

ANTHROPOLOGY OF CONSCIOUSNESS.
Society for the Anthropology of Consciousness,
Social Sciences Dept., Masa State College, 1175
Texas Ave., Grand Junction, CO 81501. TEL 970-
248-1759. *302*

ANTHROPOLOGY U C L A.
University of California at Los Angeles, Department
of Anthropology, 405 Hilgard Ave., Los Angeles, CA
90024. TEL 310-825-2055. *302*

ANTHROZOOS.
Delta Society, 289 Perimeter Rd. E., Renton, WA
98055-1329. TEL 206-226-7357. FAX 206-235-
1076. *303*

ANTI.
60 Dimocharous St., 115 21 Athens, Greece.
TEL 30-1-723-2713. FAX 30-1-722-6107. *5634*

ANTI-CANCER DRUGS.
Rapid Science Publishers, The Old Malthouse,
Paradise St., Oxford OX1 1LD, England. TEL 44-
1865-790447. FAX 44-1865-244012. *4748*

ANTI-SLAVERY REPORTER.
Anti-Slavery International, The Stableyard,
Broomgrove Rd., London SW9 9TL, England.
TEL 44-171-924-9555. FAX 44-171-738-4110.
5725

ANTIBIOTICS AND CHEMOTHERAPY.
S. Karger AG, Allschwilerstr. 10, P.O. Box, CH-4009
Basel, Switzerland. TEL 061-3061111. FAX 061-
3061234. *5399*

**ANTIBODY, IMMUNOCONJUGATES, AND
RADIOPHARMACEUTICALS.**
Mary Ann Liebert, Inc. Publishers, 2 Madison Ave.,
Larchmont, NY 10538. TEL 914-834-3100.
FAX 914-834-3688. *4748*

ANTICHTHON.
Australian Society for Classical Studies, c/o Prof.
G.R. Stanton, Ed., Dept. of Classics and Ancient
History, University of New England, Armidale, N.S.W.
2351, Australia. FAX 61-67-73-3122. *1818*

ANTIMICROBIAL AGENTS AND CHEMOTHERAPY.
American Society for Microbiology, 1325
Massachusetts Ave., N.W., Washington, DC 20005.
TEL 202-737-3600. *753*

ANTIMICROBIAL AGENTS ANNUAL.
Elsevier Science B.V., Books Division, P.O. Box 211,
1000 AE Amsterdam, Netherlands. TEL 31-20-
4853911. FAX 31-20-43537C5. *753*

**ANTIMICROBICS AND INFECTIOUS DISEASES
NEWSLETTER.**
Elsevier Science Inc., Box 945, New York, NY
10159-0945. TEL 212-633-3730. FAX 212-633-
3680. *4617*

ANTITRUST LAW JOURNAL.
American Bar Association, Antitrust Law Section,
750 N. Lake Shore Dr., Chicago, IL 60611.
TEL 312-988-5606. *3894*

ANTIVIRAL CHEMISTRY & CHEMOTHERAPY.
Blackwell Science Ltd., Osney Mead, Oxford OX2
OEL, England. TEL 44-1865-206206. FAX 44-
1865-721205. *5399*

ANTIVIRAL RESEARCH.
Elsevier Science B.V., P.O. Box 211, 1000 AE
Amsterdam, Netherlands. TEL 31-20-4853911.
FAX 31-20-4853598. *753*

ANTONIE VAN LEEUWENHOEK.
Kluwer Academic Publishers, Postbus 17, 3300 AA
Dordrecht, Netherlands. TEL 31-78-6392392
FAX 31-78-6392254. *753*

ANTROPOLOGIA PORTUGUESA.
Universidade de Coimbra, Museu e Laboratorio
Antropologico, 3000 Coimbra, Portugal. TEL 351-
39-23491. FAX 351-39-23491. *303*

ANUARIO ESTATISTICO DOS TRANSPORTES.
Empresa Brasileira de Planejamento de Transportes,
G E I P O T, SAN Quadra 3 Blocos N-O, 70040-920
Brasilia DF, Brazil. FAX 061-224-8642. *6713*

ANXIETY.
John Wiley & Sons, Inc. Journals, 605 Third Ave.,
New York, NY 10158. TEL 212-850-6645.
FAX 212-850-6021. *5827*

ANXIETY, STRESS AND COPING.
Harwood Academic Publishers, c/o International
Publishers Distributor, P.O. Box 3054, Langhorne,
PA 19047-3054. TEL 215-750-2642. FAX 215-
750-6343. *5827*

APERIODICITY AND ORDER.
Academic Press, Inc., 525 B St., Ste. 1900, San
Diego, CA 92101-4495. TEL 619-231-6616.
FAX 619-699-6715. *4542*

APHASIOLOGY.
Taylor & Francis Ltd., 1 Gunpowder Sq., London
EC4A 3DE, England. TEL 44-171-583-0490.
FAX 44-171-583-0585. *4825*

APIDOLOGIE.
Editions Scientifiques et Medicales Elsevier, 141 rue
de Javel, 75747 Paris, France. TEL 33-1-
45589022. *721*

APOPTOSIS.
Rapid Science Publishers, 2-6 Boundary Row, London SE1 8HN, England. TEL 44-171-865-0198. FAX 44-171-410-6600. *711*

APOSTROPHE.
Mr. Pillow's Press, 41 Canute Rd., Faversham, Kent ME13 8SH, England. TEL 01795-536185. *4300*

APOTHECARY.
Health Care Marketing Services, H C M S Inc., Box AP, Los Altos, CA 94023-0179. TEL 415-941-3955. FAX 415-941-2303. *5399*

APOTHEEKMANAGEMENT.
Mediselect B.V., Postbus 28091, 3828 ZH Hoogland, Netherlands. TEL 31-33-4808020. FAX 31-33-4805881. *5399*

APPLICABLE ANALYSIS.
Gordon and Breach Science Publishers, c/o International Publishers Distributor, P.O. Box 3054, Langhorne, PA 19047-3054. TEL 215-750-2642. FAX 215-750-6343. *4354*

APPLICATIONES MATHEMATICAE.
Polska Akademia Nauk, Instytut Matematyczny, Dzial Wydawnictw, Ul. Sniadeckich 8, P.O. Box 137, 00-950 Warsaw, Poland. TEL 48-22-6282471. FAX 48-22-6293997. *4355*

APPLICATIONS OF FIBONACCI NUMBERS.
Kluwer Academic Publishers, Postbus 17, 3300 AA Dordrecht, Netherlands. TEL 31-78-6392392. FAX 31-78-6392254. *4355*

APPLIED ACOUSTICS.
Elsevier Science Ltd., P.O. Box 800, Kidlington, Oxford OX5 1DX, England. TEL 44-1865-843000. FAX 44-1865-843010. *5613*

APPLIED AND ENVIRONMENTAL MICROBIOLOGY.
American Society for Microbiology, 1325 Massachusetts Ave., N.W., Washington, DC 20005. TEL 202-737-3600. *753*

APPLIED ANIMAL BEHAVIOUR SCIENCE.
Elsevier Science B.V., P.O.Box 211, 1000 AE Amsterdam, Netherlands. TEL 31-20-4853911. FAX 31-20-4853598. *798*

APPLIED ARTIFICIAL INTELLIGENCE.
Taylor & Francis Inc., 1900 Frost Rd., Ste. 101, Bristol, PA 19007-1598. TEL 215-785-5800. FAX 215-785-5515. *2005*

APPLIED BIOCHEMISTRY AND BIOTECHNOLOGY.
Humana Press Inc., 999 Riverview Dr., Ste. 208, Totowa, NJ 07512-1165. TEL 201-256-1699. FAX 201-256-8341. *630*

APPLIED BIOCHEMISTRY AND MICROBIOLOGY.
Maik Nauka - Interperiodica, Mezhdunarodnyi Otdel, Ul. Profsoyuznaya, 90, 117864 Moscow, Russia. TEL 7-095-3360066. FAX 7-095-3360066. *630*

APPLIED CARDIOPULMONARY PATHOPHYSIOLOGY.
Kluwer Academic Publishers, Postbus 17, 3300 AA Dordrecht, Netherlands. TEL 31-78-6392392. FAX 31-78-6392254. *785*

APPLIED CATALYSIS A: GENERAL.
Elsevier Science B.V., P.O. Box 211, 1000 AE Amsterdam, Netherlands. TEL 31-20-4853911. FAX 31-20-4853598. *2633*

APPLIED CATALYSIS B: ENVIRONMENTAL.
Elsevier Science B.V., P.O. Box 211, 1000 AE Amsterdam, Netherlands. TEL 31-20-4853911. FAX 31-20-4853598. *2633*

APPLIED CATEGORICAL STRUCTURES.
Kluwer Academic Publishers, Postbus 17, 3300 AA Dordrecht, Netherlands. TEL 31-78-6392392. FAX 31-78-6392254. *4407*

APPLIED CLAY SCIENCE.
Elsevier Science B.V., P.O. Box 211, 1000 AE Amsterdam, Netherlands. TEL 31-20-4853911. FAX 31-20-4853598. *2224*

APPLIED COGNITIVE PSYCHOLOGY.
John Wiley & Sons Ltd., Journals, Baffins Ln., Chichester, W. Sussex PO19 1UD, England. TEL 44-1243-779777. FAX 44-1243-843232. *5827*

APPLIED COMPOSITE MATERIALS.
Kluwer Academic Publishers, Postbus 17, 3300 AA Dordrecht, Netherlands. TEL 31-78-6392392. FAX 31-78-6392254. *2729*

APPLIED COMPUTATIONAL ELECTROMAGNETICS SOCIETY JOURNAL.
Applied Computational Electromagnetics Society, Inc., c/o Prof. Richard W. Adler, Naval Postgraduate School, Code EC-AB, 833 Dyer Rd., Rm. 437, Monterey, CA 93943. TEL 408-646-1111. FAX 408-649-0300. *5582*

APPLIED COMPUTATIONAL ELECTROMAGNETICS SOCIETY NEWSLETTER.
Applied Computational Electromagnetics Society, Inc., c/o Prof. Richard W. Adler, Naval Postgraduate School, Code EC-AB, 833 Dyer Rd., Rm. 437, CA 93943. TEL 408-646-1111. FAX 408-649-0300. *5582*

APPLIED ECONOMICS.
Chapman & Hall, Journals Department 2-6 Boundary Row, London SE1 8HN, England. TEL 44-171-8650066. FAX 44-171-5229623. *893*

APPLIED ECONOMICS LETTERS.
Chapman & Hall, Journals Department 2-6 Boundary Row, London SE1 8HN, England. TEL 44-171-8650066. FAX 44-171-5229623. *893*

APPLIED ENERGY.
Elsevier Science Ltd., P.O. Box 800, Kidlington, Oxford OX5 1DX, England. TEL 44-1865-843000. FAX 44-1865-843010. *2540*

APPLIED ENGINEERING IN AGRICULTURE.
American Society of Agricultural Engineers, 2950 Niles Rd., St. Joseph, MI 49085-9659. TEL 616-429-0300. FAX 616-429-3852. *98*

APPLIED ENTOMOLOGY AND PHYTOPATHOLOGY.
Plant Pests and Diseases Research Institute, P.O. Box 1454, Tehran 19395, Iran. TEL 98-21-2403012. *721*

APPLIED ERGONOMICS.
Butterworth - Heinemann, Part of the Reed Elsevier group, Linacre House, Jordan Hill, Oxford OX2 8DP, England. *2589*

APPLIED FINANCIAL ECONOMICS.
Chapman & Hall, Journals Department 2-6 Boundary Row, London SE1 8HN, England. TEL 44-171-8650066. FAX 44-171-5229623. *1174*

APPLIED GEOCHEMISTRY.
Elsevier Science Ltd., Pergamon, P.O. Box 800, Kidlington, Oxford OX5 1DX, England. TEL 44-1865-843000. FAX 44-1865-843010. *2224*

APPLIED GEOGRAPHY.
Butterworth - Heinemann, Part of the Reed Elsevier group, Linacre House, Jordan Hill, Oxford OX2 8DP, England. TEL 44-1865-310366. FAX 44-1865-310898. *3247*

APPLIED H.R.M. RESEARCH.
Society of I-O Graduates, Department of Psychology, Radford University, Radford, VA 24142. TEL 703-831-5513. *5827*

APPLIED INTELLIGENCE.
Kluwer Academic Publishers Boston, Box 358, Accord Sta., Hingham, MA 02018-0358. TEL 617-871-6600. FAX 617-871-6528. *2005*

APPLIED MATHEMATICAL FINANCE.
Chapman & Hall, Journals Department 2-6 Boundary Row, London SE1 8HN, England. TEL 44-171-8650066. FAX 44-171-5229623. *4355*

APPLIED MATHEMATICAL MODELLING.
Elsevier Science Inc., Box 945, New York, NY 10159-0945. TEL 212-633-3730. FAX 212-633-3680. *4407*

APPLIED MATHEMATICS.
Gordon & Breach Science Publishers, c/o International Publishers Distributor, P.O. Box 3054, Langhorne, PA 19047-3054. TEL 215-750-2642. FAX 215-750-2642. *4355*

APPLIED MATHEMATICS AND COMPUTATION.
Elsevier Science Inc., Box 945, New York, NY 10159-0945. TEL 212-633-3730. FAX 212-633-3680. *4355*

APPLIED MATHEMATICS AND MECHANICS.
Academic Press, Inc., 525 B St., Ste. 1900, San Diego, CA 92101-4495. TEL 619-231-0926. FAX 619-699-6715. *4355*

APPLIED MATHEMATICS AND OPTIMIZATION.
Springer-Verlag, Science Journals, 175 Fifth Ave., New York, NY 10010. TEL 212-460-1500. FAX 212-473-6272. *4355*

APPLIED MATHEMATICS LETTERS.
Elsevier Science Ltd., Pergamon, P.O. Box 800, Kidlington, Oxford OX5 1DX, England. TEL 44-1865-843000. FAX 44-1865-843010. *4356*

APPLIED MEASUREMENT IN EDUCATION.
Lawrence Erlbaum Associates, Inc., 10 Industrial Dr., Mahwah, NJ 07430-2262. TEL 201-236-9500. FAX 201-236-0072. *2312*

APPLIED MECHANICS REVIEWS.
American Society of Mechanical Engineers, 22 Law Dr., Fairfield, NJ 07007-2300. *2624*

APPLIED NEUROPSYCHOLOGY.
Munksgaard International Publishers Ltd., 35 Noerre Soegade, P.O. Box 1248, DK-1016 Copenhagen K, Denmark. TEL 45-33-127030. FAX 45-33-129387. *4825*

APPLIED NUMERICAL MATHEMATICS.
North-Holland P.O. Box 211, 1000 AE Amsterdam, Netherlands. TEL 31-20-4853911. FAX 31-20-4853598. *4407*

APPLIED OCEAN RESEARCH.
Elsevier Science Ltd., P.O. Box 800, Kidlington, Oxford OX5 1DX, England. TEL 44-1865-843000. FAX 44-1865-843010. *2290*

APPLIED OPTICS.
Optical Society of America, Inc., 2010 Massachusetts Ave., N.W., Washington, DC 20036-1023. TEL 202-223-8130. *5601*

APPLIED PSYCHOLINGUISTICS AND COMMUNICATION DISORDERS.
Plenum Publishing Corp., 233 Spring St., New York, NY 10013-1578. TEL 212-620-8000. FAX 212-463-0742. *4053*

APPLIED PSYCHOLOGICAL MEASUREMENT.
Applied Psychological Measurement, Inc., 2455 Teller Rd., Thousand Oaks, CA 91320. TEL 805-449-0721. FAX 805-499-0871. *5827*

APPLIED PSYCHOLOGY.
Taylor & Francis Ltd., Psychology Press, 1 Gunpowder Sq., London EC4A 3DE, England. TEL 44-171-5830490. FAX 44-171-5830585. *5827*

APPLIED PSYCHOPHYSIOLOGY AND BIOFEEDBACK.
Plenum Publishing Corp., 233 Spring St., New York, NY 10013-1578. TEL 212-620-8000. FAX 212-463-0742. *5827*

APPLIED RADIATION AND ISOTOPES.
Elsevier Science Ltd., Pergamon, P.O. Box 800, Kidlington, Oxford OX5 1DX. TEL 44-1865-843000. FAX 44-1865-843010. *5593*

APPLIED RADIOLOGY.
1301 W. Park Ave., Ocean, NJ 07712-3151. TEL 908-695-0600. FAX 908-695-9501. *4873*

APPLIED SCIENTIFIC RESEARCH.
Kluwer Academic Publishers, Postbus 17, 3300 AA Dordrecht, Netherlands. TEL 31-78-6392392. FAX 31-78-6392254. *6226*

APPLIED SOIL ECOLOGY.
Elsevier Science B.V., P.O. Box 211, 1000 AE Amsterdam, Netherlands. TEL 31-20-4853911. FAX 31-20-4853598. *211*

APPLIED SOLAR ENERGY.
Allerton Press, Inc., 150 Fifth Ave., New York, NY 10011. TEL 212-924-3950. FAX 212-463-9684. *2585*

APPLIED SOLID STATE SCIENCE.
Academic Press, Inc., 525 B St., Ste. 1900, San Diego, CA 92101-4495. TEL 619-231-0926. FAX 619-669-6715. *2683*

APPLIED SPECTROSCOPY.
Society for Applied Spectroscopy, 201B Broadway St., Frederick, MD 21701. TEL 301-694-8122. FAX 301-694-6860. *5601*

APPLIED SPECTROSCOPY REVIEWS.
Marcel Dekker Journals, 270 Madison Ave., New York, NY 10016. TEL 212-696-9000. FAX 212-685-4540. *5601*

APPLIED STOCHASTIC MODELS AND DATA ANALYSIS.
John Wiley & Sons Ltd., Journals, Baffins Ln., Chichester, W. Sussex PO19 1UD, England. TEL 44-1243-779777. FAX 44-1243-843232. *4356*

APPLIED SUPERCONDUCTIVITY.
Elsevier Science Ltd., Pergamon, P.O. Box 800, Kidlington, Oxford OX5 1DX, England. TEL 44-1865-843000. FAX 44-1865-843010. *2683*

APPLIED SURFACE SCIENCE.
North-Holland P.O. Box 211, 1000 AE Amsterdam, Netherlands. TEL 31-20-4853911. FAX 31-20-4853598. *4949*

APPLIED THERMAL ENGINEERING.
Elsevier Science Ltd., Pergamon, P.O. Box 800, Kidlington, Oxford OX5 1DX, England. TEL 44-1865-843000. FAX 44-1865-843010. *5583*

APPLIED VIROLOGY RESEARCH.
Plenum Publishing Corp., 233 Spring St., New York, NY 10013-1578. TEL 212-620-8000. FAX 212-463-0742. *754*

APPRAISAL JOURNAL.
Appraisal Institute, 875 N. Michigan Ave., Ste. 2400, Chicago, IL 60611-1980. TEL 312-335-4100. FAX 312-353-4400. *6018*

APPROPRIATE TECHNOLOGY.
Intermediate Technology Publications Ltd., 103-105 Southampton Row, London WC1B 4HH, England. TEL 44-171-436-9761. FAX 44-171-436-2013. *187*

APPROXIMATION THEORY AND ITS APPLICATIONS.
Baltzer Science Publishers B.V., Asterweg 1A, 1031 HL Amsterdam, Netherlands. TEL 31-20-6370061. FAX 31-20-6323654. *4356*

APUNTES DE INGENIERIA.
Pontificia Universidad Catolica de Chile, Escuela de Ingenieria, Casilla 306, Correo 22, Santiago, Chile. TEL 562-552-2375. FAX 562-552-4054. *2589*

AQUA.
Blackwell Science Ltd., Osney Mead, Oxford OX2 0EL, England. TEL 44-1865-206206. FAX 44-1865-721205. *6962*

AQUACULTURAL ENGINEERING.
Elsevier Science Ltd., P.O. Box 800, Kidlington, Oxford OX5 1DX, England. TEL 44-1865-843000. FAX 44-1865-843010. *2925*

AQUACULTURE.
Elsevier Science B.V., P.O. Box 211, 1000 AE Amsterdam, Netherlands. TEL 31-20-4853911. FAX 31-20-4853598. *2926*

AQUACULTURE INTERNATIONAL.
Chapman & Hall, Journals Department 2-6 Boundary Row, London SE1 8HN, England. TEL 44-171-8650066. FAX 44-171-8659623. *2926*

AQUACULTURE IRELAND.
P.O. Box 12, B.I.M. Bldg., Crofton Rd., Dun Laoghaire, Co. Dublin, Ireland. TEL 01-2841544. FAX 01-2841123. *2926*

AQUACULTURE NUTRITION.
Blackwell Science Ltd., Osney Mead, Oxford OX2 0EL, England. TEL 44-1865-206206. FAX 44-1865-721205. *2926*

AQUACULTURE RESEARCH.
Blackwell Science Ltd., Osney Mead, Oxford OX2 0EL, England. TEL 44-1865-206206. FAX 44-1865-721205. *2926*

AQUARIUM SCIENCES AND CONSERVATION.
Chapman & Hall, Journals Department 2-6 Boundary Row, London SE1 8HN, England. TEL 44-171-8650066. FAX 44-171-5229623. *2926*

AQUATIC BOTANY.
Elsevier Science B.V., P.O. Box 211, 1000 AE Amsterdam, Netherlands. TEL 31-20-4853911. FAX 31-20-4853598. *670*

AQUATIC CONSERVATION: MARINE AND FRESHWATER ECOSYSTEMS.
John Wiley & Sons Ltd., Journals, Baffins Ln., Chichester, W. Sussex PO19 1UD, England. TEL 44-1243-779777. FAX 44-1243-843232. *2120*

AQUATIC GEOCHEMISTRY.
Kluwer Academic Publishers, Postbus 17, 3300 AA Dordrecht, Netherlands. TEL 31-78-6392392. FAX 31-78-6392254. *2204*

AQUATIC MAMMALS.
European Associat on for Aquatic Mammals, Hawaii Institute of Marine Biology, Box 1106, Kailua, HI 96734. TEL 808-236-4001. FAX 808-247-5831. *798*

AQUATIC PLANT STUDIES.
Elsevier Science B.V., Books Division, P.O. Box 211, 1000 AE Amsterdam, Netherlands. TEL 31-20-4853911. FAX 31-20-4853705. *670*

AQUATIC TOXICOLOGY.
Elsevier Science B.V., P.O. Box 211, 1000 AE Amsterdam, Netherlands. TEL 31-20-4853911. FAX 31-20-4853598. *2842*

AQUILO. SERIE BOTANICA.
Societas Amicorum Naturae Ouluensis, Department of Botany, Univers ty of Oulu, Linnanmaa, FIN-90570 Oulu. Finland. FAX 981-553-1500. *670*

ARABIAN ARCHAEOLOGY AND EPIGRAPHY.
Munksgaard Internrational Publishers Ltd., 35 Noerre Soegade, F.O. Box 2148, DK-1016 Copenhagen K, Denmark. TEL 45-33-127030. FAX 45-33-129387. *340*

ARABIAN JOURNAL FOR SCIENCE AND ENGINEERING.
King Fahd Univers ty of Petroleum and Minerals, P.O. Box 5033, Dhahran 31231, Saudi Arabia. FAX 966-3-860-5458. *2589*

ARABICA.
E.J. Brill, P.O. Box 9000, 2300 PA Leiden, Netherlands. TEL 31-71-5353500. FAX 31-71-5317532. *5278*

ARBEITEN ZUR GESCHICHTE DES ANTIKEN JUDENTUMS UND DES URCHRISTENTUMS.
E.J. Brill, P.O. Box 9000, 2300 PA Leiden, Netherlands. TEL 31-71-5353500. FAX 31-71-5317532. *5122*

ARBEJDERHISTORIE.
Selskabet til Forskning i Arbejderbevaegelsens Historie, Noerrebrogade 66 D, DK-2200 Copenhagen N, Denmark. TEL 45-35-361522. FAX 45-35-363222. *1362*

ARBEJDSMILJOE.
Arbejdsmiljoefondet, Vermundsgade 38, 2100 Copenhagen. Denmark. TEL 45-39-16-05-00. FAX 45-39-16-05-80. *5245*

ARBETARHISTORIA.
Arbetarroerelsens Arkiv och Bibliotek, P.O. Box 1124, S-111 81 Stockholm, Sweden. TEL 46-84-54-65-00. FAX 8-21-55-60. *3717*

ARCHAEOASTRONOMY.
Center for Archaeoastronomy, Box X, College Park, MD 20740-1024. TEL 301-864-6637. *340*

ARCHAEOASTRONOMY.
Science History Publications Ltd., 16 Rutherford Rd., Cambridge CB2 2HH, England. TEL 44-1223-565532. *475*

ARCHAEOLOGIA.
Society of Antiquaries of London, Burlington House, London W1V 0HS, England. FAX 44-171-287-6967. *340*

ARCHAEOLOGIA JAPONICA.
Japanese Archaeclogical Association, Hirai 5-15-5aigaku Kokogaku Kenkyushitsu, Edogawa-ku, Tokyo J-132, Japan. TEL 81-3-3618-6608. FAX 81-3-3618-6625. *340*

ARCHAEOLOGICAL EXPLORATION OF SARDIS. MONOGRAPHS.
Harvard University Art Museums, Sardis Exploration Office, 7 Sumner Rd., Cambridge, MA 02138. TEL 617-495-3940. *340*

ARCHAEOLOGICAL JOURNAL.
Royal Archaeological Institute, c/o Society of Antiquaries, Burlington House, Picadilly, London W1V 0HS, England. *341*

ARCHAEOLOGICAL PROSPECTION.
John Wiley & Sons Ltd. Journals, Baffins Ln., Chichester, W. Sussex PO19 1JD, England. TEL 44-1243-779777. FAX 44-1243-843232. *341*

ARCHAEOLOGY.
Archaeological Institute of America, 135 William St., New York, NY 10038. TEL 212-732-5154. FAX 212-732-5707. *342*

ARCHEOGRAFO TRIESTINO.
Societa di Minerva, c/o Biblioteca Civica "Attilio Hortis", Piazza Attilio Hortis 4, 34123 Trieste Italy. TEL 39-40-301214. *343*

ARCHEOLOGICAL SOCIETY OF VIRGINIA. QUARTERLY BULLETIN
A S V Press, Box 70395, Richmond, VA 23255-0395. *343*

ARCHIMAGE.
Un versity of Wisconsin at Milwaukee, School of Architecture and Urban Plannirg, Box 413, Milwaukee, WI 53201. TEL 414-229-4014. *382*

ARCHITETTURA CRONACHE E STORIA.
Via Nomentana 150, 00162 Fome, Italy. TEL 39-6-86320684. FAX 39-6-6603662. *385*

ARCHIVES DES SCIENCES ET COMPTE RENDU DES SEANCES DE LA SOCIETE DE PHYSIQUE ET D'HISTOIRE NATURELLE DE GENEVE.
Societe de Physique et d'Histoire Naturelle de Geneve, Museum d'Histoire Naturelle de Geneve, Case Postale 6434, CH 1211 Geneva 6, Switzerland. TEL 41-22-7359130. FAX 41-22-7353445. *6227*

ARCHIVES ET BIBLIOTHEQUES DE BELGIQUE.
Archives et Bibliotheques de Belgique a.s.b.l., Rue de Ruysbroeck, 2-6, B-1000 Brussels, Belgium. *3394*

ARCHIVES INTERNATIONALES D'HISTOIRE DES IDEES.
Kluwer Academic Publishers, Postbus 17, 3300 AA Dordrecht, Netherlands. TEL 31-78-6392392. FAX 31-78-6392254. *5468*

ARCHIVES OF ANDROLOGY.
Taylor & Francis Inc., 1900 Frost Rd., Ste. 101, Bristol, PA 19007-1598. TEL 215-785-5800. FAX 215-785-5515. *1428*

ARCHIVES OF ASIAN ART.
As a Society, 725 Park Ave., New York, NY 10021-5088. TEL 212-517-8315. FAX 212-288-6400. *411*

ARCHIVES OF BIOCHEMISTRY AND BIOPHYSICS.
Academic Press, Inc., Journal Division, 525 B St., Ste. 1900, San Diego, CA 92101-4495. TEL 619-230-1840. FAX 619-699-6800. *630*

ARCHIVES OF CLINICAL NEUROPSYCHOLOGY.
Elsevier Science Ltd., Pergamon, P.O. Box 800, Kidlington, Oxford OX5 1DX, England. TEL 44-1865-843000. FAX 44-1865-843010. *4825*

ARCHIVES OF DERMATOLOGY.
American Medical Association, 515 N. State St., Chicago, IL 60610. TEL 312-464-5000. FAX 617-667-4948. *4658*

ARCHIVES OF DISEASE IN CHILDHOOD.
B M J Publishing Group, B.M.A. House, Tavistock Sq., London WC1H 9JR, England. TEL 44-171-383-6270. FAX 44-171-383-6402. *4802*

ARCHIVES OF DISEASE IN CHILDHOOD. FETAL AND NEONATAL EDITION.
B M J Publishing Group, B.M.A. House, Tavistock Sq., London WC1H 9JR, England. TEL 44-171-387-4499. FAX 44-171-383-666... *4731*

ARCHIVES OF ENVIRONMENTAL HEALTH.
Heldref Publications, 1319 Eighteenth St., N.W., Washington, DC 20036-1802. TEL 202-296-6267. FAX 202-296-5149. *4428*

ARCHIVES OF FAMILY MEDICINE.
American Medical Association, 515 N. State St., Chicago, IL 60610. TEL 312-464-5000. FAX 312-464-5831. *4428*

ARCHIVES OF GENERAL PSYCHIATRY.
American Medical Association, 515 N. State St., Chicago, IL 60610. TEL 312-464-5000. FAX 312-464-5831. *4826*

ARCHIVES OF GERONTOLOGY AND GERIATRICS.
Elsevier Science Ireland Ltd., P.O. Box 85, Limerick, Ireland. TEL 353-61-471944. FAX 353-61-472144. *3284*

ARCHIVES OF GERONTOLOGY AND GERIATRICS. SUPPLEMENT.
Elsevier Science Ireland Ltd., P.O. Box 85, Limerick, Ireland. TEL 353-61-471944. FAX 353-61-472144. *3284*

ARCHIVES OF GYNECOLOGY AND OBSTETRICS.
Springer-Verlag, Heidelberger Platz 3, 14197 Berlin, Germany. TEL 49-30-8207-0. FAX 49-30-8214091. *4731*

ARCHIVES OF HYDRO-ENGINEERING AND ENVIRONMENTAL MECHANICS.
Polska Akademia Nauk, Instytut Budownictwa Wodnego, Ul. Koscierska 7, 80-952 Gdansk-Oliwa, Poland. TEL 48-58-522011. FAX 48-58-524211. *6963*

ARCHIVES OF INSECT BIOCHEMISTRY AND PHYSIOLOGY.
John Wiley & Sons, Inc., Journals, 605 Third Ave., New York, NY 10158. TEL 212-850-6645. FAX 212-850-6021. *721*

ARCHIVES OF INTERNAL MEDICINE.
American Medical Association, 515 N. State St., Chicago, IL 60610. TEL 312-464-5000. FAX 312-464-5831. *4705*

ARCHIVES OF MEDICAL RESEARCH.
Instituto Mexicano del Seguro Social, Oficina de Bibliotecas y Divulgacion, Apdo. 73-032, 06720 Mexico D.F., Mexico. TEL 5-7611503. *4428*

ARCHIVES OF NEUROLOGY.
American Medical Association, 515 N. State St., Chicago, IL 60610. TEL 312-464-5000. FAX 312-464-5831. *4826*

ARCHIVES OF OPHTHALMOLOGY.
American Medical Association, 515 N. State St., Chicago, IL 60610. TEL 312-464-5000. FAX 312-464-5831. *4767*

ARCHIVES OF ORAL BIOLOGY.
Elsevier Science Ltd., Pergamon, P.O. Box 800, Kidlington, Oxford OX5 1DX, England. TEL 44-1865-843000. FAX 44-1865-843010. *4635*

ARCHIVES OF OTOLARYNGOLOGY - HEAD & NECK SURGERY.
American Medical Association, 515 N. State St., Chicago, IL 60610. TEL 312-464-5000. FAX 312-464-5831. *4795*

ARCHIVES OF PATHOLOGY & LABORATORY MEDICINE.
College of American Pathologists, 325 Waukegan Rd., Northfield, IL 60093-2750. TEL 708-446-8800. FAX 708-446-3563. *4428*

ARCHIVES OF PEDIATRICS & ADOLESCENT MEDICINE.
American Medical Association, 515 N. State St., Chicago, IL 60610. TEL 312-464-5000. FAX 312-464-4181. *4802*

ARCHIVES OF PHYSICAL MEDICINE AND REHABILITATION.
W.B. Saunders Co. Curtis Center, 3rd Fl., Independence Sq. W., Philadelphia, PA 19106-3399. TEL 215-238-7800. FAX 215-238-6445. *4816*

ARCHIVES OF PHYSIOLOGY AND BIOCHEMISTRY.
Swets & Zeitlinger bv, P.O. Box 825, 2160 SZ Lisse, Netherlands. TEL 31-252-435111. FAX 31-252-415888. *785*

ARCHIVES OF PSYCHIATRIC NURSING.
W.B. Saunders Co. Curtis Center, 3rd Fl., Independence Sq. W., Philadelphia, PA 19106-3399. TEL 215-238-7800. FAX 215-238-6445. *4710*

ARCHIVES OF S T D - HIV RESEARCH.
Reproductive Health Center, 78 Surfsong Rd., Kiawah Island, SC 29455. TEL 803-768-5556. FAX 803-768-6494. *4618*

ARCHIVES OF SEXUAL BEHAVIOR.
Plenum Publishing Corp., 233 Spring St., New York, NY 10013-1578. TEL 212-620-8000. FAX 212-463-0742. *4428*

ARCHIVES OF SOVIET SCIENCE SERIES: PHYSICAL SCIENCES SECTION.
Harwood Academic Publishers, c/o International Publishers Distributor, P.O. Box 3054, Langhorne, PA 19047-3054. TEL 215-750-2642. FAX 215-750-6343. *5593*

ARCHIVES OF SUICIDE RESEARCH.
Kluwer Academic Publishers, Postbus 17, 3300 AA Dordrecht, Netherlands. TEL 31-78-6392392. FAX 31-78-6392254. *5828*

ARCHIVES OF SURGERY.
American Medical Association, 515 N. State St., Chicago, IL 60610. TEL 312-464-5000. FAX 312-464-5831. *4904*

ARCHIVIO GEOBOTANICO.
Universita di Pavia, Istituto di Botanica, Via S. Epifanio 14, 27100 Pavia, Italy. *671*

ARCHIVO ESPANOL DE ARTE.
Consejo Superior de Investigaciones Cientificas (C.S.I.C.), Departamento de Historia del Arte "Diego Velazquez", Duque de Medinaceli 6, 28014 Madrid, Spain. TEL 34-1-4290626. FAX 34-1-3690940. *411*

ARCHIVOS DE MEDICINA VETERINARIA.
Universidad Austral de Chile, Facultad de Ciencias Veterinarias, Casilla 567, Valdivia, Chile. TEL 56-63-221690. FAX 56-63-221480. *6942*

ARCHIVOS DE ZOOTECNIA.
Instituto de Zootecnia, Facultad de Veterinaria, Avda. de Medina Azahara, 9, 14005 Cordoba, Spain. TEL 34-57-218743. FAX 34-57-218666. *264*

ARCHIVOS ESPANOLES DE UROLOGIA.
B O K, S.A. Ediciones, C. San Gregorio 8, 3o Pta. 4, 28004 Madrid, Spain. TEL 34-1-3196001. FAX 34-1-3197768. *4925*

ARCHIWUM MEDYCYNY SADOWEJ I KRIMINOLOGII.
Polskie Towarzystwo Medycyny Sadowej i Kryminologii, Ul. Grzegorzecka 16, 31-531 Krakow, Poland. TEL 48-12-211113. *4686*

ARCHIWUM MINERALOGICZNE.
Polska Akademia Nauk, Instytut Nauk Geologicznych, Ul. Zwirki Wigury 93, 02-089 Warsaw, Poland. TEL 48-22-221065. FAX 48-22-221065. *2224*

ARCHIWUM NAUKI O MATERIALACH.
Wydawnictwo Uniwersytetu Slaskiego, Ul. Bankowa 12B, 40-007 Katowice, Poland. TEL 48-32-596929. *2729*

ARCTIC.
Arctic Institute of North America, University of Calgary, MLT 11th Fl., 2500 University Dr. N.W., Calgary, AB T2N 1N4, Canada. TEL 403-220-7515. FAX 403-282-4609. *6227*

ARCTIC AND ALPINE RESEARCH.
University of Colorado, Institute of Arctic and Alpine Research, Campus Box 450, Boulder, CO 80309-0450. TEL 303-492-3765. FAX 303-492-6388. *6227*

ARCTIC ANTHROPOLOGY.
University of Wisconsin Press, Journal Division, 114 N. Murray St., Madison, WI 53715. TEL 608-262-4952. FAX 608-262-7560. *303*

ARCTIC MEDICAL RESEARCH.
Nordic Council for Arctic Medical Research, Aapistie 1, FIN-90220 Oulu, Finland. TEL 358-81-537-6201. FAX 358-81-537-6203. *4429*

ARENA MAGAZINE.
Arena Printing and Publications Pty. Ltd., P.O. Box 18, N. Carlton, Vic. 3054, Australia. TEL 61-3-416-0232. FAX 61-3-415-1301. *5634*

ARGONAUTA.
Associazione Malacologica Internazionale, Casella Postale 322, 00126 Acilia (Rome), Italy. TEL 39-6-5259331. *799*

ARGUMENTATION.
Kluwer Academic Publishers, Postbus 17, 3300 AA Dordrecht, Netherlands. TEL 31-78-6392392. FAX 31-78-6392254. *5468*

ARI.
Springer-Verlag, Heidelberger Platz 3, 14197 Berlin, Germany. TEL 49-30-82787358. FAX 49-30-82787448. *2224*

ARID SOIL RESEARCH AND REHABILITATION.
Taylor & Francis Ltd., 1 Gunpowder Sq., London EC4A 3DE, England. TEL 44-171-583-0490. FAX 44-171-583-0585. *211*

ARIEL.
University of Sindh, Department of English, Jamshoro, Sindh, Pakistan. TEL 92-221-771291. *4183*

ARIEL (ENGLISH EDITION).
Youval Tal Ltd., P.O. Box 2160, Jerusalem 91021, Israel. FAX 972-2-380626. *3607*

ARIZONA ARCHAEOLOGIST.
Arizona Archaeological Society, Inc., Box 9665, Phoenix, AZ 85068. TEL 602-488-9589. *344*

ARIZONA-NEVADA ACADEMY OF SCIENCE. JOURNAL.
Arizona-Nevada Academy of Science, Office of Climatology, Arizona State University, Box 871508, Tempe, AZ 85287-1508. TEL 602-965-6265. FAX 602-965-1473. *6227*

ARIZONA WILDLIFE VIEWS.
Game and Fish Department, 2221 W. Greenway Rd., Phoenix, AZ 85023. TEL 602-942-3000. *2120*

ARKANSAS BUSINESS AND ECONOMIC REVIEW.
University of Arkansas, College of Business Administration, Fayetteville, AR 72701. TEL 501-575-4151. FAX 501-575-7687. *894*

ARKANSAS QUARTERLY.
Epiphany Publications, Inc., Box 628, Guymon, OK 73942. *4132*

ARMED FORCES AND SOCIETY.
Transaction Publishers, Transaction Periodicals Consortium, Department 3092, Rutgers University, New Brunswick, NJ 08903. TEL 908-445-2280. FAX 908-445-3138. *5021*

ARMY LOGISTICIAN.
U.S. Army Logistics Management College, Ft. Lee, VA 23801-1705. TEL 804-734-6400. FAX 804-734-6401. *5022*

ARMY MEDICAL SERVICES MAGAZINE.
R A M C Historical Museum, Keogh Barracks, Ash Vale, Aldershot, Hants. GU12 5RQ, England. TEL 44-1252-340212. FAX 44-1252-340224. *5022*

ARNAZELLA.
3000 Landerholm Circle, S.E., Bellevue, WA 98007. TEL 206-641-4032. *4183*

AROIDEANA.
International Aroid Society, Box 43-1853, S. Miami, FL 33143. TEL 305-271-3767. *3044*

ARQUIVO BRASILEIRO DE MEDICINA VETERINARIA E ZOOTECNIA.
Universidade Federal de Minas Gerais, Escola de Veterinaria, Av. Antonio Carlos, 6627, C.P. 567, 30161-970 Belo Horizonte, Minas Gerais, Brazil. TEL 55-31-4418364. FAX 55-31-4412996. *6942*

ARQUIVOS DE GASTROENTEROLOGIA.
Instituto Brasileiro de Estudos e Pesquisas de Gastroenterologia, Rua Dr. Seng 320, 01331-020 Sao Paulo SP, Brazil. TEL 55-11-2882119. FAX 55-11-2892768. *4690*

ARQUIVOS DE NEURO-PSIQUIATRIA.
Associacao Arquivos Neuro-Psiquiatria Dr. Oswaldo Lange, Caixa Postal 8877, 01065-970 Sao Paulo, SP, Brazil. TEL 55-11-2898824. FAX 55-11-2898879. *4826*

ARQUIVOS DE SAUDE MENTAL DO ESTADO DE SAO PAULO.
Biblioteca do Hospital de Juqueri, Franco da Rocha E.F.S.J., CEP 07780-000 Sao Paulo, Brazil. TEL 55-11-432-5111. FAX 55-11-432-5444. *4826*

ARS DECORATIVA.
Iparmuveszeti Muzeum, Hopp Ferenc Keletazsiai Muveszeti Muzeum, Ulloi ut 33-37, 1091 Budapest 9, Hungary. TEL 36-1-2175222. FAX 36-1-2175838. *5117*

ARS HUNGARICA.
Magyar Tudomanyos Akademia, Muveszettorteneti Kutato Intezete, Uri u. 49, 1014 Budapest, Hungary. TEL 36-1-1759011. FAX 36-1-1561849. *412*

ARS LYRICA: JOURNAL OF LYRICA.
Lyrica Society for Word-Music Relations, 90 Church St., Guilford, CT 06437. TEL 203-453-1503. FAX 203-432-2522. *5140*

ARS ORIENTALIS.
Department of History of Art, Tappan Hall, University of Michigan, Ann Arbor, MI 48109-1357. TEL 313-747-3307. FAX 313-763-8976. *5278*

ART BUSINESS NEWS.
Advanstar Communications, Inc., 7500 Old Oak Blvd., Cleveland, OH 44130. TEL 216-826-2839. FAX 216-891-2726. *413*

ART DOCUMENTATION.
Art Libraries Society of North America, 4101 Lake Boone Trl., Ste. 201, Raleigh, NC 27607-7506. TEL 919-787-5181. FAX 919-787-4916. *3974*

ART LAW & ACCOUNTING REPORTER.
Texas Accountants & Lawyers for the Arts, 1540 Sul Ross, Houston, TX 77006. TEL 713-526-4876. FAX 731-526-1299. *3743*

ART NEXUS.
Arte en Colombia Ltda., Apdo. Aereo 90193, Bogota D.E., Colombia. TEL 571-2625178. FAX 571-4136335. *414*

ART PRICE INDEX INTERNATIONAL.
Sound View Press, 170 Boston Post Rd., Madison, CT 06443. TEL 203-245-2246. FAX 203-245-3589. *5820*

ART REFERENCE SERVICES QUARTERLY.
Haworth Press, Inc., 10 Alice St., Binghamton, NY 13904-1580. TEL 607-722-5857. FAX 607-722-1424. *415*

DE ARTE.
Unisa Press, Periodicals, P.O. Box 392, Pretoria 0001, South Africa. TEL 27-12-4293111. FAX 27-12-4293221. *415*

ARTERIOSCLEROSIS, THROMBOSIS AND VASCULAR BIOLOGY.
American Heart Association, 7272 Greenville Ave., Dallas, TX 75231-4596. TEL 214-706-1426. FAX 214-691-6342. *4596*

ARTERY.
Artery Publishing, 13998 West Ave., E., Fulton, MI 49052. *4596*

ARTHA-VIKAS.
Sardar Patel University, Department of Economics, Vallabh Vidyanagar, Gujarat 388 120, India. FAX 02692-35238. *1514*

ARTHRITIS AND RHEUMATISM.
Lippincott - Raven Publishers 227 E. Washington Sq., Philadelphia, PA 19106. TEL 215-238-4200. *4892*

ARTHRITIS CARE AND RESEARCH.
Arthritis Health Professions Association, 1314 Spring St., N.W., Atlanta, GA 30309. TEL 404-872-7100. *4892*

ARTHROPOD MANAGEMENT TESTS.
Entomological Society of America, 9301 Annapolis Rd., Lanham, MD 20706. TEL 301-731-4535. FAX 301-731-4538. *721*

ARTHROPODS OF FLORIDA AND NEIGHBORING LAND AREAS.
Department of Agriculture and Consumer Services, Division of Plant Industry, 1911 S.W. 34th St., Box 147100, Gainesville, FL 32614-7100. TEL 904-372-3505. FAX 904-955-2301. *721*

ARTHROSCOPY.
W.B. Saunders Co. Curtis Center, 3rd Fl., Independence Sq. W , Philadelphia, PA 19106-3399. TEL 215-238-7800. FAX 215-238-6445. *4781*

ARTIFICIAL CELLS, BLOOD SUBSTITUTES, AND IMMOBILIZATION BIOTECHNOLOGY.
Marcel Dekker Journals, 270 Madison Ave., New York, NY 10016. TEL 212-696-9000. FAX 212-685-4540. *4577*

ARTIFICIAL INTELLIGENCE.
North-Holland P.O. Box 211, 1000 AE Amsterdam, Netherlands. TEL 31-20-4853911. FAX 31-20-4853598. *2005*

ARTIFICIAL INTELLIGENCE AND LAW.
Kluwer Academic Publishers, Postbus 17, 3300 AA Dordrecht, Netherlands. TEL 31-78-6392392. FAX 31-78-6392254. *3743*

ARTIFICIAL INTELLIGENCE COMMUNICATIONS.
I O S Press, Van Diemenstraat 94, 1013 CN Amsterdam, Netherlands. TEL 31-20-6382189. FAX 31-20-6203419. *2005*

ARTIFICIAL INTELLIGENCE IN ENGINEERING.
Elsevier Science Ltd., P.O. Box 800, Kidlington, Oxford OX5 1DX, England. TEL 44-1865-843000. FAX 44-1865-343010. *2005*

ARTIFICIAL INTELLIGENCE IN MEDICINE.
Elsevier Science B.V., P.O. Box 211, 1000 AE Amsterdam, Netherlands. TEL 31-20-4853911. FAX 31-20-4853598. *4629*

ARTIFICIAL INTELLIGENCE REVIEW.
Kluwer Academic Publishers, Postbus 17, 3300 AA Dordrecht, Netherlands. TEL 31-78-6392392. FAX 31-78-6392254. *2005*

ARTIFICIAL ORGANS.
Blackwell Science Inc., 238 Main St., Cambridge, MA 02142-1413. TEL 617-876-7022. FAX 617-492-5263. *4577*

ARTIFICIAL ORGANS TODAY.
V S P, P.O. Box 346, 3700 AH Zeist, Netherlands. TEL 31-30-6925790. FAX 31-30-6932081. *4429*

ARTIFICIAL SATELLITES. PLANETARY GEODESY.
Polska Akademia Nauk, Centrum Badan Kosmicznych, Ul. Bartycka 18 a, 00-716 Warsaw, Poland. TEL 48-22-403766. FAX 48-39-121273. *2270*

ARTIST'S BOOK YEARBOOK.
Magpie Press, 1 Hermitage Cottage, Clamp Hill, Stanmore, Mddx. HA7 3JW, England. FAX 44-181-954-0670. *417*

ARTS EDUCATION POLICY REVIEW.
Heldref Publications, 1319 Eighteenth St., N.W., Washington, DC 20036-1802. TEL 202-296-6267. FAX 202-296-5149. *418*

THE ARTS IN PSYCHOTHERAPY.
Elsevier Science Ltd., P.O. Box 800, Kidlington, Oxford OX5 1DX, England. TEL 44-1865-843000. FAX 44-1865-843010. *5828*

ASCENT (KOOTENAY BAY).
Yasodhara Ashram Society, Box 9, Kootenay Bay, BC V0B 1X0, Canada. TEL 604-227-9224. FAX 604-227-9494. *5215*

ASEMKA.
University of Cape Coast, c/o Department of French, Cape Coast, Ghana. TEL 233-2441-9. *4183*

ASIA INSTITUTE. BULLETIN.
Bulletin of the Asia Institute, 3287 Bradway Blvd., Bloomfield Hills, MI 48301. TEL 810-647-7917. FAX 310-647-9223. *5278*

ASIA LIFE SCIENCES.
Rushing Water Publishers Ltd., No. 81 Diamond Jubileeville, Masaya, Bay, Laguna 4033, Philippines. TEL 9-63-94-3368. FAX 9-63-94-2721. *570*

ASIA - PACIFIC BUSINESS REVIEW.
Frank Cass, Newbury House, 890-900 Eastern Ave., Newbury Park, Ilford, Essex IG2 7HH, England. TEL 44-181-599-8866. FAX 44 181-599-0984. *894*

ASIA - PACIFIC DEFENSE FORUM.
U.S. Pacific Command (USCINCPAC), Box 64013, Camp H.M. Smith, HI 96861-4013. TEL 808-477-0760. FAX 808-477-1471. *5023*

ASIA PACIFIC JOURNAL OF HUMAN RESOURCES.
Australian Human Resources Institute, c/o Business Manager, P.O. Box 461, Mulgrave North, Vic. 3170, Australia. TEL 61-3-9344-1072. FAX 61-3-93444293. *1498*

ASIA - PACIFIC JOURNAL OF TEACHER EDUCATION.
Carfax Publishing Co., P.O. Box 25, Abingdon, Oxon. OX14 3UE, England. TEL 44-1235-401000. FAX 44-1235-401550. *2478*

ASIA PACIFIC LAW REVIEW
Pearson Professional (Hong Kong) Limited, Ste. 1808, Asian House, 1 Hennessy Rd., Wanchai, Hong Kong. TEL 852-2863-2659. FAX 852-2520-6954. *3744*

ASIA - PACIFIC POPULATION RESEARCH ABSTRACTS.
East - West Center, 1777 East-West Rd., Honolulu, HI 96848. TEL 808-944-7480. FAX 808-944-7490. *5794*

ASIA - PACIFIC POPULATION RESEARCH REPORTS.
East - West Center, 1777 East-West Rd., Honolulu, HI 96848. TEL 808-944-7480. FAX 808-944-7490. *5781*

ASIA-PACIFIC VIEWPOINT.
Blackwell Publishers Ltd., 108 Cowley Rd., Oxford OX4 1JF, England. TEL 44-1865-791100. FAX 44-1865-791347. *1301*

ASIAN AFFAIRS: AN AMERICAN REVIEW.
Heldref Publications, 1319 18th St., N.W., Washington, DC 20036-1302. TEL 202-296-6267. FAX 202-296-5149. *5741*

ASIAN AND PACIFIC DEVELOPMENT CENTRE NEWSLETTER.
Asian and Pacific Development Centre, P.O. Box 12224, 50770 Kuala Lumpur, Malaysia. TEL 03-2548088. FAX 03-2550316. *174*

ASIAN AND PACIFIC MIGRATION JOURNAL.
Scalabrini Migration Center, P.O. Box 10541, Broadway Centrum, Aurora Blvd. 1113 Quezon City, Philippines. TEL 02-724-3512. FAX 02-721-4296. *5781*

ASIAN AND PACIFIC WOMEN'S RESOURCE AND ACTION SERIES.
Asian and Pacific Development Centre, P.O. Box 12224, 50770 Kuala Lumpur, Malaysia. TEL 03-2548088. FAX 03-2550316. *6988*

ASIAN ART AND CULTURE.
Oxford University Press, Journals, 2001 Evans Rd., Cary NC 27513. TEL 919-677-0977. FAX 919-677-1714. *5278*

ASIAN GEOGRAPHER.
University of Hong Kong, Department of Geography & Geology, Pokfulam Rd., Hong Kong. TEL 852-2859-2837. FAX 852-2559-8994. *3248*

ASIAN JOURNAL OF PLANT SCIENCE.
Ranjana Malvey, Pub., 6-4-361 26A Anjarieya Swamy Colony, Bholakpur Secunderabad 500 380, India *671*

ASIAN JOURNAL OF POLITICAL SCIENCE.
National University of Singapore, Department of Political Science, 10 Kent Ridge Crescent, Singapore 119260, Singapore. TEL 65-779-6815. FAX 65-2889254. *5635*

ASIAN JOURNAL OF SURGERY.
Asian Surgical Association, Queen Mary Hospital, Hong Kong. TEL 852-2855-4080. FAX 852-2855-9950. *4904*

ASIAN LIBRARIES.
M C B University Pres Ltd., 60-62 Toller Ln., Bradford, W. Yorks BD8 9BY, England. TEL 44-1274-777700. FAX 44-1274-785200. *3975*

ASIAN PERSPECTIVES.
University of Hawaii Press, Journals Department, 2840 Kolowalu St., Honolulu, HI 96822. TEL 808-956-8833. FAX 808-988-6052. *345*

ASIAN PHILOSOPHY.
Carfax Publishing Co., P.O. Box 25, Abingdon, Oxon. OX14 3UE, England. TEL 44-1235-401000. FAX 44-1235-401550. *5468*

ASIAN STUDIES REVIEW.
Asian Studies Association of Australia, c/o Mr. Leon Comber, Monash Asia Institute, Monash University, Clayton, Vic. 3168, Australia. TEL 61-3-99054993. FAX 61-3-99055370. *3377*

ASIAN SURVEY.
University of California Press, Journals Division, 2120 Berkeley Way, No. 5812, Berkeley, CA 94720-5812. TEL 510-643-7154. FAX 510-642-9917. *5635*

ASIAN THEATRE JOURNAL.
University of Hawaii Press, Journals Department, 2840 Kolowalu St., Honolulu, HI 96822. TEL 808-956-8833. FAX 808-988-6052. *6692*

ASIAN YEARBOOK OF INTERNATIONAL LAW.
Martinus Nijhoff Publishers, Human Rights and International Law Postbus 163, 3300 AD Dordrecht, Netherlands. TEL 31-78-334911. FAX 31-78-334254. *3923*

ASOCIACION DE DEMOGRAFIA HISTORICA. BOLETIN.
Asociacion de Demografia Historica, Centre d'Estudis Demografics, Edifici E2, Universitat Autonoma de Barcelona, 08193 Bellaterra, Spain. TEL 34-3-5813060. FAX 34-3-5813061. *5781*

ASPECTS OF HOMOGENEOUS CATALYSIS: A SERIES OF ADVANCES.
Kluwer Academic Publishers, Postbus 17, 3300 AA Dordrecht, Netherlands. TEL 31-78-6392392. FAX 31-78-6392254. *1735*

ASSAPH. SECTION C. STUDIES IN THE THEATRE.
Tel Aviv University, Faculty of Visual and Performing Arts, Department of Theatre Arts, Ramat Aviv, Tel Aviv 69978, Israel. FAX 972-3-6409482. *6692*

ASSEMBLY (WEST POINT).
U.S. Military Academy, Association of Graduates, Herbert Hall, West Point, NY 10996-1607. TEL 914-446-5800. FAX 914-446-6988. *2419*

ASSESSMENT & EVALUATION IN HIGHER EDUCATION.
Carfax Publishing Co., P.O. Box 25, Abingdon, Oxon. OX14 3UE, England. TEL 44-1235-401000. FAX 44-1235-401550. *2419*

ASSESSMENT IN EDUCATION: PRINCIPLES, POLICY AND PRACTICE.
Carfax Publishing Co., P.O. Box 25, Abingdon, Oxon. OX14 3UE, England. TEL 44-1235-401000. FAX 44-1235-401550. *2313*

ASSESSMENT JOURNAL.
International Association of Assessing Officers, 130 E. Randolph, Ste. 850, Chicago, IL 60601. TEL 312-819-6110. *6019*

ASSIA.
Shaare Zadek Medical Center, Falk Schlesinger Institute for Medical Halachic Research, P.O. Box 3235, Jerusalem 91031, Israel. TEL 972-2-6555266. FAX 972-2-6523295. *4430*

ASSIA - JEWISH MEDICAL ETHICS.
Shaare Zadek Medical Center, Falk Schlesinger Institute for Medical Halachic Research, P.O. Box 3235, Jerusalem 91031, Israel. TEL 972-2-6555266. FAX 972-2-6523295. *4430*

ASSISTED REPRODUCTIVE TECHNOLOGY - ANDROLOGY.
Reproductive Health Center, 78 Surfsong Rd., Kiawah Island, SC 29455. TEL 803-768-5556. FAX 803-768-6494. *4430*

ASSIUT VETERINARY MEDICAL JOURNAL.
Assiut University, Faculty of Veterinary Medicine, Assiut, Egypt. FAX 088-333938. *6942*

ASSOCIACAO BRASILEIRA DE PSIQUIATRIA E ASOCIACION PSIQUIATRICA DE LA AMERICA LATINA. REVISTA.
Associacao Brasileira de Psiquiatria, Rua Borges Lagoa, 394, 04038-000 Sao Paulo SP, Brazil. TEL 55-11-549-6699. FAX 55-11-570-6210. *4826*

ASSOCIATION DES AMIS D'ALFRED DE VIGNY. BULLETIN.
Association des Amis d'Alfred de Vigny, 6 av. Constant-Coquelin, 75007 Paris, France. TEL 42-73-12-86. *4183*

ASSOCIATION FOR GERONTOLOGY IN HIGHER EDUCATION. BRIEF BIBLIOGRAPHY.
Association for Gerontology in Higher Education, 1001 Connecticut Ave., N.W., Ste. 410, Washington, DC 20036-5504. TEL 202-429-9277. *3299*

ASSOCIATION FOR GLOBAL STRATEGIC INFORMATION. JOURNAL.
Infonortics, Ltd., 9a High St., Calne, Wilts. SN11 0BS, England. TEL 01249-814584. FAX 01249-813656. *1128*

ASSOCIATION FOR PRESERVATION TECHNOLOGY INTERNATIONAL. BULLETIN.
Association for Preservation Technology International, Box 3511, Williamsburg, VA 23187-3511. TEL 703-373-1621. FAX 703-373-6050. *387*

ASSOCIATION FOR QUALITY IN HEALTHCARE. JOURNAL.
Association for Quality in Healthcare, 47 Southgate St., Winchester, Hants. SO23 9EH, England. *4430*

ASSOCIATION FOR RESEARCH IN NERVOUS AND MENTAL DISEASE. RESEARCH PUBLICATIONS.
Lippincott - Raven Publishers 227 E. Washington Sq., Philadelphia, PA 19105. TEL 215-238-4200. FAX 215-238-4235. *4826*

ASSOCIATION OF AMERICAN PHYSICIANS. PROCEEDINGS.
Blackwell Science Inc., 238 Main St., Cambridge, MA 02142. TEL 617-876-7022. FAX 617-492-5263. *4430*

ASSOCIATION OF NURSES IN AIDS CARE. JOURNAL.
Nursecom Inc., 1211 Locust St., Philadelphia, PA 19107. TEL 215-545-7222. FAX 215-545-8107. *4618*

ASSOCIATION OF PAEDIATRIC CHARTERED PHYSIOTHERAPISTS. JOURNAL.
Association of Paediatric Chartered Physiotherapists, 14 Bedford Row, London WC1R 4ED, England. TEL 44-171-242-1941. FAX 44-171-831-4509. *4816*

ASSOCIATION OF TEACHERS OF JAPANESE. JOURNAL.
Association of Teachers of Japanese, c/o Patricia Wetzel, Foreign Languages & Literatures, Portland State Univ., Portland, OR 97207. TEL 503-725-5277. FAX 503-725-5276. *4054*

ASSOCIAZIONE ROMANA DI ENTOMOLOGIA. BOLLETTINO.
Associazione Romana di Entomologia, c/o Museo Civico di Zoologia, Via Ulisse Aldrovandi, 18, 00197 Rome, Italy. *722*

ASTERISQUE.
Societe Mathematique de France, Institut Henri Poincare, 11 rue Pierre et Marie Curie, 75231 Paris Cedex 05, France. TEL 91-26-74-64. FAX 91-41-17-51. *4356*

THE ASTRONOMER.
16 Westminster Close, Basingstoke, Hants. RG22 4PP, England. TEL 44-1256-471074. FAX 44-1256-471074. *475*

ASTRONOMICAL AND ASTROPHYSICAL TRANSACTIONS.
Gordon and Breach Science Publishers, c/o International Publishers Distributors, P.O. Box 3054, Langhorne, PA 19047-3054. TEL 215-750-2642. FAX 215-750-6343. *475*

ASTRONOMICAL JOURNAL.
American Institute of Physics, One Physics Ellipse, College Park, MD 20740-3843. TEL 301-209-3000. *475*

ASTRONOMICAL SOCIETY OF AUSTRALIA. PUBLICATIONS.
C.S.I.R.O. Publishing, 150 Oxford St., Collingwood, Vic. 3066, Australia. TEL 61-3-96627500. FAX 61-3-96627611. *476*

ASTROPARTICLE PHYSICS.
North-Holland P.O. Box 211, 1000 AE Amsterdam, Netherlands. TEL 31-20-4853911. FAX 31-20-4853598. *477*

THE ASTROPHYSICAL JOURNAL.
University of Chicago Press, Journals Division, Box 37005, Chicago, IL 60637. TEL 773-753-3347. FAX 773-753-0811. *477*

ASTROPHYSICAL JOURNAL. SUPPLEMENT SERIES.
University of Chicago Press, Journals Division, 37005, Chicago, IL 60637. TEL 773-753-3347. FAX 773-753-0811. *477*

ASTROPHYSICAL LETTERS AND COMMUNICATIONS.
Gordon and Breach Science Publishers, c/o International Publishers Distributor, P.O. Box 3054, Langhorne, PA 19047-3054. TEL 215-750-2642. FAX 215-750-6343. *477*

ASTROPHYSICS.
Plenum Publishing Corp., Consultants Bureau, 233 Spring St., New York, NY 10013-1578. TEL 212-620-8468. FAX 212-463-0742. *477*

ASTROPHYSICS AND SPACE PHYSICS REVIEWS.
Harwood Academic Publishers, c/o International Publishers Distributor, P.O. Box 3054, Langhorne, PA 19047-3054. TEL 215-750-2642. FAX 215-750-6343. *478*

ASTROPHYSICS AND SPACE SCIENCE.
Kluwer Academic Publishers, Postbus 17, 3300 AA Dordrecht, Netherlands. TEL 31-78-6392392. FAX 31-78-6392254. *478*

ASTROPHYSICS AND SPACE SCIENCE LIBRARY.
Kluwer Academic Publishers, Postbus 17, 3300 AA Dordrecht, Netherlands. TEL 31-78-6392392. FAX 31-78-6392254. *478*

ASYMPTOTIC ANALYSIS.
I O S Press, Van Diemenstraat 94, 1013 CN Amsterdam, Netherlands. TEL 31-20-6382189. FAX 31-20-6203419. *4357*

ATHEROSCLEROSIS.
Elsevier Science Ireland Ltd., P.O. Box 85, Limerick, Ireland. TEL 353-61-471944. FAX 353-61-472144. *4596*

ATHEROSCLEROSIS REVIEWS.
Lippincott - Raven Publishers 227 E. Washington Sq., Philadelphia, PA 19106. TEL 215-238-4200. FAX 215-238-4235. *4597*

ATHLERAMA.
Federation Francaise d'Athletisme, 33 bd. Pierre de Coubertin, 75013 Paris, France. TEL 33-1-53-80-70-19. FAX 33-1-45-81-40-54. *6450*

ATLANTA HISTORY.
Atlanta Historical Society, Inc., 130 West Paces Ferry Rd., Atlanta, GA 30305-1366. TEL 404-814-4000. FAX 404-814-4186. *3460*

ATLANTIC GEOLOGY.
Atlantic Geoscience Society, c/o Acadia Centre for Estuarine Research, Box 115, Acadia University, Wolfville, NS B0P 1X0, Canada. TEL 902-542-2201. FAX 902-542-1454. *2225*

ATLANTIDE REPORT. SCIENTIFIC RESULTS OF THE DANISH EXPEDITION TO THE COASTS OF TROPICAL WEST AFRICA.
Apollo Books, Kirkeby Sand 19, DK-5771 Stenstrup, Denmark. TEL 45-62-26-37-37. FAX 45-62-26-37-80. *6228*

ATLANTIS.
Mount Saint Vincent University, 166 Bedford Hwy., Halifax, NS B3M 2J6, Canada. TEL 902-443-4450. FAX 902-445-3960. *7014*

ATLETISMO ESPANOL.
Real Federacion Espanola de Atletismo, C. Miguel Angel, 16, 28010 Madrid, Spain. TEL 34-1-3103677. FAX 34-1-3085912. *6556*

ATMOSPHERE - OCEAN.
Canadian Meteorological and Oceanographic Society, Ste. 903, 151 Slater St., Ottawa, ON K1P 5H3, Canada. TEL 613-237-3393. FAX 613-238-1677. *4991*

ATMOSPHERIC AND OCEANOGRAPHIC SCIENCES LIBRARY.
Kluwer Academic Publishers, Postbus 17, 3300 AA Dordrecht, Netherlands. TEL 31-78-6392392. FAX 31-78-6392254. *2204*

ATMOSPHERIC ENVIRONMENT.
Elsevier Science Ltd., Pergamon, P.O. Box 800, Kidlington, Oxford OX5 1DX, England. TEL 44-1865-843000. FAX 44-1865-843010. *2833*

ATMOSPHERIC RESEARCH.
Elsevier Science B.V., P.O. Box 211, 1000 AE Amsterdam, Netherlands. TEL 31-20-4853911. FAX 31-20-4853598. *4991*

ATOMIC DATA AND NUCLEAR DATA TABLES.
Academic Press, Inc., Journal Division, 525 B. St., Ste. 1900, San Diego, CA 92101-4495. TEL 619-230-1840. FAX 619-699-6800. *5593*

ATOMIC ENERGY.
Plenum Publishing Corp., Consultants Bureau, 233 Spring St., New York, NY 10013-1578. TEL 212-620-8468. FAX 212-463-0742. *2573*

ATOMIC ENERGY LEVELS AND GROTRIAN DIAGRAMS.
Elsevier Science B.V., Books Division, P.O. Box 211, 1000 AE Amsterdam, Netherlands. TEL 31-20-4853911. FAX 31-20-4853705. *5593*

ATOMIC SPECTROSCOPY.
Perkin - Elmer Corp., 761 Main Ave., Norwalk, CT 06859-0219. TEL 203-761-2532. FAX 203-761-2892. *1714*

ATOMIZATION AND SPRAYS.
Begell House Inc., 79 Madison Ave., New York, NY 10016-7892. TEL 212-725-1999. FAX 212-213-8368. *2633*

AUCKLAND INSTITUTE AND MUSEUM. RECORDS.
Auckland Institute and Museum, Private Bag 92018, Auckland 1, New Zealand. FAX 64-9-3799-956. *5118*

AUDIO-DIGEST ANESTHESIOLOGY.
Audio-Digest Foundation 1577 E. Chevy Chase Dr., Glendale, CA 91206. TEL 213-245-8505. FAX 818-240-7379. *4590*

AUDIO-DIGEST EMERGENCY MEDICINE.
Audio-Digest Foundation 1577 E. Chevy Chase Dr., Glendale, CA 91206. TEL 213-245-8505. FAX 818-240-7379. *4781*

AUDIO-DIGEST FAMILY PRACTICE.
Audio-Digest Foundation 1577 E. Chevy Chase Dr., Glendale, CA 91206. TEL 213-245-8505. FAX 818-240-7379. *4431*

AUDIO-DIGEST GASTROENTEROLOGY.
Audio-Digest Foundation 1577 E. Chevy Chase Dr., Glendale, CA 91206. TEL 213-245-8505. FAX 818-240-7379. *4690*

AUDIO-DIGEST GENERAL SURGERY.
Audio-Digest Foundation 1577 E. Chevy Chase Dr., Glendale, CA 91206. TEL 213-245-8505. FAX 818-240-7379. *4904*

AUDIO-DIGEST INTERNAL MEDICINE.
Audio-Digest Foundation 1577 E. Chevy Chase Dr., Glendale, CA 91206. TEL 213-245-8505. FAX 818-240-7379. *4705*

AUDIO-DIGEST OBSTETRICS - GYNECOLOGY.
Audio-Digest Foundation 1577 E. Chevy Chase Dr., Glendale, CA 91206. TEL 213-245-8505. FAX 818-240-7379. *4732*

AUDIO-DIGEST OPHTHALMOLOGY.
Audio-Digest Foundation 1577 E. Chevy Chase Dr., Glendale, CA 91206. TEL 213-245-8505. FAX 818-240-7379. *4767*

AUDIO-DIGEST ORTHOPAEDICS.
Audio-Digest Foundation 1577 E. Chevy Chase Dr., Glendale, CA 91206. TEL 213-245-8505. FAX 818-240-7379. *4781*

AUDIO-DIGEST OTOLARYNGOLOGY - HEAD AND NECK SURGERY.
Audio-Digest Foundation 1577 E. Chevy Chase Dr., Glendale, CA 91206. TEL 213-245-8505. FAX 818-240-7379. *4795*

AUDIO-DIGEST PEDIATRICS.
Audio-Digest Foundation 1577 E. Chevy Chase Dr., Glendale, CA 91206. TEL 213-245-8505. FAX 818-240-7379. *4803*

AUDIO-DIGEST PSYCHIATRY.
Audio-Digest Foundation 1577 E. Chevy Chase Dr., Glendale, CA 91206. TEL 213-245-8505. FAX 818-240-7379. *4826*

AUDIO-DIGEST UROLOGY.
Audio-Digest Foundation 1577 E. Chevy Chase Dr., Glendale, CA 91206. TEL 213-245-8505. FAX 818-240-7379. *4925*

AUDIO ENGINEERING SOCIETY. JOURNAL.
Audio Engineering Society, 60 E. 42nd St., New York, NY 10165. TEL 212-661-8528. FAX 212-661-7829. *5444*

AUDIO JOURNAL OF ONCOLOGY.
Chapman & Hall, Journals Department 2-6 Boundary Row, London SE1 8HN, England. TEL 44-171-8650066. FAX 44-171-5229623. *4748*

AUDIOFILE.
37 Silver St., Box 109, Portland, ME 04112-0109. TEL 207-774-7563. FAX 207-775-3744. *4184*

AUDIOLOGY.
S. Karger AG, Allschwilerstr. 10, P.O. Box, CH-4009 Basel, Switzerland. TEL 061-3061111. FAX 061-3061234. *4795*

AUDIOLOGY AND NEUROOTOLOGY.
S. Karger AG, Allschwilerstr. 10, P.O. Box, CH-4009 Basel, Switzerland. TEL 061-3061111. FAX 061-3061234. *4795*

AUDIT.
Oak Tree Press, 19 Rutland St., Cork, Ireland. TEL 021-313855. FAX 021-313496. *1040*

AUDITING.
American Accounting Association, Paul F. Gerhardt Bldg., 5717 Bessie Dr., Sarasota, FL 34233. TEL 941-921-7747. FAX 941-923-4093. *1041*

AUGUSTINIAN STUDIES.
Villanova University, Augustinian Studies, Tolentine Hall, Villanova, PA 19085. TEL 610-519-7903. FAX 610-519-6306. *6169*

AUK.
American Ornithologists' Union, c/o Frederick Sheldon, Museum of Natural History, 119 Foster Hall, Louisiana State University, Baton Rouge, LA 70803. TEL 504-388-2855. *772*

AUSTRALASIAN DRAMA STUDIES.
University of Queensland, c/o Department of English, Brisbane, Qld. 4072, Australia. TEL 61-7-33652501 FAX 61-7-3652799. *6692*

AUSTRALASIAN GAY AND LESBIAN LAW JOURNAL.
Federation Press Pty. Ltd., P.O. Box 45, Annandale, N.S.W. 2038, Australia. *3745*

AUSTRALASIAN JOURNAL OF PHILOSOPHY.
Australasian Association of Philosophy, Philosophy Dept., La Trobe University, Bundoora, Vic. 3083, Australia. TEL 61-3-4792424. FAX 61-3-4793639. *5468*

AUSTRALASIAN JOURNAL OF REGIONAL STUDIES.
Regional Science Association, Australian and New Zealand Section, c/o Linda Pink, University of New England, P.O. Box U271, Armidale, N.S.W. 2351, Australia. TEL 61-67-714838. *1175*

AUSTRALASIAN PHYSICAL & ENGINEERING SCIENCES IN MEDICINE
Australasian College of Physical Scientists and Engineers in Medicine, Physics Dept., Queensland University of Technology, G.P.O. Box 2434, Brisbane, Qld. 4001, Australia. TEL 61-7-38642591. FAX 61-7-38641521. *4677*

AUSTRALASIAN SOCIETY FOR HISTORICAL ARCHAEOLOGY. NEWSLETTER
Australasian Society for Historical Archaeology, Box 220 Holme Bldg., University of Sydney, Sydney, N.S.W. 2001, Australia. TEL 61-2-3512763. FAX 61-2-3514889. *365*

AUSTRALASIAN STUDIES IN HISTORY AND PHILOSOPHY OF SCIENCE.
Kluwer Academic Publishers, Postbus 17, 3300 AA Dordrecht, Netherlands. TEL 31-78-6392392. FAX 31-78-6392254. *6228*

AUSTRALIA - JAPAN ECONOMIC INSTITUTE. ECONOMIC BULLETIN.
Australia - Japan Economic Institute, Level 11, The Chifley Tower, Chifley Sq., Sydney, N.S.W. 2000, Australia. TEL 61-2-2333533. FAX 61-2-2338503. *895*

AUSTRALIAN ACCOUNTING REVIEW.
Australian Society of Certified Practising Accountants, 170 Queen St., Melbourne, Vic. 3000, Australia. TEL 61-3-606 9606. FAX 61-3-670-8901. *1041*

AUSTRALIAN AND NEW ZEALAND JOURNAL OF PUBLIC HEALTH.
Public Health Association of Australia, G.P.O. Box 2204, Canberra, A.C.T. 2601, Australia. TEL 61-6-2852373. FAX 61-6-2825438. *5955*

AUSTRALIAN AND NEW ZEALAND WINE INDUSTRY JOURNAL.
Winetitles, P.O. Box 1140, Marleston, S.A. 5033, Australia. TEL 61-8-2346055. FAX 61-8-2345050. *500*

AUSTRALIAN ART EDUCATION.
Australian Institute of Art Education, c/o Lee Emery, Ed., University of Melbourne, Faculty of Education, Parkville, Vic. 3052, Australia. TEL 61-3-344-8386. FAX 61-3-349-4290. *819*

AUSTRALIAN BIRDWATCHER.
Bird Observers Club of Australia, P.O. Box 185, Nunawading, Vic. 3131, Australia. TEL 61-3-98775342. FAX 61-3-98944048. *772*

AUSTRALIAN BUREAU OF AGRICULTURAL AND RESOURCE ECONOMICS. AUSTRALIAN FISHERIES SURVEYS REPORT.
Australian Bureau of Agricultural and Resource Economics, G.P.O. Box 1563, Canberra, A.C.T. 2601, Australia. TEL 61-6-2722211. FAX 61-6-2723330. *2946*

AUSTRALIAN COMPANY SECRETARY.
Chartered Institute of Company Secretaries in Australia Ltd., G.P.O. Box 1594, Sydney, N.S.W. 2001, Australia. TEL 61-2-223-5744. FAX 61-2-232-7174. *1406*

AUSTRALIAN CULTURAL HISTORY.
Deakin University, Faculty of Arts, Geelong, Vic. 3217, Australia. TEL 61-52-272695. FAX 61-52-272427. *3387*

AUSTRALIAN ECONOMIC REVIEW.
Blackwell Publishers Ltd., 108 Cowley Rd., Oxford OX4 1JF, England. TEL 44-1865-791100. FAX 44-1865-791347. *895*

AUSTRALIAN ENTOMOLOGIST.
Entomological Society of Queensland, P.O. Box 537, Indooroopilly, Qld. 4068, Australia. *722*

AUSTRALIAN FOLKLORE.
Australian Folklore Association, c/o Prof. J.S. Ryan, Ed., Dept. of English & Communication Studies, University of New England, Armidale, N.S.W. 2351, Australia. TEL 067-732601. FAX 067-732623. *2949*

AUSTRALIAN GEMMOLOGIST.
Gemmological Association of Australia, P.O. Box 477, Albany Creek, Brisbane, Qld.4035, Australia. TEL 61-7-32646854 FAX 61-7-32646854. *3694*

AUSTRALIAN HEALTH REVIEW.
Australian Hospital Association, P.O. Box 54, Deakin West, A.C.T. 2600, Australia. *3540*

AUSTRALIAN JOURNAL OF DAIRY TECHNOLOGY.
Dairy Industry Association of Australia, P.O. Box 8000, Glen Iris, Vic. 3146, Australia, Australia. FAX 61-3-92526555. *247*

AUSTRALIAN JOURNAL OF EDUCATIONAL TECHNOLOGY.
A J E T Publications Ltd., P.O. Box 772, Belconnen, A.C.T. 2616, Australia. TEL 61-6-2735405. FAX 61-6-2735403. *2479*

AUSTRALIAN JOURNAL OF EMERGENCY CARE.
Ambulance Employees Australia, 117-131 Capel St., North Melbourne, Vic. 3051, Australia. TEL 61-3-93295777. FAX 61-3-93295533. *4781*

AUSTRALIAN JOURNAL OF FRENCH STUDIES.
Monash University, Department of Romance Languages, Clayton, Vic. 3168, Australia. TEL 61-3-99052217. FAX 61-3-99052137. *4184*

AUSTRALIAN JOURNAL OF HOSPITAL PHARMACY.
Society of Hospital Pharmacists of Australia, Ste. 2, 31 Coventry St., S. Melbourne, Vic. 3205, Australia. TEL 61-3-96906733. FAX 61-3-96967634. *5401*

AUSTRALIAN JOURNAL OF LAW AND SOCIETY.
School of Law, Macquarie University, N.S.W. 2109, Australia. FAX 61-2-850-7686. *3745*

AUSTRALIAN JOURNAL OF LEARNING DISABILITIES.
Australian Resource Educators Association Inc., 4 Canterbury Rd., Toorak, Vic. 3142, Australia. TEL 61-3-98262929. FAX 61-3-98262829. *2466*

AUSTRALIAN JOURNAL OF LINGUISTICS.
Australian Linguistic Society, c/o D. Absalom, English Language Centre, University of Newcastle, N.S.W. 2308, Australia. TEL 61-49-613922. FAX 61-49-615476. *4055*

AUSTRALIAN JOURNAL OF MEDICAL HERBALISM.
National Herbalists Association of Australia, Ste. 305, 3 Smail St., Broadway, N.S.W. 2007, Australia. TEL 61-2-2116437. FAX 61-2-2116452. *289*

AUSTRALIAN JOURNAL OF NUTRITION AND DIETETICS.
Dietitians Association of Australia, P.O. Box 11, O'Connor, A.C.T. 2602, Australia. TEL 61-6-2472555. FAX 61-6-2572184. *5229*

AUSTRALIAN JOURNAL OF PHYSIOTHERAPY.
Australian Physiotherapy Association, P.o. Box 6465, Melbourne, Vic. 3004, Australia. TEL 61-3-95349400. FAX 61-3-95349199. *4816*

AUSTRALIAN JOURNAL OF SCIENCE AND MEDICINE IN SPORT.
Australian Sports Medicine Federation, P.O. Box 897, Belconnen, A.C.T. 2616, Australia. TEL 61-6-2516944. FAX 61-6-2531489. *4897*

AUSTRALIAN JOURNAL OF SOIL AND WATER CONSERVATION.
c/o Geoff Cunningham, 9 The Crest, Killara, N.S.W. 2071, Australia. TEL 61-2-4161995. FAX 61-2-4166626. *212*

AUSTRALIAN JOURNAL OF TEACHER EDUCATION.
Edith Cowan University, School of Education, Pearson St., Churchlands, W.A. 6018, Australia. TEL 61-9-2738415. FAX 61-9-3877095. *2420*

AUSTRALIAN JOURNAL ON AGEING.
Council on the Ageing (Australia), Level 2, 3 Bowen Crescent, 464 St. Kilda Rd., Melbourne, Vic. 3004, Australia. TEL 61-3-96453610. *3284*

AUSTRALIAN JOURNAL ON VOLUNTEERING.
Volunteer Centre of South Australia Inc., 155 Pirie St., Adelaide, S.A. 5000, Australia. TEL 61-8-2320199. FAX 61-8-2325161. *6362*

AUSTRALIAN LAW LIBRARIAN.
Australian Law Librarian, c/o Barbara Coat, Ed., Australian Securities Commission (S.A.), G.P.O. Box 9827, Adelaide, S.A. 5001, Australia. TEL 61-8-2028414. FAX 61-8-2028410. *3976*

AUSTRALIAN MAMMALOGY.
Australian Mammal Society Inc., c/o Dr. Graham Ross, Ed., Australian Biological Resources Study (Fauna), G.P.O. Box 636, Canberra, A.C.T. 2601, Australia. TEL 06-250-9435. FAX 06-250-9448. *799*

AUSTRALIAN MATHEMATICS TEACHER.
Australian Association of Mathematics Teachers Inc., G.P.O. Box 1729, Adelaide, S.A. 5001, Australia. TEL 61-8-3630288. FAX 61-8-3629288. *4357*

AUSTRALIAN NATIONAL UNIVERSITY. NATIONAL CENTRE FOR DEVELOPMENT STUDIES. PACIFIC ECONOMIC BULLETIN.
Australian National University, National Centre for Development Studies, Canberra, A.C.T. 0200, Australia. TEL 61-6-2494705. FAX 61-6-2572886. *1175*

AUSTRALIAN ORTHODONTIC JOURNAL.
Australian Society of Orthodontists, 28 Bramble St., Bendigo, Vic. 3550, Australia. TEL 61-54-413902. FAX 61-54-416982. *4635*

AUSTRALIAN PARKS & RECREATION.
Royal Australian Institute of Parks & Recreation, Bldg. E, National Exhibition Centre, Flemington Rd., Lyneham, A.C.T. 2602, Australia. TEL 06-241-4371. FAX 06-241-5817. *2120*

AUSTRALIAN PHARMACIST.
Pharmaceutical Society of Australia, P.O. Box 21, Curtin, A.C.T. 2605, Australia. TEL 61-6-2811366. FAX 61-6-2852869. *5401*

AUSTRALIAN POPULATION ASSOCIATION. JOURNAL.
Australian Population Association, P.O. Box 583, Indoorpilly, Qld. 4068, Australia. TEL 61-7-2494308. FAX 61-7-2354071. *5781*

AUSTRALIAN POULTRY SCIENCE SYMPOSIUM.
University of Sydney, Poultry Research Foundation, Sydney, N.S.W. 2006, Australia. TEL 61-46-550227. FAX 61-46-551331. *265*

AUSTRALIAN PRESCRIBER.
Commonwealth Department of Human Services and Health, P.O. Box 100, Woden, A.C.T. 2606, Australia. TEL 61-6-289-7038. *5401*

AUSTRALIAN PSYCHOLOGIST.
Australian Psychological Society, c/o Dr. Christian Lee, Department of Psychology, University of Newcastle, Newcastle, N.S.W. 2308, Australia. *5829*

AUSTRALIAN QUARTERLY.
Australian Institute of Political Science, Box 145, Balmain, N.S.W. 2041, Australia. TEL 61-2-8105642. FAX 61-2-8102406. *5635*

AUSTRALIAN SHORT STORIES.
Pascoe Publishing Pty. Ltd., P.O. Box 42, Apolo Bay, Vic. 3233, Australia. TEL 61-52-379227. FAX 61-52-376559. *4184*

AUSTRALIAN SOCIAL WORK.
Australian Association of Social Workers, P.O. Box 84, Hawker, Canberra, A.C.T. 2614, Australia. TEL 61-6-255-1626. FAX 61-6-255-2225. *6362*

AUSTRALIAN STRING TEACHER.
Australian String Teachers Association, 5 Oakridge Rd., Aberfoyle Park, S.A. 5159, Australia. TEL 61-8-270-2145. *5141*

AUSTRALIAN STUDIES.
Frank Cass, Newbury House, 890-900 Eastern Ave., Newbury Park, Ilford, Essex IG2 7HH, England. TEL 44-181-5998866. FAX 44-181-5990984. *3387*

AUSTRALIAN WINE RESEARCH INSTITUTE TECHNICAL REVIEW.
Australian Wine Research Institute, P.O. Box 197, Glen Osmond, S.A. 5064, Australia. TEL 61-8-3036600. FAX 61-8-3036601. *500*

AUSTRALIAN YEARBOOK OF INTERNATIONAL LAW.
Centre for International and Public Law, Faculty of Law, Australian National University, Canberra, A.C.T. 0200. TEL 61-6-2492479. FAX 61-6-2575088. *3923*

AUSTRIAN REVIEW OF INTERNATIONAL AND EUROPEAN LAW.
Kluwer Law International Postbus 85889, 2508 CN The Hague, Netherlands. TEL 31-70-3081500. FAX 31-70-3081515. *3923*

AUTOIMMUNITY.
Harwood Academic Publishers, c/o International Publishers Distributor, P.O. Box 3054, PA 19047-3054. TEL 215-750-2642. FAX 215-750-6343. *4578*

AUTOMATED REASONING SERIES.
Kluwer Academic Publishers, Postbus 17, 3300 AA Dordrecht, Netherlands. TEL 31-78-6392392. FAX 31-78-6392254. *2006*

AUTOMATED SOFTWARE ENGINEERING.
Kluwer Academic Publishers, Postbus 17, 3300 AA Dordrecht, Netherlands. TEL 31-78-6392392. FAX 31-78-6392254. *2006*

AUTOMATICA.
Elsevier Science Ltd., Pergamon, P.O. Box 800, Kidlington, Oxford OX5 1DX, England. TEL 44-1865-843000. FAX 44-1865-843010. *2012*

AUTOMATION AND REMOTE CONTROL.
Plenum Publishing Corp., Consultants Bureau, 233 Spring St., New York, NY 10013-1578. TEL 212-620-8468. FAX 212-463-0742. *2012*

AUTOMATION IN CONSTRUCTION.
Elsevier Science B.V., P.O. Box 211, 1000 AE Amsterdam, Netherlands. TEL 31-20-4853911. FAX 31-20-4853598. *2012*

AUTOMEDICA.
Gordon and Breach Science Publishers, c/o International Publishers Distributor, P.O. Box 3054, Langhorne, PA 19047-3054. TEL 215-750-2642. FAX 215-750-6343. *4629*

AUTOMOTIVE MANAGEMENT.
1 Oxted Chambers, 185-187 Station Rd. E., Oxted, Surrey RH8 0QE, England. TEL 44-1883-732000. FAX 44-1883-730933. *6775*

AUTONOMIC NERVOUS SYSTEM.
Harwood Academic Publishers, c/o International Publishers Distributor, P.O. Box 3054, Langhorne, PA 19047-3054. TEL 215-750-2642. FAX 215-750-6343. *785*

AUTONOMOUS ROBOTS.
Kluwer Academic Publishers, Postbus 17, 3300 AA Dordrecht, Netherlands. TEL 31-78-6392392. FAX 31-78-6392254. *2104*

AVANCES EN ALIMENTACION Y MEJORA ANIMAL.
Juan Vigon 3, 28003 Madrid, Spain. *265*

AVANTE.
Canadian Association for Health, Physical Education, Recreation and Dance, Place R. Tait McKenzie, 1600 James Naismith Dr., Gloucester, ON K1B 5N4, Canada. TEL 613-748-5622. FAX 613-748-5737. *5525*

AVIAN DISEASES.
American Association of Avian Pathologists, Inc., University of Pennsylvania, New Bolton Center, Kennett Sq., PA 19348-1692. TEL 610-444-4282. FAX 610-444-5387. *6942*

AVIAN PATHOLOGY.
Carfax Publishing Co., P.O. Box 25, Abingdon, Oxon. OX14 3UE, England. TEL 44-1235-401000. FAX 44-1235-401550. *6942*

AVIATION, SPACE, AND ENVIRONMENTAL MEDICINE.
Aerospace Medical Association, 320 S. Henry St., Alexandria, VA 22314-3579. TEL 703-739-2240. *4432*

AVIS 81.
Speciallaererforeningen af 1981, Aabenraa 5, 4, DK-1124 Copenhagen K, Denmark. TEL 45-33-14-50-65. FAX 45-33-91-50-01. *2466*

AVOCETTA.
Centro Italiano Studi Ornitologici, c/o Dipartimento di Biologia Animale, Via Accademia Albertina 17, 10123 Turin, Italy. FAX 39-50-24653. *799*

AVTOMATIKA I VYCHISLITEL'NAYA TEKHNIKA.
Latvian Academy of Sciences, Institute of Electronic
and Computer Science, Dzerbenes iela, 14, Riga LV-
1006, Latvia. TEL 371-2-554500. FAX 371-
8828211. *2013*

AXIOS.
Axios Newsletter, Inc., 30-32 Macaw Ave.,
Belmopan, Belize. TEL 501-8-23284. FAX 501-8-
23633. *6112*

AYLESFORD CARMELITE NEWSLETTER.
Lay Carmelite Office, 8501 Bailey Road, Darien, IL
60561. TEL 708-969-5050. FAX 708-969-5536.
6169

B & K SPORTS MAGAZINE.
B & K Sports Magazine AB, P.O. Box 45026, S-104
30 Stockholm, Sweden. TEL 46-8-34-77-00.
FAX 46-8-34-63-33. *5525*

B & P A.
Murray State University, College of Business and
Public Affairs, Murray, KY 42071. TEL 502-762-
4181. FAX 502-762-3482. *896*

B B A - BIOENERGETICS.
Elsevier Science B.V., P.O. Box 211, 1000 AE
Amsterdam, Netherlands. TEL 31-20-4853911.
FAX 31-20-4853598. *651*

B B A - BIOMEMBRANES.
Elsevier Science B.V., P.O. Box 211, 1000 AE
Amsterdam, Netherlands. TEL 31-20-4853911.
FAX 31-20-4853598. *630*

B B A - GENE STRUCTURE AND EXPRESSION.
Elsevier Science B.V., P.O. Box 211, 1000 AE
Amsterdam, Netherlands. TEL 31-20-4853911.
FAX 31-20-4853598. *738*

B B A - GENERAL SUBJECTS.
Elsevier Science B.V., P.O. Box 211, 1000 AE
Amsterdam, Netherlands. TEL 31-20-4853911.
FAX 31-20-4853598. *630*

B B A - LIPIDS & LIPID METABOLISM.
Elsevier Science B.V., P.O. Box 211, 1000 AE
Amsterdam, Netherlands. TEL 31-20-4853911.
FAX 31-20-4853598. *631*

B B A - MOLECULAR BASIS OF DISEASE.
Elsevier Science B.V., P.O. Box 211, 1000 AE
Amsterdam, Netherlands. TEL 31-20-4853911.
FAX 31-20-4853598. *4432*

B B A - MOLECULAR CELL RESEARCH.
Elsevier Science B.V., P.O. Box 211, 1000 AE
Amsterdam, Netherlands. TEL 31-20-4853911.
FAX 31-20-4853598. *651*

**B B A - PROTEIN STRUCTURE AND MOLECULAR
ENZYMOLOGY.**
Elsevier Science B.V., P.O. Box 211, 1000 AE
Amsterdam, Netherlands. TEL 31-20-4853911.
FAX 31-20-4853598. *631*

B B A - REVIEWS ON BIOMEMBRANES.
Elsevier Science B.V., P.O. Box 211, 1000 AE
Amsterdam, Netherlands. TEL 31-20-4853911.
FAX 31-20-4853598. *711*

B B A - REVIEWS ON CANCER.
Elsevier Science B.V., P.O. Box 211, 1000 AE
Amsterdam, Netherlands. TEL 31-20-4853911.
FAX 31-20-4853598. *4748*

B C - BOLETIM CINEMATOGRAFICO.
Rua Candido des Reis 114-3o, 2780 Oeiras,
Portugal. TEL 351-1-4420701. FAX 351-1-
4429781. *5093*

B.C. NATURALIST.
Federation of British Columbia Naturalists, 321-
1367 West Broadway, Vancouver, BC V6H 4A9,
Canada. TEL 604-737-3057. *6229*

B.C. VOICE.
British Columbia Voice of Women, P.O. Box 235,
Nanaimo, BC V9R 5K9, Canada. *6988*

B I C C GROUP WORLD.
B I C C plc, Devonshire House, Mayfair Pl., London
W1X 5FH, England. TEL 44-171-629-6622.
FAX 44-171-409-0070. *2653*

B J A: INTERNATIONAL JOURNAL OF ANAESTHESIA.
B M J Publishing Group, B.M.A. House, Tavistock
Sq., London WC1H 9JR, England. TEL 0171-387-
4499. FAX 0171-383-6662. *4590*

B M A NEWS REVIEW
B M J Publishing Group, B.M.A. House, Tavistock
Sq., London WC1H 9JP, England. TEL 0171-387-
4499. FAX 0171-383-6566. *4432*

B M J.
B M J Publishing Group, B.M.A. House, Tavistock
Sq., London WC1H 9JR, England. TEL 44-171-387-
4499. FAX 44-171-383-6661. *4432*

B S L BULLETIN.
Bank of Sierra Leone, Research Department, Siaka
Stevens St., P.O. Box 30, Freetown, Sierra Leone.
TEL 232-22-226501. FAX 232-22-224767. *1176*

B T TECHNOLOGY JOURNAL.
Chapman & Hall, Journals Department 2-6
Boundary Row, London SE1 8HN, England. TEL 44-
171-8650066. FAX 44-171-5229623. *1896*

B W P JOURNAL.
Oxford University Press, Oxford Journals, Walton St.,
Oxford OX2 6DP, England. TEL 44-1865-267907.
FAX 44-1865-267485. *772*

BABEL.
Australian Federation of Modern Languages
Teachers Associations, c/o Angela Scarino, Ed., 9
Stanley St., N Adelaide, S.A. 5006, Australia.
TEL 61-8-33024775. FAX 61-8-03024774. *2479*

BABY CONNECTION NEWS JOURNAL.
Parent Education Center for Infant Development,
Drawer 3350, San Antonio, TX 78265-3350.
1760

THE BAFFLER.
Box 378293, Chicago, IL 60637. TEL 312-493-
0413. *4133*

BAHA'I STUDIES.
Association for Baha'i Studies, 34 Copernicus St.,
Ottawa, ON K1N 7K4, Canada. TEL 613-233-1903.
6203

BAHA'I STUDIES REVIEW.
Association for Baha'i Studies, 27 Rutland Gate,
London SW7 1PD, England. *6045*

BAILEYA.
L. H. Bailey Hortorium, Cornell University, Ithaca, NY
14853. TEL 607-255-7781. *671*

BAILLIERE'S CLINICAL ANAESTHESIOLOGY.
Bailliere Tindall - W.B. Saunders Co. Ltd. 24-28 Oval
Rd., London NW1 7DX, England. TEL 44-171-485-
4752. FAX 44-171-267-4466. *4590*

**BAILLIERE'S CLINICAL ENDOCRINOLOGY AND
METABOLISM.**
Bailliere Tindall - W.B. Saunders Co. Ltd. 24-28 Oval
Rd., London NW1 7DX, England. TEL 44-171-485-
4752. FAX 44-171-267-4466. *4666*

BAILLIERE'S CLINICAL GASTROENTEROLOGY.
Bailliere Tindall - W.B. Saunders Co. Ltd. 24-28 Oval
Rd., London NW1 7DX, England. TEL 44-171-485-
4752. FAX 44-171-267-4466. *4690*

BAILLIERE'S CLINICAL HAEMATOLOGY.
Bailliere Tindall - W.B. Saunders Co. Ltd. 24-28 Oval
Rd., London NW1 7DX, England. TEL 44-171-485-
4752. FAX 44-171-267-4466. *4697*

BAILLIERE'S CLINICAL INFECTIOUS DISEASES.
Bailliere Tindall - W.B. Saunders Co. Ltd. 24-28 Oval
Rd., London NW1 7DX, England. TEL 44-171-485-
4752. FAX 44-171-267-4466. *4618*

**BAILLIERE'S CLINICAL OBSTETRICS AND
GYNAECOLOGY.**
Bailliere Tindall - W.B. Saunders Co. Ltd. 24-28 Oval
Rd., London NW1 7DX, England. TEL 44-171-485-
4752. FAX 44-171-267-4466. *4732*

BAILLIERE'S CLINICAL PAEDIATRICS.
Bailliere Tindall - W.B. Saunders Co. Ltd. 24-28 Oval
Rd., London NW1 7DX, England. TEL 44-171-485-
4752. FAX 44-171-267-4466. *4803*

BAILLIERE'S CLINICAL PSYCHIATRY.
Bailliere Tindall - W.B. Saunders Co. Ltd., 24-28
Oval Rd., London NW1 7DX, England. TEL 44-171-
485-4752. FAX 44-171-267-4466. *4827*

BAILLIERE'S CLINICAL RHEUMATOLOGY.
Bailliere Tindall - W.B. Saunders Co. Ltd. 24-28 Oval
Rd., London NW1 7DX, England. TEL 44-171-485-
4752. FAX 44-171-267-4466. *4893*

BAILLIERE'S HANDBOOK OF FIRST AID.
Bailliere Tindall - W.B. Saunders Co. Ltd. 24-28 Oval
Rd., London NW1 7DX, England. TEL -171-485-
4752. FAX 0171-267-4466. *4433*

BAILY'S HUNTING DIRECTORY.
Pearson Publishing, Chesterton Mill, French's Rd.,
Cambridge CB4 3NP, England. TEL 44-1223-
350555. FAX 44-1223-356484. *1586*

BAIYI KEJI.
Zhongguo Baiyi Fangzhi ranjiuhui, No. 693,
Moganshan Lu, Hangzhou, Zhejiang 310011,
People's Republic of China. TEL 36-571-8071061.
FAX 86-571-5151540. *722*

BALUNGAN.
American Gamelan Institute, Box 1052, Lebanon,
NH 03766-4052. TEL 603-448-8837. *5141*

BANACH CENTER PUBLICATIONS.
Polska Akademia Nauk, Instytut Matematyczny,
Dzial Wydawnictw, Ul. Sniadeckich 8, P.O. Box 137,
00-950 Warsaw, Poland. TEL 48-22-6282471.
FAX 48-22-6293997. *4357*

BANBER HAYASTANI ARKHIVNERI.
Arkhivnoe Upravlenie pri Sovete Ministrov Armenii,
Ul. Rachiia Kochara 5, Erevan 375033, Armenia.
TEL 7-885-225355. *3396*

BANDAOTI XUEBAO.
Science Press, Marketing and Sales Department, 16
Donghuangchenggen North St., Beijing 100717,
People's Republic of China. TEL 4010642.
FAX 4019810. *2508*

BANGLADESH JOURNAL OF ZOOLOGY.
Zoological Society of Bangladesh, c/o Dept. of
Zoology, University of Draka, Draka 1000,
Bangladesh. TEL 880-2-868333. FAX 880-2-
865583. *800*

BANK OF VALLETTA REVIEW.
Bank of Valletta, Zachary St., Valletta VLT 04, Malta.
TEL 356-313134. FAX 356-313139. *896*

BANKING LAW ANTHOLOGY.
International Library Law Book Publishers, Inc.,
4301 N. Fairfax Rd., Ste 875, Arlington, VA
22203. TEL 703-528-1000. FAX 703-528-6060.
3748

BANKING LAW JOURNAL.
Warren, Gorham & Lamont, One Penn Plaza, New
York, NY 10119. TEL 212-971-5000. FAX 212-
971-5113. *1069*

BAO PO.
Wuhan Gongye Daxue, Bao Po Bianjibu, 14 Luoshi
Lu, Wuchang, Wuhan, Hubei 430070, People's
Republic of China. *2633*

BAPTIST QUARTERLY.
Baptist Historical Society, 28 Dowthorpe Hill, Earls
Barton, Northampton NN6 0PE, England. TEL 44-
1604-811170. FAX 44-1604-811170. *6135*

BARIATRICIAN.
American Society of Bariatric Physicians, 5600 S.
Quebec, Ste. 109A, Englewood, CO 80111-2208.
TEL 303-779-4833. *5230*

BARRON FAMILY NEWSLETTER.
Family Heritage Publications, 1886 Rice Blvd.,
Fairborn, OH 45324-3158. TEL 513-372-2744.
3075

BARTONIA.
Philadelphia Botanical Club, c/o Academy of Natural
Sciences of Philadelphia 1900 Benjamin Franklin
Pkwy., Philadelphia, PA 19103. TEL 215-299-
1000. *672*

BASEBALL QUARTERLY REVIEWS.
H O K Enterprises, Box 9343, Schenectady, NY
12309. TEL 518-399-7890. *6497*

BASIC AND APPLIED SOCIAL PSYCHOLOGY.
Lawrence Erlbaum Associates, Inc., 10 Industrial Dr., Mahwah, NJ 07430-2262. TEL 201-236-9500. FAX 201-236-0072. *5829*

BASIC AND CLINICAL CARDIOLOGY SERIES.
Marcel Dekker, Inc., 270 Madison Ave., New York, NY 10016. TEL 212-696-9000. FAX 212-685-4540. *4597*

BASIC & CLINICAL ENDOCRINOLOGY.
Marcel Dekker, Inc., 270 Madison Ave., New York, NY 10016. TEL 212-696-9000. FAX 212-685-4540. *4666*

BASIC LEGAL DOCUMENTS ON REGIONAL ENVIRONMENTAL COOPERATION.
Martinus Nijhoff Publishers, Human Rights and International Law Postbus 163, 3300 AD Dordrecht, Netherlands. TEL 31-78-334911. FAX 31-78-334254. *3923*

BASIC LIFE SCIENCES.
Plenum Publishing Corp., 233 Spring St., New York, NY 10013-1578. TEL 212-620-8000. FAX 212-463-0742. *570*

BASIN RESEARCH.
Blackwell Science Ltd., Osney Mead, Oxford OX2 0EL, England. TEL 44-1865-206206. FAX 44-1865-721205. *2204*

DER BAYERISCHE INTERNIST.
Juergen Hartmann Verlag GmbH, Seefeld 18, 91093 Hessdorf-Klebheim, Germany. TEL 49-9135-7123-0. FAX 49-9135-712340. *4433*

BAYLOR LARIAT.
Baylor University, Lariat, Box 97353, Waco, TX 76798. TEL 817-755-1711. FAX 817-755-1321. *1858*

BEADS.
Society of Bead Researchers, 1600 Liverpool Ct., Ottawa, ON K1A 0M5, Canada. TEL 613-990-4814. FAX 613-952-1756. *304*

BEAM MODIFICATION OF MATERIALS.
Elsevier Science B.V., Books Division, P.O. Box 211, 1000 AE Amsterdam, Netherlands. TEL 31-20-4853911. FAX 31-20-4853705. *5602*

BEAUFORTIA.
Universiteit van Amsterdam, Instituut voor Systematisch en Populatie Biologie (Zoologisch Museum), P.O. Box 94766, 1090 GT Amsterdam, Netherlands. TEL 31-20-5256901. FAX 31-20-5255402. *800*

BEAUTY INC.
Beauty & Barber Supply Institute, Inc., 11811 N. Tatum Blvd., Ste. 1085, Phoeniz, AZ 85028-1618. TEL 602-404-1800. FAX 602-404-8900. *490*

BEBIDAS MEXICANAS.
Alfa Editores Tecnicos S.A., Libertad No. 107-402, 03660 Mexico DF, Mexico. TEL 525-579-3333. FAX 525-532-9504. *500*

BEE WORLD.
International Bee Research Association, 18 North Rd., Cardiff CF1 3DY, Wales. TEL 44-1222-372409. FAX 44-1222-665522. *100*

BEEKEEPING & DEVELOPMENT.
Bees for Development, Troy, Monmouth, Gwent NP5 4AB, Wales. TEL 44-1600-716167. FAX 44-1600-761167. *100*

BE'EMMET.
Beit Berl College, Yemima Center for Study and Teaching of Children's Literature, Beit Berl, Doar Beit Berl 44905. Israel. TEL 972-52-906400. FAX 972-52-454104. *4185*

BEER-SHEVA.
Ben Gurion University of the Negev Press, P.O. Box 653, Beersheva, Israel. FAX 972-7-472913. *346*

BEETHOVEN FORUM.
University of Nebraska Press, 312 N. 14th St., Box 880484, Lincoln, NE 68588-0484. TEL 402-472-3581. FAX 402-472-6214. *5142*

THE BEHAVIOR ANALYST.
Association for Behavior Analysis, 213 West Hall, Western Michigan University, Kalamazoo, MI 49008-5052. TEL 616-387-8354. FAX 616-387-8341. *5829*

BEHAVIOR AND PHILOSOPHY.
Cambridge Center for Behavioral Studies, 675 Massachusetts Ave., Cambridge, MA 02139-3309. TEL 617-491-9020. FAX 617-491-1072. *5829*

BEHAVIOR AND SOCIAL ISSUES.
Cambridge Center for Behavioral Studies, 675 Massachusetts Ave., Cambridge, MA 02139-3309. TEL 617-491-9020. FAX 617-491-1072. *5829*

BEHAVIOR GENETICS.
Plenum Publishing Corp., 233 Spring St., New York, NY 10013-1578. TEL 212-620-8000. FAX 212-463-0742. *738*

BEHAVIOR RESEARCH METHODS, INSTRUMENTS, AND COMPUTERS.
Psychonomic Society, Inc., 1710 Fortview Rd., Austin, TX 78704. TEL 512-462-2442. *5829*

BEHAVIOR THERAPY.
Association for Advancement of Behavior Therapy, 305 Seventh Ave., Ste. 16A, New York, NY 10001. *5829*

BEHAVIORAL & SOCIAL SCIENCES LIBRARIAN.
Haworth Press, Inc., 10 Alice St., Binghamton, NY 13904. TEL 607-722-5857. FAX 607-722-1424. *3977*

BEHAVIORAL BRAIN RESEARCH.
Elsevier Science B.V., P.O. Box 211, 1000 AE Amsterdam, Netherlands. TEL 31-20-4853911. FAX 31-20-4853598. *4827*

BEHAVIORAL ECOLOGY.
Oxford University Press, Journals, 2001 Evans Rd., Cary, NC 27513. TEL 919-677-0977. FAX 919-677-1714. *570*

BEHAVIORAL INTERVENTIONS.
John Wiley & Sons Ltd., Journals, Baffins Ln., Chichester, W. Sussex PO19 1UD, England. TEL 44-1243-779777. FAX 44-1243-843232. *4827*

BEHAVIORAL MEDICINE.
Heldref Publications, 1319 Eighteenth St., N.W., Washington, DC 20036-1802. TEL 202-396-6267. FAX 202-296-5149. *5830*

BEHAVIORAL NEUROSCIENCE.
American Psychological Association, 750 First St., N.E., Washington, DC 20002-4242. TEL 202-336-5600. FAX 202-336-5568. *5830*

BEHAVIOUR.
E.J. Brill, P.O. Box 9000, 2300 PA Leiden, Netherlands. TEL 31-71-5353500. FAX 31-71-5317532. *800*

BEHAVIOUR AND INFORMATION TECHNOLOGY.
Taylor & Francis Ltd., 1 Gunpowder Sq., London EC4A 3DE, England. TEL 44-171-583-0490. FAX 44-171-583-0585. *5830*

BEHAVIOUR RESEARCH AND THERAPY.
Elsevier Science Ltd., Pergamon, P.O. Box 800, Kidlington, Oxford OX5 1DX, England. TEL 44-1865-843000. FAX 44-1865-843010. *5830*

BEHAVIOURAL PROCESSES.
Elsevier Science B.V., P.O. Box 211, 1000 AE Amsterdam, Netherlands. TEL 31-20-4853911. FAX 31-20-4853598. *4827*

BEIJING YIKE DAXUE XUEBAO.
Beijing Yike Daxue, Xueyuan Lu, Beijing 100083, People's Republic of China. TEL 861-2091551. FAX 861-2015681. *4433*

BEITRAEGE ZUR INFUSIONSTHERAPIE UND TRANSFUSIONSMEDIZIN.
S. Karger AG, Allschwilerstr. 10, P.O. Box, CH-4009 Basel, Switzerland. TEL 061-3061111. FAX 061-3061234. *4433*

BEITRAEGE ZUR INTENSIV- UND NOTFALLMEDIZIN.
S. Karger AG, Allschwilerstr. 10, P.O. Box, CH-4009 Basel, Switzerland. TEL 061-3061111. FAX 061-3061234. *4433*

BEITRAEGE ZUR NAMENFORSCHUNG.
Universitaetsverlag C. Winter Heidelberg GmbH, Hans-Bunte-Str. 18, 69123 Heidelberg, Germany. TEL 49-6221-770260. FAX 49-6221-770269. *4056*

BEITRAEGE ZUR UROLOGIE.
S. Karger AG, Allschwilerstr. 10, P.O. Box, CH-4009 Basel, Switzerland. TEL 061-3061111. FAX 061-3061234. *4925*

BELGIAN JOURNAL OF BOTANY.
Societe Royale de Botanique de Belgique, Chaussee de Wavre 1850, B-1160 Brussels, Belgium. TEL 32-2-2693905. FAX 32-2-2701567. *672*

BELGISCHE FRUITREVUE.
Prov. Pomologische Vereniging Van Oost-Vlaanderen v.z.w., c/o M. Albert Vereecken, Ed., Boonstraat 12, 9220 Hamme, Belgium. TEL 32-52-477485. FAX 32-52-481193. *3045*

BELL LABS TECHNICAL JOURNAL.
Bell Labs, 700 Mountain Ave., Rm. 3C-420A, Murray Hill, NJ 07974. TEL 908-582-4834. FAX 908-582-4430. *1943*

BELTSVILLE SYMPOSIA IN AGRICULTURAL RESEARCH.
Kluwer Academic Publishers, Postbus 17, 3300 AA Dordrecht, Netherlands. TEL 31-78-6392392. FAX 31-78-6392254. *101*

BENJAMINS TRANSLATION LIBRARY.
John Benjamins Publishing Co., Amsteldijk 44, P.O. Box 75577, 1070 AN Amsterdam, Netherlands. TEL 31-20-6738156. FAX 31-20-6792956. *4056*

BERCEO.
Instituto de Estudios Riojanos, C. Muro de la Mata, 8 principal, 26071 Logrono, Spain. TEL 34-41-262064. FAX 34-41-246667. *3608*

BEREAVEMENT CARE.
Cruse - Bereavement Care, 126 Sheen Rd., Richmond, Surrey TW9 1UR, England. TEL 0181-940-4818. FAX 0181-940-7638. *6362*

BERGEY'S MANUAL OF DETERMINATIVE BACTERIOLOGY.
Williams and Wilkins, Book Division, 351 W. Camden St., Baltimore, MD 21201. TEL 410-528-4000. FAX 410-528-4312. *754*

BERICHTE NATURWISSENSCHAFTLICH - MEDIZINISCHEN VEREINS IN INNSBRUCK.
Naturwissenschaftlich - Medizinischer Verein in Innsbruck, Technikerstr. 25, A-6020 Innsbruck, Austria. TEL 43-512-5076142. FAX 43-512-2185358. *571*

BERKELEY JOURNAL OF EMPLOYMENT AND LABOR LAW.
University of California Press, Journals Division, 2120 Berkeley Way, No. 5812, Berkeley, CA 94720-5812. TEL 510-643-7154. FAX 510-642-9917. *1365*

BERKELEY JOURNAL OF INTERNATIONAL LAW.
University of California Press, Journals Division, 2120 Berkeley Way, No. 5812, Berkeley, CA 94720-5812. TEL 510-643-7154. FAX 510-642-9917. *3924*

BERKELEY PLANNING JOURNAL.
University of California at Berkeley, Department of City and Regional Planning, Graduate Students, 228 Wurster Hall, Berkeley, CA 94720. TEL 415-642-3256. FAX 510-643-9576. *3577*

BERKELEY TECHNOLOGY LAW JOURNAL.
University of California Press, Journals Division, 2120 Berkeley Way, No. 5812, Berkeley, CA 94720-5812. TEL 510-643-7154. FAX 510-642-9917. *3749*

BERKELEY WOMEN'S LAW JOURNAL.
University of California Press, Journals Division, 2120 Berkeley Way, No. 5812, Berkeley, CA 94720-5812. TEL 510-643-7154. FAX 510-642-9917. *3749*

BERKSHIRE ARCHAEOLOGICAL JOURNAL.
Berkshire Archaeological Society, 28 Holmes Rd., Reading, Berks, England. *346*

BERNHARD-HARMS-VORLESUNGEN.
Institut fuer Weltwirtschaft, Duesternbrooker Weg 120, 24105 Kiel, Germany. TEL 49-431-8814305. FAX 49-431-8814520. *1179*

BERNOULLI.
Chapman & Hall, Journals Department 2-6 Boundary Row, London SE1 8HN, England. TEL 44-171-8650066. FAX 44-171-5229623. *4357*

BERYTUS ARCHEOLOGICAL STUDIES.
American University of Beirut, Faculty of Arts and Sciences, A U B Museum, Beirut, Lebanon. FAX 873-1450231. *346*

BEST BOOK CATALOG IN THE WORLD.
Loompanics Unlimited, Box 1197, Port Townsend, WA 98368. TEL 360-385-5087. FAX 360-385-7785. *517*

BEST OF LONG RANGE PLANNING.
Elsevier Science Ltd., Books Division, P.O. Box 800, Kidlington, Oxford OX5 1DK. TEL 44-1865-843000. FAX 44-1865-843010. *1407*

BEST READ GUIDE.
Box 1958, 77 Finlay Rd., Orleans, MA 02653. TEL 508-240-1212. FAX 508-240-2912. *6870*

BEST'S LOSS CONTROL ENGINEERING MANUAL.
A.M. Best Co., Ambest Rd., Oldwick, NJ 08858. TEL 908-439-2200. FAX 908-439-3296. *3642*

BEST'S UNDERWRITING NEWSLETTER.
A.M. Best Co., Ambest Rd., Oldwick, NJ 08858. TEL 908-439-2200. FAX 908-439-3296. *3643*

BESTUURSDINAMIKA.
Suider-Afrika Instituut vir Bestuurswetenskaplikes, c/o Dept. Ondernemingsbestuur, Privaatsak X1, Matieland 7602, South Africa. TEL 27-21-8082222. FAX 27-21-8082226. *1407*

BESTUURSFORUM.
Christen Democratisch Appel (CDA), Bestuurdersvereniging, Dr. Kuyperstraat 5, 2514 BA The Hague, Netherlands. TEL 31-70-3424890. FAX 31-70-3643417. *5893*

BESTUURSKUNDE.
Vuga Uitgeverij B.V., Postbus 16400, 2500 BK The Hague, Netherlands. TEL 31-70-3614011. FAX 31-70-3632338. *5893*

BETTER ROADS.
William O. Dannhausen, Pub., Box 558, Park Ridge, IL 60068. TEL 312-693-7710. FAX 847-696-3445. *2653*

BEYOND WORDS.
Wycliffe Bible Translators Australia, Graham Rd., Kangaroo Ground, Vic. 3097, Australia. TEL 61-3-97122777. FAX 61-3-97122799. *6046*

BIBLE TODAY.
Liturgical Press, St. John's Abbey, Collegeville, MN 56321-7500. TEL 320-363-2213. FAX 800-445-5899. *6047*

BIBLICAL INTERPRETATION.
E.J. Brill, P.O. Box 9000, 2300 PA Leiden, Netherlands. TEL 31-71-5353500. FAX 31-71-5317532. *6047*

BIBLICAL INTERPRETATION SERIES.
E.J. Brill, P.O. Box 9000, 2300 PA Leiden, Netherlands. TEL 31-71-5353500. FAX 31-71-5317532. *6047*

BIBLICAL THEOLOGY BULLETIN.
Biblical Theology Bulletin, Inc., Box 1038, S. Orange, NJ 07079. TEL 201-761-9770. FAX 201-325-7136. *6047*

BIBLIOGRAPHICAL SOCIETY OF AUSTRALIA AND NEW ZEALAND. BULLETIN.
Bibliographical Society of Australia & New Zealand, c/o State Library of Victoria, 328 Swanston St., Melbourne, Vic. 3000, Australia. TEL 61-3-565-2953. FAX 61-3-565-2952. *5988*

BIBLIOGRAPHICAL SOCIETY OF CANADA. PAPERS.
Bibliographical Society of Canada, P.O. Box 575, Sta. "P", Toronto, ON M5S 2T1, Canada. *520*

BIBLION.
Greenwood Press, Inc. 88 Post Rd. W., Box 5007, Westport, CT 06881. TEL 203-226-3571. FAX 203-222-1502. *3978*

BIBLIOTECA ITALIANA.
University of California Press, 2120 Berkeley Way, Berkeley, CA 94720. TEL 510-642-4247. FAX 510-643-7127. *4186*

BIBLIOTHECA CARDIOLOGICA.
S. Karger AG, Allschwilerstr. 10, P.O. Box, CH-4009 Basel, Switzerland. TEL 061-3061111. FAX 061-3061234. *4597*

BIBLIOTHECA NUTRITIO ET DIETA.
S. Karger AG, Allschwilerstr. 10, P.O. Box, CH-4009 Basel, Switzerland. TEL 061-3061111. FAX 061-3061234. *5230*

BIBLIOTHECA PSYCHIATRICA.
S. Karger AG, Allschwilerstr. 10, P.O. Box, CH-4009 Basel, Switzerland. TEL 061-3061111. FAX 061-3061234. *4827*

BIJEN.
Bijen. Postbus 198, 6720 AD Bennekom, Netherlands. TEL 31-317-422422. FAX 31-317-424180. *102*

BILDGEBUNG.
S. Karger AG, Allschwilerstr. 10, P.O. Box, CH-4009 Basel, Switzerland. TEL 061-3061111. FAX 061-3061234. *4873*

BILINGUAL RESEARCH JOURNAL.
National Association for Bilingual Education, c/o Andrea B. Bermudez, Ed., Research Centre for Language & Culture, University of Houston - Clear Lake, 2700 Bay Area Blvd., Houston, TX 77058-1098. *4057*

BILINGUAL REVIEW.
Bilingual Review Press, Hispanic Research Center, Arizona State University, Tempe, AZ 85287-2702. TEL 502-965-3867. FAX 602-965-8309. *4057*

BINARY: COMPUTING IN MICROBIOLOGY.
Academic Press Ltd. 24-28 Oval Rd., London NW1 7DX, England. TEL 44-171-267-4466. FAX 44-171-482-2293. *754*

BINGDUXUE ZAZHI.
Science Press, Marketing and Sales Department, 16 Donghuangchenggen North St., Beijing 100717, People's Republic of China. TEL 4010642. FAX 4019810. *754*

BIO.
A B E S, Av. Beira-Mar, 216-13 andar, 20021-060 Rio de Janeiro, RJ, Brazil. TEL 55-21-2103221. FAX 55-21-2626838. *2653*

BIO-MEDICAL MATERIALS AND ENGINEERING.
I O S Press, Van Diemenstraat 94, 1013 CN Amsterdam, Netherlands. TEL 31-20-6382189. FAX 31-20-5203419. *626*

BIO-REGULADORES.
Springer-Verlag Iberica S.A., C. Provenca, 388 1a, 08025 Barcelona, Spain. TEL 34-3-4570227. FAX 34-3-4571502. *626*

BIOACTIVE MOLECULES.
Elsevier Science B.V., Books Division, P.O. Box 211, 1000 AE Amsterdam, Netherlands. TEL 31-20-4853911. FAX 31-20-4853705. *652*

BIOCATALYSIS AND BIOTRANSFORMATION.
Harwood Academic Publishers, c/o International Publishers Distributor, P.O. Box 3054, Langhorne, PA 19047-3054. TEL 215-750-2642. FAX 215-750-6343. *657*

BIOCELL.
Centro Regional de Investigaciones Cientificas y Tecnologicas, Casilla de Correo 131, 5500 Mendoza, Argentina. TEL 54-61-205020 ext. 2670. FAX 54-61-380232. *768*

BIOCHEMICAL AND BIOPHYSICAL RESEARCH COMMUNICATIONS.
Academic Press, Inc., Journal Division, 525 B St., Ste. 1900, San Diego, CA 92101-4495. TEL 619-230-1840. FAX 619-699-6800. *631*

BIOCHEMICAL AND MOLECULAR MEDICINE.
Academic Press, Inc., Journal Division, 525 B. St., Ste. 1900, San Diego, CA 92101-4495. TEL 619-230-1840. FAX 619-699-6800. *631*

BIOCHEMICAL EDUCATION.
Elsevier Science Ltd., Pergamon, P.O. Box 800, Kidlington, Oxford OX5 1DX, England. TEL 44-1865-843000. FAX 44-1865-843010. *631*

BIOCHEMICAL GENETICS.
Plenum Publishing Corp., 233 Spring St., New York, NY 10013-1578. TEL 212-620-8000. FAX 212-463-0742. *631*

BIOCHEMICAL JOURNAL.
Portland Press Ltd., 59 Portland Place, London W1N 3AJ, England. TEL 44-171-580-5530. FAX 44-171-323-1136. *632*

BIOCHEMICAL PHARMACOLOGY.
Elsevier Science Inc., Box 945, New York, NY 10159-0945. TEL 212-633-3730. FAX 212-633-3680. *5401*

BIOCHEMICAL SOCIETY SYMPOSIUM.
Portland Press Ltd., 59 Portland Pl., London W1N 3AJ, England. TEL 44-171-580-5530. FAX 44-171-323-1136. *632*

BIOCHEMICAL SOCIETY TRANSACTIONS.
Portland Press Ltd., 59 Portland Place, London W1N 3AJ, England. TEL 44-171-580-5530. FAX 44-171-323-1136. *632*

BIOCHEMICAL SYSTEMATICS AND ECOLOGY.
Elsevier Science Ltd., Pergamon, P.O. Box 800, Kidlington, Oxford OX5 1DX, England. TEL 44-1865-843000. FAX 44-1865-843010. *632*

BIOCHEMISTRY.
Maik Nauka - Interperiodica, Mezhdunarodnyi Otdel, Ul. Profsoyuznaya, 90, 117864 Moscow, Russia. TEL 7-095-3360060. FAX 212-463-0742. *632*

BIOCHEMISTRY AND CELL BIOLOGY.
National Research Council of Canada, Research Journals, Ottawa, ON K1A 0R6, Canada. TEL 613-993-9084. FAX 613-952-7656. *633*

BIOCHEMISTRY & MOLECULAR BIOLOGY OF FISHES.
Elsevier Science B.V., Books Division, P.O. Box 211, 1000 AE Amsterdam, Netherlands. TEL 31-20-4853911. FAX 31-20-4853705. *800*

BIOCHEMISTRY OF THE ELEMENTS.
Plenum Publishing Corp., 233 Spring St., New York, NY 10013-1578. TEL 212-620-8000. FAX 212-463-0742. *633*

BIOCHEMISTRY: SERIES OF MONOGRAPHS.
John Wiley & Sons, Inc., Journals, 605 Third Ave., New York, NY 10158-0012. TEL 212-850-6000. *633*

BIOCHIMICA ET BIOPHYSICA ACTA.
Elsevier Science B.V., P.O. Box 211, 1000 AE Amsterdam, Netherlands. TEL 31-20-4853911. FAX 31-20-4853598. *633*

BIOCHIMIE.
Editions Scientifiques et Medicales Elsevier, 141 rue de Javel, 75747 Paris, France. TEL 33-1-45589022. FAX 33-1-45589421. *633*

BIOCONTROL SCIENCE AND TECHNOLOGY.
Carfax Publishing Co. P.O. Box 25, Abingdon, Oxon. OX14 3UE, England. TEL 44-1235-401000. FAX 44-1235-401550. *213*

BIOCYCLE.
J G Press, Inc., 419 State Ave., Emmaus, PA 18049. TEL 610-967-4135. *2850*

BIODEGRADATION.
Kluwer Academic Publishers, Postbus 17, 3300 AA Dordrecht, Netherlands. TEL 31-78-6392392. FAX 31-78-6392254. *2850*

BIODIVERSITY AND CONSERVATION.
Chapman & Hall, Journals Department 2-6 Boundary Row, London SE1 8HN, England. TEL 44-171-8650066. FAX 44-171-5229623. *2121*

BIODRUGS.
Adis International Limited, Private Bag 65901, Mairangi Bay, Auckland 10, New Zealand. TEL 64-9-479-8100. FAX 215-741-5251. *5401*

BIOELECTROCHEMISTRY AND BIOENERGETICS.
Elsevier Science S.A., P.O. Box 564, CH-1001 Lausanne 1, Switzerland. TEL 41-21-3207381. FAX 41-21-3235444. *633*

BIOELECTROMAGNETICS.
John Wiley & Sons, Inc., Journals, 605 Third Ave., New York, NY 10158. TEL 212-850-6645. FAX 212-850-6021. *652*

BIOETHICS YEARBOOK.
Kluwer Academic Publishers, Postbus 17, 3300 AA Dordrecht, Netherlands. TEL 31-78-6392392. FAX 31-78-6392254. *6048*

BIOFACTORS.
I O S Press, Van Diemenstraat 94, 1013 CN Amsterdam, Netherlands. TEL 31-20-6382189. FAX 31-20-6203419. *633*

BIOFOULING.
Harwood Academic Publishers, c/o International Publishers Distributor, P.O. Box 3054, Langhorne, PA 19047-3054. TEL 215-750-2642. FAX 215-750-6343. *2842*

BIOGENIC AMINES.
V S P, P.O. Box 346, 3700 AH Zeist, Netherlands. TEL 31-30-6925790. FAX 31-30-6932081. *633*

BIOGEOCHEMISTRY.
Kluwer Academic Publishers, Postbus 17, 3300 AA Dordrecht, Netherlands. TEL 31-78-6392392. FAX 31-78-6392254. *634*

BIOGRAPHY (HONOLULU).
University of Hawaii Press, Journals Department, 2840 Kolowalu St., Honolulu, HI 96822. TEL 808-956-8833. FAX 808-988-6052. *554*

BIOLOGIA ACUATICA.
Instituto de Limnologia, Casilla de Correo 712, 1900 La Plata, Argentina. TEL 54-1-2375864. FAX 54-1-2377799. *572*

BIOLOGIA OGGI.
Associazione Nazionale Laureati in Scienze Biologiche, Via Guglielmo degli Ubertini, 64, 00176 Rome, Italy. TEL 39-6-21707494. *572*

BIOLOGIA PLANTARUM.
Kluwer Academic Publishers, Postbus 17, 3300 AA Dordrecht, Netherlands. TEL 31-78-6392392. FAX 31-78-6392254. *672*

BIOLOGIA & CLINICA HEMATOLOGICA.
Springer-Verlag Iberica S.A., C. Provenza 388, 1a, 08025 Barcelona, Spain. TEL 34-3-4570227. FAX 34-3-4571502. *4698*

BIOLOGICAL BULLETIN.
Science Press, Marketing and Sales Department, 16 Donghuangchenggen North St., Beijing 100717, People's Republic of China. TEL 4010642. FAX 4012180. *572*

BIOLOGICAL BULLETIN.
Marine Biological Laboratory, Woods Hole, MA 02543. TEL 508-289-7428. FAX 508-457-1924. *572*

BIOLOGICAL CONSERVATION.
Elsevier Science Ltd., P.O. Box 800, Kidlington, Oxford OX5 1DX, England. TEL 44-1865-843000. FAX 44-1865-843010. *2121*

BIOLOGICAL MAGNETIC RESONANCE.
Plenum Publishing Corp., 233 Spring St., New York, NY 10013-1578. TEL 212-620-8000. FAX 212-463-0742. *5543*

BIOLOGICAL PSYCHIATRY.
Elsevier Science Inc., Box 945, New York, NY 10159-0945. TEL 212-633-3730. FAX 212-633-3680. *4828*

BIOLOGICAL PSYCHOLOGY.
North-Holland P.O. Box 211, 1000 AE Amsterdam, Netherlands. TEL 31-20-4853911. FAX 31-20-4853598. *5831*

BIOLOGICAL REGULATION & DEVELOPMENT.
Plenum Publishing Corp., 233 Spring St., New York, NY 10013-1578. TEL 212-620-8000. FAX 212-463-0742. *634*

BIOLOGICAL RESEARCH.
Sociedad de Biologia de Chile, Casilla 16164, Santiago 9, Chile. TEL 56-2-6862850. FAX 56-2-2225515. *572*

BIOLOGICAL SCIENCE REPORT.
U.S. National Biological Service, Information Transfer Center, 1201 Oak Ridge Dr., Ste. 200, Ft. Collins, CO 80525-5589. TEL 970-226-9401. FAX 970-226-9455. *573*

BIOLOGICAL SCIENCES REVIEW.
Philip Allan Publishers Ltd., Market Pl., Deddington, Oxon. OX15 0SE, England. TEL 44-1869-338652. FAX 44-1869-338803. *573*

BIOLOGICAL SIGNALS.
S. Karger AG, Allschwilerstr. 10, P.O. Box, CH-4009 Basel, Switzerland. TEL 061-3061111. FAX 061-3061234. *634*

BIOLOGICAL SOCIETY OF WASHINGTON. PROCEEDINGS.
Biological Society of Washington, National Museum of Natural History, Smithsonian Institution, Washington, DC 20560. TEL 202-786-2550. *573*

BIOLOGICAL TRACE ELEMENT RESEARCH.
Humana Press Inc., 999 Riverview Dr., Ste. 208, Totowa, NJ 07512. TEL 201-256-1699. FAX 201-256-8341. *634*

BIOLOGY AND PHILOSOPHY.
Kluwer Academic Publishers, Postbus 17, 3300 AA Dordrecht, Netherlands. TEL 31-78-6392392. FAX 31-78-6392254. *574*

BIOLOGY OF REPRODUCTION.
Society for the Study of Reproduction, 1526 Jefferson St., Madison, WI 53711-2106. TEL 608-256-2777. FAX 608-256-4610. *738*

BIOLOGY OF THE CELL.
Editions Scientifiques et Medicales Elsevier, 141 rue de Javel, 75747 Paris, France. TEL 33-1-45589022. FAX 33-1-45589421. *711*

BIOLOGY OF THE NEONATE.
S. Karger AG, Allschwilerstr. 10, P.O. Box, CH-4009 Basel, Switzerland. TEL 061-3061111. FAX 061-3061234. *4732*

BIOMASS & BIOENERGY.
Elsevier Science Ltd., Pergamon, P.O. Box 800, Kidlington, Oxford OX5 1DX, England. TEL 44-1865-843000. FAX 44-1865-843010. *2541*

BIOMATERIALS.
Butterworth - Heinemann, Part of the Reed Elsevier group, Linacre House, Jordan Hill, Oxford OX2 8DP, England. TEL 44-1865-310366. FAX 44-1865-310898. *4434*

BIOMATERIALS SCIENCE AND ENGINEERING.
Mary Ann Liebert, Inc. Publishers, 2 Madison Ave., Larchmont. TEL 914-834-3100. FAX 914-834-3688. *657*

BIOMEDICAL AND CLINICAL ASPECTS OF COENZYME Q.
Elsevier Science B.V., Books Division, P.O. Box 211, 1000 AE Amsterdam, Netherlands. TEL 31-20-4853911. FAX 31-20-4853705. *785*

BIOMEDICAL AND ENVIRONMENTAL SCIENCES.
Zhongguo Yufang Yixue Kexueyuan, 27 Nanwei Rd., Beijing 100050, People's Republic of China. TEL 4377008. *4434*

BIOMEDICAL ENGINEERING.
Plenum Publishing Corp., Consultants Bureau, 233 Spring St., New York, NY 10013-1578. TEL 212-620-8468. FAX 212-463-0742. *4434*

BIOMEDICAL ENGINEERING AND COMPUTATION SERIES.
Harwood Academic Publishers, c/o International Publishers Distributor, P.O. Box 3054, Langhorne, PA 19047-3054. TEL 215-750-2642. FAX 215-750-6343. *626*

BIOMEDICAL INSTRUMENTATION & TECHNOLOGY.
Hanley & Belfus, Inc., 210 S. 13th St., Philadelphia, PA 19107. TEL 215-546-7293. FAX 215-790-9330. *4435*

BIOMEDICAL MARKET NEWSLETTER.
David G. Anast, Ed.& Pub., 3237 Idaho Pl., Costa Mesa, CA 92626-2207. TEL 714-434-9500. FAX 714-434-9755. *1454*

BIOMEDICAL PEPTIDES, PROTEINS & NUCLEIC ACIDS.
Mayflower Worldwide Ltd., P.O. Box 13, Kingswinford, W. Midlands DY6 0HQ, England. TEL 44-1384-279324. FAX 44-1384-294463. *634*

BIOMEDICAL SCIENCES INSTRUMENTATION.
Instrument Society of America, 67 Alexander Dr., Box 12277, Research Triangle Park, NC 27709. TEL 919-549-8411. FAX 919-549-8288. *4435*

BIOMEDICINE AND PHARMACOTHERAPY.
Editions Scientifiques et medicales Elsevier, 141 rue de Javel, 75747 Paris, France. TEL 33-1-45589026. FAX 33-1-45589421. *4435*

BIOMEMBRANES.
Plenum Publishing Corp., 233 Spring St., New York, NY 10013-1578. TEL 212-620-8000. FAX 212-463-0742. *711*

BIOMETRICS.
International Biometric Society, 808 17th St., N.W., Washington, DC 20006-3910. TEL 202-223-9669. FAX 202-223-9569. *6594*

BIOMIMETICS.
Plenum Publishing Corp., 233 Spring St., New York, NY 10013-1578. TEL 212-620-8000. FAX 212-463-0742. *626*

BIOORGANIC & MEDICINAL CHEMISTRY LETTERS.
Elsevier Science Ltd., Pergamon, P.O. Box 800, Kidlington, Oxford OX5 1DX, England. TEL 44-1865-843000. FAX 44-1865-843010. *1735*

BIOORGANIC CHEMISTRY.
Academic Press, Inc., Journal Division, 525 B St., Ste. 1900, San Diego, CA 92101-4495. TEL 619-230-1840. FAX 619-699-6800. *1735*

BIOPHYSICAL CHEMISTRY.
Elsevier Science B.V., P.O. Box 211, 1000 AE Amsterdam, Netherlands. TEL 31-20-4853911. FAX 31-20-4853598. *652*

BIOPHYSICAL JOURNAL.
Biophysical Society, 9650 Rockville Pike, Bethesda, MD 20814-3998. TEL 301-571-8338. FAX 301-530-7133. *652*

BIOPHYSICAL SOCIETY. ANNUAL MEETING. ABSTRACTS.
Biophysical Society, 9650 Rockville Pike, Bethesda, MD 20814-3998. TEL 301-571-8338. FAX 301-530-7133. *616*

BIOPHYSICS.
Elsevier Science Ltd., Pergamon, P.O. Box 800, Kidlington, Oxford OX5 1DX, England. TEL 44-1865-843000. FAX 44-1865-843010. *652*

BIOPOLYMERS.
John Wiley & Sons, Inc., Journals, 605 Third Ave., New York, NY 10158. TEL 212-692-6645. FAX 212-850-6021. *1735*

BIOPROCESS TECHNOLOGY SERIES.
Marcel Dekker, Inc., 270 Madison Ave., New York, NY 10016. TEL 212-696-9000. FAX 212-685-4540. *574*

BIOPSY INTERPRETATION SERIES.
Lippincott - Raven Publishers, 227 E. Washington Sq., Philadelphia, PA 19106. TEL 215-238-4200. FAX 215-238-4235. *4435*

BIORESOURCE TECHNOLOGY.
Elsevier Science Ltd., P.O. Box 800, Kidlington, Oxford OX5 1DX, England. TEL 44-1865-843000. FAX 44-1865-843010. *657*

BIORHEOLOGY.
Elsevier Science Ltd., Pergamon, P.O. Box 800, Kidlington, Oxford OX5 1DX, England. TEL 44-1865-843000. FAX 44-1865-843010. *653*

BIOSAFETY.
Science Reviews Ltd., P.O. Box 81, Northwood, Middlesex HA6 3DY, England. TEL 44-1923-823586. FAX 44-1923-825006. *574*

BIOSCIENCE.
American Institute of Biological Sciences, 1444 Eye St., N.W., Ste. 200, Washington, DC 20005. TEL 202-628-1500. FAX 202-628-1509. *574*

BIOSCIENCE, BIOTECHNOLOGY, AND BIOCHEMISTRY.
Japan Society for Bioscience, Biotechnology, and Agrochemistry, 2-4-16 Yayoi, Bunkyo-ku, Tokyo 113, Japan. TEL 03-3811-8789. FAX 03-3815-1920. *574*

BIOSCIENCE REPORTS.
Plenum Publishing Corp., 233 Spring St., New York, NY 10013-1578. TEL 212-620-8000. FAX 212-463-0742. *634*

BIOSENSORS AND BIOELECTRONICS.
Elsevier Science Ltd., P.O. Box 800, Kidlington, Oxford OX5 1DX, England. TEL 44-1865-843000. FAX 44-1865-843010. *657*

BIOSEPARATION.
Kluwer Academic Publishers, Postbus 17, 3300 AA Dordrecht, Netherlands. TEL 31-78-6392392. FAX 31-78-6392254. *657*

BIOSPECTROSCOPY.
John Wiley & Sons, Inc., Journals, 605 Third Ave., New York, NY 10158. TEL 212-850-6645. FAX 212-850-6021. *1714*

BIOSYNTHETIC PRODUCTS FOR CANCER CHEMOTHERAPY.
Elsevier Science B.V., Books Division, P.O. Box 211, 1000 AE Amsterdam, Netherlands. TEL 31-20-4853911. FAX 31-20-4853705. *4749*

BIOSYSTEMS.
Elsevier Science Ireland Ltd., P.O. Box 85, Limerick, Ireland. TEL 353-61-471944. FAX 353-61-472144. *575*

BIOTECHNIC AND HISTOCHEMISTRY.
Williams & Wilkins, 351 W. Camden St., Baltimore, MD 21201. TEL 410-528-4000. FAX 410-528-4312. *768*

BIOTECHNOLOGY ADVANCES.
Elsevier Science Inc., Box 945, New York, NY 10159-0945. TEL 212-633-3730. FAX 212-633-3680. *658*

BIOTECHNOLOGY AND APPLIED BIOCHEMISTRY.
Portland Press Ltd., 59 Portland Place, London W1N 3AJ, England. TEL 44-171-580-5530. FAX 44-171-323-1136. *658*

BIOTECHNOLOGY AND BIOENGINEERING.
John Wiley & Sons, Inc., Journals, 605 Third Ave., New York, NY 10158-0012. TEL 212-850-6645. FAX 212-850-6021. *658*

BIOTECHNOLOGY ANNUAL REVIEW.
Elsevier Science B.V., P.O. Box 211, 1000 AE Amsterdam, Netherlands. TEL 31-20-4853911. FAX 31-20-4853705. *658*

BIOTECHNOLOGY EDUCATION.
Helix Publishing, 1 Howard Ct., 94-96 Blackheath Hill, Greenwich, London SE10 8AF, England. *659*

BIOTECHNOLOGY LETTERS.
Chapman & Hall, Journals Department 2-6 Boundary Row, London SE1 8HN, England. TEL 44-171-8560066. FAX 44-171-5229623. *659*

BIOTECHNOLOGY PROGRESS.
American Chemical Society, 1155 16th St., N.W., Washington, DC 20036. TEL 800-333-9511. FAX 614-447-3671. *659*

BIOTECHNOLOGY TECHNIQUES.
Chapman & Hall, Journals Department 2-6 Boundary Row, London SE1 8HN, England. TEL 44-171-8560066. FAX 44-171-5229323. *659*

BIOTHERAPY.
Kluwer Academic Publishers, Postbus 17, 3300 AA Dordrecht, Netherlands. TEL 31-78-6392392. FAX 31-78-6392254. *659*

BIOTHERAPY.
Japanese Journal of Cancer and Chemotherapy Publishers, Inc., 8-9, Yaesu 1-chome, Chuo-ku, Tokyo 103, Japan. TEL 81-3-3278-0052. FAX 81-3-3281-0435. *659*

BIOTROPICA.
Association for Tropical Biology, Inc., c/o Dr. Julie S. Denslow, Exec. Dir., Dept. of Plant Biology, Lousiana State University, Baton Rouge, LA 70803. TEL 504-388-8411. FAX 504-388-8459. *575*

BIRD STUDY.
British Trust for Ornithology, The Nunnery, Nunnery Pl., Thetford, Norwich IP24 2PU, England. *773*

BIRMINGHAM POETRY REVIEW.
English Department, University of Alabama, Birmingham, AL 35294. TEL 205-934-8573. FAX 205-975-8125. *4301*

BIRTH DEFECTS INSTITUTE SYMPOSIA.
Academic Press, Inc., 525 B St., Ste. 1900, San Diego, CA 92101-4495. TEL 619-231-0926. FAX 619-699-6715. *4436*

BISON WORLD.
National Bison Association, 4701 Marion St., Ste. 100, Denver, CO 80216. TEL 303-292-2833. FAX 303-292-2564. *266*

BLACK ICE.
University of Colorado, English Department, Box 494, Boulder, CO 80309. TEL 303-492-8938. *4187*

BLACK MUSIC RESEARCH JOURNAL.
Center for Black Music Research, Columbia College Chicago, 600 S. Michigan Ave., Chicago, IL 60605. TEL 312-663-1600. FAX 312-663-9019. *5143*

BLACK TRAVELER MAGAZINE.
A & E Publishing, Inc., 11631 Victory Blvd., Ste. 201, N. Hollywood, CA 91606. TEL 818-753-9198. FAX 818-753-8405. *6870*

BLAKES REPORT ON INTELLECTUAL PROPERTY.
Blake, Cassels & Graydon, Box 25, Commerce Court West, Toronto, Ont. M5L 1A9, Canada. TEL 416-863-5840. FAX 416-863-2653. *3750*

BLIKI.
Natturufraedistofnun Islands, Hlemmur 3, P.O. Box 5320, 125 Reykjavik, Iceland. TEL 354-562-9822. FAX 354-562-0815. *774*

BLOOD.
W.B. Saunders Co Curtis Center, 3rd Fl., Independence Sq. W., Philadelphia, PA 19106-3399. TEL 215-238-7800. FAX 215-238-6445. *4698*

BLOOD CELLS, MOLECULES, AND DISEASES.
Academic Press, Inc., Journal Division, 525 B St., Ste. 1900, San Diego, CA 92101. TEL 619-230-1840. FAX 619-699-6800. *4698*

BLOOD PRESSURE MONITORING.
Rapid Science Publishing, 2-6 Boundary Row, London SE1 8HN England. TEL 44-171-865-0198. FAX 44-171-410-6600. *4597*

BLOOD PURIFICATION.
S. Karger AG, Allschwilerstr. 10, P.O. Box, CH-4009 Basel, Switzerland. TEL 061-3061111. FAX 061-3061234. *4698*

BLOOD THERAPY JOURNAL INTERNATIONAL.
Institute of Haematology, 11, 6-B Pusa Road, New Delhi 110 005, India. TEL 91-11-2246228. FAX 91-11-2247189. *4698*

BLOODSONGS.
Bambada Press, P.O. Box 7530, St. Kilda Rd., Melbourne, Vic. 3004, Australia. TEL 61-3-95762919. *4325*

BLUE BOOK OF CANADIAN BUSINESS.
Canadian Newspaper Services International Ltd., 90 Nolan Court 21, Markham, ON L3R 4L9, Canada. TEL 905-946-9588. FAX 905-946-9590. *1179*

BLUMEA.
Rijksherbarium - Hortus Botanicus, Publications Department, P.O. Box 9514, 2300 RA Leiden, Netherlands. *673*

BLUMEA. SUPPLEMENT.
Rijksherbarium - Hortus Botanicus, Publications Department, P.O. Box 9514, 2300 RA Leiden, Netherlands. *673*

BOCHUMER PHILOSOPHISCHES JAHRBUCH FUER ANTIKE UND MITTELALTER.
John Benjamins Publishing Co., Amsteldijk 44, P.O. Box 75577, 1070 AN Amsterdam, Netherlands. TEL 31-20-6762325. FAX 31-20-6792956. *5469*

BODY CONTOURING SURGERY.
Field & Wood, Medical Periodicals, Inc., Box 975, Blue Bell, PA 19422. TEL 610-828-4010. FAX 215-482-0226. *4505*

BOGAZICI JOURNAL: REVIEW OF SOCIAL, ECONOMIC AND ADMINISTRATIVE SCIENCES.
Bogazici Universitesi, Bebek, 80815 Istanbul, Turkey. TEL 90-212-2631500. FAX 90-212-2656479. *6316*

BOGTRYKKERNE - DISTRIKTSBLADENE.
Dansk Bogtrykker- og Presseforening, City Vest, P.O. Box 1559, DK-8220 Brabrand, Denmark. *5808*

BOIS ET FORETS DES TROPIQUES.
C I R A D - Foret, B.P. 5035, 34032 Montpellier cedex 1, France. TEL 67-74-58-00. *3011*

BOLETIN CHILENO DE PARASITOLOGIA.
Universidad de Chile, Departamento de Parasitologia, Casilla No. 9183, Santiago, Chile. TEL 56-2-7370081 ext. 5340 *4618*

BOLETIN DE FILOLOGIA.
Universidad de Chile, Departamento de Linguistica, Casilla 10136, Correo Central, Santiago, Chile. TEL 56-2-6787027. FAX 56-2-2716823. *4057*

BOLI YU TANGCI.
Zhongguo Qinggong Zonghui, Boli Tangci Yanjiusuo, No 6, Lane 365, Xinhua Lu, Shanghai 200052, People's Republic of China. TEL 2403230. *1652*

BOLLETTARIO.
Associazione Culturale "Le Avanguardie", Corso Camalchiaro 26-A, 41100 Modena, Italy. TEL 39-59-211791. *4188*

BOLLETTINO DEI CHIMICI IGIENISTI.
S.E.F. Editoriale S.r.l., Via Ausonio 12, 20123 Milan, Italy. TEL 63755. *1665*

BOLLETTINO DEL LAVORO E DEI TRIBUTI.
Casa Editrice Edis s.r.l. Via S. Franca 60, 29100 Piacenza, Italy. TEL 39-523-325684. FAX 39-523-336782. *3751*

BOLLETTINO DI PSICOLOGIA APPLICATA.
Organizzazioni Speciali Via Scipione Ammirato 37, 50136 Florence, Italy. TEL 39-55-672580. FAX 39-55-669446. *5831*

BOLLETTINO DI ZOOLOGIA AGRARIA E DI BACHICOLTURA.
Universita degli Studi di Milano, Istituto di Entomologia Agraria, Via Celoria 2, 20133 Milan, Italy. TEL 39-2-2362880. FAX 39-2-26680320. *722*

BOLLETTINO MALACOLOGICO.
Societa Italiana di Malacologia c/o Acquario Civico, Viale Gadio 2, 20121 Milan, Italy. FAX 39-2-800001. *800*

BOND LAW REVIEW.
Bond University, Law School, Robina, Qld. 4211, Australia. TEL 61-7-55951060. FAX 61-7-55952246. *3751*

BONE.
Elsevier Science Inc., Box 945, New York, NY 10159-0945. TEL 212-633-3730. FAX 212-633-3680. *4781*

THE BONE AND MINERAL RESEARCH ANNUAL.
Elsevier Science B.V., Books Division, P.O. Box 211, 1000 AE Amsterdam, Netherlands. TEL 31-20-4853911. FAX 31-20-4853705. *4781*

BOOK TRADE IN CANADA.
Ampersand Communications Inc., 5606 Scobie Crescent, Manotick, ON K4M 1B7, Canada. TEL 613-692-2080. FAX 613-692-1419. *5990*

BOOKS AT IOWA.
Friends of the University of Iowa Libraries, Iowa City, IA 52242. TEL 319-335-5921. FAX 319-335-5900. *3981*

BOOKS IN LIBRARY AND INFORMATION SCIENCE SERIES.
Marcel Dekker, Inc., 270 Madison Ave., New York, NY 10016. TEL 212-696-9000. FAX 212-685-4540. *4037*

BOOKS IN SOILS PLANTS AND THE ENVIRONMENT SERIES.
Marcel Dekker, Inc., 270 Madison Ave., New York, NY 10016. TEL 212-696-9000. FAX 212-685-4540. *213*

BOPUXUE ZAZHI.
Zhongguo Kexueyuan, Wuhan Wuli Yanjiusuo, P.O. Box 71010, Xiaohongshan, Wuchang-qu, Wuhan, Hubei 430071, People's Republic of China. TEL 86-27-786-7791. FAX 86-27-788-5291. *5602*

BORDER HEALTH.
Pan American Health Organization, El Paso Field Office, 6006 N. Mesa, Ste. 600, El Paso, TX 79912. TEL 915-581-6645. FAX 915-833-4768. *5956*

BORDER STATES.
American Studies Association, Kentucky-Tennessee Chapter, c/o Michael Dunne, Sarah Howell, Eds., Department of English, Middle Tennessee State University, Murfreesboro, TN 37132. TEL 615-898-2649. *3461*

BORDERLINES: STUDIES IN AMERICAN CULTURE.
University of Wales Press, 6 Gwennyth St., Cathays, Cardiff CF2 4YD, Wales. TEL 44-1222-231919. FAX 44-1222-230908. *4188*

BOSO NO KONCHU.
Chibaken Konchu Danwakai, c/o Mr. Yasutoshi Matsui, 3-102, 427-5 Nedo, Kashiwa-shi, Chiba-ken 277, Japan. *722*

BOSTON STUDIES IN APPLIED ECONOMICS.
Kluwer Academic Publishers, Postbus 17, 3300 AA Dordrecht, Netherlands. TEL 31-78-6392392. FAX 31-78-6392254. *1248*

BOSTON STUDIES IN THE PHILOSOPHY OF SCIENCE.
Kluwer Academic Publishers, Postbus 17, 3300 AA Dordrecht, Netherlands. TEL 31-78-6392392. FAX 31-78-6392254. *6231*

BOTANICA COMPLUTENSIS.
Universidad Complutense de Madrid, Departamento de Biologia Vegetal, Ciudad Universitaria, 28040 Madrid, Spain. TEL 34-1-3944402. FAX 34-1-3945034. *673*

THE BOTANICAL REVIEW.
New York Botanical Garden, Scientific Publications Department, Bronx, NY 10458-5126. TEL 718-817-8721. FAX 718-817-8842. *674*

BOUILLABAISSE.
Alpha Beat Press, 31 Waterloo St., New Hope, PA 18938. TEL 215-862-0299. *4134*

BOUNDARY ELEMENTS COMMUNICATIONS.
Computational Mechanics Publications, Ashurst Lodge, Ashurst, Southampton, Hants. SO40 7AA. TEL 44-1703-293223. FAX 44-1703-292853. *2625*

BOUNDARY-LAYER METEOROLOGY.
Kluwer Academic Publishers, Postbus 17, 3300 AA Dordrecht, Netherlands. TEL 31-78-6392392. FAX 31-78-6392254. *4992*

BOUNDARY 2.
Duke University Press, Box 90660, Durham, NC 27708-0660. TEL 919-687-3600. FAX 919-688-4574. *4188*

BRAHMS STUDIES.
University of Nebraska Press, 312 N. 14th St., Box 880484, Lincoln, NE 68588-0484. TEL 402-472-3581. FAX 402-472-6213. *5144*

BRAIN AND COGNITION.
Academic Press, Inc., Journal Division, 525 B St., Ste. 1900, San Diego, CA 92101-4495. TEL 619-230-1840. FAX 619-699-6800. *5831*

BRAIN AND DEVELOPMENT.
Elsevier Science B.V., P.O. Box 211, 1000 AE Amsterdam, Netherlands. TEL 31-20-4853911. FAX 31-20-4853598. *4828*

BRAIN AND LANGUAGE.
Academic Press, Inc., Journal Division, 525 B St., Ste. 1900, San Diego, CA 92101-4495. TEL 619-230-1840. FAX 619-699-6800. *5831*

BRAIN, BEHAVIOR AND EVOLUTION.
S. Karger AG, Allschwilerstr. 10, P.O. Box, CH-4009 Basel, Switzerland. TEL 061-3061111. FAX 061-3061234. *4828*

BRAIN, BEHAVIOR, AND IMMUNITY.
Academic Press, Inc., Journal Division, 525 B St., Ste. 1900, San Diego, CA 92101-4495. TEL 619-230-1840. FAX 619-699-6800. *4579*

BRAIN INJURY.
Taylor & Francis Ltd., 1 Gunpowder Sq., London EC4A 3DE, England. TEL 44-171-583-0490. FAX 44-171-583-0585. *4828*

BRAIN RESEARCH BULLETIN.
Elsevier Science Inc., Box 945, New York, NY 10159-0945. TEL 212-633-3730. FAX 212-633-3680. *4829*

BRAIN TOPOGRAPHY.
Human Sciences Press, Inc. 233 Spring St., New York, NY 10013-1578. TEL 212-620-8000. FAX 212-463-0742. *4829*

BRANCHING OUT FROM ST. CLAIR COUNTY, ILLINOIS.
Marissa Historical and Genealogical Society, Box 47, Marissa, IL 62257. TEL 618-295-3337. *3076*

BRASIL - BRAZIL.
Brown University, Department of Portuguese and Brazilian Studies, Box O, Providence, RI 02912. TEL 401-863-3042. FAX 401-863-7261. *4134*

BRAVO.
Bravo Editions, c/o John Edwin Cowen, Pub., 1081 Trafalgar St., Teaneck, NJ 07666. TEL 201-836-5922. *4302*

BRAZIL. SERVICO NACIONAL DE APRENDIZAGEM COMERCIAL. BOLETIM TECNICO.
Servico Nacional de Aprendizagem Comercial, Rua Dona Mariana, 48, 7 andar, Botafogo, 22280 Rio de Janeiro RJ, Brazil. FAX 55-21-2860645. *2316*

BRAZIL BUSINESS BRIEF.
Brazilian Chamber of Commerce, 32 Green St., London W1Y 3FD, England. TEL 44-171-499-0186. FAX 44-171-493-4621. *6870*

BRAZILIAN JOURNAL OF GENETICS.
Sociedade Brasileira de Genetica, Departamento de Genetica, Faculdade de Medicina de Ribeirao Preto, 14049-900 Riberao Preto SP, Brazil. TEL 55-16-6331610. FAX 55-16-6338631. *738*

BRAZILIAN JOURNAL OF PHYSICS.
Sociedade Brasileira de Fisica, Universidade de Sao Paulo, Instituto de Fisica, Rua do Mateo, Travessa R 187, 05508-900 Sao Paulo SP, Brazil. TEL 81-271-0111. FAX 081-2710359. *5543*

BREAD OF LIFE.
C.C.S.O. Bread of Life Renewal Centre, P.O. Box 395, Hamilton, ON L8N 3H8, Canada. TEL 416-529-4496. FAX 416-529-5373. *6171*

BREAST CANCER.
Field & Wood, Medical Periodicals, Inc., Box 975, Blue Bell, PA 19422. TEL 610-828-4010. FAX 215-482-0226. *4749*

BREAST CANCER RESEARCH AND TREATMENT.
Kluwer Academic Publishers Boston, Box 358, Accord Sta., Hingham, MA 02018-0358. TEL 617-871-6600. FAX 617-871-6528. *4749*

BREAST DISEASE.
Elsevier Science Inc., Box 945, New York, NY 10159-0945. TEL 212-633-3730. FAX 212-633-3680. *4436*

BREASTFEEDING REVIEW.
Nursing Mothers' Association of Australia, P.O. Box 231, Nunawading, Vic. 3131, Australia. TEL 61-3-98775011. FAX 61-3-9894-3270. *5230*

BREEDING SCIENCE.
Japanese Society of Breeding, c/o Faculty of Agriculture, University of Tokyo, Bunkyo-ku, Tokyo 113, Japan. TEL 03-3812-2111. FAX 03-3815-5851. *738*

BRETAGNE ECONOMIQUE.
Edition Bretagne Economique, 1 rue du General Guillaudot, 35044 Rennes Cedex, France. TEL 99-25-41-37. FAX 99-63-35-28. *1133*

BREWINGTECHNIQUES.
New Wine Press, Inc., 1127 Lincoln St., Eugene, OR 97401. TEL 541-687-2993. FAX 541-687-8534. *503*

BRILL'S INDOLOGICAL LIBRARY.
E.J. Brill, P.O. Box 9000, 2300 PA Leiden, Netherlands. TEL 31-71-5353500. FAX 31-71-5317532. *5280*

BRILL'S JAPANESE STUDIES LIBRARY.
E.J. Brill, P.O. Box 9000, 2300 PA Leiden, Netherlands. TEL 31-71-5353500. FAX 31-71-5317532. *5280*

BRILL'S SERIES IN JEWISH STUDIES.
E.J. Brill, P.O. Box 9000, 2300 PA Leiden, Netherlands. TEL 31-71-5353500. FAX 31-71-5317532. *6123*

BRILL'S STUDIES IN EPISTEMOLOGY, PSYCHOLOGY AND PSYCHIATRY.
E.J. Brill, P.O. Box 9000, 2300 PA Leiden, Netherlands. TEL 31-71-5353500. FAX 31-71-5317532. *5469*

BRILL'S STUDIES IN INTELLECTUAL HISTORY.
E.J. Brill, P.O. Box 9000, 2300 PA Leiden, Netherlands. TEL 31-71-5353500. FAX 31-71-5317532. *3608*

BRIMLEYANA.
North Carolina State Museum of Natural Sciences, 102 N. Salisbury St., Box 29555, Raleigh, NC 27626-0555. TEL 919-733-7450. *801*

BRITANNIA.
Society for the Promotion of Roman Studies, 31-34 Gordon Sq., London WC1H 0PP, England. TEL 44-171-387-8157. *3400*

BRITISH ACTUARIAL JOURNAL.
Institute of Actuaries, Staple Inn Hall, High Holborn, London WC1E 7QJ, England. TEL 44-171-242-0106. FAX 44-171-405-2482. *3643*

BRITISH ARACHNOLOGICAL SOCIETY. BULLETIN.
British Arachnological Society, c/o Dr. P. Merrett, Ed., 6 Hillcrest, Swanage, Dorset BH19 2HS, England. *801*

BRITISH ARCHAEOLOGICAL ASSOCIATION. JOURNAL.
W.S. Maney & Son Ltd., Hudson Rd., Leeds LS9 7DL, England. TEL 01532-497481. FAX 01532-486983. *347*

BRITISH ASSOCIATION FOR IMMEDIATE CARE. JOURNAL.
British Association for Immediate Care, 7 Black Horse Ln., Ipswich, Suffolk IP1 2EF, England. TEL 01473-218407. FAX 01473-280585. *4782*

BRITISH ASSOCIATION OF TEACHERS OF THE DEAF. JOURNAL.
British Association of Teachers of the Deaf, 41 The Orchard, Leven, N. Humberside HU17 5QA, England. TEL 44-1964-544243. *3311*

BRITISH ASTRONOMICAL ASSOCIATION. HANDBOOK.
British Astronomical Association, Burlington House, Piccadilly, London W1V 9AG, England. TEL 44-171-734-4145. *478*

BRITISH COLUMBIA. MINISTRY OF AGRICULTURE, FISHERIES AND FOOD. ANNUAL STATISTICS (YEAR).
Ministry of Agriculture, Fisheries and Food, Public Affairs Branch, Windsor Court, 808 Douglas St., Victoria, BC V8W 2Z7, Canada. TEL 604-387-7169. FAX 604-387-9105. *169*

BRITISH COLUMBIA GEOGRAPHICAL SERIES: OCCASIONAL PAPERS IN GEOGRAPHY.
University of British Columbia, Geography Department, 1984 West Mall, Rm. 217, Vancouver, BC V6T 1Z2, Canada. TEL 604-822-3511. FAX 604-822-6150. *3249*

BRITISH COLUMBIA MEDICAL JOURNAL.
British Columbia Medical Association, 115-1665 W. Broadway, Vancouver, BC V6J 5A4, Canada. TEL 604-736-5551. FAX 604-733-7317. *4436*

BRITISH DENTAL JOURNAL.
British Dental Association, 64 Wimpole St., London W1M 8AL, England. TEL 0171-935-0875. FAX 0171-224-0603. *4636*

BRITISH EDUCATIONAL RESEARCH JOURNAL.
Carfax Publishing Co., P.O. Box 25, Abingdon, Oxon. OX14 3UE, England. TEL 44-1235-400100. FAX 44-1235-401550. *2316*

BRITISH ELECTIONS AND PARTIES YEARBOOK.
Frank Cass, Newbury House, 890-900 Eastern Ave., Newbury Park, Ilford, Essex IG2 7HH, England. TEL 44-181-599-8866. FAX 44-181-599-0984. *5637*

BRITISH HOMOEOPATHIC JOURNAL.
Faculty of Homoeopathy, 2 Powis Pl., Great Ormond St., London WC1N 3HT, England. TEL 0171-833-1197. FAX 0171-278-7900. *4612*

BRITISH JOURNAL FOR THE HISTORY OF SCIENCE.
Cambridge University Press, Edinburgh Bldg., Shaftesbury Rd., Cambridge CB2 2RU, England. TEL 44-1223-312393. FAX 44-1223-315052. *6231*

THE BRITISH JOURNAL FOR THE PHILOSOPHY OF SCIENCE.
Oxford University Press, Oxford Journals, Walton St., Oxford OX2 6DP, England. TEL 44-1865-267907. FAX 44-1865-267773. *6231*

THE BRITISH JOURNAL OF AESTHETICS.
Oxford University Press, Oxford Journals, Walton St., Oxford OX2 6DP, England. TEL 44-1865-267907. FAX 44-1865-267773. *421*

BRITISH JOURNAL OF AUDIOLOGY.
Whurr Publishers Ltd., 19b Compton Terrace, London N1 2UN, England. TEL 44-171-359-5979. FAX 44-171-226-5290. *3311*

BRITISH JOURNAL OF BIOMEDICAL SCIENCE.
Royal Society of Medicine Press Ltd., 1 Wimpole St., London W1M 8AE, England. TEL 0171-290-2900. FAX 0171-290-2929. *4677*

BRITISH JOURNAL OF CANADIAN STUDIES.
British Association for Canadian Studies, 21 George Sq., Edinburgh EH8 9LD, Scotland. TEL 44-131-662-1117. FAX 44-131-662-1118. *6316*

BRITISH JOURNAL OF CLINICAL PHARMACOLOGY.
Blackwell Science Ltd., Osney Mead, Oxford OX2 OEL, England. TEL 44-1865-206206. FAX 44-1865-721205. *5402*

BRITISH JOURNAL OF CLINICAL PRACTICE.
Medicom (UK) Ltd., The Quadrant, 118 London Rd., Kingston-upon-Thames, Surrey KT2 6QJ, England. TEL 44-181-541-5666. FAX 44-181-541-4746. *4437*

BRITISH JOURNAL OF CLINICAL PRACTICE. SYMPOSIUM SUPPLEMENT.
Medicom (UK) Ltd., The Quadrant, 118 London Rd., Kingston-upon-Thames, Surrey KT2 6QJ, England. TEL 44-181-541-5666. FAX 44-181-541-4746. *4437*

BRITISH JOURNAL OF CLINICAL PSYCHOLOGY.
British Psychological Society, St. Andrew's House, 48 Princess Rd. E., Leicester LE1 7DR, England. TEL 44-116-254-9568. FAX 44-116-247-0787. *5831*

BRITISH JOURNAL OF CLINICAL RESEARCH.
Brookwood Medical Publications, Orchard House, Brookwood, Surrey GU24 OAT, England. TEL 44-1483-797975. FAX 44-1483-797915. *4437*

BRITISH JOURNAL OF DERMATOLOGY.
Blackwell Science Ltd., Osney Mead, Oxford OX2 OEL, England TEL 44-1865-206206. FAX 44-1865-721205. *4659*

BRITISH JOURNAL OF DEVELOPMENTAL DISABILITIES.
S E F A (Publications) Ltd., The Globe, 4 Great William St., Stratford-upon-Avon CV37 6RY, England. *2456*

BRITISH JOURNAL OF DEVELOPMENTAL PSYCHOLOGY.
British Psychological Society, St. Andrew's House, 48 Princess Rd. E. Leicester LE1 7DR, England. TEL 44-116-254-9568. FAX 44-116-247-0787. *5832*

BRITISH JOURNAL OF EDUCATIONAL PSYCHOLOGY.
British Psychological Society, St. Andrew's House, 48 Princess Rd. E. Leicester LE1 7DR, England. TEL 44-116-254-9568. FAX 44-116-247-0787. *5832*

BRITISH JOURNAL OF EDUCATIONAL STUDIES.
Blackwell Publishers Ltd., 108 Cowley Rd., Oxford OX4 1JF, England. TEL 44-1865-791100. FAX 44-1865-791347. *2316*

BRITISH JOURNAL OF EDUCATIONAL TECHNOLOGY.
Blackwell Publishers Ltd., 108 Cowley Rd., Oxford OX4 1FH, England. TEL 44-1865-244083. FAX 44-1865-381381. *2480*

BRITISH JOURNAL OF ETHNOMUSICOLOGY.
British Forum for Ethnomusicology, c/o Centre of Music Studies, School of Oriental and African Studies, Thornhaugh St., London WC1H 0XG, England. FAX 44-171-436-3844. *5145*

BRITISH JOURNAL OF GUIDANCE AND COUNSELLING.
Carfax Publishing Co., P.O. Box 25, Abingdon, Oxon OX14 3UE, England. TEL 44-1235-401000. FAX 44-1235-401550. *5263*

BRITISH JOURNAL OF HAEMATOLOGY.
Blackwell Science Ltd., Osney Mead, Oxford OX2 OEL, England. TEL 44-1865-206206. FAX 44-1865-721205. *4698*

BRITISH JOURNAL OF HEALTH PSYCHOLOGY.
British Psychological Society, St. Andrew's House, 48 Princess Rd. E., Leicester LE1 7DR, England. TEL 44-116-254-9568. FAX 44-116-247-0787. *5832*

BRITISH JOURNAL OF IN-SERVICE EDUCATION.
Triangle Journals Ltd., P.O. Box 65, Wallingford, Oxon. OX10 0YG, England. TEL 44-1491-838013. FAX 44-1491-834968. *2480*

BRITISH JOURNAL OF INDUSTRIAL RELATIONS.
Blackwell Publishers Ltd., 108 Cowley Rd., Oxford OX4 1JF, England. TEL 44-1865-791100. FAX 44-1865-791347. *1365*

BRITISH JOURNAL OF MANAGEMENT.
Blackwell Publishers Ltd., 108 Cowley Rd., Oxford OX4 1JF, England. TEL 44-1865-791100. FAX 44-1865-791347. *1408*

BRITISH JOURNAL OF MATHEMATICAL AND STATISTICAL PSYCHOLOGY.
British Psychological Society, St. Andrew's House, 48 Princess Rd. E., Leicester LE1 7DR, England. TEL 44-116-254-9568. FAX 44-116-247-0787. *5832*

BRITISH JOURNAL OF MEDICAL ECONOMICS.
Brookwood Medical Publications, Orchard House, Brookwood, Surrey GU24 OAT, England. TEL 44-1483-797975. FAX 44-1483-797915. *4437*

BRITISH JOURNAL OF MEDICAL PSYCHOLOGY.
British Psychological Society, St. Andrew's House, 48 Princess Rd. E., Leicester LE1 7DR, England. TEL 44-116-254-9568. FAX 44-116-247-0787. *5832*

BRITISH JOURNAL OF NEUROSURGERY.
Carfax Publishing Co., P.O. Box 25, Abingdon, Oxon. OX14 3UE, England. TEL 44-1235-401000. FAX 44-1235-401550. *4905*

BRITISH JOURNAL OF OBSTETRICS & GYNAECOLOGY.
Blackwell Science Ltd., Osney Mead, Oxford OX2 OEL, England. TEL 44-1865-206206. FAX 44-1865-721205. *4733*

BRITISH JOURNAL OF OCCUPATIONAL THERAPY.
College of Occupational Therapists Ltd., 6-8 Marshalsea Rd., Southwark, London SE1 1HL, England. TEL 44-171-357-6480. FAX 44-171-378-8095. *4437*

BRITISH JOURNAL OF OPHTHALMOLOGY.
B M J Publishing Group, B.M.A. House, Tavistock Sq., London WC1H 9JR, England. TEL 44-171-383-6270. FAX 44-171-383-6402. *4767*

BRITISH JOURNAL OF PHYSICAL EDUCATION. RESEARCH SUPPLEMENT.
Physical Education Association of the United Kingdom, Ste. 5, 10 Churchill Sq., Kings Hill, W. Malling, Kent ME19 4DU, England. TEL 44-1732-875888. FAX 44-1732-875777. *2481*

BRITISH JOURNAL OF PHYTOTHERAPY.
School of Phytotherapy, Bucksteep Manor, Bodle St. Green, Near Hailsham, E. Sussex BN27 4RJ, England. TEL 44-1323-833812. FAX 44-1323-833869. *289*

BRITISH JOURNAL OF PSYCHIATRY.
Royal College of Psychiatrists, 17 Belgrave Sq., London SW1X 8PG, England. TEL 44-171-235-8857. FAX 44-171-245-1231. *4829*

BRITISH JOURNAL OF PSYCHOLOGY.
British Psychological Society, St. Andrew's House, 48 Princess Rd. E., Leicester LE1 7DR, England. TEL 44-166-254-9568. FAX 44-166-247-0737. *5832*

BRITISH JOURNAL OF RELIGIOUS EDUCATION.
Christian Education Movement, Royal Bldgs., Victoria St., Derby DE1 1GW, England. TEL 44-1332-296655. FAX 44-1332-343253. *6048*

BRITISH JOURNAL OF RHEUMATOLOGY.
Oxford University Press, Oxford Journals, Walton St., Oxford OX2 6DP, England. TEL 01865-267907. FAX 01865-267773. *2893*

BRITISH JOURNAL OF SOCIAL PSYCHOLOGY.
British Psychological Society, St. Andrew's House, 48 Princess Rd. E., Leicester LE1 7DR, England. TEL 44-116-2549568. FAX 44-116-2470787. *5832*

BRITISH JOURNAL OF SOCIOLOGY OF EDUCATION.
Carfax Publishing Co., P.O. Box 25, Abingdon. Oxon. OX14 3UE, England. TEL 44-1235-401000. FAX 44-1235-401550. *2317*

BRITISH JOURNAL OF SPORTS MEDICINE.
B M J Publishing Group, B.M.A. House, Tavistock Sq., London WC1H 9JP, England. TEL 44-171-383-6270. FAX 44-171-383-6402. *4897*

BRITISH JOURNAL OF SURGERY.
Blackwell Science Ltd., Osney Mead, Oxford OX2 OEL, England. TEL 44-1865-206206. FAX 44-1865-721205. *4905*

BRITISH JOURNAL OF UROLOGY.
Blackwell Science Ltd., Osney Mead, Oxford OX2 OEL, England. TEL 44-1865-206206. FAX 44-1865-721205. *4925*

BRITISH POULTRY SCIENCE.
Carfax Publishing Co., P.O. Box 25, Abingdon. Oxon. OX14 3UE, England. TEL 44-1235-401000. FAX 44-1235-401550. *267*

BRITISH PSYCHOLOGICAL SOCIETY. EDUCATION SECTION. REVIEW.
British Psychological Society, St. Andrew's House, 48 Princess Rd. E., Leicester LE1 7DR, England. TEL 44-116-254-9568. FAX 44-116-247-0787. *2317*

BRITISH SCHOOL AT ATHENS. ANNUAL.
British School at Athens, 31-34 Gordon Sq., London WC1H OPY, England. TEL 44-171-387-8029. FAX 44-171-383-0781. *347*

BRITISH VETERINARY JOURNAL.
Bailliere Tindall - W.B. Saunders Co. Ltd. 24-28 Oval Rd., London NW1 7DX, England. TEL 44-171-485-4752. FAX 44-171-267-4466. *6943*

BRITTONIA.
New York Botanical Garden, Scientific Publications Department, Bronx, NY 10458-5126. TEL 718-871-8721. FAX 718-817-8842. *674*

BROMATOLOGIA I CHEMIA TOKSYKOLOGICZNA.
Polskie Towarzystwo Farmaceutyczne, Ul. Dluga 16, 00-238 Warsaw, Poland. TEL 48-22-310241. *5402*

BROMELIAD SOCIETY. JOURNAL.
Bromeliad Society, Inc., 720 Millertown Rd., Auburn, CA 95603. TEL 407-896-3722. *675*

BRONCHIAL MUCOLOGY SERIES.
Lippincott - Raven Publishers 227 E. Washington Sq., New York, NY 10036. TEL 212-930-9500. FAX 212-869-3495. *4886*

BROOKHAVEN SYMPOSIA IN BIOLOGY.
Plenum Publishing Corp., 233 Spring St., New York, NY 10013-1578. TEL 212-620-8000. FAX 212-463-0742. *575*

BROWN BOVERI SYMPOSIA. PROCEEDINGS.
Plenum Publishing Corp., 233 Spring St., New York, NY 10013-1578. TEL 212-620-8000. FAX 212-463-0742. *2685*

BRUNSWICKAN.
University of New Brunswick, Student Union, P.O. Box 4400, Fredericton, NB E3B 5A3, Canada. TEL 506-453-4983. FAX 506-458-4958. *1859*

BRUSSELS SPROUT.
6944 S.E. 33rd St., Mercer Island, WA 98040-3324. TEL 206-232-3239. *4302*

BRYN MAWR CLASSICAL REVIEW.
Bryn Mawr Commentaries, Inc., Bryn Mawr College, Thomas Library, Bryn Mawr, PA 19010. TEL 215-526-5384. FAX 215-526-7475. *1819*

BRYN MAWR MEDIEVAL REVIEW.
Bryn Mawr Commentaries, Inc., Bryn Mawr College, Thomas Library, Bryn Mawr, PA 19010. TEL 215-526-5384. *3400*

BRYN MAWR REVIEWS.
Bryn Mawr Commentaries, Inc., Bryn Mawr College, Thomas Library, Bryn Mawr, PA 19010. TEL 215-526-5384. *3400*

BRYOLOGIST.
American Bryological & Lichenological Society, c/o Robert J. Thomas, Sec.-Treas., Department of Biology, Bates College, Lewiston, ME 04240. TEL 207-786-6105. FAX 207-786-6035. *675*

BUDAPEST STUDIES IN ARABIC.
Eotvos Lorand University, Chair for Arabic Studies, Muzeum kit. 4-b, 1088 Budapest, Hungary. *4057*

BUDDHIST - CHRISTIAN STUDIES.
University of Hawaii Press, Journals Department, 2840 Kolowalu St., Honolulu, HI 96822. TEL 808-956-8833. FAX 808-988-6052. *6109*

BUENA VISTA TODAY.
Buena Vista University, 610 W. Fourth St., Storm Lake, IA 50588. TEL 712-749-2120. FAX 712-749-1459. *1859*

BUILDING ACOUSTICS.
Multi-Science Publishing Co. Ltd., 107 High St., Brentwood, Essex CM14 4RX, England. TEL 44-1277-224632. FAX 44-1277-223453. *5614*

BUILDING AND ENVIRONMENT.
Elsevier Science Ltd., Pergamon, P.O. Box 800, Kidlington, Oxford OX5 1DX, England. TEL 44-1865-843000. FAX 44-1865-843010. *839*

BUILDING RESEARCH AND INFORMATION.
Chapman & Hall, Journals Department 2-6 Boundary Row, London SE1 8HN, England. TEL 44-171-8650066. FAX 44-171-5229623. *841*

BULLAN.
Hertford College, Oxford OX1 3BW, England. TEL 44-1865-58236. *3400*

BULLDADA.
Box 80204, Indianapolis, IN 46280-0204. TEL 317-875-7149. *4135*

BULLETIN DE LA COMMUNICATION PARLEE.
Institut de la Communication Parlee, Universite Stendhal, B.P. 25 X, 38040 Grenoble Cedex, France. TEL 33-76-57-47-10. FAX 33-76-57-48-26. *4058*

BULLETIN DES SOCIETES CHIMIQUES BELGES.
Comite van Beheer van het Bulletin v.z.w., Krijgslaan 281, S-12, B-9000 Ghent, Belgium. TEL 32-9-2644831. FAX 32-9-2644992. *1666*

BULLETIN DU CANCER.
Editions Scientifiques et Medicales Elsevier, 141 rue de Javel, 75747 Paris, France. TEL 33-1-45589026. FAX 33-1-45589421. *4749*

BULLETIN DU CANCER - RADIOTHERAPIE.
Editions Scientifiques et Medicales Elsevier, 141 rue de Javel, 75747 Paris, France. TEL 33-1-45589026. FAX 33-1-45589421. *4749*

BULLETIN FOR BIBLICAL RESEARCH.
Institute for Biblical Research, Box 275, Winona Lake, IN 46590-0275. TEL 219-269-2011. FAX 219-269-6788. *6049*

BULLETIN OF BEEF CATTLE SCIENCE.
Showado Publishing Company, c/o Department of Animal Science, College of Agriculture, Kyoto University, Kyoto 606, Japan. TEL 75-753-6054. FAX 075-753-6344. *267*

BULLETIN OF CONCERNED ASIAN SCHOLARS.
Bulletin of Concerned Asian Scholars, Inc., 3239 Ninth St., Boulder, CO 80304-2112. TEL 303-449-7439. *5743*

BULLETIN OF ECONOMIC RESEARCH.
Blackwell Publishers Ltd., 108 Cowley Rd., Oxford OX4 1JF, England. TEL 44-1865-791100. FAX 44-1865-791347. *899*

BULLETIN OF ENVIRONMENTAL CONTAMINATION AND TOXICOLOGY.
Springer-Verlag, Life Science Journals, 175 Fifth Ave., New York, NY 10010. TEL 212-460-1500. FAX 212-473-6272. *2843*

BULLETIN OF EXPERIMENTAL BIOLOGY AND MEDICINE.
Plenum Publishing Corp., Consultants Bureau, 233 Spring St., New York, NY 10013-1578. TEL 212-620-8468. FAX 212-463-0742. *575*

THE BULLETIN OF HISTORICAL RESEARCH IN MUSICAL EDUCATION.
University of Kansas, M E M T Division, 311 Baily Hall, Lawrence, KS 66045-2344. TEL 913-864-4784. FAX 913-864-5076. *5145*

BULLETIN OF INFORMATICS AND CYBERNETICS.
Tokei Kagaku Kenkyukai, c/o Kyushu University 33, 10-1, Hakozaki 6-chome, Higashi-ku, Fukuoka 812, Japan. TEL 81-92-642-2697. FAX 81-92-642-2698. *4358*

BULLETIN OF LATIN AMERICAN RESEARCH.
Elsevier Science Ltd., Pergamon, P.O. Box 800, Kidlington, Oxford OX5 1DX, England. TEL 44-1865-843000. FAX 44-1865-843010. *6316*

BULLETIN OF MARINE SCIENCE.
Rosenstiel School of Marine and Atmospheric Science, 4600 Rickenbacker Causeway, Miami, FL 33149. TEL 305-361-4190. *2291*

BULLETIN OF MATHEMATICAL BIOLOGY.
Elsevier Science Inc., Box 945, New York, NY 10159-0945. TEL 212-633-3730. FAX 212-633-3680. *575*

THE BULLETIN OF SCIENCE, TECHNOLOGY & SOCIETY.
S T S Press, 102 Materials Research Laboratory, Pennsylvania State University, University Park, PA 16802. TEL 814-865-1137. FAX 814-863-7040. *6231*

BULLETIN OF THE BELGIAN MATHEMATICAL SOCIETY - SIMON STEVIN.
Belgian Mathematical Society, c/o Prof. Jules Leroy, Sec., Campus Plaine, C.P. 218-01, Bd. du Triomphe, 1050 Brussels, Belgium. TEL 32-2-6505845. FAX 32-2-6505867. *4358*

BULLETIN OF THE CANTIGUEIROS.
Society of the Cantigueiros de Santa Maria, Department of Romance Languages - ML 377, University of Cincinnati, Cincinnati, OH 45221. TEL 513-556-1836. FAX 513-556-2577. *6049*

BULLETIN OF THE COMEDIANTES.
University of California at Riverside, Department of Spanish & Portuguese, Riverside, CA 92521-0222. TEL 909-787-7334. FAX 909-787-2294. *4189*

BULLETIN OF ZOOLOGICAL NOMENCLATURE.
International Commission on Zoological Nomenclature, c/o Natural History Museum, Cromwell Rd., London. TEL 44-171-938-9387. *801*

BULLETIN SUBTERRANEA BRITANNICA.
C N H S S Ltd., 96A Brighton Rd., S. Croydon, Surrey CR2 6AD, England. TEL 0181-654-8507. FAX 0181-656-9755. *348*

BULLETINS OF AMERICAN PALEONTOLOGY.
Paleontological Research Institution, 1259 Trumansburg Rd., Ithaca, NY 14850-1398. TEL 607-273-6623. FAX 607-273-6620. *5312*

BUNYAN STUDIES.
Open University, Faculty of Arts, Parsifal College, 527 Finchley Rd., London NW3 7BG, England. TEL 44-171-794-0575. FAX 44-171-433-6196. *4189*

BURLINGTON MAGAZINE.
Burlington Magazine Publications Ltd., 14-16 Duke's Rd., London WC1H 9AD, England. TEL 44-171-388-1228. FAX 44-171-388-1230. *421*

BURNS.
Butterworth - Heinemann, Part of the Reed Elsevier group, Linacre House, Jordan Hill, Oxford OX2 8DP, England. TEL 44-1865-310366. FAX 44-1865-310898. *4782*

BUSINESS & ECONOMIC REPORT & KANSAS ECONOMIC INDICATORS.
Wichita State University, W. Frank Barton School of Business, Wichita, KS 67260-0121. TEL 316-689-3225. FAX 316-689-3950. *1180*

BUSINESS & PROFESSIONAL ETHICS JOURNAL.
Box 15017, Gainesville, FL 32604. TEL 904-392-2084. FAX 904-392-5577. *5470*

BUSINESS AND SOCIETY.
Sage Publications, Inc., 2455 Teller Rd., Thousand Oaks, CA 91320. TEL 805-499-0721. FAX 805-499-0871. *899*

BUSINESS CHANGE AND RE-ENGINEERING.
John Wiley & Sons Ltd., Journals, Baffins Ln., Chichester, W. Sussex PO19 1UD, England. TEL 44-1243-779777. FAX 44-1243-843232. *1408*

BUSINESS COMPUTER DIGEST.
Association of Computer Users, Box 2189, Berkeley, CA 94702-0189. TEL 303-241-0125. *1152*

BUSINESS ESPIONAGE REPORT.
Business Espionage Controls & Countermeasures Association (BECCA), Box 55582, Seattle, WA 98155-0582. TEL 206-364-4672. FAX 206-367-3316. *1266*

BUSINESS ETHICS.
Blackwell Publishers Ltd., 108 Cowley Rd., Oxford OX4 1JF, England. TEL 44-1865-791100. FAX 44-1865-791347. *901*

BUSINESS, GROWTH & PROFITABILITY.
Henry Stewart Publications, Russell House, 28-30 Little Russell St., London WC1A 2HN, England. TEL 44-171-404-3040. FAX 44-171-404-2081. *1573*

BUSINESS HISTORY.
Frank Cass, Newbury House, 890-900 Eastern Ave., Newbury Park, Ilford, Essex IG2 7HH, England. TEL 44-181-599-8866. FAX 44-181-599-0984. *901*

BUSINESS LIBRARY REVIEW.
Gordon and Breach Science Publishers, c/o International Publishers Distributor, P.O. Box 3054, Langhorne, PA 19047-3054. TEL 215-750-2642. FAX 215-750-6343. *1072*

BUSINESS STUDIES ON THE U.S.S.R.
Gordon and Breach Science Publishers, c/o International Publishers Distributor, P.O. Box 3054, Langhorne, PA 19047-3054. TEL 215-750-2642. FAX 215-750-6343. *1267*

BUSINESS TRAVELLER.
Perry Publications (Holdings) PLC, 22 Redan Pl., London W2 4SZ, England. TEL 44-171-229-7799. FAX 44-171-229-9441. *6971*

BUSINESS VALUATION REVIEW.
American Society of Appraisers, Business Valuation Committee, Box 101923, Denver, CO 80250. TEL 303-758-6148. *1073*

BUSSEI KENKYU.
Bussei Kenkyu Kankokai, c/o Kyoto Daigaku Yukawa Kinenkan, Kitashirakawa Oiwake-cho, Sakyo-ku, Kyoto 606, Japan. TEL 075-722-3540. FAX 075-722-6339. *5543*

BUTSURI KYOIKU.
Physics Education Society of Japan, P.O. Box 29, Koishikawa Yubbinkyoku, Tokyo 112, Japan. TEL 81-3-3942-0875. *5543*

BUTSURIGAKUSHI.
Butsurigakushi Kenkyukai, c/o Tomohiro Hyodo, Faculty of Business Administration, Ritsumeikan University, 56-1 Toji-in Kitamachi, Kita-ku, Kyoto 603-77, Japan. TEL 81-75-465-1111. FAX 81-75-465-7883. *5543*

BYZANTINA AUSTRALIENSIA.
Australian Association for Byzantine Studies, University of Sydney, Department of Modern Greek, Sydney, N.S.W. 2006, Australia. TEL 61-2-3513658. FAX 61-2-3513543. *3401*

BYZANTINA NEERLANDICA.
E.J. Brill, P.O. Box 9000, 2300 PA Leiden, Netherlands. TEL 31-71-5353500. FAX 31-71-5317532. *3401*

BYZANTINE AND MODERN GREEK STUDIES.
c/o Prof. Anthony Bryer, Centre for Byzantine, Ottoman and Modern Greek Studies, University of Birmingham, P.O. Box 363, Birmingham B15 2TT, England. TEL 44-121-414-5775. FAX 44-121-414-3656. *3401*

BYZANTINOSLAVICA.
John Benjamins Publishing Co., Amsteldijk 44, P.O. Box 75577, 1070 AN Amsterdam, Netherlands. TEL 31-20-6738156. FAX 31-20-6792956. *5280*

C A L I C O JOURNAL.
Computer Assisted Language & Instruction Consortium, 014 Language Bldg., Box 90267, Duke University, Durham, NC 27708-0267. TEL 919-660-3180. FAX 919-660-3183. *2404*

C A L M SCIENCE.
Department of Conservation and Land Management, P.O. Box 104, Como, W.A. 6152, Australia. TEL 61-9-334-0333. FAX 61-9-334-8296. *2122*

C A T M O G.
Environmental Publications, c/o R.A. Cullington, School of Environmental Sciences, University of East Anglia, Norwich NR4 7TJ, England. TEL 44-1603-592560. FAX 44-1603-507719. *3249*

C A U T BULLETIN.
Canadian Association of University Teachers, 2675 Queensview Dr., Ottawa, ON K2B 8K2, Canada. TEL 613-820-2270. FAX 613-820-2417. *2421*

C B M S - N S F REGIONAL CONFERENCE SERIES IN APPLIED MATHEMATICS.
Society for Industrial and Applied Mathematics, 3600 University City Science Center, Philadelphia, PA 19104-2688. TEL 215-382-9800. FAX 215-386-7999. *4358*

C C L.
Canadian Children's Press, University of Guelph, Department of English, Guelph, ON N1G 2W1, Canada. TEL 519-824-4120. FAX 519-837-1315. *5992*

C E D E J EGYPTE - MONDE ARABE.
Centre d'Etudes et de Documentation Economique, Juridique et Sociale. 14 Sharia Gameyet al-Nisr, Mohandessin, Cairo. Egypt. TEL 3611932. FAX 3493518. *5638*

C E M S BUSINESS REVIEW.
Kluwer Academic Publishers Boston, Box 358, Accord Sta., Hingham, MA 02018-0358. TEL 617-871-6600. FAX 617-871-6528. *1409*

C E P S PAPERS.
Centre for European Policy Studies, Place du Congres 1, 1000 Brussels, Belgium. TEL 32-2-2182247. FAX 32-2-2293911. *5743*

C E P S WORKING DOCUMENTS.
Centre for European Policy Studies, Place du Congres 1, 1000 Brussels, Belgium. TEL 32-2-2182247. FAX 32-2-2293911. *5743*

C E U PRIVATIZATION REPORTS.
Central European University Press, Nador u. 9, 1051 Budapest, Hungary. TEL 36-1-1762333. FAX 36-1-1762778. *1248*

C H R I A NEWS.
Committee for Health Rights in the Americas, 474 Valencia St., Ste. 120, San Francisco, CA 94103-3415. TEL 415-431-7760. FAX 415-431-7768. *1302*

C I M A QUESTIONS AND SUGGESTED ANSWERS.
Chartered Institute of Management Accountants, 63 Portland Pl., London W1N 4AB, England. TEL 44-171-917-9229. FAX 44-171-631-5309. *1042*

C I M BULLETIN.
Canadian Institute of Mining, Metallurgy & Petroleum, Xerox Tower, 3400 de Maisonneuve Blvd. W., Ste. 1210, Montreal, PQ H3Z 3B8, Canada. TEL 514-939-2710. FAX 514-939-2714. *5059*

C I R M.
Centro Internazionale Radio-Medico, Via Architettura 41, 00144 Rome, Italy. TEL 39-6-5923331. FAX 39-6-5923333. *4438*

C I S NEWS.
Chemical Information Systems, Inc., 810 Glen Eagles Ct., Ste. 300, Baltimore, MD 21286-2203. TEL 410-321-8440. FAX 410-296-0712. *1723*

C L A O JOURNAL.
Kellner-McCaffery Associates, Inc., 150 Fifth Ave., New York, NY 10011. TEL 212-741-0280. *4768*

C M A J.
Canadian Medical Association, P.O. Box 8650, Ottawa, ON K1G 0G8, Canada. TEL 613-731-9331. FAX 613-523-0937. *4438*

C N L.
Colonial Newsletter Foundation, Inc., Box 4411, Huntsville, AL 35815. TEL 205-881-8678. *5223*

C N S DRUGS.
Adis International Limited, Private Bag 65901, Mairangi Bay, Auckland 10, New Zealand. TEL 64-9-479-8100. FAX 64-9-479-8145. *5403*

C N S: THE JOURNAL FOR ADVANCED NURSING PRACTICE.
Williams & Wilkins, 351 W. Camden St., Baltimore, MD 21201. TEL 410-528-4000. FAX 410-528-4312. *4711*

C O R E.
Carfax Publishing Co., P.O. Box 25, Abingdon, Oxon. OX14 3UE, England. TEL 44-1235-401000. FAX 44-1235-401550. *2317*

C O S P A R INFORMATION BULLETIN.
Elsevier Science Ltd., Pergamon, P.O. Box 800, Kidlington, Oxford OX5 1DX, England. TEL 44-1865-843000. FAX 44-1865-843010. *60*

C T L R.
Sweet & Maxwell, Mill St. Oxford OX2 0JU, England. TEL 44-1865-249248. FAX 44-1865-792301. *1897*

C THEORY.
Concordia University, 1455 de Maisonneuve West, Montreal, PQ H3G 1M8, Canada. TEL 514-282-9298. FAX 514-987-9724. *5E38*

C U N Y FORUM.
City University of New York, Ph.D. Program in Linguistics, Graduate Center, 33 W. 42nd St., New York, NY 10036-8099. TEL 212-642-2154. FAX 212-642-2595. *4059*

C W I MONOGRAPHS.
Elsevier Science B.V., Books Division, P.O. Box 211, 1000 AE Amsterdam, Netherlands. TEL 31-20-4853911. *4408*

CA - A CANCER JOURNAL FOR CLINICIANS.
Lippincott - Raven Publishers 227 E. Washington Sq., Philadelphia, PA 19106. TEL 215-238-4200. *4749*

CACTACEAS Y SUCULENTAS MEXICANAS.
Sociedad Mexicana de Cactologia, A.C., 2da. de Juarez, No. 42, Colonia San Alvaro, 02090 Mexico, D.F. Mexico. TEL 3411796. *675*

CADERNOS DO PATRIMONIO CULTURAL.
Secretaria Municipal de Cultura, Departamento Geral do Patrimonio Cultural, Rua Afonso Cavalcanti, 455, sala 207, 20211-110 Cidade Nova, Rio de Janeiro RJ Brazil. TEL 55-21-2734095. FAX 55-21-5032158. *6317*

CADUCEUS.
S I U School of Medicine, Department of the Medical Humanities, The Pearson Museum, Box 19230, Springfield, IL 62794-9230. FAX 217-782-9132. *5119*

CAHIER TECHNIQUE DU BIOLOG STE.
Centre National des Biologistes, 80, Av. du Maine, 75014 Paris, France. TEL 43-22-97-70. FAX 43-21-73-12. *576*

CAHIERS DE DROIT EUROPEEN.
Bruylant, 67 rue de la Regence 1000 Brussels, Belgium. TEL 32-2-5123845. FAX 32-2-5117202. *3925*

CAHIERS DE L'IROISE.
Societe d'Etudes de Brest et du Leon, Rue des Archives, 29200 Brest, France. *3401*

CAHIERS DE LINGUISTIQUE ASIE ORIENTALE.
Centre de Recherches Linguistiques sur l'Asie Orientale, 54 bd. Raspail, 75006 Paris, France. TEL 49-54-24-35. FAX 49-54-26-71. *4059*

CAHIERS DE MEDECINE DU TRAVAIL.
Association Professionnelle Belge des Medecins du Travail, Ave. de Venus 14, 1410 Waterloo, Belgium. TEL 32-2-3547775. FAX 32-2-3510451. *5246*

CAHIERS ELISABETHAINS.
Universite de Montpellier (Universite Paul Valery), Centre d'Etudes et de Recherches Elisabethaines, B.P. 5043, Route de Mende, 34032 Montpellier, France. TEL 67-14-24-49. FAX 67-14-24-65. *3401*

CAHIERS HENRI BOSCO.
Amitie Henri Bosco, Palais Aurore, 33 bd. Tzarewitch, 06000 Nice, France. *4190*

CAHIERS HOSPITALIERS.
Berger - Levrault, 5 rue Auguste-Comte, 75006 Paris, France. TEL 44071494. FAX 44071525. *3541*

CAHIERS LINGUISTIQUES D'OTTAWA.
University of Ottawa, Department of Linguistics, P.O. Box 450, Stn. A, Ottawa, ON K1N 6N5, Canada. TEL 613-564-4207. FAX 613-564-9067. *4059*

CAHIERS SOCIALE GESCHIEDENIS.
Uitgeverij Verloren, Larenseweg 123, 1221 CL Hilversum, Netherlands. TEL 31-35-6859856. FAX 31-35-6836557. *3401*

CALCIFIED TISSUE INTERNATIONAL.
Springer-Verlag, Medical Journals, 175 Fifth Ave., New York, NY 10010. TEL 212-460-1500. FAX 212-473-6272. *4666*

CALCUTTA HISTORICAL JOURNAL.
K.P. Bagchi & Company, 286 B.B. Ganpuli St., Calcutta 700 012, India. TEL 91-33-26-7474. FAX 91-33-2482973. *3378*

CALIFORNIA ACADEMY OF SCIENCES. ACADEMY NEWSLETTER.
California Academy of Sciences, Golden Gate Park, San Francisco, CA 94118. TEL 415-750-7142. *5119*

CALIFORNIA ACADEMY OF SCIENCES. MEMOIRS.
California Academy of Sciences, Golden Gate Park, San Francisco, CA 94118. TEL 415-750-7243. *576*

CALIFORNIA ACADEMY OF SCIENCES. PROCEEDINGS.
California Academy of Sciences, Golden Gate Park, San Francisco, CA 94118. TEL 415-750-7243. *576*

CALIFORNIA CHIROPRACTIC ASSOCIATION JOURNAL.
California Chiropractic Association, 7801 Folsom Blvd., Ste. 375, Sacramento, CA 95826. TEL 916-387-0177. FAX 916-387-6222. *4612*

CALIFORNIA COOPERATIVE OCEANIC FISHERIES INVESTIGATIONS REPORTS.
California Cooperative Oceanic Fisheries Investigations, Scripps Institution of Oceanography, University of California, La Jolla, CA 92093-0227. TEL 619-534-4236. FAX 619-534-6500. *2928*

CALIFORNIA FAMILY PHYSICIAN.
California Academy of Family Physicians, 114 Sansome St., Ste. 1305, San Francisco, CA 94104-3824. TEL 415-394-9121. FAX 415-394-9119. *4439*

CALIFORNIA HISTORY (SAN FRANCISCO).
California Historical Society, 678 Mission St., San Francisco, CA 94103. TEL 415-357-1848. *3462*

CALIFORNIA INSECT SURVEY. BULLETIN.
University of California Press, 2120 Berkeley Way, Berkeley, CA 94720. TEL 510-642-4247. FAX 510-643-7127. *722*

CALIFORNIA LAW REVIEW.
University of California Press, Journals Division, 2120 Berkeley Way, No. 5812, Berkeley, CA 94720-5812. TEL 510-643-7154. FAX 510-642-9917. *3755*

CALIFORNIA MANAGEMENT REVIEW.
University of California at Berkeley, S549 Haas School of Business, Ste. 1900, Berkeley, CA 94720-1900. TEL 510-642-7159. FAX 510-642-1318. *1410*

CALIFORNIA NATURAL HISTORY GUIDES.
University of California Press, 2120 Berkeley Way, Berkeley, CA 94720. TEL 510-642-4247. FAX 510-643-7127. *576*

CALIFORNIA READER.
California Reading Association, 3186 Airway Ave., Ste. D, Costa Mesa, CA 92626-4650. TEL 714-880-5605. FAX 714-435-0269. *2481*

CALIFORNIA SCHOOLS.
California School Board Association, 3100 Beacon Blvd., Box 1660, W. Sacramento, CA 95819. TEL 916-371-4691. FAX 916-371-3407. *2317*

CALIFORNIA SERIES ON SOCIAL CHOICE & POLITICAL ECONOMY.
University of California Press, 2120 Berkeley Way, Berkeley, CA 94720. TEL 510-643-7127. FAX 510-643-7127. *5639*

CALIFORNIA STUDIES IN THE HISTORY OF ART.
University of California Press, 2120 Berkeley Way, Berkeley, CA 94720. TEL 510-642-4247. FAX 510-643-7127. *422*

CALIFORNIA STUDIES IN THE HISTORY OF SCIENCE.
University of California Press, 2120 Berkeley Way, Berkeley, CA 94720. TEL 510-642-4247. FAX 510-643-7127. *6232*

CALIFORNIA STUDIES IN 19TH CENTURY MUSIC.
University of California Press, 2120 Berkeley Way, Berkeley, CA 94720. TEL 510-642-4247. FAX 510-643-7127. *5146*

CALIFORNIA VETERINARIAN.
California Veterinary Medical Association, 5231 Madison Ave., Sacramento, CA 95841. TEL 916-344-4985. FAX 916-344-6147. *6943*

CALPHAD.
Elsevier Science Ltd., Pergamon, P.O. Box 800, Kidlington, Oxford OX5 1DX, England. TEL 44-1865-843000. FAX 44-1865-843010. *1723*

CALVIN THEOLOGICAL JOURNAL.
Calvin Theological Seminary, 3233 Burton St. S.E., Grand Rapids, MI 49546. TEL 616-957-6010. FAX 616-957-8621. *6136*

CALYX.
Calyx, Inc., Box B, Corvallis, OR 97339. TEL 541-753-9384. FAX 541-753-0515. *422*

CAMBRIDGE ANTIQUARIAN SOCIETY. PROCEEDINGS.
Cambridge Antiquarian Society, Museum of Archaeology and Anthropology, Downing St., Cambridge CB2 3DZ, England. FAX 01223-333503. *3402*

CAMBRIDGE ARCHAEOLOGICAL JOURNAL.
Cambridge University Press, Edinburgh Bldg., Shaftesbury Rd., Cambridge CB2 2RU, England. TEL 44-1223-312393. FAX 44-1223-315052. *348*

CAMBRIDGE JOURNAL OF EDUCATION.
Carfax Publishing Co., P.O. Box 25, Abingdon, Oxon. OX14 3UE, England. TEL 44-1235-401000. FAX 44-1235-401550. *2422*

CAMBRIDGE LECTURE NOTES IN PHYSICS.
University of Cambridge, Press Syndicate, The Pitt Bldg., Trumpington St., Cambridge CB2 1RP, England. TEL 44-1223-315052. *5543*

CAMDEN HISTORY REVIEW.
Camden History Society, c/o Local Studies and Archive Center, Holborn Library, 32-38 Theobalds Rd., London WCIX 8PA, England. TEL 44-171-435-2088. FAX 44-171-794-6695. *3402*

CAMPI IMMAGINABILI.
Marra Editore, c/o Bosco Sottano, Pal "Domus Apta", 87100 Cosenza, Italy. TEL 0984-394265. *3609*

CANADA. CANADIAN WILDLIFE FEDERATION. PUBLICATION LIST.
Canadian Wildlife Federation, 2740 Queensview Dr., Ottawa, ON K2B 1A2, Canada. TEL 613-721-2286. FAX 613-721-2902. *2122*

CANADA. INDIAN AND NORTHERN AFFAIRS CANADA. MINES AND MINERAL ACTIVITIES (YEAR).
Indian and Northern Affairs Canada, Mineral Resoures Directorate, Rm. 603, Ottawa, ON K1A 0H4, Canada. TEL 819-994-6447. FAX 819-953-9066. *5059*

CANADA: THE STATE OF THE FEDERATION.
Institute of Intergovernmental Relations, Queen's University, Kingston, ON K7L 3N6, Canada. TEL 603-545-2080. FAX 603-545-6868. *5639*

CANADIAN ADMINISTRATOR.
University of Alberta, Department of Educational Policy Studies, Edmonton, AB T6G 2H1, Canada. TEL 403-492-5241. FAX 403-492-2024. *2455*

CANADIAN - AMERICA PUBLIC POLICY.
Canadian - American Center, 154 College Ave., Orono, ME 04473-1591. TEL 207-581-4220. FAX 207-581-4223. *5744*

CANADIAN ASSOCIATION OF RADIOLOGISTS. JOURNAL.
Canadian Medical Association, P.O. Box 8650, Ottawa, ON K1G 0G8, Canada. TEL 613-731-9331. FAX 613-523-0937. *4873*

CANADIAN BULLETIN OF MEDICAL HISTORY.
Wilfrid Laurier University Press, 75 University Ave. W., Waterloo, ON N2L 3C5, Canada. TEL 519-884-0710. FAX 519-725-1399. *4439*

CANADIAN CATHOLIC HISTORICAL STUDIES.
Canadian Catholic Historical Association, c/o Rev. Edward Jackman, 355 Church St., Toronto, ON M5B 1Z8, Canada. TEL 416-977-1500. FAX 416-977-6063. *6171*

CANADIAN CHIROPRACTIC ASSOCIATION. JOURNAL.
Canadian Chiropractic Association, 1396 Eglinton Ave. W., Toronto, ON M6C 2E4, Canada. TEL 416-781-5656. FAX 416-781-7344. *4612*

CANADIAN CHURCH HISTORICAL SOCIETY JOURNAL.
Canadian Church Historical Society, c/o Archives, Anglican Church of Canada, 600 Jarvis St., Toronto, ON M4Y 2J6, Canada. TEL 416-924-9192. FAX 416-968-7983. *6050*

CANADIAN DENTAL ASSOCIATION. JOURNAL.
Canadian Dental Association, 1815 Alta Vista Dr., Ottawa, ON K1G 3Y6, Canada. TEL 613-523-1770. FAX 613-523-7736. *4636*

CANADIAN DENTAL HYGIENISTS ASSOCIATION. PROBE.
Canadian Dental Hygienists Association, 96 Centrepointe Dr., Nepean, ON K2G 6B1, Canada. TEL 613-224-5515. FAX 613-224-7283. *4636*

CANADIAN DIETETIC ASSOCIATION. JOURNAL.
Canadian Dietetic Association, 480 University Ave., Ste. 601, Toronto, ON M5G 1V2, Canada. TEL 416-596-0857. FAX 416-596-0603. *5230*

CANADIAN EMERGENCY NEWS.
Pendragon Publishing Ltd., Box 68010, 7750 Ranchview Dr., N.W., Calgary, AB T3G 3N8, Canada. TEL 403-547-5748. FAX 403-547-5749. *4782*

CANADIAN ENTOMOLOGIST.
Entomological Society of Canada, 393 Winston Ave., Ottawa, ON K2A 1Y8, Canada. TEL 613-725-2619. FAX 613-725-9349. *722*

CANADIAN ETHNIC STUDIES.
Canadian Ethnic Studies Association, Research Centre for Canadian Ethnic Studies, University of Calgary, 2500 University Dr., N.W., Calgary, AB T2N 1N4, Canada. TEL 403-220-7257. FAX 403-284-5467. *2870*

CANADIAN FAMILY PHYSICIAN.
College of Family Physicians of Canada, 2630 Skymark Ave., Mississauga, ON L4W 5A4, Canada. TEL 905-629-0900. FAX 905-629-0893. *4439*

CANADIAN FOLKLORE.
Folklore Studies Association of Canada, c/o Universite Laval, Cite Universitaire, Quebec, PQ G1K 7P4, Canada. TEL 418-656-7200. FAX 418-656-2019. *2950*

CANADIAN GEMMOLOGIST.
Canadian Gemmological Association, 1767 Avenue Rd., North York, ON M5M 3Y8, Canada. TEL 416-785-0962. FAX 416-785-9043. *3694*

THE CANADIAN GEOGRAPHER.
Canadian Association of Geographers, Burnside Hall, McGill University, 805 Sherbrooke St. W., Montreal, PQ H3A 2K6, Canada. TEL 514-398-4946. *3250*

CANADIAN GEOGRAPHIC.
Royal Canadian Geographical Society, 39 McArthur Ave., Vanier, ON K1L 8L7, Canada. TEL 613-745-4629. FAX 613-744-0947. *3119*

CANADIAN GEOTECHNICAL JOURNAL.
National Research Council of Canada, Research Journals, Ottawa, ON K1A 0R6, Canada. TEL 613-993-9084. FAX 613-952-7656. *2205*

CANADIAN ISSUES.
Association for Canadian Studies, P.O. Box 8888, Sta. Centre Ville, Montreal, PQ H3C 3P8, Canada. TEL 514-987-7784. FAX 514-987-8210. *3609*

CANADIAN JEWISH STUDIES.
Canadian Jewish Historical Society, c/o Dept. of Religion, Concordia U., 1455 de Maisonneuve Blvd. W., Montreal, PQ H3G 1M8, Canada. TEL 514-848-2066. FAX 514-848-4541. *2870*

CANADIAN JOURNAL FOR THE STUDY OF ADULT EDUCATION.
Canadian Association for the Study of Adult Education, Department of Adult Education, Ontario Institute for Studies in Education, 252 Bloor St. W., 7-107, Toronto, ON M5S 1V6, Canada. *2397*

CANADIAN JOURNAL OF ADMINISTRATIVE SCIENCES.
Administrative Sciences Association of Canada, Faculty of Commerce and Administration, Concordia University, 1455 de Maisonneuve Blvd. W., Montreal, PQ H3G 1M8, Canada. TEL 514-848-2719. FAX 514-848-2839. *906*

CANADIAN JOURNAL OF ANAESTHESIA.
Canadian Anaesthetists' Society, 1 Eglinton Ave., E., Ste. 208, Toronto, ON M4P 3A1, Canada. TEL 416-480-0602. FAX 416-480-0320. *4591*

CANADIAN JOURNAL OF APPLIED PHYSIOLOGY.
Human Kinetics Publishers, Inc., Box 5076, Champaign, IL 61825-5076. TEL 217-351-5076. FAX 217-351-2674. *6455*

CANADIAN JOURNAL OF ARCHAEOLOGY.
Canadian Archaeological Association, c/o Bjorn Simonsen, Secy.-Treas., 352 Viaduct Ave. W., R.R. 3, Victoria, BC V8X 3X1, Canada. TEL 604-479-1147. FAX 604-381-3890. *349*

CANADIAN JOURNAL OF BOTANY.
National Research Council of Canada, Research Journals, Ottawa, ON K1A 0R6, Canada. TEL 613-993-9084. FAX 613-952-7656. *675*

CANADIAN JOURNAL OF CARDIOLOGY.
Pulsus Group Inc., 2902 S. Sheridan Way, Oakville, ON L6J 7L6, Canada. TEL 905-829-4770. FAX 905-829-4799. *4597*

CANADIAN JOURNAL OF CARDIOVASCULAR NURSING.
Canadian Council of Cardiovascular Nurses, 160 George St., Ste. 200, Ottawa, ON K1N 9M2, Canada. TEL 613-241-4361. FAX 416-241-3278. *4711*

CANADIAN JOURNAL OF CHEMISTRY.
National Research Council of Canada, Research Journals, Ottawa, ON K1A 0R6, Canada. TEL 613-993-9084. FAX 613-952-7656. *1667*

CANADIAN JOURNAL OF CIVIL ENGINEERING.
National Research Council of Canada, Research Journals, Ottawa, ON K1A 0R6, Canada. TEL 613-993-9084. FAX 613-952-7656. *2654*

CANADIAN JOURNAL OF COMMUNICATION.
Wilfrid Laurier University Press, 75 University Ave. W., Waterloo, ON N2L 3C5, Canada. TEL 519-884-0710. FAX 519-725-1399. *1957*

CANADIAN JOURNAL OF DERMATOLOGY.
Rodar Publishing Inc., 8102 Trans Canada Hwy., St. Laurent, PQ H4S 1Z4, Canada. TEL 514-333-5350. *4659*

CANADIAN JOURNAL OF DIABETES CARE.
Canadian Diabetes Association, 15 Toronto St., Ste. 1001, Toronto, ON M5C 2E3, Canada. TEL 416-363-3373. FAX 416-363-3393. *4666*

CANADIAN JOURNAL OF EARTH SCIENCES.
National Research Council of Canada, Research Journals, Ottawa, ON K1A 0R6, Canada. TEL 613-993-9084. FAX 613-952-7656. *2205*

CANADIAN JOURNAL OF EDUCATIONAL COMMUNICATION.
Association for Media and Technology in Education in Canada (AMTEC), 3 - 1750 The Queensway, Ste. 1318, Etobicoke, ON M9C 5H5, Canada. TEL 403-492-3994. FAX 403-492-3179. *2482*

CANADIAN JOURNAL OF FISHERIES AND AQUATIC SCIENCES.
National Research Council of Canada, Research Journals, Ottawa, ON K1A 0R6, Canada. TEL 613-993-9084. FAX 613-952-7656. *2928*

CANADIAN JOURNAL OF FOREST RESEARCH.
National Research Council of Canada, Research Journals, Ottawa, ON K1A 0R6, Canada. TEL 613-993-9084. FAX 613-952-7656. *3012*

CANADIAN JOURNAL OF GASTROENTEROLOGY.
Pulsus Group Inc., 2902 S. Sheridan Way, Oakville, ON L6J 7L6, Canada. TEL 905-829-4770. FAX 905-829-4799. *4690*

CANADIAN JOURNAL OF HISTORY.
University of Saskatchewan, 707 Arts Bldg., 9 Campus Dr., Saskatoon, SK S7N 5A5, Canada. TEL 306-966-5792. FAX 306-966-5852. *3339*

CANADIAN JOURNAL OF HOSPITAL PHARMACY.
Canadian Society of Hospital Pharmacists, 1145 Hunt Club Rd., Ste. 350, Ottawa, ON K1V 0Y3, Canada. TEL 613-736-9733. FAX 613-736-5660. *5403*

CANADIAN JOURNAL OF HUMAN SEXUALITY.
Sex Information and Education Council of Canada, 850 Coxwell Ave., East York, ON M4C 5R1, Canada. TEL 416-466-5304. FAX 416-778-0785. *5833*

CANADIAN JOURNAL OF INFECTION CONTROL.
Pulsus Group Inc., 2902 S. Sheridan Way, Oakville, ON L6J 7L6, Canada. TEL 905-829-4770. FAX 905-829-4799. *4619*

CANADIAN JOURNAL OF INFECTIOUS DISEASES.
Pulsus Group Inc., 2902 S. Sheridan Way, Oakville, ON L6J 7L6, Canada. TEL 905-829-4770. FAX 905-829-4799. *4619*

CANADIAN JOURNAL OF IRISH STUDIES.
Canadian Association for Irish Studies, c/o Memorial University of Newfoundland, Dept. of English, St. John, NF A1C 5S7, Canada. FAX 306-966-8839. *3609*

CANADIAN JOURNAL OF LINGUISTICS.
Canadian Linguistic Association, c/o Dept. de Linguistique, UQAM, C.P. 8888, Succ. Centre-Ville, Montreal, PQ H3C 3P8, Canada. TEL 514-987-3000. FAX 514-987-4652. *4060*

CANADIAN JOURNAL OF MARKETING RESEARCH.
Professional Marketing Research Society, 2175 Sheppard Ave. E., Ste. 110, Willowdale, ON M2J 1W8, Canada. TEL 416-493-4080. *1458*

CANADIAN JOURNAL OF MICROBIOLOGY.
National Research Council of Canada, Research Journals, Ottawa, ON K1A 0R6, Canada. TEL 613-993-9084. FAX 613-952-7656. *755*

CANADIAN JOURNAL OF NATIVE EDUCATION.
University of Alberta, Educational Policy Studies, 4-116 Education North, Edmonton, AB T6G 2H1, Canada. TEL 403-465-3480. FAX 403-492-2024. *2318*

CANADIAN JOURNAL OF NETHERLANDIC STUDIES.
Canadian Association for the Advancement of Netherlandic Studies, Department of French, University of Windsor, Windsor, ON N9B 3P4, Canada. TEL 519-253-4232. FAX 971-36487050. *4192*

CANADIAN JOURNAL OF NEUROLOGICAL SCIENCES.
Canadian Journal of Neurological Sciences, Inc., P.O. Box 4220, Sta. C, Calgary, AB T2T 5N1, Canada. TEL 403-229-9575. FAX 403-229-1661. *4830*

CANADIAN JOURNAL OF NURSING ADMINISTRATION.
Health Media Inc., 14453 29A Ave., White Rock, BC V4A 9K8, Canada. TEL 604-535-7933. *4711*

THE CANADIAN JOURNAL OF NURSING RESEARCH.
McGill University, School of Nursing, 3506 University St., Montreal, PQ H3A 2A7, Canada. TEL 514-392-4160. FAX 514-398-8455. *4711*

CANADIAN JOURNAL OF PEDIATRICS.
Rodar Publishing Inc., 8102 Trans Canada Hwy., St. Laurent, PQ H4S 1Z4, Canada. TEL 514-333-5350. FAX 514-457-2679. *4803*

CANADIAN JOURNAL OF PHILOSOPHY.
University of Calgary Press, 2500 University Dr., N.W., Calgary, AB T2N 1N4, Canada. TEL 403-220-7578. FAX 403-282-0085. *5470*

CANADIAN JOURNAL OF PHYSICS.
National Research Council of Canada, Research Journals, Ottawa, ON K1A 0R6, Canada. TEL 613-993-9084. FAX 613-952-7656. *5544*

CANADIAN JOURNAL OF PHYSIOLOGY AND PHARMACOLOGY.
National Research Council of Canada, Research Journals, Ottawa, ON K1A 0R6, Canada. TEL 613-993-9084. FAX 613-952-7656. *786*

CANADIAN JOURNAL OF POLITICAL SCIENCE.
Canadian Political Science Association, 1 Stewart St., Ste. 205, Ottawa, ON K1N 6H7, Canada. TEL 613-564-4026. FAX 613-230-2746. *5640*

CANADIAN JOURNAL OF PROGRAM EVALUATION.
University of Calgary Press, 2500 University Dr. N.W. Calgary, AB T2N 1N4, Canada. TEL 403-220-7573. FAX 403-282-0035. *5895*

CANADIAN JOURNAL OF PSYCHIATRY.
Canadian Psychiatric Association, 237 Argyle Ave., Ste. 200, Ottawa, ON K2P 1B8, Canada. TEL 613-234-2815. FAX 613-234-9857. *4830*

CANADIAN JOURNAL OF PSYCHOANALYSIS.
Canadian Psychoanalytic Society, 7000 Cote des Neiges, Montreal, PQ H3S 2C1, Canada. TEL 514-738-6105. FAX 514-735-6393. *4830*

CANADIAN JOURNAL OF PUBLIC HEALTH.
Canadian Public Health Association, 1565 Carling Ave. Ste. 400, Ottawa, ON K1Z 8R1, Canada. TEL 613-725-3769. FAX 613-725-9826. *5956*

CANADIAN JOURNAL OF REGIONAL SCIENCE.
University of New Brunswick, Department of Economics, P.O. Box 4400, Fredericton, NB E3B 5A3, Canada. TEL 506-447-3206. FAX 506-453-4514. *1249*

CANADIAN JOURNAL OF SOCIOLOGY.
University of Toronto Press, Journals Department, 5201 Dufferin St., Downsview, ON M3H 5T8. TEL 416-667-7781. FAX 416-667-7881. *6407*

CANADIAN JOURNAL OF UNIVERSITY CONTINUING EDUCATION.
Canadian Association for University Continuing Education, c/o Ken Clements, Exec. Director, 320-350 Albert St., Ottawa, ON K1P 1B1, Canada. TEL 613-563-1236. FAX 613-563-7739. *2422*

CANADIAN JOURNAL OF VETERINARY RESEARCH.
Canadian Veterinary Medical Association, 339 Booth St., Ottawa, ON K1R 7K1, Canada. TEL 613-236-1162. FAX 613-236-9631. *6343*

CANADIAN JOURNAL OF ZOOLOGY.
National Research Council of Canada, Research Journals, Ottawa, ON K1A 0R6, Canada. TEL 613-993-9084. FAX 613-952-7656. *801*

CANADIAN JOURNAL ON AGING
Canadian Association on Gerontology, MacKinnon Bldg., Rm. 039, University of Guelph, Guelph, ON N1G 2W1, Canada. TEL 519-824-4120 ext. 6925. FAX 519-837-9953. *3285*

CANADIAN LEADER.
Canyouth Publications Ltd., Box 5112, Station F, Ottawa, ON K2C 3H4, Canada. TEL 613-224-5131. FAX 613-224-3571. *1762*

CANADIAN MARITIME BIBLIOGRAPHY.
Memorial University of Newfoundland, Maritime Studies Research Unit, St. John's, NF A1C 5S7, Canada. TEL 709-737-3424. FAX 709-737-4569. *6738*

CANADIAN MATHEMATICAL SOCIETY. CONFERENCE PROCEEDINGS.
American Mathematical Society, Box 6248, Providence, RI 02940-6248. TEL 401-455-4000. *4359*

CANADIAN METALLURGICAL QUARTERLY.
Elsevier Science Ltd., Pergamon, P.O. Box 800, Kidlington, Oxford OX5 1DX, England. TEL 44-1865-843000. FAX 44-1865-843010. *4951*

CANADIAN MODERN LANGUAGE REVIEW.
University of Toronto Press, Journals Department, 5201 Dufferin St., North York, ON M3H 5T8, Canada. TEL 416-667-7781. FAX 416-667-7881. *4060*

CANADIAN MUSIC EDUCATOR.
Canadian Music Educators Association, Faculty of Education, Memorial University of Newfoundland, St. John's, NF A1B 3X8, Canada. TEL 709-737-7603. FAX 709-737-2345. *5147*

CANADIAN ONCOLOGY NURSING JOURNAL.
Pappin Communications, The Victoria Centre, 84 Isabella St., Pembroke, ON K8A 5S5, Canada. TEL 613-735-0952. FAX 613-735-7983. *4711*

CANADIAN ORAL HISTORY ASSOCIATION. FORUM.
Canadian Oral History Association, Box 2064, Sta. "D", Ottawa, ON K1P 5W3, Canada. TEL 613-996-6996. FAX 613-995-6575. *3462*

CANADIAN PHARMACEUTICAL JOURNAL.
Keith Healthcare Communications, 21 Concourse Gate, No. 13, Nepean, ON K2E 7S4, Canada. TEL 613-727-1364. FAX 613-727-3757. *5403*

CANADIAN PLANT DISEASE SURVEY.
Agriculture and Agri-Food Canada, Information and Planning Services, Neatby Bldg., Rm. 1135, Ottawa, ON K1A OC6, Canada. TEL 613-995-7084. *676*

CANADIAN POETRY.
c/o Department of English, University of Western Ontario, London, ON N6A 3K7, Canada. TEL 519-661-3403. *4302*

CANADIAN PROPERTY MANAGEMENT.
MediaEdge Communications Inc., 33 Fraser Ave., Ste. 208, Toronto, ON M6K 3J9, Canada. TEL 416-588-6220. FAX 416-588-5217. *6022*

CANADIAN PUBLIC POLICY.
University of Toronto Press, Journals Department, 5201 Dufferin St., Downsview, ON M3H 5T8, Canada. TEL 416-667-7781. FAX 416-667-7881. *1182*

CANADIAN RAILWAY MODELLER.
28103-1453 Henderson Hwy., Winnipeg, MB R2G 4E9, Canada. TEL 204-668-0168. FAX 204-668-0168. *3503*

CANADIAN RESPIRATORY JOURNAL.
Pulsus Group Inc., 2902 S. Sheridan Way, Oakville, ON L6J 7L6, Canada. TEL 905-829-4770. FAX 905-829-4799. *4886*

CANADIAN REVIEW OF AMERICAN STUDIES.
University of Calgary Press, 2500 University Dr., N.W., Calgary, AB T2N 1N4, Canada. TEL 403-220-7578. FAX 403-282-0085. *3463*

CANADIAN REVIEW OF ART EDUCATION RESEARCH AND ISSUES.
Canadian Society for Education Through Art, 1487 Parish La., Oakville, ON L6M 2Z6, Canada. *2318*

THE CANADIAN REVIEW OF SOCIOLOGY AND ANTHROPOLOGY.
Canadian Sociology and Anthropology Association, Concordia University, 1455 bd. de Maisonneuve W., Montreal, PQ H3G 1M8, Canada. TEL 514-848-8780. FAX 514-848-4539. *6408*

CANADIAN REVIEW OF STUDIES IN NATIONALISM.
Canadian Review of Studies in Nationalism, Inc., c/o University of Prince Edward Island, Charlottetown, PE C1A 4P3, Canada. TEL 902-566-0527. FAX 902-628-4323. *3339*

CANADIAN SOCIAL WORK REVIEW.
Canadian Association of Schools of Social Work, 30 Rosemount Ave., Ste. 100-B, Ottawa, ON K1Y 1P4, Canada. TEL 613-722-2974. FAX 613-722-5661. *6364*

CANADIAN SOCIETY FOR COMPUTATIONAL STUDIES OF INTELLIGENCE. PROCEEDINGS OF THE BIENNIAL CONFERENCE.
Morgan Kaufmann Publishers, Inc., 340 Pine St., 6th Fl., San Francisco, CA 94104-3205. TEL 415-392-2665. FAX 415-982-2665. *2006*

CANADIAN SOCIETY FOR MECHANICAL ENGINEERING. TRANSACTIONS.
Canadian Society for Mechanical Engineering, Dept. of Mechanical Engineering, University of Alberta, Rm. 4-9 Mec.E. Bldg., Edmonton, AB T6G 2G8, Canada. TEL 403-492-9616. FAX 403-492-2200. *2751*

CANADIAN STUDIES UPDATE.
Association for Canadian Studies in the U S, One Dupont Circle, Ste. 620, Washington, DC 20036. TEL 202-887-6375. FAX 202-296-8379. *2422*

CANADIAN VETERINARY JOURNAL.
Canadian Veterinary Medical Association, 339 Booth St., Ottawa, ON K1R 7K1, Canada. TEL 613-236-1162. FAX 613-236-9681. *6943*

CANADIAN WATER RESOURCES JOURNAL.
Canadian Water Resources Association, Membership Service Office, P.O. Box 1329, Cambridge, ON N1R 7G6, Canada. TEL 519-888-1211. FAX 579-746-2031. *6964*

CANBERRA ANTHROPOLOGY.
Australian National University, Research School of Pacific and Asian Studies, Canberra, A.C.T. 0200, Australia. TEL 61-6-2490769. FAX 61-6-2494896. *305*

CANBERRA CYCLIST.
Pedal Power A.C.T., Inc., G.P.O. Box 581, Canberra, A.C.T. 2601, Australia. TEL 06-248-7995. FAX 06-207-3199. *6521*

CANBERRA PAPERS ON STRATEGY AND DEFENSE.
Strategic and Defence Studies Centre, Australian National University, Canberra, A.C.T. 0200, Australia. TEL 61-6-2438537. FAX 61-6-2480816. *5025*

CANCER.
John Wiley & Sons, Inc., Journals, 605 Third Ave., New York, NY 10158. TEL 212-850-6645. FAX 212-850-6021. *4749*

CANCER AND METASTASIS REVIEWS.
Kluwer Academic Publishers Boston, Box 358, Accord Sta., Hingham, MA 02018-0358. TEL 617-871-6600. FAX 617-871-6528. *4750*

CANCER BIOCHEMISTRY BIOPHYSICS.
Gordon and Breach Science Publishers, c/o International Publishers Distributor, P.O. Box 3054, Langhorne, PA 19047-3054. TEL 215-750-2642. FAX 215-750-6343. *4750*

CANCER BIOTHERAPY & RADIOPHARMACEUTICALS.
Mary Ann Liebert, Inc. Publishers, 2 Madison Ave., Larchmont, NY 10538. TEL 914-834-3100. FAX 914-834-3688. *4750*

CANCER CHEMOTHERAPY AND BIOLOGICAL RESPONSE MODIFIERS.
Elsevier Science B.V., Books Division, P.O. Box 211, 1000 AE Amsterdam, Netherlands. TEL 31-20-4853911. FAX 31-20-4853705. *4750*

CANCER CONTROL.
Moffitt Cancer Center, 12902 Magnolia Dr., Tampa, FL 33612. TEL 813-632-1349. FAX 813-632-1380. *4750*

CANCER DETECTION AND PREVENTION.
Blackwell Science Inc., 238 Main St., Cambridge, MA 02142. TEL 617-876-7022. FAX 617-492-5263. *4750*

CANCER EPIDEMIOLOGY, BIOMARKERS & PREVENTION.
American Association for Cancer Research, Public Ledger Bldg., 150 S. Independence Mall West, Ste. 816, Philadelphia, PA 19106-3483. TEL 215-440-9300. FAX 215-440-9354. *4750*

CANCER FORUM.
Australian Cancer Society, Inc., G.P.O. Box 4708, Sydney, N.S.W. 2000, Australia. FAX 61-2-356-4558. *4750*

CANCER GENE THERAPY.
Appleton & Lange, Journal Division Box 120041, Stamford, CT 06912-0041. TEL 203-406-4500. *4751*

CANCER GENETICS & CYTOGENETICS.
Elsevier Science Inc., Box 945, New York, NY 10159-0945. TEL 212-633-3730. FAX 212-633-3680. *4751*

CANCER INVESTIGATION.
Marcel Dekker Journals, 270 Madison Ave., New York, NY 10016. TEL 212-696-9000. FAX 212-685-4540. *4751*

THE CANCER JOURNAL FROM SCIENTIFIC AMERICAN.
Scientific American, Inc., 415 Madison Ave., New York, NY 10017-1111. TEL 212-754-0550. FAX 212-980-3062. *4751*

CANCER LETTERS.
Elsevier Science Ireland Ltd., P.O. Box 85, Limerick, Ireland. TEL 353-61-471944. FAX 353-61-472144. *4751*

CANCER MOLECULAR BIOLOGY.
Ain Shams Medical Faculty, Oncology Diagnostic Unit, Abbassia, Cairo, Egypt. TEL 20-2-2858940. FAX 20-2-2859928. *4751*

CANCER NURSING.
Lippincott - Raven Publishers 227 E. Washington Sq., Philadelphia, PA 19106. TEL 215-238-4200. *4711*

CANCER PRACTICE.
Lippincott - Raven Publishers 227 E. Washington Square, Philadelphia, PA 19106. TEL 215-238-4200. *4751*

CANCER PREVENTION INTERNATIONAL.
Cognizant Communication Corporation, 3 Hartsdale Rd., Elmsford, NY 10523-3701. TEL 914-592-7720. FAX 914-592-8981. *4751*

CANCER RESEARCH.
American Association for Cancer Research, Public Ledger Bldg., 150 S. Independence Mall West, Ste. 816, Philadelphia, PA 19106. TEL 215-440-9300. FAX 215-440-9354. *4752*

CANCER TOPICS.
Eurocommunica Publications, 4 Bersted Mews, Bersted St., Bognor Regis, W. Sussex PO22 9RR, England. TEL 01234-823180. FAX 01234-823180. *4752*

CANCER TOPICS ABSTRACTS SERVICE.
Eurocommunica Publications, 4 Bersted Mews, Bersted St., Bognor Regis, W. Sussex PO22 9RR, England. TEL 01243-823180. FAX 01243-823180. *4551*

CANCER TREATMENT AND RESEARCH.
Kluwer Academic Publishers, Postbus 17, 3300 AA Dordrecht, Netherlands. TEL 31-78-6392392. FAX 31-78-6392254. *4752*

CANINE PRACTICE.
Veterinary Practice Publishing Co., 7 Ashley Ave. S., Santa Barbara, CA 93103-9989. TEL 805-965-1028. FAX 805-965-0722. *6944*

CANSANG TONGBAO.
Zhejiang Cansang Xuehui, Huajiachi, Hangzhou, Zhejiang 310029, People's Republic of China. TEL 86-571-6041733. FAX 86-571-6049815. *106*

CAPISCUM & EGGPLANT NEWSLETTER.
Universita di Torino, Plant Breeding and Seed Production, Via P. Giuria 15, 10126 Turin, Italy. TEL 39-11-657300. FAX 39-11-6502754. *3047*

CARBOHYDRATE POLYMERS.
Elsevier Science Ltd., P.O. Box 800, Kidlington, Oxford OX5 1DX, England. TEL 44-1865-843000. FAX 44-1865-843010. *1736*

CARBOHYDRATE RESEARCH.
Elsevier Science Ltd., P.O. Box 800, Kidlington, Oxford OX5 1DX, England. TEL 44-1865-843000. FAX 44-1865-843010. *1736*

CARBON.
Elsevier Science Ltd., Pergamon, P.O. Box 800, Kidlington, Oxford OX5 1DX, England. TEL 44-1865-843000. FAX 44-1865-843010. *1736*

CARBONATES AND EVAPORITES.
Northeastern Science Foundation, Inc., 15 Third St., Box 746, Troy, NY 12181-0746. TEL 518-273-3247. *2227*

CARCINOGENESIS.
Lippincott - Raven Publishers 227 E. Washington Sq., Philadelphia, PA 19106. TEL 215-238-4200. FAX 215-238-4235. *4752*

CARD TALK.
American Business Card Club, Box 460297, Aurora, CO 80046-0297. TEL 303-690-6496. *33*

CARDIFF BUSINESS SCHOOL. DISCUSSION PAPER SERIES IN FINANCIAL AND BANKING ECONOMICS.
Cardiff Business School, University of Wales, Aberconway Bldg., Colum Dr., Cardiff CF1 3EU, Wales. TEL 44-1222-874417. FAX 44-1222-874419. *1074*

LA CARDIOLOGIA NELLA PRATICA CLINICA.
Springer-Verlag Milan, Via Podgora 4, 20122 Milan, Italy. TEL 39-2-55194656. FAX 39-2-55193360. *4597*

CARDIOLOGY.
S. Karger AG, Allschwilerstr. 10, P.O. Box, CH-4009 Basel, Switzerland. TEL 061-3061111. FAX 061-3061234. *4598*

CARDIOLOGY REVIEW.
M R A Publications, Inc., 2 Greenwich Office Park, Greenwich, CT 06831-5154. TEL 203-629-3550. FAX 203-629-2536. *4598*

CARDIOLOGY UPDATE.
Elsevier Science Inc., Box 945, New York, NY 10159-0945. TEL 212-633-3730. FAX 212-633-3680. *4598*

CARDIOVASCULAR AND INTERVENTIONAL RADIOLOGY.
Springer-Verlag, Medical Journals, 175 Fifth Ave., New York, NY 10010. TEL 212-460-1500. FAX 212-473-6272. *4874*

CARDIOVASCULAR CASES.
Erasmus Publishing B.V., Mathenesserlaan 332, 3021 HZ Rotterdam, Netherlands. TEL 31-10-4777277. FAX 31-10-4779586. *4598*

CARDIOVASCULAR DRUG REVIEWS.
Neva Press Inc., Box 347, Branford, CT 06405. TEL 203-272-5338. FAX 203-272-5338. *4598*

CARDIOVASCULAR DRUGS AND THERAPY.
Kluwer Academic Publishers Boston, Box 358, Accord Sta., Hingham, MA 02018-0358. TEL 617-871-6300. FAX 617-871-6528. *4598*

CARDIOVASCULAR NURSING.
American Heart Association, 7272 Greenville Ave., Dallas, TX 75231-4596. TEL 214-706-1310. FAX 214-691-6342. *4711*

CARDIOVASCULAR PATHOLOGY.
Elsevier Science Inc., Box 945, New York, NY 10159-0945. TEL 212-633-3730. FAX 212-633-3680. *4599*

CARDIOVASCULAR RESEARCH.
Elsevier Science B.V., P.O. Box 211, 1000 AE Amsterdam, Netherlands. TEL 31-20-4853911. FAX 31-20-4853598. *4599*

CARDIOVASCULAR REVIEWS & REPORTS.
LeJacq Communications, Inc., 777 W. Putnam Ave., Greenwich, CT 06830-5014. TEL 203-531-0450. FAX 203-531-0533. *4599*

CARDIOVASCULAR SURGERY.
American Heart Association, 7272 Greenville Ave., Dallas, TX 75231-4596. TEL 214-706-1310. FAX 214-691-6342. *4599*

CARDIOVASCULAR SURGERY.
Butterworth - Heinemann, Part of the Reed Elsevier group, Linacre House, Jordan Hill, Oxford OX2 8DP, England. TEL 44-1865-310366. FAX 44-1865-310898. *4599*

CARDOZO STUDIES IN LAW AND LITERATURE.
Jacob Burns Institute for Advanced Legal Studies, Cardoza School of Law, Yeshiva University, 55 Fifth Ave., New York, NY 10003. TEL 212-790-0370. FAX 212-790-0345. *3758*

CARE OF THE CRITICALLY ILL.
Mosby Europe Journals Ltd., Lynton House, 7-12 Tavistock Sq., London WC1H 9LB, England. TEL 071-388-7676. FAX 071-344-0020. *4782*

CAREERS & COLLEGES.
E.M. Guild, Inc., 989 Ave. of the Americas, 6th Fl., New York, NY 10018. TEL 212-563-4688. FAX 212-967-2531. *5264*

CARIB-LATIN ENERGY CONSULTANT.
Carib-Latin Energy Consultants Ltd., P.O. Box 3074, St. James P.O., Trinidad & Tobago, W.I. TEL 809-637-9038. FAX 809-637-9038. *2541*

CARIBBEAN GEOGRAPHY.
University of the West Indies, Department of Geography, Mona, Kingston 7, Jamaica, W.I. TEL 809-977-2659. FAX 809-977-2660. *3250*

CARIBBEAN JOURNAL OF SCIENCE.
University of Puerto Rico, College of Arts and Science, Box 5000, Mayaguez, PR 00681-5000. TEL 809-265-5427. FAX 809-265-1225. *576*

CARIBBEAN LAW REVIEW.
University of the West Indies, Cave Hill Campus, St. Michael, Barbados, W.I. TEL 809-425-1310. FAX 809-424-1788. *3758*

CARIBBEAN STUDIES (NEW YORK).
Gordon & Breach Science Publishers, c/o International Publishers Distributor, P.O. Box 3054, Langhorne, PA 19047-3054. TEL 215-750-2642. FAX 215-750-6343. *3463*

THE CARIBBEAN WRITER.
University of the Virgin Islands, RR 2, Box 10,000, Kingshill, St. Croix, VI 00850. TEL 809-692-4152. FAX 809-692-4026. *4192*

CARIES RESEARCH.
S. Karger AG, Allschwilerstr. 10, P.O. Box, CH-4009 Basel, Switzerland. TEL 061-3061111. FAX 061-3061234. *4636*

CARL NEWELL JACKSON LECTURES.
Harvard University Press, 79 Garden St., Cambridge, MA 02138. TEL 617-495-2600. FAX 617-495-5898. *2950*

CARLETON GERMANIC PAPERS.
Carleton University, Department of Modern Languages, 1125 Colonel By Drive, Ottawa, ON K1S 5B6, Canada. TEL 613-520-2116. FAX 613-520-3544. *4192*

CARNEGIE-ROCHESTER CONFERENCE SERIES ON PUBLIC POLICY.
North-Holland, P.O. Box 211, 1000 AE Amsterdam, Netherlands. TEL 31-20-4853911. FAX 31-20-4853598. *907*

THE CAROLINA QUARTERLY.
University of North Carolina at Chapel Hill, Greenlaw Hall CB 3520, Chapel Hill, NC 27599-3520. TEL 919-962-0244. *4192*

THE CARTOGRAPHIC JOURNAL.
British Cartographic Society, Centre for Remote Sensing and Mapping Science, Department of Geography, University of Aberdeen, Elphinstone Rd., Aberdeen AB24 3UF, Scotland. TEL 44-1224-272324. FAX 44-1224-272331. *3280*

CARTOGRAPHIC PERSPECTIVES.
North American Cartographic Information Society, Box 399, Milwaukee, WI 53201. FAX 414-229-3981. *3250*

CARTOGRAPHY.
Mapping Sciences Institute Australia, G.P.O. Box 6836, E. Perth, W.A. 6892, Australia. TEL 61-9-3517566. FAX 61-9-3512703. *3250*

CASTANEA.
Southern Appalachian Botanical Society, Department of Biology, University of North Carolina at Charlotte, Charlotte, NC 28223. TEL 704-547-4065. FAX 704-547-3128. *676*

CAT WORLD.
Cat World Ltd., 64 Great Eastern St., London EC2A 3QR, England. TEL 44-171-7395052. FAX 44-171-7398053. *5388*

CAT WORLD ANNUAL.
Cat World Ltd., 10 Western Rd., Shoreham-by-Sea, W. Sussex BN43 5WD, England. TEL 01273-462000. FAX 01273-455994. *5388*

CATALOGING & CLASSIFICATION QUARTERLY.
Haworth Press, Inc., 10 Alice St., Binghamton, NY 13904. TEL 607-722-5857. FAX 607-722-1424. *3984*

CATALOGUE OF PALAEARCTIC DIPTERA.
Elsevier Science B.V., Books Division, P.O. Box 211, 1000 AE Amsterdam, Netherlands. TEL 31-20-4853911. FAX 31-20-43537C5. *723*

CATALYSIS BY METAL COMPLEXES.
Kluwer Academic Publishers, Postbus 17, 3300 AA Dordrecht, Netherlands. TEL 31-78-6392392. FAX 31-78-6392254. *736*

CATALYSIS REVIEWS: SCIENCE AND ENGINEERING.
Marcel Dekker Journals, 270 Madison Ave., New York, NY 10016. TEL 212-696-9000. FAX 212-685-4540. *1748*

CATALYSIS TODAY.
Elsevier Science B.V., P.O. Box 211, 1000 AE Amsterdam, Netherlands. TEL 31-20-4853911. FAX 31-20-4853598. *2634*

THE CATALYST (WESTMINSTER).
National Council on Community Services & Continuing Education, c/o Sue Hartman, Professional Development Program, Front Range Community College, 3645 W. 112th Ave., Westminster, CO 80031. *2397*

CATALYST FOR ENVIRONMENT - ENERGY.
Catalyst for Environment, Energy, 63 Copse Rd., Madison, CT 06443-2608. TEL 212-685-8310. *2779*

CATENA.
Elsevier Science B.V., P.O. Box 211, 1000 AE Amsterdam, Netherlands. TEL 31-20-4853911. FAX 31-20-4853598. *2227*

CATHEDRA.
Yad Izhak Ben-Zvi, P.O. Box 7660, Jerusalem 91076, Israel. TEL 972-2-637268. FAX 972-2-638310. *3495*

CATHETERIZATION AND CARDIOVASCULAR DIAGNOSIS.
John Wiley & Sons, Inc., Journals, 605 Third Ave., New York, NY 10158. TEL 212-850-6645. FAX 212-850-6021. *4599*

CATHOLIC NEAR EAST MAGAZINE.
Catholic Near East Welfare Association, 1011 First Ave., New York, NY 10022-4195. TEL 212-826-1480. FAX 212-826-8979. *6173*

CATHOLIC WORKMAN.
Box 47, New Prague, MN 56071. TEL 612-758-2229. FAX 612-758-6221. *6175*

CAUDA PAVONIS.
Washington State University, Department of English, Pullman, WA 99164. TEL 509-335-3023. FAX 509-335-2582. *4193*

CAUSE - EFFECT MAGAZINE.
C A U S E, 4830 Pearl E. Cir., Ste. 302E, Boulder, CO 80301. TEL 303-449-4430. FAX 303-440-0461. *2404*

CEIBA.
Escuela Agricola Panamericana, Adpo. 93, Tegucigalpa D.C., Honduras. TEL 504-76-6140. FAX 504-76-6242. *156*

CELEBRITY ACCESS: THE DIRECTORY (YEAR).
Celebrity Access Publications, 20 Sunnyside Ave., Ste. A241, Mill Valley, CA 94941. TEL 415-389-8133. *5095*

CELEHIS.
Universidad Nacional de Mar del Plata, Centro de Letras Hispanoamericanas, Funes 3250, 7600 Mar del Plata, Argentina. TEL 54-3423-513906. *4193*

CELESTIAL MECHANICS AND DYNAMICAL ASTRONOMY.
Kluwer Academic Publishers, Postbus 17, 3300 AA Dordrecht, Netherlands. TEL 31-78-6392392. FAX 31-78-6392254. *478*

CELESTINESCA.
Michigan State University, Department of Romance Languages, E. Lansing, MI 48324. TEL 517-335-8350. FAX 517-432-3844. *4193*

CELL.
Cell Press, 50 Church St., Cambridge, MA 02138.
TEL 617-661-7060. *712*

CELL AND CHROMOSOME RESEARCH JOURNAL.
University of Calcutta, Centre of Advanced Studies
in Botany, 35 Ballygunge Circular Rd., Calcutta 700
019, India. FAX 4754772. *712*

CELL BIOCHEMISTRY AND BIOPHYSICS.
Humana Press Inc., 999 Riverview Dr., Ste. 208,
Totowa, NJ 07512. TEL 201-256-1699. FAX 201-
256-8341. *635*

CELL BIOLOGY AND TOXICOLOGY.
Kluwer Academic Publishers, Postbus 17, 3300 AA
Dordrecht, Netherlands. TEL 31-78-6392392.
FAX 31-78-6392254. *2843*

CELL GROWTH & DIFFERENTIATION.
American Association for Cancer Research, Public
Ledger Bldg., 150 S. Independence Mall West, Ste.
816, Philadelphia, PA 19106. TEL 215-440-9300.
FAX 215-440-9354. *4753*

CELL MEMBRANES, METHODS AND REVIEWS.
Plenum Publishing Corp., 233 Spring St., New York,
NY 10013-1578. TEL 212-620-8000. FAX 212-
463-0742. *577*

CELL MOTILITY AND THE CYTOSKELETON.
John Wiley & Sons, Inc., Journals, 605 Third Ave.,
New York, NY 10158. TEL 212-850-6645.
FAX 212-850-6021. *713*

CELL PROLIFERATION.
Blackwell Science Ltd., Osney Mead, Oxford OX2
0EL, England. TEL 44-1865-206206. FAX 44-
1865-721205. *713*

CELL RESEARCH.
Science Press, Marketing and Sales Department, 16
Donghuangchenggen North St., Beijing 100717,
People's Republic of China. TEL 4010642.
FAX 4019810. *577*

CELL TRANSPLANTATION.
Elsevier Science Inc., Box 945, New York, NY
10159-0945. TEL 212-633-3730. FAX 212-633-
3680. *635*

CELL VISION.
Eaton Publishing Co., 154 E. Central St., Natick, MA
01760. TEL 508-655-8282. FAX 508-655-9910.
577

CELLS AND MATERIALS.
Scanning Microscopy International, Inc., 1034
Alabam Dr., Elk Grove Village, IL 60007-2920.
TEL 708-529-6677. FAX 708-980-6698. *4440*

CELLULAR AND MOLECULAR BIOLOGY.
C M B, 1 av. du Pave Neuf, 93160 Noisy-le-Grand,
France. TEL 33-1-45923719. FAX 33-1-
43042030. *713*

CELLULAR AND MOLECULAR LIFE SCIENCES.
Birkhaeuser Verlag, P.O. Box 133, CH-4010 Basel,
Switzerland. TEL 41-61-2050730. FAX 41-61-
2050791. *577*

CELLULAR & MOLECULAR NEUROBIOLOGY.
Plenum Publishing Corp., 233 Spring St., New York,
NY 10013-1578. TEL 212-620-8000. FAX 212-
463-0742. *4830*

CELLULAR IMMUNOLOGY.
Academic Press, Inc., Journal Division, 525 B St.,
Ste. 1900, San Diego, CA 92101-4495. TEL 619-
230-1840. FAX 619-699-6800. *4579*

CELLULAR NEUROBIOLOGY.
Academic Press, Inc., 525 B St., Ste. 1900, San
Diego, CA 92101-4495. TEL 619-231-0926.
FAX 619-699-6715. *577*

CELLULAR PHYSIOLOGY AND BIOCHEMISTRY.
S. Karger AG, Allschwilerstr. 10, P.O. Box, CH-4009
Basel, Switzerland. TEL 061-3061111. FAX 061-
3061234. *635*

CELLULAR POLYMERS.
R A P R A Technology Ltd., Shawbury, Shrewsbury,
Shrops. SY4 4NR, England. TEL 44-1939-250383.
FAX 44-1939-251118. *5618*

CELLULAR SIGNALLING.
Elsevier Science Inc., Box 945, New York, NY
10159-0945. TEL 212-633-3730. FAX 212-633-
3680. *713*

CELLULOSE.
Chapman & Hall, Journals Department 2-6
Boundary Row, London SE1 8HN, England. TEL 44-
171-8650066. FAX 44-171-5229623. *676*

CEMENT AND CONCRETE COMPOSITES.
Elsevier Science Ltd., P.O. Box 800, Kidlington,
Oxford OX5 1DX, England. TEL 44-1865-843000.
FAX 44-1865-843010. *844*

CEMENT AND CONCRETE RESEARCH.
Elsevier Science Ltd., Pergamon, P.O. Box 800,
Kidlington, Oxford OX5 1DX, England. TEL 44-1865-
843000. FAX 44-1865-843010. *844*

CENTAURUS.
Munksgaard International Publishers Ltd., 35
Noerre Soegade, P.O. Box 2148, DK-1016
Copenhagen K, Denmark. TEL 45-33-127030.
FAX 45-33-129387. *6233*

CENTENNIAL REVIEW.
Michigan State University, College of Arts & Letters,
312 Linton Hall, E. Lansing, MI 48824-1044.
TEL 517-355-1905. FAX 517-336-1858. *3609*

CENTER FOCUS.
Center of Concern, 3700 13th St., N.E.,
Washington, DC 20017. TEL 202-635-2757.
FAX 202-832-9494. *6408*

CENTER FOR CHILDREN'S BOOKS. BULLETIN.
University of Illinois at Urbana-Champaign, Graduate
School of Library and Information Science,
Publications Office, 501 E. Daniel St., Champaign, IL
61820-6211. TEL 217-244-0324. FAX 217-333-
5603. *526*

CENTO.
Centre College, Box 745, Danville, KY 40422.
TEL 606-238-5533. FAX 606-236-7925. *1861*

CENTRAL ASIA MONITOR.
Institute for Democratic Development, R.R. 2, Box
6880, Fair Haven, VT 05743. TEL 802-537-4361.
FAX 802-537-4362. *5640*

CENTRAL ASIAN SURVEY.
Carfax Publishing Co., P.O. Box 25, Abingdon, Oxon.
OX14 3UE, England. TEL 44-1235-401000.
FAX 44-1235-401550. *5641*

CENTRAL STATES ARCHAEOLOGICAL JOURNAL.
Central States Archaeological Societies, Inc., 646
Knierim Pl., Kirkwood, MO 63122. TEL 314-821-
7675. *349*

**CENTRAL STATES CONFERENCE ON THE TEACHING
OF FOREIGN LANGUAGES. EDUCATION SERIES.**
National Textbook Co., 4255 W. Touhy Ave.,
Lincolnwood, IL 60646. TEL 708-679-5500.
FAX 708-679-2494. *4060*

**CENTRE CULTUREL CALOUSTE GULBENKIAN.
ACTES DES COLLOQUES.**
Centre Culturel Gulbenkian, Fondation Calouste
Gulbenkian (Lisbonne), 51 av. d'Iena, 75116 Paris,
France. TEL 1-53-23-93-93. FAX 1-53-23-93-99.
3610

CENTRE D'ETUDES DE L'ASIE DE L'EST. CAHIERS.
Universite de Montreal, Faculte des Arts et des
Sciences, C.P. 6128, Succ. A, Montreal, PQ H3C
3J7, Canada. TEL 514-343-5970. FAX 514-343-
7716. *5281*

**CENTRE FOR EUROPEAN POLICY STUDIES.
FINANCIAL MARKETS UNIT. RESEARCH REPORT.**
Centre for European Policy Studies, Place du
Congres 1, 1000 Brussels, Belgium. TEL 32-2-
2182247. FAX 32-2-2293911. *1076*

CENTRE FOR MEDICINES RESEARCH WORKSHOP.
Kluwer Academic Publishers, Postbus 17, 3300 AA
Dordrecht, Netherlands. TEL 31-78-6392392.
FAX 31-78-6392254. *5403*

**CENTRO DE INVESTIGACIONES HISTORICAS Y
ESTETICAS. BOLETIN.**
Universidad Central de Venezuela, Facultad de
Arquitectura y Urbanismo, Caracas, Venezuela.
FAX 58-2-7526718. *389*

**CENTRO DE INVESTIGACIONES PENALES Y
CRIMINOLOGICAS. REVISTA.**
Universidad de los Andes, Centro de Investigaciones
Penales y Criminologicas, Apdo. 730, Merida 5101,
Venezuela. FAX 58-74-402055. *2160*

CENTRO NAVAL. BOLETIN.
Centro Naval Argentina, Florida 826, 1St, 1005
Buenos Aires, Argentina. TEL 54-1-311-0041.
FAX 54-1-322-5791. *5025*

CERAMICA PER L'ARCHITETTURA.
Gruppo Editoriale Faenza Editrice S.p.A., Via Pier. de
Crescenzi, 44, Faenza, Italy. TEL 39-546-663488.
FAX 39-546-660440. *1654*

CERAMICS INTERNATIONAL.
Elsevier Science Ltd., P.O. Box 800, Kidlington,
Oxford OX5 1DX, England. TEL 44-1865-843000.
FAX 44-1865-843010. *1654*

CEREBRAL CORTEX.
Oxford University Press, Journals, 2001 Evans Rd.,
Cary, NC 27513. TEL 919-677-0977. FAX 919-
677-1714. *4830*

**CEREBROVASCULAR AND BRAIN METABOLISM
REVIEWS.**
Lippincott - Raven Publishers, 227 E. Washington
Sq., Philadelphia, PA 19106. TEL 215-238-4200.
4830

CEREBROVASCULAR DISEASES.
S. Karger AG, Allschwilerstr. 10, P.O. Box, CH-4009
Basel, Switzerland. TEL 061-3061111. FAX 061-
3061234. *4830*

CERVANTES.
Cervantes Society of America, Pomona College,
Claremont, CA 91711. TEL 909-621-8937.
FAX 909-621-8065. *4193*

CERVANTES SOCIETY OF AMERICA. BULLETIN.
Cervantes Society of America (Granville), Denison
University, Granville, OH 43023. TEL 614-587-
6228. *4193*

CEYLON JOURNAL OF MEDICAL SCIENCE.
University of Colombo, Faculty of Medicine, Kynsey
Rd., Colombo 8, Sri Lanka. TEL 01-583043.
FAX 01-586432. *4440*

CEYLON MEDICAL JOURNAL.
Sri Lanka Medical Association, Wijerama House, 6
Wijerama Mawatha, Colombo 7, Sri Lanka.
TEL 941-693324. FAX 941-698802. *4440*

THE CHALLENGE.
Pakistan Anti-Tuberculosis Association, Block No.
55, Rm. 8, Pakistan Secretariat, Karachi, Pakistan.
TEL 92-21-5688011. *4887*

CHALLENGE (ARMONK).
M.E. Sharpe, Inc., 80 Business Park Dr., Armonk,
NY 10504. TEL 914-273-1800. FAX 914-273-
2106. *908*

CHALLENGE (ATLANTA).
Morehouse Research Institute, 830 Westview Dr.,
S.W., Atlanta, GA 30314. *2871*

THE CHALLENGE (BANNING).
Cancer Federation, Box 1298, Banning, CA 92220-
0009. TEL 909-849-4325. FAX 909-849-0156.
4753

CHANCE.
Springer-Verlag, Science Journals, 175 Fifth Ave.,
New York, NY 10010. TEL 212-460-1612.
FAX 212-473-6272. *6598*

CHANGE (WASHINGTON).
Heldref Publications, 1319 18th St., N.W.,
Washington, DC 20036-1802. TEL 202-296-6267.
FAX 202-296-5149. *2423*

CHANGES.
John Wiley & Sons Ltd., Journals, Baffins Ln.,
Chichester, W. Sussex PO19 1UD, England. TEL 44-
1243-779777. FAX 44-1243-843232. *6365*

CHANGJIANG KEXUEYUAN YUANBAO.
Changjiang Kexueyuan, Jiu Wan Fang, Zhao Jia Tiao,
Wuhan, Hubei 430010, People's Republic of China.
TEL 86-27-2829904. FAX 86-27-2829726. *2742*

CHAOS.
American Institute of Physics, One Physics Ellipse, College Park, MD 20740-3843. TEL 301-209-3000. *5544*

CHAOS, SOLITONS AND FRACTALS.
Elsevier Science Ltd., Pergamon, P.O. Box 800, Kidlington, Oxford OX5 1DX, England. TEL 44-1865-843000. FAX 44-1865-843010. *4359*

CHARLES ELIOT NORTON LECTURES.
Harvard University Press, 79 Garden St., Cambridge, MA 02138. TEL 617-495-2600. FAX 617-495-5898. *3610*

CHARLES LAMB BULLETIN.
Charles Lamb Society, c/o Duncan Wu, Ed., Department of English Literature, University of Glasgow, Glasgow, Scotland. TEL 44-141-339-8855. *4194*

CHARTERED ACCOUNTANTS JOURNAL OF NEW ZEALAND.
New Zealand Society of Accountants, Cigna House, 40 Mercer St., Wellington, New Zealand. FAX 64-4-4998033. *1044*

CHARTERED INSTITUTION OF WATER AND ENVIRONMENTAL MANAGEMENT. JOURNAL.
Chartered Institution of Water and Environmental Management, 15 John St., London WC1N 2EB, England. TEL 44-171-831-3110. FAX 44-171-405-4967. *6964*

CHARTERED INSURANCE INSTITUTE. SOCIETY OF FELLOWS. JOURNAL.
Chartered Insurance Institute, Society of Fellows, 20 Aldermanbury, London EC2V 7HY, England. TEL 44-171-606-3835. FAX 44-171-726-0131. *3645*

CHAUCER REVIEW.
Pennsylvania State University Press, 820 N. University Dr., Ste. C, University Park, PA 16802-1003. TEL 814-865-1327. FAX 814-863-1408. *4194*

CHEMECA - AUSTRALASIAN CONFERENCE ON CHEMICAL ENGINEERING. PROCEEDINGS.
Institution of Chemical Engineers in Australia, P.O. Box 542, Collaroy, N.S.W. 2097, Australia. TEL 61-2-982-7245. FAX 61-2-982-1065. *2634*

CHEMIA ANALITYCZNA.
Instytut Chemii Fizycznej, Ul. Kasprzaka 44-52, 01-224 Warsaw, Poland. TEL 48-22-221-085. FAX 48-22-225-996. *1714*

CHEMICAL ANALYSIS.
John Wiley & Sons, Inc., 605 Third Ave., New York, NY 10158-0012. TEL 212-850-6000. FAX 212-850-6088. *1714*

CHEMICAL AND PETROLEUM ENGINEERING.
Plenum Publishing Corp., Consultants Bureau, 233 Spring St., New York, NY 10013-1578. TEL 212-620-8468. FAX 212-463-0742. *2634*

CHEMICAL COMMUNICATIONS.
Royal Society of Chemistry, Thomas Graham House, Science Park, Milton Rd., Cambridge CB4 4WF, England. TEL 44-1223-420066. FAX 44-1223-423429. *1668*

CHEMICAL EDUCATOR.
Springer-Verlag, 175 Fifth Ave., New York, NY 10010. TEL 212-460-1500. FAX 212-473-6272. *1668*

CHEMICAL ENGINEER.
Institution of Chemical Engineers, George E. Davis Bldg., 165-189 Railway Terr., Rugby, Warks CV21 3HQ, England. TEL 44-1788-578214. FAX 44-1788-547262. *2635*

CHEMICAL ENGINEERING.
McGraw-Hill Companies, 1221 Ave. of the Americas, New York, NY 10020. TEL 212-512-2197. *2635*

CHEMICAL ENGINEERING AND PROCESSING.
Elsevier Science S.A., P.O. Box 564, CH-1001 Lausanne 1, Switzerland. TEL 41-21-3207381. FAX 41-21-3235444. *2635*

CHEMICAL ENGINEERING: CONCEPTS AND REVIEWS.
Gordon & Breach Science Publishers, c/o International Publishers Distributor, P.O. Box 3054, Langhorne, PA 19047-3054. TEL 215-750-2642. FAX 215-750-6343. *2635*

CHEMICAL ENGINEERING EDUCATION.
American Society for Engineering Education, Chemical Engineering Division, 227 Chemical Engineering Bldg., Box 116005, Gainesville, FL 32611-6005. TEL 904-392-0857. FAX 904-392-9513. *2635*

CHEMICAL ENGINEERING JOURNAL AND BIOCHEMICAL ENGINEERING JOURNAL.
Elsevier Science S.A., P.O. Box 564, CH-1001 Lausanne 1, Switzerland. TEL 41-21-3207381. FAX 41-21-3235444. *2636*

CHEMICAL ENGINEERING MONOGRAPHS.
Elsevier Science B.V., Books Division, P.O. Box 211, 1000 AE Amsterdam, Netherlands. TEL 31-20-4853911. FAX 31-20-4853705. *2636*

CHEMICAL ENGINEERING PROGRESS.
American Institute of Chemical Engineers, 345 E. 47th St., New York NY 10017. TEL 212-705-7663. FAX 212-752-3294. *2636*

CHEMICAL ENGINEERING RESEARCH & DESIGN.
Institution of Chemical Engineers, George E. Davis Bldg., 165-189 Railway Terr., Rugby, Warks. CV21 3HQ, England. TEL 44-1788-578214. FAX 44-1788-560833. *2536*

CHEMICAL ENGINEERING SCIENCE.
Elsevier Science Ltd., Pergamon, P.O. Box 800, Kidlington, Oxford OX5 1GDX, England. TEL 44-1865-843000. FAX 44-1865-843010. *2636*

CHEMICAL GEOLOGY.
Elsevier Science B.V., P.O. Box 211, 1000 AE Amsterdam, Netherlands. TEL 31-20-4853911. FAX 31-20-4353598. *2205*

CHEMICAL IMMUNOLOGY.
S. Karger AG Allschwilerstr. 10, P.O. Box, CH-4009 Basel, Switzerland. TEL 061-3061111. FAX 061-3061234. *4579*

THE CHEMICAL INTELLIGENCER.
Springer-Verlag, Life Science Journals, 175 Fifth Ave., New York, NY 10010. TEL 212-460-1500. FAX 212-473-6272. *1668*

CHEMICAL PHYSICS.
North-Holland P.O. Box 211, 1000 AE Amsterdam, Netherlands. TEL 31-20-4853911. FAX 31-20-4853598. *1749*

CHEMICAL PHYSICS LETTERS.
North-Holland P.O. Box 211, 1000 AE Amsterdam, Netherlands. TEL 31-20-4853911. FAX 31-20-4853598. *1749*

CHEMICAL PHYSICS OF SOLID SURFACES.
Elsevier Science B.V., Books Division, P.O. Box 211, 1000 AE Amsterdam, Netherlands. TEL 31-20-4853911. FAX 31-20-4853705. *1749*

CHEMICAL PHYSICS REPORTS.
Gordon and Breach Science Publishers, c/o International Publishers Distributor, P.O. Box 3054, Langhorne, PA 19047-3054. TEL 215-750-2642. FAX 215-750-6343. *5544*

CHEMICAL RESEARCH IN TOXICOLOGY.
American Chemical Society, 1155 16th St., N.W., Washington, DC 20036. TEL 800-333-9511. FAX 614-447-3671. *2843*

CHEMICAL SOCIETY OF ETHIOPIA. BULLETIN.
Chemical Society of Ethiopia, P.O. Box 32934, Addis Ababa, Ethiopia. TEL 251-1-121201. FAX 251-1-551244. *1669*

CHEMICAL SUBSTANCES CONTROL.
The Bureau of National Affairs, Inc., 1231 25th St., N.W., Washington, DC 20037. TEL 202-452-4200. FAX 202-822-8092. *1669*

CHEMICAL THERMODYNAMICS.
Elsevier Science B.V., Books Division, P.O. Box 211, 1000 AE Amsterdam, Netherlands. TEL 31-20-4853911. FAX 31-20-4853705. *5544*

CHEMICALLY MODIFIED SURFACES.
Gordon & Breach Science Publishers, c/o International Publishers Distributor, P.O. Box 3054, Langhorne, PA 19047-3054. TEL 215-750-2642. FAX 215-750-6343. *1749*

CHEMICALS IN AGRICULTURE.
Elsevier Science B.V., Books Division, P.O. Box 211, 1000 AE Amsterdam, Netherlands. TEL 31-20-4853911. FAX 31-20-4853705. *215*

CHEMICO-BIOLOGICAL INTERACTIONS.
Elsevier Science Ireland Ltd., P.O. Box 85, Limerick, Ireland. TEL 353-61-471944. FAX 353-61-472144. *2843*

CHEMIST.
American Institute of Chemists, Inc., 501 Wythe St., Alexandria, VA 22314. TEL 703-836-2090. FAX 703-836-2091. *1670*

CHEMISTRY AND BIOCHEMISTRY OF AMINO ACIDS, PEPTIDES, AND PROTEINS.
Marcel Dekker, Inc., 270 Madison Ave., New York, NY 10016. TEL 212-696-9000. FAX 212-685-4540. *635*

CHEMISTRY & BIOLOGY.
Current Biology Ltd., 402 Market St., Ste. 700, Philadelphia, PA 19106 FAX 215-574-2270. *660*

CHEMISTRY AND ECOLOGY.
Gordon and Breach Science Publishers, c/o International Publishers Distributor, PO. Box 3054, Langhorne, PA 19047-3054. TEL 215-750-2642. FAX 215-750-6343. *1670*

CHEMISTRY AND PHYSICS OF CARBON: A SERIES OF ADVANCES.
Marcel Dekker, Inc., 270 Madison Ave., New York, NY 10016. TEL 212-695-9000. FAX 212-685-4540. *1736*

CHEMISTRY AND PHYSICS OF LIPIDS.
Elsevier Science Ireland Ltd., P.O. Box 85, Limerick, Ireland. TEL 353-61-471944. FAX 353-61-472144. *636*

CHEMISTRY AND TECHNOLOGY OF FUELS AND OILS.
Plenum Publishing Corp., Consultants Bureau, 233 Spring St., New York, NY 10013-1578. TEL 212-762-8468. FAX 212-463-0742. *5352*

CHEMISTRY OF FUNCTIONAL GROUPS.
John Wiley & Sons, Inc., 605 Third Ave., New York, NY 10158. TEL 212-850-6000. FAX 212-850-6088. *1671*

CHEMISTRY OF HETEROCYCLIC COMPOUNDS (NEW YORK, 1951).
John Wiley & Sons, Inc., 605 Third Ave., New York, NY 10158. TEL 212-850-6000. FAX 212-850-6088. *1737*

CHEMISTRY OF HETEROCYCLIC COMPOUNDS (NEW YORK, 1965).
Plenum Publishing Corp., Consultants Bureau, 233 Spring St., New York, NY 10013-1578. TEL 212-620-8468. FAX 212-463-0742. *1737*

CHEMISTRY OF NATURAL COMPOUNDS.
Plenum Publishing Corp., Consultants Bureau, 233 Spring St., New York, NY 10013-1578. TEL 212-620-8468. FAX 212-463-0742. *1737*

CHEMISTRY REVIEWS.
Harwood Academic Publishers c/o International Publishers Distributor, P.O. Box 3054, Langhorne, PA 19047-3054. TEL 215-750-2642. FAX 215-750-6343. *1671*

CHEMISTS AND CHEMISTRY.
Kluwer Academic Publishers, Postbus 17, 3300 AA Dordrecht, Netherlands. TEL 31-78-6392392. FAX 31-78-6392254. *1671*

CHEMOMETRICS AND INTELLIGENT LABORATORY SYSTEMS.
Elsevier Science B.V., P.O. Box 211, 1000 AE Amsterdam, Netherlands. TEL 31-20-4853911. FAX 31-20-4853598 *1724*

CHEMOSPHERE.
Elsevier Science Ltd., Pergamon, P.O. Box 800, Kidlington, Oxford OX5 1DX, England. TEL 44-1865-843000. FAX 44-1865-843010. *2843*

CHEMOTHERAPY.
S. Karger AG, Allschwilerstr. 10, P.O. Box, CH-4009 Basel, Switzerland. TEL 061-3061111. FAX 061-3061234. *5404*

CHEMUNG HISTORICAL JOURNAL.
Chemung County Historical Society, 415 E. Water St., Elmira, NY 14901. TEL 607-734-4167. FAX 607-734-1565. *3463*

CHENGSHI JINRONG LUNTAN.
Chengshi Jinrong Luntan Bianjibu, 15 Cuiwei Rd., Haidian, Beijing 100036, People's Republic of China. TEL 86-10-8185253. FAX 86-10-8217853. *1076*

CHENJI XUEBAO.
Science Press, Marketing and Sales Department, 16 Donghuangchenggen North St., Beijing 100717, People's Republic of China. TEL 4010642. FAX 4019810. *2228*

CHESHIRE AND WIRRAL BIRD REPORT.
Cheshire - Wirral Ornithological Society, 113 Nantwich Rd., Middlewich, Ches. CW10 9 HD, England. *774*

CHEST.
American College of Chest Physicians, 3300 Dundee Rd., Northbrook, IL 60062. TEL 847-498-1400. FAX 849-498-5460. *4887*

CHETHAM SOCIETY PUBLICATIONS - REMAINS, HISTORICAL AND LITERARY, CONNECTED WITH THE PALATINE COUNTIES OF LANCASTER AND CHESTER.
Carnegie Publishing Ltd., 18 Maynard St., Preston, Lancs. PR2 2AL, England. TEL 01772-881246. FAX 01772-881442. *3403*

CHICAGO ARTISTS' NEWS.
Chicago Artists' Coalition, 11 E. Hubbard St., 7th Fl., Chicago, IL 60611. TEL 312-670-2060. FAX 312-670-2521. *423*

CHICAGO GUIDES TO WRITING, EDITING, AND PUBLISHING.
University of Chicago Press, 5801 S. Ellis Ave., Chicago, IL 60637. TEL 312-702-7899. *5993*

CHICAGO HISTORY OF AMERICAN CIVILIZATION.
University of Chicago Press, 5801 S. Ellis Ave., Chicago, IL 60637. TEL 312-702-7899. *3464*

CHICAGO HISTORY OF AMERICAN RELIGION.
University of Chicago Press, 5801 S. Ellis Ave., Chicago, IL 60637. TEL 312-702-7899. *6051*

CHICAGO JOURNAL OF THEORETICAL COMPUTER SCIENCE.
M I T Press, 55 Hayward St., Cambridge, MA 02142-1399. TEL 617-253-2889. FAX 617-258-6779. *1983*

CHICAGO LECTURES IN MATHEMATICS.
University of Chicago Press, 5801 S. Ellis Ave., Chicago, IL 60637. TEL 312-702-7899. *4359*

CHICAGO LECTURES IN PHYSICS.
University of Chicago Press, 5801 S. Ellis Ave., Chicago, IL 60637. TEL 312-702-7899. *5544*

CHICAGO MEDICINE.
Chicago Medical Society, 515 N. Dearborn, Chicago, IL 60610. TEL 312-670-2550. FAX 312-670-3646. *4441*

CHICAGO STUDIES IN THE HISTORY OF JUDAISM.
University of Chicago Press, 5801 S. Ellis Ave., Chicago, IL 60637. TEL 312-702-7899. *6123*

CHIEFTAIN.
Black Hawk College, Quad Cities Campus, 6600 34th Ave., Moline, IL 61265. FAX 309-792-5976. *1861*

CHIKEI.
Nihon Chikeigaku Rengo, Kyoto Daigaku Bosai Kenkyujo, Chikei Dojo Saigai Kenkyu Bumon, Gokanosho, Uji-shi, Kyoto 611, Japan. TEL 81-774-32-6041. FAX 81-774-32-4115. *2228*

CHILD ABUSE & NEGLECT.
Elsevier Science Ltd., Pergamon, P.O. Box 800, Kidlington, Oxford OX5 1DX, England. TEL 44-1865-843000. FAX 44-1865-843010. *1762*

CHILD AND ADOLESCENT SOCIAL WORK JOURNAL.
Human Sciences Press, Inc. 233 Spring St., New York, NY 10013-1578. TEL 212-620-8000. FAX 212-463-0742. *6408*

CHILD & FAMILY BEHAVIOR THERAPY.
Haworth Press, Inc., 10 Alice St., Binghamton, NY 13904. TEL 607-722-5857. FAX 607-722-1424. *5834*

CHILD AND YOUTH CARE FORUM.
Human Sciences Press, Inc. 233 Spring St., New York, NY 10013-1578. TEL 212-620-8000. FAX 212-463-0742. *1763*

CHILD & YOUTH SERVICES.
Haworth Press, Inc., 10 Alice St., Binghamton, NY 13904. TEL 607-722-5857. FAX 607-722-1424. *6366*

CHILD CARE FOCUS.
Manitoba Child Care Association, 364 McGregor St., Winnipeg, MB R2W 4X3, Canada. TEL 204-586-8587. FAX 204-589-5613. *1763*

CHILD: CARE, HEALTH AND DEVELOPMENT.
Blackwell Science Ltd., Osney Mead, Oxford OX2 OEL, England. TEL 44-1865-206206. FAX 44-1865-721205. *4804*

CHILD DEVELOPMENT.
University of Chicago Press, Journals Division, Box 37005, Chicago, IL 60637. TEL 773-753-3347. FAX 773-753-0811. *1763*

CHILD DEVELOPMENT ABSTRACTS AND BIBLIOGRAPHY.
University of Chicago Press, Journals Division, 5720 S. Woodlawn Ave., Chicago, IL 60637. TEL 773-753-3347. FAX 773-753-0811. *1782*

CHILD MALTREATMENT.
Sage Publications, Inc., 2455 Teller Rd., Thousand Oaks, CA 91320. TEL 805-499-0721. FAX 805-499-0871. *1763*

CHILD NEUROPSYCHOLOGY.
Swets & Zeitlinger bv, P.O. Box 825, 2160 SZ Lisse, Netherlands. TEL 31-252-435111. FAX 31-252-415888. *5834*

CHILD NURTURANCE.
Plenum Publishing Corp., 233 Spring St., New York, NY 10013-1578. TEL 212-620-8000. FAX 212-463-0742. *1763*

CHILD PSYCHIATRY AND HUMAN DEVELOPMENT.
Human Sciences Press, Inc. 233 Spring St., New York, NY 10013-1578. TEL 212-620-8000. FAX 212-463-0742. *4831*

CHILD PSYCHOLOGY AND PSYCHIATRY REVIEW.
Cambridge University Press, Edinburgh Bldg., Shaftesbury Rd., Cambridge CB2 2RU, England. TEL 44-1223-312393. FAX 44-1223-315052. *5834*

CHILD STUDY JOURNAL.
State University of New York at Buffalo, Behavioral and Humanistic Studies, Bacon Hall 306, 1300 Elmwood Ave., Buffalo, NY 14222-1095. TEL 716-878-5302. FAX 716-878-5833. *2319*

CHILDHOOD.
Sage Publications Ltd., 6 Bonhill St., London EC2A 4PU, England. TEL 44-171-374-0645. FAX 44-171-374-8741. *1763*

CHILDREN AND YOUTH SERVICES REVIEW.
Elsevier Science Ltd., Pergamon, P.O. Box 800, Kidlington, Oxford OX5 1DX, England. TEL 44-1865-843000. FAX 44-1865-843010. *1764*

CHILDREN, CHURCHES AND DADDIES.
Scars Publications and Design, 3255 W. Belden, Ste. 3E, Chicago, IL 60647-2559. *4136*

CHILDREN'S BOOK AND PLAY REVIEW.
Brigham Young University, Harold B. Lee Library, 5042-J HBLL, Provo, UT 84602. TEL 801-378-6685. FAX 801-378-6708. *1787*

CHILDREN'S BOOK INSIDER.
Children's Book Insider, Box 1030, Fairplay, CO 80440-1030. TEL 719-836-0394. *5993*

CHILDREN'S ENVIRONMENTS.
Chapman & Hall, Journals Department 2-6 Boundary Row, London SE1 8HN, England. TEL 44-171-8650066. FAX 44-171-5229623. *5834*

CHILDREN'S HOSPITAL QUARTERLY.
Human Sciences Press, Inc. 233 Spring St., New York, NY 10013. TEL 212-620-8000. FAX 212-463-0742. *4804*

CHILDREN'S LANGUAGE.
Lawrence Erlbaum Associates, Inc., 10 Industrial Dr., Mahwah, NJ 07430-2262. TEL 201-236-9500. FAX 201-236-0072. *4061*

CHILDREN'S LEGAL RIGHTS JOURNAL.
William S. Hein & Co., Inc., 1285 Main St., Buffalo, NY 14209. TEL 716-882-2600. FAX 716-883-8100. *3918*

CHILDREN'S LITERATURE IN EDUCATION.
Human Sciences Press, Inc. 233 Spring St., New York, NY 10013. TEL 212-620-8000. FAX 212-463-0742. *1765*

CHILDREN'S SOCIAL & ECONOMICS EDUCATION.
Multilingual Matters Ltd., Frankfurt Lodge, Clevedon Hall, Victoria Rd., Clevedon, Avon BS21 7SJ, England. TEL 44-1275-876519. FAX 44-1275-343096. *2319*

CHILDRIGHT.
Children's Legal Centre Ltd., University of Essex, Wivenhoe Park, Colchester, Essex CO4 3SQ. TEL 44-1206-872477. FAX 44-1206-873428. *1765*

CHILD'S NERVOUS SYSTEM.
Springer-Verlag, Heidelberger Platz 3, 14197 Berlin, Germany. TEL 49-30-8207-0. FAX 49-30-8214091. *4831*

CHILTON'S REVIEW OF OPTOMETRY.
Chilton Co., Chilton Way, Radnor, PA 19089. TEL 215-964-4370. *4768*

CHIMICA ACTA TURCICA.
Istanbul Universitesi, Muhendislik Fakultesi Dekanligi, 34850 Avcilar - Istanbul, Turkey. TEL 90-212-5911998. FAX 90-212-5911997. *1672*

CHIMICA OGGI.
Teknoscienze s.r.l., Via Aurelio Saffi, 23, 20123 Milan, Italy. TEL 39-2-4818118. FAX 39-2-4818070. *1672*

CHINA CENTER OF ADVANCED SCIENCE AND TECHNOLOGY SERIES.
Gordon & Breach Science Publishers, c/o International Publishers Distributor, P.O. Box 3054, Langhorne, PA 19047-3054. TEL 215-750-2642. FAX 215-750-6343. *6233*

CHINA INFORMATION.
Rijksuniversiteit te Leiden, Sinologisch Instituut, Postbus 9515, 2300 RA Leiden, Netherlands. TEL 31-71-5272516. FAX 31-71-5272615. *5281*

CHINA OCEAN ENGINEERING.
China Ocean Press, International Cooperation Department, Haimao Dalou, 1 Fuxingmenwai Dajie, Beijing 100860, People's Republic of China. TEL 8032211. FAX 8033515. *2592*

CHINA REPORT.
Sage Publications India Pvt. Ltd., P.O. Box 4215, New Delhi 110 048. TEL 91-11-644-4958. FAX 91-11-647-2426. *5745*

CHINA STEEL TECHNICAL REPORT.
China Steel Corporation, R & D Department, No. 1 Chungkang Rd., Lin Hai Industrial District, Hsiaokang, Kaohsiung, Taiwan, Republic of China. TEL 07-8021111. FAX 07-8022432. *4952*

CHINESE ASTRONOMY AND ASTROPHYSICS.
Elsevier Science Ltd., Pergamon, P.O. Box 800, Kidlington, Oxford OX5 1DX, England. TEL 44-1865-843000. FAX 44-1865-843010. *479*

CHINESE CHEMICAL LETTERS.
Chinese Chemical Society, P.O. Box 2709, Beijing 100080, People's Republic of China. TEL 86-10-6256-8157. FAX 86-10-6256-8157. *1672*

Refereed

CHINESE ECONOMIC STUDIES.
M.E. Sharpe, Inc., 80 Business Park Dr., Armonk, NY 10504. TEL 914-273-1800. FAX 914-273-2106. *908*

CHINESE EDUCATION AND SOCIETY.
M.E. Sharpe, Inc., 80 Business Park Dr., Armonk, NY 10504. TEL 914-273-1800. FAX 914-273-2106. *2319*

CHINESE ENVIRONMENTAL SCIENCE.
Chinese Society for Environmental Sciences, No.115, Xizhimennei Nanxiaojie, Beijing 100035, People's Republic of China. TEL 6066498. FAX 6020031. *2780*

CHINESE GEOGRAPHICAL SCIENCE.
Science Press, Marketing and Sales Department, 16 Donghuangchenggen North St., Beijing 100717, People's Republic of China. TEL 4010642. FAX 4019810. *2228*

CHINESE JOURNAL OF ACOUSTICS.
Science Press, Marketing and Sales Department, 16 Donghuangchenggen North St., Beijing 100717, People's Republic of China. TEL 4010642. FAX 4019810. *5614*

CHINESE JOURNAL OF ADMINISTRATION.
National Chengchi University, Center for Public and Business Administration Education, 187 Chin Hua St., Taipei, Taiwan, Republic of China. TEL 886-2-3940690. FAX 886-2-3975219. *1410*

CHINESE JOURNAL OF ATMOSPHERIC SCIENCES.
Allerton Press, Inc., 150 Fifth Ave., New York, NY 10011. TEL 212-924-3950. FAX 212-463-9684. *4992*

CHINESE JOURNAL OF BIOTECHNOLOGY.
Allerton Press, Inc., 150 Fifth Ave., New York, NY 10011. TEL 212-924-3950. FAX 212-463-9684. *660*

CHINESE JOURNAL OF BOTANY.
Science Press, Marketing and Sales Department, 16 Donghuangchenggen North St., Beijing 100717, People's Republic of China. TEL 4010642. FAX 4019810. *676*

CHINESE JOURNAL OF CANCER RESEARCH.
Beijing Institute for Cancer Research, Da-Hong-Luo-Chang Street, Western District, Beijing, People's Republic of China. TEL 861-603-1122. FAX 861-602-3658. *4753*

CHINESE JOURNAL OF CHEMISTRY.
Science Press, Marketing and Sales Department, 16 Donghuangchenggen North St., Beijing 100717, People's Republic of China. TEL 4010642. FAX 4019810. *1672*

CHINESE JOURNAL OF GEOCHEMISTRY.
Science Press, Marketing and Sales Department, 16 Donghuangchenggen North St., Beijing 100717, People's Republic of China. TEL 4010642. FAX 4019810. *2228*

CHINESE JOURNAL OF GEOPHYSICS.
Allerton Press, Inc., 150 Fifth Ave., New York, NY 10011. TEL 212-924-3950. FAX 212-463-9684. *2271*

CHINESE JOURNAL OF LASERS.
Science Press, Marketing and Sales Department, 16 Donghuangchenggen North St., Beijing 100717, People's Republic of China. *5602*

CHINESE JOURNAL OF MECHANICAL ENGINEERING.
China Machine Press, 1 Nanjie, Baiwanzhuang, Beijing 100037, People's Republic of China. TEL 8610-8326677. FAX 8610-8326337. *2751*

CHINESE JOURNAL OF MICROBIOLOGY AND IMMUNOLOGY.
Chinese Society of Microbiology, National Taiwan University, College of Medicine, Jen-Ai Rd., Taipei, Taiwan, Republic of China. *755*

CHINESE JOURNAL OF OCEANOLOGY AND LIMNOLOGY.
Science Press, Marketing and Sales Department, 16 Donghuangchenggen North St., Beijing 100717, People's Republic of China. TEL 4010642. FAX 4019810. *2291*

CHINESE JOURNAL OF PHYSIOLOGICAL SCIENCES.
Science Press Marketing and Sales Department, 16 Donghuangchenggen North St., Beijing 100717, People's Republic of China. TEL 4010642. FAX 4019810. *786*

CHINESE JOURNAL OF POLYMER SCIENCE.
Science Press Marketing and Sales Department, 16 Donghuangchenggen North St., Beijing 100717, People's Republic of China. TEL 4010642. FAX 4019810. *1737*

CHINESE JOURNAL OF PSYCHOLOGY.
Chinese Psychological Association, c/o Department of Psychology, National Taiwan University, Taipei 10764, Taiwan, Republic of China. FAX 886-2-3629909. *5834*

CHINESE LAW AND GOVERNMENT.
M.E. Sharpe, Inc., 80 Business Park Dr., Armonk, NY 10504. TEL 914-273-1800. FAX 914-273-2106. *3759*

CHINESE LITERATURE: ESSAYS, ARTICLES, REVIEWS.
c/o Dept. of Comparative Literature, Ballantine Hall Rm. 402, Inciana University, Bloomington, IN 47405. TEL 812-855-7070. *4195*

CHINESE MEDICAL JOURNAL.
Chinese Medical Association, P.O. Box 2258, 42 Dongsi Xidajie, Beijing 100710, People's Republic of China. TEL 5133311. *4441*

CHINESE MEDICAL SCIENCES JOURNAL.
Chinese Academy of Medical Sciences (CAMS), 9 Dong Dan San Tiao, Beijing 100730, People's Republic of China. TEL 5133074. FAX 5124876. *4441*

CHINESE MUSIC.
Chinese Music Society of North America, One Heritage Plaza, Box 5275, Woodridge, IL 60517-0275. TEL 630-910-1551. FAX 630-910-1561. *5148*

CHINESE PHYSICS LETTERS.
Allerton Press, Inc., 150 Fifth Ave., New York, NY 10011. TEL 212-924-3950. FAX 212-463-9684. *5544*

CHINESE SCIENCE BULLETIN.
Science Press, Marketing and Sales Department, 16 Donghuangchenggen Beijie, Beijing, People's Republic of China. TEL 4010642. FAX 4019810. *6234*

CHINESE SOCIOLOGY AND ANTHROPOLOGY.
M.E. Sharpe, Inc., 80 Business Park Dr., Armonk, NY 10504. TEL 914-273-1800. FAX 914-273-2106. *6408*

CHINESE STUDIES IN HISTORY.
M.E. Sharpe, Inc. 80 Business Park Dr., Armonk, NY 10504 TEL 914-273-1800. FAX 914-273-2106. *3340*

CHINESE STUDIES IN PHILOSOPHY.
M.E. Sharpe, Inc., 80 Business Park Dr., Armonk, NY 10504 TEL 914-273-1800. FAX 914-273-2106. *5471*

CHINOPERL PAPERS.
Conference on Chinese Oral and Performing Literature, c/o Ball Yung, Music Department, University of Pittsburgh, Pittsburgh, PA 15260. TEL 412-624-4061. FAX 412-624-4186. *5281*

CHIRALITY.
John Wiley & Sons, Inc., Journals, 605 Third Ave., New York, NY 10158. TEL 212-850-6645. FAX 212-850-6021. *755*

CHIRON REVIEW.
Chiron Review Press, 522 E. South Ave., St. John, KS 67576-2212. TEL 316-549-3933. *4303*

CHIROPODY - PODIATRY COMMENT.
Association of Chiropodists and Podiatrists, 42 Velsheda Rd., Shirley, Solihull, W. Midlands B90 2JN, England. TEL 44-121-745-1552. *4816*

CHIROPODY REVIEW.
Institute of Chiropodists, 27 Wright St., Southport, Merseyside PR9 0TL, England. TEL 44-1704-546141. FAX 44-1704-500477. *4905*

CHIROPRACTIC HISTORY.
Association for the History of Chiropractic, 1000 Brady St., Davenport, IA 52803 TEL 319-326-9894. FAX 319-326-9897. *4612*

CHIROPRACTIC JOURNAL OF AUSTRALIA.
Chiropractors' Association of Australia, P.O. Box 748, Wagga Wagga, N.S.W. 2650, Australia. TEL 61-69-213238. FAX 61-69-262556. *4612*

CHIROPRACTIC TECHNIQUE.
Williams & Wilkins, 351 W. Camden St., Baltimore, MD 21201. TEL 410-528-4000. FAX 410-528-4312. *4612*

CHIRURGIA.
Edizioni Minerva Medica, Corso Bramante 83-85, 10126 Turin, Italy. TEL 39-11-578282. FAX 39-11-3121736. *4905*

CHIRURGIA DEL PIEDE.
Edizioni Minerva Medica, Corso Bramante 83-85, Turin 10126, Italy. TEL 39-11-678282. FAX 39-11-3121736. *4906*

CHIRURGIA TRIVENETA.
Ospedale Civile Maggiore, I Divisione Chirurgia Generale, Piazzale Stefani 1, 37126 Verona, Italy. TEL 045-8072410. FAX 045-8072057. *4906*

CHIRURGIE.
Masson - Periodiques, Villa Laromiguiere, 75005 Paris, France. TEL 1-40-46-62-00. FAX 1-40-46-62-01. *4906*

CHIRURGISCHE GASTROENTEROLOGIE.
S. Karger AG, Allschwilerstr. 10, P.O. Box, CH-4009 Basel, Switzerland. TEL 061-3061111. FAX 061-3061234. *4690*

CHOICE (MIDDLETOWN).
Choice, 100 Riverview Ctr., Middletown, CT 06457. TEL 203-347-6933. FAX 203-346-8586. *6013*

CHOICES IN CARDIOLOGY.
Choices Publishing Group, Inc. 129 Washington St., Hoboken, NJ 07030. TEL 201-792-1900. FAX 201-792-3955. *599*

CHONGQING HUANJING KEXUE.
Chongqing Huanjing Kexue Xuehui, 212 Renmin Lu, Chongqing, Sichuan 630015, People's Republic of China. TEL 86-811-3568871. FAX 86-811-3850021. *2780*

CHOONPA IGAKU.
Nihon Choonpa Igakkai, Hongo 3-23-1, Crosevia Hongo 3F, Bunkyo-ku, Tokyo 113, Japan. TEL 03-3313-5540. FAX 03-3816-7544. *4874*

CHORAL JOURNAL.
American Choral Directors Association, Box 6310, Lawton, OK 73506-0310. TEL 405-355-8161. FAX 405-248-1465. *5148*

CHOREOGRAPHY AND DANCE.
Harwood Academic Publishers, c/o International Publishers Distributor P.O. Box 3054, Langhorne, PA 19047-3054. TEL 215-750-2642. FAX 215-750-6343. *2187*

CHRISTIAN BIOETHICS.
Swets & Zeitlinger bv P.O. Box 825, 2160 SZ Lisse, Netherlands. TEL 31-252-435111. FAX 31-252-415888. *4441*

CHRISTIAN MEDICAL COLLEGE VELLORE ALUMNI JOURNAL.
Christian Medical College, Alumni Association, Vellore 632 002, Tamil Nadu, India. TEL 91-416-22603. FAX 91-416-32788. *4441*

CHRISTIAN MONTHLY.
Apostolic Lutheran Book Concern, Box 2126, Battle Ground, WA 98604-2126. TEL 360-687-4416. *6138*

CHRISTIAN OBSERVER.
Christian Observer, Inc., 9400 Fairview Ave., Manassas, VA 22111-5802. TEL 703-335-2844. FAX 703-368-4817. *6138*

CHRISTIAN SCHOLAR'S REVIEW.
c/o Calvin College, G and Rapids, MI 49546. *5052*

CHRISTIAN WEEK.
Fellowship for Print Witness Inc., Box 725, Winnipeg, MB R3C 2K3, Canada. TEL 204-943-1147. FAX 204-947-5632. *6138*

CHRISTIANITY AND LITERATURE.
Conference on Christianity and Literature, West Georgia College, Carrollton, GA 30118-2200. TEL 206-836-6512. *4136*

CHROMATOGRAPHIA.
Friedr. Vieweg und Sohn Verlagsgesellschaft mbH, Postfach 1546, 65005 Wiesbaden, Germany. TEL 49-611-7878389. FAX 49-611-7878439. *1715*

CHROMATOGRAPHIC SCIENCE SERIES.
Marcel Dekker, Inc., 270 Madison Ave., New York, NY 10016. TEL 212-696-9000. FAX 212-685-4540. *1715*

CHROMATOGRAPHY ABSTRACTS.
Royal Society of Chemistry, Thomas Graham House, Science Park, Milton Rd., Cambridge CB4 4WF, England. TEL 44-1223-420066. FAX 44-1223-423429. *1707*

CHROMOSOME RESEARCH.
Rapid Science Publishers, The Old Malthouse, Paradise St., Oxford OX1 1LD, England. TEL 44-1865-790447. FAX 44-1865-244012. *739*

CHRONICA DERMATOLOGICA.
Istituto Dermopatico dell'Immacolata, Via Monti di Creta, 104, 00167 Rome, Italy. FAX 39-6-66464437. *4659*

CHRONOBIOLOGY INTERNATIONAL.
Marcel Dekker Journals, 270 Madison Ave., New York, NY 10016. TEL 212-696-9000. FAX 212-685-4540. *578*

CHUBAN FAXING YANJIU.
China Book Publishing House, No. A-7, Xirongxian Hutong, Xicheng-qu, Beijing 100031, People's Republic of China. TEL 010-6059539. *5993*

CHUGOKU SHIKOKU NO NOGYO KISHO.
Nihon Nogyo Kisho Gakkai, Chugoku Shikoku Shibu, c/o Research Institute for Bioresources, Okayama University, Kurashiki 710, Japan. TEL 086-434-1239. FAX 086-421-0699. *4992*

CHUNG-WAI LITERARY MONTHLY.
c/o Department of Foreign Languages, National Taiwan University, Roosevelt Rd. Sec. 4, Taipei 106, Taiwan, Republic of China. TEL 886-2-3630231. FAX 886-2-3639395. *4195*

CHURCH ADVOCATE.
Churches of God, General Conference, Box 926, Findlay, OH 45839. TEL 419-424-1961. FAX 419-424-3433. *6053*

CH4 ENERGIA METANO.
Associazione Tecnica Italiana del Gas, Via Palmieri 25, 10138 Turin, Italy. TEL 39-11-4345965. FAX 39-11-4472990. *5352*

CIENCIA AGRONOMICA.
Universidade Federal do Ceara, Centro de Ciencias Agrarias, Av. Mister Hull, Caixa Postal 12168, 60355 Fortaleza, Ceara, Brazil. TEL 55-85-243-9668. FAX 55-85-243-9513. *107*

CIENCIA DEL SUELO.
Asociacion Argentina de la Ciencia del Suelo, J. Ramirez de Velasco 847, 1414 Buenos Aires, Argentina. TEL 54-1-7718968. *216*

CIENCIA RURAL.
Universidade Federal de Santa Maria, Centro de Ciencias Rurais, Campus Universitario, 97119-900 Santa Maria, Rio Grande do Sul, Brazil. TEL 55-55-226-2347. *107*

CIENCIAS MARINAS.
Universidad Autonoma de Baja California, Instituto de Investigaciones Oceanologicas, Apdo. Postal 453, Ensenada, Baja California, Mexico. TEL 617-45451. FAX 617-45303. *2292*

CINCINNATI CLASSICAL STUDIES. NEW SERIES.
E.J. Brill, P.O. Box 9000, 2300 PA Leiden, Netherlands. TEL 31-71-5353500. FAX 31-71-5317532. *1819*

CINEMA JOURNAL.
University of Texas Press, Journals Division, Box 7819, Austin, TX 78713. TEL 512-471-4531. FAX 512-320-0668. *5096*

CINESIOLOGIE.
Syndicat National des Medecins du Sport, 1 rue d'Alsace, 49100 Angers, France. TEL 33-1-41-88-35-35. FAX 33-1-41-88-13-55. *4897*

CIRCLE (NEW YORK).
Jewish Community Centers Association of North America, 15 E. 26th St., New York, NY 10010-1579. TEL 212-532-4949. FAX 212-481-4174. *2872*

CIRCULATION (DALLAS).
American Heart Association, 7272 Greenville Ave., Dallas, TX 75231-4596. TEL 214-706-1310. FAX 214-691-6342. *4599*

CIRCULATION RESEARCH.
American Heart Association, 7272 Greenville Ave., Dallas, TX 75231-4596. TEL 214-706-1310. FAX 214-691-6342. *4599*

CIRENCESTER EXCAVATIONS.
Cotswold Archaeological Trust, Cirencester Excavation Committee, Corinium Museum, Park St., Cirencester, Glos. GL7 2BX, England. TEL 01285-643625. FAX 01285-644641. *349*

CISTERCIAN STUDIES QUARTERLY.
Cistercian Studies Quarterly, Santa Rita Abbey, HC 1, Box 929, Sonoita, AZ 85637-9705. TEL 520-455-5595. *6053*

CITIES.
Butterworth - Heinemann, Part of the Reed Elsevier group, Linacre House, Jordan Hill, Oxford OX2 8DP, England. TEL 44-1865-310366. FAX 44-1865-310898. *5939*

CIUDAD Y TERRITORIO: ESTUDIOS TERRITORIALES.
Ministerio de Obras Publicas, Transportes y Medio Ambiente, Direccion General para la Vivienda, el Urbanismo y la Arquitectura, Paseo de la Castellana, 67, 28071 Madrid, Spain. TEL 34-1-5975883. FAX 34-1-5975884. *5939*

CIVIL ENGINEERING.
South African Institution of Civil Engineers, P.O. Box 93495, Yeoville 2143, South Africa. TEL 27-11-648-1184. FAX 27-11-648-7427. *2655*

CIVIL ENGINEERING (NEW YORK).
American Society of Civil Engineers, 345 E. 47th St., New York, NY 10017-2398. TEL 212-705-7288. FAX 212-980-4681. *2655*

CIVIL ENGINEERING PRACTICE.
Boston Society of Civil Engineers Section, Engineering Center, 1 Walnut St., Boston, MA 02108. TEL 617-227-5551. *2655*

CIVIL ENGINEERING SURVEYOR.
Surco Ltd., 26 Market St., Altrincham, Cheshire WA14 1PF, England. TEL 0161-928-8074. FAX 0161-941-6134. *2655*

CIVIL RIGHTS MONITOR.
Leadership Conference on Education Fund, 1629 K St., Ste. 1010, Washington, DC 20006. TEL 202-466-3434. *3881*

CLARINET.
International Clarinet Association, College of Music, University of North Texas, Denton, TX 76203. TEL 817-565-4096. FAX 817-565-2002. *5149*

CLASS: CLASSIFICATION LITERATURE AUTOMATED SEARCH SERVICE.
Classification Society of North America, c/o William H.E. Day, P.O. Box 17, Port Midland, NS B0W 2V0, Canada. TEL 902-649-2996. *4359*

CLASSICAL ANTIQUITY.
University of California Press, Journals Division, 2120 Berkeley Way, No. 5812, Berkeley, CA 94720-5812. TEL 510-643-7154. FAX 510-642-9917. *1820*

CLASSICAL BULLETIN.
Bolchazy - Carducci Publishers, Inc., 1000 Brown St., Unit 101, Wauconda, IL 60084. TEL 847-526-4344. FAX 847-526-2867. *1820*

CLASSICAL PHILOLOGY.
University of Chicago Press, Journals Division, Box 37005, Chicago, IL 60637. TEL 773-753-3347. FAX 773-753-0811. *1820*

CLASSICAL WORLD.
Duquesne University, Department of Classics, Pittsburgh, PA 15282-1704. TEL 412-396-6450. FAX 412-396-5197. *1820*

THE CLASSICIST.
Transaction Publishers, Transaction Periodicals Consortium, Department 3092, Rutgers University, New Brunswick, NJ 08903. TEL 908-445-2280. FAX 908-445-3138. *389*

CLASSICS IN THE HISTORY AND PHILOSOPHY OF SCIENCE.
Gordon and Breach Science Publishers, c/o International Publishers Distributors, P.O. Box 3054, Langhorne, PA 19047-3054. TEL 215-750-2642. FAX 215-750-6343. *6234*

CLASSICS IN URBAN HISTORY.
University of California Press, 2120 Berkeley Way, Berkeley, CA 94720. TEL 510-642-4247. FAX 510-643-7127. *3579*

CLASSICS OF SOVIET MATHEMATICS.
Gordon and Breach Science Publishers, c/o International Publishers Distributor, P.O. Box 3054, Langhorne, PA 19047-3054. TEL 215-750-2642. FAX 215-750-6343. *4359*

CLASSICUM.
Classical Association of New South Wales, c/o H. Tarrant, Ed., Dept. of Classics, University of Newcastle, N.S.W. 2308, Australia. FAX 61-49-21-6947. *1820*

THE CLEARING HOUSE.
Heldref Publications, 1319 Eighteenth St., N.W., Washington, DC 20036-1802. TEL 202-296-6267. FAX 202-296-5149. *2320*

CLEFT PALATE - CRANIOFACIAL JOURNAL.
Decker Periodicals, P.O. Box 620, LCD 1, Hamilton, ON L8N 3K7, Canada. TEL 905-522-7017. FAX 905-522-7839. *4906*

CLEVELAND CLINIC JOURNAL OF MEDICINE.
Cleveland Clinic Educational Foundation, 9500 Euclid Ave., EE37, Cleveland, OH 44195. TEL 216-444-2662. FAX 216-444-9385. *4442*

CLIMATIC CHANGE.
Kluwer Academic Publishers, Postbus 17, 3300 AA Dordrecht, Netherlands. TEL 31-78-6392392. FAX 31-78-6392254. *4993*

CLINICA CHIMICA ACTA.
Elsevier Science B.V., P.O. Box 211, 1000 AE Amsterdam, Netherlands. TEL 31-20-4853911. FAX 31-20-4853598. *4442*

CLINICAL ANATOMY.
John Wiley & Sons, Inc., Journals, 605 Third Ave., New York, NY 10158. TEL 212-850-6645. FAX 212-850-6021. *578*

CLINICAL AND BIOCHEMICAL ANALYSIS.
Marcel Dekker, Inc., 270 Madison Ave., New York, NY 10016. TEL 212-696-9000. FAX 212-685-4540. *636*

CLINICAL AND DIAGNOSTIC LABORATORY IMMUNOLOGY.
American Society for Microbiology, 1325 Massachusetts Ave., N.W., Washington, DC 20005. TEL 202-942-9319. FAX 202-942-9346. *4579*

CLINICAL AND DIAGNOSTIC VIROLOGY.
Elsevier Science B.V., P.O. Box 211, 1000 AE Amsterdam, Netherlands. TEL 31-20-4853911. FAX 31-20-4853598. *4619*

CLINICAL AND EXPERIMENTAL ALLERGY.
Blackwell Science Ltd., Osney Mead, Oxford OX2 OEL, England. TEL 44-1865-206206. FAX 44-1865-721205. *4579*

CLINICAL AND EXPERIMENTAL DERMATOLOGY.
Blackwell Science Ltd., Osney Mead, Oxford OX2 OEL, England. TEL 44-1865-206206. FAX 44-1865-206219. *4659*

CLINICAL AND EXPERIMENTAL HYPERTENSION.
Marcel Dekker Journals, 270 Madison Ave., New York, NY 10016. TEL 212-696-9000. FAX 212-685-4540. *4600*

CLINICAL AND EXPERIMENTAL IMMUNOLOGY.
Blackwell Science Ltd., Osney Mead, Oxford OX2 0EL, England. TEL 44-1865-206206. FAX 44-1865-721205. *4579*

CLINICAL AND EXPERIMENTAL OBSTETRICS AND GYNECOLOGY.
Studi Ostetrico Ginecologici s.r.l., Galleria Storione 2-A, 35128 Padua, Italy. TEL 39-49-8758644. FAX 39-49-8752018. *4733*

CLINICAL AND INVESTIGATIVE MEDICINE.
Canadian Medical Association, Montreal General Hospital, 1650 Cedar Ave., Montreal, PQ H3G 1A4, Canada. TEL 514-933-9770. *4442*

CLINICAL AND LABORATORY HAEMATOLOGY.
Blackwell Science Ltd., Osney Mead, Oxford OX2 0EL, England. TEL 44-1865-206206. FAX 44-1865-206219. *4699*

CLINICAL ASPECTS OF BIOMEDICINE.
Elsevier Science B.V., Books Division, P.O. Box 211, 1000 AE Amsterdam, Netherlands. TEL 31-20-4853911. FAX 31-20-4853705. *4442*

CLINICAL BIOCHEMISTRY.
Elsevier Science Inc., Box 945, New York, NY 10159-0945. TEL 212-633-3730. FAX 212-633-3680. *636*

CLINICAL BIOMECHANICS.
Butterworth - Heinemann, Part of the Reed Elsevier group, Linacre House, Jordan Hill, Oxford OX2 8DP, England. TEL 44-1865-310366. FAX 44-1865-310898. *4612*

CLINICAL CANCER RESEARCH.
American Association for Cancer Research, Public Ledger Bldg., 150 S. Independence Mall West, Ste. 816, Philadelphia, PA 19106. TEL 215-440-9300. FAX 215-440-9354. *4753*

CLINICAL CARDIOLOGY.
Clinical Cardiology Publishing Company, Inc., Box 832, Mahwah, NJ 07430-0832. TEL 201-818-1010. FAX 201-818-0086. *4600*

CLINICAL CHEMISTRY.
American Association for Clinical Chemistry, Inc., 2101 L St. N.W., Ste. 202, Washington, DC 20037-1526. TEL 800-892-1400. FAX 202-887-5093. *4443*

CLINICAL CHEMISTRY AND ENZYMOLOGY COMMUNICATIONS.
Harwood Academic Publishers, c/o International Publishers Distributor, P.O. Box 3054, Langhorne, PA 19047-3054. TEL 215-750-2642. FAX 215-750-6343. *636*

CLINICAL DIABETES.
American Diabetes Association, 1660 Duke St., Alexandria, VA 22314. TEL 703-549-1500. FAX 703-836-7439. *4666*

CLINICAL DRUG INVESTIGATION.
Adis International Limited, Private Bag 65901, Mairangi Bay, Auckland 10, New Zealand. TEL 64-9-479-8100. FAX 64-9-479-8145. *5404*

CLINICAL DYSMORPHOLOGY.
Chapman & Hall, Journals Department 2-6 Boundary Row, London SE1 8HN, England. TEL 44-171-8650066. FAX 44-171-5229623. *787*

CLINICAL ELECTROENCEPHALOGRAPHY.
American Medical Electroencephalographic Association, 850 Elm Grove Rd., Ste. 11, Elm Grove, WI 53122. TEL 414-797-7800. *4831*

CLINICAL ENDOCRINOLOGY.
Blackwell Science Ltd., Osney Mead, Oxford OX2 0EL, England. TEL 44-1865-206206. FAX 44-1865-721205. *4666*

CLINICAL ENGINEERING SERIES.
Academic Press, Inc., 525 B St., Ste. 1900, San Diego, CA 92101-4495. TEL 619-231-0926. FAX 619-699-6715. *4443*

CLINICAL EYE AND VISION CARE.
Elsevier Science Ireland Ltd., P.O. Box 85, Limerick, Ireland. TEL 353-61-471944. FAX 353-61-472144. *4768*

CLINICAL GENETICS.
Munksgaard International Publishers Ltd., 35 Noerre Soegace, P.O. Box 2148, DK-1016 Copenhagen K, Denmark. TEL 45-33-127030. FAX 45-33-129387. *739*

CLINICAL GERONTOLOGIST.
Haworth Press, Inc., 10 Alice St., Binghamton, NY 13904. TEL 607-722-5857. FAX 607-722-1424. *3285*

CLINICAL HEMORHEOLOGY.
I O S Press, Van Diemenstraat 94, 1013 CN Amsterdam, Netherlands. TEL 31-20-6382189. FAX 31-20-6203419. *4699*

CLINICAL IMAGING.
Elsevier Science Inc., Box 945, New York, NY 10159-0945. TEL 212-633-3730. FAX 212-633-3680. *4874*

CLINICAL IMMUNOLOGY NEWSLETTER.
Elsevier Science Inc., Box 945, New York, NY 10159-0945. TEL 212-633-3730. FAX 212-633-3680. *4579*

CLINICAL INFANT REPORTS. MONOGRAPH.
International Universities Press, Inc., 59 Boston Post Rd., Box 1524, Madison, CT 06443-1524. TEL 203-245-4000. *4804*

CLINICAL INFECTIOUS DISEASES.
University of Chicago Press, Journals Division, Box 37005, Chicago, IL 60637. TEL 312-753-3347. FAX 312-753-0811. *4619*

CLINICAL JOURNAL OF PAIN.
Lippincott - Raven Publishers 227 E. Washington Sq., Philadelphia, PA 19106. TEL 215-238-4200. *4831*

CLINICAL JOURNAL OF SPORT MEDICINE.
Lippincott - Raven Publishers 227 E. Washington Sq., Philadelphia, PA 19106. TEL 215-238-4200. FAX 212-869-3495. *4897*

CLINICAL KINESIOLOGY.
American Kinesiotherapy Association, c/o Dr. John Drowatzky, Ed., University of Toledo, Dept. of Health Promotion & Human Peformance, 2801 W. Bancroft, Toledo, OH 43606. TEL 419-537-2747. FAX 419-530-4759. *4816*

CLINICAL LABORATORY.
Verlag Klinisches Labor, Im Breitspiel 15, 69126 Heidelberg, Germany. TEL 49-6221-3432133. FAX 49-6221-300291. *4678*

CLINICAL LABORATORY MANAGEMENT REVIEW.
Williams & Wilkins, 351 W, Camden St., Baltimore, MD 21201-2436. TEL 410-528-4000. FAX 410-528-4312. *4678*

CLINICAL LABORATORY METHODS AND TECHNIQUES.
Field & Wood, Medical Periodicals, Inc., Box 975, Blue Bell, PA 19422. TEL 610-828-4010. FAX 610-482-0226. *4678*

CLINICAL LABORATORY PRODUCT COMPARISON SYSTEM.
E C R I, 5200 Butler Pike, Plymouth Meeting, PA 19462. TEL 610-825-6000. FAX 610-834-1275. *4678*

CLINICAL LINGUISTICS & PHONETICS.
Taylor & Francis Ltd., 1 Gunpowder Sq., London EC4A 3DE, England. TEL 44-171-583-0490. FAX 44-171-583-0585. *4831*

CLINICAL MEDICAL ETHICS.
Kluwer Academic Publishers, Postbus 17, 3300 AA Dordrecht, Netherlands. TEL 31-78-6392392. FAX 31-78-6392254. *4443*

CLINICAL MOLECULAR PATHOLOGY.
B M J Publishing Group, B.M.A. House, Tavistock Sq., London WC1H 9JR, England. TEL 44-171-387-4499. FAX 44-171-383-6661. *4678*

CLINICAL NEUROLOGY AND NEUROSURGERY.
Elsevier Science B.V., P.O. Box 211, 1000 AE Amsterdam, Netherlands. TEL 31-20-4853911 FAX 31-20-4853598. *4831*

CLINICAL NEUROPHARMACOLOGY.
Lippincott - Raven Publishers 227 E. Washington Sq., Philadelphia, PA 19106. TEL 215-238-4200. *5405*

CLINICAL NEUROPHYSIOLOGY UPDATES.
Elsevier Science B.V., Books Division, P.O. Box 211, 1000 AE Amsterdam, Netherlands. TEL 31-20-4853911. FAX 31-20-4853705. *4832*

CLINICAL NEUROSCIENCE.
John Wiley & Sons, Inc., Journals, 605 Third Ave., New York, NY 10158. TEL 212-850-6645. FAX 212-850-6021. *4332*

CLINICAL NUCLEAR MEDICINE.
Lippincott - Raven Publishers 227 E. Washington Sq., Philadelphia, PA 19106. TEL 215-238-4200. *4874*

CLINICAL NURSING RESEARCH.
Sage Publications, Inc., 2455 Teller Rd., Thousand Oaks, CA 91320. TEL 805-499-0721. FAX 805-499-0871. *4712*

CLINICAL OBSTETRICS AND GYNECOLOGY.
Lippincott - Raven Publishers 227 E. Washington Sq., Philadelphia, PA 19106. TEL 215-238-4200. *4733*

CLINICAL ONCOLOGY ALERT.
American Health Consultants, Inc., 3525 Piedmont Rd., N.E., Bldg. 6, Ste. 400, Atlanta, GA 30305. TEL 404-262-7436. *4753*

CLINICAL ORAL IMPLANTS RESEARCH.
Munksgaard International Publishers Ltd., 35 Noerre Soegade, P.O. Box 2148, DK-1016 Copenhagen K, Denmark. TEL 45-33-127030. FAX 45-33-129387. *4637*

CLINICAL ORAL INVESTIGATIONS.
Springer-Verlag, Heidelberger Platz 3, 14197 Berlin, Germany. TEL 49-30-82787358. FAX 49-30-82787448. *4637*

CLINICAL ORTHOPAEDIC SOCIETY. JOURNAL.
John Wiley & Sons, Inc., Journals, 605 Third Ave., New York, NY 10158. TEL 212-850-6645. FAX 212-850-6021. *2782*

CLINICAL ORTHOPAEDICS AND RELATED RESEARCH.
Lippincott - Raven Publishers 227 E. Washington Sq., Philadelphia, PA 19106. TEL 215-238-4200. *4782*

CLINICAL OTOLARYNGOLOGY AND ALLIED SCIENCES.
Blackwell Science Ltd., Osney Mead, Oxford OX2 0EL, England. TEL 44-1865-206206. FAX 44-1865-721205. *4796*

CLINICAL PEDIATRICS.
Westminster Publications Inc., 708 Glen Cove Ave., Glen Head, NY 11545. TEL 516-759-0025. FAX 516-759-5524. *4804*

CLINICAL PEDIATRICS SERIES.
Marcel Dekker, Inc., 270 Madison Ave., New York, NY 10016. TEL 212-696-9000. FAX 212-685-4540. *4804*

CLINICAL PERFORMANCE AND QUALITY HEALTH CARE.
Slack, Inc., 6900 Grove Rd., Thorofare, NJ 08086-9447. TEL 609-848-1000. *4443*

CLINICAL PHARMACOKINETICS.
Adis International Limited, Private Bag 65901, Mairangi Bay, Auckland 10, New Zealand. TEL 64-9-479-8100. FAX 64-9-479-8145. *5405*

CLINICAL PHARMACOLOGY & THERAPEUTICS.
Mosby - Year Book, Inc. 11830 Westline Industrial Dr., St. Louis, MO 63146-3318. TEL 314-872-8370. FAX 314-432-1380. *5405*

CLINICAL PHYSIOLOGY.
Blackwell Science Ltd. Osney Mead, Oxford OX2 0EL, England. TEL 44-1865-206206. FAX 44-1865-721205. *4443*

CLINICAL PRACTICE OF GYNECOLOGY.
Elsevier Science Inc., Box 945, New York, NY 10159-0945. TEL 212-633-3730. FAX 212-633-3680. *4733*

THE CLINICAL PSYCHOLOGIST.
American Psychological Association, Division of Clinical Psychology, Box 22727, Oklahoma City, OK 73123-1727. TEL 405-721-2792. *5834*

CLINICAL PSYCHOLOGY & PSYCHOTHERAPY.
John Wiley & Sons Ltd., Journals, Baffins Ln., Chichester, W. Sussex PO19 1UD, England. TEL 44-1243-779777. FAX 44-1243-843232. *5835*

CLINICAL PSYCHOLOGY FORUM.
British Psychological Society, St. Andrew's House, 48 Princess Rd. E., Leicester LE1 7DR, England. TEL 44-116-254-9568. FAX 44-116-247-0787. *5835*

CLINICAL PSYCHOLOGY REVIEW.
Elsevier Science Ltd., Pergamon, P.O. Box 800, Kidlington, Oxford OX5 1DX, England. TEL 44-1865-843000. FAX 44-1865-843010. *5835*

CLINICAL RADIOLOGY.
Blackwell Science Ltd., Osney Mead, Oxford OX2 0EL, England. TEL 44-1865-206206. FAX 44-1865-721205. *4874*

CLINICAL RESEARCH AND REGULATORY AFFAIRS.
Marcel Dekker Journals, 270 Madison Ave., New York, NY 10016. TEL 212-696-9000. FAX 212-685-4540. *5405*

CLINICAL REVIEWS IN ALLERGY & IMMUNOLOGY.
Humana Press Inc., 999 Riverview Dr., Ste. 208, Totowa, NJ 07512. TEL 201-256-1699. FAX 201-256-8341. *4580*

CLINICAL SCIENCE.
Portland Press Ltd., 59 Portland Place, London W1N 3AJ, England. TEL 44-171-580-5530. FAX 44-171-323-1136. *4443*

CLINICAL SOCIAL WORK JOURNAL.
Human Sciences Press, Inc. 233 Spring St., New York, NY 10013-1578. TEL 212-620-8000. FAX 212-463-0742. *6367*

CLINICAL SOCIOLOGY REVIEW.
Sociological Practice Association, c/o Hugh McCain, Jacksonville State University, Jacksonville, AL 36265-9982. TEL 205-782-5540. FAX 205-782-5541. *6409*

CLINICAL SUPERVISOR.
Haworth Press, Inc., 10 Alice St., Binghamton, NY 13904. TEL 607-722-5857. FAX 607-722-1424. *6367*

CLINICAL SURVEYS IN ENDOCRINOLOGY.
Plenum Publishing Corp., 233 Spring St., New York, NY 10013-1578. TEL 212-620-8000. FAX 212-463-0742. *4666*

CLINICAL THERAPEUTICS.
Excerpta Medica, Inc., Core Publishing Division 105 Raider Blvd., Belle Mead, NJ 08502-1510. TEL 908-874-8550. FAX 908-874-5633. *4444*

CLINICAL TRANSPLANTATION.
Munksgaard International Publishers Ltd., 35 Noerre Soegade, P.O. Box 2148, DK-1016 Copenhagen K, Denmark. TEL 45-33-127030. FAX 45-33-129387. *4907*

CLINICIAN REVIEWS.
Clinicians Publishing Group, 4 Brighton Rd., Clifton, NJ 07012. TEL 201-916-1000. FAX 201-916-0021. *4444*

CLINICS IN DERMATOLOGY.
Elsevier Science Inc., Box 945, New York, NY 10159-0945. TEL 212-633-3730. FAX 212-633-3680. *4659*

CLIO (FORT WAYNE).
Indiana University, English Department, 2101 Coliseum Blvd. E., Fort Wayne, IN 46805. TEL 219-481-6753. FAX 219-481-6985. *3340*

CLIONET.
James Cook University of North Queensland, Department of History and Politics, P.O., Townsville, 4811 Qld., Australia. TEL 61-77-814170. FAX 61-77-814487. *3340*

CLOSED-END FUND DIGEST.
Madent Publishing, Inc., 1224 Coast Village Circle, Ste. 11, Santa Barbara, CA 93108. TEL 805-565-5651. *1325*

CLYDESDALE STUD BOOK.
Clydesdale Society of Great Britain and Ireland, Castlepark, The Castleton, Auchterarder, Perthshire PH3 1JR, Scotland. TEL 44-1764-664925. *6545*

COAL PREPARATION.
Gordon & Breach Science Publishers, c/o International Publishers Distributor, P.O. Box 3054, Langhorne, PA 19047-3054. TEL 215-750-2642. FAX 215-750-6343. *5060*

COAL SCIENCE AND TECHNOLOGY.
Elsevier Science B.V., Books Division, P.O. Box 211, 1000 AE Amsterdam, Netherlands. TEL 31-20-4853911. FAX 31-20-4853705. *5061*

COASTAL ENGINEERING.
Elsevier Science B.V., P.O. Box 211, 1000 AE Amsterdam, Netherlands. TEL 31-20-4853911. FAX 31-20-4853598. *2656*

COASTAL MANAGEMENT.
Taylor & Francis Inc., 1900 Frost Rd., Ste. 101, Bristol, PA 19007. TEL 215-785-5800. FAX 215-785-5515. *2292*

COASTAL RESEARCH.
Florida State University, Geology Department, Tallahassee, FL 32306-3026. TEL 904-644-5860. FAX 904-644-4214. *2292*

COCUK SAGLIGI VE HASTALIKLARI DERGISI.
Turkish and International Children's Center, P.O. Box 66, Samanpazari, 06240 Ankara, Turkey. TEL 90-312-3242326. FAX 90-312-3112253. *4804*

COELACANTH.
Border Historical Society, c/o East London Museum, P.O. Box 11021, Southernwood 5213, South Africa. TEL 27-431-22623. *3371*

COGITO.
Carfax Publishing Co., P.O. Box 25, Abingdon, Oxon. OX14 3UE, England. TEL 44-1235-401000. FAX 44-1235-401550. *5471*

COGNITION.
Elsevier Science B.V., P.O. Box 211, 1000 AE Amsterdam, Netherlands. TEL 31-20-4853911. FAX 31-20-4853598. *5835*

COGNITION AND EMOTION.
Taylor & Francis Ltd., Psychology Press, 1 Gunpowder Sq., London EC4A 3DE, England. TEL 44-171-5830490. FAX 44-171-5830585. *5835*

COGNITION AND INSTRUCTION.
Lawrence Erlbaum Associates, Inc., 10 Industrial Dr., Mahwah, NJ 07430-2262. TEL 201-236-9500. FAX 201-236-0072. *5835*

COGNITION AND LANGUAGE.
Plenum Publishing Corp., 233 Spring St., New York, NY 10013-1578. TEL 212-620-8000. FAX 212-463-0742. *4061*

COGNITIVA.
Aprendizaje, S.L., Ctra. de Canillas 138, 16C, 28043 Madrid, Spain. TEL 388-38-74. FAX 300-35-27. *5835*

COGNITIVE AND BEHAVIORAL PRACTICE.
Association for Advancement of Behavior Therapy, 305 Seventh Ave., Ste. 16A, New York, NY 10001-6008. TEL 212-647-1890. FAX 212-647-1865. *5835*

COGNITIVE BRAIN RESEARCH.
Elsevier Science B.V., P.O. Box 211, 1000 AE Amsterdam, Netherlands. TEL 31-20-4853911. FAX 31-20-4853598. *4832*

COGNITIVE LINGUISTICS.
Walter de Gruyter und Co., Mouton de Gruyter, Genthiner Str. 13, 10785 Berlin, Germany. TEL 49-30-26005-0. FAX 49-30-26005-251. *4061*

COGNITIVE NEUROPSYCHOLOGY.
Taylor & Francis Ltd., Psychology Press, 1 Gunpowder Sq., London EC4A 3DE, England. TEL 44-171-5830490. FAX 44-171-5830585. *5836*

COGNITIVE PSYCHOLOGY.
Academic Press, Inc., Journal Division, 525 B St., Ste. 1900, San Diego, CA 92101-4495. TEL 619-230-1840. FAX 619-699-6800. *5836*

COGNITIVE SCIENCE SERIES (CAMBRIDGE).
Harvard University Press, 79 Garden St., Cambridge, MA 02138. TEL 617-495-2600. FAX 617-495-5898. *5836*

COGNITIVE SCIENCE SERIES: TECHNICAL MONOGRAPHS AND EDITED COLLECTIONS.
Lawrence Erlbaum Associates, Inc., 10 Industrial Dr., Mahwah, NJ 07430-2262. TEL 201-236-9500. FAX 201-236-0072. *5836*

COGNITIVE THERAPY AND RESEARCH.
Plenum Publishing Corp., 233 Spring St., New York, NY 10013-1578. TEL 212-620-8000. FAX 212-463-0742. *5836*

COHESION AND STRUCTURE.
Elsevier Science B.V., Books Division, P.O. Box 211, 1000 AE Amsterdam, Netherlands. TEL 31-20-4853911. FAX 31-20-4853705. *5544*

COLD REGIONS SCIENCE AND TECHNOLOGY.
Elsevier Science B.V., P.O. Box 211, 1000 AE Amsterdam, Netherlands. TEL 31-20-4853911. FAX 31-20-4853598. *6648*

COLEGIO BRASILEIRO DE CIRURGIOES. REVISTA.
Colegio Brasileiro de Cirurgioes, R. Visconde de Silva, 52, 3o andar, 22271-090 Rio de Janeiro, RJ, Brazil. TEL 55-21-5379164. FAX 55-21-2862595. *4907*

COLEOPTERISTS BULLETIN.
Coleopterists Society (Natchez), c/o Edward Zuccaro, Treas., Box 767, Natchez, MS 39121. TEL 601-442-2824. FAX 601-442-2866. *723*

COLLABORATIVE COMPUTING.
Chapman & Hall, Journals Department 2-6 Boundary Row, London SE1 8HN, England. TEL 44-171-8650066. FAX 44-171-5229623. *2035*

COLLECTANEA MATHEMATICA.
Universidad de Barcelona, Gran Via de les Corts Catalanes 585, 08071 Barcelona, Spain. FAX 34-3-4021601. *4359*

COLLECTION AGENCY REPORT.
First Detroit Corp., Box 5025, Warren, MI 48090-5025. TEL 810-573-0045. FAX 810-573-9219. *1077*

COLLECTION MANAGEMENT.
Haworth Press, Inc., 10 Alice St., Binghamton, NY 13904. TEL 607-722-5857. FAX 607-722-1424. *3986*

COLLECTIONS (COLUMBIA).
Columbia Museum of Art, 1112 Bull St., Columbia, SC 29201. TEL 803-799-2810. FAX 803-343-2219. *5120*

COLLECTORS CLUB PHILATELIST.
Collectors Club, Inc., 22 E. 35th St., New York, NY 10016-0559. TEL 212-683-0559. FAX 2120-481-1269. *5455*

COLLEGE & UNDERGRADUATE LIBRARIES.
Haworth Press, Inc., 10 Alice St., Binghamton, NY 13904. TEL 800-342-9678. FAX 607-722-1424. *3986*

COLLEGE E S L.
City University of New York, Office of Academic Affairs, Instructional Resource Center, 535 E. 80th St., New York, NY 10021. TEL 212-794-5444. *2482*

COLLEGE LITERATURE.
West Chester University, 554 New Main, West Chester, PA 19383. TEL 610-436-2901. FAX 610-436-3150. *4197*

COLLEGE MATHEMATICS JOURNAL.
Mathematical Association of America, 1529 18th St. N.W., Washington, DC 20036. TEL 202-387-5200. *4359*

COLLEGE MUSIC SYMPOSIUM.
College Music Society, 202 W. Spruce St., Missoula, MT 59802. TEL 406-721-9616. FAX 406-721-9419. *5150*

COLLEGE STUDENT AFFAIRS JOURNAL.
University of North Carolina at Chapel Hill, General Administration, Box 2688, Chapel Hill, NC 27515-2688. TEL 919-962-1000. FAX 919-962-0488. *1863*

COLLEGE TEACHING.
Heldref Publications, 1319 Eighteenth St., N.W., Washington, DC 20036-1802. TEL 202-296-6267. FAX 202-296-5149. *2424*

COLLOIDS AND SURFACES A: PHYSICOCHEMICAL AND ENGINEERING ASPECTS.
Elsevier Science B.V., P.O. Box 211, 1000 AE Amsterdam, Netherlands. TEL 31-20-4853911. FAX 31-20-4853598. *1749*

COLLOIDS AND SURFACES B: BIOINTERFACES.
Elsevier Science B.V., P.O. Box 211, 1000 AE Amsterdam, Netherlands. TEL 31-20-4853911. FAX 31-20-4853598. *1749*

COLLOQUIA MATHEMATICA SOCIETATIS JANOS BOLYAI.
Elsevier Science B.V., Books Division, P.O. Box 211, 1000 AE Amsterdam, Netherlands. TEL 31-20-4853911. FAX 31-20-4853705. *4360*

COLLOQUIUM MATHEMATICUM.
Polska Akademia Nauk, Instytut Matematyczny, Dzial Wydawnictw, Ul. Sniadeckich 8, P.O. Box 8, 00-950 Warsaw, Poland. TEL 48-22-6282471. FAX 48-22-6293997. *4360*

COLLOQUIUM ON THE HISTORY OF LANDSCAPE ARCHITECTURE. PAPERS.
Dumbarton Oaks, Research Library and Collection, 1703 32nd St., N.W., Washington, DC 20007. TEL 202-339-6431. *389*

COLLOQUY (MILFORD).
Frequency Marketing Inc., Box 3920, Milford, OH 45150-3920. TEL 513-248-9184. FAX 513-248-9084. *1459*

COLOMBIA: CIENCIA Y TECNOLOGIA.
Colciencias, Transversal 9a No. 133-28, P.O. Box 051580, Bogota, Colombia. TEL 2169800. FAX 6251788. *6235*

COLONIAL LATIN AMERICAN HISTORICAL REVIEW.
Spanish Colonial Research Center, Zimmerman Library, University of New Mexico, Albuquerque, NM 87131. TEL 505-277-1370. FAX 505-277-4603. *3464*

COLONIAL WATERBIRDS.
Colonial Waterbird Society, Oakland University, Rochester, MI 48309. TEL 810-370-3222. *774*

COLOR RESEARCH AND APPLICATION.
John Wiley & Sons, Inc., Journals, 605 Third Ave., New York, NY 10158. TEL 212-850-6645. FAX 212-850-6021. *2639*

COLORADO DENTAL ASSOCIATION. JOURNAL.
Colorado Dental Association, 3690 S. Yosemite, Ste. 100, Denver, CO 80237-1808. TEL 303-740-6900. FAX 303-740-7989. *4637*

COLORADO MEDICINE.
Colorado Medical Society, 7800 E. Dorado Pl., Englewood, CO 80111. TEL 303-779-5455. FAX 303-771-8657. *4444*

COLORADO PROSPECTOR.
Alan J. Kania, Ed. & Pub., Box 623, Parker, CO 80134-0623. TEL 303-841-0609. *3465*

COLTELLI, CHE PASSIONE!
Phenix Editions, Casella Postale 519, 20101 Milan, Italy. TEL 39-2-48402857. FAX 39-2-48402857. *3505*

COLUMBIA (NEW YORK, 1975).
Columbia University, School of the Arts, 404 Dodge Hall, Columbia University, New York, NY 10027. TEL 212-854-4391. *4137*

COLUMBIA BIOLOGICAL SERIES.
Columbia University Press, 562 W. 113th St., New York, NY 10025. TEL 212-666-1000. *578*

COLUMBIA REVIEW.
Columbia University, Columbia Review, 101 Ferris Booth Hall, New York, NY 10027. TEL 212-854-3611. *4197*

COLUMBIA SERIES IN MOLECULAR BIOLOGY.
Columbia University Press, 562 W. 113th St., New York, NY 10025. TEL 212-666-1000. *713*

COLUMBIA STUDIES IN THE CLASSICAL TRADITION.
E.J. Brill, P.O. Box 9000, 2300 PA Leiden, Netherlands. TEL 31-71-5353500. FAX 31-71-5317532. *182*

COMBUSTION AND FLAME.
Elsevier Science Inc., Box 945, New York, NY 10159-0945. TEL 212-633-3730. FAX 212-633-3680. *2593*

COMBUSTION, EXPLOSION, AND SHOCK WAVES.
Plenum Publishing Corp., Consultants Bureau, 233 Spring St., New York, NY 10013-1578. TEL 212-620-8468. FAX 212-463-0742. *2639*

COMBUSTION SCIENCE AND TECHNOLOGY.
Gordon & Breach Science Publishers, c/o International Publishers Distributor, P.O. Box 3054, Langhorne, PA 19047-3054. TEL 215-750-2642. FAX 215-750-2642. *1750*

COMBUSTION THEORY AND MODELLING.
I O P Publishing Ltd., Technoc House, Redcliffe Way, Bristol, Avon BS1 6NX, England. TEL 44-117-9297481. FAX 44-117-9294318. *5583*

COMITATUS.
University of California at Los Angeles, Center for Medieval and Renaissance Studies, 212 Royce Hall, 405 Hilgard Ave., Los Angeles, CA 90024-1485. TEL 310-825-1880. FAX 310-825-0655. *4197*

COMMENTS ON ASTROPHYSICS.
Gordon & Breach Science Publishers, c/o International Publishers Distributor, P.O. Box 3054, Langhorne, PA 19047-3054. TEL 215-750-2642. FAX 215-750-6343. *479*

COMMERCIAL INVESTMENT REAL ESTATE JOURNAL.
Commercial Investment Real Estate Institute, 430 N. Michigan Ave., Chicago, IL 60611-4092. TEL 312-321-4470. FAX 312-321-4530. *6022*

COMMON MARKET LAW REVIEW.
Kluwer Law International, Postbus 85889, 2508 CN The Hague, Netherlands. TEL 31-70-3081500. FAX 31-78-3081515. *3926*

COMMON SENSE.
Edinburgh Conference of Socialist Economists, Southern District Office, P.O. Box 311, Edinburgh EH9 1SF, Scotland. *1249*

COMMONWEALTH NOVEL IN ENGLISH.
B S C Center for International Understanding, Bluefield St. College, Humanities, Bluefield, WV 24701-2198. TEL 304-325-7747. FAX 304-327-4036. *4197*

COMMONWEALTH SCIENTIFIC AND INDUSTRIAL RESEARCH ORGANISATION. DIVISION OF WATER RESOURCES. DIVISIONAL REPORT.
C.S.I.R.O., Division of Water Resources, G.P.O. Box 1666, Canberra, A.C.T. 2601, Australia. FAX 61-6-2465800. *2285*

COMMONWEALTH SCIENTIFIC AND INDUSTRIAL RESEARCH ORGANISATION. DIVISION OF WATER RESOURCES. WATER RESOURCES SERIES.
C.S.I.R.O., Division of Water Resources, G.P.O. Box 1666, Canberra, A.C.T. 2601, Australia. FAX 61-6-2465800. *2285*

COMMUNICARE.
Southern African Communication Association, Department of Communication Rand Afrikaans University, P.O. Box 524, Auckland Park 2006, South Africa. TEL 27-11-4892139. FAX 27-11-4892426. *1898*

COMMUNICATIO.
Unisa Press, Periodicals P.O. Box 392, Pretoria 0001, South Africa. TEL 27-12-4296565. FAX 27-12-4293346. *1898*

COMMUNICATION & COGNITION.
Communication and Cognition, Blandijnberg 2, 9000 Ghent, Belgium. TEL 32-9-2643952. FAX 32-9-2644197. *1898*

COMMUNICATION AND THE HUMAN CONDITION.
Gordon & Breach Science Publishers, c/o International Publishers Distributor, P.O. Box 3054, Langhorne, PA 19047-3054. TEL 215-750-2642. FAX 215-750-6343. *4197*

COMMUNICATION EDUCATION.
Speech Communication Association, 5105 Backlick Rd., Bldg. E., Annandale, VA 22003. TEL 703-750-0533. FAX 703-914-9171. *2483*

COMMUNICATION RESEARCH TRENDS.
Centre for the Study of Communication and Culture, 321 N. Spring Ave., Box 56907, St. Louis, MO 63156-0907. TEL 314-977-7290. FAX 314-977-7296. *1899*

THE COMMUNICATION REVIEW.
Gordon and Breach Science Publishers, c/o International Publishers Distributor, P.O. Box 3054, Langhorne, PA 19047-3054. TEL 215-750-2643. FAX 215-750-6343. *1899*

COMMUNICATION STUDIES.
Baylor University, Waco, TX 76798. TEL 405-332-8000. FAX 405-332-1623. *1899*

COMMUNICATION THEORY.
Guilford Publications, Inc., 72 Spring St., 4th Fl., New York, NY 10012. TEL 212-431-9800. FAX 212-966-6708. *4062*

COMMUNICATIONS IN ALGEBRA.
Marcel Dekker Journals, 270 Madison Ave., New York, NY 10016. TEL 212-696-9000. FAX 212-685-4540. *4360*

COMMUNICATIONS IN ANALYSIS AND GEOMETRY.
International Press, Box 2872, Cambridge, MA 02238-2872. TEL 617-491-0329. FAX 617-495-2180. *4360*

COMMUNICATIONS IN NUMERICAL METHODS IN ENGINEERING.
John Wiley & Sons Ltd., Journals, Baffins Ln., Chichester, W. Sussex PO19 1UD, England. TEL 44-1243-779777. FAX 44-1243-843232. *4360*

COMMUNICATIONS IN PARTIAL DIFFERENTIAL EQUATIONS.
Marcel Dekker Journals, 270 Madison Ave., New York, NY 10016. TEL 212-696-9000. FAX 212-685-4540. *4360*

COMMUNICATIONS IN SCIENCE AND DEVELOPMENT RESEARCH
Prof. Dr. A.M. Balba Group for Soil and Water Research, College of Agriculture, University of Alexandria, El-Shatby, Alexandria 21545. TEL 03-5975405. FAX 03-5954684. *6235*

COMMUNICATIONS IN SOIL SCIENCE AND PLANT ANALYSIS.
Marcel Dekker Journals, 270 Madison Ave., New York, NY 10016. TEL 212-696-9000. FAX 212-685-4540. *217*

COMMUNICATIONS IN STATISTICS. PART A: THEORY AND METHODS.
Marcel Dekker Journals, 270 Madison Ave., New York, NY 10016. TEL 212-696-9000. FAX 212-685-4540. *6600*

COMMUNICATIONS IN STATISTICS. PART B: SIMULATION AND COMPUTATION.
Marcel Dekker Journals, 270 Madison Ave., New York, NY 10016. TEL 212-696-9000. FAX 212-685-4540. *6600*

COMMUNICATIONS IN THEORETICAL PHYSICS.
Baltzer Science Publishers B.V., Asterweg 1A, 1031 HL Amsterdam, Netherlands. TEL 31-20-6370061. FAX 31-20-6323651. *5545*

COMMUNICATIONS OF C O L I P S.
Chinese and Oriental Languages Information Processing Society, c/o Dept. of Information Systems & Computer Science, National University of Singapore, Kent Ridge, Singapore 0511, Singapore. TEL 65-772-2782. FAX 65-779-4580. *4128*

COMMUNICATIONS ON PURE AND APPLIED MATHEMATICS.
John Wiley & Sons, Inc., Journals, 605 Third Ave., New York, NY 10158. TEL 212-850-6645. FAX 212-850-6021. *4360*

THE COMMUNICATOR (ALBANY).
New York State Public Employees Federation, 1168-70 Troy-Schenectady Rd., Box 12414, Albany, NY 12212-2414. TEL 518-785-1900. FAX 518-785-1814. *1367*

COMMUNIO.
Communio, Inc., Box 4557, Washington, DC 20017-0557. TEL 202-526-0251. FAX 202-526-1934. *6177*

COMMUNIQUE (COLUMBUS, 1967).
Business Professionals of America, 5454 Cleveland Ave., Columbus, OH 43231-4021. TEL 614-895-7277. FAX 614-895-1165. *1492*

COMMUNIST AND POST-COMMUNIST STUDIES.
Butterworth - Heinemann, Part of the Reed Elsevier group, Linacre House, Jordan Hill, Oxford OX2 8DP, England. TEL 44-1865-310366. FAX 44-1865-310898. *5643*

COMMUNIST ECONOMIES AND ECONOMIC TRANSFORMATION.
Carfax Publishing Co., P.O. Box 25, Abingdon, Oxon. OX14 3UE, England. TEL 44-1235-401000. FAX 44-1235-401550. *1249*

COMMUNITY ALTERNATIVES.
Human Service Associates, Inc., 336 N. Robert St., Ste. 1520, St. Paul, MN 55101. TEL 612-224-8967. FAX 612-224-6057. *6319*

COMMUNITY & JUNIOR COLLEGE LIBRARIES.
Haworth Press, Inc., 10 Alice St., Binghamton, NY 13904. TEL 607-722-5857. FAX 607-722-1424. *3986*

COMMUNITY COLLEGE JOURNAL OF RESEARCH AND PRACTICE.
Taylor & Francis Inc., 1900 Frost Rd., Ste. 101, Bristol, PA 19007-1598. TEL 215-785-5800. FAX 215-785-5515. *2397*

COMMUNITY COLLEGE REVIEW.
North Carolina State University, Department of Adult and Community College Education, Box 7801, Raleigh, NC 27695-7801. TEL 919-515-6248. FAX 919-515-4039. *2425*

COMMUNITY DENTISTRY AND ORAL EPIDEMIOLOGY.
Munksgaard International Publishers Ltd., 35 Noerre Soegade, P.O. Box 2148, DK-1016 Copenhagen K, Denmark. TEL 45-33-127030. FAX 45-33-129387. *4637*

COMMUNITY LEADER BRIEFINGS.
City Leaders Institute, 3045 Thayen Pl., Boise, ID 83709-3953. TEL 208-887-6326. FAX 208-887-6015. *5939*

COMMUNITY MENTAL HEALTH JOURNAL.
Human Sciences Press, Inc. 233 Spring St., New York, NY 10013-1578. TEL 212-620-8000. FAX 212-463-0742. *6368*

THE COMPARATIST.
Southern Comparative Literature Association, Comparatist, c/o Marcel Cornis-Pope, Ed., Department of English, Virginia Commonwealth University, Richmond, VA 23284-2005. TEL 804-828-4530. FAX 804-828-2171. *4197*

COMPARATIVE BIOCHEMISTRY AND PHYSIOLOGY. PART A: COMPARATIVE PHYSIOLOGY.
Elsevier Science Inc., Box 945, New York, NY 10159-0945. TEL 212-633-3730. FAX 212-633-3680. *636*

COMPARATIVE BIOCHEMISTRY AND PHYSIOLOGY. PART B: COMPARATIVE BIOCHEMISTRY.
Elsevier Science Inc., Box 945, New York, NY 10159-0945. TEL 212-633-3730. FAX 212-633-3680. *636*

COMPARATIVE BIOCHEMISTRY AND PHYSIOLOGY. PART C: COMPARATIVE PHARMACOLOGY & TOXICOLOGY.
Elsevier Science Inc., Box 945, New York, NY 10159-0945. TEL 212-989-5800. FAX 212-633-3990. *637*

COMPARATIVE CIVILIZATIONS REVIEW.
International Society for the Comparative Study of Civilizations, Dept. of History & Political Science, University of Missouri - Rolla, Rolla, MO 65401. TEL 314-341-4815. FAX 314-341-6127. *6319*

COMPARATIVE DRAMA.
Western Michigan University, Department of English, Kalamazoo, MI 49008-3851. TEL 616-387-2576. FAX 616-387-8750. *4197*

COMPARATIVE EDUCATION.
Carfax Publishing Co., P.O. Box 25, Abingdon, Oxon. OX14 3UE, England. TEL 44-1235-401000. FAX 44-1235-401550. *2321*

COMPARATIVE EDUCATION REVIEW.
University of Chicago Press, Journals Division, Box 37005, Chicago, IL 60637. TEL 773-702-3347. FAX 773-753-0811. *2321*

COMPARATIVE HAEMATOLOGY INTERNATIONAL.
Springer-Verlag London Ltd., Sweetapple House, Catteshall Rd., Godalming, Surrey GU7 3DJ, England. TEL 44-1483-418800. FAX 44-1483-415144. *4699*

COMPARATIVE IMMUNOLOGY, MICROBIOLOGY AND INFECTIOUS DISEASES.
Elsevier Science Ltd., Pergamon, P.O. Box 800, Kidlington, Oxford OX5 1DX, England. TEL 44-1865-843000. FAX 44-1865-843010. *755*

COMPARATIVE LAW YEARBOOK.
Martinus Nijhoff Publishers, Human Rights and International Law Postbus 163, 3300 AD Dordrecht, Netherlands. TEL 31-78-334911. FAX 31-78-334254. *3926*

COMPARATIVE LITERATURE.
University of Oregon, Comparative Literature, 1223 Friendly Hall, Eugene, OR 97403-1233. TEL 503-346-4022. FAX 503-346-4030. *4198*

COMPARATIVE LITERATURE STUDIES.
Pennsylvania State University Press, 820 N. University Dr., Ste. C, University Park, PA 16802-1003. TEL 814-865-1327. FAX 814-863-1408. *4198*

COMPARATIVE POLITICS.
City University of New York, Political Science Program, 33 W. 42nd St., New York, NY 10036. TEL 212-642-2377. *5643*

COMPARATIVE STRATEGY.
Taylor & Francis Inc., 1900 Frost Rd., Ste. 101, Bristol, PA 19007. TEL 215-785-5800. FAX 215-785-5515. *5643*

COMPARATIVE STUDIES IN RELIGION & SOCIETY.
University of California Press, 2120 Berkeley Way, Berkeley, CA 94720. TEL 510-642-4247. FAX 510-643-7127. *6054*

COMPARATIVE STUDIES OF HEALTH SYSTEMS & MEDICAL CARE.
University of California Press, 2120 Berkeley Way, Berkeley, CA 94720. TEL 510-642-4247. FAX 510-643-7127. *4445*

COMPARATIVE STUDIES ON MUSLIM SOCIETIES.
University of California Press, 2120 Berkeley Way, Berkeley, CA 94720. TEL 510-642-4247. FAX 510-643-7127. *6116*

COMPARATIVE URBAN AND COMMUNITY RESEARCH.
Transaction Publishers, Transaction Periodicals Consortium, Department 3092, Rutgers University, New Brunswick, NJ 08903. TEL 908-445-2280. FAX 908-445-3138. *3579*

COMPARE.
Carfax Publishing Co., P.O. Box 25, Abingdon, Oxon. OX14 3UE, England. TEL 44-1235-401000. FAX 44-1235-401550. *2321*

COMPENDIUM OF CONTINUING EDUCATION IN DENTISTRY.
Dental Learning Systems Co., Inc., P.O. Box 505, Jamesburg, NJ 08831-0505. TEL 908-656-1143. FAX 908-656-1146. *4637*

COMPETITIVE INTELLIGENCE REVIEW.
John Wiley & Sons, Inc., Journals, 605 Third Ave., New York, NY 10158. TEL 212-850-6645. FAX 212-850-6021. *1411*

COMPETITIVENESS REVIEW.
American Society for Competitiveness, Box 1658, Indiana, PA 15705. TEL 412-357-5759. FAX 412-357-5743. *1270*

COMPLEMENTARY MEDICINE INTERNATIONAL.
Prime National Corp., 470 Boston Post Rd., Weston, MA 02193. TEL 617-899-2702. FAX 617-899-4900. *290*

COMPLEX VARIABLES: THEORY AND APPLICATION.
Gordon and Breach Science Publishers, c/o International Publishers Distributor, P.O. Box 3054, Langhorne, PA 19047-3054. TEL 215-750-2642. FAX 215-750-6343. *4360*

COMPLEXITY (NEW YORK).
John Wiley & Sons, Inc., Journals, 605 Third Ave., New York, NY 10158. TEL 212-850-6645. FAX 212-850-6021. *2593*

COMPLEXITY INTERNATIONAL.
c/o School of Information Techonology, Charles Sturt University, Panorama Ave., Bathurst, N.S.W. 2795, Australia. TEL 61-63-384272. FAX 61-63-384649. *2054*

COMPOSITE INTERFACES.
V S P, P.O. Box 346, 3700 AH Zeist, Netherlands. TEL 31-30-6925790. FAX 31-30-6932081. *5545*

COMPOSITE MATERIALS SERIES.
Elsevier Science B.V., Books Division, P.O. Box 211, 1000 AE Amsterdam, Netherlands. TEL 31-20-4853911. FAX 31-20-4853705. *2729*

COMPOSITE STRUCTURES.
Elsevier Science Ltd., P.O. Box 800, Kidlington, Oxford OX5 1DX, England. TEL 44-1865-843000. FAX 44-1865-843010. *2656*

COMPOSITES PART A: APPLIED SCIENCE AND MANUFACTURING.
Elsevier Science Ltd., Pergamon, P.O. Box 800, Kidlington, Oxford OX5 1DX, England. TEL 44-1865-843000. FAX 44-1865-843010. *2729*

COMPOSITES PART B: ENGINEERING.
Elsevier Science Ltd., Pergamon, P.O. Box 800, Kidlington, Oxford OX5 1DX, England. TEL 44-1865-843000. FAX 44-1865-843010. *2593*

COMPOSITES SCIENCE AND TECHNOLOGY.
Elsevier Science Ltd., P.O. Box 800, Kidlington, Oxford OX5 1DX, England. TEL 44-1865-843000. FAX 44-1865-843010. *6648*

COMPOSITIO MATHEMATICA.
Kluwer Academic Publishers, Postbus 17, 3300 AA Dordrecht, Netherlands. TEL 31-78-6392392. FAX 31-78-6392254. *4361*

COMPOSITION STUDIES - FRESHMAN ENGLISH NEWS.
Texas Christian University, Box 297700, Ft. Worth, TX 76129. TEL 817-921-7221. FAX 817-921-7702. *2483*

COMPOST SCIENCE & UTILIZATION.
J G Press, Inc., 419 State Ave., Emmaus, PA 18049. TEL 610-967-4135. *2851*

COMPREHENSIVE ANALYTICAL CHEMISTRY.
Elsevier Science B.V., Books Division, P.O. Box 211, 1000 AE Amsterdam, Netherlands. TEL 31-20-4853911. FAX 31-20-4853705. *1715*

COMPREHENSIVE BIOCHEMISTRY.
Elsevier Science B.V., Books Division, P.O. Box 211, 1000 AE Amsterdam, Netherlands. TEL 31-20-4853911. FAX 31-20-4853705. *637*

COMPREHENSIVE CHEMICAL KINETICS.
Elsevier Science B.V., Books Division, P.O. Box 211, 1000 AE Amsterdam, Netherlands. TEL 31-20-4853911. FAX 31-20-4853705. *1750*

COMPREHENSIVE ENDOCRINOLOGY.
Lippincott - Raven Publishers 227 E. Washington Sq., Philadelphia, PA 19106. TEL 215-238-4200. FAX 215-238-4235. *4666*

COMPREHENSIVE IMMUNOLOGY.
Plenum Publishing Corp., 233 Spring St., New York, NY 10013-1578. TEL 212-620-8000. FAX 212-463-0742. *4580*

COMPREHENSIVE PSYCHIATRY.
W.B. Saunders Co. Curtis Center, 3rd Fl., Independence Sq. W., Philadelphia, PA 19106-3399. TEL 215-238-7800. FAX 215-238-6445. *4832*

COMPREHENSIVE PSYCHOTHERAPY.
Gordon & Breach Science Publishers, c/o International Publishers Distributor, P.O. Box 3054, Langhorne, PA 19047-3054. TEL 215-750-2642. FAX 215-750-6343. *5837*

COMPREHENSIVE THERAPY.
American Society of Contemporary Medicine and Surgery, 4711 Golf Rd., Ste. 408, Skokie, IL 60076. TEL 847-568-1500. FAX 847-568-1527. *4445*

COMPUTATIONAL ACOUSTICS.
Elsevier Science B.V., Books Division, P.O. Box 211, 1000 AE Amsterdam, Netherlands. TEL 31-20-4853911. FAX 31-20-4853705. *5581*

COMPUTATIONAL & MATHEMATICAL ORGANIZATION THEORY.
Kluwer Academic Publishers Boston, Box 358, Accord Sta., Hingham, MA 02018-0358. TEL 617-871-6600. FAX 617-871-6528. *4408*

COMPUTATIONAL ECONOMICS.
Kluwer Academic Publishers, Postbus 17, 3300 AA Dordrecht, Netherlands. TEL 31-78-6392392. FAX 31-78-6392254. *1152*

COMPUTATIONAL GEOMETRY.
North-Holland P.O. Box 211, 1000 AE Amsterdam, Netherlands. TEL 31-20-4853911. FAX 31-20-4853598. *4408*

COMPUTATIONAL GEOSCIENCES.
Baltzer Science Publishers B.V., Asterweg 1a, 1031 HL Amsterdam, Netherlands. TEL 31-20-6370061. FAX 31-20-6323651. *2222*

COMPUTATIONAL IMAGING AND VISION.
Kluwer Academic Publishers, Postbus 17, 3300 AA Dordrecht, Netherlands. TEL 31-78-6392392. FAX 31-78-6392254. *2026*

COMPUTATIONAL INTELLIGENCE.
Elsevier Science B.V., P.O. Box 211, 1000 AE Amsterdam, Netherlands. TEL 31-20-4853911. FAX 31-20-4853598. *2006*

COMPUTATIONAL LINGUISTICS.
M I T Press, 55 Hayward St., Cambridge, MA 02142. TEL 617-253-2889. FAX 617-577-1545. *4129*

COMPUTATIONAL MATERIALS SCIENCE.
Elsevier Science B.V., P.O. Box 211, 1000 AE Amsterdam, Netherlands. TEL 31-20-4853911. FAX 31-20-4853598. *2730*

COMPUTATIONAL MATHEMATICS AND APPLICATIONS.
Academic Press, Inc., 525 B St., Ste. 1900, San Diego, CA 92101-4495. TEL 619-231-0926. FAX 619-699-6715. *2060*

COMPUTATIONAL MATHEMATICS AND MATHEMATICAL PHYSICS.
Elsevier Science Ltd., Pergamon, P.O. Box 800, Kidlington, Oxford OX5 1DX, England. TEL 44-1865-843000. FAX 44-1865-843010. *4361*

COMPUTATIONAL MATHEMATICS AND MODELING.
Plenum Publishing Corp., Consultants Bureau, 233 Spring St., New York, NY 10013-1578. TEL 212-620-8000. FAX 212-463-0742. *4408*

COMPUTATIONAL MECHANICS ADVANCES.
Elsevier Science S.A., P.O. Box 564, CH-1001 Lausanne 1, Switzerland. TEL 41-21-3207381. FAX 41-21-3235444. *4408*

COMPUTATIONAL OPTIMIZATION AND APPLICATIONS.
Kluwer Academic Publishers Boston, Box 358, Accord Sta., Hingham, MA 02018-0358. TEL 617-871-6600. FAX 617-871-6528. *4409*

COMPUTATIONAL POLYMER SCIENCE.
Polymer Research Associates, Inc., 9200 Montgomery Rd., Ste. 23B, Cincinnati, OH 45242. TEL 513-891-7030. FAX 513-891-5867. *5629*

COMPUTATIONAL STATISTICS.
Physica-Verlag GmbH und Co., Postfach 105280, 69042 Heidelberg, Germany. TEL 49-6221-487492. FAX 49-6221-487177. *6600*

COMPUTATIONAL STATISTICS AND DATA ANALYSIS.
North-Holland P.O. Box 211, 1000 AE Amsterdam, Netherlands. TEL 31-20-4853911. FAX 31-20-4853598. *4409*

COMPUTER-AIDED CHEMICAL ENGINEERING.
Elsevier Science B.V., Books Division, P.O. Box 211, 1000 AE Amsterdam, Netherlands. TEL 31-20-4853911. FAX 31-20-4853705. *2677*

COMPUTER-AIDED DESIGN.
Butterworth - Heinemann, Part of the Reed Elsevier group, Linacre House, Jordan Hill, Oxford OX2 8DP, England. TEL 44-1865-310366. FAX 44-1865-310898. *2026*

COMPUTER-AIDED DESIGN OF ELECTRONIC CIRCUITS.
Elsevier Science B.V., Books Division, P.O. Box 211, 1000 AE Amsterdam, Netherlands. TEL 31-20-4853911. FAX 31-20-4853705. *2677*

COMPUTER-AIDED GEOMETRIC DESIGN.
North-Holland P.O. Box 211, 1000 AE Amsterdam, Netherlands. TEL 31-20-4853911. FAX 31-20-4853598. *2026*

COMPUTER APPLICATIONS IN ENGINEERING EDUCATION.
John Wiley & Sons, Inc., Journals, 605 Third Ave., New York, NY 10158. TEL 212-850-6645. FAX 212-850-6021. *2678*

COMPUTER AUDIT UPDATE.
Elsevier Science Ltd., P.O. Box 800, Kidlington, Oxford OX5 1DX, England. TEL 44-1865-843000. FAX 44-1865-843010. *2049*

COMPUTER COMMUNICATIONS.
Elsevier Science B.V., P.O. Box 211, 1000 AE Amsterdam, Netherlands. TEL 31-20-4853911. FAX 31-20-4853598. *2068*

COMPUTER DESIGN AND ARCHITECTURE SERIES.
Elsevier Science Inc., Box 945, New York, NY 10159-0945. TEL 212-633-3730. FAX 212-633-3680. *2018*

COMPUTER GRAPHICS FORUM.
Blackwell Publishers Ltd., 108 Cowley Rd., Oxford OX4 1JF, England. TEL 44-1865-791100. FAX 44-1865-791347. *2026*

COMPUTER-INTEGRATED MANUFACTURING SYSTEMS.
Butterworth - Heinemann, Part of the Reed Elsevier group, Linacre House, Jordan Hill, Oxford OX2 8DP, England. TEL 44-1865-310366. FAX 44-1865-310898. *2678*

COMPUTER LANGUAGES.
Elsevier Science Ltd., Pergamon, P.O. Box 800, Kidlington, Oxford OX5 1DX, England. TEL 44-1865-843000. FAX 44-1865-843010. *2043*

COMPUTER LAW & SECURITY REPORT.
Elsevier Science Ltd., P.O. Box 800, Kidlington, Oxford OX5 1DX. England. TEL 44-1865-843000. FAX 44-1865-843010. *2049*

COMPUTER METHODS AND PROGRAMS IN BIOMEDICINE.
Elsevier Science Ireland Ltd., P.O. Box 85, Limerick, Ireland. TEL 353-61-471944. FAX 353-61-472144. *4630*

COMPUTER METHODS IN APPLIED MECHANICS AND ENGINEERING.
Elsevier Science S.A., P.O. Box 564, CH-1001 Lausanne 1, Switzerland. TEL 41-21-3207381. FAX 41-21-3235444. *2678*

COMPUTER METHODS IN THE GEOSCIENCES.
Elsevier Science Ltd., Books Division, P.O. Box 800, Kidlington, Oxford OX5 1DX, England. TEL 44-1865-843000. FAX 44-1865-843010. *6305*

COMPUTER MUSIC JOURNAL.
M I T Press, 55 Hayward St., Cambridge, MA 02142. TEL 617-253-2889. FAX 617-258-6779. *5210*

COMPUTER NETWORKS AND I S D N SYSTEMS.
North-Holland P.O. Box 211, 1000 AE Amsterdam, Netherlands. TEL 31-20-4853911. FAX 31-20-4853598. *2036*

COMPUTER PHYSICS COMMUNICATIONS.
North-Holland P.O. Box 211, 1000 AE Amsterdam, Netherlands. TEL 31-20-4853911. FAX 31-20-4853598. *5582*

COMPUTER STANDARDS AND INTERFACES.
Elsevier Science B.V., P.O. Box 211, 1000 AE Amsterdam, Netherlands. TEL 31-20-4853911. FAX 31-20-4853598. *986*

COMPUTER STUDIES: COMPUTERS IN EDUCATION.
Dushkin Publishing Group, Sluice Dock, Guilford, CT 06437-9989. TEL 203-453-4351. FAX 203-453-6000. *2404*

COMPUTER SUPPORTED COOPERATIVE WORK.
Kluwer Academic Publishers, Postbus 17, 3300 AA Dordrecht, Netherlands. TEL 31-78-6392392. FAX 31-78-6392254. *5319*

COMPUTERIZED MEDICAL IMAGING AND GRAPHICS.
Elsevier Science Ltd., Pergamon, P.O. Box 800, Kidlington, Oxford OX5 1DX, England. TEL 44-1865-843000. FAX 44-1865 843010. *4630*

COMPUTERS AND ARTIFICIAL INTELLIGENCE.
Slovenska Akademia Vied, Ustav Technickej Kybernetiky, Dubravska cesta 9, 842 37 Bratislava, Slovakia. TEL 42-7-374703. FAX 42-7-371004. *2006*

COMPUTERS AND BIOMEDICAL RESEARCH.
Academic Press, Inc., Journal Division, 525 B. St., Ste. 1900, San Diego, CA 92101-4495. TEL 619-230-1840. FAX 619-699-6800. *4630*

COMPUTERS & CHEMICAL ENGINEERING.
Elsevier Science Ltd., Pergamon, P.O. Box 800, Kidlington, Oxford OX5 1DX, England. TEL 44-1865-843000. FAX 44-1865-843010. *1724*

COMPUTERS & CHEMISTRY.
Elsevier Science Ltd., Pergamon, P.O. Box 800, Kidlington, Oxford OX5 1DX, England. TEL 44-1865-843000. FAX 44-1865-843010. *1724*

COMPUTERS & EDUCATION.
Elsevier Science Ltd., Pergamon, P.O. Box 800, Kidlington, Oxford OX5 1DX, England. TEL 44-1865 843000. FAX 44-1865-843010. *2404*

COMPUTERS & ELECTRICAL ENGINEERING.
Elsevier Science Ltd., Pergamon, P.O. Box 800, Kidlington, Oxford OX5 1DX, England. TEL 44-1865-843000. FAX 44-1865-843010. *2678*

COMPUTERS AND ELECTRONICS IN AGRICULTURE.
Elsevier Science B.V., P.O. Box 211, 1000 AE Amsterdam, Netherlands. TEL 31-20-4853911. FAX 31-20-4853598 *207*

COMPUTERS & FLUIDS.
Elsevier Science Ltd., Pergamon, P.O. Box 800, Kidlington, Oxford OX5 1DX, England. TEL 44-1865-843000. FAX 44-1865-843010. *2678*

COMPUTERS & GEOSCIENCES.
Elsevier Science Ltd., Pergamon, P.O. Box 800, Kidlington, Oxford OX5 1DX, England. TEL 44-1865-843000. FAX 44-1865-843010. *2222*

COMPUTERS AND GEOTECHNICS.
Elsevier Science Ltd., P.O. Box 800, Kidlington, Oxford OX5 1DX, England. TEL 44-1865-843000. FAX 44-1865-843010. *2678*

COMPUTERS & GRAPHICS.
Elsevier Science Ltd., Pergamon, P.O. Box 800, Kidlington, Oxford OX5 1DX, England. TEL 44-1865-843000. FAX 44-1865-843010. *2027*

COMPUTERS & INDUSTRIAL ENGINEERING.
Elsevier Science Ltd., Pergamon, P.O. Box 800, Kidlington, Oxford OX5 1DX, England. TEL 44-1865-843000. FAX 44-1865-843010. *2678*

COMPUTERS & MATHEMATICS WITH APPLICATIONS.
Elsevier Science Ltd., Pergamon, P.O. Box 800, Kidlington, Oxford OX5 1DX, England. TEL 44-1865-843000. FAX 44-1865-843010. *4409*

COMPUTERS & OPERATIONS RESEARCH.
Elsevier Science Ltd., Pergamon, P.O. Box 800, Kidlington, Oxford OX5 1DX, England. TEL 44-1865-843000. FAX 44-1865-843010. *1987*

COMPUTERS & SECURITY.
Elsevier Science Ltd., P.O. Box 800, Kidlington, Oxford OX5 1DX, England. TEL 44-1865-843000. FAX 44-1865-843010. *2050*

COMPUTERS & STRUCTURES.
Elsevier Science Ltd., Pergamon, P.O. Box 800, Kidlington, Oxford OX5 1DX, England. TEL 44-1865-843000. FAX 44-1865-843010. *2679*

COMPUTERS AND THE HISTORY OF ART.
Harwood Academic Publishers, c/o International Publishers Distributor, P.O. Box 3054, Langhorne, PA 19047-3054. TEL 215-750-2642. FAX 215-750-6343. *463*

COMPUTERS AND THE HUMANITIES.
Kluwer Academic Publishers, Postbus 17, 3300 AA Dordrecht, Netherlands. TEL 31-78-6392392. FAX 31-78-6392254. *3633*

COMPUTERS, ENVIRONMENT AND URBAN SYSTEMS.
Elsevier Science Ltd., Pergamon, P.O. Box 800, Kidlington, Oxford OX5 1DX, England. TEL 44-1865-843000. FAX 44-1865-843010. *2832*

COMPUTERS IN BIOLOGY AND MEDICINE.
Elsevier Science Ltd., Pergamon, P.O. Box 800, Kidlington, Oxford OX5 1DX, England. TEL 44-1865-843000. FAX 44-1865-843010. *710*

COMPUTERS IN EDUCATION JOURNAL.
American Society for Engineering Education, Computers in Education Division, Box 68, Port Royal Sq., Port Royal, VA 22535. TEL 804-742-5611. FAX 804-742-5030. *2405*

COMPUTERS IN HUMAN BEHAVIOR.
Elsevier Science Ltd., Pergamon, P.O. Box 800, Kidlington, Oxford OX5 1DX, England. TEL 44-1865-843000. FAX 44-1865-843010. *6443*

COMPUTERS IN HUMAN SERVICES.
Haworth Press, Inc., 10 Alice St., Binghamton, NY 13904. TEL 607-722-5857. FAX 607-722-1424. *6443*

COMPUTERS IN INDUSTRY.
North-Holland P.O. Box 211, 1000 AE Amsterdam, Netherlands. TEL 31-20-4853911. FAX 31-20-4853598. *1153*

COMPUTERS IN MUSIC RESEARCH.
Wisconsin Center for Music Technology, School of Music, University of Wisconsin, Madison, WI 53706. TEL 608-263-1900. *5210*

COMPUTERS IN PHYSICS.
American Institute of Physics, One Physics Ellipse, College Park, MD 20740-3843. TEL 301-209-3000. *5582*

COMPUTERS IN THE SCHOOLS.
Haworth Press, Inc., 10 Alice St., Binghamton, NY 13904. TEL 607-722-5857. FAX 607-722-1424. *2405*

COMPUTERWORLD HONG KONG.
I D G Communications (HK) Ltd., Mount Parker House, Ste. 1011-15, 1111 King's Rd., Quarry Bay, Hong Kong. TEL 852-2861-3238. FAX 852-2861-0953. *2031*

COMPUTING IN BIOMEDICINE.
Elsevier Science B.V., Books Division, P.O. Box 211, 1000 AE Amsterdam, Netherlands. TEL 31-20-4853911. FAX 31-20-4853705. *4630*

COMPUTING SYSTEMS.
M I T Press, 55 Hayward St., Cambridge, MA 02142-1399. TEL 617-253-2889. FAX 617-258-6779. *2043*

CONCEPTS AND TRANSFORMATION.
John Benjamins Publishing Co., Amsteldijk 44, P.O. Box 75577, 1070 AN Amsterdam, Netherlands. TEL 31-20-6762325. FAX 31-20-6792956. *1500*

CONCEPTS IN IMMUNOPATHOLOGY.
S. Karger AG, Allschwilerstr. 10, P.O. Box, CH-4009 Basel, Switzerland. TEL 061-3061111. FAX 061-3061234. *4666*

CONCEPTS IN MAGNETIC RESONANCE.
John Wiley & Sons, Inc., Journals, 605 Third Ave., New York, NY 10158-0012. TEL 212-850-6347. FAX 212-850-6021. *4874*

CONCEPTS IN PEDIATRIC NEUROSURGERY.
S. Karger AG, Allschwilerstr. 10, P.O. Box, CH-4009 Basel, Switzerland. TEL 061-3061111. FAX 061-3061234. *4832*

LA CONCHIGLIA.
Conchiglia, Via C. Federici 1, 00147 Rome, Italy. TEL 39-6-5110192. FAX 39-6-5110192. *802*

CONCISE.
Airworthy Publications International Ltd., Bassfield South, Manchester Rd., Walmersley, Bury, Lancs. BL9 5LY, England. TEL 44-1706-828811. FAX 44-1706-828300. *61*

CONCORDIA JOURNAL.
Ovid Bell Press, Inc., 801 Demun, Clayton, MO 63105. TEL 314-721-5934. FAX 314-721-5902. *6054*

CONCORDIA TORCH.
Concordia Mutual Life Association, 3041 Woodcreek Dr., Downers Grove, IL 60515. TEL 708-971-8000. FAX 708-971-9332. *3646*

CONCURRENCY: PRACTICE AND EXPERIENCE.
John Wiley & Sons Ltd., Journals, Baffins Ln., Chichester, W. Sussex PO19 1UD, England. TEL 44-1243-779777. FAX 44-1243-843232. *2043*

CONCURRENT ENGINEERING: RESEARCH AND APPLICATIONS.
Technomic Publishing Co., Inc., 851 New Holland Ave., Box 3535, Lancaster, PA 17604. TEL 717-291-5609. FAX 717-295-45638. *2020*

CONCURRENT SYSTEMS ENGINEERING SERIES.
I O S Press, Van Diemenstraat 94, 1013 CN Amsterdam, Netherlands. TEL 31-20-6382189. FAX 31-20-6203419. *2020*

CONDENSED MATTER NEWS.
Gordon & Breach Science Publishers, c/o International Publishers Distributor, P.O. Box 3054, Langhorne, PA 19047-3054. TEL 215-750-2642. FAX 215-750-6343. *2686*

CONDENSED MATTER THEORIES.
Plenum Publishing Corp., 233 Spring St., New York, NY 10013-1578. TEL 212-620-8000. FAX 212-463-0742. *5545*

THE CONDUCTOR.
National Association of Brass Band Conductors, Marrey, 7 Carr View Rd., Hepworth, Huddersfield HD7 7HN, England. TEL 44-1484-683793. FAX 44-1484-608512. *5150*

CONFERENCE ON REMOTE SYSTEMS TECHNOLOGY. PROCEEDINGS.
American Nuclear Society, 555 N. Kensington Ave., La Grange Park, IL 60525. TEL 708-352-6611. FAX 708-352-0499. *2104*

CONFIDENTIAL A-I-R LETTER.
Air Incident Research, Box 4745, East Lansing, MI 48826. TEL 517-336-9375. FAX 517-336-9375. *2160*

CONFRONTATION.
Long Island University, C.W. Post College, Dept. of English, Greenvale, NY 11548. TEL 516-299-2391. FAX 516-299-2735. *4198*

CONGENITAL ANOMALIES.
Nihon Senten Ijo Gakkai, Kinki University School of Medicine, Osaka-Sayama-shi, Osaka 589, Japan. TEL 0723-66-0221. FAX 0723-66-0206. *4445*

CONGRESSUS NUMERANTIUM.
Utilitas Mathematica Publishing Inc., Box 7, University Centre, University of Manitoba, Winnipeg, MB R3T 2N2, Canada. TEL 204-474-8675. *4361*

CONNECTICUT ACADEMY OF ARTS AND SCIENCES. TRANSACTIONS.
Connecticut Academy of Arts and Sciences, Box 208211, New Haven, CT 06520-8211. TEL 203-432-3113. FAX 203-432-5712. *3610*

CONNECTICUT SUPPLEMENT.
Commission on Official Legal Publications, Office of Production and Distribution, 111 Phoenix Ave., Enfield, CT 06082. TEL 203-741-3027. FAX 203-745-2178. *3764*

CONNECTICUT WARBLER.
Connecticut Ornithological Association, Inc., 314 Unquowa Rd., Fairfield, CT 06430-5018. TEL 203-259-2623. *774*

CONNECTION SCIENCE.
Carfax Publishing Co., P.O. Box 25, Abingdon, Oxon. OX14 3UE, England. TEL 44-1235-401000. FAX 44-1235-401550. *2006*

CONNECTIVE TISSUE RESEARCH.
Gordon and Breach Science Publishers, c/o International Publishers Distributor, P.O. Box 3054, Langhorne, PA 19047-3054. TEL 215-750-2642. FAX 215-750-6343. *713*

THE CONRADIAN.
Editions Rodopi B.V., Keizersgracht 302-304, 1016 EX Amsterdam, Netherlands. TEL 31-20-6227507. FAX 31-20-6380948. *4198*

CONSCIOUSNESS AND COGNITION.
Academic Press, Inc., Journal Division, 525 B St., Ste. 1900, San Diego, CA 92101-4495. TEL 619-230-1840. FAX 619-699-6800. *5837*

CONSCIOUSNESS AND SELF-REGULATION: ADVANCES IN RESEARCH AND THEORY.
Plenum Publishing Corp., 233 Spring St., New York, NY 10013-1578. TEL 212-620-8000. FAX 212-463-0742. *5837*

CONSERVATION AND MANAGEMENT OF ARCHAEOLOGICAL SITES.
James & James (Science Publishers) Ltd., Waterside House, 47 Kentish Town Rd., London NW1 8NZ, England. TEL 44-171-284-3833. FAX 44-171-284-3737. *350*

CONSERVATIVE JUDAISM.
Rabbinical Assembly, 3080 Broadway, New York, NY 10027. TEL 212-678-8060. FAX 212-749-9166. *6123*

CONSERVER.
British Trust for Conservation Volunteers, 36 St. Mary's St., Wallingford, Oxon. OX10 0EU, England. TEL 44-1491-839766. FAX 44-1491-839646. *2124*

CONSPECTUS FLORAE ORIENTALIS.
Israel Academy of Sciences and Humanities, 43 Jabotinski St., P.O. Box 4040, Jerusalem 91040, Israel. TEL 972-2-636211. FAX 972-2-666059. *677*

CONSTELLATIONS.
Blackwell Publishers Ltd., 108 Cowley Rd., Oxford OX4 1JF, England. TEL 44-1865-791100. FAX 44-1865-791347. *5644*

CONSTITUTIONAL POLITICAL ECONOMY.
Kluwer Academic Publishers Boston, Box 358, Accord Sta., Hingham, MA 02018-0358. TEL 617-871-6600. FAX 617-871-6528. *3891*

CONSTRUCTION AND BUILDING MATERIALS.
Butterworth - Heinemann, Part of the Reed Elsevier group, Linacre House, Jordan Hill, Oxford OX2 8DP, England. TEL 44-1865-310366. FAX 44-1865-310898. *847*

CONSTRUCTION MANAGEMENT AND ECONOMICS.
Chapman & Hall, Journals Department 2-6 Boundary Row, London SE1 8HN, England. TEL 44-171-8650066. FAX 44-171-5229623. *849*

CONSTRUCTIVE APPROXIMATION.
Springer-Verlag, Science Journals, 175 Fifth Ave., New York, NY 10010. TEL 212-460-1500. FAX 212-473-6272. *4361*

CONSULTANT (GREENWICH).
Cliggott Publishing Co., 55 Holly Hill Ln., Box 4010, Greenwich, CT 06831. TEL 203-661-0600. *4445*

CONSUMER CURRENTS.
Consumers International, Regional Office for Asia and Pacific, P.O. Box 1045, 10830 Penang, Malaysia. TEL 604-229-1296. FAX 604-228-6506. *2150*

CONSUMER INTERESTS ANNUAL.
American Council on Consumer Interests, c/o Anita Metzen, Exec. Dir., 240 Stanley Hall, University of Missouri, Columbia, MO 65211. TEL 573-882-3817. FAX 573-884-6571. *2150*

CONTACT (ALDERSHOT).
Officers' Christian Union, Havelock House, Barrack Rd., Aldershot GU11 3NP, England. TEL 44-1252-311221. FAX 44-1252-311222. *6055*

CONTACT DERMATITIS.
Munksgaard International Publishers Ltd., 35 Noerre Soegade, P.O. Box 2148, DK-1016 Copenhagen K, Denmark. TEL 45-33-127030. FAX 45-33-129387. *4659*

CONTEMPORARY ACCOUNTING RESEARCH.
Canadian Academic Accounting Association, 223 Scurfield Hall, Faculty of Management, University of Calgary, Calgary. AB T2N 1N4, Canada. TEL 403-220-8517. FAX 403-282-0095. *1045*

CONTEMPORARY ANALYSES IN EDUCATION.
Taylor & Francis Ltd., Rankine Rd., Basingstoke, Hants. RF24 OPR, England. *2321*

CONTEMPORARY BRITISH HISTORY.
Frank Cass, Newbury House, 890-900 Eastern Ave., Newbury Park, Ilford, Essex 1G2 7HH, England. TEL 44-181-599-8866. FAX 44-181-599-0984. *3405*

CONTEMPORARY CONCEPTS IN PHYSICS.
Harwood Academic Publishers, P.O. Box 3054, Langhorne, PA 19047-3054. TEL 215-750-2642. FAX 215-750-6343. *5545*

CONTEMPORARY ECONOMIC POLICY.
Western Economic Association International, 7400 Center Ave., Ste. 109, Huntington Beach, CA 92647-3039. TEL 714-898-3222. *911*

CONTEMPORARY ENDOCRINOLOGY.
Plenum Publishing Corp., 233 Spring St., New York, NY 10013-1578. TEL 212-620-8000. FAX 212-463-0742. *4666*

CONTEMPORARY FAMILY THERAPY.
Human Sciences Press, Inc. 233 Spring St., New York, NY 10013-1578. TEL 212-620-8000. FAX 212-463-0742. *5837*

CONTEMPORARY FRENCH CIVILIZATION.
Montana State University, Department of Modern Languages, Bozeman, MT 59717. TEL 406-994-6447. FAX 406-994-2893. *3405*

CONTEMPORARY GERIATRIC MEDICINE.
Plenum Publishing Corp., 233 Spring St., New York, NY 10013-1578. TEL 212-620-8000. FAX 212-463-0742. *3285*

CONTEMPORARY GERONTOLOGY.
Springer Publishing Company, 536 Broadway, New York, NY 10012-3955. TEL 212-431-4370. FAX 212-941-7842. *3285*

CONTEMPORARY HEMATOLOGY - ONCOLOGY.
Plenum Publishing Corp., 233 Spring St., New York, NY 10013-1578. TEL 212-620-8000. FAX 212-463-0742611. *4699*

CONTEMPORARY HYPNOSIS.
Whurr Publishers Ltd., 19b Compton Terrace, London N1 2UN, England. TEL 44-171-359-5979. FAX 44-171-226-5290. *4704*

CONTEMPORARY INTERNAL MEDICINE.
Appleton & Lange Box 120041, Stamford, CT 06912-0041. TEL 203-406-4500. FAX 203-406-4603. *4705*

CONTEMPORARY ISSUES IN GENETICS AND EVOLUTION.
Kluwer Academic Publishers, Postbus 17, 3300 AA Dordrecht, Netherlands. TEL 31-78-6392392. FAX 31-78-6392254. *739*

CONTEMPORARY ISSUES IN RISK ANALYSIS.
Plenum Publishing Corp., 233 Spring St., New York, NY 10013-1578. TEL 212-620-8000. FAX 212-463-0742. *5957*

CONTEMPORARY JEWRY.
Association for the Sociological Study of Jewry, Box 5302, Connecticut College, New London, CT 06320. TEL 360-439-2241. FAX 860-439-5332. *2873*

CONTEMPORARY MATHEMATICS.
American Mathematical Society, Box 6248, Providence, FI 02940-6248. TEL 401-455-4000. *4361*

CONTEMPORARY METABOLISM.
Plenum Publishing Corp., 233 Spring St., New York, NY 10013-1578. TEL 212-620-8000. FAX 212-463-0742. *4666*

CONTEMPORARY MUSIC REVIEW.
Harwood Academic Publishers, c/o International Publishers Distributor, P.O. Box 3054, Langhorne, PA 19047-3054. TEL 215-750-2642. FAX 215-750-6343. *5151*

CONTEMPORARY MUSIC STUDIES.
Harwood Academic Publishers, c/o International Publishers Distributor, P.O. Box 3054, PA 19047-3054. TEL 215-750-2642. FAX 215-750-6343. *5151*

CONTEMPORARY NEPHROLOGY.
Plenum Publishing Corp., 233 Spring St., New York, NY 10013-1578. TEL 212-620-8000. FAX 212-463-0742. *4925*

CONTEMPORARY NEUROLOGY SERIES.
F.A. Davis Company, 1915 Arch St., Philadelphia, PA 19103. FAX 215-568-5065. *4832*

CONTEMPORARY OB-GYN.
Medical Economics, 5 Paragon Dr., Montvale, NJ 07645. FAX 201-358-7260. *4734*

CONTEMPORARY ORTHOPAEDICS.
Bobit Publishing Company, 2512 Artesia Blvd., Redondo Beach, CA 90278-3210. TEL 310-376-8788. FAX 310-376-9043. *4782*

THE CONTEMPORARY PACIFIC.
University of Hawaii Press, Journals Department, 2840 Kolowalu St, Honolulu, HI 96822. TEL 808-956-8833. FAX 808-988-6052. *3110*

CONTEMPORARY PHILOSOPHY.
Kluwer Academic Publishers, Postbus 17, 3300 AA Dordrecht, Netherlands. TEL 31-78-6392392. FAX 31-78-6392254. *5471*

CONTEMPORARY PHYSICS.
Taylor & Francis Ltd., 1 Gunpowder Sq., London EC4A 3DE, England. TEL 44-171-583-0490. FAX 44-171-583-0585. *5545*

CONTEMPORARY PSYCHOANALYSIS.
William Alanson White Psychoanalytic Institute, 20 W. 74th St., New York, NY 10023. TEL 212-873-0725. FAX 212-362-6967. *5837*

CONTEMPORARY PSYCHOLOGY.
American Psychological Association, 750 First St., N.E., Washington, DC 20002-4242. TEL 202-336-5600. FAX 202-336-5568. *5837*

CONTEMPORARY REVIEWS IN OBSTETRICS AND GYNAECOLOGY.
Parthenon Publishing Group, Casterton Hall, Carnforth, Lancs. LA6 2LA, England. TEL 44-152-427-2084. FAX 44-152-427-1587. *4734*

CONTEMPORARY SECURITY POLICY.
Frank Cass, Newbury House, 890-900 Eastern Ave., Newbury Park, Ilford, Essex 1G2 7HH, England. TEL 44-181-599-8866. FAX 44-181-599-0984. *5745*

CONTEMPORARY SOCIAL PSYCHOLOGY.
Society for the Advancement of Social Psychology, Department of Psychology, Mercer University, 1400 Coleman Ave., Macon, GA 31207-0001. TEL 912-752-2972. FAX 912-752-2955. *5837*

CONTEMPORARY SOUTH ASIA.
Carfax Publishing Co., P.O. Box 25, Abingdon, Oxon. OX14 3UE, England. TEL 44-1238-401000. FAX 44-1235-401550. *5645*

CONTEMPORARY SURGERY.
Bobit Publishing Company, 2512 Artesia Blvd., Recondo Beach, CA 90278-3210. TEL 310-376-8788. FAX 310-376-9043. *4907*

CONTEMPORARY THEATRE REVIEW.
Harwood Academic Publishers, P.O. Box 3054, Langhorne, PA 19047-3054. TEL 215-750-2642. FAX 215-750-6343. *5694*

CONTEMPORARY THEATRE STUDIES.
Harwood Academic Publishers, c/o International Publishers Distributor, P.O. Box 3054, Langhorne, PA 19047-3054. TEL 215-750-2642. FAX 215-750-6343. *6694*

CONTEMPORARY TOPICS IN IMMUNOBIOLOGY.
Plenum Publishing Corp., 233 Spring St., New York, NY 10013-1578. TEL 212-620-8000. FAX 212-463-0742. *4580*

CONTEMPORARY TOPICS IN INFORMATION TRANSFER.
Elsevier Science B.V., Books Division, P.O. Box 211, 1000 AE Amsterdam, Netherlands. TEL 31-20-4853911. FAX 31-20-4853705. *2080*

CONTEMPORARY TOPICS IN MOLECULAR IMMUNOLOGY.
Plenum Publishing Corp., 233 Spring St., New York, NY 10013-1578. TEL 212-620-8047. FAX 212-463-0742. *4580*

CONTEMPORARY TOPICS IN PURE AND APPLIED CONDENSED MATTER SCIENCE.
Gordon and Breach Science Publishers, c/o International Publishers Distributor, P.O. Box 3054, Langhorne, PA 19047-3054. TEL 215-750-2642. FAX 215-750-6343. *5545*

CONTEMPORARY WALES.
University of Wales Press, 6 Gwennyth St., Cathays, Cardiff CF2 4YD, Wales. TEL 44-1222-231919. FAX 44-1222-230908. *6319*

CONTEXT SOUTH.
Context South Foundation, c/o David Breeden, Ed., Box 4504, 2100 Memorial Blvd., Kerrville, TX 78028-5611. TEL 501-972-6095. *4304*

CONTEXTS OF LEARNING
Swets & Zeitlinger bv, P.O. Box 825, 2160 SZ Lisse, Netherlands. TEL 31-252-435111. FAX 31-252-415888. *2321*

CONTINENTAL SHELF RESEARCH.
Elsevier Science Ltd., Pergamon, P.O. Box 800, Kidlington, Oxford OX5 1DX, England. TEL 44-1865-843000. FAX 44-1865-8430 0. *2292*

CONTINUUM.
Edith Cowan University, 2 Bradford St., Mount Lawley, W.A. 6050, Australia. TEL 61-9-3706219. FAX 61-9-3706668. *5297*

CONTINUUM (CHICAGO).
American Hospital Association, 1 N. Franklin, Chicago, IL 60606. TEL 312-445-3616. FAX 312-445-3708. *3542*

CONTRACEPTION.
Elsevier Science Inc., Box 945, New York, NY 10159-0945. TEL 212-633-3730. FAX 212-633-3680. *826*

CONTRACEPTIVE TECHNOLOGY UPDATE.
American Health Consultants, Inc., 3525 Piedmont Rd., N.E., Bldg. 6, Ste. 400, Atlanta, GA 30305. TEL 404-262-7436. FAX 800-284-3291. *826*

CONTRIBUTIONS FROM THE NEW YORK BOTANICAL GARDEN.
New York Botanical Garden, Scientific Publications Department, Bronx, NY 10458-5126. TEL 718-817-8721. FAX 718-817-8842. *677*

CONTRIBUTIONS IN MARINE SCIENCE - MONOGRAPHIC SERIES.
University of Texas at Austin, Marine Science Institute, 750 Channelview Dr., Port Aransas, TX 78373. TEL 512-749-6723. FAX 512-749-6725. *578*

CONTRIBUTIONS IN SCIENCE.
Natural History Museum of Los Angeles County, 900 Exposition Blvd., Los Angeles, CA 90007. TEL 213-744-3330. FAX 213-742-0730. *6235*

CONTRIBUTIONS ON ENTOMOLOGY, INTERNATIONAL.
Associated Publishers, Box 140103, Gainesville, FL 32614-0103. TEL 352-371-4071. FAX 352-371-4071. *723*

CONTRIBUTIONS TO BIBLICAL EXEGESIS AND THEOLOGY.
Kok Pharos Publishing House, Postbus 5016, 8260 AG Kampen, Netherlands. TEL 31-38-3392555. FAX 31-38-3327331. *6055*

CONTRIBUTIONS TO ECONOMIC ANALYSIS.
Elsevier Science B.V., Books Division, P.O. Box 211, 1000 AE Amsterdam, Netherlands. TEL 31-20-4853911. FAX 31-20-4853705. *1249*

CONTRIBUTIONS TO EPIDEMIOLOGY AND BIOSTATISTICS.
S. Karger AG, Allschwilerstr. 10, P.O. Box, CH-4009 Basel, Switzerland. TEL 061-3061111. FAX 061-3061234. *5957*

CONTRIBUTIONS TO GYNECOLOGY AND OBSTETRICS.
S. Karger AG, Allschwilerstr. 10, P.O. Box, CH-4009 Basel, Switzerland. TEL 061-3061111. FAX 061-3061234. *4734*

CONTRIBUTIONS TO HUMAN DEVELOPMENT.
S. Karger AG, Allschwilerstr. 10, CH-4009 Basel, Switzerland. TEL 061-3061111. FAX 061-3061234. *4445*

CONTRIBUTIONS TO MICROBIOLOGY AND IMMUNOLOGY.
S. Karger AG, Allschwilerstr. 10, P.O. Box, CH-4009 Basel, Switzerland. TEL 061-3061111. FAX 061-3061234. *4580*

CONTRIBUTIONS TO MINERALOGY AND PETROLOGY.
Springer-Verlag, Heidelberger Platz 3, 14197 Berlin, Germany. TEL 49-30-8207-0. FAX 49-30-8214091. *2229*

CONTRIBUTIONS TO NEPALESE STUDIES.
Tribhuvan University, Research Centre for Nepal and Asian Studies, Kirtipur, Nepal. TEL 977-1-231740. FAX 977-1-227184. *3378*

CONTRIBUTIONS TO NEPHROLOGY.
S. Karger AG, Allschwilerstr. 10, P.O. Box, CH-4009 Basel, Switzerland. TEL 061-3061111. FAX 061-3061234. *4926*

CONTRIBUTIONS TO ONCOLOGY.
S. Karger AG, Allschwilerstr. 10, CH-4009 Basel, Switzerland. TEL 061-3061111. FAX 061-3061234. *4753*

CONTRIBUTIONS TO PHENOMENOLOGY.
Kluwer Academic Publishers, Postbus 17, 3300 AA Dordrecht, Netherlands. TEL 31-78-6392392. FAX 31-78-6392254. *5471*

CONTRIBUTIONS TO PRIMATOLOGY.
S. Karger AG, Allschwilerstr. 10, P.O. Box, CH-4009 Basel, Switzerland. TEL 061-3061111. FAX 061-3061234. *802*

CONTRIBUTIONS TO THE HISTORY OF LABOR AND SOCIETY.
E.J. Brill, P.O. Box 9000, 2300 PA Leiden, Netherlands. TEL 31-71-5353500. FAX 31-71-5317532. *3719*

CONTRIBUTIONS TO THE SOCIOLOGY OF JEWISH LANGUAGES.
E.J. Brill, P.O. Box 9000, 2300 PA Leiden, Netherlands. TEL 31-71-5353500. FAX 31-71-5317532. *4062*

CONTRIBUTIONS TO ZOOLOGY.
Universiteit van Amsterdam, Commissie voor de Artis Bibliotheek, Plantage Middenlaan 45A, 1018 DC Amsterdam, Netherlands. *802*

CONTROL.
British Production and Inventory Control Society, University of Warwick Science Park, Sir William Lyons Rd., Coventry, Warks. CV4 7EZ, England. TEL 44-1203-692266. FAX 44-1203-692305. *1412*

CONTROL AND COMPUTERS.
International Association of Science and Technology for Development, 4500 16th Ave., N.W., Ste. 80, Calgary, AB T3B 0M6, Canada. TEL 403-288-1195. FAX 403-247-6851. *2014*

CONTROL AND CYBERNETICS.
Polish Academy of Sciences, Systems Research Institute, Ul. Newelska 6, 01-447 Warsaw, Poland. TEL 48-22-364103. FAX 48-22-372772. *2060*

CONTROL ENGINEERING PRACTICE.
Elsevier Science Ltd., Pergamon, P.O. Box 800, Kidlington, Oxford OX5 1DX, England. TEL 44-1865-843000. FAX 44-1865-843010. *2679*

CONTROLLED CLINICAL TRIALS.
Elsevier Science Inc., Box 945, New York, NY 10159-0945. TEL 212-633-3730. FAX 212-633-3680. *4679*

CONTROLLED RELEASE SERIES.
Elsevier Science B.V., Books Division, P.O. Box 211, 1000 AE Amsterdam, Netherlands. TEL 31-20-4853911. FAX 31-20-4853705. *1737*

CONTROVERSIES IN CLINICAL OPHTHALMOLOGY.
Field & Wood, Medical Periodicals, Inc., Box 975, Blue Bell, PA 19422. TEL 610-828-4010. FAX 610-482-0226. *4768*

CONVERGENCE.
International Council for Adult Education, 720 Bathurst St., Ste. 500, Toronto, ON M5S 2R4, Canada. TEL 416-588-1211. FAX 416-588-5725. *2398*

CONVULSIVE THERAPY.
Lippincott - Raven Publishers 227 E. Washington Sq., Philadelphia, PA 19106. TEL 215-238-4200. *4832*

COOPERATION AND CONFLICT.
Sage Publications Ltd., 6 Bonhill St., London EC2A 4PU, England. TEL 44-171-374-0645. FAX 44-171-374-8741. *5745*

COOPERATIVES ET DEVELOPPEMENT.
Centre Interuniversitaire de Recherche d'Information et d'Enseignement sur les Cooperatives, 5255 av. Decelles, Montreal, PQ H3T 1V6, Canada. TEL 514-340-6016. FAX 514-340-6995. *1159*

COORDINATION CHEMISTRY REVIEWS.
Elsevier Science S.A., P.O. Box 564, CH-1001 Lausanne 1, Switzerland. TEL 41-21-3207381. FAX 41-21-3235444. *1673*

COPEIA.
American Society of Ichthyologists and Herpetologists, c/o Dean A. Hendrickson, Sec., A S I H - Texas Natural History Collection, University of Texas - R4000, Austin, TX 78712-1100. TEL 512-471-0998. FAX 512-471-8775. *802*

COR ET VASA.
Praha Publishing Ltd., Anglicka 19, 120 00 Prague 2, Czech Republic. TEL 42-2-66312615. FAX 42-2-24247568. *4600*

CORAX.
Zum Brook 16, 24238 Bauersdorf, Germany. TEL 49-4384-1537. *775*

CORE JOURNALS IN CARDIOLOGY.
Excerpta Medica P.O. Box 548, 1000 AM Amsterdam, Netherlands. TEL 31-20-4853507. FAX 31-20-4853222. *4552*

CORE JOURNALS IN CLINICAL NEUROLOGY.
Excerpta Medica P.O. Box 548, 1000 AM Amsterdam, Netherlands. TEL 31-20-4853507. FAX 31-20-4853222. *4552*

CORE JOURNALS IN DERMATOLOGY.
Excerpta Medica P.O. Box 548, 1000 AM Amsterdam, Netherlands. TEL 31-20-4853507. FAX 31-20-4853222. *4552*

CORE JOURNALS IN GASTROENTEROLOGY.
Excerpta Medica P.O. Box 548, 1000 AM Amsterdam, Netherlands. TEL 31-20-4853507. FAX 31-20-4853222. *4552*

CORE JOURNALS IN OBSTETRICS - GYNECOLOGY.
Excerpta Medica P.O. Box 548, 1000 AM Amsterdam, Netherlands. TEL 31-20-4853507. FAX 31-20-4853222. *4552*

CORE JOURNALS IN OPHTHALMOLOGY.
Excerpta Medica P.O. Box 548, 1000 AM Amsterdam, Netherlands. TEL 31-20-4853507. FAX 31-20-4853222. *4553*

CORE JOURNALS IN PEDIATRICS.
Excerpta Medica P.O. Box 548, 1000 AM Amsterdam, Netherlands. TEL 31-20-4853507. FAX 31-20-4853222. *4553*

CORELLA.
Australian Bird Study Association, P.O. Box A313, S. Sydney, N.S.W. 2000, Australia. TEL 61-2-2318166. FAX 61-2-2517231. *775*

LE CORMORAN.
Groupe Ornithologique Normand, Universite de Caen, 14032 Caen Cedex, France. TEL 31-43-52-56. FAX 31-93-27-07. *775*

CORNEA.
Lippincott - Raven Publishers 227 E. Washington Sq., Philadelphia, PA 19106. TEL 215-238-4200. *4768*

CORNELL BIENNIAL ELECTRICAL ENGINEERING CONFERENCE.
Cornell University, School of Electrical Engineering, Phillips Hall, Ithaca, NY 14853. *2686*

THE CORNELL HOTEL & RESTAURANT ADMINISTRATION QUARTERLY.
Elsevier Science Inc., Box 945, New York, NY 10159-0945. TEL 212-633-3730. FAX 212-633-3680. *3560*

CORNELL LINGUISTIC CONTRIBUTIONS.
E.J. Brill, P.O. Box 9000, 2300 PA Leiden, Netherlands. TEL 31-71-5353500. FAX 31-71-5317532. *4062*

CORNELL MODERN INDONESIA PROJECT PUBLICATIONS.
Cornell University, Cornell Modern Indonesia Project, 640 Stewart Ave., Ithaca, NY 14850. TEL 607-255-4359. FAX 607-277-1904. *5282*

CORNELL PHONETICS LABORATORY. WORKING PAPERS.
C L C Publications, Cornell University, Morrill Hall, Ithaca, NY 14853. TEL 607-255-1105. FAX 607-255-2044. *4062*

CORNELL WORKING PAPERS IN LINGUISTICS.
C L C Publications, Cornell University, Morrill Hall, Ithaca, NY 14853-4701. TEL 607-255-1105. FAX 607-255-2044. *4062*

CORNISH ARCHAEOLOGY.
Cornwall Archaeological Society, c/o Royal Institution of Cornwall, River St., Truro, Cornwall, England. *350*

CORPORATE AND BUSINESS LAW JOURNAL.
Adelaide Law Review Association, c/o Department of Law, University of Adelaide, Adelaide, S.A. 5005, Australia. TEL 61-8-303-4440. FAX 61-8-303-4344. *3899*

CORPORATE GOVERNANCE.
Blackwell Publishers Ltd., 108 Cowley Rd., Oxford OX4 1JF, England. TEL 44-1865-791100. FAX 44-1865-791347. *911*

CORPORATE REPUTATION REVIEW.
Henry Stewart Publications, Russell House, 28-30 Little Russell St., London WC1A 2HN, England. TEL 44-171-404-3040. *1412*

CORRECTIVE AND SOCIAL PSYCHIATRY AND JOURNAL OF BEHAVIORAL TECHNOLOGY METHODS AND THERAPY.
Martin Psychiatric Research Foundation, Box 3365, Fairfield, CA 94533-0587. FAX 7078640910. *5838*

CORRELATION.
Astrological Association of Great Britain, 396 Caledonian Rd., London N1 1DN, England. *472*

CORRIERE DEI CIECHI.
Unione Italiana dei Ciechi, Via Borgognona 38, Rome, Italy. TEL 396-69988375. FAX 396-6786815. *3318*

CORROSION.
N A C E International, Box 218340, Houston, TX 77218. TEL 713-492-0535. FAX 713-492-8254. *2752*

CORROSION ABSTRACTS.
N A C E International, Box 218340, Houston, TX 77218. TEL 713-492-0535. FAX 713-492-8254. *2625*

CORROSION MANAGEMENT.
Impact Company Publications, Media House, 55 Old Rd., Leighton Buzzard, Beds. LU7 7RB, England. TEL 44-1525-370013. FAX 44-1525-382487. *2730*

CORROSION SCIENCE.
Elsevier Science Ltd., Pergamon, P.O. Box 800, Kidlington, Oxford OX5 1DX, England. TEL 44-1865-843000. FAX 44-1865-843010. *4953*

COSMETIC SCIENCE AND TECHNOLOGY SERIES.
Marcel Dekker, Inc., 270 Madison Ave., New York, NY 10016. TEL 212-696-9000. FAX 212-685-4540. *4446*

COSMIC RESEARCH.
Maik Nauka - Interperiodica, Mezhdunarodnyi Otdel, Ul. Profsoyuznaya 90, Moscow 117864, Russia. TEL 7-095-3360066. FAX 7-095-3660666. *2594*

COUNCIL FOR RESEARCH IN MUSIC EDUCATION. BULLETIN.
University of Illinois at Urbana-Champaign, School of Music, 1114 W. Nevada, Urbana, IL 61801. TEL 217-333-1027. FAX 217-244-4585. *5151*

COUNSELLING.
British Association for Counselling, 1 Regent Pl., Rugby, Warks. CV21 2PJ, England. TEL 01788-550899. FAX 01788-562189. *5838*

COUNSELLING PSYCHOLOGY QUARTERLY.
Carfax Publishing Co., P.O. Box 25, Abingdon, Oxon. OX14 3UE, England. TEL 44-1235-401000. FAX 44-1235-401550. *5838*

THE COUNSELOR (ARLINGTON).
National Association of Alcoholism and Drug Abuse Counselors, 1911 Fort Myer Dr., Ste. 900, Arlington, VA 22209-1603. TEL 703-741-7686. FAX 703-741-7648. *2195*

COUNSELOR PREPARATION (YEAR).
Accelerated Development Inc., 3812 W. Kilgore Ave., Muncie, IN 47304-4811. TEL 317-284-7511. FAX 317-284-2535. *2322*

COUNTY COMPASS.
National Organization of Black County Officials, 440 First St., N.W., Ste. 500, Washington, DC 20001. TEL 202-347-6953. FAX 202-393-6596. *2874*

COUP D'OEIL OPHTALMOLOGIQUE.
Editions et Regarde Attentivement, 68 bd. des Poilus, 44300 Nantes, France. TEL 40-68-96-06. FAX 40-68-98-76. *4769*

THE COURIER (BROCKTON).
Courier Publishing Co. (Brockton), Box 1878, Brockton, MA 02403. TEL 508-587-0975. FAX 508-858-5537. *3505*

COWBOY ARTISTS OF AMERICA NEWSLETTER.
Cowboy Artists of America Museum, 1550 Bandera Hwy., Box 1716, Kerrville, TX 78029. TEL 210-896-2553. FAX 210-896-2556. *5120*

CRANIO: JOURNAL OF CRANIOMANDIBULAR PRACTICE.
Chroma Inc., Box 8887, Chatanooga, TN 37414. TEL 800-624-4141. FAX 615-490-0791. *4446*

CRAZYHORSE.
Crazyhorse Association, Department of English, University of Arkansas at Little Rock, 2801 S. University, Little Rock, AR 72204. TEL 501-569-3161. *4199*

CREATION - EVOLUTION.
National Center for Science Education, Box 9477, Berkeley, CA 94709-0477. TEL 510-526-1674. FAX 510-526-1675. *6235*

CREATION RESEARCH SOCIETY QUARTERLY.
Creation Research Society, Box 8263, St. Joseph, MO 64508-8263. *6235*

CREATIVE NONFICTION.
Box 81536, Pittsburgh, PA 15217-0336. TEL 412-422-8404. FAX 412-422-8405. *4199*

CREATIVE NURSING.
Creative Nursing Management, Inc., Box 8286, Minneapolis, MN 55408. TEL 612-823-0637. FAX 612-339-2065. *4712*

CREATIVITY AND INNOVATION MANAGEMENT.
Blackwell Publishers Ltd., 108 Cowley Rd., Oxford OX4 1JF, England. TEL 44-1865-791100. FAX 44-1865-791347. *912*

CREDIT CONTROL.
House of Words Ltd., 7 Greding Walk, Hutton, Brentwood, Essex CM13 2UF, England. TEL 44-1277-225402. FAX 44-1277-201554. *1080*

CRIME AND JUSTICE.
University of Chicago Press, Journals Division, Box 37005, Chicago, IL 60637. TEL 773-753-3347. FAX 773-753-0811. *2161*

CRIME, LAW AND SOCIAL CHANGE.
Kluwer Academic Publishers, Postbus 17, 3300 AA Dordrecht, Netherlands. TEL 31-78-6392392. FAX 31-78-6392254. *2161*

CRIMINAL BEHAVIOUR AND MENTAL HEALTH.
Whurr Publishers Ltd., 19b Compton Terrace, London N1 2UN, England. TEL 44-171-359-5979. FAX 44-171-226-5290. *4833*

CRIMINAL JUSTICE (CHICAGO).
A B A Press 750 N. Lake Shore Dr., Chicago, IL 60611-4497. TEL 312-988-6076. FAX 312-988-6281. *3908*

CRIMINAL JUSTICE ETHICS.
Institute for Criminal Justice Ethics, John Jay College, 899 10th Ave., New York, NY 10019. TEL 212-237-8033. FAX 212-237-8901. *5471*

CRIMINAL LAW BULLETIN.
Warren, Gorham & Lamont, One Penn Plaza, New York, NY 10119. TEL 212-971-5000. FAX 212-971-5113. *3908*

CRIMINAL LAW FORUM.
Rutgers University, School of Law, Camden, 5th & Penn Streets, Camden, NJ 08102. TEL 609-757-6352. FAX 609-757-6487. *3908*

CRIMSON.
Vampire Guild, 82 Rip Croft, Portland, Dorset DT5 2EE, England. TEL 44-1305-822826. *4326*

CRITICAL CARE MEDICINE.
Williams & Wilkins, 351 W. Camden St., Baltimore, MD 21201. TEL 410-528-4000. FAX 410-528-4312. *4446*

CRITICAL CARE NURSE.
American Association of Critical Care Nurses, 101 Columbia, Aliso Viejo, CA 92656. TEL 714-362-2000. *4712*

CRITICAL INQUIRY.
University of Chicago Press, Journals Division, Box 37005, Chicago, IL 60637. TEL 773-753-3347. FAX 773-753-0811. *4138*

CRITICAL ISSUES IN DEVELOPMENTAL & BEHAVIORAL PEDIATRICS.
Plenum Publishing Corp. 233 Spring St., New York, NY 10013-1578. TEL 212-620-8000. FAX 212-463-0742. *5838*

CRITICAL MATRIX.
Princeton University, Program in Women's Studies, 113 Dickinson Hall, Princeton University, Princeton, NJ 08544-1017. TEL 609-258-5430. FAX 609-258-1833. *7015*

CRITICAL QUARTERLY.
Blackwell Publishers Ltd., 108 Cowley Rd., Oxford OX4 1JF, England. TEL 44-1865-791100. FAX 44-1865-791347. *4200*

CRITICAL REVIEW.
Charles Sturt University, School of Humanities and Social Sciences, Locked Bag 673, Wagga Wagga, N.S.W. 2678, Australia. TEL 61-69-332249. FAX 61-69-332792. *4200*

CRITICAL REVIEW OF BOOKS IN RELIGION.
Scholars Press, Box 15399, Atlanta, GA 30333-0399. TEL 404-727-2320. FAX 404-727-2345. *6055*

CRITICAL REVIEWS IN BIOCHEMISTRY AND MOLECULAR BIOLOGY.
C R C Press, Inc., 2000 Corporate Blvd., N.W., Boca Raton, FL 33431. TEL 407-994-0555. FAX 407-998-9784. *637*

CRITICAL REVIEWS IN BIOMEDICAL ENGINEERING.
Begell House Inc., 79 Madison Ave., Ste. 1205, New York, NY 10016-7892 TEL 212-725-1999. FAX 212-213-8368. *626*

CRITICAL REVIEWS IN BIOTECHNOLOGY.
C R C Press, Inc., 2000 Corporate Blvd., N.W., Boca Raton, FL 33431. TEL 407-994-0555. FAX 407-998-9784. *630*

CRITICAL REVIEWS IN CLINICAL LABORATORY SCIENCES.
C R C Press, Inc., 2000 Corporate Blvd., N.W., Boca Raton, FL 33431 TEL 407-994-0555. FAX 407-998-9784. *4446*

CRITICAL REVIEWS IN DIAGNOSTIC IMAGING.
C R C Press, Inc., 2000 Corporate Blvd., N.W., Boca Raton, FL 33431. TEL 407-994-0555. FAX 407-998-9784. *4874*

CRITICAL REVIEWS IN IMMUNOLOGY.
Begell House Inc., 79 Madison Ave., Ste. 1205, New York, NY 10016-7892 TEL 212-213-8368. FAX 212-725-1999. *4580*

CRITICAL REVIEWS IN MICROBIOLOGY.
C R C Press, Inc., 2000 Corporate Blvd., N.W., Boca Raton, FL 33431. TEL 407-994-0555. FAX 407-998-9784. *755*

CRITICAL REVIEWS IN ONCOLOGY - HEMATOLOGY.
Elsevier Science Ireland Ltd., P.O. Box 85, Limerick, Ireland. TEL 353-61-471944. FAX 353-61-472144. *4754*

CRITICAL REVIEWS IN PLANT SCIENCES.
C R C Press, Inc., 2000 Corporate Blvd., N.W., Boca Raton, FL 33431. TEL 407-994-0555. FAX 407-998-9784. *217*

CRITICAL REVIEWS IN TOXICOLOGY.
C R C Press, Inc., 2000 Corporate Blvd., N.W., Boca Raton, FL 33431. TEL 407-994-0555. FAX 407-998-9784. *2844*

CRITICAL STUDIES.
Editions Rodopi B.V., Keizersgracht 302-304, 1016 EX Amsterdam, Netherlands. TEL 31-20-6227507. FAX 31-20-6380948. *4200*

CRITICAL STUDIES IN MASS COMMUNICATION.
Speech Communication Association, 5105 Backlick Rd., Bldg. E., Annandale, VA 22003. TEL 703-750-0533. FAX 703-914-9471. *1959*

CRITIQUE OF ANTHROPOLOGY.
Sage Publications Ltd., 6 Bonhill St., London EC2A 4PU, England. TEL 44-171-374-0645. FAX 44-171-374-8741. *306*

CRITIQUE: STUDIES IN MODERN FICTION.
Heldref Publications, 1319 Eighteenth St., N.W., Washington, DC 20036-1802. TEL 202-296-6267. FAX 202-296-5149. *4200*

CROATIAN MEDICAL JOURNAL.
Pabst Science Publishers, Am Eichengrund 28, 49525 Lengerich, Germany. TEL 49-5484-308. FAX 49-5484-550. *4446*

CROISSANCE PERSONNELLE.
Publications Neomag Inc., P.O. Box 339, Bellefeuille, PQ J0R 1A0, Canada. TEL 514-565-9256. FAX 514-565-2797. *4938*

CROP PROTECTION.
Butterworth - Heinemann, Part of the Reed Elsevier group, Linacre House, Jordan Hill, Oxford OX2 8DP, England. TEL 44-1865-310366. FAX 44-1865-310898. *2639*

CROSS-CULTURAL RESEARCH.
Sage Publications, Inc., 2455 Teller Rd., Thousand Oaks, CA 91320. TEL 805-499-0721. FAX 805-499-0871. *6320*

CRUCIFERAE NEWSLETTER.
European Association for Research on Plant Breeding, INRA - Station d'Amelioration des Plantes, B.P. 29, 35650 Le Rheu, France. TEL 99-28-51-00. FAX 99-28-51-20. *109*

CRUSTACEANA.
E.J. Brill, P.O. Box 9000, 2300 PA Leiden, Netherlands. TEL 31-71-5353500. FAX 31-71-5317532. *802*

CRUSTACEANA. SUPPLEMENTS.
E.J. Brill, P.O. Box 9000, 2300 PA Leiden, Netherlands. TEL 31-71-5353500. FAX 31-71-5317532. *802*

CRYO - LETTERS.
7 Wootton Way, Cambridge CB3 9LX, England. TEL 44-1223-42092. FAX 44-1223-420502. *787*

CRYOBIOLOGY.
Academic Press, Inc., Journal Division, 525 B St., Ste. 1900, San Diego, CA 92101-4495. TEL 619-230-1840. FAX 619-699-6800. *653*

CRYOGENICS.
Butterworth - Heinemann, Part of the Reed Elsevier group, Linacre House, Jordan Hill, Oxford OX2 8DP, England. TEL 44-1865-310366. FAX 44-1865-310898. *5584*

CRYSTALLOGRAPHY REVIEWS.
Gordon & Breach Science Publishers, c/o International Publishers Distributor, P.O. Box 3054, Langhorne, PA 19047-3054. TEL 215-750-2642. FAX 215-750-6343. *1725*

CUADERNOS DE BIOESTADISTICA Y SUS APLICACIONES INFORMATICAS.
Universidad de Zaragoza, Facultad de Medicina, Domingo Miral, s-n, 50009 Zaragoza, Spain. TEL 34-76-761703. FAX 34-76-761704. *618*

CUADERNOS DE ECONOMIA.
Pontificia Universidad Catolica de Chile, Instituto de Economia, Casilla 76, Correo 17, Santiago, Chile. TEL 56-2-6864314. FAX 56-2-5521310. *912*

CUBA. MINISTERIO DE LA INDUSTRIA LIGERA. REVISTA CIENCIA Y TECNICA.
Ministerio de la Industria Ligera, Empedrado 302, esq. a Aguiar, Havana 10100, Cuba. TEL 60-3111. *6235*

CUIHUA XUEBAO.
Science Press, Marketing and Sales Department, 16 Donghuangchenggen North St., Beijing 100717, People's Republic of China. TEL 4010642. FAX 4019810. *1731*

CULTURA Y EDUCACION.
Aprendizaje, S.L., Crta. de Canillas, 138, 28043 Madrid, Spain. TEL 388-38-74. FAX 300-35-27. *4063*

CULTURAL DIVERSITY AND MENTAL HEALTH.
John Wiley & Sons, Inc., Journals, 605 Third Ave., New York, NY 10158. TEL 212-850-6645. FAX 212-850-6021. *6410*

CULTURAL DYNAMICS.
Sage Publications Ltd., 6 Bonhill St., London EC2A 4PU, England. TEL 44-171-374-0645. FAX 44-171-374-8741. *5472*

CULTURAL PERSPECTIVES ON THE AMERICAN SOUTH.
Gordon & Breach Science Publishers, c/o International Publishers Distributor, P.O. Box 3054, Langhorne, PA 19047-3054. TEL 215-750-2642. FAX 215-750-6343. *3466*

CULTURAL TRENDS.
Carfax Publishing Co., P.O. Box 25, Abingdon, Oxon. OX14 3UE, England. TEL 44-1235-401000. FAX 44-1235-401550. *425*

CULTURE, ILLNESS AND HEALING.
Kluwer Academic Publishers, Postbus 17, 3300 AA Dordrecht, Netherlands. TEL 31-78-6392392. FAX 31-78-6392254. *307*

CULTURE, MEDICINE AND PSYCHIATRY.
Kluwer Academic Publishers, Postbus 17, 3300 AA Dordrecht, Netherlands. TEL 31-78-6392392. FAX 31-78-6392254. *307*

CULTURE WARS MAGAZINE.
Ultramontane Associates, Inc., 206 Marquette Ave., South Bend, IN 46617. TEL 219-289-9786. FAX 219-289-1461. *5660*

CULTURES, BELIEFS, AND TRADITIONS.
E.J. Brill, P.O. Box 9000, 2300 PA Leiden, Netherlands. TEL 31-71-5353500. FAX 31-71-5317532. *6056*

CUORE.
Casa Editrice Scientifica Internazionale Periodici s.a.s., Via Cremona 19, 00161 Rome, Italy. TEL 39-6-44290783. FAX 39-6-44241-598. *4600*

CURRENT (PACIFIC GROVE).
National Marine Education Association, Box 51215, Pacific Grove, CA 93950. TEL 408-648-4841. *578*

CURRENT (WASHINGTON, 1960).
Heldref Publications, 1319 18th St., N.W., Washington, DC 20036-1802. TEL 202-296-6267. FAX 202-296-5149. *2322*

CURRENT AGRICULTURAL RESEARCH.
Association of Agricultural Scientists, College of Agriculture Bldg., O.U.A.T., Bhubaneswar 751003, India. *110*

CURRENT ANTHROPOLOGY.
University of Chicago Press, Journals Division, Box 37005, Chicago, IL 60637. TEL 773-753-3347. FAX 773-753-0811. *307*

CURRENT AWARENESS PROFILE ON QUANTUM CHEMISTRY.
Indiana University, QCPE, Creative Arts 181, Bloomington, IN 47405. TEL 812-855-4784. FAX 812-855-5539. *1673*

CURRENT BIOLOGY.
Current Biology Ltd., 800 Market St., Ste. 700, Philadelphia, PA 19106. TEL 800-552-5866. FAX 215-574-2270. *619*

CURRENT CHEMICAL CONCEPTS.
Academic Press, Inc., 525 B St., Ste. 1900, San Diego, CA 92101-4495. TEL 619-231-0926. FAX 619-669-6715. *1673*

CURRENT CLINICAL PRACTICE.
Elsevier Science B.V., Books Division, P.O. Box 211, 1000 AE Amsterdam, Netherlands. TEL 31-20-4853911. FAX 31-20-4853705. *4446*

CURRENT ENDOCRINOLOGY.
Elsevier Science B.V., Books Division, P.O. Box 211, 1000 AE Amsterdam, Netherlands. TEL 31-20-4853911. FAX 31-20-4853705. *4667*

CURRENT HISTOPATHOLOGY.
Kluwer Academic Publishers, Postbus 17, 3300 AA Dordrecht, Netherlands. TEL 31-78-6392392. FAX 31-78-6392254. *4705*

CURRENT ISSUES IN MIDDLE LEVEL EDUCATION.
West Georgia College, School of Education, Carrollton, GA 30118. TEL 770-836-6560. FAX 770-836-6729. *2322*

CURRENT ISSUES IN PRODUCTION ECOLOGY.
Kluwer Academic Publishers, Postbus 17, 3300 AA Dordrecht, Netherlands. TEL 31-78-6392392. FAX 31-78-6392254. *6648*

CURRENT MAMMALOGY.
Plenum Publishing Corp., 233 Spring St., New York, NY 10013-1578. TEL 212-620-8000. FAX 212-463-0742. *803*

CURRENT MANAGEMENT OF PAIN.
Kluwer Academic Publishers, Postbus 17, 3300 AA Dordrecht, Netherlands. TEL 31-78-6392392. FAX 31-78-6392254. *4833*

CURRENT MEDICINAL CHEMISTRY.
Bentham Science Publishers, 7436 S.W. 117 Ave., Box 130, Miami, FL 33183. FAX 305-596-5120. *1673*

CURRENT MICROBIOLOGY.
Springer-Verlag, Life Science Journals, 175 Fifth Ave., New York, NY 10010. TEL 212-460-1500. FAX 212-473-6272. *756*

CURRENT ORGANIC CHEMISTRY.
Bentham Science Publishers, 7436 S.W. 117 Ave., Box 130, Miami, FL 33183. FAX 305-596-5120. *1737*

CURRENT ORNITHOLOGY.
Plenum Publishing Corp., 233 Spring St., New York, NY 10013-1578. TEL 212-620-8000. FAX 212-463-0742. *775*

CURRENT PHARMACEUTICAL DESIGN.
Bentham Science Publishers, 7436 S.W. 117 Ave., Box 130, Miami, FL 33183. FAX 305-596-5120. *5406*

CURRENT PHYSICS - SOURCES AND COMMENTS.
Elsevier Science B.V., Books Division, P.O. Box 211, 1000 AE Amsterdam, Netherlands. TEL 31-20-4853911. FAX 31-20-4853705. *5545*

CURRENT PLANT SCIENCE AND BIOTECHNOLOGY IN AGRICULTURE.
Kluwer Academic Publishers, Postbus 17, 3300 AA Dordrecht, Netherlands. TEL 31-78-6392392. FAX 31-78-6392254. *660*

CURRENT PROBLEMS IN DERMATOLOGY.
S. Karger AG, Allschwilerstr. 10, P.O. Box, CH-4009 Basel, Switzerland. TEL 061-3061111. FAX 061-3061234. *4660*

CURRENT PSYCHOLOGY (NEW BRUNSWICK).
Transaction Publishers, Transaction Periodicals Consortium, Department 3092, Rutgers University, New Brunswick, NJ 08903. TEL 908-445-2280. FAX 908-445-3138. *5839*

CURRENT RESEARCH IN THE PLEISTOCENE.
Oregon State University, Center for the Study of First Americans, Corvallis, OR 97331-6510. TEL 503-737-4595. *350*

CURRENT STATUS OF CLINICAL CARDIOLOGY.
Kluwer Academic Publishers, Postbus 17, 3300 AA Dordrecht, Netherlands. TEL 31-78-6392392. FAX 31-78-6392254. *4601*

CURRENT STUDIES IN HEMATOLOGY AND BLOOD TRANSFUSION.
S. Karger AG, Allschwilerstr. 10, P.O. Box, CH-4009 Basel, Switzerland. TEL 061-3061111. FAX 061-3061234. *4699*

CURRENT STUDIES IN LIBRARIANSHIP.
Clarion University, Department of Library Science, Clarion, PA 16214. TEL 814-226-2314. FAX 814-226-2150. *3987*

CURRENT SURGERY.
Williams & Wilkins, 351 W. Camden St., Baltimore, MD 21201. TEL 410-528-4000. FAX 410-528-4312. *4907*

CURRENT THERAPEUTIC RESEARCH.
Excerpta Medica, Inc., Core Publishing Division 105 Raider Blvd., Belle Mead, NJ 08502-1510. TEL 908-874-8550. FAX 908-874-5611. *4447*

CURRENT TOPICS IN BIOENERGETICS.
Academic Press, Inc., 525 B St., Ste. 1900, San Diego, CA 92101-4495. TEL 619-231-0926. FAX 619-699-6715. *653*

CURRENT TOPICS IN CARDIOLOGY.
Elsevier Science B.V., Books Division, P.O. Box 211, 1000 AE Amsterdam, Netherlands. TEL 31-20-4853911. FAX 31-20-4853705. *4601*

CURRENT TOPICS IN CELLULAR REGULATION.
Academic Press, Inc. 525 B St., Ste. 1900, San Diego, CA 92101-4495. TEL 619-231-0926. FAX 619-699-6715. *579*

CURRENT TOPICS IN CHINESE SCIENCE. SECTION A: PHYSICS.
Gordon & Breach Science Publishers, c/o International Publishers Distributore, P.O. Box 3054, Langhorne, PA 19047-3054. TEL 215-750-2642. FAX 215-750-6343. *5546*

CURRENT TOPICS IN CHINESE SCIENCE. SECTION B: CHEMISTRY.
Gordon & Breach Science Publishers, c/o International Publishers Distributor, P.O. Box 3054, Langhorne, PA 19047-3054. TEL 215-750-2642. FAX 215-750-6343. *1673*

CURRENT TOPICS IN CHINESE SCIENCE. SECTION C: MATHEMATICS.
Gordon & Breach Science Publishers, c/o International Publishers Distributor, P.O. Box 3054, Langhorne, PA 19047-3054. TEL 215-750-2642. FAX 215-750-6343. *4361*

CURRENT TOPICS IN CHINESE SCIENCE. SECTION D: BIOLOGY.
Gordon & Breach Science Publishers, c/o International Publishers Distributor, P.O. Box 3054, Langhorne, PA 19047-3054. TEL 215-750-2642. FAX 215-750-6343. *579*

CURRENT TOPICS IN CHINESE SCIENCE. SECTION E: ASTRONOMY.
Gordon & Breach Science Publishers, c/o International Publishers Distributor, P.O. Box 3054, Langhorne, PA 19047-3054. TEL 215-750-2642. FAX 215-750-6343. *479*

CURRENT TOPICS IN CHINESE SCIENCE. SECTION F: EARTH SCIENCE.
Gordon & Breach Science Publishers, c/o International Publishers Distributor, P.O. Box 3054, Langhorne, PA 19047-3054. TEL 215-750-2642. FAX 215-750-6343. *2206*

CURRENT TOPICS IN CHINESE SCIENCE. SECTION G: MEDICAL SCIENCE.
Gordon & Breach Science Publishers, c/o International Publishers Distributor, P.O. Box 3054, Langhorne, PA 19047-3054. TEL 215-750-2642. FAX 215-750-6343. *4447*

CURRENT TOPICS IN DEVELOPMENTAL BIOLOGY.
Academic Press, Inc., 525 B St., Ste. 1900, San Diego, CA 92101-4495. TEL 619-231-0926. FAX 619-699-6715. *579*

CURRENT TOPICS IN ENVIRONMENTAL AND TOXICOLOGICAL CHEMISTRY.
Gordon & Breach Science Publishers, c/o International Publishers Distributor, P.O. Box 3054, Langhorne, PA 19047-3054. TEL 215-750-2642. FAX 215-750-6343. *2844*

CURRENT TOPICS IN EXPERIMENTAL ENDOCRINOLOGY.
Academic Press, Inc., 525 B St., Ste. 1900, San Diego, CA 92101-4495. TEL 619-231-0926. FAX 619-699-6715. *4667*

CURRENT TOPICS IN GENERAL THORACIC SURGERY.
Elsevier Science B.V., Books Division, P.O. Box 211, 1000 AE Amsterdam, Netherlands. TEL 31-20-4853911. FAX 31-20-4853705. *4907*

CURRENT TOPICS IN MATERIALS SCIENCE.
Elsevier Science B.V., Books Division, P.O. Box 211, 1000 AE Amsterdam, Netherlands. TEL 31-20-4853911. FAX 31-20-4853705. *5546*

CURRENT TOPICS IN MEMBRANES AND TRANSPORT.
Academic Press, Inc., 525 B St., Ste. 1900, San Diego, CA 92101-4495. TEL 619-231-0926. FAX 619-699-6715. *713*

CURRENT TOPICS IN NUTRITION AND DISEASE.
John Wiley & Sons, Inc., Journals, 605 Third Ave., New York, NY 10158. TEL 212-475-7700. *5231*

CURRENT TOPICS IN OBSTETRICS & GYNAECOLOGY.
Elsevier Science B.V., Books Division, P.O. Box 211, 1000 AE Amsterdam, Netherlands. TEL 31-20-4853911. FAX 31-20-4853705. *4734*

CURRENT TOPICS IN PULMONARY PHARMACOLOGY AND TOXICOLOGY.
Elsevier Science B.V., Books Division, P.O. Box 211, 1000 AE Amsterdam, Netherlands. TEL 31-20-4853911. FAX 31-20-4853705. *5406*

CURRENT TOPICS IN REMOTE SENSING.
Gordon and Breach Science Publishers, c/o International Publishers Distributor, P.O. Box 3054, Langhorne, PA 19047-3054. TEL 215-750-2642. FAX 215-750-6343. *3252*

CURRENT TOPICS IN VETERINARY MEDICINE AND ANIMAL SCIENCE.
Kluwer Academic Publishers, Postbus 17, 3300 AA Dordrecht, Netherlands. TEL 31-78-6392392. FAX 31-78-6392254. *6944*

CURRENTS IN EMERGENCY CARDIAC CARE.
American Heart Association, Citizen CPR Foundation, 7272 Greenville Ave., Dallas, TX 75231-4596. TEL 214-706-1310. FAX 214-691-6342. *4601*

CURRICULUM AND TEACHING.
James Nicholas Publishers, P.O. Box 244, Albert Park, Vic. 3206, Australia. TEL 61-3-696-5545. FAX 61-3-699-2040. *2483*

CURRICULUM INQUIRY.
Blackwell Publishers, 238 Main St., Cambridge, MA 02142. TEL 617-547-7110. FAX 617-547-0789. *2483*

CURRICULUM STUDIES.
Triangle Journals Ltd., P.O. Box 65, Wallingford, Oxon. OX10 0YG, England. TEL 44-1491-838013. FAX 44-1491-834968. *2484*

CURSUS.
Universite de Montreal, Ecole de Bibliotheconomie et des Sciences de l'Information, C.P. 6128, succ. Centre Ville, Montreal PQ H3C 3J7, Canada. *3987*

CURTIN UNIVERSITY. SCHOOL OF ENVIRONMENTAL BIOLOGY. BULLETIN.
Curtin University, School of Environmental Biology, Bentley, W.A., Australia. TEL 61-9-3517964. FAX 61-9-3512495. *579*

CURTIN UNIVERSITY OF TECHNOLOGY. MULGA RESEARCH CENTRE JOURNAL.
Curtin University of Technology, Mulga Research Centre, Kent St., Bentley, W.A. 6102, Australia. TEL 61-9-3517915. FAX 61-9-3512495. *579*

CURTIS'S BOTANICAL MAGAZINE.
Blackwell Publishers Ltd., 108 Cowley Rd., Oxford OX4 1JF, England. TEL 44-1865-791100. FAX 44-1865-791347. *3048*

CUTIS.
Quadrant HealthCom, 105 Raider Blvd., Belle Mead, NJ 08502-1510. TEL 908-874-0707. FAX 908-874-5611. *4660*

CYBERNETICS AND SYSTEMS (BRISTOL).
Taylor & Francis Inc., 1900 Frost Rd., Ste. 101, Bristol, PA 19007-1598. TEL 215-785-5800. FAX 215-785-5515. *2061*

CYBERNETICS AND SYSTEMS (NEW YORK).
Gordon & Breach Science Publishers, c/o International Publishers Distributor, P.O. Box 3054, Langhorne, PA 19047-3054. TEL 215-750-2642. FAX 215-750-6343. *2061*

CYBERNETICS AND SYSTEMS ANALYSIS.
Plenum Publishing Corp., Consultants Bureau, 233 Spring St., New York, NY 10013-1578. TEL 212-620-8468. FAX 212-463-0742. *2061*

CYTOGENETICS AND CELL GENETICS.
S. Karger AG, Allschwilerstr. 1C, P.O. Box, CH-4009 Basel, Switzerland. TEL 061-3061111. FAX 061-3061234. *739*

CYTOKINE AND GROWTH FACTOR REVIEWS.
Elsevier Science Ltd., Pergamon, P.O. Box 800, Kidington, Oxford OX5 1DX, England. TEL 44-1865-843000. FAX 44-1865-843010. *714*

CYTOKINES.
S. Karger AG, Allschwilerstr. 1C, P.O. Box, CH-4009 Basel, Switzerland. TEL 061-3061111. FAX 061-3061234. *756*

CYTOKINES AND MOLECULAR THERAPY.
Martin Dunitz Ltd., 7-9 Pratt St., Camden, London NW1 0AE, England. TEL 44-171-4822202. FAX 44-171-2670159 *4580*

CYTOMETRY (NEW YORK).
John Wiley & Sons, Inc., Journals, 605 Third Ave., New York, NY 10158. TEL 212-850-6645. FAX 212-850-6021. *714*

CYTOPATHOLOGY.
Blackwell Science Ltd., Osney Mead, Oxford OX2 0EL, England. TEL 44-1865-206206. FAX 44-1855-721205. *714*

CYTOTECHNOLOGY.
Kluwer Academic Publishers, Postbus 17, 3300 AA Dordrecht, Netherlands. TEL 31-78-6392392. FAX 31-78-6392254. *560*

CZECHOSLOVAK JOURNAL OF PHYSICS.
Plenum Publishing Corp., 233 Spring St., New York, NY 10013-1578. TEL 212-620-8000. FAX 212-463-0742. *5546*

CZECHOSLOVAK MATHEMATICAL JOURNAL.
Plenum Publishing Corp., 233 Spring St., New York, NY 10013-1578. TEL 212-620-8000. FAX 212-463-0742. *4361*

D C A M M REPORT.
Danish Center for Applied Mathematics and Mechanics, Department of Solid Mechanics, Technical University of Denmark, Lyngby, Denmark. *4361*

D N A AND CELL BIOLOGY.
Mary Ann Liebert, Inc. Publishers, 2 Madison Ave., Larchmont, NY 10538. TEL 914-834-3100. FAX 914-834-3688. *637*

D N A SEQUENCE.
Harwood Academic Publishers, c/o International Publishers Distributor, P.O. Box 3054, Langhorne, PA 19047-3054. TEL 215-750-2642. FAX 215-750-6343. *740*

D S P & MULTIMEDIA TECHNOLOGY.
Golden Gate Enterprises, Inc., Box 1603, Los Altos, CA 94023. TEL 415-969-6920. FAX 415-969-0222. *2510*

D W P S.
Aston Business School, 11th Fl., S. Wing, Aston University, Aston Triangle, Birmingham B4 7ET, England. *1413*

DADI GOUZAO YU CHENGKUANGXUE.
Science Press, Marketing and Sales Department, 16 Donghuangchenggen North St., Beijing 100717, People's Republic of China. TEL 4010642. FAX 4019810. *2229*

DAILY MISSISSIPPIAN.
Farley Hall, University, MS 38677. TEL 601-232-7118. FAX 601-232-5703. *1865*

DAIMON.
Universidad de Murcia Servicio de Publicaciones, Santo Cristo 1, 30080 Murcia, Spain. TEL 34-68-363012. FAX 34-68-363414. *5472*

DAIRY STATISTICS.
Livestock Improvement Corporation Ltd., Cnr. Ruakura & Morrinsville Rds., Private Bag 3016, Hamilton, New Zealand. TEL 64-7-8560700. FAX 64-7-8562429. *171*

DALHOUSIE REVIEW.
Dalhousie University Press Ltd., Sir James Dunn Bldg., Ste. 314, Halifax NS B3H 3J5, Canada. TEL 902-494-2541. FAX 902-494-1665. *4139*

DALHOUSIE UNIVERSITY. SCHOOL OF LIBRARY AND INFORMATION STUDIES. OCCASIONAL PAPERS.
Dalhousie University, School of Library and Information Studies, Halifax, NS B3H 3J5, Canada. TEL 902-494-3656. FAX 902-494-2451. *3988*

DALTON TRANSACTIONS.
The Royal Society of Chemistry, Thomas Graham House, Science Park, Milton Rd., Cambridge CB4 4WF, England. TEL 44-1223-420066. FAX 44-1223-423623. *1731*

DANA-REPORT.
Scandinavian Science Press Ltd. Universiteitsparken 15, 1260 Copenhagen, Denmark. *2292*

DANCE CRITICS ASSOCIATION. NEWSLETTER.
Dance Critics Association, Box 1882, Old Chelsea Sta., New York, NY 10011. TEL 212-343-3584. *2187*

DANCE INTERNATIONAL.
Vancouver Ballet Society, 1415 Barclay St., Vancouver, BC V6G 1J6, Canada. TEL 604-681-1525. FAX 604-681-7732. *2188*

DANDELION ARTS MAGAZINE.
Fern Publications, Casa Alba, 24 Frosty Hollow, E. Hunsbury, Northants. NN4 0SY, England. TEL 44-1604-701730. FAX 44-1604-702288. *4140*

DANGDAI WAIGUO WENXUE.
Nanjing Daxue, Waiguo Wenxue Yanjiusuo, Hankou Lu, Nanjing 210093, People's Republic of China. TEL 86-25-6637551. FAX 86-25-3325737. *4201*

DANISH REVIEW OF GAME BIOLOGY.
Ministry of the Environment, National Environmental Research Institute, Kaloe, 8410 Roende, Denmark. TEL 89-20-1400. FAX 89-20-1514. *803*

DANTE STUDIES.
State University of New York Press, State University Plaza, Albany, NY 12246. TEL 518-472-5000. FAX 518-472-5038. *4201*

DAQI KEXUE.
Science Press, Marketing and Sales Department, 16 Donghuangchenggen North St., Beijing 100717, People's Republic of China. TEL 4010642. FAX 4019810. *4993*

DARWINIANA.
Instituto de Botanica Darwinion, Labarden y del Campo, Casilla de Correo 22, San Isidro 1642, Buenos Aires, Argentina. TEL 742-8534. FAX 541-747-4748. *678*

DASEINSANALYSE.
S. Karger AG, Allschwilerstr. 10, P.O. Box, CH-4009 Basel, Switzerland. TEL 061-3061111. FAX 061-3061234. *4833*

DATA & KNOWLEDGE ENGINEERING.
North-Holland P.O. Box 211, 1000 AE Amsterdam, Netherlands. TEL 31-20-4853911. FAX 31-20-4853598. *1988*

DATA HANDLING IN SCIENCE AND TECHNOLOGY.
Elsevier Science B.V., Books Division, P.O. Box 211, 1000 AE Amsterdam, Netherlands. TEL 31-20-4853911. FAX 31-20-4853705. *2065*

DATA MANAGEMENT REVIEW.
Powell Publishing, Inc., 19380 Emerald Dr., Brookfield, WI 53045-3617. TEL 414-792-9696. FAX 414-792-9777. *2065*

DATA SECURITY LETTER.
Trusted Information Systems, Inc., 3060 Rte. 97, Glenwood, MD 21738. TEL 301-854-6889. FAX 301-854-5363. *2050*

DAUGHTERS OF THE AMERICAN REVOLUTION MAGAZINE.
National Society of the Daughters of the American Revolution, 1776 D St., N.W., Washington, DC 20006. TEL 202-879-3286. FAX 202-879-3283. *3466*

DAXUE HUAXUE.
Zhongguo Huaxue Xuehui, Daxue Huaxue Bianjibu, Beijing University, Chemistry Bldg., Haidian-qu, Beijing 100871, People's Republic of China. TEL 861-6275-1721. FAX 861-6275-4096. *1673*

DAY CARE AND EARLY EDUCATION.
Human Sciences Press, Inc. 233 Spring St., New York, NY 10013-1578. TEL 212-620-8000. FAX 212-463-0742. *6369*

DAYLILY JOURNAL.
American Hemerocallis Society, Inc., 6635 Highway E, Edgerton, MO 64444. TEL 816-227-3384. *3048*

DAZIRAN TANSUO.
Sichuan Kexue Jishu Chubanshe, 3, Yandao Jie, Chengdu, Sichuan 610012, People's Republic of China. TEL 86-28-666-4688. *6236*

DE MONTFORT UNIVERSITY. LEICESTER BUSINESS SCHOOL. OCCASIONAL PAPER.
De Montfort University, Leicester Business School, Scraptcroft, Leicester LE7 9SU, England. TEL 0116-257-7780. FAX 0116-257-7795. *913*

DEAD OF NIGHT.
Dead of Night Publications, 916 Shaker Rd., Ste. 228, Longmeadow, MA 01106-2416. *4326*

DEAD SEA DISCOVERIES.
E.J. Brill, P.O. Box 9000, 2300 PA Leiden, Netherlands. TEL 31-71-5353500. FAX 31-71-5317532. *6056*

DEANOTATIONS.
11919 Moss Point Lane, Reston, VA 20194. TEL 703-471-7907. *4304*

DEATH STUDIES.
Taylor & Francis Inc., 1900 Frost Rd., Ste. 101, Bristol, PA 19007-1598. TEL 215-785-5800. FAX 215-785-5515. *5839*

DEBATTE.
Carfax Publishing Co., P.O. Box 25, Abingdon, Oxon OX14 3UE, England. TEL 44-1235-401000. FAX 44-1235-401550. *3406*

DECISION.
Postfach 651180, 22371 Hamburg, Germany. FAX 49-40-5604523. *4202*

DECISION SUPPORT SYSTEMS.
North-Holland P.O. Box 211, 1000 AE Amsterdam, Netherlands. TEL 31-20-4853911. FAX 31-20-4853598. *1413*

DEEP-SEA RESEARCH. PART 1: OCEANOGRAPHIC RESEARCH PAPERS.
Elsevier Science Ltd., Pergamon, P.O. Box 800, Kidlington, Oxford OX5 1DX, England. TEL 44-1865-843000. FAX 44-1865-843010. *2293*

DEEP-SEA RESEARCH. PART 2: TOPICAL STUDIES IN OCEANOGRAPHY.
Elsevier Science Ltd., Pergamon, P.O. Box 800, Kidlington, Oxford OX5 1DX, England. TEL 44-1865-843000. FAX 44-1865-843010. *2293*

DEEP SOUTH GENEALOGICAL QUARTERLY.
Mobile Genealogical Society, Box 6224, Mobile, AL 36660. TEL 334-626-6573. *3080*

DEFENCE SCIENCE JOURNAL.
Defence Scientific Information & Documentation Centre (DESIDOC), Metcalfe House, New Delhi 110 054, India. TEL 011-239975. FAX 011-2919151. *5028*

DEFENSE TRANSPORTATION JOURNAL.
National Defense Transportation Association, 50 South Pickett St., No. 220, Alexandria, VA 22304-3008. TEL 703-751-5011. FAX 703-823-8761. *6716*

DEIR EL-BAHARI.
Polska Akademia Nauk, Zaklad Archeologii Srodziemnomorskiej, Palac Kultury i Nauki, p. 2105, 00-901 Warsaw, Poland. TEL 48-22-248593. FAX 48-22-6207651. *351*

DEL CONDOMINIUM LIFE.
Del Property Management Inc., 4800 Dufferin St., Downsview, ON M3H 5S9, Canada. TEL 416-736-2552. FAX 416-661-8923. *3676*

DELAWARE HISTORY.
Historical Society of Delaware, 505 Market St., Wilmington, DE 19801. TEL 302-655-7161. FAX 302-655-7844. *3466*

DELAWARE JOURNAL OF CORPORATE LAW.
Widener University, School of Law, Box 7286, Wilmington, DE 19803. TEL 302-477-2145. FAX 302-477-2042. *3900*

DELAWARE MEDICAL JOURNAL.
Medical Society of Delaware, 1925 Lovering Ave., Wilmington, DE 19806-2147. TEL 302-658-7596. FAX 302-658-9669. *4448*

DELAWARE VALLEY RAIL PASSENGER.
Delaware Valley Association of Railroad Passengers, Box 7505, Philadelphia, PA 19010-7505. TEL 215-673-6445. FAX 215-885-7448. *6810*

DELOS.
Harold P. Hanson, Ed. & Pub., 215 Williamson Hall, Gainesville, FL 32611. TEL 904-377-1560. FAX 904-392-0542. *4202*

DELTA BUSINESS REVIEW.
Northeast Louisiana University, Center for Business & Economic Research, Monroe, LA 71209-0101. TEL 318-342-1215. FAX 318-342-1209. *913*

DELTA KAPPA GAMMA BULLETIN.
Delta Kappa Gamma Society International, Box 1589, Austin, TX 78767-1589. TEL 512-478-5748. FAX 512-478-3961. *2426*

DELTA RESEARCH MONOGRAPH.
Massey University, Education Faculty, Palmerston N., New Zealand. FAX 64-6-35505635. *2323*

DELTION BIBLIKON MELETON.
Artos Zoes Publications, 28 Bouboulinas Str., 2nd fl., Athens 106 82, Greece. TEL 30-1-8824-547. *6057*

DEMENTIA.
S. Karger AG, Allschwilerstr. 10, P.O. Box, CH-4009 Basel, Switzerland. TEL 061-3061111. FAX 061-3061234. *4833*

DEMOCRACY AND EDUCATION.
Institute for Democracy in Education, Ohio University, College of Education, 313 McCracken Hall, Athens, OH 45701-2979. TEL 614-593-4531. FAX 614-593-0177. *2323*

DEMOCRACY & NATURE.
Aigis Publications, 1449 W. Littleton Blvd., Ste. 200, Littleton, CO 80120. TEL 303-730-6232. FAX 303-798-6568. *2781*

DEMOCRATIZATION.
Frank Cass, Newbury House, 890-900 Eastern Ave., Newbury Park, Ilford, Essex IG2 7HH, England. TEL 44-181-599-8866. FAX 44-181-599-0984. *5746*

DEMOGRAPHIC MONOGRAPHS.
Gordon & Breach Science Publishers, c/o International Publishers Distributor, P.O. Box 3054, Langhorne, PA 19047-3054. TEL 215-750-2642. FAX 215-750-6343. *5783*

DEMOS.
Harwood Academic Publishers, c/o International Publishers Distributor, P.O. Box 3054, Langhorne, PA 19047-3054. TEL 215-750-2642. FAX 215-750-6343. *2874*

DENRYOKU TO KISHO.
Denryoku Kisho Renrakukai, Nihon Kisho Kyokai, Nanbu Bldg., 2-7 Nishiki-cho, Kanda, Chiyoda-ku, Tokyo 101, Japan. TEL 81-3-3295-1521. FAX 81-3-3295-7835. *4993*

DENTAL COMPUTER NEWSLETTER.
Andent, Inc., 1000 North Ave., Waukegan, IL 60085. TEL 847-223-5077. *4630*

DENTAL HEALTH.
British Dental Hygienists' Association, St. Luke, Maywood Dr., Portsmouth Rd., Camberley, Surrey GU15 1LH, England. TEL 44-1276-677156. FAX 44-1276-671072. *4638*

DENTAL LAB MANAGEMENT TODAY.
Dental Lab Publications, Inc., 731 Main St., No. A2, Monrue, CT 06788-2872. TEL 203-459-2888. FAX 203-459-2889. *4638*

DENTAL MATERIALS.
Academy of Dental Materials, 3302 Gaston Ave., Dallas, TX 75246. TEL 214-828-8378. FAX 214-874-4503. *4639*

DENTAL REVIEW.
MediMedia Asia 1501 Tung Sun Commercial Centre, 194-200 Lockhart Rd., Wanchai, Hong Kong. TEL 852-2511-0765. FAX 852-2507-3817. *4639*

DENTALHYGIENE.
Swiss Dental Hygienists' Association, Oberstadt 11, CH-6204 Sempach, Switzerland. TEL 41-41-4627065. FAX 41-41-4627061. *4639*

DENTO-MAXILLO-FACIAL RADIOLOGY.
Stockton Press Houndmills, Basingstoke, Hants, RG21 6XS, England. *4875*

THE DEPARTMENT CHAIR.
Anker Publishing Company, Inc., 176 Ballville Rd., Box 249, Bolton, MA 01740-0249. TEL 508-779-6190. FAX 508-779-6366. *2456*

DEPRESSION.
John Wiley & Sons, Inc., Journals, 605 Third Ave., New York, NY 10158. TEL 212-850-6645. FAX 212-850-6021. *5839*

DEPRESSION AND STRESS.
International Universities Press, Inc., 59 Boston Post Rd., Box 1524, Madison, CT 06443-1524. TEL 203-245-4000. FAX 203-245-0775. *5839*

DERIVATIVES USE, TRADING & REGULATION.
Henry Stewart Publications, Russell House, 28-30 Little Russell St., London WC1A 2HN, England. TEL 44-171-404-3040. FAX 44-171-404-2081. *1327*

DERMATOLOGIA.
Obsidiana Editores, S.A., Czda. de Tlalpan 2365, Col. Ciudad Jardin, 04370 Mexico DF, Mexico. TEL 6899133. *4660*

DERMATOLOGIC SURGERY.
Elsevier Science Inc., Box 945, New York, NY 10159-0945. TEL 212-633-3730. FAX 212-633-3680. *4908*

DERMATOLOGY.
S. Karger AG, Allschwilerstr. 10, P.O. Box, CH-4009 Basel, Switzerland. TEL 061-3061111. FAX 061-3061234. *4660*

DERMATOLOGY.
Marcel Dekker, Inc., 270 Madison Ave., New York, NY 10016. TEL 212-696-9000. FAX 212-685-4540. *4660*

DERMATOLOGY NURSING.
Jannetti Publications, Inc., East Holly Ave., Box 56, Pitman, NJ 08071-0056. TEL 609-256-2300. FAX 609-589-7463. *4660*

DESALINATION.
Elsevier Science B.V., P.O. Box 211, 1000 AE Amsterdam, Netherlands. TEL 31-20-4853911. FAX 31-20-4853598. *6965*

DESARROLLO TECNOLOGICO.
Universidad Nacional Autonoma de Mexico, Instituto de Investigaciones en Matematicas Aplicadas y en Sistemas, Apdo. Postal 20-726, Del. V.A. Obregon, 01000 Mexico D.F., Mexico. TEL 622-35-62. FAX 550-00-47. *6649*

DESERT BIGHORN COUNCIL. TRANSACTIONS.
Desert Bighorn Council, c/o Brighorn Institute, 51000 Highway 74, Palm Desert, CA 92260. TEL 702-646-3401. *2125*

DESIGN AUTOMATION FOR EMBEDDED SYSTEMS.
Kluwer Academic Publishers, Postbus 17, 3300 AA Dordrecht, Netherlands. TEL 31-78-6392392. FAX 31-78-6392254. *2054*

DESIGN, CODES AND CRYPTOGRAPHY.
Kluwer Law International Postbus 85889, 2508 CN The Hague, Netherlands. TEL 31-70-3081500. FAX 31-70-3081515. *4362*

DESIGN ISSUES.
M I T Press, 55 Hayward St., Cambridge, MA 02142. TEL 617-235-2889. FAX 617-258-6779. *426*

DESIGN NEWS.
Cahners Publishing Company (Newton), Division of Reed Elsevier Inc., 275 Washington St., Newton, MA 02158-1630. TEL 617-964-3030. FAX 617-558-4402. *6649*

DESIGN STUDIES.
Butterworth - Heinemann, Part of the Reed Elsevier group, Linacre House, Jordan Hill, Oxford OX2 8DP, England. TEL 44-1865-310366. FAX 44-1865-310898. *391*

DESTINATION CALGARY.
Calgary Convention & Visitors Bureau, 237 Eighth Ave., S.E., Calgary, AB T2G 0K8, Canada. TEL 403-750-8510. FAX 403-262-3809. *6877*

DEUS LOCI.
James A. Brigham, Ed. & Pub., c/o Department of English, Okanagan University College, Kelowna, B.C. V1Y 4X8, Canada. TEL 604-762-5445. *4202*

DEUTSCHER RAT FUER LANDESPFLEGE. SCHRIFTENREIHE.
Deutscher Rat fuer Landespflege, Konstantinstr. 110, 53179 Bonn, Germany. TEL 0228-331097. FAX 0228-334727. *2782*

DEVELOPMENT AND CHANGE.
Blackwell Publishers Ltd., 108 Cowley Rd., Oxford OX4 1JF, England. TEL 44-1865-791100. FAX 44-1865-791347. *1304*

DEVELOPMENT DISABILITIES BULLETIN.
University of Alberta, Developmental Disabilities Centre, 6-123D Education North, Edmonton, AB T6G 2H1, Canada. TEL 403-492-4505. FAX 403-492-1318. *4834*

DEVELOPMENT, GENES AND EVOLUTION.
Springer-Verlag, Heidelberger Platz 3, 14197 Berlin, Germany. TEL 49-30-28787358. FAX 49-30-82787448. *579*

DEVELOPMENT, GROWTH AND DIFFERENTIATION.
Blackwell Science Pty Ltd, P.O. Box 378, Carlton South, Vic. 3053, Australia. TEL 61-3-93470300. FAX 61-3-93493016. *579*

DEVELOPMENT IN PRACTICE.
Oxfam, 274 Banbury Rd., Oxford OX2 7DZ, England. TEL 44-1865-313196. FAX 44-1865-313117. *1305*

DEVELOPMENT POLICY REVIEW.
Blackwell Publishers Ltd., 108 Cowley Rd., Oxford OX4 1JF, England. TEL 44-1865-791100. FAX 44-1865-791347. *1305*

DEVELOPMENTAL AND COMPARATIVE IMMUNOLOGY.
Elsevier Science Ltd., Pergamon, P.O. Box 800, Kidlington, Oxford OX5 1DX, England. TEL 44-1865-843000. FAX 44-1865-843010. *4580*

DEVELOPMENTAL BIOLOGY.
Academic Press, Inc., Journal Division, 525 B St., Ste. 1900, San Diego, CA 92101-4495. TEL 619-230-1840. FAX 619-699-6800. *580*

DEVELOPMENTAL BRAIN DYSFUNCTION.
S. Karger AG, Allschwilerstr. 10, P.O. Box, CH-4009 Basel, Switzerland TEL 061-3061111. FAX 061-3061234. *4834*

DEVELOPMENTAL DYNAMICS.
John Wiley & Sons, Inc., Journals, 605 Third Ave., New York, NY 10158. TEL 212-850-6645. FAX 212-850-6021. *580*

DEVELOPMENTAL GENETICS.
John Wiley & Sons, Inc., Journals, 605 Third Ave., New York, NY 10158. TEL 212-850-6645. FAX 212-850-6021. *740*

DEVELOPMENTAL IMMUNOLOGY.
Harwood Academic Publishers, c/o International Publisher Distributor, P.O. Box 3054, Langhorne, PA 19047-3054. TEL 215-750-2642. FAX 215-750-6343. *4580*

DEVELOPMENTAL MEDICINE AND CHILD NEUROLOGY.
Mac Keith Press, 526-529 High Holborn House, 52-54 High Holborn, London WC1V 6RL, England. TEL 44-171-405-5355. FAX 44-171-405-5365. *4805*

DEVELOPMENTAL NEUROPSYCHOLOGY.
Lawrence Erlbaum Associates, Inc., 10 Industrial Dr., Mahwah, NJ 07430-2262. TEL 201-236-9500. FAX 201-236-0072. *5840*

DEVELOPMENTAL NEUROSCIENCE.
S. Karger AG, Allschwilerstr. 10, P.O. Box, CH-4009 Basel, Switzerland. TEL 061-3061111. FAX 061-3061234. *4834*

DEVELOPMENTAL PSYCHOBIOLOGY.
John Wiley & Sons, Inc., Journals, 605 Third Ave., New York, NY 10158-0012. TEL 212-850-6645. FAX 212-850-6021. *530*

DEVELOPMENTAL PSYCHOLOGY.
American Psychological Association, 750 First St., N.E., Washington, DC 20002-4242. TEL 202-336-5600. FAX 202-336-5568. *5840*

DEVELOPMENTAL REVIEW.
Academic Press, Inc., Journal Division, 525 B St., Ste. 1900, San Diego, CA 92101-4495. TEL 619-230-1840. FAX 619-699-6800. *5840*

DEVELOPMENTS IN AGRICULTURAL AND MANAGED FOREST ECOLOGY.
Elsevier Science B.V., Books Division, P.O. Box 211, 1000 AE Amsterdam, Netherlands. TEL 31-20-4853911. FAX 31-20-43537C5. *3013*

DEVELOPMENTS IN AGRICULTURAL ECONOMICS.
Elsevier Science B.V., Books Division, P.O. Box 211, 1000 AE Amsterdam, Netherlands. TEL 31-20-4853911. FAX 31-20-43537C5. *189*

DEVELOPMENTS IN AGRICULTURAL ENGINEERING.
Elsevier Science B.V., Books Division, P.O. Box 211, 1000 AE Amsterdam, Netherlands. TEL 31-20-4853911. FAX 31-20-43537C5. *219*

DEVELOPMENTS IN ANIMAL AND VETERINARY SCIENCES.
Elsevier Science B.V., Books Division, P.O. Box 211, 1000 AE Amsterdam, Netherlands. TEL 31-20-4853911. FAX 31-20-4853705. *6945*

DEVELOPMENTS IN AQUACULTURE AND FISHERIES SCIENCE.
Elsevier Science B.V., Books Division, P.O. Box 211, 1000 AE Amsterdam, Netherlands. TEL 31-20-4853911. FAX 31-20-4853705. *803*

DEVELOPMENTS IN ATMOSPHERIC SCIENCE.
Elsevier Science B.V., Books Division, P.O. Box 211, 1000 AE Amsterdam, Netherlands. TEL 31-20-4853911. FAX 31-20-4853705. *4994*

DEVELOPMENTS IN BIOCHEMISTRY.
Elsevier Science B.V., Books Division, P.O. Box 211, 1000 AE Amsterdam, Netherlands. TEL 31-20-4853911. FAX 31-20-4853705. *637*

DEVELOPMENTS IN BIOENERGETICS AND BIOMEMBRANES.
Elsevier Science B.V., Books Division, P.O. Box 211, 1000 AE Amsterdam, Netherlands. TEL 31-20-4853911. FAX 31-20-4853705. *626*

DEVELOPMENTS IN BIOGEOCHEMISTRY.
Kluwer Academic Publishers, Postbus 17, 3300 AA Dordrecht, Netherlands. TEL 31-78-6392392. FAX 31-78-6392254. *2206*

DEVELOPMENTS IN BIOLOGICAL STANDARDIZATION.
S. Karger AG, Allschwilerstr. 10, P.O. Box, CH-4009 Basel, Switzerland. TEL 061-3061111. FAX 061-3061234. *5013*

DEVELOPMENTS IN BIOMECHANICS.
Kluwer Academic Publishers, Postbus 17, 3300 AA Dordrecht, Netherlands. TEL 31-78-6392392. FAX 31-78-6392254. *787*

DEVELOPMENTS IN BUSINESS SIMULATION & EXPERIENTIAL EXERCISES.
Oklahoma State University, Stillwater, College of Business Administration, Stillwater, OK 74078. TEL 405-744-8647. FAX 405-744-5180. *2051*

DEVELOPMENTS IN CANCER RESEARCH.
Elsevier Science B.V., Books Division, P.O. Box 211, 1000 AE Amsterdam, Netherlands. TEL 31-20-4853911. FAX 31-20-4853705. *4754*

DEVELOPMENTS IN CARDIOVASCULAR MEDICINE.
Kluwer Academic Publishers, Postbus 17, 3300 AA
Dordrecht, Netherlands. TEL 31-78-6392392.
FAX 31-78-6392254. *4601*

DEVELOPMENTS IN CIVIL AND FOUNDATION ENGINEERING.
Kluwer Academic Publishers, Postbus 17, 3300 AA
Dordrecht, Netherlands. TEL 31-78-6392392.
FAX 31-78-6392254. *2657*

DEVELOPMENTS IN CIVIL ENGINEERING.
Elsevier Science B.V., Books Division, P.O. Box 211,
1000 AE Amsterdam, Netherlands. TEL 31-20-
4853911. FAX 31-20-4853705. *2657*

DEVELOPMENTS IN CLINICAL BIOCHEMISTRY.
Kluwer Academic Publishers, Postbus 17, 3300 AA
Dordrecht, Netherlands. TEL 31-78-6392392.
FAX 31-78-6392254. *637*

DEVELOPMENTS IN CRITICAL CARE MEDICINE AND ANESTHESIOLOGY.
Kluwer Academic Publishers, Postbus 17, 3300 AA
Dordrecht, Netherlands. TEL 31-78-6392392.
FAX 31-78-6392254. *4591*

DEVELOPMENTS IN CROP SCIENCE.
Elsevier Science B.V., Books Division, P.O. Box 211,
1000 AE Amsterdam, Netherlands. TEL 31-20-
4853911. FAX 31-20-4853705. *219*

DEVELOPMENTS IN EARTH SURFACE PROCESSES.
Elsevier Science B.V., Books Division, P.O. Box 211,
1000 AE Amsterdam, Netherlands. TEL 31-20-
4853911. FAX 31-20-4853705. *2230*

DEVELOPMENTS IN ECONOMIC GEOLOGY.
Elsevier Science B.V., Books Division, P.O. Box 211,
1000 AE Amsterdam, Netherlands. TEL 31-20-
4853911. FAX 31-20-4853705. *2230*

DEVELOPMENTS IN ENDOCRINOLOGY (AMSTERDAM).
Elsevier Science B.V., Books Division, P.O. Box 211,
1000 AE Amsterdam, Netherlands. TEL 31-20-
4853911. FAX 31-20-4853705. *4667*

DEVELOPMENTS IN ENVIRONMENTAL BIOLOGY OF FISHES.
Kluwer Academic Publishers, Postbus 17, 3300 AA
Dordrecht, Netherlands. TEL 31-78-6392392.
FAX 31-78-6392254. *803*

DEVELOPMENTS IN ENVIRONMENTAL ECONOMICS.
Elsevier Science B.V., Books Division, P.O. Box 211,
1000 AE Amsterdam, Netherlands. TEL 31-20-
4853911. FAX 31-20-4853705. *2782*

DEVELOPMENTS IN ENVIRONMENTAL MODELLING.
Elsevier Science B.V., Books Division, P.O. Box 211,
1000 AE Amsterdam, Netherlands. TEL 31-20-
4853911. FAX 31-20-4853705. *2832*

DEVELOPMENTS IN FOOD PRESERVATION.
Elsevier Science Ltd., Books Division, P.O. Box 800,
Kidlington, Oxford OX5 1DX, England. TEL 44-1865-
843000. FAX 44-1865-843010. *2965*

DEVELOPMENTS IN FOOD PROTEINS.
Elsevier Science Ltd., Books Division, P.O. Box 800,
Kidlington, Oxford OX5 1DX, England. TEL 44-1865-
843000. FAX 44-1865-843010. *2965*

DEVELOPMENTS IN FOOD SCIENCE.
Elsevier Science B.V., Books Division, P.O. Box 211,
1000 AE Amsterdam, Netherlands. TEL 31-20-
4853911. FAX 31-20-4853705. *1737*

DEVELOPMENTS IN GASTROENTEROLOGY.
Kluwer Academic Publishers, Postbus 17, 3300 AA
Dordrecht, Netherlands. TEL 31-78-6392392.
FAX 31-78-6392254. *4690*

DEVELOPMENTS IN GEOCHEMISTRY.
Elsevier Science B.V., Books Division, P.O. Box 211,
1000 AE Amsterdam, Netherlands. TEL 31-20-
4853911. FAX 31-20-4853705. *2230*

DEVELOPMENTS IN GEOMATHEMATICS.
Elsevier Science B.V., Books Division, P.O. Box 211,
1000 AE Amsterdam, Netherlands. TEL 31-20-
4853911. FAX 31-20-4853705. *2271*

DEVELOPMENTS IN GEOTECHNICAL ENGINEERING.
Elsevier Science B.V., Books Division, P.O. Box 211,
1000 AE Amsterdam, Netherlands. TEL 31-20-
4853911. FAX 31-20-4853705. *2657*

DEVELOPMENTS IN GEOTECTONICS.
Elsevier Science B.V., Books Division, P.O. Box 211,
1000 AE Amsterdam, Netherlands. TEL 31-20-
4853911. FAX 31-20-4853705. *2230*

DEVELOPMENTS IN HEMATOLOGY AND IMMUNOLOGY.
Kluwer Academic Publishers, Postbus 17, 3300 AA
Dordrecht, Netherlands. TEL 31-78-6392392.
FAX 31-78-6392254. *4699*

DEVELOPMENTS IN HYDROBIOLOGY.
Kluwer Academic Publishers, Postbus 17, 3300 AA
Dordrecht, Netherlands. TEL 31-78-6392392.
FAX 31-78-6392254. *580*

DEVELOPMENTS IN IMMUNOLOGY.
Elsevier Science B.V., Books Division, P.O. Box 211,
1000 AE Amsterdam, Netherlands. TEL 31-20-
4853911. FAX 31-20-4853705. *580*

DEVELOPMENTS IN INDUSTRIAL MICROBIOLOGY SERIES.
Elsevier Science B.V., Books Division, P.O. Box 211,
1000 AE Amsterdam, Netherlands. TEL 31-20-
4853911. FAX 31-20-4853705. *756*

DEVELOPMENTS IN INTERNATIONAL LAW.
Martinus Nijhoff Publishers, Human Rights and
International Law Postbus 163, 3300 AD
Dordrecht, Netherlands. TEL 31-78-334911.
FAX 31-78-334254. *3928*

DEVELOPMENTS IN LANDSCAPE MANAGEMENT AND URBAN PLANNING.
Elsevier Science B.V., Books Division, P.O. Box 211,
1000 AE Amsterdam, Netherlands. TEL 31-20-
4853911. FAX 31-20-4853705. *3581*

DEVELOPMENTS IN MARINE BIOLOGY.
Elsevier Science B.V., Books Division, P.O. Box 211,
1000 AE Amsterdam, Netherlands. TEL 31-20-
4853911. FAX 31-20-4853705. *2293*

DEVELOPMENTS IN MARINE TECHNOLOGY.
Elsevier Science B.V., Books Division, P.O. Box 211,
1000 AE Amsterdam, Netherlands. TEL 31-20-
4853911. FAX 31-20-4853705. *2752*

DEVELOPMENTS IN MEDICAL VIROLOGY.
Kluwer Academic Publishers, Postbus 17, 3300 AA
Dordrecht, Netherlands. TEL 31-78-6392392.
FAX 31-78-6392254. *4619*

DEVELOPMENTS IN MINERAL PROCESSING.
Elsevier Science B.V., Books Division, P.O. Box 211,
1000 AE Amsterdam, Netherlands. TEL 31-20-
4853911. FAX 31-20-4853705. *2230*

DEVELOPMENTS IN MOLECULAR AND CELLULAR BIOCHEMISTRY.
Kluwer Academic Publishers, Postbus 17, 3300 AA
Dordrecht, Netherlands. TEL 31-78-6392392.
FAX 31-78-6392254. *637*

DEVELOPMENTS IN MOLECULAR VIROLOGY.
Kluwer Academic Publishers, Postbus 17, 3300 AA
Dordrecht, Netherlands. TEL 31-78-6392392.
FAX 31-78-6392254. *756*

DEVELOPMENTS IN NANOTECHNOLOGY.
Gordon and Breach Science Publishers, c/o
International Publishers Distributor, P.O. Box 3054,
Langhorne, PA 19047-3054. TEL 215-750-2642.
FAX 215-750-6343. *5546*

DEVELOPMENTS IN NEPHROLOGY.
Kluwer Academic Publishers, Postbus 17, 3300 AA
Dordrecht, Netherlands. TEL 31-78-6392392.
FAX 31-78-6392254. *4926*

DEVELOPMENTS IN NEUROSCIENCE.
Elsevier Science B.V., Books Division, P.O. Box 211,
1000 AE Amsterdam, Netherlands. TEL 31-20-
4853911. FAX 31-20-4853705. *4834*

DEVELOPMENTS IN NUCLEAR MEDICINE.
Kluwer Academic Publishers, Postbus 17, 3300 AA
Dordrecht, Netherlands. TEL 31-78-6392392.
FAX 31-78-6392254. *4875*

DEVELOPMENTS IN ONCOLOGY.
Kluwer Academic Publishers, Postbus 17, 3300 AA
Dordrecht, Netherlands. TEL 31-78-6392392.
FAX 31-78-6392254. *4754*

DEVELOPMENTS IN OPHTHALMOLOGY.
S. Karger AG, Allschwilerstr. 10, P.O. Box, CH-4009
Basel, Switzerland. TEL 061-3061111. FAX 061-
3061234. *4769*

DEVELOPMENTS IN ORIENTED POLYMERS.
Elsevier Science Ltd., Books Division, P.O. Box 800,
Kidlington, Oxford OX5 1DX, England. TEL 44-1865-
843000. FAX 44-1865-843010. *1737*

DEVELOPMENTS IN PALAEONTOLOGY AND STRATIGRAPHY.
Elsevier Science B.V., Books Division, P.O. Box 211,
1000 AE Amsterdam, Netherlands. TEL 31-20-
4853911. FAX 31-20-4853705. *5313*

DEVELOPMENTS IN PETROLEUM ENGINEERING.
Elsevier Science Ltd., Books Division, P.O. Box 800,
Kidlington, Oxford OX5 1DX, England. TEL 44-1865-
843000. FAX 44-1865-843010. *5353*

DEVELOPMENTS IN PETROLEUM SCIENCE.
Elsevier Science B.V., Books Division, P.O. Box 211,
1000 AE Amsterdam, Netherlands. TEL 31-20-
4853911. FAX 31-20-4853705. *5353*

DEVELOPMENTS IN PETROLOGY.
Elsevier Science B.V., Books Division, P.O. Box 211,
1000 AE Amsterdam, Netherlands. TEL 31-20-
4853911. FAX 31-20-4853705. *2230*

DEVELOPMENTS IN PHARMACOLOGY.
Kluwer Academic Publishers, Postbus 17, 3300 AA
Dordrecht, Netherlands. TEL 31-78-6392392.
FAX 31-78-6392254. *5407*

DEVELOPMENTS IN PLANT AND SOIL SCIENCES.
Kluwer Academic Publishers, Postbus 17, 3300 AA
Dordrecht, Netherlands. TEL 31-78-6392392.
FAX 31-78-6392254. *219*

DEVELOPMENTS IN PLANT BREEDING.
Kluwer Academic Publishers, Postbus 17, 3300 AA
Dordrecht, Netherlands. TEL 31-78-6392392.
FAX 31-78-6392254. *678*

DEVELOPMENTS IN PLANT GENETICS AND BREEDING.
Elsevier Science B.V., Books Division, P.O. Box 211,
1000 AE Amsterdam, Netherlands. TEL 31-20-
4853911. FAX 31-20-4853705. *627*

DEVELOPMENTS IN PLANT PATHOLOGY.
Kluwer Academic Publishers, Postbus 17, 3300 AA
Dordrecht, Netherlands. TEL 31-78-6392392.
FAX 31-78-6392254. *678*

DEVELOPMENTS IN PRECAMBRIAN GEOLOGY.
Elsevier Science B.V., Books Division, P.O. Box 211,
1000 AE Amsterdam, Netherlands. TEL 31-20-
4853911. FAX 31-20-4853705. *2230*

DEVELOPMENTS IN PSYCHIATRY.
Elsevier Science B.V., Books Division, P.O. Box 211,
1000 AE Amsterdam, Netherlands. TEL 31-20-
4853911. FAX 31-20-4853705. *4834*

DEVELOPMENTS IN RUBBER TECHNOLOGY.
Elsevier Science Ltd., Books Division, P.O. Box 800,
Kidlington, Oxford OX5 1DX, England. TEL 44-1865-
843000. FAX 44-1865-843010. *6215*

DEVELOPMENTS IN SEDIMENTOLOGY.
Elsevier Science B.V., Books Division, P.O. Box 211,
1000 AE Amsterdam, Netherlands. TEL 31-20-
4853911. FAX 31-20-4853705. *2230*

DEVELOPMENTS IN SOIL SCIENCE.
Elsevier Science B.V., Books Division, P.O. Box 211,
1000 AE Amsterdam, Netherlands. TEL 31-20-
4853911. FAX 31-20-4853705. *219*

DEVELOPMENTS IN SOLID EARTH GEOPHYSICS.
Elsevier Science B.V., Books Division, P.O. Box 211,
1000 AE Amsterdam, Netherlands. TEL 31-20-
4853911. FAX 31-20-4853705. *2272*

DEVELOPMENTS IN STRUCTURAL GEOLOGY.
Elsevier Science B.V., Books Division, P.O. Box 211,
1000 AE Amsterdam, Netherlands. TEL 31-20-
4853911. FAX 31-20-4853705. *2230*

Refereed

DEVELOPMENTS IN SURGERY.
Kluwer Academic Publishers, Postbus 17, 3300 AA Dordrecht, Netherlands. TEL 31-78-6392392. FAX 31-78-6392254. *4908*

DEVELOPMENTS IN TOXICOLOGY AND ENVIRONMENTAL SCIENCE.
Elsevier Science B.V., Books Division, P.O. Box 211, 1000 AE Amsterdam, Netherlands. TEL 31-20-4853911. FAX 31-20-4853705. *2844*

DEVELOPMENTS IN TRANSPORT STUDIES.
Kluwer Academic Publishers, Postbus 17, 3300 AA Dordrecht, Netherlands. TEL 31-78-6392392. FAX 31-78-6392254. *6716*

DEVELOPMENTS IN VETERINARY MEDICINE.
Kluwer Academic Publishers, Postbus 17, 3300 AA Dordrecht, Netherlands. TEL 31-78-6392392. FAX 31-78-6392254. *6945*

DEVELOPMENTS IN VOLCANOLOGY.
Elsevier Science B.V., Books Division, P.O. Box 211, 1000 AE Amsterdam, Netherlands. TEL 31-20-4853911. FAX 31-20-4853705. *2272*

DEVELOPMENTS IN WATER SCIENCE.
Elsevier Science B.V., Books Division, P.O. Box 211, 1000 AE Amsterdam, Netherlands. TEL 31-20-4853911. FAX 31-20-4853705. *6965*

DEVIANT BEHAVIOR.
Taylor & Francis Inc., 1900 Frost Rd., Ste. 101, Bristol, PA 19007-1598. TEL 215-785-5800. FAX 215-785-5515. *6411*

DEVON HISTORIAN.
Devon History Society, c/o Devon & Exeter Institution, 7 The Close, Exeter, Devon EX1 1EZ, England. *3406*

DEVONSHIRE ASSOCIATION FOR THE ADVANCEMENT OF SCIENCE, LITERATURE AND ART. REPORT AND TRANSACTIONS.
Devonshire Association, 7 Cathedral Close, Exeter, Devon EX1 1EZ, England. TEL 44-1392-52461. *426*

DIABETES.
Finnish Diabetes Association, Kirjoniementie 15, 33680 Tampere, Finland. TEL 358-31-28-60-111. FAX 358-31-3600-462. *4667*

DIABETES.
American Diabetes Association, 1660 Duke St., Alexandria, VA 22314. TEL 703-549-1500. FAX 703-836-7439. *4667*

DIABETES ANNUAL.
Elsevier Science B.V., Books Division, P.O. Box 211, 1000 AE Amsterdam, Netherlands. TEL 31-20-4853911. FAX 31-20-4853705. *4667*

DIABETES CARE.
American Diabetes Association, 1660 Duke St., Alexandria, VA 22314. TEL 703-549-1500. FAX 703-836-7439. *4667*

DIABETES - METABOLISM REVIEWS.
John Wiley & Sons Ltd., Journals, Baffins Ln., Chichester, W. Sussex PO19 1UD, England. TEL 44-1243-779777. FAX 44-1243-843232. *4668*

DIABETES PREVENTION AND THERAPY.
John Wiley & Sons Ltd., Journals, Baffins Ln., Chichester, W. Sussex PO19 1UD, England. TEL 44-1243-779777. FAX 44-1243-843232. *4668*

DIABETES RESEARCH AND CLINICAL PRACTICE.
Elsevier Science Ireland Ltd., P.O. Box 85, Limerick, Ireland. TEL 353-61-471944. FAX 353-61-472144. *4668*

DIABETES SELF-MANAGEMENT.
R.A. Rapaport Publishing, Inc., 150 W. 22nd St., New York, NY 10011. TEL 212-989-0200. FAX 212-989-4786. *4668*

DIABETES SPECTRUM.
American Diabetes Association, 1660 Duke St., Alexandria, VA 22314. TEL 703-549-1500. FAX 703-836-7439. *4668*

DIABETIC MEDICINE.
John Wiley & Sons Ltd., Journals, Baffins Ln., Chichester, W. Sussex PO19 1UD, England. TEL 44-1243-779777. FAX 44-1243-843232. *4668*

THE DIABETIC TRAVELER.
Box 8223 - RW, Stamford, CT 06905. TEL 203-327-5832. *4669*

DIAGNOSTIC CYTOPATHOLOGY.
John Wiley & Sons, Inc., Journals, 605 Third Ave., New York, NY 10158. TEL 212-850-6645. FAX 212-850-6021. *714*

DIAGNOSTIC IMAGING & RADIOLOGY PRODUCT COMPARISON SYSTEM.
E C R I, 5200 Butler Pike, Plymouth Meeting, PA 19462. TEL 610-825-6000. FAX 610-834-1275. *4875*

DIAGNOSTIC MICROBIOLOGY AND INFECTIOUS DISEASE.
Elsevier Science Inc., Box 945, New York, NY 10159-0945. TEL 212-633-3730. FAX 212-633-3680. *756*

DIAGNOSTIC MOLECULAR PATHOLOGY.
Lippincott - Raven Publishers 227 E. Washington Sq., Philadelphia, PA 19106. TEL 215-238-4200. *4448*

DIAGNOSTIC ONCOLOGY.
S. Karger AG, Allschwilerstr. 10, P.O. Box, CH-4009 Basel, Switzerland. TEL 061-306-1111. FAX 061-306-1234. *4754*

DIALECTICAL ANTHROPOLOGY.
Kluwer Academic Publishers, Postbus 17, 3300 AA Dordrecht, Netherlands. TEL 31-78-6392392. FAX 31-78-6392254. *307*

DIALOGAS.
Polilogas, Artakalnio 31, 2055 Vilnius, Lithuania. TEL 370-2-748943. FAX 370-2-748943. *2323*

DIALOGOS.
Frank Cass, Newbury House, 890-900 Eastern Ave., Newbury Park, Ilford, Essex IG2 7HH, England. TEL 44-181-599-8866. FAX 44-181-599-0984. *1821*

DIALOGOS.
Universidad de Puerto Rico, Departamento de Filosofia, Box 21572, U.P.R. Station, San Juan, PR 00931. TEL 809-764-0000 ext. 2072. FAX 809-764-5899. *5473*

DIALOGUE (WATERLOO).
Wilfrid Laurier University Press, 75 University Ave. W., Waterloo, ON N2L 3C5, Canada. TEL 519-884-0710. FAX 519-725-1399. *5473*

DIALOGUE & ALLIANCE.
International Religious Foundation, Inc. (IRF), 4 W. 43rd St., New York, NY 10036. TEL 212-869-6023. FAX 212-869-6424. *6057*

DIALYSE JOURNAL.
Pabst Science Publishers, Am Eichengrund 28, 49525 Lengerich. Germany. TEL 49-5484-308. FAX 49-5484-550. *4926*

DIALYSIS & TRANSPLANTATION.
Creative Age Publications, 7628 Densmore Ave., Van Nuys, CA 91406-2088. TEL 818-782-7328. FAX 818-782-7450. *4926*

DIAMOND AND RELATED MATERIALS.
Elsevier Science S.A., P.O. Box 564, CH-1001 Lausanne 1 Switzerland. TEL 41-21-3207381. FAX 41-21-3235444. *1726*

DIAMOND DEPOSITIONS SCIENCE AND TECHNOLOGY.
Superconductivity Publications, 828 Livingston Ave., North Brunswick, NJ 08902-2356. TEL 908-846-2002. FAX 908-846-2050. *5546*

DIAMOND FILMS AND TECHNOLOGY.
M Y U, Scientific Publishing Division, 2-32-3 Sendagi, Bunkyo-ku, Tokyo 113, Japan. TEL 81-3-3821-2930. FAX 81-3-3827-8547. *2752*

DIANZI KEXUE XUEKAN.
Science Press, Marketing and Sales Department, 16 Donghuangchenggen North St., Beijing 100717, People's Republic of China. TEL 4010642. FAX 4019810. *2511*

DIASPORA: A JOURNAL OF TRANSNATIONAL STUDIES.
University of Toronto Press, Journals Department, 5201 Duffering St., Toronto, ON M3H 5T8, Canada. TEL 416-667-7781. FAX 416-667-7881. *6320*

DIATRIBE.
University of Southampton, Centre for Language & Cultural Theory, Highfield, Southampton SO17 1BJ, England. *3611*

DICENGXUE ZAZHI.
Science Press, Marketing and Sales Department, 16 Donghuangchenggen North St. Beijing 100717, People's Republic of China. TEL 4010642. FAX 4019810. *2230*

DIER - EN - ARTS.
Transmondial B.V., Baron van Nagellstr. 27, 3781 AP Voorthuizen, Netherlands. TEL 31-342-473135. FAX 31-342-473154. *5945*

DIFFERENTIAL AND INTEGRAL EQUATIONS.
Khayyam Publishing Company, Inc., Box 429, Athens, OH 45701. TEL 614-592-6136. FAX 614-592-1252. *4362*

DIFFERENTIAL EQUATIONS.
Plenum Publishing Corp., Consultants Bureau, 233 Spring St., New York, NY 100 3-1578. TEL 212-620-8468. FAX 212-463-0742. *4362*

DIFFERENTIAL EQUATIONS AND DYNAMICAL SYSTEMS.
Research Square Publications, Plot No.20, H. No.13-481, Alakapuri, Saroornagar Post, Hyderabad 500035, India. TEL 91-40879023. *4362*

DIFFERENTIAL GEOMETRY AND ITS APPLICATIONS.
North-Holland P.O. Box 211, 1000 AE Amsterdam, Netherlands. TEL 31-20-4853911. FAX 31-20-4853598. *4362*

DIGEST OF MIDDLE EAST STUDIES.
University of Wisconsin at Milwaukee, Milwaukee School of Library and Information Science, Box 413, Milwaukee, WI 53201. TEL 414-229-4707. FAX 414-229-4848. *5283*

DIGESTION.
S. Karger AG, Allschwilerstr. 10, P.O. Box, CH-4009 Basel, Switzerland. TEL 061-3061111. FAX 061-3061234. *4690*

DIGESTIVE DISEASES.
S. Karger AG, Allschwilerstr. 10, P.O. Box, CH-4009 Basel, Switzerland. TEL 061-3061111. FAX 061-3061234. *4691*

DIGESTIVE DISEASES AND SCIENCES.
Plenum Publishing Corp., 233 Spring St., New York, NY 10013-1578. TEL 212-620-8000. FAX 212-463-0742. *4691*

DIGESTIVE SURGERY.
S. Karger AG, Allschwilerstr. 10, P.O. Box, CH-4009 Basel, Switzerland. TEL 061-3061111. FAX 061-3061234. *4908*

DIGITAL TECHNICAL JOURNAL.
Digital Equipment Corporation LJ02/D10, 30 Porter Rd., Littleton, MA 01460-1446. TEL 508-486-2538. FAX 508-436-2444. *2020*

DILI JIAOYU.
Di i Jiaoyu Bianjibu, 12 Tianchen Lu, Shapingba, Chongqing, Sichuan 630047, People's Republic of China. TEL 86-811-53 -1155. FAX 86-811-531-0333. *3252*

DILI KEXUE.
Science Press, Marketing and Sales Department, 16 Donghuangchenggen North St, Beijing 100717, People's Republic of China. TEL 4010642. FAX 4019810. *3252*

DILI XUEBAO.
Science Press, Marketing and Sales Department, 16 Donghuangchenggen Beijie, Beijing 100707, People's Republic of China. TEL 4010642. FAX 4012180. *3252*

DILI YANJIU.
Science Press, Marketing and Sales Department, 16 Donghuangchenggen North St., Beijing 100717, People's Republic of China. TEL 4010642. FAX 4019810. *3252*

DIME NOVEL ROUND-UP.
J. Randolph Cox, Ed. & Pub., P.O. Box 226, Dundas, MN 55019-0226. TEL 507-645-3598. FAX 507-646-3734. *5994*

DIMENSIONS OF CRITICAL CARE NURSING.
Hall Johnson Communications, Inc., 9737 W. Ohio Ave., Lakewood, CO 80226. TEL 303-988-0056. *4713*

DINE ISRAEL.
Tel Aviv University, Faculty of Law, Ramat Aviv, Tel Aviv 69978, Israel. *3769*

DIONYSOS.
Seattle University, Addiction Studies Program, Broadway and Madison, Seattle, WA 98122-4490. TEL 206-296-5350. FAX 206-296-5997. *2196*

DIOTIMA.
Evanghelos A. Moutsopoulos, Ed. & Pub., 40 Ypsilantou St., 115 21 Athens, Greece. TEL 30-1-725-1212. FAX 30-1-722-7322. *5473*

DIPLOMACY & STATECRAFT.
Frank Cass, Newbury House, 890-900 Eastern Ave., Newbury Park, Ilford, Essex IG2 7HH, England. TEL 44-181-599-8866. FAX 44-181-599-0984. *3406*

DIPLOMATIC HISTORY.
Blackwell Publishers, 238 Main St., Cambridge, MA 02142. TEL 617-547-7110. FAX 617-547-0789. *3341*

DIQIU HUAXUE.
Science Press, Marketing and Sales Department, 16 Donghuangchenggen North St., Beijing 100717, People's Republic of China. TEL 4010642. FAX 4019810. *2230*

DIQIU WULI XUEBAO.
Science Press, Marketing and Sales Department, 16 Donghuangchenggen North St., Beijing 100717, People's Republic of China. TEL 4010642. FAX 4019810. *2272*

DIRASAT. ADMINISTRATIVE SCIENCES.
University of Jordan, Deanship of Academic Research, Amman, Jordan. TEL 962-6-843555. FAX 962-6-840263. *1414*

DIRASAT. AGRICULTURAL SCIENCES.
University of Jordan, Deanship of Academic Research, Amman, Jordan. TEL 962-6-843555. FAX 962-6-840263. *111*

DIRASAT. EDUCATIONAL SCIENCES.
University of Jordan, Deanship of Academic Research, Amman, Jordan. TEL 962-6-843555. FAX 962-6-840263. *2324*

DIRASAT. HUMAN AND SOCIAL SCIENCES.
University of Jordan, Deanship of Academic Research, Amman, Jordan. TEL 962-6-843555. FAX 962-6-840263. *3612*

DIRASAT. NATURAL AND ENGINEERING SCIENCES.
University of Jordan, Deanship of Academic Research, Amman, Jordan. TEL 962-6-843555. FAX 962-6-840263. *6237*

DIRASAT. SHARI'A AND LAW SCIENCES.
University of Jordan, Deanship of Academic Research, Amman, Jordan. TEL 962-843555. FAX 962-6-840263. *3769*

DIRASAT ARABIYAT.
Dar at-Tali'at, P.O. Box 111813, Beirut, Lebanon. TEL 961-1-314659. FAX 961-1-309470. *5662*

DIRECTIONS.
New Zealand Automobile Association, 342 Lambton Quay, P.O. Box 1, Wellington, New Zealand. TEL 64-4-4738738. FAX 64-4-4712080. *3196*

DIRECTIONS IN MENTAL HEALTH COUNSELING.
Hatherleigh Company Ltd., 420 E. 51st St., New York, NY 10022. TEL 212-355-0882. FAX 212-308-7930. *5840*

DIRECTIONS IN PSYCHIATRY.
Hatherleigh Company Ltd., 420 E. 51st St., New York, NY 10022. TEL 212-355-0882. FAX 212-308-7930. *4834*

DIRECTORY OF PHILIPPINE GARMENT & TEXTILE EXPORTERS.
Garments and Textile Export Board, Market Development Division, P.O. Box 1771 MCC - New Solid Bldg., 357 Gil J. Puyat Ave. Ext., Makati, Metro Manila, Philippines. TEL 632-8904651. FAX 632-8904653. *1833*

DISABILITY AND REHABILITATION.
Taylor & Francis Ltd., 1 Gunpowder Sq., London EC4A 3DE, England. TEL 44-171-583-0490. FAX 44-171-583-0585. *3304*

DISABILITY & SOCIETY.
Carfax Publishing Co., P.O. Box 25, Abingdon, Oxon. OX14 3UE, England. TEL 44-1235-401000. FAX 44-1235-401550. *3316*

DISABILITY RAG & RESOURCE.
Advocado Press, Box 145, Louisville, KY 40201. TEL 502-459-5343. *3304*

DISASTERS.
Blackwell Publishers Ltd., 108 Cowley Rd., Oxford OX4 1JF, England. TEL 44-1865-791100. FAX 44-1865-791347. *1305*

DISCLOSURE (LEXINGTON).
University of Kentucky, Committee on Social Theory, c/o Dept. of Philosophy, University of Kentucky, Lexington, KY 40506-0027. TEL 606-257-6035. FAX 606-257-2931. *6320*

DISCOURSE.
Carfax Publishing Co., P.O. Box 25, Abingdon, Oxon. OX14 3UE, England. TEL 44-1235-401000. FAX 44-1235-401550. *2456*

DISCOURSE & SOCIETY.
Sage Publications Ltd., 6 Bonhill St., London EC2A 4PU, England. TEL 44-171-374-0645. FAX 44-171-374-8741. *5840*

DISCOVERIES IN PHARMACOLOGY.
Elsevier Science B.V., Books Division, P.O. Box 211, 1000 AE Amsterdam, Netherlands. TEL 31-20-4853911. FAX 31-20-4853705. *5407*

DISCOVERY.
Vancouver Natural History Society, Box 3021, Vancouver, BC V6B 3X5, Canada. TEL 604-737-3074. FAX 604-433-8100. *6237*

DISCOVERY (NEW HAVEN).
Peabody Museum of Natural History, Yale University, 170 Whitney Ave., Box 208118, New Haven, CT 06520-8118. TEL 203-432-3786. FAX 203-432-9816. *6237*

DISCOVERY AND INNOVATION.
Academy Science Publishers, P.O. Box 14798, Nairobi, Kenya. TEL 254-2-884401. FAX 254-2-884406. *637*

DISCOVERY Y M C A.
Y M C A of the U S A, 101 N. Wacker Dr., Chicago, IL 60606-1718. TEL 312-977-0031. FAX 312-977-9063. *6370*

DISCRETE & COMPUTATIONAL GEOMETRY.
Springer-Verlag, Science Journals, 175 Fifth Ave., New York, NY 10010. TEL 212-460-1500. FAX 212-473-6272. *4362*

DISCRETE AND CONTINUOUS DYNAMICAL SYSTEMS.
Department of Mathematics, Southwest Missouri State University, Springfield, MO 65804. TEL 417-836-5112. FAX 417-836-5610. *4362*

DISCRETE APPLIED MATHEMATICS.
North-Holland P.O. Box 211, 1000 AE Amsterdam, Netherlands. TEL 31-20-4853911. FAX 31-20-4853598. *4362*

DISCRETE EVENT DYNAMIC SYSTEMS: THEORY AND APPLICATIONS.
Kluwer Academic Publishers Boston, Box 358, Accord Sta., Hingham, MA 02018-0358. TEL 617-871-6600. FAX 617-871-6528. *2052*

DISCRETE MATHEMATICS.
North-Holland P.O. Box 211, 1000 AE Amsterdam, Netherlands. TEL 31-20-4853911. FAX 31-20-4853598. *4363*

DISCRETE MATHEMATICS AND APPLICATIONS.
V S P, P.O. Box 346, 3700 AH Zeist, Netherlands. TEL 31-30-6925790. FAX 31-30-6932081. *4363*

DISCUSSION PAPER IN ECONOMICS AND ECONOMETRICS.
University of Nottingham, Department of Economics, University Park, Nottingham NG7 2RD, England. TEL 0115-9515480. FAX 0115-9514159. *914*

DISEASE MARKERS.
ASFRA B.V., Voorhaven 33, 1135 BL Edam, Netherlands. TEL 31-2993-72751. FAX 31-2993-72877. *4754*

DISEASES OF THE COLON AND RECTUM.
Williams & Wilkins, 351 W. Camden St., Baltimore, MD 21201. TEL 410-528-4000. FAX 410-528-4312. *4908*

DISIJI YANJIU.
Science Press, Marketing and Sales Department, 16 Donghuangchenggen North St., Beijing 100717, People's Republic of China. TEL 4010642. FAX 4019810. *2231*

DISLOCATIONS IN SOLIDS.
Elsevier Science B.V., Books Division, P.O. Box 211, 1000 AE Amsterdam, Netherlands. TEL 31-20-4853911. FAX 31-20-4853705. *5546*

DISPLAYS.
Elsevier Science B.V., P.O. Box 211, 1000 AE Amsterdam, Netherlands. TEL 31-20-4853911. FAX 31-20-4853598. *2027*

DISSERTATIONES MATHEMATICAE.
Polska Akademia Nauk, Instytut Matematyczny, Dzial Wydawnictw, Ul. Sniadeckich 8, P.O. Box 137, 00-950 Warsaw, Poland. TEL 48-22-6282471. FAX 48-22-6293997. *4363*

DISSOCIATION.
International Society for the Study of Multiple Personality and Dissociation, 5700 Old Orchard Rd., 1st Fl., Skokie, IL 60077. *5840*

DISTRIBUTED AND PARALLEL DATABASES.
Kluwer Academic Publishers Boston, Box 358, Accord Sta., Hingham, MA 02018-0358. TEL 617-871-6600. FAX 617-871-6528. *2065*

DIWEN WULI XUEBAO.
Science Press, Marketing and Sales Department, 16 Donghuangchenggen North St., Beijing 100717, People's Republic of China. TEL 4010642. FAX 4019810. *5584*

DIZHEN DIZHI.
Guojia Dizhen-ju, Dizhi Yanjiusuo, Qijia Huozi, Deshengmenwai, Beijing 100029, People's Republic of China. TEL 86-1-2023377. FAX 86-1-2028617. *2272*

DIZHEN GONGCHENG YU GONGCHENG ZHENDONG.
Science Press, Marketing and Sales Department, 16 Donghuangchenggen North St., Beijing 100717, People's Republic of China. TEL 4010642. FAX 4019810. *2272*

DIZHEN XUEBAO.
Science Press, Marketing and Sales Department, 16 Donghuangchenggen North St., Beijing 100717, People's Republic of China. TEL 4010642. FAX 4019810. *2272*

DIZHI KEXUE.
Science Press, Marketing and Sales Department, 16 Donghuangchenggen North St., Beijing 100717, People's Republic of China. TEL 4010642. FAX 4019810. *2231*

DIZHI XUEBAO.
Science Press, Marketing and Sales Department, 16 Donghuangchenggen North St., Beijing 100717, People's Republic of China. TEL 4010642. FAX 4019810. *2231*

DOCUMENTA.
Documentatiecentrum voor Dramatische Kunst v.z.w., Rozier 44, 9000 Gent, Belgium. TEL 32-9-2643696. FAX 32-9-2644184. *6695*

DOCUMENTA ET MONUMENTA ORIENTIS ANTIQUI.
E.J. Brill, P.O. Box 9000, 2300 PA Leiden, Netherlands. TEL 31-71-5353500. FAX 31-71-5317532. *3495*

DOCUMENTA OPHTHALMOLOGICA.
Kluwer Academic Publishers, Postbus 17, 3300 AA Dordrecht, Netherlands. TEL 31-78-6392392. FAX 31-78-6392254. *4769*

DOCUMENTA OPHTHALMOLOGICA PROCEEDINGS SERIES.
Kluwer Academic Publishers, Postbus 17, 3300 AA Dordrecht, Netherlands. TEL 31-78-6392392. FAX 31-78-6392254. *4769*

DOCUMENTACAO DE ESTUDOS EM LINGUISTICA TEORICA E APLICADA.
Editora da Pontificia Universidade Catolica de Sao Paulo, Departamento de Linguistica, Rua Monte Alegre, 984, 05014-001 Sao Paulo SP, Brazil. TEL 55-11-629598. FAX 55-11-624920. *4064*

DOCUMENTOS DE ARQUITECTURA NACIONAL Y AMERICANA.
Instituto Argentino de Investigaciones de Historia de la Arquitectura y del Urbanismo, Casilla de Correo 120, Sucursal 48B, 1448 Buenos Aires, Argentina. FAX 54-1-8119249. *392*

DOHNE BULLETIN.
Oos-Kaapstreek, Departement van Landbou-ontwikkeling, Privaatsak X15, Stutterheim 4930, South Africa. TEL 27-436-31240. FAX 27-436-32890. *111*

DOKKYO JOURNAL OF MEDICAL SCIENCES.
Dokkyo University School of Medicine, Dokkyo Medical Society, Mibu, Tochigi 321-02, Japan. TEL 282-86-1111. FAX 282-86-5678. *4450*

DOKLADY BIOCHEMISTRY.
Maik Nauka - Interperiodica, Mezhdunarodnyi Otdel, Ul. Profsoyuznaya, 90, 117864 Moscow, Russia. TEL 7-095-3360066. FAX 7-095-3360066. *637*

DOKLADY BIOLOGICAL SCIENCES.
Maik Nauka - Interperiodica, Mezhdunarodnyi Otdel, Ul. Profsoyuznaya, 90, 117864 Moscow, Russia. TEL 7-095-3360066. FAX 7-095-3360066. *580*

DOKLADY BIOPHYSICS.
Maik Nauka - Interperiodica, Mezhdunarodnyi Otdel, Ul. Profsoyuznaya, 90, 117864 Moscow, Russia. TEL 7-095-3360066. FAX 7-095-3360066. *653*

DOKLADY BOTANICAL SCIENCES.
Interperiodica, Ul. Profsoyuznaya 90, Moscow 117864, Russia. TEL 7-095-3360066. FAX 7-095-3360066. *678*

DOKLADY CHEMICAL TECHNOLOGY.
Maik Nauka - Interperiodica, Mezhdunarodnyi Otdel, Ul. Profsoyuznaya, 90, 117864 Moscow, Russia. TEL 7-095-3360066. FAX 7-095-3360066. *2639*

DOKLADY CHEMISTRY.
Maik Nauka - Interperiodica, Mezhdunarodnyi Otdel, Ul. Profsoyznaya, 90, 117864 Moscow, Russia. TEL 7-095-3360066. FAX 7-095-23360066. *1674*

DOKLADY PHYSICAL CHEMISTRY.
Maik Nauka - Interperiodica, Mezhdunarodnyi Otdel, Ul. Profsoyuznaya, 90, 117864 Moscow, Russia. TEL 7-095-3360066. FAX 7-095-3360066. *1750*

DOMESTIC ANIMAL ENDOCRINOLOGY.
Elsevier Science Inc., Box 945, New York, NY 10159-0945. TEL 212-633-3730. FAX 212-633-3680. *6945*

DONGNAN DAXUE XUEBAO.
Dongnan Daxue, 2 Sipailou, Nanjing, Jiangsu 210018, People's Republic of China. TEL 86-25-3361361. FAX 86-25-7712719. *6237*

DONGWU FENLEI XUEBAO.
Science Press, Marketing and Sales Department, 16 Donghuangchenggen North St., Beijing 100717, People's Republic of China. TEL 4010642. FAX 4019810. *803*

DONGWU XUEBAO.
Science Press, Marketing and Sales Department, 16 Donghuangchenggen North St., Beijing 100717, People's Republic of China. TEL 4010642. FAX 4019810. *804*

DONGWUXUE ZAZHI.
Science Press, Marketing and Sales Department, 16 Donghuangchenggen Beijie, Beijing 100707, People's Republic of China. TEL 4010642. FAX 4012180. *804*

DOSHISHA DAIGAKU RIKOGAKU KENKYU HOKOKU.
Doshisha University, Science and Engineering Research Institute, Tanabe-cho, Tsuzukigun, Kyoto 610-03, Japan. FAX 774-65-6804. *2595*

DOWN SYNDROME NEWS.
National Down Syndrome Congress, 1605 Chantilly Dr., NE, Ste 250, Atlanta, GA 30324-3269. TEL 404-633-1555. FAX 404-633-2817. *4834*

DOWN'S SYNDROME: RESEARCH AND PRACTICE.
University of Portmouth, Sarah Duffen Centre, Belmont St., Southsea, Hants PO5 1NA, England. TEL 44-1705-824261. FAX 44-1705-824265. *4834*

DREAM NETWORK.
1337 Powerhouse Ln., Ste. 22, Moab, UT 84532. TEL 801-259-5936. FAX 801-259-5936. *5216*

DREAM SWITCHBOARD.
Dream Switchboard, Box 8032, Hicksville, NY 11802-8032. TEL 516-796-9455. FAX 516-731-2395. *2324*

DREAMING.
Human Sciences Press, Inc. 233 Spring St., New York, NY 10013. TEL 212-620-8000. FAX 212-463-0742. *787*

DRUG ABUSE.
Swedish Council for Information on Alcohol and other Drugs (CAN), Information and Documentation Center, P.O. Box 27302, S-102 54 Stockholm, Sweden. FAX 46-8-661-64-84. *2196*

DRUG AND ALCOHOL DEPENDENCE.
Elsevier Science Ireland Ltd., P.O. Box 85, Limerick, Ireland. TEL 353-61-471944. FAX 353-61-472144. *2196*

DRUG AND ALCOHOL REVIEW.
Carfax Publishing Co., P.O. Box 25, Abingdon, Oxon. OX14 3UE, England. TEL 44-1235-401000. FAX 44-1235-401550. *2196*

DRUG AND CHEMICAL TOXICOLOGY.
Marcel Dekker Journals, 270 Madison Ave., New York, NY 10016. TEL 212-696-9000. FAX 212-685-4540. *5407*

DRUG AND CHEMICAL TOXICOLOGY SERIES.
Marcel Dekker, Inc., 270 Madison Ave., New York, NY 10016. TEL 212-696-9000. FAX 212-685-4540. *5407*

DRUG DELIVERY.
Taylor & Francis Inc., 1900 Frost Rd., Ste. 101, Bristol, PA 19007-1598. TEL 215-785-5800. FAX 215-785-5515. *5408*

DRUG DESIGN AND DISCOVERY.
Harwood Academic Publishers, c/o International Publishers Distributor, P.O. Box 3054, Langhorne, PA 19047-3054. TEL 215-750-2642. FAX 215-750-6343. *5408*

DRUG DEVELOPMENT AND INDUSTRIAL PHARMACY.
Marcel Dekker Journals, 270 Madison Ave., New York, NY 10016. TEL 212-696-9000. FAX 212-685-4540. *5408*

DRUG DEVELOPMENT RESEARCH.
John Wiley & Sons, Inc., Journals, 605 Third Ave., New York, NY 10158. TEL 212-850-6645. FAX 212-850-6021. *5408*

DRUG DISCOVERY TODAY.
Elsevier Science Ltd., Oxford Fulfilment Centre, P.O. Box 800, Kidlington, Oxford OX5 1DX, England. TEL 44-1865-843000. FAX 44-1865-843010. *5408*

DRUG INDUCED DISORDERS.
Elsevier Science B.V., Books Division, P.O. Box 211, 1000 AE Amsterdam, Netherlands. TEL 31-20-4853911. FAX 31-20-4853705. *5408*

DRUG INFORMATION JOURNAL.
Drug Information Association, Box 3113, Maple Glen, PA 19002. TEL 215-628-2288. FAX 215-641-1229. *5408*

DRUG METABOLISM AND DISPOSITION.
Williams & Wilkins, 351 W. Camden St., Baltimore, MD 21201. TEL 410-528-4000. FAX 410-528-4312. *5409*

DRUG METABOLISM REVIEWS.
Marcel Dekker Journals, 270 Madison Ave., New York, NY 10016. TEL 212-696-9000. FAX 212-685-4540. *4450*

DRUG SAFETY.
Adis International Limited, Private Bag 65901, Mairangi Bay, Auckland 10, New Zealand. TEL 64-9-479-8100. FAX 64-9-479-8145. *5409*

DRUGS.
Adis International Limited, Private Bag 65901, Mairangi Bay, Auckland 10, New Zealand. TEL 64-9-479-8100. FAX 64-9-479-8145. *5409*

DRUGS & AGING.
Adis International Limited, Private Bag 65901, Mairangi Bay, Auckland 10, New Zealand. TEL 64-9-479-8100. FAX 64-9-479-8145. *5409*

DRUGS & SOCIETY.
Haworth Press, Inc., 10 Alice St., Binghamton, NY 13904. TEL 607-722-5857. FAX 607-722-1424. *2196*

DRUGS AND THE PHARMACEUTICAL SCIENCES.
Marcel Dekker, Inc., 270 Madison Ave., New York, NY 10016. TEL 212-696-9000. FAX 212-685-4540. *5410*

DRUGS & THERAPY PERSPECTIVES.
Adis International Limited, Private Bag 65901, Mairangi Bay, Auckland 10, New Zealand. TEL 64-9-479-8100. FAX 64-9-479-8145. *5410*

DRUGS: EDUCATION, PREVENTION & POLICY.
Carfax Publishing Co., P.O. Box 25, Abingdon, Oxon. OX14 3UE, England. TEL 44-1235-401000. FAX 44-1235-401550. *2195*

DRYING TECHNOLOGY.
Marcel Dekker Journals, 270 Madison Ave., New York, NY 10016. TEL 212-696-9000. FAX 212-685-4540. *1750*

DUBLIN SEMINAR FOR NEW ENGLAND FOLKLIFE. ANNUAL PROCEEDINGS.
Boston University, Scholarly Publications, 985 Commonwealth Ave., Boston, MA 02215. TEL 617-353-4106. *2950*

DUKE MATHEMATICAL JOURNAL.
Duke University Press, Box 90660, Durham, NC 27708-0660. TEL 919-687-3600. FAX 919-688-4574. *4363*

DUMERILIA.
A A L R A M, c/o Alain Dubois, 25 rue Cuvier, 75005 Paris, France. TEL 33-1-40793487. *804*

DUNIA WANITA.
Jalan Brigjen, Katamso No. 1 Medan 20151, Indonesia. TEL 62-550858. FAX 62-510025. *6991*

DUODECIMAL BULLETIN.
Dozenal Society of America, c/o Math Department, Nassau Community College, Garden City, NY 11530. TEL 516-669-0273. *4363*

DUQUESNE STUDIES. LANGUAGE AND LITERATURE SERIES.
Duquesne University Press, 600 Forbes Ave., Pittsburgh, PA 15282. TEL 412-396-6610. FAX 412-396-5984. *4065*

DURBAN MUSEUM NOVITATES.
Durban Natural Science Museum, P.O. Box 4085, Durban 4000, South Africa. TEL 27-31-3006211. FAX 27-31-3006302. *804*

DUTCH BIRDING.
Stichting Dutch Birding Association, Postbus 75611, 1070 AP Amsterdam, Netherlands. TEL 31-23-5378024. FAX 31-23-5376749. *775*

DYES AND PIGMENTS.
Elsevier Science Ltd., P.O. Box 800, Kidlington, Oxford OX5 1DX, England. TEL 44-1865-843000. FAX 44-1865-843010. *1674*

DYMAT JOURNAL.
Editions de Physique, B.P. 112, Z.I. de Courteboeuf, 7 av. du Hoggar, 91944 Les Ulis Cedex, France. TEL 69-07-36-88. FAX 69-28-84-91. *2730*

DYNAMIC ECONOMICS: THEORY AND APPLICATIONS (SERIES).
Elsevier Science B.V., Books Division, P.O. Box 211, 1000 AE Amsterdam, Netherlands. TEL 31-20-4853911. FAX 31-20-4853705. *915*

DYNAMIC NUTRITION RESEARCH.
S. Karger AG, Allschwilerstr. 10, P.O. Box, CH-4009 Basel, Switzerland. TEL 061-3061111. FAX 061-3061234. *5231*

DYNAMICAL PROPERTIES OF SOLIDS.
Elsevier Science B.V., Books Division, P.O. Box 211, 1000 AE Amsterdam, Netherlands. TEL 31-20-4853911. FAX 31-20-4853705. *5587*

DYNAMICS AND CONTROL.
Kluwer Academic Publishers Boston, Box 358, Accord Sta., Hingham, MA 02018-0358. TEL 617-871-6600. FAX 617-871-6528. *2055*

DYNAMICS AND STABILITY OF SYSTEMS.
Carfax Publishing Co., P.O. Box 25, Abingdon, Oxon. OX14 3UE, England. TEL 44-1235-401000. FAX 44-1235-41550. *1989*

DYNAMICS OF ATMOSPHERES AND OCEANS.
Elsevier Science B.V., P.O. Box 211, 1000 AE Amsterdam, Netherlands. TEL 31-20-4853911. FAX 31-20-4853598. *4994*

DYSLEXIA.
John Wiley & Sons Ltd., Journals, Baffins Ln., Chichester, W. Sussex PO19 1UD, England. TEL 44-1243-779777. FAX 44-1243-843232. *4834*

DYSPHAGIA.
Springer-Verlag, Medical Journals, 175 Fifth Ave., New York, NY 10010. TEL 212-460-1500. FAX 212-473-6272. *4796*

E A A EXPERIMENTER.
Experimental Aircraft Association, Inc., Box 3086, Oshkosh, WI 54903-3086. TEL 414-426-4800. FAX 414-426-4828. *63*

E A R.
University of Edinburgh, Department of Architecture, 20 Chambers St., Edinburgh EH1 1JZ, Scotland. FAX 0131-650-8019. *392*

E A R SE L ADVANCES IN REMOTE SENSING.
European Association of Remote Sensing Laboratories, 2 av. Rapp, 75340 Paris Cedex 07, France. TEL 45-56-73-60. FAX 45-56-73-61. *2207*

E A: THE JOURNAL OF THE NATIONAL ASSOCIATION OF ENROLLED AGENTS.
National Association of Enrolled Agents, 200 Orchard Ridge Dr., Ste. 302, Gaithersburg, MD 20878-1978. TEL 301-212-9608. FAX 301-990-1611. *1542*

E D I LAW REVIEW.
Kluwer Law International Postbus 85889, 2508 CN The Hague, Netherlands. TEL 31-70-3081500. FAX 31-70-3081515. *2069*

E D T N A - E R C A JOURNAL.
European Dialysis and Transplant Nurses Association, European Renal Care Association, P.O. Box 3052, CH-6002 Luzern, Switzerland. *4926*

E E: EVALUATION ENGINEERING.
Nelson Publishing Co., 2504 N. Tamiami Trail, Nokomis, FL 34275-3476. TEL 813-966-9521. FAX 813-966-2590. *2512*

E H E NEWS.
Exceptional Human Experience Network, Inc., 414 Rockledge Rd., New Bern, NC 28562-9553. TEL 919-636-8734. FAX 919-636-8371. *5330*

E H P SUPPLEMENTS.
U.S. Department of Health and Human Services, National Institute of Environmental Health Sciences, Box 12233, Research Triangle Park, NC 27709. TEL 919-541-3406. FAX 919-541-0273. *2782*

E - LAB.
Massachusetts Institute of Technology, Energy Laboratory, Rm. E40-479, Cambridge, MA 01239-4307. TEL 617-253-3405. FAX 617-253-8013. *2543*

E LAW.
Murdoch University, School of Law, Perth, W.A. 6150, Australia. FAX 61-9-3106671. *3772*

E N E A NOTIZIARIO - ENERGIA E INNOVAZIONE.
Ente per le Nuove Tecnologie, l'Energie e l'Ambiente, Viale Regina Margherita 125, 00198 Rome, Italy. TEL 06-85282401. FAX 06-85285875. *2543*

E P A NEWSLETTER.
European Photochemistry Association, Stiftstr. 34-36, 45470 Muelheim, Germany. TEL 0208-30643672. FAX 0208-30643951. *1750*

E P E JOURNAL.
E P E Association, Secretariat S R B E, Av. de la Plaine 2, 1050 Brussels, Belgium. TEL 32-2-6292819. FAX 32-2-6293620. *2512*

E P P O BULLETIN.
Blackwell Science Ltd., Osney Mead, Oxford OX2 OEL, England. TEL 44-1865-206206. FAX 44-1865-721205. *219*

E P S I G NEWS.
Electronic Publishing Special Interest Group, c/o GCARI, 100 Daingerfield Rd., Alexandria, VA 22314. TEL 703-519-8184. FAX 703-548-2867. *5995*

E P S L ONLINE.
Elsevier Science B.V., P.O. Box 211, 1000 AE Amsterdam, Netherlands. TEL 31-20-4853911. FAX 31-20-4853705. *2207*

E S C W A POPULATION BULLETIN.
United Nations Publications, Rm. DC2-853, New York, NY 10017. TEL 212-963-8302. FAX 212-963-3489. *5783*

EAR AND HEARING.
Williams & Wilkins, 351 W. Camden St., Baltimore, MD 21201. TEL 410-528-4000. FAX 410-528-4312. *4796*

EAR, NOSE AND THROAT JOURNAL.
Medquest Communications, Inc., 629 Euclid Ave., Ste. 500, Cleveland, OH 44114-3003. TEL 216-522-9700. FAX 216-522-9707. *4796*

EARLY AMERICAN LITERATURE.
University of North Carolina Press, Box 2288, Chapel Hill, NC 27515-2288. TEL 919-966-3561. FAX 800-272-6817. *4204*

EARLY CHILD DEVELOPMENT AND CARE.
Gordon and Breach Science Publishers, c/o International Publishers Distributor, P.O. Box 3054, Langhorne, PA 19047-3054. TEL 215-750-2642. FAX 215-750-6343. *1766*

EARLY CHILDHOOD EDUCATION JOURNAL.
Human Sciences Press, Inc. 233 Spring St., New York, NY 10013-1578. TEL 212-620-8000. FAX 212-463-0742. *2325*

EARLY DEVELOPMENT AND PARENTING.
John Wiley & Sons Ltd., Journals, Baffins Ln., Chichester, W. Sussex PO19 1UD, England. TEL 44-1243-779777. FAX 44-1243-843232. *5841*

EARLY HUMAN DEVELOPMENT.
Elsevier Science Ireland Ltd., P.O. Box 85, Limerick, Ireland. TEL 353-61-471944. FAX 353-61-472144. *4735*

EARLY KEYBOARD JOURNAL.
Southeastern Historical Keyboard Society, Box 32022, Charlotte, NC 28232-2022. TEL 704-334-3468. FAX 704-334-3468. *5155*

EARLY KEYBOARD STUDIES NEWSLETTER.
Westfield Center for Early Keyboard Studies, One Cottage St., Easthampton, MA 01027. TEL 413-527-7664. FAX 413-527-7689. *5155*

EARLY PREGNANCY BIOLOGY & MEDICINE.
Parthenon Publishing Group, Casterton Hall, Carnforth, Lancs. LA6 2LA, England. TEL 44-152-427-2084. FAX 44-152-427-1587. *4735*

EARLY SCIENCE AND MEDICINE.
E.J. Brill, P.O. Box 9000, 2300 PA Leiden, Netherlands. TEL 31-71-5353500. FAX 31-71-5317532. *4450*

EARTH AND PLANETARY SCIENCE LETTERS.
Elsevier Science B.V., P.O. Box 211, 1000 AE Amsterdam, Netherlands. TEL 31-20-4853911. FAX 31-20-4853598. *2207*

EARTH, MOON AND PLANETS.
Kluwer Academic Publishers, Postbus 17, 3300 AA Dordrecht, Netherlands. TEL 31-78-6392392. FAX 31-78-6392254. *479*

EARTH OBSERVATION AND REMOTE SENSING.
Harwood Academic Publishers, c/o International Publishers Distributor, P.O. Box 3054, Langhorne, PA 19047-3054. TEL 215-750-2642. FAX 215-750-6343. *2595*

EARTH SCIENCE REVIEWS.
Elsevier Science B.V., P.O. Box 211, 1000 AE Amsterdam, Netherlands. TEL 31-20-4853911. FAX 31-20-4853598. *2207*

EARTH SURFACE PROCESSES AND LANDFORMS.
John Wiley & Sons Ltd., Journals, Baffins Ln., Chichester, W. Sussex PO19 1UD, England. TEL 44-1243-779777. FAX 44-1243-843232. *2231*

EARTHQUAKES AND VOLCANOES.
U.S. Geological Survey, 12201 Sunrise Valley Dr., Reston, VA 22092. TEL 202-648-4000. *2272*

EARTHSONG.
Heard Museum, 22 E. Monte Vista Rd., Phoenix, AZ 85004-1480. TEL 602-252-8840. FAX 602-252-9757. *5121*

EAST AFRICAN AGRICULTURAL AND FORESTRY JOURNAL.
Kenya Agricultural Research Institute, P.O. Box 30148, Nairobi, Kenya. TEL 254-2-444144. *112*

THE EAST AFRICAN MEDICAL JOURNAL.
Kenya Medical Association House, Chyulu Rd., P.O. Box 41632, Nairobi, Kenya. TEL 254-2-712010. FAX 254-2-724617. *4450*

EAST AND CENTRAL AFRICAN JOURNAL OF SURGERY.
Association of Surgeons of East Africa, P.O. Box 320159, Woodlands, Lusaka, Zambia. TEL 260-1-230710. FAX 260-1-250753. *4908*

EAST ANGLIAN ARCHAEOLOGY. REPORT.
Norfolk Field Archaeology Division, Union House, Gressenhall, Dereham, Norfolk NR20 4DR, England. TEL 44-1362-860528. FAX 44-1362-860951. *352*

EAST EUROPEAN MEDICAL JOURNAL.
Edit Dan Publishing Co., P.O. Box 209, 600 Iasi 1, Rumania. TEL 40-98-135778. FAX 40-98-117607. *4450*

EAST EUROPEAN POLITICS & SOCIETIES.
University of California Press, Journals Division, 2120 Berkeley Way, No. 5812, Berkeley, CA 94720-5812. TEL 510-643-7154. FAX 510-642-9917. *5663*

EAST TEXAS HISTORICAL JOURNAL.
East Texas Historical Association, Box 6223, SFA Sta., Nacogdoches, TX 75962. TEL 405-468-2407. FAX 409-468-2190. *3467*

EAST - WEST CENTER OCCASIONAL PAPERS: POPULATION SERIES.
East - West Center, 1777 East-West Rd., Honolulu, HI 96848. TEL 808-944-7480. FAX 808-944-7490. *5783*

EAST-WEST FILM JOURNAL.
East-West Center, 1777 East-West Rd., Honolulu, HI 96848. *5099*

EAST-WEST JOURNAL OF NUMERICAL MATHEMATICS.
V S P, P.O. Box 346, 3700 AH Zeist, Netherlands. TEL 31-30-6925790. FAX 31-30-6932081. *4409*

EAST-WEST PERSPECTIVES.
Kluwer Academic Publishers, Postbus 17, 3300 AA Dordrecht, Netherlands. TEL 31-78-6392392. FAX 31-78-6392254. *5748*

EASTERN AFRICA SOCIAL SCIENCE RESEARCH REVIEW.
Organization for Social Science Research in Eastern Africa, P.O. Box 31971, Addis Ababa, Ethiopia. TEL 251-1-1197505. FAX 251-1-551399. *6321*

EASTERN ART REPORT.
Eastern Art Publishing, Acre House, 69-76 Long Acre, Covent Garden, London WC2E 9JH, England. TEL 44-81-392-1122. FAX 44-81-392-1422. *427*

EASTERN BUDDHIST.
Eastern Buddhist Society, Otani University, Koyama, Kita-ku, Kyoto 603, Japan. TEL 81-75-431-4390. *6109*

EASTERN CHALLENGE.
International Missions, Inc., Box 14866, Reading, PA 19612-4866. TEL 610-375-0300. FAX 610-375-6862. *6142*

EASTERN EUROPEAN ECONOMICS.
M.E. Sharpe, Inc., 80 Business Park Dr., Armonk, NY 10504. TEL 914-273-1800. FAX 914-273-2106. *915*

EASTERN PHARMACIST.
507 Ashok Bhawan, 93, Nehru Place, New Delhi 110019, India. TEL 6433315. *5410*

ECCLESIASTICAL LAW JOURNAL.
Ecclesiastical Law Society, 1 The Sanctuary, Westminster, London SW1P 3JT, England. TEL 44-171-222-5381. *6058*

ECHOCARDIOGRAPHY.
Futura Publishing Company, Inc., 135 Bedford Rd., Box 418, Armonk, NY 10504. TEL 914-273-1014. FAX 914-273-1015. *4601*

ECHOES.
Echoes of Service, 1 Widcombe Cresc., Bath, Avon BA2 6AQ, England. TEL 44-1225-310893. FAX 44-1225-480134. *6142*

ECHOS DU MONDE CLASSIQUE.
University of Calgary Press, 2500 University Dr. N.W., Calgary, AB T2N 1N4, Canada. TEL 403-220-7578. FAX 403-282-0085. *1821*

ECO DEL MANTE.
Guerrero 701 Ote., 89800 Mante, Tamaulipas, Mexico. TEL 91-123-22420. FAX 91-123-24784. *3192*

ECOGRAPHY.
Munksgaard International Publishers Ltd., 35 Noerre Soegade, P.O. Box 2148, DK-1016 Copenhagen K, Denmark. TEL 45-33-127030. FAX 45-33-129387. *2784*

ECOL NEWS.
Minneapolis Public Library and Information Center, 300 Nicollet Mall, Minneapolis, MN 55401. TEL 612-372-6570. *2784*

ECOLOGIA EN BOLIVIA.
Instituto de Ecologia, Casilla 10077, La Paz, Bolivia. TEL 591-2-792582. FAX 591-2-797511. *581*

ECOLOGICAL APPLICATIONS.
Ecological Society of America, 2010 Massachusetts Ave., N.W., Ste. 400, Washington, DC 20036. TEL 202-833-8773. FAX 202-833-8775. *2784*

ECOLOGICAL ECONOMICS.
Elsevier Science B.V., P.O. Box 211, 1000 AE Amsterdam, Netherlands. TEL 31-20-4853911. FAX 31-20-4853598. *2784*

ECOLOGICAL ENGINEERING.
Elsevier Science B.V., P.O. Box 211, 1000 AE Amsterdam, Netherlands. TEL 31-20-4853911. FAX 31-20-4853598. *2784*

ECOLOGICAL ENTOMOLOGY.
Blackwell Science Ltd., Osney Mead, Oxford OX2 0EL, England. TEL 44-1865-206206. FAX 44-1865-7212C5. *724*

ECOLOGICAL MODELLING.
Elsevier Science B.V., P.O. Box 211, 1000 AE Amsterdam, Netherlands. TEL 31-20-4853911. FAX 31-20-4353598. *2832*

ECOLOGICAL MONOGRAPHS.
Ecological Society of America, 2010 Massachusetts Ave., N.W., Ste. 400, Washington, DC 20036. TEL 202-833-8773. FAX 202-833-8775. *2784*

ECOLOGICAL PSYCHOLOGY.
Lawrence Erlbaum Associates, Inc., 10 Industrial Dr., Mahwah, NJ 07430-2262. TEL 201-236-9500. FAX 201-236-0072. *5841*

ECOLOGY.
Ecological Society of America, 2010 Massachusetts Ave., N.W., Ste. 400, Washington, DC 20036. TEL 202-833-8773. FAX 202-833-8775. *2785*

ECOLOGY & ENVIRONMENT.
Kluwer Academic Publishers, Postbus 17, 3300 AA Dordrecht, Netherlands. TEL 31-78-6392392. FAX 31-78-6392254. *2785*

ECOLOGY, ECONOMY & ENVIRONMENT.
Kluwer Academic Publishers, Postbus 17, 3300 AA Dordrecht, Netherlands. TEL 31-78-6392392. FAX 31-78-6392254. *2785*

ECOLOGY LAW QUARTERLY.
University of California Press, Journals Division, 2120 Berkeley Way, No. 5812, Berkeley, CA 94720-5812. TEL 510-643-7154. FAX 510-642-9917. *3772*

ECOLOGY OF FOOD AND NUTRITION.
Gordon and Breach Science Publishers, c/o International Publishers Distributor, P.O. Box 3054, Langhorne, PA 19047-3054. TEL 215-750-2642. FAX 215-750-6343. *5231*

ECOLOGY OF FRESHWATER FISH.
Munksgaard International Publishers Ltd., 35 Noerre Soegade, P.O. Box 2148, DK-1016 Copenhagen K, Denmark. TEL 45-33-127030. FAX 45-33-129387. *804*

ECONOMETRICA.
Blackwell Publishers Ltd., 108 Cowley Rd., Oxford OX4 1JF, England. TEL 44-1865-791100. FAX 44-1865-791347. *916*

ECONOMIA CAFETERA.
Federacion Nacional de Cafeteros de Colombia, Estudios y Proyectos Basicos Cafeteros, Calle 73 No. 8-13, piso 10 B, Bogota D.E., Colombia. TEL 57-1-3451088. FAX 57-1-2171021. *190*

ECONOMIA E SOCIOLOGIA.
Instituto Superior Economico e Social, Rua Vasco da Gama 15, 7000 Evora, Portugal. TEL 23327. *1205*

ECONOMIA EM REVISTA.
Universidade Estadual de Maringa, Departamento de Economia, Av. Colombo 5790, 87020-900 Maringa PR, Brazil. TEL 55-442262727. FAX 55-442232675. *916*

ECONOMIC AFFAIRS.
Blackwell Publishers Ltd., 108 Cowley Rd., Oxford OX4 1JF, England. TEL 44-1865-791100. FAX 44-1865-791347. *917*

ECONOMIC & FINANCIAL COMPUTING.
European Economics and Financial Centre, Publications Department, P.O. Box 2498, London W2 4LE, England. TEL 0171-229-0402. FAX 0171-221-5118. *1153*

ECONOMIC & FINANCIAL MODELLING.
European Economics and Finacial Centre, Publications Department, P.O. Box 2498, London W2 4LE, England. TEL 44-171-229-0402. FAX 44-171-221-5118. *1153*

ECONOMIC & FINANCIAL REVIEW.
European Economics and Financial Centre, P.O. Box 2498, London W2 4LE, England. TEL 0171-229-0402. FAX 0171-221-5118. *917*

ECONOMIC AND INDUSTRIAL DEMOCRACY.
Sage Publications Ltd., 6 Bonhill St., London EC2A 4PU, England. TEL 44-171-374-0645. FAX 44-171-374-8741. *5664*

ECONOMIC BOTANY.
New York Botanical Garden, Scientific Publications Department, Bronx, NY 10458-5126. TEL 718-817-8721. FAX 718-817-8842. *678*

ECONOMIC DESIGN.
North-Holland P.O. Box 211, 1000 AE Amsterdam, Netherlands. TEL 31-20-4853911. FAX 31-20-4853598. *1253*

ECONOMIC DEVELOPMENT AND CULTURAL CHANGE.
University of Chicago Press, Journals Division, Box 37005, Chicago, IL 60637. TEL 773-753-3347. FAX 773-753-0811. *1305*

ECONOMIC HISTORY REVIEW.
Blackwell Publishers Ltd., 108 Cowley Rd., Oxford OX4 1JF, England. TEL 44-1865-791100. FAX 44-1865-791347. *1253*

ECONOMIC INQUIRY.
Western Economic Association International, 7400 Center Ave., Ste. 109, Huntington Beach, CA 92547. TEL 714-898-3222. *918*

ECONOMIC JOURNAL.
Blackwell Publishers Ltd., 108 Cowley Rd., Oxford OX4 1JF, England. TEL 44-1865-791100. FAX 44-1865-791347. *918*

ECONOMIC MICROBIOLOGY.
Academic Press, Inc., 525 B St., Ste. 1900, San Diego, CA 92101-4495. TEL 619-231-0926. FAX 619-699-6715. *756*

ECONOMIC MODELLING.
Butterworth - Heinemann, Part of the Reed Elsevier group, Linacre House, Jordan Hill, Oxford OX2 8DP, England. TEL 44-1865-310366. FAX 44-1865-310898. *918*

ECONOMIC OUTLOOK.
Pakistan Press International, Press Centre, Shahrah-e-Kamal Ataturk, Karachi, Pakistan. TEL 92-21-2635751. FAX 92-21-2631125. *1206*

ECONOMIC OUTLOOK.
Blackwell Publishers Ltd., 108 Cowley Rd., Oxford OX4 1JF, England. TEL 44-1865-791100. FAX 44-1865-791347. *1206*

ECONOMIC POLICY.
Blackwell Publishers Ltd., 108 Cowley Rd., Oxford OX4 1JF, England. TEL 44-1865-791100. FAX 44-1865-791347. *918*

ECONOMIC REVIEW OF AGRICULTURE.
Ministry of Agriculture, Development Planning Division, P.O. Box 30028, Nairobi, Kenya. TEL 254-2-718870. *190*

ECONOMIC SYSTEMS - JOICE.
Physica-Verlag GmbH and Co. Postfach 105280, 69042 Heidelberg, Germany. TEL 49-6221-487492. FAX 49-6221-487177. *1272*

ECONOMIC SYSTEMS RESEARCH.
Carfax Publishing Co., P.O. Box 25, Abingdon, Oxon. OX14 3UE, England. TEL 44-1235-401000. FAX 44-1235-401550. *1253*

ECONOMICA.
Blackwell Publishers Ltd., 108 Cowley Rd., Oxford OX4 1JF, England. TEL 44-1865-791100. FAX 44-1865-791347. *919*

ECONOMICS & POLITICS.
Blackwell Publishers Ltd., 108 Cowley Rd., Oxford OX4 1JF, England. TEL 44-1865-791100. FAX 44-1865-791347. *1253*

ECONOMICS LETTERS.
Elsevier Science S.A., P.O. Box 564, CH-1001 Lausanne 1, Switzerland. TEL 41-21-3207381. FAX 41-21-3235444 *1253*

ECONOMICS OF EDUCATION REVIEW.
Elsevier Science Ltd., Pergamon, P.O. Box 800, Kidlington, Oxford OX5 1DX, England. TEL 44-1865-843000. FAX 44-1865-843010. *2456*

ECONOMICS OF INNOVATION AND NEW TECHNOLOGY.
Harwood Academic Publishers, c/o International Publishers Distributor, P.O. Box 3054, Langhorne, PA 19047-3054. TEL 215-750-2642. FAX 215-750-6343. *6650*

ECONOMICS OF PLANNING.
Kluwer Academic Publishers, Postbus 17, 3300 AA Dordrecht, Netherlands. TEL 31-78-6392392. FAX 31-78-6392254. *1207*

ECONOMICS OF SCIENCE, TECHNOLOGY AND INNOVATION.
Kluwer Academic Publishers, Postbus 17, 3300 AA Dordrecht, Netherlands. TEL 31-78-6392392. FAX 31-78-6392254. *6650*

ECONOMIE ET SOCIALISME.
Centre d'Etudes et de Recherches Aziz Belal, B.P. 6330, Rabat, Morocco. TEL 77-62-17. FAX 77-38-89. *1207*

ECONOMIE RURALE.
Societe Francaise d'Economie Rurale, 16 rue Claude Bernard, 75231 Paris Cedex 05, France. TEL 47-07-47-86. FAX 44-08-18-42. *190*

DE ECONOMIST.
Kluwer Academic Publishers, Postbus 17, 3300 AA Dordrecht, Netherlands. TEL 31-78-6392392. FAX 31-78-6392254. *919*

ECONOMY & ENVIRONMENT.
Kluwer Academic Publishers, Postbus 17, 3300 AA Dordrecht, Netherlands. TEL 31-78-6392392. FAX 31-78-6392254. *2785*

ECOSYSTEMS OF THE WORLD.
Elsevier Science B.V., Books Division, P.O. Box 211, 1000 AE Amsterdam, Netherlands. TEL 31-20-4853911. FAX 31-20-4853705. *2785*

ECOTOXICOLOGY.
Chapman & Hall, Journals Department 2-6 Boundary Row, London SE1 8HN, England. TEL 44-171-8650066. FAX 44-171-5229623. *2844*

ECOTOXICOLOGY AND ENVIRONMENTAL SAFETY.
Academic Press, Inc., Journal Division, 525 B St., Ste. 1900, San Diego, CA 92101-4495. TEL 619-250-1840. FAX 619-699-6800. *2844*

ECQUID NOVI.
Institute for Communication Research, Potchefstroom University, Potchefstroom 2520, South Africa. TEL 27-148-2991648. FAX 27-148-2991651. *3703*

ECUMENE.
Arnold 338 Euston Rd., London NW1 3BH, England. TEL 44-171-873-6000. FAX 44-171-873-6325. *2786*

EDINBURGH REVIEW.
Edinburgh University Press, 22 George Sq., Edinburgh EH8 9LF, Scotland. TEL 44-131-650-6207. FAX 44-131-662-0053. *4141*

EDMUNDITE.
Society of St. Edmund, P.O. Box 399, Mystic, CT 06355-0399. TEL 203-536-7540. *6179*

EDUCACION (HAVANA).
Editorial Pueblo y Educacion, Av. 3ra A No. 4601, entre 46 y 60, Playa, Havana, Cuba. TEL 236192. FAX 537-330844. *2326*

EDUCACION SUPERIOR Y SOCIEDAD.
Unesco - C R E S A L C, Apdo. 68394, Caracas 1062-A, Venezuela. TEL 582-283-1333. FAX 582-283-1411. *2427*

EDUCATION AND AGEING.
Association for Educational Gerontology, c/o Centre for Social Gerontology, University of Keele, Keele, Staffs. ST5 5BG, England. *2398*

EDUCATION AND SOCIETY.
James Nicholas Publishers, P.O. Box 244, Albert Park, Vic. 3206, Australia. TEL 03-696-5545. FAX 613-699-2040. *2327*

EDUCATION AND SOCIETY IN THE MIDDLE AGES AND RENAISSANCE.
E.J. Brill, P.O. Box 9000, 2300 PA Leiden, Netherlands. TEL 31-71-5353500. FAX 31-71-5317532. *3408*

EDUCATION AND TREATMENT OF CHILDREN.
Pressley Ridge Schools, 530 Marshall Ave., Pittsburgh, PA 15214. TEL 412-321-6995. FAX 412-321-5313. *2485*

EDUCATION ECONOMICS.
Carfax Publishing Co., P.O. Box 25, Abingdon, Oxon. OX14 3UE, England. TEL 44-1235-401000. FAX 44-1235-401550. *2456*

EDUCATION ET FRANCOPHONIE.
Association Canadienne d'Education de Langue Francaise, 268 rue Marie-de-l'Incarnation, Quebec, PQ G1N 3G4, Canada. TEL 418-681-4661. FAX 418-681-3389. *2328*

EDUCATION FOR LIBRARY AND INFORMATION SERVICES: AUSTRALIA.
Australian Library and Information Association, P.O. Box E441, Queen Victoria Terrace, A.C.T. 2600, Australia. TEL 61-6-285-1877. FAX 61-6-282-2249. *3991*

EDUCATION INTERNATIONAL QUARTERLY MAGAZINE.
Education International, Bd. E. Jacqmain 155, 8th Fl., 1210 Brussels, Belgium. TEL 32-2-2240611. FAX 32-2-2240606. *2328*

EDUCATION LIBRARIES.
Special Library Association, Education Division, c/o Concordia University, 7141 Sherbrooke St. W., TA 7079, Montreal, PQ H4B 1R6, Canada. TEL 514-848-2543. FAX 514-848-3492. *3991*

EDUCATION MARKETING.
Heist, 2 College Close, Beckett Park Campus, Leeds LS6 3QS, England. TEL 44-113-283-3184. FAX 44-113-283-3187. *2457*

EDUCATION RESEARCH AND PERSPECTIVES.
University of Western Australia, Department of Education, Nedlands, W.A. 6009, Australia. TEL 61-9-3802385. FAX 61-9-3801052. *2428*

EDUCATION TODAY.
Pitman Publishing, 128 Long Acre, London WC2E 9AN, England. TEL 0171-379-7383. FAX 0171-240-5771. *2329*

EDUCATION 3-13.
Pitman Publishing, 128 Long Acre, London WC2E 9AN, England. TEL 0171-379-7383. FAX 0171-240-5771. *2329*

EDUCATIONAL ACTION RESEARCH.
Triangle Journals Ltd., P.O. Box 65, Wallingford, Oxon. OX10 0YG, England. TEL 44-1491-838013. FAX 44-1491-834968. *2485*

EDUCATIONAL ADMINISTRATION QUARTERLY.
Corwin Press, Inc. 2455 Teller Rd., Thousand Oaks, CA 91320. TEL 805-499-0721. FAX 805-499-0871. *2457*

EDUCATIONAL & CHILD PSYCHOLOGY.
British Psychological Society, Division of Educational and Child Psychology, St. Andrew's House, 48 Princess Rd. E., Leicester LE1 7DR, England. *5841*

EDUCATIONAL AND PSYCHOLOGICAL MEASUREMENT.
Sage Publications Inc., 2455 Teller Rd., Thousand Oaks, CA 91320. TEL 805-499-0721. FAX 805-499-0871. *5841*

EDUCATIONAL CONSIDERATIONS.
Kansas State University, College of Education, Bluemont Hall 313, Manhattan, KS 66506. TEL 913-532-5543. FAX 913-532-7304. *2330*

EDUCATIONAL EVALUATION & POLICY ANALYSIS.
American Educational Research Association, 1230 17th St., N.W., Washington, DC 20036-3078. TEL 202-223-9485. FAX 202-775-1824. *2330*

EDUCATIONAL FORUM.
Kappa Delta Pi International Honor Society in Education, Box A, West Lafayette, IN 47906-0576. TEL 317-743-1705. FAX 317-743-2202. *2428*

EDUCATIONAL GERONTOLOGY.
Taylor & Francis Inc., 1900 Frost Rd., Ste. 101, Bristol, PA 19007-1598. TEL 215-785-5800. FAX 215-785-5515. *2398*

EDUCATIONAL MANAGEMENT & ADMINISTRATION.
Sage Publications Ltd., 6 Bonhill St., London EC2A 4PU, England. TEL 44-171-374-9645. FAX 44-171-374-8741. *2457*

EDUCATIONAL MEASUREMENT: ISSUES AND PRACTICE.
National Council on Measurement in Education, 1230 17th St. N.W., Washington, DC 20036-3078. TEL 202-223-9318. FAX 202-775-1824. *2330*

EDUCATIONAL PHILOSOPHY AND THEORY.
Philosophy of Education Society of Australasia, c/o Prof. Jim Walker, Ed., Faculty of Education, UWS Nepean, P.O. Box 10, Kingwood, N.S.W. 2747, Australia. TEL 61-47-360214. FAX 61-47-360400. *2330*

EDUCATIONAL PLANNING.
International Society for Educational Planning, Memphis State University, Bldg. 48, South Campus, Memphis, TN 38152. *2330*

EDUCATIONAL POLICY.
Corwin Press, Inc. 2455 Teller Rd., Thousand Oaks, CA 91320. TEL 805-499-0721. FAX 805-499-0871. *2330*

EDUCATIONAL PRACTICE AND THEORY.
James Nicholas Publishers, P.O. Box 244, Albert Park, Vic. 3206, Australia. TEL 61-3-696-5545. FAX 613-699-2040. *2330*

EDUCATIONAL PSYCHOLOGIST.
Lawrence Erlbaum Associates, Inc., 10 Industrial Dr., Mahwah, NJ 07430-2262. TEL 201-236-9500. FAX 201-236-0072. *5841*

EDUCATIONAL PSYCHOLOGY.
Carfax Publishing Co., P.O. Box 25, Abingdon, Oxon. OX14 3UE, England. TEL 44-1235-401000. FAX 44-1235-401550. *5841*

EDUCATIONAL PSYCHOLOGY IN PRACTICE.
Pitman Publishing, 128 Long Acre, London WC2E 9AN, England. TEL 0171-379-7383. FAX 0171-240-5771. *5841*

EDUCATIONAL PSYCHOLOGY REVIEW.
Plenum Publishing Corp., 233 Spring St., New York, NY 10013-1578. TEL 212-620-8000. FAX 212-463-0742. *2330*

EDUCATIONAL RESEARCH AND EVALUATION.
Swets & Zeitlinger bv, P.O. Box 825, 2160 SZ Lisse, Netherlands. TEL 31-252-435111. FAX 31-252-415888. *2331*

EDUCATIONAL RESEARCH QUARTERLY.
113 Greenbriar Dr., W. Monroe, LA 71291. TEL 318-274-2355. *2331*

EDUCATIONAL RESEARCHER.
American Educational Research Association, 1230 17th St. N.W., Washington, DC 20036-3078. TEL 202-223-9485. FAX 202-775-1824. *2331*

EDUCATIONAL REVIEW.
Carfax Publishing Co., P.O. Box 25, Abingdon, Oxon. OX14 3UE, England. TEL 44-1235-401000. FAX 44-1235-401550. *2331*

EDUCATIONAL STUDIES.
Carfax Publishing Co., P.O. Box 25, Abingdon, Oxon. OX14 3UE, England. TEL 44-1235-401000. FAX 44-1235-401550. *2331*

EDUCATIONAL STUDIES IN MATHEMATICS.
Kluwer Academic Publishers, Postbus 17, 3300 AA Dordrecht, Netherlands. TEL 31-78-6392392. FAX 31-78-6392254. *4363*

EDUCATIONAL TECHNOLOGY RESEARCH & DEVELOPMENT.
Association for Educational Communications and Technology, 1025 Vermont Ave. N.W., Ste. 820, Washington, DC 20005-3516. TEL 202-347-7834. FAX 202-347-7839. *2485*

Refereed

EDUQUER & FORMER.
Institut Superieur de Pedagogie de la Region de Bruxelles - Capitale, Bd. de Waterloo 100-103, 1000 Brussels, Belgium. TEL 32-2-5428351. FAX 32-2-5428390. *2332*

EFFECTIVE MANAGEMENT SERIES.
Blackwell Publishers Ltd., 108 Cowley Rd., Oxford OX4 1JF, England. TEL 44-1865-791100. FAX 44-1865-791347. *1415*

EGYPTIAN JOURNAL OF DAIRY SCIENCE.
Egyptian Society of Dairy Science, National Research Centre, Sharia Tahrir, Dokki, Cairo, Egypt. TEL 20-2-701211. FAX 20-2-700931. *250*

EIDOS.
University of Waterloo, Philosophy Graduate Student Association, Dept. of Philosophy, Waterloo, ON N2L 3G1, Canada. TEL 519-885-1211. *5473*

EIDOS: STUDIES IN CLASSICAL KINDS.
University of California Press, 2120 Berkeley Way, Berkeley, CA 94720. TEL 510-642-4247. FAX 510-643-7127. *1821*

EIGHTEENTH-CENTURY STUDIES.
Johns Hopkins University Press, Journals Publishing Division, 2715 N. Charles St., Baltimore, MD 21218-4319. TEL 410-516-6987. FAX 410-516-6968. *3341*

THE EINSTEIN QUARTERLY.
Springer-Verlag, Medical Journals, 175 Fifth Ave., New York, NY 10010. TEL 212-460-1500. FAX 212-473-6272. *581*

EIRENE.
John Benjamins Publishing Co., Amsteldijk 44, P.O. Box 75577, 1070 AN Amsterdam, Netherlands. TEL 31-20-6738156. FAX 31-20-6792956. *1821*

EKONOMIA.
Cyprus Economic Society, P.O. Box 8724, Nicosia, Cyprus. *1254*

EKONOMIKA UKRAINY.
Vidavnitstvo Presa Ukrainy, Peremogy pr., 50, 252047 Kiev 47, Ukraine. TEL 380-44-4418214. FAX 044-2908663. *1254*

ELECTORAL STUDIES.
Butterworth - Heinemann, Part of the Reed Elsevier group, Linacre House, Jordan Hill, Oxford OX2 8DP, England. TEL 44-1865-310366. FAX 44-1865-310898. *5664*

ELECTRIC MACHINES AND POWER SYSTEMS.
Taylor & Francis Inc., 1900 Frost Rd., Ste. 101, Bristol, PA 19007-1598. TEL 215-785-5800. FAX 215-785-5515. *2691*

ELECTRIC POWER SYSTEMS RESEARCH.
Elsevier Science S.A., P.O. Box 564, CH-1001 Lausanne 1, Switzerland. TEL 41-21-3207381. FAX 41-21-3235444. *2691*

ELECTRICAL TECHNOLOGY.
Elsevier Science Ltd., Pergamon, P.O. Box 800, Kidlington, Oxford OX5 1DX, England. TEL 44-1865-843000. FAX 44-1865-843010. *2693*

ELECTRICIDADE.
Empresa Editorial Electrotecnica Edel, Ltda., Rua de Dona Estefania 48, 3 Esq, 1000 Lisbon, Portugal. TEL 351-1-528608. FAX 351-1-3561640. *2694*

ELECTRO- AND MAGNETOBIOLOGY.
Marcel Dekker Journals, 270 Madison Ave., New York, NY 10016. TEL 212-696-9000. FAX 212-685-4540. *653*

ELECTRO-TECHNOLOGY.
Society of Electronic Engineers, Box 9324, LRDE, DRDO Complex, CV Raman Nagar, Bangalore 560 093, India. TEL 91-080-5280903. FAX 91-080-5282916. *2694*

ELECTROANALYTICAL CHEMISTRY: A SERIES OF ADVANCES.
Marcel Dekker, Inc., 270 Madison Ave., New York, NY 10016. TEL 212-696-9000. FAX 212-685-4540. *1715*

ELECTROCHEMICAL SCIENCE AND TECHNOLOGY OF POLYMERS.
Elsevier Science Ltd., Books Division, P.O. Box 800, Kidlington, Oxford OX5 1DX, England. TEL 44-1865-843000. FAX 44-1865-843010. *1728*

ELECTROCHIMICA ACTA.
Elsevier Science Ltd., Pergamon, P.O. Box 800, Kidlington, Oxford OX5 1DX, England. TEL 44-1865-843000. FAX 44-1865-843010. *1729*

ELECTROCOMPONENT SCIENCE MONOGRAPHS.
Gordon & Breach Science Publishers, c/o International Publishers Distributor, P.O. Box 3054, Langhorne, PA 19047-3054. TEL 215-750-2642. FAX 215-750-6343. *2694*

ELECTROENCEPHALOGRAPHY AND CLINICAL NEUROPHYSIOLOGY INCLUDING EVOKED POTENTIALS AND ELECTROMYOGRAPHY AND MOTOR CONTROL.
Elsevier Science Ireland Ltd., P.O. Box 85, Limerick, Ireland. TEL 353-61-471944. FAX 353-61-472144. *4835*

ELECTROENCEPHALOGRAPHY AND CLINICAL NEUROPHYSIOLOGY. SUPPLEMENTS.
Elsevier Science B.V., Books Division, P.O. Box 211, 1000 AE Amstercam, Netherlands. TEL 31-20-4853911. FAX 31-20-4853705. *4835*

ELECTROMAGNETIC WAVES.
Elsevier Science B.V., Books Division, P.O. Box 211, 1000 AE Amsterdam, Netherlands. TEL 31-20-4853911. FAX 31-20-4853705. *5547*

ELECTROMAGNETICS.
Taylor & Francis Inc., 1900 Frost Rd., Ste. 101, Bristol, PA 19007-1598. TEL 215-758-5800. FAX 215-758-5515. *2694*

ELECTROMECHANICAL BENCH REFERENCE.
Barks Publications, Inc., 400 N. Michigan Ave., Chicago, IL 60611-4198. TEL 312-321-9440. FAX 312-321-1238. *2694*

ELECTROMYOGRAPHY AND MOTOR CONTROL.
Elsevier Science Ireland Ltd., P.O. Box 85, Limerick, Ireland. TEL 353-61-471944. FAX 353-61-472144. *4835*

ELECTRON MICROSCOPY IN BIOLOGY AND MEDICINE.
Kluwer Academic Publishers, Postbus 17, 3300 AA Dordrecht, Netherlands. TEL 31-78-6392392. FAX 31-78-6392254. *769*

ELECTRONIC ANTIQUITY.
University of Tasmania, Department of Classics, Hobart, Tasmania 7001, Australia. TEL 61-02-202-294. FAX 61-02-202-288. *1821*

ELECTRONIC GREEN JOURNAL.
University of Idaho Library, University of Idaho Library, Moscow, ID 83844. TEL 208-885-6631. FAX 208-885-6817. *2786*

ELECTRONIC JOURNAL OF SOCIOLOGY.
University of Alberta, Department of Sociology, Edmonton, AB T6G 2H4, Canada. *6411*

ELECTRONIC JOURNAL OF STRATEGIC INFORMATION SYSTEMS.
University of Sheffield, Information Studies Department, 211 Portobello St., Regents Court, Rm. 315, Sheffield S10 2UH, England. TEL 44-742-768555. FAX 44-742-780300. *2080*

ELECTRONIC PRODUCTION.
Angel Business Communications Ltd., Kingsland House, 361-373 City Rd., London EC1V 1LR, England. TEL 44-171-417-7400. FAX 44-171-417-7500. *2515*

ELECTRONIC PUBLISHING.
John Wiley & Sons Ltd., Journals, Baffins Ln., Chichester, W. Sussex PO19 1UD, England. TEL 44-1243-779777. FAX 44-1243-843232. *6016*

ELECTRONICS COOLING.
Flomerics Ltd., 13 Uxbridge Rd., Kingston-upon-Thames, Surrey KT1 2LH, England. TEL 0181-547-3418. FAX 0181-547-3419. *2516*

ELECTRONICS LETTERS.
I.E.E., Michael Faraday House, Six Hills Way, Stevenage, Herts. SG1 2AY, England. TEL 44-1438-313311. FAX 44-1438-742840. *2516*

ELECTRONICS LETTERS ONLINE.
I.E.E., Michael Faraday House, Six Hills Way, Stevenage, Herts. SG1 2AY, England. TEL 44-1438-313311. FAX 44-1438-742840. *2516*

ELEKTRONIKK BRANSJEN.
Elektronikk Forbundet, Brynsengvn. 2, P.O. Box 6322, Etterstad, N-0604 Oslo, Norway. TEL 47-22-72-21-40. FAX 47-22-72-21-21. *2518*

ELEKTRONNOE MODELIROVANIE.
Akademiya Nauk Ukrainy, Institut Problem Modelirovaniya v Energetike, Ul. Generala Naumova, 15, Kiev 252680, Ukraine. TEL 38-44-4441466. FAX 38-44-4440586. *2052*

THE ELEMENTARY SCHOOL JOURNAL.
University of Chicago Press, Journals Division, Box 37005, Chicago, IL 60637. TEL 773-753-3347. FAX 773-753-0811. *3332*

ELEVATORI.
Vo pe Editore, Via di Vittorio 21A, 20060 Vignate, Italy. TEL 39-2-95360116. FAX 39-2-95360418. *6716*

THE ELIZABETHAN REVIEW.
123-60 83rd Ave., Kew Gardens, NY 11415. TEL 718-575-9656. *3408*

ELLEN GLASGOW NEWSLETTER.
Ellen Glasgow Society, c/o Prof. Catherine Rainwater, School of Humanities, St. Edwards University, 3001 S. Congress Ave., Austin, TX 78704-6489. TEL 512-837-6579. *4206*

ELSEVIER HANDLING AND PROCESSING OF SOLIDS SERIES.
Elsevier Science Ltd., Books Division, P.O. Box 800, Kidlington, Oxford OX5 1DX, England. TEL 44-1865-843000. FAX 44-1865-843010. *2742*

ELSEVIER OCEANOGRAPHY SERIES.
Elsevier Science B.V., Books Division, P.O. Box 211, 1000 AE Amsterdam, Netherlands. TEL 31-20-4853911. FAX 31-20-4853705. *2293*

ELSEVIER SERIES IN FORENSIC AND POLICE SCIENCE.
Elsevier Science B.V., Books Division, P.O. Box 211, 1000 AE Amsterdam, Netherlands. TEL 31-20-4853911. FAX 31-20-4853705. *4686*

ELSEVIER SERIES IN PRACTICAL ASPECTS OF CRIMINAL & FORENSIC INVESTIGATION.
Elsevier Science B.V., Books Division, P.O. Box 211, 1000 AE Amsterdam, Netherlands. TEL 31-20-4853911. FAX 31-20-4853705. *4686*

EM ABERTO.
Instituto Nacional de Estudos e Pesquisas Educacionais, Campus da UnB, Acesso Sul, 70910-900 Brasilia, DF, Brazil. TEL 061-347-8970. FAX 061-273-3233. *2332*

EMERGENCY LIBRARIAN.
Ken Haycock & Associates, Inc., 284 - 810 W. Broadway, Vancouver, BC V5Z 4C9, Canada. TEL 604-925-0266. FAX 604-925-0566. *3991*

EMERGENCY MEDICAL SERVICES.
Summer Communications Inc., Attn.: Barbara Feiner, 7526 Densmore Ave. Van Nuys, CA 91406. TEL 818-786-4367. FAX 818-786-9246. *4783*

EMERGENCY PRODUCT BUYER.
C M E Communications, Inc., 20854 Dalton Rd., P.O. Box 507, Sutton W, ON L0E 1L0, Canada. TEL 416-722-9839. FAX 416-722-9687. *4908*

EMERGENCY RADIOLOGY.
Williams & Wilkins, 351 W. Camden St., Baltimore, MD 21201. TEL 410-528-8555. FAX 410-528-8596. *4875*

EMIRATES JOURNAL FOR ENGINEERING RESEARCH.
United Arab Emirates University, Faculty of Engineering, P.O. Box 17555, Al-Ain, United Arab Emirates. TEL 971-3-637833. FAX 971-3-632382. *2595*

EMIRATES MEDICAL JOURNAL.
Emirates Medical Association, P.O. Box 6600, Dubai, United Arab Emirates. TEL 971-4-377377. FAX 971-4-344082. *4451*

EMOTION.
Academic Press, Inc., 525 B St., Ste. 1900, San Diego, CA 92101-4495. TEL 619-231-0926. FAX 619-699-6715. *5841*

EMOTIONS AND BEHAVIOR. MONOGRAPH.
International Universities Press, Inc., 59 Boston Post Rd., Box 1524, Madison, CT 06443-1524. TEL 203-245-4000. *4835*

EMPATHY.
Gay and Lesbian Adovcacy Research Project, Inc., Box 5085, Columbia, SC 29250. TEL 803-791-1607. *3530*

EMPIRE STATE MASON.
Grand Lodge Free and Accepted Masons of the State of New York, Committee on Publications, 37 Oliver St., Lockport, NY 14094-4615. TEL 716-434-4946. FAX 716-434-4946. *1849*

EMPIRICAL ECONOMICS.
Physica-Verlag GmbH und Co., Postfach 105280, 69042 Heidelberg, Germany. TEL 49-6221-487492. FAX 49-6221-487177. *920*

EMPIRICAL SOFTWARE ENGINEERING.
Kluwer Academic Publishers Boston, Box 358, Accord Sta., Hingham, MA 02018-0358. TEL 617-871-6600. FAX 617-871-6528. *2109*

EMPLOYEE ASSISTANCE QUARTERLY.
Haworth Press, Inc., 10 Alice St., Binghamton, NY 13904. TEL 607-722-5857. FAX 607-722-1424. *1501*

EMPLOYEE RESPONSIBILITIES AND RIGHTS JOURNAL.
Plenum Publishing Corp., 233 Spring St., New York, NY 10013-1578. TEL 212-620-8000. FAX 212-463-0742. *1371*

EMPRESA BRASILEIRA DE PESQUISA AGROPECUARIA. CENTRO NACIONAL DE PESQUISA DE FLORESTAS. DOCUMENTO.
Empresa Brasileira de Pesquisa Agropecuaria, Centro Nacional de Pesquisa de Florestas, Caixa Postal 3319, 83411-000 Curitaba PR, Brazil. TEL 55-41-7661313. FAX 55-41-7661276. *3014*

ENCAPSULATOR.
Monash Medical Centre, Pharmacy Department, 246 Clayton Rd., Clayton, Vic. 3168, Australia. TEL 61-3-95502596. FAX 61-3-95502595. *5410*

ENCOUNTERS.
Islamic Foundation, Markfield Dawah Centre, Ratby Lane, Markfield, Leicester LE6 0RN, England. TEL 01530-244944. FAX 01530-244946. *6059*

ENCUENTRO.
Universidad Centroamericana, Apdo. 69, 70352 Managua, Nicaragua. TEL 505-2-670352. FAX 505-2-670106. *6322*

ENCYCLIA.
Utah Academy of Sciences, Arts, and Letters, c/o Thomas F. Rogers, Ed., 4089A JKHB, Brigham Young University, Provo, UT 84602. TEL 801-378-3385. FAX 802-378-4649. *6239*

ENDEAVOUR.
Elsevier Science Ltd., Pergamon, P.O. Box 800, Kidlington, Oxford OX5 1DX, England. TEL 44-1865-843000. FAX 44-1865-843010. *6239*

ENDOCRINE JOURNAL.
Japan Endocrine Society, Department of Veterinary Physiology, Veterinary Medical Science, University of Tokyo, 1-1-1 Yayoi Bunkyo-ku, Tokyo 113, Japan. FAX 011-81-3-815-4266. *4669*

ENDOCRINE PATHOLOGY.
Humana Press Inc., 999 Riverview Dr., Ste. 208, Totowa, NJ 07512. TEL 201-256-1699. FAX 201-256-8341. *4669*

ENDOCRINE RESEARCH.
Marcel Dekker Journals, 270 Madison Ave., New York, NY 10016. TEL 212-696-9000. FAX 212-685-4540. *4669*

THE ENDOCRINOLOGIST.
Williams & Wilkins, 351 W. Camden St., Baltimore, MD 21201. TEL 410-528-4000. FAX 410-528-4312. *4670*

ENDOCRINOLOGY.
Endocrine Society, 4350 East West Hwy., Ste. 500, Bethesda, MD 20814-4410. TEL 301-941-0200. FAX 301-941-0259. *4670*

ENDOCRINOLOGY AND METABOLISM.
Bailliere Tindall - W.B. Saunders Co. Ltd. 24-28 Oval Rd., London NW1 7DX, England. TEL 44-171-485-4752. FAX 44-171-267-4466. *4670*

ENDOCRINOLOGY AND METABOLISM. SUPPLEMENT.
Bailliere Tindall - W.B. Saunders Co. Ltd. 24-28 Oval Rd., London NW1 7DX, England. TEL 44-171-485-4752. FAX 44-171-267-4466. *4670*

ENDOCURIETHERAPY - HYPERTHERMIA ONCOLOGY.
Endocurietherapy Research Foundation, 2801 Atlantic Ave., Long Beach, CA 90801. TEL 310-933-2929. FAX 310-933-0301. *4755*

ENDODONTICS & DENTAL TRAUMATOLOGY.
Munksgaard International Publishers Ltd., 35 Noerre Soegade, P.O. Box 2148, DK-1016 Copenhagen K, Denmark. TEL 45-33-127030. FAX 45-33-129387. *4640*

ENDOSURGERY.
Edizioni Minerva Medica, Corso Bramante 83-85, 10126 Turin, Italy. TEL 39-11-678282. FAX 39-11-31217364. *4908*

ENERGY.
Elsevier Science Ltd., Pergamon, P.O. Box 800, Kidlington, Oxford OX5 1DX, England. TEL 44-1865-843000. FAX 44-1865-843010. *2544*

ENERGY AND BUILDINGS.
Elsevier Science S.A., P.O. Box 564, CH-1001 Lausanne 1, Switzerland. TEL 41-21-3207381. FAX 41-21-3235444. *2545*

ENERGY AND ENGINEERING SCIENCE.
Gordon & Breach Science Publishers, c/o International Publishers Distributor, P.O. Box 3054, Langhorne, PA 19047-3054. TEL 215-750-2642. FAX 215-750-6343. *2545*

ENERGY & ENVIRONMENT.
Multi-Science Publishing Co. Ltd., 107 High St., Brentwood, Essex CM14 4RX, England. TEL 44-1277-224632. FAX 44-1277-223453. *2545*

ENERGY CONVERSION AND MANAGEMENT.
Elsevier Science Ltd., Pergamon, P.O. Box 800, Kidlington, Oxford OX5 1DX, England. TEL 44-1865-843000. FAX 44-1865-843010. *2545*

ENERGY ECONOMICS.
Butterworth - Heinemann, Part of the Reed Elsevier group, Linacre House, Jordan Hill, Oxford OX2 8DP, England. TEL 44-1865-310366. FAX 44-1865-310898. *2546*

ENERGY IN WORLD AGRICULTURE.
Elsevier Science B.V., Books Division, P.O. Box 211, 1000 AE Amsterdam, Netherlands. TEL 31-20-4853911. FAX 31-20-4853705. *2546*

ENERGY JOURNAL.
International Association for Energy Economics, 28790 Chagrin Blvd., Ste. 210, Cleveland, OH 44122. TEL 216-464-5365. *2547*

ENERGY POLICY.
Butterworth - Heinemann, Part of the Reed Elsevier group, Linacre House, Jordan Hill, Oxford OX2 8DP, England. TEL 44-1865-310366. FAX 44-1865-310898. *2547*

ENERGY RESEARCH.
Elsevier Science B.V., Books Division, P.O. Box 211, 1000 AE Amsterdam, Netherlands. TEL 31-20-4853911. FAX 31-20-4853705. *2547*

ENERGY SOURCES.
Taylor & Francis Inc., 1900 Frost Rd., Ste. 101, Bristol, PA 19007-1598. TEL 215-785-5800. FAX 215-785-5515. *2548*

ENERGY STUDIES REVIEW.
McMaster University, Institute for Energy Studies, Hamilton, ON L8S 4M4, Canada. TEL 905-525-9140. FAX 905-521-8232. *2548*

ENFERMEDADES INFECCIOSAS Y MICROBIOLOGIA.
Obsidiana Editores, S.A., Czda. de Tlalpan 2365, Col. Ciudad Jardin, 04370 Mexico DF, Mexico. TEL 6899133. *4619*

ENGENHARIA AGRICOLA.
Brazilian Agricultural Engineering Society, Departamento de Engenharia Rural, Faculdade de Ciencias Agronomicas-UNESP, Rodovia Carlos Tonnani, km 5, 14870-000 Jaboticabal SP, Brazil. TEL 55-16-3233341. *112*

ENGINEER - I.M.E. NEWS.
Institution of Mechanical Engineers (India), Janmabhoomi Chambers, 3rd Fl., 29 W. Hirachand Marg, Ballard Estate, Bombay 400 038, India. TEL 91-22-2612885. FAX 91-22-2614815. *2753*

ENGINEERING ANALYSIS WITH BOUNDARY ELEMENTS.
Elsevier Science Ltd., P.O. Box 800, Kidlington, Oxford OX5 1DX, England. TEL 44-1865-843000. FAX 44-1865-843010. *2753*

ENGINEERING APPLICATIONS OF ARTIFICIAL INTELLIGENCE.
Elsevier Science Ltd., Pergamon, P.O. Box 800, Kidlington, Oxford OX5 1DX, England. TEL 44-1865-843000. FAX 44-1865-843010. *2007*

ENGINEERING APPLICATIONS OF SYSTEMS RELIABILITY AND RISK ANALYSIS.
Kluwer Academic Publishers, Postbus 17, 3300 AA Dordrecht, Netherlands. TEL 31-78-6392392. FAX 31-78-6392254. *2021*

ENGINEERING CONSTRUCTION AND ARCHITECTURAL MANAGEMENT.
Blackwell Science Ltd., Osney Mead, Oxford OX2 0EL, England. TEL 44-1865-206206. FAX 44-1865-721205. *854*

ENGINEERING DESIGN & AUTOMATION.
John Wiley & Sons, Inc., Journals, 605 Third Ave., New York, NY 10158. TEL 212-850-6645. FAX 212-850-6021. *2104*

ENGINEERING DESIGN GRAPHICS JOURNAL.
American Society for Engineering Education, Engineering Design Graphics Division, c/o Mary A. Sadowski, Ed., 1419 Knoy Hall, Purdue University, W. Lafayette, IN 47907-1419. TEL 317-494-8206. FAX 317-494-9267. *6650*

ENGINEERING FAILURE ANALYSIS.
Elsevier Science Ltd., Pergamon, P.O. Box 800, Kidlington, Oxford OX5 1DX, England. TEL 44-1865-843000. FAX 44-1865-843010. *2730*

ENGINEERING FRACTURE MECHANICS.
Elsevier Science Ltd., Pergamon, P.O. Box 800, Kidlington, Oxford OX5 1DX, England. TEL 44-1865-843000. FAX 44-1865-843010. *2731*

ENGINEERING GEOLOGY.
Elsevier Science B.V., P.O. Box 211, 1000 AE Amsterdam, Netherlands. TEL 31-20-4853911. FAX 31-20-4853598. *2659*

ENGINEERING OPTIMIZATION.
Gordon & Breach Science Publishers, c/o International Publishers Distributor, P.O. Box 3054, Langhorne, PA 19047-3054. TEL 215-750-2642. FAX 215-750-6343. *2597*

ENGINEERING PLASTICS.
R A P R A Technology Ltd., Shawbury, Shrewsbury, Shrops. SY4 4NR, England. TEL 44-1939-250383. FAX 44-1939-251118. *5619*

ENGINEERING SCIENCE AND EDUCATION JOURNAL.
Institution of Electrical Engineers, Michael Faraday House, Six Hills Way, Stevenage, Herts. SG1 2AY, England. TEL 44-1438-313311. FAX 44-1438-742792. *2697*

ENGINEERING SCIENCE AND TECHNOLOGY.
University of Malaya, Lembah Pantai, 59100 Kuala Lumpur, Malaysia. FAX 603-755-3466. *2597*

ENGINEERING SIMULATION.
Gordon and Breach Science Publishers, c/o International Publishers Distributor, P.O. Box 3054, Langhorne, PA 19047-3054. TEL 215-750-2642. FAX 215-750-6343. *2519*

ENGINEERING STRUCTURES.
Elsevier Science Ltd., P.O. Box 800, Kidlington, Oxford OX5 1DX, England. TEL 44-1865-843000. FAX 44-1865-843010. *2659*

ENGLERA.
Botanischer Garten und Botanisches Museum Berlin-Dahlem, Koenigin-Luise-Str. 6-8, 14191 Berlin, Germany. TEL 49-30-83006-0. FAX 49-30-83006186. *679*

ENGLISH.
The English Association, University of Leicester, University Rd., Leicester LE1 7RH, England. TEL 44-116-252-3982. FAX 44-116-252-2301. *4206*

ENGLISH FOR SPECIFIC PURPOSES.
Elsevier Science Ltd., Pergamon, P.O. Box 800, Kidlington, Oxford OX5 1DX, England. TEL 44-1865-843000. FAX 44-1865-843010. *4066*

ENGLISH IN AUSTRALIA.
Australian Association for the Teaching of English, P.O. Box 3203, Norwood, S.A. 5067, Australia. TEL 61-8-3322845. FAX 61-8-3330394. *4066*

ENGLISH IN EDUCATION.
National Association for the Teaching of English, Broadfield Business Centre, 50 Broadfield Rd., Sheffield S8 OXJ, England. TEL 44-1142-555419. FAX 44-1142-555296. *2486*

ENGLISH LANGUAGE AND LINGUISTICS.
Cambridge University Press, Edinburgh Bldg., Shaftesbury Rd., Cambridge CB2 2RU, England. TEL 44-1223-312393. FAX 44-1223-315052. *4066*

ENGLISH LANGUAGE NOTES.
University of Colorado, English Language Notes, CB 226, Boulder, CO 80309. TEL 303-492-7176. FAX 303-492-3521. *4206*

ENGLISH LITERATURE IN TRANSITION, 1880-1920.
Robert Langenfeld, Ed. & Pub., Department of English, University of North Carolina, Greensboro, NC 27412-5001. TEL 910-334-5446. FAX 910-334-3281. *4206*

ENGLISH MONARCHS SERIES.
University of California Press, 2120 Berkeley Way, Berkeley, CA 94720. TEL 510-642-4247. FAX 510-643-7127. *3408*

ENGLISH QUARTERLY.
Canadian Council of Teachers of English, 340 Education, University of Manitoba, Winnipeg, MB R3T 2N2, Canada. TEL 204-474-8564. FAX 204-275-5962. *2486*

ENGLISH STUDIES.
Swets & Zeitlinger bv, P.O. Box 825, 2160 SZ Lisse, Netherlands. TEL 31-252-435111. FAX 31-252-415888. *4066*

ENGLISH STUDIES IN CANADA.
Association of Canadian College and University Teachers of English, Department of English, Carleton University, 1125 Colonel By Dr., Ottawa, ON K1S 5B6, Canada. TEL 613-788-2600. FAX 613-788-3544. *4206*

ENTERPRISE SYSTEMS JOURNAL.
Cardinal Business Media, Inc., 12225 Greenville Ave., Ste. 700, Dallas, TX 75243-9338. TEL 214-669-9000. FAX 214-669-9909. *2073*

ENTOMOLOGIA EXPERIMENTALIS ET APPLICATA.
Kluwer Academic Publishers, Postbus 17, 3300 AA Dordrecht, Netherlands. TEL 31-78-6392392. FAX 31-78-6392254. *724*

ENTOMOLOGICA FENNICA.
Entomologica Fennica ry, c/o Institute of Zoology, P.O. Box 17, FIN-00014 University of Helsinki, Finland. FAX 358-0-635017. *724*

ENTOMOLOGICAL NEWS.
American Entomological Society, Academy of Natural Sciences, 1900 Benjamin Franklin Pkwy., Philadelphia, PA 19103-1195. TEL 215-561-3978. FAX 215-299-1028. *724*

ENTOMOLOGICAL REVIEW.
Scripta Technica, Inc. 8555 16th St., Ste. 220, Silver Spring, MD 20910. TEL 301-588-0484. FAX 301-588-5278. *724*

ENTOMOLOGICAL SOCIETY OF AMERICA. ANNALS.
Entomological Society of America, 9301 Annapolis Rd., Lanham, MD 20706. TEL 301-731-4535. FAX 301-731-4538. *725*

ENTOMOLOGICAL SOCIETY OF BRITISH COLUMBIA. JOURNAL.
Entomological Society of British Columbia, c/o R.G. Bennett, Ministry of Forests, Seed Pest Management, 7380 Puckle Rd., Saanichton, BC V8M 1W4, Canada. TEL 604-652-6593. FAX 604-652-4204. *725*

ENTOMOLOGICAL SOCIETY OF CANADA. MEMOIRS.
Entomological Society of Canada, 393 Winston Ave., Ottawa, ON K2A 1Y8, Canada. TEL 613-725-2619. FAX 613-725-9349. *725*

ENTOMOLOGICAL SOCIETY OF MANITOBA. PROCEEDINGS.
Entomological Society of Manitoba, Inc., 195 Dafoe Rd., Winnipeg, MB R3T 2M9, Canada. TEL 204-945-8444. *725*

ENTOMOLOGICAL SOCIETY OF ONTARIO. PROCEEDINGS.
Entomological Society of Ontario, University of Guelph, Dept. of Environmental Biology, Guelph, ON N1G 2W1, Canada. TEL 519-824-4120. FAX 519-837-0442. *725*

ENTOMOLOGICAL SOCIETY OF WASHINGTON. MEMOIRS.
Entomological Society of Washington, c/o Dept. of Entomology, Smithsonian Institution NHB 168, Washington, DC 20560. *725*

ENTOMOLOGICAL SOCIETY OF WASHINGTON. PROCEEDINGS.
Entomological Society of Washington, c/o Dept. of Entomology, Smithsonian Institution NHB 168, Washington, DC 20560. *725*

ENTOMOLOGISK TIDSKRIFT.
Sveriges Entomologiska Foerening, c/o Ola Atlegrim, Trattgraend 24, S-906 25 Umeaa, Sweden. TEL 46-90-18-77-89. FAX 46-90-16-68-17. *725*

ENTOMONOGRAPH.
E.J. Brill, P.O. Box 9000, 2300 PA Leiden, Netherlands. TEL 31-71-5353500. FAX 31-71-5317532. *726*

ENTOURAGE.
Roeher Institute, Kinsmen Bldg., York University, 4700 Keele St., North York, ON M3J 1P3, Canada. TEL 416-661-9611 FAX 416-661-5701. *3305*

ENTREPRENEURSHIP & REGIONAL DEVELOPMENT.
Taylor & Francis Ltd., Rankine Rd., Basingstoke, Hants. RG24 8PR, England. TEL 44-1256-840366. FAX 44-1256-479438. *921*

ENTREPRENEURSHIP, INNOVATION AND CHANGE.
Plenum Publishing Corp., 233 Spring St., New York, NY 10013-1578. TEL 212-620-8000. FAX 212-463-0742. *1416*

ENVIRONMENT (WASHINGTON).
Heldref Publications, 1319 Eighteenth St., N.W., Washington, DC 20036-1802. TEL 202-296-6267. FAX 202-296-5149 *2787*

ENVIRONMENT & ASSESSMENT.
Kluwer Academic Publishers, Postbus 17, 3300 AA Dordrecht, Netherlands. TEL 31-78-6392392. FAX 31-78-6392254. *2787*

ENVIRONMENT AND DEVELOPMENT ECONOMICS.
Cambridge University Press, Edinburgh Bldg., Shaftesbury Rd., Cambridge CB2 2RU, England. TEL 44-1223-312393. FAX 44-1223-315052. *2787*

ENVIRONMENT & MANAGEMENT.
Kluwer Academic Publishers, Postbus 17, 3300 AA Dordrecht, Netherlands. TEL 31-78-6392392. FAX 31-78-6392254. *2787*

ENVIRONMENT AND PLANNING A.
Pion Ltd., 207 Brondesbury Park, London NW2 5JN, England. TEL 44-181-459-0066. FAX 44-181-451-6454. *3582*

ENVIRONMENT AND PLANNING B: PLANNING & DESIGN.
Pion Ltd., 207 Brondesbury Park, London NW2 5JN, England. TEL 44-181-459-0066. FAX 44-181-451-6454. *3582*

ENVIRONMENT AND PLANNING C: GOVERNMENT & POLICY.
Pion Ltd., 207 Brondesbury Park, London NW2 5JN, England. TEL 44-181-459-0066. FAX 44-181-451-6454. *5900*

ENVIRONMENT AND PLANNING D: SOCIETY & SPACE.
Pion Ltd., 207 Brondesbury Park, London NW2 5JN, England. TEL 44-181-459-0066. FAX 44-181-451-6454. *3582*

ENVIRONMENT AND URBANIZATION.
International Institute for Environment and Development (IIED), 3 Endsleigh St., London WC1H ODD, England. TEL 44-171-388-2117. FAX 44-171-388-2826. *2787*

ENVIRONMENT INTERNATIONAL.
Elsevier Science Ltd., Pergamon, P.O. Box 800, Kidlington, Oxford OX5 1DX, England. TEL 44-1865-843000. FAX 44-1865-843010. *2788*

ENVIRONMENT SOUTH AUSTRALIA.
Conservation Council of South Australia, Conservation Centre, 120 Wakefield St., Adelaide, S.A. 5000, Australia. TEL 61-8-2235155. FAX 61-8-2324782. *2788*

ENVIRONMENTAL AND ECOLOGICAL STATISTICS.
Chapman & Hall, Journals Department 2-6 Boundary Row, London SE1 8HN, England. TEL 44-171-8650066. FAX 44-171-5229623. *2829*

ENVIRONMENTAL AND ENGINEERING GEOLOGY.
Association of Engineering Geologists, 323 Boston Post Rd., Ste. 2D, Box 132, Sudbury, MA 01776. TEL 508-443-4639. *2232*

ENVIRONMENTAL AND EXPERIMENTAL BOTANY.
Elsevier Science Ltd., Pergamon, P.O. Box 800, Kidlington, Oxford OX5 1DX, England. TEL 44-1865-843000. FAX 44-1865-843010. *679*

ENVIRONMENTAL AND MOLECULAR MUTAGENESIS.
John Wiley & Sons, Inc., Journals, 605 Third Ave., New York, NY 10158. TEL 212-850-6645. FAX 212-850-6021. *740*

ENVIRONMENTAL AND RESOURCE ECONOMICS.
Kluwer Academic Publishers, Postbus 17, 3300 AA Dordrecht, Netherlands. TEL 31-78-6392392. FAX 31-78-6392254. *2789*

ENVIRONMENTAL BIOLOGY OF FISHES.
Kluwer Academic Publishers, Postbus 17, 3300 AA Dordrecht, Netherlands. TEL 31-78-6392392. FAX 31-78-6392254. *804*

ENVIRONMENTAL CARCINOGENESIS & ECOTOXICOLOGY REVIEWS.
Marcel Dekker Journals, 270 Madison Ave., New York, NY 10016. TEL 212-696-9000. FAX 212-685-4540. *2844*

ENVIRONMENTAL CONSERVATION.
Cambridge University Press, Edinburgh Bldg., Shaftesbury Rd., Cambridge CB2 2RU, England. TEL 44-1223-312393. FAX 44-1223-315052. *2789*

ENVIRONMENTAL EDUCATION AND INFORMATION.
University of Salford, Environmental Resources Unit, Newton Bldg., Salford M5 4WT, England. TEL 44-161-745-5221. FAX 44-161-745-5999. *2790*

ENVIRONMENTAL EDUCATION RESEARCH.
Carfax Publishing Co., P.O. Box 25, Abingdon, Oxon. OX14 3UE, England. TEL 44-1235-401000. FAX 44-1235-401550. *2486*

ENVIRONMENTAL ENTOMOLOGY.
Entomological Society of America, 9301 Annapolis
Rd., Lanham, MD 20706. TEL 301-731-4535.
FAX 301-731-4538. *726*

ENVIRONMENTAL ETHICS.
Environmental Philosophy, Inc., Center for
Environmental Philosophy, University of North
Texas, Box 13496, Denton, TX 76203-6496.
TEL 817-565-2727. FAX 817-565-4448. *5474*

ENVIRONMENTAL FLUID MECHANICS.
Kluwer Academic Publishers, Postbus 17, 3300 AA
Dordrecht, Netherlands. TEL 31-78-6392392.
FAX 31-78-6392254. *2208*

ENVIRONMENTAL GEOCHEMISTRY AND HEALTH.
Chapman & Hall, Journals Department 2-6
Boundary Row, London SE1 8HN, England. TEL 44-
171-8560066. FAX 44-171-5229623. *2790*

ENVIRONMENTAL HEALTH PERSPECTIVES.
U.S. Department of Health and Human Services,
National Institute of Environmental Health Sciences,
Box 12233, Research Triangle Park, NC 27709.
TEL 919-541-3406. FAX 919-541-0273. *2790*

ENVIRONMENTAL HISTORY.
Forest History Society, 701 Vickers Ave., Durham,
NC 27701-3147. TEL 919-682-9319. *2126*

ENVIRONMENTAL LAW ANTHOLOGY.
International Library Law Book Publishers, Inc.,
4301 N. Fairfax Dr., Ste. 875, Arlington, VA
22203. TEL 703-528-1000. FAX 703-528-6060.
3775

ENVIRONMENTAL MANAGEMENT (NEW YORK).
Springer-Verlag, Life Science Journals, 175 Fifth
Ave., New York, NY 10010. TEL 212-460-1500.
FAX 212-473-6272. *2791*

ENVIRONMENTAL MEDICINE.
Nagoya Daigaku, Kankyo Igaku Kenkyujo, Furo-cho,
Chikusa-ku, Nagoya 464-01, Japan. TEL 81-52-
789-3873. FAX 81-52-789-3876. *4452*

ENVIRONMENTAL MODELING & ASSESSMENT.
Baltzer Science Publishers B.V., Asterweg 1a, 1031
HL Amsterdam, Netherlands. TEL 31-20-6370061.
FAX 31-20-6323651. *2832*

ENVIRONMENTAL MODELLING & SOFTWARE.
Elsevier Science Ltd., P.O. Box 800, Kidlington,
Oxford OX5 1DX, England. TEL 44-1865-843000.
FAX 44-1865-843010. *2832*

ENVIRONMENTAL MONITORING AND ASSESSMENT.
Kluwer Academic Publishers, Postbus 17, 3300 AA
Dordrecht, Netherlands. TEL 31-78-6392392.
FAX 31-78-6392254. *2792*

ENVIRONMENTAL POLITICS.
Frank Cass, Newbury House, 890-900 Eastern Ave.,
Newbury Park, Ilford, Essex 1G2 7HH, England.
TEL 44-181-599-8866. FAX 44-181-599-0984.
5748

ENVIRONMENTAL POLLUTION.
Elsevier Science Ltd., P.O. Box 800, Kidlington,
Oxford OX5 1DX, England. TEL 44-1865-843000.
FAX 44-1865-843010. *2835*

ENVIRONMENTAL PROFESSIONAL.
Blackwell Science Inc., 238 Main St., Cambridge,
MA 02142. TEL 617-876-7022. FAX 617-492-
5263. *2793*

ENVIRONMENTAL PROTECTION.
Stevens Publishing Corporation, 3700 J.H. Kultgen
Frwy., Waco, TX 76706. TEL 817-776-9000.
FAX 817-776-9018. *2793*

ENVIRONMENTAL PROTECTION BULLETIN.
Institution of Chemical Engineers, 165-189 Railway
Terr., Rugby, Warks. CV21 3HQ, England.
TEL 01788-578214. FAX 01788-560833. *2640*

**ENVIRONMENTAL RADIATION SURVEILLANCE IN
WASHINGTON STATE. ANNUAL REPORT.**
Department of Health, Division of Radiation
Protection, Box 47827, Olympia, WA 98504-7827.
TEL 206-586-3306. FAX 206-753-1496. *2793*

ENVIRONMENTAL RESEARCH.
Academic Press, Inc., Journal Division, 525 B St.,
Ste. 1900, San Diego, CA 92101-4495. TEL 619-
230-1840. FAX 619-699-6800. *2793*

ENVIRONMENTAL REVIEWS.
National Research Council of Canada, Research
Journals, Ottawa, ON K1A 0R6, Canada. TEL 613-
993-9084. FAX 613-952-7656. *2794*

ENVIRONMENTAL SCIENCE AND TECHNOLOGY.
Kluwer Academic Publishers, Postbus 17, 3300 AA
Dordrecht, Netherlands. TEL 31-78-6392392.
FAX 31-78-6392254. *2794*

ENVIRONMENTAL SCIENCE RESEARCH.
Plenum Publishing Corp., 233 Spring St., New York,
NY 10013-1578. TEL 212-620-8000. FAX 212-
463-0742. *2794*

ENVIRONMENTAL SCIENCES.
M Y U, Scientific Publishing Division, 2-32-3
Sendagi, Bunkyo-ku, Tokyo 113, Japan. *2794*

ENVIRONMENTAL TECHNOLOGY.
Adams - Green Industry Publishing, Inc., Adams
Trade Press, 2100 Powers Ferry Rd., N.W., Ste.
405, Atlanta, GA 30339-5014. TEL 770-937-
0222. FAX 770-937-0303. *2795*

ENVIRONMENTAL TOPICS.
Gordon and Breach Science Publishers, c/o
International Publishers Distributor, P.O. Box 3054,
Langhorne, PA 19047-3054. TEL 215-750-2642.
FAX 215-750-6343. *2795*

ENVIRONMENTAL TOXICOLOGY AND CHEMISTRY.
Society of Environmental Toxicology and Chemistry,
1010 N. 12th St., Pensacola, FL 32501-3370.
TEL 904-469-1500. FAX 904-469-9778. *2845*

**ENVIRONMENTAL TOXICOLOGY AND
PHARMACOLOGY.**
Elsevier Science B.V., P.O. Box 211, 1000 AE
Amsterdam, Netherlands. TEL 31-20-4853911.
FAX 31-20-4853598. *2845*

**ENVIRONMENTAL TOXICOLOGY AND WATER
QUALITY.**
John Wiley & Sons, Inc., Journals, 605 Third Ave.,
New York, NY 10158-0012. TEL 212-850-6645.
FAX 212-850-6021. *2845*

ENVIRONMENTAL VALUES.
White Horse Press, 10 High St., Knapwell,
Cambridge CB3 8NR, England. TEL -1954-267527.
FAX 44-1954-267527. *2795*

THE ENVIRONMENTALIST.
Chapman & Hall, Journals Department 2-6
Boundary Row, London SE1 8HN, England. TEL 44-
171-8560066. FAX 44-171-5229623. *2795*

ENVIRONMENTS.
University of Waterloo, Faculty of Environmental
Studies, Waterloo, ON N2L 3G1, Canada. TEL 519-
888-4567. FAX 519-746-2031. *2795*

ENVIRONMETRICS.
John Wiley & Sons Ltd., Journals, Baffins Ln.,
Chichester, W. Sussex PO19 1UD, England. TEL 44-
1243-779777. FAX 44-1243-843232. *2795*

ENZYME AND MICROBIAL TECHNOLOGY.
Elsevier Science Inc., Box 945, New York, NY
10159-0945. TEL 212-633-3730. FAX 212-633-
3680. *661*

ENZYME AND PROTEIN.
S. Karger AG, Allschwilerstr. 10, P.O. Box, CH-4009
Basel, Switzerland. TEL 061-3061111. FAX 061-
3061234. *638*

ENZYME ENGINEERING.
New York Academy of Sciences, 2 E. 63rd St., New
York, NY 10021. TEL 212-838-0230. *638*

EOS.
American Geophysical Union, 2000 Florida Ave.,
N.W., Washington, DC 20009. TEL 202-462-6900.
FAX 202-328-0566. *2272*

EPIDEMIOLOGICAL NEWS BULLETIN.
Ministry of Health, Committee on Epidemic
Diseases, Quarantine & Epidemiology Dept., 40
Scotts Rd., Environment Bldg., Singapore 0922,
Singapore. TEL 65-732-9758. FAX 65-731-9866.
4619

EPILEPSIA.
Lippincott - Raven Publishers 227 E. Washington
Sq., Philadelphia, PA 19106. TEL 215-238-4200.
4835

EPILEPSY RESEARCH.
Elsevier Science B.V., P.O. Box 211, 1000 AE
Amsterdam, Netherlands. TEL 31-20-4853911.
FAX 31-20-4853598. *4835*

EPILEPSY RESEARCH SUPPLEMENTS.
Elsevier Science B.V., Books Division, P.O. Box 211,
1000 AE Amsterdam, Netherlands. TEL 31-20-
4853911. FAX 31-20-4853705. *4836*

EPISODES (NOTTINGHAM).
International Union of Geological Sciences, c/o
British Geological Survey, Keyworth, Nottingham
NG12 5GG, England. TEL 44-1602-363100.
FAX 44-1602-363474. *2232*

EPISTEME.
Kluwer Academic Publishers, Postbus 17, 3300 AA
Dordrecht, Netherlands. TEL 31-78-6392392.
FAX 31-78-6392254. *6239*

EQUINE ATHLETE.
Veterinary Practice Publishing Co., 7 Ashley Ave. S.,
Santa Barbara, CA 93103-9989. TEL 805-965-
1028. FAX 805-965-0722. *6945*

EQUINE PRACTICE.
Veterinary Practice Publishing Co., 7 Ashley Ave. S.,
Santa Barbara, CA 93103-9989. TEL 805-965-
1028. FAX 805-965-0722. *6945*

EQUINE REPRODUCTION (NO.).
Society for the Study of Reproduction, 1526
Jefferson St., Madison, WI 53711-2106. TEL 608-
256-2777. FAX 608-256-4610. *740*

EQUIVALENCIAS.
Fundacion Fernando Rielo, Jorge Juan 102, 2nd B,
28009 Madrid, Spain. TEL 575-4091. *4305*

ERASMUS OF ROTTERDAM SOCIETY YEARBOOK.
Erasmus of Rotterdam Society, 1015 Patterson
Office Tower, Lexington, KY 40506-0027. TEL 606-
257-5710. FAX 606-257-3743. *5474*

ERGONOMIA.
Polska Akademia Nauk, Komitet Ergonomii, Ul. Sw.
Jana 28, 31-018 Krakow, Poland. FAX 48-12-
222791. *6239*

ERGONOMICS.
Taylor & Francis Ltd., 1 Gunpowder Sq., London
EC4A 3DE, England. TEL 44-171-583-0490.
FAX 44-171-583-0585. *2598*

ERGONOMICS ABSTRACTS.
Taylor & Francis Ltd., 1 Gunpowder Sq., London
EC4A 3DE, England. TEL 44-171-583-0490.
FAX 44-171-583-0585. *2627*

ERGONOMICS IN DESIGN.
Human Factors and Ergonomics Society, Box 1369,
Santa Monica, CA 90406-1369. TEL 310-394-
1811. FAX 310-394-2410. *2598*

ERKENNTNIS.
Kluwer Academic Publishers, Postbus 17, 3300 AA
Dordrecht, Netherlands. TEL 31-78-6392392.
FAX 31-78-6392254. *5474*

ERNEST BLOCH LECTURES.
University of California Press, 2120 Berkeley Way,
Berkeley, CA 94720. TEL 510-642-4247.
FAX 510-643-7127. *2428*

ERYTHROPOIESIS.
Adis International Ltd., Chowley Oak Ln., Tattenhall,
Chester, Ches. CH3 9GA, England. TEL 44-1829-
771155. FAX 44-1829-770330. *4699*

ERZIEHERBRIEF.
Arbeitsgemeinschaft Sudetendeutscher Lehrer und
Erzieher e.V., Hochstr. 8, 81669 Munich, Germany.
TEL 49-89-480003-28. *5748*

ESPACIO ABIERTO.
Universidad del Zulia, Consejo de Desarollo Cientifico y Humanistico, Av. Universidad (Calle 60) 25-266, Sector Grano de Oro, Maracaibo, Venezuela. TEL 58-61-515131. FAX 58-61-528934. *6412*

ESPRIT CREATEUR.
University of Kentudy, 1015 Patterson, Lexington, KY 40506-0001. TEL 606-257-7557. FAX 606-257-3743. *4207*

ESSAYS AND MONOGRAPHS IN COLORADO HISTORY.
Colorado Historical Society, 1300 Broadway, Denver, CO 80203. TEL 303-866-5784. *3467*

ESSAYS IN BIOCHEMISTRY.
Portland Press Ltd., 59 Portland Place, London W1N 3AJ, England. TEL 44-171-580-5530. FAX 44-171-323-1136. *638*

ESSAYS IN CHEMISTRY.
Academic Press, Inc., 525 B St., Ste. 1900, San Diego, CA 92101-4495. TEL 619-231-0926. FAX 619-699-6715. *1675*

ESSAYS IN ECONOMIC AND BUSINESS HISTORY.
Ohio State University, Department of History, 106 Dulles Hall, 230 W. 17th Ave., OH 43210-1367. TEL 614-292-2674. FAX 614-292-2282. *1254*

ESSAYS IN HISTORY.
University of Virginia, Corcoran Department of History, Charlottesville, VA 22903. TEL 804-924-7146. *3342*

ESSAYS IN THEATRE.
University of Guelph, Department of Drama, Guelph, ON N1G 2W1, Canada. TEL 519-824-4120. FAX 519-824-0560. *6696*

ESTACION EXPERIMENTAL DE AULA DEI. ANALES.
Estacion Experimental de Aula Dei, Apdo. de Correos 202, C. Montanana 177, 50081 Zaragoza, Spain. TEL 34-76-576511. FAX 34-76-575620. *219*

ESTATE PLANNING (NEW YORK).
Warren, Gorham & Lamont, One Penn Plaza, New York, NY 10119. TEL 212-971-5000. FAX 212-971-5113. *3914*

ESTHETIC DENTISTRY UPDATE (PHILADELPHIA).
W.B. Saunders Co. The Curtis Center, 3rd Fl., Independence Sq. W., Philadelphia, PA 19106-3399. TEL 215-238-7807. FAX 215-238-6445. *4641*

ESTRENO.
350 N. Burrowes Bldg., University Park, PA 16802. TEL 814-238-0270. FAX 814-863-7944. *6696*

ESTUARIES.
Estuarine Research Federation, 490 Chippingwood Dr., No. 2, Port Republic, MD 20676-2140. TEL 318-475-5443. FAX 318-475-5675. *582*

ESTUDIOS DE ECONOMIA.
Universidad de Chile, Facultad de Ciencias Economicas y Administrativas, Av. Ranacagua 257, Santiago, Chile. FAX 562-634-7342. *921*

ESTUDIOS DE PSICOLOGIA.
Aprendizaje, S.L., Ctr. de Canillas 138, 2o 16C, 28043 Madrid, Spain. TEL 388-38-74. FAX 300-35-27. *5842*

ESTUDIOS GEOLOGICOS.
Museo Nacional de Ciencias Naturales, J. Gutierrez Abascal 2, 28006 Madrid, Spain. FAX 341-5645078. *2208*

ESTUDIOS INTERDISCIPLINARIOS DE AMERICA LATINA Y EL CARIBE.
University of Tel Aviv, Aranne School of History, Ramat Aviv 69978, Israel. FAX 972-3-6409457. *3612*

ESTUDIOS INTERNACIONALES.
Universidad de Chile, Instituto de Estudios Internacionales, Condell 249, Casilla 14187, Suc. 21, Santiago 9, Chile. TEL 56-2-2745377. FAX 56-2-2740155. *5748*

ESTUDIOS JALISCIENSES.
Colegio de Jaliscc, 5 de mayo 321, 45100 Zapopan, Jal., Mexico. TEL 633-2196. FAX 633-2154. *3612*

ESTUDIOS OCEANOLOGICOS.
Universidad de Artofagasta, Facultad de Recursos del Mar, Casilla 170, Antofagasta, Chile. FAX 56-55-247542. *2294*

ESTUDIOS SOBRE LAS CULTURAS CONTEMPORANEAS.
Universidad de Cclima, Centro Universitario de Investigaciones Sociales, Av. 25 de Julio 965, 28045 Colima, Col., Mexico. TEL 52-331-41133. FAX 52-331-30397. *3612*

ESTUDOS AFRO-ASIATICOS.
Sociedade Brasileira de Instrucao, Centro de Estudos Afro-Asiaticos, Rua da Assembleia, 10 Conj. 501, 20011-000 Rio de Janeiro, Brazil. TEL 55-21-5312636. FAX 55-21-5312155. *6322*

ETHEL BROWNING'S TOXICITY AND METABOLISM OF INDUSTRIAL SOLVENTS.
Elsevier Science B.V., Books Division, P.O. Box 211, 1000 AE Amsterdam, Netherlands. TEL 31-20-4853911. FAX 31-20-4853705. *2845*

ETHICS (CHICAGO).
University of Chicago Press, Journals Division, Box 37005, Chicago, IL 60637. TEL 773-753-3347. FAX 773-753-0811. *5474*

ETHICS & BEHAVIOR.
Lawrence Erlbaum Associates, Inc., 10 Industrial Dr., Mahwah, NJ 07430-2262. TEL 201-236-9500. FAX 201-236-0072. *5842*

ETHICS & INTERNATIONAL AFFAIRS (JOURNAL).
Carnegie Council on Ethics and International Affairs, c/o Matthew Mattern, Ed., Merrill House, 170 E. 64th St., New York, NY 10021-7478. TEL 212-838-4120. FAX 212-752-2432. *5748*

ETHICS AND MEDICS.
Pope John XXIII Medical-Moral Research and Education Center, 186 Forbes Rd., Braintree, MA 02184. TEL 617-848-6965. FAX 617-849-1309. *5475*

ETHIOPIAN REVIEW.
P.O. Box 98499, Atlanta, CA 30359. TEL 404-325-8411. FAX 404-325-8411. *6322*

ETHNIC HISTORY OF CHICAGO.
University of Illinois Press, 1325 S. Oak St., Champaign, IL 61820. TEL 217-333-0950. FAX 217-244-8082. *2877*

ETHNIC STUDIES REPORT.
International Centre for Ethnic Studies, 554-1 Peradeniya Rc., Kandy, Sri Lanka. TEL 08-34892. FAX 08-34892. *2877*

ETHNICITY & DISEASE.
International Society on Hypertension in Blacks, 2045 Manchester St., N.E., Atlanta, GA 30324-4110. TEL 404-875-6263. FAX 404-875-6334. *4452*

ETHNOBOTANY.
Deep Publications, A-3-27A DDA Flats, Paschim Vihar, New Delhi 110063, India. TEL 91-11-5579514. FAX 91-11-5437621. *679*

ETHNOHISTORY.
Duke University Press, Box 90660, Durham, NC 27708-0660. TEL 919-687-3600. FAX 919-688-4574. *308*

ETHNOLOGY.
University of Pittsburgh, Department of Anthropology, Pittsburgh, PA 15260. TEL 412-648-7503. FAX 412-648-5911. *308*

ETHNOMUSICOLOGY.
Society for Ethnomusicology, Morrison Hall 005, Indiana University, Bloomington, IN 47405-2501. TEL 812-855-5672. FAX 812-855-6673. *5156*

ETHNOS.
Folkens Museum Etnografiska, P.O. Box 27140, 102 52 Stockholm, Sweden. FAX 08-6665070. *308*

ETNOLOSKA TRIBINA.
Institut za Etnologiju i Folkloristiku, Ul. Kralja Zvonimira 17, 41000 Zagreb Croatia. TEL 385-41-440880. *309*

ETOLOGIA.
Sociedad Espanola de Etologia, c/o Museu de Zoologia, Apdo. 593, 03080 Barcelona, Spain. TEL 343-3196912. FAX 343-3104999. *805*

ETRUSCAN STUDIES.
Wayne State University Press, 4809 Woodward Ave., Detroit, MI 48201-1309. TEL 313-577-6120. FAX 313-577-6131. *1821*

ETTORE MAJORANA INTERNATIONAL SCIENCE SERIES. PHYSICAL SCIENCES.
Plenum Publishing Corp., 233 Spring St., New York, NY 10013-1578. TEL 212-620-8000. FAX 212-463-0742. *6239*

LES ETUDES CLASSIQUES.
Facultes Notre-Dame de la Paix, Faculte de Philosophie et Lettres, Rue de Bruxelles, 61, B-5000 Namur, Belgium. TEL 32-81-724189. FAX 32-81-724203. *1821*

ETUDES FRANCOPHONES.
University of Southwestern Louisiana, Conseil International d'Etudes Francophones, Box 43331, Lafayette, LA 70504-3331. TEL 318-482-6811. FAX 318-482-5446. *2377*

ETUDES MONGOLES ET SIBERIENNES.
Laboratoire d'Ethnologie et de Sociologie Comparative, Universite de Paris X, 200 av. de la Republique, 92001 Nanterre, France. TEL 40-97-75-22. FAX 40-97-71-17. *309*

ETUDES SUR LE JUDAISME MEDIEVAL.
E.J. Brill, P.O. Box 9000 2300 PA Leiden, Netherlands. TEL 31-71-5353500. FAX 31-71-5317532. *6124*

EUPHYTICA.
Kluwer Academic Publishers, Postbus 17, 3300 AA Dordrecht, Netherlands. TEL 31-78-6392392. FAX 31-78-6392254. *220*

EURESIS - CAHIERS ROUMAINS D'ETUDES LITTERAIRES.
Editura Univers, Piata Presei Libere 1, 79739 Bucharest, Rumania. TEL 40-1-2226629. FAX 40-1-2225652. *4208*

EURO COURSES. ADVANCED SCIENTIFIC TECHNIQUES.
Kluwer Academic Publishers, Postbus 17, 3300 AA Dordrecht, Netherlands. TEL 31-78-6392392. FAX 31-78-6392254. *5650*

EURO COURSES. CHEMICAL AND ENVIRONMENTAL SCIENCES.
Kluwer Academic Publishers, Postbus 17, 3300 AA Dordrecht, Netherlands. TEL 31-78-6392392. FAX 31-78-6392254. *2795*

EURO COURSES. COMPUTER AND INFORMATION SCIENCE.
Kluwer Academic Publishers, Postbus 17, 3300 AA Dordrecht, Netherlands. TEL 31-78-6392392. FAX 31-78-6392254. *1989*

EURO COURSES. ENVIRONMENTAL IMPACT ASSESSMENT.
Kluwer Academic Publishers, Postbus 17, 3300 AA Dorcrecht, Netherlands. TEL 31-78-6392392. FAX 31-78-6392254. *2795*

EURO COURSES. ENVIRONMENTAL MANAGEMENT.
Kluwer Academic Publishers, Postbus 17, 3300 AA Dordrecht, Netherlands. TEL 31-78-6392392. FAX 31-78-6392254. *2796*

EURO COURSES. HEALTH PHYSICS AND RADIATION PROTECTION.
Kluwer Academic Publishers, Postbus 17, 3300 AA Dordrecht, Netherlands. TEL 31-78-6392392. FAX 31-78-6392254. *2575*

EURO COURSES. NUCLEAR SCIENCE AND TECHNOLOGY.
Kluwer Academic Publishers, Postbus 17, 3300 AA Dordrecht, Netherlands. TEL 31-78-6392392. FAX 31-78-6392254. *2575*

EURO COURSES. RELIABILITY AND RISK ANALYSIS.
Kluwer Academic Publishers, Postbus 17, 3300 AA Dordrecht, Netherlands. TEL 31-78-6392392. FAX 31-78-6392254. *6650*

EURO COURSES. REMOTE SENSING.
Kluwer Academic Publishers, Postbus 17, 3300 AA Dordrecht, Netherlands. TEL 31-78-6392392. FAX 31-78-6392254. *6650*

EURO COURSES. TECHNOLOGICAL INNOVATION.
Kluwer Academic Publishers, Postbus 17, 3300 AA Dordrecht, Netherlands. TEL 31-78-6392392. FAX 31-78-6392254. *6650*

EURO-LATIN AMERICAN RELATIONS.
Kluwer Academic Publishers, Postbus 17, 3300 AA Dordrecht, Netherlands. TEL 31-78-6392392. FAX 31-78-6392254. *5749*

EUROBIOLOGISTE.
Centre National des Biologistes, 80 Av. du Maine, 75014 Paris, France. TEL 43-22-97-70. FAX 43-21-73-12. *638*

EUROPA MEDICOPHYSICA.
Edizioni Minerva Medica, Corso Bramante 83-85, 10126 Turin, Italy. TEL 39-11-678282. FAX 39-11-3121736. *4817*

EUROPE - ASIA STUDIES.
Carfax Publishing Co., P.O. Box 25, Abingdon, Oxon. OX14 3UE, England. TEL 44-1235-401000. FAX 44-1235-401550. *922*

EUROPE IN THE MIDDLE AGES.
Elsevier Science B.V., Books Division, P.O. Box 211, 1000 AE Amsterdam, Netherlands. TEL 31-20-4853911. FAX 31-20-4853705. *3409*

EUROPEAN ACADEMY OF DERMATOLOGY AND VENEREOLOGY. JOURNAL.
Elsevier Science B.V., P.O. Box 211, 1000 AE Amsterdam, Netherlands. TEL 31-20-4853911. FAX 31-20-4853598. *4661*

EUROPEAN ACADEMY OF DERMATOLOGY AND VENEREOLOGY. JOURNAL. SUPPLEMENT.
Elsevier Science B.V., Books Division, P.O. Box 211, 1000 AE Amsterdam, Netherlands. TEL 31-20-4853911. FAX 31-20-4853705. *4661*

EUROPEAN APPLIED RESEARCH REPORTS: NUCLEAR SCIENCE AND TECHNOLOGY SECTION.
Harwood Academic Publishers, c/o International Publishers Distributor, P.O. Box 3054, Langhorne, PA 19047-3054. TEL 215-750-2642. FAX 215-750-6343. *5594*

EUROPEAN APPLIED RESEARCH REPORTS SPECIAL TOPICS SERIES.
Harwood Academic Publishers, c/o International Publishers Distributor, P.O. Box 3054, Langhorne, PA 19047-3054. TEL 215-750-2642. FAX 215-750-6343. *5594*

EUROPEAN BREWERY CONVENTION. PROCEEDINGS OF THE INTERNATIONAL CONGRESS.
I R L Press Ltd. Walton St., Oxford OX2 6 DP, England. TEL 44-1865-56767. FAX 44-1865-56646. *504*

THE EUROPEAN BUSINESS JOURNAL.
Whurr Publishers Ltd., 19b Compton Terrace, London N1 2UN, England. TEL 44-171-359-5979. FAX 44-171-226-5290. *922*

EUROPEAN CANCER NEWS.
Kluwer Academic Publishers, Postbus 17, 3300 AA Dordrecht, Netherlands. TEL 31-78-6392392. FAX 31-78-6392254. *4755*

EUROPEAN CERAMIC SOCIETY. JOURNAL.
Elsevier Science Ltd., P.O. Box 800, Kidlington, Oxford OX5 1DX, England. TEL 44-1865-843000. FAX 44-1865-843010. *1655*

EUROPEAN CHILD & ADOLESCENT PSYCHIATRY.
Dr. Dietrich Steinkopff Verlag, Saalbaustr. 12, 64283 Darmstadt. TEL 49-6151-1745-0. FAX 49-6151-174510. *4836*

EUROPEAN COMMUNICATION POLICY RESEARCH SERIES.
I O S Press, Van Diemenstraat 94, 1013 CN Amsterdam, Netherlands. TEL 31-20-6382189. FAX 31-20-6203419. *1903*

EUROPEAN COMMUNITIES ENVIRONMENTAL POLICY SERIES.
Martinus Nijhoff Publishers, Human Rights and International Law Postbus 17, 3300 AA Dordrecht, Netherlands. TEL 31-78-334911. FAX 31-78-334254. *2796*

EUROPEAN CONVENTION ON HUMAN RIGHTS. YEARBOOK.
Martinus Nijhoff Publishers, Human Rights and International Law Postbus 163, 3300 AD Dordrecht, Netherlands. TEL 31-78-334911. FAX 31-78-334254. *5727*

EUROPEAN EARLY CHILDHOOD EDUCATION RESEARCH JOURNAL.
Amber Publishing, Worcester College of Higher Education, Henwick Grove, Worcester WR2 6AJ, England. TEL 44-1905-855000. FAX 44-1905-855000. *2333*

EUROPEAN EATING DISORDERS REVIEW.
John Wiley & Sons Ltd., Journals, Baffins Ln., Chichester, W. Sussex PO19 1UD, England. TEL 44-1243-779777. FAX 44-1243-843232. *5842*

EUROPEAN ECONOMIC PERSPECTIVES.
Centre for Economic Policy Research, 25 Old Burlington St., London W1X 1LB, England. TEL 0171-734-9110. FAX 0171-734-8760. *1254*

EUROPEAN ECONOMIC REVIEW.
North-Holland P.O. Box 211, 1000 AE Amsterdam, Netherlands. TEL 31-20-4853911. FAX 31-20-4853598. *922*

EUROPEAN EDUCATION.
M.E. Sharpe, Inc., 80 Business Park Dr., Armonk, NY 10504. TEL 914-273-1800. FAX 914-273-2106. *2333*

EUROPEAN ENVIRONMENTAL LAW REVIEW.
Kluwer Law International Postbus 85889, 2508 CN The Hague, Netherlands. TEL 31-70-3081500. FAX 31-70-3081515. *3776*

EUROPEAN FINANCE REVIEW.
Kluwer Academic Publishers Boston, Box 358, Accord Sta., Hingham, MA 02018-0358. TEL 617-871-6600. FAX 617-871-6528. *1086*

EUROPEAN FINANCIAL MANAGEMENT.
Blackwell Publishers Ltd., 108 Cowley Rd., Oxford OX4 1JF, England. TEL 44-1865-791100. FAX 44-1865-791347. *1086*

EUROPEAN FINANCIAL SERVICES LAW.
Kluwer Law International Postbus 85889, 2508 CN The Hague, Netherlands. TEL 31-70-30815003. FAX 31-70-3081515. *1086*

EUROPEAN FOREIGN AFFAIRS REVIEW.
Kluwer Law International Postbus 85889, 2508 CN The Hague, Netherlands. TEL 31-70-3081500. FAX 31-70-3081515. *5749*

EUROPEAN HISTORY QUARTERLY.
Sage Publications Ltd., 6 Bonhill St., London EC2A 4PU, England. TEL 44-171-374-0645. FAX 44-171-374-8741. *3409*

EUROPEAN JOURNAL OF AGRICULTURAL EDUCATION AND EXTENSION.
P.O. Box 194, 6700 AD Wageningen, Netherlands. TEL 31-317-484018. FAX 31-317-485123. *113*

EUROPEAN JOURNAL OF ANAESTHESIOLOGY.
Blackwell Science Ltd., Osney Mead, Oxford OX2 OEL, England. TEL 44-1865-206206. FAX 44-1865-721205. *4591*

EUROPEAN JOURNAL OF CANCER.
Elsevier Science Ltd., Pergamon, P.O. Box 800, Kidlington, Oxford OX5 1DX, England. TEL 44-1865-843000. FAX 44-1865-843010. *4755*

EUROPEAN JOURNAL OF CANCER. PART B: ORAL ONCOLOGY.
Elsevier Science Ltd., Pergamon, P.O. Box 800, Kidlington, Oxford OX5 1DX, England. TEL 44-1865-843000. FAX 44-1865-843010. *4755*

EUROPEAN JOURNAL OF CANCER CARE (ENGLISH EDITION).
Blackwell Science Ltd., Osney Mead, Oxford OX2 OEL, England. TEL 44-1865-206206. FAX 44-1865-721205. *4755*

EUROPEAN JOURNAL OF CHIROPRACTIC.
European Chiropractors' Union, c/o Simon Leyson, Ed., 16 Uplands Crescent, Swansea SA2 0PB, Wales. *4613*

EUROPEAN JOURNAL OF CLINICAL INVESTIGATION.
Blackwell Science Ltd., Osney Mead, Oxford OX2 OEL, England. TEL 44-1865-206206. FAX 44-1865-721205. *4452*

EUROPEAN JOURNAL OF CLINICAL MICROBIOLOGY & INFECTIOUS DISEASES.
M M V Medizin Verlag, Neumarkter Str. 18, 81673 Munich, Germany. TEL 49-89-43189-0. FAX 49-89-43189633. *756*

EUROPEAN JOURNAL OF CLINICAL RESEARCH.
Brookwood Medical Publications, Orchard House, Brookwood, Surrey GU24 0AT, England. TEL 44-1483-797975. FAX 44-1483-797915. *4453*

EUROPEAN JOURNAL OF COGNITIVE PSYCHOLOGY.
Taylor & Francis Ltd., Psychology Press, 1 Gunpowder Sq., London EC4A 3DE, England. TEL 44-171-5830490. FAX 44-171-5830585. *5842*

EUROPEAN JOURNAL OF COMMUNICATION.
Sage Publications Ltd., 6 Bonhill St., London EC2A 4PU, England. TEL 44-171-374-0645. FAX 44-171-374-8741. *1903*

THE EUROPEAN JOURNAL OF DEVELOPMENT RESEARCH.
Frank Cass, Newbury House, 890-900 Eastern Ave., Newbury Park, Ilford, Essex IG2 7HH, England. TEL 44-181-599-8666. FAX 44-181-599-0984. *1306*

EUROPEAN JOURNAL OF DISORDERS OF COMMUNICATION.
Whurr Publishers Ltd., 19b Compton Terrace, London N1 2UN, England. TEL 44-171-359-5979. FAX 44-171-226-5290. *2468*

EUROPEAN JOURNAL OF EDUCATION.
Carfax Publishing Co., P.O. Box 25, Abingdon, Oxon. OX14 3UE, England. TEL 44-1235-401000. FAX 44-1235-401550. *2333*

EUROPEAN JOURNAL OF EMERGENCY MEDICINE.
Chapman & Hall, Journals Department 2-6 Boundary Row, London SE1 8HN, England. TEL 44-171-8650066. FAX 44-171-5229623. *4783*

EUROPEAN JOURNAL OF ENGINEERING EDUCATION.
Carfax Publishing Co., P.O. Box 25, Abingdon, Oxon. OX14 3UE, England. TEL 44-1235-401000. FAX 44-1235-401550. *2598*

EUROPEAN JOURNAL OF ENGLISH STUDIES.
Swets & Zeitlinger bv, P.O. Box 825, 2160 SZ Lisse, Netherlands. TEL 31-252-435111. FAX 31-252-415888. *4209*

EUROPEAN JOURNAL OF ENTOMOLOGY.
Academy of Sciences of the Czech Republic, Institute of Entomology, Branisovska 31, 37005 Ceske Budejovice, Czech Republic. TEL 42-38-817213. FAX 42-38-43624. *726*

EUROPEAN JOURNAL OF EPIDEMIOLOGY.
Kluwer Academic Publishers, Postbus 17, 3300 AA Dordrecht, Netherlands. TEL 31-78-6392392. FAX 31-78-6392254. *4453*

THE EUROPEAN JOURNAL OF FINANCE.
Chapman & Hall, Journals Department 2-6 Boundary Row, London SE1 8HN, England. TEL 44-171-8650066. FAX 44-171-5229623. *1086*

EUROPEAN JOURNAL OF FOREST PATHOLOGY.
Blackwell Wissenschaft, Kurfuerstendamm 57, 10707 Berlin, Germany. TEL 49-30-32790634. FAX 49-30-32790610. *3014*

THE EUROPEAN JOURNAL OF GENERAL PRACTICE.
Mediselect B.V., Postbus 28091, 3828 ZH Hoogland, Netherlands. TEL 31-33-4808020. FAX 31-33-4805881. *4453*

EUROPEAN JOURNAL OF GENETICS IN SOCIETY.
European Bioethical Research, 191 Leith Walk, Edinburgh EH6 8NX, Scotland. TEL 44-131-554-8869. FAX 44-131-1236-451299. *5475*

EUROPEAN JOURNAL OF GYNECOLOGICAL ONCOLOGY.
Studi Ostetrico Ginecologici s.r.l., Galleria Storione 2-A, 35128 Padua, Italy. TEL 39-49-8758644. FAX 39-49-8752018. *4755*

EUROPEAN JOURNAL OF HAEMATOLOGY.
Munksgaard International Publishers Ltd., 35 Noerre Soegade, P.O. Box 2148, DK-1016 Copenhagen K, Denmark. TEL 45-33-127030. FAX 45-33-129387. *4699*

EUROPEAN JOURNAL OF HAEMATOLOGY. SUPPLEMENTUM.
Munksgaard International Publishers Ltd., P.O. Box 2148, DK-1016 Copenhagen K, Denmark. TEL 45-33-127030. FAX 45-33-129387. *4699*

EUROPEAN JOURNAL OF HEALTH LAW.
Kluwer Law International Postbus 85889, 2508 CN The Hague, Netherlands. TEL 31-70-3081500. FAX 31-70-3081515. *4453*

EUROPEAN JOURNAL OF HUMAN GENETICS.
S. Karger AG, Allschwilerstr. 10, P.O. Box, CH-4009 Basel, Switzerland. TEL 061-3061111. FAX 061-3061234. *740*

EUROPEAN JOURNAL OF IMMUNOGENETICS.
Blackwell Science Ltd., Osney Mead, Oxford OX2 0EL, England. TEL 44-1865-206206. FAX 44-1865-721205. *740*

EUROPEAN JOURNAL OF INTERNATIONAL RELATIONS.
Sage Publications Ltd., 6 Bonhill St., London EC2A 4PU, England. TEL 44-171-374-0645. FAX 44-171-374-8741. *5749*

EUROPEAN JOURNAL OF LAW AND ECONOMICS.
Kluwer Academic Publishers Boston, Box 358, Accord St., Hingham, MA 02018-0358. TEL 617-871-6600. FAX 617-871-6528. *922*

EUROPEAN JOURNAL OF MECHANICAL ENGINEERING.
Societe Belge des Mecaniciens, 21 rue des Drapiers, B-1050 Brussels, Belgium. TEL 32-2-5118286. *2754*

EUROPEAN JOURNAL OF MEDICINAL CHEMISTRY.
Editions Scientifiques et Medicales Elsevier, 141 rue de Javel, 75747 Paris, France. TEL 33-1-45589022. FAX 33-1-45589421. *638*

EUROPEAN JOURNAL OF MINERALOGY.
E. Schweizerbart'sche Verlagsbuchhandlung, Johannesstr. 3A, 70176 Stuttgart, Germany. TEL 49-711-625001. FAX 49-711-625005. *5062*

EUROPEAN JOURNAL OF NEUROLOGY.
Rapid Science Publishers, 2-6 Boundary Row, London SE1 8HN, England. TEL 44-171-865-0198. FAX 44-171-410-6600. *4836*

EUROPEAN JOURNAL OF OBSTETRICS & GYNECOLOGY AND REPRODUCTIVE BIOLOGY.
Elsevier Science Ireland Ltd., P.O. Box 85, Limerick, Ireland. TEL 353-61-471944. FAX 353-61-472144. *4735*

EUROPEAN JOURNAL OF OPERATIONAL RESEARCH.
North-Holland P.O. Box 211, 1000 AE Amsterdam, Netherlands. TEL 31-20-4853911. FAX 31-20-4853598. *1416*

EUROPEAN JOURNAL OF ORAL SCIENCES.
Munksgaard International Publishers Ltd., 35 Noerre Soegade, P.O. Box 2148, DK-1016 Copenhagen K, Denmark. TEL 45-33-127030. FAX 45-33-129387. *4641*

EUROPEAN JOURNAL OF PARAPSYCHOLOGY.
Koestler Chair of Parapsychology, Dept. of Psychology, Univ. of Edinburgh, 7 George Sq., Edinburgh EH8 9JZ, Scotland. TEL 44-131-650-3348. FAX 44-131-650-3461. *5330*

EUROPEAN JOURNAL OF PHARMACEUTICAL SCIENCES.
Elsevier Science B.V., P.O. Box 211, 1000 AE Amsterdam, Netherlands. TEL 31-20-4853911. FAX 31-20-4853598. *5411*

EUROPEAN JOURNAL OF PHARMACOLOGY.
Elsevier Science B.V., P.O. Box 211, 1000 AE Amsterdam, Netherlands. TEL 31-20-4853911. FAX 31-20-4853598. *5411*

EUROPEAN JOURNAL OF PHARMACOLOGY. MOLECULAR PHARMACOLOGY SECTION.
Elsevier Science B.V., P.O. Box 211, 1000 AE Amsterdam, Netherlands. TEL 31-20-4853911. FAX 31-20-4853598. *5412*

EUROPEAN JOURNAL OF PHILOSOPHY.
Blackwell Publishers Ltd., 108 Cowley Rd., Oxford OX4 1JF, England. TEL 44-1865-791100. FAX 44-1865-791347 *5475*

EUROPEAN JOURNAL OF PLANT PATHOLOGY.
Kluwer Academic Publishers, Postbus 17, 3300 AA Dordrecht, Netherlands. TEL 31-78-6392392. FAX 31-78-6392254. *679*

EUROPEAN JOURNAL OF POLITICAL ECONOMY.
North-Holland P.O. Box 211, 1000 AE Amsterdam, Netherlands. TEL 31-20-4853911. FAX 31-20-4853598. *1401*

EUROPEAN JOURNAL OF POLITICAL RESEARCH.
Kluwer Academic Publishers, Postbus 17, 3300 AA Dordrecht, Netherlands. TEL 31-78-6392392. FAX 31-78-6392254. *5665*

EUROPEAN JOURNAL OF POPULATION.
Kluwer Academic Publishers, Postbus 17, 3300 AA Dordrecht, Netherlands. TEL 31-78-6392392. FAX 31-78-6392254. *5798*

EUROPEAN JOURNAL OF PSYCHIATRY.
University of Zaragoza, P.O. Box 6029, Avda. S. Juan Bosco 15, 50009 Zaragoza. TEL 76-559795. *4836*

EUROPEAN JOURNAL OF PSYCHOLOGY OF EDUCATION.
Instituto Superior de Psicologia Aplicada, Rua Jardim do Tabaco, 44, 1100 Lisbon, Portugal. TEL 351-1-8863184. FAX 351-1-8860954. *2333*

EUROPEAN JOURNAL OF PURCHASING AND SUPPLY MANAGEMENT.
Butterworth - Heinemann, Part of the Reed Elsevier group, Linacre House, Jordan Hill, Oxford OX2 8DP, England. TEL 44-1865-310366. FAX 44-1865-310898. *1465*

EUROPEAN JOURNAL OF RADIOLOGY.
Elsevier Science Ireland Ltd., P.O. Box 85, Limerick, Ireland. TEL 353-61-471944. FAX 353-61-472144. *4875*

EUROPEAN JOURNAL OF SOCIAL PSYCHOLOGY.
John Wiley & Sons Ltd., Journals, Baffins Ln., Chichester, W. Sussex PO19 1UD, England. TEL 44-1243-779777. FAX 44-1243-843232. *5843*

EUROPEAN JOURNAL OF SOIL SCIENCE.
Blackwell Science Ltd., Osney Mead, Oxford OX2 0EL, England. TEL 44-1865-206206. FAX 44-1865-721205. *220*

EUROPEAN JOURNAL OF TEACHER EDUCATION.
Carfax Publishing Co., P.O. Box 25, Abingdon, Oxon. OX14 3UE, England. TEL 44-1235-401000. FAX 44-1235-401550. *2333*

EUROPEAN JOURNAL OF ULTRASOUND.
Elsevier Science Ireland Ltd., P.O. Box 85, Limerick, Ireland. TEL 353-61-471944. FAX 353-61-472144. *4875*

EUROPEAN JUDAISM.
Berg Publishers, 150 Cowley Rd., Oxford OX4 1JJ, England. TEL 01865-245104. FAX 01865-791165. *6124*

THE EUROPEAN LEGACY.
M I T Press, 55 Hayward St., Cambridge, MA 02142. TEL 617-253-2889. FAX 617-258-5028. *5475*

EUROPEAN MANAGEMENT JOURNAL.
Elsevier Science Ltd., Pergamon, P.O. Box 800, Kidlington, Oxford OX5 1DX, England. TEL 44-1865-843000. FAX 44-1865-843010. *1416*

EUROPEAN MASS SPECTROSCOPY.
I M Publications, 6 Charlton Mill, Charlton, Chichester, W. Sussex PO18 0HY, England. TEL 44-1243-811334. FAX 44-1243-811711. *1715*

EUROPEAN MATERIALS RESEARCH SOCIETY. MONOGRAPHS.
Elsevier Science B.V., Books Division, P.O. Box 211, 1000 AE Amsterdam, Netherlands. TEL 31-20-4853911. FAX 31-20-4853705 *2731*

EUROPEAN MATERIALS RESEARCH SOCIETY. SYMPOSIA PROCEEDINGS.
Elsevier Science B.V., Books Division, P.O. Box 211, 1000 AE Amsterdam, Netherlands. TEL 31-20-4853911. FAX 31-20-4853705. *2731*

EUROPEAN NEUROLOGY.
S. Karger AG, Allschwilerstr. 10, P.O. Box, CH-4009 Basel, Switzerland. TEL 061-3061111. FAX 061-3061234. *4836*

EUROPEAN NEUROPSYCHOPHARMACOLOGY.
Elsevier Science B.V., P.O. Box 211, 1000 AE Amsterdam, Netherlands. TEL 31-20-4853911. FAX 31-20-4853598. *4836*

EUROPEAN ORGANIZATION FOR RESEARCH ON TREATMENT OF CANCER. MONOGRAPH SERIES.
Lippincott - Raven Publishers 227 E. Washington Sq., Philadelphia, PA 19106. TEL 215-238-4200. FAX 215-238-4235. *4755*

EUROPEAN PHYSICAL EDUCATION REVIEW.
North Western Counties Physical Education Association, Driffield Rd., Nafferton, Driffield, E. Yorks YO25 0JL, England. TEL 44-1377-254231. FAX 44-1377-256861. *2486*

EUROPEAN PLANNING STUDIES.
Carfax Publishing Co., P.O. Box 25, Abingdon, Oxon. OX14 3UE, England. TEL 44-1235-401000. FAX 44-1235-401550. *3582*

EUROPEAN POLYMER JOURNAL.
Elsevier Science Ltd., Pergamon, P.O. Box 800, Kidlington, Oxford OX5 1DX, England. TEL 44-1865-843000. FAX 44-1865-843010. *1738*

EUROPEAN PSYCHIATRY.
Editions Scientifiques et Medicales Elsevier, 141 rue de Javel, 75747 Paris, France. TEL 33-1-45589026. FAX 33-1-45589421. *4836*

EUROPEAN PUBLIC LAW.
Kluwer Law International Postbus 85889, 2508 CN The Hague, Netherlands. TEL 31-70-3081500. FAX 31-70-3081515. *3950*

EUROPEAN RESEARCH IN REGIONAL SCIENCE.
Pion Ltd., 207 Brondesbury Park, London NW2 5JN, England. TEL 44-181-459-0066. FAX 44-181-451-6454. *3582*

EUROPEAN RESEARCH LIBRARY COOPERATION.
Ligue des Bibliotheques Europeenes de Recherche, Secretariat, Skindergade 27 I, 1159 Copenhagen K, Denmark. TEL 45-33-93-52-22. FAX 45-33-91-95-96. *3992*

THE EUROPEAN RESPIRATORY JOURNAL.
Munksgaard International Publishers Ltd., 35 Noerre Soegade, P.O. Box 2148, DK-1016 Copenhagen K, Denmark. TEL 45-33-127030. FAX 45-33-129387. *4887*

EUROPEAN RESPIRATORY REVIEW.
Munksgaard International Publishers Ltd., 35 Noerre Soegade, P.O. Box 2148, DK-2148 Copenhagen K, Denmark. TEL 45-33-127030. FAX 45-33-129387. *4887*

EUROPEAN REVIEW.
John Wiley & Sons Ltd., Journals, Baffins Ln., Chichester, W. Sussex PO19 1UD, England. TEL 44-1243-779777. FAX 44-1243-843232. *6240*

EUROPEAN REVIEW OF ECONOMIC HISTORY.
Cambridge University Press Edinburgh Bldg., Shaftesbury Rd., Cambridge CB2 2RU, England. TEL 44-1223-312393. FAX 44-1223-315052. *1254*

EUROPEAN REVIEW OF HISTORY.
Carfax Publishing Co., P.O. Box 25, Abingdon, Oxon. OX14 3UE, England. TEL 44-1235-401000. FAX 44-1235-401550. *3409*

EUROPEAN REVIEW OF PRIVATE LAW.
Kluwer Law International Postbus 85889, 2508 CN The Hague, Netherlands. TEL 31-70-3081500. FAX 31-70-3081515. *3930*

EUROPEAN REVIEW OF SOCIAL PSYCHOLOGY.
John Wiley & Sons Ltd., Journals, Baffins Ln., Chichester, W. Sussex PO19 1UD, England. TEL 44-1243-779777. FAX 44-1243-843232. *5843*

EUROPEAN SECURITY.
Frank Cass, Newbury House, 890-900 Eastern Ave., Newbury Park, Ilford, Essex 1G2 7HH, England. TEL 44-181-599-8866. FAX 44-181-599-0984. *5749*

EUROPEAN SPINE JOURNAL.
Springer-Verlag, Heidelberger Platz 3, 14197 Berlin, Germany. TEL 49-30-8207-0. FAX 49-30-8214091. *4909*

EUROPEAN STUDIES IN LAW.
Elsevier Science B.V., Books Division, P.O. Box 211, 1000 AE Amsterdam, Netherlands. TEL 31-20-4853911. FAX 31-20-4853705. *3776*

EUROPEAN STUDIES IN PHILOSOPHY OF MEDICINE.
Kluwer Academic Publishers, Postbus 17, 3300 AA Dordrecht, Netherlands. TEL 31-78-6392392. FAX 31-78-6392254. *4453*

EUROPEAN STUDIES JOURNAL.
University of Northern Iowa, Department of Modern Languages, Cedar Falls, IA 50614-0504. TEL 319-273-2749. FAX 319-273-2921. *3409*

EUROPEAN STUDIES ON MULTILINGUALISM.
Swets & Zeitlinger bv, P.O. Box 825, 2160 SZ Lisse, Netherlands. TEL 31-252-435111. FAX 31-252-415888. *4068*

EUROPEAN SURGICAL RESEARCH.
S. Karger AG, Allschwilerstr. 10, P.O. Box, CH-4009 Basel, Switzerland. TEL 061-3061111. FAX 061-3061234. *4909*

EUROPEAN UROLOGY.
S. Karger AG, Allschwilerstr. 10, P.O. Box, CH-4009 Basel, Switzerland. TEL 061-3061111. FAX 061-3061234. *4926*

EUROPEAN WATER POLLUTION CONTROL.
Elsevier Science B.V., P.O. Box 211, 1000 AE Amsterdam, Netherlands. TEL 31-20-4853911. FAX 31-20-4853598. *2836*

EVALUATION AND PROGRAM PLANNING.
Elsevier Science Ltd., Pergamon, P.O. Box 800, Kidlington, Oxford OX5 1DX, England. TEL 44-1865-843000. FAX 44-1865-843010. *6323*

EVELYN WAUGH NEWSLETTER AND STUDIES.
Evelyn Waugh Society, Nassau Community College, State University of New York, Department of English, Garden City, NY 11530. TEL 516-572-7792. *4209*

THE EVERGREEN CHRONICLES.
Box 8939, Minneapolis, MN 55408-0939. TEL 612-649-4982. *4209*

EVOKED POTENTIALS.
Elsevier Science Ireland Ltd., P.O. Box 85, Limerick, Ireland. TEL 353-61-471944. FAX 353-61-472144. *4837*

EVOLUTION.
Allen Press, Inc., 1041 New Hampshire Ave., Box 1897, Lawrence, KS 66044-8897. FAX 913-843-1274. *740*

EVOLUTION OF COMMUNICATION.
John Benjamins Publishing Co., Amsteldijk 44, P.O. Box 75577, 1070 AN Amsterdam, Netherlands. TEL 31-20-6762325. FAX 31-20-6792956. *4068*

EVOLUTIONARY ANTHROPOLOGY.
John Wiley & Sons, Inc., Journals, 605 Third Ave., New York, NY 10158-0012. TEL 212-850-6000. FAX 212-850-6088. *309*

EVOLUTIONARY BIOLOGY.
Plenum Publishing Corp., 233 Spring St., New York, NY 10013-1578. TEL 212-620-8000. FAX 212-463-0742. *741*

EVOLUTIONARY COMPUTATION.
M I T Press, 55 Hayward St., Cambridge, MA 02142. TEL 617-253-2889. FAX 617-577-1545. *710*

EVOLUTIONARY ECOLOGY.
Chapman & Hall, Journals Department 2-6 Boundary Row, London SE1 8HN, England. TEL 44-171-8650066. FAX 44-171-5229623. *2796*

EVOLUTIONARY MONOGRAPHS.
University of Chicago, Department of Ecology and Evolution, 1101 E. 57th St., Chicago, IL 60637. TEL 312-702-9475. *582*

EVOLUTIONARY THEORY.
University of Chicago, Department of Ecology and Evolution, 1101 E. 57th St., Chicago, IL 60637. TEL 312-702-9475. *582*

THE EXAMINER (RALEIGH).
Society of Financial Examiners, 4101 Lake Boone Trail, No. 201, Raleigh, NC 27607. TEL 919-787-5181. FAX 919-787-4961. *1046*

EXCEPTIONAL CHILDREN.
Council for Exceptional Children, 1920 Association Dr., Reston, VA 22091. TEL 703-620-3660. FAX 703-264-9494. *1767*

EXCEPTIONAL HUMAN EXPERIENCE.
Exceptional Human Experience Network, Inc., 414 Rockledge Rd., New Bern, NC 28562. TEL 919-636-8734. FAX 919-636-8371. *5334*

EXCEPTIONALITY EDUCATION CANADA.
University of Calgary Press, 2500 University Dr. N.W., Calgary, AB T2N 1N4, Canada. TEL 403-220-7578. FAX 403-282-0085. *2468*

EXCHANGE.
E.J. Brill, P.O. Box 9000, 2300 PA Leiden, Netherlands. TEL 31-71-5353500. FAX 31-71-5317532. *6061*

EXECUTIVE ENGINEER.
Institution of Incorporated Executive Engineers, Wix Hill House, W. Housley, Surrey KT24 6DZ, England. TEL 44-1483-222383. FAX 44-1483-211109. *2599*

EXECUTIVE HOUSEKEEPING TODAY.
National Executive Housekeepers Association, 1001 Eastwind Dr., Ste. 301, Westerville, OH 43081. TEL 614-895-7166. FAX 614-895-1248. *5248*

EXECUTIVE SYSTEMS INTERNATIONAL.
Business Intelligence Publishing, 25 Prospect Rd., Southborough, Tunbridge Wells, Kent TN4 0EL, England. TEL 01892-517340. FAX 01892-517476. *1154*

EXEMPLARIA.
Medieval and Renaissance Texts and Studies, LNG 99, Box 6000, State University of New York, Binghamton, NY 13902-6000. TEL 607-777-6758. FAX 607-777-2408. *4209*

EXLIBRISKUNST UND GRAPHIK. JAHRBUCH.
Deutsche Exlibris-Gesellschaft e.V., Ringstr. 109, 78465 Konstanz, Germany. TEL 49-7533-6882. FAX 49-7533-6882. *428*

EXPEDITION.
University of Pennsylvania Museum, 33rd & Spruce Sts., Philadelphia, PA 19104-6324. TEL 215-898-0023. FAX 215-898-0657. *309*

EXPERIMENTAL & APPLIED ACAROLOGY.
Chapman & Hall, Journals Department 2-6 Boundary Row, London SE1 8HN, England. TEL 44-171-8560066. FAX 44-171-5229623. *582*

EXPERIMENTAL AND CLINICAL IMMUNOGENETICS.
S. Karger AG, Allschwilerstr. 10, P.O. Box, CH-4009 Basel, Switzerland. TEL 061-3061111. FAX 061-3061234. *741*

EXPERIMENTAL AND MOLECULAR MEDICINE.
Korean Society of Medical Biochemistry and Molecular Biology, No. 12 KOFST, 635-4 Yeoksam-dong, Kangnam-gu, Seoul 135-703, S. Korea. TEL 82-2-565-1621. FAX 82-2-565-1622. *639*

EXPERIMENTAL AND MOLECULAR PATHOLOGY.
Academic Press, Inc., Journal Division, 525 B St., Ste. 1900, San Diego, CA 92101-4495. TEL 619-230-1840. FAX 619-699-6800. *4453*

EXPERIMENTAL ASTRONOMY.
Kluwer Academic Publishers, Postbus 17, 3300 AA Dordrecht, Netherlands. TEL 31-78-6392392. FAX 31-78-6392254. *480*

EXPERIMENTAL CELL RESEARCH.
Academic Press, Inc., Journal Division, 525 B St., Ste. 1900, San Diego, CA 92101-4495. TEL 619-230-1840. FAX 619-699-6800. *714*

EXPERIMENTAL DERMATOLOGY.
Munksgaard International Publishers Ltd., 35 Noerre Soegade, P.O. Box 2148, DK-1016 Copenhagen K, Denmark. TEL 45-33-127030. FAX 45-33-129387. *4661*

EXPERIMENTAL EYE RESEARCH.
Academic Press Ltd. 24-28 Oval Rd., London NW1 7DX, England. TEL 44-171-267-4466. FAX 44-171-482-2293. *4769*

EXPERIMENTAL GERONTOLOGY.
Elsevier Science Inc., Box 945, New York, NY 10159-0945. TEL 212-633-3730. FAX 212-633-3680. *3286*

EXPERIMENTAL HEAT TRANSFER.
Taylor & Francis Inc., 1900 Frost Rd., Ste. 101, Bristol, PA 19007-1598. TEL 215-785-5800. FAX 215-785-5515. *5584*

EXPERIMENTAL LUNG RESEARCH.
Taylor & Francis Inc., 1900 Frost Rd., Ste. 101, Bristol, PA 19007-1598. TEL 215-785-5800. FAX 215-785-5515. *4887*

EXPERIMENTAL MATHEMATICS.
A.K. Peters, Ltd., 289 Linden St., Wellesley, MA 02181. TEL 617-235-2210. FAX 617-235-2404. *4364*

EXPERIMENTAL MECHANICS.
Sage Publications, Inc., Sage Science Press, 2455 Teller Rd., Thousand Oaks, CA 91320. TEL 805-499-0721. FAX 805-499-0871. *2731*

EXPERIMENTAL METHODS IN THE PHYSICAL SCIENCES.
Academic Press, Inc., 525 B St., Ste. 1900, San Diego, CA 92101-4495. TEL 619-231-0926. FAX 619-699-6715. *5547*

EXPERIMENTAL NEPHROLOGY.
S. Karger AG, Allschwilerstr. 10, P.O. Box, CH-4009 Basel, Switzerland. TEL 061-3061111. FAX 061-3061235. *4926*

EXPERIMENTAL NEUROLOGY.
Academic Press, Inc., Journal Division, 525 B St., Ste. 1900, San Diego, CA 92101-4495. TEL 619-230-1840. FAX 619-699-6800. *4837*

EXPERIMENTAL PARASITOLOGY.
Academic Press, Inc., Journal Division, 525 B St., Ste. 1900, San Diego, CA 92101-4495. TEL 619-230-1840. FAX 619-699-6800. *4620*

EXPERIMENTAL TECHNIQUES.
Society for Experimental Mechanics, 7 School St., Bethel, CT 06801. TEL 203-790-6373. FAX 203-790-4472. *2731*

EXPERIMENTAL THERMAL AND FLUID SCIENCE.
Elsevier Science Inc., Box 945, New York, NY 10159-0945. TEL 212-633-3730. FAX 212-633-3680. *2599*

EXPERIMENTAL VIROLOGY.
Academic Press, Inc., 525 B St., Ste. 1900, San Diego, CA 92101-4495. TEL 619-231-0926. FAX 619-699-6715. *756*

EXPERT OPINION IN INVESTIGATIONAL DRUGS.
Ashley Publications Ltd., First Fl., The Library, 1 Shepherds Hill, Highgate, London N6 5QJ, England. TEL 44-181-347-5030. FAX 44-181-181-5040. *5412*

EXPERT OPINION ON THERAPEUTIC PATENTS.
Ashley Publications Ltd., First Fl., The Library, 1 Shepherds Hill, Highgate, London N6 5QJ, England. TEL 44-181-347-5030. FAX 44-181-347-5040. *5412*

EXPERT SYSTEMS WITH APPLICATIONS.
Elsevier Science Ltd., Pergamon, P.O. Box 800, Kidlington, Oxford OX5 1DX, England. TEL 44-1865-843000. FAX 44-1865-843010. *2055*

EXPLICACION DE TEXTOS LITERARIOS.
California State University, Sacramento, Department of Foreign Languages, 6000 J St., Sacramento, CA 95819-6087. TEL 916-454-6011. FAX 916-278-5502. *4209*

THE EXPLICATOR.
Heldref Publications, 1319 Eighteenth St., N.W., Washington, DC 20036-1802. TEL 202-296-6267. FAX 202-296-5149. *4209*

EXPLORATION & MINING GEOLOGY.
Elsevier Science Ltd., Pergamon, P.O. Box 800, Kidlington, Oxford OX5 1DX, England. TEL 44-1865-843000. FAX 44-1865-843010. *2232*

EXPLORATIONS.
University of Alaska Southeast, English Department, 11120 Glacier Hwy., Juneau, AK 99801-8761. TEL 907-465-6418. FAX 907-465-6406. *4209*

EXPLORATIONS IN ETHNIC STUDIES.
National Association for Ethnic Studies, Inc., Dept. of English, Arizona State University, Tempe, AZ 85287-0302. TEL 602-965-2197. FAX 602-965-3451. *2878*

EXPLORATIONS IN KNOWLEDGE.
Sombourne Press, 294 Leigh Rd., Chandlers Ford, Hants. SO5 3AU, England. TEL 01703-269687. *5475*

EXPLORATIONS IN RENAISSANCE CULTURE.
Southwest Missouri State University, Department of English, Springfield, MO 65804. TEL 417-836-5107. FAX 417-836-6940. *3613*

EXPLORER (LAKE WORTH).
Atlantic Coast District Dental Association, 5700 Lake Worth Rd., Ste. 206, Lake Worth, FL 33463. TEL 407-968-7714. FAX 407-968-4834. *4641*

EXPLORING THE ROMAN WORLD.
University of California Press, 2120 Berkeley Way, Berkeley, CA 94720. TEL 510-642-4247. FAX 510-643-7127. *1821*

EXPOSURE (DALLAS).
Society for Photographic Education, Box 222116, Dallas, TX 75222-2116. TEL 817-272-2845. FAX 817-272-2846. *5511*

EXPRESSIONS (GREENVILLE).
Box 4064, Greenville, DE 19807. TEL 610-869-4060. FAX 610-869-4060. *4305*

EXQUISITE CORPSE.
Illinois State University, Campus Box 4241, Normal, IL 61790-4241. *4142*

EXTRAPOLATION.
Kent State University Press, Box 5190, Kent, OH 44242-0001. TEL 330-672-7913. FAX 330-672-3104. *4326*

EXTREMOPHILES.
Springer-Verlag Tokyo, 3-13, Hongo 3-chome, Bunkyo-ku, Tokyo 113, Japan. TEL 03-38120331. FAX 03-38120719. *661*

EYE ON IMPROVEMENT.
Institute for Healthcare Improvement, Box 38100, Cleveland, OH 44138-0100. TEL 216-235-8580. FAX 216-235-2714. *3543*

EYE SCIENCE.
Sun Yat-sen University of Medical Sciences, Zhongshan Ophthalmic Center, 54 Xianlie Rd., Guangzhou, Guangdong 510060, People's Republic of China. *4769*

EYEOPENER.
Rye Eye Publishing Inc, 380 Victoria, Rm. A-54, Toronto, ON M5B 1W7, Canada. TEL 416-595-1490. FAX 416-595-1374. *1867*

F A M - FIRE AND MATERIALS.
John Wiley & Sons Ltd., Journals, Baffins Ln., Chichester, W. Sussex PO19 1UD, England. TEL 44-1243-779777. FAX 44-1243-843232. *1750*

F A R M S REVIEW OF BOOKS.
Foundation for Ancient Research and Mormon Studies; Box 7113, University Sta., Provo, UT 84602. TEL 801-378-3295. FAX 801-373-5342. *6205*

F A S E B JOURNAL.
Federation of American Societies for Experimental Biology, 9650 Rockville Pike, Bethesda, MD 20814. TEL 301-530-7100. FAX 301-571-1855. *582*

F E E M SERIES ON ECONOMICS, ENERGY AND ENVIRONMENT.
Kluwer Academic Publishers, Postbus 17, 3300 AA Dordrecht, Netherlands. TEL 31-78-6392392. FAX 31-78-6392254. *2549*

F E M S. IMMUNOLOGY AND MEDICAL MICROBIOLOGY.
Elsevier Science B.V., P.O. Box 211, 1000 AE Amsterdam, Netherlands. TEL 31-20-4853911. FAX 31-20-4853598. *757*

F E M S. MICROBIOLOGY.
Elsevier Science B.V., P.O. Box 211, 1000 AE Amsterdam, Netherlands. TEL 31-20-4853911. FAX 31-20-4853598. *757*

F E M S. MICROBIOLOGY ECOLOGY.
Elsevier Science B.V., P.O. Box 211, 1000 AE Amsterdam, Netherlands. TEL 31-20-4853911. FAX 31-20-4853598. *757*

F E M S. MICROBIOLOGY LETTERS.
Elsevier Science B.V., P.O. Box 211, 1000 AE Amsterdam, Netherlands. TEL 31-20-4853911. FAX 31-20-4853598. *757*

F E M S. MICROBIOLOGY REVIEWS.
Elsevier Science B.V., P.O. Box 211, 1000 AE Amsterdam, Netherlands. TEL 31-20-4853911. FAX 31-20-4853598. *757*

F E M S SYMPOSIUM.
Plenum Publishing Corp., 233 Spring St., New York, NY 10013-1578. TEL 212-620-8000. FAX 212-463-0742. *757*

F F COMMUNICATIONS.
Suomalainen Tiedeakatemia, Mariankatu 5, FIN-00170 Helsinki, Finland. *2951*

F M R A NEWS.
American Society of Farm Managers and Rural Appraisers, 950 S. Cherry St., Ste. 508, Denver, CO 80222-2664. TEL 303-758-3513. FAX 303-758-0190. *191*

F P R D I JOURNAL.
Forest Products Research and Development Institute, College, Laguna 4031, Philippines. TEL 63-94-2360. FAX 63-94-3630. *3034*

F R I BULLETIN.
Forest Research Institute, Private Bag 3020, Rotorua, New Zealand *3014*

LE FABLIER.
Societe des Amis de Jean de la Fontaine, Musee Jean de la Fontaine, B.P. 284, 02400 Chateau-Thierry, France. TEL 23690560. *4209*

FABRIMETAL MAGAZINE.
Fabrimetal A.S.B.L., 21 rue des Drapiers, 1050 Brussels, Belgium. TEL 32-2-510-2311. FAX 32-2-510-2301. *4554*

FACIES.
Universitaet Erlangen - Nuernberg, Institut fuer Palaeontologie, Loewenichstr. 28, 91054 Erlangen, Germany. TEL 49-9131-852622. FAX 49-9131-852690. *2203*

FACTS.
African Oxygen Ltd., Box 5404, Johannesburg 2000, South Africa. TEL 27-11-490-0400. FAX 27-11-493-8828. *2595*

FAHRENHEIT 451.
Alpha Beat Press, 31 Waterloo St., New Hope, PA 18938. TEL 215-862-0299. *5727*

FAILURE & LESSONS LEARNED IN INFORMATION TECHNOLOGY MANAGEMENT.
Cognizant Communication Corporation, 3 Hartsdale Rd., Elmsford, NY 10523. TEL 914-592-7720. FAX 914-592-8981. *2020*

FALK SYMPOSIUM.
Kluwer Academic Publishers, Postbus 17, 3300 AA Dordrecht, Netherlands. TEL 31-78-6392392. FAX 31-78-6392254. *4554*

FALMER.
University of Sussex Society, Alumni Office, Sussex House, Falmer, Brighton BN1 9RH, England. TEL 44-1273-678258. FAX 44-1273-678335. *1868*

FAMILIA CRISTIANA.
Ediciones Paulinas, S.A., Apdo. 69-766, 04460 Coyoacan, Mexico D.F., Mexico. TEL 525-5491454. FAX 525-6709392. *6180*

FAMILIES IN SOCIETY.
Families International, Inc., 11700 W. Lake Park Dr., Milwaukee, WI 53224. TEL 414-359-1040. FAX 414-359-1074. *6371*

FAMILY BUSINESS REVIEW.
Jossey-Bass Inc., Publishers, 350 Sansome St., 5th Fl., San Francisco, CA 94104. TEL 415-433-1767. FAX 415-433-0499. *1575*

FAMILY ECONOMICS AND NUTRITION REVIEW.
U.S. Department of Agriculture, Center for Nutrition Policy and Promotion, 1120 20th St., N.W., Ste. 200, North Lobby, Washington, DC 20036. TEL 202-606-4816. FAX 202-208-2321. *3522*

FAMILY MEDIATION.
National Family Mediation, 9 Tavistock Pl., London WC1H 9SN, England. TEL 44-171-383-5993. FAX 44-171-383-5994. *6372*

FAMILY PLANNING PERSPECTIVES.
Alan Guttmacher Institute, 120 Wall St., New York, NY 10005. TEL 212-248-1111. FAX 212-248-1951. *4735*

FAMILY PRACTICE RECERTIFICATION.
M R A Publications, Inc., 2 Greenwich Office Park, Greenwich, CT 06831-5154. TEL 203-629-3550. FAX 203-629-2536. *4454*

FAMILY RESEARCH REPORT.
Family Research Institute, Inc., Box 62640, Colorado Springs, CO 80962. TEL 303-681-3113. FAX 303-681-3724. *3531*

FAMILY VIOLENCE & SEXUAL ASSAULT BULLETIN.
Family Violence & Sexual Assualt Institute, 1310 Clinic Dr., Tyler, TX 75701. TEL 903-595-6600. FAX 903-595-6799. *6372*

FAR EAST JOURNAL OF MATHEMATICAL SCIENCES.
Pushpa Publishing House, VIJAYA NIWAS, 198, Mumfordganj, Allahabad 2 1 002, India. TEL 532-64078. FAX 532-623221. *4364*

FARADAY DISCUSSIONS.
The Royal Society of Chemistry, Thomas Graham House, Science Park, Milton Rd., Cambridge CB4 4WF, England. TEL 44-1223-420066. FAX 44-1223-423429. *1750*

FARADAY TRANSACTIONS.
The Royal Society of Chemistry, Thomas Graham House, Science Park, Milton Rd., Cambridge CB4 4WF, England. TEL 44-1223-420066. FAX 44-1223-423623. *1751*

FARAVID.
Pohjois-Suomen Historiallinen Yhdistys, Oulun Yliopisto, Historian Laitos, Postilokero 111, FIN-90571 Oulu, Finland. FAX 358-81-5533315. *3410*

FARM GATE.
North Waterloo Publishing, 15 King St., Elmira, ON N3B 2R1, Canada. TEL 519-669-5155. FAX 519-669-5928. *115*

FARM TIMES, INCORPORATED.
Farm Times, Box 158, Rupert, ID 83350. TEL 208-436-1111. FAX 208-436-9455. *115*

FASCIST.
Box 6381, Minneapolis, MN 55406. *4142*

FAT TUESDAY.
Fat Tuesday Productions, 560 Manada Gap Rd., Grantville, PA 17028. TEL 717-469-7159. *4210*

FATIGUE & FRACTURE OF ENGINEERING MATERIALS AND STRUCTURES.
Structural Integrity Research Institute, University of Sheffield, Sheffield S1 3JD, England. TEL 44-114-282-5239. FAX 44-114-275-3671. *2599*

FAUNA ENTOMOLOGICA SCANDINAVICA.
E.J. Brill, P.O. Box 9000, 2300 PA Leiden, Netherlands. TEL 31-71-5353500. FAX 31-71-5317532. *727*

FAUNA NORVEGICA SERIES A. NORWEGIAN FAUNA EXCEPT ENTOMOLOGY AND ORNITHOLOGY.
Norsk Institutt for Naturforskning (NINA), c/o Kjetil Bevanger, Tungasletta 2, N-7005 Trondheim, Norway. TEL 47-73-58-05-00. FAX 47-73-91-54-33. *805*

FAUNA PALAESTINA.
Israel Academy of Sciences and Humanities, 43 Jabotinsky St., P.O. Box 4040, 91040 Jerusalem, Israel. TEL 972-2-636211. FAX 972-2-666059. *805*

FAUNA SLODKOWODNA POLSKI.
Wydawnictwo Naukowe P W N, Ul. Miodowa 10, 00-251 Warsaw, Poland. TEL 48-22-260207. FAX 48-22-267163. *805*

FAUX TITRE.
Editions Rodopi B.V., Keizersgracht 302-304, 1016 EX Amsterdam, Netherlands. TEL 31-20-6227507. FAX 31-20-6380948. *4142*

FEDERAL BENEFITS FOR VETERANS AND DEPENDENTS.
U.S. Department of Veterans Affairs, Office of Public Affairs, 810 Vermont Ave., Washington, DC 20420. *3648*

FEDERAL INFORMATION PROCESSING STANDARDS PUBLICATION.
U.S. National Institute of Standards and Technology, Gaithersburg, MD 20899. TEL 301-975-3058. *5013*

FEDERAL RESERVE BANK OF MINNEAPOLIS. QUARTERLY REVIEW.
Federal Reserve Bank of Minneapolis, 250 Marquette Ave., Minneapolis, MN 55401-2171. TEL 612-340-2341. FAX 612-340-2366. *1088*

FEDERAL SENTENCING REPORTER.
University of California Press, Journals Division, 2120 Berkeley Way, No. 5812, Berkeley, CA 94720-5812. TEL 510-643-7154. FAX 510-642-9917. *2164*

FELINE PRACTICE.
Veterinary Practice Publishing Co., 7 Ashley Ave. S., Santa Barbara, CA 93103-9989. TEL 805-965-1028. FAX 805-965-0722. *6946*

FELLOWSHIP.
Fellowship of Reconciliation, 521 N. Broadway, Box 271, Nyack, NY 10960. TEL 914-358-4601. FAX 914-358-4924. *5666*

FEMALE PATIENT: PRACTICAL OB-GYN MEDICINE.
Quadrant HealthCom, 105 Raider Blvd., Belle Mead, NJ 08502-1510. TEL 908-874-0707. FAX 908-874-5611. *4735*

FEMINARIA.
C.C. 402, 1000 Buenos Aires, Argentina. TEL 54-1-5683029. *7016*

FEMINISM & PSYCHOLOGY.
Sage Publications Ltd., 6 Bonhill St., London EC2A 4PU, England. TEL 44-171-374-0645. FAX 44-171-374-8741. *5844*

FEMINIST LEGAL STUDIES.
Deborah Charles Publications, 173 Mather Ave., Liverpool L18 6JZ, England. TEL 0151-724-2500. FAX 0151-729-0371. *3778*

FENGJING MINGSHENG.
Hangzhou Yuanlin Wenwu Guanliju, 12 Jiangyuan Nong, Xiaoying Xiang, Hangzhou, Zhejiang 310003, People's Republic of China. TEL 86-571-711944. FAX 86-571-7027890. *6881*

FERN GAZETTE.
British Pteridological Society, c/o Botany Department, Natural History Museum, Cromwell Rd., London SW7 5BD, England. TEL 44-171-938-9497. *680*

FERNSTROM FOUNDATION SERIES.
Elsevier Science B.V., Books Division, P.O. Box 211, 1000 AE Amsterdam, Netherlands. TEL 31-20-4853911. FAX 31-20-4853705. *4455*

FERROELECTRICITY AND RELATED PHENOMENA.
Gordon & Breach Science Publishers, c/o International Publishers Distributor, P.O. Box 3054, Langhorne, PA 19047-3054. TEL 215-750-2642. FAX 215-750-6343. *2698*

FERROELECTRICS.
Gordon and Breach Science Publishers, c/o International Publishers Distributor, P.O. Box 3054, Langhorne, PA 19047-3054. TEL 215-750-2642. FAX 215-750-6343. *5547*

FERROELECTRICS LETTERS.
Gordon & Breach Science Publishers, c/o International Publishers Distributors, P.O. Box 3054, Langhorne, PA 19047-3054. TEL 215-750-2642. FAX 215-750-6343. *2698*

FERTILITY AND STERILITY.
American Society for Reproductive Medicine, 1209 Montgomery Hwy., Birmingham, AL 35216-2809. TEL 205-978-5000. FAX 205-978-5005. *4735*

FERTILIZER SCIENCE AND TECHNOLOGY SERIES.
Marcel Dekker, Inc., 270 Madison Ave., New York, NY 10016. TEL 212-696-9000. FAX 212-658-4540. *221*

FESTIVAL MANAGEMENT & EVENT TOURISM.
Cognizant Communication Corporation, 3 Hartsdale Rd., Elmsford, NY 10523-3701. TEL 914-592-7720. FAX 914-592-8981. *6881*

FETAL AND MATERNAL MEDICINE REVIEW.
Cambridge University Press, Edinburgh Bldg., Shaftebury Rd., Cambridge CB2 2RU, England. TEL 44-1223-312393. FAX 44-1223-315052. *4736*

FETAL DIAGNOSIS AND THERAPY.
S. Karger AG, Allschwilerstr. 10, P.O. Box, CH-4009 Basel, Switzerland. TEL 061-3061111. FAX 061-3061234. *4736*

FIBER AND INTEGRATED OPTICS.
Taylor & Francis Inc., 1900 Frost Rd., Ste. 101, Bristol, PA 19007. TEL 215-785-5800. FAX 215-785-5515. *5602*

THE FIBONACCI QUARTERLY.
Fibonacci Association, c/o South Dakota State University, Computer Science Dept., Box 2201, Brookings, SD 57007-1596. TEL 605-688-5719. FAX 605-688-5878. *4364*

FIBRE CHEMISTRY.
Plenum Publishing Corp., Consultants Bureau, 233 Spring St., New York, NY 10013-1578. TEL 212-620-8468. FAX 212-463-0742. *6677*

FICHTE-STUDIEN.
Editions Rodopi B.V., Keizersgracht 302-304, 1016 EX Amsterdam, Netherlands. TEL 31-20-6227507. FAX 31-20-6380948. *5475*

FIDES ET HISTORIA.
Conference on Faith and History, c/o Richard V. Pierard, Dept. of History, Indiana State University, Terre Haute, IN 47809. TEL 812-232-2707. *3342*

FIELD.
Oberlin College, Rice Hall, Oberlin, OH 44074. TEL 216-775-8408. FAX 216-775-8124. *4306*

FIELD CROPS RESEARCH.
Elsevier Science B.V., P.O. Box 211, 1000 AE Amsterdam, Netherlands. TEL 31-20-4853911. FAX 31-20-4853598. *221*

FIELD GUIDE TO FOSSILS.
Palaeontological Association, c/o Andy King, Environmental Impacts Team, Northminster House, Peterborough PE1 1UA, England. *5313*

FIELD STUDIES.
Field Studies Council, Central Services, Preston Montford, Montford Bridge, Shrewsbury, Shrops. SY4 1HW, England. TEL 01743-850674. FAX 01743-850178. *2796*

FIELDIANA: ANTHROPOLOGY.
Field Museum Press, Roosevelt Rd. at Lake Shore Dr., Chicago, IL 60605-2498. TEL 312-922-9410. FAX 312-427-7269. *309*

FIELDIANA: BOTANY.
Field Museum Press, Roosevelt Rd. at Lake Shore Dr., Chicago, IL 60605-2498. TEL 312-922-9410. FAX 312-427-7269. *680*

FIELDIANA: GEOLOGY.
Field Museum Press, Roosevelt Rd. at Lake Shore Dr., Chicago, IL 60605-2498. TEL 312-922-9410. FAX 312-427-7269. *2232*

FIELDIANA: ZOOLOGY.
Field Museum Press, Roosevelt Rd. at Lake Shore Dr., Chicago, IL 60605-2498. TEL 312-922-9410. FAX 312-427-7269. *805*

FILM HISTORIA.
Promocions, Publicacions Universitaries, Marques del Campo Sagrado, 16, 08015 Barcelona, Spain. TEL 34-3-4420391. *5101*

FILM HISTORY.
John Libbey Media, University of Luton, 75 Castle St., Luton, Bedfordshire LU1 3AJ, England. TEL 44-1582-743297. FAX 44-1582-743298. *5101*

FILM QUARTERLY.
University of California Press, Journals Division, 2120 Berkeley Way, No. 5812, Berkeley, CA 94720-5812. TEL 510-643-7154. FAX 510-642-9917. *5102*

FILOLOGIA ANTICA E MODERNA.
Universita degli Studi della Calabria, Dipartimento di Filologia, 87036 Arcavacata di Rende (Cosenza), Italy. TEL 39-984-493128. FAX 39-984-493163. *4210*

FILTRATION & SEPARATION.
Elsevier Science Ltd., P.O. Box 800, Kidlington, Oxford OX5 1DX, England. TEL 44-1865-843000. FAX 44-1865-843010. *2640*

FINANCE AND STOCHASTICS.
Springer-Verlag, Heidelberger Platz 3, 14197 Berlin, Germany. TEL 49-30-82787358. FAX 49-30-82787448. *1089*

FINANCE INDIA.
Indian Institute of Finance, P.O. Box 8486, Ashok Vihar, Delhi 110052, India. TEL 91-7125791. FAX 91-9234472. *1089*

FINANCIAL ACCOUNTABILITY & MANAGEMENT.
Blackwell Publishers Ltd., 108 Cowley Rd., Oxford OX4 1JF, England. TEL 44-1865-791100. FAX 44-1865-791347. *1544*

FINANCIAL AND MONETARY POLICY STUDIES.
Kluwer Academic Publishers, Postbus 17, 3300 AA Dordrecht, Netherlands. TEL 31-78-6392392. FAX 31-78-6392254. *1089*

FINANCIAL ENGINEERING AND THE JAPANESE MARKETS.
Kluwer Academic Publishers, Postbus 17, 3300 AA Dordrecht, Netherlands. TEL 31-78-6392392. FAX 31-78-6392254. *1129*

FINANCIAL EXECUTIVE.
Financial Executives Institute, 10 Madison Ave., Box 1938, Morristown, NJ 07962-1938. TEL 201-898-4621. FAX 201-267-4031. *1418*

FINANCIAL HISTORY REVIEW.
Cambridge University Press, The Edinburgh Bldg., Shaftesbury Rd., Cambridge CB2 2RU, England. TEL 44-1223-312393. FAX 44-1223-315052. *1090*

FINANCIAL MANAGEMENT.
Financial Management Association, University of South Florida, College of Business, Tampa, FL 33620. TEL 813-974-2084. FAX 813-974-3318. *1418*

FINANCIAL PRACTICE AND EDUCATION.
Financial Management Association, Univ. of South Florida, College of Bus. Admin. 3331, Tampa, FL 33620. TEL 813-974-2084. FAX 813-974-3318. *1091*

FINANCIAL REVIEW (STATESBORO).
Eastern Finance Association, c/o Univ. of Tennessee, 426 Stokley Management Ctr., Knoxville, TN 37996-0540. TEL 423-974-1713. FAX 423-974-1716. *1091*

FINITE ELEMENTS IN ANALYSIS AND DESIGN.
North-Holland P.O. Box 211, 1000 AE Amsterdam, Netherlands. TEL 31-20-4853911. FAX 31-20-4853598. *2679*

FINITE FIELDS AND THEIR APPLICATIONS.
Academic Press, Inc., Journal Division, 525 B St., Ste. 1900, San Diego, CA 92101-4495. TEL 619-230-1840. FAX 619-688-6800. *4364*

FIRE AUSTRALIA.
Australian Fire Protection Association Pty. Ltd., P.O. Box 456, Canberwell, Vic. 3124, Australia. *2919*

FIRE SAFETY JOURNAL.
Elsevier Science Ltd., P.O. Box 800, Kidlington, Oxford OX5 1DX, England. TEL 44-1865-843000. FAX 44-1865-843010. *2920*

FIRE TECHNOLOGY.
National Fire Protection Association, 1 Batterymarch Park, Quincy, MA 02269. TEL 617-984-7562. FAX 617-984-7010. *2920*

FIREWEED.
Fireweed Inc., Box 279, Sta. B, Toronto, ON M5T 2W2, Canada. TEL 416-504-1339. *6994*

FIRST BREAK.
Blackwell Science Ltd., Osney Mead, Oxford OX2 0EL, England. TEL 44-1865-206206. FAX 44-1865-721205. *2273*

FIRST MONDAY.
Munksgaard International Publishers Ltd., Noerre Soegade 35, P.O. Box 2148, DK-1016 Copenhagen, Denmark. TEL 45-33-127030. *2037*

FIRUDO BAIOROJISUTO.
Gunma Yagai Seibutsu Gakkai, c/o Mr. S. Saito, Gunma Pref. Women's University, 1395 Kaminote, Tamamuramachi, Sawa-gun, Gunma-ken 370-11, Japan. TEL 0270-65-8511. FAX 0270-65-9538. *583*

FISCAL STUDIES.
Institute of Fiscal Studies, 7 Ridgmount St., London WC1E 7AE, England. TEL 44-171-636-3784. FAX 44-171-323-4780. *1545*

FISH AND SHELLFISH IMMUNOLOGY.
Academic Press Ltd. 24-28 Oval Rd., London NW1 7DX, England. TEL 44-171-267-4466. FAX 44-171-482-2293. *583*

FISHERIES.
American Fisheries Society, 5410 Grosvenor Ln., Ste. 110, Bethesda, MD 20814-2199. TEL 301-897-8616. FAX 301-897-8096. *2931*

FISHERIES OCEANOGRAPHY.
Blackwell Science Ltd., Osney Mead, Oxford OX2 0EL, England. TEL 44-1865-206206. FAX 44-1865-721205. *2931*

FISHERIES RESEARCH.
Elsevier Science B.V., P.O. Box 211, 1000 AE Amsterdam, Netherlands. TEL 31-20-4853911. FAX 31-20-4853598. *2931*

FISHERY BULLETIN.
U.S. National Marine Fisheries Service, Scientific Publications Office, 7600 Sandpoint Way, N.E., Bin C15700, Seattle, WA 98115. TEL 206-526-6107. FAX 206-526-6426. *2932*

FISHERY TECHNOLOGY.
Society of Fisheries Technologists (India), Matsyapuri P.O., Cochin 682029, India. TEL 91-484-666845. FAX 91-484-668212. *2932*

FISICA DE LA TIERRA.
Universidad Complutense de Madrid, Facultad de Fisica, Academia 4, 28014 Madrid, Spain. *2273*

FITOPATOLOGIA.
Asociacion Latinoamericana de Fitopatologia, Apdo. 1558, Lima 100, Peru. FAX 51-1-4351570. *680*

FITOSSANIDADE.
Fitossanitaristas do Ceara, Rua Livreiro Edesio, 612-401, 60135-620 Fortaleza, Ceara, Brazil. TEL 55-85-2571242. FAX 55-85-2438442. *680*

FIZIK TEDAVI REHABILITASYON DERGISI.
Turkiye Fiziksel Tip ve Rehabilitasyon Dernegi, Capa, 34390 Istanbul, Turkey. TEL 90-212-6330505. FAX 90-212-6321144. *4817*

FLAGSCAN.
Canadian Flag Association, 50 Heathfield Dr., Scarborough, ON M1M 3B1, Canada. TEL 416-267-9618. FAX 415-267-9618. *3083*

FLANNERY O'CONNOR BULLETIN.
Georgia College, Department of English and Speech, Box 44, Milledgeville, GA 31061. TEL 912-453-4581. *4211*

FLETCHER FORUM OF WORLD AFFAIRS.
Fletcher School of Law and Diplomacy, Tufts University, Medford, MA 02155. TEL 617-623-3610. FAX 617-627-3979. *5750*

FLORA MALESIANA. SERIES 1: SPERMATOPHYTA.
Rijksherbarium - Hortus Botanicus, Publications Department, P.O. Box 9514, 2300 RA Leiden, Netherlands. *581*

FLORA MALESIANA. SERIES 2: PTERIDOPHYTA.
Rijksherbarium - Hortus Botanicus, Publications Department, P.O. Box 9514, 2300 RA Leiden, Netherlands. *681*

FLORA MALESIANA BULLETIN.
Rijksherbarium - Hortus Botanicus, Publications Department, P.O. Box 9514, 2300 RA Leiden, Netherlands. *681*

FLORA NEOTROPICA.
New York Botanical Garden, Scientific Publications Department, Bronx, NY 10458-5126. TEL 718-817-8721. FAX 718-817-8842. *681*

FLORA OG FAUNA.
Naturhistorisk Forening for Jylland, c/o Thomas Secher Jensen, Afdeling for Zoologi, Aarhus Universitet, bygn. 135, DK-8000 Aarhus C, Denmark. TEL 45-89-42-27-58. FAX 45-86-12-51-75. *6240*

FLORA PALAESTINA.
Israel Academy of Sciences and Humanities, 43 Jabotinsky St., P.O Box 4040, Jerusalem 91040, Israel. *681*

FLORA POLSKA: GRZYBY (MYCOTA).
Polska Akademia Nauk, Instytut Botaniki im. W. Szafera, Ul. Lubicz 46, 31-512 Krakow, Poland. TEL 48-12-215144. FAX 48-12-219790. *681*

FLORESTA.
Fundacao de Pesquisas Florestais do Parana, Caixa Postal 4088 82501-970 Curitiba, PR, Brazil. TEL 55-41-352-2443. FAX 55-41-253-2332. *3014*

FLORIDA ANTHROPOLOGIST.
Florida Anthropological Society, Inc., Box 82255, Tampa, FL 33682-2255. TEL 813-821-7600. FAX 813-822-2368. *309*

FLORIDA EDUCATIONAL RESEARCH COUNCIL. RESEARCH BULLETIN.
Florida Educational Research Council, Inc., Box 506, Sanibel, FL 33957. TEL 813-472-4397. *2335*

FLORIDA ENTOMOLOGIST.
Florida Entomological Society, 1321 N.W. 31st Dr., Gainesville, FL 32605. TEL 813-324-5502. FAX 904-374-5852. *727*

FLORIDA FAMILY PHYSICIAN.
Journalistic, Inc., 4905 Pine Cone Dr., Durham, NC 27707. TEL 919-489-1916. FAX 919-489-4767. *4455*

FLORIDA FIELD NATURALIST.
Florida Ornithological Society, Florida State Museum, University of Florida, Gainesville, FL 32611. TEL 904-376-6481. *776*

FLORIDA GEOGRAPHER.
Florida Society of Geographers, c/o College of Liberal Arts, Florida Atlantic Univ. 2912 College Ave., Davie, FL 33314. TEL 305-476-4580. FAX 305-476-4582. *3254*

FLORIDA GROCER.
Florida Grocer Publications, Inc., Box 430760, S. Miami, FL 33243-0760. TEL 305-441-1138. FAX 305-661-6720. *3034*

FLORIDA JOURNAL OF ANTHROPOLOGY.
University of Florida, Department of Anthropology, 1350 GPA, Gainesville, FL 32611. TEL 904-392-2031. FAX 904-392-6929. *310*

FLORIDA LIBRARIES.
Florica Library Association 1135 W. Morse Blvd., No. 201, Winter Park, FL 32789-3788. TEL 407-647-8839. FAX 407-629-2502. *3993*

FLORIDA MEDICAL ASSOCIATION. JOURNAL.
Florida Medical Association, Inc., Box 2411, Jacksonville, FL 32203. TEL 904-356-1571. FAX 904-353-1247. *4435*

FLORIDA MOSQUITO CONTROL ASSOCIATION. JOURNAL.
Florida Mosquito Control Association, Inc., Box 11857, Jacksonville, FL 32239-1867. TEL 904-743-4482. FAX 904-743-6879 *727*

FLORIDA MUSIC DIRECTOR.
Florida Music Educators Association, c/o Vicki Miazga, Man. Ed., 207 Office Plaza Dr., Tallahassee, FL 32301. TEL 904-878-6844. FAX 904-942-1793. *5158*

FLORIDA READING QUARTERLY.
Florida Reading Association, 11775 Raintree Dr., Tampa, FL 33617-2706. TEL 813-988-0442. FAX 813-988-0442. *2335*

FLORIDA SCIENTIST.
Florida Academy of Sciences, Inc., Box 33012, Indialantic, FL 32903-0012. TEL 407-723-6835. *6240*

FLORIDA STATE UNIVERSITY RESEARCH IN REVIEW.
Florida State University, Office of Graduate Studies and Research, 109 HME R-23, Tallahassee, FL 32306. TEL 904-644-8634. *6240*

FLOW MEASUREMENT AND INSTRUMENTATION.
Butterworth - Heinemann Part of the Reed Elsevier group, Linacre House, Jordan Hill, Oxford OX2 8DP, England. TEL 44-1865-310366. FAX 44-1865-310898. *3634*

FLUID DYNAMICS.
Plenum Publishing Corp. Consultants Bureau, 233 Spring St., New York, NY 10013-1578. TEL 212-620-8468. FAX 212-463-0742. *5588*

FLUID DYNAMICS RESEARCH.
North-Holland P.O. Box 211, 1000 AE Amsterdam, Netherlands. TEL 31-20-4853911. FAX 31-20-4853598. *2743*

FLUID MECHANICS AND ITS APPLICATIONS.
Kluwer Academic Publishers, Postbus 17, 3300 AA Dordrecht, Netherlands. TEL 31-78-6392392. FAX 31-78-6392254. *5588*

FLUID MECHANICS OF ASTROPHYSICS AND GEOPHYSICS.
Gordon & Breach Science Publishers, c/o International Publishers Distributor, P.O. Box 3054, Langhorne, PA 19047-3054. TEL 215-750-2542. FAX 215-750-6343. *5588*

FLUID PHASE EQUILIBRIA.
Elsevier Science B.V., P.O. Box 211, 1000 AE Amsterdam, Netherlands. TEL 31-20-4853911. FAX 31-20-4853598. *1751*

FLUID POWER JOURNAL
Innovative Designs and Publishing, 4544 Pheasant Run, Bethlehem, PA 18017-9512. TEL 610-694-0650. FAX 610-694-0611. *2743*

FLUORIDE.
International Society for Fluoride Research, 81 A Landscape Rd., Mount Eden, Auckland, New Zealand. TEL 64-9-6307114. *4564*

FOCUS (GAITHERSBURG).
Life Technologies, Inc., Box 6009, Gaithersburg, MD 20884-9980. TEL 301-840-8000. *741*

FOCUS (WESTFIELD).
Westfield State College, Public Affairs Office, Western Ave., Westfield, MA 01086. TEL 413-572-5208. FAX 413-572-4843. *1868*

FOCUS ON AUTISM AND OTHER DEVELOPMENTAL DISABILITIES.
Pro-Ed Inc., 8700 Shoal Creek Blvd., Austin, TX 78757-6897. TEL 512-451-3246. FAX 512-451-8542. *4837*

FOCUS: SOCIAL AND PREVENTIVE MEDICINE.
Community Health Services Association, 455-2nd Ave. N., Saskatoon, SK S7K 2C2, Canada. TEL 306-664-4289. FAX 306-664-4120. *5960*

FOLIA BIOLOGICA.
Polska Akademia Nauk, Instytut Systematyki i Ewolucji Zwierzat, Ul. Slawkowska 17, 31-016 Krakow, Poland. TEL 48-12-227006. FAX 48-12-224294. *583*

FOLIA BIOTHEORETICA.
Kluwer Academic Publishers, Postbus 17, 3300 AA Dordrecht, Netherlands. TEL 31-78-6392392. FAX 31-78-6392254. *583*

FOLIA ENTOMOLOGICA MEXICANA.
Sociedad Mexicana de Entomologia, A.C., Consejo Editorial Folia Entomologica Mexicana, Apdo. Postal 63, 91000 Xalapa, Veracruz, Mexico. FAX 28-187809. *727*

FOLIA FORESTALIA.
Metsantutkimuslaitos, Unioninkatu 40 A, FIN-00170 Helsinki, Finland. TEL 358-0-857051. FAX 358-0-625308. *3014*

FOLIA GEOBOTANICA ET PHYTOTAXONOMICA.
Opulus Press AB, P.O. Box 25137, S-750 25 Uppsala, Sweden. TEL 46-18-320662. FAX 46-18-321368. *682*

FOLIA HISTOCHEMICA ET CYTOBIOLOGICA.
Polskie Towarzystwo Histochemikow i Cytochemikow, c/o P.O. Box 843, 30-960 Krakow 1, Poland. TEL 48-12-227027. *715*

FOLIA HORTICULTURAE.
Polskie Towarzystwo Nauk Ogrodniczych, Al. 29 Listopada 54, 31-425 Krakow, Poland. FAX 48-12-111322. *682*

FOLIA MORPHOLOGICA.
Polskie Towarzystwo Anatomiczne, c/o Akademia Medyczna w Poznaniu, Zaklad Anatomii, Ul. Swiecickiego 6, 60-781 Poznan, Poland. TEL 48-61-699181. FAX 48-61-658985. *583*

FOLIA NEUROPATHOLOGICA.
Stowarzyszenie Neuropatologow Polskish, Ul. Dworkowa 3, 00-784 Warsaw, Poland. TEL 48-22-496793. FAX 48-22-496973. *4837*

FOLIA OPHTHALMOLOGICA JAPONICA.
Association of Folia Ophthalmologica Japonica, 302-3-6- Mihogaoka, Ibaraki 567, Japan. TEL 81-726-23-7878. FAX 81-726-23-6060. *4770*

FOLIA PARASITOLOGICA.
Academy of Sciences of the Czech Republic, Parasitological Institute, Branisovska 31, 37005 Ceske Budejovice, Czech Republic. TEL 0042-38-41158. *4620*

FOLIA PHARMACOLOGICA JAPONICA.
Japanese Pharmacological Society, Editorial Office, Kantohya Bldg., Gokomachi-Ebisugawa, Nakagyo-ku, Kyoto 604, Japan. TEL 075-252-4641. FAX 075-252-4618. *5414*

FOLIA PHONIATRICA ET LOGOPAEDICA.
S. Karger AG, Allschwilerstr. 10, P.O. Box, CH-4009 Basel, Switzerland. TEL 061-3061111. FAX 061-3061234. *4796*

FOLIA PRIMATOLOGICA.
S. Karger AG, Allschwilerstr. 10, P.O. Box, CH-4009 Basel, Switzerland. TEL 061-3061111. FAX 061-3061234. *805*

FOLIA ZOOLOGICA.
Academy of Sciences of the Czech Republic, Institute of Landscape Ecology, Kvetna 8, 60365 Brno, Czech Republic. TEL 42-5-43321306. FAX 42-5-43211346. *805*

FOLKLORE & SOCIETY.
University of Illinois Press, 1325 S. Oak St., Champaign, IL 61820. TEL 217-333-0950. FAX 217-244-8082. *2951*

FOLKLORE FORUM.
Folklore Publications Group, Inc., 504 N. Fess, Bloomington, IN 47405. TEL 812-855-1027. *2952*

FOLKTALES OF THE WORLD.
University of Chicago Press, 5801 S. Ellis Ave., Chicago, IL 60637. TEL 312-702-7899. *2952*

FONDAZIONE LUIGI MICHELETTI. ANNALI.
Fondazione Luigi Micheletti, Via Cairoli, 9, 25122 Brescia, Italy. TEL 39-30-48578. FAX 39-30-45203. *3410*

FONTANUS.
McGill University Libraries, McLennan Library Bldg., 3459 McTavish St., Montreal, PQ H3A 1Y1, Canada. TEL 514-398-4740. FAX 514-398-7356. *3613*

FOOD ADDITIVES AND CONTAMINANTS.
Taylor & Francis Ltd., 1 Gunpowder Sq., London EC4A 3DE, England. TEL 44-171-583-0490. FAX 44-171-583-0585. *5414*

FOOD AND AGRICULTURAL IMMUNOLOGY.
Carfax Publishing Co., P.O. Box 25, Abingdon, Oxon. OX14 3UE, England. TEL 44-1235-401000. FAX 44-1235-401550. *583*

FOOD AND BIOPRODUCTS PROCESSING.
Institution of Chemical Engineers, George E. Davis Bldg., 165-189 Railway Terr., Rugby, CV21 3HQ, England. TEL 44-1788-78214. FAX 44-1788-578214. *661*

FOOD AND CHEMICAL TOXICOLOGY.
Elsevier Science Ltd., Pergamon, P.O. Box 800, Kidlington, Oxford OX5 1DX, England. TEL 44-1865-843000. FAX 44-1865-843010. *2845*

FOOD AND FOODWAYS.
Harwood Academic Publishers, c/o International Publishers Distributor, P.O. Box 3054, Langhorne, PA 19047-3054. TEL 215-750-2642. FAX 215-750-6343. *5232*

FOOD AND NUTRITION IN HISTORY AND ANTHROPOLOGY.
Gordon & Breach Science Publishers, c/o International Publishers Distributor, P.O. Box 3054, Langhorne, PA 19047-3054. TEL 215-750-2642. FAX 215-750-6343. *310*

FOOD BIOTECHNOLOGY.
Marcel Dekker Journals, 270 Madison Ave., New York, NY 10016. TEL 212-969-9000. FAX 212-685-4540. *661*

FOOD CHEMISTRY.
Elsevier Science Ltd., P.O. Box 800, Kidlington, Oxford OX5 1DX, England. TEL 44-1865-843000. FAX 44-1865-843010. *1675*

FOOD CONTROL.
Butterworth.- Heinemann, Part of the Reed Elsevier group, Linacre House, Jordan Hill, Oxford OX2 8DP, England. TEL 44-1865-310366. FAX 44-1865-310898. *2969*

FOOD HYGIENIC SOCIETY OF JAPAN. JOURNAL.
Food Hygienic Society of Japan, 2-6-1 Jingumae, Shibuya-ku, Tokyo 150, Japan. FAX 03-3470-2933. *5960*

FOOD POLICY.
Butterworth - Heinemann, Part of the Reed Elsevier group, Linacre House, Jordan Hill, Oxford OX2 8DP, England. TEL 44-1865-310366. FAX 44-1865-310898. *191*

FOOD QUALITY AND PREFERENCE.
Elsevier Science Ltd., P.O. Box 800, Kidlington, Oxford OX5 1DX, England. TEL 44-1865-843000. FAX 44-1865-843010. *2972*

FOOD RESEARCH INTERNATIONAL.
Elsevier Science Ltd., P.O. Box 800, Kidlington, Oxford OX5 1DX, England. TEL 44-1865-843000. FAX 44-1865-843010. *2972*

FOOD SCIENCE AND TECHNOLOGY SERIES.
Marcel Dekker, Inc., 270 Madison Ave., New York, NY 10016. TEL 212-696-9000. FAX 212-685-4540. *2972*

FOOD STRUCTURE.
Scanning Microscopy International, Inc., Box 66507, AMF O'Hare, Chicago, IL 60666-0507. TEL 312-529-6677. FAX 312-980-6698. *5233*

FOOD TECHNOLOGIST.
New Zealand Institute of Food Science and Technology, P.O. Box 35-187, Browns Bay, Auckland, New Zealand. TEL 64-4-4726722. FAX 64-9-4726722. *2973*

THE FOOT.
Churchill Livingstone Robert Stevenson House, 1-3 Baxter's Pl., Leith Walk, Edinburgh EH1 3AF, Scotland. TEL 0131-556-2424. FAX 0131-535-1704. *4783*

FOOT AND ANKLE CLINICS.
W.B. Saunders Co. Curtis Center, 3rd Fl., Independence Sq. W., Philadelphia, PA 19106-3399. TEL 215-238-7800. FAX 212-238-6445. *4784*

FOOT & ANKLE INTERNATIONAL.
Williams & Wilkins, 351 W. Camden St., Baltimore, MD 21201. TEL 410-528-4000. FAX 410-528-4312. *4784*

FOR THE RECORD (VALLEY FORGE).
Great Valley Publishing, Box 2224, Valley Forge, PA 19482. TEL 610-917-9300. FAX 610-917-9186. *4456*

FOREIGN LANGUAGE ANNALS.
American Council on the Teaching of Foreign Languages, Inc., 6 Executive Plaza, Yonkers, NY 10701-6801. TEL 914-963-8830. FAX 914-963-1275. *4069*

FORENSIC SCIENCE INTERNATIONAL.
Elsevier Science Ireland Ltd., P.O. Box 85, Limerick, Ireland. TEL 353-61-471944. FAX 353-61-472144. *4686*

FORENSISCHE PSYCHIATRIE UND PSYCHOTHERAPIE.
Pabst Science Publishers, Am Eichengrund 28, 49525 Lengerich, Germany. TEL 49-5484-308. FAX 49-5484-550. *5844*

FOREST & LANDSCAPE RESEARCH.
Danish Forest and Landscape Research Institute, Hoersholm Kongevej 11, DK-2970 Hoersholm, Denmark. TEL 45-45-76-32-00. FAX 45-45-76-32-33. *3014*

FOREST ECOLOGY AND MANAGEMENT.
Elsevier Science B.V., P.O. Box 211, 1000 AE Amsterdam, Netherlands. TEL 31-20-4853911. FAX 31-20-4853598. *3014*

FOREST GENETICS RESEARCH INSTITUTE. RESEARCH REPORT.
Forest Genetics Research Institute, P.O. Box 24, Suwon, Kyonggi-do 441-350, S. Korea. TEL 0331-290-1114. FAX 0331-292-4458. *3015*

FOREST SCIENCE.
Society of American Foresters, 5400 Grosvenor Ln., Bethesda, MD 20814. TEL 301-897-8720. FAX 301-897-3690. *3015*

FORESTS & PEOPLE.
Louisiana Forestry Association, Drawer 5067, Alexandria, LA 71307. TEL 318-443-2558. *3016*

FORMA.
K T K Scientific Publishers, 14-17 Midorigaoka 2-chome, Meguro-ku, Tokyo 152, Japan. *4365*

FORMAL LINGUISTICS SERIES.
Kluwer Academic Publishers, Postbus 17, 3300 AA Dordrecht, Netherlands. TEL 31-78-6392392. FAX 31-78-6392254. *4069*

FORMAL METHODS IN SYSTEM DESIGN.
Kluwer Academic Publishers Boston, Box 358, Accord Sta., Hingham, MA 02018-0358. TEL 617-871-6600. FAX 617-871-6528. *2055*

FORO HISPANICO.
Editions Rodopi B.V., Keizersgracht 302-304, 1016 EX Amsterdam, Netherlands. TEL 31-20-6227507. FAX 31-20-6380948. *4211*

FORT.
Fortress Study Group, c/o Athanassios Migos, Ed., Nearchos, 9 Rock Park, Rock Ferry, Wirral L42 1PJ, England. TEL 44-151-644-0761. FAX 44-151-707-2953. *5031*

FORT HARE PAPERS.
Fort Hare University Press, Private Bag X1314, Alice 5700, South Africa. TEL 27-404-22011. FAX 27-404-31255. *6241*

FORTSCHRITTE IN DER GEOLOGIE VON RHEINLAND UND WESTFALEN.
Geologisches Landesamt Nordrhein-Westfalen, Postfach 1080, 47710 Krefeld, Germany. TEL 49-2151-8971. FAX 49-2151-897505. *2233*

FORUM (SANTA ROSA).
Polebridge Press, 2120 Bluebell Dr., Box 6144, Santa Rosa, CA 95406. TEL 707-523-1323. FAX 707-523-1350. *6062*

FORUM FOR APPLIED RESEARCH AND PUBLIC POLICY.
University of Tennessee at Knoxville, Energy, Environment and Resources Center, 600 Henley St., Ste. 311, Knoxville, TN 37996-4134. TEL 423-974-4251. FAX 423-974-8491. *2797*

FORUM FOR READING.
University of Pittsburgh, School of Education, 5T01 Forbes Quadrangle, Pittsburgh, PA 15260. *2487*

FORUM FOR SOCIAL ECONOMICS.
Association for Social Economics, Department of Economics, Saint Louis University, 3674 Lindell Blvd., St. Louis, MO 63108. TEL 314-977-3814. FAX 314-977-3897. *1255*

FORUM ITALICUM.
State University of New York at Stony Brook, Center for Italian Studies, Stony Brook, NY 11794-3359. TEL 516-632-7444. *4211*

FORUM OF EDUCATION.
Sydney University, Faculty of Education, Sydney, N.S.W. 2066, Australia. TEL 61-2-3514799. FAX 61-2-3514580. *2429*

FORUM: TRENDS IN EXPERIMENTAL AND CLINICAL MEDICINE.
Scuola Superiore di Oncologia e Scienze Biomediche, Piazza della Vittoria 15-1, 16121 Genova, Italy. TEL 39-10-5458611. FAX 39-10-541761. *4679*

FOUNDATION.
Science Fiction Foundation, University of Reading, Department of History, Faculty of Letters and Social Sciences, Whiteknights, Reading RG6 6AA, England. TEL 44-1734-318145. *4327*

FOUNDATIONS OF NEUROLOGICAL SURGERY.
Kluwer Academic Publishers, Postbus 17, 3300 AA Dordrecht, Netherlands. TEL 31-78-6392392. FAX 31-78-6392254. *4838*

FOUNDATIONS OF NEUROLOGY.
Kluwer Academic Publishers, Postbus 17, 3300 AA Dordrecht, Netherlands. TEL 31-78-6392392. FAX 31-78-6392254. *4838*

FOUNDATIONS OF NEUROPSYCHOLOGY.
Kluwer Academic Publishers, Postbus 17, 3300 AA Dordrecht, Netherlands. TEL 31-78-6392392. FAX 31-78-6392254. *4838*

FOUNDATIONS OF PHYSICS.
Plenum Publishing Corp., 233 Spring St., New York, NY 10013-1578. TEL 212-620-8000. FAX 212-463-0742. *5548*

FOUNDATIONS OF PHYSICS LETTERS.
Plenum Publishing Corp., 233 Spring St., New York, NY 10013-1578. TEL 212-620-8000. FAX 212-463-0742. *5548*

FOUNDATIONS OF SCIENCE.
Kluwer Academic Publishers, Postbus 17, 3300 AA Dordrecht, Netherlands. TEL 31-78-6392392. FAX 31-78-6392254. *6241*

FOUR SEASONS (BERKELEY).
East Bay Regional Park District, Tilden Regional Park, Botanic Garden, Berkeley, CA 94708-2396. TEL 510-841-3732. FAX 510-848-6025. *682*

FRA FYSIKKENS VERDEN.
Universitetet i Oslo, P.O. Box 1048 Blindern, N-0316 Oslo, Norway. TEL 47-22-85-64-28. FAX 47-22-85-64-22. *5548*

FRAGMENTA FLORISTICA ET GEOBOTANICA.
Polska Akademia Nauk, Instytut Botaniki im. W. Szafera, Ul. Lubicz 46, 31-512 Krakow, Poland. TEL 48-12-215144. FAX 48-12-219790. *682*

FRAGMENTA FLORISTICA ET GEOBOTANICA. SERIES POLONICA.
Polska Akademia Nauk, Instytut Botaniki im. W. Szafera, Ul. Lubicz 46, 31-512 Krakow, Poland. TEL 48-12-215144. FAX 48-12-219790. *682*

FRAMES ARCHITETTURA DEI SERRAMENTI.
Gruppo Editoriale Faenza Editrice S.p.A., Via Pier. de Crescenzi, 44 48018 Faenza RA, Italy. TEL 39-546-663488 FAX 39-546-660440. *856*

FRANCHISE NEWS.
Consultants America Corporation, 3820 Premier Ave., Memphis, TN 38118. TEL 901-368-3333. FAX 901-368-1144. *1466*

FRANKLIN INSTITUTE. JOURNAL.
Elsevier Science Ltd., Pergamon, P.O. Box 800, Kidlington, Oxford OX5 1DX, England. TEL 44-1865-843000. FAX 44-1865-843010. *5548*

FREE INQUIRY.
Council for Secular Humanism, Box 664, Buffalo, NY 14226. TEL 716-636-1425. FAX 716-636-1733. *5476*

FREE INQUIRY IN CREATIVE SOCIOLOGY.
Oklahoma State University, Department of Sociology, 006 Classroom Bldg., Stillwater, OK 74078. TEL 405-744-6125. FAX 405-744-5780. *6414*

FREE RADICAL BIOLOGY & MEDICINE.
Elsevier Science Inc., Box 945, New York, NY 10159-0945. TEL 212-633-3730. FAX 212-633-3680. *653*

FREE RADICAL RESEARCH.
Harwood Academic Publishers, P.O. Box 3054, Langhorne, PA 19047-3054. TEL 215-750-2642. FAX 215-750-6343. *639*

FRENCH FORUM.
French Forum Publishers Inc., Box 130, Nicholasville, KY 40340. TEL 606-885-1446. FAX 606-257-3743. *4144*

FRENCH LITERATURE SERIES.
University of South Carolina, Department of French & Classics, Columbia, SC 29208. TEL 803-777-4881. FAX 803-777-0454. *4293*

FRESH INK.
Naugatuck Valley Community-Technical College, Student Senate, c/o Gloria D. Pond, Advisor, 750 Chase Pkwy., Waterbury, CT 06708. TEL 203-596-8603. *4212*

FRESHWATER BIOLOGY.
Blackwell Science Ltd., Osney Mead, Oxford OX2 0EL, England. TEL 44-1865-206206. FAX 44-1865-721205. *584*

IL FRIULI MEDICO.
Tipografia Editorice A. Pellegrini, Via della Vigna 24-A, 33100 Udine, Italy. TEL 39-432-559400. FAX 39-432-559420. *4456*

FRONESIS.
Ediluz, Apdo. 526, Maracaibo 4011, Venezuela. TEL 58-61-424738. FAX 58-61-423913. *5477*

FRONTIERS: A JOURNAL OF WOMEN STUDIES.
Frontiers Editorial Collective, Wilson 12, Washington State University, Pullman, WA 99164-4007. TEL 509-335-7258. FAX 509-335-4377. *7016*

FRONTIERS IN APPLIED MATHEMATICS.
Society for Industrial and Applied Mathematics, 3600 University City Science Center, Philadelphia, PA 19104-2688. TEL 215-382-9800. FAX 215-386-7999. *4365*

FRONTIERS IN DIABETES.
S. Karger AG, Allschwilerstr. 10, P.O. Box, CH-4009 Basel, Switzerland. TEL 061-3061111. FAX 061-3061234. *4670*

FRONTIERS IN HEADACHE RESEARCH.
Lippincott - Raven Publishers 227 E. Washington sq., Phialdelphia, PA 19106. TEL 215-238-4200. FAX 215-238-4235. *4436*

FRONTIERS IN METABOLISM.
Portland Press Ltd., 59 Portland Pl., London W1N 3AJ, England. TEL 44-171-580-5530. FAX 44-171-323-1136. *639*

FRONTIERS IN NEUROBIOLOGY.
Portland Press Ltd., 59 Portland Place, London W1N 3AJ, England. TEL 44-171-580-5530. FAX 44-171-323-1136. *639*

FRONTIERS IN NEUROENDOCRINOLOGY.
Academic Press, Inc., 525 B. St., Ste. 1900, San Diego, CA 92101-4495 TEL 619-230-1840. FAX 619-699-6800. *4670*

FRONTIERS OF GASTROINTESTINAL RESEARCH.
S. Karger AG, Allschwilerstr. 10, P.O. Box, CH-4009 Basel, Switzerland. TEL 061-3061111. FAX 061-3061234. *4691*

FRONTIERS OF HORMONE RESEARCH.
S. Karger AG, Allschwilerstr. 10 P.O. Box, CH-4009 Basel, Switzerland. TEL 061-3061111. FAX 061-3061234. *4670*

FRONTIERS OF ORAL PHYSIOLOGY.
S. Karger AG, Allschwilerstr. 10 P.O. Box, CH-4009 Basel, Switzerland. TEL 061-3061111. FAX 061-3061234. *4642*

FRONTIERS OF RADIATION THERAPY AND ONCOLOGY.
S. Karger AG, Allschwilerstr. 10, P.O. Box, CH-4009 Basel, Switzerland. TEL 061-3061111. FAX 061-3061234. *4876*

FRUIT VARIETIES JOURNAL.
American Pomological Society, c/o Dr. Robert M. Crassweller, Bus. Mgr., 103 Tyson Bldg., University Park, PA 16802. TEL 814-863-6163. FAX 814-863-6139. *3050*

FRUITS.
Editions Scientifiques et Medicales Elsevier, 141 rue de Javel, 75747 Paris Cedex 15, France. TEL 33-1-45589022. FAX 33-1-45589421. *3050*

FU JEN STUDIES.
Fu Jen University, College of Foreign Languages & Literatures, 24205 Hsi-chuang, Taipei, Taiwan, Republic of China. TEL 386-2-903-111. FAX 886-2-9021327. *4212*

FUEL
Butterworth - Heinemann, Part of the Reed Elsevier group, Linacre House, Jordan Hill, Oxford OX2 8DP, England. TEL 44-1865-310366. FAX 44-1865-310898. *5355*

FUEL AND ENERGY ABSTRACTS.
Butterworth - Heinemann, Part of the Reed Elsevier group, Linacre House, Jordan Hill, Oxford OX2 8DP, England. TEL 44-1865-310366. FAX 44-1865-310898. *5382*

FUEL PROCESSING TECHNOLOGY.
Elsevier Science B.V., P.O. Box 211, 1000 AE Amsterdam, Netherlands. TEL 31-20-4853911. FAX 31-20-4853598. *5355*

FUEL SCIENCE AND TECHNOLOGY INTERNATIONAL.
Marcel Dekker, Inc., 270 Madison Ave., New York, NY 10016. TEL 212-696-9000. FAX 212-685-4540. *2599*

FUJIAN JIANZHU.
Fujian Tumu Jianzhu Xuehui, 240 Beida Rd., Fuzhou, Fujian 350001, People's Republic of China. TEL 86-591-7855358 *393*

FUKUYAMA DAIGAKU FUZOKU NAIKAI SEIBUTSU SHIGEN KENKYUJO HOKOKU.
Fukuyama Daigaku, Fuzoku Naikai Seibutsu Shigen Kenkyujo, Ohamacho, Innoshima-shi, Hiroshima-ken 722-21, Japan. TEL 0849-36-2111. FAX 0849-36-2023. *2294*

FULLERENE SCIENCE AND TECHNOLOGY.
Marcel Dekker, Inc., 270 Madison Ave., New York, NY 10016. TEL 212-696-9000. FAX 212-685-4540. *1751*

FUNCTION.
Monash University, Department of Mathematics, Wellington Road, Clayton, Vic. 3168, Australia. TEL 61-3-9032723. FAX 61-3-9032227. *4365*

FUNCTIONAL ANALYSIS AND ITS APPLICATIONS.
Plenum Publishing Corp., Consultants Bureau, 233 Spring St., New York, NY 10013-1578. TEL 212-620-8468. FAX 212-463-0742. *4365*

FUNCTIONAL ECOLOGY.
Blackwell Science Ltd., Osney Mead, Oxford OX2 0EL, England. TEL 44-1865-206206. FAX 44-1865-721205. *2128*

FUNDAMENTA INFORMATICAE.
I O S Press, Van Diemenstraat 94, 1013 CN Amsterdam, Netherlands. TEL 31-20-6382189. FAX 31-20-6203419. *4409*

FUNDAMENTA MATHEMATICAE.
Polska Akademia Nauk, Instytut Matematyczny, Dzial Wydawnictw, Ul. Sniadeckich 8, P.O. Box 137, 00-950 Warsaw, Poland. TEL 48-22-6282471. FAX 48-22-6293997. *4365*

FUNDAMENTAL AND APPLIED TOXICOLOGY.
Academic Press, Inc., Journal Division, 525 B St., Ste. 1900, San Diego, CA 92101-4495. TEL 619-230-1840. FAX 619-699-6800. *2845*

FUNDAMENTAL AND CLINICAL PHARMACOLOGY.
Editions Scientifiques et Medicales Elsevier, 141 rue de Javel, 75747 Paris, France. TEL 33-1-45589026. FAX 33-1-45589421. *5414*

FUNDAMENTAL ASPECTS OF POLLUTION CONTROL AND ENVIRONMENTAL SCIENCE.
Elsevier Science B.V., Books Division, P.O. Box 211, 1000 AE Amsterdam, Netherlands. TEL 31-20-4853911. FAX 31-20-4853705. *2836*

FUNDAMENTAL ISSUES IN ARCHAEOLOGY.
Plenum Publishing Corp., 233 Spring St., New York, NY 10013-1578. TEL 212-620-8000. FAX 212-463-0742. *354*

FUNDAMENTAL MATERIALS RESEARCH.
Plenum Publishing Corp., 233 Spring St., New York, NY 10013-1578. TEL 212-620-8000. FAX 212-463-0742. *2731*

FUNDAMENTAL STUDIES IN COMPUTER SCIENCE.
Elsevier Science B.V., Books Division, P.O. Box 211, 1000 AE Amsterdam, Netherlands. TEL 31-20-4853911. FAX 31-20-4853705. *1990*

FUNDAMENTAL STUDIES IN ENGINEERING.
Elsevier Science B.V., Books Division, P.O. Box 211, 1000 AE Amsterdam, Netherlands. TEL 31-20-4853911. FAX 31-20-4853705. *2600*

FUNDAMENTAL THEORIES OF PHYSICS.
Kluwer Academic Publishers, Postbus 17, 3300 AA Dordrecht, Netherlands. TEL 31-78-6392392. FAX 31-78-6392254. *5549*

FUNDAMENTALS OF COSMIC PHYSICS.
Gordon and Breach Science Publishers, c/o International Publishers Distributor, P.O. Box 3054, Langhorne, PA 19048-3054. TEL 215-750-2642. FAX 215-750-6343. *480*

FUNDAMENTALS OF PURE AND APPLIED ECONOMICS SERIES.
Harwood Academic Publishers, c/o International Publishers Distributor, P.O. Box 3054, Langhorne, PA 19047-3054. TEL 215-750-2642. FAX 215-750-6343. *1255*

FUNGAL GENETICS AND BIOLOGY.
Academic Press, Inc., Journal Division, 525 B St., Ste. 1900, San Diego, CA 92101-4495. TEL 619-230-1840. FAX 619-699-6800. *682*

FUSION ENGINEERING AND DESIGN.
Elsevier Science S.A., P.O. Box 564, CH-1001 Lausanne 1, Switzerland. TEL 41-21-3207381. FAX 41-21-3235444. *2754*

FUSION TECHNOLOGY.
American Nuclear Society, 555 N. Kensington Ave., La Grange Park, IL 60525. TEL 708-352-6611. *2576*

FUTURES.
Butterworth - Heinemann, Part of the Reed Elsevier group, Linacre House, Jordan Hill, Oxford OX2 8DP, England. TEL 44-1865-310366. FAX 44-1865-310898. *1213*

FUTURICS.
Minnesota Futurists, 365 Summit Ave., St. Paul, MN 55102. TEL 612-290-2846. FAX 612-290-2847. *6414*

FUZZY SETS AND SYSTEMS.
North-Holland P.O. Box 211, 1000 AE Amsterdam, Netherlands. TEL 31-20-4853911. FAX 31-20-4853598. *4365*

G W U M C. DEPARTMENT OF BIOCHEMISTRY. ANNUAL SPRING SYMPOSIA SERIES.
Plenum Publishing Corp., 233 Spring St., New York, NY 10013-1578. TEL 212-620-8000. FAX 212-463-0742. *639*

GACETA LABORAL.
Universidad del Zulia, Facultad de Ciencias Juridicas y Politicas, Ciudad Universitaria, Nucleo Humanistico, Apdo. Postal 526, Maracaibo, Venezuela. *3782*

GACETA RURAL.
Gestora Editoral Rural, S.L., Avda. de Ramon y Cajal 5, 28016 Madrid, Spain. TEL 34-1-3440462. FAX 34-1-3440463. *119*

GAIT AND POSTURE.
Elsevier Science B.V., P.O. Box 211, 1000 AE Amsterdam, Netherlands. TEL 31-20-4853911. FAX 31-20-4853598. *4457*

GALAXIA.
Asociacion Argentina de Quimicos y Coloristas Textiles, Bulnes 1425, 1176 Buenos Aires, Argentina. TEL 541-963-0394. *6677*

GALILEAN ELECTRODYNAMICS.
Howard C. Hayden, Ed. & Pub., Box 545, Storrs, CT 06268-0545. TEL 203-486-0436. FAX 203-429-7775. *5549*

GALLOWAY PRESS.
Galloway Press, 647 Fouth St., Berthoud, CO 80513. TEL 970-532-0797. FAX 970-532-0797. *271*

GAMMA.
Nederlandse Vereniging van Radiologisch Laboranten, Catharijnesingel 73, 3511 GM Utrecht, Netherlands. *4876*

GANGUANG CAILIAO.
Huagong Bu, Ganguang Cailiao Xinxi Zhan, c/o Zhongguo Lekai Jiaopian Gongsi, Jianshe Rd., Baoding, Hebei 071054, People's Republic of China. TEL 86-312-3033279. FAX 86-312-3033279. *1675*

GANGUANG KEXUE YU GUANGHUAXUE.
Science Press, Marketing and Sales Department, 16 Donghuangchenggen North St., Beijing 100717, People's Republic of China. TEL 4010642. FAX 4019810. *5512*

GANN MONOGRAPHS ON CANCER RESEARCH.
Gakkai Shuppan Senta, 2-10, Hongo 6-chome, Bunkyo-ku, Tokyo 113, Japan. *4756*

GANSU SHEHUI KEXUE.
Gansu Sheng Shehui Kexueyuan, Shi Li Dian, Lanzhou, Gansu 730070, People's Republic of China. TEL 86-931-7668021. *6325*

GAOFENZI XUEBAO.
Science Press, Marketing and Sales Department, 16 Donghuangchenggen North St., Beijing 100717, People's Republic of China. TEL 4010642. FAX 4019810. *1751*

GAONENG WULI YU HE WULI.
Science Press, Marketing and Sales Department, 16 Donghuangchenggen North St., Beijing 100717, People's Republic of China. TEL 4010642. FAX 4109810. *5594*

GARDENS' BULLETIN, SINGAPORE.
National Parks Board, Singapore Botanic Gardens, Cluny Rd., Singapore 1025, Singapore. TEL 4741165. FAX 4754295. *682*

GAS.
Stichting Tijdschrift Openbare Gasvoorziening, Postbus 220, 7300 AE Apeldoorn, Netherlands. TEL 31-55-5393226. FAX 31-55-5393228. *5356*

GAS AKTUELL.
Messer Griesheim GmbH, 47793 Krefeld, Germany. TEL 49-2151-379434. FAX 49-2151-379116. *2640*

GAS INDUSTRIES MAGAZINE.
Gas Industries Inc., Box 558, Park Ridge, IL 60068. TEL 312-693-3682. FAX 847-696-3445. *5356*

GAS SEPARATION AND PURIFICATION.
Butterworth - Heinemann, Part of the Reed Elsevier group, Linacre House, Jordan Hill, Oxford OX2 8DP, England. TEL 44-1865-310366. FAX 44-1865-310898. *2641*

GASSHO.
Dharmanet International, Box 4951, Berkeley, CA 94704-4951. TEL 510-620-0936. *6110*

GASTROENTEROLOGY.
W.B. Saunders Co. Curtis Center, 3rd Fl., Independence Sq. W., Philadelphia, PA 19106-3399. TEL 215-238-7800. FAX 215-238-6445. *4692*

GASTROENTEROLOGY AND ENDOSCOPY NEWS.
McMahon Group, 148 W. 24th St., New York, NY 10011. TEL 212-620-4600. FAX 212-620-5928. *4692*

GASTROENTEROLOGY & HEPATOLOGY SERIES.
Marcel Dekker, Inc., 270 Madison Ave., New York, NY 10016. TEL 212-696-9000. FAX 212-685-4540. *4692*

GASTROINTESTINAL ENDOSCOPY.
Mosby - Year Book, Inc. 11830 Westline Industrial Dr., St. Louis, MO 63146-3318. TEL 314-872-8370. FAX 314-432-1380. *4692*

GAY AND LESBIAN MEDICAL ASSOCIATION. JOURNAL.
Plenum Publishing Corp., 233 Spring St., New York, NY 10013-1578. TEL 212-620-8000. FAX 212-463-0742. *4458*

GAZELLA. ANNUAL REPORT AND SCIENTIFIC ARTICLES.
Zoologicka Zahrada v Praze, 171 00 Prague, Czech Republic. TEL 42-2-66410480. FAX 42-2-870369. *806*

GAZETA NIEDZIELNA.
Veritas Foundation Publication Centre, 63 Jeddo Rd., London WI2 9EE, England. TEL 44-181-749-4957. FAX 44-181-749-4965. *3206*

GAZETTE.
Kluwer Academic Publishers, Postbus 17, 3300 AA Dordrecht, Netherlands. TEL 31-78-6392392. FAX 31-78-6392254. *3704*

GAZI MEDICAL JOURNAL.
Gazi Universitesi, Tip Fakultesi Dekanligi, 06500 Besevler, Ankara, Turkey. TEL 90-312-2141000. FAX 90-312-2124647. *4458*

GAZI UNIVERSITESI ECZACILIK FAKULTESI DERGISI.
Gazi Universitesi, Eczacilik Fakultesi, 06330 Etiler - Ankara, Turkey. TEL 90-312-2227225. FAX 90-312-2235018. *5414*

GEFAHRSTOFFE - REINHALTUNG DER LUFT.
Springer-Verlag, Heidelberger Platz 3, 14197 Berlin, Germany. TEL 49-30-8207-0. FAX 49-30-8214091. *2836*

GEKKAN CHIIKI IGAKU.
Chiiki Iryo Shinko Kyokai, Hibiya-dai Bldg., 13F., 1-2-2 Uchisaiwai-cho, Chiyoda-ku, Tokyo 100, Japan. TEL 81-3-3580-8471. FAX 81-3-3580-8472. *4458*

GEKKAN GASORIN STUTANDO.
Gekkan Gasorin Sutandosha, 3-2-3 Shinbashi, Minato-ku, Tokyo 105, Japan. TEL 81-3-3502-5941. FAX 81-3-3502-5940. *5357*

GELDERS ERFGOED.
Stichting Gelders Oudheidkundig Contact, Postbus 4040, 7200 BA Zutphen, Netherlands. TEL 31-575-511826. FAX 31-575-543223. *3412*

GELFAND MATHEMATICAL SEMINARS.
Birkhauser Boston, 675 Massachusetts Ave., Cambridge, MA 02139. TEL 617-876-2333. FAX 617-876-1272. *4366*

GEMS OF GENEALOGY.
Bay Area Genealogical Society, Inc., c/o Lisa Youngblood, Box 283, Green Bay, WI 54305-0283. *3084*

GENDER AND EDUCATION.
Carfax Publishing Co., P.O. Box 25, Abingdon, Oxon. OX14 3UE, England. TEL 44-1235-401000. FAX 44-1235-401550. *2336*

GENDER AND HISTORY.
Blackwell Publishers Ltd., 108 Cowley Rd., Oxford OX4 1JF, England. TEL 44-1865-791100. FAX 44-1865-791347. *3343*

GENDER, PLACE AND CULTURE.
Carfax Publishing Co., P.O. Box 25, Abingdon, Oxon. OX14 3UE, England. TEL 44-1235-401000. FAX 44-1235-401550. *7016*

GENDER, WORK AND ORGANIZATION.
Blackwell Publishers Ltd., 108 Cowley Rd., Oxford OX4 1JF, England. TEL 44-1865-791100. FAX 44-1865-791347. *1419*

GENE.
Elsevier Science B.V., P.O. Box 211, 1000 AE Amsterdam, Netherlands. TEL 31-20-4853911. FAX 31-20-4853598. *741*

GENE AMPLIFICATION AND ANALYSIS SERIES.
Elsevier Science B.V., Books Division, P.O. Box 211, 1000 AE Amsterdam, Netherlands. TEL 31-20-4853911. FAX 31-20-4853705. *741*

GENEESMIDDELENBULLETIN.
Stichting Geneesmiddelenbulletin, Lomanlaan 85, 3526 XC Utrecht, Netherlands. TEL 31-30-2802660. *5414*

GENERAL AND COMPARATIVE ENDOCRINOLOGY.
Academic Press, Inc., Journal Division, 525 B St., Ste. 1900, San Diego, CA 92101-4495. TEL 619-230-1840. FAX 619-699-6800. *4671*

GENERAL DENTISTRY.
Academy of General Dentistry, 211 E. Chicago Ave., Ste. 1200, Chicago, IL 60611. TEL 312-440-4300. FAX 312-440-0559. *4642*

GENERAL HOSPITAL PSYCHIATRY.
Elsevier Science Inc., Box 945, New York, NY 10159-0945. TEL 212-633-3730. FAX 212-633-3680. *4838*

GENERAL MOTORS SYMPOSIA SERIES.
Plenum Publishing Corp., 233 Spring St., New York, NY 10013-1578. TEL 212-620-8000. FAX 212-463-0742. *6786*

GENERAL PHARMACOLOGY.
Elsevier Science Inc., Box 945, New York, NY 10159-0945. TEL 212-633-3730. FAX 212-633-3680. *5415*

GENERAL RELATIVITY AND GRAVITATION.
Plenum Publishing Corp., 233 Spring St., New York, NY 10013-1578. TEL 212-620-8000. FAX 212-463-0742. *5549*

GENES & DEVELOPMENT.
Cold Spring Harbor Laboratory Press, Publications Department, Box 100, Cold Spring Harbor, NY 11724. TEL 800-843-4388. FAX 516-349-1946. *741*

GENES & GENETIC SYSTEMS.
Genetics Society of Japan, c/o National Institute of Genetics, 1111 Yata, Mishima-shi, Shizuoka-ken 411, Japan. TEL 81-849-36-2111. FAX 81-849-36-2024. *741*

GENES, CHROMOSOMES & CANCER.
John Wiley & Sons, Inc., Journals, 605 Third Ave., New York, NY 10158. TEL 212-850-6645. FAX 212-850-6021. *742*

GENESIS OF BEHAVIOR.
Plenum Publishing Corp., 233 Spring St., New York, NY 10013-1578. TEL 212-620-8000. FAX 212-463-0742. *4538*

GENETIC ANALYSIS, BIOMOLECULAR ENGINEERING.
Elsevier Science B.V., P.O. Box 211, 1000 AE Amsterdam, Netherlands. TEL 31-20-4853911. FAX 31-20-4853598. *661*

GENETIC DISORDER.
Box 151362, San Diego, CA 92175. *4144*

THE GENETIC ENGINEER AND BIOTECHNOLOGIST.
Carfax Publishing Co., P.O. Box 25, Abingdon, Oxon. OX14 3UE, England. TEL 44-1235-401000. FAX 44-1235-401550. *627*

GENETIC ENGINEERING.
Plenum Publishing Corp., 233 Spring St., New York, NY 10013-1578. TEL 212-620-8000. FAX 212-463-0742. *742*

GENETIC ENGINEERING AND BIOTECHNOLOGY YEARBOOK.
Elsevier Science B.V., Books Division, P.O. Box 211, 1000 AE Amsterdam, Netherlands. TEL 31-20-4853911. FAX 31-20-4853705. *742*

GENETIC EPIDEMIOLOGY.
John Wiley & Sons, Inc., Journals, 605 Third Ave., New York, NY 10158. TEL 212-850-6645. FAX 212-850-6021. *742*

GENETIC EPISTEMOLOGIST.
Jean Piaget Society, Department of Psychology, Franklin and Marshall College, Box 3003, Lancaster, PA 17604. *5845*

GENETIC RESOURCES AND CROP EVOLUTION.
Kluwer Academic Publishers, Postbus 17, 3300 AA Dordrecht, Netherlands. TEL 31-78-6392392. FAX 31-78-6392254. *683*

GENETIC, SOCIAL, AND GENERAL PSYCHOLOGY MONOGRAPHS.
Heldref Publications, 1319 Eighteenth St., N.W., Washington, DC 20036-1802. TEL 202-296-6267. FAX 202-296-5149. *5845*

GENETICA.
Kluwer Academic Publishers, Postbus 17, 3300 AA Dordrecht, Netherlands. TEL 31-78-6392392. FAX 31-78-6392254. *742*

GENETICS.
Genetics Society of America, 9650 Rockville Pike, Bethesda, MD 20814. TEL 301-571-1825. FAX 301-530-7001. *742*

GENETICS, SELECTION, EVOLUTION.
Editions Scientifiques et Medicales Elsevier, 141 rue de Javel, 75747 Paris, France. TEL 33-1-45589022. FAX 33-1-45589421. *743*

GENEVA PAPERS ON RISK AND INSURANCE THEORY.
Kluwer Academic Publishers Boston, Box 358, Accord Sta., Hingham, MA 02018-0358. TEL 617-871-6600. FAX 617-871-6528. *3649*

GENGO TO KYOIKU NO KENKYU.
Saitama Daigaku Kyoiku Gakubu, Kyoiku Gakubu, Takenaga Laboratory, 255, Shimo Okubo, Urawa-shi 338, Japan. TEL 048-858-3175. FAX 048-858-3690. *2488*

GENITOURINARY MEDICINE.
B M J Publishing Group, B.M.A. House, Tavistock Sq., London WC1H 9JR, England. TEL 44-171-387-4499. FAX 44-171-383-6402. *4661*

GENOME.
National Research Council of Canada, Research Journals, Ottawa, ON K1A 0R6, Canada. TEL 613-993-9084. FAX 513-952-7656. *743*

GENOME PRIORITY REPORTS.
S. Karger AG, Allschwilerst. 10, P.O. Box, CH-4009 Basel, Switzerland. TEL 061-306-111. FAX 061-3061234. *743*

GENOME RESEARCH.
Cold Spring Harbor Laboratory Press, Publications Department, Box 100, Cold Spring Harbor, NY 11724. TEL 800-843-4388. FAX 516-349-1946. *758*

GENOMICS.
Academic Press, Inc., Journal Division, 525 B St., Ste. 1900, San Diego, CA 92101-4495. TEL 619-230-1840. FAX 619-699-6800. *743*

GENTES.
Lega Missionaria Studenti, Via M. Massimo, 7, 00144 Rome, Italy. TEL 39-6-5439628. FAX 39-6-5910803. *6063*

THE GENTLE SURVIVALIST.
Laura Martin-Buhler Co., Box 4004, St. George, UT 84770. *5217*

GEOARCHAEOLOGY.
John Wiley & Sons, Inc., Journals, 605 Third Ave., New York, NY 10158-0012. TEL 212-850-6645. FAX 212-850-6021. *354*

GEOBOTANY.
Kluwer Academic Publishers, Postbus 17, 3300 AA Dordrecht, Netherlands. TEL 31-78-6392392. FAX 31-78-6392254. *2234*

GEOCHIMICA ET COSMOCHIMICA ACTA.
Elsevier Science Ltd., Pergamon, P.O. Box 800, Kidlington, Oxford OX5 1DX, England. TEL 44-1865-843000. FAX 44-1865-843010. *2234*

GEODERMA.
Elsevier Science B.V., P.O. Box 211, 1000 AE Amsterdam, Netherlands. TEL 31-20-4853911. FAX 31-20-4853598. *223*

GEOFISICA INTERNACIONAL.
Universidad Nacional Autonoma de Mexico, Instituto de Geofisica, Circuito Exterior, Ciudad Universitaria, Mexico 20, D.F., Mexico. TEL 525-622-4113. FAX 525-550-2486. *2273*

GEOFORUM.
Elsevier Science Ltd., Pergamon, P.O. Box 800, Kidlington, Oxford OX5 1DX, England. TEL 44-1865-843000. FAX 44-1865-843010. *3256*

GEOGRAFICKY CASOPIS.
Slovenska Akademia Vied, Geograficky Ustav, Stefanikova 49, 814 73 Bratislava, Slovakia. TEL 42-7-495587. FAX 42-7-491340. *3256*

GEOGRAPHICAL ANALYSIS.
Ohio State University Press, 1070 Carmack Rd., Columbus, OH 43210. TEL 614-292-6930. FAX 614-292-2065. *3257*

GEOGRAPHICAL JOURNAL OF ZIMBABWE.
Geographical Association of Zimbabwe, c/o University of Zimbabwe, Dept. of Geography, P.O. Box MP 167, Mt. Pleasant, Harare, Zimbabwe. TEL 263-4-303211. FAX 263-4-335249. *3257*

GEOGRAPHICAL REVIEW OF INDIA.
Geographical Society of India, c/o Calcutta University, Geography Department, 35 Ballygunge Circular Rd., Calcutta 700 019, India. TEL 475-3681. *3258*

GEOGRAPHY TEACHERS ASSOCIATION OF NEW SOUTH WALES. GEOGRAPHY BULLETIN.
Geography Teachers Association of New South Wales, P.O. Box 602, Gladesville, N.S.W. 2111, Australia. TEL 61-2-817-3647. FAX 61-2-817-4592. *3259*

GEOINFORMATICA.
Kluwer Academic Publishers Boston, Box 358, Accord Sta., Hingham, MA 02018-0358. TEL 617-871-6600. FAX 617-871-6528. *2222*

GEOJOURNAL.
Kluwer Academic Publishers, Postbus 17, 3300 AA Dordrecht, Netherlands. TEL 31-78-6392392. FAX 31-78-6392254. *3259*

GEOJOURNAL LIBRARY.
Kluwer Academic Publishers, Postbus 17, 3300 AA
Dordrecht, Netherlands. TEL 31-78-6392392.
FAX 31-78-6392254. *2234*

GEOLINGUISTICS.
American Society of Geolinguistics, 485 Brooklawn
Ave., Fairfield, CT 06432-1805. TEL 203-333-
8920. *4071*

GEOLOGI.
Danmarks og Groenlands Geologiske
Undersoegelse, Thoravej 8, DK-2400 Copenhagen
NV, Denmark. *2235*

GEOLOGIA SUDETICA.
Polska Akademia Nauk, Instytut Nauk
Geologicznych, Ul. Zwirki i Wigury 93, 02-089
Warsaw, Poland. TEL 48-22-221065. FAX 48-22-
221065. *2235*

GEOLOGICA CARPATHICA - CLAYS.
Vydavatel'stvo S A P, s.r.o., P.O. Box 57, Nam.
Slobody 6, 810 05 Bratislava, Slovakia. TEL 42-7-
211729. *2235*

GEOLOGICA ULTRAIECTINA.
Universiteit Utrecht, Faculteit Aardwetenschappen,
Budapestlaan 4, 3584 CD Utrecht, Netherlands.
TEL 31-30-2534994. FAX 31-30-2535030. *2235*

GEOLOGICAL SOCIETY OF AMERICA. BULLETIN.
Geological Society of America, 3300 Penrose Pl.,
Box 9140, Boulder, CO 80301. TEL 303-447-
2020. FAX 303-447-1133. *2236*

**GEOLOGICAL SOCIETY OF AMERICA. SPECIAL
PAPERS.**
Geological Society of America, 3300 Penrose Pl.,
Box 9140, Boulder, CO 80301. TEL 303-447-
2020. FAX 303-447-1133. *2236*

GEOLOGICAL SOCIETY OF INDIA. JOURNAL.
Geological Society of India, Post Box 1922,
Gavipuran, Bangalore 560 019, India. TEL 080-
6613352. *2237*

**GEOLOGICKA SLUZBA SLOVENSKEJ REPUBLIKY.
GEOLOGICKE PRACE. SPRAVY.**
Geologicka Sluzba Slovenskej Republiky, Mlynska
Dolina 1, 817 04 Bratislava, Slovakia. TEL 42-7-
3705111. FAX 42-7-3705451. *2238*

GEOLOGIE EN MIJNBOUW.
Kluwer Academic Publishers, Postbus 17, 3300 AA
Dordrecht, Netherlands. TEL 31-78-6392392.
FAX 31-78-6392254. *2238*

GEOLOGY (BOULDER).
Geological Society of America, 3300 Penrose Pl.,
Box 9140, Boulder, CO 80301. TEL 303-447-
2020. FAX 303-447-1133. *2239*

GEOLOGY OF GREENLAND SURVEY BULLETIN.
Danmarks og Groenlands Geologiske
Undersoegelse, Thoravej 8, DK-2400 Copenhagen
NV, Denmark. TEL 45-31-10-66-00. FAX 45-31-19-
68-68. *2240*

GEOLOGY OF THE PACIFIC OCEAN.
Harwood Academic Publishers, c/o International
Publishers Distributor, P.O. Box 3054, Langhorne,
PA 19047-3054. TEL 215-750-2642. FAX 215-
750-6343. *2240*

GEOLOGY REVIEWS.
Harwood Academic Publishers, c/o International
Publishers Distributor, P.O. Box 3054, Langhorne,
PA 19047-3054. TEL 215-750-2642. FAX 215-
750-6343. *2240*

GEOLOGY TODAY.
Blackwell Science Ltd., Osney Mead, Oxford OX2
OEL, England. TEL 44-1865-206206. FAX 44-
1865-721205. *2240*

GEOMAGNETISM AND AERONOMY.
American Geophysical Union, 2000 Florida Ave.,
N.W., Washington, DC 20009. TEL 202-462-6900.
FAX 202-328-0566. *2273*

GEOMETRIAE DEDICATA.
Kluwer Academic Publishers, Postbus 17, 3300 AA
Dordrecht, Netherlands. TEL 31-78-6392392.
FAX 31-78-6392254. *4366*

GEOMICROBIOLOGY JOURNAL.
Taylor & Francis Inc., 1900 Frost Rd., Ste. 101,
Bristol, PA 19007-1598. TEL 215-785-5800.
FAX 215-785-5515. *758*

GEOMORPHOLOGY.
Elsevier Science B.V., P.O. Box 211, 1000 AE
Amsterdam, Netherlands. TEL 31-20-4853911.
FAX 31-20-4853598. *2240*

**GEOPHYSICAL AND ASTROPHYSICAL FLUID
DYNAMICS.**
Gordon and Breach Science Publishers, c/o
International Publishers Distributors, P.O. Box 3054,
Langhorne, PA 19047-3054. TEL 215-750-2642.
FAX 215-750-6343. *2273*

GEOPHYSICAL JOURNAL.
Gordon and Breach Science Publishers, c/o
International Publishers Distributor, P.O. Box 3054,
Langhorne, PA 90471-3054. TEL 215-750-2642.
FAX 215-750-6343. *2274*

GEOPHYSICAL JOURNAL INTERNATIONAL.
Blackwell Science Ltd., Osney Mead, Oxford OX2
OEL, England. TEL 44-1865-206206. FAX 44-
1865-721205. *2274*

GEOPHYSICAL PROSPECTING.
Blackwell Science Ltd., Osney Mead, Oxford OX2
OEL, England. TEL 44-1865-206206. FAX 44-
1865-721205. *2274*

GEOPHYSICAL RESEARCH LETTERS.
American Geophysical Union, 2000 Florida Ave.,
N.W., Washington, DC 20009. TEL 202-462-6900.
FAX 202-328-0566. *2274*

GEOPHYSICS.
Society of Exploration Geophysicists, Box 702740,
Tulsa, OK 74170-2740. TEL 918-493-3516.
2274

GEOPHYSICS AND ASTROPHYSICS MONOGRAPHS.
Kluwer Academic Publishers, Postbus 17, 3300 AA
Dordrecht, Netherlands. TEL 31-78-6392392.
FAX 31-78-6392254. *480*

GEOPHYTOLOGY.
Palaeobotanical Society, 53 University Rd., Lucknow
7, India. TEL 0522-74291. FAX 0522-246169.
5314

GEOPOLITICS AND INTERNATIONAL BOUNDARIES.
Frank Cass, Newbury House, 890-900 Eastern Ave.,
Newbury Park, Ilford, Essex IG2 7HH, England.
TEL 44-181-5990984. FAX 44-181-5998866.
5751

GEORGE ELIOT - GEORGE HENRY LEWES STUDIES.
Dr. W. Baker, Ed. & Pub., Department of English,
Northern Illinois University, Dekalb, IL 60115.
TEL 815-753-1857. FAX 815-753-2003. *4144*

GEORGE HERBERT JOURNAL.
c/o Sidney Gottlieb, Ed., English Department, Sacred
Heart University, 5151 Park Ave., Fairfield, CT
06432. TEL 203-371-7810. *4306*

GEORGETOWN REVIEW.
Georgetown College, Box 6309, Southern Sta.,
Hattiesburg, MS 39406-6309. TEL 601-583-6940.
FAX 601-583-6940. *4213*

GEORGIA ANCHORAGE.
Georgia Ports Authority, Box 2406, Savannah, GA
31402. TEL 912-964-3811. FAX 912-964-3921.
6834

GEORGIA JOURNAL OF SCIENCE.
Georgia Academy of Science, c/o Norris O'Dell, Ed.,
Medical College of Georgia, Augusta, GA 30912.
TEL 706-272-4516. FAX 706-272-4588. *6242*

GEORGIA LIBRARIAN.
Georgia Library Association, Box 39, Young Harris,
GA 30582-0039. TEL 404-827-8725. FAX 404-
669-2705. *3994*

GEORGIA MUSIC NEWS.
Georgia Music Educators Association, c/o Mary
Leglar, Ed., University of Georgia School of Music,
Athens, GA 30602. TEL 706-542-2763. FAX 706-
542-2773. *5159*

GEORGIAN MATHEMATICAL JOURNAL.
Plenum Publishing Corp., 233 Spring St., New York,
NY 10013-1578. TEL 212-620-8000. FAX 212-
463-0742. *4366*

**GEOSCIENCE INFORMATION SOCIETY.
PROCEEDINGS.**
Geoscience Information Society, c/o American
Geological Institute, 4220 King St., Alexandria, VA
22302. *2209*

GEOTECHNICAL AND GEOLOGICAL ENGINEERING.
Chapman & Hall, Journals Department 2-6
Boundary Row, London SE1 8HN, England. TEL 44-
171-8650066. FAX 44-171-522-9623. *5063*

GEOTECHNICAL TESTING JOURNAL.
American Society for Testing and Materials, 100
Barr Harbor Dr., W. Conshohocken, PA 19428-
2959. TEL 610-832-9500. FAX 610-832-9555.
2660

GEOTECHNIK.
Verlag Glueckauf GmbH, Postfach 185620, 45206
Essen, Germany. TEL 49-2054-924122. FAX 49-
2054-924129. *2600*

GEOTECHNIQUE.
Thomas Telford Services Ltd., Thomas Telford
House, 1 Heron Quay, London E14 4JD, England.
TEL 44-171-987-6999. FAX 44-171-538-9620.
2660

GEOTEXTILES AND GEOMEMBRANES.
Elsevier Science Ltd., P.O. Box 800, Kidlington,
Oxford OX5 1DX, England. TEL 44-1865-843000.
FAX 44-1865-843010. *654*

GEOTHERMAL SCIENCE AND TECHNOLOGY.
Gordon & Breach Science Publishers, c/o
International Publishers Distributor, P.O. Box 3054,
Langhorne, PA 19047-3054. TEL 215-750-2642.
FAX 215-750-6343. *2241*

GEOTHERMICS.
Elsevier Science Ltd., Pergamon, P.O. Box 800,
Kidlington, Oxford OX5 1DX, England. TEL 44-1865-
843000. FAX 44-1865-843010. *2209*

GERIATRIC NEPHROLOGY AND UROLOGY.
Kluwer Academic Publishers, Postbus 17, 3300 AA
Dordrecht, Netherlands. TEL 31-78-6392392.
FAX 31-78-6392254. *4927*

GERIATRICS.
Advanstar Communications, Inc., 7500 Old Oak
Blvd., Cleveland, OH 44130. TEL 216-826-2839.
FAX 216-891-2726. *3287*

GERIATRIE FUER DIE TAEGLICHE PRAXIS.
S. Karger AG, Allschwilerstr. 10, P.O. Box, CH-4009
Basel, Switzerland. TEL 061-3061111. FAX 061-
3061234. *3287*

GERMAN HISTORY.
Arnold 338 Euston Rd., London NW1 3BH, England.
TEL 44-171-873-6000. FAX 44-171-873-6325.
3412

GERMAN JOURNAL OF OPHTHALMOLOGY.
Springer-Verlag, Heidelberger Platz 3, 14197
Berlin, Germany. TEL 49-30-8207-0. FAX 49-30-
8214091. *4770*

GERMAN LIFE.
Zeitgeist Publishing, 1 Corporate Dr., Grantsville,
MD 21536. TEL 301-895-3859. FAX 301-895-
5029. *3144*

GERMAN LIFE AND LETTERS.
Blackwell Publishers Ltd., 108 Cowley Rd., Oxford
OX4 1JF, England. TEL 44-1865-791100. FAX 44-
1865-791347. *4213*

GERMAN POLITICS.
Frank Cass, Newbury House, 890-900 Eastern Ave.,
Newbury Park, Ilford, Essex, England. TEL 44-181-
599-8866. FAX 44-181-599-0984. *5751*

GERMAN POLITICS & SOCIETY.
University of California at Berkeley, German Center,
247 Moses Hall, Berkeley, CA 94720-2324.
TEL 510-642-4065. FAX 510-643-7062. *5669*

GERMAN QUARTERLY.
American Association of Teachers of German, Inc., 112 Haddontowne Ct., Ste. 104, Cherry Hill, NJ 08034. TEL 609-795-5553. FAX 609-795-9398. *4071*

GERMANIC NOTES AND REVIEWS.
Department of Modern and Classical Languages, Bemidji State University, Bemidji, MN 56601. TEL 218-751-6265. FAX 218-751-2958. *4071*

GERMANIC REVIEW.
Heldref Publications, 1319 Eighteenth St., N.W., Washington, DC 20036-1802. TEL 202-296-6267. FAX 202-296-5149. *4071*

GERMANO-SLAVICA.
University of Waterloo, Department of Germanic and Slavic Languages and Literature, Waterloo, ON N2L 3G1, Canada. TEL 519-885-1211. FAX 519-746-5243. *4213*

GERMANTOWN CRIER.
Germantown Historical Society, 5501 Germantown Ave., Philadelphia, PA 19144-2291. TEL 215-844-0514. FAX 215-844-2831. *3469*

GERODONTOLOGY.
F D I World Dental Press Ltd., 7 Carlisle St., London W1V 5RG, England. TEL 0171-935-7852. FAX 0171-486-0183. *4642*

GERONTOLOGIST.
Gerontological Society of America, 1275 K St., N.W., Ste. 350, Washington, DC 20005-4006. TEL 202-842-1275. FAX 202-842-1150. *3288*

GERONTOLOGY.
S. Karger AG, Allschwilerstr. 10, P.O. Box, CH-4009 Basel, Switzerland. TEL 061-3061111. FAX 061-3061234. *3288*

GERONTOLOGY & GERIATRICS EDUCATION.
Haworth Press, Inc., 10 Alice St., Binghamton, NY 13904. TEL 607-722-5857. FAX 607-722-1424. *3288*

GESELLSCHAFT FUER NIEDERSAECHSISCHE KIRCHENGESCHICHTE. JAHRBUCH.
Buchdruckerei Rihn, Industriestr. 16, 32819 Blomberg, Germany. *3413*

GESHER.
World Jewish Congress, P.O. Box 4293, Jerusalem 91042, Israel. TEL 972-2-635262. FAX 972-2-635544. *2879*

GHANA JOURNAL OF AGRICULTURAL SCIENCE.
National Science and Technology Press, P.O. Box M.32, Accra, Ghana. *119*

GHANA JOURNAL OF SCIENCE.
National Science and Technology Press, Box M. 32, Accra, Ghana. TEL 233-21-777651. FAX 223-21-777355. *6242*

GIFTED CHILD QUARTERLY.
National Association for Gifted Children, 1707 L St., N.W., Ste. 550, Washington, DC 20036-4201. TEL 202-785-4268. *1768*

GIFU PREFECTURAL FISHERIES EXPERIMENTAL STATION. REPORT.
Gifu Prefectural Fisheries Experimental Station, 2605, Hane, Hagiwara-cho, Mashita-gun, Gifu 509-25, Japan. TEL 0576-52-3111. FAX 0576-52-4354. *2933*

GIFUKEN SHOKUBUTSU KENKYUKAISHI.
Gifuken Shokubutsu Kenkyukai, Gifu Daigaku Kyoikugakubu, Seibutsugaku Kyoshitsu Shokubutsu, Bunrui Kenkyushitsu, Yanagido, Gifu-shi, Gifu-ken 501-11, Japan. TEL 058-293-2258. FAX 058-293-2207. *683*

GINECOLOGIA CLINICA E ONCOLOGICA.
Tipografia Editrice La Garangola, Via Montona 6, 35137 Padua, Italy. TEL 39-49-8750550. FAX 39-49-8751743. *4736*

GIORNALE ITALIANO DI CHIRURGIA VASCOLARE.
Edizioni Minerva Medica, Corso Bramante 83-85, 10126 Turin, Italy. TEL 011-678282. FAX 011-3121736. *4910*

GISTER EN VANDAG.
South African Society for History Teaching, c/o P.H. Kapp, Ed., P.O. Box 5341, Uniedal 7612, South Africa. TEL 27-21-8082186. FAX 27-21-8084336. *3343*

GLACIAL GEOLOGY AND GEOMORPHOLOGY.
John Wiley & Sons Ltd., Journals, Baffins Ln., Chichester, W. Sussex PO19 1UD, England. TEL 44-1243-779777. FAX 44-1243-843232. *2209*

GLACIOLOGY AND QUATERNARY GEOLOGY.
Kluwer Academic Publishers, Postbus 17, 3300 AA Dordrecht, Netherlands. TEL 31-78-6392392. FAX 31-78-6392254. *2241*

GLASGOW INTRODUCTORY GUIDES TO FRENCH LITERATURE.
University of Glasgow, French and German Publications, Modern Languages Bldg., Glasgow G12 8QL, Scotland. TEL 44-141-330-4599. FAX 44-141-330-4234. *4213*

GLASGOW NATURALIST.
Glasgow Natural History Society, c/o Dr. J.R. Downie, Ed., Graham Kerr (Zoology) Bldg., University of Glasgow, Glasgow G12 8QQ, Scotland. TEL 44-141-330-5157. FAX 44-141-330-5971. *584*

GLASRA.
National Botanic Gardens, Glasnevin, Dublin 9, Ireland. TEL 8374388. FAX 8360080. *683*

GLASS AND CERAMICS.
Plenum Publishing Corp., Consultants Bureau, 233 Spring St., New York, NY 10013-1578. TEL 212-620-8468. FAX 212-463-0742. *1656*

GLASS PHYSICS AND CHEMISTRY.
Maik Nauka - Interperiodica, Mezhdunarodnyi Otdel, Ul. Profsoyuznaya, 90, 117864 Moscow, Russia. TEL 7-095-3360056. FAX 7-095-3360666. *1657*

GLASS SCIENCE AND TECHNOLOGY.
Deutsche Glastechnische Gesellschaft e.V., Mendelssohnstr. 75-77, 60325 Frankfurt a.M., Germany. TEL 49-69-749088. FAX 49-69-749719. *1657*

GLASS SCIENCE AND TECHNOLOGY.
Elsevier Science B.V., Books Division, P.O. Box 211, 1000 AE Amsterdam, Netherlands. TEL 31-20-4853911. FAX 31-20-4853705. *1657*

GLEAMS.
Glaucoma Research Foundation, 490 Post, Ste. 830, San Francisco, CA 94102. TEL 415-986-3162. FAX 415-936-3763. *4770*

GLIA.
John Wiley & Sons, Inc., Journals, 605 Third Ave., New York, NY 10158. TEL 212-850-6645. FAX 212-850-6021. *4838*

GLOBAL AND PLANETARY CHANGE.
Elsevier Science B.V., P.O. Box 211, 1000 AE Amsterdam, Netherlands. TEL 31-20-4853911. FAX 31-20-4853598. *2241*

GLOBAL ATMOSPHERE AND OCEAN SYSTEM.
Gordon and Breach Science Publishers, c/o International Publishers Distributor, P.O. Box 3054, Langhorne, PA 19047-3054. TEL 215-750-2642. FAX 215-750-6343. *2294*

GLOBAL BIOGEOCHEMICAL CYCLES.
American Geophysical Union, 2000 Florida Ave., N.W., Washington DC 20009. TEL 202-462-6900. FAX 202-328-0556. *6242*

GLOBAL CHANGE BIOLOGY.
Blackwell Science Ltd., Osney Mead, Oxford OX2 0EL, England. TEL 44-1865-206206. FAX 44-1865-721205. *584*

GLOBAL GOVERNANCE.
Lynne Rienner Publishers, 1800 30th St., Ste. 314, Boulder, CO 80301. TEL 303-444-6684. FAX 303-444-0824. *5752*

GLOBO.
Ringier Publishing GmbH, Gustav-Heinemann-Ring 212, 81739 Munich, Germany. TEL 49-89-63818134. FAX 49-89-63818169. *6888*

GLOBULUS.
Polygon Verlag, Am Aschweg 57 85114 Buxheim, Germany. TEL 49-8458-8281. FAX 49-8458-4746. *6242*

GLYCOCONJUGATE JOURNAL.
Chapman & Hall, Journals Department 2-6 Boundary Row, London SE1 8HN, England. TEL 44-171-8650066. FAX 44-171-5229623. *639*

GNOSIS.
Concordia University, Philosophy Department, 1455 de Maisonneuve Blvd. W. Montreal, PQ H3G 1M8, Canada. TEL 514-848-2300. *5477*

GOLDEN ROOTS OF THE MOTHER LODE.
Tuolumne County Genealogical Society, Box 3956, Sonora, CA 95370. TEL 209-532-1317. *3086*

GOLF NEWS.
Golf News, s.r.l., Via Scarlatti, 30, 20124 Milan, Italy. TEL 39-2-6692299. FAX 39-2-6692306. *6504*

GONGCHENG RE-WULI XUEBAO.
Science Press, Marketing and Sales Department, 16 Donghuangchenggen North St., Beijing 100717, People's Republic of China. TEL 4010642. FAX 4012180. *5584*

GONGYE JIANZHU.
Yejin-bu, Jianzhu Yanjiu Zongyuan, 33 Xitucheng Lu, Haidian-qu, Beijing 100038, People's Republic of China. TEL 86-10-6201-5599. FAX 86-10-6201-1361. *856*

GOOD CLINICAL PRACTICE JOURNAL.
Brookwood Medical Publications, Orchard House, Brookwood, Surrey GU24 0AT, England. TEL 44-1483-797975. FAX 44-1483-797915. *4460*

GORTANIA.
Comune di Udine, Museo Friulano di Storia Naturale, Via Grazzano 1, 33100 Udine, Italy. TEL 39-432-510221. FAX 39-432-271578. *2209*

THE GOSPEL HERALD AND SUNDAY SCHOOL TIMES.
Union Gospel Press, Box 6059 Cleveland, OH 44101. TEL 216-749-2100. FAX 216-459-1337. *6064*

GOVERNMENT ACCOUNTANTS JOURNAL.
Association of Government Accountants, 2200 Mount Vernon Ave., Alexandria, VA 22301-1314. TEL 703-684-6931. FAX 703-548-9367. *1047*

GOVERNMENT AND OPPOSITION.
London School of Economics and Political Science, Houghton St., London WC2, England. TEL 0171-405-5991. FAX 0171-242-0392. *5669*

GOVERNMENT INFORMATION QUARTERLY.
J A I Press Inc., 55 Old Post Rd., No. 2, Box 1678, Greenwich, CT 06836-1678. TEL 203-661-7602. FAX 203-661-0792. *3994*

GRACE AND TRUTH.
St. Joseph's Theological Institute, Private Bag 6004, Hilton 3245, South Africa. TEL 27-331-433293. FAX 27-331-431232. *6181*

GRADIVA.
c/o S. Morandina, Man. Ed., Department of French and Italian, State University of New York at Stony Brook, Stony Brook, NY 11794-3359. TEL 516-632-7448. FAX 516-632-9612. *4214*

GRADUATE WOMEN.
Australian Federation of University Women, A.F.U.W. Federal Council, Dymocks Bldg., 428 George St., Sydney, N.S.W. 2000, Australia. TEL 61-2-2351335. FAX 61-2-2351335. *6996*

GRAELLSIA.
Museo Nacional de Ciencias Naturales, Jose Gutierrez Abascal 2, 28006 Madrid, Spain. TEL 34-1-4111328. FAX 34-1-5645078. *806*

GRAIL: AN ECUMENICAL JOURNAL.
Novalis, St. Paul University, 223 Main St., Ottawa, ON K1S 1C4, Canada. TEL 613-236-1393. FAX 613-782-3004. *6064*

GRAND TIMES.
Grand Times Publishing, Inc., 403 Village Dr., El Cerrito, CA 94530-3355. TEL 510-527-4337. *3288*

GRANTHALAYA VIJNANA.
P. Kaula Endowment for Library and Information Science, C-239 Indira Nagar, Lucknow 226 016, India. *3994*

GRAPHICS INTERFACE. PROCEEDINGS - COMPTES RENDUS.
Canadian Information Processing Society, 430 King St., W., Ste. 106, Toronto, ON M5V 1L5, Canada. TEL 416-593-4040. FAX 416-593-5184. *2037*

GRASS AND FORAGE SCIENCE.
Blackwell Science Ltd., Osney Mead, Oxford OX2 OEL, England. TEL 44-1865-206206. FAX 44-1865-721205. *120*

GRASSLANDS REVIEW.
Box 626, Berea, OH 44017. *4214*

GRAVESIANA.
Nene College, Department of English, Northampton, England. *4214*

THE GREAT CIRCLE.
Australian Association of Maritime History, c/o G.R. Henning, Ed., Dept. of Economic History, University of New England, Armidale, N.S.W. 2351, Australia. TEL 61-67-732702. FAX 61-67-73-3596. *3343*

GREAT LAKES ENTOMOLOGIST.
Michigan Entomological Society, c/o Dept. of Entomology, Michigan State Univ., East Lansing, MI 48824. TEL 517-321-2192. *728*

GREAT LAKES FISHERY COMMISSION. SPECIAL PUBLICATION.
Great Lakes Fishery Commission, 2100 Commonwealth Blvd., Ste. 209, Ann Arbor, MI 48105-1563. TEL 313-662-3209. FAX 313-741-2010. *2934*

GREAT LAKES FISHERY COMMISSION (UNITED STATES AND CANADA) TECHNICAL REPORT SERIES.
Great Lakes Fishery Commission, 2100 Commonwealth Blvd., Ste. 209, Ann Arbor, MI 48105-1563. TEL 313-662-3209. FAX 313-741-2010. *2934*

GREAT LAKES GEOGRAPHER.
University of Western Ontario, Department of Geography, London, ON N6A 3K7, Canada. TEL 519-661-3423. FAX 519-661-3750. *3260*

GREAT PLAINS QUARTERLY.
University of Nebraska at Lincoln, Center for Great Plains Studies, 1214 Oldfather Hall, Lincoln, NE 68588-0313. TEL 402-472-6058. FAX 402-472-0463. *3469*

GREATER HOUSTON DENTAL SOCIETY. JOURNAL.
Greater Houston Dental Society, One Greenway Plaza, Ste. 110, Houston, TX 77046. TEL 713-961-4337. FAX 713-961-3617. *4642*

GREENER MANAGEMENT INTERNATIONAL.
Greenleaf Publishing, 8-10 Broomhall Rd., Sheffield S10 2DR, England. TEL 44-114-266-3789. FAX 44-114-267-9403. *2799*

GREGORIOS O PALAMAS.
Metropolis Thessalonikes, P.O. Box 10335, Thessaloniki, Greece. FAX 30-31-230-722. *3414*

GRIFFITHIANA.
Cineteca del Friuli, Via Osoppo 26, 33014 Gemona, Italy. TEL 39-432-980458. FAX 39-432-970542. *5104*

GRIST ON-LINE.
Box 20805, Columbus Circle Sta., New York, NY 18023. TEL 212-787-2861. *4307*

GROSS REPORT.
John E. Gross, Ed. & Pub., 1 Crossfield Ave., W. Nyack, NY 10994. TEL 914-358-7019. FAX 914-358-8074. *1002*

GROUND WATER.
Ground Water Publishing Co., 2600 Ground Water Way, Columbus, OH 43219. TEL 614-337-8229. *2285*

GROUND WATER MONITORING & REMEDIATION.
Ground Water Publishing Co., 2600 Ground Water Way, Columbus, OH 43219. TEL 614-337-8229. *2285*

GROUP DECISION AND NEGOTIATION.
Kluwer Academic Publishers, Postbus 17, 3300 AA Dordrecht, Netherlands. TEL 31-78-6392392. FAX 31-78-6392254. *1420*

GROUPE D'ETUDE DES RYTHMES BIOLOGIQUES. BULLETIN.
Societe Francophone de Chronobiologie, c/o Institut de Physiologie, Universite Louis Pasteur, 4 rue Kirschleger, 67085 Strasbourg Cedex, France. TEL 88-35-87-68. FAX 88-24-3334. *584*

GROWTH AND CHANGE.
Blackwell Publishers, 238 Main St., Cambridge, MA 02141. TEL 617-547-7110. FAX 617-547-0789. *1521*

GROWTH, DEVELOPMENT & AGING.
Growth Publishing Co., Inc., Box 42, Bar Harbor, ME 04609-0042. TEL 207-288-3533. FAX 207-288-5079. *585*

GROWTH FACTORS.
Harwood Academic Publishers, c/o International Publishing Distributor, P.O. Box 3054, Langhorne, PA 19047-3054. TEL 215-750-2642. FAX 215-750-6343. *788*

GROWTH REGULATION.
Churchill Livingstone Robert Stevenson House, 1-3 Baxter's Pl., Leith Walk, Edinburgh EH1 3AF, Scotland. TEL 44-131-5562424. FAX 44-131-5351704. *4671*

GRUNDTVIG STUDIER.
Grundtvig-Selskabet af 8. September 1947, c/o Kirkeligt Samfund, Vartorv, Farvergade 27, DK-1463 Copenhagen K, Denmark. TEL 45-33-13-76-70. *6146*

GUANG TONGXIN JISHU.
Guilin Institute of Optical Communications, P.O. Box 5, Guilin, Guangxi 541004, People's Republic of China. TEL 0773-5813838. FAX 0773-5812724. *1904*

GUANGDONG MINZU XUEYUAN XUEBAO.
Guangdong Minzu Xueyuan, Shipai, Guangzhou, Guangdong 510633, People's Republic of China. TEL 86-20-8551-5722. FAX 86-20-8551-5901. *6325*

GUANGPUXUE YU GUANGPU FENXI.
Beijing University Press, Haidian-qu, Beijing 100871, People's Republic of China. TEL 86-10-2182998. FAX 86-10-2181051. *5603*

GUILD NEWS.
Graphic Artists Guild, 11 W. 20th St., 8th Fl., New York, NY 10011-3704. TEL 212-463-7730. FAX 212-463-8779. *431*

GUISUANYAN XUEBAO.
Chinese Ceramic Society, Guojia Jiancaiju Nei (Inside National Bureau of Bldg. Materials), Baiwanzhuang, Beijing 100831, People's Republic of China. TEL 861-8311144. FAX 861-8313364. *1731*

GUJIZHUI DONGWU XUEBAO.
Science Press, Marketing and Sales Department, 16 Donghuangchenggen North St., Beijing 100717, People's Republic of China. TEL 4010642. FAX 4019810. *5314*

GULDEN PASSER.
Vereeniging der Antwerpsche Bibliophielen, Museum Plantin-Moretus, Vrijdagmarkt 22-23, 2000 Antwerp, Belgium. TEL 32-3-2330294. FAX 32-3-2262516. *5997*

GULF OF MEXICO SCIENCE.
Marine Environmental Sciences Consortium of Alabama, c/o Dauphin Island Sea Lab, Box 369-370, Dauphin Island, AL 36528. TEL 334-460-6351. FAX 334-460-7357. *2294*

GULF RESEARCH REPORTS.
Gulf Coast Research Laboratory, P.O. Box 7000, Ocean Springs, MS 39566-7000. TEL 601-872-4200. FAX 601-872-4204. *2294*

GULHANE ASKERI TIP AKADEMISI BULTEN.
Gulhane Askeri Tip Akademisi, 06018 Etlik - Ankara, Turkey. TEL 90-312-3212353. FAX 90-312-3234923. *4460*

GUO MORUO XUEKAN.
Guo Moruo Xuekan Qikanshe, Dafo Si Nei, Leshan, Sichuan 614003, People's Republic of China. TEL 86-833-2139721. *556*

GUOJI GUANGBO DIANSHI JISHU.
Guangbo Yingshi Bu, Keji Xinxi Yanjiuso, P.O. Box 2116, Beijing 100866, People's Republic of China. TEL 86-10-6092081. FAX 86-10-6092040. *1905*

GUOSHU KEXUE.
Zhongguo Nongye Kexueyuan, Zhengzhou Guoshu Yanjiusuo, Nanjiao, Zhengzhou, Henan 450004, People's Republic of China. TEL 86-371-633-5740. FAX 86-371-633-5771. *3055*

GUSHENGWU XUEBAO.
Science Press, Marketing and Sales Department, 16 Donghuangchenggen North St., Beijing 100717, People's Republic of China. TEL 4010642. FAX 4019810. *5314*

GUT.
B M J Publishing Group, B.M.A. House, Tavistock Sq., London WC1H 9JR, England. TEL 44-171-387-4499. FAX 44-171-383-6661. *4693*

GUTI DIANZIXUE YANJIU YU JINZHAN.
Nanjing Dianzi Qijian Yanjiusuo, 524 Zhongshan Donglu, P.O. Box 1601, Nanjing, Jiangsu 210016, People's Republic of China. TEL 86-25-4414155. FAX 86-25-4617126. *2520*

GYNAECOLOGICAL ENDOSCOPY.
Blackwell Science Ltd., Osney Mead, Oxford OX2 OEL, England. TEL 44-1865-206206. FAX 44-1865-721205. *4736*

GYNAEKOLOGISCH - GEBURTSHILFLICHE RUNDSCHAU.
S. Karger AG, Allschwilerstr. 10, P.O. Box, CH-4009 Basel, Switzerland. TEL 061-3061111. FAX 061-3061234. *4737*

GYNECOLOGIC AND OBSTETRIC INVESTIGATION.
S. Karger AG, Allschwilerstr. 10, P.O. Box, CH-4009 Basel, Switzerland. TEL 061-3061111. FAX 061-3061234. *4737*

GYNECOLOGIC ENDOSCOPY.
Elsevier Science B.V., Books Division, P.O. Box 211, 1000 AE Amsterdam, Netherlands. TEL 31-20-4853911. FAX 31-20-4853705. *4737*

GYNECOLOGIC ONCOLOGY.
Academic Press, Inc., Journal Division, 525 B St., Ste. 1900, San Diego, CA 92101-4495. TEL 619-230-1840. FAX 619-699-6800. *4737*

GYNECOLOGICAL ENDOCRINOLOGY.
Parthenon Publishing Group, Casterton Hall, Carnforth, Lancs. LA6 2LA, England. TEL 44-152-427-2084. FAX 44-152-427-1587. *4671*

GYNECOLOGIE INTERNATIONALE.
Presence et Communication Medicales, 11 rue de Rome, 75008 Paris, France. TEL 44-70-75-00. FAX 44-70-75-09. *4737*

GYOBYO KENKYU.
Japanese Society of Fish Pathology, c/o Dept. of Fisheries, Faculty of Agriculture, University of Tokyo, Yayoi 1-1-1, Bunkyo-ku, Tokyo 113, Japan. TEL 81-3-3812-2111. FAX 81-3-3813-2776. *806*

GYPSY LORE SOCIETY. JOURNAL.
Gypsy Lore Society, 5607 Greenleaf Rd., Cheverly, MD 20785. TEL 301-341-1261. FAX 301-341-1261. *310*

H A L - P C USER JOURNAL.
Houston Area League of P C Users, Inc., 1200 Post Oak Blvd. No. 106, Houston, TX 77056-3104. TEL 713-963-4155. FAX 713-623-4251. *2095*

H C I LETTERS.
Springer-Verlag London Ltd., Sweetapple House, Cattashall Rd., Godalming, Surrey GU7 3DJ, England. TEL 44-1483-418800. FAX 44-1483-415144. *1990*

H E C FORUM.
Kluwer Academic Publishers, Postbus 17, 3300 AA Dordrecht, Netherlands. TEL 31-78-6392392. FAX 31-78-6392254. *3544*

H L Q THREE RIVERS RESOURCE GUIDE FOR HOLISTIC LIVING.
H L Q Associates, Box 86054, Pittsburgh, PA 15221-0054. TEL 412-242-9355. *290*

H P B SURGERY.
Harwood Academic Publishers, P.O. Box 3054, Langhorne, PA 19047-3054. TEL 215-750-2642. FAX 215-750-6343. *4910*

HABERSHAM REVIEW.
Box 10, Demorest, GA 30535. TEL 404-778-3000. FAX 706-776-2811. *4215*

HABITAT INTERNATIONAL.
Elsevier Science Ltd., Pergamon, P.O. Box 800, Kidlington, Oxford OX5 1DX, England. TEL 44-1865-843000. FAX 44-1865-843010. *2799*

HACETTEPE BULLETIN OF NATURAL SCIENCES AND ENGINEERING.
Hacettepe Universitesi, Fen Fakultesi, 06532 Beytepe, Ankara, Turkey. FAX 90-4-2352531. *6243*

HACETTEPE DIS HEKIMLIGI FAKULTESI DERGISI.
Hacettepe Universitesi, Dis Hekimligi Fakultesi, Yayin Kurulu Sekreterligi, 06100 Sihhiye - Ankara, Turkey. TEL 90-312-3116461. FAX 90-312-3091138. *4642*

HACETTEPE FEN VE MUHENDISLIK BILIMLERI DERGISI. SERI A: BIYOLOJI.
Hacettepe Universitesi, Fen Fakultesi, 06532 Beytepe, Ankara, Turkey. FAX 90-212-2352531. *585*

HAEMATOLOGIA.
V S P, P.O. Box 346, 3700 AH Zeist, Netherlands. TEL 31-30-6925790. FAX 31-30-6932081. *4700*

HAEMOPHILIA.
Blackwell Science Ltd., Osney Mead, Oxford OX2 0EL, England. TEL 44-1865-206206. FAX 44-1865-721205. *4700*

HAEMOSTASIS.
S. Karger AG, Allschwilerstr. 10, P.O. Box, CH-4009 Basel, Switzerland. TEL 061-3061111. FAX 061-3061234. *4700*

HAGIOGRAPHICA.
N.V. Brepols, Steenweg op Tielen 68, 2300 Turnhout, Belgium. TEL 32-14-402500. FAX 32-14-428919. *6181*

HAGUE YEARBOOK OF INTERNATIONAL LAW.
Kluwer Academic Publishers, Postbus 17, 3300 AA Dordrecht, Netherlands. TEL 31-78-6392392. FAX 31-78-6392254. *3931*

HAGUE-ZAGREB ESSAYS.
Kluwer Academic Publishers, Postbus 17, 3300 AA Dordrecht, Netherlands. TEL 31-78-6392392. FAX 31-78-6392254. *3931*

HAIKIBUTSU GAKKAISHI.
Japan Society of Waste Management Experts, 2F 13-11 Shiba 5-chome, Minato-ku, Tokyo 108, Japan. TEL 81-3-3769-5099. FAX 81-3-3769-1492. *2852*

HAIYANG XUEBAO.
China Ocean Press, International Cooperation Department, Haimao Dalou, 1 Fuxingmenwai Dajie, Beijing 100860, People's Republic of China. TEL 8032211. FAX 8033515. *2295*

HAIYANG YU HUZHAO.
Science Press, Marketing and Sales Department, 16 Donghuangchenggen Beijie, Beijing 100707, People's Republic of China. TEL 4010642. FAX 4019810. *2295*

HALCYON.
Nevada Humanities Committee, Box 8029, Reno, NV 89507. TEL 702-784-6755. FAX 702-784-6266. *3613*

HAMBURGISCHES ZOOLOGISCHES MUSEUM UND INSTITUT. MITTEILUNGEN.
Universitaet Hamburg, Zoologisches Institut, Martin-Luther-King-Platz 3, 20146 Hamburg, Germany. TEL 49-4123-3960. FAX 49-4123-3937. *806*

HAMLET STUDIES.
R.W. Desai Publishing Company Ltd., Rangoon Villa, 1-10 W. Patel Nagar, New Delhi 110 008, India. TEL 574-7399. *4216*

HAMPSHIRE FIELD CLUB AND ARCHAEOLOGICAL SOCIETY PROCEEDINGS.
Hampshire Field Club, c/o A.C. King, King Alfred's College, Winchester SO22 4NR, England. TEL 44-1962-841515. *355*

HANDAI KAGAKU NETSUGAKU REPOTO.
Osaka Daigaku, Rigakubu, 1-1, Machikaneyamacho, Toyonaka-shi, Osaka 560, Japan. TEL 81-6-850-5523. FAX 81-6-850-5526. *1751*

HANDBOOK OF ANXIETY.
Elsevier Science B.V., Books Division, P.O. Box 211, 1000 AE Amsterdam, Netherlands. TEL 31-20-4853911. FAX 31-20-4853705. *5846*

HANDBOOK OF AROMA RESEARCH.
Kluwer Academic Publishers, Postbus 17, 3300 AA Dordrecht, Netherlands. TEL 31-78-6392392. FAX 31-78-6392254. *2975*

HANDBOOK OF BEHAVIORAL NEUROBIOLOGY.
Plenum Publishing Corp., 233 Spring St., New York, NY 10013-1578. TEL 212-620-8000. FAX 212-463-0742. *4839*

HANDBOOK OF CHEMICAL NEUROANATOMY.
Elsevier Science B.V., Books Division, P.O. Box 211, 1000 AE Amsterdam, Netherlands. TEL 31-20-4853911. FAX 31-20-4853705. *4839*

HANDBOOK OF CLINICAL NEUROLOGY.
Elsevier Science B.V., Books Division, P.O. Box 211, 1000 AE Amsterdam, Netherlands. TEL 31-20-4853911. FAX 31-20-4853705. *4839*

HANDBOOK OF COMPOSITES.
Elsevier Science B.V., Books Division, P.O. Box 211, 1000 AE Amsterdam, Netherlands. TEL 31-20-4853911. FAX 31-20-4853705. *1751*

HANDBOOK OF ELECTROENCEPHALOGRAPHY AND CLINICAL NEUROPHYSIOLOGY.
Elsevier Science B.V., Books Division, P.O. Box 211, 1000 AE Amsterdam, Netherlands. TEL 31-20-4853911. FAX 31-20-4853705. *4839*

HANDBOOK OF ENDOTOXIN.
Elsevier Science B.V., Books Division, P.O. Box 211, 1000 AE Amsterdam, Netherlands. TEL 31-20-4853911. FAX 31-20-4853705. *5415*

HANDBOOK OF ENVIRONMENTAL ISOTOPE GEOCHEMISTRY.
Elsevier Science B.V., Books Division, P.O. Box 211, 1000 AE Amsterdam, Netherlands. TEL 31-20-4853911. FAX 31-20-4853705. *2210*

HANDBOOK OF EXPLORATION GEOCHEMISTRY.
Elsevier Science B.V., Books Division, P.O. Box 211, 1000 AE Amsterdam, Netherlands. TEL 31-20-4853911. FAX 31-20-4853705. *2242*

HANDBOOK OF HYPERTENSION.
Elsevier Science B.V., Books Division, P.O. Box 211, 1000 AE Amsterdam, Netherlands. TEL 31-20-4853911. FAX 31-20-4853705. *4461*

HANDBOOK OF INFLAMMATION.
Elsevier Science B.V., Books Division, P.O. Box 211, 1000 AE Amsterdam, Netherlands. TEL 31-20-4853911. FAX 31-20-4853705. *4461*

HANDBOOK OF LIPID RESEARCH.
Plenum Publishing Corp., 233 Spring St., New York, NY 10013-1578. TEL 212-620-8000. FAX 212-463-0742. *1738*

HANDBOOK OF NATURAL PRODUCTS DATA.
Elsevier Science B.V., Books Division, P.O. Box 211, 1000 AE Amsterdam, Netherlands. TEL 31-20-4853911. FAX 31-20-4853705. *1676*

HANDBOOK OF NATURAL TOXINS.
Marcel Dekker, Inc., 270 Madison Ave., New York, NY 10016. TEL 212-696-9000. FAX 212-685-4540. *4461*

HANDBOOK OF NEUROPSYCHOLOGY.
Elsevier Science B.V., Books Division, P.O. Box 211, 1000 AE Amsterdam, Netherlands. TEL 31-20-4853911. FAX 31-20-4853705. *4839*

HANDBOOK OF NUMERICAL ANALYSIS.
Elsevier Science B.V., Books Division, P.O. Box 211, 1000 AE Amsterdam, Netherlands. TEL 31-20-4853911. FAX 31-20-4853705. *4366*

HANDBOOK OF PAPER SCIENCE.
Elsevier Science B.V., Books Division, P.O. Box 211, 1000 AE Amsterdam, Netherlands. TEL 31-20-4853911. FAX 31-20-4853705. *5322*

HANDBOOK OF PHYSIOLOGY.
American Physiological Society, 9650 Rockville Pike, Bethesda, MD 20814. TEL 301-530-7164. FAX 301-571-8313. *728*

HANDBOOK OF PLASMA PHYSICS.
Elsevier Science B.V., Books Division, P.O. Box 211, 1000 AE Amsterdam, Netherlands. TEL 31-20-4853911. FAX 31-20-4853705. *5549*

HANDBOOK OF POWDER TECHNOLOGY.
Elsevier Science B.V., Books Division, P.O. Box 211, 1000 AE Amsterdam, Netherlands. TEL 31-20-4853911. FAX 31-20-4853705. *2661*

HANDBOOK OF PSYCHOLOGY AND HEALTH SERIES.
Lawrence Erlbaum Associates, Inc., 10 Industrial Dr., Mahwah, NJ 07430-2262. TEL 201-236-9500. FAX 201-236-0072. *5346*

HANDBOOK OF SCHIZOPHRENIA.
Elsevier Science B.V., Books Division, P.O. Box 211, 1000 AE Amsterdam, Netherlands. TEL 31-20-4853911. FAX 31-20-4853705. *4839*

HANDBOOK OF SEMICONDUCTORS.
Elsevier Science B.V., Books Division, P.O. Box 211, 1000 AE Amsterdam, Netherlands. TEL 31-20-4853911. FAX 31-20-4853705. *2520*

HANDBOOK OF SOIL MECHANICS.
Elsevier Science B.V., Books Division, P.O. Box 211, 1000 AE Amsterdam, Netherlands. TEL 31-20-4853911. FAX 31-20-4853705. *2210*

HANDBOOK OF STRATA-BOUND AND STRATIFORM ORE DEPOSITS.
Elsevier Science B.V., Books Division, P.O. Box 211, 1000 AE Amsterdam, Netherlands. TEL 31-20-4853911. FAX 31-20-4853705. *2243*

HANDBOOK OF THE SPINAL CORD.
Marcel Dekker, Inc., 270 Madison Ave., New York, NY 10016. TEL 212-696-9000. FAX 212-685-4540. *4461*

HANDBOOK ON FERROMAGNETIC MATERIALS.
Elsevier Science B.V., Books Division, P.O. Box 211, 1000 AE Amsterdam, Netherlands. TEL 31-20-4853911. FAX 31-20-4853705. *4957*

HANDBOOK ON SYNCHROTRON RADIATION.
Elsevier Science B.V., Books Division, P.O. Box 211, 1000 AE Amsterdam, Netherlands. TEL 31-20-4853911. FAX 31-20-4853705. *3634*

HANDBOOK ON THE PHYSICS AND CHEMISTRY OF RARE EARTHS.
Elsevier Science B.V., Books Division, P.O. Box 211, 1000 AE Amsterdam, Netherlands. TEL 31-20-4853911. FAX 31-20-4853705. *5549*

HANDBOOK ON THE PHYSICS AND CHEMISTRY OF THE ACTINIDES.
Elsevier Science B.V., Books Division, P.O. Box 211, 1000 AE Amsterdam, Netherlands. TEL 31-20-4853911. FAX 31-20-4853705. *5549*

HANDBOOKS IN ECONOMICS.
Elsevier Science B.V., Books Division, P.O. Box 211, 1000 AE Amsterdam, Netherlands. TEL 31-20-4853911. FAX 31-20-4853705. *1255*

HANDBOOKS IN OPERATIONS RESEARCH AND MANAGEMENT SCIENCE.
Elsevier Science B.V., Books Division, P.O. Box 211, 1000 AE Amsterdam, Netherlands. TEL 31-20-4853911. FAX 31-20-4853705. *1990*

HANDBUCH DER ORIENTALISTIK.
E.J. Brill, P.O. Box 9000, 2300 PA Leiden, Netherlands. TEL 31-71-5353500. FAX 31-71-5317532. *5284*

HANDBUCH DER ORIENTALISTIK. 1. ABTEILUNG. DER NAHE UND DER MITTLERE OSTEN.
E.J. Brill, P.O. Box 9000, 2300 PA Leiden, Netherlands. TEL 31-71-5353500. FAX 31-71-5317532. *5284*

HANDBUCH DER ORIENTALISTIK. 2. ABTEILUNG. INDIEN.
E.J. Brill, P.O. Box 9000, 2300 PA Leiden, Netherlands. TEL 31-71-5353500. FAX 31-71-5317532. *5284*

HANDBUCH DER ORIENTALISTIK. 3. ABTEILUNG. INDONESIEN, MALAYSIA UND DIE PHILIPPINEN.
E.J. Brill, P.O. Box 9000, 2300 PA Leiden, Netherlands. TEL 31-71-5353500. FAX 31-71-5317532. *5284*

HANDBUCH DER ORIENTALISTIK. 4. ABTEILUNG. CHINA.
E.J. Brill, P.O. Box 9000, 2300 PA Leiden, Netherlands. TEL 31-71-5353500. FAX 31-71-5317532. *5284*

HANDBUCH DER ORIENTALISTIK. 5. ABTEILUNG. JAPAN.
E.J. Brill, P.O. Box 9000, 2300 PA Leiden, Netherlands. TEL 31-71-5353500. FAX 31-71-5317532. *5284*

HANDBUCH DER ORIENTALISTIK. 8. ABTEILUNG. HANDBOOK OF URALIC STUDIES.
E.J. Brill, P.O. Box 9000, 2300 PA Leiden, Netherlands. TEL 31-71-5353500. FAX 31-71-5317532. *5284*

HARROWSMITH COUNTRY LIFE.
T M Communications, Ferry Rd., Charlotte, VT 05445. TEL 802-425-3961. FAX 802-425-3307. *3055*

HART BULLETIN.
Misset P.O. Box 1110, 3600 BC Maarssen, Netherlands. TEL 31-346-558222. FAX 31-346-554287. *4602*

HARVARD AIDS INSTITUTE SERIES ON GENE REGULATION OF HUMAN RETROVIRUSES.
Lippincott - Raven Publishers 227 E. Washington Sq., Philadelphia, PA 19106. TEL 215-238-4200. FAX 215-238-4235. *743*

HARVARD ARMENIAN TEXTS AND STUDIES.
Harvard University Press, 79 Garden St., Cambridge, MA 02138. TEL 617-495-2600. FAX 617-495-5898. *3495*

HARVARD BOOKS IN BIOPHYSICS.
Harvard University Press, 79 Garden St., Cambridge, MA 02138. TEL 617-495-2600. FAX 617-495-5898. *654*

HARVARD EAST ASIAN SERIES.
Harvard University Press, 79 Garden St., Cambridge, MA 02138. TEL 617-495-2600. FAX 617-495-5898. *3379*

HARVARD ECONOMIC STUDIES.
Harvard University Press, 79 Garden St., Cambridge, MA 02138. TEL 617-495-2600. FAX 617-495-5898. *927*

HARVARD HISTORICAL MONOGRAPHS.
Harvard University Press, 79 Garden St., Cambridge, MA 02138. TEL 617-495-2600. FAX 617-495-5898. *3343*

HARVARD HISTORICAL STUDIES.
Harvard University Press, 79 Garden St., Cambridge, MA 02138. TEL 617-495-2600. FAX 617-495-5898. *3344*

THE HARVARD JOURNAL OF WORLD AFFAIRS.
Harvard University, John F. Kennedy School of Government, 273 Taubman Bldg., 79 John F. Kennedy St., Cambridge, MA 02138. TEL 617-496-0517. FAX 617-496-9027. *5752*

HARVARD PAPERS IN BOTANY.
Harvard University Herbaria, 22 Divinity Ave., Cambridge, MA 02138. TEL 617-495-2360. FAX 617-495-9484. *684*

HARVARD PUBLICATIONS IN MUSIC.
Harvard University, Department of Music, Music Bldg. G6, Cambridge, MA 02138. TEL 617-495-2791. FAX 617-496-8081. *5162*

HARVARD REVIEW OF PSYCHIATRY.
Mosby, Journal Subscription Services 11830 Westline Industrial Dr., St. Louis, MO 63146-3318. TEL 314-453-4351. FAX 314-432-1158. *4839*

HARVARD STUDIES IN BUSINESS HISTORY.
Harvard University Press, 79 Garden St., Cambridge, MA 02138. TEL 617-495-2600. FAX 617-495-5898. *1255*

HARVARD STUDIES IN CLASSICAL PHILOLOGY.
Harvard University, Department of the Classics, Boylston 320, Cambridge, MA 02138. TEL 617-496-6720. FAX 617-495-4027. *4072*

HARVARD STUDIES IN COMPARATIVE LITERATURE.
Harvard University Press, 79 Garden St., Cambridge, MA 02138. TEL 617-495-2600. FAX 617-495-5898. *4216*

HARVARD STUDIES IN URBAN HISTORY.
Harvard University Press, 79 Garden St., Cambridge, MA 02138. TEL 617-495-2600. FAX 617-495-5898. *3583*

HARVARD UKRAINIAN STUDIES.
Harvard University, Ukrainian Research Institute, 1583 Massachusetts Ave., Cambridge, MA 02138. TEL 617-495-4243. FAX 617-495-8097. *3414*

HARVARD UNIVERSITY. RUSSIAN RESEARCH CENTER. STUDIES.
Harvard University Press, 79 Garden St., Cambridge, MA 02138. TEL 617-495-2600. FAX 617-495-5898. *3414*

HARVARD - YENCHING INSTITUTE. STUDIES.
Harvard University Press, 79 Garden St., Cambridge, MA 02138. TEL 617-495-2600. FAX 617-495-5898. *3379*

HARVEY LECTURES.
Academic Press, Inc., 525 B St., Ste. 1900, San Diego, CA 92101-4495. TEL 619-231-0926. FAX 619-699-6715. *4462*

DER HAUTARZT.
Springer-Verlag, Heidelberger Platz 3, 14197 Berlin, Germany. TEL 49-30-8207-0. FAX 49-30-8214091. *4662*

HAVSFISKELABORATORIET. MEDDELANDE.
National Board of Fisheries, Institute of Marine Research, Box 4, 453 21 Lysekil, Sweden. TEL 46-523-14180. FAX 46-523-13977. *2934*

HAWAII INSTITUTE OF MARINE BIOLOGY. TECHNICAL REPORTS.
Hawaii Institute of Marine Biology, Box 1346, Kaneohe, HI 96744. TEL 808-237-7401. FAX 808-247-6634. *585*

HAWAII MEDICAL JOURNAL.
Hawaii Medical Association, 1360 S. Beretania St., 2nd Fl., Honolulu, HI 96814. TEL 808-536-7702. FAX 808-528-2376. *4462*

HAWAIIAN ENTOMOLOGICAL SOCIETY. PROCEEDINGS.
Hawaiian Entomological Society, c/o Entomology Dept., Bishop Museum, 1525 Bernice St., Honolulu, HI 96817. TEL 808-956-7076. FAX 808-956-2428. *728*

HAYDN SOCIETY JOURNAL.
Haydn Society, University of Lancaster, Music Department, Bailrigg, Lancaster LA1 4YW, England. TEL 44-1524-593777. FAX 44-1524-847298. *5162*

HE JISHU.
Science Press, Marketing and Sales Department, 16 Donghuangchenggen North St., Beijing 100717, People's Republic of China. TEL 4010642. FAX 4019810. *2577*

HE WULI DONGTAI.
He Wuli Dongtai Bianjibu, P.O. Box 31, Lanzhou, Gansu 730000, People's Republic of China. TEL 86-931-8828960. FAX 86-931-8881100. *5594*

HEAD & NECK.
John Wiley & Sons, Inc., Journals, 605 Third Ave., New York, NY 10158. TEL 212-692-6645. FAX 212-850-6021. *4910*

HEADACHE QUARTERLY.
Headache Quarterly, 467 W. Demming Pl., Ste 500, Chicago, Madison, IL 60614. *4462*

HEALTH AFFAIRS.
Project Hope, 7500 Old Georgetown Rd., No. 600, Bethesda, MD 20814-6133. TEL 301-656-7401. FAX 301-654-2845. *5961*

HEALTH & ENVIRONMENT DIGEST.
Freshwater Foundation, 725 County Rd. 6, Wayzata, MN 55391. TEL 612-449-0092. FAX 612-449-0592. *2800*

HEALTH & PLACE.
Elsevier Science Ltd., Pergamon, P.O. Box 800, Kidlington, Oxford OX5 1DX, England. TEL 44-1865-843000. FAX 44-1865-843010. *3260*

HEALTH AND SOCIAL CARE IN THE COMMUNITY.
Blackwell Science Ltd., Osney Mead, Oxford OX2 0EL, England. TEL 44-1865-206206. FAX 44-1865-721205. *5962*

HEALTH CARE ANALYSIS.
John Wiley & Sons Ltd., Journals, Baffins Ln., Chichester, W. Sussex PO19 1UD, England. TEL 44-1243-779777. FAX 44-1243-843232. *4463*

HEALTH CARE RISK REPORT.
Eclipse Group Ltd., 18-20 Highbury Pl., London N5 1QP, England. TEL 44-171-354-5858. FAX 44-171-354-8106. *3545*

HEALTH COMMUNICATION.
Lawrence Erlbaum Associates, Inc., 10 Industrial Dr., Mahwah, NJ 07430-2262. TEL 201-236-9500. FAX 201-236-0072. *5962*

HEALTH DEVICES.
E C R I, 5200 Butler Pike, Plymouth Meeting, PA 19462. TEL 610-825-6000. FAX 610-834-1275. *4463*

HEALTH DEVICES ALERTS.
E C R I, 5200 Butler Pike, Plymouth Meeting, PA 19462. TEL 610-825-6000. FAX 610-834-1275. *4565*

HEALTH DEVICES INSPECTION & PREVENTIVE MAINTENANCE SYSTEM.
E C R I, 5200 Butler Pike, Plymouth Meeting, PA 19462. TEL 610-825-6000. FAX 610-834-1275. *4463*

HEALTH DEVICES SOURCEBOOK.
E C R I, 5200 Butler Pike, Plymouth Meeting, PA 19462. TEL 610-825-6000. FAX 610-834-1275. *4463*

HEALTH ECONOMICS.
John Wiley & Sons Ltd., Journals, Baffins Ln., Chichester, W. Sussex PO19 1UD, England. TEL 44-1243-779777. FAX 44-1243-843232. *4463*

HEALTH EDUCATION & BEHAVIOR.
Sage Publications, Inc., 2455 Teller Rd., Thousand Oaks, CA 91320. TEL 805-499-0721. FAX 805-499-0871. *4463*

HEALTH EDUCATION RESEARCH.
Oxford University Press, Oxford Journals, Walton St., Oxford OX2 6DP, England. TEL 01865-267907. FAX 01865-267773. *6375*

HEALTH INFORM.
Infolink, Box 306, 31 Albany Post Rd., Montrose, NY 10548. TEL 914-736-1565. FAX 914-736-3806. *290*

HEALTH JOURNAL.
Madison Publishing, 263 Summer St., Boston, MA 02210. TEL 617-428-4600. FAX 617-428-4626. *5529*

HEALTH LAW JOURNAL.
Health Law Institute, 457 Law Centre, University of Alberta, Edmonton, AB T6G 2H5, Canada. TEL 403-492-8343. FAX 403-492-4924. *3787*

HEALTH MARKETING QUARTERLY.
Haworth Press, Inc., 10 Alice St., Binghamton, NY 13904. TEL 607-722-5857. FAX 607-722-1424. *5962*

HEALTH MATRIX: JOURNAL OF LAW-MEDICINE.
Case Western Reserve University, School of Law, 11075 East Blvd., Cleveland, OH 44106-7148. TEL 216-368-3304. FAX 216-368-3310. *3787*

HEALTH PHYSICS.
Williams & Wilkins, 351 W. Camden St., Baltimore, MD 21201. TEL 410-528-4000. FAX 410-528-4312. *4464*

HEALTH POLICY.
Elsevier Science Ireland Ltd., P.O. Box 85, Limerick, Ireland. TEL 353-61-471944. FAX 353-61-472144. *5963*

HEALTH POLICY MONOGRAPHS.
Elsevier Science B.V., Books Division, P.O. Box 211, 1000 AE Amsterdam, Netherlands. TEL 31-20-4853911. FAX 31-20-4853705. *5963*

HEALTH PROGRESS.
Catholic Health Association of the United States, 4455 Woodson Rd., St. Louis, MO 63134-3797. TEL 314-427-2500. FAX 314-427-0029. *3545*

HEALTH PSYCHOLOGY.
American Psychological Association, 750 First St., N.E., Washington, DC 20002-4242. TEL 202-336-5600. FAX 202-336-5568. *5846*

HEALTH SERVICES MANAGEMENT RESEARCH.
Churchill Livingstone Robert Stevenson House, 1-3 Baxter's Pl., Leith Walk, Edinburgh EH1 3AF, Scotland. TEL 44-131-5562424. FAX 44-131-5351704. *4464*

HEALTH SERVICES RESEARCH.
Health Administration Press, 1 North Franklin St., Ste. 1700, Chicago, IL 60606. TEL 312-424-2800. FAX 312-424-0014. *3545*

HEALTH, SOCIETY AND CULTURE.
Gordon & Breach Science Publishers, c/o International Publishers Distributor, P.O. Box 3054, Langhorne, PA 19047-3054. TEL 215-750-2642. FAX 215-750-6343. *6415*

HEALTH TECHNOLOGY MANAGEMENT.
E C R I, 5200 Butler Pike, Plymouth Meeting, PA 19462. TEL 610-825-6000. FAX 610-834-1275. *4464*

HEALTH TECHNOLOGY TRENDS.
E C R I, 5200 Butler Pike, Plymouth Meeting, PA 19462. TEL 610-825-6000. FAX 610-834-1275. *4464*

HEALTH VISITOR.
Professional & Scientific Publications, BMA House, Tavistock Sq., London WC1H 9JR, England. TEL 0171-383-6640. FAX 0171-383-6662. *4714*

HEALTHCARE ENVIRONMENTAL MANAGEMENT SYSTEM.
E C R I, 5200 Butler Pike, Plymouth Meeting, PA 19462. TEL 610-825-6000. FAX 610-834-1275. *4465*

HEALTHCARE HAZARDOUS MATERIALS MANAGEMENT.
E C R I, 5200 Butler Pike, Plymouth Meeting, PA 19462. TEL 610-834-1275. FAX 610-834-1275. *4465*

HEALTHCARE MANAGEMENT FORUM.
Canadian College of Health Service Executives, 350 Sparks St., Ste. 402, Ottawa, ON K1R 7S8, Canada. TEL 613-235-7218. FAX 613-235-5451. *3546*

HEARING RESEARCH.
Elsevier Science B.V., P.O. Box 211, 1000 AE Amsterdam, Netherlands. TEL 31-20-4853911. FAX 31-20-4853598. *4797*

HEART.
B M J Publishing Group, B.M.A. House, Tavistock Sq., London WC1H 9JR, England. TEL 0171-383-6270. FAX 0171-383-6402. *4602*

HEART & LUNG.
Mosby - Year Book, Inc. 11830 Westline Industrial Dr., St. Louis, MO 63146-3318. TEL 314-872-8370. FAX 314-432-1380. *4714*

HEART FAILURE REVIEWS.
Kluwer Academic Publishers Boston, Box 358, Accord Sta., Hingham, MA 02018-0358. TEL 617-871-6600. FAX 617-871-6528. *4603*

HEAT TRANSFER ENGINEERING.
Taylor & Francis Inc., 1900 Frost Rd., Ste. 101, Bristol, PA 19007-1598. TEL 215-785-5800. FAX 215-785-5515. *2641*

HEATHER NOTES.
Northeast Heather Society, Box 101, Highland View, Alstead, NH 03602-0101. TEL 603-835-6165. *3055*

HEAVY VEHICLE SYSTEMS.
Inderscience Enterprises Ltd., World Trade Centre Bldg., 110 Ave. Lousis Casai, Case Postale 306, CH-1215 Geneva-Aeroport, Switzerland. FAX 41-22-7910885. *6718*

HEBEI ZHONGYI.
Hebei Yixue Kexueyuan, Qingbao Yanjiusuo, 62 Qingyuan St. Shijiazhuang, Hebei 050021, People's Republic of China. TEL 86-311-5812687. FAX 86-311-5819161. *290*

HEBREW STUDIES.
National Association of Professors of Hebrew, 1346 Van Hise Hall, 1220 Linden Dr., University of Wisconsin-Madison, Madison, WI 53706. TEL 608-262-3204. FAX 608-262-9417. *4073*

HECATE.
Hecate Press, c/o English Dept., Univ. of Queensland, St. Lucia, Qld. 4067, Australia. TEL 61-7-365-3146. FAX 61-7-365-2799. *7017*

HEELAL.
Vereniging voor Sterrenkunde v.z.w., Brieversweg 147, 8310 Brugge, Belgium. TEL 32-50-358872. *480*

HEEMKRING OKEGEM. MEDEDELINGEN.
Heemkring Okegem, Idevoordelaan 27, 9400 Ninove-Okegem, Belgium. *3414*

HEGEL SOCIETY OF AMERICA. PROCEEDINGS.
State University of New York Press, State University Plaza, Albany, NY 12246. TEL 518-472-5000. FAX 518-472-5038. *5477*

HEIMEN.
Landslaget for Lokalhistorie, Historisk Institutt, N-7055 Dragvoll, Norway. TEL 47-73-59-64-33. FAX 47-73-59-64-41. *3415*

HELIOCENTRIC NET.
Box 68817, Seattle, WA 98168. TEL 206-242-8236. FAX 206-243-2882. *4146*

HELLENIC JOURNAL OF CARDIOLOGY.
Hellenic Cardiological Society, 6 Potamianou, 115 28 Athens, Greece. TEL 30-1-722-1633. FAX 30-1-722-6139 *4603*

HELLENIC JOURNAL OF GASTROENTEROLOGY.
Beta Medical Publishers Ltd., Adrianiou 3, 115 25 Athens, Greece. TEL 30-1-7232-302. FAX 30-1-7232-302. *4693*

HELLENIKA.
Foereningen Svenska Atheninstitutets Vanner, P.O. Box 14124, S-104 41 Stockholm, Sweden. TEL 46-8-6632102. *356*

HELLENISTIC CULTURE & SOCIETY.
University of California Press, 2120 Berkeley Way, Berkeley, CA 94720. TEL 510-642-4247. FAX 510-643-7127. *1822*

HELMINTHOLOGIA.
Slovak Academy of Sciences, Parasitological Institute, Hlinkova 3, 04001 Kosice, Slovakia. TEL 42-95-6331411. FAX 42-95-3631414. *807*

THE HELPER.
Herpes Resource Center, Box 13827, Research Triangle Park, NC 27709. TEL 919-361-8488. FAX 919-361-8425. *4631*

HEMATOLOGIE.
Johr Libbey Eurotext, 127 ave. de la Republique, 92120 Montrouge, France. TEL 33-1-46730660. FAX 33-1-40840999. *4700*

HEMATOLOGY.
Harwood Academic Publishers, c/o Internationa Publishers Distributor, P.O. Box 3054, Langhorne, PA 19047-3054. TEL 215-750-2642. FAX 215-750-6343. *4700*

HEMATOLOGY - ONCOLOGY CLINICS OF NORTH AMERICA.
W.B. Saunders Co. Curtis Center, 3rd Fl., Independence Sq. W., Philadelphia, PA 19106-3399. TEL 215-238-7800. FAX 215-238-6445. *4756*

HEMATOLOGY SERIES.
Marcel Dekker, Inc., 270 Madison Ave., New York, NY 10016. TEL 212-695-9000. FAX 212-658-4540. *4701*

HEMATOPATHOLOGY AND MOLECULAR HEMATOLOGY.
Marcel Dekker Journals 270 Madison Ave., New York, NY 10016. TEL 212-696-9000. FAX 212-685-4540. *4701*

THE HEMINGWAY REVIEW.
University of Idaho Press, c/o Susan F. Beegel Ed., 180 Polpis Rd., Nantucket, MA 02554. TEL 508-325-7157. *4217*

HEMOGLOBIN.
Marcel Dekker Journals, 270 Madison Ave., New York, NY 10016. TEL 212-695-9000. FAX 212-685-4540. *4701*

HEPATOLOGY.
W.B. Saunders Co., Curtis Center, 3rd Fl., Independence Sq. W., Philadelphia, PA 19106-3399. TEL 215-238-7800. FAX 215-238-6445. *4593*

HERALD OF LIBRARY SCIENCE.
P. Kaula Endowment for Library and Information Science, C-239 Indira Nagar, Lucknow 226 016, India. *3995*

HEREDITY.
Blackwell Science Ltd., Osney Mead, Oxford OX2 0EL, England. TEL 44-1865-206206. FAX 44-1865-721205. *744*

HERITAGE (LAWRENCEVILLE).
Gwinnett Historical Society, Inc., Box 261, Lawrenceville, GA 30246. TEL 770-822-5174. *3470*

HERITAGE CANADA.
Heritage Canada, 412 MacLaren, Ottawa, ON K2P 0M8, Canada. TEL 613-237-1066. FAX 613-237-5987. *394*

HERPETOLOGICAL REVIEW.
Society for the Study of Amphibians and Reptiles, Box 626, Hays, KS 67501-0526. *807*

HERVORMDE TEOLOGIESE STUDIES.
Universiteit van Pretoria, Fakulteit Teologie, Afdeling A, Pretoria 0002, South Africa. TEL 27-12-4203156. FAX 27-12-420-2887. *6065*

HESPERIA.
American School of Classical Studies at Athens, 6-8 Charlton St., Princeton, NJ 08540-5232. TEL 609-683-0800. FAX 609-924-0578. *356*

HESPERIS - TAMUDA.
Universite Mohammed V, Faculte des Lettres et des Sciences Humaines, B.P. 1040, Rabat, Rabat, Morocco. TEL 212-7-771889. FAX 212-7-772068. *5285*

HETEROCYCLES.
Japan Institute of Heterocyclic Chemistry, 1-1-7-804 Motoakasaka, Minato-ku, Tokyo 107, Japan. TEL 03-3404-5019. FAX 03-3497-9370. *1738*

HETEROFONIA.
Centro Nacional de Investigacion, Documentacion e Informacion Musical, Liverpool 16, Col. Juarez, 06600 Mexico, D.F., Mexico. TEL 52-5-5466140. *5162*

HETEROGENEOUS CHEMISTRY REVIEWS.
John Wiley & Sons, Inc., Journals, 605 Third Ave., New York, NY 10158-0012. TEL 212-850-6645. FAX 212-850-6021. *1676*

HEYTHROP JOURNAL.
Blackwell Publishers Ltd., 108 Cowley Rd., Oxford OX4 1JF, England. TEL 44-1865-791100. FAX 44-1865-791347. *6065*

HIGH ENERGY CHEMISTRY.
Maik Nauka - Interperiodica, Mezhdunarodnyi Otdel, Ul. Prosoyuznaya, 90, 117864 Moscow, Russia. TEL 7-095-3360066. FAX 7-095-3360666. *1751*

HIGH ENERGY PHYSICS AND NUCLEAR PHYSICS.
Allerton Press, Inc., 150 Fifth Ave., New York, NY 10011. TEL 212-924-3950. FAX 212-463-9684. *5594*

HIGH PERFORMANCE.
Art in the Public Interest, Box 68, Saxapahaw, NC 27340-0068. TEL 910-376-8404. FAX 910-376-3228. *432*

HIGH PRESSURE RESEARCH.
Gordon & Breach Science Publishers, c/o International Publishers Distributor, P.O. Box 3054, Langhorne, PA 19047-3054. TEL 215-750-2642. FAX 215-750-6343. *5588*

HIGH SCHOOL JOURNAL.
University of North Carolina Press, Box 2288, Chapel Hill, NC 27515-2288. TEL 919-966-3561. FAX 800-272-6817. *2339*

HIGH TEMPERATURE.
Maik Nauka - Interperiodica, Mezhdunarodnyi Otdel, Ul. Profsoyuznaya, 90, 117864 Moscow, Russia. TEL 7-095-231-2164. FAX 7-095-233-5590. *5584*

HIGH TEMPERATURE MATERIALS SCIENCE.
Humana Press Inc., 999 Riverview Dr., Ste. 208, Totowa, NJ 07512. TEL 201-256-1699. FAX 201-256-8341. *1751*

HIGH TEMPERATURES - HIGH PRESSURES.
Pion Ltd., 207 Brondesbury Park, London NW2 5JN, England. TEL 44-181-459-0069. FAX 44-181-451-6454. *5584*

HIGHER EDUCATION.
Kluwer Academic Publishers, Postbus 17, 3300 AA Dordrecht, Netherlands. TEL 31-78-6392392. FAX 31-78-6392254. *2430*

HIGHER EDUCATION QUARTERLY.
Blackwell Publishers Ltd., 108 Cowley Rd., Oxford OX4 1JF, England. TEL 44-1865-791100. FAX 44-1865-791347. *2431*

HIGHER EDUCATION RESEARCH AND DEVELOPMENT. RESEARCH PAPERS.
Higher Education Research & Development Society of Australasia Inc. (Queensland), P.O. Box 25, Abingdon, Oxon OX14 3UE, England. *2339*

HIGHER EDUCATION REVIEW.
Tyrrell Burgess Associates Ltd., 34 Sandilands, Croydon CRO 5DB, England. TEL 44-181-656-1770. *2431*

HIGHLIGHTS OF AGRICULTURAL RESEARCH.
Alabama Agricultural Experiment Station, 110 Comer Hall, Auburn University, AL 36849. TEL 334-844-4877. *121*

HIKOBIA.
Hikobia Botanical Club, c/o Laboratory of Plant Taxonomy & Ecology, Dept. of Biological Science, Faculty of Science, Hiroshima University, 5-1, Kagamiyama 1-chome, Higashi-hiroshima-shi 739, Japan. TEL 81-824-24-7451. FAX 81-824-24-0734. *684*

HIMACHAL JOURNAL OF AGRICULTURAL RESEARCH.
H.P. Agriculture University, Himachal Pradesh Krishi Vishvavidyalaya, Palampur 176 062, Himachal Pradesh, India. TEL 0189-30406. FAX 01894-30311. *122*

HIMALAYAN JOURNAL.
Himalayan Club, P.O. Box 1905, Bombay 400 001, India. TEL 91-22-495-0772. FAX 91-22-495-8804. *6565*

HIMALAYAN JOURNAL OF ENVIRONMENT AND ZOOLOGY.
Indian Academy of Environmental Sciences, c/o Dept. of Zoology, Gurukula Kangri University, Hardwar 249404, India. TEL 0133-425793. *2800*

HIMALAYAN PLANT JOURNAL.
Primulaceae Books, P.O. Box No. 6, Kalimpong-Darjeeling 734 301, West Bengal, India. TEL 91-3552-55673. FAX 91-3552-55673. *3055*

HINDU - CHRISTIAN STUDIES BULLETIN.
Centre for Studies in Religion and Society, University of Victoria, P.O. Box 3045, Victoria, BC V8W 3P4, Canada. TEL 604-721-6325. FAX 604-721-6234. *6114*

THE HIPPOCAMPUS.
John Wiley & Sons, Inc., Journals, 605 Third Ave., New York, NY 10158. TEL 212-850-6645. FAX 202-850-6021. *4466*

HIRAM POETRY REVIEW.
Hiram College, English Department, Box 162, Hiram, OH 44234. TEL 216-569-5330. FAX 216-569-5449. *4307*

HIROSHIMA SHUDO DAIGAKU RINSHO SHINRIGAKU KENKYU.
Hiroshima Shudo Daigaku, Shinrigaku Kyoshitsu, 1717, Otsuka, Numatacho, Asaminami-ku, Hiroshima-shi 731-31, Japan. TEL 81-82-830-1139. FAX 81-82-848-6633. *5846*

HISPAMERICA.
c/o Saul Sosnowski, Ed. & Pub., 5 Pueblo Ct., Gaithersburg, MD 20878. TEL 301-948-3494. *4217*

HISPANIA.
American Association of Teachers of Spanish and Portuguese, Inc., Georgetown University, Spanish Dept., Washington, DC 20057-0989. TEL 617-832-3779. *4073*

HISPANIC AMERICAN HISTORICAL REVIEW.
Duke University Press, Box 90660, Durham, NC 27708-0660. TEL 919-687-3600. FAX 919-688-4574. *3470*

HISPANIC JOURNAL.
Indiana University of Pennsylvania, Department of Spanish and Classical Languages, 462 Sutton Hall, Indiana, PA 15705. TEL 412-357-7528. FAX 412-357-2514. *2882*

THE HISTOCHEMICAL JOURNAL.
Chapman & Hall, Journals Department 2-6 Boundary Row, London SE1 8HN, England. TEL 44-171-8650066. FAX 44-171-5229623. *715*

HISTOIRE DES SCIENCES ET DES TECHNIQUES.
Gordon and Breach Science Publishers, c/o International Publishers Distributor, P.O. Box 3054, Langhorne, PA 19047-3054. TEL 215-750-2642. FAX 215-750-6343. *6244*

HISTOIRE SOCIALE.
University of Toronto Press, Journals Department, 5201 Dufferin St., Downsview, ON M3H 5T8, Canada. TEL 416-667-7781. FAX 416-667-7881. *3344*

HISTOPATHOLOGY.
Blackwell Science Ltd., Osney Mead, Oxford OX2 OEL, England. TEL 44-1865-206206. FAX 44-1865-721205. *4756*

HISTORIA.
Historical Association of South Africa, Department of History & Cultural History, University of Pretoria, Pretoria 0002, South Africa. TEL 27-12-4202323. FAX 27-12-432185. *3344*

HISTORIA (BUDAPEST).
Foundation Historia, Uri u. 53, 1014 Budapest I, Hungary. TEL 36-1-1560457. *3415*

HISTORIA, CIENCIAS, SAUDE - MANGUINHOS.
Fundacao Oswaldo Cruz, Avda. Brasil 4365, 21045-360 Rio de Janeiro RJ, Brazil. TEL 55-21-2809241. FAX 55-21-598-4437. *3344*

HISTORIA MATHEMATICA.
Academic Press, Inc., Journal Division, 525 B St., Ste. 1900, San Diego, CA 92101-4495. TEL 619-230-1840. FAX 619-699-6800. *4367*

HISTORIA MEDICINAE VETERINARIAE.
Historia Medicinae Veterinariae, Soendergade 39, 4130 Viby Sjaelland, Denmark. *6946*

THE HISTORIAN (EAST LANSING).
Michigan State University Press, Manly Miles Bldg., Ste. 25, 1405 S. Harrison Rd., East Lansing, MI 48823-5202. TEL 517-432-9543. FAX 517-336-2611. *3345*

HISTORIC BRASS SOCIETY JOURNAL.
Historic Brass Society, Inc., 148 W. 23rd St., No. 2A, New York, NY 10011. TEL 212-627-3820. FAX 212-627-3820. *5162*

HISTORIC BRASS SOCIETY NEWSLETTER.
Historic Brass Society, Inc., 148 West 23rd St., No. 2A, New York, NY 10011. TEL 212-627-3820. FAX 212-627-3820. *5162*

HISTORIC MADISON.
Historic Madison, Inc., of Wisconsin, Box 2721, Madison, WI 53701-2721. TEL 608-238-8664. *3471*

HISTORIC SOCIETY OF LANCASHIRE AND CHESHIRE. TRANSACTIONS.
Historic Society of Lancashire and Cheshire, c/o Department of History, Manchester University, Manchester M13 9PL, England. *3416*

HISTORICAL ARCHAEOLOGY.
Society for Historical Archaeology, Box 30446, Tucson, AZ 85751. TEL 520-886-8006. FAX 520-886-0182. *356*

HISTORICAL BIOLOGY.
Harwood Academic Publishers, c/o International Publishers Distributor, PO. Box 3054, Langhorne, PA 19047-3054. TEL 215-750-2642. FAX 215-750-6343. *5314*

HISTORICAL FOOTNOTES (STONINGTON).
Stonington Historical Society, Box 103, Stonington, CT 06378. TEL 203-535-1131. *3471*

HISTORICAL JOURNAL OF FILM, RADIO AND TELEVISION.
Carfax Publishing Co., P.O. Box 25, Abingdon, Oxon. OX14 3UE, England. TEL 44-1235-401000. FAX 44-1235-401550. *3345*

HISTORICAL METALLURGY.
Historical Metallurgy Society Ltd., Rock House, Bowens Hill, Coleford, Glos. GL16 8DH, England. TEL 44-1594-833778. *4957*

HISTORICAL METHODS.
Heldref Publications, 1319 Eighteenth St., N.W., Washington, DC 20036-1802. TEL 202-296-6267. FAX 202-296-5149. *3345*

HISTORICAL REFLECTIONS.
Alfred University, Division of Human Studies, Kanakadea Hall, Alfred, NY 14802. TEL 607-871-2217. *3345*

HISTORICAL RESEARCH.
Blackwell Publishers Ltd., 108 Cowley Rd., Oxford OX4 1JF, England. TEL 44-1865-791100. FAX 44-1865-791347. *3345*

HISTORICAL REVIEW OF BERKS COUNTY.
Historical Society of Berks County, 940 Centre Ave., Reading, PA 19601. TEL 215-375-4375. FAX 610-375-4376. *3471*

HISTORICAL STUDIES IN THE PHYSICAL AND BIOLOGICAL SCIENCES.
University of California Press, Journals Division, 2120 Berkeley Way, No. 5812, Berkeley, CA 94720-5812. TEL 510-643-7154. FAX 510-642-9917. *6245*

HISTORISK TIDSKRIFT.
Svenska Historiska Foereningen, P.O.Box 5405, S-114 84 Stockholm, Sweden. TEL 08-783-2502. FAX 08-7832515. *3417*

HISTORISK TIDSSKRIFT.
Danske Historiske Forening, Institut for Historie, Njalsgade 102, Tr. 15, DK-2300 Copenhagen S, Denmark. TEL 45-35-32-82-44. FAX 45-35-32-82-41. *3417*

HISTORY.
Blackwell Publishers Ltd., 108 Cowley Rd., Oxford OX4 1JF, England. TEL 44-1865-791100. *3346*

HISTORY AND ANTHROPOLOGY.
Harwood Academic Publishers, c/o International Publishers Distributor, P.O. Box 3054, Langhorne, PA 19047-3054. TEL 215-750-2642. FAX 215-750-6343. *311*

HISTORY AND COMPUTING (EDINBURGH).
Edinburgh University Press, 22 George Sq., Edinburgh EH8 9LF, Scotland. TEL 44-131-650-6207. FAX 44-131-662-0053. *1991*

HISTORY AND PHILOSOPHY OF LOGIC.
Taylor & Francis Ltd., 1 Gunpowder Sq., London EC4A 3DE, England. TEL 44-171-583-0490. FAX 44-171-583-0585. *5478*

HISTORY AND PHILOSOPHY OF THE LIFE SCIENCES.
Taylor & Francis Ltd., 1 Gunpowder Sq., London EC4A 3DE, England. TEL 44-171-583-0490. FAX 44-171-583-0585. *585*

HISTORY AND TECHNOLOGY.
Harwood Academic Publishers, c/o International Publishers Distributor, P.O. Box 3054, Langhorne, PA 19047-3054. TEL 215-750-2642. FAX 215-750-6343. *3346*

HISTORY AND THEORY.
Blackwell Publishers, 238 Main St., Cambridge, MA 02142. TEL 617-547-7110. FAX 617-547-0789. *3346*

HISTORY OF BIBLICAL INTERPRETATION SERIES.
E.J. Brill, P.O. Box 9000, 2300 PA Leiden, Netherlands. TEL 31-71-5353500. FAX 31-71-5317532. *6066*

HISTORY OF EDUCATION.
Taylor & Francis Ltd., Rankine Rd., Basingstoke, Hants. RG24 8PR, England. TEL 44-1256-840366. FAX 44-1256-479438. *2339*

HISTORY OF EDUCATION QUARTERLY.
Indiana University, School of Education, Bloomington, IN 47405. FAX 812-856-8440. *2339*

HISTORY OF EUROPEAN IDEAS.
Elsevier Science Ltd., Pergamon, P.O. Box 800, Kidlington, Oxford OX5 1DX, England. TEL 44-1865-843000. FAX 44-1865-843010. *5478*

HISTORY OF HIGHER EDUCATION ANNUAL.
Pennsylvania State University, Higher Education Program, 403 S. Allen St., Ste. 115, University Park, PA 16801-5202. TEL 814-863-3784. *2431*

HISTORY OF MATHEMATICS.
American Mathematical Society, Box 6248, Providence, RI 02940-6248. TEL 401-455-4000. *4367*

HISTORY OF PHOTOGRAPHY.
Taylor & Francis Ltd., Rankine Rd., Basingstoke, Hants. RG24 8PR, England. TEL 44-1256-840366. FAX 44-1256-479438. *5513*

HISTORY OF POLITICAL ECONOMY.
Duke University Press, Box 90660, Durham, NC 27708-0660. TEL 919-687-3600. FAX 919-688-4574. *1255*

HISTORY OF POLITICAL THOUGHT.
Imprint Academic, P.O. Box 1, Thorverton, Exeter, Devon EX 5YX, England. TEL 44-1392-841600. FAX 44-1392-841478. *5671*

HISTORY OF RELIGIONS.
University of Chicago Press, Journals Division, Box 37005, Chicago, IL 60637. TEL 773-753-3347. FAX 773-753-0811. *6066*

HISTORY OF SCIENCE.
Science History Publications Ltd., 16 Rutherford Rd., Cambridge CB2 2HH, England. TEL 44-1223-565532. FAX 44-1223-565532. *6245*

HISTORY OF THE HUMAN SCIENCES.
Sage Publications Ltd., 6 Bonhill St., London EC2A 4PU, England. TEL 44-171-374-0645. FAX 44-171-374-8741. *6326*

HISTORY: REVIEWS OF NEW BOOKS.
Heldref Publications, 1319 Eighteenth St., N.W., Washington, DC 20036-1802. TEL 202-296-6267. FAX 202-296-5149. *3347*

HITCHCOCK ANNUAL.
Hitchcock Annual Corporation, Box 2568, New London, NH 03257. TEL 614-427-3156. *5104*

HOBART PAPERBACKS.
Institute of Economic Affairs, 2 Lord North St., London SW1P 3LB, England. TEL 44-171-799-3745. FAX 44-171-799-2137. *1255*

HOBART PAPERS.
Institute of Economic Affairs, 2 Lord North St., London SW1P 3LB, England. TEL 44-171-799-3745. FAX 44-171-799-2137. *928*

HOKKAIDO UNIVERSITY. FACULTY OF SCIENCE. JOURNAL. SERIES 4: GEOLOGY AND MINERALOGY.
Hokkaido University, Faculty of Science, Nishi-8-chome, Kita-10-jo, Kita-ku, Sapporo 060, Japan. TEL 011-706-3225. FAX 011-716-0394. *2243*

HOKURIKU GEKA GAKKAI ZASSHI.
Hokuriku Geka Gakkai, Kanazawa Daigaku Igakubu Dai 1 Gekagaku Kyoshitsu, 13-1, Takaramachi, Kanazawa-shi, Ishikawa-ken 920, Japan. FAX 81-762-22-6833. *4910*

HOLISTIC EDUCATION REVIEW.
Psychology Press, Inc., Box 328, Brandon, VT 05733-0328. TEL 802-247-8312. FAX 802-247-8312. *2339*

HOLISTIC LIFE
New York Institute for Holistic Life, Box 302, Bronx, NY 10458. TEL 718-364-2202. FAX 718-364-2202. *290*

HOLOCAUST AND GENOCIDE STUDIES.
Oxford University Press, Journals, 2001 Evans Rd., Cary, NC 27513. TEL 919-677-0977. FAX 919-677-1714. *3417*

HOLOCAUST STUDIES SERIES.
Kluwer Academic Publishers, Postbus 17, 3300 AA Dordrecht, Netherlands. TEL 31-78-6392392. FAX 31-78-6392254. *3418*

HOME AND COUNTRY.
National Federation of Women's Institutes, 104 New Kings Rd., Fulham, London SW6 4LY, England. TEL 44-171-731-5777. FAX 44-171-736-4061. *6997*

HOME ECONOMICS INSTITUTE OF AUSTRALIA. JOURNAL.
Home Economics Institute of Australia Inc., Q U T, Kelvin Grove Campus, Locked Bag No. 2, Red Hill, Qld., 4059, Australia. TEL 61-7-864-3522. FAX 61-7-864-3369. *3523*

HOME ECONOMIST JOURNAL.
Institute of Home Economics, 21 Portland Pl., London W1N 3AF England. TEL 44-171-436-5677. *3523*

HOME ENERGY.
Energy Auditor and Retrofitter, Inc., 2124 Kittredge St., No. 95, Berkeley, CA 94704. TEL 510-524-5405. *2550*

HOME HEALTH CARE SERVICES QUARTERLY.
Haworth Press, Inc., 10 Alice St., Binghamton, NY 13904. TEL 607-722-5857. FAX 607-722-1424. *3547*

HOME SCHOOL MARKET GUIDE.
Bluestocking Press, Dept. U, Box 1014, Placerville, CA 95667. FAX 916-642-9222. *2339*

HOME SCHOOL RESEARCHER.
National Home Education Research Institute, 5000 Deer Park Dr., S.E., Salem OR 97301-9330. TEL 503-375-7019. FAX 503-585-4316. *2340*

HOMELIFE.
Society of St. Paul, Inc., MCPO Box 1722, 1299 Makati, Metro Manila, Philippines. FAX 632-890-7131. *3205*

HOMEOSTASIS.
Collegium Internationale Activitatis Nervosae Superioris, c/o Institute of Hygiene and Epidemiology, Srobarova 48, 10042 Prague 10, Czech Republic. *4840*

HOMES & LIVING.
H B M Publishing, 33 Brisbane St., E. Perth, W.A. 6000, Australia. TEL 09 228-9334. FAX 09-227-8337. *858*

HONG KONG MEDICAL JOURNAL.
Hong Kong Academy of Medicine, 9th Fl., Multicentre Block A, Pamela Youde Nethersole Eastern Hospital, 3 Lok Man Rd, Chaiwan, Hong Kong. TEL 852-2515-5739. FAX 852-2505-3194. *4467*

HONG KONG PSYCHOLOGICAL SOCIETY. BULLETIN.
Hong Kong Psychological Society Ltd., c/o Department of Education Studies, Hong Kong Baptist University, Kowloon Tong, Hong Kong. FAX 852-2339-7894. *846*

HONYU DOBUTSU SHIKEN BUNKAKAI KAIHO.
Nihon Kankyo Hen'igen Gakkai, Honyu Dobutsu Shiken Bunkakai, Shokuhin Yakuhin Anzen Senta Hadano Kenkyujo, 729-5 Ochiai, Hadano-shi, Kanagawa-ken 257, Japan. *724*

THE HOOK.
Tailhook Association, 9696 Businesspark Ave., San Diego, CA 92131-1643 TEL 619-689-9227. FAX 619-578-8839. *5033*

HOPSCOTCH.
Bluffton News Printing and Publishing Co., Box 164, 103 N. Main St., Bluffton, OH 45817-0164. TEL 419-358-4610. FAX 419-358-5027. *1794*

HORIZONS.
Haifa University, Department of Geography, Mount Carmel, Haifa 31905, Israel. FAX 972-4-246814. *3261*

HORIZONS (VILLANOVA).
Villanova University, Villanova, PA 19085. TEL 610-519-7302. *6182*

HORMONE RESEARCH.
S. Karger AG, Allschwilerstr. 10, P.O. Box, CH-4009 Basel, Switzerland. TEL 061-3061111. FAX 061-3061234. *4671*

HORMONES AND BEHAVIOR.
Academic Press, Inc., Journal Division, 525 B St., Ste. 1900, San Diego, CA 92101-4495. TEL 619-230-1840. FAX 619-699-6800. *4671*

HOROLOGICAL TIMES.
American Watchmakers Institute, 701 Enterprise Dr., Harrison, OH 45030-1696. TEL 513-367-9302. FAX 513-367-1414. *3696*

THE HORTICULTURIST.
Institute of Horticulture, 14-15 Belgrave Sq., London SW1X 8PS, England. TEL 44-171-245-6943. *3057*

HOSPICE JOURNAL.
Haworth Press, Inc., 10 Alice St., Binghamton, NY 13904. TEL 607-722-5857. FAX 607-722-1424. *3547*

EL HOSPITAL (CINCINNATI).
Salud Publications International Inc., 2724 Erie Ave., Ste. B, Cincinnati OH 45208-2125. TEL 513 533-5470. FAX 513-533-5474. *4467*

HOSPITAL MEDICINE.
Quadrant HealthCom, 105 Raider Blvd., Belle Mead, NJ 08502-1510. TEL 908-874-0707. FAX 908-874-5611. *4467*

HOSPITAL PHYSICIAN.
Turner White Communications, Inc., 125 Strafford Ave., Ste. 220, Wayne, PA 19087-3391. TEL 610-975-4541. FAX 610-975-4564. *4467*

HOSPITAL PRACTICE.
McGraw-Hill Companies (Minneapolis), 4530 W. 77th St., Minneapolis, MN 55434. TEL 612-835-3222. FAX 612-835-3460. *4467*

HOSPITAL PRODUCT COMPARISON SYSTEM.
E C R I, 5200 Butler Pike, Plymouth Meeting, PA 19462. TEL 610-825-6000. FAX 610-834-1275. *3549*

HOSPITAL RISK CONTROL.
E C R I, 5200 Butler Pike, Plymouth Meeting, PA 19462. TEL 610-825-6000. FAX 610-834-1275. *3549*

HOSPITAL TOPICS.
Heldref Publications, 1319 Eighteenth St., N.W., Washington, DC 20036. TEL 202-296-6267. FAX 202-296-5149. *3549*

HOTEL EXCLUSIV.
Am Wingertsberg 24, 76857 Waldhambach, Germany. TEL 49-6346-6431. FAX 49-6346-6518. *3564*

LES HOUCHES SUMMER SCHOOL PROCEEDINGS.
Elsevier Science B.V., Books Division, P.O. Box 211, 1000 AE Amsterdam, Netherlands. TEL 31-20-4853911. FAX 31-20-4853705. *5550*

HOUSING POLICY DEBATE.
Federal National Mortgage Association, 3900 Wisconsin Ave., N.W., Washington, DC 20016-2899. TEL 202-752-4422. FAX 202-752-4933. *3584*

HOUSING STUDIES.
Carfax Publishing Co., P.O. Box 25, Abingdon, Oxon. OX14 3UE, England. TEL 44-1235-401000. FAX 44-1235-401550. *3585*

HOUSTON JOURNAL OF MATHEMATICS.
University of Houston, Department of Mathematics, Houston, TX 77204-3476. TEL 713-743-3475. FAX 713-743-3505. *4367*

HOUSTON REVIEW: HISTORY AND CULTURE OF THE GULF COAST.
Houston Metropolitan Research Center, Houston Public Library, 500 McKinney, Houston, TX 77002. TEL 713-247-1661. *3472*

HUAN BOHAI JINGJI LIAOWANG.
Huan Bohai Diqu Jingji Xinxi Xiehui, 39 Youyi Lu, Hexi Qu, Tianjin 300201, People's Republic of China. TEL 86-22-835-4219. FAX 86-22-835-4270. *929*

HUANG ZHONG.
Wuhan Yiyue Xueyuan, No. 255, Jiefang Lu, Wuchang, Wuhan, Hubei 430060, People's Republic of China. TEL 027-8872571. *5163*

HUANJING HUAXUE.
Science Press, Marketing and Sales Department, 16 Donghuangchenggen North St., Beijing 100717, People's Republic of China. TEL 4010642. FAX 4012180. *1676*

HUANJING KEXUE.
Science Press, Marketing and Sales Department, 16 Donghuangchenggen North St., Beijing 100717, People's Republic of China. TEL 4010642. FAX 4019810. *2800*

HUANJING KEXUE XUEBAO.
Science Press, Marketing and Sales Department, 16 Donghuangchenggen North St., Beijing 100717, People's Republic of China. TEL 4010642. FAX 4019810. *2800*

HUANJING YAOGAN.
Science Press, Marketing and Sales Department, 16 Donghuangchenggen North St., Beijing 100717, People's Republic of China. TEL 4010642. FAX 4019810. *3261*

HUAXUE XUEBAO.
Science Press, Marketing and Sales Department, 16 Donghuangchenggen North St., Beijing 100717, People's Republic of China. TEL 4010642. FAX 4019810. *1677*

HUBBUB.
5344 S.E. 38th, Portland, OR 97202. TEL 503-775-0370. *4308*

HUEBNER SERIES IN RISK AND INSURANCE.
Kluwer Academic Publishers, Postbus 17, 3300 AA Dordrecht, Netherlands. TEL 31-78-6392392. FAX 31-78-6392254. *3650*

HUISARTS EN WETENSCHAP.
Bohn Stafleu van Loghum B.V. Postbus 246, 3990 GA Houten, Netherlands. TEL 31-3403-95711. FAX 31-3403-50903. *4467*

HUMAN ANTIBODIES AND HYBRIDOMAS.
Forefront Publishing Group, 5 River Rd., Ste. 113, Wilton, CT 06897-4069. TEL 203-834-0631. FAX 203-834-0940. *4581*

HUMAN BEHAVIOR AND ENVIRONMENT.
Plenum Publishing Corp., 233 Spring St., New York, NY 10013-1578. TEL 212-620-8000. FAX 212-463-0742. *5846*

HUMAN BIOLOGY (DETROIT).
Wayne State University Press, 4809 Woodward Ave., Detroit, MI 48201-1309. TEL 313-577-6120. FAX 313-577-6131. *585*

HUMAN BRAIN MAPPING.
John Wiley & Sons, Inc., Journals, 605 Third Ave., New York, NY 10158. TEL 212-850-6645. FAX 212-850-6021. *4840*

HUMAN - COMPUTER INTERACTION (MAHWAH).
Lawrence Erlbaum Associates, Inc., 10 Industrial Dr., Mahwah, NJ 07430-2262. TEL 201-236-9500. FAX 201-236-0072. *1991*

HUMAN DEVELOPMENT.
S. Karger AG, Allschwilerstr. 10, P.O. Box, CH-4009 Basel, Switzerland. TEL 061-3061111. FAX 061-3061234. *5847*

HUMAN ECOLOGY (NEW YORK).
Plenum Publishing Corp., 233 Spring St., New York, NY 10013-1578. TEL 212-620-8000. FAX 212-463-0742. *311*

HUMAN FACTORS.
Human Factors and Ergonomics Society, Box 1369, Santa Monica, CA 90406-1369. TEL 310-394-1811. FAX 310-394-2410. *2601*

HUMAN FACTORS AND ERGONOMICS SOCIETY ANNUAL MEETING. PROCEEDINGS.
Human Factors and Ergonomics Society, Box 1369, Santa Monica, CA 90406-1369. TEL 310-394-1811. FAX 310-394-2410. *2601*

HUMAN FACTORS IN ERGONOMICS AND MANUFACTURING.
John Wiley & Sons, Inc., Journals, 605 Third Ave., New York, NY 10158. TEL 212-850-6645. FAX 212-850-6021. *2747*

HUMAN FACTORS IN INFORMATION TECHNOLOGY.
Elsevier Science B.V., Books Division, P.O. Box 211, 1000 AE Amsterdam, Netherlands. TEL 31-20-4853911. FAX 31-20-4853705. *2081*

HUMAN GEOGRAPHY.
Human Geographical Society of Japan, Kinkichiho-Hatsumei Center, 14 Yoshida Kawara-cho, Sakyo-ku, Kyoto 606, Japan. TEL 81-75-751-7687. FAX 81-75-751-7687. *3261*

HUMAN HEREDITY.
S. Karger AG, Allschwilerstr. 10, P.O. Box, CH-4009 Basel, Switzerland. TEL 061-3061111. FAX 061-3061234. *744*

HUMAN IMMUNOLOGY.
Elsevier Science Inc., Box 945, New York, NY 10159-0945. TEL 212-633-3730. FAX 212-633-3680. *4581*

HUMAN MOVEMENT SCIENCE.
North-Holland P.O. Box 211, 1000 AE Amsterdam, Netherlands. TEL 31-20-4853911. FAX 31-20-4853598. *4468*

HUMAN MUTATION.
John Wiley & Sons, Inc., Journals, 605 Third Ave., New York, NY 10158-0012. TEL 212-850-6645. FAX 212-850-6021. *744*

HUMAN NUTRITION.
Plenum Publishing Corp., 233 Spring St., New York, NY 10013-1578. TEL 212-620-8468. FAX 212-463-0742. *5234*

HUMAN ORGANIZATION.
Society for Applied Anthropology, Box 24083, Oklahoma City, OK 73124-0084. TEL 405-843-5113. *311*

HUMAN PARASITIC DISEASES.
Elsevier Science B.V., Books Division, P.O. Box 211, 1000 AE Amsterdam, Netherlands. TEL 31-20-4853911. FAX 31-20-4853705. *4621*

HUMAN PATHOLOGY.
W.B. Saunders Co. Curtis Center, 3rd Fl., Independence Sq. W., Philadelphia, PA 19106-3399. TEL 215-238-7800. FAX 215-238-6445. *4468*

HUMAN PERFORMANCE.
Lawrence Erlbaum Associates, Inc., 10 Industrial Dr., Mahwah, NJ 07430-2262. TEL 201-236-9500. FAX 201-236-0072. *5847*

HUMAN PHYSIOLOGY.
Maik Nauka - Interperiodica, Mezhdunarodnyi Otdel, Ul. Profsoyuznaya, 90, 117864 Moscow, Russia. TEL 7-095-3360066. FAX 7-095-3360066. *788*

HUMAN PSYCHOPHARMACOLOGY: CLINICAL AND EXPERIMENTAL.
John Wiley & Sons Ltd., Journals, Baffins Ln., Chichester, W. Sussex PO19 1UD, England. TEL 44-1243-779777. FAX 44-1243-843232. *4840*

HUMAN RELATIONS.
Plenum Publishing Corp., 233 Spring St., New York, NY 10013-1578. TEL 212-260-8000. FAX 212-463-0742. *6326*

HUMAN RIGHTS IN DEVELOPING COUNTRIES YEARBOOK.
Kluwer Law International Postbus 85889, 2508 CN The Hague, Netherlands. TEL 31-70-3081500. FAX 31-70-3081515. *5729*

HUMAN RIGHTS LAW AND PRACTICE.
Brooker's Limited, Level 1 - Telecom Networks House, 68-86 Jervois Quay, Wellington, New Zealand. TEL 64-4-4998178. FAX 64-4-4998173. *3891*

HUMAN STUDIES.
Kluwer Academic Publishers, Postbus 17, 3300 AA Dordrecht, Netherlands. TEL 31-78-6392392. FAX 31-78-6392254. *5478*

HUMAN SYSTEMS.
University of Leeds, Department of Psychology, Leeds Family Therapy & Research Centre, Leeds LS2 9JT, England. TEL 44-113-2335728. FAX 44-113-2335700. *5847*

HUMANE MEDICINE.
Multimed, 1120 Finch Ave. W., Ste. 601, Downsville, ON M3J 3H7, Canada. TEL 416-650-0610. FAX 416-650-6039. *4468*

THE HUMANISTIC PSYCHOLOGIST.
American Psychological Association, Division of Humanistic Psychology, Psychology Dept., W. Georgia College, Carrollton, GA 30118. TEL 770-836-4578. FAX 770-836-6791. *5847*

HUMANITIES COLLECTIONS.
Haworth Press, Inc., 10 Alice St., Binghamton, NY 13904-1580. TEL 607-722-5857. FAX 607-722-1424. *3996*

HUME PAPERS ON PUBLIC POLICY.
Edinburgh University Press, 22 George Sq., Edinburgh EH8 9LF, Scotland. TEL 44-131-650-6207. FAX 44-131-662-0053. *5905*

HUME STUDIES.
Hume Society, 338 Orson Spencer Hall, University of Utah, Salt Lake City, UT 84112. TEL 801-581-8161. FAX 801-585-5195. *5479*

HUNAN JIAOYU XUEYUAN XUEBAO.
Hunan Jiaoyu Xueyuan, Xuebao Bianjibu, Zuojialong, Changsha, Hunan 410012, People's Republic of China. *2432*

HURRICANE ALICE.
Hurricane Alice Foundation, Rhode Island College, Dept. of English, Providence, RI 02908. TEL 401-456-8377. FAX 401-456-8379. *6997*

HUSSERL STUDIES.
Kluwer Academic Publishers, Postbus 17, 3300 AA Dordrecht, Netherlands. TEL 31-78-6392392. FAX 31-78-6392254. *5479*

HUSSERLIANA.
Kluwer Academic Publishers, Postbus 17, 3300 AA Dordrecht, Netherlands. TEL 31-78-6392392. FAX 31-78-6392254. *5479*

HYBRIDOMA.
Mary Ann Liebert, Inc. Publishers, 2 Madison Ave., Larchmont, NY 10538. TEL 914-834-3100. FAX 914-834-3688. *4581*

HYDRO REVIEW.
H C I Publications, 410 Archibald St., Kansas City, MO 64111-3046. TEL 816-931-1311. FAX 816-931-2015. *2572*

HYDROBIOLOGIA.
Kluwer Academic Publishers, Postbus 17, 3300 AA Dordrecht, Netherlands. TEL 31-78-6392392. FAX 31-78-6392254. *586*

HYDROCARBON TECHNOLOGY INTERNATIONAL.
Sterling Publications Ltd. 86-88 Edgware Rd., London W2 2YW, England. TEL 0171-915-9623. FAX 0171-258-0624. *5359*

HYDROGEN TODAY.
American Hydrogen Association, 216 S. Clark Dr., Ste. 103, Tempe, AZ 85281. TEL 602-921-0433. FAX 602-967-6601. *2572*

HYDROGEOLOGY JOURNAL.
Verlag Heinz Heise GmbH und Co. KG, Helstorferstr. 7, 30625 Hannover, Germany. TEL 49-511-5352-0. FAX 49-511-5352-294. *2286*

HYDROLOGICAL PROCESSES: AN INTERNATIONAL JOURNAL.
John Wiley & Sons Ltd., Journals, Baffins Ln., Chichester, W. Sussex PO19 1UD, England. TEL 44-1243-779777. FAX 44-1243-843232. *2286*

HYDROLOGICAL SCIENCE AND TECHNOLOGY.
American Institute of Hydrology, 2499 Rice St., Ste. 135, St. Paul, MN 55113-3724. TEL 612-484-8169. FAX 612-484-8357. *6969*

HYDROLOGICAL SCIENCES JOURNAL.
I A H S Press, Wallingford, Oxon. OX10 8BB, England. TEL 01491-692442. FAX 01491-692424. *2286*

HYDROMETALLURGY.
Elsevier Science B.V., P.O. Box 211, 1000 AE Amsterdam, Netherlands. TEL 31-20-4853911. FAX 31-20-4853598. *4957*

HYDROTECHNICAL CONSTRUCTION.
Plenum Publishing Corp., Consultants Bureau, 233 Spring St., New York, NY 10013-1578. TEL 212-620-8000. FAX 212-463-0742. *2661*

HYGIENE & MEDIZIN - INFECTION CONTROL AND HEALTHCARE.
M H P Verlag GmbH, Ostring 13, 65205 Wiesbaden, Germany. TEL 49-6122-7709131. FAX 49-6122-76331. *4468*

HYMN SOCIETY OF GREAT BRITAIN AND IRELAND. BULLETIN.
Hymn Society of Great Britain and Ireland, c/o Rev. Michael Garland, St. Nicholas Rectory, Curdworth, Sutton Coldfield, W. Midlands B76 9ES, England. TEL 44-1675-470384. *5163*

HYPERTENSION.
American Heart Association, 7272 Greenville Ave., Dallas, TX 75231-4596. TEL 214-706-1310. FAX 214-691-6342. *4603*

HYPERTENSION IN PREGNANCY.
Marcel Dekker Journals, 270 Madison Ave., New York, NY 10016. TEL 212-696-9000. FAX 212-685-4540. *4603*

I A B M C P NEWSLETTER.
International Academy of Behavioral Medicine, Counseling and Psychotherapy, 13140 Coit Rd., Ste. 307, Dallas, TX 75240. TEL 214-437-3370. FAX 214-437-1190 *5847*

I B M JOURNAL OF RESEARCH AND DEVELOPMENT.
International Business Machines Corp., Box 218, Yorktown Heights, NY 10598. TEL 914-945-3836. *1991*

I B M SYSTEMS JOURNAL.
International Business Machines Corp., Box 218, Yorktown Heights, NY 10598. TEL 914-945-3836. *2055*

I C A S A NEWS
International Consortium for Agricultural Systems Applications (ICASA), University of Hawaii, 2500 Dole St., Krauss 22 Honolulu, HI 96822. TEL 808-956-8858. FAX 808-956-3421. *224*

I C A S E - L A R C INTERDISCIPLINARY SERIES IN SCIENCE.
Kluwer Academic Publishers, Postbus 17, 3300 AA Dordrecht, Netherlands. TEL 31-78-6392392. FAX 31-78-6392254. *6246*

I C L TECHNICAL JOURNAL.
I C L plc., Lovelace Rd., Bracknell, Berks. RG12 4SN, England. TEL 44-1344-472000. FAX 44-1344-473000. *1991*

I C S A JOURNAL.
International Customer Service Association, 401 N. Michigan Ave., Chicago, IL 60611-4267. TEL 312-321-6800. FAX 312-321-6869. *929*

I C U M S A METHODS BOOK.
I C U M S A Publications, c/o British Sugar Technical Centre, Norwich Research Park, Colney, Norwich NR4 7UB, England. TEL 01493-751678. FAX 01493-751807. *2976*

I D U G SOLUTIONS JOURNAL.
Powell Publishing, Inc., 19380 Emerald Dr., Brookfield, WI 53045-3617. TEL 414-792-9696. FAX 414-792-9777. *2110*

I E E E DESIGN & TEST OF COMPUTERS.
I E E E Computer Society, 10662 Los Vaqueros Circle, Box 3014, Los Alamitos, CA 90720-1264. TEL 714-821-8380. *2021*

I E E E JOURNAL OF TECHNOLOGY COMPUTER AIDED DESIGN.
Institute of Electrical and Electronics Engineers, Inc., 345 E. 47th St., New York, NY 10017-2394. *2029*

I E E E PARALLEL & DISTRIBUTED TECHNOLOGY.
I E E E Computer Society Press, 10662 Los Vaqueros Circle, Box 3014, Los Alamitos, CA 90720-1264. TEL 714-821-8380. *2019*

I E E PROCEEDINGS - CIRCUITS, DEVICES AND SYSTEMS.
I.E.E., Michael Faraday House, Six Hills Way, Stevenage, Herts. SG1 2AY, England. TEL 44-1438-313311. FAX 44-1438-742840. *2705*

I F A C WORKSHOP SERIES.
Elsevier Science Ltd., Books Division, P.O. Box 800, Kidlington, Oxford OX2 1DX, England. TEL 44-1865-843000. FAX 44-1865-843010. *2755*

I G B P GLOBAL CHANGE REPORT.
Royal Swedish Academy of Sciences, International Geosphere-Biosphere Programme, P.O. Box 50005, S-104 05 Stockholm, Sweden. TEL 46-8-16-64-48. FAX 46-8-16-64-05. *2243*

I G C C NEWSLETTER.
Institute on Global Conflict and Cooperation, University of California, San Diego, 9500 Gilman Dr., Dept. C518, La Jolla, CA 92093-0518. TEL 619-534-1979. FAX 619-534-7655. *5753*

I I E TRANSACTIONS.
Chapman & Hall, Journals Department 2-6 Boundary Row, London SE1 8HN, England. TEL 44-171-8560066. FAX 44-171-5229623. *2747*

I L A R JOURNAL.
Institute of Laboratory Animal Resources, 2101 Constitution Ave., N.W., Washington, DC 20418. TEL 202-334-2590. FAX 202-334-1687. *4680*

I L S A JOURNAL OF INTERNATIONAL AND COMPARATIVE LAW.
International Law Students Association, Tillar House, 2223 Massachusetts Ave. N.W., Washington, DC 20008. TEL 305-423-5325. FAX 305-423-5327. *3932*

I P O ANNUAL PROGRESS REPORT.
Instituut voor Perceptie Onderzoek, P.O. Box 513, 5600 MB Eindhoven, Netherlands. TEL 31-40-773873. FAX 31-40-773876. *4074*

I R B REVISTA.
Instituto de Resseguros do Brasil Secretaria Geral da Presidencia, Av. Marechal Camara 171-8, Rio de Janeiro, Brazil. TEL 55-21-2720317. FAX 55-21-2405261. *3651*

I S A TRANSACTIONS.
Elsevier Science B.V., P.C. Box 211, 1000 AE Amsterdam, Netherlands. TEL 31-20-4853911. FAX 31-20-4853598. *2502*

I S K C O N WORLD REVIEW.
International Society for Krishna Consciousness, Box 238, Alachua, FL 32616. TEL 904-462-5054. FAX 904-462-5056. *6207*

I S L A: A JOURNAL OF MICRONESIAN STUDIES.
University of Guam Press, UOG Station, Mangilao, Guam 96923. TEL 671-734-9401. FAX 617-734-3676. *6327*

I S P R S JOURNAL OF PHOTOGRAMMETRY AND REMOTE SENSING.
Elsevier Science B.V., P.C. Box 211, 1000 AE Amsterdam, Netherlands. TEL 31-20-4853911. FAX 31-20-4853598. *2261*

I T C JOURNAL.
International Institute for Aerospace Survey and Earth Sciences, P.O. Box 6, 7500 AA Enschede, Netherlands. TEL 31-53-4874282. FAX 31-53-4874400. *3261*

I T E A PRODUCCION ANIMAL.
Asociacion Interprofesional para el Desarrollo Agrario, Montanana 177, Apdo. 727, 50080 Zaragoza, Spain. TEL 34-76-576311. FAX 34-76-575501. *272*

I T E A PRODUCCION VEGETAL.
Asociacion Interprofesional para el Desarrollo Agrario, Montanana 177, Apdo. 727, 50080 Zaragoza, Spain. TEL 34-76-576311. FAX 34-76-575501. *224*

I T G JOURNAL.
International Trumpet Guild, Drawer 2025, Columbia, SC 29202. *5163*

I T L REVIEW OF APPLIED LINGUISTICS.
Katholieke Universiteit Leuven, Instituut Toegepaste Linguistiek, Blijde Inkomststraat 21, P.O. Box 33, 3000 Leuven, Belgium. TEL 32-16-325030. FAX 32-16-324767. *4074*

I T TRAINING.
51 High St., Ruislip, Middx. HA4 7BG, England. TEL 0895-622112. FAX 0895-621582. *1505*

I U P STRESS AND HEALTH SERIES.
International Universities Press, Inc., 59 Boston Post Rd., Box 1524, Madison, CT 06443-1524. TEL 203-245-4000. *840*

I W G O NEWSLETTER.
International Working Group on Ostrinia Nubilalis, Trunnerstr. 5, A-1020 Vienna, Austria. TEL 01-21113250. *224*

IBARAKI DAIGAKU KYO IKUGAKUBU KIYO. SHIZEN KAGAKU.
Ibaraki Daigaku, Kyoikugakubu, 1-1, Bunkyo 2-chome, Mito-shi, Ibaraki-ken 310, Japan. TEL 81-29-228-8282. FAX 81-29-228-8329. *6246*

IBERIAN STUDIES.
University of Keele, Centre for Iberian Studies, Keele, Staffs. ST5 5BG, England. TEL 44-1782-621111. FAX 44-1782-613347. *6327*

ICARUS (SAN DIEGO).
Academic Press, Inc., Journal Division, 525 B St., Ste. 1900, San Diego, CA 92101-4495. TEL 619-230-1840. FAX 619-699-6800. *481*

ICHNOS.
Harwood Academic Publishers, c/o International Publishers Distributor, P.O. Box 3054, Langhorne, PA 19047-3054. TEL 215-750-2642. FAX 215-750-6343. *586*

ICON.
Frank Cass, Newbury House, 890-900 Eastern Ave., Newbury Park, Ilford, Essex IG2 7HH, England. TEL 44-181-5998866. FAX 44-181-5990984. *6653*

ICONOGRAPHY OF RELIGIONS.
E.J. Brill, P.O. Box 9000, 2300 PA Leiden, Netherlands. TEL 31-71-5353500. FAX 31-71-5317532. *432*

ICONOGRAPHY OF RELIGIONS. SECTION 2, NEW ZEALAND.
E.J. Brill, P.O. Box 9000, 2300 PA Leiden, Netherlands. TEL 31-71-5353500. FAX 31-71-5317532. *432*

ICONOGRAPHY OF RELIGIONS. SECTION 5, AUSTRALIA.
E.J. Brill, P.O. Box 9000, 2300 PA Leiden, Netherlands. TEL 31-71-5353500. FAX 31-71-5317532. *432*

ICONOGRAPHY OF RELIGIONS. SECTION 7, AFRICA.
E.J. Brill, P.O. Box 9000, 2300 PA Leiden, Netherlands. TEL 31-71-5353500. FAX 31-71-5317532. *433*

ICONOGRAPHY OF RELIGIONS. SECTION 8, ARCTIC PEOPLES.
E.J. Brill, P.O. Box 9000, 2300 PA Leiden, Netherlands. TEL 31-71-5353500. FAX 31-71-5317532. *433*

ICONOGRAPHY OF RELIGIONS. SECTION 9, SOUTH AMERICA.
E.J. Brill, P.O. Box 9000, 2300 PA Leiden, Netherlands. TEL 31-71-5353500. FAX 31-71-5317532. *433*

ICONOGRAPHY OF RELIGIONS. SECTION 10, NORTH AMERICA.
E.J. Brill, P.O. Box 9000, 2300 PA Leiden, Netherlands. TEL 31-71-5353500. FAX 31-71-5317532. *433*

ICONOGRAPHY OF RELIGIONS. SECTION 11, ANCIENT AMERICA.
E.J. Brill, P.O. Box 9000, 2300 PA Leiden, Netherlands. TEL 31-71-5353500. FAX 31-71-5317532. *433*

ICONOGRAPHY OF RELIGIONS. SECTION 12, EAST AND CENTRAL ASIA.
E.J. Brill, P.O. Box 9000, 2300 PA Leiden, Netherlands. TEL 31-71-5353500. FAX 31-71-5317532. *433*

ICONOGRAPHY OF RELIGIONS. SECTION 13, INDIAN RELIGIONS.
E.J. Brill, P.O. Box 9000, 2300 PA Leiden, Netherlands. TEL 31-71-5353500. FAX 31-71-5317532. *433*

ICONOGRAPHY OF RELIGIONS. SECTION 14, IRAN.
E.J. Brill, P.O. Box 9000, 2300 PA Leiden, Netherlands. TEL 31-71-5353500. FAX 31-71-5317532. *433*

ICONOGRAPHY OF RELIGIONS. SECTION 15, MESOPOTAMIA AND THE NEAR EAST.
E.J. Brill, P.O. Box 9000, 2300 PA Leiden, Netherlands. TEL 31-71-5353500. FAX 31-71-5317532. *433*

ICONOGRAPHY OF RELIGIONS. SECTION 16, EGYPT.
E.J. Brill, P.O. Box 9000, 2300 PA Leiden, Netherlands. TEL 31-71-5353500. FAX 31-71-5317532. *433*

ICONOGRAPHY OF RELIGIONS. SECTION 17, GREECE AND ROME.
E.J. Brill, P.O. Box 9000, 2300 PA Leiden, Netherlands. TEL 31-71-5353500. FAX 31-71-5317532. *433*

ICONOGRAPHY OF RELIGIONS. SECTION 19, ANCIENT EUROPE.
E.J. Brill, P.O. Box 9000, 2300 PA Leiden, Netherlands. TEL 31-71-5353500. FAX 31-71-5317532. *433*

ICONOGRAPHY OF RELIGIONS. SECTION 20, MANICHAEISM.
E.J. Brill, P.O. Box 9000, 2300 PA Leiden, Netherlands. TEL 31-71-5353500. FAX 31-71-5317532. *433*

ICONOGRAPHY OF RELIGIONS. SECTION 21, MANDAEISM.
E.J. Brill, P.O. Box 9000, 2300 PA Leiden, Netherlands. TEL 31-71-5353500. FAX 31-71-5317532. *433*

ICONOGRAPHY OF RELIGIONS. SECTION 22, ISLAM.
E.J. Brill, P.O. Box 9000, 2300 PA Leiden, Netherlands. TEL 31-71-5353500. FAX 31-71-5317532. *433*

ICONOGRAPHY OF RELIGIONS. SECTION 23, JUDAISM.
E.J. Brill, P.O. Box 9000, 2300 PA Leiden, Netherlands. TEL 31-71-5353500. FAX 31-71-5317532. *433*

ICONOGRAPHY OF RELIGIONS. SECTION 24, CHRISTIANITY.
E.J. Brill, P.O. Box 9000, 2300 PA Leiden, Netherlands. TEL 31-71-5353500. FAX 31-71-5317532. *434*

ICONOGRAPHY OF RELIGIONS. SUPPLEMENTS.
E.J. Brill, P.O. Box 9000, 2300 PA Leiden, Netherlands. TEL 31-71-5353500. FAX 31-71-5317532. *434*

IDAHO ACADEMY OF SCIENCE. JOURNAL.
Idaho Academy of Science, c/o Phil Anderson, Exec. Dir., 909 Lucille Ave., Pocatello, ID 83201-2542. TEL 208-526-3395. *6246*

IDAHO CURRENTS.
Department of Water Resources, Box 83720, Boise, ID 83720-0098. TEL 208-327-7982. FAX 208-327-7866. *2550*

IDAHO YESTERDAYS.
Idaho State Historical Society, 450 N. Fourth St., Boise, ID 83702. TEL 208-334-3428. FAX 208-334-3198. *3472*

IDENTITIES.
Gordon and Breach Science Publishers, c/o International Publishers Distributor, P.O. Box 3054, Langhorne, PA 19047-3054. TEL 215-750-2642. FAX 215-750-6343. *2883*

IDESIA.
Universidad de Tarapaca, Instituto de Agronomia, Casilla 6-D, Arica, Chile. TEL 56-58-224157. FAX 56-58-226737. *123*

IHERINGIA. SERIE ZOOLOGIA.
Fundacao Zoobotanica do Rio Grande do Sul, Museu de Ciencias Naturais, Caixa Postal 1188, 90690-000 Porto Alegre, RS, Brazil. *808*

ILLINOIS. NATURAL HISTORY SURVEY. BIOLOGICAL NOTES.
Department of Natural Resources, Natural History Survey, Natural Resources Bldg., 607 E. Peabody Dr., Champaign, IL 61820. TEL 217-244-2115. FAX 217-333-4949. *586*

ILLINOIS. NATURAL HISTORY SURVEY. BULLETIN.
Department of Natural Resources, Natural History Survey Division, Natural Resources Bldg., 607 E. Peabody Dr., Champaign, IL 61820. TEL 217-244-2115. FAX 217-333-4949. *586*

ILLINOIS. STATE MUSEUM. INVENTORY OF THE COLLECTIONS.
Illinois State Museum, Springfield, IL 62706. TEL 217-782-7386. FAX 217-782-1254. *5123*

ILLINOIS. STATE MUSEUM. POPULAR SCIENCE SERIES.
Illinois State Museum, Springfield, IL 62706. TEL 217-782-7386. FAX 217-782-1254. *6246*

ILLINOIS. STATE MUSEUM. RESEARCH SERIES. PAPERS IN ANTHROPOLOGY.
Illinois State Museum, Springfield, IL 62706. TEL 217-782-7386. FAX 217-782-1254. *312*

ILLINOIS. STATE MUSEUM. SCIENTIFIC PAPERS SERIES.
Illinois State Museum, Springfield, IL 62706. TEL 217-782-7386. FAX 217-782-1254. *6246*

ILLINOIS BIOLOGICAL MONOGRAPHS.
University of Illinois Press, 1325 S. Oak St., Champaign, IL 61820. TEL 217-333-0950. FAX 217-244-8082. *586*

ILLINOIS ENGLISH BULLETIN.
University of Illinois at Urbana-Champaign, English Department, 608 Wright St., Urbana, IL 61801. TEL 217-333-1006. FAX 217-333-4321. *2489*

ILLINOIS GEOGRAPHICAL SOCIETY. BULLETIN.
Illinois Geographical Society, c/o Michael Sublett, Illinois State University, Campus Box 4400, Normal, IL 61790-4400. TEL 309-438-7649. FAX 309-438-5310. *3261*

ILLINOIS HISTORICAL JOURNAL.
Illinois Historic Preservation Agency, Old State Capitol, Springfield, IL 62701. TEL 217-782-4836. *3472*

ILLINOIS JOURNAL OF MATHEMATICS.
University of Illinois Press, 1325 S. Oak St., Champaign, IL 61820. TEL 217-333-0950. FAX 217-244-8082. *4368*

ILLINOIS MEDIEVAL MONOGRAPH SERIES.
University of Illinois Press, 1325 S. Oak St., Champaign, IL 61820. TEL 217-333-0950. FAX 217-244-8082. *3418*

ILLINOIS SCHOOL RESEARCH AND DEVELOPMENT.
Illinois Association for Supervision and Curriculum Development, College of Education 5300, Illinois State University, Normal, IL 61790-5300. TEL 309-438-8294. FAX 309-438-3813. *2489*

ILLINOIS SPEECH AND THEATRE ASSOCIATION. JOURNAL.
Illinois Speech and Theatre Association, Bradley University, Peoria, IL 61625. TEL 309-677-2364. FAX 309-677-2330. *1906*

ILLINOIS STATE ACADEMY OF SCIENCE. TRANSACTIONS.
Illinois State Academy of Sciences, Illinois State Museum, Springfield, IL 62706. TEL 217-782-6436. FAX 217-782-1254. *6246*

ILLINOIS STEWARD.
Illinois Stewardship Committee, W503 Turner Hall, 1102 S. Goodwin Ave., Urbana, IL 61801. TEL 217-333-2778. FAX 217-244-3219. *2130*

ILLINOIS STUDIES IN ANTHROPOLOGY.
University of Illinois Press, 1325 S. Oak St., Champaign, IL 61820. TEL 217-333-0950. FAX 217-244-8082. *312*

ILLUSTRATED CASE REPORTS IN GASTROENTEROLOGY.
Chapman & Hall, Journals Department 2-6 Boundary Row, London SE1 8HN, England. TEL 44-171-8650066. FAX 44-171-5229323. *4693*

IMAGE & TEXT.
University of Pretoria, Faculty of Arts: Visual Art & Art History, Pretoria 0002, South Africa. TEL 27-12-420-2286. FAX 27-12-420-3686. *434*

IMAGE AND VISION COMPUTING.
Elsevier Science B.V., P.O. Box 211, 1000 AE Amsterdam, Netherlands. TEL 31-20-4853911. FAX 31-20-4853598. *2028*

IMAGE: JOURNAL OF NURSING SCHOLARSHIP.
Sigma Theta Tau International Honor Society of Nursing, 550 W. North St., Indianapolis, IN 46202. TEL 317-634-8171. FAX 317-634-8188. *4715*

IMAGE PROCESSING.
European Technology Publishing, Preston Barn, Preston Ln., Ramsbury, Malborough, Wilts. SN8 2HF, England. TEL 44-1632-520788. FAX 44-1672-520789. *5603*

IMAGE TECHNOLOGY.
British Kinematograph Sound and Television Society, G3-71 Victoria House, Vernon Pl., London WC1B 4DA, England. TEL 44-171-242-8400. FAX 44-171-405-3560. *5105*

IMAGINATION, COGNITION AND PERSONALITY.
Baywood Publishing Co., Inc., 26 Austin Ave., Box 337, Amityville, NY 11701. TEL 516-691-1270. FAX 516-691-1770. *5847*

IMAGING ABSTRACTS.
Pira International, Randalls Rd., Leatherhead, Surrey KT22 7RU, England. TEL 44-1372-802050. FAX 44-1372-802239. *5523*

IMAGING AND CLINICAL ANATOMY.
S. Karger AG, Allschwilerstr. 10, P.O. Box, CH-4009 Basel, Switzerland. TEL 061-3061111. FAX 061-3061234. *4469*

IMAGO MUNDI.
International Society for the History of Cartography, 285 Nether St., London N3 1PD, England. TEL 44-181-346-5112. *3261*

IMMIGRANTS AND MINORITIES.
Frank Cass, Newbury House, 890-900 Eastern Ave., Newbury Park, Ilford, Essex IG2 7HH, England. TEL 44-181-599-8866. FAX 44-181-599-0984. *5785*

IMMIGRATION AND NATIONALITY LAW REVIEW.
William S. Hein & Co., Inc., 1285 Main St., Buffalo, NY 14209. TEL 716-882-2600. FAX 800-882-7571. *3932*

IMMUNITY.
Cell Press, 50 Church St., Cambridge, MA 02138. TEL 617-661-7060. FAX 617-661-7061. *4581*

THE IMMUNOASSAY KIT DIRECTORY. SERIES A: CLINICAL CHEMISTRY.
Kluwer Academic Publishers, Postbus 17, 3300 AA Dordrecht, Netherlands. TEL 31-78-6392392. FAX 31-78-6392254. *4581*

IMMUNOLOGIC RESEARCH.
Humana Press Inc., 999 Riverview Dr., Ste. 208, Totowa, NJ 07512-1165. TEL 201-256-1699. FAX 201-256-8341. *4582*

IMMUNOLOGICAL INVESTIGATIONS.
Marcel Dekker Journals, 270 Madison Ave., New York, NY 10016. TEL 212-696-9000. FAX 212-685-4540. *4582*

IMMUNOLOGICAL REVIEWS.
Munksgaard International Publishers Ltd., 35 Noerre Soegade, P.O. Box 2148, DK-1016 Copenhagen K, Denmark. TEL 45-33-127030. FAX 45-33-129387. *4582*

IMMUNOLOGY.
Blackwell Science Ltd., Osney Mead, Oxford OX2 0EL, England. TEL 44-1865-206206. FAX 44-1865-721205. *4582*

IMMUNOLOGY AND MEDICINE.
Kluwer Academic Publishers, Postbus 17, 3300 AA Dordrecht, Netherlands. TEL 31-78-6392392. FAX 31-78-6392254. *4582*

IMMUNOLOGY LETTERS.
Elsevier Science B.V., P.O. Box 211, 1000 AE Amsterdam, Netherlands. TEL 31-20-4853911. FAX 31-20-4853598. *4583*

IMMUNOLOGY SERIES.
Marcel Dekker, Inc., 270 Madison Ave., New York, NY 10016. TEL 212-696-9000. FAX 212-685-4540. *4583*

IMMUNOLOGY TODAY (REFERENCE EDITION).
Elsevier Science Ltd., P.O. Box 800, Kidlington, Oxford OX5 1DX, England. TEL 44-1865-843000. FAX 44-1865-843010. *4583*

IMMUNOPHARMACOLOGY.
Elsevier Science B.V., P.O. Box 211, 1000 AE Amsterdam, Netherlands. TEL 31-20-4853911. FAX 31-20-4853598. *4583*

IMMUNOPHARMACOLOGY AND IMMUNOTOXICOLOGY.
Marcel Dekker Journals, 270 Madison Ave., New York, NY 10016. TEL 212-696-9000. FAX 212-685-4540. *5417*

IMMUNOTECHNOLOGY.
Elsevier Science B.V., P.O. Box 211, 1000 AE Amsterdam, Netherlands. TEL 31-20-4853911. FAX 31-20-4853598. *4583*

IMPACT ASSESSMENT.
International Association for Impact Assessment, Box 5256, Fargo, ND 58105. TEL 919-964-2338. FAX 919-964-2340. *6653*

IMPLANT DENTISTRY.
Williams & Wilkins, 351 W. Camden St., Baltimore, MD 21201. TEL 410-528-4000. FAX 410-528-4312. *4643*

IMPRESSIONS (DALLAS).
Miller Freeman Inc. (San Francisco) 13760 Noel Rd., Ste. 500, Dallas, TX 75240. TEL 214-239-3060. FAX 214-419-7825. *1841*

IN DIE SKRIFLIG.
Buro vir Wetenskaplike Tydskrifte, Private Bag X6001, Potchefstroom 2520, South Africa. TEL 27-148-2991769. FAX 27-148-2991562. *6147*

IN OTHER WORDS.
Wycliffe Bible Translators, Inc., Box 2727, Huntington Beach, CA 92647. TEL 714-969-4600. FAX 714-969-4661. *6067*

IN SESSION: PSYCHOTHERAPY IN PRACTICE.
John Wiley & Sons, Inc., Journals, 605 Third Ave., New York, NY 10158. TEL 212-850-6645. FAX 212-850-6021. *5847*

IN SITU.
Marcel Dekker Journals, 270 Madison Ave., New York, NY 10016. TEL 212-696-9000. FAX 212-685-4540. *2602*

IN TOUCH (LONDON, ONTARIO).
University of Western Ontario, Information Technology Services, Natural Sciences Centre, London, ON N6A 3K7, Canada. TEL 519-661-2151. FAX 519-661-3486. *1992*

IN VITRO CELLULAR & DEVELOPMENTAL BIOLOGY - ANIMAL.
Society for In Vitro Biology, 8815 Centre Park Dr., Ste. 210, Columbia, MD 21045. TEL 410-992-0946. FAX 410-992-0949. *758*

IN VITRO CELLULAR & DEVELOPMENTAL BIOLOGY - PLANT.
Society for In Vitro Biology, 8815 Centre Park Dr., Ste. 210, Columbia, MD 21045. TEL 410-992-0946. FAX 410-992-0949. *758*

IN VITRO REPORT.
Society for In Vitro Biology, 8815 Centre Park Dr., Ste. 210, Columbia, MD 21045. TEL 410-992-0946. FAX 410-992-0949. *758*

INDAGATIONES MATHEMATICAE.
North-Holland P.O. Box 211, 1000 AE Amsterdam, Netherlands. TEL 31-20-4853911. FAX 31-20-4853598. *4368*

INDEX OF ARTICLES ON JEWISH STUDIES.
Jewish National and University Library, P.O. Box 34165, Jerusalem 91341, Israel. TEL 972-2-585039. FAX 972-2-511771. *2917*

INDIAN ACADEMY OF MATHEMATICS. JOURNAL.
Indian Academy of Mathematics, 15 Kaushaliya Puri, Chitawad Rd., Indore 452001, India. TEL 91-731-400464. FAX 91-731-401389. *4368*

INDIAN CERAMIC SOCIETY. TRANSACTIONS.
Indian Ceramic Society, c/o Central Glass and Ceramic Research Institute, Calcutta 700032, India. TEL 473-3496. FAX 473-0957. *1657*

INDIAN CHEMICAL ENGINEER.
Indian Institute of Chemical Engineers, P.O. Box 17001, Raja S C Mullick Rd., Calcutta 700 032, India. TEL 9133-473-4670. *2642*

INDIAN CHEMICAL SOCIETY. JOURNAL.
Indian Chemical Society, 92 Acharya Prafulla Chandra Rd., Calcutta 700009, India. TEL 330-350-3478. *1677*

INDIAN DEFENCE REVIEW.
Lancer International, B-3 Gulmohar Park, New Delhi 110 049, India. TEL 655652. FAX 6862077. *5033*

INDIAN ECONOMIC AND SOCIAL HISTORY REVIEW.
Sage Publications India Pvt. Ltd., P.O. Box 4215, New Delhi 110 048, India. TEL 91-11-644-4958. FAX 91-11-647-2426. *6328*

INDIAN ECONOMIC JOURNAL.
Indian Economic Association, c/o Dynaram Electronics & Computers, No. 20 1st Fl., South Cross Rd., Bosavanagadi, Bangalore 560004, India. TEL 91-80-627010. FAX 91-80-500440. *930*

INDIAN FERN JOURNAL.
Indian Fern Society, c/o S.S. Bir, Ed., Department of Botany, Punjabi University Patiala 147 002, India. TEL 0175-822250. *685*

INDIAN GEOGRAPHICAL JOURNAL.
Indian Geographical Society, c/o Dept. of Geography, University of Madras Chepauk, Madras 600 005, India. TEL 91-44-568778. FAX 91-44-566693. *3261*

INDIAN JOURNAL OF ANIMAL NUTRITION.
Animal Nutrition Society of India, National Dairy Research Institute, Karnal 132 001 (Haryana), India. TEL 2832. *273*

INDIAN JOURNAL OF COMPARATIVE ANIMAL PHYSIOLOGY.
Indian Society for Comparative Animal Physiologists, Dept. of Zoology, Sri Venkateswara University, Tirupati 517502, India. TEL 91-8574-24166. FAX 91-8574-24111. *808*

INDIAN JOURNAL OF DENTAL RESEARCH.
Indian Society for Dental Research, 1-40, Port Trust Colony, Thirusulam, Madras 600 100, India. TEL 403522. *4643*

INDIAN JOURNAL OF EARTH SCIENCES.
Indian Society of Earth Sciences, Department of Geology, Presidency College, Calcutta 700 073, India. TEL 033-241-1903. *2210*

INDIAN JOURNAL OF FINANCE AND RESEARCH.
Indian Financial Management Association, 116-D Pocket IV, Mayur Vihar, New Delhi 110 091, India. TEL 2250164. *1100*

INDIAN JOURNAL OF GENDER STUDIES.
Sage Publications India Pvt. Ltd., P.O. Box 4215, New Delhi 110 048, India. TEL 91-11-6444958. FAX 91-11-6472426. *7017*

INDIAN JOURNAL OF HETEROCYCLIC CHEMISTRY.
C-85, Sector B, Aliganj Scheme, Lucknow 226 020, India. TEL 73421. *1679*

INDIAN JOURNAL OF MALARIOLOGY.
Indian Council of Medical Research, Malaria Research Center, 22, Sham Nath Marg, Delhi 110 054, India. TEL 91-11-2528455. FAX 91-11-7234234. *4621*

INDIAN JOURNAL OF MEDICAL RESEARCH. SECTION A: INFECTIOUS DISEASES.
Indian Council of Medical Research, Division of Publication & Information, P.O. Box 4911, Ansari Nagar, New Delhi 110 029, India. TEL 91-11-6963980. FAX 91-11-6868662. *4470*

INDIAN JOURNAL OF NATURAL RUBBER RESEARCH.
Rubber Research Institute of India, Kottayam 586 009, Kerala, India. TEL 91-481-578316. FAX 91-481-578317. *6216*

INDIAN JOURNAL OF NUTRITION AND DIETETICS.
Avinashilingam Institute for Home Science and Higher Education for Women, c/o Rajammal P. Devadas, Ed., Coimbatore 641 043, India. TEL 40241. *5234*

INDIAN JOURNAL OF PHARMACOLOGY.
Indian Pharmacologial Society, Department of Pharmacology, Jipmer, Pondicherry 605006, India. TEL 413-36380. FAX 413-38132. *5417*

INDIAN JOURNAL OF PHYSIOLOGY AND PHARMACOLOGY.
Association of Physiologists and Pharmacologists of India, Department of Physiology, All India Institute of Medical Sciences, Ansari Nagar, New Delhi 110 029, India. *788*

INDIAN JOURNAL OF PLASTIC SURGERY.
Association of Plastic Surgeons of India, Garga Hospital, Swarnambika Layout, Coimbatore 641 009, India. TEL 91-422-32050. FAX 91-422-438433. *4910*

INDIAN JOURNAL OF RURAL TECHNOLOGY.
Department of Rural Development, Council for Advancement of People's Action and Rural Technology (CAPART), D-58 Pankha Rd., New Delhi 110058, India. TEL 464-7954. FAX 464-8607. *6653*

INDIAN JOURNAL OF TRAINING & DEVELOPMENT.
Indian Society for Training & Development, B-41, Institutional Area, Behind Qutab Hotel, New Delhi 110016, India. TEL 011-6867710. FAX 011-6867607. *1505*

INDIAN ODONATOLOGY.
International Odonatological Society, D-f, Saraswati Nagar, Jodhpur 342 005, India. TEL 40766. *728*

INDIAN POTATO ASSOCIATION. JOURNAL.
Indian Potato Association, Central Potato Research Institute, Simla 171 001, India. TEL 0177-72182. FAX 0177-5016. *225*

INDIAN PSYCHOLOGICAL ABSTRACTS AND REVIEWS.
Sage Publications India Pvt. Ltd., P.O. Box 4215, New Delhi 110 048, India. TEL 91-11-644-4958. FAX 91-11-647-2426. *5889*

INDIAN SCIENCE CRUISER.
Institute of Science, Education and Culture, 42-B Syed Amir Ali Avenue, Calcutta 700 017, India. TEL 247-7985. *6247*

INDIAN THOUGHT.
E.J. Brill, P.O. Box 9000, 2300 PA Leiden, Netherlands. TEL 31-71-5353500. FAX 31-71-5317532. *5479*

INDIANA ACADEMY OF SCIENCE. PROCEEDINGS.
Indiana Academy of Science, 140 N. Senate Ave., Indianapolis, IN 46204. TEL 317-232-3686. *6247*

INDIANA CENTER ON GLOBAL CHANGE AND WORLD PEACE. OCCASIONAL PAPER SERIES.
Indiana Center on Global Change and World Peace, Indiana University, 1217 E. Atwater, Bloomington, IN 47405. TEL 812-855-8859. FAX 812-855-3209. *2801*

INDIANA DENTAL ASSOCIATION. JOURNAL.
Indiana Dental Association, Box 2467, Indianapolis, IN 46206-2467. TEL 317-634-2610. FAX 317-634-2612. *4643*

THE INDIANA HISTORIAN.
Indiana Historical Bureau, 140 N. Senate, Rm. 408, Indianapolis, IN 46204-2296. TEL 317-232-2535. FAX 317-232-3728. *2341*

INDIANA UNIVERSITY MATHEMATICS JOURNAL.
Indiana University, Department of Mathematics, Rawles Hall 115, Bloomington, IN 47405. TEL 812-855-2252. FAX 812-855-0046. *4368*

INDIGENOUS KNOWLEDGE AND DEVELOPMENT MONITOR.
Centre for International Research and Advisory Networks (CIRAN), P.O. Box 29777, 2502 LT The Hague, Netherlands. TEL 31-70-4260324. FAX 317-0-4260329. *1309*

INDIGENOUS WOMAN.
Indigenous Women's Network, Box 174, Lake Elmo, MN 55042. *6416*

INDO-IRANIAN JOURNAL.
Kluwer Academic Publishers, Postbus 17, 3300 AA Dordrecht, Netherlands. TEL 31-78-6392392. FAX 31-78-6392254. *5285*

INDO-PACIFIC FISHES.
Bishop Museum Press, 1525 Bernice St., Box 19000-A, Honolulu, HI 96817. TEL 808-848-4135. *808*

INDOLOGICA TAURINENSIA.
Association Internationale pour les Etudes Sanskrites, c/o C E S M E O, Via Cavour 17, 10123 Turin, Italy. TEL 33-1-44-27-10-98. *5285*

INDONESIA HUMAN RIGHTS CAMPAIGN. OCCASIONAL REPORTS.
Indonesia Human Rights Campaign, 111 Northwood Rd., Thornton Heath, Surrey CR7 8HW, England. TEL 0181-771-2904. FAX 0181-653-0322. *5730*

INDOOR AIR.
Munksgaard International Publishers Ltd., 35 Noerre Soegade, P.O. Box 2148, DK-1016 Copenhagen K, Denmark. TEL 45-33-127030. FAX 45-33-129387. *5964*

INDOOR ENVIRONMENT.
S. Karger AG, Allschwilerstr. 10, P.O. Box, CH-4009 Basel, Switzerland. TEL 061-3061111. FAX 061-3061234. *4583*

INDUSTRIA ALIMENTARIA.
Alfa Editores Tecnicos S.A., Libertad No. 107-402, 03660 Mexico DF, Mexico. TEL 525-579-3333. FAX 525-532-9504. *2976*

INDUSTRIAL AND LABOR RELATIONS REVIEW.
Cornell University, New York State School of Industrial and Labor Relations, Ithaca, NY 14853-3901. TEL 607-255-2732. FAX 607-255-8016. *1378*

INDUSTRIAL CHEMISTRY LIBRARY.
Elsevier Science B.V., Books Division, P.O. Box 211, 1000 AE Amsterdam, Netherlands. TEL 31-20-4853911. FAX 31-20-4853705. *1678*

INDUSTRIAL CROPS AND PRODUCTS.
Elsevier Science B.V., P.O. Box 211, 1000 AE Amsterdam, Netherlands. TEL 31-20-4853911. FAX 31-20-4853598. *225*

INDUSTRIAL LABORATORY.
Plenum Publishing Corp., Consultants Bureau, 233 Spring St., New York, NY 10013-1578. TEL 212-620-8468. FAX 212-463-0742. *6653*

INDUSTRIAL MARKETING MANAGEMENT.
Elsevier Science Inc., Box 945, New York, NY 10159-0945. TEL 212-633-3730. FAX 212-633-3680. *1468*

INDUSTRIAL RELATIONS JOURNAL.
Blackwell Publishers Ltd., 108 Cowley Rd., Oxford OX4 1JF, England. TEL 44-1865-791100. FAX 44-1865-791347. *1378*

INDUSTRIAL SAFETY SERIES.
Elsevier Science B.V., Books Division, P.O. Box 211, 1000 AE Amsterdam, Netherlands. TEL 31-20-4853911. FAX 31-20-4853705. *5251*

INDUSTRIAL SELLING.
Institute of Industrial Selling, c/o European Marketing Association, 18 St. Peters Steps, Brixham, Devon, England. *1468*

INDUSTRIE MANAGEMENT.
G I T O Verlag, Kellenzeile 50A, 13437 Berlin, Germany. TEL 49-30-3142118. FAX 49-30-4148270. *1992*

INDUSTRIELLE BEZIEHUNGEN.
Rainer Hampp Verlag, Meringerzellerstr. 16, 86415 Mering, Germany. TEL 49-8233-4783. FAX 49-8233-30755. *1379*

INDUSTRY AND HIGHER EDUCATION.
In Print Publishing Ltd., 9 Beaufort Terr., Brighton BN2 2SU, England. TEL 44-1273-682836. FAX 44-1273-620958. *2432*

INDUSTRY OF FREE CHINA.
Publishing Committee of Industry of Free China, 9th Fl., No. 87 Nanking E. Rd., Sec. 2, Taipei, Taiwan 10408, Republic of China. TEL 886-2-522-5404. FAX 886-2-562-2950. *931*

INFANCIA Y APRENDIZAJE.
Aprendizaje, S.L., Crta. de Canillas, 138, 28043 Madrid, Spain. TEL 388-38-74. FAX 300-35-27. *5848*

INFANT BEHAVIOR AND DEVELOPMENT.
Ablex Publishing Corporation, 355 Chestnut St., Norwood, NJ 07648. TEL 201-767-8455. FAX 201-767-6717. *5848*

INFANT MENTAL HEALTH JOURNAL.
John Wiley & Sons, Inc., Journals, 605 Third Ave., New York, NY 10158-0012. TEL 212-850-6645. FAX 212-850-6021. *4806*

INFANT - TODDLER INTERVENTION.
Singular Publishing Group, Inc., 401 W. A St., 325, San Diego, CA 92101-7901. FAX 800-774-8398. *4806*

INFECTION AND IMMUNITY.
American Society for Microbiology, 1325 Massachusetts Ave., N.W., Washington, DC 20005. TEL 202-737-3600. *4583*

INFECTION CONTROL & HOSPITAL EPIDEMIOLOGY.
Slack, Inc., 6900 Grove Rd., Thorofare, NJ 08086-9447. TEL 609-848-1000. FAX 609-853-5991. *4621*

INFECTION CONTROL & STERILIZATION TECHNOLOGY.
Mayworm Associates, Inc., 507 N. Milwaukee Ave., Libertyville, IL 60048. TEL 847-680-7878. FAX 847-680-8180. *4621*

INFECTIOUS AGENTS AND DISEASE.
Lippincott - Raven Publishers, 227 E. Washington Sq., Philadelphia, PA 19106. TEL 215-238-4200. *4622*

INFECTIOUS DISEASES IN OBSTETRICS AND GYNECOLOGY.
John Wiley & Sons, Inc., Journals, 605 Third Ave., New York, NY 10158. TEL 212-850-6645. FAX 212-850-6021. *4738*

INFEKTOLOGIIA.
Natsionalen Tsentar po Zarasni i Parasitni Bolesti, Bul. Yanko Sakazov 26, 1504 Sofia, Bulgaria. TEL 395-2-4347399. FAX 359-2-442260. *4622*

INFERTILITY.
c/o Dr. Louis A. Mucelli, Ed., 614 2nd Ave., Ste. H, New York, NY 10016. TEL 212-684-4242. FAX 212-684-4290. *4738*

INFLAMMATION.
Plenum Publishing Corp., 233 Spring St., New York, NY 10013-1578. TEL 212-620-8000. FAX 212-463-0742. *4471*

INFLAMMATION AND DRUG THERAPY SERIES.
Kluwer Academic Publishers, Postbus 17, 3300 AA Dordrecht, Netherlands. TEL 31-78-6392392. FAX 31-78-6392254. *5417*

INFLAMMOPHARMACOLOGY.
Kluwer Academic Publishers, Postbus 17, 3300 AA Dordrecht, Netherlands. TEL 31-78-6392392. FAX 31-78-6392254. *5417*

INFORMAL LOGIC.
Department of Philosophy, University of Windsor, Windsor, ON N9B 3P4, Canada. TEL 519-253-4232. FAX 519-973-7050. *5479*

INFORMATICA Y AUTOMATICA.
Asociacion Espanola de Informatica y Automatica, Hortaleza, 104, 28004 Madrid, Spain. TEL 34-1-3192565. FAX 34-1-3083028. *2015*

INFORMATION AND MANAGEMENT.
North-Holland P.O. Box 211, 1000 AE Amsterdam, Netherlands. TEL 31-20-4853911. FAX 31-20-4853598. *2066*

INFORMATION AND SOFTWARE TECHNOLOGY.
Elsevier Science B.V., P.O. Box 211, 1000 AE Amsterdam, Netherlands. TEL 31-20-4853911. FAX 31-20-4853598. *2075*

INFORMATION AND SYSTEMS ENGINEERING.
I O S Press, Van Diemenstraat 94, 1013 CN Amsterdam, Netherlands. TEL 31-20-6382189. FAX 31-20-6203419. *2707*

INFORMATION BULLETIN ON VARIABLE STARS.
Hungarian Academy of Sciences, Konkoly Observatory, Box 67, 1525 Budapest, Hungary. *481*

INFORMATION ECONOMICS AND POLICY.
North-Holland P.O. Box 211, 1000 AE Amsterdam, Netherlands. TEL 31-20-4853911. FAX 31-20-4853598. *1906*

INFORMATION EXCHANGE.
National Sudden Infant Death Syndrome Resource Center, 2070 Chain Bridge Rd., Ste. 450, Vienna, VA 22182-2536. TEL 703-821-8955. FAX 703-821-2098. *4806*

INFORMATION INFRASTRUCTURE AND POLICY.
I O S Press, Van Diemenstraat 94, 1013 CN Amsterdam, Netherlands. TEL 31-20-6382189. FAX 31-20-6203419. *2081*

INFORMATION LAW SERIES.
Kluwer Law International Postbus 85889, 2508 CN The Hague, Netherlands. TEL 31-70-3081500. FAX 31-70-3081515. *3791*

INFORMATION NETWORK AND DATA COMMUNICATION.
Elsevier Science B.V., Books Division, P.O. Box 211, 1000 AE Amsterdam, Netherlands. TEL 31-20-4853911. FAX 31-20-4853705. *2037*

INFORMATION PROCESSING & MANAGEMENT.
Elsevier Science Ltd., Pergamon, P.O. Box 800, Kidlington, Oxford OX5 1DX, England. TEL 44-1865-843000. FAX 44-1865-843010. *3999*

INFORMATION PROCESSING LETTERS.
North-Holland P.O. Box 211, 1000 AE Amsterdam, Netherlands. TEL 31-20-4853911. FAX 31-20-4853598. *2075*

INFORMATION PROCESSING SOCIETY OF JAPAN. TRANSACTIONS.
Information Processing Society of Japan, 7th Fl., Shibaura-Maekawa Bldg., 3-16-20, Shibaura, Minato-ku, Tokyo 108, Japan. TEL 81-3-5404-3535. FAX 81-3-5484-3534. *2075*

INFORMATION RESOURCES MANAGEMENT JOURNAL.
Idea Group Publishing, 4811 Jonestown Rd., Ste. 230, Harrisburg, PA 17109-1751. TEL 717-541-9150. FAX 717-541-9159. *1423*

INFORMATION SERVICES & USE.
I O S Press, Van Diemenstraat 94, 1013 CN Amsterdam, Netherlands. TEL 31-20-6382189. FAX 31-20-6203419. *2082*

THE INFORMATION SOCIETY.
Taylor & Francis Inc., 1900 Frost Rd., Ste. 101, Bristol, PA 19007-1598. TEL 215-785-5800. FAX 215-785-5515. *2082*

INFORMATION SYSTEMS.
Elsevier Science Ltd., Pergamon, P.O. Box 800, Kidlington, Oxford OX5 1DX, England. TEL 44-1865-843000. FAX 44-1865-843010. *4044*

INFORMATION SYSTEMS JOURNAL.
Blackwell Science Ltd., Osney Mead, Oxford OX2 OEL, England. TEL 44-1865-206206. FAX 44-1865-721205. *2082*

INFORMATION TECHNOLOGY AND LIBRARIES.
American Library Association, 50 E. Huron St, Chicago, IL 60611-2795. TEL 312-944-6780. FAX 312-440-9374. *4044*

INFORMATION TECHNOLOGY AND PUBLIC POLICY.
Parliamentary Information Technology Committee, W. Heaton, Old Hillside Rd., Winchester, Hants SO22 5LN, England. TEL 44-1962-868900. *3999*

INFORMATION TECHNOLOGY AND THE LAW.
Kluwer Law International Postbus 85889, 2508 CN The Hague, Netherlands. TEL 31-70-3081500. FAX 31-70-3081515. *3876*

INFORMATION TECHNOLOGY, EDUCATION AND SOCIETY.
James Nicholas Publishers, P.O. Box 244, Alberst Park, Vic. 3206, Australia. TEL 61-3-6965545. FAX 61-3-6992040. *2082*

INFORMATION TECHNOLOGY FOR DEVELOPMENT.
I O S Press, Van Diemenstraat 94, 1013 CN Amsterdam, Netherlands. TEL 31-20-6382189. FAX 31-20-6203419. *1309*

INFORMATION TECHNOLOGY REPORT.
U.S. National Biological Service, Information Transfer Center, c/o Managing Editor, 1201 Oak Ridge Dr., Ste. 200, Ft. Collins, CO 80525-5589. TEL 970-226-9401. FAX 970-226-9455. *710*

INFORMATORE DI VETERINARIA E ZOOTECNIA.
Organizzazione Editoriale Medico Farmaceutica, Via Edolo 42, 20125 Milan, Italy. TEL 39-2-675051. FAX 39-2-67505223. *6947*

INFORMAZIONI SUI FARMACI.
Farmacie Comunali Riunite di Reggio Emilia, Servizio Informazione e Documentazione Scientifica, Via Doberdo 9, 42100 Reggio Emilia, Italy. TEL 39-522-543450. FAX 39-522-550146. *5418*

INFRARED PHYSICS AND TECHNOLOGY.
Elsevier Science B.V., P.O. Box 211, 1000 AE Amsterdam, Netherlands. TEL 31-20-4853911. FAX 31-20-4853598. *5604*

INFUSIONSTHERAPIE UND TRANSFUSIONSMEDIZIN.
S. Karger AG, Allschwilerstr. 10, P.O. Box, CH-4009 Basel, Switzerland. TEL 061-3061111. FAX 061-3061234. *4701*

INGEGNERIA ALIMENTARE - CONSERVE ANIMALI.
G M Editoriale s.a.s., Via Lanzone 22, 20123 Milan, Italy. TEL 39-2-8055531. FAX 39-2-72010095. *2977*

INGENIERIA HIDRAULICA EN MEXICO.
Instituto Mexicano de Tecnologia del Agua, Apdo. Postal No. 202, C.P. 65500, CIVAC, Morelos, Mexico. TEL 52-73-194000 ext. 553. FAX 52-73-194341. *6970*

INHALATION TOXICOLOGY.
Taylor & Francis Inc., 1900 Frost Rd., Ste. 101, Bristol, PA 19007-1598. TEL 215-785-5800. FAX 215-785-5515. *2846*

INITIATIVES.
National Association for Women in Education, 1325 18th St., N.W., No. 210, Washington, DC 20036-6511. TEL 202-659-9330. FAX 202-457-0946. *2458*

INJURY.
Butterworth - Heinemann, Part of the Reed Elsevier group, Linacre House, Jordan Hill, Oxford OX2 8DP, England. TEL 44-1865-310366. FAX 44-1865-310898. *4784*

INJURY PREVENTION.
B M J Publishing Group, B.M.A. House, Tavistock Sq., London WC1H 9JR, England. TEL 44-171-387-4499. FAX 44-171-383-6661. *4806*

INKS: CARTOON AND COMIC ARTS STUDIES.
Ohio State University Press, 1070 Carmack Rd., Columbus, OH 43210-1002. TEL 614-292-6930. FAX 614-292-2065. *434*

INNER VOICE.
A F S E E E, Box 11615, Eugene, OR 97440. TEL 541-484-2692. FAX 541-484-3004. *3019*

INNOVANT.
Sentrum vir Mensilike Ontwikkeling in Psigososiele Konteks - CEMCO, Department of Psychology, University of Pretoria, Lynnwood Rd., Brooklyn 0181, South Africa. TEL 27-12-4203430. FAX 27-12-4202404. *5848*

INNOVATION (ABINGDON).
Carfax Publishing Co., P.O. Box 25, Abingdon, Oxon. OX14 3UE, England. TEL 44-1235-401000. FAX 44-1235-401550. *6328*

INNOVATIVE HIGHER EDUCATION.
Human Sciences Press, Inc. 233 Spring St., New York, NY 10013-1578. TEL 212-620-8000. FAX 212-463-0742. *2432*

INORGANIC MATERIALS.
Maik Nauk - Interperiodica, Mezhdunarodnyi Otdel, Ul. Profsoyuznaya, 90, 117864 Moscow, Russia. TEL 7-095-3360066. FAX 7-095-3360066. *1731*

INORGANIC SYNTHESES SERIES.
John Wiley & Sons, Inc., Journals, 605 Third Ave., New York, NY 10158-0012. TEL 212-850-6645. *1752*

INORGANICA CHIMICA ACTA.
Elsevier Science S.A., P.O. Box 564, CH-1001 Lausanne 1, Switzerland. TEL 41-21-3207381. FAX 41-21-3235444. *1731*

INQUIRY (ROCHESTER).
Blue Cross and Blue Shield of the Rochester Area, Box 25399, Rochester, NY 14625. TEL 716-264-9122. *4471*

INSECT BIOCHEMISTRY AND MOLECULAR BIOLOGY.
Elsevier Science Ltd., Pergamon, P.O. Box 800, Kidlington, Oxford OX5 1DX, England. TEL 44-1865-843000. FAX 44-1865-843010. *728*

INSECT MOLECULAR BIOLOGY.
Blackwell Science Ltd., Osney Mead, Oxford OX2 OEL, England. TEL 44-1865-206206. FAX 44-1865-721205. *728*

INSECTA MUNDI.
Center for Systematic Entomology, Box 140429 Gainesville, FL 32614. *728*

INSECTS OF VIRGINIA.
Virginia Polytechnic Institute and State University, Department of Entomology, Blacksburg, VA 24061-0319. TEL 703-231-6341. *729*

INSIDE ARTS.
Association of Performing Arts Presenters, 1112 16th St., N.W., Ste. 400, Washington, DC 20035. TEL 202-833-2787. FAX 202-833-1543. *6697*

INSIDE THE VATICAN.
Urbi et Orbi Communications, 3050 Gap Knob Rd., New Hope, KY 40052. TEL 502-325-3061. FAX 502-325-3091. *6182*

INSIGHT (NORTHAMPTON).
British Institute of Non-Destructive Testing, 1 Spencer Parade, Northampton NN1 5AA, England. TEL 44-1604-30124. FAX 44-1604-231489. *4958*

INSIGHT - JOURNAL OF THE AMERICAN SOCIETY OF OPHTHALMIC REGISTERED NURSES.
Mosby - Year Book, Inc. 11830 Westline Industrial Dr., St. Louis, MO 63146-3318. TEL 314-872-8370. FAX 314-432-1350. *4770*

INSTITUT DE LA COMMUNICATION PARLEE. RAPPORT DE RECHERCHE.
Institut de la Communication Parlee, Universite Stendhal, B.P. 25 X, 38040 Grenoble Cedex 9 France. TEL 76-82-43-37. FAX 76-82-43-35. *4075*

INSTITUT FUER ALLGEMEINE BOTANIK UND BOTANISCHER GARTEN MITTEILUNGEN.
Universitaet Hamburg, Institut fuer Allgemeine Botanik und Botanischer Garten, Ohnhorststr. 18, 22609 Hamburg, Germany. FAX 49-40-82282254. *685*

INSTITUT FUER WELTWIRTSCHAFT. ANNUAL REPORT.
Institut fuer Weltwirtschaft, Duesternbrooker Weg 120, 24105 Kiel, Germany. TEL 49-431-8814305. FAX 49-431-8814520. *1216*

INSTITUT PASTEUR. ANNALES. ACTUALITES.
Editions Scientifiques et Medicales Elsevier, 141 rue de Javel, 75747 Paris, France. TEL 33-1-45589022. FAX 33-1-45589421. *759*

INSTITUT PASTEUR. BULLETIN.
Editions Scientifiques et Medicales Elsevier, 141 rue de Javel, 75747 Paris, France. TEL 33-1-45589022. FAX 33-1-45589421. *4622*

INSTITUTE OF ECONOMIC AFFAIRS. OCCASIONAL PAPERS.
Institute of Economic Affairs, 2 Lord North St. London SW1P 3LB, England. TEL 44-171-799-3745. FAX 44-171-799-2137. *932*

INSTITUTE OF ECONOMIC AFFAIRS. RESEARCH MONOGRAPHS.
Institute of Economic Affairs, 2 Lord North St., London SW1P 3LB, England. TEL 44-171-799-3745. FAX 44-171-799-2137. *932*

INSTITUTE OF ENVIRONMENTAL SCIENCES. JOURNAL.
Institute of Environmental Sciences, 940 E. Northwest Hwy., Mt. Prospect, IL 60056. TEL 847-255-1561. FAX 847-255-1699. *2802*

INSTITUTE OF HEALTH EDUCATION. JOURNAL.
Institute of Health Education, 9 Elm Ridge Dr, Hale Barns, Altrincham, Ches. WA15 0JE, England. TEL 44-161-980-8276. FAX 44-161-980-7446. *2341*

INSTITUTE OF MATHEMATICAL GEOGRAPHY. MONOGRAPH SERIES.
Institute of Mathematical Geography, 2790 Briarcliff, Ann Arbor, MI 48105-1429. TEL 313-761-1231. *4369*

INSTITUTE OF MEASUREMENT AND CONTROL. TRANSACTIONS.
Institute of Measurement and Control, 87 Gower St., London WC1E 6AA, England. TEL 44-171-387-4949. FAX 44-171-388-8431. *3635*

INSTITUTE OF MEDICINE OF CHICAGO. PROCEEDINGS.
Institute of Medicine of Chicago, 332 S. Michigan Ave., Chicago, IL 60604-4022. TEL 312-663-0040. FAX 312-663-9058. *4471*

INSTITUTE OF METAL FINISHING. TRANSACTIONS.
Institute of Metal Finishing, Exeter House, 48 Holloway Head, Birmingham B1 1NQ, England. TEL 44-121-622-7387. FAX 44-121-666-6316. *4958*

INSTITUTE OF ROMANCE STUDIES. JOURNAL.
Institute of Romance Studies, Publications Office, Senate House, Malet St., London WC1E 7HU, England. TEL 44-171-636-8000. FAX 44-171-436-4533. *4075*

INSTITUTE OF STATISTICAL MATHEMATICS. ANNALS.
Kluwer Academic Publishers, Postbus 17, 3300 AA Dordrecht, Netherlands. TEL 31-78-6392392. FAX 31-78-6392254. *4369*

INSTITUTION OF CHEMISTS (INDIA). JOURNAL.
Institution of Chemists (India), 11-4, Dr. Biresh Guha Road, Calcutta 700 017, India. TEL 40-3832. *1678*

INSTITUTION OF CIVIL ENGINEERS. PROCEEDINGS. CIVIL ENGINEERING.
Thomas Telford Services Ltd., Thomas Telford House, 1 Heron Quay, London E14 4JD, England. TEL 44-171-987-6999. FAX 44-171-538-9620. *2662*

INSTITUTION OF CIVIL ENGINEERS. PROCEEDINGS. GEOTECHNICAL ENGINEERING.
Thomas Telford Services Ltd., Thomas Telford House, 1 Heron Quay, London E14 4JD, England. TEL 44-171-987-6999. FAX 44-171-538-9620. *2662*

INSTITUTION OF CIVIL ENGINEERS. PROCEEDINGS. MUNICIPAL ENGINEER.
Thomas Telford Services Ltd., Thomas Telford House, 1 Heron Quay, London E14 4JD, England. TEL 44-171-987-6999. FAX 44-171-538-9620. *2662*

INSTITUTION OF CIVIL ENGINEERS. PROCEEDINGS. STRUCTURES AND BUILDINGS.
Thomas Telford Services Ltd., Thomas Telford House, 1 Heron Quay, London E14 4JD, England. TEL 44-171-987-6999. FAX 44-171-538-9620. *2663*

INSTITUTION OF CIVIL ENGINEERS. PROCEEDINGS. TRANSPORT.
Thomas Telford Services Ltd., Thomas Telford House, 1 Heron Quay, London E14 4JD, England. TEL 44-171-987-6999. FAX 44-171-538-9620. *2663*

INSTITUTION OF CIVIL ENGINEERS. PROCEEDINGS. WATER, MARITIME AND ENERGY.
Thomas Telford Services Ltd., Thomas Telford House, 1 Heron Quay, London E14 4JD, England. TEL 44-171-987-6999. FAX 44-171-538-9620. *2663*

INSTITUTION OF ELECTRONICS AND TELECOMMUNICATION ENGINEERS. JOURNAL.
Institution of Electronics and Telecommunication Engineers, 2, Institutional Area, Lodi Rd., New Delhi 110 003, India. TEL 11-4631850. *1907*

INSTITUTION OF ENGINEERS (INDIA). TEXTILE ENGINEERING DIVISION. JOURNAL.
Institution of Engineers (India), 8 Gokhale Rd., Calcutta 700 020, India. TEL 033-288334. FAX 033-288345. *6679*

INSTITUTION OF MECHANICAL ENGINEERS. PROCEEDINGS. PART J: JOURNAL OF ENGINEERING TRIBOLOGY.
Mechanical Engineering Publications Ltd., Northgate Ave., Bury St. Edmunds, Suffolk IP32 6BW, England. TEL 01284-763277. FAX 01284-704006. *2757*

INSTITUTO ADOLFO LUTZ. REVISTA.
Instituto Adolfo Lutz, Av. Dr. Arnaldo 355, C.P. 7027, 01246-902 Sao Paulo SP, Brazil. TEL 55-11-8510111. FAX 55-11-8533505. *640*

INSTITUTO DE INVESTIGACION TEXTIL Y DE COOPERACION INDUSTRIAL. BOLETIN INTEXTER.
Instituto de Investigacion Textil y de Cooperacion Industrial, Colon 15, 08222 Terrassa, Spain. TEL 34-3-7398277. FAX 34-3-7398272. *6679*

INSTITUTO DE LA PATAGONIA. ANALES. CIENCIAS SOCIALES.
Universidad de Magallanes, Instituto de la Patagonia, Casilla de Correo 113-D, Punta Arenas, Magallanes, Chile. TEL 56-61-212913. FAX 56-61-212973. *3473*

INSTITUTO NACIONAL DE CANCEROLOGIA DE MEXICO. REVISTA.
Editorial Cultura Medica S.A., Casma 576, Col. Lindavista 2C, 07300 Mexico, D.F., Mexico. TEL 525-6280429. FAX 525-57346662. *4757*

INSTITUTO NACIONAL DE MEDICINA LEGAL DE COLOMBIA. REVISTA.
Instituto Nacional de Medicina Legal y Ciencias Forenses, Division de Desarrollo Tecnologico y Normalizacion, Calle 7A, 12-61 Bogota, DC, Colombia. TEL 571-2-339883. FAX 571-2-338534. *4686*

INSTITUTO POLITECNICO NACIONAL. ESCUELA NACIONAL DE CIENCIAS BIOLOGICAS. ANALES.
Instituto Politecnico Nacional, Escuela Nacional de Ciencias Biologicas, Carpio y Plan de Ayala, Col. Santo Tomas, Apdo. Postal 42-186, 11340, Mexico, D.F., Mexico. FAX 525-3963503. *640*

INSTITUTUL DE STUDII SI PROIECTARI ENERGETICE. BULETINUL.
Institutul de Studii si Proiectari Energetice, Bd. Lacul Tei nr. 1, Sector 2, 72301 Bucarest 30, Rumania. TEL 401-2107080. FAX 401-2103620. *2551*

INSTRUCTIONAL SCIENCE.
Kluwer Academic Publishers, Postbus 17, 3300 AA Dordrecht, Netherlands. TEL 31-78-6392392. FAX 31-78-6392254. *2342*

INSTRUCTIONAL STRATEGIES: AN APPLIED RESEARCH SERIES.
Delta Pi Epsilon Graduate Business Education Society, National Office, Box 4340, Little Rock, AR 72214. TEL 501-562-1233. FAX 501-562-1293. *2489*

INSTRUMENTATION, CONTROLS, AND AUTOMATION IN THE POWER INDUSTRY.
Instrument Society of America, 67 Alexander Dr., Box 12277, Research Triangle Park, NC 27709. TEL 919-549-8411. FAX 919-549-8288. *3635*

INSTRUMENTATION FOR THE PROCESS INDUSTRIES.
Instrument Society of America, 67 Alexander Dr., Box 12277, Research Triangle Park, NC 27709. TEL 919-549-8411. FAX 919-549-8288. *3635*

INSTRUMENTATION SCIENCE & TECHNOLOGY.
Marcel Dekker Journals, 270 Madison Ave., New York, NY 10016. TEL 212-696-9000. FAX 212-685-4540. *1716*

INSTRUMENTS AND EXPERIMENTAL TECHNIQUES.
Maik Nauka - Interperiodica, Mezhdunarodnyi Otdel, Ul. Profsoyuznaya, 90, 117864 Moscow, RU. TEL 7-095-3360066. FAX 7-095-3360066. *3635*

INSTYTUT MEDYCYNY MORSKIEJ I TROPIKALNEJ W GDYNI. BULLETIN.
Instytut Medycyny Morskiej i Tropikalnej w Gdyni, Ul. Powstania Styczniowego 9B, 81-519 Gdynia-Radlowo, Poland. TEL 48-58-223011. FAX 48-58-223354. *4622*

INSTYTUT METALURGII ZELAZA. PRACE.
Instytut Metalurgii Zelaza, Ul. K. Miarki 12, 44-100 Gliwice, Poland. TEL 48-32-314051. FAX 48-32-313594. *4958*

INSTYTUT TECHNOLOGII DREWNA. PRACE.
Instytut Technologii Drewna, Ul. Winiarska 1, 60-654 Poznan, Poland. TEL 48-61-224081. FAX 48-61-224372. *886*

INSURANCE BROKER.
National Insurance Brokers Association, 2 Jocelyn Ct., Doncaster East, Vic. 3109, Australia. TEL 61-3-848-9540. FAX 61-3-848-6908. *3652*

INSURANCE INSTITUTE OF CANADA. PERSPECTIVES.
Insurance Institute of Canada, 18 King St. E., 6th Fl., Toronto, ON M5C 1C4, Canada. TEL 416-362-8586. FAX 416-362-1126. *3652*

INSURANCE LAW ANTHOLOGY.
International Library Law Book Publishers, Inc., 4301 N. Fairfax Dr., Ste 875, Arlington, VA 22203. TEL 703-528-1000. FAX 703-528-6060. *3653*

INSURANCE: MATHEMATICS & ECONOMICS.
North-Holland P.O. Box 211, 1000 AE Amsterdam, Netherlands. TEL 31-20-4853911. FAX 31-20-4853598. *3653*

INSURANCE SERIES.
Elsevier Science B.V., Books Division, P.O. Box 211, 1000 AE Amsterdam, Netherlands. TEL 31-20-4853911. FAX 31-20-4853705. *3653*

INTEGRAL.
Eastman School of Music, 26 Gibbs St., Rochester, NY 14604. TEL 716-274-1000. FAX 716-274-1088. *5164*

INTEGRATED COMPUTER-AIDED ENGINEERING.
John Wiley & Sons, Inc., Journals, 605 Third Ave., New York, NY 10158. TEL 212-850-6645. FAX 212-850-6021. *2021*

INTEGRATED FERROELECTRICS.
Gordon and Breach Science Publishers, c/o International Publishers Distributor, P.O. Box 3054, Langhorne, PA 19047-3054. TEL 215-750-2642. FAX 215-750-6343. *2708*

INTEGRATED PEST MANAGEMENT REVIEWS.
Chapman & Hall, Journals Department 2-6 Boundary Row, London SE1 8HN, England. TEL 44-171-8650066. FAX 44-171-5229623. *226*

INTEGRATION.
Elsevier Science B.V., P.O. Box 211, 1000 AE Amsterdam, Netherlands. TEL 31-20-4853911. FAX 31-20-4853598. *2078*

INTEGRATIVE PSYCHIATRY.
International Universities Press, Inc., 59 Boston Post Rd., Box 1523, CT 06443-1524. TEL 203-245-4000. FAX 203-245-0775. *4841*

INTELLECTUAL PROPERTY LAW (NEW YORK).
Harwood Academic Publishers, c/o International Publishers Distributor, P.O. Box 3054, Langhorne, PA 19047-3054. TEL 215-750-2462. FAX 215-750-6343. *5340*

INTELLIGENCE (NORWOOD).
Ablex Publishing Corporation, 355 Chestnut St., Norwood, NJ 07648. TEL 201-767-8455. FAX 201-767-6717. *5849*

INTELLIGENCE AND NATIONAL SECURITY.
Frank Cass, Newbury House, 890-900 Eastern Ave., Newbury Park, Ilford, Essex 1G2 7HH, England. TEL 44-181-599-8866. FAX 44-181-599-0984. *5754*

INTENSIV.
Georg Thieme Verlag, Ruedigerstr. 14, 70469 Stuttgart, Germany. TEL 0711-8931443. FAX 0711-8931258. *4472*

INTERACTING WITH COMPUTERS.
Elsevier Science B.V., P.O. Box 211, 1000 AE Amsterdam, Netherlands. TEL 31-20-4853911. FAX 31-20-4853598. *1993*

INTER-AMERICAN TROPICAL TUNA COMMISSION. BULLETIN.
Inter-American Tropical Tuna Commission, c/o Scripps Institution of Oceanography, 8604 La Jolla Shores Dr., La Jolla, CA 92037-1508. TEL 619-546-7100. FAX 619-546-7133. *2936*

INTERCHANGE.
Kluwer Academic Publishers, Postbus 17, 3300 AA Dordrecht, Netherlands. TEL 31-78-6392392. FAX 31-78-6392254. *2342*

INTERCULTURAL COMMUNICATION STUDIES.
Institute for Cross-Cultural Research, Trinity University, No. 418, 715 Stadium Dr., San Antonio, TX 78212-7200. TEL 210-736-7369. FAX 210-494-4435. *6417*

INTERDISCIPLINARY CONTRIBUTIONS TO ARCHAEOLOGY.
Plenum Publishing Corp., 233 Spring St., New York, NY 10013-1578. TEL 212-620-8000. FAX 212-463-0742. *357*

INTERDISCIPLINARY TOPICS IN GERONTOLOGY.
S. Karger AG, Allschwilerstr. 10, P.O. Box, CH-4009 Basel, Switzerland. TEL 061-3061111. FAX 061-3061234. *3289*

INTEREST GROUP IN PURE AND APPLIED LOGICS. BULLETIN.
Interest Group in Pure and Applied Logics, c/o Max-Planck-Institut fuer Informatik, Im Stadtwald, 66123 Saarbruecken, Germany. *5480*

INTERFACE: BRADFORD STUDIES IN LANGUAGE, CULTURE AND SOCIETY.
University of Bradford, Department of Modern Languages, Bradford, W. Yorks. BD7 1DP, England. TEL 44-1274-733466. FAX 44-1274-385590. *4220*

INTERFACE SCIENCE.
Kluwer Academic Publishers Boston, Box 358, Accord Sta., Hingham, MA 02018-0358. TEL 617-871-6600. FAX 617-871-6528. *1752*

INTERFACES: LINGUISTICS, PSYCHOLOGY AND HEALTH THERAPEUTICS.
Providence College Press, Providence, RI 02918. *4075*

INTERMETALLICS.
Elsevier Science Ltd., P.O. Box 800, Kidlington, Oxford OX5 1DX, England. TEL 44-1865-843000. FAX 44-1865-843010. *4958*

INTERNATIONAL ACADEMY FOR BIOMEDICAL AND DRUG RESEARCH.
S. Karger AG, Allschwilerstr. 10, P.O. Box, CH-4009 Basel, Switzerland. TEL 061-3061111. FAX 061-3061234. *5418*

INTERNATIONAL ADVANCES IN NONDESTRUCTIVE TESTING.
Gordon & Breach Science Publishers, c/o International Publishers Distributor, P.O. Box 3054, Langhorne, PA 19047-3054. TEL 215-750-2642. FAX 215-750-6343. *2732*

INTERNATIONAL AGROPHYSICS.
Foundation for Development of Agrophysical Research, Ul. Doswiadczalna 4, P.O. Box 121, 20-236 Lublin, Poland. TEL 48-81-450-61. FAX 48-81-450-67. *226*

INTERNATIONAL ANGIOLOGY.
Edizioni Minerva Medica, Corso Bramante 83-85, 10126 Turin, Italy. TEL 39-11-678282. FAX 39-11-3121736. *4604*

INTERNATIONAL ANNALS OF ADOLESCENT PSYCHIATRY.
University of Chicago Press, Journals Division, Box 37005, Chicago, IL 60637. TEL 773-753-3347. FAX 773-753-0811. *4841*

INTERNATIONAL ANTIVIRAL NEWS.
MediTech Media Ltd., 125 High Holborn, London WC1V 6QA, England. TEL 44-171-404-7151. FAX 44-171-404-6946. *4583*

INTERNATIONAL APPLIED MECHANICS.
Plenum Publishing Corp., Consultants Bureau, 233 Spring St., New York, NY 10013-1578. TEL 212-620-8468. FAX 212-463-0742. *2732*

INTERNATIONAL ARCHIVES OF ALLERGY AND IMMUNOLOGY.
S. Karger AG, Allschwilerstr. 10, P.O. Box, CH-4009 Basel, Switzerland. TEL 061-3061111. FAX 061-3061234. *4584*

INTERNATIONAL ASSOCIATION OF ENGINEERING GEOLOGY. BULLETIN.
A I G I, Laboratoire Central des Ponts et Chaussees, 58 bd. Lefebvre, 75732 Paris Cedex 15, France. FAX 40-43-54-98. *2244*

INTERNATIONAL ASTRONOMICAL UNION. GENERAL ASSEMBLY. HIGHLIGHTS.
Kluwer Academic Publishers, Postbus 17, 3300 AA Dordrecht, Netherlands. TEL 31-78-6392392. FAX 31-78-6392254. *481*

INTERNATIONAL ASTRONOMICAL UNION. PROCEEDINGS OF SYMPOSIA.
Kluwer Academic Publishers, Postbus 17, 3300 AA Dordrecht, Netherlands. TEL 31-78-6392392. FAX 31-78-6392254. *481*

INTERNATIONAL ASTRONOMICAL UNION. TRANSACTIONS.
Kluwer Academic Publishers, Postbus 17, 3300 AA Dordrecht, Netherlands. TEL 31-78-6392392. FAX 31-78-6392254. *481*

INTERNATIONAL BIODETERIORATION & BIODEGRADATION.
Elsevier Science Ltd., P.O. Box 800, Kidlington, Oxford OX5 1DX, England. TEL 44-1865-843000. FAX 44-1865-843010. *662*

INTERNATIONAL BIODETERIORATION SYMPOSIUM. PROCEEDINGS.
Elsevier Science Ltd., Books Division, P.O. Box 800, Kidlington, Oxford OX5 1DX, England. TEL 44-1865-843000. FAX 44-1865-843010. *662*

INTERNATIONAL BUSINESS REVIEW.
Elsevier Science Ltd., Pergamon, P.O. Box 800, Kidlington, Oxford OX5 1DX, England. TEL 44-1865-843000. FAX 44-1865-843010. *932*

INTERNATIONAL CATALOGUING AND BIBLIOGRAPHIC CONTROL.
International Federation of Library Associations, UBCIM Programme, c/o Deutsche Bibliothek, 4-8 Zeppelinallee, 60325 Frankfurt a.M., Germany. TEL 49-69-7410906. FAX 49-69-7566224. *4000*

INTERNATIONAL CHRISTIAN UNIVERSITY. LANGUAGE RESEARCH BULLETIN.
International Christian University, Division of Languages, 3-10-2 Osawa, Mitaka, Tokyo 181, Japan. TEL 0422-33-3214. FAX 0412-33-9887. *4075*

INTERNATIONAL COMET QUARTERLY.
International Comet Quarterly, Smithsonian Astrophysical Observatory, M.S.18, 60 Garden St., Cambridge, MA C2138. TEL 617-495-7440. *482*

INTERNATIONAL COMMISSION ON RADIOLOGICAL PROTECTION. ANNALS.
Elsevier Science Ltd., Pergamon, P.O. Box 800, Kidlington, Oxford OX5 1DX, England. TEL 44-1865-843000. FAX 44-1865-843010. *4877*

INTERNATIONAL COMMUNICATIONS IN HEAT AND MASS TRANSFER.
Elsevier Science Ltd., Pergamon, P.O. Box 800, Kidlington, Oxford OX5 1DX, England. TEL 44-1865-843000. FAX 44-1865-843010. *2757*

INTERNATIONAL CONFERENCE ON BASEMENT TECTONICS. PROCEEDINGS.
Kluwer Academic Publishers, Postbus 17, 3300 AA Dordrecht, Netherlands. TEL 31-78-6392392. FAX 31-78-6392254. *2210*

INTERNATIONAL CONFERENCE ON COMPUTER COMMUNICATIONS. (PROCEEDINGS).
Elsevier Science Inc., Box 945, New York, NY 10159-0945. TEL 212-633-3730. FAX 212-633-3680. *2069*

INTERNATIONAL CONFERENCE ON VERY LARGE DATA BASES. PROCEEDINGS.
Morgan Kaufmann Publishers, Inc., 340 Pine St., 6th Fl., San Francisco, CA 94104-3205. TEL 415-392-2665. FAX 415-982-2665. *2066*

INTERNATIONAL CONGRESS FOR STEREOLOGY. PROCEEDINGS.
International Society for Stereology, c/o Dr. Aurora Astudillo, Sec.-Treas., Tatiana, Univ. de Oviedo, Ed. Quimicas, Julian Claveria s-n, 33006 Oviedo, Spain. TEL 34-85-103658. *2732*

INTERNATIONAL CONGRESS OF OPHTHALMOLOGY. ABSTRACTS.
International Federation of Ophthalmological Societies, c/o Dr. Bruce E. Spivey, Northwestern Healthcare Network, 980 N. Michigan Ave., Ste. 1500, Chicago, IL 60611. *4770*

INTERNATIONAL CONGRESS ON COMBUSTION ENGINES. PROCEEDINGS.
International Council on Combustion Engines, c/o V D M A e.V., Lyoner Strasse 18, 60528 Frankfurt, Germany. TEL 49-69-6603-1567. FAX 49-69-6603-1566. *2757*

INTERNATIONAL CONGRESS SERIES.
Elsevier Science B.V., Books Division, P.O. Box 211, 1000 AE Amsterdam, Netherlands. TEL 31-20-4853911. FAX 31-20-43537C5. *6248*

INTERNATIONAL CONTACT LENS CLINIC.
Elsevier Science Inc., Box 945, New York, NY 10159-0945. TEL 212-633-3730. FAX 212-633-3680. *4771*

INTERNATIONAL CRISIS BEHAVIOR.
University of California Press, 2120 Berkeley Way, Berkeley, CA 94720. TEL 510-642-4247. FAX 510-643-7127. *5755*

INTERNATIONAL CRYOGENICS MONOGRAPH SERIES.
Plenum Publishing Corp., 233 Spring St., New York, NY 10013-1578. TEL 212-620-8000. FAX 212-463-0742. *5584*

INTERNATIONAL DAIRY JOURNAL.
Elsevier Science Ltd., P.O. Box 800, Kidlington, Oxford OX5 1DX, England. TEL 44-1865-843000. FAX 44-1865-843010. *251*

INTERNATIONAL DEFENCE NEWSLETTER.
I T X Publishing, P.O. Box 28, Twickenham, Middx. TW1 1EH, England. TEL 44-181-8927471. FAX 44-181-7442704. *5034*

INTERNATIONAL DENTAL JOURNAL.
F D I World Dental Press Ltd., 7 Carlisle St., London W1V 5RG, England. TEL 0171-935-7852. FAX 0171-486-0183. *4643*

INTERNATIONAL DERIVE JOURNAL.
Research Information Ltd., 222 Maylands Ave., Hemel Hempstead, Herts. HP2 7TD, England. TEL 44-1442-213222. FAX 44-1442-259395. *2020*

INTERNATIONAL ECONOMIC DEVELOPMENT LAW.
Kluwer Law International Postbus 85889, 2508 CN The Hague, Netherlands. TEL 31-70-3081500. FAX 31-70-3081515. *3934*

INTERNATIONAL ECONOMIC JOURNAL.
Department of International Economics, College of Social Sciences, Seoul University, Seoul 151-742, S Korea. TEL 82-2-880-6394. FAX 82-2-876-0357. *1217*

INTERNATIONAL ECONOMIC REVIEW.
University of Pennsylvania, Department of Economics, 3718 Locust Walk, Philadelphia, PA 19104-6297. TEL 215-898-5841. FAX 215-573-2072. *932*

INTERNATIONAL EDUCATION.
University of Tennessee at Knoxville, College of Education, 212 Claxton, Knoxville, TN 37996-3400. TEL 423-974-4252. FAX 423-974-8718. *2451*

INTERNATIONAL EMERGENCY MANAGEMENT AND ENGINEERING CONFERENCE. PROCEEDINGS.
Society for Computer Simulation, Box 17900, San Diego, CA 92177. TEL 619-277-3888. FAX 609-277-3930. *2052*

INTERNATIONAL ENDODONTIC JOURNAL.
Blackwell Science Ltd. Osney Mead, Oxford OX2 0EL, England. TEL 01365-206206. FAX 01865-721205. *4643*

INTERNATIONAL ENVIRONMENTAL LAW AND POLICY.
Kluwer Academic Publishers, Postbus 17, 3300 AA Dordrecht, Netherlands. TEL 31-78-6392392. FAX 31-78-6392254. *2803*

THE INTERNATIONAL EXECUTIVE.
John Wiley & Sons, Inc., Journals, 605 Third Ave., New York, NY 10158. TEL 212-850-6645 FAX 212-850-6021 *1281*

INTERNATIONAL FAMILY PLANNING PERSPECTIVES.
Alan Guttmacher Institute, 120 Wall St., New York, NY 10005. TEL 212-248-1111. FAX 212-248-1951. *4738*

INTERNATIONAL FEDERATION FOR INFORMATION AND DOCUMENTATION. PROCEEDINGS OF CONGRESS.
Elsevier Science B.V., Books Division, P.O. Box 211, 1000 AE Amsterdam, Netherlands. TEL 31-20-4853911. FAX 31-20-4853705. *4000*

INTERNATIONAL FIBER SCIENCE AND TECHNOLOGY SERIES.
Marcel Dekker, Inc., 270 Madison Ave., New York, NY 10016. TEL 212-696-9000. FAX 212-685-4540. *1739*

INTERNATIONAL FICTION REVIEW.
University of New Brunswick, Department of German, Russian, Fredericton, NB E3B 5A3, Canada. TEL 506-453-4636. *4220*

INTERNATIONAL GAS TURBINE INSTITUTE TECHNOLOGY REPORT. LAND, SEA & AIR.
International Gas Turbine Institute, 5801 Peachtree Dunwoody Rd., N.E., Ste. 100, Atlanta, GA 30342-1503. TEL 404-847-0072. FAX 404-847-0151. *4339*

INTERNATIONAL HEPATOLOGY COMMUNICATIONS.
Elsevier Science Ireland Ltd., P.O. Box 85, Limerick, Ireland. TEL 353-61-471944. FAX 353-61-472144. *4693*

THE INTERNATIONAL INFORMATION AND LIBRARY REVIEW.
Academic Press Ltd. 24-28 Oval Rd., London NW1 7DX, England. TEL 44-171-482-2293. FAX 44-171-482-2293. *4000*

INTERNATIONAL INFORMATION, COMMUNICATION AND EDUCATION.
P. Kaula Endowment for Library and Information Science, C-239, Indira Nagar, Lucknow 226 016, India. *4001*

INTERNATIONAL INSTRUMENTATION SYMPOSIUM.
Instrument Society of America, 67 Alexander Dr., Box 12277, Research Triangle Park, NC 27709. TEL 919-549-8411. FAX 919-549-8288. *69*

INTERNATIONAL INTERACTIONS.
Gordon and Breach Science Publishers, c/o International Publishers Distributor, P.O. Box 3054, Langhorne, PA 19047-3054. TEL 215-750-2642. FAX 215-750-6343. *5755*

INTERNATIONAL JOINT CONFERENCE ON ARTIFICIAL INTELLIGENCE. PROCEEDINGS.
Morgan Kaufmann Publishers, 340 Pine St., 6th Fl., San Francisco, CA 94104. TEL 415-392-2665. FAX 415-982-2665. *2008*

INTERNATIONAL JOURNAL.
Canadian Institute of International Affairs, 5 Devonshire Place, Toronto, ON M5S 2C8, Canada. TEL 416-979-1851. FAX 416-979-8575. *5755*

INTERNATIONAL JOURNAL FOR CONSUMER SAFETY.
Aeolus Press Postbus 740, 4116 ZJ Buren, Netherlands. TEL 31-344-572055. FAX 31-344-572562. *2152*

INTERNATIONAL JOURNAL FOR HOUSING SCIENCE AND ITS APPLICATIONS.
Ural and Associates, Inc., Box 340525, Coral Gables, FL 33134. TEL 305-348-3797. FAX 305-446-9462. *3586*

INTERNATIONAL JOURNAL FOR JOINING OF MATERIALS.
J O M Institute, D T U - Helsingoer, Rasmus Knudsens Vej 50, DK-3000 Helsingoer, Denmark. TEL 45-49-21-66-22. FAX 45-49-21-33-24. *4987*

INTERNATIONAL JOURNAL FOR MICROCIRCUITS AND ELECTRONIC PACKAGING.
International Society for Hybrid Microelectronics, 1850 Centennial Park Dr., Ste. 105, Reston, VA 22091-1517. TEL 703-758-1060. FAX 703-758-1066. *2524*

INTERNATIONAL JOURNAL FOR NUMERICAL AND ANALYTICAL METHODS IN GEOMECHANICS.
John Wiley & Sons Ltd., Journals, Baffins Ln., Chichester, W. Sussex PO19 1UD, England. TEL 44-1243-779777. FAX 44-1243-843232. *2664*

INTERNATIONAL JOURNAL FOR PARASITOLOGY.
Elsevier Science Ltd., Pergamon, P.O. Box 800, Kidlington, Oxford OX5 1DX, England. TEL 44-1865-843000. FAX 44-1865-843010. *4623*

INTERNATIONAL JOURNAL FOR PHILOSOPHY OF RELIGION.
Kluwer Academic Publishers, Postbus 17, 3300 AA Dordrecht, Netherlands. TEL 31-78-6392392. FAX 31-78-6392254. *6068*

INTERNATIONAL JOURNAL FOR QUALITY IN HEALTH CARE.
Elsevier Science Ltd., Pergamon, P.O. Box 800, Kidlington, Oxford OX5 1DX, England. TEL 44-1865-843000. FAX 44-1865-843010. *4472*

INTERNATIONAL JOURNAL FOR THE ADVANCEMENT OF COUNSELLING.
Kluwer Academic Publishers, Postbus 17, 3300 AA Dordrecht, Netherlands. TEL 31-78-6392392. FAX 31-78-6392254. *2342*

INTERNATIONAL JOURNAL FOR THE PSYCHOLOGY OF RELIGION.
Lawrence Erlbaum Associates, Inc., 10 Industrial Dr., Mahwah, NJ 07430-2262. TEL 201-236-9500. FAX 201-236-0072. *6068*

INTERNATIONAL JOURNAL FOR THE SEMIOTICS OF LAW.
Deborah Charles Publications, 173 Mather Ave., Liverpool L18 6JZ, England. TEL 0151-724-2500. FAX 0151-729-0371. *3792*

INTERNATIONAL JOURNAL OF ACTIVE CONTROL.
Multi-Science Publishing Co. Ltd., 107 High St., Brentwood, Essex CM14 4RX, England. TEL 44-1277-224632. FAX 44-1277-223453. *5614*

INTERNATIONAL JOURNAL OF ADAPTIVE CONTROL AND SIGNAL PROCESSING.
John Wiley & Sons Ltd., Journals, Baffins Ln., Chichester, W. Sussex PO19 1UD, England. TEL 44-1243-779777. FAX 44-1243-843232. *2709*

INTERNATIONAL JOURNAL OF ADHESION AND ADHESIVES.
Butterworth - Heinemann, Part of the Reed Elsevier group, Linacre House, Jordan Hill, Oxford OX2 8DP, England. TEL 44-1865-310366. FAX 44-1865-310898. *5620*

INTERNATIONAL JOURNAL OF ADOLESCENCE AND YOUTH.
A B Academic Publishers, P.O. Box 42, Bicester, Oxon. OX6 7NW, England. TEL 44-1869-320949. *1769*

INTERNATIONAL JOURNAL OF ADULT ORTHODONTICS AND ORTHOGNATHIC SURGERY.
Quintessence Publishing Co., Inc., 551 Kimberly Dr., Carol Stream, IL 60188-1881. TEL 708-682-3223. FAX 708-682-3288. *4644*

INTERNATIONAL JOURNAL OF ADVANCED MANUFACTURING TECHNOLOGY.
Springer-Verlag London Ltd., Sweetapple House, Catteshall Rd., Godalming, Surrey GU7 3DJ, England. TEL 44-1483-418800. FAX 44-1483-415144. *2757*

INTERNATIONAL JOURNAL OF ADVERTISING.
Blackwell Publishers Ltd., 108 Cowley Rd., Oxford OX4 1JF, England. TEL 44-1865-791100. FAX 44-1865-791347. *38*

INTERNATIONAL JOURNAL OF AGING & HUMAN DEVELOPMENT.
Baywood Publishing Co., Inc., 26 Austin Ave., Box 337, Amityville, NY 11701. TEL 516-691-1270. FAX 516-691-1770. *3289*

INTERNATIONAL JOURNAL OF AMERICAN LINGUISTICS.
University of Chicago Press, Journals Division, Box 37005, Chicago, IL 60637. TEL 773-753-3347. FAX 773-753-0811. *4076*

INTERNATIONAL JOURNAL OF ANDROLOGY.
Blackwell Science Ltd., Osney Mead, Oxford OX2 0EL, England. TEL 44-1865-206206. FAX 44-1865-721205. *4927*

INTERNATIONAL JOURNAL OF ANGIOLOGY.
Springer-Verlag, Medical Journals, 175 Fifth Ave., New York, NY 10010. TEL 212-460-1500. FAX 212-473-6272. *4604*

INTERNATIONAL JOURNAL OF ANIMAL SCIENCES.
Nitasha Publications, 921, Sector 14, Sonepat, 131001 Haryana, India. *274*

INTERNATIONAL JOURNAL OF ANTIMICROBIAL AGENTS.
Elsevier Science B.V., P.O. Box 211, 1000 AE Amsterdam, Netherlands. TEL 31-20-4853911. FAX 31-20-4853598. *759*

INTERNATIONAL JOURNAL OF APPLIED ELECTROMAGNETICS AND MECHANICS.
I O S Press, Van Diemenstraat 94, 1013 CN Amsterdam, Netherlands. TEL 31-20-6382189. FAX 31-20-6203419. *2709*

INTERNATIONAL JOURNAL OF APPROXIMATE REASONING.
Elsevier Science Inc., Box 945, New York, NY 10159-0945. TEL 212-633-3730. FAX 212-633-3680. *2008*

INTERNATIONAL JOURNAL OF ARTS MEDICINE.
I J A M, M M B Music, Inc., Contemporary Arts Bldg., 3526 Washington Ave., St. Louis, MO 63103-1019. TEL 314-531-9635. FAX 314-531-8384. *4473*

INTERNATIONAL JOURNAL OF AVIATION PSYCHOLOGY.
Lawrence Erlbaum Associates, Inc., 10 Industrial Dr., Mahwah, NJ 07430-2262. TEL 201-236-9500. FAX 201-236-0072. *69*

INTERNATIONAL JOURNAL OF BEHAVIORAL DEVELOPMENT.
Taylor & Francis Ltd., Psychology Press, 1 Gunpowder Sq., London EC4A 3DE, England. TEL 44-171-5830490. FAX 44-171-5830585. *5849*

INTERNATIONAL JOURNAL OF BIO-MEDICAL COMPUTING.
Elsevier Science Ireland Ltd., P.O. Box 85, Limerick, Ireland. TEL 353-61-471944. FAX 353-61-472144. *4631*

INTERNATIONAL JOURNAL OF BIOCHEMISTRY & CELL BIOLOGY.
Elsevier Science Ltd., Pergamon, P.O. Box 800, Kidlington, Oxford OX5 1DX, England. TEL 44-1865-843000. FAX 44-1865-843010. *640*

INTERNATIONAL JOURNAL OF BIOLOGICAL MACROMOLECULES.
Elsevier Science B.V., P.O. Box 211, 1000 AE Amsterdam, Netherlands. TEL 31-20-4853911. FAX 31-20-4853598. *640*

INTERNATIONAL JOURNAL OF BIOSOCIAL AND MEDICAL RESEARCH.
Life Sciences Press, Box 1174, Tacoma, WA 98401-1174. TEL 206-922-0442. FAX 206-922-0479. *5234*

INTERNATIONAL JOURNAL OF CANADIAN STUDIES.
International Council for Canadian Studies, 325 Dalhousie, S-800, Ottawa, ON K1N 7G2, Canada. TEL 613-789-7834. FAX 613-789-7830. *6417*

INTERNATIONAL JOURNAL OF CANCER.
John Wiley & Sons, Inc., Journals, 605 Third Ave., New York, NY 10158. TEL 212-850-6645. FAX 212-850-6021. *4757*

INTERNATIONAL JOURNAL OF CARDIAC IMAGING.
Kluwer Academic Publishers, Postbus 17, 3300 AA Dordrecht, Netherlands. TEL 31-78-6392392. FAX 31-78-6392254. *4604*

INTERNATIONAL JOURNAL OF CARDIOLOGY.
Elsevier Science Ireland Ltd., P.O. Box 85, Limerick, Ireland. TEL 353-61-471944. FAX 353-61-472144. *4604*

INTERNATIONAL JOURNAL OF CHEMICAL KINETICS.
John Wiley & Sons, Inc., Journals, 605 Third Ave., New York, NY 10158. TEL 212-850-6645. FAX 212-850-6021. *1752*

INTERNATIONAL JOURNAL OF CHILDBIRTH EDUCATION.
International Childbirth Education Association, Box 20048, Minneapolis, MN 55420-0048. TEL 612-854-8660. FAX 612-854-8772. *4738*

THE INTERNATIONAL JOURNAL OF CHILDREN'S RIGHTS.
Kluwer Law International Postbus 85889, 2508 CN The Hague, Netherlands. TEL 31-70-3081500. FAX 31-70-3081515. *5730*

INTERNATIONAL JOURNAL OF CLINICAL MONITORING AND COMPUTING.
Kluwer Academic Publishers, Postbus 17, 3300 AA Dordrecht, Netherlands. TEL 31-78-6392392. FAX 31-78-6392254. *4591*

INTERNATIONAL JOURNAL OF CLINICAL ONCOLOGY.
Churchill Livingstone Japan, Churchill Bldg., 2-8-16 Yutenji, Meguro-ku, Tokyo 153, Japan. TEL 81-3-5721-0442. FAX 81-3-5721-0415. *4757*

INTERNATIONAL JOURNAL OF COAL GEOLOGY.
Elsevier Science B.V., P.O. Box 211, 1000 AE Amsterdam, Netherlands. TEL 31-20-4853911. FAX 31-20-4853598. *2245*

INTERNATIONAL JOURNAL OF COMMERCE AND MANAGEMENT.
Indiana University of Pennsylvania, College of Business, Indiana, PA 15705. TEL 412-357-5759. FAX 412-357-5743. *1424*

INTERNATIONAL JOURNAL OF COMMUNICATION SYSTEMS.
John Wiley & Sons Ltd., Journals, Baffins Ln., Chichester, W. Sussex PO19 1UD, England. TEL 44-1243-779777. FAX 44-1243-843232. *2709*

THE INTERNATIONAL JOURNAL OF COMPARATIVE LABOUR LAW AND INDUSTRIAL RELATIONS.
Kluwer Law International Postbus 85889, 2508 CN The Hague, Netherlands. TEL 31-70-3081500. FAX 31-70-3081515. *3792*

INTERNATIONAL JOURNAL OF COMPARATIVE SOCIOLOGY.
E.J. Brill, P.O. Box 9000, 2300 PA Leiden, Netherlands. TEL 31-71-5353500. FAX 31-71-5317532. *6417*

INTERNATIONAL JOURNAL OF COMPUTER INTEGRATED MANUFACTURING.
Taylor & Francis Ltd., 1 Gunpowder Sq., London EC4A 3DE, England. TEL 44-171-583-0490. FAX 44-171-583-0585. *1155*

INTERNATIONAL JOURNAL OF COMPUTER MATHEMATICS.
Gordon and Breach Science Publishers, c/o International Publishers Distributor, P.O. Box 3054, Langhorne, PA 19047-3054. TEL 215-750-2642. FAX 215-750-6343. *4410*

INTERNATIONAL JOURNAL OF COMPUTER SYSTEMS SCIENCE AND ENGINEERING.
C R L Publishing Ltd., P.O. Box 31, Market Harborough, Leics. LE16 9RQ, England. TEL 44-8158-525382. FAX 44-1858-525635. *2056*

INTERNATIONAL JOURNAL OF COMPUTERS FOR MATHEMATICAL LEARNING.
Kluwer Academic Publishers, Postbus 17, 3300 AA Dordrecht, Netherlands. TEL 31-78-6392392. FAX 31-78-6392254. *4410*

INTERNATIONAL JOURNAL OF CONTEMPORARY HOSPITALITY MANAGEMENT.
M C B University Press Ltd., 60-62 Toller Ln., Bradford, W. Yorks BD8 9BY, England. TEL 44-1274-777700. FAX 44-1274-785200. *3565*

INTERNATIONAL JOURNAL OF CONTROL.
Taylor & Francis Ltd., 1 Gunpowder Sq., London EC4A 3DE, England. TEL 44-171-583-0490. FAX 44-171-583-0585. *2605*

INTERNATIONAL JOURNAL OF COSMETIC SCIENCE.
Chapman & Hall, Journals Department 2-6 Boundary Row, London SE1 8HN, England. TEL 44-171-8650066. FAX 44-171-5229623. *496*

INTERNATIONAL JOURNAL OF DAMAGE MECHANICS.
Technomic Publishing Co., Inc., 851 New Holland Ave., Box 3535, Lancaster, PA 17604. TEL 717-291-5609. FAX 717-295-4538. *2757*

INTERNATIONAL JOURNAL OF DERMATOLOGY.
Blackwell Science Ltd., Osney Mead, Oxford OX2 OEL, England. TEL 44-1865-206206. FAX 44-1865-721205. *4662*

INTERNATIONAL JOURNAL OF DEVELOPMENTAL BIOLOGY.
Universidad del Pais Vasco, Facultad de Medicina, Dep. de Biologia Celular, 48940 Lejona (Vizcaya), Spain. TEL 34-4-4647700. FAX 34-4-4801314. *587*

INTERNATIONAL JOURNAL OF DEVELOPMENTAL NEUROSCIENCE.
Elsevier Science Ltd., Pergamon, P.O. Box 800, Kidlington, Oxford OX5 1DX, England. TEL 44-1865-843000. FAX 44-1865-843010. *4841*

INTERNATIONAL JOURNAL OF DISCRIMINATION AND THE LAW.
A B Academic Publishers, P.O. Box 42, Bicester, Oxon. OX6 7VW, England. TEL 44-1869-320949. *5730*

INTERNATIONAL JOURNAL OF DRUG POLICY.
Whurr Publishers Ltd., 19b Compton Terrace, London N1 2UN, England. TEL 44-171-359-5979. FAX 44-171-226-5290. *2197*

INTERNATIONAL JOURNAL OF EATING DISORDERS.
John Wiley & Sons, Inc., Journals, 605 Third Ave., New York, NY 10158. TEL 212-850-6645. FAX 212-850-6021. *5234*

INTERNATIONAL JOURNAL OF ECOLOGY AND ENVIRONMENTAL SCIENCES.
International Scientific Publications 50-B Pocket C, Sidhartha Extension, New Delhi 110 014, India. TEL 91-11-6912169. *2803*

INTERNATIONAL JOURNAL OF EDUCATIONAL DEVELOPMENT.
Elsevier Science Ltd., Pergamon, P.O. Box 800, Kidlington, Oxford OX5 1DX, England. TEL 44-1865-843000. FAX 44-1865-843010. *2343*

INTERNATIONAL JOURNAL OF EDUCATIONAL REFORM.
Technomic Publishing Co., Inc., 851 New Holland Ave., Box 3535, Lancaster, PA 17604. TEL 717-291-5609. FAX 717-295-4538. *2343*

INTERNATIONAL JOURNAL OF EDUCATIONAL RESEARCH.
Elsevier Science Ltd., Pergamon, P.O. Box 800, Kidlington, Oxford OX5 1DX, England. TEL 44-1865-843000. FAX 44-1865-843010. *2451*

INTERNATIONAL JOURNAL OF EDUCOLOGY.
Educology Research Associates, P.O. Box 216, Terrigal, N.S.W. 2260, Australia. TEL 61-43-653120. FAX 61-43-652871. *2399*

INTERNATIONAL JOURNAL OF ELECTRICAL POWER & ENERGY SYSTEMS.
Butterworth - Heinemann, Part of the Reed Elsevier group, Linacre House, Jordan Hill, Oxford OX2 8DP, England. TEL 44-1865-310366. FAX 44-1865-310898. *2709*

INTERNATIONAL JOURNAL OF ELECTRONICS.
Taylor & Francis Ltd., 1 Gunpowder Sq., London EC4A 3DE, England. TEL 44-171-583-0490. FAX 44-171-583-0585. *2524*

INTERNATIONAL JOURNAL OF ENERGY RESEARCH.
John Wiley & Sons Ltd., Journals, Baffins Ln., Chichester, W. Sussex PO19 1UD, England. TEL 44-1243-779777. FAX 44-1243-843232. *2552*

INTERNATIONAL JOURNAL OF ENGINEERING EDUCATION.
Tempus Publications, Berliner Tor 21, 20099 Hamburg, Germany. TEL 49-40-24883014. FAX 49-40-24882847. *2605*

INTERNATIONAL JOURNAL OF ENGINEERING SCIENCE.
Elsevier Science Ltd., Pergamon, P.O. Box 800, Kidlington, Oxford OX5 1DX, England. TEL 44-1865-843000. FAX 44-1865-843010. *2605*

INTERNATIONAL JOURNAL OF ENVIRONMENTAL ANALYTICAL CHEMISTRY.
Gordon and Breach Science Publishers, c/o International Publishers Distributors, P.O. Box 3054, Langhorne, PA 19047-3054. TEL 215-750-2642. FAX 215-750-6343. *1716*

INTERNATIONAL JOURNAL OF ENVIRONMENTAL STUDIES. SECTIONS A & B.
Gordon and Breach Science Publishers, c/o International Publishers Distributor, P.O. Box 3054, Langhorne, PA 19047-3054. TEL 215-750-2642. FAX 215-750-6343. *2504*

INTERNATIONAL JOURNAL OF EXPERIMENTAL PATHOLOGY.
Blackwell Science Ltd., Osney Mead, Oxford OX2 OEL, England. TEL 44-1865-206206. FAX 44-1865-721205. *4473*

INTERNATIONAL JOURNAL OF FATIGUE.
Butterworth - Heinemann, Part of the Reed Elsevier group, Linacre House, Jordan Hill, Oxford OX2 8DP, England. TEL 44-1865-310366. FAX 44-1865-310898. *2732*

INTERNATIONAL JOURNAL OF FERTILITY AND MENOPAUSAL STUDIES.
M S P (Medical Science Publishing) International, Inc., 405 Main St., Port Washington, NY 11050. TEL 516-944-7340. FAX 516-944-8663. *4473*

INTERNATIONAL JOURNAL OF FINANCE.
205 Rabbit Run Dr., Cherry Hill, NJ 08003-1427. TEL 609-424-2262. FAX 609-424-6007. *1102*

INTERNATIONAL JOURNAL OF FLEXIBLE MANUFACTURING SYSTEMS.
Kluwer Academic Publishers Boston, Box 358, Accord Sta., Hingham, MA 02018-0358. TEL 617-871-6600. FAX 617-871-6528. *2732*

INTERNATIONAL JOURNAL OF FOOD MICROBIOLOGY.
Elsevier Science B.V., P.O. Box 211, 1000 AE Amsterdam, Netherlands. TEL 31-20-4853911. FAX 31-20-4853598. *759*

INTERNATIONAL JOURNAL OF FOOD SCIENCE AND TECHNOLOGY.
Blackwell Science Ltd., Osney Mead, Oxford OX2 OEL, England. TEL 44-1865-206206. FAX 44-1865-721205. *2978*

INTERNATIONAL JOURNAL OF FORECASTING.
North-Holland P.O. Box 211, 1000 AE Amsterdam, Netherlands. TEL 31-20-4853911. FAX 31-20-4853598. *1217*

INTERNATIONAL JOURNAL OF FRACTURE.
Kluwer Academic Publishers, Postbus 17, 3300 AA Dordrecht, Netherlands. TEL 31-78-6392392. FAX 31-78-6392254. *2733*

INTERNATIONAL JOURNAL OF GENERAL SYSTEMS.
Gordon and Breach Science Publishers, c/o International Publishers Distributors, P.O. Box 3054, Langhorne, PA 19047-3054. TEL 215-750-2642. FAX 215-750-6343. *2056*

INTERNATIONAL JOURNAL OF GEOGRAPHICAL INFORMATION SYSTEMS.
Taylor & Francis Ltd., 1 Gunpowder Sq., London EC4A 3DE, England. TEL 44-171-583-0490. FAX 44-171-583-0585. *3231*

INTERNATIONAL JOURNAL OF GROUP PSYCHOTHERAPY.
Guilford Publications, Inc., 72 Spring St., 4th Fl., New York, NY 10012. TEL 212-431-9800. FAX 212-966-6708. *5849*

INTERNATIONAL JOURNAL OF GROUP TENSIONS.
Human Sciences Press, Inc. 233 Spring St., New York, NY 10013-1578. TEL 212-620-8000. FAX 212-463-0742. *5850*

Refereed

INTERNATIONAL JOURNAL OF GYNAECOLOGY AND OBSTETRICS.
Elsevier Science Ireland Ltd., P.O. Box 85, Limerick, Ireland. TEL 353-61-471944. FAX 353-61-472144. *4738*

INTERNATIONAL JOURNAL OF GYNECOLOGICAL PATHOLOGY.
Lippincott - Raven Publishers 227 E. Washington Sq., Philadelphia, PA 19106. TEL 215-238-4200. *4738*

INTERNATIONAL JOURNAL OF HEALTH PLANNING AND MANAGEMENT.
John Wiley & Sons Ltd., Journals, Baffins Ln., Chichester, W. Sussex PO19 1UD, England. TEL 44-1243-779777. FAX 44-1243-843232. *6377*

INTERNATIONAL JOURNAL OF HEALTH SERVICES.
Baywood Publishing Co., Inc., 26 Austin Ave., Box 337, Amityville, NY 11701. TEL 516-691-1270. FAX 516-691-1770. *5965*

INTERNATIONAL JOURNAL OF HEAT AND FLUID FLOW.
Elsevier Science Inc., Box 945, New York, NY 10159-0945. TEL 212-633-3730. FAX 212-633-3680. *5585*

INTERNATIONAL JOURNAL OF HEAT AND MASS TRANSFER.
Elsevier Science Ltd., Pergamon, P.O. Box 800, Kidlington, Oxford OX5 1DX, England. TEL 44-1865-843000. FAX 44-1865-843010. *2757*

INTERNATIONAL JOURNAL OF HEMATOLOGY.
Elsevier Science Ireland Ltd., P.O. Box 85, Limerick, Ireland. TEL 353-61-471944. FAX 353-61-472144. *4701*

INTERNATIONAL JOURNAL OF HERITAGE STUDIES.
Intellect, Earl Richards Rd. N., Exeter, Devon EX2 6AS. TEL 44-1392-475101. FAX 44-1392-475110. *3348*

INTERNATIONAL JOURNAL OF HISTORICAL ARCHAEOLOGY.
Plenum Publishing Corp., 233 Spring St., New York, NY 10013-1578. TEL 212-620-8000. FAX 212-463-0742. *357*

INTERNATIONAL JOURNAL OF HOSPITALITY MANAGEMENT.
Elsevier Science Ltd., Pergamon, P.O. Box 800, Kidlington, Oxford OX5 1DX, England. TEL 44-1865-843000. FAX 44-1865-843010. *3566*

INTERNATIONAL JOURNAL OF HUMAN RIGHTS.
Frank Cass, Newbury House, 890-900 Eastern Ave., Newbury Park, Ilford, Essex IG2 7HH, England. TEL 44-181-5998866. FAX 44-181-5990984. *5730*

INTERNATIONAL JOURNAL OF HUMANITIES AND PEACE.
Vasant V. Merchant, Ed. & Pub., IJHP Journal, 1436 Evergreen Drive, Flagstaff, AZ 86001. TEL 602-774-4793. *3615*

INTERNATIONAL JOURNAL OF HYDROGEN ENERGY.
Elsevier Science Ltd., Pergamon, P.O. Box 800, Kidlington, Oxford OX5 1DX, England. TEL 44-1865-843000. FAX 44-1865-843010. *2552*

INTERNATIONAL JOURNAL OF HYPERTHERMIA.
Taylor & Francis Ltd., 1 Gunpowder Sq., London EC4A 3DE, England. TEL 44-171-583-0490. FAX 44-171-583-0585. *4757*

INTERNATIONAL JOURNAL OF IBERIAN STUDIES.
Intellect, Earl Richards Rd. N., Exeter, Devon EX2 6AS, England. TEL 44-1392-475110. FAX 44-1392-475110. *3419*

INTERNATIONAL JOURNAL OF IMAGING SYSTEMS AND TECHNOLOGY.
John Wiley & Sons, Inc., Journals, 605 Third Ave., New York, NY 10158-0012. TEL 212-850-6645. FAX 212-850-6021. *5551*

INTERNATIONAL JOURNAL OF IMMUNOPATHOLOGY AND PHARMACOLOGY.
Biomedical Research Press, s.a.s., c/o Universita di Chieti, Depto. di Immunologia, Via dei Vestini, Chieti, Italy. TEL 39-871-355293. FAX 39-871-561635. *4584*

INTERNATIONAL JOURNAL OF IMMUNOPHARMACOLOGY.
Elsevier Science Ltd., Pergamon, P.O. Box 800, Kidlington, Oxford OX5 1DX, England. TEL 44-1865-843000. FAX 44-1865-843010. *5418*

INTERNATIONAL JOURNAL OF IMPACT ENGINEERING.
Elsevier Science Ltd., Pergamon, P.O. Box 800, Kidlington, Oxford OX5 1DX, England. TEL 44-1865-843000. FAX 44-1865-843010. *2605*

INTERNATIONAL JOURNAL OF INDUSTRIAL ERGONOMICS.
Elsevier Science B.V., P.O. Box 211, 1000 AE Amsterdam, Netherlands. TEL 31-20-4853911. FAX 31-20-4853598. *2605*

INTERNATIONAL JOURNAL OF INDUSTRIAL ORGANIZATION.
North-Holland P.O. Box 211, 1000 AE Amsterdam, Netherlands. TEL 31-20-4853911. FAX 31-20-4853598. *1424*

INTERNATIONAL JOURNAL OF INFORMATION MANAGEMENT.
Butterworth - Heinemann, Part of the Reed Elsevier group, Linacre House, Jordan Hill, Oxford OX2 8DP, England. TEL 44-1865-310366. FAX 44-1865-301898. *2082*

INTERNATIONAL JOURNAL OF INFRARED AND MILLIMETER WAVES.
Plenum Publishing Corp., 233 Spring St., New York, NY 10013-1578. TEL 212-620-8000. FAX 212-463-0742. *5604*

INTERNATIONAL JOURNAL OF INSECT MORPHOLOGY AND EMBRYOLOGY.
Elsevier Science Ltd., Pergamon, P.O. Box 800, Kidlington, Oxford OX5 1DX, England. TEL 44-1865-843000. FAX 44-1865-843010. *729*

INTERNATIONAL JOURNAL OF INSTRUCTIONAL MEDIA.
Westwood Press, Inc., 23 E. 22nd St., 4th Fl., New York, NY 10010. TEL 212-420-8008. FAX 212-353-8291. *2490*

INTERNATIONAL JOURNAL OF INTELLIGENT SYSTEMS.
John Wiley & Sons, Inc., Journals, 605 Third Ave., New York, NY 10158. TEL 212-570-6645. FAX 212-850-6021. *2008*

INTERNATIONAL JOURNAL OF INTELLIGENT SYSTEMS IN ACCOUNTING, FINANCE & MANAGEMENT.
John Wiley & Sons Ltd., Journals, Baffins Ln., Chichester, W. Sussex PO19 1UD, England. TEL 44-1243-779777. FAX 44-1243-843232. *1155*

INTERNATIONAL JOURNAL OF INTENSIVE CARE.
Greycoat Publishing, 1 Harley St., London W1N 1DA, England. TEL 44-171-637-1828. FAX 44-171-637-3020. *4473*

INTERNATIONAL JOURNAL OF INTERCULTURAL RELATIONS.
Elsevier Science Ltd., Pergamon, P.O. Box 800, Kidlington, Oxford OX5 1DX, England. TEL 44-1865-843000. FAX 44-1865-843010. *6417*

INTERNATIONAL JOURNAL OF LAW AND PSYCHIATRY.
Elsevier Science Ltd., Pergamon, P.O. Box 800, Kidlington, Oxford OX5 1DX, England. TEL 44-1865-843000. FAX 44-1865-843010. *3793*

INTERNATIONAL JOURNAL OF LEPROSY AND OTHER MYCOBACTERIAL DISEASES.
International Leprosy Association, One ALM Way, Greenville, SC 29601. TEL 864-271-7040. FAX 864-271-7062. *4623*

INTERNATIONAL JOURNAL OF LIFELONG EDUCATION.
Taylor & Francis Ltd., Rankine Rd., Basingstoke, Hants. RG24 8PR, England. TEL 44-1256-840366. FAX 44-1256-479438. *2399*

INTERNATIONAL JOURNAL OF MACHINE TOOLS & MANUFACTURE.
Elsevier Science Ltd., Pergamon, P.O. Box 800, Kidlington, Oxford OX5 1DX, England. TEL 44-1865-843000. FAX 44-1865-843010. *2748*

INTERNATIONAL JOURNAL OF MANAGEMENT.
P.O. Box 982, Poole, Dorset BH12 5YF, England. *1424*

INTERNATIONAL JOURNAL OF MARINE AND COASTAL LAW.
Kluwer Law International Postbus 85889, 2508 CN The Hague, Netherlands. TEL 31-70-3081500. FAX 31-70-3081515. *3957*

INTERNATIONAL JOURNAL OF MARITIME HISTORY.
Maritime Economic History Association, c/o Memorial University of Newfoundland, Maritime Studies Research Unit, St. John's, NF A1C 5S7, Canada. TEL 709-737-8424. FAX 709-737-8427. *6837*

INTERNATIONAL JOURNAL OF MASS SPECTROMETRY AND ION PROCESSES.
Elsevier Science B.V., P.O. Box 211, 1000 AE Amsterdam, Netherlands. TEL 31-20-4853911. FAX 31-20-4853598. *5604*

INTERNATIONAL JOURNAL OF MATHEMATICAL AND STATISTICAL SCIENCES.
Berkeley - Cambridge Press, Box 947, Carmichael, CA 95609-0947. *4369*

INTERNATIONAL JOURNAL OF MATHEMATICAL EDUCATION IN SCIENCE AND TECHNOLOGY.
Taylor & Francis Ltd., Rankine Rd., Basingstoke, Hants. RG24 8PR, England. TEL 44-1256-840366. FAX 44-1256-47943. *4370*

INTERNATIONAL JOURNAL OF MECHANICAL SCIENCES.
Elsevier Science Ltd., Pergamon, P.O. Box 800, Kidlington, Oxford OX5 1DX, England. TEL 44-1865-843000. FAX 44-1865-843010. *2733*

INTERNATIONAL JOURNAL OF MENTAL HEALTH.
M.E. Sharpe, Inc., 80 Business Park Dr., Armonk, NY 10504. TEL 914-273-1800. FAX 913-273-2106. *5850*

INTERNATIONAL JOURNAL OF MICROCIRCULATION: CLINICAL & EXPERIMENTAL.
S. Karger AG, Altschwilerstr. 10, P.O. Box, CH-4009 Basel, Switzerland. TEL 061-3061111. FAX 061-3061234. *4473*

INTERNATIONAL JOURNAL OF MICROGRAPHICS & OPTICAL TECHNOLOGY.
Research Information Ltd., 222 Maylands Ave., Hemel Hempstead, Herts. HP2 7TD, England. TEL 44-1442-213222. FAX 44-1442-259395. *4045*

INTERNATIONAL JOURNAL OF MICROWAVE AND MILLIMETER-WAVE COMPUTER AIDED ENGINEERING.
John Wiley & Sons, Inc., Journals, 605 Third Ave., New York, NY 10158. TEL 212-692-6645. FAX 212-850-6021. *2680*

INTERNATIONAL JOURNAL OF MINERAL PROCESSING.
Elsevier Science B.V., P.O. Box 211, 1000 AE Amsterdam, Netherlands. TEL 31-20-4853911. FAX 31-20-4853598. *5066*

INTERNATIONAL JOURNAL OF MULTIPHASE FLOW.
Elsevier Science Ltd., Pergamon, P.O. Box 800, Kidlington, Oxford OX5 1DX, England. TEL 44-1865-843000. FAX 44-1865-843010. *2758*

INTERNATIONAL JOURNAL OF NETWORK MANAGEMENT.
John Wiley & Sons Ltd., Journals, Baffins Ln., Chichester, W. Sussex PO19 1UD, England. TEL 44-1243-779777. FAX 44-1243-843232. *1907*

INTERNATIONAL JOURNAL OF NEURAL NETWORK.
Information Today, Inc., 143 Old Marlton Pike, Medford, NJ 08055. TEL 609-654-6266. FAX 609-654-4309. *2008*

INTERNATIONAL JOURNAL OF NEURORADIOLOGY.
Lippincott - Raven Publishers 227 E. Washington Sq., Philadelphia, PA 19106. TEL 215-238-4200. *4877*

INTERNATIONAL JOURNAL OF NEUROSCIENCE.
Gordon and Breach Science Publishers, c/o International Publishers Distributor, P.O. Box 3054, Langhorne, PA 19047-3054. TEL 215-750-2642. FAX 215-750-6343. *4841*

INTERNATIONAL JOURNAL OF NON-LINEAR MECHANICS.
Elsevier Science Ltd., Pergamon, P.O. Box 800, Kidlington, Oxford OX5 1DX, England. TEL 44-1865-843000. FAX 44-1865-843010. *2733*

INTERNATIONAL JOURNAL OF NURSING STUDIES.
Elsevier Science Ltd., Pergamon, P.O. Box 800, Kidlington, Oxford OX5 1DX, England. TEL 44-1865-843000. FAX 44-1865-843010. *4715*

INTERNATIONAL JOURNAL OF OBSTETRIC ANESTHESIA.
Churchill Livingstone Robert Stevenson House, 1-3 Baxter's Pl., Leith Walk, Edinburgh EH1 3AF, Scotland. TEL 0131-556-2424. FAX 0131-535-1704. *4738*

INTERNATIONAL JOURNAL OF OCCUPATIONAL AND ENVIRONMENTAL HEALTH.
Hanley and Belfus Inc., 210 S. 13th St., Philadelphia, PA 19107. TEL 215-546-4995. FAX 215-790-9330. *5251*

INTERNATIONAL JOURNAL OF OCCUPATIONAL MEDICINE AND ENVIRONMENTAL HEALTH.
Instytut Medycyny Pracy im. Jerzego Nofera, Ul. Sw. Teresy 8, P.O. Box 199, 90-950 Lodz, Poland. TEL 48-42-314718. FAX 48-42-348331. *5251*

INTERNATIONAL JOURNAL OF OCCUPATIONAL MEDICINE, IMMUNOLOGY AND TOXICOLOGY.
Princeton Scientific Publishing Co., Inc., Box 2155, Princeton, NJ 08543. TEL 609-683-4750. FAX 609-683-0838. *5251*

INTERNATIONAL JOURNAL OF OFFENDER THERAPY AND COMPARATIVE CRIMINOLOGY.
Sage Publications, Inc., 2455 Teller Rd., Thousand Oaks, CA 91320. TEL 805-499-0721. FAX 805-499-0871. *2166*

INTERNATIONAL JOURNAL OF OFFSHORE AND POLAR ENGINEERING.
International Society of Offshore and Polar Engineers, Box 1107, Golden, CO 80402-1107. TEL 303-273-3673. FAX 303-420-3760. *2758*

INTERNATIONAL JOURNAL OF ONCOLOGY.
Demetrios A. Spandidos, Ed. & Pub., Editorial Office, 1, S. Merkouri St., Athens 116 35, Greece. TEL 30-1-722-6469. FAX 30-1-752-3866. *4757*

INTERNATIONAL JOURNAL OF OPTOELECTRONICS.
Taylor & Francis Ltd., 1 Gunpowder Sq., London EC4A 3DE, England. TEL 44-171-583-0490. FAX 44-171-583-0585. *5604*

INTERNATIONAL JOURNAL OF ORAL & MAXILLOFACIAL IMPLANTS.
Quintessence Publishing Co., Inc., 551 Kimberly Dr., Carol Stream, IL 60188-1881. TEL 708-682-3223. FAX 708-682-3288. *4644*

INTERNATIONAL JOURNAL OF ORAL & MAXILLOFACIAL SURGERY.
Munksgaard International Publishers Ltd., 35 Noerre Soegade, P.O. Box 2148, DK-1016 Copenhagen K, Denmark. TEL 45-33-127030. FAX 45-33-129387. *4644*

INTERNATIONAL JOURNAL OF OSTEOARCHAEOLOGY.
John Wiley & Sons Ltd., Journals, Baffins Ln., Chichester, W. Sussex PO19 1UD, England. TEL 44-1243-779777. FAX 44-1243-843232. *313*

INTERNATIONAL JOURNAL OF PAEDIATRIC DENTISTRY.
Blackwell Science Ltd., Osney Mead, Oxford OX2 OEL, England. TEL 44-1865-206206. FAX 44-1865-721205. *4644*

INTERNATIONAL JOURNAL OF PANCREATOLOGY.
Humana Press Inc., 999 Riverview Dr., Ste. 208, Totowa, NJ 07512. TEL 201-256-1699. FAX 201-256-8341. *4672*

INTERNATIONAL JOURNAL OF PARALLEL PROGRAMMING.
Plenum Publishing Corp., 233 Spring St., New York, NY 10013-1578. TEL 212-620-8000. FAX 212-463-0742. *2045*

INTERNATIONAL JOURNAL OF PATTERN RECOGNITION AND ARTIFICIAL INTELLIGENCE.
World Scientific Publishing Co. Pte. Ltd., Farrer Rd., P.O. Box 128, Singapore 9128, Singapore. TEL 3825663. FAX 3825919. *2028*

INTERNATIONAL JOURNAL OF PEDIATRIC OTORHINOLARYNGOLOGY.
Elsevier Science Ireland Ltd., P.O. Box 85, Limerick, Ireland. TEL 353-61-471944. FAX 353-61-472144. *4797*

INTERNATIONAL JOURNAL OF PEPTIDE & PROTEIN RESEARCH.
Munksgaard International Publishers Ltd., 35 Noerre Soegade, P.O. Box 2148, DK-1016 Copenhagen K, Denmark. TEL 45-33-127030. FAX 45-33-129387. *641*

INTERNATIONAL JOURNAL OF PERIODONTICS & RESTORATIVE DENTISTRY.
Quintessence Publishing Co., Inc., 551 Kimberly Dr., Carol Stream, IL 60188-1881. TEL 708-682-3223. FAX 708-682-3288. *4644*

INTERNATIONAL JOURNAL OF PEST MANAGEMENT.
Taylor & Francis Ltd., 1 Gunpowder Sq., London EC4A 3DE, England. TEL 44-171-583-0490. FAX 44-171-583-0585. *227*

INTERNATIONAL JOURNAL OF PHARMACEUTICS.
Elsevier Science B.V., P.O. Box 211, 1000 AE Amsterdam, Netherlands. TEL 31-20-4853911. FAX 31-20-4853598. *5418*

INTERNATIONAL JOURNAL OF PLANT SCIENCES.
University of Chicago Press, Journals Division, Box 37005, Chicago, IL 60637. TEL 773-753-3347. FAX 773-753-0811. *686*

INTERNATIONAL JOURNAL OF PLASTICITY.
Elsevier Science Ltd., Pergamon, P.O. Box 800, Kidlington, Oxford OX5 1DX, England. TEL 44-1865-843000. FAX 44-1865-843010. *2733*

INTERNATIONAL JOURNAL OF POLITICAL ECONOMY.
M.E. Sharpe, Inc., 80 Business Park Dr., Armonk, NY 10504. TEL 914-273-1800. FAX 914-273-2106. *5674*

INTERNATIONAL JOURNAL OF POLITICS, CULTURE, AND SOCIETY.
Human Sciences Press, Inc. 233 Spring St., New York, NY 10013. TEL 212-620-8000. FAX 212-463-0742. *5755*

INTERNATIONAL JOURNAL OF POLYMERIC MATERIALS.
Gordon and Breach Science Publishers, c/o International Publishers Distributor, P.O. Box 3054, Langhorne, PA 19047-3054. TEL 215-750-2642. FAX 215-750-6343. *2643*

INTERNATIONAL JOURNAL OF POPULATION GEOGRAPHY.
John Wiley & Sons Ltd., Journals, Baffins Ln., Chichester, W. Sussex PO19 1UD, England. TEL 44-1243-779777. FAX 44-1243-843232. *5786*

INTERNATIONAL JOURNAL OF PRESSURE VESSELS AND PIPING.
Elsevier Science Ltd., P.O. Box 800, Kidlington, Oxford OX5 1DX, England. TEL 44-1865-843000. FAX 44-1865-843010. *2758*

INTERNATIONAL JOURNAL OF PRIMATOLOGY.
Plenum Publishing Corp., 233 Spring St., New York, NY 10013-1578. TEL 212-620-8000. FAX 212-463-0742. *808*

INTERNATIONAL JOURNAL OF PRODUCTION ECONOMICS.
Elsevier Science B.V., P.O. Box 211, 1000 AE Amsterdam, Netherlands. TEL 31-20-4853911. FAX 31-20-4853598. *2748*

INTERNATIONAL JOURNAL OF PROJECT MANAGEMENT.
Butterworth - Heinemann, Part of the Reed Elsevier group, Linacre House, Jordan Hill, Oxford OX2 8DP, England. TEL 44-1865-310366. FAX 44-1865-310898. *1155*

INTERNATIONAL JOURNAL OF PROSTHODONTICS.
Quintessence Publishing Co., Inc., 551 Kimberly Dr., Carol Stream, IL 60188-1881. TEL 708-682-3223. FAX 708-682-3288. *4644*

INTERNATIONAL JOURNAL OF PSYCHIATRY IN MEDICINE.
Baywood Publishing Co., Inc., 26 Austin Ave., Box 337, Amityville, NY 11701. TEL 516-691-1270. FAX 516-691-1770. *4842*

INTERNATIONAL JOURNAL OF PSYCHO-ANALYSIS.
Institute of Psychoanalysis, 63 New Cavendish St., London W1M 7RD, England. TEL 0171-323-5312. FAX 0171-580-4952. *5850*

INTERNATIONAL JOURNAL OF PSYCHOPHYSIOLOGY.
Elsevier Science B.V., P.O. Box 211, 1000 AE Amsterdam, Netherlands. TEL 31-20-4853911. FAX 31-20-4853598. *5850*

INTERNATIONAL JOURNAL OF PUNJAB STUDIES.
Sage Publications India Pvt. Ltd., Box 4215, New Delhi 110 048, India. TEL 91-11-644-4958. FAX 91-11-647-2426. *5329*

INTERNATIONAL JOURNAL OF QUALITATIVE STUDIES IN EDUCATION.
Taylor & Francis Ltd., Rankine Rd., Basingstoke, Hants RG24 8PR, England. TEL 44-1256-840366. FAX 44-1256-479438. *2343*

INTERNATIONAL JOURNAL OF QUANTUM CHEMISTRY.
John Wiley & Sons, Inc., Journals, 605 Third Ave., New York, NY 10158. TEL 212-850-6645. FAX 212-850-6021. *1578*

INTERNATIONAL JOURNAL OF RADIATION BIOLOGY.
Taylor & Francis Ltd., 1 Gunpowder Sq., London EC4A 3DE, England. TEL 44-171-583-0490. FAX 44-171-583-0585. *4757*

INTERNATIONAL JOURNAL OF RADIATION: ONCOLOGY - BIOLOGY - PHYSICS.
Elsevier Science Inc., Box 945, New York, NY 10159-0945. TEL 212-633-3730. FAX 212-633-3680. *5595*

INTERNATIONAL JOURNAL OF RADIOACTIVE MATERIALS TRANSPORT.
Nuclear Technology Publishing P.O. Box 7, Ashford, Kent TN23 1YW, England. TEL 44-1233-641683. FAX 44-1233-610021. *6720*

INTERNATIONAL JOURNAL OF REFRACTORY METALS AND HARD MATERIALS.
Elsevier Science Ltd., P.O. Box 800, Kidlington, Oxford OX5 1DX, England. TEL 44-1865-843000. FAX 44-1865-843010 *4953*

INTERNATIONAL JOURNAL OF REFRIGERATION.
Butterworth - Heinemann, Part of the Reed Elsevier group, Linacre House, Jordan Hill, Oxford OX2 8DP, England. TEL 44-1865-310366. FAX 44-1865-310898. *3330*

INTERNATIONAL JOURNAL OF REHABILITATION AND HEALTH.
Plenum Publishing Corp., 233 Spring St., New York, NY 10013-1578. TEL 212-620-8000. FAX 212-463-0742. *3305*

INTERNATIONAL JOURNAL OF REHABILITATION RESEARCH.
Chapman & Hall, Journals Department 2-6 Boundary Row, London SE1, England. TEL 44-171-8650066. FAX 44-171-5229623. *3305*

INTERNATIONAL JOURNAL OF REMOTE SENSING.
Taylor & Francis Ltd., 1 Gunpowder Sq., London EC4A 3DE, England. TEL 44-171-583-0490. FAX 44-171-583-0585. *2211*

INTERNATIONAL JOURNAL OF RESEARCH IN MARKETING.
North-Holland P.O. Box 211, 1000 AE Amsterdam, Netherlands. TEL 31-20-4853911. FAX 31-20-4853598. *1469*

INTERNATIONAL JOURNAL OF RISK AND SAFETY IN MEDICINE.
I O S Press, Van Diemenstraat 94, 1013 CN Amsterdam, Netherlands. TEL 31-20-6382189. FAX 31-20-6203419 *4474*

INTERNATIONAL JOURNAL OF ROBOTICS RESEARCH.
M I T Press, 55 Hayward St., Cambridge, MA 02142. TEL 617-253-2889. FAX 617-577-1545. *2105*

INTERNATIONAL JOURNAL OF ROCK MECHANICS & MINING SCIENCES.
Elsevier Science Ltd., Pergamon, P.O. Box 800, Kidlington, Oxford OX5 1DX, England. TEL 44-1865-843000. FAX 44-1865-843010. *5066*

INTERNATIONAL JOURNAL OF RURAL STUDIES.
International Task Force for the Rural Poor, Amarpurkashi Rural Polytechnic, P.O. Bilari 202411, District Moradabad (U.P.), India. TEL 91-5926-41267. *6417*

INTERNATIONAL JOURNAL OF S T D & AIDS.
Royal Society of Medicine Press Ltd., 1 Wimpole St., London W1M 8AE, England. TEL 0171-290-2900. FAX 0171-290-2929. *4623*

INTERNATIONAL JOURNAL OF SALT LAKE RESEARCH.
Kluwer Academic Publishers, Postbus 17, 3300 AA Dordrecht, Netherlands. TEL 31-78-6392392. FAX 31-78-6392254. *6970*

INTERNATIONAL JOURNAL OF SCIENCE EDUCATION.
Taylor & Francis Ltd., Rankine Rd., Basingstoke, Hants. RG24 8PR, England. TEL 01256-840366. FAX 01256-479438. *2343*

INTERNATIONAL JOURNAL OF SELECTION AND ASSESSMENT.
Blackwell Publishers Ltd., 108 Cowley Rd., Oxford OX4 1JF, England. TEL 44-1865-791100. FAX 44-1865-791347. *1505*

INTERNATIONAL JOURNAL OF SLAVIC LINGUISTICS AND POETICS.
Slavica Publishers, Inc., Box 14388, Columbus, OH 43214. TEL 614-268-4002. FAX 614-268-0106. *4076*

INTERNATIONAL JOURNAL OF SOCIAL SCIENCES.
Box 98029, S. Common Post, 2150 Burnhamthorpe Rd., Mississauga, ON L5L 3A0, Canada. FAX 516-277-2875. *6329*

INTERNATIONAL JOURNAL OF SOCIOLOGY.
M.E. Sharpe, Inc., 80 Business Park Dr., Armonk, NY 10504. TEL 914-273-1800. FAX 914-273-2106. *6417*

INTERNATIONAL JOURNAL OF SOLAR ENERGY.
Harwood Academic Publishers, c/o International Publishers Distributor, P.O. Box 3054, Langhorne, PA 19047-3054. TEL 215-750-2642. FAX 215-750-6343. *2585*

INTERNATIONAL JOURNAL OF SOLIDS AND STRUCTURES.
Elsevier Science Ltd., Pergamon, P.O. Box 800, Kidlington, Oxford OX5 1DX, England. TEL 44-1865-843000. FAX 44-1865-843010. *5588*

INTERNATIONAL JOURNAL OF SPACE STRUCTURES.
Multi-Science Publishing Co. Ltd., 107 High St., Brentwood, Essex CM14 4RX, England. TEL 44-1277-224632. FAX 44-1277-223453. *860*

INTERNATIONAL JOURNAL OF SPEECH TECHNOLOGY.
Kluwer Academic Publishers, Postbus 17, 3300 AA Dordrecht, Netherlands. TEL 31-78-6392392. FAX 31-78-6392254. *4129*

INTERNATIONAL JOURNAL OF SPORT NUTRITION.
Human Kinetics Publishers, Inc., Box 5076, Champaign, IL 61825-5076. TEL 217-351-5076. FAX 217-351-2674. *5235*

INTERNATIONAL JOURNAL OF STRESS MANAGEMENT.
Human Sciences Press, Inc. 233 Spring St., New York, NY 10013. TEL 212-620-8000. FAX 212-463-0742. *4474*

INTERNATIONAL JOURNAL OF STRUCTURES.
Nem Chand & Bros., Civil Lines, Roorkee 247667, India. TEL 01332-72258. *2664*

INTERNATIONAL JOURNAL OF SUPERCOMPUTER APPLICATIONS AND HIGH-PERFORMANCE COMPUTING.
Sage Publications, Inc., Sage Science Press, 2455 Teller Rd., Thousand Oaks, CA 91320. TEL 805-499-0721. FAX 805-499-0871. *2111*

INTERNATIONAL JOURNAL OF SURGICAL PATHOLOGY.
Churchill Livingstone, 650 Ave. of the Americas, New York, NY 10011. TEL 212-206-5000. FAX 212-727-7808. *4910*

INTERNATIONAL JOURNAL OF SUSTAINABLE DEVELOPMENT AND WORLD ECOLOGY.
Parthenon Publishing Group, Casterton Hall, Carnforth, Lancs. LA6 2LA, England. TEL 44-152-427-2084. FAX 44-152-427-1587. *2804*

INTERNATIONAL JOURNAL OF SYSTEMATIC BACTERIOLOGY.
American Society for Microbiology, 1325 Massachusetts Ave., N.W., Washington, DC 20005. TEL 202-737-3600. *759*

INTERNATIONAL JOURNAL OF SYSTEMS SCIENCE.
Taylor & Francis Ltd., 1 Gunpowder Sq., London EC4A 3DE, England. TEL 44-171-583-0490. FAX 44-171-583-0585. *2605*

THE INTERNATIONAL JOURNAL OF TECHNICAL COOPERATION.
Frank Cass, Newbury House, 890-900 Eastern Ave., Newbury Park, Ilford, Essex IG2 7HH, England. TEL 44-181-559-8866. FAX 44-181-599-0984. *1310*

INTERNATIONAL JOURNAL OF TECHNOLOGY ADVANCES.
Box 98029, S. Common Post, 2150 Burnhamthorpe Rd., Mississauga, ON L5L 3A0, Canada. FAX 516-277-2875. *6654*

INTERNATIONAL JOURNAL OF TECHNOLOGY AND DESIGN EDUCATION.
Kluwer Academic Publishers, Postbus 17, 3300 AA Dordrecht, Netherlands. TEL 31-78-6392392. FAX 31-78-6392254. *2490*

INTERNATIONAL JOURNAL OF THE CLASSICAL TRADITION.
Transaction Publishers, Transaction Periodicals Consortium, Department 3092, Rutgers University, New Brunswick, NJ 08903. TEL 908-445-2280. FAX 908-445-3138. *1823*

INTERNATIONAL JOURNAL OF THE ECONOMICS OF BUSINESS.
Carfax Publishing Co., P.O. Box 25, Abingdon, Oxon. OX14 3UE, England. TEL 44-1235-401000. FAX 44-1235-401550. *933*

THE INTERNATIONAL JOURNAL OF THE HISTORY OF SPORT.
Frank Cass, Newbury House, 890-900 Eastern Ave., Newbury Park, Ilford, Essex IG2 7HH, England. TEL 44-181-599-8866. FAX 44-181-599-0984. *6465*

INTERNATIONAL JOURNAL OF THE LEGAL PROFESSION.
Carfax Publishing Co., P.O. Box 25, Abingdon, Oxon. OX14 3UE, England. TEL 44-1235-401000. FAX 44-1235-401550. *3793*

INTERNATIONAL JOURNAL OF THEORETICAL PHYSICS.
Plenum Publishing Corp., 233 Spring St., New York, NY 10013-1578. TEL 212-620-8000. FAX 212-463-0742. *5551*

INTERNATIONAL JOURNAL OF THERMOPHYSICS.
Plenum Publishing Corp., 233 Spring St., New York, NY 10013-1578. TEL 212-620-8000. FAX 212-463-0742. *5585*

INTERNATIONAL JOURNAL OF THYMOLOGY.
Thymus Medizinischer Fachbuchverlag, Rudolf-Huch-Str. 14, 38667 Bad Harzburg, Germany. TEL 49-5322-960532. FAX 49-5322-3017. *4672*

INTERNATIONAL JOURNAL OF TRAINING & DEVELOPMENT.
Blackwell Publishers Ltd., 108 Cowley Rd., Oxford OX4 1JF, England. TEL 44-1865-791100. FAX 44-1865-791347. *1505*

INTERNATIONAL JOURNAL OF TRAUMA NURSING.
Mosby - Year Book, Inc. 11830 Westline Industrial Dr., St.Louis, MO 63146. TEL 314-872-8370. FAX 314-872-9164. *4716*

INTERNATIONAL JOURNAL OF UNIVERSITY ADULT EDUCATION.
International Congress of University Adult Education, c/o John F. Morris, Sec. Treas., Dept. of Extension and Summer Session, Univ. of New Brunswick, Box 4400, Fredericton, NB E3B 5A3, Canada. TEL 506-453-4646. FAX 506-453-3572. *2400*

INTERNATIONAL JOURNAL OF URBAN AND REGIONAL RESEARCH.
Blackwell Publishers Ltd., 108 Cowley Rd., Oxford OX4 1JF, England. TEL 44-1865-791100. FAX 44-1865-791347. *3586*

INTERNATIONAL JOURNAL OF UROLOGY.
Churchill Livingstone Japan, Churchill Bldg., 2-8-16 Yutenji, Meguro-ku, Tokyo 153, Japan. TEL 81-3-5721-0442. FAX 81-3-5721-0415. *4927*

INTERNATIONAL JOURNAL OF VALUE-BASED MANAGEMENT.
Kluwer Academic Publishers Boston, Box 358, Accord Sta., Hingham, MA 02018-0358. TEL 617-871-6600. FAX 617-871-6528. *1425*

INTERNATIONAL JOURNAL OF VISUAL COMPUTING.
Intellect, Earl Richards Rd. N., Exeter, Devon EX2 6AS, England. TEL 44-1392-475110. FAX 44-1392-475110. *463*

INTERNATIONAL JOURNAL OF VOCATIONAL EDUCATION AND TRAINING.
International Vocational Education and Training Association, 676-B Enterprise Dr., Lewis Center, OH 43035. TEL 614-847-9550. FAX 614-847-9844. *2451*

INTERNATIONAL JOURNAL OF WATER JET TECHNOLOGY.
International Society of Water Jet Technology, Box 46039, 2339 Ogilvie Rd., Glouchester, ON K1J 9M7, Canada. TEL 613-993-2731. FAX 613-952-1395. *2744*

INTERNATIONAL JOURNAL OF WATER RESOURCES DEVELOPMENT.
Carfax Publishing Co., P.O. Box 25, Abingdon, Oxon. OX14 3UE, England. TEL 44-1235-401000. FAX 44-1235-401550. *6971*

INTERNATIONAL JOURNAL OF WIRELESS INFORMATION NETWORKS.
Plenum Publishing Corp., 233 Spring St., New York, NY 10013-1578. TEL 212-620-8000. FAX 212-463-0742. *1907*

INTERNATIONAL JOURNAL ON DIGITAL LIBRARIES.
Springer-Verlag, Heidelberger Platz 3, 14197 Berlin, Germany. TEL 49-30-82787358. FAX 49-30-82787448. *4045*

THE INTERNATIONAL JOURNAL ON HYDROPOWER & DAMS.
Aqua-Media International Ltd., Westmead House, Westmead Rd., Sutton, Surrey SM1 4JH, England. TEL 44-181-643-4727. FAX 44-181-643-8200. *2572*

INTERNATIONAL JOURNAL ON MINORITY AND GROUP RIGHTS.
Kluwer Law International Postbus 85889, 2508 CN The Hague, Netherlands. TEL 31-70-3081500. FAX 31-70-3081515. *5730*

INTERNATIONAL LABOR AND WORKING CLASS HISTORY.
Cambridge University Press, Edinburgh Bldg., Shaftesbury Rd., Cambridge CB2 2RU, England. TEL 44-1223-312393. FAX 44-1223-315052. *1380*

INTERNATIONAL LABOUR LAW REPORTS.
Kluwer Academic Publishers, Postbus 17, 3300 AA Dordrecht, Netherlands. TEL 31-78-6392392. FAX 31-78-6392254. *3793*

INTERNATIONAL LAW IN ASIAN PERSPECTIVE.
Martinus Nijhoff Publishers, Human Rights and International Law Postbus 163, 3300 AD Dordrecht, Netherlands. TEL 31-78-334911. FAX 31-78-334254. *3935*

INTERNATIONAL LAW IN JAPANESE PERSPECTIVE.
Martinus Nijhoff Publishers, Human Rights and International Law Postbus 163, 3300 AD Dordrecht, Netherlands. TEL 31-78-334911. FAX 31-78-334254. *3935*

INTERNATIONAL LAW PRACTICUM.
New York State Bar Association, International Law and Practice Section, 1 Elk St., Albany, NY 12207-1096. TEL 518-463-3200. FAX 518-463-8844. *3935*

INTERNATIONAL LECTURE SERIES IN COMPUTER SCIENCE.
Academic Press, Inc., 525 B St., Ste. 1900, San Diego, CA 92101-4495. TEL 619-231-0926. FAX 619-699-6715. *1993*

INTERNATIONAL MEDICAL JOURNAL.
Japan International Cultural Exchange Foundation, 2-15-5-207 Shoto, Shibuya-ku, Tokyo 150, Japan. TEL 81-3-3424-9090. FAX 81-3-3424-9119. *4474*

INTERNATIONAL MIGRATION REVIEW.
Center for Migration Studies, 209 Flagg Pl., Staten Island, NY 10304-1199. TEL 718-351-8800. FAX 718-667-4598. *5786*

INTERNATIONAL NEGOTIATION REVIEW.
Kluwer Law International Postbus 85889, 2508 CN The Hague, Netherlands. TEL 31-70-3081500. FAX 31-78-3081515. *3936*

INTERNATIONAL NEUROPSYCHOLOGICAL SOCIETY. JOURNAL.
Cambridge University Press, Edinburgh Bldg., Shaftesbury Rd., Cambridge CB2 2RU, England. TEL 44-1223-312393. FAX 44-1223-315052. *4842*

INTERNATIONAL OPHTHALMOLOGY.
Kluwer Academic Publishers, Postbus 17, 3300 AA Dordrecht, Netherlands. TEL 31-78-6392392. FAX 31-78-6392254. *4771*

INTERNATIONAL ORGANIZATION.
M I T Press, 55 Hayward St., Cambridge, MA 02142. TEL 617-253-2889. FAX 617-577-1545. *5755*

INTERNATIONAL ORGANIZATION AND THE EVOLUTION OF WORLD SOCIETY.
Kluwer Academic Publishers, Postbus 17, 3300 AA Dordrecht, Netherlands. TEL 31-78-6392392. FAX 31-78-6392254. *3936*

INTERNATIONAL ORGANIZATIONS AND THE LAW OF THE SEA (YEAR).
Kluwer Academic Publishers, Postbus 17, 3300 AA Dordrecht, Netherlands. TEL 31-78-6392392. FAX 31-78-6392254. *3957*

INTERNATIONAL PEACEKEEPING.
Frank Cass, Newbury House, 890-900 Eastern Ave., Newbury Park, Ilford, Essex 1G2 7HH, England. TEL 44-181-599-8866. FAX 44-181-599-0984. *5756*

INTERNATIONAL PEACEKEEPING.
Kluwer Law International Postbus 85889, 2508 CN The Hague, Netherlands. TEL 31-70-3081500. FAX 31-70-3081515. *5756*

INTERNATIONAL PHILOSOPHICAL QUARTERLY.
Foundation for International Philosophical Exchange, Fordham University, Bronx, NY 10458. TEL 718-817-4776. FAX 718-817-4785. *5480*

INTERNATIONAL PLAY JOURNAL.
Chapman & Hall, Journals Department 2-6 Boundary Row, London SE1 8HN, England. TEL 44-171-8650066. FAX 44-171-5229623. *5850*

INTERNATIONAL POETRY.
International Writers and Artists Association, Bluffton College, Bluffton, OH 45817. TEL 419-358-3418. FAX 419-358-3323. *4308*

INTERNATIONAL POLITICAL SCIENCE REVIEW.
Sage Publications Ltd., 6 Bonhill St., London EC2A 4PU, England. TEL 44-171-374-0645. FAX 44-171-374-8741. *5756*

INTERNATIONAL POLITICS.
Kluwer Law International Postbus 85889, 2508 CN The Hague, Netherlands. TEL 31-70-3081500. FAX 31-70-3031515. *6329*

INTERNATIONAL PROGRESS IN URETHANES.
Technomic Publishing Co., Inc., 851 New Holland Ave., Box 3535, Lancaster, PA 17604. TEL 717-291-5609. FAX 717-295-4538. *5620*

INTERNATIONAL PSYCHOGERIATRICS.
Springer Publishing Company, 536 Broadway, New York, NY 10012-3955. TEL 212-431-4370. FAX 212-941-7842. *4842*

INTERNATIONAL PUBLIC RELATIONS REVIEW.
International Public Relations Association, Ste. 1007, South Tower 175 Bloor St. E., Toronto ON M4W 3R8. TEL 416-968-7311. FAX 416-968-6281. *38*

INTERNATIONAL QUARTERLY OF COMMUNITY HEALTH EDUCATION.
Baywood Publishing Co., Inc., 26 Austin Ave., Box 337, Amityville, NY 11701. TEL 516-691-1270. FAX 516-691-1770. *5966*

INTERNATIONAL REGIONAL SCIENCE REVIEW.
West Virginia University, Regional Research Institute, Morgantown, WV 26506-6825. TEL 304-293-2896. FAX 304-293-6699. *6329*

INTERNATIONAL RESEARCH IN GEOGRAPHICAL AND ENVIRONMENTAL EDUCATION.
Multilingual Matters Ltd., Frankfurt Lodge, Clevedon Hall, Victoria Rd., Clevedon, Avon BS21 7SJ, England. TEL 44-1275-876519. FAX 44-1275-343096. *3262*

INTERNATIONAL REVIEW OF ADMINISTRATIVE SCIENCES.
Sage Publications Ltd., 6 Bonhill St., London EC2A 4PU, England. TEL 44-171-374-0645. FAX 44-171-374-8741. *5907*

INTERNATIONAL REVIEW OF CHILD NEUROLOGY SERIES.
Lippincott - Raven Publishers 227 E. Washington Sq., Philadelphia, PA 19106. TEL 215-238-4200. FAX 215-238-4235. *4842*

INTERNATIONAL REVIEW OF CHINESE LINGUISTICS.
John Benjamins Publishing Co., Amsteldijk 44, P.O. Box 75577, 1070 AN Amsterdam, Netherlands. TEL 31-20-6762325. FAX 31-20-6792956. *4076*

INTERNATIONAL REVIEW OF CYTOLOGY.
Academic Press, Inc., 525 B St., Ste. 1900, San Diego, CA 92101-4495. TEL 619-231-0926. FAX 619-699-6715. *715*

INTERNATIONAL REVIEW OF ECONOMICS AND FINANCE.
J A I Press Inc., 55 Old Post Rd., No. 2, Box 1678, Greenwich, CT 06836-1678. TEL 203-661-7602. FAX 203-661-0792. *1217*

INTERNATIONAL REVIEW OF EDUCATION.
Kluwer Academic Publishers, Postbus 17, 3300 AA Dordrecht, Netherlands. TEL 31-78-6392392. FAX 31-78-6392254. *2343*

INTERNATIONAL REVIEW OF EXPERIMENTAL PATHOLOGY.
Academic Press, Inc., 525 B St., Ste. 1900, San Diego, CA 92101-4495. TEL 619-231-0926. FAX 619-699-6715. *4474*

INTERNATIONAL REVIEW OF FINANCIAL ANALYSIS.
J A I Press Inc., 55 Old Post Rd., No. 2, Box 1678, Greenwich, CT 06836-1678. TEL 203-661-7602. FAX 203-661-0792. *1103*

INTERNATIONAL REVIEW OF INDUSTRIAL AND ORGANIZATIONAL PSYCHOLOGY.
John Wiley & Sons Ltd., Journals, Baffins Ln., Chichester, W. Sussex PO19 1UD, England. TEL 44-1243-779777. FAX 44-1243-843232. *5850*

INTERNATIONAL REVIEW OF LAW AND ECONOMICS.
Elsevier Science Inc., Box 945, New York, NY 10159-0945. TEL 212-633-3730. FAX 212-633-3680. *3793*

INTERNATIONAL REVIEW OF LAW, COMPUTERS & TECHNOLOGY.
Carfax Publishing Co., P.O. Box 25, Abingdon, Oxon. OX14 3UE, England. TEL 44-1235-401000. FAX 44-1235-401550. *5889*

INTERNATIONAL REVIEW OF NEUROBIOLOGY.
Academic Press, Inc., 525 B St., Ste. 1900, San Diego, CA 92101-4495. TEL 619-231-0926. FAX 619-699-6715. *4842*

INTERNATIONAL REVIEW OF PSYCHIATRY.
Carfax Publishing Co., P.O. Box 25, Abingdon, Oxon. OX14 3UE, England. TEL 44-1235-401000. FAX 44-1235-401550. *4842*

INTERNATIONAL REVIEW OF RESEARCH IN MENTAL RETARDATION.
Academic Press, Inc., 525 B St., Ste. 1900, San Diego, CA 92101-4495. TEL 619-231-0926. FAX 619-699-6715. *4842*

INTERNATIONAL REVIEW OF SOCIAL HISTORY.
Cambridge University Press, Edinburgh Bldg., Shaftesbury Rd., Cambridge CB2 2RU, England. TEL 44-1223-312393. FAX 44-1223-315052. *3348*

INTERNATIONAL REVIEW OF SOCIOLOGY.
Carfax Publishing Co., P.O. Box 25, Abingdon, Oxon. OX14 3UE, England. TEL 44-1235-401000. FAX 44-1235-401550. *5418*

INTERNATIONAL REVIEWS IN PHYSICAL CHEMISTRY.
Taylor & Francis Ltd., 1 Gunpowder Sq., London EC4A 3DE, England. TEL 44-171-583-0490. FAX 44-171-583-0585. *1752*

INTERNATIONAL REVIEWS OF IMMUNOLOGY.
Harwood Academic Publishers, c/o International Publishers Distributor, P.O. Box 3054, Langhorne, PA 19047-3054. TEL 215-750-2642. FAX 215-750-6343. *4584*

INTERNATIONAL SATELLITE SYMPOSIUM ON ACUTE RENAL FAILURE. PROCEEDINGS.
International Society of Nephrology, Commission on Acute Renal Failure, Hippokration General Hospital, 50 Papanastasiou St., 543 42 Thessaloniki, Greece. TEL 30-31-835955. FAX 30-31-861111. *4927*

INTERNATIONAL SCHOOL OF PHYSICS "ENRICO FERMI". PROCEEDINGS.
I O S Press, Van Diemenstraat 94, 1013 CN Amsterdam, Netherlands. TEL 31-20-6382189. FAX 31-20-6203419. *5552*

INTERNATIONAL SECURITY.
M I T Press, 55 Hayward St., Cambridge, MA 02142. TEL 617-253-2889. FAX 617-577-1545. *5756*

INTERNATIONAL SERIES IN ECONOMIC MODELING.
Kluwer Academic Publishers, Postbus 17, 3300 AA Dordrecht, Netherlands. TEL 31-78-6392392. FAX 31-78-6392254. *1155*

INTERNATIONAL SERIES IN INTELLIGENT TECHNOLOGIES.
Kluwer Academic Publishers, Postbus 17, 3300 AA Dordrecht, Netherlands. TEL 31-78-6392392. FAX 31-78-6392254. *2008*

INTERNATIONAL SERIES IN QUANTITATIVE MARKETING.
Kluwer Academic Publishers, Postbus 17, 3300 AA Dordrecht, Netherlands. TEL 31-78-6392392. FAX 31-78-6392254. *1469*

INTERNATIONAL SERIES IN SOCIAL WELFARE
Kluwer Academic Publishers, Postbus 17, 3300 AA Dordrecht, Netherlands. TEL 31-78-6392392. FAX 31-78-6392254. *6377*

INTERNATIONAL SERIES OF MONOGRAPHS ON CHEMISTRY.
Oxford University Press, Walton St., Oxford OX2 6DP, England. TEL 44-1865-56767. FAX 44-1865-56646. *1678*

INTERNATIONAL SERIES OF MONOGRAPHS ON PHYSICS.
Oxford University Press, Walton St., Oxford OX2 6DP, England. TEL 44-1865-56767. FAX 44-1865-56646. *5552*

INTERNATIONAL SMALL BUSINESS JOURNAL.
Woodcock Publications Ltd., P.O. Box 1, Macclesfield, Cheshire SK10 4YQ, England. TEL 44-1625-528516. FAX 44-1625-532644. *1576*

INTERNATIONAL SOCIAL SCIENCE JOURNAL.
Blackwell Publishers Ltd., 108 Cowley Road, Oxford OX4 1JF, England. TEL 44-1865-791100. FAX 44-1865-791347. *6330*

INTERNATIONAL SOCIAL WORK.
Sage Publications Ltd., 6 Bonhill St., London EC2A 4PU, England. TEL 44-171-374-0645. FAX 44-171-374-8741. *6377*

INTERNATIONAL SOCIETY FOR RESPIRATORY PROTECTION. JOURNAL.
International Society for Respiratory Protection, 2090 Eola Dr., N.W., Salem, OR 97304-4443. TEL 503-588-1382. *4888*

INTERNATIONAL SOCIETY FOR TERRAIN-VEHICLE SYSTEMS. PROCEEDINGS OF INTERNATIONAL CONFERENCE.
International Society for Terrain-Vehicle Systems, c/o Dr. Ronald A. Liston, USACRREL, 72 Lyme Rd., Hanover, NH 03755-1290. TEL 603-646-4362. *2664*

INTERNATIONAL SOCIETY OF CITRICULTURE. PROCEEDINGS.
International Society of Citriculture, c/o Prof. C.W. Coggins Jr., Department of Botany and Plant Sciences, University of California, Riverside, CA 92521. TEL 909-787-4412. FAX 909-787-4437. *126*

INTERNATIONAL SOCIETY ON OPTICS WITHIN LIFE SCIENCES. SERIES (PROCEEDINGS).
Elsevier Science B.V., Books Division, P.O. Box 211, 1000 AE Amsterdam, Netherlands. TEL 31-20-4853911. FAX 31-20-4853705. *588*

INTERNATIONAL SOCIOLOGY.
Sage Publications Ltd., 6 Bonhill St., London EC2A 4PU, England. TEL 44-171-374-0645. FAX 44-171-374-8741. *6418*

INTERNATIONAL STRAITS OF THE WORLD.
Kluwer Academic Publishers, Postbus 17, 3300 AA Dordrecht, Netherlands. TEL 31-78-6392392. FAX 31-78-6392254. *5756*

INTERNATIONAL STUDIES.
Sage Publications India Pvt. Ltd., P.O. Box 4215, New Delhi 110 048, India. TEL 91-11-644-4958. FAX 91-11-647-2426. *5756*

INTERNATIONAL STUDIES IN ECONOMICS AND ECONOMETRICS.
Kluwer Academic Publishers, Postbus 17, 3300 AA Dordrecht, Netherlands. TEL 31-78-6392392. FAX 31-78-6392254. *933*

INTERNATIONAL STUDIES IN EDUCATIONAL ACHIEVEMENT.
Elsevier Science Ltd., Pergamon, P.O. Box 800, Kidlington, Oxford OX5 1DX, England. TEL 44-1865-843000. FAX 44-1865-843010. *2343*

INTERNATIONAL STUDIES IN GLOBAL CHANGE.
Harwood Academic Publishers, c/o International Publishers Distributor, P.O. Box 3054, Langhorne, PA 19047-3054. TEL 215-750-2642. FAX 215-750-6343. *1425*

INTERNATIONAL STUDIES IN HUMAN RIGHTS.
Kluwer Academic Publishers, Postbus 17, 3300 AA Dordrecht, Netherlands. TEL 31-78-6392392. FAX 31-78-6392254. *5730*

INTERNATIONAL STUDIES IN SOCIOLOGY AND SOCIAL ANTHROPOLOGY.
E.J. Brill, P.O. Box 9000, 2300 PA Leiden, Netherlands. TEL 31-71-5353500. FAX 31-71-5317532. *6418*

INTERNATIONAL STUDIES IN SOCIOLOGY OF EDUCATION.
Triangle Journals Ltd., P.O. Box 65, Wallingford, Oxon. OX10 0YG, England. TEL 44-1491-838013. FAX 44-1491-834968. *2490*

INTERNATIONAL STUDIES IN THE PHILOSOPHY OF SCIENCE.
Carfax Publishing Co., P.O. Box 25, Abingdon, Oxon. OX14 3UE, England. TEL 44-1235-401000. FAX 44-1235-401550. *5480*

INTERNATIONAL STUDIES IN THE SERVICE ECONOMY.
Kluwer Academic Publishers, Postbus 17, 3300 AA Dordrecht, Netherlands. TEL 31-78-6392392. FAX 31-78-6392254. *1523*

INTERNATIONAL STUDIES OF MANAGEMENT AND ORGANIZATION.
M.E. Sharpe, Inc., 80 Business Park Dr., Armonk, NY 10504. TEL 914-273-1800. FAX 914-273-2106. *1425*

INTERNATIONAL STUDIES ON TERRORISM.
Kluwer Academic Publishers, Postbus 17, 3300 AA Dordrecht, Netherlands. TEL 31-78-6392392. FAX 31-78-6392254. *5757*

INTERNATIONAL STUDIES QUARTERLY.
Blackwell Publishers, 238 Main St., Cambridge, MA 02142. TEL 617-547-7110. FAX 617-547-0789. *5757*

INTERNATIONAL SURGERY.
Edizioni Minerva Medica, Corso Bramante 83-85, 10126 Turin, Italy. TEL 39-11-678282. FAX 39-11-3121736. *4911*

INTERNATIONAL SYMPOSIA ON THE PHARMACOLOGY OF THERMOREGULATION.
S. Karger AG, Allschwilerstr. 10, P.O. Box, CH-4009 Basel, Switzerland. TEL 061-3061111. FAX 061-3061234. *5419*

INTERNATIONAL SYMPOSIUM ON ATOMIC, MOLECULAR AND SOLID-STATE THEORY, COLLISION PHENOMENA AND COMPUTATIONAL METHODS. PROCEEDINGS.
John Wiley & Sons, Inc., 605 Third Ave., New York, NY 10158. TEL 212-850-6000. *1679*

INTERNATIONAL SYMPOSIUM ON COMPUTER HARDWARE DESCRIPTION LANGUAGES. PROCEEDINGS.
Institute of Electrical and Electronics Engineers, Inc., 345 E. 47th St., New York, NY 10017-2394. TEL 212-705-7366. *2078*

INTERNATIONAL SYMPOSIUM ON QUANTUM BIOLOGY AND QUANTUM PHARMACOLOGY. PROCEEDINGS.
John Wiley & Sons, Inc., 605 Third Ave., New York, NY 10158. TEL 212-850-6000. FAX 212-850-6088. *588*

INTERNATIONAL TAX AND PUBLIC FINANCE.
Kluwer Academic Publishers Boston, Box 358, Accord Sta., Hingham, MA 02018-0358. TEL 617-871-6600. FAX 617-871-6528. *1549*

INTERNATIONAL TELEMETERING CONFERENCE.
Instrument Society of America, 67 Alexander Dr., Box 12277, Research Triangle Park, NC 27709. TEL 919-549-8411. FAX 919-549-8288. *1908*

THE INTERNATIONAL TRADE JOURNAL.
Taylor & Francis Inc., 1900 Frost Rd., Bristol, PA 19007-1598. TEL 215-785-5800. FAX 215-785-5515. *1281*

INTERNATIONAL TRADE LAW AND REGULATION.
Sweet & Maxwell, Mill St., Oxford OX2 0JU, England. TEL 44-1865-249248. FAX 44-1865-792301. *3936*

INTERNATIONAL TRANSACTIONS IN OPERATIONAL RESEARCH.
Elsevier Science Ltd., Pergamon, P.O. Box 800, Kidlington, Oxford OX5 1DX, England. TEL 44-1865-843000. FAX 44-1865-843010. *1993*

INTERNATIONAL UROGYNECOLOGY JOURNAL.
Springer-Verlag London Ltd., Sweetapple House, Catteshall Rd., Godalming, Surrey GU7 3DJ, England. TEL 44-1483-418800. FAX 44-1483-415144. *4739*

INTERNATIONAL UROLOGY AND NEPHROLOGY.
Akademiai Kiado, Publishing House of the Hungarian Academy of Sciences, P.O. Box 245, H-1519 Budapest, Hungary. TEL 181-2134. FAX 166-6466. *4927*

INTERNATIONAL VISUAL LITERACY ASSOCIATION. ANNUAL CONFERENCE READINGS.
International Visual Literacy Association (Blacksburg), c/o Barbara I. Clark, Gonzaga University, E. 502 Boone AD 25, Spokane, WA 99258-0001. *2490*

INTERNATIONAL WESTERN GEOGRAPHICAL SERIES.
University of Victoria, Department of Geography, Victoria, BC V8W 3P5, Canada. TEL 604-721-7327. FAX 604-721-6216. *3263*

INTERNATIONAL WHALING COMMISSION. REPORT. SPECIAL ISSUE.
International Whaling Commission, Red House, Station Rd., Histon, Cambs. CB4 4NP, England. TEL 01223-233971. FAX 01223-232876. *2936*

INTERNATIONAL WOLF.
International Wolf Center, 5930 Brooklyn Blvd., Minneapolis, MN 55429. TEL 612-560-7374. FAX 612-569-7368. *2131*

INTERNATIONAL WORKSHOP ON H D T V. PROCEEDINGS.
Elsevier Science B.V., Books Division, P.O. Box 211, 1000 AE Amsterdam, Netherlands. TEL 31-20-4853911. FAX 31-20-4853705. *1928*

INTERNATIONAL YEARBOOK OF RURAL PLANNING.
Elsevier Science Ltd., Books Division, P.O. Box 800, Kidlington, Oxford OX5 1DX, England. TEL 44-1865-843000. FAX 44-1865-843010. *3586*

INTERNATIONALE STIFTUNG MOZARTEUM. MITTEILUNGEN.
Internationale Stiftung Mozarteum, Schwarzstr. 26, Postfach 34, A-5024 Salzburg, Austria. TEL 43-662-88940-10. FAX 43-662-882419. *5166*

L'INTERNISTA.
P C A Publishing, Via Clerici 12, 20032 Brusuglio di Corman (MI), Italy. TEL 39-2-66300802. FAX 39-2-6151239. *4706*

INTERPRETATION (FLUSHING).
Queens College, Flushing, NY 11367-1597. TEL 718-997-5542. *5674*

INTERPRETING.
John Benjamins Publishing Co., Amsteldijk 44, P.O. Box 75577, 1070 AN Amsterdam, Netherlands. TEL 31-20-6762325. FAX 31-20-6792956. *4076*

INTERPRETING THE PAST.
University of California Press, 2120 Berkeley Way, Berkeley, CA 94720. TEL 510-642-4247. FAX 510-643-7127. *358*

INTERSCIENCE CONFERENCE ON ANTIMICROBIAL AGENTS AND CHEMOTHERAPY. PROGRAM AND ABSTRACTS.
American Society for Microbiology, 1325 Massachusetts Ave., N.W., Washington, DC 20005-4171. TEL 202-737-3600. *759*

INTERVENTION IN SCHOOL AND CLINIC.
Pro-Ed Inc., 8700 Shoal Creek Blvd., Austin, TX 78757-6897. TEL 512-451-3246. FAX 512-451-8542. *2470*

INTERVENTIONAL CARDIOLOGY.
Kluwer Academic Publishers, Postbus 17, 3300 AA Dordrecht, Netherlands. TEL 31-78-6392392. FAX 31-78-6392254. *4604*

INTERVIROLOGY.
S. Karger AG, Allschwilerstr. 10, P.O. Box, CH-4009 Basel, Switzerland. TEL 061-3061111. FAX 061-3061234. *760*

INTI.
Inti Publications, Box 20657, Cranston, RI 02920. TEL 401-865-2490. FAX 401-865-2057. *4220*

INVASION AND METASTASIS.
S. Karger AG, Allschwilerstr. 10, P.O. Box, CH-4009 Basel, Switzerland. TEL 061-3061111. FAX 061-3061234. *715*

INVENTIONES MATHEMATICAE.
Springer-Verlag, Heidelberger Platz 3, 14197 Berlin, Germany. TEL 49-30-8207-0. FAX 49-30-8214091. *4370*

INVERTEBRATE NEUROSCIENCE.
S U B I S, Mansion House, 19 Kingfield Rd.,
Sheffield S11 9AS, England. TEL 44-114-2554433.
FAX 44-114-2554626. *729*

INVESTIGACION BIBLIOTECOLOGICA.
Universidad Nacional Autonoma de Mexico, Centro
Universitario de Investigaciones Bibliotecologicas,
Torre II de Humanidades, pisos 12 y 13, Ciudad
Universitaria, 04510 Mexico, D.F., Mexico. TEL 525-
6230352. FAX 525-5507461. *4001*

INVESTIGATIONAL NEW DRUGS.
Kluwer Academic Publishers Boston, Box 358,
Accord Sta., Hingham, MA 02018-0358. TEL 617-
871-6600. FAX 617-871-6528. *5419*

**INVESTIGATIVE OPHTHALMOLOGY & VISUAL
SCIENCE.**
Lippincott - Raven Publishers 227 E. Washington
Sq., Philadelphia, PA 19106. TEL 215-238-4200.
4771

INVESTIGATIVE RADIOLOGY.
Lippincott - Raven Publishers 227 E. Washington
Sq., Philadelphia, PA 19106. TEL 215-238-4200.
4877

INVITATION.
Islamic Information Center of America, Box 4052,
Des Plaines, IL 60016. TEL 847-541-8141.
FAX 847-824-8436. *6117*

ION EXCHANGE AND SOLVENT EXTRACTION.
Marcel Dekker, Inc., 270 Madison Ave., New York,
NY 10016. TEL 212-696-9000. FAX 212-685-
4540. *1752*

IOWA ACADEMY OF SCIENCE. JOURNAL.
Iowa Academy of Science, 175 Baker Hall,
University of Northern Iowa, Cedar Falls, IA 50614.
TEL 319-273-2021. *6249*

IOWA ARCHITECT.
Mauck & Associates, 303 Locust St., Ste. 200, Des
Moines, IA 50309. TEL 515-243-4010. FAX 515-
243-6011. *396*

IOWA ENGLISH BULLETIN.
Iowa Council of Teachers of English Language Arts,
130 Baker Hall, English Dept., University of
Northern Iowa, Cedar Falls, IA 50614. TEL 319-
273-2729. FAX 319-273-5807. *2490*

IOWA JOURNAL OF COMMUNICATION.
Iowa Communication Association, c/o Marvin D.
Jensen, Dept. of Communication Studies, University
of Northern Iowa, Cedar Falls, IA 50614. TEL 319-
273-2593. FAX 319-273-2731. *1908*

IOWA P T A BULLETIN.
Iowa Congress of Parents and Teachers, 610 Merle
Hay Towers, Des Moines, IA 50310. *2344*

IOWA STATE UNIVERSITY VETERINARIAN.
Iowa State University, College of Veterinary
Medicine, Ames, IA 50011. TEL 515-294-0867.
6948

IRAN.
British Institute of Persian Studies, c/o British
Academy, 20-21 Cornwall Terrace, London NW1
4QP, England. TEL 44-171-920-0823. *3496*

IRAN AGRICULTURAL RESEARCH.
Shiraz University, College of Agriculture, Shiraz, Iran.
TEL 98-71-28193. FAX 98-71-28193. *126*

**IRANIAN JOURNAL OF CHEMISTRY AND CHEMICAL
ENGINEERING (INTERNATIONAL ENGLISH
EDITION).**
Jihad Danishgahi, P.O. Box 14155-4364, Tehran,
Iran. TEL 98-21-6497572. FAX 98-21-6400730.
1679

IRANIAN JOURNAL OF PLANT PATHOLOGY.
Iranian Phytopathological Society, Box 19395-
1454, Teheran, Iran. TEL 98-21-2400645. FAX 98-
21-2400645. *686*

IRANIAN JOURNAL OF SCIENCE AND TECHNOLOGY.
Shiraz University, School of Engineering, Shiraz,
Iran. TEL 98-71-672060. FAX 98-71-672060.
6249

IRANIAN MATHEMATICAL SOCIETY. BULLETIN.
Iranian Mathematical Society, P.O. Box 13145-418,
Teheran, Iran. FAX 98-21-8847275. *4370*

IRANIAN STUDIES.
Society for Iranian Studies, Middle East Center, Box
353650, University of Washington, Seattle, WA
98195. TEL 206-543-4227. FAX 206-685-0668.
5286

IRANICA ANTIQUA.
Editions Peeters s.p.r.l., Bondgenotenlaan 153,
3000 Leuven, Belgium. TEL 32-16-235170.
FAX 32-16-228500. *358*

THE IRISH ASTRONOMICAL JOURNAL.
Armagh Observatory, College Hill, Armagh BT61
9DG, N. Ireland. TEL 44-1861-522928. FAX 44-
1861-527174. *432*

IRISH BIBLICAL STUDIES.
Irish Biblical Studies, 26 College Green, Belfast BT7
1JT, Northern Ireland. TEL 44-1232-325374.
FAX 44-1232-325397. *6068*

IRISH BIRDS.
Irish Wildbird Conservancy, Ruttledge House, 8
Longford Pl., Monkstown, Co. Dublin, Ireland.
TEL 01-2804322. FAX 01-2844407. *777*

IRISH CATHOLIC DIRECTORY.
Veritas Book Co. Ltd., Veritas House, 7-8 Lower
Abbey St., Dublin, Ireland. *6183*

IRISH ECONOMIC AND SOCIAL HISTORY.
Economic and Social History Society of Ireland,
History Department, University College, Belfield,
Dublin 4, Ireland. TEL 0353-17068376. FAX 0353-
12837022. *3419*

IRISH GEOGRAPHY.
Geographical Society of Ireland, Department of
Geography, St. Patrick's College, Maynooth, County
Kildare, Ireland. TEL 01-7083684. FAX 01-
6289063. *3263*

IRISH IN BRITAIN DIRECTORY.
Brent Irish Advisory Service, 76 Salisbury Rd.,
London NW6 6NY, England. TEL 44-171-328-
1188. FAX 44-171-328-1198. *2885*

IRISH JOURNAL OF PSYCHOLOGICAL MEDICINE.
MedMedia Ltd., P.O. Box 86, Blackrock, Co. Dublin,
Ireland. TEL 353-1-2803967. FAX 353-1-
2807076. *1842*

IRISH JOURNAL OF SOCIOLOGY.
Sociological Association of Ireland, Department of
Political Science and Sociology, University College
Galway, Galway, Ireland. TEL 091-24411. *6418*

THE IRISH NATURALISTS' JOURNAL.
Irish Naturalists' Journal Ltd., School of Biology and
Biochemistry, Queen's University, Belfast BT7 1NN,
N. Ireland. TEL 44-1232-335793. FAX 44-1232-
236505. *6249*

IRON GAME HISTORY.
University of Texas at Austin, McLean Sport History
Fellowship, Rm. 217, Gregory Gymnasium, Austin,
TX 78712. TEL 512-447-3635. FAX 512-443-
0381. *6507*

IRRIGATION AND DRAINAGE SYSTEMS.
Kluwer Academic Publishers, Postbus 17, 3300 AA
Dordrecht, Netherlands. TEL 31-78-6392392.
FAX 31-78-6392254. *204*

ISELYA.
X Club, Department of Biological Science, Nicholls
State University, Thibodaux, LA 70310. *686*

ISIS.
University of Chicago Press, Journals Division, Box
37005, Chicago, IL 60637. TEL 773-753-3347.
FAX 773-753-0811. *6249*

ISLAM AND CHRISTIAN - MUSLIM RELATIONS.
Carfax Publishing Co., P.O. Box 25, Abingdon, Oxon.
OX14 3UE, England. TEL 44-1235-401000.
FAX 44-1235-401550. *6118*

ISLAMIC ACADEMY OF SCIENCES. JOURNAL.
Anadolu Health and Research Foundation,
Mithatpasa Caddesi 66-5, Kizilay, 06420 Ankara,
Turkey. TEL 90-312-4250319. FAX 90-312-
4259487. *6249*

ISLAMIC HISTORY AND CIVILIZATION.
E.J. Brill, P.O. Box 9000, 2300 PA Leiden,
Netherlands. TEL 31-71-3353500. FAX 31-71-
5317532. *6118*

ISLAMIC LAW & SOCIETY.
E.J. Brill, P.O. Box 9000, 2300 PA Leiden,
Netherlands. TEL 31-71-3353500. FAX 31-71-
5317532. *6118*

ISLAMIC PHILOSOPHY, THEOLOGY AND SCIENCE.
E.J. Brill, P.O. Box 9000, 2300 PA Leiden,
Netherlands. TEL 31-71-3353500. FAX 31-71-
5317532. *6118*

ISLAMIC THOUGHT AND SCIENTIFIC CREATIVITY.
Organization of Islamic Conference, Standing
Committee on Scientific and Technological Co-
operation (COMSTECH), 3 Constitution Ave., Sector
G-5, Islamabad 44000, Pakistan. TEL 92-51-
220681. FAX 92-51-220265. *6118*

THE ISLAND ARC.
Blackwell Science Pty Ltd, P.O. Box 378, Carlton
South, Vic. 3053, Australia. TEL 61-3-93470300.
FAX 61-3-93493016. *245*

ISLAND MAGAZINE.
Prince Edward Island Museum and Heritage
Foundation, 2 Kent St., Charlottetown, PE C1A
1M6, Canada. TEL 902-368-6604. FAX 902-368-
6608. *3473*

ISLAND PARENT MAGAZINE.
Krayenhoff-Holland Enterprises Ltd., 941 Kings Rd.,
Victoria, BC V8T 1W7, Canada. TEL 604-388-
6905. FAX 604-388-4391. *2152*

ISOLATION AND PURIFICATION.
Gordon & Breach Science Publishers, c/o
International Publishers Distributor, P.O. Box 3054,
Langhorne, PA 19047-3054. TEL 215-750-6343.
FAX 215-750-6343. *1716*

ISOTOPES IN ORGANIC CHEMISTRY.
Elsevier Science B.V., Books Division, P.O. Box 211,
1000 AE Amsterdam, Netherlands. TEL 31-20-
4853911. FAX 31-20-4853705. *1739*

**ISOTOPES IN THE PHYSICAL AND BIOMEDICAL
SCIENCES.**
Elsevier Science B.V., Books Division, P.O. Box 211,
1000 AE Amsterdam, Netherlands. TEL 31-20-
4853911. FAX 31-20-4853705. *1679*

**ISPRA COURSES ON ENERGY SYSTEMS AND
TECHNOLOGY.**
Kluwer Academic Publishers, Postbus 17, 3300 AA
Dordrecht, Netherlands. TEL 31-78-6392392.
FAX 31-78-6392254. *2578*

**ISPRA COURSES ON NUCLEAR ENGINEERING AND
TECHNOLOGY SERIES**
Harwood Academic Publishers, c/o International
Publishers Distributor, P.O. Box 3054, Langhorne,
PA 19047-3054. TEL 215-750-2642. FAX 215-
750-6343. *2578*

ISRAEL AFFAIRS.
Frank Cass, 890-900 Eastern Ave., Newbury Park,
Ilford, Essex IG2 7HH, England. TEL 44-181-599-
8866. FAX 44-181-599-0984. *5757*

**ISRAEL ANNUAL CONFERENCE ON AEROSPACE
SCIENCES. PROCEEDINGS.**
Technion - Israel Institute of Technology, Faculty of
Aerospace Engineering, Technion City, Haifa 32000,
Israel. TEL 972-4-8292260. FAX 972-4-8231848.
70

ISRAEL JOURNAL OF CHEMISTRY.
Laser Pages Publishing (1992) Ltd., P.O. Box
50257, Jerusalem 91502, Israel. TEL 972-2-
370699. FAX 972-2-370625. *1679*

ISRAEL JOURNAL OF EARTH SCIENCES.
Laser Pages Publishing (1992) Ltd., P.O. Box
50257, Jerusalem 91502, Israel. TEL 972-2-
370699. FAX 972-2-370625. *2211*

ISRAEL JOURNAL OF ENTOMOLOGY.
Entomological Society of Israel, P.O. Box 6, Bet
Dagan 50200, Israel. TEL 972-3-9683520.
FAX 972-3-9604180. *730*

Refereed

ISRAEL JOURNAL OF MEDICAL SCIENCES.
Israel Journal of Medical Sciences, 2 Etzel St., French Hill, Jerusalem 97853, Israel. TEL 972-2-817727. FAX 972-2-815722. *4475*

ISRAEL JOURNAL OF OBSTETRICS & GYNECOLOGY.
Menachem Horowitz Publishing, 22 Shlomzion Hamalca St., Tel Aviv 62276, Israel. TEL 972-3-448676. FAX 972-3-449422. *4739*

ISRAEL JOURNAL OF PLANT SCIENCES.
Laser Pages Publishing (1992) Ltd., P.O. Box 52507, Jerusalem 91502, Israel. TEL 972-2-370699. FAX 972-2-370625. *686*

ISRAEL JOURNAL OF ZOOLOGY.
Laser Pages Publishing (1992) Ltd., P.O. Box 50257, Jerusalem 91502, Israel. TEL 972-2-370699. FAX 972-2-370625. *809*

ISRAEL ORIENTAL STUDIES.
E.J. Brill, P.O. Box 9000, 2300 PA Leiden, Netherlands. TEL 31-71-5353500. FAX 31-71-5317532. *5286*

ISRAEL SOCIAL SCIENCE RESEARCH.
Hubert H. Humphrey Institute for Social Ecology, Ben-Gurion University of the Negev, P.O. Box 653, Beersheva 84105, Israel. TEL 972-7-461112. FAX 972-7-271536. *6330*

ISRAEL STUDIES IN MUSICOLOGY.
Israel Musicology Society, P.O. Box 503, Jerusalem, Israel. *5166*

ISRAELI JOURNAL OF AQUACULTURE - BAMIDGEH.
c/o Department of Animal Sciences, Faculty of Agriculture, Hebrew University of Jerusalem, P.O. Box 12, Rehovot 76100, Israel. TEL 972-8-481302. FAX 972-8-465763. *2936*

ISSUES IN ACCOUNTING EDUCATION.
American Accounting Association, Paul F. Gerhardt Bldg., 5717 Bessie Dr., Sarasota, FL 33583-2399. TEL 941-921-7747. FAX 941-923-4093. *1048*

ISSUES IN APPLIED LINGUISTICS.
University of California at Los Angeles, Department of TESL and Applied Linguistics, 3300 Rolfe Hall, Box 951531, Los Angeles, CA 90024-1531. *4076*

ISSUES IN BIOMEDICINE.
S. Karger AG, Allschwilerstr. 10, P.O. Box, CH-4009 Basel, Switzerland. TEL 061-3061111. FAX 061-3061234. *588*

ISSUES IN BUSINESS ETHICS.
Kluwer Academic Publishers, Postbus 17, 3300 AA Dordrecht, Netherlands. TEL 31-78-6392392. FAX 31-78-6392254. *5481*

ISSUES IN CHILD ABUSE ACCUSATIONS.
Institute for Psychological Therapies, 13200 Cannon City Blvd., Northfield, MN 55057. TEL 507-645-8881. FAX 507-645-8883. *1769*

ISSUES IN COMPREHENSIVE PEDIATRIC NURSING.
Taylor & Francis Inc., 1900 Frost Rd., Ste. 101, Bristol, PA 19007-1598. TEL 215-785-5800. FAX 215-785-5515. *4716*

ISSUES IN CRIMINOLOGICAL AND LEGAL PSYCHOLOGY.
British Psychological Society, Division of Criminological and Legal Psychology, St. Andrew's House, 48 Princess Rd. E., Leicester LE1 7DR, England. TEL 44-116-254-9568. FAX 44-116-247-0787. *5851*

ISSUES IN INTEGRATIVE STUDIES.
Association for Integrative Studies, c/o Prof. William H. Newell, Exec. Dir., School of Interdisciplinary Studies, Miami University, Oxford, OH 45056. TEL 513-529-2213. FAX 513-529-5849. *2344*

ISSUES IN LAW AND MEDICINE.
National Legal Center for the Medically Dependent and Disabled, Inc., Box 1586, Terre Haute, IN 47808-1586. TEL 812-232-0103. *4475*

ISSUES IN MENTAL HEALTH NURSING.
Taylor & Francis Inc., 1900 Frost Rd., Ste. 101, Bristol, PA 19007-1598. TEL 215-785-5800. FAX 215-785-5515. *4716*

ISSUES IN SOCIAL WORK EDUCATION.
Association of Teachers in Social Work Education, Department of Sociological Studies, University of Sheffield, Sheffield S10 2TN, England. TEL 44-114-276-8555. FAX 44-114-276-8125. *6378*

ISSUES IN WRITING.
University of Wisconsin at Stevens Point, Department of English, Stevens Point, WI 54481. TEL 715-346-4477. FAX 715-346-4215. *3705*

ISTITUTO ITALIANO DI NUMISMATICA. ANNALI.
Istituto Italiano di Numismatica, Palazzo Barberini, Via Quattro Fontane 13, 00195 Rome, Italy. TEL 39-6-4743603. FAX 39-6-4743603. *5225*

ISTITUTO RICERCHE PESCA MARITTIMA. QUADERNI.
Istituto Ricerche sulla Pesca Marittima, Molo Mandracchio, 60100 Ancona, Italy. TEL 39-71-5314. FAX 39-71-55313. *2937*

ISTITUTO SPERIMENTALE TALASSOGRAFICO DI TRIESTE. PUBBLICAZIONE.
Consiglio Nazionale delle Ricerche, Istituto Sperimentale Talassografico di Trieste, Viale Romolo Gessi, 2, 34123 Trieste, Italy. TEL 39-40-305312. FAX 39-40-308941. *2297*

ISTITUTO STORICO ITALIANO PER IL MEDIO EVO E ARCHIVIO MURATORIANO. BULLETTINO.
Istituto Storico Italiano per il Medio Evo, Palazzo Borromini, Piazza dell'Orologio 4, 00186 Rome, Italy. FAX 39-6-6877059. *3420*

ISTMICA.
Universidad Nacional, Facultad de Filosofia y Letras, Apdo. 86, 3000 Heredia, Costa Rica. TEL 506-237-6363 ext. 429. *3616*

ISTMO.
Centros Culturales de Mexico, A.C., Goya 73-303, 03910 Mexico D.F., Mexico. TEL 525-5631963. FAX 525-5636435. *3193*

ITALIAN AMERICANA.
University of Rhode Island, College of Continuing Education, 80 Washington St., Providence, RI 02903-1803. TEL 401-277-5306. FAX 401-277-5100. *2885*

ITALIAN JOURNAL OF INTELLECTIVE IMPAIRMENT.
GISSTIMMAI Editore, Via Liberta 21, 61039 S. Costanza, Italy. TEL 39-721-950234. *4842*

ITALIAN JOURNAL OF MINERAL & ELECTROLYTE METABOLISM.
Edizioni Minerva Medica, Corso Bramante 83-85, 10126 Turin, Italy. TEL 39-11-678282. FAX 39-11-3121736. *4476*

ITALIAN QUARTERLY.
Rutgers University, Department of Italian, 84 College Ave., New Brunswick, NJ 08903. TEL 908-932-7031. *4221*

ITALIAN STUDIES IN LAW.
Kluwer Academic Publishers, Postbus 17, 3300 AA Dordrecht, Netherlands. TEL 31-78-6392392. FAX 31-78-6392254. *3794*

ITALY ITALY.
Italy Italy Corp. s.r.l., Via Michele Mercati 51, 00197 Rome, Italy. TEL 39-6-3221150. FAX 39-6-3223869. *6894*

ITINERA GEOBOTANICA.
Universidad de Leon, Secretariado de Publicaciones, Campus de Verganza, s-n, 24007 Leon, Spain. TEL 34-87-291558. FAX 34-87-291558. *686*

IURIS SCRIPTA HISTORICA.
Koninklijke Academie voor Wetenschappen, Letteren en Schone Kunsten van Belgie, 1 Hertogsstraat, B-1000 Brussels, Belgium. *3794*

IYO DENSHI TO SEITAI KOGAKU.
Gakkaishi Kanko Senta, 4-16, Yayoi 2-chome, Bunkyo-ku, Tokyo 113, Japan. *4476*

J A M A: THE JOURNAL OF THE AMERICAN MEDICAL ASSOCIATION.
American Medical Association, 515 N. State St., Chicago, IL 60610. TEL 312-464-5000. FAX 312-464-4184. *4476*

J A O A: JOURNAL OF THE AMERICAN OSTEOPATHIC ASSOCIATION.
American Osteopathic Association, 142 E. Ontario St., Chicago, IL 60611. TEL 312-280-5800. FAX 312-280-5893. *4613*

J A R D - JOURNAL OF AGE RELATED DISORDERS.
Medical Media C C, P.O. Box 581, 1620 Kempton Park, South Africa. TEL 27-11-9756439. FAX 27-11-9702532. *3289*

J A S T.
American Studies Association of Turkey, c/o Dr. Irem Balkir, Dept. of English, Bilkent Universitesi, 06553 Ankara, Turkey. FAX 90-312-2664934. *3473*

J E T: JOURNAL OF EDUCATIONAL THOUGHT.
University of Calgary, Faculty of Education, Rm. 1304 Education Tower, Calgary, AB T2N 1N4, Canada. TEL 403-220-5629. FAX 403-282-5849. *2344*

J G R: JOURNAL OF GEOPHYSICAL RESEARCH.
American Geophysical Union, 2000 Florida Ave., N.W., Washington, DC 20009. TEL 202-462-6900. FAX 202-328-0566. *4999*

J G R: JOURNAL OF GEOPHYSICAL RESEARCH: OCEANS.
American Geophysical Union, 2000 Florida Ave., N.W., Washington, DC 20009. TEL 202-462-6900. FAX 202-328-0566. *2276*

J G R: JOURNAL OF GEOPHYSICAL RESEARCH: SOLID EARTH.
American Geophysical Union, 2000 Florida Ave., N.W., Washington, DC 20009. TEL 202-462-6900. FAX 202-328-0566. *2276*

J I S S I: INTERNATIONAL JOURNAL OF SCIENTOMETRICS AND INFORMETRICS.
Brzark Information Systems (P) Ltd., 112 Humayun Pur, Safdarjung Enclave, New Delhi 110 029, India. TEL 91-11-688-2366. FAX 91-33-551-2180. *4001*

J L B SMITH INSTITUTE OF ICHTHYOLOGY. ICHTHYOLOGICAL BULLETIN.
J L B Smith Institute of Ichthyology, Private Bag 1015, Grahamstown 6140, South Africa. TEL 27-461-27124. FAX 27-461-22403. *809*

J L B SMITH INSTITUTE OF ICHTHYOLOGY. SPECIAL PUBLICATION.
J L B Smith Institute of Ichthyology, Private Bag 1015, Grahamstown 6140, South Africa. TEL 27-461-27124. FAX 27-461-22403. *809*

J P S.
Polynesian Society, Inc., c/o Maori Dept., University of Auckland, Auckland, New Zealand. *313*

THE J. PAUL GETTY MUSEUM JOURNAL.
J. Paul Getty Museum, 17985 Pacific Coast Highway, Malibu, CA 90265. TEL 310-459-7611. FAX 310-454-8156. *5123*

J R A - THE SUPPLEMENTARY SERIES.
1216 Bending Rd., Ann Arbor, MI 48103. TEL 313-623-7162. FAX 313-662-3240. *359*

J S A E REVIEW.
Elsevier Science B.V., P.O. Box 211, 1000 AE Amsterdam, Netherlands. TEL 31-20-4853911. FAX 31-20-4853598. *6789*

J U F NEWS.
Jewish United Fund - Jewish Federation of Metropolitan Chicago, One S. Franklin St., Rm. 701, Chicago, IL 60606. TEL 312-357-4848. FAX 312-855-2470. *6378*

JACKSONVILLE MEDICINE.
Duval County Medical Society, 515 Lomax St., Jacksonville, FL 32204. TEL 904-355-6561. FAX 904-353-5848. *4476*

JAHRBUCH FUER ANTISEMITISMUSFORSCHUNG.
Campus Verlag, Heerstr. 149, 60488 Frankfurt a.M., Germany. TEL 069-97651610. FAX 069-97651678. *6330*

JAMAICAN JOURNAL OF SCIENCE AND TECHNOLOGY.
Scientific Research Council, P.O. Box 350, Kingston 6, Jamaica, W.I. TEL 809-927-1771. FAX 809-927-5347. *6250*

JAMES JOYCE QUARTERLY.
Academic Publications (Tulsa), 600 S. College Ave., Tulsa, OK 74104. TEL 918-631-2501. FAX 918-631-2033. *4222*

JAMI'AT AL-IMARAT AL-ARABIYYAH AL-MUTTAHIDAH. KULLIYYAT AL-AADAAB. MAJALLAH.
Jami'at al-Imarat al-Arabiyyah al-Muttahidah, Kulliyyat al-Aadaab, P.O. Box 17771, Al-Ain, United Arab Emirates. TEL 678007. FAX 671612. *3616*

JAPAN AND THE WORLD ECONOMY.
North-Holland P.O. Box 211, 1000 AE Amsterdam, Netherlands. TEL 31-20-4853911. FAX 31-20-4853598. *1256*

JAPAN ORTHODONTIC SOCIETY. JOURNAL.
Japan Orthodontic Society, c/o Oral health Association of Japan, 1-44-2 Komagome, Toshima-ku, Tokyo 170, Japan. TEL 81-3-3947-8891. FAX 81-3-3947-8341. *4644*

JAPAN SOCIETY OF LIBRARY SCIENCE. ANNALS.
Japan Society of Library Science, c/o Office of Library and Information Science, Faculty of Sociology, Tokyo University, 28-20 Hakusan 5-chome, Bunkyo-ku, Tokyo 112, Japan. TEL 81-3-3945-7444. *4001*

JAPANESE ECONOMIC REVIEW.
Blackwell Publishers Ltd., 108 Cowley Rd., Oxford OX4 1JF, England. TEL 44-1865-791100. FAX 44-1865-791347. *934*

JAPANESE ECONOMIC STUDIES.
M.E. Sharpe, Inc., 80 Business Park Dr., Armonk, NY 10504. TEL 914-273-1800. FAX 914-273-2106. *934*

JAPANESE JOURNAL OF CHEMOTHERAPY.
Nihon Kagaku Ryoho Gakkai, 2-20-8 Kamiosaki, Shinagawa-ku, Tokyo 141, Japan. TEL 81-3-3493-7129. FAX 81-3-5434-0843. *5420*

JAPANESE JOURNAL OF MEDICAL SCIENCE AND BIOLOGY.
National Institute of Health, 23-1, Toyama 1-chome, Shinjuku-ku, Tokyo 162, Japan. *4477*

JAPANESE JOURNAL OF OPHTHALMOLOGY.
University of Tokyo, School of Medicine, Department of Ophthalmology, 7-3-1 Hongo, Bunkyo-ku, Tokyo 113, Japan. TEL 81-3-3815-5411. FAX 81-3-3817-0798. *4771*

JAPANESE JOURNAL OF PHARMACOLOGY.
Japanese Pharmacological Society, Editorial Office, Kantohya Bld., Gokomachi-Ebisugawa, Nakagyo-ku, Kyoto 604, Japan. TEL 075-252-4641. FAX 075-252-4618. *5420*

JAPANESE JOURNAL OF PHYCOLOGY (JAPANESE EDITION).
Japanese Society of Phycology, c/o Division of Biological Sciences, Graduate School of Science, Hokkaido University, Sapporo 060, Japan. TEL 81-11-706-2745. FAX 81-11-746-1512. *686*

JAPANESE JOURNAL OF PHYSICAL FITNESS AND SPORTS MEDICINE.
Japanese Society of Physical Fitness and Sports Medicine, 3-25-8 Nishi-Shibashi, Minato-ku, Tokyo 105, Japan. *5531*

JAPANESE JOURNAL OF PHYSIOLOGY.
Center for Academic Publications Japan, 2-4-16 Yayoi, Bunkyo-ku, Tokyo 113, Japan. TEL 03-3817-5821. FAX 03-3817-5830. *789*

JAPANESE SOCIETY OF COMPUTATIONAL STATISTICS. JOURNAL.
Japanese Society of Computational Statistics, University of Tsukuba, Institute of Policy and Planning Sciences, 1-1-1 Tennodai, Tsukuba, Ibaraki 305, Japan. TEL 0298-53-5008. FAX 0298-55-3849. *6613*

JAPANOPHILE.
Japanophile, Box 223, Okemos, MI 48864. TEL 517-669-2109. *5286*

JAVA REPORT.
Sigs Publications, Inc., 71 W. 23rd St., 3rd Fl., New York, NY 10010-4102. TEL 212-274-0640. FAX 212-274-0646. *2045*

JAWETZ, MELNICK & ADELBERG'S MEDICAL MICROBIOLOGY.
Appleton & Lange Box 120041, Stamford, CT 06912-0041. TEL 203-406-4500. *760*

JEFFERSONIANA.
Virginia Museum of Natural History, 1001 Douglas Ave., Martinsville, VA 24112. TEL 540-666-8631. FAX 540-632-6487. *6250*

JERSEY AT HOME.
Royal Jersey Agricultural and Horticultural Society, Springfield, St Helier, Jersey JE2 4LF, Channel Islands. TEL 44-1534-37227. FAX 44-1534-24692. *251*

JERUSALEM SYMPOSIA ON QUANTUM CHEMISTRY AND BIOCHEMISTRY.
Kluwer Academic Publishers, Postbus 17, 3300 AA Dordrecht, Netherlands. TEL 31-78-6392392. FAX 31-78-6392254. *1752*

JEWISH AFFAIRS.
South African Jewish Board of Deputies, P.O. Box 87557, Houghton 2041, South Africa. TEL 27-11-4861434. FAX 27-11-6464940. *2886*

JEWISH CURRENTS.
Association for Promotion of Jewish Secularism, Inc., 22 E. 17th St., Rm. 601, New York, NY 10003. TEL 212-924-5740. *2887*

JEWISH JURISPRUDENCE SERIES.
Harwood Academic Publishers, c/o International Publishers Distributor, P.O. Box 3054, Langhorne, PA 19047-3054. TEL 215-750-2642. FAX 215-750-6343. *3795*

JEWISH LAW ANNUAL.
Harwood Academic Publishers, c/o International Publishers Distributor, P.O. Box 3054, Langhorne, PA 19047-3054. TEL 215-750-2642. FAX 215-750-6343. *3795*

JEWISH LAW IN CONTEXT.
Harwood Academic Publishers, c/o International Publishers Distributor, P.O. Box 3054, Langhorne, PA 19047-3054. TEL 215-750-2642. FAX 215-750-6343. *3795*

JEWISH REPORTER.
Jewish Federation of Las Vegas, 3909 S. Maryland Pkwy., Ste. 400, Las Vegas, NV 89119-7520. TEL 702-732-0556. FAX 702-732-3228. *2888*

JEWISH STAR (EDISON).
Jewish Federation of Greater Middlesex County, 100 Metroplex Dr., Edison, NJ 08817. TEL 908-985-1234. FAX 908-935-3295. *2888*

JIANGSU CHUANBO.
Jiangsu Sheng Chuanbo Sheji Yanjiusuo, 37 Zhengdong Road, Zhenjiang, Jiangsu 212003, People's Republic of China. TEL 86-511-4422493. FAX 86-511-4424389. *6838*

JIANGSU NONGYE XUEBAO.
Jiangsu Sheng Nongye Kexueyuan, Xiaolingwei, Nanjing, Jiangsu 210014, People's Republic of China. *128*

JIAOYU YANJIU.
Jiaoyu Yanjiu Zazhishe, 46, Beisanhuan Zhonglu, Beijing 100088, People's Republic of China. TEL 86-10-6201-1873. FAX 86-10-6203-3132. *2345*

JINGJI GUANLI WENZHAI.
Jingji Guanli Wenzhai Bianjibu, No. 11, Rendinghu Beixiang, Huangshi Dajie, Beijing 100011, People's Republic of China TEL 86-10-6201-5945. FAX 86-10-6618-0323. *1425*

JINKO KOKYU.
Nihon Kokyurhyohou Igakkai, Fukushima Kenritsu Ika Daigaku Masuikagaku Kyoshitsu, 1, Hikarigaoka, Fukushima-shi, Fukushima-ken 960-12, Japan. TEL 81-245-48-0828. FAX 81-245-48-0828. *4888*

JINSHU KEXUE YU GONGYI
Harbin Gongye Daxue, 165, Dazhi Jie, Harbin, Heilongjiang 150001, People's Republic of China. TEL 86-451-3621000. FAX 86-451-321048. *4961*

JINSHU XUEBAO.
Science Press, Marketing and Sales Department, 16 Donghuangchenggen North St., Beijing 100707, People's Republic of China. TEL 4010642. FAX 4012180. *4961*

JIOSINSETIKKUSU SHINPOJUMU HAPPYO RONBUNSHU.
Kokusai Jiosinsetikkusu Gakkai, Nihon Shibu, Doshitsu Kogakkai, 2-23, Kanda Awaji-cho, Chiyoda-ku, Tokyo 101, Japan. TEL 81-3-3251-7661. FAX 81-3-3251-6688. *2245*

JISHU KAIFA YU YINJIN.
Fujiansheng Keji Xinxi Yanjiusuo 11 Hudong Lu, Fuzhou, Fujian 350003, People's Republic of China. TEL 86-591-7850828. FAX 86-591-7856468. *6655*

JISUAN JIEGOU LIXUE JIQI YINGYONG.
Dalian Ligong Daxue, P.O. Box 320, Dalian, Liaoning 116023, People's Republic of China. TEL 86-411-4708405. FAX 86-411-4671039. *2759*

JISUAN SHUXUE.
Science Press, Marketing and Sales Department, 16 Donghuangchenggen North St., Beijing 100717, People's Republic of China. TEL 4010642. FAX 4019810. *4371*

JISUANJI XUEBAO.
Science Press, Marketing and Sales Department, 16 Donghuangchenggen North St., Beijing 100717, People's Republic of China. TEL 4010642. FAX 4019810. *2118*

JISUANJI YANJIU YU FAZHAN.
Science Press, Marketing and Sales Department, 16 Donghuangchenggen North St., Beijing 100717, People's Republic of China. TEL 4010642. FAX 4019810. *2021*

JISUANJI YU YINGYONG HUAXUE.
Science Press, Marketing and Sales Department, 16 Donghuangchenggen North St., Beijing 100717, People's Republic of China. TEL 4010642. FAX 4019810. *1724*

JOB PRATIQUE MAGAZINE.
23 rue des Appenins, 75017 Paris, France. TEL 42-28-59-00. FAX 42-28-24-58. *5269*

JOGGING - LE GRANDE CORSA.
Publimaster s.r.l., Via Winckelmann 2, 20146 Milan, Italy. TEL 39-2-424191 FAX 39-2-47710278. *6466*

JOHN DONNE JOURNAL: STUDIES IN THE AGE OF DONNE.
North Carolina State University, Department of English, Box 8105, Raleigh, NC 27695-8105. TEL 919-515-4148. FAX 919-515-1836. *4223*

JOHN RYLANDS UNIVERSITY LIBRARY OF MANCHESTER. BULLETIN.
John Rylands University Library, Manchester M13 9PP, England. FAX 44-161-273-7488. *3616*

JOHNS HOPKINS A P L TECHNICAL DIGEST.
Johns Hopkins University, Applied Physics Laboratory, Johns Hopkins Rd. Laurel, MD 20723. TEL 301-953-5625. FAX 301-953-1093. *5552*

JOHO SHORI.
Information Processing Society of Japan, 7th Fl., Shibaura-Maekawa Bldg., 3-16-20, Shibaura, Minato-ku, Tokyo 108, Japan. TEL 81-3-5484-3535. FAX 81-3-5484-3534. *2075*

JOINT CENTER FOR URBAN STUDIES. PUBLICATIONS.
Harvard University Press, 79 Garden St., Cambridge, MA 02138 TEL 617-495-2600. FAX 617-495-5898. *2586*

JONG HOLLAND.
Stichting Jong Holland Postbus 6642, 3002 AP Rotterdam, Netherlands. TEL 31-10-4254122. FAX 31-10-4254122. *436*

JORDEMODERN.
Svenska Barnmorskefoerbundet, Ostermalmsg. 19, 114 26 Stockholm, Sweden. TEL 46-8-10-70-88. FAX 46-8-24-49-46. *4739*

JOSHI EIYO DAIGAKU KIYO.
Joshi Eiyo Daigaku, 24-3, Komagome 3-chome, Toshima-ku, Tokyo 170, Japan. *5235*

JOURNAL ASIATIQUE.
Editions Peeters s.p.r.l., Bondgenotenlaan 153, 3000 Leuven, Belgium. TEL 32-16-235170. FAX 32-16-228500. *5287*

JOURNAL DE CHIMIE PHYSIQUE ET DE PHYSICO-CHIMIE BIOLOGIQUE.
Editions Scientifiques et Medicales Elsevier, 141 rue de Javel, 75747 Paris, France. TEL 33-1-45589022. FAX 33-1-45589421. *1752*

JOURNAL DE PEDIATRIE ET DE PUERICULTURE.
Editions Scientifiques et Medicales Elsevier, 141 rue de Javel, 75747 Paris, France. TEL 33-1-45589026. FAX 33-1-45589421. *4478*

JOURNAL DES TRIBUNAUX.
Larcier, Rue des Minimes 39, 1000 Brussels, Belgium. TEL 32-2-5480711. FAX 32-2-5139009. *3795*

JOURNAL FOR CONTEMPORARY HISTORY.
University of the Orange Free State, Institute for Contemporary History, P.O. Box 2320, Bloemfontein 9300, South Africa. TEL 27-51-4012250. FAX 27-51-4473416. *5758*

JOURNAL FOR EAST EUROPEAN MANAGEMENT STUDIES.
Rainer Hampp Verlag, Meringerzellerstr. 16, 86415 Mering, Germany. TEL 49-8233-4783. FAX 49-8233-30755. *1426*

JOURNAL FOR GENERAL PHILOSOPHY OF SCIENCE.
Kluwer Academic Publishers, Postbus 17, 3300 AA Dordrecht, Netherlands. TEL 31-78-6392392. FAX 31-78-6392254. *6251*

JOURNAL FOR RESEARCH IN MATHEMATICS EDUCATION.
National Council of Teachers of Mathematics, 1906 Association Dr., Reston, VA 22091. TEL 703-620-9840. FAX 703-476-2970. *4371*

JOURNAL FOR STUDIES IN ECONOMICS AND ECONOMETRICS.
University of Stellenbosch, Bureau for Economic Research, Private Bag 5050, University, Stellenbosch 7599, South Africa. TEL 27-21-8872810. FAX 27-21-8899225. *1256*

JOURNAL FOR THE EDUCATION OF THE GIFTED.
Prufrock Press, Box 8813, Waco, TX 76714. FAX 800-340-0333. *2470*

JOURNAL FOR THE HISTORY OF ASTRONOMY.
Science History Publications Ltd., 16 Rutherford Rd., Cambridge CB2 2HH, England. TEL 44-1223-565532. FAX 44-1223-565532. *482*

JOURNAL FOR THE PROFESSIONAL COUNSELOR.
New York Counseling Association, Box 12636, Albany, NY 12212-2636. TEL 518-235-2026. *2345*

JOURNAL FOR THE SCIENTIFIC STUDY OF RELIGION.
Society for the Scientific Study of Religion, c/o Ralph Hood, Department of Psychology, University of Tennessee, Chattanooga, TN 37403. TEL 423-755-4262. *6070*

JOURNAL FOR THE STUDY OF JUDAISM. SUPPLEMENT.
E.J. Brill, P.O. Box 9000, 2300 PA Leiden, Netherlands. TEL 31-71-5353500. FAX 31-71-5317532. *6126*

JOURNAL FOR THE STUDY OF JUDAISM IN THE PERSIAN, HELLENISTIC AND ROMAN PERIOD.
E.J. Brill, P.O. Box 9000, 2300 PA Leiden, Netherlands. TEL 31-71-5353500. FAX 31-71-5317532. *6126*

JOURNAL FOR THE STUDY OF RELIGION.
Association for the Study of Religion in Southern Africa, c/o Dept. of Religious Studies, University of Natal, Pietermaritzburg 3201, South Africa. TEL 27-331-2605571. *6070*

JOURNAL FOR THE THEORY OF SOCIAL BEHAVIOUR.
Blackwell Publishers Ltd., 108 Cowley Rd, Oxford OX4 1JF, England. TEL 44-1865-791100. FAX 44-1865-791347. *5851*

JOURNAL FOR VOCATIONAL SPECIAL NEEDS EDUCATION.
National Association of Vocational Education Special Needs Personnel, 624 Aderhold Hall, University of Georgia, Athens, GA 30602-7162. TEL 706-542-4461. FAX 706-542-4054. *2470*

JOURNAL FOR WEAVERS, SPINNERS & DYERS.
Association of Guilds of Weavers, Spinners & Dyers, 33 Fennel Gardens, Lymington SO41 9FS, England. TEL 44-1590-670625. *6680*

JOURNAL FUER ANAESTHESIE UND INTENSIVBEHANDLUNG.
Pabst Science Publishers, Am Eichengrund 28, 49525 Lengerich, Germany. TEL 49-5484-308. FAX 49-5484-550. *4591*

JOURNAL FUER BETRIEBSWIRTSCHAFT.
Linde Verlag Wien GmbH, Scheydgasse 24, A-1210 Vienna, Austria. TEL 43-1-313364692. FAX 43-1-31336712. *1426*

JOURNAL FUER DAS NEPHROLOGISCHE TEAM.
Pabst Science Publishers, Am Eichengrund 28, 49525 Lengerich, Germany. TEL 49-5484-308. FAX 49-5484-550. *4928*

JOURNAL INTERNATIONAL MEDICAL SCIENCES ACADEMY.
International Medical Sciences Academy, National Medical Library Bldg., Ansari Nagar, Ring Rd., New Delhi 110 029, India. TEL 6964660. *4478*

JOURNAL OF ABDOMINAL SURGERY.
American Society of Abdominal Surgeons, 675 Main St., Melrose, MA 02176. TEL 617-665-6102. *4911*

JOURNAL OF ABNORMAL CHILD PSYCHOLOGY.
Plenum Publishing Corp., 233 Spring St., New York, NY 10013-1578. TEL 212-620-8000. FAX 212-463-0742. *5851*

JOURNAL OF ABNORMAL PSYCHOLOGY.
American Psychological Association, 750 First St., N.E., Washington, DC 20002-4242. TEL 202-336-5600. FAX 202-336-5568. *5852*

THE JOURNAL OF ACADEMIC LIBRARIANSHIP.
J A I Press Inc., 55 Old Post Rd. No. 2, Box 1678, Greenwich, CT 06836-1678. TEL 203-661-7602. FAX 203-661-0792. *4002*

JOURNAL OF ACCIDENT AND EMERGENCY MEDICINE.
B M J Publishing Group, B.M.A. House, Tavistock Sq., London WC1H 9JR, England. TEL 44-171-383-6270. FAX 44-171-383-6402. *4911*

JOURNAL OF ACCOUNTING AND ECONOMICS.
North-Holland P.O. Box 211, 1000 AE Amsterdam, Netherlands. TEL 31-20-4853911. FAX 31-20-4853598. *1049*

JOURNAL OF ACCOUNTING AND PUBLIC POLICY.
Elsevier Science Inc., Box 945, New York, NY 10159-0945. TEL 212-633-3730. FAX 212-633-3680. *1049*

JOURNAL OF ACCOUNTING EDUCATION.
Elsevier Science Ltd., Pergamon, P.O. Box 800, Kidlington, Oxford OX5 1DX, England. TEL 44-1865-843000. FAX 44-1865-843010. *1049*

JOURNAL OF ACCOUNTING LITERATURE.
University of Florida, Accounting Research Center, Fisher School of Accounting-267 BUS, College of Business Administration, Gainsville, FL 32611. TEL 904-392-0155. *1049*

JOURNAL OF ACQUIRED IMMUNE DEFICIENCY SYNDROMES AND HUMAN RETROVIROLOGY.
Lippincott - Raven Publishers 227 E. Washington Sq., Philadelphia, PA 19106. TEL 215-238-4200. *4623*

JOURNAL OF ACTUARIAL PRACTICE.
Absalom Press, Inc., Box 22098, Lincoln, NE 68542-2098. TEL 402-421-8149. FAX 402-421-8149. *3655*

JOURNAL OF ADDICTIVE DISEASES.
Haworth Press, Inc., 10 Alice St., Binghamton, NY 13904. TEL 607-722-5857. FAX 607-722-1424. *2198*

JOURNAL OF ADHESION.
Gordon and Breach Science Publishers, c/o International Publishers Distributor, P.O. Box 3054, Langhorne, PA 19047-3054. TEL 215-750-2642. FAX 215-750-6343. *5553*

JOURNAL OF ADHESION SCIENCE AND TECHNOLOGY.
V S P, P.O. Box 346, 3700 AH Zeist, Netherlands. TEL 31-30-6925790. FAX 31-30-6932081. *5621*

JOURNAL OF ADOLESCENT AND ADULT LITERACY.
International Reading Association, Inc., 800 Barksdale Rd., Box 8139, Newark, DE 19714-8139. TEL 302-731-1600. FAX 302-731-1057. *2345*

JOURNAL OF ADOLESCENT HEALTH.
Elsevier Science Inc., Box 945, New York, NY 10159-0945. TEL 212-633-3730. FAX 212-633-3680. *4478*

JOURNAL OF ADOLESCENT RESEARCH.
Sage Publications, Inc., 2455 Teller Rd., Thousand Oaks, CA 91320. TEL 805-499-0721. FAX 805-499-0871. *1770*

JOURNAL OF ADULT DEVELOPMENT.
Plenum Publishing Corp., 233 Spring St., New York, NY 10013-1578. TEL 212-620-8468. FAX 212-463-0742. *5852*

JOURNAL OF ADVANCED MATERIALS.
Intercontact Science, Leninskii Prospekt 49, 117911 Moscow, Russia. TEL 095-135-62-97. FAX 095-135-86-80. *2734*

JOURNAL OF ADVANCED NURSING.
Blackwell Science Ltd., Osney Mead, Oxford OX2 OEL, England. TEL 44-1865-206206. FAX 44-1865-721205. *4716*

JOURNAL OF ADVANCEMENT IN MEDICINE.
Human Sciences Press, Inc. 233 Spring St., New York, NY 10013-1578. TEL 212-620-8000. FAX 212-807-1047. *4478*

JOURNAL OF AEROSOL SCIENCE.
Elsevier Science Ltd., Pergamon, P.O. Box 800, Kidlington, Oxford OX5 1DX, England. TEL 44-1865-843000. FAX 44-1865-843010. *5300*

JOURNAL OF AEROSPACE ENGINEERING.
American Society of Civil Engineers, 345 E. 47th St., New York, NY 10017-2398. TEL 212-705-7288. FAX 212-980-4681. *2664*

JOURNAL OF AESTHETIC EDUCATION.
University of Illinois Press, 1325 S. Oak St., Champaign, IL 61820. TEL 217-333-0950. FAX 217-244-8082. *2345*

JOURNAL OF AFFECTIVE DISORDERS.
Elsevier Science B.V., P.O. Box 211, 1000 AE Amsterdam, Netherlands. TEL 31-20-4853911. FAX 31-20-4853598. *4843*

JOURNAL OF AFRICAN AMERICAN MEN.
Transaction Publishers, Transaction Periodicals Consortium, Department 3092, Rutgers University, New Brunswick, NJ 08903. TEL 908-445-2280. FAX 908-445-3138. *4947*

JOURNAL OF AFRICAN EARTH SCIENCES (AND THE MIDDLE EAST).
Elsevier Science Ltd., Pergamon, P.O. Box 800, Kidlington, Oxford OX5 1DX, England. TEL 44-1865-843000. FAX 44-1865-843010. *2245*

JOURNAL OF AFRICAN STUDIES.
Japan Association of Africanists, c/o Dogura & Co. Ltd., 1-8 Nishihanaikecho, Koyama, Kita-ku, Kyoto 603, Japan. TEL 075-451-4844. FAX 075-441-0436. *3373*

JOURNAL OF AFRO-LATIN AMERICAN STUDIES AND LITERATURES.
c/o Dept. of Modern Languages & Literatures, Howard University, 2400 Sixth St., N.W. - Locke Hall, Washington, DC 20059. TEL 202-806-6758. *3616*

JOURNAL OF AGING AND ETHNICITY.
Springer Publishing Company, 536 Broadway, New York, NY 10012-3955. TEL 212-431-4370. FAX 212-941-7842. *3289*

JOURNAL OF AGING AND HEALTH.
Sage Publications, Inc., 2455 Teller Rd., Thousand Oaks, CA 91320. TEL 805-499-0721. FAX 805-499-0871. *3289*

JOURNAL OF AGING & IDENTITY.
Human Sciences Press, Inc. 233 Spring St., New York, NY 10013-1578. TEL 212-620-8000. FAX 212-463-0742. *3289*

JOURNAL OF AGING & SOCIAL POLICY.
Haworth Press, Inc., 10 Alice St., Binghamton, NY 13904. TEL 607-722-5857. FAX 607-722-1424. *3290*

JOURNAL OF AGRICULTURAL AND ENVIRONMENTAL ETHICS.
Kluwer Academic Publishers. Postbus 17, 3300 AA Dordrecht, Netherlands. TEL 31-78-6392392. FAX 31-78-6392254. *5481*

JOURNAL OF AGRICULTURAL AND FOOD CHEMISTRY.
American Chemical Society, 1155 16th St., N.W., Washington, DC 20036. TEL 800-333-9511. FAX 614-447-3671. *228*

JOURNAL OF AGRICULTURAL & FOOD INFORMATION.
Haworth Press, Inc., 10 Alice St., Binghamton, NY 13904-1580. TEL 607-722-5857. FAX 607-722-1424. *128*

JOURNAL OF AGRICULTURAL & RESOURCE ECONOMICS.
Western Agricultual Economics Association, Utah State Univ., Economics Dept., Logan, UT 84322-3530. TEL 801-797-2294. FAX 801-797-2701. *194*

JOURNAL OF AGROMEDICINE.
Haworth Press, Inc., 10 Alice St., Binghamton, NY 13904. TEL 607-722-5857. FAX 607-722-1424. *5252*

JOURNAL OF AIR TRANSPORT MANAGEMENT.
Butterworth - Heinemann, Part of the Reed Elsevier group, Linacre House, Jordan Hill, Oxford OX2 8DP, England. TEL 44-1865-310366. FAX 44-1865-310398. *1426*

JOURNAL OF AIRCRAFT.
American Institute of Aeronautics and Astronautics, Inc., 370 L'Enfant Promenade, S.W., Washington, DC 20024. TEL 202-646-7400. *71*

JOURNAL OF ALCOHOL AND DRUG EDUCATION.
American Alcohol and Drug Information Foundation (Lansing), c/o M I C A P, Box 10212, Lansing, MI 48901. TEL 517-484-2636. FAX 517-484-0444. *2198*

JOURNAL OF ALGEBRA.
Academic Press, Inc., Journal Division, 525 B St., Ste. 1900, San Diego, CA 92101-4495. TEL 619-230-1840. FAX 619-699-5800. *4371*

JOURNAL OF ALGEBRAIC COMBINATORICS.
Kluwer Academic Publishers Boston, Box 358, Accord Sta., Hingham, MA 02018-0358. TEL 617-871-6600. FAX 617-871-6528. *4371*

JOURNAL OF ALGERIAN STUDIES.
Frank Cass, Newbury House, 890-900 Eastern Ave., Newbury Park, Ilford, Essex IG2 7HH, England. TEL 44-181-5998866. FAX 44-181-5990984. *3496*

JOURNAL OF ALGORITHMS.
Academic Press, Inc., Journal Division, 525 B St., Ste. 1900, San Diego, CA 92101-4495. TEL 619-230-1840. FAX 619-699-5800. *4410*

THE JOURNAL OF ALLERGY AND CLINICAL IMMUNOLOGY
Mosby - Year Book, Inc. 11830 Westline Industrial Dr., St. Louis, MO 63146-3318. TEL 314-872-8370. FAX 314-872-9164. *4584*

JOURNAL OF ALLIED HEALTH.
University of Illinois at Chicago, College of Associated Health Professions (M-C 518), 808 S. Wood St., Chicago, IL 60612. TEL 312-413-9180. FAX 312-413-0086 *5966*

JOURNAL OF ALLOYS AND COMPOUNDS.
Elsevier Science S.A., P.O. Box 564, CH-1001 Lausanne 1, Switzerland. TEL 41-21-3207381. FAX 41-21-3235444. *4961*

JOURNAL OF AMBULATORY CARE MARKETING.
Haworth Press Inc., 10 Alice St., Binghamton, NY 13904. TEL 607-722-5857. FAX 607-722-1424. *4785*

JOURNAL OF AMBULATORY MONITORING.
Taylor & Francis Ltd., 1 Gunpowder Sq., London EC4A 3DE, England. TEL 44-171-583-0490. FAX 44-171-583-0585. *4605*

JOURNAL OF AMERICAN COLLEGE HEALTH.
Heldref Publications 1319 Eighteenth St., N.W., Washington, DC 20036-1802. TEL 202-296-6267. FAX 202-296-5149. *5531*

JOURNAL OF AMERICAN CULTURE.
Popular Press, Bowling Green State University, Bowling Green, OH 43403. TEL 419-372-2981. *3616*

JOURNAL OF AMERICAN DRAMA AND THEATRE.
C A S T A, City University of New York, Graduate School, 33 W. 42nd St., New York, NY 10036. TEL 212-642-2445. FAX 212-642-2221. *6697*

JOURNAL OF AMERICAN INDIAN EDUCATION.
Arizona State University, Center for Indian Education, College of Education, Box 871311, Tempe, AZ 85287-1311. TEL 602-965-6292. FAX 602-965-8115. *2889*

JOURNAL OF ANALYTIC SOCIAL WORK.
Haworth Press, Inc. 10 Alice St., Binghamton, NY 13904. TEL 607-722-5857. FAX 607-722-1424. *6378*

JOURNAL OF ANALYTICAL AND APPLIED PYROLYSIS.
Elsevier Science B.V., P.O. Box 211, 1000 AE Amsterdam, Netherlands. TEL 31-20-4853911. FAX 31-20-4853598. *1680*

JOURNAL OF ANALYTICAL ATOMIC SPECTROMETRY.
The Royal Society of Chemistry, Thomas Graham House, Science Park, Milton Rd., Cambridge CB4 4WF, England. TEL 44-1223-420066. FAX 44-1223-423429. *1716*

JOURNAL OF ANALYTICAL CHEMISTRY.
Maik Nauka - Interperiodica, Mezhdunarodnyi Otdel, Ul. Profsoyuznaya, 90, 117864 Moscow, Russia. TEL 7-095-33600664. FAX 7-095-3360666. *1716*

JOURNAL OF ANALYTICAL TOXICOLOGY.
Preston Publications, Inc., 7800 Merrimac Ave., Box 48312, Niles, IL 60714. TEL 847-965-0566. FAX 847-965-7639. *2846*

JOURNAL OF ANDROLOGY.
American Society of Andrology, c/o Dept. of Urology Research, Guggenheim 1711, Mayo Clinic, 200 First St., S.W., Rochester, MN 55905. TEL 507-284-2423. FAX 507-284-2384. *4478*

JOURNAL OF ANIMAL AND FEED SCIENCES.
Polska Akademia Nauk, Instytut Fizjologii i Zywienia Zwierzat im. Jana Kielanowskiego, 00-110 Jablonna, Poland, Poland. TEL 48-22-7824175. FAX 48-22-7742038. *275*

JOURNAL OF ANIMAL ECOLOGY.
Blackwell Science Ltd., Osney Mead, Oxford OX2 0EL, England. TEL 44-1865-206206. FAX 44-1865-721205. *589*

JOURNAL OF ANIMAL SCIENCE.
American Society of Animal Science, 1111 N. Dunlap Ave., Savoy, IL 61874. TEL 217-356-3182. FAX 217-393-4119. *275*

JOURNAL OF ANIMAL SCIENCE. SUPPLEMENT. BIENNIAL SYMPOSIUM ON ANIMAL REPRODUCTION.
American Society of Animal Science, 1111 N. Dunlap Ave., Savoy, IL 61874. TEL 217-356-3192. FAX 217-398-4119. *275*

JOURNAL OF ANTHROPOLOGICAL ARCHAEOLOGY.
Academic Press, Inc., Journal Division, 525 B St., Ste. 1900, San Diego, CA 92101-4495. TEL 619-230-1840. FAX 619-699-6859. *313*

JOURNAL OF ANTHROPOLOGICAL RESEARCH.
University of New Mexico Department of Anthropology, Albuquerque, NM 87131. TEL 505-277-4544. FAX 505-277-0874. *313*

JOURNAL OF ANXIETY DISORDERS.
Elsevier Science Ltd., Pergamon, P.O. Box 800, Kidlington, Oxford OX5 1DX, England. TEL 44-1365-843000. FAX 44-1865-843010. *5852*

JOURNAL OF APICULTURAL RESEARCH.
International Bee Research Association, 18 North Rd., Cardiff CF1 3DY, Wales. TEL 44-1222-372409. FAX 44-1222-665522. *129*

JOURNAL OF APPALACHIAN STUDIES.
West Virginia University, Regional Research Institute, Box 6825, Morgantown, WV 26506. TEL 304-293-8541. FAX 304-293-6699. *6418*

JOURNAL OF APPLIED ANIMAL RESEARCH.
Garuda Scientific Publicators, 151 Janakpuri, P.O. Box 6, Izatnagar 243 122, India. TEL 91-581-479723. FAX 91-581-450147. *810*

JOURNAL OF APPLIED ANIMAL WELFARE SCIENCE.
American Society for the Prevention of Cruelty to Animals, 424 E. 92nd St., New York, NY 10128. *296*

JOURNAL OF APPLIED AQUACULTURE.
Haworth Press, Inc., Food Products Press, 10 Alice St., Binghamton, NY 13904. TEL 607-722-5857. FAX 607-722-6362. *2337*

JOURNAL OF APPLIED BEHAVIOR ANALYSIS.
Society for the Experimental Analysis of Behavior, Inc. (Lawrence), c/o Department of Human Development, University of Kansas, Lawrence, KS 66045. TEL 913-843-0008. *5852*

JOURNAL OF APPLIED BEHAVIORAL RESEARCH.
Bellwether Publishing, Ltd., 8640 Guilford Rd., Ste. 200, Columbia, MD 21046. TEL 410-290-3870. FAX 410-290-8726. *5552*

JOURNAL OF APPLIED BIOMECHANICS.
Human Kinetics Publishers, Inc., Box 5076, Champaign, IL 61825-5076. TEL 217-351-5076. FAX 217-351-2674. *4598*

JOURNAL OF APPLIED BUSINESS RESEARCH.
Western Academic Press, Box 620760, Littleton, CO 80162. TEL 303-904-4750. FAX 303-978-0413. *935*

JOURNAL OF APPLIED COMMUNICATION RESEARCH.
Speech Communication Association, 5105 Backlick Rd., Bldg. E, Annandale, VA 22003. TEL 703-750-0533. FAX 703-914-9471. *1908*

JOURNAL OF APPLIED CRYSTALLOGRAPHY.
Munksgaard International Publishers Ltd., 35 Noerre Soegade, P.O. Box 2143, DK-1016 Copenhagen K, Denmark. TEL 45-33-127030 FAX 45-33-129387. *1726*

JOURNAL OF APPLIED DEVELOPMENTAL PSYCHOLOGY.
Ablex Publishing Corporation, 355 Chestnut St., Norwood, NJ 07648. TEL 201 767-8455. FAX 201-767-6717. *5352*

JOURNAL OF APPLIED ECOLOGY.
Blackwell Science Ltd., Osney Mead, Oxford OX2 0EL, England. TEL 44-1865-206206. FAX 44-1865-721205. *589*

JOURNAL OF APPLIED ELECTROCHEMISTRY.
Chapman & Hall, Journals Department 2-6 Boundary Row, London SE1 8HN, England. TEL 44-171-8650066. FAX 44-171-5229623. *1729*

JOURNAL OF APPLIED FIRE SCIENCE.
Baywood Publishing Co., Inc., 26 Austin Ave., Box 337, Amityville, NY 11701. TEL 516-691-1270. FAX 516-691-1770. *2921*

JOURNAL OF APPLIED GEOPHYSICS.
Elsevier Science B.V., P.O. Box 211, 1000 AE Amsterdam, Netherlands. TEL 31-20-4853911. FAX 31-20-4853598. *2277*

JOURNAL OF APPLIED GERONTOLOGY.
Sage Publications, Inc., 2455 Teller Rd., Thousand Oaks, CA 91320. TEL 805-499-0721. FAX 805-499-0871. *3290*

JOURNAL OF APPLIED MANAGEMENT STUDIES.
Carfax Publishing Co., P.O. Box 25, Abingdon, Oxon. OX14 3UE, England. TEL 44-1235-401000. FAX 44-1235-401550. *1426*

JOURNAL OF APPLIED MATHEMATICS AND MECHANICS.
Elsevier Science Ltd., Pergamon, P.O. Box 800, Kidlington, Oxford OX5 1GB, England. TEL 44-1865-843000. FAX 44-1865-843010. *2734*

JOURNAL OF APPLIED MECHANICS AND TECHNICAL PHYSICS.
Plenum Publishing Corp., Consultants Bureau, 233 Spring St., New York, NY 10013-1578. TEL 212-620-8468. FAX 212-463-0742. *2734*

JOURNAL OF APPLIED METEOROLOGY.
American Meteorological Society, 45 Beacon St., Boston, MA 02108-3693. TEL 617-227-2425. FAX 617-742-8718. *5000*

JOURNAL OF APPLIED MICROBIOLOGY.
Blackwell Science Ltd., Osney Mead, Oxford OX2 0EL, England. TEL 44-1865-206206. FAX 44-1865-721205. *760*

JOURNAL OF APPLIED NUTRITION.
International Academy of Nutrition and Preventive Medicine, Box 18433, Asheville, NC 28814-0433. TEL 704-258-3243. *5235*

JOURNAL OF APPLIED PHYCOLOGY.
Kluwer Academic Publishers, Postbus 17, 3300 AA Dordrecht, Netherlands. TEL 31-78-6392392. FAX 31-78-6392254. *760*

JOURNAL OF APPLIED PHYSIOLOGY.
American Physiological Society, 9650 Rockville Pike, Bethesda, MD 20814. TEL 301-530-7164. FAX 301-571-8313. *789*

JOURNAL OF APPLIED POLYMER SCIENCE. SYMPOSIA.
John Wiley & Sons, Inc., 605 Third Ave., New York, NY 10158. TEL 212-692-6000. FAX 212-850-6088. *2643*

JOURNAL OF APPLIED PROBABILITY.
Applied Probability Trust, School of Mathematics, University of Sheffield, Sheffield S3 7RH, England. TEL 44-114-282-4269. FAX 44-114-272-9782. *4372*

JOURNAL OF APPLIED PSYCHOLOGY.
American Psychological Association, 750 First St., N.E., Washington, DC 20002-4242. TEL 202-336-5600. FAX 202-336-5568. *5852*

JOURNAL OF APPLIED RECREATION RESEARCH.
Wilfrid Laurier University Press, 75 University Ave. W., Waterloo, ON N2L 3C5, Canada. TEL 519-884-1970. FAX 519-725-1399. *3964*

JOURNAL OF APPLIED SCIENCE IN SOUTHERN AFRICA.
University of Zimbabwe Publications, P.O. Box MP 203, Mt. Pleasant, Harare, Zimbabwe. TEL 263-4-303211. FAX 263-4-333407. *6251*

JOURNAL OF APPLIED SOCIAL PSYCHOLOGY.
V.H. Winston & Son, Inc., c/o Bellwether Publishing, Ltd., 8640 Guilford Rd., Ste. 200, Columbia, MD 21046. TEL 410-290-3870. FAX 410-290-8726. *5853*

JOURNAL OF APPLIED SPECTROSCOPY.
Plenum Publishing Corp., Consultants Bureau, 233 Spring St., New York, NY 10013-1578. TEL 212-620-8468. FAX 212-463-0742. *5604*

JOURNAL OF APPLIED SPORT PSYCHOLOGY.
Association for the Advancement of Applied Sport Psychology, c/o Joan L. Duda, Editor, Dept. of HKLS, Lambert 113, Purdue University, West Lafayette, IN 47907. TEL 317-494-5827. FAX 317-496-1239. *4898*

JOURNAL OF APPLIED STATISTICS.
Carfax Publishing Co., P.O. Box 25, Abingdon, Oxon. OX14 3UE, England. TEL 44-1235-401000. FAX 44-1235-401550. *6614*

JOURNAL OF APPROXIMATION THEORY.
Academic Press, Inc., Journal Division, 525 B St., Ste. 1900, San Diego, CA 92101-4495. TEL 619-230-1840. FAX 619-699-6800. *4372*

JOURNAL OF AQUACULTURE IN THE TROPICS.
Oxford & I.B.H. Publishing Co. Pvt. Ltd., 66 Janpath, New Delhi 110 001, India. FAX 91-11-3322639. *2937*

JOURNAL OF AQUARICULTURE AND AQUATIC SCIENCES.
The Written Word, 7601 E. Forest Lake Dr., N.W., Parkville, MO 64152. TEL 816-842-5936. FAX 816-474-5597. *589*

JOURNAL OF AQUATIC ANIMAL HEALTH.
American Fisheries Society, 5410 Grosvenor Ln., Ste. 110, Bethesda, MD 20814-2199. TEL 301-897-8616. FAX 301-897-8096. *2937*

JOURNAL OF AQUATIC ECOSYSTEM HEALTH.
Kluwer Academic Publishers, Postbus 17, 3300 AA Dordrecht, Netherlands. TEL 31-78-6392392. FAX 31-78-6392254. *2805*

JOURNAL OF AQUATIC FOOD PRODUCT TECHNOLOGY.
Haworth Press, Inc., Food Products Press, 10 Alice St., Binghamton, NY 13904-1580. TEL 800-342-9678. FAX 607-722-6362. *2979*

JOURNAL OF AQUATIC PLANT MANAGEMENT.
Aquatic Plant Management Society, Inc., Box 121086, Clermont, FL 34712-1086. TEL 202-547-5437. FAX 202-547-5645. *687*

JOURNAL OF ARABIC LITERATURE.
E.J. Brill, P.O. Box 9000, 2300 PA Leiden, Netherlands. TEL 31-71-5353500. FAX 31-71-5317532. *4223*

JOURNAL OF ARACHNOLOGY.
American Arachnological Society, c/o Norman I. Platnick, Secretary, American Museum of Natural History, Central Park W. at 79th St., New York, NY 10024. TEL 212-769-5612. FAX 212-769-5277. *730*

JOURNAL OF ARCHAEOLOGICAL METHOD AND THEORY.
Plenum Publishing Corp., 233 Spring St., New York, NY 10013-1578. TEL 212-620-8000. FAX 212-463-0742. *359*

JOURNAL OF ARCHAEOLOGICAL RESEARCH.
Plenum Publishing Corp., 233 Spring St., New York, NY 10013-1578. TEL 212-620-8000. FAX 212-463-0742. *359*

JOURNAL OF ARCHITECTURAL AND PLANNING RESEARCH.
Locke Science Publishing Company, Inc., 117 West Harrison Bldg., Ste. 640-L221, Chicago, IL 60605. *396*

JOURNAL OF ARCHITECTURAL CONSERVATION.
Donhead Publishing Ltd., 28 Southdean Gardens, Wimbledon, London SW19 6NU, England. TEL 44-181-789-0138. FAX 44-181-789-9114. *396*

JOURNAL OF ARCHITECTURAL EDUCATION.
M I T Press, 55 Hayward St., Cambridge, MA 02142. TEL 617-253-2889. FAX 617-577-1545. *396*

JOURNAL OF ART AND DESIGN EDUCATION.
Blackwell Publishers Ltd., 108 Cowley Rd., Oxford OX4 1DF, England. TEL 44-1865-791100. FAX 44-1865-791347. *2491*

JOURNAL OF ARTHROPLASTY.
Churchill Livingstone, 650 Ave. of the America, New York, NY 10011. TEL 212-206-5040. FAX 212-727-7808. *4785*

JOURNAL OF ARTIFICIAL INTELLIGENCE IN EDUCATION.
Association for the Advancement of Computing in Education, Box 2966, Charlottesville, VA 22902-2966. TEL 804-973-3987. *2406*

JOURNAL OF ARTS MANAGEMENT, LAW, AND SOCIETY.
Heldref Publications, 1319 Eighteenth St., N.W., Washington, DC 20036-1802. TEL 202-296-6267. FAX 202-296-5149. *3796*

JOURNAL OF ASIA - PACIFIC BUSINESS.
Haworth Press, Inc., 10 Alice St., Binghamton, NY 13904. TEL 607-722-5857. FAX 607-722-1424. *1287*

JOURNAL OF ASIAN AND AFRICAN STUDIES.
E.J. Brill, P.O. Box 9000, 2300 PA Leiden, Netherlands. TEL 31-71-5353500. FAX 31-71-5317532. *6419*

JOURNAL OF ASIAN BUSINESS.
Association for Asian Studies, 130 Lane Hall, Ann Arbor, MI 48109-1290. TEL 313-763-4508. FAX 313-747-2083. *1218*

JOURNAL OF ASIAN MARTIAL ARTS.
Via Media Publishing Co., 821 W. 24th St., Erie, PA 16502. TEL 814-455-9517. FAX 814-838-7811. *5287*

JOURNAL OF ASIAN PACIFIC COMMUNICATION.
Multilingual Matters Ltd., Frankfurt Lodge, Clevedon Hall, Victoria Rd., Clevedon, Avon BS21 7SJ, England. TEL 44-1275-876519. FAX 44-1275-343096. *1908*

JOURNAL OF ASSISTED REPRODUCTION AND GENETICS.
Plenum Publishing Corp., 233 Spring St., New York, NY 10013-1578. TEL 212-620-8000. FAX 212-463-0742. *4739*

JOURNAL OF ASTHMA (NEW YORK).
Marcel Dekker Journals, 270 Madison Ave., New York, NY 10016. FAX 212-685-4540. *4888*

JOURNAL OF ATHLETIC TRAINING.
National Athletic Trainers Association, Inc., 2952 N. Stemmons Fwy., Dallas, TX 75247-6117. TEL 800-879-6282. FAX 214-637-2206. *4898*

JOURNAL OF ATMOSPHERIC AND OCEANIC TECHNOLOGY.
American Meteorological Society, 45 Beacon St., Boston, MA 02108-3693. TEL 617-227-2425. FAX 617-742-8718. *5000*

JOURNAL OF ATMOSPHERIC AND SOLAR - TERRESTRIAL PHYSICS.
Elsevier Science Ltd., Pergamon, P.O. Box 800, Kidlington, Oxford OX5 1DX, England. TEL 44-1865-843000. FAX 44-1865-843010. *2277*

JOURNAL OF ATMOSPHERIC CHEMISTRY.
Kluwer Academic Publishers, Postbus 17, 3300 AA Dordrecht, Netherlands. TEL 31-78-6392392. FAX 31-78-6392254. *1680*

JOURNAL OF AUDIOLOGICAL MEDICINE.
Whurr Publishers Ltd., 19b Compton Terrace, London N1 2UN, England. TEL 44-171-359-5979. FAX 44-171-226-5290. *4797*

JOURNAL OF AUDIOVISUAL MEDIA IN MEDICINE.
Carfax Publishing Co., P.O. Box 25, Abingdon, Oxon OX14 3UE, England. TEL 44-1235-401000. FAX 44-1235-401550. *4479*

JOURNAL OF AUSTRALIAN POLITICAL ECONOMY.
Australian Political Economy Movement, P.O. Box 76, Wentworth Bldg., University of Sydney, N.S.W. 2006. TEL 61-2-6923063. FAX 61-2-5523105. *1219*

JOURNAL OF AUTISM AND DEVELOPMENTAL DISORDERS.
Plenum Publishing Corp., 233 Spring St., New York, NY 10013-1578. TEL 212-620-8000. FAX 212-463-0742. *4843*

JOURNAL OF AUTOMATED REASONING.
Kluwer Academic Publishers, Postbus 17, 3300 AA Dordrecht, Netherlands. TEL 31-78-6392392. FAX 31-78-6392254. *2008*

JOURNAL OF AUTOMATIC CHEMISTRY.
Taylor & Francis Ltd., 1 Gunpowder Sq., London EC4A 3DE, England. TEL 44-171-583-0490. FAX 44-171-583-0585. *6305*

JOURNAL OF AUTONOMIC PHARMACOLOGY.
Blackwell Science Ltd., Osney Mead, Oxford OX2 OEL, England. TEL 44-1865-206206. FAX 44-1865-721205. *5420*

JOURNAL OF AVIAN BIOLOGY.
Munksgaard International Publishers Ltd., 35 Noerre Soegade, P.O. Box 2148, DK-1016 Copenhagen K, Denmark. TEL 45-33-127030. FAX 45-33-129387. *777*

JOURNAL OF AVIAN MEDICINE AND SURGERY.
Association of Avian Veterinarians, Box 618372, Orlando, FL 32861-8372. TEL 407-521-6101. FAX 407-521-6401. *6948*

JOURNAL OF BACTERIOLOGY.
American Society for Microbiology, 1325 Massachusetts Ave., N.W., Washington, DC 20005. TEL 202-737-3600. *760*

JOURNAL OF BAHA'I STUDIES.
Association for Baha'i Studies, 34 Copernicus St., Ottawa, ON K1N 7K4, Canada. TEL 613-233-1903. FAX 613-233-3644. *6207*

JOURNAL OF BANKING AND FINANCE.
North-Holland P.O. Box 211, 1000 AE Amsterdam, Netherlands. TEL 31-20-4853911. FAX 31-20-4853598. *1104*

JOURNAL OF BASIC WRITING.
City University of New York, Office of Academic Affairs, Instructional Resource Center, 535 E. 80th St., New York, NY 10021. TEL 212-794-5445. FAX 212-794-5706. *2433*

JOURNAL OF BECKETT STUDIES.
Florida State University, Department of English, Tallahasse, FL 32306. TEL 904-664-6038. FAX 904-644-0811. *4223*

JOURNAL OF BEHAVIOR THERAPY AND EXPERIMENTAL PSYCHIATRY.
Elsevier Science Ltd., Pergamon, P.O. Box 800, Kidlington, Oxford OX5 1DX, England. TEL 44-1865-843000. FAX 44-1865-843010. *4843*

JOURNAL OF BEHAVIORAL EDUCATION.
Human Sciences Press, Inc. 233 Spring St., New York, NY 10013. TEL 212-620-8000. FAX 212-463-0742. *5853*

JOURNAL OF BEHAVIORAL MEDICINE.
Plenum Publishing Corp., 233 Spring St., New York, NY 10013-1578. TEL 212-620-8000. FAX 212-463-0742. *4843*

JOURNAL OF BEHAVIORAL OPTOMETRY.
Optometric Extension Program, 1921 Carnegie Ave., Ste. 3L, Santa Ana, CA 92705-5510. TEL 714-250-8070. FAX 714-250-8157. *4771*

JOURNAL OF BIBLICAL ETHICS IN MEDICINE.
Biblical Medical Ethics, Inc., Box 13231, Florence, SC 29504. TEL 803-665-6853. *4479*

JOURNAL OF BIG BEND STUDIES.
Sul Ross State University, Center for Big Bend Studies, Box C-71, Alpine, TX 79832. TEL 915-837-8179. *3474*

JOURNAL OF BIOACTIVE AND COMPATIBLE POLYMERS.
Technomic Publishing Co., Inc., 851 New Holland Ave., Box 3535, Lancaster, PA 17604. TEL 717-291-5609. FAX 717-295-4538. *641*

JOURNAL OF BIOCHEMICAL AND BIOPHYSICAL METHODS.
Elsevier Science B.V., P.O. Box 211, 1000 AE Amsterdam, Netherlands. TEL 31-20-4853911. FAX 31-20-4853598. *641*

JOURNAL OF BIOENERGETICS AND BIOMEMBRANES.
Plenum Publishing Corp., 233 Spring St., New York, NY 10013-1578. TEL 212-620-8000. FAX 212-463-0742. *654*

JOURNAL OF BIOGEOGRAPHY.
Blackwell Science Ltd., Osney Mead, Oxford OX2 OEL, England. TEL 44-1865-206206. FAX 44-1865-721205 *3263*

JOURNAL OF BIOLOGICAL CHEMISTRY.
American Society for Biochemistry and Molecular Biology, Inc., Box 630591, Baltimore, MD 21263. *641*

JOURNAL OF BIOLOGICAL EDUCATION.
Institute of Biology, 20-22 Queensberry Pl., London SW7 2DZ, England. TEL 44-171-581-8333. FAX 44-171-823-9409. *589*

JOURNAL OF BIOLOGICAL PHOTOGRAPHY.
Biological Photographic Association, Inc., 1819 Peachtree St., N.E., Ste. 620, Atlanta, GA 30309-1849. TEL 404-351-6300. FAX 404-351-3348. *589*

JOURNAL OF BIOLOGICAL PHYSICS.
Kluwer Academic Publishers, Postbus 17, 3300 AA Dordrecht, Netherlands. TEL 31-78-6392392. FAX 31-78-6392254. *654*

JOURNAL OF BIOLOGICAL RHYTHMS.
Sage Publications, Inc., Sage Science Press, 2455 Teller Rd., Thousand Oaks, CA 91320. TEL 805-499-0721. FAX 805-499-0871. *4843*

JOURNAL OF BIOMATERIALS APPLICATIONS.
Technomic Publishing Co., Inc., 851 New Holland Ave., Box 3535, Lancaster, PA 17604. TEL 717-291-5609. FAX 717-295-4538. *5621*

JOURNAL OF BIOMATERIALS SCIENCE. POLYMER EDITION.
V S P, P.O. Box 346, 3700 AH Zeist, Netherlands. TEL 31-30-6925790. FAX 31-30-6932081. *662*

JOURNAL OF BIOMECHANICAL ENGINEERING.
American Society of Mechanical Engineers, 22 Law Dr., Fairfield, NJ 07007-2300. *4479*

JOURNAL OF BIOMECHANICS.
Elsevier Science Ltd., Pergamon, P.O. Box 800, Kidlington, Oxford OX5 1DX, England. TEL 44-1865-843000. FAX 44-1865-843010. *4479*

JOURNAL OF BIOMEDICAL MATERIALS RESEARCH.
John Wiley & Sons, Inc., Journals, 605 Third Ave., New York, NY 10158. TEL 212-850-6645. FAX 212-850-6021. *662*

JOURNAL OF BIOMEDICAL SCIENCE.
S. Karger AG, Allschwilerstr. 10, P.O. Box, CH-4009 Basel, Switzerland. TEL 41-61-3061111. FAX 41-61-3061234. *4479*

JOURNAL OF BIOPHARMACEUTICAL STATISTICS.
Marcel Dekker Journals, 270 Madison Ave., New York, NY 10016. TEL 212-696-9000. FAX 212-685-4540. *5420*

JOURNAL OF BIOSOCIAL SCIENCE.
Cambridge University Press, Edinburgh Bldg., Shaftesbury Rd., Cambridge CB2 2RU, England. TEL 44-1223-312393. FAX 44-1223-315052. *745*

JOURNAL OF BIOTECHNOLOGY.
Elsevier Science B.V., P.O. Box 211, 1000 AE Amsterdam, Netherlands. TEL 31-20-4853911. FAX 31-20-4853598. *662*

JOURNAL OF BIOTECHNOLOGY IN HEALTHCARE.
Henry Stewart Publications, Russell House, 28-30 Little Russell St., London WC1A 2HN, England. TEL 44-171-404-3040. FAX 44-171-486-7083. *663*

JOURNAL OF BONE AND JOINT SURGERY: AMERICAN VOLUME.
Journal of Bone and Joint Surgery, Inc., 20 Pickering St., Needham, MA 02192-3157. TEL 617-449-9738. *4785*

JOURNAL OF BONE AND JOINT SURGERY: BRITISH VOLUME.
British Editorial Society of Bone and Joint Surgery, 22 Buckingham St., London WC2N 6ET, England. TEL 0171-782-0010. FAX 0171-782-0995. *4785*

JOURNAL OF BRITISH STUDIES.
University of Chicago Press, Journals Division, Box 37005, Chicago, IL 60637. TEL 773-753-3347. FAX 773-753-0811. *3421*

JOURNAL OF BRONCHOLOGY.
Lippincott - Raven Publishers 227 E. Washington Sq., Philadelphia, PA 19106. TEL 215-238-4200. *4888*

JOURNAL OF BRYOLOGY.
W.S. Maney & Son Ltd., Hudson Rd., Leeds LS9 7DL, England. TEL 01532-497481. FAX 01532-486983. *687*

JOURNAL OF BUDDHIST ETHICS.
University of London, Goldsmiths London SE14, England. TEL 44-171-919-7497 FAX 44-171-919-7398. *6110*

JOURNAL OF BURN CARE & REHABILITATION.
Mosby - Year Book, Inc. 11830 Westline Industrial Dr., St. Louis, MO 63146-3318. TEL 314-872-8370. FAX 314-432-1380. *4479*

THE JOURNAL OF BUSINESS (CHICAGO).
University of Chicago Press, Journals Division, Box 37005, Chicago, IL 60637. TEL 312-753-3347. FAX 312-753-0811. *935*

JOURNAL OF BUSINESS AND ECONOMIC PERSPECTIVES.
University of Tennessee at Martin, School of Business Administration, 113 Business Administration Bldg., Martin, TN 38238-5015. TEL 901-587-7226. FAX 901-537-7241. *935*

JOURNAL OF BUSINESS AND ECONOMIC STUDIES.
Fairfield University, School of Business, Fairfield, CT 06430. TEL 203-254-4070. FAX 203-254-4105. *935*

JOURNAL OF BUSINESS & FINANCE LIBRARIANSHIP.
Haworth Press, Inc., 10 Alice St., Binghamton, NY 13904. TEL 607-722-5857. FAX 607-722-1424. *4002*

JOURNAL OF BUSINESS & PSYCHOLOGY.
Human Sciences Press, Inc. 233 Spring St., New York, NY 10013-1578. TEL 212-620-8000. FAX 212-463-0742. *5853*

JOURNAL OF BUSINESS ETHICS.
Kluwer Academic Publishers, Postbus 17, 3300 AA Dordrecht, Netherlands. TEL 31-78-6392392. FAX 31-78-6392254. *935*

JOURNAL OF BUSINESS FINANCE & ACCOUNTING.
Blackwell Publishers Ltd., 108 Cowley Rd., Oxford OX4 1JF, England. TEL 44-1865-791100. FAX 44-1865-791347. *1049*

JOURNAL OF BUSINESS FORECASTING METHODS AND SYSTEMS.
Graceway Publishing Co., Box 670159, Flushing, NY 11367-0159. TEL 718-463-3914. FAX 718-544-9086. *935*

JOURNAL OF BUSINESS RESEARCH.
Elsevier Science Inc., Box 945, New York, NY 10159-0945. TEL 212-633-3730. FAX 212-633-3680. *1426*

JOURNAL OF BUSINESS-TO-BUSINESS MARKETING.
Haworth Press, Inc., 10 Alice St., Binghamton, NY 13904-1580. TEL 607-722-5857. FAX 607-722-1424. *1470*

JOURNAL OF BUSINESS VENTURING.
Elsevier Science Inc., Box 945, New York, NY 10159-0945. TEL 212-633-3730. FAX 212-633-3680. *935*

JOURNAL OF CALIFORNIA AND GREAT BASIN ANTHROPOLOGY.
California State University, Bakersfield, Department of Sociology - Anthropology, 9001 Stockdale Hwy., Bakersfield, CA 93311. TEL 805-664-3153. *313*

JOURNAL OF CALIFORNIA LAW ENFORCEMENT.
California Peace Officers Association, 1455 Response Rd., Ste. 190, Sacramento, CA 95815. TEL 916-923-1825. FAX 916-263-6090. *2166*

JOURNAL OF CANADIAN ART HISTORY.
Concordia University, 1455 boul. de Maisonneuve Ouest, S-VA 432, Montreal, PQ H3G 1M8, Canada. TEL 514-848-4699. FAX 514-848-8627. *436*

JOURNAL OF CANADIAN PETROLEUM TECHNOLOGY.
Canadian Institute of Mining, Metallurgy and Petroleum, Petroleum Society, 101 6 Ave., S.W., Ste. 320, Calgary, AB T2P 3P4, Canada. TEL 403-237-5112. FAX 403-262-4792. *5361*

JOURNAL OF CANADIAN POETRY.
Borealis Press Limited, 9 Ashburn Dr., Nepean, ON K2E 6N4, Canada. TEL 613-224-6837. FAX 613-829-7783. *4308*

JOURNAL OF CANCER EDUCATION.
Hanley & Belfus, Inc., 210 S. 13th St., Philadelphia, PA 19107. TEL 215-546-7293. FAX 215-790-9330. *4758*

JOURNAL OF CANCER RESEARCH AND CLINICAL ONCOLOGY.
Springer-Verlag, Heidelberger Platz 3, 14197 Berlin, Germany. TEL 49-30-8207-0. FAX 49-30-8214091. *4758*

JOURNAL OF CARBOHYDRATE CHEMISTRY.
Marcel Dekker Journals, 270 Madison Ave., New York, NY 10016. TEL 212-696-9000. FAX 212-685-4540. *1680*

JOURNAL OF CARDIAC FAILURE.
Churchill Livingstone, 650 Ave. of the Americas, New York, NY 10011. TEL 212-206-5040. FAX 212-727-7808. *4605*

JOURNAL OF CARDIAC SURGERY.
Futura Publishing Company, Inc., 135 Bedford Rd., Box 418, Armonk, NY 10504-0418. TEL 914-273-1014. FAX 914-273-1015. *4605*

JOURNAL OF CARDIOPULMONARY REHABILITATION.
Lippincott - Raven Publishers 227 E. Washington Sq., Philadelphia, PA 19106. TEL 215-238-4200. *4605*

JOURNAL OF CARDIOTHORACIC AND VASCULAR ANESTHESIA.
W.B. Saunders Co. The Curtis Center, 3rd Fl., Independence Sq. W., Philadelphia, PA 19106-3399. TEL 215-238-7800. FAX 215-238-6445. *4605*

JOURNAL OF CARDIOVASCULAR DIAGNOSIS AND PROCEDURES.
Mary Ann Liebert, Inc. Publishers, 2 Madison Ave., Larchmont, NY 10538. TEL 914-834-3100. FAX 914-834-3688. *4605*

JOURNAL OF CARDIOVASCULAR ELECTROPHYSIOLOGY.
Futura Publishing Company, Inc., 135 Bedford Rd., Box 418, Armonk, NY 10504-0418. TEL 914-273-1014. FAX 914-273-1015. *4605*

JOURNAL OF CARDIOVASCULAR PHARMACOLOGY.
Lippincott - Raven Publishers 227 E. Washington Sq., Philadelphia, PA 19106. TEL 215-238-4200. *5420*

JOURNAL OF CARDIOVASCULAR RISK.
Rapid Science Publishers, 2-6 Boundary Row, London SE1 8HN, England. TEL 44-171-865-0198. FAX 44-171-410-6600. *4606*

JOURNAL OF CARDIOVASCULAR SURGERY.
Edizioni Minerva Medica, Corso Bramante 83-85, 10126 Turin, Italy. TEL 011-678282. FAX 011-3121736. *4606*

JOURNAL OF CAREER ASSESSMENT.
Psychological Assessment Resources, Inc., 16204 N. Florida Ave., Lutz, FL 33549. TEL 813-968-3003. FAX 813-968-2598. *5853*

JOURNAL OF CAREER DEVELOPMENT.
Human Sciences Press, Inc. 233 Spring St., New York, NY 10013-1578. TEL 212-620-8000. FAX 212-463-0742. *5270*

JOURNAL OF CASE MANAGEMENT.
Springer Publishing Company, 536 Broadway, New York, NY 10012-3955. TEL 212-431-4370. FAX 212-941-7842. *4479*

JOURNAL OF CATALYSIS.
Academic Press, Inc., Journal Division, 525 B St., Ste. 1900, San Diego, CA 92101-4495. TEL 619-230-1840. FAX 619-699-6800. *1753*

JOURNAL OF CATARACT AND REFRACTIVE SURGERY.
American Society of Cataract and Refractive Surgery, 4000 Legato Rd., Ste. 850, Fairfax, VA 22033-4003. TEL 703-591-2220. FAX 703-591-0614. *4771*

JOURNAL OF CELL BIOLOGY.
Rockefeller University Press, 222 E. 70th St., New York, NY 10021. TEL 212-327-8572. FAX 212-327-7944. *715*

JOURNAL OF CELLULAR BIOCHEMISTRY.
John Wiley & Sons, Inc., Journals, 605 Third Ave., New York, NY 10158. TEL 212-850-6645. FAX 212-850-6021. *716*

JOURNAL OF CELLULAR BIOCHEMISTRY. SUPPLEMENT.
John Wiley & Sons, Inc., Journals, 605 Third Ave., New York, NY 10158. TEL 212-850-6645. FAX 212-850-6021. *716*

JOURNAL OF CELLULAR PATHOLOGY.
Oxford University Press, Oxford Journals, Walton St., Oxford OX2 6DP, England. TEL 44-1865-267907. FAX 44-1865-267485. *716*

JOURNAL OF CELLULAR PHYSIOLOGY.
John Wiley & Sons, Inc., Journals, 605 Third Ave., New York, NY 10158. TEL 212-850-6645. FAX 212-850-6021. *789*

JOURNAL OF CELLULAR PLASTICS.
Technomic Publishing Co., Inc., 851 New Holland Ave., Box 3535, Lancaster, PA 17604. TEL 717-291-5609. FAX 717-295-4538. *5621*

JOURNAL OF CEREBRAL BLOOD FLOW AND METABOLISM.
Lippincott - Raven Publishers 227 E. Washington Sq., Philadelphia, PA 19106. TEL 215-238-4200. *4844*

JOURNAL OF CHEMICAL CRYSTALLOGRAPHY.
Plenum Publishing Corp., 233 Spring St., New York, NY 10013-1578. TEL 212-620-8000. FAX 212-463-0742. *1726*

JOURNAL OF CHEMICAL DEPENDENCY TREATMENT.
Haworth Press, Inc., 10 Alice St., Binghamton, NY 13904. TEL 607-722-5857. FAX 607-722-1424. *2198*

JOURNAL OF CHEMICAL ECOLOGY.
Plenum Publishing Corp., 233 Spring St., New York, NY 10013-1578. TEL 212-620-8000. FAX 212-463-0742. *2805*

JOURNAL OF CHEMICAL EDUCATION.
American Chemical Society, c/o Dept. of Chemistry, Montana State University, Bozeman, MT 59717-0340. TEL 406-994-5393. FAX 406-994-5407. *1680*

JOURNAL OF CHEMICAL EDUCATION: SOFTWARE. SERIES B.
American Chemical Society, Division of Chemical Education, Inc., c/o Dept. of Chemistry, Univ. of Wisconsin at Madison, 1101 University Ave., Madison, WI 53706-1396. TEL 608-262-5753. FAX 608-265-8094. *2406*

JOURNAL OF CHEMICAL EDUCATION: SOFTWARE. SERIES C.
American Chemical Society, Division of Chemical Education, Inc., c/o Dept. of Chemistry, Univ. of Wisconsin at Madison, 1101 University Ave., Madison, WI 53706-1396. TEL 608-262-5163. FAX 608-265-8094. *2406*

JOURNAL OF CHEMICAL EDUCATION: SOFTWARE. SERIES D.
American Chemical Society, Division of Chemical Education, Inc., c/o Dept. of Chemistry, Univ. of Wisconsin at Madison, 1101 University Ave., Madison, WI 53706-1396. TEL 608-262-5153. FAX 608-265-8094. *2406*

JOURNAL OF CHEMICAL EDUCATION: SOFTWARE. SPECIAL ISSUE SERIES.
American Chemical Society, Division of Chemical Education, Inc., c/o Dept. of Chemistry, Univ. of Wisconsin at Madison, 1101 University Ave., Madison, WI 53706-1396. TEL 608-262-5153. FAX 608-265-8094. *2406*

JOURNAL OF CHEMICAL INFORMATION AND COMPUTER SCIENCES.
American Chemical Society, 1155 16th St. N.W., Washington, DC 20036. TEL 800-333-9511. FAX 614-447-3671. *1724*

JOURNAL OF CHEMICAL NEUROANATOMY.
Elsevier Science B.V., P.O. Box 211, 1000 AE Amsterdam, Netherlands. TEL 31-20-4853911. FAX 31-20-4853598. *4844*

JOURNAL OF CHEMICAL PHYSICS.
American Institute of Physics, One Physics Ellipse, College park, MD 20740-3843. TEL 301-209-3000. FAX 516-349-9704. *5553*

JOURNAL OF CHEMICAL RESEARCH.
The Royal Society of Chemistry, Thomas Graham House, Science Park, Milton Rd., Cambridge CB4 4WF, England. TEL 44-1223-420066. FAX 44-1223-423429. *1681*

JOURNAL OF CHEMICAL TECHNOLOGY AND BIOTECHNOLOGY.
John Wiley & Sons Ltd., Journals, Baffins Ln., Chichester, W. Sussex PO19 1UD, England. TEL 44-1243-779777. FAX 44-1243-843232. *663*

JOURNAL OF CHEMICAL VAPOR DEPOSITION.
Technomic Publishing Co., Inc., 851 New Holland Ave., Box 3535, Lancaster, PA 17604. TEL 717-291-5609. FAX 717-295-4538. *1726*

JOURNAL OF CHEMOMETRICS.
John Wiley & Sons Ltd., Journals, Baffins Ln., Chichester, W. Sussex PO19 1UD, England. TEL 44-1243-779777. FAX 44-1243-843232. *1717*

JOURNAL OF CHEMOTHERAPY.
E I F T srl, Via XX Settembre 102, 50129 Florence, Italy. TEL 39-55-486147. FAX 39-55-474426. *4758*

JOURNAL OF CHILD AND ADOLESCENT GROUP THERAPY.
Human Sciences Press, Inc. 233 Spring St., New York, NY 10013. TEL 212-620-8000. FAX 212-463-0742. *4844*

JOURNAL OF CHILD AND ADOLESCENT PSYCHIATRIC NURSING.
Nursecom, Inc., 1211 Locust St., Philadelphia, PA 19107. TEL 215-545-7222. FAX 215-545-1807. *4716*

JOURNAL OF CHILD & ADOLESCENT SUBSTANCE ABUSE.
Haworth Press, Inc., 10 Alice St., Binghamton, NY 13904. TEL 607-722-5857. FAX 607-722-1424. *2198*

JOURNAL OF CHILD AND FAMILY STUDIES.
Human Sciences Press, Inc. 233 Spring St., New York, NY 10013-1578. TEL 212-620-8000. FAX 212-463-0742. *5853*

JOURNAL OF CHILD NEUROLOGY.
Decker Periodicals, P.O. Box 620, LCD 1, Hamilton, ON L8N 3K7, Canada. TEL 905-522-7017. FAX 905-522-7839. *4844*

JOURNAL OF CHILD PSYCHOLOGY & PSYCHIATRY & ALLIED DISCIPLINES.
Cambridge University Press, Edinburgh Bldg., Shaftesbury Rd., Cambridge CB2 2RU, England. TEL 44-1223-312393. FAX 44-1223-315052. *5853*

JOURNAL OF CHILD SEXUAL ABUSE.
Haworth Press, Inc., 10 Alice St., Binghamton, NY 13904-1580. TEL 607-722-5857. FAX 607-722-1424. *6378*

JOURNAL OF CHINESE LINGUISTICS.
Project on Linguistic Analysis, 2222 Piedmont Ave., Berkeley, CA 94720. TEL 510-642-5939. *4078*

JOURNAL OF CHINESE LINGUISTICS MONOGRAPH SERIES.
Project on Linguistic Analysis, 2222 Piedmont Ave., Berkeley, CA 94720. TEL 510-642-5939. *4078*

JOURNAL OF CHINESE RELIGIONS.
Society for the Study of Chinese Religions, c/o Linda Penkwer, Treas., Department of Religious Studies, 2604 CL, University of Pittsburgh, Pittsburgh, PA 15260. TEL 412-624-2277. FAX 412-624-5994. *6207*

JOURNAL OF CHROMATOGRAPHY.
Elsevier Science B.V., P.O. Box 211, 1000 AE Amsterdam, Netherlands. TEL 31-20-4853911. FAX 31-20-4853598. *1717*

JOURNAL OF CHROMATOGRAPHY - BIOMEDICAL APPLICATIONS.
Elsevier Science B.V., P.O. Box 211, 1000 AE Amsterdam, Netherlands. TEL 31-20-4853911. FAX 31-20-4853598. *1681*

JOURNAL OF CHROMATOGRAPHY LIBRARY.
Elsevier Science B.V., Books Division, P.O. Box 211, 1000 AE Amsterdam, Netherlands. TEL 31-20-4853911. FAX 31-20-4853705. *1717*

JOURNAL OF CHRONIC FATIGUE SYNDROME.
Haworth Press, Inc., 10 Alice St., Binghamton, NY 13904. FAX 607-722-1424. *4479*

JOURNAL OF CLASSIFICATION.
Springer-Verlag, Science Journals, 175 Fifth Ave., New York, NY 10010. TEL 212-460-1500. FAX 212-473-6272. *4372*

JOURNAL OF CLEANER PRODUCTION.
Butterworth - Heinemann, Part of the Reed Elsevier group, Linacre House, Jordan Hill, Oxford OX2 8DP, England. TEL 44-1865-310366. FAX 44-1865-310898. *2748*

JOURNAL OF CLIMATE.
American Meteorological Society, 45 Beacon St., Boston, MA 02108-3693. TEL 617-227-2425. FAX 617-742-8718. *5000*

JOURNAL OF CLINICAL ANESTHESIA.
Elsevier Science Inc., Box 945, New York, NY 10159-0945. TEL 212-633-3730. FAX 212-633-3680. *4592*

JOURNAL OF CLINICAL APHERESIS.
John Wiley & Sons, Inc., Journals, 605 Third Ave., New York, NY 10158. TEL 212-850-6645. FAX 212-850-6021. *4928*

JOURNAL OF CLINICAL CHILD PSYCHOLOGY.
Lawrence Erlbaum Associates, Inc., 10 Industrial Dr., Mahwah, NJ 07430-2262. TEL 201-236-9500. FAX 201-236-0072. *5853*

JOURNAL OF CLINICAL ENDOCRINOLOGY AND METABOLISM.
Endocrine Society, 4350 East West Hwy., Ste. 500, Bethesda, MD 20814-4410. TEL 301-941-0200. FAX 301-941-0259. *4672*

JOURNAL OF CLINICAL ENGINEERING.
Lippincott - Raven Publishers 227 E. Washington Sq., Philadelphia, PA 19106-3780. TEL 215-238-4200. *627*

JOURNAL OF CLINICAL EPIDEMIOLOGY.
Elsevier Science Inc., Box 945, New York, NY 10159-0945. TEL 212-633-3730. FAX 212-633-3680. *4480*

JOURNAL OF CLINICAL ETHICS.
The Journal of Clinical Ethics, Inc., 107 E. Church St., Frederick, MD 21701. TEL 301-694-8561. *4480*

JOURNAL OF CLINICAL GASTROENTEROLOGY.
Lippincott - Raven Publishers 227 E. Washington Sq., Philadelphia, PA 19106. TEL 215-238-4200. *4694*

JOURNAL OF CLINICAL GEROPSYCHOLOGY.
Plenum Publishing Corp., 233 Spring St., New York, NY 10013-1578. TEL 212-620-8000. FAX 212-463-0742. *3290*

JOURNAL OF CLINICAL IMMUNOLOGY.
Plenum Publishing Corp., 233 Spring St., New York, NY 10013-1578. TEL 212-620-8000. FAX 212-463-0742. *4584*

JOURNAL OF CLINICAL INVESTIGATION.
Rockefeller University Press, 222 E. 70th St., New York, NY 10021. TEL 212-327-8572. FAX 212-327-7944. *4480*

JOURNAL OF CLINICAL LABORATORY ANALYSIS.
John Wiley & Sons, Inc., Journals, 605 Third Ave., New York, NY 10158. TEL 212-850-6645. FAX 212-850-6021. *4681*

JOURNAL OF CLINICAL LIGAND ASSAY.
Kellner-McCaffery Associates, Inc., 150 Fifth Ave., Ste. 840, New York, NY 10011. TEL 212-741-0280. *4584*

JOURNAL OF CLINICAL MICROBIOLOGY.
American Society for Microbiology, 1325 Massachusetts Ave., N.W., Washington, DC 20005. TEL 202-737-3600 *760*

JOURNAL OF CLINICAL MONITORING.
Kluwer Academic Publishers, Postbus 17, 3300 AA Dordrecht. TEL 31-78-6392392. FAX 31-78-6392254. *4280*

JOURNAL OF CLINICAL NEUROPHYSIOLOGY.
Lippincott - Raven Publishers 227 E. Washington Sq., Philadelphia, PA 19106. TEL 215-238-4200. *4844*

JOURNAL OF CLINICAL NURSING.
Blackwell Science Ltd., Osney Mead, Oxford OX3 0EL, England. TEL 44-1865-206206. FAX 44-1865-721205. *4717*

JOURNAL OF CLINICAL ONCOLOGY.
W.B. Saunders Co. Curtis Center, 3rd Fl., Independence Sq. W., Philadelphia, PA 19106-3399. TEL 215-238-7800. FAX 215-238-6445. *4758*

JOURNAL OF CLINICAL ORTHODONTICS.
J C O Inc., 1828 Pearl St., Boulder, CO 80302. FAX 303-443-9356. *4645*

JOURNAL OF CLINICAL OUTCOMES MANAGEMENT.
Turner White Communications, Inc., 125 Strafford Ave., Ste. 220, Wayne, PA 19087-3391. TEL 610-975-4541. FAX 610-975-4564. *4480*

JOURNAL OF CLINICAL PATHOLOGY.
B M J Publishing Group, B.M.A. House, Tavistock Sq., London WC1H 9JR, England. TEL 44-171-383-6270. FAX 44-171-383-6402. *4480*

JOURNAL OF CLINICAL PEDIATRIC DENTISTRY.
Tufts University, School of Dental Medicine, Dept. of Pediatric Dentistry, 1 Kneeland St., Boston, MA 02111. TEL 617-956-6902. FAX 205-995-1588. *4645*

JOURNAL OF CLINICAL PERIODONTOLOGY.
Munksgaard International Publishers Ltd., 35 Noerre Soegade, P.O. Box 2148, DK-1016 Copenhagen K, Denmark. TEL 45-33-127030. FAX 45-33-129387. *4645*

JOURNAL OF CLINICAL PHARMACOLOGY.
Lippincott - Raven Publishers 227 E. Washington Sq., Philadelphia, PA 19106. TEL 215-238-4200. *5421*

JOURNAL OF CLINICAL PHARMACY AND THERAPEUTICS.
Blackwell Science Ltd., Osney Mead, Oxford OX2 0EL, England. TEL 44-1865-206206. FAX 44-1865-721205. *5421*

JOURNAL OF CLINICAL PSYCHIATRY.
Physicians Postgraduate Press, Inc., Box 240008, Memphis, TN 38124. TEL 901-682-1001. FAX 901-682-6992. *4844*

JOURNAL OF CLINICAL PSYCHOANALYSIS.
International Universities Press, Inc., 59 Boston Post Rd., Box 1524, Madison, CT 06443-1524. TEL 203-245-4000. FAX 203-245-0775. *5853*

JOURNAL OF CLINICAL PSYCHOLOGY.
John Wiley & Sons, Inc., Journals, 605 Third Ave., New York, NY 10158-0012. TEL 212-850-6645. FAX 212-850-6021. *5854*

JOURNAL OF CLINICAL PSYCHOLOGY IN MEDICAL SETTINGS.
Plenum Publishing Corp., 233 Spring St., New York, NY 10013-1578. TEL 212-620-8000. FAX 212-463-0742. *5854*

JOURNAL OF CLINICAL PSYCHOPHARMACOLOGY.
Williams & Wilkins, 351 W Camden St., Baltimore, MD 21201. TEL 410-528-4000. FAX 410-528-4312. *5421*

JOURNAL OF CLINICAL ULTRASOUND.
John Wiley & Sons, Inc., Journals, 605 Third Ave., New York, NY 10158. TEL 212-850-6645. FAX 212-850-6021. *4877*

JOURNAL OF CLUSTER SCIENCE.
Plenum Publishing Corp., 233 Spring St., New York, NY 10013-1578. TEL 212-620-8000. FAX 212-463-0742. *1681*

JOURNAL OF COASTAL RESEARCH.
Coastal Education & Research Foundation, Box 21087, Royal Palm Beach, FL 33421-0187. TEL 305-565-1051. FAX 305-565-1051. *2297*

JOURNAL OF COATED FABRICS.
Technomic Publishing Co., Inc., 851 New Holland Ave., Box 3535, Lancaster, PA 17604. TEL 717-291-5609. FAX 717-295-4538. *6680*

JOURNAL OF COGNITIVE NEUROSCIENCE.
M I T Press, 55 Hayward St., Cambridge, MA 02142. TEL 617-253-2839. FAX 617-577-1545. *4844*

JOURNAL OF COGNITIVE PSYCHOTHERAPY.
Springer Publishing Company, 536 Broadway, New York, NY 10012-3955. TEL 212-431-4370. FAX 212-941-7842. *5854*

JOURNAL OF COLD REGIONS ENGINEERING.
American Society of Civil Engineers, 345 E. 47th St., New York, NY 10017-2398. TEL 212-705-7288. FAX 212-980-4681. *2665*

JOURNAL OF COLLEGE & UNIVERSITY FOODSERVICE.
Haworth Press, Inc., Food Products Press, 10 Alice St., Binghamton, NY 13904-1580. FAX 607-722-6362. *2979*

JOURNAL OF COLLEGE AND UNIVERSITY STUDENT HOUSING.
Association of College and University Housing Officers' International, 364 West Lane Ave., Ste. C, Columbus, OH 43201-1062. TEL 614-292-0099. FAX 614-292-3205. *2133*

JOURNAL OF COLLEGE STUDENT DEVELOPMENT.
American College Personnel Association, One Dupont Circle, Ste. 300, Washington, DC 20036-1110. TEL 202-835-2272. FAX 202-296-3286. *5854*

JOURNAL OF COLLEGE STUDENT PSYCHOTHERAPY.
Haworth Press, Inc., 10 Alice St, Binghamton, NY 13904. TEL 607-722-5857. FAX 607-722-1424. *5854*

JOURNAL OF COLLOID AND INTERFACE SCIENCE.
Academic Press, Inc., Journal Division, 525 B St., Ste. 1900, San Diego, CA 92101-4495. TEL 619-230-1840. FAX 619-699-6800. *1753*

JOURNAL OF COMBINATORIAL DESIGNS.
John Wiley & Sons, Inc. Journals, 605 Third Ave., New York, NY 10158. TEL 212-850-6645. FAX 212-850-6021. *4372*

JOURNAL OF COMBINATORIAL MATHEMATICS AND COMBINATORIAL COMPUTING.
Charles Babbage Research Centre, Box 272, St. Norbert Postal Sta., Winnipeg, MB R3V 1L6, Canada. TEL 204-772-2612. *4372*

JOURNAL OF COMBINATORIAL OPTIMIZATION.
Kluwer Academic Publishers, Postbus 17, 3300 AA Dordrecht, Netherlands. TEL 31-78-6392392. FAX 31-78-6392254. *4410*

JOURNAL OF COMBINATORIAL THEORY. SERIES A.
Academic Press, Inc., Journal Division, 525 B St., Ste. 1900, San Diego, CA 92101-4495. TEL 619-230-1840. FAX 619-699-6800. *4372*

JOURNAL OF COMBINATORIAL THEORY. SERIES B.
Academic Press, Inc., Journal Division, 525 B St., Ste. 1900, San Diego, CA 92101-4490. TEL 619-230-1840. FAX 619-699-6800. *4372*

JOURNAL OF COMMON MARKET STUDIES.
Blackwell Publishers Ltd., 108 Cowley Rd., Oxford OX4 1JF, England. TEL 44-1865-791100. FAX 44-1865-791347. *5676*

THE JOURNAL OF COMMONWEALTH & COMPARATIVE POLITICS.
Frank Cass, Newbury House, 890-900 Eastern Ave., Newbury Park, Ilford, Essex 1G2 7HH, England. TEL 44-181-599-8866. FAX 44-181-599-0984. *5758*

JOURNAL OF COMMUNICATION.
Oxford University Press, Journals, 2001 Evans Rd., Cary, NC 27513. TEL 919-677-0977. FAX 919-677-1714. *1908*

JOURNAL OF COMMUNICATION DISORDERS.
Elsevier Science Inc., Box 945, New York, NY 10159-0945. TEL 212-633-3730. FAX 212-633-3990. *5854*

JOURNAL OF COMMUNICATION MANAGEMENT.
Henry Stewart Publications, Russell House, 28-30 Little Russell St., London WC1A 2HN, England. TEL 44-171-404-3040. FAX 44-171-404-2081. *1426*

JOURNAL OF COMMUNIST STUDIES AND TRANSITION POLITICS.
Frank Cass, Newbury House, 890-900 Eastern Ave., Newbury Park, Ilford, Essex 1G2 7HH, England. TEL 44-181-599-8866. FAX 44-181-599-0984. *5758*

JOURNAL OF COMMUNITY AND APPLIED SOCIAL PSYCHOLOGY.
John Wiley & Sons Ltd., Journals, Baffins Ln., Chichester, W. Sussex PO19 1UD, England. TEL 44-1243-779777. FAX 44-1243-843232. *5854*

JOURNAL OF COMMUNITY HEALTH.
Human Sciences Press, Inc. 233 Spring St., New York, NY 10013-1578. TEL 212-620-8000. FAX 212-463-0742. *4480*

JOURNAL OF COMMUNITY HEALTH NURSING.
Lawrence Erlbaum Associates, Inc., 10 Industrial Dr., Mahwah, NJ 07430-2262. TEL 201-236-9500. FAX 201-236-0072. *4717*

JOURNAL OF COMMUNITY NURSING.
P T M Publishers Ltd., 282 High St., Sutton, Surrey SM1 1PQ, England. TEL 0181-642-0162. FAX 0181-643-2275. *4717*

JOURNAL OF COMMUNITY PSYCHOLOGY.
John Wiley & Sons, Inc., Journals, 605 Third Ave., New York, NY 10158-0012. TEL 212-850-6645. FAX 212-850-6021. *5854*

JOURNAL OF COMPARATIVE FAMILY STUDIES.
University of Calgary, Department of Sociology, 2500 University Dr. N.W., Calgary, AB T2N 1N4, Canada. TEL 403-220-7317. FAX 403-282-9298. *6419*

THE JOURNAL OF COMPARATIVE GERMAN LINGUISTICS.
Kluwer Academic Publishers, Postbus 17, 3300 AA Dordrecht, Netherlands. TEL 31-78-6392392. FAX 31-78-6392254. *4078*

THE JOURNAL OF COMPARATIVE NEUROLOGY.
John Wiley & Sons, Inc., Journals, 605 Third Ave., New York, NY 10158. TEL 212-850-6645. FAX 212-850-6021. *4844*

JOURNAL OF COMPARATIVE PHYSICAL AND EDUCATION SPORT.
Verlag Karl Hofmann, Postfach 1360, 73603 Schorndorf, Germany. TEL 49-7181-402-0. FAX 49-7181-402111. *6466*

JOURNAL OF COMPARATIVE PSYCHOLOGY.
American Psychological Association, 750 First St., N.E., Washington, DC 20002-4242. TEL 202-336-5600. FAX 202-336-5568. *5854*

JOURNAL OF COMPARATIVE RELIGION.
Universal Publications (a division of S T C), P.O. Box 7305, Ottawa, ON K1L 8E4, Canada. TEL 613-831-1052. FAX 613-831-8452. *6070*

JOURNAL OF COMPARATIVE SOCIOLOGY AND ETHICS.
S T C, P.O. Box 7305, Ottawa, ON K1L 8E4, Canada. TEL 613-831-1052. FAX 613-831-8452. *6419*

JOURNAL OF COMPLEXITY.
Academic Press, Inc., Journal Division, 525 B St., Ste. 1900, San Diego, CA 92101-4495. TEL 619-230-1840. FAX 619-699-6800. *4410*

JOURNAL OF COMPOSITE MATERIALS.
Technomic Publishing Co., Inc., 851 New Holland Ave., Box 3535, Lancaster, PA 17604. TEL 717-291-5609. FAX 717-295-4538. *2734*

JOURNAL OF COMPOSITES TECHNOLOGY AND RESEARCH.
American Society for Testing and Materials, 100 Barr Harbor Dr., W. Conshohocken, PA 19428-2959. TEL 610-832-9500. FAX 610-832-9555. *2759*

JOURNAL OF COMPUTATIONAL AND APPLIED MATHEMATICS.
North-Holland P.O. Box 211, 1000 AE Amsterdam, Netherlands. TEL 31-20-4853911. FAX 31-20-4853598. *4372*

JOURNAL OF COMPUTATIONAL BIOLOGY.
Mary Ann Liebert, Inc. Publishers, 2 Madison Ave., Larchmont, NY 10538. TEL 914-834-3100. FAX 914-834-3688. *589*

JOURNAL OF COMPUTATIONAL CHEMISTRY.
John Wiley & Sons, Inc., Journals, 605 Third Ave., New York, NY 10158. TEL 212-850-6645. FAX 212-850-6021. *1681*

JOURNAL OF COMPUTATIONAL MATHEMATICS.
Science Press, Marketing and Sales Department, 16 Donghuangchenggen North St., Beijing 100717, People's Republic of China. TEL 4010642. FAX 4019810. *4372*

JOURNAL OF COMPUTATIONAL NEUROSCIENCE.
Kluwer Academic Publishers, Postbus 17, 3300 AA Dordrecht, Netherlands. TEL 31-78-6392392. FAX 31-78-6392254. *4845*

JOURNAL OF COMPUTATIONAL PHYSICS.
Academic Press, Inc., Journal Division, 525 B St., Ste. 1900, San Diego, CA 92101-4495. TEL 619-230-1840. FAX 619-699-6800. *5582*

JOURNAL OF COMPUTER-AIDED MATERIALS DESIGN.
E S C O M Science Publishers BV, P.O. Box 214, 2300 AE Leiden, Netherlands. TEL 31-71-127052. FAX 31-71-121772. *1724*

JOURNAL OF COMPUTER AND SYSTEM SCIENCES.
Academic Press, Inc., Journal Division, 525 B St., Ste. 1900, San Diego, CA 92101-4495. TEL 619-230-1840. FAX 619-699-6800. *1994*

JOURNAL OF COMPUTER ASSISTED LEARNING.
Blackwell Science Ltd., Osney Mead, Oxford OX2 OEL, England. TEL 44-1865-206206. FAX 44-1865-721205. *2020*

JOURNAL OF COMPUTER-ASSISTED MICROSCOPY.
Plenum Publishing Corp., 233 Spring St., New York, NY 10013-1578. TEL 212-620-8000. FAX 212-463-0742. *2052*

JOURNAL OF COMPUTER ASSISTED TOMOGRAPHY.
Lippincott - Raven Publishers 227 E. Washington Sq., Philadelphia, PA 19106. TEL 215-237-4200. *4878*

JOURNAL OF COMPUTER INFORMATION SYSTEMS.
International Association for Computer Information Systems, 217 College of Business, Oklahoma State University, Stillwater, OK 74075. TEL 405-744-5090. FAX 405-744-5180. *2056*

JOURNAL OF COMPUTER SCIENCE AND TECHNOLOGY.
Science Press, Marketing and Sales Department, 16 Donghuangchenggen North St., Beijing 100717, People's Republic of China. TEL 4010642. FAX 4019810. *2118*

JOURNAL OF COMPUTERS IN MATHEMATICS AND SCIENCE TEACHING.
Association for the Advancement of Computing in Education, Box 2966, Charlottesville, VA 22902-2966. TEL 804-973-3987. *4410*

JOURNAL OF COMPUTING IN CHILDHOOD EDUCATION.
Association for the Advancement of Computing in Education, Box 2966, Charlottesville, VA 22902-2966. TEL 804-973-3987. *2406*

JOURNAL OF COMPUTING IN HIGHER EDUCATION.
Norris Publishers, Box 2593, Amherst, MA 01004-2593. TEL 413-545-4232. FAX 413-545-3203. *2406*

JOURNAL OF COMPUTING IN TEACHER EDUCATION.
International Society for Technology in Education, 1787 Agate St., Eugene, OR 97403-1923. TEL 541-346-4414. FAX 541-346-5890. *2406*

JOURNAL OF CONFEDERATE HISTORY.
Southern Heritage Press, Box 347163, Atlanta, GA 30334. TEL 404-963-6776. *5036*

JOURNAL OF CONSCIOUSNESS STUDIES.
Imprint Academic, P.O. Box 1, Thorverston, Exeter, Devon EX5 5YX, England. TEL 44-1392-841600. FAX 44-1392-841478. *5854*

JOURNAL OF CONSTRUCTIONAL STEEL RESEARCH.
Elsevier Science Ltd., P.O. Box 800, Kidlington, Oxford OX5 1DX, England. TEL 44-1865-843000. FAX 44-1865-843010. *2665*

JOURNAL OF CONSTRUCTIVIST PSYCHOLOGY.
Taylor & Francis Inc., 1900 Frost Rd., Ste. 101, Bristol, PA 19007-1598. TEL 215-785-5800. FAX 215-785-5515. *5855*

JOURNAL OF CONSULTING AND CLINICAL PSYCHOLOGY.
American Psychological Association, 750 First St., N.E., Washington, DC 20002-4242. TEL 202-336-5600. FAX 202-336-5568. *5855*

JOURNAL OF CONSUMER AFFAIRS.
American Council on Consumer Interests, 240 Stanley Hall, University of Missouri, Columbia, MO 65211. TEL 573-882-3817. FAX 573-884-6571. *2153*

JOURNAL OF CONSUMER POLICY.
Kluwer Academic Publishers, Postbus 17, 3300 AA Dordrecht, Netherlands. TEL 31-78-6392392. FAX 31-78-6392254. *2153*

JOURNAL OF CONSUMER PSYCHOLOGY.
Lawrence Erlbaum Associates, Inc., 10 Industrial Dr., Mahwah, NJ 07430-2262. TEL 201-236-9500. FAX 201-236-0072. *39*

JOURNAL OF CONSUMER RESEARCH.
University of Chicago Press, Journals Division, Box 37005, Chicago, IL 60637. TEL 312-753-3347. FAX 312-753-0811. *1470*

JOURNAL OF CONSUMER STUDIES & HOME ECONOMICS.
Blackwell Science Ltd., Osney Mead, Oxford OX2 OEL, England. TEL 01865-206206. FAX 01865-721205. *2153*

JOURNAL OF CONTAMINANT HYDROLOGY.
Elsevier Science B.V., P.O. Box 211, 1000 AE Amsterdam, Netherlands. TEL 31-20-4853911. FAX 31-20-4853598. *2837*

JOURNAL OF CONTEMPORARY HEALTH LAW AND POLICY.
Catholic University of America, Columbus School of Law, Washington, DC 20064. TEL 202-319-5732. FAX 202-319-4313. *4480*

JOURNAL OF CONTEMPORARY HISTORY.
Sage Publications Ltd., 6 Bonhill St., London EC2A 4PU, England. TEL 44-171-374-0645. FAX 44-171-374-8741. *3349*

JOURNAL OF CONTEMPORARY NEUROLOGY.
M I T Press, 55 Hayward St., Cambridge, MA
02142. TEL 617-253-2889. FAX 617-258-6779.
4845

JOURNAL OF CONTEMPORARY PSYCHOTHERAPY.
Human Sciences Press, Inc. 233 Spring St., New
York, NY 10013-1578. TEL 212-620-8000.
FAX 212-463-0742. *5855*

JOURNAL OF CONTEMPORARY RELIGION.
Carfax Publishing Co., P.O. Box 25, Abingdon, Oxon.
OX14 3UE, England. TEL 44-1235-401000.
FAX 44-1235-401550. *6071*

**JOURNAL OF CONTINGENCIES AND CRISIS
MANAGEMENT.**
Blackwell Publishers Ltd., 108 Cowley Rd., Oxford
OX4 1JF, England. TEL 44-1865-791100. FAX 44-
1865-791347. *1427*

**JOURNAL OF CONTINUING EDUCATION IN
NURSING.**
Slack, Inc., 6900 Grove Rd., Thorofare, NJ 08086-
9447. TEL 609-848-1000. FAX 609-853-5991.
4717

**JOURNAL OF CONTINUING EDUCATION IN THE
HEALTH PROFESSIONS.**
Decker Periodicals, P.O. Box 620, LCD 1, Hamilton,
ON L8N 3K7, Canada. TEL 905-522-7017.
FAX 905-522-7839. *4480*

JOURNAL OF CONTINUING HIGHER EDUCATION.
Association for Continuing Higher Education
(University Park), 506 Keller Bldg., University Park,
PA 16802. TEL 814-863-7752. FAX 814-863-
2765. *2400*

JOURNAL OF CONTROLLED RELEASE.
Elsevier Science B.V., P.O. Box 211, 1000 AE
Amsterdam, Netherlands. TEL 31-20-4853911.
FAX 31-20-4853598. *642*

**JOURNAL OF COORDINATION CHEMISTRY.
SECTIONS A & B.**
Gordon and Breach Science Publishers, c/o
International Publishers Distributor, P.O. Box 3054,
Langhorne, PA 19047-3054. TEL 215-750-2642.
FAX 215-750-6343. *1681*

JOURNAL OF CORPORATE FINANCE.
North-Holland P.O. Box 211, 1000 AE Amsterdam,
Netherlands. TEL 31-20-4853911. FAX 31-20-
4853598. *1104*

JOURNAL OF CORRECTIONAL HEALTH CARE.
National Commission on Correctional Health Care,
2105 N. Southport, Ste. 200, Chicago, IL 60614-
4017. TEL 312-528-0818. FAX 312-528-4915.
4481

JOURNAL OF COST ANALYSIS.
Society of Cost Estimating and Analysis, 101 S.
Whiting St., Ste. 201, Alexandria, VA 22304.
TEL 703-751-8069. FAX 703-461-7328. *1050*

JOURNAL OF COUNSELING PSYCHOLOGY.
American Psychological Association, 750 First St.,
N.E., Washington, DC 20002-4242. TEL 202-336-
5600. FAX 202-336-5568. *5855*

JOURNAL OF COUPLES THERAPY.
Haworth Press, Inc., 10 Alice St., Binghamton, NY
13904. TEL 607-722-5857. FAX 607-722-1424.
5855

JOURNAL OF CRANIO-MAXILLOFACIAL TRAUMA.
Montage Media Corp., 70 Hilltop Rd., Ramsey, NJ
07446. TEL 201-236-0700. FAX 201-236-1339.
4911

**JOURNAL OF CRANIOFACIAL GENETICS AND
DEVELOPMENTAL BIOLOGY.**
Munksgaard International Publishers Ltd., P.O. Box
2148, DK-1016 Copenhagen K, Denmark. TEL 45-
33-127030. FAX 45-33-129387. *745*

JOURNAL OF CRANIOFACIAL SURGERY.
Little, Brown and Company, Medical Journals, 34
Beacon St., Boston, MA 02108. TEL 617-859-
5500. FAX 617-859-0629. *4911*

JOURNAL OF CRIMINAL JUSTICE.
Elsevier Science Ltd., Pergamon, P.O. Box 800,
Kidlington, Oxford, OX5 1DX, England. TEL 44-
1865-843000. FAX 44-1865-843010. *3911*

**JOURNAL OF CRIMINAL JUSTICE AND POPULAR
CULTURE.**
State University of New York at Albany, School of
Criminal Justice, 135 Western Ave., Albany, NY
12222. TEL 518-442-5210. *3911*

JOURNAL OF CRISIS NEGOTIATIONS.
Texas Association of Hostage Negotiators, c/o Dr.
James L. Greenstone, Ed., Box 670292, Dallas, TX
75367-0292. TEL 214-361-0209. FAX 214-361-
6545. *2167*

JOURNAL OF CRITICAL CARE.
W.B. Saunders Co. Curtis Center, 3rd Fl.,
Independence Sq. W., Philadelphia, PA 19106-
3399. TEL 215-238-7800. FAX 215-238-6445.
4786

JOURNAL OF CRITICAL ILLNESS.
Cliggott Publishing Co., 55 Holly Hill Lane, Box
4010, Greenwich, CT 06831. TEL 203-661-0600.
4481

JOURNAL OF CROSS-CULTURAL GERONTOLOGY.
Kluwer Academic Publishers, Postbus 17, 3300 AA
Dordrecht, Netherlands. TEL 31-78-6392392.
FAX 31-78-6392254. *3290*

JOURNAL OF CRUSTACEAN BIOLOGY.
Crustacean Society, 810 E. 10th St., Box 1897,
Lawrence, KS 66044. TEL 913-843-1221.
FAX 913-843-1274. *810*

JOURNAL OF CRYPTOLOGY.
Springer-Verlag, Science Journals, 175 Fifth Ave.,
New York, NY 10010. TEL 212-460-1500.
FAX 212-474-6272. *4373*

JOURNAL OF CRYSTAL GROWTH.
North-Holland P.O. Box 211, 1000 AE Amsterdam,
Netherlands. TEL 31-20-4853911. FAX 31-20-
4853598. *1726*

JOURNAL OF CULTURAL DIVERSITY.
Tucker Publications, Inc., Box 580, Lisle, IL 60532.
TEL 708-969-3809. FAX 708-969-3895. *4717*

JOURNAL OF CULTURAL ECONOMICS.
Kluwer Academic Publishers, Postbus 17, 3300 AA
Dordrecht, Netherlands. TEL 31-78-6392392.
FAX 31-78-6392254. *1256*

JOURNAL OF CURRICULUM STUDIES.
Taylor & Francis Ltd., Rankine Rd., Basingstoke,
Hants. RG24 8PR, England. TEL 44-1256-
840366. FAX 44-1256-479438. *2491*

**JOURNAL OF CUSTOMER SERVICE IN MARKETING
& MANAGEMENT.**
Haworth Press, Inc., 10 Alice St., Binghamton, NY
13904-1580. TEL 607-722-5857. FAX 607-722-
6362. *936*

JOURNAL OF CUTANEOUS PATHOLOGY.
Munksgaard International Publishers Ltd., 35
Noerre Soegade, P.O. Box 2148, DK-1016
Copenhagen K, Denmark. TEL 45-33-127030.
FAX 45-33-129387. *4662*

JOURNAL OF CYTOLOGY AND GENETICS.
Society of Cytologists and Geneticists, Department
of Botany, Bangalore University, Bangalore 560
056, India. TEL 3355036. *745*

**THE JOURNAL OF DATA MINING AND KNOWLEDGE
DISCOVERY.**
Kluwer Academic Publishers Boston, Box 358,
Accord Sta., Hingham, MA 02018-0358. TEL 617-
871-6600. FAX 617-871-6528. *2083*

JOURNAL OF DATABASE MANAGEMENT.
Idea Group Publishing, 4811 Jonestown Rd., Ste.
230, Harrisburg, PA 17109-1751. TEL 717-541-
9150. FAX 717-541-9159. *2066*

THE JOURNAL OF DATABASE MARKETING.
Henry Stewart Publications, Russell House, 28-30
Little Russell St., London WC1A 2HN, England.
TEL 44-171-404-3040. FAX 44-171-404-2081.
1155

**THE JOURNAL OF DEAF STUDIES AND DEAF
EDUCATION.**
Oxford University Press, Journals, 2001 Evans Rd.,
Cary, NC 27513. TEL 919-677-0977. FAX 919-
677-1714. *3313*

THE JOURNAL OF DEMENTIA CARE.
Hawker Publications, 140 Battersea Park Rd.,
London SW11 4NB, England. TEL 44-171-720-
2108. FAX 44-171-498-5023. *4845*

JOURNAL OF DENTAL HYGIENE.
American Dental Hygienists' Association, 444 N
Michigan Ave., Ste. 3400, Chicago, IL 60611.
TEL 312-440-8900. FAX 312-440-8929. *4645*

JOURNAL OF DENTAL RESEARCH.
American Association for Dental Research, 1619
Duke St., Alexandria, VA 22314-3406. TEL 703-
548-0066. FAX 703-543-1883. *4645*

JOURNAL OF DENTISTRY.
Butterworth - Heinemann, Part of the Reed Elsevier
group, Linacre House, Jordan Hill, Oxford OX2 8DP,
England. TEL 44-1865-310366. FAX 44-1865-
310898. *4645*

JOURNAL OF DENTISTRY FOR CHILDREN.
American Society of Dentistry for Children, 875 N.
Michigan Ave., Ste. 4040 Chicago, IL 60611-
1901. TEL 312-943-1244. FAX 312-943-5341.
4645

JOURNAL OF DERMATOLOGICAL SCIENCE.
Elsevier Science Ireland Ltd., P.C. Box 85, Limerick,
Ireland. TEL 353-61-471944. FAX 353-61-
472144. *4662*

JOURNAL OF DESIGN & MANUFACTURING.
Chapman & Hall, Journals Department 2-6
Boundary Row, London SE1 8HN, England. TEL 44-
171-8650066. FAX 44-171-5229623. *2759*

JOURNAL OF DEVELOPING AREAS.
Western Illinois University, Morgan Hall 232,
Macomb, IL 61455. TEL 309-298-1108. FAX 309-
298-2865. *1310*

JOURNAL OF DEVELOPING SOCIETIES.
E.J. Brill, P.O. Box 9000, 2300 PA Leiden,
Netherlands. TEL 31-71-5353500. FAX 31-71-
5317532. *6331*

JOURNAL OF DEVELOPMENT ECONOMICS.
North-Holland P.O. Box 211, 1000 AE Amsterdam,
Netherlands. TEL 31-20-4853911. FAX 31-20-
4853598. *1310*

THE JOURNAL OF DEVELOPMENT STUDIES.
Frank Cass, Newbury House, 890-900 Eastern Ave.,
Newbury Park, Ilford, Essex IG2 7HH, England.
TEL 44-181-599-8866 FAX 44-181-599-0984.
1310

**JOURNAL OF DEVELOPMENTAL AND BEHAVIORAL
PEDIATRICS.**
Williams & Wilkins, 351 W. Camden St., Baltimore,
MD 21201. TEL 410-528-4000. FAX 410-528-
4312. *4807*

**JOURNAL OF DEVELOPMENTAL AND PHYSICAL
DISABILITIES.**
Plenum Publishing Corp. 233 Spring St., New York,
NY 10013-1578. TEL 212-620-8000. FAX 212-
463-0742. *3305*

JOURNAL OF DHARMA.
Dharmaram College, Centre for the Study of World
Religions, Bangalore 560 029, India. TEL 80-
5536866. FAX 80-5536046. *6071*

JOURNAL OF DIABETES AND ITS COMPLICATIONS.
Elsevier Science Inc., Box 945, New York, NY
10159-0945. TEL 212-633-3730. FAX 212-633-
3680. *4672*

JOURNAL OF DIAGNOSTIC MEDICAL SONOGRAPHY.
Lippincott - Raven Publishers 227 E. Washington
Sq., Philadelphia, PA 19106. TEL 215-238-4200.
4878

JOURNAL OF DIARRHOEAL DISEASES RESEARCH.
International Centre for Diarrhoeal Disease
Research, Bangladesh, C.P.O. Box 128, Dhaka
1000, Bangladesh. TEL 600171-78. FAX 880-2-
883116. *4567*

JOURNAL OF DIFFERENTIAL EQUATIONS.
Academic Press, Inc., Journal Division, 525 B St.,
Ste. 1900, San Diego, CA 92101-4495. TEL 619-
230-1840. FAX 619-699-6800. *4373*

JOURNAL OF DIGITAL IMAGING.
W.B. Saunders Co. The Curtis Center, 3rd Fl., Independence Sq. W., Philadelphia, PA 19106-3399. TEL 215-238-7800. FAX 215-238-6445. *4878*

JOURNAL OF DIRECT & INTERACTIVE MARKETING.
John Wiley & Sons, Inc., Journals, 605 Third Ave., New York, NY 10158. TEL 212-850-6645. FAX 212-850-6021. *1470*

JOURNAL OF DISABILITY POLICY STUDIES.
University of Arkansas, Department of Rehabilitation Education and Research, 346 N. West Ave., Fayetteville, AR 72701. TEL 501-575-3656. FAX 501-575-3253. *3306*

JOURNAL OF DISPERSION SCIENCE AND TECHNOLOGY.
Marcel Dekker Journals, 270 Madison Ave., New York, NY 10016. TEL 212-696-9000. FAX 212-685-4540. *1753*

JOURNAL OF DISTANCE EDUCATION.
Canadian Association for Distance Education, One Stewart St., Ste. 205, Ottawa, ON K1N 6H7, Canada. FAX 613-230-2746. *2491*

JOURNAL OF DIVORCE & REMARRIAGE.
Haworth Press, Inc., 10 Alice St., Binghamton, NY 13904. TEL 607-722-5857. FAX 607-722-1424. *4414*

JOURNAL OF DRUG DEVELOPMENT AND CLINICAL PRACTICE.
Gardiner - Caldwell Communications Ltd., Old Ribbon Mill, Pitt St., Macclesfield, Ches. SK11 7PT, England. TEL 44-1625-618507. FAX 44-1625-614161. *5421*

JOURNAL OF DRUG EDUCATION.
Baywood Publishing Co., Inc., 26 Austin Ave., Box 337, Amityville, NY 11701. TEL 516-691-1270. FAX 516-691-1770. *2198*

JOURNAL OF DRUG ISSUES.
Journal of Drug Issues Inc., Box 4021, Leon Sta., Tallahassee, FL 32315. TEL 904-668-6669. *2198*

JOURNAL OF DYNAMIC SYSTEMS, MEASUREMENT AND CONTROL.
American Society of Mechanical Engineers, 22 Law Dr., Fairfield, NJ 07007-2300. *2734*

JOURNAL OF DYNAMICAL AND CONTROL SYSTEMS.
Plenum Publishing Corp., 233 Spring St., New York, NY 10013-1578. TEL 212-620-8000. FAX 212-463-0742. *2748*

JOURNAL OF DYNAMICS AND DIFFERENTIAL EQUATIONS.
Plenum Publishing Corp., 233 Spring St., New York, NY 10013-1578. TEL 212-620-8000. FAX 212-463-0742. *4373*

JOURNAL OF EARLY ADOLESCENCE.
Sage Publications, Inc., 2455 Teller Rd., Thousand Oaks, CA 91320. TEL 805-499-0721. FAX 805-499-0871. *1770*

JOURNAL OF EARLY CHRISTIAN STUDIES.
Johns Hopkins University Press, Journals Publishing Division, 2715 N. Charles St., Ste. 750, Baltimore, MD 21218-4319. TEL 410-516-6987. FAX 410-516-6968. *6071*

JOURNAL OF EARLY MODERN HISTORY.
E.J. Brill, P.O. Box 9000, 2300 PA Leiden, Netherlands. TEL 31-71-5353566. FAX 31-71-5317532. *3349*

JOURNAL OF EARLY SOUTHERN DECORATIVE ARTS.
Museum of Early Southern Decorative Arts, P.O. Box 10310, Winston-Salem, NC 27108-0310. TEL 910-721-7360. FAX 910-721-7367. *333*

JOURNAL OF EAST AFRICAN NATURAL HISTORY.
East Africa Natural History Society, P.O. Box 44486, Nairobi, Kenya. TEL 254-2-742161. FAX 254-2-741424. *590*

JOURNAL OF EAST ASIAN LINGUISTICS.
Kluwer Academic Publishers, Postbus 17, 3300 AA Dordrecht, Netherlands. TEL 31-78-6392392. FAX 31-78-6392254. *4078*

JOURNAL OF EAST - WEST BUSINESS.
Haworth Press, Inc., 10 Alice St., Binghamton, NY 13904-1580. TEL 607-722-5857. FAX 607-722-1424. *1257*

JOURNAL OF EASTERN AFRICAN RESEARCH & DEVELOPMENT.
Gideon S. Were Press, P.O. Box 10622, Nairobi, Kenya. TEL 254-2-331135. FAX 254-2-331135. *3373*

JOURNAL OF ECOBIOLOGY.
Palani Paramount Publications, 69D, Anna Nagar, Palani 624 602, India. TEL 04545-42332. FAX 04545-42199. *590*

JOURNAL OF ECOLOGY.
Blackwell Science Ltd., Osney Mead, Oxford OX2 OEL, England. TEL 44-1865-206206. FAX 44-1865-721205. *590*

JOURNAL OF ECONOMETRICS.
Elsevier Science S.A., P.O. Box 564, CH-1001 Lausanne 1, Switzerland. TEL 41-21-3207381. FAX 41-21-3235444. *1257*

JOURNAL OF ECONOMIC BEHAVIOR & ORGANIZATION.
North-Holland P.O. Box 211, 1000 AE Amsterdam, Netherlands. TEL 31-20-4853911. FAX 31-20-4853598. *936*

JOURNAL OF ECONOMIC DYNAMICS AND CONTROL.
North-Holland P.O. Box 211, 1000 AE Amsterdam, Netherlands. TEL 31-20-4853911. FAX 31-20-4853598. *1257*

THE JOURNAL OF ECONOMIC EDUCATION.
Heldref Publications, 1319 18th St., N.W., Washington, DC 20036-1802. TEL 202-296-6267. FAX 202-296-5149. *936*

JOURNAL OF ECONOMIC ENTOMOLOGY.
Entomological Society of America, 9301 Annapolis Rd., Lanham, MD 20706. TEL 301-731-4535. FAX 301-731-4538. *730*

JOURNAL OF ECONOMIC GROWTH.
Kluwer Academic Publishers Boston, Box 358, Accord Sta., Hingham, MA 02018-0358. TEL 617-871-6600. FAX 617-871-6528. *1257*

JOURNAL OF ECONOMIC INTEGRATION.
Sejong University, Institute for International Economics, Seongdong-ku, Seoul 143-747, S. Korea. TEL 02-460-0338. FAX 02-460-0338. *936*

JOURNAL OF ECONOMIC PSYCHOLOGY.
North-Holland P.O. Box 211, 1000 AE Amsterdam, Netherlands. TEL 31-20-4853911. FAX 31-20-4853598. *1471*

JOURNAL OF ECONOMIC SURVEYS.
Blackwell Publishers Ltd., 108 Cowley Rd., Oxford OX4 1JF, England. TEL 44-1865-791100. FAX 44-1865-791347. *936*

JOURNAL OF ECONOMICS AND BUSINESS.
Elsevier Science Inc., Box 945, New York, NY 10159-0945. TEL 212-633-3730. FAX 212-633-3680. *936*

JOURNAL OF ECONOMICS AND FINANCE.
University of Southern Mississippi, Southern Sta., Box 5076, Hattiesburg, MS 39406-5076. TEL 601-266-4691. FAX 601-266-5992. *936*

JOURNAL OF ECONOMICS & MANAGEMENT STRATEGY.
M I T Press, 55 Hayward St., Cambridge, MA 02142-9902. TEL 617-253-2889. FAX 617-577-1545. *1257*

JOURNAL OF ECOTOXICOLOGY & ENVIRONMENTAL MONITORING.
Palani Paramount Publications, 69D, Anna Nagar, Palani 624 602, India. TEL 04545-42332. FAX 04545-42199. *2846*

JOURNAL OF ECUMENICAL STUDIES.
Temple University, 022-38, 1114 W. Berks St., Rm. 511, Philadelphia, PA 19122-6090. TEL 215-204-7714. FAX 215-204-4569. *6071*

JOURNAL OF EDUCATION AND PSYCHOLOGY.
Sardar Patel University, Department of Education, Vallabh Vidyanagar, Pin 388 120, India. TEL 02792-30379. *2346*

JOURNAL OF EDUCATION FINANCE.
A S B O International, 11461 N. Shore Dr., Reston, VA 22090. TEL 703-478-0405. FAX 703-478-0205. *2459*

JOURNAL OF EDUCATION FOR BUSINESS.
Heldref Publications, 1319 18th St., N.W., Washington, DC 20036-1802. TEL 202-296-6267. FAX 202-296-5149. *937*

JOURNAL OF EDUCATION FOR LIBRARY AND INFORMATION SCIENCE.
Association for Library and Information Science Education, 4101 Lake Boone Tr., Ste. 201, Raleigh, NC 27607. TEL 919-787-5181. *4002*

JOURNAL OF EDUCATION FOR STUDENTS PLACED AT RISK.
Lawrence Erlbaum Associates, Inc., 10 Industrial Ave., Mahwah, NJ 07430-2262. TEL 201-236-9500. FAX 201-236-0072. *2491*

JOURNAL OF EDUCATION FOR TEACHING.
Carfax Publishing Co., P.O. Box 25, Abingdon, Oxon. OX14 3UE, England. TEL 44-1235-401000. FAX 44-1235-401550. *2434*

JOURNAL OF EDUCATION POLICY.
Taylor & Francis Ltd., Rankine Rd., Basingstoke, Hants RG24 8PR, England. TEL 44-1256-840366. FAX 44-1256-479438. *2459*

JOURNAL OF EDUCATIONAL AND BEHAVIORAL STATISTICS.
American Educational Research Association, 1230 17th St., N.W., Washington, DC 20036-3078. TEL 202-223-9485. FAX 202-775-1824. *2390*

JOURNAL OF EDUCATIONAL AND PSYCHOLOGICAL CONSULTATION.
Lawrence Erlbaum Associates, Inc., 10 Industrial Dr., Mahwah, NJ 07430-2262. TEL 201-236-9500. FAX 201-236-0072. *2346*

JOURNAL OF EDUCATIONAL COMPUTING RESEARCH.
Baywood Publishing Co., Inc., 26 Austin Ave., Box 337, Amityville, NY 11701. TEL 516-691-1270. FAX 516-691-1770. *2406*

JOURNAL OF EDUCATIONAL MEASUREMENT.
National Council on Measurement in Education, 1230 17th St., N.W., Washington, DC 20036-3078. TEL 202-223-9318. FAX 202-775-1824. *2346*

JOURNAL OF EDUCATIONAL MEDIA.
Carfax Publishing Co., P.O. Box 25, Abingdon, Oxon. OX14 3UE, England. TEL 44-1235-401000. FAX 44-1235-401550. *1963*

JOURNAL OF EDUCATIONAL MULTIMEDIA AND HYPERMEDIA.
Association for the Advancement of Computing in Education, Box 2966, Charlottesville, VA 22902-2966. TEL 804-973-3987. *2406*

JOURNAL OF EDUCATIONAL PSYCHOLOGY.
American Psychological Association, 750 First St., N.E., Washington, DC 20002-4242. TEL 202-336-5600. FAX 202-336-5568. *5855*

JOURNAL OF EDUCATIONAL RELATIONS.
Educational Communication Center, Box 657, 1830 Walnut St., Camp Hill, PA 17011. TEL 717-761-6620. *1909*

THE JOURNAL OF EDUCATIONAL RESEARCH.
Heldref Publications, 1319 18th St., N.W., Washington, DC 20036-1802. TEL 202-296-6267. FAX 202-296-5149. *2346*

JOURNAL OF EDUCATIONAL TECHNOLOGY SYSTEMS.
Baywood Publishing Co., Inc., 26 Austin Ave., Box 337, Amityville, NY 11701. TEL 516-691-1270. FAX 516-691-1770. *2407*

JOURNAL OF ELASTICITY.
Kluwer Academic Publishers, Postbus 17, 3300 AA Dordrecht, Netherlands. TEL 31-78-6392392. FAX 31-78-6392254. *2734*

JOURNAL OF ELASTOMERS AND PLASTICS.
Technomic Publishing Co. Inc., 851 New Holland Ave., Box 3535, Lancaster, PA 17604. TEL 717-291-5609. FAX 717-295-4538. *5621*

JOURNAL OF ELDER ABUSE & NEGLECT.
Haworth Press, Inc., 10 Alice St., Binghamton, NY 13904. TEL 607-722-5857. FAX 607-722-1424. *3290*

JOURNAL OF ELECTROANALYTICAL CHEMISTRY.
Elsevier Science S.A., P.O. Box 564, CH-1001 Lausanne 1, Switzerland. TEL 41-21-3207381. FAX 41-21-3235444. *1717*

JOURNAL OF ELECTROCARDIOLOGY.
Churchill Livingstone, 650 Ave. of the Americas, New York, NY 10011. TEL 212-206-5040. FAX 212-727-7808. *4606*

JOURNAL OF ELECTROCERAMICS.
Kluwer Academic Publishers Boston, Box 358, Accord Sta., Hingham, MA 02018-0358. TEL 617-871-6600. FAX 617-871-6528. *2734*

JOURNAL OF ELECTROMAGNETIC WAVES AND APPLICATIONS.
V S P, P.O. Box 346, 3700 AH Zeist, Netherlands. TEL 31-30-6925790. FAX 31-30-6932081. *5553*

JOURNAL OF ELECTROMYOGRAPHY AND KINESIOLOGY.
Butterworth - Heinemann, Part of the Reed Elsevier group, Linacre House, Jordan Hill, Oxford OX2 8DP, England. TEL 44-1865-310366. FAX 44-1865-310398. *590*

JOURNAL OF ELECTRON SPECTROSCOPY AND RELATED PHENOMENA.
Elsevier Science B.V., P.O. Box 211, 1000 AE Amsterdam, Netherlands. TEL 31-20-4853911. FAX 31-20-4853598. *5605*

JOURNAL OF ELECTRONIC PACKAGING.
American Society of Mechanical Engineers, 22 Law Dr., Fairfield, NJ 07007-2300. *2525*

JOURNAL OF ELECTRONIC TESTING.
Kluwer Academic Publishers Boston, Box 358, Accord Sta., Hingham, MA 02018-0358. TEL 617-871-6600. FAX 617-871-6528. *2710*

JOURNAL OF ELECTRONICS (CHINA).
Science Press, Marketing and Sales Department, 16 Donghuangchenggen North St., Beijing 100717, People's Republic of China. TEL 4010642. FAX 4019810. *2525*

JOURNAL OF ELECTRONICS MANUFACTURING.
Chapman & Hall, Journals Department 2-6 Boundary Row, London SE1 8HN, England. TEL 44-171-8650066. FAX 44-171-5229623. *2525*

JOURNAL OF ELECTROPHYSIOLOGICAL TECHNOLOGY.
Electrophysiological Technologists' Association, c/o E.E.G. Department, St. Bartholomew's Hospital, W. Smithfield, London EC1A 7BE, England. TEL 44-171-601-8859. FAX 44-171-601-7875. *654*

JOURNAL OF ELECTROSTATICS.
Elsevier Science B.V., P.O. Box 211, 1000 AE Amsterdam, Netherlands. TEL 31-20-4853911. FAX 31-20-4853598. *2710*

JOURNAL OF ELECTROTOPOGRAPHY.
Electrotopograph Corporation, Box 98, Eldred, PA 16731. TEL 814-225-3296. *5553*

JOURNAL OF EMERGENCY MEDICINE.
Elsevier Science Inc., Box 945, New York, NY 10159-0945. TEL 212-633-3730. FAX 212-633-3680. *4786*

JOURNAL OF EMOTIONAL AND BEHAVIORAL DISORDERS.
Pro-Ed Inc., 8700 Shoal Creek Blvd., Austin, TX 78757-6897. TEL 512-451-3246. FAX 512-451-8542. *4845*

JOURNAL OF EMPIRICAL FINANCE.
North-Holland P.O. Box 211, 1000 AE Amsterdam, Netherlands. TEL 31-20-4853911. FAX 31-20-4853598. *1104*

JOURNAL OF END USER COMPUTING.
Idea Group Publishing, 4811 Jonestown Rd., Ste. 230, Harrisburg, PA 17109-1751. TEL 717-541-9150. FAX 717-541-9159. *2088*

THE JOURNAL OF ENDODONTICS.
Williams & Wilkins, 351 W. Camden St., Baltimore, MD 21201. TEL 410-528-4000. FAX 410-528-4312. *4645*

JOURNAL OF ENDOUROLOGY.
Mary Ann Liebert, Inc. Publishers, 2 Madison Ave., Larchmont, NY 10538. TEL 914-834-3100. FAX 914-834-2688. *4928*

JOURNAL OF ENDOVASCULAR SURGERY.
Futura Publishing Company, Inc., 135 Bedford Rd., Box 418, Armonk, NY 10504-0418. TEL 914-273-1014. FAX 914-273-1015. *4912*

JOURNAL OF ENERGY AND NATURAL RESOURCES LAW.
Kluwer Law International Postbus 85889, 2508 CN The Hague, Netherlands. TEL 31-70-3081500. FAX 31-70-3081515. *3796*

JOURNAL OF ENERGY, HEAT AND MASS TRANSFER.
Regional Centre for Energy, Heat and Mass Transfer for Asia and the Pacific, Madras 60036, India. TEL 91-44-235-1365. FAX 91-44-235-3094. *2553*

JOURNAL OF ENERGY IN SOUTHERN AFRICA.
Energy Research Institute, Information Service, P.O. Box 207, Plumstead 7801, South Africa. TEL 27-21-705-0120. FAX 27-21-705-6266. *2553*

JOURNAL OF ENERGY RESOURCES TECHNOLOGY.
American Society of Mechanical Engineers, 22 Law Dr., Fairfield, NJ 07007-2300. *2553*

JOURNAL OF ENGINEERING AND TECHNOLOGY MANAGEMENT.
Elsevier Science B.V., P.O. Box 211, 1000 AE Amsterdam, Netherlands. TEL 31-20-4853911. FAX 31-20-4853598. *1427*

JOURNAL OF ENGINEERING DESIGN.
Carfax Publishing Co., P.O. Box 25, Abingdon, Oxon. OX14 3UE, England. TEL 44-1235-401000. FAX 44-1235-401550. *2606*

JOURNAL OF ENGINEERING MATERIALS AND TECHNOLOGY.
American Society of Mechanical Engineers, 22 Law Dr., Fairfield, NJ 07007-2300. *2734*

JOURNAL OF ENGINEERING MATHEMATICS.
Kluwer Academic Publishers, Postbus 17, 3300 AA Dordrecht, Netherlands. TEL 31-78-6392392. FAX 31-78-6392254. *2607*

JOURNAL OF ENGINEERING MECHANICS.
American Society of Civil Engineers, 345 E. 47th St., New York, NY 10017-2398. TEL 212-705-7288. FAX 212-930-4681. *2665*

JOURNAL OF ENGINEERING TECHNOLOGY.
American Society for Engineering Education, Engineering Technology Division, c/o Richard M. Moore, Ed., Oregon Institute of Technology, 7726 S.E. Harmony Rd., Portland, OR 97222. TEL 503-725-3066. FAX 503-725-5925. *2607*

JOURNAL OF ENGLISH AND GERMANIC PHILOLOGY.
University of Illinois Press, 1325 S. Oak St., Champaign, IL 61820. TEL 217-333-0950. FAX 217-244-8082. *4078*

JOURNAL OF ENTOMOLOGICAL SCIENCE.
Georgia Entomological Society, Inc., c/o G. David Buntin, Department of Entomology, Georgia Experiment Station, Griffin, GA 30223-1797. TEL 404-228-7288. FAX 404-228-7287. *730*

JOURNAL OF ENTREPRENEURSHIP.
Sage Publications India Pvt. Ltd., P.O. Box 4215, New Delhi 110 048, India. TEL 91-11-644-4958. FAX 91-11-647-2426. *1427*

JOURNAL OF ENVIRONMENTAL BIOLOGY.
711, Civil Lines (South), Muzaffarnagar 251 001, India. TEL 0131-405306. *2805*

THE JOURNAL OF ENVIRONMENTAL EDUCATION.
Heldref Publications, 1319 Eighteenth St., N.W., Washington, DC 20036-1802. TEL 202-296-6267. *2805*

JOURNAL OF ENVIRONMENTAL ENGINEERING.
American Society of Civil Engineers, 345 E. 47th St., New York, NY 10017-2398. TEL 212-705-7288. FAX 212-980-4681. *2805*

JOURNAL OF ENVIRONMENTAL HEALTH.
National Environmental Health Association, 720 S. Colorado Blvd., No. 970 S. Tower, Denver, CO 80222-1925. TEL 303-756-9090. FAX 303-691-9490. *2805*

JOURNAL OF ENVIRONMENTAL HORTICULTURE.
Horticultural Research Institute, 1250 I St., N.W., Ste. 500, Washington, DC 20005. FAX 202-789-1893. *3058*

JOURNAL OF ENVIRONMENTAL PATHOLOGY, TOXICOLOGY AND ONCOLOGY.
Begell House Inc., 79 Madison Ave., Ste. 1205, New York, NY 10016-7892. TEL 212-725-1999. FAX 212-213-8368. *2346*

JOURNAL OF ENVIRONMENTAL PLANNING AND MANAGEMENT.
Carfax Publishing Co., P.O. Box 25, Abingdon, Oxon. OX14 3UE, England. TEL 44-1235-401000. FAX 44-1235-401550. *3586*

JOURNAL OF ENVIRONMENTAL POLYMER DEGRADATION.
Plenum Publishing Corp., 233 Spring St., New York, NY 10013-1578. TEL 212-620-8000. FAX 212-463-0742. *642*

JOURNAL OF ENVIRONMENTAL QUALITY.
American Society of Agronomy, Inc., 677 S. Segoe Rd., Madison, WI 53711. TEL 608-273-8080. FAX 608-273-2021. *2806*

JOURNAL OF ENVIRONMENTAL RADIOACTIVITY.
Elsevier Science Ltd., P.O. Box 800, Kidlington, Oxford OX5 1DX, England. TEL 44-1865-843000. FAX 44-1865-843010. *2806*

JOURNAL OF ENVIRONMENTAL SCIENCE AND HEALTH. PART A: ENVIRONMENTAL SCIENCE AND ENGINEERING AND TOXICOLOGY.
Marcel Dekker Journals 270 Madison Ave., New York, NY 10016. TEL 212-696-9000. FAX 212-685-4540. *2846*

JOURNAL OF ENVIRONMENTAL SCIENCE AND HEALTH. PART B: PESTICIDES, FOOD CONTAMINANTS, AND AGRICULTURAL WASTES.
Marcel Dekker Journals 270 Madison Ave., New York, NY 10016. TEL 212-696-9000. FAX 212-685-4540. *2806*

JOURNAL OF ENVIRONMENTAL SYSTEMS.
Baywood Publishing Co., Inc., 26 Austin Ave., Box 337, Amityville, NY 11701. TEL 516-691-1270. FAX 516-691-1770. *2306*

JOURNAL OF ENZYME INHIBITION.
Harwood Academic Publishers, c/o International Publishers Distributor, P.O. Box 3054, Langhorne, PA 19047-3054. TEL 215-750-2462. FAX 215-750-6343. *642*

JOURNAL OF EPIDEMIOLOGY & COMMUNITY HEALTH.
B M J Publishing Group, B.M.A. House, Tavistock Sq., London WC1H 9JR, England. TEL 44-171-383-6270. FAX 44-171-383-6402. *4481*

JOURNAL OF EPILEPSY.
Elsevier Science Inc., Box 945, New York, NY 10159-0945. TEL 212-633-3730. FAX 212-633-3680. *4845*

THE JOURNAL OF ETHICS.
Kluwer Academic Publishers, Postbus 17, 3300 AA Dordrecht, Netherlands. TEL 31-78-6392392. FAX 31-78-6392254. *5482*

JOURNAL OF ETHICS, LAW, AND AGING.
Springer Publishing Company, 536 Broadway, New York, NY 10012-3955. TEL 212-431-4370. FAX 212-941-7842. *3290*

JOURNAL OF ETHNOBIOLOGY.
Society of Ethnobiology, c/o Gayle Fritz, Anthropology - CB1114, Washington University, St. Louis, MO 63130-4899. TEL 314-935-8588. FAX 314-935-8535. *590*

JOURNAL OF ETHNOPHARMACOLOGY.
Elsevier Science Ireland Ltd., P.O. Box 85, Limerick, Ireland. TEL 353-61-471944. FAX 353-61-472144. *5421*

THE JOURNAL OF EUKARYOTIC MICROBIOLOGY.
Allen Press, Inc., 1041 New Hampshire Ave., Box 1897, Lawrence, KS 66044. TEL 913-843-1221. FAX 913-843-1274. *810*

JOURNAL OF EUROMARKETING.
Haworth Press, Inc., 10 Alice St., Binghamton, NY 13904. TEL 607-722-5857. FAX 607-722-1424. *1471*

JOURNAL OF EUROMED PHARMACY.
University of Malta, Department of Pharmacy, Msida, Malta. TEL 356-343764. FAX 356-340427. *5421*

JOURNAL OF EUROPEAN SOCIAL POLICY.
Longman Group UK Ltd., Longman House, Burnt Mill, Harlow, Essex CM20 2JE, England. TEL 44-1279-426721. FAX 44-1279-431059. *5759*

JOURNAL OF EVOLUTIONARY BIOCHEMISTRY AND PHYSIOLOGY.
Maik Nauka - Interperiodica, Mezhdunarodnyi Otdel, Ul. Profsoyuznaya, 90, 117864 Moscow, Russia. TEL 7-095-3360066. FAX 7-095-3360066. *642*

JOURNAL OF EXPERIMENTAL & THEORETICAL ARTIFICIAL INTELLIGENCE.
Taylor & Francis Ltd., 1 Gunpowder Sq., London EC4A 3DE, England. TEL 44-171-583-0490. FAX 44-171-583-0585. *2008*

JOURNAL OF EXPERIMENTAL BIOLOGY.
Company of Biologists Ltd., Bidder Bldg., 140 Cowley Rd., Cambridge CB4 4DL, England. TEL 44-1223-426164. FAX 44-1223-423353. *590*

JOURNAL OF EXPERIMENTAL CHILD PSYCHOLOGY.
Academic Press, Inc., Journal Division, 525 B St., Ste. 1900, San Diego, CA 92101-4495. TEL 619-230-1840. FAX 619-699-6800. *5856*

JOURNAL OF EXPERIMENTAL EDUCATION.
Heldref Publications, 1319 18th St., N.W., Washington, DC 20036-1802. TEL 202-296-6267. FAX 202-296-5149. *2492*

JOURNAL OF EXPERIMENTAL MARINE BIOLOGY AND ECOLOGY.
Elsevier Science B.V., P.O. Box 211, 1000 AE Amsterdam, Netherlands. TEL 31-20-4853911. FAX 31-20-4853598. *590*

JOURNAL OF EXPERIMENTAL MEDICINE.
Rockefeller University Press, 222 E. 70th St., New York, NY 10021. TEL 212-327-8572. FAX 212-327-7944. *4681*

JOURNAL OF EXPERIMENTAL PSYCHOLOGY: ANIMAL BEHAVIOR PROCESSES.
American Psychological Association, 750 First St., N.E., Washington, DC 20002-4242. TEL 202-336-5600. FAX 202-336-5568. *5856*

JOURNAL OF EXPERIMENTAL PSYCHOLOGY: APPLIED.
American Psychological Association, 750 First St., N.E., Washington, DC 20002-4242. TEL 202-336-5600. FAX 202-336-5568. *5856*

JOURNAL OF EXPERIMENTAL PSYCHOLOGY: GENERAL.
American Psychological Association, 750 First St., N.E., Washington, DC 20002-4242. TEL 202-336-5600. FAX 202-336-5568. *5856*

JOURNAL OF EXPERIMENTAL PSYCHOLOGY: HUMAN PERCEPTION AND PERFORMANCE.
American Psychological Association, 750 First St., N.E., Washington, DC 20002-4242. TEL 202-336-5600. FAX 202-336-5568. *5856*

JOURNAL OF EXPERIMENTAL PSYCHOLOGY: LEARNING, MEMORY, AND COGNITION.
American Psychological Association, 750 First St., N.E., Washington, DC 20002-4242. TEL 202-336-5600. FAX 202-336-5568. *5856*

JOURNAL OF EXPERIMENTAL SOCIAL PSYCHOLOGY.
Academic Press, Inc., Journal Division, 525 B St., Ste. 1900, San Diego, CA 92101-4495. TEL 619-230-1840. FAX 619-699-6800. *5856*

JOURNAL OF EXPERIMENTAL THERAPEUTICS AND ONCOLOGY.
Rapid Science Publishers, 2-6 Boundary Row, London SE1 8HN, England. TEL 44-171-865-0198. FAX 44-171-410-6600. *4759*

JOURNAL OF EXPERIMENTAL ZOOLOGY.
John Wiley & Sons, Inc., Journals, 605 Third Ave., New York, NY 10158. TEL 212-850-6645. FAX 212-850-6021. *810*

JOURNAL OF EXPERIMENTAL ZOOLOGY. SUPPLEMENT.
John Wiley & Sons, Inc., Journals, 605 Third Ave., New York, NY 10158-0012. TEL 212-850-6645. FAX 212-850-6021. *810*

JOURNAL OF EXTENSION (ASCII EDITION).
Virginia Tech, 233 Smyth Hall, Blacksburg, VA 24061-0452. TEL 703-231-7880. *2346*

JOURNAL OF EYE TRAUMA.
Field & Wood, Medical Periodicals, Inc., Box 975, Blue Bell, PA 19422. TEL 610-828-4010. FAX 215-482-0226. *4772*

JOURNAL OF FAMILY AND CONSUMER SCIENCES.
American Association of Family and Consumer Sciences, 1555 King St., Alexandria, VA 22314. TEL 703-706-4600. FAX 703-706-4663. *3524*

JOURNAL OF FAMILY AND ECONOMIC ISSUES.
Human Sciences Press, Inc. 233 Spring St., New York, NY 10013-1578. TEL 212-620-8000. FAX 212-463-0742. *5856*

JOURNAL OF FAMILY LIFE.
72 Philip St., Albany, NY 12202. TEL 518-432-1578. FAX 518-462-6836. *6419*

JOURNAL OF FAMILY NURSING.
Sage Publications, Inc., 2455 Teller Rd., Thousand Oaks, CA 91320. TEL 805-499-0721. FAX 805-499-0871. *4717*

JOURNAL OF FAMILY PRACTICE.
Appleton & Lange, Journal Division Box 120041, Stamford, CT 06912-0041. TEL 203-406-4500. *4481*

JOURNAL OF FAMILY PSYCHOTHERAPY.
Haworth Press, Inc., 10 Alice St., Binghamton, NY 13904. TEL 607-722-5857. FAX 607-722-1424. *5857*

JOURNAL OF FAMILY SOCIAL WORK.
Haworth Press, Inc., 10 Alice St., Binghamton, NY 13904. TEL 607-722-5857. FAX 607-722-1424. *6379*

JOURNAL OF FAMILY STUDIES.
La Trobe University Press, Bundoora, Vic. 3085, Australia. TEL 61-3-94791460. FAX 61-3-94702011. *4414*

JOURNAL OF FAMILY THERAPY.
Blackwell Publishers Ltd., 108 Cowley Rd., Oxford OX4 1JF, England. TEL 44-1865-791100. FAX 44-1865-791347. *4845*

JOURNAL OF FAMILY VIOLENCE.
Plenum Publishing Corp., 233 Spring St., New York, NY 10013-1578. TEL 212-620-8000. FAX 212-463-0742. *2167*

JOURNAL OF FASHION MARKETING AND MANAGEMENT.
Henry Stewart Publications, Russell House, 28-30 Little Russell St., London WC1A 2HN, England. TEL 44-171-404-3040. FAX 44-171-404-2081. *1471*

JOURNAL OF FEMINIST FAMILY THERAPY.
Haworth Press, Inc., 10 Alice St., Binghamton, NY 13904. TEL 607-722-5857. FAX 607-722-1424. *7017*

JOURNAL OF FERMENTATION AND BIOENGINEERING.
Society of Fermentation and Bioengineering, Japan, c/o Osaka Daigaku Kogakubu, 2-1 Yamadaoka, Suita-shi, Osaka-fu 565, Japan. TEL 81-6-877-5111. FAX 81-6-879-2034. *627*

JOURNAL OF FIELD ARCHAEOLOGY.
Boston University, Journal of Field Archaeology, 675 Commonwealth Ave., Boston, MA 02215. TEL 617-353-2357. FAX 617-353-6800. *360*

JOURNAL OF FILM AND VIDEO.
University Film and Video Association (Atlanta), c/o Georgia State University, Department of Communication, Atlanta, GA 30303. TEL 404-651-3200. FAX 404-651-1409. *5106*

JOURNAL OF FINANCIAL ECONOMICS.
Elsevier Science S.A., P.O. Box 564, CH-1001 Lausanne 1, Switzerland. TEL 41-21-3207381. FAX 41-21-3235444. *937*

JOURNAL OF FINANCIAL INTERMEDIATION.
Academic Press, Inc., Journal Division, 525 B St., Ste. 1900, San Diego, CA 92101-4495. TEL 619-230-1840. FAX 619-699-6800. *1257*

JOURNAL OF FINANCIAL MANAGEMENT AND ANALYSIS.
Om Sai Ram Centre for Financial Management Research, 15 Prakash Co-operative Housing Society, Relief Rd., Santacruz (W.), Bombay 400 054, India. TEL 91-22-6121715. *1105*

JOURNAL OF FINANCIAL PLANNING TODAY.
New Directions Publications, Inc., Box 6097, W. Palm Beach, FL 33405. TEL 407-434-0100. FAX 407-641-4801. *1105*

JOURNAL OF FINANCIAL REGULATION AND COMPLIANCE.
Henry Stewart Publications, Russell House, 28-30 Little Russell St., London WC1A 2HN, England. TEL 44-171-404-3040. FAX 44-171-404-2081. *1105*

JOURNAL OF FINANCIAL SERVICES RESEARCH.
Kluwer Academic Publishers Boston, Box 358, Accord Sta., Hingham, MA 02018-0358. TEL 617-871-6300. FAX 617-871-6528. *1105*

JOURNAL OF FIRE SCIENCES.
Technomic Publishing Co., Inc., 851 New Holland Ave., Box 3535, Lancaster, PA 17604. TEL 717-291-5609. FAX 717-295-4538. *2921*

JOURNAL OF FISH DISEASES.
Blackwell Science Ltd., Osney Mead, Oxford OX2 OEL, England. TEL 44-1865-206206. FAX 44-1865-721205. *2937*

JOURNAL OF FLOW VISUALIZATION AND IMAGE PROCESSING.
Begell House Inc., 79 Madison Ave., New York, NY 10016-7892. TEL 212-725-1999. FAX 212-213-8368. *2760*

JOURNAL OF FLUENCY DISORDERS.
Elsevier Science Inc., Box 945, New York, NY 10159-0945. TEL 212-633-3730. FAX 212-633-3680. *5857*

JOURNAL OF FLUID CONTROL.
Delbridge Publishing Co., P.O. Box 2694, Saratoga, CA 95070-0694. TEL 408-446-3131. FAX 408-446-3131. *2760*

JOURNAL OF FLUIDS ENGINEERING.
American Society of Mechanical Engineers, 22 Law Dr., Fairfield, NJ 07007-2300. *2744*

JOURNAL OF FLUORESCENCE.
Plenum Publishing Corp., 233 Spring St., New York, NY 10013-1578. TEL 212-620-8000. FAX 212-463-0742. *1731*

JOURNAL OF FLUORINE CHEMISTRY.
Elsevier Science S.A., P.O. Box 564, CH-1001 Lausanne 1, Switzerland. TEL 41-21-3207381. FAX 41-21-3235444. *1732*

JOURNAL OF FOLKLORE RESEARCH.
Indiana University, Folklore Institute, 504 North Fess, Bloomington, IN 47405. TEL 812-855-8049. FAX 812-855-4008. *2953*

JOURNAL OF FOOD ENGINEERING.
Elsevier Science Ltd., P.O. Box 800, Kidlington, Oxford OX5 1DX, England. TEL 44-1865-843000. FAX 44-1865-843010. *2980*

JOURNAL OF FOOD PRODUCTS MARKETING.
Haworth Press, Inc., 10 Alice St., Binghamton, NY 13904. TEL 607-722-5857. FAX 607-722-1424. *2980*

JOURNAL OF FOOD PROTECTION.
International Association of Milk, Food and Environmental Sanitarians, Inc., 6200 Aurora Ave., Ste. 200 W, Des Moines, IA 50322. TEL 515-276-3344. FAX 515-276-8655. *5967*

JOURNAL OF FOOD SCIENCE AND TECHNOLOGY.
Association of Food Scientists and Technologists (India), Central Executive Committee, CFTRI Campus, Mysore 570 013, India. TEL 28157. FAX 521747. *2980*

JOURNAL OF FOOT AND ANKLE SURGERY.
Williams & Wilkins, 351 W. Camden St., Baltimore, MD 21201. TEL 410-528-4000. FAX 410-528-4312. *4912*

JOURNAL OF FORAMINIFERAL RESEARCH.
Cushman Foundation for Foraminiferal Research, Invertebrate Paleontology, Museum of Comparative Zoology, Harvard University, Cambridge, MA 02138. *5314*

JOURNAL OF FORECASTING.
John Wiley & Sons Ltd., Journals, Baffins Ln., Chichester, W. Sussex PO19 1UD, England. TEL 44-1243-779777. FAX 44-1243-843232. *1427*

JOURNAL OF FORENSIC ECONOMICS.
National Association of Forensic Economics, Box 30067, Kansas City, MO 64112. TEL 816-235-2833. FAX 816-235-5263. *1257*

JOURNAL OF FORENSIC IDENTIFICATION.
International Association for Identification, Box 2423-0247, Alameda, CA 94501. TEL 510-865-2174. FAX 510-865-2167. *4687*

JOURNAL OF FORENSIC MEDICINE.
Ministry of Justice, Institute of Forensic Sciences, 1347 West Guangfu Rd., Shanghai 200063, People's Republic of China. TEL 021-2440148. FAX 021-2442691. *4687*

JOURNAL OF FORENSIC SCIENCES.
American Society for Testing and Materials, 100 Barr Harbor Dr., W. Conshohocken, PA 19428-2959. TEL 610-832-9500. FAX 610-832-9555. *4687*

JOURNAL OF FORESTRY.
Society of American Foresters, 5400 Grosvenor Ln., Bethesda, MD 20814. TEL 301-897-8720. FAX 301-897-3690. *3020*

JOURNAL OF FRESHWATER ECOLOGY.
Oikos Publishers, Inc., Box 2558, La Crosse, WI 54602-2558. TEL 608-526-9577. FAX 608-526-9477. *2287*

JOURNAL OF FUNCTIONAL ANALYSIS.
Academic Press, Inc., Journal Division, 525 B St., Ste. 1900, San Diego, CA 92101-4495. TEL 619-230-1840. FAX 619-699-6800. *4373*

JOURNAL OF FUNCTIONAL AND LOGIC PROGRAMMING.
M I T Press, 55 Hayward St., Cambridge, MA 02142-1399. TEL 617-253-2889. FAX 617-258-6779. *2045*

JOURNAL OF FUSION ENERGY.
Plenum Publishing Corp., 233 Spring St., New York, NY 10013-1578. TEL 212-620-8000. FAX 212-463-0742. *2578*

JOURNAL OF GAMBLING STUDIES.
Human Sciences Press, Inc. 233 Spring St., New York, NY 10013-1578. TEL 212-620-8000. FAX 212-463-0742. *4845*

JOURNAL OF GARDEN HISTORY.
Taylor & Francis Ltd., 1 Gunpowder Sq., London EC4A 3DE, England. TEL 44-171-583-0490. FAX 44-171-583-0585. *3059*

JOURNAL OF GAY & LESBIAN PSYCHOTHERAPY.
Haworth Press, Inc., 10 Alice St., Binghamton, NY 13904. TEL 607-722-5857. FAX 607-722-1424. *3533*

JOURNAL OF GAY & LESBIAN SOCIAL SERVICES.
Haworth Press, Inc., 10 Alice St., Binghamton, NY 13904-1580. TEL 607-722-5857. FAX 607-722-1424. *6379*

JOURNAL OF GAY, LESBIAN & BISEXUAL IDENTITY.
Human Sciences Press, Inc. 233 Spring St., New York, NY 10013-1578. TEL 212-620-8000. FAX 212-643 0742. *3533*

THE JOURNAL OF GEMMOLOGY.
Gemmological Association and Gem Testing Laboratory of Great Britain, 27 Greville St., London EC1N 8SU, England. TEL 44-171-404-3334. FAX 44-171-404-8843. *3697*

JOURNAL OF GENDER, CULTURE AND HEALTH.
Plenum Publishing Corp., 233 Spring St., New York, NY 10013-1578. TEL 212-620-8000. FAX 212-463-0742. *2481*

JOURNAL OF GENDER STUDIES.
Carfax Publishing Co., P.O. Box 25, Abingdon, Oxon. OX14 3UE, England. TEL 44-1235-401000. FAX 44-1235-401550. *7017*

JOURNAL OF GENERAL EDUCATION.
Pennsylvania State University Press, 820 N. University Dr. Ste. C, University Park, PA 16802-1003. TEL 814-865-1327. FAX 814-863-1408. *2346*

JOURNAL OF GENERAL INTERNAL MEDICINE.
Blackwell Science Inc., 238 Main St., Cambridge, MA 02142. TEL 617-876-7000. *4707*

JOURNAL OF GENERAL PHYSIOLOGY.
Rockefeller University Press, 222 E. 70th St., New York, NY 10021. TEL 212-327-8572. FAX 212-327-7944. *789*

THE JOURNAL OF GENERAL PSYCHOLOGY.
Heldref Publications, 1319 Eighteenth St., N.W., Washington, DC 20036. TEL 202-296-6267. FAX 202-296-5149. *5857*

JOURNAL OF GENETIC COUNSELING.
Human Sciences Press, Inc. 233 Spring St., New York, NY 10013-1578. TEL 212-620-8432. FAX 212-463-0742. *5857*

THE JOURNAL OF GENETIC PSYCHOLOGY.
Heldref Publications, 1319 Eighteenth St., N.W., Washington, DC 20036-1802. TEL 202-296-6267. FAX 202-296-5149. *5857*

JOURNAL OF GENETICS & BREEDING.
Istituto Sperimentale per la Cerealicoltura, Via Cassia, 176, 00191 Rome, Italy. TEL 39-6-3295705. FAX 39-6-36306022. *129*

JOURNAL OF GEOCHEMICAL EXPLORATION.
Elsevier Science B.V., P.O. Box 211, 1000 AE Amsterdam, Netherlands. TEL 31-20-4853911. FAX 31-20-4853598. *2211*

JOURNAL OF GEODYNAMICS.
Elsevier Science Ltd., Pergamon, P.O. Box 800, Kidlington, Oxford OX5 1DX, England. TEL 44-1865-843000. FAX 44-1865-843010. *2277*

JOURNAL OF GEOGRAPHICAL SCIENCE.
National Taiwan University, Department of Geography, National Taiwan University, Taipei, Taiwan, Republic of China. TEL 886-2-3629908. FAX 886-2-3622911. *3263*

JOURNAL OF GEOGRAPHY IN HIGHER EDUCATION.
Carfax Publishing Co., P.O. Box 25, Abingdon, Oxon. OX14 3UE, England. TEL 44-1235-401000. FAX 44-1235-401550. *3264*

JOURNAL OF GEOLOGY.
University of Chicago Press, Journals Division, Box 37005, Chicago, IL 60637. TEL 312-753-3347. FAX 312-753-0811. *2246*

JOURNAL OF GEOMETRY AND PHYSICS.
North-Holland P.O. Box 211, 1000 AE Amsterdam, Netherlands. TEL 31-20-4853911. FAX 31-20-4853598. *4373*

JOURNAL OF GEOSCIENCE EDUCATION.
National Association of Geoscience Teachers, Inc., Box 5443, Bellingham, WA 98227-5443. TEL 360-650-3587. FAX 360-650-7302. *2246*

JOURNAL OF GEOSCIENCES.
Osaka City University, Department of Geosciences, Faculty of Science, 3-3-138 Sugimoto, Sumiyoshi-ku, Osaka 558, Japan. TEL 81-6-605-2587. FAX 81-6-605-2522. *2211*

JOURNAL OF GEOTECHNICAL ENGINEERING.
American Society of Civil Engineers, 345 E. 47th St., New York, NY 10017-2398. TEL 212-705-7288. FAX 212-980-4681. *2665*

JOURNAL OF GERIATRIC DERMATOLOGY.
Health Management Publications, Inc., 950 W Valley Rd., Ste. 2800, Wayne, PA 19037. TEL 215-337-4466. FAX 215-337-0890. *3290*

JOURNAL OF GERIATRIC DRUG THERAPY.
Haworth Press, Inc., 10 Alice St., Binghamton, NY 13904. TEL 607-722-5857. FAX 607-722-1424. *5421*

JOURNAL OF GERIATRIC PSYCHIATRY.
International Universities Press, Inc., 59 Boston Post Rd., Box 1524, Madison, CT 06443-1524. TEL 203-245-4000. FAX 203-245-0775. *4845*

JOURNAL OF GERONTOLOGICAL NURSING.
Slack, Inc., 6900 Grove Rd., Thorofare, NJ 08086-9447. TEL 609-848-1000. FAX 609-853-5991. *3290*

JOURNAL OF GERONTOLOGICAL SOCIAL WORK.
Haworth Press, Inc., 10 Alice St., Binghamton, NY 13904. TEL 607-722-5857. FAX 607-722-1424. *3290*

JOURNAL OF GLAUCOMA.
Lippincott - Raven Publishers 227 E. Washington Sq., Philadelphia, PA 19106. TEL 215-238-4200. *4772*

JOURNAL OF GLOBAL BUSINESS.
Association for Global Business, Box 1381, Harrisonburg, VA 22801. TEL 540-433-7403. FAX 540-433-7403. *937*

JOURNAL OF GLOBAL MARKETING.
Haworth Press, Inc., 10 Alice St., Binghamton, NY 13904. TEL 607-722-9678. FAX 607-722-1424. *1471*

JOURNAL OF GLOBAL OPTIMIZATION.
Kluwer Academic Publishers, Postbus 17, 3300 AA Dordrecht, Netherlands. TEL 31-78-6392392. FAX 31-78-6392254. *6306*

JOURNAL OF GOVERNMENT INFORMATION.
Elsevier Science Ltd., Pergamon, P.O. Box 800, Kidington, Oxford OX5 1DX, England. TEL 44-1865-843000. FAX 44-1865-843010. *5908*

JOURNAL OF GRAPH THEORY.
John Wiley & Sons, Inc., Journals, 605 Third Ave., New York, NY 10158. TEL 212-850-6645. FAX 212-850-6021. *4373*

JOURNAL OF GRAPHICS TOOLS.
A.K. Peters, Ltd., 289 Linden St., Wellesley, MA 02181. TEL 617-235-2210. FAX 617-235-2404. *2028*

JOURNAL OF GREAT LAKES RESEARCH.
International Association for Great Lakes Research, c/o Thomas J. Murphy, Ed., Dept. of Chemistry, DePaul University, 1036 W. Belden Ave., Chicago, IL 60614. TEL 312-325-7422. FAX 312-325-7421. *2807*

JOURNAL OF GROUP PSYCHOTHERAPY, PSYCHODRAMA & SOCIOMETRY.
Heldref Publications, 1319 Eighteenth St., N.W., Washington, DC 20036 1802. TEL 202-296-6267. FAX 202-296-5149. *5857*

JOURNAL OF GUIDANCE, CONTROL, AND DYNAMICS.
American Institute of Aeronautics and Astronautics, Inc., 370 L'Enfant Promenade, S.W., Washington, DC 20024. TEL 202-646-7400. *71*

JOURNAL OF GYNECOLOGIC SURGERY.
Mary Ann Liebert, Inc. Publishers, 2 Madison Ave., Larchmont, NY 10538. TEL 914-834-3100. FAX 914-834-3688. *4739*

JOURNAL OF GYNECOLOGIC TECHNIQUES.
Churchill Livingstone, 650 Ave. of the Americas, New York, NY 10011. TEL 212-206-5040. FAX 212-727-7808. *4739*

JOURNAL OF HAND SURGERY: AMERICAN VOLUME.
Churchill Livingstone 650 Ave. of the Americas, New York, NY 10011. TEL 212-206-5040. FAX 212-727-7808. *4912*

JOURNAL OF HAND THERAPY.
Hanley & Belfus, Inc., 210 S. 13th St., Philadelphia, PA 19107. TEL 215-546-7293. FAX 215-790-9330. *4817*

JOURNAL OF HAZARDOUS MATERIALS.
Elsevier Science B.V., P.O. Box 211, 1000 AE Amsterdam, Netherlands. TEL 31-20-4853911. FAX 31-20-4853598. *2854*

JOURNAL OF HEAD TRAUMA REHABILITATION.
Aspen Publishers, Inc., 200 Orchard Ridge Dr., Gaithersburg, MD 20878. FAX 301-417-7550. *4786*

JOURNAL OF HEALTH AND HUMAN SERVICES ADMINISTRATION.
Southern Public Administration Education Foundation, Pennsylvania State University at Harrisburg, Division of Public Affairs, Middletown, PA 17057. TEL 717-948-6363. FAX 717-540-1383. *3551*

JOURNAL OF HEALTH AND SOCIAL BEHAVIOR.
American Sociological Association, 1722 N St., N.W., Washington, DC 20036. TEL 202-833-3410. FAX 202-785-0146. *6419*

JOURNAL OF HEALTH & SOCIAL POLICY.
Haworth Press, Inc., 10 Alice St., Binghamton, NY 13904. TEL 607-722-5857. FAX 607-722-1424. *6379*

JOURNAL OF HEALTH CARE CHAPLAINCY.
Haworth Press, Inc., 10 Alice St., Binghamton, NY 13904. TEL 607-722-5857. FAX 607-722-1424. *5531*

JOURNAL OF HEALTH CARE FOR THE POOR AND UNDERSERVED.
Sage Publications, Inc., 2455 Teller Rd., Thousand Oaks, CA 91320. TEL 805-499-0721. FAX 805-499-0721. *4481*

JOURNAL OF HEALTH COMMUNICATION.
Taylor & Francis Inc., 1900 Frost Rd., Ste. 101, Bristol, PA 19007-1598. TEL 215-785-5800. FAX 215-785-5515. *4481*

JOURNAL OF HEALTH ECONOMICS.
North-Holland P.O. Box 211, 1000 AE Amsterdam, Netherlands. TEL 31-20-4853911. FAX 31-20-4853598. *5967*

JOURNAL OF HEALTH EDUCATION.
American Alliance for Health, Physical Education, Recreation, and Dance, 1900 Association Dr., Reston, VA 22091. TEL 703-476-3400. FAX 703-476-9527. *2492*

JOURNAL OF HEALTH POLITICS, POLICY AND LAW.
Duke University Press, Box 90660, Durham, NC 27708-0660. TEL 919-687-3600. FAX 919-687-4574. *4481*

JOURNAL OF HEALTHCARE RESOURCE MANAGEMENT.
Mayworm Associates, Inc., 507 N. Milwaukee Ave., Libertyville, IL 60048-2018. TEL 847-680-7878. FAX 847-680-8180. *3551*

JOURNAL OF HEALTHCARE RISK MANAGEMENT.
American Hospital Association, One North Franklin, Chicago, IL 60606. TEL 312-422-3989. FAX 312-422-4580. *3551*

THE JOURNAL OF HEART AND LUNG TRANSPLANTATION.
Mosby - Year Book, Inc. 11830 Westline Industrial Dr., St. Louis, MO 63146-3318. TEL 314-872-8370. FAX 314-432-1380. *4912*

JOURNAL OF HEART VALVE DISEASE.
I C R Publishers Ltd., 9 West End Ct., West End Ave., Pinner, Middx. HA5 1BP, England. TEL 44-1923-836873. *4606*

JOURNAL OF HEAT TRANSFER.
American Society of Mechanical Engineers, 22 Law Dr., Fairfield, NJ 07007-2300. *2760*

JOURNAL OF HELLENIC STUDIES.
Society for the Promotion of Hellenic Studies, 31-34 Gordon Sq., London WC1H OPP, England. TEL 44-171-387-7495. *1823*

JOURNAL OF HELMINTHOLOGY.
CAB International, Wallingford, Oxon OX10 8DE, England. TEL 44-1491-832111. FAX 44-1491-826090. *4623*

JOURNAL OF HEMATOTHERAPY.
Mary Ann Liebert, Inc. Publishers, 2 Madison Ave., Larchmont, NY 10538. TEL 914-834-3100. FAX 914-834-3688. *4701*

JOURNAL OF HEPATOLOGY.
Munksgaard International Publishers Ltd., 35 Noerre Soegade, P.O. Box 2148, DK-1016 Copenhagen K, Denmark. TEL 45-33-127030. FAX 45-33-129387. *4694*

JOURNAL OF HERBS, SPICES & MEDICINAL PLANTS.
Haworth Press, Inc., 10 Alice St., Binghamton, NY 13904. TEL 607-722-5857. FAX 607-722-1424. *3059*

JOURNAL OF HEREDITY.
Oxford University Press, Journals, 2001 Evans Rd., Cary, NC 27513. TEL 919-677-0977. FAX 919-677-1714. *746*

JOURNAL OF HERPETOLOGY.
Society for the Study of Amphibians and Reptiles, Box 626, Hays, KS 67601-0626. *810*

JOURNAL OF HEURISTICS.
Kluwer Academic Publishers Boston, Box 358, Accord Sta., Hingham, MA 02018-0358. TEL 617-871-6600. FAX 617-871-6528. *5482*

JOURNAL OF HIGH SPEED NETWORKS.
I O S Press, Van Diemenstraat 94, 1013 CN Amsterdam, Netherlands. TEL 31-20-6382189. FAX 31-20-6203419. *2039*

THE JOURNAL OF HIGHER CRITICISM.
Institute for Higher Critical Studies, Drew University Theological School, 36 Madison Ave., Madison, NJ 07940. TEL 201-408-3000. *6071*

JOURNAL OF HIGHER EDUCATION.
Ohio State University Press, 1070 Carmack Rd., Columbus, OH 43210. TEL 614-292-6930. *2434*

JOURNAL OF HISTOCHEMISTRY AND CYTOCHEMISTRY.
Histochemical Society, P.O. Box 1023, Planetarium Station, New York, NY 10024-1023. TEL 212-362-1801. FAX 212-874-8313. *716*

JOURNAL OF HISTORICAL SOCIOLOGY.
Blackwell Publishers Ltd., 108 Cowley Rd., Oxford OX4 1JF, England. TEL 44-1865-791100. FAX 44-1865-791347. *6420*

JOURNAL OF HISTOTECHNOLOGY.
National Society for Histotechnology, 4201 Northview Dr., Ste. 502, Bowie, MD 20716-1073. TEL 301-262-6221. FAX 301-262-9188. *716*

JOURNAL OF HIV - AIDS PREVENTION & EDUCATION FOR ADOLESCENTS & CHILDREN.
Haworth Press, Inc., 10 Alice St., Binghamton, NY 13904-1580. FAX 607-722-6362. *4624*

THE JOURNAL OF HOLOCAUST EDUCATION.
Frank Cass, Newbury House, 890-900 Eastern Ave., Newbury Park, Ilford, Essex 1G2 7HH, England. TEL 44-181-599-8866. FAX 44-181-599-0984. *3422*

JOURNAL OF HOMOSEXUALITY.
Haworth Press, Inc., 10 Alice St., Binghamton, NY 13904. TEL 607-722-5857. FAX 607-722-1424. *3533*

JOURNAL OF HOSPITAL MARKETING.
Haworth Press, Inc., 10 Alice St., Binghamton, NY 13904. TEL 607-722-5857. FAX 607-722-1424. *1471*

JOURNAL OF HOSPITALITY & LEISURE MARKETING.
Haworth Press, Inc., 10 Alice St., Binghamton, NY 13904-1580. TEL 607-722-5857. FAX 607-722-1424. *3566*

JOURNAL OF HOUSING FOR THE ELDERLY.
Haworth Press, Inc., 10 Alice St., Binghamton, NY 13904. TEL 607-722-5857. FAX 607-722-1424. *3291*

JOURNAL OF HOUSING RESEARCH.
Federal National Mortgage Association, 3900 Wisconsin Ave., N.W., Washington, DC 20016-2899. TEL 202-752-4422. FAX 202-752-4933. *3586*

JOURNAL OF HUMAN ECOLOGY.
Kamla-Raj Enterprises, 2273 Gali Bari Paharwali, Chawri Bazar, Delhi 110 006, India. TEL 3284126. *2807*

JOURNAL OF HUMAN JUSTICE.
Human Justice Collective, Dept. of Anthropology and Sociology, U. of British Columbia, 6303 N.W. Marine Dr., Vancouver, BC V6T 2B2, Canada. TEL 604-228-2240. *6420*

JOURNAL OF HUMAN LACTATION.
Human Sciences Press, Inc. 233 Spring St., New York, NY 10013. TEL 212-620-8000. FAX 212-463-0742. *4740*

JOURNAL OF HUMAN NUTRITION AND DIETETICS.
Blackwell Science Ltd., Osney Mead, Oxford OX2 OEL, England. TEL 44-1865-206206. FAX 44-1865-721205. *5235*

JOURNAL OF HUMAN VALUES.
Sage Publications India Pvt. Ltd., P.O. Box 4215, New Delhi 110 048, India. TEL 91-11-644-4958. FAX 91-11-647-2426. *5482*

JOURNAL OF HYDRAULIC ENGINEERING (NEW YORK).
American Society of Civil Engineers, 345 E. 47th St., New York, NY 10017-2398. TEL 212-705-7288. FAX 212-980-4681. *2665*

JOURNAL OF HYDRODYNAMICS.
China Ocean Press, International Cooperation Department, Haimao Dalou, 1 Fuxingmenwai Dajie, Beijing 100860, People's Republic of China. TEL 8032211. FAX 8033515. *5554*

JOURNAL OF HYDROLOGY.
Elsevier Science B.V., P.O. Box 211, 1000 AE Amsterdam, Netherlands. TEL 31-20-4853911. FAX 31-20-4853598. *2287*

JOURNAL OF HYDROLOGY. NEW ZEALAND.
New Zealand Hydrological Society, P.O. Box 12-300, Wellington, New Zealand. TEL 64-3-3256701. FAX 64-3-3252418. *2287*

JOURNAL OF IMAGE GUIDED SURGERY.
John Wiley & Sons, Inc., Journals, 605 Third Ave., New York, NY 10158-0012. TEL 212-850-6645. FAX 212-850-6021. *4912*

THE JOURNAL OF IMAGING SCIENCE AND TECHNOLOGY.
Society for Imaging Science and Technology, 7003 Kilworth Ln., Springfield, VA 22151. TEL 703-642-9090. FAX 703-642-9094. *5514*

JOURNAL OF IMMUNOASSAY.
Marcel Dekker Journals, 270 Madison Ave., New York, NY 10016. TEL 212-696-9000. FAX 212-685-4540. *5421*

JOURNAL OF IMMUNOLOGICAL METHODS.
Elsevier Science B.V., P.O. Box 211, 1000 AE Amsterdam, Netherlands. TEL 31-20-4853911. FAX 31-20-4853598. *4584*

JOURNAL OF IMMUNOLOGY.
American Association of Immunologists, 9650 Rockville Pike, Bethesda, MD 20814. TEL 301-530-7178. FAX 301-571-1831. *4585*

JOURNAL OF IMMUNOTHERAPY WITH EMPHASIS ON TUMOR IMMUNOLOGY.
Lippincott - Raven Publishers 227 E. Washington Sq., Philadelphia, PA 19106. TEL 215-238-4200. FAX 215-238-4235. *4585*

THE JOURNAL OF IMPERIAL AND COMMONWEALTH HISTORY.
Frank Cass, Newbury House, 890-900 Eastern Ave., Newbury Park, Ilford, Essex IG2 7HH, England. TEL 44-181-599-8866. FAX 44-181-599-0984. *3349*

JOURNAL OF INCLUSION PHENOMENA AND MOLECULAR RECOGNITION IN CHEMISTRY.
Kluwer Academic Publishers, Postbus 17, 3300 AA Dordrecht, Netherlands. TEL 31-78-6392392. FAX 31-78-6392254. *1753*

JOURNAL OF INDIAN PHILOSOPHY.
Kluwer Academic Publishers, Postbus 17, 3300 AA Dordrecht, Netherlands. TEL 31-78-6392392. FAX 31-78-6392254. *5482*

JOURNAL OF INDIGENOUS STUDIES.
Gabriel Dumont Institute of Native Studies and Applied Research, 505 - 23rd St., E., Saskatoon, SK S7K 4K7, Canada. TEL 306-934-4941. FAX 306-244-0252. *314*

JOURNAL OF INDIVIDUAL EMPLOYMENT RIGHTS.
Baywood Publishing Co., Inc., 26 Austin Ave., Box 337, Amityville, NY 11701. TEL 516-691-1270. FAX 516-691-1770. *1382*

JOURNAL OF INDO-EUROPEAN STUDIES.
Institute for the Study of Man, Box 34070, N.W., Washington, DC 20043. TEL 202-371-2700. FAX 202-371-1523. *6331*

JOURNAL OF INDUSTRIAL ECONOMICS.
Blackwell Publishers Ltd., 108 Cowley Rd., Oxford OX4 1JF, England. TEL 44-1865-791100. FAX 44-1865-791347. *937*

JOURNAL OF INDUSTRIAL MICROBIOLOGY.
Stockton Press Houndmills, Basingstoke, Hampshire RG21 2XS, England. TEL 01256-817245. FAX 01256-28339. *663*

JOURNAL OF INDUSTRIAL RELATIONS.
Industrial Relations Society of Australia, c/o Braham Dabscheck, Ed., School of Industrial Relations and Organisational Behaviour, Univ.of N.S.W., Sydney, N.S.W. 2052, Australia. TEL 61-2-3852148. FAX 61-2-6628531. *1382*

JOURNAL OF INFECTION AND CHEMOTHERAPY.
Churchill Livingstone Japan, Churchill Bldg., 2-8-16 Yutenji, Meguro-ku, Tokyo 153, Japan. TEL 81-3-5721-0442. FAX 81-5721-0415. *5422*

JOURNAL OF INFECTIOUS DISEASE PHARMACOTHERAPY.
Haworth Press, Inc., Pharmaceutical Products Press, 10 Alice St., Binghamton, NY 13904. TEL 607-722-5857. FAX 607-722-6362. *5422*

JOURNAL OF INFECTIOUS DISEASES.
University of Chicago Press, Journals Division, Box 37005, Chicago, IL 60637. TEL 312-753-3347. FAX 312-753-0811. *4624*

JOURNAL OF INFLAMMATION.
John Wiley & Sons, Inc., Journals, 605 Third Ave., New York, NY 10158. TEL 212-850-6645. FAX 212-850-6021. *4606*

JOURNAL OF INFORMATION & OPTIMIZATION SCIENCES.
Analytic Publishing Co., F-23 Model Town, Delhi-110009, India. TEL 7129726. *4374*

JOURNAL OF INFORMATION SCIENCE - PRINCIPLES AND PRACTICE.
Bowker - Saur Ltd., A member of the Reed Elsevier plc group, Maypole House, Maypole Rd., E. Grinstead, W. Sussex RH19 1HU, England. TEL 44-1342-330100. FAX 44-1342-330192. *4002*

JOURNAL OF INFORMATION TECHNOLOGY.
Chapman & Hall, Journals Department 2-6 Boundary Row, London SE1 8HN, England. TEL 44-171-8650066. FAX 44-171-5229623. *4002*

JOURNAL OF INFORMATION TECHNOLOGY FOR TEACHER EDUCATION.
Triangle Journals Ltc., P.O. Box 65, Wallingford, Oxon. OX10 0YG, England. TEL 44-1491-838013. FAX 44-1491-334958. *2492*

JOURNAL OF INHERITED METABOLIC DISEASE.
Kluwer Academic Publishers, Postbus 17, 3300 AA Dordrecht, Netherlands. TEL 31-78-6392392. FAX 31-78-6392254. *4807*

JOURNAL OF INORGANIC AND ORGANOMETALLIC POLYMERS.
Plenum Publishing Corp., 233 Spring St., New York, NY 10013-1578. TEL 212-620-8000. FAX 212-463-0742. *1739*

JOURNAL OF INORGANIC BIOCHEMISTRY.
Elsevier Science Inc. Box 945, New York, NY 10159-0945. TEL 212-633-3730. FAX 212-633-3680. *642*

JOURNAL OF INSECT BEHAVIOR.
Plenum Publishing Corp., 233 Spring St., New York, NY 10013-1578. TEL 212-620-8000. FAX 212-463-0742. *731*

JOURNAL OF INSECT PHYSIOLOGY.
Elsevier Science Ltd., Pergamon, P.O. Box 800, Kidlington, Oxford CX5 1DX, England. TEL 44-1865-843000. FAX 44-1865-843010. *731*

JOURNAL OF INSURANCE REGULATION.
National Association of Insurance Commissioners, 120 W. 12th St., Kansas City, MO 64105. TEL 816-374-7259. *3655*

JOURNAL OF INTELLECTUAL DISABILITY RESEARCH.
Blackwell Science Ltd., Osney Mead, Oxford OX2 0EL, England. TEL 44-1865-206206. FAX 44-1865-721205. *4845*

JOURNAL OF INTELLIGENT AND FUZZY SYSTEMS.
John Wiley & Sons, Inc., Journals, 605 Third Ave., New York, NY 10158. TEL 212-850-6645. FAX 212-850-6021. *4374*

JOURNAL OF INTELLIGENT AND ROBOTIC SYSTEMS.
Kluwer Academic Publishers, Postbus 17, 3300 AA Dordrecht, Netherlands. TEL 31-78-6392392. FAX 31-78-6392254. *2009*

JOURNAL OF INTELLIGENT INFORMATION SYSTEMS.
Kluwer Academic Publishers Boston, Box 358, Accord Sta., Hingham, MA 02018-0358. TEL 617-871-6600. FAX 617-871-6528. *2009*

JOURNAL OF INTELLIGENT MANUFACTURING.
Chapman & Hall, Journals Department 2-6 Boundary Row, London SE1 8HN, England. TEL 44-171-8650066. FAX 44-171-5229624. *2016*

JOURNAL OF INTELLIGENT MATERIAL SYSTEMS AND STUCTURES.
Technomic Publishing Co., Inc., 851 New Holland Ave., Box 3535, Lancaster, PA 17604. TEL 717-291-5609. FAX 717-295-4538. *6251*

JOURNAL OF INTENSIVE CARE MEDICINE.
Blackwell Science Inc., 238 Main St., Cambridge, MA 02142-1413. TEL 617-876-7022. FAX 617-492-5263. *4482*

JOURNAL OF INTERAMERICAN STUDIES AND WORLD AFFAIRS.
University of Miami, North - South Center Publications, Box 248205, Coral Gables, FL 33124-3027. TEL 305-284-8914. FAX 305-284-5083. *5759*

JOURNAL OF INTERDISCIPLINARY HISTORY.
MIT Press, 55 Hayward St., Cambridge, MA 02142. TEL 617-253-2889. FAX 617-577-1545. *3349*

JOURNAL OF INTERDISCIPLINARY STUDIES.
Institute for Interdisciplinary Research, 2828 Third St., Ste. 11, Santa Monica, CA 90405-4150. TEL 310-396-0517. *3617*

JOURNAL OF INTERFERON & CYTOKINE RESEARCH.
Mary Ann Liebert, Inc. Publishers, 2 Madison Ave., Larchmont, NY 10538. TEL 914-834-3100. FAX 914-834-3688. *4585*

JOURNAL OF INTERIOR DESIGN.
Interior Design Educators Council Inc., c/o Denise Guerin, University of Minnesota, 240 McNeal Hall, 1985 Buford Ave., St. Paul, MN 55108. TEL 612-626-1257. FAX 612-624-2750. *3679*

JOURNAL OF INTERLIBRARY LOAN, DOCUMENT DELIVERY & INFORMATION SUPPLY.
Haworth Press, Inc., 10 Alice St., Binghamton, NY 13904. TEL 607-722-5857. FAX 607-722-1424. *4002*

JOURNAL OF INTERNAL MEDICINE.
Blackwell Science Ltd., Osney Mead, Oxford OX2 0EL, England. TEL 44-1865-206206. FAX 44-1865-721205. *4707*

JOURNAL OF INTERNATIONAL BUSINESS STUDIES.
University of Western Ontario, Western Business School, London, ON N6A 3K7, Canada. TEL 519-661-4031. FAX 519-66-3700. *937*

JOURNAL OF INTERNATIONAL CONSUMER MARKETING.
Haworth Press, Inc., 10 Alice St. Binghamton, NY 13904. TEL 607-722-5857. FAX 607-722-1424. *1471*

JOURNAL OF INTERNATIONAL DEVELOPMENT.
John Wiley & Sons Ltd., Journals, Baffins Ln., Chichester, W. Sussex PO19 1UD, England. TEL 44-1243-779777. FAX 44-1243-843232. *6331*

JOURNAL OF INTERNATIONAL ECONOMICS.
North-Holland P.O. Box 211, 1000 AE Amsterdam, Netherlands. TEL 31-20-4853911. FAX 31-20-4853598. *937*

JOURNAL OF INTERNATIONAL FINANCIAL MANAGEMENT AND ACCOUNTING.
Blackwell Publishers Ltd. 108 Cowley Rd., Oxford OX4 1JF, England. TEL 44-1865-791100. *1105*

JOURNAL OF INTERNATIONAL FOOD & AGRIBUSINESS MARKETING.
Haworth Press, Inc., 10 Alice St., Binghamton, NY 13904. TEL 607-722-5857. FAX 607-722-1424. *194*

JOURNAL OF INTERNATIONAL HOSPITALITY, LEISURE AND TOURISM MANAGEMENT.
Haworth Press, Inc., Food Products Press, 10 Alice St., Binghamton, NY 13904. TEL 607-722-6362. FAX 800-895-0582. *366*

JOURNAL OF INTERNATIONAL INFORMATION MANAGEMENT.
International Information Management Association, Department of Information and Decision Sciences, California State University, San Bernardino, CA 92407. TEL 909-880-5186. FAX 909-880-5994. *1427*

JOURNAL OF INTERNATIONAL MANAGEMENT.
John Wiley & Sons, Inc., Journals, 605 Third Ave., New York, NY 10158. TEL 212-850-6645. FAX 212-820-6021. *1427*

JOURNAL OF INTERNATIONAL MARKETING.
Michigan State University Press Manly Miles Bldg., Ste. 25, 1405 S. Harrison Rd., East Lansing, MI 48823-5202. TEL 517-355-9543. FAX 517-432-2611. *1471*

JOURNAL OF INTERNATIONAL MEDICAL RESEARCH.
Cambridge Medical Publications Ltd., Wicker House, High St., Worthing, W. Sussex BN11 1DJ, England. TEL 01903-205884. FAX 01903-234862. *4482*

JOURNAL OF INTERNATIONAL MONEY AND FINANCE.
Butterworth - Heinemann, Part of the Reed Elsevier group, Linacre House, Jordan Hill, Oxford OX2 8DP, England. TEL 44-1865-310366. FAX 44-1865-310898. *1105*

JOURNAL OF INTERNATIONAL SELLING & SALES MANAGEMENT.
European Marketing Association, 18 St. Peters Steps, Brixham, Devon, England. *1471*

JOURNAL OF INTERNATIONAL STUDIES.
Sophia University, Institute of International Relations, 7-1 Kioi-cho, Chiyoda-ku, Tokyo 102, Japan. TEL 03-3238-3561. FAX 03-3238-3592. *5759*

JOURNAL OF INTERPROFESSIONAL CARE.
Carfax Publishing Co., P.O. Box 25, Abingdon, Oxon. OX14 3UE, England. TEL 44-1235-401000. FAX 44-1235-401550. *4482*

JOURNAL OF INTERVENTIONAL CARDIAC ELECTROPHYSIOLOGY.
Kluwer Academic Publishers, Postbus 17, 3300 AA Dordrecht, Netherlands. TEL 31-78-6392392. FAX 31-78-6392254. *4606*

JOURNAL OF INTERVENTIONAL CARDIOLOGY.
Futura Publishing Company, Inc., 135 Bedford Rd., Box 418, Armonk, NY 10504-0418. TEL 914-273-1014. FAX 914-273-1015. *4606*

JOURNAL OF INTRAVENOUS NURSING.
J.B. Lippincott Co., E. Washington Sq., Philadelphia, PA 19106. TEL 215-238-4200. *4717*

JOURNAL OF INVASIVE CARDIOLOGY.
Health Management Publications, Inc., 950 W Valley Rd., Ste. 2800, Wayne, PA 19087. TEL 215-337-4466. FAX 215-337-0890. *4606*

JOURNAL OF INVERSE AND ILL-POSED PROBLEMS.
V S P, P.O. Box 346, 3700 AH Zeist, Netherlands. TEL 31-30-6925790. FAX 31-30-6932081. *4374*

JOURNAL OF INVERTEBRATE PATHOLOGY.
Academic Press, Inc., Journal Division, 525 B St., Ste. 1900, San Diego, CA 92101-4495. TEL 619-230-1840. FAX 619-699-6800. *731*

JOURNAL OF INVESTIGATIVE DERMATOLOGY.
Blackwell Science Inc., 238 Main St., Cambridge, MA 02142. TEL 617-876-7022. FAX 617-492-5263. *4663*

JOURNAL OF INVESTIGATIVE MEDICINE.
Slack, Inc., 6900 Grove Rd., Thorofare, NJ 08086-9447. TEL 609-848-1000. FAX 609-853-5991. *4687*

JOURNAL OF INVESTIGATIVE SURGERY.
Taylor & Francis Inc., 1900 Frost Rd., Ste. 101, Bristol, PA 19007. TEL 215-785-5800. FAX 215-785-5515. *4912*

JOURNAL OF IRRIGATION AND DRAINAGE.
American Society of Civil Engineers, 345 E. 47th St., New York, NY 10017-2398. TEL 212-705-7288. FAX 212-980-4681. *2665*

THE JOURNAL OF ISRAELI HISTORY.
Frank Cass, Newbury House, 890-900 Eastern Ave., Newbury Park, Ilford, Essex 1G2 7HH, England. TEL 44-181-599-8866. FAX 44-181-599-0984. *3497*

JOURNAL OF JAPANESE STUDIES.
Society for Japanese Studies, University of Washington, Box 353650, Seattle, WA 98195-3650. TEL 206-543-9302. FAX 206-685-0668. *5287*

JOURNAL OF JEWISH COMMUNAL SERVICE.
Jewish Communal Service Association, 3084 State Hwy. 27, Ste. 9, Kendall Park, NJ 08824-1657. TEL 908-821-1871. FAX 908-821-5335. *6379*

JOURNAL OF JEWISH THOUGHT AND PHILOSOPHY.
Harwood Academic Publishers, c/o International Publishers Distributor, P.O. Box 3054, Langhorne, PA 19047-3054. TEL 215-750-2642. FAX 215-750-6343. *6126*

JOURNAL OF LABELLED COMPOUNDS AND RADIOPHARMACEUTICALS.
John Wiley & Sons Ltd., Journals, Baffins Ln., Chichester, W. Sussex PO19 1UD, England. TEL 44-1243-779777. FAX 44-1243-843232. *1717*

JOURNAL OF LABOR ECONOMICS.
University of Chicago Press, Journals Division, Box 37005, Chicago, IL 60637. TEL 312-753-3347. FAX 312-753-0811. *1050*

JOURNAL OF LABOR RESEARCH.
George Mason University, Department of Economics, MSN 3G4, 4400 University Dr., Fairfax, VA 22030-4444. TEL 703-993-1155. FAX 703-993-1133. *1382*

THE JOURNAL OF LABORATORY AND CLINICAL MEDICINE.
Mosby - Year Book, Inc. 11830 Westline Industrial Dr., St. Louis, MO 63146. TEL 314-872-8370. FAX 314-432-1380. *4681*

JOURNAL OF LANGUAGE FOR INTERNATIONAL BUSINESS.
American Graduate School of International Management, Modern Language Department, 15249 N. 59th Ave., Glendale, AZ 85306-6012. TEL 602-978-7249. FAX 602-439-1435. *4079*

JOURNAL OF LASER APPLICATIONS.
Chapman & Hall, Journals Department 2-6 Boundary Row, London SE1 8HN, England. TEL 44-171-8650066. FAX 44-171-5229623. *5605*

JOURNAL OF LATIN AMERICAN LORE.
University of California at Los Angeles, Latin American Center, 10343 Bunche Hall, Box 951447, Los Angeles, CA 90095-1447. TEL 310-825-6634. FAX 310-206-6859. *2953*

JOURNAL OF LAW AND ECONOMICS.
University of Chicago Press, Journals Division, Box 37005, Chicago, IL 60637. TEL 312-753-3347. FAX 312-753-0811. *3797*

JOURNAL OF LAW, ECONOMICS, AND ORGANIZATION.
Oxford University Press, Journals, 2001 Evans Rd., Cary, NC 27513. TEL 919-677-0977. FAX 919-677-1714. *3797*

THE JOURNAL OF LAW, MEDICINE & ETHICS.
American Society of Law, Medicine & Ethics, 765 Commonwealth Ave., Ste. 1634, Boston, MA 02215. TEL 617-262-4990. FAX 617-437-7596. *3797*

JOURNAL OF LEADERSHIP STUDIES.
Baker College, Center for Graduate Studies, 1050 W. Bristol Rd., Flint, MI 48507. TEL 810-766-4105. FAX 810-766-4399. *1428*

JOURNAL OF LEARNING DISABILITIES.
Pro-Ed Inc., 8700 Shoal Creek Blvd., Austin, TX 78757-6897. TEL 512-451-3246. FAX 512-451-8542. *2470*

THE JOURNAL OF LEGAL HISTORY.
Frank Cass, Newbury House, 890-900 Eastern Ave., Newbury Park, Ilford, Essex 1G2 7HH, England. TEL 44-181-599-8866. FAX 44-181-599-0984. *3349*

THE JOURNAL OF LEGAL MEDICINE.
Taylor & Francis Inc., 1900 Frost Rd., Ste. 101, Bristol, PA 19007-1598. TEL 215-785-5800. FAX 215-785-5515. *4482*

JOURNAL OF LEGAL STUDIES.
University of Chicago Press, Journals Division, Box 37005, Chicago, IL 60637. TEL 312-753-3347. FAX 312-753-0811. *3798*

THE JOURNAL OF LEGISLATIVE STUDIES.
Frank Cass, 890-900 Eastern Ave., Newbury Park, Ilford, Essex IG2 7HH, England. TEL 44-181-599-8866. FAX 44-181-599-0984. *5759*

JOURNAL OF LESBIAN STUDIES.
Haworth Press, Inc., 10 Alice St., Binghamton, NY 13904-1580. FAX 607-722-6362. *3534*

JOURNAL OF LIBRARY ADMINISTRATION.
Haworth Press, Inc., 10 Alice St., Binghamton, NY 13904. TEL 607-722-5857. FAX 607-722-1424. *4003*

JOURNAL OF LIE THEORY.
Heldermann Verlag, Langer Graben 13d, 32657 Lemgo, Germany. TEL 49-5261-10226. FAX 49-5261-15264. *4374*

JOURNAL OF LIGHTWAVE TECHNOLOGY.
Institute of Electrical and Electronics Engineers, Inc., 345 E. 47th St., New York, NY 10017-2394. TEL 908-981-0060. FAX 908-981-9667. *5605*

JOURNAL OF LIMITED LIABILITY COMPANIES.
Warren, Gorham & Lamont, One Penn Plaza, New York, NY 10119-4098. TEL 212-971-5423. FAX 212-971-5113. *1551*

JOURNAL OF LIPID MEDIATORS AND CELL SIGNALING.
Elsevier Science B.V., P.O. Box 211, 1000 AE Amsterdam, Netherlands. TEL 31-20-4853911. FAX 31-20-4853598. *642*

JOURNAL OF LIPID RESEARCH.
Federation of American Societies for Experimental Biology, 9650 Rockville Pike, Bethesda, MD 20814. TEL 301-530-7100. FAX 301-571-1855. *642*

JOURNAL OF LIPOSOME RESEARCH.
Marcel Dekker Journals, 270 Madison Ave., New York, NY 10016. TEL 212-696-9000. FAX 212-685-4540. *5422*

JOURNAL OF LIQUID CHROMATOGRAPHY & RELATED TECHNOLOGIES.
Marcel Dekker Journals, 270 Madison Ave., New York, NY 10016. TEL 212-696-9000. FAX 212-685-4540. *1681*

JOURNAL OF LITERARY STUDIES.
University of South Africa, Department of Literary Theory, P.O. Box 392, Pretoria 0001, South Africa. TEL 27-12-4296058. FAX 27-12-4293221. *4224*

JOURNAL OF LOGIC, LANGUAGE AND INFORMATION.
Kluwer Academic Publishers, Postbus 17, 3300 AA Dordrecht, Netherlands. TEL 31-78-6392392. FAX 31-78-6392254. *4079*

JOURNAL OF LOGIC PROGRAMMING.
Elsevier Science Inc., Box 945, New York, NY 10159-0945. TEL 212-633-3730. FAX 212-633-3680. *2045*

JOURNAL OF LONG TERM HOME HEALTH CARE.
Springer Publishing Company, 536 Broadway, New York, NY 10012-3955. TEL 212-431-4370. FAX 212-941-7842. *3551*

JOURNAL OF LOSS PREVENTION IN THE PROCESS INDUSTRIES.
Butterworth - Heinemann, Part of the Reed Elsevier group, Linacre House, Jordan Hill, Oxford OX2 8DP, England. TEL 44-1865-310366. FAX 44-1865-310898. *2644*

JOURNAL OF LOW FREQUENCY NOISE & VIBRATION.
Multi-Science Publishing Co. Ltd., 107 High St., Brentwood, Essex CM14 4RX, England. TEL 44-1277-224632. FAX 44-1277-223453. *5615*

JOURNAL OF LOW TEMPERATURE PHYSICS.
Plenum Publishing Corp., 233 Spring St., New York, NY 10013-1578. TEL 212-620-8000. FAX 212-463-0742. *5585*

JOURNAL OF LUMINESCENCE.
North-Holland P.O. Box 211, 1000 AE Amsterdam, Netherlands. TEL 31-20-4853911. FAX 31-20-4853598. *5605*

JOURNAL OF MACROMOLECULAR SCIENCE: PART A - PURE AND APPLIED CHEMISTRY.
Marcel Dekker Journals, 270 Madison Ave., New York, NY 10016. TEL 212-696-9000. FAX 212-685-4540. *1739*

JOURNAL OF MACROMOLECULAR SCIENCE: PART B - PHYSICS.
Marcel Dekker Journals, 270 Madison Ave., New York, NY 10016. TEL 212-696-9000. FAX 212-685-4540. *5554*

JOURNAL OF MACROMOLECULAR SCIENCE: PART C - REVIEWS IN MACROMOLECULAR CHEMISTRY AND PHYSICS.
Marcel Dekker Journals, 270 Madison Ave., New York, NY 10016. TEL 212-696-9000. FAX 212-685-4540. *1739*

JOURNAL OF MAGNETIC RESONANCE IMAGING.
Williams & Wilkins, 351 W. Camden St., Baltimore, MD 21201-2436. TEL 410-528-4000. FAX 410-528-4312. *4878*

JOURNAL OF MAGNETIC RESONANCE - SERIES A.
Academic Press, Inc., Journal Division, 525 B St., Ste. 1900, San Diego, CA 92101-4495. TEL 619-230-1840. FAX 619-699-6800. *5554*

JOURNAL OF MAGNETISM AND MAGNETIC MATERIALS.
North-Holland P.O. Box 211, 1000 AE Amsterdam, Netherlands. TEL 31-20-4853911. FAX 31-20-4853598. *5554*

JOURNAL OF MAGNETOHYDRODYNAMICS AND PLASMA RESEARCH.
Nova Science Publishers, Inc., 6080 Jericho Tpke., Ste. 207, Commack, NY 11725-2808. TEL 516-499-3103. FAX 516-499-3146. *5585*

JOURNAL OF MAHARASHTRA AGRICULTURAL UNIVERSITIES.
Poona Agricultural College, Poona 411 005, India. TEL 327033. *129*

JOURNAL OF MAINTENANCE IN THE ADDICTIONS.
Haworth Press, Inc., 10 Alice St., Binghamton, NY 13904-1580. FAX 607-722-6362. *2198*

JOURNAL OF MAMMALIAN EVOLUTION.
Plenum Publishing Corp., 233 Spring St., New York, NY 10013-1578. TEL 212-620-8000. FAX 212-807-1047. *811*

JOURNAL OF MAMMALOGY.
American Society of Mammalogists, c/o Dr. H. Duane Smith, Sec.-Treas., Monte L. Bean Life Science Museum, Brigham Young University, Provo, UT 84602. TEL 801-378-2492. *811*

JOURNAL OF MAMMARY GLAND BIOLOGY AND NEOPLASIA.
Plenum Publishing Corp., 233 Spring St., New York, NY 10013-1578. TEL 212-620-8000. FAX 212-463-0742. *4740*

JOURNAL OF MANAGEMENT CONSULTING.
858 Longview Rd., Burlingame, CA 94010-6974. TEL 415-342-1954. FAX 415-344-5005. *1428*

JOURNAL OF MANAGEMENT INFORMATION SYSTEMS.
M.E. Sharpe, Inc., 80 Business Park Dr., Armonk, NY 10504. TEL 914-273-1800. FAX 914-273-2106. *2083*

JOURNAL OF MANAGEMENT STUDIES.
Blackwell Publishers Ltd., 108 Cowley Rd., Oxford OX4 1JF, England. TEL 44-1865-791100. FAX 44-1865-791347. *1428*

JOURNAL OF MANAGERIAL ISSUES.
Pittsburg State University, Department of Economics, Finance & Banking, 1701 S. Broadway, Pittsburg, KS 66762-7533. TEL 316-235-4547. FAX 316-235-4578. *1428*

JOURNAL OF MANIPULATIVE AND PHYSIOLOGICAL THERAPEUTICS.
Williams & Wilkins, 351 W. Camden St., Baltimore, MD 21201. TEL 410-528-4000. FAX 410-528-4312. *4613*

JOURNAL OF MANUFACTURING SYSTEMS.
Elsevier Science Ltd., P.O. Box 800, Kidlington, Oxford OX5 1DX, England. TEL 44-1865-843000. FAX 44-1865-843010. *2056*

JOURNAL OF MARINE AND ATMOSPHERIC RESEARCH.
Cochin University of Science and Technology, School of Marine Sciences, Fine Arts Ave., Cochin 682 016, India. *2297*

JOURNAL OF MARINE BIOTECHNOLOGY.
Springer-Verlag, Life Science Journals, 175 Fifth Ave., New York, NY 10010. TEL 212-460-1500. FAX 212-473-6272. *663*

JOURNAL OF MARINE RESEARCH.
Sears Foundation for Marine Research, Kline Geology Laboratory, Yale University, Box 208109, New Haven, CT 06520-8109. TEL 203-432-3154. *2297*

JOURNAL OF MARINE SYSTEMS.
Elsevier Science B.V., P.O. Box 211, 1000 AE Amsterdam, Netherlands. TEL 31-20-4853911. FAX 31-20-4853598. *2298*

JOURNAL OF MARKET - FOCUSED MANAGEMENT.
Kluwer Academic Publishers Boston, Box 358, Accord Sta., Hingham, MA 02018-0358. TEL 617-871-6600. FAX 617-871-6528. *1429*

JOURNAL OF MARKETING CHANNELS.
Haworth Press, Inc., 10 Alice St., Binghamton, NY 13904. TEL 607-722-5857. FAX 607-722-1424. *1472*

JOURNAL OF MARKETING COMMUNICATIONS.
Chapman & Hall, Journals Department 2-6 Boundary Row, London SE1 8HN, England. TEL 44-171-8650066. FAX 44-171-5229623. *1472*

JOURNAL OF MARKETING FOR HIGHER EDUCATION.
Haworth Press, Inc., 10 Alice St., Binghamton, NY 13904. TEL 607-722-5857. FAX 607-722-1424. *1472*

JOURNAL OF MASS MEDIA ETHICS.
Lawrence Erlbaum Associates, Inc., 10 Industrial Dr., Mahwah, NJ 07430-2262. TEL 201-236-9500. FAX 201-236-0072. *1909*

JOURNAL OF MASS SPECTROMETRY.
John Wiley & Sons Ltd., Journals, Baffins Ln., Chichester, W. Sussex PO19 1UD, England. TEL 44-1243-779777. FAX 44-1243-843232. *1718*

JOURNAL OF MATERIALS ENGINEERING AND PERFORMANCE.
A S M International, Materials Division, Materials Park, OH 44073-0022. TEL 216-338-5151. FAX 216-338-4634. *2734*

JOURNAL OF MATERIALS IN CIVIL ENGINEERING: PROPERTIES, APPLICATIONS, DURABILITY.
American Society of Civil Engineers, 345 E. 47th St., New York, NY 10017-2398. TEL 212-705-7288. FAX 212-980-4681. *2666*

JOURNAL OF MATERIALS PROCESSING AND MANUFACTURING SCIENCE.
Technomic Publishing Co., Inc., 851 New Holland Ave., Box 3535, Lancaster, PA 17604. TEL 717-291-5609. FAX 717-295-4538. *6655*

JOURNAL OF MATERIALS PROCESSING TECHNOLOGY.
Elsevier Science S.A., P.O. Box 564, CH-1001 Lausanne 1, Switzerland. TEL 41-21-3207381. FAX 41-21-3235444. *2760*

JOURNAL OF MATERIALS SCIENCE.
Chapman & Hall, Journals Department 2-6 Boundary Row, London SE1 8HN, England. TEL 44-171-8650066. FAX 44-171-5229623. *2735*

JOURNAL OF MATERIALS SCIENCE & TECHNOLOGY.
Chinese Society for Metals (Shenyang), 72 Wenhua Rd., Shenyang 110015, People's Republic of China. TEL 86-24-384-3531. FAX 86-24-389-1320. *4961*

JOURNAL OF MATERIALS SCIENCE LETTERS.
Chapman & Hall, Journals Department 2-6 Boundary Row, London SE1 8HN, England. TEL 44-171-8650066. FAX 44-171-5229623. *2735*

JOURNAL OF MATERIALS SCIENCE: MATERIALS IN ELECTRONICS.
Chapman & Hall, Journals Department 2-6 Boundary Row, London SE1 8HN, England. TEL 44-171-8650066. FAX 44-171-5229623. *2735*

JOURNAL OF MATERIALS SCIENCE: MATERIALS IN MEDICINE.
Chapman & Hall, Journals Department 2-6 Boundary Row, London SE1 8HN, England. TEL 44-171-8650066. FAX 44-171-5229623. *2735*

JOURNAL OF MATERIALS SYNTHESIS AND PROCESSING.
Plenum Publishing Corp., 233 Spring St., New York, NY 10013-1578. TEL 212-620-8000. FAX 212-463-0172. *2735*

JOURNAL OF MATERNAL - FETAL INVESTIGATION.
Springer-Verlag, Medical Journals, 175 Fifth Ave., New York, NY 10010. TEL 212-460-1500. FAX 212-473-6272. *4740*

THE JOURNAL OF MATERNAL - FETAL MEDICINE.
John Wiley & Sons, Inc., Journals, 605 Third Ave., New York, NY 10158-0012. TEL 212-850-6645. FAX 212-850-6021. *4740*

JOURNAL OF MATHEMATICAL ANALYSIS AND APPLICATIONS.
Academic Press, Inc., Journal Division, 525 B St., Ste. 1900, San Diego, CA 92101-4495. TEL 619-230-1840. FAX 619-699-5800. *4374*

JOURNAL OF MATHEMATICAL BEHAVIOR.
Ablex Publishing Corporation, 355 Chestnut St., Norwood, NJ 07648. TEL 201-767-8455. FAX 201-767-6717. *4374*

JOURNAL OF MATHEMATICAL BIOLOGY.
Springer-Verlag, Heidelberger Platz 3, 14197 Berlin, Germany. TEL 49-30-8207-0. FAX 49-30-8214091. *590*

JOURNAL OF MATHEMATICAL ECONOMICS.
Elsevier Science S.A., P.O. Box 564, CH-1001 Lausanne 1, Switzerland. TEL 41-21-3207381. FAX 41-21-3235444. *1258*

JOURNAL OF MATHEMATICAL IMAGING AND VISION.
Kluwer Academic Publishers Boston, Box 358, Accord Sta., Hingham, MA 02018-0358. TEL 617-871-6600. FAX 617-871-6528 *4410*

JOURNAL OF MATHEMATICAL PHYSICS.
American Institute of Physics, One Physics Ellipse, College Park, MD 20740-3843. TEL 301-209-3000. *5554*

JOURNAL OF MATHEMATICAL PSYCHOLOGY.
Academic Press, Inc., Journal Division, 525 B St., Ste. 1900, San Diego, CA 92101-4495. TEL 619-230-1840. FAX 619-699-5800. *5858*

JOURNAL OF MATHEMATICAL SCIENCES.
Plenum Publishing Corp. Consultants Bureau, 233 Spring St., New York, NY 10013-1578. TEL 212-620-8468. FAX 212-463-0742. *4374*

JOURNAL OF MATHEMATICAL SOCIOLOGY.
Gordon and Breach Science Publishers, c/o International Publishers Distributor, P.O. Box 3054, Langhorne, PA 19047-3054. TEL 215-750-2624. FAX 215-750-6343. *6420*

JOURNAL OF MAYAN LINGUISTICS.
Geoscience Publications, Box 16010, Baton Rouge, LA 70893-6010. TEL 504-388-6245. FAX 504-388-4420. *4079*

JOURNAL OF MECHANICAL DESIGN.
American Society of Mechanical Engineers, 22 Law Dr., Fairfield, NJ 07007-2300. TEL 800-843-2763. *2760*

JOURNAL OF MEDIA ECONOMICS.
Lawrence Erlbaum Associates, Inc., 10 Industrial Dr., Mahwah, NJ 07430-2262. TEL 201-236-9500. FAX 201-236-0072. *1909*

JOURNAL OF MEDICAL & VETERINARY MYCOLOGY.
Blackwell Science Ltd., Osney Mead, Oxford OX2 0EL, England. TEL 44-1865-206206. FAX 44-1865-721205. *4624*

JOURNAL OF MEDICAL AND VETERINARY MYCOLOGY. SUPPLEMENT.
Blackwell Science Ltd., Osney Mead, Oxford OX2 0EL, England. TEL 01865-240201. FAX 01865-721205. *4624*

JOURNAL OF MEDICAL BIOGRAPHY.
Royal Society of Medicine Press Ltd., 1 Wimpole St., London W1M 8AE, England. TEL 0171-290-2900. FAX 0171-290-2929. *557*

JOURNAL OF MEDICAL ENGINEERING & TECHNOLOGY.
Taylor & Francis Ltd., 1 Gunpowder Sq., London EC4A 3DE, England. TEL 44-171-583-0490. FAX 44-171-583-0585. *4483*

JOURNAL OF MEDICAL ENTOMOLOGY.
Entomological Society of America, 9301 Annapolis Rd., Lanham, MD 20706. TEL 301-731-4535. FAX 301-731-4538. *4524*

JOURNAL OF MEDICAL ETHICS.
B M J Publishing Group, B.M.A. House, Tavistock Sq., London WC1H 9JR, England. TEL 44-171-383-6270. FAX 44-171-383-6402. *4483*

JOURNAL OF MEDICAL GENETICS.
B M J Publishing Group, B.M.A. House, Tavistock Sq., London WC1H 9JR, England. TEL 44-171-383-6270. FAX 44-171-383-6402. *746*

JOURNAL OF MEDICAL HUMANITIES.
Human Sciences Press, Inc. 233 Spring St., New York, NY 10013-1578. TEL 212-620-8000. FAX 212-463-0742. *4483*

JOURNAL OF MEDICAL PRIMATOLOGY.
Munksgaard International Publishers Ltd., P.O. Box 2148, DK-1016 Copenhagen K, Denmark. TEL 45-33-127030. FAX 45-33-129387. *811*

JOURNAL OF MEDICAL SCREENING.
B M J Publishing Group, B.M.A. House, Tavistock Sq., London WC1H 9JR, England. TEL 44-171-383-6270. FAX 44-171-383-6402. *4624*

JOURNAL OF MEDICAL SYSTEMS.
Plenum Publishing Corp., 233 Spring St., New York, NY 10013-1578. TEL 212-620-8000. FAX 212-463-0742. *4631*

JOURNAL OF MEDICAL VIROLOGY.
John Wiley & Sons, Inc., Journals, 605 Third Ave., New York, NY 10158. TEL 212-850-6645. FAX 212-850-6021. *4483*

JOURNAL OF MEDICINAL CHEMISTRY.
American Chemical Society, 1155 16th St., N.W., Washington, DC 20036. TEL 800-333-9511. FAX 614-447-3671. *5422*

JOURNAL OF MEDICINE.
P J D Publications Ltd., Box 966, Westbury, NY 11590. TEL 516-626-0650. FAX 516-626-5546. *4483*

THE JOURNAL OF MEDICINE AND PHILOSOPHY.
Kluwer Academic Publishers, Postbus 17, 3300 AA Dordrecht, Netherlands. TEL 31-78-6392392. FAX 31-78-6392254. *4483*

JOURNAL OF MEDIEVAL AND EARLY MODERN STUDIES.
Duke University Press, Box 90660, Durham, NC 27708-0660. TEL 919-687-3600. FAX 919-688-4574. *3617*

JOURNAL OF MEDIEVAL HISTORY.
Elsevier Science B.V., P.O. Box 211, 1000 AE Amsterdam, Netherlands. TEL 31-20-4853911. FAX 31-20-4853598. *3422*

JOURNAL OF MEDIEVAL LATIN.
N.V. Brepols, Steenweg op Tielen 68, 2300 Turnhout, Belgium. TEL 32-14-402500. FAX 32-14-428919. *4079*

JOURNAL OF MEDITERRANEAN STUDIES.
University of Malta Services Ltd., Msida MSD 06, Malta. TEL 356-343572. *3617*

JOURNAL OF MEMBRANE BIOLOGY.
Springer-Verlag, Life Science Journals, 175 Fifth Ave., New York, NY 10010. TEL 212-460-1500. FAX 212-473-6272. *716*

JOURNAL OF MEMBRANE SCIENCE.
Elsevier Science B.V., P.O. Box 211, 1000 AE Amsterdam, Netherlands. TEL 31-20-4853911. FAX 31-20-4853598. *1753*

JOURNAL OF MENNONITE STUDIES.
University of Winnipeg, Winnipeg, MB R3B 2E9, Canada. TEL 204-786-9104. FAX 204-786-1824. *6148*

JOURNAL OF MEN'S STUDIES.
Box 32, Harriman, TN 37748-0032. *4947*

JOURNAL OF MENTAL HEALTH.
Carfax Publishing Co., P.O. Box 25, Abingdon, Oxon. OX14 3UE, England. TEL 44-1235-401000. FAX 44-1235-401550. *4846*

JOURNAL OF MENTAL HEALTH ADMINISTRATION.
Sage Publications, Inc., 2455 Teller Rd., Thousand Oaks, CA 91320. TEL 805-499-0721. FAX 805-499-0871. *5967*

JOURNAL OF MENTAL HEALTH AND AGING.
Springer Publishing Company, 536 Broadway, New York, NY 10012-3955. TEL 212-431-4370. FAX 212-941-7842. *3291*

JOURNAL OF METAMORPHIC GEOLOGY.
Blackwell Science Inc., 238 Main St., Cambridge, MA 02142-1413. TEL 617-876-7022. FAX 617-492-5263. *2246*

JOURNAL OF METEOROLOGY.
Artetech Publishing Co., Chateau de Blanchelande, 50250 Neufmesnil, France. TEL 33-33-47-38-23. FAX 33-33-47-16-39. *5000*

JOURNAL OF MICROBIOLOGICAL METHODS.
Elsevier Science B.V., P.O. Box 211, 1000 AE Amsterdam, Netherlands. TEL 31-20-4853911. FAX 31-20-4853598. *761*

JOURNAL OF MICROCOLUMN SEPARATIONS.
John Wiley & Sons, Inc., Journals, 605 Third Ave., New York, NY 10158-0012. TEL 212-850-6645. FAX 212-850-6021. *1718*

JOURNAL OF MICROELECTRONIC SYSTEMS INTEGRATION.
Plenum Publishing Corp., 233 Spring St., New York, NY 10013-1578. TEL 212-620-8000. FAX 212-463-0742. *2711*

JOURNAL OF MICROENCAPSULATION.
Taylor & Francis Ltd., 1 Gunpowder Sq., London EC4A 3DE, England. TEL 44-171-583-0490. FAX 44-171-583-0585. *5422*

JOURNAL OF MICROSCOPY.
Blackwell Science Ltd., Osney Mead, Oxford OX2 0EL, England. TEL 44-1865-206206. FAX 44-1865-721205. *769*

JOURNAL OF MICROSCOPY RESEARCH AND TECHNIQUE.
John Wiley & Sons, Inc., Journals, 605 Third Ave., New York, NY 10158. TEL 212-850-6645. FAX 212-850-6021. *590*

JOURNAL OF MICROWAVE POWER AND ELECTROMAGNETIC ENERGY.
International Microwave Power Institute, 10210 Leatherleaf Ct., Manassas, VA 22111-4245. TEL 703-257-1415. *2711*

JOURNAL OF MILITARY HISTORY.
Society for Military History, c/o Virginia Military Institute, Lexington, VA 24450. TEL 540-464-7468. FAX 540-464-5229. *5036*

JOURNAL OF MIND AND BEHAVIOR.
Institute of Mind & Behavior, Box 522, Village Sta., New York, NY 10014. TEL 212-595-4853. *5858*

JOURNAL OF MINING AND GEOLOGY.
Nigerian Mining and Geosciences Society, University of Ibadan, Department of Geology, Ibadan, Oyo State, Nigeria. TEL 234-2-8101100. *5067*

JOURNAL OF MINING SCIENCE.
Plenum Publishing Corp., Consultants Bureau, 233 Spring St., New York, NY 10013-1578. TEL 212-620-8468. FAX 212-463-0742. *5067*

JOURNAL OF MINISTRY IN ADDICTION & RECOVERY.
Haworth Press, Inc., 10 Alice St., Binghamton, NY 13904. TEL 607-722-5857. FAX 607-722-1424. *6071*

JOURNAL OF MINISTRY MARKETING & MANAGEMENT.
Haworth Press, Inc., 10 Alice St., Binghamton, NY 13904. TEL 607-722-5857. FAX 607-722-1424. *6071*

JOURNAL OF MODERN HISTORY.
University of Chicago Press, Journals Division, Box 37005, Chicago, IL 60637. TEL 312-753-3347. FAX 312-753-0811. *3349*

JOURNAL OF MODERN OPTICS.
Taylor & Francis Ltd., 1 Gunpowder Sq., London EC4A 3DE, England. TEL 44-171-583-0490. FAX 44-171-583-0585. *5605*

JOURNAL OF MOLECULAR CATALYSIS A: CHEMICAL.
Elsevier Science B.V., P.O. Box 211, 1000 AE Amsterdam, Netherlands. TEL 31-20-4853911. FAX 31-20-4853598. *1753*

JOURNAL OF MOLECULAR CATALYSIS B: ENZYMATIC.
Elsevier Science B.V., P.O. Box 211, 1000 AE Amsterdam, Netherlands. TEL 31-20-4853911. FAX 31-20-4853598. *1753*

JOURNAL OF MOLECULAR EVOLUTION.
Springer-Verlag, Life Science Journals, 175 Fifth Ave., New York, NY 10010. TEL 212-460-1500. FAX 212-473-6272. *746*

JOURNAL OF MOLECULAR GRAPHICS.
Elsevier Science Inc., Box 945, New York, NY 10159-0945. TEL 212-633-3730. FAX 212-633-3680. *2029*

JOURNAL OF MOLECULAR LIQUIDS.
Elsevier Science B.V., P.O. Box 211, 1000 AE Amsterdam, Netherlands. TEL 31-20-4853911. FAX 31-20-4853598. *1754*

JOURNAL OF MOLECULAR NEUROSCIENCE.
Humana Press Inc., 999 Riverview Dr., Ste. 208, Totowa, NJ 07512. TEL 201-256-1699. FAX 201-256-8341. *4846*

JOURNAL OF MOLECULAR RECOGNITION.
John Wiley & Sons Ltd., Journals, Baffins Ln., Chichester, W. Sussex PO19 1UD, England. TEL 44-1243-779777. FAX 44-1243-843232. *642*

JOURNAL OF MOLECULAR SPECTROSCOPY.
Academic Press, Inc., Journal Division, 525 B St., Ste. 1900, San Diego, CA 92101-4495. TEL 619-230-1840. FAX 619-699-6800. *5605*

JOURNAL OF MOLECULAR STRUCTURE.
Elsevier Science B.V., P.O. Box 211, 1000 AE Amsterdam, Netherlands. TEL 31-20-4853911. FAX 31-20-4853598. *1681*

JOURNAL OF MOLECULAR STRUCTURE: THEOCHEM.
Elsevier Science B.V., P.O. Box 211, 1000 AE Amsterdam, Netherlands. TEL 31-20-4853911. FAX 31-20-4853598. *1682*

JOURNAL OF MONETARY ECONOMICS.
North-Holland P.O. Box 211, 1000 AE Amsterdam, Netherlands. TEL 31-20-4853911. FAX 31-20-4853598. *1105*

JOURNAL OF MONEY, CREDIT & BANKING.
Ohio State University Press, 1070 Carmack Rd., Columbus, OH 43210. TEL 614-292-6930. *1105*

JOURNAL OF MORAL EDUCATION.
Carfax Publishing Co., P.O. Box 25, Abingdon, Oxon. OX14 3UE, England. TEL 44-1235-401000. FAX 44-1235-401550. *5482*

JOURNAL OF MORPHOLOGY.
John Wiley & Sons, Inc., Journals, 605 Third Ave., New York, NY 10158. TEL 212-850-6645. FAX 212-850-6021. *591*

JOURNAL OF MOTOR BEHAVIOR.
Heldref Publications, 1319 Eighteenth St., N.W., Washington, DC 20036-1802. TEL 202-296-6267. FAX 202-296-5149. *5858*

JOURNAL OF MULTICULTURAL NURSING AND HEALTH.
Riley Publications, Inc., Box 889, Chautauqua Institution, Chautauqua, NY 14722. TEL 716-357-2479. FAX 716-357-3193. *4717*

JOURNAL OF MULTICULTURAL SOCIAL WORK.
Haworth Press, Inc., 10 Alice St., Binghamton, NY 13904. TEL 607-722-5857. FAX 607-722-1424. *6420*

JOURNAL OF MULTIPHASE SCIENCE AND TECHNOLOGY.
Begell House Inc., 79 Madison Ave., Ste. 1205, New York, NY 10016-7892. TEL 212-725-1999. FAX 212-213-8368. *2607*

JOURNAL OF MULTISTATE TAXATION.
Warren, Gorham & Lamont, One Penn Plaza, New York, NY 10119. TEL 212-971-5000. FAX 212-971-5113. *1552*

JOURNAL OF MULTIVARIATE ANALYSIS.
Academic Press, Inc., Journal Division, 525 B St., Ste. 1900, San Diego, CA 92101-4495. TEL 619-230-1840. FAX 619-699-6800. *4374*

JOURNAL OF MUSCLE RESEARCH AND CELL MOTILITY.
Chapman & Hall, Journals Department 2-6 Boundary Row, London SE1 8HN, England. TEL 44-171-8650066. FAX 44-171-5229623. *4484*

JOURNAL OF MUSCLE SHOALS HISTORY.
Tennessee Valley Historical Society, Box 149, Sheffield, AL 35660. TEL 205-381-2298. *3474*

THE JOURNAL OF MUSCULOSKELETAL MEDICINE.
Cliggott Publishing Co., 55 Holly Hill Ln., Box 4010, Greenwich, CT 06831. TEL 203-661-0600. *4786*

JOURNAL OF MUSCULOSKELETAL PAIN.
Haworth Press, Inc., 10 Alice St., Binghamton, NY 13904. TEL 607-722-5857. FAX 607-722-1424. *4786*

JOURNAL OF MUSIC THEORY PEDAGOGY.
University of Oklahoma, School of Music, Parrington Oval, Norman, OK 73019. TEL 405-325-2081. *5168*

JOURNAL OF MUSIC THERAPY.
National Association for Music Therapy, Inc., 8455 Colesville Rd, Ste. 930, Silver Spring, MD 20910-3392. TEL 301-589-3300. FAX 301-589-5175. *5168*

JOURNAL OF MUSICOLOGICAL RESEARCH.
Gordon and Breach Science Publishers, c/o International Publishers Distributor, P.O. Box 3054, Langhorne, PA 19047-3054. TEL 215-750-2642. FAX 215-750-6343. *5168*

JOURNAL OF MUSICOLOGY.
University of California Press, Journals Division, 2120 Berkeley Way, No. 5812, Berkeley, CA 94720-5812. TEL 510-643-7154. FAX 510-642-9917. *5168*

JOURNAL OF MYCOPATHOLOGICAL RESEARCH.
Indian Mycological Society, Department of Botany, University of Calcutta, 35 B.C. Rd., Calcutta 700 019, India. TEL 91-33-551-4189. FAX 91-33-475-3681. *687*

JOURNAL OF NARRATIVE AND LIFE HISTORY.
Lawrence Erlbaum Associates, Inc., 10 Industrial Dr., Mahwah, NJ 07430-2262. TEL 201-236-9500. FAX 201-236-0072. *4224*

JOURNAL OF NATURAL GEOMETRY.
University of London, Mathematical Research Unit, Birbeck College, 7-15 Gresse St., London W1P 1PA, England. TEL 44-171-580-7710. FAX 44-171-631-6270. *4375*

JOURNAL OF NATURAL HISTORY.
Taylor & Francis Ltd., 1 Gunpowder Sq., London EC4A 3DE, England. TEL 44-171-583-0490. FAX 44-171-583-0585. *591*

JOURNAL OF NATURAL PRODUCTS.
American Society of Pharmacognosy, Dept. L-0011, Columbus, OH 43268-0011. TEL 614-447-3776. FAX 614-447-3671. *5422*

JOURNAL OF NATURAL RESOURCES AND LIFE SCIENCES EDUCATION.
American Society of Agronomy, Inc., 677 S. Segoe Rd., Madison, WI 53711. TEL 608-273-8080. FAX 608-273-2021. *228*

JOURNAL OF NEAR-DEATH STUDIES.
Human Sciences Press, Inc. 233 Spring St., New York, NY 10013-1578. TEL 212-620-8000. FAX 212-463-0742. *5858*

JOURNAL OF NEAR EASTERN STUDIES.
University of Chicago Press, Journals Division, Box 37005, Chicago, IL 60637. TEL 312-753-3347. FAX 312-753-0811. *360*

JOURNAL OF NEAR INFRARED SPECTROSCOPY.
N I R Publications, 6 Charlton Mill, Charlton, Chichester, W. Sussex PO18 0HY, England. TEL 44-1243-811334. FAX 44-1243-811711. *1718*

JOURNAL OF NEGRO EDUCATION.
Howard University Press, Marketing Department, 2600 Sixth St., N.W., Washington, DC 20059. TEL 202-806-8120. FAX 202-806-8434. *2347*

JOURNAL OF NEGRO HISTORY.
Association for the Study of Afro-American Life and History, Inc., c/o Alton Hornsby, Jr., Ed., Dept. of History, Morehouse College, Atlanta, GA 30314. TEL 404-215-2620 FAX 404-215-2715. *2890*

JOURNAL OF NEMATOLOGY.
Society of Nematologists, c/o Dr. M. McClure, 3012 Skyview Dr., Lakeland, FL 33801-7072. TEL 815-665-4481. FAX 815-665-1297. *811*

JOURNAL OF NERVOUS AND MENTAL DISEASE.
Williams & Wilkins, 351 W. Camdaen St., Baltimore, MD 21201. TEL 410-528-4000. FAX 410-528-4312. *4846*

JOURNAL OF NETWORK AND SYSTEMS MANAGEMENT.
Plenum Publishing Corp., 233 Spring St., New York, NY 10013-1578. TEL 212-620-8000. FAX 212-463-0742. *2056*

JOURNAL OF NEURO-AIDS.
Haworth Press, Inc., 10 Alice St., Binghamton, NY 13904. TEL 607-722-5857. FAX 609-722-1424. *4846*

JOURNAL OF NEURO-ONCOLOGY.
Kluwer Academic Publishers Boston, Box 358, Accord Sta., Hingham, MA 02018-0358. TEL 617-871-6600. FAX 617-871-6528. *4759*

JOURNAL OF NEURO-OPHTHALMOLOGY.
Lippincott - Raven Publishers 227 E. Washington Sq., Philadelphia, PA 19106. TEL 215-238-4200. *4772*

JOURNAL OF NEUROBIOLOGY.
John Wiley & Sons, Inc., Journals, 605 Third Ave., New York, NY 10158. TEL 212-850-6645. FAX 212-850-6021. *790*

JOURNAL OF NEUROCHEMISTRY.
Lippincott - Raven Publishers 227 E. Washington Sq., Philadelphia, PA 19106. TEL 215-238-4200. *642*

JOURNAL OF NEUROCYTOLOGY.
Chapman & Hall, Journals Department 2-6 Boundary Row, London SE1 8HN, England. TEL 44-171-8650066. FAX 44-171-5229623. *716*

JOURNAL OF NEUROENDOCRINOLOGY.
Blackwell Science Ltd., Osney Mead, Oxford OX2 0EL, England. TEL 44-1865-206206. FAX 44-1865-721205. *4846*

JOURNAL OF NEUROGENETICS.
Harwood Academic Publishers, c/o International Publishers Distributor, P.O. Box 3054, Langhorne, PA 19047-3054. TEL 215-750-2642. FAX 215-750-6343. *4846*

JOURNAL OF NEUROIMAGING.
Little, Brown and Company, Medical Journals, 34 Beacon St., Boston, MA 02108. TEL 617-859-5500. FAX 617-267-3507. *4846*

JOURNAL OF NEUROIMMUNOLOGY.
Elsevier Science B.V., P.O. Box 211, 1000 AE Amsterdam, Netherlands. TEL 31-20-4853911. FAX 31-20-4853598. *4846*

JOURNAL OF NEUROLINGUISTICS.
Elsevier Science Ltd., Pergamon, P.O. Box 800, Kidlington, Oxford OX5 1DX, England. TEL 44-1865-843000. FAX 44-1865-843010. *4847*

JOURNAL OF NEUROLOGY, NEUROSURGERY AND PSYCHIATRY.
B M J Publishing Group, B.M.A. House, Tavistock Sq., London WC1H 9JR, England. TEL 44-171-383-6270. FAX 44-171-383-6402. *4847*

JOURNAL OF NEUROPATHOLOGY AND EXPERIMENTAL NEUROLOGY.
American Association of Neuropathologists, Inc., Box 1897, Lawrence, KS 66044-8897. *4847*

JOURNAL OF NEUROPHYSIOLOGY.
American Physiological Society, 9650 Rockville Pike, Bethesda, MD 20814. TEL 301-530-7164. FAX 301-571-3813. *790*

JOURNAL OF NEUROPSYCHIATRY AND CLINICAL NEUROSCIENCES.
American Psychiatric Press, Inc., Journals Division, 1400 K St. N.W., Ste. 1001, Washington, DC 20005. TEL 202-682-6240. FAX 202-682-6341. *4847*

JOURNAL OF NEUROSCIENCE.
Society for Neuroscience, 11 Dupont Cir., N.W., Ste. 500, Washington, DC 20036. TEL 202-462-6638. FAX 202-462-1547. *4847*

JOURNAL OF NEUROSCIENCE METHODS.
Elsevier Science B.V., P.O. Box 211, 1000 AE Amsterdam, Netherlands. TEL 31-20-4853911. FAX 31-20-4853598. *4847*

JOURNAL OF NEUROSCIENCE NURSING.
American Association of Neuroscience Nurses, 224 N. Des Plaines, Ste. 601, Chicago, IL 60661. TEL 312-993-0043. FAX 312-993-0962. *4717*

JOURNAL OF NEUROSCIENCE RESEARCH.
John Wiley & Sons, Inc., Journals, 605 Third Ave., New York, NY 10158. TEL 212-850-6645. FAX 212-850-6021. *4847*

JOURNAL OF NEUROSURGERY.
American Association of Neurological Surgeons, 1224 W. Main St., Ste. 450, Charlottesville, VA 22903. TEL 804-924-5503. FAX 804-924-2702. *4848*

JOURNAL OF NEUROSURGICAL ANESTHESIOLOGY.
Lippincott - Raven Publishers 227 E. Washington Sq., Philadelphia, PA 19106. TEL 215-238-4200. *4592*

JOURNAL OF NEUROSURGICAL SCIENCES.
Edizioni Minerva Medica, Corso Bramante 83-85, 10126 Turin, Italy. TEL 39-11-678282. FAX 39-11-3121736. *4912*

JOURNAL OF NEW ZEALAND LITERATURE.
University of Otago, Department of English, P.O. Box 56, Dunedin, New Zealand. TEL 54-3-4798636. FAX 64-3-4798558. *4224*

JOURNAL OF NON-CRYSTALLINE SOLIDS.
North-Holland P.O. Box 211, 1000 AE Amsterdam, Netherlands. TEL 31-20-4853911. FAX 31-20-4853598. *5554*

JOURNAL OF NON-NEWTONIAN FLUID MECHANICS.
Elsevier Science B.V., P.O. Box 211, 1000 AE Amsterdam, Netherlands. TEL 31-20-4853911. FAX 31-20-4853598. *5589*

JOURNAL OF NONDESTRUCTIVE EVALUATION.
Plenum Publishing Corp., 233 Spring St., New York, NY 10013-1578. TEL 212-620-8000. FAX 212-463-0742. *2735*

JOURNAL OF NONLINEAR DYNAMICS, PSYCHOLOGY, AND LIFE SCIENCES.
Human Sciences Press 233 Spring St., New York, NY 10013-1578. TEL 212-620-8000. FAX 212-463-0742. *5859*

JOURNAL OF NONLINEAR SCIENCE.
Springer-Verlag, Science Journals, 175 Fifth Ave., New York, NY 10010. TEL 212-460-1500. FAX 212-473-6272. *5555*

JOURNAL OF NONPROFIT & PUBLIC SECTOR MARKETING.
Haworth Press, Inc., 10 Alice St., Binghamton, NY 13904. TEL 607-722-5857. FAX 607-722-1424. *1472*

JOURNAL OF NONPROFIT AND VOLUNTARY SECTOR MARKETING.
Henry Stewart Publications, Russell House, 28-30 Little Russell St., London WC1A 2HN, England. TEL 44-171-404-3040 FAX 44-171-404-2081. *1472*

JOURNAL OF NONVERBAL BEHAVIOR.
Human Sciences Press, Inc. 233 Spring St., New York, NY 10013-1578. TEL 212-620-8000. FAX 212-463-0742. *5859*

JOURNAL OF NORTH AFRICAN STUDIES.
Frank Cass, Newbury House, 890-900 Eastern Ave., Newbury Park, Ilford, Essex IG2 7HH, England TEL 44-181-5998866. FAX 44-181-5990984. *3373*

JOURNAL OF NORTHERN LUZON.
Saint Mary's College of Bayombong, Nueva Vizcaya 3700, Philippines. TEL 321-2221. FAX 321-2117. *6420*

JOURNAL OF NORTHWEST SEMITIC LANGUAGES.
University of Stellenbosch, Department of Ancient Near Eastern Studies, University, 7600 Stellenbosch, South Africa. TEL 27-21-808-3203. FAX 27-21-8084336. *4079*

JOURNAL OF NUCLEAR CARDIOLOGY.
Mosby - Year Book, Inc. 11830 Westline Industrial Dr., St. Louis, MO 63146-3318. TEL 314-872-8370. FAX 314-432-1380. *4878*

JOURNAL OF NUCLEAR MATERIALS.
North-Holland P.O. Box 211, 1000 AE Amsterdam, Netherlands. TEL 31-20-4853911. FAX 31-20-4853598. *5595*

JOURNAL OF NUCLEAR MATERIALS MANAGEMENT.
Institute of Nuclear Materials Management, Inc., 60 Revere Dr., Ste. 500, Northbrook, IL 60062-1563. TEL 847-480-9573. FAX 847-480-9282. *2578*

JOURNAL OF NUCLEAR MEDICINE.
Society of Nuclear Medicine, 1850 Samuel Morse Dr., Reston, VA 22090-5316. TEL 703-708-9000. FAX 703-708-9015. *4878*

JOURNAL OF NUCLEAR MEDICINE TECHNOLOGY.
Society of Nuclear Medicine, 1850 Samuel Morse Dr., Reston, VA 22090-5316. TEL 703-708-9000. FAX 703-708-9015. *4878*

JOURNAL OF NUMBER THEORY.
Academic Press, Inc., Journal Division, 525 B St., Ste. 1900, San Diego, CA 92101-4495. TEL 619-230-1840. FAX 619-699-6800. *4375*

JOURNAL OF NURSE-MIDWIFERY.
Elsevier Science Inc., Box 945, New York, NY 10159-0945. TEL 212-633-3730. FAX 212-633-3680. *4740*

JOURNAL OF NURSING LAW.
K R M Information Services, Inc., 200 Spring St., Eau Claire, WI 54703. TEL 715-833-5208. FAX 715-836-0031. *4718*

JOURNAL OF NURSING MANAGEMENT.
Blackwell Science Ltd., Osney Mead, Oxford OX2 OEL, England. TEL 44-1865-206206. FAX 44-1865-721205. *4718*

JOURNAL OF NURSING MEASUREMENT.
Springer Publishing Company, 526 Broadway, New York, NY 10012-3955. TEL 212-431-4370. FAX 212-941-7842. *4718*

JOURNAL OF NUTRITION.
American Institute of Nutrition, 9650 Rockville Pike, Bethesda, MD 20814. TEL 301-530-7027. FAX 301-571-1892. *5235*

JOURNAL OF NUTRITION FOR THE ELDERLY.
Haworth Press, Inc., 10 Alice St., Binghamton, NY 13904. TEL 607-722-5857. FAX 607-722-1424. *3291*

JOURNAL OF NUTRITION IN RECIPE & MENU DEVELOPMENT.
Haworth Press, Inc., 10 Alice St., Binghamton, NY 13904-1580. TEL 607-722-5857. FAX 607-722-1424. *5236*

JOURNAL OF NUTRITIONAL & ENVIRONMENTAL MEDICINE.
Carfax Publishing Co., P.O. Box 25, Abingdon, Oxon. OX14 3UE, England. TEL 44-1235-401000. FAX 44-1235-401550. *5236*

JOURNAL OF NUTRITIONAL IMMUNOLOGY.
Haworth Press, Inc., 10 Alice St., Binghamton, NY 13904. TEL 607-722-5857. FAX 607-722-1424. *4585*

JOURNAL OF OBJECT - ORIENTED PROGRAMMING.
Sigs Publications, Inc., 71 W. 23rd St., New York, NY 10010-4102. TEL 212-242-7447. FAX 212-242-7574. *2045*

JOURNAL OF OBSTETRICS AND GYNAECOLOGY.
Carfax Publishing Co., P.O. Box 25, Abingdon, Oxon. OX14 3UE, England. TEL 44-1235-401000. FAX 44-1235-401550. *4740*

JOURNAL OF OCCUPATIONAL AND ENVIRONMENTAL MEDICINE.
Williams & Wilkins, 351 W. Camden St., Baltimore, MD 21201. TEL 410-528-4000. FAX 410-528-4312. *4484*

JOURNAL OF OCCUPATIONAL AND ORGANIZATIONAL PSYCHOLOGY.
British Psychological Society, St. Andrew's House, 48 Princess Rd. E., Leicester LE1 7DR, England. TEL 44-116-254-9568. FAX 44-116-247-0787. *5859*

JOURNAL OF OCCUPATIONAL HEALTH AND SAFETY: AUSTRALIA AND NEW ZEALAND.
C C H Australia Ltd., P.O. Box 230, North Ryde, N.S.W. 2113, Australia. TEL 61-1-300300224. FAX 61-2-300306224. *5252*

JOURNAL OF OCCUPATIONAL REHABILITATION.
Plenum Publishing Corp., 233 Spring St., New York, NY 10013-1578. TEL 212-620-8000. FAX 212-463-0742. *5252*

JOURNAL OF OCCUPATIONAL SCIENCE: AUSTRALIA.
c/o University of South Australia, N. Terrace, Adelaide, S.A. 5000, Australia. TEL 61-8-3022693. FAX 61-8-3022645. *6420*

JOURNAL OF OCEANOGRAPHY.
Oceanographical Society of Japan, 6-14, Minamidai 1-chome, Nakano-ku, Tokyo 164, Japan. TEL 81-3-3377-3951. FAX 81-3-3378-9419. *2298*

JOURNAL OF OFFENDER REHABILITATION.
Haworth Press, Inc., 10 Alice St., Binghamton, NY 13904. TEL 607-722-5857. FAX 607-722-1424. *2167*

JOURNAL OF OFFSHORE MECHANICS AND ARCTIC ENGINEERING.
American Society of Mechanical Engineers, 22 Law Dr., Fairfield, NJ 07007-2300. *2760*

JOURNAL OF ONCOLOGY PHARMACY PRACTICE.
Appleton & Lange, Journal Division, Box 120041, Stamford, CT 06912-0041. TEL 203-406-4500. *5422*

THE JOURNAL OF ONE-DAY SURGERY.
Newton Mann Ltd., Stretton Rd., Tansley, Matlock, Derbyshire DE4 5GE, England. TEL 44-1629-583941. FAX 4401629-580479. *4912*

JOURNAL OF OPERATIONS MANAGEMENT.
Elsevier Science B.V., P.O. Box 211, 1000 AE Amsterdam, Netherlands. TEL 31-20-4853911. FAX 31-20-4853598. *2748*

JOURNAL OF OPTIMIZATION THEORY AND APPLICATIONS.
Plenum Publishing Corp., 233 Spring St., New York, NY 10013-1578. TEL 212-620-8000. FAX 212-463-0742. *4375*

JOURNAL OF ORAL AND MAXILLOFACIAL SURGERY.
W.B. Saunders Co. Curtis Center, 3rd Fl., Independence Sq. W., Philadelphia, PA 19106-3399. TEL 215-238-7800. FAX 215-238-6445. *4646*

JOURNAL OF ORAL PATHOLOGY & MEDICINE.
Munksgaard International Publishers Ltd., 35 Noerre Soegade, P.O. Box 2148, DK-1016 Copenhagen K, Denmark. TEL 45-33-127030. FAX 45-33-129387. *4646*

JOURNAL OF ORAL REHABILITATION.
Blackwell Science Ltd., Osney Mead, Oxford OX2 OEL, England. TEL 44-1865-206206. FAX 44-1865-721205. *4646*

JOURNAL OF ORGANIC CHEMISTRY (WASHINGTON).
American Chemical Society, 1155 16th St., N.W., Washington, DC 20036. TEL 800-333-9511. FAX 614-447-3671. *1739*

JOURNAL OF ORGANIZATIONAL BEHAVIOR MANAGEMENT.
Haworth Press, Inc., 10 Alice St., Binghamton, NY 13904. TEL 607-722-5857. FAX 607-722-1424. *5859*

JOURNAL OF ORGANIZATIONAL BEHAVIOUR.
John Wiley & Sons Ltd., Journals, Baffins Ln., Chichester, W. Sussex PO19 1UD, England. TEL 44-1243-779777. FAX 44-1243-843232. *5859*

JOURNAL OF ORGANOMETALLIC CHEMISTRY.
Elsevier Science S.A., P.O. Box 564, CH-1001 Lausanne 1, Switzerland. TEL 41-21-3207381. FAX 41-21-3235444. *1740*

JOURNAL OF ORGANOMETALLIC CHEMISTRY LIBRARY.
Elsevier Science B.V., Books Division, P.O. Box 211, 1000 AE Amsterdam, Netherlands. TEL 31-20-4853911. FAX 31-20-4853705. *1682*

JOURNAL OF ORGONOMY.
Orgonomic Publications, Box 490, Princeton, NJ 08542. TEL 908-821-1144. FAX 908-821-0174. *4848*

JOURNAL OF OROFACIAL PAIN.
Quintessence Publishing Co., Inc., 551 Kimberly Dr., Carol Stream, IL 60188-1881. TEL 708-682-3223. FAX 708-682-3288. *4646*

JOURNAL OF ORTHOPAEDIC AND SPORTS PHYSICAL THERAPY.
Williams & Wilkins, 351 W. Camden St., Baltimore, MD 21201. TEL 410-528-4000. FAX 410-528-4312. *4898*

JOURNAL OF ORTHOPAEDIC RESEARCH.
Journal of Bone and Joint Surgery, Inc., 20 Pickering St., Needham, MA 02192-3145. TEL 617-734-2835. *4786*

JOURNAL OF ORTHOPAEDIC TECHNIQUES.
Stockton Press Houndmills, Basingstoke, Hampshire RG21 6XS, England. TEL 01256-817245. FAX 01256-28339. *4786*

JOURNAL OF OTOLARYNGOLOGY OF JAPAN.
Oto-Rhino-Laryngological Society of Japan, c/o Chateau Takanawa, 23-14, 3-chome, Minato-ku, Tokyo 108, Japan. TEL 03-3443-3085. FAX 03-3443-3037. *4798*

JOURNAL OF PACIFIC HISTORY.
Journal of Pacific History Inc., c/o Research School of Pacific Studies, Australian National Univ., Canberra, A.C.T. 0200, Australia. FAX 06-249-5525. *3388*

JOURNAL OF PAEDIATRICS AND CHILD HEALTH.
Blackwell Science Pty Ltd, P.O. Box 378, Carlton, Vic. 3053, Australia. TEL 61-3-93470300. FAX 61-3-93493016. *4807*

JOURNAL OF PAIN AND SYMPTOM MANAGEMENT.
Elsevier Science Inc., Box 945, New York, NY 10159-0945. TEL 212-633-3730. FAX 212-633-3680. *4592*

JOURNAL OF PALEOLIMNOLOGY.
Kluwer Academic Publishers, Postbus 17, 3300 AA Dordrecht, Netherlands. TEL 31-78-6392392. FAX 31-78-6392254. *5314*

JOURNAL OF PALEONTOLOGY.
Paleontological Society, Business Office, Box 1897, Lawrence, KS 66044-8897. TEL 913-843-1221. *5314*

JOURNAL OF PALESTINE STUDIES.
University of California Press, Journals Division, 2120 Berkeley Way, No. 5812, Berkeley, CA 94720-5812. TEL 510-643-7154. FAX 510-642-9917. *3497*

JOURNAL OF PARALLEL AND DISTRIBUTED COMPUTING.
Academic Press, Inc., Journal Division, 525 B St., Ste. 1900, San Diego, CA 92101-4495. TEL 619-230-1840. FAX 619-699-6800. *1994*

JOURNAL OF PARAPSYCHOLOGY.
Parapsychology Press, 402 N. Buchanan Blvd., Durham, NC 27701-1728. TEL 919-688-8241. FAX 919-683-4338. *5331*

JOURNAL OF PARENTERAL AND ENTERAL NUTRITION.
American Society for Parenteral and Enteral Nutrition, 8630 Fenton St., Ste. 412, Silver Spring, MD 20910-3805. TEL 301-587-6315. FAX 301-587-3323. *5236*

JOURNAL OF PEACE RESEARCH.
Sage Publications Ltd., 6 Bonhill St., London EC2A 4PU, England. TEL 44-171-374-0645. FAX 44-171-374-8741. *5759*

THE JOURNAL OF PEASANT STUDIES.
Frank Cass, Newbury House, 890-900 Eastern Ave., Newbury Park, Ilford, Essex 1G2 7HH, England. TEL 44-181-599-8866. FAX 44-181-599-0984. *6420*

JOURNAL OF PEDIATRIC GASTROENTEROLOGY AND NUTRITION.
Lippincott - Raven Publishers 227 E. Washington Sq., Philadelphia, PA 19106. TEL 215-238-4200. *4694*

JOURNAL OF PEDIATRIC HEALTH CARE.
Mosby - Year Book, Inc. 11830 Westline Industrial Dr., St. Louis, MO 63146-3318. TEL 314-872-8370. FAX 314-432-1380. *4807*

JOURNAL OF PEDIATRIC HEMATOLOGY - ONCOLOGY.
Lippincott - Raven Publishers 227 E. Washington Sq., Philadelphia, PA 19106. TEL 215-238-4200. *4759*

JOURNAL OF PEDIATRIC NURSING.
W.B. Saunders Co. Curtis Center, 3rd Fl., Independence Sq. W., Philadelphia, PA 19106-3399. TEL 215-238-7800. FAX 215-238-6445. *4718*

JOURNAL OF PEDIATRIC ONCOLOGY NURSING.
W.B. Saunders Co. The Curtis Center, 3rd Fl., Independence Sq. W., Philadelphia, PA 19106-3399. TEL 215-238-7800. FAX 215-238-6445. *4759*

JOURNAL OF PEDIATRIC OPHTHALMOLOGY AND STRABISMUS.
Slack, Inc., 6900 Grove Rd., Thorofare, NJ 08086-9447. TEL 609-848-1000. FAX 609-853-5991. *4772*

JOURNAL OF PEDIATRIC ORTHOPAEDICS.
Lippincott - Raven Publishers 227 E. Washington Sq., Philadelphia, PA 19106. TEL 215-238-4200. *4787*

JOURNAL OF PEDIATRIC ORTHOPAEDICS, PART B.
Lippincott - Raven Publishers 227 E. Washington Sq., Philadelphia, PA 19106. TEL 215-238-4200. *4787*

JOURNAL OF PEDIATRIC PSYCHOLOGY.
Plenum Publishing Corp., 233 Spring St., New York, NY 10013-1578. TEL 212-620-8000. FAX 212-463-0742. *5859*

JOURNAL OF PEDIATRIC SURGERY.
W.B. Saunders Co. Curtis Center, Independence Sq. W., Philadelphia, PA 19106-3399. TEL 215-238-7800. FAX 215-238-6445. *4913*

JOURNAL OF PEDIATRICS.
Mosby - Year Book, Inc. 11830 Westline Industrial Dr., St. Louis, MO 63146-3318. TEL 314-872-8370. FAX 314-432-1380. *4807*

JOURNAL OF PELVIC SURGERY.
Lippincott - Raven Publishers 227 E. Washington Sq., Philadelphia, PA 19106. TEL 215-238-4200. *4913*

JOURNAL OF PEPTIDE SCIENCE.
John Wiley & Sons Ltd., Journals, Baffins Ln., Chichester, W. Sussex PO19 1UD, England. TEL 44-1243-779777. FAX 44-1243-843232. *643*

THE JOURNAL OF PERFORMANCE ENHANCING DRUGS.
Whurr Publishers Ltd., 19b Compton Terrace, London N1 2UN, England. TEL 44-171-359-5979. FAX 44-171-226-5290. *5422*

JOURNAL OF PERINATOLOGY.
Mosby - Year Book, Inc. 11830 Westline Industrial Dr., St. Louis, MO 63146-3318. TEL 314-872-8370. FAX 314-432-1380. *4740*

JOURNAL OF PERIODONTAL RESEARCH.
Munksgaard International Publishers Ltd., 35 Noerre Soegade, P.O. Box 2148, DK-1016 Copenhagen K, Denmark. TEL 45-33-127030. FAX 45-33-129387. *4646*

JOURNAL OF PERIODONTOLOGY.
American Academy of Periodontology, 737 N. Michigan, Ste. 800, Chicago, IL 60611. TEL 312-573-3220. FAX 312-573-3225. *4646*

JOURNAL OF PERSONALITY.
Duke University Press, Box 90660, Durham, NC 27708-0660. TEL 919-687-3600. FAX 919-688-4574. *5859*

JOURNAL OF PERSONALITY AND SOCIAL PSYCHOLOGY.
American Psychological Association, 750 First St., N.E., Washington, DC 20002-4242. TEL 202-336-5600. FAX 202-336-5568. *5859*

JOURNAL OF PERSONALITY ASSESSMENT.
Lawrence Erlbaum Associates, Inc., 10 Industrial Dr., Mahwah, NJ 07430-2262. TEL 201-236-9500. FAX 201-236-0072. *5860*

JOURNAL OF PERSONALITY DISORDERS.
Guilford Publications, Inc., 72 Spring St., 4th Fl., New York, NY 10012. TEL 212-431-9800. FAX 212-966-6708. *5860*

JOURNAL OF PERSONNEL EVALUATION IN EDUCATION.
Kluwer Academic Publishers Boston, Box 358, Accord Sta., Hingham, MA 02018-0358. TEL 617-871-6600. FAX 617-871-6528. *2347*

JOURNAL OF PESTICIDE SCIENCE (INTERNATIONAL EDITION).
Pesticide Science Society of Japan, c/o Tamagawa University, Machida-shi, Tokyo, Japan. *2644*

JOURNAL OF PETROLEUM GEOLOGY.
Scientific Press Ltd., P.O. Box 21, Beaconsfield, Bucks. HP9 1NS, England. TEL 44-1494-675139. FAX 44-1494-670155. *5362*

JOURNAL OF PETROLEUM SCIENCE AND ENGINEERING.
Elsevier Science B.V., P.O. Box 211, 1000 AE Amsterdam, Netherlands. TEL 31-20-4853911. FAX 31-20-4853598. *5362*

JOURNAL OF PETROLEUM TECHNOLOGY.
Society of Petroleum Engineers, Inc., 222 Palisades Creek Dr., Richardson, TX 75080-2040. TEL 214-952-9393. FAX 214-952-9435. *5362*

JOURNAL OF PHARMACEUTICAL AND BIOMEDICAL ANALYSIS.
Elsevier Science B.V., P.O. Box 211, 1000 AE Amsterdam, Netherlands. TEL 31-20-4853911. FAX 31-20-4853598. *5423*

JOURNAL OF PHARMACEUTICAL CARE IN PAIN & SYMPTOM CONTROL.
Haworth Press, Inc., 10 Alice St., Binghamton, NY 13904. TEL 607-722-5857. FAX 607-722-1424. *5423*

JOURNAL OF PHARMACEUTICAL MARKETING AND MANAGEMENT.
Haworth Press, Inc., 10 Alice St., Binghamton, NY 13904. TEL 607-722-5857. FAX 607-722-1424. *5423*

JOURNAL OF PHARMACEUTICAL MEDICINE.
Chapman & Hall, 2-6 Boundary Row, London SE1 8HN, England. TEL 44-171-8650066. FAX 44-171-5229623. *5423*

JOURNAL OF PHARMACEUTICAL SCIENCES.
American Pharmaceutical Association, 2215 Constitution Ave., N.W., Washington, DC 20037. TEL 202-628-4410. FAX 202-638-3783. *5423*

JOURNAL OF PHARMACOEPIDEMIOLOGY.
Haworth Press, Inc., 10 Alice St., Binghamton, NY 13904. TEL 607-722-5857. FAX 607-722-1424. *5423*

JOURNAL OF PHARMACOKINETICS AND BIOPHARMACEUTICS.
Plenum Publishing Corp., 233 Spring St., New York, NY 10013-1578. TEL 212-620-8000. FAX 212-463-0742. *5423*

JOURNAL OF PHARMACOLOGICAL AND TOXICOLOGICAL METHODS.
Elsevier Science Inc., Box 945, New York, NY 10159-0945. TEL 212-633-3730. FAX 212-633-3680. *2847*

JOURNAL OF PHARMACOLOGY AND EXPERIMENTAL THERAPEUTICS.
Williams & Wilkins, 351 W. Camden St., Baltimore, MD 21201. TEL 410-528-4000. FAX 410-528-4312. *5423*

JOURNAL OF PHARMACY TEACHING.
Haworth Press, Inc., 10 Alice St. Binghamton, NY 13904. TEL 607-722-5857. FAX 607-722-1424. *5424*

JOURNAL OF PHARMACY TECHNOLOGY.
Harvey Whitney Books Company, Box 42696, Cincinnati, OH 45242. TEL 513-793-3555. FAX 513-793-3600. *5424*

JOURNAL OF PHASE EQUILIBRIA.
A S M International, Materials Information, Materials Park, OH 44073-0002. TEL 215-338-5151. FAX 216-338-4634. *4951*

JOURNAL OF PHILIPPINE DEVELOPMENT.
Philippine Institute for Development Studies, NEDA sa Makati Bldg., 3rd Fl., Rm. 304, 106 Amorsolo St., Legaspi Village, Makati 1229, Metro Manila, Philippines. TEL 632-893-5705. FAX 632-816-1091. *1552*

JOURNAL OF PHILOSOPHICAL LOGIC.
Kluwer Academic Publishers, Postbus 17, 3300 AA Dordrecht, Netherlands. TEL 31-78-6392392. FAX 31-78-6392254. *5482*

JOURNAL OF PHILOSOPHICAL RESEARCH.
Bowling Green State University, Philosophy Documentation Center, Bowling Green, OH 43403-0189. TEL 419-372-2419. FAX 419-372-6987. *5482*

JOURNAL OF PHILOSOPHY OF EDUCATION.
Blackwell Publishers Ltd., 108 Cowley Rd., Oxford OX4 1JF, England. TEL 44-1865-791100. FAX 44-1865-791347. *5482*

JOURNAL OF PHOTOCHEMISTRY AND PHOTOBIOLOGY, A: CHEMISTRY.
Elsevier Science S.A., P.O. Box 564, CH-1001 Lausanne 1, Switzerland. TEL 41-21-3207381. FAX 41-21-3235444. *754*

JOURNAL OF PHOTOCHEMISTRY AND PHOTOBIOLOGY, B: BIOLOGY.
Elsevier Science S.A., P.O. Box 564, CH-1001 Lausanne 1, Switzerland TEL 41-21-3207381. FAX 41-21-3235444. *643*

JOURNAL OF PHOTOGRAPHIC SCIENCE.
The Barn, Whitehall, Near Middle Marwood, Barnstaple, N. Devon EX31 4EQ, England. TEL 44-1271-72482. FAX 44-1271-24716. *5514*

JOURNAL OF PHYCOLOGY.
Allen Press, Inc., 1041 New Hampshire St., Box 1897, Lawrence, KS 66044. TEL 913-843-1221. FAX 913-843-1274. *638*

JOURNAL OF PHYSICAL AND CHEMICAL REFERENCE DATA.
American Institute of Physics, One Physics Ellipse, College Park, MD 20740-3843. TEL 301-209-3000. *1682*

JOURNAL OF PHYSICAL CHEMISTRY.
American Chemical Society, 1155 16th St., N.W., Washington, DC 20036. TEL 800-333-9511. FAX 614-447-3671. *754*

JOURNAL OF PHYSICAL OCEANOGRAPHY.
American Meteorological Society, 45 Beacon St., Boston, MA 02108-3693. TEL 617-227-2425. FAX 617-742-8718. *2298*

JOURNAL OF PHYSICAL ORGANIC CHEMISTRY.
John Wiley & Sons Ltd., Journals, Baffins Ln., Chichester, W. Sussex PO19 1UD, England. TEL 44-1243-779777. FAX 44-1243-843232. *1754*

THE JOURNAL OF PHYSICS AND CHEMISTRY OF SOLIDS.
Elsevier Science Ltd., Pergamon, P.O. Box 800, Kidlington, Oxford OX5 1DX, England. TEL 44-1865-843000. FAX 44-1865-843010. *5555*

JOURNAL OF PHYSICS OF THE EARTH.
Center for Academic Publications Japan, 2-4-16 Yayoi, Bunkyo-ku, Tokyo 113, Japan. TEL 03-3817-5821. FAX 03-5817-5820. *2277*

JOURNAL OF PHYSIOLOGY.
Cambridge University Press, Edinburgh Bldg., Shaftesbury Rd., Cambridge CB2 2RU, England. TEL 44-1223-312393. FAX 44-1223-315052. *790*

JOURNAL OF PHYSIOLOGY (PARIS).
Editions Scientifiques et Medicales Elsevier, 141 rue de Javel, 75747 Paris, France. TEL 33-1-45589022. FAX 33-1-45589421. *790*

JOURNAL OF PHYSIOLOGY AND PHARMACOLOGY.
Polskie Towarzystwo Fizjologiczne, Ul. Grzegorzecka 16, 31-531 Krakow, Poland. TEL 48-12-211006. FAX 48-12-211578. *790*

JOURNAL OF PINEAL RESEARCH.
Munksgaard International Publishers Ltd., P.O. Box 2148, DK-1016 Copenhagen K, Denmark. TEL 45-33-127030. FAX 45-33-129387. *4848*

JOURNAL OF PLANNING EDUCATION AND RESEARCH.
Association of Collegiate Schools of Planning, College of Urban and Public Affairs, University of New Orleans, New Orleans, LA 70148. TEL 504-286-7106. FAX 504-286-6272. *3587*

JOURNAL OF PLANNING LITERATURE.
Sage Publications, Inc., 2455 Teller Rd., Thousand Oaks, CA 91320. TEL 805-499-0721. FAX 805-499-0871. *3587*

JOURNAL OF PLANT BIOCHEMISTRY AND BIOTECHNOLOGY.
Society for Plant Biochemistry and Biotechnology, Division of Biochemistry, Indian Agricultural Research Institute, New Delhi 110 012, India. TEL 91-11-5750932. FAX 91-11-5750932. *643*

JOURNAL OF PLANT GROWTH REGULATION.
Springer-Verlag, Life Science Journals, 175 Fifth Ave., New York, NY 10010. TEL 212-460-1500. FAX 212-473-6272. *688*

JOURNAL OF PLANT NUTRITION.
Marcel Dekker Journals, 270 Madison Ave., New York, NY 10016. TEL 212-696-9000. FAX 212-685-4540. *688*

JOURNAL OF PLANTATION CROPS.
Indian Society for Plantation Crops, Central Plantation Crops Research Institute, Kasaragod - 671 124, Kerala, India. TEL 4995-20094. FAX 4995-22300. *228*

JOURNAL OF PLASTIC FILM AND SHEETING.
Technomic Publishing Co., Inc., 851 New Holland Ave., Box 3535, Lancaster, PA 07604. TEL 717-291-5609. FAX 717-295-4538. *5621*

JOURNAL OF POETRY THERAPY.
Human Sciences Press, Inc. 233 Spring St., New York, NY 10013-1578. TEL 212-620-8000. FAX 212-463-0742. *4309*

JOURNAL OF POLICY ANALYSIS AND MANAGEMENT.
John Wiley & Sons, Inc., Journals, 605 Third Ave., New York, NY 10158. TEL 212-850-6645. FAX 212-850-6021. *5908*

JOURNAL OF POLICY HISTORY.
Pennsylvania State University Press, 820 N. University Dr., Ste. C, University Park, PA 16802-1003. TEL 814-865-1327. FAX 814-863-1408. *3350*

JOURNAL OF POLICY MODELING.
Elsevier Science Inc., Box 945, New York, NY 10159-0945. TEL 212-633-3730. FAX 212-633-3680. *5677*

JOURNAL OF POLITICAL ECONOMY.
University of Chicago Press, Journals Division, Box 37005, Chicago, IL 60637. TEL 312-753-3347. FAX 312-753-0811. *937*

JOURNAL OF POLITICAL PHILOSOPHY.
Blackwell Publishers Ltd., 108 Cowley Rd., Oxford OX4 1JF, England. TEL 44-1865-791100. FAX 44-1865-791347. *5482*

JOURNAL OF POLITICAL SCIENCE.
College of Charleston, Department of Political Science, Charleston, SC 29424. TEL 803-953-5724. FAX 803-656-0258. *5677*

JOURNAL OF POLITICAL SCIENCE.
Government College, Department of Political Science, Lahore, Pakistan. *5677*

JOURNAL OF POLYMER MATERIALS.
Oxford & I.B.H. Publishing Co. Pvt. Ltd., 66 Janpath, New Delhi 110 001, India. FAX 91-11-3322639. *1740*

JOURNAL OF POLYMER SCIENCE. PART A: POLYMER CHEMISTRY.
John Wiley & Sons, Inc., Journals, 605 Third Ave., New York, NY 10158. TEL 212-850-6645. FAX 212-850-6021. *1740*

JOURNAL OF POLYMER SCIENCE. PART B: POLYMER PHYSICS.
John Wiley & Sons, Inc., Journals, 605 Third Ave., New York, NY 10158. TEL 212-850-6645. FAX 212-850-6021. *1740*

JOURNAL OF POLYMER SCIENCE. SYMPOSIA PROCEEDINGS.
John Wiley & Sons, Inc., Journals, 605 Third Ave., New York, NY 10158-0012. TEL 212-850-6000. FAX 212-850-6088. *1740*

JOURNAL OF POPULAR CULTURE.
Popular Press, Bowling Green State University, Bowling Green, OH 43403. TEL 419-372-7866. *4224*

JOURNAL OF POPULAR FILM AND TELEVISION.
Heldref Publications, 1319 Eighteenth St., N.W., Washington, DC 20036-1802. TEL 202-296-6267. FAX 202-296-5149. *5106*

JOURNAL OF POPULATION STUDIES.
National Taiwan University, Population Studies Center, Taipei, Taiwan, Republic of China. *5787*

JOURNAL OF POROUS MATERIALS.
Kluwer Academic Publishers, Postbus 17, 3300 AA Dordrecht, Netherlands. TEL 31-78-6392392. FAX 31-78-6392254. *2735*

JOURNAL OF PORPHYRINS AND PHTHALOCYANINES.
John Wiley & Sons Ltd., Journals, Baffins Ln., Chichester, W. Sussex PO19 1UD, England. TEL 44-1243-779777. FAX 44-1243-843232. *1682*

JOURNAL OF POST ANESTHESIA NURSING.
W.B. Saunders Co. Curtis Center, 3rd Fl., Independence Sq., Philadelphia, PA 19106-3399. TEL 215-238-7800. FAX 215-238-6445. *4718*

JOURNAL OF POST KEYNESIAN ECONOMICS.
M.E. Sharpe, Inc., 80 Business Park Dr., Armonk, NY 10504. TEL 914-273-1800. FAX 914-273-2106. *1258*

JOURNAL OF POTASSIUM RESEARCH.
Potash Research Institute of India, Sector 19, Dundahera, Gurgaon 122 001 (Haryana), India. TEL 0124-340185. *4961*

JOURNAL OF POTATO PRODUCTION & POSTHARVEST HANDLING.
Haworth Press, Inc., 10 Alice St., Binghamton, NY 13904. TEL 800-342-9678. FAX 607-722-1424. *228*

JOURNAL OF POWER SOURCES.
Elsevier Science S.A., P.O. Box 564, CH-1001 Lausanne 1, Switzerland. TEL 41-21-3207381. FAX 41-21-3235444. *2711*

JOURNAL OF PRACTICAL APPROACHES TO DEVELOPMENTAL HANDICAP.
University of Calgary, Rehabilitation Studies, c/o Rehabilitation Studies, Education Tower 4th Fl., University of Calgary, 2500 University Dr., N.W., Calgary, AB T2N 1N4, Canada. TEL 403-220-7429. FAX 403-284-5569. *2470*

JOURNAL OF PRACTICAL HYGIENE.
Montage Media Corp., 70 Hill Top Rd., Ramsey, NJ 07446. TEL 201-236-0700. FAX 201-236-1339. *4646*

JOURNAL OF PRACTICAL NURSING.
National Association for Practical Nurse Education and Service, Inc., 1400 Spring St., Ste. 310, Silver Spring, MD 20910. TEL 301-588-2491. FAX 301-588-2839. *4718*

JOURNAL OF PRAGMATICS.
North-Holland P.O. Box 211, 1000 AE Amsterdam, Netherlands. TEL 31-20-4853911. FAX 31-20-4853598. *4080*

JOURNAL OF PRE-RAPHAELITE STUDIES.
Stong College, York University, Toronto, ON M3J 1P3, Canada. TEL 416-736-5166. *4224*

JOURNAL OF PRECISION TEACHING AND CELERATION.
Standard Celeration Society, Center for Individualized Instruction, Jacksonville State University, Jacksonville, AL 36265. TEL 205-782-5570. FAX 205-782-5573. *2347*

JOURNAL OF PREVENTION AND INTERVENTION IN THE COMMUNITY.
Haworth Press, Inc., 10 Alice St., Binghamton, NY 13904. TEL 607-722-5857. FAX 607-722-1424. *5889*

JOURNAL OF PRIMARY PREVENTION.
Human Sciences Press, Inc. 233 Spring St., New York, NY 10013-1578. TEL 212-620-8000. FAX 212-463-0742. *5860*

JOURNAL OF PROCESS CONTROL.
Butterworth - Heinemann, Part of the Reed Elsevier group, Linacre House, Jordan Hill, Oxford OX2 8DP, England. TEL 44-1865-310366. FAX 44-1865-310898. *2076*

JOURNAL OF PRODUCT INNOVATION MANAGEMENT.
Elsevier Science Inc., Box 945, New York, NY 10159-0945. TEL 212-633-3730. FAX 212-633-3680. *1524*

JOURNAL OF PRODUCTIVITY ANALYSIS.
Kluwer Academic Publishers Boston, Box 358, Accord Sta., Hingham, MA 02018-0358. TEL 617-871-6600. FAX 617-871-6528. *1429*

JOURNAL OF PRODUCTS AND TOXICS LIABILITY.
Elsevier Science Ltd., Pergamon, P.O. Box 800, Kidlington, Oxford OX5 1DX, England. TEL 44-1865-843000. FAX 44-1865-843010. *3798*

JOURNAL OF PROFESSIONAL ISSUES IN ENGINEERING AND PRACTICE.
American Society of Civil Engineers, 345 E. 47th St., New York, NY 10017-2398. TEL 212-705-7288. FAX 212-980-4681. *2666*

JOURNAL OF PROFESSIONAL SERVICES MARKETING.
Haworth Press, Inc., 10 Alice St., Binghamton, NY 13904. TEL 607-722-5857. FAX 607-722-1424. *1472*

JOURNAL OF PROGRAMMING LANGUAGES.
Chapman & Hall, Journals Department 2-6 Boundary Row, London SE1 8HN, England. TEL 44-171-8650066. FAX 44-171-5229623. *2045*

JOURNAL OF PROGRESSIVE HUMAN SERVICES.
Haworth Press, Inc., 10 Alice St., Binghamton, NY 13904. TEL 607-722-5857. FAX 607-722-1424. *6379*

JOURNAL OF PROMOTION MANAGEMENT.
Haworth Press, Inc., 10 Alice St., Binghamton, NY 13904-1580. TEL 607-722-5857. FAX 607-722-1424. *39*

JOURNAL OF PROPERTY RESEARCH.
Chapman & Hall, Journals Department 2-6 Boundary Row, London SE1 8HN, England. TEL 44-171-8650066. FAX 44-171-5229623. *3587*

JOURNAL OF PROPULSION AND POWER.
American Institute of Aeronautics and Astronautics, Inc., 370 L'Enfant Promenade, S.W., Washington, DC 20024. TEL 202-646-7400. *71*

THE JOURNAL OF PROSTHETIC DENTISTRY.
Mosby - Year Book, Inc. 11830 Westline Industrial Dr., St. Louis, MO 63146-3318. TEL 314-872-8370. FAX 314-432-1380. *4646*

JOURNAL OF PROSTHETICS AND ORTHOTICS.
American Academy of Orthotists and Prosthetists, 1650 King St., Ste. 500, Alexandria, VA 22314. TEL 703-836-7116. FAX 703-836-0838. *4787*

JOURNAL OF PROSTHODONTICS.
W.B. Saunders Co. Curtis Center, 3rd Fl., Independence Sq. W., Philadelphia, PA 19106-3399. TEL 215-238-7800. FAX 215-238-6445. *4646*

JOURNAL OF PROTEIN CHEMISTRY.
Plenum Publishing Corp., 233 Spring St., New York, NY 10013-1578. TEL 212-620-8000. FAX 212-463-0742. *1740*

JOURNAL OF PSYCHIATRIC AND MENTAL HEALTH NURSING.
Blackwell Science Ltd., Osney Mead, Oxford OX2 OEL, England. TEL 44-1865-206206. FAX 44-1865-721205. *4848*

JOURNAL OF PSYCHIATRIC RESEARCH.
Elsevier Science Ltd., Pergamon, P.O. Box 800, Kidlington, Oxford OX5 1DX, England. TEL 44-1865-843000. FAX 44-1865-843010. *4848*

JOURNAL OF PSYCHOACTIVE DRUGS.
Haight-Ashbury Publications, 612 Clayton St., San Francisco, CA 94117. TEL 415-565-1904. FAX 415-864-6162. *2198*

JOURNAL OF PSYCHOEDUCATIONAL ASSESSMENT.
Psychoeducational Corporation, 505 22nd St., Knoxville, TN 37916. FAX 423-974-2135. *5860*

JOURNAL OF PSYCHOHISTORY.
Association for Psychohistory, Inc., 140 Riverside Dr., New York, NY 10024-2605. TEL 212-799-2294. *5860*

JOURNAL OF PSYCHOLINGUISTIC RESEARCH.
Plenum Publishing Corp., 233 Spring St., New York, NY 10013-1578. TEL 212-620-8000. FAX 212-463-0742. *4080*

JOURNAL OF PSYCHOLOGICAL TYPE.
Association for Psychological Type, c/o Department of Psychology, Mississippi State Univ., Box 6161, Mississippi State, MS 39762. TEL 601-325-7655. FAX 601-325-7212. *5860*

JOURNAL OF PSYCHOLOGY AND CHRISTIANITY.
Christian Association for Psychological Studies, Inc., c/o Robert R. King, Jr., Box 310400, New Braunfels, TX 78131-0400. TEL 210-629-2277. FAX 210-629-2342. *5860*

JOURNAL OF PSYCHOLOGY & HUMAN SEXUALITY.
Haworth Press, Inc., 10 Alice St., Binghamton, NY 13904. TEL 607-722-5857. FAX 607-722-1424. *5860*

JOURNAL OF PSYCHOLOGY AND JUDAISM.
Human Sciences Press, Inc. 233 Spring St., New York, NY 10013-1578. TEL 212-620-8000. FAX 212-463-0742. *5860*

JOURNAL OF PSYCHOLOGY: INTERDISCIPLINARY & APPLIED.
Heldref Publications, 1319 Eighteenth St., N.W., Washington, DC 20036-1802. TEL 202-296-6267. FAX 202-296-5149. *5861*

JOURNAL OF PSYCHOPATHOLOGY AND BEHAVIORAL ASSESSMENT.
Plenum Publishing Corp., 233 Spring St., New York, NY 10013-1578. TEL 212-620-8000. FAX 212-463-0742. *5861*

JOURNAL OF PSYCHOSOCIAL ONCOLOGY.
Haworth Press, Inc., 10 Alice St., Binghamton, NY 13904. TEL 607-722-5857. FAX 607-722-1424. *4759*

JOURNAL OF PSYCHOSOMATIC OBSTETRICS AND GYNAECOLOGY.
Parthenon Publishing Group, Casterton Hall, Casterton, Carnforth, Lancs. LA6 2LA, England. TEL 44-152-427-2084. FAX 44-152-427-1587. *4740*

JOURNAL OF PSYCHOSOMATIC RESEARCH.
Elsevier Science Inc., Box 945, New York, NY 10159-0945. TEL 212-633-3730. FAX 212-633-3680. *4848*

JOURNAL OF PSYCHOTHERAPY INTEGRATION.
Plenum Publishing Corp., 233 Spring St., New York, NY 10013-1578. TEL 212-620-8000. FAX 212-463-0742. *4848*

JOURNAL OF PUBLIC ADMINISTRATION RESEARCH AND THEORY.
Transaction Publishers, Transaction Periodicals Consortium, Department 3092, Rutgers University, New Brunswick, NJ 08903. TEL 908-445-2280. FAX 908-445-3138. *5908*

JOURNAL OF PUBLIC HEALTH MANAGEMENT AND PRACTICE.
Aspen Publishers, Inc., 200 Orchard Ridge Dr., Gaithersburg, MD 20873. FAX 301-417-7550. *5967*

JOURNAL OF PUBLIC HEALTH POLICY.
Journal of Public Health Policy, Inc., 208 Meadowood Dr., South Burlington, VT 05403. TEL 802-658-0136. FAX 802-862-4011. *5967*

JOURNAL OF PUBLIC RELATIONS RESEARCH.
Lawrence Erlbaum Associates, Inc., 10 Industrial Dr., Mahwah, NJ 07430-2262. TEL 201-236-9500. FAX 201-236-0072. *39*

JOURNAL OF PURE AND APPLIED ALGEBRA.
North-Holland P.O. Box 211, 1000 AE Amsterdam, Netherlands. TEL 31-20-4853911. FAX 31-20-4853598. *4375*

JOURNAL OF PURE AND APPLIED ULTRASONICS.
Ultrasonics Society of India, c/o Ultrasonic Section, National Physical Laboratory, Hillside Rd., New Delhi 110012, India. TEL 91-11-5781736. FAX 91-11-5752678. *5615*

JOURNAL OF QUALITY MANAGEMENT.
J A I Press Inc., 55 Old Post Rd., No. 2, Box 1678, Greenwich, CT 06836-1678. TEL 203-661-7602. FAX 203-661-0792. *1429*

JOURNAL OF QUANTITATIVE ANTHROPOLOGY.
Kluwer Academic Publishers, Postbus 17, 3300 AA Dordrecht, Netherlands. TEL 31-78-6392392. FAX 31-78-6392254. *314*

JOURNAL OF QUANTITATIVE CRIMINOLOGY.
Plenum Publishing Corp., 233 Spring St., New York, NY 10013-1578. TEL 212-620-8000. FAX 212-463-0742. *2167*

JOURNAL OF QUANTITATIVE SPECTROSCOPY AND RADIATIVE TRANSFER.
Elsevier Science Ltd., Pergamon, P.O. Box 800, Kidlington, Oxford OX5 1DX, England. TEL 44-1865-843000. FAX 44-1865-843010. *5606*

JOURNAL OF QUATERNARY SCIENCE.
John Wiley & Sons Ltd., Journals, Baffins Ln., Chichester, W. Sussex PO19 1UD, England. TEL 44-1243-779777. FAX 44-1243-843232. *2246*

JOURNAL OF RADIATION CURING.
Technology Marketing Corporation, One Technology Plaza, Norwalk, CT 06854. TEL 203-852-6800. FAX 203-853-2845. *1682*

JOURNAL OF RADIOANALYTICAL AND NUCLEAR CHEMISTRY. ARTICLES.
Elsevier Science S.A., P.O. Box 564, CH-1001 Lausanne 1. Switzerland. TEL 41-21-3207381. FAX 41-21-3235444. *1718*

JOURNAL OF RAMAN SPECTROSCOPY.
John Wiley & Sons Ltd., Journals, Baffins Ln., Chichester, W. Sussex PO19 1UD, England. TEL 44-1243-779777. FAX 44-1243-843232. *1718*

JOURNAL OF RANGE MANAGEMENT.
Society for Range Management, 1839 York St., Denver, CO 80206-1213. TEL 303-355-7070. *591*

JOURNAL OF RAPTOR RESEARCH.
Raptor Research Foundation, Inc., c/o Jim Fitzpatrick, Treas., Carpenter St. Croix Valley Nature Center, 12805 St. Croix Trail, Hastings, MN 55033. TEL 612-437-4359. FAX 612-438-2908. *777*

JOURNAL OF RATIONAL-EMOTIVE AND COGNITIVE-BEHAVIOR THERAPY.
Human Sciences Press, Inc. 233 Spring St., New York, NY 10013-1578. TEL 212-620-8000. FAX 212-463-0742. *5861*

JOURNAL OF REAL ESTATE FINANCE AND ECONOMICS.
Kluwer Academic Publishers Boston, Box 358, Accord Sta., Hingham, MA 02018-0358. TEL 617-871-6600. FAX 617-871-6528. *6028*

JOURNAL OF REAL ESTATE LITERATURE.
Kluwer Academic Publishers Boston, Box 358, Accord Sta., Hingham, MA 02018-0358. TEL 617-871-6300. FAX 617-871-6528. *6028*

JOURNAL OF REAL ESTATE PORTFOLIO MANAGEMENT.
American Real Estate Society, c/o James R. Webb, Exec. Dir., Cleveland State University, University Center, Rm. 592A, Cleveland, OH 44115. TEL 216-687-4732. FAX 216-687-9354. *6028*

JOURNAL OF REAL ESTATE RESEARCH.
American Real Estate Society, c/o James R. Webb, Cleveland State University, Dept. of Finance, College of Busines, University Center, Rm. 592A, Cleveland, OH 44115. TEL 216-687-4732. FAX 216-687-9354. *6028*

JOURNAL OF RECEPTOR AND SIGNAL TRANSDUCTION RESEARCH.
Marcel Dekker Journals, 270 Madison Ave., New York, NY 10016. TEL 212-696-9000. *643*

JOURNAL OF REFRACTIVE SURGERY.
Slack, Inc., 6900 Grove Rd., Thorofare, NJ 08086-9447. TEL 609-848-1000. FAX 609-853-5991. *4913*

JOURNAL OF REGRESSION THERAPY.
Association for Past-Life Research and Therapies, Inc., Box 20151, Riverside, CA 92516-0151. TEL 909-784-1570. FAX 909-789-8440. *5861*

JOURNAL OF REGULATORY ECONOMICS.
Kluwer Academic Publishers Boston, Box 358, Accord Sta., Hingham, MA 02018-0358. TEL 617-871-6600. FAX 617-871-6523. *1258*

JOURNAL OF REHABILITATION.
National Rehabilitation Association, 633 S. Washington St., Alexandria, VA 22314-4109. TEL 703-836-0850. FAX 703-836-0848. *6379*

JOURNAL OF REHABILITATION ADMINISTRATION.
Journal of Rehabilitation Administration, Inc., c/o Fred McFarlane, Man.Ed., Box 19891, San Diego, CA 92159. TEL 619-594-6115. FAX 619-594-4208. *1429*

JOURNAL OF REINFORCED PLASTICS & COMPOSITES.
Technomic Publishing Co., Inc., 851 New Holland Ave., Box 3535, Lancaster, PA 17604. TEL 717-291-5609. FAX 717-295-4538. *2736*

THE JOURNAL OF RELIGION.
University of Chicago Press, Journals Division, Box 37005, Chicago, IL 60637. TEL 773-753-3347. FAX 773-753-0811. *5071*

JOURNAL OF RELIGION AND HEALTH.
Human Sciences Press, Inc. 233 Spring St., New York, NY 10013-1578. TEL 212-620-8000. FAX 212-463-0742. *6072*

JOURNAL OF RELIGION IN AFRICA.
E.J. Brill, P.O. Box 9000, 2300 PA Leiden, Netherlands. TEL 31-71-5353500. FAX 31-71-5317532. *6072*

JOURNAL OF RELIGION IN DISABILITY & REHABILITATION.
Haworth Press, Inc. 10 Alice St., Binghamton, NY 13904-1580. TEL 607-722-5857. FAX 607-722-1424. *6072*

JOURNAL OF RELIGIOUS & THEOLOGICAL INFORMATION.
Haworth Press, Inc., 10 Alice St., Binghamton, NY 13904-1580. TEL 607-722-5857. FAX 607-722-1424. *6072*

JOURNAL OF RELIGIOUS GERONTOLOGY.
Haworth Press, Inc., 10 Alice St., Binghamton, NY 13904. TEL 607-722-5857. FAX 607-722-1424. *3291*

JOURNAL OF RELIGIOUS HISTORY.
Blackwell Publishers Ltd., 108 Cowley Rd., Oxford, OX4 1JF, England. TEL 44-1865-791100. FAX 44-1865-791347. *6072*

JOURNAL OF RENAL NUTRITION.
W.B. Saunders Co. Curtis Center, 3rd Fl., Independence Sq. W., Philadelphia, PA 19106-3399. TEL 215-238-7800. FAX 215-238-6445. *5236*

JOURNAL OF REPRODUCTION AND DEVELOPMENT.
Japanese Society of Animal Reproduction, c/o Dept. of Veterinary Physiology, University of Tokyo, 1-1-1 Yayoi, Bunkyo-ku, Tokyo 113, Japan. TEL 81-3-3812-2111. FAX 81-3-3815-4266. *790*

JOURNAL OF REPRODUCTIVE AND INFANT PSYCHOLOGY.
Carfax Publishing Co., P.O. Box 25, Abingdon, Oxon. OX14 3UE, England. TEL 44-1235-401000. FAX 44-1235-401550. *5861*

JOURNAL OF REPRODUCTIVE IMMUNOLOGY.
Elsevier Science Ireland Ltd., P.O. Box 85, Limerick, Ireland. TEL 353-61-471944. FAX 353-61-472144. *4585*

JOURNAL OF REPRODUCTIVE MEDICINE.
Journal of Reproductive Medicine, Inc., 8342 Olive Blvd., St. Louis, MO 63132. TEL 314-991-4440. FAX 314-991-4654. *4741*

JOURNAL OF RESEARCH AND DEVELOPMENT IN EDUCATION.
University of Georgia, College of Education, 427 Tucker Hall, Athens, GA 30602. TEL 404-542-1154. *2347*

JOURNAL OF RESEARCH IN MUSIC EDUCATION.
Music Educators National Conference, 1806 Robert Fulton Dr., Reston, VA 20191-4348. TEL 703-860-4000. FAX 703-860-4826. *5168*

JOURNAL OF RESEARCH IN PERSONALITY.
Academic Press, Inc., Journal Division, 525 B St., Ste. 1900, San Diego, CA 92101-4495. TEL 619-230-1840. FAX 619-699-6800. *5861*

JOURNAL OF RESEARCH IN PHARMACEUTICAL ECONOMICS.
Haworth Press, Inc., 10 Alice St., Binghamton, NY 13904. TEL 607-722-5857. FAX 067-722-1424. *5424*

JOURNAL OF RESEARCH IN READING.
Blackwell Publishers Ltd., 108 Cowley Rd., Oxford OX4 1JF, England. TEL 44-1865-791100. FAX 44-1865-791347. *2347*

JOURNAL OF RESEARCH IN SCIENCE TEACHING.
John Wiley & Sons, Inc., Journals, 605 Third Ave., New York, NY 10158. TEL 212-850-6645. FAX 212-850-6021. *6251*

JOURNAL OF RESEARCH ON ADOLESCENCE.
Lawrence Erlbaum Associates, Inc., 10 Industrial Dr., Mahwah, NJ 07430-2262. TEL 201-236-9500. FAX 201-236-0072. *1770*

THE JOURNAL OF RESPIRATORY DISEASES.
Cliggott Publishing Co., 55 Holly Hill Ln., Box 4010, Greenwich, CT 06831. TEL 203-661-0600. *4888*

JOURNAL OF RESTAURANT & FOODSERVICE MARKETING.
Haworth Press, Inc., 10 Alice St., Binghamton, NY 13904. TEL 607-722-5857. FAX 607-722-1424. *3566*

JOURNAL OF RETAILING AND CONSUMER SERVICES.
Butterworth - Heinemann, Part of the Reed Elsevier group, Linacre House, Jordan Hill, Oxford OX2 8DP, England. TEL 44-1865-310366. FAX 44-1865-310398. *1473*

JOURNAL OF RHEOLOGY.
American Institute of Physics, One Physics Ellipse, College Park, MD 20740-3843. TEL 301-209-3000. *5589*

JOURNAL OF RISK AND UNCERTAINTY.
Kluwer Academic Publishers Boston, Box 358, Accord Sta., Hingham, MA 02018-0358. TEL 617-871-6600. FAX 617-871-6528. *5861*

JOURNAL OF ROBOTIC SYSTEMS.
John Wiley & Sons, Inc., Journals, 605 Third Ave., New York, NY 10158. TEL 212-692-6645. FAX 212-850-6021. *2105*

JOURNAL OF RURAL HEALTH.
National Rural Health Association, 1 W. Armour Blvd., Ste. 301, Kansas City, MO 64111. TEL 816-756-3140. FAX 816-756-3144. *4484*

JOURNAL OF RURAL STUDIES.
Elsevier Science Ltd., Pergamon, P.O. Box 800, Kidlington, Oxford OX5 1DX, England. TEL 44-1865-843000. FAX 44-1865-843010. *6420*

JOURNAL OF RUSSIAN AND EAST EUROPEAN PSYCHOLOGY.
M.E. Sharpe, Inc., 80 Business Park Dr., Armonk, NY 10504. TEL 914-273-1800. FAX 914-273-2106. *5861*

JOURNAL OF RUSSIAN LASER RESEARCH.
Plenum Publishing Corp., Consultants Bureau, 233 Spring St., New York, NY 10013-1578. TEL 212-620-8468. FAX 212-463-0742. *2607*

JOURNAL OF SAFETY RESEARCH.
Elsevier Science Ltd., Pergamon, P.O. Box 800, Kidlington, Oxford OX5 1DX, England. TEL 44-1865-843000. FAX 44-1865-843010. *5252*

JOURNAL OF SAN DIEGO HISTORY.
San Diego Historical Society, Box 81825, San Diego, CA 92138. TEL 619-232-6203. FAX 619-232-6297. *3474*

JOURNAL OF SCHOOL HEALTH.
American School Health Association, Box 708, Kent, OH 44240. TEL 216-678-1601. FAX 216-678-4526. *5967*

JOURNAL OF SCHOOL LEADERSHIP.
Technomic Publishing Co., Inc., 851 New Holland Ave., Box 3535, Lancaster, PA 17604. TEL 717-291-5609. FAX 717-295-4538. *2459*

JOURNAL OF SCHOOL PSYCHOLOGY.
Elsevier Science Ltd., Pergamon, P.O. Box 800, England. TEL 44-1865-843000. FAX 44-1865-843010. *5861*

JOURNAL OF SCIENCE EDUCATION AND TECHNOLOGY.
Plenum Publishing Corp., 233 Spring St., New York, NY 10013-1578. TEL 212-620-8000. FAX 212-463-0742. *2347*

JOURNAL OF SCIENCE TEACHER EDUCATION.
Kluwer Academic Publishers, Postbus 17, 3300 AA Dordrecht, Netherlands. TEL 31-78-6392392. FAX 31-78-6392254. *2348*

JOURNAL OF SCIENCES, ISLAMIC REPUBLIC OF IRAN.
National Center for Scientific Research, 1188 Enghelab Ave., P.O. Box 13145-478, Tehran, Iran. TEL 98-21-6462778. FAX 98-21-6468180. *6251*

JOURNAL OF SCIENTIFIC COMPUTING.
Plenum Publishing Corp., 233 Spring St., New York, NY 10013-1578. TEL 212-620-8000. FAX 212-463-0742. *6306*

JOURNAL OF SCIENTIFIC EXPLORATION.
Society for Scientific Exploration, Box 5848, Stanford, CA 94309-5848. TEL 415-593-8581. FAX 415-595-4466. *6252*

JOURNAL OF SEA RESEARCH.
Netherlands Institute for Sea Research, P.O. Box 59, 1790 AB Den Burg, Texel, Netherlands. TEL 31-222-369362. FAX 31-222-319674. *2298*

JOURNAL OF SECURITY ADMINISTRATION.
B L S S, Inc., Box 164509, Miami, FL 33116-4509. TEL 305-254-7006. FAX 305-254-9662. *2183*

JOURNAL OF SEDIMENTARY RESEARCH. SECTION A: SEDIMENTARY PETROLOGY AND PROCESSES.
S E P M, 1731 E. 71st St., Tulsa, OK 74136-5108. TEL 918-793-5108. FAX 918-493-2093. *2211*

JOURNAL OF SEED TECHNOLOGY.
Association of Official Seed Analysts, Inc., Box 81152, Lincoln, NE 68501-1152. TEL 402-476-3852. *129*

JOURNAL OF SEISMOLOGY.
Kluwer Academic Publishers, Postbus 17, 3300 AA Dordrecht, Netherlands. TEL 31-78-6392392. FAX 31-78-6392254. *2277*

JOURNAL OF SERICULTURAL SCIENCE OF JAPAN.
Japanese Society of Sericultural Science, National Institute of Sericultural and Entomological Science, 1-2 Owashi, Tsukuba-shi, Ibaraki-ken 305, Japan. TEL 0298-38-6056. FAX 0298-38-6028. *731*

JOURNAL OF SEROTONIN RESEARCH.
Euroscience Press, P.O. Box 3405, London N1 0NZ, England. TEL 44-171-601-8138. FAX 44-171-601-7969. *643*

JOURNAL OF SEX EDUCATION AND THERAPY.
Guilford Publications, Inc., 72 Spring St., 4th Fl., New York, NY 10012. TEL 212-431-9800. FAX 212-966-6708. *5531*

JOURNAL OF SEX RESEARCH.
Society for the Scientific Study of Sex, Box 208, Mt. Vernon, IA 52314. TEL 319-895-8407. FAX 319-895-6203. *5862*

JOURNAL OF SHELLFISH RESEARCH.
National Shellfisheries Association, Inc., Natural Science Division, Southampton College, Southampton, NY 11968. TEL 516-287-8407. FAX 516-287-8419. *811*

JOURNAL OF SHOULDER AND ELBOW SURGERY.
Mosby - Year Book, Inc. 11830 Westline Industrial Dr., St. Louis, MO 63146-3318. TEL 314-872-8370. FAX 314-432-1380. *4913*

JOURNAL OF SINGING.
National Association of Teachers of Singing, Inc., 2800 University Blvd. N., JU Sta., Jacksonville, FL 32211. TEL 904-744-9022. FAX 904-744-9033. *5169*

JOURNAL OF SLAVIC LINGUISTICS.
Dept. of Slavic Languages, IU, Ballantine 502, Bloomington, IN 47405. TEL 812-855-2829. FAX 812-855-2107. *4080*

THE JOURNAL OF SLAVIC MILITARY STUDIES.
Frank Cass, Newbury House, 890-900 Eastern Ave., Newbury Park, Ilford, Essex 1G2 7HH, England. TEL 44-181-599-8866. FAX 44-181-599-0984. *5036*

JOURNAL OF SLEEP RESEARCH.
Blackwell Science Ltd., Osney Mead, Oxford OX2 0EL, England. TEL 44-1865-206206. FAX 44-1865-721205. *4484*

JOURNAL OF SMALL BUSINESS STRATEGY.
Small Business Institute Directors' Association, c/o Randalei Ellis, Black Hills State Univ., 1200 University, USB 9006, Spearfish, SD 57799-9006. *1577*

JOURNAL OF SMALL FRUIT & VITICULTURE.
Haworth Press, Inc., 10 Alice St., Binghamton, NY 13904. TEL 607-722-5857. FAX 607-722-1424. *229*

JOURNAL OF SOCIAL AND CLINICAL PSYCHOLOGY.
Guilford Publications, Inc., 72 Spring St., 4th Fl., New York, NY 10012. TEL 212-431-9800. FAX 212-966-6708. *5862*

JOURNAL OF SOCIAL AND PERSONAL RELATIONSHIPS.
Sage Publications Ltd., 6 Bonhill St., London EC2A 4PU, England. TEL 44-171-374-0645. FAX 44-171-374-8741. *5862*

JOURNAL OF SOCIAL BEHAVIOR AND PERSONALITY.
Select Press, Box 37, Corte Madera, CA 94976-0037. TEL 415-924-1612. FAX 415-924-7179. *5862*

JOURNAL OF SOCIAL DEVELOPMENT IN AFRICA.
School of Social Work, Private Bag 66022, Kopje, Harare, Zimbabwe. TEL 263-4-751815. FAX 263-4-751903. *6379*

JOURNAL OF SOCIAL DISTRESS AND THE HOMELESS.
Human Sciences Press, Inc. 233 Spring St., New York, NY 10013. TEL 212-620-8000. FAX 212-463-0742. *6379*

JOURNAL OF SOCIAL ISSUES.
Blackwell Publishers, 238 Main St., Cambridge, MA 02142. TEL 617-547-7110. FAX 617-547-0789. *5862*

THE JOURNAL OF SOCIAL PSYCHOLOGY.
Heldref Publications, 1319 Eighteenth St., N.W., Washington, DC 20036-1802. TEL 202-296-6267. FAX 202-296-5149. *5862*

JOURNAL OF SOCIAL SERVICE RESEARCH.
Haworth Press, Inc., 10 Alice St., Binghamton, NY 13904. TEL 607-722-5857. FAX 607-722-1424. *6380*

JOURNAL OF SOCIAL WORK EDUCATION.
Council on Social Work Education, 1600 Duke St., Alexandria, VA 22314-3421. TEL 703-683-8080. FAX 703-683-8099. *6380*

JOURNAL OF SOCIAL WORK PRACTICE.
Carfax Publishing Co., P.O. Box 25, Abingdon, Oxon. OX14 3UE, England. TEL 44-1235-401000. FAX 44-1235-401550. *6380*

JOURNAL OF SOCIOLOGY AND SOCIAL WELFARE.
Western Michigan University, School of Social Work, c/o Gary Mathews, Manag. Ed., Kalamazoo, MI 49008-5034. TEL 616-387-3198. FAX 616-387-3217. *6421*

JOURNAL OF SOFTWARE MAINTENANCE: RESEARCH AND PRACTICE.
John Wiley & Sons Ltd., Journals, Baffins Ln., Chichester, W. Sussex PO19 1UD, England. TEL 44-1243-779777. FAX 44-1243-843232. *2112*

JOURNAL OF SOFTWARE TESTING, VERIFICATION AND RELIABILITY.
John Wiley & Sons Ltd., Journals, Baffins Ln., Chichester, W. Sussex PO19 1UD, England. TEL 44-1243-779777. FAX 44-1243-843232. *2112*

JOURNAL OF SOIL AND WATER CONSERVATION.
Soil and Water Conservation Society, 7515 N.E. Ankeny Rd., Ankeny, IA 50021. TEL 515-289-2331. FAX 515-289-1227. *229*

JOURNAL OF SOIL CONTAMINATION.
C R C Press, Inc., 2000 Corporate Blvd., N.W., Boca Raton, FL 33431. TEL 407-994-0555. FAX 407-998-9784. *2837*

JOURNAL OF SOL-GEL SCIENCE AND TECHNOLOGY.
Kluwer Academic Publishers, Postbus 17, 3300 AA Dordrecht, Netherlands. TEL 31-78-6392392. FAX 31-78-6392254. *2736*

JOURNAL OF SOLAR ENERGY ENGINEERING.
American Society of Mechanical Engineers, 22 Law Dr., Fairfield, NJ 07007-2300. *2585*

JOURNAL OF SOLID STATE CHEMISTRY.
Academic Press, Inc., Journal Division, 525 B St., Ste. 1900, San Diego, CA 92101-4495. TEL 619-230-1840. FAX 619-699-6800. *1754*

JOURNAL OF SOLID WASTE TECHNOLOGY AND MANAGEMENT.
National Center for Resource Recovery and Management, c/o Dept. of Civil Engineering, Widener University, 1 University Pl., Chester, PA 19013-5792. TEL 610-499-4042. FAX 610-499-4059. *2807*

JOURNAL OF SOLUTION CHEMISTRY.
Plenum Publishing Corp., 233 Spring St., New York, NY 10013-1578. TEL 212-620-8000. FAX 212-463-0742. *1754*

JOURNAL OF SOUTH AMERICAN EARTH SCIENCES.
Elsevier Science Ltd., Pergamon, P.O. Box 800, Kidlington, Oxford OX5 1DX, England. TEL 44-1865-843000. FAX 44-1865-843010. *2211*

JOURNAL OF SOUTH-EAST ASIAN EARTH SCIENCES.
Elsevier Science Ltd., Pergamon, P.O. Box 800, Kidlington, Oxford OX5 1DX, England. TEL 44-1865-843000. FAX 44-1865-843010. *2246*

JOURNAL OF SOUTHERN AFRICAN STUDIES.
Carfax Publishing Co., P.O. Box 25, Abingdon, Oxon. OX14 3UE, England. TEL 44-1235-401000. FAX 44-1235-401550. *6332*

JOURNAL OF SOUTHERN HISTORY.
Southern Historical Association, Rice University, 6100 Main St., Houston, TX 77005-1892. TEL 713-527-3069. FAX 713-285-5207. *3474*

JOURNAL OF SOUTHWEST GEORGIA HISTORY.
Thronateeska Heritage Center, 100 Roosevelt Ave., Albany, GA 31701. TEL 912-430-4870. FAX 912-430-4830. *3474*

JOURNAL OF SPACECRAFT AND ROCKETS.
American Institute of Aeronautics and Astronautics, Inc., 370 L'Enfant Promenade, S.W., Washington, DC 20024. TEL 202-646-7400. *71*

THE JOURNAL OF SPECIAL EDUCATION.
Pro-Ed Inc., 8700 Shoal Creek Blvd., Austin, TX 78757-6897. TEL 512-451-3246. FAX 512-451-8542. *2471*

JOURNAL OF SPECIAL EDUCATION TECHNOLOGY.
Council for Exceptional Children, Technology and Media Division, c/o Herbert Rieth, Ed., Box 328, Peabody College, Nashville, TN 37203. TEL 615-322-8165. FAX 615-343-1570. *2471*

JOURNAL OF SPECULATIVE PHILOSOPHY.
Pennsylvania State University Press, 820 N. University Dr., Ste. C, University Park, PA 16802-1003. TEL 814-865-1327. FAX 814-863-1408. *5483*

JOURNAL OF SPEECH - LANGUAGE PATHOLOGY AND AUDIOLOGY.
Canadian Association of Speech - Language Pathologists and Audiologists, 2006 - 130 Albert St., Ottawa, ON K1P 5G4, Canada. TEL 613-567-9968. FAX 613-567-2859. *2471*

JOURNAL OF SPICES AND AROMATIC CROPS.
Indian Society for Spices, c/o Indian Institute of Spices Research, P.O. Box 1701, Marikunnu P.O., Calicut 673 012, Kerala, India. TEL 0495-370294. FAX 0495-370294. *229*

JOURNAL OF SPINAL CORD MEDICINE.
American Paraplegia Society, 75-20 Astoria Blvd., Jackson Heights, NY 11370-1177. TEL 718-803-3782. FAX 718-803-0414. *4817*

JOURNAL OF SPINAL DISORDERS.
Lippincott - Raven Publishers 227 E. Washington Sq., Philadelphia, PA 19106. TEL 215-238-4200. *4787*

JOURNAL OF SPIRITUAL BODYWORK.
Spiritual Massage healing Ministry, 6907 Sherman St., Philadelphia, PA 19119. TEL 215-842-0265. FAX 215-842-0265. *291*

JOURNAL OF SPORT AND EXERCISE PSYCHOLOGY.
Human Kinetics Publishers, Inc., Box 5076, Champaign, IL 61825-5076. TEL 217-351-5076. FAX 217-351-2674. *5862*

JOURNAL OF SPORT BEHAVIOR.
University of South Alabama, Department of Health, Physical Education and Leisure Services, Mobile, AL 36688. TEL 334-460-7131. FAX 334-460-7252. *6466*

JOURNAL OF SPORT MANAGEMENT.
Human Kinetics Publishers, Inc., Box 5076, Champaign, IL 61325-5076. TEL 217-351-5076. FAX 217-351-2674. *6466*

JOURNAL OF SPORT REHABILITATION.
Human Kinetics Publishers, Inc., Box 5076, Champaign, IL 61825-5076. TEL 217-351-5076. FAX 217-351-2674. *4898*

JOURNAL OF SPORTS CHIROPRACTIC AND REHABILITATION.
Williams & Wilkins, 351 W. Camden St., Baltimore, MD 21201. TEL 410-528-4000. FAX 410-528-4312. *4613*

JOURNAL OF SPORTS MEDICINE AND PHYSICAL FITNESS.
Edizioni Minerva Medica, Corso Bramante 83-85, 10126 Turin, Italy. TEL 011-678282. FAX 011-3121736. *4898*

JOURNAL OF SPORTS SCIENCES.
Chapman & Hall, Journals Department 2-6 Boundary Row, London SE1 8HN, England. TEL 44-171-8650066. FAX 44-171-5229623. *6466*

JOURNAL OF STATISTICAL COMPUTATION AND SIMULATION.
Gordon & Breach Science Publishers, c/o International Publishers Distributor, P.O. Box 3054, Langhorne, PA 19047-3054. TEL 215-750-2642. FAX 215-750-6343. *2052*

JOURNAL OF STATISTICAL PHYSICS.
Plenum Publishing Corp., 233 Spring St., New York, NY 10013-1578. TEL 212-620-8000. FAX 212-463-0742. *5556*

JOURNAL OF STATISTICAL PLANNING AND INFERENCE.
North-Holland P.O. Box 211, 1000 AE Amsterdam, Netherlands. TEL 31-20-4853911. FAX 31-20-4853598. *6614*

JOURNAL OF STEROID BIOCHEMISTRY AND MOLECULAR BIOLOGY.
Elsevier Science Ltd., Pergamon, P.O. Box 800, Kidlington, Oxford OX5 1DX, England. TEL 44-1865-843000. FAX 44-1865-843010. *643*

JOURNAL OF STORED PRODUCTS RESEARCH.
Elsevier Science Ltd., Pergamon, P.O. Box 800, Kidlington, Oxford OX5 1DX, England. TEL 44-1865-843000. FAX 44-1865-843010. *229*

JOURNAL OF STRATEGIC CHANGE.
John Wiley & Sons Ltd., Journals, Baffins Ln., Chichester, W. Sussex PO19 1UD, England. TEL 44-1243-779777. FAX 44-1243-843232. *1429*

JOURNAL OF STRATEGIC INFORMATION SYSTEMS.
Elsevier Science B.V., P.O. Box 211, 1000 AE Amsterdam, Netherlands. TEL 31-20-4853911. FAX 31-20-4853598. *2051*

JOURNAL OF STRATEGIC MARKETING.
Chapman & Hall, Journals Department 2-6 Boundary Row, London SE1 8HN, England. TEL 44-171-8650066. FAX 44-171-5229623. *1473*

THE JOURNAL OF STRATEGIC STUDIES.
Frank Cass, Newbury House, 850-900 Eastern Ave., Newbury Park, Ilford, Essex IG2 7HH, England. TEL 44-181-599-8866. FAX 44-181-599-0984. *5759*

JOURNAL OF STRENGTH AND CONDITIONING RESEARCH.
Human Kinetics Publishers, Inc. Box 5076, Champaign, IL 61825-5076. TEL 217-351-5076. FAX 217-351-2674. *4899*

JOURNAL OF STRUCTURAL BIOLOGY.
Academic Press, Inc., Journal Division, 525 B St., Ste. 1900, San Diego, CA 92101-4495. TEL 619-230-1840. FAX 619-699-6859. *591*

JOURNAL OF STRUCTURAL CHEMISTRY.
Plenum Publishing Corp., Consultants Bureau, 233 Spring St., New York, NY 10013-1578. TEL 212-620-8468. FAX 212-463-0742. *1682*

JOURNAL OF STRUCTURAL GEOLOGY.
Elsevier Science Ltd., Pergamon, P.O. Box 800, Kidlington, Oxford OX5 1DX, England. TEL 44-1865-843000. FAX 44-1865-843010. *2247*

JOURNAL OF STRUCTURAL LEARNING.
Gordon & Breach Science Publishers, c/o International Publishers Distributor, P.O. Box 3054, Langhorne, PA 19047-3054. TEL 215-750-2642. FAX 215-750-6343. *5362*

JOURNAL OF STUDIES ON ALCOHOL. SUPPLEMENT.
Alcohol Research Documentation, Inc., Box 969, Piscataway, NJ 08855. TEL 908-445-3510. FAX 908-445-5944. *2198*

JOURNAL OF SUBSTANCE ABUSE TREATMENT.
Elsevier Science Inc., Box 945, New York, NY 10159-0945. TEL 212-633-3730. FAX 212-633-3680. *2199*

JOURNAL OF SUBSTANCE MISUSE.
Churchill Livingstone Robert Stevenson House, 1-3 Baxter's Pl., Leith Walk, Edinburgh EH1 3AF, Scotland. TEL 44-131-5562424. *2199*

JOURNAL OF SUDDEN INFANT DEATH SYNDROME AND INFANT MORTALITY.
Plenum Publishing Corp., 233 Spring St., New York, NY 10013-1578. TEL 212-620-8000. FAX 212-463-0742. *4808*

JOURNAL OF SUPERCOMPUTING.
Kluwer Academic Publishers Boston, Box 358, Accord Sta., Hingham, MA 02018-0358. TEL 617-871-6300. FAX 617-871-6528. *1994*

JOURNAL OF SUPERCONDUCTIVITY.
Plenum Publishing Corp., 233 Spring St., New York, NY 10013-1578. TEL 212-620-8000. FAX 212-463-0742. *5556*

JOURNAL OF SUPERCRITICAL FLUIDS.
Polymer Research Associates, Inc., 9200 Montgomery Rd., Ste. 23B, Cincinnati, OH 45242. TEL 513-891-7030. FAX 513-891-5867. *1718*

JOURNAL OF SURGICAL ONCOLOGY.
John Wiley & Sons, Inc., Journals, 605 Third Ave., New York, NY 10158. TEL 212-850-6645. FAX 212-850-6021. *4913*

JOURNAL OF SURGICAL PATHOLOGY.
Chapman & Hall, Journals Department 2-6 Boundary Row, London SE1 8HN, England. TEL 44-171-8650066. FAX 44-171-5229623. *4485*

JOURNAL OF SURGICAL RESEARCH.
Academic Press, Inc., Journal Division, 525 B St., Ste. 1900, San Diego, CA 92101-4495. TEL 619-230-1840. FAX 619-699-6800. *4913*

JOURNAL OF SURVEYING ENGINEERING.
American Society of Civil Engineers, 345 E. 47th St., New York, NY 10017-2398. TEL 212-705-7288. FAX 212-980-4681. *2666*

JOURNAL OF SUSTAINABLE AGRICULTURE.
Haworth Press, Inc., 10 Alice St., Binghamton, NY 13904-1580. TEL 607-722-5857. FAX 607-722-1424. *2131*

JOURNAL OF SUSTAINABLE FORESTRY.
Haworth Press, Inc., 10 Alice St., Binghamton, NY 13904. TEL 607-722-5857. FAX 607-722-1424. *3020*

JOURNAL OF SWIMMING RESEARCH.
American Swimming Coaches Association, 301 S.E. 20th St., Fort Lauderdale, FL 33316. FAX 305-462-6280. *6467*

JOURNAL OF SYNCHROTRON RADIATION.
Munksgaard International Publishers Ltd., 35 Noerre Soegade, P.O. Box 1248, DK-1016 Copenhagen K, Denmark. TEL 45-33-127030. FAX 45-33-129387. *5596*

JOURNAL OF SYNTHETIC LUBRICATION.
Leaf Coppin Publishing Co., P.O. Box 111, Deal, Kent CT14 6SX, England. TEL 44-1304-360241. *5362*

JOURNAL OF SYSTEMS AND SOFTWARE.
Elsevier Science Inc., Box 945, New York, NY 10159-0945. TEL 212-633-3730. FAX 212-633-3680. *2112*

JOURNAL OF SYSTEMS ARCHITECTURE.
North-Holland P.O. Box 211, 1000 AE Amsterdam, Netherlands. TEL 31-20-4853911. FAX 31-20-4853598. *2088*

JOURNAL OF SYSTEMS ENGINEERING.
Springer-Verlag London Ltd., Sweetapple House, Catteshall Rd., Godalming, Surrey GU7 3DJ, England. TEL 44-1483-418800. FAX 44-1483-415144. *2748*

JOURNAL OF SYSTEMS ENGINEERING AND ELECTRONICS.
Science Press, Marketing and Sales Department, 16 Donghuangchenggen North St., Beijing 100717, People's Republic of China. TEL 4010642. FAX 4019810. *71*

JOURNAL OF SYSTEMS INTEGRATION.
Kluwer Academic Publishers Boston, Box 358, Accord Sta., Hingham, MA 02018-0358. TEL 617-871-6600. FAX 617-871-6528. *2057*

JOURNAL OF TARGETING, MEASUREMENT AND ANALYSIS.
Henry Stewart Publications, Russell House, 28-30 Little Russell St., London WC1A 2HN, England. TEL 44-171-404-3040. FAX 44-171-486-2081. *1524*

THE JOURNAL OF TAXATION.
Warren, Gorham & Lamont, One Penn Plaza, New York, NY 10119. TEL 212-971-5185. FAX 212-971-5113. *1552*

JOURNAL OF TEACHER EDUCATION.
Corwin Press, Inc. 2455 Teller Rd., Thousand Oaks, CA 91320. TEL 805-499-0721. FAX 805-499-0871. *2434*

JOURNAL OF TEACHING IN INTERNATIONAL BUSINESS.
Haworth Press, Inc., 10 Alice St., Binghamton, NY 13904. TEL 607-722-5857. FAX 607-722-1424. *2348*

JOURNAL OF TEACHING IN PHYSICAL EDUCATION.
Human Kinetics Publishers, Inc., Box 5076, Champaign, IL 61825-5076. TEL 217-351-5076. FAX 217-351-2674. *2492*

JOURNAL OF TEACHING IN SOCIAL WORK.
Haworth Press, Inc., 10 Alice St., Binghamton, NY 13904. TEL 607-722-5857. FAX 607-722-6362. *2492*

JOURNAL OF TECHNICAL WRITING AND COMMUNICATION.
Baywood Publishing Co., Inc., 26 Austin Ave., Box 337, Amityville, NY 11701. TEL 516-691-1270. FAX 516-691-1770. *2348*

JOURNAL OF TECHNOLOGY AND TEACHER EDUCATION.
Association for the Advancement of Computing in Education, Box 2966, Charlottesville, VA 22901-2966. TEL 804-973-3987. *2407*

JOURNAL OF TECHNOLOGY EDUCATION.
Virginia Polytechnic Institute, Technology Education Program, c/o Mark Sanders, Ed., 144 Smyth Hall, Blacksburg, VA 24061-0432. FAX 703-231-4188. *2492*

JOURNAL OF TECHNOLOGY STUDIES.
Epsilon Pi Tau, c/o Jerry Streichler, Ed., Bowling Green State University, Bowling Green, OH 43403-0305. *6655*

JOURNAL OF TECHNOLOGY TRANSFER.
Technology Transfer Society, 55 S. State Ave., Ste. 3-F2, Indianapolis, IN 46201-7876. *6655*

JOURNAL OF TERRAMECHANICS.
Elsevier Science Ltd., Pergamon, P.O. Box 800, Kidlington, Oxford OX5 1DX, England. TEL 44-1865-843000. FAX 44-1865-843010. *6721*

JOURNAL OF TESTING AND EVALUATION.
American Society for Testing and Materials, 100 Barr Harbor Dr., W. Conshohocken, PA 19428-2959. TEL 610-832-9500. FAX 610-832-9555. *2736*

JOURNAL OF THE ATMOSPHERIC SCIENCES.
American Meteorological Society, 45 Beacon St., Boston, MA 02108-3693. TEL 617-227-2425. FAX 617-742-8718. *5000*

JOURNAL OF THE AUSTRALIAN WAR MEMORIAL.
Australian War Memorial, G.P.O. Box 345, Canberra, A.C.T. 2601, Australia. TEL 61-6-2434345. FAX 61-6-2434325. *5036*

JOURNAL OF THE AUTONOMIC NERVOUS SYSTEM.
Elsevier Science B.V., P.O. Box 211, 1000 AE Amsterdam, Netherlands. TEL 31-20-4853911. FAX 31-20-4853598. *4849*

JOURNAL OF THE ECONOMIC AND SOCIAL HISTORY OF THE ORIENT.
E.J. Brill, P.O. Box 9000, 2300 PA Leiden, Netherlands. TEL 31-71-5353500. FAX 31-71-5317532. *3497*

JOURNAL OF THE FANTASTIC IN THE ARTS.
International Association for the Fantastic in the Arts, c/o Jade Seas Publishing, 1157 Temple Tr., Stow, OH 44224. TEL 216-688-2818. *4328*

JOURNAL OF THE FRESHMAN YEAR EXPERIENCE.
University of South Carolina, National Center for the Study of the Freshman Year Experience, 1728 College St., Columbia, SC 29208. TEL 803-777-6029. FAX 803-777-4699. *2434*

JOURNAL OF THE GULF AND ARABIAN PENINSULA STUDIES.
University of Kuwait, P.O. Box 17073, Al-Khaldiah 72451, Kuwait. TEL 965-4816807. FAX 965-4814295. *3497*

JOURNAL OF THE HISTORY OF BIOLOGY.
Kluwer Academic Publishers, Postbus 17, 3300 AA Dordrecht, Netherlands. TEL 31-78-6392392. FAX 31-78-6392254. *591*

JOURNAL OF THE HISTORY OF DENTISTRY.
American Academy of the History of Dentistry, c/o Aletha Kowitz, 100 S. Vail Ave., Arlington Heights, IL 60005-1866. TEL 847-670-7561. *4647*

JOURNAL OF THE HISTORY OF MEDICINE AND ALLIED SCIENCES.
Oxford University Press, Oxford Journals, Walton St., Oxford OX2 6DP, England. TEL 44-1865-267485. FAX 44-1865-267907. *4485*

JOURNAL OF THE HISTORY OF SEXUALITY.
University of Chicago Press, Journals Division, Box 37005, Chicago, IL 60637. TEL 312-753-3347. FAX 312-753-0811. *6421*

JOURNAL OF THE HISTORY OF THE BEHAVIORAL SCIENCES.
John Wiley & Sons, Inc., Journals, 605 Third Ave., New York, NY 10158-0012. TEL 212-850-6645. FAX 212-850-6021. *5863*

JOURNAL OF THE HISTORY OF THE NEUROSCIENCES.
Swets & Zeitlinger bv, P.O. Box 825, 2160 SZ Lisse, Netherlands. TEL 31-252-435111. FAX 31-252-415888. *4849*

JOURNAL OF THE LEARNING SCIENCES.
Lawrence Erlbaum Associates, Inc., 10 Industrial Dr., Mahwah, NJ 07430-2262. TEL 201-236-9500. FAX 201-236-0072. *2348*

JOURNAL OF THE MECHANICS AND PHYSICS OF SOLIDS.
Elsevier Science Ltd., Pergamon, P.O. Box 800, Kidlington, Oxford OX5 1DX, England. TEL 44-1865-843000. FAX 44-1865-843010. *5589*

JOURNAL OF THE NEUROLOGICAL SCIENCES.
Elsevier Science B.V., P.O. Box 211, 1000 AE Amsterdam, Netherlands. TEL 31-20-4853911. FAX 31-20-4853598. *4849*

JOURNAL OF THE NEUROMUSCULOSKELETAL SYSTEM.
Data Trace Publishing Company, 110 West Rd., Ste. 227, Baltimore, MD 21204-2316. TEL 410-494-4994. FAX 410-494-0515. *4849*

JOURNAL OF THE PHILOSOPHY OF SPORT.
Human Kinetics Publishers, Inc., Box 5076, Champaign, IL 61825-5076. TEL 217-351-5076. FAX 217-351-2674. *6467*

JOURNAL OF THE ROYAL ASIATIC SOCIETY.
Cambridge University Press, Edinburgh Bldg., Shaftesbury Rd., Cambridge CB2 2RU, England. TEL 44-1223-312393. FAX 44-1223-315052. *5287*

JOURNAL OF THE SCIENCE OF FOOD AND AGRICULTURE.
John Wiley & Sons Ltd., Journals, Baffins Ln., Chichester, W. Sussex PO19 1UD, England. TEL 44-1243-779777. FAX 44-1243-843232. *129*

JOURNAL OF THE THIRD WORLD SPECTRUM.
Box 44843, Washington, DC 20026-4843. TEL 202-806-7649. *5287*

JOURNAL OF THE WEST.
Journal of the West, Inc., 1531 Yuma, Box 1009, Manhattan, KS 66505-1009. TEL 913-539-1888. FAX 913-539-2233. *3475*

JOURNAL OF THEOLOGY FOR SOUTHERN AFRICA.
c/o University of Cape Town, Department of Religious Studies, Rondebosch 7700, South Africa. TEL 27-21-650-3453. FAX 27-21-650-3761. *6073*

JOURNAL OF THEORETICAL POLITICS.
Sage Publications Ltd., 6 Bonhill St., London EC2A 4PU, England. TEL 44-171-374-0645. FAX 44-171-374-8741. *5677*

JOURNAL OF THEORETICAL PROBABILITY.
Plenum Publishing Corp., 233 Spring St., New York, NY 10013-1578. TEL 212-620-8000. FAX 212-463-0742. *4375*

JOURNAL OF THEORY CONSTRUCTION AND TESTING.
Tucker Publications, Inc., Box 580, Lisle, IL 60532. TEL 708-969-3809. FAX 708-969-3895. *4719*

JOURNAL OF THERAPEUTIC HORTICULTURE.
American Horticultural Therapy Association, 362A Christopher Ave., Gaithersburg, MD 20879-3660. TEL 301-948-3010. FAX 301-869-2397. *3059*

JOURNAL OF THERMAL ANALYSIS.
Akademiai Kiado, Publishing House of the Hungarian Academy of Sciences, P.O. Box 245, H-1519 Budapest, Hungary. TEL 181-2134. FAX 166-6466. *1754*

JOURNAL OF THERMAL INSULATION AND BUILDING ENVELOPES.
Technomic Publishing Co., Inc., 851 New Holland Ave., Box 3535, Lancaster, PA 17604. TEL 717-291-5609. FAX 717-295-4538. *2608*

JOURNAL OF THERMAL SCIENCE.
Science Press, Marketing and Sales Department, 16 Donghuangchenggen North St., Beijing 100717, People's Republic of China. TEL 4010642. FAX 4019810. *5585*

JOURNAL OF THERMAL SPRAY TECHNOLOGY.
A S M International, Materials Information, Materials Park, OH 44073-0002. TEL 216-338-5151. FAX 216-338-4634. *5585*

JOURNAL OF THERMAL STRESSES.
Taylor & Francis Inc., 1900 Frost Rd., Ste. 101, Bristol, PA 19007-1598. TEL 215-785-5800. FAX 215-785-5515. *2760*

JOURNAL OF THERMOPHYSICS AND HEAT TRANSFER.
American Institute of Aeronautics and Astronautics, Inc., 370 L'Enfant Promenade, S.W., Washington, DC 20024. TEL 202-646-7400. *5556*

JOURNAL OF THERMOPLASTIC COMPOSITE MATERIALS.
Technomic Publishing Co., Inc., 851 New Holland Ave., Box 3535, Lancaster, PA 17604. TEL 717-291-5609. FAX 717-295-4538. *5621*

JOURNAL OF THIRD WORLD STUDIES.
Association of Third World Studies, Inc., Box 1232, Americus, GA 31709. TEL 912-924-8287. FAX 912-931-2270. *3350*

THE JOURNAL OF THORACIC AND CARDIOVASCULAR SURGERY.
Mosby - Year Book, Inc. 11830 Westline Industrial Dr., St. Louis, MO 63146-3318. TEL 314-872-8370. FAX 314-432-1380. *4913*

JOURNAL OF THORACIC IMAGING.
Lippincott - Raven Publishers 276 E. Washington Sq., Philadelphia, PA 19106. TEL 215-238-4200. *4878*

JOURNAL OF THROMBOSIS AND THROMBOLYSIS.
Kluwer Academic Publishers, Postbus 17, 3300 AA Dordrecht, Netherlands. TEL 31-78-6392392. FAX 31-78-6392254. *4607*

JOURNAL OF TIME SERIES ANALYSIS.
Blackwell Publishers Ltd., 108 Cowley Rd., Oxford OX4 1JF, England. TEL 44-1865-791100. FAX 44-1865-791347. *6614*

JOURNAL OF TISSUE VIABILITY.
Tissue Viability Society, c/o Wessex Rehabilitation Association, Salisbury District Hospital, Salisbury, Wilts. SP2 8BJ, England. TEL 44-1722-336262. FAX 44-1722-325904. *4663*

THE JOURNAL OF TOURISM STUDIES.
James Cook University of North Queensland, Department of Tourism, Townsville, Qld. 4811, Australia. TEL 61-77-815133. FAX 61-77-251116. *6895*

JOURNAL OF TOXICOLOGY. CLINICAL TOXICOLOGY.
Marcel Dekker Journals, 270 Madison Ave., New York, NY 10016. TEL 212-696-9000. FAX 212-685-4540. *2847*

JOURNAL OF TOXICOLOGY. CUTANEOUS AND OCULAR TOXICOLOGY.
Marcel Dekker Journals, 270 Madison Ave., New York, NY 10016. TEL 212-696-9000. FAX 212-685-4540. *5424*

JOURNAL OF TOXICOLOGY. TOXIN REVIEWS.
Marcel Dekker Journals, 270 Madison Ave., New York, NY 10016. TEL 212-696-9000. FAX 212-685-4540. *5424*

JOURNAL OF TOXICOLOGY AND ENVIRONMENTAL HEALTH.
Taylor & Francis Inc., 1900 Frost Rd., Ste. 101, Bristol, PA 19007-1598. FAX 215-785-5515. *2847*

JOURNAL OF TRACE AND MICROPROBE TECHNIQUES.
Marcel Dekker Journals, 270 Madison Ave., New York, NY 10016. TEL 212-696-9000. FAX 212-685-4540. *1718*

THE JOURNAL OF TRACE ELEMENTS IN EXPERIMENTAL MEDICINE.
John Wiley & Sons, Inc., Journals, 605 Third Ave., New York, NY 10158. TEL 212-850-6645. FAX 212-850-6021. *4681*

JOURNAL OF TRADITIONAL MEDICINES.
Chuo Insatsu Co., 1-4-5, Shimookui, Toyama 930-01, Japan. TEL 0764-32-6572. *5424*

JOURNAL OF TRAFFIC MEDICINE.
International Association for Accident and Traffic Medicine, c/o Kjell Roos, IAATM Headquarters, P.O. Box 1644, S-751 46 Uppsala, Sweden. TEL 4618-175-158. FAX 4618-175-031. *4787*

JOURNAL OF TRANSCULTURAL NURSING.
Transcultural Nursing Society, 601 N. Wenona, Bay City, MI 48706. TEL 517-684-7381. FAX 517-684-1248. *4719*

JOURNAL OF TRANSNATIONAL MANAGEMENT DEVELOPMENT.
Haworth Press, Inc., 10 Alice St., Binghamton, NY 13904-1580. TEL 607-722-5857. FAX 607-722-1424. *1287*

JOURNAL OF TRANSPLANT COORDINATION.
American Association of Critical Care Nurses, 101 Columbia, Aliso Viejo, CA 92656. TEL 714-362-2000. FAX 714-362-2020. *4913*

JOURNAL OF TRANSPORT ECONOMICS AND POLICY.
University of Bath Claverton Down, Bath BA2 7AY, England. TEL 44-1225-826302. FAX 44-1225-826767. *6721*

JOURNAL OF TRANSPORT GEOGRAPHY.
Butterworth - Heinemann, Part of the Reed Elsevier group, Linacre House, Jordan Hill, Oxford OX2 8DP, England. TEL 44-1865-310366. FAX 44-1865-310898. *2264*

JOURNAL OF TRANSPORTATION ENGINEERING.
American Society of Civil Engineers, 345 E. 47th St., New York, NY 10017-2398. TEL 212-705-7288. FAX 212-980-4681. *6721*

JOURNAL OF TRAUMA - INJURY, INFECTION AND CRITICAL CARE.
Williams & Wilkins, 351 W. Camden St., Baltimore, MD 21201 TEL 410-528-4000. FAX 410-528-4312. *4737*

JOURNAL OF TRAUMATIC STRESS.
Plenum Publishing Corp., 233 Spring St., New York, NY 10013 1578. TEL 212-620-8000. FAX 212-463-0742 *5863*

JOURNAL OF TRAVEL & TOURISM MARKETING.
Haworth Press, Inc., 10 Alice St., Binghamton, NY 13904-1580. TEL 607-722-5857. FAX 607-722-1424. *6895*

JOURNAL OF TREE FRUIT PRODUCTION.
Haworth Press, Inc., 10 Alice St., Binghamton, NY 13904-1580. TEL 607-722-5857. FAX 607-722-1424. *229*

JOURNAL OF TRIBOLOGY.
American Society of Mechanical Engineers, 22 Law Dr., Fairfield, NJ 07007-2300. *5362*

JOURNAL OF TROPICAL AGRICULTURE.
Kerala Agricultural University, College of Horticulture, Vellanikkara 680 654, Trichur, Kerala, India. TEL 91-487-21822 FAX 91-487-399019. *129*

JOURNAL OF TROPICAL FOREST PRODUCTS.
Forest Research Institute Malaysia, Kepong, 52109 Kuala Lumpur, Malaysia. *3020*

JOURNAL OF TROPICAL FOREST SCIENCE.
Forest Research Institute Malaysia, Kepong, 52109 Kuala Lumpur, Malaysia. *3020*

JOURNAL OF TROPICAL MEDICINE.
Royal Society of Tropical Medicine & Hygiene, Egyptian Branch, Tager Bldg., 1 Dzoris St., Garden City, Cairo, Egypt. TEL 3541857. *4624*

JOURNAL OF TROPICAL METEOROLOGY.
Guangzhou Redai Haiyang Qixiang Yanjiusuo, No. 6, Fujir Rd., Dongshan District, Guangzhou, Guangdong 510080, People's Republic of China. TEL 86-20-777-5231. FAX 86-20-776-5281. *5000*

JOURNAL OF TURBOMACHINERY
American Society of Mechanical Engineers, 22 Law Dr., Fairfield, NJ 07007 2300. *2760*

JOURNAL OF TURFGRASS MANAGEMENT.
Haworth Press, Inc., Food Products Press, 10 Alice St., Binghamton, NY 13904-1580. FAX 607-722-6362. *229*

JOURNAL OF UKRAINIAN STUDIES.
Canadian Institute of Ukrainian Studies, 352 Athabasca Hall, University of Alberta, Edmonton, AB T6G 2E8, Canada. TEL 416-978-8669. FAX 416-978-2672. *4224*

JOURNAL OF ULTRASOUND IN MEDICINE.
American Institute for Ultrasound in Medicine, 14750 Sweitzer Ln., Ste. 100, Laurel, MD 20707-5906. TEL 301-498-4100. FAX 301-498-4450. *4879*

JOURNAL OF UNDERGRADUATE MATHEMATICS.
Guilford College, Department of Mathematics, Greensboro, NC 27410 *4375*

JOURNAL OF UNDERGRADUATE RESEARCH IN PHYSICS.
Guilford College, Department of Physics, Guilford, NC 27410. TEL 910-316-2279. FAX 910-316-2951. *5556*

JOURNAL OF UROGENITAL PATHOLOGY.
Field & Wood, Medical Periodicals, Inc., Box 975, Blue Bell, PA 19422. TEL 610-828-4010. FAX 215-482-0226. *4928*

JOURNAL OF UROLOGIC PATHOLOGY.
Humana Press Inc., 999 Riverview Dr., Ste. 208, Totowa, NJ 07512. TEL 201-256-1699. FAX 201-256-8341. *4928*

JOURNAL OF UROLOGY.
Williams & Wilkins, 351 W. Camden St., Baltimore, MD 21201. TEL 410-528-4000. FAX 410-528-4312. *4928*

JOURNAL OF V L S I SIGNAL PROCESSING.
Kluwer Academic Publishers Boston, Box 358, Accord Sta., Hingham, MA 02018-0358. TEL 617-871-6600. FAX 617-871-6528. *2069*

JOURNAL OF VACATION MARKETING.
Henry Stewart Publications, Russell House, 28-30 Little Russell St., London WC1A 2HN, England. TEL 44-171-404-3040. FAX 44-171-404-2081. *6895*

JOURNAL OF VACUUM SCIENCE AND TECHNOLOGY. PART A. VACUUM, SURFACES AND FILMS.
American Institute of Physics, One Physics Ellipse, College Park, MD 20740-3843. TEL 301-209-3000. *5556*

JOURNAL OF VACUUM SCIENCE AND TECHNOLOGY. PART B. MICROELECTRONICS AND NANOMETER STRUCTURES.
American Institute of Physics, One Physics Ellipse, College Park, MD 20740-3843. TEL 301-209-3000. *5556*

THE JOURNAL OF VALUE INQUIRY.
Kluwer Academic Publishers, Postbus 17, 3300 AA Dordrecht, Netherlands. TEL 31-78-6392392. FAX 31-78-6392254. *5483*

JOURNAL OF VASCULAR AND INTERVENTIONAL RADIOLOGY.
Lippincott - Raven Publishers 227 E. Washington Sq., Philadelphia, PA 19106. TEL 215-238-4200. *4879*

JOURNAL OF VASCULAR NURSING.
Mosby - Year Book, Inc. 11830 Westline Industrial Dr., St. Louis, MO 63146-3318. TEL 314-872-8370. FAX 314-432-1380. *4719*

JOURNAL OF VASCULAR RESEARCH.
S. Karger AG, Allschwilerstr. 10, P.O. Box, CH-4009 Basel, Switzerland. TEL 061-3061111. FAX 061-3061234. *643*

JOURNAL OF VASCULAR SURGERY.
Mosby - Year Book, Inc. 11830 Westline Industrial Dr., St. Louis, MO 63146-3318. TEL 314-872-8370. FAX 314-432-1380. *4914*

JOURNAL OF VASCULAR TECHNOLOGY.
Society of Vascular Technology, 4601 Presidents Dr., Ste. 260, Lanham, MD 20706-4365. TEL 301-459-7550. FAX 301-459-5651. *4607*

JOURNAL OF VECTOR ECOLOGY.
Society for Vector Ecology, Box 87, Santa Ana, CA 92702. TEL 714-971-2421. FAX 714-971-3940. *731*

JOURNAL OF VEGETABLE CROP PRODUCTION.
Haworth Press, Inc., 10 Alice St., Binghamton, NY 13904. TEL 607-722-5857. FAX 607-722-1424. *229*

JOURNAL OF VEGETATION SCIENCE.
Opulus Press AB, P.O. Box 25137, S-750 25 Uppsala, Sweden. TEL 46-18-32-06-62. FAX 46-18-32-13-68. *688*

JOURNAL OF VENOMOUS ANIMALS AND TOXINS.
Universidade Estadual Paulista, Centro de Estudios de Venenos e Animais Peconhentos, Caixa Postal 577, 18618-000 Botucatu SP, Brazil. TEL 55-148-212121. FAX 55-14-8213963. *5424*

JOURNAL OF VERTEBRATE PALEONTOLOGY.
Society of Vertebrate Paleontology, W. 436 Nebraska Hall, University of Nebraska, Lincoln, NE 68588-0542. TEL 402-472-4604. FAX 402-472-8949. *5314*

JOURNAL OF VESTIBULAR RESEARCH: EQUILIBRIUM AND ORIENTATION.
Elsevier Science Inc., Box 945, New York, NY 10159-0945. TEL 212-633-3730. FAX 212-633-3680. *790*

THE JOURNAL OF VETERINARY AND CLINICAL IMMUNOLOGY.
Veterinary Practice Publishing Co., 7 Ashley Ave., S., Santa Barbara, CA 93103-3307. TEL 805-965-1028. FAX 805-965-0722. *6949*

JOURNAL OF VETERINARY EMERGENCY AND CRITICAL CARE.
V.E.C.C.S. Administration Office, 15729 San Pedro, San Antonio, TX 78232. TEL 210-826-1488. *6949*

JOURNAL OF VETERINARY INTERNAL MEDICINE.
W.B. Saunders Co. Curtis Center, 3rd Fl., Independence Sq. W., Philadelphia, PA 19106-3399. TEL 215-238-7800. FAX 215-238-6445. *6949*

JOURNAL OF VETERINARY PHARMACOLOGY AND THERAPEUTICS.
Blackwell Science Ltd., Osney Mead, Oxford OX2 0EL, England. TEL 44-1865-206206. FAX 44-1865-721205. *5425*

JOURNAL OF VIBRATION AND ACOUSTICS.
American Society of Mechanical Engineers, 22 Law Dr., Fairfield, NJ 07007-2300. TEL 800-843-2763. *2761*

JOURNAL OF VIBRATION AND CONTROL.
Sage Publications, Inc., Sage Science Press, 2455 Teller Rd., Thousand Oaks, CA 91320. TEL 805-499-0721. FAX 805-499-0871. *5615*

JOURNAL OF VINYL & ADDITIVE TECHNOLOGY.
Society of Plastics Engineers, Inc., 14 Fairfield Dr., Box 0403, Brookfield, CT 06804-0403. TEL 203-775-0471. FAX 203-775-8490. *5621*

JOURNAL OF VIRAL HEPATITIS.
Blackwell Science Ltd., Osney Mead, Oxford OX2 0EL, England. TEL 44-1865-206206. FAX 44-1865-721205. *4694*

JOURNAL OF VIROLOGICAL METHODS.
Elsevier Science B.V., P.O. Box 211, 1000 AE Amsterdam, Netherlands. TEL 31-20-4853911. FAX 31-20-4853598. *761*

JOURNAL OF VISUAL COMMUNICATION AND IMAGE REPRESENTATION.
Academic Press, Inc., Journal Division, 525 B St., Ste. 1900, San Diego, CA 92101-4495. TEL 619-230-1840. FAX 619-699-6800. *2029*

JOURNAL OF VISUAL IMPAIRMENT & BLINDNESS.
American Foundation for the Blind, Inc., 11 Penn Plaza, Ste. 300, New York, NY 10001-2018. TEL 212-502-7648. FAX 212-502-7774. *3320*

THE JOURNAL OF VISUALIZATION AND COMPUTER ANIMATION.
John Wiley & Sons Ltd., Journals, Baffins Ln., Chichester, W. Sussex PO19 1UD, England. TEL 44-1243-779777. FAX 44-1243-843232. *2029*

JOURNAL OF VOCATIONAL EDUCATION AND TRAINING.
Triangle Journals Ltd., P.O. Box 65, Wallingford, Oxon. OX10 0YG, England. TEL 44-1491-838013. FAX 44-1491-834968. *2400*

JOURNAL OF VOCATIONAL EDUCATION RESEARCH.
American Vocational Education Research Association, c/o Natalie Wysong, Center on Education & Work, 964 Educational Sciences Bldg., 1025 W. Johnson, Madison, WI 53706. TEL 608-262-8415. FAX 608-262-9197. *2492*

JOURNAL OF VOCATIONAL REHABILITATION.
Elsevier Science Ireland Ltd., P.O. Box 85, Limerick, Ireland. TEL 353-61-472144. FAX 353-61-472144. *5252*

JOURNAL OF VOICE.
Lippincott - Raven Publishers 227 E. Washington Sq., Philadelphia, PA 19106. TEL 215-238-4200. *4798*

JOURNAL OF VOLCANOLOGY AND GEOTHERMAL RESEARCH.
Elsevier Science B.V., P.O. Box 211, 1000 AE Amsterdam, Netherlands. TEL 31-20-4853911. FAX 31-20-4853598. *2277*

JOURNAL OF W O C N.
Mosby - Year Book, Inc. 11830 Westline Industrial Dr., St. Louis, MO 63146-3318. TEL 314-872-8370. FAX 314-432-1380. *4914*

JOURNAL OF WASTE MANAGEMENT & RESOURCE RECOVERY.
E P P Publications, 52 Kings Rd., Richmond, Surrey TW10 6EP, England. TEL 44-181-948-7165. FAX 44-181-747-9663. *2854*

JOURNAL OF WATER RESOURCES PLANNING AND MANAGEMENT.
American Society of Civil Engineers, 345 E. 47th St., New York, NY 10017-2398. TEL 212-705-7288. FAX 212-980-4681. *2666*

JOURNAL OF WEIGHT ENGINEERING.
International Society of Allied Weight Engineers, 5530 Aztec Dr., La Mesa, CA 91942. TEL 619-465-1367. FAX 619-465-2561. *71*

JOURNAL OF WELSH RELIGIOUS HISTORY.
Welsh Religious Historical Society, c/o Rev. Roger L. Brown, Welshpool Vicarage, Powys SY21 7DT, Wales. TEL 44-1938-553164. *6148*

JOURNAL OF WILDLIFE DISEASES.
Wildlife Disease Association, Inc., Box 1897, Lawrence, KS 66044-8897. TEL 913-843-1221. FAX 913-843-1221. *6950*

JOURNAL OF WIND ENGINEERING AND INDUSTRIAL AERODYNAMICS.
Elsevier Science B.V., P.O. Box 211, 1000 AE Amsterdam, Netherlands. TEL 31-20-4853911. FAX 31-20-4853598. *2761*

JOURNAL OF WINE RESEARCH.
Carfax Publishing Co., P.O Box 25, Abingdon, Oxon. OX14 3UE, England. TEL 44-1235-401000. FAX 44-1235-401550. *229*

JOURNAL OF WOMEN AND AGING.
Haworth Press, Inc., 10 Alice St., Binghamton, NY 13904. TEL 607-722-5857. FAX 607-722-1424. *7018*

JOURNAL OF WOMEN AND MINORITIES IN SCIENCE AND ENGINEERING.
Begell House Inc., 79 Madison Ave., New York, NY 10016-7892. TEL 212-213-8368. FAX 212-725-1999. *2608*

JOURNAL OF WOMEN'S HEALTH.
Mary Ann Liebert, Inc. Publishers, 2 Madison Ave., Larchmont, NY 10538. TEL 914-834-3100. FAX 914-834-3688. *6984*

JOURNAL OF WOOD CHEMISTRY AND TECHNOLOGY.
Marcel Dekker Journals, 270 Madison Ave., New York, NY 10016. TEL 212-696-9000. FAX 212-685-4540. *1682*

JOURNAL OF WORLD HISTORY.
University of Hawaii Press, Journals Department, 2840 Kolowalu St., Honolulu, HI 96822. TEL 808-956-8833. FAX 808-988-6052. *3350*

JOURNAL OF WORLD PREHISTORY.
Plenum Publishing Corp., 233 Spring St., New York, NY 10013-1578. TEL 212-620-8000. FAX 212-463-0742. *360*

JOURNAL OF WOUND CARE.
Macmillan Magazines Ltd., Porters South, 4-6 Crinan St., London N1 9XW, England. TEL 44-171-833-6000. FAX 44-171-843-4640. *4787*

JOURNAL OF X-RAY SCIENCE AND TECHNOLOGY.
Academic Press, Inc., Journal Division, 525 B St., Ste. 1900, San Diego, CA 92101-4495. TEL 619-230-1840. FAX 619-699-6800. *5556*

JOURNAL OF YOUTH AND ADOLESCENCE.
Plenum Publishing Corp., 233 Spring St., New York, NY 10013-1578. TEL 212-620-8000. FAX 212-463-0742. *1770*

JOURNAL OF ZOO AND WILDLIFE MEDICINE.
American Association of Zoo Veterinarians, 3400 Girard Ave., Philadelphia, PA 19104-1196. TEL 215-387-9094. FAX 215-387-2165. *6950*

JOURNAL ON EXCELLENCE IN COLLEGE TEACHING.
Miami University, O A S T, Oxford, OH 45056. TEL 513-529-6648. *2434*

JOURNALISM HISTORY.
Greenspun School of Communication, University of Nevada, Las Vegas, NV 89154-5007. TEL 702-895-3964. FAX 702-895-4805. *3706*

JUDAICA LIBRARIANSHIP.
Association of Jewish Libraries, 15 E. 26th St., Rm. 1034, New York, NY 10010-1579. TEL 212-678-8092. FAX 212-678-8998. *4003*

JUDARNA I F.D. SOVJET.
Svenska Kommitten foer Judarna i f.d. Sovjet, P.O. Box 5053, S-102 42 Stockholm, Sweden. TEL 46-8-664-53-38. FAX 46-8-664-05-91. *5731*

THE JUDGES.
Martinus Nijhoff Publishers, Human Rights and International Law Postbus 163, 3300 AH Dordrecht, Netherlands. TEL 31-78-334911. FAX 31-78-334254. *3937*

JUDICATURE.
American Judicature Society, 180 N. Michigan Ave., Ste. 600, Chicago, IL 60601-7401. *3949*

JUNTENDO MEDICAL JOURNAL.
Juntendo Medical Society, 2-1-1 Hongo, Bunkyo-ku, Tokyo 113, Japan. FAX 3814-9100. *4485*

JURIST.
Catholic University of America, Department of Canon Law, Washington, DC 20064. TEL 202-319-5439. FAX 202-319-5439. *3799*

JUVENILE AND FAMILY COURT JOURNAL.
National Council of Juvenile and Family Court Judges, Box 8970, Reno, NV 89507. TEL 702-784-6012. FAX 702-784-1084. *3919*

K - THEORY.
Kluwer Academic Publishers, Postbus 17, 3300 AA Dordrecht, Netherlands. TEL 31-78-6392392. FAX 31-78-6392254. *4375*

KAFKA SOCIETY OF AMERICA. JOURNAL.
Temple University, Department of Germanic and Slavic Languages and Literatures, AB 529, Philadelphia, PA 19122. TEL 215-787-8282. FAX 215-204-7752. *4225*

KAI TIAKI: NURSING NEW ZEALAND.
New Zealand Nurses' Organisation, P.O. Box 2128, Wellington, New Zealand. TEL 64-4-385-0847. FAX 64-4-382-9993. *4719*

KAIYO CHOSA GIJUTSU.
Kaiyo Chosa Gijutsu Gakkai, Nihon Suiro Kyokai, 3-1, Tsukiji 5-chome, Chuo-ku, Tokyo 104, Japan. TEL 81-3-3545-6255. FAX 81-3-3545-6255. *2298*

KALAMAZOO COLLEGE QUARTERLY.
Kalamazoo College, 1200 Academy St., Kalamazoo, MI 49006-3295. TEL 616-377-7304. FAX 616-337-7305. *1873*

KANAGAWA-KEN SEISHIN IGAKKAISHI.
Kanagawa Association of Psychiatry, c/o Department of Psychiatry, Yokohama City University School of Medicine, 3-9, Fukuura, Kanagawa-ku, Yoakohama 236, Japan. TEL 81-45-787-2667. FAX 81-45-783-2540. *4849*

KANARA CHAMBER OF COMMERCE & INDUSTRY JOURNAL.
Kanara Chamber of Commerce & Industry, Box 116, Bunder, Mangalore 575 001, India. TEL 420128. *1144*

KANAZAWA DAIGAKU IRYO GIJUTSU TANKI DAIGAKUBU SAGYO RYOHOGAKKA SOTSUGYO KENKYU RONBUNSHU.
Kanazawa Daigaku, Iryo Gijutsu Tanki Daigakubu, 11-80, Kodatsuno 5-chome, Kanazawa-shi, Ishikawa-ken 920, Japan. TEL 81-762-22-2211. FAX 81-762-34-4375. *4485*

KANSAS BIOLOGY TEACHER.
Emporia State University Press, 1200 Commercial, Emporia, KS 66801-5087. TEL 316-341-5614. *592*

KANSAS ENTOMOLOGICAL SOCIETY. JOURNAL.
Kansas Entomological Society, Box 1897, Lawrence, KS 66044-8897. TEL 913-843-1221. FAX 913-843-1274. *731*

KAOGU.
Science Press, Marketing and Sales Department, 16 Donghuangchenggen North St., Beijing 100717, People's Republic of China. TEL 4010642. FAX 4019810. *361*

KAOGU XUEBAO.
Science Press, Marketing and Sales Department, 16 Donghuangchenggen North St., Beijing 100717, People's Republic of China. TEL 4010642. FAX 4019810. *361*

KAPPA DELTA PI RECORD.
Kappa Delta Pi Publications, Box A, 1601 West State Street, West Lafayette, IN 47906-0576. TEL 317-743-1705. FAX 317-743-2202. *2493*

KARLSRUHER PAEDAGOGISCHE BEITRAEGE.
Paedagogischer Hochschule Karlsruhe, Bismarckstr. 10, 76133 Karlsruhe, Germany. TEL 49-721-9254014. FAX 49-721-9254000. *2493*

AL-KARMIL.
Haifa University, Institute of Middle Eastern Studies, Ha-Carmel, Haifa 31999, Israel. *4225*

KAROLINSKA INSTITUTE NOBEL CONFERENCE SERIES.
Lippincott - Raven Publishers 227 E. Washington Sq., Philadelphia, PA 19106. TEL 215-238-4200. FAX 215-238-4235. *4486*

KARSTENIA.
Finnish Mycological Society, P.O. Box 47, SF-00014 University of Helsinki, Finland. FAX 358-0-7084830. *€88*

KATACHI NO KAGAKKAIHO.
Katachi no Kagakkai, Tokyo University of Agriculture & Technology, Dept. of Mechanical System Engineering, 24-16 Nakamachi 2-chome, Koganei-shi, Tokyo 184, Japan. TEL 81-423-67-5607. FAX 81-423-57-5607. *592*

KEATS - SHELLEY JOURNAL.
Keats - Shelley Association of America, Inc., Rm. 226 New York Public Library, 5th Ave. & 42nd St., New York, NY 10018-2788. TEL 212-764-0655. FAX 212-259-2467. *4309*

KECHENG - JIAOCAI - JIAOFA.
Renmin Jiaoyu Chubanshe, 55, Shatan Houjie, Beijing 100009, People's Republic of China. TEL 4035745. FAX 4010370. *2493*

KEEP ON TRUCKIN' NEWS.
Mid-West Truckers Association, Inc., 2727 N. Dirksen Parkway, Springfield, IL 62702. TEL 217-525-0310. FAX 217-525-0342. *6858*

KEIO JOURNAL OF MEDICINE.
Keio Gijuku Daigaku, Igakubu, 35 Shinano-machi, Shinjuku-ku, Tokyo 160, Japan. TEL 81-3-3353-1211. FAX 81-3-5379-6059. *4486*

KEIRYO KOKUGO GAKKAI.
Keiryo Kokugo Gakkai, c/o Tokyo Joshi Daigaku, Zenpukuji 2-6-1, Suginami-ku, Tokyo 167, Japan. TEL 03-3395-1211. *4081*

KEIZAI KAGAKU.
Nagoya Daigaku, Keizaigakubu, Furo-cho, Chikusa-ku, Nagoya 464-01, Japan. TEL 81-52-789-2360. FAX 81-52-789-4924. *938*

KEJI GUANLI YANJIU.
Science & Technology Management Research Periodicals House, No. 100, Xianlie Zhonglu, Guangzhou Guangdong 510070, People's Republic of China. TEL 86-20-8766-8145. FAX 86-20-8777-579. *6253*

KENKALUSIKKA.
Suomen Kenkakauppiaiden Liitto r.y., Fredrikinkatu 67 E 42, FIN-00100 Helsinki 10, Finland. TEL 358-0-409-932. FAX 358-0-409-563. *6307*

KENTUCKY ACADEMY OF SCIENCE. TRANSACTIONS.
Kentucky Academy of Science, c/o J.G. Rodriguez, Exec. Sec., Box 4484, Lexington, KY 40544-4484. TEL 606-257-4902. *6253*

KENTUCKY ENGLISH BULLETIN.
Kentucky Council of Teachers of English - Language Arts, Western Kentucky University, Dept. of English, Bowling Green, KY 42101. TEL 502-745-3043. FAX 502-745-2533. *4081*

KENTUCKY MEDICAL ASSOCIATION. JOURNAL.
Kentucky Medical Association, 301 N. Hurstbourne Pkwy., Ste. 200, Louisville, KY 40222-8512. TEL 502-426-6200. FAX 502-426-6877. *4486*

KENTUCKY REVIEW.
University of Kentucky, Library Associates, Lexington, KY 40506-0039. TEL 606-257-3801. FAX 606-257-1563. *3617*

KENTUCKY SCHOOL DIRECTORY.
Department of Education Office of Communication Services, 1908 Capital Plaza Tower, 500 Mero St., 19th Fl., Frankfort, KY 40601. TEL 502-564-3421. *2413*

KERKHISTORISCHE BIJDRAGEN.
E.J. Brill, P.O. Box 9000, 2300 PA Leiden, Netherlands. TEL 31-71-5353500. FAX 31-71-5317532. *6073*

KERN INSTITUTE, LEIDEN. MEMOIRS.
E.J. Brill, P.O. Box 9000, 2300 PA Leiden, Netherlands. TEL 31-71-5353500. FAX 31-71-5317532. *5288*

KESKI-SUOMI.
Keski-Suomen Museo, P.O. Box 534, 40101 Jyvaskyla, Finland. TEL 358-14-624910. FAX 358-14-624933. *3423*

KETTENWIRK-PRAXIS.
Karl Mayer GmbH, Postfach 1120, 63166 Obertshausen, Germany. TEL 49-6104-402-0. FAX 49-6104-43574. *€681*

KEXUE TONGBAO.
Science Press, Marketing and Sales Department, 16 Donghuangchenggen North St., Beijing 100717, People's Republic of China. TEL 4010642. FAX 4019810. *6254*

KEYS TO THE FAUNA OF THE U S S R.
E.J. Brill, P.O. Box 9000, 2300 PA Leiden, Netherlands. TEL 31-71-5353500. FAX 31-71-5317532. *812*

THE KIDNEY (NEW YORK, 1968).
National Kidney Foundation, 30 East 33rd St., New York, NY 10016. TEL 212-889-2210. *4928*

KIDNEY (NEW YORK, 1992).
Springer-Verlag, Medical Journals, 175 Fifth Ave., New York, NY 10010. TEL 212-460-1500. FAX 212-473-6272. *4567*

KIDNEY DISEASES.
Marcel Dekker, Inc., 270 Madison Ave., New York, NY 10016. TEL 212-696-9000. FAX 212-685-4540. *4928*

KIDSAFE.
Child Accident Prevention Foundation of Australia, 123 Queen St., 10th Fl., Melbourne, Vic. 3000, Australia. TEL 61-3-6701319 FAX 61-3-6707616. *1771*

KIELER ARBEITSPAPIERE.
Institut fuer Weltwirtschaft, Duesternbrooker Weg 120, 24105 Kiel, Germany. TEL 49-431-8814305. FAX 49-431-8814520. *1219*

KIELER BIBLIOGRAPHIE ZU AKTUELLEN OEKONOMISCHEN THEMEN.
Institut fuer Weltwirtschaft, Duesternbrooker Weg 120, 24105 Kiel, Germany. TEL 49-431-8814305. FAX 49-43 -8814520. *1011*

KIELER DISKUSSIONSBEITRAEGE.
Institut fuer Weltwirtschaft, Duesternbrooker Weg 120, 24105 Kiel, Germany. TEL 49-431-8814305. FAX 49-431-8814520. *1219*

KIELER KURZBERICHTE.
Institut fuer Weltwirtschaft, Duesternbrooker Weg 120, 24105 Kiel, Germany. TEL 49-431-8814305. FAX 49-431-8814520. *1219*

KIELER VORTRAEGE.
Institut fuer Weltwirtschaft, Duesternbrooker Weg 120, 24105 Kiel, Germany. TEL 49-431-8814305. FAX 49-431-8814520. *1219*

KIERKEGAARDIANA.
C.A. Reitzels Forlag, Nørregade 20, DK-1165 Copenhagen K, Denmark. *5483*

KIMIKA.
Kapisanan ng mga Kimiko sa Pilipinas, P.O. Box CM70, Murphy District Rd., Santolan Rd., Quezon City, Philippines. TEL 63-2-936868. *1684*

KINEMA.
University of Waterloo, Department of Fine Arts and Film Studies, Waterloo, ON N2L 3G1, Canada. TEL 519-885-1211. FAX 519-746-4982. *5106*

KINETICS AND CATALYSIS.
Maik Nauka - Interperiodica, Mezhdunarodnyi Otdel, Ul. Profsoyuznaya, 90, 117864 Moscow, Russia. TEL 7-095-3360066. FAX 7-095-3360666. *1754*

KINETOSCOPIO.
Centro Colombo Americano, Apdo. Aereo 8734, Medellin, Colombia. TEL 574-513-4444. FAX 574-513-2666. *5106*

KING SAUD UNIVERSITY. JOURNAL. ADMINISTRATIVE SCIENCES.
King Saud University, University Libraries, P.O. Box 22480, Riyadh 11495, Saudi Arabia. TEL 966-1-4676148. FAX 966-1-4676162. *939*

KING SAUD UNIVERSITY. JOURNAL. AGRICULTURAL SCIENCES.
King Saud University, University Libraries, P.O. Box 22480, Riyadh 11495, Saudi Arabia. TEL 966-1-4676148. FAX 966-1-4676162. *130*

KING SAUD UNIVERSITY. JOURNAL. ARCHITECTURE AND PLANNING.
King Saud University, University Libraries, P.O. Box 22480, Riyadh 11495, Saudi Arabia. TEL 966-1-4676148. FAX 966-1-4676162. *3587*

KING SAUD UNIVERSITY. JOURNAL. ARTS.
King Saud University, University Libraries, P.O. Box 22480, Riyadh 11495, Saudi Arabia. TEL 966-1-4676148. FAX 966-1-4676162. *437*

KING SAUD UNIVERSITY. JOURNAL. COMPUTER AND INFORMATION SCIENCES.
King Saud University, University Libraries, P.O. Box 22480, Riyadh 11495, Saudi Arabia. TEL 966-1-4676148. FAX 966-1-4676162. *1994*

KING SAUD UNIVERSITY. JOURNAL. EDUCATIONAL SCIENCES AND ISLAMIC STUDIES.
King Saud University, University Libraries, P.O. Box 22480, Riyadh 11495, Saudi Arabia. TEL 966-1-4676148. FAX 966-1-4676162. *6119*

KING SAUD UNIVERSITY. JOURNAL. ENGINEERING SCIENCES.
King Saud University, University Libraries, P.O. Box 22480, Riyadh 11495, Saudi Arabia. TEL 966-1-4676148. FAX 966-1-4676162. *2608*

KING SAUD UNIVERSITY. JOURNAL. SCIENCE.
King Saud University, University Libraries, P.O Box 22480, Riyadh 11495, Saudi Arabia. TEL 966-1-4676148. FAX 966-1-4676162. *6254*

KING'S COLLEGE LAW JOURNAL.
King's College London, School of Law, Strand, London WC2R 2LS, England. TEL 4-171-836-5454. FAX 44-171-873-2465. *3801*

KISHO RIYO KENKYU.
Kisho Riyo Kenkyukai, Kyushu Daigaku Nogakubu Nogyo Kishogaku Kyoshitsu, 10-1, Hakozaki 6-chome, Higashi-ku, Fukuoka-shi, Fukuoka-ken 812, Japan. TEL 81-92-641-1101. FAX 81-92-641-2928. *5001*

KITAKANTO MEDICAL JOURNAL.
Kitakanto Medical Society, c/o Gumma University, School of Medicine, 3-39-22 Showa-machi, Maebashi-shi 371, Japan. TEL 81-272-20-7111. *4487*

KITANO HOSPITAL JOURNAL OF MEDICINE.
Tazuke Kofukai Foundation, Medical Research Institute, 13-3 Kamiyama-cho, Kita-ku, Osaka 530, Japan. TEL 81-6-312-1221. FAX 81-6-361-0588. *4487*

THE KIWI.
New Zealand Society of Great Britain, 24 Irwin Rd., Guildford, Surrey GU2 5PP, England. TEL 44-1483-567185. FAX 44-1483-34676. *5458*

KLUWER INTERNATIONAL SERIES IN ENGINEERING AND COMPUTER SCIENCE.
Kluwer Academic Publishers, Postbus 17, 3300 AA Dordrecht, Netherlands. TEL 31-78-6392392. FAX 31-78-6392254. *1994*

THE KLUWER INTERNATIONAL SERIES IN SOFTWARE ENGINEERING.
Kluwer Academic Publishers, Postbus 17, 3300 AA Dordrecht, Netherlands. TEL 31-78-6392392. FAX 31-78-6392254. *2112*

KLUWER NIJHOFF STUDIES IN HUMAN ISSUES.
Kluwer Academic Publishers, Postbus 17, 3300 AA Dordrecht, Netherlands. TEL 31-78-6392392. FAX 31-78-6392254. *6421*

KLUWER TEXTS IN THE MATHEMATICAL SCIENCES.
Kluwer Academic Publishers, Postbus 17, 3300 AA Dordrecht, Netherlands. TEL 31-78-6392392. FAX 31-78-6392254. *4375*

THE KNEE.
Butterworth - Heinemann, Part of the Reed Elsevier group, Linacre House, Jordan Hill, Oxford OX2 8DP, England. TEL 44-1865-310366. FAX 44-1865-310398. *791*

KNOWLEDGE-BASED SYSTEMS.
Elsevier Science B.V., P.O. Box 211, 1000 AE Amsterdam, Netherlands. TEL 31-20-4853911. FAX 31-20-4853598. *2009*

KNOWLEDGE ORGANIZATION.
Indeks Verlag, Woogstr. 36a, 60431 Frankfurt a.M., Germany. TEL 069-523690. FAX 069-520566. *4004*

KOBE WOMEN'S UNIVERSITY. FACULTY OF HOME ECONOMICS. BULLETIN.
Kobe Women's University, Faculty of Home Economics, Aoyama, Suma-ku, Kobe-shi 654, Japan. TEL 078-731-4416. FAX 078-732-5161. *3524*

KOCHI UNIVERSITY. MARINE SCIENCES AND FISHERIES. BULLETIN.
Kochi University, Usa Marine Biological Institute, Usa-cho, Tosa, Kochi 781-11, Japan. TEL 0888-56-0422. FAX 0888-56-0425. *2299*

KODALY ENVOY.
Organization of American Kodaly Educators, 1457 S. 23rd St., Fargo, ND 58103-3708. TEL 701-235-0366. FAX 701-241-7051. *5170*

KODO RYOHO KENKYU.
Nihon Kodo Ryoho Gakkai, c/o Masahiko Sogiyama, Sec.-Gen., Institute of Special Education, University of Tsukuba, 1-1-1 Tennoudai Tsukuba, Ibaraki 305, Japan. TEL 0298-53-6719. FAX 0298-53-6719. *5863*

KOEBSTADMUSEET DEN GAMLE BY.
DK-8000 Aarhus C, Denmark. TEL 86-12-31-88. FAX 86-76-06-87. *3423*

KOEDOE.
National Parks Board, P.O. Box 787, Pretoria 0001, South Africa. TEL 27-12-343-9770. FAX 27-12-343-2832. *2132*

KOERS.
Buro vir Wetenskaplike Tydskrifte, Private Bag X6001, Potchefstroom 2520, South Africa. TEL 27-148-2991769. FAX 27-148-2991562. *6074*

KOKU IGAKU JIKKENTAI HOKOKU.
Japan Air Self Defense Force, Aeromedical Laboratory, 2-10, Sakae-cho 1-chome, Tachikawa-shi, Tokyo, Japan. TEL 0245-24-4131. *4487*

KOLA.
C.P. 1602, Place Bonaventure, Montreal, PQ H5A 1H6, Canada. TEL 514-737-4629. *4226*

KON POLSKI.
Kon Polski Sp. z o.o., Zlota 63a m.6, 00-819 Warsaw, Poland. TEL 48-22-209817. FAX 48-22-243628. *6548*

KONGELIGE NORSKE VIDENSKABERS SELSKAB. SKRIFTER.
Kongelige Norske Videnskabers Selskab, Erling Skakkes gt. 47 b, N-7013 Trondheim, Norway. TEL 47-73-59-21-57. FAX 47-73-59-58-95. *6255*

KONGJIAN KEXUE XUEBAO.
Science Press, Marketing and Sales Department, 16 Donghuangchenggen North St., Beijing 100717, People's Republic of China. TEL 4010642. FAX 4019810. *72*

KONGQI DONGLIXUE XUEBAO.
Zhongguo Kongqi Dongli Yanjiu yu Fazhan Zhongxin, P.O. Box 211, Mianyang, Sichuan 621000, People's Republic of China. TEL 86-816-2466261. *5589*

KONINKLIJK NEDERLANDS GEOLOGISCH MIJNBOUWKUNDIG GENOOTSCHAP. VERHANDELINGEN.
Kluwer Academic Publishers, Postbus 17, 3300 AA Dordrecht, Netherlands. TEL 31-78-6392392. FAX 31-78-6392254. *2247*

KONINKLIJKE NEDERLANDSE AKADEMIE VAN WETENSCHAPPEN. AFDELING LETTERKUNDE. VERHANDELINGEN. NIEUWE REEKS.
Elsevier Science B.V., Books Division, P.O. Box 211, 1000 AE Amsterdam, Netherlands. TEL 31-20-4853911. FAX 31-20-4853705. *3618*

KONINKLIJKE NEDERLANDSE AKADEMIE VAN WETENSCHAPPEN. AFDELING NATUURKUNDE. VERHANDELINGEN. TWEEDE REEKS.
Elsevier Science B.V., Books Division, P.O. Box 211, 1000 AE Amsterdam, Netherlands. TEL 31-20-4853911. FAX 31-20-4853705. *6255*

DIE KONSENTRASIEKAMP-GEDENKREEKS.
Oorlogsmuseum van die Boererepublieke, Posbus 704, Bloemfontein 9300, South Africa. TEL 27-51-470079. FAX 27-51-471322. *3373*

KOREAN INSTITUTE OF METALS AND MATERIALS. JOURNAL.
Korean Institute of Metals and Materials, Rm. 605, Keoyang Bldg., 51-8 Susong-dong, Chong Ro-ku, Seuol 110-140, S. Korea. TEL 02-734-0595. FAX 02-734-0596. *4962*

KOREAN JOURNAL OF PARASITOLOGY.
Korean Society for Parasitology, c/o Dept. of Parasitology, College of Medicine, Seoul National University, Seoul 110 799, S. Korea. TEL 82-2-740-8348. FAX 82-2-765-6142. *4625*

KOREAN JOURNAL OF PHARMACOLOGY.
Society of Pharmacology, c/o Dept. of Pharmacology, College of Medicine, 28 Yunkun-dong, Chongro-ku, Seoul 110, S. Korea. TEL 02-361-5210. FAX 02-745-7996. *5425*

KOREAN SOCIETY FOR CLINICAL PHARMACOLOGY AND THERAPEUTICS. JOURNAL.
Korean Society for Clinical Pharmacology and Therapeutics, c/o Seoul National University College of Medicine, Department of Neuropsychiatry, 28 Yongon-dong, Chongno-gu, Seoul 110-744, S. Korea. TEL 740-8286. FAX 745-7996. *5425*

KOREAN SOCIETY OF OCEANOGRAPHY. JOURNAL.
Hangug Haeyang Haghoe, c/o Dept. of Oceanography, Seoul National University, Seoul 151-742, S. Korea. TEL 82-2-872-5032. FAX 82-2-872-0311. *2299*

KOREAN STUDIES.
University of Hawaii Press, Journals Department, 2840 Kolowalu St., Honolulu, HI 96822. TEL 808-956-8833. FAX 808-988-6052. *5288*

KORROZIOS FIGYELO.
V E K O R Ltd., Wartha V. u. 1, Bldg. M, 8200 Veszprem, Hungary. TEL 36-88-328514. *5308*

KOSMON VOICE.
Universal Faithists of Kosmon, Box 654, McCook, NE 69001. TEL 308-345-6369. *6208*

KOSMOS.
International Society for Astrological Research, Inc., P.O. Box 38613, Los Angeles, CA 90038-0613. TEL 805-525-0461. FAX 805-525-0461. *472*

KOSMOS.
Polskie Towarzystwo Przyrodnikow im. Kopernika, Ul. Pawinskiego 5a, 02-106 Warsaw, Poland. TEL 48-22-6584729. *592*

KOTSU KANSETSU KANSENSHO.
Nihon Kotsu Kansetsu Kansensho Kenkyukai, University of Tukuba, Dept. of Orthopaedic Surgery, 1-1-1 Tennoudai, Tsukuba-shi, Ibaraki 305, Japan. TEL 81-298-53-3219. FAX 81-298-53-3214. *4787*

KRED.
University of Kent Students' Union, Mandela Bldg., University of Kent, Canterbury, Kent CT2 7NW, England. TEL 01227-765224. FAX 01227-464625. *1874*

KREFELD IMMIGRANTS AND THEIR DESCENDANTS.
Links Genealogy Publications, 7677 Abaline Way, Sacramento, CA 95823. TEL 916-428-2245. FAX 916-428-2245. *3091*

KRONOS.
University of the Western Cape, Institute for Historical Research, Private Bag X17, Bellville 7530, South Africa. TEL 27-21-9592616. FAX 27-21-9593178. *3373*

KUNCHONG XUEBAO.
Science Press, Marketing and Sales Department, 16 Donghuangchenggen North St., Beijing 100717, People's Republic of China. TEL 4010642. FAX 4019810. *732*

KURUME MEDICAL JOURNAL.
Kurume University School of Medicine, 67 Asahi-machi, Kurume 830, Japan. TEL 942-35-3311. FAX 942-32-1665. *4488*

KYORIN IGAKKAI ZASSHI.
Kyorin Medical Society, Kyorin University, 20-2, 6-chome, Shinkawa, Mitaka-shi, Tokyo 181, Japan. FAX 0422-40-7281. *4488*

KYOTO JOURNAL.
Heian Bunka Center, 35 Minamigosho-machi, Okazaki, Sakyo-ku, Kyoto 606, Japan. TEL 075-771-6111. FAX 075-751-1196. *5288*

KYOTO PREFECTURAL UNIVERSITY OF MEDICINE. MEDICAL SOCIETY. JOURNAL.
Kyoto Prefectural University of Medicine, Kyoto Foundations for the Promotion of Medical Science, Hirokoji, Kawara-machi, Kamigyo-ku, Kyoto 602, Japan. TEL 81-75-212-5466. FAX 81-75-212-5467. *4488*

KYOTO UNIVERSITY. BIOLOGICAL LABORATORY. CONTRIBUTIONS.
Kyoto University, Faculty of General Education, Yoshida Nihonmatsucho, Sakyo-ku, Kyoto 606, Japan. TEL 81-75-753-6849. FAX 81-75-753-6864. *592*

KYUSHU UNIVERSITY. DEPARTMENT OF EARTH AND PLANETARY SCIENCES. SCIENCE REPORTS.
Kyushu University 33, Department of Earth and Planetary Sciences, 6-10-1 Hakozaki, Higashi-ku, Fukuoka 812-81, Japan. TEL 81-92-641-1101. FAX 81-92-632-2736. *2248*

L A S A FORUM.
Latin American Studies Association, William Pitt Union, 9th Fl., University of Pittsburgh, Pittsburgh, PA 15260. TEL 412-648-7929. FAX 412-624-7145. *6332*

L.E. BEACON.
L.E. Support Group, 8039 Nova Court, N. Charleston, SC 29420. TEL 803-764-1769. *4894*

L E R S MONOGRAPH SERIES.
Raven Publishers 227 E. Washington Sq., Philadelphia, PA 19106. TEL 215-238-4200. FAX 215-238-4235. *4488*

L I N Q.
James Cook University of North Queensland, Department of English, Townsville, Qld. 4811, Australia. TEL 61-77-815097. FAX 61-77-815655. *4227*

L I S P AND SYMBOLIC COMPUTATION.
Kluwer Academic Publishers Boston, Box 358, Accord Sta., Hingham, MA 02018-0358. TEL 617-871-6600. FAX 617-871-6528. *2029*

L I T: LITERATURE INTERPRETATION THEORY.
Gordon and Breach Science Publishers, c/o International Publishers Distributor, P.O. Box 3054, Langhorne, PA 19047-3054. TEL 215-750-2642. FAX 215-750-6343. *4227*

LAB ANIMAL.
Nature Publishing Co. 345 Park Ave. S., 10th Fl., New York, NY 10012-2467. *4681*

LABMEDICA INTERNATIONAL.
Globetech Publishing, 30 Cannon Rd., Wilton, CT 06897. TEL 203-762-3432. FAX 203-762-8640. *4682*

LABOR HISTORY.
Tamiment Institute, Ben Josephson Library, New York University, Bobst Library, 10th Fl., 70 Washington Sq S., New York, NY 10012. TEL 212-998-2630. FAX 212-741-6790. *1383*

LABORATORIUMS MEDIZIN.
Blackwell Wissenschaft, Kurfuerstendamm 57, 10707 Berlin, Germany. TEL 49-30-32790624. FAX 49-30-32790610. *4682*

LABORATORY ANIMAL SCIENCE.
American Association for Laboratory Animal Science, 70 Timber Creek Dr., Ste. 5, Cordova, TN 38018. TEL 901-754-8620. *4682*

LABORATORY ANIMALS.
Royal Society of Medicine Press Ltd., 1 Wimpole St., London W1M 8AE, England. TEL 0171-290-2900. FAX 0171-290-2929. *4682*

LABORATORY AUTOMATION AND INFORMATION MANAGEMENT.
Elsevier Science B.V., P.O. Box 211, 1000 AE Amsterdam, Netherlands. TEL 31-20-4853911. FAX 31-20-4853598. *6306*

LABORATORY INVESTIGATION.
Williams & Wilkins, 351 W. Camden St., Baltimore, MD 21201. TEL 410-528-4000. FAX 410-528-4312. *4682*

LABORATORY MEDICINE.
American Society of Clinical Pathologists, 2100 W. Harrison St., Chicago, IL 60612. TEL 312-738-4860. FAX 312-738-0101. *4683*

LABORATORY ROBOTICS AND AUTOMATION.
John Wiley & Sons. Inc., Journals, 605 Third Ave., New York, NY 10158-0012. TEL 212-850-6645. FAX 212-850-6021. *2016*

LABORATORY TECHNIQUES IN BIOCHEMISTRY AND MOLECULAR BIOLOGY.
Elsevier Science B.V., Books Division, P.O. Box 211, 1000 AE Amsterdam, Netherlands. TEL 31-20-4853911. FAX 31-20-4853705. *644*

LABOR'S HERITAGE.
George Meany Center for Labor Studies, 10000 New Hampshire Ave., Silver Spring, MD 20903. TEL 301-431-5457. FAX 301-431-0385. *1384*

LABOUR.
Canadian Committee on Labour History, Department of History, Memorial University of Newfoundland, St. John's, NF A1C 5S7, Canada. TEL 709-737-2144. FAX 709-737-4342. *1384*

LABOUR.
Blackwell Publishers Ltd., 108 Cowley Rd., Oxford OX4 1JF, England. TEL 44-1865-791100. FAX 44-1865-791347. *1384*

LABOUR ECONOMICS.
North-Holland P.O. Box 211, 1000 AE Amsterdam, Netherlands. TEL 31-20-4853911. FAX 31-20-4853598. *1385*

LABOUR FOCUS ON EASTERN EUROPE.
Labor Focus on Eastern Europe, 30 Bridge St., Oxford OX2 0BA, England. TEL 44-1865-723207. *1385*

LABOUR HISTORY.
Australian Society for the Study of Labour History, Faculty of Economics, Institute Bldg. HO4, University of Sydney, N.S.W., Australia. TEL 61-2-3513786. FAX 61-2-3514729. *1385*

LACKAWANNA JURIST.
Lackawanna Bar Association, 205 1 Pyramid Center, Corner Spruce and Wyoming Aves., Scranton, PA 18503. TEL 717-969-9161. FAX 717-969-9150. *3802*

LACTEOS Y CARNICOS MEXICANOS.
Alfa Editores Tecnicos S.A., Libertad No. 107-402, 03660 Mexico DF, Mexico. TEL 525-579-3333. FAX 525-5329504. *2982*

LACTIC ACID BACTERIA.
Elsevier Science Ltd., Books Division, P.O. Box 800, Kidlington, Oxford OX5 1DX, England. TEL 44-1865-843000. FAX 44-1865-843010. *761*

LAEGEMIDDELKATALOGET.
Laegemiddelkataloget, Stroedamvej 50 B, DK-2100 Copenhagen Oe, Denmark. TEL 45-39-27-44-88. FAX 45-39-27-59-10. *5426*

LE LAIT.
Editions Scientifiques et Medicales Elsevier, 141 rue de Javel, 75747 Paris, France. TEL 33-1-45589022. FAX 33-1-45589421. *251*

LAKE BIWA STUDY MONOGRAPHS.
Lake Biwa Research Institute, 1-10, Uchide-hama, Otsu-shi, Shiga-ken 520, Japan. TEL 0775-26-4800. FAX 0775-26-4803. *2237*

LAKOKRASOCHNYE MATERIALY I IKH PRIMENENIE.
Journal LKM Ltd., Scherbakovskaya, 3, VNIIK, 105318 Moscow, Russia. TEL 369-97-13. FAX 284-84-02. *5309*

LAMAR JOURNAL OF THE HUMANITIES.
Lamar University, Department of English and Foreign Languages, Box 10023, Beaumont, TX 77710. TEL 409-880-8258. *5618*

LAMMERGEYER.
Natal Parks Board, P.O. Box 662, Pietermaritzburg 3200, South Africa. TEL 27-33-471961. FAX 27-331-471037. *2132*

LANCASTER WORKING PAPERS IN POLITICAL ECONOMY. POLITICAL ECONOMY OF LOCAL GOVERNANCE SERIES.
Lancaster University, Department of Sociology, Lancaster LA1 4YL, England. TEL 01524-594178. FAX 01524-594256. *258*

THE LANCET.
The Lancet Ltd. 42 Bedford Sq. London WC1B 3SL, England. TEL 44-171-436498. FAX 44-171-4367570. *4489*

THE LANCET (NORTH AMERICAN EDITION).
The Lancet Ltd. 655 Ave. of the Americas, New York, NY 10011. TEL 212-633-3800. FAX 212-633-3850. *4489*

LAND & WATER.
Land and Water, Inc., Box 1197, Ft. Dodge, IA 50501. TEL 515-576-3191. FAX 515-576-2606. *2132*

LAND AND WATER LAW REVIEW.
University of Wyoming, College of Law, Box 3035, Laramie, WY 82071-3035. TEL 307-766-2329. FAX 307-766-4044. *3802*

LAND CONTAMINATION & RECLAMATION.
E P P Publications, 52 Kings Rd., Richmond, Surrey, TW10 6EP, England. TEL 44-181-948-7165. FAX 44-181-747-9663. *2837*

LAND DEGRADATION AND DEVELOPMENT.
John Wiley & Sons Ltd. Journals, Baffins Ln., Chichester, W. Sussex PO19 1UD, England. TEL 44-1243-779777. FAX 44-1243-843232. *2212*

LAND USE POLICY.
Butterworth - Heinemann, Part of the Reed Elsevier group, Linacre House, Jordan Hill, Oxford OX2 8DP, England. TEL 44-1865 310366. FAX 44-1865-310898. *3588*

LANDSCAPE ECOLOGY.
S P B Academic Publishing b.v., P.O. Box 11188, 1001 GD Amsterdam, Netherlands. *2808*

LANDSCAPE ISSUES.
Department of Countryside and Landscape, Cheltenham and Gloucester College of Higher Education, Francis Close Hall, Swindon Rd., Cheltenham, England. TEL 44-1242-532930. FAX 44-1242-532997. *397*

LANDSCAPE RESEARCH.
Carfax Publishing Co. P.O. Box 24, Abingdon, Oxon OX14 3UE, England. TEL 44-1235-401000. FAX 44-1235-401550. *397*

LANDSCHAFTSVERBAND WESTFALEN-LIPPE. MITTEILUNGEN DES LANDESJUGENDAMTES.
Landschaftsverband Westfalen-Lippe, Landesjugendamt, 48133 Muenster, Germany. TEL 49-251-591-3611. FAX 49-251-591-275. *6381*

LANDSCHAP.
Werkgemeenschap Landschapsecologisch Onderzoek (WLO), Postbus 23, 6700 AA Wageningen, Netherlands. TEL 1-317-477986. *2808*

LANGUAGE ACQUISITION.
Lawrence Erlbaum Associates, Inc., 10 Industrial Dr., Mahwah, NJ 07430-2262. TEL 201-236-9500. FAX 201-236-0072. *4082*

LANGUAGE AND COGNITIVE PROCESSES.
Taylor & Francis Ltd., Psychology Press, 1 Gunpowder Sq., London EC4A 3DE, England. TEL 44-171-5830490. FAX 44-171-5830585. *4083*

LANGUAGE & COMMUNICATION.
Elsevier Science Ltd., Pergamon, P.O. Box 800, Kidlington, Oxford OX5 1DX, England. TEL 44-1865-843000. FAX 44-1865-843010. *4083*

LANGUAGE AND LITERATURE.
Pitman Press, P.O. Box 791786, San Antonio, TX 78279-1786. TEL 210-736-7369. FAX 210-494-4435. *4083*

LANGUAGE, CULTURE AND CURRICULUM.
Multilingual Matters Ltd., Frankfurt Lodge, Clevedon Hall, Victoria Rd., Clevedon, Avon BS21 7SJ, England. TEL 44-1275-876519. FAX 44-1275-343096. *4083*

LANGUAGE IN SOCIETY.
Cambridge University Press, Edinburgh Bldg., Shaftesbury Rd., Cambridge CB2 2RU, England. TEL 44-1223-312393. FAX 44-1223-315052. *4084*

LANGUAGE INTERNATIONAL.
John Benjamins Publishing Co., Amsteldijk 44, P.O. Box 75577, 1070 AN Amsterdam, Netherlands. TEL 31-20-6738156. FAX 31-20-6792956. *4084*

LANGUAGE OF DANCE.
Gordon & Breach Science Publishers, c/o International Publishers Distributor, P.O. Box 3054, Langhorne, PA 19047-3054. TEL 215-750-2642. FAX 215-750-6343. *2190*

LANGUAGE QUARTERLY.
University of South Florida, College of Arts & Sciences, 4202 E. Fowler Ave., CPR 107, Tampa, FL 33620-5550. TEL 813-974-5618. FAX 813-974-5618. *4084*

LANGUAGE RESEARCH.
Soeul National University, San 56-1, Sinlim-dong, Kwanak-ku, Seoul 151-742, S. Korea. TEL 82-2-880-5485. FAX 82-2-871-6907. *4084*

LANGUAGE SCIENCES.
Elsevier Science Ltd., Pergamon, P.O. Box 800, Kidlington, Oxford OX5 1DX, England. TEL 44-1865-843000. FAX 44-1865-843010. *4084*

LANGUAGES OF DESIGN.
Penrose Press, Box 470925, San Francisco, CA 94147. *463*

LANNAN SERIES.
University of California Press, 2120 Berkeley Way, Berkeley, CA 94720. TEL 510-642-4247. FAX 510-643-7127. *4227*

LAPIS.
Christian Weise Verlag GmbH, Orleansstr. 69, 81667 Munich, Germany. TEL 49-89-4802933. FAX 49-89-6886160. *5068*

LARGE ANIMAL VETERINARIAN.
Watt Publishing Co., 122 S. Wesley Ave., Mt. Morris, IL 61054-1497. TEL 815-734-4171. *275*

LARYNGOSCOPE.
Lippincott - Raven Publishers 227 E. Washington Sq., Philadelphia, PA 19106-3780. TEL 215-238-4200. *4798*

LASER CHEMISTRY.
Harwood Academic Publishers, c/o International Publishers Distributor, P.O. Box 3054, Langhorne, PA 19047-3054. TEL 215-750-2642. FAX 215-750-6343. *5606*

LASER HANDBOOK.
Elsevier Science B.V., Books Division, P.O. Box 211, 1000 AE Amsterdam, Netherlands. TEL 31-20-4853911. FAX 31-20-4853705. *5606*

LASER SCIENCE AND TECHNOLOGY.
Harwood Academic Publishers, c/o International Publishers Distributor, P.O. Box 3054, Langhorne, PA 19047-3054. TEL 215-750-2642. FAX 215-750-6343. *5607*

LASER THERAPY.
International Laser Therapy Association, c/o 14-18 Iwaicho, Tochigi City, Tochigi 328, Japan. TEL 81-282-24-0313. FAX 81-282-22-5019. *4489*

LASERS & OPTRONICS.
Gordon Publications, Part of Cahners Publishing Company, Division of Reed Elsevier Inc., 301 Gibraltar Dr., Box 650, Morris Plains, NJ 07950-0650. TEL 201-292-5100. FAX 201-898-9281. *5607*

LASERS IN ENGINEERING.
Gordon and Breach Science Publishers, c/o International Publishers Distributor, P.O. Box 3054, Langhorne, PA 19047-3054. TEL 215-750-2642. FAX 215-750-6343. *5607*

LASERS IN SURGERY AND MEDICINE.
John Wiley & Sons, Inc., Journals, 605 Third Ave., New York, NY 10158. TEL 212-850-6645. FAX 212-850-6021. *4914*

LASERS IN THE LIFE SCIENCES.
Harwood Academic Publishers, c/o International Publishers Distributor, P.O. Box 3054, Langhorne, PA 19047-3054. TEL 215-750-2642. FAX 215-750-6343. *5607*

LATE IMPERIAL CHINA.
Johns Hopkins University Press, Journals Publishing Division, 2715 N. Charles St., MD 21218-4319. TEL 410-516-6987. FAX 410-740-6968. *3382*

LATIN AMERICAN ANTIQUITY.
Society for American Archaeology, 900 Second St., N.W., No. 12, Washington, DC 20002-3557. TEL 202-789-8200. FAX 202-789-0284. *362*

LATIN AMERICAN INDIAN LITERATURES JOURNAL.
Penn State University, McKeesport, University Dr., McKeesport, PA 15132-7698. TEL 412-675-9466. FAX 412-675-9043. *4227*

LATIN AMERICAN LITERATURE AND CULTURE.
University of California Press, 2120 Berkeley Way, Berkeley, CA 94720. TEL 510-642-4247. FAX 510-643-7127. *3476*

LATIN AMERICAN THEATRE REVIEW.
University of Kansas, Center of Latin American Studies, 107 Lippincott Hall, Lawrence, KS 66045. TEL 913-864-4141. FAX 913-864-4555. *6698*

LATINO STUDIES JOURNAL.
Department of LA and PRS, Lehman College - CUNY, Bronx, NY 10468. *5760*

LATVIJAS FIZIKAS UN TEHNISKO ZINATNU ZURNALS.
Latvijas Zinatnu Akademijas, Fizikalas Energetikas Instituts, Aizkraukles iela, 21, 1006 Riga, Latvia. TEL 371-7552011. FAX 371-7820339. *5557*

LAUREL REVIEW (MARYVILLE).
GreenTower Press, c/o William Trowbridge, Dept. of English, Northwest Missouri State University, Maryville, MO 64468. TEL 816-562-1265. *4227*

LAVAL THEOLOGIQUE ET PHILOSOPHIQUE.
Universite Laval, Faculte de Philosophie, Cite Universitaire, Quebec, PQ G1K 7P4, Canada. TEL 418-656-3816. FAX 418-656-7267. *5484*

LAW AND CRITIQUE.
Deborah Charles Publications, 173 Mather Ave., Liverpool L18 6JZ, England. TEL 0151-724-2500. FAX 0151-729-0371. *3803*

LAW AND HISTORY REVIEW.
University of Illinois Press, 1325 S. Oak St., Champaign, IL 61820. TEL 217-233-0950. FAX 217-244-8082. *3803*

LAW AND HUMAN BEHAVIOR.
Plenum Publishing Corp., 233 Spring St., New York, NY 10013-1578. TEL 212-620-8000. FAX 212-463-0742. *3803*

LAW AND PHILOSOPHY.
Kluwer Academic Publishers, Postbus 17, 3300 AA Dordrecht, Netherlands. TEL 31-78-6392392. FAX 31-78-6392254. *3803*

LAW AND PHILOSOPHY LIBRARY.
Kluwer Academic Publishers, Postbus 17, 3300 AA Dordrecht, Netherlands. TEL 31-78-6392392. FAX 31-78-6392254. *3803*

LAW AND SOCIAL INQUIRY.
University of Chicago Press, Journals Division, Box 37005, Chicago, IL 60637. TEL 773-753-3347. FAX 773-753-0811. *3803*

LAW & SOCIETY REVIEW.
Law and Society Association, Hampshire House, Box 33615, University of Massachusetts, Amherst, MA 01003-3615. TEL 413-545-4617. FAX 413-545-1640. *3804*

LAW IN EASTERN EUROPE.
Martinus Nijhoff Publishers, Human Rights and International Law, Postbus 163, 3300 AD Dordrecht, Netherlands. TEL 31-78-334228. FAX 31-78-334254. *3938*

LAW INSTITUTE JOURNAL.
Law Institute of Victoria, 470 Bourke St, Melbourne, Vic. 3000, Australia. TEL 61-3-96079478. FAX 61-3-96079451. *3804*

LAW, SOCIETY, AND POLICY.
Plenum Publishing Corp., 233 Spring St., New York, NY 10013-1578. TEL 212-620-8000. FAX 212-463-0742. *3805*

LAWRENCE BERKELEY LABORATORY. MATERIALS AND CHEMICAL SCIENCES DIVISION. ANNUAL REPORT.
University of California at Berkeley, Materials and Chemical Sciences Division, Berkeley, CA 94720. TEL 415-422-1100. *2736*

LEAD BELLY LETTER.
Lead Belly Society, Box 6679, Ithaca, NY 14851. TEL 607-273-6615. FAX 607-844-4810. *5171*

LEADER MAGAZINE.
Active Parenting Publishers, 810 Franklin Court, Ste. B, Marietta, GA 30067-8943. TEL 770-429-0565. FAX 770-429-0334. *1772*

LEADERSHIP MEDICA.
Ce.S.I.L. srl, Via Olmetto 5, 20123 Milan, Italy. TEL 39-2-878397. FAX 39-2-866576. *4489*

LEARNING AND INSTRUCTION.
Elsevier Science Ltd., Pergamon, P.O. Box 800, Kidlington, Oxford OX5 1DX, England. TEL 44-1865-843000. FAX 44-1865-843010. *2350*

LEARNING & MEMORY.
Cold Spring Harbor Laboratory Press, Publications Department, Box 100, Cold Spring Harbor, NY 11724. TEL 516-367-8492. FAX 516-349-1946. *4850*

LEARNING DISABILITY QUARTERLY.
C L D, Box 40303, Overland Park, KS 66204. TEL 913-492-8755. *2471*

LEATHERS.
Council for Leather Exports, 53 Sydenhams Rd., Periamet, Madras 600 003, India. TEL 91-44-589098. FAX 91-44-588713. *3961*

LEBENDIGE SEELSORGE.
Seelsorge Verlag Echter, Postfach 5560, 97005 Wuerzburg, Germany. TEL 49-931-6671-0. FAX 49-931-6671151. *5864*

LECTURA Y VIDA.
International Reading Association, Inc., 800 Barksdale Rd., Box 8139, Newark, DE 19714-8139. TEL 302-731-1600. FAX 302-731-1057. *4085*

LECTURES IN ECONOMICS: THEORY, INSTITUTIONS, POLICY.
Elsevier Science B.V., Books Division, P.O. Box 211, 1000 AE Amsterdam, Netherlands. TEL 31-20-4853911. FAX 31-20-4853705. *1258*

LEDELSE I DAG.
Ledernes Hovedorganisation, Vermlandsgade 63, DK-2300 Copenhagen S, Denmark. TEL 45-31-57-56-22. FAX 45-31-57-90-22. *1430*

THE LEECH.
University of the Witwatersrand Medical School, 7 York Rd., Parktown 2193, South Africa. TEL 27-11-6472451. FAX 27-11-6434318. *4489*

LEGACY (UNIVERSITY PARK).
Pennsylvania State University Press, 820 N. University Dr., Ste. C, University Park, PA 16802-1003. TEL 814-865-1327. FAX 814-863-1408. *4228*

LEGAL ABACUS.
Institute of Legal Cashiers and Administrators, 146-148 Eltham Hill, 2nd Fl., Eltham, London SE9 5DX, England. TEL 44-181-294-2887. FAX 44-181-859-1682. *3807*

LEGAL AND CRIMINOLOGICAL PSYCHOLOGY.
British Psychological Society, St. Andrew's House, 48 Princess Rd. E., Leicester LE1 7DR, England. TEL 44-116-254-9568. FAX 44-116-2470787. *5864*

LEGAL ASPECTS OF INTERNATIONAL ORGANIZATION.
Kluwer Law International Postbus 85889, 2508 CN The Hague, Netherlands. TEL 31-70-3081500. FAX 31-70-3081515. *3938*

LEGAL REFERENCE SERVICES QUARTERLY.
Haworth Press, Inc., 10 Alice St., Binghamton, NY 13904. TEL 607-722-5857. FAX 607-722-1424. *4005*

LEGAL STUDIES FORUM.
American Legal Studies Association, c/o Law, Policy and Society Program, 341 Cushing Hall, Northeastern University, Boston, MA 02114. TEL 617-437-5211. FAX 617-437-4691. *3809*

LEGAL THEORY.
Cambridge University Press, Edinburgh Bldg., Shaftesbury Rd., Cambridge CB2 2RU, England. TEL 44-1223-312393. FAX 44-1223-315052. *3809*

LEGON JOURNAL OF THE HUMANITIES.
Black Mask Ltd., P.O. Box 69, Legon, Ghana. TEL 233-21-775178. FAX 233-21-667701. *3618*

LEIDEN JOURNAL OF INTERNATIONAL LAW.
Kluwer Law International Postbus 85889, 2508 CN The Hague, Netherlands. TEL 31-70-3081500. FAX 31-70-3081515. *3938*

LEIDSE JURIDISCHE REEKS.
E.J. Brill, P.O. Box 9000, 2300 PA Leiden, Netherlands. TEL 31-71-5353500. FAX 31-71-5317532. *3809*

LEIDSE ROMANISTISCHE REEKS.
E.J. Brill, P.O. Box 9000, 2300 PA Leiden, Netherlands. TEL 31-71-5353500. FAX 31-71-5317532. *4085*

LEISURE SCIENCES.
Taylor & Francis Inc., 1900 Frost Rd., Ste. 101, Bristol, PA 19007. TEL 215-785-5800. FAX 215-785-5515. *3965*

LEISURE STUDIES.
Chapman & Hall, Journals Department 2-6 Boundary Row, London SE1 8HN, England. TEL 171-8650066. FAX 171-5229623. *3965*

LEJEUNIA.
Botanical Society in Liege, Universite de Liege, Departement de Botanique, Sart Tilman, B-4000 Liege, Belgium. TEL 32-41-663850. FAX 32-41-663840. *689*

LENGUAJE.
Universidad del Valle, Escuela de Ciencias del Lenguaje y Literatura, Apdo. Aereo 25360, Cali, Colombia. TEL 5792-3330494. FAX 5792-3398497. *4085*

LENOX AVENUE: A JOURNAL OF INTERARTISTIC INQUIRY.
Center for Black Music Research, Columbia College, 600 S. Michigan Ave., Chicago, IL 60605. TEL 312-663-1600. FAX 312-663-9019. *5171*

LEONARDO: ART SCIENCE AND TECHNOLOGY.
M I T Press, 55 Hayward St., Cambridge, MA 02142. TEL 617-253-2889. FAX 617-577-1545. *439*

LEONARDO MUSIC JOURNAL.
M I T Press, 55 Hayward St., Cambridge, MA 02142. TEL 617-253-2889. FAX 617-577-1545. *5171*

LETRAS DE DEUSTO.
Universidad de Deusto, Facultad de la Filosofia y Letras, Departamento de Publicaciones, Apdo. 1, 48080 Bilbao Spain. TEL 34-4-4453100. FAX 34-4-445-8916. *3618*

LETTERS IN APPLIED MICROBIOLOGY.
Blackwell Science Ltd., Osney Mead, Oxford OX2 0EL, England. TEL 44-1865-206206. FAX 44-1865-721205. *761*

LETTERS IN MATHEMATICAL PHYSICS.
Kluwer Academic Publishers, Postbus 17, 3300 AA Dordrecht, Netherlands. TEL 31-78-6392392. FAX 31-78-6392254. *5557*

LEUKEMIA.
Macmillan Press Ltd., Houndmills, Basingstoke, Hants RG21 2XS, England. TEL 44-1256-29242. FAX 44-1256-28339. *4702*

LEUKEMIA AND LYMPHOMA.
Harwood Academic Publishers, c/o International Publishers Distributor, P.O. Box 3054, Langhorne, PA 19047-3054. TEL 215-750-2642. FAX 215-750-6343. *4702*

LEUKEMIA RESEARCH.
Elsevier Science Ltd., Pergamon, P.O. Box 800, Kidlington, Oxford OX5 1DX, England. TEL 44-1865-843000. FAX 44-1865-843010. *4702*

LEVANT.
British School of Archaeology in Jerusalem, c/o British Academy, 20-21 Cornwall Terrace, London NW1 4QP, England. *362*

LEXINGTON THEOLOGICAL QUARTERLY.
Lexington Theological Seminary, 631 S. Limestone St., Lexington, KY 40508. FAX 606-281-6042. *6075*

LIBERTAS MATHEMATICA.
A R A Publications (Arlington), Department of Mathematics, University of Texas, Box 19408, Arlington, TX 76019. TEL 817-794-5765. FAX 817-794-5802. *4377*

LIBRARIES & CULTURE.
University of Texas Press, Journals Division, Box 7819, Austin, TX 78713. TEL 512-471-3821. FAX 512-320-0668. *4006*

LIBRARY ACQUISITIONS: PRACTICE AND THEORY.
Elsevier Science Ltd., Pergamon, P.O. Box 800, Kidlington, Oxford OX5 1DX, England. TEL 44-1865-843000. FAX 44-1865-843010. *4006*

LIBRARY & ARCHIVAL SECURITY.
Haworth Press, Inc., 10 Alice St., Binghamton, NY 13904. TEL 607-722-5857. FAX 607-722-1424. *4007*

LIBRARY AND INFORMATION SCIENCE.
Mita Society for Library and Information Science, c/o Keio University. 2-15-45 Mita, Minato-ku, Tokyo 108, Japan. TEL 03-3453-3920. FAX 03-3798-7480. *4007*

LIBRARY ASSOCIATION OF CHINA. NEWSLETTER.
Library Association of China, c/o National Central Library, 20 Chung Shan S. Rd., Taipei, Taiwan 10040, Republic of China. FAX 02-382-0747. *4007*

LIBRARY HI TECH JOURNAL.
Pierian Press, Box 1808, Ann Arbor, MI 48106. TEL 313-434-5530. FAX 313-434-6409. *4045*

LIBRARY HISTORY.
Library Association, Library History Group, 7 Ridgmount St., London WC1E 7AE, England. *4008*

LIBRARY MOSAICS.
Yenor, Inc., P.O. Box 5171, Culver City, CA 90231. TEL 310-410-1573. *4008*

LIBRARY OF ANTHROPOLOGY.
Gordon & Breach Science Publishers, c/o International Publishers Distributor, P.O. Box 3054, Langhorne, PA 19047-3054. TEL 215-750-2642. FAX 215-750-6343. *315*

LIBRARY OF PEASANT STUDIES.
Frank Cass, Newbury House, 890-900 Eastern Ave., Newbury Park, Ilford, Essex IG2 7HH, England. TEL 44-181-599-8866. FAX 44 181-599-0984. *2892*

THE LIBRARY QUARTERLY.
University of Chicago Press, Journals Division, Box 37005, Chicago, IL 60637. TEL 773-753-3347. FAX 773-753-0811. *4009*

LIBRES: LIBRARY AND INFORMATION SCIENCE RESEARCH ELECTRONIC JOURNAL.
R&D Librarian, Curtin University of Technology, GPO Box U1987, Perth, WA 6001, Australia. TEL 61-9-3513212. FAX 61-9-3512424. *4009*

LIBRI.
Munksgaard International Publishers Ltd., 35 Noerre Soegade, P.O. Box 2148, DK-1016 Copenhagen K, Denmark. TEL 45-33-127030. FAX 45-33-129387. *4209*

THE LICKING RIVER REVIEW.
Northern Kentucky University, Department of Literature and Language, 500 Landrum Academic Center, Highland Heights KY 41099. TEL 606-572-6636. FAX 606-572-5566. *4229*

LIETUVOS FIZIKOS ZHURNALAS.
Leidykla Fisica, A. Gostauto 11, 2600 Vilnius, Lithuania. TEL 370-2-619-402 FAX 370-2-618-464. *5558*

LIFE CHEMISTRY REPORTS.
Harwood Academic Publishers, c/o International Publishers Distributor, P.O. Box 3054, Langhorne, PA 19047-3054. TEL 215-750-2642. FAX 215-750-6343. *1685*

LIFE SCIENCES.
Elsevier Science Inc., Box 945, New York, NY 10159-0945. TEL 212-633-3730. FAX 212-633-3680. *6257*

LIFE SUPPORT AND BIOSPHERE SCIENCE.
Cognizant Communication Corporation, 3 Hartsdale Rd., Elmsford, NY 10523-3701. TEL 914-592-7720. FAX 914-592-8981. *593*

LIFETIME DATA ANALYSIS.
Kluwer Academic Publishers, Postbus 17, 3300 AA Dordrecht, Netherlands. TEL 31-78-6392392. FAX 31-78-6392254. *3657*

LIGHT OF CONSCIOUSNESS.
Truth Consciousness at Desert Ashram., 3403 W. Sweetwater Dr., Tucson AZ 85745-9301. TEL 520-743-0384. FAX 520-743-3394. *5218*

LIGHT OF LIFE.
Christian Digest Society of India, 21 YMCA Rd., Bombay 400 008, India. TEL 3076941. FAX 3076941. *6075*

LIGHTWORKS.
Lightworks Magazine, Inc., Box 1202, Birmingham, MI 48012-1202. TEL 810-626-8026. FAX 810-737-0046. *440*

LIMBA SI LITERATURA.
Societatea de Stiinte Filologice din Romania, Bd. Schitul Magureanu nr.1, Bucharest, cod 79664, sector 5, Rumania. TEL 615-176-92. *4086*

LIMNETICA.
Asociacion Espanola de Limnologia, Museo Nacional de Ciencias Naturales C. Jose Gutierrez Abascal, 2, 28006 Madrid, Spain. TEL 91-4649881. FAX 91-3974168. *2288*

LIMNOLOGY AND OCEANOGRAPHY.
American Society of Limnology and Oceanography, Inc., School of Oceanography, WB-10, University of Washington, Seattle, WA 98195. TEL 206-543-0952. FAX 206-543-8655. *2288*

LINCOLN LABORATORY JOURNAL.
Massachusetts Institute of Technology, Lincoln Laboratory, 244 Wood St., Lexington, MA 02173-9108. TEL 617-981-2342. *2526*

LINEAR ALGEBRA AND ITS APPLICATIONS.
Elsevier Science Inc., Box 945, New York, NY 10159-0945. TEL 212-633-3730. FAX 212-633-3680. *4377*

LINEAR AND MULTILINEAR ALGEBRA.
Gordon and Breach Science Publishers, c/o International Publishers Distributor, P.O. Box 3054, Langhorne, PA 19047-3054. TEL 215-750-2642. FAX 215-750-6343. *4377*

LINGUA.
North-Holland P.O. Box 211, 1000 AE Amsterdam, Netherlands. TEL 31-20-4853911. FAX 31-20-4853598. *4086*

LINGUISTIC ANALYSIS.
c/o David Willingham, Man. Ed., Box 95679, Seattle, WA 98145-2679. TEL 206-567-4373. FAX 206-567-5711. *4087*

LINGUISTIC BIBLIOGRAPHY.
Kluwer Academic Publishers, Postbus 17, 3300 AA Dordrecht, Netherlands. TEL 31-78-6392392. FAX 31-78-6392254. *4128*

LINGUISTIC CALCULATION.
Kluwer Academic Publishers, Postbus 17, 3300 AA Dordrecht, Netherlands. TEL 31-78-6392392. FAX 31-78-6392254. *4087*

LINGUISTIC INQUIRY.
M I T Press, 55 Hayward St., Cambridge, MA 02142. TEL 617-253-2889. FAX 617-577-1545. *4087*

LINGUISTIC TYPOLOGY.
Walter de Gruyter und Co., Genthiner Str. 13, 10785 Berlin, Germany. TEL 49-30-250050. FAX 49-30-26005222. *4087*

LINGUISTICA SILESIANA.
Polska Akademia Nauk, Oddzial w Katowicach, Ul. Graniczna 32, 40-018 Katowice, Poland. *4088*

LINGUISTICS ABSTRACTS.
Blackwell Publishers Ltd., 108 Cowley Rd., Oxford OX4 1JF, England. TEL 44-1865-791100. FAX 44-1865-791347. *4128*

LINGUISTICS AND PHILOSOPHY.
Kluwer Academic Publishers, Postbus 17, 3300 AA Dordrecht, Netherlands. TEL 31-78-6392392. FAX 31-78-6392254. *4088*

LINGUISTICS OF THE TIBETO - BURMAN AREA.
University of California at Berkeley, Department of Linguistics, 2337 Dwinelle Hall, Berkeley, CA 94720. TEL 510-643-9910. FAX 510-643-9911. *4088*

LINKS.
Southern Links Magazine Publishing Associates, 1040 William Hilton Pkwy., Ste. 200, Hilton Head Island, SC 29938. TEL 803-842-6200. FAX 803-842-6233. *6507*

LINNEAN SOCIETY OF NEW SOUTH WALES. PROCEEDINGS.
Southwood Press Pty. Ltd., P.O. Box 457, Milsons Point, N.S.W. 2061, Australia. TEL 61-2-99290253. *812*

LINNEANA BELGICA.
c/o R. Leestmans, Ed., Krabbosstraat 179, 1653 Dworp, Belgium. TEL 32-2-3803979. *732*

LINYE KEXUE.
Science Press, Marketing and Sales Department, 16 Donghuangchenggen North St., Beijing 100717, People's Republic of China. TEL 4010642. FAX 4019810. *3021*

THE LION AND THE UNICORN.
Johns Hopkins University Press, Journals Publishing Division, 2715 N. Charles St., Baltimore, MD 21218. TEL 410-516-6987. FAX 410-516-6968. *4230*

LIPID TECHNOLOGY NEWSLETTER.
P.J. Barnes & Associates, P.O. Box 345, High Wycombe HP10 9HL, England. *644*

LIPIDS.
A O C S Press, 1608 Broadmoor Dr., Box 3489, Champaign, IL 61821-0489. TEL 217-359-2344. FAX 217-351-8091. *644*

LIQUID CRYSTALS.
Taylor & Francis Ltd., 1 Gunpowder Sq., London EC4A 3DE, England. TEL 44-171-583-0490. FAX 44-171-583-0585. *1726*

LIQUID CRYSTALS TODAY.
Taylor & Francis Inc., 1900 Frost Rd., Ste. 101, Bristol, PA 19007-1598. TEL 215-785-5800. FAX 215-785-5515. *1727*

LISHI DANG'AN.
Historical Archives Magazine House, Palace Museum inside Xihuamen, Beijing 100031, People's Republic of China. TEL 86-10-6309-7399. FAX 86-10-6309-6489. *3382*

LISZT SAECULUM.
International Liszt Centre, Synaalsvaegen 5, S-161 49 Bromma, Sweden. TEL 46-8-25-17-16. FAX 46-8-25-17-36. *5171*

LITERACY LINK.
Australian Council For Adult Literacy, G.P.O. Box 2283, Canberra, A.C.T. 2601, Australia. TEL 61-7-33780438. FAX 61-7-38781404. *2400*

LITERARY CRITERION.
c/o English Dept., Bangalore University, Jnana Bharathi, Bangalore 560 056, India. TEL 3355299. *4152*

LITERARY REVIEW.
Fairleigh Dickinson University, Literary Review, 285 Madison Ave., Madison, NJ 07940. TEL 201-443-8564. *4231*

LITERATURA MEXICANA.
Universidad Nacional Autonoma de Mexico, Instituto de Investigaciones Filologicas, Ciudad Universitaria, Cir. Mario de la Cueva, 04510 Mexico DF, Mexico. *4231*

LITERATURE AND BELIEF.
Brigham Young University, College of Humanities, Center, Study of Christian Values in Literature, 3076F Jesse Knight Bldg., Provo, UT 84604-9989. TEL 801-378-3073. FAX 801-378-4720. *6075*

LITERATURE - FILM QUARTERLY.
Salisbury State University, Salisbury, MD 21801. TEL 410-543-6446. FAX 410-543-6068. *5107*

LITHOLOGY AND MINERAL RESOURCES.
Maik Nauka - Interperiodica, Mezhdunarodnyi Otdel, Ul. Profsoyuznaya, 90, 117864 Moscow, Russia. TEL 7-095-3360066. FAX 7-095-3360666. *2248*

LITHOS.
Elsevier Science B.V., P.O. Box 211, 1000 AE Amsterdam, Netherlands. TEL 31-20-4853911. FAX 31-20-4853598. *2248*

LITHUANIAN MATHEMATICAL JOURNAL.
Plenum Publishing Corp., Consultants Bureau, 233 Spring St., New York, NY 10013-1578. TEL 212-620-8468. FAX 212-463-0742. *4377*

LITHUANIAN PAPERS.
Tasmanian University, Lithuanian Studies Society, P.O. Box 777, Sandy Bay, Tas. 7005, Australia. TEL 61-02-252505. *2892*

LITURGY NEWS.
Archdiocese of Brisbane, Liturgical Commission, G.P.O. Box 282, Brisbane, Qld. 4001, Australia. TEL 61-7-32243329. FAX 61-7-32211705. *6185*

LIUTI LIXUE SHIYAN YU CELIANG.
Zhongguo Kongqi Dongli Yanjiu yu Fazhan Zhongxin, P.O. Box 211, Mianyang, Sichuan 621000, People's Republic of China. TEL 86-816-2466261. *5589*

LIVER.
Munksgaard International Publishers Ltd., 35 Noerre Soegade, P.O. Box 2148, DK-1016 Copenhagen K, Denmark. TEL 45-33-127030. FAX 45-33-129387. *4695*

LIVER TRANSPLANTATION AND SURGERY.
W.B. Saunders Co. Curtis Center, 3rd Fl., Independence Sq., W., Philadelphia, PA 19106-3399. TEL 215-238-7800. FAX 215-238-3445. *4695*

LIVERPOOL LAW REVIEW.
Deborah Charles Publications, 173 Mather Ave., Liverpool L18 6JZ, England. TEL 0151-724-2500. FAX 0151-729-0371. *3811*

LIVERPOOL STUDIES IN LANGUAGE AND DISCOURSE.
University of Liverpool, Department of English Language and Literature, Modern Languages Bldg., P.O. Box 147, Liverpool L69 3BX, England. TEL 44-151-794-2705. FAX 44-151-794-2730. *4089*

LIVESTOCK PRODUCTION SCIENCE.
Elsevier Science B.V., P.O. Box 211, 1000 AE Amsterdam, Netherlands. TEL 31-20-4853911. FAX 31-20-4853598. *276*

LIVING WORLD.
International Life Services, Inc., 2606 1-2 W. 8th St., Los Angeles, CA 90057. TEL 213-382-2156. FAX 213-382-4203. *6381*

LIVRUSTKAMMAREN.
Kungliga Livrustkammaren, Kungliga Slottet, Slottsbacken 3, S-111 30 Stockholm, Sweden. TEL 46-8-666-44-68. FAX 46-8-666-44-68. *5125*

LIXUE JINZHAN.
Zhongguo Kexueyuan, Lixue Yanjiusuo, 15 Zhongguancun Lu, Beijing 100080, People's Republic of China. TEL 2554108. FAX 86-1-2561284. *5589*

LIXUE XUEBAO.
Science Press, Marketing and Sales Department, 16 Donghuangchenggen North St., Beijing 100717, People's Republic of China. TEL 4010642. FAX 4019810. *5589*

LIXUE YU SHIJIAN.
Science Press, Marketing and Sales Department, 16 Donghuangchenggen North St., Beijing 100717, People's Republic of China. TEL 4010642. FAX 4019810. *2762*

LOCAL ECONOMY.
Pitman Publishing, 128 Long Acre, London WC2E 9AN, England. TEL 0171-379-7383. FAX 0171-240-5771. *941*

LOCAL GOVERNMENT POLICY MAKING.
Pitman Publishing, 128 Long Acre, London WC2E 9AN, England. TEL 0171-379-7383. FAX 0171-240-5771. *5945*

LOCAL GOVERNMENT STUDIES.
Frank Cass, Newbury House, 890-900 Eastern Ave., Newbury Park, Ilford, Essex IG2 7HH, England. TEL 44-181-599-8866. FAX 44-181-599-0984. *5945*

LOCATION SCIENCE.
Elsevier Science Ltd., Pergamon, P.O. Box 800, Kidlington, Oxford OX5 1DX, England. TEL 44-1865-843000. FAX 44-1865-843010. *5864*

LOEB CLASSICAL LIBRARY.
Harvard University Press, 79 Garden St., Cambridge, MA 02138. TEL 617-495-2600. FAX 617-495-5898. *4233*

LOGISTICA MANAGEMENT.
Edizioni Ritman s.r.l., Via Varesina 76, 20156 Milan, Italy. TEL 39-2-38008859. FAX 39-2-38008828. *1431*

LOGOS.
Whurr Publishers Ltd., 19b Compton Terrace, London N1 2UN, England. TEL 44-171-359-5979. FAX 44-171-226-5290. *6002*

LONDON JOURNAL.
London Journal Trust, c/o Centre for Metropolitan History, Senate House, Rm. 351, Malet St., London WC1E 7HU, England. TEL 44-171-636-0272. FAX 44-171-436-2183. *3425*

LONDON MATHEMATICAL SOCIETY. BULLETIN.
London Mathematical Society, Burlington House, Picadilly, London W1V ONL, England. TEL 44-171-437-5377. FAX 44-171-439-4629. *4377*

LONDON MATHEMATICAL SOCIETY. JOURNAL.
Cambridge University Press, Edinburgh House, Shaftesbury Rd., Cambridge CB2 2RU, England. TEL 44-1223-312393. FAX 44-1223-315052. *4377*

LONDON MATHEMATICAL SOCIETY. MONOGRAPHS.
Academic Press, Inc., 525 B St., Ste. 1900, San Diego, CA 92101-4495. TEL 619-231-0926. FAX 619-699-6715. *4377*

LONG ISLAND HISTORICAL JOURNAL.
State University of New York at Stony Brook, Department of History, Stony Brook, NY 11794-4348. TEL 516-632-7500. FAX 516-632-7367. *3476*

LONG ISLAND POSTAL HISTORIAN.
Long Island Postal History Society, 144 Hamilton Ave., Clifton, NJ 07011. TEL 201-772-1413. *1931*

LONG RANGE PLANNING.
Elsevier Science Ltd., Pergamon, P.O. Box 800, Kidlington, Oxford OX5 1DX, England. TEL 44-1865-843000. FAX 44-1865-843010. *1431*

LONGITUDINAL RESEARCH IN THE BEHAVIORAL, SOCIAL AND MEDICAL SCIENCES.
Kluwer Academic Publishers, Postbus 17, 3300 AA Dordrecht, Netherlands. TEL 31-78-6392392. FAX 31-78-6392254. *6333*

THE LONSDALE.
Vagabond Press, VIP Meguro 802, 4-1-16 Shimo-Meguro, Meguro-ku, Tokyo 153, Japan. TEL 81-3-5721-9979. FAX 81-3-5721-9979. *4310*

LOOP TRANSFORMATIONS FOR RESTRUCTURING COMPILERS.
Kluwer Academic Publishers, Postbus 17, 3300 AA Dordrecht, Netherlands. TEL 31-78-6392392. FAX 31-78-6392254. *2021*

LORIS.
Wildlife & Nature Protection Society of Sri Lanka, Chaitiya Rd., Fort, Colombo 1, Sri Lanka. TEL 25248. FAX 941-580721. *2133*

LOS ALAMOS SERIES IN BASIC AND APPLIED SCIENCES.
University of California Press, 2120 Berkeley Way, Berkeley, CA 94720. TEL 510-642-4247. FAX 510-643-7127. *6257*

LOS ANGELES.
11100 Santa Monica Blvd., 7th Fl., Los Angeles, CA 90025. TEL 310-996-6870. *3231*

LOS ANGELES LAWYER.
Los Angeles County Bar Association, Box 55020, Los Angeles, CA 90055. TEL 213-896-6503. FAX 213-623-2348. *3811*

LOSS, GRIEF & CARE.
Haworth Press, Inc., 10 Alice St., Binghamton, NY 13904. TEL 607-722-5857. FAX 607-722-1424. *5864*

LOSS PREVENTION BULLETIN.
Institution of Chemical Engineers, George E. Davis Bldg., 165-189 Railway Terr., Rugby, Warwickshire CV21 3HQ, England. TEL 44-1788-578214. FAX 44-1788-560833. *2645*

LOUISIANA ACADEMY OF SCIENCES. PROCEEDINGS.
Louisiana Academy of Sciences, c/o Dr. Brad Mc Pherson, Department of Biology, Centenary College, Shreveport, LA 71104. *6257*

LOUISIANA AGRICULTURE.
Louisiana State University, Agricultural Center, Box 25100, Baton Rouge, LA 70894-5100. TEL 504-388-2263. FAX 504-388-4524. *133*

LOUISIANA ENGLISH JOURNAL.
Louisiana Council of Teachers of English, Louisiana State University at Eunice, Box 1129, Eunice, LA 70535. TEL 318-457-7311. FAX 318-546-6620. *4089*

LOUISIANA LITERATURE.
Southeastern Louisiana University, English Department, SLU-792, Hammond, LA 70402. TEL 504-549-5022 FAX 504-549-5021. *4233*

LOUISIANA STATE MEDICAL SOCIETY. JOURNAL.
Journal of the Louisiana State Medical Society, Inc., 3501 N. Causeway Blvd., Ste. 800, Metairie, LA 70002-3625. TEL 504-832-9815. FAX 504-833-7685. *4490*

LOUVAIN STUDIES.
Katholieke Universiteit Leuven, Faculteit Godgeleerdheid, St. Michielsstraat 2, B-3000 Leuven, Belgium. TEL 32-16-283894. FAX 32-16-283858. *6076*

LOVE AND RAGE.
Box 853, New York, NY 10009-0853. TEL 718-834-9077. *5681*

LOW INTENSITY CONFLICT & LAW ENFORCEMENT.
Frank Cass, Newbury House, 890-900 Eastern Ave., Newbury Park, Ilford, Essex IG2 7HH, England. TEL 44-181-599-8366. FAX 44-181-599-0984. *5761*

LOWER EXTREMITY.
Churchill Livingstone, 650 Ave. of the Americas, New York, NY 10011. TEL 212-206-5040. FAX 212-727-7808. *4490*

LOYOLA JOURNAL OF SOCIAL SCIENCES.
Loyola College of Social Sciences, Thiruvananthapuram 695 017, India. TEL 91-471-442059. *6333*

LUBRICATION ENGINEERING.
Society of Tribologists and Lubrication Engineers, 840 Busse Hwy., Park Ridge, IL 60068-2376. TEL 847-825-5536. FAX 847-825-1456. *2762*

LUBRICATION SCIENCE.
Leaf Coppin Publishing Co., P.O. Box 111, Deal, Kent CT14 6SX, England. TEL 44-1304-360241. *5363*

LUNG.
Springer-Verlag, Medical Journals, 175 Fifth Ave., New York, NY 10010. TEL 212-460-1500. FAX 212-473-6272. *4889*

LUNG BIOLOGY IN HEALTH AND DISEASE.
Marcel Dekker, Inc., 270 Madison Ave., New York, NY 10016. TEL 212-696-9000. FAX 212-685-4540. *4889*

LUNG CANCER.
Elsevier Science Ireland Ltd., P.O. Box 85, Limerick, Ireland. TEL 353-61-471944. FAX 353-61-472144. *4759*

LUSITANIA SACRA.
Universidade Catolica Portuguesa, Centro de Estudos de Historia Religiosa, Palma de Cima, 1600 Lisbon, Portugal. TEL 351-1-7214130. FAX 351-1-7270256. *3426*

LUTRA.
Bureau V Z Z, Emmalaan 41, 3581 HP Utrecht, Netherlands TEL 31-30-2544642. *812*

LUZO - BRAZILIAN REVIEW.
University of Wisconsin Press, Journal Division, 114 N. Murray St., Madison, WI 53715. TEL 608-262-4952. FAX 608-262-7560. *4153*

LYMPHOLOGY.
International Society of Lymphology, c/o Univ. of Arizona, Dept. of Surgery - Trauma, Box 245063, Tucson, AZ 85724-5063. TEL 520-626-6118. FAX 520-626-0822. *4673*

LYNX.
A H A Books, Box 1250, Gualala, CA 95445-0767. TEL 707-882-2226. *4310*

LYON PHARMACEUTIQUE.
Editions Scientifiques et Medicales Elsevier, 141 rue de Javel, 75747 Paris, France. TEL 33-1-45589026. FAX 33-1-45589421. *5426*

LYSOSOMES IN BIOLOGY AND PATHOLOGY.
Elsevier Science B.V., Books Division, P.O. Box 211, 1000 AE Amsterdam, Netherlands. TEL 31-20-4853911. FAX 31-20-4853705. *593*

LYTS FRISIA.
Jongfryske Mienskip, Julianalaan 26, 9801 BP Zuidhorn, Netherlands. TEL 31-594-502829. *4153*

M A R D I REPORT.
Malaysian Agricultural Research & Development Institute, P.O. Box 1230, General Post Office, 50774 Kuala Lumpur, Malaysia. TEL 03-9437111. FAX 03-3664. *133*

M A R D I RESEARCH JOURNAL.
Malaysian Agricultural Research & Development Institute, P.O. Box 1230, General Post Office, 50774 Kuala Lumpur, Malaysia. TEL 03-9437111. FAX 03-9426434. *133*

M COMPUTING.
M Technology Association, 1738 Elton Rd., Ste. 205, Silver Spring, MD 20903. TEL 301-431-4070. FAX 301-431-0017. *2045*

M.D. COMPUTING (NEW YORK).
Springer-Verlag, Medical Journals, 175 Fifth Ave., New York, NY 10010. TEL 212 460-1500. FAX 212-473-4262. *4632*

M E L A NOTES.
Middle East Librarians Association, c/o Mary St. Germain, Secy., Cataloging, Suzallo Library, U. of WA, Box 352900, Seattle, WA 98195-2900. TEL 206-543-1828. FAX 206-685-8049. *4010*

M E L U S.
Society for the Study of the Multi-Ethnic Literature of the United States, 272 Bartlett Hall, Department of English, University of Massachusetts, Amherst, MA 01003. TEL 413-545-3166. FAX 413-545-3880. *4234*

M G V.
Nederlands Centrum Geestelijke Volksgezondheid, Postbus 5103, 3502 JC Utrecht, Netherlands. TEL 31-2154-82211. *4850*

M I M S IRELAND.
Medical Publications (Ireland) Ltd., 15 Harcourt St., Dublin 2, Ireland. TEL 475746. FAX 757467. *4430*

M S L A JOURNAL.
Manitoba School Library Association, c/o Manitoba Teachers' Society, 191 Harcourt St., Winnipeg, Man. R3J 3H2, Canada. TEL 204-888-7961. *2494*

M UND A REPORT.
M und A Verlag fuer Messen, Ausstellungen und Kongresse GmbH Postfach 10 528, 60015 Frankfurt a.M., Germany. TEL 49-69-759502. FAX 49-69-75951280. *40*

MCCALLUM OBSERVER.
Box 313, Lansing, IL 60438-0313. TEL 708-895-0736. *558*

MACEDONIAN TRIBUNE.
Macedonian Patriotic Organization of the U S and Canada, 124 W. Wayne, Fort Wayne, IN 46802-2505. TEL 219-422-5900. FAX 219-422-1348. *1851*

MCGILL LAW JOURNAL.
Chancellor Day Hall, 3644 Peel St., Montreal, PQ H3A 1W9, Canada. TEL 514-874-9038. FAX 514-398-7397. *3812*

MCGOLDRICK'S CANADIAN CUSTOMS GUIDE "HARMONIZED SYSTEM".
McMullin Publishers Ltd., 417 St. Pierre, Montreal, PQ H2Y 2M4, Canada. TEL 514-849-1424. FAX 514-849-9809. *289*

THE MCGUFFEY WRITER.
McGuffey Foundation School, 5128 Westgate Dr., Oxford, OH 45056. TEL 513-523-7742. FAX 513-523-5565. *1798*

MACH.
Mach, P.O. Box 5002 S-161 05 Bromma, Sweden. TEL 46008-17-88-50. FAX 46-08-17-88-55. *72*

MACHETE.
Machete Press, Box 605, Cooper Sq. Sta., New York, NY 10276. TEL 718-237-1471. *4153*

MACHINE DYNAMICS PROBLEMS.
Wydawnictwo M E T, c/o Mieczyslaw Pekalak, Ul. Piekalkiewicza 5 m.6, 00-710 Warsaw, Poland. TEL 48-22-490195. FAX 48-22-490306. *2762*

MACHINE INTELLIGENCE AND PATTERN RECOGNITION.
Elsevier Science B.V., Books Division, P.O. Box 211, 1000 AE Amsterdam, Netherlands. TEL 31-20-4853911. FAX 31-20-4853705. *2009*

MACHINE LEARNING.
Kluwer Academic Publishers Boston, Box 358, Accord Sta., Hingham, MA 02018-0358. TEL 617-871-6300. FAX 617-871-6528. *1995*

MACHINE LEARNING ONLINE.
Kluwer Academic Publishers Boston, Box 358, Accord Sta., Hingham, MA 02018-0358. TEL 617-871-6600. FAX 617-871-6528. *1995*

MACHINE TRANSLATION.
Kluwer Academic Publishers, Postbus 17, 3300 AA Dordrecht, Netherlands. TEL 31-78-6392392. FAX 31-78-6392254. *4129*

MCILVAINEA.
North American Mycological Association, 3556 Oakwood, Ann Arbor, MI 48104-5213. TEL 313-971-2552. *690*

MACROMOLECULES.
American Chemical Society, 1155 16th St., N.W., Washington, DC 20036. TEL 800-333-9511. FAX 614-447-3671. *1741*

MADISON REVIEW (TALLAHASSEE).
James Madison Institute for Public Policy, P.O. Box 13894, Tallahassee, FL 32317-3894. TEL 904-386-3131. FAX 904-386-1807. *5682*

MADRAS AGRICULTURAL JOURNAL.
Madras Agricultural Students' Union, Tamil Nadu Agricultural University Campus, Coimbatore 641 003, India. *134*

MAGAZINE OF ALBEMARLE COUNTY HISTORY.
Albemarle County Historical Society, Publications Committee, 200 Second St., N.E., Charlottesville, VA 22902. TEL 804-296-1492. FAX 804-296-4576. *3477*

MAGAZINE OF CONCRETE RESEARCH.
Thomas Telford Services Ltd., Thomas Telford House, 1 Heron Quay, London E14 4JD, England. TEL 44-171-987-6999. FAX 44-171-538-9620. *864*

MAGNES NEWS.
Judah L. Magnes Museum, 2911 Russell St., Berkeley, CA 94705. TEL 510-549-6950. FAX 510-849-3673. *5125*

MAGNETIC AND ELECTRICAL SEPARATION.
Gordon & Breach Science Publishers, c/o International Publishers Distributor, P.O. Box 3054, Langhorne, PA 19047-3054. TEL 215-750-2642. FAX 215-750-6343. *5558*

MAGNETIC RESONANCE IMAGING.
Elsevier Science Inc., Box 945, New York, NY 10159-0945. TEL 212-633-3730. FAX 212-633-3680. *4879*

MAGNETIC RESONANCE IN CHEMISTRY.
John Wiley & Sons Ltd., Journals, Baffins Ln., Chichester, W. Sussex PO19 1UD, England. TEL 44-1243-779777. FAX 44-1243-843232. *1755*

MAGNETIC RESONANCE IN MEDICINE.
Williams & Wilkins, 351 W. Camden St., Baltimore, MD 21201. TEL 410-528-4000. FAX 410-528-4312. *4880*

MAGNETIC RESONANCE MATERIALS IN PHYSICS, BIOLOGY AND MEDICINE.
Chapman & Hall, Journals Department 2-6 Boundary Row, London SE1 8HN, England. TEL 44-171-8560066. FAX 44-171-5229623. *5596*

MAGNETIC RESONANCE QUARTERLY.
Lippincott - Raven Publishers 227 E. Washington Sq., Philadelphia, PA 19106. TEL 215-238-4200. *4880*

MAGNETIC RESONANCE REVIEW.
Gordon and Breach Science Publishers, c/o International Publishers Distributor, P.O. Box 3054, Langhorne, PA 19047-3054. TEL 215-750-2642. FAX 215-750-6343. *5558*

MAGNETOHYDRODYNAMICS.
Plenum Publishing Corp., Consultants Bureau, 233 Spring St., New York, NY 10013-1578. TEL 212-620-8468. FAX 212-463-0742. *2712*

MAGNETS IN YOUR FUTURE.
L H Publishing Agency, Box 250, Ash Flat, AR 72513. TEL 501-856-3877. FAX 501-856-3590. *2712*

MAGYAR EGYHAZTORTENETI VAZLATOK.
M E T E M - International Society of Toronto for Hungarian Church History, Regis College, 15 St. Mary St., Toronto, ON M4Y 2R5, Canada. *3426*

MAGYAR PEDAGOGIA.
Jozsef Attila Tudomanyegyetem, Department of Education, Petofi sgt. 30-34, 6722 Szeged, Hungary. TEL 36-62-321034. *2352*

MAILOUT.
Mailout Trust, 9 Chapel St., Holywell Green, Halifax HX4 9AY, England. TEL 44-1422-310161. FAX 44-1422-310161. *441*

MAINE HISTORY.
Maine Historical Society, 485 Congress St., Portland, ME 04101. TEL 207-744-1822. FAX 207-775-4301. *3477*

MAINE IN PRINT.
Maine Writers & Publishers Alliance, 12 Pleasant St., Brunswick, ME 04011-1513. *4234*

MAJALAH U S U.
University of North Sumatra, Jl. Dr. Mansur, Kampus USU, Medan 20155, Indonesia. TEL 061-524033. FAX 061-520822. *2435*

MAJALLAT AL-IMARAT LIL-'ULUM AL-ZIRA'IYYAH.
United Arab Emirates University, Faculty of Agriculture, P.O. Box 17555, Al-Ain, United Arab Emirates. TEL 971-3-635647. FAX 971-3-632384. *134*

MAJALLAT AL-SHARI'AH WAL-QANUN.
United Arab Emirates University, Faculty of Law and Islamic Jurisprudence, P.O. Box 15551, Al-Ain, United Arab Emirates. TEL 643998. FAX 660655. *3813*

MAJALLAT AL-WAHDAH AL-IQTISADIYYAH AL-ARABIYYAH.
Majlis al-Wahdah al-Iqtisadiyyah al-Arabiyyah, Al-Amanah al-Aamah, P.O. Box 925100, Amman, Jordan. TEL 664329. *1258*

MAJOR HEALTH ISSUES.
Elsevier Science B.V., Books Division, P.O. Box 211, 1000 AE Amsterdam, Netherlands. TEL 31-20-4853911. FAX 31-20-4853705. *5969*

MAJORIE KINNAN RAWLINGS JOURNAL OF FLORIDA LITERATURE.
Illinois State University, Department of English, Normal, IL 61790-4240. TEL 309-438-5776. FAX 309-438-5414. *4235*

MAKING SENSE OF SCIENCE.
Portland Press Ltd., 59 Portland Pl., London W1N 3AJ, England. TEL 44-171-580-5530. FAX 44-171-323-1136. *1798*

MALAYSIAN APPLIED BIOLOGY JOURNAL.
Malaysian Society of Applied Biology, c/o Faculty of Science, Universiti Kebangsaan Malaysia, 43600 UKM, Bangi, Selangor, Malaysia. *134*

MALAYSIAN JOURNAL OF SCIENCE.
University of Malaya, Lembah Pantai, 59100 Kuala Lumpur, Malaysia. TEL 565000. *6257*

MAMMAL REVIEW.
Blackwell Science Ltd., Osney Mead, Oxford OX2 0EL, England. TEL 44-1865-206206. FAX 44-1865-721205. *813*

MAMMALIA.
Museum National d'Histoire Naturelle, Mammiferes et Oiseaux, 55 rue Buffon, 75005 Paris, France. TEL 40-79-30-69. FAX 40-79-30-63. *813*

MAMMALIAN GENOME.
Springer-Verlag, Life Science Journals, 175 Fifth Ave., New York, NY 10010. TEL 212-460-1500. FAX 212-473-6272. *593*

MAMMALIAN SPECIES.
American Society of Mammalogists, c/o Dr. H. Duane Smith, Sec.-Treas., Monte L. Bean Life Science Museum, Brigham Young University, Provo, UT 84602. TEL 801-378-2492. *813*

MAMMOGRAPHY TODAY.
Durantech Publishing Co., 3870 La Sierra Ave., Ste. 392, Riverside, CA 92505. TEL 909-243-0784. FAX 909-247-0735. *4741*

MAN AND WORLD.
Kluwer Academic Publishers, Postbus 17, 3300 AA Dordrecht, Netherlands. TEL 31-78-6392392. FAX 31-78-6392254. *5485*

MANAGEMENT AND AVOIDANCE OF COMPLICATIONS IN EYELID SURGERY.
Field & Wood, Medical Periodicals, Inc., Box 975, Blue Bell, PA 19422. TEL 610-828-4010. FAX 215-482-0226. *4914*

MANAGEMENT DEVELOPMENT.
Bangladesh Management Development Centre, Mirpur Rd., Dhaka 7, Bangladesh. TEL 802-817405-7. FAX 802-814304. *1432*

MANAGEMENT IN EDUCATION.
Pitman Publishing, 128 Long Acre, London WC2E 9AN, England. TEL 0171-379-7383. FAX 0171-240-5771. *1433*

MANAGERIAL AND DECISION ECONOMICS.
John Wiley & Sons Ltd., Journals, Baffins Ln., Chichester, W. Sussex PO19 1UD, England. TEL 44-1243-779777. FAX 44-1243-843232. *1434*

MANAGERSEMINARE.
ManagerSeminare Gerhard May Verlags GmbH, Endenicherstr. 282, 53121 Bonn, Germany. TEL 49-228-97791-0. FAX 49-228-616164. *1435*

THE MANCHESTER GEOGRAPHER.
Manchester Geographical Society, 385 Corn Exchange Buildings, Manchester M4 3HN, England. *3265*

MANCHESTER SCHOOL OF ECONOMIC AND SOCIAL STUDIES.
Blackwell Publishers Ltd., 108 Cowley Rd., Oxford OX4 1JF, England. TEL 44-1865-791100. FAX 44-1865-791347. *1259*

MANKIND QUARTERLY.
Institute for the Study of Man, Box 34070, N.W., Washington, DC 20043. TEL 202-371-2700. FAX 202-371-1523. *315*

MANOA.
University of Hawaii Press, Journals Department, 2840 Kolowalu St., Honolulu, HI 96822. TEL 808-956-8833. FAX 808-988-6052. *4235*

MANSOURA JOURNAL OF PHARMACEUTICAL SCIENCES.
University of Mansoura, Faculty of Pharmacy, University P.O. 35516, Mansoura, Egypt. *5427*

MANUAL THERAPY.
Churchill Livingstone Robert Stevenson House, 1-3 Baxter's Pl., Leith Walk, Edinburgh EH1 3AF, Scotland. TEL 44-131-5562424. FAX 44-131-5351704. *4818*

MANUFACTURING RESEARCH AND TECHNOLOGY.
Elsevier Science B.V., Books Division, P.O. Box 211, 1000 AE Amsterdam, Netherlands. TEL 31-20-4853911. FAX 31-20-4853705. *1526*

MANUFACTURING REVIEW.
American Society of Mechanical Engineers, 22 Law Dr., Fairfield, NJ 07007-2300. TEL 201-882-1170. FAX 201-882-5155. *6657*

MAP COLLECTOR.
Map Collector Publications Ltd., 48 High St., Tring, Herts. HP23 5BH, England. TEL 44-1442-824977. FAX 44-1442-827712. *3265*

MARCOLIAN.
Marietta College, Box A-20, Marietta, OH 45750-4000. TEL 614-376-4937. FAX 614-376-4810. *1876*

MARINE AND FRESHWATER BEHAVIOUR AND PHYSIOLOGY.
Gordon and Breach Science Publishers, c/o International Publishers Distributor, P.O. Box 3054, Langhorne, PA 19047-3054. TEL 215-750-2642. FAX 215-750-6343. *594*

MARINE AND PETROLEUM GEOLOGY.
Butterworth - Heinemann, Part of the Reed Elsevier group, Linacre House, Jordan Hill, Oxford OX2 8DP, England. TEL 44-1865-310366. FAX 44-1865-310898. *2249*

MARINE BIOLOGICAL ASSOCIATION OF THE UNITED KINGDOM. JOURNAL.
Cambridge University Press, Edinburgh Bldg., Shaftesbury Rd., Cambridge CB2 2RU, England. TEL 44-1223-312393. FAX 44-1223-315052. *594*

MARINE BIOLOGICAL ASSOCIATION OF THE UNITED KINGDOM. OCCASIONAL PUBLICATIONS.
Marine Biological Association of the United Kingdom, Citadel Hill, Plymouth PL1 2PB, England. TEL 44-1752-633334. FAX 44-1752-633102. *594*

MARINE BOARD OF HOBART. ANNUAL REPORT.
Marine Board of Hobart, Franklin Wharf, Tas. 7000, Australia. TEL 61-02-351000. FAX 61-02-310693. *6841*

MARINE CHEMISTRY.
Elsevier Science B.V., P.O. Box 211, 1000 AE Amsterdam, Netherlands. TEL 31-20-4853911. FAX 31-20-4853598. *2212*

MARINE ENVIRONMENTAL RESEARCH.
Elsevier Science Ltd., P.O. Box 800, Kidlington, Oxford OX5 1DX, England. TEL 44-1865-843000. FAX 44-1865-843010. *2838*

MARINE FISHERIES REVIEW.
U.S. National Marine Fisheries Service, Scientific Publications Office, 7600 Sandpoint Way, N.E., Bin C15700, Seattle, WA 98115. TEL 206-526-6107. FAX 206-526-6426. *2938*

MARINE GEODESY.
Taylor & Francis Inc., 1900 Frost Rd., Ste. 101, Bristol, PA 19007. TEL 215-785-5800. FAX 215-785-5515. *3265*

MARINE GEOLOGY.
Elsevier Science B.V., P.O. Box 211, 1000 AE Amsterdam, Netherlands. TEL 31-20-4853911. FAX 31-20-4853598. *2300*

MARINE GEOPHYSICAL RESEARCHES.
Kluwer Academic Publishers, Postbus 17, 3300 AA Dordrecht, Netherlands. TEL 31-78-6392392. FAX 31-78-6392254. *2300*

MARINE GEORESOURCES AND GEOTECHNOLOGY.
Taylor & Francis Inc., 1900 Frost Rd., Ste. 101, Bristol, PA 19007. TEL 215-785-5800. FAX 215-785-5515. *2300*

MARINE MICROPALEONTOLOGY.
Elsevier Science B.V., P.O. Box 211, 1000 AE Amsterdam, Netherlands. TEL 31-20-4853911. FAX 31-20-4853598. *5315*

MARINE ORNITHOLOGY.
African Seabird Group, P.O. Box 34113, Rhodes Gift 7707, South Africa. TEL 27-21-6503294. FAX 27-21-6503295. *778*

MARINE POLICY.
Butterworth - Heinemann, Part of the Reed Elsevier group, Linacre House, Jordan Hill, Oxon. OX2 8DP, England. TEL 44-1865-310366. FAX 44-1865-310898. *2300*

MARINE POLLUTION BULLETIN.
Elsevier Science Ltd., Pergamon, P.O. Box 800, Kidlington, Oxford OX5 1DX, England. TEL 44-1865-843000. FAX 44-1865-843010. *2838*

MARINE STRUCTURES.
Elsevier Science Ltd., P.O. Box 800, Kidlington, Oxford OX5 1DX, England. TEL 44-1865-843000. FAX 44-1865-843010. *2762*

MARINE TECHNOLOGY AND S N A M E NEWS.
Society of Naval Architects and Marine Engineers, 601 Pavonia Ave., Jersey City, NJ 07306-2907. TEL 201-798-4800. FAX 201-798-4975. *6841*

MARINE TECHNOLOGY SOCIETY JOURNAL.
Marine Technology Society, Inc., 1828 L St., N.W., Ste. 906, Washington, DC 20036-5104. TEL 202-775-5966. FAX 202-429-9417. *2300*

MARINEBLAD.
Koninklijke Vereniging van Marine-Officieren, Wassenaarseweg 2b, 2596 CH The Hague, Netherlands. TEL 31-70-3839504. FAX 31-70-3835911. *5038*

MARINER'S MIRROR.
Society for Nautical Research, Department of History, University of Exeter, Devon, England. FAX 01392-264377. *3352*

MARITIME POLICY AND MANAGEMENT.
Taylor & Francis Ltd., 1 Gunpowder Sq., London EC4A 3DE, England. TEL 44-171-583-0490. FAX 44-171-583-0585. *6842*

MARKETING AND RESEARCH TODAY.
European Society for Opinion and Marketing Research, J.J. Viottastraat 29, 1071 JP Amsterdam, Netherlands. TEL 31-20-664-2141. FAX 31-20-664-2922. *1476*

MARKETING LETTERS.
Kluwer Academic Publishers Boston, Box 358, Accord Sta., Hingham, MA 02018-0358. TEL 617-871-6600. FAX 617-871-6528. *1477*

MARKETING RESEARCH.
American Marketing Association, 250 S. Wacker Dr., Ste. 200, Chicago, IL 60606. TEL 312-648-0536. FAX 312-993-7542. *1478*

MARKETPLACE MAGAZINE.
A D D Inc., 211 N. Lynndale Dr., Ste. 8, Appleton, WI 54913-1897. TEL 414-735-5969. FAX 414-735-5970. *943*

MARMARA UNIVERSITY. FACULTY OF DENTISTRY. JOURNAL.
Marmara University, Faculty of Dentistry, Buyukciftlik Sok. No. 6, 80200 Nisantasi - Istanbul, Turkey. TEL 90-212-2483697. FAX 90-212-2465247. *4647*

MARO POLYMER NOTES.
Maro Communications, Box 37019, Tucson, AZ 85740-7019. TEL 602-322-5739. *5629*

MARRIAGE & FAMILY REVIEW.
Haworth Press, Inc., 10 Alice St., Binghamton, NY 13904. TEL 607-722-5857. FAX 607-722-1424. *6422*

MARTIN CLASSICAL LECTURES.
Princeton University Press, 41 William St., Princeton, NJ 08540. TEL 609-258-4900. FAX 609-253-6305. *1824*

MARTYRDOM AND RESISTANCE.
American Society for Yad Vashem, 48 W. 37th St. 9th Fl., New York, NY 10018-7408. TEL 212-564-9606. FAX 212-564-6395. *2893*

MARXISME AUJOURD'HUI.
Federation des Cercles le Marxisme Aujourd'hui, B.P. 9012, 64050 Pau Cedex 9, France. *5682*

MARYLAND BIRDLIFE.
Maryland Ornithological Society, Inc., Patuxent Wildlife Research, Laurel, MD 20708. TEL 301-497-5641. FAX 301-497-5624. *778*

MARYLAND ENGLISH JOURNAL.
Maryland Council of Teachers of English Language Arts, Frostburg State University, Dept. of English, Frostburg, MD 21532. TEL 301-687-4221. FAX 301-687-4495. *2494*

MARYLAND HISTORIAN.
University of Maryland, Department of History, College Park, MD 20742. TEL 301-405-4331. *3352*

MARYLAND MEDICAL JOURNAL.
Medical and Chirurgical Faculty of Maryland, 1211 Cathedral St, Baltimore, MD 21201. TEL 410-539-0872. FAX 410-547-0915. *4492*

MARYLAND POETRY REVIEW.
Maryland State Poetry and Literary Society, Drawer H, Catonsville, MD 21228. TEL 410-747-0594. *4310*

MARYLAND STATE DENTAL ASSOCIATION. JOURNAL.
Maryland State Dental Association, 6450 Dobbin Rd., Columbia Business Center, Columbia, MD 21045-4744. TEL 410-964-2880. FAX 410-964-0583. *4647*

MASONRY SOCIETY JOURNAL.
Masonry Society, 3970 Broadway St., Ste. 201-D, Boulder, CO 80304-1135. TEL 303-939-9700. FAX 303-444-3239. *864*

MASS SPECTROMETRY REVIEWS.
John Wiley & Sons, Inc., Journals, 605 Third Ave., New York, NY 10158. TEL 212-850-6645. FAX 212-850-6021. *5607*

MASSACHUSETTS INSTITUTE OF TECHNOLOGY. FLIGHT TRANSPORTATION LABORATORY. F T L REPORTS AND MEMORANDA.
Massachusetts Institute of Technology, Department of Aeronautics and Astronautics, Rm. 33-412, Cambridge, MA 02139. TEL 617-253-2424. *72*

MASSACHUSETTS INSTITUTE OF TECHNOLOGY. RESEARCH LABORATORY OF ELECTRONICS. R L E PROGRESS REPORT.
Massachusetts Institute of Technology, Research Laboratory of Electronics, Cambridge, MA 02139. TEL 617-253-2566. FAX 617-258-7864. *2712*

MASSAGE THERAPY JOURNAL.
American Massage Therapy Association, 820 Davis St., Ste. 100, Evanston, IL 60201-4444. TEL 708-864-0123. FAX 708-864-1178. *5532*

MASTER, MATE & PILOT.
International Organization of Masters, Mates & Pilots, 700 Maritime Blvd., Linthicum Heights, MD 21090. TEL 410-850-8700. FAX 410-850-0973. *3725*

MASTER'S THESES IN THE PURE AND APPLIED SCIENCES.
Plenum Publishing Corp. 233 Spring St., New York, NY 10013-1578. TEL 212-620-8000. FAX 212-463-0742. *6303*

MATCH.
Universitaet Bayreuth, Lehrstuhl II fuer Mathematik, 95540 Bayreuth, Germany. TEL 49-921-553387. FAX 49-921-553385. *685*

MATCH NEWS.
Match International Centre, 1102-200 Elgin St., Ottawa, ON K2P 1L5, Canada. TEL 613-238-1312. FAX 613-238-6867. *7001*

MATEKON.
M.E. Sharpe, Inc., 80 Business Park Dr., Armonk, NY 10504. TEL 914-273-1800. FAX 914-273-2106. *943*

MATEMATICA APLICADA E COMPUTACIONAL.
Sociedade Brasileira de Matematica Aplicada e Computacional, Rua Lauro Muller, 455 Botafogo CEP, 22290 Rio de Janero RJ, Brazil. TEL 55-21-541-2132. *4410*

MATEMATICA E LA SUA DIDATTICA.
Pitagora Scolastica, Via del Legatore 3, 40138 Bologna, Italy. FAX 39-51-535301. *4378*

MATERIAL HISTORY REVIEW.
National Museum of Science and Technology, Box 9724, Sta. T, Ottawa, ON K1G 5A3, Canada. TEL 613-990-7529. FAX 613-990-3635. *3352*

MATERIALS AND CORROSION.
V C H Verlagsgesellschaft mbH, Postfach 101161, 69451 Weinheim, Germany. TEL 49-6201-606-147. FAX 49-6201-606117. *4963*

MATERIALS & MANUFACTURING PROCESSES.
Marcel Dekker Journals, 270 Madison Ave., New York, NY 10016. TEL 212-696-9000. FAX 212-685-4540. *2763*

MATERIALS AND STRUCTURES.
International Union of Testing and Research Laboratories for Materials and Structures (RILEM), Pavillon des Jardins 61, Av. du Pres dent Wilson, 94235 Cachan Cedex, France. *864*

MATERIALS CHARACTERIZATION.
Elsevier Science Inc., Box 945, New York, NY 10159-0945. TEL 212-633-3730. FAX 212-633-3680. *4964*

MATERIALS CHEMISTRY AND PHYSICS.
Elsevier Science S.A., P.O. Box 564, CH-1001 Lausanne 1, Switzerland. TEL 41-21-3207381. FAX 41-21-3235444. *2737*

MATERIALS EVALUATION.
American Society for Nondestructive Testing, 1711 Arlingate Lane, Box 28518, Columbus, OH 43228-0158. TEL 614-274-6003. FAX 614-274-6899. *2737*

MATERIALS LETTERS.
North-Holland P.O. Box 211, 1000 AE Amsterdam, Netherlands. TEL 31-20-4853911. FAX 31-20-4853598. *5558*

MATERIALS PROCESSING: THEORY AND PRACTICES.
Elsevier Science B.V., Books Division, P.O. Box 211, 1000 AE Amsterdam, Netherlands. TEL 31-20-4853911. FAX 31-20-4853705. *5558*

MATERIALS RESEARCH BULLETIN.
Elsevier Science Ltd., Pergamon, P.O. Box 800, Kidlington, Oxford OX5 1DX, England. TEL 44-1865-843000. FAX 44-1865-843010. *1727*

MATERIALS RESEARCH SOCIETY OF JAPAN. TRANSACTIONS.
Elsevier Science B.V., Books Division, P.O. Box 211, 1000 AE Amsterdam, Netherlands. TEL 31-20-4853911. FAX 31-20-4853705. *2738*

MATERIALS SCIENCE.
Plenum Publishing Corp., Consultants Bureau, 233 Spring St., New York, NY 10013-1578. TEL 212-620-8468. FAX 212-463-0742. *2738*

MATERIALS SCIENCE AND ENGINEERING A: STRUCTURAL MATERIALS: PROPERTIES, MICROSTRUCTURES AND PROCESSING.
Elsevier Science S.A., P.O. Box 564, CH-1001 Lausanne 1, Switzerland. TEL 41-21-3207381. FAX 41-21-3235444. *2738*

MATERIALS SCIENCE AND ENGINEERING B: SOLID-STATE MATERIALS FOR ADVANCED TECHNOLOGY.
Elsevier Science S.A., P.O. Box 564, CH-1001 Lausanne 1, Switzerland. TEL 41-21-3207381. FAX 41-21-3235444. *2738*

MATERIALS SCIENCE AND ENGINEERING R: REPORTS.
Elsevier Science S.A., P.O. Box 564, CH-1001 Lausanne 1, Switzerland. TEL 41-21-3207381. FAX 41-21-3235444. *2738*

MATERIALS SCIENCE MONOGRAPHS.
Elsevier Science B.V., Books Division, F.O. Box 211, 1000 AE Amsterdam, Netherlands. TEL 31-20-4853911. FAX 31-20-4853705. *2610*

MATERIALS SCIENCE OF MINERALS AND ROCKS.
Kluwer Academic Publishers, Postbus 17, 3300 AA Dordrecht, Netherlands. TEL 31-78-6392392. FAX 31-78-6392254. *2249*

MATERIALS SCIENCE RESEARCH.
Plenum Publishing Corp., 233 Spring St., New York, NY 10013-1578. TEL 212-620-8000. FAX 212-463-0742. *2738*

MATERIALS SCIENCE RESEARCH INTERNATIONAL.
Chapman & Hall, Journals Department 2-6 Boundary Row, London SE1 8HN, England. TEL 44-171-8650066. FAX 44-171-5229623. *2738*

MATERIALS TECHNOLOGY.
Elsevier Science Inc., Box 945, New York, NY 10159-0945. TEL 212-633-3730. FAX 212-633-3680. *4964*

MATERIALY GLYATSIOLOGICHESKIKH ISSLEDOVANII.
Rossiiskaya Akademiya Nauk, Institut Geografii, Staromonetnyi St. 29, Moscow 109017, Russia. TEL 7-095-2388610. FAX 7-095-2302090. *2278*

MATERIALY ZACHODNIO-POMORSKIE.
Muzeum Narodowe, Szczecin, Staromlynska 27, 70-561 Szczecin, Poland. TEL 48-91-335066. FAX 48-91-347894. *5125*

MATERNAL AND CHILD HEALTH JOURNAL.
Plenum Publishing Corp., 233 Spring St., New York, NY 10013-1578. TEL 212-620-8000. FAX 212-463-0742. *4741*

MATHEMATICA SLOVACA.
Slovenska Akademia Vied, Matematicky Ustav, Stefanikova 49, 814 73 Bratislava, Slovakia. *4379*

MATHEMATICAL AND COMPUTER MODELLING.
Elsevier Science Ltd., Pergamon, P.O. Box 800, Kidlington, Oxford OX5 1DX, England. TEL 44-1865-843000. FAX 44-1865-843010. *4379*

MATHEMATICAL BIOSCIENCES.
Elsevier Science Inc., Box 945, New York, NY 10159-0945. TEL 212-633-3730. FAX 212-633-3680. *4380*

MATHEMATICAL CONCEPTS AND METHODS IN SCIENCE AND ENGINEERING.
Plenum Publishing Corp., 233 Spring St., New York, NY 10013-1578. TEL 212-620-8000. FAX 212-463-0742. *4380*

MATHEMATICAL ENGINEERING IN INDUSTRY.
V S P, P.O. Box 346, 3700 AH Zeist, Netherlands. TEL 31-30-6925790. FAX 31-30-6932081. *4380*

MATHEMATICAL GEOLOGY.
Plenum Publishing Corp., 233 Spring St., New York, NY 10013-1578. TEL 212-620-8000. FAX 212-463-0742. *2249*

THE MATHEMATICAL INTELLIGENCER.
Springer-Verlag, Science Journals, 175 Fifth Ave., New York, NY 10010. TEL 212-460-1500. FAX 212-473-6272. *4380*

MATHEMATICAL METHODS IN THE APPLIED SCIENCES.
John Wiley & Sons Ltd., Journals, Baffins Ln., Chichester, W. Sussex PO19 1UD, England. TEL 44-1243-779777. FAX 44-1243-843232. *4380*

MATHEMATICAL METHODS OF OPERATIONS RESEARCH.
Physica-Verlag GmbH und Co., Postfach 105280, 69042 Heidelberg, Germany. TEL 49-6221-487492. FAX 49-6221-487177. *4411*

MATHEMATICAL MODELING AND COMPUTATIONAL EXPERIMENT.
John Wiley & Sons, Inc., Journals, 605 Third Ave., New York, NY 10158. TEL 212-850-6645. FAX 212-850-6021. *4411*

MATHEMATICAL MODELLING OF SYSTEMS.
Swets & Zeitlinger bv, P.O. Box 825, 2160 SZ Lisse, Netherlands. TEL 31-252-435111. FAX 31-252-415888. *4411*

MATHEMATICAL PHYSICS, ANALYSIS AND GEOMETRY.
Kluwer Academic Publishers, Postbus 17, 3300 AA Dordrecht, Netherlands. TEL 31-78-6392392. FAX 31-78-6392254. *5559*

MATHEMATICAL PHYSICS AND APPLIED MATHEMATICS.
Kluwer Academic Publishers, Postbus 17, 3300 AA Dordrecht, Netherlands. TEL 31-78-6392392. FAX 31-78-6392254. *4381*

MATHEMATICAL PHYSICS REVIEWS.
Harwood Academic Publishers, c/o International Publishers Distributor, P.O. Box 3054, Langhorne, PA 19047-3054. TEL 215-750-2642. FAX 215-750-6343. *5559*

MATHEMATICAL PHYSICS STUDIES.
Kluwer Academic Publishers, Postbus 17, 3300 AA Dordrecht, Netherlands. TEL 31-78-6392392. FAX 31-78-6392254. *5559*

MATHEMATICAL POPULATION STUDIES.
Gordon & Breach Science Publishers, c/o International Publishers Distributor, P.O. Box 3054, Langhorne, PA 19047-3054. TEL 215-750-2642. FAX 215-750-6343. *5788*

MATHEMATICAL PROGRAMMING.
North-Holland P.O. Box 211, 1000 AE Amsterdam, Netherlands. TEL 31-20-4853911. FAX 31-20-4853598. *4411*

MATHEMATICAL REPORTS.
Harwood Academic Publishers, c/o International Publishers Distributor, P.O. Box 3054, Langhorne, PA 19047-3054. TEL 215-750-2642. FAX 215-750-6343. *4381*

MATHEMATICAL REVIEWS.
American Mathematical Society, Box 6248, Providence, RI 02940-6248. TEL 401-455-4000. *4406*

THE MATHEMATICAL SCIENTIST.
Applied Probability Trust, School of Mathematics, University of Sheffield, Sheffield S3 7RH, England. TEL 44-114-282-4269. FAX 44-114-272-9782. *4381*

MATHEMATICAL SOCIAL SCIENCES.
North-Holland P.O. Box 211, 1000 AE Amsterdam, Netherlands. TEL 31-20-4853911. FAX 31-20-4853598. *4381*

MATHEMATICAL SPECTRUM.
Applied Probability Trust, School of Mathematics, University of Sheffield, Sheffield S3 7RH, England. TEL 44-114-282-4269. FAX 44-114-272-9782. *4381*

MATHEMATICAL SURVEYS & MONOGRAPHS.
American Mathematical Society, Box 6248, Providence, RI 02940-6248. TEL 401-455-4000. *4381*

MATHEMATICS AND COMPUTER EDUCATION.
M A T Y C Journal, Inc., Box 158, Old Bethpage, NY 11804. TEL 516-822-5475. *4411*

MATHEMATICS AND COMPUTERS IN SIMULATION.
North-Holland P.O. Box 211, 1000 AE Amsterdam, Netherlands. TEL 31-20-4853911. FAX 31-20-4853598. *2052*

MATHEMATICS AND ITS APPLICATIONS.
Gordon & Breach Science Publishers, c/o International Publishers Distributor, P.O. Box 3054, Langhorne, PA 19047-3054. TEL 215-750-2642. FAX 215-750-6343. *4381*

MATHEMATICS AND ITS APPLICATIONS.
Kluwer Academic Publishers, Postbus 17, 3300 AA Dordrecht, Netherlands. TEL 31-78-6392392. FAX 31-78-6392254. *4381*

MATHEMATICS AND ITS APPLICATIONS: CHINESE SERIES.
Kluwer Academic Publishers, Postbus 17, 3300 AA Dordrecht, Netherlands. TEL 31-78-6392392. FAX 31-78-6392254. *4382*

MATHEMATICS AND ITS APPLICATIONS: EAST EUROPEAN SERIES.
Kluwer Academic Publishers, Postbus 17, 3300 AA Dordrecht, Netherlands. TEL 31-78-6392392. FAX 31-78-6392254. *4382*

MATHEMATICS AND ITS APPLICATIONS: JAPANESE SERIES.
Kluwer Academic Publishers, Postbus 17, 3300 AA Dordrecht, Netherlands. TEL 31-78-6392392. FAX 31-78-6392254. *4382*

MATHEMATICS AND ITS APPLICATIONS: SOVIET SERIES.
Kluwer Academic Publishers, Postbus 17, 3300 AA Dordrecht, Netherlands. TEL 31-78-6392392. FAX 31-78-6392254. *4382*

MATHEMATICS AND MECHANICS OF SOLIDS.
Sage Publications, Inc., Sage Science Press, 2455 Teller Rd., Thousand Oaks, CA 91320. TEL 805-499-0721. FAX 805-499-0871. *5559*

MATHEMATICS EDUCATION LIBRARY.
Kluwer Academic Publishers, Postbus 17, 3300 AA Dordrecht, Netherlands. TEL 31-78-6392392. FAX 31-78-6392254. *2352*

MATHEMATICS EDUCATION RESEARCH JOURNAL.
Mathematics Education Research Group of Australasia, c/o Dr. M. Mitchelmore, School of Education, Macquarie University, North Ryde, N.S.W. 2109, Australia. TEL 61-2-985086545. FAX 61-2-98508674. *2494*

MATHEMATICS IN SCHOOL.
Pitman Publishing, 128 Long Acre, London WC2E 9AN, England. TEL 0171-379-7383. FAX 0171-240-5771. *4382*

MATHEMATICS IN SCIENCE AND ENGINEERING.
Academic Press, Inc., 525 B St., Ste. 1900, San Diego, CA 92101-1495. TEL 619-231-0926. FAX 619-699-6715. *4382*

MATHEMATICS OF COMPUTATION.
American Mathematical Society, Box 6248, Providence, RI 02940-6248. TEL 401-455-4000. *4382*

MATHEMATICS OF OPERATIONS RESEARCH.
Institute for Operations Research and the Management Sciences, 901 Elkridge Landing Rd., Ste.400, Linthicum, MD 21090-2909. TEL 410-850-0300. *1995*

MATHEMATICS TEACHER.
National Council of Teachers of Mathematics, 1906 Association Dr., Reston, VA 22091. TEL 703-620-9840. FAX 703-476-2970. *4382*

MATHEMATICS TEACHING IN THE MIDDLE SCHOOL.
National Council of Teachers of Mathematics, 1906 Association Dr., Reston, VA 22091-1593. TEL 703-620-9840. FAX 703-476-2970. *4382*

MATHEMATISCHE GESELLSCHAFT IN HAMBURG. MITTEILUNGEN.
Mathematische Gesellschaft in Hamburg, Bundesstr. 55, 20146 Hamburg, Germany. TEL 49-40-41235138. FAX 49-40-41235117. *4383*

MATHESIS.
Universidad Nacional Autonoma de Mexico, Departamento de Matematicas, Ciudad Universitaria, Cubiculo No. 016, 04510 Mexico DF, Mexico. TEL 525-6224858. FAX 525-6224859. *4383*

MATHWARE AND SOFT COMPUTING.
Universitat Politecnica de Catalunya, E T S d'Arquitectura de Barcelona, Seccio de Matematiques i Informacion, Diagonal 649, 08028 Barcelona, Spain. FAX 34-3-4016367. *4411*

MATI.
Standards Institution of Israel, 42 Chaim Levanon St., Tel Aviv 69977, Israel. TEL 972-3-6465154. FAX 972-3-6419683. *5015*

MATTOID.
Deakin University, Deakin Literary Society, Vic. 3217, Australia. FAX 61-52-272018. *4236*

MATURITAS.
Elsevier Science Ireland Ltd., P.O. Box 85, Limerick, Ireland. TEL 353-61-471944. FAX 353-61-472144. *3293*

MAYDICA.
Istituto Sperimentale per la Cerealicoltura, Sezione di Bergamo, Via Stezzano 24, 24126 Bergamo, Italy. TEL 39-35-313132. FAX 39-35-316054. *231*

MAYNOOTH OCCASIONAL PAPERS.
St. Patrick's College, Department of Geography, Maynooth, Co. Kildare, Ireland. TEL 01-6285222. FAX 01-6289063. *3265*

MAYO CLINIC PROCEEDINGS.
Mayo Foundation for Medical Education and Research, Rochester, MN 55905. TEL 507-284-2154. FAX 507-284-0252. *4492*

MEADOWLARK.
Illinois Ornithological Society, Box 1971, Evanston, IL 60204-1971. *778*

MEASUREMENT.
Elsevier Science B.V., P.O. Box 211, 1000 AE Amsterdam, Netherlands. TEL 31-20-4853911. FAX 31-20-4853598. *5015*

MEASUREMENT TECHNIQUES.
Plenum Publishing Corp., Consultants Bureau, 233 Spring St., New York, NY 10013-1578. TEL 212-620-8468. FAX 212-463-0742. *5015*

MEASUREMENTS AND CONTROL.
Measurements & Data Corp., 2994 W. Liberty Ave., Pittsburgh, PA 15216. TEL 412-343-9666. *3637*

MEAT SCIENCE.
Elsevier Science Ltd., P.O. Box 800, Kidlington, Oxford OX5 1DX, England. TEL 44-1865-843000. FAX 44-1865-843010. *2983*

MECCANICA.
Kluwer Academic Publishers, Postbus 17, 3300 AA Dordrecht, Netherlands. TEL 31-78-6392392. FAX 31-78-6392254. *5589*

MECHANICAL ENGINEERING.
American Society of Mechanical Engineers, 22 Law Dr., Fairfield, NJ 07007-2300. *2763*

MECHANICAL ENGINEERING SERIES.
Marcel Dekker, Inc., 270 Madison Ave., New York, NY 10016. TEL 212-696-9000. FAX 212-658-4540. *2763*

MECHANICS AND MATHEMATICAL METHODS - SERIES OF HANDBOOKS.
Elsevier Science B.V., Books Division, P.O. Box 211, 1000 AE Amsterdam, Netherlands. TEL 31-20-4853911. FAX 31-20-4853705. *4383*

MECHANICS AND PHYSICS OF DISCRETE SYSTEMS.
Elsevier Science B.V., Books Division, P.O. Box 211, 1000 AE Amsterdam, Netherlands. TEL 31-20-4853911. FAX 31-20-4853705. *2763*

MECHANICS OF COMPOSITE MATERIALS.
Plenum Publishing Corp., Consultants Bureau, 233 Spring St., New York, NY 10013-1578. TEL 212-620-8468. FAX 212-463-0742. *2645*

MECHANICS OF MATERIALS.
North-Holland P.O. Box 211, 1000 AE Amsterdam, Netherlands. TEL 31-20-4853911. FAX 31-20-4853598. *2739*

MECHANICS OF STRUCTURES AND MACHINES.
Marcel Dekker Journals, 270 Madison Ave., New York, NY 10016. TEL 212-696-9000. FAX 212-685-4540. *2763*

MECHANICS OF TIME DEPENDENT MATERIALS.
Kluwer Academic Publishers, Postbus 17, 3300 AA Dordrecht, Netherlands. TEL 31-78-6392392. FAX 31-78-6392254. *5590*

MECHANICS RESEARCH COMMUNICATIONS.
Elsevier Science Ltd., Pergamon, P.O. Box 800, Kidlington, Oxford OX5 1DX, England. TEL 44-1865-843000. FAX 44-1865-843010. *2739*

MECHANIKA TEORETYCZNA I STOSOWANA.
Polskie Towarzystwo Mechaniki Teoretycznej i Stosowanej, Palac Kultury, p.309, 00-901 Warsaw, Poland. *2739*

MECHANISM AND MACHINE THEORY.
Elsevier Science Ltd., Pergamon, P.O. Box 800, Kidlington, Oxford OX5 1DX, England. TEL 44-1865-843000. FAX 44-1865-843010. *2764*

MECHANISMS OF AGEING AND DEVELOPMENT.
Elsevier Science Ireland Ltd., P.O. Box 85, Limerick, Ireland. TEL 353-61-471944. FAX 353-61-472144. *3293*

MECHANISMS OF DEVELOPMENT.
Elsevier Science Ireland Ltd., P.O. Box 85, Limerick, Ireland. TEL 353-61-471944. FAX 353-61-472144. *716*

MECHANISMS OF INORGANIC AND ORGANOMETALLIC REACTIONS.
Plenum Publishing Corp., 233 Spring St., New York, NY 10013-1578. TEL 212-620-8000. FAX 212-463-0742. *1732*

MECHATRONICS.
Elsevier Science Ltd., Pergamon, P.O. Box 800, Kidlington, Oxford OX5 1DX, England. TEL 44-1865-843000. FAX 44-1865-843010. *2764*

THE MEDAL.
British Art Medal Trust, c/o Philip Attwood, Ed., Department of Coins and Medals, British Museum, London WC1B 3DG, England. TEL 44-171-323-8260. FAX 44-171-323-3171. *5225*

MEDECIN DU QUEBEC.
Federation des Medecins Omnipraticiens du Quebec, 1440 Rue St.Catherine Ouest, Ste. 1000, Montreal, PQ H3G 1R8, Canada. TEL 514-878-1911. FAX 514-878-4455. *4492*

MEDECINE ET ENFANCE, ADOLESCENCE.
Edition et Communication Medicales, 23 rue Saint-Ferdinand, 75017 Paris France. TEL 45-74-44-65. FAX 40-55-94-13. *4808*

MEDECINE NUCLEAIRE.
Editions Scientifiques et Medicales Elsevier, 141 rue de Javel, 75747 Paris, France. TEL 33-1-45589068. FAX 33-1-45589421. *4880*

MEDECINE THERAPEUTIQUE.
John Libbey Eurotext, 127 av. de la Republique, 92120 Montrouge, France. TEL 33-1-46730660. FAX 33-1-40840999. *4493*

MEDIA.
Media & Marketing Ltd., 1002 McDonald's Bldg., 46-54 Yee Wo Street, Causeway Bay, Hong Kong. TEL 852-2577-2628. FAX 852-2576-9171. *40*

MEDIA CULTURE AND SOCIETY.
Sage Publications Ltd., 6 Bonhill St., London EC2A 4PU, England. TEL 44-171-374-0645. FAX 44-171-374-8741. *1964*

MEDIAPLUSNEWS.
Media Plus s.r.l., Via Ausonio 5, 20123 Milan, Italy. TEL 39-2-8372407. FAX 39-2-58100311. *6657*

MEDIATION QUARTERLY.
Jossey-Bass Inc., Publishers, 350 Sansome St. 5th Fl., San Francisco, CA 94104. TEL 415-433-1767. FAX 415-433-0499. *5365*

MEDICAL AND PEDIATRIC ONCOLOGY.
John Wiley & Sons, Inc. Journals, 605 Third Ave., New York, NY 10158. TEL 212-850-6645. FAX 212-850-6021. *4760*

MEDICAL AND PEDIATRIC ONCOLOGY. SUPPLEMENT.
John Wiley & Sons, Inc., Journals, 605 Third Ave., New York, NY 10158. TEL 212-850-6645. FAX 212-850-6021. *2760*

MEDICAL & SURGICAL DERMATOLOGY.
Springer-Verlag, Medical Journals, 175 Fifth Ave., New York, NY 10010. TEL 212-460-1500. FAX 212-473-6272. *4568*

MEDICAL ANTHROPOLOGY.
Gordon & Breach Science Publishers, c/o International Publishers Distributor, P.O. Box 5054, Langhorne, PA 19047-5054. TEL 215-750-2642. FAX 215-750-6343. *315*

MEDICAL ARTIFICIAL INTELLIGENCE.
Elsevier Science B.V., Books Division, P.O. Box 211, 1000 AE Amsterdam, Netherlands. TEL 31-20-4853911. FAX 31-20-4853705. *2009*

MEDICAL CARE.
Lippincott - Raven Publishers 227 E. Washington Sq., Philadelphia, PA 19106. TEL 215-238-4200. *4493*

MEDICAL CARE RESEARCH AND REVIEW.
Sage Publications, Inc. 2455 Teller Rd., Thousand Oaks, CA 91320. TEL 805-499-0721. FAX 805-499-0871. *5983*

MEDICAL DECISION MAKING.
Hanley & Belfus, Inc., 210 S. 13th St., Philadelphia, PA 19107. TEL 215-546-7293. FAX 215-790-9330. *4494*

MEDICAL DOSIMETRY.
Elsevier Science Inc., Box 945, New York, NY 10159-0945. TEL 212-633-3730. FAX 212-633-3680. *4880*

MEDICAL EDUCATION.
Blackwell Science Ltd., Osney Mead, Oxford OX2 0EL, England. TEL 44-1865-206206. FAX 44-1365-721205. *4494*

MEDICAL ENGINEERING AND PHYSICS.
Butterworth - Heinemann, Part of the Reed Elsevier group, Linacre House, Jordan Hill, Oxford OX2 8DP, England. TEL 44-1865-310366. FAX 44-1865-310898. *4494*

MEDICAL GRAND ROUNDS.
University of Texas, Southwestern Medical Center, 5323 Harry Hines Blvd., Dallas, TX 75235-9030. TEL 214-648-2635. FAX 214-648-9100. *4495*

MEDICAL HISTORY.
Professional & Scientific Publications, BMA House, Tavistock Sq., London WC1H 9JR, England. TEL 0171-383-6640. FAX 0171-383-6662. *4495*

MEDICAL IMAGE ANALYSIS.
Oxford University Press, Oxford Journals, Walton St., Oxford OX2 6DP, England. TEL 44-1865-267907. FAX 44-1865-267485. *4880*

MEDICAL INFORMATICS.
Taylor & Francis Ltd., 1 Gunpowder Sq., London EC4A 3DE, England. TEL 44-171-583-0490. FAX 44-171-583-0585. *4632*

MEDICAL JOURNAL ARMED FORCES INDIA.
Armed Forces Medical College, Pune 411 040, Maharashtra, India. TEL 673290. *4495*

MEDICAL JOURNAL OF AUSTRALIA.
Australasian Medical Publishing Co., Private Bag 901, N. Sydney, N.S.W. 2059, Australia. TEL 61-2-99548666. FAX 61-2-99567644. *4495*

MEDICAL LAW INTERNATIONAL.
A B Academic Publishers, P.O. Box 42, Bicester, Oxon. OX6 7NW, England. TEL 44-1869-320949. *3815*

MEDICAL LETTER ON DRUGS AND THERAPEUTICS (ENGLISH EDITION).
Medical Letter, Inc., 1000 Main St., New Rochelle, NY 10801. TEL 914-235-0500. FAX 914-632-1733. *5427*

MEDICAL LIBRARY ASSOCIATION. BULLETIN.
Medical Library Association, 6 N. Michigan Ave., Ste. 300, Chicago, IL 60602-4805. TEL 312-419-9094. FAX 312-419-8905. *4496*

MEDICAL MISSION NEWS.
Catholic Medical Mission Board, Inc., 10 W. 17th St., New York, NY 10011. TEL 212-242-7757. FAX 212-807-9161. *6187*

MEDICAL ONCOLOGY.
Chapman & Hall, Journals Department 2-6 Boundary Row, London SE1 8HN, England. TEL 44-171-8560066. FAX 44-171-5229623. *4760*

MEDICAL PHYSICS.
American Institute of Physics, One Physics Ellipse, College Park, MD 20740-3843. TEL 301-209-3000. *4496*

MEDICAL PHYSICS SERIES.
Academic Press, Inc., 525 B St., Ste. 1900, San Diego, CA 92101-4495. TEL 619-231-0926. FAX 619-699-6715. *4496*

MEDICAL PRINCIPLES AND PRACTICE.
S. Karger AG, Allschwilerstr. 10, P.O. Box, CH-4009 Basel, Switzerland. TEL 061-3061111. FAX 061-3061234. *4496*

MEDICAL PROBLEMS OF PERFORMING ARTISTS.
Hanley & Belfus, Inc., 210 S. 13th St., Philadelphia, PA 19107. TEL 215-546-7293. FAX 215-790-9330. *4496*

MEDICAL PROGRESS THROUGH TECHNOLOGY.
Kluwer Academic Publishers, Postbus 17, 3300 AA Dordrecht, Netherlands. TEL 31-78-6392392. FAX 31-78-6392254. *663*

MEDICAL REFERENCE SERVICES QUARTERLY.
Haworth Press, Inc., 10 Alice St., Binghamton, NY 13904. TEL 607-722-5857. FAX 607-722-1424. *4012*

MEDICAL SCIENCE RESEARCH.
Chapman & Hall, Journals Department 2-6 Boundary Row, London SE1 8HN, England. TEL 44-171-8560066. FAX 44-171-5229623. *4497*

MEDICAL SCIENCE SYMPOSIA SERIES.
Kluwer Academic Publishers, Postbus 17, 3300 AA Dordrecht, Netherlands. TEL 31-78-6392392. FAX 31-78-6392254. *4497*

MEDICAL TEACHER.
Carfax Publishing Co., P.O. Box 25, Abingdon, Oxon. OX14 3UE, England. TEL 44-1235-401000. FAX 44-1235-401550. *4498*

MEDICAL TECHNOLOGY S A.
Medical Technology News, P.O. Box 253, Rondebosch 7700, South Africa. TEL 27-21-4610054. *4683*

MEDICINA.
Fundacion Revista Medicina, Donato Alvarez 3150, 1427 Buenos Aires, Argentina. TEL 541-5236619. FAX 541-5236619. *4498*

MEDICINA.
Universidade de Sao Paulo, Faculdade de Medicina de Ribeirao Preto, Campus Universitario, Av. Bandeirantes, 3900, 14049 Ribeirao Preto, SP, Brazil. FAX 55-16-6331144. *4498*

MEDICINA DELLO SPORT.
Edizioni Minerva Medica, Corso Bramante 83-85, 10126 Turin, Italy. TEL 39-11-678282. FAX 39-11-3121736. *4899*

MEDICINA INTERNA.
Obsidiana Editores, S.A., Czda. de Tlalpan 2365, Col. Ciudad Jardin, 04370 Mexico DF, Mexico. TEL 6899133. *4707*

MEDICINA, PSICHE E ADOLESCENZA.
Centro Italiano Studi di Psicologia Medica, Viale Romagna 51, 20133 Milan, Italy. TEL 39-2-2361226. FAX 39-2-2361226. *4850*

MEDICINA TORACICA.
Masson S.p.A., Divisione Periodici, Via Statuto 2-4, 20121 Milan, Italy. TEL 39-2-63671. FAX 39-2-6367211. *4889*

MEDICINA VETERINARIA.
Pulso Ediciones S.A., Rambla del Celler, 117-119, 08190 Sant Cugat del Valles (Barcelona), Spain. TEL 34-3-5896264. *6950*

MEDICINAL CHEMISTRY RESEARCH.
Birkhaeuser, 675 Massachusetts Ave., Cambridge, MA 02139-3309. FAX 201-348-4505. *4499*

MEDICINAL RESEARCH REVIEWS.
John Wiley & Sons, Inc., Journals, 605 Third Ave., New York, NY 10158. TEL 212-850-6645. FAX 212-850-6021. *5427*

MEDICINAL RESEARCH SERIES.
Marcel Dekker, Inc., 270 Madison Ave., New York, NY 10016. TEL 212-696-9000. FAX 212-658-4540. *4499*

MEDICINE (BALTIMORE).
Williams & Wilkins, 351 W. Camden St., Baltimore, MD 21201. TEL 410-528-4000. FAX 410-528-4312. *4499*

MEDICINE AND LAW.
Yozmot Heiliger (1989) Ltd., 3 Yohanan Hasandlar St., P.O. Box 56055, Tel Aviv 61560, Israel. TEL 972-3-5284851. FAX 972-3-5285397. *3815*

MEDICINE AND SCIENCE IN SPORTS AND EXERCISE.
American College of Sports Medicine, Box 1440, Indianapolis, IN 46206-1440. TEL 317-637-9200. FAX 317-634-7817. *4899*

MEDICINE AND SOCIETY.
University of California Press, 2120 Berkeley Way, Berkeley, CA 94720. TEL 510-642-4247. FAX 510-643-7127. *4850*

MEDICINE AND SPORT SCIENCE.
S. Karger AG, Allschwilerstr. 10, P.O. Box, CH-4009 Basel, Switzerland. TEL 061-3061111. FAX 061-3061234. *4899*

MEDICINE, CONFLICT AND SURVIVAL.
Frank Cass, Newbury House, 890-900 Eastern Ave., Newbury Park, Ilford, Essex 1G2 7HH, England. TEL 44-181-599-8866. FAX 44-181-599-0984. *4499*

MEDICINE ON THE MIDWAY.
University of Chicago Hospitals, Office of Public Affairs, 5841 S. Maryland Ave., Mail Code 6063, Chicago, IL 60637. TEL 312-702-7322. FAX 312-702-3171. *1876*

MEDICINE, SCIENCE AND THE LAW.
Chiltern Publishing, 34 Aylesbury End, Beaconsfield, Bucks HP9 1LW, England. TEL 44-1494-678914. FAX 44-1494-678914. *4688*

MEDICINSKI RAZGLEDI.
Univerza v Ljubljani, Medicinska Fakulteta, Korytkova 2, 61105 Ljubljana, Slovenia. TEL 442-356. *4500*

MEDIEVAL AND RENAISSANCE AUTHORS.
E.J. Brill, P.O. Box 9000, 2300 PA Leiden, Netherlands. TEL 31-71-5353500. FAX 31-71-5317532. *4236*

MEDIEVAL AND RENAISSANCE AUTHORS AND TEXTS.
E.J. Brill, P.O. Box 9000, 2300 PA Leiden, Netherlands. TEL 31-71-5353500. FAX 31-71-5317532. *3427*

MEDIEVAL AND RENAISSANCE TEXTS.
E.J. Brill, P.O. Box 9000, 2300 PA Leiden, Netherlands. TEL 31-71-5353500. FAX 31-71-5317532. *3427*

MEDIEVAL ENCOUNTERS.
E.J. Brill, P.O. Box 9000, 2300 PA Leiden, Netherlands. TEL 31-71-5353500. FAX 31-71-5317532. *3352*

MEDIEVAL IBERIAN PENINSULA.
E.J. Brill, P.O. Box 9000, 2300 PA Leiden, Netherlands. TEL 31-71-5353500. FAX 31-71-5317532. *3427*

THE MEDIEVAL MEDITERRANEAN.
E.J. Brill, P.O. Box 9000, 2300 PA Leiden, Netherlands. TEL 31-71-5353500. FAX 31-71-5317532. *3352*

MEDIEVAL PHILOSOPHY AND THEOLOGY.
Cambridge University Press, Edinburgh Bldg., Shaftesbury Rd., Cambridge CB2 2RU, England. TEL 44-1223-312393. FAX 44-1223-315052. *5485*

MEDIFILE.
T P S Drug Information Centre, P.O. Box 31238, Braamfontein 2017, South Africa. FAX 27-11-3393819. *5427*

MEDIPHORS.
Mediphors Inc., Box 327, Bloomsburg, PA 17815. *4236*

MEDIPRESS.
Clyancourt Corporation AG, Postfach 5044, CH-6305 Zug, Switzerland. TEL 41-41-7413044. FAX 41-41-7417844. *4500*

MEDITATOR'S NEWSLETTER.
Sacred Orchard Corporation, Box 298, Harriman, NY 10926-0298. TEL 914-783-8154. *6077*

MEDITERRANEAN HISTORICAL REVIEW.
Frank Cass, Newbury House, 890-900 Eastern Ave., Newbury Park, Ilford, Essex 1G2 7HH, England. TEL 44-181-599-8866. FAX 44-181-599-0984. *3498*

MEDITERRANEAN JOURNAL OF EDUCATIONAL STUDIES.
University of Malta, Faculty of Education, Msida MSD 06, Malta. TEL 356-32902936. FAX 356-336450. *2353*

MEDITERRANEAN QUARTERLY.
Duke University Press, Box 90660, Durham, NC 27708-0660. TEL 919-687-3600. FAX 919-688-4574. *5761*

MEDIUM AEVUM.
Society for the Study of Mediaeval Languages and Literature, c/o Dr. D.G. Pattison, Hon. Treas., Magdalen College, Oxford OX1 4AU, England. TEL 44-1865-276087. *4236*

MEDSURG NURSING.
Jannetti Publications, Inc., East Holly Ave., Box 56, Pitman, NJ 08071-0056. TEL 609-256-2300. FAX 609-589-7463. *4914*

MEGADRILOGICA.
Oligochaetology Laboratory, Sir Sandford Fleming College, P.O. Box 8000, Lindsay, ON K9V 5E6, Canada. TEL 705-324-9144. FAX 705-878-9312. *813*

MEIGUO YANJIU.
Zhongguo Shehui Kexueyuan, Meiguo Yanjiusuo, No. 3, Zhangzizhong Rd., Beijing 100007, People's Republic of China. TEL 86-10-400-0071. *6334*

MEIKAI UNIVERSITY SCHOOL OF DENTISTRY. JOURNAL.
Meikai University, School of Dentistry, 1-1 Keyakidai, Sakado, Saitama 350-02, Japan. TEL 81-492-85-5511. FAX 81-492-87-6657. *4647*

MELANDERIA.
Washington State Entomological Society, Department of Entomology, Washington State University, Pullman, WA 99164-6382. TEL 509-335-3681. *732*

MELBOURNE JOURNAL OF POLITICS.
University of Melbourne, Political Science Department, Parkville, Vic. 3052, Australia. TEL 61-3-3446571. *5683*

MELBOURNE UNIVERSITY LAW REVIEW.
University of Melbourne, Law School, Parkville 3052, Victoria, Australia. FAX 61-3-3446593. *3815*

MELITA THEOLOGICA SUPPLEMENTARY SERIES.
Theology Students' Association, University of Malta, Msida MSD 04, Malta. TEL 356-333998. *6077*

MELLIAND TEXTILBERICHTE.
Melliand Textilberichte GmbH, Mainzer Landstr. 251, 60326 Frankfurt a.M., Germany. TEL 49-69-75951651. FAX 49-69-75951650. *6682*

MELVILLE SOCIETY EXTRACTS.
c/o Dennis Berthold, Department of English, Texas A&M University, College Station, TX 77843-4227. TEL 409-845-8317. FAX 409-862-2292. *4236*

MEMBRANE AND CELL BIOLOGY.
Harwood Academic Publishers, c/o International Publishers Distributor, P.O. Box 3054, Langhorne, PA 19047-3054. TEL 215-750-2642. FAX 215-750-6343. *655*

MEMBRANE SCIENCE AND TECHNOLOGY SERIES.
Elsevier Science B.V., Books Division, P.O. Box 211, 1000 AE Amsterdam, Netherlands. TEL 31-20-4853911. FAX 31-20-4853705. *644*

MEMISA MEDISCH.
Memisa Medicus Mundi, Eendrachtsweg 48, 3012 LD Rotterdam, Netherlands. FAX 31-10-4047319. *4502*

MEMOIRS ON ENTOMOLOGY, INTERNATIONAL.
Associated Publishers, Box 140103, Gainesville, FL 32614-0103. TEL 352-371-4071. FAX 352-371-4071. *732*

MEMORIE DI SCIENZE GEOLOGICHE.
Universita di Padova, Dipartimento di Geologia, Paleontologia e Geofisica, Via Giotto 1, 35137 Padua, Italy. TEL 39-49-8272056. FAX 39-49-8272070. *2249*

MEMORY AND COGNITION.
Psychonomic Society, Inc., 1710 Fortview Rd., Austin, TX 78704. TEL 512-462-2442. *5865*

MENNINGER CLINIC. BULLETIN.
Menninger Foundation, Box 829, Topeka, KS 66601-0829. TEL 913-273-7500. FAX 913-273-8625. *4851*

MENNONITISCHE GESCHICHTSBLAETTER.
Mennonitischer Geschichtsverein, Weierhof, 67295 Bolanden, Germany. *6152*

MENOPAUSE.
Lippincott - Raven Publishers 227 E. Washington Sq., Philadelphia, PA 19106. TEL 215-238-4200. *4741*

MENTAL HEALTH NURSING JOURNAL.
Community Psychiatric Nurses Association, 44 Dartford Rd., Sevenoaks, Kent TN13 3TQ, England. TEL 44-1732-455244. FAX 44-1732-457542. *4851*

MENTAL MEASUREMENTS YEARBOOK.
Buros Institute of Mental Measurements, 135 Bancroft, University of Nebraska-Lincoln, Lincoln, NE 68588-0348. TEL 402-472-6203. FAX 402-472-6207. *5865*

MENTAL RETARDATION AND DEVELOPMENTAL DISABILITIES (NEW YORK, 1970).
Plenum Publishing Corp., 233 Spring St., New York, NY 10013-1578. TEL 212-620-8000. FAX 212-463-0742. *4851*

MENTAL RETARDATION AND DEVELOPMENTAL DISABILITIES (NEW YORK, 1995).
John Wiley & Sons, Inc., Journals, 605 Third Ave., New York, NY 10158. TEL 212-850-6645. FAX 212-850-6021. *4851*

MERCER BULLETIN.
William M. Mercer Limited, BCE Place, 161 Bay St., P.O. Box 501, Toronto, ON M5J 2S5. TEL 416-868-2892. FAX 416-868-7694. *3658*

MERIDIAN.
Map and Geography Round Table, American Library Association, c/o Charles A. Seavey, Ed., School of Library Science, 1515 E. First St., Tucson, AZ 85719. TEL 602-621-3957. FAX 609-621-3279. *4012*

MERIDIONALE.
Largo Randazzo, 89048 Siderno (RC), Italy. TEL 39-964-381698. FAX 39-964-381085. *3185*

MERRILL - PALMER QUARTERLY.
Wayne State University Press, Leonard N. Simons Bldg., 4809 Woodward Ave., Detroit, MI 48201-1309. TEL 313-577-6120. FAX 313-577-6131. *5866*

MESSAGE OF THE TEACHER.
Ministry of Education, Educational Publications Division, P.O. Box 1646, Amman, Jordan. TEL 607331. FAX 666019. *2436*

METABOLIC ASPECTS OF CARDIOVASCULAR DISEASE.
Elsevier Science B.V., Books Division, P.O. Box 211, 1000 AE Amsterdam, Netherlands. TEL 31-20-4853911. FAX 31-20-4853705. *4607*

METABOLIC BRAIN DISEASE.
Plenum Publishing Corp., 233 Spring St., New York, NY 10013-1578. TEL 212-620-8000. FAX 212-463-0742. *4502*

METABOLIC, PEDIATRIC AND SYSTEMIC OPHTHALMOLOGY.
Opto Education Corp, 105 E. 90th St., New York, NY 10128. TEL 212-427-1246. *4773*

METABOLISM: CLINICAL AND EXPERIMENTAL.
W.B. Saunders Co. Curtis Center, 3rd Fl., Independence Sq. W., Philadelphia, PA 19106-3399. TEL 215-238-7800. FAX 215-238-6445. *4673*

METAL FINISHING.
Elsevier Science Inc., Box 945, New York, NY 10159-0945. TEL 212-633-3730. FAX 212-633-3680. *4965*

METAL IONS IN BIOLOGICAL SYSTEMS.
Marcel Dekker, Inc., 270 Madison Ave., New York, NY 10016. TEL 212-696-9000. FAX 212-658-4540. *1732*

METAL SCIENCE AND HEAT TREATMENT.
Plenum Publishing Corp., Consultants Bureau, 233 Spring St., New York, NY 10013-1578. TEL 212-620-8468. FAX 212-463-0742. *4966*

METALLIZED PLASTICS.
Plenum Publishing Corp., 233 Spring St., New York, NY 10013-1578. TEL 212-620-8000. FAX 212-863-0742. *1729*

METALLURGICAL AND MATERIALS TRANSACTIONS A - PHYSICAL METALLURGY AND MATERIALS SCIENCE.
A S M International, Materials Information, Materials Park, OH 44073-0002. TEL 216-338-5151. FAX 216-338-4634. *4967*

METALLURGICAL AND MATERIALS TRANSACTIONS B - PROCESS METALLURGY AND MATERIALS PROCESSING SCIENCE.
A S M International, Materials Information, Materials Park, OH 44073-0002. TEL 216-338-5151. FAX 216-338-4634. *4967*

METALLURGIST.
Plenum Publishing Corp., Consultants Bureau, 233 Spring St., New York, NY 10013-1578. TEL 212-620-8468. FAX 212-463-0742. *4967*

METAPHILOSOPHY.
Blackwell Publishers Ltd., 108 Cowley Rd., Oxford OX4 1JF, England. TEL 44-1865-791100. FAX 44-1865-791347. *5486*

METAPHOR AND SYMBOLIC ACTIVITY.
Lawrence Erlbaum Associates, Inc., 10 Industrial Dr., Mahwah, NJ 07430-2262. TEL 201-236-9500. FAX 201-236-0072. *4091*

METEORITICS AND PLANETARY SCIENCE.
Meteoritical Society, Dep. of Chemistry, University of Arkansas, Fayetteville, AR 72701. TEL 501-575-7625. FAX 501-575-7778. *433*

METEOROLOGICAL AND GEOASTROPHYSICAL ABSTRACTS.
American Meteorological Society, c/o Inforonics, Inc., 550 Newtown Rd., Littleton, MA 01460. TEL 508-486-8976. FAX 508-485-0027. *5011*

METHOD: JOURNAL OF LONERGAN STUDIES.
Lonergan Institute at Boston College, Bapst Library, Boston College, Chestnut Hill, MA 02167-3805. TEL 617-552-8095. *5486*

METHODS: A COMPANION TO METHODS IN ENZYMOLOGY.
Academic Press, Inc., Journal Division, 525 B St., Ste. 1900, San Diego, CA 92101-4495. TEL 619-230-1840. FAX 619-699-6800. *644*

METHODS AND PHENOMENA.
Elsevier Science B.V., Books Division, P.O. Box 211, 1000 AE Amsterdam, Netherlands. TEL 31-20-4853911. FAX 31-20-4853705. *6258*

METHODS IN CELL BIOLOGY.
Academic Press, Inc., 525 B St., Ste. 1900, San Diego, CA 92101-4495. TEL 619-231-0926. FAX 619-699-6715. *717*

METHODS IN CELL SCIENCE.
Kluwer Academic Publishers, Postbus 17, 3300 AA Dordrecht, Netherlands. TEL 31-78-6392392. FAX 31-78-6392254. *762*

METHODS IN COMPUTATIONAL CHEMISTRY.
Plenum Publishing Corp., 233 Spring St., New York, NY 10013-1578. TEL 212-620-8000. FAX 212-463-0742. *1724*

METHODS IN ENZYMOLOGY.
Academic Press, Inc., 525 B St., Ste. 1900, San Diego, CA 92101-4495. TEL 619-231-0926. FAX 619-699-6715. *644*

METHODS IN GEOCHEMISTRY AND GEOPHYSICS.
Elsevier Science B.V., Books Division, P.O. Box 211, 1000 AE Amsterdam, Netherlands. TEL 31-20-4853911. FAX 31-20-4853705. *2212*

METHODS IN MICROANALYSIS.
Gordon and Breach Science Publishers, c/o International Publishers Distributor, P.O. Box 3054, Langhorne, PA 19047-3054. TEL 215-750-2672. FAX 215-750-6343. *759*

METHODS IN MOLECULAR AND CELLULAR BIOLOGY.
John Wiley & Sons, Inc., Journals, 605 Third Ave., New York, NY 10158. TEL 212-850-6645. FAX 212-850-6021. *762*

METHODS IN PHYSIOLOGY SERIES.
American Physiological Society, 9650 Rockville Pike, Bethesda. TEL 301-530-7164. FAX 301-571-8313. *791*

METHODS OF BIOCHEMICAL ANALYSIS.
John Wiley & Sons, Inc., 605 Third Ave., New York, NY 10158-0012. TEL 212-850-6000. *645*

METHODS OF SURFACE CHARACTERIZATION.
Plenum Publishing Corp., 233 Spring St., New York, NY 10013-1578. TEL 212-620-8000. FAX 212-463-0742. *1729*

METMENYS.
A M & M Publications, 306 55th Place, Downers Grove, IL 60516. TEL 630-852-3887. *4237*

METRIKA.
Physica-Verlag GmbH und Co., Postfach 105280, 69042 Heidelberg, Germany. TEL 49-6221-487492. FAX 49-6221-487177. *6619*

METROECONOMICA.
Blackwell Publishers Ltd., 108 Cowley Rd., Oxford OX4 1JF, England. TEL 44-1865-791100. FAX 44-1865-791347. *944*

METRON.
Universita degli Studi di Roma, Facolta di Scienze Statistiche Demografiche ed Attuariali, Dipartimento di Statistica, Probabilita e Stat. Applicate, Piazzale Aldo Moro 5, 00185 Rome, Italy. TEL 39-6-4958308. FAX 39-6-4959241. *6619*

METROPOLITAN TORONTO POLICE ASSOCIATION. NEWS & VIEWS.
Metropolitan Toronto Police Association, 180 Yorkland Blvd., North York, ON M2J 1R5, Canada. TEL 416-491-4301. FAX 416-494-4948. *2169*

MEXICAN STUDIES.
University of California Press, Journals Division, 2120 Berkeley Way, No. 5812, Berkeley, CA 94720-5812. TEL 510-643-7154. FAX 510-642-9917. *3619*

MEYER'S DIRECTORY OF GENEALOGICAL SOCIETIES IN THE U S A & CANADA.
Libra - Pipe Creek Publications, 5179 Perry Rd., Pipe Creek, Mt. Airy, MD 21771. TEL 410-875-2824. FAX 410-875-0180. *3093*

MEYLER'S SIDE EFFECTS OF DRUGS.
Elsevier Science B.V., Books Division, P.O. Box 211, 1000 AE Amsterdam, Netherlands. TEL 31-20-4853911. FAX 31-20-4853705. *5428*

MICHIGAN ACADEMICIAN.
Michigan Academy of Science, Arts and Letters, 400 Fourth St., Ann Arbor, MI 48109-4816. TEL 313-936-2938. FAX 313-763-6927. *6258*

MICHIGAN ASSOCIATION OF SPEECH COMMUNICATION JOURNAL.
Michigan Association of Speech Communication, Communication, 585 Manoogian, Wlayne State University, Detroit, MI 48202. TEL 517-774-7896. *2472*

MICHIGAN BOTANIST.
Michigan Botanical Club, Inc., University of Michigan Herbarium, 2001 N. University Bldg., 1205 N. University Ave., Ann Arbor, MI 48109-1057. TEL 313-764-2407. *690*

MICHIGAN HISTORICAL REVIEW (MT. PLEASANT).
Clarke Historical Library, Central Michigan University, Mt. Pleasant, MI 48859. TEL 517-774-6567. FAX 517-774-4499. *3478*

MICHIGAN MONOGRAPHS IN CHINESE STUDIES.
University of Michigan, Center for Chinese Studies, 104 Lane Hall, Ann Arbor, MI 48109-1290. TEL 313-998-7181. FAX 313-936-2948. *3382*

MICHIGAN PHARMACIST.
Michigan Pharmacists Association, 815 N. Washington Ave., Lansing, MI 48906. TEL 517-484-1466. FAX 517-484-4893. *5428*

MICHIGAN READING JOURNAL.
Michigan Reading Association, c/o Robert L. Smith, 5241 Plainfield, N.E., Ste. 1, Grand Rapids, MI 49505. TEL 313-698-2098. *2353*

MICHIGAN STATE UNIVERSITY. AGRICULTURAL ECONOMICS REPORT.
Michigan State University, Department of Agricultural Economics, Reference Rm., East Lansing, MI 48824-1039. TEL 517-355-6650. FAX 517-432-1800. *196*

MICHIGAN STATE UNIVERSITY. MUSEUM PUBLICATIONS. ANTHROPOLOGICAL SERIES.
Michigan State University, Museum, East Lansing, MI 48824. TEL 517-355-2370. *315*

MICHIGAN WATER ENVIRONMENT MATTERS.
Michigan Water Environment Association, P.O. Box 82410, Rochester, MI 48308-2410. TEL 810-375-0548. FAX 810-375-0522. *6972*

MICHKAR CHAKLAEI BEYISRAEL.
Agricultural Research Organization, Volcani Center, P.O. Box 6, Bet Dagan 50250, Israel. TEL 972-3-9683215. FAX 972-3-993998. *135*

MICHMANIM.
Reuben and Edith Hecht Museum, Haifa University, Mt. Carmel, Haifa 31905, Israel. TEL 972-4-257773. FAX 972-4-240724. *363*

MICROBEAM ANALYSIS.
V C H Verlagsgesellschaft mbH, Postfach 101161, 69451 Weinheim. TEL 06201-606147. FAX 06201-606117. *1719*

MICROBIAL & COMPARATIVE GENOMICS.
Mary Ann Liebert, Inc. Publishers, 2 Madison Ave., Larchmont, NY 10538. TEL 914-834-3100. FAX 914-834-3688. *747*

MICROBIAL DRUG RESISTANCE: MECHANISM, EPIDEMIOLOGY, AND DISEASE.
Mary Ann Liebert, Inc. Publishers, 2 Madison Ave., Larchmont, NY 10538. TEL 914-834-3100. FAX 914-834-3688. *762*

MICROBIAL ECOLOGY.
Springer-Verlag, Life Science Journals, 175 Fifth Ave., New York, NY 10010. TEL 212-460-1500. FAX 212-473-6272. *762*

MICROBIOLOGICAL REVIEWS.
American Society for Microbiology, 1325 Massachusetts Ave., N.W., Washington, DC 20005. TEL 202-737-3600. *762*

MICROBIOLOGY.
Maik Nauka - Interperiodica, Mezhdunarodnyi Otdel, Ul. Profsoyuznaya, 90, 117864 Moscow, Russia. TEL 7-095-3360066. FAX 7-095-3360666. *763*

MICROBIOLOGY AND IMMUNOLOGY.
Center for Academic Publications Japan, 2-4-16 Yayoi, Bunkyo-ku, Tokyo 113, Japan. TEL 03-3817-5821. FAX 03-3817-5820. *763*

MICROBIOLOGY EUROPE.
V C H Verlagsgesellschaft mbH, Postfach 101161, 69451 Weinheim, Germany. TEL 06201-606147. FAX 06201-606117. *763*

MICROBIOLOGY SERIES.
Marcel Dekker, Inc., 270 Madison Ave., New York, NY 10016. TEL 212-889-9595. FAX 212-658-4540. *763*

MICROCHEMICAL JOURNAL.
Academic Press, Inc., Journal Division, 525 B St., Ste. 1900, San Diego, CA 92101-4495. TEL 619-230-1840. FAX 619-699-6800. *769*

MICROCIRCULATION (LONDON).
Chapman & Hall 2-6 Boundary Row, London SE1 8HN, England. TEL 44-171-8650066. FAX 44-171-5229623. *4502*

MICROCIRCULATION, ENDOTHELIUM AND LYMPHATICS.
B M A Publications, Box 562, 31 Willows Rd., Ayer, MA 01432-0562. TEL 212-270-2194. *4702*

MICROCIRCULATION REVIEWS.
Kluwer Academic Publishers, Postbus 17, 3300 AA Dordrecht, Netherlands. TEL 31-78-6392392. FAX 31-78-6392254. *791*

MICROCOMPUTERS IN CIVIL ENGINEERING.
Blackwell Publishers, 238 Main St., Cambridge, MA 02142. TEL 617-547-7110. FAX 617-547-0789. *2680*

MICROELECTRONIC ENGINEERING.
North-Holland P.O. Box 211, 1000 AE Amsterdam, Netherlands. TEL 31-20-4853911. FAX 31-20-4853598. *2527*

MICROELECTRONICS AND RELIABILITY.
Elsevier Science Ltd., Pergamon, P.O. Box 800, Kidlington, Oxford OX5 1DX, England. TEL 44-1865-843000. FAX 44-1865-843010. *2527*

MICROELECTRONICS JOURNAL.
Elsevier Science Ltd., Pergamon, P.O. Box 800, Kidlington, Oxford OX5 1DX, England. TEL 44-1865-843000. FAX 44-1865-843010. *2527*

MICRON.
Elsevier Science Ltd., Pergamon, P.O. Box 800, Kidlington, Oxford OX5 1DX, England. TEL 44-1865-843000. FAX 44-1865-843010. *769*

MICRONESICA.
University of Guam Press, UOG Station, Mangilao, Guam 96923. TEL 671-734-9430. FAX 671-735-2170. *316*

MICROPALEONTOLOGY.
American Museum of Natural History, Central Park W. at 79th St., New York, NY 10024-5192. TEL 212-769-5656. FAX 212-769-5653. *5315*

MICROPOROUS MATERIALS.
Elsevier Science B.V., P.O. Box 211, 1000 AE Amsterdam, Netherlands. TEL 31-20-4853911. FAX 31-20-4853598. *1755*

MICROPROCESSOR - BASED AND INTELLIGENT SYSTEMS ENGINEERING.
Kluwer Academic Publishers, Postbus 17, 3300 AA Dordrecht, Netherlands. TEL 31-78-6392392. FAX 31-78-6392254. *2610*

MICROPROCESSOR REPORT.
874 Gravenstein Hwy., Ste.14, Sebastopol, CA 95472. TEL 707-824-4004. FAX 707-823-0504. *2089*

MICROPROCESSORS & MICROSYSTEMS.
Elsevier Science B.V., P.O. Box 211, 1000 AE Amsterdam, Netherlands. TEL 31-20-4853911. FAX 31-20-4853598. *2089*

MICROSCOPE.
McCrone Research Institute, 2820 S. Michigan Ave., Chicago, IL 60616-3292. TEL 312-842-7100. FAX 312-842-1078. *770*

MICROSCOPICAL SOCIETY OF CANADA. BULLETIN.
Microscopical Society of Canada, Dept. of Pathology, Rm. 2V17, McMaster Univ., 1200 Main St., Hamilton, ON L8N 3Z5, Canada. TEL 905-525-9140. FAX 905-577-0198. *770*

MICROSCOPY SOCIETY OF AMERICA. JOURNAL.
Jones & Begell Publishings, 79 Madison Ave., New York, NY 10016-7892. TEL 212-725-1999. *3637*

MICROSOFT WORKS IN EDUCATION.
International Society for Technology in Education, 1787 Agate St., Eugene, OR 97403-1923. TEL 541-346-4414. FAX 541-346-5890. *2020*

MICROSURGERY.
John Wiley & Sons, Inc., Journals, 605 Third Ave., New York, NY 10158. TEL 212-850-6645. FAX 212-850-6021. *4915*

MICROSYSTEM TECHNOLOGIES.
Springer-Verlag, Heidelberger Platz 3, 14197 Berlin, Germany. TEL 49-30-8207-0. FAX 49-30-820-7448. *2022*

MICROVASCULAR RESEARCH.
Academic Press, Inc., Journal Division, 525 B St., Ste. 1900, San Diego, CA 92101-4495. TEL 619-230-1840. FAX 619-699-6800. *4607*

MICROWAVE & OPTICAL TECHNOLOGY LETTERS.
John Wiley & Sons, Inc., Journals, 605 Third Ave., New York, NY 10158. TEL 212-850-6645. FAX 212-850-6021. *5607*

MICROWAVE JOURNAL (INTERNATIONAL EDITION).
Horizon - House - Publications, Inc., 685 Canton St., Norwood, MA 02062. TEL 617-769-9750. FAX 617-762-9230. *2713*

MID-AMERICA (CHICAGO).
Loyola University of Chicago, Department of History, 6525 Sheridan Rd., Chicago, IL 60626. TEL 312-508-2230. *3478*

MID-AMERICA FOLKLORE.
Mid-America Folklore Society, c/o Lyon College, Batesville, AR 72501. TEL 501-793-9813. FAX 501-698-4346. *2954*

MID-AMERICAN JOURNAL OF BUSINESS.
Ball State University, Bureau of Business Research, Muncie, IN 47306. TEL 317-285-5926. FAX 317-285-8024. *944*

MID-AMERICAN REVIEW.
Bowling Green State University, Department of English, c/o George Looney, Ed., Bowling Green State University, Bowling Green, OH 43403. TEL 419-372-2725. *4154*

MIDDLE EAST COMMERCIAL LAW REVIEW.
Sweet & Maxwell, Mill St., Oxford OX2 0JU, England. TEL 44-1865-249248. FAX 44-1865-792301. *3939*

MIDDLE EAST FORUM.
Institute of Middle East Studies "Al Mamun" (IMSAM), c/o Prof. John Karkazis, Ed., Smirnis 1, 15772 Zografou, Greece. TEL 30-1-6123631. FAX 30-1-6123631. *5761*

MIDDLE EAST REPORT.
Middle East Research & Information Project, 1500 Massachusetts Ave., N.W., Ste. 119, Washington, DC 20005. TEL 202-223-3677. FAX 202-223-3604. *3498*

MIDDLE EASTERN STUDIES.
Frank Cass, Newbury House, 890-900 Eastern Ave., Newbury Park, Ilford, Essex IG2 7HH, England. TEL 44-181-599-8836. FAX 44-181-599-0984. *3498*

MIDDLE SCHOOL JOURNAL.
National Middle School Association, 2600 Corporate Exchange Dr., Ste. 370, Columbus, OH 43231. TEL 614-895-4730. FAX 614-895-4750. *2495*

MIDDLE STATES COUNCIL FOR THE SOCIAL STUDIES. JOURNAL.
Middle States Council for the Social Studies, Rider College, 2083 Lawrenceville Rd., Lawrenceville, NJ 08648-3099. TEL 609-896-5068. *6334*

MIDLAND CATHOLIC HISTORY.
Midland Catholic History Society, c/o Vincent Burke, 16 Brandhall Ct., Wolverhampton Rd., Warley, W. Midlands B68 8DE, England. *6187*

MIDLAND HISTORY.
University of Birmingham, School of History, Edgbaston, Birmingham B15 2TT, England. TEL 44-121-414-5759. *3428*

MIDLAND REVIEW.
Oklahoma State University, English Department, Morrill Hall, Stillwater, OK 74078. TEL 405-744-9474. *4237*

MIDWEST HISTORY OF EDUCATION SOCIETY. JOURNAL.
Midwest History of Education Society, University of Dayton, Dayton, OH 45469-0525. TEL 513-229-3328. *2353*

MIDWIVES.
Nursing Notes Ltd., 120 High Rd., E. Finchley, London N2 8AG, England. TEL 44-181-442-0801. FAX 44-181-442-0623. *4741*

MIGRATORI ALATI.
R G F di Realini Gianfranco e C. s.a.s., Via Cascine, 4, 21027 Ispra (VA), Italy. TEL 0332-781057. *778*

MIKROBIYOLOJI BULTENI.
Ankara Microbiology Society, Hacettepe University Faculty of Medicine, Dept. of Microbiology, 06100 Ankara, Turkey. TEL 90-312-3114752. FAX 90-312-3115250. *763*

MILITARY ADVOCATE.
Judge Advocates Association, 1815 H St. N.W., Ste. 408, Washington, DC 20006-3697. TEL 202-628-0979. FAX 202-775-0295. *3958*

MILITARY CHAPLAIN.
Military Chaplains Association of the United States of America, Box 42660, Washington, DC 20015-0660. TEL 717-642-6792. FAX 717-642-6792. *5039*

MILITARY HISTORY OF THE WEST.
University of North Texas Press, Journals Division, Box 13856, Denton TX 76203. TEL 817-369-8838. FAX 817-569-2288. *3478*

MILITARY MEDICINE.
Association of Military Surgeons of the U S, 9320 Old Georgetown Rd. Bethesda, MD 20814. TEL 301-897-8800. FAX 301-530-5446. *4502*

MILITARY OPERATIONS RESEARCH.
Gordon & Breach Science Publishers, c/o International Publishers Distributor, P.O. Box 3054, Langhorne, PA 19047-3054. TEL 215-750-2642. FAX 215-750-6343. *5039*

MILITARY PSYCHOLOGY.
Lawrence Erlbaum Associates, Inc., 10 Industrial Dr., Mahwah, NJ C7430-2262. TEL 201-236-9500. FAX 201-236-0072. *5866*

MILITARY SCIENCE INDEX.
Royal Military College of Science Library, Shrivenham, Swindon, Wiltshire SN6 8LA, England. TEL 44-1793-785484. FAX 44-1793-785555. *5055*

MINAMI-KYUSHU DAIGAKU ENGEIGAKUBU KENKYU HOKOKU. JINBUN SHAKAI KAGAKUKEI.
Minami-Kyushu Daigaku, Engeigakubu, Hibarigaoka, Takanabe-cho, Koyu-gun, Miyazaki-ken 884, Japan. TEL 81-983-23-0793. FAX 81-983-22-3444. *6334*

MINAMI-KYUSHU DAIGAKU ENGEIGAKUBU KENKYU HOKOKU. SHIZEN KAGAKUKEI.
Minami-Kyushu Daigaku, Engeigakubu, Hibarigaoka, Takanabe-cho, Koyu-gun, Miyazaki-ken 884, Japan. TEL 81-983-23-0793. FAX 81-983-22-3444. *3061*

MINAMI TAIHEIYO KENKYU.
Kagoshima University, Research Center for the South Pacific, 1-21-24, Korimoto, Kagoshima 890, Japan. TEL 81-99-285-7394. FAX 81-99-256-9358. *6258*

MIND & LANGUAGE.
Blackwell Publishers Ltd., 108 Cowley Rd., Oxford OX4 1JF, England. TEL 44-1865-791100. FAX 44-1865-791347. *5486*

MIND YOUR OWN BUSINESS.
Market Place Publishing Ltd., 106 Church Rd., London SE19 2UB, England. TEL 44-181-771-3614. FAX 44-181-771-4592. *1494*

MINDANAO ART & CULTURE.
Mindanao State University, Mamitua Saber Research Center, P.O. Box 5594, Iligan City 9200, Philippines. *2954*

MINDANAO STATE UNIVERSITY. U R C PROFESSIONAL PAPERS.
Mindanao State University, Mamitua Saber Research Center, P.O. Box 5594, Iligan City 9200, Philippines. *6258*

MINDS AND MACHINES.
Kluwer Academic Publishers, Postbus 17, 3300 AA Dordrecht, Netherlands. TEL 31-78-6392392. FAX 31-78-6392254. *2009*

MINERAL AND ELECTROLYTE METABOLISM.
S. Karger AG, Allschwilerstr. 10, P.O. Box, CH-4009 Basel, Switzerland. TEL 061-3061111. FAX 061-3061234. *4502*

MINERAL PROCESSING AND EXTRACTIVE METALLURGY REVIEW.
Gordon and Breach Science Publishers, c/o International Publishers Distributor, P.O. Box 3054, Langhorne, PA 19047-3054. TEL 215-750-2642. FAX 215-750-6343. *4968*

MINERALES.
Instituto de Ingenieros de Minas de Chile, Casilla 14668, Correo 21, Santiago, Chile. TEL 6953849. FAX 6972351. *5070*

THE MINERALOGICAL RECORD.
Mineralogical Record, Inc., 4631 Paseo Tubutama, Tucson, AZ 85740. FAX 520-544-0815. *3510*

MINERALS AND METALLURGICAL PROCESSING.
Society for Mining, Metallurgy and Exploration, Box 625002, Littleton, CO 80162-5002. TEL 303-973-9550. FAX 303-973-3845. *5070*

MINERALS ENGINEERING.
Elsevier Science Ltd., Pergamon, P.O. Box 800, Kidlington, Oxford OX5 1DX, England. TEL 44-1865-843000. FAX 44-1865-843010. *5070*

MINERALS RESEARCH LABORATORY NEWSLETTER.
North Carolina State University, Minerals Research Laboratory, 180 Coxe Ave., Asheville, NC 28801. TEL 704-251-6155. *5071*

MINERVA ANESTESIOLOGICA.
Edizioni Minerva Medica, Corso Bramante 83-85, 10126 Turin, Italy. TEL 39-11-678282. FAX 39-11-3121736. *4592*

MINERVA ANGIOLOGICA.
Edizioni Minerva Medica, Corso Bramante 83-85, 10126 Turin, Italy. TEL 39-11-678282. FAX 39-11-3121736. *4607*

MINERVA BIOTECNOLOGICA.
Edizioni Minerva Medica, Corso Bramante 83-85, 10126 Turin, Italy. TEL 39-11-678282. FAX 39-11-3121736. *664*

MINERVA CARDIOANGIOLOGICA.
Edizioni Minerva Medica, Corso Bramante 83-85, 10126 Turin, Italy. TEL 39-11-678282. FAX 39-11-3121736. *4607*

MINERVA CHIRURGICA.
Edizioni Minerva Medica, Corso Bramante 83-85, 10126 Turin, Italy. TEL 39-11-678282. FAX 39-11-3121736. *4915*

MINERVA ENDOCRINOLOGICA.
Edizioni Minerva Medica, Corso Bramante 83-85, 10126 Turin, Italy. TEL 39-11-678282. FAX 39-11-3121736. *4673*

MINERVA GASTROENTEROLOGICA E DIETOLOGICA.
Edizioni Minerva Medica, Corso Bramante 83-85, 10126 Turin, Italy. TEL 39-11-678282. FAX 39-11-3121736. *4695*

MINERVA GINECOLOGICA.
Edizioni Minerva Medica, Corso Bramante 83-85, 10126 Turin, Italy. TEL 39-11-678282. FAX 39-11-3121736. *4741*

MINERVA MEDICA.
Edizioni Minerva Medica, Corso Bramante 83-85, 10126 Turin, Italy. TEL 39-11-678282. FAX 39-11-3121736. *4707*

MINERVA ORTOGNATODONTICA.
Edizioni Minerva Medica, Corso Bramante 83-85, 10126 Turin, Italy. TEL 39-11-678282. FAX 39-11-3121736. *4648*

MINERVA PEDIATRICA.
Edizioni Minerva Medica, Corso Bramante 83-85, 10126 Turin, Italy. TEL 39-11-678282. FAX 39-11-3121736. *4808*

MINERVA PNEUMOLOGICA.
Edizioni Minerva Medica, Corso Bramante 83-85, 10126 Turin, Italy. TEL 39-11-678282. FAX 39-11-3121736. *4889*

MINERVA PSICHIATRICA.
Edizioni Minerva Medica, Corso Bramante 83-85, 10126 Turin, Italy. TEL 39-11-678282. FAX 39-11-3121736. *4851*

MINERVA STOMATOLOGICA.
Edizioni Minerva Medica, Corso Bramante 83-85, 10126 Turin, Italy. TEL 39-11-678282. FAX 39-11-3121736. *4648*

MINERVA UROLOGICA E NEFROLOGICA.
Edizioni Minerva Medica, Corso Bramante 83-85, 10126 Turin, Italy. TEL 39-11-678282. FAX 39-11-3121736. *4929*

MINIATURE COLLECTOR.
Scott Publishing Company (Livonia), 30595 W. Eight Mile Rd., Livonia, MI 48152-1798. TEL 810-477-6650. FAX 810-477-6795. *3510*

MINIMALLY INVASIVE THERAPY AND ALLIED TECHNOLOGIES.
Blackwell Science Ltd., Osney Mead, Oxford OX2 OEL, England. TEL 44-1865-206206. FAX 44-1865-721205. *4502*

MINING ENGINEERING.
Society for Mining, Metallurgy and Exploration, Box 625002, Littleton, CO 80162-5002. TEL 303-973-9550. FAX 303-973-3845. *5072*

MINING R & D NEWS.
C S I R, Division of Mining Technology, P.O. Box 91230, Auckland Park 2006, South Africa. *5072*

MINNESOTA ACADEMY OF SCIENCE. JOURNAL.
Minnesota Academy of Science, 408 St. Peter St., Ste. 410, St. Paul, MN 55102-1119. TEL 612-227-6361. *6259*

MINNESOTA LITERATURE.
1 Nord Circle, St. Paul, MN 55127. TEL 612-483-3904. *4237*

MINNESOTA STUDIES IN THE PHILOSOPHY OF SCIENCE.
University of Minnesota Press, 111 Third Ave., S., Ste. 290, Minneapolis, MN 55401-2520. FAX 612-627-1980. *5486*

MINOTAURO.
Gruppo Autonomo di Psicologia Analitica, Via della Consulta 50, 00184 Rome, Italy. TEL 39-6-4885304. FAX 39-6-36303643. *5866*

MINZU.
Minzu Zazhishe, 18 Wenshuyuan Jie, Chengdu, Sichuan 610017, People's Republic of China. TEL 86-28-6610665. FAX 86-28-6742119. *2895*

MIR KAMNYA.
Plus Ltd. Publishing, P.O. Box 162, 103050 Moscow, Russia. TEL 7-95-2033574. FAX 7-95-2926511. *5073*

MISCEL.LANIA ZOOLOGICA.
Museu de Zoologia, Attn: Dr. Anna Omedes, Ed., Apdo. de Correus 593, 08080 Barcelona, Spain. TEL 34-3-3196912. FAX 34-3-3104999. *813*

MISSISSIPPI COLLEGE LAW REVIEW.
Mississippi College Law Review, 151 E. Griffith St., Jackson, MS 39201. TEL 601-925-7167. FAX 601-925-7113. *3816*

MISSISSIPPI GEOLOGY.
Department of Environmental Quality, Office of Geology, Box 20307, Jackson, MS 39289. TEL 601-961-5500. FAX 601-961-5521. *2250*

MISSISSIPPI KITE.
Mississippi Ornithological Society, Box Z, Mississippi State, MS 39762. *778*

MISSISSIPPI STATE MEDICAL ASSOCIATION. JOURNAL.
Mississippi State Medical Association, 735 Riverside Dr., Box 5229, Jackson, MS 39296-5229. TEL 601-354-5433. *4503*

MISSOURI. DIVISION OF GEOLOGICAL SURVEY AND WATER RESOURCES. ENGINEERING GEOLOGY SERIES.
Department of Natural Resources, Division of Geology and Land Survey, Box 250, Rolla, MO 65401. TEL 314-368-2125. *2668*

MISSOURI. DIVISION OF HIGHWAY SAFETY (YEAR). HIGHWAY SAFETY PLAN.
Division of Highway Safety, Box 104808, Jefferson City, MO 65110-4808. TEL 314-751-4161. FAX 314-634-5977. *6823*

MISSOURI ACADEMY OF SCIENCE. TRANSACTIONS.
Missouri Academy of Science, Ophelia Parrish 113B, 100 E. Normal St., Kirksville, MO 63501-4221. TEL 816-785-4635. FAX 816-785-4045. *6259*

MISSOURI JOURNAL OF RESEARCH IN MUSIC EDUCATION.
Missouri Music Educators Association, c/o Martin J. Bergee, 140 Fine Arts. Missouri University, Columbia, MO 65211. TEL 417-887-5252. FAX 314-882-5071. *5174*

MITIGATION AND ADAPTATION STRATEGIES FOR GLOBAL CHANGE.
Kluwer Academic Publishers, Postbus 17, 3300 AA Dordrecht, Netherlands. TEL 31-78-6392392. FAX 31-78-6392254. *2810*

MITTELLATEINISCHE STUDIEN UND TEXTE.
E.J. Brill, P.O. Box 9000, 2300 PA Leiden, Netherlands. TEL 31-71-5353500. FAX 31-71-5317532. *3428*

HAMIZRAH HEHADASH.
Magnes Press, Hebrew University, Jerusalem, P.O. Box 7695, Jerusalem 91076, Israel. TEL 972-2-660341. FAX 972-2-633370. *5289*

MNEMOSYNE.
E.J. Brill, P.O. Box 9000, 2300 PA Leiden, Netherlands. TEL 31-71-5353500. FAX 31-71-5317532. *1824*

MNEMOSYNE. SUPPLEMENTS.
E.J. Brill, P.O. Box 9000, 2300 PA Leiden, Netherlands. TEL 31-71-5353500. FAX 31-71-5317532. *1824*

MOBILE NETWORKS & NOMADIC APPLICATIONS (NOMAD).
Baltzer Science Publishers B.V., Asterweg 1a, 1031 HL Amsterdam, Netherlands. TEL 31-20-6370061. FAX 31-20-6323651. *2039*

MODELLING, MEASUREMENT AND CONTROL.
A M S E Press, 16 av. de Grange Blanche, 69160 Tassin-la-Demi-Lune, France. TEL 78-34-36-04. FAX 78-34-54-17. *4411*

MODELS OF SCIENTIFIC THOUGHT.
Harwood Academic Publishers, c/o International Publishers Distributor, P.O. Box 3054, Langhorne, PA 19047-3054. TEL 215-750-2642. FAX 215-750-6343. *4092*

MODERN AGING RESEARCH.
John Wiley & Sons, Inc., Journals, 605 Third Ave., New York, NY 10158. TEL 212-475-7700. *3293*

MODERN ANALYTICAL CHEMISTRY.
Plenum Publishing Corp., 233 Spring St., New York, NY 10013-1578. TEL 212-620-8000. FAX 212-463-0742. *1719*

MODERN APPROACHES IN GEOPHYSICS.
Kluwer Academic Publishers, Postbus 17, 3300 AA Dordrecht, Netherlands. TEL 31-78-6392392. FAX 31-78-6392254. *2278*

MODERN ASPECTS OF ELECTROCHEMISTRY.
Plenum Publishing Corp., 233 Spring St., New York, NY 10013-1578. TEL 212-620-8000. FAX 212-463-0742. *1730*

MODERN AUSTRIAN LITERATURE.
International Arthur Schnitzler Research Association, c/o Donald G. Daviau, Ed., Department of Literatures and Languages, University of California, Riverside, CA 92521. TEL 909-787-5603. FAX 909-684-9202. *4238*

MODERN BIOLOGY SERIES.
Holt, Rinehart and Winston, Inc., c/o Harcourt Brace Jovanovich, 6277 Sea Harbor Dr., Orlando, FL 32887. TEL 407-345-2500. *595*

MODERN FICTION STUDIES.
Johns Hopkins University Press, Journals Publishing Division, 2715 N. Charles St., Baltimore, MD 21218-4319. TEL 410-516-6900. FAX 410-516-6968. *4238*

MODERN GEOLOGY.
Gordon and Breach Science Publishers, c/o International Publishers Distributor, P.O. Box 3054, Langhorne, PA 19047-3054. TEL 215-750-2642. FAX 215-750-6343. *2250*

MODERN GREEK STUDIES ASSOCIATION BULLETIN.
Modern Greek Studies Association, Box 1826, New Haven, CT 06508. TEL 203-392-5668. FAX 203-392-5670. *3429*

MODERN INORGANIC CHEMISTRY.
Plenum Publishing Corp., 233 Spring St., New York, NY 10013-1578. TEL 212-620-8000. FAX 212-463-0742. *1732*

MODERN LANGUAGE JOURNAL.
University of Wisconsin Press, Journal Division, 114 N. Murray St., Madison, WI 53715. TEL 608-262-4925. FAX 608-262-7560. *4092*

MODERN LOGIC.
Modern Logic Publishing, 2408 1/2 W. Lincoln Way, Ames, IA 50014-7217. TEL 515-292-1819. *4384*

MODERN MEDICINE.
Advanstar Communications, Inc., 7500 Old Oak Blvd., Cleveland, OH 44130. TEL 216-826-2839. FAX 216-891-2726. *4503*

MODERN METHODS IN PHARMACOLOGY.
John Wiley & Sons, Inc., Journals, 605 Third Ave., New York, NY 10158. TEL 212-475-7700. *5428*

MODERN MONOGRAPHS IN ANALYTICAL CHEMISTRY.
Marcel Dekker, Inc., 270 Madison Ave., New York, NY 10016. TEL 212-696-9000. FAX 212-658-4540. *1719*

MODERN NEURORADIOLOGY SERIES.
Lippincott - Raven Publishers 227 E. Washington Sq., Philadelphia, PA 19106. TEL 215-238-4200. FAX 215-238-4235. *4880*

MODERN ORTHODOX SAINTS.
Institute for Byzantine and Modern Greek Studies, 115 Gilbert Rd., Belmont, MA 02178. TEL 617-484-6595. *6112*

MODERN PATHOLOGY.
Williams & Wilkins, 351 W. Camden St., Baltimore, MD 21201. TEL 410-528-4000. FAX 410-528-4312. *4503*

MODERN PHILOLOGY.
University of Chicago Press, Journals Division, 5720 S. Woodlawn Ave., Chicago, IL 60637. TEL 773-753-3347. FAX 773-753-0811. *4092*

MODERN POETRY IN TRANSLATION.
King's College London, School of Humanities, Strand, London WC2R 2LS, England. TEL 44-171-873-2360. FAX 44-171-873-2415. *4311*

MODERN PROBLEMS IN CONDENSED MATTER SCIENCES.
Elsevier Science B.V., Books Division, P.O. Box 211, 1000 AE Amsterdam, Netherlands. TEL 31-20-4853911. FAX 31-20-4853705. *5559*

MODERN PROBLEMS OF PHARMACOPSYCHIATRY.
S. Karger AG, Allschwilerstr. 10, P.O. Box, CH-4009 Basel, Switzerland. TEL 061-3061111. FAX 061-3061234. *4851*

MODERN PSYCHOANALYSIS.
Center for Modern Psychoanalytic Studies, 16 W. 10th St., New York, NY 10011. TEL 212-260-7050. FAX 212-260-7052. *5866*

MODERN SCHOOLMAN.
Saint Louis University, 221 N. Grand, St. Louis, MO 63103. TEL 314-977-3149. *5486*

MODERN THEOLOGY.
Blackwell Publishers Ltd., 108 Cowley Rd., Oxford OX4 1JF, England. TEL 44-1865-791100. FAX 44-1865-791347. *6078*

MODERN THEORETICAL CHEMISTRY.
Plenum Publishing Corp., 233 Spring St., New York, NY 10013-1578. TEL 212-620-8000. FAX 212-463-0742. *1686*

MODERNISM - MODERNITY.
Johns Hopkins University Press, Journals Publishing Division, 2715 N. Charles St., Baltimore, MD 21218. TEL 410-516-6987. FAX 410-516-6968. *3353*

MOLECULAR AND BIOCHEMICAL PARASITOLOGY.
Elsevier Science B.V., P.O. Box 211, 1000 AE Amsterdam, Netherlands. TEL 31-20-4853911. FAX 31-20-4853598. *763*

MOLECULAR AND CELLULAR BIOCHEMISTRY.
Kluwer Academic Publishers Boston, Box 358, Accord Sta., Hingham, MA 02018-0358. TEL 617-871-6600. FAX 617-871-6528. *645*

MOLECULAR AND CELLULAR BIOLOGY.
American Society for Microbiology, 1325 Massachusetts Ave., N.W., Washington, DC 20005. TEL 202-737-3600. *763*

MOLECULAR AND CELLULAR ENDOCRINOLOGY.
Elsevier Science Ireland Ltd., P.O. Box 85, Limerick, Ireland. TEL 353-61-471944. FAX 353-61-472144. *4673*

MOLECULAR AND CELLULAR NEUROSCIENCES.
Academic Press, Inc., Journal Division, 525 B St., Ste. 1900, San Diego, CA 92101-4495. TEL 619-230-1840. FAX 619-699-6800. *4851*

MOLECULAR AND CHEMICAL NEUROPATHOLOGY.
Humana Press Inc., 999 Riverview Dr., Ste. 208, Totowa, NJ 07512. TEL 201-256-1699. FAX 201-256-8341. *4852*

MOLECULAR ASPECTS OF CELLULAR REGULATION.
Elsevier Science B.V., Books Division, P.O. Box 211, 1000 AE Amsterdam, Netherlands. TEL 31-20-4853911. FAX 31-20-4853705. *717*

MOLECULAR ASPECTS OF MEDICINE.
Elsevier Science Ltd., Pergamon, P.O. Box 800, Kidlington, Oxford OX5 1DX, England. TEL 44-1865-843000. FAX 44-1865-843010. *4503*

MOLECULAR BIOLOGY (NEW YORK).
Plenum Publishing Corp., Consultants Bureau, 233 Spring St., New York, NY 10013-1578. TEL 212-620-8468. FAX 212-463-0742. *717*

MOLECULAR BIOLOGY AND EVOLUTION.
University of Chicago Press, Journals Division, 5702 S. Woodlawn Ave., Chicago, IL 60637. TEL 773-753-3347. FAX 773-753-0811. *595*

MOLECULAR BIOLOGY OF THE CELL.
American Society for Cell Biology, 9650 Rockville Pike, Bethesda, MD 20814-3992. TEL 301-530-7153. FAX 301-571-7139. *764*

MOLECULAR BIOLOGY REPORTS.
Kluwer Academic Publishers, Postbus 17, 3300 AA Dordrecht, Netherlands. TEL 31-78-6392392. FAX 31-78-6392254. *717*

MOLECULAR BIOTECHNOLOGY.
Humana Press, Inc., 999 Riverview Dr., Ste. 208, Totowa, NJ 07512-1165. TEL 201-256-1699. FAX 201-256-8341. *664*

MOLECULAR BREEDING.
Kluwer Academic Publishers, Postbus 17, 3300 AA Dordrecht, Netherlands. TEL 31-78-6392392. FAX 31-78-6392254. *690*

MOLECULAR CARCINOGENESIS.
John Wiley & Sons, Inc., Journals, 605 Third Ave., New York, NY 10158. TEL 212-850-6645. FAX 212-850-6021. *4760*

MOLECULAR COMPARATIVE PHYSIOLOGY.
S. Karger AG, Allschwilerstr. 10, P.O. Box, CH-4009 Basel, Switzerland. TEL 061-3061111. FAX 061-3061234. *791*

MOLECULAR CRYSTALS AND LIQUID CRYSTALS SCIENCE AND TECHNOLOGY. SECTION A: MOLECULAR CRYSTALS AND LIQUID CRYSTALS.
Gordon & Breach Science Publishers, c/o International Publishers Distributor, P.O. Box 3054, Langhorne, PA 19047-3054. TEL 610-750-2642. FAX 610-750-6343. *1727*

MOLECULAR CRYSTALS AND LIQUID CRYSTALS SCIENCE AND TECHNOLOGY. SECTION B: NONLINEAR OPTICS.
Gordon and Breach Science Publishers, c/o International Publishers Distributor, P.O. Box 3054, Langhorne, PA 19047-3054. TEL 215-750-2642. FAX 215-750-6343. *5608*

MOLECULAR CRYSTALS AND LIQUID CRYSTALS SCIENCE AND TECHNOLOGY. SECTION C: MOLECULAR MATERIALS.
Gordon and Breach Science Publishers, c/o International Publishers Distributor, P.O. Box 3054, Langhorne, PA 19047-3054. TEL 215-750-2642. FAX 215-750-6343. *1727*

MOLECULAR CRYSTALS AND LIQUID CRYSTALS SCIENCE AND TECHNOLOGY. SECTION D: DISPLAY AND IMAGING.
Gordon & Breach Science Publishers, c/o International Publishers Distributor, P.O. Box 3054, Langhorne, PA 19047-3054. TEL 215-750-2642. FAX 215-750-6343. *5608*

MOLECULAR ECOLOGY.
Blackwell Science Ltd., Osney Mead, Oxford OX2 OEL. TEL 44-1365-206206. FAX 44-1865-721205. *764*

MOLECULAR ENDOCRINOLOGY.
Endocrine Society, 4350 East West Hwy., Ste. 500, Bethesda, MD 20814-4410. TEL 301-941-0200. FAX 301-941-0259. *4673*

MOLECULAR ENGINEERING.
Kluwer Academic Publishers, Postbus 17, 3300 AA Dordrecht, Netherlands. TEL 31-78-6392392. FAX 31-78-6392254. *2645*

MOLECULAR GENETICS, MICROBIOLOGY AND VIROLOGY.
Allerton Press, Inc., 150 Fifth Ave., New York, NY 10011. TEL 212-924-3950. FAX 212-463-9684. *747*

MOLECULAR IMMUNOLOGY.
Elsevier Science Ltd., Pergamon, P.O. Box 800, Kidlington, Oxford OX5 1DX, England. TEL 44-1865-843000. FAX 44-1865-843010. *645*

MOLECULAR MEDICINE.
Blackwell Science Inc., 238 Main St., Cambridge, MA 02142. TEL 617-876-7022. FAX 617-492-5263. *4503*

MOLECULAR MEMBRANE BIOLOGY.
Taylor & Francis Ltd., 1 Gunpowder Sq., London EC4A 3DE, England. TEL 44-171-583-0490. FAX 44-171-583-0585. *645*

MOLECULAR MICROBIOLOGY.
Blackwell Science Ltd., Osney Mead, Oxford OX2 OEL, England. TEL 44-1865-206206. FAX 44-1865-721205. *764*

MOLECULAR NEUROBIOLOGY.
Humana Press Inc., 999 Riverview Dr., Ste. 208, Totowa, NJ 07512. TEL 201-256-1699. FAX 201-256-8341. *4852*

MOLECULAR PHARMACOLOGY.
Williams & Wilkins, 351 W. Camden St., Baltimore, MD 21201. TEL 410-528-4000. FAX 410-528-4312. *5423*

MOLECULAR PHYLOGENETICS AND EVOLUTION.
Academic Press, Inc., Journal Division, 525 B St., Ste. 1900, San Diego, CA 92101-4495. TEL 619-230-1840. FAX 619-699-6800. *747*

MOLECULAR PHYSICS.
Taylor & Francis Ltd., 1 Gunpowder Sq., London EC4A 3DE, England. TEL 44-171-583-0490. FAX 44-171-583-0585. *1755*

MOLECULAR REPRODUCTION AND DEVELOPMENT.
John Wiley & Sons, Inc., Journals, 605 Third Ave., New York, NY 10158. TEL 212-850-6645. FAX 212-850-6021. *764*

MOLECULAR SIMULATION.
Gordon & Breach Science Publishers, c/o International Publishers Distributor, P.O. Box 3054, Langhorne, PA 19047-3054. TEL 215-750-2642. FAX 215-750-6343. *1686*

MOLECULAR STRUCTURES AND DIMENSIONS.
Kluwer Academic Publishers, Postbus 17, 3300 AA Dordrecht, Netherlands. TEL 31-78-6392392. FAX 31-78-6392254. *1727*

MOLLUSCAN RESEARCH.
Malacological Society of Australasia, Division of Invertebrate Zoology, Australian Museum, P.O. Box A285, Sydney South, N.S.W. 200, Australia, Australia. TEL 61-2-3206275. FAX 61-2-3206050. *813*

MOLOCHNO-M'YASNE SKOTARSTVO.
Akademiya Nauk Ukrainy, Institut Tvarinnitstva, P-v Kulinichi, 312120 Kharkov, Ukraine. TEL 7-0572-953181. FAX 7-0572-953066. *253*

MONALDI ARCHIVES FOR CHEST DISEASE.
PI-ME Tipografia Editrice s.r.l., Viale Sardegna 64, 27100 Pavia, Italy. TEL 322-830101. FAX 322-830294. *4889*

MONASH UNIVERSITY LAW REVIEW.
Monash University, Faculty of Law, Wellington Rd., Clayton, Vic. 3168, Australia. TEL 03-9053374. FAX 61-3-9055305. *3817*

MONDE LIBERTAIRE.
Federation Anarchiste, 145 rue Amelot, 75011 Paris France. TEL 48-05-34-08. FAX 49-29-98-59. *5684*

MONETARY AND ECONOMIC REVIEW.
F A M C Inc., 3500 J F K Pkwy., Fort Collins, CO 80525. TEL 970-223-4952. FAX 970-223-4996. *945*

MONO GEO GRAPHY.
Haifa University, Department of Geography, Mount Carmel, Haifa 31905, Israel. FAX 972-4-246814. *3265*

MONOGRAPH OF LIVING CHITONS (MOLLUSCA: POLYPLACOPHORA).
E.J. Brill, P.O. Box 9000, 2300 PA Leiden, Netherlands. TEL 31-71-5353500. FAX 31-71-5317532. *814*

MONOGRAPH SERIES ON SCHIZOPHRENIA.
International Universities Press, Inc., 59 Boston Post Rd., Box 1524, Madison, CT 06443-1524. TEL 203-245-4000. *4852*

MONOGRAPHIAE BIOLOGICAE.
Kluwer Academic Publishers, Postbus 17, 3300 AA Dordrecht, Netherlands. TEL 31-78-6392392. FAX 31-78-6392254. *595*

MONOGRAPHS AND THEORETICAL STUDIES IN SOCIOLOGY AND ANTHROPOLOGY IN HONOUR OF NELS ANDERSON.
E.J. Brill, P.O. Box 9000, 2300 PA Leiden, Netherlands. TEL 31-71-5353500. FAX 31-71-5317532. *6423*

MONOGRAPHS IN ALLERGY.
S. Karger AG, Allschwilerstr. 10, P.O. Box, CH-4009 Basel, Switzerland. TEL 061-3051111. FAX 061-3061234. *4586*

MONOGRAPHS IN ANAESTHESIOLOGY.
Elsevier Science B.V., Books Division, P.O. Box 211, 1000 AE Amsterdam, Netherlands. TEL 31-20-4853911. FAX 31-20-4853705. *4592*

MONOGRAPHS IN CLINICAL CYTOLOGY.
S. Karger AG, Allschwilerstr. 10, P.O. Box, CH-4009 Basel, Switzerland. TEL 061-3061111. FAX 061-3061234. *4504*

MONOGRAPHS IN CONTEMPORARY MATHEMATICS.
Plenum Publishing Corp., Consultants Bureau, 233 Spring St., New York, NY 10013-1578. TEL 212-620-8000. FAX 212-463-0742. *4384*

MONOGRAPHS IN CRYOGENICS.
Oxford University Press, Walton St., Oxford OX2 6DP, England. TEL 44-1865-56767. FAX 44-1865-56646. *2611*

MONOGRAPHS IN DEVELOPMENTAL BIOLOGY.
S. Karger AG, Allschwilerstr. 10, P.O. Box, CH-4009 Basel, Switzerland. TEL 061-3061111. FAX 061-3061234. *645*

MONOGRAPHS IN ELECTROANALYTICAL CHEMISTRY AND ELECTROCHEMISTRY SERIES.
Marcel Dekker, Inc., 270 Madison Ave., New York, NY 10016. TEL 212-696-9000. FAX 212-658-4540. *1730*

MONOGRAPHS IN EPIDEMIOLOGY AND BIOSTATISTICS.
Oxford University Press, Walton St., Oxford OX2 6DP, England. TEL 44-1865-56767. FAX 44-1865-56646. *5969*

MONOGRAPHS IN HUMAN GENETICS.
S. Karger AG, Allschwilerstr. 10, P.O. Box, CH-4009 Basel, Switzerland. TEL 061-3061111. FAX 061-3061234. *747*

MONOGRAPHS IN NEURAL SCIENCES.
S. Karger AG, Allschwilerstr. 10, P.O. Box, CH-4009 Basel, Switzerland. TEL 061-3061111. FAX 061-3061234. *4852*

MONOGRAPHS IN NEUROSCIENCE.
Gordon & Breach Science Publishers, c/o International Publishers Distributor, P.O. Box 3054, Langhorne, PA 19047-3054. TEL 215-750-2642. FAX 215-750-6343. *4852*

MONOGRAPHS IN OPHTHALMOLOGY.
Kluwer Academic Publishers, Postbus 17, 3300 AA Dordrecht, Netherlands. TEL 31-78-6392392. FAX 31-78-6392254. *4773*

MONOGRAPHS IN ORAL SCIENCE.
S. Karger AG, Allschwilerstr. 10, P.O. Box, CH-4009 Basel, Switzerland. TEL 061-3061111. FAX 061-3061234. *4648*

MONOGRAPHS IN PHYSICAL MEASUREMENT.
Academic Press, Inc., 525 B St., Ste. 1900, San Diego, CA 92101-4495. TEL 619-231-0926. FAX 619-699-6715. *2611*

MONOGRAPHS IN PRIMATOLOGY.
John Wiley & Sons, Inc., Journals, 605 Third Ave., New York, NY 10158. *595*

MONOGRAPHS IN PSYCHOBIOLOGY.
Gordon & Breach Science Publishers, c/o International Publishers Distributor, P.O. Box 3054, Langhorne, PA 19047-3054. TEL 215-750-2642. FAX 215-750-6343. *5866*

MONOGRAPHS IN VIROLOGY.
S. Karger AG, Allschwilerstr. 10, P.O. Box, CH-4009 Basel, Switzerland. TEL 061-3061111. FAX 061-3061234. *764*

MONOGRAPHS ON ASTRONOMICAL SUBJECTS.
Oxford University Press, Walton St., Oxford OX2 6DP, England. TEL 44-1865-56767. FAX 44-1865-56646. *483*

MONOGRAPHS ON NUMERICAL ANALYSIS.
Oxford University Press, Walton St., Oxford OX2 6DP, England. TEL 44-1865-56767. FAX 44-1865-56646. *4384*

MONOGRAPHS ON PHYSICAL BIOCHEMISTRY.
Oxford University Press, Walton St., Oxford OX2 6DP, England. TEL 44-1865-56767. FAX 44-1865-56646. *1755*

MONOGRAPHS ON SCIENCE, TECHNOLOGY, AND SOCIETY.
Oxford University Press, Walton St., Oxford OX2 6DP, England. TEL 44-1865-56767. FAX 44-1865-56646. *6658*

MONOGRAPHS ON SOIL AND RESOURCES SURVEY.
Oxford University Press, Walton St., Oxford OX2 6DP, England. TEL 44-1865-56767. FAX 44-1865-56646. *231*

MONOGRAPHS ON THE PHYSICS AND CHEMISTRY OF MATERIALS.
Oxford University Press, Walton St., Oxford OX2 6DP, England. TEL 44-1865-56767. FAX 44-1865-56646. *5559*

MONTE CARLO METHODS AND APPLICATIONS.
V S P, P.O. Box 346, 3700 AH Zeist, Netherlands. TEL 31-30-6925790. FAX 31-30-6932081. *4411*

MONUMENTA GRAECA ET ROMANA.
E.J. Brill, P.O. Box 9000, 2300 PA Leiden, Netherlands. TEL 31-71-5353500. FAX 31-71-5317532. *399*

MONUMENTA NIPPONICA.
Sophia University, 7-1 Kioi-cho, Chiyoda-ku, Tokyo 102, Japan. TEL 81-3-3238-3544. FAX 81-3-3238-5056. *5289*

MONUMENTS OF RENAISSANCE MUSIC.
University of Chicago Press, 5801 S. Ellis Ave., Chicago, IL 60637. TEL 312-702-7899. *5174*

MOOREANA.
Townsville City Council, P.O. Box 1268, Townsville, Qld. 4810, Australia. TEL 61-77-220455. FAX 61-77-253290. *691*

MOREANA.
Moreana Publications, B.P. 808, 49008 Angers Cedex 01, France. TEL 33-41-87-19-32. FAX 33-41-88-74-42. *3429*

MOROCCO.
Frank Cass, Newbury House, 890-900 Eastern Ave., Newbury Park, Ilford, Essex IG2 7HH, England. TEL 44-181-5998866. FAX 44-181-5990984. *3498*

MORRIS COUNTY FAMILY.
Kids Monthly Publications, Inc., Box 159, Westfield, NJ 07091. TEL 908-232-2913. *1773*

MOSAIC (WINNIPEG, 1967).
University of Manitoba, 208 Tier Bldg., Winnipeg, MB R3T 2N2, Canada. TEL 204-474-9763. FAX 204-261-9086. *4239*

MOSCOW PHYSICAL SOCIETY. JOURNAL.
Allerton Press, Inc., 150 Fifth Ave., New York, NY 10011. TEL 212-924-3950. FAX 212-463-9684. *5559*

MOSENODI.
Botswana Educational Research Association, University of Botswana, Private Bag 0022, Gaborone, Botswana. TEL 267-351151. FAX 267-356591. *2354*

MOST.
Kluwer Academic Publishers, Postbus 17, 3300 AA Dordrecht, Netherlands. TEL 31-78-6392392. FAX 31-78-6392254. *1259*

MOTIVATION AND EMOTION.
Plenum Publishing Corp., 233 Spring St., New York, NY 10013-1578. TEL 212-620-8000. FAX 212-463-0742. *5866*

MOUNT OLIVE REVIEW.
Mt. Olive College Pressss, 634 Henderson St., Mt. Olive, NC 28365. TEL 919-658-2502. FAX 919-658-7160. *4239*

MOUNT SINAI JOURNAL OF MEDICINE.
Mount Sinai Hospital, Committee on Medical Education and Publications, 50 E. 98th St., Box 1094, New York, NY 10029. TEL 212-241-6108. FAX 212-722-6386. *4504*

MOUNTAIN PLAINS JOURNAL OF ADULT EDUCATION.
Mountain Plains Adult Education Association, Journal, Boise Graduate Center, University of Idaho, 800 Park Blvd., Ste. 200, Boise, ID 83712. TEL 208-334-2999. FAX 208-364-4035. *2401*

MOUNTAIN RESEARCH AND DEVELOPMENT.
University of California Press, Journals Division, 2120 Berkeley Way, No. 5812, Berkeley, CA 94720-5812. TEL 510-643-7154. FAX 510-642-9917. *2213*

MOUNTAIN XPRESS.
Mountain Xpress, Inc., Box 144, Asheville, NC 28802. TEL 704-251-1333. FAX 704-251-1311. *3233*

MOVEMENT DISORDERS.
Lippincott - Raven Publishers 227 Washington Sq., Philadelphia, PA 19106. TEL 215-238-4200. *4852*

MOVEMENT THEATRE QUARTERLY.
National Movement Theatre Association, Box 1437, Portsmouth, NH 03802-1437. TEL 603-436-6660. *6699*

MOVIE.
c/o Ian Cameron, Ed. & Pub., P.O. Box 1, Moffat, Dumfriesshire DG10 9SU, Scotland. TEL 44-1683-220808. FAX 44-1683-220012. *5108*

MOVING OUT.
c/o Dayana Stetco, Wayne State University, English Department, Detroit, MI 48202. FAX 313-267-6596. *7002*

MOYO.
Ministry of Health, P.O. Box 30377, Lilongwe 3, Malawi. TEL 265-783-044. FAX 265-783-109. *3191*

MUELLERIA.
National Herbarium of Victoria, Birdwood Ave., South Yarra, Vic. 3141, Australia. TEL 61-3-96552300. FAX 61-3-96552350. *691*

MULTIBODY SYSTEM DYNAMICS.
Kluwer Academic Publishers, Postbus 17, 3300 AA Dordrecht, Netherlands. TEL 31-78-6392392. FAX 31-78-6392254. *5590*

MULTIDIMENSIONAL SYSTEMS AND SIGNAL PROCESSING.
Kluwer Academic Publishers Boston, Box 358, Accord Sta., Hingham, MA 02018-0358. TEL 617-871-6600. FAX 617-871-6528. *2057*

MULTIHULLS WORLD.
Multicoques, Centre Commercial du Nautisme, 28 A Port St. Pierre, 83400 Hyeres, France. TEL 94-38-31-09. FAX 94-38-46-74. *6537*

MULTIMEDIA TOOLS AND APPLICATIONS.
Kluwer Academic Publishers, Postbus 17, 3300 AA Dordrecht, Netherlands. TEL 31-78-6392392. FAX 31-78-6392254. *2113*

MULTINATIONAL BUSINESS REVIEW.
University of Detroit Mercy, College of Business Administration, Box 19900, Detroit, MI 48219-0900. TEL 313-993-1264. FAX 313-993-1052. *1290*

MULTINATIONAL EMPLOYER.
P.O. Box 149, Farnham, Surrey GU9 8YH, England. TEL 44-1252-726416. FAX 44-1252-713730. *945*

MULTIVARIATE BEHAVIORAL RESEARCH.
Lawrence Erlbaum Associates, Inc., 10 Industrial Dr., Mahwah, NJ 07430-2262. TEL 201-236-9500. FAX 201-236-0072. *5866*

MUNDO ELECTRONICO.
Cetisa - Boixareu S.A., Concepcion Arenal 5, 08027 Barcelona, Spain. TEL 34-3-3527061. FAX 34-3-3492350. *2528*

MUQARNAS.
E.J. Brill, P.O. Box 9000, 2300 PA Leiden, Netherlands. TEL 31-71-5353500. FAX 31-71-5317532. *443*

MUQARNAS, SUPPLEMENTS.
E.J. Brill, P.O. Box 9000, 2300 PA Leiden, Netherlands. TEL 31-71-5353500. FAX 31-71-5317532. *443*

MUSCLE & NERVE.
John Wiley & Sons, Inc., Journals, 605 Third Ave., New York, NY 10158. TEL 212-850-6645. FAX 212-850-6021. *4504*

MUSCULO-SKELETAL MANAGEMENT.
Blackwell Science Ltd., Osney Mead, Oxford OX2 OEL, England. TEL 44-1865-206206. FAX 44-1865-721205. *4788*

MUSEES.
Societe des Musees Quebecois, C.P. 8888, Succ. Centre-Ville, UQAM, Montreal, PQ H3C 3P8, Canada. TEL 514-987-3264. FAX 514-987-3379. *5126*

MUSEO CIVICO DI STORIA NATURALE DI VENEZIA. BOLLETTINO.
Museo Civico di Storia Naturale di Venezia, Fontego dei Turchi, S. Croce 1730, 30135 Venice, Italy. TEL 39-41-721852. FAX 39-41-5242592. *596*

MUSEU DE ZOOLOGIA. TREBALLS.
Museu de Zoologia, Attn: Dr. Anna Omedes, Ed., Apdo. 593, 08080 Barcelona, Spain. TEL 34-3-3196912. FAX 34-3-3104999. *814*

MUSEUM INTERNATIONAL.
Blackwell Publishers Ltd., 108 Cowley Rd., Oxford OX4 1JF, England. TEL 44-1865-791100. FAX 44-1865-791347. *5127*

MUSEUM MANAGEMENT AND CURATORSHIP.
Butterworth - Heinemann, Part of the Reed Elsevier group, Linacre House, Jordan Hill, Oxford OX2 8DP, England. TEL 44-1865-310366. FAX 44-1865-310898. *5127*

MUSEUM PRACTICE.
Museums Associations, 42 Clerkenwell Close, London EC1R OPA, England. TEL 44-171-250-1834. FAX 44-171-250-1929. *5127*

MUSIC ANALYSIS.
Blackwell Publishers Ltd., 108 Cowley Rd., Oxford OX4 1JF, England. TEL 44-1865-791100. FAX 44-1865-791347. *5175*

MUSIC IN AMERICAN LIFE.
University of Illinois Press, 1325 S. Oak St., Champaign, IL 61820. TEL 217-333-0950. FAX 217-244-8082. *5176*

MUSIC PERCEPTION.
University of California Press, Journals Division, 2120 Berkeley Way, No. 5812, Berkeley, CA 94720-5812. TEL 510-643-7154. FAX 510-642-9917. *5177*

MUSIC REFERENCE SERVICES QUARTERLY.
Haworth Press, Inc., 10 Alice St., Binghamton, NY 13904. TEL 607-722-5857. FAX 607-722-1424. *4013*

MUSIC THEORY SPECTRUM.
Society for Music Theory, College of Music, Temple University, Philadelphia, PA 19122. TEL 215-204-8316. FAX 215-204-4957. *5177*

MUSIC THERAPY PERSPECTIVES.
National Association for Music Therapy, Inc., 8455 Colesville Rd., Ste. 930, Silver Spring, MD 20910-3392. TEL 301-589-3300. FAX 301-589-5175. *5177*

MUSICK.
Vancouver Society for Early Music, 1254 W. Seventh Ave., Vancouver, BC V6H 1B6, Canada. TEL 604-732-1610. FAX 604-732-1602. *5179*

MUSICOLOGY.
Gordon & Breach Science Publishers, c/o International Publishers Distributor, P.O. Box 3054, Langhorne, PA 19047-3054. TEL 215-750-2642. FAX 215-750-6343. *5179*

MUSICUS.
Unisa Press, Periodicals, P.O. Box 392, Pretoria 0001, South Africa. TEL 27-12-4292953. FAX 27-12-4293221. *5179*

MUSIIKKI.
Suomen Musiikkitieteellinen Seura, P.O. Box 35, FIN-00014 Helsinki, Finland. FAX 358-0-1917955. *5179*

MUSLIM EDUCATION QUARTERLY.
The Islamic Academy, 23 Metcalfe Rd., Cambridge CB4 2DB, England. TEL 01223-350976. FAX 01223-350976. *6120*

THE MUSLIM NEWS.
Visitcrest Ltd., P.O. Box 380, Harrow, Middlesex HA2 6LL, England. TEL 44-171-831-0428. FAX 44-171-831-0830. *6120*

MU'TAH LIL-BUHUTH WAL-DIRASAT. AL-SILSILAH A: AL-'ULUM AL-INSANIYYAH WAL-IJTIMA'IYYAH.
Mu'tah University, Deanship of Scientific Research and Graduate Studies, P.O. Box 7, Mu'tah, Jordan. FAX 962-6-654061. *3619*

MU'TAH LIL-BUHUTH WAL-DIRASAT. AL-SILSILAH B: AL-'ULUM AL-TABI'IYYAH WAL-TATBIQIYYAH.
Mu'tah University, Deanship of Scientific Research and Graduate Studies, P.O. Box 7, Mu'tah, Jordan. FAX 962-2-654061. *6259*

MUTATION RESEARCH.
Elsevier Science B.V., P.O. Box 211, 1000 AE Amsterdam, Netherlands. TEL 31-20-4853911. FAX 31-20-4853598. *747*

MUTATION RESEARCH - D N A REPAIR.
Elsevier Science B.V., P.O. Box 211, 1000 AE Amsterdam, Netherlands. TEL 31-20-4853911. FAX 31-20-4853598. *747*

MUTATION RESEARCH - ENVIRONMENTAL MUTAGENESIS AND RELATED SUBJECTS.
Elsevier Science B.V., P.O. Box 211, 1000 AE Amsterdam, Netherlands. TEL 31-20-4853911. FAX 31-20-4853598. *748*

MUTATION RESEARCH - FUNDAMENTAL AND MOLECULAR MECHANISMS OF MUTAGENESIS.
Elsevier Science B.V. P.O. Box 211, 1000 AE Amsterdam, Netherlands. TEL 31-20-4853911. FAX 31-20-4853598. *748*

MUTATION RESEARCH - GENETIC TOXICOLOGY.
Elsevier Science B.V., P.O. Box 211, 1000 AE Amsterdam, Netherlands. TEL 31-20-4853911. FAX 31-20-4853598. *748*

MUTATION RESEARCH LETTERS.
Elsevier Science B.V., P.O. Box 211, 1000 AE Amsterdam, Netherlands. TEL 31-20-4853911. FAX 31-20-4853598. *748*

MUTATION RESEARCH - MUTATION RESEARCH GENOMICS.
Elsevier Science B.V., P.O. Box 211, 1000 AE Amsterdam, Netherlands. TEL 31-20-4853757. FAX 31-20-4853432. *748*

MUTATION RESEARCH - REVIEWS IN GENETIC TOXICOLOGY.
Elsevier Science B.V., P.O. Box 211, 1000 AE Amsterdam, Netherlands. TEL 31-20-4853911. FAX 31-20-4853598. *748*

MUZEUM ZIEMI. PRACE.
Polska Akademia Nauk, Muzeum Ziemi, Al. Na Skarpie 20-26, 00-488 Warsaw, Poland. TEL 48-22-6298061. FAX 48-22-6297497. *2251*

MYCOLOGIA.
New York Botanical Garden, Scientific Publications Department, Bronx, NY 10458-5126. TEL 718-817-8721. FAX 718-817-8842. *691*

MYCOLOGY SERIES.
Marcel Dekker, Inc., 270 Madison Ave., New York, NY 10016. TEL 212-696-9000. FAX 212-658-4540. *692*

MYCOPATHOLOGIA.
Kluwer Academic Publishers, Postbus 17, 3300 AA Dordrecht, Netherlands. TEL 31-78-6392392. FAX 31-78-6392254. *764*

MYCOTAXON.
Mycotaxon Ltd., Box 264, Ithaca, NY 14851. TEL 607-273-4357. FAX 607-273-4357. *692*

N A C T A JOURNAL.
National Association of Colleges and Teachers of Agriculture, 608 W. Vermont, Urbana, IL 61801. TEL 217-344-5738. *136*

N A C W P I JOURNAL.
Simpson Publishing Co., c/o Dr. Richard Weerts, Ed., Division of Fine Arts, Northeast Missouri State University, Kirksville, MO 63501. TEL 816-785-4442. FAX 816-785-7463. *5182*

N A F T A LAW AND POLICY SERIES.
Martinus Nijhoff Publishers, Human Rights and International Law Postbus 163, 3300 AD Dordrecht, Netherlands. FAX 31-78-392254. *3939*

N A I E C NEWSLETTER.
National Association for Industry - Education Cooperation, 235 Hendricks Blvd., Buffalo, NY 14226-3304. TEL 716-837-7047. FAX 716-834-7047. *1436*

N A T O ADVANCED SCIENCE INSTITUTES SERIES. PARTNERSHIP SUB-SERIES 4: SCIENCE AND TECHNOLOGY POLICY.
Kluwer Academic Publishers, Postbus 17, 3300 AA Dordrecht, Netherlands. TEL 31-78-6392392. FAX 31-78-6392254. *6260*

N A T O ADVANCED SCIENCE INSTITUTES SERIES A: LIFE SCIENCES.
Plenum Publishing Corp., 233 Spring St., New York, NY 10013-1578. TEL 212-620-8000. FAX 212-463-0742. *596*

N A T O ADVANCED SCIENCE INSTITUTES SERIES B: PHYSICS.
Plenum Publishing Corp., 233 Spring St., New York, NY 10013-1578. TEL 212-620-8000. FAX 212-463-0742 *5560*

N A T O ADVANCED SCIENCE INSTITUTES SERIES C: MATHEMATICAL AND PHYSICAL SCIENCES.
Kluwer Academic Publishers, Postbus 17, 3300 AA Dordrecht, Netherlands. TEL 31-78-6392392. FAX 31-78-6392254. *4384*

N A T O ADVANCED SCIENCE INSTITUTES SERIES D: BEHAVIOURAL AND SOCIAL SCIENCES.
Kluwer Academic Publishers, Postbus 17, 3300 AA Dordrecht, Netherlands. TEL 31-78-6392392. FAX 31-78-6392254. *5266*

N A T O ADVANCED SCIENCE INSTITUTES SERIES E: APPLIED SCIENCES.
Kluwer Academic Publishers, Postbus 17, 3300 AA Dordrecht, Netherlands. TEL 31-78-6392392. FAX 31-78-6392254. *6658*

N A T O ADVANCED SCIENCE INSTITUTES SERIES F: COMPUTER AND SYSTEMS SCIENCES.
Kluwer Academic Publishers, Postbus 17, 3300 AA Dordrecht, Netherlands. TEL 31-78-6392392. FAX 31-78-6392254. *2057*

N A T O ADVANCED SCIENCE INSTITUTES SERIES G: ECOLOGICAL SCIENCES.
Kluwer Academic Publishers, Postbus 17, 3300 AA Dordrecht, Netherlands. TEL 31-78-6392392. FAX 31-78-6392254. *2911*

N A T O ADVANCED SCIENCE INSTITUTES SERIES H: CELL BIOLOGY.
Kluwer Academic Publishers, Postbus 17, 3300 AA Dordrecht, Netherlands. TEL 31-78-6392392. FAX 31-78-6392254. *717*

N A T O CHALLENGES OF MODERN SOCIETY.
Plenum Publishing Corp., 233 Spring St., New York, NY 10013-1578. TEL 212-620-8000. FAX 212-463-0742. *2811*

N D T & E INTERNATIONAL.
Butterworth - Heinemann, Part of the Reed Elsevier group, Linacre House, Jordan Hill, Oxford OX2 8DP, England. TEL 44-1865-310366. FAX 44-1865-310898. *2739*

N E M L A ITALIAN STUDIES.
Prof. Umberto C. Mariani, Ed. & Pub., Rutgers Univ., Dept. of Italian, 84 College Ave., New Brunswick, NJ 08903. TEL 908-932-7536. FAX 908-932-1686. *4240*

N I P R SYMPOSIUM ON ANTARCTIC GEOSCIENCES. PROCEEDINGS.
National Institute of Polar Research, Library, 9-10, Kaga 1-chome, Itabashi-ku, Tokyo 173, Japan. TEL 81-3-3962-2214. FAX 81-3-3962-2225. *2251*

N I P R SYMPOSIUM ON ANTARCTIC METEORITES. PROCEEDINGS.
National Institute of Polar Research, Library, 9-10, Kaga 1-chome, Itabashi-ku, Tokyo 173, Japan. TEL 81-3-3962-2214. FAX 81-3-3962-2225. *2251*

N I P R SYMPOSIUM ON POLAR BIOLOGY. PROCEEDINGS.
National Institute of Polar Research, Library, 9-10, Kaga 1-chome, Itabashi-ku, Tokyo 173, Japan. TEL 81-3-3962-2214. FAX 81-3-3962-2225. *596*

N I P R SYMPOSIUM ON POLAR METEOROLOGY AND GLACIOLOGY. PROCEEDINGS.
National Institute of Polar Research, Library, 9-10, Kaga 1-chome, Itabashi-ku, Tokyo 173, Japan. TEL 81-3-3962-2214. FAX 81-3-3962-2225. *2251*

N I P R SYMPOSIUM ON UPPER ATMOSPHERE PHYSICS. PROCEEDINGS.
National Institute of Polar Research, Library, 9-10, Kaga 1-chome, Itabashi-ku, Tokyo 173, Japan. TEL 81-3-3962-2214. FAX 81-3-3962-2225. *5560*

N I S T BUILDING SCIENCE SERIES.
U.S. National Institute of Standards and Technology, Gaithersburg, MD 20899. TEL 301-975-3058. *856*

N I S T HANDBOOK.
U.S. National Institute of Standards and Technology, Gaithersburg, MD 20899. TEL 301-975-3058. *5015*

N I S T MONOGRAPH.
U.S. National Institute of Standards and Technology, Gaithersburg, MD 20899. TEL 301-975-3058. *5015*

N I S T SPECIAL PUBLICATION.
U.S. National Institute of Standards and Technology, Gaithersburg, MD 20899. TEL 301-975-3058. *5016*

N I S T TECHNICAL NOTES.
U.S. National Institute of Standards and Technology, Gaithersburg, MD 20899. TEL 301-975-3058. *5016*

N J A O P S JOURNAL.
New Jersey Association of Osteopathic Physicians and Surgeons, 1 Distribution Way, Monmouth Jct., NJ 08852-3001. TEL 908-940-9000. FAX 908-940-8899. *4614*

N L P WORLD.
Les 3 Chasseurs, CH-1413 Orzens, Switzerland. TEL 41-21-8877721. FAX 41-21-8877976. *5866*

N M C D.
Medikal Press s.r.l., Vioa Luigi Zoja 30, 20153 Milan, Italy. TEL 39-2-48202740. FAX 39-2-48201219. *5237*

N M R IN BIOMEDICINE.
John Wiley & Sons Ltd., Journals, Baffins Ln., Chichester, W. Sussex PO19 1UD, England. TEL 44-1243-779777. FAX 44-1243-843232. *4880*

N S R D S - N B S: NATIONAL STANDARD REFERENCE DATA SERIES.
U.S. National Institute of Standards and Technology, Gaithersburg, MD 20899. TEL 301-975-3058. *5016*

N Z FAMILY PHYSICIAN.
Royal New Zealand College of General Practitioners, c/o Dr. T. Turnbull, Ed., 62 Park Rd., Katikati, New Zealand. TEL 64-7-54904112. FAX 64-7-5491222. *4505*

NAG HAMMADI AND MANICHAEAN STUDIES.
E.J. Brill, P.O. Box 9000, 2300 PA Leiden, Netherlands. TEL 31-71-5353500. FAX 31-71-5317532. *6079*

NAGOYA MEDICAL JOURNAL.
Nagoya-shiritsu Daigaku, Igakubu, Kawasumi 1, Mizuho-cho, Mizuho-ku, Nagoya 467, Japan. FAX 052-851-4166. *4505*

NAGOYA SHIRITSU DAIGAKU IGAKKAI ZASSHI.
Nagoya-shiritsu Daigaku, Igakkai, 1 Kawasumi, Mizuho-cho, Mizuho-ku, Nagoya-shi, Aichi-ken 467, Japan. TEL 81-52-853-8084. FAX 81-52-842-0863. *4505*

THE NAIROBI LAW MONTHLY.
Kaibi Ltd., P.O. Box 53234, Nairobi, Kenya. TEL 254-2-330480. *3819*

NAMENKUNDLICHE INFORMATIONEN.
Universitaet Leipzig, Abteilung Deutsch-Slavische Namenforschung, Augustusplatz 9, 04109 Leipzig, Germany. TEL 0341-7192973. *4093*

NAMES.
American Name Society, c/o Wayne H. Finke, Department of Modern Languages, Baruch College, Box G-1224, 17 Lexington Ave., New York, NY 10010-5526. TEL 212-387-1570. FAX 212-387-1591. *4093*

NANJING DAXUE XUEBAO (ZIRAN KEXUE BAN).
Nanjing Daxue Chubanshe, Hankou Lu, Nanjing, Jiangsu 210008, People's Republic of China. TEL 86-25-6634651. FAX 86-25-3302728. *6261*

NANJING TIEDAO YIXUEYUAN XUEBAO.
Nanjing Tiedao Yixueyuan, 87 Dingjiaqiao, Nanjing, Jiangsu 210009, People's Republic of China. TEL 301509. FAX 3317073. *4505*

NANKYOKU SHIRYO.
National Institute of Polar Research, Library, 9-10, Kaga 1-chome, Itabashi-ku, Tokyo 173, Japan. TEL 81-3-3962-2214. FAX 81-3-3962-2225. *3266*

NANOBIOLOGY.
Gordon and Breach Science Publishers, c/o International Publishers Distribution, P.O. Box 3054, Langhorne, PA 19047-3054. TEL 215-750-2642. FAX 215-750-6343. *764*

NANONEWS.
Superconductivity Publications, 828 Livingston Ave., North Brunswick, NJ 08902-2356. TEL 908-846-2002. FAX 908-846-2050. *5560*

NANOSTRUCTURED MATERIALS.
Elsevier Science Ltd., Pergamon, P.O. Box 800, Kidlington, Oxford OX5 1DX, England. TEL 44-1865-843000. FAX 44-1865-843010. *2739*

NANOTECHNOLOGY.
I O P Publishing Ltd., Techno House, Redcliffe Way, Bristol, Avon BS1 6NX, England. TEL 44-117-929-7481. FAX 44-117-929-4318. *5560*

NAPRSTKOVO MUZEUM ASIJSKYCH, AFRICKYCH A AMERICKYCH KULTUR. ANNALS.
Naprstkovo Muzeum Asijskych, Africkych a Americkych Kultur, Betlemske nam. 1, 110 00 Prague 1, Czech Republic. TEL 442-24214537. FAX 422-24226488. *317*

NARA IGAKU ZASSHI.
Nara Igakkai, Nara Medical University, Kashihara 634, Nara, Japan. TEL 07442-2-3051. *4505*

NARRATIVE.
Ohio State University Press, 1070 Carmack Rd., Columbus, OH 43210. TEL 614-292-6930. FAX 614-292-2065. *4240*

NASIONALE MUSEUM, BLOEMFONTEIN. NAVORSINGE.
Nasionale Museum, Bloemfontein, P.O. Box 266, Bloemfontein 9300, South Africa. TEL 27-51-4479609. FAX 27-51-4479681. *6261*

NASSAU COUNTY DENTAL SOCIETY. NEWSLETTER.
Nassau County Dental Society Headquarters, 377 Oak St., No. 205, Garden City, NY 11530-6543. TEL 516-764-9620. FAX 516-227-1114. *4648*

NASSAU REVIEW.
Nassau Community College, State University of New York, Department of English, Garden City, NY 11530. TEL 516-572-7792. *4240*

NASSAUISCHE ANNALEN.
Verein fuer Nassauische Altertumskunde und Geschichtsforschung e.V., Mosbacher Str. 55, 65187 Wiesbaden, Germany. TEL 49-611-881-0. FAX 49-611-881145. *3430*

NATAL MUSEUM. ANNALS.
Natal Museum, Private Bag 9070, Pietermaritzburg 3200, South Africa. TEL 27-331-451404. FAX 27-331-450561. *815*

NATAL MUSEUM JOURNAL OF HUMANITIES.
Natal Museum, Private Bag 9070, Pietermaritzburg 3200, South Africa. TEL 27-331-451404. FAX 27-331-450561. *365*

NATHANIEL HAWTHORNE REVIEW.
Nathaniel Hawthorne Society, Dept. of English, Duquesne University, Pittsburgh, PA 15282. TEL 412-396-5165. FAX 412-396-5197. *4240*

NATIONAL (OTTAWA, 1974).
Maclean-Hunter Ltd., Business Publications Division, 777 Bay St., 5th Fl., Toronto, ON M5W 1A7, Canada. TEL 416-593-3162. *3819*

NATIONAL ACADEMY OF SCIENCES OF THE UNITED STATES OF AMERICA. PROCEEDINGS.
National Academy of Sciences, Proceedings Office, 2101 Constitution Ave., N.W., Washington, DC 20418. TEL 202-625-4725. FAX 202-625-4747. *6261*

NATIONAL ASSOCIATION OF CONSERVATION DISTRICTS. TUESDAY LETTER.
National Association of Conservation Districts, 408 E. Main St., League City, TX 77574-0855. TEL 713-332-3402. FAX 713-332-5259. *2134*

NATIONAL BOTANIC GARDENS. OCCASIONAL PAPERS.
National Botanic Gardens, Glasnevin, Dublin 9, Ireland. TEL 8374388. FAX 8360080. *692*

NATIONAL BOTANICAL INSTITUTE. REVIEW.
National Botanical Institute (Claremont), Private Bag X7, Claremont 7735, South Africa. TEL 27-21-762-1166. FAX 27-21-762-3229. *692*

NATIONAL CANCER INSTITUTE. JOURNAL.
Oxford University Press, Oxford Journals, Walton St., Oxford OX2 6DP, England. TEL 44-1865-267907. FAX 44-1865-267485. *4760*

NATIONAL CANCER INSTITUTE. JOURNAL. MONOGRAPHS.
U.S. National Cancer Institute, R. A. Bloch International Cancer Information Center, Bldg. 82, Rm. 227, Bethesda, MD 20814. TEL 301-496-4907. *4760*

NATIONAL CONFERENCE ON WEIGHTS AND MEASURES. REPORT.
U.S. National Institute of Standards and Technology, Gaithersburg, MD 20899. TEL 301-975-3058. *5016*

NATIONAL CONTRACT MANAGEMENT JOURNAL.
National Contract Management Association, 1912 Woodford Rd., Vienna, VA 22182-3728. *1436*

NATIONAL FORUM OF APPLIED EDUCATIONAL RESEARCH JOURNAL.
National Forum Journals, 4000 Locke Ln. Tr. 9, Lake Charles, LA 70605-2244. TEL 318-474-6976. *2356*

NATIONAL FORUM OF EDUCATION ADMINISTRATION AND SUPERVISION JOURNAL.
National Forum Journals, 4000 Locke Ln., Tr. 9, Lake Charles, LA 70605-2244. TEL 318-474-6976. *2460*

NATIONAL FORUM OF INSTRUCTIONAL TECHNOLOGY JOURNAL.
National Forum Journals, 4000 Locke Ln., Tr. 9, Lake Charles, LA 70605-2244. TEL 318-474-6976. *2407*

NATIONAL FORUM OF SPECIAL EDUCATION JOURNAL.
National Forum Journals, 4000 Locke Ln., Tr. 9, Lake Charles, LA 70605-2244. TEL 318-474-6976. *2472*

NATIONAL FORUM TEACHER EDUCATION JOURNAL.
National Forum Journals, 4000 Locke Ln., Tr. 9, Lake Charles, LA 70605-2244. TEL 318-474-6976. *2356*

NATIONAL GEOGRAPHICAL JOURNAL OF INDIA.
National Geographical Society of India, Banaras Hindu University, Department of Geography, Varanasi 221005, Uttar Pradesh, India. TEL 0542-310291. FAX 0542-312059. *3267*

NATIONAL INSTITUTE OF MATERIALS AND CHEMICAL RESEARCH. JOURNAL.
National Institute of Materials and Chemical Research, Ibaraki 305, Japan. TEL 81-298-54-4410. FAX 81-298-54-6233. *1686*

NATIONAL INSTITUTE OF POLAR RESEARCH. MEMOIRS. SPECIAL ISSUE.
National Institute of Polar Research, Library, 9-10, Kaga 1-chome, Itabashi-ku, Tokyo 173, Japan. TEL 81-3-3962-2214. FAX 81-3-3962-2225. *2213*

NATIONAL INSTITUTE OF STANDARDS AND TECHNOLOGY. JOURNAL OF RESEARCH.
U.S. National Institute of Standards and Technology, U.S. Department of Commerce, Gaithersburg, MD 20899. TEL 301-975-3069. *5016*

NATIONAL INSTITUTE OF WATER AND ATMOSPHERIC RESEARCH. MEMOIR.
National Institute of Water and Atmospheric Research Ltd., P.O. Box 14-901, Kilbirnie, Wellington, New Zealand. TEL 64-4-386-0300. FAX 64-4-386-2153. *2301*

NATIONAL MEDICAL ASSOCIATION. JOURNAL.
Slack, Inc., 6900 Grove Rd., Thorofare, NJ 08086-9447. TEL 609-848-1000. FAX 609-853-5991. *4506*

NATIONAL MEDICAL JOURNAL OF INDIA.
All India Institute of Medical Sciences, New Delhi 110 029, India. TEL 91-11-6863002. FAX 91-11-6862663. *4506*

NATIONAL RESEARCH COUNCIL OF THAILAND. JOURNAL.
National Research Council of Thailand, 196 Phahonyothin Rd., Chatuchak, Bangkok 10900, Thailand. TEL 66-2-579-2690. FAX 66-2-5613049. *6262*

NATIONAL SECURITY REVIEW.
National Defense College of the Philippines, Fort Bonifacio, Rizal, Philippines. *5686*

NATIONAL TAIWAN UNIVERSITY. COLLEGE OF MEDICINE. MEMOIRS.
National Taiwan University, College of Medicine, No. 1 Jen-Ai Rd. Sec. 1, Taipei, Taiwan, Republic of China. TEL 02-3970800. *4506*

NATIONAL TECHNICAL REPORT.
Matsushita Electric Industrial Co., Ltd., 3-1-1 Yakumonaka-machi, Moriguchi-shi, Osaka 570, Japan. FAX 06-906-0177. *2714*

NATIONALISM & ETHNIC POLITICS.
Frank Cass, 890-900 Eastern Ave., Newbury Park, Ilford, Essex IG2 7HH, England. TEL 44-181-599-8866. FAX 44-181-599-0984. *5763*

NATIONALITIES PAPERS.
Carfax Publishing Co., P.O. Box 25, Agingdon, Oxon. OX14 3UE, England. TEL 44-1235-401000. FAX 44-1235-401550. *6336*

NATIONS AND NATIONALISM.
Cambridge University Press, Edinburgh Bldg., Shaftesbury Rd., Cambridge CB2 2RU, England. TEL 44-1223-312393. FAX 44-1223-315052. *5686*

NATIVE PEOPLES.
Media Concepts Group, Inc., 5333 N. Seventh St., Ste. C-224, Phoenix, AZ 85014. TEL 602-252-2236. FAX 602-265-3113. *2897*

NATIVE STUDIES REVIEW.
University of Saskatchewan, Native Studies Department, 104 McLean Hall, Saskatoon, SK S7N 0W0, Canada. TEL 306-966-6216. FAX 306-966-6242. *2897*

NATURAL AREAS JOURNAL.
Natural Areas Association, Box 900, Chesterfield, MO 63006-0900. TEL 314-878-7850. FAX 314-878-3410. *2811*

NATURAL HAZARDS.
Kluwer Academic Publishers, Postbus 17, 3300 AA Dordrecht, Netherlands. TEL 31-78-6392392. FAX 31-78-6392254. *2213*

NATURAL HISTORY.
American Museum of Natural History, Central Park W. at 79th St., New York, NY 10024-5192. TEL 212-769-5500. FAX 212-769-5511. *6263*

NATURAL HISTORY MUSEUM AND INSTITUTE, CHIBA. JOURNAL.
Natural History Museum and Institute, Chiba, 955-2 Aoba-cho, Chuo-ku, Chiba 260, Japan. TEL 81-43-265-3111. FAX 81-43-266-2481. *692*

NATURAL HISTORY MUSEUM AND INSTITUTE, CHIBA. JOURNAL. SPECIAL ISSUE.
Natural History Museum and Institute, Chiba, 955-2 Aoba-cho, Chuo-ku, Chiba 260, Japan. TEL 81-43-265-3111. FAX 81-43-266-2481. *693*

NATURAL HISTORY MUSEUM OF LOS ANGELES COUNTY. SCIENCE SERIES.
Natural History Museum of Los Angeles County, 900 Exposition Blvd., Los Angeles, CA 90007. TEL 213-744-3330. FAX 213-742-0730. *6263*

NATURAL HISTORY RESEARCH.
Natural History Museum and Institute, Chiba, 955-2 Aoba-cho, Chuo-ku, Chiba 260, Japan. TEL 81-43-265-3111. FAX 81-43-266-2481. *693*

NATURAL HISTORY SOCIETY OF NORTHUMBRIA. TRANSACTIONS.
Natural History Society of Northumbria, Hancock Museum, Newcastle upon Tyne NE2 4PT, England. TEL 44-191-232-6386. *6263*

NATURAL IMMUNITY.
S. Karger AG, Allschwilerstr. 10, P.O. Box, CH-4009 Basel, Switzerland. TEL 061-3061111. FAX 061-3061234. *764*

NATURAL LANGUAGE AND LINGUISTIC THEORY.
Kluwer Academic Publishers, Postbus 17, 3300 AA Dordrecht, Netherlands. TEL 31-78-6392392. FAX 31-78-6392254. *4094*

NATURAL LANGUAGE ENGINEERING.
Cambridge University Press, Edinburgh Bldg., Shaftesury Rd., Cambridge CB22RU, England. TEL 44-1223-312393. FAX 44-1223-315052. *2046*

NATURAL LANGUAGE SEMANTICS.
Kluwer Academic Publishers, Postbus 17, 3300 AA Dordrecht, Netherlands. TEL 31-78-6392392. FAX 31-78-6392254. *4094*

NATURAL RESOURCE MANAGEMENT AND POLICY.
Kluwer Academic Publishers, Postbus 17, 3300 AA Dordrecht, Netherlands. TEL 31-78-6392392. FAX 31-78-6392254. *2135*

NATURAL RESOURCES FORUM.
Butterworth - Heinemann, Part of the Reed Elsevier group, Linacre House, Jordan Hill, Oxford OX2 8DP, England. TEL 44-1865-310366. FAX 44-1865-310898. *3267*

NATURAL RESOURCES MANAGEMENT AND POLICY.
Kluwer Academic Publishers, Postbus 17, 3300 AA Dordrecht, Netherlands. TEL 31-78-6392392. FAX 31-78-6392254. *2812*

NATURAL TOX NS.
John Wiley & Sons, Inc., Journals, 605 Third Ave., New York, NY 10158. TEL 212-692-6645. FAX 212-850-6021. *1719*

NATURE.
Macmillan Magazines Ltd., 4 Porters South, Crinan St., London N1 9XW, England. TEL 44-171-8334000. FAX 44-171-8434640. *6263*

NATURE BIOTECHNOLOGY.
Nature Publishing Co. 345 Park Ave. S., 10th Fl., New York, NY 10010-1707. TEL 212-726-9200. FAX 212-696-9006. *664*

NATURE IN AVON: PROCEEDINGS OF THE BRISTOL NATURALISTS' SOCIETY.
Bristol Naturalists Society, City Museum, Bristol BS8 1RL, England. *6263*

NATURE MED CINE.
Macmillan Magazines Ltd. Porters South, Crinan St., London N1 9SQ, England. TEL 44-171-8434962. FAX 44-171-8434998. *4506*

NATURE STRUCTURAL BIOLOGY.
MacMillan Magazines Ltd., 1234 National Press Bldg., Washington, DC 20045. TEL 202-626-2513. FAX 202-628-1609. *597*

NAUTILUS (SANIBEL ISLAND).
Bailey-Matthews Shell Museum, Box 1580, Sanibel Island, FL 33957. TEL 941-395-2233. FAX 941-395-6706. *815*

NAVAL ENGINEERS JOURNAL.
American Society of Naval Engineers, Inc., 1452 Duke St., Alexandria, VA 22314. TEL 703-836-6727. FAX 703-836-7491. *2612*

NAVAL RESEARCH LOGISTICS: AN INTERNATIONAL JOURNAL.
John Wiley & Sons, Inc., Journals, 605 Third Ave., New York, NY 10158. TEL 212-850-6645. FAX 212-850-6021. *5055*

NAVY CHAPLAIN.
U.S. Navy, Bureau of Naval Personnel, Washington, DC 20370. TEL 804-444-7665. FAX 804-445-1006. *5041*

NAZAN STUDIES IN RELIGION & CULTURE.
University of California Press, 2120 Berkeley Way, Berkeley, CA 94720. TEL 510-642-4247. FAX 510-643-7127. *5487*

NEA PAPHOS.
Polska Akademia Nauk, Zaklad Archeologii Srodziemnomorskiej, Palac Kultury i Nauki, p. 2105, 00-901 Warsaw, Poland. TEL 48-22-248593. FAX 48-22-6207651. *365*

NEBRASKA ACADEMY OF SCIENCES. TRANSACTIONS.
Nebraska Academy of Sciences, 302 Morrill Hall, 14th & U Sts., Lincoln, NE 68538-0339. FAX 402-472-8899. *6265*

NEBRASKA MUSIC EDUCATOR.
Nebraska Music Educators Association, Box 83046, Lincoln, NE 68501-3046. TEL 402-435-6913 FAX 402-474-3250. *5182*

NEDERDUITSE GEREFORMEERDE TEOLOGIESE TYDSKRIF.
Nederduitse Gereformeerde Kerk Uitgewers, P.O. Box 4539, Cape Town, South Africa. TEL 27-21-215540. FAX 27-21-4191865. *6153*

NEDERLANDS ARCHIEF VOOR KERKGESCHIEDENIS.
E.J. Brill, P.O. Box 9000, 2300 PA Leiden, Netherlands. TEL 31-71-5353500. FAX 31-71-5317532. *6079*

NEDERLANDS TIJDSCHRIFT VOOR MEDISCHE MICROBIOLOGIE.
Misset P.O. Box 1110, 3600 EC Maarssen, Netherlands. TEL 31-346-558222. FAX 31-546-554287. *764*

NEDERLANDS TIJDSCHRIFT VOOR UROLOGIE.
Misset P.O. Box 1110, 3600 EC Maarssen, Netherlands. TEL 31-346-558222. FAX 31-346-554287. *4929*

NEDERLANDSE CHEMISCHE INDUSTRIE.
Vereniging van de Nederlandse Chemische Industrie, Postbus 443, 2260 AK Leidschendam, Netherlands. TEL 31-70 3378787. FAX 31-70-3208438. *2645*

NEDERLANDSE OUDHEDEN.
Rijksdienst voor het Oudheidkundig Bodemonderzoek te Amersfoort, Kerkstraat 1, 3811 CV Amersfoort, Netherlands. TEL 31-33-4634233. FAX 31-33-4653235. *365*

NEGOTIATION JOURNAL.
Plenum Publishing Corp., 233 Spring St., New York, NY 10013-1578. TEL 212-620-8000. FAX 212-463-0742. *5763*

NEGRO EDUCATIONAL REVIEW.
Negro Educational Review, Inc., Box 70895, Florida A & M University, Jacksonville, FL 32307. TEL 904-599-8446. FAX 904-599-8446. *2356*

NEMATOLOGIA BRASILEIRA.
Sociedade Brasileira de Nematologia, Secao de Nematologia, Caixa Postal 28 13020-902 Campinas SP, Brazil. TEL 55-192-415188. FAX 55-192-314943. *815*

NEMATOLOGICA.
E.J. Brill, P.O. Box 9000, 2300 PA Leiden, Netherlands. TEL 31-71-5353500. FAX 31-71-5317532. *815*

NEMOURIA: OCCASIONAL PAPERS OF THE DELAWARE MUSEUM OF NATURAL HISTORY.
Delaware Museum of Natural History, Box 3937, Wilmington, DE 19807-0937. TEL 302-658 9111. FAX 302-658-2610. *315*

NEOMETAPHYSICAL DIGEST.
Society of Metaphysicians Ltd., Archers' Ct., Stonestile Ln., The Ridge, Hastings, E. Sussex TN35 4PG, England. TEL 44-1424-751577. FAX 44-1424-722387. *535*

NEONATAL INTENSIVE CARE.
Goldstein and Associates Publishing, Inc., 1150 Yale St., Ste. 12, Santa Monica, CA 90403-4738. TEL 213-828-1309. *4742*

NEONATAL NETWORK.
Neonatal Network, 1304 Southpoint Blvd., Ste. 280, Petaluma, CA 94954-6859. TEL 707-762-2646. FAX 707-762 0401. *4721*

NEOPHILOLOGUS.
Kluwer Academic Publishers, Postbus 17, 3300 AA Dordrecht, Netherlands. TEL 31-78-6392392. FAX 31-78-6392254. *4241*

NEOTESTAMENTICA.
New Testament Society of South Africa, c/o Department of New Testament, University of the Orange Free State, P.O. Box 339, Bloemfontein 9300, South Africa. TEL 27-51-4012667. FAX 27-51-489203. *6079*

NEPAL MEDICAL ASSOCIATION. JOURNAL.
Nepal Medical Association, Siddhi Sadan, Exhibition Road, G.P.O. Box 189, Kathmandu, Nepal. *4507*

NEPHROLOGY NEWS & ISSUES.
Nephrology News & Issues, Inc., 15150 N. Hayden Rd., Ste. 101, Scottsdale, AZ 85260-2514. TEL 602-443-4635. FAX 602-443-4528. *4929*

NEPHROLOGY NEWS & ISSUES - EUROPE.
Nephrology News & Issues, Inc., 15150 N. Hayden Rd., Ste. 101, Scottsdale, AZ 85260-2514. TEL 602-443-4635. FAX 602-443-4528. *4929*

NEPHRON.
S. Karger AG, Allschwilerstr. 10, P.O. Box, CH-4009 Basel, Switzerland. TEL 061-3061111. FAX 061-3061234. *4929*

NESTLE NUTRITION SERIES.
Lippincott - Raven Publishers 227 E. Washington Sq., Philadelphia, PA 19106. TEL 215-238-4200. FAX 215-238-4235. *5237*

NETHERLANDS INSTITUTE OF ARCHAEOLOGY AND ARABIC STUDIES IN CAIRO. PUBLICATIONS.
E.J. Brill, P.O. Box 9000, 2300 PA Leiden, Netherlands. TEL 31-71-5353500. FAX 31-71-5317532. *365*

NETHERLANDS INTERNATIONAL LAW REVIEW.
Kluwer Law International Postbus 85889, 2508 CN The Hague, Netherlands. TEL 31-70-3081500. FAX 31-70-3081515. *3939*

NETHERLANDS JOURNAL OF MEDICINE.
Elsevier Science B.V., P.O. Box 211, 1000 AE Amsterdam, Netherlands. TEL 31-20-4853911. FAX 31-20-4853598. *4707*

NETHERLANDS JOURNAL OF ZOOLOGY.
Nederlands Diekundige Vereniging, c/o Netherlands Instituut van Biologen, Nicolaas Beetsstraat 221, 3511 HG Utrecht, Netherlands. TEL 31-30-369244. *816*

NETHERLANDS MILK AND DAIRY JOURNAL.
Netherlands Association for Advancement of Dairy Science (NIZO), P.O. Box 20, 6710 BA Ede, Netherlands. TEL 31-318-659511. FAX 31-318-659522. *253*

NETHERLANDS QUARTERLY OF HUMAN RIGHTS.
Kluwer Law International Postbus 85889, 2508 CN The Hague, Netherlands. TEL 31-70-3081500. FAX 31-70-3081515. *3939*

NETHERLANDS YEARBOOK OF INTERNATIONAL LAW.
Martinus Nijhoff Publishers, Human Rights and International Law Postbus 163, 3300 AD Dordrecht, Netherlands. TEL 31-78-334267. FAX 31-78-334254. *3939*

NETSU BUSSEI.
Nihon Netsu Bussei Gakkai, Dept. of Mechanical Engineering, Nagaoka University of Technology, 1603-1 Kamitomioka-cho, Nagaoka-shi, Niigata-ken 940, Japan. TEL 81-258-46-6000. FAX 81-258-46-6972. *5586*

NETWORKS.
John Wiley & Sons, Inc., Journals, 605 Third Ave., New York, NY 10158. TEL 212-850-6645. FAX 212-850-6021. *4411*

NEUMOLOGIA Y CIRUGIA DE TORAX.
Obsidiana Editores, S.A., Czda. de Tlalpan 2365, Col. Ciudad Jardin, 04370 Mexico DF, Mexico. TEL 6899133. *4915*

NEURAL COMPUTATION.
M I T Press, 55 Hayward St., Cambridge, MA 02142. TEL 617-253-2889. FAX 617-577-1545. *2010*

NEURAL NETWORK WORLD.
V S P, P.O. Box 346, 3700 AH Zeist, Netherlands. TEL 31-30-6925790. FAX 31-30-6932081. *2010*

NEURAL NETWORKS.
Elsevier Science Ltd., Pergamon, P.O. Box 800, Kidlington, Oxford OX5 1DX, England. TEL 44-1865-843000. FAX 44-1865-843010. *2010*

NEURO-OPHTHALMOLOGY.
Aeolus Press Postbus 740, 4116 ZJ Buren, Netherlands. TEL 31-344-572055. FAX 31-344-572562. *4853*

NEUROBIOLOGIA.
Sociedade Editora da Revista Neurobiologia, Caixa Postal 651, 50001-970 Recife PE, Brazil. TEL 55-81-268-5495. FAX 39-55-81-2224359. *4853*

NEUROBIOLOGY OF AGING.
Elsevier Science Inc., Box 945, New York, NY 10159-0945. TEL 212-633-3730. FAX 212-633-3680. *791*

NEUROBIOLOGY OF DISEASE.
Academic Press, Inc., Journal Division, 525 B St., Ste. 1900, San Diego, CA 92101-4495. TEL 619-230-1840. FAX 619-699-6800. *4853*

NEUROBIOLOGY OF LEARNING AND MEMORY.
Academic Press, Inc., Journal Division, 525 B. St., Ste. 1900, San Diego, CA 92101-4495. TEL 619-230-1840. FAX 619-699-6800. *4853*

NEUROCHEMICAL RESEARCH.
Plenum Publishing Corp., 233 Spring St., New York, NY 10013-1578. TEL 212-620-8000. FAX 212-463-0742. *4853*

NEUROCHEMISTRY INTERNATIONAL.
Elsevier Science Ltd., Pergamon, P.O. Box 800, Kidlington, Oxford OX5 1DX, England. TEL 44-1865-843000. FAX 44-1865-843010. *4854*

NEUROCOMPUTING.
North-Holland P.O. Box 211, 1000 AE Amsterdam, Netherlands. TEL 31-20-4853911. FAX 31-20-4853598. *2010*

NEURODEGENERATION.
Academic Press, Inc., Journal Division, 525 B St., Ste. 1900, San Diego, CA 92101-4495. TEL 619-230-1840. FAX 619-699-6800. *4854*

NEUROENDOCRINE PERSPECTIVES.
Springer-Verlag, 175 Fifth Ave., New York, NY 10010. TEL 212-460-1500. FAX 212-473-6272. *4854*

NEUROENDOCRINOLOGY.
S. Karger AG, Allschwilerstr. 10, P.O. Box, CH-4009 Basel, Switzerland. TEL 061-3061111. FAX 061-3061234. *4673*

NEUROEPIDEMIOLOGY.
S. Karger AG, Allschwilerstr. 10, P.O. Box, CH-4009 Basel, Switzerland. TEL 061-3061111. FAX 061-3061234. *4854*

NEUROGASTROENTEROLOGY AND MOTILITY.
Blackwell Science Ltd., Osney Mead, Oxford OX2 OEL, England. TEL 44-1865-206206. FAX 44-1865-721205. *4695*

NEUROGENETICS.
Oxford University Press, Oxford Journals, Walton St., Oxford OX2 6DP, England. TEL 44-1865-267907. FAX 44-1865-267485. *4854*

NEUROIMAGE.
Academic Press, Inc., Journal Division, 525 B St., Ste. 1900, San Diego, CA 92101-4495. TEL 619-230-1840. FAX 619-699-6800. *4854*

NEUROIMMUNOMODULATION.
S. Karger AG, Allschwilerstr. 10, P.O. Box, CH-4009 Basel, Switzerland. TEL 061-3061111. FAX 061-3061234. *4586*

NEUROLOGIA MEDICO-CHIRURGICA.
SciMed Publications, c/o Sumitomo Seimei, Akasaka Bldg., 3-3-3, Akasaka, Minato-ku, Tokyo 107, Japan. *4854*

NEUROLOGICAL RESEARCH.
Forefront Publishing Group, 5 River Rd., Ste. 113, Wilton, CT 06897-4069. TEL 203-834-0631. FAX 203-834-0940. *4855*

NEUROLOGY REVIEWS.
Partners in Medical Communication, 4 Brighton Rd., Clifton, NJ 07012. TEL 201-913-1000. FAX 201-916-0021. *4855*

NEUROMUSCULAR DISORDERS.
Elsevier Science Ltd., Pergamon, P.O. Box 800, Kidlington, Oxford OX5 1DX, England. TEL 44-1865-843000. FAX 44-1865-843010. *4855*

NEUROPATHOLOGY AND APPLIED NEUROBIOLOGY.
Blackwell Science Ltd., Osney Mead, Oxford OX2 OEL, England. TEL 44-1865-206206. FAX 44-1865-721205. *4855*

NEUROPHARMACOLOGY.
Elsevier Science Ltd., Pergamon, P.O. Box 800, Kidlington, Oxford OX5 1DX, England. TEL 44-1865-843000. FAX 44-1865-843010. *5430*

NEUROPHYSIOLOGIE CLINIQUE.
Editions Scientifiques et Medicales Elsevier, 141 rue de Javel, 75747 Paris, France. TEL 33-1-45589026. FAX 33-1-45589421. *4855*

NEUROPHYSIOLOGY.
Plenum Publishing Corp., Consultants Bureau, 233 Spring St., New York, NY 10013-1578. TEL 212-620-8468. FAX 212-463-0742. *4855*

NEUROPROTECTION.
I O S Press, Van Diemenstraat 94, 1013 CN Amsterdam, Netherlands. TEL 31-20-6382189. FAX 31-20-6203419. *4856*

NEUROPSYCHIATRY, NEUROPSYCHOLOGY AND BEHAVIORAL NEUROLOGY.
Lippincott - Raven Publishers 227 E. Washington Sq., Philadelphia, PA 19106. TEL 215-238-4200. *4856*

NEUROPSYCHOBIOLOGY.
S. Karger AG, Allschwilerstr. 10, P.O. Box, CH-4009 Basel, Switzerland. TEL 061-3061111. FAX 061-3061234. *4856*

NEUROPSYCHOLOGIA.
Elsevier Science Ltd., Pergamon, P.O. Box 800, Kidlington, Oxford OX5 1DX, England. TEL 44-1865-843000. FAX 44-1865-843010. *4856*

NEUROPSYCHOLOGY.
American Psychological Association, 750 First St., N.E., Washington, DC 20002-4242. TEL 202-336-5600. FAX 202-336-5568. *4856*

NEUROPSYCHOLOGY AND COGNITION.
Kluwer Academic Publishers, Postbus 17, 3300 AA Dordrecht, Netherlands. TEL 31-78-6392392. FAX 31-78-6392254. *4856*

NEUROPSYCHOLOGY, DEVELOPMENT AND COGNITION. SECTION A: JOURNAL OF CLINICAL AND EXPERIMENTAL NEUROPSYCHOLOGY.
Swets & Zeitlinger bv, P.O. Box 825, 2160 SZ Lisse, Netherlands. TEL 31-252-435111. FAX 31-252-415888. *5867*

NEUROPSYCHOLOGY, DEVELOPMENT AND COGNITION. SECTION B: AGING, NEUROPSYCHOLOGY AND COGNITION.
Swets & Zeitlinger bv, P.O. Box 825, 2160 SZ Lisse, Netherlands. TEL 31-252-435111. FAX 31-252-415888. *5867*

NEUROPSYCHOLOGY REVIEW.
Plenum Publishing Corp., 233 Spring St., New York, NY 10013-1578. TEL 212-620-8000. FAX 212-463-0742. *4856*

NEUROPSYCHOPHARMACOLOGY.
Elsevier Science Inc., Box 945, New York, NY 10159-0945. TEL 212-633-3730. FAX 212-633-3680. *4856*

NEUROREHABILITATION.
Elsevier Science Ireland Ltd., P.O. Box 85, Limerick, Ireland. FAX 353-61-472144. *4857*

NEUROSCIENCE.
Elsevier Science Ltd., Pergamon, P.O. Box 800, Kidlington, Oxford OX5 1DX, England. TEL 44-1865-843000. FAX 44-1865-843010. *4857*

NEUROSCIENCE AND BEHAVIORAL PHYSIOLOGY.
Plenum Publishing Corp., Consultants Bureau, 233 Spring St., New York, NY 10013-1578. TEL 212-620-8468. FAX 212-463-0742. *4857*

NEUROSCIENCE AND BIOBEHAVIORAL REVIEWS.
Elsevier Science Ltd., Pergamon, P.O. Box 800, Kidlington, Oxford OX5 1DX, England. TEL 44-1865-843000. FAX 44-1865-843010. *4857*

NEUROSCIENCE LETTERS.
Elsevier Science Ireland Ltd., P.O. Box 85, Limerick, Ireland. TEL 353-61-471944. FAX 353-61-472144. *4857*

NEUROSCIENCE RESEARCH.
Elsevier Science Ireland Ltd., P.O. Box 85, Limerick, Ireland. TEL 353-61-471944. FAX 353-61-472144. *4857*

NEUROSCIENCE RESEARCH COMMUNICATONS.
John Wiley & Sons Ltd., Journals, Baffins Ln., Chichester, W. Sussex PO19 1UD, England. TEL 44-1243-779777. FAX 44-1243-843232. *4857*

NEUROSURGERY (BALTIMORE).
Williams & Wilkins, 351 W. Camden St., Baltimore, MD 21201. TEL 410-528-4000. FAX 410-528-4312. *4858*

NEUROSURGERY QUARTERLY.
Lippincott - Raven Publishers 227 E. Washington Sq., Philadelphia, PA 19106. TEL 215-238-4200. *4915*

NEUROTOXICOLOGY AND TERATOLOGY.
Elsevier Science Inc., Box 945, New York, NY 10159-0945. TEL 212-633-3730. FAX 212-633-3680. *4858*

NEUROUROLOGY AND URODYNAMICS.
John Wiley & Sons, Inc., Journals, 605 Third Ave., New York, NY 10158. TEL 212-850-6645. FAX 212-850-6021. *4929*

NEUTRON NEWS.
Gordon and Breach Science Publishers, c/o International Publishers Distributor, P.O. Box 3054, Langhorne, PA 19047-3054. TEL 215-750-2642. FAX 215-750-6343. *5596*

NEVADA LAWYER.
State Bar of Nevada, 1325 Airmotive Way, Ste. 140, Reno, NV 89502-3239. TEL 702-329-4100. FAX 702-329-0522. *3821*

THE NEW ADVOCATE.
Christopher - Gordon Publishers, Inc., 480 Washington St., Norwood, MA 02062. TEL 617-762-5577. *4241*

NEW ARCADIAN JOURNAL.
New Arcadian Press, 13 Graham Grove, Burley, Leeds LS4 2NF, England. TEL 44-113-2304608. FAX 44-1274-753236. *399*

NEW ASTRONOMY.
Elsevier Science B.V., P.O. Box 211, 1000 AE Amsterdam, Netherlands. TEL 31-20-4853911. FAX 31-20-4853705. *484*

NEW CANADIAN.
Japan Communications Inc., 524 Front St. W. 2nd Fl., Toronto, ON M5V 1B8, Canada. TEL 416-593-6118. FAX 416-593-1871. *2898*

NEW CHURCH LIFE.
General Church of the New Jerusalem, Box 277, Bryn Athyn, PA 19009. TEL 215-947-4200. FAX 215-938-2616. *6209*

NEW CITY (LONDON).
Mariapolis Ltd. Focolare Movement, 57 Twyford Ave., London W3 9PZ, England. TEL 44-181-993-6944. FAX 44-181-993-6944. *6080*

NEW CLINICAL APPLICATIONS. DERMATOLOGY.
Kluwer Academic Publishers, Postbus 17, 3300 AA Dordrecht, Netherlands. TEL 31-78-6392392. FAX 31-78-6392254. *4929*

NEW CLINICAL APPLICATIONS. NEPHROLOGY.
Kluwer Academic Publishers, Postbus 17, 3300 AA Dordrecht, Netherlands. TEL 31-78-6392392. FAX 31-78-6392254. *4929*

NEW CLINICAL APPLICATIONS IN GASTROENTEROLOGY.
Kluwer Academic Publishers, Postbus 17, 3300 AA Dordrecht, Netherlands. TEL 31-78-6392392. FAX 31-78-6392254. *4695*

NEW CLINICAL APPLICATIONS IN PAEDIATRICS.
Kluwer Academic Publishers, Postbus 17, 3300 AA Dordrecht, Netherlands. TEL 31-78-6392392. FAX 31-78-6392254. *4809*

NEW CLINICAL APPLICATIONS IN RADIOLOGY.
Kluwer Academic Publishers, Postbus 17, 3300 AA Dordrecht, Netherlands. TEL 31-78-6392392. FAX 31-78-6392254. *4881*

NEW COMPREHENSIVE BIOCHEMISTRY.
Elsevier Science B.V., Books Division, P.O. Box 211, 1000 AE Amsterdam, Netherlands. TEL 31-20-4853911. FAX 31-20-4853705. *646*

NEW DIRECTIONS IN CULTURAL ANALYSIS.
University of California Press, 2120 Berkeley Way, Berkeley, CA 94720. TEL 510-642-4247. FAX 510-643-7127. *3620*

NEW ENGLAND CLASSICAL NEWSLETTER & JOURNAL.
Classical Association of New England, Greek and Roman Studies, Fairfield University, Fairfield, CT 06430. TEL 203-254-4000. *1824*

NEW ENGLAND JOURNAL OF HISTORY.
New England History Teachers Association, Home Office, Bentley College, Waltham, MA 02254. TEL 617-441-3181. *3479*

NEW ENGLAND JOURNAL OF MEDICINE.
Massachusetts Medical Society, 10 Shattuck St., Boston, MA 02115. TEL 617-734-9800. FAX 617-893-8103. *4507*

NEW ENGLAND JOURNAL OF OPTOMETRY.
New England Council of Optometrists, 101 Tremont St., Boston, MA 02108. TEL 617-542-1233. FAX 617-542-4574. *4773*

NEW ENGLAND QUARTERLY.
New England Quarterly, Inc., Meserve Hall, 2nd Fl., Northeastern University, Boston, MA 02115. TEL 617-373-2734. FAX 617-373-2661. *4242*

NEW ENGLAND READING ASSOCIATION. JOURNAL.
New England Reading Association, Box 997, Portland, ME 04104-0997. TEL 207-772-6540. *2357*

NEW ENGLAND THEATRE JOURNAL.
New England Theatre Conference, c/o Department of Theatre, Northeastern University, 360 Huntington Ave., Boston, MA 02115. TEL 617-424-9275. *6699*

NEW EQUITABLE LIFE TAX GUIDE.
Blackwell Publishers Ltd., 108 Cowley Rd., Oxford OX4 1JF, England. TEL 44-1865-791100. FAX 44-1865-791347. *1556*

NEW ERA IN EDUCATION.
World Education Fellowship, University of Hertfordshire, Wall Hall, Aldenham, Watford, Herts WD2 8AT, England. TEL 44-1707-285677. FAX 44-1707-285616. *2357*

NEW FARMER AND GROWER.
British Organic Farmers, 86-88 Colston St., Bristol, Avon BS1 5BB, England. TEL 44-117-929-9666. FAX 44-117-925-2504. *138*

NEW FORESTS.
Kluwer Academic Publishers, Postbus 17, 3300 AA Dordrecht, Netherlands. TEL 31-78-6392392. FAX 31-78 6392254. *3021*

NEW FORMATIONS.
Lawrence & Wishart, 144a Old South Lambeth Rd., London SW8 1XX, England. TEL 0171-820-9281. FAX 0171-587-0469. *4156*

NEW HAMPSHIRE. AGRICULTURAL EXPERIMENT STATION. DURHAM. RESEARCH REPORTS.
University of New Hampshire, Agricultural Experiment Station, Durham, NH 03824. TEL 603-862-1234. *138*

NEW HAVEN STUDIES IN INTERNATIONAL LAW AND WORLD PUBLIC ORDER.
Kluwer Academic Publishers, Postbus 17, 3300 AA Dordrecht, Netherlands. TEL 31-78-6392392. FAX 31-78-6392254. *3939*

THE NEW HISTORICISM: STUDIES IN CULTURAL POETICS.
University of California Press, 2120 Berkeley Way, Berkeley, CA 94720. TEL 510-642-4247. FAX 510-643-7127. *4242*

NEW HORIZONS IN EDUCATION.
World Education Fellowship (Australia), 21 Ridgway Dr., Flagstaff Hill, S.A. 5159, Australia. TEL 61-8-2703541. *2357*

NEW HORIZONS IN THERAPEUTICS: SMITH, KLINE & FRENCH LABORATORIES RESEARCH SYMPOSIA SERIES.
Plenum Publishing Corp., 233 Spring St., New York, NY 10013-1578. TEL 212-620-8000. FAX 212-463-0742. *4507*

NEW IDEAS IN PSYCHOLOGY.
Elsevier Science Ltd., Pergamon, P.O. Box 800, Kidlington, Oxford OX5 1DX, England. TEL 44-1865-843000. FAX 44-1865-843010. *5867*

NEW JERSEY DENTAL ASSOCIATION. JOURNAL.
New Jersey Dental Association, 1 Dental Plaza, N. Brunswick, NJ 08902. TEL 903-821-9400. FAX 908-821-1082. *4548*

NEW JERSEY LAW JOURNAL.
American Lawyer Media L.P. (Newark), 238 Mulberry St., Box 20081, Newark, NJ 07101-6081. TEL 201-642-0075. FAX 201-642-0920. *3822*

NEW JERSEY MEDICINE.
Medical Society of New Jersey, 2 Princess Rd., Trenton, NJ 08648. TEL 609-393-7196. FAX 609-393-3759. *4507*

NEW JERSEY WASTEWATER TREATMENT TRUST. ANNUAL REPORT.
New Jersey Wastewater Treatment Trust, CN 425, Trenton, NJ 08625. TEL 609-292-1840. FAX 609-633-8165. *2854*

NEW LAUREL REVIEW.
Smoke Bend Publishing, 828 Lesseps St., New Orleans, LA 70117. TEL 504-947-6001. *4242*

NEW LITERATURES REVIEW.
University of Wollongong, Department of English, Northfields Ave., Wollongong, N.S.W. 2522, Australia. TEL 61-42-23677 FAX 61-42-214471. *4242*

NEW MEXICO GEOLOGICAL SOCIETY. GUIDEBOOK, FIELD CONFERENCE.
New Mexico Geological Society, Inc., Campus Station, Socorro, NM 87801. TEL 505-835-5410. *2253*

NEW NOVEL REVIEW.
Elmira College, Humanities Department, Elmira, NY 14901. TEL 607-735-1898. FAX 607-735-1758. *4242*

NEW OBSERVATIONS.
New Observations Ltd., 611 Broadway, No. 701, New York, NY 10012. TEL 212-677-8561. *444*

NEW ORLEANS REVIEW.
Loyola University, Box 195, New Orleans, LA 70118. TEL 504-865-2295. FAX 504-865-2294. *4242*

THE NEW PLANTSMAN.
Royal Horticultural Society, 80 Vincent Sq., London SW1P 2PE, England. TEL 44-171-834-4333. FAX 44-171-3630-6050. *3062*

NEW POLITICAL SCIENCE.
Caucus for a New Political Science, c/o John C. Berg, Treas., Department of Government, Suffolk University, Boston, MA 02103-2770. TEL 617-573-8126. FAX 617-367-4623. *5687*

NEW SYNTHESE HISTORICAL LIBRARY.
Kluwer Academic Publishers, Postbus 17, 3300 AA Dordrecht, Netherlands. TEL 31-78-6392392. FAX 31-78-6392254. *5487*

NEW TECHNOLOGY IN THE HUMAN SERVICES.
Computers in Teaching Initiative, Centre for Human Service Technology, University of Southampton, Department of Social Work Studies, Southampton, Hants. S09 5NH, England. TEL 44-1703-593536. FAX 44-1703-592779. *6443*

NEW TECHNOLOGY, WORK & EMPLOYMENT.
Blackwell Publishers Ltd., 108 Cowley Rd., Oxford OX4 1JF, England. TEL 44-1865-791100. FAX 44-1865-791347. *1389*

NEW TESTAMENT TOOLS AND STUDIES.
E.J. Brill, P.O. Box 9000, 2300 PA Leiden, Netherlands. TEL 31-71-5353500. FAX 31-71-5317532. *6080*

NEW TRENDS IN LIPID MEDIATORS RESEARCH.
S. Karger AG, Allschwilerstr. 10, P.O. Box, CH-4009 Basel, Switzerland. TEL 061-3061111. FAX 061-3061234. *5430*

NEW YORK ACADEMY OF SCIENCES. ANNALS.
New York Academy of Sciences, 2 E. 63rd St., New York, NY 10021. TEL 212-838-0230. *6266*

NEW YORK ACADEMY OF SCIENCES. TRANSACTIONS.
New York Academy of Sciences, 2 E. 63rd St., New York, NY 10021. *6266*

NEW YORK BOTANICAL GARDEN. MEMOIRS.
New York Botanical Garden, Scientific Publications Department, Bronx, NY 10458-5126. TEL 718-817-8721. FAX 718-817-8842. *693*

NEW YORK ECONOMIC REVIEW.
New York State Economic Association, c/o William O'Dea, Ed., Dept. of Economics and Business, SUNY-Oneonta, Oneonta, NY 13820. TEL 607-436-2127. FAX 607-436-2107. *1224*

NEW YORK ENTOMOLOGICAL SOCIETY. JOURNAL.
New York Entomological Society, c/o American Museum of Natural History, Central Park West at 79th St., New York, NY 10024-5192. TEL 212-769-5613. FAX 212-769-5277. *733*

NEW YORK FOLKLORE.
New York Folklore Society, Box 130, Newfield, NY 14867. TEL 607-273-9137. FAX 607-273-9137. *2954*

NEW YORK GENEALOGICAL AND BIOGRAPHICAL RECORD.
New York Genealogical and Biographical Society, 122 E. 58th St., New York, NY 10022-1939. TEL 212-755-8532. FAX 212-754-4218. *3095*

NEW YORK INTERNATIONAL LAW REVIEW.
New York State Bar Association, International Law and Practice Section, 1 Elk St., Albany, NY 12207-1096. TEL 518-463-3200. FAX 518-463-8844. *3939*

NEW YORK PSYCHOANALYTIC INSTITUTE. KRIS STUDY GROUP. MONOGRAPHS.
International Universities Press, Inc., 59 Boston Post Rd., Box 1524, Madison, CT 06443-1524. TEL 203-245-4000. *5867*

NEW YORK STATE NURSES ASSOCIATION. JOURNAL.
New York State Nurses Association, 46 Cornell Rd., Latham, NY 12110-1403. TEL 518-782-9400. FAX 518-782-9533. *4721*

NEW YORK UNIVERSITY JOURNAL OF INTERNATIONAL LAW AND POLITICS.
New York University, Law Publications, 110 W. Third St., New York, NY 10012. TEL 212-998-6520. FAX 212-995-4032. *3939*

NEW ZEALAND BUSINESS LAW QUARTERLY.
Brooker's Limited, Level 1 - Telecom Networks House, 68-86 Jervois Quay, Wellington, New Zealand. TEL 64-4-4998178. FAX 64-4-4998173. *3905*

NEW ZEALAND ECONOMIC PAPERS.
New Zealand Association of Economists, P.O. Box 568, Wellington, New Zealand. TEL 64-3-4798655. FAX 64-3-4798174. *947*

NEW ZEALAND JOURNAL OF AGRICULTURAL RESEARCH.
S I R Publishing, P.O. Box 399, Wellington, New Zealand. TEL 64-4-472-7421. FAX 64-4-473-1841. *138*

NEW ZEALAND JOURNAL OF BOTANY.
S I R Publishing, P.O. Box 399, Wellington, New Zealand. TEL 64-4-472-7421. FAX 64-4-473-1841. *693*

NEW ZEALAND JOURNAL OF CROP AND HORTICULTURAL SCIENCE.
S I R Publishing, P.O. Box 399, Wellington, New Zealand. TEL 64-4-472-7421. FAX 64-4-473-1841. *138*

NEW ZEALAND JOURNAL OF ECOLOGY.
New Zealand Ecological Society, Inc., P.O. Box 25-178, Christchurch, New Zealand. TEL 64-3-3256701. FAX 64-3-3252418. *597*

NEW ZEALAND JOURNAL OF FORESTRY SCIENCE.
Forest Research Institute, Private Bag 3020, Rotorua, New Zealand. TEL 64-7-347-5889. FAX 64-7-347-9380. *3022*

NEW ZEALAND JOURNAL OF FRENCH STUDIES.
Massey University, Department of European Languages, Private Bag 11-222, Palmerston North, New Zealand. TEL 64-6-3505237. FAX 64-6-3505633. *4243*

NEW ZEALAND JOURNAL OF GEOLOGY AND GEOPHYSICS.
S I R Publishing, P.O. Box 399, Wellington, New Zealand. TEL 64-4-472-7421. FAX 64-4-473-1841. *2253*

NEW ZEALAND JOURNAL OF MARINE AND FRESHWATER RESEARCH.
S I R Publishing, P.O. Box 399, Wellington, New Zealand. TEL 64-4-472-7421. FAX 64-4-473-1841. *2301*

NEW ZEALAND JOURNAL OF SPORTS MEDICINE.
Sports Medicine New Zealand, 96 Anzac Ave., P.O. Box 6398, Dunedin, New Zealand. TEL 64-3-4886390. FAX 64-3-4792557. *4899*

NEW ZEALAND JOURNAL OF TAXATION LAW AND POLICY.
Brooker's Limited, Level 1 - Telecom Networks House, 68-86 Jervois Quay, Wellington, New Zealand. TEL 64-4998178. FAX 64-4-4998173. *1556*

NEW ZEALAND JOURNAL OF ZOOLOGY.
S I R Publishing, P.O. Box 399, Wellington, New Zealand. TEL 64-4-472-7421. FAX 64-4-473-1841. *816*

NEW ZEALAND LAW REVIEW.
Legal Research Foundation, University of Auckland, Private Bag, Auckland, New Zealand. TEL 64-9-3099540. FAX 64-9-3737473. *3825*

NEW ZEALAND NATURAL SCIENCES.
University of Canterbury, Zoology Department, Private Bag 4800, Christchurch 1, New Zealand. TEL 64-3-364-2860. FAX 64-3-364-2024. *598*

NEW ZEALAND SOCIETY OF PERIODONTOLOGY. JOURNAL.
New Zealand Society of Periodontology, P.O. Box 647, Dunedin, New Zealand. TEL 64-3-4797-108. FAX 64-3-4790-673. *4649*

NEW ZEALAND STATISTICIAN.
New Zealand Statistical Association (Inc.), P.O. Box 1731, Wellington, New Zealand. TEL 64-6-350-4265. FAX 64-6-350-5611. *6621*

NEW ZEALAND VALUERS' JOURNAL.
New Zealand Institute of Valuers, P.O. Box 27-146, Willis St., Wellington, New Zealand. TEL 64-4-385-8436. FAX 64-4-382-9214. *6032*

NEW ZEALAND VETERINARY JOURNAL.
New Zealand Veterinary Association, P.O. Box 27-499, Wellington, New Zealand. TEL 64-4-471-0484. FAX 64-4-471-0494. *6951*

A NEWBERRY NEWSLETTER.
Newberry Library, 60 W. Walton St., Chicago, IL 60610. TEL 312-255-3548. *4016*

NEWFOUNDLAND. DEPARTMENT OF NATURAL RESOURCES. GEOLOGICAL SURVEY BRANCH. ORE HORIZONS.
Department of Natural Resources, P.O. Box 8700, St. John's, NF A1B 4J6, Canada. TEL 709-729-3159. FAX 709-729-3493. *5074*

NEWFOUNDLAND. DEPARTMENT OF NATURAL RESOURCES. GEOLOGICAL SURVEY. CURRENT RESEARCH.
Department of Mines and Energy, Geological Survey, P.O. Box 8700, St. John's, NF A1B 4J6, Canada. TEL 709-729-3159. FAX 709-729-3493. *5074*

NEWFOUNDLAND STUDIES.
Memorial University of Newfounland, Department of English, St. John's, NF A1C 5S7, Canada. TEL 709-737-2144. FAX 709-737-4342. *3123*

NEWPORT TRAVELER.
Traveler Publications, 172 Bellevue Ave., Ste. 319, Newport, RI 02840. TEL 401-847-0089. FAX 401-847-5267. *6903*

NEWS IN NUTRITION.
Australian Nutrition Foundation, P.O. Box 509, Ashgrove, Qld. 4060, Australia. TEL 61-7-33667375. FAX 61-7-33667379. *5238*

NEWS IN PHYSIOLOGICAL SCIENCES.
American Physiological Society, 9650 Rockville Pike, Bethesda, MD 20814. TEL 301-530-7164. FAX 301-571-3813. *791*

NEWS 3X-400.
Duke Communications International, 221 E. 29th St., Ste. 242, Loveland, CO 80538. TEL 970-663-4700. FAX 970-669-3016. *2079*

NEXUS (HAMILTON).
c/o Department of Anthropology, McMaster University, Hamilton, ON L8S 4L9, Canada. TEL 416-525-9140. *317*

NIANGJIU KEJI.
Niangjiu Keji Zazhishe, 45 Shachong Zhonglu, Guiyang, Guizhou 550002, People's Republic of China. TEL 86-851-5796163. *510*

NICARAGUA UPDATE.
Nicaragua Solidarity Campaign, 129 Seven Sisters Rd., London N7 7QG, England. TEL 44-171-272-9619. FAX 44-171-272-5476. *5688*

NICOLAUS. STUDI STORICI.
Comunita dei Padri Domenicani della Basilica Pontificia di S. Nicola, Centro Studi Nicolaiani, Largo Abate Elia, 15, 70122 Bari, Italy. TEL 080-5237247. *6189*

NIDAN.
University of Durban-Westville, Department of Hindu Studies, Private Bag X54001, Durban 4000, South Africa. TEL 27-31-820-2657. FAX 27-31-820-2383. *6115*

NIELS BOHR - COLLECTED WORKS.
Elsevier Science B.V., Books Division, P.O. Box 211, 1000 AE Amsterdam, Netherlands. TEL 31-20-4853911. FAX 31-20-4853705. *5560*

NIGERIA ENGINEER.
Nigerian Society of Engineers, Editorial Committee, National Engineering Centre, 1 Engineering Close, P.O. Box 72667, Victoria Island, Lagos State, Nigeria. TEL 234-1-2617349. FAX 234-1-2617315. *2612*

NIGERIA SOCIETY OF PHYSIOTHERAPY. JOURNAL.
Nigeria Society of Physiotherapy, Department of Physiotherapy, College of Medicine, University of Lagos, Idi-Araba, Lagos, Nigeria. FAX 234-1-837630. *4818*

NIGERIAN FIELD.
Nigerian Field Society, P.O. Box 30385, Secretariat Post Office, Ibadan, Oyo State, Nigeria. TEL 234-22-8102138. *6267*

NIHON BENTOSU GAKKAISHI.
Nihon Bentosu Gakkai, Ocean Research Institute, University of Tokyo, Minami-Dai, Nakano-ku, Tokyo 164, Japan. TEL 81-3-5351-6469. FAX 81-3-3375-6716. *598*

NIHON CONTACT LENS GAKKAISHI.
Japan Contact Lens Society, Nihon Ganka Kiyo Kai, 302 Yamamoto Bldg., 3-6 Mihogaoka, Ibaraki 567, Japan. TEL 81-726-23-7878. FAX 81-726-23-6060. *4773*

NIHON GAISHO GAKKAI ZASSHI.
Nihon Gaisho Gakkai, Teikyo Daigaku Kyumei Kyukyu Senta, 11-1, Kaga 2-chome, Itabashi-ku, Tokyo 173, Japan. TEL 81-3-3964-1211. FAX 81-3-5375-0854. *4788*

NIHON GANKA GAKKAI ZASSHI.
Nihon Ganka Gakkai, 2-4-11-402 Sarugaku-cho, Chiyoda-ku, Tokyo 101, Japan. TEL 03-3295-2360. FAX 03-3293-9384. *4773*

NIHON IDEN GAKKAI TAIKAI PUROGURAMU YOKOSHU.
Nihon Iden Gakkai, Kokuritsu Idengaku Kenkyujo, 111 Yata, Mishima-shi, Shizuoka-ken 411, Japan. *622*

NIHON KIJI MIZUTORI KYOKAISHI.
Nihon Kiji Mizutori Kyokai, 17-11 Kuwazu 3-chome, Higashisumiyoshi-ku, Osaka 546, Japan. FAX 81-06-719-2616. *779*

NIHON ONKYO GAKKAISHI.
Nihon Onkyo Gakkai, 7-7, Yoyogi 2-chome, Shibuya-ku, Tokyo 151, Japan. TEL 81-3-3379-1200. FAX 81-3-3379-1456. *5615*

NIHON OYO DOBUTSU KONCHU GAKKAI CHUGOKU SHIBU KAIHO.
Nihon Oyo Dobutsu Konchu Gakkai, Chugoku Shibu, Chugoku Nogyo Shikenjo, 12-1, Nishifukatsucho 6-chome, Fukuyama-shi, Hiroshima-ken 721, Japan. TEL 81-0849-23-4100. FAX 81-0849-24-7893. *733*

NIHON RINSHO EIYO GAKKAI ZASSHI.
Nihon Rinsho Eiyo Gakkai, c/o Nihon Gakkai Jimu Senta, 16-9 Honkomagome 5-chome, Bunkyo-ku, Tokyo 113, Japan. TEL 81-3-5814-5801. *5238*

NIHON SANFUJINKA SHINSEIJI KETSUEKI GAKKAISHI.
Japanese Society of Obstetrical, Gynecological and Neonatal Hematology, Hamamatsu University, School of Medicine, Department of Obstetrics and Gynecology, 3600 Handa-cho, Hamamatsu 431-31, Japan. TEL 053-435-2309. FAX 053-435-2308. *4742*

NIHON SEKIGAISEN GAKKAISHI.
Nihon Sekigaisen Gakkai, Nihon Gakkai Jimu Senta, 16-9, Honkomagome 5-chome, Bunkyo-ku, Tokyo 113, Japan. TEL 03-5814-5801. FAX 03-5814-5820. *5586*

NIHON SHIKA MASUI GAKKAI ZASSHI.
Nihon Shika Masui Gakkai, Osaka University, 1-8 Yamadaoka, Suita, 565 Osaka, Japan. TEL 03-3947-8891. FAX 03-3947-8341. *4592*

NIHONKAI MATHEMATICAL JOURNAL.
Niigata Daigaku, Rigakubu, c/o Dept. of mathematics, 8050, Igarashi 2, Niigata, 951-21, Japan. *4385*

NIHONKAIKU SUISAN KENKYUJO KENKYU HOKOKU.
Japan Sea National Fisheries Research Institute, 5939-22, Suido-cho 1-chome, Niigata-shi, Niigata 951, Japan. TEL 81-25-228-0451. FAX 81-25-224-0950. *2940*

NIJHOFF INTERNATIONAL PHILOSOPHY SERIES.
Kluwer Academic Publishers, Postbus 17, 3300 AA Dordrecht, Netherlands. TEL 31-78-6392392. FAX 31-78-6392254. *5488*

NIJHOFF LAW SPECIALS.
Kluwer Academic Publishers, Postbus 17, 3300 AA Dordrecht, Netherlands. TEL 31-78-6392392. FAX 31-78-6392254. *3825*

NIMBUS.
Societa Meteorologica Subalpina, V. Gioberti 88, 10128 Turin, Italy. TEL 39-11-591145. FAX 39-11-5683190. *5004*

NINETEENTH-CENTURY CONTEXTS.
Gordon & Breach Science Publishers, c/o International Publishers Distributor, P.O. Box 3054, Langhorne, PA 19047-3054. TEL 215-750-2642. FAX 215-750-6343. *4243*

NINETEENTH CENTURY FRENCH STUDIES.
State University of New York, College at Fredonia, Department of Foreign Languages, Fredonia, NY 14063. TEL 716-673-3387. FAX 716-673-1627. *4243*

NINETEENTH-CENTURY LITERATURE (BERKELEY).
University of California Press, Journals Division, 2120 Berkeley Way, No. 5812, Berkeley, CA 94720-5812. TEL 510-643-7154. FAX 510-642-9917. *4243*

19TH-CENTURY MUSIC.
University of California Press, Journals Division, 2120 Berkeley Way, No. 5812, Berkeley, CA 94720-5812. TEL 510-643-7154. FAX 510-642-9917. *5183*

NINETEENTH-CENTURY STUDIES.
Franklin Nlaishall College, Department of English, Lancaster, PA 17604. TEL 803-953-5140. FAX 803-953-7084. *4243*

NIPPON MEDICAL SCHOOL. JOURNAL.
Nippon Medical School, Medical Association, 1-1-5 Sendagi, Bunkyo-ku Tokyo 113, Japan. TEL 81-3-3822-2131. FAX 81-3-3822-3759. *4508*

NIPPON SUISAN GAKKAISHI (JAPANESE EDITION).
Japanese Society of Scientific Fisheries, c/o Tokyo University of Fisheries, 4-5-7, Konan, Minato-ku, Tokyo 108, Japan. TEL 81-3-3471-2165. FAX 81-3-3471-2054. *2940*

NIPPONDENSO TECHNICAL DISCLOSURE. JOURNAL.
Nippondenso Co., Ltd., 1-1, Showa-cho, Kariya-shi, Aichi-ken 448, Japan. FAX 566-25-4554. *2765*

NOISE & VIBRATION BULLETIN.
Multi-Science Publishing Co. Ltd., 107 High St., Brentwood, Essex CM14 4RX, England. TEL 44-1277-224632. FAX 44-1277-223453. *2830*

NOISE & VIBRATION IN INDUSTRY.
Multi-Science Publishing Co. Ltd., 107 High St., Brentwood, Essex CM14 4RX, England. TEL 44-1277-224632. FAX 44-1277-223453. *5615*

NOISE CONTROL ENGINEERING JOURNAL.
Institute of Noise Control Engineering, Department of Mechanical Engineering, Auburn University, Auburn, AL 36849-5341. TEL 205-844-3306. FAX 205-844-3307. *2765*

NOMINA AFRICANA.
Names Society of Southern Africa, c/o Dr. Lucie A. Moeller, Sec.-Treas., Onomastics Research Centre, HSRC, Private Bag X41, Pretoria 0001, South Africa. TEL 27-12-202-2164. FAX 27-12-326-5362. *4094*

NON-FERROUS METAL DATA (YEAR).
American Bureau of Metal Statistics Inc., Box 1405, Plaza Sta., 400 Plaza Dr., Secaucus, NJ 07094-0405. TEL 201-863-6900. FAX 201-863-6050. *4970*

NONDESTRUCTIVE TESTING AND EVALUATION.
Gordon and Breach Science Publishers, c/o International Publishers Distributor, P.O. Box 3054, Langhorne, PA 19047-3054. TEL 215-750-2642. FAX 215-750-6343. *2740*

NONDESTRUCTIVE TESTING MONOGRAMS AND TRACTS.
Gordon & Breach Science Publishers, c/o International Publishers Distributor, P.O. Box 3054, Langhorne, PA 19047-3054. TEL 215-750-2642. FAX 215-750-6343. *2740*

NONGYE HUANJING BAOHU.
Zhongguo Nongye Shengtai Huanjing Baohu Xiehui, 31 Kangfu Lu, Nankai Qu, Tianjin 300191, People's Republic of China. TEL 361247. *2813*

NONGYE JISHU JINGJI.
Zhongguo Nongye Jishu Jingji Yanjiuhui, 30 Baishiqiao Lu, Beijing 100081, People's Republic of China. TEL 86-10-6217-6213. FAX 86-10-6218-7545. *197*

NONGYE JIXIE XUEBAO.
Zhongguo Nongye Jixie Xuehui, 1 Bei Shatan, Dewai, Beijing 100083, People's Republic of China. TEL 86-10-6201-7131. FAX 86-10-6204-3686. *205*

NONLINEAR ANALYSIS.
Elsevier Science Ltd., Pergamon, P.O. Box 800, Kidlington, Oxford OX5 1DX, England. TEL 44-1865-843000. FAX 44-1865-843010. *2612*

NONLINEAR DYNAMICS.
Kluwer Academic Publishers, Postbus 17, 3300 AA Dordrecht, Netherlands. TEL 31-78-6392392. FAX 31-78-6392254. *2765*

NONPARAMETRIC STATISTICS.
Gordon and Breach Science Publishers, c/o International Publishers Distributor, P.O. Box 3054, Langhorne, PA 19047-3054. TEL 215-750-2642. FAX 215-750-6343. *6622*

NONPROFIT AND VOLUNTARY SECTOR QUARTERLY.
Sage Publications, Inc., 2455 Teller Rd., Thousand Oaks, CA 91320. TEL 805-499 0721. FAX 805-499-0871. *6385*

NONPROFIT MANAGEMENT AND LEADERSHIP.
Jossey-Bass Inc., Publishers, 350 Sansome St., 5th Fl., San Francisco, CA 94104. TEL 415-433-1767. FAX 415-433-0499. *1437*

THE NONPROLIFERATION REVIEW.
Monterey Institute of International Studies, Center for Nonproliferation Studies, 425 Van Buren St., Monterey, CA 93940. TEL 408-647-4193. FAX 408-647-4199. *5754*

NONRENEWABLE RESOURCES.
Plenum Publishing Corp. 233 Spring St., New York, NY 10013-1578. TEL 212-620-8000. FAX 212-463-0742. *5074*

NORDIC HYDROLOGY.
Nordic Association of Hydrology. c/o ISVA, Technical University of Denmark, Bldg. 115, DK-2800 Lyngby, Denmark. TEL 45-42-88-48-29. FAX 45-45-93-28-60. *2288*

NORDIC JOURNAL OF COMPUTING.
University of Helsinki, Department of Computer Science, P.O. Box 26, FIN-00014 University of Helsinki, Finland. TEL 358-9-70351. FAX 358-9-7084441. *1996*

NORDIC JOURNAL OF INTERNATIONAL LAW.
Kluwer Law International Postbus 85889, 2508 CN The Hague, Netherlands TEL 31-70-3081500. FAX 31-70-3081515. *5939*

NORDISK TIDSKRIFT FOR VETENSKAP, KONST OCH INDUSTRI.
Letterstedtska Foereningen Nordisk Tidskrift, P.O. Box 34037, S-100 26 Stockholm, Sweden. TEL 08-6567570. FAX 08-6567570. *4157*

NOR'EASTER (DULUTH).
Lake Superior Marine Museum Association, Box 177, Duluth, MN 55802. TEL 218-727-2497. FAX 218-720-5270. *3480*

NORMALIZACJA.
Wydawnictwa Normalizacyjne "Alfa". Ul. Elektoralna 2, 00-139 Warsaw, Poland. TEL 48-22-200241. *2612*

NOROIS.
97 av. du Recteur Pineau, 86022 Poitiers Cedex, France. TEL 49-45-32-39. FAX 49-45-32-39. *3267*

NOROPSIKIYATRI ARSIVI.
Turk Noropsikiyatri Dernegi, Istanbul Universitesi, Istanbul Tip Fakultesi, 34390 Topkapi - Istanbul, Turkey. FAX 90-212-632400. *4859*

NORSK POLARINSTITUTT. SKRIFTER.
Norsk Polarinstitutt, Middelthuns gate 29, P.O. Box 5072 Majorstua, N-0301 Oslo Norway. TEL 47-22-95-95-12. FAX 47-22-95-95-02. *2254*

NORSK VETERINAERTIDSSKRIFT.
Norske Veterinaerforening, General Birchs Gate 16, N-C454 Oslo, Norway. TEL 47-22-59-16-50. FAX 47-22-69-04-50. *6951*

NORTE.
Frente de Afirmacion Hispanista A.C., Lago Como 201, 11320 Mexico DF Mexico. TEL 525-5963328. FAX 525-5962426. *4244*

NORTH AMERICAN ARCHAEOLOGIST.
Baywood Publishing Co., Inc., 26 Austin Ave., Box 337, Amityville, NY 11701. TEL 516-691-1270. FAX 516-691-1770. *366*

NORTH AMERICAN BENTHOLOGICAL SOCIETY. JOURNAL.
North American Benthological Society, c/o Lynda Corkum, Sec., Dept. of Biological Sciences, University of Windsor, Windsor, ON N9B 3PA, Canada. TEL 519-253-4232. FAX 519-971-3609. *816*

NORTH AMERICAN BIRD BANDER.
35 Logan Hill Rd., Candor, NY 13743. *779*

NORTH AMERICAN FAUNA.
U.S. National Biological Service, Information Transfer Center, c/o Managing Editor, 1201 Oak Ridge Dr., Ste. 200, CO 80525-5589. TEL 970-226-9401. FAX 970-226-9455. *816*

NORTH AMERICAN FLORA.
New York Botanical Garden, Scientific Publications Department, Bronx, NY 10458-5126. TEL 718-817-8721. FAX 718-817-8842. *694*

NORTH AMERICAN JOURNAL OF FISHERIES MANAGEMENT.
American Fisheries Society, 5410 Grosvenor Ln., Ste. 110, Bethesda, MD 20814-2199. TEL 301-897-8616. FAX 301-897-8096. *2940*

NORTH AMERICAN MISSIONS.
Association of North American Missions, 3859 Nottingham Dr., Sarasota, FL 34235. TEL 941-955-8529. FAX 941-951-0805. *6154*

NORTH CAROLINA ENGLISH TEACHER.
North Carolina English Teachers Association, c/o Chris Gould, Ed., English Department, Univ. of North Carolina at Wilmington, Wilmington, NC 28403. TEL 910-395-3324. FAX 910-350-7011. *2497*

NORTH CAROLINA NATURALIST.
Friends of the North Carolina State Museum of Natural Sciences, Box 27647, Raleigh, NC 27611. TEL 919-733-7450. FAX 919-733-1573. *5130*

NORTH COUNTRY NATURALIST.
North County Institute for Natural Philosophy, Inc., RD No. 3, Emery Rd. Box 53, Mexico, NY 13114. TEL 315-963-4854. *6267*

NORTH DAKOTA ACADEMY OF SCIENCE. PROCEEDINGS.
North Dakota Academy of Science, Box 5567, University Sta., Fargo, ND 58105. TEL 701-231-8697. *6267*

NORTH DAKOTA HISTORY.
State Historical Society of North Dakota, North Dakota Heritage Center, Bismarck, ND 58505. TEL 701-328-2799. FAX 701-328-3710. *3480*

NORTH-HOLLAND DELTA SERIES.
Elsevier Science B.V., Books Division, P.O. Box 211, 1000 AE Amsterdam, Netherlands. TEL 31-20-4853911. FAX 31-20-4853705. *5561*

NORTH-HOLLAND LINGUISTIC SERIES.
Elsevier Science B.V., Books Division, P.O. Box 211, 1000 AE Amsterdam, Netherlands. TEL 31-20-4853911. FAX 31-20-4853705. *4095*

NORTH-HOLLAND MATHEMATICAL LIBRARY.
Elsevier Science B.V., Books Division, P.O. Box 211, 1000 AE Amsterdam, Netherlands. TEL 31-20-4853911. FAX 31-20-4853705. *4385*

NORTH-HOLLAND MATHEMATICS STUDIES.
Elsevier Science B.V., Books Division, P.O. Box 211, 1000 AE Amsterdam, Netherlands. TEL 31-20-4853911. FAX 31-20-4853705. *4386*

NORTH-HOLLAND PERSONAL LIBRARY.
Elsevier Science B.V., Books Division, P.O. Box 211, 1000 AE Amsterdam, Netherlands. TEL 31-20-4853911. FAX 31-20-4853705. *5561*

NORTH-HOLLAND SERIES IN APPLIED MATHEMATICS AND MECHANICS.
Elsevier Science B.V., Books Division, P.O. Box 211, 1000 AE Amsterdam, Netherlands. TEL 31-20-4853911. FAX 31-20-4853705. *4386*

NORTH-HOLLAND SERIES IN STATISTICS AND PROBABILITY.
Elsevier Science B.V., Books Division, P.O. Box 211, 1000 AE Amsterdam, Netherlands. TEL 31-20-4853911. FAX 31-20-4853705. *4386*

NORTH-HOLLAND SERIES IN SYSTEM SCIENCE AND ENGINEERING.
Elsevier Science B.V., Books Division, P.O. Box 211, 1000 AE Amsterdam, Netherlands. TEL 31-20-4853911. FAX 31-20-4853705. *2681*

NORTH-HOLLAND STUDIES IN TELECOMMUNICATION.
Elsevier Science B.V., Books Division, P.O. Box 211, 1000 AE Amsterdam, Netherlands. TEL 31-20-4853911. FAX 31-20-4853705. *1913*

NORTH-HOLLAND SYSTEMS AND CONTROL SERIES.
Elsevier Science B.V., Books Division, P.O. Box 211, 1000 AE Amsterdam, Netherlands. TEL 31-20-4853911. FAX 31-20-4853705. *2057*

THE NORTH STONE REVIEW.
D Station, Box 14098, Minneapolis, MN 55414. TEL 612-721-8011. *4244*

NORTH WIND.
George MacDonald Society, The Library, King's College, Strand, London WC2R 2LS, England. TEL 01994-823859. *4157*

NORTHEAST ANTHROPOLOGY.
State University of New York at Albany, Institute for Archeological Studies, c/o Department of Anthropology, Social Science Bldg. 263, Albany, NY 12222. TEL 518-442-4721. FAX 518-442-5710. *318*

NORTH EAST LABOUR HISTORY BULLETIN.
North East Labour History Society, University of Northumbria, Dept. of English and History, Lipman Bldg., Newcastle Upon Tyne NE1 8ST, England. TEL 44-191-227-3738. FAX 44-191-227-4572. *1390*

NORTH EAST LINGUISTIC SOCIETY. PROCEEDINGS.
North East Linguistic Society, c/o Graduate Linguistic Student Association, Department of Linguistics, University of Massachusetts, Amherst, MA 01003. TEL 413-545-6838. FAX 413-545-2992. *4095*

NORTH EASTERN DOCTORS CALLING.
Indian Medical Association, I.M.A. House, Indraprastha Marg, New Delhi 110 002, India. *4509*

NORTHEASTERN NEVADA HISTORICAL SOCIETY QUARTERLY.
Northeastern Nevada Historical Society, 1515 Idaho St., Elko, NV 89801. TEL 702-738-3418. FAX 702-788-9318. *3481*

NORTHERN ECONOMIC REVIEW.
University of Durham, Department of Sociology and Social Policy, Elvet Riverside, New Elvet, Durham DH1 3JT, England. TEL 44-191-3742308. FAX 44-191-3744743. *3590*

NORTHERN JOURNAL OF APPLIED FORESTRY.
Society of American Foresters, 5400 Grosvenor Ln., Bethesda, MD 20814. TEL 301-897-8720. FAX 301-897-3690. *3022*

NORTHERN MARINER.
Memorial University of Newfoundland, Maritime Research Studies Unit, St. John's, NF A1C 5S7, Canada. TEL 709-737-8424. FAX 709-737-4569. *3353*

NORTHERN MOSAIC.
Thunder Bay Multicultural Association, 17 N. Court St., Thunder Bay, ON P7A 4T4, Canada. TEL 807-345-0551. FAX 807-345-0173. *2899*

NORTHERN NEW ENGLAND REVIEW.
Franklin Pierce College, Box 60, Rindge, NH 03461. TEL 603-899-4089. FAX 603-899-6448. *4244*

NORTHERN REVIEW.
Yukon College, P.O. Box 2799, Whitehorse, YT Y1A 5K4, Canada. TEL 403-668-8773. FAX 403-668-8828. *3620*

NORTHERN SCOTLAND.
University of Aberdeen, Centre for Scottish Studies, Old Brewery, King's College, Old Aberdeen AB9 2UB, Scotland. TEL 01224-272203. FAX 01224-487048. *3431*

NORTHWEST ANTHROPOLOGICAL RESEARCH NOTES.
University of Idaho, Alfred W. Bowers Laboratory of Anthropology, Moscow, ID 83844-1111. TEL 208-885-6123. FAX 208-885-5878. *318*

NORTHWEST FOLKLORE.
c/o Scandinavian Dept., 318 Raitt Hall, DL20, University of Washington, Seattle, WA 98195. TEL 206-543-6884. FAX 206-685-9173. *2955*

NORTHWEST LITERARY FORUM.
Irvington Press, 3439 N.E. Sandy Blvd., No. 143, Portland, OR 97232. *4158*

NORTHWEST OHIO QUARTERLY.
Maumee Valley Historical Society, University of Toledo, Department of History, Toledo, OH 43606. TEL 419-530-2209. FAX 419-530-4539. *3481*

NORTHWEST SCIENCE.
Washington State University Press, Pullman, WA 99164-5910. TEL 509-335-3518. FAX 509-335-8568. *6268*

NORTHWESTERN NATURALIST.
Allen Press, 1041 New Hampshire Ave., Box 1897, Lawrence, KS 66044. TEL 913-843-0629. FAX 913-843-1274. *817*

NORTHWESTERN UNIVERSITY. ROBERT H. LURIE CANCER CENTER. JOURNAL.
Northwestern University, Robert H. Lurie Cancer Center, Olson Pavilion 8250, 303 E. Chicago Ave., Chicago, IL 60611. TEL 312-908-6346. FAX 312-908-1372. *4761*

NOTA LEPIDOPTEROLOGICA.
Apollo Books Aps, Kirkeby Sand 19, DK-5771 Stenstrup, Denmark. TEL 45-62-26-37-37. FAX 45-62-26-37-80. *733*

NOTARIUS INTERNATIONAL.
Kluwer Law International Postbus 85889, 2508 CN The Hague, Netherlands. TEL 31-70-3081500. FAX 31-70-3081515. *3940*

NOTATKI ORNITOLOGICZNE.
Polskie Towarzystwo Zoologiczne, Ul. Sienkiewicza 21, 50-335 Wroclaw, Poland. TEL 48-71-225041. FAX 48-71-222817. *779*

NOTES ON NUMERICAL FLUID MECHANICS.
Friedr. Vieweg und Sohn Verlagsgesellschaft mbH, Postfach 5829, 65048 Wiesbaden, Germany. TEL 49-611-7878357. FAX 49-611-7878420. *2745*

NOTICIARIO DE HISTORIA AGRARIA.
Universidad de Murcia, Facultad de Ciencias Economicas y Empresariales, C. Ronda de Levante, 10, 30008 Murcia, Spain. TEL 34-968-363832. FAX 34-968-363750. *140*

NOTORNIS.
Ornithological Society of New Zealand Inc., P.O. Box 12-397, Wellington, New Zealand. TEL 64-6-3546540. FAX 64-6-3546731. *779*

NOTRE DAME JOURNAL.
Notre Dame University, Cotabato City, Philippines. TEL 063-64-214312. FAX 63-64-214312. *2358*

NOTRE DAME TECHNICAL REVIEW.
University of Notre Dame, Engineering Department, 218 Cushing Mall, Notre Dame, IN 46556. TEL 219-283-3524. FAX 219-239-8007. *2613*

NOTTINGHAM FRENCH STUDIES.
Nottingham University Press, Nottingham NG7 2RD, England. TEL 44-115-951-5872. FAX 44-115-951-4998. *4244*

NOUVELLE REVUE D'ONOMASTIQUE.
Societe Francaise d'Onomastique, 87 rue Vielle-du-Temple, 75003 Paris, France. *4095*

NOVA ET VETERIS IURIS GENTIUM. SERIES A: MODERN INTERNATIONAL LAW.
Martinus Nijhoff Publishers, Human Rights and International Law Postbus 163, 3300 AD Dordrecht, Netherlands. TEL 31-78-334911. FAX 31-78-334254. *3940*

NOVA SCOTIAN INSTITUTE OF SCIENCE. PROCEEDINGS.
Nova Scotian Institute of Science, Science Services, Killam Library, Dalhousie University, Halifax, NS B3H 4H8, Canada. TEL 902-494-2384. FAX 902-494-2062. *6268*

NOVUM TESTAMENTUM.
E.J. Brill, P.O. Box 9000, 2300 PA Leiden, Netherlands. TEL 31-71-5353500. FAX 31-71-5317532. *6081*

NOVUM TESTAMENTUM. SUPPLEMENTS.
E.J. Brill, P.O. Box 9000, 2300 PA Leiden, Netherlands. TEL 31-71-5353500. FAX 31-71-5317532. *6081*

NUBIA.
Polska Akademia Nauk, Zaklad Archeologii Srodziemnomorskiej, Palac Kultury i Nauki, p. 2105, 00-901 Warsaw, Poland. TEL 48-22-248593. FAX 48-22-6207651. *366*

NUCLEAR ENERGY.
Thomas Telford Services Ltd., Thomas Telford House, 1 Heron Quay, London E14 4JD, England. TEL 44-171-987-6999. FAX 44-171-538-9620. *2580*

NUCLEAR ENGINEERING AND DESIGN.
Elsevier Science S.A., P.O. Box 546, CH-1001 Lausanne 1, Switzerland. TEL 41-21-3207381. FAX 41-21-3235444. *2740*

NUCLEAR INSTRUMENTS & METHODS IN PHYSICS RESEARCH. SECTION A. ACCELERATORS, SPECTROMETERS, DETECTORS, AND ASSOCIATED EQUIPMENT.
North-Holland P.O. Box 211, 1000 AE Amsterdam, Netherlands. TEL 31-20-4853911. FAX 31-20-4853598. *5597*

NUCLEAR INSTRUMENTS & METHODS IN PHYSICS RESEARCH. SECTION B. BEAM INTERACTIONS WITH MATERIALS AND ATOMS.
North-Holland P.O. Box 211, 1000 AE Amsterdam, Netherlands. TEL 31-20-4853911. FAX 31-20-4853598. *5597*

NUCLEAR MEDICINE AND BIOLOGY.
Elsevier Science Inc., Box 945, New York, NY 10159-0945. TEL 212-633-3730. FAX 212-633-3680. *4881*

NUCLEAR MEDICINE ANNUAL.
Lippincott - Raven Publishers 227 E. Washington Sq., Philadelphia, PA 19106. TEL 215-238-4200. FAX 215-238-4235. *4881*

NUCLEAR MEDICINE COMMUNICATIONS.
Chapman & Hall, Journals Department 2-6 Boundary Row, London SE1 8HN, England. TEL 44-171-8650066. FAX 44-171-522-9623. *4881*

NUCLEAR PHYSICS NEWS.
Gordon and Breach Science Publishers, c/o International Publishers Distributor, P.O. Box 3054, Langhorne, PA 19047-3054. TEL 215-750-2642. FAX 215-750-6343. *5597*

NUCLEAR PHYSICS, SECTION A.
North-Holland P.O. Box 211, 1000 AE Amsterdam, Netherlands. TEL 31-20-4853911. FAX 31-20-4853598. *5597*

NUCLEAR PHYSICS, SECTION B.
North-Holland P.O. Box 211, 1000 AE Amsterdam, Netherlands. TEL 31-20-4853911. FAX 31-20-4853598. *5597*

NUCLEAR PHYSICS, SECTION B, PROCEEDINGS SUPPLEMENTS.
North-Holland P.O. Box 211, 1000 AE Amsterdam, Netherlands. TEL 31-20-4853911. FAX 31-20-4853598. *5597*

NUCLEAR SCIENCE AND ENGINEERING.
American Nuclear Society, 555 N. Kensington Ave., La Grange Park, IL 60525. TEL 708-352-6611. *2581*

NUCLEAR SCIENCE AND TECHNIQUES.
Science Press, Marketing and Sales Department, 16 Donghuangchenggen North St., Beijing 100717, People's Republic of China. TEL 4010642. FAX 4019810. *5597*

NUCLEAR SCIENCE APPLICATIONS - SECTION B: IN DEPTH REVIEWS.
Harwood Academic Publishers, c/o International Publishers Distributor, P.O. Box 3054, Langhorne, PA 19047-3054. TEL 215-750-2642. FAX 215-750-6343. *5597*

NUCLEAR SCIENCE RESEARCH CONFERENCE SERIES.
Harwood Academic Publishers, c/o International Publishers Distributor, P.O. Box 3054, Langhorne, PA 19047-3054. TEL 215-750-2642. FAX 215-750-6343. *5598*

NUCLEOTECNICA.
Comision Chilena de Energia Nuclear, Amunategui 95, Casilla 188-D, Santiago, Chile. TEL 56-2-6990070. FAX 56-2-6991618. *2581*

NUCLEUS.
University of Calcutta, Department of Botany, 35 Ballygunj Circular Rd., Calcutta 19, West Bengal, India. TEL 4753681. FAX 4405802. *717*

NUEVO TEXTO CRITICO.
Stanford University, Department of Spanish and Portuguese, Stanford, CA 94305-2014. TEL 415-725-0112. FAX 415-723-0482. *4245*

NUKLEONIKA.
Polska Akademia Nauk, Instytut Chemii i Techniki Jadrowej, Ul. Dorodna 16, 03-195 Warsaw, Poland. TEL 48-22-110656. FAX 48-22-111532. *2582*

NUMBER ONE.
Volunteer State Community College, Humanities Division, 1480 Nashville Pike, Gallatin, TN 37066. TEL 615-452-8600. *4312*

NUMEN.
E.J. Brill, P.O. Box 9000, 2300 PA Leiden, Netherlands. TEL 31-71-5353500. FAX 31-71-5317532. *6081*

NUMEN SUPPLEMENTS.
E.J. Brill, P.O. Box 9000, 2300 PA Leiden, Netherlands. TEL 31-71-5353500. FAX 31-71-5317532. *6081*

NUMERICAL FUNCTIONAL ANALYSIS AND OPTIMIZATION.
Marcel Dekker Journals, 270 Madison Ave., New York, NY 10016. TEL 212-696-9000. FAX 212-685-4540. *4386*

NUMERICAL HEAT TRANSFER PART A: APPLICATIONS.
Taylor & Francis Inc., 1900 Frost Rd., Ste. 101, Bristol, PA 19007-1598. TEL 215-785-5800. FAX 215-785-5515. *2765*

NUMERICAL HEAT TRANSFER PART B: FUNDAMENTALS.
Taylor & Francis Inc., 1900 Frost Rd., Ste. 101, Bristol, PA 19007-1598. TEL 215-785-5800. FAX 215-785-5515. *2765*

NUMERICAL LINEAR ALGEBRA.
John Wiley & Sons Ltd., Journals, Baffins Ln., Chichester, W. Sussex PO19 1UD, England. TEL 44-1243-779777. FAX 44-1243-843232. *4386*

NUMERICAL METHODS FOR PARTIAL DIFFERENTIAL EQUATIONS: AN INTERNATIONAL JOURNAL.
John Wiley & Sons, Inc., Journals, 605 Third Ave., New York, NY 10158. TEL 212-850-6645. FAX 212-850-6021. *4386*

NUMISMATICA E ANTICHITA CLASSICHE.
Amici dei Quadern Ticinesi di Numismatica e Antichita Classiche, Secretariat, C.P. 3157, CH-6901 Lugano, Switzerland. TEL 41-91-6061606. *5226*

THE NURSE PRACTITIONER.
Springhouse Corporation 1111 Bethlehem Pike, Box 908, Springhouse, PA 19477. TEL 215-646-8700. *4722*

NURSE PRACTITIONERS' PRESCRIBING REFERENCE.
Prescribing Reference, Inc., 53 Park Pl., Ste. 1010, New York, NY 10007. TEL 212-766-7200. FAX 212-732-2360. *5431*

NURSE RESEARCHER.
R C N Publishing Co., Viking House, 17-19 Peterborough Rd., Harrow, Middlesex HA1 2AX, England. TEL 0181-423-1066. FAX 0181-423-3867. *4722*

THE NURSE, THE PATIENT AND THE LAW.
Cox Publications, Box 20316, Billings, MT 59104-0316. TEL 406-256-8822. *4722*

NURSE TO NURSE.
Registered Nurses Association of Nova Scotia, 120 Eileen Stubbs Ave., Ste. 104, Dartmouth, NS B3B 1Y1, Canada. TEL 902-468-9744. FAX 902-468-9510. *4722*

NURSING AND HEALTH SCIENCE EDUCATION.
James Nicholas Publishers, P.O. Box 244, Albert Park, Vic. 3206, Australia. TEL 61-3-6965545. FAX 61-3-6992040. *4723*

NURSING CONNECTIONS.
Washington Hospital Center, Division of Nursing, 110 Irving St., N.W., Washington, DC 20010. TEL 202-877-3048. FAX 202-877-8082. *4723*

NURSING DIAGNOSIS.
Nursecom, Inc., 1211 Locust St., Philadelphia, PA 19107. TEL 215-545-7222. FAX 215-545-8107. *4723*

NURSING ECONOMICS.
Jannetti Publications, Inc. East Holly Ave., Box 56, Pitman, NJ 08071-0056. TEL 609-256-2300 FAX 609-589-7463. *4723*

NURSING ETHICS.
Arnold 338 Euston Rd., London NW1 3BH, England. TEL 44-171-873-6000. FAX 44-171-873-6325. *4723*

NURSING FORUM.
Nursecom Inc., 1211 Locust St., Philadelphia, PA 19107. TEL 215-545-7222. FAX 215-545-8107. *4723*

NURSING LEADERSHIP FORUM.
Springer Publishing Company, 536 Broadway, New York, NY 10012-3955. TEL 212-431-4370. FAX 212-941-7842. *4724*

NURSING MANAGEMENT
Springhouse Corporation 1111 Bethlehem Pike, Box 908, Springhouse, PA 19477. TEL 215-646-8700. *4724*

NURSING MANAGEMENT
R C N Publishing Co., Viking House, 17-19 Peterborough Rd., Harrow-on-the-Hill, Middlesex HA1 2AX, England. TEL 0181-423-1066. FAX 0181-423-3867. *4724*

NURSING NEWS.
South African Nursing Association, P.O. Box 1280, Pretoria 0001, South Africa. TEL 27-12-3432315. FAX 27-12-3440750. *4724*

NURSING NEWS (CONCORD).
New Hampshire Nurses Association, 48 West St., Concord, NH 03301. TEL 603-225-3783. FAX 603-228-6672. *4724*

NURSING SCIENCE QUARTERLY.
Chestnut House Publications, Box 22492, Pittsburgh, PA 15222. TEL 412-391-8585. FAX 412-391-8458. *4724*

NUTRICIA SYMPOSIA.
Kluwer Academic Publishers, Postbus 17, 3300 AA Dordrecht, Netherlands. TEL 31-78-6392392. FAX 31-78-6392254. *5238*

NUTRIENT CYCLING IN AGROECOSYSTEMS.
Kluwer Academic Publishers, Postbus 17, 3300 AA Dordrecht, Netherlands. TEL 31-78-6392392. FAX 31-78-6392254. *233*

NUTRITION.
Elsevier Science Inc., Box 945, New York, NY 10159-0945. TEL 212-533-3730. FAX 212-633-3680. *5238*

NUTRITION AND CANCER.
Lawrence Erlbaum Associates, Inc., 10 Industrial Dr., Mahwah, NJ 07430-2262. TEL 201-236-9500. FAX 201-236-0072. *4761*

NUTRITION AND THE BRAIN.
Lippincott - Raven Publishers 227 E. Washington Sq., Philadelphia, PA 19106. TEL 215-238-4200. FAX 215-238-4235. *5238*

NUTRITION RESEARCH.
Elsevier Science Inc., Box 945, New York, NY 10159-0945. TEL 212-633-3730. FAX 212-633-3680. *5239*

NUTTALL ORNITHOLOGICAL CLUB. PUBLICATIONS.
Nuttall Ornithological Club, c/o Museum of Comparative Zoology, Harvard University, Cambridge, MA 02138. TEL 617-495-2471. *779*

O C L.
John Libbey Eurotext, 127 av. de la Republique, 92120 Montrouge, France. TEL 33-1-46730660. FAX 33-1-40840999. *1742*

O D T U GELISME DERGISI.
Orta Dogu Teknik Universitesi, Iktisadi ve Idari Bilimler Fakultesi, Department of Economics, Balgat 06531 Ankara, Turkey. TEL 90-312-2102006. FAX 90-312-2101244. *1259*

O I E REVUE SCIENTIFIQUE ET TECHNIQUE.
Office International des Epizooties, 12 rue de Prony, 75017 Paris, France. TEL 33-1-44-15-18-88. FAX 33-1-42-67-09-87. *6951*

O N A NEWS.
Ontario Nurses' Association, 85 Grenville St., Ste. 600, Toronto, ON M5S 3A2, Canada. TEL 416-964-8833. FAX 416-964-8864. *4725*

O N S NURSING SCAN IN ONCOLOGY.
Nursecom, Inc., 1211 Locust St., Philadelphia, PA 19107. TEL 215-545-7222. FAX 215-545-8107. *4570*

O P A L.
Ontario Puppetry Association, c/o 62-6770 Glen Erin, Mississauga ON L5N 2L1, Canada. TEL 416-861-0202. *6700*

O P E C REVIEW.
Blackwell Publishers Ltd., 108 Cowley Rd., Oxford OX4 1JF, England. TEL 44-1865-791100. FAX 44-1865-791347. *5367*

O R L.
S. Karger AG, Allschwilerstr. 10, P.O. Box, CH-4009 Basel, Switzerland. TEL 061-3061111. FAX 061-3061234. *4798*

O R L - HEAD AND NECK NURSING.
Health Information Publications, Inc., 1719 Rte. 10, 220, Parsippany, NJ 07054. TEL 914-762-6498. FAX 914-762-0239. *4798*

O R T E S O L JOURNAL.
Portland State University, Applied Linguistics Department, Portland, OR 97207. TEL 503-725-4088. FAX 503-725-4882. *4096*

O S M T ADVOCATE.
Ontario Society of Medical Technologists, 234 Eglinton Ave. E., Ste. 600, Toronto, Ont. M4P 1K5, Canada. *4684*

OBESITY RESEARCH.
North American Association for the Study of Obesity, c/o Pennington Biomedical Research Center, 6400 Perkins Rd., Baton Rouge, LA 70808. TEL 504-763-0934. *4509*

OBJECT.
Centre for Contemporary Craft, Level 4, 88 George St., The Rocks, Sydney, N.S.W. 2000, Australia. TEL 61-2-2479126. FAX 61-2-2472641. *469*

OBJECT-ORIENTED SYSTEMS.
Chapman & Hall, Journals Department 2-6 Boundary Row, London SE1 8HN, England. TEL 44-171-8650066. FAX 44-171-5229623. *2046*

OBSERVATORY.
c/o Dr. D.J. Stickland, Space and Astrophysics Div., Rutherford Appleton Laboratory, Chilton, Didcot, Oxon OX11 0QX, England. FAX 44-1235-445848. *484*

OBSIDIAN II: BLACK LITERATURE IN REVIEW.
North Carolina State University, English Department, Box 8105, Raleigh, NC 27695-8105. TEL 919-515-4150. *4245*

OBSTETRIC ANESTHESIA DIGEST.
Lippincott - Raven Publishers 227 E. Washington Sq., Philadelphia, PA 19106. TEL 215-238-4200. *4592*

OBSTETRICS AND GYNECOLOGY.
Elsevier Science Inc., Box 945, New York, NY 10159-0945. TEL 212-633-3730. FAX 212-633-3680. *4743*

OBSTETRICS AND GYNECOLOGY CLINICS OF NORTH AMERICA.
W.B. Saunders Co. Curtis Center, 3rd Fl., Independence Sq. W., Philadelphia, PA 19106-3399. TEL 215-238-7800. FAX 215-238-6445. *4743*

OCCASIONAL PAPERS IN ANTHROPOLOGY.
Pennsylvania State University, Department of Anthropology, 409 Carpenter Bldg., University Park, PA 16802. TEL 814-865-2509. FAX 814-863-1474. *318*

OCCASIONAL PAPERS IN EDUCATION AND INTERDISCIPLINARY STUDIES.
University of Southampton, School of Education, Southampton SO9 5NH, England. TEL 44-1703-592414. FAX 44-1703-593939. *2439*

OCCASIONAL PAPERS IN ENTOMOLOGY.
Department of Food and Agriculture, Division of Plant Industry, 1220 N St., Sacramento, CA 95814. TEL 916-445-5421. *733*

OCCASIONAL PAPERS ON ISLANDS AND SMALL STATES.
Foundation for International Studies, Islands and Small States Institute, St. Paul's St., Valletta VLT 07, Malta. TEL 356-230551. FAX 356-230551. *5765*

OCCUPATIONAL AND ENVIRONMENTAL MEDICINE.
B M J Publishing Group, B.M.A. House, Tavistock Sq., London WC1H 9JR, England. TEL 44-171-383-6270. FAX 44-171-383-6402. *5254*

OCCUPATIONAL ERGONOMICS.
Chapman & Hall, Journals Department 2-6 Boundary Row, London SE1 8HN, England. TEL 44-171-8650066. FAX 44-171-5229623. *5254*

OCCUPATIONAL HEALTH.
Aldwych Publishing plc., 230-234 Long Ln., London SE1 4QE, England. *4725*

OCCUPATIONAL HEALTH & SAFETY.
Stevens Publishing Corporation, 3700 J.H. Kultgen Frwy., Waco, TX 76706. TEL 817-776-9000. FAX 817-776-9018. *5255*

OCCUPATIONAL MEDICINE.
Rapid Science Publishers, 2-6 Boundary Row, London SE1 8HN, England. TEL 44-171-865-0198. FAX 44-171-410-6600. *5255*

OCCUPATIONAL MEDICINE (PHILADELPHIA).
Hanley & Belfus, Inc., 210 S. 13th St., Philadelphia, PA 19107. TEL 215-546-7293. FAX 215-790-9330. *5255*

OCCUPATIONAL PROGRAMS IN CALIFORNIA PUBLIC COMMUNITY COLLEGES.
Leo A. Meyer Associates, Inc., 23850 Clawiter Rd., Ste. 1, Hayward, CA 94545. TEL 510-785-1091. FAX 510-785-1099. *2414*

OCCUPATIONAL SAFETY AND HEALTH SERIES (NEW YORK).
Marcel Dekker, Inc., 270 Madison Ave., New York, NY 10016. TEL 212-696-9000. FAX 212-658-4540. *5971*

OCCUPATIONAL THERAPY IN HEALTH CARE.
Haworth Press, Inc., 10 Alice St., Binghamton, NY 13904. TEL 607-722-5857. FAX 607-722-1424. *4510*

OCCUPATIONAL THERAPY IN MENTAL HEALTH.
Haworth Press, Inc., 10 Alice St., Binghamton, NY 13904. TEL 607-722-5857. FAX 607-722-1424. *4859*

OCCUPATIONAL THERAPY INTERNATIONAL.
Whurr Publishers Ltd., 19b Compton Terrace, London N1 2UN, England. TEL 44-171-359-5979. FAX 44-171-226-5290. *5256*

OCCUPATIONAL THERAPY JOURNAL OF RESEARCH.
Slack, Inc., 6900 Grove Rd., Thorofare, NJ 08086-9447. TEL 609-848-1000. FAX 609-853-5991. *4510*

OCEAN & COASTAL MANAGEMENT.
Elsevier Science Ltd., P.O. Box 800, Kidlington, Oxford OX5 1DX, England. TEL 44-1865-843000. FAX 44-1865-843010. *2302*

OCEAN DEVELOPMENT AND INTERNATIONAL LAW.
Taylor & Francis Inc., 1900 Frost Rd., Ste. 101, Bristol, PA 19007-1598. TEL 215-785-5800. FAX 215-785-5515. *2302*

OCEAN DRILLING PROGRAM. SCIENTIFIC RESULTS. PROCEEDINGS. PART B: SCIENTIFIC RESULTS.
Texas A&M University, Ocean Drilling Program, 1000 Discovery Dr., College Station, TX 77845-9547. TEL 409-845-2016. FAX 409-845-4857. *2302*

OCEAN ENGINEERING.
Elsevier Science Ltd., Pergamon, P.O. Box 800, Kidlington, Oxford OX5 1DX, England. TEL 44-1865-843000. FAX 44-1865-843010. *2302*

OCEAN YEARBOOK.
University of Chicago Press, Journals Division, Box 37005, Chicago, IL 60637. TEL 773-753-3347. FAX 773-753-0811. *2303*

OCEANIC LINGUISTICS.
University of Hawaii Press, Journals Department, 2840 Kolowalu St., Honolulu, HI 96822. TEL 808-956-8833. FAX 808-988-6052. *4096*

OCEANOGRAPHIC LITERATURE REVIEW.
Elsevier Science Ltd., Pergamon, P.O. Box 800, Kidlington, Oxford OX5 1DX, England. TEL 44-1865-843000. FAX 44-1865-843010. *2220*

OCEANOGRAPHIC RESEARCH INSTITUTE. INVESTIGATIONAL REPORT.
Oceanographic Research Institute, P.O. Box 10712, Marine Parade, Durban 4056, South Africa. TEL 27-31-373536. FAX 27-31-372132. *817*

OCEANOGRAPHIC SCIENCES LIBRARY.
Kluwer Academic Publishers, Postbus 17, 3300 AA Dordrecht, Netherlands. TEL 31-78-6392392. FAX 31-78-6392254. *2303*

OCEANOGRAPHY.
Oceanography Society, 4052 Timber Ridge Dr., Virginia Beach, VA 23455. TEL 804-464-0131. FAX 804-683-5550. *2303*

OCEANS. CONFERENCE RECORD.
Institute of Electrical and Electronics Engineers, Inc., 345 E. 47th St., New York, NY 10017-2394. TEL 212-705-7900. FAX 212-705-7682. *2613*

OCULAR IMMUNOLOGY AND INFLAMMATION.
Aeolus Press Postbus 740, 4116 ZJ Buren, Netherlands. TEL 31-344-572055. FAX 31-344-572562. *4773*

OCULAR INFECTIOUS DISEASES.
Field & Wood, Medical Periodicals, Inc., Box 975, Blue Bell, PA 19422. TEL 610-828-4010. FAX 215-482-0226. *4773*

ODONTOLOGO.
Asociacion Odontologica Panamena, Apdo. 6777, Zona 5, Panama, Panama. TEL 507-269-1603. FAX 507-269-3749. *4650*

OEKOLOGIEPOLITIK.
Oekologisch - Demokratische Partei, Bundesgeschaeftsstelle, Marienstr. 41, 40210 Duesseldorf, Germany. TEL 49-211-134375. FAX 49-211-134376. *2137*

OESTERREICHISCHE GEOGRAPHISCHE GESELLSCHAFT. MITTEILUNGEN.
Oesterreichische Geographische Gesellschaft, Karl-Schweighofer-Gasse 3, A-1070 Vienna, Austria. TEL 43-1-5237974. FAX 43-1-5237974. *3268*

OESTERREICHISCHE GEOLOGISCHE GESELLSCHAFT. MITTEILUNGEN.
Oesterreichische Geologische Gesellschaft, c/o Geological Survey of Austria, Rasumofskygasse 23, Postfach 127, A-1031 Vienna, Austria. TEL 01-712567443. FAX 01-712567456. *2254*

OFFENE SYSTEME.
Springer-Verlag, Heidelberger Platz 3, 14197 Berlin, Germany. TEL 49-30-8207-0. FAX 49-30-8214091. *2114*

OFFICE SYSTEMS RESEARCH JOURNAL.
Office Systems Research Association, Southwest Missouri State University, 901 S. National Ave., Springfield, MO 65804-0089. TEL 417-836-6319. FAX 417-836-6337. *1996*

OH CALCUTTA.
Aditi Nath Roy, Ed. & Pub., CB-168, Sector 1, Salt Lake, Calcutta 700 064, India. TEL 374502. *3174*

OHIO AGRICULTURAL RESEARCH AND DEVELOPMENT CENTER, WOOSTER. RESEARCH BULLETIN.
Ohio State University, Ohio Agricultural Research and Development Center, Wooster, 1680 Madison Ave., Wooster, OH 44691-4096. TEL 216-263-3777. *141*

OHIO AGRICULTURAL RESEARCH AND DEVELOPMENT CENTER, WOOSTER. RESEARCH CIRCULAR.
Ohio State University, Ohio Agricultural Research and Development Center, Wooster, 1680 Madison Ave., Wooster, OH 44691-4096. TEL 216-263-3777. *141*

OHIO BIOLOGICAL SURVEY. BULLETIN. NEW SERIES.
Ohio Biological Survey, 1315 Kinnear Rd., Columbus, OH 43212. TEL 614-292-9645. FAX 614-688-4322. *599*

OHIO BIOLOGICAL SURVEY. MISCELLANEOUS CONTRIBUTIONS.
Ohio Biological Survey, 1315 Kinnear Rd., Columbus, OH 43212. TEL 614-292-9645. FAX 614-688-4322. *599*

THE OHIO JOURNAL OF SCIENCE.
Ohio Academy of Science, 1500 W. Third Ave., Ste. 223, Columbus, OH 43212. TEL 614-488-2228. *6269*

OHIO READING TEACHER.
International Reading Association, Inc., Ohio Council, 401 McGuffey Hall, Miami University, Oxford, OH 45056. TEL 513-529-6451. *2359*

OHIO STATE UNIVERSITY. BYRD POLAR RESEARCH CENTER. CONTRIBUTION SERIES.
Ohio State University, Byrd Polar Research Center, 125 S. Oval Mall, Columbus, OH 43210-1308. TEL 614-292-6531. *6269*

OIKOS.
Munksgaard International Publishers Ltd., 35 Noerre Soegade, P.O. Box 2148, DK-1016 Copenhagen K, Denmark. TEL 45-33-127030. FAX 45-33-129387. *2813*

OIL AND ENERGY TRENDS.
Blackwell Publishers Ltd., 108 Cowley Rd., Oxford OX4 1JF, England. TEL 44-1865-791110. FAX 44-1865-791347. *2555*

OIL AND ENERGY TRENDS: ANNUAL STATISTICAL REVIEW.
Blackwell Publishers Ltd., 108 Cowley Rd., Oxford OX4 1JF, England. TEL 44-1865-791100. FAX 44-1865-791347. *2564*

OIL SHALE.
Estonian Academy of Sciences, Institute of Chemistry, Akadeemia 15, 0026 Tallinn, Estonia. TEL 3722-537084. FAX 3722-536371. *5074*

OILFIELD REVIEW.
Oilfield Review Services, Long Barn, New Russia Hall, Chester Rd., Tattenhall CH3 9AH, England. *5369*

OKAJIMA'S FOLIA ANATOMICA JAPONICA.
Okajima Foria Anatomica Yaponika Henshubu, c/o Keio University, School of Medicine, Dept. of Anatomy, 35, Shinano-machi, Shinjuku-ku, Tokyo 160, Japan. TEL 81-3-3353-1211. FAX 81-3-5379-1977. *599*

OKLAHOMA ACADEMY OF SCIENCE. PROCEEDINGS.
Oklahoma Academy of Science, c/o Edward N. Nelson, Exec. Sec.-Treas., Box 70195, Tulsa, OK 74170-1915. TEL 914-495-6944. FAX 918-495-6033. *6269*

OKLAHOMA GEOLOGICAL SURVEY. CIRCULAR.
Oklahoma Geological Survey, 100 E. Boyd, Rm. N-131, Norman, OK 73019. TEL 405-325-3031. FAX 405-325-7069. *2255*

OKLAHOMA GEOLOGICAL SURVEY. SPECIAL PUBLICATION SERIES.
Oklahoma Geological Survey, 100 E. Boyd, Rm. N-131, Norman, OK 73019. TEL 405-325-3031. FAX 405-325-7069. *2255*

OKLAHOMA GEOLOGY NOTES.
Oklahoma Geological Survey, 100 E. Boyd, Rm N-131, Norman, OK 73019. TEL 405-325-3031. FAX 405-325-7069. *2255*

OLD TESTAMENT ESSAYS.
Serva Publishers, P.O. Box 30043, Sunnyside 0132, Transvaal, South Africa. *6082*

OLD YORK ROAD HISTORICAL SOCIETY BULLETIN.
Old York Road Historical Society, c/o Jenkintown Library, York and Vista Rds., Jenkintown, PA 19046. TEL 215-884-0593. *3482*

OLIFANT.
University of Virginia, Department of French, Charlottesville, VA 22903. TEL 804-924-4627. *4313*

OLYMPIKA.
Centre for Olympic Studies, Thames Hall, University of Western Ontario, London, ON N6A 3K7, Canada. TEL 519-679-2111. FAX 519-661-2008. *6474*

OMEGA.
Elsevier Science Ltd., Pergamon, P.O. Box 800, Kidlington, Oxford OX5 1DX, England. TEL 44-1865-843000. FAX 44-1865-843010. *1438*

OMEGA: JOURNAL OF DEATH AND DYING.
Baywood Publishing Co., Inc., 26 Austin Ave., Box 337, Amityville, NY 11701. TEL 516-691-1270. FAX 516-691-1770. *5868*

OMETECA.
Ometeca Institute, Box 38, New Brunswick, NJ 08903-0038. TEL 908-435-0152. FAX 908-932-6916. *3621*

OMNI.
Omni International, Ltd. 277 Park Ave., 4th Fl., New York, NY 10172. TEL 212-702-6000. FAX 212-702-6282. *6269*

ON - STAGE STUDIES.
University of Colorado, Department of Theatre & Dance, Box 261, Boulder, CO 80309-0261. TEL 303-492-7355. FAX 303-492-7722. *6700*

ON THE LEVEL.
Family Planning N.S.W., 328-336 Liverpool Rd., Ashfield, N.S.W. 2131, Australia. TEL 61-2-716-6099. *6424*

ONCOLOGY.
S. Karger AG, Allschwilerstr. 10, P.O. Box, CH-4009 Basel, Switzerland. TEL 061-3061111. FAX 061-3061234. *4761*

ONCOLOGY NURSING FORUM.
Oncology Nursing Press, Inc., 501 Holiday Dr., Pittsburgh, PA 15220-2749. TEL 412-921-7373. FAX 412-921-2131. *4725*

ONCOLOGY REPORTS.
Demetrios A. Spandidos, Ed. & Pub., Editorial Office, 1, S. Merkouri St., Athens 116 35, Greece. TEL 30-1-722-6469. FAX 30-1-752-3866. *4762*

ONCOLOGY RESEARCH.
Elsevier Science Inc., Box 945, New York, NY 10159-0945. TEL 212-633-3730. FAX 212-633-3680. *4762*

ONCOLOGY TIMES.
Lippincott - Raven Publishers 227 E. Washington Sq., Philadelphia, PA 19106. TEL 215-238-4200. *4762*

ONDERSTEPOORT JOURNAL OF VETERINARY RESEARCH.
Agricultural Research Council, Onderstepoort Veterinary Institute, Private Bag X5, Onderstepoort 0110, South Africa. TEL 27-12-5299101. FAX 27-12-5299318. *6951*

ONION RIVER REVIEW.
Box 7345, York, PA 17404-0345. *4159*

ONKOLOGIE.
S. Karger AG, Allschwilerstr. 10, P.O. Box, CH-4009 Basel, Switzerland. TEL 061-3061111. FAX 061-3061234. *4762*

THE ONLINE JOURNAL OF CURRENT CLINICAL TRIALS.
Chapman & Hall, Journals Department 2-6 Boundary Row, London SE1 8HN, England. TEL 44-171-8650066. FAX 44-171-5229623. *4511*

ONLINE JOURNAL OF KNOWLEDGE SYNTHESIS FOR NURSING.
Sigma Theta Tau International Honor Society of Nursing, 550 W. North St., Indianapolis, IN 46202. TEL 317-634-8171. FAX 317-634-8188. *4725*

ONOMA.
International Centre of Onomastics, Blijde-Inkomststraat 21, P.O. Box 33, 3000 Leuven, Belgium. FAX 32-16-325025. *4096*

ONOMASTICA CANADIANA.
Canadian Society for the Study of Names, c/o Prof. W. Ahrens, Dept. of Languages, Literatures and Linguistics, York University, North York, ON M3J 1P3, Canada. TEL 416-736-5016. FAX 416-736-5483. *4096*

ONS GEESTELIJK ERF.
Editions Peeters s.p.r.l., Bondgenotenlaan 153, 3000 Leuven, Belgium. TEL 32-16-235170. FAX 32-16-228500. *6082*

ONTARIO ARCHAEOLOGY.
Ontario Archaeological Society, 126 Willowdale Ave., North York, ON M2N 4Y2, Canada. *367*

ONTARIO MATHEMATICS GAZETTE.
Ontario Association for Mathematics Education, 112 Peter St. N., Orillia, ON L3V 4Z2, Canada. TEL 705-326-3375. *4387*

ONTARIO MUSEUM ANNUAL.
Ontario Museum Association, George Brown House, 50 Baldwin St., Toronto, ON M5T 1L4, Canada. TEL 416-348-8672. FAX 416-348-0438. *5130*

OPEN.
c/o C. Van Schendel, Keizersgracht 802III, 1017 ED Amsterdam, Netherlands. TEL 31-20-6224322. FAX 31-20-6384860. *4018*

OPEN ECONOMIES REVIEW.
Kluwer Academic Publishers, Postbus 17, 3300 AA Dordrecht, Netherlands. TEL 31-78-6392392. FAX 31-78-6392254. *1259*

OPEN HOUSE INTERNATIONAL.
Open House International Association, c/o NBS Services, Mansion House Chambers, The Close, Newcastle-upon-Tyne NE1 3RE, England. TEL 44-191-2329594. FAX 44-191-2329594. *3590*

OPEN SYSTEMS & INFORMATION DYNAMICS.
Kluwer Academic Publishers, Postbus 17, 3300 AA Dordrecht, Netherlands. TEL 31-78-6392392. FAX 31-78-6392254. *3083*

OPENBAAR BESTUUR.
Samsom H.D. Tjeenk Willink B.V. Postbus 316, 2400 AH Alphen aan den Rijn, Netherlands. TEL 31-1720-66822. FAX 31-1720-66639. *5914*

OPERA JOURNAL.
National Opera Association, Inc.. Department of Music, University of Nevada - Las Vegas, 4505 Maryland Pkwy., Las Vegas, NV 89154-5025. TEL 702-895-1665. FAX 702-895-4194. *5185*

OPERA QUARTERLY.
Duke University Press, Box 90660, Durham, NC 27708-0660. TEL 919-687-3600. FAX 919-688-4571. *5185*

OPERATING ROOM RISK MANAGEMENT.
E C R I, 5200 Butler Pike, Plymouth Meeting, PA 19462. TEL 610-825-6000. FAX 610-834-1275. *4916*

OPERATIONS RESEARCH.
Institute for Operations Research and the Management Sciences, 901 Elkridge Landing Rd., Ste. 400, Linthicum, MD 21090-2909. TEL 410-850-0300. FAX 410-684-2963. *1996*

OPERATIONS RESEARCH COMPUTER SCIENCE INTERFACE.
Kluwer Academic Publishers, Postbus 17, 3300 AA Dordrecht, Netherlands. TEL 31-78-6392392. FAX 31-78-6392254. *1996*

OPERATIONS RESEARCH LETTERS.
North-Holland P.O. Box 211, 1000 AE Amsterdam, Netherlands. TEL 31-20-4853911. FAX 31-20-4853598. *6269*

OPERATIVE TECHNIQUES IN ORTHOPAEDICS.
W.B. Saunders Co. Curtis Center, 3rd Fl., Independence Sq. W., Philadelphia, PA 19106-3399. TEL 215-238-7862. FAX 215-238-6445. *4789*

OPERATIVE TECHNIQUES IN OTOLARYNGOLOGY - HEAD AND NECK SURGERY.
W.B. Saunders Co. Curtis Center, 3rd Fl., Independence Sq. W., Philadelphia, PA 19106-3399. TEL 215-238-7800. *4799*

OPERATIVE TECHNIQUES IN PLASTIC AND RECONSTRUCTIVE SURGERY.
W.B. Saunders Co. Curtis Center, 3rd Fl., Independence Sq. W., Philadelphia, PA 19106-3399. TEL 215-238-7800. FAX 215-238-6445. *4916*

OPHTHALMIC AND PHYSIOLOGICAL OPTICS.
Butterworth - Heinemann, Part of the Reed Elsevier group, Linacre House, Jordan Hill, Oxford OX2 8DP, England. *4774*

OPHTHALMIC EPIDEMIOLOGY.
Aeolus Press Postbus 740, 4116 ZJ Buren, Netherlands. TEL 31-344-572055. FAX 31-344-572562. *4774*

OPHTHALMIC GENETICS.
Aeolus Press Postbus 740, 4116 ZJ Buren, Netherlands. TEL 31-344-572055. FAX 31-344-572562. *4774*

OPHTHALMIC PLASTIC AND RECONSTRUCTIVE SURGERY.
Lippincott - Raven Publishers 227 E. Washington Sq., Philadelphia, PA 19106. TEL 215-238-4200. *4774*

OPHTHALMIC RESEARCH.
S. Karger AG, Allschwilerstr. 10, P.O. Box, CH-4009 Basel, Switzerland. TEL 061-3061111. FAX 061-3061234. *4774*

OPHTHALMOLOGICA.
S. Karger AG, Allschwilerstr. 10, P.O. Box, CH-4009 Basel, Switzerland. TEL 061-3061111. FAX 061-3061234. *4775*

OPHTHALMOLOGY.
Lippincott - Raven Publishers 227 E. Washington Sq., Philadelphia, PA 19106. TEL 215-238-4200. *4775*

OPPORTUNISTIC PATHOGENS.
Elsevier Science B.V., P.O. Box 211, 1000 AE Amsterdam, Netherlands. TEL 31-20-4853911. FAX 31-20-4853598. *4625*

OPTICAL AND QUANTUM ELECTRONICS.
Chapman & Hall, Journals Department 2-6 Boundary Row, London SE1 8HN, England. TEL 44-171-8650066. FAX 44-171-5229623. *2529*

OPTICAL FIBER TECHNOLOGY.
Academic Press, Inc., Journal Division, 525 B St., Ste. 1900, San Diego, CA 92101-4495. TEL 619-699-6715. FAX 619-231-6616. *5608*

OPTICAL MATERIALS.
North-Holland P.O. Box 211, 1000 AE Amsterdam, Netherlands. TEL 31-20-4853911. FAX 31-20-4853598. *5609*

OPTICAL PHYSICS AND ENGINEERING.
Plenum Publishing Corp., 233 Spring St., New York, NY 10013-1578. TEL 212-620-8000. FAX 212-463-0742. *5609*

OPTICAL SOCIETY OF AMERICA. JOURNAL PART A.
Optical Society of America, Inc., 2010 Massachusetts Ave., N.W., Washington, DC 20036-1023. TEL 202-223-8130. *5609*

OPTICAL SOCIETY OF AMERICA. JOURNAL PART B.
Optical Society of America, Inc., 2010 Massachusetts Ave., N.W., Washington, DC 20036-1023. TEL 202-223-8130. *5609*

OPTICAL WAVE SCIENCES AND TECHNOLOGY.
Elsevier Science B.V., Books Division, P.O. Box 211, 1000 AE Amsterdam, Netherlands. TEL 31-20-4853911. FAX 31-20-4853705. *5609*

OPTICS AND LASER TECHNOLOGY.
Butterworth - Heinemann, Part of the Reed Elsevier group, Linacre House, Jordan Hill, Oxford OX2 8DP, England. TEL 44-1865-310366. FAX 44-1865-310898. *5609*

OPTICS AND LASERS IN ENGINEERING.
Elsevier Science Ltd., P.O. Box 800, Kidlington, Oxford OX5 1DX, England. TEL 44-1865-843000. FAX 44-1865-843010. *5609*

OPTICS AND SPECTROSCOPY.
Optical Society of America, Inc., 2010 Massachusetts Ave., N.W., Washington, DC 20036-1023. TEL 202-223-8130. FAX 202-223-1096. *5610*

OPTICS COMMUNICATIONS.
North-Holland P.O. Box 211, 1000 AE Amsterdam, Netherlands. TEL 31-20-4853911. FAX 31-20-4853598. *5610*

OPTIMAL CONTROL APPLICATIONS AND METHODS.
John Wiley & Sons Ltd., Journals, Baffins Ln., Chichester, W. Sussex PO19 1UD, England. TEL 44-1243-779777. FAX 44-1243-843232. *2017*

OPTOMETRY AND VISION SCIENCE.
Williams & Wilkins, 351 W. Camden St., Baltimore, MD 21201. TEL 410-528-4000. FAX 410-528-4312. *4776*

OPTOMETRY CLINICS.
Appleton & Lange, Journal Division Box 120041, Stamford, CT 06912-0041. TEL 203-406-4500. *4776*

OPUSCULA ZOOLOGICA FLUMINENSIA.
Flumserberg Scientific Publishers, Casa d'Uors, Postfach 34, CH-8896 Flumserberg, Switzerland. TEL 081-332214. *817*

B'OR HA'TORAH.
Shamir, Association of Religious Professionals from the Former Soviet Union in Israel, 6 David Yellin St., P.O. Box 5749, Jerusalem, Israel. TEL 972-2-385702. FAX 972-2-385118. *6128*

ORAL HISTORY.
University of Essex, Department of Sociology, Wivenhoe Park, Colchester CO4 3SQ, England. TEL 44-1206-873333. FAX 44-1206-873410. *3433*

ORAL MICROBIOLOGY AND IMMUNOLOGY.
Munksgaard International Publishers Ltd., 35 Noerre Soegade, P.O. Box 2148, DK-1016 Copenhagen K, Denmark. TEL 45-33-127030. FAX 45-33-129387. *765*

ORAL SURGERY, ORAL MEDICINE, ORAL PATHOLOGY, ORAL RADIOLOGY, AND ENDODONTICS.
Mosby - Year Book, Inc. 11830 Westline Industrial Dr., St. Louis, MO 63146-3318. TEL 314-872-8370. FAX 314-432-1380. *4650*

ORAL TRADITION.
Slavica Publishers, Inc., Box 14388, Columbus, OH 43214. TEL 614-268-4002. FAX 614-268-0106. *2955*

ORALPROPHYLAXE.
Zahnaerztlicher Fach-Verlag GmbH, Mont-Cenis-Str. 5, 44623 Herne, Germany. TEL 49-2323-593141. FAX 49-2323-593135. *4650*

THE ORATORY.
St. Joseph's Oratory, 3800 Queen Mary Rd., Montreal, PQ H3V 1H6, Canada. TEL 514-733-8211. FAX 514-733-9735. *6190*

ORBIS LITTERARUM.
Munksgaard International Publishers Ltd., 35 Noerre Soegade, P.O. Box 2148, DK-1016 Copenhagen K, Denmark. TEL 45-33-127030. FAX 45-33-129387. *4246*

ORBIT.
Aeolus Press Postbus 740, 4116 ZJ Buren, Netherlands. TEL 31-344-572055. FAX 31-344-572562. *4776*

THE ORCHARD.
United Jewish Appeal, Rabbinic Cabinet, 99 Park Ave., Ste. 300, New York, NY 10016. TEL 212-880-1418. FAX 212-867-1074. *6128*

ORCHID DIGEST.
Orchid Digest Corporation, c/o Robert Schuler, Executive Director, Box 1216, Redlands, CA 92373-0402. *3063*

ORDER.
Kluwer Academic Publishers, Postbus 17, 3300 AA Dordrecht, Netherlands. TEL 31-78-6392392. FAX 31-78-6392254. *4387*

ORE GEOLOGY REVIEWS.
Elsevier Science B.V., P.O. Box 211, 1000 AE Amsterdam, Netherlands. TEL 31-20-4853911. FAX 31-20-4853598. *2255*

OREGON GEOLOGY.
Department of Geology and Mineral Industries, 800 N.E. Oregon St., No. 28, Ste. 965, Portland, OR 97232-2109. TEL 503-731-4100. FAX 503-731-4066. *2255*

OREGON STATE UNIVERSITY. FOREST RESEARCH LABORATORY. RESEARCH CONTRIBUTION.
Oregon State University, Forest Research Laboratory, Corvallis, OR 97331. TEL 541-737-4271. *3022*

ORGANIC CHEMISTRY.
Academic Press, Inc., 525 B St., Ste. 1900, San Diego, CA 92101-4495. TEL 619-231-0926. FAX 619-699-6715. *1742*

ORGANIC ELECTRONIC SPECTRAL DATA.
John Wiley & Sons, Inc., 605 Third Ave., New York, NY 10158. TEL 212-850-6000. FAX 212-850-6088. *1719*

ORGANIC GEOCHEMISTRY.
Elsevier Science Ltd., Pergamon, P.O. Box 800, Kidlington, Oxford OX5 1DX, England. TEL 44-1865-843000. FAX 44-1865-843010. *1742*

ORGANIC PHOTOCHEMISTRY: A SERIES OF ADVANCES.
Marcel Dekker, Inc., 270 Madison Ave., New York, NY 10016. TEL 212-696-9000. FAX 212-685-4540. *1742*

ORGANIC PREPARATIONS AND PROCEDURES INTERNATIONAL.
Organic Preparations and Procedures, Inc., Box 9, Newton Highlands, MA 02161. *1742*

ORGANIC REACTION MECHANISMS. ANNUAL SURVEY.
John Wiley & Sons, Inc., 605 Third Ave., New York, NY 10158. TEL 212-850-6000. FAX 212-860-6088. *1742*

ORGANIC REACTIONS.
John Wiley & Sons, Inc., 605 Third Ave., New York, NY 10158. TEL 212-850-6000. FAX 212-850-6088. *1742*

ORGANIC SYNTHESES.
John Wiley & Sons, Inc., 605 Third Ave., New York, NY 10158. TEL 212-850-6000. FAX 212-850-6088. *1743*

Refereed

ORGANIZATION & ENVIRONMENT.
Sage Publications, Inc., 2455 Teller Rd., Thousand Oaks, CA 91320. TEL 805-499-0721. FAX 805-499-0871. *5256*

ORGANIZATION DEVELOPMENT JOURNAL.
Organization Development Institute (Cleveland), 781 Beta Dr., Ste. K, Cleveland, OH 44143. TEL 216-461-4333. FAX 216-729-9319. *1438*

ORGANIZING.
St. Joseph's University Press, 5600 City Ave., Philadelphia, PA 19131. TEL 215-878-4253. FAX 215-879-3148. *6386*

ORGANOMETALLIC SYNTHESES.
Academic Press, Inc., 525 B St., Ste. 1900, San Diego, CA 92101-4495. TEL 619-231-0926. FAX 619-699-6715. *4970*

ORGANOMETALLICS.
American Chemical Society, 1155 16th St., N.W., Washington, DC 20036. TEL 800-333-9511. FAX 614-447-3671. *1743*

ORIENS.
E.J. Brill, P.O. Box 9000, 2300 PA Leiden, Netherlands. TEL 31-71-5353500. FAX 31-71-5317532. *5291*

ORIENTAL INSECTS.
Associated Publishers, Box 140103, Gainesville, FL 32614-0103. TEL 352-371-4071. FAX 352-371-4071. *733*

ORIENTAL NOTES AND STUDIES.
Magnes Press, Hebrew University, Jerusalem, P.O. Box 7695, Jerusalem 91076, Israel. TEL 972-2-660341. FAX 972-2-633370. *3499*

ORIENTAL SOCIETY OF AUSTRALIA. JOURNAL.
Oriental Society of Australia, University of Sydney, School of Asian Studies, Sydney, N.S.W. 2006, Australia. FAX 61-2-351-2319. *5291*

ORIENTALIA LOVANIENSIA ANALECTA.
Editions Peeters s.p.r.l., Bondgenotenlaan 153, 3000 Leuven, Belgium. TEL 32-16-235170. FAX 32-16-228500. *5291*

ORIENTALIA RHENO-TRAIECTINA.
E.J. Brill, P.O. Box 9000, 2300 PA Leiden, Netherlands. TEL 31-71-5353500. FAX 31-71-5317532. *5291*

ORIENTATION SCOLAIRE ET PROFESSIONNELLE.
Institut National d'Etude du Travail et d'Orientation Professionnelle, 41 rue Gay Lussac, 75005 Paris, France. TEL 33-1-44-10-7848. FAX 33-1-43-54-1091. *5868*

ORIGINS OF LIFE AND EVOLUTION OF THE BIOSPHERE.
Kluwer Academic Publishers, Postbus 17, 3300 AA Dordrecht, Netherlands. TEL 31-78-6392392. FAX 31-78-6392254. *599*

ORION.
Operations Research Society of South Africa, P.O. Box 850, Groenkloof 0027, South Africa. *1996*

ORIS MEDICINA.
Diade s.r.l., Via Ausonio 5, 20123 Milan, Italy. TEL 39-2-8372407. FAX 39-2-58100311. *4511*

ORNIS FENNICA.
Finnish Ornithological Society, University of Helsinki, Department of Ecology and Systematics, Division of Population Biology, P.O. Box 17, SF-00014 Helsinki, Finland. TEL 358-81-5531214. FAX 358-81-5531227. *779*

ORNIS HUNGARICA.
Hungarian Ornithological and Nature Conservation Society, Kolto u. 21, 1121 Budapest, Hungary. *779*

L'OROPTERO.
Istituto Regionale Studi Ottici e Optometrici, Piazza della Liberta 17, 50059 Vinci (Fi), Italy. TEL 39-571-567923. FAX 39-571-56520. *4776*

ORTHOPAEDIC NURSING JOURNAL.
Jannetti Publications, Inc., East Holly Ave., Box 56, Pitman, NJ 08071-0056. TEL 609-256-2300. FAX 609-589-7463. *4725*

ORTHOPAEDICS INTERNATIONAL EDITION.
Slack, Inc., 6900 Grove Rd., Thorofare, NJ 08086-9447. TEL 609-848-1000. *4789*

ORTHOPEDIC CLINICS OF NORTH AMERICA.
W.B. Saunders Co. Curtis Center, 3rd Fl., Independence Sq. W., Philadelphia, PA 19106-3399. TEL 215-238-7800. FAX 215-238-6445. *4789*

ORTHOPEDICS.
Slack, Inc., 6900 Grove Rd., Thorofare, NJ 08086-9447. TEL 609-848-1000. FAX 609-853-5991. *4789*

ORYX.
Blackwell Science Ltd., Osney Mead, Oxford OX2 OEL, England. TEL 44-1865-206206. FAX 44-1865-721205. *2137*

OSAKA CITY UNIVERSITY. FACULTY OF ENGINEERING. MEMOIRS.
Osaka City University, Faculty of Engineering, 3-138 Sugimoto 3-chome, Sumiyoshi-ku, Osaka 558, Japan. *2613*

OSAKA TOSEKI KENKYUKAI KAISHI.
Osaka Toseki Kenkyukai, Osaka Shiritsu Daigaku Igakubu Hinyokika Kyoshitsu, 5-7, Asahimachi 1-chome, Abeno-ku, Osaka 545, Japan. TEL 81-6-645-2166. FAX 81-6-647-4426. *4930*

OSIRIS (CHICAGO).
University of Chicago Press, Journals Division, Box 37005, Chicago, IL 60637. TEL 773-753-3347. FAX 773-753-0811. *6270*

OSIRIS (DEERFIELD).
Box 297, Deerfield, MA 01342. TEL 413-774-4027. *4313*

OSMANIA PAPERS IN LINGUISTICS.
Osmania University, Department of Linguistics, Hyderabad 500 007, Andhra Pradesh, India. TEL 868951. *4097*

OSNABRUECKER NATURWISSENSCHAFTLICHE MITTEILUNGEN.
Naturwissenschaftlicher Verein Osnabrueck, Am Schoelerberg 8, 49082 Osnabrueck, Germany. TEL 49-541-5600332. FAX 49-541-5600337. *6270*

OSO.
Stichting Instituut ter Bevordering van de Surinamistiek, Koperslagershoek 13, 3981 SB Bunnik, Netherlands. TEL 31-30-6567543. FAX 31-30-253466. *318*

OSTEOPATHIC PROGRESS.
American Osteopathic Healthcare Association, 5301 Wisconsin Ave., N.W., Ste. 630, Washington, DC 20015-2015. TEL 202-686-1700. FAX 202-686-7615. *3554*

OTHER REALITIES.
Undena Publications, Box 97, Malibu, CA 90265. TEL 805-746-5870. FAX 805-746-2728. *318*

OTHER VOICES.
Other Voices, Inc., University of Illinois at Chicago, Department of English MC 162, 601 S. Morgan St., Chicago, IL 60607-7120. TEL 312-413-2209. *4247*

OTOLARYNGOLOGY - HEAD AND NECK SURGERY.
Mosby - Year Book, Inc. 11830 Westline Industrial Dr., St. Louis, MO 63146-3318. TEL 314-872-8370. FAX 314-432-1380. *4799*

THE OTOLARYNGOLOGY JOURNAL CLUB JOURNAL.
Lippincott - Raven Publishers 227 E. Washington Sq., Philadelphia, PA 19106. TEL 215-238-4200. *4570*

OTORINOLARINGOLOGICA.
Edizioni Minerva Medica, Corso Bramante 83-85, 10126 Turin, Italy. TEL 39-11-678282. FAX 39-11-3121736. *4799*

OTTAWA LAW REVIEW.
University of Ottawa, Faculty of Law, 57 rue Louis Pasteur, Ottawa, ON K1N 6N5, Canada, Canada. TEL 613-564-2919. FAX 613-564-9800. *3830*

THE OTTOMAN EMPIRE AND ITS HERITAGE.
E.J. Brill, P.O. Box 9000 2300 PA Leiden, Netherlands. TEL 31-71-5353500. FAX 31-71-5317532. *3499*

OUDTESTAMENTISCHE STUDIEN.
E.J. Brill, P.O. Box 9000 2300 PA Leiden, Netherlands. TEL 31-71-5353500. FAX 31-71-5317532. *6082*

OUR VOICE (NEW YORK).
Our Voice, 365 W. 25th St., Ste. 13E, New York, NY 10001-5816. TEL 212-929-4299. FAX 212-929-4099. *4799*

OUTLOOK ON AGRICULTURE.
CAB International, Wallingford, Oxon. OX10 8DE, England. TEL 44-1491-832111. FAX 44-1491-833508. *142*

OVULATION METHOD RESEARCH AND REFERENCE CENTRE OF AUSTRALIA. BULLETIN.
Ovulation Method Research and Reference Centre of Australia, Billings Family Life Centre, 27 Alexandra Parade, N. Fitzroy, Melbourne, Vic. 3068, Australia. TEL 61-3-9481722 FAX 61-3-94824208. *828*

OXFORD BULLETIN OF ECONOMICS AND STATISTICS.
Blackwell Publishers Ltd., 108 Cowley Rd., Oxford OX4 1JF, England. TEL 44-1865-791100. FAX 44-1865-791347. *950*

OXFORD DEVELOPMENT STUDIES.
Carfax Publishing Co., P.O. Box 25, Abingdon, Oxon. OX14 3UE, England. TEL 44-1235-401000. FAX 44-1235-401550. *1312*

OXFORD JOURNAL OF ARCHAEOLOGY.
Blackwell Publishers Ltd. 108 Cowley Rd., Oxford OX4 1JF, England. TEL 44-1865-791100. FAX 44-1865-791347. *367*

OXFORD LITERARY REVIEW.
Department of English Studies, University of Stirling, Stirling FK9 4LA, England. *4247*

OXFORD MATHEMATICAL MONOGRAPHS.
Oxford University Press Walton St., Oxford OX2 6DP, England. TEL 44-1865-56767. FAX 44-1865-56646. *4387*

OXFORD MONOGRAPHS ON BIOGEOGRAPHY.
Oxford University Press Walton St., Oxford OX2 6UP, England. TEL 44-1365-56767. FAX 44-1865-56646. *600*

OXFORD MONOGRAPHS ON GEOLOGY AND GEOPHYSICS.
Oxford University Press Walton St., Oxford OX2 6DP, England. TEL 44-1365-56767. FAX 44-1865-56646. *2256*

OXFORD MONOGRAPHS ON MEDICAL GENETICS.
Oxford University Press, Walton St., Oxford OX2 6DP, England. TEL 44-1365-56767. FAX 44-1865-56646. *4512*

OXFORD MONOGRAPHS ON METEOROLOGY AND PHYSICAL OCEANOGRAPHY.
Oxford University Press, Walton St., Oxford OX2 6DP, England. TEL 44-1865-56767. FAX 44-1865-56646. *5004*

OXFORD NEUROLOGICAL MONOGRAPHS.
Oxford University Press, Walton St., Oxford OX2 6DP, England. TEL 44-1865-56767. FAX 44-1865-56646. *4859*

OXFORD REVIEW OF EDUCATION.
Carfax Publishing Co., P.O. Box 25, Abingdon, Oxon. OX14 3UE, England. TEL 44-1235-401000. FAX 44-1235-401550. *2360*

OXFORD REVIEWS OF REPRODUCTIVE BIOLOGY.
Oxford University Press, Oxford Journals, Walton St., Oxford OX2 6DP, England. TEL 44-1865-56767. FAX 44-1865-56646. *817*

OXFORD STUDIES IN ANCIENT PHILOSOPHY.
Oxford University Press Walton St., Oxford OX2 6DP, England. TEL 44-1865-56767. FAX 44-1865-56646. *5489*

OXFORD STUDIES IN COMPARATIVE EDUCATION.
Triangle Journals Ltd., P.O. Box 65, Wallingford, Oxon. OX10 0YG, England. TEL 44-1491-838013. FAX 44-1491-834968. *2360*

OXIDATION OF METALS.
Plenum Publishing Corp., 233 Spring St., New York, NY 10013-1578. TEL 212-620-8000. FAX 212-463-0742. *1755*

OYEN ECHO.
109 6 Ave. E., P.O. Box 420, Oyen, AB T0J 2J0, Canada. TEL 403-664-3622. FAX 403-664-3622. *3124*

OYO YAKURI.
Oyo Yakuri Kenkyukai, C.P.O. Box 180, Sendai 980-91, Japan. TEL 022-267-3810. FAX 022-222-0515. *5431*

OZ CLARK'S WINE GUIDE (YEAR).
Websters Wine Guide Ltd., Axe & Bottle Ct., 70 Newcomen St., London SE1 1YT, England. TEL 44-171-407-5956. FAX 44-171-407-6437. *510*

OZONE: SCIENCE AND ENGINEERING.
Lewis Publishers, Inc., Journals Department, 2000 Corporate Blvd., N.W., Boca Raton, FL 33431. TEL 407-994-0555. FAX 407-997-0949. *2646*

P A C E.
Futura Publishing Company, Inc., 135 Bedford Rd., Box 418, Armonk, NY 10504-0418. TEL 914-273-1014. FAX 914-973-1015. *4608*

P & T.
Quadrant HealthCom, 105 Raider Blvd., Belle Mead, NJ 08052-1510. TEL 908-874-0707. FAX 908-874-5611. *5431*

P - FORM.
Randolph Street Gallery, 756 N. Milwaukee Ave., Chicago, IL 60622. TEL 312-666-7737. FAX 312-666-8986. *447*

P I D S RESEARCH PAPER SERIES.
Philippine Institute for Development Studies, NEDA sa Makati Bldg., 3rd Fl., Rm. 304, 106 Amorsolo St., Legaspi Village, Makati 1229, Metro Manila, Philippines. TEL 632-8935705. FAX 632-8161091. *1312*

P L I WARWICK JOURNAL OF PHILISOPHY.
University of Warwick, Department of Philosophy, Coventry CV4 7AL, England. TEL 44-1203-523421. FAX 44-1203-523019. *5489*

P S A JOURNAL.
Photographic Society of America, Inc., 3000 United Founders Blvd., No. 103, Oklahoma City, OK 73112-3940. TEL 405-843-1437. FAX 405-843-1438. *5516*

P S: POLITICAL SCIENCE & POLITICS.
American Political Science Association, 1527 New Hampshire Ave., N.W., Washington, DC 20036. TEL 202-483-2512. FAX 202-483-2657. *5690*

PACIFIC BASIN FINANCE JOURNAL.
North-Holland P.O. Box 211, 1000 AE Amsterdam, Netherlands. TEL 31-20-4853911. FAX 31-20-4853598. *1114*

PACIFIC COAST PHILOLOGY.
Pacific Ancient and Modern Language Association, c/o Cyndia Clegg, Ed., Dept. of Humanities, Pepperdine University, Malibu, CA 90263-4225. TEL 310-456-4435. *4248*

PACIFIC HISTORICAL REVIEW.
University of California Press, Journals Division, 2120 Berkeley Way, No. 5812, Berkeley, CA 94720-5812. TEL 510-643-7154. FAX 510-642-9917. *3482*

PACIFIC JOURNAL OF MATHEMATICS.
International Press, Pacific Journal of Mathematics, Mathematics Department, University of California, Los Angeles, CA 90095-1555. FAX 310-206-6673. *4387*

PACIFIC NORTHWEST QUARTERLY.
University of Washington, 4045 Brooklyn Ave., N.E., JA-15, Seattle, WA 98105-6261. TEL 206-543-2992. *3482*

PACIFIC NORTHWESTERNER.
Westerners, Spokane Corral, Box 14707, Spokane, WA 99210-1717. TEL 509-928-9540. *3483*

PACIFIC PHILOSOPHICAL QUARTERLY.
Blackwell Publishers Ltd., 108 Cowley Rd., Oxford OX4 1JF, England. TEL 44-1865-791100. FAX 44-1865-791347. *5489*

PACIFIC SCIENCE.
University of Hawaii Press, Journals Department, 2840 Kolowalu St., Honolulu, HI 96822. TEL 808-956-8833. FAX 808-988-6052. *6270*

PACIFIC SCIENCE ASSOCIATION. INFORMATION BULLETIN.
Pacific Science Association, Box 17801, Honolulu, HI 96817. TEL 808-848-4139. FAX 808-841-8968. *6270*

PACIFIC SEABIRDS.
Pacific Seabird Group, 4505 University Way, N.E., Box 179, Seattle, WA 98105. *780*

PACIFIC STUDIES.
Brigham Young University, Hawaii Campus, Box 1829, Laie, HI 96762. TEL 808-293-3667. FAX 808-293-3645. *6337*

PACIFIC TOURISM REVIEW.
Cognizant Communication Corporation, 3 Hartsdale Rd., Elmsford, NY 10523. TEL 914-592-7720. FAX 914-592-8981. *6906*

PAEDAGOGICA HISTORICA.
Universiteit Gent, A. Baertsoenkaai 3, 9000 Ghent, Belgium. TEL 32-9-2240224. FAX 32-9-2259311. *2360*

PAEDIATRIC & PERINATAL EPIDEMIOLOGY.
Blackwell Science Ltd., Osney Mead, Oxford OX2 0EL, England. TEL 44-1865-206206. FAX 44-1865-721205. *4809*

PAEDIATRIC NURSING.
R C N Publishing Co., Viking House, 17-19 Peterborough Rd., Harrow-on-the-Hill, Middlesex HA1 2AX, England. TEL 0181-423-1066. FAX 0181-423-3867. *4725*

PAIDEUSIS.
Canadian Philosophy of Education Society, c/o Prof. Don Cochrane, Manag.Ed., University of Saskatchewan, Dept. of Educational Foundations, Saskatoon, SK S7N 0W0, Canada. FAX 306-966-7020. *5489*

PAIN.
Elsevier Science B.V., P.O. Box 211, 1000 AE Amsterdam, Netherlands. TEL 31-20-4853911. FAX 31-20-4853598. *4860*

PAIN AND HEADACHE.
S. Karger AG, Allschwilerstr. 10, P.O. Box, CH-4009 Basel, Switzerland. TEL 061-3061111. FAX 061-3061234. *4860*

THE PAIN CLINIC.
V S P, P.O. Box 346, 3700 AH Zeist, Netherlands. TEL 31-30-6925790. FAX 31-30-6932081. *4593*

PAIN DIGEST.
Springer-Verlag, Medical Journals, 175 Fifth Ave., New York, NY 10010. TEL 212-460-1575. FAX 212-473-6272. *4593*

PAIN FORUM.
Churchill Livingstone, 650 Ave. of the Americas, New York, NY 10011. TEL 212-206-5040. FAX 212-206-7808. *4860*

PAIN RESEARCH AND CLINICAL MANAGEMENT.
Elsevier Science B.V., Books Division, P.O. Box 211, 1000 AE Amsterdam, Netherlands. TEL 31-20-4853911. FAX 31-20-4853705. *4512*

PAINT TITLES.
Paint Research Association, 8 Waldegreave Rd., Teddington, Middlesex TW118LD, England. TEL 44-181-977-4427. FAX 44-181-943-4705. *5311*

PAKISTAN CONGRESS OF ZOOLOGY. PROCEEDINGS.
Zoological Society of Pakistan, c/o Department of Zoology, University of the Punjab, New Campus, Lahore, Pakistan. TEL 92-42-5868376. *817*

PAKISTAN JOURNAL OF APPLIED ECONOMICS.
University of Karachi, Applied Economics Research Centre, P.O. Box 8403, Karachi 75270, Pakistan. TEL 92-21-474749. FAX 92-21-471634. *1228*

PAKISTAN JOURNAL OF BOTANY.
Pakistan Botanical Society, Dept. of Botany, University of Karachi, Karachi 75270, Pakistan. TEL 92-21-447867. FAX 92-21-466896. *695*

PAKISTAN JOURNAL OF HYDROCARBON RESEARCH.
Hydrocarbon Development Institute of Pakistan, 230 Nizamuddin Rd. F 7-4, P.O. Box 1308, Islamabad, Pakistan. TEL 92-51-823690. FAX 92-51-828773. *5370*

PAKISTAN JOURNAL OF NEMATOLOGY.
Pakistan Nematological Society, National Nematological Research Centre, University of Karachi, Karachi 75270, Pakistan. FAX 92-21-466896. *817*

PAKISTAN JOURNAL OF PHARMACEUTICAL SCIENCES.
University of Karachi, Faculty of Pharmacy, Karachi 75270, Pakistan. *5432*

PAKISTAN JOURNAL OF ZOOLOGY.
Zoological Society of Pakistan, c/o Department of Zoology, University of the Punjab, New Campus, Lahore, Pakistan. TEL 92-42-5868376. *817*

PAKISTAN VETERINARY JOURNAL.
University of Agriculture, Faculty of Veterinary Science, Faisalabad 38040, Pakistan. TEL 92-41-624607. FAX 92-41-610200. *6952*

PAKPHYTON.
Agriculturalists, Breeders and Botanists' Club of Pakistan, Department of Botany, University of the Punjab, Quaid-e-Azam Campus, Lahore 54590, Pakistan. TEL 92-42-5869939. FAX 92-42-5868313. *695*

PALAEOGEOGRAPHY, PALAEOCLIMATOLOGY, PALAEOECOLOGY.
Elsevier Science B.V., P.O. Box 211, 1000 AE Amsterdam, Netherlands. TEL 31-20-4853911. FAX 31-20-4853598. *5316*

PALAEONTOGRAPHICA AMERICANA.
Paleontological Research Institution, 1259 Trumansburg Rd., Ithaca, NY 14850. TEL 607-273-6623. FAX 607-273-6620. *5316*

PALAEONTOLOGIA CATHAYANA.
Science Press, Marketing and Sales Department, 16 Donghuangchenggen North St., Beijing 100717, People's Republic of China. TEL 4010642. FAX 4012180. *5316*

PALAEONTOLOGY.
Blackwell Publishers Ltd., 108 Cowley Rd., Oxford OX4 1JF, England. TEL 44-1865-791100. FAX 44-1865-791347. *5316*

PALAIOS.
S E P M, 1731 E. 71st. St., Tulsa, OK 74136-5108. TEL 918-493-3361. FAX 918-493-2093. *5317*

PALEOBIOLOGY.
Paleontological Society, Business Office, Box 1897, Lawrence, KS 66044-8897. TEL 913-843-1221. *5317*

PALEOBIOS.
University of California at Berkeley, Museum of Paleontology, Berkeley, CA 94720. TEL 510-642-1821. FAX 510-642-1822. *5317*

PALEOCEANOGRAPHY.
American Geophysical Union, 2000 Florida Ave., N.W., Washington, DC 20009. TEL 202-462-6900. FAX 202-328-0566. *6271*

PALEONTOLOGICAL JOURNAL.
Scripta Technica, Inc. 8555 16th St., Ste. 220, Silver Spring, MD 20910. TEL 301-588-0484. FAX 301-588-5278. *5317*

PALESTINE YEARBOOK OF INTERNATIONAL LAW.
Al-Shaybani Society of International Law, P.O. Box 4247, 1702 Nicosia, Cyprus. TEL 357-2-429396. FAX 357-2-312104. *3940*

PALLIATIVE CARE TODAY.
C C T Healthcare Communications Ltd., 50-52
Union St., London SE1 1TD, England. TEL 0171-
407-9731. FAX 0171-407-7083. *4762*

PALMYRE.
Polska Akademia Nauk, Zaklad Archeologii
Srodziemnomorskiej, Palac Kultury i Nauki, p.
2105, 00-901 Warsaw, Poland. TEL 48-22-
248593. FAX 48-22-6207651. *367*

PALYNOLOGY.
American Association of Stratigraphic Palynologists
Foundation, c/o Vaughn M. Bryant, Jr., Palynology
Laboratory, Anthropology Bldg., Texas A & M
University, College Station, TX 77843-4352.
TEL 409-845-5242. FAX 409-845-4070. *5317*

**PAN AMERICAN JOURNAL OF ORGAN
REPLACEMENT THERAPIES.**
Field & Wood, Medical Periodicals, Inc., Box 975,
Blue Bell, PA 19422. TEL 610-828-4010.
FAX 215-482-0226. *4930*

PAN-PACIFIC ENTOMOLOGIST.
Pacific Coast Entomological Society, c/o California
Academy of Sciences, Golden Gate Park, San
Francisco, CA 94118-4599. TEL 415-750-7227.
FAX 415-750-7228. *733*

PANCREAS.
Lippincott - Raven Publishers 227 E. Washington
Sq., Philadelphia, PA 19106. TEL 215-238-4200.
4674

PANMINERVA MEDICA.
Edizioni Minerva Medica, Corso Bramante 83-85,
10126 Turin, Italy. TEL 39-11-678282. FAX 39-
11-3121736. *4512*

PAPERS IN COMPARATIVE STUDIES.
Ohio State University, Division of Comparative
Studies in the Humanities, 308 Dulles Hall, 230 W.
17th Ave., Columbus, OH 43210-1311. TEL 614-
292-2559. FAX 614-292-6707. *4249*

PAPERS IN REGIONAL SCIENCE.
Regional Science Association International, 1-3
Observatory, 901 S. Mathews, Univ. of Illinois,
Urbana, IL 61801-3681. TEL 217-333-8904.
FAX 217-244-1785. *6337*

PAPERS ON LANGUAGE AND LITERATURE.
Southern Illinois University at Edwardsville,
Edwardsville, IL 62026. TEL 618-692-2119.
FAX 618-692-3509. *4249*

PAPYROLOGICA LUGDUNO-BATAVA.
E.J. Brill, P.O. Box 9000, 2300 PA Leiden,
Netherlands. TEL 31-71-5353500. FAX 31-71-
5317532. *4249*

PARA.DOXA.
Delta Productions, Box 2237, Vashon, WA 98070.
TEL 206-567-4373. *4249*

PARADOXIST LITERARY MOVEMENT.
Paradoxist Literary Association, 2456 S. Rose Peak
Dr., Tucson, AZ 85710-6122. TEL 520-886-7413.
4249

PARAGRAPH.
Edinburgh University Press, 22 George Sq.,
Edinburgh EH8 9LF, Scotland. TEL 44-131-650-
6207. FAX 44-131-662-0053. *4249*

**PARALLEL AND DISTRIBUTED SIMULATION
WORKSHOP. PROCEEDINGS.**
Society for Computer Simulation, Box 17900, San
Diego, CA 92177. TEL 619-277-3888. FAX 619-
277-3930. *2053*

PARALLEL COMPUTING.
North-Holland P.O. Box 211, 1000 AE Amsterdam,
Netherlands. TEL 31-20-4853911. FAX 31-20-
4853598. *2058*

PARAMETERS (CARLISLE BARRACKS).
U.S. Army War College, Carlisle Barracks, PA
17013-6050. TEL 717-245-4943. FAX 717-245-
4721. *5043*

PARAPSYCHOLOGY, NEW AGE AND THE OCCULT.
Reference Press International, Box 812726, Boca
Raton, FL 33481-2726. TEL 407-994-3499.
FAX 407-994-3699. *5219*

PARASITE.
Princeps Editions, 64 Av. Charles de Gaulle, F
92130 Issy-les-Moulineaux, France. TEL 33-1-
46382414. FAX 33-1-40957215. *4626*

PARASITE IMMUNOLOGY.
Blackwell Science Ltd., Osney Mead, Oxford OX2
OEL, England. TEL 44-1865-206206. FAX 44-
1865-721205. *4626*

PARASITOLOGIA AL DIA.
Sociedad Chilena de Parasitologia, Casilla 50470,
Santiago 1, Chile. FAX 56-2-5416840. *765*

PARASITOLOGY TODAY.
Elsevier Science Ltd., P.O. Box 800, Kidlington,
Oxford OX5 1DX, England. TEL 44-1865-843000.
FAX 44-1865-843010. *4626*

PARASITOLOGY TODAY (REFERENCE EDITION).
Elsevier Science Ltd., P.O. Box 800, Kidlington,
Oxford OX5 1DX, England. TEL 44-1865-843000.
FAX 44-1865-843010. *4626*

PARDES.
Editions Le Cerf, 24 bd. Saint-Michel, 75006 Paris,
France. *6128*

PARENTESI.
Associazaione Culturale Parentesi, S.S. 114 Pal Iles,
98125 Messina, Italy. TEL 39-90-692568. FAX 39-
90-692568. *3185*

PARERGON.
Australian and New Zealand Association for
Medieval and Renaissance Studies, University of
Sydney, Department of English, Sydney, N.S.W.
2006, Australia. FAX 02-692-2434. *4249*

PARISH AND COMMUNITY LIBRARIES NEWS.
Catholic Library Association, Parish Section, Box
16321, St. Paul, MN 55116. FAX 612-690-2131.
4019

PARKINSONISM AND RELATED DISORDERS.
Elsevier Science Ltd., P.O. Box 800, Kidlington,
Oxford OX5 1DX, England. TEL 44-1865-843000.
FAX 44-1865-843010. *4860*

PARLIAMENTARY HISTORY.
Edinburgh University Press, 22 George Sq.,
Edinburgh EH8 9LF, Scotland. TEL 44-131-650-
6207. FAX 44-131-662-0053. *3354*

PARNASSOS.
Parnassos Literary Society, 8 St. George Karytsis
Sq., 105 61 Athens, Greece. TEL 30-1-322-1917.
FAX 30-1-324-9398. *3621*

PARTICLE ACCELERATORS.
Gordon and Breach Science Publishers, c/o
International Publishers Distributor, P.O. Box 3054,
Langhorne, PA 19047-3054. TEL 215-750-2642.
FAX 215-7850-6343. *5598*

PARTICLE WORLD.
Gordon and Breach Science Publishers, c/o
International Publishers Distributor, P.O. Box 3054,
Langhorne, PA 19047-3054. TEL 215-750-2642.
FAX 215-750-6343. *5561*

PARTICULATE SCIENCE AND TECHNOLOGY.
Taylor & Francis Inc., 1900 Frost Rd., Ste. 101,
Bristol, PA 19007-1598. TEL 215-785-5800.
FAX 215-785-5515. *2646*

PARTISAN REVIEW.
Partisan Review, Inc., 236 Bay State Rd., Boston,
MA 02215. TEL 617-353-4260. FAX 617-353-
7444. *4160*

PASSAGES NORTH.
c/o Northern Michigan Univ., 1401 Presque Isle
Ave., Marquette, MI 49829. TEL 906-227-1203.
4250

PAST IMPERFECT.
University of Alberta, History Graduate Students
Association, c/o History Dept., 2-28 Tory Bldg.,
Edmonton, AB T6G 2H4, Canada. TEL 403-492-
4568. FAX 403-492-9125. *3354*

PASTORAL CARE IN EDUCATION.
Blackwell Publishers Ltd., 108 Cowley Rd., Oxford
OX4 1JF, England. TEL 44-1865-791100. FAX 44-
1865-791347. *2361*

PASTORAL PSYCHOLOGY.
Human Sciences Press, Inc. 233 Spring St., New
York, NY 10013-1578. TEL 212-620-8000.
FAX 212-463-0742. *5859*

PATHOBIOLOGY.
S. Karger AG, Allschwilerstr. 10, P.O. Box, CH-4009
Basel, Switzerland. TEL 061-3061111. FAX 061-
3061234. *4513*

PATHOLOGY: STATE OF THE ART REVIEWS.
Hanley & Belfus, Inc., 210 S. 13th St., Philadelphia,
PA 19107. TEL 215-545-7293. FAX 215-790-
9330. *4514*

PATHOPHYSIOLOGY.
Elsevier Science B.V., P.O. Box 211, 1000 AE
Amsterdam, Netherlands. TEL 31-20-4853911.
FAX 31-20-4853598. *792*

PATIENT EDUCATION AND COUNSELING.
Elsevier Science Ireland Ltd., P.O. Box 85, Limerick,
Ireland. TEL 353-61-471944. FAX 353-61-
472144. *5972*

PATOLOGIA.
Obstetricia Editores, S.A., Czda. de Tlalpan 2365,
Col. Ciudad Jardin, 04370 Mexico DF, Mexico.
TEL 6899133. *600*

PATOLOGO CLINICO.
A I P A C Service s.r.l., Via Luigi Ungarelli 23,
00162 Rome, Italy. TEL 39-6-8500007. FAX 39-6-
8600042. *4514*

PATTERN RECOGNITION.
Elsevier Science Ltd., Pergamon P.O. Box 800,
Kidlington, Oxford OX5 1DX, England. TEL 44-1865-
843000. FAX 44-1865-843010. *2029*

PATTERN RECOGNITION AND IMAGE ANALYSIS.
Maik Nauka - Interperiodica, Mezhdunarodnyi Otdel,
Ul. Profsoyuznaya, 90, 117864 Moscow, Russia.
TEL 7-095-3360066. FAX 7-095-3360066. *4387*

PATTERN RECOGNITION LETTERS.
North-Holland P.O. Box 211, 1000 AE Amsterdam,
Netherlands. TEL 31-20-4853911. FAX 31-20-
4853598. *2029*

PATTERNS OF PREJUDICE.
Sage Publications Ltd., 6 Bonhill St., London EC2A
4PU, England. TEL 44-171-374-0645. FAX 44-
171-374-8741. *5733*

PAUL ANTHONY BRICK LECTURES.
University of Missouri Press, 2910 LeMone Blvd.,
Columbia, MO 65202. TEL 314-882-7641.
FAX 314-884-4498. *5489*

**PAWA EREKUTORONIKUSU KENKYUKAI
RONBUNSHI.**
Pawa Erekutoronikusu Kenkyukai, c/o Center for
Academic Societies Japan, Osaka, 14th Fl., Senri
Life Science Center Bldg., 1-4-2 Shinsenrihigashi-
machi, Toyonaka 565, Japan. TEL 81-6-879-7982.
FAX 81-6-879-7984. *3529*

PEABODY JOURNAL OF EDUCATION.
Lawrence Erlbaum Associates, Inc., 10 Industrial Dr.,
Mahwah, NJ 07430-2262. TEL 201-236-9500.
FAX 201-236-0072. *2361*

PEACHTREE MAGAZINE.
C S Publishers, Inc., 120 Interstate N. Pkwy. E.,
Ste. 445, Atlanta, GA 30339. TEL 770-956-1207.
FAX 770-988-8972. *3235*

PE'AMIM.
Ben Zvi Institute for the Study of Jewish
Communities in the East, P.O. Box 7504, Jerusalem
91076, Israel. TEL 972-2-639204. FAX 972-2-
638310. *3499*

PEDAGOGIEKJOERNAAL.
University of Pretoria, Faculty of Education, Pretoria
0002, South Africa. TEL 27-12-4202272. FAX 27-
12-3422914. *2361*

PEDAGOGISCH TIJDSCHRIFT.
Institute of Psychology, Tiensestraat 102, B-3000
Leuven, Belgium. TEL 32-16-326102. FAX 32-16-
326000. *2361*

PEDIATRIA POLSKA.
Wydawnictwo Medyczne Urban i Partner, Ul. Marii
Sklodowskiej-Curie 55-61, 50-950 Wroclaw,
Poland. TEL 48-71-225497. FAX 48-71-224391.
4810

PEDIATRIC ALLERGY AND IMMUNOLOGY.
Munksgaard International Publishers Ltd., 35
Noerre Soegade, P.O. Box 2148, DK-1016
Copenhagen K, Denmark. TEL 45-33-127030.
FAX 45-33-129387. *4810*

**PEDIATRIC ALLERGY AND IMMUNOLOGY.
SUPPLEMENTUM.**
Munksgaard International Publishers Ltd., 35 Norre
Soegade, P.O. Box 2148, DK-1016 Copenhagen,
Denmark. TEL 45-33-127030. FAX 45-33-129387.
4810

PEDIATRIC AND ADOLESCENT ENDOCRINOLOGY.
S. Karger AG, Allschwilerstr. 10, P.O. Box, CH-4009
Basel, Switzerland. TEL 061-3061111. FAX 061-
3061234. *4674*

PEDIATRIC AND ADOLESCENT MEDICINE.
S. Karger AG, Allschwilerstr. 10, P.O. Box, CH-4009
Basel, Switzerland. TEL 061-3061111. FAX 061-
3061234. *4811*

PEDIATRIC CARDIOLOGY.
Springer-Verlag, Medical Journals, 175 Fifth Ave.,
New York, NY 10010. TEL 212-460-1500.
FAX 212-473-6272. *4608*

PEDIATRIC DENTISTRY.
American Academy of Pediatric Dentistry, 211 E.
Chicago Ave., Ste. 700, Chicago, IL 60611-2616.
TEL 312-337-2169. FAX 312-337-6329. *4651*

PEDIATRIC DERMATOLOGY.
Blackwell Science Inc., 238 Main St., Cambridge,
MA 02142-1413. TEL 617-876-7022. FAX 617-
492-5263. *4664*

PEDIATRIC EMERGENCY & CRITICAL CARE.
Riverpress, Inc., Box 23, Jersey City, NJ 07303-
0023. TEL 201-434-5073. FAX 201-434-7230.
4572

PEDIATRIC EMERGENCY CARE.
Williams & Wilkins, 351 W. Camden St., Baltimore,
MD 21201. TEL 410-528-4000. FAX 410-528-
4312. *4811*

PEDIATRIC EXERCISE SCIENCE.
Human Kinetics Publishers, Inc., Box 5076,
Champaign, IL 61825-5076. TEL 217-351-5076.
FAX 217-351-2674. *4811*

PEDIATRIC HEMATOLOGY & ONCOLOGY.
Taylor & Francis Inc., 1900 Frost Rd., Ste. 101,
Bristol, PA 19007-1598. TEL 215-785-5800.
FAX 215-785-5515. *4811*

PEDIATRIC HEMATOLOGY - ONCOLOGY SERIES.
Lippincott - Raven Publishers 227 E. Washington
Sq., Philadelphia, PA 19106. TEL 215-238-4200.
FAX 215-238-4235. *4762*

THE PEDIATRIC INFECTIOUS DISEASE JOURNAL.
Williams & Wilkins, 351 W. Camden St., Baltimore,
MD 21201. TEL 410-528-4000. FAX 410-528-
4312. *4811*

PEDIATRIC NEUROLOGY.
Elsevier Science Inc., Box 945, New York, NY
10159-0945. TEL 212-633-3730. FAX 212-633-
3680. *4811*

PEDIATRIC NEUROSURGERY.
S. Karger AG, Allschwilerstr. 10, P.O. Box, CH-4009
Basel, Switzerland. TEL 061-3061111. FAX 061-
3061234. *4860*

PEDIATRIC NURSING.
Jannetti Publications, Inc., East Holly Ave., Box 56,
Pitman, NJ 08071-0056. TEL 609-256-2300.
FAX 609-589-7463. *4725*

PEDIATRIC PATHOLOGY & LABORATORY MEDICINE.
Taylor & Francis Inc., 1900 Frost Rd., Ste. 101,
Bristol, PA 19007-1598. TEL 215-785-5800.
FAX 215-785-5515. *4812*

PEDIATRIC PHYSICAL THERAPY.
Williams & Wilkins, 351 W. Camden St., Baltimore,
MD 21201. TEL 410-528-4000. FAX 410-528-
4312. *4812*

PEDIATRIC PRIMARY CARE.
Riverpress, Inc., Box 23, Jersey City, NJ 07303-
0023. TEL 201-434-5073. FAX 201-434-7230.
4572

PEDIATRIC PULMONOLOGY.
John Wiley & Sons, Inc., Journals, 605 Third Ave.,
New York, NY 10158. TEL 212-850-6645.
FAX 212-850-6021. *4812*

PEDIATRIC RESEARCH.
Williams & Wilkins, 351 W. Camden St., Baltimore,
MD 21201. TEL 410-528-4000. FAX 410-528-
4312. *4812*

PEDIATRIC REVIEWS AND COMMUNICATIONS.
Harwood Academic Publishers, c/o International
Publishers Distributor, P.O. Box 3054, Langhorne,
PA 19047-3054. TEL 215-750-2642. FAX 215-
750-6343. *4812*

PEDIATRICS IN REVIEW.
American Academy of Pediatrics, 141 Northwest
Point Blvd., Box 927, Elk Grove Village, IL 60009-
0927. TEL 847-228-5005. FAX 847-228-5097.
4812

PEDOLOGIST.
Japanese Society of Pedology, c/o National Institute
of Agro-Environmental Sciences, 3-1-1 Kannondai,
Tsukuba, Ibaraki 305, Japan. TEL 0298-38-8275.
FAX 0298-38-8199. *234*

PEDOSPHERE.
Science Press, Marketing and Sales Department, 16
Donghuangchenggen North St., Beijing 100717,
People's Republic of China. TEL 4010642.
FAX 4019810. *2214*

PENN SOUNDS.
Composer Services Inc., 345 S. 19th St.,
Philadelphia, PA 19103. TEL 215-985-0963.
5187

PENNSYLVANIA ACADEMY OF SCIENCE. JOURNAL.
Pennsylvania Academy of Science, c/o Dr. S.K.
Majumdar, Ed., Dept. of Biology, Lafayette College,
Easton, PA 18042. TEL 610-250-5464. FAX 610-
250-6557. *6271*

PENNSYLVANIA DENTAL JOURNAL.
Pennsylvania Dental Association, Box 3341,
Harrisburg, PA 17105. TEL 717-234-5941.
FAX 717-232-7169. *4651*

PENNSYLVANIA FOLKLIFE.
Pennsylvania Folklife Society, Box 92, Collegeville,
PA 19426. TEL 215-489-4111. *3483*

PENNSYLVANIA GENEALOGICAL MAGAZINE.
Genealogical Society of Pennsylvania, 1305 Locust
St., Philadelphia, PA 19107. TEL 215-545-0391.
FAX 215-545-0936. *3097*

PENNSYLVANIA GEOGRAPHER.
University of Pittsburgh at Johnstown, Department
of Geography, Johnstown, PA 15904. TEL 814-
269-2994. FAX 814-269-7255. *3268*

PENNSYLVANIA HISTORY.
Pennsylvania Historical Association, Weaver Bldg.,
Penn State University, State College, PA 16802.
TEL 814-865-1367. *3483*

**PENNSYLVANIA MAGAZINE OF HISTORY AND
BIOGRAPHY.**
Historical Society of Pennsylvania, 1300 Locust St.,
Philadelphia, PA 19107. TEL 215-732-6201.
FAX 215-732-2680. *3483*

**PENNSYLVANIA OSTEOPATHIC MEDICAL
ASSOCIATION. JOURNAL.**
Pennsylvania Osteopathic Medical Association, 1330
Eisenhower Blvd., Harrisburg, PA 17111. TEL 717-
939-9318. FAX 717-939-7255. *4514*

THE PENTAGON.
Kappa Mu Epsilon, c/o Larry Scott, Bus. Manager,
Div. of Mathematics & Computer Science, Emporia
State University, Emporia, KS 66801. TEL 316-
341-5638. FAX 316-341-6055. *4387*

PEOPLE SEARCHING NEWS.
Adoption Education Resources, Box 100444, Palm
Bay, FL 32910-0444. TEL 407-768-2222.
FAX 407-728-7999. *6387*

PEPPERDINE LAW REVIEW.
Pepperdine University, School of Law, 24255
Pacific Coast Hwy., Mailbu, CA 90263-4694.
TEL 310-456-4694. FAX 310-317-7283. *3832*

PEPTIDES.
Elsevier Science Inc., Box 945, New York, NY
10159-0945. TEL 212-633-3730. FAX 212-633-
3680. *646*

PERCEPTION.
Pion Ltd., 207 Brondesbury Park, London NW2
5JN, England. TEL 44-181-459-0066. FAX 44-
181-451-6454. *5869*

PERCEPTION & PSYCHOPHYSICS.
Psychonomic Society, Inc., 1710 Fortview Rd.,
Austin, TX 78704. TEL 512-462-2442. *5869*

PERCEPTUAL AND MOTOR SKILLS.
Dr. C.H. Ammons & Dr. R.B. Ammons, Eds. &
Pubs., Box 9229, Missoula, MT 59807. *5869*

PERFORMANCE EVALUATION.
North-Holland P.O. Box 211, 1000 AE Amsterdam,
Netherlands. TEL 31-20-4853911. FAX 31-20-
4853598. *1997*

PERGAMON UNIFIED ENGINEERING SERIES.
Elsevier Science Ltd., Books Division, P.O. Box 800,
Kidlington, Oxford OX3 0BW, England. TEL 44-
1865-843000. FAX 44-1865-843010. *2614*

PERIODICA MATHEMATICA HUNGARICA.
Kluwer Academic Publishers, Postbus 17, 3300 AA
Dordrecht, Netherlands. TEL 31-78-6392392.
FAX 31-78-6392254. *4387*

PERIODICA POLYTECHNICA. ARCHITECTURE.
Budapesti Muszaki Egyetem, Periodica Polytechnica,
1521 Budapest, Hungary. TEL 36-1-4631469.
FAX 36-1-4632141. *400*

**PERIODICA POLYTECHNICA. CHEMICAL
ENGINEERING.**
Budapesti Muszaki Egyetem, Periodica Polytechnica,
1521 Budapest, Hungary. TEL 36-1-4631469.
FAX 36-1-4632141. *2646*

PERIODICA POLYTECHNICA. CIVIL ENGINEERING.
Budapesti Muszaki Egyetem, Periodica Polytechnica,
1521 Budapest, Hungary. TEL 36-1-4631469.
FAX 36-1-4632141. *2670*

**PERIODICA POLYTECHNICA. ELECTRICAL
ENGINEERING.**
Budapesti Muszaki Egyetem, Periodica Polytechnica,
1521 Budapest, Hungary. TEL 36-1-4631469.
FAX 36-1-4632141. *2715*

**PERIODICA POLYTECHNICA. HUMANITIES AND
SOCIAL SCIENCES.**
Budapesti Muszaki Egyetem, Periodica Polytechnica,
1521 Budapest, Hungary. TEL 36-1-4631469.
FAX 36-1-4632141. *3621*

**PERIODICA POLYTECHNICA. MECHANICAL
ENGINEERING.**
Budapesti Muszaki Egyetem, Periodica Polytechnica,
1521 Budapest, Hungary. TEL 36-1-4631469.
FAX 36-1-4632141. *2766*

**PERIODICA POLYTECHNICA. TRANSPORT
ENGINEERING.**
Budapesti Muszaki Egyetem, Periodica Polytechnica,
1521 Budapest, Hungary. TEL 36-1-4631469.
FAX 36-1-4632141. *6725*

PERIODONTOLOGY.
Australian Society of Periodontology, Dept. of
Dentistry, University of Queensland, Brisbane, Qld.
4000, Australia. TEL 61-7-365-8055. FAX 61-7-
365-8199. *4651*

PERIODONTOLOGY 2000.
Munksgaard International Publishers Ltd., 35
Noerre Soegade, P.O. Box 2148, DK-1016
Copenhagen K, Denmark. TEL 45-33-127030.
FAX 45-33-129387. *4651*

PERITO AGRARIO.
IACICO s.r.l., Via A. Poliziano 80, 00184 Rome, Italy. TEL 39-6-4873183. FAX 39-6-4873144. *143*

PERMAFROST AND PERIGLACIAL PROCESSES.
John Wiley & Sons Ltd., Journals, Baffins Ln., Chichester, W. Sussex PO19 1UD, England. TEL 44-1243-779777. FAX 44-1243-843232. *2256*

PERSIMMON HILL.
National Cowboy Hall of Fame and Western Heritage Center, 1700 N.E. 63rd St., Oklahoma City, OK 73111. TEL 405-478-2250. FAX 405-478-4714. *3483*

PERSONAL RELATIONSHIPS.
Cambridge University Press, The Edinburgh Bldg., Shaftesbury Rd., Cambridge CB2 2RU, England. TEL 44-1223-312393. FAX 44-1223-315052. *5889*

PERSONALITY AND INDIVIDUAL DIFFERENCES.
Elsevier Science Ltd., Pergamon, P.O. Box 800, Kidlington, Oxford OX5 1DX, England. TEL 44-1865-843000. FAX 44-1865-843010. *5869*

PERSONALITY, PSYCHOPATHOLOGY AND PSYCHOTHERAPY.
Academic Press, Inc., 525 B St., Ste. 1900, San Diego, CA 92101-4495. TEL 619-231-0926. FAX 619-699-6715. *5869*

PERSONNEL POLICIES IN EUROPE.
P-E International plc, Park House, Wick Rd., Egham, Surrey TW20 0HW, England. TEL 44-1784-434411. FAX 44-1784-476369. *1509*

PERSONNEL PSYCHOLOGY.
Personnel Psychology, Inc., 745 Haskins Rd., Ste. A, Bowling Green, OH 43402-1600. TEL 419-352-1562. FAX 419-352-2645. *5870*

PERSONNEL, TRAINING AND EDUCATION.
Library Association, Personnel, Training and Education Group, 14 Aireville Ave., Bradford BD9 4ET, England. FAX 01274-594685. *4019*

PERSOONIA.
Rijksherbarium - Hortus Botanicus, Publications Department, P.O. Box 9514, 2300 RA Leiden, Netherlands. *695.*

PERSPECTIVAS EM CIENCIA DA INFORMACAO.
Universidade Federal de Minas Gerais, Escola de Biblioteconomia, Caixa Postal 1606, 30161-970 Belo Horizonte MG, Brazil. TEL 55-31-4995227. FAX 55-31-4995200. *4019*

PERSPECTIVE OF PHYSICS.
Gordon & Breach Science Publishers, c/o International Publishers Distributor, P.O. Box 3054, Langhorne, PA 19047-3054. TEL 215-750-2642. FAX 215-750-6343. *5561*

PERSPECTIVES (COLUMBUS).
Association for General and Liberal Studies, Ohio Dominican College, 1216 Sunbury Rd., Columbus, OH 43219-2099. TEL 614-251-4663. FAX 614-252-0776. *2362*

PERSPECTIVES (TORONTO).
Gerontological Nursing Association, P.O. Box 368, Station "K", Toronto, ON M4P 2G7, Canada. TEL 416-767-4454. FAX 416-591-6812. *3294*

PERSPECTIVES IN ARTIFICIAL INTELLIGENCE.
Academic Press, Inc., 525 B St., Ste. 1900, San Diego, CA 92101-4495. TEL 619-231-6616. FAX 619-699-6715. *2010*

PERSPECTIVES IN BIOLOGY AND MEDICINE.
University of Chicago Press, Journals Division, Box 37005, Chicago, IL 60637. TEL 773-753-3347. FAX 773-753-0811. *4514*

PERSPECTIVES IN BIOMECHANICS.
Harwood Academic Publishers, c/o International Publishers Distributor, P.O. Box 3054, Langhorne, PA 19047-3054. TEL 215-750-2642. FAX 215-750-6343. *600*

PERSPECTIVES IN COMPUTING.
Academic Press, Inc., 525 B St., Ste. 1900, San Diego, CA 92101-4495. TEL 619-231-6616. FAX 619-699-6715. *1997*

PERSPECTIVES IN CONDENSED MATTER PHYSICS.
Kluwer Academic Publishers, Postbus 17, 3300 AA Dordrecht, Netherlands. TEL 31-78-6392392. FAX 31-78-6392254. *5561*

PERSPECTIVES IN DRUG DISCOVERY AND DESIGN.
E S C O M Science Publishers BV, P.O. Box 214, 2300 AE Leiden, Netherlands. TEL 31-71-127052. FAX 31-71-121772. *5432*

PERSPECTIVES IN EDUCATION AND DEAFNESS.
Gallaudet University Pre-College Programs, KDES PAS-6, 800 Florida Ave., N.E., Washington, DC 20002-3695. TEL 202-651-5340. FAX 202-651-5708. *2473*

PERSPECTIVES IN ENERGY.
Pion Ltd., 207 Brondesbury Park, London NW2 5JN, England. TEL 44-181-459-0066. FAX 44-181-451-6454. *2555*

PERSPECTIVES IN ETHOLOGY.
Plenum Publishing Corp., 233 Spring St., New York, NY 10013-1578. TEL 212-620-8000. FAX 212-463-0742. *817*

PERSPECTIVES IN HYPERTENSION SERIES.
Lippincott - Raven Publishers 227 E. Washington Sq., Philadelphia, PA 19106. TEL 215-238-4200. FAX 215-238-4235. *4608*

PERSPECTIVES IN IMMUNOLOGY.
Academic Press, Inc., 525 B St., Ste. 1900, San Diego, CA 92101-4495. TEL 619-231-0926. FAX 619-699-6715. *4586*

PERSPECTIVES IN LAW AND PSYCHOLOGY.
Plenum Publishing Corp., 233 Spring St., New York, NY 10013-1578. TEL 212-620-8000. FAX 212-463-0742. *3332*

PERSPECTIVES IN MATHEMATICS.
Academic Press, Inc., 525 B St., Ste. 1900, San Diego, CA 92101-4495. TEL 619-231-6616. FAX 619-699-6715. *4388*

PERSPECTIVES IN MEDICAL VIROLOGY.
Elsevier Science B.V. Books Division, P.O. Box 211, 1000 AE Amsterdam, Netherlands. TEL 31-20-4853911. FAX 31-20-4853705. *765*

PERSPECTIVES IN MEXICAN AMERICAN STUDIES.
University of Arizona, Mexican American Studies & Research Center, Douglass Bldg., Rm. 315, Tucson, AZ 85721. TEL 520-621-7551. FAX 602-621-7966. *2902*

PERSPECTIVES IN NEUROLINGUISTICS, NEUROPSYCHOLOGY, AND PSYCHOLINGUISTICS.
Academic Press, Inc. 525 B St., Ste. 1900, San Diego, CA 92101-4495. TEL 619-231-6616. FAX 619-699-6715. *4860*

PERSPECTIVES IN PEDIATRIC PATHOLOGY.
S. Karger AG, Allschwilerstr. 10, P.O. Box, CH-4009 Basel, Switzerland. TEL 061-3061111. FAX 061-3061234. *4813*

PERSPECTIVES IN PHYSICS.
Academic Press, Inc., 525 B St., Ste. 1900, San Diego, CA 92101-4495. TEL 619-231-6616. FAX 619-699-6715. *5561*

PERSPECTIVES IN PSYCHIATRIC CARE.
Nursecom Inc., 1211 Locust St., Philadelphia, PA 19107. TEL 215-545-7222. FAX 215-545-8107. *4725*

PERSPECTIVES IN PSYCHOTHERAPY.
Gordon & Breach Science Publishers, c/o International Publishers Distributor, P.O. Box 3054, Langhorne, PA 19047-3054. TEL 215-750-2642. FAX 215-750-6343. *5870*

PERSPECTIVES IN VERTEBRATE SCIENCE.
Kluwer Academic Publishers, Postbus 17, 3300 AA Dordrecht, Netherlands. TEL 31-78-6392392. FAX 31-78-6392254. *817*

PERSPECTIVES OF NEW MUSIC.
Perspectives of New Music, Inc., University of Washington, Music, Box 353450, Seattle, WA 98195-3450. TEL 206-543-0196. FAX 206-543-9285. *5188*

PERSPECTIVES ON MEDICAL RESEARCH.
Medical Research Modernization Committee, Box 2751, New York, NY 10163. TEL 216-832-3904. FAX 216-283-6702. *4634*

PERSPECTIVES ON POLITICAL SCIENCE.
Heldref Publications, 1319 18th St, N.W., Washington, DC 20036-1802. TEL 202-296-6267. FAX 202-296-5149. *5692*

PERSPECTIVES ON SCIENCE: HISTORICAL, PHILOSOPHICAL, SOCIAL.
University of Chicago Press, Journals Division, Box 37005, Chicago, IL 60637. TEL 773-702-7600. FAX 773-753-0811. *6271*

PERSPECTIVES ON SOUTHERN AFRICA.
University of California Press, 2120 Berkeley Way, Berkeley, CA 94720. TEL 510-642-4247. FAX 510-643-7127. *5692*

PERTANIKA JOURNAL OF SCIENCE AND TECHNOLOGY.
Universiti Pertanian Malaysia Press, Serdang, Selangor, Malaysia. TEL 03-9433740. FAX 03-9433404. *6271*

PERTANIKA JOURNAL OF SOCIAL SCIENCE AND HUMANITIES.
Universiti Pertanian Malaysia Press, Serdang, Selangor, Malaysia. TEL 03-9433740. FAX 03-9433404. *6337*

PERTANIKA JOURNAL OF TROPICAL AGRICULTURAL SCIENCE.
Universiti Pertanian Malaysia Press, Serdang, Selangor, Malaysia. FAX 03-9483745. *144*

PESARO CITTA E CONTA.
Societa Pesarese di Studi Storici, Via Abbati 30, Casella 9, 61100 Pesaro, Italy. TEL 39-721-34411. *3434*

PESHITTA INSTITUTE, LEIDEN. MONOGRAPHS.
E.J. Brill, P.O. Box 9000, 2300 PA Leiden, Netherlands. TEL 31-71-5353500. FAX 31-71-5317532. *6128*

PESQUISA E PLANEJAMENTO ECONOMICO.
Instituto de Pesquisa Economica Aplicada, Av. Presidente Antonio Carlos, 51, 13 andar, 20020-010 Rio de Janeiro, RJ, Brazil. TEL 55-21-2205533. FAX 55-21-2401920. *1528*

PEST CONTROL.
Advanstar Communications, Inc., 7500 Old Oak Blvd., Cleveland, OH 44130. TEL 216-243-8100. FAX 216-891-2675. *234*

PESTICIDE BIOCHEMISTRY AND PHYSIOLOGY.
Academic Press, Inc., Journal Division, 525 B St. Ste. 1900, San Diego, CA 92101-4495. TEL 619-230-1840. FAX 619-699-5800. *234*

PESTICIDE SCIENCE.
John Wiley & Sons Ltd., Journals, Baffins Ln., Chichester, W. Sussex PO19 1UD, England. TEL 44-1243-779777. FAX 44-1243-843232. *235*

PETROLE ET TECHNIQUES.
Association Francaise des Techniciens et des Professionels du Petrole (A F T P), 92038 Paris la Defense, France. TEL 33-1-47-17-67-32. FAX 33-1-47-17-67-44. *5370*

PETROLEUM CHEMISTRY.
Elsevier Science Ltd., Pergamon, P.O. Box 800, Kidlington, Oxford OX5 1DX, England. TEL 44-1865-843000. FAX 44-1865-843010. *5371*

PETROLEUM ENGINEERING AND DEVELOPMENT STUDIES.
Kluwer Academic Publishers, Postbus 17, 3300 AA Dordrecht, Netherlands. TEL 31-78-6392392. FAX 31-78-6392254. *5371*

PETROLOGY AND STRUCTURAL GEOLOGY.
Kluwer Academic Publishers, Postbus 17, 3300 AA Dordrecht, Netherlands. TEL 31-78-6392392. FAX 31-78-6392254. *2256*

PHAENOMENOLOGICA.
Kluwer Academic Publishers, Postbus 17, 3300 AA Dordrecht, Netherlands. TEL 31-78-6392392. FAX 31-78-6392254. *5430*

PHARMA SELECTA.
Stichting Pharma Selecta, Postbus 122, 8430 Oosterwolde, Netherlands. TEL 31-5160-15908. *5433*

PHARMACEUTICA ACTA HELVETIAE.
Elsevier Science B.V., P.O. Box 211, 1000 AE Amsterdam, Netherlands. TEL 31-20-4853911. FAX 31-20-4853598. *5433*

PHARMACEUTICAL CHEMISTRY JOURNAL.
Plenum Publishing Corp., Consultants Bureau, 233 Spring St., New York, NY 10013-1578. TEL 212-620-8468. FAX 212-463-0742. *5433*

PHARMACEUTICAL DEVELOPMENT AND TECHNOLOGY.
Marcel Dekker Journals, 270 Madison Ave., New York, NY 10016. TEL 212-696-9000. FAX 212-685-4540. *5433*

PHARMACEUTICAL MEDICINE (LONDON).
Chapman & Hall, Journals Department 2-6 Boundary Row, London SE1 8HN, England. TEL 0171-865-0066. FAX 0171-522-9623. *5434*

PHARMACEUTICAL RESEARCH.
Plenum Publishing Corp., 233 Spring St., New York, NY 10013-1578. TEL 212-620-8000. FAX 212-463-0742. *5434*

PHARMACEUTICAL TECHNOLOGY.
Advanstar Communications, Inc., 7500 Old Oak Blvd., Cleveland, OH 44130. TEL 216-826-2839. FAX 216-891-2726. *5435*

PHARMACEUTICAL TECHNOLOGY EUROPE - BIOPHARM.
Advanstar Communications, Advanstar House, Park West, Sealand Rd., Chester CH1 4RN, England. TEL 44-1244-378888. FAX 44-1244-370512. *5435*

PHARMACIST'S LETTER.
Therapeutic Research Center, 2453 Grand Canal Blvd., Ste. A, Box 8190, Stockton, CA 95208. TEL 209-472-2240. FAX 209-472-2249. *5435*

PHARMACOCHEMISTRY LIBRARY.
Elsevier Science B.V., Books Division, P.O. Box 211, 1000 AE Amsterdam, Netherlands. TEL 31-20-4853911. FAX 31-20-4853705. *5435*

PHARMACOECONOMICS.
Adis International Limited, Private Bag 65901, Mairangi Bay, Auckland 10, New Zealand. TEL 64-9-479-8100. FAX 64-9-479-8145. *5436*

PHARMACOEPIDEMIOLOGY AND DRUG SAFETY.
John Wiley & Sons Ltd., Journals, Baffins Ln., Chichester, W. Sussex PO19 1UD, England. TEL 44-1243-779777. FAX 44-1243-843232. *5436*

PHARMACOGENETICS.
Chapman & Hall, Journals Department 2-6 Boundary Row, London SE1 8HN, England. TEL 44-171-8650066. FAX 44-171-5229623. *749*

PHARMACOLOGICAL REVIEWS.
Williams & Wilkins, 351 W. Camden St., Baltimore, MD 21201. TEL 410-528-4000. FAX 410-528-4312. *5436*

PHARMACOLOGY.
S. Karger AG, Allschwilerstr. 10, P.O. Box, CH-4009 Basel, Switzerland. TEL 061-3061111. FAX 061-3061234. *5436*

PHARMACOLOGY AND THE SKIN.
S. Karger AG, Allschwilerstr. 10, P.O. Box, CH-4009 Basel, Switzerland. TEL 061-3061111. FAX 061-3061234. *4664*

PHARMACOLOGY AND THERAPEUTICS.
Elsevier Science Inc., Box 945, New York, NY 10159-0945. TEL 212-633-3730. FAX 212-633-3680. *5436*

PHARMACOLOGY & TOXICOLOGY.
Munksgaard International Publishers Ltd., 35 Noerre Soegade, P.O. Box 2148, DK-1016 Copenhagen K, Denmark. TEL 45-33-127030. FAX 45-33-129387. *5436*

PHARMACOLOGY & TOXICOLOGY. SUPPLEMENTUM.
Munksgaard International Publishers Ltd., 35 Noerre Soegade, P.O. Box 2148, DK-1016 Copenhagen K, Denmark. TEL 45-33-127030. FAX 45-33-129387. *2847*

PHARMACOLOGY, BIOCHEMISTRY AND BEHAVIOR.
Elsevier Science Inc., Box 945, New York, NY 10159-0945. TEL 212-633-3730. FAX 212-633-3680. *647*

PHARMACOTHERAPY.
Pharmacotherapy Publications, Inc., New England Medical Center - Box 806, 750 Washington St., Boston, MA 02111. TEL 617-636-5390. FAX 617-636-5318. *5437*

PHARMACY CADENCE.
P A S Pharmacy - Association Services, Box 6565, Athens, GA 30604. TEL 706-613-0100. FAX 706-613-0200. *5437*

DIE PHARMAZIE.
Govi Pharmazeutischer Verlag GmbH, Ginnheimerstr. 26, 65760 Eschborn, Germany. TEL 49-6196-928262. FAX 49-6196-928203. *5438*

PHAROS (MENLO PARK).
Alpha Omega Alpha Honor Medical Society, 525 Middlefield Rd., Ste. 130, Menlo Park, CA 94025. TEL 415-329-0291. FAX 415-329-1618. *4515*

PHASE TRANSITION PHENOMENA.
Elsevier Science B.V., Books Division, P.O. Box 211, 1000 AE Amsterdam, Netherlands. TEL 31-20-4853911. FAX 31-20-4853705. *5562*

PHASE TRANSITIONS.
Gordon and Breach Science Publishers, c/o International Publishers Distributor, P.O. Box 3054, Langhorne, PA 19047-3054. TEL 215-750-2642. FAX 215-750-6343. *5562*

PHILADELPHIA MEDICINE.
Philadelphia County Medical Society, 2100 Spring Garden St., Philadelphia, PA 19130. TEL 215-563-5343. FAX 215-563-3627. *4515*

THE PHILIPPINE ENTOMOLOGIST.
Philippine Association of Entomologists, c/o Department of Entomology, University of the Philippines at Los Banos, College, Laguna 4031, Philippines. TEL 536-94-2225. FAX 536-94-2721. *734*

PHILIPPINE JOURNAL OF VETERINARY MEDICINE.
University of the Philippines Los Banos, College of Veterinary Medicine, Los Banos, Laguna 4031, Philippines. TEL 94-536-2730. FAX 94-536-2727. *6952*

PHILIPPINE QUARTERLY OF CULTURE AND SOCIETY.
San Carlos Publications, P.O. Box 182, 6000 Cebu City, Philippines. FAX 6332-54341. *3621*

PHILIPS JOURNAL OF RESEARCH.
Elsevier Science Ltd., P.O. Box 800, Kidlington, Oxford OX5 1DX, England. TEL 44-1865-843000. FAX 44-1865-843010. *2614*

PHILOSOPHIA ANTIQUA.
E.J. Brill, P.O. Box 9000, 2300 PA Leiden, Netherlands. TEL 31-71-5353500. FAX 31-71-5317532. *5490*

PHILOSOPHIA MATHEMATICA.
University of Toronto Press, Journals Department, 5201 Dufferin St., Downsview, ON M3H 5T8, Canada. TEL 416-667-7838. FAX 416-667-7881. *5490*

PHILOSOPHIA PATRUM.
E.J. Brill, P.O. Box 9000, 2300 PA Leiden, Netherlands. TEL 31-71-5353500. FAX 31-71-5317532. *6084*

PHILOSOPHIA PERENNIS.
Society for Aristotelian Sudies, c/o Robert Augros, Treas., Box 1643, St. Anselm College, 100 St. Anselm Dr., Manchester, NH 03102. TEL 603-641-7065. *5490*

PHILOSOPHICAL INQUIRY.
Artistotelian University, P.O. Box 84, Thessaloniki, Greece. TEL 30-31-992-519. *5491*

PHILOSOPHICAL INVESTIGATIONS.
Blackwell Publishers Ltd., 108 Cowley Rd., Oxford OX4 1JF, England. TEL 44-1865-791100. FAX 44-1865-791347. *5491*

PHILOSOPHICAL MAGAZINE A: PHYSICS OF CONDENSED MATTER, DEFECTS AND MECHANICAL PROPERTIES.
Taylor & Francis Ltd., 1 Gunpowder Sq., London EC4A 3DE, England. TEL 44-171-583-0490. FAX 44-171-583-0585. *5562*

PHILOSOPHICAL MAGAZINE LETTERS.
Taylor & Francis Ltd., 1 Gunpowder Sq., London EC4A 3DE, England. TEL 44-171-583-0490. FAX 44-171-583-0585. *5562*

PHILOSOPHICAL PAPERS.
c/o Dept. of Philosophy, University of the Witwatersrand, P.O. Wits, Johannesburg 2050, South Africa. TEL 716-2757. FAX 403-1174. *5491*

PHILOSOPHICAL PROBLEMS TODAY.
Kluwer Academic Publishers, Postbus 17, 3300 AA Dordrecht, Netherlands. TEL 31-78-6392392. FAX 31-78-6392254. *5491*

PHILOSOPHICAL PSYCHOLOGY.
Carfax Publishing Co., P.O. Box 25, Abingdon, Oxon. OX14 3UE, England. TEL 44-1235-401000. FAX 44-1235-401550. *5870*

PHILOSOPHICAL QUARTERLY.
Blackwell Publishers Ltd., 108 Cowley Rd., Oxford OX4 1JF, England. TEL 44-1865-791100. FAX 44-1865-791347. *5491*

PHILOSOPHICAL STUDIES.
Kluwer Academic Publishers, Postbus 17, 3300 AA Dordrecht, Netherlands. TEL 31-78-6392392. FAX 31-78-6392254. *5491*

PHILOSOPHICAL STUDIES SERIES.
Kluwer Academic Publishers, Postbus 17, 3300 AA Dordrecht, Netherlands. TEL 31-78-6392392. FAX 31-78-6392254. *5491*

PHILOSOPHY AND EDUCATION.
Kluwer Academic Publishers, Postbus 17, 3300 AA Dordrecht, Netherlands. TEL 31-78-6392392. FAX 31-78-6392254. *5492*

PHILOSOPHY AND MEDICINE.
Kluwer Academic Publishers, Postbus 17, 3300 AA Dordrecht, Netherlands. TEL 31-78-6392392. FAX 31-78-6392254. *5492*

PHILOSOPHY AND PHENOMENOLOGICAL RESEARCH.
International Phenomenological Society, Brown University, Box 1947, Providence, RI 02912. TEL 401-863-3215. FAX 401-863-2719. *5492*

PHILOSOPHY AND RELIGION.
E.J. Brill, P.O. Box 9000, 2300 PA Leiden, Netherlands. TEL 31-71-5353500. FAX 31-71-5317532. *5492*

PHILOSOPHY AND RHETORIC.
Pennsylvania State University Press, 820 N. University Dr., Ste. C, University Park, PA 16802-1003. TEL 814-865-1327. FAX 814-863-1408. *5492*

PHILOSOPHY & SOCIAL ACTION.
Committee of Concerned Indian Philosophers for Social Action, M-120 Greater Kailash 1, New Delhi 110 048, India. TEL 091-11-641-5365. FAX 091-11-647-4646. *6338*

PHILOSOPHY AND SOCIAL CRITICISM.
Sage Publications Ltd., 6 Bonhill St., London EC2A 4PU, England. TEL 44-171-374-0645. FAX 44-171-374-8741. *3622*

PHILOSOPHY AND TECHNOLOGY.
Kluwer Academic Publishers, Postbus 17, 3300 AA Dordrecht, Netherlands. TEL 31-78-6392392. FAX 31-78-6392254. *6660*

PHILOSOPHY EAST AND WEST.
University of Hawaii Press, Journals Department, 2840 Kolowalu St., Honolulu, HI 96822. TEL 808-956-8833. FAX 808-988-6052. *5493*

PHILOSOPHY OF HISTORY AND CULTURE.
E.J. Brill, P.O. Box 9000, 2300 PA Leiden, Netherlands. TEL 31-71-5353500. FAX 31-71-5317532. *5493*

PHILOSOPHY OF MUSIC EDUCATION REVIEW.
Indiana University, School of Music, Music Education Department, Sycamore Hall 405, Bloomington, IN 47405. TEL 812-855-2051. FAX 812-855-4936. *5188*

PHILOSOPHY OF SCIENCE.
University of Chicago Press, Journals Division, Box 37005, Chicago, IL 60637. TEL 773-753-3347. FAX 773-753-0811. *6272*

PHILOSOPHY, PSYCHIATRY & PSYCHOLOGY.
Johns Hopkins University Press, Journals Publishing Division, 2715 N. Charles St., Baltimore, MD 21218. TEL 410-516-6980. FAX 410-516-6968. *5493*

PHOENIX FICTION.
University of Chicago Press, 5801 S. Ellis Ave., Chicago, IL 60637. TEL 312-702-7899. *4250*

PHOENIX POETS.
University of Chicago Press, 5801 S. Ellis Ave., Chicago, IL 60637. TEL 708-702-7899. *4314*

PHONETICA.
S. Karger AG, Allschwilerstr. 10, P.O. Box, CH-4009 Basel, Switzerland. TEL 061-3061111. FAX 061-3061234. *4098*

PHOSPHORUS, SULPHUR AND SILICON AND THE RELATED ELEMENTS.
Gordon and Breach Science Publishers, c/o International Publishers Distributor, P.O. Box 3054, Langhorne, PA 19047-3054. TEL 215-750-2642. FAX 215-750-6343. *1732*

PHOTO ELECTRONIC IMAGING.
Professional Photographers of America, 57 Forsyth St., N.W., Ste. 1600, Atlanta, GA 30303. TEL 404-522-8600. FAX 404-614-6405. *5517*

PHOTOCHEMICAL & PHOTOBIOLOGICAL REVIEWS.
Plenum Publishing Corp., 233 Spring St., New York, NY 10013-1578. TEL 212-620-8000. FAX 212-463-0742. *1687*

PHOTOCHEMISTRY.
C R C Press, Inc., TEL 407-994-0555. FAX 407-998-9784. *1755*

PHOTOCHEMISTRY AND PHOTOBIOLOGY.
American Society for Photobiology, BioTech Park, Ste. 9, 1021 15th St., Augusta, GA 30901. TEL 706-721-2601. FAX 706-721-3048. *1688*

PHOTODERMATOLOGY, PHOTOIMMUNOLOGY & PHOTOMEDICINE.
Munksgaard International Publishers Ltd., 35 Noerre Soegade, P.O. Box 2148, DK-1016 Copenhagen K, Denmark. TEL 45-33-127030. FAX 45-33-129387. *4664*

PHOTOGRAMMETRIC RECORD.
Photogrammetric Society, Department of Photogrammetry & Surveying, University College London, Gower St., London WC1E 6BT, England. TEL 44-171-387-7050. FAX 44-171-380-0453. *3269*

PHOTOSYNTHESIS RESEARCH.
Kluwer Academic Publishers, Postbus 17, 3300 AA Dordrecht, Netherlands. TEL 31-78-6392392. FAX 31-78-6392254. *792*

PHOTOSYNTHETICA.
Kluwer Academic Publishers, Postbus 17, 3300 AA Dordrecht, Netherlands. TEL 31-78-6392392. FAX 31-78-6392254. *695*

PHOTOVISION.
Arte y Proyectos Editoriales, S.L., Apdo. 164, 41710 Utrera (Seville), Spain. TEL 95-486-28-95. *5519*

PHUKET MARINE BIOLOGICAL CENTER. RESEARCH BULLETIN.
Phuket Marine Biological Center, P.O. Box 60, Phuket 83000, Thailand. TEL 076-391128. FAX 076-391127. *600*

PHYCOLOGIA.
International Phycological Society, c/o Prof. M. Chihara, 3-19-7 Fuse-shin-machi, Kashiwa City 277, Japan. TEL 81-33-409-0589. *695*

PHYCOLOGICAL RESEARCH.
Blackwell Science Pty Ltd, P.O. Box 378, Carlton South, Vic. 3053, Australia. TEL 61-3-93470300. FAX 61-3-93493016. *695*

PHYSICA A - STATISTICAL AND THEORETICAL PHYSICS.
North-Holland P.O. Box 211, 1000 AE Amsterdam, Netherlands. TEL 31-20-4853911. FAX 31-20-4853598. *5562*

PHYSICA B - PHYSICS OF CONDENSED MATTER.
North-Holland P.O. Box 211, 1000 AE Amsterdam, Netherlands. TEL 31-20-4853911. FAX 31-20-4853598. *5562*

PHYSICA C - SUPERCONDUCTIVITY.
North-Holland P.O. Box 211, 1000 AE Amsterdam, Netherlands. TEL 31-20-4853911. FAX 31-20-4853598. *5562*

PHYSICA D - NONLINEAR PHENOMENA.
North-Holland P.O. Box 211, 1000 AE Amsterdam, Netherlands. TEL 31-20-4853911. FAX 31-20-4853598. *5563*

PHYSICAL ACOUSTICS: PRINCIPLES AND METHODS.
Academic Press, Inc., 525 B St., Ste. 1900, San Diego, CA 92101-4495. TEL 619-231-0926. FAX 619-699-6715. *5615*

PHYSICAL & OCCUPATIONAL THERAPY IN GERIATRICS.
Haworth Press, Inc., 10 Alice St., Binghamton, NY 13904. TEL 607-722-5857. FAX 607-722-1424. *3294*

PHYSICAL & OCCUPATIONAL THERAPY IN PEDIATRICS.
Haworth Press, Inc., 10 Alice St., Binghamton, NY 13904. TEL 607-722-5857. FAX 607-722-1424. *4813*

PHYSICAL GEOGRAPHY.
V.H. Winston & Son, Inc., c/o Bellwether Publishing, Ltd., 8640 Guilford Rd., Ste. 200, Columbia, MD 21046. TEL 410-290-3870. FAX 410-290-8726. *2214*

PHYSICAL MEDICINE & REHABILITATION.
Hanley & Belfus, Inc., 210 S. 13th St., Philadelphia, PA 19107. TEL 215-546-7293. FAX 215-790-9330. *4818*

PHYSICAL REVIEW A.
American Physical Society, One Physics Ellipse, College Park, MD 20740-3844. TEL 301-209-3202. *5563*

PHYSICAL REVIEW B (CONDENSED MATTER).
American Physical Society, One Physics Ellipse, College Park, MD 20740-3844. TEL 301-209-3202. *5563*

PHYSICAL REVIEW C (NUCLEAR PHYSICS).
American Physical Society, One Physics Ellipse, College Park, MD 20740-3843. TEL 301-209-3000. *5598*

PHYSICAL REVIEW ABSTRACTS.
American Physical Society, One Physics Ellipse, College Park, MD 20740-3844. TEL 301-209-3202. *5580*

PHYSICAL REVIEW LETTERS.
American Physical Society, One Physics Ellipse, College Park, MD 20740-3844. TEL 301-209-3202. *5563*

PHYSICAL SCIENCES DATA.
Elsevier Science B.V. Books Division, P.O. Box 211, 1000 AE Amsterdam, Netherlands. TEL 31-20-4853911. FAX 31-20-4853705. *5563*

PHYSICAL THERAPY.
American Physical Therapy Association, 1111 N. Fairfax St., Alexandria, VA 22314-1488. TEL 703-684-2782. FAX 703-684-7343. *4819*

PHYSICIAN ASSISTANT.
Springhouse Corporation, 1111 Bethlehem Pike, Box 908, Springhouse, PA 19477. TEL 215-646-8700. *4515*

PHYSICIAN ASSISTANTS' PRESCRIBING REFERENCE.
Prescribing Reference, Inc., 53 Park Pl., Ste. 1010, New York, NY 10007. TEL 212-766-7200. FAX 212-732-2360. *5439*

PHYSICIAN EXECUTIVE.
American College of Physician Executives, Two Urban Centre, Ste. 200, 4890 W. Kennedy Blvd., Tampa, FL 33609. TEL 813-287-2000. FAX 813-287-8993. *3554*

PHYSICS: A SERIES OF MONOGRAPHS & TRACTS.
Harwood Academic Publishers, c/o International Publishers Distributor, P.O. Box 3054, Langhorne, PA 19047-3054. TEL 215-750-2642. FAX 215-750-6343. *5563*

PHYSICS AND CHEMISTRY OF LIQUIDS.
Gordon and Breach Science Publishers, c/o International Publishers Distributor, P.O. Box 3054, Langhorne, PA 19047-3054. TEL 215-750-2642. FAX 215-750-6343. *5530*

PHYSICS AND CHEMISTRY OF MATERIALS WITH LOW-DIMENSIONAL STRUCTURES.
Kluwer Academic Publishers, Postbus 17, 3300 AA Dordrecht, Netherlands. TEL 31-78-6392392. FAX 31-78-6392254. *5390*

PHYSICS AND CHEMISTRY OF THE EARTH.
Elsevier Science Ltd., Pergamon, P.O. Box 800, Kidlington, Oxford OX5 1DX, England. TEL 44-1865-843000. FAX 44-1865-843010. *2214*

PHYSICS, CHEMISTRY AND MECHANICS OF SURFACES.
Gordon & Breach Science Publishers, c/o International Publishers Distributor, P.O. Box 3054, Langhorne, PA 19047-3054. TEL 215-750-2642. FAX 215-750-6343. *2736*

PHYSICS EDUCATION.
I O P Publishing Ltd., Techno House, Redcliffe Way, Bristol, Avon BS1 6NX, England. TEL 44-117-929-7481. FAX 44-117-929-4318. *5564*

PHYSICS EDUCATION.
New Age International Pvt. Ltd., Journals Division, 4835-24 Ansari Rd., Daryaganj, New Delhi 110 002, India. TEL 3276802 *5564*

PHYSICS ESSAYS.
c/o Alft, Inc., 189 Deveault St., Unit 7, Hull, QC J8Z 1S7, Canada. FAX 819-770-3862. *5564*

PHYSICS IN CANADA.
Canadian Association of Physicists, 151 Slater St., Ste. 903, Ottawa, ON K1P 5H3, Canada. TEL 613-237-3392. FAX 613-238-1677. *5564*

PHYSICS LETTERS. SECTION A: GENERAL, ATOMIC AND SOLID STATE PHYSICS.
North-Holland P.O. Box 211, 1000 AE Amsterdam, Netherlands. TEL 31-20-4853911. FAX 31-20-4853598. *5598*

PHYSICS LETTERS. SECTION B: NUCLEAR, ELEMENTARY PARTICLE AND HIGH-ENERGY PHYSICS.
North-Holland P.O. Box 211, 1000 AE Amsterdam, Netherlands. TEL 31-20-4853911. FAX 31-20-4853598. *5598*

PHYSICS OF FLUIDS.
American Institute of Physics, One Physics Ellipse, College Park, MD 20740-3843. TEL 301-209-3000. *5564*

PHYSICS OF METALS.
Gordon and Breach Science Publishers, c/o International Publishers Distributor, P.O. Box 3054, Langhorne, PA 19046-3054. TEL 215-750-2642. FAX 215-750-6343. *4970*

PHYSICS OF METALS AND METALLOGRAPHY.
Maik Nauka - Interperiodica, Mezhdunarodnyi Otdel, Ul. Profsoyuznaya, 90, 117864 Moscow, Russia. TEL 7-095-3360066. FAX 7-095-3360066. *4970*

PHYSICS OF PARTICLES AND NUCLEI.
American Institute of Physics, One Physics Ellipse, College Park, MD 20740-3843. TEL 301-209-3000. *5599*

PHYSICS OF PLASMAS.
American Institute of Physics, One Physics Ellipse, College Park, MD 20740-3843. TEL 301-209-3000. *5564*

PHYSICS OF THE EARTH AND PLANETARY INTERIORS.
Elsevier Science B.V., P.O. Box 211, 1000 AE Amsterdam, Netherlands. TEL 31-20-4853911. FAX 31-20-4853598. *2279*

PHYSICS OF THIN FILMS; ADVANCES IN RESEARCH AND DEVELOPMENT.
Academic Press, Inc., 525 B St., Ste. 1900, San Diego, CA 92101-4495. TEL 619-231-0926. FAX 619-699-6715. *5564*

PHYSICS REPORTS.
North-Holland P.O. Box 211, 1000 AE Amsterdam, Netherlands. TEL 31-20-4853911. FAX 31-20-4853598. *5565*

PHYSICS REPORTS REPRINTS BOOK SERIES.
Elsevier Science B.V., Books Division, P.O. Box 211, 1000 AE Amsterdam, Netherlands. TEL 31-20-4853911. FAX 31-20-4853705. *5565*

PHYSICS REVIEWS.
Harwood Academic Publishers, c/o International Publishers Distributor, P.O. Box 3054, Langhorne, PA 19047-3054. TEL 215-750-2642. FAX 215-750-6343. *5565*

PHYSICS TODAY.
American Institute of Physics, One Physics Ellipse, College Park, MD 20740-3843. TEL 301-209-3037. *5565*

PHYSIOLOGIA PLANTARUM.
Munksgaard International Publishers Ltd., 35 Noerre Soegade, P.O. Box 2148, DK-1016 Copenhagen K, Denmark. TEL 45-33-127030. FAX 45-33-129387. *696*

PHYSIOLOGICAL CHEMISTRY AND PHYSICS AND MEDICAL N M R.
Pacific Press, Box 1452 Melville, NY 11747. TEL 516-694-2929. FAX 516-249-3734. *655*

PHYSIOLOGICAL ENTOMOLOGY.
Blackwell Science Ltd., Osney Mead, Oxford OX2 0EL, England. TEL 44-1865-206206. FAX 44-1865-721205. *734*

PHYSIOLOGICAL REVIEWS.
American Physiological Society, 9650 Rockville Pike, Bethesda, MD 20814. TEL 301-530-7164. FAX 301-571-8313. *792*

PHYSIOLOGICAL ZOOLOGY.
University of Chicago Press, Journals Division, Box 37005, Chicago, IL 60637. TEL 773-753-3347. FAX 773-753-0811. *817*

PHYSIOLOGIST.
American Physiological Society, 9650 Rockville Pike, Bethesda, MD 20814. TEL 301-530-7164. FAX 301-571-8313. *792*

PHYSIOLOGY AND BEHAVIOR.
Elsevier Science Inc., Box 945, New York, NY 10159-0945. TEL 212-633-3730. FAX 212-633-3680. *792*

PHYSIOTHERAPY.
Chartered Society of Physiotherapy, 14 Bedford Row, London WC1R 4ED, England. TEL 44-171-306-6662. FAX 44-171-306-6667. *4819*

PHYSIOTHERAPY RESEARCH INTERNATIONAL.
Whurr Publishers Ltd., 19b Compton Terrace, London N1 2UN, England. TEL 44-171-359-5979. FAX 44-171-226-5290. *4819*

PHYSIOTHERAPY THEORY AND PRACTICE.
Taylor & Francis Ltd., Psychology Press, 1 Gunpowder Sq., London EC4A 3DE, England. TEL 44-171-5830490. FAX 44-171-5830585. *4819*

PHYSIS.
Asociacion Argentina de Ciencias Naturales, Universidad de Buenos Aires, Facultad de Ciencias Exactas y Naturales, Departamento de Biologia, Ciudad Universitaria, 1428 Buenos Aires, Argentina. TEL 54-1-9828370. FAX 54-1-9824494. *818*

PHYTOCHEMICAL ANALYSIS.
John Wiley & Sons Ltd., Journals, Baffins Ln., Chichester, W. Sussex PO19 1UD, England. TEL 44-1243-779777. FAX 44-1243-843232. *647*

PHYTOCHEMISTRY.
Elsevier Science Ltd., Pergamon, P.O. Box 800, Kidlington, Oxford OX5 1DX, England. TEL 44-1865-843000. FAX 44-1865-843010. *696*

PHYTOLOGIA.
c/o Michael J. Warnock, Ed., 185 Westridge Dr., Huntsville, TX 77340. TEL 409-295-5410. FAX 409-291-0009. *696*

PHYTOMA ESPANA.
Agropubli S.L., Blasco Ibanlez 24, 2a, 46010 Valencia, Spain. TEL 6-393-39-49. FAX 6-360-57-79. *235*

PHYTOPATHOLOGIA POLONICA.
Polskie Towarzystwo Fitopatologiczne, Ul. Wojska Polskiego 71 c, 60-625 Poznan, Poland. TEL 48-61-487713. FAX 48-61-487145. *696*

PHYTOPATHOLOGY.
A P S Press, 3340 Pilot Knob Rd., St. Paul, MN 55121-2097. TEL 612-454-7250. FAX 612-454-0766. *697*

PHYTOPROTECTION.
Societe de Protection des Plantes du Quebec, 430 bvd. Gouin, St-Jean-sur-Richelieu, PQ J3B 3E6, Canada. TEL 514-346-4494. FAX 514-346-7740. *235*

PHYTOTHERAPY RESEARCH.
John Wiley & Sons Ltd., Journals, Baffins Ln., Chichester, W. Sussex PO19 1UD, England. TEL 44-1243-779777. FAX 44-1243-843232. *697*

PI MU EPSILON JOURNAL.
Pi Mu Epsilon, c/o Robert S. Smith, Mathematics Department, Miami University, Oxford, OH 45056. *4388*

PICTISH ARTS SOCIETY JOURNAL.
Pictish Arts Society, 27 George Sq., Edinburgh EH8 9LD, Scotland. *3435*

PICTURA NOVA.
N.V. Brepols, Steenweg op Tielen 68, 2300 Turnhout, Belgium. TEL 32-14-402500. FAX 32-14-428919. *447*

PIECEWORK.
Interweave Press, Inc., 201 E. Fourth St., Loveland, CO 80537. TEL 970-669-7672. FAX 970-667-8317. *5213*

PIG IRON.
Pig Iron Press, Box 237, Youngstown, OH 44501. TEL 330-747-6932. *4251*

PIGMENT CELL.
S. Karger AG, Allschwilerstr. 10, P.O. Box, CH-4009 Basel, Switzerland. TEL 061-3061111. FAX 061-3061234. *749*

PIGMENT CELL RESEARCH.
Munksgaard International Publishers Ltd., P.O. Box 2148, DK-1016 Copenhagen K, Denmark. TEL 45-33-127030. FAX 45-33-129387. *718*

PING PONG.
Henry Miller Memorial Library, Hwy. 1, Big Sur, CA 93920. TEL 408-667-2574. FAX 408-667-2574. *4251*

PINTER REVIEW: ANNUAL ESSAYS.
University of Tampa, Box 11F, Tampa, FL 33606. *6700*

PIONEER.
Regional Synod of Canada Inc., Reformed Church in America, R.R. 4, Cambridge, ON N1R 5S5, Canada. TEL 519-622-1777. FAX 519-622-1993. *6155*

PITTSBURGH SERIES IN PHILOSOPHY & HISTORY OF SCIENCE.
University of California Press, 2120 Berkeley Way, Berkeley, CA 94720. TEL 510-642-4247. FAX 510-643-7127. *5493*

PLAINS ANTHROPOLOGIST.
Plains Anthropological Society, c/o Lawrence Tomsyck, 410 Wedgewood Dr., Lincoln, NE 68510. TEL 402-488-3813. *319*

PLAN.
Foereningen foer Samhaellsplanering, P.O. Box 15013, S-800 15 Gaevle, Sweden. TEL 46-26-68-75-00. FAX 46-26-61-15-36. *3591*

PLANETARY AND SPACE SCIENCE.
Elsevier Science Ltd., Pergamon, P.O. Box 800, Kidlington, Oxford OX5 1DX, England. TEL 44-1865-843000. FAX 44-1865-843010. *485*

PLANNING IN LONDON.
Land Research Unit Ltd., The Studio, Crown Reach, 149a Grosvenor Rd., London SW1V 3JY, England. TEL 44-171-834-9471. FAX 44-171-834-9470. *3591*

PLANNING PERSPECTIVES.
Chapman & Hall, Journals Department 2-6 Boundary Row, London SE1 8HN, England. TEL 44-171-8650066. FAX 44-171-5229623. *3355*

PLANNING PRACTICE AND RESEARCH.
Carfax Publishing Co., P.O. Box 25, Abingdon, Oxon. OX14 3UE, England. TEL 44-1235-401000. FAX 44-1235-401550. *3591*

PLANT AND SOIL.
Kluwer Academic Publishers, Postbus 17, 3300 AA Dordrecht, Netherlands. TEL 31-78-6392392. FAX 31-78-6392254. *697*

PLANT CELL.
American Society of Plant Physiologists, 15501 Monona Dr., Rockville, MD 20855. TEL 301-251-0560. FAX 301-279-2996. *697*

PLANT, CELL AND ENVIRONMENT.
Blackwell Science Ltd., Osney Mead, Oxford OX2 0EL, England. TEL 44-1865-206206. FAX 44-1865-721205. *600*

PLANT CELL, TISSUE AND ORGAN CULTURE.
Kluwer Academic Publishers, Postbus 17, 3300 AA Dordrecht, Netherlands. TEL 31-78-6392392. FAX 31-78-6392254. *601*

PLANT DISEASE.
A P S Press, 3340 Pilot Knob Rd., St. Paul, MN 55121-2097. TEL 612-454-7250. FAX 612-454-0766. *236*

PLANT ECOLOGY.
Kluwer Academic Publishers, Postbus 17, 3300 AA Dordrecht, Netherlands. TEL 31-78-6392392. FAX 31-78-6392254. *698*

PLANT FOODS FOR HUMAN NUTRITION.
Kluwer Academic Publishers, Postbus 17, 3300 AA Dordrecht, Netherlands. TEL 31-78-6392392. FAX 31-78-6392254. *5240*

PLANT GROWTH REGULATION.
Kluwer Academic Publishers, Postbus 17, 3300 AA Dordrecht, Netherlands. TEL 31-78-6392392. FAX 31-78-6392254. *698*

THE PLANT JOURNAL FOR CELL AND MOLECULAR BIOLOGY.
Blackwell Science Ltd., Osney Mead, Oxford OX2 0EL, England. TEL 44-1865-206206. FAX 44-1865-721205. *698*

PLANT MOLECULAR BIOLOGY.
Kluwer Academic Publishers, Postbus 17, 3300 AA Dordrecht, Netherlands. TEL 31-78-6392392. FAX 31-78-6392254. *601*

PLANT PATHOLOGY.
Blackwell Science Ltd., Osney Mead, Oxford OX2 0EL, England. TEL 44-1865-206206. FAX 44-1865-721205. *698*

PLANT PHYSIOLOGY.
American Society of Plant Physiologists, 15501 Monona Dr., Rockville, MD 20855. TEL 301-251-0560. FAX 301-279-2996. *698*

PLANT PROTECTION QUARTERLY.
R.G. & F.J. Richardson, Ed. & Pub., P.O. Box 1108,
Frankston, Vic. 3199, Australia. TEL 61-3-
97873804. FAX 61-3-97754245. *236*

PLANT SCIENCE.
Elsevier Science Ireland Ltd., P.O. Box 85, Limerick,
Ireland. TEL 353-61-471944. FAX 353-61-
472144. *699*

PLANT TISSUE CULTURE.
Bangladesh Association for Plant Tissue Culture,
University of Dhaka, Department of Botany, Dhaka-
1000, Bangladesh. TEL 880-2-506378. FAX 880-
2-865583. *699*

PLANT VARIETIES AND SEEDS.
National Institute of Agricultural Botany, Huntingdon
Rd., Cambridge CB3 0LE, England. TEL 44-1223-
276381. FAX 44-1223-277602. *236*

THE PLANTAGENET CONNECTION.
Heliotrope Communications, Box 1401, Arvada, CO
80001. TEL 303-657-2723. *3435*

PLANTER.
Incorporated Society of Planters, P.O. Box 10262,
50708 Kuala Lumpur, Malaysia. TEL 3-242-5561.
FAX 3-242-6898. *144*

PLASMA CHEMISTRY & PLASMA PROCESSING.
Plenum Publishing Corp., 233 Spring St., New York,
NY 10013-1578. TEL 212-620-8000. FAX 212-
463-0742. *2646*

PLASMA DEVICES AND OPERATIONS.
Gordon and Breach Science Publishers, c/o
International Publishers Directory, P.O. Box 3054,
Langhorne, PA 19046-3054. TEL 215-750-2642.
FAX 215-750-6343. *5566*

PLASMA PHYSICS AND CONTROLLED FUSION.
I O P Publishing Ltd., Techno House, Redcliffe Way,
Bristol, Avon BS1 6NX, England. TEL 44-117-929-
7481. FAX 44-117-929-4318. *5566*

PLASMA SOURCES SCIENCE AND TECHNOLOGY.
I O P Publishing Ltd., Techno House, Redcliffe Way,
Bristol, Avon BS1 6NX, England. TEL 44-117-929-
7481. FAX 44-117-929-4318. *5566*

PLASMA TECHNOLOGY.
Elsevier Science B.V., Books Division, P.O. Box 211,
1000 AE Amsterdam, Netherlands. TEL 31-20-
4853911. FAX 31-20-4853705. *5566*

PLASMAS AND POLYMERS.
Plenum Publishing Corp., 233 Spring St., New York,
NY 10013-1578. TEL 212-620-8000. FAX 212-
463-0742. *1743*

PLASMID.
Academic Press, Inc., Journal Division, 525 B St.,
Ste. 1900, San Diego, CA 92101-4495. TEL 619-
230-1840. FAX 619-699-6800. *601*

PLASTIC AND RECONSTRUCTIVE SURGERY.
Williams & Wilkins, 351 W. Camden St., Baltimore,
MD 21201. TEL 410-528-4000. FAX 410-528-
4312. *4917*

PLASTICS ENGINEERING SERIES.
Marcel Dekker, Inc., 270 Madison Ave., New York,
NY 10016. TEL 212-696-9000. FAX 212-685-
4540. *5624*

PLASTICS IN BUILDING CONSTRUCTION.
Technomic Publishing Co., Inc., 851 New Holland
Ave., Box 3535, Lancaster, PA 17604. TEL 717-
291-5609. FAX 717-295-45388. *869*

**PLASTICS, RUBBER & COMPOSITES PROCESSING
AND APPLICATIONS.**
Institute of Materials, 1 Carlton House Terr., London
SW1Y 5DB, England. TEL 44-171-839-4071.
FAX 44-171-839-2078. *5625*

PLASTICULTURE.
International Committee for Plastics in Agriculture,
65 rue de Prony, 75854 Paris Cedex 17, France.
TEL 44-01-16-48. FAX 44-01-16-55. *5626*

PLAYTIMES.
Playgroup Association of Queensland, 396 Milton
Rd., Auchenflower, Qld. 4066, Australia. TEL 61-7-
3718253. FAX 61-7-8700569. *1776*

PLEIN SOLEIL.
Association Diabete Quebec Inc., 5635 rue
Sherbrooke E., Montreal, PQ H1N 1A2, Canada.
TEL 514-259-3422. FAX 514-259-9286. *4674*

POETICS.
North-Holland P.O. Box 211, 1000 AE Amsterdam,
Netherlands. TEL 31-20-4853911. FAX 31-20-
4853598. *4252*

POETICS TODAY.
Duke University Press, Box 90660, Durham, NC
27708-0660. TEL 919-687-3600. FAX 919-688-
4574. *4161*

POETRY.
Poetry Publications, Jasnal, 2nd Fl., Old Christian
St., Berhampur 760 001, India. *4315*

POETRY MOTEL.
1228 E. Third St., Duluth, MN 55805-2319.
4316

POLAR RESEARCH.
Norwegian Polar Institute, Middelthuns gate 29,
P.O. Box 5072 Majorstua, N-0301 Oslo, Norway.
TEL 47-22-95-95-00. FAX 47-22-95-95-01. *6272*

POLARFORSCHUNG.
Deutsche Gesellschaft fuer Polarforschung e.V., c/o
Alfred-Wegener-Institut fuer Polar- und
Meeresforschung, Postfach 120161, 27515
Bremerhaven, Germany. TEL 49-471-4831200.
FAX 49-471-4831149. *2214*

POLEN.
Universidad de Cordoba, Departamento de Biologia
Vegetal y Ecologia, Avda. de San Alberto Magno s-n,
14004 Cordoba, Spain. TEL 57-218599. FAX 57-
218598. *699*

POLICING AND SOCIETY.
Harwood Academic Publishers, c/o International
Publishers Distributor, P.O. Box 3054, Langhorne,
PA 19047-3054. TEL 215-750-2642. FAX 215-
750-6343. *2173*

POLICY.
Centre for Independent Studies, Box 92, St.
Leonards, N.S.W. 2065, Australia. TEL 61-2-438-
4377. FAX 61-2-439-7310. *951*

**POLICY ANALYSIS RESEARCH UNIT. DISCUSSION
PAPER.**
Glasgow Caledonian University, Policy Analysis
Research Unit. Cowcaddens Rd., Glasgow G4 0BA,
Scotland. TEL 0141-331-3319. FAX 0141-331-
3293. *5915*

POLICY AND POLITICS.
The Policy Press, Rodney Lodge, Grange Rd.,
Bristol, Avon BS8 4EA, England. TEL 44-117-
9741117. FAX 44-117-9737308. *3592*

POLICY FORUM.
University of Illinois at Urbana-Champaign, Institute
of Government and Public Affairs, 1007 W. Nevada
St., Urbana, IL 61801. TEL 217-333-3340.
FAX 217-244-4817. *5915*

POLICY SCIENCES.
Kluwer Academic Publishers, Postbus 17, 3300 AA
Dordrecht, Netherlands. TEL 31-78-6392392.
FAX 31-78-6392254. *5693*

POLIMERY W MEDYCYNIE.
Akademia Medyczna we Wroclawiu, Zaklad Chirurgii
Eksperymentalnej i Badania Biomaterialow, Ul.
Poniatowskiego 2, 50-326 Wroclaw, Poland.
TEL 48-71-226310. FAX 48-71-215729. *1743*

POLISH BOTANICAL STUDIES.
Polska Akademia Nauk, Instytut Botaniki im. W.
Szafera, Ul. Lubicz 46, 31-512 Krakow, Poland.
TEL 48-12-215144. FAX 48-12-219790. *699*

POLISH BOTANICAL STUDIES. GUIDEBOOK SERIES.
Polska Akademia Nauk, Instytut Botaniki im. W.
Szafera, Ul. Lubicz 46, 31-512 Krakow, Poland.
TEL 48-12-215144. FAX 48-12-219790. *699*

**POLISH JOURNAL OF FOOD AND NUTRITION
SCIENCES.**
Polska Akademia Nauk, Instytut Rozrodu Zwierzat i
Badan Zywnosci, Ul. J. Tuwima 10, 10-718 Olsztyn-
Kortowo, Poland. TEL 48-89-237670. FAX 48-89-
237824. *2987*

POLISH JOURNAL OF IMMUNOLOGY.
Polskie Towarzystwo Immunologiczne, c/o
Samodzielna Pracownia Immunologii, Centrum
Zdrowia Dziecka, Al. Dzieci Polskich 20, 07-736
Warsaw, Poland. TEL 48-22-157156. FAX 48-22-
157159. *4586*

POLISH JOURNAL OF PATHOLOGY.
Polskie Towarzystwo Patologow, Ul. Grzegorzecka
16, 31-531 Krakow, Poland. TEL 48-12-211564.
FAX 48-12-215210. *4573*

POLISH MUSIC HISTORY SERIES.
Friends of Polish Music, University of Southern
California, School of Music, Los Angeles, CA 90089-
0851. TEL 213-877-1906. FAX 318-509-8435.
5189

POLISH REVIEW.
Polish Institute of Arts and Sciences of America,
Inc., 208 E. 30th St., New York, NY 10016.
TEL 212-686-4164. FAX 212-545-1130. *3206*

POLITICAL BEHAVIOR.
Plenum Publishing Corp., 233 Spring St., New York,
NY 10013-1578. TEL 212-620-8000. FAX 212-
463-0742. *5694*

POLITICAL CHRONICLE.
Florida Political Science Association, St. Leo College,
Institute of Political Science, Box 2127, Saint Leo,
FL 33574. *5694*

POLITICAL COMMUNICATION.
Taylor & Francis Inc., 1900 Frost Rd., Ste. 101,
Bristol, PA 19007. TEL 215-785-5800. FAX 215-
785-5515. *5694*

POLITICAL CROSSROADS.
James Nicholas Publishers, P.O. Box 244, Albert
Park Vic. 3206, Australia. TEL 61-3-6965545.
FAX 61-3-6992040. *5694*

POLITICAL GEOGRAPHY.
Butterworth - Heinemann, Part of the Reed Elsevier
group, Linacre House, Jordan Hill, Oxford OX2 8DP,
England. TEL 44-1865-310366 FAX 44-1865-
310398. *5695*

POLITICAL PSYCHOLOGY.
Blackwell Publishers, 238 Main St., Cambridge, MA
02142. TEL 617-547-7110. FAX 617-547-0789.
5695

POLITICAL QUARTERLY.
Blackwell Publishers Ltd. 108 Cowley Rd., Oxford
OX4 1JF, England. TEL 44-1865-791100. FAX 44-
1865-791347. *5695*

POLITICAL RESEARCH QUARTERLY.
University of Utah, 252 Orson Spencer Hall, Salt
Lake City, UT 84112. *5695*

POLITICAL SCIENCE QUARTERLY.
Academy of Political Science, 475 Riverside Dr.,
Ste. 1274, New York, NY 10115-1274. TEL 212-
870-2500. FAX 212-870-2202. *5697*

POLITICAL STUDIES.
Blackwell Publishers Ltd. 108 Cowley Rd., Oxford
OX4 1JF, England. TEL 44-1865-791100. FAX 44-
1865-791347. *5697*

POLITICAL THEORY NEWSLETTER.
Australian National University, Research School of
Social Sciences, Canberra A.C.T 0200, Australia.
FAX 61-6-2493051. *5697*

POLITICKA EKONOMIE.
Vysoka Skola Ekonomicka, Nam. W. Churchilla 4,
130 67 Prague 3, Czech Republic. TEL 42-2-
24095819. FAX 42-2-24220675. *951*

POLITICS.
Blackwell Publishers Ltd., 108 Cowley Rd., Oxford
OX4 1JF, England. TEL 44-1865-791100. FAX 44-
1865-791347. *5697*

POLITICS AND SOCIETY.
Sage Publications, Inc., 2455 Teller Rd., Thousand
Oaks, CA 91320. TEL 805-499-0721. FAX 805-
499-0871. *5697*

POLITICS AND THE LIFE SCIENCES.
Beech Tree Publishing, 10 Watford Close, Guildford,
Surrey GU1 2EP, England. TEL 44-1483-67497.
FAX 44-1483-67497. *4517*

POLITIK UND GESELLSCHAFT. WUERZBURGER UNIVERSITAETSSCHRIFTEN.
Ergon-Verlag, Grombuehlstr. 7, 97080 Wuerzburg, Germany. TEL 0931-280084. FAX 0931-282872. *5698*

POLITIKON.
Staatkundige Vereniging van Suid Afrika, P.O. Box 1041, Florida 1710, South Africa. FAX 27-11-7825500. *5698*

POLSKIE PISMO ENTOMOLOGICZNE.
Polskie Towarzystwo Entomologiczne, Ul. Sienkiewicza 21, 50-335 Wroclaw, Poland. TEL 48-71-225041. *734*

POLSKIE TOWARZYSTWO JEZYKOZNAWCZE. BIULETYN.
Wydawnictwo Energia, sp. z o.o., Ul. Szturmowa 1, 02-678 Warsaw, Poland. TEL 48-22-470053. *4099*

POLYCYCLIC AROMATIC COMPOUNDS.
Gordon and Breach Science Publishers, c/o International Publishers Distributor, P.O. Box 3054, Langhorne, PA 19047-3054. TEL 215-750-2642. FAX 215-750-6343. *1744*

POLYHEDRON.
Elsevier Science Ltd., Pergamon, P.O. Box 800, Kidlington, Oxford OX5 1DX, England. TEL 44-1865-843000. FAX 44-1865-843010. *1732*

POLYMER.
Elsevier Science Ltd., Part of the Reed Elsevier group, Langford Ln., Kidlington, Oxford OX5 3DR, England. TEL 44-1865-843000. FAX 44-1865-843010. *1744*

POLYMER BLENDS, ALLOYS AND INTERPENETRATING POLYMER NETWORKS ABSTRACTS.
Technomic Publishing Co., Inc., 851 New Holland Ave., Box 3535, Lancaster, PA 17604. TEL 717-291-5609. FAX 717-295-4538. *1711*

POLYMER CONTENTS.
Elsevier Science Ltd., P.O. Box 800, Kidlington, Oxford OX5 1DX, England. TEL 44-1865-843000. FAX 44-1865-843010. *2629*

POLYMER DEGRADATION AND STABILITY.
Elsevier Science Ltd., P.O. Box 800, Kidlington, Oxford OX5 1DX, England. TEL 44-1865-843000. FAX 44-1865-843010. *1744*

POLYMER ENGINEERING AND SCIENCE.
Society of Plastics Engineers, Inc., 14 Fairfield Dr., Box 403, Brookfield, CT 06804-0403. TEL 203-775-0471. FAX 203-775-8490. *2647*

POLYMER GELS AND NETWORKS.
Elsevier Science Ltd., P.O. Box 800, Kidlington, Oxford OX5 1DX, England. TEL 44-1865-843000. FAX 44-1865-843010. *2647*

POLYMER INTERNATIONAL.
John Wiley & Sons Ltd., Journals, Baffins Ln., Chichester, W. Sussex PO19 1UD, England. TEL 44-1243-779777. FAX 44-1243-843232. *5626*

POLYMER MONOGRAPHS.
Gordon & Breach Science Publishers, c/o International Publishers Distributor, P.O. Box 3054, Langhorne, PA 19047-3054. TEL 215-750-2642. FAX 215-750-6343. *1744*

POLYMER NEWS.
Gordon and Breach Science Publishers, c/o International Publishers Distributor, P.O. Box 3054, Langhorne, PA 19047-3054. TEL 215-750-2642. FAX 215-750-6343. *1744*

POLYMER-PLASTICS TECHNOLOGY AND ENGINEERING.
Marcel Dekker Journals, 270 Madison Ave., New York, NY 10016. TEL 212-696-9000. FAX 212-685-4540. *1744*

POLYMER REACTION ENGINEERING.
Marcel Dekker, Inc., 270 Madison Ave., New York, NY 10016. TEL 212-696-9000. FAX 212-685-4540. *2647*

POLYMER SCIENCE.
Maik Nauka - Interperiodica, Ul. Profsoyuznaya, 90, 117864 Moscow, Russia. TEL 7-095-3360066. FAX 7-095-3360666. *1744*

POLYMER SCIENCE AND TECHNOLOGY.
Plenum Publishing Corp., 233 Spring St., New York, NY 10013-1578. TEL 212-620-8000. FAX 212-463-0742. *1744*

POLYMER SCIENCE LIBRARY.
Elsevier Science B.V., Books Division, P.O. Box 211, 1000 AE Amsterdam, Netherlands. TEL 31-20-4853911. FAX 31-20-4853705. *1689*

POLYMER TESTING.
Elsevier Science Ltd., P.O. Box 800, Kidlington, OX5 1DX, England. TEL 44-1865-843000. FAX 44-1865-843010. *5626*

POLYMER THERAPEUTICS.
I O S Press, Van Diemenstraat 94, 1013 CN Amsterdam, Netherlands. TEL 31-20-6382189. FAX 31-20-6203419. *5439*

POLYMER YEARBOOK.
Harwood Academic Publishers, c/o International Publishers Distributor, P.O. Box 3054, Langhorne, PA 19047-3054. TEL 215-750-2642. FAX 215-750-6343. *1689*

POLYMERIC MATERIALS SCIENCE AND ENGINEERING.
American Chemical Society, Division of Polymeric Materials Science & Engineering, 1155 16th St., N.W., Washington, DC 20036. *1744*

POLYMERS AND POLYMER COMPOSITES.
R A P R A Technology Ltd., Shawbury, Shrewsbury, Shrops. SY4 4NR, England. TEL 44-1939-250383. FAX 44-1939-251118. *5626*

POLYTECHNICAL UNIVERSITY OF BUCHAREST. SCIENTIFIC BULLETIN. SERIES A: APPLIED MATHEMATICS AND PHYSICS.
Universitatea Politehnica Bucuresti, Biblioteca Centrala, Splaiul Independentei 313, 77206 Bucharest 16, Rumania. TEL 40-1-6317185. FAX 40-1-3120188. *4388*

POMPEBLEDEN.
Stichting Algemiene Fryske Underrjocht Kommisje, P.B. 53, 8900 AB Leeuwarden, Netherlands. TEL 31-58-2138045. FAX 31-58-2159475. *4099*

POPULAR CULTURE IN LIBRARIES.
Haworth Press, Inc., 10 Alice St., Binghamton, NY 13904-1580. TEL 607-722-5857. FAX 607-722-1424. *4020*

POPULATION AND ENVIRONMENT.
Human Sciences Press, Inc. 233 Spring St., New York, NY 10013-1578. TEL 212-620-8000. FAX 212-463-0742. *5870*

POPULATION RESEARCH AND POLICY REVIEW.
Kluwer Academic Publishers, Postbus 17, 3300 AA Dordrecht, Netherlands. TEL 31-78-6392392. FAX 31-78-6392254. *5790*

PORTICUS.
University of Rochester, Memorial Art Gallery, 500 University Ave., Rochester, NY 14607. TEL 716-473-7720. FAX 716-473-6266. *5131*

PORTLAND PRESS PROCEEDINGS.
Portland Press Ltd., 59 Portland Place, London W1N 3AJ, England. TEL 44-171-580-5530. FAX 44-171-323-1136. *4684*

PORTLAND PRESS RESEARCH MONOGRAPH.
Portland Press Ltd., 59 Portland Place, London W1N 3AJ, England. TEL 44-171-580-5530. FAX 44-171-323-1136. *647*

PORTUGUESE STUDIES REVIEW.
International Conference Group on Portugal, Univ. of New Hampshire, Dept. of History, HSCC 408, Durham, NH 03824. TEL 603-862-3018. FAX 603-868-6935. *3622*

POSITIVE OUTLOOK.
AIDS Training, Information & Counselling Centre (ATICC), 42 Havelock Rd., Pietermaritzburg 3201, South Africa. TEL 27-331-942111. FAX 27-331-423245. *4627*

POSITIVITY.
Kluwer Academic Publishers, Postbus 17, 3300 AA Dordrecht, Netherlands. TEL 31-78-6392392. FAX 31-78-6392254. *4388*

POST-MEDIEVAL ARCHAEOLOGY.
Society for Post-Medieval Archaeology, c/o Dr. Paul Courtney, 20 Lytton Rd., Leicester LE2 1WJ, England. TEL 44-1533-707999. *368*

POST SCRIPT (COMMERCE).
Post Script, Inc., Department of Literature and Languages, East Texas State University, Commerce, TX 75429. TEL 903-886-5260. FAX 903-886-5980. *3622*

POSTEPY ASTRONOMII.
Polskie Towarzystwo Astronomiczne, Ul. Bartycka 18, 00-716 Warsaw, Poland. TEL 48-22-410041. FAX 48-22-410046. *485*

POSTEPY BIOLOGII KOMORKI.
Fundacja Postepu Biologii Komorki, Ul. Marymoncka 99, 01-813 Warsaw, Poland. TEL 48-22-340344. FAX 48-22-370470. *718*

POSTGRADUATE MEDICINE.
McGraw-Hill Companies (Minneapolis), 4530 W. 77th St., Minneapolis, 609-426-7070, MN 55435. TEL 612-835-3222. *4518*

POSTHARVEST BIOLOGY AND TECHNOLOGY.
Elsevier Science B.V., P.O. Box 211, 1000 AE Amsterdam, Netherlands. TEL 31-20-4853911. FAX 31-20-4853598. *664*

POSTHORN.
Scandinavian Collectors Club, 2316 Lakeview Dr., Fergus Falls, MN 56537-3903. TEL 218-739-3260. *5461*

POSTMODERN CULTURE.
Oxford University Press, Journals, 2001 Evans Rd., Cary, NC 27513. TEL 919-677-0977. FAX 919-677-1714. *4252*

POTENTIAL ANALYSIS.
Kluwer Academic Publishers, Postbus 17, 3300 AA Dordrecht, Netherlands. TEL 31-78-6392392. FAX 31-78-6392254. *4388*

POTPOURRI.
Potpourri Publications, Box 8278, Prairie Village, KS 66208. TEL 913-642-1503. FAX 913-642-3128. *4161*

POULTRY AND AVIAN BIOLOGY REVIEWS.
Science and Technology Letters, P.O. Box 81, Northwood, Middlesex HA6 3DY, England. TEL 44-1923-823586. FAX 44-1923-825066. *280*

POULTRY SCIENCE SYMPOSIUM SERIES.
Carfax Publishing Co., P.O. Box 25, Abingdon, Oxon. OX14 3UE, England. TEL 44-1235-401000. FAX 44-1235-401550. *281*

POVIJESNI PRILOZI.
Institut za Suvremenu Povijest, Opaticka 10, 41000 Zagreb, Croatia. *3355*

POWDER METALLURGY SCIENCE & TECHNOLOGY.
Powder Metallurgy Development Centre Pvt. Ltd., P-26 Laxminagar, Saidabad, Hyderabad 500 659, India. TEL 91-40-4065951. FAX 91-40-248141. *4971*

POWDER TECHNOLOGY.
Elsevier Science S.A., P.O. Box 564, CH-1001 Lausanne 1, Switzerland. TEL 41-21-3207381. FAX 41-21-3235444. *2648*

POWER (NEW YORK).
McGraw-Hill Companies, 1221 Ave. of the Americas, New York, NY 10020. TEL 212-512-2000. *2767*

POWER INTERNATIONAL.
Lincoln Publications Ltd., 28 Centre Point House, St. Giles High St., London WC2 8LW, England. TEL 44-171-240-5562. FAX 44-171-497-2811. *2555*

POWYS NOTES.
Powys Society of North America, Dept. of English, Valparaiso University, Valparaiso, IN 46383. *4252*

POWYS REVIEW.
c/o Belinda Humfrey, Ed., Department of English, University of Wales, Lampeter, Dyfed SA48 7ED, Wales. TEL 44-1570-424764. FAX 44-1570-423634. *4253*

POZNAN STUDIES IN THE PHILOSOPHY OF THE SCIENCES AND THE HUMANITIES.
Editions Rodopi B.V., Keizersgracht 302-304, 1016 EX Amsterdam, Netherlands. TEL 31-20-6227507. FAX 31-20-6380948. *5493*

PRACHYA PRATIBHA.
Birla Institute of Art and Music, Prachya Niketan, Birla Museum, P.O. Vallabh Bhavan, Bhopal 462004, India. TEL 0755-551388. *5292*

PRACTICAL DIABETOLOGY.
R.A. Rapaport Publishing, Inc., 150 W. 22nd St., New York, NY 10011. TEL 212-989-0200. FAX 212-989-4786. *4674*

PRACTICAL GASTROENTEROLOGY.
Shugar Publishing, 32 Mill Rd., Westhampton Beach, NY 11978-0947. TEL 516-288-4404. FAX 516-288-4435. *4695*

PRACTICAL METHODS IN ELECTRON MICROSCOPY.
Elsevier Science B.V., Books Division, P.O. Box 211, 1000 AE Amsterdam, Netherlands. TEL 31-20-4853911. FAX 31-20-4853705. *770*

THE PRACTICAL REAL ESTATE LAWYER.
American Law Institute - American Bar Association, Committee on Continuing Professional Education, 4025 Chestnut St., Philadelphia, PA 19104. TEL 215-243-1604. FAX 215-243-1664. *3834*

PRACTICAL SPECTROSCOPY SERIES.
Marcel Dekker, Inc., 270 Madison Ave., New York, NY 10016. TEL 212-696-9000. FAX 212-685-4540. *1719*

PRACTITIONER'S HANDBOOKS ON THE WORLD COURT.
Kluwer Law International Postbus 85889, 2508 CN The Hague, Netherlands. TEL 31-70-3081500. FAX 31-70-3081515. *3940*

PRAESENTATIONSHAEFTE.
Danske Sprog- og Litteraturselskab, Frederiksholms Kanal 18 A, DK-1220 Copenhagen K, Denmark. TEL 45-33-13-06-60. FAX 45-33-14-06-08. *4253*

PRAGMATICS & COGNITION.
John Benjamins Publishing Co., Amsteldijk 44, P.O. Box 75577, 1070 AN Amsterdam, Netherlands. TEL 31-20-6738156. FAX 31-20-6792956. *4130*

PRAGUE CONFERENCE ON INFORMATION THEORY, STATISTICAL DECISION FUNCTIONS, RANDOM PROCESSES. TRANSACTIONS.
Kluwer Academic Publishers, Postbus 17, 3300 AA Dordrecht, Netherlands. TEL 31-78-6392392. FAX 31-78-6392254. *2083*

PRAGUE ECONOMIC PAPERS.
Vysoka Skola Ekonomicka, Nam. W. Churchilla 4, 130 67 Prague 3, Czech Republic. TEL 42-2-24095819. FAX 42-2-24220657. *952*

PRAIRIE FORUM.
Canadian Plains Research Center, University of Regina, Regina, SK S4S 0A2, Canada. TEL 306-585-4795. FAX 306-585-4699. *2815*

PRAIRIE NATURALIST.
Box 4050, Emporia, KS 66801-5087. TEL 701-328-5368. FAX 701-328-5363. *6272*

PRAJNAN (PUNE).
National Institute of Bank Management, NIBM Post Office, Kondhwe Khurd, Pune 411 048, India. TEL 0212-673080. FAX 0212-674478. *1116*

PRAXISREPORT PSYCHOLOGISCHE THERAPIEN UND PSYCHOTHERAPIEN.
Psychomedia Verlags GmbH, Postfach 465, 12214 Berlin, Germany. TEL 49-30-4927200. FAX 49-30-7749176. *5870*

PRE- AND PERI-NATAL PSYCHOLOGY JOURNAL.
Human Sciences Press, Inc. 233 Spring St., New York, NY 10013-1578. TEL 212-620-8000. FAX 212-463-0742. *4744*

PRE-VUE ENTERTAINMENT MAGAZINE.
National Pre-Vue Network, 7825 Fay Ave., La Jolla, CA 92037. TEL 619-456-5577. FAX 619-542-0114. *5110*

PRECAMBRIAN RESEARCH.
Elsevier Science B.V. P.O. Box 211, 1000 AE Amsterdam, Netherlands. TEL 31-20-4853911. FAX 31-20-4853593. *2257*

PRECISION ENGINEERING.
Elsevier Science Inc., Box 945, New York, NY 10159-0945. TEL 212-633-3730. FAX 212-633-3680. *2615*

PREHISTORIC SOCIETY, LONDON. PROCEEDINGS.
Prehistoric Society, Institute of Archaeology, 31-34 Gordon Sq., London WC1H 0PY, England. *368*

PREHOSPITAL AND DISASTER MEDICINE.
Jems Publishing Co. Inc., Box 2789, Carlsbad, CA 92018. TEL 619-431-9797. FAX 619-431-8176. *4518*

PRENATAL AND NEONATAL MEDICINE.
Parthenon Publishing Group, Casterton Hall, Carnforth, Lancs. LA6 2LA, England. TEL 44-152-427-2084. FAX 44-152-427-1587. *4744*

PRENATAL DIAGNOSIS.
John Wiley & Sons Ltd., Journals, Baffins Ln., Chichester, W. Sussex PO19 1UD, England. TEL 44-1243-779777. FAX 44-1243-843232. *4744*

PRENSA DEL RIOJA.
Chile 9, 1o, 26005 Logrono, Spain. TEL 34-41-221968. FAX 34-41-223110. *510*

PREPARATIVE BIOCHEMISTRY AND BIOTECHNOLOGY.
Marcel Dekker Journals, 270 Madison Ave., New York, NY 10016. TEL 212-696-9000. FAX 212-685-4540. *647*

PRESCRIBER.
A & M Publishing Ltd., Alexandra House, First Fl., 1-5 Alexandra Terr., Guildford, Surrey GU1 3DA, England. TEL 44-1483-34888. FAX 44-1483-33316. *5439*

PRESCRIBER'S LETTER.
Therapeutic Research Center, 2453 Grand Canal Blvd., Ste. A, Box 8190, Stockton, CA 95208. TEL 209-472-2240. FAX 209-472-2249. *5439*

PRESCRIBING REFERENCE FOR OBSTETRICIANS AND GYNECOLOGISTS.
Prescribing Reference, Inc., 53 Park Pl., Ste. 1010, New York, NY 10007. TEL 212-766-7200. FAX 212-732-2360. *5439*

PRESCRIBING REFERENCE FOR PEDIATRICIANS.
Prescribing Reference, Inc., 53 Park Pl., Ste. 1010, New York, NY 10007. TEL 212-766-7200. FAX 212-732-2360. *5439*

PRESCRIRE INTERNATIONAL.
Association Mieux Prescrire, BP 459, 75527 Paris Cedex 11, France. TEL 33-1-47-00-94-45. FAX 33-1-48-07-87-32. *5440*

PRESIDENTIAL STUDIES QUARTERLY.
Center for the Study of the Presidency, 208 E. 75th St., New York, NY 10021. TEL 212-249-1200. FAX 212-628-9503. *5699*

LA PRESSE MEDICALE.
Masson - Periodiques, Villa Laromiguiere, 75005 Paris, France. TEL 40-46-62-00. FAX 40-46-62-01. *4519*

PREVENTING SCHOOL FAILURE.
Heldref Publications, 1319 Eighteenth St., N.W., Washington, DC 20036-1802. TEL 202-296-6267. FAX 202-296-5149. *2473*

PREVENTIVE MEDICINE.
Academic Press, Inc., Journal Division, 525 B St., Ste. 1900, San Diego, CA 92101-4495. TEL 619-230-1840. FAX 619-699-6800. *4519*

PREVENTIVE VETERINARY MEDICINE.
Elsevier Science B.V., P.O. Box 211, 1000 AE Amsterdam, Netherlands. TEL 31-20-4853911. FAX 31-20-4853593. *6952*

PREVIEWS OF HEAT AND MASS TRANSFER.
Rumford Publishing Co., Inc., Box 5370, Chicago, IL 60680. *2629*

PRIMARY CARDIOLOGY.
P W Communications, Inc., 400 Plaza Dr., Secaucus, NJ 07094. TEL 201-865-7500. *4608*

PRIMARY CARE UPDATE FOR OB - GYNS.
Elsevier Science Inc., Box 945, New York, NY 10159-0945. TEL 212-633-3730. FAX 212-633-3680. *4744*

PRIMARY FILE.
Primary File Publishing, 61 Gray's Inn Rd., London WC1X 8TZ, England. TEL 44-171-404-2776. FAX 44-171-404-2766. *3498*

PRIMARY SCIENCE REVIEW.
Association for Science Education, College Ln., Hatfield, Herts. AL10 9AA, England. TEL 44-1707-267411. FAX 44-1707-256532. *6273*

PRIMARY SENSORY NEURON.
V S P, P.O. Box 346, 3700 AH Zeist, Netherlands. TEL 31-30-6925790. FAX 31-30-6932081. *4861*

PRIMARY SOURCES & ORIGINAL WORKS.
Haworth Press, Inc., 10 Alice St., Binghamton, NY 13904. TEL 607-722-5857. FAX 607-722-1424. *4020*

PRIMARY SOURCES IN PHENOMENOLOGY.
Kluwer Academic Publishers, Postbus 17, 3300 AA Dordrecht, Netherlands. TEL 31-78-6392392. FAX 31-78-6392254. *5493*

PRIMUS.
Dept. of Mathematics, U.S. Military Academy, West Point, NY 10996-9902. TEL 914-938-3200. FAX 914-938-2409. *4339*

PRINCETON HISTORY.
Historical Society of Princeton, 158 Nassau St., Princeton, NJ 08542. TEL 609-921-6748. *3484*

PRINCETON MATHEMATICAL SERIES.
Princeton University Press, 41 William St., Princeton, NJ 08540. TEL 609-258-4900. FAX 509-258-6305. *4339*

THE PRINCETON PAPERS.
Markus Wiener Publishers, Inc., 114 Jefferson Rd., Princeton, NJ 08540. TEL 609-921-1141. FAX 609-921-1140. *3239*

PRINCETON SERIES IN PHYSICS.
Princeton University Press, 41 William St., Princeton, NJ 08540. TEL 609-258-4900. FAX 609-258-6305. *5557*

PRINCETON UNIVERSITY LIBRARY CHRONICLE.
Princeton University Library, 1 Washington Rd., Princeton, NJ 08544. TEL 609-258-3184. FAX 609-258-4105. *3622*

PRINCIPIA CYBERNETICA NEWSLETTER.
Principia Cybernetica Project, c/o Free University of Brussels, Pleinlaan 2, 1050 Brussels, Belgium. TEL 32-2-6412525. FAX 32-2-6412489. *2063*

PRISM INTERNATIONAL.
University of British Columbia, Creative Writing Department, E462-1866 Main Mall, Vancouver BC V6T 1Z1, Canada. TEL 604-822-2514. FAX 604-822-3616. *4253*

THE PRISON JOURNAL.
Sage Publications, Inc., 2455 Teller Rd., Thousand Oaks, CA 91320. TEL 805-499-0721. FAX 805-499-0871. *2174*

PROBABILISTIC ENGINEERING MECHANICS.
Elsevier Science Ltd., P.O. Box 800, Kidlington, Oxford OX5 1DX, England. TEL 44-1865-843000. FAX 44-1865-843010. *2768*

PROBABILITY AND MATHEMATICAL STATISTICS.
Academic Press, Inc., 525 B St., Ste. 1900, San Diego, CA 92101-4495. TEL 619-231-0926. FAX 619-699-6715. *4389*

PROBLEME DER AEGYPTOLOGIE.
E.J. Brill, P.O. Box 900C, 2300 PA Leiden, Netherlands. TEL 31-71-5353500. FAX 31-71-5317532. *5292*

PROBLEMS IN ECONOMIC TRANSITION.
M.E. Sharpe, Inc., 80 Business Park Dr., Armonk, NY 10504. TEL 914-273-1800. FAX 914-273-2106. *952*

PROBLEMS IN GENERAL SURGERY.
Lippincott - Raven Publishers 227 E. Washington Sq., Philadelphia, PA 19106. TEL 215-238-4200. *4918*

PROBLEMS IN PRIVATE INTERNATIONAL LAW.
Elsevier Science B.V., Books Division, P.O. Box 211, 1000 AE Amsterdam, Netherlands. TEL 31-20-4853911. FAX 31-20-4853705. *3940*

PROBLEMS OF DESERT DEVELOPMENT.
Allerton Press, Inc., 150 Fifth Ave., New York, NY 10011. TEL 212-924-3950. FAX 212-463-9684. *2815*

PROBLEMS OF INDUSTRIAL PSYCHIATRIC MEDICINE SERIES.
Human Sciences Press, Inc. 233 Spring St., New York, NY 10013-1578. TEL 212-620-8000. FAX 212-463-0742. *5871*

PROBLEMS OF INFORMATION TRANSMISSION.
Plenum Publishing Corp., Consultants Bureau, 233 Spring St., New York, NY 10013-1578. TEL 212-620-8468. FAX 212-463-0742. *2070*

PROBLEMS OF POST-COMMUNISM.
M.E. Sharpe, Inc., 80 Business Park Dr., Armonk, NY 10504. TEL 914-273-1800. FAX 914-273-2106. *5700*

PROBLEMY PROJEKTOWE PRZEMYSLU I BUDOWNICTWA.
Przedsiebiorstwo Inzynierskie "Biprohut", Sp. z o.o., Ul. Dubois 16, 44-100 Gliwice, Poland. TEL 48-32-316011. FAX 48-32-312435. *4971*

PROCESS BIOCHEMISTRY.
Elsevier Science Ltd., P.O. Box 800, Kidlington, Oxford OX5 1DX, England. TEL 44-1865-843000. FAX 44-1865-843010. *665*

PROCESS CONTROL AND QUALITY.
Elsevier Science B.V., P.O. Box 211, 1000 AE Amsterdam, Netherlands. TEL 31-20-4853911. FAX 31-20-4853598. *5017*

PROCESS MEASUREMENT & CONTROL.
Elsevier Science B.V., Books Division, P.O. Box 211, 1000 AE Amsterdam, Netherlands. TEL 31-20-4853911. FAX 31-20-4853705. *2648*

PROCESS METALLURGY.
Elsevier Science B.V., Books Division, P.O. Box 211, 1000 AE Amsterdam, Netherlands. TEL 31-20-4853911. FAX 31-20-4853705. *4971*

PROCESS SAFETY AND ENVIRONMENTAL PROTECTION.
Institution of Chemical Engineers, George E. Davis Bldg., 165-189 Railway Terr., Rugby, Warks. CV21 3HQ, England. TEL 44-1788-78214. FAX 44-1788-578214. *2648*

PROCESS SIMULATION & MODELING.
Elsevier Science B.V., Books Division, P.O. Box 211, 1000 AE Amsterdam, Netherlands. TEL 31-20-4853911. FAX 31-20-4853705. *2053*

PROCESS TECHNOLOGY PROCEEDINGS.
Elsevier Science B.V., Books Division, P.O. Box 211, 1000 AE Amsterdam, Netherlands. TEL 31-20-4853911. FAX 31-20-4853705. *2749*

PRODUCTION AND OPERATIONS MANAGEMENT.
Production and Operations Management Society, University of Baltimore, 1420 N. Charles St., Baltimore, MD 21201. TEL 410-837-4976. FAX 410-837-5675. *1441*

PRODUCTION PLANNING & CONTROL.
Taylor & Francis Ltd., Rankine Rd., Basingstoke, Hants. RG24 8PR, England. TEL 44-1256-840366. FAX 44-1256-479438. *2681*

PROFESSIONAL EDUCATOR.
Auburn University, College of Education, 3084 Haley Ctr., Auburn, AL 36849-5218. TEL 334-844-5979. FAX 334-844-5785. *2499*

PROFESSIONAL ETHICS.
Box 15017, Gainesville, FL 32604. TEL 904-392-2084. FAX 904-392-5575. *5494*

THE PROFESSIONAL MANAGER.
Institute of Mangement Foundation, 2 Savoy Ct., 3rd. Fl., Strand, London WC2R OEZ, England. TEL 44-171-497-0580. FAX 44-171-497-0463. *1441*

PROFESSIONAL PSYCHOLOGY: RESEARCH AND PRACTICE.
American Psychological Association, 750 First St., N.E., Washington, DC 20002-4242. TEL 202-336-5600. FAX 202-336-5568. *5871*

PROFESSIONAL SPEAKER.
National Speakers Association, 1500 S. Priest Dr., Tempe, AZ 85281-6203. TEL 602-968-2552. FAX 602-968-0911. *4100*

PROFILE OF THE WORLDWIDE SEMICONDUCTOR INDUSTRY.
Elsevier Science Ltd., Books Division, P.O. Box 800, Kidlington, Oxford OX5 1DX, England. TEL 44-1865-843000. FAX 44-1865-843010. *2530*

PROFILES.
Kluwer Academic Publishers, Postbus 17, 3300 AA Dordrecht, Netherlands. TEL 31-78-6392392. FAX 31-78-6392254. *5494*

PROGRAMMING AND COMPUTER SOFTWARE.
Maik Nauka - Interperiodica, Mezhdunarodnyi Otdel, Ul. Profsayuznaya, 90, 117864 Moscow, Russia. TEL 7-095-3360666. FAX 7-095-3360666. *2046*

PROGRES EN UROLOGIE.
Progres en Urologie S.A.R.L., 7 bd. Flandrin, 75116 Paris, France. TEL 33-1-45-03-31-96. FAX 33-1-45-04-72-89. *4930*

PROGRESS AND TOPICS IN CYTOGENETICS.
John Wiley & Sons, Inc., Journals, 605 Third Ave., New York, NY 10158. TEL 212-475-7700. *749*

PROGRESS IN AEROSPACE SCIENCES.
Elsevier Science Ltd., Pergamon, P.O. Box 800, Kidlington, Oxford OX5 1DX, England. TEL 44-1865-843000. FAX 44-1865-843010. *75*

PROGRESS IN AIDS PATHOLOGY.
Field & Wood, Medical Periodicals, Inc., Box 975, Blue Bell, PA 19422. TEL 610-828-4010. FAX 215-482-0226. *4627*

PROGRESS IN APPLIED MICROCIRCULATION.
S. Karger AG, Allschwilerstr. 10, P.O. Box, CH-4009 Basel, Switzerland. TEL 061-3061111. FAX 061-3061234. *4608*

PROGRESS IN BASIC AND CLINICAL PHARMACOLOGY.
S. Karger AG, Allschwilerstr. 10, P.O. Box, CH-4009 Basel, Switzerland. TEL 061-3061111. FAX 061-3061234. *5440*

PROGRESS IN BIOCHEMICAL PHARMACOLOGY.
S. Karger AG, Allschwilerstr. 10, P.O. Box, CH-4009 Basel, Switzerland. TEL 061-3061111. FAX 061-3061234. *5440*

PROGRESS IN BIOMEDICAL ENGINEERING.
Elsevier Science B.V., Books Division, P.O. Box 211, 1000 AE Amsterdam, Netherlands. TEL 31-20-4853911. FAX 31-20-4853705. *628*

PROGRESS IN BIOPHYSICS & MOLECULAR BIOLOGY.
Elsevier Science Ltd., Pergamon, P.O. Box 800, Kidlington, Oxford OX5 1DX, England. TEL 44-1865-843000. FAX 44-1865-843010. *655*

PROGRESS IN BIOTECHNOLOGY.
Elsevier Science B.V., Books Division, P.O. Box 211, 1000 AE Amsterdam, Netherlands. TEL 31-20-4853911. FAX 31-20-4853705. *665*

PROGRESS IN BRAIN RESEARCH.
Elsevier Science B.V., Books Division, P.O. Box 211, 1000 AE Amsterdam, Netherlands. TEL 31-20-4853911. FAX 31-20-4853705. *4861*

PROGRESS IN CANCER RESEARCH AND THERAPY.
Lippincott - Raven Publishers 227 E. Washington Sq., Philadelphia, PA 19106. TEL 215-238-4200. FAX 215-238-4235. *4763*

PROGRESS IN CARDIOVASCULAR DISEASES.
W.B. Saunders Co. Curtis Center, 3rd Fl., Independence Sq. W., Philadelphia, PA 19106-3399. TEL 215-238-7800. FAX 215-238-6445. *4608*

PROGRESS IN CARDIOVASCULAR NURSING.
Medquest Communications, Inc., 629 Euclid Ave., Ste. 500, Cleveland, OH 44114-3003. TEL 216-522-9700. FAX 216-522-9707. *4608*

PROGRESS IN CELL RESEARCH.
Elsevier Science B.V., Books Division, P.O. Box 211, 1000 AE Amsterdam, Netherlands. TEL 31-20-4853911. FAX 31-20-4853705. *718*

PROGRESS IN CLINICAL AND BIOLOGICAL RESEARCH.
John Wiley & Sons, Inc., Journals, 605 Third Ave., New York, NY 10158. TEL 212-475-7700. *4520*

PROGRESS IN CRYSTAL GROWTH AND CHARACTERIZATION OF MATERIALS.
Elsevier Science Ltd., Pergamon, P.O. Box 800, Kidlington, Oxford OX5 1DX, England. TEL 44-1865-843000. FAX 44-1865-843010. *1727*

PROGRESS IN ENDOCRINE RESEARCH AND THERAPY.
Lippincott - Raven Publishers 227 E. Washington Sq., Phialdelphia, PA 19106. TEL 215-238-4200. FAX 215-238-4235. *4674*

PROGRESS IN ENERGY AND COMBUSTION SCIENCE.
Elsevier Science Ltd., Pergamon, P.O. Box 800, Kidlington, Oxford OX5 1DX, England. TEL 44-1865-843000. FAX 44-1865-843010. *2556*

PROGRESS IN EXPERIMENTAL TUMOR RESEARCH.
S. Karger AG, Allschwilerstr. 10, P.O. Box, CH-4009 Basel, Switzerland. TEL 061-3061111. FAX 061-3061234. *4763*

PROGRESS IN FILTRATION AND SEPARATION.
Elsevier Science B.V., Books Division, P.O. Box 211, 1000 AE Amsterdam, Netherlands. TEL 31-20-4853911. FAX 31-20-4853705. *1689*

PROGRESS IN HORMONE BIOCHEMISTRY.
Kluwer Academic Publishers, Postbus 17, 3300 AA Dordrecht, Netherlands. TEL 31-78-6392392. FAX 31-78-6392254. *647*

PROGRESS IN INDUSTRIAL MICROBIOLOGY.
Elsevier Science B.V., Books Division, P.O. Box 211, 1000 AE Amsterdam, Netherlands. TEL 31-20-4853911. FAX 31-20-4853705. *765*

PROGRESS IN INORGANIC CHEMISTRY.
John Wiley & Sons, Inc., 605 Third Ave., New York, NY 10158. TEL 212-850-6000. FAX 212-850-6088. *1733*

PROGRESS IN LIPID RESEARCH.
Elsevier Science Ltd., Pergamon, P.O. Box 800, Kidlington, Oxford OX5 1DX, England. TEL 44-1865-843000. FAX 44-1865-843010. *1745*

PROGRESS IN LIVER DISEASE.
W.B. Saunders Co. Curtis Center, 3rd Fl., PA 19106-3399. TEL 215-238-7800. FAX 215-238-6445. *4695*

PROGRESS IN LOW TEMPERATURE PHYSICS.
Elsevier Science B.V., Books Division, P.O. Box 211, 1000 AE Amsterdam, Netherlands. TEL 31-20-4853911. FAX 31-20-4853705. *5586*

PROGRESS IN MATERIALS SCIENCE.
Elsevier Science Ltd., Pergamon, P.O. Box 800, Kidlington, Oxford OX5 1DX, England. TEL 44-1865-843000. FAX 44-1865-843010. *2740*

PROGRESS IN MEDICAL VIROLOGY.
S. Karger AG, Allschwilerstr. 10, P.O. Box, CH-4009 Basel, Switzerland. TEL 061-3061111. FAX 061-3061234. *4627*

PROGRESS IN MEDICINAL CHEMISTRY.
Elsevier Science B.V., Books Division, P.O. Box 211, 1000 AE Amsterdam, Netherlands. TEL 31-20-4853911. FAX 31-20-4853705. *1689*

Refereed

PROGRESS IN MOLECULAR AND SUBCELLULAR BIOLOGY.
Springer-Verlag, 175 Fifth Ave., New York, NY 10010. TEL 212-460-1500. FAX 212-473-6272. *718*

PROGRESS IN MUTATION RESEARCH.
Elsevier Science B.V., Books Division, P.O. Box 211, 1000 AE Amsterdam, Netherlands. TEL 31-20-4853911. FAX 31-20-4853705. *749*

PROGRESS IN NEURO-PSYCHOPHARMACOLOGY AND BIOLOGICAL PSYCHIATRY.
Elsevier Science Inc., Box 945, New York, NY 10159-0945. TEL 212-633-3730. FAX 212-633-3680. *5440*

PROGRESS IN NEUROBIOLOGY.
Elsevier Science Ltd., Pergamon, P.O. Box 800, Kidlington, Oxford OX5 1DX, England. TEL 44-1865-843000. FAX 44-1865-843010. *602*

PROGRESS IN NEUROLOGICAL SURGERY.
S. Karger AG, Allschwilerstr. 10, P.O. Box, CH-4009 Basel, Switzerland. TEL 061-3061111. FAX 061-3061234. *4861*

PROGRESS IN NEUROPATHOLOGY.
Lippincott - Raven Publishers 227 E. Washington Sq., Philadelphia, PA 19106. TEL 215-238-4200. FAX 215-238-4235. *4861*

PROGRESS IN NUCLEAR ENERGY.
Elsevier Science Ltd., Pergamon, P.O. Box 800, Kidlington, Oxford OX5 1DX, England. TEL 44-1865-843000. FAX 44-1865-843010. *2582*

PROGRESS IN NUCLEAR MAGNETIC RESONANCE SPECTROSCOPY.
Elsevier Science B.V., P.O. Box 211, 1000 AE Amsterdam, Netherlands. TEL 31-20-4853911. FAX 31-20-4853598. *1720*

PROGRESS IN NUCLEIC ACID RESEARCH AND MOLECULAR BIOLOGY.
Academic Press, Inc., 525 B St., Ste. 1900, San Diego, CA 92101-4495. TEL 619-231-0926. FAX 619-699-6715. *602*

PROGRESS IN OBESITY RESEARCH (YEAR).
John Libbey Media, University of Luton, 75 Castle St., Luton, Bedfordshire LU1 3AJ, England. TEL 44-1582-743297. FAX 44-1582-743298. *4520*

PROGRESS IN OCEANOGRAPHY.
Elsevier Science Ltd., Pergamon, P.O. Box 800, Kidlington, Oxford OX5 1DX, England. TEL 44-1865-843000. FAX 44-1865-843010. *2304*

PROGRESS IN OPTICS.
Elsevier Science B.V., Books Division, P.O. Box 211, 1000 AE Amsterdam, Netherlands. TEL 31-20-4853911. FAX 31-20-4853705. *5611*

PROGRESS IN ORGANIC COATINGS.
Elsevier Science S.A., P.O. Box 564, CH-1001 Lausanne 1, Switzerland. TEL 41-21-3207381. FAX 41-21-3235444. *5310*

PROGRESS IN PAPER RECYCLING.
Doshi & Associates Inc., Box 2771, Appleton, WI 54913-2771. TEL 414-832-9101. FAX 414-832-0870. *5325*

PROGRESS IN PARTICLE AND NUCLEAR PHYSICS.
Elsevier Science Ltd., Pergamon, P.O. Box 800, Kidlington, Oxford OX5 1DX, England. TEL 44-1865-843000. FAX 44-1865-843010. *5599*

PROGRESS IN PEDIATRIC CARDIOLOGY.
Elsevier Science Ireland Ltd., P.O. Box 85, Limerick, Ireland. TEL 353-31-471944. FAX 353-61-472144. *4609*

PROGRESS IN PHOTOVOLTAICS.
John Wiley & Sons Ltd., Journals, Baffins Ln., Chichester, W. Sussex PO19 1UD, England. TEL 44-1243-779777. FAX 44-1243-843232. *2556*

PROGRESS IN PHYCOLOGICAL RESEARCH.
Elsevier Science B.V., Books Division, P.O. Box 211, 1000 AE Amsterdam, Netherlands. TEL 31-20-4853911. FAX 31-20-4853705. *700*

PROGRESS IN PHYSICAL ORGANIC CHEMISTRY.
John Wiley & Sons, Inc., 605 Third Ave., New York, NY 10158. TEL 212-850-6000. FAX 212-850-6088. *1756*

PROGRESS IN PLANNING.
Elsevier Science Ltd., Pergamon, P.O. Box 800, Kidlington, Oxford OX5 1DX, England. TEL 44-1865-843000. FAX 44-1865-843010. *3592*

PROGRESS IN POLYMER SCIENCE.
Elsevier Science Ltd., Pergamon, P.O. Box 800, Kidlington, Oxford OX5 1DX, England. TEL 44-1865-843000. FAX 44-1865-843010. *1745*

PROGRESS IN PSYCHOBIOLOGY AND PHYSIOLOGICAL PSYCHOLOGY.
Academic Press, Inc., 525 B St., Ste. 1900, San Diego, CA 92101-4495. TEL 619-231-0926. FAX 619-699-6715. *5871*

PROGRESS IN QUANTUM ELECTRONICS.
Elsevier Science Ltd., Pergamon, P.O. Box 800, Kidlington, Oxford OX5 1DX, England. TEL 44-1865-843000. FAX 44-1865-843010. *2530*

PROGRESS IN REACTION KINETICS.
Elsevier Science Ltd., Pergamon, P.O. Box 800, Kidlington, Oxford OX5 1DX, England. TEL 44-1865-843000. FAX 44-1865-843010. *1756*

PROGRESS IN REPRODUCTIVE BIOLOGY AND MEDICINE.
S. Karger AG, Allschwilerstr. 10, P.O. Box, CH-4009 Basel, Switzerland. TEL 061-3061111. FAX 061-3061234. *4727*

PROGRESS IN RESPIRATION RESEARCH.
S. Karger AG, Allschwilerstr. 10, P.O. Box, CH-4009 Basel, Switzerland. TEL 061-3061111. FAX 061-3061234. *4890*

PROGRESS IN RETINAL AND EYE RESEARCH.
Elsevier Science Ltd., Pergamon, P.O. Box 800, Kidlington, Oxford OX5 1DX, England. TEL 44-1865-843000. FAX 44-1865-843010. *4777*

PROGRESS IN RUBBER AND PLASTICS TECHNOLOGY.
R A P R A Technology Ltd., Shawbury, Shrewsbury, Shrops. SY4 4NR, England. TEL 44-1939-250383. FAX 44-1939-251118. *6218*

PROGRESS IN SOLID STATE CHEMISTRY.
Elsevier Science Ltd., Pergamon, P.O. Box 800, Kidlington, Oxford OX5 1DX, England. TEL 44-1865-843000. FAX 44-1865-843010. *1756*

PROGRESS IN SURFACE AND MEMBRANE SCIENCE.
Academic Press, Inc., 525 B St., Ste. 1900, San Diego, CA 92101-4495. TEL 619-231-0926. FAX 619-699-6715. *1756*

PROGRESS IN SURFACE SCIENCE.
Elsevier Science Ltd., Pergamon, P.O. Box 800, Kidlington, Oxford OX5 1DX, England. TEL 44-1865-843000. FAX 44-1865-843010. *5567*

PROGRESS IN SURGERY.
S. Karger AG, Allschwilerstr. 10, P.O. Box, CH-4009 Basel, Switzerland. TEL 061-3061111. FAX 061-3061234. *4918*

PROGRESS IN SURGICAL PATHOLOGY.
Field & Wood, Medical Periodicals, Inc., Box 975, Blue Bell, PA 19422. TEL 610-828-4010. FAX 215-482-0226. *4520*

PROGRESS IN THEORETICAL ORGANIC CHEMISTRY.
Elsevier Science B.V., Books Division, P.O. Box 211, 1000 AE Amsterdam, Netherlands. TEL 31-20-4853911. FAX 31-20-4853705. *1745*

PROGRESS IN VETERINARY NEUROLOGY.
Veterinary Practice Publishing Co., 7 Ashley Ave., S., Santa Barbara, CA 93103-9989. TEL 805-965-1028. FAX 805-965-0722. *6952*

PROGRESSIVE FISH-CULTURIST.
American Fisheries Society, 5410 Grosvenor Lane, Ste. 110, Bethesda, MD 20814-2199. TEL 301-897-8616. FAX 301-897-8096. *2941*

PROJECT APPRAISAL.
Beech Tree Publishing, 10 Watford Close, Guildford, Surrey GU1 2EP, England. TEL 44-1483-67497. FAX 44-1483-67497. *1348*

PROJECT MANAGEMENT JOURNAL.
P M I Communications, 40 Colonial Sq., Sylva, NC 28779. TEL 704-586-3715. FAX 704-586-4020. *1441*

PROJECTS IN METAL.
Village Press, Inc., 2779 Aero Park Dr., Traverse City, MI 49686. TEL 616-946-3712. FAX 616-946-3289. *4345*

PROMAX INTERNATIONAL.
Promotion & Marketing Executives in the Electronic Media, 2029 Century Pk. E., Ste. 555, Los Angeles, CA 90067-2906. TEL 310-788-7600. FAX 310-788-7616. *1967*

PROMETHEUS.
Carfax Publishing Co., Abingdon, Oxon. OX14 3UE, England. TEL 44-1235-401000. FAX 44-1235-401550. *1914*

PROSE STUDIES.
Frank Cass, Newbury House, 890-900 Eastern Ave., Newbury Park, Ilford, Essex 1G2 7HH, England. TEL 44-181-599-8666. FAX 44-181-599-0984 *4254*

PROSECUTOR.
National District Attorneys Association, 99 Canal Center Plaza, Ste. 510, Alexandria, VA 22314. TEL 703-549-9222. *3835*

PROSPECT.
National Centre for English Language Teaching and Research, Macquarie University, New South Wales 2109, Australia. TEL 61-2-850-7573. FAX 61-2-850-7849. *2401*

PROSPERO.
Triangle Journals Ltd., P.O. Box 65, Wallingford, Oxon. OX10 0YG, England. TEL 44-1491-838013. FAX 44-1491-834968. *2499*

PROSPETTIVE SOCIALI E SANITARIE.
Istituto per la Ricerca Sociale, Via XX Settembre 24, 20123 Milan, Italy. TEL 39-2-48010483. FAX 39-2-48008495. *6387*

PROSTAGLANDINS.
Elsevier Science Inc., Box 945, New York, NY 10159-0945. TEL 212-633-3730. FAX 212-633-3680. *4674*

PROSTAGLANDINS, LEUKOTRIENES AND CANCER.
Kluwer Academic Publishers, Postbus 17, 3300 AA Dordrecht, Netherlands. TEL 31-73-6392392. FAX 31-78-6392254. *4753*

THE PROSTATE.
John Wiley & Sons, Inc., Journals, 605 Third Ave., New York, NY 10158. TEL 212-850-6645. FAX 212-850-6021. *4520*

PROSTHETICS AND ORTHOTICS INTERNATIONAL.
International Society for Prosthetics and Orthotics, Borgervaenget 5, DK-2100 Copenhagen OE, Denmark. TEL 45-31-20-72-60. FAX 45-31-18-16-69. *4790*

PROTECTING CHILDREN.
American Humane Association, Children's Division, 63 Inverness Dr. E., Englewood, CO 80112-5117. TEL 303-792-9900. FAX 303-792-5333. *6388*

PROTECTION OF METALS.
Maik Nauka - Interperiodica, Mezhdunarodnyi Otdel, Ul. Profsoyuznaya 90, Moscow 117864, Russia. TEL 7-095-231-2164. FAX 7-095-233-5590. *4972*

PROTEIN AND PEPTIDE LETTERS.
Bentham Science Publishers, 7435 S.W. 117 Ave., Box 130, Miami, FL 33183. FAX 305-596-5120. *648*

PROTEIN ENGINEERING.
Oxford University Press, Oxford Journals, Walton St., Oxford OX2 6DP, England. TEL 01865-267907. FAX 01865-267773. *649*

PROTEIN EXPRESSION AND PURIFICATION.
Academic Press, Inc., Journal Division, 525 B St., Ste. 1900, San Diego, CA 92101-4495. TEL 619-230-1840. FAX 619-699-6800. *648*

PROTEIN SCIENCE.
Cambridge University Press, Edinburgh Bldg., Shaftesbury Rd., Cambridge CB2 2RU, England. TEL 44-1223-312393. FAX 44-1223-315052. *648*

PROTEINS: STRUCTURE, FUNCTION, AND GENETICS.
John Wiley & Sons, Inc., Journals, 605 Third Ave., New York, NY 10158. TEL 212-850-6645. FAX 212-850-6021. *602*

PROTEUS.
Shippensburg University, Shippensburg, PA 17257. TEL 717-532-1206. FAX 717-532-1253. *3236*

PROVENANCE.
Society of Georgia Archivists, Box 80631, Athens, GA 30608. TEL 706-542-7123. *3484*

PROYECCIONES.
Universidad Catolica del Norte, Departamento de Matematicas, Avda. Angamos 0610, Casilla 1280, Antofagasta, Chile. TEL 241148. FAX 241724. *4389*

PRUDENTIA.
University of Auckland, Department of Classic and Ancient History, Attn: Dr. T.C. Gilmour, Private Bag, Auckland, New Zealand. TEL 3737-999. FAX 3732-878. *3355*

PRZEGLAD ANTROPOLOGICZNY.
Polskie Towarzystwo Antropologiczne, Ul. Marymoncka 34, 01-813 Warsaw, Poland. *319*

PSEUDEPIGRAPHA VETERIS TESTAMENTI GRAECE.
E.J. Brill, P.O. Box 9000, 2300 PA Leiden, Netherlands. TEL 31-71-5353500. FAX 31-71-5317532. *6085*

PSICHIATRIA E PSICOTERAPIA ANALITICA.
Universita degli Studi di Roma II, Cattedra di Clinica Psychiatrica, Via Trionfale 11224, 00135 Rome, Italy. TEL 39-6-30818097. *4861*

PSICOLOGIA: TEORIA E PESQUISA.
Universidade de Brasilia, Instituto de Psicologia, Campus Universitario, 70910-900 Brasilia DF, Brazil. TEL 55-61-2746455. FAX 55-61-2736378. *5872*

PSICOTHEMA: REVISTA DE PSICOLOGIA.
Universidad de Oviedo, Facultad de Psicologia, C. San Francisco 3, 33003 Oviedo, Spain. TEL 34-85-104486. FAX 34-85-104488. *5872*

PSIONIC MEDICINE.
Psionic Medical Society, Garden Cottage, Beacon Hill Park, Hindhead, Surrey GU26 6HU, England. *4520*

PSIQUIATRIA PUBLICA.
Jarpyo Editores, S.A., Antonio Lopez Aguado 4, 28029 Madrid, Spain. TEL 34-1-3144338. FAX 34-1-3144499. *4862*

PSYCHE.
Cambridge Entomological Club, 26 Oxford St., Cambridge, MA 02138. TEL 617-495-2464. FAX 617-495-5667. *734*

PSYCHE.
Monash University, Department of Computer Science, Clayton Vic. 3168, Australia. TEL 61-3-94271242. FAX 61-3-99055146. *5872*

PSYCHIATRIA POLSKA.
Polskie Towarzystwo Psychiatryczne, Ul. Lenartowicza 14, 31-138 Krakow, Poland. TEL 48-12-331203. FAX 48-12-334067. *4862*

PSYCHIATRIC BULLETIN.
Royal College of Psychiatrists, 17 Belgrave Sq., London SW1X 8PG, England. TEL 44-171-235-8857. FAX 44-171-245-1231. *4862*

PSYCHIATRIC GENETICS.
Rapid Science Publishers, The Old Malthouse, Paradise St., Oxford OX1 1LD, England. TEL 44-1865-790447. FAX 44-1865-244012. *749*

PSYCHIATRIC QUARTERLY.
Human Sciences Press, Inc. 233 Spring St., New York, NY 10013-1578. TEL 212-620-8000. FAX 212-463-0742. *4863*

PSYCHIATRIC REHABILITATION JOURNAL.
Boston University, 930 Commonwealth Ave., Boston, MA 02215. TEL 617-353-3549. FAX 617-353-9209. *5872*

PSYCHIATRIC SERVICES.
American Psychiatric Association, 1400 K St., N.W., Washington, DC 20005. TEL 202-682-6070. FAX 202-682-6114. *4863*

PSYCHIATRIC TIMES.
C M E Inc., 1924 E. Deere Ave., Santa Ana, CA 92705-5723. TEL 800-447-4474. FAX 714-250-1245. *4863*

PSYCHIATRY.
Guilford Publications, Inc., 72 Spring St., 4th Fl., New York, NY 10012. TEL 212-431-9800. FAX 212-966-6708. *4863*

PSYCHIATRY PSYCHOLOGY AND LAW.
Australian Academic Press Pty. Ltd., 32 Jeays St., Bowen Hills, Qld. 4006, Australia. TEL 61-7-2571176. *4863*

PSYCHIATRY RESEARCH.
Elsevier Science Ireland Ltd., P.O. Box 85, Limerick, Ireland. TEL 353-61-471944. FAX 353-61-472144. *4863*

PSYCHIATRY RESEARCH: NEUROIMAGING SECTION.
Elsevier Science Ireland Ltd., P.O. Box 85, Limerick, Ireland. TEL 353-61-471944. FAX 353-61-472144. *4864*

PSYCHIC STUDIES.
Gordon & Breach Science Publishers, c/o International Publishers Distributor, P.O. Box 3054, Langhorne, PA 19047-3054. TEL 215-750-2642. FAX 215-750-6343. *5332*

PSYCHO-ONCOLOGY.
John Wiley & Sons Ltd., Journals, Baffins Ln., Chichester, W. Sussex PO19 1UD, England. TEL 44-1243-779777. FAX 44-1243-843232. *4763*

PSYCHOANALYSIS AND CONTEMPORARY THOUGHT.
International Universities Press, Inc., 59 Boston Post Rd., Box 1524, Madison, CT 06443-1524. TEL 203-245-4000. FAX 203-245-0775. *4864*

PSYCHOANALYTIC PSYCHOLOGY.
Lawrence Erlbaum Associates, Inc., 10 Industrial Dr., Mahwah, NJ 07430-2262. TEL 201-236-9500. FAX 201-236-0072. *5873*

PSYCHOANALYTIC REVIEW.
Guilford Publications, Inc., 72 Spring St., 4th Fl., New York, NY 10012. TEL 212-431-9800. FAX 212-966-6708. *5873*

PSYCHOBIOLOGY.
Psychonomic Society, Inc., 1710 Fortview Rd., Austin, TX 78704. TEL 512-462-2442. *5873*

PSYCHOLOGICA BELGICA.
Societe Belge de Psychologie, Tiensestraat 102, 3000 Leuven, Belgium. TEL 32-16-326013. FAX 32-16-326000. *5873*

PSYCHOLOGICAL ASSESSMENT.
American Psychological Association, 750 First St., N.E., Washington, DC 20002-4242. TEL 202-336-5600. FAX 202-336-5568. *5873*

PSYCHOLOGICAL BULLETIN.
American Psychological Association, 750 First St., N.E., Washington, DC 20002-4242. TEL 202-336-5500. FAX 202-336-5568. *5873*

PSYCHOLOGICAL INQUIRY.
Lawrence Erlbaum Associates, Inc., 10 Industrial Dr., Mahwah, NJ 07430-2262. TEL 201-236-9500. FAX 201-236-0072. *5873*

PSYCHOLOGICAL ISSUES.
International Universities Press, Inc., 59 Boston Post Rd., Box 1524, Madison, CT 06443-1524. TEL 203-245-4000. *5874*

THE PSYCHOLOGICAL RECORD.
Kenyon College, Gambier, OH 43022-9623. TEL 614-427-5377. FAX 614-427-4950. *5874*

PSYCHOLOGICAL REPORTS.
Dr. C.H. Ammons & Dr. R.B. Ammons, Eds. & Pubs., Box 9229, Missoula, MT 59807. *5874*

PSYCHOLOGICAL RESEARCH BULLETIN.
Lunds Universitet, Department of Psychology, Paradisgatan 5 P, 223 50 Lund, Sweden. TEL 46-46-2228770. FAX 46-46-2224209. *5874*

PSYCHOLOGICAL REVIEW.
American Psychological Association, 750 First St., N.E., Washington, DC 20002-4242. TEL 202-336-5600. FAX 202-336-5568. *5874*

PSYCHOLOGIE MEDICALE.
Societe de Presse Medicale, 14 rue Drout, 75009 Paris, France. TEL 48-24-96-93. FAX 42-47-00-44. *4864*

PSYCHOLOGISCHE BEITRAEGE.
Pabst Science Publishers, Am Eichengrund 28, 49525 Lengerich, Germany. FAX 35-5484-308. *5875*

THE PSYCHOLOGIST.
British Psychological Society, St. Andrew's House, 48 Princess Rd. E., Leicester LE1 7DR, England. TEL 44-166-254-9568. FAX 44-166-247-0787. *5875*

PSYCHOLOGY.
Institute for Leadership and Organization Effectiveness, 1409 Mt. Ayre, Bowling Green, KY 42101. FAX 614-292-7999. *5875*

PSYCHOLOGY AND DEVELOPING SOCIETIES.
Sage Publications India Pvt. Ltd., P.O. Box 4215, New Delhi 110 048, India. TEL 91-11-744-4958. FAX 91-11-647-2426. *5875*

PSYCHOLOGY & HEALTH.
Harwood Academic Publishers, c/o International Publishers Distributor, P.O. Box 3054, Langhorne, PA 19047-3054. TEL 215-750-2642. FAX 215-750-6343. *5875*

PSYCHOLOGY & MARKETING.
John Wiley & Sons, Inc., Journals, 605 Third Ave., New York, NY 10158. TEL 212-850-6645. FAX 212-850-6021. *5875*

PSYCHOLOGY BULLETIN.
Psychology Resource Centre, Private Bag X17, Bellville 7535, South Africa. TEL 27-21-959-2283. FAX 27-21-959-3515. *5876*

PSYCHOLOGY GRADUATE STUDENT JOURNAL.
c/o School of Psychology, University of Ottawa, 145 Jean Jacques Lussier, Ottowa ON K1N 6N5, Canada. *5876*

PSYCHOLOGY, HEALTH & MEDICINE.
Carfax Publishing Co., P.O. Box 25, Abingdon, Oxon. OX14 3UE, England. TEL 44-1235-401000. FAX 44-1235-401550. *5876*

PSYCHOLOGY IN THE SCHOOLS.
John Wiley & Sons, Inc., Journals, 605 Third Ave., New York, NY 10158-0012. TEL 212-850-6645. FAX 212-850-6021. *5876*

PSYCHOLOGY OF MUSIC.
Society for Research in Psychology of Music and Music Education, Department of Psychology, The University, Leicester LE1 7RH, England. TEL 44-116-2522155. FAX 44-116-2522067. *5189*

PSYCHOLOGY OF WOMEN QUARTERLY.
Cambridge University Press, Edinburgh Bldg., Shaftesbury Rd., Cambridge CB2 2RU, England. TEL 44-1223-312393. FAX 44-1223-315052. *5876*

PSYCHOLOGY, PUBLIC POLICY, AND LAW.
American Psychological Association, 750 First St., N.E., Washington, DC 20002-4242. TEL 202-336-5600. FAX 202-336-5568. *5876*

PSYCHOLOGY TODAY.
Sussex Publishers Inc., 49 E. 21st St., 11th Fl., New York, NY 10010. TEL 212-260-7210. FAX 212-260-7445. *5876*

PSYCHONEUROENDOCRINOLOGY.
Elsevier Science Ltd., Pergamon, P.O. Box 800, Kidlington, Oxford OX5 1DX, England. TEL 44-1865-843000. FAX 44-1865-843010. *4864*

PSYCHONOMIC BULLETIN & REVIEW.
Psychonomic Society, Inc., 1710 Fortview Rd., Austin, TX 78704. TEL 512-462-2442. FAX 512-462-1101. *5877*

PSYCHOPATHOLOGY.
S. Karger AG, Allschwilerstr. 10, P.O. Box, CH-4009 Basel, Switzerland. TEL 061-3061111. FAX 061-3061234. *4864*

PSYCHOPHARMACOLOGY.
Elsevier Science B.V., Books Division, P.O. Box 211, 1000 AE Amsterdam, Netherlands. TEL 31-20-4853911. FAX 31-20-4853705. *5440*

PSYCHOPHYSIOLOGY.
Cambridge University Press, Edinburgh Bldg., Shaftesbury Rd., Cambridge CB2 2RU, England. TEL 44-1223-312393. FAX 44-1223-315052. *4520*

PSYCHOPOETICA.
Psychopoetica Publications, University of Hull, Dept. of Psychology, Hull HU6 7RX, England. TEL 44-1482-465581. FAX 44-1482-465599. *4317*

PSYCHOSOMATIC MEDICINE.
Williams & Wilkins, 351 W. Camden St., Baltimore, MD 21201. TEL 410-528-4000. FAX 410-528-4312. *4865*

PSYCHOSOMATICS.
American Psychiatric Press, Inc., Journals Division, 1400 K St., N.W., Ste. 1101, Washington, DC 20005. TEL 202-682-6240. FAX 202-682-6341. *4865*

PSYCHOTHERAPY.
American Psychological Association, Division of Psychotherapy, 3900 E. Camelback Rd., Ste. 200, Phoenix, AZ 85018. TEL 602-912-5329. *4865*

PSYCHOTHERAPY AND PSYCHOSOMATICS.
S. Karger AG, Allschwilerstr. 10, P.O. Box, CH-4009 Basel, Switzerland. TEL 061-3061111. FAX 061-3061234. *4865*

PSYCHOTHERAPY IN PRIVATE PRACTICE.
Haworth Press, Inc., 10 Alice St., Binghamton, NY 13904. TEL 607-722-5857. FAX 607-722-1424. *5877*

THE PSYCHOTHERAPY PATIENT.
Haworth Press, Inc., 10 Alice St., Binghamton, NY 13904. TEL 607-722-5857. FAX 607-722-1424. *5877*

PSYCHOTHERAPY RESEARCH.
Guilford Publications, Inc., 72 Spring St., 4th Fl., New York, NY 10012. TEL 212-431-9800. FAX 212-966-6708. *5877*

PSYCOLOQUY.
c/o Cognitive Sciences Centre, Dept. of Psychology, Univ. of Southhampton, Highfield, Southampton SO17 1BJ, England. *5877*

PTERIDOLOGIA.
American Fern Society, Inc., c/o Dr. David B. Lellinger, 326 West St., N.W., Vienna, VA 22180-4151. *700*

PUBLIC ADMINISTRATION.
Blackwell Publishers Ltd., 108 Cowley Rd., Oxford OX4 1JF, England. TEL 44-1865-791100. FAX 44-1865-791347. *5916*

PUBLIC ADMINISTRATION AND DEVELOPMENT.
John Wiley & Sons Ltd., Journals, Baffins Ln., Chichester, W. Sussex PO19 1UD, England. TEL 44-1243-779777. FAX 44-1243-843232. *1313*

PUBLIC ADMINISTRATION QUARTERLY.
Southern Public Administration Education Foundation, c/o Dr. Jack Rabin, Pennsylvania State University at Harrisburg, Division of Public Affairs, Middletown, PA 17057. TEL 717-948-6363. FAX 717-540-1383. *5916*

PUBLIC & ACCESS SERVICES QUARTERLY.
Haworth Press, Inc., 10 Alice St., Binghamton, NY 13904-1580. TEL 607-722-5857. FAX 607-722-1424. *4020*

PUBLIC CHOICE.
Kluwer Academic Publishers, Postbus 17, 3300 AA Dordrecht, Netherlands. TEL 31-78-6392392. FAX 31-78-6392254. *953*

PUBLIC CULTURE.
University of Chicago Press, Journals Division, Box 37005, Chicago, IL 60637. TEL 773-753-3347. FAX 773-753-0811. *4162*

PUBLIC HEALTH REVIEWS.
Technosdar Ltd., P.O. Box 31684, Tel Aviv 61316, Israel. TEL 972-3-5607418. FAX 972-3-5604932. *5973*

THE PUBLIC HISTORIAN.
University of California Press, Journals Division, 2120 Berkeley Way, No. 5812, Berkeley, CA 94720-5812. TEL 510-643-7154. FAX 510-642-9917. *3355*

PUBLIC LIBRARY QUARTERLY.
Haworth Press Inc., 10 Alice St., Binghamton, NY 13904. TEL 607-722-5857. FAX 607-722-1424. *4021*

THE PUBLIC MANAGER.
Bureaucrat, Inc., 12007 Titian Way, Potomac, MD 20854. TEL 301-279-9445. FAX 301-251-5872. *5917*

PUBLIC MONEY AND MANAGEMENT.
Blackwell Publishers Ltd., 108 Cowley Rd., Oxford OX4 1JF, England. TEL 44-1865-791100. FAX 44-1865-791347. *5917*

PUBLIC OPINION QUARTERLY.
University of Chicago Press, Journals Division, Box 37005, Chicago, IL 60637. TEL 773-753-3347. FAX 773-753-0811. *5701*

PUBLIC POLICY ISSUES IN RESOURCE MANAGEMENT.
University of Washington Press, Box 50096, Seattle, WA 98105. TEL 206-543-4050. *1529*

PUBLIC PRODUCTIVITY AND MANAGEMENT REVIEW.
Sage Publications, Inc., 2455 Teller Rd., Thousand Oaks, CA 91320. TEL 805-499-0721. FAX 805-499-0871. *5917*

PUBLIC TREASURER.
L G C Communications, 33-39 Bowling Green Ln., London EC1R 0DA, England. TEL 44-171-505-8400. FAX 44-171-837-2725. *1559*

PUBLIC UTILITIES LAW ANTHOLOGY.
International Library Law Book Publishers, Inc., 4301 N. Fairfax Rd., Ste. 875, Arlington, VA 22203. TEL 703-528-1000. FAX 703-528-6060. *3836*

PUBLICACIONS MATEMATIQUES.
Universitat Autonoma de Barcelona, Departamento de Matematicas, Apartat Postal 53, 08193 Bellterra (Barcelona), Spain. TEL 34-3-5811304. FAX 34-3-5812790. *4389*

PUBLICATIONS ON OCEAN DEVELOPMENT.
Kluwer Academic Publishers, Postbus 17, 3300 AA Dordrecht, Netherlands. TEL 31-78-6392392. FAX 31-78-6392254. *2304*

PUBLISHING TECHNOLOGY REVIEW.
Pira International, Randalls Rd., Leatherhead, Surrey KT22 7RU, England. TEL 44-1372-802050. FAX 44-1372-802239. *6006*

PUFF.
Odsgard Reklame - Marketing ApS, Hovedvejen 182, DK-2600 Glostrup, Denmark. TEL 45-43-45-34-91. FAX 45-43-43-13-28. *871*

PULA.
National Institute of Development Research and Documentation, University of Botswana, Private Bag 0022, Gaborore, Botswana. TEL 267-356364. FAX 267-357573. *5768*

PULMONARY PERSPECTIVES.
American College of Chest Physicians, 3300 Dundee Rd., Northbrook, IL 60062. TEL 847-498-1400. FAX 847-498-5460. *4890*

PULMONARY REVIEWS.
Partners in Medical Communication, 4 Brighton Rd., Clifton, NJ 07012. TEL 201-916-1000. FAX 201-916-0021. *4890*

PULPIT HELPS.
Advancing the Ministries of the Gospel International, 6815 Shallowford Rd., Chattanooga, TN 37422-1755. FAX 615-894-6863. *6035*

PUNJAB UNIVERSITY JOURNAL OF ZOOLOGY.
University of the Punjab, Department of Zoology Quaid-e-Azam Campus, Lahore 54590, Pakistan. TEL 92-42-5864028. *818*

PURABHILEKH - PURATATVA.
Directorate of Archives, Archaeology and Museum, Rua de Ourem, Panaji-Goa 403 001, India. TEL 226692. *3383*

PURE AND APPLIED MATHEMATICS.
Academic Press, Inc., 525 B St., Ste. 1900, San Diego, CA 92101-4495. TEL 619-231-0926. FAX 619-699-6715. *4389*

PURE AND APPLIED MATHEMATICS: A WILEY INTERSCIENCE SERIES OF TEXTS, MONOGRAPHS AND TRACTS.
John Wiley & Sons, Inc., Wiley Interscience Journals, 605 Third Ave., New York, NY 10158-0012. TEL 212-850-6418. *4389*

PURE AND APPLIED MATHEMATICS SERIES.
Marcel Dekker, Inc., 270 Madison Ave., New York, NY 10016. TEL 212-696-9000. FAX 212-685-4540. *4389*

PUSH AND PULL.
Keighley & Worth Valley Railway, Haworth Sta., Keighley, W. Yorks. BD22 8NJ, England. TEL 44-1535-645214. FAX 44-1535-647317. *6815*

PUTTERIDGE BURY MANAGEMENT REVIEW.
University of Luton, Putteridge Bury, Hitchin Rd., Luton, Beds. LU2 8LE, England. TEL 01582-482555. FAX 01582-483689. *1441*

PYNCHON NOTES.
c/o Bernard Duyfhuizen, Man. Ed., English Dept., Univ. of Wisconsin, Eau Claire, WI 54702-4004. TEL 715-836-3165. FAX 715-836-2380. *4254*

THE PYROTECHNIC LITERATURE SERIES.
Journal of Pyrotechnic, Inc., 1775 Blair Rd., Whitewater, CO 81527-9513. TEL 970-245-0692. FAX 970-245-0692. *2649*

THE PYROTECHNIC REFERENCE SERIES.
Pyrotechnic Journal, Inc., 1775 Blair Rd., Whitewater, CO 81527-9513. TEL 970-245-0692. FAX 970-245-0692. *2649*

PYROTECHNICA.
Pyrotechnica Publications, 2302 Tower Dr., Austin, TX 78703. TEL 512-476-4062. FAX 512-476-4062. *2649*

Q J I.
Louisiana State University Shreveport, 1 University Pl., Shreveport, LA 71115-2399. TEL 318-797-5235. FAX 318-797-5358. *5701*

QIANGJIGUANG YU LIZISHU
Qiang Jiguang yu Lizishu Journal Agency, P.O. Box 511-5, Chengdu, Sichuan 610003, People's Republic of China. TEL 86-316-25839. *2582*

QIXIANG XUEBAO.
China Meteorological Press, 46 Baishiqiao Rd., West Suburb, Beijing 100081, People's Republic of China. TEL 86-10-217-2277. *5005*

QUADERNI DI COOPERAZIONE SANITARIA.
Amici di Raoul Follereau, Via Borselli 4, 40135 Bologna, Italy. TEL 39-51-433402. FAX 39-51-434046. *4627*

QUADERNI FRIULANI DI ARCHEOLOGIA.
Societa Friulana di Archeologia, c/o Civici Musei, 33100 Castello di Udine, Italy. TEL 39-432-26560. *369*

QUADRANT.
Christian Research, Vision Bldg., 4 Footscray Rd., Eltham, London SE9 2TZ, England. TEL 44-181-294-1989. FAX 44-181-294-00.4. *6108*

QUAERENDO.
E.J. Brill, P.O. Box 9000, 2300 PA Leiden, Netherlands. TEL 31-71-5353500. FAX 31-71-5317532. *6006*

QUAKER HISTORY.
Friends Historical Association, Haverford College Library, Haverford, PA 19041. TEL 610-896-1161. *6211*

QUALITATIVE INQUIRY.
Sage Publications, Inc., 2455 Teller Rd., Thousand Oaks, CA 91320. TEL 805-499-0721. FAX 805-499-0871. *6339*

QUALITATIVE SOCIOLOGY.
Human Sciences Press, Inc. 233 Spring St., New York, NY 10013-1578. TEL 212-620-8000. FAX 212-463-0742. *6425*

QUALITIQUE.
Editions Labeau, 9 rue Albert Einstein, 77420 Champs-sur-Marne, France. TEL 64-68-21-93. FAX 64-68-79-04. *953*

QUALITY AND QUANTITY.
Kluwer Academic Publishers, Postbus 17, 3300 AA Dordrecht, Netherlands. TEL 31-78-6392392. FAX 31-78-6392254. *6426*

QUALITY AND RELIABILITY ENGINEERING INTERNATIONAL.
John Wiley & Sons Ltd., Journals, Baffins Ln., Chichester, W. Sussex PO19 1UD, England. TEL 44-1243-779777. FAX 44-1243-843232. *2717*

QUALITY ENGINEERING.
Marcel Dekker Journals, 270 Madison Ave., New York, NY 10016. TEL 212-696-9000. FAX 212-685-4540. *2616*

QUALITY IN HEALTH CARE.
B M J Publishing Group, B.M.A. House, Tavistock Sq., London WC1H 9JR, England. TEL 44-171-383-6270. FAX 44-171-383-6402. *4521*

QUALITY OF LIFE NEWSLETTER.
M A P I Research Institute, 27 rue de la Villette, 69003 Lyon, France. TEL 33-72-136667. FAX 33-72136668. *4521*

QUALITY PROGRESS.
American Society for Quality Control, 611 E. Wisconsin Ave., Box 3005, Milwaukee, WI 53201-3005. TEL 414-272-8575. FAX 414-272-1734. *2616*

QUANTITATIVE GEOLOGY AND GEOSTATISTICS.
Kluwer Academic Publishers, Postbus 17, 3300 AA Dordrecht, Netherlands. TEL 31-78-6392392. FAX 31-78-6392254. *2257*

QUANTUM (NEW YORK).
Springer-Verlag, Science Journals, 175 Fifth Ave., New York, NY 10010. TEL 212-460-1500. FAX 212-473-6272. *6273*

QUARTERLY ACCOUNT.
Money Advice Association, Gresham House, 1st Fl., 24 Holborn Viaduct, London EC1A 2BN, England. TEL 44-171-236-3566. *953*

QUARTERLY JOURNAL OF ADMINISTRATION.
Obafemi Awolowo University Press Ltd., Periodicals Department, University P.O. Box 1044, Ile-Ife, Osun State, Nigeria. TEL 234-36-230290-9. FAX 234-2-8101963. *5918*

QUARTERLY JOURNAL OF BUSINESS AND ECONOMICS.
University of Nebraska at Lincoln, College of Business Administration, CBA Bldg., Lincoln, NE 68588-0407. TEL 402-472-3309. FAX 402-472-9777. *953*

QUARTERLY JOURNAL OF EXPERIMENTAL PSYCHOLOGY. SECTION A: HUMAN EXPERIMENTAL PSYCHOLOGY.
Taylor & Francis Ltd., Psychology Press, 1 Gunpowder Sq., London EC4A 3DE, Engand. TEL 44-171-5830490. FAX 44-171-5830585. *5878*

QUARTERLY JOURNAL OF EXPERIMENTAL PSYCHOLOGY. SECTION B: COMPARATIVE AND PHYSIOLOGICAL PSYCHOLOGY.
Taylor & Francis Ltd., Psychology Press, 1 Gunpowder Sq., London EC4A 3DE, England. TEL 44-171-5830490. FAX 44-171-5830585. *5878*

THE QUARTERLY JOURNAL OF MUSIC TEACHING AND LEARNING.
University of Northern Colorado, School of Music, 123 Frazier Hall, Greeley, CO 80639. TEL 970-351-2254. FAX 970-351-1923. *5190*

QUARTERLY JOURNAL OF NUCLEAR MEDICINE.
Edizioni Minerva Medica, Corso Bramante 83-85, 10126 Turin, Italy. TEL 39-11-678282. FAX 39-11-3121736. *4882*

THE QUARTERLY JOURNAL OF SPEECH.
Speech Communication Association, 5105 Backlick Rd., Bldg. E., Annandale, VA 22003. TEL 703-750-0533. FAX 703-914-9471. *2365*

QUARTERLY OF APPLIED MATHEMATICS.
Brown University, Department of Mathamatics, 182 George St., Providence, RI 02940. *4390*

QUARTERLY REVIEW OF BIOLOGY.
University of Chicago Press, Journals Division, 5720 S. Woodlawn Ave., Chicago, IL 60637. TEL 773-753-3347. FAX 773-753-0811. *602*

QUARTERLY REVIEW OF FILM AND VIDEO.
Harwood Academic Publishers, c/o International Publishers Distributor, P.O. Box 3054, Langhorne, PA 19047-3054. TEL 215-750-2642. FAX 215-750-6343. *5111*

QUARTERLY REVIEW OF LITERATURE POETRY SERIES.
26 Haslet Ave., Princeton, NJ 08540. TEL 609-921-6976. FAX 609-258-2230. *4317*

QUARTERLY WEST.
University of Utah, Quarterly West, 317 Olpin Union, Salt Lake City, UT 84112. TEL 801-581-3938. *4255*

QUATERNARIO.
Associazione Italiana per lo Studio del Quaternario, c/o Dr. Ravazzi, Dipto. Scienze Terra, Piazza Cittadella 4, 24129 Bergamo, Italy. TEL 39-35-248051. *2215*

QUATERNARY INTERNATIONAL.
Elsevier Science Ltd., Pergamon, P.O. Box 800, Kidlington, Oxford OX5 1DX, England. TEL 44-1865-843000. FAX 44-1865-843010. *2257*

QUATERNARY RESEARCH.
Academic Press, Inc., Journal Division, 525 B St., Ste. 1900, San Diego, CA 92101-4495. TEL 619-230-1840. FAX 619-699-6800. *2257*

QUATERNARY SCIENCE REVIEWS.
Elsevier Science Ltd., Pergamon, P.O. Box 800, Kidlington, Oxford OX5 1DX, England. TEL 44-1865-843000. FAX 44-1865-843010. *2258*

QUEBEC STUDIES.
American Council for Quebec Studies, c/o Robert Schartzwald, Ed., French and Italian Dept., Univ. of Massachusetts, Amherst, MA 01003. TEL 413-545-6704. FAX 413-545-4778. *4255*

QUEEN CITY HERITAGE.
Cincinnati Historical Society, The Museum Center, Cincinnati Union Terminal, 1301 Western Ave., Cincinnati, OH 45203-1129. TEL 513-287-7058. FAX 513-287-7095. *3485*

QUEEN'S QUARTERLY.
Queen's Quarterly, Queen's University, Kingston, ON K7L 3N6, Canada. TEL 613-545-2667. FAX 613-545-6822. *3124*

QUEENSLAND UNIVERSITY OF TECHNOLOGY LAW JOURNAL.
Queensland University of Technology, Faculty of Law, George St., Brisbane, Qld. 4001, Australia. TEL 61-7-8642707. FAX 61-7-8641519. *3837*

QUERY.
Saskatchewan Reading Council, 4742 McTavish St., Regina, SK S4S 6N6, Canada. TEL 306-585-1439. *2365*

QUEST.
Quest, P.O. Box 9114, 9703 LC Groningen, Netherlands. TEL 31-50-3637509. FAX 31-50-3637100. *5494*

QUEST (CHAMPAIGN).
Human Kinetics Publishers, Inc., Box 5076, Champaign, IL 61825-5076. TEL 217-351-5076. FAX 217-351-2674. *2499*

QUEST (GRAND RAPIDS).
CSPACE Press, Box 9331, Grand Rapids, MI 49509-0331. TEL 616-452-5500. FAX 616-452-5538. *75*

QUESTIIO.
Institut d'Estadistica de Catalunya, Via Laietana 58, 08003 Barcelona, Spain. TEL 34-3-4121730. FAX 34-3-4123145. *6625*

QUFO.
Societas Upsaliensis, Institute of Earth Science, Quaternary Geology, Norbyvaegen 18 B, S-752 36 Uppsala, Sweden. TEL 46-18-18-25-00. FAX 46-18-18-25-91. *2258*

QUI PARLE.
University of California at Berkeley, Doreen B. Townsend Center for the Humanities, 460 Stephens Hall, Berkeley, CA 94720. TEL 510-643-9670. FAX 510-643-5284. *3623*

QUINCY BUSINESS NEWS.
John R. Graham, Inc., 40 Oval Rd., Ste. 2, Quincy, MA 02170-3813. TEL 617-328-0069. FAX 617-471-1504. *954*

QUINTESSENCE INTERNATIONAL.
Quintessence Publishing Co., Inc., 551 Kimberly Dr., Carol Stream, IL 60188-1881. TEL 708-682-3223. FAX 708-682-3288. *4652*

QUIPU.
Sociedad Latinoamericana de Historia de las Ciencias y la Tecnologia, Apdo. Postal 21-873, CP 04000 Mexico, DF, Mexico. TEL 525-6221864. FAX 525-6596406. *6274*

R A I R O RECHERCHE OPERATIONNELLE.
Dunod, 15 rue Gossin, 92543 Montrouge Cedex, France. TEL 33-1-40-92-65-00. FAX 33-1-40-92-65-97. *2063*

R A P R A ABSTRACTS.
R A P R A Technology Ltd., Shawbury, Shrewsbury, Shrops. SY4 4NR, England. TEL 44-1939-250383. FAX 44-1939-251118. *6220*

R A P R A REVIEW REPORTS.
R A P R A Technology Ltd., Shawbury, Shrewsbury, Shrops. SY4 4ND, England. TEL 44-1939-250383. FAX 44-1939-251118. *5629*

R & D MANAGEMENT.
Blackwell Publishers Ltd., 108 Cowley Rd., Oxford OX4 1JF, England. TEL 44-1865-791100. FAX 44-1865-791347. *1442*

R B M - REVUE EUROPEENNE DE TECHNOLOGIE BIOMEDICALE.
Editions Scientifiques et Medicales Elsevier, 141 rue de Javel, 75747 Paris, France. TEL 33-1-45589067. FAX 33-1-45589421. *665*

R N A.
Cambridge University Press, Edinburgh Bldg., Shaftesbury Rd., Cambridge CB2 2RU, England. TEL 44-1223-312393. FAX 44-1223-315052. *648*

R Q.
Tullis Russell & Co. Ltd., Auchmuty & Rothes Paper Mills, Markinch, Glenrothes, Fife KY7 6PB, Scotland. TEL 44-1592-753311. FAX 44-1592-610371. *3158*

R Q.
American Library Association, 50 E. Huron St., Chicago, IL 60611-2795. TEL 800-545-2433. FAX 312-440-9374. *4021*

R R T: THE CANADIAN JOURNAL OF RESPIRATORY THERAPY.
Canadian Medical Association, P.O. Box 8650, 1867 Alta Vista Dr., Ottawa, ON K1G 0G8, Canada. TEL 613-731-9331. FAX 613-523-0937. *4890*

R S G.
Uitgeverij Isidoro B.V., Scheltuslaan 53, 2273 DM Voorburg, Netherlands. TEL 31-70-3864430. FAX 31-70-3862372. *6476*

R S R.
Pierian Press, Box 1808, Ann Arbor, MI 48106. TEL 313-434-5530. FAX 313-434-6409. *4021*

RACE, SEX & CLASS.
University of Wisconsin - Superior, Center for Research on Race, Sex and Class, Sandquist Hall 318, Superior, WI 54880. *7019*

RACHUNKOWOSC.
Rachunkowosc Sp. z o.o., Ul. Tamka 18, lokal 29, 00-349 Warsaw, Poland. TEL 48-22-265621. FAX 48-22-265621. *1053*

RACING & FOOTBALL OUTLOOK.
Outlook Press Ltd., Kemp House, 152-160 City Rd., London EC1N 2NP, England. TEL 44-171-490-1212. FAX 44-171-608-3299. *6476*

RADIATION EFFECTS AND DEFECTS IN SOLIDS.
Gordon & Breach Science Publishers, c/o International Publishers Distributor, P.O. Box 3054, Langhorne, PA 19047-3054. TEL 215-750-2642. FAX 215-750-6343. *5599*

RADIATION MEASUREMENTS.
Elsevier Science Ltd., Pergamon, P.O. Box 800, Kidlington, Oxford OX5 1DX, England. TEL 44-1865-843000. FAX 44-1865-843010. *5599*

RADIATION PHYSICS AND CHEMISTRY.
Elsevier Science Ltd., Pergamon, The Boulevard, Langford Ln., Kidlington, Oxford OX5 1GB, England. TEL 44-1865-843000. FAX 44-1865-843010. *5599*

RADIATION PROTECTION DOSIMETRY.
Nuclear Technology Publishing, P.O. Box 7, Ashford, Kent TN23 1JW, England. TEL 44-1233-641683. FAX 44-1233-610021. *5600*

RADIATION PROTECTION MANAGEMENT.
R S A Publications, 19 Pendleton Dr., Box 19, Hebron, CT 06248. TEL 203-228-0824. FAX 203-228-4402. *5257*

RADIATION RESEARCH.
Kluge Carden Jennings, 1224 W. Main St., Ste. 200, Charlottesville, VA 22903-2858. TEL 804-979-4913. *5600*

RADIATION THERAPIST.
American Society of Radiologic Technologists, 15000 Central Ave., S.E., Albuquerque, NM 87123. TEL 505-298-4500. FAX 505-298-5063. *4882*

RADICAL AMERICA.
Alternative Education Project, Inc., One Summer St., Somerville, MA 02143. TEL 617-628-6585. FAX 617-628-6585. *5702*

RADICAL PHILOSOPHY.
Radical Philosophy Ltd., c/o Jean Grimshaw, North View, Dundry Lane, Dundry, Bristol BS18 8JG, England. TEL 01272-642986. *5494*

RADICAL TEACHER.
Boston Women's Teachers' Group, Box 102, Cambridge, MA 02142. *2365*

RADIO RIVISTA.
Ediradio, Via Scarlatti 31, 20124 Milan, Italy. TEL 2-6692894. FAX 2-66714809. *1939*

RADIO SCIENCE.
American Geophysical Union, 2000 Florida Ave., N.W., Washington, DC 20009. TEL 202-462-6900. FAX 202-328-0566. *2280*

RADIOACTIVE WASTE MANAGEMENT AND ENVIRONMENTAL RESTORATION.
Harwood Academic Publishers, c/o International Publishers Distributor, P.O. Box 3054, Langhorne, PA 19047-3054. TEL 215-750-2642. FAX 215-750-6343. *2855*

RADIOACTIVE WASTE MANAGEMENT HANDBOOK.
Harwood Academic Publishers, c/o International Publishers Distributor, P.O. Box 3054, Langhorne, PA 19047-3054. TEL 215-750-2642. FAX 215-750-6343. *2855*

RADIOACTIVE WASTE MANAGEMENT SERIES.
Harwood Academic Publishers, c/o International Publishers Distributor, P.O. Box 3054, Langhorne, PA 19047-3054. TEL 215-750-2642. FAX 215-750-6343. *2855*

RADIOCARBON.
University of Arizona, Department of Geosciences, 4717 E. Ft. Lowell Rd., Tucson, AZ 85712. TEL 520-881-0857. FAX 520-881-0554. *6274*

RADIOCHEMISTRY.
Maik Nauka - Interperiodica, Mezhdunarodnyi Otdel, Ul. Profsoyuznaya, 90, 117864 Moscow, Russia. TEL 7-095-3360066. FAX 7-095-3360666. *1756*

RADIOLOGIA BRASILEIRA.
Colegio Brasileiro de Radiologia, Departamento da Associacao Medica Brasileira, Av. Paulista, 491, 13a andar, 01311-909 Sao Paulo, Brazil. TEL 55-11-285-4022. *4882*

RADIOLOGIA MEDICA.
Edizioni Minerva Medica, Corso Bramante 83-85, 10126 Turin, Italy. TEL 39-11-678282. FAX 39-11-3121736. *4833*

RADIOLOGIC TECHNOLOGY.
American Society of Radiologic Technologists, 15000 Central Ave. S.E., Albuquerque, NM 87123-3917. TEL 505-298-4500. FAX 505-298-5063. *4883*

RADIOLOGY ONCOLOGY INVESTIGATIONS.
John Wiley & Sons, Inc., Journals, 605 Third Ave., New York, NY 10158. TEL 212-850-6645. FAX 212-850-6021. *4763*

RADIONIC JOURNAL.
Radionic Association Ltd., Baerlein House, Goose Green, Deddington, Banbury, Oxon OX15 0SZ, England. TEL 44-1869-338852. FAX 44-1869-338852. *4522*

RADIONUCLIDES IN NEPHROUROLOGY.
Field & Wood, Medical Periodicals, Inc., Box 975, Blue Bell, PA 19422. TEL 610-828-4010. FAX 215-482 0226. *4883*

RADIOPHARMACY AND RADIOPHARMACOLOGY YEARBOOK SERIES.
Gordon & Breach Science Publishers, c/o International Publishers Distributor, P.O. Box 3054, Langhorne, PA 19047-3054. TEL 215-750-2642. FAX 215-750-6343. *5441*

RADIOPHYSICS AND QUANTUM ELECTRONICS.
Plenum Publishing Corp., Consultants Bureau, 233 Spring St., New York, NY 10013-1578. TEL 212-620-8468. FAX 212-463-0742. *2531*

RADIOTHERAPY AND ONCOLOGY.
Elsevier Science Ireland Ltd., P.O. Box 85, Limerick, Ireland. TEL 353-61-471944. FAX 353-61-472144. *4833*

RAILWATCH.
Railway Development Society, 4 Christchurch Sq., London E9 7HU, England. TEL 44-181-985-8548. FAX 44-181-985-8212. *6816*

RAILWAY AND CANAL HISTORICAL SOCIETY JOURNAL.
Railway and Canal Historical Society, Fron Fawnog, Hafod Rd., Gwernymynydd Mold, Clwyd CH75JE, Wales. *6816*

RAILWAYS AFRICA.
Rail-Link C C, P.O. Box 4794, 2125 Randburg, Transvaal, South Africa. TEL 27-11-463-4330. FAX 27-11-463-4224. *6817*

THE RAMANUJAN JOURNAL.
Kluwer Academic Publishers, Postbus 17, 3300 AH Dordrecht, Netherlands. TEL 31-78-6392392. FAX 31-78-6392254. *4390*

RAMUS.
Aureal Publications, P.O. Box 49, Bendigo North, Vic. 3550, Australia. FAX 61-54-447970. *1825*

RAND JOURNAL OF ECONOMICS.
Rand Corporation, Publications Department, 1700 Main St., Box 2138, Santa Monica, CA 90407-2138. TEL 310-393-0411. FAX 310-393-4818. *954*

RANDOM MATERIALS AND PROCESSES.
Elsevier Science B.V., Books Division, P.O. Box 211, 1000 AE Amsterdam, Netherlands. TEL 31-20-4853911. FAX 31-20-4353705. *5567*

RANDOM OPERATORS AND STOCHASTIC EQUATIONS.
V S P, P.O. Box 346, 3700 AH Zeist, Netherlands. TEL 31-30-6925790. FAX 31-30-6932081. *4390*

RANDOM STRUCTURES & ALGORITHMS.
John Wiley & Sons, Inc., Journals, 605 Third Ave., New York, NY 10158. TEL 212-850-6645. FAX 212-850-6021. *4390*

RANGIFER.
Nordisk Organ for Reinforskning (NOR), c/o NVH, Institute of Arctic Veterinary Medicine, N-9005 Tromsoe, Norway. TEL 47-77-63-43-10. FAX 47-77-68-44-11. *818*

RANLIAO HUAXUE XUEBAO.
Science Press, Marketing and Sales Department, 16 Donghuangchenggen North St., Beijing 100717, People's Republic of China. TEL 4010642. FAX 4019810. *2649*

THE RAOUL WALLENBERG INSTITUTE HUMAN RIGHTS STUDIES.
Kluwer Law International Postbus 85889, 2508 CN The Hague, Netherlands. TEL 31-78-3381500. FAX 31-70-3051515. *5734*

RAPA NUI JOURNAL.
Easter Island Foundation Box 6774, Los Osos, CA 93412-6774. TEL 805-528-6279. FAX 805-534-9301. *319*

RAPID COMMUNICATIONS IN MASS SPECTROMETRY.
John Wiley & Sons Ltd., Journals, Baffins Ln., Chichester, W. Sussex PO19 1UD, England. TEL 44-1243-779777. FAX 44-1243-843232. *5611*

RARE COIN REVIEW.
Bowers and Merena Galleries, Inc., Box 1224, Wolfeboro, NH 03894. TEL 603-596-5095. FAX 603-569-5319. *5227*

RARE EARTH BULLETIN.
Multi-Science Publishing Co. Ltd., 107 High St., Brentwood, Essex CM14 4RX, England. TEL 44-1277-224632. FAX 44-1277-223453. *4972*

RASSEGNA MEDICO-CHIRURGICA.
Mess, Viale Mellusi 134, 32100 Benevento, Italy. TEL 39-824-311311. *4522*

RATIO.
Blackwell Publishers Ltd. 108 Cowley Rd., Oxford OX4 1JF, England. TEL 44-1865-791100. FAX 44-1865-791347. *5494*

RAVEN: A JOURNAL OF VEXILLOLOGY.
North American Vexillological Association, 1977 N. Olden St. Ext., Ste. 225, Trenton, NJ 08618-2193. *3099*

RAVEN CHRONICLES.
Raven Chronicles, Box 95918, University Sta., Seattle, WA 98145. TEL 206-328-1676. FAX 206-543-0411. *4163*

RAVEN PRESS SERIES IN PHYSIOLOGY.
Lippincott - Raven Publishers 227 E. Washington Sq., Philadelphia, PA 19106. TEL 215-238-4200. FAX 215-238-4235. *793*

RAW MATERIALS REPORT.
Raavarugruppen Ekonomisk Foerening, P.O. Box 44062, S-100 73 Stockolm, Sweden. TEL 46-8-7440065. FAX 46-8-7440066. *1313*

LA RAZA LAW JOURNAL.
University of California Press, Journals Division, 2120 Berkeley Way, No. 5812, Berkeley, CA 94720-5812. TEL 510-643-7154. FAX 510-642-9917. *3838*

RE: A L
Stephen F. Austin State University, School of Liberal Arts, Box 13007, SFA Sta., Nacogdoches, TX 75962. TEL 409-468-2059. *3623*

REACTION KINETICS AND CATALYSIS LETTERS.
Elsevier Science B.V., P.O. Box 211, 1000 AE
Amsterdam, Netherlands. TEL 31-20-4853911.
FAX 31-20-4853598. *1756*

REACTIVE AND FUNCTIONAL POLYMERS.
Elsevier Science B.V., P.O. Box 211, 1000 AE
Amsterdam, Netherlands. TEL 31-20-4853911.
FAX 31-20-4853598. *2649*

**REACTIVITY AND STRUCTURE: CONCEPTS OF
ORGANIC CHEMISTRY.**
Springer-Verlag, 175 Fifth Ave., New York, NY
10010. TEL 212-460-1500. FAX 212-473-6272.
1745

READING.
Blackwell Publishers Ltd., 108 Cowley Rd., Oxford
OX4 1JF, England. TEL 44-1865-791100. FAX 44-
1865-791347. *2366*

READING AND WRITING.
Kluwer Academic Publishers, Postbus 17, 3300 AA
Dordrecht, Netherlands. TEL 31-78-6392392.
FAX 31-78-6392254. *4102*

**READING AND WRITING QUARTERLY: OVERCOMING
LEARNING DIFFICULTIES.**
Taylor & Francis Inc., 1900 Frost Rd., Ste. 101,
Bristol, PA 19007-1598. TEL 215-785-5800.
FAX 215-785-5515. *2473*

READING IN POLITICAL ECONOMY.
Institute of Economic Affairs, 2 Lord North St.,
London SW1P 3LB, England. TEL 44-171-799-
3745. FAX 44-171-799-2137. *954*

THE READING PROFESSOR.
International Reading Association, Special Interest
Group Professors of Reading Teacher Educators, c/
o Dr. Larry Kenney, Ed., College of Education,
Winther Hall 2035, University of Wisconsin,
Whitewater, Whitewater, WI 53190. TEL 414-472-
4677. *2440*

READING PSYCHOLOGY.
Taylor & Francis Inc., 1900 Frost Rd., Ste. 101,
Bristol, PA 19007-1598. TEL 215-785-5800.
FAX 215-785-5515. *2499*

READING RESEARCH AND INSTRUCTION.
College Reading Association, c/o Dr. Gary L.
Shaffer, 83 Sharon St., Harrisonburg, VA 22801-
2715. TEL 540-434-2951. *2499*

READING RESEARCH QUARTERLY.
International Reading Association, Inc., 800
Barksdale Rd., Box 8139, Newark, DE 19714-
8139. TEL 302-731-1600. FAX 302-731-1057.
2366

READING TEACHER.
International Reading Association, Inc., 800
Barksdale Rd., Box 8139, Newark, DE 19714-
8139. TEL 302-731-1600. FAX 301-731-1057.
2499

READING THE PAST.
University of California Press, 2120 Berkeley Way,
Berkeley, CA 94720. TEL 510-642-4247.
FAX 510-643-7127. *4102*

REAL ACADEMIA DE FARMACIA. ANALES.
Real Academia de Farmacia, Calle de Farmacia 11,
28004 Madrid, Spain. TEL 915-31-03-07. FAX 91-
531-03-06. *5441*

REAL ACADEMIA GALEGA DE CIENCIAS. REVISTA.
Real Academia Galega de Ciencias, Rua do Franco
2, 15702 Santiago de Compostela, Spain. TEL 91-
582049. FAX 91-582049. *6274*

REAL ESTATE ECONOMICS.
Edward Bros., 2500 S. State St., Ann Arbor, MI
48106. TEL 313-769-1004. FAX 313-769-7653.
6034

REAL ESTATE LAW JOURNAL.
Warren, Gorham & Lamont, One Penn Plaza, New
York, NY 10119. TEL 212-971-5000. FAX 212-
971-5113. *3838*

REAL ESTATE RESEARCH ISSUES.
Kluwer Academic Publishers, Postbus 17, 3300 AA
Dordrecht, Netherlands. TEL 31-78-6392392.
FAX 31-78-6392254. *6035*

REAL ESTATE REVIEW.
Warren, Gorham & Lamont, One Penn Plaza, New
York, NY 10119. TEL 212-971-5000. FAX 212-
971-5240. *6035*

REAL ESTATE TAX DIGEST.
Matthew Bender & Co., Inc., 2 Park Ave., New York,
NY 10016. TEL 518-487-3000. FAX 518-462-
3788. *6035*

REAL-TIME SAFETY CRITICAL SYSTEMS.
Elsevier Science B.V., P.O. Box 211, 1000 AE
Amsterdam, Netherlands. TEL 31-20-4853911.
FAX 31-20-4853598. *2058*

REAL-TIME SYSTEMS.
Kluwer Academic Publishers Boston, Box 358,
Accord Sta., Hingham, MA 02018-0358. TEL 617-
871-6600. FAX 617-871-6528. *2058*

RECALL.
C T I Modern Languages, The University of Hull,
School of European Languages & Cultures,
Cottingham Rd., Hull HU6 7RX, England. TEL 44-
1482-466373. FAX 44-1482-473816. *4130*

**RECENT ACHIEVEMENTS IN RESTORATIVE
NEUROLOGY.**
S. Karger AG, Allschwilerstr. 10, P.O. Box, CH-4009
Basel, Switzerland. TEL 061-3061111. FAX 061-
3061234. *4865*

RECENT ADVANCES IN EPILEPSY.
Churchill Livingstone Robert Stevenson House, 1-3
Baxter's Pl., Leith Walk, Edinburgh EH1 3AF,
Scotland. TEL 44-131-556-2424. FAX 44-131-
459-1177. *4865*

RECENT DEVELOPMENTS IN ALCOHOLISM.
Plenum Publishing Corp., 233 Spring St., New York,
NY 10013-1578. TEL 212-620-8000. FAX 212-
463-0742. *2200*

RECENT ECONOMIC THOUGHT.
Kluwer Academic Publishers, Postbus 17, 3300 AA
Dordrecht, Netherlands. TEL 31-78-6392392.
FAX 31-78-6392254. *1260*

**RECENT PROGRESS IN HORMONE RESEARCH.
PROCEEDINGS OF THE LAURENTIAN HORMONE
CONFERENCE.**
Academic Press, Inc., 525 B St., Ste. 1900, San
Diego, CA 92101-4495. TEL 619-231-0926.
FAX 619-699-6715. *4675*

**RECENT PROGRESS IN SURFACE MEMBRANE
SCIENCE.**
Academic Press, Inc., 525 B St., Ste. 1900, San
Diego, CA 92101-4495. TEL 619-231-0926.
FAX 619-699-6715. *1757*

RECEPTORS AND SIGNAL TRANSDUCTION.
Humana Press Inc., 999 Riverview Dr., Ste. 208,
Totowa, NJ 07512. TEL 201-256-1699. FAX 201-
256-8341. *648*

RECHERCHES FEMINISTES.
Universite Laval, Groupe de Recherche
Multidisciplinaire Feministe, 3e etage, 2336 Chemin
Ste-Foy, Quebec, Que. G1K 7P4, Canada. TEL 418-
656-5421. FAX 418-656-3266. *7019*

RECLAIMING CHILDREN AND YOUTH.
Pro-Ed Inc., 8700 Shoal Creek Blvd., Austin, TX
78757-6897. TEL 512-451-3246. FAX 512-451-
8542. *5878*

RECONSTRUCTION SURGERY AND TRAUMATOLOGY.
S. Karger AG, Allschwilerstr. 10, P.O. Box, CH-4009
Basel, Switzerland. TEL 061-3061111. FAX 061-
3061234. *4918*

THE RECORD (NORTHBRIDGE).
P.O. Box 75, Leederville, W.A. 6902, Australia.
TEL 61-9-2277080. FAX 61-9-2277087. *6193*

RECORD (NORWOOD).
Factory Mutual Engineering Corp., 1151 Boston-
Providence Turnpike, Norwood, MA 02062.
TEL 617-255-4657. FAX 617-255-4672. *2923*

**RECORDS OF EARLY ENGLISH DRAMA
NEWSLETTER.**
McMaster University, English Department, Hamilton
ON L8S 4L9, Canada. TEL 905-525-9140.
FAX 905-577-6930. *6701*

RECUEIL DES TRAVAUX CHIMIQUES DES PAYS-BAS.
Elsevier Science B.V., P.O. Box 211, 1000 AE
Amsterdam, Netherlands. TEL 31-20-4853911.
FAX 31-20-4853598. *1690*

RED CROSS, RED CRESCENT.
International Federation of Red Cross and Red
Crescent Societies, P.O. Box 372, CH-1211 Geneva
19, Switzerland. TEL 41-22-7304222. FAX 41-22-
7530395. *6388*

REDAI HAIYANG.
Science Press, Marketing and Sales Department, 16
Donghuangchenggen North St., Beijing 100717,
People's Republic of China. TEL 4010642.
FAX 4019810. *2304*

REDAI QIXIANG XUEBAO.
Guangzhou Redai Haiyang Qixiang Yanjiusuo, No. 6,
Fujin Rd., Dongshan District, Guangzhou,
Guangdong 510080, People's Republic of China.
TEL 86-20-777-5231. FAX 86-20-776-5281.
5005

REDOUBT.
University of Canberra, c/o Sally Clarke, Ed., P.O.
Box 1, Belconnen, A.C.T. 2614, Australia. TEL 61-6-
2012945. FAX 61-6-2015300. *4163*

REFERENCE LIBRARIAN.
Haworth Press, Inc., 10 Alice St., Binghamton, NY
13904. TEL 607-722-5857. FAX 607-722-1424.
4022

**REFLECTIONS: NARRATIVES OF PROFESSIONAL
HELPING.**
University Press, California State University at Long
Beach, c/o Dept. of Social Work, Long Beach, CA
90840-0902. TEL 310-985-4626. FAX 310-985-
5514. *6388*

REFLECTIONS ON HIGHER EDUCATION.
Higher Education Foundation, Westminster College,
Oxford OX2 9AT, England. TEL 44-1865-247644.
FAX 44-1865-251847. *2441*

REFRACTORIES AND INDUSTRIAL CERAMICS.
Plenum Publishing Corp., Consultants Bureau, 233
Spring St., New York, NY 10013-1578. TEL 212-
620-8468. FAX 212-463-0742. *1659*

REGENT ONLINE JOURNAL OF COMMUNICATION.
Regent University, College of Communication and
the Arts, School of Communication Studies, Virginia
Beach, VA 23464-9800. TEL 804-523-7943.
FAX 804-424-7051. *5111*

REGIONAL AND FEDERAL STUDIES.
Frank Cass, Newbury House, 890-900 Eastern Ave.,
Newbury Park, Ilford, Essex IG2 7HH, England.
TEL 44-181-599-8866. FAX 44-181-599-0984.
5768

REGIONAL DEVELOPMENT STUDIES.
United Nations Centre for Regional Development,
Nagono 1-47-1, Nakamura-ku, Nagoya 450, Japan.
TEL 052-561-9377. FAX 052-561-9375. *1314*

THE REGIONAL REVIEW.
Yorkshire and Humberside Regional Research
Observatory, University of Leeds, School of
Geography, Leeds LS2 9JT, England. TEL 44-113-
233-3336. FAX 44-113-233-3308. *6274*

REGIONAL SCIENCE & URBAN ECONOMICS.
North-Holland P.O. Box 211, 1000 AE Amsterdam,
Netherlands. TEL 31-20-4853911. FAX 31-20-
4853598. *3593*

REGIONAL STUDIES.
Carfax Publishing Co., P.O. Box 25, Abingdon, Oxon.
OX14 3UE, England. TEL 44-1235-401000.
FAX 44-1235-401550. *3593*

THE REGIONALIST.
Institute of Community and Area Development,
University of Georgia, 1234 S. Lumpkin St., Athens,
GA 30602-3552. TEL 706-542-3350. FAX 706-
542-6189. *5918*

**REGULATED RIVERS: RESEARCH AND
MANAGEMENT.**
John Wiley & Sons Ltd., Journals, Baffins Ln.,
Chichester, W. Sussex PO19 1UD, England. TEL 44-
1243-779777. FAX 44-1243-843232. *6974*

REGULATORY PEPTIDES.
Elsevier Science B.V., P.O. Box 211, 1000 AE
Amsterdam, Netherlands. TEL 31-20-4853911.
FAX 31-20-4853598. *1745*

REGULATORY TOXICOLOGY AND PHARMACOLOGY.
Academic Press, Inc., Journal Division, 525 B St.,
Ste. 1900, San Diego, CA 92101-4495. TEL 619-
230-1840. FAX 619-699-6800. *2848*

REHAB & COMMUNITY CARE MANAGEMENT.
B C S Communications Ltd., 101 Thorncliffe Park
Dr., Toronto, ON M4H 1M2, Canada. TEL 416-421-
7944. FAX 416-421-0966. *4819*

REHABILITACIA.
F. Liecreh, Cervenova 34, 811 03 Bratislava,
Slovakia. TEL 42-7-5314700. FAX 42-7-5314700.
4522

REHABILITATION EDUCATION.
Elliott & Fitzpatrick, Inc., 1135 Cedar Shoals Dr.,
Athens, GA 30605. TEL 706-548-8161. FAX 706-
546-8417. *2474*

REHABILITATION PSYCHOLOGY.
Springer Publishing Company, 536 Broadway, New
York, NY 10012-3955. TEL 212-431-4370.
FAX 212-941-7842. *5878*

REIMPRESSION.
Gordon & Breach Science Publishers, c/o
International Publishers Distributor, P.O. Box 3054,
Langhorne, PA 19047-3054. TEL 215-750-2642.
FAX 215-750-2642. *4257*

RELIABILITY ASSESSMENT.
North American Electric Reliability Council,
Princeton Forrestal Village, 116-290 Village Blvd.,
Princeton, NJ 08540-5731. TEL 609-452-8060.
2570

RELIABILITY ENGINEERING AND SYSTEM SAFETY.
Elsevier Science Ltd., P.O. Box 800, Kidlington,
Oxford OX5 1DX, England. TEL 44-1865-843000.
FAX 44-1865-843010. *2616*

RELIABILITY PHYSICS.
Institute of Electrical and Electronics Engineers, Inc.,
345 E. 47th St., New York, NY 10017-2394.
TEL 212-705-7900. FAX 212-705-7682. *5580*

RELIABLE COMPUTING.
Kluwer Academic Publishers, Postbus 17, 3300 AA
Dordrecht, Netherlands. TEL 31-78-6392392.
FAX 31-78-6392254. *2022*

RELIGION.
Academic Press Ltd. 24-28 Oval Rd., London NW1
7DX, England. TEL 44-171-267-4466. FAX 44-
171-482-2293. *6087*

RELIGION AND AMERICAN CULTURE.
Indiana University Press, Journal Division, 601 N.
Morton St., Bloomington, IN 47404. TEL 812-855-
9449. FAX 812-855-8507. *6087*

RELIGION & PUBLIC EDUCATION.
Webster University, 470 E. Lockwood, Webster
Groves, MO 63119. TEL 314-968-7135. *2366*

RELIGION & THEOLOGY.
Unisa Press, Periodicals, P.O. Box 392, Pretoria
0001, South Africa. TEL 27-12-4292953. FAX 27-
12-4293221. *6087*

RELIGION, STATE AND SOCIETY: THE KESTON JOURNAL.
Carfax Publishing Co., P.O. Box 25, Abingdon, Oxon.
OX14 3UE, England. TEL 44-1235-401000.
FAX 44-1235-401550. *6088*

RELIGIONS IN THE GRAECO-ROMAN WORLD.
E.J. Brill, P.O. Box 9000, 2300 PA Leiden,
Netherlands. TEL 31-71-5353500. FAX 31-71-
5317532. *6088*

REMEDIAL AND SPECIAL EDUCATION.
Pro-Ed Inc., 8700 Shoal Creek Blvd., Austin, TX
78757-6897. TEL 512-451-3246. FAX 512-451-
8542. *2474*

REMOTE SENSING OF EARTH RESOURCES AND ENVIRONMENT.
Kluwer Academic Publishers, Postbus 17, 3300 AA
Dordrecht, Netherlands. TEL 31-78-6392392.
FAX 31-78-6392254. *2215*

REMOTE SENSING OF ENVIRONMENT.
Elsevier Science Inc., Box 945, New York, NY
10159-0945. TEL 212-633-3730. FAX 212-633-
3680. *3271*

REMOTE SENSING REVIEWS.
Harwood Academic Publishers, c/o International
Publishers Distributor, P.O. Box 3054, Langhorne,
PA 19047-3054. TEL 215-750-2642. FAX 215-
750-6343. *2616*

RENAISSANCE AND REFORMATION.
University of Guelph, Department of French Studies,
Guelph, ON N1G 2W1, Canada. TEL 519-824-
4120. FAX 519-763-9572. *4257*

RENAL FAILURE.
Marcel Dekker Journals, 270 Madison Ave., New
York, NY 10016. TEL 212-696-9000. FAX 212-
685-4540. *4930*

RENAL PHYSIOLOGY AND BIOCHEMISTRY.
S. Karger AG, Allschwilerstr. 10, P.O. Box, CH-4009
Basel, Switzerland. TEL 061-3061111. FAX 061-
3061234. *4930*

RENASCENCE.
Marquette University Renascence, Brookshall, Box
1881, Milwaukee, WI 53201-1881. TEL 414-288-
6725. *4257*

RENDITIONS.
Chinese University of Hong Kong, Research Centre
for Translation, Shatin, New Territories, Hong Kong.
TEL 852-26097407. FAX 852-26035149. *5292*

RENEWABLE ENERGY.
Elsevier Science Ltd., Pergamon, P.O. Box 800,
Kidlington, Oxford CX5 1DX, England. TEL 44-1865-
843000. FAX 44-1865-843010. *2557*

RENEWABLE RESOURCES JOURNAL.
Renewable Natural Resources Foundation, 5430
Grosvenor Ln., Bethesda, MD 20814. TEL 301-
493-9101. FAX 301-493-6148. *2817*

RENEWAL NEWS.
Presbyterian Renewal Publications, Box 429, Black
Mountain, NC 28711-0429. TEL 704-669-7373.
FAX 704-669-4880. *6158*

RENLEIXUE XUEBAO.
Science Press, Marketing and Sales Department, 16
Donghuangchenggen North St., Beijing 100717,
People's Republic of China. TEL 4010642.
FAX 4019810. *320*

RENWEN JI SHEHUI KEXUE JIKAN.
Academia Sinica, Sun Yat-Sen Institute for Social
Sciences and Philosophy, Nankang, Taipei, Taiwan
11529, Republic of China. TEL 886-2-782-1693.
FAX 886-2-785-4160. *5495*

REPORT ON OBJECT ANALYSIS AND DESIGN.
Sigs Publications, Inc., 71 W. 23rd St., New York,
NY 10010-4102. TEL 212-242-7447. FAX 212-
242-7574. *2046*

REPORT PSYCHOLOGIE.
Deutscher Psychologen Verlag GmbH, Heilsbachstr.
22, 53123 Bonn, Germany. TEL 49-228-98731-0.
FAX 49-228-9873170. *5878*

REPORTS ON MATHEMATICAL PHYSICS.
Elsevier Science Ltd., Pergamon, P.O. Box 800,
Kidlington, Oxford CX5 1DX, England. TEL 44-1865-
843000. FAX 44-1865-843010. *5567*

REPORTS ON PROGRESS IN PHYSICS.
I O P Publishing Ltd., Techno House, Redcliffe Way,
Bristol, Avon BS1 6NX, England. TEL 44-117-929-
7481. FAX 44-117-929-4318. *5568*

REPORTS ON RESEARCH ASSISTED BY THE PETROLEUM RESEARCH FUND.
American Chemical Society, 1155 16th St., N.W.,
Washington, DC 20036. TEL 202-872-4600.
FAX 202-872-4615. *5374*

REPRESENTATION: JOURNAL OF REPRESENTATIVE DEMOCRACY.
The Arthur McDougall Fund, 6 Chancel St., London
SE1 0UU, England. TEL 44-171-620-1080.
FAX 44-171-928-4366. *5702*

REPRESENTATIONS.
University of California Press, Journals Division,
2120 Berkeley Way, No. 5812, Berkeley, CA
94720-5812. TEL 510-643-7154. FAX 510-642-
9917. *3623*

REPRESENTATIVE RESEARCH IN SOCIAL PSYCHOLOGY.
University of North Carolina at Chapel Hill,
Department of Psychology, Davie Hall, Campus Box
3270, Chapel Hill, NC 27599-3270. TEL 919-962-
7635. FAX 919-962-2537. *5878*

REPRODUCTION BULLETIN.
Andrews Paper & Chemical Co., Inc., 1 Channel Dr.,
Box 509, Port Washington, NY 11050. TEL 516-
767-2800. FAX 516-767-1632. *5818*

REPRODUCTION, NUTRITION, DEVELOPMENT.
Editions Scientifiques et Medicales Elsevier, 141 rue
de Javel, 75747 Paris, France. TEL 33-1-
45539022. FAX 33-1-45589421. *603*

REPRODUCTIVE TOXICOLOGY.
Elsevier Science Inc., Box 945, New York, NY
10159-0945. TEL 212-633-3730. FAX 212-633-
3680. *2848*

REPUBLIC OF CHINA. NATIONAL SCIENCE COUNCIL. PROCEEDINGS. PART B: LIFE SCIENCES.
National Science Council, 106 Ho-Ping E. Rd., Sec.
2, Taipei, Taiwan 106, Republic of China. TEL 2-
737-7594. FAX 2-737-7248. *4523*

REQUIREMENTS FOR CERTIFICATION OF TEACHERS, COUNSELORS, LIBRARIANS, ADMINISTRATORS FOR ELEMENTARY SCHOOLS, SECONDARY SCHOOLS, JUNIOR COLLEGES.
University of Chicago Press, 5801 S. Ellis Ave.,
Chicago, IL 60637. TEL 312-702-7899. *2462*

RES PUBLICA.
Deborah Charles Publications, 173 Mather Ave.
Liverpool L18 6JZ, England. TEL 44-151-724-
2500. FAX 44-151-729-0371. *5495*

RESEARCH ADVANCES IN ALCOHOL & DRUG PROBLEMS.
Plenum Publishing Corp., 233 Spring St., New York,
NY 10013-1578. TEL 212-620-8000. FAX 212-
463-0742. *2200*

RESEARCH AND CLINICAL CENTER FOR CHILD DEVELOPMENT. ANNUAL REPORT.
Hokkaido University, Research and Clinical Center
for Child Development, Nishi 7-chome, Kita 11-jo,
Kita-ku, Sapporo-shi 060, Japan. TEL 81-11-706-
2607. FAX 81-11-706-4946. *776*

RESEARCH & DEVELOPMENT.
Cahners Publishing Company (Des Plaines), Division
of Reed Elsevier Inc., 1350 E. Touhy Ave., Box
5080, Des Plaines, IL 60018-5080. TEL 847-635-
8800. FAX 847-390-2618. *6662*

RESEARCH AND TEACHING IN DEVELOPMENTAL EDUCATION.
New York College Learning Skills Association, Finger
Lakes Community College, 4355 Lake Shore Dr.,
Canandaigua, NY 14424. TEL 716-394-3500.
FAX 716-394-5005. *2367*

RESEARCH COMMUNICATIONS IN ALCOHOL & SUBSTANCES OF ABUSE.
P J D Publications Ltd., Box 966, Westbury, NY
11590. TEL 516-626-0650. FAX 516-626-5546.
5441

RESEARCH COMMUNICATIONS IN MOLECULAR PATHOLOGY AND PHARMACOLOGY.
P J D Publications Ltd., Box 966, Westbury, NY
11590. TEL 516-626-0650. *4523*

RESEARCH COMMUNICATIONS IN PSYCHOLOGY, PSYCHIATRY AND BEHAVIOR.
P J D Publications Ltd., Box 966, Westbury, NY
11590. TEL 516-626-0650. FAX 516-626-5546.
5879

RESEARCH EVALUATION.
Beech Tree Publishing, 10 Watford Close, Guildford,
Surrey GU1 2EP, England. TEL 44-1483-67497.
FAX 44-1483-67497. *6275*

RESEARCH GROUP FOR EUROPEAN MIGRATION PROBLEMS. PUBLICATIONS.
Kluwer Academic Publishers, Postbus 17, 3300 AA Dordrecht, Netherlands. TEL 31-78-6392392. FAX 31-78-6392254. *5791*

RESEARCH IN DEVELOPMENTAL DISABILITIES.
Elsevier Science Ltd., Pergamon, P.O. Box 800, Kidlington, Oxford OX5 1DX, England. TEL 44-1865-843000. FAX 44-1865-843010. *4866*

RESEARCH IN EXPERIMENTAL MEDICINE.
Springer-Verlag, Heidelberger Platz 3, 14197 Berlin, Germany. TEL 49-30-8207-0. FAX 49-30-8214091. *4684*

RESEARCH IN HIGHER EDUCATION.
Human Sciences Press, Inc. 233 Spring St., New York, NY 10013. TEL 212-620-8000. FAX 212-463-0742. *2462*

RESEARCH IN IMMUNOLOGY.
Editions Scientifiques et Medicales Elsevier, 141 rue de Javel, 75747 Paris, France. TEL 33-1-45589022. FAX 33-1-45589421. *4586*

RESEARCH IN MICROBIOLOGY.
Editions Scientifiques et Medicales Elsevier, 141 rue de Javel, 75747 Paris, France. TEL 33-1-45589022. FAX 33-1-45589421. *765*

RESEARCH IN MIDDLE LEVEL EDUCATION QUARTERLY.
National Middle School Association, 2600 Corporate Exchange Dr., Ste. 370, Columbus, OH 43231. TEL 614-895-4730. FAX 614-895-4750. *2500*

RESEARCH IN NONDESTRUCTIVE EVALUATION.
Springer-Verlag, Science Journals, 175 Fifth Ave., New York, NY 10010. TEL 212-460-1500. FAX 212-473-6272. *2617*

RESEARCH IN NURSING & HEALTH.
John Wiley & Sons, Inc., Journals, 605 Third Ave., New York, NY 10158. TEL 212-850-6645. FAX 212-850-6021. *4727*

RESEARCH IN PHILOSOPHY AND TECHNOLOGY.
J A I Press Inc., 55 Old Post Rd., No. 2, Box 1678, Greenwich, CT 06836-1678. TEL 203-661-7602. *5495*

RESEARCH IN POST-COMPULSORY EDUCATION.
Triangle Journals Ltd., P.O. Box 65, Wallingford, Oxon. OX10 0YG, England. TEL 44-1491-838013. FAX 44-1491-834968. *2441*

RESEARCH IN SCIENCE & TECHNOLOGICAL EDUCATION.
Carfax Publishing Co., P.O. Box 25, Abingdon, Oxon. OX14 3UE, England. TEL 44-1235-401000. FAX 44-1235-401550. *2367*

RESEARCH IN SCIENCE EDUCATION.
Australasian Science Education Research Association, c/o C.J. McRobbie, Ed., Center for Mathematics & Science Education, Queensland University of Technology, Locked Bag No. 2, Red Hill, Brisbane, Qld. 4059, Australia. TEL 61-7-8643643. FAX 61-3-8643333. *2500*

RESEARCH IN THE SOCIAL SCIENTIFIC STUDY OF RELIGION.
J A I Press Inc., 55 Old Post Rd., No. 2, Box 1678, Greenwich, CT 06836-1678. TEL 203-661-7602. *6089*

RESEARCH IN VIROLOGY.
Editions Scientifiques et Medicales Elsevier, 141 rue de Javel, 75747 Paris, France. TEL 33-1-45589022. FAX 33-1-45589421. *4627*

RESEARCH IN YORUBA: LANGUAGE & LITERATURE.
Department of African Language and Literature, Obafemi Awolowo University, Ile-Ife, Osun State, Nigeria. *4102*

RESEARCH METHODS IN NEUROCHEMISTRY.
Plenum Publishing Corp., 233 Spring St., New York, NY 10013-1578. TEL 212-620-8000. FAX 212-463-0742. *649*

RESEARCH MONOGRAPHS IN CELL AND TISSUE PHYSIOLOGY.
Elsevier Science B.V., Books Division, P.O. Box 211, 1000 AE Amsterdam, Netherlands. TEL 31-20-4853911. FAX 31-20-4853705. *4523*

RESEARCH MONOGRAPHS IN IMMUNOLOGY.
Elsevier Science B.V., Books Division, P.O. Box 211, 1000 AE Amsterdam, Netherlands. TEL 31-20-4853911. FAX 31-20-4853705. *4586*

RESEARCH NOTES IN ARTIFICIAL INTELLIGENCE.
Morgan Kaufmann Publishers, Inc., 340 Pine St., 6th Fl., San Francisco, CA 94104-3205. TEL 415-392-2665. FAX 415-982-2665. *2010*

RESEARCH NOTES IN MATHEMATICS.
John Wiley & Sons, Inc., Journals, 605 Third Ave., New York, NY 10158-0012. TEL 212-850-6000. FAX 212-850-6088. *4391*

RESEARCH ON CHEMICAL INTERMEDIATES.
V S P, P.O. Box 346, 3700 AH Zeist, Netherlands. TEL 31-30-6925790. FAX 31-30-6932081. *1690*

RESEARCH ON TECHNOLOGICAL INNOVATION, MANAGEMENT AND POLICY.
J A I Press Inc., 55 Old Post Rd., No. 2, Box 1678, Greenwich, CT 06836-1678. TEL 203-661-7602. *6662*

RESEARCH PAPERS IN GEOGRAPHY.
University of Newcastle, Department of Geography, Newcastle, N.S.W. 2308, Australia. TEL 61-49-215080. FAX 61-49-215877. *3271*

RESEARCH PAPERS IN MANAGEMENT STUDIES.
University of Cambridge, Judge Institute of Management Studies, Mill Ln., Cambridge CB2 1RX, England. *1511*

RESEARCH POLICY.
North-Holland P.O. Box 211, 1000 AE Amsterdam, Netherlands. TEL 31-20-4853911. FAX 31-20-4853598. *6275*

RESIDENTIAL TREATMENT FOR CHILDREN & YOUTH.
Haworth Press, Inc., 10 Alice St., Binghamton, NY 13904. TEL 607-722-5857. FAX 607-722-1424. *1776*

RESIDENTS' PRESCRIBING REFERENCE.
Prescribing Reference, Inc., 53 Park Pl., Ste. 1010, New York, NY 10007. TEL 212-766-7200. FAX 212-732-2360. *5441*

RESOURCE AND ENERGY ECONOMICS.
North-Holland P.O. Box 211, 1000 AE Amsterdam, Netherlands. TEL 31-20-4853911. FAX 31-20-4853598. *2557*

RESOURCE MANAGEMENT AND OPTIMIZATION.
Harwood Academic Publishers, c/o International Publishers Distributor, P.O. Box 3054, Langhorne, PA 19047-3054. TEL 215-750-2642. FAX 215-750-6343. *2140*

RESOURCE SHARING & INFORMATION NETWORKS.
Haworth Press, Inc., 10 Alice St., Binghamton, NY 13904. TEL 607-722-5857. FAX 607-722-1424. *4022*

RESOURCES (NASHVILLE).
F I S I - Madison Financial Box 40726, Nashville, TN 37204. TEL 615-371-2658. *2155*

RESOURCES, CONSERVATION AND RECYCLING.
Elsevier Science B.V., P.O. Box 211, 1000 AE Amsterdam, Netherlands. TEL 31-20-4853911. FAX 31-20-4853598. *2857*

RESOURCES FOR AMERICAN LITERARY STUDY.
Pennsylvania State University Press, 820 N. University Dr., Ste. C, University Park, PA 16802-1003. TEL 814-865-1327. FAX 814-863-1408. *4257*

RESOURCES IN AGING.
Demko Publishing, 21946 Pine Trace, Boca Raton, FL 33428. TEL 407-482-6271. *3295*

RESOURCES POLICY.
Butterworth - Heinemann, Part of the Reed Elsevier group, Linacre House, Jordan Hill, Oxford OX2 8DP, England. TEL 44-1865-310366. FAX 44-1865-310898. *2557*

RESPIRATION.
S. Karger AG, Allschwilerstr. 10, P.O. Box, CH-4009 Basel, Switzerland. TEL 061-3061111. FAX 061-3061234. *4890*

RESPIRATION PHYSIOLOGY.
Elsevier Science B.V., P.O. Box 211, 1000 AE Amsterdam, Netherlands. TEL 31-20-4853911. FAX 31-20-4853598. *793*

RESPONSE (FAIRFAX).
National Association for Search and Rescue, 4500 Southgate Pl., Ste. 100, Chantilly, VA 22021-1714. TEL 703-352-1349. FAX 703-352-0309. *4790*

RESPONSE TO THE VICTIMIZATION OF WOMEN AND CHILDREN.
Response, Inc., 4938 Hampden Ln., No. 255, Bethesda, MD 20814-2962. TEL 301-951-0039. *7006*

RESTAURATOR.
Munksgaard International Publishers Ltd., 35 Noerre Soegade, P.O. Box 2148, DK-1016 Copenhagen K, Denmark. TEL 45-33-127030. FAX 45-33-129387. *4022*

RESTORATION & EIGHTEENTH CENTURY THEATRE RESEARCH.
Loyola University of Chicago, Department of English, 6525 N. Sheridan Rd., Chicago, IL 60626. FAX 312-508-8696. *4257*

RESTORATION AND MANAGEMENT NOTES.
University of Wisconsin Press, Journal Division, 114 N. Murray St., Madison, WI 53715. TEL 608-262-4952. FAX 608-262-7560. *2140*

RESTORATION QUARTERLY.
Restoration Quarterly Corporation, ACU Station, Box 8227, Abilene, TX 79699. TEL 915-674-3781. FAX 915-674-3776. *6089*

RESTORATION: STUDIES IN ENGLISH LITERARY CULTURE, 1660-1700.
Tennessee Technological University, Department of the College of Arts and Sciences, Cookeville, TN 38505. TEL 615-372-3119. FAX 615-372-6142. *4258*

RESTORATIVE NEUROLOGY AND NEUROSCIENCE.
Elsevier Science Ireland Ltd., P.O. Box 85, Limerick, Ireland. TEL 353-61-471944. FAX 353-61-472144. *4866*

RESTORICA.
Simon van der Stel Foundation, P.O. Box 12293, Centrahil 6006, South Africa. TEL 27-41-562849. FAX 27-41-562849. *403*

RESUSCITATION.
Elsevier Science Ireland Ltd., P.O. Box 85, Limerick, Ireland. TEL 353-61-471944. FAX 353-61-472144. *4891*

RETAIL SYSTEMS ALERT.
Ardea Research Corp., 77 Oak St., Ste. 201, Box 332, Newton Upper Falls, MA 02164. TEL 617-527-8102. FAX 617-527-8102. *2076*

RETINA.
Lippincott - Raven Publishers 227 E. Washington Sq., Philadelphia, PA 19105. TEL 215-238-4200. *4777*

REUMATISMO.
Societa Italiana di Reumatologia (S.I.R.), C.so Plebisciti 9, 20129 Milano, Italy. TEL 39-2-7382330. FAX 39-2-7385763. *4895*

REUMATOLOGIA.
Instytut Reumatologiczny, Ul. Spartanska 1, 02-637 Warsaw, Poland. TEL 48-22-444241. FAX 48-22-449522. *4895*

REUSE - RECYCLE.
Technomic Publishing Co. Inc., 851 New Holland Ave., Box 3535, Lancaster, PA 17604. TEL 717-291-5609. FAX 717-295-4538. *2857*

REVEIL MISSIONNAIRE.
Missionnaires de la Consolata, 2505 W. bd. Gouin, Montreal, PQ H3M 1B5, Canada. TEL 514-334-1910. FAX 514-332-1940. *6089*

REVIEW (BINGHAMTON).
Fernand Braudel Center for the Study of Economies, Historical Systems, and Civilizations, Box 6000, Binghamton University, Binghamton, NY 13902-6000. TEL 607-777-4924. FAX 607-777-4315. *1260*

REVIEW (WASHINGTON).
Heldref Publications, 1319 Eighteenth St., N.W., Washington, DC 20036-1802. TEL 202-296-6267. *3322*

REVIEW FOR RELIGIOUS.
Jesuits of the Missouri Province, 3601 Lindell Blvd., St. Louis, MO 63108. TEL 314-977-7363. FAX 314-977-7362. *6194*

REVIEW OF ACCOUNTING STUDIES.
Kluwer Academic Publishers Boston, Box 358, Accord Sta., Hingham, MA 02018-0358. TEL 617-871-6600. FAX 617-871-6528. *1053*

REVIEW OF AFRICAN POLITICAL ECONOMY.
Carfax Publishing Co., P.O. Box 25, Abingdon, Oxon. OX14 3UE, England. TEL 44-1235-401000. FAX 44-1235-401550. *5769*

REVIEW OF AGRICULTURAL ECONOMICS.
Review of Agricultural Economics, c/o Department of Agricultural Economics, Kansas State University, Manhattan, KS 66506-4011. TEL 913-532-4488. FAX 913-532-6925. *198*

THE REVIEW OF ARCHAEOLOGY.
Review of Archaeology, Inc., 10 Liberty St., Salem, MA 01970. TEL 508-745-1876. FAX 508-745-8303. *369*

REVIEW OF AUSTRIAN ECONOMICS.
Kluwer Academic Publishers Boston, Box 358, Accord Sta., Hingham, MA 02018-0358. TEL 617-871-6600. FAX 617-871-6528. *1260*

REVIEW OF BUSINESS.
St. John's University, College of Business Administration, Bent Hall, 8000 Utopia Pkwy., NY 11439. TEL 718-990-6768. FAX 718-990-1868. *955*

REVIEW OF CENTRAL AND EAST EUROPEAN LAW.
Kluwer Law International Postbus 85889, 2508 CN The Hague, Netherlands. TEL 31-70-3081500. FAX 31-70-3081515. *3841*

REVIEW OF CONSTITUTIONAL STUDIES.
Centre for Constitutional Studies, Rm. 459, Law Centre, University of Alberta, Edmonton, AB T6G 2H5, Canada. TEL 403-492-5681. FAX 403-492-9959. *3892*

THE REVIEW OF CONTEMPORARY FICTION.
Review of Contemporary Fiction, Inc., 4241 Illinois State University, Normal, IL 61790-4241. TEL 309-438-7555. FAX 309-437-7422. *4258*

REVIEW OF DERIVATIVES RESEARCH.
Kluwer Academic Publishers Boston, Box 358, Accord Sta., Hingham, MA 02018-0358. TEL 617-871-6600. FAX 617-871-6528. *1119*

THE REVIEW OF ECONOMICS AND STATISTICS.
M I T Press, 55 Hayward St., Cambridge, MA 02142-1399. TEL 617-577-1545. FAX 617-258-6779. *955*

THE REVIEW OF EDUCATION - PEDAGOGY - CULTURAL STUDIES.
Gordon and Breach Science Publishers, c/o International Publishers Distributor, P.O. Box 3054, Langhorne, PA 19047-3054. TEL 215-750-2642. FAX 215-750-6343. *2393*

REVIEW OF EDUCATIONAL RESEARCH.
American Educational Research Association, 1230 17th St., N.W., Washington, DC 20036-3078. TEL 202-223-9485. FAX 202-775-1824. *2367*

REVIEW OF EMPLOYMENT TOPICS.
Labour Relations Agency, Windsor House, 9-15 Bedford St., Belfast BT2 7NU, N. Ireland. TEL 44-1232-321442. FAX 44-1232-330827. *1393*

REVIEW OF EXISTENTIAL PSYCHOLOGY AND PSYCHIATRY.
Humanities Press, 165 First Ave., Atlantic Highlands, NJ 07716-1289. TEL 908-872-1441. FAX 908-872-0717. *5879*

REVIEW OF FINANCIAL ECONOMICS.
J A I Press Inc., Box 1678, 55 Old Post Rd., No. 2, Greenwich, CT 06836-1678. TEL 203-661-7602. FAX 203-661-0792. *955*

REVIEW OF FINANCIAL STUDIES.
Oxford University Press, Journals, 2001 Evans Rd., Cary, NC 27513. TEL 919-677-0977. FAX 919-677-1714. *1119*

REVIEW OF INCOME AND WEALTH.
International Association for Research in Income and Wealth, New York University, Dept. of Economics, 269 Mercer St., Rm. 700, New York, NY 10003. TEL 212-998-8917. FAX 212-366-5067. *1402*

REVIEW OF INDUSTRIAL ORGANIZATION.
Kluwer Academic Publishers, Postbus 17, 3300 AA Dordrecht, Netherlands. TEL 31-78-6392392. FAX 31-78-6392254. *1260*

REVIEW OF INTERNATIONAL ECONOMICS.
Blackwell Publishers Ltd., 108 Cowley Rd., Oxford OX4 1JF, England. TEL 44-1865-791100. FAX 44-1865-791347. *955*

REVIEW OF ISLAMIC ECONOMICS.
Islamic Foundation, Markfield Dawah Centre, Ratby Lane, Markfield, Leicester LE67 9RN, England. TEL 01530-244944. FAX 01530-244946. *1238*

REVIEW OF LAW & SOCIAL CHANGE.
New York University, Review of Law & Social Change, 110 W. Third St., New York, NY 10012. TEL 212-998-6370. FAX 212-995-4032. *3841*

REVIEW OF PALAEOBOTANY AND PALYNOLOGY.
Elsevier Science B.V., P.O. Box 211, 1000 AE Amsterdam, Netherlands. TEL 31-20-4853911. FAX 31-20-4853598. *5318*

THE REVIEW OF POLICY ISSUES.
Sheffield Hallam University, Unit 7, Sheffield Science Park, Howard St., Sheffield S1 2LX, England. TEL 44-114-2534462. FAX 44-114-2534467. *956*

REVIEW OF QUANTITATIVE FINANCE AND ACCOUNTING.
Kluwer Academic Publishers Boston, Box 358, Accord Sta., Hingham, MA 02018-0358. FAX 617-871-6528. *1053*

REVIEW OF REGIONAL STUDIES.
Southern Regional Science Association, 505A Stokely Management Center, The University of Tennessee, Knoxville, TN 37996-0550. TEL 615-974-3303. FAX 615-974-4601. *3593*

REVIEW OF RESEARCH IN EDUCATION.
American Educational Research Association, 1230 17th St., N.W., Washington, DC 20036-3078. TEL 202-223-9485. FAX 202-775-1824. *2500*

REVIEW OF SCIENTIFIC INSTRUMENTS.
American Institute of Physics, One Physics Ellipse, College Park, MD 20740-3843. TEL 301-209-3000. *3637*

REVIEW OF SCOTTISH CULTURE.
Tuckwell Press, The Mill House, Phantassie, E. Linton, E. Lothian EH40 3DG, Scotland. TEL 44-1620-860164. *2905*

REVIEW OF SOCIAL ECONOMY.
Routledge, 11 New Fetter Ln., London EC4P 4EE, England. TEL 44-171-583-9855. FAX 44-171-842-2298. *956*

REVIEWS IN ANTHROPOLOGY.
Gordon and Breach Science Publishers, c/o International Publishers Distributor, P.O. Box 3054, Langhorne, PA 19047-3054. TEL 215-750-2642. FAX 215-750-6343. *320*

REVIEWS IN CANCER EPIDEMIOLOGY.
Elsevier Science B.V., Books Division, P.O. Box 211, 1000 AE Amsterdam, Netherlands. TEL 31-20-4853911. FAX 31-20-4853705. *4763*

REVIEWS IN CONTEMPORARY PHARMACOTHERAPY.
Marius Press, P.O. Box 15, Carnforth LA6 1HW, England. TEL 44-1524-733027. FAX 44-1524-736659. *5442*

REVIEWS IN ENGINEERING GEOLOGY.
Geological Society of America, 3300 Penrose Pl., Box 9140, Boulder, CO 80301. TEL 303-447-2020. FAX 303-447-1133. *2671*

REVIEWS IN FISH BIOLOGY AND FISHERIES.
Chapman & Hall, Journals Department 2-6 Boundary Row, London SE1 8HN, England. TEL 44-171-8650066. FAX 44-171-5229623. *819*

REVIEWS IN MEDICAL MICROBIOLOGY.
Chapman & Hall, Journals Department Boundary Row, London SE1 8HN, England. TEL 44-171-8650066. FAX 44-171-5229323. *766*

REVIEWS IN MEDICAL VIROLOGY.
John Wiley & Sons Ltd., Journals, Baffins Ln., Chichester, W. Sussex PO19 1UD, England. TEL 44-1243-779777. FAX 44-1243-843232. *766*

REVIEWS IN PARTICULATE MATERIALS.
Metal Powder Industries Federation, 105 College Rd. E., Princeton, NJ 08540. TEL 609-987-8523. FAX 609-987-8523. *4972*

REVIEWS IN PERINATAL MEDICINE.
Lippincott - Raven Publishers 227 E. Washington Sq., Philadelphia, PA 19106. TEL 215-238-4200. FAX 215-238-4235. *4715*

REVIEWS IN TOXICOLOGY.
I O S Press, Van Diemenstraat 94, 1013 CN Amsterdam, Netherlands. TEL 31-20-6382189. FAX 31-20-6203419. *2348*

REVIEWS OF GEOPHYSICS.
American Geophysical Union, 2000 Florida Ave., N.W., Washington, DC 20009. TEL 202-462-6900. FAX 202-328-0566. *2230*

REVIEWS OF HEMATOLOGY.
P J D Publications Ltd., Box 966, Westbury, NY 11590. TEL 516-626-0650. FAX 516-626-5546. *4702*

REVIEWS OF MODERN PHYSICS.
American Physical Society, One Physics Ellipse, College Park, MD 20740-3844. TEL 301-209-3202. *5568*

REVIEWS OF OCULOMOTOR RESEARCH.
Elsevier Science B.V., Books Division, P.O. Box 211, 1000 AE Amsterdam, Netherlands. TEL 31-20-4853911. FAX 31-20-4853705. *4777*

REVIEWS OF PHYSIOLOGY, BIOCHEMISTRY AND PHARMACOLOGY.
Springer-Verlag, 175 Fifth Ave., New York, NY 10010. TEL 212-460-1500. FAX 212-473-6272. *793*

REVIEWS OF PLASMA PHYSICS.
Plenum Publishing Corp., Consultants Bureau, 233 Spring St., New York, NY 10013-1578. TEL 212-620-8000. FAX 212-463-0742. *5568*

REVIEWS OF REPRODUCTION.
Journals of Reproduction & Fertility Ltd., 22 Newmarket Rd., Cambridge CB5 8DT, England. TEL 44-1223-351809. FAX 44-1223-359754. *793*

REVIEWS ON HETEROATOM CHEMISTRY.
M Y U, Scientific Publishing Division, 2-32-3 Sendagi, Bunkyo-ku, Tokyo 113, Japan. TEL 03-3821-2930. FAX 03-3827-8547. *1690*

REVISION: A JOURNAL OF CONSCIOUSNESS AND TRANSFORMATION.
Heldref Publications, 1319 Eighteenth St., N.W., Washington, DC 20036-1802. TEL 202-296-6267. FAX 202-296-5149. *5220*

REVISTA A M R I G S.
Asscciacao Medica do Rio Grande do Sul, Av. Ipiranga, 5311, 90620 Porto Alegre RS, Brazil. TEL 55-51-3392899. FAX 55-51-3392998. *4523*

REVISTA ARGENTINA DE MICROBIOLOGIA.
Asociacion Argentina de Microbiologia, Bulnes 44, P.B. B, 1176 Buenos Aires, Argentina. TEL 54-1-9828557. FAX 54-1-9828557. *766*

REVISTA BRASILEIRA DE ENTOMOLOGIA.
Sociedade Brasileira de Entomologia, Caixa Postal 9063, 01065-970 Sao Paulo SP, Brazil. TEL 55-11-274-3455 ext. 60. FAX 55-11-2743690. *734*

REVISTA BRASILEIRA DE ESTUDOS PEDAGOGICOS.
Instituto Nacional de Estudos e Pesquisas Educacionais, Campus da UnB, Acesso Sul, 70910-900 Brasilia DF, Brazil. TEL 55-61-347-8970. FAX 55-61-273-3233. *2367*

REVISTA BRASILEIRA DE FISIOLOGIA VEGETAL.
Sociedade Brasileira de Fisiologia Vegetal, Cx. Postal 0281, 70359-9700 Brasilis DF, Brazil. FAX 55-61-556744. *701*

REVISTA BRASILEIRA DE OTO-RINO-LARINGOLOGIA.
Sociedade Brasileira de Otorrinolaringologia, Rua Visconde de Piraja 330, Grupo 510, 22410 Rio de Janeiro RJ, Brazil. TEL 55-21-2870893. FAX 55-21-2870893. *4800*

REVISTA BRASILEIRA DE PESQUISAS MEDICAS E BIOLOGICAS.
c/o Eduardo Moacy Krieger, Faculdade de Medicina de Ribeirao Preto, Campus de Ribeirao Preto, 14049-900 Ribeirao Preto SP, Brazil. TEL 55-16-633-3825. *4524*

REVISTA CERES.
Universidade Federal de Vicosa, 36570-000 Vicosa, Minas Gerais, Brazil. TEL 55-31-8992136. FAX 55-31-8992205. *147*

REVISTA CHILENA DE HISTORIA Y GEOGRAFIA.
Sociedad Chilena de Historia y Geografia, Londres 65, Casilla 1386, Santiago, Chile. TEL 6382489. *3485*

REVISTA CHILENA DE LITERATURA.
Universidad de Chile, Facultad de Filosofia y Humanidades, Casilla 10136, Santiago, Chile. TEL 56-2-6787022. FAX 56-2-2716823. *4258*

REVISTA COLOMBIANA DE MATEMATICAS.
Sociedad Colombiana de Matematicas, Apdo. Aereo No. 25-21, Bogota, Colombia. FAX 2686465. *4391*

REVISTA CUBANA DE CIENCIA AGRICOLA.
Instituto de Ciencia Animal, Tulipan No. 1011 e-47 y Loma, Nuevo Vedado, Havana, Cuba. TEL 9-9180. FAX 33-5382. *147*

REVISTA DE AGRICULTURA.
Caixa Postal 60, 13400-970 Piracicaba, Sao Paulo, Brazil. TEL 0194-22-3604. *147*

REVISTA DE ANTROPOLOGIA.
Universidade de Sao Paulo, Faculdade de Filosofia, Letras e Ciencias Humanas, C.P. 8105, 01065-970 Sao Paulo SP, Brazil. TEL 55-11-8183726. FAX 55-11-8183163. *320*

REVISTA DE BIOLOGIA MARINA.
Universidad de Valparaiso, Instituto de Oceanologia, Casilla 13-D, Vina del Mar, Chile. TEL 56-32-833214. FAX 56-32-833214. *604*

REVISTA DE CRITICA LITERARIA LATINOAMERICANA.
Latinoamericana Editores, 4319 Dwinelle Hall, University of California, Department of Spanish and Portuguese, Berkeley, CA 94720-2590. TEL 510-883-9443. FAX 510-883-9443. *4258*

REVISTA DE ESTUDIOS COLOMBIANOS.
Association of North American Colombianists, c/o James Alstrum, Secy., Illinois State U., Dept. of For. Lang., Normal, IL 61761. TEL 309-438-7620. FAX 309-438-8038. *3485*

REVISTA DE ESTUDIOS HISPANICOS.
University of Puerto Rico, Seminario de Estudios Hispanicos "Federico de Onis", P.O. Box 21787, Rio Piedras, PR 00931. TEL 809-764-0000 ext. 3673. FAX 809-763-5899. *3623*

REVISTA DE ESTUDIOS REGIONALES.
Universidad Nacional de Cuyo, Facultad de Filosofia y Letras, Centro Universitario, Parque Gral. San Martin, CC 345, 5500 Mendoza, Argentina. TEL 54-61-253010. FAX 54-61-380457. *6341*

REVISTA DE FILOSOFIA.
Universidad del Zulia, Centro de Estudios Filosoficos, Edif. Viyaluz, Av. 4 esq. Calle 74, 8o piso, Maracaibo, Zulia, Venezuela. TEL 58-61-596840. *5496*

REVISTA DE GASTROENTEROLOGIA DE MEXICO.
Obsidiana Editores, S.A., Czda. de Tlalpan 2365, Col. Ciudad Jardin, 04370 Mexico DF, Mexico. TEL 6899133. *4696*

REVISTA DE GASTROENTEROLOGIA DEL PERU.
Sociedad de Gastroenterologia del Peru, Casilla Postal 14, 0028 Lima, Peru. TEL 51-1-4492467. FAX 51-1-4729055. *4696*

REVISTA DE MARINA.
Armada de Chile, Casilla 220, Valparaiso, Chile. TEL 56-32-281222. FAX 56-32-281223. *5045*

REVISTA DE MEDICINA SI FARMACIE.
Universitatea de Medicina si Farmacie din Targu Mures, Str. Gh. Marinescu Nr. 38, 4300 Targu-Mures, Rumania. TEL 40-65-113127. FAX 40-65-164407. *4524*

REVISTA DE MICROBIOLOGIA.
Sociedade Brasileira de Microbiologia, c/o Luiz Rachid Trabulsi, Ed., Depto. de Microbiologia, Instituto de Ciencias Biomedicas USP, Av. Prof. Lineu Prestes, 1374, 05508-900 Sao Paulo, SP, Brazil. TEL 55-11-8139647. FAX 55-11-81396747. *766*

REVISTA DE PSICOLOGIA SOCIAL.
Aprendizaje, S.L., Ctra. de Canillas 138, 16 C, 28043 Madrid, Spain. TEL 388-38-74. FAX 300-35-27. *5879*

REVISTA DE SAUDE PUBLICA.
Universidade de Sao Paulo, Faculdade de Saude Publica, Av. Dr. Arnaldo 715, 01246-904 Sao Paulo, Brazil. TEL 55-11-2809163. *5974*

REVISTA ESPANOLA DE ECONOMIA AGRARIA.
Ministerio de Agricultura, Pesca y Alimentacion, Centro de Publicaciones, Paseo de la Infanta Isabel 1, 28071 Madrid, Spain. TEL 34-1-3475551. FAX 34-1-3475722. *199*

REVISTA FORESTAL CENTROAMERICANA.
Centro Agronomico Tropical de Investigacion y Ensenanza, Area de Comunicacion e Informatica, Catie 7170, Turrialba, Costa Rica. TEL 506-556-6784. FAX 506-556-6282. *3024*

REVISTA IBEROAMERICANA DE MICOLOGIA.
Asociacion Espanola de Micologia, C. Industria 241-249, 1o 1a Escalera Izq., 08026 Barcelona, Spain. TEL 34-3-4551100. FAX 34-3-4550918. *701*

REVISTA MATEMATICA IBEROAMERICANA.
Real Sociedad Matematica Espanola, c/o Departamento de Matematicas, Universidad Autonoma de Madrid, 28049 Madrid, Spain. TEL 34-1-397-4930. FAX 34-1-397-4889. *4391*

REVISTA MEDICA DE CHILE.
Sociedad Medica de Santiago, Clasificador 168, Correo 55, Santiago 9, Chile. TEL 56-2-2748985. FAX 56-2-3413068. *4525*

REVISTA MEXICANA DE ASTRONOMIA Y ASTROFISICA.
Universidad Nacional Autonoma de Mexico, Instituto de Astronomia, Apdo. Postal 70-264, 04510 Mexico DF, Mexico. FAX 525-616-0653. *485*

REVISTA MEXICANA DE FISICA.
Sociedad Mexicana de Fisica, A.C., Apdo. 70-348, Coyoacan, 04511 Mexico, D.F., Mexico. TEL 525-622-4848. *5568*

REVISTA MEXICANA DE OFTALMOLOGIA.
Sociedad Mexicana de Oftalmologia, Boston, No. 99, Col. Noche Buena, 03720 Mexico D.F., Mexico. *4777*

REVISTA MINELOR.
Directia Generala Strategia Industriei Miniere si Geologiei, Calea Victoriei 220, Sector 1, 71104 Bucharest, Rumania. TEL 40-1-6505020. *5077*

REVISTA MUSICAL CHILENA.
Universidad de Chile, Facultad de Artes, Compania 1264, Casilla 2100, Santiago, Chile. TEL 56-2-6781337. FAX 56-2-6711435. *5192*

REVISTA PADURILOR.
R.A. Romsilva, Bd. Magheru nr.31, etaj. 1, sector 1, 70162 Bucharest, Rumania. TEL 40-1-6592020. FAX 40-1-2228428. *3024*

REVISTA PORTUGUESA DE ESTOMATOLOGIA E CIRURGIA MAXILO-FACIAL.
Sociedade Portuguesa de Estomatologia e Medicina Dentaria, Av. Rainha D. Amelia 36, 1600 Lisbon, Portugal. TEL 351-1-7593948. *4653*

REVISTA TIEMPO Y ESPACIO.
Universidad del Bio-Bio, Departamento de Historia, Geografia y Ciencias Sociales, Casilla 447, Chillan, Chile. TEL 56-42-214417. FAX 56-42-214417. *3356*

REVISTA UNIMAR.
Universidade Estadual de Maringa, Av. Colombo, 3690, 87020-900 Maringa PR, Brazil. TEL 55-442-224378. FAX 55-442-232676. *2441*

REVMATOLOGIIA.
Tsentar za Informatsiia po Meditsina, 1, Sv. Georgi Sofiiski St., 1431 Sofia, Bulgaria. TEL 359-2-522342. FAX 359-2-522393. *4895*

REVOLUTION: THE JOURNAL OF NURSE EMPOWERMENT.
A.D. Von Publishers, Inc., 56 McArthur Ave., Staten Island, NY 10312. FAX 718-317-0858. *4727*

REVOLUTIONARY RUSSIA.
Frank Cass, Newbury House, 890-900 Eastern Ave., Newbury Park, Ilford, Essex 1G2 7HH, England. TEL 44-181-599-8866. FAX 44-181-599-0984. *3438*

REVUE AGRICOLE ET SUCRIERE DE MAURICE.
Societe de Technologie Agricole et Sucriere de l'Ile Maurice, c/o M.S.I.R.I., Reduit, Mauritius. TEL 230-4541061. FAX 230-4541971. *238*

REVUE ANDRE MALRAUX REVIEW.
c/o Dr. Robert S. Thornberry, Ed., University of Alberta, Dept. of Romance Languages, Edmonton, AB T6G 2E6, Canada. TEL 403-492-1997. FAX 403-439-9393. *4259*

REVUE ARACHNOLOGIQUE.
J.C. Ledoux, Ed. & Pub., 43 rue Paul Bert, 30390 Aramon, France. *604*

REVUE BELGE D'HISTOIRE CONTEMPORAINE.
Jan Dhondt Foundation v.z.w., Blandijnberg 2, 9000 Ghent, Belgium. TEL 32-9-2644007. FAX 32-9-2644189. *3356*

REVUE CANADIENNE D'ETUDES CINEMATOGRAPHIQUES.
Film Studies Association of Canada, c/o School for Studies in Art & Culture, Film Studies, Carleton University, 1125 Colonel by Drive, Ottawa, ON K1S 5B6, Canada. TEL 613-520-2600. FAX 613-520-3575. *5111*

REVUE D'HISTOIRE DE L'AMERIQUE FRANCAISE.
Institut d'Histoire de l'Amerique Francaise, 261 Avenue Bloomfield, Montreal, PQ H2V 3R6, Canada. TEL 514-278-2232. FAX 514-271-6369. *3486*

REVUE D'INTEGRATION EUROPEENNE.
Canadian Council for European Affairs, c/o Department of Political Studies, University of Saskatchewan, Saskatoon, SK S7N 0W0, Canada. TEL 306-966-5231. FAX 306-966-5250. *5769*

REVUE DE BIO-MATHEMATIQUE.
Editions Europeennes, 11 bis Ave. de la Providence, 92160 Antony, France. *4391*

REVUE DE DROIT COMMERCIAL BELGE.
Kluwer Rechtswetenschappen Belgie Kouterveld 2, 1831 Diegem, Belgium. FAX 32-2-7232121. *3842*

REVUE DE LA CERAMIQUE ET DU VERRE.
61 rue Marconi, B.P. 3, 62880 Vendin-le-Vieil, France. TEL 21-79-44-44. FAX 21-79-44-45. *1659*

REVUE DE MATHEMATIQUES SPECIALES.
Librairie Vuibert, 20 rue Berbier du Mets, 75647 Paris cedex 13, France. TEL 33-1-44-08-49-00. FAX 33-1-44-08-49-29. *4391*

REVUE DE MICROPALEONTOLOGIE.
Maison de la Geologie, B.P. 11705, 75224 Paris Cedex 05, France. *5318*

REVUE DE QUMRAN.
J. Gabalda et Cie, 18 rue P.et M. Curie, 75005 Paris, France. *6090*

REVUE DES COLLECTIVITES LOCALES ET L'EQUIPEMENT.
Publications Periodique Professionnelles, 38 rue Claude Terrasse, 75016 Paris, France. TEL 33-1-44-14-60-60. FAX 33-1-44-14-60-61. *5950*

REVUE DES ETUDES GEORGIENNES ET CAUCASIENNES.
Editions Peeters s.p.r.l., Bondgenotenlaan 153, 3000 Leuven, Belgium. TEL 32-16-235170. FAX 32-16-228500. *3438*

REVUE DES QUESTIONS SCIENTIFIQUES.
Societe Scientifique de Bruxelles, Rue de Bruxelles 61, B-5000 Namur, Belgium. TEL 32-81-724464. FAX 32-81-724502. *6275*

REVUE EUROPEENE DE PSYCHOLOGIE APPLIQUEE.
Swets & Zeitlinger bv, P.O. Box 825, 2160 SZ Lisse, Netherlands. TEL 31-252-435111. FAX 31-252-415888. *5880*

REVUE EUROPEENNE DES MIGRATIONS INTERNATIONALES.
Association pour l'Etude des Migrations Internationales (AEMI), 95 Av. du Recteur-Pineau, 86022 Poitiers Cedex, France. TEL 49-45-32-57. FAX 49-45-33-22. *5791*

REVUE FRANCAISE D'ACUPUNCTURE.
Association Francaise d'Acupuncture, Tour CIT, 3 rue de l'Arrivee, 75749 Paris Cedex 15, France. TEL 43-20-26-26. FAX 43-20-54-46. *292*

REVUE FRANCAISE D'AQUARIOLOGIE, HERPETOLOGIE.
Musee de Zoologie, 34 rue Sainte-Catherine, 54000 Nancy, France. *819*

REVUE FRANCAISE D'ETUDES AMERICAINES.
Association Francaise d'Etudes Americaines, 14 rue Corvisart, 75013 Paris, France. TEL 1-44-08-51-70. *6427*

REVUE GENERALE DE THERMIQUE.
Editions Scientifiques et Medicales Elsevier, 141 rue de Javel, 75747 Paris, France. TEL 33-1-45589000. FAX 33-1-45-589419. *5586*

REVUE HELLENIQUE DE DROIT INTERNATIONAL.
Hellenic Institute of International and Foreign Law, 73 Solonos St., 106079 Athens, Greece. TEL 30-1-3615-646. FAX 30-1-3619-777. *3941*

REVUE INTERNATIONALE DE POLICE CRIMINELLE.
International Criminal Police Organization (Interpol), Secretariat General, 200 quai Charles de Gaulle, 69006 Lyon, France. TEL 72-44-70-00. FAX 72-44-71-63. *2175*

REVUE MEDICALE DE BRUXELLES.
Association des Medecins Anciens Etudiants de l'Universite Libre de Bruxelles (A.M.U.B.), Route de Lennik 808, Bte. 612, 1070 Brussels, Belgium. TEL 32-2-555-6062. FAX 32-2-555-6117. *4525*

REVUE MEDICALE DE LIEGE.
Institut de Medecine, 13 rue Alex Bouvy, 4020 Liege, Belgium. TEL 32-41-437572. FAX 32-41-437572. *4525*

REVUE ROMANE.
Munksgaard International Publishers Ltd., 35 Noerre Soegade, P.O. Box 2148, DK-1016 Copenhagen K, Denmark. TEL 45-33-127030. FAX 45-33-129387. *4103*

REVUE SVETOVEJ LITERATURY.
Slovak Society of Literary Translations, Laurinska 2, 815 08 Bratislava, Slovakia. TEL 42-7-5334016. FAX 42-7-5331294. *4164*

RHETORIC REVIEW.
University of Arizona, Department of English, Rhetoric Review, Tuscon, AZ 85721. TEL 602-621-3371. FAX 602-621-7397. *2441*

RHETORICA.
University of California Press, Journals Division, 2120 Berkeley Way, No. 5812, Berkeley, CA 94720-5812. TEL 510-643-7154. FAX 510-642-9917. *4104*

RHEUMATOLOGY.
S. Karger AG, Allschwilerstr. 10, P.O. Box, CH-4009 Basel, Switzerland. TEL 061-3061111. FAX 061-3061234. *4895*

RHINOLOGY.
International Rhinologic Society, c/o Journal Rhinology, Postbus 85500, 3508 GA Utrecht, Netherlands. TEL 31-30-2506645. FAX 31-30-2541922. *4300*

RHODORA.
New England Botanical Club, Inc., 22 Divinity Ave., Cambridge, MA 02138. TEL 603-862-3222. FAX 603-862-4757. *701*

RIHABIRITESHON IGAKU.
Japanese Association of Rehabilitation Medicine, 1-1-17 Komone. Itabashi-ku, Tokyo, Japan. TEL 81-3-5966-2031. FAX 81-3-5966-2033. *4820*

RIJKSINSTITUUT VOOR OORLOGSDOCUMENTATIE. MONOGRAFIEEN.
Kluwer Academic Publishers, Postbus 17, 3300 AA Dordrecht, Netherlands. TEL 31-78-6392392. FAX 31-78-6392254. *3439*

RIKUSUI SEIBUTSUGAKUHO.
Nara Rikusui Seibutsu Kenkyukai, c/o Nara Joshi Daigaku Rigakubu, Seibutsugaku Kyoshitsu, Kitauoyanish-machi Nara-shi, Nara-ken 630, Japan. TEL 0742-20-3424. *604*

RIO BRAVO.
University of Texas - Pan American, Center for International Studies, LA 102, Edinburg, TX 78539. TEL 210-381-3572. FAX 210-316-7012. *5770*

RIRON TO HOHO.
Japanese Association for Mathematical Sociology, Osaka University, Faculty of Human Sciences, 1-2, Yamadaoka, Suita 565, Japan. TEL 81-6-879-8068. FAX 81-6-879-8068. *6428*

RISK ANALYSIS.
Plenum Publishing Corp., 233 Spring St., New York, NY 10013-1578. TEL 212-620-8000. FAX 212-463-0742. *4391*

RISK, DECISION AND POLICY.
Chapman & Hall, Journals Department 2-6 Boundary Row, London SE1 8HN, England. TEL 44-171-8650066. FAX 44-171-5229623. *1444*

RISK: HEALTH, SAFETY & ENVIRONMENT.
Franklin Pierce Law Center, 2 White St., Concord, NH 03301. TEL 603-228-1541. FAX 603-224-3342. *5975*

RIVASGODAYA.
Asociacion Espanola de Fitosociologia, c/o Univ. Complutense, Fac. de Farmacia, Dep. de Biologia Vegetal II, 28040 Madrid, Spain. TEL 34-1-3941769. FAX 34-1-3941774. *1914*

RIVEON LEBANKAUT.
Association of Banks in Israel, P.O. Box 2258, Tel Aviv 61021, Israel. TEL 972-3-5609019. FAX 972-3-5660317. *1119*

RIVERS.
S E L & Associates, 19 Old Town Square, Ste. 238, Ft. Collins, CO 80524-2471. TEL 970-224-1220. FAX 970-482-0251. *6974*

RIVISTA.
British-Italian Society, 21-22 Grosvenor St., London W1X 9FE, England. TEL 44-171-495-5536. *5770*

RIVISTA DI NEURORADIOLOGIA.
Edizioni del Centauro, Via del Pratello 8, 40122 Bologna, Italy. TEL 39-337-532604. *4884*

RIVISTA DI PEDIATRIA PREVENTIVA E SOCIALE.
Edizioni Minerva Medica, Corso Bramante 83-85, 10126 Turin, Italy. TEL 39-11-678282. FAX 39-11-3121736. *4314*

RIVISTA DI STORIA DELL'AGRICOLTURA.
Accademia dei Georgofili, Logge Uffizi Corti, 50122 Florence, Italy. TEL 39-55-212114. FAX 39-55-2302754. *148*

RIVISTA ITALIANA DI ANALISI TRANSAZIONALE E METODOLOGIE PSICOTERAPEUTICHE.
Societa Italiana di Metodologie Psicoterapeutiche e Analisi Transazionale, Via F. Nicolai 70, 00136 Rome, Italy. TEL 39-6-3544043. FAX 39-6-35402495. *5880*

RIVISTA ITALIANA DI PALEONTOLOGIA E STRATIGRAFIA.
Universita degli Studi di Milano, Dipartimento di Scienze della Terra, Via Mangiagalli 34, 20133 Milan, Italy. TEL 39-2-23698232. FAX 39-2-70638261. *5318*

RIVISTA ITALIANA ESSENZE, PROFUMI, PIANTE OFFICINALI, AROMI, SAPONI, AEROSOL, COSMETICI.
Istituto Tetrahedron, Via Capitan di Mozzo, 12, 24030 Mozzo (BG), Italy. TEL 39-35-468511. FAX 39-35-463803. *493*

RIVISTA MARITTIMA.
Stato Maggiore della Marina, Via Romeo Romei 5, 00136 Rome, Italy. FAX 39-6-35804304. *5046*

ROBINSON JEFFERS NEWSLETTER.
California State University, Department of English, 1250 Bellflower Blvd., Long Beach, CA 90840. TEL 310-985-4235. FAX 310-985-2369. *4318*

ROBOTICS AND AUTONOMOUS SYSTEMS.
North-Holland P.O. Box 211, 1000 AE Amsterdam, Netherlands. TEL 31-20-4853911. FAX 31-20-4853598. *2106*

ROBOTICS AND COMPUTER-INTEGRATED MANUFACTURING.
Elsevier Science Ltd., Pergamon P.O. Box 800, Kidlington, Oxford OX5 1DX, England. TEL 44-1865-843000. FAX 44-1865-843010. *2106*

ROCHESTER STUDIES IN ECONOMICS AND POLICY ISSUES.
Kluwer Academic Publishers, Postbus 17, 3300 AA Dordrecht, Netherlands. TEL 31 78-6392392. FAX 31-78-6392254. *1261*

ROCK ART RESEARCH.
Archaeological Publications, P.O. Box 216, Caulfield South, Vic. 3162, Australia, TEL 61-3-95230549. FAX 61-3-95230549. *220*

ROCK GARDEN.
Scottish Rock Garden Club, 43 Rubislaw Park Crescent, Aberdeen AB1 8BT, Scotland. TEL 44-1224-314533. *3066*

ROCKFORD REVIEW.
Rockford Writers' Guild, Box 858, Rockford, IL 61105. *4260*

ROCKS AND MINERALS.
Heldref Publications, 1319 Eighteenth St., N.W., Washington, DC 20036-1802. TEL 202-296-6267. FAX 202-296-5149. *5077*

ROCKY MOUNTAIN JOURNAL OF MATHEMATICS.
Rocky Mountain Mathematics Consortium, Arizona State University, Department of Mathematics, Tempe, AZ 85287. TEL 502-955-3788. *4391*

ROCKY MOUNTAIN MEDIEVAL AND RENAISSANCE ASSOCIATION. JOURNAL.
Rocky Mountain Medieval and Renaissance Association, c/o Nancy Spatz, Treasurer, Department of History, University of Northern Colorado, Greeley, CO 80639. TEL 970-351-2199. *3439*

ROCKY MOUNTAIN REVIEW OF LANGUAGE AND LITERATURE.
Rocky Mountain Modern Language Association, Department of English, Boise State University, Boise, ID 83725. TEL 208-385-1233. FAX 208-385-4373. *4260*

RODD'S CHEMISTRY OF CARBON COMPOUNDS.
Elsevier Science B.V., Books Division, P.O. Box 211, 1000 AE Amsterdam, Netherlands. TEL 31-20-4853911. FAX 31-20-4853705. *1745*

RODD'S CHEMISTRY OF CARBON COMPOUNDS. SUPPLEMENTS TO THE SECOND EDITION.
Elsevier Science B.V., Books Division, P.O. Box 211, 1000 AE Amsterdam, Netherlands. TEL 31-20-4853911. FAX 31-20-4853705. *1745*

ROEPER REVIEW.
Roeper School, Box 329, Bloomfield Hills, MI 48303. TEL 810-642-1500. FAX 810-642-1500. *2368*

ROMANCE PHILOLOGY.
University of California Press, Journals Division, 2120 Berkeley Way, No. 5812, Berkeley, CA 94720-5812. TEL 510-643-7154. FAX 510-642-9117. *4104*

ROMANCE WRITERS' REPORT.
Romance Writers of America, Inc., R W A Headquarters, 13700 Veterans Memorial Pkwy., Ste. 315, Houston, TX 77014-1023. TEL 713-440-6885. FAX 713-440-7510. *4296*

ROMANIAN CIVILIZATION.
Center for Romanian Studies, Oficiul Postal I, Casuta Postala 108, 6600 Iasi, Rumania. TEL 40-32-210274. *3440*

ROMANIAN JOURNAL OF METEOROLOGY.
National Institute of Meteorology and Hydrology, 97 Bucuresti-Ploiesti Hwy., 71581 Bucharest, Rumania. TEL 40-1-6793240. FAX 40-1-3129843. *5005*

ROMANIAN JOURNAL OF PETROLOGY.
Institutul Geologic al Romaniei, Str. Caransebes Nr. 1, 78344 Bucharest, Rumania. TEL 665-66-25. FAX 401-3-12-84-44. *2259*

ROMANIAN JOURNAL OF PHYSICS.
Editura Academiei Romane, Calea Victoriei 125, 79717 Bucharest, Rumania. TEL 40-1-6807040. *5568*

ROMANIAN PHYSICAL SOCIETY. NATIONAL CONFERENCE FOR PHYSICS. ABSTRACTS.
Institutul de Fizica Atomica, P.O. Box MG-6, Bucharest-Magurele, Rumania. TEL 40-1-6807040. FAX 40-1-6122247. *5600*

ROMANICA GANDENSIA.
Blandijnberg 2, 9000 Gent, Belgium. TEL 32-9-2644045. FAX 32-9-2644174. *4104*

ROMATOLOJI VE TIBBI REHABILITASYON DERGISI.
Turk Tibbi Rehabilitasyon Kurumu Dernegi, Hacettepe Universitesi, Tip Fakultesi, 06100 Hacettepe - Ankara, Turkey. TEL 90-312-3105769. FAX 90-312-3105769. *4896*

ROSSICA OLOMUCENSIA.
Universita Palackeho, Filozoficka Fakulta, Krizkovskeho 10, 771 47 Olomouc, Czech Republic. TEL 42-28-5508371. FAX 42-28-26476. *4105*

ROSSICA SOCIETY OF RUSSIAN PHILATELY JOURNAL.
Rossica Society of Russian Philately, Inc., c/o Kennedy Wilson, Ed., 7415 Venice St., Falls Church, VA 22043. *5462*

THE ROUND TABLE.
Carfax Publishing Co., P.O. Box 25, Abingdon, Oxon. OX14 3UE, England. TEL 44-1235-401000. FAX 44-1235-401550. *5770*

ROUNDALAB JOURNAL.
International Association of Round Dance Teachers, Inc., 2970 Yorkway, Baltimore, MD 21222-5356. TEL 410-285-6884. *2191*

ROYAL ASTRONOMICAL SOCIETY. MONTHLY NOTICES.
Blackwell Science Ltd., Osney Mead, Oxford OX2 0EL, England. TEL 44-1865-206206. FAX 44-1865-721205. *485*

ROYAL CALEDONIAN CURLING CLUB. ANNUAL.
Royal Caledonian Curling Club, Cairnie House, Ave. K, Ingliston Showground, Newbridge, Midlothian EH28 2NB, Scotland. TEL 44-131-333-3003. FAX 44-131-333-3323. *6478*

ROYAL COLLEGE OF PHYSICIANS AND SURGEONS OF CANADA. ANNALS.
Royal College of Physicians & Surgeons of Canada, 774 Echo Dr., Ottawa, ON K1S 5N8, Canada. TEL 613-730-6200. FAX 613-730-8830. *4527*

ROYAL COLLEGE OF PHYSICIANS OF EDINBURGH. PROCEEDINGS.
Royal College of Physicians of Edinburgh, 9 Queen St., Edinburgh EH2 1JQ, Scotland. TEL 0131-225-7324. FAX 0131-220-3939. *4527*

ROYAL COLLEGE OF PHYSICIANS OF LONDON. JOURNAL.
Royal College of Physicians, 11 St. Andrews Pl., Regents Park, London NW1 4LE, England. TEL 44-171-935-1174. FAX 44-171-487-5218. *4527*

ROYAL COLLEGE OF SURGEONS OF EDINBURGH. JOURNAL.
Blackwell Science Ltd., Osney Mead, Oxford OX2 0EL, England. TEL 44-1865-206206. FAX 44-1865-721205. *4918*

ROYAL INSTITUTE OF PHILOSOPHY CONFERENCE.
Kluwer Academic Publishers, Postbus 17, 3300 AA Dordrecht, Netherlands. TEL 31-78-6392392. FAX 31-78-6392254. *5497*

ROYAL MUSICAL ASSOCIATION. R.M.A. RESEARCH CHRONICLE.
Royal Musical Association, c/o Rachel Segal, Department of Music, Leeds University, 14 Cromer Terrace, Leeds LS2 9JR, England. TEL 49-113-233-2583. *5194*

ROYAL NAVAL MEDICAL SERVICE. JOURNAL.
Institute of Naval Medicine, Alverstoke, Gosport, Hants. PO12 2DL, England. TEL 44-1705-768110. FAX 44-1705-768106. *4527*

ROYAL NETHERLANDS ACADEMY OF SCIENCES. PROCEEDINGS.
North-Holland P.O. Box 211, 1000 AE Amsterdam, Netherlands. TEL 31-20-4853911. FAX 31-20-4853598. *6276*

ROYAL SOCIETY OF CANADA. TRANSACTIONS.
Royal Society of Canada, 225 Metcalfe St., Ste 308, Ottawa, ON K2P 1P9, Canada. TEL 613-991-6990. FAX 613-991-6996. *6276*

ROYAL SOCIETY OF CHEMISTRY. JOURNAL: PERKIN TRANSACTIONS 1.
The Royal Society of Chemistry, Thomas Graham House, Science Park, Milton Rd., Cambridge CB4 4WF, England. TEL 44-1223-420066. FAX 44-1223-423623. *1746*

ROYAL SOCIETY OF CHEMISTRY. JOURNAL: PERKIN TRANSACTIONS 2.
The Royal Society of Chemistry, Thomas Graham House, Science Park, Milton Rd., Cambridge CB4 4WF, England. TEL 44-1223-420066. FAX 44-1223-423623. *1757*

ROYAL SOCIETY OF EDINBURGH. PROCEEDINGS. SECTION A (MATHEMATICS).
Royal Society of Edinburgh, 22 George St., Edinburgh EH2 2PQ, Scotland. TEL 44-131-225-6057. FAX 44-131-220-6889. *4392*

ROYAL SOCIETY OF EDINBURGH. TRANSACTIONS. (EARTH SCIENCES).
Royal Society of Edinburgh, 22 George St., Edinburgh EH2 2PQ, Scotland. TEL 44-131-225-6057. FAX 44-131-220-6889. *2215*

ROYAL SOCIETY OF HEALTH JOURNAL.
Royal Society of Health, R S H House, 38A St., George's Dr., London SW1V 4BH, England. TEL 44-171-630-0121. FAX 44-171-976-6847. *6390*

ROYAL SOCIETY OF LONDON. NOTES AND RECORDS.
Royal Society of London, 6 Carlton House Terrace, London SW1Y 5AG, England. TEL 44-171-839-5561. FAX 44-171-976-1837. *6276*

ROYAL SOCIETY OF LONDON. PHILOSOPHICAL TRANSACTIONS. SERIES A. PHYSICAL SCIENCES AND ENGINEERING.
Royal Society of London, 6 Carlton House Terrace, London SW1Y 5AG, England. TEL 44-171-839-5561. FAX 44-171-976-1837. *5569*

ROYAL SOCIETY OF LONDON. PHILOSOPHICAL TRANSACTIONS. SERIES B. BIOLOGICAL SCIENCES.
Royal Society of London, 6 Carlton House Terrace, London SW1Y 5AG, England. TEL 44-171-839-5561. FAX 44-171-976-1837. *605*

ROYAL SOCIETY OF LONDON. PROCEEDINGS. SERIES A. MATHEMATICAL AND PHYSICAL SCIENCES.
Royal Society of London, 6 Carlton House Terrace, London SW1Y 5AG, England. TEL 44-171-839-5561. FAX 44-171-976-1837. *4392*

ROYAL SOCIETY OF LONDON. PROCEEDINGS. SERIES B. BIOLOGICAL SCIENCES.
Royal Society of London, 6 Carlton House Terrace, London SW1Y 5AG, England. TEL 44-171-839-5561. FAX 44-171-976-1837. *605*

ROYAL SOCIETY OF MEDICINE. JOURNAL.
Royal Society of Medicine Press Ltd., 1 Wimpole St., London W1M 8AE, England. TEL 0171-290-2900. FAX 0171-290-2929. *4527*

ROYAL SOCIETY OF NEW SOUTH WALES. JOURNAL AND PROCEEDINGS.
Royal Society of New South Wales, P.O. Box 1525, Macquarie Centre, N.S.W. 2113, Australia. TEL 02-887-4448. *6276*

ROYAL SOCIETY OF NEW ZEALAND. JOURNAL.
S I R Publishing, P.O. Box 399, Wellington, New Zealand. TEL 64-4-472-7421. FAX 64-4-473-1841. *6277*

ROYAL SOCIETY OF QUEENSLAND. PROCEEDINGS.
Royal Society of Queensland, P.O. Box 21, St. Lucia, Queensland 4067, Australia. TEL 07-870-1697. *6277*

ROYAL SOCIETY OF SOUTH AFRICA. TRANSACTIONS.
Royal Society of South Africa, P.D. Hahn Building, P.O. Box 594, Cape Town 8000, South Africa. TEL 27-21-650-2543. FAX 27-21-650-3726. *6277*

ROYAL SOCIETY OF SOUTH AUSTRALIA. TRANSACTIONS.
Royal Society of South Australia Inc., S.A. Museum, North Terrace, Adelaide, S.A. 5000, Australia. TEL 61-8-223-5360. *6277*

ROYAL SOCIETY OF TASMANIA, HOBART. PAPERS AND PROCEEDINGS.
Royal Society of Tasmania, Box 1166M, Hobart, Tas. 7001, Australia. TEL 61-362-350777. FAX 61-362-347139. *6277*

ROYAL SOCIETY OF TROPICAL MEDICINE AND HYGIENE. TRANSACTIONS.
Royal Society of Tropical Medicine and Hygiene, Manson House, 26 Portland Pl., London W1N 4EY, England. TEL 44-171-580-2127. FAX 44-171-436-1389. *4627*

ROYAL SOCIETY OF WESTERN AUSTRALIA. JOURNAL.
Royal Society of Western Australia, Inc., c/o Western Australian Museum, Perth, W.A. 6000, Australia. TEL 61-9-3802235. FAX 61-9-3801029. *6277*

ROYAL STATISTICAL SOCIETY. JOURNAL. SERIES A: STATISTICS IN SOCIETY.
Blackwell Publishers Ltd., 108 Cowley Road, Oxford OX4 1JF, England. TEL 44-1865-791100. FAX 44-1865-791347. *6626*

ROYAL STATISTICAL SOCIETY. JOURNAL. SERIES B: METHODOLOGICAL.
Blackwell Publishers Ltd., 108 Cowley Road, Oxford OX4 1JF, England. TEL 44-1865-791100. FAX 44-1865-791347. *6626*

ROYAL STATISTICAL SOCIETY. JOURNAL. SERIES C: APPLIED STATISTICS.
Blackwell Publishers Ltd., 108 Cowley Rd., Oxford OX4 1JF, England. TEL 44-1865-791100. FAX 44-1865-791347. *6626*

ROZPRAWY HYDROTECHNICZNE.
Polska Akademia Nauk, Instytut Budownictwa Wodnego, Ul. Koscierska 7, 80-952 Gdansk-Oliwa, Poland. *6974*

RUAH.
Power of Poetry, c/o Dominican School of Philosophy & Theology, 2401 Ridge Rd., Berkeley, CA 94709. TEL 510-849-2030. FAX 510-849-1372. *4318*

RUCH FILOZOFICZNY.
Polskie Towarzystwo Filozoficzne, c/o Uniwersytet Mikolaja Kopernika, Instytut Filozofii, Ul. Podmurna 74, 87-100 Torun, Poland. TEL 48-56-21157. FAX 48-56-21157. *5497*

RUDARSKO-METALURSKI ZBORNIK.
Univerza v Ljubljani, Fakulteta za Naravoslovje in Tehnologijo, Askerceva 20, P.O. Box 594, 61001 Ljubljana, Slovenia. TEL 386-61-1254121. FAX 386-61-1258114. *5077*

RUECKERT STUDIEN.
Ergon-Verlag, Grombuehlstr. 7, 97080 Wuerzburg, Germany. TEL 0931-280084. FAX 0931-282872. *4261*

RUNA.
Universidad de Buenos Aires, Facultad de Filosofia y Letras, Museo Etnografico Juan B. Ambrosetti, Moreno 350, 1091 Buenos Aires, Argentina. TEL 54-1-331-7788. *321*

RUPAMBARA.
22B Pratapaditya Rd., Calcutta 26, India. TEL 466-4269. *4261*

RURAL ROOTS.
Prince Albert Daily Herald, 30-10th St., P.O. Box 550, Prince Albert, SK S6V 5R9, Canada. TEL 306-764-4276. FAX 306-763-3331. *149*

RUSSELL REVIEW.
Russell Review Partnership, P.O. Box 179, Russell, New Zealand. TEL 64-9-4037431. FAX 64-9-4038009. *3389*

RUSSIA AND HER NEIGHBORS.
Highgate Road Social Science Research Station, Inc., 32 Highgate Rd., Berkeley, CA 94707. TEL 510-525-3248. FAX 510-525-3313. *321*

RUSSIAN ACADEMY OF SCIENCE. IZVESTIYA. MATHEMATICS.
Turpin Distribution Services Ltd., Blackhorse Rd., Letchworth, Herts. SG6 1HN, England. TEL 44-1462-672555. FAX 44-1462-480947. *4392*

RUSSIAN ACADEMY OF SCIENCE. LEBEDEV PHYSICS INSTITUTE. PROCEEDINGS.
Nova Science Publishers, Inc., 6080 Jericho Tpke., Ste. 207, Commack, NY 11725-2808. TEL 516-499-3103. *5611*

RUSSIAN ACADEMY OF SCIENCES. BIOLOGY BULLETIN.
Maik Nauka - Interperiodica, Mezhdunarodnyi Otdel, Ul. Prosoyuznaya, 90, 117864 Moscow, Russia. TEL 7-095-3360066. FAX 7-095-3360666. *605*

RUSSIAN ACADEMY OF SCIENCES. COLLOID JOURNAL.
Maik Nauka - Interperiodica, Mezhdunarodnyi Otdel, Ul. Profsoyuznaya, 90, 117864 Moscow, Russia. TEL 7-095-3360066. FAX 7-095-3360666. *1757*

RUSSIAN ACADEMY OF SCIENCES. INSTITUTE OF GENERAL PHYSICS. PROCEEDINGS.
Nova Science Publishers, Inc., 6080 Jericho Tpke. Ste. 207, Commack, NY 11725-2808. TEL 516-499-3103. *5569*

RUSSIAN ACADEMY OF SCIENCES. MATHEMATICAL NOTES.
Plenum Publishing Corp., Consultants Bureau, 233 Spring St., New York, NY 10013-1578. TEL 212-620-8468. FAX 212-463-0742. *4392*

RUSSIAN AND EAST EUROPEAN FINANCE AND TRADE.
M.E. Sharpe, Inc., 80 Business Park Dr., Armonk, NY 10504. TEL 914-273-1800. FAX 914-273-2106. *1294*

RUSSIAN CHEMICAL BULLETIN.
Plenum Publishing Corp., Consultants Bureau, 233 Spring St., New York, NY 10013-1578. TEL 212-620-8468. FAX 212-463-0742. *1691*

RUSSIAN ECONOMIC TRENDS.
Whurr Publishers Ltd., 19b Compton Terr., London N1 2UN, England. TEL 44-171-359-5979. FAX 44-171-226-5290. *1239*

RUSSIAN EDUCATION AND SOCIETY.
M.E. Sharpe, Inc., 80 Business Park Dr., Armonk, NY 10504. TEL 914-273-1800. FAX 914-273-2106. *2369*

RUSSIAN ELECTROCHEMISTRY.
Maik Nauka - Interperiodica, Mezhdunarodnyi Otdel, Ul. Profsoyuznaya, 90, 117864 Moscow, Russia. TEL 7-095-3360065. FAX 7-095-3360666. *1730*

RUSSIAN JOURNAL OF APPLIED CHEMISTRY.
Maik Nauka - Interperiodica, Mezhdunarodnyi Otdel, Ul. Profsoyuznaya, 90, 117864 Moscow, Russia. TEL 7-095-3360065. FAX 7-095-3360666. *2649*

RUSSIAN JOURNAL OF BIOORGANIC CHEMISTRY.
Maik Nauka - Interperiodica, Mezhdunarodnyi Otdel, Ul. Profsoyuznaya, 90, 117864 Moscow, Russia. TEL 7-095-3360066. FAX 7-095-3360666. *1746*

RUSSIAN JOURNAL OF COMPUTATIONAL MECHANICS.
John Wiley & Sons, Inc., Journals, 605 Third Ave., New York, NY 10158. TEL 212-850-6645. FAX 212-850-6021. *5591*

RUSSIAN JOURNAL OF COORDINATION CHEMISTRY.
Maik Nauka - Interperiodica, Mezhdunarodyi Otdel, Ul. Profsoyuznaya, 90, 117864 Moscow, Russia. TEL 7-095-3360066. FAX 7-095-3360666. *1691*

RUSSIAN JOURNAL OF DEVELOPMENTAL BIOLOGY.
Maik Nauka - Interperiodica, Mezhdunarodnyi Otdel, Ul. Profsoyuznaya, 90, 117864 Moscow, Russia. TEL 7-095-3360066. FAX 7-095-3360666. *749*

RUSSIAN JOURNAL OF ECOLOGY.
Maik Nauka - Interperiodica, Mezhdunarodnyi Otdel, Ul. Profsoyuznaya, 90, 117864 Moscow, Russia. TEL 7-095-3360066. FAX 7-095-3360666. *2818*

RUSSIAN JOURNAL OF ENGINEERING THERMOPHYSICS.
Begell House Inc., 79 Madison Ave., New York, NY 10016-7892. TEL 212-725-1999. FAX 212-213-8368. *5569*

RUSSIAN JOURNAL OF GENERAL CHEMISTRY.
Maik Nauka - Interperiodica, Mezhdunarodnyi Otdel, Ul. Profsoyuznaya, 90, 17864 Moscow, Russia. TEL 7-095-3360066. FAX 7-095-3360666. *1691*

RUSSIAN JOURNAL OF GENETICS.
Maik Nauka - Interperiodica, Mezhdunarodnayi Otdel, Ul. Profsoyuznaya, 90, 117864 Moscow, Russia. TEL 7-095-3360066. FAX 7-095-3360666. *749*

RUSSIAN JOURNAL OF MARINE BIOLOGY.
Maik Nauka - Interperiodica, Mezhdunarodnyi Otdel, Ul. Profsoyuznaya, 90, 117864 Moscow, Russia. TEL 7-095-3360066. FAX 7-095-3360666. *605*

RUSSIAN JOURNAL OF MATHEMATICAL PHYSICS.
John Wiley & Sons, Inc., Journals, 605 Third Ave., New York, NY 10158. TEL 212-850-6645. FAX 212-850-6021. *5569*

RUSSIAN JOURNAL OF NONDESTRUCTIVE TESTING.
Plenum Publishing Corp., Consultants Bureau, 233 Spring St., New York, NY 10013-1578. TEL 212-620-8468. FAX 212-463-0742. *1691*

RUSSIAN JOURNAL OF NUMERICAL ANALYSIS AND MATHEMATICAL MODELLING.
V S P, P.O. Box 346, 3700 AH Zeist, Netherlands. TEL 31-30-6925790. FAX 31-30-6932081. *4392*

RUSSIAN JOURNAL OF ORGANIC CHEMISTRY.
Maik Nauka Interperiodica, Mezhdunarodnyi Otdel, Ul. Profsoyuznaya, 90, 117864 Moscow, Russia. TEL 7-095-3360066. FAX 7-095-3360666. *1746*

RUSSIAN JOURNAL OF PLANT PHYSIOLOGY.
Maik Nauka - Interperiodica, Mezhdunarodnyi Otdel, Ul. Profsoyuznaya, 90, 117864 Moscow, Russia. TEL 7-095-3360066. FAX 7-095-3360666. *702*

RUSSIAN LINGUISTICS.
Kluwer Academic Publishers, Postbus 17, 3300 AA Dordrecht, Netherlands. TEL 31-78-6392392. FAX 31-78-6392254. *4105*

RUSSIAN LITERATURE.
North-Holland P.O. Box 211, 1000 AE Amsterdam, Netherlands. TEL 31-20-4853911. FAX 31-20-4853598. *4261*

RUSSIAN MICROELECTRONICS.
Maik Nauk - Interperiodica, Mezhdunarodnyi Otdel, Ul. Profsoyuznaya, 90, 117864 Moscow, Russia. TEL 7-095-33600664. FAX 7-095-3360666. *253*

RUSSIAN PHYSICS JOURNAL.
Plenum Publishing Corp., Consultants Bureau, 233 Spring St., New York, NY 10013-1578. TEL 212-620-8468. FAX 212-463-0742. *5569*

RUSSIAN POLITICS AND LAW.
M.E. Sharpe, Inc., 80 Business Park Dr., Armonk, NY 10504. TEL 914-273-1800. FAX 914-273-2106. *3844*

RUSSIAN POLITICS AND SOCIETY.
James Nicholas Publishers, P.O. Box 244, Albert Park. Vic. 3206, Australia. TEL 61-3-6965545. FAX 61-3-6992040. *5770*

THE RUSSIAN REVIEW.
Ohio State University Press, 1070 Carmack Rd., Columbus, OH 43210. TEL 617-292-6930. FAX 617-292-2065. *3441*

RUSSIAN SERIES ON SOCIAL HISTORY.
Kluwer Academic Publishers, Postbus 17, 3300 AA Dordrecht, Netherlands. TEL 31-78-6392392. FAX 31-78-6392254. *3441*

RUSSIAN SOCIAL SCIENCE REVIEW.
M.E. Sharpe, Inc., 80 Business Park Dr., Armonk, NY 10504. TEL 914-273-1800. FAX 914-273-2106. *5705*

RUSSIAN STUDIES IN HISTORY.
M.E. Sharpe, Inc., 80 Business Park Dr., Armonk, NY 10504. TEL 914-273-1800. FAX 914-273-2106. *3357*

RUSSIAN STUDIES IN LITERATURE.
M.E. Sharpe, Inc., 80 Business Park Dr., Armonk, NY 10504. TEL 914-273-1800. FAX 914-273-2106. *4261*

RUSSIAN STUDIES IN PHILOSOPHY.
M.E. Sharpe, Inc., 80 Business Park Dr., Armonk, NY 10504. TEL 914-273-1800. FAX 914-273-2106. *5497*

RUSSKOE VOZROZHDENIE
St. Seraphim Foundation, 53 Duane Ln., Demarest, NJ 07627-1304. TEL 201-768-5424. FAX 201-768-3436. *6113*

S A F E SYMPOSIUM PROCEEDINGS.
S A F E Association, 107 Music City Circle, Ste. 112, Nashville, TN 37214. TEL 615-902-0056. FAX 615-902-0077. *73*

S A Q: THE SOUTH ATLANTIC QUARTERLY.
Duke University Press, Box 90660, Durham, NC 27708-0660. TEL 919-687-3600. FAX 919-688-4574. *4164*

S A W E NEWSLETTER.
Society of Allied Weight Engineers, Inc., 5530 Aztec Dr., La Mesa, CA 91942-2110. TEL 619-465-1367. FAX 619-465-2551. *75*

S B A N E ENTERPRISE.
Smaller Business Association of New England, 204 Second Ave., Waltham, MA 02154. TEL 617-890-9070. FAX 617-890-4557. *1578*

S C I PSYCHOSOCIAL PROCESS.
American Association of Spinal Cord Injury Psychologists and Social Workers, 75-20 Astoria Blvd., Jackson Heights, NY 11370-1177. TEL 718-803-3782. FAX 718-803-0414. *5880*

S E C O L A S ANNALS.
Southeastern Council on Latin American Studies, L.B 8106, Georgia Southern University, Statesboro, GA 30460. TEL 912-681-5929. FAX 912-681-0824. *3486*

S E R EN EL 2000.
Hipolito Yrigoyen 1994, 2do. 4, 1089 Buenos Aires, Argentina. TEL 54-1-9510712. *5046*

SIAM - AMS PROCEEDINGS.
American Mathematical Society, Box 6248, Providence, RI 02940-6248. TEL 401-455-4000. *4392*

S I A M JOURNAL ON APPLIED MATHEMATICS.
Society for Industrial and Applied Mathematics, 3600 University City Science Center, Philadelphia, PA 19104-2688. TEL 215-382-9800. FAX 215-386-7999. *4393*

S I A M JOURNAL ON COMPUTING.
Society for Industrial and Applied Mathematics, 3600 University City Science Center, Philadelphia, PA 19104-2688. TEL 215-382-9800. FAX 215-386-7999. *4412*

S I A M JOURNAL ON CONTROL AND OPTIMIZATION.
Society for Industrial and Applied Mathematics, 3600 University City Science Center, Philadelphia, PA 19104-2688. TEL 215-382-9800. FAX 215-386-7999. *4393*

S I A M JOURNAL ON DISCRETE MATHEMATICS.
Society for Industrial and Applied Mathematics, 3600 University City Science Center, Philadelphia, PA 19104-2688. TEL 215-382-9800. FAX 215-386-7998. *4393*

S I A M JOURNAL ON MATHEMATICAL ANALYSIS.
Society for Industrial and Applied Mathematics, 3600 University City Science Center, Philadelphia, PA 19104-2688. TEL 215-382-9800. FAX 215-386-7999. *4393*

S I A M JOURNAL ON MATRIX ANALYSIS AND APPLICATIONS.
Society for Industrial and Applied Mathematics, 3600 University City Science Center, Philadelphia, PA 19104-2688. TEL 215-382-9800. FAX 215-386-7999. *4393*

S I A M JOURNAL ON NUMERICAL ANALYSIS.
Society for Industrial and Applied Mathematics, 3600 University City Science Center, Philadelphia, PA 19104-2688. TEL 215-382-9800. FAX 215-386-7999. *4393*

S I A M JOURNAL ON OPTIMIZATION.
Society for Industrial and Applied Mathematics, 3600 University City Science Center, Philadelphia, PA 19104-2688. TEL 215-382-9800. FAX 215-386-7999. *4393*

S I A M JOURNAL ON SCIENTIFIC COMPUTING.
Society for Industrial and Applied Mathematics, 3600 University City Science Center, Philadelphia, PA 19104-2688. TEL 215-382-9800. FAX 215-386-7999. *4393*

S I A M NEWS.
Society for Industrial and Applied Mathematics, 3600 University City Science Center, Philadelphia, PA 19104-2688. TEL 215-382-9800. FAX 215-386-7999. *4393*

S I A M REPORTS.
Society for Industrial and Applied Mathematics, 3600 University City Science Center, Philadelphia, PA 19104-2688. TEL 215-382-9800. FAX 213-386-9800. *4393*

S I A M REVIEW.
Society for Industrial and Applied Mathematics, 3600 University City Science Center, Philadelphia, PA 19104-2688. TEL 215-382-9800. FAX 215-386-7999. *4394*

S I A - SURFACE AND INTERFACE ANALYSIS.
John Wiley & Sons Ltd., Journals, Baffins Ln., Chichester, W. Sussex PO19 1UD, England. TEL 44-1243-779777. FAX 44-1243-843232. *1720*

S I D A - E T S.
Obsidiana Editores, S.A., Czda. de Tlalpan 2365, Col. Ciudad Jardin, 04370 Mexico DF, Mexico. TEL 6899133. *4628*

S I E C C A N NEWSLETTER.
Sex Information and Education Council of Canada, 850 Coxwell Ave., East York, ON M4C 5R1, Canada. TEL 416-446-5304. FAX 416-778-0785. *5880*

S L D.
New Paradigm Press, 5413 Neilwoods Dr., Knoxville, TN 37919. TEL 423-588-8878. *4262*

S M P T E JOURNAL.
Society of Motion Picture and Television Engineers, 595 W. Hartsdale Ave., White Plains, NY 10607-1824. TEL 914-761-1100. FAX 914-761-3115. *5111*

S P E DRILLING & COMPLETION.
Society of Petroleum Engineers, Inc., Box 833836, Richardson, TX 75083-3836. TEL 214-952-9393. FAX 214-952-9435. *5374*

S P E FORMATION EVALUATION.
Society of Petroleum Engineers, Inc., Box 833836, Richardson, TX 75083-3836. TEL 214-952-9393. FAX 214-952-9435. *5374*

S P E PRODUCTION & FACILITIES.
Society of Petroleum Engineers, Inc., Box 833836, Richardson, TX 75083-3836. TEL 214-952-9393. FAX 214-952-9435. *5375*

S P E RESERVOIR ENGINEERING.
Society of Petroleum Engineers, Inc., Box 833836, Richardson, TX 75083-3836. TEL 214-952-9393. FAX 214-952-9435. *5375*

S R A T E JOURNAL.
Southeastern Regional Association of Teacher Educators, c/o Scott Hopkins, Ed., Department of Curriculum and Instruction, College of Education, University of South Alabama, Mobile, AL 36688-0002. TEL 205-380-2895. *2369*

S S A JOURNAL.
Congnizant Communication Corporation, 3 Hartsdale Rd., Elmsford, NY 10523-3701. TEL 914-592-7720. FAX 914-592-8981. *5257*

S T A R.
U.S. National Aeronautics and Space Administration, National Technology Transfer Center, c/o Wheeling Jesuit University, 316 Washington Ave., Wheeling, WV 26003. TEL 304-243-2440. FAX 304-243-4390. *83*

S T O P PRESS.
Society to Overcome Pollution (Stop) Inc., 651 Notre Dame St. W., Ste. 130, Montreal, PQ, H3C 1H92, Canada. TEL 514-393-9559. FAX 514-393-9588. *2840*

SADO MARINE BIOLOGICAL STATION. REPORT.
Niigata Daigaku, Rigakubu Fuzoku Sado Rinkai Jikkenjo, 2-8050 Igarashi, Niigata 950-21, Japan. TEL 0259-75-2012. FAX 0259-75-2012. *605*

SAFE & VAULT TECHNOLOGY.
Safe & Vault Technicians Association, 3003 Live Oak St., Dallas, TX 75204-6189. TEL 214-827-7233. FAX 214-827-1810. *2183*

THE SAFETY & HEALTH PRACTITIONER.
Paramount Publishing Ltd., 17-21 Shenley Rd., Borehamwood, Herts. WD6 1RT, England. TEL 44-181-207-5599. FAX 44-181-207-2598. *5975*

SAFETY RESOURCES.
Gulf Atlantic Communications Corporation, Inc., Box 407000, Ft. Lauderdale, FL 33340-7000. TEL 954-489-4070. FAX 954-489-4079. *5258*

SAFETY SCIENCE.
Elsevier Science B.V., P.O. Box 211, 1000 AE Amsterdam, Netherlands. TEL 31-20-4853911. FAX 31-20-4853598. *5258*

SAGAMORE ARMY MATERIALS RESEARCH CONFERENCE. PROCEEDINGS.
Plenum Publishing Corp., 233 Spring St., New York, NY 10013-1578. TEL 212-620-8000. FAX 212-463-0742. *5047*

SAGE SERIES IN WRITTEN COMMUNICATION.
Sage Publications, Inc., 2455 Teller Rd., Thousand Oaks, CA 91320. TEL 805-499-0721. FAX 805-499-0871. *1915*

SAGGI.
Masson S.p.A., Divisione Periodici, Via Statuto 2-4, 20121 Milan, Italy. TEL 39-2-63671. FAX 39-2-6367211. *4867*

SAGYOSEN.
Nihon Sagyosen Kyokai, 9-7, Yaesu 2-chome, Chuo-ku, Tokyo 104, Japan. TEL 81-3-3271-5618. FAX 81-3-3281-2975. *6847*

ST. CATHERINE'S CONFERENCE REPORT.
King George VI and Queen Elizabeth Foundation of St. Catharine's, Cumberland Lodge, The Great Park, Windsor, Berkshire SL4 2HP, England. TEL 44-1784-432316. FAX 44-1784-438507. *6390*

ST. JOHN'S JOURNAL OF MEDICINE.
St. John's Medical College, Alumni Association, c/o Dr. S.V. Srikishna, Gen. Sec., Robert Koch Bhavan, 1st Fl., St. John's Medical College, Bangalore 560 034, India. TEL 565435. *4527*

ST. JOHN'S REVIEW.
St. John's College, Annapolis, MD 21404. TEL 410-263-2371. FAX 410-263-4828. *2442*

SAKKELET.
Nemzeti Sport Kft., c/o Andras Ozsvath, Ed., Falk Miksa u.10, 1005 Budapest 5, Hungary. TEL 36-1-1312790. FAX 36-1-1319738. *6479*

SALAMANDER.
Salamander, Inc., 48 Ackers Ave., Brookline, MA 02146. TEL 617-232-4647. *4165*

SALMAGUNDI.
Skidmore College, Saratoga Springs, NY 12866. TEL 518-581-7400. FAX 518-581-7400. *3624*

SALUD MENTAL.
Instituto Mexicana de Psiquiatria, Calz. Mexico-Xochimilco, No. 101, Col. San L. Huipulco, Del. Tlalpan, 14370 Mexico DF, Mexico. TEL 525-6552811 ext. 144. FAX 525-6550411. *4867*

SALUD PUBLICA DE MEXICO.
Instituto Nacional de Salud Publica, Secretaria de Salud, Av. Universidad, 665, Planta Baja, Col. Santa Maria Ahuacatitlad, 62508 Cuernavaca, Morelos, Mexico. TEL 52-73-110111. FAX 52-73-175745. *5975*

SAN DIEGO SOCIETY OF NATURAL HISTORY. PROCEEDINGS.
San Diego Society of Natural History, San Diego Natural History Museum Library, Box 1390, San Diego, CA 92112. TEL 619-232-3821. FAX 619-232-0248. *6278*

SAN JOAQUIN AGRICULTURAL LAW REVIEW.
San Joaquin College of Law, 3385 E. Shields Ave., Fresno, CA 93726. TEL 209-225-5953. FAX 209-225-4322. *3846*

SANANJALKA.
Suomen Kielen Seura, Fennicum, Henrikinkatu 3, 20500 Turku, Finland. FAX 358-21-3336360. *4106*

SANS LAISSE.
Editions Cynofil, BP 28, 15 rue Reclosiere, 39160 Saint-Amour, France. TEL 84-44-30-73. FAX 84-48-80-33. *5394*

SANTE MENTALE AU QUEBEC.
Revue Sante Mentale au Quebec, C.P. 548, Succ. Place d'Armes, Montreal, PQ H2Y 3H3, Canada. TEL 514-523-0607. FAX 514-523-0797. *5880*

SAPIENZA.
Editrice Domenicana Italiana, Via Luigi Palmieri, 19, 80133 Naples, Italy. TEL 39-81-459003. FAX 39-81-5526670. *5497*

SARCOMA.
Carfax Publishing Co., P.O. Box 25, Abingdon, Oxon OX14 3UE, England. TEL 44-1235-401000. FAX 44-1235-401550. *4764*

SASKATCHEWAN HISTORY.
Saskatchewan Archives Board, Murray Building, Univ. of Saskatchewan, 3 Campus Dr., Saskatoon, SK S7N 5A4, Canada. TEL 306-933-8326. FAX 306-933-7305. *3487*

SASKATCHEWAN LAW REVIEW.
University of Saskatchewan, College of Law, Law Building, Saskatoon, SK S7N 0W0, Canada. TEL 306-966-5869. FAX 306-966-5900. *3846*

SASKATCHEWAN MEDICAL JOURNAL.
University of Saskatchewan, Division of Continuing Medical Education, Box 60001, RPO University, Saskatoon, SK S7N 4J8, Canada. TEL 306-966-7787. FAX 306-966-7673. *4528*

SATHER CLASSICAL LECTURES.
University of California Press, 2120 Berkeley Way, Berkeley, CA 94720. TEL 510-642-4247. FAX 510-643-7127. *1825*

SAUDI HEART JOURNAL.
King Abdul Aziz University Hospital, P.O. Box 6615, Jeddah 21452, Saudi Arabia. TEL 966-2-6697043. FAX 966-2-6697043. *4609*

SAUDI MEDICAL JOURNAL.
Saudi Arabian Armed Forces Ministry of Defence and Aviation, Medical Services Department, P.O. Box 7897, Riyadh 11159, Saudi Arabia. TEL 966-1-4777714. FAX 966-1-4777194. *4528*

SAURIA.
Terrariengemeinschaft Berlin e.V., Planetenstr. 45, 12057 Berlin, Germany. TEL 030-6847140. *819*

THE SAVERS AND INVESTORS GUIDE.
Wisebuy Publications, 25 West Cottages, London NW6 1RJ, England. TEL 44-171-433-1121. *1351*

SAYBROOK REVIEW.
Saybrook Institute, Graduate School and Research Center, 450 Pacific, 3rd. Fl., San Francisco, CA 94133. TEL 415-433-9200. FAX 415-433-9271. *5880*

SCANDINAVIAN CONFERENCE ON ARTIFICIAL INTELLIGENCE.
I O S Press, Van Diemenstraat 94, 1013 CN Amsterdam, Netherlands. TEL 31-20-6382189. FAX 31-20-6203419. *2011*

SCANDINAVIAN JOURNAL OF CLINICAL & LABORATORY INVESTIGATION.
Scandinavian University Press, P.O. Box 2959 Toeyen, N-0608 Oslo, Norway. TEL 47-22-57-54-00. FAX 47-22-57-53-53. *4684*

SCANDINAVIAN JOURNAL OF DEVELOPMENT ALTERNATIVES AND AREA STUDIES.
Bethany Books, Sweden, P.O. Box 7444, S-103 91 Stockholm, Sweden. *6343*

SCANDINAVIAN JOURNAL OF ECONOMICS.
Blackwell Publishers Ltd., 108 Cowley Rd., Oxford OX4 1JF, England. TEL 44-1865-791100. FAX 44-1165-791347. *958*

SCANDINAVIAN JOURNAL OF EDUCATIONAL RESEARCH.
Carfax Publishing Co., P.O. Box 25, Abingdon, Oxon. OX14 3UE, England. TEL 44-1235-401000. FAX 44-1235-401550. *2369*

SCANDINAVIAN JOURNAL OF IMMUNOLOGY.
Blackwell Science Ltd., Osney Mead, Oxford OX2 0EL, England. TEL 44-1865-206206. FAX 44-1865-721205. *4587*

SCANDINAVIAN JOURNAL OF MANAGEMENT.
Elsevier Science Ltd., Pergamon, P.O. Box 800, Kidlington, Oxford OX5 1DX, England. TEL 44-1865-843000. FAX 44-1865-843010. *1444*

SCANDINAVIAN JOURNAL OF MEDICINE & SCIENCE IN SPORTS.
Munksgaard International Publishers Ltd., P.O. Box 2148, DK-1016 Copenhagen K, Denmark. TEL 45-33-127030. FAX 45-33-129387. *4900*

SCANDINAVIAN JOURNAL OF METALLURGY.
Munksgaard International Publishers Ltd., 35 Noerre Soegade, P.O. Box 2148, DK-1016 Copenhagen K, Denmark. TEL 45-33-127030. FAX 45-33-129387. *4973*

SCANDINAVIAN JOURNAL OF OCCUPATIONAL THERAPY.
Scandinavian University Press, P.O. Box 2959 Toeyen, N-0608 Oslo, Norway. TEL 47-22-57-54-00. FAX 47-22-57-53-53. *4528*

SCANDINAVIAN JOURNAL OF SOCIAL WELFARE.
Munksgaard International Publishers Ltd., 35 Noerre Soegade, P.O. Box 2148, DK-1016 Copenhagen K, Denmark. TEL 45-33-127030. FAX 45-33-129387. *6391*

SCANDINAVIAN JOURNAL OF STATISTICS.
Blackwell Publishers Ltd., 108 Cowley Rd., Oxford OX4 1JF, England. TEL 44-1865-791100. FAX 44-1865-791347. *6627*

THE SCANDINAVIAN PSYCHOANALYTIC REVIEW.
Munksgaard International Publishers Ltd., 35 Noerre Soegade, P.C. Box 2148, DK-1016 Copenhagen K, Denmark. TEL 45-33-127030. FAX 45-33-129387. *4867*

SCANDINAVIAN STUDIES (PROVO).
Society for the Advancement of Scandinavian Study, c/o Office of Sec. Treas., 3003 JKHB, Brigham Young University, Provo, UT 84602-6118. TEL 801-378-5598. FAX 801-378-4649. *4263*

SCANDO-SLAVICA.
Munksgaard International Publishers Ltd., 35 Noerre Soegade, P.O. Box 2148, DK-1016 Copenhagen K, Denmark. TEL 45-33-129387. *4106*

SCANNING MICROSCOPY.
Scanning Microscopy International, Inc., Box 66507, AMF O'Hare, Chicago, IL 60666-0507. TEL 708-529-6677. FAX 708-980-6698. *771*

SCARP.
University of Wollongong, Faculty of Creative Arts, Northfields Ave., Wollongong, N.S.W. 2522, Australia. TEL 61-42-213867. FAX 61-42-213301. *4319*

SCHIZOPHRENIA BULLETIN.
U.S. Public Health Service, National Institute of Mental Health, 5600 Fishers Ln., Rockville, MD 20857. TEL 301-443-9772. *4867*

SCHIZOPHRENIA RESEARCH.
Elsevier Science B.V., P.O. Box 211, 1000 AE Amsterdam, Netherlands. TEL 31-20-4853911. FAX 31-20-4853598. *4868*

SCHOLARLY INQUIRY FOR NURSING PRACTICE.
Springer Publishing Company, 536 Broadway, New York, NY 10012-3955. TEL 212-431-4370. FAX 212-941-7842. *4728*

SCHOLIA.
University of Natal (Durban), Department of Classics, Private Bag X10, Dalbridge 4014, South Africa. TEL 27-31-2602312. FAX 27-31-2602698. *1825*

SCHOOL EFFECTIVENESS AND SCHOOL IMPROVEMENT.
Swets & Zeitlinger bv, P.O. Box 825, 2160 SZ Lisse, Netherlands. TEL 31-252-435111. FAX 31-252-415888. *2370*

SCHOOL FOOD SERVICE RESEARCH REVIEW.
American School Food Service Association, 1600 Duke St., 7th Fl., Alexandria, VA 22314-3436. TEL 703-739-3900. FAX 703-739-3915. *2990*

SCHOOL LEADERSHIP & MANAGEMENT.
Carfax Publishing Co., P.O. Box 25, Abingdon, Oxon OX14 3UE, England. TEL 44-1235-401000. FAX 44-1235-401550. *2463*

SCHOOL LIBRARIES IN CANADA.
Canadian School Library Association, 602-200 Elgin St., Ottawa, Ont. K2P 1L5, Canada. TEL 613-232-9625. FAX 613-563-9895. *4025*

SCHOOL OF INTERNATIONAL STUDIES. PUBLICATIONS ON ASIA.
University of Washington Press, Box 50096, Seattle, WA 98105. TEL 206-543-4050. *3384*

SCHOOL OF INTERNATIONAL STUDIES. PUBLICATIONS ON RUSSIA AND EASTERN EUROPE.
University of Washington Press, Box 50096, Seattle, WA 98105. TEL 206-543-4050. *5705*

SCHOOL PSYCHOLOGY INTERNATIONAL.
Sage Publications Ltd., 6 Bonhill St., London EC2A 4PU, England. TEL 44-171-374-0645. FAX 44-171-374-8741. *2501*

SCHOOL PSYCHOLOGY QUARTERLY.
Guilford Publications, Inc., 72 Spring St., 4th Fl., New York, NY 10012. TEL 212-431-9800. FAX 212-966-6708. *5881*

SCHOOL SCIENCE AND MATHEMATICS.
School Science and Mathematics Association, Weniger Hall 237, Oregon State U., Cornwallis, OR 97331-6508. TEL 541-737-4031. FAX 541-737-1817. *2370*

SCHOOL SOCIAL WORK JOURNAL.
Illinois Association of School Social Workers, Box 634, Algonquin, IL 60102. TEL 847-948-7515. FAX 847-831-5100. *2474*

SCHULINTERN.
Ministerium fuer Kultus und Sport, Schlossplatz 4, 70173 Stuttgart, Germany. TEL 49-711-2792800. FAX 49-711-2792810. *2501*

SCHUYLER COUNTY HISTORICAL SOCIETY. JOURNAL.
Schuyler County Historical Society, Gray Brick Museum, Montour Falls, NY 14865. TEL 607-535-9741. *3487*

SCHWEIZER NATURSCHUTZ.
Schweizerischer Bund fuer Naturschutz, Postfach, CH-4020 Basel, Switzerland. TEL 41-61-3179191. FAX 41-61-3179266. *6278*

SCHWEIZER STRAHLER.
Schweizer Vereinigung der Strahler und Mineraliensammler (S V S M), Postfach 101, CH-3608 Thun, Switzerland. TEL 41-33-364996. *5073*

DER SCHWEIZER TREUHAENDER.
Treuhand-Kammer, Postfach 892, CH-8025 Zurich, Switzerland. TEL 41-1-2677575. FAX 41-1-2677555. *1054*

SCIENCE.
American Association for the Advancement of Science, 1200 New York Ave., N.W., Washington, DC 20005. TEL 202-326-6417. *6279*

SCIENCE ACTIVITIES.
Heldref Publications, 1319 Eighteenth St., N.W., Washington, DC 20036-1802. TEL 202-296-6267. FAX 202-296-5149. *2371*

SCIENCE & EDUCATION.
Kluwer Academic Publishers, Postbus 17, 3300 AA Dordrecht, Netherlands. TEL 31-78-6392392. FAX 31-78-6392254. *6279*

SCIENCE AND ENGINEERING ETHICS.
Opragen Publications, P.O. Box 54, Guildford, Surrey GU1 2YF, England. TEL 44-1483-560074. FAX 44-1483-560074. *5279*

SCIENCE AND GLOBAL SECURITY.
Gordon & Breach Science Publishers, c/o International Publishers Distributor, P.O. Box 3054, Langhorne, PA 19047-3054. TEL 215-750-2642. FAX 215-750-6343. *6279*

SCIENCE AND GLOBAL SECURITY MONOGRAPH SERIES.
Gordon and Breach Science Publishers, c/o International Publishers Distributor, P.O. Box 3054, Langhorne, PA 19047-3054. TEL 215-750-2642. FAX 215-750-6343. *5770*

SCIENCE AND ITS CONCEPTUAL FOUNDATIONS.
University of Chicago Press, 5801 S. Ellis Ave., Chicago, IL 60637. TEL 312-702-7899. *6279*

SCIENCE AND PHILOSOPHY.
Kluwer Academic Publishers, Postbus 17, 3300 AA Dordrecht, Netherlands. TEL 31-78-6392392. FAX 31-78-6392254. *6279*

SCIENCE AND PRACTICE OF SURGERY SERIES.
Marcel Dekker, Inc., 270 Madison Ave., New York, NY 10016. TEL 212-696-9000. FAX 212-685-4540. *4919*

SCIENCE AND PUBLIC POLICY.
Beech Tree Publishing, 10 Watford Close, Guildford, Surrey GU1 2EP, England. TEL 44-1483-67497. FAX 44-1483-67497. *6279*

SCIENCE & SOCIETY.
Guilford Publications, Inc., 72 Spring St., 4th Fl., New York, NY 10012. TEL 212-431-9800. FAX 212-966-6708. *5706*

SCIENCE & TECHNOLOGY LIBRARIES.
Haworth Press, Inc., 10 Alice St., Binghamton, NY 13904. TEL 607-722-5857. FAX 607-722-1424. *4025*

SCIENCE AS CULTURE.
Free Association Books, 26 Freegrove Rd., London N7, England. TEL 0171-609-0507. FAX 0171-609-4837. *6280*

SCIENCE COMMUNICATION.
Sage Publications, Inc., 2455 Teller Rd., Thousand Oaks, CA 91320. TEL 805-499-0721. FAX 805-499-0871. *1915*

SCIENCE EDUCATION.
John Wiley & Sons, Inc., Journals, 605 Third Ave., New York, NY 10158. TEL 212-850-6645. FAX 212-850-6021. *6280*

SCIENCE ET COMPORTEMENT.
Association Scientifique pour la Modification du Comportement, 309 rue Godin, Repentigny, PQ J6A 5Z8, Canada. TEL 514-253-8200. FAX 514-585-9935. *5881*

SCIENCE ET SPORTS.
Editions Scientifiques et Medicales Elsevier, 141 rue de Javel, 75747 Paris, France. TEL 33-1-45589026. FAX 33-1-45589421. *4900*

SCIENCE FICTION.
University of Western Australia, Department of English, c/o Dr. Van Ikin, Ed., Nedlands, W.A. 6907, Australia. TEL 61-9-380-2280. FAX 61-9-380-1030. *4331*

SCIENCE-FICTION STUDIES.
S F - T H, Inc., c/o Prof. Arthur B. Evans, Ed., DePauw University, Greencastle, IN 46135-0037. TEL 317-658-4758. FAX 317-658-4856. *4331*

SCIENCE IN CHINA. SERIES A: MATHEMATICS, PHYSICS, ASTRONOMY & TECHNOLOGICAL SCIENCES.
Science Press, Marketing and Sales Department, 16 Donghuangchenggen North St., Beijing 100717, People's Republic of China. TEL 4010642. FAX 4019810. *6281*

SCIENCE IN CHINA. SERIES B: CHEMISTRY, LIFE SCIENCES & EARTH SCIENCES.
Science Press, Marketing and Sales Department, 16 Donghuangchenggen North St., Beijing 100717, People's Republic of China. TEL 4010642. FAX 4019810. *6281*

SCIENCE IN NEW GUINEA.
University of Papua New Guinea, Faculty of Science, P.O. Box 320, University, Papua New Guinea. FAX 260-369. *6281*

SCIENCE OF ADVANCED MATERIAL AND PROCESS ENGINEERING SERIES.
Society for the Advancement of Material and Process Engineering, Box 2459, Covina, CA 91722. TEL 818-331-0616. FAX 818-332-8929. *2741*

SCIENCE OF COMPUTER PROGRAMMING.
North-Holland P.O. Box 211, 1000 AE Amsterdam, Netherlands. TEL 31-20-4853911. FAX 31-20-4853598. *2046*

THE SCIENCE OF THE TOTAL ENVIRONMENT.
Elsevier Science B.V., P.O. Box 211, 1000 AE Amsterdam, Netherlands. TEL 31-20-4853911. FAX 31-20-4853598. *2818*

SCIENCE PROGRESS.
Science Reviews Ltd., P.O. Box 81, Northwood, Middlesex HA6 3DY, England. TEL 44-1923-823586. FAX 44-1923-825066. *6282*

SCIENCE, TECHNOLOGY & DEVELOPMENT.
Frank Cass, Newbury House, 890-900 Eastern Ave., Newbury Park, Ilford, Essex IG2 7HH, England. TEL 44-181-599-8866. FAX 44-181-599-0984. *1314*

SCIENCE, TECHNOLOGY & SOCIETY.
Sage Publications India Pvt. Ltd., P.O. Box 4215, New Delhi 110 048, India. TEL 91-11-6444958. FAX 91-11-6472426. *6282*

SCIENCELAND.
Komat Inc., 501 Fifth Ave., Ste. 2108, New York, NY 10017. TEL 212-490-2180. FAX 212-490-2187. *1805*

THE SCIENCES.
New York Academy of Sciences, 2 E. 63rd St., New York, NY 10021. *6283*

SCIENCES DE LA SOCIETE.
Presses Universitaires du Mirail, 56, rue du Taur, 31000 Toulouse, France. TEL 33-61-22-58-31. FAX 33-61-21-84-20. *6343*

SCIENTIA. SERIES A: MATHEMATICAL SCIENCES.
Universidad Tecnica Federico Santa Maria, Casilla 110-V, Valparaiso, Chile. TEL 0056-32-626364. FAX 0056-32-660504. *4394*

SCIENTIA GEOLOGICA SINICA.
Science Press, Marketing and Sales Department, 16 Donghuangchenggen North St., Beijing 100717, People's Republic of China. *2260*

SCIENTIA HORTICULTURAE.
Elsevier Science B.V., P.O. Box 211, 1000 AE Amsterdam, Netherlands. TEL 31-20-4853911. FAX 31-20-4853598. *3066*

SCIENTIA IRANICA.
Sharif University of Technology, P.O. Box 11365-8639, Tehran, Iran. TEL 98-21-6005419. FAX 98-21-6012983. *6283*

SCIENTIA MARINA.
Consejo Superior de Investigaciones Cientificas (C.S.I.C.), Instituto de Ciencias del Mar, Passeig Joan de Borbo, s-n, 08039 Barcelona, Spain. TEL 34-3-2216450. FAX 34-3-2217340. *2305*

SCIENTIA PAEDAGOGICA EXPERIMENTALIS.
State University Ghent, Labo Pedagogiek, Blandijnberg 2, B-9000 Gent, Belgium. TEL 32-9-2643952. FAX 32-9-2646498. *2371*

SCIENTIFIC AMERICAN.
Scientific American, Inc., 415 Madison Ave., New York, NY 10017-1111. TEL 212-754-0550. FAX 212-754-1138. *6283*

SCIENTIFIC AMERICAN MEDICINE.
Scientific American, Inc., 415 Madison Ave., New York, NY 10017-1111. TEL 212-754-0550. FAX 212-754-1138. *4529*

SCIENTIFIC AND APPLIED PHOTOGRAPHY.
Gordon & Breach Science Publishers, c/o International Publishers Distributor, P.O. Box 3054, Langhorne, PA 19047-3054. TEL 215-750-2642. FAX 215-750-6343. *5520*

SCIENTIFIC PROGRAMMING: TOOLS & TECHNIQUES.
John Wiley & Sons, Inc., Journals, 605 Third Ave., New York, NY 10158. TEL 212-850-6645. FAX 212-850-6021. *2114*

SCIENTIFIC REPORTS OF CETACEAN RESEARCH.
Institute of Cetacean Research, Tokyo Suisan Bldg., 4-18 Toyomi-cho, Chuo-ku, Tokyo 104, Japan. TEL 81-3-3536-6521. FAX 81-3-3536-6522. *819*

SCIENTOMETRICS.
Elsevier Science B.V., P.O. Box 211, 1000 AE Amsterdam, Netherlands. TEL 31-20-4853911. FAX 31-20-4853598. *6284*

SCOPUS.
East Africa Natural History Society, Ornithological Sub-Committee, P.O. Box 15194, Nairobi, Kenya. TEL 254-2-891419. *781*

SCOTIA.
Old Dominion University, Department of History, Arts and Letters Building, Norfolk, VA 23529. TEL 804-683-3949. FAX 804-683-3241. *3442*

SCOTLANDS.
Edinburgh University Press, 22 George Sq., Edinburgh EH8 9LF, Scotland. TEL 44-131-650-6207. FAX 44-131-662-0053. *2907*

SCOTTISH AFFAIRS.
Unit for the Study of Government in Scotland, 31 Buccleuch Pl., Edinburgh EH8 9JT, Scotland. TEL 0131-650-4197. FAX 0131-668-3263. *5706*

SCOTTISH BIRDS.
Scottish Ornithologists Club, 21 Regent Terrace, Edinburgh EH7 5BT, Scotland. TEL 44-131-556-6042. *781*

SCOTTISH CHURCH HISTORY SOCIETY. RECORDS.
Scottish Church History Society, 1 Denham Green Terrace, Edinburgh EH5 3PG, Scotland. TEL 44-131-552-4059. FAX 44-131-552-4059. *6092*

SCOTTISH ECONOMIC AND SOCIAL HISTORY.
22 George Sq., Edinburgh EH8 9LF, Scotland. TEL 44-131-650-4223. FAX 44-131-662-0053. *6343*

SCOTTISH FORESTRY.
Royal Scottish Forestry Society, The Stables, Dalkeith Country Park, Dalkeith, Midlothian EH22 2NA, Scotland. TEL 44-131-660-9480. FAX 44-131-660-9490. *3024*

SCOTTISH HISTORICAL REVIEW.
Edinburgh University Press, 22 George Sq., Edinburgh EH8 9LF, Scotland. TEL 44-131-650-6207. FAX 44-131-662-0053. *3358*

SCOTTISH JOURNAL OF ADULT AND CONTINUING EDUCATION.
Scottish Community Education Council, Marketing and Public Affairs Unit, Rosebery House, 9 Haymarket Terrace, Edinburgh EH12 5EZ, Scotland. TEL 44-131-313-2488. FAX 44-131-313-6800. *2402*

SCOTTISH JOURNAL OF POLITICAL ECONOMY.
Blackwell Publishers Ltd., 108 Cowley Rd., Oxford OX4 1JF, England. TEL 44-1865-791100. FAX 44-1865-791347. *959*

SCOTTISH PLANNING AND ENVIRONMENTAL LAW.
Planning Exchange, Tontine House, 8 Gordon St., Glasgow G1 3PL, Scotland. TEL 44-141-248-8541. FAX 44-141-248-8277. *3847*

SCOTTISH WILDLIFE.
Scottish Wildlife Trust, Cramond House, Kirk Cramond, Cramond Glebe Rd., Edinburgh EH4 6NS, Scotland. TEL 44-131-312-7765. FAX 44-131-312-8705. *2140*

SCREAM FACTORY.
Deadline Press, Box 2808, Apache Junction, AZ 85217. TEL 408-353-4450. *4331*

SCREENING.
Elsevier Science Ireland Ltd., P.O. Box 85, Limerick, Ireland. TEL 353-61-471944. FAX 353-61-472144. *4745*

THE SCRIBE.
University of Bridgeport, Student Center, 244 University Ave., Bridgeport, CT 06601. TEL 203-576-4382. FAX 203-576-4941. *1885*

SCRIPPS INSTITUTION OF OCEANOGRAPHY. BULLETIN.
University of California Press, 2120 Berkeley Way, Berkeley, CA 94720. TEL 510-642-4247. FAX 510-643-7127. *2305*

SCRIPTA MATERIALIA.
Elsevier Science Ltd., Pergamon, P.O. Box 800, Kidlington, Oxford OX5 1DX, England. TEL 44-1865-843000. FAX 44-1865-843010. *4974*

SCRIPTURA.
University of Stellenbosch, Department of Religion, 7602 Matieland, South Africa. TEL 27-21-8082117. FAX 27-21-8082031. *6159*

SEA TECHNOLOGY.
Compass Publications, Inc. (Arlington), Ste. 1000, 1117 N. 19th St., Arlington, VA 22209. TEL 703-524-3136. FAX 703-841-0852. *2618*

SEABIRD.
Seabird Group, c/o R.S.P.B., The Lodge, Sandy, Beds. SG19 2DL, England. *781*

SEATTLE UNIVERSITY LAW REVIEW.
Seattle University, School of Law, 950 Broadway Plaza, Tacoma, WA 98402. TEL 206-591-2995. FAX 206-591-6313. *3847*

SECURE COMPUTING.
West Coast Publishing Ltd., William Knox House, Britannic Way, Llandarcy, Swansea SA10 6EL, Wales. TEL 44-1792-324000. FAX 44-1792-324001. *2051*

Refereed

SECURITIES REGULATION LAW JOURNAL.
Warren, Gorham & Lamont, One Penn Plaza, New York, NY 10119. TEL 212-971-5000. FAX 212-971-5113. *1351*

SECURITY DIALOGUE.
Sage Publications Ltd., 6 Bonhill St., London EC2A 4PU, England. TEL 44-171-374-0645. FAX 44-171-374-8741. *5706*

SECURITY JOURNAL.
Elsevier Science Ireland Ltd., P.O. Box 85, Limerick, Ireland. TEL 353-61-471944. FAX 353-61-472144. *2184*

SECURITY STUDIES.
Frank Cass, Newbury House, 890-900 Eastern Ave., Newbury Park, Ilford, Essex IG2 7HH, England. TEL 44-181-599-8866. FAX 44-181-599-0984. *5771*

SEDIMENTARY BASINS OF THE WORLD.
Elsevier Science B.V., Books Division, P.O. Box 211, 1000 AE Amsterdam, Netherlands. TEL 31-20-4853911. FAX 31-20-4853705. *2215*

SEDIMENTARY GEOLOGY.
Elsevier Science B.V., P.O. Box 211, 1000 AE Amsterdam, Netherlands. TEL 31-20-4853911. FAX 31-20-4853598. *2260*

SEDIMENTOLOGY.
Blackwell Science Ltd., Osney Mead, Oxford OX2 OEL, England. TEL 44-1865-206206. FAX 44-1865-721205. *2260*

SEDIMENTOLOGY AND PETROLEUM GEOLOGY.
Kluwer Academic Publishers, Postbus 17, 3300 AA Dordrecht, Netherlands. TEL 31-78-6392392. FAX 31-78-6392254. *5375*

SEEMEILE.
Seemeile Verlag, Sunneberg 3, CH-8634 Hombrechtikon, Switzerland. TEL 01-55424387. FAX 01-7806211. *6540*

SEI MARIANNA IKA DAIGAKU KIYO. IPPAN KYOIKU.
St. Marianna University School of Medicine, 2-16-1 Sugao Miyamae-ku, Kawasaki-shi 216, Japan. TEL 81-44-977-8111. FAX 81-44-977-9835. *2416*

SEIBUTSU BUTSURI.
Nihon Seibutsu Butsuri Gakkai, Rearize Inc., 4-1-4 Hongo, Bunkyo-ku, Tokyo 133, Japan. TEL 81-52-783-0901. FAX 81-52-789-2989. *655*

SEIBUTSU KANKYO CHOSETSU.
Nihon Seibutsu Kankyo Chosetsu Gakkai, Tokyo Daigaku Nogakubu, Nogyo Kogakka Kankyo Chosetsu Kogaku Kenkyushitsu, 1-1 Yayoi 1-chome, Bunkyo-ku, Tokyo 113. TEL 81-3-3812-2111. FAX 81-3-3813-2437. *606*

SEIBUTSU KYOIKU.
Nihon Seibutsu Kyoiku Gakkai, Tokyo Gakugei Daigaku Seibutsugaku Kyositsu, 1-1 Nukui Kitamachi 4-chome, Koganei-shi, Tokyo 184, Japan. *606*

SEISMOLOGICAL RESEARCH LETTERS.
Seismological Society of America, 201 Plaza Professional Bldg., El Cerrito, CA 94530-4003. TEL 510-525-5474. FAX 510-525-7204. *2281*

SEISMOLOGICAL SOCIETY OF AMERICA. BULLETIN.
Seismological Society of America, 201 Plaza Professional Bldg., El Cerrito, CA 94530. TEL 510-525-5474. FAX 510-525-7204. *2281*

SEIZURE.
W.B. Saunders Co. Ltd. 24-28 Oval Rd., London NW1 7DX, England. TEL 0171-267-4466. FAX 0171-482-2293. *4868*

SELECTA (CORVALLIS).
Pacific Northwest Council for Languages, c/o Foreign Languages & Literatures, Oregon State Univ., 210 Kidder Hall, Corvallis, OR 97331-4603. TEL 541-737-3945. FAX 541-737-3563. *4107*

SELECTED REPORTS IN ETHNOMUSICOLOGY.
University of California at Los Angeles, Department of Ethnomusicology and Systematic Musicology, Box 951657, Los Angeles, CA 90095-1657. TEL 213-825-5947. FAX 213-206-4738. *5196*

SELECTED TABLES IN MATHEMATICAL STATISTICS.
American Mathematical Society, Box 6248, Providence, RI 02940-6248. TEL 401-455-4000. *4394*

SELECTED TOPICS IN MASS SPECTROMETRY.
Plenum Publishing Corp., 233 Spring St., New York, NY 10013-1578. TEL 212-620-8000. FAX 212-463-0742. *1720*

SELECTED TOPICS IN SOLID STATE PHYSICS.
Elsevier Science B.V., Books Division, P.O. Box 211, 1000 AE Amsterdam, Netherlands. TEL 31-20-4853911. FAX 31-20-4853705. *5569*

SELECTED TOPICS IN SUPERCONDUCTIVITY.
Plenum Publishing Corp., 233 Spring St., New York, NY 10013-1578. TEL 212-620-8000. FAX 212-463-0742. *5570*

SELECTION AND DEVELOPMENT REVIEW.
British Psychological Society, St Andrew's House, 48 Princess Rd. E., Leicester LE1 7DR, England. TEL 44-166-254-9568. FAX 44-166-247-0787. *1444*

SEL'SKOKHOZYAISTVENNAYA LITERATURA.
Rossiiskaya Akademiya Sel'skokhozyaistvennykh Nauk, Tsentral'naya Nauchnaya Sel'skokhozyaistvennaya Biblioteka, Orlikov per. 3, 107804 Moscow, Russia. TEL 7-095-2078972. FAX 7-095-2075662. *180*

SEMIGROUP FORUM.
Springer-Verlag, Science Journals, 175 Fifth Ave., New York, NY 10010. TEL 212-460-1500. FAX 212-473-6272. *4394*

SEMINARS IN ARTHRITIS & RHEUMATISM.
W.B. Saunders Co. Curtis Center, 3rd Fl., Independence Sq. W., Philadelphia, PA 19106-3399. TEL 215-238-7800. FAX 215-238-6445. *4896*

SEMINARS IN CELL AND DEVELOPMENTAL BIOLOGY.
Academic Press Ltd. 24-28 Oval Rd., London NW1 7DX, England. TEL 44-171-267-4466. FAX 44-171-482-2293. *718*

SEMINARS IN DIALYSIS.
Blackwell Science Inc., 238 Main St., Cambridge, MA 02142-1413. TEL 617-876-7022. FAX 617-492-5263. *4930*

SEMINARS IN NEUROLOGICAL SURGERY.
Lippincott - Raven Publishers 227 E. Washington Sq., Philadelphia, PA 19106. TEL 215-238-4200. FAX 215-238-4235. *4919*

SEMINARS IN SURGICAL ONCOLOGY.
John Wiley & Sons, Inc., Journals, 605 Third Ave., New York, NY 10158. TEL 212-850-6645. FAX 212-850-6021. *4764*

SEMINARS IN VETERINARY MEDICINE AND SURGERY: SMALL ANIMAL.
W.B. Saunders Co. Curtis Center, 3rd Fl., Independence Sq. W., Philadelphia, PA 19106-3399. TEL 215-238-7800. FAX 215-238-6445. *6954*

SEMIOTIC REVIEW OF BOOKS.
Victoria University, 73 Queen's Park Crescent E., Toronto, ON M5S 1K7, Canada. TEL 416-585-4456. FAX 416-535-4584. *3625*

SEMITIC STUDY SERIES.
E.J. Brill, P.O. Box 9000, 2300 PA Leiden, Netherlands. TEL 31-71-5353500. FAX 31-71-5317532. *4107*

THE SENIOR MESSENGER.
City of Vancouver, Box 1995, Vancouver, WA 98668. TEL 360-596-8016. FAX 360-696-8942. *3296*

SENSORS.
Helmers Publishing, Inc., 174 Concord St., Box 874, Peterborough, NH 03458-0874. TEL 603-924-9631. FAX 603-924-2076. *3638*

SENSORS AND ACTUATORS: A PHYSICAL.
Elsevier Science S.A., P.O. Box 564, CH-1001 Lausanne 1, Switzerland. TEL 41-21-3207381. FAX 41-21-3235444. *5583*

SENSORS AND ACTUATORS: B CHEMICAL.
Elsevier Science S.A., P.O. Box 564, CH-1001 Lausanne 1, Switzerland. TEL 41-21-3207381. FAX 41-21-3235444. *730*

SENSORS AND MATERIALS.
M Y U, Scientific Publishing Division, 2-32-3 Sendagi, Bunkyo-ku, Tokyo 113, Japan. *5570*

SENSORY SYSTEMS.
Plenum Publishing Corp. Consultants Bureau, 233 Spring St., New York, NY 10013-1578. TEL 212-620-8468. FAX 212-463-0742. *5881*

SEPARATION AND PURIFICATION METHODS.
Marcel Dekker Journals, 270 Madison Ave., New York, NY 10016. TEL 212-696-9000. FAX 212-685-4540. *1720*

SEPARATION SCIENCE AND TECHNOLOGY.
Marcel Dekker Journals, 270 Madison Ave., New York, NY 10016. TEL 212-696-9000. FAX 212-685-4540. *1720*

SEPARATIONS TECHNOLOGY.
Elsevier Science Ireland Ltd., P.O. Box 85, Limerick, Ireland. TEL 353-61-471944. FAX 353-61-472144. *2650*

SEPIA.
Kawabata Press, Knill Cross House, Knill Cross, Millbrook, Torpoint, Cornwall, England. *4319*

SEPSIS.
Kluwer Academic Publishers Boston, Box 358, Accord Sta., Hingham, MA 02018-0358. TEL 617-871-6600. FAX 617-871-6528. *4628*

SERIALS LIBRARIAN.
Haworth Press, Inc., 10 Alice St., Binghamton, NY 13904-1580. TEL 607-722-5857. FAX 607-722-1424. *4026*

SERIALS REVIEW.
J A I Press Inc., 55 Old Post Rd. No.2, Box 1678, Greenwich, CT 06836-1678. TEL 203-661-7602. FAX 203-661-0792. *4026*

SERIE D'ECRITURE.
Burning Deck, 71 Elmgrove Ave., Providence, RI 02906. TEL 401-351-0015. *4319*

SERIE MEMORIA VIVA DA EDUCACAO BRASILERA.
Instituto Nacional de Estudos e Pesquisas Educacionais, Campus da UNB, Acesso Sul - Ala Norte, 70910-900 Brasilia, Brazil. TEL 55-61-347-8970. FAX 55-61-273-2232. *2371*

SERIES ENTOMOLOGICA.
Kluwer Academic Publishers, Postbus 17, 3300 AA Dordrecht, Netherlands. TEL 31-78-6392392. FAX 31-78-6392254. *734*

SERIES IN DEATH EDUCATION, AGING, AND HEALTH CARE.
Taylor & Francis Inc., 1900 Frost Rd., Ste. 101, Bristol, PA 19007-1598. TEL 215-785-5800 FAX 215-785-5515. *5381*

SERIES IN FOOD MATERIAL SCIENCE.
Kluwer Academic Publishers, Postbus 17, 3300 AA Dordrecht, Netherlands. TEL 31-78-6392392. FAX 31-78-6392254. *2990*

SERIES IN INTERNATIONAL BUSINESS AND ECONOMICS.
Elsevier Science Ltd., Books Division, P.O. Box 800, Kidlington, Oxford OX2 0DX, England. TEL 44-1865-843000. FAX 44-1865-8430410. *1239*

SERIES IN RADIOLOGY.
Kluwer Academic Publishers, Postbus 17, 3300 AA Dordrecht, Netherlands. TEL 31-78-6392392 FAX 31-78-6392254. *1884*

THE SERVICE INDUSTRIES JOURNAL.
Frank Cass, Newbury House, 890-900 Eastern Ave., Newbury Park, Ilford, Essex IG2 7HH, England. TEL 44-181-599-8866. FAX 44-181-599-0934. *959*

SET-VALUED ANALYSIS.
Kluwer Academic Publishers, Postbus 17, 3300 AA Dordrecht, Netherlands. TEL 31-78-6392392 FAX 31-78-6392254. *4395*

SETGUULCH.
Press Institute of Mongolia, P.O. Box 46-600, Ulaanbaatar, Mongolia. TEL 977-1-313912. FAX 977-1-313912. *3711*

SETO MARINE BIOLOGICAL LABORATORY. PUBLICATIONS.
Kyoto University, Faculty of Science, Seto Marine Biological Laboratory, Shirahama-cho, Nishimuro-gun, Wakayama-ken 649-22, Japan. TEL 0739-42-3515. FAX 0739-42-4518. *607*

SETTORE CULTURA E SPETTACOLO. RASSEGNA DI STUDI E DI NOTIZIE.
Settore Cultura e Spettacolo, Civiche Raccolte d'Arte Applicata ed Incisioni, Castello Sforzesco, 20121 Milan, Italy. FAX 39-2-8693071. *452*

SEVENTEENTH CENTURY FRENCH STUDIES.
Society for Seventeenth-Century French Studies, French Department, The University, Glasgow G12 8QL, Scotland. TEL 44-140-339-8855. FAX 44-140-330-4234. *4264*

SEVENTEENTH - CENTURY NEWS.
Texas A & M University, Department of English, College Station, TX 77843-4227. TEL 409-845-3400. FAX 409-862-2292. *4264*

SEWANEE MEDIAEVAL STUDIES.
University of the South, Sewanee Mediaeval Colloquium, Office of Communications, 735 University Ave., Sewanee, TN 37383-1000. TEL 615-598-1531. *3442*

SEX ROLES.
Plenum Publishing Corp., 233 Spring St., New York, NY 10013-1578. TEL 212-620-8000. FAX 212-463-0742. *5882*

SEXUAL ABUSE.
Plenum Publishing Corp., 233 Spring St., New York, NY 10013-1578. TEL 212-620-8000. FAX 212-463-0742. *5882*

SEXUAL AND MARITAL THERAPY.
Carfax Publishing Co., P.O. Box 25, Abingdon, Oxon. OX14 3UE, England. TEL 44-1235-401000. FAX 44-1235-401550. *5882*

SEXUAL PLANT REPRODUCTION.
Springer-Verlag, Heidelberger Platz 3, 14197 Berlin, Germany. TEL 49-30-8207-0. FAX 49-30-8214091. *703*

SEXUALITY AND DISABILITY.
Human Sciences Press, Inc. 233 Spring St., New York, NY 10013-1578. TEL 212-620-8000. FAX 212-463-0742. *4530*

SEXUALLY TRANSMITTED DISEASES.
Lippincott - Raven Publishers 227 E. Washington Sq., Philadelphia, PA 19106. TEL 215-238-4200. *4664*

SHAKESPEARE BULLETIN.
Lafayette College, English Department, Easton, PA 18042. TEL 610-250-5245. FAX 610-559-4006. *6702*

SHAKESPEARE IN SOUTHERN AFRICA.
Rhodes University, Institute for the Study of English in Africa, P.O. Box 94, Grahamstown 6140, South Africa. TEL 27-461-26093. FAX 27-461-25642. *4264*

THE SHANDEAN.
The Shandean, P.O. Box 71851, 1008 EB Amsterdam, Netherlands. FAX 31-20-4445405. *4265*

SHANDI YANJIU.
Science Press, Marketing and Sales Department, 16 Donghuangchenggen North Ave., Beijing 100717, People's Republic of China. TEL 4010642. FAX 4019810. *2260*

SHANDONG SHIDA XUEBAO (SHEHUI KEXUE BAN).
Shandong Shifan Daxue, Xuebao Bianjibu, Wenhua Donglu, Jinan, Shandong 250014, People's Republic of China. TEL 86-531-2961064. *6343*

SHANGHAI DANG'AN.
684 Gubei Rd., Shanghai 200335, People's Republic of China. TEL 86-21-62751700. FAX 86-21-62752867. *4027*

SHAW.
Pennsylvania State University Press, 820 N. University Dr., Ste. C, University Park, PA 16802-1003. TEL 814-865-1327. FAX 814-863-1408. *4266*

SHENGLI KEXUE JINZHAN.
Zhongguo Shengli Xuehui, 38 Xueyuan Rd., Beijing Medical University, Beijing 100083, People's Republic of China. TEL 861-209-1150. FAX 861-202-9252. *794*

SHENGLI XUEBAO.
Science Press, Marketing and Sales Department, 16 Donghuangchenggen North St., Beijing 100717, People's Republic of China. TEL 4010642. FAX 4019810. *794*

SHENGTAI XUEBAO.
Science Press, Marketing and Sales Department, 16 Donghuangchenggen North St., Beijing 100717, People's Republic of China. TEL 4010642. FAX 4019810. *2819*

SHENGTAIXUE ZAZHI.
Zhongguo Shengtaixue Xuehui, 72, Wenhua Lu, Shenyang, Liaoning 110015, People's Republic of China. TEL 86-24-391-6249. FAX 86-24-384-313. *2819*

SHENGWU GONGCHENG XUEBAO.
Science Press, Marketing and Sales Department, 16 Donghuangchenggen North St., Beijing 100717, People's Republic of China. TEL 4010642. FAX 4019810. *665*

SHENGWU HUAXUE YU SHENGWU WULI JINZHAN.
Science Press, Marketing and Sales Department, 16 Donghuangchenggen North St., Beijing 100717, People's Republic of China. TEL 4010642. FAX 4019810. *649*

SHENGWU HUAXUE ZAZHI.
Beijing Yike Daxue, Shengwu Huaxue yu Fenzi Shengwuxue Xi, No. 38, Xueyuan Lu, Beijing 100083, People's Republic of China. TEL 8610-2091416. FAX 8610-2015681. *649*

SHENGXUE XUEBAO.
Science Press, Marketing and Sales Department, 16 Donghuangchenggen North St., Beijing 100717, People's Republic of China. TEL 4010642. FAX 4019810. *5616*

SHENYANG YAOKE DAXUE XUEBAO.
Shenyang Yaoke Daxue, Xuebao Bianjibu, 103 Wenhua Rd., Shenyang, Liaoning 110015, People's Republic of China. TEL 3843711. *5443*

SHIJIE DIANXIN.
Youdian-bu, Keji Qingbao Zhongxin, 40 Xueyuan Rd., Haidian, Beijing 100083, People's Republic of China. TEL 86-10-6203-3106. FAX 86-10-6203-3106. *1915*

SHILAP.
Sociedad Hispano-Luso-Americana de Lepidopterologia, Apdo. 331, 28080 Madrid, Spain. FAX 34-1-4475609. *734*

SHIN BOEI RONSHU.
Boei Gakkai, Daini-Matsuda Bldg., 7-8-7, Roppongi, Minato-ku, Tokyo 106, Japan. TEL 81-3-3713-2469. FAX 81-3-3713-2723. *5047*

SHINKEI GANKA.
Nihon Shinkei Ganka Gakkai, Kitasato Daigaku Igakubu Ganka, 15-1, Kitasato 1-chome, Sagamihara-shi, Kanagawa-ken 228, Japan. FAX 81-427-78-2357. *4777*

SHINKO PANTEC GIHO.
Shinko Pantec Co. Ltd., 1-4, 1-chome, Murotani, Nishi-ku, Kobe-shi, Hyogo-ken 651-22, Japan. TEL 81-078-992-6525. FAX 81-078-992-6504. *2769*

SHINKO TEKUNO GIHO.
Shinko Tekuno K.K., 10-26, Wakihamacho 2-chome, Chuo-ku, Kobe-shi, Hyogo-ken 651, Japan. TEL 81-78-393-5001. FAX 81-78-393-5011. *2769*

SHIYONG ZHONGLIU ZAZHI.
Zhejiang Yike Daxue, 157 Yan'an Lu, Hangzhou, Zhejiang 310006, People's Republic of China. TEL 722700. *4764*

SHIYOU HUAGONG.
Ministry of Chemical Industry, Beijing Research Institute of Chemical Industry, P.O. Box 1442, Hepingli, Beijing, People's Republic of China. TEL 86-10-6429-5032. FAX 86-10-6422-8661. *5375*

SHIYOU KANTAN YU KAIFA.
Shiyou Kantan yu Kaifa Bianjibu, No. 20 Xueyuan Lu, P.O. Box 910, Beijing 100083, People's Republic of China. TEL 86-10-6209-7424. FAX 86-10-6209-7181. *5375*

SHIYOU LIANZHI YU HUAGONG.
Shiyou Lianzhi yu Huagong Bianjibu, 18 Xueyuan Rd., Beijing 100083, People's Republic of China. TEL 86-10-2019183. FAX 86-10-2017429. *5376*

SHIYOU ZHUANTAN JISHU.
Shiyou Zhuantan Jishu Bianjibu, 35 Dongfeng Donglu, Dezhou, Shandong 253005, People's Republic of China. TEL 86-534-262-2554. FAX 86-534-262-2468. *5376*

SHOCK.
BioMedical Press, 1021 15th St., Ste. 9, Augusta, GA 30901. TEL 706-722-7511. FAX 706-721-3048. *4531*

SHOCK AND VIBRATION.
John Wiley & Sons, Inc., Journals, 605 Third Ave., New York, NY 10158. TEL 212-850-6645. FAX 212-850-6021. *5616*

SHORT STORY.
University of Texas, Brownsville, Department of English, 80 Ft. Brown, Brownsville, TX 78520. TEL 210-544-8239. *4166*

SHOUDU YIKE DAXUE.
Shoudu Yike Daxue, You'anmenwai, Beijing 100054, People's Republic of China. TEL 86-10-6305-1258. FAX 86-10-6329-1972. *4531*

SHOULEI XUEBAO.
Science Press, Marketing and Sales Department, 16 Donghuangchenggen North St., Beijing 100717, People's Republic of China. TEL 4010642. FAX 4019810. *820*

SHUICHAN KEJI QINGBAO.
Shanghai Shuichan Xuehui, 265 Jiamusi Lu, Shanghai 200433, People's Republic of China. TEL 5483215. FAX 5489502. *2943*

SHUISHENG SHENGWU XUEBAO.
Science Press, Marketing and Sales Department, 16 Donghuangchenggen North St., Beijing 100717, People's Republic of China. TEL 4010642. FAX 4019810. *607*

SHU'UN IJTIMA'IYYAH.
Sociological Association of the U A E, P.O. Box 3745, Sharjah, United Arab Emirates. TEL 971-6-548161. FAX 971-6-522267. *6429*

SHUXUE DE SHIJIAN YU RENSHI.
Science Press, Marketing and Sales Department, 16 Donghuangchenggen North St., Beijing 100717, People's Republic of China. TEL 4010642. FAX 4019810. *4395*

SHUXUE XUEBAO.
Science Press, Marketing and Sales Department, 16 Donghuangchenggen North St., Beijing 100717, People's Republic of China. TEL 4010642. FAX 4019810. *4395*

SHUZHI JISUAN YU JISUANJI YINGYONG.
Science Press, Marketing and Sales Department, 16 Donghuangchenggen North St., Beijing 100717, People's Republic of China. TEL 4010642. FAX 4019810. *6306*

SIBERIAN MATHEMATICAL JOURNAL.
Plenum Publishing Corp., Consultants Bureau, 233 Spring St., New York, NY 10013-1578. TEL 212-620-8468. FAX 212-463-0742. *4396*

SIBOGA EXPEDITION.
E.J. Brill, P.O. Box 9000, 2300 PA Leiden, Netherlands. TEL 31-71-5353500. FAX 31-71-5317532. *607*

Refereed

SIDA: CONTRIBUTIONS TO BOTANY.
Botanical Research Institute of Texas, Inc., 509 Pecan St., Fort Worth, TX 76102-4060. TEL 817-332-4441. FAX 817-332-4112. *703*

SIDE EFFECTS OF DRUGS ANNUAL.
Elsevier Science B.V., Books Division, P.O. Box 211, 1000 AE Amsterdam, Netherlands. TEL 31-20-4853911. FAX 31-20-4853705. *5443*

SIDOR HOY INTERNACIONAL.
C.V.G. Siderurgica del Orinoco C.A. (Sidor), Gerencia Corporativa de Asuntos Publicos, Matanzas - Edo. Bolivar, Venezuela. TEL 58-86-907535. FAX 58-86-907536. *4974*

SIGLO XX.
Society of Spanish and Spanish-American Studies, Department of Spanish and Portuguese, University of Colorado, Campus Box 278, Boulder, CO 80309-0278. TEL 303-492-5900. FAX 303-492-3699. *4266*

SIGNAL PROCESSING.
Elsevier Science B.V., P.O. Box 211, 1000 AE Amsterdam, Netherlands. TEL 31-20-4853911. FAX 31-20-4853598. *2046*

SIGNAL PROCESSING: IMAGE COMMUNICATION.
Elsevier Science B.V., P.O. Box 211, 1000 AE Amsterdam, Netherlands. TEL 31-20-4853911. FAX 31-20-4853598. *2070*

SIGNO Y SENA.
Universidad de Buenos Aires, Instituto de Linguistica, 25 de Mayo 221, 1002 Buenos Aires, Argentina. TEL 54-1-3431196. FAX 54-1-343-2733. *4108*

SIGNS: JOURNAL OF WOMEN IN CULTURE AND SOCIETY.
University of Chicago Press, Journals Division, Box 37005, Chicago, IL 60637. TEL 773-753-3347. FAX 773-753-0811. *7019*

SILHOUETTE.
McMaster Students Union, Rm. 406, Hamilton Hall, 1280 Main St. W., Hamilton, ON L8S 4K1, Canada. TEL 905-525-9140. FAX 905-523-0107. *4166*

SILNICNI OBZOR.
Nakladatelstvi Silnicni Spolecnosti, Novotneho Lavka 5, 116 68 Prague 1, Czech Republic. TEL 42-2-21082388. FAX 42-2-24227836. *6825*

SILVER.
Silver Magazine Inc., Box 9690, Rancho Santa Fe, CA 92067. TEL 619-756-1054. FAX 619-756-9928. *335*

SIMON'S TOWN HISTORICAL SOCIETY BULLETIN.
Simon's Town Historical Society, P.O. Box 56, Simon's Town 7995, South Africa. *3375*

SIMPLIFIED SPELLING SOCIETY. JOURNAL.
Simplified Spelling Society, 61 Valentine Rd., Birmingham B14 7AJ, England. TEL 44-121-689-2597. FAX 44-121-359-6153. *4108*

SIMULATION (SAN DIEGO).
Society for Computer Simulation, Box 17900, San Diego, CA 92117-7900. TEL 619-277-3888. FAX 619-277-3930. *2053*

SIMULATION PRACTICE AND THEORY.
Elsevier Science B.V., P.O. Box 211, 1000 AE Amsterdam, Netherlands. TEL 31-20-4853911. FAX 31-20-4853598. *2053*

SIMULATION SERIES.
Society for Computer Simulation, Box 17900, San Diego, CA 92177. TEL 619-277-3888. FAX 619-277-3930. *2053*

SINERGIE.
Consorzio Universitario Economia Industriale e Manageriale, Via S. Cristoforo 4, 37129 Verona, Italy. TEL 39-45-597655. FAX 39-45-597550. *1445*

SINET.
Addis Ababa University, Faculty of Science, P.O. Box 31226, Addis Ababa, Ethiopia. TEL 251-1-553177. FAX 251-1-552112. *6286*

SINGAPORE JOURNAL OF TROPICAL GEOGRAPHY.
Blackwell Publishers Ltd., 108 Cowley Rd., Oxford OX4 1JF, England. TEL 44-1865-791100. FAX 44-1865-791347. *3273*

SINGAPORE LITERATURE.
Singapore Literature Society, 122B Sims Ave., Singapore 1438, Singapore. TEL 65-7477134. FAX 65-7428701. *4267*

SINGAPORE NATIONAL INSTITUTE OF CHEMISTRY. BULLETIN.
Singapore National Institute of Chemistry, c/o Department of Chemistry, National University of Singapore, Kent Ridge, Singapore 0511, Singapore. TEL 65-772-2914. FAX 65-779-1691. *1692*

SINGAPORE PAEDIATRIC JOURNAL.
Singapore Paediatric Society, c/o Department of Paediatrics, National University Hospital, Lower Kent Ridge Rd., Singapore 119074, Singapore. TEL 7724112. *4814*

SINICA LEIDENSIA.
E.J. Brill, P.O. Box 9000, 2300 PA Leiden, Netherlands. TEL 31-71-5353500. FAX 31-71-5317532. *3384*

SINN UND FORM.
Aufbau-Verlag Berlin und Weimar, Franzoesische Str. 32, 10117 Berlin, Germany. TEL 030-22350. FAX 030-2298637. *4267*

SINO - JAPANESE STUDIES.
University of California at Santa Barbara, History Department, Santa Barbara, CA 93106. TEL 805-893-4065. FAX 805-893-8795. *3384*

SIR THOMAS BROWNE INSTITUTE. PUBLICATIONS. NEW SERIES.
E.J. Brill, P.O. Box 9000, 2300 PA Leiden, Netherlands. TEL 31-71-5353500. FAX 31-71-5317532. *3442*

SIXTEENTH CENTURY JOURNAL.
Sixteenth Century Journal Publishers, Inc., Truman State University, MC 111L, Kirksville, MO 63501. TEL 816-785-4665. FAX 816-785-4181. *3442*

SJOGREN'S SYNDROME FOUNDATION INC.
Sjogren's Syndrome Foundation Inc., c/o Rita M. May, Exec. Dir., 333 N. Broadway, Ste. 2000, NY 11753-2007. TEL 516-933-6365. FAX 516-933-6368. *4587*

SKEPTIC.
Skeptics Society, 2761 N. Marengo Ave., Altadena, CA 91001. TEL 818-794-3119. FAX 818-794-1301. *5333*

SKIN PHARMACOLOGY.
S. Karger AG, Allschwilerstr. 10, P.O. Box, CH-4009 Basel, Switzerland. TEL 061-3061111. FAX 061-30161234. *5443*

SKIN RESEARCH AND TECHNOLOGY.
Munksgaard International Publishers Ltd., 35 Noerre Soegade, P.O. Box 1248, DK-1016 Copenhagen K, Denmark. TEL 45-33-127030. FAX 45-33-129337. *4665*

SKYDD & SAEKERHET.
Svenska Stoeldskyddsfoereningen, S-115 87 Stockholm, Sweden. TEL 46-8-783-7450. FAX 46-8-663-9652. *2185*

SKYWINGS.
British Hang Gliding and Paragliding Association Ltd., Old Schoolroom, Loughborough Rd., Leicester LE4 5PJ, England. TEL 44-114-267-9227. *6576*

SLANT: A JOURNAL OF POETRY.
University of Central Arkansas, Box 5063, Conway, AR 72035. TEL 501-450-5107. *4319*

SLAVE AND POST-SLAVE SOCIETIES AND CULTURES.
Frank Cass Newbury House, 890-900 Eastern Ave., Newbury Park, Ilford, Essex 1G2 7HH, England. TEL 44-181-599-8866. FAX 44-181-599-0984. *6429*

SLAVERY & ABOLITION.
Frank Cass Newbury House, 890-900 Eastern Ave., Newbury Park, Ilford, Essex 1G2 7HH, England. TEL 44-181-599-8866. FAX 44-181-599-0984. *6429*

SLAVICA LUNDENSIA.
Lunds Universitet, Slaviska Institutionen, Finngatan 12, S-223 62 Lund, Sweden. TEL 46-222-88-21. FAX 46-222-88-25. *4108*

SLAVONICA.
University of Manchester, Arts Bldg., Manchester M13 9PL, England. TEL 0161-275-3138. FAX 0161-275-3031. *4267*

SLIPSTREAM (NIAGARA FALLS).
Slipstream Publications, Box 2071, Niagara Falls, NY 14301. TEL 716-282-2616. *4319*

SLOAN MANAGEMENT REVIEW.
Massachusetts Institute of Technology, Sloan School of Management, 292 Main St., E38-120, Cambridge, MA 02139. TEL 617-253-7170. FAX 617-253-5584. *1445*

SLOVAK GEOLOGICAL MAGAZINE.
Geologicka Sluzaba Slovenskej Republiky, Mlynska Dolina 1, 817 04 Bratislava, Slovakia. TEL 42-7-3705111. FAX 42-7-371940. *2216*

SLOVENSKE DIVADLO.
Slovenska Akademia Vied, Kabinet Divadla a Filmu, Dubravska cesta 9, 813 64 Bratislava, Slovakia. TEL 42-7-377193. FAX 42-7-373567. *6702*

SLOVENSKO ETNOLOSKO DRUSTVO. GLASNIK.
Slovensko Etnolosko Drustvo, Zavetiska 5, 61000 Ljubljana, Slovenia. TEL 386-61-262782. FAX 386-61-1231220. *3443*

SLOVENSKY NARODOPIS.
Slovenska Akademia Vied, Ustav Etnologie, Jakubovo nam. 12, 813 64 Bratislava, Slovakia. TEL 42-7-5334925. FAX 42-7 361312. *2908*

SMALL BUSINESS ADVISOR.
Small Business Advisors Inc., Box 436, Woodmere, NY 11598. TEL 516-374-1387. FAX 516-374-1387. *1579*

SMALL BUSINESS ECONOMICS.
Kluwer Academic Publishers, Postbus 17, 3300 AA Dordrecht, Netherlands. TEL 31-78-6392392. FAX 31-78-6392254. *1579*

SMALL BUSINESS FORUM.
University of Wisconsin Small Business Development Center, 432 North Lake St., Madison, WI 53706. TEL 608-263-7843. FAX 608-263-7830. *1579*

SMALL BUSINESS, MARKETING AND SOCIETY.
James Nicholas Publishers, P.O. Box 224, Alber Park, Vic. 3206, Australia. TEL 61-3-6965545. FAX 61-3-6992040. *1579*

SMALL ENTERPRISE DEVELOPMENT.
Intermediate Technology Publications Ltd., 103-105 Southampton Row, London WC1B 4HH, England. TEL 44-171-436-9761. FAX 44-171-436-2013. *1580*

SMALL POND MAGAZINE OF LITERATURE.
Napoleon St. Cyr, Ed. & Pub., Box 664, Stratford, CT 06497. TEL 203-378-4066. *4267*

SMALL RUMINANT RESEARCH.
Elsevier Science B.V., P.O. Box 211, 1000 AE Amsterdam, Netherlands. TEL 31-20-4853911. FAX 31-20-4853598. *284*

SMALL WARS AND INSURGENCIES.
Frank Cass, Newbury House, 890-900 Eastern Ave. Newbury Park, Ilford, Essex 1G2 7HH, England. TEL 44-181-599-8866. FAX 44-181-599-0984. *5771*

SMARANDACHE NOTIONS.
Erhus University Press, 13333 Colossal Cave Rd., Box 722, Vail, AZ 85641. *4396*

SMITH COLLEGE STUDIES IN SOCIAL WORK.
Smith College, School for Social Work, Lilly Hall, Northampton, MA 01063. TEL 413-585-7984. FAX 413-585-7994. *5392*

SMOKE.
Windows Project, 40 Canning St., Liverpool L8 7NP England. TEL 0151-729-3688. *4320*

SOCIAL AND ECONOMIC STUDIES.
University of the West Indies, Institute of Social and Economic Research, Mona Campus, Kingston 7, Jamaica, W.I. TEL 809-927-1020. FAX 809-927-2409. *6345*

SOCIAL AND LEGAL STUDIES.
Sage Publications Ltd., 6 Bonhill St., London EC2A 4PU, England. TEL 44-171-374-0645. FAX 44-171-374-8741. *6429*

SOCIAL ANTHROPOLOGY.
Cambridge University Press, Edinburgh Bldg., Shaftesbury Rd., Cambridge CB2 2RU, England. TEL 44-1223-312393. FAX 44-1223-315052. *322*

SOCIAL BEHAVIOR AND PERSONALITY.
Society for Personality Research (Inc.), P.O. Box 1539, Palmerston North, New Zealand. TEL 64-6-355-5736. FAX 64-6-355-5736. *5882*

SOCIAL BIOLOGY.
Society for the Study of Social Biology, Box 2349, Port Angeles, WA 98362. TEL 608-233-1487. *750*

SOCIAL COGNITION.
Guilford Publications, Inc., 72 Spring St., 4th Fl., New York, NY 10012. TEL 212-431-9800. FAX 212-966-6708. *5882*

SOCIAL COMPASS.
Sage Publications Ltd., 6 Bonhill St., London EC2A 4PU, England. TEL 44-171-374-0645. FAX 44-171-374-8741. *6430*

THE SOCIAL CREDITER.
K R P Publications Ltd., P.O. Box 13855, Edinburgh EH15 1YD, Scotland. TEL 44-131-657-4740. *5707*

SOCIAL DEVELOPMENT.
Blackwell Publishers Ltd., 108 Cowley Rd., Oxford OX4 1JF, England. TEL 44-1865-791100. FAX 44-1865-791347. *6430*

SOCIAL DIMENSIONS OF ECONOMICS.
Kluwer Academic Publishers, Postbus 17, 3300 AA Dordrecht, Netherlands. TEL 31-78-6392392. FAX 31-78-6392254. *1261*

SOCIAL, ECONOMIC AND POLITICAL STUDIES OF THE MIDDLE EAST.
E.J. Brill, P.O. Box 9000, 2300 PA Leiden, Netherlands. TEL 31-71-5353500. FAX 31-71-5317532. *3499*

SOCIAL EDUCATION.
National Council for the Social Studies, 3501 Newark St., N.W., Washington, DC 20016. TEL 202-966-7840. *6345*

SOCIAL EPISTEMOLOGY.
Taylor & Francis Ltd., Rankine Rd., Basingstoke, Hants. RG24 8PR, England. TEL 44-1256-840366. FAX 44-1256-479438. *5498*

SOCIAL FORCES.
University of North Carolina Press, Box 2288, Chapel Hill, NC 27515-2288. TEL 919-966-3561. FAX 919-966-3829. *6430*

SOCIAL INDICATORS RESEARCH.
Kluwer Academic Publishers, Postbus 17, 3300 AA Dordrecht, Netherlands. TEL 31-78-6392392. FAX 31-78-6392254. *6430*

SOCIAL JUSTICE.
Global Options, Box 40601, San Francisco, CA 94140. TEL 415-550-1703. *5771*

SOCIAL JUSTICE RESEARCH.
Plenum Publishing Corp., 233 Spring St., New York, NY 10013-1578. TEL 212-620-8000. FAX 212-463-0742. *6430*

SOCIAL NETWORKS.
North-Holland P.O. Box 211, 1000 AE Amsterdam, Netherlands. TEL 31-20-4853911. FAX 31-20-4853598. *6345*

SOCIAL ORDERS SERIES.
Harwood Academic Publishers, c/o International Publishers Distributor, P.O. Box 3054, Langhorne, PA 19047-3054. TEL 215-750-2642. FAX 215-750-6343. *6430*

SOCIAL PATHOLOGY.
Harrow and Heston Publishers, 1830 Western Ave., Albany, NY 12203. TEL 518-456-4894. FAX 518-456-4894. *6431*

SOCIAL POLICY AND ADMINISTRATION.
Blackwell Publishers Ltd., 108 Cowley Rd., Oxford OX4 1JF, England. TEL 44-1865-791100. FAX 44-1865-791347. *6431*

SOCIAL POLITICS.
Oxford University Press, Oxford Journals, Walton St., Oxford OX2 6DP, England. TEL 44-1865-267907. FAX 44-1865-267485. *7019*

SOCIAL PROBLEMS.
University of California Press, Journals Division, 2120 Berkeley Way, Berkeley, CA 94720. TEL 510-643-7154. FAX 510-642-9917. *6431*

SOCIAL PSYCHOLOGICAL APPLICATIONS TO SOCIAL ISSUES.
Plenum Publishing Corp., 233 Spring St., New York, NY 10013-1578. TEL 212-620-8000. FAX 212-463-0742. *5883*

SOCIAL PSYCHOLOGY OF EDUCATION.
Kluwer Academic Publishers, Postbus 17, 3300 AA Dordrecht, Netherlands. TEL 31-78-6392392. FAX 31-78-6392254. *2373*

SOCIAL SCIENCE & MEDICINE.
Elsevier Science Ltd., Pergamon, P.O. Box 800, Kidlington, Oxford OX5 1DX, England. TEL 44-1865-843000. FAX 44-1865-843010. *4532*

SOCIAL SCIENCE COMPUTER REVIEW.
Sage Publications, Inc., 2455 Teller Rd., Thousand Oaks, CA 91320. *2408*

SOCIAL SCIENCE HISTORY.
Duke University Press, Box 90660, Durham, NC 27708-0660. TEL 919-687-3600. FAX 919-688-4574. *6345*

SOCIAL SCIENCE INFORMATION.
Sage Publications Ltd., 6 Bonhill St., London EC2A 4PU, England. TEL 44-171-374-0645. FAX 44-171-374-8741. *6345*

SOCIAL SCIENCES IN HEALTH.
Arnold 338 Euston Rd., London NW1 3BH, England. TEL 44-171-873-6000. FAX 44-171-873-6325. *5976*

SOCIAL SEMIOTICS.
Carfax Publishing Co., P.O. Box 25, Abingdon, Oxon OX14 3UE, England. TEL 44-1235-401000. FAX 44-1235-401550. *5499*

SOCIAL SERVICE REVIEW.
University of Chicago Press, Journals Division, Box 37005, Chicago, IL 60637. TEL 773-753-3347. FAX 773-753-0811. *6393*

THE SOCIAL STUDIES.
Heldref Publications, 1319 Eighteenth St., N.W., Washington, DC 20036-1802. TEL 202-296-6267. FAX 202-296-5149. *2373*

SOCIAL STUDIES OF SCIENCE.
Sage Publications Ltd., 6 Bonhill St., London EC2A 4PU, England. TEL 44-171-374-0645. FAX 44-171-374-8741. *6286*

SOCIAL WORK.
University of Stellenbosch, Department of Social Work, B.J. Vorster Bldg., Stellenbosch 7600, South Africa. TEL 27-21-8082070. FAX 27-21-8084336. *6393*

SOCIAL WORK AND CHRISTIANITY.
North American Association of Christians in Social Work, Box 7090, St. Davids, PA 19087-7090. TEL 610-687-5777. *6393*

SOCIAL WORK IN EUROPE.
Russell House Publishing Ltd., 38 Silver St., Lyme Regis, Dorset DT7 3HS, England. TEL 44-1297-443948. FAX 44-1297-443948. *6393*

SOCIAL WORK IN HEALTH CARE.
Haworth Press, Inc., 10 Alice St., Binghamton, NY 13904. TEL 607-722-5857. FAX 607-722-1424. *6394*

SOCIAL WORK WITH GROUPS.
Haworth Press, Inc., 10 Alice St., Binghamton, NY 13904. TEL 607-722-5857. FAX 607-722-1424. *6394*

SOCIAL WORKER.
Myropen Publications Ltd., 383 Parkdale Ave., Ste. 402, Ottawa, ON K1Y 4R4, Canada. TEL 613-729-6668. FAX 613-729-9608. *6394*

SOCIALE WETENSCHAPPEN.
Tilburg University, Faculty of Social Sciences, Postbus 90153, 5000 LE Tilburg, Netherlands. FAX 31-13-4662370. *6346*

SOCIALIST STANDARD.
Socialist Party of Great Britain, 52 Clapham High St., London SW4 7UN, England. TEL 44-171-622-3811. FAX 44-171-720-3665. *5708*

SOCIALIST STUDIES.
Societe for Socialist Studies, University College, No. 448, University of Manitoba, Winnipeg, MB R3T 2M8, Canada. TEL 204-474-9119. FAX 204-261-0021. *5708*

SOCIEDAD ARGENTINA PARA LA INVESTIGACION DE PRODUCTOS AROMATICOS. ANALES.
Sociedad Argentina para la Investigacion de Productos Aromaticos, Libertad 1079, 2o piso, 1012 Buenos Aires, Argentina. TEL 54-1-383-2360. *498*

SOCIEDAD BOTANICA DE MEXICO. BOLETIN.
Sociedad Botanica de Mexico, A.C., Apdo. Postal 70-385, Del. Coyoacan; Ciudad Universitaria, 04510 Mexico D.F., Mexico. *703*

SOCIEDAD ESPANOLA DE MINERALOGIA. BOLETIN.
Sociedad Espanola de Mineralogia, Alenza 1, 28003 Madrid, Spain. TEL 34-1-4417138. FAX 34-58-243368. *5078*

SOCIEDAD ESPANOLA DE QUIMICA CLINICA. REVISTA.
Ediciones Mayo, S.A., Muntaner, 374-376, 4o, 08006 Barcelona, Spain. TEL 34-3-2090255. FAX 34-3-2020643. *1692*

SOCIEDAD MATEMATICA MEXICANA. BOLETIN.
Sociedad Matematica Mexicana, Apdo. Postal 14-170, 07000 Mexico, D.F., Mexico. TEL 525-747-7103. FAX 525-747-7104. *4396*

SOCIEDAD MICOLOGICA DE MADRID. BOLETIN.
Sociedad Micologica de Madrid, c/o Real Jardin Botanico, Claudio Moyano 1, 28014 Madrid, Spain. FAX 34-1-4200157. *703*

SOCIEDAD QUIMICA DE MEXICO. REVISTA.
Sociedad Quimica de Mexico, Mar del Norte 5, Col. San Alvaro, Deleg. Azcapotzalco, 02090 Mexico, D.F., Mexico. TEL 52-5-3860255. FAX 52-5-3862905. *1692*

SOCIEDADE BRASILEIRA DE MATEMATICA. BOLETIM, NOVA SERIE.
Springer-Verlag, 175 Fifth Ave., New York, NY 10010. TEL 212-460-1500. FAX 212-473-6272. *4396*

SOCIEDADE ENTOMOLOGICA DO BRASIL. ANAIS.
Sociedade Entomologica do Brasil, EMBRAPA - CNPSo, Caixa Postal 231, 86001-970 Londrina, Parana, Brazil. TEL 55-43-3204253. FAX 55-43-3204253. *735*

SOCIEDADE PARANAENSE DE MATEMATICA. BOLETIM.
Sociedade Paranaense de Matematica, Caixa Postal 19081, 81531-990 Curitiba, Parana, Brazil. FAX 55-41-2674236. *4396*

SOCIETAS PRO FAUNA ET FLORA FENNICA. MEMORANDA.
Societas pro Fauna et Flora Fennica, P.O. Box 17, FIN-00014 University of Helsinki, Finland. *608*

SOCIETE AMERICAINE DE PHILOSOPHIE DE LANGUE FRANCAISE. BULLETIN.
Societe Americaine de Philosophie de Langue Francaise, c/o Northern Illinois University, 635 Joanne Lane, DeKalb, IL 60115. TEL 815-753-6463. FAX 815-753-6302. *5499*

SOCIETE BELGE D'ETUDES GEOGRAPHIQUES. BULLETIN.
Societe Belge d'Etudes Geographiques, De Croylaan 42, 3001 Heverlee, Belgium. TEL 32-16-322427. FAX 32-6-322980. *3273*

SOCIETE BELGE DE GEOLOGIE. BULLETIN.
Societe Belge de Geologie, 13 rue Jenner, 1000 Brussels, Belgium. TEL 32-2-6270410. FAX 32-2-6477359. *2261*

SOCIETE BELGE DE PHOTOGRAMMETRIE - TELEDETECTION ET CARTOGRAPHIE. BULLETIN TRIMESTRIEL.
Societe Belge de Photogrammetrie-Teledetection et Cartographie, C.A.E.-Tour Finances, Bte. 38, 50 bd. du Jardin Botanique, B-1010 Brussels, Belgium. TEL 32-2-2103575. *3274*

SOCIETE CHIMIQUE DE FRANCE. BULLETIN.
Editions Scientifiques et Medicales Elsevier, 141 rue de Javel, 75747 Paris, France. TEL 33-1-45589022. FAX 33-1-45589421. *1692*

SOCIETE DES SCIENCES MEDICALES DU GRAND-DUCHE DE LUXEMBOURG. BULLETIN.
Societe des Sciences Medicales du Grand-Duche de Luxembourg, Centre Hospitalier de Luxembourg, 4 rue Barble, L-1210 Luxembourg, Luxembourg. TEL 352-4411-2024. FAX 352-441209. *4532*

SOCIETE FRANCAISE DE CHIMIE. ANNUAIRE.
Societe Francaise de Chimie, 250 rue St. Jacques, 75005 Paris, France. *1692*

SOCIETE FRANCAISE DE PHOTOGRAMMETRIE ET DE TELEDETECTION. BULLETIN.
Societe Francaise de Photogrammetrie et de Teledetection, B.P. 68, 2 ave. Pasteur, 94160 Saint Mande, France. TEL 33-1-43-98-80-73. FAX 33-1-43-98-85-41. *3274*

SOCIETE FRANCAISE DU VIDE. PROCEEDINGS.
Societe Francaise du Vide, 19 rue du Renard, 75004 Paris, France. TEL 33-1-53-01-90-30. FAX 33-1-42-78-63-20. *5570*

SOCIETE GEOLOGIQUE DE BELGIQUE. ANNALES.
Societe Geologique de Belgique, Universite de Liege, 7 Place du Vingt-Aout, 4000 Liege, Belgium. TEL 32-41-665395. FAX 32-41-665700. *2261*

SOCIETE GEOLOGIQUE DE FRANCE. BULLETIN.
Societe Geologique de France, 77 rue Claude Bernard, 75005 Paris, France. TEL 43-31-77-35. FAX 45-35-79-10. *2261*

SOCIETE GEOLOGIQUE DE FRANCE. MEMOIRES.
Societe Geologique de France, 77 rue Claude-Bernard, 75005 Paris, France. TEL 43-31-77-35. FAX 45-35-79-10. *2261*

SOCIETE GEOLOGIQUE DE NORMANDIE ET DES AMIS DU MUSEUM DU HAVRE. BULLETIN TRIMESTRIEL.
Editions du Museum du Havre, Place du Vieux Marche, 76600 le Havre, France. TEL 33-35-41-37-28. FAX 33-35-42-12-40. *2261*

SOCIETE THEOPHILE GAUTIER. BULLETIN.
University Paul Valery, B.P. 5043, 34032 Montpellier Cedex 1, France. TEL 33-67-56-52-25. FAX 33-67-14-20-52. *4268*

SOCIETE ZOOLOGIQUE DE FRANCE. BULLETIN.
Societe Zoologique de France, 195 rue Saint-Jacques, 75005 Paris, France. TEL 40-9-31-10. *820*

SOCIETE ZOOLOGIQUE DE FRANCE. MEMOIRES.
Societe Zoologique de France, 195 rue Saint Jacques, 75005 Paris, France. TEL 40-79-31-10. *820*

SOCIETY.
Transaction Publishers, Transaction Periodicals Consortium, Department 3092, Rutgers University, New Brunswick, NJ 08903. TEL 908-445-2280. FAX 908-445-3138. *6347*

SOCIETY & ANIMALS.
White Horse Press, 10 High St., Knapwell, Cambridge CB3 8NR, England. TEL 44-1954-267527. FAX 44-1954-267527. *298*

SOCIETY AND CULTURE IN EAST-CENTRAL EUROPE.
University of California Press, 2120 Berkeley Way, Berkeley, CA 94720. TEL 510-643-7127. FAX 510-643-7127. *3444*

SOCIETY AND NATURAL RESOURCES.
Taylor & Francis Ltd., 1 Gunpowder Sq., London EC4A 3DE, England. TEL 44-171-583-0490. FAX 44-171-583-0585. *2819*

SOCIETY FOR APPLIED BACTERIOLOGY. SYMPOSIUM SERIES.
Academic Press, Inc., 525 B St., Ste. 1900, San Diego, CA 92101-4495. TEL 619-231-0926. FAX 619-699-6719. *766*

SOCIETY FOR APPLIED BACTERIOLOGY. TECHNICAL SERIES.
Academic Press, Inc., 525 B St., Ste. 1900, San Diego, CA 92101-4495. TEL 619-231-0926. FAX 619-699-6715. *766*

SOCIETY FOR COMPUTER SIMULATION. TRANSACTIONS.
Society for Computer Simulation, Box 17900, San Diego, CA 92177. TEL 619-277-3888. FAX 619-277-3930. *2053*

SOCIETY FOR EXISTENTIAL ANALYSIS. JOURNAL.
Society for Existential Analysis, c/o School of Psychotherapy and Counselling, Regent's College, Inner Circle, Regent's Park, London NW1 4NS, England. TEL 44-171-487-7406. *5883*

SOCIETY FOR EXPERIMENTAL BIOLOGY AND MEDICINE. PROCEEDINGS.
Blackwell Science Inc., 238 Main St., Cambridge, MA 02142. TEL 617-876-7022. FAX 617-492-5263. *608*

SOCIETY FOR GYNECOLOGIC INVESTIGATION. JOURNAL.
Elsevier Science Inc., Box 945, New York, NY 10159-0945. TEL 212-633-3730. FAX 212-633-3680. *4746*

SOCIETY FOR IN VITRO BIOLOGY. MONOGRAPH SERIES.
Society for In Vitro Biology, 8815 Centre Park Dr., Ste. 210, Columbia MD 21045. TEL 410-992-0946. FAX 410-992-0949. *767*

SOCIETY FOR IN VITRO BIOLOGY. PROCEEDINGS.
Society for In Vitro Biology, 8815 Centre Park Dr., Ste. 210, Columbia MD 21045. TEL 410-992-0946. FAX 410-992-0949. *767*

SOCIETY FOR INFORMATION DISPLAY. SYMPOSIUM DIGEST.
Society for Information Display, 1526 Brookhollow Dr., Ste. 82, Santa Ana, CA 92705-5421. TEL 714-545-1526. FAX 714-545-1547. *2618*

SOCIETY FOR PIRANDELLO STUDIES. YEARBOOK.
Society for Pirandello Studies, School of Languages, University of Kent, Canterbury CT2 7NF, England. FAX 44-1227-475476. *4268*

SOCIETY FOR RESEARCH IN CHILD DEVELOPMENT. MONOGRAPHS.
University of Chicago Press, Journals Division, Box 37005, Chicago, IL 60637. TEL 773-753-3347. FAX 773-753-0811. *1778*

SOCIETY FOR SPANISH AND PORTUGUESE HISTORICAL STUDIES. BULLETIN.
Society for Spanish and Portuguese Historical Studies, c/o William D. Phillips, Jr., Gen. Sec., History Department, University of Minnesota, Minneapolis, MN 55455. TEL 612-624-2800. FAX 612-624-7096. *3444*

SOCIETY FOR THE SCIENTIFIC STUDY OF RELIGION. MONOGRAPH SERIES.
Society for the Scientific Study of Religion, 1365 Stone Hall, Sociology Dept., Purdue Univ., West Lafayette, IN 47907-1365. TEL 317-494-6286. *6093*

SOCIETY FOR THE STUDY OF ARCHITECTURE IN CANADA. BULLETIN.
Society for the Study of Architecture in Canada, Box 2302, Sta. D, Ottawa, ON K1P 5W5, Canada. *404*

SOCIETY FOR THE STUDY OF HUMAN BIOLOGY. SYMPOSIUM SERIES.
Cambridge University Press, Edinburgh Bldg., Shaftesbury Rd., Cambridge CB2 2RU, England. TEL 44-1223-312393. FAX 44-1223-315052. *794*

SOCIETY OF ACTUARIES. TRANSACTIONS (GENERAL).
Society of Actuaries, 475 N. Martingale, Ste. 800, Schaumburg, IL 60173-2226. TEL 708-706-3500. FAX 708-706-3599. *3656*

SOCIETY OF ARCHIVISTS. JOURNAL.
Carfax Publishing Co., P.O. Box 25, Abingdon, Oxon. OX14 3UE, England. TEL 44-1235-401000. FAX 44-1235-401550. *4027*

SOCIETY OF DEPRECIATION PROFESSIONALS. JOURNAL.
Society of Depreciation Professionals, 3421 M St., N.W., Ste. 218, Washington, DC 20007-3516. TEL 202-362-0680. FAX 202-956-2283. *1055*

SOCIETY OF EXPLORATION GEOPHYSICISTS. SPECIAL PUBLICATIONS (SYMPOSIA) SERIES.
Society of Exploration Geophysicists, Box 702740, Tulsa, OK 74170-2740. TEL 918-493-3516. *2281*

SOCIETY OF LEATHER TECHNOLOGISTS AND CHEMISTS. JOURNAL.
Society of Leather Technologists and Chemists, 1 Edges Court, Moulton, Northampton NN3 7UJ, England. TEL 01604-647318. FAX 01604-35932. *3961*

SOCIETY OF PEDIATRIC NURSES. JOURNAL.
Nursecom Inc., 1211 Locust St., Philadelphia, PA 19107. TEL 215-545-7222. FAX 215-545-8107. *4728*

SOCIETY OF PETROLEUM ENGINEERS. REPRINT SERIES.
Society of Petroleum Engineers, Inc., Box 833836, Richardson, TX 75083-3836. TEL 214-952-9393. FAX 214-952-9435. *5376*

SOCIETY OF PETROLEUM ENGINEERS. TRANSACTIONS.
Society of Petroleum Engineers, Inc., Box 833836, Richardson, TX 75083-3836. TEL 214-952-9393. FAX 214-952-9435. *5376*

SOCIETY OF THE PLASTICS INDUSTRY. URETHANE DIVISION. CONFERENCE PROCEEDINGS.
Technomic Publishing Co. Inc., 851 New Holland Ave. Box 3535, Lancaster, PA 17604. TEL 717-291-5609. FAX 717-295-4538. *5627*

SOCIO-ECONOMIC PLANNING SCIENCES.
Elsevier Science Ltd., Pergamon, P.O. Box 800, Kidlington, Oxford OX5 1DX, England. TEL 44-1865-843000. FAX 44-1865-543010. *5920*

SOCIOBIOLOGY.
California State University, Chico, Department of Biological Sciences, Chico CA 95926. TEL 916-898-5116. FAX 916-895-4363. *608*

SOCIOLOGIA RURALIS.
Blackwell Publishers Ltd. 108 Cowley Rd., Oxford OX4 1JF, England. TEL 44-1865-791100. FAX 44-1865-791347. *6432*

SOCIOLOGICAL FORUM.
Plenum Publishing Corp. 233 Spring St., New York, NY 10013-1578. TEL 212-620-8000. FAX 212-463-0742. *6432*

SOCIOLOGICAL IMAGINATION.
Wisconsin Sociological Association, University of Wisconsin at Whitewater, Department of Sociology, Whitewater, WI 53190. TEL 414-472-1133. FAX 414-472-5238. *6432*

SOCIOLOGICAL PAPERS.
Sociological Institute for Community Studies, Bar-Ilan University, Ramat Gan 52900, Israel. TEL 972-3-5344449. FAX 972-3-5351825. *6433*

SOCIOLOGICAL QUARTERLY.
University of California Press, Journals Division, 2120 Berkeley Way, No. 5812, Berkely, CA 94720-5812. TEL 510-643-7154. FAX 510-642-9917. *6433*

SOCIOLOGICAL RESEARCH.
M.E. Sharpe, Inc., 80 Business Park Dr., Armonk, NY 10504. TEL 914-273-1800. FAX 914-273-2106. *6433*

SOCIOLOGICAL RESEARCH ONLINE.
Sage Publications Ltd., 6 Bonhill St., London EC2 4PU, England. TEL 44-171-374-0645. FAX 44-171-374-8741. *6433*

SOCIOLOGICAL REVIEW.
Blackwell Publishers Ltd., 108 Cowley Rd., Oxford OX4 1JF, England. TEL 44-1865-791100. FAX 44-1865-791347. *6433*

SOCIOLOGICAL SPECTRUM.
Taylor & Francis Inc., 1900 Frost Rd., Ste. 101, Bristol, PA 19007-1598. TEL 215-785-5800. FAX 215-785-5515. *6433*

SOCIOLOGICAL VIEWPOINTS.
Pennsylvania Sociological Society, c/o University of Scranton, Scranton, PA 18510-4605. TEL 717-941-7425. FAX 717-941-6369. *6434*

SOCIOLOGY OF HEALTH AND ILLNESS.
Blackwell Publishers Ltd., 108 Cowley Rd., Oxford OX4 1JF, England. TEL 44-1865-791100. FAX 44-1865-791347. *6435*

SOCIOLOGY OF SPORT JOURNAL.
Human Kinetics Publishers, Inc., Box 5076, Champaign, IL 61825-5076. TEL 217-351-5076. FAX 217-351-2674. *6435*

SOCIOLOGY OF THE SCIENCES. YEARBOOK.
Kluwer Academic Publishers, Postbus 17, 3300 AA Dordrecht, Netherlands. TEL 31-78-6392392. FAX 31-78-6392254. *6287*

SOCIOLOGY OF THE SCIENCES MONOGRAPHS.
Kluwer Academic Publishers, Postbus 17, 3300 AA Dordrecht, Netherlands. TEL 31-78-6392392. FAX 31-78-6392254. *6435*

SOFIISKI UNIVERSITET. GEOLOGO-GEOGRAFSKI FAKULTET. GEOLOGIIA. GODISHNIK.
Izdatelstvo Sv. Kliment Ohridski, 125 Tsarigradsko Shosse Blvd., Bl.4, 1113 Sofia, Bulgaria. FAX 359-2-703216. *2261*

SOFTWARE - CONCEPTS & TOOLS.
Springer-Verlag, Heidelberger Platz 3, 14197 Berlin, Germany. TEL 49-30-8207-0. FAX 49-30-8214091. *2047*

SOFTWARE DEVELOPMENT MONITOR.
Elsevier Science Ltd., P.O. Box 800, Kidlington, Oxford OX5 1DX, England. TEL 44-1865-843000. FAX 44-1865-843010. *2115*

SOFTWARE FUTURES.
A P T Data Group plc., 12 Sutton Row, 4th Fl., London W1V 5FH, England. TEL 44-171-528-7083. FAX 44-171-439-1105. *2115*

SOFTWARE: PRACTICE & EXPERIENCE.
John Wiley & Sons Ltd., Journals, Baffins Ln., Chichester, W. Sussex PO19 1UD, England. TEL 44-1243-779777. FAX 44-1243-843232. *2116*

SOFTWARE PROCESS IMPROVEMENT AND PRACTICE.
John Wiley & Sons Ltd., Journals, Baffins Ln., Chichester, W. Sussex PO19 1UD, England. TEL 44-1243-779777. FAX 44-1243-843232. *2116*

SOFTWARE QUALITY JOURNAL.
Chapman & Hall, Journals Department 2-6 Boundary Row, London SE1 8HN, England. TEL 44-171-8650066. FAX 44-171-5229623. *2116*

SOIL & ENVIRONMENT.
Kluwer Academic Publishers, Postbus 17, 3300 AA Dordrecht, Netherlands. TEL 31-78-6392392. FAX 31-78-6392254. *2819*

SOIL AND TILLAGE RESEARCH.
Elsevier Science B.V., P.O. Box 211, 1000 AE Amsterdam, Netherlands. TEL 31-20-4853911. FAX 31-20-4853598. *152*

SOIL BIOLOGY & BIOCHEMISTRY.
Elsevier Science Ltd., Pergamon, P.O. Box 800, Kidlington, Oxford OX5 1DX, England. TEL 44-1865-843000. FAX 44-1865-843010. *608*

SOIL DYNAMICS AND EARTHQUAKE ENGINEERING.
Elsevier Science Ltd., P.O. Box 800, Kidlington, Oxford OX5 1DX, England. TEL 44-1865-843000. FAX 44-1865-843010. *2281*

SOIL MECHANICS AND FOUNDATION ENGINEERING.
Plenum Publishing Corp., Consultants Bureau, 233 Spring St., New York, NY 10013-1578. TEL 212-620-8468. FAX 212-463-0742. *2672*

SOIL SCIENCE.
Williams & Wilkins, 351 W. Camden St., Baltimore, MD 21201. TEL 410-528-4000. FAX 410-528-4312. *240*

SOIL SCIENCE SOCIETY OF AMERICA. JOURNAL.
Soil Science Society of America, 677 S. Segoe Rd., Madison, WI 53711. TEL 608-273-8080. FAX 608-273-2021. *240*

SOIL TECHNOLOGY.
Elsevier Science B.V., P.O. Box 211, 1000 AE Amsterdam, Netherlands. TEL 31-20-4853911. FAX 31-20-4853598. *241*

SOIL USE AND MANAGEMENT.
CAB International, Wallingford, Oxon. OX10 8DE, England. TEL 01491-832111. FAX 44-1491-833508. *241*

SOLAR ENERGY.
Elsevier Science Ltd., Pergamon, P.O. Box 800, Kidlington, Oxford OX5 1DX, England. TEL 44-1865-843000. FAX 44-1865-843010. *2586*

SOLAR ENERGY MATERIALS AND SOLAR CELLS.
Elsevier Science B.V., P.O. Box 211, 1000 AE Amsterdam, Netherlands. TEL 31-20-4853911. FAX 31-20-4853598. *2586*

SOLAR PHYSICS.
Kluwer Academic Publishers, Postbus 17, 3300 AA Dordrecht, Netherlands. TEL 31-78-6392392. FAX 31-78-6392254. *486*

SOLAR SYSTEM RESEARCH.
Maik Nauka - Interperiodica, Mezhdunarodnyi Otdel, Ul. Profsoyuznaya, 90, 117864 Moscow, Russia. TEL 7-095-3360066. FAX 7-095-3360066. *486*

SOLICITOR'S JOURNAL.
Canadian Bar Association, New Brunswick Branch, 1133 Regent St., Ste. 206, Fredericton, NB E3B 3Z2, Canada. TEL 506-458-8536. FAX 506-451-1421. *3849*

SOLID EARTH SCIENCES LIBRARY.
Kluwer Academic Publishers, Postbus 17, 3300 AA Dordrecht, Netherlands. TEL 31-78-6392392. FAX 31-78-6392254. *2216*

SOLID FUEL CHEMISTRY.
Allerton Press, Inc., 150 Fifth Ave., New York, NY 10011. TEL 212-924-3950. FAX 212-463-9684. *2650*

SOLID MECHANICS AND ITS APPLICATIONS.
Kluwer Academic Publishers, Postbus 17, 3300 AA Dordrecht, Netherlands. TEL 31-78-6392392. FAX 31-78-6392254. *5591*

SOLID STATE COMMUNICATIONS.
Elsevier Science Ltd., Pergamon, P.O. Box 800, Kidlington, Oxford OX5 1DX, England. TEL 44-1865-843000. FAX 44-1865-843010. *5571*

SOLID-STATE ELECTRONICS.
Elsevier Science Ltd., Pergamon, P.O. Box 800, Kidlington, Oxford OX5 1DX, England. TEL 44-1865-843000. FAX 44-1865-843010. *2532*

SOLID STATE IONICS.
North-Holland P.O. Box 211, 1000 AE Amsterdam, Netherlands. TEL 31-20-4853911. FAX 31-20-4853598. *5571*

SOLID STATE NUCLEAR MAGNETIC RESONANCE.
Elsevier Science B.V., P.O. Box 211, 1000 AE Amsterdam, Netherlands. TEL 31-20-4853911. FAX 31-20-4853598. *1720*

SOLID STATE PHYSICS: ADVANCES IN RESEARCH AND APPLICATIONS.
Academic Press, Inc., 525 B St., Ste. 1900, San Diego, CA 92101-4495. TEL 619-231-0926. FAX 619-699-6715. *5571*

SOLID-STATE SCIENCE AND TECHNOLOGY LIBRARY.
Kluwer Academic Publishers, Postbus 17, 3300 AA Dordrecht, Netherlands. TEL 31-78-6392392. FAX 31-78-6392254. *2532*

SOLID STATE TECHNOLOGY.
PennWell Publishing Co. (Nashua), 10 Tara Blvd., 5th Fl., Nashua, NH 03062-2801. TEL 603-891-0123. FAX 609-891-0597. *2533*

SOLOS E ROCHAS.
Associacao Brasileira de Mecanica dos Solos, I P T, Predio Geotecnica, Cidade Universitaria, Caixa Postal 7141, 01064-970 Sao Paulo, Brazil. TEL 55-11-2687325. FAX 55-11-2687325. *2619*

SOLSTICE: AN ELECTRONIC JOURNAL OF GEOGRAPHY AND MATHEMATICS.
Institute of Mathematical Geography, 2790 Briarcliff, Ann Arbor, MI 48105-1429. TEL 313-761-1231. *4396*

SOLUBILITY DATA SERIES.
Oxford University Press, Oxford Journals, Walton St., Oxford OX2 6DB, England. TEL 44-1865-56767. FAX 44-1865-267985. *1693*

SOLUCIONES AVANZADAS.
Xview, S.A. de C.V., Tuxpan 2, Desp. 603, Col. Roma Sur, 06760 Mexico DF, Mexico. TEL 574-5316. FAX 574-5318. *1156*

SOLVENT EXTRACTION AND ION EXCHANGE.
Marcel Dekker Journals, 270 Madison Ave., New York, NY 10016. TEL 212-696-9000. FAX 212-685-4540. *1720*

SOMATIC CELL AND MOLECULAR GENETICS.
Plenum Publishing Corp., 233 Spring St., New York, NY 10013-1578. TEL 212-620-8000. FAX 212-463-0742. *750*

SOMATOSENSORY AND MOTOR RESEARCH.
Carfax Publishing Co., P.O. Box 25, Abingdon, Oxon OX14 3UE. TEL 44-1235-401000. FAX 44-1235-401550. *794*

SOMMERFELTIA.
University of Oslo, Botanical Garden and Museum, Trondheimsveien 23B, N-0562 Oslo, Norway. TEL 47-22-85-16-29. FAX 47-22-85-18-35. *704*

SONIC ARTS NETWORK JOURNAL.
Sonic Arts Network, Francis House, Francis St., London SW1P 1DE, England. TEL 0171-828-9796. FAX 0171-233-5159. *5198*

SONOMA COUNTY PHYSICIAN.
Sonoma County Medical Association, 3033 Cleveland Ave., Santa Rosa, CA 95403. TEL 707-525-4325. FAX 707-525-4289. *4532*

SONOMA MANDALA.
Sonoma State University, English Department, Rohnert Park, CA 94928. TEL 717-664-3902. FAX 707-664-2505. *4268*

SONS OF NORWAY VIKING.
Sons of Norway, 1455 W. Lake St., Minneapolis, MN 55408. TEL 612-827-3611. FAX 612-827-0658. *2909*

SOPHIA.
Society for Philosophy of Religion and Philosophical Theology, Dept. of Philosophy, P.O. Box 4230, Melbourne University, Vic. 3052, Australia. TEL 61-3-3444778. FAX 61-3-3444280. *5499*

SOSHIKI BAIYO KENKYU.
Nihon Soshiki Baiyo Gakkai, Research Institute for Functional Peptides, 4-3-32 Shimojo-machi, Yamagata-shi, Yamagata-ken 990, Japan. TEL 0236-46-2525. FAX 0236-46-2526. *718*

SOURCE (SEATTLE).
Church Council of Greater Seattle, 4759 15 Ave., N.E., 3rd Fl., Seattle, WA 98105-4404. TEL 206-525-1213. FAX 206-525-1218. *6094*

SOURCE: NOTES IN THE HISTORY OF ART.
Ars Brevis Foundation, Inc., 1 E. 87th St., Ste. 8A, New York, NY 10128. TEL 212-369-1667. FAX 212-360-6494. *453*

SOUTH AFRICA. SEA FISHERIES RESEARCH INSTITUTE. INVESTIGATIONAL REPORT.
Sea Fisheries Research Institute, Private Bag X2, Rogge Bay 8012, Cape Town, South Africa. TEL 27-21-4023911. FAX 27-21-252920. *2943*

SOUTH AFRICAN ASSOCIATION FOR MARINE BIOLOGICAL RESEARCH. BULLETIN.
South African Association for Marine Biological Research, P.O. Box 10712, Marine Parade 4056, South Africa. TEL 27-31-373536. FAX 27-31-372132. *608*

SOUTH AFRICAN BANKER.
Institute of Bankers in South Africa, P.O. Box 61420, Marshalltown 2107, South Africa. TEL 27-11-8321371. *1121*

SOUTH AFRICAN COMPUTER JOURNAL.
Computer Society of South Africa, P.O. Box 1714, Halfway House 1685, South Africa. TEL 27-12-420-2504. FAX 27-12-436454. *1998*

SOUTH AFRICAN FAMILY PRACTICE.
South African Academy of Family Practice - Primary Care, P.O. Box 2731, Rivonia 2128, South Africa. TEL 27-11-8076605. FAX 27-11-8076611. *4532*

SOUTH AFRICAN FORESTRY JOURNAL.
Southern African Institute of Forestry, P.O. Box 1022, Pretoria 0001, South Africa. TEL 27-12-473479. FAX 27-12-473479. *3025*

SOUTH AFRICAN GEOGRAPHICAL JOURNAL.
South African Society of Geographers, c/o Dept. of Environmental & Geographical Science, University of Cape Town, Rondebosch 7700, South Africa. TEL 27-21-6502877. FAX 27-21-6503791. *3274*

SOUTH AFRICAN HISTORICAL JOURNAL.
South African Historical Society, c/o University of South Africa, Department of History, P.O. Box 392, Pretoria 0001, South Africa. TEL 27-12-4296272. FAX 27-12-4293221. *3375*

SOUTH AFRICAN INSTITUTE OF MINING AND METALLURGY. JOURNAL.
South African Institute of Mining and Metallurgy, P.O. Box 61127, Marshalltown 2107, South Africa. TEL 27-11-8341273. FAX 27-11-8385923. *4974*

SOUTH AFRICAN JOURNAL OF AFRICAN LANGUAGES.
Foundation for Education, Science & Technology, P.O. Box 1758, Pretoria 0001, South Africa. TEL 27-12-3226404. FAX 27-12-3207803. *4109*

SOUTH AFRICAN JOURNAL OF ANIMAL SCIENCE.
Foundation for Education, Science & Technology, P.O. Box 1758, Pretoria 0001, South Africa. TEL 27-12-3226404. FAX 27-12-3207803. *284*

SOUTH AFRICAN JOURNAL OF BOTANY.
Foundation for Education, Science & Technology, P.O. Box 1758, Pretoria 0001, South Africa. TEL 27-12-3226404. FAX 27-12-3207803. *704*

SOUTH AFRICAN JOURNAL OF BUSINESS MANAGEMENT.
Foundation for Education, Science & Technology, P.O. Box 1758, Pretoria 0001, South Africa. TEL 27-12-3226404. FAX 27-12-3207803. *1446*

SOUTH AFRICAN JOURNAL OF CHEMISTRY.
Foundation for Education, Science & Technology, P.O. Box 1758, Pretoria 0001, South Africa. TEL 27-12-3226404. FAX 27-12-3207803. *1693*

SOUTH AFRICAN JOURNAL OF COMMUNICATION DISORDERS.
South African Speech - Language - Hearing Association, P.O. Box 600, Wits 2050, South Africa. TEL 27-11-4031892. FAX 27-11-4036689. *4800*

SOUTH AFRICAN JOURNAL OF ECONOMIC HISTORY.
Economic History Society of Southern Africa, University of South Africa, Economics Department, P.O. Box 392, Pretoria 0001, South Africa. TEL 27-12-4294502. FAX 27-12-4293433. *1261*

SOUTH AFRICAN JOURNAL OF ETHNOLOGY.
Foundation for Education, Science & Technology, P.O. Box 1758, Pretoria 0001, South Africa. TEL 27-12-3226404. FAX 27-12-3207803. *322*

SOUTH AFRICAN JOURNAL OF GEOLOGY.
Foundation for Education, Science & Technology, P.O. Box 1758, Pretoria 0001, South Africa. TEL 27-12-3226404. FAX 27-12-3207803. *2262*

SOUTH AFRICAN JOURNAL OF LABOUR RELATIONS.
University of South Africa, Graduate School of Business Leadership, P.O. Box 392, Pretoria 0001, South Africa. TEL 27-11-6520343. FAX 27-11-6520299. *1395*

SOUTH AFRICAN JOURNAL OF LIBRARY AND INFORMATION SCIENCE.
Foundation for Education, Science & Technology, P.O. Box 1758, Pretoria 0001, South Africa. TEL 27-12-3226404. FAX 27-12-3207803. *4028*

SOUTH AFRICAN JOURNAL OF LINGUISTICS.
Foundation for Education, Science & Technology, P.O. Box 1758, Pretoria 0001, South Africa. TEL 27-12-3226404. FAX 27-12-3207803. *4109*

SOUTH AFRICAN JOURNAL OF MARINE SCIENCE.
Sea Fisheries Research Institute, Private Bag X2, Rogge Bay 8012, Cape Town, South Africa. TEL 27-21-4023911. FAX 27-21-252920. *2944*

SOUTH AFRICAN JOURNAL OF MUSIC THERAPY.
Music Therapy Society of Southern Africa, P.O. Box 361, Florida Hills 1716, South Africa. TEL 27-11-672-2111. *5199*

SOUTH AFRICAN JOURNAL OF PHILOSOPHY.
Foundation for Education, Science & Technology, P.O. Box 1758, Pretoria 0001, South Africa. TEL 27-12-3226404. FAX 27-12-3207803. *5499*

SOUTH AFRICAN JOURNAL OF PLANT AND SOIL.
Foundation for Education, Science & Technology, P.O. Box 1758, Pretoria 0001, South Africa. TEL 27-12-3226404. FAX 27-12-3207803. *241*

SOUTH AFRICAN JOURNAL OF PSYCHOLOGY.
Foundation for Education, Science & Technology, P.O. Box 1758, Pretoria 0001, South Africa. TEL 27-12-3226404. FAX 27-12-3207803. *5883*

SOUTH AFRICAN JOURNAL OF SCIENCE.
Foundation for Research Development, P.O. Box 2600, Pretoria 0001, South Africa. TEL 27-12-8414076. FAX 27-12-8042679. *6287*

SOUTH AFRICAN JOURNAL OF ZOOLOGY.
Foundation for Education, Science & Technology, P.O. Box 1758, Pretoria 0001, South Africa. TEL 27-12-3226404. FAX 27-12-3207803. *820*

SOUTH AFRICAN MUSEUM. ANNALS.
South African Museum, P.O. Box 61, Cape Town 8000, South Africa. TEL 27-21-243330. FAX 27-21-246716. *609*

SOUTH AFRICAN PHILATELIST.
Philatelic Federation of Southern Africa, P.O. Box 2789, Cape Town 8000, South Africa. FAX 27-21-238763. *5462*

SOUTH AFRICAN SOCIETY OF PATHOLOGISTS. CONGRESS BROCHURE.
South Africa Society of Pathologists, P.O. Box 2034, Pretoria 0001, South Africa. TEL 27-12-3283600. *4937*

SOUTH AFRICAN VETERINARY ASSOCIATION. SCIENTIFIC JOURNAL.
South African Veterinary Association, P.O. Box 25033, Monument Park, 0105 Pretoria, South Africa. TEL 27-12-3461150. FAX 27-12-3462929. *6954*

SOUTH ASIA: JOURNAL OF SOUTH ASIAN STUDIES.
South Asian Studies Association, c/o Department of History, University of New England, Armidale, N.S.W. 2351, Australia. TEL 61-67-732479. FAX 61-67-733520. *3384*

SOUTH ASIAN ANTHROPOLOGIST.
Sarat Chandra Roy Institute of Anthropological Studies, House No. H I-98, Harmu Housing Colony, Harmu, Ranchi 834 012, Bihar, India. TEL 91-651-307824. *322*

SOUTH ASIAN REVIEW.
South Asian Literary Association, c/o Univ. of North Florida, Jacksonville, FL 32224. TEL 904-646-2580. *4268*

SOUTH ASIAN SOCIAL SCIENTIST.
South Asian Social Scientists Association, Department of Anthropology, University of Madras, Tamil Nadu, Madras 600 025, India. TEL 568778. *5293*

SOUTH ASIAN SURVEY.
Sage Publications India Pvt. Ltd., P.O. Box 4215, New Delhi 110 048, India. TEL 91-11-644-4958. FAX 91-11-647-2426. *3354*

SOUTH CAROLINA HISTORICAL ASSOCIATION. PROCEEDINGS.
South Carolina Historical Association, USCA History Department, 171 University Pkwy., Aiken, SC 29801. TEL 803-641-3223. *3489*

SOUTH CAROLINA MEDICAL ASSOCIATION. JOURNAL.
South Carolina Medical Association, Box 11188, Columbia, SC 29211. TEL 803-798-6207. FAX 803-772-6783. *4532*

SOUTH CENTRAL REVIEW.
South Central Modern Language Association, Department of English, Texas A & M University, College Station, TX 77843-4227. TEL 409-845-7041. FAX 409-862-2292. *4269*

SOUTH DAKOTA JOURNAL OF MEDICINE.
South Dakota State Medical Association, 1323 S. Minnesota Ave., Sioux Falls, SD 57105. TEL 605-336-1965. FAX 605-336-0270. *4533*

SOUTH DAKOTA MUNICIPALITIES.
South Dakota Municipal League, 214 E. Capitol, Pierre, SD 57501. TEL 605-224-8654. FAX 605-224-8655. *5950*

SOUTH EUROPEAN SOCIETY & POLITICS.
Frank Cass, Newbury House, 890-900 Eastern Ave., Newbury Park, Ilford, Essex IG2 7HH, England. TEL 44-181-899-8866. FAX 44-181-599-0984. *5772*

SOUTH INDIA CHURCHMAN.
Church of South India, c/o Christian Literature Society, Box 501, Park Town, Madras 600003, India. TEL 044-852-1566. *5212*

SOUTH EAST ASIA RESEARCH.
In Print Publishing Ltd., 9 Beaufort Terr., Brighton BN2 2SU, England. TEL 44-1273-682836. FAX 44-1273-620958. *5709*

SOUTHEASTERN ASSOCIATION OF FISH AND WILDLIFE AGENCIES. PROCEEDINGS.
Southeastern Association of Fish and Wildlife Agencies, c/o Robert M. Brantly, Exec. Sec., 7221 Covey Trace, Tallahassee, FL 32303. TEL 904-893-1204. *2944*

SOUTHEASTERN GEOGRAPHER.
Association of American Geographers, Southeastern Division, University of Georgia, Department of Geography, Athens, GA 30602. TEL 706-542-2350. FAX 706-542-2388. *3274*

SOUTHEASTERN GEOLOGY.
Duke University, Geology Department, Box 90233, Durham, NC 27708-0233. TEL 919-684-5321. FAX 919-684-5833. *2262*

SOUTHEASTERN POLITICAL REVIEW.
Georgia Southern University, Department of Political Science, Landrum Box 8101, Statesboro, GA 30460-8101. TEL 912-681-5698. FAX 912-764-6466. *5709*

SOUTHERN AFRICA JOURNAL OF MATHEMATICS AND SCIENCE.
University of Botswana, Department of Mathematics and Science Education, Private Bag 0022, Gaborone, Botswana. TEL 267-351151. FAX 267-256591. *4396*

SOUTHERN AFRICAN FIELD ARCHAEOLOGY.
Albany Museum, Somerset St., Grahamstown 6140, South Africa. TEL 27-461-22312. FAX 27-461-22398. *374*

SOUTHERN AFRICAN JOURNAL OF AQUATIC SCIENCES.
Southern African Society of Aquatic Scientists, c/o F.C. de Moor, Albany Museum, Somerset St., Grahamstown 6140. TEL 27-461-22318. FAX 27-461-22398. *609*

SOUTHERN AFRICAN JOURNAL OF EPIDEMIOLOGY AND INFECTION.
P.O. Box 1038, Johannesburg 2000, South Africa. TEL 27-11-4899021. FAX 27-11-4899012. *4665*

SOUTHERN BUSINESS & ECONOMIC JOURNAL.
Auburn University at Montgomery, School of Business, 7300 University Dr., Montgomery, AL 36117-3596. TEL 334-244-3523. FAX 334-244-3792. *961*

SOUTHERN CALIFORNIA ACADEMY OF SCIENCES. BULLETIN.
Southern California Academy of Sciences, 1041 New Hampshire Ave., Box 1897, Lawrence, KS 66044-8897. FAX 913-843-1274. *6288*

SOUTHERN CALIFORNIA QUARTERLY.
Historical Society of Southern California, 200 East Ave., No. 43, Los Angeles, CA 90031. TEL 213-222-0546. *3488*

THE SOUTHERN COLLEGIATE ACCOUNTANT.
Savannah State College, School of Business, Box 20359, Savannah, GA 31404. TEL 912-927-9560. FAX 912-356-2874. *1055*

SOUTHERN ECONOMIC JOURNAL.
University of North Carolina at Chapel Hill, Southern Economic Association, 300 Hanes Hall, CB 3540, Chapel Hill, NC 27514. TEL 919-966-5261. FAX 919-932-5469. *961*

SOUTHERN FOLKLORE.
University Press of Kentucky, 663 S. Limestone St., Lexington, KY 40508-4008. TEL 606-257-8439. FAX 606-257-2984. *2956*

SOUTHERN HISTORY.
Southern History Society, c/o R.A.E. Wells, Ed., Department of History, Christ Church College, Canterbury CT1 1QU, England. TEL 44-1227-767700. FAX 01273-643128. *3445*

SOUTHERN ILLINOIS UNIVERSITY LAW JOURNAL.
Southern Illinois University at Carbondale, School of Law, Lesar Law Bldg., Carbondale, IL 62901. TEL 618-453-8721. FAX 618-453-8769. *3850*

SOUTHERN JOURNAL OF APPLIED FORESTRY.
Society of American Foresters, 5400 Grosvenor Ln., Bethesda, MD 20814. TEL 301-897-8720. FAX 301-897-3690. *3025*

SOUTHERN JOURNAL OF OPTOMETRY.
Southern Council of Optometrists, 4661 N. Shallowford Rd., Atlanta, GA 30338. TEL 404-451-8206. FAX 770-451-3156. *4778*

SOUTHERN LITERARY JOURNAL.
University of North Carolina Press, Box 2288, Chapel Hill, NC 27515-2288. TEL 919-966-3561. FAX 800-272-6817. *4269*

SOUTHERN MEDICAL JOURNAL.
Southern Medical Association, 35 Lakeshore Dr., Box 190088, Birmingham, AL 35219-0088. TEL 205-945-1840. FAX 205-945-1548. *4533*

SOUTHERN ORTHOPAEDIC ASSOCIATION. JOURNAL.
Southern Orthopaedic Association, 35 Lake Shore Dr., Box 190088, Birmingham, AL 35219-0088. FAX 205-945-1548. *4791*

SOUTHERN POETRY REVIEW.
Central Piedmont Community College, Charlotte, NC 28235. *4320*

SOUTHERN STARS.
Royal Astronomical Society of New Zealand (Inc.), P.O. Box 3181, Wellington, New Zealand. TEL 64-4-472-8167. FAX 64-4-472-8320. *487*

SOUTHERN STUDIES.
Northwestern State University of Louisiana, Southern Studies Institute, Natchitoches, LA 71497. TEL 318-357-5507. FAX 318-357-6153. *6347*

SOUTHWEST JOURNAL OF LINGUISTICS.
University of North Texas and Linguistics Association of the Southwest, University of North Texas, Department of English, Denton, TX 76203-3827. TEL 505-277-7416. FAX 505-277-6355. *4110*

SOUTHWEST JOURNAL ON AGING.
Southwest Society on Aging, University of North Texas, Box 13438, Denton, TX 76203. TEL 817-565-2823. FAX 817-565-4914. *3297*

SOUTHWEST PHILOSOPHY REVIEW. JOURNAL.
Southwestern Philosophical Society, Department of Philoshy, Wittenberg Univ., Box 720, Springfield, OH 45501-0720. *5499*

SOUTHWESTERN ENTOMOLOGIST.
Southwestern Entomological Society, 17360 Coit Rd., Dallas, TX 75252. TEL 214-952-9222. *735*

SOUTHWESTERN ENTOMOLOGIST. SUPPLEMENT.
Southwestern Entomological Society, 17360 Coit Rd., Dallas, TX 75252. TEL 214-952-9222. *735*

SOUTHWESTERN MASS COMMUNICATION JOURNAL.
Southwest Education Council for Journalism and Mass Communication, P.O. Box 1930, Arkansas State University, State University, AR 72467. *3711*

SOUTHWESTERN NATURALIST.
Southwestern Association of Naturalists, c/o Dr. Paula Williamson, Treas., Biology Department, Southwest Texas State University, 601 University Dr., San Marcos, TX 78666. TEL 512-245-2178. FAX 512-245-8095. *6288*

SOUTHWESTERN STUDIES. MONOGRAPHS.
Texas Western Press, University of Texas at El Paso, El Paso, TX 79968-0633. TEL 915-747-5688. FAX 915-747-7515. *3489*

SOVIET AND POST SOVIET REVIEW.
Charles Schlacks Jr., Publisher, c/o University of California, CMTS, GFS 344, Los Angeles, CA 90089-1694. FAX 213-740-5810. *3445*

SOVIET SCIENTIFIC REVIEWS. SECTION F: PHYSIOLOGY AND GENERAL BIOLOGY REVIEWS.
Harwood Academic Publishers, P.O. Box 3054, Langhorne, PA 19047-3054. TEL 215-750-2642. FAX 215-750-6343. *794*

SOVIET SCIENTIFIC REVIEWS SUPPLEMENT SERIES. SECTION C: PHYSICOCHEMICAL BIOLOGY.
Harwood Academic Publishers, c/o International Publishers Distributor, P.O. Box 3054, Langhorne, PA 19047-3054. TEL 215-750-2642. FAX 215-750-6343. *649*

SOVIET STUDIES.
Harwood Academic Publishers, c/o International Publishers Distributor, P.O. Box 3054, Langhorne, PA 19047-3054. TEL 215-750-2642. FAX 215-750-6343. *6435*

SOVIETICA. PUBLICATIONS AND MONOGRAPHS.
Kluwer Academic Publishers, Postbus 17, 3300 AA Dordrecht, Netherlands. TEL 31-78-6392392. FAX 31-78-6392254. *3445*

SOW'S EAR POETRY REVIEW.
19535 Pleasant View Dr., Abingdon, VA 24211-6827. TEL 540-628-2651. *4320*

SPACE FORUM.
Harwood Academic Publishers, c/o International Publishers Distributor, P.O. Box 3054, Langhorne, PA 19047-3054. TEL 215-750-2642. FAX 215-750-6343. *78*

SPACE POLICY.
Butterworth - Heinemann, Part of the Reed Elsevier group, Linacre House, Jordan Hill, Oxford OX2 8DP, England. TEL 44-1865-310366. FAX 44-1865-310898. *78*

SPACE SCIENCE REVIEWS.
Kluwer Academic Publishers, Postbus 17, 3300 AA Dordrecht, Netherlands. TEL 31-78-6392392. FAX 31-78-6392254. *487*

SPACE TECHNOLOGY.
Elsevier Science Ltd., Pergamon, P.O. Box 800, Kidlington, Oxford OX5 1DX, England. TEL 44-1865-843000. FAX 44-1865-843010. *6664*

SPACE TECHNOLOGY LIBRARY.
Kluwer Academic Publishers, Postbus 17, 3300 AA Dordrecht, Netherlands. TEL 31-78-6392392. FAX 31-78-6392254. *78*

SPAN.
South Pacific Association for Commonwealth Literature and Language Studies, University of Waikato, Dept. of English, Private Bag 3105, Hamilton, New Zealand. *4269*

SPANISH YEARBOOK OF INTERNATIONAL LAW.
Martinus Nijhoff Publishers, Human Rights and International Law Postbus 163, 3300 AD Dordrecht, Netherlands. TEL 31-78-334911. FAX 31-78-334254. *3942*

SPATIAL VISION.
V S P, P.O. Box 346, 3700 AH Zeist, Netherlands. TEL 31-30-6925790. FAX 31-30-6932081. *4412*

SPECIAL ASPECTS OF EDUCATION.
Gordon & Breach Science Publishers, c/o International Publishers Distributor, P.O. Box 3054, Langhorne, PA 19047-3054. TEL 215-750-2642. FAX 215-750-6343. *2373*

SPECIAL CARE IN DENTISTRY.
Federation of Special Care Organizations in Dentistry, 211 E. Chicago Ave., Chicago, IL 60611. TEL 312-440-2661. *4654*

SPECIAL SERVICES IN THE SCHOOLS.
Haworth Press, Inc., 10 Alice St., Binghamton, NY 13904. TEL 607-722-5857. FAX 607-722-1424. *2475*

SPECIAL TOPICS IN SUPERCOMPUTING.
Elsevier Science B.V., Books Division, P.O. Box 211, 1000 AE Amsterdam, Netherlands. TEL 31-20-4853911. FAX 31-20-4853705. *2059*

SPECIALIST.
Doctor Publications (Pvt) Ltd., P.O. Box 8766, Raja Ghazanfar Ali Rd., Saddar, Karachi, Pakistan. TEL 92-21-5688791. FAX 92-21-5689860. *4533*

LO SPECIALISTA.
Ansid - Edit s.r.l., Viale Monte Ceneri 58, 20155 Milan, Italy. TEL 39-2-33003971. FAX 39-2-39215800. *6801*

SPECIFIER REPORTS.
Rensselaer Polytechnic Institute, Lighting Research Center, Greene Bldg., Rm. 115, Troy, NY 12180-3590. TEL 518-276-8716. FAX 518-276-2999. *874*

SPECTROCHIMICA ACTA. PART A: MOLECULAR AND BIOMOLECULAR SPECTROSCOPY.
Elsevier Science B.V., P.O. Box 211, 1000 AE Amsterdam, Netherlands. TEL 31-20-4853911. FAX 31-20-4853598. *1721*

SPECTROCHIMICA ACTA. PART B: ATOMIC SPECTROSCOPY.
Elsevier Science B.V., P.O. Box 211, 1000 AE Amsterdam, Netherlands. TEL 31-20-4853911. FAX 31-20-4853598. *1721*

SPECTROSCOPY.
I O S Press, Van Diemenstraat 94, 1013 CN Amsterdam, Netherlands. TEL 31-20-6382189. FAX 31-20-6203419. *649*

SPECTROSCOPY LETTERS.
Marcel Dekker Journals, 270 Madison Ave., New York, NY 10016. TEL 212-696-9000. FAX 212-685-4540. *5612*

SPECTRUM (GREENBELT).
National Association of Black Accountants, 7249A Hanover Pkwy, Greenbelt, MD 20770-3653. TEL 301-474-6222. *1055*

SPECULATIONS IN SCIENCE AND TECHNOLOGY.
Chapman & Hall, Journals Department 2-6 Boundary Row, London SE1 8HN, England. TEL 44-171-8560066. FAX 44-171-5229623. *6288*

SPEECH AND DRAMA.
Society of Teachers of Speech and Drama, 4 Fane Rd., Oxford OX3 0SA, England. TEL 44-1865-728304. *6703*

SPEECH COMMUNICATION.
North-Holland P.O. Box 211, 1000 AE Amsterdam, Netherlands. TEL 31-20-4853911. FAX 31-20-4853598. *4110*

SPEEDHORSE - RACING REPORT.
Speedhorse, Inc., Box 1000, Norman, OK 73070-1000. TEL 405-573-1050. FAX 405-573-1059. *6552*

SPEKTRUM DER AUGENHEILKUNDE.
Springer-Verlag, Sachsenplatz 4-6, P.O. Box 89, A-1201 Vienna, Austria. TEL 43-1-3302415. FAX 43-1-3302415. *4778*

SPILL SCIENCE & TECHNOLOGY BULLETIN.
Elsevier Science Ltd., Pergamon, P.O. Box 800, Kidlington, Oxford OX5 1DX, England. TEL 44-1865-843000. FAX 44-1865-843010. *2840*

SPILL TECHNOLOGY NEWSLETTER.
Environment Canada, Technology Development and Technical Services Branch, Ottawa, ON K1A 0H3, Canada. TEL 613-990-7297. *6288*

SPINAL CORD INJURY LIFE.
National Spinal Cord Injury Association, 545 Concord Ave., No. 29, Cambridge, MA 02138-1122. TEL 617-935-2722. *3316*

SPINE (PHILADELPHIA, 1986).
Hanley & Belfus, Inc., 210 S. 13th St., Philadelphia, PA 19107. TEL 215-546-7293. FAX 215-790-9330. *4792*

SPOON RIVER POETRY REVIEW.
Illinois State University, Unit for Contemporary Literature, Normal, IL 61790-4241. TEL 309-438-7906. *4320*

SPORT HISTORY REVIEW.
University of Windsor, Faculty of Human Kinetics, Windsor, ON N9B 3P4, Canada. TEL 519-253-4232. *6483*

SPORT MARKETING QUARTERLY.
Fitness Information Technology Inc., Box 4425, University Ave., Morgantown, WV 26504-4425. TEL 304-599-3482. FAX 304-599-3482. *6483*

THE SPORT PSYCHOLOGIST.
Human Kinetics Publishers, Inc., Box 5076, Champaign, IL 61825-5076. TEL 217-351-5076. FAX 217-351-2674. *5883*

SPORT SCIENCE REVIEW.
Human Kinetics Publishers, Inc., Box 5076, Champaign, IL 61825-5076. TEL 217-351-5076. FAX 217-351-3674. *4900*

SPORTPARACHUTIST.
Koninklijke Nederlandse Vereniging voor Luchtvaart, Afdeling Parachutespringen, Jozef Israelsplein 8, 2596 AS The Hague, Netherlands. TEL 31-70-3245457. FAX 31-70-3240230. *6578*

THE SPORTS HISTORIAN.
British Society of Sports History, c/o Benny J. Peiser, Membership Sec., Dept. of Human Sciences, Liverpool John Moores Univ., Byrom St., Liverpool L3 3AF, England. *6485*

SPORTS MEDICINE.
Adis International Limited, Private Bag 65901, Mairangi Bay, Auckland 10, New Zealand. TEL 64-9-479-8100. FAX 64-9-479-8145. *4900*

SPORTS MEDICINE IN PRIMARY CARE.
Phys Ed Fitness Ltd., Box 717, Decatur, GA 30031-0717. TEL 404-377-0300. FAX 404-377-0604. *4901*

SPORTS MEDICINE, TRAINING AND REHABILITATION.
Harwood Academic Publishers, c/o International Publishers Distributor, P.O. Box 3054, Langhorne, PA 19047-3054. TEL 215-750-2642. FAX 215-750-6343. *4901*

SPRAAK OCH STIL.
Adolf Noreen-saellskapet foer Svensk Spraak- och Stilforskning, PO Box 513, S-751 20 Uppsala, Sweden. TEL 46-18-18-12-82. FAX 46-18-18-12-72. *4110*

SPRING JOURNAL.
Box 583, Putnam, CT 06260. TEL 203-974-3428. FAX 203-974-3195. *5883*

SPRINGFIELD PARENT.
Box 4732, Springfield, MO 65808. TEL 417-869-9800. FAX 417-831-5471. *1778*

SPRINGS.
Spring Manufacturers Institute, Inc., 2001 Midwest Rd., Ste. 106, Oak Brook, IL 60521-1335. TEL 708-495-8588. FAX 708-495-8595. *2769*

SPUR.
World Development Movement, 25 Beehive Pl., London SW9 7QR, England. TEL 44-171-737-6215. FAX 44-171-274-8232. *1315*

SRI VENKATESWARA UNIVERSITY. ORIENTAL JOURNAL.
Sri Venkateswara University, Oriental Research Institute, Tirupati 517502, District Chittoor, India. TEL 91-8574-24166. FAX 91-8574-24111. *3385*

STADLER GENETICS SYMPOSIUM. PROCEEDINGS.
Plenum Publishing Corp., 233 Spring St., New York, NY 10013-1578. TEL 212-620-8000. FAX 212-463-0742. *750*

STAFFORDSHIRE ARCHAEOLOGICAL AND HISTORICAL SOCIETY. TRANSACTIONS.
Staffordshire Archaeological and Historical Society, William Salt Library, Eastgate St., Stafford ST16 2LZ, England. *374*

STANDARDS ACTIVITIES OF ORGANIZATIONS IN THE U.S.
U.S. National Institute of Standards and Technology, Gaithersburg, MD 20899. TEL 301-975-3058. *5018*

STANFORD NURSE.
Stanford Health Services, Division of Patient Care Services, Center for Education and Professional Development, 300 Pasteur Dr., Ste. NOB, Stanford, CA 94305. *4728*

STATE FORESTS OF NEW SOUTH WALES. FOREST RESEARCH AND DEVELOPMENT DIVISION. RESEARCH PAPERS.
State Forests of New South Wales, Forest Research and Development Division, 121-131 Oratava Ave., W. Pennant Hills, N.S.W. 2125, Australia. TEL 61-2-8720111. FAX 61-2-8716941. *3026*

STATEMENT (FORT COLLINS).
Colorado Language Arts Society, Co. State Univ., English Dept., Eddy Bldg., Fort Collins, CO 80523. TEL 303-491-5264. FAX 303-491-5601. *2502*

STATISTICA NEERLANDICA.
Blackwell Publishers Ltd., 108 Cowley Rd., Oxford OX4 1JF, England. TEL 44-1865-791100. FAX 44-1865-791347. *6634*

STATISTICAL AND SOCIAL INQUIRY SOCIETY OF IRELAND. JOURNAL.
Statistical and Social Inquiry Society of Ireland, c/o Central Statistics Office, Ardee Rd., Rathmines, Dublin 6, Ireland. TEL 01-4977144. FAX 01-4972360. *6634*

STATISTICAL SCIENCE.
Institute of Mathematical Statistics, 3401 Investment Blvd., Ste. 7, Hayward, CA 94545-3819. TEL 510-783-8141. FAX 510-783-4131. *6635*

THE STATISTICIAN.
Blackwell Publishers Ltd., 108 Cowley Rd., Oxford OX4 1DF, England. TEL 44-1865-791100. FAX 44-1865-791347. *6636*

STATISTICS.
Gordon & Breach Science Publishers, c/o International Publishers Distributor, P.O. Box 3054, Langhorne, PA 19047-3054. TEL 215-750-2642. FAX 215-750-6343. *6636*

STATISTICS AND COMPUTING.
Chapman & Hall Journals Department 2-6 Boundary Row, London SE1 8HN, England. TEL 44-171-8650066. FAX 44-171-5229623. *6636*

STATISTICS & PROBABILITY LETTERS.
North-Holland P.O. Box 211, 1000 AE Amsterdam, Netherlands. TEL 31-20-4853911. FAX 31-20-4853598. *6636*

STATISTICS IN MEDICINE.
John Wiley & Sons Ltd., Journals, Baffins Ln., Chichester, W. Sussex PO19 1UD, England. TEL 44-1243-779777. FAX 44-1243-843232. *4575*

STATUTES AND DECISIONS: THE LAWS OF THE U S S R & ITS SUCCESSOR STATES.
M.E. Sharpe, Inc., 80 Business Park Dr., Armonk, NY 10504. TEL 914-273-1300. FAX 914-273-2106. *3853*

STEEL INDIA.
Steel Authority of India Ltd. R & D Centre for Iron & Steel, Ranchi 834 002, India. FAX 0651-300023. *4975*

STEINE SPRECHEN.
Oesterreichische Gesellschaft fuer Denkmal und Ortsbildpflege, Karlsplatz 5, A-1010 Vienna, Austria. TEL 43-1-587-96630. FAX 43-1-5232374. *2142*

STEM CELLS.
AlphaMed Press, Inc., 410C S. Kettering Blvd., Dayton, OH 45439-2092. TEL 513-293-8508. FAX 513-293-7652. *771*

STEPHEN CRANE STUDIES.
Virginia Polytechnic Institute and State University, Department of English, Blacksburg, VA 24061-0112. TEL 540-231-5932. FAX 540-231-5692. *4320*

STEREOCHEMISTRY OF ORGANOMETALLIC AND INORGANIC COMPOUNDS.
Elsevier Science B.V., Books Division, P.O. Box 211, 1000 AE Amsterdam, Netherlands. TEL 31-20-4853911. FAX 31-20-4853705. *1721*

STEREOTACTIC AND FUNCTIONAL NEUROSURGERY.
S. Karger AG, Allschwilerstr 10, P.O. Box, CH-4009 Basel, Switzerland. TEL 061-3061111. FAX 061-3061234. *4920*

STEROIDS.
Elsevier Science Inc., Box 945, New York, NY 10159-0945. TEL 212-633-3730. FAX 212-633-3680. *650*

STOCHASTIC ANALYSIS AND APPLICATIONS.
Marcel Dekker Journals, 270 Madison Ave., New York, NY 10016. TEL 212-696-9000. FAX 212-685-4540. *4397*

STOCHASTIC PROCESSES AND THEIR APPLICATIONS.
North-Holland P.O. Box 211, 1000 AE Amsterdam, Netherlands. TEL 31-20-4853911. FAX 31-20-4853598. *4397*

STOCHASTICS AND STOCHASTICS REPORTS.
Gordon and Breach Science Publishers, c/o International Publishers Distributor, P.O. Box 3054, Langhorne, PA 19047-3054. TEL 215-750-2642. FAX 215-750-6343. *4397*

STOCHASTICS MONOGRAPHS.
Gordon & Breach Science Publishers, c/o International Publishers Distributor, P.O. Box 3054, Langhorne, PA 19047-3054. TEL 215-750-2642. FAX 215-750-6343. *4397*

STOCHASTIK IN DER SCHULE.
Verein zur Foerderung des Schulischen Statistikunterrichts e.V., Kammannstr. 13, 58097 Hagen, Germany. *6637*

STRABISMUS.
Aeolus Press Postbus 740, 4116 ZJ Buren, Netherlands. TEL 31-344-52055. FAX 31-344-572562. *4778*

STRATEGIC AND DEFENCE STUDIES CENTRE. WORKING PAPERS.
Strategic and Defence Studies Centre, Australian National University, Canberra, A.C.T. 0200, Australia. TEL 61-6-2438537. FAX 61-6-2480815. *5049*

STRATEGIC MANAGEMENT JOURNAL.
John Wiley & Sons Ltd., Journals, Baffins Ln., Chichester, W. Sussex PO19 1UD, England. TEL 44-1243-779777. FAX 44-1243-843232. *1446*

STRENGTH OF MATERIALS.
Plenum Publishing Corp., Consultants Bureau, 233 Spring St., New York, NY 10013-1578. TEL 212-620-8468. FAX 212-463-0742. *2741*

STRESS AND EMOTION.
Taylor & Francis, 1900 Frost Rd., Ste. 101, Bristol, PA 19007-1598. TEL 215-785-5800. FAX 215-785-5515. *5883*

STRESS MEDICINE.
John Wiley & Sons Ltd., Journals, Baffins Ln., Chichester, W. Sussex PO19 1UD, England. TEL 44-1243-779777. FAX 44-1243-843232. *4869*

STRIAE.
Societas Upsaliensis, Institute of Earth Sciences, Quaternary Geology, Norbyvaegen 18 B, S-752 36 Uppsala, Sweden. TEL 46-18-18-25-00. FAX 46-18-18-25-91. *2263*

STRIOLAE.
Societas Upsaliensis, Institute of Earth Sciences, Quaternary Geology, Norbyvaegen 18 B, S-752 36 Uppsala, Sweden. TEL 46-18-18-25-00. FAX 46-18-18-25-91. *2263*

STROKE.
American Heart Association, 7272 Greenville Ave., Dallas, TX 75231-4596. TEL 214-706-1310. FAX 214-691-6342. *4609*

STRUCTURAL CHANGE AND ECONOMIC DYNAMICS.
Elsevier Science B.V., P.O. Box 211, 1000 AE Amsterdam, Netherlands. TEL 31-20-4853911. FAX 31-20-4853598. *1261*

STRUCTURAL CHEMISTRY.
Plenum Publishing Corp., 233 Spring St., New York, NY 10013-1578. FAX 212-463-0742. *1693*

STRUCTURAL DESIGN OF TALL BUILDINGS.
John Wiley & Sons Ltd., Journals, Baffins Ln., Chichester, W. Sussex PO19 1UD, England. TEL 44-1243-779777. FAX 44-1243-843232. *2673*

STRUCTURAL ENGINEER.
Structural Engineers Trading Organisation Ltd., 11 Upper Belgrave St., London SW1X 8BH, England. TEL 44-171-235-4535. FAX 44-171-235-4294. *2673*

STRUCTURAL ENGINEERING REVIEW.
Elsevier Science Ltd., Pergamon, P.O. Box 800, Kidlington, Oxford OX5 1DX, England. TEL 44-1865-843000. FAX 44-1865-843010. *2673*

STRUCTURAL SAFETY.
Elsevier Science B.V., P.O. Box 211, 1000 AE Amsterdam, Netherlands. TEL 31-20-4853911. FAX 31-20-4853598. *2674*

STRUCTURE.
Current Biology Ltd., 400 Market St., Ste. 700, Philadelphia, PA 19106. FAX 215-574-2270. *609*

STRUCTURE REPORTS. SECTION A: METALS AND INORGANIC COMPOUNDS.
Kluwer Academic Publishers, Postbus 17, 3300 AA Dordrecht, Netherlands. TEL 31-78-6392392. FAX 31-78-6392254. *1727*

THE STUDEBAKER FAMILY.
Studebaker Family National Association, 6555 S. State Rt. 202, Tipp City, OH 45371-9444. TEL 513-667-4451. FAX 513-667-9322. *3103*

STUDI BRESCIANI.
Fondazione Luigi Micheletti, Via Cairoli 9, 25122 Brescia, Italy. TEL 39-30-48578. FAX 39-30-45203. *3446*

STUDI PIEMONTESI.
Centro Studi Piemontesi, Via O. Revel 15, 10121 Turin, Italy. TEL 39-11-537486. FAX 39-11-534777. *4271*

STUDIA AD CORPUS HELLENISTICUM NOVI TESTAMENTI.
E.J. Brill, P.O. Box 9000, 2300 PA Leiden, Netherlands. TEL 31-71-5353500. FAX 31-71-5317532. *6095*

STUDIA BIBLICA.
E.J. Brill, P.O. Box 9000, 2300 PA Leiden, Netherlands. TEL 31-71-5353500. FAX 31-71-5317532. *6095*

STUDIA CANONICA.
Saint Paul University, Faculty of Canon Law, 223 Main St., Ottawa, ON K1S 1C4, Canada. TEL 613-236-1393. FAX 613-782-3005. *6095*

STUDIA COPERNICANA - BRILL SERIES.
E.J. Brill, P.O. Box 9000, 2300 PA Leiden, Netherlands. TEL 31-71-5353500. FAX 31-71-5317532. *487*

STUDIA CROATICA.
Instituto Croata Latinoamericano de Cultura, Zapata 234-3E, 1426 Buenos Aires, Argentina. TEL 54-1-771-4954. *2909*

STUDIA ET DOCUMENTA AD IURA ORIENTIS ANTIQUI PERTINENTIA.
E.J. Brill, P.O. Box 9000, 2300 PA Leiden, Netherlands. TEL 31-71-5353500. FAX 31-71-5317532. *5293*

STUDIA FORESTALIA SUECICA.
Swedish University of Agricultural Sciences, Research Information Centre, Box 7057, S-750 07 Uppsala, Sweden. FAX 46-18-67-35-20. *3026*

STUDIA GEOLOGICA POLONICA.
Polska Akademia Nauk, Instytut Nauk Geologicznych, Al. Zwirki i Wigury 93, 02-089 Warsaw, Poland. TEL 48-22-221065. FAX 48-22-221065. *2263*

STUDIA GEOPHYSICA ET GEODAETICA.
Plenum Publishing Corp., 233 Spring St., New York, NY 10013-1578. TEL 212-620-8000. FAX 212-463-0742. *2282*

STUDIA HISTORICA SEPTENTRIONALIA.
Pohjois-Suomen Historiallinen Yhdistys, Oulun Yliopisto, Historian Laitos, Postilokero 111, FIN-90571 Oulu, Finland. FAX 358-81-553-33-15. *3447*

STUDIA HUMANITATIS.
E.J. Brill, P.O. Box 9000, 2300 PA Leiden, Netherlands. TEL 31-71-5353500. FAX 31-71-5317532. *3447*

STUDIA IMAGOLOGICA.
Editions Rodopi B.V., Keizersgracht 302-304, 1016 EX Amsterdam, Netherlands. TEL 31-20-6227507. FAX 31-20-6380948. *4271*

STUDIA IN VETERIS TESTAMENTI PSEUDEPIGRAPHA.
E.J. Brill, P.O. Box 9000, 2300 PA Leiden, Netherlands. TEL 31-71-5353500. FAX 31-71-5317532. *6095*

STUDIA LINGUISTICA.
Blackwell Publishers Ltd., 108 Cowley Rd., Oxford OX4 1JF, England. TEL 44-1865-791100. FAX 44-1865-791347. *4112*

STUDIA LITURGICA.
Societas Liturgica, Box 597, Notre Dame, IN 46556. *6095*

STUDIA LOGICA.
Kluwer Academic Publishers, Postbus 17, 3300 AA Dordrecht, Netherlands. TEL 31-78-6392392. FAX 31-78-6392254. *5500*

STUDIA MATHEMATICA.
Polska Akademia Nauk, Instytut Matematyczny, Dzial Wydawnictw, Ul. Sniadeckich 8, P.O. Box 137, 00-950 Warsaw, Poland. TEL 48-22-6282471. FAX 48-22-6293997. *4397*

STUDIA MORALIA.
Editiones Academiae Alfonsianae, Via Merulana 31, C.P. 2458, 00100 Rome, Italy. FAX 39-6-4465887. *6095*

STUDIA MUSICOLOGICA NORVEGICA.
Scandinavian University Press, P.O. Box 2959 Toeyen, NO-0608 Oslo, Norway. *5200*

STUDIA ORIENTALIA LUNDENSIA.
Lund University Press, P.O. Box 141, S-221 00 Lund, Sweden. TEL 46-46-31-20-00. FAX 46-46-30-53-38. *5294*

STUDIA SILENSIA.
Abadia de Santo Domingo de Silos, Libreria de la Abadia, 09610 Burgos, Spain. TEL 34-47-390068. FAX 34-47-390033. *6095*

STUDIA Z FILOLOGII POLSKIEJ I SLOWIANSKIEJ.
Polska Akademia Nauk, Instytut Slawisyki, Al. Ujazdowskie 18, m.16, 00-478 Warsaw, Poland. TEL 48-22-6243729. FAX 48-22-6290075. *4113*

STUDIEN UND TEXTE ZUR GEISTESGESCHICHTE DES MITTELALTERS.
E.J. Brill, P.O. Box 9000, 2300 PA Leiden, Netherlands. TEL 31-71-5353500. FAX 31-71-5317532. *5500*

STUDIEN ZUR KINDERPSYCHOANALYSE. JAHRBUCH.
Oesterreichische Studiengesellschaft fuer Kinderpsychoanalyse, Robert-Bosch-Breite 6, 37079 Goettingen, Germany. TEL 49-551-6959-0. FAX 49-551-695917. *5884*

STUDIEN ZUR PROBLEMGESCHICHTE DER ANTIKEN UND MITTELALTERLICHEN PHILOSOPHIE.
E.J. Brill, P.O. Box 9000, 2300 PA Leiden, Netherlands. TEL 31-71-5353500. FAX 31-71-5317532. *5500*

STUDIES AND RESEARCHES IN VETERINARY MEDICINE.
Pasteur National Institute of Veterinary Medicine, 333 Giulesti Rd., 77826 Bucharest 6, Rumania. TEL 40-1-2206920. FAX 40-1-2206915. *6954*

STUDIES IN AMERICAN FICTION.
Northeastern University, Department of English, Boston, MA 02115. TEL 617-437-3687. *4272*

STUDIES IN AMERICAN HUMOR.
American Humor Studies Association (New Haven), c/o Joseph Alvarez, Sec., Box 35009, Central Piedmont Community College, Charlotte, NC 28235-5009. *4168*

STUDIES IN AMERICAN JEWISH LITERATURE.
Studies in American Jewish Literature, Inc., 117 Burrowes Bldg., University Park, PA 16802. TEL 814-863-3753. FAX 814-863-7285. *2909*

STUDIES IN ANALYTICAL CHEMISTRY.
Elsevier Science B.V., Books Division, P.O. Box 211, 1000 AE Amsterdam, Netherlands. TEL 31-20-4853911. FAX 31-20-4853705. *1721*

STUDIES IN ANCIENT MEDICINE.
E.J. Brill, P.O. Box 9000, 2300 PA Leiden, Netherlands. TEL 31-71-5353500. FAX 31-71-5317532. *4534*

STUDIES IN ANTHROPOLOGY AND HISTORY.
Harwood Academic Publishers, c/o International Publishers Distributor, PO. Box 3054, Langhorne, PA 19047-3054. TEL 215-750-2642. FAX 215-750-6343. *3360*

STUDIES IN APPLIED ELECTROMAGNETICS AND MECHANICS.
I O S Press, Van Diemenstraat 94, 1013 CN Amsterdam, Netherlands. TEL 31-20-6382189. FAX 31-20-6203419. *2720*

STUDIES IN APPLIED MATHEMATICS (CAMBRIDGE).
Blackwell Publishers, 238 Main St., Cambridge, MA 02142. TEL 617-547-7110. *4397*

STUDIES IN APPLIED MECHANICS.
Elsevier Science B.V., Books Division, P.O. Box 211, 1000 AE Amsterdam, Netherlands. TEL 31-20-4853911. FAX 31-20-4853705. *5592*

STUDIES IN ARABIC LITERATURE.
E.J. Brill, P.O. Box 9000, 2300 PA Leiden, Netherlands. TEL 31-71-5353500. FAX 31-71-5317532. *4272*

STUDIES IN ASIAN ART AND ARCHAEOLOGY.
E.J. Brill, P.O. Box 9000, 2300 PA Leiden, Netherlands. TEL 31-71-5353500. FAX 31-71-5317532. *5294*

STUDIES IN ASTRONAUTICS.
Elsevier Science B.V., Books Division, P.O. Box 211, 1000 AE Amsterdam, Netherlands. TEL 31-20-4853911. FAX 31-20-4853705. *79*

STUDIES IN AUSTRIAN ECONOMICS.
Kluwer Academic Publishers, Postbus 17, 3300 AA Dordrecht, Netherlands. TEL 31-78-6392392. FAX 31-78-6392254. *1261*

STUDIES IN AUTOMATION AND CONTROL.
Elsevier Science B.V., Books Division, P.O. Box 211, 1000 AE Amsterdam, Netherlands. TEL 31-20-4853911. FAX 31-20-4853705. *2018*

STUDIES IN AVIAN BIOLOGY.
Cooper Ornithological Society, Inc. (Riverside), Department of Biology, University of California at Riverside, Riverside, CA 92521. FAX 909-787-4286. *781*

STUDIES IN BAYESIAN ECONOMETRICS AND STATISTICS.
Elsevier Science B.V., Books Division, P.O. Box 211, 1000 AE Amsterdam, Netherlands. TEL 31-20-4853911. FAX 31-20-4853705. *1261*

STUDIES IN BILINGUALISM.
John Benjamins Publishing Co., Amsteldijk 44, P.O. Box 75577, 1070 AN Amsterdam, Netherlands. TEL 31-20-6738156. FAX 31-20-6792956. *4114*

STUDIES IN BUSINESS AND SOCIETY.
University of Chicago Press, 5801 S. Ellis Ave., Chicago, IL 60637. TEL 312-702-7899. *962*

STUDIES IN CENTRAL AND EAST ASIAN RELIGIONS.
Seminar for Buddhist Studies, 11 Hallandsgade, I.TV, 2300 Copenhagen S., Denmark. TEL 45-35-32-25-96. FAX 45-35-32-25-95. *6111*

STUDIES IN CHRISTIAN MISSION.
E.J. Brill, P.O. Box 9000, 2300 PA Leiden, Netherlands. TEL 31-71-5353500. FAX 31-71-5317532. *6096*

STUDIES IN COMPARATIVE ECONOMIC POLICIES.
Elsevier Science B.V., Books Division, P.O. Box 211, 1000 AE Amsterdam, Netherlands. TEL 31-20-4853911. FAX 31-20-4853705. *1261*

STUDIES IN COMPARATIVE LITERATURE (CHAPEL HILL).
University of North Carolina Press, Box 2288, Chapel Hill, NC 27515-2288. TEL 919-966-3561. FAX 919-966-3829. *4272*

STUDIES IN COMPUTATIONAL MATHEMATICS.
Elsevier Science B.V., Books Division, P.O. Box 211, 1000 AE Amsterdam, Netherlands. TEL 31-20-4853911. FAX 31-20-4853705. *4398*

STUDIES IN COMPUTER AND COMMUNICATIONS SYSTEMS.
I O S Press, Van Diemenstraat 94, 1013 CN Amsterdam, Netherlands. TEL 31-20-6382189. FAX 31-20-6203419. *1929*

STUDIES IN COMPUTER SCIENCE AND ARTIFICIAL INTELLIGENCE.
Elsevier Science B.V., Books Division, P.O. Box 211, 1000 AE Amsterdam, Netherlands. TEL 31-20-4853911. FAX 31-20-4853705. *2011*

STUDIES IN CONFLICT AND TERRORISM.
Taylor & Francis Inc., 1900 Frost Rd., Ste. 101, Bristol, PA 19007. TEL 215-785-5800. FAX 215-785-5515. *5773*

STUDIES IN CONSERVATION.
International Institute for Conservation of Historic and Artistic Works, 6 Buckingham St., London WC2N 6BA, England. TEL 44-171-839-5975. FAX 44-171-976-1564. *454*

STUDIES IN CONTEMPORARY HISTORY.
Kluwer Academic Publishers, Postbus 17, 3300 AA Dordrecht, Netherlands. TEL 31-78-6392392. FAX 31-78-6392254. *3448*

STUDIES IN CYBERNETICS.
Gordon & Breach Science Publishers, c/o International Publishers Distributor, P.O. Box 3054, Langhorne, PA 19047-3054. TEL 215-750-2642. FAX 215-750-6343. *2063*

STUDIES IN DANCE HISTORY.
A Cappella Books, Inc., 106 W. Franklin Ave., 814 N. Franklin St., Chicago, IL 60610-3109. TEL 609-737-6525. FAX 609-737-3787. *2191*

STUDIES IN DEMOGRAPHY.
University of California Press, 2120 Berkeley Way, Berkeley, CA 94720. TEL 510-643-7127. FAX 510-643-7127. *5792*

STUDIES IN DEVELOPMENT AND PLANNING.
Kluwer Academic Publishers, Postbus 17, 3300 AA Dordrecht, Netherlands. TEL 31-78-6392392. FAX 31-78-6392254. *1315*

STUDIES IN DISCOURSE AND GRAMMAR.
John Benjamins Publishing Co., Amsteldijk 44, P.O. Box 75577, 1070 AN Amsterdam, Netherlands. TEL 31-20-6738156. FAX 31-20-6792956. *4114*

STUDIES IN EAST EUROPEAN THOUGHT.
Kluwer Academic Publishers, Postbus 17, 3300 AA Dordrecht, Netherlands. TEL 31-78-6392392. FAX 31-78-6392254. *5710*

STUDIES IN ECONOMIC ORGANIZATION.
Kluwer Academic Publishers, Postbus 17, 3300 AA Dordrecht, Netherlands. TEL 31-78-6392392. FAX 31-78-6392254. *1262*

STUDIES IN ECONOMICS AND FINANCE.
University of North Carolina at Charlotte, Economics Department, Charlotte, NC 28223-0001. TEL 704-547-4130. FAX 704-547-4130. *1262*

STUDIES IN EDUCATIONAL EVALUATION.
Elsevier Science Ltd., Pergamon, P.O. Box 800, Kidlington, Oxford OX5 1DX, England. TEL 44-1865-843000. FAX 44-1865-843010. *2375*

STUDIES IN ELECTRICAL AND ELECTRONIC ENGINEERING.
Elsevier Science B.V., Books Division, P.O. Box 211, 1000 AE Amsterdam, Netherlands. TEL 31-20-4853911. FAX 31-20-4853705. *2720*

STUDIES IN ENGLISH LITERATURE.
English Literary Society of Japan, 501 Kenkyusha Bldg., 9 Surugadai 2-chome, Kanda, Chiyoda-ku, Tokyo 101, Japan. TEL 03-3293-7528. FAX 03-3233-3398. *4272*

STUDIES IN ENVIRONMENTAL SCIENCE.
Elsevier Science B.V., Books Division, P.O. Box 211, 1000 AE Amsterdam, Netherlands. TEL 31-20-4853911. FAX 31-20-4853705. *2820*

STUDIES IN FERTILITY AND STERILITY.
Kluwer Academic Publishers, Postbus 17, 3300 AA Dordrecht, Netherlands. TEL 31-78-6392392. FAX 31-78-6392254. *794*

STUDIES IN GENDER AND CULTURE.
Gordon & Breach Science Publishers, c/o International Publishers Distributor, P.O. Box 3054, Langhorne, PA 19047-3054. TEL 215-750-2642. FAX 215-750-6343. *6436*

STUDIES IN GREEK AND ROMAN RELIGION.
E.J. Brill, P.O. Box 9000, 2300 PA Leiden, Netherlands. TEL 31-71-5353500. FAX 31-71-5317532. *6096*

STUDIES IN HIGH ENERGY PHYSICS SERIES.
Harwood Academic Publishers, c/o International Publishers Distributor, P.O. Box 3054, Langhorne, PA 19047-3054. TEL 215-750-2642. FAX 215-750-6343. *5571*

STUDIES IN HIGHER EDUCATION.
Carfax Publishing Co., P.O. Box 25, Abingdon, Oxon. OX14 3UE, England. TEL 44-1235-401000. FAX 44-1235-401550. *2443*

STUDIES IN HISTORY.
Sage Publications India Pvt. Ltd., P.O. Box 4215, New Delhi 110 048, India. TEL 91-11-644-4958. FAX 91-11-647-2426. *3385*

STUDIES IN HISTORY AND PHILOSOPHY OF SCIENCE.
Elsevier Science Ltd., Pergamon, P.O. Box 800, Kidlington, Oxford OX5 1DX, England. TEL 44-1865-843000. FAX 44-1865-843010. *6289*

STUDIES IN HISTORY AND PHILOSOPHY OF SCIENCE PART B: STUDIES IN HISTORY AND PHILOSOPHY OF MODERN PHYSICS.
Elsevier Science Ltd., Pergamon, P.O. Box 800, Kidlington, Oxford OX5 1DX, England. TEL 44-1865-843000. FAX 44-1865-843010. *5571*

STUDIES IN HISTORY OF MEDICINE AND SCIENCE.
Jamia Hamdard, Hamdard Nagar, New Delhi 110 062, India. TEL 91-11-698-4685. FAX 91-11-698-8874. *4534*

STUDIES IN HOGG AND HIS WORLD.
James Hogg Society, Department of English Studies, University of Stirling, Stirling FK9 4LA, Scotland. *4272*

STUDIES IN HUMAN SOCIETY.
E.J. Brill, P.O. Box 9000, 2300 PA Leiden, Netherlands. TEL 31-71-5353500. FAX 31-71-5317532. *6436*

STUDIES IN INDUSTRIAL ORGANIZATION.
Kluwer Academic Publishers, Postbus 17, 3300 AA Dordrecht, Netherlands. TEL 31-78-6392392. FAX 31-78-6392254. *1262*

STUDIES IN INFECTIOUS DISEASES RESEARCH.
University of Chicago Press, 5801 S. Ellis Ave., Chicago, IL 60637. TEL 312-702-7899. *4628*

STUDIES IN INFORMATICS AND CONTROL.
Research Institute for Informatics, 8-10 Averescu Ave., 71316 Bucharest 1, Rumania. TEL 40-1-2223778. FAX 40-1-3128539. *4047*

STUDIES IN INORGANIC CHEMISTRY.
Elsevier Science B.V., Books Division, P.O. Box 211, 1000 AE Amsterdam, Netherlands. TEL 31-20-4853911. FAX 31-20-4853705. *1733*

STUDIES IN INTERFACE SCIENCE.
Elsevier Science B.V., Books Division, P.O. Box 211, 1000 AE Amsterdam, Netherlands. TEL 31-20-4853911. FAX 31-20-4853705. *5572*

STUDIES IN INTERNATIONAL ECONOMICS.
Elsevier Science B.V., Books Division, P.O. Box 211, 1000 AE Amsterdam, Netherlands. TEL 31-20-4853911. FAX 31-20-4853705. *962*

STUDIES IN INTERRELIGIOUS DIALOGUE.
Kok Pharos Publishing House, Postbus 5019, 8260 AG Kampen, Netherlands. TEL 31-38-3392565. FAX 31-38-3327331. *6096*

STUDIES IN ISLAMIC LAW & SOCIETY.
E.J. Brill, P.O. Box 9000, 2300 PA Leiden, Netherlands. TEL 31-71-5353500. FAX 31-71-5317532. *6121*

STUDIES IN JUDAISM IN LATE ANTIQUITY.
E.J. Brill, P.O. Box 9000, 2300 PA Leiden, Netherlands. TEL 31-71-5353500. FAX 31-71-5317532. *6129*

STUDIES IN JUDAISM IN MODERN TIMES.
E.J. Brill, P.O. Box 9000, 2300 PA Leiden, Netherlands. TEL 31-71-5353500. FAX 31-71-5317532. *6129*

STUDIES IN LANGUAGE.
John Benjamins Publishing Co., Amsteldijk 44, P.O. Box 75577, 1070 AN Amsterdam, Netherlands. TEL 31-20-6738156. FAX 31-20-6792956. *4114*

STUDIES IN LATIN AMERICAN POPULAR CULTURE.
c/o Charles M. Tatum, Modern Language Bldg. 345, University of Arizona, Tucson, AZ 85721. TEL 602-621-1044. FAX 602-621-5594. *6436*

STUDIES IN LEGAL HISTORY.
University of North Carolina Press, Box 2288, Chapel Hill, NC 27515-2288. TEL 919-966-3561. FAX 919-966-3829. *3854*

STUDIES IN LINGUISTICS AND PHILOSOPHY.
Kluwer Academic Publishers, Postbus 17, 3300 AA Dordrecht, Netherlands. TEL 31-78-6392392. FAX 31-78-6392254. *5884*

STUDIES IN LOCATIONAL ANALYSIS.
International Institute of Interdisciplinary Studies in Environmental Management, Locational Decisions & Regional Planning, c/o J. Karkazis, Smirnis 1, 15772 Zografou, Greece. TEL 30-1-6123-631. FAX 30-1-6123-631. *3595*

STUDIES IN LOGIC AND COMPUTATION.
Oxford University Press, Walton St., Oxford OX2 6DP, England. TEL 44-1865-56767. FAX 44-1865-56646. *4398*

STUDIES IN LOGIC AND THE FOUNDATIONS OF MATHEMATICS.
Elsevier Science B.V., Books Division, P.O. Box 211, 1000 AE Amsterdam, Netherlands. TEL 31-20-4853911. FAX 31-20-4853705. *4398*

STUDIES IN MANAGEMENT SCIENCE AND SYSTEMS.
Elsevier Science B.V., Books Division, P.O. Box 211, 1000 AE Amsterdam, Netherlands. TEL 31-20-4853911. FAX 31-20-4853705. *1446*

STUDIES IN MATHEMATICAL AND MANAGERIAL ECONOMICS.
Elsevier Science B.V., Books Division, P.O. Box 211, 1000 AE Amsterdam, Netherlands. TEL 31-20-4853911. FAX 31-20-4853705. *1446*

STUDIES IN MATHEMATICAL PHYSICS.
Elsevier Science B.V., Books Division, P.O. Box 211, 1000 AE Amsterdam, Netherlands. TEL 31-20-4853911. FAX 31-20-4853705. *5572*

STUDIES IN MATHEMATICS (WASHINGTON).
Mathematical Association of America, 1529 Eighteenth St., N.W., Washington, DC 20036. TEL 202-387-5200. *4398*

STUDIES IN MATHEMATICS AND ITS APPLICATIONS.
Elsevier Science B.V., Books Division, P.O. Box 211, 1000 AE Amsterdam, Netherlands. TEL 31-20-4853911. FAX 31-20-4853705. *4398*

STUDIES IN MECHANICAL ENGINEERING.
Elsevier Science B.V., Books Division, P.O. Box 211, 1000 AE Amsterdam, Netherlands. TEL 31-20-4853911. FAX 31-20-4853705. *2770*

STUDIES IN MEDIEVAL AND REFORMATION THOUGHT.
E.J. Brill, P.O. Box 9000, 2300 PA Leiden, Netherlands. TEL 31-71-5353500. FAX 31-71-5317532. *6096*

STUDIES IN MELANESIAN ANTHROPOLOGY.
University of California Press, 2120 Berkeley Way, Berkeley, CA 94720. TEL 510-642-4247. FAX 510-643-7127. *323*

STUDIES IN MODERN THERMODYNAMICS.
Elsevier Science B.V., Books Division, P.O. Box 211, 1000 AE Amsterdam, Netherlands. TEL 31-20-4853911. FAX 31-20-4853705. *1757*

STUDIES IN MONETARY ECONOMICS.
Elsevier Science B.V., Books Division, P.O. Box 211, 1000 AE Amsterdam, Netherlands. TEL 31-20-4853911. FAX 31-20-4853705. *1122*

STUDIES IN NATURAL LANGUAGE AND LINGUISTIC THEORY.
Kluwer Academic Publishers, Postbus 17, 3300 AA Dordrecht, Netherlands. TEL 31-78-6392392. FAX 31-78-6392254. *4114*

STUDIES IN NATURAL PRODUCTS CHEMISTRY.
Elsevier Science B.V., Books Division, P.O. Box 211, 1000 AE Amsterdam, Netherlands. TEL 31-20-4853911. FAX 31-20-4853705. *1693*

STUDIES IN NEW MUSIC RESEARCH.
Swets & Zeitlinger bv, P.O. Box 825, 2160 SZ Lisse, Netherlands. TEL 31-252-435111. FAX 31-252-415888. *2035*

STUDIES IN NONLINEAR DYNAMICS AND ECONOMETRICS.
M I T Press, 55 Hayward St., Cambridge, MA 02142-1399. TEL 617-253-2889. FAX 617-258-6779. *4398*

STUDIES IN OPERATIONAL REGIONAL SCIENCE.
Kluwer Academic Publishers, Postbus 17, 3300 AA Dordrecht, Netherlands. TEL 31-78-6392392. FAX 31-78-6392254. *1262*

STUDIES IN OPERATIONS RESEARCH.
Gordon & Breach Science Publishers, c/o International Publishers Distributor, P.O. Box 3054, Langhorne, PA 19047-3054. TEL 215-750-2642. FAX 215-750-6343. *1998*

STUDIES IN ORGANIC CHEMISTRY.
Elsevier Science B.V., Books Division, P.O. Box 211, 1000 AE Amsterdam, Netherlands. TEL 31-20-4853911. FAX 31-20-4853705. *1746*

STUDIES IN PHILOLOGY.
University of North Carolina Press, Box 2288, Chapel Hill, NC 27515-2288. TEL 919-966-3561. FAX 800-272-6817. *4114*

STUDIES IN PHILOSOPHY AND EDUCATION.
Kluwer Academic Publishers, Postbus 17, 3300 AA Dordrecht, Netherlands. TEL 31-78-6392392. FAX 31-78-6392254. *2375*

STUDIES IN PHILOSOPHY AND RELIGION.
Kluwer Academic Publishers, Postbus 17, 3300 AA Dordrecht, Netherlands. TEL 31-78-6392392. FAX 31-78-6392254. *5501*

STUDIES IN PHYSICAL AND THEORETICAL CHEMISTRY.
Elsevier Science B.V., Books Division, P.O. Box 211, 1000 AE Amsterdam, Netherlands. TEL 31-20-4853911. FAX 31-20-4853705. *1757*

STUDIES IN PHYSIOLOGY.
Portland Press Ltd., 59 Portland Place, London W1N 3AJ, England. TEL 44-171-580-5530. FAX 44-171-323-1136. *794*

STUDIES IN PLANT SCIENCE.
Elsevier Science B.V., Books Division, P.O. Box 211, 1000 AE Amsterdam, Netherlands. TEL 31-20-4853911. FAX 31-20-4853705. *704*

STUDIES IN POLITICAL ECONOMY.
Politecon, Box 4729, Station E, Ottawa, ON K1S 5H9, Canada. TEL 613-788-2600. *5710*

STUDIES IN POLYMER SCIENCE.
Elsevier Science B.V., Books Division, P.O. Box 211, 1000 AE Amsterdam, Netherlands. TEL 31-20-4853911. FAX 31-20-4853705. *1693*

STUDIES IN POPULAR CULTURE.
Popular Culture Association in the South, c/o Dennis Hall, Ed., University of Louisville, Department of English, Louisville, KY 40292. *6436*

STUDIES IN PRE-COLUMBIAN ART AND ARCHAEOLOGY.
Dumbarton Oaks, Publications Office, 1703 32nd St., N.W., Washington, DC 20007. TEL 202-339-6431. *375*

STUDIES IN PRODUCTION AND ENGINEERING ECONOMICS.
Elsevier Science B.V., Books Division, P.O. Box 211, 1000 AE Amsterdam, Netherlands. TEL 31-20-4853911. FAX 31-20-4853705. *962*

STUDIES IN PRODUCTIVITY ANALYSIS.
Kluwer Academic Publishers, Postbus 17, 3300 AA Dordrecht, Netherlands. TEL 31-78-6392392. FAX 31-78-6392254. *1447*

STUDIES IN PROOF THEORY.
Elsevier Science B.V., Books Division, P.O. Box 211, 1000 AE Amsterdam, Netherlands. TEL 31-20-4853911. FAX 31-20-4853705. *4398*

STUDIES IN PSYCHOANALYTIC THEORY.
Texas Christian University, Box 32875, Ft. Worth, TX 76129. TEL 817-921-7221. FAX 817-921-7702. *5884*

STUDIES IN PUBLIC CHOICE.
Kluwer Academic Publishers, Postbus 17, 3300 AA Dordrecht, Netherlands. TEL 31-78-6392392. FAX 31-78-6392254. *1262*

STUDIES IN REGIONAL AND URBAN PLANNING.
International Institute of Interdisciplinary Studies in Environmental Management, Locational Decisions & Regional Planning, c/o Prof. John Karkazis, Ed., Smirnis 1, 15772 Zografou, Greece. TEL 30-1-6123-631. FAX 30-1-6123-631. *3595*

STUDIES IN REGIONAL SCIENCE AND URBAN ECONOMICS.
Elsevier Science B.V., Books Division, P.O. Box 211, 1000 AE Amsterdam, Netherlands. TEL 31-20-4853911. FAX 31-20-4853705. *1241*

STUDIES IN RISK AND UNCERTAINTY.
Kluwer Academic Publishers, Postbus 17, 3300 AA Dordrecht, Netherlands. TEL 31-78-6392392. FAX 31-78-6392254. *1262*

STUDIES IN SECOND LANGUAGE ACQUISITION.
Cambridge University Press, Edinburgh Bldg., Shaftesbury Rd., Cambridge CB2 2RU, England. TEL 44-1223-312393. FAX 44-1223-315052. *4114*

STUDIES IN SEMITIC LANGUAGES AND LINGUISTICS.
E.J. Brill, P.O. Box 9000, 2300 PA Leiden, Netherlands. TEL 31-71-5353500. FAX 31-71-5317532. *4114*

STUDIES IN SOCIAL HISTORY.
Kluwer Academic Publishers, Postbus 17, 3300 AA Dordrecht, Netherlands. TEL 31-78-6392392. FAX 31-78-6392254. *6348*

STUDIES IN SOCIAL LIFE.
Kluwer Academic Publishers, Postbus 17, 3300 AA Dordrecht, Netherlands. TEL 31-78-6392392. FAX 31-78-6392254. *6437*

STUDIES IN SPEECH PATHOLOGY AND CLINICAL LINGUISTICS.
John Benjamins Publishing Co., Amsteldijk 44, P.O. Box 75577, 1070 AN Amsterdam, Netherlands. TEL 31-20-6738156. FAX 31-20-6792956. *4869*

STUDIES IN SPELEOLOGY.
William Pengelly Cave Studies Trust Ltd., 107 Andover Rd., Newbury, Berks. RG14 6JH, England. TEL 44-1202-721164. *2263*

STUDIES IN STATISTICAL MECHANICS.
Elsevier Science B.V., Books Division, P.O. Box 211, 1000 AE Amsterdam, Netherlands. TEL 31-20-4853911. FAX 31-20-4853705. *5592*

STUDIES IN SURFACE SCIENCE AND CATALYSIS.
Elsevier Science B.V., Books Division, P.O. Box 211, 1000 AE Amsterdam, Netherlands. TEL 31-20-4853911. FAX 31-20-4853705. *5592*

STUDIES IN TEXTILE AND COSTUME HISTORY.
E.J. Brill, P.O. Box 9000, 2300 PA Leiden, Netherlands. TEL 31-71-5353500. FAX 31-71-5317532. *3360*

STUDIES IN THE AGE OF CHAUCER.
Ohio State University, Department of English, 421 Denney Hall, 164 W. 17th Ave., Columbus, OH 43210. TEL 614-292-2061. FAX 614-292-1599. *4273*

STUDIES IN THE DECORATIVE ARTS.
Bard Graduate Center for Studies in the Decorative Arts, 18 W. 86th St., New York, NY 10024. TEL 212-501-3058. FAX 212-501-3089. *454*

STUDIES IN THE DEVELOPMENT OF MODERN MATHEMATICS.
Gordon and Breach Science Publishers, c/o International Publishing Distributor, P.O. Box 3054, Langhorne, PA 19047-3054. TEL 215-750-2643. FAX 215-750-6343. *4398*

STUDIES IN THE GERMANIC LANGUAGES AND LITERATURES.
University of North Carolina Press, Box 2288, Chapel Hill, NC 27515-2288. TEL 919-966-3561. FAX 919-966-3829. *4273*

STUDIES IN THE HISTORY AND PHILOSOPHY OF MATHEMATICS.
Elsevier Science B.V., Books Division, P.O. Box 211, 1000 AE Amsterdam, Netherlands. TEL 31-20-4853911. FAX 31-20-4853705. *4398*

STUDIES IN THE HISTORY OF CHRISTIAN THOUGHT.
E.J. Brill, P.O. Box 9000, 2300 PA Leiden, Netherlands. TEL 31-71-5353500. FAX 31-71-5317532. *6096*

STUDIES IN THE HISTORY OF LEIDEN UNIVERSITY.
E.J. Brill, P.O. Box 9000, 2300 PA Leiden, Netherlands. TEL 31-71-5353500. FAX 31-71-5317532. *3448*

STUDIES IN THE HUMANITIES (INDIANA).
Indiana University of Pennsylvania, English Department, Indiana, PA 15705. TEL 412-357-2322. FAX 412-357-3056. *3626*

STUDIES IN TROPICAL OCEANOGRAPHY.
Office of the Bulletin of Marine Science, 4600 Rickenbacker Causeway, Miami, FL 33149-1098. TEL 305-361-4190. *2306*

STUDIES IN TWENTIETH CENTURY LITERATURE.
Kansas State University, Department of Modern Languages, Eisenhower 104, Manhattan, KS 66506-1003. TEL 913-532-6760. FAX 913-532-7004. *4273*

STUDIES IN U S NATIONAL SECURITY.
Kluwer Academic Publishers, Postbus 17, 3300 AA Dordrecht, Netherlands. TEL 31-78-6392392. FAX 31-78-6392254. *5049*

STUDIES IN VISUAL INFORMATION PROCESSING.
Elsevier Science B.V., Books Division, P.O. Box 211, 1000 AE Amsterdam, Netherlands. TEL 31-20-4853911. FAX 31-20-4853705. *4869*

STUDIES IN WIND ENGINEERING AND INDUSTRIAL ENGINEERING.
Elsevier Science B.V., Books Division, P.O. Box 211, 1000 AE Amsterdam, Netherlands. TEL 31-20-4853911. FAX 31-20-4853705. *2749*

STUDIES OF CLASSICAL INDIA.
Kluwer Academic Publishers, Postbus 17, 3300 AA Dordrecht, Netherlands. TEL 31-78-6392392. FAX 31-78-6392254. *5501*

STUDIES ON CHINA.
University of California Press, 2120 Berkeley Way, Berkeley, CA 94720. TEL 510-642-4247. FAX 510-643-7127. *3385*

STUDIES ON RELIGION IN AFRICA.
E.J. Brill, P.O. Box 9000, 2300 PA Leiden, Netherlands. TEL 31-71-5353500. FAX 31-71-5317532. *6096*

STUDIES ON THE MORPHOLOGY AND SYSTEMATICS OF SCALE INSECTS.
Virginia Polytechnic Institute and State University, Department of Entomology, Blacksburg, VA 24061-0319. TEL 703-231-6341. *735*

STUDIES ON THE TEXTS OF THE DESERT OF JUDAH.
E.J. Brill, P.O. Box 9000, 2300 PA Leiden, Netherlands. TEL 31-71-5353500. FAX 31-71-5317532. *6130*

STUDIME FILOLOGJIKE.
Academia e Shkencave e RPSSH, Instituti i Gjuhesise dhe i Letersise, Rruga N. Frasheri 7, Tirana, Albania. TEL 355-42-3514. FAX 355-42-3514. *4115*

STUDIO.
Studio, Givat Haviva, M.P. Menashe 37850, Israel. TEL 972-6-309263. FAX 972-6-373335. *454*

STUDIO (ALBURY).
Studio, 727 Peel St., Albury, N.S.W. 2640, Australia. TEL 61-6-211135. *4274*

STUDIO ONE.
College of Saint Benedict, St. Joseph, MN 56374. *4320*

STYLE (DEKALB).
Northern Illinois University, Department of English, DeKalb, IL 60115. TEL 815-753-0611. FAX 815-753-1824. *4274*

SUB-SAHARAN NEWSBRIEF.
Centre for Development Analysis (CDA), P.O. Box 73399, Lynnwood Ridge 0040, South Africa. TEL 27-12-471303. FAX 27-12-475055. *1315*

SUBCELLULAR BIOCHEMISTRY.
Plenum Publishing Corp., 233 Spring St., New York, NY 10013-1578. TEL 212-620-8000. FAX 212-463-0742. *650*

SUBNUCLEAR SERIES.
Plenum Publishing Corp., 233 Spring St., New York, NY 10013-1578. TEL 212-620-8000. FAX 212-463-0742. *5572*

SUBSTANCE ABUSE.
Plenum Publishing Corp., 233 Spring St., New York, NY 10013-1578. TEL 212-620-8000. FAX 212-463-0742. *2201*

SUBSTANCE USE AND MISUSE.
Marcel Dekker Journals, 270 Madison Ave., New York, NY 10016. TEL 212-696-9000. FAX 212-685-4540. *2201*

SUBTLE ENERGIES.
International Society for the Study of Subtle Energies and Energy Medicine, 356 Goldco Circle, Golden, CO 80401. TEL 303-278-2228. FAX 303-279-3539. *293*

SUCHT.
Neuland Verlagsgesellschaft mbH, Markt 24-26, 21502 Geesthacht, Germany. TEL 49-4152-81342. FAX 49-4152-81343. *2201*

SUDANIC AFRICA.
University of Bergen, Centre for Middle Eastern and Islamic Studies, Parkv. 22A, N-5007 Bergen, Norway. TEL 47-5558-2711. FAX 47-5558-9891. *3375*

SUFFOLK INSTITUTE OF ARCHAEOLOGY AND HISTORY. PROCEEDINGS.
Suffolk Institute of Archaeology and History, c/o E.A. Martin, Hon. Secy., Oak Tree Farm, Finborough Rd., Hitcham, Ipswich, Suffolk IP7 7LS, England. TEL 44-1449-741266. *375*

SUFFOLK TRANSNATIONAL LAW REVIEW.
Suffolk University Law School, Suffolk Transnational Law Review, 41 Temple St., Boston, MA 02114-4280. TEL 617-573-8610. *3854*

SUFFOLK UNIVERSITY LAW REVIEW.
Joe Christensen, Inc. (Boston), Beacon Hill, 41 Temple St., Boston, MA 02114. TEL 617-573-8180. FAX 617-723-5847. *3854*

SUGAR SERIES.
Elsevier Science B.V., Books Division, P.O. Box 211, 1000 AE Amsterdam, Netherlands. TEL 31-20-4853911. FAX 31-20-4853705. *2992*

SUI YUAN WEN HSIEN.
Association of Fellow Provincials of Sui Yuan, 101 Fourth St., Chung Yang Rd., Hsin Tien, Taipei Hsien, Taiwan 23127, Republic of China. TEL 886-2-219-6633. *2910*

SUICIDE AND LIFE-THREATENING BEHAVIOR.
Guilford Publications, Inc., 72 Spring St., 4th Fl., New York, NY 10012. TEL 212-431-9800. FAX 212-966-6708. *5884*

SULFUR LETTERS.
Harwood Academic Publishers, c/o International Publishers Distributor, P.O. Box 3054, Langhorne, PA 19047-3054. TEL 215-750-2642. FAX 215-750-6343. *1693*

SULFUR REPORTS.
Harwood Academic Publishers, c/o International Publishers Distributor, P.O. Box 3054, Langhorne, PA 19047-3054. TEL 215-750-2642. FAX 215-750-6343. *1693*

SULPHUR IN AGRICULTURE.
Sulphur Institute, 1140 Connecticut Ave., N.W., Ste. 612, Washington DC 20036. TEL 202-331-9660. FAX 202-293-2940. *154*

SUMMARIES OF B F R L FIRE RESEARCH IN-HOUSE AND GRANTS (YEAR).
U.S. National Institute of Standards and Technology, Fire Research Information Services, Bldg. 224, Rm. A252, Gaithersburg, MD 20899. TEL 301-975-6862. *2923*

SUO.
Suoseura, Unioninkatu 40, SF-00170 Helsinki, Finland. FAX 358-41-677405. *3026*

SUOMEN ANTROPOLOGI.
Suomen Antropologinen Seura, P.O. Box 13, SF-00014 University of Helsinki, Finland. FAX 358-0-19123006. *323*

SUOMEN LAAKARILEHTI.
Suomen Laakariliitto, Makelankatu 2, 00500 Helsinki, Finland. TEL 358-90-393-0795. *4534*

SUPERCOMPUTER.
ASFRA B.V., Voorhaven 33, 1135 BL Edam, Netherlands. TEL 31-2993-72751. FAX 31-2993-72877. *2063*

SUPRAMOLECULAR CHEMISTRY.
Gordon & Breach Science Publishers, c/o International Publishers Distributor, P.O. Box 3054, Langhorne, PA 19047-3054. TEL 215-750-2642. FAX 215-750-6343. *1694*

SUPRAMOLECULAR SCIENCE.
Butterworth - Heinemann, Part of the Reed Elsevier group, Linacre House, Jordan Hill, Oxford OX2 8DP, England. TEL 44-1865-310366. FAX 44-1865-310398. *5572*

SUPREME COURT REVIEW.
University of Chicago Press, Journals Division, Box 37005, Chicago IL 60637. TEL 773-753-3347. FAX 773-753-0811. *3954*

SURFACE AND COATINGS TECHNOLOGY.
Elsevier Science S.A., P.O. Box 564, CH-1001 Lausanne 1, Switzerland. TEL 41-21-3207381. FAX 41-21-3235444. *1721*

SURFACE AND COLLOID SCIENCE.
Plenum Publishing Corp., 233 Spring St., New York, NY 10013-1578. TEL 212-620-8000. FAX 212-463-0742. *1758*

SURFACE COATINGS.
Elsevier Science Ltd., Books Division, P.O. Box 800, Kidlington, Oxford OX5 1DX, England. TEL 44-1865-843000. FAX 44-1865-843010. *5310*

SURFACE SCIENCE.
North-Holland P.O. Box 211, 1000 AE Amsterdam, Netherlands. TEL 31-20-4853911. FAX 31-20-4853598. *5572*

SURFACE SCIENCE REPORTS.
North-Holland P.O. Box 211, 1000 AE Amsterdam, Netherlands. TEL 31-20-4853911. FAX 31-20-4853598. *5572*

SURFACTANT SCIENCE SERIES.
Marcel Dekker, Inc., 270 Madison Ave., New York, NY 10016. TEL 212-696-9000. FAX 212-685-4540. *1694*

SURGERY.
Mosby - Year Book, Inc. 11830 Westline Industrial Dr., St. Louis, MO 63146-3318. TEL 314-872-8370. FAX 314-432-1380. *4920*

SURGICAL ENDOSCOPY.
Springer-Verlag, Medical Journals, 175 Fifth Ave., New York, NY 10010. TEL 212-460-1500. FAX 212-473-6272. *4921*

SURGICAL LAPAROSCOPY AND ENDOSCOPY.
Lippincott - Raven Publishers 227 E. Washington Sq., Philadelphia, PA 19106. TEL 215-238-4200. *4921*

SURGICAL NEUROLOGY.
Elsevier Science Inc., Box 945, New York, NY 10159-0945. TEL 212-633-3730. FAX 212-633-3680. *4921*

SURGICAL ONCOLOGY.
Blackwell Science Ltd., Osney Mead, Oxford OX2 0EL, England. TEL 44-1865-206206. FAX 44-1865-721205. *4764*

SURGICAL PATHOLOGY.
Field & Wood, Medical Periodicals, Inc., Box 975, Blue Bell, PA 19422. TEL 610-828-4010. FAX 215-482-0226. *4535*

SURGICAL PRACTICE NEWS.
McMahon Publishing Co., 83 Peaceable St., West Redding, CT 06896. TEL 203-944-9343. *4921*

SURGICAL RESEARCH COMMUNICATIONS.
Harwood Academic Publishers, c/o International Publishers Distributor, P.O. Box 3054, Langhorne, PA 19047-3054. TEL 215-750-2642. FAX 215-750-6343. *4921*

SURGICAL UPDATE.
American Association of Oral and Maxillofacial Surgeons, 9700 W. Bryn Mawr Ave., Rosemont, IL 60018 TEL 708-678-6200 FAX 708-678-6286. *4655*

SURVEY OF OPHTHALMOLOGY.
Survey of Ophthalmology, Inc., 7 Kent St., Ste. 4, Brookline, MA 02146. TEL 617-566-2138. FAX 617-566-4019. *4575*

SURVEYS IN GEOPHYSICS.
Kluwer Academic Publishers, Postbus 17, 3300 AA Dordrecht, Netherlands. TEL 31-78-6392392. FAX 31-78-6392254. *2282*

SURVEYS IN HIGH ENERGY PHYSICS.
Harwood Academic Publishers, c/o International Publishers Distributor, P.O. Box 3054, Langhorne, PA 19047-3054. TEL 215-750-2642. FAX 215-750-6343. *5573*

SUSSEX RECORD SOCIETY.
Sussex Record Society, Barbican House, Lewes BN7 1YE, England. TEL 44-1243 533911. FAX 44-1243-533959. *3449*

SUZHOU DAXUE XUEBAO (ZHEXUE SHEHUI KEXUE BAN).
Suzhou Daxue, 1 Shizi Jie, Suzhou, Jiangsu 215006, People's Republic of China. TEL 0512-5223614. FAX 0512-5231918. *6348*

SUZUGAMINE JOSHI TANDAI KENKYU SHUHO. SHIZEN KAGAKU.
Suzugamine Joshi Tanki Daigaku, 6-8 Inokuchi 4-chome, Nishi-ku, Hiroshima-shi, Hiroshima-ken 733, Japan. TEL 082-278-1103. FAX 082-277-0301. *6289*

SVENSK FLYGHISTORISK TIDSKRIFT.
Svensk Flyghistorisk Foerening, P.O. Box 308, S-101 26 Stockholm, Sweden. *79*

SVENSK VETERINAERTIDNING.
Sveriges Veterinaerfoerbund, P.O. Box 12 709, S-112 94 Stockholm, Sweden. TEL 08-654-2480. FAX 08-6517082. *6954*

SVENSKA LINNE-SALLSKAPET AARSSKRIFT.
Linne-Sallskapet, Kungshuset, S-222 22 Lund, Sweden. TEL 46-46-2227589. FAX 46-46-2224606. *705*

SVETSAREN.
Esab AB, Marketing Communications, P.O. Box 8004, S-402 77 Goeteborg, Sweden. FAX 46-31-509-390. *4988*

SWAMY BOTANICAL CLUB. JOURNAL.
Swamy Botanical Club, c/o Dr. K.V. Krishnamurthy, Dept. of Plant Sciences, Bharathidasan University, Tiruchirapalli 620 024, India. TEL 0431-60351. FAX 0431-96245. *705*

SWEDISH BOOK REVIEW.
Swedish-English Literary Translators Association, University of Wales, Lampeter SA48 7ED, Wales. TEL 44-1570-422351. FAX 44-1570-423782. *6010*

SWISS - AMERICAN HISTORICAL SOCIETY. REVIEW.
Swiss - American Historical Society, c/o Erdmann Schmocker, 6440 N. Bosworth Ave., Chicago, IL 60626. TEL 312-262-8336. *3361*

SWISS SURGERY.
Hans Huber AG, Laenggassstr. 76, CH-3000 Bern 9, Switzerland. TEL 41-31-3004500. FAX 41-31-3004590. *4922*

SYCAMORE REVIEW.
Purdue University, Department of English, W. Lafayette, IN 47907. TEL 317-494-3783. FAX 317-494-3780. *4275*

SYMBOLA ET EMBLEMATA.
E.J. Brill, P.O. Box 9000, 2300 PA Leiden, Netherlands. TEL 31-71-5353500. FAX 31-71-5317532. *454*

SYMPLOKE.
Ballantine 402, Indiana University, Bloomington, IN 47405. TEL 813-855-7070. FAX 812-885-2688. *3627*

SYMPOSIA FOUNDATION MERIEUX.
Elsevier Science B.V., Books Division, P.O. Box 211, 1000 AE Amsterdam, Netherlands. TEL 31-20-4853911. FAX 31-20-4853705. *4535*

SYMPOSIA MATHEMATICA.
Academic Press, Inc., 525 B St., Ste. 1900, San Diego, CA 92101-4495. TEL 619-231-0926. FAX 619-699-6715. *4399*

SYMPOSIUM.
Heldref Publications, 1319 Eighteenth St., N.W., Washington, DC 20036-1802. TEL 202-296-6267. FAX 202-296-5149. *4275*

SYMPOSIUM (INTERNATIONAL) ON COMBUSTION.
Combustion Institute, 5001 Baum Blvd., Pittsburgh, PA 15213. TEL 412-387-1366. FAX 412-687-0340. *1758*

SYMPOSIUM ON COMPUTER APPLICATIONS IN MEDICAL CARE. PROCEEDINGS.
American Medical Informatics Association, 4915 St. Elmo Ave., Ste. 302, Bethesda, MD 20814. TEL 301-657-1291. FAX 301-657-1296. *4632*

SYMPOSIUM ON COMPUTER ARITHMETIC. PROCEEDINGS.
I E E E Computer Society Press, 10662 Los Vaqueros Circle, Los Alamitos, CA 90720-1264. TEL 714-821-8380. FAX 714-821-4641. *2063*

SYMPOSIUM ON FUSION ENGINEERING. PROCEEDINGS.
Institute of Electrical and Electronics Engineers, Inc., 345 E. 47th St., New York, NY 10017-2394. TEL 212-705-7900. FAX 212-705-7682. *2583*

SYNAPSE (NEW YORK).
John Wiley & Sons, Inc., Journals, 605 Third Ave., New York, NY 10158. TEL 212-850-6645. FAX 212-850-6021. *4869*

SYNCHROTRON RADIATION NEWS.
Gordon & Breach Science Publishers, c/o International Publishers Distributor, P.O. Box 3054, Langhorne, PA 19047-3054. TEL 215-750-2642. FAX 215-750-6343. *5600*

SYNERGY.
A F L Deeson Partnership Ltd., Ewell House, Faversham, Kent ME13 8UP, England. TEL 44-1795-535468. FAX 44-1795-535469. *4885*

SYNOPSES OF THE BRITISH FAUNA.
Backhuys Publishers - Universal Book Services, P.O. Box 321, 2300 AH Leiden, Netherlands. TEL 31-71-5170208. FAX 31-71-5171856. *821*

SYNTAX IN THE SCHOOLS.
Assembly for the Teaching of English Grammar, One College Ave., Williamsport, PA 17701. TEL 717-326-3761. *2502*

SYNTHESE.
Kluwer Academic Publishers, Postbus 17, 3300 AA Dordrecht, Netherlands. TEL 31-78-6392392. FAX 31-78-6392254. *5501*

SYNTHESE LIBRARY.
Kluwer Academic Publishers, Postbus 17, 3300 AA Dordrecht, Netherlands. TEL 31-78-6392392. FAX 31-78-6392254. *5501*

SYNTHESIS (KNOXVILLE).
New Paradigm Press, 5413 Neilwoods Dr., Knoxville, TN 37919. TEL 423-588-8878. *4275*

SYNTHESIS AND REACTIVITY IN INORGANIC AND METALORGANIC CHEMISTRY.
Marcel Dekker Journals, 270 Madison Ave., New York, NY 10016. TEL 212-696-9000. FAX 212-685-4540. *1758*

SYNTHETIC COMMUNICATIONS.
Marcel Dekker Journals, 270 Madison Ave., New York, NY 10016. TEL 212-696-9000. FAX 212-685-4540. *1746*

SYNTHETIC METALS.
Elsevier Science S.A., P.O. Box 564, CH-1001 Lausanne 1, Switzerland. TEL 41-21-3207381. FAX 41-21-3235444. *2741*

SYNTHETIC METHODS OF ORGANIC CHEMISTRY.
S. Karger AG, Allschwilerstr. 10, P.O. Box, CH-4009 Basel, Switzerland. TEL 061-3061111. FAX 061-3061234. *1746*

SYRACUSE CHEMIST.
American Chemical Society, Syracuse Section, c/o David Orser, Ed., General Electric Co., Electronics Park, Bldg. 6, Rm. 305, Syracuse, NY 13221. *1694*

SYRACUSE UNIVERSITY LIBRARY ASSOCIATES COURIER.
Syracuse University Library Associates, 600 Bird Library, Syracuse, NY 13244-2010. TEL 315-443-2130. FAX 315-443-2671. *3627*

SYSTEM.
Elsevier Science Ltd., Pergamon, P.O. Box 800, Kidlington, Oxford OX5 1DX, England. TEL 44-1865-843000. FAX 44-1865-843010. *2502*

SYSTEM DYNAMICS.
System Dynamics Society of India, c/o Dept. of Industrial Engineering & Management, Indian Institute of Technology, Kharagpur 721 302, India. TEL 91-2221-2224. FAX 91-3222-2303. *2619*

SYSTEM DYNAMICS REVIEW.
John Wiley & Sons Ltd., Journals, Baffins Ln., Chichester, W. Sussex PO19 1UD, England. TEL 44-1243-779777. FAX 44-1243-843232. *1447*

SYSTEMATIC BIOLOGY.
Allen Press, c/o National Museum of Natural History, NHB 163, Washington, DC 20560. TEL 913-843-1234. FAX 205-460-7357. *821*

SYSTEMATIC BOTANY.
American Society of Plant Taxonomists, Department of Biology, Saint Mary's College, Notre Dame, IN 46556. TEL 219-284-4674. FAX 219-284-4716. *705*

SYSTEMATIC BOTANY MONOGRAPHS.
American Society of Plant Taxonomists (Ann Arbor), University of Michigan Herbarium, N. University Bldg., Ann Arbor, MI 48109-1057. TEL 313-747-2812. FAX 313-763-0369. *705*

SYSTEMATIC ENTOMOLOGY.
Blackwell Science Ltd., Osney Mead, Oxford OX2 0EL, England. TEL 44-1865-206206. FAX 44-1865-721205. *736*

SYSTEMATIC PARASITOLOGY.
Kluwer Academic Publishers, Postbus 17, 3300 AA Dordrecht, Netherlands. TEL 31-78-6392392. FAX 31-78-6392254. *609*

SYSTEMS AND CONTROL LETTERS.
North-Holland P.O. Box 211, 1000 AE Amsterdam, Netherlands. TEL 31-20-4853911. FAX 31-20-4853598. *2059*

SYSTEMS PRACTICE.
Plenum Publishing Corp., 233 Spring St., New York, NY 10013-1578. TEL 212-620-8000. FAX 212-463-0742. *1447*

SYSTEMS RESEARCH.
John Wiley & Sons Ltd., Journals, Baffins Ln., Chichester, W. Sussex PO19 1UD, England. TEL 44-1243-779777. FAX 44-1243-843232. *2059*

SYSTEMS RESEARCH IN PHYSIOLOGY.
Gordon & Breach Science Publishers, c/o International Publishers Distributor, P.O. Box 3054, Langhorne, PA 19047-3054. TEL 215-750-2642. FAX 215-750-6343. *5884*

SYSTEMS SCIENCE AND MATHEMATICAL SCIENCES.
Science Press, Marketing and Sales Department, 16 Donghuangchenggen North St., Beijing 100717, People's Republic of China. *4399*

THE SYSTEMS THINKER.
Pegasus Communications, Inc., Box 120, Kendal Sq., Cambridge, MA 02142. TEL 617-576-1231. FAX 617-576-3114. *1447*

SZKOLA ZAWODOWA.
Szkola Zawodowa, Ul. Smulikowskiego 6-8, 00-389 Warsaw, Poland. TEL 48-22-261011. *2375*

T A H P E R D JOURNAL.
Texas Association for Health, Physical Education, Recreation and Dance, 6300 La Calma Dr., No. 100, Austin, TX 78752. TEL 512-459-1299. FAX 512-459-1290. *5536*

T A P P I COATING CONFERENCE.
Technical Association of the Pulp and Paper Industry, Inc., Technology Park - Atlanta, Box 105113, Atlanta, GA 30348. TEL 770-446-1400. FAX 770-446-6947. *5327*

T A P P I ENGINEERING CONFERENCE PROCEEDINGS (YEAR).
Technical Association of the Pulp and Paper Industry, Inc., Technology Park - Atlanta, Box 105113, Atlanta, GA 30348. TEL 770-446-1400. FAX 770-446-6947. *2619*

T A P P I FINISHING AND CONVERTING CONFERENCE. PROCEEDINGS (YEAR).
Technical Association of the Pulp and Paper Industry, Inc., Technology Park - Atlanta, Box 105113, Atlanta, GA 30348. TEL 770-446-1400. FAX 770-446-6947. *5327*

T A P P I HOT MELT CONFERENCE (YEAR).
Technical Association of the Pulp and Paper Industry, Inc., Technology Park - Atlanta, Box 105113, Atlanta, GA 30348. TEL 770-446-1400. FAX 770-446-6947. *5327*

T A P P I INTERNATIONAL CORRUGATED CONTAINERS CONFERENCE. PROCEEDINGS.
Technical Association of the Pulp and Paper Industry, Inc., Technology Park - Atlanta, Box 105113, Atlanta, GA 30348. TEL 770-446-1400. FAX 770-446-6947. *5327*

T A P P I INTERNATIONAL ENVIRONMENTAL CONFERENCE. PROCEEDINGS.
Technical Association of the Pulp and Paper Industry, Inc., Technology Park - Atlanta, Box 105113, Atlanta, GA 30348. TEL 770-446-1400. FAX 770-446-6947. *2821*

T A P P I INTERNATIONAL PROCESS & PRODUCT QUALITY CONFERENCE PROCEEDINGS (YEAR).
Technical Association of the Pulp and Paper Industry, Inc., Technology Park - Atlanta, Box 105113, Atlanta, GA 30348. TEL 770-446-1400. FAX 770-446-6947. *5327*

T A P P I JOURNAL.
Technical Association of the Pulp and Paper Industry, Inc., Technology Park - Atlanta, Box 105113, Atlanta, GA 30348. TEL 770-446-1400. FAX 770-446-6947. *5327*

T A P P I NONWOOD PLANT FIBER PULPING PROGRESS REPORT.
Technical Association of the Pulp and Paper Industry, Inc., Technology Park - Atlanta, Box 105113, Atlanta, GA 30348. TEL 770-446-1400. FAX 770-446-6947. *5327*

T A P P I NONWOVENS CONFERENCE. PROCEEDINGS (YEAR).
Technical Association of the Pulp and Paper Industry, Inc., Technology Park - Atlanta, Box 105113, Atlanta, GA 30348. TEL 770-446-1400. FAX 770-446-6947. *5327*

T A P P I PAPERMAKERS CONFERENCE.
Technical Association of the Pulp and Paper Industry, Inc., Technology Park - Atlanta, Box 105113, Atlanta, GA 30348. TEL 770-446-1400. FAX 770-446-6947. *5327*

T A P P I POLYMERS, LAMINATIONS & COATINGS CONFERENCE. PROCEEDINGS (YEAR).
Technical Association of the Pulp and Paper Industry, Inc., Technology Park - Atlanta, Box 105113, Atlanta, GA 30348. TEL 770-446-1400. FAX 770-446-6947. *5327*

T A P P I PROCEEDINGS (YEAR).
Technical Association of the Pulp and Paper Industry, Inc., Technology Park - Atlanta, Box 105113, Atlanta, GA 30348. TEL 770-446-1400. FAX 770-446-6947. *5327*

T A P P I PROCESS CONTROL CONFERENCE. PROCEEDINGS (YEAR).
Technical Association of the Pulp and Paper Industry, Inc., Technology Park - Atlanta, Box 105113, Atlanta, GA 30348. TEL 770-446-1400. FAX 770-446-6947. *5327*

T A P P I PULPING CONFERENCE. PROCEEDINGS.
Technical Association of the Pulp and Paper Industry, Inc., Technology Park - Atlanta, Box 105113, Atlanta, GA 30348. TEL 770-446-1400. FAX 770-446-6947. *5327*

T A P P I TEST METHODS.
Technical Association of the Pulp and Paper Industry, Inc., Technology Park - Atlanta, Box 105113, Atlanta, GA 30348. TEL 770-446-1400. FAX 770-446-6947. *5327*

T E S O L MATTERS.
Teachers of English to Speakers of Other Languages, 1600 Cameron St., Ste. 300, Alexandria, VA 22314-2751. TEL 703-836-0774. FAX 703-836-7864. *4116*

T I M S STUDIES IN THE MANAGEMENT SCIENCES.
Elsevier Science B.V., Books Division, P.O. Box 211, 1000 AE Amsterdam, Netherlands. TEL 31-20-4853911. FAX 31-20-4853705. *1157*

T M A JOURNAL.
Treasury Management Association, 7315 Wisconsin Ave., Ste. 1250W, Bethesda, MD 20814. TEL 301-907-2862. FAX 301-907-2864. *1123*

T R C SPECTRAL DATA - INFRARED.
Thermodynamics Research Center, Texas Engineering Experiment Station, Texas A & M University System, College Station, TX 77843-3111. TEL 409-845-4940. FAX 409-847-8590. *1721*

T R C SPECTRAL DATA - ULTRAVIOLET.
Thermodynamics Research Center, Texas Engineering Experiment Station, Texas A & M University System, College Station, TX 77843-3111. TEL 409-845-4940. FAX 409-847-8590. *1722*

T R C SPECTRAL DATA - 13 C NUCLEAR MAGNETIC RESONANCE.
Thermodynamics Research Center, Texas Engineering Experiment Station, Texas A & M University System, College Station, TX 77843-3111. TEL 409-845-4940. FAX 409-847-8590. *1722*

T R C THERMODYNAMIC TABLES - HYDROCARBONS.
Thermodynamics Research Center, Texas Engineering Experiment Station, Texas A & M University System, College Station, TX 77843-3111. TEL 409-845-4940. FAX 409-847-8590. *1758*

T R C THERMODYNAMIC TABLES - NON-HYDROCARBONS.
Thermodynamics Research Center, Texas Engineering Experiment Station, Texas A & M University System, College Station, TX 77843-3111. TEL 409-845-4940. FAX 409-847-8590. *1722*

T SQUARED NEWSLETTER.
Technology Transfer Society, 23 Main St., Franklin, IN 46131. TEL 317-738-3908. FAX 317-738-3980. *6665*

T W TAGUNGSREGIONEN.
T W Tagungswirtschaft GmbH, M und A Verlag fuer Messen, Ausstellunger und Kongresse GmbH, Mainzer Landstr. 251, 60326 Frankfurt a.M., Germany. TEL 069-759502. FAX 069-75951909. *4937*

TAAL EN TONGVAL.
Seminarie Vlaamse Dialektologie te Gent, Blandijnberg 2, B-9000 Gent, Belgium. TEL 32-9-2644075. FAX 32-9-2644170. *4116*

TAKAHE.
Takahe Collective Trust, P.O. Box 13-335, Christchurch 1, New Zealand. TEL 64-3-3598133. *4275*

TALANTA.
Elsevier Science B.V., P.O. Box 211, 1000 AE Amsterdam, Netherlands. TEL 31-20-4853911. FAX 31-20-4853598. *1722*

TALISMAN.
Box 3157, Jersey City, NJ 07303-3157. TEL 201-938-0698. *4321*

TALKING POLITICS.
Politics Association, 64 W. Hill Dr., Dartford, Kent DA1 3EA, England. TEL 44-1322-275145. *5711*

TALLER DE LETRAS.
Pontificia Universidad Catolica de Chile, Instituto de Letras, Jaime Guzman Errazuriz 3300, Campus Oriente U.C., Casilla 6277, Correo 22, Santiago, Chile. TEL 562-274-4041 ext. 5189. FAX 562-2233125. *4275*

TAMAQUA.
Parkland College, Humanities Department, 2400 W. Bradley Ave., Champaign, IL 61821-1899. TEL 217-351-2380. FAX 217-373-3899. *4169*

TAMKANG JOURNAL OF MATHEMATICS.
Tamkang University Press, Tamsui, Taipei, Taiwan 25137, Republic of China. TEL 886-2-621-5656. FAX 886-2-620-2613. *4399*

TAMPA REVIEW.
University of Tampa Press, 401 W. Kennedy Blvd., Tampa, FL 33606-1490. TEL 813-253-3333. FAX 813-258-7593. *4321*

T'ANG STUDIES.
T'ang Studies Society, c/o Prof. Michael R. Drompp, Rhodes College, Department of History, 2000 N. Pkwy., Memphis, TN 38112. TEL 901-726-3655. FAX 901-726-3727. *5294*

TANMIAT AL-RAFIDAIN.
Majallat Tanmiat al-Rafidain P.O. Box 78, Mosul, Iraq. TEL 814433. *5924*

TAOIST RESOURCES.
Indiana University, East Asian Studies Center, Memorial Hall W 207, Indiana University, Bloomington, IN 47405. TEL 812-855-3765. FAX 812-855-7762. *6213*

TAPOL.
Indonesia Human Rights Campaign, 111 Northwood Rd., Thornton Heath, Surrey CR7 8HW, England. TEL 0131-771-2904. FAX 0181-653-0322. *5736*

TARGET.
John Benjamins Publishing Co., Amsteldijk 44, P.O. Box 75577, 1070 AN Amsterdam, Netherlands. TEL 31-20-6738156. FAX 31-20-6792956. *4116*

TARGET ORGAN TOXICOLOGY SERIES.
Lippincott - Raven Publishers, 227 E. Washington Sq., Philadelphia, PA 19106. TEL 215-238-4200. FAX 215-238-4235. *2843*

TASKS FOR VEGETATION SCIENCE.
Kluwer Academic Publishers, Postbus 17, 3300 AA Dordrecht, Netherlands. TEL 31-78-6392392. FAX 31-78-6392254. *705*

TASMANIA. DEPARTMENT OF PRIMARY INDUSTRY AND FISHERIES. MARINE RESOURCES DIVISION TECHNICAL REPORT.
Department of Primary Industry and Fisheries, Marine Resources Division, P.O. Box 619F, Hobart Tas. 7001, Australia. TEL 61-02-278035. *2944*

TASMANIAN NATURALIST.
Tasmanian Field Naturalist Club, Inc., G.P.O. Box 68A, Hobart, Tas. 7001, Australia. TEL 61-02-337870. FAX 61-02-337594. *609*

TASMANIAN TRAVELWAYS.
Creative Publications Pty., Ltd., 71-75 Paterson St., Launceston, Tas. 7250, Australia. *6914*

TAUBMAN LECTURES IN JEWISH STUDIES.
California University Press, 2120 Berkeley Way, Berkeley, CA 94720. TEL 510-643-7127. FAX 510-643-7127. *6132*

TAWAGOTO.
Hohm Press, Box 4272, Prescott, AZ 86302. TEL 602-778-9189. FAX 520-717-1779. *6213*

TAXATION FOR LAWYERS.
Warren, Gorham & Lamont, One Penn Plaza, New York, NY 10119. TEL 212-971-5000. FAX 212-971-5240. *1568*

TAXATION IN AUSTRALIA (BLUE EDITION).
Taxation Institute of Australia, 7th Fl., 64 Castlereagh St., Sydney, N.S.W. 2000, Australia. TEL 61-2-2323422. FAX 61-2-2216953. *1568*

TAXATION IN AUSTRALIA (RED EDITION).
Taxation Institute of Australia, 7th Fl., 64 Castlereagh St., Sydney, N.S.W. 2000, Australia. TEL 61-2-7323422. FAX 61-2-2216953. *1568*

TAXATION PRACTITIONER.
Chartered Institute of Taxation, 12 Upper Belgrave St., London SW1X 8BB, England. TEL 0171-235-9381. FAX 0171-235-2562. *1568*

TAXON.
International Association for Plant Taxonomy, Botanischer Garten & Botanisches Museum, Koenigin-Luise-Str. 6-8, 14191 Berlin, Germany. TEL 49-30-8316010. FAX 49-30 83006218. *705*

TAYLOR.
Taylor University, 500 W. Reade Ave., Upland, IN 46989. TEL 317-998-2751. FAX 317-998-4910. *2443*

TE REO.
Linguistic Society of New Zealand, c/o University of Auckland, English Dept., Private Bag 92019, Auckland 1, New Zealand. TEL 64-9-3737999. FAX 64-9-3737449. *4116*

TEACHER EDUCATION AND PRACTICE.
Texas Association of Colleges of Teacher Education, c/o Lamar University, College of Education and Human Development, Beaumont, TX 77710. *2443*

TEACHER IN ZIMBABWE.
Zimbabwe Publishing House, P.O. Box 350, Harare, Zimbabwe. TEL 263-4-497548. FAX 263-4-497554. *2376*

TEACHING AND LEARNING IN MEDICINE.
Lawrence Erlbaum Associates, Inc., 10 Industrial Dr., Mahwah, NJ 07430-2262. TEL 201-236-9500. FAX 201-236-0072. *4536*

TEACHING AND LEARNING: THE JOURNAL OF NATURAL INQUIRY.
University of North Dakota, Box 7189, Univ. Sta., Grand Forks, ND 58202-7189. TEL 701-777-3146. FAX 701-777-4393. *2503*

TEACHING & TEACHER EDUCATION.
Elsevier Science Ltd., Pergamon, P.O. Box 800, Kidlington, Oxford OX5 1DX, England. TEL 44-1865-843000. FAX 44-1865-843010. *2503*

TEACHING AND TRAINING IN GERIATRIC MEDICINE.
S. Karger AG, Allschwilerstr. 10, P.O. Box, CH-4009 Basel, Switzerland. TEL 061-3061111. FAX 061-3061234. *3297*

TEACHING BUSINESS ETHICS.
Kluwer Academic Publications, Postbus 17, 3300 AA Dordrecht, Netherlands. TEL 31-78-6392392. FAX 31-78-9392254. *5502*

TEACHING CHILDREN MATHEMATICS.
National Council of Teachers of Mathematics, 1906 Association Dr., Reston, VA 22091-1593. TEL 703-620-9840. FAX 703-476-2970. *4399*

TEACHING EARTH SCIENCES.
Institute of Earth Studies, University of Wales, Aberstwyth, Dyfed SY23 3DB, Wales. TEL 44-1970-622639. FAX 44-1970-622659. *2264*

TEACHING ELEMENTARY PHYSICAL EDUCATION.
Human Kinetics Publishers, Inc., Box 5076, Champaign, IL 61825-5076. TEL 217-351-5076. FAX 217-351-2674. *2503*

TEACHING EXCEPTIONAL CHILDREN.
Council for Exceptional Children, 1920 Association Dr., Reston, VA 22091. TEL 703-620-3660. FAX 703-264-9494. *2476*

TEACHING HISTORY: A JOURNAL OF METHODS.
Emporia State University, Division of Social Sciences, Box 4032, Emporia, KS 66801. TEL 316-341-5579. FAX 316-341-5143. *2504*

TEACHING OF PSYCHOLOGY.
Lawrence Erlbaum Associates, Inc., 10 Industrial Dr., Mahwah, NJ 07430-2262. TEL 201-236-9500. FAX 201-236-0072. *5884*

TEACHING PROFESSOR.
Magna Publications, Inc., 2718 Dryden Dr., Madison, WI 53704-3006. TEL 608-246-3580. FAX 608-249-0355. *2444*

TEACHING PUBLIC ADMINISTRATION.
Sheffield Business School, Policy Research Centre, Unit 7, Science Park, Howard St., Sheffield S1 2LX, England. TEL 44-114-253-4460. FAX 44-114-253-4467. *2504*

TEACHING STATISTICS.
Teaching Statistics Trust, RSS Centre for Statistical Education, University of Nottingham, Nottingham N97 2RD, England. TEL 44-115-951-4911. FAX 44-115-951-4951. *2394*

TECHNICA.
Comite National de la Bijouterie, Horlogerie, Joaillerie, Orfevrerie, Blvd. de Smet de Naeyer 290a, 1090 Brussels, Belgium. TEL 32-2-4282245. FAX 32-2-4283078. *3698*

TECHNICAL ANALYSIS OF STOCKS & COMMODITIES.
Technical Analysis, Inc., 4757 California Ave., S.W., Seattle, WA 98116-4499. TEL 206-938-0570. FAX 206-938-1307. *1355*

TECHNICAL COMMUNICATION QUARTERLY.
University of Minnesota, Rhetoric Department, 201 Haecker Hall, St. Paul, MN 55108. TEL 612-624-9729. FAX 612-624-3167. *2504*

TECHNICAL SERVICES QUARTERLY.
Haworth Press, Inc., 10 Alice St., Binghamton, NY 13904. TEL 607-722-5857. FAX 607-722-1424. *4029*

TECHNIKA POSZUKIWAN GEOLOGICZNYCH, GEOSYNOPTYKA I GEOTERMIA.
Polska Akademia Nauk, Centrum Podstawowych Problemow Gospodarki Surowcami Mineralnymi i Energia, Ul. Jozefa Wybickiego 7, 31-261 Krakow, Poland. TEL 48-12-322435. FAX 48-12-323534. *2264*

TECHNIQUES AND INSTRUMENTATION IN ANALYTICAL CHEMISTRY.
Elsevier Science B.V., Books Division, P.O. Box 211, 1000 AE Amsterdam, Netherlands. TEL 31-20-4853911. FAX 31-20-4853705. *1722*

TECHNIQUES IN ORTHOPAEDICS.
Lippincott - Raven Publishers 227 Washington Sq., Philadelphia, PA 19106. TEL 215-238-4200. *4792*

TECHNIQUES IN THE BEHAVIORAL AND NEURAL SCIENCES.
Elsevier Science B.V., Books Division, P.O. Box 211, 1000 AE Amsterdam, Netherlands. TEL 31-20-4853911. FAX 31-20-4853705. *4870*

TECHNIQUES OF CHEMISTRY.
John Wiley & Sons, Inc., 605 Third Ave., New York, NY 10158. TEL 212-850-6000. FAX 212-850-6088. *1694*

TECHNIQUES OF PHYSICS.
Academic Press, Inc., 525 B St., Ste. 1900, San Diego, CA 92101-4495. TEL 619-231-0926. FAX 619-699-6715. *5573*

TECHNISCHE UNIVERSITEIT EINDHOVEN. FACULTEIT DER WISKUNDE EN INFORMATICA. E U T REPORTS - W S K.
Technische Universiteit Eindhoven, Faculteit der Wiskunden Informatica, Postbus 513, 5600 MB Eindhoven, Netherlands. *4399*

TECHNOLOGICAL FORECASTING AND SOCIAL CHANGE.
Elsevier Science Inc., Box 945, New York, NY 10159-0945. TEL 212-633-3730. FAX 212-633-3680. *6666*

TECHNOLOGY ANALYSIS & STRATEGIC MANAGEMENT.
Carfax Publishing Co., P.O. Box 25, Abingdon, Oxon. OX14 3UE, England. TEL 44-1235-401000. FAX 44-1235-401550. *6667*

TECHNOLOGY AND CULTURE.
University of Chicago Press, Journals Division, Box 37005, Chicago, IL 60637. TEL 773-753-3347. FAX 773-753-0811. *6667*

TECHNOLOGY AND DISABILITY.
Elsevier Science Ireland Ltd., P.O. Box 85, Limerick, Ireland. TEL 353-61-471944. FAX 353-61-472144. *3308*

TECHNOLOGY AND HEALTH CARE.
I O S Press, Van Diemenstraat 94, 1013 CN Amsterdam, Netherlands. TEL 31-20-6382189. FAX 31-20-6203419. *4536*

TECHNOLOGY FOR ALASKAN TRANSPORTATION.
Alaska Transportation Technology Transfer Program, DOT & PF T2 Program, 2301 Peger Rd., Fairbanks, AK 99709-5399. TEL 907-451-5320. FAX 907-451-2313. *6728*

TECHNOLOGY FOR ANESTHESIA.
E C R I, 5200 Butler Pike, Plymouth Meeting, PA 19462. TEL 610-825-6000. FAX 610-834-1275. *4593*

TECHNOLOGY FOR CARDIOLOGY.
E C R I, 5200 Butler Pike, Plymouth Meeting, PA 19462. TEL 610-825-6000. FAX 610-834-1275. *4610*

TECHNOLOGY FOR CRITICAL CARE NURSES.
E C R I, 5200 Butler Pike, Plymouth Meeting, PA 19462. TEL 610-825-6000. FAX 610-834-1274. *4729*

TECHNOLOGY FOR EMERGENCY CARE NURSES.
E C R I, 5200 Butler Pike, Plymouth Meeting, PA 19462. TEL 610-825-6000. FAX 610-834-1275. *4729*

TECHNOLOGY FOR RESPIRATORY THERAPY.
E C R I, 5200 Butler Pike, Plymouth Meeting, PA 19462. TEL 610-825-6000. FAX 610-834-1275. *4892*

TECHNOLOGY IN SOCIETY.
Elsevier Science Ltd., Pergamon, P.O. Box 800, Kidlington, Oxford OX5 1DX, England. TEL 44-1865-843000. FAX 44-1865-843010. *6437*

TECHNOLOGY MANAGEMENT.
Elsevier Science Inc., Box 945, New York, NY 10159-0945. TEL 212-633-3730. FAX 212-633-3680. *6667*

TECHNOLOGY, RISK AND SOCIETY.
Kluwer Academic Publishers, Postbus 17, 3300 AA Dordrecht, Netherlands. TEL 31-78-6392392. FAX 31-78-6392254. *1262*

TECHNOLOGY TRANSFER SOCIETY. INTERNATIONAL SYMPOSIUM PROCEEDINGS.
Technology Transfer Society, 23 N. Main St., Franklin, IN 46131. TEL 317-738-3908. FAX 317-738-3908. *1448*

TECHNOMETRICS.
American Statistical Association, 1429 Duke St., Alexandria, VA 22314-3402. TEL 703-684-1221. FAX 703-684-2037. *2620*

TECHNOVATION.
Elsevier Science Ltd., P.O. Box 800, Kidlington, Oxford OX5 1DX, England. TEL 44-1865-843000. FAX 44-1865-843010. *6668*

TECHTRENDS.
Association for Educational Communications and Technology, 1025 Vermont Ave., N.W., Ste. 820, Washington, DC 20005-3516. TEL 202-347-7834. FAX 202-347-7839. *2504*

TECNOLOGIA DE ALIMENTOS.
Asociacion de Tecnologos Alimentos de Mexico, Mar del Norte 5, San Alvaro, Atzcapozalco, 02090 Mexico DF, Mexico. TEL 525-3861368. FAX 525-3861952. *2992*

TECNOLOGIA Y CONSTRUCCION.
Instituto de Desarrollo Experimental de la Construccion, Apdo. Postal 47169, Caracas 1041-A, Venezuela. TEL 58-2-6931269. FAX 58-2-6931183. *877*

TECTONOPHYSICS.
Elsevier Science B.V., P.O. Box 211, 1000 AE Amsterdam, Netherlands. TEL 31-20-4853911. FAX 57-20-4853598. *2282*

TEHUDA.
Weizman Institute of Science, Department of Science Teaching, Rehovot 76100, Israel. TEL 972-8-342981. FAX 972-8-344174. *5573*

TEKI HISTORYCZNE.
Polish Historical Society in Great Britain, 20 Princes Gate, London SW7 1QA, England. *3450*

TEKNIK DERGI.
Turkish Chamber of Civil Engineers, Selanik Caddesi 19-1, Kizilay 06650 Ankara, Turkey. TEL 90-312-4337626. FAX 90-312-4170632. *2674*

TELECOMMUNICATION JOURNAL OF AUSTRALIA.
Telecommunication Society of Australia Ltd., P.O. Box 4050, Melbourne, Vic. 3001, Australia. TEL 61-3-96390906. FAX 61-3-96391515. *1917*

TELECOMMUNICATIONS POLICY.
Butterworth - Heinemann, Part of the Reed Elsevier group, Linacre House, Jordan Hill, Oxford OX2 8DP, England. TEL 44-1865-310366. FAX 44-1865-310898. *1917*

TELEKTRONIKK.
Telenor AS, P.O. Box 83, N-2007 Kjeller, Norway. TEL 47-63-84-84-00. FAX 47-63-81-00-76. *1918*

TELEMATICS AND INFORMATICS.
Elsevier Science Ltd., Pergamon, P.O. Box 800, Kidlington, Oxford OX5 1DX, England. TEL 44-1865-843000. FAX 44-1865-843010. *1918*

TELETRAFFIC SCIENCE AND ENGINEERING.
Elsevier Science B.V., Books Division, P.O. Box 211, 1000 AE Amsterdam, Netherlands. TEL 31-20-4853911. FAX 31-20-4853705. *1930*

TELLUS. SERIES A: DYNAMIC METEOROLOGY AND OCEANOGRAPHY.
Munksgaard International Publishers Ltd., P.O. Box 2148, DK-1016 Copenhagen K, Denmark, Denmark. TEL 45-33-127030. FAX 45-33-129387. *2283*

TELLUS. SERIES B: CHEMICAL AND PHYSICAL METEOROLOGY.
Munksgaard International Publishers Ltd., 35 Noerre Soegade, P.O. Box 2148, DK-1016 Copenhagen K, Denmark. TEL 45-33-127030. FAX 45-33-129387. *2283*

TEMPORARY CULTURE.
Box 43072, Upper Montclair, NJ 07043-7072. *4332*

TEMPUS.
University of Queensland, Anthropology Museum, St. Lucia, Qld. 4072, Australia. TEL 61-7-33652674. FAX 61-7-33654696. *324*

TENNESSEE ACADEMY OF SCIENCE. JOURNAL.
Tennessee Academy of Science, 2001 Craven Ln., Prairie Peninsula, Hixson, TN 37343. TEL 615-251-1573. *6290*

TENNESSEE HISTORICAL QUARTERLY.
Tennessee Historical Society, War Memorial Bldg., Nashville, TN 37243. TEL 615-741-8934. FAX 615-741-8937. *3489*

TENNESSEE NURSE.
Tennessee Nurses Association, 545 Mainstream Dr., Ste. 405, Nashville, TN 37228-1201. TEL 615-254-0350. FAX 615-254-0303. *4729*

TENNESSEE REGISTER.
Diocese of Nashville, 2400 21st Ave. S., Nashville, TN 37212-5302. TEL 615-783-0770. FAX 615-292-8411. *6198*

TENNESSEE TOWN AND CITY.
Tennessee Municipal League, 226 Capitol Blvd., Nashville, TN 37219. TEL 615-255-6416. FAX 615-255-7428. *5951*

TENNESSEE WILDLIFE.
Wildlife Resources Agency, Box 40747, Nashville, TN 37204. TEL 615-781-6504. FAX 615-741-4606. *821*

TENSO.
Societe Guilhem IX, c/o Classical & Modern Languages, University of Louisville, Louisville, KY 40292. TEL 502-852-6686. FAX 502-852-8885. *4276*

TERATOGENESIS, CARCINOGENESIS, AND MUTAGENESIS.
John Wiley & Sons, Inc., Journals, 605 Third Ave., New York, NY 10158. TEL 212-850-6645. FAX 212-850-6021. *4536*

TERATOLOGY.
John Wiley & Sons, Inc., Journals, 605 Third Ave., New York, NY 10158. TEL 212-850-6645. FAX 212-850-6021. *610*

TERMINOLOGY.
John Benjamins Publishing Co., Amsteldijk 44, P.O. Box 75577, 1070 AN Amsterdam, Netherlands. TEL 31-20-6762325. FAX 31-20-6792956. *4117*

TERRA E SOLE.
IACICO S.r.L., Via A. Poliziano 80, 00184 Rome, Italy. TEL 39-6-4873183. FAX 39-6-4873144. *156*

TERRA NOVA.
Blackwell Science Ltd., Osney Mead, Oxford OX2 OEL, England. TEL 44-1865-206206. FAX 44-1865-721205. *2216*

TERRAIN.
Ministere de la Culture 65 rue de Richelieu, 75002 Paris, France. TEL 40-15-85-27. FAX 40-15-87-33. *324*

TERRORISM AND POLITICAL VIOLENCE.
Frank Cass, Newbury House, 890-900 Eastern Ave., Newbury Park, Ilford, Essex 1G2 7HH, England. TEL 44-181-599-8866. FAX 44-181-599-0984. *5773*

TETRAHEDRON.
Elsevier Science Ltd., Pergamon, P.O. Box 800, Kidlington, Oxford OX5 1DX, England. TEL 44-1865-843000. FAX 44-1865-843010. *1747*

TETRAHEDRON: ASYMMETRY.
Elsevier Science Ltd., Pergamon, P.O. Box 800, Kidlington, Oxford OX5 1DX, England. TEL 44-1865-843000. FAX 44-1865-843010. *1747*

TETRAHEDRON LETTERS.
Elsevier Science Ltd., Pergamon, P.O. Box 800, Kidlington, Oxford OX5 1DX, England. TEL 44-1865-843000. FAX 44-1865-843010. *1747*

TEXAS A & M UNIVERSITY. COLLEGE OF GEOSCIENCES. CONTRIBUTIONS IN OCEANOGRAPHY.
Texas A & M University, Department of Oceanography, College Sta., TX 77843. TEL 409-845-7327. FAX 409-845-6331. *2306*

TEXAS CHILD CARE.
Department of Human Services, Self-Support Services, 701 W. 51st St., Box 149030, E-311, Austin, TX 78714-9030. TEL 512-450-4562. FAX 512-441-6633. *1779*

TEXAS HEART INSTITUTE JOURNAL.
Texas Heart Institute, Publications & Communications, MC 1-194, Box 20345, Houston, TX 77225-0345. TEL 713-794-6630. FAX 713-791-3714. *4610*

TEXAS JOURNAL OF POLITICAL STUDIES.
Sam Houston State University, Department of Government, San Angelo, TX 76909-0896. TEL 409-294-1462. FAX 409-294-3622. *5712*

TEXAS JOURNAL OF SCIENCE.
Texas Academy of Science, c/o Texas Tech University, The Museum, Box 4499, Lubbock, TX 79409. TEL 806-742-2487. *6290*

TEXAS TALK.
Arc of Texas, Box 5368, Austin, TX 78763-5368. TEL 512-454-6694. FAX 512-454-4956. *3308*

TEXAS TECH LAW REVIEW.
Texas Tech University, School of Law, Lubbock, TX 79409-0004. TEL 806-742-3789. FAX 806-742-1629. *3857*

TEXT AND PERFORMANCE QUARTERLY.
Speech Communication Association, 5105 Backlick Rd., Bldg. E., Annandale, VA 22003. TEL 703-750-0533. FAX 703-914-9471. *4277*

TEXT TECHNOLOGY.
Wright State University, Lake Campus, 7600 State Rt. 703, Celina, OH 45322-2952. TEL 419-586-0358. FAX 419-586-0368. *3712*

TEXTIEL BEHEER.
Stichting Vakblad Textielreiniging, Rembrandtlaan 67, 3723 BH Bilthoven Netherlands. FAX 31-30-2286885. *1829*

TEXTILE CHEMIST AND COLORIST.
American Association of Textile Chemists and Colorists, One Davis Dr., Box 12215, Research Triangle Park, NC 27709-2215. TEL 919-549-8141. FAX 919-549-8933. *6686*

TEXTILE MUSEUM JOURNAL.
Textile Museum, 2320 S St. N.W., Washington, DC 20008. TEL 202-667-044 L FAX 202-483-0994 *6687*

TEXTILE RESEARCH JOURNAL.
Textile Research Institute, 601 Prospect Ave., Box 625, Princeton, NJ 08542. TEL 609-924-3150. FAX 609-683-7836. *6687*

TEXTILE SCIENCE AND TECHNOLOGY.
Elsevier Science B.V., Books Division, P.O. Box 211, 1000 AE Amsterdam, Netherlands. TEL 31-20-4853911. FAX 31-20-4853705. *6687*

TEXTS ON COMPUTATIONAL MECHANICS.
Elsevier Science B.V., Books Division, P.O. Box 211, 1000 AE Amsterdam, Netherlands. TEL 31-20-4853911. FAX 31-20-4853705. *2771*

TEXTUAL STUDIES IN CANADA.
University College of the Cariboo, English Department, Box 3010, Kamloops, BC V2C 5N3, Canada TEL 604-828-5000 FAX 604-828-5086. *4169*

TEXTURE.
Texture Press, 3760 Cedar Ridge Dr., Norman, OK 73072. TEL 405-366-7730 FAX 405-364-3627. *4321*

TEXTURES AND MICROSTRUCTURES.
Gordon & Breach Science Publishers, c/o International Publishers Distributor, P.O. Box 3054 Langhorne, PA 19047-3054 TEL 215-750-2642. FAX 215-750-6343. *2264*

THEATRE ANNUAL.
College of William and Mary Department of Theatre and Speech, Williamsburg, VA 23187. TEL 804-221-2668. FAX 804-221-1287. *6705*

THEATRE HISTORY STUDIES.
Mid-America Theatre Association, Theatre Program, Central College, Pella, IA 50219. TEL 515-628-5234. FAX 515-628-5316. *6705*

THEATRE STUDIES.
Ohio State University, Theatre Research Institute, 1430 Lincoln Tower, 1800 Cannon Dr., Columbus, OH 43210. TEL 614-292-6614. FAX 614-292-3222. *6706*

THEATRE SURVEY.
American Society for Theatre Research, c/o Gordon Armstrong, Sec., Dept. of Fine Arts Ctr., Univ. of Rhode Island, Kingston, RI 02881-0824. *6706*

THEATRE TOPICS.
Johns Hopkins University Press, Journals Publishing Division, 2715 N. Charles St. Baltimore, MD 21218. TEL 410-516-6987. FAX 410-516-6968. *6706*

THEMIS.
Zeta Tau Alpha, International Office, 3450 Founders Rd., Indianapolis, IN 46268. TEL 317-872-0540. FAX 371-876-3948. *1888*

THEOLOGICAL STUDIES.
Theological Studies, Inc., Georgetown University, 37th and O Sts., N.W., Washington, DC 20057. TEL 202-338-0754. FAX 202-687-7679. *6098*

THEOLOGY AND MEDICINE.
Kluwer Academic Publishers, Postbus 17, 3300 AA Dordrecht, Netherlands. TEL 31-78-6392392. FAX 31-78-6392254. *6095*

THEOLOGY & PUBLIC POLICY.
Churches' Center for Theology and Public Policy, 4500 Massachusetts Ave. N.W., Washington, DC 20016-5690. TEL 202-885-3648. *6099*

THEORETICAL AND APPLIED FRACTURE MECHANICS.
Elsevier Science B.V., P.O. Box 211, 1000 AE Amsterdam, Netherlands. TEL 31-20-4853911. FAX 31-20-4853598. *5592*

THEORETICAL AND EXPERIMENTAL BIOLOGY.
Academic Press, Inc., 525 B St., Ste 1900, San Diego, CA 92101-4495. TEL 619-231-0962. FAX 619-699-6715. *610*

THEORETICAL AND EXPERIMENTAL CHEMISTRY.
Plenum Publishing Corp., Consultants Bureau, 233 Spring St., New York, NY 10013-1578. TEL 212-620-8468. FAX 212-463-0742. *1694*

THEORETICAL AND MATHEMATICAL PHYSICS.
Plenum Publishing Corp., Consultants Bureau, 233 Spring St., New York, NY 10013-1578. TEL 212-620-8468. FAX 212-463-0742. *5573*

THEORETICAL CHEMISTRY.
Academic Press, Inc., 525 B St., Ste. 1900, San Diego, CA 92101-4495. TEL 619-231-0926. FAX 619-699-6715. *1694*

THEORETICAL COMPUTER SCIENCE.
North-Holland P.O. Box 211, 1000 AE Amsterdam, Netherlands. TEL 31-20-4853911. FAX 31-20-4853598. *2118*

THEORETICAL FOUNDATION OF CHEMICAL ENGINEERING.
Maik Nauka - Interperiodica, Mezhdunarodnyi Otdel, Ul. Profsoyuznaya, 90, 117864 Moscow, Russia. TEL 7-095-3360066. FAX 7-095-3360666. *2650*

THEORETICAL MEDICINE.
Kluwer Academic Publishers, Postbus 17, 3300 AA Dordrecht, Netherlands. TEL 31-78-6392392. FAX 31-78-6392254. *4537*

THEORETICAL POPULATION BIOLOGY.
Academic Press, Inc., Journal Division, 525 B St., Ste. 1900, San Diego, CA 92101-4495. TEL 619-230-1840. FAX 619-699-6800. *610*

THEORIA.
University of Natal Press, P.O. Box 375, Pietermaritzburg 3200, South Africa. TEL 27-331-260226. FAX 27-331-260599. *3627*

THEORIA.
Centro de Analisis, Logica e Informatica Juridica, Universidad del Pais Vasco, Servicio Editorial, Apdo. 1397, 48080 Bilbao, Spain. TEL 34-43-291725. FAX 34-4-4801314. *5502*

THEORY AND APPLICATIONS OF TRANSPORT IN POROUS MEDIA.
Kluwer Academic Publishers, Postbus 17, 3300 AA Dordrecht, Netherlands. TEL 31-78-6392392. FAX 31-78-6392254. *5573*

THEORY AND DECISION.
Kluwer Academic Publishers, Postbus 17, 3300 AA Dordrecht, Netherlands. TEL 31-78-6392392. FAX 31-78-6392254. *6349*

THEORY AND DECISION LIBRARY. SERIES A: PHILOSOPHY AND METHODOLOGY OF THE SOCIAL SCIENCES.
Kluwer Academic Publishers, Postbus 17, 3300 AA Dordrecht, Netherlands. TEL 31-78-6392392. FAX 31-78-6392254. *6349*

THEORY AND DECISION LIBRARY. SERIES B: MATHEMATICAL AND STATISTICAL METHODS.
Kluwer Academic Publishers, Postbus 17, 3300 AA Dordrecht, Netherlands. TEL 31-78-6392392. FAX 31-78-6392254. *4400*

THEORY AND DECISION LIBRARY. SERIES C: GAME THEORY, MATHEMATICAL PROGRAMMING AND OPERATIONS RESEARCH.
Kluwer Academic Publishers, Postbus 17, 3300 AA Dordrecht, Netherlands. TEL 31-78-6392392. FAX 31-78-6392254. *4412*

THEORY AND DECISION LIBRARY. SERIES D: SYSTEM THEORY, KNOWLEDGE ENGINEERING AND PROBLEM SOLVING.
Kluwer Academic Publishers, Postbus 17, 3300 AA Dordrecht, Netherlands. TEL 31-78-6392392. FAX 31-78-6392254. *2064*

THEORY & PRACTICE OF OBJECT BASED SYSTEMS.
John Wiley & Sons, Inc., Journals, 605 Third Ave., New York, NY 10158. TEL 212-850-6645. FAX 212-850-6021. *2011*

THEORY & PSYCHOLOGY.
Sage Publications Ltd., 6 Bonhill St., London EC2A 4PU, England. TEL 44-171-374-0645. FAX 44-171-374-8741. *5885*

THEORY AND RESEARCH IN BEHAVIORAL PEDIATRICS.
Plenum Publishing Corp., 233 Spring St., New York, NY 10013-1578. TEL 202-620-8000. FAX 212-463-0742. *5885*

THEORY AND SOCIETY.
Kluwer Academic Publishers, Postbus 17, 3300 AA Dordrecht, Netherlands. TEL 31-78-6392392. FAX 31-78-6392254. *6438*

THEORY CULTURE & SOCIETY.
Sage Publications Ltd., 6 Bonhill St., London EC2A 4PU, England. TEL 44-171-374-0645. FAX 44-171-374-8741. *6438*

THEORY INTO PRACTICE.
Ohio State University, College of Education, 172 Arps Hall, 1945 N. High St., Columbus, OH 43210-1172. TEL 614-292-3407. FAX 614-688-3942. *2377*

THEORY OF COMPUTING SYSTEMS.
Springer-Verlag, Science Journals, 175 Fifth Ave., New York, NY 10010. TEL 212-460-1500. FAX 212-473-6272. *2118*

THEORY OF PROBABILITY AND ITS APPLICATIONS.
Society for Industrial and Applied Mathematics, 3600 University City Science Center, Philadelphia, PA 19104-2688. TEL 215-382-9800. FAX 215-386-7999. *4400*

THEOSOPHICAL HISTORY.
c/o Department of Religious Studies, California State University, Fullerton, CA 92634-9480. TEL 714-773-3727. FAX 714-449-5820. *3361*

THEOSOPHY IN AUSTRALIA.
Theosophical Society in Australia, 484 Kent St., Sydney, N.S.W. 2000, Australia. TEL 61-2-264-7056. FAX 61-2-264-5857. *6213*

THERAPEUTIC DRUG MONITORING.
Lippincott - Raven Publishers 227 Washington Sq., Philadelphia, PA 19106. TEL 215-238-4200. *5444*

THERAPEUTIC IMMUNOLOGY.
Blackwell Science Ltd., Osney Mead, Oxford OX2 0EL, England. TEL 44-1865-206206. FAX 44-1865-721205. *4587*

THERIOGENOLOGY.
Elsevier Science Inc., Box 945, New York, NY 10159-0945. TEL 212-633-3730. FAX 212-633-3680. *6954*

THERMOCHIMICA ACTA.
Elsevier Science B.V., P.O. Box 211, 1000 AE Amsterdam, Netherlands. TEL 31-20-4853911. FAX 31-20-4853598. *1758*

THERMODYNAMICS AT TEXAS A & M.
Thermodynamics Research Center, Texas Engineering Experiment Station, Texas A & M University System, College Station, TX 77843. TEL 409-845-4940. FAX 409-847-8590. *1758*

THERMOPHYSICAL PROPERTIES.
Nihon Netsu Bussei Gakkai, Nagaoka Gijutsu Kagaku Daigaku, Kikaikei, 1603 Kamitomioka-cho, Nagaoka-shi, Niigata-ken 940-21, Japan. TEL 81-258-46-6000. FAX 81-258-46-6972. *5586*

THETA.
Crewe & Alsager Faculty of M M U, Crewe, Ches. CW1 1DU, England. TEL 44-161-247-5089. FAX 44-161-247-6370. *4400*

THIN FILMS SCIENCE AND TECHNOLOGY.
Elsevier Science B.V., Books Division, P.O. Box 211, 1000 AE Amsterdam, Netherlands. TEL 31-20-4853911. FAX 31-20-4853705. *5574*

THIN SOLID FILMS.
Elsevier Science S.A., P.O. Box 564, CH-1001 Lausanne 1, Switzerland. TEL 41-21-3207381. FAX 41-21-3235444. *5574*

THIN-WALLED STRUCTURES.
Elsevier Science Ltd., P.O. Box 800, Kidlington, Oxford OX5 1DX, England. TEL 44-1865-843000. FAX 44-1865-843010. *2771*

THE THIRD ALTERNATIVE.
T T A Press, 5 Martins Ln., Witcham, Ely, Cambs. CB6 2LB, England. TEL 44-1353-777931. *4332*

THIRD TEXT.
Kala Press, P.O. Box 3509, London NW6 3PJ, England. TEL 0171-372-0826. *455*

THIRD WORLD LEGAL STUDIES (YEAR).
International Third World Legal Studies Association, c/o Valparaiso University, School of Law, Valparaiso, IN 46383. TEL 219-465-7830. FAX 219-465-7872. *3943*

THIRD WORLD LIBRARIES.
Rosary College, Graduate School of Library and Information Science, 7900 W. Division, River Forest, IL 60305. TEL 708-524-6866. FAX 708-524-6657. *4030*

THIRD WORLD QUARTERLY.
Carfax Publishing Co., P.O. Box 25, Abingdon, Oxon. OX14 3UE, England. TEL 44-1235-401000. FAX 44-1235-401550. *1315*

THIRTIETH DISTRICT DENTAL SOCIETY, FRESNO, CALIFORNIA. BULLETIN.
Fresno-Madera Dental Society, 371 E. Bullard Ave., Ste. 120, Fresno, CA 93710-5217. TEL 209-438-7284. FAX 209-438-7287. *4655*

THIS WORLD: RELIGION AND PUBLIC LIFE.
Transaction Publishers, Transaction Periodicals Consortium, Department 3092, Rutgers University, New Brunswick, NJ 08903. TEL 908-445-2280. FAX 908-445-3138. *6099*

THOMAS HARDY JOURNAL.
Thomas Hardy Society Ltd., c/o Simon Curtis, Ed., 25 Hawthorn Grove, Heaton Moor, Stockport SK4 4HZ, England. TEL 44-161-4329075. *4277*

THOMAS WOLFE REVIEW.
Thomas Wolfe Society, c/o John S. Phillipson, Ed., Department of English, University of Akron, Akron, OH 44325. TEL 216-972-7470. *4278*

THOMIST.
Thomist Press, 487 Michigan Ave., N.E., Washington, DC 20017. TEL 202-529-5300. FAX 202-636-4460. *6198*

THOMSON'S CONSTRUCTION AUSTRALIA.
Thomson Business Publishing, 47 Chippen St., Chippendale, N.S.W. 2008, Australia. TEL 02-699-2411. FAX 02-698-3920. *877*

THORAX.
B M J Publishing Group, B.M.A. House, Tavistock Sq., London WC1H 9JR, England. TEL 44-171-383-6270. FAX 44-171-383-6402. *4537*

THOUGHTS FOR ALL SEASONS.
Valley Press, 478 N.E. 56th St., Miami, FL 33137-2621. TEL 305-756-8800. *4278*

THRESHOLDS IN EDUCATION.
Thresholds in Education Foundation, Box 771, Dekalb, IL 60115. TEL 815-753-9357. FAX 815-753-8750. *2377*

THROMBOSIS RESEARCH.
Elsevier Science Ltd., Pergamon, P.O. Box 800, Kidlington, Oxford OX5 1DX, England. TEL 44-1865-843000. FAX 44-1865-843010. *4610*

THUNDER BAY HISTORICAL MUSEUM SOCIETY. PAPERS AND RECORDS.
Thunder Bay Historical Museum Society, 425 Donald St., E., Thunder Bay, ON P7E 5V1, Canada. TEL 807-623-0801. FAX 807-622-6880. *3490*

THYMUS.
Kluwer Academic Publishers, Postbus 17, 3300 AA Dordrecht, Netherlands. TEL 31-78-6392392. FAX 31-78-6392254. *4587*

THYMUS UPDATE.
Harwood Academic Publishers, c/o International Publishers Distributor, P.O. Box 3054, Langhorne, PA 19047-3054. TEL 215-750-2642. FAX 215-750-6343. *4587*

TIANJIN DAXUE XUEBAO.
Tianjin Daxue, Qilitai, Nankai Qu, Tianjin 300072, People's Republic of China. TEL 022-3359116. FAX 022-3358706. *6290*

TIANJIN FANGZHI GONGXUEYUAN XUEBAO.
Tianjin Fangzhi Gongxueyuan, 63 Chenglinzhuang Rd., Tianjin 300160, People's Republic of China. TEL 86-22-4344477. FAX 86-22-4344572. *6688*

TIANJIN UNIVERSITY. TRANSACTIONS.
Tianjin Daxue, Qilitai, Nankai Qu, Tianjin 300072, People's Republic of China. TEL 022-3359116. FAX 022-3358706. *6291*

TIANRANQI GONGYE.
Tianranqi Gongye Zazhishe, No.3, Sec. 1, Fuqing Lu, Chengdu, Sichuan 610051, People's Republic of China. TEL 86-28-3324911. FAX 86-28-3358727. *5378*

TIANTI WULI XUEBAO.
Science Press, Marketing and Sales Department, 16 Donghuangchenggen North St., Beijing 100717, People's Republic of China. TEL 4010642. FAX 4019810. *487*

TIANWEN XUEBAO.
Science Press, Marketing and Sales Department, 16 Donghuangchenggen North St., Beijing 100717, People's Republic of China. TEL 4010642. FAX 4019810. *487*

TIANWENXUE JINZHAN.
Science Press, Marketing and Sales Department, 16 Donghuangchenggen North St., Beijing 100717, People's Republic of China. TEL 4010642. FAX 4019810. *487*

THE TIE (SCHAUMBURG).
College of Chaplains, Inc., 1701 E. Woodfield Rd., Ste. 311, Schaumburg, IL 60173. FAX 847-240-1015. *6099*

TIEDAO YIXUE.
Nanjing Tiedao Yixueyuan, 87 Dingjiaqiao, Nanjing, Jiangsu 210009, People's Republic of China. TEL 3301508. FAX 3317073. *4537*

TIJDSCHRIFT LANDINRICHTING.
Stichting Tijdschrift Landinrichting, P.O. Box 20021, 3502 LA Utrecht, Netherlands. TEL 31-30-858722. FAX 31-30-858999. *243*

TIJDSCHRIFT VOOR FERTILITEITSONDERZOEK.
Excerpta Medica Medical Communications b.v. P.O. Box 1126, 1000 BC Amsterdam, Netherlands. TEL 31-20-5153350. FAX 31-20-5153354. *4746*

TIJDSCHRIFT VOOR GENEESKUNDE.
Tijdschrift voor Geneeskunde A.S.B.L., De Pintelaan 185, 9000 Ghent, Belgium. TEL 32-9-2403330. FAX 32-9-2403390. *4537*

TIJDSCHRIFT VOOR INTEGRALE GENEESKUNDE.
Stichting Tijdschrift voor Integrale Geneeskunde, Tooropstraat 181, 6521 NM Nijmegen, Netherlands. TEL 31-80-601688. *293*

TIJDSCHRIFT VOOR MEDISCHE INFORMATICA.
Vereniging voor Medische en Biologische Informatieverwerking, c/o Erasmus University EE2116, Postbus 1738, 3000 DR Rotterdam, Netherlands. FAX 31-10-4362882. *4632*

TIJDSCHRIFT VOOR NUCLEAIRE GENEESKUNDE.
Stichting ter Bevordering van de Nucleaire Geneeskunde, c/o Paula A. Boeijen, Ouderkerkerdijk 37, 1096 CR Amsterdam, Netherlands. TEL 31-20-6657723. FAX 31-20-6636494. *4885*

TIJDSCHRIFT VOOR RECHTSGESCHIEDENIS.
Kluwer Law International Postbus 85889, 2508 CN The Hague, Netherlands. TEL 31-70-3081500. FAX 31-70-3081515. *3858*

TIJDSCHRIFT VOOR SOCIALE GEZONDHEIDSZORG.
Stichting Journals for Public Health and Science, Admiraal Helfrichlaan 1, 3527 KV Utrecht, Netherlands. TEL 31-30-2913252. FAX 31-30-2913242. *4537*

TIJDSCHRIFT VOOR THEOLOGIE.
Theologisch Faculteit, Postbus 9103, 6500 HD Nijmegen, Netherlands. TEL 31-80-772077. *6198*

TIME & SOCIETY.
Sage Publications Ltd., 6 Bonhill St., London EC2A 4PU, England. TEL 44-171-374-0645. FAX 44-171-374-8741. *6438*

TISSUE & CELL.
Churchill Livingstone Robert Stevenson House, 1-3 Baxter's Pl., Leith Walk, Edinburgh EH1 3AF, Scotland. TEL 0131-556-2424. FAX 0131-535-1704. *719*

TISSUE ANTIGENS.
Munksgaard International Publishers Ltd., 35 Noerre Soegade, F.O. Box 2148, DK-1016 Copenhagen K, Denmark. TEL 45-33-127030. FAX 45-33-129387. *4538*

TISSUE ENGINEERING.
Mary Ann Liebert, Inc. Publishers, 2 Madison Ave., Larchmont, NY 10538. TEL 914-834-3100. FAX 914-834-3688. *719*

TOBACCO CONTROL.
B M J Publishing Group, B.M.A. House, Tavistock Sq., London WC1H 9JR, England. TEL 44-171-383-6270. FAX 44-171-383-6402. *6711*

TODAY'S C P A.
Texas Society of C P A's, 1421 W. Mockingbird Ln., Ste. 100, Dallas, TX 75247-4957. TEL 214-689-6000. FAX 214-639-6046. *1056*

TODAY'S CHRISTIAN DOCTOR.
Christian Medical & Dental Society, 501 Fifth St., King Bldg., 3rd Fl., Bristol, TN 37620. TEL 615-844-1000. FAX 615-844-1005. *4538*

TODAY'S F D A.
Florida Dental Association, 1111 E. Tennessee St., Tallahassee, FL 32308-5914. TEL 904-681-3629. FAX 904-561-0504. *4656*

TODAY'S LIFE SCIENCE.
Reed Business Publishing Pty. Ltd. P.O. Box 5487, W. Chatswood, N.S.W. 2057, Australia. TEL 61-2-699-2411. FAX 61-2-698-3920. *6291*

TODAY'S WOMAN IN BUSINESS.
E M C Marketing Associates, 113 Old Black River Rd., P.O. Box 1291, Saint John, NB E2L 4H8, Canada. TEL 506-558-0754. FAX 506-633-0868. *964*

TOHKAI SEIKEI GEKA GAISHO KENKYU KAISHI.
Tohkai Seikei Geka Gaisho Kenkyukai, Gifu Kenritsu Tajimi Byoin Seikei Geka, 5-161, Maebatacho, Tajimi-shi, Gifu-ken 507, Japan. TEL 0572-22-5311. FAX 0572-25-1246. *4792*

TOHKAI SEKITSUI GEKA.
Tohkai Sekitsui Geka Konwakai, Gifu Kenritsu Tajimi Byoin, 5-161, Maebbatacho, Tajimi-shi, Gifuken 507, Japan. TEL 0572-22-5311. FAX 0572-25-1246. *4792*

TOHOKU MATHEMATICAL JOURNAL.
Tohoku Daigaku, Suugaku Kyoushitsu, Aramaki aza Aoba, Aoba-ku, Sendai-shi, Miyagi-ken 980-77, Japan. FAX 022-217-6400. *4400*

TOHOKU NO NOGYO KISHO.
Nihon Nogyo Kisho Gakkai, Tohoku Shibu, Norin Suisansho Tohoku Nogyo Shikenjo, 4 Akahira, Shimokuriyagawa, Morioka-shi, Iwate-ken 020-01, Japan. TEL 81-195-43-3461. FAX 81-196-41-7794. *5007*

TOKUSHIMA JOURNAL OF EXPERIMENTAL MEDICINE.
Tokushima Daigaku, Igakubu, 18-15 Kuramoto-cho 3-chome, Tokushima-shi, Tokushima-ken 770, Japan. TEL 0886-33-7081. FAX 0886-33-7082. *4685*

TOKYO DAIGAKU TEION SENTA DAYORI.
Tokyo Daigaku, Teion Senta, 11-16, Yayoi 2-chome, Bunkyo-ku, Tokyo 113, Japan. TEL 03-3812-2111. FAX 03-3815-8389. *5586*

TOKYO JOSHI IKA DAIGAKU ZASSHI.
Tokyo Joshi Ika Daigaku Gakkai, c/o Library, 8-1 Kawada-cho, Shinjuku-ku, Tokyo 162, Japan. *4538*

TOKYO METROPOLITAN UNIVERSITY. BULLETIN OF NATURAL HISTORY.
Tokyo Toritsu Daigaku, Rigakubu, 1-1, Minami-osawa, Hachioji-shi, Tokyo 192-03, Japan. *6291*

TOLEDO MEDICINE.
Academy of Medicine of Toledo and Lucas County, 4428 Secor Rd., Toledo, OH 43623. TEL 419-473-3200. FAX 419-475-6744. *4538*

TONGJI MEDICAL UNIVERSITY. JOURNAL.
Tongji Medical University, c/o Prof. Liu Xunfang, Wuhan, Hubei 430030, People's Republic of China. TEL 01-506-6688. FAX 01-506-3101. *4538*

TOP RAIL.
B L A Group Ltd., 5-8 Hardwick St., London EC1R 4RB, England. TEL 44-171-278-7603. FAX 44-171-278-6246. *6916*

TOPICS (CAMBRIDGE).
E R Consultants, Compass House, 80 Newmarket Rd., Cambridge CB5 8DZ, England. TEL 01223-315944. FAX 01223-322565. *1396*

TOPICS IN CATALYSIS.
Baltzer Science Publishers B.V., Asterweg 1A, 1031 HL Amsterdam, Netherlands. TEL 31-20-6370061. FAX 31-20-6323651. *1695*

TOPICS IN CHEMICAL ENGINEERING.
Gordon & Breach Science Publishers c/o International Publishers Distributor, P.O. Box 3054, Langhorne, PA 19047-3054. TEL 215-750-2642. FAX 215-750-6343. *2650*

TOPICS IN CHEMICAL MUTAGENESIS.
Plenum Publishing Corp., 233 Spring St., New York NY 10013-1578. TEL 212-620-8000. FAX 212-463-0742. *650*

TOPICS IN CLINICAL CHIROPRACTIC.
Aspen Publishers, Inc., 200 Orchard Ridge Dr., Gaithersburg, MD 20878. FAX 301-417-7550. *4614*

TOPICS IN COMPUTER MATHEMATICS.
Gordon & Breach Science Publishers c/o International Publishers Distributor, P.O. Box 3054, Langhorne, PA 19047-3054. TEL 215-750-2642. FAX 215-750-6343. *4412*

TOPICS IN DISCRETE MATHEMATICS.
Elsevier Science B.V., Books Division, P.O. Box 211, 1000 AE Amsterdam, Netherlands. TEL 31-20-4853911. FAX 31-20-4853705. *4400*

TOPICS IN EARLY CHILDHOOD SPECIAL EDUCATION.
Pro-Ed Inc., 8700 Shoal Creek Blvd., Austin, TX 78757-6897. TEL 512-451-3246. FAX 512-451-8542. *2476*

TOPICS IN ENVIRONMENTAL HEALTH.
Elsevier Science B.V., Books Division, P.O. Box 211, 1000 AE Amsterdam, Netherlands. TEL 31-20-4853911. FAX 31-20-4853705. *610*

TOPICS IN F-ELEMENT CHEMISTRY.
Kluwer Academic Publishers, Postbus 17, 3300 AA Dordrecht, Netherlands. TEL 31-78-6392392. FAX 31-78-6392254. *1733*

TOPICS IN GASTROENTEROLOGY.
Plenum Publishing Corp., 233 Spring St., New York, NY 10013-1578. TEL 212-620-8000. FAX 212-463-0742. *4696*

TOPICS IN GEOBIOLOGY.
Plenum Publishing Corp., 233 Spring St., New York, NY 10013-1578. TEL 212-620-8000. FAX 212-463-0742. *2265*

TOPICS IN INCLUSION SCIENCE.
Kluwer Academic Publishers, Postbus 17, 3300 AA Dordrecht, Netherlands. TEL 31-78-6392392. FAX 31-78-6392254. *1747*

TOPICS IN INORGANIC AND GENERAL CHEMISTRY.
Elsevier Science B.V., Books Division P.O. Box 211, 1000 AE Amsterdam, Netherlands. TEL 31-20-4853911. FAX 31-20-4853705. *1733*

TOPICS IN MAGNETIC RESONANCE IMAGING.
Lippincott - Raven Publishers 227 Washington Sq., Philadelphia, PA 19106. TEL 215-238-4200. *4885*

TOPICS IN MOLECULAR ORGANIZATION AND ENGINEERING.
Kluwer Academic Publishers, Postbus 17, 3300 AA Dordrecht, Netherlands. TEL 31-78-6392392. FAX 31-78-6392254. *2652*

TOPICS IN MOLECULAR PHARMACOLOGY.
Elsevier Science B.V., Books Division, P.O. Box 211,
1000 AE Amsterdam, Netherlands. TEL 31-20-
4853911. FAX 31-20-4853705. *5445*

TOPICS IN NEUROSURGERY.
Kluwer Academic Publishers, Postbus 17, 3300 AA
Dordrecht, Netherlands. TEL 31-78-6392392.
FAX 31-78-6392254. *4870*

TOPICS IN PHILOSOPHY.
University of California Press, 2120 Berkeley Way,
Berkeley, CA 94720. TEL 510-642-4247.
FAX 510-643-7127. *5503*

TOPICS IN PHOTOSYNTHESIS.
Elsevier Science B.V., Books Division, P.O. Box 211,
1000 AE Amsterdam, Netherlands. TEL 31-20-
4853911. FAX 31-20-4853705. *610*

TOPICS IN RENAL MEDICINE.
Kluwer Academic Publishers, Postbus 17, 3300 AA
Dordrecht, Netherlands. TEL 31-78-6392392.
FAX 31-78-6392254. *4931*

**TOPICS IN SAFETY, RISK, RELIABILITY AND
QUALITY.**
Kluwer Academic Publishers, Postbus 17, 3300 AA
Dordrecht, Netherlands. TEL 31-78-6392392.
FAX 31-78-6392254. *5259*

TOPICS IN STEREOCHEMISTRY.
John Wiley & Sons, Inc., 605 Third Ave., New York,
NY 10158. TEL 212-850-6000. FAX 212-850-
6088. *1695*

TOPICS IN STROKE REHABILITATION.
Aspen Publishers, Inc., 200 Orchard Ridge Dr., Ste.
200, Gaithersburg, MD 20878. *4610*

TOPICS IN THE NEUROSCIENCES.
Kluwer Academic Publishers, Postbus 17, 3300 AA
Dordrecht, Netherlands. TEL 31-78-6392392.
FAX 31-78-6392254. *4870*

TOPOI.
Kluwer Academic Publishers, Postbus 17, 3300 AA
Dordrecht, Netherlands. TEL 31-78-6392392.
FAX 31-78-6392254. *5503*

TOPOLOGY.
Elsevier Science Ltd., Pergamon, P.O. Box 800,
Kidlington, Oxford OX5 1DX, England. TEL 44-1865-
843000. FAX 44-1865-843010. *4400*

TOPOLOGY AND ITS APPLICATIONS.
North-Holland P.O. Box 211, 1000 AE Amsterdam,
Netherlands. TEL 31-20-4853911. FAX 31-20-
4853598. *4401*

TOPOLOGY PROCEEDINGS.
Auburn University, Mathematics Department,
Auburn, AL 36830. TEL 334-844-6566. FAX 334-
884-6555. *4401*

THE TORCH (VALPARAISO).
Valparaiso University, 816 Union St., Valparaiso, IN
46383. TEL 219-464-5426. *1889*

TORONTO JOURNAL OF THEOLOGY.
Wilfrid Laurier University Press, 75 University Ave.
W., Waterloo, ON N2L 3C5, Canada. TEL 519-884-
0710. FAX 519-725-1399. *6100*

**TORQUAY NATURAL HISTORY SOCIETY.
TRANSACTIONS AND PROCEEDINGS.**
Torquay Natural History Society, The Museum,
Babbacombe Rd., Torquay TQ1 1HG, England.
TEL 44-1803-293975. *6291*

TOTAL QUALITY MANAGEMENT.
Carfax Publishing Co., P.O. Box 25, Abingdon, Oxon.
OX14 3UE, England. TEL 44-1235-401000.
FAX 44-1235-401550. *1449*

TOUCHSTONE (SPRING).
Touchstone Press, Box 8308, Spring, TX 77387-
8308. *4321*

T'OUNG PAO.
E.J. Brill, P.O. Box 9000, 2300 PA Leiden,
Netherlands. TEL 31-71-5353500. FAX 31-71-
5317532. *5294*

T'OUNG PAO. MONOGRAPHIES.
E.J. Brill, P.O. Box 9000, 2300 PA Leiden,
Netherlands. TEL 31-71-5353500. FAX 31-71-
5317532. *5295*

TOURISM ANALYSIS.
Cognizant Communication Corporation, 3 Hartsdale
Rd., Elmsford, NY 10523. TEL 914-592-7720.
FAX 914-592-8981. *6918*

TOURISM ECONOMICS.
In Print Publishing Ltd., 9 Beaufort Terr., Brighton
BN2 2SU, England. TEL 44-1273-682836. FAX 44-
1273-620958. *6918*

TOURISM MANAGEMENT.
Butterworth - Heinemann, Part of the Reed Elsevier
group, Linacre House, Jordan Hill, Oxford OX2 8DP,
England. TEL 44-1865-310366. FAX 44-1865-
310898. *6918*

TOWARD AN ELECTRONIC PATIENT RECORD.
Medical Records Institute, Box 289, Newtonville, MA
02160. TEL 617-964-3923. FAX 617-964-3926.
4632

**TOWSON STATE JOURNAL OF INTERNATIONAL
AFFAIRS.**
Towson State University, Department of Political
Science, Baltimore, MD 21204. TEL 410-830-
3526. FAX 410-830-2960. *5774*

TOXIC SUBSTANCE MECHANISMS.
Taylor & Francis Inc., 1900 Frost Rd., Ste. 101,
Bristol, PA 19007-1598. TEL 215-785-5800.
FAX 215-785-5515. *2857*

TOXICOLOGIC PATHOLOGY.
Society of Toxicologic Pathologists, c/o Dr. Carl L.
Alden, Ed., G.D. Searle & Co., 4901 Searle Pky.,
Skokie, IL 60077. TEL 708-982-7379. FAX 708-
982-7374. *2848*

**TOXICOLOGICAL AND ENVIRONMENTAL
CHEMISTRY.**
Gordon and Breach Science Publishers, c/o
International Publishers Distributor, P.O. Box 3054,
Langhorne, PA 19047-3054. TEL 215-750-2642.
FAX 215-750-6343. *2848*

TOXICOLOGY AND APPLIED PHARMACOLOGY.
Academic Press, Inc., Journal Division, 525 B St.,
Ste. 1900, San Diego, CA 92101-4495. TEL 619-
230-1840. FAX 619-699-6800. *2849*

TOXICOLOGY AND INDUSTRIAL HEALTH.
Princeton Scientific Publishing Co., Inc., Box 2155,
Princeton, NJ 08543. TEL 609-683-4750.
FAX 609-683-0838. *2849*

TOXICOLOGY IN VITRO.
Elsevier Science Ltd., Pergamon, P.O. Box 800,
Kidlington, Oxford OX5 1DX, England. TEL 44-1865-
843000. FAX 44-1865-843010. *2849*

TOXICOLOGY LETTERS.
Elsevier Science Ireland Ltd., P.O. Box 85, Limerick,
Ireland. TEL 353-61-471944. FAX 353-61-
472144. *2849*

TOXICOLOGY METHODS.
Taylor & Francis Inc., 1900 Frost Rd., Ste. 101,
Bristol, PA 19007-1598. TEL 215-785-5800.
FAX 215-785-5515. *2849*

TOXICON.
Elsevier Science Ltd., Pergamon, P.O. Box 800,
Kidlington, Oxford OX5 1DX, England. TEL 44-1865-
843000. FAX 44-1865-843010. *5445*

TRACE ANALYSIS.
Academic Press, Inc., 525 B St., Ste. 1900, San
Diego, CA 92101-4495. TEL 619-231-0926.
FAX 619-699-6715. *5977*

TRACE METALS IN THE ENVIRONMENT.
Elsevier Science B.V., Books Division, P.O. Box 211,
1000 AE Amsterdam, Netherlands. TEL 31-20-
4853911. FAX 31-20-4853705. *2849*

TRACE SUBSTANCES IN ENVIRONMENTAL HEALTH.
Science Reviews Ltd., 18 Oaklands Gate,
Northwood, Mddx. HA6 3AA, England. TEL 44-
1923-823586. FAX 44-1923-825066. *2849*

TRACES OF INDIANA AND MIDWESTERN HISTORY.
Indiana Historical Society, 315 W. Ohio, Indianapolis,
IN 46202-3299. TEL 317-232-1878. FAX 317-
233-3109. *3490*

TRADESHOW REPORT INTERNATIONAL.
M und A Verlag fuer Messen, Ausstellungen und
Kongresse GmbH Postfach 101528, 60015
Frankfurt a.M., Germany. TEL 49-69-759502.
FAX 49-69-75951880. *1297*

**TRADITIONAL DWELLINGS AND SETTLEMENTS
REVIEW.**
International Association for the Study of Traditional
Environments, Center for Environmental Design
Research, 390 Wurster Hall, Department of
Architecture, University of California, Berkeley, CA
94720. TEL 510-642-2896. FAX 510-643-5571.
405

TRAITEMENT DU SIGNAL.
Groupe de Recherche et d'Etude de Traitement du
Signal et des Images (GRETSI), B.P. 46, 38402
Saint-Martin d'Heres, France. TEL 76-82-62-74.
FAX 76-82-63-84. *5574*

TRAJECTA.
Postbus 9100, 6500 HA Nijmegen, Netherlands.
6199

TRANSAFRICAN JOURNAL OF HISTORY.
Gideon S. Were Press, P.O. Box 10622, Nairobi,
Kenya. TEL 254-2-331135. FAX 254-2-331135.
3361

TRANSCULTURAL PSYCHIATRIC RESEARCH REVIEW.
McGill University, Department of Psychiatry, 1033
Pine Ave. W., Montreal, PQ H3A 1A1, Canada.
TEL 514-398-7302. FAX 514-398-4370. *4870*

TRANSFORMATION OF THE CLASSICAL HERITAGE.
University of California Press, 2120 Berkeley Way,
Berkeley, CA 94720. TEL 510-642-4247.
FAX 510-613-7127. *1826*

TRANSFUSION MEDICINE.
Blackwell Science Ltd., Osney Mead, Oxford OX2
0EL, England. TEL 44-1865-206206. FAX 44-
1865-721205. *4703*

TRANSFUSION SCIENCE.
Elsevier Science Ltd., Pergamon, P.O. Box 800,
Kidlington, Oxford OX5 1DX, England. TEL 44-1865-
843000. FAX 44-1865-843010. *4703*

TRANSGENIC RESEARCH.
Chapman & Hall, Journals Department 2-6
Boundary Row, London SE1 8HN, England. TEL 44-
171-8650066. FAX 44-171-5229623. *750*

TRANSGRESSIONS.
University of Newcastle, Geography Department,
Daysh Bldg., Newcastle NE1 7RU, England. TEL 44-
191-222-6439. FAX 44-191-222-5421. *3596*

TRANSITION METAL CHEMISTRY.
Chapman & Hall, Journals Department 2-6
Boundary Row, London SE1 8HN, England. TEL 44-
171-8650066. FAX 44-171-5229623. *4978*

TRANSLATION AND LITERATURE.
Edinburgh University Press, 22 George Sq.,
Edinburgh EH8 9LF, Scotland. TEL 44-131-650-
6207. FAX 44-131-662-0053. *4118*

TRANSLATION REVIEW.
American Literary Translators Association, University
of Texas at Dallas, Box 830688, Richardson, TX
75083-0688. TEL 214-883-2093. FAX 214-883-
6303. *4118*

TRANSLATIONS OF MATHEMATICAL MONOGRAPHS.
American Mathematical Society, Box 6248,
Providence, RI 02940-6248. TEL 401-455-4000.
4401

THE TRANSLATOR.
St. Jerome Publishing, 2 Maple Rd. W., Brooklands,
Manchester M23 9HH, England. TEL 44-161-973-
9856. *4118*

**TRANSNATIONAL CORPORATIONS AND
TRANSBORDER DATA FLOWS.**
Elsevier Science B.V., Books Division, P.O. Box 211,
1000 AE Amsterdam, Netherlands. TEL 31-20-
4853911. FAX 31-20-4853705. *1157*

Refereed

TRANSNATIONAL ORGANIZED CRIME.
Frank Cass, 890-900 Eastern Ave., Newbury Park, Ilford, Essex IG2 7HH, England. TEL 44-181-599-8866. FAX 44-181-599-0984. *5774*

TRANSPLANTATION.
Williams & Wilkins, 351 W. Camden St., Baltimore, MD 21201. TEL 410-528-4000. FAX 410-528-4312. *4922*

TRANSPLANTATION PROCEEDINGS.
Appleton & Lange, Journal Division Box 120041, Stamford, CT 06912-0041. TEL 203-406-4500. *4922*

TRANSPLANTATION REVIEWS.
W.B. Saunders Co. Curtis Center, 3rd Fl., Independence Sq. W., Philadelphia, PA 19106-3399. TEL 215-238-7800. FAX 215-238-6445. *4922*

TRANSPLANTATION 2006.
R.G. Landes Company, Medical Intelligence Unit, Box 4858, Austin, TX 78765. TEL 512-863-7762. FAX 512-863-0081. *4922*

TRANSPLANTATIONSMEDIZIN.
Pabst Science Publishers, Am Eichengrund 28, 49525 Lengerich, Germany. TEL 49-5484-308. FAX 49-5484-550. *4922*

TRANSPORT IN POROUS MEDIA.
Kluwer Academic Publishers, Postbus 17, 3300 AA Dordrecht, Netherlands. TEL 31-78-6392392. FAX 31-78-6392254. *1695*

TRANSPORT MANAGEMENT.
Institute of Transport Administration, 32 Palmerston Rd., Southampton SO14 1LL, England. FAX 44-1703-634165. *6730*

TRANSPORT POLICY.
Butterworth - Heinemann, Part of the Reed Elsevier group, Linacre House, Jordan Hill, Oxford OX2 8DP, England. TEL 44-1865-310366. FAX 44-1865-310898. *6730*

TRANSPORT PROCESSES IN ENGINEERING.
Elsevier Science B.V., Books Division, P.O. Box 211, 1000 AE Amsterdam, Netherlands. TEL 31-20-4853911. FAX 31-20-4853705. *2771*

TRANSPORT REVIEWS.
Taylor & Francis Ltd., 1 Gunpowder Sq., London EC4A 3DE, England. TEL 44-171-583-0490. FAX 44-171-583-0585. *6730*

TRANSPORT THEORY AND STATISTICAL PHYSICS.
Marcel Dekker Journals, 270 Madison Ave., New York, NY 10016. TEL 212-696-9000. FAX 212-685-4540. *5574*

TRANSPORTATION.
Kluwer Academic Publishers, Postbus 17, 3300 AA Dordrecht, Netherlands. TEL 31-78-6392392. FAX 31-78-6392254. *6731*

TRANSPORTATION PLANNING AND TECHNOLOGY.
Gordon and Breach Science Publishers, c/o International Publishers Distributor, P.O. Box 3054, Langhorne, PA 19047-3054. TEL 215-750-2642. FAX 215-750-6343. *6731*

TRANSPORTATION RESEARCH. PART A: POLICY & PRACTICE.
Elsevier Science Ltd., Pergamon, P.O. Box 800, Kidlington, Oxford OX5 1DX, England. TEL 44-1865-843000. FAX 44-1865-843010. *6732*

TRANSPORTATION RESEARCH. PART B: METHODOLOGICAL.
Elsevier Science Ltd., Pergamon, P.O. Box 800, Kidlington, Oxford OX5 1DX, England. TEL 44-1865-843000. FAX 44-1865-843010. *6732*

TRANSPORTATION RESEARCH. PART C: EMERGING TECHNOLOGIES.
Elsevier Science Ltd., Pergamon, P.O. Box 800, Kidlington, Oxford OX5 1DX, England. TEL 44-1865-843000. FAX 44-1865-843010. *6732*

TRANSPORTATION RESEARCH, ECONOMICS AND POLICY.
Kluwer Academic Publishers, Postbus 17, 3300 AA Dordrecht, Netherlands. TEL 31-78-6392392. FAX 31-78-6392254. *6732*

TRANSPORTATION RESEARCH RECORD.
U.S. National Research Council, Transportation Research Board, 2101 Constitution Ave., N.W., Washington, DC 20418. TEL 202-334-3213. FAX 202-334-2519. *6826*

TRANSPORTATION STUDIES.
Gordon & Breach Science Publishers, c/o International Publishers Distributor, P.O. Box 3054, Langhorne, PA 19047-3054. TEL 215-750-2642. FAX 215-750-6343. *6732*

TRANSPORTS URBAINS.
Groupement pour l'Etude des Transports Urbains Modernes, 173 rue Armand Silvestre, 92400 Courbevoie, France. *6733*

TRAPANANDA.
Co-Austral y Chile Futuro, 21 de Mayo, 466, Coyhaique, Chile. *3490*

TRAUMA QUARTERLY.
V S P, P.O. Box 346, 3700 AH Zeist, Netherlands. TEL 31-30-6925790. FAX 31-30-6932081. *4922*

TRAVEL INDUSTRY WORLD YEARBOOK.
Child & Waters, Inc., Box 610, Rye, NY 10580-0811. TEL 914-921-0988. *6932*

TREATISE ON MATERIALS SCIENCE & TECHNOLOGY.
Academic Press, Inc., 525 B St., Ste. 1900, San Diego, CA 92101-4495. TEL 619-231-0926. FAX 619-699-6715. *2741*

TREE PHYSIOLOGY.
Heron Publishing, 202-3994 Shelbourne St., Victoria, BC V8N 3E2, Canada. TEL 604-721-9921. FAX 604-721-9924. *706*

TREE PLANTERS' NOTES.
U.S. Forest Service, 201 14th St., S.W., Washington, DC 20250. *3027*

TRENCHLESS TECHNOLOGY.
Trenchless Technology, Inc., 1770 Main St., Box 190, Peninsula, OH 44264. TEL 216-467-7588. FAX 216-468-2289. *2621*

TRENDS IN ANALYTICAL CHEMISTRY.
Elsevier Science B.V., P.O. Box 211, 1000 AE Amsterdam, Netherlands. TEL 31-20-4853911. FAX 31-20-4853598. *1722*

TRENDS IN ANALYTICAL CHEMISTRY: REFERENCE EDITION.
Elsevier Science B.V., Books Division, P.O. Box 211, 1000 AE Amsterdam, Netherlands. TEL 31-20-4853911. FAX 31-20-4853705. *1723*

TRENDS IN BIOCHEMICAL SCIENCES.
Elsevier Science Ltd., P.O. Box 800, Kidlington, Oxford OX5 1DX, England. TEL 44-1865-843000. FAX 44-1865-843010. *650*

TRENDS IN BIOCHEMICAL SCIENCES (REFERENCE EDITION).
Elsevier Science Ltd., P.O. Box 800, Kidlington, Oxford OX5 1DX, England. TEL 44-1865-843000. FAX 44-1865-843010. *650*

TRENDS IN BIOTECHNOLOGY.
Elsevier Science Ltd., P.O. Box 800, Kidlington, Oxford OX5 1DX, England. TEL 44-1865-843000. FAX 44-1865-843010. *665*

TRENDS IN BIOTECHNOLOGY (REFERENCE EDITION).
Elsevier Science Ltd., P.O. Box 800, Kidlington, Oxford OX5 1DX, England. TEL 44-1865-843000. FAX 44-1865-843010. *665*

TRENDS IN CARDIOVASCULAR MEDICINE.
Elsevier Science Inc., Box 945, New York, NY 10159-0945. TEL 212-633-3730. FAX 212-633-3680. *4610*

TRENDS IN CELL BIOLOGY.
Elsevier Science Ltd., P.O. Box 800, Kidlington, Oxford OX5 1DX, England. TEL 44-1865-843000. FAX 44-1865-843010. *719*

TRENDS IN CELL BIOLOGY (REFERENCE EDITION).
Elsevier Science Ltd., P.O. Box 800, Kidlington, Oxford OX5 1DX, England. TEL 44-1865-843000. FAX 44-1865-843010. *719*

TRENDS IN ECOLOGY AND EVOLUTION.
Elsevier Science Ltd., P.O. Box 800, Kidlington, Oxford OX5 1DX, England. TEL 44-1865-843000. FAX 44-1865-843010. *511*

TRENDS IN ECOLOGY AND EVOLUTION (REFERENCE EDITION).
Elsevier Science Ltd., P.O. Box 800, Kidlington, Oxford OX5 1DX, England. TEL 44-1865-843000. FAX 44-1865-843010. *511*

TRENDS IN ENDOCRINOLOGY AND METABOLISM.
Elsevier Science Inc., Box 945, New York, NY 10159-0945. TEL 212-633-3730. FAX 212-633-3680. *4675*

TRENDS IN FOOD SCIENCE AND TECHNOLOGY.
Elsevier Science Ltd., P.O Box 800, Kidlington, Oxford OX5 1DX, England. TEL 44-1865-843000. FAX 44-1865-843010. *2993*

TRENDS IN FOOD SCIENCE AND TECHNOLOGY (REFERENCE EDITION).
Elsevier Science Ltd., P.O. Box 800, Kidlington, Oxford OX5 1DX, England. TEL 44-1865-843000. FAX 44-1865-843010. *2993*

TRENDS IN GENETICS.
Elsevier Science Ltd., P.O. Box 800, Kidlington, Oxford OX5 1DX, England. TEL 44-1865-843000. *750*

TRENDS IN GENETICS (REFERENCE EDITION).
Elsevier Science Ltd., P.O. Box 800, Kidlington, Oxford OX5 1DX, England. TEL 44-1865-843000. FAX 44-1865-843010. *750*

TRENDS IN GLYCOSCIENCE AND GLYCOTECHNOLOGY.
F C C A, 3-10-1 Koufudai, Fujishiro-cho, Kitasoma-gun, Ibaraki-ken 300-15, Japan. TEL 81-297-837635. FAX 81-297-837545. *1747*

TRENDS IN MICROBIOLOGY.
Elsevier Science Ltd., P.O. Box 800, Kidlington, Oxford OX5 1DX, England. TEL 44-1865-843000. FAX 44-1865-843010. *757*

TRENDS IN MICROBIOLOGY (REFERENCE EDITION).
Elsevier Science Ltd., P.O. Box 800, Kidlington, Oxford OX5 1DX, England. TEL 44-1865-843000. FAX 44-1865-843010. *757*

TRENDS IN NEUROSCIENCES.
Elsevier Science Ltd., P.O. Box 800, Kidlington, Oxford OX5 1DX, England. TEL 44-1865-843000. FAX 44-1865-843010. *4870*

TRENDS IN NEUROSCIENCES (REFERENCE EDITION).
Elsevier Science Ltd., P.O. Box 800, Kidlington, Oxford OX5 1DX, England. TEL 44-1865-843000. FAX 44-1865-843010. *4870*

TRENDS IN PHARMACOLOGICAL SCIENCES.
Elsevier Science Ltd., P.O. Box 800, Kidlington, Oxford OX5 1DX, England. TEL 44-1865-843000. FAX 44-1865-843010. *5445*

TRENDS IN PHARMACOLOGICAL SCIENCES (REFERENCE EDITION).
Elsevier Science Ltd., P.O. Box 800, Kidlington, Oxford OX5 1DX, England. TEL 44-1865-843000. FAX 44-1865-843010. *5445*

TRENDS IN POLYMER SCIENCE.
Elsevier Science Ltd., P.O. Box 800, Kidlington, Oxford OX5 1DX, England. TEL 44-1865-843000. FAX 44-1865-843010. *2651*

TRENDS IN POLYMER SCIENCE (REFERENCE EDITION).
Elsevier Science Ltd., P.O. Box 800, Kidlington, Oxford OX5 1DX, England. TEL 44-1865-843000. FAX 44-1865-843010. *2651*

TRI-STATE BLUEGRASS ASSOCIATION BAND AND FESTIVAL GUIDE.
Tri-State Bluegrass Association R.R. 1, Kahoka, MO 63445. TEL 314-853-4344. *5203*

TRIBHUVAN UNIVERSITY. NATURAL HISTORY MUSEUM JOURNAL.
Tribhuvan University, Natural History Museum, Swoyambhu, Kathmandu, Nepal. *706*

TRIBOLOGY INTERNATIONAL.
Butterworth - Heinemann, Part of the Reed Elsevier group, Linacre House, Jordan Hill, Oxford OX2 8DP, England. TEL 44-1865-310366. FAX 44-1865-310898. *2772*

TRIBOLOGY LETTERS.
Baltzer Science Publishers B.V., Asterweg 1a, 1031 HL Amsterdam, Netherlands. TEL 31-20-6370061. FAX 31-20-6323651. *2741*

TRIBOLOGY SERIES.
Elsevier Science B.V., Books Division, P.O. Box 211, 1000 AE Amsterdam, Netherlands. TEL 31-20-4853911. FAX 31-20-4853705. *2772*

TRIBOLOGY TRANSACTIONS.
Society of Tribologists and Lubrication Engineers, 840 Busse Hwy., Park Ridge, IL 60068-2376. TEL 847-825-5536. FAX 847-825-1456. *2651*

TRIBUNAL DE JUSTICA DO ESTADO DO RIO GRANDE DO SUL. REVISTA DE JURISPRUDENCIA.
Tribuna de Justica, Praca Marechal Deodoro, 55, 5o andar, 90010-908 Porto Alegre RS, Brazil. TEL 55-51-2282444 ext. 1550. *3859*

TRIBUTARY (TRENTON).
New Jersey Wastewater Treatment Trust, CN 425, Trenton, NJ 08625. TEL 609-292-1840. FAX 609-633-8165. *2858*

TRISOMY 21.
Eterna International, Inc., Box 5731, Hauppauge, NY 11788-0154. *4815*

TROPHOBLAST RESEARCH.
Plenum Publishing Corp., 233 Spring St., New York, NY 10013-1578. TEL 212-620-8000. FAX 212-463-0742. *4746*

TROPICAL AGRICULTURE.
University of the West Indies, Imperial College of Tropical Agriculture, St. Augustine, Trinidad & Tobago, W.I. TEL 809-645-3640. FAX 809-662-1182. *157*

TROPICAL AGRICULTURIST.
Department of Agriculture, No. 1, Sarasavi Mawatha, P.O. Box 05, Peradeniya, Sri Lanka. TEL 94-8-88136. FAX 94-8-88030. *157*

TROPICAL ANIMAL HEALTH AND PRODUCTION.
Edinburgh University Press, 22 George Sq., Edinburgh EH8 9LF, Scotland. TEL 44-131-650-6207. FAX 44-131-662-0053. *6955*

TROPICAL DOCTOR.
Royal Society of Medicine Press Ltd., 1 Wimpole St., London W1M 8AE, England. TEL 0171-290-2900. FAX 0171-290-2929. *4628*

TROPICAL ECOLOGY.
International Society for Tropical Ecology, Dept. of Botany, Banaras Hindu University, Varanasi 221 005, India. TEL 91-542-312989. FAX 91-542-312059. *706*

TROPICAL FRUIT NEWS.
Rare Fruit Council International, Inc., Box 561914, Miami, FL 33156. TEL 813-474-6133. *3068*

TROPICAL LEPIDOPTERA.
Association for Tropical Lepidoptera, Box 141210, Gainesville, FL 32614-1210. TEL 352-372-3505. FAX 352-373-3249. *736*

TROPICAL MEDICINE.
Nagasaki Daigaku, Nettai Igaku Kenkyujo, 12-4 Sakamoto-machi, Nagasaki 852, Japan. *4628*

TROPICAL MEDICINE & INTERNATIONAL HEALTH.
Blackwell Science Ltd., Osney Mead, Oxford OX2 0EL, England. TEL 44-1865-206206. FAX 44-1865-721205. *5977*

TROPICAL SCIENCE.
Whurr Publishers Ltd., 19b Compton Terrace, London N1 2UN, England. TEL 44-171-359-5979. FAX 44-171-226-5290. *157*

TROPICAL VETERINARIAN.
University of Ibadan, Faculty of Veterinary Medicine, Ibadan, Oyo State, Nigeria. FAX 234-2-8103043. *6955*

TROPICULTURA.
A G C D - A B O S, Rue du Trone 4, Bte. 404, 1050 Brussels, Belgium. TEL 32-2-5190377. *243*

TRUCKERS - U S A.
Horizon Media, Box 3168, Tuscaloosa, AL 35403-3168. TEL 205-758-3070. *6863*

THE TS A G I JOURNAL.
Begell House Inc., 79 Madison Ave., New York, NY 10016-7892. TEL 212-725-1999. FAX 212-213-8368. *79*

TSAFON.
1 place du Temple, 59000 Lille, France. TEL 33-1-20-57-53-99. FAX 33-1-20-91-91-71. *6130*

TSITOLOGIYA.
Izdatel'stvo Nauka, S.-Peterburgskoe Otdelenie, Mendeleevskaya liniya, 1, 199034 St. Petersburg B-34, Russia. *719*

TSUDA REVIEW.
Tsuda College, 2-1-1 Tsuda-machi, Kodaira-shi, Tokyo 187, Japan. TEL 0423-42-5111. FAX 0423-41-2444. *4279*

TUBERCLE AND LUNG DISEASE.
Churchill Livingstone Robert Stevenson House, 1-3 Baxter's Pl., Leith Walk, Edinburgh EH1 3AF, Scotland. TEL 44-131-556-2424. FAX 44-131-535-1704. *4892*

TUHINGA: RECORDS OF THE MUSEUM OF NEW ZEALAND TE PAPA TONGAREWA.
Museum of New Zealand, Board of Trustees, Buckle St., P.O. Box 467, Wellington, New Zealand. TEL 64-4-385-9609. FAX 64-4-385-6035. *5134*

TUIJIN JISHU.
Zhongguo Hangtian Gongye Zonggongsi, Di 3 Yanjiuyuan, 31 Yanjiusho, P.O. Box 7208-26, Beijing 100074, People's Republic of China. TEL 86-10-6837-6141. FAX 86-10-6837-4052. *79*

TULANE STUDIES IN GEOLOGY AND PALEONTOLOGY.
Tulane University, Department of Geology, New Orleans, LA 70118. TEL 504-865-5198. *2265*

TULANE STUDIES IN ZOOLOGY AND BOTANY.
Tulane University, Department of E.E.O. Biology, New Orleans, LA 70118. TEL 504-865-5191. FAX 504-862-8706. *822*

TULSA STUDIES IN WOMEN'S LITERATURE.
University of Tulsa, Tulsa Studies in Women's Literature, 600 S. College Ave., Tulsa, OK 74104-3189. TEL 918-631-2503. FAX 918-584-0623. *4279*

TUMOR BIOLOGY.
S. Karger AG, Allschwilerstr. 10, P.O. Box, CH-4009 Basel, Switzerland. TEL 061-3061111. FAX 061-3061234. *4765*

TUMOR DIAGNOSIS.
Field & Wood, Medical Periodicals, Inc., Box 975, Blue Bell, PA 19422. TEL 610-828-4010. FAX 215-482-0226. *4765*

TUMOR TARGETING.
Chapman & Hall, Journals Department 2-6 Boundary Row, London SE1 8HN, England. TEL 44-171-8650066. FAX 44-171-5229623. *4765*

LA TUNISIE MEDICALE.
Societe Tunisienne des Sciences Medicales, 16 Rue Touraine, 1002 Tunis - Belvedere, Tunisia. TEL 790-924. *4539*

TUNNELLING AND UNDERGROUND SPACE TECHNOLOGY.
Elsevier Science Ltd., Pergamon, P.O. Box 800, Kidlington, Oxford OX5 1DX, England. TEL 44-1865-843000. FAX 44-1865-843010. *2621*

TURANG XUEBAO.
Science Press, Marketing and Sales Department, 16 Donghuangchenggen North St., Beijing 100717, People's Republic of China. TEL 4010642. FAX 4019810. *2216*

TURBOMACHINERY INTERNATIONAL.
Turbomachinery International Publications Box 5550, Norwalk, CT 06856. TEL 203-853-6015. FAX 203-852-8175. *2772*

TURBULENCE.
Wydawnictwo Politechniki Czestochowskiej, Ul. Dabrowskiego 69, 42-200 Czestochowa, Poland. TEL 48-34-250974. FAX 48-34-612385. *5018*

TURK VETERINERLIK VE HAYVANCILIK DERGISI.
Scientific and Technical Research Council of Turkey - TUBITAK, Ataturk Bulvari, No. 221, Kavaklidere, 06100 Ankara, Turkey. TEL 90-312-4685300. FAX 90-312-4271336. *6955*

TURKIC LANGUAGES.
Harrassowitz Verlag, Taunusstr. 14, 65183 Wiesbaden, Germany. TEL 49-611-530555. FAX 49-611-530559. *4118*

TURKISH CHAMBER OF CIVIL ENGINEERS. DIGEST (YEAR).
Turkish Chamber of Civil Engineers, Selanik Caddesi 19-1, Kizilay 06650 Ankara, Turkey. TEL 90-312-4337626. FAX 90-312-4170632. *2631*

TURKISH JOURNAL OF AGRICULTURE AND FORESTRY.
Scientific and Technical Research Council of Turkey - TUBITAK, Ataturk Bulvari, No. 221, Kavaklidere, 06100 Ankara, Turkey. TEL 90-312-4685300. FAX 90-312-4271336. *157*

TURKISH JOURNAL OF BIOLOGY.
Scientific and Technical Research Council of Turkey - TUBITAK, Ataturk Bulvari, No. 221, Kavaklidere, 06100 Ankara, Turkey. TEL 90-312-4685300. FAX 90-312-4271336. *611*

TURKISH JOURNAL OF BOTANY.
Scientific and Technical Research Council of Turkey - TUBITAK, Ataturk Bulvari, No. 221, Kavaklidere, 06100 Ankara, Turkey. TEL 90-312-4685300. FAX 90-312-4271336. *706*

TURKISH JOURNAL OF CANCER.
Turkish Association for Cancer Research and Control, Atac Sokak No. 21, 06420 Yenisehir, Ankara, Turkey. TEL 90-312-3092908. FAX 90-312-4313958. *4765*

TURKISH JOURNAL OF CHEMISTRY.
Scientific and Technical Research Council of Turkey - TUBITAK, Ataturk Bulvari, No. 221, Kavaklidere, 06100 Ankara, Turkey. TEL 90-312-4685300. FAX 90-312-4271336. *1695*

TURKISH JOURNAL OF EARTH SCIENCES.
Scientific and Technical Research Council of Turkey - TUBITAK, Ataturk Bulvari, No. 221, Kavaklidere, 06100 Ankara, Turkey. TEL 90-312-4685300. FAX 90-312-4271336. *2216*

TURKISH JOURNAL OF ELECTRICAL ENGINEERING AND COMPUTER SCIENCES.
Scientific and Technical Research Council of Turkey - TUBITAK, Ataturk Bulvari, No. 221, Kavaklidere, 06100 Ankara, Turkey. TEL 90-312-4685300. FAX 90-312-4271336. *1999*

TURKISH JOURNAL OF ENGINEERING AND ENVIRONMENTAL SCIENCES.
Scientific and Technical Research Council of Turkey - TUBITAK, Ataturk Bulvari, No. 221, Kavaklidere, 06100 Ankara, Turkey. TEL 90-312-4685300. FAX 90-312-4271336. *2621*

TURKISH JOURNAL OF GASTROENTEROLOGY.
Turkish Society of Gastroenterology, Bayindir Sokak 17-7, 06420 Kizilay - Ankara, Turkey. TEL 90-312-4354373. *4696*

TURKISH JOURNAL OF MATHEMATICS.
Scientific and Technical Research Council of Turkey - TUBITAK, Ataturk Bulvari, No. 221, Kavaklidere, 06100 Ankara, Turkey. TEL 90-312-4685300. FAX 90-312-4271336. *4401*

TURKISH JOURNAL OF MEDICAL SCIENCES.
Scientific and Technical Research Council of Turkey - TUBITAK, Ataturk Bulvari, No. 221, Kavaklidere, 06100 Ankara, Turkey. TEL 90-312-4685300. FAX 90-312-4271336. *4539*

TURKISH JOURNAL OF NUCLEAR SCIENCES.
Turkiye Atom Enerjisi Kurumu - T A E K, 06530
Ankara, Turkey. TEL 90-312-2876013. FAX 90-
312-2878761. *2584*

TURKISH JOURNAL OF PEDIATRICS.
Turkish and International Children's Center, P.O. Box
66, Samanpazari, 06240 Ankara, Turkey. TEL 90-
312-3242326. FAX 90-312-3112253. *4815*

TURKISH JOURNAL OF PHYSICS.
Scientific and Technical Research Council of Turkey
- TUBITAK, Ataturk Bulvari, No. 221, Kavaklidere,
06100 Ankara, Turkey. TEL 90-312-4685300.
FAX 90-312-4271336. *5574*

TURKISH JOURNAL OF ZOOLOGY.
Scientific and Technical Research Council of Turkey
- TUBITAK, Ataturk Bulvari, No. 221, Kavaklidere,
06100 Ankara, Turkey. TEL 90-312-4685300.
FAX 90-312-4271336. *822*

TWELVE STEP RAG.
Families Anonymous, Inc., Box 3475, Culver City,
CA 90231-3475. TEL 310-313-5800. FAX 310-
313-6841. *2201*

**TWENTIETH CENTURY JAPAN: THE EMERGENCE OF
A WORLD POWER.**
University of California Press, 2120 Berkeley Way,
Berkeley, CA 94720. TEL 510-642-4247.
FAX 510-643-7127. *3385*

TYDSKRIF VIR ISLAMKUNDE.
Rand Afrikaans University, Centre for Islamic
Studies, P.O. Box 524, Auckland Park 2006, South
Africa. *6121*

TYDSKRIF VIR LETTERKUNDE.
Foundation for Education, Science and Technology,
P.O. Box 1758, Pretoria 0001, South Africa.
TEL 27-12-322-6404. FAX 27-12-320-7803.
4280

TYDSKRIF VIR SKOONLUG.
National Association for Clean Air, P.O. Box 5777,
Johannesburg 2000, South Africa. TEL 27-11-
6462210. FAX 27-11-6462210. *2840*

U C L A FORUM IN MEDICAL SCIENCES.
Academic Press, Inc., 525 B St., Ste. 1900, San
Diego, CA 92101-4495. TEL 619-231-0926.
FAX 619-699-6715. *4540*

U C L A HISTORICAL JOURNAL.
University of California at Los Angeles, Graduate
Students Association, Department of History, Los
Angeles, CA 90095-1473. TEL 310-825-4601.
FAX 310-206-9630. *3362*

U C L A JOURNAL OF DANCE ETHNOLOGY.
University of California at Los Angeles, Department
of Dance, Dance Bldg. 124, Los Angeles, CA
90095-1608. TEL 310-825-3951. FAX 310-825-
7507. *2191*

**U C L A SYMPOSIUM SERIES ON MOLECULAR AND
CELLULAR BIOLOGY.**
John Wiley & Sons, Inc., Journals, 605 Third Ave.,
New York, NY 10158. TEL 212-475-7700. *611*

U K NATURE CONSERVATION.
Joint Nature Conservation Committee, Monkstone
House, City Rd., Peterborough PE1 1JY, England.
2143

U N R I S D DISCUSSION PAPER SERIES.
United Nations Research Institute for Social
Development, Reference Centre, Palais des Nations,
1211 Geneva 10, Switzerland. TEL 41-22-798-
8400. FAX 41-22-740-0791. *6350*

U R I S A JOURNAL.
University of Wisconsin Press, Journal Division, c/o
Institute for Environmental Studies, WARF Bldg.,
Rm. 1048, 610 Walnut St., Madison, WI 53705.
TEL 608-263-6843. *2143*

U S M C A RESEARCH JOURNAL.
University of Southern Mindanao, College of
Agriculture, Kabacan, Cotabato 9407, Philippines.
6669

U S PHARMACIST.
Jobson Publishing, Inc., 100 Ave. of the Americas,
New York, NY 10013-1678. TEL 212-274-7000.
FAX 212-431-0500. *5446*

U T S REVIEW.
University of Technology, Sydney, Faculty of
Humanities and Social Sciences, P.O. Box 123,
Broadway, N.S.W. 2007, Australia. TEL 61-2-
95142728. FAX 61-2-3301596. *6350*

UDITVANI.
Jugsalai, Jamshedpur 831006 (Bihar), India.
TEL 431042. *3179*

UIT.
Vlaamse Toeristenbond, Vlaamse
Automobilistenbond, Sint-Jakobsmarkt 45, B-2000
Antwerp, Belgium. TEL 32-3-2203400. FAX 32-3-
2340598. *6923*

UKRAINIAN MATHEMATICAL JOURNAL.
Plenum Publishing Corp., Consultants Bureau, 233
Spring St., New York, NY 10013-1578. TEL 212-
620-8468. FAX 212-463-0742. *4401*

ULAM QUARTERLY.
Gordon and Breach Science Publishers, c/o
International Publishers Distributor, P.O. Box 3054,
Langhorne, PA 19047-3054. TEL 215-750-2642.
FAX 215-750-6343. *4401*

ULSTER MEDICAL JOURNAL.
Ulster Medical Society, c/o Queens University
Medical Library, Institute of Clinical Science,
Grosvenor Rd., Belfast BT12 6BA, Northern Ireland.
TEL 44-1232-322043. FAX 44-1232-247068.
4540

ULTIMATE REALITY AND MEANING.
University of Toronto Press, Journals Department,
5201 Dufferin St., Downsview, ON M3H 5T8,
Canada. TEL 416-667-7781. FAX 416-667-7881.
5503

ULTIMO BUSCADERO.
Ultimo Buscadero S.r.., Casella Postale 239,
21013 Gallarate (VA), Italy. TEL 39-331-771027.
5203

ULTRA SCIENTIST OF PHYSICAL SCIENCES.
P.O. Box 93, G.P.O., Ehopal 462 001, India.
TEL 91-755-540624. FAX 91-755-510334. *6292*

ULTRAMICROSCOPY.
North-Holland P.O. Box 211, 1000 AE Amsterdam,
Netherlands. TEL 31-20-4853911. FAX 31-20-
4853598. *771*

ULTRASONICS.
Elsevier Science B.V., P.O. Box 211, 1000 AE
Amsterdam, Netherlands. TEL 31-20-4853911.
FAX 31-20-4853598. *5616*

ULTRASONICS SONOCHEMISTRY.
Elsevier Science B.V., P.O. Box 211, 1000 AE
Amsterdam, Netherlands. TEL 31-20-4853911.
FAX 31-20-4853598. *5616*

ULTRASOUND IN MEDICINE & BIOLOGY.
Elsevier Science Inc., Box 945, New York, NY
10159-0945. TEL 212-633-3730. FAX 212-633-
3680. *611*

ULTRASOUND IN OBSTETRICS & GYNECOLOGY.
Parthenon Publishing Group, Casterton Hall,
Carnforth, Lancs. LA6 2LA, England. TEL 44-152-
427-2084. FAX 44-152-427-1587. *4746*

ULTRASOUND QUARTERLY.
Lippincott - Raven Publishers 227 E. Washington
Sq., Philadelphia, PA 19106. TEL 215-238-4200.
4885

ULTRASTRUCTURAL PATHOLOGY.
Taylor & Francis Inc., 1900 Frost Rd., Ste. 101,
Bristol, PA 19007-1598. TEL 215-785-5800.
FAX 215-785-5515. *719*

ULUSAL CERRAHI DERGISI.
Turkish Surgical Society, Guzelbahce Sok. 35-7,
80200 Nisantasi - Istanbul, Turkey. TEL 90-212-
2475295. FAX 90-212-2470835. *4922*

UNA'S LECTURES.
University of California Press, 2120 Berkeley Way,
Berkeley, CA 94720. TEL 510-643-7127.
FAX 510-643-7127. *3628*

THE UNDERGROUND WINE JOURNAL.
Wine Journal Enterprises, Inc., 1654 Amberwood
Dr., Ste. A, South Pasadena, CA 91031. TEL 818-
441-6617. FAX 818-44 -6765. *512*

UNDERSEA & HYPERBARIC MEDICINE.
Undersea and Hyperbaric Medical Society, Inc.,
10531 Metropolitan Ave. Kensington, MD 20895.
TEL 301-942-2980. FAX 301-942-7804. *4540*

UNDERSTANDING CHEMICAL REACTIVITY.
Kluwer Academic Publishers, Postbus 17, 3300 AA
Dordrecht, Netherlands. TEL 31-78-6392392.
FAX 31-78-6392254. *1695*

UNDERSTANDING MAGAZINE.
Dionysia Press, 20A Montgomery St., Edinburgh
EH7 5JS, Scotland. TEL 44-131-478-0089. *4280*

UNESCO GENERAL HISTORY OF AFRICA.
University of California Press, 2120 Berkeley Way,
Berkeley, CA 94720. TEL 510-777-4726.
FAX 510-643-7127. *3376*

UNFORGETTABLE FIRE.
Jordan O'Neill, Ed. & Pub., 530 Riverside Dr., No.
5G, New York, NY 10027 *7008*

UNI MAGAZIN HANNOVER.
Universitaet Hannover, Pressestelle, Postfach 6009,
30060 Hannover, Germany. TEL 49-511-
7625355. FAX 49-511-7625391. *6669*

UNICIENCIA.
Universidad Nacional, Facultad de Ciencias Exactas
y Naturales, Apdo. 86, 3000 Heredia, Costa Rica.
TEL 506-2376363. FAX 506-2376427. *6292*

UNIFORM LAW REVIEW.
Kluwer Law International Postbus 35889, 2508 CN
The Hague, Netherlands. TEL 31-70-3081500.
FAX 31-70-3081515. *3693*

UNION MATEMATICA ARGENTINA. REVISTA.
Union Matematica Argentina, Ciudad Universitaria,
5000 Cordoba, Argentina. TEL 54-51-690068.
FAX 54-51-615693. *4401*

**UNITARIAN UNIVERSALIST HISTORICAL SOCIETY.
PROCEEDINGS.**
Unitarian Universalist Historical Society, c/o Conrad
Wright, Harvard Divinity School, Andover Hall,
Cambridge, MA 02138. TEL 617-495-9766.
6163

**U.S. FOREST SERVICE. GENERAL TECHNICAL
REPORT N E.**
U.S. Forest Service, Northeastern Forest Experiment
Station, 359 Main Rd., Delaware, OH 43015.
TEL 614-368-0124. FAX 614-368 0152. *3028*

U.S. FOREST SERVICE. RESOURCE BULLETIN N E.
U.S. Forest Service, Northeastern Forest Experiment
Station, 359 Main Rd., Delaware, OH 43015.
TEL 614-368-0124. FAX 614-368-0152. *3028*

**U.S. NATIONAL CENTER FOR HEALTH STATISTICS.
MONTHLY VITAL STATISTICS REPORT.**
U.S. National Center for Health Statistics, Data
Dissemination Branch, 6525 Belcrest Rd.,
Hyattsville, MD 20782. TEL 301-436-8500. *5806*

**U.S. NATIONAL MARINE FISHERIES SERVICE.
TECHNICAL REPORT.**
U.S. National Marine Fisheries Service, Scientific
Publications Office, 7600 Sandpoint Way, N.E., Bin
C15700, Seattle, WA 98115 TEL 206-526-6107.
FAX 206-526-6426. *2945*

**UNITED STATES IN THE WORLD: FOREIGN
PERSPECTIVES.**
University of Chicago Press, 5801 S. Ellis Ave.,
Chicago, IL 60637. TEL 312-702-7899. *5776*

**UNIVERSIDAD CENTRAL DE VENEZUELA. CENTRO
DE ESTUDIOS DEL DESARROLLO. CUADERNOS
DEL C E N D E S.**
Universidad Central de Venezuela, Centro de
Estudios del Desarrollo, Apdo. Postal 6622, Caracas
1010-A, Venezuela. TEL 7523266. FAX 582-
7512691. *6438*

**UNIVERSIDAD CENTRAL DE VENEZUELA. FACULTAD
DE AGRONOMIA. REVISTA.**
Universidad Central de Venezuela, Facultad de
Agronomia, Apdo. 4579, Maracay, Edo. Aragua
2101, Venezuela. TEL 58-43-462212. *159*

UNIVERSIDAD CENTRAL DE VENEZUELA. INSTITUTO DE ESTUDIOS HISPANOAMERICANOS. ANUARIO.
Universidad Central de Venezuela, Instituto de Estudios Hispanoamericanos, Centro Comercial Los Chaguaramos, piso 3, Caracas 1041 A, Venezuela. TEL 58-2-6930502. FAX 58-2-6930508. *3490*

UNIVERSIDAD COMPLUTENSE DE MADRID. REVISTA MATEMATICA.
Editorial Complutense de Madrid, Donoso Cortes 65, 28015 Madrid, Spain. TEL 34-1-3946372. FAX 34-1-3946382. *4402*

UNIVERSIDAD DE ANTIOQUIA. REVISTA.
Universidad de Antioquia, Departamento de Publicaciones, Bloque 22, Cuidad Universitaria, Apdo. Aereo 1226, Medellin, Colombia. TEL 57-4-2105010. FAX 57-4-2638282. *3628*

UNIVERSIDAD DE GUADALAJARA. INSTITUTO DE BOTANICA. BOLETIN.
Universidad de Guadalajara, Instituto de Botanica, Apdo. Postal 139, 45110 Zapopan, Jalisco, Mexico. TEL 52-3-6820003. FAX 52-3-6264635. *706*

UNIVERSIDAD DE MURCIA. ANALES DE PSICOLOGIA.
Universidad de Murcia, Servicio de Publicaciones, Santo Cristo 1, 30080 Murcia, Spain. TEL 34-68-363014. FAX 34-68-363414. *5886*

UNIVERSIDAD DE PUERTO RICO. REVISTA JURIDICA.
Universidad de Puerto Rico, Escuela de Derecho, P.O. Box 23349, San Juan, PR 00931-3349. TEL 787-764-0000 ext. 2443. FAX 787-764-2675. *3955*

UNIVERSIDAD DE ZULIA. FACULTAD DE CIENCIAS VETERINARIAS. REVISTA CIENTIFICA.
Universidad del Zulia, Facultad de Ciencias Veterinarias, Apdo. 15252, Maracaibo 4003-A, Venezuela. TEL 58-61-596158. FAX 58-61-425176. *6955*

UNIVERSIDAD DE ZULIA. FACULTAD DE INGENIERIA. REVISTA TECNICA.
Universidad del Zulia, Facultad de Ingenieria, Apdo. 10-482, Correo Bella Vista, Maracaibo, Venezuela. TEL 58-61-525732. FAX 58-61-525732. *2622*

UNIVERSIDAD NACIONAL DE ASUNCION. FACULTAD DE CIENCIAS EXACTAS Y NATURALES. MEMORIA.
Universidad Nacional de Asuncion, Facultad de Ciencias Exactas y Naturales, Casilla de Correo 1039, Asuncion, Paraguay. TEL 595-21-585601. FAX 595-21-585600. *6293*

UNIVERSIDAD NACIONAL DE LA PLATA. FACULTAD DE AGRONOMIA. REVISTA.
Universidad Nacional de la Plata, Facultad de Agronomia, C.C. 31, Calle 60 y 119, 1900 La Plata, Argentina. TEL 54-21-38168. FAX 54-21-252346. *159*

UNIVERSIDADE DE SAO PAULO. FACULDADE DE EDUCACAO. REVISTA.
Universidade de Sao Paulo, Faculdade de Educacao, Av. da Universidade, 308, 05508-900 Sao Paulo SP, Brazil. TEL 55-11-8183525. FAX 55-11-818-3148. *2380*

UNIVERSIDADE DE SAO PAULO. REVISTA DE FARMACIA E BIOQUIMICA.
Universidade de Sao Paulo, Faculdade de Ciencias Farmaceuticas, C.P. 66083, 05389-970 Sao Paulo, Brazil. TEL 55-11-8137251. FAX 55-11-2128194. *5446*

UNIVERSIDADE FEDERAL DO RIO DE JANEIRO. INSTITUTO DE MATEMATICA. ESTUDOS E COMUNICACOES.
Universidade Federal do Rio de Janeiro, Instituto de Matematica, C.P. 68530, 21945-970 Rio de Janeiro, RJ, Brazil. TEL 55-21-5900940. FAX 55-21-2901095. *4402*

UNIVERSIDADE FEDERAL DO RIO DE JANEIRO. INSTITUTO DE MATEMATICA. MEMORIAS DE MATEMATICA.
Universidade Federal do Rio de Janeiro, Instituto de Matematica, C.P. 68530, 21945-970 Rio de Janeiro, RJ, Brazil. TEL 55-21-5900940. FAX 55-21-2901095. *4406*

UNIVERSIDADE FEDERAL DO RIO DE JANEIRO. INSTITUTO DE MATEMATICA. TEXTOS DE METODOS MATEMATICOS.
Universidade Federal do Rio de Janeiro, Instituto de Matematica, C.P. 68.530, 21945-970 Rio de Janeiro, RJ, Brazil. TEL 55-21-5900940. FAX 55-21-2901095. *4402*

UNIVERSITA DEGLI STUDI DI GENOVA. ISTITUTO DI ARCHEOLOGIA E FILOLOGIA CLASSICA "F. DELLA CORTE". PUBBLICAZIONI.
Universita degli Studi di Genova, Istituto di Archeologia e Filologia Classica "F. Della Corte", Via Balbi 4, 3p, 16126 Genoa, Italy. TEL 209-97-22. *4119*

UNIVERSITA DEGLI STUDI DI MODENA. SEMINARIO MATEMATICO E FISICO. ATTI.
Universita degli Studi di Modena, Seminario Matematico e Fisico, Via Campi 213-b, 41100 Modena, Italy. TEL 39-59-364496. FAX 39-59-370513. *4402*

UNIVERSITAS COMENIANA. ACTA MATHEMATICA.
Univerzita Komenskeho, Matematicko-fizikalna Fakulta, Mlynska dlina, 842 15 Bratislava, Slovakia. TEL 42-7-725741. FAX 42-7-725882. *4402*

UNIVERSITE DE BORDEAUX II. CAHIERS ETHNOLOGIQUES.
Presses Universitaires de Bordeaux, 3 place de la Victoire, 33000 Bordeaux, France. TEL 54-31-33-14. FAX 56314694. *325*

UNIVERSITE DE BORDEAUX III. CENTRE DE RECHERCHES SUR L'AMERIQUE ANGLOPHONE. ANNALES.
Maison des Sciences de l'Homme d'Aquitaine, Esplanade des Antilles, Domaine Universitaire, 33405 Talence Cedex, France. TEL 56-84-68-00. FAX 56-84-68-10. *4281*

UNIVERSITE DE PARIS VI (PIERRE ET MARIE CURIE). INSTITUT DE STATISTIQUE. PUBLICATIONS.
Universite de Paris VI (Pierre et Marie Curie), Institut de Statistique, 4, Place Jussieu, 75230 Paris Cedex 05, France. *4406*

UNIVERSITE DE REIMS. INSTITUT DE GEOGRAPHIE. TRAVAUX.
Universite de Reims, Institut de Geographie, 57 rue Pierre Taittinger, 51096 Reims, France. TEL 26-05-36-81. FAX 26-05-36-82. *3276*

UNIVERSITE DES SCIENCES HUMAINES DE STRASBOURG. CENTRE DE RECHERCHE SUR LE PROCHE ORIENT ET LA GRECE ANTIQUES. TRAVAUX.
E.J. Brill, P.O. Box 9000, 2300 PA Leiden, Netherlands. TEL 31-71-5353500. FAX 31-71-5317532. *1826*

UNIVERSITEIT VAN STELLENBOSCH. ANNALE.
Universiteit van Stellenbosch, Private Bag X1, Matieland 7602, Stellenbosch. TEL 27-21-80804587. FAX 27-21-8084499. *6293*

UNIVERSITY OF ALASKA. ANTHROPOLOGICAL PAPERS.
University of Alaska Fairbanks, Department of Anthropology, Box 757720, 310 Eielson Bldg., Fairbanks, AK 99775-7720. TEL 907-474-7288. FAX 907-474-7453. *325*

UNIVERSITY OF ALASKA. BIOLOGICAL PAPERS.
University of Alaska at Fairbanks, Institute of Arctic Biology, 308 Irving, Fairbanks, AK 99775-0180. TEL 907-474-7658. FAX 907-474-6967. *612*

UNIVERSITY OF ARIZONA. ANTHROPOLOGICAL PAPERS.
University of Arizona Press, 1230 N. Park Ave., Tucson, AZ 85719. TEL 602-621-1441. *325*

UNIVERSITY OF ARKANSAS. LECTURE NOTES IN THE MATHEMATICAL SCIENCES.
John Wiley & Sons, Inc., 605 Third Ave., New York, NY 10158. TEL 212-850-6000. FAX 212-850-6088. *4403*

UNIVERSITY OF BRADFORD. DEVELOPMENT AND PROJECT PLANNING CENTRE. RESEARCH MONOGRAPH.
University of Bradford, Development and Project Planning Centre, The Library, Bradford, W. Yorks. BD1 1DP, England. *1316*

UNIVERSITY OF BRITISH COLUMBIA LAW REVIEW.
University of British Columbia Law Review Society, Faculty of Law, Vancouver, BC V6T 1Z2, Canada. TEL 604-822-3066. FAX 604-822-4633. *3862*

UNIVERSITY OF CAIRO. FACULTY OF MEDICINE. MEDICAL JOURNAL.
University of Cairo, Faculty of Medicine, Manyal University Hospital, Kasr El-Aini Post, Cairo, Egypt. TEL 726-0595. *4541*

UNIVERSITY OF CALIFORNIA AT BERKELEY. CENTER FOR CHINESE STUDIES. SERIES.
University of California Press, 2120 Berkeley Way, Berkeley, CA 94720. TEL 510-642-4247. FAX 510-643-7127. *3386*

UNIVERSITY OF CALIFORNIA AT BERKELEY. CENTER FOR JAPANESE STUDIES. SERIES.
University of California Press, 2120 Berkeley Way, Berkeley, CA 94720. TEL 510-642-4247. FAX 510-643-4247. *3188*

UNIVERSITY OF CALIFORNIA AT LOS ANGELES. CENTER FOR MEDIEVAL AND RENAISSANCE STUDIES. CONTRIBUTIONS.
University of California Press, 2120 Berkeley Way, Berkeley, CA 94720. TEL 510-642-4247. FAX 510-643-7127. *3362*

UNIVERSITY OF CALIFORNIA AT LOS ANGELES. CENTER FOR MEDIEVAL AND RENAISSANCE STUDIES. PUBLICATIONS.
University of California Press, 2120 Berkeley Way, Berkeley, CA 94720. TEL 510-642-4247. FAX 510-643-7127. *3362*

UNIVERSITY OF CALIFORNIA AT LOS ANGELES. CENTER FOR THE STUDY OF COMPARATIVE FOLKLORE AND MYTHOLOGY. PUBLICATIONS.
University of California Press, 2120 Berkeley Way, Berkeley, CA 94720. TEL 510-642-4247. FAX 510-643-7127. *2957*

UNIVERSITY OF CALIFORNIA AT LOS ANGELES. CLARK LIBRARY PROFESSORSHIP. MONOGRAPHIC SERIES.
University of California Press, 2120 Berkeley Way, Berkeley, CA 94720. TEL 510-642-4247. FAX 510-643-7127. *3629*

UNIVERSITY OF CALIFORNIA AT LOS ANGELES. LATIN AMERICAN CENTER. LATIN AMERICAN STUDIES SERIES.
Latin American Studies Center Publications, University of California, Los Angeles, Box 951447, 10343 Bunche Hall, Los Angeles, CA 90095-1447. *3491*

UNIVERSITY OF CALIFORNIA, DAVIS. CENTERS FOR WATER AND WILDLAND RESOURCES. CONTRIBUTIONS.
University of California, Davis, Centers for Water and Wildland Resources, Davis, CA 95616. TEL 916-752-8070. FAX 916-752-8086. *6976*

UNIVERSITY OF CALIFORNIA PUBLICATIONS. ANTHROPOLOGICAL RECORDS.
University of California Press, 2120 Berkeley Way, Berkeley, CA 94720. TEL 510-642-4247. FAX 510-643-7127. *325*

UNIVERSITY OF CALIFORNIA PUBLICATIONS. CLASSICAL STUDIES.
University of California Press, 2120 Berkeley Way, Berkeley, CA 94720. TEL 510-642-4247. FAX 510-643-7127. *1826*

UNIVERSITY OF CALIFORNIA PUBLICATIONS. FOLKLORE & MYTHOLOGY STUDIES.
University of California Press, 2120 Berkeley Way, Berkeley, CA 94720. TEL 510-642-4247. FAX 510-643-7127. *2957*

UNIVERSITY OF CALIFORNIA PUBLICATIONS. NEAR EASTERN STUDIES.
University of California Press, 2120 Berkeley Way, Berkeley, CA 94720. TEL 510-642-4247. FAX 510-643-7127. *3386*

UNIVERSITY OF CALIFORNIA PUBLICATIONS IN ANTHROPOLOGY.
University of California Press, 2120 Berkeley Way, Berkeley, CA 94720. TEL 510-642-4247. FAX 510-643-7127. *325*

Refereed

UNIVERSITY OF CALIFORNIA PUBLICATIONS IN BOTANY.
University of California Press, 2120 Berkeley Way, Berkeley, CA 94720. TEL 510-642-4247. FAX 510-643-7127. *707*

UNIVERSITY OF CALIFORNIA PUBLICATIONS IN ENTOMOLOGY.
University of California Press, 2120 Berkeley Way, Berkeley, CA 94720. TEL 510-642-4247. FAX 510-643-7127. *736*

UNIVERSITY OF CALIFORNIA PUBLICATIONS IN GEOGRAPHY.
University of California Press, 2120 Berkeley Way, Berkeley, CA 94720. TEL 510-642-4247. FAX 510-643-7127. *3276*

UNIVERSITY OF CALIFORNIA PUBLICATIONS IN GEOLOGICAL SCIENCES.
University of California Press, 2120 Berkeley Way, Berkeley, CA 94720. TEL 510-642-4247. FAX 510-643-7127. *2217*

UNIVERSITY OF CALIFORNIA PUBLICATIONS IN LINGUISTICS.
University of California Press, 2120 Berkeley Way, Berkeley, CA 94720. TEL 510-642-4247. FAX 510-643-7127. *4120*

UNIVERSITY OF CALIFORNIA PUBLICATIONS IN MODERN PHILOLOGY.
University of California Press, 2120 Berkeley Way, Berkeley, CA 94720. TEL 510-642-4247. FAX 510-643-7127. *4120*

UNIVERSITY OF CALIFORNIA PUBLICATIONS IN ZOOLOGY.
University of California Press, 2120 Berkeley Way, Berkeley, CA 94720. TEL 510-642-4247. FAX 510-643-7127. *822*

UNIVERSITY OF CHICAGO. GEOGRAPHY RESEARCH PAPERS.
University of Chicago Press, 5801 S. Ellis Ave., Chicago, IL 60637. TEL 800-621-2736. FAX 312-660-2235. *3276*

UNIVERSITY OF CHICAGO STUDIES IN LIBRARY SCIENCE.
University of Chicago Press, 5801 S. Ellis Ave., Chicago, IL 60637. TEL 312-702-7899. *4032*

UNIVERSITY OF COLORADO. INSTITUTE OF ARCTIC AND ALPINE RESEARCH. OCCASIONAL PAPERS.
University of Colorado, Institute of Arctic and Alpine Research, Campus Box 450, Boulder, CO 80309-0450. TEL 303-492-3765. FAX 303-492-6388. *6293*

UNIVERSITY OF CONNECTICUT. INSTITUTE OF WATER RESOURCES. REPORT SERIES.
University of Connecticut, Institute of Water Resources, Storrs, CT 06269-4018. TEL 203-486-0335. *6976*

UNIVERSITY OF DAYTON REVIEW.
University of Dayton Press, 300 College Park Ave., Dayton, OH 45469-1539. TEL 513-229-2449. FAX 513-229-4330. *3629*

UNIVERSITY OF DELAWARE. DISASTER RESEARCH CENTER. REPORT SERIES.
University of Delaware, Disaster Research Center, Newark, DE 19716. TEL 302-831-6618. FAX 302-831-2091. *5978*

UNIVERSITY OF FLORIDA. SCHOOL OF FOREST RESOURCES & CONSERVATION. COOPERATIVE FOREST GENETICS RESEARCH PROGRAM. PROGRESS REPORT.
University of Florida, School of Forest Resources & Conservation, Gainesville, FL 32601. TEL 904-392-1792. *3028*

UNIVERSITY OF GHANA LAW JOURNAL.
University of Ghana, Faculty of Law, Legon, Ghana. TEL 233-21-775304. *3862*

UNIVERSITY OF HAWAII. WATER RESOURCES RESEARCH CENTER. TECHNICAL REPORT.
University of Hawaii, Water Resources Research Center, 2540 Dole St., Honolulu, HI 96822. TEL 808-956-7847. FAX 808-956-5044. *6976*

UNIVERSITY OF IDAHO ANTHROPOLOGICAL MONOGRAPHS.
University of Idaho, Alfred W. Bowers Laboratory of Anthropology, Moscow, ID 83844-1111. TEL 208-885-6123. *325*

UNIVERSITY OF ILLINOIS. SCHOOL OF ARCHITECTURE - BUILDING RESEARCH COUNCIL. RESEARCH REPORT.
University of Illinois at Urbana-Champaign, School of Architecture, One E. St. Mary's Rd., Champaign, IL 61820. TEL 217-333-1801. FAX 217-244-2204. *878*

UNIVERSITY OF ILLINOIS AT URBANA-CHAMPAIGN. ENGINEERING EXPERIMENT STATION. SUMMARY OF ENGINEERING RESEARCH.
University of Illinois at Urbana-Champaign, College of Engineering, 112 Engineering Hall, 1308 W. Green St., Urbana, IL 61801. TEL 217-333-1510. *2622*

UNIVERSITY OF ILLINOIS AT URBANA-CHAMPAIGN. WATER RESOURCES CENTER. RESEARCH REPORT.
University of Illinois at Urbana-Champaign, Water Resources Center, 1101 W. Peabody Dr., Rm. 278, Urbana, IL 61801. TEL 217-333-0536. FAX 217-244-8583. *6976*

UNIVERSITY OF KANSAS. DEPARTMENT OF ANTHROPOLOGY. PUBLICATIONS IN ANTHROPOLOGY.
University of Kansas Libraries, Exchange & Gifts Department, Level 2W Watson Library, Lawrence, KS 66045. TEL 913-864-3746. *325*

UNIVERSITY OF KANSAS. MUSEUM OF NATURAL HISTORY. MISCELLANEOUS PUBLICATIONS.
University of Kansas, Museum of Natural History, 602 Dyche Hall, Lawrence, KS 66045-2454. TEL 913-864-4540. FAX 913-864-5335. *612*

UNIVERSITY OF KANSAS. MUSEUM OF NATURAL HISTORY. MONOGRAPHS.
University of Kansas, Museum of Natural History, 602 Dyche Hall, Lawrence, KS 66044-2454. TEL 913-864-4540. FAX 913-864-5335. *612*

UNIVERSITY OF KANSAS. MUSEUM OF NATURAL HISTORY. OCCASIONAL PAPERS.
University of Kansas, Museum of Natural History, 602 Dyche Hall, Lawrence, KS 66045-2454. *6293*

UNIVERSITY OF KANSAS. MUSEUM OF NATURAL HISTORY. SPECIAL PUBLICATIONS.
University of Kansas, Museum of Natural History, 602 Dyche Hall, Lawrence, KS 66045-2454. *612*

UNIVERSITY OF KANSAS. PALEONTOLOGICAL CONTRIBUTIONS. NEW SERIES.
University of Kansas, Paleontological Institute, 121 Lindley Hall, Lawrence, KS 66045. TEL 913-864-3338. FAX 913-864-5276. *5319*

UNIVERSITY OF LONDON. SCHOOL OF ORIENTAL AND AFRICAN STUDIES. BULLETIN.
Oxford University Press, Oxford Journals, Walton St., Oxford OX2 6DP, England. TEL 01865-267907. FAX 01865-267773. *3629*

UNIVERSITY OF MANCHESTER. DEPARTMENT OF COMPUTER SCIENCE. TECHNICAL REPORT SERIES.
University of Manchester, Department of Computer Science, Oxford Rd., Manchester M13 9PL, England. TEL 44-161-275-6130. FAX 44-161-275-6236. *2059*

UNIVERSITY OF MEMPHIS. ANTHROPOLOGICAL RESEARCH CENTER. OCCASIONAL PAPERS.
University of Memphis, Anthropological Research Center, Memphis, TN 38152. TEL 901-678-2618. FAX 901-678-2069. *325*

UNIVERSITY OF MICHIGAN. DIVISION OF RESEARCH DEVELOPMENT AND ADMINISTRATION. RESEARCH NEWS.
University of Michigan, Division of Research Development and Administration, 3003 S. State St., Ann Arbor, MI 48109-1274. TEL 313-763-5587. FAX 313-763-4053. *2447*

UNIVERSITY OF MICHIGAN. HERBARIUM. CONTRIBUTIONS.
University of Michigan, Herbarium, North University Building, Ann Arbor, MI 48109-1057. TEL 313-764-2407. FAX 313-763-0369. *707*

UNIVERSITY OF MICHIGAN. MUSEUM OF PALEONTOLOGY. CONTRIBUTIONS.
University of Michigan, Museum of Paleontology, 1529 Ruthven Museums Bldg., 1109 Geddes Rd., Ann Arbor, MI 48109-1079. TEL 313-764-0489. *5319*

UNIVERSITY OF MICHIGAN. MUSEUM OF PALEONTOLOGY. PAPERS ON PALEONTOLOGY.
University of Michigan, Museum of Paleontology, 1529 Ruthven Museums Bldg., 1109 Geddes Rd., Ann Arbor, MI 48109-1079. TEL 313-764-0489. *5319*

UNIVERSITY OF MICHIGAN. MUSEUM OF ZOOLOGY. MISCELLANEOUS PUBLICATIONS.
University of Michigan, Museum of Zoology, Ann Arbor, MI 48109-1079. TEL 313-764-0476. FAX 313-763-4080. *822*

UNIVERSITY OF MICHIGAN. MUSEUM OF ZOOLOGY. OCCASIONAL PAPERS.
University of Michigan, Museum of Zoology, Ann Arbor, MI 48109-1079. TEL 313-764-0476. FAX 313-763-4080. *822*

UNIVERSITY OF MICHIGAN. MUSEUMS OF ART AND ARCHAEOLOGY. BULLETIN.
Kelsey Museum of Archaeology, Department of the History of Art, 434 S. State St., Ann Arbor, MI 48109-1390. TEL 313-747-3307. FAX 313-763-8976. *5134*

UNIVERSITY OF MISSOURI AT COLUMBIA. MUSEUM OF ANTHROPOLOGY. MISCELLANEOUS PUBLICATIONS IN ANTHROPOLOGY.
University of Missouri at Columbia, Museum of Anthropology, 104 Swallow Hall, Columbia, MO 65211. TEL 314-882-3573. *325*

UNIVERSITY OF MISSOURI MONOGRAPHS IN ANTHROPOLOGY.
University of Missouri at Columbia, Museum of Anthropology, 104 Swallow Hall, Columbia, MO 65211. TEL 314-882-3573. *325*

UNIVERSITY OF NEVADA. DESERT RESEARCH INSTITUTE. TECHNICAL REPORT.
University of Nevada, Desert Research Institute, Social Sciences Center, Box 60220, Reno, NV 89506. TEL 702-673-7303. *6294*

UNIVERSITY OF NEW MEXICO. INSTITUTE OF METEORITICS. SPECIAL PUBLICATION.
University of New Mexico, Institute of Meteoritics, Albuquerque, NM 87131. TEL 505-277-2747. FAX 505-277-3577. *488*

UNIVERSITY OF NORTH DAKOTA. INSTITUTE FOR ECOLOGICAL STUDIES. RESEARCH REPORT.
Institute for Ecological Studies, University of North Dakota, Box 8278, University Sta., Grand Forks, ND 58202. TEL 701-777-2851. *2824*

UNIVERSITY OF OREGON ANTHROPOLOGICAL PAPERS.
University of Oregon, Department of Anthropology, Eugene, OR 97403-1218. TEL 503-346-5102. FAX 503-346-0668. *325*

UNIVERSITY OF OTAGO MEDICAL SCHOOL. PROCEEDINGS.
Otago Medical School Research Society, P.O. Box 913, Dunedin, New Zealand. TEL 64-3-4797570. FAX 64-3-4790401. *4541*

UNIVERSITY OF SOUTH CAROLINA. BELLE W. BARUCH LIBRARY IN MARINE SCIENCE AND COASTAL RESEARCH. COLLECTED PAPERS.
University of South Carolina Press, c/o Robin Sumner, Rights & Permissions, Columbia, SC 29208. TEL 803-777-5243. *2307*

UNIVERSITY OF SOUTH FLORIDA. INTERNATIONAL BIOMEDICAL SYMPOSIA SERIES.
Plenum Publishing Corp., 233 Spring St., New York, NY 10013-1578. TEL 212-620-8000. FAX 212-463-0742. *612*

UNIVERSITY OF SUSSEX. CENTRE FOR CONTINUING EDUCATION. OCCASIONAL PAPER.
University of Sussex, Centre for Continuing Education, Falmer, Brighton, Sussex BN1 9RG, England. TEL 44-1273-678025. FAX 44-1273-678848. *3362*

UNIVERSITY OF TASMANIA. CENTRE FOR ENVIRONMENTAL STUDIES. OCCASIONAL PAPER.
University of Tasmania, Centre for Environmental Studies, G.P.O. Box 252C, Hobart, Tas. 7001, Australia. FAX 61-02-202989. *2824*

UNIVERSITY OF TASMANIA. CENTRE FOR ENVIRONMENTAL STUDIES. PROJECT REPORT.
University of Tasmania, Centre for Environmental Studies, G.P.O. Box 252C, Hobart, Tas. 7001, Australia. FAX 61-02-202989. *2144*

UNIVERSITY OF TEXAS AT AUSTIN. BUREAU OF ECONOMIC GEOLOGY. ANNUAL REPORT.
University of Texas at Austin, Bureau of Economic Geology, Attn. S. Doenges, Box X, University Sta., Austin, TX 78713-8924. TEL 512-471-7721. FAX 512-471-0140. *2265*

UNIVERSITY OF TEXAS AT AUSTIN. BUREAU OF ECONOMIC GEOLOGY. GEOLOGICAL CIRCULAR.
University of Texas at Austin, Bureau of Economic Geology, Attn.: S. Doenges, Box X, University Sta., Austin, TX 78713-8924. TEL 512-471-7721. FAX 512-471-0140. *2266*

UNIVERSITY OF TEXAS AT AUSTIN. BUREAU OF ECONOMIC GEOLOGY. GUIDEBOOK.
University of Texas at Austin, Bureau of Economic Geology, Attn.: S. Doenges, Box X, University Sta., Austin, TX 78713-8924. TEL 512-471-7721. FAX 512-471-0140. *2266*

UNIVERSITY OF TEXAS AT AUSTIN. BUREAU OF ECONOMIC GEOLOGY. MINERAL RESOURCE CIRCULARS.
University of Texas at Austin, Bureau of Economic Geology, Attn.: S. Doenges, Box X, University Sta., Austin, TX 78713-8924. TEL 512-471-7721. FAX 512-471-0140. *2266*

UNIVERSITY OF TEXAS AT AUSTIN. BUREAU OF ECONOMIC GEOLOGY. OTHER PUBLICATIONS.
University of Texas at Austin, Bureau of Economic Geology, Attn.: S. Doenges, Box X, University Sta., Austin, TX 78713-8924. TEL 512-471-7721. FAX 512-471-0140. *2266*

UNIVERSITY OF TEXAS AT AUSTIN. BUREAU OF ECONOMIC GEOLOGY. REPORT OF INVESTIGATIONS.
University of Texas at Austin, Bureau of Economic Geology, Attn.: S. Doenges, Box X, University Sta., Austin, TX 78713-8924. TEL 512-471-7721. FAX 512-471-0140. *2266*

UNIVERSITY OF TEXAS AT AUSTIN. CENTER FOR RESEARCH IN WATER RESOURCES. TECHNICAL REPORT SERIES.
University of Texas at Austin, Center for Research in Water Resources, J.J. Pickle Research Campus, Austin, TX 78712. TEL 512-471-3131. FAX 512-471-0072. *6976*

THE UNIVERSITY OF TEXAS LIFETIME HEALTH LETTER.
University of Texas, Houston Health Science Center, 7000 Fannin St., Houston, TX 77030. TEL 713-792-4265. FAX 713-794-4738. *5537*

UNIVERSITY OF THE WITWATERSRAND. INSTITUTE FOR ADVANCED SOCIAL RESEARCH. SEMINAR PAPERS.
University of the Witwatersrand, Institute for Advanced Social Research, Private Bag 3, Wits 2050, South Africa. FAX 27-11-7168030. *6351*

UNIVERSITY OF TOKYO. OCEAN RESEARCH INSTITUTE. BULLETIN.
University of Tokyo, Ocean Research Institute, 15-1 Minami-Dai 1-chome, Nakano-ku, Tokyo 164, Japan. TEL 81-3-5351-6342. FAX 81-3-3375-6716. *2307*

UNIVERSITY OF TORONTO MEDICAL JOURNAL.
University of Toronto, Medical Society, Medical Sciences Bldg., Toronto, ON M5S 1A1, Canada. TEL 416-978-8730. *4541*

UNIVERSITY OF UTAH ANTHROPOLOGICAL PAPERS.
University of Utah Press, 101 University Services Bldg., Salt Lake City, UT 84112. TEL 801-581-6771. *325*

UNIVERSITY OF WESTERN ONTARIO SERIES IN PHILOSOPHY OF SCIENCE.
Kluwer Academic Publishers, Postbus 17, 3300 AA Dordrecht, Netherlands. TEL 31-78-6392392. FAX 31-78-6392254. *5504*

UNIVERSITY OF WYOMING. CONTRIBUTIONS TO GEOLOGY.
University of Wyoming, Department of Geology and Geophysics, Box 3006, University Sta., Laramie, WY 82071. TEL 307-766-3386. FAX 307-766-6679. *2266*

UNMANNED SYSTEMS.
Association for Unmanned Vehicle Systems International, 1735 N. Lynn St., Ste. 950, Arlington, VA 22209-2229. TEL 703-524-6646. FAX 703-524-2303. *5051*

UPDATE (SOUTH AFRICAN EDITION).
George Warman Publications (Pty.) Ltd., P.O. Box 704, Cape Town 8000, South Africa. TEL 27-21-245320. FAX 27-21-261332. *4541*

UPPELDI OG MENNTUN.
Rannsoknarstofnun Kennarahaskola Islands, Stakkahlid, 105 Rekjavik, Iceland. TEL 354-568-3827. FAX 354-563-3833. *2380*

UPPER INDIA MOTORIST.
Automobile Association of Upper India, C-8, Institutional Area, South of IIT, New Delhi 110 016, India. TEL 3312323. FAX 6866302. *6805*

THE UPPERCRUST.
Upper Crust Publications, 361 Virginia St., Crystal Lake, IL 60014. TEL 815-459-1000. *3527*

URBAN ACADEMIC LIBRARIAN.
Library Association of the City University of New York, Hunter College Library, 695 Park Ave., New York, NY 10021. TEL 212-772-4168. *4034*

URBAN AFFAIRS (NEWARK).
Urban Affairs Association, University of Delaware, Newark, DE 19716. *3597*

URBAN AFFAIRS REVIEW.
Sage Publications, Inc., 2455 Teller Rd., Thousand Oaks, CA 91320. TEL 805-499-0721. FAX 805-499-0871. *3597*

URBAN ANTHROPOLOGY AND STUDIES OF CULTURAL SYSTEMS AND WORLD ECONOMIC DEVELOPMENT.
Institute Incorporated, 56 Centennial Ave., Brockport, NY 14420. TEL 716-637-6531. *326*

URBAN DESIGN AND PRESERVATION QUARTERLY.
American Planning Association, Urban Design and Preservation, 1776 Massachusetts Ave. N.W., Washington, DC 20036. *3597*

URBAN DESIGN INTERNATIONAL.
Chapman & Hall, Journals Department 2-6 Boundary Row, London SE1 8HN, England. TEL 44-171-8650066. FAX 44-171-5229623. *3597*

URBAN EDUCATION.
Corwin Press, Inc. 2455 Teller Rd., Thousand Oaks, CA 91320. TEL 805-499-0721. FAX 805-499-0871. *2381*

URBAN HISTORY REVIEW.
Becker Associates, Box 507, Sta. Q, Toronto, ON M4T 2M5, Canada. TEL 416-483-7282. FAX 416-489-1713. *3491*

URBAN POLICY & RESEARCH.
Urban Policy and Research, Planning Policy and Landscape RMIT, P.O. Box 2476V, Melbourne, Vic. 3001, Australia. TEL 61-3-4293316. FAX 61-3-6601855. *3598*

THE URBAN REVIEW.
Human Sciences Press, Inc. 233 Spring St., New York, NY 10013. TEL 212-620-8000. FAX 212-463-0742. *2381*

URBAN STUDIES.
Carfax Publishing Co., P.O. Box 25, Abingdon, Oxon OX14 3UE, England. TEL 44-1235-401000. FAX 44-1235-401550. *3598*

URETHANE ABSTRACTS.
Technomic Publishing Co., Inc., 851 New Holland Ave., Box 3535, Lancaster, PA 17604. TEL 717-291-5609. FAX 717-295-4538. *5628*

URO-GRAM.
Society of Urologic Nurses and Associates, Box 56, Pitman, NJ 08071-0056. TEL 609-256-2335. FAX 609-589-7463. *4931*

UROLOGIA INTERNATIONALIS.
S. Karger AG, Allschwilerstr. 10, P.O. Box, CH-4009 Basel, Switzerland. TEL 061-3061111. FAX 061-3061234. *4931*

UROLOGIC NURSING.
Mosby - Year Book, Inc. 11830 Westline Industrial Dr., St. Louis, MO 63146-3318. TEL 314-872-8370. FAX 314-432-1380. *4931*

UROLOGIC ONCOLOGY.
Elsevier Science Inc., Box 945, New York, NY 10159-0945. TEL 212-633-3730. FAX 212-633-3680. *4765*

UROLOGY.
Excerpta Medica, Inc. 105 Raider Blvd., Belle Meade, NJ 08502. TEL 908-874-8550. FAX 908-874-8419. *4932*

US WURK.
Fries Instituut, Postbus 716, 9700 AS Groningen, Netherlands. FAX 31-50-634900. *4122*

USER MODELLING AND USER-ADAPTED INTERACTION.
Kluwer Academic Publishers, Postbus 17, 3300 AA Dordrecht, Netherlands. TEL 31-78-6392392. FAX 31-78-6392254. *2408*

UTAH GENEALOGICAL ASSOCIATION. GENEALOGICAL JOURNAL.
Utah Genealogical Association, Box 1144, Salt Lake City, UT 84110. TEL 801-531-2091. *3104*

UTAH GEOLOGICAL ASSOCIATION. ANNUAL GUIDEBOOK.
Utah Geological Association, Box 520100, Salt Lake City, UT 84152-0100. TEL 801-537-3300. *2266*

UTAH GEOLOGICAL SURVEY. BULLETIN.
Utah Geological Survey, 1594 W. North Temple, Ste. 3410, Box 14600, Salt Lake City, UT 84114-6100. TEL 801-537-3300. FAX 801-537-3400. *2266*

UTAH GEOLOGICAL SURVEY. SURVEY NOTES.
Utah Geological Survey, 1594 W. North Temple, Ste. 3410, Box 146100, Salk Lake City, UT 84114-6100. TEL 801-537-3300. FAX 801-537-2400. *2267*

UTAH HISTORICAL QUARTERLY.
State Historical Society, 300 Rio Grande, Salt Lake City, UT 84101. TEL 801-533-3500. FAX 801-533-3504. *3491*

UTILITIES LAW REVIEW.
John Wiley & Sons Ltd., Journals, Baffins Ln., Chichester, W. Sussex PO19 1UD, England. TEL 44-1243-779777. FAX 44-1243-843232. *3864*

UTILITIES POLICY.
Butterworth - Heinemann, Part of the Reed Elsevier group, Linacre House, Jordan Hill, Oxford OX2 8DP, England. TEL 44-1865-310366. FAX 44-1865-310898. *2722*

UTRECHT STUDIES IN AIR AND SPACE LAW.
Kluwer Academic Publishers, Postbus 17, 3300 AA Dordrecht, Netherlands. TEL 31-78-6392392. FAX 31-78-6392254. *3864*

V F A PROFIL.
Profil Verlag GmbH, Scheideweg 160B, 26127 Oldenburg, Germany. TEL 49-441-93023-0. FAX 49-441-9302320. *406*

V H L FAMILY FORUM.
V H L Family Alliance, 171 Clinton Rd., Brookline, MA 02146. TEL 617-232-5946. FAX 617-734-8233. *4871*

V I C MEDICAL UPDATE.
Vitamin Information Centre, P.O. Box 182, Isando 1600, South Africa. TEL 27-11-9741887. FAX 27-11-3924034. *5242*

V I E R BULLETIN.
Victorian Institute of Educational Research, c/o Kevin Hall, Ed., Faculty of Education, University of Melbourne, Parkville, Vic. 3052, Australia. TEL 61-3-344-8418. FAX 61-3-347-2468. *2381*

V O REALITES.
Parti Suisse du Travail, Case Postale 366, CH-1211 Geneva 4, Switzerland. TEL 022-3206335. FAX 022-3200587. *3731*

VAARD I NORDEN.
Sygeplejerskerners Samarbejde i Norden, P.O. Box 2681, St. Hanshaugen, N-131 Oslo 1, Norway. TEL 47-22-38-20-00. FAX 47-22-38-54-47. *4729*

VACATION INDUSTRY REVIEW.
Interval International, 6262 Sunset Dr., Penthouse 1, S. Miami, FL 33143. TEL 305-666-1861. FAX 305-663-2220. *6924*

VACCINE.
Elsevier Science Ltd., Oxford Fulfilment Centre, P.O. Box 800, Kidlington, Oxford OX5 1DX, England. TEL 44-1865-843000. FAX 44-1865-843010. *4587*

VACUUM.
Elsevier Science Ltd., Pergamon, P.O. Box 800, Kidlington, Oxford OX5 1DX, England. TEL 44-1865-843000. FAX 44-1865-843010. *5576*

VALLEY WOMEN'S VOICE.
University of Massachusetts, 321 Student Union, Amherst, MA 01003. TEL 413-545-2436. *7009*

VALOER.
Foereningen Valoer, Konstvetenskapliga Institutionen, Slottet, Soedra tornet, inngaang HO, S-752 37 Uppsala, Sweden. TEL 46-18-182888. FAX 46-18-182892. *458*

VAN TAAL TOT TAAL.
Nederlands Genootschap van Vertalers, P.O. Box 8138, 3503 RC Utrecht, Netherlands. TEL 31-30-2588366. FAX 31-30-2588787. *4122*

VANDERBILT UNIVERSITY. DEPARTMENT OF ENVIRONMENTAL AND WATER RESOURCES ENGINEERING. TECHNICAL REPORTS.
Vanderbilt University, Department of Civil & Environmental Engineering, Box 6304, Sta. B, Nashville, TN 37235. TEL 615-322-2720. *2824*

VANDERBILT UNIVERSITY PUBLICATIONS IN ANTHROPOLOGY.
Vanderbilt University Publications in Anthropology, Box 1532, Sta. B, Nashville, TN 37235. TEL 615-322-7522. FAX 615-343-0230. *326*

VANGUARD.
Vanguard Publications, P.O. Box 2269, London E6 3RF, England. TEL 44-181-471-6872. FAX 44-181-592-3009. *5715*

VASCULUM.
Northern Naturalists Union, Sunderland Museum & Art Gallery, Borough Rd., Sunderland, Tyne and Wear SR1 1PP, England. TEL 44-191-565-0723. FAX 44-191-565-0713. *6294*

VECTEUR ENVIRONNEMENT.
Association Quebecoise des Techniques de l'Environnement, 911 rue Jean-Talon Est, Montreal, PQ H2R 1V5, Canada. TEL 514-270-7110. FAX 514-270-7154. *2824*

VELIGER.
California Malacozoological Society, Inc., Department of Invertebrate Zoology, Santa Barbara Museum of Natural History, 2559 Puesta del Sol Rd., Santa Barbara, CA 93105. TEL 802-682-4711. FAX 805-963-9679. *822*

VENEZUELAN LITERATURE AND ARTS JOURNAL.
Hamline University Press, Hamline University, Mail Stop 50, 1536 Hewitt Ave., St. Paul, MN 55104-1284. TEL 612-641-2001. FAX 612-641-2956. *4282*

VERA LEX.
Pace University, Costello House, Pleasantville, NY 10570-2799. TEL 914-773-3945. FAX 914-773-3541. *5505*

VERGILIUS.
Vergilian Society of America, Box 817, Oxford, OH 45056. TEL 803-777-2765. FAX 803-777-0454. *1827*

VERHALTENSTHERAPIE.
S. Karger AG, Allschwilerstr. 10, P.O. Box, CH-4009 Basel, Switzerland. TEL 061-3061111. FAX 061-3061234. *4871*

VERSES.
Cader Publishing, Ltd., 36915 Ryan Rd., Sterling Heights, MI 48310. TEL 810-795-3635. FAX 810-795-9875. *4282*

VESTNIK.
Vestnik Information Agency, 6100 Park Heights Ave., Baltimore, MD 21215. TEL 410-358-0900. FAX 410-358-3867. *3453*

VETERANS FOR PEACE JOURNAL.
Veterans for Peace, Inc., Box 3881, Portland, ME 04104. TEL 207-773-1431. FAX 207-773-0804. *5777*

VETERINARIA E ZOOTECNIA.
Universidade Estadual Paulista, Av. Vicente Ferreira 1278, Caixa Postal 71, 17515-901 Marilla SP, Brazil. TEL 55-144-222504. FAX 55-144-222504. *6956*

VETERINARY & COMPARATIVE OPHTHALMOLOGY.
Veterinary Practice Publishing Co., 7 Ashley Ave. S., Santa Barbara, CA 93103-9989. TEL 805-965-1028. FAX 805-965-0722. *6957*

VETERINARY AND COMPARATIVE ORTHOPAEDICS AND TRAUMATOLOGY.
F.K. Schattauer Verlagsgesellschaft mbH, Lenzhalde 3, 70192 Stuttgart, Germany. TEL 49-711-22987-0. FAX 49-711-22987-50. *6957*

VETERINARY AND HUMAN TOXICOLOGY.
Comparative Toxicology Laboratories, Publication Office, Kansas State University, Manhattan, KS 66506-5606. TEL 913-532-4334. FAX 913-532-4481. *2850*

VETERINARY CLINICAL NUTRITION.
Veterinary Practice Publishing Co., 7 Ashley Ave. S., Santa Barbara, CA 93103-3397. TEL 805-965-1028. FAX 805-965-0722. *6957*

VETERINARY CLINICAL PATHOLOGY.
Veterinary Practice Publishing Co., 7 Ashley Ave. S., Santa Barbara, CA 93103-9989. TEL 805-965-1028. FAX 805-965-0722. *6957*

VETERINARY DERMATOLOGY.
Blackwell Science Ltd., Osney Mead, Oxford OX2 OEL, England. TEL 44-1865-206206. FAX 44-1865-721205. *6957*

VETERINARY IMMUNOLOGY AND IMMUNOPATHOLOGY.
Elsevier Science B.V., P.O. Box 211, 1000 AE Amsterdam, Netherlands. TEL 31-20-4853911. FAX 31-20-4853598. *6958*

VETERINARY INSTITUTE, PULAWY. BULLETIN.
Instytut Weterynarii, c/o Krystyna Ciemiega-Wilczynska, Sec., Al. Partyzantow 57, 24-100 Pulawy, Poland. TEL 48-81-863051. FAX 48-81-862595. *6958*

VETERINARY MEDICAL JOURNAL GIZA.
Cairo University, Faculty of Veterinary Medicine, Giza, Cairo, Egypt. *6958*

VETERINARY MEDICINE.
Veterinary Medicine Publishing Co. 15333 W. 95th, Lenexa, KS 66219 TEL 913-492-4300. FAX 913-492-4157. *6958*

VETERINARY MICROBIOLOGY.
Elsevier Science B.V., P.O. Box 211, 1000 AE Amsterdam, Netherlands. TEL 31-20-4853911. FAX 31-20-4853598. *6958*

VETERINARY PARASITOLOGY.
Elsevier Science B.V., P.O. Box 211, 1000 AE Amsterdam, Netherlands. TEL 31-20-4853911. FAX 31-20-4853598. *6958*

VETERINARY PATHOLOGY.
Waverly Press, Inc. 351 W. Camden St., Baltimore, MD 21201. TEL 410-528-4000. FAX 410-528-4412. *6958*

VETERINARY PRACTICE STAFF.
Veterinary Practice Publishing Co., Box 4457, Santa Barbara, CA 93104-4457. TEL 805-965-1028. FAX 805-965-0722. *6959*

VETERINARY QUARTERLY.
Koninklijke Nederlandse Maatschappij voor Diergeneeskunde, Julianalaan 10 Postbus 14301, 3508 SB Utrecht, Netherlands. TEL 31-50-2510111. FAX 31-30-25 1787 *6959*

VETERINARY RADIOLOGY & ULTRASOUND.
American College of Veterinary Radiology, c/o Lucinda Ayres, 2520 Beechridge Rd., Raleigh, NC 27608. TEL 919-881-4155. FAX 919-821-9578. *6959*

VETERINARY RESEARCH.
Editions Scientifiques et Medicales Elsevier, 141 rue de Javel, 75747 Paris, France. TEL 33-1-45589022. FAX 33-1-45389421. *6959*

VETERINARY RESEARCH COMMUNICATIONS.
Kluwer Academic Publishers, Postbus 17, 3300 AA Dordrecht, Netherlands. TEL 31-78-6392392. FAX 31-78-6392254. *6959*

VETERINARY SURGERY.
W.B. Saunders Co. Curtis Center, 3rd Fl., Independence Sq. W., Philadelphia, PA 19106-3399. TEL 215-238-7800. FAX 215-238-6445. *6959*

VETERINER HEKIMLERI DERNEGI DERGISI.
Turk Veteriner Hekimleri Dernegi, Saglik Sok. 21-3, Yenisehir, Ankara, Turkey. *6959*

VETUS TESTAMENTUM.
E.J. Brill, P.O. Box 9000, 2300 PA Leiden, Netherlands. TEL 31-71-5353500. FAX 31-71-5317532. *6101*

VETUS TESTAMENTUM. SUPPLEMENTS.
E.J. Brill, P.O. Box 9000, 2300 PA Leiden, Netherlands. TEL 31-71-5353500. FAX 31-71-5317532. *6101*

VEXILOLOGIE.
Vexilologicky Klub, Pod Lipami 53, 130 00 Prague, Czech Republic. *3105*

VIANDES ET PRODUITS CARNES.
Association pour le Developpement de l'Institut de la Viande, 2 rue Chappe, 63039 Clermont-Ferrand Cedex 2, France. TEL 33-4-73907297. FAX 33-4-73921777. *286*

VIATOR.
N.V. Brepols, Steenweg op Tielen 68, 2300 Turnhout, Belgium. TEL 32-14-402500. FAX 32-14-428919. *3363*

VIBRATIONAL SPECTRA AND STRUCTURE.
Elsevier Science B.V., Books Division, P.O. Box 211, 1000 AE Amsterdam, Netherlands. TEL 31-20-4853911. FAX 31-20-4853705. *1758*

VIBRATIONAL SPECTROSCOPY.
Elsevier Science B.V., P.O. Box 211, 1000 AE Amsterdam, Netherlands. TEL 31-20 4853911. FAX 31-20-4853598. *1696*

VICTORIA, AUSTRALIA. GEOLOGICAL SURVEY. REPORT.
Geological Survey of Victoria, Energy and Minerals, Victoria, P.O. Box 2145, MDC, Fitzroy, Vic. 3065, Australia. TEL 61-3-941270C0. FAX 51-3-94127803. *2267*

VICTORIAN LITERATURE AND CULTURE.
Cambridge University Press, Edinburgh Bldg., Shaftesbury Rd., Cambridge CB2 2RU, England. TEL 44-1223-312393. FAX 44-1223-315052. *4283*

VICTORIAN REVIEW.
Victorian Studies Association of Western Canada,
c/o Prof. Chris Hosgood, Ed., Dept. of History,
University of Lethbridge, Lethbridge, AB T1K 3M4,
Canada. TEL 403-329-2543. FAX 403-329-5109.
4283

VICTORIANS INSTITUTE JOURNAL.
University of North Carolina Press, Box 2288, NC
27515-2288. TEL 919-966-3561. FAX 919-966-
3829. *4171*

LE VIDE: SCIENCE, TECHNIQUE ET APPLICATIONS.
Societe Francaise du Vide, 19 rue du Renard,
75004 Paris, France. TEL 33-1-53-01-90-30.
FAX 33-1-42-78-63-20. *5576*

VIDEO INDUSTRY STATISTICAL REPORT.
Corbell Publishing, 4676 Admiralty Way, Ste. 300,
Marina Del Rey, CA 90292. TEL 310-574-5337.
FAX 310-574-5383. *1926*

VIDEO JOURNAL OF COLOR FLOW IMAGING.
Dynamedia, Inc., 2 Fulham Court, Silver Spring, MD
20902-3016. TEL 301-649-6886. FAX 301-649-
3447. *4885*

VIDEO JOURNAL OF ECHOCARDIOGRAPHY.
Dynamedia, Inc., 2 Fulham Court, Silver Spring, MD
20902-3016. TEL 301-649-6886. FAX 301-649-
3447. *4611*

VIDEOMAKER.
Videomaker Inc., Box 4591, Chico, CA 95927.
TEL 916-891-8410. FAX 916-891-8443. *1980*

VIE ET MILIEU.
Universite de Paris VI (Pierre et Marie Curie),
Laboratoire Arago, 66650 Banyuls sur Mer, France.
TEL 33-1-68-88-73-27. FAX 33-1-68-88-16-99.
613

VIENNA CIRCLE COLLECTION.
Kluwer Academic Publishers, Postbus 17, 3300 AA
Dordrecht, Netherlands. TEL 31-78-6392392.
FAX 31-78-6392254. *560*

VIET NAM GENERATION.
Viet Nam Generation, Inc., 18 Center Rd.,
Woodbridge, CT 06525-1630. TEL 203-387-6882.
FAX 203-389-3104. *3491*

VIGILIAE CHRISTIANAE.
E.J. Brill, P.O. Box 9000, 2300 PA Leiden,
Netherlands. TEL 31-71-5353500. FAX 31-71-
5317532. *6102*

VIGILIAE CHRISTIANAE. SUPPLEMENT.
E.J. Brill, P.O. Box 9000, 2300 PA Leiden,
Netherlands. TEL 31-71-5353500. FAX 31-71-
5317532. *6102*

VILLES EN PARALLELE.
Universite de Paris X - Nanterre, Laboratoire de
Geographie Urbaine, 200 av. de la Republique,
92001 Nanterre Cedex, France. TEL 33-1-40-97-
73-67. FAX 33-1-40-97-76-16. *3278*

VINYAR TENGWAR.
Elvish Linguistic Fellowship, 2509 Ambling Circle,
Crofton, MD 21114. TEL 410-721-5690. *4283*

**VIOLA D'AMORE SOCIETY OF AMERICA.
NEWSLETTER.**
Viola d'Amore Society of America, 39-23 47th St.,
Sunnyside, NY 11104. TEL 718-729-3138. *5204*

VIOLENCE AGAINST WOMEN.
Sage Publications, Inc., 2455 Teller Rd., Thousand
Oaks, CA 91320. TEL 805-499-0721. FAX 805-
499-0871. *6439*

VIOLENCE AND VICTIMS.
Springer Publishing Company, 536 Broadway, New
York, NY 10012-3955. TEL 212-431-4370.
FAX 212-941-7842. *6439*

VIRAL IMMUNOLOGY.
Mary Ann Liebert, Inc. Publishers, 2 Madison Ave.,
Larchmont, NY 10538. TEL 914-834-3100.
FAX 914-834-3688. *4588*

**VIRGINIA. WATER RESOURCES RESEARCH CENTER.
BULLETIN.**
Water Resources Research Center, Virginia
Polytechnic Institute and State University, 617 N.
Main St., Blacksburg, VA 24060. TEL 703-231-
8036. *6977*

VIRGINIA BUILDER.
Mid-Atlantic Trade Exposition Inc., 2117 Smith Ave.,
Chesapeake, VA 23320. TEL 804-420-2434.
FAX 804-424-5954. *878*

VIRGINIA ENVIRONMENTAL LAW JOURNAL.
Virginia Environmental Law Journal, University of
Virginia, School of Law, Charlottesville, VA 22901.
TEL 804-924-3683. FAX 804-924-7536. *3866*

VIRGINIA EPISCOPALIAN.
Episcopal Diocese of Virginia, 110 W. Franklin,
Richmond, VA 23220. TEL 804-643-8451.
FAX 804-644-6928. *6164*

VIRGINIA GEOGRAPHER.
Virginia Geographical Society, c/o Donald Zeigler,
Ed., Old Dominion Univ., Norfolk, VA 23529-0088.
FAX 804-683-3241. *3278*

VIRGINIA JOURNAL OF INTERNATIONAL LAW.
Virginia Journal of International Law Association,
University of Virginia, School of Law, 580 Massie
Rd., Charlottesville, VA 22901. TEL 804-924-
3415. FAX 804-924-7536. *3944*

VIRGINIA JOURNAL OF SCIENCE.
Virginia Academy of Science, c/o James H. Martin,
J.S. Reynolds Community College, Box 85622,
Richmond, VA 23285-5622. TEL 804-371-3064.
6295

**VIRGINIA POLYTECHNIC INSTITUTE AND STATE
UNIVERSITY. DEPARTMENT OF ENTOMOLOGY.
OCCASIONAL PAPERS.**
Virginia Polytechnic Institute and State University,
Department of Entomology, Blacksburg, VA 24061-
0319. TEL 703-231-6341. *736*

VIRGINIA TAX REVIEW.
Virginia Tax Review Association, University of
Virginia, School of Law, Charlottesville, VA 22901.
TEL 804-924-4726. FAX 804-924-7536. *1570*

VIRGINIA TECH RESEARCH.
Virginia Polytechnic Institute and State University,
Research and Graduate Studies, 312 Sandy Hall,
Blacksburg, VA 24061-0325. TEL 540-231-5646.
FAX 540-231-3714. *2448*

VIRITTAAJAA.
Kotikielen Seura, Castrenianum, P.O. Box 3, FIN-
00014, University of Helsinki, Finland. FAX 358-0-
19123329. *4122*

VIROLOGY.
Academic Press, Inc., Journal Division, 525 B St.,
Ste. 1900, San Diego, CA 92101-4495. TEL 619-
230-1840. FAX 619-688-6800. *767*

VIRUS GENES.
Kluwer Academic Publishers Boston, Box 358,
Accord Sta., Hingham, MA 02018-0358. TEL 617-
871-6600. FAX 617-871-6528. *767*

VIRUS INFECTIONS OF VERTEBRATES.
Elsevier Science B.V., Books Division, P.O. Box 211,
1000 AE Amsterdam, Netherlands. TEL 31-20-
4853911. FAX 31-20-4853705. *6960*

VIRUS RESEARCH.
Elsevier Science B.V., P.O. Box 211, 1000 AE
Amsterdam, Netherlands. TEL 31-20-4853911.
FAX 31-20-4853598. *767*

VISIBLE RELIGION.
E.J. Brill, P.O. Box 9000, 2300 PA Leiden,
Netherlands. TEL 31-71-5353500. FAX 31-71-
5317532. *6102*

VISION RESEARCH.
Elsevier Science Ltd., Pergamon, P.O. Box 800,
Kidlington, Oxford OX5 1DX, England. TEL 44-1865-
843000. FAX 44-1865-843010. *4779*

VISTAS IN ASTRONOMY.
Elsevier Science Ltd., Pergamon, P.O. Box 800,
Kidlington, Oxford OX5 1DX, England. TEL 44-1865-
843000. FAX 44-1865-843010. *488*

VISUAL ANTHROPOLOGY.
Harwood Academic Publishers, c/o International
Publishers Distributor, P.O. Box 3054, Langhorne,
PA 19047-3054. TEL 215-750-2642. FAX 215-
750-6343. *326*

VISUAL LITERACY REVIEW.
International Visual Literacy Association (Blacksburg),
c/o Barbara I. Clark, Gonzaga university, E. 502
Boone AD 25, Spokane, WA 99258-0001. *2505*

VISUAL RESOURCES.
Gordon & Breach Science Publishers, c/o
International Publishers Distributor, P.O. Box 3054,
Langhorne, PA 19047-3054. TEL 215-750-2642.
FAX 215-750-6343. *458*

**VITAMINS AND HORMONES: ADVANCES IN
RESEARCH AND APPLICATIONS.**
Academic Press, Inc. 525 B St., Ste. 1900, San
Diego, CA 92101-4495. TEL 619-231-0926.
FAX 619-699-6715. *5447*

VIVARIUM.
E.J. Brill, P.O. Box 9000, 2300 PA Leiden,
Netherlands. TEL 31-71-5353500. FAX 31-71-
5317532. *3454*

VIVEK.
National Centre for Software Technology, Gulmohar
Cross Rd. No. 9, Juhu, Bombay 400 049, India.
TEL 91-22-620-1606. FAX 91-22-621-0139.
2011

VOCE DELL'EMIGRANTE.
Comitato Regionale Emigranti Abruzzesi, Vico
Sportello, 10, Casella Postale 7, 67035 Pratola
Peligna (AQ), Italy. TEL 39-864-53147. FAX 39-
864-52785. *2913*

VODOHOSPODARSKY CASOPIS.
Slovenska Akademia Vied, Ustav Hydrologie,
Racianska 75, P.O. Box 94, 830 08 Bratislava,
Slovakia. TEL 42-7-253000. FAX 42-7-259404.
2289

VOICES (BURNSVILLE).
Rural Southern Voice for Peace, 1898 Hannah
Branch Rd., Burnsville, NC 28714. TEL 704-675-
5933. FAX 704-675-9335. *6352*

VOICES (DECAUTUR).
American Academy of Psychotherapists, Box 607,
Decautur, GA 30031. TEL 404-299-6336.
FAX 404-299-0206. *5886*

VOICES IN ITALIAN AMERICANA.
Bordighera, Inc., c/o Purdue University, Dept. of Foreign
Languages and Literatures, 1359 Stanley Coulter
Hall, W. Lafayette, IN 47907-1359. TEL 317-494-
3839. FAX 317-496-1700. *4172*

VOICES - ISRAEL.
Voices Israel Group of Poets in English, c/o Mark
Levinson, Ed., P.O. Box 5780, Herzliya 46157,
Israel. TEL 972-52-552411. *4322*

VOLCANOLOGY & SEISMOLOGY.
Gordon & Breach Science Publishers, c/o
International Publishers Distributor, P.O. Box 3054,
Langhorne, PA 19047-3054. TEL 215-750-2642.
FAX 215-750-6343. *2283*

VOLKSKUNDE IN NIEDERSACHSEN.
Volker Schmerse Text- und Bildgestaltung, Postfach
110335, 37048 Goettingen, Germany. TEL 49-
551-46335. FAX 49-551-47550. *2958*

VOLKSKUNDIG BULLETIN.
Uitgeverij S U N, Postbus 1609, 6501 BP
Nijmegen, Netherlands. TEL 31-24-3221700.
FAX 31-24-3235493. *326*

VOLUME REVERSAL SURVEY.
Almarco L C C, Box 1451, Sedona, AZ 86339.
TEL 602-282-1275. FAX 602-282-6364. *1358*

VOX (ALBUQUERQUE).
Cleave Press, 2118 Central S.E., Ste. 6,
Albuquerque, NM 87106. TEL 505-243-3492.
4172

VOX HOSPITII.
Misset P.O. Box 1110, 3600 BC Maarssen,
Netherlands. TEL 31-346-558222. FAX 31-346-
554287. *4543*

VOX SANGUINIS.
S. Karger AG, Allschwilerstr. 10, P.O. Box, CH-4009 Basel, Switzerland. TEL 061-3061111. FAX 061-3061234. *4588*

VOXAIR.
Canadian Forces Base Winnipeg, Westwin, MB R3J 0T0, Canada. TEL 204-889-3963. FAX 204-885-4176. *5052*

VRIJETIJDSTUDIES.
Uitgeverij Boom, P.O. Box 400, 7940 AK Meppel, Netherlands. TEL 31-522-257012. FAX 31-522-253864. *3968*

VSTRECHI.
Encounters, 7738 Woodbine Ave., Philadelphia, PA 19151. TEL 215-477-6172. *4322*

VYTAPENI, VETRANI, INSTALACE.
Spolecnost pro Techniku Prostredi, Novotneho Lavka 5, 116 68 Prague 1, Czech Republic. TEL 42-2-21082201. FAX 42-2-21082201. *3334*

VYZVOL'NYI SHLYAKH.
Ukrainian Information Service Ltd., 200 Liverpool Rd., London N1 1LF, England. TEL 44-171-607-6266. *4172*

W C C I FORUM.
World Council for Curriculum and Instruction, c/o Estela Matriano, WCCI Exec. Dir., University of Cincinnati, Cincinnati, OH 45221-0002. TEL 513-556-3573. FAX 513-556-2483. *2453*

W E A LEGEND.
Wilderness Education Association, Colorado State University, Department of Natural Resource Recreation and Tourism, Colorado State University, Ft. Collins, CO 80523. TEL 970-223-6252. FAX 970-223-6252. *2145*

W H Y.
World Hunger Year, 505 Eigth Ave., 21st Fl., New York, NY 10018-6582. TEL 212-629-8850. FAX 212-465-9274. *6398*

W P S PROFESSIONAL HANDBOOK SERIES.
Western Psychological Services, 12031 Wilshire Blvd., Los Angeles, CA 90025. TEL 310-478-2061. FAX 310-478-7838. *5887*

W Z B PAPERS.
Wissenschaftszentrum Berlin fuer Sozialforschung, Reichpietschufer 50, 10785 Berlin, Germany. TEL 49-30-25491-0. FAX 49-30-25491684. *6352*

WAIKATO LAW REVIEW.
University of Waikato, School of Law, Private Bag 3105, Hamilton, New Zealand. TEL 64-7-8384167. FAX 64-7-8384417. *3867*

WALLACE STEVENS JOURNAL.
Wallace Stevens Society, Inc., Box 5750 Clarkson University, Potsdam, NY 13699-5750. TEL 315-268-3987. FAX 315-268-3983. *4322*

WAR AND SOCIETY.
University of New South Wales, Department of History, University College, Australian Defence Force Academy, Campbell, A.C.T. 2600, Australia. TEL 61-6-2688879. FAX 61-6-2688879. *3363*

WAR IN HISTORY.
Arnold 338 Euston Rd., London NW1 3BH, England. TEL 44-171-873-6000. FAX 44-171-873-6325. *5053*

WAR, LITERATURE, AND THE ARTS.
U.S. Air Force Academy, Department of English, HQ USAFA-DFENG, 2354 Fairchild Dr., Ste. 6D35, USAF Academy, CO 80840-6242. TEL 719-472-3930. FAX 719-472-3132. *4284*

WARM EARTH.
Warm Earth Publishing, Kiah Cottage, Kenilworth, Qld. 4754, Australia. TEL 61-74-460457. *3069*

WASCANA REVIEW.
University of Regina, Regina, SK S4S 0A2, Canada. TEL 306-584-4302. FAX 306-585-4827. *4284*

WASHINGTON ACADEMY OF SCIENCES. JOURNAL.
Washington Academy of Sciences, 1200 New York Ave., N.W., 8th Fl., Washington, DC 20005. FAX 202-326-8975. *6295*

WASHINGTON HISTORY.
Historical Society of Washington, D.C., 1307 New Hampshire N W., Washington, DC 20036-1507. TEL 202-785-2473. FAX 202-331-1979. *3492*

WASHINGTON INTERNATIONAL.
1090 Vermont Ave. N.W., Ste. 700, Washington, DC 20005. TEL 202-223-3180. FAX 301-946-0779. *6926*

WASHINGTON STATE UNIVERSITY. MATHEMATICS NOTES.
Washington State University, Department of Pure and Applied Mathematics, Pullman, WA 99164-3113. TEL 509-335-8518. *4404*

WASMANN JOURNAL OF BIOLOGY.
University of San Francisco, Biology Department, San Francisco, CA 94117. TEL 415-666-6381. *613*

WASTE MANAGEMENT.
Elsevier Science Ltd., Pergamon, P.O. Box 800, Kidlington, Oxford OX5 1DX, England. TEL 44-1865-843000. FAX 44-1865-843010. *2858*

WATCH MAGAZINE.
Watch Magazines Inc., 245-401 Richmond St. W., Toronto, ON M5V 1X3, Canada. TEL 416-595-1313. FAX 416-595-1312. *1811*

WATER ENVIRONMENT RESEARCH.
Water Environment Federation, 601 Wythe St., Alexandria, VA 22314-1994. TEL 703-684-2400. FAX 703-684-2492. *2841*

WATER INTERNATIONAL.
International Water Resources Association, University of Illinois, 1101 W. Peabody Dr., Urbana, IL 61801. TEL 217-333-6275. FAX 217-244-6633. *6978*

WATER LAW.
John Wiley & Sons Ltd., Journals, Baffins Ln., Chichester, W. Sussex PO19 1UD, England. TEL 44-1243-779777. FAX 44-1243-843232. *6979*

WATER POLLUTION: A SERIES OF MONOGRAPHS.
Academic Press. Inc., 525 B St., Ste. 1900, San Diego, CA 92101-4495. TEL 619-231-0926. FAX 619-699-6715. *6979*

WATER QUALITY INTERNATIONAL.
Elsevier Science Ltd., Pergamon, P.O. Box 800, Kidlington, Oxford OX5 1DX, England. TEL 44-1865-843000. FAX 44-1865-843010. *2841*

WATER QUALITY RESEARCH JOURNAL OF CANADA.
National Water Research Institute, 867 Lakeshore Rd., Box 5050, Burlington, ON L7R 4L7, Canada. TEL 905-336-4884. FAX 905-336-6444. *2841*

WATER RESEARCH.
Elsevier Science Ltd., Pergamon, P.O. Box 800, Kidlington, Oxford OX5 1DX, England. TEL 44-1865-843000. FAX 44-1865-843010. *6979*

WATER RESOURCES.
Maik Nauka - Interperiodica, Mezhdunarodnyi Otdel, Ul. Profsoyuznaya, 90, 117864 Moscow, Russia. TEL 7-095-3360066. FAX 7-095-3360666. *6980*

WATER RESOURCES BULLETIN.
American Water Resources Association, 950 Herndon Pkwy., Ste. 300, Herndon, VA 22070-5531. TEL 703-904-1225. FAX 703-904-1228. *6980*

WATER RESOURCES MANAGEMENT.
Kluwer Academic Publishers, Postbus 17, 3300 AA Dordrecht, Netherlands. TEL 31-78-6392392. FAX 31-78-6392254. *6980*

WATER S.A.
Water Research Commission, P.O. Box 824, Pretoria 0001, South Africa. *6980*

WATER SCIENCE AND TECHNOLOGY.
Elsevier Science Ltd., Pergamon, P.O. Box 800, Kidlington, Oxford OX5 1DX, England. TEL 44-1865-843000. FAX 44-1865-843010. *6981*

WATER SCIENCE AND TECHNOLOGY LIBRARY.
Kluwer Academic Publishers, Postbus 17, 3300 AA Dordrecht, Netherlands. TEL 31-78-6392392. FAX 31-78-6392254. *6981*

WATER TREATMENT.
China Ocean Press, International Cooperation Department, Haimao Dalou, 1 Fuxingmenwai Dajie, Beijing 100860, People's Republic of China. TEL 8032211. FAX 8033515. *6981*

WATERLINES.
Intermediate Technology Publications Ltd., 103-105 Southampton Row, London WC1B 4HH, England. TEL 44-171-436-9761. FAX 44-171-436-2013. *6981*

WATERLOO HISTORICAL SOCIETY. ANNUAL VOLUME.
Waterloo Historical Society, 85 Queen St. N., Kitchener, ON N2H 2H1 Canada. FAX 519-570-1360. *3492*

WAVE MOTION.
North-Holland P.O. Box 211, 1000 AE Amsterdam, Netherlands. TEL 31-20-4853911. FAX 31-20-4853598. *5576*

WAY STATION MAGAZINE.
1319 S. Logan St., Lansing, MI 48910. *4284*

WEAR.
Elsevier Science S.A., P.O Box 564, CH-1001 Lausanne 1, Switzerland. TEL 41-21-3207381. FAX 41-21-3235444. *2772*

WEATHERWISE.
Heldref Publications, 1319 Eighteenth St., N.W., Washington, DC 20036-1802. TEL 202-296-6267. FAX 202-296-5149. *5008*

WEBER STUDIES: AN INTERDISCIPLINARY HUMANITIES JOURNAL.
Weber State University, Ogden, UT 84408-1214. TEL 801-626-6473. FAX 801-625-7130. *3630*

WECHSELWIRKUNG.
Remember e.G., Mariabrunnstr. 48, 52064 Aachen, Germany. TEL 0241-405930. FAX 0241-408461. *6670*

WEED RESEARCH.
Blackwell Science Ltd., Osney Mead, Oxford OX2 0EL, England. TEL 44-1865-206206. FAX 44-1865-721205. *245*

WEED SCIENCE.
Weed Science Society of America, 1508 W. University, Champaign, IL 61821-3133. TEL 217-352-4212. FAX 217-352-4241. *245*

WEEKLY BULLETIN.
Magyar Tavirati Iroda, Pl. Naphegy ter. 8, 1016 Budapest, Hungary. TEL 36-1-1756722. FAX 36-1-1188297. *3164*

WEIMAR AND NOW: GERMAN CULTURAL CRITICISM.
University of California Press, 2120 Berkeley Way, Berkeley, CA 94720. TEL 510-642-4247. FAX 510-643-7127. *4284*

WEISHENGWU XUEBAO.
Science Press, Marketing and Sales Department, 16 Donghuangchenggen North St., Beijing 100717, People's Republic of China. TEL 4019810. FAX 4019810. *768*

WEITI GUSHENGWU XUEBAO.
Science Press, Marketing and Sales Department, 16 Donghuangchenggen North St., Beijing 100717, People's Republic of China. TEL 4019810. FAX 4019810. *768*

WEIXING XIAOSHUO XUANKAN.
Weixing Xiaoshuo Xuankan Zazhishe No.5, Xinwei Lu, Nanchang, Jiangxi 330022, People's Republic of China TEL 0791-8332782. FAX 0791-8331282. *4284*

WELDING AND SURFACING REVIEWS.
Harwood Academic Publishers c/o International Publishers Distributor, P.O. Box 3054, Langhorne, PA 19047-3054. TEL 215-750-2642. FAX 215-750-6343. *4988*

WELDING IN THE WORLD.
Elsevier Science Ltd., Pergamon, P.O. Box 800, Kidlington, Oxford OX5 1DX, England. TEL 44-1865-843000. FAX 44-1865-843010. *4989*

WELSH HISTORY REVIEW.
University of Wales Press, 6 Gwennyth St., Cathays, Cardiff CF2 4YD, Wales. TEL 44-1222-231919. FAX 44-1222-230908. *3363*

WELSH JOURNAL OF EDUCATION.
University of Wales Press, 6 Gwennyth St., Cathays, Cardiff CF2 4YD, Wales. TEL 44-1222-231919. FAX 44-1222-230908. *2382*

DIE WELT DES ISLAMS.
E.J. Brill, P.O. Box 9000, 2300 PA Leiden, Netherlands. TEL 31-71-5353500. FAX 31-71-5317532. *5296*

DE WERELD VAN HET JONGE KIND.
Uitgeverij Dijkstra bv, Postbus 24018, 3502 MA Utrecht, Netherlands. TEL 31-30-803321. FAX 31-30-803844. *2382*

WERTHEIM PUBLICATIONS IN INDUSTRIAL RELATIONS.
Harvard University, J.F.K. School of Government, Cambridge, MA 02138. TEL 617-495-4157. FAX 617-495-5898. *1399*

WEST AFRICAN JOURNAL OF EDUCATIONAL AND VOCATIONAL MEASUREMENT.
West African Examinations Council, Test Development and Research Division, P.M.B. 1076, Yaba, Lagos State, Nigeria. TEL 234-1-861711. *5887*

WEST COAST MAGAZINE.
Festival Business Centre, Unit F8, 150 Brand St., Glasgow G51 1DH, Scotland. TEL 44-141-314-0017. *4173*

WEST EUROPEAN POLITICS.
Frank Cass, Newbury House, 890-900 Eastern Ave., Newbury Park, Ilford, Essex 1G2 7HH. TEL 44-181-599-8866. FAX 44-181-599-0954. *5778*

WEST INDIAN MEDICAL JOURNAL.
University of the West Indies, Faculty of Medical Sciences, Mona Campus, Kingston 7, Jamaica, W.I. TEL 809-927-1214. FAX 809-927-2556. *4543*

WEST VIRGINIA ACADEMY OF SCIENCE. PROCEEDINGS.
West Virginia Academy of Science, Marshall University, 400 Hal Greer Blvd., Huntington, WV 25755. TEL 304-696-2338. FAX 304-696-3243. *6295*

WEST VIRGINIA MEDICAL JOURNAL.
West Virginia State Medical Association, 4307 MacCorkle Ave., Box 4106, Charleston, WV 25364. TEL 304-925-0342. FAX 304-925-0345. *4543*

WESTERN AMERICAN LITERATURE.
Western Literature Association, Utah State University, English Department, Logan, UT 84322-3200. TEL 801-797-1603. FAX 801-797-4099. *4285*

WESTERN AUSTRALIAN NATURALIST.
Western Australian Naturalists' Club Inc., P.O. Box 156, Nedlands, W.A. 6009, Australia. FAX 61-9-2728688. *6296*

WESTERN BIRDS.
Western Field Ornithologists, c/o Dorothy Myers, 6011 Saddletree Ln., Yorba Linda, CA 92686. TEL 714-779-2201. *782*

WESTERN JOURNAL OF COMMUNICATION.
Western States Communication Association, c/o Dennis Alexander, Department of Communication, University of Utah, Salt Lake City, UT 84112. TEL 801-581-6526. FAX 801-585-6255. *4123*

WESTERN JOURNAL OF MEDICINE.
California Medical Association, Box 7690, 221 Main St., San Francisco, CA 94105. TEL 415-882-5179. FAX 415-882-5116. *4543*

WESTERN PHARMACOLOGY SOCIETY. PROCEEDINGS.
Western Pharmacology Society, Inc., University of Arizona, Department of Pharmacology, College of Medicine, Tuscon, AZ 85724. TEL 602-626-7843. FAX 602-626-6883. *5447*

WESTMINSTER MAGAZINE.
Westminster College, Office of Communication Services, New Wilmington, PA 16172. TEL 412-946-7226. FAX 412-946-7187. *1894*

WESTMINSTER STUDIES IN EDUCATION.
Carfax Publishing Co., P.O. Box 25, Abingdon, Oxon. OX14 3UE, England. TEL 44-1235-401000. FAX 44-1235-401550. *2382*

WESTWIND (LOS ANGELES).
University of California at Los Angeles, A-265 Murphy Hall, 405 Hilgard Ave., Los Angeles, CA 90095. TEL 310-206-1225. *459*

WETLANDS.
Society of Wetlands Scientists, Box 1897, Lawrence, KS 66044. TEL 913-843-1235. FAX 913-843-1274. *6982*

WETLANDS ECOLOGY AND MANAGEMENT.
S P B Academic Publishing b.v., P.O. Box 11188, 1001 GD Amsterdam, Netherlands. *6982*

WHAT'S NEW IN FOREST RESEARCH.
Forest Research Institute, Private Bag 3020, Rotorua, New Zealand. TEL 64-7-347-5899. FAX 64-7-347-9380. *3029*

WHISPERING WIND.
Jack Heriard, Ed. & Pub., Box 1390, Folsom, LA 70437-1390. TEL 504-796-5433. *2915*

WHITE RIBBON BULLETIN.
M & D Printing Co., R.I. Box 43, Lowpoint, IL 61545. TEL 309-443-5275. FAX 309-364-3355. *2202*

WHITE RIVER VALLEY HISTORICAL QUARTERLY.
White River Valley Historical Society, Box 555, Point Lookout, MO 65726. *3493*

WIADOMOSCI BOTANICZNE.
Polska Akademia Nauk, Instytut Botaniki im. W. Szafera, Ul. Lubicz 46, 31-512 Krakow, Poland. TEL 48-12-215144. FAX 48-12-219790. *708*

WIES I ROLNICTWO.
Polska Akademia Nauk, Instytut Rozwoju Wsi i Rolnictwa, Ul. Nowy Swiat 72, 00-330 Warsaw, Poland. TEL 48-22-269436. FAX 48-22-266371. *201*

WILD CAT.
Cat Survival Trust, The Centre, Codicote Rd., Welwun, Herts AL6 9TU, England. TEL 44-143-871-6873. FAX 44-143-871-7535. *2145*

WILDERNESS AND ENVIRONMENTAL MEDICINE.
Chapman & Hall, Journals Department 2-6 Boundary Row, London SE1 8HN, England. TEL 44-171-8650066. FAX 44-171-5229623. *4901*

WILDERNESS MEDICINE NEWSLETTER.
Box 3150, Conway, NH 03818. TEL 603-447-6711. FAX 603-447-2310. *4544*

WILDERNESS NEWS.
Wilderness Society, 130 Davey St., Hobart, Tas. 7000, Australia. TEL 61-02-349799. *2825*

WILDLIFE BEHAVIOR AND ECOLOGY.
University of Chicago Press, 5801 S. Ellis Ave., Chicago, IL 60637. TEL 312-702-7899. *614*

WILDLIFE CONSERVATION.
Wildlife Conservation Society, Wildlife Conservation Park, Bronx, NY 10460. TEL 718-220-5121. FAX 718-584-2625. *2146*

WILDLIFE GUARDIAN.
League against Cruel Sports Ltd., Sparling House, 83-87 Union St., London SE1 1SG, England. FAX 44-171-403-4532. *298*

WILDLIFE RESCUE.
Wildlife Rescue Association of British Columbia, 5216 Glencarin Dr., Burnaby, BC V5B 3C1, Canada. TEL 604-526-7275. FAX 604-524-2890. *2146*

WILEY SERIES IN GEOTECHNICAL ENGINEERING.
John Wiley & Sons, Inc., 605 Third Ave., New York, NY 10158. TEL 212-850-6000. FAX 212-850-6088. *245*

WILLDENOWIA.
Botanischer Garten und Botanisches Museum Berlin-Dahlem, Koenigin-Luise-Str. 6-8, 14191 Berlin, Germany. TEL 49-30-83006194. FAX 49-30-83006186. *708*

WILLIAM CARLOS WILLIAMS REVIEW.
William Carlos Williams Society, University of Texas at Austin, Department of English, PAR 108, Austin, TX 78712-1164. TEL 512-471-7842. FAX 512-471-4909. *4286*

WILLIAMS ALUMNI REVIEW.
Williams College, Society of Alumni, Mears House, 75 Park St., Box 38, Williamstown, MA 01267. TEL 413-597-4151. FAX 413-597-4158. *1894*

WIND ENGINEERING.
Multi-Science Publishing Co. Ltd., 107 High St., Brentwood, Essex CM14 4RX, England. TEL 44-1277-224632. FAX 44-1277-223453. *2587*

WINDOW FASHIONS.
G & W McNamara Publishing, Inc., 4225 White Bear Pky., Ste. 400, St. Paul, MN 55110-3349. TEL 612-293-1544. FAX 612-653-4308. *3693*

WINDSOR REVIEW.
University of Windsor, Faculty of Arts, Windsor, ON N9B 3P4, Canada. TEL 519-253-4232. FAX 519-973-7050. *4173*

WINTERTHUR PORTFOLIO.
University of Chicago Press, Journals Division, Box 37005, Chicago, IL 60637. TEL 773-753-3347. FAX 773-753-0811. *5135*

WIRELESS PERSONAL COMMUNICATIONS.
Kluwer Academic Publishers, Postbus 17, 3300 AA Dordrecht, Netherlands. TEL 31-78-6392392. FAX 31-78-6392254. *1942*

WIRELESS TELECOM.
275 Slater St., Ste. 2004, Ottawa, ON K1P 5H9, Canada. TEL 613-233-4888. FAX 613-233-2032. *1921*

WISCONSIN ARCHEOLOGIST.
Wisconsin Archeological Society, Box 1292, Milwaukee, WI 53201. TEL 414-229-4273. *379*

WISCONSIN ARCHITECT.
Wisconsin Architect, Inc., 321 S. Hamilton St., Madison, WI 53703-3606. TEL 608-257-8477. *406*

WISCONSIN BLUE BOOK.
Department of Administration, Document Sales, 202 S. Thornton Ave., Box 7840, Madison, WI 53707. TEL 608-266-3358. *5928*

WISCONSIN MEDICAL JOURNAL.
State Medical Society of Wisconsin, 330 E. Lakeside St., Box 1109, Madison, WI 53701. TEL 608-257-6781. FAX 608-283-5401. *4544*

WITNESS (FARMINGTON HILLS).
Oakland Community College, 27055 Orchard Lake Rd., Farmington Hills, MI 48334. TEL 810-471-7740. *4173*

WOMAN IN HISTORY.
Monument Press (Las Colinas), Box 160361, Las Colinas, TX 75016-9998. TEL 214-686-5332. FAX 214-685-5332. *7010*

WOMEN & CRIMINAL JUSTICE.
Haworth Press, Inc., 10 Alice St., Binghamton, NY 13904. TEL 607-722-5857. FAX 607-722-1424. *3914*

WOMEN & HEALTH.
Haworth Press, Inc., 10 Alice St., Binghamton, NY 13904. TEL 607-722-5857. FAX 607-722-1424. *6986*

WOMEN AND LANGUAGE.
George Mason University, Communication Department, 4400 University Dr., Fairfax, VA 22030-4444. TEL 703-993-1099. FAX 703-993-1096. *4123*

WOMEN & POLITICS (BINGHAMTON).
Haworth Press, Inc., 10 Alice St., Binghamton, NY 13904. TEL 607-722-5857. FAX 607-722-1424. *5717*

WOMEN & THERAPY.
Haworth Press, Inc., 10 Alice St., Binghamton, NY 13904. TEL 607-722-5857. FAX 607-722-1424. *5887*

WOMEN IN CONTEXT.
Plenum Publishing Corp., 233 Spring St., New York, NY 10013-1578. TEL 212-620-8000. FAX 212-463-0742. *6986*

WOMEN IN CULTURE AND SOCIETY.
University of Chicago Press, 5801 S. Ellis Ave., Chicago, IL 60637. TEL 312-702-7899. *7011*

WOMEN IN GERMAN YEARBOOK.
University of Nebraska Press, 312 N. 14th St., Box 880484, Lincoln, NE 68588-0484. TEL 402-472-3581. FAX 402-472-6214. *7021*

WOMEN OF NOTE QUARTERLY.
Vivace Press, N.W. 310 Wawawai Rd., Pullman, WA 99163-2959. TEL 509-334-4660. FAX 509-334-3551. *5205*

WOMEN WITH WHEELS.
Susan Frissell, Ed. & Pub., 1718 Northfield Sq., Ste. A, Northfield, IL 60093. TEL 847-501-3519. *6807*

WOMEN'S EDUCATION.
Canadian Congress for Learning Opportunities for Women, 47 Main St., Toronto, ON M4E 2V6, Canada. TEL 416-699-1909. FAX 416-699-2145. *7012*

WOMEN'S HEALTH ISSUES.
Elsevier Science Inc., Box 945. New York, NY 10159-0945. TEL 212-633-3730. FAX 212-633-3680. *6986*

WOMEN'S HISTORY REVIEW.
Triangle Journals Ltd., P.O. Box 65, Wallingford, Oxon. OX10 0YG, England. TEL 44-1491-838013. FAX 44-1491-834968. *7021*

WOMEN'S STUDIES (NEW YORK).
Gordon and Breach Science Publishers, c/o International Publishers Distributor, P.O. Box 3054, Langhorne, PA 19047-3054. TEL 215-750-2642. FAX 215-750-6343. *7021*

WOMEN'S STUDIES IN COMMUNICATION.
Organization for Research on Women and Communication, c/o Sharon Downey, Department of Speech Comm., CSU, 1250 Bellflower Blvd., Long Beach, CA 90840-2407. TEL 310-985-4301. FAX 310-985-4259. *7021*

WOMEN'S STUDIES INTERNATIONAL FORUM.
Elsevier Science Ltd., Pergamon, P.O. Box 800, Kidlington, Oxford OX5 1DX, England. TEL 44-1865-843000. FAX 44-1865-843010. *7021*

WOMEN'S STUDIES QUARTERLY.
Feminist Press at the City University of New York, 311 E. 94th St., New York, NY 10128-5603. TEL 212-360-5790. FAX 212-348-1241. *7021*

WOMEN'S WORLD.
Isis - Women's International Cross-Cultural Exchange (WICCE), P.O. Box 4934, Kampala, Uganda. TEL 256-41-266007. FAX 256-41-268676. *7022*

WOMEN'S WRITING.
Triangle Journals Ltd., P.O. Box 65, Wallingford, Oxon. OX10 0YG, England. TEL 44-1491-838013. FAX 44-1491-834968. *7022*

WOMENWISE.
Concord Feminist Health Center, 38 S. Main St., Concord, NH 03301. TEL 603-225-2739. FAX 603-668-6255. *6986*

WOMYN'S WORDS.
Women's Energy Bank, Inc., Box 15548, St. Petersburg, FL 33733-5548. TEL 813-823-5333. *7022*

WOOL TECHNOLOGY AND SHEEP BREEDING.
University of New South Wales, Department of Wool and Animal Science, Sydney, N.S.W. 2052, Australia. TEL 61-2-3854481. FAX 61-2-3855953. *287*

WOOLF STUDIES ANNUAL.
Pace University Press, 1 Pace Plaza, New York, NY 10038. TEL 212-346-1405. FAX 212-346-1754. *4286*

WORD & IMAGE.
Taylor & Francis Ltd., 1 Gunpowder Sq., London EC4A 3DE, England. TEL 44-171-5830490. FAX 44-171-5830585. *4173*

WORD & SPIRIT.
St. Bede's Publications, Box 545, Rte. 32, Petersham, MA 01366. TEL 508-724-3407. FAX 508-724-3574. *6201*

WORD IN ACTION.
British and Foreign Bible Society, Stonehill Green, Westlea, Swindon, Wilts. SN5 7DG, England. TEL 44-1793-418100. FAX 44-1793-418118. *6104*

WORD OF MOUTH (SAN FRANCISCO).
c/o Delta Dental Plan of CA, Box 7736, San Francisco, CA 94120. TEL 415-972-8300. *4657*

WORK.
Elsevier Science Ireland Ltd., P.O. Box 85, Limerick, Ireland. TEL 353-61-471944. FAX 353-61-472144. *5260*

WORK AND STRESS.
Taylor & Francis Ltd., 1 Gunpowder Sq., London EC4A 3DE, England. TEL 44-171-583-0490. FAX 44-171-583-0585. *5887*

WORKING MOMS AND DADS.
Corporate Marketing and Publishing Inc., Box 12217, Tucson, AZ 85732-2217. TEL 520-790-4044. *1780*

WORKING PAPERS ON WOMEN IN INTERNATIONAL DEVELOPMENT.
Michigan State University, Office of Women in International Development, 202 International Center, E. Lansing, MI 48824-1035. TEL 517-353-5040. FAX 517-353-7254. *1317*

WORKING - PARTY REPORTS.
Centre for European Policy Studies, Place du Congres 1, 1000 Brussels, Belgium. TEL 32-2-2182247. FAX 32-2-2293911. *5778*

WORKS AND DAYS.
Indiana University of Pennsylvania, English Department, 110 Leonard Hall, Indiana, PA 15705. TEL 412-357-6486. FAX 412-357-6213. *4286*

WORLD AFFAIRS (WASHINGTON).
Heldref Publications, 1319 Eighteenth St., N.W., Washington, DC 20036-1802. TEL 202-296-6267. FAX 202-296-5149. *5778*

WORLD ANIMAL SCIENCE.
Elsevier Science B.V., Books Division, P.O. Box 211, 1000 AE Amsterdam, Netherlands. TEL 31-20-4853911 FAX 31-20-4853705. *823*

WORLD AQUACULTURE SOCIETY. JOURNAL.
World Aquaculture Society, 143 J M Parker Coliseum, Louisiana State University, Baton Rouge, LA 70803. TEL 504-388-3137. FAX 504-388-3493. *2308*

THE WORLD BANK ECONOMIC REVIEW.
World Bank, 1818 H St., N.W., Washington, DC 20433. TEL 202-477-1155. FAX 202-522-2627. *1246*

WORLD BANK RESEARCH OBSERVER.
World Bank, 1818 H St. N.W., Washington, DC 20433. TEL 202-473-1155. FAX 202-522-2627. *1127*

WORLD CERAMICS ABSTRACTS.
Ceram Research Ltd., Queens Rd., Penkhull, Stoke-on-Trent, Staffs. ST4 7LQ, England. *1662*

WORLD CROP PESTS.
Elsevier Science B.V., Books Division, P.O. Box 211, 1000 AE Amsterdam, Netherlands. TEL 31-20-4853911. FAX 31-20-4853705. *246*

WORLD DEVELOPMENT.
Elsevier Science Ltd., Pergamon, P.O. Box 800, Kidlington, Oxford OX5 1DX, England. TEL 44-1865-843000. FAX 44-1865-843010. *1318*

THE WORLD ECONOMY.
Blackwell Publishers Ltd., 108 Cowley Rd., Oxford OX4 1JF, England. TEL 44-1865-791100. FAX 44-1865-791347. *971*

WORLD ENGLISHES.
Blackwell Publishers Ltd., 108 Cowley Rd., Oxford OX4 1JF, England. TEL 44-1865-791100. FAX 44-1865-791347. *4124*

WORLD FUTURES.
Gordon and Breach Science Publishers, c/o International Publishers Distributor, P.O. Box 3054, Langhorne, PA 19047-3054. TEL 215-750-2642. FAX 215-750-6343. *5526*

WORLD HOSPITALS AND HEALTH SERVICES.
International Hospital Federation, 4 Abbots Pl., London NW6 4NP, England. TEL 0171-372-7181. FAX 0171-328-7433. *3356*

WORLD JOURNAL OF PSYCHOSYNTHESIS.
World Journal Press, Box 859, E. Lansing, MI 48823. TEL 517-372-4660. FAX 517-372-9959. *4871*

WORLD JOURNAL OF SURGERY.
Springer-Verlag, Medical Journals, 175 Fifth Ave., New York, NY 10010. TEL 212-460-1500. FAX 212-473-6272. *4923*

WORLD LITERATURE WRITTEN IN ENGLISH.
National Institute of Education, Division of Literature and Drama, Bukit Timah Rd., Singapore 1025, Singapore. FAX 4692427. *4287*

THE WORLD OF A S P.
American Self-Protection Association, 825 Greengate Oval, Sagamore Hills, OH 44067. TEL 216-467-7110. FAX 216-457-6834. *6492*

THE WORLD OF TRIBAL ARTS.
Tribarts Inc., 2166 Market St., Ste. 644, San Francisco, CA 94114. TEL 415-677-7917. FAX 415-413-8321. *5136*

WORLD PATENT INFORMATION.
Elsevier Science Ltd., Pergamon, P.O. Box 800, Kidlington, Oxford OX5 1DX, England. TEL 44-1865-843000. FAX 44-1865-843010. *5346*

WORLD POLITICS (BALTIMORE).
Johns Hopkins University Press, Journals Publishing Division 2715 N. Charles St., Baltimore, MD 21218-4319. TEL 410-516-6987. FAX 410-516-6968. *5779*

WORLD RESOURCE REVIEW.
22 W. 381 75th St., Naperville, IL 60565-9245. TEL 630-910-1551. FAX 630-910-1561. *2826*

WORLD REVIEW OF NUTRITION AND DIETETICS.
S. Karger AG, Allschwilerstr. 10, P.O. Box, CH-4009 Basel, Switzerland. TEL 061-3061111. FAX 061-3061234. *5243*

WORLD SURFACE COATING ABSTRACTS.
Paint Research Association, 8 Waldegrave Rd., Teddington, Middlesex TW11 8LD, England. TEL 44-181-977-4427. FAX 44-181-943-4705. *5312*

WORLD SURVEY OF CLIMATOLOGY.
Elsevier Science B.V., Books Division, P.O. Box 211, 1000 AE Amsterdam, Netherlands. TEL 31-20-4853911. FAX 31-20-4853705. *5010*

WORLDPLAST.
Field & Wood, Medical Periodicals, Inc., Box 975, Blue Bell, PA 19422. TEL 610-828-4010. FAX 215-482-0226. *4923*

WORLD'S POULTRY SCIENCE JOURNAL.
Butterworth - Heinemann, Part of the Reed Elsevier group, Linacre House, Jordan Hill, Oxford OX2 8DP, England. TEL 44-1865-310366. FAX 44-1865-310898. *287*

WORLDWIDE LIVING COSTS.
P-E International plc, Park House, Wick Rd., Egham, Surrey TW20 0HW, England. TEL 44-1784-434411. FAX 44-1784-476369. *1571*

WOUND BALLISTICS REVIEW.
International Wound Ballistics Association, Box 701, El Segundo, CA 90245. TEL 310-640-6065. *4688*

WOUND REPAIR AND REGENERATION.
Mosby - Year Book, Inc. 11830 Westline Industrial Dr., St. Louis, MO 63146-3318. TEL 800-325-4177. FAX 314-432-1380. *4793*

WRITING LAB NEWSLETTER.
Purdue University, Department of English, 1356 Heavelon, West Lafayette, IN 47907-1356. TEL 317-494-7268. FAX 317-494-3780. *2506*

WUJI CAILIAO XUEBAO.
Science Press, Marketing and Sales Department, 16 Donghuangchenggen North St., Beijing 100717, People's Republic of China. TEL 4010642. FAX 4019810. *1733*

WULI.
Science Press, Marketing and Sales Department, 16 Donghuangchenggen North St., Beijing 100717, People's Republic of China. TEL 4010642. FAX 4019810. *5576*

WULI XUEBAO.
Science Press, Marketing and Sales Department, Donghuangchenggen North St., Beijing 100717, People's Republic of China. TEL 4010642. FAX 4019810. *5577*

WUTAISHAN YANJIU.
Wutaishan Yanjiuhui, 38, Bingzhou Nanlu, Taiyuan, Shanxi 030006, People's Republic of China. TEL 0351-7075841. *3364*

WYOMING ARCHAEOLOGIST.
Wyoming Archaeological Society, Inc., 1617 Westridge Terr., Casper, WY 82604. TEL 307-268-2212. FAX 307-268-2224. *379*

X R S - X-RAY SPECTROMETRY.
John Wiley & Sons Ltd., Journals, Baffins Ln., Chichester, W. Sussex PO19 1UD, England. TEL 44-1243-779777. FAX 44-1243-843232. *5612*

XENOBIOTICA.
Taylor & Francis Ltd., 1 Gunpowder Sq., London EC4A 3DE, England. TEL 44-171-583-0490. FAX 44-171-583-0585. *651*

XENOTRANSPLANTATION.
Munksgaard International Publishers Ltd., 35 Noerre Soegade, P.O. Box 2148, DK-1016 Copenhagen K, Denmark. TEL 45-33-127030. FAX 45-33-129387. *4923*

XIANDAI BINGQI.
Xiandai Bingqi Zazhishe, P.O. Box 2413-8, Beijing 100081, People's Republic of China. TEL 86-10-68414477. FAX 86-10-68413642. *5054*

XIANDAI GUOJI GUANXI.
Xiandai Guoji Guanxi Yanjiusuo, No. A-2, Wanshousi, Haidian, Beijing 100081, People's Republic of China. TEL 86-10-6879-7796. FAX 86-10-6841-8641. *5779*

XIBEI SHI-DI.
Lanzhou Daxue, Sichou zhi Lu Wenhua Kaifa Jingying Zhongxin, Lanzhou, Gansu 730000, People's Republic of China. TEL 8825500. FAX 8885076. *3386*

XIBU TANKUANG GONGCHENG.
Xibu Tankuang Gongcheng Bianjibu, 16 Youhao Beilu, Urumqi, Xinjiang 830000, People's Republic of China. TEL 86-991-4818457. FAX 86-991-4841517. *5082*

XINLI XUEBAO.
Science Press, Marketing and Sales Department, 16 Donghuangchenggen North St., Beijing 100717, People's Republic of China. TEL 4010642. FAX 4019810. *5887*

XITONG GONGCHENG XUEBAO.
Tianjin Daxue, Qilitai, Nankai Qu, Tianjin 300072, People's Republic of China. FAX 022-7388657. *2623*

XITONG KEXUE YU SHUXUE.
Science Press, Marketing and Sales Department, 16 Donghuangchenggen North St., Beijing 100717, People's Republic of China. TEL 4010642. FAX 4019810. *2060*

YAD VASHEM STUDIES.
Rubin Mass Ltd., P.O. Box 990, Jerusalem 91009, Israel. TEL 972-2-277863. FAX 972-2-277864. *6131*

THE YALE - CHINA REVIEW.
Yale China Association, Box 208223, Yale Sta., New Haven, CT 06520. TEL 203-432-0880. *2453*

YALE DAILY NEWS.
Yale Daily News Publishing, Co., Inc., 202 York St., New Haven, CT 06511-4804. TEL 203-432-2424. FAX 203-432-7425. *1894*

YALE JOURNAL OF BIOLOGY AND MEDICINE.
Yale Journal of Biology and Medicine, Inc., 333 Cedar St., New Haven, CT 06510. TEL 203-785-4251. FAX 203-785-6309. *4545*

YALE JOURNAL OF CRITICISM.
Johns Hopkins University Press, Journals Publishing Division, 2715 N. Charles St., Baltimore, MD 21218-4319. TEL 410-516-6987. FAX 410-516-6968. *4289*

YALE UNIVERSITY. DEPARTMENT OF ANTHROPOLOGY. PUBLICATIONS IN ANTHROPOLOGY.
Yale University, Department of Anthropology, Box 208277, New Haven, CT 06520. TEL 203-432-3670. FAX 203-432-3669. *326*

YANSHI LIXUE YU GONGCHENG XUEBAO.
Chinese Academy of Sciences, Institute of Rock and Soil Mechanics, Wuhan, Hubei 430071, People's Republic of China. TEL 86-27-786-9250. FAX 86-27-786-2413. *5592*

YANSHI XUEBAO.
Science Press, Marketing and Sales Department, 16 Donghuangchenggen North St., Beijing 100717, People's Republic of China. TEL 4010642. FAX 4019810. *2269*

YANTU LIXUE.
Zhongguo Kexueyuan, Wuhan Yantu Lixue Yanjiusuo, Xiaohongshan, Wuhan, Hubei 430071, People's Republic of China. TEL 813712. *5592*

YAOWU FENXI ZAZHI.
Chinese Medical Association, P.O. Box 2258, 42 Dongsi Xidajie, Beijing 100710, People's Republic of China. TEL 1-550394. *5448*

YASO.
Yagai Shokubutsu Kenkyukai, c/o Mr. Nobushige Kato, 1-18 Wakaba, Shinjuku-ku, Tokyo 160, Japan. TEL 03-3357-9090. *708*

YEAR IN IMMUNOLOGY.
S. Karger AG, Allschwilerstr. 10, P.O. Box, CH-4009 Basel, Switzerland. TEL 061-3061111. FAX 061-3061234. *4588*

THE YEARBOOK OF LANGLAND STUDIES.
Colleagues Press Inc., Box 4007, East Lansing, MI 48826. TEL 704-298-8904. FAX 704-298-3044. *4323*

YEARBOOK OF MORPHOLOGY.
Kluwer Academic Publishers, Postbus 17, 3300 AA Dordrecht, Netherlands. TEL 31-78-6392392. FAX 31-78-6392254. *4124*

YEARBOOK OF SUBSTANCE USE AND ABUSE.
Human Sciences Press, Inc. 233 Spring St., New York, NY 10013-1578. TEL 212-620-8000. FAX 212-463-0742. *2202*

YEAST.
John Wiley & Sons Ltd., Journals, Baffins Ln., Chichester, W. Sussex PO19 1UD, England. TEL 44-1243-779777. FAX 44-1243-843232. *666*

YEATS ELIOT REVIEW.
Murphy Newsletter Services, 8524 Asher Ave., Little Rock, AR 72204. TEL 501-562-6619. *4323*

YICHUAN XUEBAO.
Science Press, Marketing and Sales Department, 16 Donghuangchenggen North St., Beijing 100717, People's Republic of China. TEL 4010642. FAX 4019810. *751*

YINGXIANG JISHU.
Quanguo Qinggong Ganguang Cailiao Keji Qingbaozhan, 20 Dongting Lu, Hexi Qu, Tianjin 300220, People's Republic of China. TEL 840654. FAX 86-22-8342934. *5522*

YINGYONG SHENGXUE.
Science Press, Marketing and Sales Department, 16 Donghuangchenggen North St., Beijing 100717, People's Republic of China. TEL 4010642. FAX 4019810. *5617*

YINGYONG SHUXUE HE LIXUE.
Chongqing Jiaotong Xueyuan, 107 Dahuang Lu, Chongqing, Sichuan 630042, People's Republic of China. TEL 86-811-881-3708. *4404*

YINGYONG SHUXUE XUEBAO.
Science Press, Marketing and Sales Department, 16 Donghuangchenggen North St., Beijing 100717, People's Republic of China. TEL 4010642. FAX 4019810. *4404*

YINGYU SHIJIE.
Commercial Press, P.O. Box 1504, Beijing 100005, People's Republic of China. TEL 525-7190. FAX 513-5899. *4124*

YISHU BAIJIA.
Jiangsu Sheng Wenhua Yishu Yanjiusuo, 1 Qingdao Lu, Nanjing, Jiangsu 210008, People's Republic of China. TEL 86-25-6632175. *460*

YOGA AND TOTAL HEALTH.
Yoga Institute, Prabhat Colony, Santa Cruz East, Bombay 400 055, India. TEL 22-6122185. *5506*

YOGA - MIMAMSA.
Kaivalyadhama Institution, Lonavla 410 403, District Puna, Maharashtra, India. TEL 91-2114-73039. FAX 91-2114-71983. *5506*

YONSEI MEDICAL JOURNAL.
Yonsei University, College of Medicine, C.P.O. Box 8044, Seoul, S. Korea. TEL 82-2-361-5061. FAX 82-2-393-4945. *4546*

YORK RESEARCH PAPERS IN LINGUISTICS.
University of York, Department of Language and Linguistic Science, Heslington, York YO1 5DD, England. TEL 44-1904-432650. FAX 44-1904-432652. *4125*

YOU!
Veritas Communications Inc., 31194 La Baya Dr., Ste. 200, Westlake Village, CA 91362-4022. TEL 818-991-1813. FAX 818-991-2024. *1813*

YOUJI HUAXUE.
Science Press, Marketing and Sales Department, 16 Donghuangchenggen North St., Beijing 100717, People's Republic of China. TEL 4010642. FAX 4019810. *1747*

YOUR HEALTH & FITNESS.
General Learning Communications, Health Communications Group, 60 Revere Dr., Northbrook, IL 60062-1563. TEL 847-205-3000. FAX 847-564-8197. *5538*

YOUTH THEATRE JOURNAL.
American Alliance for Theatre & Education, Theatre Department, Arizona State University, Box 852002, Tempe, AZ 85287-2002. TEL 602-965-6064. FAX 602-965-5361. *6708*

YUGOSLAV JOURNAL OF OPERATIONS RESEARCH.
University of Belgrade, Faculty of Organizational Sciences, Jove Ilica 154, 11000 Belgrade, Yugoslavia. TEL 38-11-465855. FAX 38-11-461221. *2000*

YUNNAN MINZU XUEYUAN XUEBAO.
Yunnan Minzu Xueyuan, Lianhua Chi, Kunming, Yunnan 650031, People's Republic of China. TEL 86-871-5154458. *5296*

Z BADAN NAD POLSKIMI KSIEGOZBIORAMI HISTORYCZNYMI.
Uniwersytet Warszawski, Instytut Bibliotekoznawstwa i Informacji Naukowej, Nowy Swiat 69, 00-046 Warsaw, Poland. TEL 48-22-268569. FAX 48-22-268569. *4036*

ZAMBEZIA: THE JOURNAL OF THE UNIVERSITY OF ZIMBABWE.
University of Zimbabwe, Publications Office, P.O. Box MP 203, Mt. Pleasant, Harare, Zimbabwe. TEL 263-4-303211. FAX 263-4-333407. *6354*

ZAOCHUAN JISHU.
Zhongguo Chuanbo Gongye Zonggongsi, Chuanbo Gongyi Yanjiusuo, P.O. Box 032-201, Shanghai 200032, People's Republic of China. TEL 86-21-6439-9626. FAX 86-21-6439-0908. *6853*

ZAOZHI HUAXUE PIN.
China Papermaking Chemicals Industry Association, 7 Shihuiba, Changbanxiang, Hangzhou, Zhejiang Province 310014, People's Republic of China. TEL 86-571-8315561. *5328*

ZEITSCHRIFT FUER HAUTKRANKHEITEN H UND G.
Blackwell Wissenschaft, Kurfuerstendamm 57, 10707 Berlin, Germany. TEL 49-30-32790624. FAX 49-30-32790610. *4665*

ZEITSCHRIFT FUER NATURFORSCHUNG. SECTION A: A JOURNAL OF PHYSICAL SCIENCES.
Verlag der Zeitschrift fuer Naturforschung, Postfach 2645, 72016 Tuebingen, Germany. TEL 49-7071-31555. FAX 49-7071-360571. *5577*

ZEITSCHRIFT FUER NATURFORSCHUNG. SECTION B: A JOURNAL OF CHEMICAL SCIENCES.
Verlag der Zeitschrift fuer Naturforschung, Postfach 2645, 72016 Tuebingen, Germany. TEL 49-7071-31555. FAX 49-7071-360571. *1734*

ZEITSCHRIFT FUER NATURFORSCHUNG. SECTION C: A JOURNAL OF BIOSCIENCES.
Verlag der Zeitschrift fuer Naturforschung, Postfach 2645, 72016 Tuebingen, Germany. TEL 49-7071-31555. FAX 49-7071-360571. *614*

ZEITSCHRIFT FUER PARAPSYCHOLOGIE UND GRENZGEBIETE DER PSYCHOLOGIE.
Wissenschaftliche Gesellschaft zur Foederung der Parapsychologie e.V., Hildastr. 64, 79102 Freiburg, Germany. TEL 49-761-77202. *5334*

ZEITSCHRIFT FUER RELIGIONS- UND GEISTESGESCHICHTE.
E.J. Brill, P.O. Box 9000, 2300 PA Leiden, Netherlands. TEL 31-71-5353500. FAX 31-71-5317532. *6105*

ZEITSCHRIFT FUER RELIGIONS- UND GEISTESGESCHICHTE. BEIHEFTE.
E.J. Brill, P.O. Box 9000, 2300 PA Leiden, Netherlands. TEL 31-71-5353500. FAX 31-71-5317532. *6106*

ZENTRALSTERILISATION - CENTRAL SERVICE.
M H P Verlag GmbH, Ostring 13, 65205 Wiesbaden, Germany. TEL 49-6122-7709131. FAX 49-6122-76331. *4546*

ZEOLITES.
Elsevier Science Inc., Box 945, New York, NY 10159-0945. TEL 212-633-3730. FAX 212-633-3680. *1723*

ZHENJUN XUEBAO.
Science Press, Marketing and Sales Department, 16 Donghuangchenggen North St., Beijing 100717, People's Republic of China. TEL 4109810. FAX 4109810. *708*

ZHIWU BAOHU.
Zhongguo Zhiwu Baohu Xuehui, Zhongguo Nongke Yuan, Zhibao Suo, 2 Yuanmingyuan Xilu, Beijing 100094, People's Republic of China. TEL 86-10-6258-1177. FAX 86-10-6258-3080. *708*

ZHIWU BINGLI XUEBAO.
Zhongguo Zhiwu Bingli Xuehui, Department of Plant Protection, Beijing University of Agriculture, Beijing 100094, People's Republic of China. TEL 86-10-2582244. FAX 86-10-2582332. *709*

ZHIWU FENLEI XUEBAO.
Science Press, Marketing and Sales Department, 16 Donghuangchenggen North St., Beijing 100717, People's Republic of China. TEL 4109810. FAX 4019810. *709*

ZHIWU SHENGLI XUEBAO.
Science Press, Marketing and Sales Department, 16 Donghuangchenggen North St., Beijing 100717, People's Republic of China. TEL 4010642. FAX 4019810. *709*

ZHIWU SHENGTAI XUEBAO.
Science Press, Marketing and Sales Department, 16 Donghuangchenggen North St., Beijing 100717, People's Republic of China. TEL 86-10-6401-9815. FAX 86-10-6401-9810. *709*

ZHIWU XUEBAO.
Science Press, Marketing and Sales Department, 16 Donghuangchenggen North St., Beijing 100717, People's Republic of China. TEL 4010642. FAX 4019810. *709*

ZHIWU ZIYUAN YU HUANJING.
Zhiwu Ziyuan yu Huanjing Bianjibu, Zhongshan Mengwai, Nanjing, Jiangsu 210014, People's Republic of China. TEL 86-25-443-2128. FAX 86-25-443-2074. *709*

ZHIWUXUE TONGBAO.
Zhongguo Kexueyuan, Zhiwu Yanjiusuo, 141 Xizhimenwai Dajie, Beijing 100044, People's Republic of China. TEL 893831. *709*

ZHIYE YU JIANKANG.
Tianjin Institute of Industrial Hygiene and Occupational Diseases, 221 Ma Chang Rd., Hexi District, Tianjin 300204, People's Republic of China. TEL 3283432 *5980*

ZHONGGUO BINGLI SHENGLI ZAZHI.
Zhongguo Bingli Shengli Xuehui, Jinan University, Shipai, Guangzhou, Guangdong 510632, People's Republic of China. TEL 5516511. FAX 5516941. *4546*

ZHONGGUO GANGCHANGBING ZAZHI.
Zhongguo Gangchangbing Zazhi Bianjibu, No. 42, Wenhua Xilu, Jinan, Shandong 250011, People's Republic of China. TEL 0531-2963276. *4697*

ZHONGGUO HAIYANG PINGTAI.
China State Shipbuilding Corporation, Shipbuilding Technology Research Institute, P.O. Box 032-201, No. 851, Zhongshan Nan 2 Lu, Shanghai 200032, People's Republic of China. TEL 021-64399626. FAX 021-64390908. *5381*

ZHONGGUO HANGTIAN.
Hangtian Gongye Zong Gongsi, Keji Qingbao-suo, P.O. Box 1408, 1 Binhe Lu, Hepingli, Beijing 100013, People's Republic of China. TEL 86-10-837-3440. FAX 81-10-422-7606. *82*

ZHONGGUO HUANJING KEXUE.
Chinese Society for Environmental Sciences, No.115, Xizhimennei Nanxiaojie, Beijing 100035, People's Republic of China. TEL 6066498. FAX 6020031. *2827*

ZHONGGUO KANGFU YIXUE ZAZHI.
Zhongguo Kangfu Yixuehui, Zhongri Youhao Yiyuan, Yinghuayuan East St., Beijing 100029, People's Republic of China. TEL 86-10-422-1122. FAX 86-10-421-7749. *4546*

ZHONGGUO KEXUE A.
Science Press, Marketing and Sales Department, 16 Donghuangchenggen North St., Beijing 100717, People's Republic of China. TEL 4010642. FAX 4109810. *6298*

ZHONGGUO KEXUE B.
Science Press, Marketing and Sales Department, 16 Donghuangchenggen North St., Beijing 100717, People's Republic of China. TEL 4010642. FAX 4019810. *6298*

ZHONGGUO MIANYIXUE ZAZHI.
Jilin Sheng Weisheng Ting, Fu 2, Dong Minzhu Dajie, Changchun, Jilin 130061, People's Republic of China. TEL 825027. *4588*

ZHONGGUO NONGYE QIXIANG.
Zhongguo Nongye Kexueyuan, 30 Baishiqiao Lu, Beijing 100081, People's Republic of China. TEL 8314433. *5011*

ZHONGGUO SHENGWU FANGZHI.
Zhongguo Nongye Kexueyuan, 30 Baishiqiao Lu, Beijing 100081, People's Republic of China. TEL 86-10-8314433. FAX 86-10-8323182. *614*

ZHONGGUO SHIYONG ERKE ZAZHI.
Zhongguo Shiyong Yixue Zazhishe, 44-1, Jixian St., Heping District, Shenyang Liaoning 110005, People's Republic of China. TEL 86-24-3394597. FAX 86-24-3391212. *6315*

ZHONGGUO SHIYONG FUKE YU CHANKE ZAZHI.
Zhongguo Shiyong Yixue Zazhishe, 44-1, Jixian St., Heping District, Shenyang Liaoning 110005, People's Republic of China. TEL 86-24-3394474. FAX 86-24-3391212. *4747*

ZHONGGUO SHIYONG NEIKE ZAZHI.
Zhongguo Shiyong Yixue Zazhishe, 44-1, Jixian St., Heping District, Shenyang Liaoning 110005, People's Republic of China. TEL 86-24-3395218. FAX 86-24-3391212. *4708*

ZHONGGUO SHIYONG WAIKE ZAZHI.
Zhongguo Shiyong Yixue Zazhishe, 44-1, Jixian St., Heping District, Shenyang Liaoning 110005, People's Republic of China. TEL 85-24-3395362. FAX 96-24-3391212. *4723*

ZHONGGUO XIAODUXUE ZAZHI.
Zhonghua Yufang Yixuehu (Fengtai), 20 Dongdajie, Fengtai, Beijing 100071, People's Republic of China. TEL 86-1-6688-8229. FAX 86-1-6688-8229 *4547*

ZHONGGUO XINLI WEISHENG ZAZHI.
Beijing Yike Daxue, Jingshen Weisheng Yanjiusuo, 38 Huayuan Beilu, Beijing 100083, People's Republic of China. TEL 861-2010890. FAX 861-2027314. *5888*

ZHONGGUO XIUFU CHONGJIAN WAIKE ZAZHI.
Zhongguo Xiufu Chongjian Waike Zazhi Bianjibu, Huaxi Yike Daxue Fushu Diyi Yiyuan Nei, 37 Guoxue Xiang, Chengdu, Sichuan 610041, People's Republic of China. TEL 86-28-5551255. FAX 86-28-5559438. *4924*

ZHONGGUO YAOLI XUEBAO.
Science Press, Marketing and Sales Department, 16 Donghuangchenggen Beijie, Beijing 100707, People's Republic of China. TEL 4010642. FAX 4012180. *5448*

ZHONGGUO YINGYONG SHENGLIXUE ZAZHI.
Zhongguo Yingyong Shenglixue Zazhi Bianjibu, 27 Taiping Rd., Beijing 100850 People's Republic of China. FAX 861-8213044. *794*

ZHONGGUO YIXUE KEXUEYUAN XUEBAO.
Chinese Academy of Medical Sciences (CAMS), 9 Dong Dan San Tiao, Beijing 100730, People's Republic of China. TEL 86-1-5133074. *4547*

ZHONGGUO ZIXINGCHE.
Bicycle Information Centre of China, China Bicycle Association, No.6, Alley 360, Anyuan Road, Shanghai 200060, People's Republic of China. TEL 021-2584696. FAX 021-2550918. *6531*

ZHONGHUA SHENJING WAIKE ZAZHI.
Beijing Neurosurgical Institute No.6, Tiantan Xili, Beijing 100050, People's Republic of China. TEL 86-10-5113169. FAX 86-10-7018349. *4872*

ZHONGHUA YANDIBING ZAZH.
West China University of Medical Sciences, First Teaching Hospital, No. 37, Guoxue Xiang, Chengdu, Sichuan 610041, People's Republic of China. TEL 86-28-5551255. FAX 86-28-5583252. *4779*

ZHONGHUA YINGCAI.
Zhonghua Yingcai Huabaoshe, 3 Fuyou St., Beijing 100032, People's Republic of China. TEL 81-10-309-5986. FAX 86-10-309-5508. *3131*

ZHONGSHAN.
Zhongshan Bianjibu, 2 Yihe Lu, Nanjing, Jiangsu 210024, People's Republic of China. TEL 86-25-6638819. *4291*

ZHONGWEN XINXI.
Zhongguo Zhongwen Xinxi Xuehui, P.O. Box 263, Chendu Keji Daxue - Chengdu University of Science and Technology, Chengdu, Sichuan Province, People's Republic of China. TEL 028-581554. *4036*

ZHONGXUE YUWEN.
Hubei Daxue, Zhongwen Xi, Baojia'an, Wuchang-qu, Wuhan, Hubei 430062, People's Republic of China. TEL 86-27-6811903. FAX 86-27-6814263. *4126*

ZIDONGHUA XUEBAO.
Science Press, Marketing and Sales Department, 16
Donghuangchenggen North St., Beijing 100717,
People's Republic of China. TEL 4010642.
FAX 4019810. *2018*

ZIMBABWE JOURNAL OF EDUCATIONAL RESEARCH.
University of Zimbabwe, Faculty of Education, P.O.
Box MP 167, Mount Pleasant, Harare, Zimbabwe.
TEL 263-4-303271. FAX 263-4-333407. *2385*

ZIMBABWE VETERINARY JOURNAL.
Zimbabwe Veterinary Journal, P.O. Box CY168,
Causeway, Harare, Zimbabwe. TEL 263-4-495859.
FAX 263-4-495859. *6960*

ZION.
Historical Society of Israel, P.O. Box 4179,
Jerusalem 91041, Israel. TEL 972-2-637171.
FAX 972-2-662135. *2916*

ZIRAN ZIYUAN XUEBAO.
Science Press, Marketing and Sales Department, 16
Donghuangchenggen North St., Beijing 100717,
People's Republic of China. TEL 4010642.
FAX 4019810. *2217*

ZOO BIOLOGY.
John Wiley & Sons, Inc., Journals, 605 Third Ave.,
New York, NY 10158. TEL 212-850-6645.
FAX 212-850-6021. *824*

ZOOLOGICA POLONIAE.
Polskie Towarzystwo Zoologiczne, Ul. Sienkiewicza
21, 50-335 Wroclaw, Poland. TEL 48-71-225041.
FAX 48-71-222817. *824*

ZOOLOGICA SCRIPTA.
Elsevier Science Ltd., Pergamon, P.O. Box 800,
Kidlington, Oxford OX5 1DX, England. TEL 44-1865-
843000. FAX 44-1865-843010. *824*

ZOOLOGICAL SCIENCE.
Zoological Society of Japan, Toshin Bldg., 2-27-2
Hongo, Bunkyo-ku, Tokyo 113, Japan. TEL 81-3-
3812-2111. FAX 81-3-3816-1965. *825*

ZOOLOGICAL SOCIETY OF LONDON. SYMPOSIA.
Oxford University Press, Walton St., Oxford OX2
6DP, England. TEL 44-1865-56767. FAX 44-1865-
56646. *825*

ZOOLOGY IN THE MIDDLE EAST.
Max Kasparek Verlag, Bleichstr. 1, 69120
Heidelberg, Germany. TEL 49-6221-475069.
FAX 49-6221-471858. *825*

ZUID - AFRIKA.
Zuid - Afrikaansche Stichting Moederland,
Keizersgracht 141, 1015 CK Amsterdam,
Netherlands. TEL 31-20-6249318. FAX 31-20-
6382596. *5720*

ZUOWU XUEBAO.
Science Press, Marketing and Sales Department, 16
Donghuangchenggen North St., Beijing 100717,
People's Republic of China. TEL 4010642.
FAX 4019810. *247*

ZUOWU ZAZHI.
Zhongguo Zuowu Xuehui, Zhongguo Nongye
Kexueyuan, 30 Baishiqiao Lu, Beijing 100081,
People's Republic of China. TEL 891731. *165*

ZYGON.
Blackwell Publishers, 238 Main St., Cambridge, MA
02142. FAX 617-547-0789. *6106*

ZYGOTE.
Cambridge University Press, Edinburgh Bldg.,
Shaftsbury Rd., Cambridge CB2 2RU, England.
TEL 44-1223-312393. FAX 44-1223-315052.
615

ZYMURGY.
American Homebrewers Association Inc., Box 1679,
Boulder, CO 80306-1679. TEL 303-447-0816.
FAX 303-447-2825. *514*

9-1-1 MAGAZINE.
Official Publications, Inc., Box 11788, Santa Ana,
CA 92711-1788. TEL 714-544-7776. FAX 714-
838-9233. *2179*

16 DE ABRIL.
Ministerio de Salud Publica, Instituto Superior de
Ciencias Medicas de la Habana, Calle G s-n, e. 25 y
27, Plaza de la Revolucion, 10400 Vedado,
Havana, Cuba. TEL 308942. FAX 537-333063.
4547

21ST CENTURY AFRO REVIEW.
I A A S Publishers, Inc., 7676 New Hampshire Ave.,
Langley Park, MD 20783. TEL 301-499-6308.
FAX 301-499-4298. *2917*

50 PLUS NEWS MAGAZINE.
Box 230, Hartland, WI 53029-0230. TEL 414-367-
5303. FAX 414-367-9517. *3298*

Serials Available on CD-ROM

A B C.
Prensa Espanola S.A., Juan I Luca de Tena, 7,
28027 Madrid, Spain. TEL 34-1-3399000. FAX 34-
1-3208711. *3215*

A B C BELGE POUR LE COMMERCE ET L'INDUSTRIE.
A B C Belge pour le Commerce et l'Industrie B.V.,
Ave. de l'Heliport 21, 1000 Brussels, Belgium.
TEL 32-2-2015414. FAX 32-2-2015471. *1582*

**A B C DER DEUTSCHEN WIRTSCHAFT -
QUELLENWERK FUR EINKAUF-VERKAUF.**
A B C Publishing Group, Postfach 100262, 64202
Darmstadt, Germany. TEL 49-6151-3892-0.
FAX 49-6151-33164. *1582*

A B C EUROP PRODUCTION.
A B C Publishing Group, Postfach 100262, 64202
Darmstadt, Germany. TEL 49-6151-3892-0.
FAX 49-6151-33164. *1263*

**A B C LUXEMBOURGEOIS POUR LE COMMERCE ET
L'INDUSTRIE.**
A B C Belge pour le Commerce et l'Industrie B.V.,
Ave. de l'Heliport 21, 1000 Brussels, Belgium.
TEL 32-2-2015414. FAX 32-2-2015271. *1582*

A B C POL SCI.
A B C-Clio, 130 Cremona, Box 1911, Santa
Barbara, CA 93116-1911. TEL 805-968-1911.
FAX 805-685-9685. *5720*

A B I - INFORM.
U M I Company 300 N. Zeeb Rd., Ann Arbor, MI
48106. TEL 313-761-4700. FAX 800-864-0019.
Producer(s): University Microfilms International.
973

A B I X: AUSTRALASIAN BUSINESS INTELLIGENCE.
Business Intelligence Australia, McConnell Dowell
House, 627 Chapel St., S. Yarra, Vic. 3141,
Australia. TEL 61-3-98279088. FAX 61-3-
98279099. *973*

A E S I S QUARTERLY.
Australian Mineral Foundation, 63 Conyngham St.,
Glenside, S.A. 5065, Australia. TEL 61-8-3790444.
FAX 61-8-3794634. *5082*

A F P - DOC SUR C D - R O M.
Chadwyck-Healey France S.A., 50 rue de Paradis,
75010 Paris, France. TEL 33-1-44838181.
FAX 33-1-44838183.
Available only on CD-ROM. Producer(s): Chadwyck-
Healey Inc.. *3699*

A F P SCIENCES.
Agence France Presse, 13 Place de la Bourse, B.P.
20, 75061 Paris Cecex 2, France. TEL 40-41-46-
46.
Producer(s): Chadwyck-Healey Inc.. *4416*

A F P SCIENCES SUR C D - R O M.
Chadwyck-Healey France S.A., 50 rue de Paradis,
75010 Paris, France. TEL 33-1-44838181.
FAX 33-1-44838183.
Available only on CD-ROM. Producer(s): Chadwyck-
Healey Inc.. *6221*

A H F S DRUG INFORMATION.
American Society of Health-System Pharmacists,
7272 Wisconsin Ave., Bethesda, MD 20814.
TEL 301-657-3000. FAX 301-657-1641.
Producer(s): SilverPlatter Information, Inc.. *5396*

A I A A JOURNAL.
American Institute of Aeronautics and Astronautics,
Inc., 370 L'Enfant Promenade, S.W., Washington,
DC 20024. TEL 202-646-7400. *51*

A L I S A.
Australian Clearing House for Library & Information
Science, Library, St. Bernards Rd., Magill, S.A.
5072, Australia. TEL 61-8-3024457. FAX 61-8-
3024695. *4036*

(YEAR) A R R L PERIODICALS C D - R O M.
American Radio Relay League, Inc., 225 Main St.,
Newington, CT 06111. TEL 860-594-0200.
FAX 860-594-0303.
Available only on CD-ROM. *1933*

A S F A AQUACULTURE ABSTRACTS.
Cambridge Scientific Abstracts, 7200 Wisconsin
Ave., 6th Fl., Bethesda, MD 20814. TEL 301-961-
6750. FAX 301-961-6720.
Producer(s): NISC, SilverPlatter Information, Inc..
2946

A S F A MARINE BIOTECHNOLOGY ABSTRACTS.
Cambridge Scientific Abstracts, 7200 Wisconsin
Ave., 6th Fl., Bethesda, MD 20814. TEL 301-961-
6750. FAX 301-961-6720.
Producer(s): Knight-Ridder, Inc., NISC, SilverPlatter
Information, Inc.. *615*

**A S S I A: APPLIED SOCIAL SCIENCES INDEX &
ABSTRACTS.**
Bowker - Saur Ltd., A member of the Reed Elsevier
plc group, Maypole House, Maypole Rd., E.
Grinstead, W. Sussex RH19 1HU, England. TEL 44-
1342-330100. FAX 44-1342-330191.
Producer(s): Bowker - Saur Ltd.. *6355*

A S S I A PLUS.
Bowker - Saur Ltd., A member of the Reed Elsevier
plc group, Maypole House, Maypole Rd., E.
Grinstead, W. Sussex RH19 1HU, England. TEL 44-
1342-330100. FAX 44-1342-330191.
Available only on CD-ROM. Producer(s): Bowker -
Saur Ltd.. *6355*

A S T I S BIBLIOGRAPHY.
Arctic Science & Technology Information System,
Arctic Institute of North America, University of
Calgary, 2500 University Dr. N.W., Calgary, AB T2N
1N4, Canada. TEL 403-220-4036. *2217*

A S T I S CURRENT AWARENESS BULLETIN.
Arctic Science & Technology Information System,
Arctic Institute of North America, University of
Calgary, 2500 University Dr. N.W., Calgary, AB T2N
1N4, Canada. TEL 403-284-7515. FAX 403-282-
4609. *6671*

A S T I S OCCASIONAL PUBLICATIONS.
Arctic Science & Technology Information System,
University of Calgary, 2500 University Dr. N.W.,
Calgary, AB T2N 1N4, Canada. TEL 403-220-
4036. FAX 403-282-4609. *6221*

A TO ZOO.
R.R. Bowker, A Division of Reed Elsevier plc group,
121 Chanlon Rd., New Providence, NJ 07974.
TEL 908-464-6800. FAX 908-665-6688.
Producer(s): Bowker Electronic Publishing
(Children's Reference PLUS). *515*

ABSTRACTS IN BIOCOMMERCE.
BioCommerce Data Ltd., Prudential Bldgs., 95 High
St., Slough, Berks. SL1 1DH, England. TEL 44-
1753-511777. FAX 44-1753-512239. *615*

ABSTRACTS OF WORKING PAPERS IN ECONOMICS.
Cambridge University Press, Edinburgh Bldg.,
Shaftesbury Rd., Cambridge CB2 2RU, England.
TEL 44-1223-312393. FAX 44-1223-315052.
973

ABYA YALA NEWS.
South and Meso American Indian Rights Center, Box
28703, Oakland, CA 94604-8703. TEL 510-834-
4263. FAX 510-834-4264. *2860*

ACADEMIA SINICA. BOTANICAL BULLETIN.
Academia Sinica, Institute of Botany, Nankang,
Taipei, Taiwan 11529, Republic of China. TEL 886-
2-782-1605. FAX 886-2-782-7954. *666*

CD-ROM

ACADEMIC ABSTRACTS C D - R O M.
EBSCO Publishing 10 Estes St., Box 682, Ipswich, MA 01938. TEL 508-356-6500. FAX 508-356-6565. *2*

ACADEMIC INDEX.
Information Access Company 362 Lakeside Dr., Foster City, CA 94404. TEL 415-378-5200. FAX 415-378-5369. *3631*

ACADEMY OF MEDICINE, SINGAPORE. ANNALS.
Academy of Medicine, Singapore, 16 College Road, 01-01 College of Medicine Bldg., Singapore 0316, Singapore. TEL 2245166. FAX 2255155. *4417*

ACCESS: THE SUPPLEMENTARY INDEX TO PERIODICALS.
John Gordon Burke Publisher, Inc., Box 1492, Evanston, IL 60204-1492. TEL 847-866-8625. FAX 847-866-6639.
Producer(s): SilverPlatter Information, Inc.. *2*

ACCOUNTANCY.
Institute of Chartered Accountants in England and Wales, P.O. Box 433, Moorgate Pl., London EC2P 2BJ, England. TEL 44-171-833-3291. *1037*

ACCOUNTING AND TAX INDEX.
U M I Company 300 N. Zeeb Rd., Ann Arbor, MI 48106. TEL 313-761-4700. FAX 800-864-0019. *973*

ACCOUNTING FOR GOVERNMENT CONTRACTS: FEDERAL ACQUISITION REGULATION.
Matthew Bender & Co., Inc., 2 Park Ave., New York, NY 10016. TEL 518-487-3000. FAX 518-462-3788. *1038*

ACKNOWLEDGE THE WINDOW LETTER.
Mendham Technology Group, 144 Talmadge Rd., Box 11, Mendham, NJ 07945. TEL 201-543-2273. FAX 201-543-6033. *2084*

ACQUISITION OF GREATER DAYTON.
Hannover Publishing Co., Inc., 6356 Far Hills Ave., Dayton, OH 45459-2782. TEL 513-291-1100. FAX 513-436-3426.
Producer(s): University Microfilms International. *6018*

ACTORS C D - R O M.
Spotlight, 7 Leicester Pl., London WC2H 7BP, England. TEL 44-171-437-7631. FAX 44-171-437-5881.
Available only on CD-ROM. *6691*

ACTRESSES C D - R O M.
Spotlight, 7 Leicester Pl., London WC2H 7BP, England. TEL 44-171-437-7631. FAX 44-171-437-5881.
Available only on CD-ROM. *6691*

ACTUALIDAD ECONOMICA.
Recoletos 1, 7o, 28001 Madrid, Spain. TEL 34-1-3373220. FAX 34-1-5768150.
Producer(s): Chadwyck-Healey Inc.. *1172*

ACTUALIDAD ECONOMICA EN C D - R O M.
Chadwyck-Healey Ltd., The Quorum, Barnwell Rd., Cambridge CB5 8SW, England. TEL 44-1223-215512. FAX 44-1223-215514.
Available only on CD-ROM. Producer(s): Chadwyck-Healey Inc.. *891*

ADOLESCENCE.
Libra Publishers, Inc., 3089C Clairemont Dr., Ste. 383, San Diego, CA 92117. TEL 619-571-1414. *1759*

ADRESSBUCH FUER DEN DEUTSCHSPRACHIGEN BUCHHANDEL C D - R O M.
Buchhaendler-Vereinigung GmbH, Postfach 100442, 60004 Frankfurt a.M., Germany. TEL 49-69-1306-0. FAX 49-69-1306201.
Available only on CD-ROM. *5986*

ADVANCES (KALAMAZOO).
Fetzer Institute, 9292 West KL Ave., Kalamazoo, MI 49009-9398. TEL 616-375-2000. FAX 616-372-2163. *4420*

ADVERTISER & AGENCY RED BOOKS PLUS.
National Register Publishing, A Division of Reed Elsevier Inc., 121 Chanlon Rd., New Providence, NJ 07974. TEL 908-464-6800. FAX 908-665-6688.
Producer(s): Bowker Electronic Publishing. *30*

AFRIQUE MEDICALE.
B.P. 1826, Dakar, Senegal. TEL 23-48-80. FAX 22-56-30. *4421*

AGEINFO C D - R O M.
Centre for Policy on Ageing, 25-31 Ironmonger Row, London EC1V 3QP, England. TEL 44-171-253-1787. FAX 44-171-490-4206.
Available only on CD-ROM. *3298*

AGRI-INDUSTRY EUROPE.
Europe Information Service, Rue de Geneve, 6, 1140 Brussels, Belgium. TEL 32-2-2426020. FAX 32-2-2429410. *87*

AGRICULTURAL & ENVIRONMENTAL BIOTECHNOLOGY ABSTRACTS.
Cambridge Scientific Abstracts, 7200 Wisconsin Ave., 6th Fl., Bethesda, MD 20814. TEL 301-961-6700. FAX 301-961-6720.
Producer(s): Knight-Ridder, Inc., NISC, SilverPlatter Information, Inc.. *166*

AGRICULTURE AND ENVIRONMENT FOR DEVELOPING COUNTRIES.
Koninklijk Instituut voor de Tropen, Mauritskade 63, 1092 AD Amsterdam, Netherlands. TEL 31-20-5688298. FAX 31-20-6654423.
Producer(s): SilverPlatter Information, Inc.. *166*

AGRO LIBREX.
Madex, Ul. Grunwaldzka 11, 60-782 Poznan, Poland. TEL 48-61-666066. FAX 48-61-659643.
Available only on CD-ROM. *6299*

AGROFORESTRY ABSTRACTS.
CAB International, Wallingford, Oxon. OX10 8DE, England. TEL 01491-832111. FAX 01491-833508. *3030*

AHWAZ UNIVERSITY OF MEDICAL SCIENCES. SCIENTIFIC MEDICAL JOURNAL.
Ahwaz University of Medical Sciences, P.O. Box 189, Ahwaz, Iran. TEL 98-61-32036. FAX 98-61-61544. *4422*

AIDS.
Rapid Science Publishers, 2-6 Boundary Row, London SE1 8HN, England. TEL 44-171-865-0198. FAX 44-171-410-6600. *4615*

THE AIDS LEADER.
Modus Operandi, P.O. Box HP346, Leeds LS6 1UL, England. TEL 44-127-4521511. FAX 44-127-4521512. *5953*

AIDS - S T D HEALTH PROMOTION EXCHANGE.
Koninklijk Instituut voor de Tropen, Mauritskade 63, 1092 AD Amsterdam, Netherlands. TEL 31-20-5688711. FAX 31-20-5688286. *4617*

AIR CONDITIONING & HEATING SERVICE & REPAIR - DOMESTIC CARS, LIGHT TRUCKS & VANS.
Mitchell International, Inc., 9889 Willow Creek Rd., Box 26260, San Diego, CA 92196-0260. TEL 800-648-8010. FAX 619-578-4752. *6768*

AIR CONDITIONING & HEATING SERVICE & REPAIR - IMPORTED CARS & TRUCKS.
Mitchell International, Inc., 9889 Willow Creek Rd., Box 26260, San Diego, CA 92196-0260. TEL 800-878-6550. FAX 619-578-4752. *6768*

AIR UNIVERSITY LIBRARY INDEX TO MILITARY PERIODICALS.
U.S. Air Force, Air University Library, Maxwell AFB, AL 36112-6424. TEL 334-953-2504. FAX 334-953-1192. *5054*

ALABAMA BUSINESS DIRECTORY.
American Business Directories 5711 S. 86th Cir., Box 27347, Omaha, NE 68127. TEL 402-593-4600. FAX 401-331-5481. *1583*

ALAMEDA COUNTY COMMERCE AND INDUSTRY DIRECTORY.
Database Publishing Company, 1590 S. Lewis St., Anaheim, CA 92805-6423. TEL 714-778-6400. FAX 714-778-6811. *1583*

ALASKA BUSINESS DIRECTORY.
American Business Directories 5711 S. 86th Cir., Box 27347, Omaha, NE 68127. TEL 402-593-4600. FAX 402-331-5481. *1583*

ALASKA COURT RULES, STATE AND FEDERAL.
West Publishing Corp., 620 Opperman Dr., Eagan, MN 55123. TEL 612-687-8000. FAX 612-387-7302. *3945*

ALASKA MANUFACTURERS REGISTER.
Manufacturers' News, Inc., 1633 Central St., Evanston, IL 60201-1569. TEL 847-864-7000. FAX 847-332-1100. *1583*

ALLOYS INDEX.
Cambridge Scientific Abstracts, 7200 Wisconsin Ave., 6th fl., Bethesda, MD 20814. TEL 301-961-6750. FAX 301-961-6720.
Producer(s): Knight-Ridder, Inc.. *4980*

ALMANAQUE ABRIL.
Editora Abril, S.A., Rua do Curtume, 571, Bl. A, 6o andar, 05066-900 Sao Paulo, SP, Brazil. TEL 011-871-6020. FAX 011-871-6334. *2535*

ALTERNATIVE PRESS INDEX.
Alternative Press Center, Inc., Box 33109, Baltimore, MD 21218. TEL 410-243-2471. FAX 410-235-5325.
Producer(s): NISC. *4175*

AMERICA.
America Press Inc., 106 W. 56th St., New York, NY 10019. TEL 212-581-4640. FAX 212-399-3596.
Producer(s): University Microfilms International. *6167*

AMERICA: HISTORY AND LIFE. ANNUAL INDEX.
A B C-Clio, 130 Cremona, Box 1911, Santa Barbara, CA 93116-1911. TEL 805-968-1911. FAX 805-685-9685. *3364*

AMERICA: HISTORY AND LIFE. ARTICLE ABSTRACTS AND CITATIONS OF REVIEWS AND DISSERTATIONS COVERING THE UNITED STATES AND CANADA.
A B C-Clio, 130 Cremona, Box 1911, Santa Barbara, CA 93116-1911. TEL 805-968-1911. FAX 805-685-9685. *3364*

AMERICAN ACADEMY OF PEDIATRICS. COMMITTEE ON INFECTIOUS DISEASES. REPORT (YEAR).
American Academy of Pediatrics, 141 Northwest Point Blvd., Box 927, Elk Grove Village, IL 60009-0927. TEL 708-228-5005. FAX 708-228-1281. *4802*

AMERICAN ASSOCIATION OF TEXTILE CHEMISTS AND COLORISTS. TECHNICAL MANUAL (YEAR).
American Association of Textile Chemists and Colorists, One Davis Dr., Box 12215, Research Triangle Park, NC 27709-2215. TEL 919-549-8141. FAX 919-549-8933. *6673*

AMERICAN BOOK TRADE DIRECTORY.
R.R. Bowker, A Division of Reed Elsivier Inc., 121 Chanlon Rd., New Providence, NJ 07974. TEL 908-464-6800. FAX 908-665-6688.
Producer(s): Bowker Electronic Publishing. *5986*

THE AMERICAN BUSINESS DISC.
American Business Directories 5711 S. 86th Circle, Box 27347, Omaha, NE 68127. TEL 402-593-4523. FAX 402-331-6681.
Available only on CD-ROM. *1583*

AMERICAN COLLEGE OF CARDIOLOGY. JOURNAL.
Elsevier Science Inc., Box 945, New York, NY 10159-0945. TEL 212-633-3730. FAX 212-633-3680. *4594*

AMERICAN CRAFT.
American Craft Council, 72 Spring St., New York, NY 10012. TEL 212-274-0630. FAX 212-274-0650.
Producer(s): University Microfilms International. *464*

AMERICAN DOCTORAL DISSERTATIONS.
U M I Company 300 N. Zeeb Rd., Ann Arbor, MI 48106. TEL 313-761-4700. FAX 800-864-0019.
Producer(s): University Microfilms International. *2419*

AMERICAN FAMILY PHYSICIAN.
American Academy of Family Physicians, 8880 Ward Pkwy., Kansas City, MO 64114. TEL 816-333-9700. FAX 816-333-0303. *4423*

CD-ROM

AMERICAN JOURNAL OF CRITICAL CARE.
American Association of Critical Care Nurses, 101 Columbia, Aliso Viejo, CA 92656. TEL 714-362-2000. FAX 714-362-2020.
Producer(s): SilverPlatter Information, Inc.. *4709*

AMERICAN JOURNAL OF INTERNATIONAL LAW.
American Society of International Law, 2223 Massachusetts Ave., N.W., Washington, DC 20008-2864. TEL 202-939-6000. FAX 202-797-7133.
Producer(s): University Microfilms International. *3922*

AMERICAN LIBRARY DIRECTORY.
R.R. Bowker, A Division of Reed Elsevier Inc., 121 Chanlon Rd., New Providence, NJ 07974. TEL 908-464-6800. FAX 908-665-6688.
Producer(s): Bowker Electronic Publishing. *3972*

AMERICAN MANUFACTURERS DIRECTORY.
American Business Directories 5711 S. 86th Circle, Box 27347, Omaha, NE 68127. TEL 402-593-4600. FAX 402-331-5481. *1584*

AMERICAN MEN AND WOMEN OF SCIENCE.
R.R. Bowker, A Division of Reed Elsevier Inc., 121 Chanlon Rd., New Providence, NJ 07974. TEL 908-464-6800. FAX 908-665-6688.
Producer(s): Bowker Electronic Publishing. *554*

AMERICAN PUBLIC OPINION DATA.
Opinion Research Service, 7200 Wisconsin Ave., Ste. 704, Bethesda, MD 20814-4811. *3224*

AMERICAN PUBLIC OPINION INDEX.
Opinion Research Service, 7200 Wisconsin Ave., Ste. 704, Bethesda, MD 20814-4811. *6441*

AMERICAN SOCIETY OF MECHANICAL ENGINEERS. TRANSACTIONS.
American Society of Mechanical Engineers, 22 Law Dr., Fairfield, NJ 07007-2300. FAX 201-882-8113. *2750*

AMERICAN SPECTATOR.
2020 N. 14th St., Ste. 750, Box 549, Arlington, VA 22201. TEL 703-243-3733. FAX 703-243-6814. *4131*

AMERICAN STATISTICS INDEX.
Congressional Information Service, Inc., A member of the LEXIS NEXIS family, 4520 East-West Hwy., Bethesda, MD 20814-3389. TEL 301-654-1550. FAX 301-654-4033. *6585*

AMERICAS.
Americas Magazine, 19th St. & Constitution Ave., N.W., Ste. 300, Washington, DC 20006. TEL 202-458-3278. FAX 202-458-6217. *3607*

AMERICA'S CORPORATE FINANCE DIRECTORY.
National Register Publishing, A Division of Reed Elsevier Inc., 121 Chanlon Rd., New Providence, NJ 07974. TEL 908-464-6800. FAX 908-665-2870.
Producer(s): Bowker Electronic Publishing. *1584*

AMIGA GAMES.
Computec Verlag, Isarstr. 32-34, 90451 Nuernberg, Germany. TEL 49-911-96832-0. FAX 49-911-6426333. *2022*

AMIGA PLUS C D - R O M.
I C P - Innovativ Presse GmbH, Wendelsteinstr. 3, 85591 Vaterstetten, Germany. TEL 49-8106-33954. FAX 49-8106-34238.
Available only on CD-ROM. *2022*

ANALYTICAL ABSTRACTS.
The Royal Society of Chemistry, Thomas Graham House, Science Park, Milton Rd., Cambridge CB4 4WF, England. TEL 44-1223-420066. FAX 44-1223-423429.
Producer(s): SilverPlatter Information, Inc. *1697*

ANDERSON'S LAWRITER UNREPORTED OHIO APPELLATE CASES.
Anderson Publishing Co., 2035 Reading Rd., Cincinnati, OH 45202. TEL 513-421-4142. FAX 513-562-8116.
Available only on CD-ROM. *3741*

ANIMAL BEHAVIOR ABSTRACTS.
Cambridge Scientific Abstracts, 7200 Wisconsin Ave., 6th Fl., Bethesda, MD 20814. TEL 301-961-6750. FAX 301-961-6720.
Producer(s): NISC, SilverPlatter Information, Inc.. *615*

ANNALS OF HEALTH LAW.
Loyola University Chicago, School of Law, One E. Pearson St., Chicago, IL 60611. TEL 312-915-6304. FAX 312-915-7201. *3741*

ANNALS OF INTERNAL MEDICINE.
American College of Physicians, Independence Mall W., Sixth St. at Race, Philadelphia, PA 19106-1572. TEL 215-351-2400. FAX 215-351-2644. *4705*

ANNOTATED BIBLIOGRAPHY OF ENGLISH STUDIES.
Swets & Zeitlinger bv, P.O. Box 825, 2160 SZ Lisse, Netherlands. TEL 31-252-435111. FAX 31-252-415888
Available only on CD-ROM. *4291*

ANNUAIRE TELEXPORT.
Chambre de Commerce et d'Industrie de Paris (CEDIP), 2 place de la Bourse, 75002 Paris, France. *1131*

ANNUARIO DEI DEPUTATI E SENATORI DEL PARLAMENTO REPUBBLICANO.
Editoriale Italiana, Via Vigliena 10, 00192 Rome, Italy. TEL 39-6-32301777. FAX 39-6-3211359. *5892*

ANNUARIO GENERALE ITALIANO.
Guida Monaci S.p.A., Via Vitorchiano 107, 00189 Rome, Italy. TEL 39-6-3288805. FAX 39-6-3275693. *1162*

ANTARCTIC BIBLIOGRAPHY.
U.S. Library of Congress, Washington, DC 20540. TEL 202-707-1181.
Producer(s): NISC (Arctic & Antarctic Regions). *6299*

ANTHROPOLOGICAL LITERATURE.
Harvard University, Tozzer Library, 21 Divinity Ave., Cambridge, MA 02138. TEL 617-495-2253. FAX 617-496-2741. *327*

ANTHROPOLOGY TODAY.
Royal Anthropological Institute of Great Britain and Ireland, 50 Fitzroy St., London W1P 5HS, England. TEL 44-171-387-0455. FAX 44-171-383-4235. *302*

ANTI-CANCER DRUGS.
Rapid Science Publishers, The Old Malthouse, Paradise St., Oxford OX1 1LD, England. TEL 44-1865-790447. FAX 44-1865-244012. *4748*

ANTIMICROBIAL AGENTS AND CHEMOTHERAPY.
American Society for Microbiology, 1325 Massachusetts Ave., N.W., Washington, DC 20005. TEL 202-737-3600. *753*

ANTIOCH REVIEW.
Antioch Review, Inc., Box 148, Yellow Springs, OH 45387. TEL 513-767-6389. *4132*

ANUARIO DE ESTUDIOS AMERICANOS.
Consejo Superior de Investigaciones Cientificas (C.S.I.C.), Escuela de Estudios Hispano Americanos, Calle Alfonso XII, 16, 41002 Seville, Spain. TEL 34-54-4223445. FAX 34-54-4224331. *3459*

ANUARIO HISPANO.
T I Y M Publishing Company, Inc., 1489 Chain Bridge Rd., Ste. 200, McLean, VA 22101. TEL 703-734-1632. FAX 703-356-0787. *5262*

APPLIED AND ENVIRONMENTAL MICROBIOLOGY.
American Society for Microbiology, 1325 Massachusetts Ave., N.W., Washington, DC 20005. TEL 202-737-3600. *753*

APPLIED PHYSICS LETTERS.
American Institute of Physics, One Physics Ellipse, College Park, MD 20740-3843. TEL 301-209-3000. *5542*

APPLIED SCIENCE & TECHNOLOGY INDEX.
H.W. Wilson Co., 950 University Ave., Bronx, NY 10452. TEL 718-588-8400. FAX 718-590-1617.
Producer(s): SilverPlatter Information, Inc., H.W. Wilson. *2624*

AQUALINE ABSTRACTS.
W R C plc, P.O. Box 85, Frankland Rd., Blagrove, Swindon, Wilts SN5 8YF England. *6982*

AQUATIC BIOLOGY, AQUACULTURE & FISHERIES RESOURCES.
National Information Services Corporation (NISC), Ste. 6, Wyman Towers, 3100 St. Paul St., Baltimore, MD 21218. TEL 410-243-0797. FAX 410-243-0982.
Available only on CD-ROM. Producer(s): NISC. *615*

AQUATIC SCIENCES & FISHERIES ABSTRACTS. PART 1: BIOLOGICAL SCIENCES AND LIVING RESOURCES.
Cambridge Scientific Abstracts, 7200 Wisconsin Ave., 6th Fl., Bethesda, MD 20814. TEL 301-951-6750. FAX 301-961-6720.
Producer(s): NISC, SilverPlatter Information, Inc. *6982*

AQUATIC SCIENCES & FISHERIES ABSTRACTS. PART 2: OCEAN TECHNOLOGY, POLICY AND NON-LIVING RESOURCES.
Cambridge Scientific Abstracts, 7200 Wisconsin Ave., 6th Fl., Bethesda, MD 20814. TEL 301-961-6750. FAX 301-961-6720.
Producer(s): NISC, SilverPlatter Information, Inc. *6983*

AQUATIC SCIENCES & FISHERIES ABSTRACTS. PART 3: AQUATIC POLLUTION AND ENVIRONMENTAL QUALITY.
Cambridge Scientific Abstracts, 7200 Wisconsin Ave., 6th Fl., Bethesda, MD 20814. TEL 301-961-6700. FAX 301-961-6720.
Producer(s): Knight-Ridder Inc. (Environmental Management), NISC, SilverPlatter Information, Inc.. *2946*

ARAB STUDIES QUARTERLY.
Association of Arab-American University Graduates, Inc., 2121 Wisconsin Ave., N.W., Ste. 310, Washington, DC 20007-2258. TEL 202-337-7717. FAX 202-337-3302. *2864*

ARBEITSRECHTLICHE PRAXIS C D - R O M.
C.H. Beck'sche Verlagsbuchhandlung, Wilhelmstr. 9, 80801 Munich, Germany. TEL 49-89-38189338. FAX 49-89-38189398.
Available only on CD-ROM. *1362*

ARCHITECTURAL PUBLICATIONS INDEX ON DISC.
R I B A Publications, Finsbury Mission, 39 Moreland St., London EC1V 8BB, England. TEL 44-171-251-0791. FAX 44-171-608-2275.
Available only on CD-ROM. *407*

ARCHIVES OF ENVIRONMENTAL HEALTH.
Heldref Publications, 1319 Eighteenth St., N.W., Washington, DC 20036-1802. TEL 202-296-6267. FAX 202-296-5149.
Producer(s): University Microfilms International. *4428*

ARCHIVES OF FAMILY MEDICINE.
American Medical Association, 515 N. State St., Chicago, IL 60610. TEL 312-464-5000. FAX 312-464-5831. *4428*

ARCHIVES OF GENERAL PSYCHIATRY.
American Medical Association, 515 N. State St., Chicago, IL 60610. TEL 312-464-5000. FAX 312-464-5831. *4826*

ARCHIVES OF INTERNAL MEDICINE.
American Medical Association, 515 N. State St., Chicago, IL 60610. TEL 312-464-5000. FAX 312-464-5831. *4705*

ARCHIVES OF NEUROLOGY.
American Medical Association, 515 N. State St., Chicago, IL 60610. TEL 312-464-5000. FAX 312-464-5831. *4826*

ARCHIVES OF OPHTHALMOLOGY.
American Medical Association, 515 N. State St., Chicago, IL 60610. TEL 312-464-5000. FAX 312-464-5831. *4767*

ARCHIVES OF OTOLARYNGOLOGY - HEAD & NECK SURGERY.
American Medical Association, 515 N. State St., Chicago, IL 60610. TEL 312-464-5000. FAX 312-464-5831. *4795*

ARCHIVES OF PEDIATRICS & ADOLESCENT MEDICINE.
American Medical Association, 515 N. State St., Chicago, IL 60610. TEL 312-464-5000. FAX 312-464-4181. *4802*

ARCHIVES OF SURGERY.
American Medical Association, 515 N. State St., Chicago, IL 60610. TEL 312-464-5000. FAX 312-464-5831. *4904*

ARCTIC & ANTARCTIC REGIONS (COLD REGIONS).
National Information Services Corporation (NISC), Ste. 6, Wyman Towers, 3100 St. Paul St., Baltimore, MD 21218. TEL 410-243-0797. FAX 410-243-0982.
Available only on CD-ROM. Producer(s): NISC. *2217*

ARGENTINA. INSTITUTO NACIONAL DE ESTADISTICA Y CENSOS. ANUARIO ESTADISTICO.
Instituto Nacional de Estadistica y Censos, Avda. Julio A. Roca, 609 P.B., 1067 Buenos Aires, Argentina. TEL 54-1-3499662. FAX 54-1-3499621. *5794*

ARIZONA BUSINESS DIRECTORY.
American Business Directories 5711 S. 86th Circle, Box 27347, Omaha, NE 68127. TEL 402-593-4600. FAX 402-331-5481. *1585*

ARIZONA INDUSTRIAL DIRECTORY.
Phoenix Chamber of Commerce, 201 N. Central Ave., 27th Fl., Phoenix, AZ 85073. TEL 602-495-2195. FAX 602-495-8913. *1585*

ARKANSAS BUSINESS DIRECTORY.
American Business Directories 5711 S. 86th Circle, Box 27347, Omaha, NE 68127. TEL 402-593-4600. FAX 402-331-5481. *1585*

ARKANSAS HISTORICAL QUARTERLY.
Arkansas Historical Association, University of Arkansas, Department of History, Old Main 416, Fayetteville, AR 72701. TEL 501-575-5884. FAX 501-575-2642. *3460*

ARKANSAS MANUFACTURERS REGISTER.
Manufacturers' News, Inc., 1633 Central St., Evanston, IL 60201-1569. TEL 847-864-7000. FAX 847-332-1100. *1585*

ARQUIVOS DE NEURO-PSIQUIATRIA.
Associacao Arquivos Neuro-Psiquiatria Dr. Oswaldo Lange, Caixa Postal 8877, 01065-970 Sao Paulo, SP, Brazil. TEL 55-11-2898824. FAX 55-11-2898879. *4826*

ART INDEX.
H.W. Wilson Co., 950 University Ave., Bronx, NY 10452. TEL 718-588-8400. FAX 718-590-1617. Producer(s): SilverPlatter Information, Inc., H.W. Wilson (WILSONDISC). *462*

THE ART NEWSPAPER (INTERNATIONAL EDITION).
Umberto Allemandi & Co. Publishing, 27-29 Vauxhall Grove, London SW815Y, England. TEL 44-171-7353331. FAX 44-171-7353332. *414*

ARTBIBLIOGRAPHIES MODERN.
A B C - Clio Ltd., 35A Great Clarendon St., Oxford OX2 6AT, England. TEL 44-1865-311350. FAX 44-1865-311358. *462*

ARTS & HUMANITIES CITATION INDEX.
Institute for Scientific Information, 3501 Market St., Philadelphia, PA 19104. TEL 215-386-0100. FAX 215-386-2991.
Producer(s): Institute for Scientific Information (A&HCI/CDE). *462*

ARTS EDUCATION POLICY REVIEW.
Heldref Publications, 1319 Eighteenth St., N.W., Washington, DC 20036-1802. TEL 202-296-6267. FAX 202-296-5149.
Producer(s): University Microfilms International. *418*

ASIAN AFFAIRS: AN AMERICAN REVIEW.
Heldref Publications, 1319 18th St., N.W., Washington, DC 20036-1802. TEL 202-296-6267. FAX 202-296-5149.
Producer(s): University Microfilms International. *5741*

ASIAN CLASSICS INPUT PROGRAM.
Asian Classics Input Program, 1911 Marmary Rd., Gaithersburg, MD 20878-1839. TEL 301-948-5569. FAX 301-294-7870. *6109*

ASIAN MANAGEMENT EDUCATION DIRECTORY.
E M D Centre, Naarderstraat 296, 1272 NT Huizen, Netherlands. TEL 31-35-6951111. FAX 31-35-6951900. *1406*

ASIANWEEK.
Pan Asia Venture Capital Corporation, 809 Sacramento St., San Francisco, CA 94108. TEL 415-397-0220. FAX 415-397-7258. *2865*

ASSOCIATIONS YELLOW BOOK.
Leadership Directories, Inc., 104 Fifth Ave., 2nd Fl., New York, NY 10011. TEL 212-627-4140. FAX 212-645-0931.
Producer(s): Chadwyck-Healey Inc.. *1585*

THE ATLANTA CONSTITUTION AND JOURNAL INDEX.
U M I Company 300 N. Zeeb Rd., Ann Arbor, MI 48106-1346. TEL 313-761-4700. FAX 800-864-0019. *3714*

THE ATLANTIC MONTHLY.
Atlantic Monthly Co., 745 Boylston St., Boston, MA 02116. TEL 617-536-9500.
Producer(s): University Microfilms International. *4133*

AUDUBON.
National Audubon Society, 700 Broadway, New York, NY 10003. TEL 212-979-3126. FAX 212-477-9069.
Producer(s): University Microfilms International. *2120*

AUSTRALIA. BUREAU OF STATISTICS. HISTORICAL PUBLICATIONS ON C D - R O M.
Australian Bureau of Statistics, P.O. Box 10, Belconnen, A.C.T. 2616, Australia.
Available only on CD-ROM. *6589*

AUSTRALIAN & NEW ZEALAND JOURNAL OF SOCIOLOGY.
Longman Australia, 95 Coventry St., S. Melbourne, Vic. 3205, Australia. TEL 61-3-96970657. FAX 61-3-96992041. *6406*

AUSTRALIAN ARCHITECTURAL PERIODICALS INDEX.
Stanton Library, Reader Services Department, P.O. Box 12, N. Sydney, N.S.W. 2059, Australia. TEL 61-2-99368400. FAX 61-2-99368440. *407*

AUSTRALIAN ART AUCTION RECORDS.
Australian Art Sales, P.O. Box 50, Sutherland, N.S.W. 2232, Australia. TEL 61-2-267-7363. *419*

AUSTRALIAN CASE CITATOR.
L B C Information Services, 50 Waterloo Rd., N. Ryde, N.S.W. 2113, Australia. TEL 61-2-99366444. FAX 62-2-8889706. *3946*

AUSTRALIAN CATALOGUE OF NEW FILMS AND VIDEOS.
Australian Catalogue, P.O. Box 204, Albert Park, Vic. 3206, Australia. TEL 61-3-525-5302. FAX 61-3-537-2325. *5093*

AUSTRALIAN CORPORATIONS & SECURITIES LAW REPORTER.
C C H Australia Ltd., P.O. Box 230, North Ryde, N.S.W. 2113, Australia. TEL 61-1-300300224. FAX 61-1-300306224. *3894*

AUSTRALIAN DIGEST.
L B C Information Services, 50 Waterloo Rd., N. Ryde, N.S.W. 2113, Australia. TEL 61-2-99366444. FAX 61-2-8889706. *3745*

AUSTRALIAN FAMILY AND SOCIETY ABSTRACTS.
Australian Institute of Family Studies, 300 Queen St., Melbourne, Vic. 3000, Australia. TEL 61-3-2147888. FAX 61-3-2147839. *6441*

AUSTRALIAN FAMILY LAW & PRACTICE.
C C H Australia Ltd., P.O. Box 230, North Ryde, N.S.W. 2113, Australia. TEL 61-1-300306224. FAX 61-2-300306224. *3917*

AUSTRALIAN FEDERAL TAX REPORTER.
C C H Australia Ltd., P.O. Box 230, North Ryde, N.S.W. 2113, Australia. TEL 61-1-300300224. FAX 61-1-300306224. *1535*

AUSTRALIAN INCOME TAX LEGISLATION.
C C H Australia Ltd., P.O. Box 230, North Ryde, N.S.W. 2113, Australia. TEL 61-1-300300224. FAX 61-1-300306224. *1535*

AUSTRALIAN INCOME TAX RULINGS.
C C H Australia Ltd., P.O. Box 230, North Ryde, N.S.W. 2113, Australia. TEL 61-1-300300224. FAX 61-1-300306224. *3745*

AUSTRALIAN LEGAL MONTHLY DIGEST.
L B C Information Services, 50 Waterloo Rd., N. Ryde, N.S.W. 2113, Australia. TEL 61-2-99366444. FAX 61-2-8889706. *3946*

AUTORIDADES DE LA BIBLIOTECA NACIONAL DE ESPANA EN C D - R O M.
Biblioteca Nacional de Espana, Paeo de Recoletos 20, 28001 Madrid, Spain.
Available only on CD-ROM. Producer(s): Chadwyck-Healey Inc.. *517*

AVIATION WEEK & SPACE TECHNOLOGY.
McGraw-Hill Companies, Aviation Week Group (New York), 1221 Ave. of the Americas, New York, NY 10020. TEL 212-512-2000. FAX 212-512-4225. *58*

AZ B - ARIZONA BUSINESS.
Arizona State University, Center for Business Research, College of Business, Box 874406, Tempe, AZ 85287-4406. TEL 602-965-3961. FAX 602-965-5458. *896*

B D I DEUTSCHLAND LIEFERT.
Verlag W. Sachon, Schloss Mindelburg, 87714 Mindelheim, Germany. TEL 49-8261-999-0. FAX 49-8261-999180. *1265*

B H I PLUS.
Bowker - Saur Ltd., A member of the Reed Elsevier plc group, Maypole House, Maypole Rd., E. Grinstead, W. Sussex RH19 1HU, England. TEL 44-1342-330100. FAX 44-1342-330191.
Available only on CD-ROM. Producer(s): Bowker - Saur Ltd.. *3631*

B I B TELEVISION PROGRAMMING SOURCE BOOKS.
North American Publishing Co., 401 N. Broad St., Philadelphia, PA 19108. TEL 215-238-5300. FAX 215-238-5457. *1954*

B I R D.
Centre International de l'Enfance, Chateau de Longchamp, Bois de Boulogne, 75016 Paris, France. TEL 1-45-20-79-92. FAX 1-45-25-73-67. *1782*

B M J.
B M J Publishing Group, B.M.A. House, Tavistock Sq., London WC1H 9JR, England. TEL 44-171-387-4499. FAX 44-171-383-6661. *4432*

B N A'S EMPLOYEE BENEFITS LIBRARY ON C D.
The Bureau of National Affairs, Inc., 1231 25th St., N.W., Washington, DC 20037. TEL 202-452-4200. FAX 202-822-8092.
Available only on CD-ROM. *1364*

B N B ON C D - R O M.
British Library, National Bibliographic Service, Boston Spa, Wetherby, W. Yorks. LS23 7BQ, England. TEL 44-1937-546585. FAX 44-1937-546586.
Available only on CD-ROM. Producer(s): Chadwyck-Healey Inc.. *517*

B N I.
Primary Source Media, P.O. Box 45, Reading RG1 8HF, England. TEL 44-1734-583247. FAX 44-1734-591325.
Available only on CD-ROM. *3714*

B S I STANDARDS CATALOGUE.
British Standards Institution, Linford Wood, Milton Keynes, Bucks. MK14 6LE, England. TEL 44-1908-220022. FAX 44-1908-320856. *5012*

BAHRAIN MEDICAL BULLETIN.
P.O. Box 32159, Manama, Bahrain. TEL 973-279472. *4433*

BAHRAIN MEDICAL SOCIETY. JOURNAL.
Bahrain Medical Society, P.O. Box 26136, Manama, Bahrain. TEL 973-742666. *4433*

BANGLADESH JOURNAL OF BOTANY.
Bangladesh Botanical Society, c/o Department of Botany, University of Dhaka, Dhaka 1000, Bangladesh. TEL 505848. *672*

CD-ROM

BANGLADESH MEDICAL RESEARCH COUNCIL BULLETIN.
Bangladesh Medical Research Council, Mokakhali, Dhaka 1212, Bangladesh. *4433*

BANK LETTER.
Institutional Investor Newsletters, 477 Madison Ave., New York, NY 10022. TEL 212-224-3233. FAX 212-224-3353. *1065*

BANKRUPTCY CODE, RULES AND FORMS.
West Publishing Corp., 620 Opperman Dr., Eagan, MN 55123. TEL 612-687-7000. FAX 612-687-7302. *3748*

BANKRUPTCY EVIDENCE MANUAL.
West Publishing Corp., 620 Opperman Dr., Eagan, MN 55123-1308. TEL 612-687-8000. FAX 612-687-7302. *3748*

BARRON'S PROFILES OF AMERICAN COLLEGES.
Barron's Educational Series, Inc., 250 Wireless Blvd., Hauppauge, NY 11788. TEL 516-434-3311. *2409*

BEHAVIORAL MEDICINE.
Heldref Publications, 1319 Eighteenth St., N.W., Washington, DC 20036-1802. TEL 202-396-6267. FAX 202-296-5149. Producer(s): University Microfilms International. *5830*

BEHAVIOURAL NEUROLOGY.
Rapid Science Publishers, 2-6 Boundary Row, London SE1 8HN, England. TEL 44-171-865-0198. FAX 44-171-410-6600. *4827*

BEHAVIOURAL PHARMACOLOGY.
Rapid Science Publishers, The Old Malthouse, Paradise St., Oxford OX1 1LD, England. TEL 44-1865-790447. FAX 44-1865-244012. *5401*

DIE BEKLEIDUNGS- UND WAESCHE-INDUSTRIE UND IHRE HELFER.
Industrieschau-Verlagsgesellschaft mbH, Postfach 100262, 64202 Darmstadt, Germany. TEL 49-6151-38920. FAX 49-6151-33164. *1831*

BESPRECHUNGEN ANNOTATIONEN.
Einkaufszentrale fuer Bibliotheken, Bismarckstr. 3, 72764 Reutlingen, Germany. TEL 07121-144-0. FAX 07121-144280. *3978*

BEST BOOKS FOR CHILDREN.
R.R. Bowker, A Division of Reed Elsevier Inc., 121 Chanlon Rd., New Providence, NJ 07974. TEL 908-464-6800. FAX 908-665-6688. Producer(s): Bowker Electronic Publishing. *1761*

BEST'S INSURANCE REPORTS: LIFE - HEALTH.
A.M. Best Co., Ambest Rd., Oldwick, NJ 08858. TEL 908-439-2200. FAX 908-439-3296. *3642*

BEST'S INSURANCE REPORTS: PROPERTY - CASUALTY.
A.M. Best Co., Ambest Rd., Oldwick, NJ 08858. TEL 908-439-2200. FAX 908-439-3296. *3642*

BEST'S UNDERWRITING GUIDE.
A.M. Best Co., Ambest Rd., Oldwick, NJ 08858. TEL 908-439-2200. FAX 908-439-3296. *3643*

BIBLIOGRAFIA BRASILEIRA DE ENERGIA NUCLEAR.
Comissao Nacional de Energia Nuclear, Centro de Informacoes Nucleares, Rua General Severiano 90, Botafogo, 22294-900 Rio de Janeiro RJ, Brazil. TEL 55-21-5462440. FAX 55-21-5462447. *2561*

BIBLIOGRAFIA BRASILEIRA DE ODONTOLOGIA.
Universidade de Sao Paulo, Faculdade de Odontologia, Av. Prof. Lineu Prestes, 2227, Caixa Postal 8216, 05508-900 Sao Paulo SP, Brazil. TEL 55-11-8187861. FAX 55-11-8187413. *4549*

BIBLIOGRAFIA ESPANOLA DESDE 1976 EN C D - R O M.
Biblioteca Nacional de Espana, Paseo de Recoletos 20, 28001 Madrid, Spain. Available only on CD-ROM. Producer(s): Chadwyck-Healey Inc.. *518*

BIBLIOGRAFIA GENERALE DELLA LINGUA E DELLA LETTERATURA ITALIANA.
Salerno Editrice, Via di Donna Olimpia 20, 00152 Rome, Italy. TEL 39-6-58205688. FAX 39-6-58238241. *518*

BIBLIOGRAFIA LATINOAMERICANA: PART I.
Universidad Nacional Autonoma de Mexico, Centro de Informacion Cientifica y Humanistica, Apdo. Postal 70-392, C.P. 04510 Mexico, D.F., Mexico. TEL 525-6223958. FAX 525-6162557. *518*

BIBLIOGRAFIA LATINOAMERICANA: PART II.
Universidad Nacional Autonoma de Mexico, Centro de Informacion Cientifica y Humanistica, Apdo. Postal 70-392, C.P. 04510 Mexico, D.F., Mexico. TEL 525-6223958. FAX 525-6162557. *518*

BIBLIOGRAFIA NACIONAL PORTUGUESA EM C D - R O M.
Chadwyck-Healey Ltd., The Quorum, Barnwell Rd., Cambridge CB5 8SW, England. TEL 44-1223-215512. FAX 44-1223-215514. Available only on CD-ROM. Producer(s): Chadwyck-Healey Inc.. *518*

BIBLIOGRAFIA NAZIONALE ITALIANA.
Istituto Centrale per il Catalogo Unico delle Biblioteche Italiane e per le Informazioni Bibliografiche, Viale del Castro Pretorio, 105, Rome, Italy. Producer(s): Chadwyck-Healey Inc.. *519*

BIBLIOGRAPHIA MEDICA CECHOSLOVACA.
Narodn Lekarska Knihovna, Sokolska 31, 121 32 Prague 2, Czech Republic. TEL 42-2-24915775. FAX 42-2-24924625. *4549*

BIBLIOGRAPHIE NATIONALE FRANCAISE. LIVRES.
Bibliotheque Nationale de France, Quai Francois Mauriac, 75706 Paris Cedex 13, France. TEL 33-1-47038610. FAX 33-1-47038586. Producer(s): Chadwyck-Healey Inc.. *521*

BIBLIOGRAPHIE NATIONALE FRANCAISE. PUBLICATIONS EN SERIE.
Bibliotheque Nationale de France, Quai Francois Mauriac, 75706 Paris Cedex 13, France. TEL 33-1-47038610. FAX 33-1-47038586. Producer(s): Chadwyck-Healey Inc.. *521*

BIBLIOGRAPHIE NATIONALE FRANCAISE. PUBLICATIONS OFFICIELLES.
Bibliotheque Nationale de France, Quai Francois Mauriac, 75706 Paris Cedex 13, France. TEL 33-1-47038610. FAX 33-1-47038586. Producer(s): Chadwyck-Healey Inc.. *521*

BIBLIOGRAPHY AND INDEX OF GEOLOGY.
American Geological Institute, 4220 King St., Alexandria, VA 22302-1502. TEL 703-379-2480. FAX 703-379-7563. Producer(s): SilverPlatter Information, Inc. (GeoRef). *2218*

BIBLIOGRAPHY OF AGRICULTURE.
Oryx Press, 4041 N. Central Ave., No. 700, Phoenix, AZ 85012-3397. TEL 602-265-2651. FAX 602-265-6250. Producer(s): SilverPlatter Information, Inc.. *169*

BIBLIOGRAPHY OF BIOETHICS.
Kennedy Institute of Ethics, National Reference Center for Bioethics Literature, Georgetown University, Box 571212, Washington, DC 20057-1212. TEL 202-687-6738. FAX 202-687-6770. Producer(s): SilverPlatter Information, Inc.. *4549*

BIBLIOGRAPHY OF ECONOMIC GEOLOGY.
Geosystems, P.O. Box 40, Didcot, Oxon. OX11 9BX, England. TEL 44-1235-813913. Producer(s): NISC (Geosearch). *2218*

BIBLIOGRAPHY OF EDUCATION THESES IN AUSTRALIA.
Australian Council for Educational Research, Private Bag 55, Camberwell, Vic. 3124, Australia. TEL 61-3-92775555. FAX 61-3-92775500. *2386*

BIBLIOGRAPHY OF SYSTEMATIC MYCOLOGY.
CAB International, International Mycological Institute, Wallingford, Oxon. OX10 8DE, England. TEL 44-1491-832111. FAX 44-1491-833508. *615*

BIBLIOGRAPHY ON COLD REGIONS SCIENCE & TECHNOLOGY.
U.S. Army Cold Regions Research and Engineering Laboratory, 72 Lyme Rd., Hanover, NH 03755-1290. TEL 603-646-4221. FAX 603-646-4712. Producer(s): NISC (Arctic & Antarctic Regions). *2625*

BIBLIOTHECA SACRA.
Dallas Theological Seminary, 3909 Swiss Ave., Dallas, TX 75204. TEL 214-824-3094. FAX 214-841-3532. *6136*

BILLBOARD HISTORY OF ROCK 'N ROLL.
B P I Communications, Inc. (New York), 1515 Broadway, New York, NY 10036. TEL 212-764-7300. FAX 212-944-1719. Available only on CD-ROM. *5143*

BIOCHEMISTRY AND BIOPHYSICS CITATION INDEX.
Institute for Scientific Information, 3501 Market St., Philadelphia, PA 19104. TEL 215-386-0100. FAX 215-386-2991. *616*

BIOENGINEERING ABSTRACTS.
Cambridge Scientific Abstracts, 7200 Wisconsin Ave., 6th Fl., Bethesda, MD 20814. TEL 301-961-6700. FAX 301-961-6720. Producer(s): Knight-Ridder Inc. (Biotechnology & Bioengineering). *2625*

BIOGRAPHY AND GENEALOGY MASTER INDEX.
Gale Research Inc., 835 Penobscot Bldg., Detroit, MI 48226. TEL 313-961-2242. FAX 313-961-6083. *563*

BIOGRAPHY INDEX.
H.W. Wilson Co., 950 University Ave., Bronx, NY 10452. TEL 718-588-8400. FAX 718-590-1617. Producer(s): SilverPlatter Information, Inc., H.W. Wilson (WILSONDISC). *563*

BIOLOGICAL ABSTRACTS.
BIOSIS, 2100 Arch St., Philadelphia, PA 19103-1399. TEL 215-587-4847. FAX 215-587-2016. Producer(s): SilverPlatter Information, Inc.. *616*

BIOLOGICAL ABSTRACTS - R R M.
BIOSIS, 2100 Arch St., Philadelphia, PA 19103-1399. TEL 215-587-4847. FAX 215-587-2016. *616*

BIOLOGICAL & AGRICULTURAL INDEX.
H.W. Wilson Co., 950 University Ave., Bronx, NY 10452. TEL 718-588-8400. FAX 718-590-1617. Producer(s): SilverPlatter Information, Inc., H.W. Wilson (WILSONDISC). *616*

BIOLOGY DIGEST.
Plexus Publishing, Inc., 143 Old Marlton Pike, Medford, NJ 08055. TEL 609-654-6500. FAX 609-654-4309. *616*

BIOMEDICAL AND ENVIRONMENTAL SCIENCES.
Zhongguo Yufang Yixue Ke xueyuar, 27 Nanwei Rd., Beijing 100050, People's Republic of China. TEL 4377008. Available only on CD-ROM. Producer(s): SilverPlatter Information, Inc.. *4434*

BIOMEDICAL ENGINEERING CITATION INDEX.
Institute for Scientific Information, 3501 Market St., Philadelphia, PA 19104. TEL 215-386-0100. FAX 215-386-2991. *4550*

BIOMETALS.
Rapid Science Publishers, 2-6 Boundary Row, London SE1 8HN, England. TEL 44-171-865-0198. FAX 44-171-410-6600. *654*

BIOTECHNOLOGY ABSTRACTS.
Derwent Publications Ltd., Derwent House, 14 Great Queen St., London WC2B 5DF, England. TEL 44-171-3442800. *617*

BIOTECHNOLOGY CITATION INDEX.
Institute for Scientific Information, 3501 Market St., Philadelphia, PA 19104. TEL 215-386-0100. FAX 215-386-2991. *617*

BIRKNER (YEAR) - EUROPEAN AND INTERNATIONAL PAPERWORLD.
Birkner & Co. Verlag, Winsbergring 38, 22525 Hamburg, Germany. TEL 040-85303502. FAX 040-85308381. *5320*

BLENDER.
25 W. 39th St., Ste. 900, New York, NY 10018. TEL 212-302-2626. FAX 212-302-2635. Available only on CD-ROM. *5143*

BLIND WELFARE.
National Association for the Blind, India, 11 Khan Abdul Gaffar Khan Rd., Worli Seaface, Bombay 400 025, India. TEL 91-22-493-6930. FAX 91-22-493-2539. *3317*

BLOOD COAGULATION AND FIBRINOLYSIS.
Rapid Science Publishers, The Old Malthouse, Paradise St., Oxford OX1 1LD, England. TEL 44-1865-790447. FAX 44-1865-244012. *4698*

BLUE SKY LAW REPORTS.
Commerce Clearing House, Inc., 2700 Lake Cook Rd., Riverwoods, IL 60015. TEL 847-267-7000. FAX 800-224-8299. *3750*

BOERNEBIBLIOTEKSKATALOG. BOEGER & TIDSSKRIFTER. EMNEKATALOG.
Dansk BiblioteksCenter as, Tempovej 7-11, DK-2750 Ballerup, Denmark. TEL 45-44-867777. FAX 45-44-867892. *522*

BOERNEBIBLIOTEKSKATALOG. BOEGER & TIDSSKRIFTER. FORFATTERKATALOG.
Dansk BiblioteksCenter as, Tempovej 7-11, DK-2750 Ballerup, Denmark. TEL 45-44-867777. FAX 45-44-867892. *522*

BOERNEBIBLIOTEKSKATALOG. BOEGER & TIDSSKRIFTER. TITELKATALOG.
Dansk BiblioteksCenter as, Tempovej 7-11, DK-2750 Ballerup, Denmark. TEL 45-44-867777. FAX 45-44-867892. *522*

BOERNEBIBLIOTEKSKATALOG. GRAMMOFONPLADER, KASSETTEBAAND.
Dansk BiblioteksCenter as, Tempovej 7-11, DK-2750 Ballerup, Denmark. TEL 45-44-867777. FAX 45-44-867892. *5207*

BOERNEBIBLIOTEKSKATALOG. LYDBOEGER, BOG & BAAND.
Dansk BiblioteksCenter as, Tempovej 7-11, DK-2750 Ballerup, Denmark. TEL 45-44-867777. FAX 45-44-867892. *1782*

BOLETIN OFICIAL DEL ESTADO.
Boletin Oficial del Estado, Trafalgar, 27, 28071 Madrid, Spain. TEL 34-1-5382297. FAX 34-1-5382275. *5894*

BOND INFORMATION DATABASE SERVICE.
Moody's Investors Service 99 Church St., New York, NY 10007. TEL 212-553-0300. FAX 212-553-4700. *2071*

BOOK OF THE STATES.
The Council of State Governments, 3560 Iron Works Pike, Box 11910, Lexington, KY 40578-1910. TEL 606-244-8000. FAX 606-244-8001. *5894*

BOOK REVIEW DIGEST.
H.W. Wilson Co., 950 University Ave., Bronx, NY 10452. TEL 718-588-8400. FAX 718-590-1617. Producer(s): K.G. Saur Verlag, H.W. Wilson (WILSONDISC). *4134*

BOOKS & PERIODICALS ONLINE.
Library Alliance, Inc., Box 77232, Washington, DC 20013-8232. TEL 202-682-6418. *523*

BOOKS IN PRINT.
R.R. Bowker, A Division of Reed Elsevier Inc., 121 Chanlon Rd., New Providence, NJ 07974. TEL 908-464-6800. FAX 908-665-3502. Producer(s): Bowker Electronic Publishing (Books in Print PLUS). *523*

BOOKS IN PRINT PLUS.
R.R. Bowker, A Division of Reed Elsevier Inc., 121 Chanlon Rd., New Providence, NJ 07974. TEL 908-665-2866. FAX 908-665-3528. Available only on CD-ROM. Producer(s): Bowker Electronic Publishing (Books in Print PLUS). *523*

BOOKS IN PRINT SUPPLEMENT.
R.R. Bowker, A Division of Reed Elsevier Inc., 121 Chanlon Rd., New Providence, NJ 07974. TEL 908-464-6800. FAX 908-665-3502. Producer(s): Bowker Electronic Publishing (Books in Print PLUS). *523*

BOOKS IN PRINT WITH BOOK REVIEWS PLUS.
R.R. Bowker, A Division of Reed Elsevier Inc., 121 Chanlon Rd., New Providence, NJ 07974. TEL 908-665-2866. FAX 908-665-3528. Available only on CD-ROM. Producer(s): Bowker Electronic Publishing (Books in Print PLUS). *523*

BOOKS OUT-OF-PRINT.
R.R. Bowker, A Division of Reed Elsevier Inc., 121 Chanlon Rd., New Providence, NJ 07974. TEL 908-464-6800. FAX 908-665-3502. Producer(s): Bowker Electronic Publishing (Books Out-of-Print PLUS). *523*

BOOKS OUT-OF-PRINT PLUS.
R.R. Bowker, A Division of Reed Elsevier Inc., 121 Chanlon Rd., New Providence, NJ 07974. TEL 908-665-2866. FAX 908-665-3528. Producer(s): Bowker Electronic Publishing (Books Out-of-Print PLUS). *523*

BOOKS OUT-OF-PRINT WITH BOOK REVIEWS PLUS.
R.R. Bowker, A Division of Reed Elsevier Inc., 121 Chanlon Rd., New Providence, NJ 07974. TEL 908-665-2866. FAX 908-665-3528. Producer(s): Bowker Electronic Publishing (Books Out-of-Print with Book Reviews PLUS). *523*

BOSTON SPA CONFERENCES ON C D - R O M.
British Library, Document Supply Centre, Boston Spa, Wetherby, W. Yorks. LS23 7BQ, England. TEL 44-1937-546080. FAX 44-1937-546286. Available only on CD-ROM. *524*

BOSTON SPA SERIALS ON C D - R O M.
British Library, Document Supply Centre, Boston Spa, Wetherby, W. Yorks. LS23 7BQ, England. TEL 44-1937-546061. FAX 44-1937-546286. Available only on CD-ROM. *524*

THE BOWKER ANNUAL LIBRARY AND BOOK TRADE ALMANAC.
R.R. Bowker, A Division of Reed Elsevier Inc., 121 Chanlon Rd., New Providence, NJ 07974. TEL 908-464-6800. FAX 908-665-6688. Producer(s): Bowker Electronic Publishing. *3981*

BOWKER - WHITAKER GLOBAL BOOKS IN PRINT PLUS.
R.R. Bowker, A Division of Reed Elsevier Inc., 121 Chanlon Rd., New Providence, NJ 07974. TEL 908-665-2866. FAX 908-665-3528. Producer(s): Bowker Electronic Publishing (Books In Print PLUS). *524*

BOWKER'S COMPLETE VIDEO DIRECTORY.
R.R. Bowker, A Division of Reed Elsevier Inc., 121 Chanlon Rd., New Providence, NJ 07974. TEL 908-464-6800. FAX 908-665-6688. Producer(s): Bowker Electronic Publishing. *1975*

BOWKER'S LAW BOOKS AND SERIALS IN PRINT.
R.R. Bowker, A Division of Reed Elsevier Inc., 121 Chanlon Rd., New Providence, NJ 07974. TEL 908-464-6800. FAX 908-665-3502. *3874*

BRASILIA MEDICA.
Associacao Medica de Brasilia, EQS 713-913, Modulo E, 70930 Brasilia, D.F., Brazil. TEL 061-245-1408. FAX 061-245-2501. *4436*

BRITANNICA BOOK OF THE YEAR.
Encyclopaedia Britannica, Inc., 310 S. Michigan Ave., Chicago, IL 60604. TEL 312-347-7000. FAX 312-347-7914. *2536*

BRITISH EDUCATION INDEX.
British Education Index, Brotherton Library, University of Leeds, Leeds LS2 9JT, England. TEL 44-113-233-5525. FAX 44-113-233-5524. *2386*

BRITISH HUMANITIES INDEX.
Bowker - Saur Ltd., A member of the Reed Elsevier plc group, Maypole House, Maypole Rd., E. Grinstead, W. Sussex RH19 1HU, England. TEL 44-1342-330100. FAX 44-1342-330191. Producer(s): Bowker - Saur Ltd.. *3632*

BRITISH NATIONAL BIBLIOGRAPHY.
British Library, National Bibliographic Service, Boston Spa, Wetherby, W. Yorks. LS23 7BQ, England. TEL 44-1937-546613. FAX 44-1937-546586. *524*

BRITISH PHARMACOPOEIA: MAIN EDITION.
H.M.S.O., 51 Nine Elms Ln., London SW8 5DR, England. TEL 44-171-873-0011. FAX 44-171-873-8247. *5402*

BRITISH PHARMACOPOEIA: VETERINARY EDITION.
H.M.S.O., 51 Nine Elms Ln., London SW8 5DR, England. TEL 44-171-873-0011. FAX 44-171-873-8247. *6943*

BRITISH STANDARDS MICROFILE.
Technical Indexes Ltd., Willoughby Rd., Bracknell, Berkshire RG12 8DW, England. TEL 44-1344-426311. FAX 44-1344-424971. *2591*

BROADCASTING IN THE U K.
Key Note Ltd., Field House, 72 Oldfield Rd., Hampton, Middlesex TW12 2HQ, England. TEL 44-181-783-0755. FAX 44-181-783-1940. *1934*

BULLETIN OF THE ATOMIC SCIENTISTS.
Educational Foundation for Nuclear Science, 6042 S. Kimbark Ave., Chicago, IL 60637. TEL 312-702-2555. FAX 312-702-0725. Producer(s): University Microfilms International. *5743*

DIE BURGER.
P.O. Box 692, Cape Town 8000, South Africa. TEL 27-21-4062222. FAX 27-21-4062913. *3212*

BURTON GROUP NEWS ANALYSIS.
Burton Group, Box 3448, Salt Lake City, UT 84110-3448. TEL 801-943-1966. FAX 801-943-2425. *1983*

BURTON GROUP REPORT.
Burton Group, Box 3448, Salt Lake City, UT 84110-3448. TEL 801-943-1966. FAX 801-943-2425. *1983*

BUSINESS DATELINE.
U M I Comapny (Louisville), 620 S. Third St., Louisville, KY 40202-2475. *900*

BUSINESS ECONOMICS.
National Association of Business Economists, 1233 20th St., N.W., Ste. 505, Washington, DC 20036-2304. TEL 202-463-6223. FAX 202-463-6239. *900*

BUSINESS FINLAND.
Helsinki Media Special Magazines, P.O. Box 16, FIN-00381 Helsinki, Finland. TEL 358-0-120-5911. FAX 358-0-120-5959. *1589*

BUSINESS HISTORY.
Frank Cass, Newbury House, 890-900 Eastern Ave., Newbury Park, Ilford, Essex 1G2 7HH, England. TEL 44-181-599-8866. FAX 44-181-599-0984. *901*

BUSINESS INFORMATION REVIEW.
Headland Business Information Customer Services Department, Maypole House, Maypole Rd., E. Grinstead, W. Sussex RH19 1HU, England. TEL 44-1342-330-100. FAX 44-1342-330-191. *1589*

BUSINESS JOURNAL (SACRAMENTO).
City Media, Inc., 821 Marquette Ave., Ste. 2000, Minneapolis, MN 55402. Producer(s): University Microfilms International. *902*

BUSINESS MEXICO.
American Chamber of Commerce of Mexico, A.C., Lucerna 78, Col. Juarez, Del. Cuauhtemoc, 0600 Mexico DF, Mexico. TEL 724-3800. FAX 703-2911. Producer(s): University Microfilms International. *1134*

BUSINESS PERIODICALS INDEX.
H.W. Wilson Co., 950 University Ave., Bronx, NY 10452. TEL 718-588-8400. FAX 718-590-1617. Producer(s): SilverPlatter Information, Inc., H.W. Wilson (WILSONDISC). *985*

BUSINESS PUBLICATION ADVERTISING SOURCE.
S R D S L.P. 1700 Higgins Rd., Des Plaines, IL 60018. TEL 847-375-5000. FAX 847-375-5001. *48*

THE BUSINESS WHO'S WHO AUSTRALIAN PRODUCTS AND TRADENAMES GUIDE.
Dun & Bradstreet Marketing Pty. Ltd., 19 Havilan St., Chatswood, N.S.W. 2065, Australia. TEL 61-2-9352700. FAX 61-2-9352777. *1457*

CD-ROM

BYTE.
McGraw-Hill Companies, Byte Publications, One Phoenix Mill Ln., Peterborough, NH 03458. TEL 603-924-9281. FAX 603-924-2550. *2054*

C C H FEDERAL TAX WEEKLY.
Commerce Clearing House, Inc., 2700 Lake Cook Rd., Riverwoods, IL 60015. TEL 847-267-7000. FAX 800-224-8299. *1537*

C - C PLUS PLUS USERS JOURNAL.
R & D Publications, Inc. 1601 W. 23rd St., Ste. 200, Lawrence, KS 66046. TEL 913-841-1631. FAX 913-841-2624. *2043*

C D - I H L.
International Committee of the Red Cross, Public Information Division, 19 avenue de la Paix, CH-1202 Geneva, Switzerland. TEL 022-7302885. FAX 022-7332057.
Available only on CD-ROM. *3924*

C D - M A R C BIBLIOGRAPHIC.
U.S. Library of Congress, Cataloging Distribution Service, Washington, DC 20541-5017. TEL 202-707-6100. FAX 202-707-1334.
Available only on CD-ROM. *525*

C D - M A R C BIBLIOGRAPHIC. ENGLISH ONLY.
U.S. Library of Congress, Cataloging Distribution Service, Washington, DC 20541-5017. TEL 202-707-6100. FAX 202-707-1334.
Available only on CD-ROM. *525*

C D - M A R C BIBLIOGRAPHIC. ENGLISH ONLY. CURRENT YEARS.
U.S. Library of Congress, Cataloging Distribution Service, Washington, DC 20541-5017. TEL 202-707-6100. FAX 202-707-1334.
Available only on CD-ROM. *525*

C D - M A R C NAMES.
U.S. Library of Congress, Cataloging Distribution Service, Washington, DC 20541-5017. TEL 202-707-6100. FAX 202-707-1334.
Available only on CD-ROM. *525*

C D - M A R C SERIALS.
U.S. Library of Congress, Cataloging Distribution Service, Washington, DC 20541-5017. TEL 202-707-6100. FAX 202-707-1334.
Available only on CD-ROM. *525*

C D - M A R C SUBJECTS.
U.S. Library of Congress, Cataloging Distribution Service, Washington, DC 20541-5017. TEL 202-707-6100. FAX 202-707-1334.
Available only on CD-ROM. *525*

C D MONACI.
Guida Monaci S.p.A., Via Vitorchiano 107, 00189 Rome, Italy. TEL 39-6-3331333. FAX 39-6-3335555.
Available only on CD-ROM. *1590*

C D P FILE.
U.S. Centers for Disease Control, National Center for Chronic Disease Prevention and Health Promotion, 4770 Burford Hwy., N.E., MS K-50, Atlanta, GA 30341-3724. TEL 404-488-5705. FAX 404-488-5739.
Available only on CD-ROM. *5956*

C D - R O M DIRECTORY.
T F P L Publishing, 17-18 Britton St., London EC1M 5NQ, England. TEL 44-171-251-5522. FAX 44-171-251-8318. *2013*

C D - R O M SOURCEBOOK.
Disc Company, 21 Red Maple Rd., Hilton Head Island, SC 29928. TEL 703-237-0682. FAX 703-532-5447. *4042*

C D - R O M SPORTWISSENSCHAFT.
Czwalina Verlag, Postfach 730240, 22122 Hamburg, Germany. TEL 49-40-6794300. FAX 49-40-67943030.
Available only on CD-ROM. *6493*

C D - R O M S IN PRINT.
Gale Research Inc., 835 Penobscot Bldg., Detroit, MI 48226. TEL 313-961-2242. FAX 313-961-7806. *2001*

C I S INDEX TO PUBLICATIONS OF THE UNITED STATES CONGRESS.
Congressional Information Service, Inc., A member of the LEXIS-NEXIS family, 4520 East-West Hwy., Bethesda, MD 20814. TEL 301-654-1550. FAX 301-654-4033. *5930*

C L A S E.
Universidad Nacional Autonoma de Mexico, Centro de Informacion Cientifica y Humanistica, Apdo. Postal 70-392, C.P. 04510 Mexico, D.F., Mexico. TEL 525-6223958. FAX 525-6162557. *6356*

C M A J.
Canadian Medical Association, P.O. Box 8650, Ottawa, ON K1G 0C8, Canada. TEL 613-731-9331. FAX 613-523-0937. *4438*

C R I S P: BIOMEDICAL RESEARCH INFORMATION ON C D - R O M.
U.S. Government Printing Office, c/o Superintendent of Documents, Washington, DC 20242.
Available only on CD-ROM. *626*

C S A NEUROSCIENCES ABSTRACTS.
Cambridge Scientific Abstracts, 7200 Wisconsin Ave., 6th Fl., Bethesda, MD 20814. TEL 301-961-6750. FAX 301-961-6720.
Producer(s): SilverPlatter Information, Inc.. *4551*

C T I PLUS.
Bowker - Saur Ltd., A member of the Reed Elsevier plc group, Maypole House, Maypole Rd., E. Grinstead, W. Sussex RH19 1HU, England. TEL 44-1342-330100. FAX 44-1342-330191.
Available only on CD-ROM. Producer(s): Bowker - Saur Ltd.. *6671*

C U S I P MASTER DIRECTORY.
Standard & Poor's 25 Broadway, New York, NY 10004. TEL 212-208-8000. *1324*

CALCIUM AND CALCIFIED TISSUE ABSTRACTS.
Cambridge Scientific Abstracts, 7200 Wisconsin Ave., 6th Fl., Bethesda, MD 20814. TEL 301-961-6750. FAX 301-961-5720.
Producer(s): SilverPlatter Information, Inc.. *618*

CALIFORNIA BUSINESS DIRECTORY.
American Business Directories 5711 S. 86th Circle, Box 27347, Omaha, NE 68127. TEL 402-593-4600. FAX 402-331-5481. *1590*

CALIFORNIA MANUFACTURERS REGISTER.
Database Publishing Company, 1590 S. Lewis St., Anaheim, CA 92805-6423. TEL 714-778-6400. FAX 714-778-6811. *1590*

CALIFORNIA TAX ANALYSIS.
Commerce Clearing House, Inc., 2700 Lake Cook Rd., Riverwoods, IL 60015. TEL 847-267-7000. FAX 800-224-8299. *1537*

CALIFORNIA WEEKLY EXPLORER.
California Weekly Explorer, Inc., 285 E. Main St., Ste. 3, Tustin, CA 92630. TEL 714-730-5991. FAX 714-730-3548.
Available only on CD-ROM. *1786*

CANADA STATUTE CITATOR.
Canada Law Book Inc., 240 Edward St., Aurora, ON L4G 3S9, Canada. TEL 905-841-6472. FAX 905-841-5085. *3756*

CANADIAN EDUCATION INDEX.
Micromedia Ltd., 20 Victoria St., Toronto, ON M5C 2N8, Canada. TEL 416-362-5211. FAX 416-362-6161. *2387*

CANADIAN INDEX.
Micromedia Ltd., 20 Victoria St., Toronto, ON M5C 2N8, Canada. TEL 416-362-5211. FAX 416-362-6161.
Producer(s): Knight-Ridder, Inc., SilverPlatter Information, Inc.. *987*

CANADIAN JOURNAL OF ANAESTHESIA.
Canadian Anaesthetists' Society, 1 Eglinton Ave., E., Ste. 208, Toronto, ON M4P 3A1, Canada. TEL 416-480-0602. FAX 416-480-0320. *4591*

CANADIAN JOURNAL OF HISTORY.
University of Saskatchewan, 707 Arts Bldg., 9 Campus Dr., Saskatoon, SK S7N 5A5, Canada. TEL 306-966-5792. FAX 306-966-5852.
Producer(s): H.W. Wilson. *3339*

CANADIAN LITERARY PERIODICALS INDEX.
Reference Press, P.O. Box, Teeswater, ON N0G 2S0, Canada. TEL 519-392-6634. *4175*

CANADIAN PERIODICAL INDEX.
Gale Research Inc., 835 Penobscot Bldg., Detroit, MI 48226. TEL 313-961-2242. FAX 313-961-7085. *8*

CANADIAN RESEARCH INDEX, MICROLOG.
Micromedia Ltd., 20 Victoria St., Toronto, ON M5C 2N8, Canada. TEL 416-362-5211. FAX 416-362-6161. *8*

CANADIAN STANDARDS ASSOCIATION E - CODE ELECTRICAL SAFETY STANDARDS.
Canadian Standards Association, 178 Rexdale Blvd., Toronto, ON M9W 1R3, Canada. TEL 416-747-4044. FAX 416-747-2475. *5012*

CANCER.
John Wiley & Sons, Inc., Journals 605 Third Ave., New York, NY 10158. TEL 212-850-6645. FAX 212-850-6021. *4749*

CANCER CAUSES & CONTROL.
Rapid Science Publishers, The Old Malthouse, Paradise St., Oxford OX1 1LD, England. TEL 44-1865-790447. FAX 44-1865-244012. *4750*

CAP-AUX-DIAMANTS.
Editions Cap-aux-Diamants Inc., C.P. 609, Haute Ville, PQ G1R 4S2, Canada. TEL 418-656-5040. FAX 418-656-7282. *3463*

CAPITAL CHANGES REPORTS.
Commerce Clearing House, Inc., 2700 Lake Cook Rd., Riverwoods, IL 60015. TEL 847-267-7000. FAX 800-224-8299. *1537*

CAR AND DRIVER BUYERS GUIDE.
Hachette Filipacchi Magazines, Inc., 1633 Broadway, New York, NY 10019. TEL 212-767-6000. FAX 212-267-5619. *6779*

CARNETEC.
Marketing and Technology Group, Inc., 1415 N. Dayton St., Chicago, IL 60622. TEL 312-266-3311. FAX 312-266-3363. *2963*

CATALOGO COLETIVO DE ANAIS DE EVENTOS.
Comissao Nacional de Energia Nuclear, Centro de Informacoes Nucleares, Rua General Severiano, 90 Botafogo, 22294-900 Rio de Janeiro RJ, Brazil. TEL 55-21-5462467. FAX 55-21-5462447. *6300*

CATALOGO COLETIVO NACIONAL DE PUBLICACOES PERIODICAS (IN MICROFICHES).
Instituto Brasileiro de Informacao em Ciencia e Tecnologia, SAS Quadra 5, Lote 6, Bloco H, 70070-000 Brasilia D.F., Brazil. TEL 2176161. FAX 2252677. *526*

CATALOGO DEI LIBRI IN COMMERCIO.
Editrice Bibliografica S.p.A., Viale Vittorio Veneto 24, 20124 Milan, Italy. TEL 02-29006965. FAX 02-654624. *526*

CATALOGO DEI LIBRI IN COMMERCIO - C D - R O M.
Informazioni Editoriale, Via Carlo Poma 1, 20129 Milan, Italy. TEL 39-2-70129293. FAX 39-2-70129424.
Available only on CD-ROM. Producer(s): K.G. Saur Verlag. *526*

CATALOGUE AFNOR (NORMES FRANCAISES).
Association Francaise de Normalisation, Tour Europe, 92049 Paris La Defense, Cedex, France. TEL 42-91-55-55. FAX 42-91-56-56. *5012*

CATALOGUE OF BRITISH OFFICIAL PUBLICATIONS NOT PUBLISHED BY H.M.S.O.
Chadwyck-Healey Ltd., The Quorum, Barnwell Rd., Cambridge CB5 8SW, England. TEL 01223-215512. FAX 01223-215513.
Producer(s): Chadwyck-Healey Inc.. *526*

CATCHWORD AND TRADE NAME INDEX.
Bowker - Saur Ltd., A member of the Reed Elsevier plc group, Maypole House, Maypole Rd., E. Grinstead, W. Sussex RH19 1HU, England. TEL 44-1342-330100. FAX 44-1342-330191.
Producer(s): Bowker - Saur Ltd. (CTI Plus). *6671*

CATHOLIC INSIGHT.
Life Ethics Information Centre, P.O. Box 625, Adelaide Station, 36 Adelaide St., E., Toronto, ON M5C 2J8, Canada. TEL 416-368-4558. FAX 416-368-8575. *3119*

CENSUS OF AGRICULTURE: FINAL REPORTS.
U.S. Bureau of the Census, Customer Services, Washington, DC 20233. TEL 301-457-4100. FAX 301-457-4714. *170*

CENSUS OF CONSTRUCTION INDUSTRIES: FINAL REPORTS.
U.S. Bureau of the Census, Customer Services, Washington, DC 20233. TEL 301-457-4100. FAX 301-457-4714. *844*

CENSUS OF CONSTRUCTION INDUSTRIES: PRELIMINARY REPORTS.
U.S. Bureau of the Census, Customer Services, Washington, DC 20233. TEL 301-457-4100. FAX 301-457-4714. *881*

CENSUS OF MANUFACTURES: FINAL REPORTS.
U.S. Bureau of the Census, Customer Services, Washington, DC 20233. TEL 301-457-4100. FAX 301-457-4714. *988*

CENSUS OF MANUFACTURES: PRELIMINARY REPORTS.
U.S. Bureau of the Census, Customer Services, Washington, DC 20233. TEL 301-457-4100. FAX 301-457-4714. *988*

CENSUS OF MINERAL INDUSTRIES: FINAL REPORTS.
U.S. Bureau of the Census, Customer Services, Washington, DC 20233. TEL 301-457-4100. FAX 301-457-4714. *5059*

CENSUS OF MINERAL INDUSTRIES: PRELIMINARY REPORTS.
U.S. Bureau of the Census, Customer Services, Washington, DC 20233. TEL 301-457-4100. FAX 301-457-4714. *5059*

CENSUS OF RETAIL TRADE: FINAL REPORTS.
U.S. Bureau of the Census, Customer Services, Washington, DC 20233. TEL 301-457-4100. FAX 301-457-4714. *988*

CENSUS OF SERVICE INDUSTRIES: FINAL REPORTS.
U.S. Bureau of the Census, Customer Services, Washington, DC 20233. TEL 301-457-4100. FAX 301-457-4714. *988*

CENSUS OF TRANSPORTATION, COMMUNICATIONS, AND UTILITIES: FINAL REPORTS.
U.S. Bureau of the Census, Customer Services, Washington, DC 20233. TEL 301-457-4100. FAX 301-457-4714. *6715*

CENSUS OF WHOLESALE TRADE: FINAL REPORTS.
U.S. Bureau of the Census, Customer Services, Washington, DC 20233. TEL 301-457-4100. FAX 301-457-4714. *988*

CENTRAL AFRICAN JOURNAL OF MEDICINE.
Central African Journal of Medicine Co., P.O. Box A195, Avondale, Harare, Zimbabwe. TEL 263-4-791631. *4440*

CERAMIC ABSTRACTS.
American Ceramic Society, 735 Ceramic Pl., Westerville, OH 43081. TEL 614-890-6136. FAX 614-899-6109.
Producer(s): NISC. *1661*

CERAMIC ABSTRACTS (C D - R O M).
National Information Services Corporation (NISC), Ste. 6, Wyman Towers, 3100 St. Paul St., Baltimore, MD 21218. TEL 410-243-0797. FAX 410-243-0982.
Available only on CD-ROM. Producer(s): NISC. *1661*

CEYLON MEDICAL JOURNAL.
Sri Lanka Medical Association, Wijerama House, 6 Wijerama Mawatha, Colombo 7, Sri Lanka. TEL 941-693324. FAX 941-698802. *4440*

THE CHALLENGE.
Pakistan Anti-Tuberculosis Association, Block No. 55, Rm. 8, Pakistan Secretariat, Karachi, Pakistan. TEL 92-21-5688011. *4887*

CHANGE (WASHINGTON).
Heldref Publications, 1319 18th St., N.W., Washington, DC 20036-1802. TEL 202-296-6267. FAX 202-296-5149.
Producer(s): University Microfilms International. *2423*

CHEM SOURCES INTERNATIONAL.
Chemical Sources International, Inc., Box 1824, Clemson, SC 29633. TEL 803-646-7840. FAX 803-646-9938. *1592*

CHEM SOURCES U S A.
Chemical Sources International, Inc., Box 1824, Clemson, SC 29633-1824. TEL 803-646-7840. FAX 803-646-9938. *1592*

CHEMICAL ABSTRACTS.
Chemical Abstracts Service 2540 Olentangy River Rd., Box 3012, Columbus, OH 43210-0012. TEL 614-447-3600. FAX 614-447-3713. *1706*

CHEMICAL HAZARDS IN INDUSTRY.
The Royal Society of Chemistry, Thomas Graham House, Science Park, Milton Rd., Cambridge CB4 4WF, England. TEL 44-1223-420066. FAX 44-1223-423429.
Producer(s): Knight-Ridder, Inc.. *5247*

CHEMINFORM.
V C H Verlagsgesellschaft mbH, Postfach 101161, 69451 Weinheim, Germany. TEL 49-6201-606-147. FAX 49-6201-606117. *1707*

DIE CHEMISCHE INDUSTRIE UND IHRE HELFER.
Industrie-Verlagsgesellschaft mbH, Berliner Allee 8, 64295 Darmstadt, Germany. TEL 06151-38920. FAX 06151-33164. *2638*

CHEMISTRY & BIOLOGY.
Current Biology Ltd., 400 Market St., Ste. 700, Philadelphia, PA 19106. FAX 215-574-2270. *660*

CHEMISTRY CITATION INDEX.
Institute for Scientific Information, 3501 Market St., Philadelphia, PA 19104. TEL 215-386-0100. FAX 215-386-2991. *1707*

CHEMORECEPTION ABSTRACTS.
Cambridge Scientific Abstracts, 7200 Wisconsin Ave., 6th Fl., Bethesda, MD 20814. TEL 301-961-6750. FAX 301-961-6720.
Producer(s): SilverPlatter Information, Inc.. *1707*

CHICAGO AREA BUSINESS DIRECTORY.
American Business Directories 5711 S. 86th Circle, Box 27347, Omaha, NE 68127. TEL 402-593-4600. FAX 402-331-5481. *1592*

THE CHICAGO TRIBUNE INDEX.
U M I Company 300 N. Zeeb Rd., Ann Arbor, MI 48106-1346. TEL 313-761-4700. FAX 800-864-0019. *3714*

CHICANO DATABASE ON C D - R O M.
University of California at Berkeley, Chicano Studies Library Publications Unit, c/o Lillian Castillo-Speed, 3404 Dwinelle Hall, Berkeley, CA 94720. TEL 510-642-3859. FAX 510-642-6453.
Available only on CD-ROM. *2872*

CHICANO INDEX.
University of California at Berkeley, Chicano Studies Library Publication Unit, 3404 Dwinelle Hall, Berkeley, CA 94702. TEL 510-642-3859. FAX 510-642-6456. *2917*

CHILD ABUSE & NEGLECT C D - R O M.
National Information Services Corporation (NISC), Ste. 6, Wyman Towers, 3100 St. Paul St., Baltimore, MD 21218. TEL 410-243-0797. FAX 410-243-0982.
Available only on CD-ROM. Producer(s): NISC. *1762*

CHILDREN'S BOOKS IN PRINT.
R.R. Bowker, A Division of Reed Elsevier Inc., 121 Chanlon Rd., New Providence, NJ 07974. TEL 908-464-6800. FAX 908-665-6688.
Producer(s): Bowker Electronic Publishing (Books in Print PLUS). *527*

CHILDREN'S REFERENCE PLUS.
R.R. Bowker, A Division of Reed Elsevier Inc., 121 Chanlon Rd., New Providence, NJ 07974. TEL 908-665-2866. FAX 908-665-3528.
Available only on CD-ROM. Producer(s): Bowker Electronic Publishing. *527*

CHINESE JOURNAL OF MICROBIOLOGY AND IMMUNOLOGY.
Chinese Society of Microbiology, National Taiwan University, College of Medicine, Jen-Ai Rd., Taipei, Taiwan, Republic of China. *755*

CHINESE NATIONAL BIBLIOGRAPHY.
National Central Library, 20 Chung Shan S. Rd., Taipei, Taiwan 10040, Republic of China. TEL 886-2-3619132. FAX 886-2-311-0155.
Available only on CD-ROM. *4038*

CHOICE (MIDDLETOWN).
Choice, 100 Riverview Ctr., Middletown, CT 06457. TEL 203-347-6933. FAX 203-346-8586.
Producer(s): SilverPlatter Information, Inc.. *6013*

CHOICES: A CORE COLLECTION FOR YOUNG RELUCTANT READERS.
John Gordon Burke Publisher, Inc., Box 1492, Evanston, IL 60204-1492. TEL 847-866-8625. FAX 847-866-6639.
Producer(s): SilverPlatter Information, Inc.. *1787*

CHRISTIAN CENTURY.
Christian Century Foundation, 407 S. Dearborn St., Chicago, IL 60605. TEL 312-427-5380.
Producer(s): University Microfilms International. *6051*

CHRISTIAN SCIENCE MONITOR INDEX.
U M I Company 300 N. Zeeb Rd., Ann Arbor, MI 48106-1346. TEL 313-761-4700. FAX 800-864-0019. *3714*

CHROMOSOME RESEARCH.
Rapid Science Publishers, The Old Malthouse, Paradise St., Oxford OX1 1LD, England. TEL 44-1865-790447. FAX 44-1865-244012. *739*

CHRONICLE FINANCIAL AID GUIDE.
Chronicle Guidance Publications, Inc., Box 1190, Moravia, NY 13118. TEL 315-497-0330. FAX 315-497-3359. *2423*

CHRONICLE FOUR-YEAR COLLEGE DATABOOK.
Chronicle Guidance Publications, Inc., Box 1190, Moravia, NY 13118. TEL 315-497-0330. FAX 315-497-3359. *2410*

CHRONICLE OF LATIN AMERICAN ECONOMIC AFFAIRS.
University of Latin America, Latin American Institute, 801 Yale N.E., Albuquerque, NM 87131-1016. TEL 505-277-6839. FAX 505-277-5989.
Producer(s): NISC (Latin American Studies - Vol.2). *1183*

CHRONICLE TWO-YEAR COLLEGE DATABOOK.
Chronicle Guidance Publications, Inc., Box 1190, Moravia, NY 13118. TEL 315-497-0330. FAX 315-497-3359. *2410*

CHRONICLE VOCATIONAL SCHOOL MANUAL.
Chronicle Guidance Publications, Inc., Box 1190, Moravia, NY 13118. TEL 315-497-0330. FAX 315-497-3359. *2410*

CLASSICA ET MEDIAEVALIA.
Museum Tusculanum Press, University of Copenhagen, Njalsgade 92, DK-2300 Copenhagen S, Denmark. TEL 45-35-32-91-09. FAX 45-35-32-91-13. *1820*

CLASSIFIED DIRECTORY OF WISCONSIN MANUFACTURERS.
W M C Service Corporation, 501 E. Washington Ave., Box 352, Madison, WI 53701-0352. TEL 608-258-3400. FAX 608-258-3413. *1592*

THE CLEARING HOUSE.
Heldref Publications, 1319 Eighteenth St., N.W., Washington, DC 20036-1802. TEL 202-296-6267. FAX 202-296-5149.
Producer(s): University Microfilms International. *2320*

CLINICAL AND DIAGNOSTIC LABORATORY IMMUNOLOGY.
American Society for Microbiology, 1325 Massachusetts Ave., N.W., Washington, DC 20005. TEL 202-942-9319. FAX 202-942-9346. *4579*

CLINICAL AND EXPERIMENTAL IMMUNOLOGY.
Blackwell Science Ltd., Osney Mead, Oxford OX2 OEL, England. TEL 44-1865-206206. FAX 44-1865-721205. *4579*

CLINICAL AND EXPERIMENTAL METASTASIS.
Rapid Science Publishers, The Old Malthouse, Paradise St., Oxford OX1 1LD, England. TEL 44-1865-790447. FAX 44-1865-244012. *4753*

CLINICAL AUTONOMIC RESEARCH.
Rapid Science Publishers, The Old Malthouse, Paradise St., Oxford OX1 1LD, England. TEL 44-1865-790447. FAX 44-1865-244012. *4443*

CLINICAL LABORATORY.
Verlag Klinisches Labor, Im Breitspiel 15, 69126 Heidelberg, Germany. TEL 49-6221-3432133. FAX 49-6221-300291. *4678*

CLINICAL LABORATORY PRODUCT COMPARISON SYSTEM.
E C R I, 5200 Butler Pike, Plymouth Meeting, PA 19462. TEL 610-825-6000. FAX 610-834-1275. Producer(s): Knight-Ridder, Inc.. *4678*

CLINICAL MICROBIOLOGY REVIEWS.
American Society for Microbiology, 1325 Massachusetts Ave., N.W., Washington, DC 20005. TEL 202-737-3600. *755*

CLOTHING AND TEXTILE ARTS INDEX.
Box 1300, Monument, CO 80132. TEL 719-488-3716. *1838*

COAL HIGHLIGHTS.
I E A Coal Research, Gemini House, 10-18 Putney Hill, London SW15 6AA, England. TEL 44-181-780-0111. FAX 44-181-780-1746. *2542*

COAL WEEK.
McGraw-Hill Companies, Energy & Business Newsletters, 1221 Ave. of the Americas, 36th Fl., New York, NY 10020. TEL 212-512-6410. Producer(s): SilverPlatter Information, Inc. (McGraw-Hill Energy Library). *5061*

COAL WEEK INTERNATIONAL.
McGraw-Hill Companies, Energy & Business Newsletters, 1221 Ave. of the Americas, 36th Fl., New York, NY 10020. TEL 212-512-6410. Producer(s): SilverPlatter Information, Inc. (McGraw-Hill Energy Library). *5061*

CODE OF FEDERAL REGULATIONS.
U.S. Office of the Federal Register, National Archives and Records Administration, 8th St. and Pennsylvania Ave., N.W., Washington, DC 20408. TEL 202-523-5230. *3760*

COLLEGE BLUE BOOK.
Macmillan Publishing Company, 866 Third Ave., New York, NY 10022. TEL 212-702-4296. *2410*

COLLEGE CATALOG COLLECTION.
Career Guidance Foundation, 8090 Engineer Rd., San Diego, CA 92111. FAX 619-278-8960. *2424*

COLLEGE OF AGRICULTURAL, CONSUMER AND ENVIRONMETAL SCIENCES. RESEARCH PROGRESS.
University of Illinois at Urbana-Champaign, College of Agricultural, Consumer and Environmental Sciences, 47 Mumford Hall, 1301 W. Gregory Dr., Urbana, IL 61801. TEL 217-244-2830. *108*

COLLEGE TEACHING.
Heldref Publications, 1319 Eighteenth St., N.W., Washington, DC 20036-1802. TEL 202-296-6267. FAX 202-296-5149. Producer(s): University Microfilms International. *2424*

COLORADO BUSINESS DIRECTORY.
American Business Directories 5711 S. 86th Circle, Box 27347, Omaha, NE 68127. TEL 402-593-4600. FAX 402-331-5481. *1593*

COLOUR INDEX.
Society of Dyers and Colourists, Perkin House, P.O. Box 244, Bradford, W. Yorks BD1 2JB, England. TEL 44-1274-7215138. FAX 44-1274-392888. *6675*

COMERCIO EXTERIOR.
Banco Nacional de Comercio Exterior, S.A., Gerencia de la Revista Comercio Exterior, Camino a Santa Teresa 1679, Col. Jardines del Pedregal, 01900 Mexico D.F., Mexico. TEL 525-3276220. FAX 525-3276214. *1269*

COMMERCIO E SERVIZI.
Maggioli Editore, Vale Vespucci 12-n, 47037 Rimini, Italy. TEL 0541-626777. FAX 0541-622020. *3898*

COMMONWEAL.
Commonweal Foundation, 15 Dutch St., New York, NY 10038. TEL 212-732-0800. Producer(s): University Microfilms International. *4137*

COMMONWEALTH STATUTES ANNOTATIONS.
L B C Information Services, 50 Waterloo Rd., N. Ryde, N.S.W. 2113, Australia. TEL 61-2-99366444. FAX 61-2-8889706. *3946*

COMMUNICATIONS COMPANIES ANALYSIS. MANUFACTURERS VOLUME.
M D I S Publications Ltd., MDIS House, City Fields Business Park, City Fields Way, Chichester, W. Sussex PO20 6FS, England. TEL 44-1243-533322. FAX 44-1243-533418. *1899*

COMMUNICATIONS COMPANIES ANALYSIS. OPERATORS VOLUME.
M D I S Publications Ltd., MDIS House, City Fields Business Park, City Fields Way, Chichester, W. Sussex PO20 6FS, England. TEL 44-1243-533322. FAX 44-1243-533418. *1899*

COMMUNICATIONS MARKETS ANALYSIS.
M D I S Publications Ltd., MDIS House, City Fields Business Park, City Fields Way, Chichester, W. Sussex PO20 6FS, England. TEL 44-1243-533322. FAX 44-1243-533418. *1900*

COMMUNICATIONS OF C O L I P S.
Chinese and Oriental Languages Information Processing Society, c/o Dept. of Information Systems & Computer Science, National University of Singapore, Kent Ridge, Singapore 0511, Singapore. TEL 65-772-2782. FAX 65-779-4580. *4128*

COMMUNITY CURRENTS.
Community Development Foundation, 60 Highbury Grove, London N5 2AG, England. TEL 0171-226-5375. FAX 0171-704-0313. *6400*

COMPACTMATH - COMPACT MATHEMATICS LIBRARY.
Springer-Verlag, Heidelberger Platz 3, 14197 Berlin, Germany. TEL 49-30-8207-0. FAX 49-30-8214091. Available only on CD-ROM. *4405*

COMPANY DATABASE CD.
Herold Business Data GmbH, Guntramsdorferstr. 105, A-2340 Moedling, Austria. TEL 02236-401. FAX 02236-4018. Available only on CD-ROM. *1593*

COMPENDIUM OF PHARMACEUTICALS AND SPECIALTIES.
Canadian Pharmaceutical Association, 1785 Alta Vista Dr., Ottawa, ON K1G 3Y6, Canada. TEL 613-523-7877. FAX 613-523-0445. *5405*

COMPENSATION AND WORKING CONDITIONS.
U.S. Bureau of Labor Statistics, 441 G St., N.W., Washington, DC 20212. TEL 202-655-4000. *1184*

COMPLETE DIRECTORY OF LARGE PRINT BOOKS AND SERIALS.
R.R. Bowker, A Division of Reed Elsevier Inc., 121 Chanlon Rd., New Providence, NJ 07974. TEL 908-464-6800. FAX 908-655-3502. Producer(s): Bowker Electronic Publishing. *3309*

COMPLIANCE OFFICER'S MANAGEMENT MANUAL.
Sheshunoff Information Services Inc., 505 Barton Springs Rd., Ste. 1100, Austin, TX 78704. TEL 512-472-2244. *1078*

COMPREHENSIVE MEDLINE.
EBSCO Publishing 10 Estes St., Box 682, Ipswich, MA 01938. TEL 508-356-6565. FAX 508-356-6565. Available only on CD-ROM. *4552*

COMPUTER ABSTRACTS.
M C B University Press Ltd., Anbar Abstracts, 60-62 Toller Ln., Bradford, W. Yorks BD8 9BY, England. TEL 01274-499821. FAX 01274-547143. *2001*

COMPUTER AND COMMUNICATIONS TECHNOLOGY DOCUMENTS MICROFILE.
Technical Indexes Ltd., Willoughby Rd., Bracknell, Berkshire RG12 8DW, England. TEL 44-1344-426311. FAX 44-1344-424971. *1926*

COMPUTER & CONTROL ABSTRACTS.
INSPEC, I.E.E., Michael Faraday House, Six Hills Way, Stevenage, Herts. SG1 2AY, England. TEL 44-1438-313311. FAX 44-1438-742840. Producer(s): University Microfilms International. *2001*

COMPUTER SELECT.
Computer Library, One Park Ave., New York, NY 10016. TEL 212-503-4400. FAX 212-503-4414. Available only on CD-ROM. *2001*

THE COMPUTER USERS YEAR BOOK.
V N U Business Publications BV, VNU House, 32-34 Broadwick St., London W1A 2HG, England. *2054*

CONFEDERATE VETERAN.
Sons of Confederate Veterans, P.O. Box 41828, Houston, TX 77241-1828. TEL 713-373-1199. *3463*

CONFIDENTIAL REPORT FOR ATTORNEYS.
Confidential Report for Attorneys, Box 1476, Oceanside, CA 92051. TEL 619-721-3622. FAX 619-721-3683. *3763*

CONGRESSIONAL STAFF DIRECTORY.
Staff Directories Ltd., Box 62, Mount Vernon, VA 22121. TEL 703-739-0900. FAX 703-739-0234. *5644*

CONGRESSIONAL YELLOW BOOK.
Leadership Directories, Inc. 104 Fifth Ave., 2nd Fl., New York, NY 10011. TEL 212-627-4140. FAX 212-645-0931. Producer(s): Chadwyck-Healey Inc. *5898*

CONNECTICUT BUSINESS DIRECTORY.
American Business Directories 5711 S. 86th Cir., Box 27347, Omaha, NE 68127. TEL 402-593-4600 FAX 402-331-5481. *1593*

CONNECTICUT RULES OF COURT, STATE AND FEDERAL.
West Publishing Corp., 620 Opperman Dr., Eagan, MN 55123. TEL 612-687-3000. FAX 612-687-7302. *3946*

CONSIGLIO DI STATO.
Casa Editrice Italedi, Piazza Cavour 19, 00193 Rome, Italy. TEL 39-6-3213803. *3764*

CONSOLIDATED FEDERAL FUNDS REPORT.
U.S. Bureau of the Census, Customer Services, Washington, DC 20233. TEL 301-457-4100. FAX 301-457-4714. *5899*

CONSOLIDATED TREATIES & INTERNATIONAL AGREEMENTS: UNITED STATES CURRENT DOCUMENT SERVICE.
Oceana Publications, Inc., 75 Main St., Dobbs Ferry, NY 10522. TEL 914-693-8100. FAX 914-693-0402. *3927*

CONSUMER HEALTH AND NUTRITION INDEX.
Oryx Press, 4041 N. Central Ave., No. 700, Phoenix, AZ 85012-3397. TEL 602-265-2651. FAX 602-265-6250. Producer(s): NISC (Consumers Reference Disc). *5243*

CONSUMER MAGAZINE AND AGRI-MEDIA SOURCE.
S R D S L.P. 1700 Higgins Rd., Des Plaines, IL 60018. TEL 847-375-5000 FAX 847-375-5001. *48*

CONSUMER REPORTS.
Consumers Union of the United States, Inc., 101 Truman Ave., Yonkers, NY 10703-1057. TEL 914-378-2000. FAX 914-378-2500. *2150*

CONSUMERS INDEX.
Pierian Press, Box 1808, Ann Arbor, MI 48106. TEL 313-434-5530. FAX 313-434-5409. Producer(s): NISC (Consumers Reference Disc). *2156*

CONSUMERS REFERENCE DISC.
National Information Services Corporation (NISC), Ste. 6, Wyman Towers, 3100 St. Paul St., Baltimore, MD 21218. TEL 410-243-0797. FAX 410-243-0982.
Available only on CD-ROM. Producer(s): NISC. *2156*

CONSUMER'S RESEARCH MAGAZINE.
Consumers' Research, Inc., 800 Maryland Ave., N.E., Washington, DC 20002. TEL 202-546-1713. FAX 202-546-1638.
Producer(s): University Microfilms International. *2151*

CONTRA COSTA COUNTY COMMERCE AND INDUSTRY DIRECTORY.
Database Publishing Company, 1590 S. Lewis St., Anaheim, CA 92805-6423. TEL 714-778-6400. FAX 714-778-6811. *1594*

COREL MAGAZINE.
Omray Inc., 9801 Anderson Mill Rd., Ste. 207, Austin, TX 78750. TEL 512-250-1700. FAX 512-219-3156. *2027*

CORPORATE AFFILIATIONS PLUS.
National Register Publishing, A Division of Reed Elsevier Inc., 121 Chanlon Rd., New Providence, NJ 07974. TEL 908-464-6800. FAX 908-771-7704. Available only on CD-ROM. Producer(s): Bowker Electronic Publishing. *1594*

CORPORATE DIRECTORY OF US PUBLIC COMPANIES.
Walker's Western Research, 1650 Borel Pl., Ste. 130, San Mateo, CA 94402. TEL 415-341-1110. FAX 415-341-2351. *1326*

CORPORATE FINANCING WEEK.
Institutional Investor Newsletters, 477 Madison Ave., New York, NY 10022. TEL 212-224-3233. FAX 212-224-3353. *1079*

CORPORATE REPORT MINNESOTA.
City Media, Inc., 821 Marquette Ave., Ste. 2000, Minneapolis, MN 55402-2000. TEL 612-359-2100. FAX 612-359-2110.
Producer(s): University Microfilms International. *1412*

CORPORATE YELLOW BOOK.
Leadership Directories, Inc., 104 Fifth Ave., 2nd Fl., New York, NY 10011. TEL 212-627-4140. FAX 212-645-0931.
Producer(s): Chadwyck-Healey Inc.. *1412*

CORPTECH DIRECTORY OF TECHNOLOGY COMPANIES.
Corporate Technology Information Services Inc., 12 Alfred St., Ste. 200, Woburn, MA 01801. TEL 617-932-3939. FAX 617-932-6335. *1594*

CORPUS CHRISTIANORUM. CONTINUATIO MEDIAEVALIS.
N.V. Brepols, Steenweg op Tielen 68, 2300 Turnhout, Belgium. TEL 32-14-402500. FAX 32-14-428919. *6177*

CORPUS CHRISTIANORUM. SERIES LATINA.
N.V. Brepols, Steenweg op Tielen 68, 2300 Turnhout, Belgium. TEL 32-14-402500. FAX 32-14-428919. *6177*

CORROSION ABSTRACTS.
N A C E International, Box 218340, Houston, TX 77218. TEL 713-492-0535. FAX 713-492-8254. *2625*

COUNTRY FORECASTS (NEW YORK).
Economist Intelligence Unit, 111 W. 57th St., New York, NY 10019. TEL 212-554-0600. FAX 212-586-1182. *5650*

COUNTRY REPORT. BOLIVIA.
Economist Intelligence Unit, 111 W. 57th St., New York, NY 10019. TEL 212-554-0600. FAX 212-586-1182.
Producer(s): Knight-Ridder, Inc., SilverPlatter Information, Inc.. *1188*

COUNTRY REPORT. BULGARIA, ALBANIA.
Economist Intelligence Unit, 111 W. 57th St., New York, NY 10019. TEL 212-554-0600. FAX 212-586-1182.
Producer(s): Knight-Ridder, Inc., SilverPlatter Information, Inc.. *1188*

COUNTRY REPORT. PERU.
Economist Intelligence Unit, 111 W. 57th St., New York, NY 10019. TEL 212-554-0600. FAX 212-586-1182.
Producer(s): Knight-Ridder, Inc., SilverPlatter Information, Inc.. *1194*

COUNTRY REPORTS.
Economist Intelligence Unit, 111 W. 57th St., New York, NY 10019. TEL 212-554-0600. FAX 212-586-1182. *1197*

COUNTY AND CITY DATA BOOK.
U.S. Bureau of the Census, Customer Services, Washington, DC 20233. TEL 301-457-4100. FAX 301-457-4714. *6601*

COUNTY AND CITY EXTRA.
Bernan Press, 4611-F Assembly Dr., Lanham, MD 20706-4391. TEL 301-459-7666. FAX 301-459-0056. *6601*

COUNTY BUSINESS PATTERNS.
U.S. Bureau of the Census, Customer Services, Washington, DC 20233. TEL 301-457-4100. FAX 301-457-4714. *991*

CRAWFORD'S DIRECTORY OF CITY CONNECTIONS.
Miller Freeman Information Services Riverbank House, Angel Ln., Tonbridge, Kent TN9 1SE, England. TEL 01732-362666. FAX 01732-367301. *1080*

CRIMINAL JUSTICE ABSTRACTS.
Willow Tree Press, Inc., 124 Willow Tree Rd., Monsey, NY 10952. TEL 914-354-9139. FAX 914-362-8376.
Producer(s): SilverPlatter Information, Inc.. *2179*

CRITIQUE: STUDIES IN MODERN FICTION.
Heldref Publications, 1319 Eighteenth St., N.W., Washington, DC 20036-1802. TEL 202-296-6267. FAX 202-296-5149.
Producer(s): University Microfilms International. *4200*

CROATIAN MEDICAL JOURNAL.
Pabst Science Publishers, Am Eichengrund 28, 49525 Lengerich, Germany. TEL 49-5484-308. FAX 49-5484-550. *4446*

CROSS CURRENTS (NEW ROCHELLE).
Association for Religion and Intellectual Life, College of New Rochelle, New Rochelle, NY 10805-2339. TEL 914-654-5425. FAX 914-654-5925. *6056*

CUADERNOS DE HISTORIA DEL ARTE.
Universidad Nacional de Cuyo, Facultad de Filosofia y Letras, Centro Universitario, Parque General San Martin, 5500 Mendoza, Argentina. TEL 54-61-230915. FAX 54-61-380457. *425*

CULTIVOS TROPICALES.
Instituto Nacional de Ciencias Agricolas, Gaveta Postal No. 1, San Jose de las Lajas, Havana 32700, Cuba. TEL 064-63290. FAX 53-7-333295. *218*

CUMULATIVE BOOK INDEX.
H.W. Wilson Co., 950 University Ave., Bronx, NY 10452. TEL 718-588-8400. FAX 718-590-1617.
Producer(s): SilverPlatter Information, Inc., H.W. Wilson. *528*

CUMULATIVE INDEX TO NURSING & ALLIED HEALTH LITERATURE.
C I N A H L Information Systems, 1509 Wilson Terrace, Box 871, Glendale, CA 91209-0871. TEL 818-409-8005. FAX 818-546-5679.
Producer(s): C I N A H L, SilverPlatter Information, Inc.. *4553*

CURRENT (WASHINGTON, 1960).
Heldref Publications, 1319 18th St., N.W., Washington, DC 20036-1802. TEL 202-296-6267. FAX 202-296-5149.
Producer(s): University Microfilms International. *2322*

CURRENT BIOGRAPHY YEARBOOK.
H.W. Wilson Co., 950 University Ave., Bronx, NY 10452. TEL 718-588-8400. FAX 718-590-1716.
Producer(s): H.W. Wilson (WILSONDISC). *555*

CURRENT BIOTECHNOLOGY.
The Royal Society of Chemistry, Thomas Graham House, Science Park, Milton Rd., Cambridge CB4 4WF, England. TEL 44-1223-420066. FAX 44-1223-423429.
Producer(s): Knight-Ridder, Inc.. *619*

CURRENT CONTENTS: AGRICULTURE, BIOLOGY & ENVIRONMENTAL SCIENCES.
Institute for Scientific Information, 3501 Market St., Philadelphia, PA 19104. TEL 215-386-0100. FAX 215-386-2991. *171*

CURRENT CONTENTS: CLINICAL MEDICINE.
Institute for Scientific Information, 3501 Market St., Philadelphia, PA 19104. TEL 215-386-0100. FAX 215-386-2991. *4554*

CURRENT CONTENTS: LIFE SCIENCES.
Institute for Scientific Information, 3501 Market St., Philadelphia, PA 19104. TEL 215-386-0100. FAX 215-386-2291. *619*

CURRENT CONTENTS: PHYSICAL, CHEMICAL & EARTH SCIENCES.
Institute for Scientific Information, 3501 Market St., Philadelphia, PA 19104. TEL 215-386-0100. FAX 215-386-2291. *1708*

CURRENT HEALTH 2.
Weekly Reader Corporation, 245 Long Hill Rd., Box 2791, Middletown, CT 06457-9291. FAX 609-786-3360.
Producer(s): University Microfilms International. *5526*

CURRENT HISTORY.
Current History, Inc., 4225 Main St., Philadelphia, PA 19127. TEL 215-482-4464. FAX 215-482-9197. *5660*

CURRENT INDEX TO JOURNALS IN EDUCATION.
Oryx Press, 4041 N. Central Ave., No. 700, Phoenix, AZ 85012-3397. TEL 602-265-2651. FAX 602-265-6250.
Producer(s): NISC (ERIC on CD-ROM), OCLC, SilverPlatter Information, Inc. (ERIC). *2387*

CURRENT MATHEMATICAL PUBLICATIONS.
American Mathematical Society, Box 6248, Providence, RI 02940-6248. TEL 401-455-4000.
Producer(s): SilverPlatter Information, Inc. (MathDisc). *4405*

CURRENT MEDICAL DIAGNOSIS AND TREATMENT.
Appleton & Lange Box 120041, Stamford, CT 06912-0041. TEL 203-406-4500. *4446*

CURRENT OPINION IN ANAESTHESIOLOGY.
Rapid Science Publishers, 2-6 Boundary Row, London SE1 8HN, England. TEL 44-171-865-0198. FAX 44-171-410-6600. *4556*

CURRENT OPINION IN BIOTECHNOLOGY.
Current Biology Ltd., 400 Market St., Ste. 700, Philadelphia, PA 19106. TEL 800-552-5866. FAX 215-574-2270. *660*

CURRENT OPINION IN CARDIOLOGY.
Rapid Science Publishers, 2-6 Boundary Row, London SE1 8HN, England. TEL 44-171-865-0198. FAX 44-171-410-6600. *4556*

CURRENT OPINION IN CELL BIOLOGY.
Current Biology Ltd., 400 Market St., Ste. 700, Philadelphia, PA 19106. FAX 215-574-2270. *619*

CURRENT OPINION IN COSMETIC DENTISTRY.
Rapid Science Publishers, 2-6 Boundary Row, London SE1 8HN, England. TEL 44-171-865-0198. FAX 44-171-410-6600. *4557*

CURRENT OPINION IN CRITICAL CARE.
Rapid Science Publishers, 2-6 Boundary Row, London SE1 8HN, England. TEL 44-171-865-0198. FAX 44-171-865-0198. *4782*

CURRENT OPINION IN DERMATOLOGY.
Rapid Science Publishers, 2-6 Boundary Row, London SE1 8HN, England. TEL 44-171-865-0198. FAX 44-171-410-6600. *4660*

CURRENT OPINION IN ENDOCRINOLOGY & DIABETES.
Rapid Science Publishers, 2-6 Boundary Row, London SE1 8HN, England. TEL 44-171-865-0198. FAX 44-171-410-6600. *4667*

CURRENT OPINION IN GASTROENTEROLOGY.
Rapid Science Publishers, 2-6 Boundary Row,
London SE1 8HN, England. TEL 44-171-865-0198.
FAX 44-171-410-6600. *4557*

CURRENT OPINION IN GENETICS & DEVELOPMENT.
Current Biology Ltd., 400 Market St., Ste. 700,
Philadelphia, PA 19106. TEL 800-552-5866.
FAX 215-574-2270. *620*

CURRENT OPINION IN HEMATOLOGY.
Rapid Science Publishers, 2-6 Boundary Row,
London SE1 8HN, England. TEL 44-171-865-0198.
FAX 44-171-410-6600. *4699*

CURRENT OPINION IN IMMUNOLOGY.
Current Biology Ltd., 400 Market St., Ste. 700,
Philadelphia, PA 19106. FAX 215-574-2270.
4557

CURRENT OPINION IN INFECTIOUS DISEASES.
Rapid Science Publishers, 2-6 Boundary Row,
London SE1 8HN, England. TEL 44-171-865-0198.
FAX 44-171-410-6600. *4557*

CURRENT OPINION IN LIPIDOLOGY.
Rapid Science Publishers, 2-6 Boundary Row,
London SE1 8HN, England. TEL 44-171-410-6600.
FAX 44-171-410-6600. *4557*

**CURRENT OPINION IN NEPHROLOGY &
HYPERTENSION.**
Rapid Science Publishers, 2-6 Boundary Row,
London SE1 8HN, England. TEL 44-171-865-0198.
FAX 44-171-865-0198. *4557*

CURRENT OPINION IN NEUROBIOLOGY.
Current Biology, Ltd., 400 Market St., Ste. 700,
Philadelphia, PA 19106. TEL 800-552-5866.
FAX 215-574-2270. *620*

CURRENT OPINION IN NEUROLOGY.
Rapid Science Publishers, 2-6 Boundary Row,
London SE1 8HN, England. TEL 44-171-865-0198.
FAX 44-171-410-6600. *4557*

**CURRENT OPINION IN OBSTETRICS &
GYNECOLOGY.**
Rapid Science Publishers, 2-6 Boundary Row,
London SE1 8HN, England. TEL 44-171-865-0198.
FAX 44-171-410-6600. *4557*

CURRENT OPINION IN ONCOLOGY.
Rapid Science Publishers, 2-6 Boundary Row,
London SE1 8HN, England. TEL 44-171-865-0198.
FAX 44-171-410-6600. *4557*

CURRENT OPINION IN OPHTHALMOLOGY.
Rapid Science Publishers, 2-6 Boundary Row,
London SE1 8HN, England. TEL 44-171-865-0198.
FAX 44-171-410-6600. *4558*

CURRENT OPINION IN ORTHOPEDICS.
Rapid Science Publishers, 2-6 Boundary Row,
London SE1 8HN, England. TEL 44-171-865-0198.
FAX 44-171-410-6600. *4558*

**CURRENT OPINION IN OTOLARYNGOLOGY & HEAD
AND NECK SURGERY.**
Rapid Science Publishers, 2-6 Boundary Row,
London SE1 8HN, England. TEL 44-171-865-0198.
FAX 44-171-410-6600. *4796*

CURRENT OPINION IN PEDIATRICS.
Rapid Science Publishers, 2-6 Boundary Row,
London SE1 8HN, England. TEL 44-171-865-0198.
FAX 44-171-410-6600. *4558*

CURRENT OPINION IN PERIODONTOLOGY.
Rapid Science Publishers, 2-6 Boundary Row,
London SE1 8HN, England. TEL 44-171-865-0198.
FAX 44-171-410-6600. *4558*

CURRENT OPINION IN PSYCHIATRY.
Rapid Science Publishers, 2-6 Boundary Row,
London SE1 8HN, England. TEL 44-171-865-0198.
FAX 44-171-410-6600. *4558*

CURRENT OPINION IN PULMONARY MEDICINE.
Rapid Science Publishers, 2-6 Boundary Row,
London SE1 8HN, England. TEL 44-171-865-0198.
FAX 44-171-410-6600. *4887*

CURRENT OPINION IN RHEUMATOLOGY.
Rapid Science Publishers, 2-6 Boundary Row,
London SE1 8HN, England. TEL 44-171-865-0198.
FAX 44-171-410-6600. *4558*

CURRENT OPINION IN STRUCTURAL BIOLOGY.
Current Biology Ltd., 400 Market St., Ste. 700,
Philadelphia, PA 19106. TEL 800-552-5866.
FAX 215-574-2270. *620*

CURRENT OPINION IN SURGICAL INFECTIONS.
Rapid Science Publishers, 2-6 Boundary Row,
London SE1 8HN, England. TEL 44-171-865-0198.
FAX 44-171-410-6600. *4907*

CURRENT OPINION IN UROLOGY.
Rapid Science Publishers, 2-6 Boundary Row,
London SE1 8HN, England. TEL 44-171-865-0198.
FAX 44-171-410-6600. *4558*

CURRENT PROTOCOLS IN HUMAN GENETICS.
John Wiley & Sons, Inc., Journals, 605 Third Ave.,
New York, NY 10158. TEL 212-850-6645.
FAX 212-850-6021. *739*

CURRENT PROTOCOLS IN IMMUNOLOGY.
John Wiley & Sons, Inc., Journals, 605 Third Ave.,
New York, NY 10158. TEL 212-850-6645.
FAX 212-850-6021. *4580*

CURRENT PROTOCOLS IN MOLECULAR BIOLOGY.
John Wiley & Sons, Inc., Journals, 605 Third Ave.,
New York, NY 10158. TEL 212-850-6645.
FAX 212-850-6021. *578*

**CURRENT RESEARCH IN LIBRARY & INFORMATION
SCIENCE.**
Bowker - Saur Ltd., A member of the Reed Elsevier
plc group, Maypole House, Maypole Rd., E.
Grinstead, W. Sussex RH19 1HU, England. TEL 44-
1342-330100. FAX 44-1342-330191.
Producer(s): Bowker - Saur Ltd.. *3987*

CURRENT SURGICAL DIAGNOSIS & TREATMENT.
Appleton & Lange Box 120041t St., Stamford, CT
06912-0041. TEL 203-406-4500. *4907*

CURRENT TECHNOLOGY INDEX.
Bowker - Saur Ltd., A member of the Reed Elsevier
plc group, Maypole House, Maypole Rd., E.
Grinstead, W. Sussex RH19 1HU, England. TEL 44-
1342-330100. FAX 44-1342-330191.
Producer(s): Bowker - Saur Ltd.. *6671*

CURRENT THOUGHTS & TRENDS.
Box 35004, Colorado Springs, CO 80935-3504.
TEL 719-531-3585. FAX 719-598-7128. *6107*

CYMBIOSIS.
Cymbiosis, Inc., 6201 W. Sunset Blvd., Ste. 80,
Hollywood, CA 90028-8704. TEL 213-463-3808.
FAX 213-463-5426. *5152*

**CYPRUS. AGRICULTURAL RESEARCH INSTITUTE.
AGRICULTURAL ECONOMICS REPORT.**
Ministry of Agriculture, Natural Resources and the
Environment, Agricultural Research Institute,
Nicosia, Cyprus. TEL 357-2-305101. FAX 357-2-
316770. *189*

**CYPRUS. AGRICULTURAL RESEARCH INSTITUTE.
ANNUAL REVIEW.**
Ministry of Agriculture, Natural Resources and the
Environment, Agricultural Research Institute,
Nicosia, Cyprus. TEL 357-2-305101. FAX 357-2-
316770. *110*

**CYPRUS. AGRICULTURAL RESEARCH INSTITUTE.
MISCELLANEOUS REPORTS.**
Ministry of Agriculture, Natural Resources and the
Environment, Agricultural Research Institute,
Nicosia, Cyprus. TEL 357-2-305101. FAX 357-2-
316770. *110*

**CYPRUS. AGRICULTURAL RESEARCH INSTITUTE.
TECHNICAL BULLETIN.**
Ministry of Agriculture, Natural Resources and the
Environment, Agricultural Research Institute,
Nicosia, Cyprus. TEL 357-2-305101. FAX 357-2-
316770. *110*

C2C ABSTRACTS: JAPAN - ANALYTICAL CHEMISTRY.
Scan C2C, 1001 Pennsylvania Ave., N.W., No.
1300, Washington, DC 20024-2505. TEL 800-
525-3865. FAX 202-863-3855.
Producer(s): Knight-Ridder, Inc.. *1708*

C2C ABSTRACTS: JAPAN - CERAMICS.
Scan C2C, 1001 Pennsylvania Ave., N.W.,
No.1300, Washington, DC 20024-2505. TEL 800-
525-3865. FAX 202-863-3855.
Producer(s): Knight-Ridder, Inc.. *1661*

**C2C ABSTRACTS: JAPAN - CHEMICAL
ENGINEERING.**
Scan C2C, 1001 Pennsylvania Ave., N.W., No.
1300, Washington, DC 20024-2505. TEL 800-
525-3865. FAX 202-863-3855.
Producer(s): Knight-Ridder, Inc.. *2626*

C2C ABSTRACTS: JAPAN - CRYSTALLOGRAPHY.
Scan C2C, 1001 Pennsylvania Ave., N.W., No.
1300, Washington, DC 20024-2505. TEL 800-
525-3865. FAX 202-863-3855.
Producer(s): Knight-Ridder, Inc.. *1708*

C2C ABSTRACTS: JAPAN - HYDROCARBONS.
Scan C2C, 1001 Pennsylvania Ave., N.W., No.
1300, Washington, DC 20024-2505. TEL 800-
525-3865. FAX 202-863-3855.
Producer(s): Knight-Ridder, Inc.. *1708*

C2C ABSTRACTS: JAPAN - INORGANIC CHEMISTRY.
Scan C2C, 1001 Pennsylvania Ave., N.W., No.
1300, Washington, DC 20024-2505. TEL 800-
525-3865. FAX 202-863-3855.
Producer(s): Knight-Ridder, Inc.. *1708*

C2C ABSTRACTS: JAPAN - MATERIALS SCIENCE.
Scan C2C, 1001 Pennsylvania Ave., N.W., No.
1300, Washington, DC 20024-2505. TEL 800-
525-3865. FAX 202-863-3855.
Producer(s): Knight-Ridder, Inc.. *2626*

C2C ABSTRACTS: JAPAN - METALS.
Scan C2C, 1001 Pennsylvania Ave., N.W., No.
1300 Washington, DC 20024-2505. TEL 800-
525-3865. FAX 202-863-3855.
Producer(s): Knight-Ridder Inc.. *4981*

C2C ABSTRACTS: JAPAN - ORGANIC CHEMISTRY.
Scan C2C, 1001 Pennsylvania Ave., N.W., No.
1300, Washington, DC 20024-2505. TEL 800-
525-3865. FAX 202-863-3855.
Producer(s): Knight-Ridder, Inc.. *1708*

C2C ABSTRACTS: JAPAN - PHYSICAL CHEMISTRY.
Scan C2C, 1001 Pennsylvania Ave., N.W., No.
1300, Washington, DC 20024-2505. TEL 800-
525-3865. FAX 202-863-3855.
Producer(s): Knight-Ridder, Inc.. *1708*

C2C ABSTRACTS: JAPAN - PLASTICS.
Scan C2C, 1001 Pennsylvania Ave., N.W., No.
1300, Washington, DC 20024-2505. TEL 800-
525-3865. FAX 202-863-3855.
Producer(s): Knight-Ridder, Inc.. *5528*

C2C ABSTRACTS: JAPAN - POLYMER CHEMISTRY.
Scan C2C, 1001 Pennsylvania Ave., N.W., No.
1300, Washington, DC 20024-2505. TEL 800-
525-3865. FAX 202-863-3855.
Producer(s): Knight-Ridder, Inc.. *1708*

C2C ABSTRACTS: JAPAN - SURFACE CHEMISTRY.
Scan C2C, 1001 Pennsylvania Ave., N.W., No.
1300, Washington, DC 20024-2505. TEL 800-
525-3865. FAX 202-863-3855.
Producer(s): Knight-Ridder, Inc.. *1708*

C2C ABSTRACTS: JAPAN - TEXTILES
Scan C2C, 1001 Pennsylvania Ave., N.W., No.
1300, Washington, DC 20024-2025. TEL 800-
525-3865. FAX 202-863-3855.
Producer(s): Knight-Ridder, Inc.. *6690*

C2C CURRENTS: JAPAN - CHEMISTRY.
Scan C2C, 1001 Pennsylvania Ave., N.W., No.
1300, Washington, DC 20024-2025. TEL 800-
525-3865. FAX 202-863-3855.
Producer(s): Knight-Ridder, Inc.. *1709*

C2C CURRENTS: JAPAN - COMPUTERS.
Scan C2C, 1001 Pennsylvania Ave., N.W., No.
1300, Washington, DC 20024-2025. TEL 800-
525-3865. FAX 202-863-3855.
Producer(s): Knight-Ridder, Inc.. *2002*

C2C CURRENTS: JAPAN - ELECTRONICS.
Scan C2C, 1001 Pennsylvania Ave., N.W., No.
1300, Washington, DC 20024-2505. TEL 800-
525-3865. FAX 202-863-3855.
Producer(s): Knight-Ridder, Inc.. *2510*

C2C CURRENTS: JAPAN - MATERIALS.
Scan C2C, 1001 Pennsylvania Ave., N.W., No.
1300, Washington, DC 20024-2505. TEL 800-
525-3865. FAX 202-863-3855.
Producer(s): Knight-Ridder, Inc.. *2626*

D L A P S.
U.S. Defense Logistics Agency, 8725 John J.
Kingman Rd., Ste. 2533, Fort Belvoir, VA 22060-
6221.
Available only on CD-ROM. *5931*

**D M S MARKET INTELLIGENCE REPORTS:
AIRBORNE ELECTRONICS.**
Forecast International Inc. - D M S, 22 Commerce
Rd., Newtown, CT 06470. TEL 203-426-0800.
FAX 203-426-0223. *2510*

**D M S MARKET INTELLIGENCE REPORTS:
AIRBORNE RETROFIT AND MODERNIZATION.**
Forecast International Inc. - D M S, 22 Commerce
Rd., Newtown, CT 06470. TEL 203-426-0800.
FAX 203-426-1964. *62*

**D M S MARKET INTELLIGENCE REPORTS:
AIRCRAFT: CIVIL AND MILITARY.**
Forecast International - D M S, 22 Commerce Rd.,
Newtown, CT 06470. TEL 203-426-0800.
FAX 203-426-0223. *62*

**D M S MARKET INTELLIGENCE REPORTS: "AN"
EQUIPMENT.**
Forecast International Inc. - D M S, 22 Commerce
Rd., Newtown, CT 06470. TEL 203-426-0800.
FAX 203-426-0223. *5026*

**D M S MARKET INTELLIGENCE REPORTS: ANTI-
SUBMARINE WARFARE.**
Forecast International Inc. - D M S, 22 Commerce
Rd., Newtown, CT 06470. TEL 203-426-0800.
FAX 203-426-0233. *5026*

D M S MARKET INTELLIGENCE REPORTS: C 3 I.
Forecast International Inc. - D M S, 22 Commerce
Rd., Newtown, CT 06470. TEL 203-426-0800.
FAX 203-426-0223. *5026*

**D M S MARKET INTELLIGENCE REPORTS: CIVIL
AIRCRAFT.**
Forecast International Inc. - D M S, 22 Commerce
Rd., Newtown, CT 06470. TEL 203-426-0800.
FAX 203-426-0223. *62*

**D M S MARKET INTELLIGENCE REPORTS: DEFENSE
AND AEROSPACE COMPANIES.**
Forecast International Inc. - D M S, 22 Commerce
Rd., Newtown, CT 06470. TEL 203-426-0800.
FAX 203-426-2033. *5026*

**D M S MARKET INTELLIGENCE REPORTS: ELECTRO-
OPTICAL SYSTEMS.**
Forecast International Inc. - D M S, 22 Commerce
Rd., Newtown, CT 06470. TEL 203-426-0800.
FAX 203-426-0223. *2510*

**D M S MARKET INTELLIGENCE REPORTS:
ELECTRONIC SYSTEMS.**
Forecast International Inc. - D M S, 22 Commerce
Rd., Newtown, CT 06470. TEL 203-426-0800.
FAX 203-426-0223. *5027*

**D M S MARKET INTELLIGENCE REPORTS:
ELECTRONIC WARFARE.**
Forecast International Inc. - D M S, 22 Commerce
Rd., Newtown, CT 06470. TEL 203-426-0800.
FAX 203-426-0223. *5027*

**D M S MARKET INTELLIGENCE REPORTS: FOREIGN
MILITARY MARKETS: ASIA, AUSTRALIA & PACIFIC
RIM.**
Forecast International Inc. - D M S, 22 Commerce
Rd., Newtown, CT 06470. TEL 203-426-0800.
FAX 203-426-0223. *5027*

**D M S MARKET INTELLIGENCE REPORTS: FOREIGN
MILITARY MARKETS: LATIN AMERICA &
CARIBBEAN.**
Forecast International Inc. - D M S, 22 Commerce
Rd., Newtown, CT 06470. TEL 203-426-0800.
FAX 203-426-0233. *5027*

**D M S MARKET INTELLIGENCE REPORTS: FOREIGN
MILITARY MARKETS: MIDDLE EAST & AFRICA.**
Forecast International Inc. - D M S, 22 Commerce
Rd., Newtown, CT 06470. TEL 203-426-0800.
FAX 203-426-0233. *5027*

**D M S MARKET INTELLIGENCE REPORTS: FOREIGN
MILITARY MARKETS: N A T O & EUROPE.**
Forecast International Inc. - D M S, 22 Commerce
Rd., Newtown, CT 06470. TEL 203-426-0800.
FAX 203-426-2033. *5027*

**D M S MARKET INTELLIGENCE REPORTS: GAS
TURBINE.**
Forecast International Inc. - D M S, 22 Commerce
Rd., Newtown, CT 06470. TEL 203-426-0800.
FAX 203-426-0223. *5027*

**D M S MARKET INTELLIGENCE REPORTS:
INTERNATIONAL CONTRACTORS.**
Forecast International Inc. - D M S, 22 Commerce
Rd., Newtown, CT 06470. TEL 203-426-0800.
FAX 203-426-0223. *5027*

**D M S MARKET INTELLIGENCE REPORTS: LAND
AND SEA-BASED ELECTRONICS.**
Forecast International Inc. - D M S, 22 Commerce
Rd., Newtown, PA 06470. TEL 203-426-0800.
FAX 203-426-0223. *2510*

**D M S MARKET INTELLIGENCE REPORTS: MILITARY
AIRCRAFT.**
Forecast International Inc. - D M S, 22 Commerce
Rd., Newtown, CT 06470. TEL 203-426-0800.
FAX 203-426-0223. *5027*

**D M S MARKET INTELLIGENCE REPORTS: MILITARY
FORCE STRUCTURES OF THE WORLD.**
Forecast International Inc. - D M S, 22 Commerce
Rd., Newtown, CT 06470. TEL 203-426-0800.
FAX 203-426-0223. *5027*

**D M S MARKET INTELLIGENCE REPORTS: MILITARY
VEHICLES.**
Forecast International Inc. - D M S, 22 Commerce
Rd., Newtown, CT 06470. TEL 203-426-0800.
FAX 203-426-0223. *5027*

D M S MARKET INTELLIGENCE REPORTS: MISSILES.
Forecast International Inc. - D M S, 22 Commerce
Rd., Newtown, CT 06470. TEL 203-426-0800.
FAX 203-426-1964. *5027*

**D M S MARKET INTELLIGENCE REPORTS:
ORDNANCE & MUNITIONS.**
Forecast International Inc. - D M S, 22 Commerce
Rd., Newtown, CT 06470. TEL 203-426-0800.
FAX 203-426-0233. *5027*

D M S MARKET INTELLIGENCE REPORTS: RADAR.
Forecast International Inc. - D M S, 22 Commerce
Rd., Newtown, CT 06470. TEL 203-426-0800.
FAX 203-426-0233. *5027*

**D M S MARKET INTELLIGENCE REPORTS: SPACE
SYSTEMS.**
Forecast International Inc. - D M S, 22 Commerce
Rd., Newtown, CT 06470. TEL 203-426-0800.
FAX 203-426-0233. *5027*

**D M S MARKET INTELLIGENCE REPORTS: U S
DEFENSE BUDGET.**
Forecast International Inc. - D M S, 22 Commerce
Rd., Newtown, CT 06470. TEL 203-426-0800.
FAX 203-426-0223. *5027*

**D M S MARKET INTELLIGENCE REPORTS:
UNMANNED VEHICLES.**
Forecast International Inc. - D M S, 22 Commerce
Rd., Newtown, CT 06470. TEL 203-426-0800.
FAX 203-426-0233. *5027*

**D M S MARKET INTELLIGENCE REPORTS:
WARSHIPS.**
Forecast International Inc. - D M S, 22 Commerce
Rd., Newtown, CT 06470. TEL 203-426-0800.
FAX 203-426-0223. *5027*

**D M S MARKET INTELLIGENCE REPORTS: WORLD
AIRLINE MAINTENANCE.**
Forecast International Inc. - D M S, 22 Commerce
St., Newtown, CT 06470. TEL 203-426-0800.
FAX 203-426-0223. *62*

**D M S MARKET INTELLIGENCE REPORTS: WORLD
COMMERCIAL AIRCRAFT - ENGINE ORDERS &
OPTIONS.**
Forecast International Inc. - D M S, 22 Commerce
Rd., Newtown, CT 06470. TEL 203-426-0800.
FAX 203-426-0223. *62*

DAILY MAIL.
Associated Newspaper Holdings PLC, 2 Derry St.,
Kensington, London W8 5TT, England. TEL 44-171-
938-6000. FAX 44-171-938-4890.
Producer(s): Chadwyck-Healey Inc.. *3154*

DAILY TELEGRAPH.
Telegraph plc., 1 Canada Sq., Canary Wharf, London
E14 5DT, England. TEL 44-171-538-5000.
FAX 44-171-538-6242.
Producer(s): Chadwyck-Healey Inc.. *3154*

DAKAR MEDICAL.
Societe Medicale d'Afrique Noire de Langue
Francaise, B.P. 450, Dakar, Senegal. *4447*

DANISH YEARBOOK OF PHILOSOPHY.
Museum Tusculanum Press, University of
Copenhagen, Njalsgade 92, DK-2300 Copenhagen
S, Denmark. TEL 45-35-32-91-09. FAX 45-35-32-
91-13. *5472*

DANSK ARTIKELINDEKS: AVISER OG TIDSSKRIFTER.
Dansk BiblioteksCenter as, Tempovej 7-11, DK-
2750 Ballerup, Denmark. TEL 45-44-867777.
FAX 45-44-867892. *3714*

DANSK LYDFORTEGNELSE.
Dansk BiblioteksCenter as, Tempovej 7-11, DK-
2750 Ballerup, Denmark. TEL 45-44-867777.
FAX 45-44-867892. *5208*

DANSKE KOMMUNER.
Kommunernes Landsforening, Gyldenloevesgade 11,
1600 Copenhagen V, Denmark. TEL 45-31-
122788. FAX 45-31-122785. *5940*

**DATA BASE OF DEFINED CONTRIBUTION AND
DEFINED BENEFIT PLANS.**
Judy Diamond Associates, Inc., 1730 M St., N.W.,
Ste. 1025, Washington, DC 20036. TEL 202-728-
0840. FAX 202-728-0845. *3647*

DATA-INFO.
Marketons B.V., Postbus 1310, 6501 BH Nijmegen,
Netherlands. TEL 31-24-3224200. FAX 31-24-
3603176. *2032*

DATAPRO SOFTWARE FINDER.
Datapro Information Services Group 600 Delran
Pkwy., Delran, NJ 08075.
Available only on CD-ROM. *2109*

DATAWORLD.
Faulkner Information Services, Inc., 114 Cooper
Center, 7905 Browning Rd., Pennsauken, NJ
08109-4319. TEL 609-662-2070. FAX 609-662-
3380. *2073*

DAYTON BUSINESS REPORTER.
Hannover Publishing Co., Inc., 6356 Far Hills Ave.,
Dayton, OH 45459-2782. TEL 513-291-1100.
FAX 513-436-3426.
Producer(s): University Microfilms International.
913

LES DEBROUILLARDS.
Publications BLD, 3995 rue Sainte-Catherine Est,
Montreal, PQ H1W 2G7, Canada. TEL 514-522-
1304. FAX 514-522-1761. *1789*

DEFENCE DOCUMENTS MICROFILE.
Technical Indexes Ltd., Willoughby Rd., Bracknell,
Berks. RG12 8DW, England. TEL 44-1344-
426311. FAX 44-1344-424971. *5028*

DEFENSE COUNSEL JOURNAL.
International Association of Defense Counsel, 1 N.
Franklin St., Ste. 2400, Chicago, IL 60606-3401.
TEL 312-368-1494. FAX 312-368-1854.
Producer(s): University Microfilms International.
3882

DELAWARE BUSINESS DIRECTORY.
American Business Directories 5711 S. 86th Circle,
Box 27347, Omaha, NE 68127. TEL 402-593-
4600. FAX 402-331-5481. *1595*

DELAWARE MANUFACTURERS REGISTER.
Manufacturers' News, Inc., 1633 Central St.,
Evanston, IL 60201-1569. TEL 847-864-7000.
FAX 847-332-1100. *1595*

DELAWARE REPORTER.
West Publishing Corp., 620 Opperman Dr., Eagan,
MN 55123. TEL 612-687-8000. FAX 612-687-
7302. *3767*

DELPHI INFORMANT.
Informant Communications Group, Inc., 10519 E.
Stockton Blvd., Ste 142, Elk Grove, CA 95624-
9704. TEL 916-686-6610. FAX 916-686-8497.
2043

DESIGN AND APPLIED ARTS INDEX.
Design Documentation, Old Manor Lodge, Bodiam, Robertsbridge, E. Sussex TN32 5UJ, England. TEL 0580-830877. FAX 0435-863184. *462*

DESIGN NEWS O E M DIRECTORY.
Cahners Publishing Company (Newton), Division of Reed Elsevier Inc., 275 Washington St., Newton, MA 02158-1630. TEL 617-964-3030. FAX 617-558-4402.
Available only on CD-ROM. *4337*

DEUTSCH - DEUTSCHE RECHTS ZEITSCHRIFT.
C.H. Beck'sche Verlagsbuchhandlung, Wilhelmstr. 9, 80801 Munich, Germany. TEL 089-38189338. FAX 089-38189398. *3768*

DEUTSCHE FACHPRESSE C D - R O M.
Buchhaendler-Vereinigung GmbH, Postfach 100442, 60004 Frankfurt a.M., Germany. TEL 49-69-1306-0. FAX 49-69-1306201.
Available only on CD-ROM. *529*

DEUTSCHE NATIONALBIBLIOGRAPHIE (C D - R O M AKTUELL).
Buchhaendler-Vereinigung GmbH, Postfach 100442, 60004 Frankfurt a.M., Germany. TEL 49-69-1306-243. FAX 49-69-1306201.
Available only on CD-ROM. Producer(s): Chadwyck-Healey Inc.. *529*

DEUTSCHE NATIONALBIBLIOGRAPHIE MUSIK C D - R O M.
Buchhaendler-Vereinigung GmbH, Postfach 100442, 60004 Frankfurt a.M., Germany. TEL 49-69-1306-0. FAX 49-69-1306201.
Available only on CD-ROM. *5208*

DEVOIR.
2050 rue de Bleury, 9e etage, Montreal, PQ H3A 3M9, Canada. TEL 514-985-3333. *3120*

DHAKA UNIVERSITY STUDIES. PART B: SCIENCE.
University of Dhaka, Ramna, Dhaka 1000, Bangladesh. *6237*

DIAGNOSTIC IMAGING & RADIOLOGY PRODUCT COMPARISON SYSTEM.
E C R I, 5200 Butler Pike, Plymouth Meeting, PA 19462. TEL 610-825-6000. FAX 610-834-1275. Producer(s): Knight-Ridder, Inc.. *4875*

DIALOG ONDISC CHEMICAL BUSINESS NEWSBASE.
The Royal Society of Chemistry, Thomas Graham House, Science Park, Milton Rd., Cambridge CB4 4WF, England. TEL 01223-420066. FAX 01223-423623.
Available only on CD-ROM. *1673*

DIALOG ONDISC ENVIRONMENTAL CHEMISTRY, HEALTH AND SAFETY.
The Royal Society of Chemistry, Thomas Graham House, Science Park, Milton Rd., Cambridge CB4 4WF, England. TEL 01223-420066. FAX 01223-423623.
Available only on CD-ROM. *2844*

DICTIONNAIRE JOLY SOCIETES.
G L N - Joly Editions, 1 av. Franklin D. Roosevelt, 75008 Paris, France. TEL 44-95-16-20. FAX 45-63-89-39. *1413*

DICTIONNAIRE VIDAL.
O.V.P. - Editions du Vidal, 11 rue Quentin Bauchart, 75008 Paris, France. TEL 47-23-90-91. FAX 47-20-72-89. *5407*

DIGITAL NEWS & REVIEW.
Cahners Publishing Company (Newton), Division of Reed Elsevier Inc., 275 Washington St., Newton, MA 02158-1630. TEL 617-964-3030. FAX 617-558-4759. *2086*

DIODE D.A.T.A. DIGEST.
D.A.T.A. Business Publishing 15 Inverness Way E., Box 6510, Englewood, CO 80155-6510. FAX 303-799-4082. *2511*

DIRECTORY OF AMERICAN RESEARCH AND TECHNOLOGY.
R.R. Bowker, A Division of Reed Elsevier Inc., 121 Chanlon Rd., New Providence, NJ 07974. TEL 908-464-6800. FAX 908-665-6688.
Producer(s): Bowker Electronic Publishing. *6649*

DIRECTORY OF CALIFORNIA TECHNOLOGY COMPANIES.
Database Publishing Company, 1590 S. Lewis St., Anaheim, CA 92805-6423. TEL 714-778-6400. FAX 714-778-6811. *1597*

DIRECTORY OF CALIFORNIA WHOLESALERS AND SERVICE COMPANIES.
Database Publishing Company, 1590 S. Lewis St., Anaheim, CA 92805-6423. TEL 714-778-6400. FAX 714-778-6811 *1597*

DIRECTORY OF CHAIN RESTAURANT OPERATORS (YEAR).
C S G Information Services 3922 Coconut Palm Dr., Tampa, FL 33619. TEL 813-664-6800. FAX 813-664-6882. *1597*

DIRECTORY OF CHEMICAL PRODUCERS - CANADA.
S R I International, Process Industries Division, Chemical Marketing Research Center, Menlo Park, CA 94025. TEL 415-859-3627. FAX 415-859-4623. *1673*

DIRECTORY OF CHEMICAL PRODUCERS - CHINA.
S R I International, Process Industries Division, Chemical Marketing Research Center, Menlo Park, CA 94025. TEL 415-859-3627. FAX 415-859-4623. *1673*

DIRECTORY OF CHEMICAL PRODUCERS - EAST ASIA.
S R I International, Process Industries Division, Chemical Marketing Research Center, Menlo Park, CA 94025. TEL 415-859-3627. FAX 415-859-4623. *1673*

DIRECTORY OF CHEMICAL PRODUCERS - MEXICO.
S R I International, Process Industries Division, Chemical Marketing Research Center, Menlo Park, CA 94025. TEL 415-859-3627. FAX 415-859-4623. *1673*

DIRECTORY OF CHEMICAL PRODUCERS - MIDDLE EAST.
S R I International, Process Industries Division, Chemical Marketing Research Center, Menlo Park, CA 94025. TEL 415-859-3627. FAX 415-859-4623. *1673*

DIRECTORY OF CHEMICAL PRODUCERS - SOUTH AMERICA.
S R I International, Process Industries Division, Chemical Marketing Research Center, Menlo Park, CA 94025. TEL 415-859-3627. FAX 415-859-4623. *1673*

DIRECTORY OF CHEMICAL PRODUCERS - UNITED STATES.
S R I International, Process Industries Division, Chemical Marketing Research Center, Menlo Park, CA 94025. TEL 415-859-3627. FAX 415-859-4623. *1674*

DIRECTORY OF CHEMICAL PRODUCERS - WESTERN EUROPE.
S R I International, Process Industries Division, Chemical Marketing Research Center, Menlo Park, CA 94025. TEL 415-859-3627. FAX 415-859-4623. *1674*

DIRECTORY OF COMPUTER RETAILERS, DEALERS & DISTRIBUTORS (YEAR).
C S G Information Services 3922 Coconut Palm Dr., Tampa, FL 33619. TEL 813-664-6800. FAX 813-664-6882. *2034*

DIRECTORY OF CORPORATE AFFILIATIONS.
National Register Publishing, A Division of Reed Elsevier Inc., 121 Chanlon Rd., New Providence, NJ 07974. TEL 908-464-6800. FAX 908-771-7704. Producer(s): Bowker Electronic Publishing. *1598*

DIRECTORY OF ENGINEERING GRADUATE STUDIES AND RESEARCH.
American Society for Engineering Education, 1818 N St., N.W., Ste. 600, Washington, DC 20036. TEL 202-331-3500. FAX 202-265-8504. *2594*

DIRECTORY OF FLORIDA INDUSTRIES.
Harris InfoSource International, 2057 E. Aurora Rd., Twinsburg, OH 44087-1999. TEL 216-425-9000. FAX 216-425-7150. *1599*

DIRECTORY OF HISTORY DEPARTMENTS AND ORGANIZATIONS (YEAR).
American Historical Association, 400 A St., S.E., Washington, DC 20003-3389. TEL 202-544-2422. FAX 202-544-8307. *2411*

DIRECTORY OF LIBRARIES IN CANADA.
Micromedia Ltd., 20 Victoria St., Toronto, ON M5C 2N8, Canada. TEL 416-362-5211. FAX 416-362-6161. *3989*

DIRECTORY OF LOUISIANA MANUFACTURERS.
Harris InfoSource International, 2057 Aurora Rd., Twinsburg, OH 44087. TEL 216-425-9000. FAX 800-643-5997. *1621*

DIRECTORY OF RESEARCH GRANTS.
Oryx Press, 4041 N. Central Ave., No. 700, Phoenix, AZ 85012-3397. TEL 602-265-2651. FAX 602-265-6250.
Producer(s): Knight-Ridder, Inc.. *2427*

DIRECTORY OF TEXAS MANUFACTURERS.
University of Texas at Austin, Bureau of Business Research, Box 7459, Austin, TX 78713. TEL 512-471-1616. FAX 512-471-1063. *1602*

DIRECTORY OF U.S. SUBSIDIARIES OF BRITISH COMPANIES.
British - American Chamber of Commerce, 52 Vanderbilt Ave., Ste. 20, New York, NY 10017-3808. TEL 212-661-4060. *1139*

DIRECTORY OF UNITED STATES EXPORTERS.
Journal of Commerce, Inc. 2 World Trade Center, 27th Fl., New York, NY 10048-0203. TEL 212-837-7000. FAX 212-837-7035. *1271*

DISCONTINUED DISCRETE SEMICONDUCTORS D.A.T.A. DIGEST.
D.A.T.A. Business Publishing 15 Inverness Way E., Box 6510, Englewood, CO 30155-6510. FAX 303-799-4082. *2511*

DISCONTINUED I CS D.A.T.A. DIGEST.
D.A.T.A. Business Publishing 15 Inverness Way E., Box 6510, Englewood, CO 80155-6510. FAX 303-799-4082. *2511*

DISSERTATION ABSTRACTS INTERNATIONAL. SECTION A: HUMANITIES AND SOCIAL SCIENCES.
U M I Company 300 N. Zeeb Rd., Ann Arbor, MI 48106. TEL 313-761-4700. FAX 300-864-0019. Producer(s): University Microfilms International. *3632*

DISSERTATION ABSTRACTS INTERNATIONAL. SECTION B: PHYSICAL SCIENCES AND ENGINEERING.
U M I Company 300 N. Zeeb Rd., Ann Arbor, MI 48106. TEL 313-761-4700. FAX 800-864-0019 Producer(s): University Microfilms International. *6301*

DISSERTATION ABSTRACTS INTERNATIONAL. SECTION C: WORLDWIDE.
U M I Company 300 N. Zeeb Rd., Ann Arbor, MI 48106 TEL 313-761-4700 FAX 800-864-0019. Producer(s): University Microfilms International. *3632*

DISSERTATION ABSTRACTS ON DISC.
U M I Company 300 N. Zeeb Rd., Ann Arbor, MI 48016-1304. TEL 313-761-4700. FAX 800-864-0019.
Producer(s): University Microfilms International. *3632*

DISTRIBUTED COMPUTING MONITOR.
Patricia Seybold Group, 148 State St., 7th Fl., Boston, MA 02109. TEL 617-742-5200. FAX 617-742-1028. *2055*

DOMESTIC CARS SERVICE & REPAIR.
Mitchell International, Inc., 9389 Willow Creek Rd., Box 26260, San Diego, CA 92196-0260. FAX 619-578-4752. *6783*

DOMESTIC LIGHT TRUCKS & VANS SERVICE & REPAIR.
Mitchell International, Inc., 9389 Willow Creek Rd., Box 26260, San Diego, CA 92196-0260. TEL 800-648-8010. FAX 619-578-4752. *6783*

CD-ROM

DOMINION TAX CASES.
C C H Canadian Ltd., 6 Garamond Ct., North York, ON M3C 1Z5, Canada. TEL 416-441-2992. FAX 416-444-9011. *1542*

DOWNSTATE ILLINOIS BUSINESS DIRECTORY.
American Business Directories 5711 S. 86th Circle, Box 27347, Omaha, NE 68127. TEL 402-593-4600. FAX 402-331-5481. *1603*

DRUG DATA REPORT.
J.R. Prous, S.A. International Publishers, Apdo. de Correos 540, 08080 Barcelona, Spain. TEL 343-459-2220. FAX 343-458-1535. *5408*

DRUG NEWS & PERSPECTIVES.
J.R. Prous, S.A. International Publishers, Apdo. de Correos 540, 08080 Barcelona, Spain. TEL 343-459-2220. FAX 343-458-1535. *5409*

DRUGS OF THE FUTURE.
J.R. Prous, S.A. International Publishers, Apdo. de Correos 540, 08080 Barcelona, Spain. TEL 343-459-2220. FAX 343-458-1535. *5410*

DRYDEN OBSERVER.
Alex Wilson Coldstream Ltd., Colonization St., Dryden, ON P8N 2Y9, Canada. FAX 807-223-2907. *3120*

DUQUESNE LAW REVIEW.
Duquesne University, Duquesne School of Law, 900 Locust St., Pittsburgh, PA 15282. TEL 412-396-6297. FAX 412-396-6294. *3772*

E D I FORUM.
E D I Group, Ltd., Box 710, Oak Park, IL 60302. TEL 708-848-0135. FAX 708-848-0270. *2068*

E E M.
Hearst Business Publishing UTP Division, Attn. Georgeann Amsler, Mktg. Mgr., 645 Stewart Ave., Garden City, NY 11530. TEL 516-227-1300. FAX 516-227-1453. *2512*

E FOR ENVIRONMENT.
R.R. Bowker, A Division of Reed Elsevier Inc., 121 Chanlon Rd., New Providence, NJ 07974. TEL 908-464-6800. FAX 908-665-6688. *2782*

E I S.
Cambridge Scientific Abstracts, 7200 Wisconsin Ave., 6th Fl., Bethesda, MD 20814. TEL 301-961-6750. FAX 301-961-6720. Producer(s): Knight-Ridder, Inc., NISC, SilverPlatter Information, Inc.. *2828*

E I U NEWSLETTERS.
Economist Intelligence Unit, 111 W. 57th St., New York, NY 10019. TEL 212-554-0600. FAX 212-586-1182. *915*

E M F - E M I CONTROL.
E E C Press, 6193 Finchingfield Rd., Gainesville, VA 22065. TEL 540-347-0030. FAX 540-347-5813. *6649*

E R I C ON C D - R O M.
National Information Services Corporation (NISC), Ste. 6, Wyman Towers, 3100 St. Paul St., Batimore, MD 21218. TEL 410-243-0797. FAX 410-243-0982. Available only on CD-ROM. Producer(s): NISC. *2388*

E U D I S E D - EUROPEAN EDUCATIONAL RESEARCH YEARBOOK.
K.G. Saur Verlag KG, A member of the Reed Elsevier plc group, Ortlerstr. 8, 81373 Munich, Germany. TEL 49-89-76902-0. FAX 49-89-76902150. *2388*

E Z A - ENTSCHEIDUNGSSAMMLUNG ZUM ARBEITSRECHT.
Luchterhand Verlag, Heddesdorferstr. 31, 56564 Neuwied, Germany. TEL 49-2631-801-0. FAX 49-2631-801204. *3900*

EARTHQUAKE ENGINEERING ABSTRACTS DATABASE.
University of California at Berkeley, Earthquake Engineering Research Center, 1301 S. 46th St., Richmond, CA 94804-4698. TEL 510-231-9401. FAX 510-231-9461. Producer(s): NISC (Earthquakes and the Built Environment Index). *2627*

EARTHQUAKE HISTORY OF THE UNITED STATES.
U.S. National Geophysical Data Center, 325 Broadway, Boulder, CO 80303-3328. TEL 303-497-6826. FAX 303-497-6513. *2272*

THE EAST AFRICAN MEDICAL JOURNAL.
Kenya Medical Association House, Chyulu Rd., P.O. Box 41632, Nairobi, Kenya. TEL 254-2-712010. FAX 254-2-724617. *4450*

EBONY.
Johnson Publishing Co., Inc., 820 S. Michigan Ave., Chicago, IL 60605. TEL 312-322-9200. FAX 312-322-9375. Producer(s): University Microfilms International. *2876*

ECO DEL MANTE.
Guerrero 701 Ote., 89800 Mante, Tamaulipas, Mexico. TEL 91-123-22420. FAX 91-123-24784. *3192*

ECOLOGY ABSTRACTS.
Cambridge Scientific Abstracts, 7200 Wisconsin Ave., 6th Fl., Bethesda, MD 20814. TEL 301-961-6750. FAX 301-961-6720. Producer(s): NISC, SilverPlatter Information, Inc.. *2828*

ECONOMIC REPORT OF THE PRESIDENT.
U.S. Executive Office of the President, Council of Economic Advisers, Washington, DC 20500. TEL 202-395-7332. *1206*

THE ECONOMIST.
Economist Newspaper Ltd., 25 St. James's St., London SW1A 1HG, England. TEL 44-171-830-7000. FAX 44-171-839-2968. Producer(s): Chadwyck-Healey Inc.. *1207*

ECONOMIST. ANNUAL INDEX.
Economist Newspaper Ltd., 25 St. James's St., London SW1A 1HG, England. TEL 44-171-830-7000. FAX 44-171-839-2968. Producer(s): Chadwyck-Healey Inc.. *1207*

THE ECONOMIST ON C D - R O M.
Chadwyck-Healey Ltd., The Quorum, Barnwell Rd., Cambridge CB5 8SW, England. TEL 44-1223-215512. FAX 44-1223-215514. Available only on CD-ROM. Producer(s): Chadwyck-Healey Inc.. *1208*

EDITOR & PUBLISHER INTERNATIONAL YEAR BOOK.
Editor & Publisher Co., Inc., 11 W. 19th St., New York, NY 10011. TEL 212-675-4380. FAX 212-929-1259. *1902*

EDITOR & PUBLISHER MARKET GUIDE.
Editor & Publisher Co., Inc., 11 W. 19th St., New York, NY 10011. TEL 212-675-4380. FAX 212-929-1259. *1463*

THE EDMONTON JOURNAL.
P.O. Box 2421, Edmonton, AB T5J 2S6, Canada. TEL 403-429-5100. FAX 403-429-5500. *3120*

THE EDUCATION DIGEST.
Prakken Publications, Inc., Box 8623, Ann Arbor, MI 48107. TEL 313-769-1211. FAX 313-769-8383. Producer(s): University Microfilms International. *2328*

EDUCATION ET FRANCOPHONIE.
Association Canadienne d'Education de Langue Francaise, 268 rue Marie-de-l'Incarnation, Quebec, PQ G1N 3G4, Canada. TEL 418-681-4661. FAX 418-681-3389. *2328*

EDUCATION INDEX.
H.W. Wilson Co., 950 University Ave., Bronx, NY 10452. TEL 718-590-8400. FAX 718-590-1617. Producer(s): SilverPlatter Information, Inc., H.W. Wilson (WILSONDISC). *2388*

EGYPTIAN JOURNAL OF FOOD SCIENCE.
National Information and Documentation Centre (NIDOC), Tahrir St., Dokki, Awqaf P.O., Cairo, Egypt. TEL 20-2-701696. *5231*

EGYPTIAN JOURNAL OF PHARMACEUTICAL SCIENCES.
National Information and Documentation Centre (NIDOC), Tahrir St., Dokki, Awqaf P.O., Cairo, Egypt. TEL 20-2-701696. *5410*

EGYPTIAN JOURNAL OF VETERINARY SCIENCE.
National Information and Documentation Centre (NIDOC), Tahrir St., Dokki, Awqaf P.O., Cairo, Egypt. TEL 20-2-701696. *6945*

EGYPTIAN ORTHOPAEDIC JOURNAL.
Egyptian Orthopaedic Association, P.O. Box 4, Alexandria 21111, Egypt. TEL 20-3-4225626. *4783*

EINKAUFEN IN EUROPA CD.
Herold Business Data GmbH, Guntramsdorferstr. 105, A-2340 Moedling, Austria. TEL 02236-4010. FAX 02236-4018. Available only on CD-ROM. *1463*

EINKAUFS DATA.
Herold Business Data GmbH, Guntramsdorferstr. 105, A-2340 Moedling, Austria. TEL 02236-401. FAX 02236-4018. *1464*

EINKAUFS 1X1 DER DEUTSCHEN INDUSTRIE.
Deutscher Adressbuch Verlag, Arheilger Weg 17, 64380 Rossdorf, Germany. TEL 06154-699500. FAX 06154-6995490. *1607*

DIE EISEN, BLECH UND METALL VERARBEITENDE INDUSTRIE, STAHLVERFORMUNG UND IHRE HELFER.
Industrieschau-Verlagsgesellschaft mbH, Postfach 100262, 64202 Darmstadt, Germany. TEL 49-6151-38920. FAX 49-6151-33164. *4954*

DIE EISEN-, STAHL- UND N E METALL-INDUSTRIE UND IHRE HELFER.
Industrieschau-Verlagsgesellschaft mbH, Postfach 100262, 64202 Darmstadt, Germany. TEL 49-6151-38920. FAX 49-6151-33164. *4954*

ELECTRE BIBLIO.
Electre, 35 rue Gregoire-de-Tours, 75006 Paris, France. TEL 44-41-28-00. FAX 44-41-28-65. Available only on CD-ROM. *6014*

ELECTRIC UTILITY WEEK.
McGraw-Hill, Inc., 1221 Ave. of the Americas, New York, NY 10020. TEL 212-512-6410. Producer(s): SilverPlatter Information, Inc. (McGraw-Hill Energy Library). *2691*

ELECTRIC UTILITY WEEK'S DEMAND-SIDE REPORT.
McGraw-Hill, Inc., 1221 Ave. of the Americas, New York, NY 10020. TEL 212-512-6410. Producer(s): SilverPlatter Information, Inc. (McGraw-Hill Energy Library). *2568*

ELECTRICAL & ELECTRONICS ABSTRACTS.
INSPEC, I.E.E., Michael Faraday House, Six Hill Way, Stevenage, Herts. SG1 2AY, England. TEL 44-1438-313311. FAX 44-1438-742840. *2627*

ELECTRICAL COMPONENT LOCATOR - DOMESTIC CARS, LIGHT TRUCKS & VANS.
Mitchell International, Inc., 9889 Willow Creek Rd., Box 26260, San Diego, CA 92196-0260. TEL 619-578-6550. FAX 619-578-4752. *6784*

ELECTRICAL COMPONENT LOCATOR - IMPORTED CARS, LIGHT TRUCKS & VANS.
Mitchell International, Inc., 9889 Willow Creek Rd., Box 26260, San Diego, CA 92196-0260. TEL 800-648-8010. FAX 619-578-4752. *6784*

ELECTRO.
Societe Nouvelle d'Editions Publicitaires, 16, Av. de Verdun, 75010 Paris, France. *2513*

ELECTRONIC ENGINEERING INDEX.
Technical Indexes Ltd., Willoughby Rd., Bracknell, Berks RG12 8DW, England. TEL 44-1344-426311. FAX 44-1344-424971. *2514*

ELECTRONIC JOURNAL OF THEORETICAL CHEMISTRY.
John Wiley & Sons Ltd., Journals, Baffins Ln., Chichester, W. Sussex PO19 1UD, England. TEL 44-1243-779777. FAX 44-1243-843232. *1715*

ELECTRONIC QUALITY ASSURANCE DOCUMENTS.
Technical Indexes Ltd., Willoughby Rd., Bracknell, Berkshire RG12 8DW, England. TEL 44-1344-426311. FAX 44-1344-424971. *2515*

DIE ELEKTRO-INDUSTRIE, ELEKTRONIK UND IHRE HELFER.
Industrieschau-Verlagsgesellschaft mbH, Postfach 100262, 64202 Darmstadt, Germany. TEL 49-6151-3892-0. FAX 49-6151-33164. *2518*

ELEMENTARY SCHOOL LIBRARY COLLECTION.
Brodart Co., 500 Arch St., Williamsport, PA 17705. FAX 717-326-6769. *3991*

EL-HI TEXTBOOKS AND SERIALS IN PRINT.
R.R. Bowker, A Division of Reed Elsevier Inc., 121 Chanlon Rd., New Providence, NJ 07974. TEL 908-464-6800. FAX 908-665-3502.
Producer(s): Bowker Electronic Publishing. *2388*

ELSEVIER SCIENCE. CATALOGUE - BOOKS.
Elsevier Science B.V., P.O. Box 211, 1000 AE Amsterdam, Netherlands. TEL 31-20-4853911. FAX 31-20-4853598. *6238*

ELSEVIER SCIENCE. CATALOGUE - JOURNALS.
Elsevier Science B.V., P.O. Box 211, 1000 AE Amsterdam, Netherlands. TEL 31-20-4853911. FAX 31-20-4853598. *6238*

ELSEVIER SCIENCE. CATALOGUE ON C D - R O M.
Elsevier Science B.V., P.O. Box 211, 1000 AE Amsterdam, Netherlands. TEL 31-20-4853911. FAX 31-20-4853598.
Available only on CD-ROM. *6238*

EMIRATES MEDICAL JOURNAL.
Emirates Medical Association, P.O. Box 6600, Dubai, United Arab Emirates. TEL 971-4-377377. FAX 971-4-344082. *4451*

EMPLOYEE BENEFITS MANAGEMENT.
Commerce Clearing House, Inc., 2700 Lake Cook Rd., Riverwoods, IL 60015. TEL 847-267-7000. FAX 800-224-8299. *1415*

EMPLOYMENT AND EARNINGS: UNITED STATES.
U.S. Bureau of Labor Statistics, 2 Massachusetts Ave., N.E., Washington, DC 20212. TEL 202-655-4000. *1208*

EMPLOYMENT LAW CASES.
Incomes Data Services Ltd., 193 St. John St., London EC1V 4LS, England. TEL 0171-250-3434. FAX 0171-608-0949.
Available only on CD-ROM. *1372*

ENCYCLOPEDIA OF ASSOCIATIONS.
Gale Research Inc., 835 Penobscot Bldg., Detroit, MI 48226. TEL 313-961-2242. FAX 313-961-6083. *2536*

ENCYCLOPEDIA OF SOCIAL WORK.
N A S W Press, 750 First St., N.E., Ste. 700, Washington, DC 20002-4241. TEL 202-408-8600. FAX 202-336-8312. *6370*

ENGINEERED MATERIALS ABSTRACTS.
Cambridge Scientific Abstracts, 7200 Wisconsin Ave., Bethesda, MD 20814. TEL 301-961-6750. FAX 301-961-6720.
Producer(s): Knight-Ridder, Inc.. *2627*

ENGINEERING INDEX ANNUAL.
Engineering Information, Inc., Castle Point on the Hudson, Hoboken, NJ 07030. TEL 201-216-8500. FAX 201-216-8532.
Producer(s): Knight-Ridder, Inc. (COMPENDEX PLUS CD-ROM). *2627*

ENGINEERING INDEX MONTHLY.
Engineering Information Inc., Castle Point on the Hudson, Hoboken, NJ 07030. TEL 201-216-8500. FAX 201-216-8532.
Producer(s): Knight-Ridder, Inc. (COMPENDEX PLUS CD-ROM). *2627*

ENSEMBLE.
Banque Internationale d'Information sur les Etats Francophones, 25 Eddy, Hull, ON K1A 0M5, Canada. TEL 819-997-3857. FAX 819-953-8439.
Available only on CD-ROM. *3992*

ENTOMOLOGY ABSTRACTS.
Cambridge Scientific Abstracts, 7200 Wisconsin Ave., 6th Fl., Bethesda, MD 20814. TEL 301-961-6750. FAX 301-961-6720.
Producer(s): NISC, SilverPlatter Information, Inc.. *620*

ENTREPRENEURSHIP: THEORY AND PRACTICE.
Baylor University, Hankamer School of Business, John F. Baugh Center for Entrepreneurship, BU Box 98011, Waco, TX 76798-8011. TEL 817-755-2265. FAX 817-755-2271. *1575*

ENVIRONMENT (WASHINGTON).
Heldref Publications, 1319 Eighteenth St., N.W., Washington, DC 20036-1802. TEL 202-296-6267. FAX 202-296-5149.
Producer(s): University Microfilms International. *2787*

ENVIRONMENT ABSTRACTS.
Congressional Information Service, Inc., A member of the LEXIS NEXIS family, 4520 East-West Hwy., Bethesda, MD 20814-3389. TEL 301-654-1550. FAX 301-654-4033. *2829*

ENVIRONMENT ABSTRACTS ANNUAL.
Congressional Information Service, Inc., A member of the LEXIS-NEXIS family, 4520 East-West Hwy., Ste. 800, Bethesda, MD 20814-3389. TEL 301-654-1550. FAX 301-654-4033. *2829*

ENVIRONMENT AND ECOLOGY.
M K K Publications, 91A Ananda Palit Rd., Calcutta, West Bengal 700 014, India. TEL 91-33-828220. *2787*

ENVIRONMENTAL ACTION.
Environmental Action Foundation, 6930 Carroll Ave., Ste. 600, Takoma Park, MD 20912. TEL 301-891-1106. FAX 301-891-2218.
Producer(s): University Microfilms International. *2788*

ENVIRONMENTAL HEALTH BRIEFING.
Barbour Index, New Lodge Drift Rd., Windsor, Berks. SL4 4RQ, England. TEL 01344-884121. FAX 01344-884112. *5958*

ENVIRONMENTAL PERIODICALS BIBLIOGRAPHY.
International Academy at Santa Barbara, 800 Garden St., Ste. D, Santa Barbara, CA 93101-1552. TEL 805-965-5010. FAX 805-965-6071.
Producer(s): NISC. *2829*

ENVIRONMENTAL PERIODICALS BIBLIOGRAPHY (C D - R O M).
National Information Services Corporation (NISC), Ste. 6, Wyman Towers, 3100 St. Paul St., Baltimore, MD 21218. TEL 410-243-0797. FAX 410-243-0982.
Available only on CD-ROM. Producer(s): NISC. *2829*

EPIDEMIOLOGICAL NEWS BULLETIN.
Ministry of Health, Committee on Epidemic Diseases, Quarantine & Epidemiology Dept., 40 Scotts Rd., Environment Bldg., Singapore 0922, Singapore. TEL 65-732-9758. FAX 65-731-9866. *4619*

ERGA.
Instituto Nacional de Seguridad e Higiene en el Trabajo, Ministerio de Trabajo y Seguridad Social, Calle Dulcet 2-10, 08034 Barcelona, Spain. FAX 34-3-2803642. *5260*

ERGONOMICS ABSTRACTS.
Taylor & Francis Ltd., 1 Gunpowder Sq., London EC4A 3DE, England. TEL 44-171-583-0490. FAX 44-171-583-0585. *2627*

ESSAY AND GENERAL LITERATURE INDEX.
H.W. Wilson Co., 950 University Ave., Bronx, NY 10452. TEL 718-588-8400. FAX 718-590-1617.
Producer(s): SilverPlatter Information, Inc., H.W. Wilson (WILSONDISC). *4293*

ESSENTIAL ECOLOGY, ZOOLOGY & PLANT SCIENCE ABSTRACTS.
National Information Services Corporation (NISC), Ste. 6, Wyman Towers, 3100 St. Paul St., Baltimore, MD 21218. TEL 410-243-0797. FAX 410-243-0982.
Available only on CD-ROM. Producer(s): NISC. *620*

ESSENTIAL FISHERIES ABSTRACTS.
National Information Services Corporation (NISC), Ste. 6, Wyman Towers, 3100 St. Paul St., Baltimore, MD 21218. TEL 410-243-0797. FAX 410-243-0982.
Available only on CD-ROM. Producer(s): NISC. *2947*

ESSENTIAL FORESTRY & WILDFIRE ABSTRACTS.
National Information Services Corporation (NISC), Ste. 6, Wyman Towers, 3100 St. Paul St., Baltimore, MD 21218. TEL 410-243-0797. FAX 410-243-0982.
Available only on CD-ROM. Producer(s): NISC. *3031*

ESSENTIAL ORNITHOLOGICAL ABSTRACTS.
National Information Services Corporation (NISC), Ste. 6, Wyman Towers, 3100 St. Paul St., Baltimore, MD 21218. TEL 410-243-0797. FAX 410-243-0982.
Available only on CD-ROM. Producer(s): NISC. *620*

ESSENTIAL WILDLIFE & CONSERVATION BIOLOGY ABSTRACTS.
National Information Services Corporation (NISC), Ste. 6, Wyman Towers, 3100 St. Paul St., Baltimore, MD 21218. TEL 410-243-0797. FAX 410-243-0982.
Available only on CD-ROM. Producer(s): NISC. *620*

ESTUARIES AND COASTAL WATERS OF THE BRITISH ISLES.
Plymouth Marine Laboratory, Citadel Hill, Plymouth PL1 2PB, England. TEL 44-1752-222772. FAX 44-1752-226865.
Producer(s): NISC (Oceanographic & Marine Resources). *620*

ETHIOPIAN MEDICAL JOURNAL.
Ethiopian Medical Association, P.O. Box 3472, Addis Ababa, Ethiopia. TEL 158174. *4452*

EURO-EAST.
Europe Information Service, Rue de Geneve, 6, 1140 Brussels, Belgium. TEL 32-2-242-6020. FAX 32-2-242-9410. *5743*

EURO O S H.
Chapman & Hall, 2-6 Boundary Row, London SE1 8HN, England. TEL 44-171-365-0066. FAX 44-171-5220101.
Available only on CD-ROM. *5248*

EUROCAT.
Chadwyck-Healey Ltd., The Quorum, Barnwell Rd., Cambridge CB5 8SW, England. TEL 44-1223-215512. FAX 44-1223-215514.
Available only on CD-ROM. Producer(s): Chadwyck-Healey Inc.. *5901*

EUROMONEY.
Euromoney Publications plc., Nestor House, Playhouse Yard, London EC4V 5EX, England. TEL 44-171-779-8935. FAX 44-171-779-8541. *1086*

EUROPAEISCHES PATENTAMT AMTSBLATT.
European Patent Office, Schottenfeldgasse 29, Postfach 82, A-1072 Vienna, Austria. TEL 01-521264051. FAX 01-521254192. *5338*

EUROPAGES.
Euredit s.a., 9, Avenue de Fredland, 75008 Paris, France. TEL 1-53-77-54-00. FAX 42-89-34-73. *1608*

EUROPE ENERGY.
Europe Information Service, Rue de Geneve, 6, 1140 Brussels, Belgium. TEL 32-2-242-6020. FAX 32-2-242-9410. *2548*

EUROPE ENVIRONMENT.
Europe Information Service, Rue de Geneve, 6, 1140 Brussels, Belgium. TEL 32-2-242-6020. FAX 32-2-242-9410. *2796*

EUROPEAN BOOK WORLD.
Andersor Rand Ltd., Scotts Bindery, Russell Ct., Cambridge CB2 1HL, England. TEL 44-1223-566640. FAX 44-1223-566643. *5995*

EUROPEAN CONVERTING INDUSTRY DIRECTORY.
Kingland House, 361 City Rd., London EC1V 1LR, England. TEL 44-171-417-7400. FAX 44-171-417-7500. *5321*

EUROPEAN JOURNAL OF BIOCHEMISTRY.
Springer-Verlag, Heidelberger Platz 3, 14197 Berlin, Germany. TEL 49-30-8207-0. FAX 49-30-8214091. *638*

CD-ROM

EUROPEAN JOURNAL OF BIOCHEMISTRY (C D - R O M).
Springer-Verlag, Heidelberger Platz 3, 14197 Berlin, Germany. TEL 49-30-8207-0. FAX 49-30-8214091.
Available only on CD-ROM. *638*

EUROPEAN JOURNAL OF CANCER PREVENTION.
Rapid Science Publishers, The Old Malthouse, Paradise St., Oxford OX1 1LD, England. TEL 44-1865-790447. FAX 44-1865-244012. *4755*

EUROPEAN JOURNAL OF GASTROENTEROLOGY AND HEPATOLOGY.
Rapid Science Publishers, 2-6 Boundary Row, London SE1 8HN, England. TEL 44-171-865-0198. FAX 44-171-410-6600. *4691*

EUROPEAN JOURNAL OF NEUROLOGY.
Rapid Science Publishers, 2-6 Boundary Row, London SE1 8HN, England. TEL 44-171-865-0198. FAX 44-171-410-6600. *4836*

EUROPEAN MANAGEMENT EDUCATION DIRECTORY.
E M D Centre, Naarderstraat 296, 1272 NT Huizen, Netherlands. TEL 31-35-6951111. FAX 31-35-6951900. *1416*

EUROPEAN MEDIA ART FESTIVAL.
International Experimental Film Workshop, Postfach 1861, 49008 Osnabrueck, Germany. TEL 49-541-21658. FAX 49-541-28327. *5100*

EUROPEAN REPORT.
Europe Information Service, Rue de Geneve, 6, 1140 Brussels, Belgium. TEL 32-2-242-6020. FAX 32-2-242-9410. *1087*

EUROPEAN SOCIAL POLICY.
Europe Information Service, Rue de Geneve, 6, 1140 Brussels, Belgium. TEL 32-2-242-6020. FAX 32-2-242-9410. *5749*

EUROPEAN TAXATION.
I B F D Publications B.V., P.O. Box 20237, 1000 HE Amsterdam, Netherlands. TEL 31-20-6267726. FAX 31-20-6228658. *1543*

EUROPEAN TAXATION DATA BASE ON C D - R O M.
I B F D Publications B.V., P.O. Box 20237, 1000 HE Amsterdam, Netherlands. TEL 31-20-6267726. FAX 31-20-6228658.
Available only on CD-ROM. *1543*

EXCEPTIONAL CHILD EDUCATION RESOURCES.
Council for Exceptional Children, 1920 Association Dr., Reston, VA 22091-1589. TEL 703-620-3660. FAX 703-264-9494.
Producer(s): SilverPlatter Information, Inc.. *2389*

EXCERPTA MEDICA ABSTRACT JOURNALS.
Excerpta Medica P.O. Box 548, 1000 AM Amsterdam, Netherlands. TEL 31-20-4853507. FAX 31-20-4853222.
Producer(s): SilverPlatter Information, Inc. (Excerpta Medica Library Service). *4559*

EXCERPTA MEDICA. SECTION 1: ANATOMY, ANTHROPOLOGY, EMBRYOLOGY & HISTOLOGY.
Excerpta Medica P.O. Box 548, 1000 AM Amsterdam, Netherlands. TEL 31-20-4853507. FAX 31-20-4853222.
Producer(s): SilverPlatter Information, Inc.. *4559*

EXCERPTA MEDICA. SECTION 2: PHYSIOLOGY.
Excerpta Medica P.O. Box 548, 1000 AM Amsterdam, Netherlands. TEL 31-20-4853507. FAX 31-20-4853222.
Producer(s): SilverPlatter Information, Inc.. *4560*

EXCERPTA MEDICA. SECTION 3: ENDOCRINOLOGY.
Excerpta Medica P.O. Box 548, 1000 AM Amsterdam, Netherlands. TEL 31-20-4853507. FAX 31-20-4853222.
Producer(s): SilverPlatter Information, Inc.. *4560*

EXCERPTA MEDICA. SECTION 4: MICROBIOLOGY: BACTERIOLOGY, MYCOLOGY, PARASITOLOGY AND VIROLOGY.
Excerpta Medica P.O. Box 548, 1000 AM Amsterdam, Netherlands. TEL 31-20-4853507. FAX 31-20-4853222.
Producer(s): SilverPlatter Information, Inc.. *4560*

EXCERPTA MEDICA. SECTION 5: GENERAL PATHOLOGY AND PATHOLOGICAL ANATOMY.
Excerpta Medica P.O. Box 548, 1000 AM Amsterdam, Netherlands. TEL 31-20-4853507. FAX 31-20-4853222.
Producer(s): SilverPlatter Information, Inc.. *4560*

EXCERPTA MEDICA. SECTION 6: INTERNAL MEDICINE.
Excerpta Medica P.O. Box 548, 1000 AM Amsterdam, Netherlands. TEL 31-20-4853507. FAX 31-20-4853222.
Producer(s): SilverPlatter Information, Inc.. *4560*

EXCERPTA MEDICA. SECTION 7: PEDIATRICS AND PEDIATRIC SURGERY.
Excerpta Medica P.O. Box 548, 1000 AM Amsterdam, Netherlands. TEL 31-20-4853507. FAX 31-20-4853222.
Producer(s): SilverPlatter Information, Inc.. *4560*

EXCERPTA MEDICA. SECTION 8: NEUROLOGY AND NEUROSURGERY.
Excerpta Medica P.O. Box 548, 1000 AM Amsterdam, Netherlands. TEL 31-20-4853507. FAX 31-20-4853222.
Producer(s): SilverPlatter Information, Inc.. *4560*

EXCERPTA MEDICA. SECTION 9: SURGERY.
Excerpta Medica P.O. Box 548, 1000 AM Amsterdam, Netherlands. TEL 31-20-4853507. FAX 31-20-4853222.
Producer(s): SilverPlatter Information, Inc.. *4561*

EXCERPTA MEDICA. SECTION 10: OBSTETRICS AND GYNECOLOGY.
Excerpta Medica P.O. Box 548, 1000 AM Amsterdam, Netherlands. TEL 31-20-4853507. FAX 31-20-4853222.
Producer(s): SilverPlatter Information, Inc.. *4561*

EXCERPTA MEDICA. SECTION 11: OTORHINOLARYNGOLOGY.
Excerpta Medica P.O. Box 548, 1000 AM Amsterdam, Netherlands. TEL 31-20-4853507. FAX 31-20-4853222.
Producer(s): SilverPlatter Information, Inc.. *4561*

EXCERPTA MEDICA. SECTION 12: OPHTHALMOLOGY.
Excerpta Medica P.O. Box 548, 1000 AM Amsterdam, Netherlands. TEL 31-20-4853507. FAX 31-20-4853222.
Producer(s): SilverPlatter Information, Inc.. *4561*

EXCERPTA MEDICA. SECTION 13: DERMATOLOGY AND VENEREOLOGY.
Excerpta Medica P.O. Box 548, 1000 AM Amsterdam, Netherlands. TEL 31-20-4853507. FAX 31-20-4853222.
Producer(s): SilverPlatter Information, Inc.. *4561*

EXCERPTA MEDICA. SECTION 14: RADIOLOGY.
Excerpta Medica P.O. Box 548, 1000 AM Amsterdam, Netherlands. TEL 31-20-4853507. FAX 31-20-4853222.
Producer(s): SilverPlatter Information, Inc.. *4561*

EXCERPTA MEDICA. SECTION 15: CHEST DISEASES, THORACIC SURGERY AND TUBERCULOSIS.
Excerpta Medica P.O. Box 548, 1000 AM Amsterdam, Netherlands. TEL 31-20-4853507. FAX 31-20-4853222.
Producer(s): SilverPlatter Information, Inc.. *4561*

EXCERPTA MEDICA. SECTION 16: CANCER.
Excerpta Medica P.O. Box 548, 1000 AM Amsterdam, Netherlands. TEL 31-20-4853507. FAX 31-20-4853222.
Producer(s): SilverPlatter Information, Inc.. *4562*

EXCERPTA MEDICA. SECTION 17: PUBLIC HEALTH, SOCIAL MEDICINE AND EPIDEMIOLOGY.
Excerpta Medica P.O. Box 548, 1000 AM Amsterdam, Netherlands. TEL 31-20-4853507. FAX 31-20-4853222.
Producer(s): SilverPlatter Information, Inc.. *5982*

EXCERPTA MEDICA. SECTION 18: CARDIOVASCULAR DISEASES AND CARDIOVASCULAR SURGERY.
Excerpta Medica P.O. Box 548, 1000 AM Amsterdam, Netherlands. TEL 31-20-4853507. FAX 31-20-4853222.
Producer(s): SilverPlatter Information, Inc.. *4562*

EXCERPTA MEDICA. SECTION 19: REHABILITATION AND PHYSICAL MEDICINE.
Excerpta Medica P.O. Box 548, 1000 AM Amsterdam, Netherlands. TEL 31-20-4853507. FAX 31-20-4853222.
Producer(s): SilverPlatter Information, Inc.. *4562*

EXCERPTA MEDICA. SECTION 20: GERONTOLOGY AND GERIATRICS.
Excerpta Medica P.O. Box 548, 1000 AM Amsterdam, Netherlands. TEL 31-20-4853507. FAX 31-20-4853222.
Producer(s): SilverPlatter Information, Inc.. *3299*

EXCERPTA MEDICA. SECTION 21: DEVELOPMENTAL BIOLOGY AND TERATOLOGY.
Excerpta Medica P.O. Box 548, 1000 AM Amsterdam, Netherlands. TEL 31-20-4853507. FAX 31-20-4853222.
Producer(s): SilverPlatter Information, Inc.. *4562*

EXCERPTA MEDICA. SECTION 22: HUMAN GENETICS.
Excerpta Medica P.O. Box 548, 1000 AM Amsterdam, Netherlands. TEL 31-20-4853507. FAX 31-20-4853222.
Producer(s): SilverPlatter Information, Inc.. *621*

EXCERPTA MEDICA. SECTION 23: NUCLEAR MEDICINE.
Excerpta Medica P.O. Box 548, 1000 AM Amsterdam, Netherlands. TEL 31-20-4853507. FAX 31-20-4853222.
Producer(s): SilverPlatter Information, Inc.. *4562*

EXCERPTA MEDICA. SECTION 24: ANESTHESIOLOGY.
Excerpta Medica P.O. Box 548, 1000 AM Amsterdam, Netherlands. TEL 31-20-4853507. FAX 31-20-4853222.
Producer(s): SilverPlatter Information, Inc.. *4562*

EXCERPTA MEDICA. SECTION 25: HEMATOLOGY.
Excerpta Medica P.O. Box 548, 1000 AM Amsterdam, Netherlands. TEL 31-20-4853507. FAX 31-20-4853222.
Producer(s): SilverPlatter Information, Inc.. *4562*

EXCERPTA MEDICA. SECTION 26: IMMUNOLOGY, SEROLOGY AND TRANSPLANTATION.
Excerpta Medica P.O. Box 548, 1000 AM Amsterdam, Netherlands. TEL 31-20-4853507. FAX 31-20-4853222.
Producer(s): SilverPlatter Information, Inc.. *4563*

EXCERPTA MEDICA. SECTION 27: BIOPHYSICS, BIO-ENGINEERING AND MEDICAL INSTRUMENTATION.
Excerpta Medica P.O. Box 548, 1000 AM Amsterdam, Netherlands. TEL 31-20-4853507. FAX 31-20-4853222.
Producer(s): SilverPlatter Information, Inc.. *4563*

EXCERPTA MEDICA. SECTION 28: UROLOGY AND NEPHROLOGY.
Excerpta Medica P.O. Box 548, 1000 AM Amsterdam, Netherlands. TEL 31-20-4853507. FAX 31-20-4853222.
Producer(s): SilverPlatter Information, Inc.. *4563*

EXCERPTA MEDICA. SECTION 29: CLINICAL AND EXPERIMENTAL BIOCHEMISTRY.
Excerpta Medica P.O. Box 548, 1000 AM Amsterdam, Netherlands. TEL 31-20-4853507. FAX 31-20-4853222.
Producer(s): SilverPlatter Information, Inc.. *4563*

EXCERPTA MEDICA. SECTION 30: CLINICAL AND EXPERIMENTAL PHARMACOLOGY.
Excerpta Medica P.O. Box 548, 1000 AM Amsterdam, Netherlands. TEL 31-20-4853507. FAX 31-20-4853222.
Producer(s): SilverPlatter Information, Inc.. *5450*

EXCERPTA MEDICA. SECTION 31: ARTHRITIS AND RHEUMATISM.
Excerpta Medica P.O. Box 548, 1000 AM Amsterdam, Netherlands. TEL 31-20-4853507. FAX 31-20-4853222.
Producer(s): SilverPlatter Information, Inc.. *4563*

EXCERPTA MEDICA. SECTION 32: PSYCHIATRY.
Excerpta Medica P.O. Box 548, 1000 AM Amsterdam, Netherlands. TEL 31-20-4853507. FAX 31-20-4853222.
Producer(s): SilverPlatter Information, Inc.. *4563*

CD-ROM

EXCERPTA MEDICA. SECTION 33: ORTHOPEDIC SURGERY.
Excerpta Medica P.O. Box 548, 1000 AM Amsterdam, Netherlands. TEL 31-20-4853507. FAX 31-20-4853222.
Producer(s): SilverPlatter Information, Inc.. *4563*

EXCERPTA MEDICA. SECTION 35: OCCUPATIONAL HEALTH AND INDUSTRIAL MEDICINE.
Excerpta Medica P.O. Box 548, 1000 AM Amsterdam, Netherlands. TEL 31-20-4853507. FAX 31-20-4853222.
Producer(s): SilverPlatter Information, Inc.. *4563*

EXCERPTA MEDICA. SECTION 36: HEALTH POLICY, ECONOMICS AND MANAGEMENT.
Excerpta Medica P.O. Box 548, 1000 AM Amsterdam, Netherlands. TEL 31-20-4853507. FAX 31-20-4853222.
Producer(s): SilverPlatter Information, Inc.. *3557*

EXCERPTA MEDICA. SECTION 38: ADVERSE REACTIONS TITLES.
Excerpta Medica P.O. Box 548, 1000 AM Amsterdam, Netherlands. TEL 31-20-4853507. FAX 31-20-4853222.
Producer(s): SilverPlatter Information, Inc.. *4564*

EXCERPTA MEDICA. SECTION 40: DRUG DEPENDENCE, ALCOHOL ABUSE AND ALCOHOLISM.
Excerpta Medica P.O. Box 548, 1000 AM Amsterdam, Netherlands. TEL 31-20-4853507. FAX 31-20-4853222.
Producer(s): SilverPlatter Information, Inc.. *2202*

EXCERPTA MEDICA. SECTION 46: ENVIRONMENTAL HEALTH AND POLLUTION CONTROL.
Excerpta Medica P.O. Box 548, 1000 AM Amsterdam, Netherlands. TEL 31-20-4853507. FAX 31-20-4853222.
Producer(s): SilverPlatter Information, Inc.. *2829*

EXCERPTA MEDICA. SECTION 48: GASTROENTEROLOGY.
Excerpta Medica P.O. Box 548, 1000 AM Amsterdam, Netherlands. TEL 31-20-4853507. FAX 31-20-4853222.
Producer(s): SilverPlatter Information, Inc.. *4564*

EXCERPTA MEDICA. SECTION 49: FORENSIC SCIENCE ABSTRACTS.
Excerpta Medica P.O. Box 548, 1000 AM Amsterdam, Netherlands. TEL 31-20-4853507. FAX 31-20-4853222.
Producer(s): SilverPlatter Information, Inc.. *4564*

EXCERPTA MEDICA. SECTION 50: EPILEPSY ABSTRACTS.
Excerpta Medica P.O. Box 548, 1000 AM Amsterdam, Netherlands. TEL 31-20-4853507. FAX 31-20-4853222.
Producer(s): SilverPlatter Information, Inc.. *4564*

EXCERPTA MEDICA. SECTION 52: TOXICOLOGY.
Excerpta Medica P.O. Box 548, 1000 AM Amsterdam, Netherlands. TEL 31-20-4853507. FAX 31-20-4853222.
Producer(s): SilverPlatter Information, Inc.. *2830*

EXECUTIVE SPEECHES.
Executive Speaker Co., Box 292437, Dayton, OH 45429. TEL 513-294-8493. FAX 513-294-6044. *923*

EXEGY.
A B C-Clio, 130 Cremona Dr., Box 1911, Santa Barbara, CA 93116-1911. TEL 805-968-1911. FAX 805-685-5685. *3228*

EXEMPT ORGANIZATION MASTER LIST ON CD-ROM.
Tax Analysts, 6830 N. Fairfax Dr., Arlington, VA 22213. FAX 703-533-4444.
Available only on CD-ROM. *1543*

EXPANSION.
Recoletos 1, 5o, 28001 Madrid, Spain. TEL 34-1-3373220. FAX 34-1-5756502.
Producer(s): Chadwyck-Healey Inc.. *923*

EXPANSION EN C D - R O M.
Chadwyck-Healey Ltd., The Quorum, Barnwell Rd., Cambridge CB5 8SW, England. TEL 44-1223-215512. FAX 44-1223-215514.
Available only on CD-ROM. Producer(s): Chadwyck-Healey Inc.. *923*

L'EXPERT AUTOMOBILE.
Societe d'Edition de l'Expertise Automobile et Materiel Industriel, 19 rue des Filles du Calvaire, 75140 Paris Cedex 03, France. TEL 16-1-42-77-32-50. FAX 16-1-40-27-02-63. *6784*

EXPERTS CONTACT DIRECTORY.
Gale Research Inc., 835 Penobscot Bldg., Detroit, MI 48226. TEL 313-961-2242. FAX 313-961-6083. *1867*

THE EXPLICATOR.
Heldref Publications 1319 Eighteenth St., N.W., Washington, DC 20036-1802. TEL 202-296-6267. FAX 202-296-5149.
Producer(s): University Microfilms International. *4209*

F R A N C I S. 519: PHILOSOPHIE.
Centre National de la Recherche Scientifique, Institut de l'Information Scientifique et Technique, 2 allee du Parc de Brabois, 54514 Vandoeuvre-les-Nancy Cedex, France. TEL 83-50-46-00. FAX 83-50-46-50. *5507*

F R A N C I S. 520: SCIENCES DE L'EDUCATION.
Centre National de la Recherche Scientifique, Institut de l'Information Scientifique et Technique, 2 allee du Parc de Brabois, 54514 Vandoeuvre-les-Nancy Cedex, France. TEL 83-50-46-00. FAX 83-50-46-50. *2389*

F R A N C I S. 521: SOCIOLOGIE.
Centre National de la Recherche Scientifique, Institut de l'Information Scientifique et Technique, 2 allee du Parc de Brabois, 54514 Vandoeuvre-les-Nancy Cedex, France TEL 83-50-46-00. FAX 83-50-46-50. *6441*

F R A N C I S. 522: HISTOIRE DES SCIENCES ET DE TECHNIQUES.
Centre National de la Recherche Scientifique, Institut de l'Information Scientifique et Technique, 2 allee du Parc de Brabois, 54514 Vandoeuvre-les-Nancy Cedex, France. TEL 83-50-46-00. FAX 83-50-46-50. *3366*

F R A N C I S. 523: HISTOIRE ET SCIENCES DE LA LITTERATURE.
Centre National de la Recherche Scientifique, Institut de l'Information Scientifique et Technique, 2 allee du Parc de Brabois, 54514 Vandoeuvre-les-Nancy Cedex, France. TEL 83-50-46-00. FAX 83-50-46-50. *4293*

F R A N C I S. 524: SCIENCES DU LANGAGE.
Centre National de la Recherche Scientifique, Institut de l'Information Scientifique et Technique, 2 allee du Parc de Brabois, 54514 Vandoeuvre-les-Nancy Cedex, France. TEL 83-50-46-00. FAX 83-50-46-50. *4127*

F R A N C I S. 525: PREHISTOIRE ET PROTOHISTOIRE.
Centre National de la Recherche Scientifique, Institut de l'Information Scientifique et Technique, 2 allee du Parc de Brabois, 54514 Vandoeuvre-les-Nancy Cedex, France. TEL 83-50-46-00. FAX 83-50-46-50. *380*

F R A N C I S. 526: ART ET ARCHEOLOGIE.
Centre National de la Recherche Scientifique, Institut de l'Information Scientifique et Technique, 2 allee du Parc de Brabois, 54514 Vandoeuvre-les-Nancy Cedex, France. TEL 83-50-46-00. FAX 83-50-46-50. *462*

F R A N C I S. 527: HISTOIRE ET SCIENCES DES RELIGIONS.
Centre National de la Recherche Scientifique, Institut de l'Information Scientifique et Technique, 2 allee du Parc de Brabois, 54514 Vandoeuvre-les-Nancy Cedex, France. TEL 83-50-46-00. FAX 83-50-46-50. *6107*

F R A N C I S. 528: BIBLIOGRAPHIE INTERNATIONALE DE SCIENCE ADMINISTRATIVE.
Centre National de la Recherche Scientifique, Institut de l'Information Scientifique et Technique, 2 allee du Parc de Brabois, 54514 Vandoeuvre-les-Nancy Cedex, France. TEL 83-50-46-00. FAX 83-50-46-50. *997*

F R A N C I S. 529: ETHNOLOGIE.
Centre National de la Recherche Scientifique, Institut de l'Information Scientifique et Technique, 2 allee du Parc de Brabois. 54514 Vandoeuvre-les-Nancy Cedex, France. TEL 83-50-46-00. FAX 83-50-46-50. *328*

F R A N C I S. 531: BIBLIOGRAPHIE GEOGRAPHIQUE INTERNATIONALE.
Centre National de la Recherche Scientifique, Institut de l'Information Scientifique et Technique, 2 allee du Parc de Brabois, 54514 Vandoeuvre-les-Nancy Cedex, France. TEL 83-50-46-00. FAX 83-50-46-50. *3279*

F R A N C I S. 603: INFORMATIQUE ET SCIENCES JURIDIQUES.
Centre National de la Recherche Scientifique, Institut de l'Information Scientifique et Technique, 2 allee du Parc de Brabois, 54514 Vandoeuvre-les-Nancy Cedex, France. TEL 83-50-46-00. FAX 83-50-46-50. *3889*

F R A N C I S. 617: E C O L O C.
Centre National de la Recherche Scientifique, Institut de l'Information Scientifique et Technique, 2 allee du Parc de Brabois, 54514 Vandoeuvre-les-Nancy Cedex, France. TEL 83-50-46-00. FAX 83-50-46-50. *997*

FACTS ON FILE WORLD NEWS DIGEST WITH INDEX.
Facts on File, Inc., 460 Park Ave. S., New York, NY 10016. TEL 212-683-2244. *3342*

FAMILY PRACTICE RECERTIFICATION.
M R A Publications, Inc., 2 Greenwich Office Park, Greenwich, CT 06831-5154. TEL 203-629-3550. FAX 203-629-2536. *4454*

FAMILY RELATIONS.
National Council on Family Relations, 3989 Central Ave., N.E., Ste. 550, Minneapolis, MN 55421-3921. TEL 612-781-9331. FAX 612-781-9348.
Producer(s): NISC. *6413*

FAMILY STUDIES DATABASE.
National Information Services Corporation (NISC), Ste. 6, Wyman Towers, 3100 St. Paul St., MD 21218. TEL 410-243-0797. FAX 410-243-0982. Available only on CD-ROM. Producer(s): NISC. *4415*

FAMILY THERAPY.
Libra Publishers, Inc., 3089C Clairemont Dr., Ste. 383, San Diego, CA 92117. TEL 619-571-1414. *4837*

FAULKNER'S ENTERPRISE NETWORKING.
Faulkner Information Services, Inc., 114 Cooper Center, 7905 Browning Rd., Pennsauken, NJ 08109-4319. TEL 609-662-2070. FAX 609-662-3380. *2069*

FAULKNER'S LOCAL AREA NETWORKING.
Faulkner Information Services, Inc., 114 Cooper Center, 7905 Browning Rd., Pennsauken, NJ 08109-4319. TEL 609-662-2070. FAX 609-662-3380. *2086*

FAULKNER'S MICROCOMPUTERS AND SOFTWARE.
Faulkner Information Services, Inc., 114 Cooper Center, 7905 Browning Rd., Pennsauken, NJ 08109-4319. TEL 609-662-2070. FAX 609-662-3380. *2086*

FAULKNER'S TELECOMMUNICATIONS WORLD.
Faulkner Information Services, Inc., 114 Cooper Center, 7905 Browning Rd., Pennsauken, NJ 08109-4319. TEL 609-662-2070. FAX 609-662-3380. *1945*

FEDERAL BANKING LAW REPORTS.
Commerce Clearing House, Inc., 2700 Lake Cook Rd., Riverwoods, IL 60015. TEL 847-267-7000. FAX 800-224-8299. *1087*

FEDERAL CRIMINAL CODE AND RULES.
West Publishing Corp., 620 Opperman Dr., Eagan, MN 55123. TEL 612-687-7000. FAX 612-687-7302. *3910*

FEDERAL ESTATE AND GIFT TAX REPORTS.
Commerce Clearing House, Inc., 2700 Lake Cook Rd., Riverwoods, IL 60015. TEL 847-267-7000. FAX 800-224-8299. *3915*

CD-ROM

FEDERAL EXCISE TAX REPORTS.
Commerce Clearing House, Inc., 2700 Lake Cook Rd., Riverwoods, IL 60015. TEL 847-267-7000. FAX 800-224-8299. *1543*

FEDERAL LABOR LAWS.
West Publishing Corp., 620 Opperman Dr., Eagan, MN 55123. TEL 612-687-7000. FAX 612-687-7602. *3778*

FEDERAL REGIONAL YELLOW BOOK.
Leadership Directories, Inc., 104 Fifth Ave., 2nd Fl., New York, NY 10011. TEL 212-627-4140. FAX 212-645-0931.
Producer(s): Chadwyck-Healey Inc.. *5901*

FEDERAL REGISTER.
U.S. Office of the Federal Register, National Archives and Records Administration, Washington, DC 20408. TEL 202-523-5230. *5901*

FEDERAL SECURITIES LAW REPORTS.
Commerce Clearing House, Inc., 2700 Lake Cook Rd., Riverwoods, IL 60015. TEL 312-583-8500. *3778*

FEDERAL SENTENCING GUIDELINES MANUAL.
West Publishing Corp., 620 Opperman Dr., Eagan, MN 55123. TEL 612-687-8000. FAX 612-687-7302. *3910*

FEDERAL SOCIAL SECURITY LAWS.
West Publishing Corp., 620 Opperman Dr., Eagan, MN 55123. TEL 612-687-7000. FAX 612-687-7302. *3648*

FEDERAL STAFF DIRECTORY.
Staff Directories Ltd., Box 62, Mount Vernon, VA 22121. TEL 703-739-0900. FAX 703-739-0234. *5902*

FEDERAL TAX COORDINATOR 2D.
Research Institute of America, Inc., 90 Fifth Ave., New York, NY 10011. TEL 212-645-4800. FAX 212-337-4279. *1544*

FEDERAL TAX GUIDE REPORTS.
Commerce Clearing House, Inc., 2700 Lake Cook Rd., Riverwoods, IL 60015. TEL 847-267-7000. FAX 800-224-8299. *1544*

FEDERAL TECHNOLOGY REPORT.
McGraw-Hill Companies, Energy & Business Newsletters, 1221 Ave. of the Americas, 36th Fl., New York, NY 10020. TEL 212-512-6410.
Producer(s): SilverPlatter Information, Inc. (McGraw-Hill Energy Library). *2549*

FEDERAL YELLOW BOOK.
Leadership Directories, Inc., 104 Fifth Ave., 2nd Fl., Ste. 1000, New York, NY 10011. TEL 212-627-4140. FAX 212-645-0931.
Producer(s): Chadwyck-Healey Inc.. *5902*

FILIERA CARNE.
Essepiesse s.r.l., Via G. Galilei 14, 21024 Milan, Italy. TEL 39-2-29003814. *2968*

FILM & VIDEO FINDER.
Plexus Publishing, Inc., 143 Old Marlton Pike, Medford, NJ 08055-8750. TEL 609-654-4888. FAX 609-654-4309.
Producer(s): SilverPlatter Information, Inc.. *2389*

FILM COMMENT.
Film Society of Lincoln Center, 70 Lincoln Center Plaza, New York, NY 10023-6595. TEL 212-875-5610. FAX 212-875-5636.
Producer(s): University Microfilms International. *5101*

FILM INDEX INTERNATIONAL.
Chadwyck-Healey Ltd., The Quorum, Barnwell Rd., Cambridge CB5 8SW, England. TEL 44-1223-215512. FAX 44-1223-215514.
Available only on CD-ROM. Producer(s): Chadwyck-Healey Inc.. *5101*

FILMSTRIP AND SLIDE SET FINDER.
Plexus Publishing, Inc., 143 Old Marlton Pike, Medford, NJ 08055-8750. TEL 609-654-6500. FAX 609-654-4309. *2389*

FINANCIAL AND ESTATE PLANNING.
Commerce Clearing House, Inc., 2700 Lake Cook Rd., Riverwoods, IL 60015. TEL 847-267-7000. FAX 800-224-8299. *1089*

FINANCIAL TIMES (FRANKFURT EDITION).
Financial Times (Europe) GmbH, Nibelungenplatz 3, 60318 Frankfurt a.M., Germany. TEL 069-156850. FAX 069-5964481.
Producer(s): Chadwyck-Healey Inc.. *1092*

FINANCIAL TIMES (LONDON, 1888).
Financial Times, One Southwark Bridge, London SE1 9HL, England. TEL 44-171-873-3000. FAX 44-171-263-9764.
Producer(s): Chadwyck-Healey Inc.. *1092*

FINANCIAL TIMES (NORTH AMERICAN EDITION).
F T Publications Inc., 14 E. 60th St., New York, NY 10022. TEL 212-752-7400. FAX 212-319-0704.
Producer(s): Chadwyck-Healey Inc.. *1092*

FINANCIAL TIMES ON C D - R O M.
Chadwyck-Healey Ltd., The Quorum, Barnwell Rd., Cambridge CB5 8SW, England. TEL 44-1223-215512. FAX 44-1223-215514.
Available only on CD-ROM. Producer(s): Chadwyck-Healey Inc.. *1092*

FINANCIAL YELLOW BOOK.
Leadership Directories, Inc., 104 Fifth Ave., 2nd Fl., New York, NY 10011. TEL 212-627-4140. FAX 212-645-0931.
Producer(s): Chadwyck-Healey Inc.. *1418*

DE FINANCIEEL EKONOMISCHE TIJD.
Uitgeversbedrijf Tijd n.v., Franklin Building, Posthoflei 3, 2600 Berchem (Antwerp), Belgium. TEL 32-3-2860211. FAX 32-3-2860310. *924*

EL FINANCIERO INTERNATIONAL EDITION.
El Financiero International, Inc., Lago Bolsena 176, Col. Anahuac, 11320 Mexico DF, Mexico. TEL 525-227-7600. FAX 525-227-7634. *1092*

FINDEX (YEAR).
Euromonitor, 60-61 Britton St., London EC1M 5NA, England. TEL 44-171-251-8024. FAX 44-171-608-3149.
Producer(s): SilverPlatter Information, Inc.. *998*

FIRMEN DER NEUEN BUNDESLAENDER.
Verlag Hoppenstedt GmbH, Havelstr. 9, 64295 Darmstadt, Germany. TEL 49-6151-380-0. FAX 49-6151-380-360. *1520*

FIRMENHANDBUCH CHEMISCHE INDUSTRIE. BUNDESREPUBLIK DEUTSCHLAND.
E C O N Verlag GmbH, Postfach 300321, 40403 Duesseldorf, Germany. TEL 49-211-4359746. FAX 49-211-4359781. *1610*

FIRST MONDAY.
Munksgaard International Publishers Ltd., Noerre Soegade 35, P.O. Box 2148, DK-1016 Copenhagen, Denmark. TEL 45-33-127030. *2037*

FISH & FISHERIES WORLDWIDE.
National Information Services Corporation (NISC), Ste. 6, Wyman Towers, 3100 St. Paul St., Baltimore, MD 21218. TEL 410-243-0797. FAX 410-243-0982.
Available only on CD-ROM. Producer(s): NISC. *2947*

FISHERIES REVIEW.
U.S. National Biological Service, Information Transfer Center, 1201 Oak Ridge Dr., Ste. 200, Ft. Collins, CO 80525-5589. TEL 303-226-9401.
Producer(s): NISC (Fish & Fisheries Worldwide). *2947*

FLORIDA BUSINESS DIRECTORY.
American Business Directories 5711 S. 86th Circle, Box 27347, Omaha, NE 68127. TEL 402-593-4600. FAX 402-331-5481. *1610*

FOCUS ON EXCEPTIONAL CHILDREN.
Love Publishing Co., Box 22353, Denver, CO 80222. TEL 303-757-2579. FAX 303-782-5683. *2468*

FOOD SCIENCE AND TECHNOLOGY ABSTRACTS.
International Food Information Service (I F I S Publishing), Lane End House, Shinfield, Reading, Berks. RG2 9BB, England. TEL 01734-883895. FAX 01734-885065.
Producer(s): SilverPlatter Information, Inc. (COMPU-INFO). *2996*

FOREIGN AFFAIRS.
Council on Foreign Relations, Inc., 58 E. 68th St., New York, NY 10021. TEL 212-734-0400.
Producer(s): University Microfilms International. *5750*

FOREIGN POLICY (WASHINGTON).
Carnegie Endowment for International Peace, 2400 N St., N.W., Ste. 700, Washington, DC 20037. TEL 202-862-7940. *5750*

FORLAGSSERIEKATALOG FOR BOERNE- OG SKOLEBIBLIOTEKER.
Dansk BiblioteksCenter as, Tempovej 7-11, DK-2750 Ballerup, Denmark. TEL 45-44-867777. FAX 45-44-867892. *2389*

FORO ITALIANO.
Zanichelli Editore S.p.A., Via Irnerio, 34, 40126 Bologna, Italy. TEL 39-51-293111. FAX 39-51-249782. *3781*

FORTHCOMING BOOKS.
R.R. Bowker, A Division of Reed Elsevier Inc., 121 Chanlon Rd., New Prvidence, NJ 07974. TEL 908-464-6800. FAX 908-665-3502.
Producer(s): Bowker Electronic Publishing (Books in Print PLUS). *531*

FORTUNE MAGAZINE.
Time Inc. Time & Life Bldg., Rockefeller Center, New York, NY 10020-1393. TEL 212-522-1212.
Producer(s): University Microfilms International. *1419*

FOXTALK.
Pinnacle Publishing, Inc., Box 888, Kent, WA 98035-0888. TEL 206-251-1900. FAX 206-251-5057. *2044*

FRANKFURT C D - R O M.
Buchhaendler-Vereinigung GmbH, Postfach 100442, 60004 Frankfurt a.M., Germany. TEL 49-69-1306-0. FAX 49-69-1306201.
Available only on CD-ROM. *1611*

FRONTIERS IN NETWORKING.
Academic Press, Inc, Journal Division, 525 B St., Ste. 1900, San Diego, CA 92101-4495. TEL 619-230-1840.
Available only on CD-ROM. *2037*

FUJIAN ZHONGYI YAO.
Fujian Zhongyi Xueyuan, 282 Wusi Lu, Fuzhou, Fujian 350003, People's Republic of China. TEL 0591-7841296. FAX 0591-7842524. *290*

G S A TODAY.
Geological Society of America, 3300 Penrose Pl., Box 9140, Boulder, CO 80301. TEL 303-447-2020. FAX 303-447-1133. *2233*

GALE'S LITERARY INDEX C D - R O M.
Gale Research Inc., 835 Penobscot Bldg., Detroit, MI 48226. *4212*

GAS & LIQUID CHROMATOGRAPHY LITERATURE - ABSTRACTS & INDEX.
Preston Publications, Inc., Box 48312, Niles, IL 60714. TEL 847-965-0566. FAX 847-965-7639. *1709*

GAZETTE.
250 rue St-Antoine O., Montreal, PQ H2Y 3R7, Canada. *3121*

GEFAHRGUT - DANGEROUS GOODS C D - R O M.
Springer-Verlag, Heidelberger Platz 3, 14197 Berlin, Germany. TEL 49-30-8207-0. FAX 49-30-8214091.
Available only on CD-ROM. *6756*

GENBANK.
U.S. National Center for Biotechnology Information, National Library of Medicine, Bldg. 38A, Rm. 8N-803, 8600 Rockville Pike, Bethesda, MD 20894. TEL 301-496-2475. FAX 301-480-2233.
Available only on CD-ROM. *710*

GENERAL LAWS OF MASSACHUSETTS. OFFICIAL EDITION (YEAR).
West Publishing Corp., 620 Opperman Dr., Eagan, MN 55123. TEL 612-687-8000. FAX 612-687-7302. *3948*

GENERAL SCIENCE INDEX.
H.W. Wilson Co., 950 University Ave., Bronx, NY 10452. TEL 718-588-8400. FAX 718-590-1617. Producer(s): SilverPlatter Information, Inc., H.W. Wilson (WILSONDISC). *6301*

GENETIC, SOCIAL, AND GENERAL PSYCHOLOGY MONOGRAPHS.
Heldref Publications, 1319 Eighteenth St., N.W., Washington, DC 20036-1802. TEL 202-296-6267. FAX 202-296-5149. Producer(s): University Microfilms International. *5845*

GENETICS ABSTRACTS.
Cambridge Scientific Abstracts, 7200 Wisconsin Ave., 6th Fl., Bethesda, MD 20814. TEL 301-961-6750. FAX 301-961-6720. Producer(s): SilverPlatter Information, Inc.. *621*

GEO KATALOG (YEAR). VOLUME 1. TOURISTISCHE VEROEFFENTLICHUNGEN.
GeoCenter Verlagsvertrieb GmbH, Neumarkterstr. 18, 81673 Munich, Germany. TEL 49-89-43189-0. FAX 49-89-43189555. *3255*

THE GEOGRAPHICAL JOURNAL.
Royal Geographical Society, 1 Kensington Gore, London SW7 2AR, England. TEL 44-171-589-5466. FAX 44-171-584-4447. Producer(s): University Microfilms International. *3257*

GEOLOGICAL SOCIETY OF AMERICA. BULLETIN.
Geological Society of America, 3300 Penrose Pl., Box 9140, Boulder, CO 80301. TEL 303-447-2020. FAX 303-447-1133. *2236*

GEOLOGY (BOULDER).
Geological Society of America, 3300 Penrose Pl., Box 9140, Boulder, CO 80301. TEL 303-447-2020. FAX 303-447-1133. *2239*

GEOPHYSICS.
Society of Exploration Geophysicists, Box 702740, Tulsa, OK 74170-2740. TEL 918-493-3516. *2274*

GEORGIA ADVANCE SHEETS.
Darby Printing Co., 6215 Purdue Dr., S.W., Atlanta, GA 30336-2827. TEL 404-344-2665. FAX 404-346-3332. *3783*

GEORGIA BUSINESS DIRECTORY.
American Business Directories 5711 S. 86th Circle, Box 27347, Omaha, NE 68127. TEL 402-593-4600. FAX 402-331-5481. *1612*

GEORGIA COURT RULES AND PROCEDURE, STATE AND FEDERAL.
West Publishing Corp., 620 Opperman Dr., Eagan, MN 55123. TEL 612-687-8000. FAX 612-687-7602. *3948*

GEOROM.
National Information Services Corporation (NISC), Ste. 6, Wyman Towers, 3100 St. Paul St., Baltimore, MD 21218. TEL 410-243-0797. FAX 410-243-0982. Available only on CD-ROM. Producer(s): NISC. *2219*

GEOSCIENCE DOCUMENTATION.
Geosystems, P.O. Box 40, Didcot, Oxon. OX11 9BX, England. TEL 44-1235-813913. Producer(s): NISC (Geosearch). *2219*

GEOSOURCES.
Geosystems, P.O. Box 40, Didcot, Oxon. OX11 9BS, England. TEL 44-1385-813913. Producer(s): NISC (Geosearch). *2219*

GEOTECHNICAL ABSTRACTS.
Research Resources, Inc., Geotext Services, 8819 Sundale Dr., Silver Spring, MD 20910. TEL 301-589-2070. FAX 301-589-4129. *2628*

GEOTITLES.
Geosystems, P.O. Box 40, Didcot, Oxon. OX11 9BX, England. TEL 44-1235-813913. Producer(s): NISC (Geosearch). *2219*

GERMAN AND EAST EUROPEAN BOOKS IN PRINT.
Buchhaendler-Vereinigung GmbH, Postfach 100442, 60004 Frankfurt a.M., Germany. TEL 49-69-1306-0. FAX 49-69-1306201. Available only on CD-ROM. *531*

GERMAN LIFE.
Zeitgeist Publishing, 1 Corporate Dr., Grantsville, MD 21536. TEL 301-895-3859. FAX 301-895-5029. *3144*

GERMANIC REVIEW.
Heldref Publications, 1319 Eighteenth St., N.W., Washington, DC 20036-1802. TEL 202-296-6267. FAX 202-296-5149. Producer(s): University Microfilms International. *4071*

GEWERBLICHER RECHTSSCHUTZ UND URHEBERRECHT.
V C H Verlagsgesellschaft mbH, Postfach 101161, 69451 Weinheim, Germany. TEL 06201-606-147. FAX 06201-606117. *5339*

GEWERBLICHER RECHTSSCHUTZ UND URHEBERRECHT. INTERNATIONALER TEIL.
V C H Verlagsgesellschaft mbH, Postfach 101161, 69451 Weinheim, Germany. TEL 06201-606-147. FAX 06201-606117. *5339*

DIE GIESSEREI-INDUSTRIE UND IHRE HELFER.
Industrieschau-Verlagsgesellschaft mbH, Postfach 100262, 64202 Darmstadt, Germany. TEL 49-6151-38920. FAX 49-6151-33164. *4956*

GIFTED EDUCATION REVIEW.
Peak Educational Resources, Inc., Box 2278, Evergreen, CO 80437-2278. TEL 303-670-8350. *2469*

GINECOLOGIA Y OBSTETRICIA DE MEXICO.
Asociacion Mexicana de Ginecologia y Obstetricia, Ave. Amsterdam 214-PH2, Col. Hipodromo, Deleg. Cuauhtemoc, 06100 Mexico D.F., Mexico. TEL 5645463. FAX 2641745. *4736*

GIURISPRUDENZA ITALIANA.
Unione Tipografico Editrice Torinese, Corso Raffaello 28, 10125 Turin, Italy. TEL 39-11-65291. FAX 39-11-6529394. *3784*

GLOBAL COMPANY HANDBOOK.
C I F A R Publications, Inc., 3490 US Hwy 1, BLO12, Princeton, NJ 08540-5920. TEL 609-520-9333. FAX 609-520-0905. *1277*

THE GLOBE AND MAIL.
Globe and Mail Publishing, 444 Front St., W., Toronto, ON M5V 2S9, Canada. TEL 416-585-5600. FAX 416-585-5275. *3121*

GNOMON.
C.H. Beck'sche Verlagsbuchhandlung, Wilhelmstr. 9, 80801 Munich, Germany. TEL 49-89-38189-338. FAX 49-89-38189-398. *1822*

GORDON'S (YEAR) INTERNATIONAL PHOTOGRAPHY PRICE ANNUAL.
Gordon's Art Reference, Inc., 1840 Eighth St., S., Naples, FL 33940. TEL 941-434-6842. FAX 941-434-6969. *5513*

GORDON'S PRINT PRICE ANNUAL (YEAR).
Gordon's Art Reference, Inc., 1840 Eighth St., S., Naples, FL 33940. TEL 941-434-6842. FAX 941-434-6969. *430*

GOVERNMENT AFFAIRS YELLOW BOOK.
Leadership Directories, Inc., 104 Fifth Ave., 2nd Fl., New York, NY 10011. TEL 212-627-4140. FAX 212-645-0931. Producer(s): Chadwyck-Healey Inc.. *5903*

GOVERNMENT COMPUTER NEWS.
Cahners Publishing Company (Silver Spring), Division of Reed Elsevier Inc., 8601 Georgia Ave., Ste. 300, Silver Spring, MD 20910. TEL 301-650-2000. FAX 301-650-2111. *5935*

GOVERNMENT CONTRACTOR.
Federal Publications Inc., 1120 20th St., N.W., Ste. 500 S., Washington, DC 20036. TEL 202-337-7000. FAX 202-659-2233. *3784*

GOVERNMENT CONTRACTS REPORTS.
Commerce Clearing House, Inc., 2700 Lake Cook Rd., Riverwoods, IL 60015. TEL 847-267-7000. FAX 800-224-8299. *3795*

GRADUATE MEDICAL EDUCATION DIRECTORY (YEARS).
American Medical Association, 515 N. State St., Chicago, IL 60610. TEL 312-464-5000. FAX 312-464-5600. *2429*

GRADUATE STUDIES.
Hobsons Publishing plc., Bateman St., Cambridge CB2 1LZ, England. TEL 44-1223-460366. FAX 44-1223-301506. *2429*

THE GRAMOPHONE CLASSICAL CATALOGUE.
Retail Establishment Data Publishing Ltd., Paulton House, 8 Shepherdess Walk, London N1 7LR, England. TEL 0171-490-0049. FAX 0171-253-1308. *5160*

THE GRAMOPHONE CLASSICAL GOOD C D GUIDE.
Gramophone Publications Ltd., 177-179 Kenton Rd., Harrow, Mddx. HA3 0HA, England. TEL 44-181-907-4476. FAX 44-181-907-0073. *5160*

GRAVITY (YEAR).
U.S. National Geophysical Data Center, 325 Broadway, Boulder, CO 80303-3328. TEL 303-497-6836. FAX 303-497-6513. Available only on CD-ROM. *2275*

GREAT BRITAIN. HOUSE OF COMMONS. PARLIAMENTARY DEBATES.
H.M.S.O., 51 Nine Elms Ln. London SW8 5DR, England. TEL 44-171-873-0011. FAX 44-171-873-8247. Producer(s): Chadwyck-Healey Inc. *5669*

GREAT BRITAIN. HOUSE OF COMMONS. PARLIAMENTARY DEBATES (C D - R O M EDITION).
Chadwyck-Healey Ltd., The Quorum, Barnwell Rd., Cambridge CB5 8SW, England. TEL 44-1223-215512. FAX 44-1223-215514. Available only on CD-ROM. Producer(s): Chadwyck-Healey Inc. *5670*

GREAT BRITAIN. HOUSE OF LORDS. PARLIAMENTARY DEBATES.
H.M.S.O., P.O. Box 276, London SW8 5DT, England. TEL 44-171-873-0011. FAX 44-171-873-8463. Producer(s): Chadwyck-Healey Inc.. *5670*

GREAT BRITAIN. HOUSE OF LORDS. PARLIAMENTARY DEBATES (C D - R O M EDITION).
Chadwyck-Healey Ltd., The Quorum, Barnwell Rd., Cambridge CB5 8SW, England. TEL 44-1223-215512. FAX 44-1223-215514. Available only on CD-ROM. Producer(s): Chadwyck-Healey Inc. *5670*

GREAT BRITAIN. NATURAL RESOURCES INSTITUTE. BULLETIN.
Natural Resources Institute, Central Ave., Chatham Maritime, Kent ME4 4TB, England. TEL 44-1634-880088. FAX 44-1634-880066. *120*

THE GUARDIAN (MANCHESTER).
Guardian Newspapers Ltd. 164 Deansgate, Manchester M60 2RR, England. TEL 44-161-832-7200. FAX 44-161-876-5362. Producer(s): Chadwyck-Healey Inc.. *3155*

THE GUARDIAN ON C D - R O M.
Chadwyck-Healey Ltd., The Quorum, Barnwell Rd., Cambridge CB5 8SW, England. TEL 44-1223-215512. FAX 44-1223-215514. Available only on CD-ROM. Producer(s): Chadwyck-Healey Inc.. *3155*

GUIDA DELLE REGIONI D'ITALIA.
SISPR - Societa Italiana per lo Studio dei Problemi Regionali, Via della Scrofa 14, 00186 Rome, Italy. TEL 39-6-6879852. FAX 39-6-6867537. *1613*

GUIDE TO NEW AUSTRALIAN BOOKS.
D.W. Thorpe, A member of the Reed Elsevier plc group, 18 Salmon St., Port Melbourne, Vic. 3207, Australia. TEL 03-9245-7370 FAX 03-9245-7395. *533*

GUIDELINES.
Bibliographic Services, P.O. Box 961, Mount Waverley, Vic. 3149, Australia. *4038*

H C F A'S LAWS, REGULATIONS, AND MANUALS (C D - R O M).
U.S. Health Care Financing Administration, Department of Health and Human Services, C-3-11-07, 7500 Security Blvd., Baltimore, MD 21244. TEL 410-786-6572. FAX 410-786-5768. Available only on CD-ROM. *3544*

H T F S DIGEST.
A.E.A. Technology, Harwell Bldg. 392.7, Didcot, Oxon OX11 ORA, England. TEL 44-1235-432862. FAX 44-1235-831981. *2641*

HAMDARD ISLAMICUS.
Hamdard Foundation, Nazimabad No. 3, Karachi 74600, Pakistan. TEL 92-21-6616001. FAX 92-21-6641766. *6117*

HAMDARD MEDICUS.
Hamdard Foundation, Nazimabad No. 3, Karachi 74600, Pakistan. TEL 92-21-6616001. FAX 92-21-6641766. *4461*

HANDBOEK VAN DE NEDERLANDSE PERS EN PUBLICITEIT.
Nijgh Periodieken B.V., Postbus 122, 3100 AC Schiedam, Netherlands. TEL 31-10-4274100. FAX 31-10-4739911. *37*

HANDBOOK OF LABOR STATISTICS.
U.S. Bureau of Labor Statistics, 441 G St., N.W., Washington, DC 20212. TEL 202-655-4000. *1214*

HANDBOOK OF LATIN AMERICAN STUDIES: A SELECTED AND ANNOTATED GUIDE TO RECENT PUBLICATIONS.
University of Texas Press, Journals Division, Box 7819, Austin, TX 78713. TEL 512-471-4278. Producer(s): NISC (Latin American Studies - Vol.1). *3366*

HANDBOOK ON INJECTABLE DRUGS.
American Society of Health-System Pharmacists, 7272 Wisconsin Ave., Bethesda, MD 20814. TEL 301-657-3000. FAX 301-657-8817. *5415*

HANDBUCH DER AUSLANDSZOELLE.
Mendel Verlag, Robensstr. 39, 52070 Aachen, Germany. TEL 49-241-154355. FAX 49-241-154355. *1278*

HANDBUCH DER STEUERVERANLAGUNGEN: EINKOMMENSTEUER, KOERPERSCHAFTSTEUER, GEWERBESTEUER, UMSATZSTEUER.
C.H. Beck'sche Verlagsbuchhandlung, Wilhelmstr. 9, 80801 Munich, Germany. TEL 089-38189-338. FAX 089-38189-398. *1547*

HARPER'S MAGAZINE.
Harpers Magazine Foundation, 666 Broadway, New York, NY 10012-2317. TEL 212-614-6500. FAX 212-228-5889. Producer(s): University Microfilms International. *4145*

HARRIS CONNECTICUT MANUFACTURERS DIRECTORY.
InfoSource International, 2057-2 Aurora Rd., Twinsburg, OH 44087. TEL 216-425-9000. FAX 800-643-5997. *1613*

HARRIS DELAWARE MANUFACTURERS DIRECTORY.
InfoSource International, 2057-2 Aurora Rd., Twinsburg, OH 44087. TEL 216-425-9000. FAX 800-643-5997. *1613*

HARRIS GEORGIA MANUFACTURERS DIRECTORY.
InfoSource International, 2057-2 Aurora Rd., Twinsburg, OH 44087. TEL 216-425-9000. FAX 800-643-5997. *1613*

HARRIS ILLINOIS INDUSTRIAL DIRECTORY (YEAR).
InfoSource International, 2057-2 Aurora Rd., Twinsburg, OH 44087. TEL 216-426-7150. *1613*

HARRIS INDIANA INDUSTRIAL DIRECTORY (YEAR).
InfoSource International, 2057-2 Aurora Rd., Twinsburg, OH 44087. TEL 216-425-7150. *1613*

HARRIS KENTUCKY INDUSTRIAL DIRECTORY (YEAR)
.
InfoSource International, 2057-2 Aurora Rd., Twinsburg, OH 44087. TEL 216-425-9000. FAX 216-425-7150. *1613*

HARRIS MASSACHUSSETTS MANUFACTURERS DIRECTORY.
InfoSource International, 2057-2 Aurora Rd., Twinsburg, OH 44087. TEL 216-425-9000. FAX 800-643-5997. *1614*

HARRIS MICHIGAN INDUSTRIAL DIRECTORY (YEAR).
InfoSource International, 2057-2 Aurora Rd., Twinsburg, OH 44087. TEL 216-425-9000. FAX 216-425-7150. *1614*

HARRIS MISSOURI DIRECTORY OF MANUFACTURERS.
InfoSource International, 2057-2 Aurora Rd., Twinsburg, OH 44087. TEL 216-425-9000. FAX 216-425-7150. *1614*

HARRIS NATIONAL MANUFACTURERS DIRECTORY (YEAR).
InfoSource International, 2057 Aurora Rd., Twinsburg, OH 44087. TEL 216-425-9000. FAX 216-425-7150. *1614*

HARRIS NATIONAL MANUFACTURERS DIRECTORY MIDWEST EDITION (YEAR).
InfoSource International, 2057 Aurora Rd., Twinsburg, OH 44087. TEL 216-425-9000. FAX 216-425-7150. *1614*

HARRIS NATIONAL MANUFACTURERS DIRECTORY NORTHEAST EDITION (YEAR).
InfoSource International, 2057 Aurora Rd., Twinsburg, OH 44087. TEL 216-425-9000. FAX 216-425-7150. *1614*

HARRIS NATIONAL MANUFACTURERS DIRECTORY SOUTHEAST EDITION (YEAR).
InfoSource International, 2057 Aurora Rd., Twinsburg, OH 44087. TEL 216-425-9000. FAX 216-425-7150. *1614*

HARRIS NEW ENGLAND MANUFACTURERS DIRECTORY.
InfoSource Internaional, 2057-2 Aurora Rd., Twinsburg, OH 44087. TEL 216-425-9000. FAX 800-643-5997. *1614*

HARRIS OHIO INDUSTRIAL DIRECTORY (YEAR).
InfoSource International, 2057-2 Aurora Rd., Twinsburg, OH 44087. TEL 216-425-9000. FAX 216-425-7150. *1614*

HARRIS RHODE ISLAND MANUFACTURERS DIRECTORY.
Harris Publishing Co. (Twinsburg), 2057-2 Aurora Rd., Twinsburg, OH 44087. TEL 216-425-9000. FAX 800-643-5997. *1614*

HARRIS SOUTH CAROLINA MANUFACTURERS DIRECTORY.
InfoSource International, 2057-2 Aurora Rd., Twinsburg, OH 44087. TEL 216-425-9000. FAX 800-643-5997. *1614*

HARRIS TEXAS MANUFACTURERS DIRECTORY.
InfoSource International, 2057-2 Aurora Rd., Twinsburg, OH 44087. TEL 216-425-9000. FAX 800-643-5997. *1614*

HARRIS WEST VIRGINIA MANUFACTURING DIRECTORY (YEAR).
Harris Publishing Co. (Twinsburg), 2057-2 Aurora Rd., Twinsburg, OH 44087. TEL 216-425-7150. *1614*

HASTINGS COMMUNICATIONS AND ENTERTAINMENT LAW JOURNAL (COMM - ENT).
University of California at San Francisco, Hastings College of the Law, 200 McAllister St., San Francisco, CA 94102-4978. TEL 415-565-4731. FAX 415-565-4814. *3786*

HASTINGS CONSTITUTIONAL LAW QUARTERLY.
University of California at San Francisco, Hastings College of the Law, 200 McAllister St., San Francisco, CA 94102-4978. TEL 415-565-4726. FAX 415-565-4814. *3891*

HASTINGS INTERNATIONAL AND COMPARATIVE LAW REVIEW.
University of California at San Francisco, Hastings College of the Law, 200 McAllister St., San Francisco, CA 94102-4978. TEL 415-565-4730. FAX 415-565-4814. *3931*

HASTINGS LAW JOURNAL.
University of California at San Francisco, Hastings College of the Law, 200 McAllister St., San Francisco, CA 94102-4978. TEL 415-565-4727. FAX 415-565-4814. *3786*

HASTINGS WOMEN'S LAW JOURNAL.
University of California at San Francisco, Hastings College of the Law, 200 McAllister St., San Francisco, CA 94102. TEL 415-565-4870. FAX 415-464-4814. *3786*

HAWAII BUSINESS DIRECTORY.
American Business Directories 5711 S. 86th Circle, Box 27347, Omaha, NE 68127. TEL 402-593-4600. FAX 402-331-5481. *1614*

HAWAII MANUFACTURERS REGISTER.
Manufacturers' News, Inc., 1633 Central St., Evanston, IL 60201-1569. TEL 847-864-7000. FAX 847-332-1100. *1614*

HAWKEYE (LA PLATA).
Charles County Community College, Box 910, Mitchell Rd., La Plata, MD 20646-0910. TEL 301-934-2251. FAX 301-934-7698. *1871*

AL-HAYAT.
Al Hayat Publishing Company Ltd., Kensington Centre, 66 Hammersmith Rd., London W14 84T, England. TEL 44-171-602-9988. FAX 44-171-602-4225. *3194*

HAZARDOUS WASTE BUSINESS.
McGraw-Hill Companies, Energy & Business Newsletters, 1221 Ave. of the Americas, 36th Fl., New York, NY 10020. TEL 212-521-6410. Producer(s): SilverPlatter Information, Inc. (McGraw-Hill Energy Library). *2852*

HEALTH AND POPULATION: PERSPECTIVES AND ISSUES.
National Institute of Health and Family Welfare, New Mehrauli Rd., Munirka, New Delhi 110 067, India. *827*

HEALTH AND SAFETY SCIENCE ABSTRACTS.
Cambridge Scientific Abstracts, 7200 Wisconsin Ave., 6th Fl., Bethesda, MD 20814. TEL 301-961-6750. FAX 301-961-6720. Producer(s): Knight-Ridder, Inc. (Toxicology & Pharmacology), NISC (Health & Safety - Risk Abstracts), SilverPlatter Information, Inc. (PolTox1). *5982*

HEALTH DEVICES ALERTS.
E C R I, 5200 Butler Pike, Plymouth Meeting, PA 19462. TEL 610-825-6000. FAX 610-834-1275. *4565*

HEALTH INDEX.
Information Access Company 362 Lakeside Dr., Foster City, CA 94404. TEL 415-378-5200. FAX 415-378-5369. *4565*

HEALTH INDUSTRY QUICKSOURCE.
QuickSource Press, 10 Pelham Ave., Nanuet, NY 10954-3428. *4565*

HEALTH MANPOWER MANAGEMENT.
M C B University Press Ltd., 60-62 Toller Ln., Bradford, W. Yorks BD8 9BY, England. TEL 44-1274-777700. FAX 44-1274-785200. *1420*

HEALTHCARE FINANCIAL MANAGEMENT.
Healthcare Financial Management Association, Two Westbrook Corporate Center, Ste. 700, Westchester, IL 60154. TEL 708-531-9600. FAX 708-531-0032. *3546*

HEBEI SHIFAN DAXUE XUEBAO (SHEHUI KEXUE BAN).
Hebei Shifan Daxue, Yuhua Lu, Shijiazhuang, Hebei 050016, People's Republic of China. TEL 86-311-6049941. FAX 86-311-6049413. *6325*

HEBEI SHIFAN DAXUE XUEBAO (ZIRAN KEXUE BAN).
Hebei Shifan Daxue, Yuhua Donglu, Shijiazhuang, Hebei 050016, People's Republic of China. TEL 86-311-6049941. FAX 86-311-6049413. *6244*

HEHAI DAXUE XUEBAO.
Hehai Daxue, 1 Xikang Rd., Nanjing, Jiangsu 210024, People's Republic of China. TEL 86-25-6632106. FAX 86-25-3315375. *2285*

CD-ROM

HELLENIC JOURNAL OF GASTROENTEROLOGY.
Beta Medical Publishers Ltd., Adrianiou 3, 115 25 Athens, Greece. TEL 30-1-7232-302. FAX 30-1-7232-302. *4693*

THE HEMINGWAY REVIEW.
University of Idaho Press, c/o Susan F. Beegel, Ed., 180 Polpis Rd., Nantucket, MA 02554. TEL 508-325-7157.
Producer(s): University Microfilms International. *4217*

HERALD EXPRESS.
Herald Express Publications Ltd., Barton Hill Rd., Torquay, Devon TQ2 8JN, England. TEL 44-1803-676000. FAX 44-1803-676299. *3156*

HEWLETT-PACKARD JOURNAL.
Hewlett Packard Co. (Palo Alto), 3000 Hanover St., Palo Alto, CA 94304. TEL 415-857-2387. FAX 415-857-2157. *2087*

HISPANIA.
American Association of Teachers of Spanish and Portuguese, Inc., Georgetown University, Spanish Dept., Washington, DC 20057-0989. TEL 617-832-3779. *4073*

HISPANIC AMERICAN PERIODICALS INDEX.
Latin American Studies Center Publications, University of California, Los Angeles, Box 951447, 10347 Bunche Hall, Los Angeles, CA 90095-1447. TEL 310-825-0810. FAX 310-206-2634.
Producer(s): NISC (Latin American Studies - Vol.1). *3366*

HISPANIC REVIEW.
University of Pennsylvania, Romance Languages Department, Philadelphia, PA 19104-6305. TEL 215-898-7420. FAX 215-898-0933. *4073*

HISTORICAL ABSTRACTS. PART A: MODERN HISTORY ABSTRACTS, 1450-1914.
A B C-Clio, 130 Cremona, Box 1911, Santa Barbara, CA 93116-1911. TEL 805-968-1911. FAX 805-685-9685. *3366*

HISTORICAL ABSTRACTS. PART B: TWENTIETH CENTURY ABSTRACTS, 1914 TO THE PRESENT.
A B C-Clio, 130 Cremona, Box 1911, Santa Barbara, CA 93116-1911. TEL 805-968-1911. FAX 805-685-9685. *3366*

HISTORICAL ABSTRACTS. PART B: TWENTIETH CENTURY ABSTRACTS, 1914 TO THE PRESENT. ANNUAL INDEX.
A B C-Clio, 130 Cremona, Box 1911, Santa Barbara, CA 93116-1911. TEL 805-968-1911. FAX 805-685-9685. *3367*

HISTORICAL METHODS.
Heldref Publications, 1319 Eighteenth St., N.W., Washington, DC 20036-1802. TEL 202-296-6267. FAX 202-296-5149.
Producer(s): University Microfilms International. *3345*

HISTORY AND THEORY.
Blackwell Publishers, 238 Main St., Cambridge, MA 02142. TEL 617-547-7110. FAX 617-547-0789.
Producer(s): University Microfilms International, H.W. Wilson. *3346*

HISTORY: REVIEWS OF NEW BOOKS.
Heldref Publications, 1319 Eighteenth St., N.W., Washington, DC 20036-1802. TEL 202-296-6267. FAX 202-296-5149.
Producer(s): University Microfilms International. *3347*

HISTORY TODAY.
History Today Ltd., 20 Old Compton St., London W1V 5PE, England. TEL 44-171-439-8315.
Producer(s): University Microfilms International. *3347*

HOLLAND EXPORTS.
A B C voor Handel en Industrie C.V., P.O. Box 190, 2000 AD Haarlem, Netherlands. TEL 31-23-5319031. FAX 31-23-5327033. *1278*

HOME POWER.
Home Power, Inc., Box 520, Ashland, OR 97520-0520. TEL 916-475-0830. FAX 916-475-3179. *2550*

HOOVER'S GUIDE TO THE BOOK BUSINESS.
Reference Press, Inc., Box 140375, Austin, TX 78714-0375. TEL 512-454-7778. FAX 512-454-9401. *1615*

HOOVER'S GUIDE TO THE TOP NEW YORK COMPANIES.
Reference Press, Inc., Box 140375, Austin, TX 78714-0375. TEL 512-454-7778. FAX 512-454-9401. *1615*

HOOVER'S GUIDE TO THE TOP SOUTHERN CALIFORNIA COMPANIES.
Reference Press, Inc., Box 140375, Austin, TX 78714-0375. TEL 512-454-7778. FAX 512-454-9401. *1615*

HOOVER'S HANDBOOK OF AMERICAN BUSINESS.
Reference Press Inc., Box 140375, Austin, TX 78714-0375. TEL 512-454-7778. FAX 512-454-9401. *1615*

HOOVER'S HANDBOOK OF EMERGING COMPANIES.
Reference Press, Inc., Box 140375, Austin, TX 78714-0375. TEL 512-454-7778. FAX 512-454-9401. *1615*

HOOVER'S HANDBOOK OF WORLD BUSINESS.
Reference Press Inc., Box 140375, Austin, TX 78714-0375. TEL 512-454-7778. FAX 512-454-9401. *1615*

HOPPENSTEDT VADEMECUM DER INVESTMENTFONDS.
Verlag Hoppenstedt GmbH, Havelstr. 9, 64295 Darmstadt, Germany. TEL 49-6151-380-0. FAX 49-6151-380-360. *1333*

HOPSCOTCH.
Bluffton News Printing and Publishing Co., Box 164, 103 N. Main St., Bluffton, OH 45817-0164. TEL 419-358-4610. FAX 419-358-5027. *1794*

HORIZONTES (SAN FRANCISCO).
Horizontes, 2601 Mission St., Ste. 900, San Francisco, CA 94110. TEL 415-641-6051. FAX 415-282-3320. *2882*

HORTICULTURAL ABSTRACTS.
CAB International, Wallingford, Oxon. OX10 8DE, England. TEL 44-1491-832111. FAX 44-1491-833508. *3070*

HOSPITAL ADMINISTRATION.
Indian Hospital Association, B-401, Sarita Vihar, New Delhi 110044, India. TEL 6835648. *3547*

HOSPITAL PRODUCT COMPARISON SYSTEM.
E C R I, 5200 Butler Pike, Plymouth Meeting, PA 19462. TEL 610-825-6000. FAX 610-834-1275.
Producer(s): Knight-Ridder, Inc.. *3549*

HOSPITAL TOPICS.
Heldref Publications, 1319 Eighteenth St., N.W., Washington, DC 20036. TEL 202-296-6267. FAX 202-296-5149.
Producer(s): University Microfilms International. *3549*

HUMAN RESOURCES MANAGEMENT.
Commerce Clearing House, Inc., 2700 Lake Cook Rd., Riverwoods, IL 60015. TEL 847-267-7000. FAX 800-224-8299. *1376*

HUMAN RESOURCES MANAGEMENT - COMPENSATION.
Commerce Clearing House, Inc., 2700 Lake Cook Rd., Riverwoods, IL 60015. TEL 847-267-7000. FAX 800-224-8299. *1504*

HUMAN RESOURCES MANAGEMENT - EMPLOYEE RELATIONS.
Commerce Clearing House, Inc., 4025 W. Peterson Ave., Riverwoods, IL 60015. TEL 847-267-7000. FAX 800-224-8299. *1504*

HUMAN RESOURCES MANAGEMENT - EQUAL EMPLOYMENT OPPORTUNITY.
Commerce Clearing House, Inc., 2700 Lake Cook Rd., Riverwoods, IL 60015. TEL 847-267-7000. FAX 847-224-8299. *1504*

HUMAN RESOURCES MANAGEMENT - O S H A COMPLIANCE.
Commerce Clearing House, Inc., 2700 Lake Cook Rd., Riverwoods, IL 60015. TEL 847-267-7000. FAX 800-224-8299. *5250*

HUMAN RESOURCES MANAGEMENT - PERSONNEL PRACTICES - COMMUNICATIONS.
Commerce Clearing House, Inc., 2700 Lake Cook Rd., Riverwoods, IL 60015. TEL 847-267-7000. FAX 800-224-8299. *1504*

HUMANITIES INDEX.
H.W. Wilson Co., 950 University Ave., Bronx, NY 10452. TEL 718-588-8400. FAX 718-590-1617.
Producer(s): H.W. Wilson (WILSONDISC). *3632*

HYDROGEN TODAY.
American Hydrogen Association, 216 S. Clark Dr., Ste. 103, Tempe, AZ 85281. TEL 602-921-0433. FAX 602-967-6601. *2572*

HYDROTITLES.
Geosystems, P.O. Box 40, Didcott, Oxon. OX11 9BX, England. TEL 44-1235-813913.
Producer(s): NISC (HydroROM). *2219*

I A R C MONOGRAPHS ON THE EVALUATION OF CARCINOGENIC RISK OF CHEMICALS TO HUMANS.
I A R C Press, 150, cours Albert Thomas, 69372 Lyon Cedex 08, France. TEL 33-72-738485. FAX 33-72-738302. *4736*

I C MASTER.
Hearst Business Publishing UTP Division, 645 Stewart Ave., Garden City, NY 11530. TEL 516-227-1300. FAX 516-227-1453. *2521*

I D F DIRECTORY.
International Diabetes Federation, 1 rue Defacqz, 1000 Brussels, Belgium. TEL 32-2-5385511. FAX 32-2-5385514. *4671*

I E E REVIEW.
I.E.E., Michael Faraday House, Six Hills Way, Stevenage, Herts. SG1 2AY, England. TEL 44-1438-313311. FAX 44-1438-742840.
Producer(s): University Microfilms International. *2707*

I I C.
V C H Verlagsgesellschaft mbH, Postfach 101161, 69451 Weinheim, Germany. TEL 06201-606-147. FAX 06201-606117. *5339*

I N I S ATOMINDEX.
International Atomic Energy Agency, Wagramerstrasse 5, Box 100, A-1400 Vienna, Austria. TEL 43-1-2060-22529. FAX 43-1-2060-29302.
Producer(s): SilverPlatter Information, Inc. (INIS). *5579*

I R S LETTER RULINGS AND TECHNICAL ADVICE MEMORANDUMS (1980-1995).
Tax Analysts, 6830 N. Fairfax Dr., Arlington, VA 22213. FAX 703-533-4444. *1548*

I R S PUBLICATIONS.
Commerce Clearing House, Inc., 2700 Lake Cook Rd., Riverwoods, IL 60015. TEL 847-267-7000. FAX 800-224-8299. *1548*

I S S N COMPACT.
International Centre for the Registration of Serials, I S S N International Centre, 20 rue Bachaumont, 75002 Paris, France. TEL 33-1-44-88-22-20. FAX 33-1-40-26-32-43.
Available only on CD-ROM. *534*

I S S N REGISTER (MICROFICHE EDITION).
International Centre for the Registration of Serials, I S S N International Centre, 20 rue Bachaumont, 75002 Paris, France. TEL 33-1-44-88-22-20. FAX 33-1-40-26-32-43. *534*

I S S N REGISTER (TAPE EDITION).
International Centre for the Registration of Serials, I S S N International Center, 20 rue Bachaumont, 75002 Paris, France. TEL 33-1-44-88-22-20. FAX 33-1-40-26-32-43. *534*

IBERLEX.
Boletin Oficial del Estado, Trafalgar, 27, 28071 Madrid, Spain. TEL 34-1-5382297. FAX 34-1-5382275. *3891*

IDAHO BUSINESS DIRECTORY.
American Business Directories, 5711 S. 86th Circle, Box 27347, Omaha, NE 68127. TEL 402-593-4600. FAX 402-331-5481. *1615*

IDAHO MANUFACTURERS REGISTER.
Database Publishing Company, 1590 S. Lewis St., Anaheim, CA 92805. TEL 714-778-6400. FAX 714-778-6811. *1616*

IGAKU CHUO ZASSHI.
Igaku Chuo Zasshi Kankokai, 5-18, Takaido Higashi 2-chome, Suginami-ku, Tokyo 168, Japan. *4469*

ILLINOIS BUSINESS DIRECTORY.
American Business Directories 5711 S. 86th Circle, Box 27347, Omaha, NE 68127. TEL 402-593-4600. FAX 402-331-5481. *1616*

ILLINOIS FAMILY LAWS AND COURT RULES.
West Publishing Corp., 620 Opperman Dr., Eagan, MN 55123. TEL 612-687-8000. FAX 612-687-7302. *3919*

ILLINOIS RESEARCH.
University of Illinois at Urbana-Champaign, College of Agricultural, Consumer and Environmental Sciences, 47 Mumford Hall, 1301 W. Gregory Dr., IL 61801. TEL 217-244-2830. *123*

ILLINOIS STATISTICAL ABSTRACT.
University of Illinois at Urbana-Champaign, Bureau of Economic and Business Research, 428 Commerce Bldg., W., 1206 S. Sixth St., Champaign, IL 61820. TEL 217-333-2331. FAX 217-233-7410. *6609*

ILOLEX C D - R O M.
Kluwer Law International, Postbus 85889, 2508 CN The Hague, Netherlands. TEL 31-70-3081500. FAX 31-70-3081515.
Available only on CD-ROM. *1377*

IMAGING.
Rapid Science Publishers, The Old Malthouse, Paradise St., Oxford OX1 1LD, England. TEL 44-1865-790447. FAX 44-1865-244012. *4876*

IMMIGRATION BRIEFINGS.
Federal Publications Inc., 1120 20th St., N.W., Ste. 500 S., Washington, DC 20036. TEL 202-337-7000. FAX 202-659-2233. *3891*

IMMUNOLOGY ABSTRACTS.
Cambridge Scientific Abstracts, 7200 Wisconsin Ave., 6th Fl., Bethesda, MD 20814. TEL 301-961-6750. FAX 301-961-6720.
Producer(s): SilverPlatter Information, Inc.. *4566*

IMPORTED CARS, LIGHT TRUCKS & VANS SERVICE & REPAIR.
Mitchell International, Inc., 9889 Willow Creek Rd., Box 26260, San Diego, CA 92196-0260. TEL 800-648-8010. FAX 619-578-4752. *6788*

THE INDEPENDENT.
Newspaper Publishing plc., 40 City Rd., London EC1Y 2DB, England. TEL 44-171-293-1222. FAX 44-171-293-1435.
Producer(s): Chadwyck-Healey Inc.. *3156*

THE INDEPENDENT INDEX.
Primary Source Media, P.O. Box 45, Reading RG1 8HF, England. TEL 44-1734-583247. FAX 44-1734-591325. *3715*

THE INDEPENDENT ON C D - R O M.
Chadwyck-Healey Ltd., The Quorum, Barnwell Rd., Cambridge CB5 8SW, England. TEL 44-1223-215512. FAX 44-1223-215514.
Available only on CD-ROM. Producer(s): Chadwyck-Healey Inc.. *3156*

THE INDEPENDENT ON SUNDAY.
Newspaper Publishing plc., 40 City Rd., London EC1Y 2DB, England. TEL 44-171-293-1222. FAX 44-171-293-1435.
Producer(s): Chadwyck-Healey Inc.. *3156*

INDEPENDENT POWER REPORT.
McGraw-Hill Companies, Energy & Business Newsletters, 1221 Ave. of the Americas, 36th Fl., New York, NY 10020. TEL 212-512-6410. Producer(s): SilverPlatter Information, Inc. (McGraw-Hill Energy Library). *2551*

INDEX: FOREIGN BROADCAST INFORMATION SERVICE DAILY REPORTS: AFRICA SUB-SAHARA.
NewsBank, Inc., 58 Pine St., New Canaan, CT 06840-5426. TEL 203-966-1100. FAX 203-966-6254. *5721*

INDEX: FOREIGN BROADCAST INFORMATION SERVICE DAILY REPORTS: CHINA.
NewsBank, Inc., 58 Pine St., New Canaan, CT 06840-5426. TEL 203-966-1100. FAX 203-966-6254. *5721*

INDEX: FOREIGN BROADCAST INFORMATION SERVICE DAILY REPORTS: EAST ASIA.
NewsBank, Inc., 58 Pine St., New Canaan, CT 06840-5426. TEL 203-966-1100. FAX 203-966-6254. *5721*

INDEX: FOREIGN BROADCAST INFORMATION SERVICE DAILY REPORTS: EASTERN EUROPE.
NewsBank, Inc., 58 Pine St., New Canaan, CT 06840-5426. TEL 203-966-1100. FAX 203-966-6254. *5721*

INDEX: FOREIGN BROADCAST INFORMATION SERVICE DAILY REPORTS: LATIN AMERICA.
NewsBank, Inc., 58 Pine St., New Canaan, CT 06840-5426. TEL 203-966-1100. FAX 203-966-6254. *5722*

INDEX: FOREIGN BROADCAST INFORMATION SERVICE DAILY REPORTS: NEAR EAST AND SOUTH ASIA.
NewsBank, Inc., 58 Pine St., New Canaan, CT 06840-5426. TEL 203-966-1100. FAX 203-966-6254. *5722*

INDEX: FOREIGN BROADCAST INFORMATION SERVICE DAILY REPORTS: WESTERN EUROPE.
NewsBank, Inc., 58 Pine St., New Canaan, CT 06840-5426. TEL 203-966-1100. FAX 203-966-6254. *5722*

INDEX: FOREIGN BROADCAST INFORMATION SERVICE REPORTS: CENTRAL EURASIA.
NewsBank, Inc., 58 Pine St., New Canaan, CT 06840-5426. TEL 203-966-1100. FAX 203-966-6254.
Available only on CD-ROM. *5722*

INDEX MEDICUS.
U.S. National Library of Medicine, 8600 Rockville Pike, Bethesda, MD 20894.
Producer(s): Cambridge Scientific Abstracts (Compact Cambridge MEDLINE), Knight-Ridder, Inc. (DIALOG OnDisc MEDLINE), SilverPlatter Information, Inc. (MEDLINE). *4566*

INDEX NEW ZEALAND.
National Library of New Zealand, P.O. Box 1467, Wellington, New Zealand. TEL 64-4-4743098. FAX 64-4-4753124. *15*

INDEX TO BOOK REVIEWS IN RELIGION.
American Theological Library Association, 820 Church St., Ste. 300, Evanston, IL 60201-5613. TEL 847-869-7788. FAX 847-869-8513. *6107*

INDEX TO CHINESE PERIODICALS.
National Central Library, 20 Chung Shan S. Rd., Taipei, Taiwan 10040, Republic of China. TEL 886-2-361-9132. FAX 886-2-311-0155.
Available only on CD-ROM. *15*

INDEX TO DENTAL LITERATURE.
American Dental Association, 211 E. Chicago Ave., Chicago, IL 60611. TEL 312-440-2500. FAX 312-440-2550.
Producer(s): Cambridge Scientific Abstracts (Compact Cambridge MEDLINE), Knight-Ridder, Inc. (DIALOG OnDisc MEDLINE), SilverPlatter Information, Inc. (MEDLINE). *4566*

INDEX TO FOREIGN LEGAL PERIODICALS.
University of California Press, Journals Division, 2120 Berkeley Way, No. 5812, Berkeley, CA 94720-5812. TEL 510-643-7154. FAX 510-642-9917.
Producer(s): SilverPlatter Information, Inc.. *3876*

INDEX TO HEBREW PERIODICALS (C D - R O M EDITION).
University of Haifa Library, Haifa 31905, Israel. FAX 972-4-257753.
Available only on CD-ROM. *534*

INDEX TO HOUSE OF COMMONS PARLIAMENTARY PAPERS.
Chadwyck-Healey Ltd., The Quorum, Barnwell Rd., Cambridge CB5 8SW, England. TEL 44-1223-215512. FAX 44-1223-215514.
Producer(s): Chadwyck-Healey Inc.. *5722*

INDEX TO INTERNATIONAL STATISTICS.
Congressional Information Service, Inc., A member of the LEXIS-NEXIS family, 4520 East-West Hwy., Bethesda, MD 20814-3389. TEL 301-654-1550. FAX 301-654-4033. *6609*

INDEX TO LEGAL PERIODICALS & BOOKS.
H.W. Wilson Co., 950 University Ave., Bronx, NY 10452. TEL 718-588-8400. FAX 718-590-1617. Producer(s): SilverPlatter Information, Inc., H.W. Wilson (WILSONDISC). *3876*

INDEX TO SCIENTIFIC & TECHNICAL PROCEEDINGS.
Institute for Scientific Information, 3501 Market St., Philadelphia, PA 19104. TEL 215-386-0100. FAX 215-386-2991.
Producer(s): Institute for Scientific Information. *6302*

INDEX TO SOCIAL SCIENCES & HUMANITIES PROCEEDINGS.
Institute for Scientific Information, 3501 Market St., Philadelphia, PA 19104. TEL 215-386-0100. FAX 215-386-2991.
Producer(s): Institute for Scientific Information. *6357*

INDEX TO SOUTH AFRICAN PERIODICALS.
State Library, P.O. Box 397, Pretoria 0001, South Africa. TEL 27-12-21-8931. FAX 27-12-325-5984. *6014*

INDIAN JOURNAL OF CANCER.
Indian Cancer Society, 74 Jerbai Wadia Rd., Parel, Bombay 400 012, India. TEL 22-412-5238. *4757*

INDIAN JOURNAL OF CHEST DISEASES AND ALLIED SCIENCES.
University of Delhi, Vallabhbhai Patel Chest Institute, P.O. Box 2101, Delhi 110 007, India. TEL 7257102. *4706*

INDIAN JOURNAL OF DERMATOLOGY, VENEREOLOGY AND LEPROLOGY.
Indian Association of Dermatologists, Venereologists and Leprologists, c/o Dr. Gurmohan Singh, Ed., New D-7, Banaras Hindu University, Varanasi 221 005, India. TEL 0542-310845. *4662*

INDIAN JOURNAL OF LEPROSY.
Indian Leprosy Association, 1, Red Cross Road, New Delhi 110 001, India. TEL 3714748. *4621*

INDIAN JOURNAL OF MALARIOLOGY.
Indian Council of Medical Research, Malaria Research Center, 22, Sham Nath Marg, Delhi 110 054, India. TEL 91-11-2528455. FAX 91-11-7234234. *4621*

INDIAN JOURNAL OF MEDICAL RESEARCH. SECTION A: INFECTIOUS DISEASES.
Indian Council of Medical Research, Division of Publication & Information, P.O. Box 4911, Ansari Nagar, New Delhi 110 029, India. TEL 91-11-6963980. FAX 91-11-6868662. *4470*

INDIAN JOURNAL OF NUTRITION AND DIETETICS.
Avinashilingam Institute for Home Science and Higher Education for Women, c/o Rajammal P. Devadas, Ed., Coimbatore 641 043, India. TEL 40241. *5234*

INDIAN JOURNAL OF OPHTHALMOLOGY.
All India Ophthalmological Society, c/o L.V. Prasad Eye Institute, Road No. 2, Banjara Hills 500 034, Hyderabad, India. *4770*

INDIAN JOURNAL OF PATHOLOGY & MICROBIOLOGY.
Indian Association of Pathologists and Microbiologists, Department of Laboratory Medicine, Safdarjung Hospital, New Delhi 110029, India. TEL 011-668433. *4470*

INDIAN JOURNAL OF PHARMACEUTICAL SCIENCES.
Indian Pharmaceutical Association, Kalina Santacruz East, Bombay 400098, India. *5417*

INDIAN JOURNAL OF PHARMACOLOGY.
Indian Pharmacologial Society, Department of Pharmacology, Jipmer, Pondicherry 605006, India. TEL 413-36380. FAX 413-38132. *5417*

CD-ROM

INDIAN JOURNAL OF PHYSIOLOGY AND PHARMACOLOGY.
Association of Physiologists and Pharmacologists of India, Department of Physiology, All India Institute of Medical Sciences, Ansari Nagar, New Delhi 110 029, India. *788*

INDIAN JOURNAL OF PSYCHIATRY.
Indian Psychiatric Society, K.G.'s Medical College, B 104-2 Niralanagar, Lucknow 226 020, India. TEL 91-416-22603. FAX 91-416-22788. *4840*

INDIAN JOURNAL OF RADIOLOGY & IMAGING.
Indian Radiological & Imaging Association, 13 Bheemanna Mudali Garden St., Madras 600018, India. TEL 91-22-412-1521. FAX 91-22-382-9595. *4876*

INDIANA BUSINESS DIRECTORY.
American Business Directories 5711 S. 86th Circle, Box 27347, Omaha, NE 68127. TEL 402-593-4600. FAX 402-331-5481. *1616*

INDICE DE LA LITERATURA DENTAL EN CASTELLANO.
Asociacion Odontologica Argentina, Junin 959, Buenos Aires, Argentina. TEL 541-9611062. FAX 541-9611110. *4566*

INDICE ESPANOL DE CIENCIA Y TECNOLOGIA.
Centro de Informacion y Documentacion Cientifica (Cindoc), Joaquin Costa 22, 28002 Madrid, Spain. TEL 34-1-5635482. FAX 34-1-5642644. *6302*

INDICE ESPANOL DE CIENCIAS SOCIALES. SERIES A: PSYCHOLOGY AND EDUCATIONAL SCIENCES.
Centro de Informacion y Documentacion Cientifica (Cindoc), Pinar, 25, 28006 Madrid, Spain. TEL 34-1-4111098. FAX 34-1-5645069. *5889*

INDICE ESPANOL DE CIENCIAS SOCIALES. SERIES B: ECONOMICS, SOCIOLOGY AND POLITICAL SCIENCE.
Centro de Informacion y Documentacion Cientifica (Cindoc), Pinar, 25, 3, 28006 Madrid, Spain. TEL 34-1-4111098. FAX 34-1-5645069. *1005*

INDICE ESPANOL DE CIENCIAS SOCIALES. SERIES C: LAW.
Centro de Informacion y Documentacion Cientifica (Cindoc), Pinar, 25, 3, 28006 Madrid, Spain. TEL 34-1-4111098. FAX 34-1-5645069. *3876*

INDICE ESPANOL DE CIENCIAS SOCIALES. SERIES D: SCIENCE AND SCIENTIFIC INFORMATION.
Centro de Informacion y Documentacion Cientifica (Cindoc), Pinar, 25, 3, 28006 Madrid, Spain. TEL 34-1-4111098. FAX 34-1-5645069. *6302*

INDICE ESPANOL DE CIENCIAS SOCIALES. SERIES E: URBAN PLANNING.
Centro de Informacion y Documentacion Cientifica (Cindoc), Pinar, 25, 3, 28006 Madrid, Spain. TEL 34-1-4111098. FAX 34-1-5645069. *3602*

INDICE ESPANOL DE HUMANIDADES. SERIES A: ART.
Centro de Informacion y Documentacion Cientifica (Cindoc), Pinar, 25, 3, 28006 Madrid, Spain. TEL 34-3-4111098. FAX 34-1-5645069. *463*

INDICE ESPANOL DE HUMANIDADES. SERIES B: HISTORICAL SCIENCES.
Centro de Informacion y Documentacion Cientifica (Cindoc), Pinar 25, 3, 28006 Madrid, Spain. TEL 34-1-4111098. FAX 34-1-5645069. *3367*

INDICE ESPANOL DE HUMANIDADES. SERIES C: LINGUISTICS AND LITERATURE.
Centro de Informacion y Documentacion Cientifica (Cindoc), Pinar 25, 3, 28006 Madrid, Spain. TEL 34-1-4111098. FAX 34-1-5645069. *4127*

INDICE ESPANOL DE HUMANIDADES. SERIES D: PHILOSOPHY.
Centro de Informacion y Documentacion Cientifica (Cindoc), Pinar, 25, 3, 28006 Madrid, Spain. TEL 34-1-4111098. FAX 34-1-5645069. *5507*

INDICE MEDICO ESPANOL.
Generalitat Valenciana, Conselleria de Sanitat i Consum, Avda. Blasco Ibanez - 17, 46010 Valencia, Spain. TEL 96-361-06-54. FAX 96-3613975. *4566*

INDIVIDUALS WITH DISABILITIES EDUCATION LAW REPORTER.
L R P Publications 747 Dresher Rd., Box 980, Horsham, PA 19044-0980. TEL 215-784-0941. FAX 215-784-9639. *2469*

INDUSTRIAL AND COMMERCIAL TRAINING.
M C B University Press Ltd., 60-62 Toller Ln., Bradford, W. Yorks BD8 9BY, England. TEL 44-1274-777700. FAX 44-1274-785200. *1505*

INDUSTRIAL CASES REPORTS.
Incorporated Council of Law Reporting for England and Wales, 3 Stone Bldgs., Lincoln's Inn, London WC2A 3XN, England. TEL 44-171-242-6471. FAX 44-171-831-5247. *3902*

INDUSTRIAL ENERGY BULLETIN.
McGraw-Hill Companies, Energy & Business Newsletters, 1221 Ave. of the Americas, 36th Fl., New York, NY 10020. TEL 212-512-2000. Producer(s): SilverPlatter Information, Inc. (McGraw-Hill Energy Library). *2551*

INDUSTRIAL MANAGEMENT & DATA SYSTEMS.
M C B University Press Ltd., 60-62 Toller Ln., Bradford, W. Yorks ED8 9BY, England. TEL 44-1274-777700. FAX 44-1274-785200. *1155*

INDUSTRIAL NEWS (IAEGER).
Box 180, Iaeger, WV 24844. TEL 304-938-2142. *931*

INDUSTRY GROUP MARKET VALUES.
Standard & Poor's 25 Broadway, New York, NY 10004. TEL 212-203-8000. *1334*

INFECTION AND IMMUNITY.
American Society for Microbiology, 1325 Massachusetts Ave., N.W., Washington, DC 20005. TEL 202-737-3600. *4583*

INFORMATIE.
Kluwer Bedrijfswetenschappen B.V. Postbus 23, 7400 GA Deventer, Netherlands. TEL 31-570-648932. FAX 31-570-611504. *1992*

INFORMATORE DI VETERINARIA E ZOOTECNIA.
Organizzazione Editoriale Medico Farmaceutica, Via Edolo 42, 20125 Milan, Italy. TEL 39-2-675051. FAX 39-2-67505223. *6947*

INGRAM - BOOKS IN PRINT PLUS.
R.R. Bowker, A Division of Reed Elsevier Inc., 121 Chanlon Rd., New Providence, NJ 07974. TEL 908-665-2866. FAX 908-665-3528. Available only on CD-ROM. Producer(s): Bowker Electronic Publishing (Books In Print PLUS). *535*

INGRAM - BOOKS IN PRINT PLUS WITH BOOK REVIEWS PLUS.
R.R. Bowker, A Division of Reed Elsevier Inc., 121 Chanlon Rd., New Providence, NJ 07974. TEL 908-665-2866. FAX 908-665-3528. Available only on CD-ROM. Producer(s): Bowker Electronic Publishing (Books In Print PLUS). *535*

INPHARMA WEEKLY.
Adis International Limited, Private Bag 65901, Mairangi Bay, Auckland 10, New Zealand. TEL 64-9-479-8100. FAX 64-9-479-8145. Producer(s): SilverPlatter Information, Inc.. *5450*

INSIDE CONFERENCES ON C D - R O M.
British Library, Document Supply Centre, Boston Spa, Weatherby, W. Yorks. LS23 7BQ, England. TEL 44-1937-546080. FAX 44-1937-546286. Available only on CD-ROM. *535*

INSIDE ENERGY WITH FEDERAL LANDS.
McGraw-Hill Companies, Energy & Business Newsletters, 1221 Ave. of the Americas, 36th Fl., New York, NY 10020. TEL 212-512-6410. Producer(s): SilverPlatter Information, Inc. (McGraw-Hill Energy Library). *2551*

INSIDE F E R C.
McGraw-Hill Companies, 1221 Ave. of the Americas, New York, NY 10020. Producer(s): SilverPlatter Information, Inc. (McGraw-Hill Energy Library). *2551*

INSIDE F E R C'S GAS MARKET REPORT.
McGraw-Hill Companies, Energy & Business Newsletters, 1221 Ave. of the Americas, 36th Fl., New York, NY 10020. TEL 212-512-6410. Producer(s): SilverPlatter Information, Inc. (McGraw-Hill Energy Library) *5360*

INSIDE INFORMATION ON C D - R O M.
British Library, Document Supply Centre, Boston Spa, Wetherby, W. Yorks. LS23 7BQ, England. TEL 44-1937-546080. FAX 44-1937-546080. Available only on CD-ROM. *535*

INSIDE N R C.
McGraw-Hill Companies, Energy and Business Newsletters, 1221 Ave. of the Americas, 36th Fl., New York, NY 10020. Producer(s): SilverPlatter Information, Inc. (McGraw-Hill Energy Library). *2577*

INSIGHT ON THE NEWS.
Washington Times Corporation, 3600 New York Ave., N.E., Washington, DC 20002. TEL 202-636-8800. FAX 202-529-2434. *3230*

INSTITUT PASTEUR DE TUNIS. ARCHIVES.
Institut Pasteur de Tunis, 13 Place Pasteur, B.P. 74, 1002 Tunis Belvedere, Tunisia. TEL 216-1-283022. FAX 216-1-79-333. *4471*

INSTITUTE OF MANAGEMENT INTERNATIONAL DATABASES PLUS.
Bowker - Saur Ltd., A member of the Reed Elsevier plc group, Maypole House, Maypole Rd., E. Grinstead, W. Sussex RH19 1HU, England. TEL 44-1342-330100. FAX 44-1342-330191. Available only on CD-ROM. Producer(s): Bowker - Saur Ltd.. *1423*

INSTITUTIONAL INVESTOR.
Institutional Investor, Inc., 488 Madison Ave., New York, NY 10022. TEL 212-224-3570. FAX 212-224-3592. *1334*

INSTITUTIONAL INVESTOR INTERNATIONAL EDITION.
Institutional Investor, Inc., 488 Madison Ave., New York, NY 10022. TEL 212-224-3570. FAX 212-224-3592. *1334*

INSTITUTO DE CARDIOLOGIA DE MEXICO. ARCHIVOS.
Instituto Nacional de Cardiologia "Ignacio Chavez", Oficina de Publicaciones, Juan Badiano No.1, Tlalpan, 14080 Mexico D.F. Mexico. TEL 52-5-5732911 ext. 310. FAX 52-5-5730994. *4604*

INSTITUTO NACIONAL DE CANCEROLOGIA DE MEXICO. REVISTA.
Editorial Cultura Medica S.A., Casma 576, Col. Lindavista 2C, 07300 Mexico, D.F. Mexico. TEL 525-6280429. FAX 525-57346662. *4757*

INSTITUTO NACIONAL DE ENFERMEDADES RESPIRATORIAS. REVISTA.
Instituto Nacional de Enfermedades Respiratorias, Clz. Tlalpan 4502, Col. Seccion XVI, 14082 Mexico DF, Mexico. *4888*

INSURANCE PERIODICALS INDEX.
N I L S Publishing Company, 21625 Prairie St., Box 2507, Chatsworth, CA 91311. TEL 818-998-8830. FAX 818-718-8482. *3671*

INTEGRATED CIRCUITS. DIGITAL.
D.A.T.A. Business Publishing 15 Inverness Way E., Box 6510, Englewood, CO 80155-6510. FAX 303-799-4032. *2524*

INTEGRATED WASTE MANAGEMENT.
McGraw-Hill Companies, Energy & Business Newsletters, 1221 Ave. of the Americas, 36th Fl., New York, NY 10020. TEL 212-512-6410. Producer(s): SilverPlatter Information, Inc. (McGraw-Hill Energy Library). *2853*

INTERFACE I CS D.A.T.A. DIGEST.
D.A.T.A. Business Publishing 15 Inverness Way E., Box 6510, Englewood, CO 80155-6510. FAX 303-799-4082. *2524*

INTERNATIONAL AEROSPACE ABSTRACTS.
American Institute of Aeronautics and Astronautics, 3370 L'Enfant Promedade, S.W., Washington, DC 20024. TEL 202-646-7400. FAX 202-646-7508. Producer(s): Knight-Ridder, Inc. (OnDisc Aerospace Database). *82*

INTERNATIONAL ATOMIC ENERGY AGENCY. SAFETY SERIES.
International Atomic Energy Agency, Wagramerstr. 5, P.O. Box 100, A-1400 Vienna, Austria. TEL 43-1-2060-22529. FAX 43-1-2060-29302. *5965*

INTERNATIONAL BOOKS IN PRINT.
K.G. Saur Verlag KG, A member of the Reed Elsevier plc group, Ortlerstr. 8, 81373 Munich, Germany. TEL 49-89-76902-0. FAX 49-89-76902150.
Producer(s): K.G. Saur Verlag. *535*

INTERNATIONAL BOOKS IN PRINT PLUS.
K.G. Saur Verlag KG, A member of the Reed Elsevier plc group, Ortlerstr. 8, 81373 Munich, Germany. TEL 49-89-76902-0. FAX 49-89-76902150.
Available only on CD-ROM. Producer(s): K.G. Saur Verlag. *536*

INTERNATIONAL BUILDING SCIENCE & CONSTRUCTION ABSTRACTS.
C I T I S Ltd., 2 Rosemount Terrace, Blackrock, Dublin, Ireland. TEL 353-1-2886227. FAX 353-1-2885971. *883*

INTERNATIONAL CIVIL ENGINEERING ABSTRACTS.
C I T I S Ltd., 2 Rosemount Terrace, Blackrock, Dublin, Ireland. TEL 353-1-2886227. FAX 353-1-885-971. *2628*

INTERNATIONAL CLINICAL PSYCHOPHARMACOLOGY.
Rapid Science Publishers, The Old Malthouse, Paradise St., Oxford OX1 1LD, England. TEL 44-1865-790447. FAX 44-1865-244012. *5849*

INTERNATIONAL DIRECTORY OF DESIGN.
Penrose Press, Box 470925, San Francisco, CA 94147. TEL 415-567-4157. FAX 415-567-4165. *435*

INTERNATIONAL ECONOMIC INSIGHTS.
Institute for International Economics, 11 Dupont Circle N.W., Ste. 620, Washington, DC 20036-1207. TEL 202-328-9000. FAX 202-328-5432. *1217*

INTERNATIONAL EXAMINER.
622 S. Washington, Seattle, WA 98104. *2884*

INTERNATIONAL FILMARCHIVE C D - R O M.
International Federation of Film Archives (F I A F), 6 Nottingham St., London W1M 3RB, England. TEL 0171-224-1203. FAX 0171-224-0991. Available only on CD-ROM. *5116*

INTERNATIONAL FINANCIAL STATISTICS.
International Monetary Fund, Publications Unit, 700 19th St., N.W., Washington, DC 20431. TEL 202-623-7430. FAX 202-623-7201. *1006*

INTERNATIONAL FREQUENCY LIST.
International Telecommunication Union, Radiocommunication Bureau, Place des Nations, CH-1211 Geneva 20, Switzerland. TEL 41-22-730-5801. FAX 41-22-730-5785. *1963*

INTERNATIONAL HOSPITALITY AND TOURISM DATABASE C D - R O M.
Consortium of Hospitality Research Information Services (CHRIS), Attn. Karen Bobbett, Sha Library, Statler Hall, Ithaca, NY 14853-6902. TEL 607-254-4656. FAX 607-255-0021.
Available only on CD-ROM. *3574*

INTERNATIONAL INDEX TO FILM PERIODICALS.
International Federation of Film Archives (F I A F), 6 Nottingham St., London W1M 3RB, England. TEL 0171-224-1203. FAX 0171-224-0991. *5116*

INTERNATIONAL INDEX TO TELEVISION PERIODICALS.
International Federation of Film Archives (F I A F), 6 Nottingham St., London W1M 3RB, England. TEL 0171-224-1203. FAX 0171-224-0991. *1924*

INTERNATIONAL JOURNAL OF BANK MARKETING.
M C B University Press Ltd., 60-62 Toller Ln., Bradford, W. Yorks BD8 9BY, England. TEL 44-1274-777700. FAX 44-1274-785200. *1102*

INTERNATIONAL JOURNAL OF OPERATIONS AND PRODUCTION MANAGEMENT.
M C B University Press Ltd., 60-62 Toller Ln., Bradford, W. Yorks BD8 9BY, England. TEL 44-1274-777700. FAX 44-1274-785200. *1424*

INTERNATIONAL JOURNAL OF PHYSICAL DISTRIBUTION & LOGISTICS MANAGEMENT.
M C B University Press Ltd., 60-62 Toller Ln., Bradford, W. Yorks BD8 9BY, England. TEL 44-1274-777700. FAX 44-1274-785200. *6858*

INTERNATIONAL JOURNAL OF PUNJAB STUDIES.
Sage Publications India Pvt. Ltd., Box 4215, New Delhi 110 048, India. TEL 91-11-644-4958. FAX 91-11-647-2426.
Producer(s): SilverPlatter Information, Inc.. *6329*

INTERNATIONAL JOURNAL OF RETAIL & DISTRIBUTION MANAGEMENT.
M C B University Press Ltd., 60-62 Toller Ln., Bradford, W. Yorks BD8 9BY, England. TEL 44-1274-777700. FAX 44-1274-785200. *1469*

INTERNATIONAL JOURNAL OF SOCIAL ECONOMICS.
M C B University Press Ltd., 60-62 Toller Ln., Bradford, W. Yorks BD8 9BY, England. TEL 44-1274-777700. FAX 44-1274-785200. *933*

INTERNATIONAL JOURNAL OF SYSTEMATIC BACTERIOLOGY.
American Society for Microbiology, 1325 Massachusetts Ave., N.W., Washington, DC 20005. TEL 202-737-3600. *759*

INTERNATIONAL LITERARY MARKET PLACE.
R.R. Bowker, A Division of Reed Elsevier Inc., New Providence, NJ 07974. TEL 908-464-6800. FAX 908-665-6688.
Producer(s): Bowker Electronic Publishing. *5999*

INTERNATIONAL MARKETING DATA AND STATISTICS (YEAR).
Euromonitor, 60-61 Britton St., London EC1M 5QU, England. TEL 44-171-251-8024. FAX 44-171-608-3149. *1006*

INTERNATIONAL MARKETING REVIEW.
M C B University Press Ltd., 60-62 Toller Ln., Bradford, W. Yorks BD8 9BY, England. TEL 44-1274-777700. FAX 44-1274-785200. *1469*

INTERNATIONAL MEDICAL JOURNAL.
Japan International Cultural Exchange Foundation, 2-15-5-207 Shoto, Shibuya-ku, Tokyo 150, Japan. TEL 81-3-3424-9090. FAX 81-3-3424-9119. *4474*

INTERNATIONAL MEDIEVAL BIBLIOGRAPHY.
International Medieval Bibliography, International Medieval Institute, Parkinson 103, University of Leeds, Leeds LS2 9JT, England. TEL 44-113-2333614. FAX 44-113-2333616. *3367*

INTERNATIONAL NEW PRODUCT REPORT.
Mintel International Group Ltd., 18-19 Long Ln., London EC1A 9HE, England. TEL 44-171-606-4533. FAX 44-171-606-5932. *3006*

INTERNATIONAL NURSING INDEX.
American Journal of Nursing Co., 555 W. 57th St., New York, NY 10019. TEL 212-582-8820.
Producer(s): Cambridge Scientific Abstracts (Compact Cambridge MEDLINE), Knight-Ridder, Inc. (DIALOG OnDisc MEDLINE), SilverPlatter Information, Inc. (MEDLINE). *4566*

INTERNATIONAL PACKAGING ABSTRACTS.
Pira International, Randalls Rd., Leatherhead, Surrey KT22 7RU, England. TEL 44-1372-802050. FAX 44-1372-802239.
Producer(s): Knight-Ridder, Inc.. *5305*

INTERNATIONAL PHARMACEUTICAL ABSTRACTS.
American Society of Health-System Pharmacists, 7272 Wisconsin Ave., Bethesda, MD 20814. TEL 301-657-3000. FAX 301-657-1641.
Producer(s): SilverPlatter Information, Inc.. *5450*

INTERNATIONAL SATELLITE DIRECTORY.
Design Publishers, 800 Siesta Way, Sonoma, CA 95476-4413. *69*

INTERNATIONAL SEMICONDUCTOR DIRECTORY D.A.T.A. DIGEST: MASTER TYPE LOCATOR.
D.A.T.A. Business Publishing 15 Inverness Way E., Box 6510, Englewood, CO 80155-6510. FAX 303-799-0381. *2525*

INTERNATIONALE BIBLIOGRAPHIE DER REZENSIONEN WISSENSCHAFTLICHER LITERATUR.
Zeller Verlag GmbH, Postfach 1949, 49009 Osnabrueck, Germany. TEL 49-541-4045914. FAX 49-541-41255. *6302*

INTERNATIONALE BIBLIOGRAPHIE DER ZEITSCHRIFTENLITERATUR AUS ALLEN GEBIETEN DES WISSENS.
Zeller Verlag GmbH, Postfach 1949, 49009 Osnabrueck, Germany. TEL 49-541-4045914. FAX 49-541-41255. *536*

INTERPRETER RELEASES.
Federal Publications Inc., 1120 20th St., N.W., Ste. 500 S., Washington, DC 20036. TEL 202-337-7000. FAX 202-659-2233. *3891*

INTLEC C D - R O M.
Chadwyck-Healey Inc., 1101 King St., Alexandria, VA 22314. TEL 703-683-4890. FAX 703-683-7589.
Available only on CD-ROM. Producer(s): Chadwyck-Healey Inc.. *1218*

IOWA BUSINESS DIRECTORY.
American Business Directories 5711 S. 86th Circle, Box 27347, Omaha, NE 68127. TEL 402-593-4600. FAX 402-331-5481. *1618*

IOWA RULES OF COURT, STATE AND FEDERAL.
West Publishing Corp., 620 Opperman Dr., Eagan, MN 55123. TEL 612-687-8000. FAX 612-687-7302. *3948*

IRANIAN JOURNAL OF PUBLIC HEALTH.
Iranian Public Health Association, University of Teheran, Teheran, Iran. *5966*

J A M A: THE JOURNAL OF THE AMERICAN MEDICAL ASSOCIATION.
American Medical Association, 515 N. State St., Chicago, IL 60610. TEL 312-464-5000. FAX 312-464-4184. *4476*

J A R AMENDMENT SERVICE TO REGULATORY DOCUMENTS.
Joint Aviation Authorities, J A A Headquarters, Saturnusstraat 8-10, P.O. Box 3000, 2130 KA Hoofddorp, Netherlands. TEL 31-23-5679700. FAX 31-23-5621714. *6760*

J & W BANKING INTERNATIONAL. INTERNATIONAL BANKING AND FINANCE COMMUNICATIONS DIRECTORY.
Telex - Verlag Jaeger & Waldmann GmbH, Birkenweg 8-10, 64295 Darmstadt, Germany. TEL 49-6151-3302-0. FAX 49-6151-3302-50. *1946*

J & W TELEFAX INTERNATIONAL. INTERNATIONAL FAX DIRECTORY.
Telex - Verlag Jaeger & Waldmann GmbH, Birkenweg 8-10, 64295 Darmstadt, Germany. TEL 49-6151-3302-0. FAX 49-6151-3302-50. *1946*

J & W TELEX INTERNATIONAL. INTERNATIONAL TELEX AND TELETEX DIRECTORY.
Telex - Verlag Jaeger & Waldmann GmbH, Birkenweg 8-10, 64295 Darmstadt, Germany. TEL 49-6151-3302-0. FAX 49-6151-3302-50. *1946*

J & W TRAVEL INTERNATIONAL.
Telex - Verlag Jaeger & Waldmann GmbH, Birkenweg 8-10, 64295 Darmstadt, Germany. TEL 49-6151-3302-0. FAX 49-6151-3302-50. *1946*

JAHRBUCH FUER BERGBAU, ERDOEL UND ERDGAS, PETROCHEMIE, ELEKTRIZITAET, UMWELTSCHUTZ.
Verlag Glueckauf GmbH, Postfach 185620, 45206 Essen, Germany. TEL 49-2054-92412023. FAX 49-2054-924129. *5067*

JANE'S AIRCRAFT UPGRADES.
Jane's Information Group, Sentinel House, 163 Brighton Rd., Coulsdon, Surrey CR5 2NH, England. TEL 44-181-700-3700. FAX 44-181-700-3788. *70*

JANE'S ALL THE WORLD'S AIRCRAFT.
Jane's Information Group, Sentinel House, 163
Brighton Rd., Coulsdon, Surrey CR5 2NH, England.
TEL 44-181-700-3700. FAX 44-181-700-3788.
70

JANE'S ARMOUR AND ARTILLERY.
Jane's Information Group, Sentinel House, 163
Brighton Rd., Coulsdon, Surrey CR5 2NH, England.
TEL 44-181-700-3700. FAX 44-181-700-3788.
5034

JANE'S ARMOUR AND ARTILLERY UPGRADES.
Jane's Information Group, Sentinel House, 163
Brighton Rd., Coulsdon, Surrey CR5 2NH, England.
TEL 44-181-700-3700. FAX 44-181-700-3788.
5034

JANE'S AVIONICS.
Jane's Information Group, Sentinel House, 163
Brighton Rd., Coulsdon, Surrey CR5 2NH, England.
TEL 44-181-700-3700. FAX 44-181-700-3788.
70

JANE'S C 4 I SYSTEMS.
Jane's Information Group, Sentinel House, 163
Brighton Rd., Coulsdon, Surrey CR5 2NH, England.
TEL 44-181-700-3700. FAX 44-181-700-3788.
5034

JANE'S FIGHTING SHIPS.
Jane's Information Group, Sentinel House, 163
Brighton Rd., Coulsdon, Surrey CR5 2NH, England.
TEL 44-181-700-3700. FAX 44-181-700-3788.
5035

JANE'S HIGH-SPEED MARINE TRANSPORTATION.
Jane's Information Group, Sentinel House, 163
Brighton Rd., Coulsdon, Surrey CR5 2NH, England.
TEL 44-181-700-3700. FAX 44-181-700-3788.
6838

JANE'S INFANTRY WEAPONS.
Jane's Information Group, Sentinel House, 163
Brighton Rd., Coulsdon, Surrey CR5 2NH, England.
TEL 44-181-700-3700. FAX 44-181-700-3788.
5035

JANE'S INTERNATIONAL A B C AEROSPACE DIRECTORY.
Jane's Information Group, Sentinel House, 163
Brighton Rd., Coulsdon, Surrey CR5 2NH, England.
TEL 44-181-700-3700. FAX 44-181-700-3788.
1618

JANE'S INTERNATIONAL DEFENCE DIRECTORY.
Jane's Information Group, Sentinel House, 163
Brighton Rd., Coulsdon, Surrey CR5 2NH, England.
TEL 44-181-700-3700. FAX 44-181-700-3788.
5035

JANE'S LAND-BASED AIR DEFENCE.
Jane's Information Group, Sentinel House, 163
Brighton Rd., Coulsdon, Surrey CR5 2NH, England.
TEL 44-181-700-3700. FAX 44-181-700-3788.
5035

JANE'S MILITARY COMMUNICATIONS.
Jane's Information Group, Sentinel House, 163
Brighton Rd., Coulsdon, Surrey CR5 2NH, England.
TEL 44-181-700-3700. FAX 44-181-700-3788.
5035

JANE'S MILITARY VEHICLES AND LOGISTICS.
Jane's Information Group, Sentinel House, 163
Brighton Rd., Coulsdon, Surrey CR5 2NH, England.
TEL 44-18700-3700. FAX 44-181-700-3788.
5035

JANE'S N B C PROTECTION EQUIPMENT.
Jane's Information Group, Sentinel House, 163
Brighton Rd., Coulsdon, Surrey CR5 2NH, England.
TEL 44-181-700-3700. FAX 44-181-700-3788.
5035

JANE'S NAVAL WEAPON SYSTEM.
Jane's Information Group, Sentinel House, 163
Brighton Rd., Coulsdon, Surrey CR5 2NH, England.
TEL 44-181-700-3700. FAX 44-181-700-3788.
5035

JANE'S POLICE AND SECURITY EQUIPMENT.
Jane's Information Group, Sentinel House, 163
Brighton Rd., Coulsdon, Surrey CR5 2NH, England.
TEL 44-181-700-3700. FAX 44-181-700-3788.
2182

JANE'S RADAR AND ELECTRONIC WARFARE SYSTEMS.
Jane's Information Group, Sentinel House, 163
Brighton Rd., Coulsdon, Surrey CR5 2NH, England.
TEL 44-181-700-3700. FAX 44-181-700-3788.
5035

JANE'S SIMULATION AND TRAINING SYSTEMS.
Jane's Information Group, Sentinel House, 163
Brighton Rd., Coulsdon, Surrey CR5 2NH, England.
TEL 44-181-700-3700. FAX 44-181-700-3788.
5035

JANE'S SPACE DIRECTORY.
Jane's Information Group, Sentinel House, 163
Brighton Rd., Coulsdon, Surrey CR5 2NH, England.
TEL 44-181-700-3700. FAX 44-181-700-3788.
70

JANE'S UNDERWATER WARFARE SYSTEMS.
Jane's Information Group, Sentinel House, 163
Brighton Rd., Coulsdon, Surrey CR5 2NH, England.
TEL 44-181-700-3700. FAX 44-181-700-3788.
5036

JANE'S URBAN TRANSPORT SYSTEMS.
Jane's Information Group, Sentinel House, 163
Brighton Rd., Coulsdon, Surrey CR5 2NH, England.
TEL 44-181-700-3700. FAX 44-181-700-3788.
6720

JANE'S WORLD RAILWAYS.
Jane's Information Group, Sentinel House, 163
Brighton Rd., Coulsdon, Surrey CR5 2NH, England.
TEL 44-181-700-3700. FAX 44-181-700-3788.
6812

JAPAN ELECTRONICS BUYERS' GUIDE.
Dempa Publications, Inc., 1-11-15, Higashi
Gotanda, Shinagawa-ku, Tokyo 141, Japan. TEL 81-
3-3445-6111. FAX 81-3-3445-6101.
Available only on CD-ROM. 1618

JAPAN TIMES.
Japan Times Ltc., 5-4 Shibaura 4-chome, Minato-ku,
Tokyo 108, Japan. TEL 03-3453-5242. FAX 03-
3452-1298. 3187

JAPANESE NATIONAL BIBLIOGRAPHY WEEKLY LIST.
National Diet Library, 1-10-1 Nagata-cho, Chiyoda-
ku, Tokyo 100, Japan. TEL 03-3581-2331.
FAX 03-3597-9104. 536

JAPANESE PERIODICALS INDEX. SCIENCE AND TECHNOLOGY.
National Diet Library, 1-10-1 Nagata-cho, Chiyoda-
ku, Tokyo 100, Japan TEL 03-3581-2331.
FAX 03-3597-9104. 6302

THE JERUSALEM POST.
Jerusalem Post, P.O. Box 81, Jerusalem 91000,
Israel. TEL 972-2-315666. FAX 972-2-389017.
3182

THE JERUSALEM POST (EDITION FRANCAISE).
Jerusalem Post, P.O. Box 81, Jerusalem 91000,
Israel. TEL 972-2-315666. FAX 972-2-389017.
3182

THE JERUSALEM POST (INTERNATIONAL EDITION).
Jerusalem Post, P.O. Box 81, Jerusalem 91000,
Israel. TEL 972-2-315666. FAX 972-2-389017.
3182

JET.
Johnson Publishing Co. Inc., 820 S. Michigan Ave.,
Chicago, IL 60605-2190. TEL 312-322-9200.
Producer(s): University Microfilms International.
3230

JIANGHAN KAOGU.
Archaeological Insitute of Hubei Province, Tian'e
Cun, Donghu Lu, Wuchang-qu, Wuhan, Hubei
430077, People's Republic of China. TEL 86-10-
27-6813122. 359

JOHANSENS RECOMMENDED HOTELS, COUNTRY HOUSES & INNS IN GREAT BRITAIN & IRELAND C D - R O M.
Hobsons Publishing Plc, Bateman St., Cambridge
CB2 1LZ, England. TEL 44-1223-354551. FAX 44-
1223-321454.
Available only on CD-ROM. 3566

JOHANSENS RECOMMENDED HOTELS IN EUROPE.
Hobsons Publishing Plc, Bateman St., Cambridge
CB2 1LZ, England. TEL 44-1223-354551. FAX 44-
1223-321454. 3566

JOINT AVIATION AUTHORITIES. CERTIFICATION INFORMATION - PROCEDURES.
Joint Aviation Authorities, J A A Headquarters,
Saturnusstraat 8-10, P.O. Box 3000, 2130 KA
Hoofddorp, Netherlands. TEL 31-23-5679700.
FAX 31-23-5621714. 6761

JOINT AVIATION AUTHORITIES. GENERAL INFORMATION - PROCEDURES. INFORMATION LEAFLETS.
Joint Aviation Authorities, J A A Headquarters,
Saturnusstraat 8-10, P.O. Box 3000, 2130 KA
Hoofddorp, Netherlands. TEL 31-23-5679700.
FAX 31-23-5621714. 6761

JOINT AVIATION AUTHORITIES. MAINTENANCE INFORMATION - PROCEDURES.
Joint Aviation Authorities, J A A Headquarters,
Saturnusstraat 8-10, P.O. Box 3000, 2130 KA
Hoofddorp, Netherlands. TEL 31-23-5679700.
FAX 31-23-5621714. 6761

JOINT AVIATION AUTHORITIES. REGULATORY DOCUMENTS.
Joint Aviation Authorities, J A A Headquarters,
Saturnusstraat 8-10, P.O. Box 3000, 2130 KA
Hoofddorp, Netherlands. TEL 31-23-5679700.
FAX 31-23-5621714. 6761

JORDAN MEDICAL JOURNAL.
Jordan Medical Association P.O. Box 915, Amman,
Jordan. 4477

JOURNAL OF ADVERTISING
American Academy of Advertising, Clemson
University, College of Commerce & Industry, 245
Sirrine Hall, Clemson, SC 29634-1325. 38

JOURNAL OF AMERICAN COLLEGE HEALTH.
Heldref Publications, 1319 Eighteenth St., N.W.,
Washington, DC 20036-1802. TEL 202-296-6267.
FAX 202-296-5149.
Producer(s): University Microfilms International.
5531

JOURNAL OF APPLIED PHYSICS.
American Institute of Physics, One Physics Ellipse,
College Park, MD 20740-3843. TEL 301-209-
3000. 5553

JOURNAL OF ARTS MANAGEMENT, LAW, AND SOCIETY.
Heldref Publications, 1319 Eighteenth St., N.W.,
Washington, DC 20036-1802. TEL 202-296-6267.
FAX 202-296-5149.
Producer(s): University Microfilms International.
3796

JOURNAL OF BACTERIOLOGY.
American Society for Microbiology, 1325
Massachusetts Ave., N.W., Washington, DC 20005.
TEL 202-737-3600. 760

JOURNAL OF BLACKS IN HIGHER EDUCATION.
CH II Publishers, Inc., 200 W 57th St., New York,
NY 10019. TEL 212-399-1084. FAX 212-245-
1973. 2889

JOURNAL OF BONE AND JOINT SURGERY: BRITISH VOLUME.
British Editorial Society of Bone and Joint Surgery,
22 Buckingham St., London WC2N 5ET, England.
TEL 0171-782-0010. FAX 0171-782-0995. 4785

JOURNAL OF BUSINESS FORECASTING METHODS AND SYSTEMS.
Graceway Publishing Co., Box 670159, Flushing,
NY 11367-0159. TEL 718-463-3914. FAX 718-
544-9086. 935

JOURNAL OF CHEMICAL EDUCATION. SOFTWARE. SPECIAL ISSUE SERIES.
American Chemical Society, Division of Chemical
Education, Inc., c/o Dept. of Chemistry, Univ. of
Wisconsin at Madison, 1101 University Ave.,
Madison, WI 53706-1396. TEL 608 262-5153.
FAX 608-265-8094. 2406

JOURNAL OF CHEMICAL PHYSICS.
American Institute of Physics, One Physics Ellipse,
College park, MD 20740-3843. TEL 301-209-
3000. FAX 516-349-9704. 5553

JOURNAL OF CLINICAL MICROBIOLOGY.
American Society for Microbiology, 1325 Massachusetts Ave., N.W., Washington, DC 20005. TEL 202-737-3600. *760*

JOURNAL OF COMPARATIVE FAMILY STUDIES.
University of Calgary, Department of Sociology, 2500 University Dr. N.W., Calgary, AB T2N 1N4, Canada. TEL 403-220-7317. FAX 403-282-9298. *6419*

JOURNAL OF COMPARATIVE RELIGION.
Universal Publications (a division of S T C), P.O. Box 7305, Ottawa, ON K1L 8E4, Canada. TEL 613-831-1052. FAX 613-831-8452. *6070*

JOURNAL OF CONSUMER MARKETING.
M C B University Press Ltd., 60-62 Toller Ln., Bradford, W. Yorks BD8 9BY, England. TEL 44-1274-777700. FAX 44-1274-785200. *1470*

JOURNAL OF CONSUMER RESEARCH.
University of Chicago Press, Journals Division, Box 37005, Chicago, IL 60637. TEL 312-753-3347. FAX 312-753-0811. *1470*

JOURNAL OF CORPORATION LAW.
University of Iowa, College of Law, 190 Boyd Law Bldg., Iowa City, IA 52242-1113. TEL 319-335-9061. FAX 319-335-9019. *3903*

. THE JOURNAL OF DEVELOPMENT STUDIES.
Frank Cass, Newbury House, 890-900 Eastern Ave., Newbury Park, Ilford, Essex 1G2 7HH, England. TEL 44-181-599-8866. FAX 44-181-599-0984. *1310*

THE JOURNAL OF ECONOMIC EDUCATION.
Heldref Publications, 1319 18th St., N.W., Washington, DC 20036-1802. TEL 202-296-6267. FAX 202-296-5149.
Producer(s): University Microfilms International. *936*

JOURNAL OF ECONOMIC LITERATURE.
American Economic Association, 2014 Broadway, Ste. 305, Nashville, TN 37203. TEL 615-322-2595.
Producer(s): SilverPlatter Information, Inc.. *1010*

JOURNAL OF ECONOMIC STUDIES.
M C B University Press Ltd., 60-62 Toller Ln., Bradford, W. Yorks BD8 9BY, England. TEL 44-1274-777700. FAX 44-1274-785200. *936*

JOURNAL OF EDUCATION FOR BUSINESS.
Heldref Publications, 1319 18th St., N.W., Washington, DC 20036-1802. TEL 202-296-6267. FAX 202-296-5149.
Producer(s): University Microfilms International. *937*

JOURNAL OF EDUCATIONAL ADMINISTRATION.
M C B University Press Ltd., 60-62 Toller Ln., Bradford, W. Yorks BD8 9BY, England. TEL 44-1274-777700. FAX 44-1274-785200. *2459*

THE JOURNAL OF EDUCATIONAL RESEARCH.
Heldref Publications, 1319 18th St., N.W., Washington, DC 20036-1802. TEL 202-296-6267. FAX 202-296-5149.
Producer(s): University Microfilms International. *2346*

THE JOURNAL OF ENVIRONMENTAL EDUCATION.
Heldref Publications, 1319 Eighteenth St., N.W., Washington, DC 20036-1802. TEL 202-296-6267. Producer(s): University Microfilms International. *2805*

JOURNAL OF EVOLUTIONARY PSYCHOLOGY.
Institute for Evolutionary Psychology, 5117 Forbes Ave., Pittsburgh, PA 15213. TEL 412-621-7057. *5856*

JOURNAL OF EXPERIMENTAL EDUCATION.
Heldref Publications, 1319 18th St., N.W., Washington, DC 20036-1802. TEL 202-296-6267. FAX 202-296-5149.
Producer(s): University Microfilms International. *2492*

JOURNAL OF FAMILY WELFARE.
Family Planning Association of India, Bajaj Bhavan, Nariman Point, Bombay 400021, India. TEL 91-22-202-9080. FAX 91-22-202-9038. *827*

THE JOURNAL OF GENERAL PSYCHOLOGY.
Heldref Publications, 1319 Eighteenth St., N.W., Washington, DC 20036. TEL 202-296-6267. FAX 202-296-5149.
Producer(s): University Microfilms International. *5857*

THE JOURNAL OF GENETIC PSYCHOLOGY.
Heldref Publications, 1319 Eighteenth St., N.W., Washington, DC 20036-1802. TEL 202-296-6267. FAX 202-296-5149.
Producer(s): University Microfilms International. *5857*

JOURNAL OF GROUP PSYCHOTHERAPY, PSYCHODRAMA & SOCIOMETRY.
Heldref Publications, 1319 Eighteenth St., N.W., Washington, DC 20036-1802. TEL 202-296-6267. FAX 202-296-5149.
Producer(s): University Microfilms International. *5857*

JOURNAL OF HIGHER EDUCATION.
Ohio State University Press, 1070 Carmack Rd., Columbus, OH 43210. TEL 614-292-6930. Producer(s): University Microfilms International. *2434*

JOURNAL OF MANAGEMENT CONSULTING.
858 Longview Rd., Burlingame, CA 94010-6974. TEL 415-342-1954. FAX 415-344-5005. *1428*

JOURNAL OF MANAGEMENT HISTORY.
M C B University Press Ltd., 60-62 Toller Ln., Bradford, W. Yorks BD8 9BY, England. TEL 44-1274-777700. FAX 44-1274-785200. *1428*

JOURNAL OF MANAGEMENT IN MEDICINE.
M C B University Press Ltd., 60-62 Toller Ln., Bradford, W. Yorks BD8 9BY, England. TEL 44-1274-777700. FAX 44-1274-785200. *4482*

JOURNAL OF MARKETING PRACTICE: APPLIED MARKETING SCIENCE.
M C B University Press Ltd., 60-62 Toller Ln., Bradford, W. Yorks BD8 9BY, England. TEL 44-1274-777700. FAX 44-1274-785200. *1472*

JOURNAL OF MARRIAGE AND THE FAMILY.
National Council on Family Relations, 3989 Central Ave., N.E., Ste. 550, Minneapolis, MN 55421-3921. TEL 612-781-9331. FAX 612-781-9348. Producer(s): NISC. *6420*

JOURNAL OF MATERIALS SCIENCE.
Chapman & Hall, Journals Department 2-6 Boundary Row, London SE1 8HN, England. TEL 44-171-8650066. FAX 44-171-5229623. *2735*

JOURNAL OF MATERIALS SCIENCE LETTERS.
Chapman & Hall, Journals Department 2-6 Boundary Row, London SE1 8HN, England. TEL 44-171-8650066. FAX 44-171-5229623. *2735*

JOURNAL OF MONEY, CREDIT & BANKING.
Ohio State University Press, 1070 Carmack Rd., Columbus, OH 43210. TEL 614-292-6930. Producer(s): University Microfilms International. *1105*

JOURNAL OF MOTOR BEHAVIOR.
Heldref Publications, 1319 Eighteenth St., N.W., Washington, DC 20036-1802. TEL 202-296-6267. FAX 202-296-5149.
Producer(s): University Microfilms International. *5858*

JOURNAL OF OBSTETRICS AND GYNAECOLOGY.
University of Tokyo Press, 3-1, Hongo 7-chome, Bunkyo-ku, Tokyo 113, Japan. *4740*

JOURNAL OF OBSTETRICS AND GYNAECOLOGY OF INDIA.
Federation of Obstetric & Gynaecological Societies of India, Purandare Griha, 31 C, Dr. N.A. Purandare Marg, Bombay 400 007, India. TEL 811-04-46. *4740*

JOURNAL OF ORGANIZATIONAL CHANGE MANAGEMENT.
M C B University Press Ltd., 60-62 Toller Ln., Bradford, W. Yorks BD8 9BY, England. TEL 44-1274-777700. FAX 44-1274-785200. *1429*

JOURNAL OF ORTHOPAEDIC RHEUMATOLOGY.
Rapid Science Publishers, The Old Malthouse, Paradise St., Oxford OX1 1LD, England. TEL -1865-790447. FAX -1865-244012. *4894*

JOURNAL OF POPULAR FILM AND TELEVISION.
Heldref Publications, 1319 Eighteenth St., N.W., Washington, DC 20036-1802. TEL 202-296-6267. FAX 202-296-5149.
Producer(s): University Microfilms International. *5106*

JOURNAL OF POPULATION, HEALTH AND SOCIAL WELFARE.
Korea Institute for Health and Social Affairs, San 42-14, Bulgwang-Dong, Eunpyung-Ku, Seoul 122 040, S. Korea. TEL 02-355-8003. FAX 02-352-9129. *6379*

JOURNAL OF PORTFOLIO MANAGEMENT.
Institutional Investor Journals, 488 Madison Ave., New York, NY 10022. TEL 212-224-3185. FAX 212-224-3527. *1338*

JOURNAL OF POSTGRADUATE MEDICINE.
Seth G.S. Medical College and K.E.M. Hospital, Staff Society, Dept. of Nephrology, Bombay 400012, India. TEL 4132118. *4484*

JOURNAL OF PROPERTY FINANCE.
M C B University Press Ltd., 60-62 Toller Ln., Bradford, W. Yorks BD8 9BY, England. TEL 44-1274-777700. FAX 44-1274-785200. *6028*

JOURNAL OF PROTECTIVE COATINGS AND LININGS.
Technology Publishing Co., 2100 Wharton St., Ste. 31, Pittsburgh, PA 15203. TEL 412-431-8300. FAX 412-431-5428. *5308*

JOURNAL OF REGIONAL AND LOCAL STUDIES.
c/o Univeristy of Humberside, Inglemire Ave., Hull HU6 7LU, England. FAX 01482-449624. *3422*

JOURNAL OF SERVICES MARKETING.
M C B University Press Ltd., 60-62 Toller Ln., Bradford, W. Yorks BD8 9BY, England. TEL 44-1274-777700. FAX 44-1274-785200. *1473*

JOURNAL OF SPORT BEHAVIOR.
University of South Alabama, Department of Health, Physical Education and Leisure Services, Mobile, AL 36688. TEL 334-460-7131. FAX 334-460-7252. Producer(s): University Microfilms International. *6466*

JOURNAL OF TECHNOLOGY TRANSFER.
Technology Transfer Society, 55 S. State Ave., Ste. 3-F2, Indianapolis, IN 46201-7876. *6655*

JOURNAL OF TRAUMA - INJURY, INFECTION AND CRITICAL CARE.
Williams & Wilkins, 351 W. Camden St., Baltimore, MD 21201. TEL 410-528-4000. FAX 410-528-4312. *4787*

JOURNAL OF VACUUM SCIENCE AND TECHNOLOGY. PART A. VACUUM, SURFACES AND FILMS.
American Institute of Physics, One Physics Ellipse, College Park, MD 20740-3843. TEL 301-209-3000. *5556*

JOURNAL OF VACUUM SCIENCE AND TECHNOLOGY. PART B. MICROELECTRONICS AND NANOMETER STRUCTURES.
American Institute of Physics, One Physics Ellipse, College Park, MD 20740-3843. TEL 301-209-3000. *5556*

JOURNAL OF VIROLOGY.
American Society for Microbiology, 1325 Massachusetts Ave., N.W., Washington, DC 20005. TEL 202-737-3600. *761*

JUDICIAL STAFF DIRECTORY.
Staff Directories Ltd., Box 62, Mount Vernon, VA 22121. TEL 703-739-0900. FAX 703-739-0234. *3949*

JUDICIAL YELLOW BOOK.
Leadership Directories, Inc., 104 Fifth Ave., 2nd Fl., New York, NY 10011. TEL 212-627-4140. FAX 212-645-0931.
Producer(s): Chadwyck-Healey Inc.. *3798*

JUTA - STATE LIBRARY INDEX TO THE GOVERNMENT GAZETTE.
Juta & Co. Ltd., P.O. Box 14373, Kenwyn 7790, South Africa. TEL 27-21-7975101. FAX 27-21-7970121. *5932*

JUTA'S STATUTES OF SOUTH AFRICA.
Juta & Co. Ltd., P.O. Box 14373, Kenwyn 7790, South Africa. TEL 27-21-7975101. FAX 27-21-7970121. *3800*

KAIJO HOANCHO. SUIROBU KANSOKU HOKOKU. KAIYO HEN.
Kaijo Hoancho, Suirobu, 3-1, Tsukiji 5-chome, Chuo-ku, Tokyo 104, Japan. FAX 81-3-3545-2885. *2287*

KANSAS BUSINESS DIRECTORY.
American Business Directories 5711 S. 86th Circle, Box 27347, Omaha, NE 68127. TEL 402-593-4600. FAX 402-331-5481. *1619*

KANSAS MANUFACTURERS REGISTER.
Manufacturers' News, Inc., 1633 Central St., Evanston, IL 60201-1569. TEL 847-864-7000. FAX 847-332-1100. *1619*

KATALOG FOR SKOLEBIBLIOTEKER. SKOLEBIBLIOTEKARENS.
Dansk BiblioteksCenter as, Tempovej 7-11, DK-2750 Ballerup, Denmark. TEL 45-44-867777. FAX 45-44-867892. *537*

KATALOG FOR SKOLEBIBLIOTEKER. TITELKATALOG.
Dansk BiblioteksCenter as, Tempovej 7-11, DK-2750 Ballerup, Denmark. TEL 45-44-867777. FAX 45-44-867892. *537*

KELLY'S DIRECTORY.
Kelly's Directories Part of the Reed Elsevier group, Windsor Court, E. Grinstead House, E. Grinstead, W. Sussex RH19 1XB, England. TEL 01342-326972. FAX 01342-335747. *1619*

KENTUCKY ATTORNEY GENERAL OPINIONS.
Banks - Baldwin Law Publishing Co., Box 318063, Cleveland, OH 44131-8063. TEL 216-520-5600. FAX 216-520-5655. *3949*

KENTUCKY BUSINESS DIRECTORY.
American Business Directories 5711 S. 86th Circle, Box 27347, Omaha, NE 68127. TEL 402-593-4600. FAX 402-331-5481. *1619*

KENTUCKY RULES OF COURT, STATE AND FEDERAL.
West Publishing Corp., 620 Opperman Dr., Eagan, MN 55123. TEL 612-687-8000. FAX 612-687-7302. *3949*

KEY ABSTRACTS - BUSINESS AUTOMATION.
INSPEC, I.E.E., Michael Faraday House, Six Hill Way, Stevenage, Herts. SG1 2AY, England. TEL 44-1438-313311. FAX 44-1438-742840. Producer(s): Knight-Ridder, Inc.. *2002*

KEY NOTE MARKET REPORT: ACCOUNTANCY.
Key Note Ltd., Field House, 72 Oldfield Rd., Hampton, Middlesex TW12 2HQ, England. TEL 44-181-783-0755. FAX 44-181-783-1940. *1050*

KEY NOTE MARKET REPORT: ADHESIVES.
Key Note Ltd., Field House, 72 Oldfield Rd., Hampton, Middlesex TW12 2HQ, England. TEL 44-181-783-0755. FAX 44-181-783-1940. *2644*

KEY NOTE MARKET REPORT: ADVERTISING AGENCIES.
Key Note Ltd., Field House, 72 Oldfield Rd., Hampton, Middlesex TW12 2HQ, England. TEL 44-181-783-0755. FAX 44-181-783-1940. *39*

KEY NOTE MARKET REPORT: AEROSPACE.
Key Note Ltd., Field House, 72 Oldfield Rd., Hampton, Middlesex TW12 2HQ, England. TEL 44-181-783-0755. FAX 44-181-783-1940. *71*

KEY NOTE MARKET REPORT: AFTER DINNER DRINKS.
Key Note Ltd., Field House, 72 Oldfield Rd., Hampton, Middlesex TW12 2HQ, England. TEL 44-181-783-0755. FAX 44-181-783-1940. *507*

KEY NOTE MARKET REPORT: AGRICULTURAL MACHINERY.
Key Note Ltd., Field House, 72 Oldfield Rd., Hampton, Middlesex TW12 2HQ, England. TEL 44-181-783-0755. FAX 44-181-783-1940. *205*

KEY NOTE MARKET REPORT: AGROCHEMICALS & FERTILIZERS.
Key Note Ltd., Field House, 72 Oldfield Rd., Hampton, Middlesex TW12 2HQ, England. TEL 44-181-783-0755. FAX 44-181-783-1940. *229*

KEY NOTE MARKET REPORT: AIRLINES.
Key Note Ltd., Field House, 72 Oldfield Rd., Hampton, Middlesex TW12 2HQ, England. TEL 44-181-783-0755. FAX 44-181-783-1940. *6761*

KEY NOTE MARKET REPORT: AIRPORTS.
Key Note Ltd., Field House, 72 Oldfield Rd., Hampton, Middlesex TW12 2HQ, England. TEL 44-181-783-0755. FAX 44-181-783-1940. *6761*

KEY NOTE MARKET REPORT: ANIMAL FEEDSTUFFS.
Key Note Ltd., Field House, 72 Oldfield Rd., Hampton, Middlesex TW12 2HQ, England. TEL 44-181-783-0755. FAX 44-181-783-1940. *259*

KEY NOTE MARKET REPORT: AUTOMATIC VENDING.
Key Note Ltd., Field House, 72 Oldfield Rd., Hampton, Middlesex TW12 2HQ, England. TEL 44-181-783-0755. FAX 44-181-783-1940. *1473*

KEY NOTE MARKET REPORT: AUTOPARTS.
Key Note Ltd., Field House, 72 Oldfield Rd., Hampton, Middlesex TW12 2HQ, England. TEL 44-181-783-0755. FAX 44-181-783-1940. *6790*

KEY NOTE MARKET REPORT: BABY PRODUCTS.
Key Note Ltd., Field House, 72 Oldfield Rd., Hampton, Middlesex TW12 2HQ, England. TEL 44-181-783-0755. FAX 44-181-783-1940. *1771*

KEY NOTE MARKET REPORT: BATHS & SANITARYWARE.
Key Note Ltd., Field House, 72 Oldfield Rd., Hampton, Middlesex TW12 2HQ, England. TEL 44-181-783-0755. FAX 44-181-783-1940. *492*

KEY NOTE MARKET REPORT: BETTING & GAMING.
Key Note Ltd., Field House, 72 Oldfield Rd., Hampton, Middlesex TW12 2HQ, England. TEL 44-181-783-0755. FAX 44-181-783-1940. *6467*

KEY NOTE MARKET REPORT: BICYCLES.
Key Note Ltd., Field House, 72 Oldfield Rd., Hampton, Middlesex TW12 2HQ, England. TEL 44-181-783-0755. FAX 44-181-783-1940. *6524*

KEY NOTE MARKET REPORT: BISCUITS & CAKES.
Key Note Ltd., Field House, 72 Oldfield Rd., Hampton, Middlesex TW12 2HQ, England. TEL 44-181-783-0755. FAX 44-181-783-1940. *3000*

KEY NOTE MARKET REPORT: BOOK PUBLISHING.
Key Note Ltd., Field House, 72 Oldfield Rd., Hampton, Middlesex TW12 2HQ, England. TEL 44-181-783-0755. FAX 44-181-783-1940. *6000*

KEY NOTE MARKET REPORT: BOOKSELLING.
Key Note Ltd., Field House, 72 Oldfield Rd., Hampton, Middlesex TW12 2HQ, England. TEL 44-181-783-0755. FAX 44-181-783-1940. *6000*

KEY NOTE MARKET REPORT: BOTTLED WATERS.
Key Note Ltd., Field House, 72 Oldfield Rd., Hampton, Middlesex TW12 2HQ, England. TEL 44-181-783-0755. FAX 44-181-783-1940. *507*

KEY NOTE MARKET REPORT: BREAD BAKERS.
Key Note Ltd., Field House, 72 Oldfield Rd., Hampton, Middlesex TW12 2HQ, England. TEL 44-181-783-0755. FAX 44-181-783-1940. *3000*

KEY NOTE MARKET REPORT: BREAKFAST CEREALS.
Key Note Ltd., Field House, 72 Oldfield Rd., Hampton, Middlesex TW12 2HQ, England. TEL 44-181-783-0755. FAX 44-181-783-1940. *2981*

KEY NOTE MARKET REPORT: BREWERIES & THE BEER MARKET.
Key Note Ltd., Field House, 72 Oldfield Rd., Hampton, Middlesex TW12 2HQ, England. TEL 44-181-783-0755. FAX 44-181-783-1940. *507*

KEY NOTE MARKET REPORT: BRICKS & TILES.
Key Note Ltd., Field House, 72 Oldfield Rd., Hampton, Middlesex TW12 2HQ England. TEL 44-181-783-0755. FAX 44-181-783-1940. *862*

KEY NOTE MARKET REPORT: BROWN GOODS.
Key Note Ltd., Field House, 72 Oldfield Rd., Hampton, Middlesex TW12 2HQ. England. TEL 44-181-783-0755. FAX 44-181-783-1940. *2526*

KEY NOTE MARKET REPORT: BUILDING CONTRACTING.
Key Note Ltd., Field House, 72 Oldfield Rd., Hampton, Middlesex TW12 2HQ, England. TEL 44-181-783-0755. FAX 44-181-783-1940. *862*

KEY NOTE MARKET REPORT: BUILDING MATERIALS.
Key Note Ltd., Field House, 72 Oldfield Rd., Hampton, Middlesex TW12 2HQ, England. TEL 44-181-783-0755. FAX 44-181-783-1940. *862*

KEY NOTE MARKET REPORT: BUILDING SOCIETIES.
Key Note Ltd., Field House, 72 Oldfield Rd., Hampton, Middlesex TW12 2HQ, England. TEL 44-181-783-0755. FAX 44-181-783-1940. *862*

KEY NOTE MARKET REPORT: BUS & COACH OPERATORS.
Key Note Ltd., Field House, 72 Oldfield Rd., Hampton, Middlesex TW12 2HQ, England. TEL 44-181-783-1940. *6721*

KEY NOTE MARKET REPORT: BUSINESS PRESS.
Key Note Ltd., Field House, 72 Oldfield Rd., Hampton, Middlesex TW12 2HQ, England. TEL 44-181-783-1940. *939*

KEY NOTE MARKET REPORT: BUSINESS TRAVEL.
Key Note Ltd., Field House, 72 Oldfield Rd., Hampton, Middlesex TW12 2HQ, England. TEL 44-181-783-0755. FAX 44-181-783-1940. *6896*

KEY NOTE MARKET REPORT: C D - R O M.
Key Note Ltd., Field House, 72 Oldfield Rd., Hampton, Middlesex TW12 2HQ, England. TEL 44-181-783-0755. FAX 44-181-783-1940. *1928*

KEY NOTE MARKET REPORT: C T N'S.
Key Note Ltd., Field House, 72 Oldfield Rd., Hampton, Middlesex TW12 2HQ, England. TEL 44-181-783-1940. *1106*

KEY NOTE MARKET REPORT: CABLE AND SATELLITE T V.
Key Note Ltd., Field House, 72 Oldfield Rd., Hampton, Middlesex TW12 2HQ, England. TEL 44-181-783-1940. *1963*

KEY NOTE MARKET REPORT: CAMERAS & CAMCORDERS.
Key Note Ltd., Field House, 72 Oldfield Rd., Hampton, Middlesex TW12 2HQ, England. TEL 44-181-783-1940. *5514*

KEY NOTE MARKET REPORT: CAMPING & CARAVANNING.
Key Note Ltd., Field House, 72 Oldfield Rd., Hampton, Middlesex TW12 2HQ, England. TEL 44-181-783-1940. *3964*

KEY NOTE MARKET REPORT: CANNED FOODS.
Key Note Ltd., Field House, 72 Oldfield Rd., Hampton, Middlesex TW12 2HQ, England. TEL 44-181-783-1940. *2981*

KEY NOTE MARKET REPORT: CAR DEALERS.
Key Note Ltd., Field House, 72 Oldfield Rd., Hampton, Middlesex TW12 2HQ, England. TEL 44-181-783-1940. *6790*

KEY NOTE MARKET REPORT: CARPETS & FLOORCOVERINGS.
Key Note Ltd., Field House, 72 Oldfield Rd., Hampton, Middlesex TW12 2HQ, England. TEL 44-181-783-1940. *3689*

KEY NOTE MARKET REPORT: CASH & CARRY OUTLETS.
Key Note Ltd., Field House, 72 Oldfield Rd., Hampton, Middlesex TW12 2HQ, England. TEL 44-181-783-1940. *1473*

KEY NOTE MARKET REPORT: CHARITIES.
Key Note Ltd., Field House, 72 Oldfield Rd., Hampton, Middlesex TW12 2HQ, England. TEL 44-181-783-1940. *6380*

KEY NOTE MARKET REPORT: CHEMICAL INDUSTRY.
Key Note Ltd., Field House, 72 Oldfield Rd.,
Hampton, Middlesex TW12 2HQ, England. TEL 44-
181-783-0755. FAX 44-181-783-1940. *2644*

KEY NOTE MARKET REPORT: CHILDRENSWEAR.
Key Note Ltd., Field House, 72 Oldfield Rd.,
Hampton, Middlesex TW12 2HQ, England. TEL 44-
181-783-0755. FAX 44-181-783-1940. *1834*

KEY NOTE MARKET REPORT: CHILLED FOODS.
Key Note Ltd., Field House, 72 Oldfield Rd.,
Hampton, Middlesex TW12 2HQ, England. TEL 44-
181-783-0755. FAX 44-181-783-1940. *2981*

KEY NOTE MARKET REPORT: CHINA & EARTHENWARE.
Key Note Ltd., Field House, 72 Oldfield Rd.,
Hampton, Middlesex TW12 2HQ, England. TEL 44-
181-783-0755. FAX 44-181-783-1940. *1658*

KEY NOTE MARKET REPORT: CIDER.
Key Note Ltd., Field House, 72 Oldfield Rd.,
Hampton, Middlesex TW12 2HQ, England. TEL 44-
181-783-0755. FAX 44-181-783-1940. *508*

KEY NOTE MARKET REPORT: CIGARETTES & TOBACCO.
Key Note Ltd., Field House, 72 Oldfield Rd.,
Hampton, Middlesex TW12 2HQ, England. TEL 44-
181-783-0755. FAX 44-181-783-1940. *6709*

KEY NOTE MARKET REPORT: CIVIL ENGINEERING.
Key Note Ltd., Field House, 72 Oldfield Rd.,
Hampton, Middlesex TW12 2HQ, England. TEL 44-
181-783-0755. FAX 44-181-783-1940. *2667*

KEY NOTE MARKET REPORT: CLOTHING MANUFACTURING.
Key Note Ltd., Field House, 72 Oldfield Rd.,
Hampton, Middlesex TW12 2HQ, England. TEL 44-
181-783-0755. FAX 44-181-783-1940. *1834*

KEY NOTE MARKET REPORT: CLOTHING RETAILING.
Key Note Ltd., Field House, 72 Oldfield Rd.,
Hampton, Middlesex TW12 2HQ, England. TEL 44-
181-783-0755. FAX 44-181-783-1940. *1834*

KEY NOTE MARKET REPORT: COMMERCIAL RADIO.
Key Note Ltd., Field House, 72 Oldfield Rd.,
Hampton, Middlesex TW12 2HQ, England. TEL 44-
181-783-0755. FAX 44-181-783-1940. *1937*

KEY NOTE MARKET REPORT: COMMERCIAL T V.
Key Note Ltd., Field House, 72 Oldfield Rd.,
Hampton, Middlesex TW12 2HQ, England. TEL 44-
181-783-0755. FAX 44-181-783-1940. *1963*

KEY NOTE MARKET REPORT: COMMERCIAL VEHICLES.
Key Note Ltd., Field House, 72 Oldfield Rd.,
Hampton, Middlesex TW12 2HQ, England. TEL 44-
181-783-0755. FAX 44-181-783-1940. *6790*

KEY NOTE MARKET REPORT: COMPUTER SERVICES.
Key Note Ltd., Field House, 72 Oldfield Rd.,
Hampton, Middlesex TW12 2HQ, England. TEL 44-
181-783-0755. FAX 44-181-783-1940. *2032*

KEY NOTE MARKET REPORT: COMPUTER SOFTWARE.
Key Note Ltd., Field House, 72 Oldfield Rd.,
Hampton, Middlesex TW12 2HQ, England. TEL 44-
181-783-0755. FAX 44-181-783-1940. *2112*

KEY NOTE MARKET REPORT: CONFECTIONERY.
Key Note Ltd., Field House, 72 Oldfield Rd.,
Hampton, Middlesex TW12 2HQ, England. TEL 44-
181-783-0755. FAX 44-181-783-1940. *3000*

KEY NOTE MARKET REPORT: CONSUMER MAGAZINES.
Key Note Ltd., Field House, 72 Oldfield Rd.,
Hampton, Middlesex TW12 2HQ, England. TEL 44-
181-783-0755. FAX 44-181-783-1940. *6000*

KEY NOTE MARKET REPORT: CONTRACEPTIVES.
Key Note Ltd., Field House, 72 Oldfield Rd.,
Hampton, Middlesex TW12 2HQ, England. TEL 44-
181-783-0755. FAX 44-181-783-1940. *827*

KEY NOTE MARKET REPORT: CONTRACT CATERING.
Key Note Ltd., Field House, 72 Oldfield Rd.,
Hampton, Middlesex TW12 2HQ, England. TEL 44-
181-783-0755. FAX 44-171-783-1940. *3566*

KEY NOTE MARKET REPORT: CONTRACT CLEANING.
Key Note Ltd., Field House, 72 Oldfield Rd.,
Hampton, Middlesex TW12 2HQ, England. TEL 44-
181-783-0755. FAX 44-181-783-1940. *1828*

KEY NOTE MARKET REPORT: CONVENIENCE RETAILING.
Key Note Ltd., Field House, 72 Oldfield Rd.,
Hampton, Middlesex TW12 2HQ, England. TEL 44-
181-783-0755. FAX 44-181-783-1940. *1473*

KEY NOTE MARKET REPORT: COSMETICS & FRAGRANCES.
Key Note Ltd., Field House, 72 Oldfield Rd.,
Hampton, Middlesex TW12 2HQ, England. TEL 44-
181-783-0755. FAX 44-181-783-1940. *496*

KEY NOTE MARKET REPORT: COURIER & EXPRESS SERVICES.
Key Note Ltd., Field House, 72 Oldfield Rd.,
Hampton, Middlesex TW12 2HQ, England. TEL 44-
181-783-0755. FAX 44-181-783-1940. *1931*

KEY NOTE MARKET REPORT: CREDIT & OTHER FINANCE CARDS.
Key Note Ltd., Field House, 72 Oldfield Rd.,
Hampton, Middlesex TW12 2HQ, England. TEL 44-
181-783-0755. FAX 44-181-783-1940. *1106*

KEY NOTE MARKET REPORT: DEBT MANAGEMENT & FACTORING.
Key Note Ltd., Field House, 72 Oldfield Rd.,
Hampton, Middlesex TW12 2HQ, England. TEL 44-
181-783-0755. FAX 44-181-783-1940. *1106*

KEY NOTE MARKET REPORT: DEFENCE EQUIPMENT.
Key Note Ltd., Field House, 72 Oldfield Rd.,
Hampton, Middlesex TW12 2HQ, England. TEL 44-
181-783-0755. FAX 44-181-783-1940. *5037*

KEY NOTE MARKET REPORT: DIRECT MARKETING.
Key Note Ltd., Field House, 72 Oldfield Rd.,
Hampton, Middlesex TW12 2HQ, England. TEL 44-
181-783-0755. FAX 44-181-783-1940. *1473*

KEY NOTE MARKET REPORT: DISPOSABLE PAPER PRODUCTS.
Key Note Ltd., Field House, 72 Oldfield Rd.,
Hampton, Middlesex TW12 2HQ, England. TEL 44-
181-783-0755. FAX 44-181-783-1940. *5323*

KEY NOTE MARKET REPORT: DISTILLERS (WHISKY).
Key Note Ltd., Field House, 72 Oldfield Rd.,
Hampton, Middlesex TW12 2HQ, England. TEL 44-
181-783-0755. FAX 44-181-783-1940. *508*

KEY NOTE MARKET REPORT: DOMESTIC HEATING.
Key Note Ltd., Field House, 72 Oldfield Rd.,
Hampton, Middlesex TW12 2HQ, England. TEL 44-
181-783-0755. FAX 44-181-783-1940. *3330*

KEY NOTE MARKET REPORT: DRY BATTERIES.
Key Note Ltd., Field House, 72 Oldfield Rd.,
Hampton, Middlesex TW12 2HQ, England. TEL 44-
181-783-0755. FAX 44-181-783-1940. *5582*

KEY NOTE MARKET REPORT: ELECTRICAL CONTRACTING.
Key Note Ltd., Field House, 72 Oldfield Rd.,
Hampton, Middlesex TW12 2HQ, England. TEL 44-
181-783-0755. FAX 44-181-783-1940. *2711*

KEY NOTE MARKET REPORT: ELECTRONIC COMPONENT DISTRIBUTION.
Key Note Ltd., Field House, 72 Oldfield Rd.,
Hampton, Middlesex TW12 2HQ, England. TEL 44-
181-783-0755. FAX 44-181-783-1940. *2526*

KEY NOTE MARKET REPORT: ELECTRONIC COMPONENT MANUFACTURERS.
Key Note Ltd., Field House, 72 Oldfield Rd.,
Hampton, Middlesex TW12 2HQ, England. TEL 44-
181-783-0755. FAX 44-181-783-1940. *2526*

KEY NOTE MARKET REPORT: ELECTRONIC GAMES.
Key Note Ltd., Field House, 72 Oldfield Rd.,
Hampton, Middlesex TW12 2HQ, England. TEL 44-
181-783-0755. FAX 44-181-783-1940. *2024*

KEY NOTE MARKET REPORT: EMPLOYMENT AGENCIES.
Key Note Ltd., Field House, 72 Oldfield Rd.,
Hampton, Middlesex TW12 2HQ, England. TEL 44-
181-783-0755. FAX 44-181-783-1940. *5270*

KEY NOTE MARKET REPORT: EQUIPMENT LEASING.
Key Note Ltd., Field House, 72 Oldfield Rd.,
Hampton, Middlesex TW12 2HQ, England. TEL 44-
181-783-0755. FAX 44-181-783-1940. *1577*

KEY NOTE MARKET REPORT: ESTATE AGENTS.
Key Note Ltd., Field House, 72 Oldfield Rd.,
Hampton, Middlesex TW12 2HQ, England. TEL 44-
181-783-0755. FAX 44-181-783-1940. *3915*

KEY NOTE MARKET REPORT: ETHNIC FOODS.
Key Note Ltd., Field House, 72 Oldfield Rd.,
Hampton, Middlesex TW12 2HQ, England. TEL 44-
181-783-0755. FAX 44-181-783-1940. *2981*

KEY NOTE MARKET REPORT: EXHIBITIONS AND CONFERENCE ORGANISERS.
Key Note Ltd., Field House, 72 Oldfield Rd.,
Hampton, Middlesex TW12 2HQ, England. TEL 44-
181-783-0755. FAX 44-181-783-1940. *4935*

KEY NOTE MARKET REPORT: FAST FOOD AND HOME DELIVERY OUTLETS.
Key Note Ltd., Field House, 72 Oldfield Rd.,
Hampton, Middlesex TW12 2HQ, England. TEL 44-
181-783-0755. FAX 44-181-783-1940. *2981*

KEY NOTE MARKET REPORT: FIBRES.
Key Note Ltd., Field House, 72 Oldfield Rd.,
Hampton, Middlesex TW12 2HQ, England. TEL 44-
181-783-0755. FAX 44-181-783-1940. *6681*

KEY NOTE MARKET REPORT: FINANCE HOUSES.
Key Note Ltd., Field House, 72 Oldfield Rd.,
Hampton, Middlesex TW12 2HQ, England. TEL 44-
181-783-0755. FAX 44-181-783-1940. *1106*

KEY NOTE MARKET REPORT: FIRE PROTECTION EQUIPMENT.
Key Note Ltd., Field House, 72 Oldfield Rd.,
Hampton, Middlesex TW12 2HQ, England. TEL 44-
181-783-0755. FAX 44-181-783-1940. *2921*

KEY NOTE MARKET REPORT: FOOD FLAVOURINGS & INGREDIENTS.
Key Note Ltd., Field House, 72 Oldfield Rd.,
Hampton, Middlesex TW12 2HQ, England. TEL 44-
181-783-0755. FAX 44-181-783-1940. *2981*

KEY NOTE MARKET REPORT: FOOTWEAR.
Key Note Ltd., Field House, 72 Oldfield Rd.,
Hampton, Middlesex TW12 2HQ, England. TEL 44-
181-783-0755. FAX 44-181-783-1940. *6307*

KEY NOTE MARKET REPORT: FREIGHT FORWARDING.
Key Note Ltd., Field House, 72 Oldfield Rd.,
Hampton, Middlesex TW12 2HQ, England. TEL 44-
181-783-0755. FAX 44-181-783-1940. *6721*

KEY NOTE MARKET REPORT: FROZEN FOODS.
Key Note Ltd., Field House, 72 Oldfield Rd.,
Hampton, Middlesex TW12 2HQ, England. TEL 44-
181-783-0755. FAX 44-181-783-1940. *2981*

KEY NOTE MARKET REPORT: FRUIT & VEGETABLES.
Key Note Ltd., Field House, 72 Oldfield Rd.,
Hampton, Middlesex TW12 2HQ, England. TEL 44-
181-783-0755. FAX 44-181-783-1940. *3006*

KEY NOTE MARKET REPORT: FRUIT JUICES & HEALTH DRINKS.
Key Note Ltd., Field House, 72 Oldfield Rd.,
Hampton, Middlesex TW12 2HQ, England. TEL 44-
181-783-0755. FAX 44-181-783-1940. *508*

KEY NOTE MARKET REPORT: GARDEN EQUIPMENT.
Key Note Ltd., Field House, 72 Oldfield Rd.,
Hampton, Middlesex TW12 2HQ, England. TEL 44-
181-783-0755. FAX 44-181-783-1940. *3059*

KEY NOTE MARKET REPORT: GIFTWARE.
Key Note Ltd., Field House, 72 Oldfield Rd.,
Hampton, Middlesex TW12 2HQ, England. TEL 44-
181-783-0755. FAX 44-181-783-1940. *3301*

KEY NOTE MARKET REPORT: GLASSWARE.
Key Note Ltd., Field House, 72 Oldfield Rd.,
Hampton, Middlesex TW12 2HQ, England. TEL 44-
181-783-0755. FAX 44-181-783-1940. *1658*

KEY NOTE MARKET REPORT: GREETINGS CARDS.
Key Note Ltd., Field House, 72 Oldfield Rd.,
Hampton, Middlesex TW12 2HQ, England. TEL 44-
181-783-0755. FAX 44-181-783-1940. *3301*

KEY NOTE MARKET REPORT: HAND LUGGAGE & LEATHER GOODS.
Key Note Ltd., Field House, 72 Oldfield Rd., Hampton, Middlesex TW12 2HQ, England. TEL 44-181-783-0755. FAX 44-181-783-1940. *3960*

KEY NOTE MARKET REPORT: HEALTH CLUBS AND LEISURE CENTRES.
Key Note Ltd., Field House, 72 Oldfield Rd., Hampton, Middlesex TW12 2HQ, England. TEL 44-181-783-0755. FAX 44-181-783-1940. *6467*

KEY NOTE MARKET REPORT: HEALTH FOODS.
Key Note Ltd., Field House, 72 Oldfield Rd., Hampton, Middlesex TW12 2HQ, England. TEL 44-181-783-0755. FAX 44-181-783-1940. *2981*

KEY NOTE MARKET REPORT: HEATING, VENTILATING & AIR CONDITIONING.
Key Note Ltd., Field House, 72 Oldfield Rd., Hampton, Middlesex TW12 2HQ, England. TEL 44-181-783-0755. FAX 44-181-783-1940. *3330*

KEY NOTE MARKET REPORT: HOME FURNISHINGS.
Key Note Ltd., Field House, 72 Oldfield Rd., Hampton, Middlesex TW12 2HQ, England. TEL 44-181-783-0755. FAX 44-181-783-1940. *3689*

KEY NOTE MARKET REPORT: HOME LEISURE.
Key Note Ltd., Field House, 72 Oldfield Rd., Hampton, Middlesex TW12 2HQ, England. TEL 44-181-783-0755. FAX 44-181-783-1940. *3964*

KEY NOTE MARKET REPORT: HOME SHOPPING.
Key Note Ltd., Field House, 72 Oldfield Rd., Hampton, Middlesex TW12 2HQ, England. TEL 44-181-783-0755. FAX 44-181-783-1940. *1473*

KEY NOTE MARKET REPORT: HORTICULTURAL RETAILING.
Key Note Ltd., Field House, 72 Oldfield Rd., Hampton, Middlesex TW12 2HQ, England. TEL 44-181-783-0755. FAX 44-181-783-1940. *3059*

KEY NOTE MARKET REPORT: HOT DRINKS.
Key Note Ltd., Field House, 72 Oldfield Rd., Hampton, Middlesex TW12 2HQ, England. TEL 44-181-783-0755. FAX 44-181-783-1940. *508*

KEY NOTE MARKET REPORT: HOTELS.
Key Note Ltd., Field House, 72 Oldfield Rd., Hampton, Middlesex TW12 2HQ, England. TEL 44-181-783-0755. FAX 44-181-783-1940. *3566*

KEY NOTE MARKET REPORT: HOUSEBUILDING.
Key Note Ltd., Field House, 72 Oldfield Rd., Hampton, Middlesex TW12 2HQ, England. TEL 44-181-783-0755. FAX 44-181-783-1940. *862*

KEY NOTE MARKET REPORT: HOUSEHOLD APPLIANCES (WHITE GOODS).
Key Note Ltd., Field House, 72 Oldfield Rd., Hampton, Middlesex TW12 2HQ, England. TEL 44-181-783-0755. FAX 44-181-783-1940. *3690*

KEY NOTE MARKET REPORT: HOUSEHOLD FURNITURE.
Key Note Ltd., Field House, 72 Oldfield Rd., Hampton, Middlesex TW12 2HQ, England. TEL 44-181-783-0755. FAX 44-181-783-1940. *3690*

KEY NOTE MARKET REPORT: ICE-CREAMS & FROZEN DESSERTS.
Key Note Ltd., Field House, 72 Oldfield Rd., Hampton, Middlesex TW12 2HQ, England. TEL 44-181-783-0755. FAX 44-181-783-1940. *2981*

KEY NOTE MARKET REPORT: INDUSTRIAL FASTENERS.
Key Note Ltd., Field House, 72 Oldfield Rd., Hampton, Middlesex TW12 2HQ, England. TEL 44-181-783-0755. FAX 44-181-783-1940. *2736*

KEY NOTE MARKET REPORT: INDUSTRIAL PUMPS.
Key Note Ltd., Field House, 72 Oldfield Rd., Hampton, Middlesex TW12 2HQ, England. TEL 44-181-783-0755. FAX 44-181-783-1940. *2744*

KEY NOTE MARKET REPORT: INDUSTRIAL VALVES.
Key Note Ltd., Field House, 72 Oldfield Rd., Hampton, Middlesex TW12 2HQ, England. TEL 44-181-783-0755. FAX 44-181-783-1940. *2748*

KEY NOTE MARKET REPORT: INSULATION PRODUCTS.
Key Note Ltd., Field House, 72 Oldfield Rd., Hampton, Middlesex TW12 2HQ, England. TEL 44-181-783-0755. FAX 44-181-783-1940. *862*

KEY NOTE MARKET REPORT: JEWELLERY, WATCHES & FASHION ACCESSORIES.
Key Note Ltd., Field House, 72 Oldfield Rd., Hampton, Middlesex TW12 2HQ, England. TEL 44-181-783-0755. FAX 44-181-783-1940. *3697*

KEY NOTE MARKET REPORT: KITCHENWARE.
Key Note Ltd., Field House, 72 Oldfield Rd., Hampton, Middlesex TW12 2HQ, England. TEL 44-181-783-0755. FAX 44-181-783-1940. *3690*

KEY NOTE MARKET REPORT: LIGHTING EQUIPMENT.
Key Note Ltd., Field House, 72 Oldfield Rd., Hampton, Middlesex TW12 2HQ, England. TEL 44-181-783-0755. FAX 44-181-783-1940. *3690*

KEY NOTE MARKET REPORT: LINGERIE.
Key Note Ltd., Field House, 72 Oldfield Rd., Hampton, Middlesex TW12 2HQ, England. TEL 44-181-783-0755. FAX 44-181-783-1940. *1834*

KEY NOTE MARKET REPORT: LOW ALCOHOL DRINKS.
Key Note Ltd., Field House, 72 Oldfield Rd., Hampton, Middlesex TW12 2HQ, England. TEL 44-181-783-0755. FAX 44-181-783-1940. *508*

KEY NOTE MARKET REPORT: MACHINE TOOLS.
Key Note Ltd., Field House, 72 Oldfield Rd., Hampton, Middlesex TW12 2HQ, England. TEL 44-181-783-0755. FAX 44-181-783-1940. *2749*

KEY NOTE MARKET REPORT: MANAGEMENT CONSULTANTS.
Key Note Ltd., Field House, 72 Oldfield Rd., Hampton, Middlesex TW12 2HQ, England. TEL 44-181-783-0755. FAX 44-181-783-1940. *1429*

KEY NOTE MARKET REPORT: MEAT & MEAT PRODUCTS.
Key Note Ltd., Field House, 72 Oldfield Rd., Hampton, Middlesex TW12 2HQ, England. TEL 44-181-783-0755. FAX 44-181-783-1940. *2981*

KEY NOTE MARKET REPORT: MECHANICAL HANDLING.
Key Note Ltd., Field House, 72 Oldfield Rd., Hampton, Middlesex TW12 2HQ, England. TEL 44-181-783-0755. FAX 44-181-783-1940. *2761*

KEY NOTE MARKET REPORT: MEDICAL EQUIPMENT.
Key Note Ltd., Field House, 72 Oldfield Rd., Hampton, Middlesex TW12 2HQ, England. TEL 44-181-783-0755. FAX 44-181-783-1940. *4486*

KEY NOTE MARKET REPORT: MILK & DAIRY PRODUCTS.
Key Note Ltd., Field House, 72 Oldfield Rd., Hampton, Middlesex TW12 2HQ, England. TEL 44-181-783-0755. FAX 44-181-783-1940. *251*

KEY NOTE MARKET REPORT: MORTGAGE FINANCE.
Key Note Ltd., Field House, 72 Oldfield Rd., Hampton, Middlesex TW12 2HQ, England. TEL 44-181-783-0755. FAX 44-181-783-1940. *1106*

KEY NOTE MARKET REPORT: NEWSPAPERS.
Key Note Ltd., Field House, 72 Oldfield Rd., Hampton, Middlesex TW12 2HQ, England. TEL 44-181-783-0755. FAX 44-181-783-1940. *3707*

KEY NOTE MARKET REPORT: O T C PHARMACEUTICALS.
Key Note Ltd., Field House, 72 Oldfield Rd., Hampton, Middlesex TW12 2HQ, England. TEL 44-181-783-1940. FAX 44-181-783-1940. *5425*

KEY NOTE MARKET REPORT: OFF-LICENSE TRADE.
Key Note Ltd., Field House, 72 Oldfield Rd., Hampton, Middlesex TW12 2HQ, England. TEL 44-181-783-0755. FAX 44-181-783-1940. *1524*

KEY NOTE MARKET REPORT: OFFICE FURNITURE.
Key Note Ltd., Field House, 72 Oldfield Rd., Hampton, Middlesex TW12 2HQ, England. TEL 44-181-783-0755. FAX 44-181-783-1940. *1494*

KEY NOTE MARKET REPORT: OPHTHALMIC GOODS & SERVICES.
Key Note Ltd., Field House, 72 Oldfield Rd., Hampton, Middlesex TW12 2HQ, England. TEL 44-181-783-1940. *4772*

KEY NOTE MARKET REPORT: OWN BRANDS.
Key Note Ltd., Field House, 72 Oldfield Rd., Hampton, Middlesex TW12 2HQ, England. TEL 44-181-783-0755. FAX 44-181-783-1940. *1474*

KEY NOTE MARKET REPORT: PACKAGING (GLASS).
Key Note Ltd., Field House, 72 Oldfield Rd., Hampton, Middlesex TW12 2HQ, England. TEL 44-181-783-0755. FAX 44-181-783-1940. *5301*

KEY NOTE MARKET REPORT: PACKAGING (METALS & AEROSOLS).
Key Note Ltd., Field House, 72 Oldfield Rd., Hampton, Middlesex TW12 2HQ, England. TEL 44-181-783-0755. FAX 44-181-783-1940. *5301*

KEY NOTE MARKET REPORT: PACKAGING (PAPER & BOARD).
Key Note Ltd., Field House, 72 Oldfield Rd., Hampton, Middlesex TW12 2HQ, England. TEL 44-181-783-0755. FAX 44-181-783-1940. *5301*

KEY NOTE MARKET REPORT: PACKAGING (PLASTICS).
Key Note Ltd., Field House, 72 Oldfield Rd., Hampton, Middlesex TW12 2HQ, England. TEL 44-181-783-1940. *5301*

KEY NOTE MARKET REPORT: PAINTS & VARNISHES.
Key Note Ltd., Field House, 72 Oldfield Rd., Hampton, Middlesex TW12 2HQ, England. TEL 44-181-783-1940. *5308*

KEY NOTE MARKET REPORT: PASSENGER SHIPPING.
Key Note Ltd., Field House, 72 Oldfield Rd., Hampton, Middlesex TW12 2HQ, England. TEL 44-181-783-0755. FAX 44-181-783-1940. *6838*

KEY NOTE MARKET REPORT: PERISHABLE FAST-MOVING CONSUMER GOODS.
Key Note Ltd., Field House, 72 Oldfield Rd., Hampton, Middlesex TW12 2HQ, England. TEL 44-181-783-1940. *2981*

KEY NOTE MARKET REPORT: PET FOODS.
Key Note Ltd., Field House, 72 Oldfield Rd., Hampton, Middlesex TW12 2HQ, England. TEL 44-181-783-1940. *5391*

KEY NOTE MARKET REPORT: PHOTOCOPIERS & FAX MACHINES.
Key Note Ltd., Field House, 72 Oldfield Rd., Hampton, Middlesex TW12 2HQ, England. TEL 44-181-783-1940. *1494*

KEY NOTE MARKET REPORT: PHOTOGRAPHIC SERVICES.
Key Note Ltd., Field House, 72 Oldfield Rd., Hampton, Middlesex TW12 2HQ, England. TEL 44-181-783-1940. *5514*

KEY NOTE MARKET REPORT: PLANT HIRE.
Key Note Ltd., Field House, 72 Oldfield Rd., Hampton, Middlesex TW12 2HQ, England. TEL 44-181-783-1940. *1219*

KEY NOTE MARKET REPORT: PLASTICS PROCESSING.
Key Note Ltd., Field House, 72 Oldfield Rd., Hampton, Middlesex TW12 2HQ, England. TEL 44-181-783-0755. FAX 44-181-783-1940. *5621*

KEY NOTE MARKET REPORT: PREMIUM LAGERS, BEERS AND CIDERS.
Key Note Ltd., Field House, 72 Oldfield Rd., Hampton, Middlesex TW12 2HQ, England. TEL 44-181-783-0755. FAX 44-181-783-1940. *508*

KEY NOTE MARKET REPORT: PRESCRIBED PHARMACEUTICALS.
Key Note Ltd., Field House, 72 Oldfield Rd., Hampton, Middlesex TW12 2HQ, England. TEL 44-181-783-0755. FAX 44-181-783-1940. *5425*

KEY NOTE MARKET REPORT: PRINTED CIRCUITS.
Key Note Ltd., Field House, 72 Oldfield Rd., Hampton, Middlesex TW12 2HQ, England. TEL 44-181-783-0755. FAX 44-181-783-1940. *2018*

CD-ROM

KEY NOTE MARKET REPORT: PRINTING.
Key Note Ltd., Field House, 72 Oldfield Rd.,
Hampton, Middlesex TW12 2HQ, England. TEL 44-
181-783-0755. FAX 44-181-783-1940. *5814*

KEY NOTE MARKET REPORT: PRISON SERVICES.
Key Note Ltd., Field House, 72 Oldfield Rd.,
Hampton, Middlesex TW12 2HQ, England. TEL 44-
181-783-0755. FAX 44-181-783-1940. *2183*

**KEY NOTE MARKET REPORT: PRIVATE
HEALTHCARE.**
Key Note Ltd., Field House, 72 Oldfield Rd.,
Hampton, Middlesex TW12 2HQ, England. TEL 44-
181-783-0755. FAX 44-181-783-1940. *4486*

KEY NOTE MARKET REPORT: PROCESS PLANT.
Key Note Ltd., Field House, 72 Oldfield Rd.,
Hampton, Middlesex TW12 2HQ, England. TEL 44-
181-783-0755. FAX 44-181-783-1940. *1524*

KEY NOTE MARKET REPORT: PUBLIC HOUSES.
Key Note Ltd., Field House, 72 Oldfield Rd.,
Hampton, Middlesex TW12 2HQ, England. TEL 44-
181-783-0755. FAX 44-181-783-1940. *3567*

KEY NOTE MARKET REPORT: READY MEALS.
Key Note Ltd., Field House, 72 Oldfield Rd.,
Hampton, Middlesex TW12 2HQ, England. TEL 44-
181-783-0755. FAX 44-181-783-1940. *2981*

KEY NOTE MARKET REPORT: RESTAURANTS.
Key Note Ltd., Field House, 72 Oldfield Rd.,
Hampton, Middlesex TW12 2HQ, England. TEL 44-
181-783-0755. FAX 44-181-783-1940. *3567*

**KEY NOTE MARKET REPORT: RETAIL BRANCH
BANKING.**
Key Note Ltd., Field House, 72 Oldfield Rd.,
Hampton, Middlesex TW12 2HQ, England. TEL 44-
181-783-0755. FAX 44-181-783-1940. *1106*

**KEY NOTE MARKET REPORT: RETAIL CHEMISTS &
DRUG STORES.**
Key Note Ltd., Field House, 72 Oldfield Rd.,
Hampton, Middlesex TW12 2HQ, England. TEL 44-
181-783-0755. FAX 44-181-783-1940. *5425*

KEY NOTE MARKET REPORT: ROAD HAULAGE.
Key Note Ltd., Field House, 72 Oldfield Rd.,
Hampton, Middlesex TW12 2HQ, England. TEL 44-
181-783-0755. FAX 44-181-783-1940. *6858*

**KEY NOTE MARKET REPORT: RUBBER
MANUFACTURING & PROCESSING.**
Key Note Ltd., Field House, 72 Oldfield Rd.,
Hampton, Middlesex TW12 2HQ, England. TEL 44-
181-783-0755. FAX 44-181-783-1940. *6217*

**KEY NOTE MARKET REPORT: SAUCES AND
SPREADS.**
Key Note Ltd., Field House, 72 Oldfield Rd.,
Hampton, Middlesex TW12 2HQ, England. TEL 44-
181-783-0755. FAX 44-181-783-1940. *2981*

**KEY NOTE MARKET REPORT: SCIENTIFIC
INSTRUMENTS.**
Key Note Ltd., Field House, 72 Oldfield Rd.,
Hampton, Middlesex TW12 2HQ, England. TEL 44-
181-783-0755. FAX 44-181-783-1940. *3636*

**KEY NOTE MARKET REPORT: SCRAP METAL
PROCESSING.**
Key Note Ltd., Field House, 72 Oldfield Rd.,
Hampton, Middlesex TW12 2HQ, England. TEL 44-
181-783-0755. FAX 44-181-783-1940. *4962*

**KEY NOTE MARKET REPORT: SELF-ASSEMBLY
FURNITURE.**
Key Note Ltd., Field House, 72 Oldfield Rd.,
Hampton, Middlesex TW12 2HQ, England. TEL 44-
181-783-0755. FAX 44-181-783-1940. *3690*

KEY NOTE MARKET REPORT: SHOP FITTING.
Key Note Ltd., Field House, 72 Oldfield Rd.,
Hampton, Middlesex TW12 2HQ, England. TEL 44-
181-783-0755. FAX 44-181-783-1940. *1474*

**KEY NOTE MARKET REPORT: SHOWERS & SHOWER
ACCESSORIES.**
Key Note Ltd., Field House, 72 Oldfield Rd.,
Hampton, Middlesex TW12 2HQ, England. TEL 44-
181-783-0755. FAX 44-181-783-1940. *3690*

KEY NOTE MARKET REPORT: SLIMMING MARKET.
Key Note Ltd., Field House, 72 Oldfield Rd.,
Hampton, Middlesex TW12 2HQ, England. TEL 44-
181-783-0755. FAX 44-181-783-1940. *1524*

**KEY NOTE MARKET REPORT: SMALL DOMESTIC
ELECTRICAL APPLIANCES.**
Key Note Ltd., Field House, 72 Oldfield Rd.,
Hampton, Middlesex TW12 2HQ, England. TEL 44-
181-783-0755. FAX 44-181-783-1940. *2526*

KEY NOTE MARKET REPORT: SNACK FOODS.
Key Note Ltd., Field House, 72 Oldfield Rd.,
Hampton, Middlesex TW12 2HQ, England. TEL 44-
181-783-0755. FAX 44-181-783-1940. *2981*

**KEY NOTE MARKET REPORT: SOAPS &
DETERGENTS.**
Key Note Ltd., Field House, 72 Oldfield Rd.,
Hampton, Middlesex TW12 2HQ, England. TEL 44-
181-783-0755. FAX 44-181-783-1940. *1828*

**KEY NOTE MARKET REPORT: SOFT DRINKS
(CARBONATES & CONCENTRATES).**
Key Note Ltd., Field House, 72 Oldfield Rd.,
Hampton, Middlesex TW12 2HQ, England. TEL 44-
181-783-0755. FAX 44-181-783-1940. *508*

**KEY NOTE MARKET REPORT: SPORTS CLOTHING
AND FOOTWEAR.**
Key Note Ltd., Field House, 72 Oldfield Rd.,
Hampton, Middlesex TW12 2HQ, England. TEL 44-
181-783-0755. FAX 44-181-783-1940. *1834*

KEY NOTE MARKET REPORT: SPORTS EQUIPMENT.
Key Note Ltd., Field House, 72 Oldfield Rd.,
Hampton, Middlesex TW12 2HQ, England. TEL 44-
181-783-0755. FAX 44-181-783-1940. *6467*

**KEY NOTE MARKET REPORT: STATIONERY
(PERSONAL & OFFICE).**
Key Note Ltd., Field House, 72 Oldfield Rd.,
Hampton, Middlesex TW12 2HQ, England. TEL 44-
181-783-0755. FAX 44-181-783-1940. *1494*

**KEY NOTE MARKET REPORT: STEEL
STOCKHOLDING.**
Key Note Ltd., Field House, 72 Oldfield Rd.,
Hampton, Middlesex TW12 2HQ, England. TEL 44-
181-783-0755. FAX 44-181-783-1940. *1338*

**KEY NOTE MARKET REPORT: SUPERMARKETS &
SUPERSTORES.**
Key Note Ltd., Field House, 72 Oldfield Rd.,
Hampton, Middlesex TW12 2HQ, England. TEL 44-
181-783-0755. FAX 44-181-783-1940. *2981*

KEY NOTE MARKET REPORT: T V & VIDEO RENTAL.
Key Note Ltd., Field House, 72 Oldfield Rd.,
Hampton, Middlesex TW12 2HQ, England. TEL 44-
181-783-0755. FAX 44-181-783-1940. *2526*

**KEY NOTE MARKET REPORT:
TELECOMMUNICATIONS.**
Key Note Ltd., Field House, 72 Oldfield Rd.,
Hampton, Middlesex TW12 2HQ, England. TEL 44-
181-783-0755. FAX 44-181-783-1940. *1909*

KEY NOTE MARKET REPORT: TIMBER & JOINERY.
Key Note Ltd., Field House, 72 Oldfield Rd.,
Hampton, Middlesex TW12 2HQ, England. TEL 44-
181-783-0755. FAX 44-181-783-1940. *3035*

KEY NOTE MARKET REPORT: TOILETRIES.
Key Note Ltd., Field House, 72 Oldfield Rd.,
Hampton, Middlesex TW12 2HQ, England. TEL 44-
181-783-0755. FAX 44-181-783-1940. *492*

**KEY NOTE MARKET REPORT: TOURIST
ATTRACTIONS.**
Key Note Ltd., Field House, 72 Oldfield Rd.,
Hampton, Middlesex TW12 2HQ, England. TEL 44-
181-783-0755. FAX 44-181-783-1940. *6896*

KEY NOTE MARKET REPORT: TOYS & GAMES.
Key Note Ltd., Field House, 72 Oldfield Rd.,
Hampton, Middlesex TW12 2HQ, England. TEL 44-
181-783-0755. FAX 44-181-783-1940. *3301*

KEY NOTE MARKET REPORT: TRAINING.
Key Note Ltd., Field House, 72 Oldfield Rd.,
Hampton, Middlesex TW12 2HQ, England. TEL 44-
181-783-0755. FAX 44-181-783-1940. *2400*

**KEY NOTE MARKET REPORT: TRAVEL AGENTS &
OVERSEAS TOUR OPERATORS.**
Key Note Ltd., Field House, 72 Oldfield Rd.,
Hampton, Middlesex TW12 2HQ, England. TEL 44-
181-783-0755. FAX 44-181-783-1940. *6896*

**KEY NOTE MARKET REPORT: VEHICLE LEASING &
HIRE.**
Key Note Ltd., Field House, 72 Oldfield Rd.,
Hampton, Middlesex TW12 2HQ, England. TEL 44-
181-783-0755. FAX 44-181-783-1940. *6790*

KEY NOTE MARKET REPORT: VEHICLE SECURITY.
Key Note Ltd., Field House, 72 Oldfield Rd.,
Hampton, Middlesex TW12 2HQ, England. TEL 44-
181-783-0755. FAX 44-181-783-1940. *6790*

KEY NOTE MARKET REPORT: VIDEO RETAIL & HIRE.
Key Note Ltd., Field House, 72 Oldfield Rd.,
Hampton, Middlesex TW12 2HQ, England. TEL 44-
181-783-0755. FAX 44-181-783-1940. *1977*

KEY NOTE MARKET REPORT: WALLCOVERINGS.
Key Note Ltd., Field House, 72 Oldfield Rd.,
Hampton, Middlesex TW12 2HQ, England. TEL 44-
181-783-0755. FAX 44-181-783-1940. *3679*

**KEY NOTE MARKET REPORT: WASTE
MANAGEMENT.**
Key Note Ltd., Field House, 72 Oldfield Rd.,
Hampton, Middlesex TW12 2HQ, England. TEL 44-
181-783-0755. FAX 44-181-783-1940. *2854*

KEY NOTE MARKET REPORT: WATER UTILITIES.
Key Note Ltd., Field House, 72 Oldfield Rd.,
Hampton, Middlesex TW12 2HQ, England. TEL 44-
181-783-0755. FAX 44-181-783-1940. *6971*

KEY NOTE MARKET REPORT: WINDOWS & DOORS.
Key Note Ltd., Field House, 72 Oldfield Rd.,
Hampton, Middlesex TW12 2HQ, England. TEL 44-
181-783-0755. FAX 44-181-783-1940. *3690*

KEY NOTE MARKET REPORT: WINE.
Key Note Ltd., Field House, 72 Oldfield Rd.,
Hampton, Middlesex TW12 2HQ, England. TEL 44-
181-783-0755. FAX 44-181-783-1940. *508*

**KEY NOTE MARKET REPORT: WOMEN'S
MAGAZINES.**
Key Note Ltd., Field House, 72 Oldfield Rd.,
Hampton, Middlesex TW12 2HQ, England. TEL 44-
181-783-0755. FAX 44-181-783-1940. *6998*

**KEY NOTE MARKET REVIEW: CORPORATE SERVICES
IN THE U K.**
Key Note Ltd., Field House, 72 Oldfield Rd.,
Hampton, Middlesex TW12 2HQ, England. TEL 44-
181-783-0755. FAX 44-181-783-1940. *1619*

**KEY NOTE MARKET REVIEW: D I Y & HOME
IMPROVEMENTS.**
Key Note Ltd., Field House, 72 Oldfield Rd.,
Hampton, Middlesex TW12 2HQ, England. TEL 44-
181-783-0755. FAX 44-181-783-1940. *3679*

**KEY NOTE MARKET REVIEW: ENERGY INDUSTRY IN
THE U K.**
Key Note Ltd., Field House, 72 Oldfield Rd.,
Hampton, Middlesex TW12 2HQ, England. TEL 44-
181-783-0755. FAX 44-181-783-1940. *2553*

**KEY NOTE MARKET REVIEW: GREY MARKET IN THE
U K.**
Key Note Ltd., Field House, 72 Oldfield Rd.,
Hampton, Middlesex TW12 2HQ, England. TEL 44-
181-783-0755. FAX 44-181-783-1940. *1474*

KEY NOTE MARKET REVIEW: MULTIMEDIA IN U K.
Key Note Ltd., Field House, 72 Oldfield Rd.,
Hampton, Middlesex TW12 2HQ, England. TEL 44-
181-783-0755. FAX 44-181-783-1940. *1928*

**KEY NOTE MARKET REVIEW: PASSENGER TRAVEL
IN U K.**
Key Note Ltd., Field House, 72 Oldfield Rd.,
Hampton, Middlesex TW12 2HQ, England. TEL 44-
181-783-0755. FAX 44-181-783-1940. *6896*

**KEY NOTE MARKET REVIEW: PERSONAL FINANCE
IN THE U K.**
Key Note Ltd., Field House, 72 Oldfield Rd.,
Hampton, Middlesex TW12 2HQ, England. TEL 44-
181-783-0755. FAX 44-181-783-1940. *1106*

CD-ROM

KEY NOTE MARKET REVIEW: RETAILING IN THE U K.
Key Note Ltd., Field House, 72 Oldfield Rd., Hampton, Middlesex TW12 2HQ, England. TEL 44-181-783-0755. FAX 44-181-783-1940. *1474*

KEY NOTE MARKET REVIEW: U K CATERING MARKET.
Key Note Ltd., Field House, 72 Oldfield Rd., Hampton, Middlesex TW12 2HQ, England. TEL 44-181-783-0755. FAX 44-181-783-1940. *3567*

KEY NOTE MARKET REVIEW: U K CHEMICAL INDUSTRY.
Key Note Ltd., Field House, 72 Oldfield Rd., Hampton, Middlesex TW12 2HQ, England. TEL 44-181-783-0755. FAX 44-181-783-1940. *1683*

KEY NOTE MARKET REVIEW: U K CLOTHING & FOOTWEAR.
Key Note Ltd., Field House, 72 Oldfield Rd., Hampton, Middlesex TW12 2HQ, England. TEL 44-181-783-0755. FAX 44-181-783-1940. *1834*

KEY NOTE MARKET REVIEW: U K COMPUTER MARKET.
Key Note Ltd., Field House, 72 Oldfield Rd., Hampton, Middlesex TW12 2HQ, England. TEL 44-181-783-0755. FAX 44-181-783-1940. *2032*

KEY NOTE MARKET REVIEW: U K CONSTRUCTION INDUSTRY.
Key Note Ltd., Field House, 72 Oldfield Rd., Hampton, Middlesex TW12 2HQ, England. TEL 44-181-783-0755. FAX 44-181-783-1940. *862*

KEY NOTE MARKET REVIEW: U K DEFENCE INDUSTRY.
Key Note Ltd., Field House, 72 Oldfield Rd., Hampton, Middlesex TW12 2HQ, England. TEL 44-181-783-0755. FAX 44-181-783-1940. *5037*

KEY NOTE MARKET REVIEW: U K DISTRIBUTION.
Key Note Ltd., Field House, 72 Oldfield Rd., Hampton, Middlesex TW12 2HQ, England. TEL 44-181-783-0755. FAX 44-181-783-1940. *1524*

KEY NOTE MARKET REVIEW: U K DRINKS MARKET.
Key Note Ltd., Field House, 72 Oldfield Rd., Hampton, Middlesex TW12 2HQ, England. TEL 44-181-783-0755. FAX 44-181-783-1940. *508*

KEY NOTE MARKET REVIEW: U K EDUCATION INDUSTRY.
Key Note Ltd., Field House, 72 Oldfield Rd., Hampton, Middlesex TW12 2HQ, England. TEL 44-181-783-0755. FAX 44-181-783-1940. *2459*

KEY NOTE MARKET REVIEW: U K FOOD MARKET.
Key Note Ltd., Field House, 72 Oldfield Rd., Hampton, Middlesex TW12 2HQ, England. TEL 44-181-783-0755. FAX 44-181-783-1940. *2981*

KEY NOTE MARKET REVIEW: U K HEALTHCARE.
Key Note Ltd., Field House, 72 Oldfield Rd., Hampton, Middlesex TW12 2HQ, England. TEL 44-181-783-0755. FAX 44-181-783-1940. *4486*

KEY NOTE MARKET REVIEW: U K HOUSEHOLD MARKET - FURNITURE, FITTINGS & DECOR.
Key Note Ltd., Field House, 72 Oldfield Rd., Hampton, Middlesex TW12 2HQ, England. TEL 44-181-783-0755. FAX 44-181-783-1940. *3690*

KEY NOTE MARKET REVIEW: U K HOUSEHOLD MARKET - HOUSEHOLD APPLIANCES AND HOUSEWARES.
Key Note Ltd., Field House, 72 Oldfield Rd., Hampton, Middlesex TW12 2HQ, England. TEL 44-181-783-0755. FAX 44-181-783-1940. *3690*

KEY NOTE MARKET REVIEW: U K INSURANCE MARKET.
Key Note Ltd., Field House, 72 Oldfield Rd., Hampton, Middlesex TW12 2HQ, England. TEL 44-181-783-0755. FAX 44-181-783-1940. *3655*

KEY NOTE MARKET REVIEW: U K LEISURE AND RECREATION.
Key Note Ltd., Field House, 72 Oldfield Rd., Hampton, Middlesex TW12 2HQ, England. TEL 44-181-783-0755. FAX 44-181-783-1940. *3964*

KEY NOTE MARKET REVIEW: U K MOTOR INDUSTRY.
Key Note Ltd., Field House, 72 Oldfield Rd., Hampton, Middlesex TW12 2HQ, England. TEL 44-181-783-0755. FAX 44-181-783-1940. *6790*

KEY NOTE MARKET REVIEW: U K OFFICE EQUIPMENT.
Key Note Ltd., Field House, 72 Oldfield Rd., Hampton, Middlesex TW12 2HQ, England. TEL 44-181-783-0755. FAX 44-181-783-1940. *1494*

KEY NOTE MARKET REVIEW: U K PACKAGING INDUSTRY.
Key Note Ltd., Field House, 72 Oldfield Rd., Hampton, Middlesex TW12 2HQ, England. TEL 44-181-783-0755. FAX 44-181-783-1940. *5301*

KEY NOTE MARKET REVIEW: U K PET MARKET.
Key Note Ltd., Field House, 72 Oldfield Rd., Hampton, Middlesex TW12 2HQ, England. TEL 44-181-783-0755. FAX 44-181-783-1940. *1474*

KEY NOTE MARKET REVIEW: U K PHARMACEUTICAL INDUSTRY.
Key Note Ltd., Field House, 72 Oldfield Rd., Hampton, Middlesex TW12 2HQ, England. TEL 44-181-783-0755. FAX 44-181-783-1940. *5425*

KEY NOTE MARKET REVIEW: U K PUBLISHING.
Key Note Ltd., Field House, 72 Oldfield Rd., Hampton, Middlesex TW12 2HQ, England. TEL 44-181-783-0755. FAX 44-181-783-1940. *6000*

KEY NOTE MARKET REVIEW: U K SECURITY MARKET.
Key Note Ltd., Field House, 72 Oldfield Rd., Hampton, Middlesex TW12 2HQ, England. TEL 44-181-783-0755. FAX 44-181-783-1940. *2183*

KEY NOTE MARKET REVIEW: U K SOFT DRINKS.
Key Note Ltd., Field House, 72 Oldfield Rd., Hampton, Middlesex TW12 2HQ, England. TEL 44-181-783-0755. FAX 44-181-783-1940. *508*

KEY NOTE MARKET REVIEW: U K SPORTS MARKET.
Key Note Ltd., Field House, 72 Oldfield Rd., Hampton, Middlesex TW12 2HQ, England. TEL 44-181-783-0755. FAX 44-181-783-1940. *6467*

KEY NOTE MARKET REVIEW: U K TELECOMMUNICATIONS.
Key Note Ltd., Field House, 72 Oldfield Rd., Hampton, Middlesex TW12 2HQ, England. TEL 44-181-783-0755. FAX 44-181-783-1940. *1909*

KEY NOTE MARKET REVIEW: U K TOILETRIES & COSMETICS MARKET
Key Note Ltd., Field House, 72 Oldfield Rd., Hampton, Middlesex TW12 2HQ, England. TEL 44-181-783-0755. FAX 44-181-783-1940. *497*

KEY NOTE MARKET REVIEW: U K TRAVEL & TOURISM.
Key Note Ltd., Field House, 72 Oldfield Rd., Hampton, Middlesex TW12 2HQ, England. TEL 44-181-783-0755. FAX 44-181-783-1940. *6896*

KEY NOTE MARKET REVIEW: U K WEDDING MARKET.
Key Note Ltd., Field House, 72 Oldfield Rd., Hampton, Middlesex TW12 2HQ, England. TEL 44-181-783-0755. FAX 44-181-783-1940. *4414*

KEY NOTE MARKET REVIEW: WHOLESALING IN THE U K.
Key Note Ltd., Field House, 72 Oldfield Rd., Hampton, Middlesex TW12 2HQ, England. TEL 44-181-783-0755. FAX 44-181-783-1940. *1474*

KEY NOTE MARKET REVIEW: YOUTH MARKET IN THE U.K.
Key Note Ltd., Field House, 72 Oldfield Rd., Hampton, Middlesex TW12 2HQ, England. TEL 44-181-783-0755. FAX 44-181-783-1940. *39*

KEY NOTE REPORT: FURNITURE.
Key Note Publications Ltd., Field House, 72 Oldfield Rd., Hampton, Middlesex TW12 2HQ, England. TEL 0181-783-0755. FAX 0181-783-1720. *3690*

KEY NOTE REPORT: PRINTING INKS.
Key Note Publications Ltd., Field House, 72 Oldfield Rd., Hampton, Middlesex TW12 2HQ, England. TEL 0181-783-0755. FAX 0181-783-1720. *5814*

KING ABDULAZIZ MEDICAL JOURNAL.
King Abdul Aziz University, College of Medicine and Allied Sciences, P.O. Box 1540, Jeddah 21441, Saudi Arabia. *4486*

KIPLINGER'S PERSONAL FINANCE MAGAZINE.
Kiplinger Washington Editors, Inc., 1729 H St., N.W., Washington, DC 20006. TEL 202-887-6400. FAX 202-331-1206.
Producer(s): University Microfilms International. *1106*

KNACK.
N.V. R M G Bd. Louis Schmidt 97, 1040 Brussels, Belgium. TEL 32-2-7361.75. FAX 32-2-7344018. *3115*

KNJIZNICA.
Zveza Bibliotekarskih Drustev Slovenije, Turjaska 1, Ljubljana, Slovenia. TEL 061-150-131. *4004*

KOMPASS.
Forlaget Kompass Danmark, Oeveroedvej 5, DK-2840 Holte, Denmark. TEL 45-45-41-21-00. FAX 45-45-41-06-65. *1620*

KOMPASS AUSTRALIA.
Peter Isaacson Publications Pty. Ltd., 46-50 Porter St., Prahran, Vic. 3181, Australia. TEL 61-3-2457777. FAX 61-3-2457840. *1620*

KOMPASS BELGIUM.
Editus Belgium S.A., Av. Moliere 256, 1060 Brussels, Belgium. TEL 32-2-3459070. FAX 32-2-3473340. *1620*

KOMPASS ITALIA.
Kompass Italia S.p.A., Via Seruais, 125, 10146 Turin, Italy.
Producer(s): SilverPlatter Information, Inc.. *1620*

KOMPASS SELECT EXPORT. BUILDING CONSTRUCTION, CONTRACTORS.
Forlaget Kompass-Danmark, Oeveroedvej 5, DK-Holte, Denmark. TEL 45-45-41-21-00. FAX 45-45-41-06-65. *862*

KOMPASS SELECT EXPORT. BUSINESS SERVICES.
Forlaget Kompass-Danmark, Oeveroedvej 5, DK-2840 Holte, Denmark. TEL 45-45-41-21-00. FAX 45-45-41-21-00. *1258*

KOMPASS SELECT EXPORT. CHEMICAL INDUSTRY.
Forlaget Kompass Danmark, Oeveroedvej 5, DK-2840 Holte, Denmark. TEL 45-45-41-21-00. FAX 45-45-41-21-00. *1634*

KOMPASS SELECT EXPORT. ELECTRICAL AND ELECTRONIC EQUIPMENT.
Kompas-Danmark, Oeveroedvej 5, DK-2840 Holte, Denmark. TEL 45-45-41-21-00. FAX 45-45-41-21-00. *2526*

KOMPASS SELECT EXPORT. FOOD INDUSTRY.
Forlaget Kompass Danmark, Oeveroedvej 5, DK-2840 Holte, Denmark. TEL 45-45-41-21-00. FAX 45-45-41-21-00. *2982*

KOMPASS SELECT EXPORT. MACHINE INDUSTRY.
Forlaget Kompass Danmark, Oeveroedvej 5, DK-2840 Holte, Denmark. TEL 45-45-41-06-65. *4342*

KOMPASS SELECT EXPORT. METAL PRODUCTS.
Oeveroedvej 5, DK-2840 Holte, Denmark. TEL 45-45-41-21-00. FAX 45-45-41-06-65. *4962*

KOMPASS SELECT EXPORT. PAPER INDUSTRY, GRAPHIC ARTS.
Forlaget Kompass Danmark, Oeverroedevej 5, DK-2840 Holte, Denmark. TEL 45-45-41-21-00. FAX 45-45-41-06-65. *5323*

KOMPASS SELECT EXPORT. RUBBER INDUSTRY, PLASTICS INDUSTRY.
Forlaget Kompass Danmark, Oeveroedvej 5, DK-2840 Holte, Denmark. TEL 45-45-41-21-00. FAX 45-45-41-06-65. *6217*

KOMPASS SELECT EXPORT. SCIENTIFIC AND INDUSTRIAL INSTRUMENTS, WATCH INDUSTRY.
Forlaget Kompass Danmark, Oeveroedvej 5, DK-2840 Holte, Denmark. TEL 45-45-41-21-00. FAX 45-45-41-06-65. *3636*

KOMPASS SELECT EXPORT. TEXTILES, CLOTHING, FOOTWEAR AND LEATHER GOODS.
Forlaget Kompass Danmark, Oeveroedvej 5, DK-2840 Holte, Denmark. TEL 45-45-41-21-00. FAX 45-45-41-06-65. *6681*

KOMPASS SELECT EXPORT. TRANSPORT EQUIPMENT.
Forlaget Kompass Danmark, Oeveroedvej 5, DK-2840 Holte, Denmark. TEL 45-45-41-21-00. FAX 45-45-41-06-65. *6721*

KOMPASS SELECT EXPORT. WOOD INDUSTRY.
Kompass-Danmark, Oeveroedvej 5, DK-2840 Holte, Denmark. TEL 45-45-41-21-00. FAX 45-45-41-06-65. *3690*

KOMPASS SOUTH AFRICA.
SAFTO, Publishing Division, P.O. Box 782706, Sandton 2146, South Africa. TEL 27-11-883-3737. FAX 27-11-883-6569. *1621*

KOMPASS SVERIGE.
Kompass Sverige AB, Torsgatan 21, S-113 90 Stockholm, Sweden, Sweden. FAX 46-8-7363022. *1621*

KOMPASS UNITED KINGDOM.
Kompass Part of the Reed Elsevier group, Windsor Ct., E. Grinstead House, E. Grinstead, W. Sussex RH19 1XD, England. TEL 01342-326972. FAX 01342-335992. *1621*

KONZERNE IN SCHAUBILDERN.
Verlag Hoppenstedt GmbH, Havelstr. 9, 64295 Darmstadt, Germany. TEL 49-6151-380-0. FAX 49-6151-380360. *1621*

KOREA POLICY SERIES.
Korean Overseas Information Service, 82-1 Sejongnoo, Chongno-gu, Seoul 110-050, S. Korea. TEL 739-4481. FAX 736-2199. *5678*

KOREAN NURSE.
Korean Nurses' Association, 88-7 Sanglim-Dong, Choong Ku, Seoul, S. Korea. *4719*

KORRESPONDENZ ABWASSER.
Gesellschaft zur Foerderung der Abwassertechnik, Postfach 1165, 53758 Hennef, Germany. TEL 49-2242-8720. FAX 49-2242-872151. *2808*

DIE KUNSTSTOFF-INDUSTRIE UND IHRE HELFER.
Industrieschau-Verlagsgesellschaft mbH, Postfach 100262, 64202 Darmstadt, Germany. TEL 49-6151-3892-0. FAX 49-6151-33164. *5622*

L I L A C S · C D · R O M.
Latin American and Caribbean Center on Health Sciences Information (BIREME), Rua Botucatu, 862, Vila Clementino, 04023-901 Sao Paulo SP, Brazil. TEL 011-5492611. FAX 011-5711919. Available only on CD-ROM. *4567*

L I S A: LIBRARY & INFORMATION SCIENCE ABSTRACTS.
Bowker - Saur Ltd., A member of the Reed Elsevier plc group, Maypole House, Maypole Rd., E. Grinstead, W. Sussex RH19 1HU, England. TEL 44-1342-330100. FAX 44-1342-330191. Producer(s): Bowker - Saur Ltd.. *4039*

L I S A PLUS.
Bowker - Saur Ltd., A member of the Reed Elsevier plc group, Maypole House, Maypole Rd., E. Grindstead, W. Sussex RH19 1HU, England. TEL 44-1342-330100. FAX 44-1342-330191. Available only on CD-ROM. Producer(s): Bowker - Saur Ltd.. *4039*

LABORATORY HAZARDS BULLETIN.
The Royal Society of Chemistry, Thomas Graham House, Science Park, Milton Rd., Cambridge CB4 4WF, England. TEL 44-1223-420066. FAX 44-1223-423429.
Producer(s): Knight-Ridder, Inc.. *5252*

LAMY FISCAL.
Lamy S.A., 187-189 quai de Valmy, 75490 Paris, France. TEL 44-72-13-43. FAX 44-72-13-95. *3802*

LAMY SOCIAL.
Lamy S.A., 187-189 quai de Valmy, 75490 Paris, France. TEL 44-72-13-43. FAX 44-72-13-95. *3802*

THE LANCET.
The Lancet Ltd. 42 Bedford Sq., London WC1B 3SL, England. TEL 44-171-4364981. FAX 44-171-4367570. *4489*

THE LANCET (NORTH AMERICAN EDITION).
The Lancet Ltd. 655 Ave. of the Americas, New York, NY 10011. TEL 212-633-3800. FAX 212-633-3850. *4489*

LANDES- UND KOMMUNALVERWALTUNG.
C.H. Beck'sche Verlagsbuchhandlung, Wilhelmstr. 9, 80801 Munich, Germany. TEL 089-38189338. FAX 089-38189398. *5909*

THE LATEST AND BEST OF T E S S.
Educational Products Information Exchange (EPIE) Institute, 103-3 W. Montauk Hwy., No. 3, Hampton Bays, NY 11946-4006. TEL 516-728-9100. FAX 516-728-9228.
Available only on CD-ROM. *2112*

LATIN AMERICAN RESEARCH REVIEW.
Latin American Studies Association (Albuquerque), c/o University of New Mexico, 801 Yale N.E., Albuquerque, NM 87131-1016. TEL 505-277-5985. FAX 505-277-5989. *6333*

LATIN AMERICAN STUDIES. VOLUME 1.
National Information Services Corporation (NISC), Ste. 6, Wyman Towers, 3100 St. Paul St., Baltimore, MD 21218. TEL 410-243-0797. FAX 410-243-0982.
Available only on CD-ROM. Producer(s): NISC. *3367*

LATIN AMERICAN STUDIES. VOLUME 2.
National Information Services Corporation (NISC), Ste. 6, Wyman Towers, 3100 St. Paul St., Baltimore, MD 21218. TEL 410-243-0797. FAX 410-243-0982.
Available only on CD-ROM. Producer(s): NISC. *3367*

LATIN AMERICAN TAXATION DATA BASE ON C D - R O M.
I B F D Publications B.V., P.O. Box 20237, 1000 HE Amsterdam, Netherlands. TEL 31-20-6267726. FAX 31-20-6228658.
Available only on CD-ROM. *1553*

LAW FIRMS YELLOW BOOK.
Leadership Directories, Inc., 104 Fifth Ave., 2nd Fl., New York, NY 10011. TEL 212-627-4140. FAX 212-645-0931.
Producer(s): Chadwyck-Healey Inc.. *3804*

LAWS AFFECTING CHILDREN WITH SPECIAL NEEDS.
L R P Publications 747 Dresher Rd., Box 980, Horsham, PA 19044-0980. FAX 215-784-9639. *6381*

LAWYERS' LIABILITY REVIEW.
Timeline Publishing Co., Inc., Box 1435, Bellevue, WA 98009. TEL 206-462-7714. FAX 206-462-0411. *3806*

LEADERSHIP DIRECTORIES ON C D - R O M.
Chadwyck-Healey Inc., 1101 King St., Alexandria, VA 22314. TEL 703-683-7589. FAX 703-683-7589.
Available only on CD-ROM. Producer(s): Chadwyck-Healey Inc.. *5909*

THE LEADING EDGE (TULSA).
Society of Exploration Geophysicists, Box 702740, Tulsa, OK 74170-2740. TEL 918-493-3516. *2278*

THE LEARNING ORGANIZATION.
M C B University Press Ltd., 60-62 Toller Ln., Bradford, W. Yorks BD8 9BY, England. TEL 44-1274-777700. FAX 44-1274-785200. *1506*

LEGALTRAC.
Information Access Company, 362 Lakeside Dr., Foster City, CA 94404. TEL 415-378-5200. FAX 415-378-5369. *3877*

LEISURE INTELLIGENCE.
Mintel International Group Ltd., 18-19 Long Ln., London EC1A 9HE, England. TEL 44-171-606-4533. FAX 44-171-606-5932. *3965*

LEITSATZKARTEI DES DEUTSCHEN RECHTS.
C.H. Beck'sche Verlagsbuchhandlung, Wilhelmstr. 9, 80801 Munich, Germany. TEL 49-89-38189338. FAX 49-89-38189398.
Available only on CD-ROM. *3809*

LETTERATURA ITALIANA. AGGIORNAMENTO BIBLIOGRAFICO.
Alcione Edizioni s.r.l., Corso Italia 31, C.P. 554, Trieste, Italy. TEL 39-40-366069. *4294*

LIBRARIAN CAREER DEVELOPMENT.
M C B University Press Ltd., 60-62 Toller Ln., Bradford, W. Yorks BD8 9BY, England. TEL 44-1274-777700. FAX 44-1274-785200. *4006*

LIBRARY LITERATURE.
H.W. Wilson Co., 950 University Ave., Bronx, NY 10452. TEL 718-588-8400. FAX 718-590-1617. Producer(s): SilverPlatter Information, Inc., H.W. Wilson (WILSONDISC). *4040*

LIBRARY MANAGEMENT.
M C B University Press Ltd., 60-62 Toller Ln., Bradford, W. Yorks BD8 9BY, England. TEL 44-1274-777700. FAX 44-1274-785200. *4008*

LIBRARY REVIEW.
M C B University Press Ltd., 60-62 Toller Ln., Bradford, W. Yorks BD8 9BY, England. TEL 44-1274-777700. FAX 44-1274-785200. *4009*

LIBROS EN VENTA EN HISPANOAMERICA Y ESPANA.
Melcher Ediciones, c/o Margaret Melcher, Box 6000, San Juan, PR 00906. TEL 809-724-1352. FAX 809-724-2886.
Producer(s): K.G. Saur Verlag. *538*

LIBROS EN VENTA EN HISPANOAMERICA Y ESPANA PLUS.
R.R. Bowker, A Division of Reed Elsevier plc group, 121 Chanlon Rd., New Providence, NJ 07974. TEL 908-665-2866. FAX 908-665-3528.
Available only on CD-ROM. Producer(s): Bowker Electronic Publishing. *538*

LIBROS ESPANOLES EN VENTA.
Ministerio de Cultura, Centro del Libro y de la Lectura, C. Santiago Rusinol, 8, 28040 Madrid, Spain. TEL 536-88-30. FAX 553-99-90. *538*

LIEFERN UND LEISTEN.
Deutscher Adressbuch Verlag, Arheilger Weg 17, 64380 Rossdorf, Germany. TEL 06154-699500. FAX 06154-6995490. *1622*

LIFE (NEW YORK).
Time Inc. Time & Life Bldg., Rockefeller Center, 1271 Ave. of the Americas, New York, NY 10020. TEL 212-522-1212. FAX 212-522-1863.
Producer(s): University Microfilms International, H.W. Wilson. *3231*

LINCHUANG PIFUKE ZAZHI.
Jiangsu Sheng Renmin Yiyuan, 300 Guangzhou Lu, Nanjing, Jiangsu 210029, People's Republic of China. TEL 86-25-303836. FAX 86-25-6612555. *4663*

LINEAR I CS D.A.T.A. DIGEST.
D.A.T.A. Business Publishing 15 Inverness Way E., Box 6510, Englewood, CO 80155-6510. FAX 303-799-4082. *2527*

LINGUISTICS AND LANGUAGE BEHAVIOR ABSTRACTS.
Sociological Abstracts, Inc., Box 22206, San Diego, CA 92192-0206. TEL 619-695-8803. FAX 619-695-0416.
Producer(s): NISC, SilverPlatter Information, Inc.. *4128*

LITERARY MARKET PLACE.
R.R. Bowker, A Division of Reed Elsevier Inc., 121 Chanlon Rd., New Providence, NJ 07974. TEL 908-464-6800. FAX 908-665-6688.
Producer(s): Bowker Electronic Publishing. *6001*

LITERARY REVIEW.
Fairleigh Dickinson University, Literary Review, 285 Madison Ave., Madison, NJ 07940. TEL 201-443-8564. *4231*

LITERATURE - FILM QUARTERLY.
Salisbury State University, Salisbury, MD 21801. TEL 410-543-6446. FAX 410-543-6068. *5107*

LIVRES DISPONIBLES.
Editions du Cercle de la Librairie, 35 rue Gregoire de Tours, 75006 Paris Cedex 06, France. *538*

LODGING, RESTAURANT AND TOURISM INDEX.
Hotel and Institutional Management Institute, Purdue University, West Lafayette, IN 47907-1002. TEL 317-494-2914. *3574*

THE LOS ANGELES TIMES INDEX.
U M I Company 300 N. Zeeb Rd., Ann Arbor, MI 48106-1346. TEL 313-761-4700. FAX 800-864-0019. *3715*

LOUISIANA BUSINESS DIRECTORY.
American Business Directories 5711 S. 86th Circle, Box 27347, Omaha, NE 68127. TEL 402-593-4600. FAX 402-331-5481. *1623*

LOUISIANA RULES OF COURT, FEDERAL.
West Publishing Corp., 620 Opperman Dr., Eagan, MN 55123. TEL 612-687-8000. FAX 612-687-7302. *3950*

LUCKNOW LIBRARIAN.
Uttar Pradesh Library Association, Lucknow Branch, U.P. Library Association, P.O. Box 446, Lucknow 226 001, India. *4010*

M D R'S SCHOOL DIRECTORIES.
Market Data Retrieval, Inc., 16 Progress Dr., Box 2117, Shelton, CT 06484-1117. TEL 203-926-4800. FAX 203-929-5253. *2413*

M L A INTERNATIONAL BIBLIOGRAPHY OF BOOKS AND ARTICLES ON THE MODERN LANGUAGES AND LITERATURES.
Modern Language Association of America, 10 Astor Place, New York, NY 10003. TEL 212-475-9500. FAX 212-477-9863.
Producer(s): SilverPlatter Information, Inc.. *4294*

MCGOLDRICK'S CANADIAN CUSTOMS GUIDE "HARMONIZED SYSTEM".
McMullin Publishers Ltd., 417 St. Pierre, Montreal, PQ H2Y 2M4, Canada. TEL 514-849-1424. FAX 514-849-9809. *1289*

MACINTOSH PRODUCT REGISTRY.
Redgate Communications Corp., 660 Beachland Blvd., Vero Beach, FL 32963. TEL 407-231-6904. FAX 407-231-7872. *2097*

MACINTOSH TIPS & TRICKS.
Giles Road Press, Box 212, Harrington Park, NJ 07640-0212. TEL 201-767-7001. FAX 201-767-7457. *2097*

MACLEAN'S.
Maclean Hunter Ltd., Maclean Hunter Bldg., 777 Bay St., Toronto, ON M5W 1A7, Canada. TEL 416-596-5386. FAX 416-596-7730.
Producer(s): University Microfilms International. *3123*

MACTECH MAGAZINE.
Xplain Corporation, Box 5200, West Lake, CA 90025. TEL 805-494-9797. FAX 805-494-9798. *2097*

MAGAZINE ARTICLE SUMMARIES.
EBSCO Publishing 10 Estes St., Box 682, Ipswich, MA 01938. TEL 508-356-6500. FAX 508-356-6565. *18*

MAGAZINE INDEX.
Information Access Company 362 Lakeside Dr., Foster City, CA 94404. TEL 415-378-5200. FAX 415-378-5369. *6015*

MAGYAR NEMZETI BIBLIOGRAFIA. KONYVEK.
Orszagos Szechenyi Konyvtar, Budavari Palota F epulet, 1827 Budapest, Hungary. TEL 36-1-1556967. FAX 36-1-2020804.
Available only on CD-ROM. *539*

MAGYAR NEMZETI BIBLIOGRAFIA. KONYVEK BIBLIOGRAFIAJA.
Orszagos Szechenyi Konyvtar, Budavari Palota F epulet, 1827 Budapest, Hungary. TEL 36-1-156-8497. FAX 36-1-202-0804. *539*

THE MAIL ON C D - R O M.
Chadwyck-Healey Ltd., The Quorum, Barnwell Rd., Cambridge CB5 8SW, England. TEL 44-1223-215512. FAX 44-1223-215514.
Available only on CD-ROM. Producer(s): Chadwyck-Healey Inc.. *3157*

THE MAIL ON SUNDAY.
Associated Newspaper Holdings PLC, Northcliffe House, 2 Derry St., Kensington, London W8 5TS. TEL 44-171-938-6000. FAX 44-171-938-4980.
Producer(s): Chadwyck-Healey Inc.. *3157*

MAINE BAR DIRECTORY.
Tower Publishing Co., 588 Saco Rd., Standish, ME 04084-6239. TEL 207-642-5400. FAX 207-642-5463. *3812*

MAINE BUSINESS DIRECTORY.
American Business Directories 5711 S. 86th Circle, Box 27347, Omaha, NE 68127. TEL 402-593-4600. FAX 402-331-5481. *1623*

AL-MAJALLAH AL-TIBBIYYAH AL-MISRIYYAH AL-JADIDAH.
Egyptian Junior Medical Doctors Association, Medical Information and Publishing Center, c/o Egyptian Medical Association, 42 Sharia Kasr El-Aini, Cairo, Egypt. *4491*

MAJALLAH-I DANISHKADAH-I DAMPIZISHKI.
University of Teheran, Faculty of Veterinary Medicine, Azadi Ave., P.O. Box 14155-6453, Tehran, Iran. *6950*

MAKERERE MEDICAL JOURNAL.
Makerere University Medical Students' Association (MUMSA), P.O. Box 7072, Kampala, Uganda. *4491*

MANAGERIAL AUDITING JOURNAL.
M C B University Press Ltd., 60-62 Toller Ln., Bradford, W. Yorks ED8 9BY, England. TEL 44-1274-777700. FAX 44-1274-785200. *1434*

MANAGING SERVICE QUALITY.
M C B University Press Ltd., 60-62 Toller Ln., Bradford, W. Yorks ED8 9BY, England. TEL 44-1274-777700. FAX 44-1274-785200. *1435*

MANITOBA CO-OPERATOR.
Manitoba Pool Elevators, 220 Portage Ave., P.O. Box 9800, Sta. Main, Winnipeg, MB R3C 3K7, Canada. TEL 204-934-0401. FAX 204-934-0480. *134*

MANSOURA JOURNAL OF PHARMACEUTICAL SCIENCES.
University of Mansoura, Faculty of Pharmacy, University P.O. 35516, Mansoura, Egypt. *5427*

MANUFACTURING SUPPLIES & FABRICS.
Asian Sources Media Group, G.P.O. Box 12367, Hong Kong. TEL 852-2555-4777. *1835*

MARINE POLLUTION RESEARCH TITLES.
Plymouth Marine Laboratory, Citadel Hill, Plymouth PL1 2PB, England. TEL 44-1752-222772. FAX 44-1752-226865.
Producer(s): NISC (Oceanographic & Marine Resources). *2830*

MARINE TECHNOLOGY ABSTRACTS ON C D - R O M.
Institute of Marine Engineers, The Memorial Bldg., 76 Mark Ln., London EC3R 7JN, England. TEL 44-171-481-8493. FAX 44-171-488-1854.
Available only on CD-ROM. *6742*

MARINEFACTS.
Running End Ltd., Box 257, Crownsville, MD 21032-0257. TEL 410-923-1325. *6536*

MARKET INTELLIGENCE.
Mintel International Group Ltd., 18-19 Long Ln., London EC1A 9HE, England. TEL 44-171-606-4533. FAX 44-171-606-5932. *1475*

MARKETING ADRESS DATA CD.
Herold Business Data GmbH, Guntramsdorferstr. 105, A-2340 Moedling, Austria. TEL 02236-401. FAX 02236-4018.
Available only on CD-ROM. *1624*

MARKETING INTELLIGENCE & PLANNING.
M C B University Press Ltd., 60-62 Toller Ln., Bradford, W. Yorks BD8 9BY, England. TEL 44-1274-777700. FAX 44-1274-785200. *1477*

MARKETING SERIES.
Natural Resources Institute, Central Ave., Chatham Maritime, Kent ME4 4TB, England. TEL 44-1634-880088. FAX 44-1634-880066. *1478*

MARLY - RECHTSPRECHUNG ZUM COMPUTERRECHT.
C.H. Beck'sche Verlagsbuchhandlung, Wilhelmstr. 9, 80801 Munich, Germany. TEL 49-89-38189338. FAX 49-89-38189398.
Available only on CD-ROM. *2051*

MARTINDALE-HUBBELL LAW DIRECTORY.
Martindale-Hubbell, A Division of Reed Elsevier Inc., 121 Chanlon Rd., New Providence, NJ 07974. FAX 908-464-3553.
Producer(s): Bowker Electronic Publishing. *3814*

MARTINDALE-HUBBELL LAW DIRECTORY ON C D - R O M.
Martindale-Hubbell, A Division of Reed Elsevier Inc., 121 Chanlon Rd., New Providence, NJ 07974. FAX 908-464-3553.
Available only on CD-ROM. Producer(s): Bowker Electronic Publishing. *3814*

MARYLAND BUSINESS DIRECTORY.
American Business Directories 5711 S. 86th Circle, Box 27347, Omaha, NE 68127. TEL 402-593-4600. FAX 402-331-5481. *1625*

MARYLAND - D.C. MANUFACTURERS REGISTER.
Manufacturers' News, Inc., 1633 Central St., Evanston, IL 60201-1563. TEL 847-864-7000. FAX 847-332-1100. *1625*

MASSACHUSETTS BUSINESS DIRECTORY.
American Business Directories 5711 S. 86th Circle, Omaha, NE 68127. TEL 402-593-4600. FAX 402-331-5481. *1625*

MASTERS ABSTRACTS INTERNATIONAL.
U M I Company 300 N. Zeeb Rd., Ann Arbor, MI 48106. TEL 313-761-4700. FAX 800-864-0019.
Producer(s): University Microfilms International. *2391*

MATERIALS SCIENCE CITATION INDEX.
Institute for Scientific Information, 3501 Market St., Philadelphia, PA 19104. TEL 215-386-0100. FAX 215-386-0100. *2629*

MATHEMATICAL REVIEWS.
American Mathematical Society, Box 6248, Providence, RI 02940-6248. TEL 401-455-4000.
Producer(s): SilverPlatter Information, Inc. (MathDisc). *4406*

A MATTER OF FACT: STATEMENTS CONTAINING STATISTICS ON CURRENT SOCIAL, ECONOMIC AND POLITICAL ISSUES.
Pierian Press, Box 1808, Ann Arbor, MI 48106. TEL 313-434-5530. FAX 313-434-6409.
Producer(s): NISC, SilverPlatter Information, Inc.. *3352*

MAYO CLINIC PROCEEDINGS.
Mayo Foundation for Medical Education and Research, Rochester, MN 55905. TEL 507-284-2154. FAX 507-284-0252. *4492*

MEALEY'S LITIGATION REPORT: INSURANCE.
Mealey Publications, Inc., Box 446, Wayne, PA 19087. TEL 610-688-6565. FAX 610-688-7552. *3885*

MEALEY'S LITIGATION REPORT: INSURANCE INSOLVENCY.
Mealey Publications, Inc., Box 446, Wayne, PA 19087. TEL 610-688-6565. FAX 610-688-7552. *3885*

MECHANICAL ENGINEERING ABSTRACTS.
Cambridge Scientific Abstracts, 7200 Wisconsin Ave., 6th Fl., Bethesda, MD 20814. TEL 301-961-6700. FAX 301-961-6720.
Producer(s): SilverPlatter Information, Inc.. *2629*

MEDECINE ET ENFANCE, ADOLESCENCE.
Edition et Communication Medicales, 23 rue Saint-Ferdinand, 75017 Paris, France. TEL 45-74-44-65. FAX 40-55-94-13. *4808*

MEDIATORS OF INFLAMMATION.
Rapid Science Publishers, The Old Malthouse, Paradise St., Oxford OX1 1LD, England. TEL 44-1865-790447. FAX 44-1865-244012. *4493*

CD-ROM

MEDICAL AND HEALTH CARE BOOKS AND SERIALS IN PRINT.
R.R. Bowker, A Division of Reed Elsevier Inc., 121 Chanlon Rd., New Providence, NJ 07974. TEL 908-464-6800. FAX 908-665-3502. *4568*

MEDICAL AND HEALTHCARE MARKETPLACE GUIDE.
Investment Dealers' Digest, 2 World Trade Center, 18th Fl., New York, NY 10048. TEL 212-432-0045. FAX 212-321-2336. *1625*

MEDICAL & PHARMACEUTICAL BIOTECHNOLOGY ABSTRACTS.
Cambridge Scientific Abstracts, 7200 Wisconsin Ave., 6th Fl., Bethesda, MD 20814. TEL 301-961-6700. FAX 301-961-6720.
Producer(s): Knight-Ridder, Inc. (Biotechnology & Bioengineering), SilverPlatter Information, Inc.. *4568*

MEDICAL JOURNAL ARMED FORCES INDIA.
Armed Forces Medical College, Pune 411 040, Maharashtra, India. TEL 673290. *4495*

MEDICAL JOURNAL OF THE ISLAMIC REPUBLIC OF IRAN.
National Center for Scientific Research, 1188 Enghelab Ave., P.O. Box 13145-554, Tehran 13158, Iran. TEL 98-21-6462778. FAX 98-21-6468180. *4495*

MEDLINE PROFESSIONAL - C D.
SilverPlatter Information, Inc., 100 River Ridge Dr., Norwood, MA 02062-5026. TEL 617-769-2599. FAX 617-769-8763.
Available only on CD-ROM. *4568*

MELANOMA RESEARCH.
Rapid Science Publishers, The Old Malthouse, Paradise St., Oxford OX1 1LD, England. TEL 44-1865-790447. FAX 44-1865-244012. *4760*

MEMORY I CS D.A.T.A. DIGEST.
D.A.T.A. Business Publishing 15 Inverness Way E., Box 6510, Englewood, CO 80155-6510. FAX 303-799-4082. *2527*

MENDELEEV COMMUNICATIONS.
The Royal Society of Chemistry, Thomas Graham House, Science Park, Milton Rd., Cambridge CB4 4WF, England. TEL 44-1223-420066. FAX 44-1223-423429. *1686*

MENNONITE REPORTER.
Mennonite Publishing Service, 3-312 Marsland Drive, Waterloo, ON N2J 3Z1, Canada. TEL 519-884-3810. FAX 519-884-3331. *6152*

MENTAL MEASUREMENTS YEARBOOK.
Buros Institute of Mental Measurements, 135 Bancroft, University of Nebraska-Lincoln, Lincoln, NE 68588-0348. TEL 402-472-6203. FAX 402-472-6207. *5865*

MERCADO DE VALORES.
Nacional Financiera, S.N.C., Subdireccion de Informacion Tecnica y Publicaciones, Insurgentes Sur 1971, Nivel Fuente, Col. Guadalupe Inn, 01020 Mexico, D.F., Mexico. TEL 525-3256047. *1341*

METALS ABSTRACTS.
Cambridge Scientific Abtracts, 7200 Wisconsin Ave., Bethesda, MD 20814. TEL 301-961-6750. FAX 301-961-6720.
Producer(s): Knight-Ridder, Inc.. *4984*

METALS ABSTRACTS INDEX.
Cambridge Scientific Abstracts, 7200 Wisconsin Ave., Bethesda, MD 20814. TEL 301-961-6750. FAX 301-961-6720.
Producer(s): Knight-Ridder, Inc.. *4984*

METEOROLOGICAL AND GEOASTROPHYSICAL ABSTRACTS.
American Meteorological Society, c/o Inforonics, Inc., 550 Newtown Rd., Littleton, MA 01460. TEL 508-486-8976. FAX 508-486-0027. *5011*

MEYLER'S SIDE EFFECTS OF DRUGS.
Elsevier Science B.V., Books Division, P.O. Box 211, 1000 AE Amsterdam, Netherlands. TEL 31-20-4853911. FAX 31-20-4853705.
Producer(s): SilverPlatter Information, Inc. (SEDBASE). *5428*

MICHIGAN BUSINESS DIRECTORY.
American Business Directories 5711 S. 86th Circle, Box 27347, Omaha, NE 68127. TEL 402-593-4600. FAX 402-331-5481. *1626*

MICROBIAL & COMPARATIVE GENOMICS.
Mary Ann Liebert, Inc. Publishers, 2 Madison Ave., Larchmont, NY 10538. TEL 914-834-3100. FAX 914-834-3688. *747*

MICROBIOLOGICAL REVIEWS.
American Society for Microbiology, 1325 Massachusetts Ave., N.W., Washington, DC 20005. TEL 202-737-3600. *762*

MICROBIOLOGY ABSTRACTS: SECTION A. INDUSTRIAL & APPLIED MICROBIOLOGY.
Cambridge Scientific Abstracts, 7200 Wisconsin Ave., 6th Fl., Bethesda, MD 20814. TEL 301-961-6750. FAX 301-961-6720.
Producer(s): NISC, SilverPlatter Information, Inc.. *621*

MICROBIOLOGY ABSTRACTS: SECTION B. BACTERIOLOGY.
Cambridge Scientific Abstracts, 7200 Wisconsin Ave., 6th Fl., Bethesda, MD 20814. TEL 301-961-6750. FAX 301-961-6720.
Producer(s): SilverPlatter Information, Inc.. *621*

MICROBIOLOGY ABSTRACTS: SECTION C. ALGOLOGY, MYCOLOGY AND PROTOZOOLOGY.
Cambridge Scientific Abstracts, 7200 Wisconsin Ave., 6th Fl., Bethesda, MD 20814. TEL 301-961-6750. FAX 301-961-6720.
Producer(s): NISC, SilverPlatter Information, Inc.. *622*

MICROCOMPUTER ABSTRACTS.
Information Today, Inc., 143 Old Marlton Pike, Medford, NJ 08055. TEL 609-654-6266. FAX 609-654-4309.
Producer(s): SilverPlatter Information, Inc.. *2003*

MICROPROCESSOR I C'S D.A.T.A. DIGEST.
D.A.T.A. Business Publishing 15 Inverness Way E., Box 6510, Englewood, CO 80155-6510. FAX 303-799-4082. *2089*

MICROPROCESSOR REPORT.
874 Gravenstein Hwy., Ste.14, Sebastopol, CA 95472. TEL 707-824-4004. FAX 707-823-0504. *2089*

MIDDLE EASTERN STUDIES.
Frank Cass, Newbury House, 890-900 Eastern Ave., Newbury Park, Ilford, Essex 1G2 7HH, England. TEL 44-181-599-8836. FAX 44-181-599-0984. *3498*

MIDLIFE WOMAN.
MidLife Women's Network, 5129 Logan Ave. S., Minneapolis, MN 55419-1019. TEL 612-915-0020. FAX 612-925-5430. *7001*

MIETRECHT VOLLTEXT C D - R O M.
C.H. Beck'sche Verlagsbuchhandlung, Wilhelmstr. 9, 80801 Munich, Germany. TEL 49-89-38189338. FAX 49-89-38189398.
Available only on CD-ROM. *3816*

MILITARY SPECIFICATIONS AND STANDARDS SERVICES NUMERIC INDEX.
Information Handling Services, 15 Inverness Way East, Englewood, CO 80150. TEL 303-790-0600. FAX 303-799-4085. *5040*

MILLION DOLLAR DIRECTORY.
Dun and Bradstreet Information Services 3 Sylvan Way, Parsippany, NJ 07054-3896. TEL 201-605-6000.
Producer(s): Dun & Bradstreet Information Services. *1626*

MINERALOGICAL ABSTRACTS.
Mineralogical Society, 41 Queen's Gate, London SW7 5HR, England. TEL 44-171-584-7516. FAX 44-171-823-8021. *5084*

MINNESOTA BUSINESS DIRECTORY.
American Business Directories 5711 S. 86th Circle, Box 27347, Omaha, NE 68127. TEL 402-593-4600. FAX 402-331-5481. *1627*

MINNESOTA STATUTES.
Office of Revisor of Statutes, 700 State Office Bldg., St. Paul, MN 55155. TEL 612-296-2868. *3950*

MINNESOTA STATUTES ON C D - R O M.
Office of Revisor of Statutes, 700 State Office Bldg., St. Paul, MN 55155. TEL 612-296-2868.
Available only on CD-ROM. *3950*

MINT MUSEUM MEMBERNEWS.
Mint Museum of Art, 2730 Randolph Rd., Charlotte, NC 28207. TEL 704-337-2000. FAX 704-337-2101. *5126*

MISSISSIPPI BUSINESS DIRECTORY.
American Business Directories 5711 S. 86th Circle, Box 27347, Omaha, NE 68127. TEL 402-593-4600. FAX 402-331-5481. *1627*

MISSISSIPPI MANUFACTURERS REGISTER.
Manufacturers' News, Inc., 1633 Central St., Evanston, IL 60201-1569. TEL 847-864-7000. FAX 847-332-1100. *1627*

MISSOURI BUSINESS DIRECTORY.
American Business Directories 5711 S. 86th Circle, Box 27347, Omaha, NE 68127. TEL 402-593-4600. FAX 402-331-5481. *1627*

MITTELSTAENDISCHE UNTERNEHMEN.
Verlag Hoppenstedt GmbH, Havelstr. 9, 64295 Darmstadt, Germany. TEL 49-6151-380-0. FAX 49-6151-380-360. *1526*

DIE MOEBEL-INDUSTRIE UND IHRE HELFER.
Industrieschau-Verlagsgesellschaft mbH, Postfach 100262, 64202 Darmstadt, Germany. TEL 49-6151-3892-0. FAX 49-6151-33164. *3691*

MOLECULAR AND CELLULAR BIOLOGY.
American Society for Microbiology, 1325 Massachusetts Ave., N.W., Washington, DC 20005. TEL 202-737-3600. *763*

MOLECULES.
Springer-Verlag, Heidelberger Platz 3, 14197 Berlin, Germany. TEL 49-30-8207-0. *1742*

LE MONDE.
Le Monde S.A., 21 rue Claude Bernard, 75005 Paris, France. TEL 42-17-2000. FAX 42-17-2121. *3139*

LE MONDE INDEX.
Primary Source Media, P.O. Box 45, Reading RG1 8HF, England. TEL 44-1734-583247. FAX 44-1734-591325. *3715*

MONEY (NEW YORK).
Time Inc. Time & Life Bldg., Rockefeller Center, 1271 Ave. of the Americas, New York, NY 10020. TEL 212-522-1212.
Producer(s): University Microfilms International. *2153*

MONEY MANAGEMENT LETTER.
Institutional Investor Newsletters, 477 Madison Ave., New York, NY 10022. TEL 212-224-3233. FAX 212-224-3353. *1341*

MONTANA BUSINESS DIRECTORY.
American Business Directories 5711 S. 86th Circle, Box 27347, Omaha, NE 68127. TEL 402-593-4600. FAX 402-331-5481. *1627*

MONTHLY CATALOG OF UNITED STATES GOVERNMENT PUBLICATIONS.
U.S. Government Printing Office, Superintendent of Documents, Washington, DC 20402-9341.
Producer(s): SilverPlatter Information, Inc., H.W. Wilson. *5932*

MONTHLY LABOR REVIEW.
U.S. Bureau of Labor Statistics, 2 Massachusettes Ave., N.E., Washington, DC 20212. TEL 202-606-5902. *1223*

MOODY'S COMPANY DATA.
Moody's Investors Service 99 Church St., New York, NY 10007-0300. TEL 212-553-0300. FAX 212-553-4700.
Available only on CD-ROM. *1156*

MOODY'S INTERNATIONAL COMPANY DATA.
Moody's Investors Service 99 Church St., New York, NY 10007. TEL 212-553-0300. FAX 212-553-4700.
Available only on CD-ROM. *1342*

MORNINGSTAR MUTUAL FUNDS ONDISC.
Morningstar, Inc., 225 W. Wacker Dr., Chicago, IL 60606. TEL 312-696-6000. FAX 312-696-6001. Available only on CD-ROM. *1343*

MOTHER AND CHILD.
Maternity & Child Welfare Association of Pakistan, MCH House, 30-F, Gulberg-II, Lahore 54666, Pakistan. TEL 92-42-874621. *7002*

MOTHER JONES.
Foundation for National Progress, 731 Market St., Ste. 600, San Francisco, CA 94103. TEL 415-665-6637. FAX 415-665-6696.
Producer(s): University Microfilms International. *4155*

MOTOR BUSINESS INTERNATIONAL.
Economist Intelligence Unit, 111 W. 57th St., New York, NY 10019. TEL 212-554-0600. FAX 212-586-1182. *6793*

MOTOR TREND.
Petersen Publishing Co., 6420 Wilshire Blvd., Los Angeles, CA 90048. TEL 213-782-2220. FAX 213-782-2866.
Producer(s): University Microfilms International. *6794*

MULTI-STATE SALES TAX GUIDE.
Commerce Clearing House, Inc., 2700 Lake Cook Rd., Riverwoods, IL 60015. TEL 847-267-7000. FAX 800-224-8299. *1555*

MULTIMEDIA COMPUTING & PRESENTATIONS.
Multimedia Computing Corporation, P.O. Box 60369, Sunnyvale, CA 94088-0369. TEL 408-737-7575. FAX 408-739-8019. *2113*

MULTIMEDIA MONITOR.
Future Systems, Inc., Box 26, Falls Church, VA 22040. TEL 703-241-1799. FAX 703-532-0529. *2057*

MULTIMEDIA WORLD.
I D G Communications Inc. (San Francisco), 501 Second St., San Francisco, CA 94107. TEL 415-281-8650. FAX 415-281-3915. *2098*

MULTIMEDIA WORLD LIVE!
I D G Communications Inc. (San Francisco), 501 Second St., San Francisco, CA 94107. TEL 415-281-8650. FAX 415-281-3915. Available only on CD-ROM. *2098*

THE MULTIMEDIA YEARBOOK.
Interactive Media Publications, Ltd., 104A St. John St., London EC1M 4EH, England. TEL 44-171-490-1185. FAX 44-171-490-4706. *1929*

MULTINATIONAL BUSINESS REVIEW.
University of Detroit Mercy, College of Business Administration, Box 19900, Detroit, MI 48219-0900. TEL 313-993-1264. FAX 313-993-1052.
Producer(s): University Microfilms International. *1290*

MULTISTATE CORPORATE INCOME TAX GUIDE.
Commerce Clearing House, Inc., 2700 Lake Cook Rd., Riverwoods, IL 60015. TEL 312-583-8500. FAX 800-224-8299. *1555*

MUNDO HISPANICO.
Mundo Hispanico, Inc., Box 13808, Sta. K, Atlanta, GA 30324-0808. TEL 404-881-0441. FAX 404-881-6085. *2896*

MUNICIPAL YELLOW BOOK.
Leadership Directories, Inc., 104 Fifth Ave., 2nd Fl., New York, NY 10011. TEL 212-627-4140. FAX 212-645-0931.
Producer(s): Chadwyck-Healey Inc.. *5947*

MUSE, MUSIC SEARCH.
National Information Services Corporation (NISC), Ste. 6, Wyman Towers, 3100 St. Paul St., Baltimore, MD 21218. TEL 410-243-0797. FAX 410-243-0982.
Available only on CD-ROM. Producer(s): NISC. *5208*

MUSI - KEY.
10260 N. Alder Spring Dr., Tucson, AZ 85737-9477. TEL 520-742-0880. FAX 520-742-1881. *5174*

MUSIC INDEX.
Harmonie Park Press, 23630 Pinewood, Warren, MI 48091-4759. TEL 810-755-3080. FAX 810-755-4213.
Producer(s): Knight-Ridder, Inc.. *5209*

N A B E INDUSTRY SURVEY.
National Association of Business Economists, 1233 20th St., N.W., Ste. 505, Washington, DC 20036-2304. TEL 202-463-6223. FAX 202-462-6239. *1223*

N A B E OUTLOOK & POLICY SURVEY.
National Association of Business Economists, 1233 20th St., N.W., Ste. 505, Washington, DC 20036-2304. TEL 202-463-6223. FAX 202-463-6239. *1223*

N C J R S DOCUMENT RETRIEVAL INDEX.
U.S. National Institute of Justice, National Criminal Justice Reference Service, Box 6000, Department F, Rockville, MD 20850. TEL 301-251-5500. FAX 301-251-5212. *2180*

N E L M INDEX SERIES.
National English Literary Museum, Private Bag 1019, Grahamstown 6140, South Africa. TEL 27-461-27042. FAX 27-461-22582.
Producer(s): NISC. *4294*

N I O S H T I C DATABASE.
U.S. National Technical Information Service, 5285 Port Royal Rd., Springfield, VA 22161. TEL 703-487-4630. *5253*

N J W - RECHTSPRECHUNGS-REPORT ZIVILRECHT.
C.H. Beck'sche Verlagsbuchhandlung, Wilhelmstr. 9, 80801 Munich, Germany. TEL 089-38189-338. FAX 089-38189-398. *3886*

N O S P - MIKRO.
University of Oslo Library, N O S P - Centre, N-0242 Oslo, Norway. TEL 47-22-859181. FAX 47-22-859050. *540*

N T I S BIBLIOGRAPHIC DATA BASE.
U.S. National Technical Information Service, 5285 Port Royal Rd., Springfield, VA 22161. TEL 703-487-4630.
Producer(s): Knight-Ridder, Inc., OCLC, SilverPlatter Information, Inc.. *6017*

N V W Z RECHTSPRECHUNGS REPORT VERWALTUNGSRECHT.
C.H. Beck'sche Verlagsbuchhandlung, Wilhelmstr. 9, 80801 Munich, Germany. TEL 089-38189-338. FAX 089-38189398. *3818*

DIE NAHRUNGS- UND GENUSSMITTEL-INDUSTRIE UND IHRE HELFER.
Industrieschau-Verlagsgesellschaft mbH, Postfach 100262, 64202 Darmstadt, Germany. TEL 49-6151-38920. FAX 49-6151-33164. *2985*

NANJING SHEHUI KEXUE.
Nanjing Shehui Kexuejie Lianhehui, 35 Jinxianghe Lu, Nanjing, Jiangsu 210008, People's Republic of China. TEL 86-25-3611547. *6335*

THE NATION.
The Nation Company, L.P., 72 Fifth Ave., New York, NY 10011. TEL 212-242-8400. FAX 212-463-9712.
Producer(s): University Microfilms International. *4155*

NATIONAL CIVIC REVIEW
National Civic League, Inc., 1445 Market St., Ste. 300, Denver, CO 80202-1728. TEL 303-571-4343.
Producer(s): University Microfilms International. *5947*

NATIONAL CONTEST JOURNAL.
American Radio Relay League, Inc., 25 Main St., Newington, CT 06111. TEL 860-594-0200. FAX 860-594-0303. *1937*

NATIONAL DIRECTORY OF MAGAZINES.
Oxbridge Communications, Inc., 150 Fifth Ave., New York, NY 10011. TEL 212-741-0231. FAX 212-633-2938. *541*

NATIONAL DIRECTORY OF MAILING LISTS.
Oxbridge Communications, Inc., 150 Fifth Ave., Ste. 302, New York, NY 10011. TEL 212-741-0231. FAX 212-633-2938. *1628*

NATIONAL ENGLISH LITERARY MUSEUM. BIBLIOGRAPHIC SERIES.
National English Literary Museum, Private Bag 1019, Grahamstown 6140, South Africa. TEL 27-461-27042. FAX 27-461-22582. *4294*

NATIONAL MEDICAL JOURNAL OF INDIA.
All India Institute of Medical Sciences, New Delhi 110 029, India. TEL 91-11-6863002. FAX 91-11-6862663. *4506*

NATIONAL NEWSPAPER INDEX.
Information Access Company 362 Lakeside Dr., Foster City, CA 94404. TEL 415-378-5200. FAX 415-378-5369. *3715*

NATIONAL REVIEW.
National Review, Inc., 150 E. 35th St., New York, NY 10016. TEL 212-679-7330. FAX 212-696-0309.
Producer(s): University Microfilms International. *5685*

NATION'S BUSINESS.
U.S. Chamber of Commerce, 1615 H St., N.W., Washington, DC 20062-2000. TEL 202-463-5650. FAX 202-887-3437.
Producer(s): University Microfilms International. *1146*

NATURAL HISTORY.
American Museum of Natural History, Central Park W. at 79th St., New York, NY 10024-5192. TEL 212-769-5500. FAX 212-769-5511.
Producer(s): University Microfilms International. *6263*

NEBRASKA BUSINESS DIRECTORY.
American Business Directories 5711 S. 86th Circle, Box 27347, Omaha, NE 68127. TEL 402-593-4600 FAX 402-331-5481. *1629*

NEBRASKA MANUFACTURERS REGISTER.
Manufacturers' News, Inc., 1633 Central St., Evanston, IL 60201-1569. TEL 847-864-7000. FAX 847-332-1100. *1629*

NETWORK WORLD.
Network World Inc., 161 Worcester Rd., 5th Fl., Framingham, MA 01701. TEL 508-875-6400. FAX 508-879-3167. *2041*

NEUE JURISTISCHE WOCHENSCHRIFT.
C.H. Beck'sche Verlagsbuchhandlung, Wilhelmstr. 9, 80801 Munich, Germany. TEL 49-89-38189-338. FAX 49-89-38189-398. *3821*

NEUE WIRTSCHAFTS-BRIEFE.
Verlag Neue Wirtschafts-Briefe GmbH, Eschstr. 22, 44629 Herne, Germany. TEL 49-2323-141-0. FAX 49-2323-141123. *1555*

NEUE ZEITSCHRIFT FUER STRAFRECHT.
C.H. Beck'sche Verlagsbuchhandlung, Wilhelmstr. 9, 80801 Munich, Germany. TEL 49-89-38189-338. FAX 49-89-38189-398. *3712*

NEUE ZEITSCHRIFT FUER VERWALTUNGSRECHT.
C.H. Beck'sche Verlagsbuchhandlung, Wilhelmstr. 9, 80801 Munich, Germany. TEL 49-89-38189-338. FAX 49-89-38189-398. *3951*

NEUE ZUERCHER ZEITUNG.
Neue Zuercher Zeitung, Falkenstr. 11, CH-8021 Zurich, Switzerland. TEL 41-1-2581-11. FAX 41-1-2581675. *3219*

NEUROCASE.
Oxford University Press, Oxford Journals, Walton St., Oxford OX2 6DP, England. TEL 01865-267907. FAX 01865-267773. *4853*

NEUROLOGY INDIA.
Neurological Society of India, Dept. of Neurology, Post-graduate Institute of Medical Education & Research, Chandigarh 160 012, India. TEL 0172-541032. *4855*

NEUROREPORT.
Rapid Science Publishers, The Old Malthouse, Paradise St., Oxford OX1 1LD, England. TEL 44-1865-790447. FAX 44-1865-244012. *4857*

NEUROSCIENCE CITATION INDEX.
Institute for Scientific Information, 3501 Market St., Philadelphia, PA 19104. TEL 215-386-0100. FAX 215-386-2991. *4569*

CD-ROM

NEVADA BUSINESS DIRECTORY.
American Business Directories 5711 S. 86th Circle, Box 27347, Omaha, NE 68127. TEL 402-593-4600. FAX 402-331-5481. *1630*

NEW ENGLAND JOURNAL OF MEDICINE.
Massachusetts Medical Society, 10 Shattuck St., Boston, MA 02115. TEL 617-734-9800. FAX 617-893-8103. *4507*

NEW ENGLAND WATER WORKS ASSOCIATION. JOURNAL.
New England Water Works Association, 64 Dilla St., Milford, MA 01757-1104. TEL 508-478-6996. FAX 508-634-8643.
Producer(s): Knight-Ridder, Inc.. *6973*

NEW HAMPSHIRE BUSINESS DIRECTORY.
American Business Directories 5711 S. 86th Circle, Box 27347, Omaha, NE 68127. TEL 402-593-4600. FAX 402-331-5481. *1630*

NEW JERSEY BUSINESS DIRECTORY.
American Business Directories 5711 S. 86th Circle, Box 27347, Omaha, NE 68127. TEL 402-593-4600. FAX 402-331-5481. *1630*

NEW JERSEY MANUFACTURERS DIRECTORY.
InfoSource International, 2057-2 Aurora Rd., Twinsburg, OH 44087. TEL 216-425-9000. FAX 800-6423-5997. *1630*

NEW JERSEY RULES OF COURT, STATE AND FEDERAL.
West Publishing Corp., 620 Opperman Dr., Eagan, MN 55123. TEL 612-687-8000. FAX 612-687-7302. *3951*

NEW LIBRARY WORLD.
M C B University Press Ltd., 60-62 Toller Ln., Bradford, W. Yorks BD8 9BY, England. TEL 44-1274-777700. FAX 44-1274-785200. *4016*

NEW MEXICO BUSINESS DIRECTORY.
American Business Directories 5711 S. 86th Circle, Box 27347, Omaha, NE 68127. TEL 402-593-4600. FAX 402-331-5481. *1630*

NEW MEXICO REPORTS.
West Publishing Corp., 620 Opperman Dr., Eagan, MN 55123. TEL 612-687-8000. FAX 612-687-7302. *3823*

NEW PERSPECTIVES QUARTERLY.
Blackwell Publishers, 238 Main St., Cambridge, MA 02142. TEL 617-547-7110. FAX 617-547-0789. *5687*

NEW PRODUCT LAUNCH LETTER.
IMSWORLD Publications Ltd., 7 Harewood Ave., London NW1 6JB, England. TEL 0171-393-5000. FAX 0171-393-5900. *5430*

THE NEW REPUBLIC.
1220 19th St., N.W., Washington, DC 20036. TEL 202-331-7494. FAX 202-331-0275.
Producer(s): University Microfilms International. *4156*

NEW SCIENTIST.
I P C Magazines, Specialist Magazine Group King's Reach Tower, Stamford St., London SE1 9LS, England. TEL 44-171-261-5000. FAX 44-1444-445599.
Producer(s): Bowker - Saur Ltd.. *6266*

NEW YORK BUSINESS DIRECTORY.
American Business Directories 5711 S. 86th Circle, Box 27347, Omaha, NE 68127. TEL 402-593-4600. FAX 402-331-5481. *1630*

NEW YORK LAW JOURNAL.
New York Law Publishing Co., 345 Park Ave. S., New York, NY 10010. TEL 212-779-9200. *3823*

NEW YORK MANUFACTURERS DIRECTORY.
InfoSource International, 2057-2 Aurora Rd., Twinsburg, OH 44087. TEL 216-425-9000. FAX 800-643-5997. *1630*

NEW YORK METRO BUSINESS DIRECTORY.
American Business Directories 5711 S. 86th Circle, Box 27347, Omaha, NE 68127. TEL 402-593-4600. FAX 402-331-5481. *1630*

THE NEW YORK TIMES.
New York Times Company, 229 W. 43rd St., New York, NY 10036, TEL 212-556-1234. FAX 212-556-4603.
Producer(s): University Microfilms International. *3234*

THE NEW YORK TIMES INDEX.
U M I Company 300 N. Zeeb Rd., Ann Arbor, MI 48106. TEL 313-761-4700. FAX 800-864-0019. *3715*

NEW ZEALAND BUSINESS WHO'S WHO.
New Zealand Financial Press Ltd., P.O. Box 1881, Auckland 1, New Zealand. TEL 64-9-3071287. FAX 64-9-3732734. *1630*

NEWS FROM INDIAN COUNTRY.
Indian Country Communications, Rte. 2, Box 2900-A, Hayward, WI 54843. TEL 715-634-5226. FAX 715-634-3243. *2898*

NEWS MEDIA YELLOW BOOK.
Leadership Directories, Inc., 104 Fifth Ave., 2nd Fl., New York, NY 10011. TEL 212-627-4140. FAX 212-645-0931.
Producer(s): Chadwyck-Healey Inc.. *1631*

NEWSBANK REVIEW OF THE ARTS: FILM AND TELEVISION.
NewsBank, Inc., 58 Pine St., New Canaan, CT 06840-5426. TEL 203-966-1100. FAX 203-966-6254. *5109*

NEWSMAKERS.
Gale Research Inc., 835 Penobscot Bldg., Detroit, MI 48226. TEL 319-961-2242. FAX 313-221-7086. *558*

NEWSPAPER ABSTRACTS.
U M I Company (Louisville) 620 S. Third St., Louisville, KY 40202-2475. *3715*

NEWSWEEK.
Newsweek, Inc. 251 W. 57th St., New York, NY 10019. TEL 212-445-4000. *3234*

NIEMAN REPORTS.
Nieman Foundation, Harvard University, 1 Francis Ave., Cambridge, MA 02138. TEL 617-495-2237. FAX 617-495-8976.
Producer(s): University Microfilms International. *3709*

NIGERIAN JOURNAL OF NUTRITIONAL SCIENCES.
Ibadan University Press, University of Ibadan, Ibadan, Oyo State, Nigeria. *5238*

NIGERIAN JOURNAL OF PAEDIATRICS.
Ibadan University Press, University of Ibadan, Ibadan, Oyo State, Nigeria. *4809*

NIGERIAN MEDICAL JOURNAL.
Nigerian Medical Association, P.O. Box 1108, Lagos, Nigeria. TEL 234-1-801500. FAX 231-1-837630. *4508*

NIHON SHIKA MASUI GAKKAI ZASSHI.
Nihon Shika Masui Gakkai, Osaka University, 1-8 Yamadaoka, Suita, 565 Osaka, Japan. TEL 03-3947-8891. FAX 03-3947-8341. *4592*

NIKKEI MULTIMEDIA.
Nikkei Business Publications, Inc. 2-7-6 Hirakawa-cho, Chiyoda-ku, Tokyo 102, Japan. TEL 03-5210-8502. FAX 03-5210-8119. *4046*

NINETEENTH CENTURY BIBLIOGRAPHIC RECORDS.
Chadwyck-Healey Ltd., The Quorum, Barnwell Rd., Cambridge CB5 8SW, England. TEL 44-1223-215512. FAX 44-1223-215514.
Available only on CD-ROM. Producer(s): Chadwyck-Healey Inc.. *542*

NON-PRESCRIPTION DRUG REFERENCE FOR HEALTH CARE PROFESSIONAL.
Canadian Pharmaceutical Association, 1785 Alta Vista Dr., Ottawa, ON K1G 3Y6, Canada. TEL 613-523-7877. *5430*

NONFERROUS METALS ALERT.
Cambridge Scientific Abstracts, 7200 Wisconsin Ave., Bethesda, MD 20814. TEL 301-961-6750. FAX 301-961-6720.
Producer(s): Knight-Ridder, Inc.. *4984*

NONGYE JIXIE XUEBAO.
Zhongguo Nongye Jixie Xuehui, 1 Bei Shatan, Dewai, Beijing 100083, People's Republic of China. TEL 86-10-6201-7131. FAX 86-10-6204-3686. *205*

NONWOVENS ABSTRACTS.
Pira International, Randalls Rd., Leatherhead, Surrey KT22 7RU, England. TEL 44-1372-802050. FAX 44-1372-802239.
Producer(s): Knight-Ridder, Inc.. *5629*

NORSK SKATTELOVSAMLING.
Jacob Jaroey, Vraasgt. 18, N-3701 Skien, Norway. TEL 47-35-59-92-26. *1557*

NORTH CAROLINA BUSINESS DIRECTORY.
American Business Directories 5711 S. 86th Circle, Box 27347, Omaha, NE 68127. TEL 402-593-4600. FAX 402-331-5481. *1631*

NORTH CAROLINA MANUFACTURERS DIRECTORY.
Harris InfoSource International, 2057-2 Aurora Rd., Twinsburg, OH 44087. TEL 216-425-9000. FAX 800-643-5997. *1631*

NORTH CAROLINA MANUFACTURERS REGISTER.
Manufacturers' News, Inc., 1633 Central St., Evanston, IL 60201-1569. TEL 847-864-7000. FAX 847-332-1100. *1631*

NORTH DAKOTA BUSINESS DIRECTORY.
American Business Directories 5711 S. 86th Circle, Box 27347, Omaha, NE 68127. TEL 402-593-4600. FAX 402-331-5481. *1631*

NORTH DAKOTA LAW REVIEW.
University of North Dakota, School of Law, Box 9003, Grand Forks, ND 58201. TEL 701-777-2941. FAX 701-777-2217. *3826*

NORTH DAKOTA MANUFACTURERS REGISTER.
Manufacturers' News, Inc., 1633 Central St., Evanston, IL 60201-1569. TEL 847-864-7000. FAX 847-332-1100. *1631*

NORTHEAST POWER REPORT.
McGraw-Hill Companies, Energy & Business Newsletters, 1221 Ave. of the Americas, 36th Fl., New York, NY 10020. TEL 212-512-6410. FAX 212-512-2723.
Producer(s): SilverPlatter Information, Inc. (McGraw-Hill Energy Library). *2570*

NORTHERN CALIFORNIA BUSINESS DIRECTORY.
American Business Directories 5711 S. 86th Circle, Box 27347, Omaha, NE 68127. TEL 402-593-4600. FAX 402-331-5481. *1631*

NORTHERN CALIFORNIA BUSINESS DIRECTORY AND BUYERS GUIDE.
Database Publishing Company, 1590 S. Lewis St., Anaheim, CA 92805-6423. TEL 714-778-6400. FAX 714-778-6811. *1631*

NOTIMEX ON C D - R O M.
National Information Services Corporation (NISC), Ste. 6, Wyman Towers, 3100 St. Paul St., Baltimore, MD 21218. TEL 410-243-0797. FAX 410-243-0982.
Available only on CD-ROM. Producer(s): NISC. *3715*

NOTISUR.
University of New Mexico, Latin American Institute, 801 Yale N.E., Albuquerque, NM 87131-1016. TEL 505-277-6839. FAX 505-277-5989.
Producer(s): NISC (Latin American Studies - Vol.2). *5689*

NUCLEARFUEL.
McGraw-Hill Companies, 1221 Ave. of the Americas, New York, NY 10020.
Producer(s): SilverPlatter Information, Inc. (McGraw-Hill Energy Library). *2581*

NUCLEIC ACIDS ABSTRACTS.
Cambridge Scientific Abstracts, 7200 Wisconsin Ave., 6th Fl., Bethesda, MD 20814. TEL 301-961-6750. FAX 301-961-6720.
Producer(s): SilverPlatter Information, Inc.. *622*

NUCLEIC ACIDS RESEARCH.
Oxford University Press, Oxford Journals, Walton St., Oxford OX2 6DP, England. TEL 44-1865-267907. FAX 44-1865-267485. *646*

NUCLEONICS WEEK.
McGraw-Hill Companies, Energy & Business Newsletters, 1221 Ave. of the Americas, 36th Fl., New York, NY 10020. TEL 212-512-6410. Producer(s): SilverPlatter Information, Inc. (McGraw-Hill Energy Library) *2554*

NUEVA SOCIEDAD.
Editorial Nueva Sociedad Ltda., Apdo. 61712, Chacao, Caracas 1060-A, Venezuela. TEL 58-2-2651849. FAX 58-2-2673397. *5689*

NURSING BIBLIOGRAPHY.
Royal College of Nursing, Library and Information Services, 20 Cavendish Sq., London W1M 0AB, England. TEL 44-171-409-3333. FAX 44-171-491-3859. *4569*

NUTRITION HEALTH REVIEW.
Vegetus Publications, Box 406, Haverford, PA 19041. TEL 610-896-1853. FAX 610-896-1857. *5239*

NYERE DANSK FAGLITTERATUR.
Dansk BiblioteksCenter as, Tempovej 7-11, DK-2750 Ballerup, Denmark. TEL 45-44-867777. FAX 45-44-867892. *542*

O J C D.
Chadwyck-Healey Ltd., The Quorum, Barnwell Rd., Cambridge CB5 8SW, England. TEL 44-1223-215512. FAX 44-1223-215514. Available only on CD-ROM. Producer(s): Chadwyck-Healey Inc.. *5765*

THE OBSERVER.
Guardian Newspapers Ltd. 164 Deansgate, Manchester M60 2RR, England. TEL 44-161-832-7200. FAX 44-161-831-5362. Producer(s): Chadwyck-Healey Inc.. *3158*

OCCUPATIONAL OUTLOOK HANDBOOK.
U.S. Bureau of Labor Statistics, 2 Massachusetts Ave., N.E., Washington, DC 20212. TEL 202-606-5701. *5271*

OCCUPATIONAL OUTLOOK QUARTERLY.
U.S. Bureau of Labor Statistics, 2 Massachusetts Ave., N.E., Washington, DC 20212. TEL 202-606-5701. *5272*

OCEANIC ABSTRACTS.
Cambridge Scientific Abstracts, 7200 Wisconsin Ave., 6th Fl., Bethesda, MD 20814. TEL 301-961-6750. FAX 301-961-6720. Producer(s): NISC. *2220*

OCEANOGRAPHIC & MARINE RESOURCES.
National Information Services Corporation (NISC), Ste. 6, Wyman Towers, 3100 St. Paul St., Baltimore, MD 21218. TEL 410-243-0797. FAX 410-243-0982. Available only on CD-ROM. Producer(s): NISC. *2220*

OCEANOGRAPHIC LITERATURE REVIEW.
Elsevier Science Ltd., Pergamon, P.O. Box 800, Kidlington, Oxford OX5 1DX, England. TEL 44-1865-843000. FAX 44-1865-843010. Producer(s): NISC (Oceanographic & Marine Resources). *2220*

OFFICIAL A B M S DIRECTORY OF BOARD CERTIFIED MEDICAL SPECIALISTS.
Marquis Who's Who, A Division of Reed Elsevier Inc., 121 Chanlon Rd., New Providence, NJ 07974. TEL 908-464-6800. FAX 908-665-6688. Producer(s): Bowker Electronic Publishing. *4510*

OFFICIAL INDEX TO THE FINANCIAL TIMES.
Primary Source Media, P.O. Box 45, Reading RG1 8HF, England. TEL 44-1734-583247. FAX 44-1734-591325. *1019*

OFFICIAL IOWA MANUFACTURERS DIRECTORY.
InfoSource International, 2057-2 Aurora Rd., Twinsburg, OH 44087. TEL 216-425-9000. FAX 800-643-5997. *1632*

OFFICIAL JOURNAL OF THE EUROPEAN COMMUNITIES. C SERIES: INFORMATION AND NOTICES (ENGLISH EDITION).
Office for Official Publications of the European Communities, L-2985 Luxembourg, Luxembourg. Producer(s): Chadwyck-Healey Inc.. *5765*

OFFICIAL JOURNAL OF THE EUROPEAN COMMUNITIES. L & C: LEGISLATION AND COMPETITION.
Office for Official Publications of the European Communities, L-2985 Luxembourg, Luxembourg. Producer(s): Chadwyck-Healey Inc.. *5765*

OHIO ATTORNEY GENERAL OPINIONS.
Banks - Baldwin Law Publishing Co., Box 318063, Cleveland, OH 44131-8063. TEL 216-520-5600. FAX 216-520-5655. *3952*

OHIO BUSINESS DIRECTORY.
American Business Directories 5711 S. 86th Circle, Box 27347, Omaha, NE 68127. TEL 402-593-4600. FAX 402-331-5481. *1632*

OHIO RULES OF COURT, STATE AND FEDERAL.
West Publishing Corp., 620 Opperman Dr., Eagan, MN 55123. TEL 612-687-8000. FAX 612-687-7302. *3952*

OHIO STATE LAW JOURNAL.
Ohio State University, College of Law, 55 W. 12th Ave., Columbus, OH 43210-1391. TEL 614-292-6829. *3828*

OKLAHOMA BUSINESS DIRECTORY.
American Business Directories 5711 S. 86th Circle, Box 27347, Omaha, NE 68127. TEL 402-593-4600. FAX 402-331-5481. *1632*

ON THE LEVEL.
Family Planning N.S.W., 328-336 Liverpool Rd., Ashfield, N.S.W. 2131, Australia. TEL 61-2-716-6099. *6424*

ONCOGENES AND GROWTH FACTORS ABSTRACTS.
Cambridge Scientific Abstracts, 7200 Wisconsin Ave., 6th Fl., Bethesda, MD 20814. TEL 301-961-6750. FAX 301-961-6720. Producer(s): SilverPlatter Information, Inc.. *4570*

ONEDISC.
Tax Analysts, 6830 N. Fairfax Dr., Arlington, VA 22213. FAX 703-533-4444. Available only on CD-ROM. *1557*

ONLINE HOTLINE NEWS SERVICE.
Information Intelligence, Inc., Box 31098, Phoenix, AZ 85046. TEL 602-996-2283. Available only on CD-ROM. *2041*

THE ONLINE JOURNAL OF CURRENT CLINICAL TRIALS.
Chapman & Hall, Journals Department 2-6 Boundary Row, London SE1 8HN, England. TEL 44-171-8650066. FAX 44-171-5229623. *4511*

ONLINE LIBRARIES AND MICROCOMPUTERS.
Information Intelligence, Inc., Box 31098, Phoenix, AZ 85046. TEL 602-996-2283. *4046*

ONLINE NEWSLETTER.
Information Intelligence Inc., Box 31098, Phoenix, AZ 85046. TEL 602-996-2283. *2041*

ONTARIO STATUTE CITATOR.
Canada Law Book Inc., 240 Edward St., Aurora, ON L4G 3S9, Canada. TEL 905-841-6472. FAX 905-841-5085. *3830*

OPEN INFORMATION SYSTEMS.
Patricia Seybold Group, 148 State St., 7th Fl., Boston, MA 02109. TEL 617-742-5200. FAX 617-742-1028. *2057*

OPTICAL AND QUANTUM ELECTRONICS.
Chapman & Hall, Journals Department 2-6 Boundary Row, London SE1 8HN, England. TEL 44-171-8650066. FAX 44-171-5229623. *2529*

OPTOELECTRONICS D.A.T.A. DIGEST.
D.A.T.A. Business Publishing 15 Inverness Way E., Box 6510, Englewood, CO 80155-6510. FAX 303-799-4082. *2529*

ORACLE INFORMANT.
Informant Communications Group, Inc., 10519 E. Stockton Blvd., Ste. 142, Elk Grove, CA 95624-9704. TEL 916-686-6610. FAX 916-686-8497. *2114*

ORANGE COUNTY BUSINESS AND INDUSTRIAL DIRECTORY.
Database Publishing Company, 1590 S. Lewis St., Anaheim, CA 92805-6423. TEL 714-778-6400. FAX 714-778-6811. *1632*

OREGON BUSINESS DIRECTORY.
American Business Directories 5711 S. 86th Circle, Box 27347, Omaha, NE 68127. TEL 402-593-4600. FAX 402-331-5481. *1633*

ORGANISED SOUND.
Cambridge University Press, Edinburgh Bldg., Shaftesbury Rd., Cambridge CB2 2RU, England. TEL 44-1223-312393. FAX 44-1223-315052. *5185*

OUTDOOR LIFE.
Times Mirror Magazines, Inc., 2 Park Ave., New York, NY 10016. TEL 212-779-5000. FAX 212-686-6877. Producer(s): University Microfilms International. *6572*

OXBRIDGE DIRECTORY OF NEWSLETTERS.
Oxbridge Communications, Inc., 150 Fifth Ave., New York, NY 10011. TEL 212-741-0231. FAX 212-633-2938. *543*

P A I S INTERNATIONAL IN PRINT.
Public Affairs Information Service, Inc., 521 W. 43rd St., 5th Fl., New York, NY 10036-4396. TEL 212-736-6629. FAX 212-643-2848. Producer(s): Public Affairs Information Service, Inc. (PAIS ON CD-ROM), SilverPlatter Information, Inc. (PAIS INTERNATIONAL ON SILVERPLATTER). *1020*

P A I S SELECT.
Public Affairs Information Service, Inc., 521 W. 43rd St., New York, NY 10036-4396. TEL 212-736-6629. Available only on CD-ROM. *5722*

P A S C A L. E 11: PHYSIQUE ATOMIQUE ET MOLECULAIRE. PLASMAS.
Centre National de la Recherche Scientifique, Institut de l'Information Scientifique et Technique, 2 allee du Parc de Brabois, 54514 Vandoeuvre-Les-Nancy Cedex, France. TEL 83-50-46-00. FAX 83-50-46-50. *5579*

P A S C A L. E 12: ETAT CONDENSE.
Centre National de la Recherche Scientifique, Institut de l'Information Scientifique et Technique, 2 allee du Parc de Brabois, 54514 Vandoeuvre-Les-Nancy Cedex, France. TEL 83-50-46-00. FAX 83-50-46-50. *5579*

P A S C A L. E 13: STRUCTURE DES LIQUIDES ET DES SOLIDES - CRISTALLOGRAPH E.
Centre National de la Recherche Scientifique, Institut de l'Information Scientifique et Technique, 2 allee du Parc de Brabois, 54514 Vandoeuvre-Les-Nancy Cedex, France. TEL 83-50-46-00. FAX 83-50-46-50. *1710*

P A S C A L. E 18: CHROMATOGRAPHIE.
Centre National de la Recherche Scientifique, Institut de l'Information Scientifique et Technique, 2 allee du Parc de Brabois, 54514 Vandoeuvre-les-Nancy Cedex, France. TEL 83-50-46-00. FAX 83-50-46-50. *1710*

P A S C A L. E 20: ELECTRONIQUE ET TELECOMMUNICATIONS.
Centre National de la Recherche Scientifique, Institut de l'Information Scientifique et Technique, 2 allee du Parc de Brabois, 54514 Vandoeuvre-Les-Nancy Cedex, France. TEL 83-50-46-00. FAX 83-50-46-50. *2529*

P A S C A L. E 27: METHODES DE FORMATION ET TRAITEMENT DES IMAGES.
Centre National de la Recherche Scientifique, Institut de l'Information Scientifique et Technique, 2 allee du Parc de Brabois, 54514 Vandoeuvre-Les-Nancy Cedex, France. TEL 83-50-46-00. FAX 83-50-46-50. *5579*

P A S C A L. E 30: MICROSCOPIE ELECTRONIQUE ET DIFFRACTION ELECTRONIQUE.
Centre National de la Recherche Scientifique, Institut de l'Information Scientifique et Technique, 2 allee du Parc de Brabois, 54514 Vandoeuvre-Les-Nancy Cedex, France. TEL 83-50-46-00. FAX 83-50-46-50. *622*

CD-ROM

P A S C A L. E 32: METROLOGIE ET APPAREILLAGE EN PHYSIQUE ET PHYSICOCHIMIE.
Centre National de la Recherche Scientifique, Institut de l'Information Scientifique et Technique, 2 allee du Parc de Brabois, 54514 Vandoeuvre-les-Nancy Cedex, France. TEL 83-50-46-00. FAX 83-50-46-50. *5019*

P A S C A L. E 33. INFORMATIQUE.
Centre National de la Recherche Scientifique, Institut de l'Information Scientifique et Technique, 2 allee du Parc de Brabois, 54514 Vandoeuvre-Les-Nancy Cedex, France. TEL 83-50-46-00. FAX 83-50-46-50. *2003*

P A S C A L. E 34. ROBOTIQUE, AUTOMATIQUE ET AUTOMATISATION DES PROCESSUS INDUSTRIELS.
Centre National de la Recherche Scientifique, Institut de l'Information Scientifique et Technique, 2 allee du Parc de Brabois, 54514 Vandoeuvre-Les-Nancy Cedex, France. TEL 83-50-46-00. FAX 83-50-46-50. *2003*

P A S C A L. E 36: POLLUTION DE L'EAU, DE L'AIR ET DU SOL - DECHETS - BRUIT.
Centre National de la Recherche Scientifique, Institut de l'Information Scientifique et Technique, 2 allee du Parc de Brabois, 54514 Vandoeuvre-Les-Nancy. France. TEL 83-50-46-00. FAX 83-50-46-50. *2830*

P A S C A L. E 48: ENVIRONNEMENT COSMIQUE TERRESTRE, ASTRONOMIE ET GEOLOGIE EXTRATERRESTRE.
Centre National de la Recherche Scientifique, Institut de l'Information Scientifique et Technique, 2 allee du Parc de Brabois, 54514 Vandoeuvre-Les-Nancy, France. TEL 83-50-46-00. FAX 83-50-46-50. *2220*

P A S C A L. E 49: METEOROLOGIE, GLACIOLOGIE, PHYSIQUE DES OCEANS.
Centre National de la Recherche Scientifique, Institut de l'Information Scientifique et Technique, 2 allee du Parc de Brabois, 54514 Vandoeuvre-Les-Nancy Cedex, France. TEL 83-50-46-00. FAX 83-50-46-50. *5011*

P A S C A L. E 58: GENETIQUE.
Centre National de la Recherche Scientifique, Institut de l'Information Scientifique et Technique, 2 allee du Parc de Brabois, 54514 Vandoeuvre-Les-Nancy Cedex, France. TEL 83-50-46-00. FAX 83-50-46-50. *623*

P A S C A L. E 61: MICROBIOLOGIE: BACTERIOLOGIE, VIROLOGIE, MYCOLOGIE, PROTOZOAIRES PATHOGENES.
Centre National de la Recherche Scientifique, Institut de l'Information Scientifique et Technique, 2 allee du Parc de Brabois, 54514 Vandoeuvre-Les-Nancy Cedex, France. TEL 83-50-46-00. FAX 83-50-46-50. *623*

P A S C A L. E 62: IMMUNOLOGIE.
Centre National de la Recherche Scientifique, Institut de l'Information Scientifique et Technique, 2 allee du Parc de Brabois, 54514 Vandoeuvre-Les-Nancy Cedex, France. TEL 83-50-46-00. FAX 83-50-46-50. *623*

P A S C A L. E 63: TOXICOLOGIE.
Centre National de la Recherche Scientifique, Institut de l'Information Scientifique et Technique, 2 allee du Parc de Brabois, 54514 Vandoeuvre-Les-Nancy Cedex, France. TEL 83-50-46-00. FAX 83-50-46-50. *2831*

P A S C A L. E 64: ENDOCRINOLOGIE HUMAINE ET EXPERIMENTALE. ENDOCRINOPATHIES.
Centre National de la Recherche Scientifique, Institut de l'Information Scientifique et Technique, 2 allee du Parc de Brabois, 54514 Vandoeuvre-Les-Nancy Cedex, France. TEL 83-50-46-00. FAX 83-50-46-50. *4570*

P A S C A L. E 65: PSYCHOLOGIE, PSYCHOPATHOLOGIE, PSYCHIATRIE.
Centre National de la Recherche Scientifique, Institut de l'Information Scientifique et Technique, 2 allee du Parc de Brabois, 54514 Vandoeuvre-Les-Nancy Cedex, France. TEL 83-50-46-00. FAX 83-50-46-50. *4570*

P A S C A L. E 68: GENETIQUE HUMAINE.
Centre National de la Recherche Scientifique, Institut de l'Information Scientifique et Technique, 2 allee du Parc de Brabois, 54514 Vandoeuvre-les-Nancy Cedex, France. TEL 83-50-46-00. FAX 83-50-46-50. *623*

P A S C A L. E 71: OPHTALMOLOGIE.
Centre National de la Recherche Scientifique, Institut de l'Information Scientifique et Technique, 2 allee du Parc de Brabois, 54514 Vandoeuvre-Les-Nancy Cedex, France. TEL 83-50-46-00. FAX 83-50-46-50. *4570*

P A S C A L. E 72: OTORHINOLARYNGOLOGIE. STOMATOLOGIE. PATHOLOGIE CERVICOFACIALE.
Centre National de la Recherche Scientifique, Institut de l'Information Scientifique et Technique, 2 allee du Parc de Brabois, 54514 Vandoeuvre-les-Nancy. France. TEL 83-50-46-00. FAX 83-50-46-50. *4571*

P A S C A L. E 73: DERMATOLOGIE. MALADIES SEXUELLEMENT TRANSMISSIBLES.
Centre National de la Recherche Scientifique, Institut de l'Information Scientifique et Technique, 2 allee du Parc de Brabois, 54514 Vandoeuvre-les-Nancy. France. TEL 83-50-46-00. FAX 83-50-46-50. *4571*

P A S C A L. E 74: PNEUMOLOGIE.
Centre National de la Recherche Scientifique, Institut de l'Information Scientifique et Technique, 2 allee du Parc de Brabois, 54514 Vandoeuvre-les-Nancy Cedex, France. TEL 83-50-46-00. FAX 83-50-46-50. *4571*

P A S C A L. E 75: CARDIOLOGIE ET APPAREIL CIRCULATOIRE.
Centre National de la Recherche Scientifique, Institut de l'Information Scientifique et Technique, 2 allee du Parc de Brabois, 54514 Vandoeuvre-les-Nancy Cedex, France. TEL 83-50-46-00. FAX 83-50-46-50. *4571*

P A S C A L. E 76: GASTROENTEROLOGIE, FOIE, PANCREAS, ABDOMEN.
Centre National de la Recherche Scientifique, Institut de l'Information Scientifique et Technique, 2 allee du Parc de Brabois, 54514 Vandoeuvre-les-Nancy Cedex, France. TEL 83-50-46-00. FAX 83-50-46-50. *4571*

P A S C A L. E 77: NEPHROLOGIE. VOIES URINAIRES.
Centre National de la Recherche Scientifique, Institut de l'Information Scientifique et Technique, 2 allee du Parc de Brabois, 54514 Vandoeuvre-les-Nancy Cedex, France. TEL 83-50-46-00. FAX 83-50-46-50. *4571*

P A S C A L. E 78: NEUROLOGIE.
Centre National de la Recherche Scientifique, Institut de l'Information Scientifique et Technique, 2 allee du Parc de Brabois, 54514 Vandoeuvre-les-Nancy Cedex, France. TEL 83-50-46-00. FAX 83-50-46-50. *4571*

P A S C A L. E 79: PATHOLOGIE ET PHYSIOLOGIE OSTEOARTICULAIRES.
Centre National de la Recherche Scientifique, Institut de l'Information Scientifique et Technique, 2 allee du Parc de Brabois, 54514 Vandoeuvre-les-Nancy Cedex, France. TEL 83-50-46-00. FAX 83-50-46-50. *4571*

P A S C A L. E 80: HEMATOLOGIE.
Centre National de la Recherche Scientifique, Institut de l'Information Scientifique et Technique, 2 allee du Parc de Brabois, 54514 Vandoeuvre-les-Nancy Cedex, France. TEL 83-50-46-00. FAX 83-50-46-50. *4571*

P A S C A L. E 82: GYNECOLOGIE, OBSTETRIQUE, ANDROLOGIE.
Centre National de la Recherche Scientifique, Institut de l'Information Scientifique et Technique, 2 allee du Parc de Brabois, 54514 Vandoeuvre-les-Nancy Cedex, France. TEL 83-50-46-00. FAX 83-50-46-50. *4571*

P A S C A L. E 83: ANESTHESIE ET REANIMATION.
Centre National de la Recherche Scientifique, Institut de l'Information Scientifique et Technique, 2 allee du Parc de Brabois, 54514 Vandoeuvre-les-Nancy Cedex, France. TEL 83-50-46-00. FAX 83-50-46-50. *4571*

P A S C A L. E 84: GENIE BIOMEDICAL. INFORMATIQUE BIOMEDICALE.
Centre National de la Recherche Scientifique, Institut de l'Information Scientifique et Technique, 2 allee du Parc de Brabois, 54514 Vandoeuvre-les-Nancy Cedex, France. TEL 83-50-46-00. FAX 83-50-46-50. *4572*

P A S C A L. E 89: CANCER.
Centre National de la Recherche Scientifique, Institut de l'Information Scientifique et Technique, 2 allee du Parc de Brabois, 54514 Vandoeuvre-les-Nancy Cedex, France. TEL 83-50-46-00. FAX 83-50-46-50. *4572*

P A S C A L. F 10: MECANIQUE, ACOUSTIQUE ET TRANSFERT DE CHALEUR.
Centre National de la Recherche Scientifique, Institut de l'Information Scientifique et Technique, 2 allee du Parc de Brabois, 54514 Vandoeuvre-Les-Nancy Cedex, France. TEL 83-50-46-00. FAX 83-50-46-50. *5580*

P A S C A L. F 16: CHIMIE ANALYTIQUE, MINERALE ET ORGANIQUE.
Centre National de la Recherche Scientifique, Institut de l'Information Scientifique et Technique, 2 allee du Parc de Brabois, 54514 Vandoeuvre-Les-Nancy Cedex, France. TEL 83-50-46-00. FAX 83-50-46-50. *1710*

P A S C A L. F 17: CHIMIE GENERALE, MINERALE ET ORGANIQUE.
Centre National de la Recherche Scientifique, Institut de l'Information Scientifique et Technique, 2 allee du Parc de Brabois, 54514 Vandoeuvre-Les-Nancy Cedex, France. TEL 83-50-46-00. FAX 83-50-46-50. *1710*

P A S C A L. F 23: GENIE CHIMIQUE. INDUSTRIES CHIMIQUE ET PARACHIMIQUE.
Centre National de la Recherche Scientifique, Institut de l'Information Scientifique et Technique, 2 allee du Parc de Brabois, 54514 Vandoeuvre-Les-Nancy Cedex, France. TEL 83-50-46-00. FAX 83-50-46-50. *1710*

P A S C A L. F 24: POLYMERES - PEINTURES - BOIS.
Centre National de la Recherche Scientifique, Institut de l'Information Scientifique et Technique, 2 allee du Parc de Brabois, 54514 Vandoeuvre-Les-Nancy Cedex, France. TEL 83-50-46-00. FAX 83-50-46-50. *1711*

P A S C A L. F 40: MINERALOGIE. GEOCHIMIE. GEOLOGIE EXTRATERRESTRE.
Centre National de la Recherche Scientifique, Institut de l'Information Scientifique et Technique, 2 allee du Parc de Brabois, 54514 Vandoeuvre-Les-Nancy Cedex, France. TEL 83-50-46-00. FAX 83-50-46-50. *2220*

P A S C A L. F 41: GISEMENTS METALLIQUES ET NON METALLIQUES.
Centre National de la Recherche Scientifique, Institut de l'Information Scientifique et Technique, 2 allee du Parc de Brabois, 54514 Vandoeuvre-Les-Nancy Cedex, France. TEL 83-50-46-00. FAX 83-50-46-50. *5084*

P A S C A L. F 42: ROCHES CRISTALLINES.
Centre National de la Recherche Scientifique, Institut de l'Information Scientifique et Technique, 2 allee du Parc de Brabois, 54514 Vandoeuvre-Les-Nancy Cedex, France. TEL 83-50-46-00. FAX 83-50-46-50. *2220*

P A S C A L. F 43: ROCHES SEDIMENTAIRES. GEOLOGIE MARINE.
Centre National de la Recherche Scientifique, Institut de l'Information Scientifique et Technique, 2 allee du Parc de Brabois, 54514 Vandoeuvre-Les-Nancy Cedex, France. TEL 83-50-46-00. FAX 83-50-46-50. *2220*

P A S C A L. F 44: STRATIGRAPHIE, GEOLOGIE REGIONALE, GEOLOGIE GENERALE.
Centre National de la Recherche Scientifique, Institut de l'Information Scientifique et Technique, 2 allee du Parc de Brabois, 54514 Vandoeuvre-Les-Nancy Cedex, France. TEL 83-50-46-00. FAX 83-50-46-50. *2220*

P A S C A L. F 45: TECTONIQUE, GEOPHYSIQUE INTERNE.
Centre National de la Recherche Scientifique, Institut de l'Information Scientifique et Technique, 2 allee du Parc de Brabois, 54514 Vandoeuvre-Les-Nancy Cedex, France. TEL 83-50-46-00. FAX 83-50-46-50. *2220*

P A S C A L. F 46: HYDROLOGIE. GEOLOGIE DE L'INGENIEUR. FORMATIONS SUPERFICIELLES.
Centre National de la Recherche Scientifique, Institut de l'Information Scientifique et Technique, 2 allee du Parc de Brabois, 54514 Vandoeuvre-Les-Nancy Cedex, France. TEL 83-50-46-00. FAX 83-50-46-50. *2221*

P A S C A L. F 47: PALEONTOLOGIE.
Centre National de la Recherche Scientifique, Institut de l'Information Scientifique et Technique, 2 allee du Parc de Brabois, 54514 Vandoeuvre-Les-Nancy Cedex, France. TEL 83-50-46-00. FAX 83-50-46-50. *5319*

P A S C A L. F 52: BIOCHIMIE - BIOPHYSIQUE - MOLECULAIRE - BIOLOGIE MOLECULAIRE ET CELLULAIRE.
Centre National de la Recherche Scientifique, Institut de l'Information Scientifique et Technique, 2 allee du Parc de Brabois, 54514 Vandoeuvre-Les-Nancy Cedex, France. TEL 83-50-46-00. FAX 83-50-46-50. *623*

P A S C A L. F 53: ANATOMIE ET PHYSIOLOGIE DES VERTEBRES.
Centre National de la Recherche Scientifique, Institut de l'Information Scientifique et Technique, 2 allee du Parc de Brabois, 54514 Vandoeuvre-Les-Nancy Cedex, France. TEL 83-50-46-00. FAX 83-50-46-50. *623*

P A S C A L. F 54: REPRODUCTION DES VERTEBRES, EMBRYOLOGIE DES VERTEBRES ET DES INVERTEBRES.
Centre National de la Recherche Scientifique, Institut de l'Information Scientifique et Technique, 2 allee du Parc de Brabois, 54514 Vandoeuvre-Les-Nancy Cedex, France. TEL 83-50-46-00. FAX 83-50-46-50. *4572*

P A S C A L. F 55: BIOLOGIE VEGETALE.
Centre National de la Recherche Scientifique, Institut de l'Information Scientifique et Technique, 2 allee du Parc de Brabois, 54514 Vandoeuvre-Les-Nancy Cedex, France. TEL 83-50-46-00. FAX 83-50-46-50. *623*

P A S C A L. F 56: ECOLOGIE ANIMALE, VEGETALE ET MICROBIENNE. ETHOLOGIE ANIMALE.
Centre National de la Recherche Scientifique, Institut de l'Information Scientifique et Technique, 2 allee du Parc de Brabois, 54514 Vandoeuvre-Les-Nancy Cedex, France. TEL 83-50-46-00. FAX 83-50-46-50. *623*

P A S C A L. F 70: PHARMACOLOGIE. TRAITEMENTS MEDICAMENTEUX.
Centre National de la Recherche Scientifique, Institut de l'Information Scientifique et Technique, 2 allee du Parc de Brabois, 54514 Vandoeuvre-Les-Nancy Cedex, France. TEL 83-50-46-00. FAX 83-50-46-50. *5451*

P A S C A L. T 205: SCIENCES DE L'INFORMATION. DOCUMENTATION.
Centre National de la Recherche Scientifique, Institut de l'Information Scientifique et Technique, 2 allee du Parc de Brabois, 54514 Vandoeuvre-Les-Nancy Cedex, France. TEL 83-50-46-00. FAX 83-50-46-50. *4040*

P A S C A L. T 215: BIOTECHNOLOGIES.
Centre National de la Recherche Scientifique, Institut de l'Information Scientifique et Technique, 2 allee du Parc de Brabois, 54514 Vandoeuvre-les-Nancy Cedex, France. TEL 83-50-46-00. FAX 83-50-46-50. *4572*

P A S C A L. T 230: ENERGIE.
Centre National de la Recherche Scientifique, Institut de l'Information Scientifique et Technique, 2 allee du Parc de Brabois, 54514 Vandoeuvre-Les-Nancy Cedex, France. TEL 83-50-46-00. FAX 83-50-46-50. *5580*

P A S C A L. T 235: MEDECINE TROPICALE.
Centre National de la Recherche Scientifique, Institut de l'Information Scientifique et Technique, 2 allee du Parc de Brabois, 54514 Vandoeuvre-Les-Nancy Cedex, France. TEL 83-50-46-00. FAX 83-50-46-50. *4572*

P A S C A L. T 240: METAUX - METALLURGIE.
Centre National de la Recherche Scientifique, Institut de l'Information Scientifique et Technique, 2 allee du Parc de Brabois, 54514 Vandoeuvre-Les-Nancy Cedex, France. TEL 83-50-46-00. FAX 83-50-46-50. *4984*

P A S C A L. T 260: ZOOLOGIE FONDAMENTALE ET APPLIQUEE DES INVERTEBRES.
Centre National de la Recherche Scientifique, Institut de l'Information Scientifique et Technique, 2 allee du Parc de Brabois, 54514 Vandoeuvre-Les-Nancy Cedex, France. TEL 83-50-46-00. FAX 83-50-46-50. *623*

P A S C A L. T 280: SCIENCES AGRONOMIQUES ET FORESTIERES: PRODUCTIONS VEGETALES.
Centre National de la Recherche Scientifique, Institut de l'Information Scientifique et Technique, 2 allee du Parc de Brabois, 54514 Vandoeuvre-Les-Nancy Cedex, France. TEL 83-50-46-00. FAX 83-50-46-50. *178*

P A S C A L. T 295: BATIMENT. TRAVAUX PUBLICS.
Centre National de la Recherche Scientifique, Institut de l'Information Scientifique et Technique, 2 allee du Parc de Brabois, 54514 Vandoeuvre-les-Nancy Cedex, France. TEL 83-50-46-00. FAX 83-50-46-50. *2629*

P A S C A L. V.4 SCIENCES DE LA TERRE.
Centre National de la Recherche Scientifique, Institut de l'Information Scientifique et Technique, 2 allee du Parc de Brabois, 54514 Vandoeuvre-les-Nancy Cedex, France. TEL 83-50-46-00. FAX 83-50-46-50. *2221*

P C ACTION.
Computec Verlag, Isarstr. 32-34, 90451 Nuernberg, Germany. TEL 49-911-96832-0. FAX 49-911-6426333. *2024*

P C GAMES.
Computec Verlag, Isarstr. 32-34, 90451 Nuernberg, Germany. TEL 49-911-96832-0. FAX 49-911-6426333. *2024*

P C GAMES.
E M A P - Images, Priory Ct., 30-32 Farringdon Ln., London EC1R 3AU, England. TEL 44-171-972-6700. FAX 44-171-972-6710. *2024*

P C GAMES PLUS.
Computec Verlag, Osarstr. 32-34, 90451 Nuernberg, Germany. TEL 49-911-96832-0. FAX 49-911-6426333. *2024*

P C LETTER.
155 Bovet Rd., Ste. 800, San Mateo, CA 94402-3115. TEL 800-432-2478. FAX 415-312-0547. *2048*

P C REVIEW.
E M A P - Images, Priory Ct., 30-32 Ferringdon Ln., London EC1R 3AU, England. TEL 44-171-972-6710. FAX 44-171-972-6710. *2090*

P C WEEK.
Ziff-Davis Publishing Co. (Medford), One Park Ave., New York, NY 10016-5146. TEL 212-503-5100. *2101*

P R PLANNER - EUROPE.
Media Information Ltd., Hale House, 290-296 Green Lanes, London N13 5TP, England. FAX 44-181-886-0703. *1633*

PACIFIC TELECOMMUNICATIONS COUNCIL. CONFERENCE PROCEEDINGS.
Pacific Telecommunications Council, 2454 S. Beretania St., Ste. 302, Honolulu, HI 96826-1596. TEL 808-941-3789. FAX 808-944-4874. *1948*

PAEDIATRICA INDONESIANA.
Indonesian Society of Pediatrician, c/o Dept. of Child Health, Medical School, University of Indonesia, Jalan Salemba 6, Jakarta 10430, Indonesia. TEL 62-21-314-8610. FAX 61-21-390-7743. *4809*

PAKISTAN JOURNAL OF BIOCHEMISTRY.
Pakistan Society of Biochemists, Institute of Chemistry, University of Funjab, Lahore 54590, Pakistan. *646*

PAKISTAN JOURNAL OF CLINICAL PSYCHOLOGY.
University of Karachi, Institute of Clinical Psychology, 118, Block 2C, Abul Asar Hafeez Jalindhri Rd., Gulistan-e-Janhar, Karachi 75290, Pakistan. TEL 92-21-8113584. *5868*

PAKISTAN JOURNAL OF HEALTH.
College of Community Medicine, 6 Birdwood Rd., Lahore, Pakistan. TEL 92-42-7583945. FAX 92-42-7586395. *5972*

PAKISTAN JOURNAL OF OTOLARYNGOLOGY.
Pakistan Society of Otolaryngology, c/o Dr. M.H.A. Beg, F.R.C.S., Modern Ear Nose and Throat Hospital, B-10 Block 13-A, Opposite PIA Plaentarium, University Rd., Karachi 74400, Pakistan. TEL 92-21-4971762. FAX 92-21-4971753. *4799*

PAKISTAN JOURNAL OF PHARMACEUTICAL SCIENCES.
University of Karachi, Faculty of Pharmacy, Karachi 75270, Pakistan. *5432*

PAKISTAN JOURNAL OF PSYCHOLOGY.
University of Karachi, Institute of Clinical Psychology, 118, Block 2C, Abul Asar Hafeez Jalindhri Rd., Gulistan-e-Janhar, Karachi 75290, Pakistan. TEL 92-21-8113584. *5868*

PAKISTAN MEDICAL ASSOCIATION. JOURNAL.
Pakistan Medical Association, P.M.A. House, Aga Khan III Rd., Karachi 74400, Pakistan. TEL 92-21-7214632. FAX 92-21-7226443. *4512*

PAPERBASE ABSTRACTS.
Pira International, Randalls Rd., Leatherhead, Surrey KT22 7RU, England. TEL 44-1372-802050. FAX 44-1372-802239.
Producer(s): Knight-Ridder, Inc.. *5329*

PAPERBOUND BOOKS IN PRINT.
R.R. Bowker, A Division of Reed Elsevier Inc., 121 Chanlon Rd., New Providence, NJ 07974. TEL 908-464-6800. FAX 908-665-3502.
Producer(s): Bowker Electronic Publishing. *543*

PARENTS.
Gruner & Jahr U.S.A. Publishing, 110 Fifth Ave., New York, NY 10011. TEL 212-463-1600.
Producer(s): University Microfilms International. *1775*

PARKER DIRECTORY OF CALIFORNIA ATTORNEYS.
Parker Directory of California Attorneys, A Division of Reed Elsevier Inc., 12233 W. Olympic Blvd., Ste. 236, Los Angeles, CA 90064. TEL 310-207-9448. FAX 310-207-9448. *3831*

PATOLOGIA.
Obsidiana Editores, S.A., Czda. de Talpan 2365, Col. Ciudad Jardin, 04370 Mexico DF, Mexico. TEL 6899133. *600*

PAYROLL MANAGEMENT GUIDE.
Commerce Clearing House, Inc., 2700 Lake Cook Rd., Riverwoods, IL 60015. TEL 847-267-7000. FAX 800-224-8299. *1114*

PEACE CORPS TIMES.
U.S. Peace Corps, 1990 K St., N.W. Washington, DC 20526. TEL 202-254-3371. FAX 202-606-3110. *1313*

PEDIATRICS (ENGLISH EDITION).
American Academy of Pediatrics, 141 Northwest Point Blvd., Box 927, Elk Grove Village, IL 60009-0927. TEL 847-228-5005. FAX 847-228-5097. *4812*

PENNSYLVANIA BUSINESS DIRECTORY.
American Business Directories 5711 S. 86th Circle, Box 27347, Omaha, NE 68127. TEL 402-593-4600. FAX 402-331-5481. *1633*

PENNSYLVANIA RULES OF COURT, STATE AND FEDERAL.
West Publishing Corp., 620 Opperman Dr., Eagan, MN 55123. TEL 612-687-8000. FAX 612-687-7302. *3952*

PENSION PLAN GUIDE.
Commerce Clearing House, Inc., 2700 Lake Cook Rd., Riverwoods, IL 60015. TEL 847-267-7000. FAX 800-224-8299. *3661*

PERIODICA. INDICE DE REVISTAS LATINOAMERICANAS EN CIENCIAS.
Universidad Nacional Autonoma de Mexico, Centro de Informacion Cientifica y Humanistica, Apdo. Postal 70-392, C.P. 04510 Mexico, D.F., Mexico. TEL 525-6223958. FAX 525-6162557. *6303*

PERIODICAL ABSTRACTS.
U M I Company 300 N. Zeeb Rd., Ann Arbor, MI 48106. TEL 313-761-4700. FAX 800-864-0019. *22*

THE PERRYMAN TEXAS LETTER.
Texas Economic Publishers, Inc., 510 N. Valley Mills Dr., Ste. 300, Waco, TX 76710-6076. TEL 817-751-7411. FAX 817-751-7855. *1228*

PERSONAL FINANCE INTELLIGENCE.
Mintel International Group Ltd., 18-19 Long Ln., London EC1A 9HE, England. TEL 44-171-606-4533. FAX 44-171-606-5932. *1115*

PERSONNEL REVIEW.
M C B University Press Ltd., 60-62 Toller Ln., Bradford, W. Yorks BD8 9BY, England. TEL 44-1274-777700. FAX 44-1274-785200. *1509*

PERSPECTIVES OF NEW MUSIC.
Perspectives of New Music, Inc., University of Washington, Music, Box 353450, Seattle, WA 98195-3450. TEL 206-543-0196. FAX 206-543-9285. *5188*

PERSPECTIVES ON POLITICAL SCIENCE.
Heldref Publications, 1319 18th St, N.W., Washington, DC 20036-1802. TEL 202-296-6267. FAX 202-296-5149.
Producer(s): University Microfilms International. *5692*

PETERSON'S GUIDE TO GRADUATE AND PROFESSIONAL PROGRAMS: AN OVERVIEW (YEAR) (BOOK 1).
Peterson's Guides, Inc., 202 Carnegie Center, Box 2123, Princeton, NJ 08543-2123. TEL 609-243-9111. FAX 609-243-9150.
Producer(s): SilverPlatter Information, Inc. (PETERSON'S GRADLINE). *2415*

PETERSON'S GUIDE TO GRADUATE PROGRAMS IN BUSINESS, EDUCATION, HEALTH, AND LAW (YEAR) (BOOK 6).
Peterson's Guides, Inc., 202 Carnegie Center, Box 2123, Princeton, NJ 08543-2123. TEL 609-243-9111. FAX 609-243-9150.
Producer(s): SilverPlatter Information, Inc. (PETERSON'S GRADLINE). *2415*

PETERSON'S GUIDE TO GRADUATE PROGRAMS IN ENGINEERING AND APPLIED SCIENCES (YEAR) (BOOK 5).
Peterson's Guides, Inc., 202 Carnegie Center, Box 2123, Princeton, NJ 08543-2123. TEL 609-243-9111. FAX 609-243-9150.
Producer(s): SilverPlatter Information, Inc. (PETERSON'S GRADLINE). *2415*

PETERSON'S GUIDE TO GRADUATE PROGRAMS IN THE BIOLOGICAL AND AGRICULTURAL SCIENCES (YEAR) (BOOK 3).
Peterson's Guides, Inc., 202 Carnegie Center, Box 2123, Princeton, NJ 08543-2123. TEL 609-243-9111. FAX 609-243-9150.
Producer(s): SilverPlatter Information, Inc. (PETERSON'S GRADLINE). *2415*

PETERSON'S GUIDE TO GRADUATE PROGRAMS IN THE HUMANITIES AND SOCIAL SCIENCES (YEAR) (BOOK 2).
Peterson's Guides, Inc., 202 Carnegie Center, Box 2123, Princeton, NJ 08543-2123. TEL 609-243-9111. FAX 609-243-9150.
Producer(s): SilverPlatter Information, Inc. (PETERSON'S GRADLINE). *2415*

PETERSON'S GUIDE TO GRADUATE PROGRAMS IN THE PHYSICAL SCIENCES AND MATHEMATICS (YEAR) (BOOK 4).
Peterson's Guides, Inc., 202 Carnegie Center, Box 2123, NJ 08543-2123. TEL 609-243-9111. FAX 609-243-9150.
Producer(s): SilverPlatter Information, Inc. (PETERSON'S GRADLINE). *2415*

PETROLEUM ABSTRACTS.
University of Tulsa, Information Services Division, 600 S. College Ave., Tulsa, OK 74104-3189. TEL 918-631-2297. FAX 918-599-9361. Producer(s): Knight-Ridder, Inc.. *5384*

PHARMACEUTICAL COMPANIES ANALYSIS.
M D I S Publications, MDIS House, City Fields Business Park, City Fields Way, Chichester, W. Sussex PO20 6FS, England. TEL 44-1243-533322. FAX 44-1243-533418. *5433*

PHARMACEUTICAL COMPANY PROFILES.
IMSWORLD Publications Ltd., 7 Harewood Ave., London NW1 6JB, England. TEL 0171-393-5000. FAX 0171-393-5900. *5433*

PHILIPPINE DENTAL ASSOCIATION. JOURNAL.
Philippine Dental Association, Ayala Ave. corner Kamagong St., Makati, Metro Manila, Philippines. TEL 818-6144. FAX 816-3034. *4652*

PHILIPPINE JOURNAL OF INTERNAL MEDICINE.
Philippine College of Physicians, Facilities Central Bldg., 548 Shaw Blvd., Mandaluyong, Metro Manila, Philippines. TEL 2-780233. *4707*

PHILIPPINE JOURNAL OF NUTRITION.
Philippine Association of Nutrition, c/o Nutrition Foundation of the Philippines, 107 E. Rodriguez, Sr. Blvd., Quezon City, Philippines. *5240*

PHILIPPINE JOURNAL OF OPHTHALMOLOGY.
Philippine Society of Ophthalmology, Philippine General Hospital, Taft Ave., Manila 1000, Philippines. *4776*

PHILIPPINE JOURNAL OF SURGICAL SPECIALTIES.
Philippine College of Surgeons, c/o Philippine Medical Association, PMA Bldg., North Ave., Quezon City, Philippine. *4917*

PHILOSOPHER'S INDEX.
Philosopher's Information Center, 1616 E. Wooster St., Box P, Bowling Green, OH 43402. TEL 419-353-8830. FAX 419-353-8784. *5507*

PHONOLOG REPORTER.
Trade Service Corporation, 10996 Torreyana Rd., Box 85007, San Diego, CA 92186-9982. TEL 619-457-5920. FAX 619-457-1320. *5209*

PHYSICIANS' DESK REFERENCE.
Medical Economics Publishing Co., Inc., 5 Paragon Dr., Montvale, NJ 07645. TEL 201-357-7200. FAX 201-573-1045. *4516*

PHYSICIANS' DESK REFERENCE FOR NONPRESCRIPTION DRUGS.
Medical Economics Publishing Co., Inc., 5 Paragon Dr., Montvale, NJ 07645. TEL 201-358-7200. FAX 201-573-1045. *4516*

PHYSICIANS' GENRX.
Mosby - Year Book, Inc., 11830 Westline Industrial Dr., St. Louis, MO 63146-3318. TEL 314-872-8370. FAX 314-432-1380. *4516*

PHYSICS ABSTRACTS.
INSPEC, I.E.E., Michael Faraday House, Six Hills Way, Stevenage, Herts. SG1 2AY, England. TEL 44-1438-313311. FAX 44-1438-742840. Producer(s): University Microfilms International. *5580*

PHYSICS - USPEKHI.
Turpin Distribution Services Ltd., Blackhorse Rd., Letchworth, Herts. SG6 1HN, England. TEL 44-1462-672555. FAX 44-1462-489047. *5565*

PINKERTON EYE ON TRAVEL.
Pinkerton Risk Assessment Services, 200 N. Glebe Rd., No. 1011, Arlington, VA 22203-3728. TEL 703-525-6111. FAX 703-525-2454. *6907*

PLANT TISSUE CULTURE.
Bangladesh Association for Plant Tissue Culture, University of Dhaka, Department of Botany, Dhaka-1000, Bangladesh. TEL 880-2-506378. FAX 880-2-865583.
Available only on CD-ROM. *699*

PLASTICS D.A.T.A. DIGEST.
D.A.T.A. Business Publishing 15 Inverness Way E., Box 6510, Englewood, CO 80155-6510. FAX 303-799-4082. *5624*

PLOUGHSHARES.
Ploughshares, Inc., Emerson College, 100 Beacon St., Boston, MA 02116. TEL 617-824-8753.
Producer(s): University Microfilms International, H.W. Wilson. *4251*

POEMFINDER.
Roth Publishing, Inc., 185 Great Neck Rd., Great Neck, NY 11021. TEL 516-466-3676. FAX 516-829-7746.
Available only on CD-ROM. *4294*

POINT DE REPERE.
Services Documentaires Multimedia Inc., 75 Port Royal E., No. 300, Montreal, PQ H3L 3T1, Canada. TEL 514-382-0895. FAX 514-384-9139. *22*

POLAR AND GLACIOLOGICAL ABSTRACTS.
Cambridge University Press, Edinburgh Bldg., Shaftesbury Rd., Cambridge CB2 2RU, England. TEL 44-1223-312393. FAX 44-1223-315052. *2221*

POLITICAL RISK SERVICES ON C D - R O M.
Political Risk Services, Box 248, E. Syracuse, NY 13057-0248. TEL 315-431-0511. FAX 315-431-0200.
Available only on CD-ROM. *5767*

POLITICAL RISK YEARBOOK.
Political Risk Services, Box 248, E. Syracuse, NY 13057-0248. TEL 315-431-0511. FAX 315-431-0200. *1115*

POLLING THE NATIONS.
Opinion Research Service, 7200 Wisconsin Ave., Ste. 704, Bethesda, MD 20814-4811.
Available only on CD-ROM. *6442*

POLLUTION ABSTRACTS.
Cambridge Scientific Abstracts, 7200 Wisconsin Ave., 6th Fl., Bethesda, MD 20814. TEL 301-961-6750. FAX 301-961-6720.
Producer(s): Knight-Ridder, Inc. (Environmental Management), NISC, SilverPlatter Information, Inc. (POLTOX1). *2831*

POLYMERS, CERAMICS, COMPOSITES ALERT.
Cambridge Scientific Abstracts, 7200 Wisconsin Ave., Bethesda, MD 20814. TEL 301-961-6750. FAX 301-961-6720.
Producer(s): Knight-Ridder, Inc.. *5629*

POPULAR.
2413 Dundas St. W., Toronto, ON M6P 1X3, Canada. TEL 416-531-2495. FAX 416-531-7187. *2903*

POPULAR MECHANICS.
Hearst Corp., Popular Mechanics, 959 Eighth Ave., New York, NY 10019. TEL 212-649-2100.
Producer(s): University Microfilms International. *6661*

POPULAR SCIENCE.
Times Mirror Magazines, Inc., 2 Park Ave., New York, NY 10016. TEL 212-779-5000.
Producer(s): University Microfilms International. *6661*

POPULATION INDEX.
Princeton University, Office of Population Research, 21 Prospect Ave., Princeton, NJ 08544-2091. TEL 609-258-4949. FAX 609-258-1039.
Producer(s): SilverPlatter Information, Inc.. *5803*

PORTFOLIO LETTER.
Institutional Investor Newsletters, 477 Madison Ave., New York, NY 10022. TEL 212-224-3233. FAX 212-224-3353. *1347*

POWDER DIFFRACTION FILE SEARCH MANUAL. HANAWALT METHOD. INORGANIC.
Joint Committee on Powder Diffraction Standards, International Centre for Diffraction Data, Newton Sq. Corp. Camp, 12, Newton Square, PA 19073. TEL 215-328-9400. FAX 215-328-2503. *1719*

POWDER DIFFRACTION FILE SEARCH MANUAL. ORGANIC.
Joint Committee on Powder Diffraction Standards, International Centre for Diffraction Data, 12 Campus Blvd., Newtown Square, PA 19073. TEL 610-325-9814. FAX 610-325-9823. *1744*

POWER ENGINEERING JOURNAL.
I.E.E., Michael Faraday House, Six Hills Way, Stevenage, Herts. SG1 2AG, England. TEL 44-1438-313311. FAX 44-1438-742840.
Producer(s): University Microfilms International. *2717*

PREDICASTS F & S INDEX INTERNATIONAL.
Information Access Company 362 Lakeside Dr., Foster City, CA 94404. TEL 415-378-5200. FAX 415-378-5369. *1022*

PRENSA LIBRE.
Prensa Libre, S.A., 13 Calle 9-31, Zona 1, 01001 Guatemala, Guatemala. TEL 502-2-305096. FAX 502-2-301347. *3162*

PRESENCE MAGAZINE.
Presence Magazine Inc., 2715 Cote Ste-Catherine, Montreal, PQ H3T 1B6, Canada. TEL 514-739-9797. FAX 514-739-1664. *6085*

PREVENTING SCHOOL FAILURE.
Heldref Publications, 1319 Eighteenth St., N.W., Washington, DC 20036-1802. TEL 202-296-6267. FAX 202-296-5149.
Producer(s): University Microfilms International. *2473*

PRINT MEDIA PRODUCTION SOURCE.
S R D S L.P. 1700 Higgins Rd., Des Plaines, IL 60018. TEL 847-375-5000. FAX 847-375-5001. *50*

PRIVATISATION INTERNATIONAL.
Privatisation International Ltd., Butlers Wharf Business Centre, Ste. 404, 45 Curlew St., London SE1 2ND, England. TEL 44-171-378-1620. FAX 44-171-403-7876. *952*

PROARBEIT.
Bundesanstalt fuer Arbeit, Institut fuer Arbeitsmarkt- und Berufsforschung, Regensburgerstr. 104, 90327 Nuernberg, Germany. TEL 49-911-1793011. FAX 49-911-1791147. *1023*

PROCESS AND CHEMICAL ENGINEERING.
The Royal Society of Chemistry, Thomas Graham House, Science Park, Milton Rd., Cambridge CB4 4WF, England. TEL 44-1223-420066. FAX 44-1223-423429.
Producer(s): Knight-Ridder, Inc.. *2630*

PRODUCER PRICE INDEXES.
U.S. Bureau of Labor Statistics, 2 Massachusetts Ave., N.E., Washington, DC 20212. TEL 202-655-4000. *1236*

PRODUCTIVITY MEASURES FOR SELECTED INDUSTRIES.
U.S. Bureau of Labor Statistics, 441 G St., N.W., Washington, DC 20212. TEL 202-523-9244. *1236*

PROJECT FINANCE INTERNATIONAL.
I F R Publishing 11 New Fetter Ln., London EC4A 1JN, England. TEL 44-171-815-3900. FAX 44-171-815-3856. *1116*

PROMAX INTERNATIONAL.
Promotion & Marketing Executives in the Electronic Media, 2029 Century Pk. E., Ste. 555, Los Angeles, CA 90067-2906. TEL 310-788-7600. FAX 310-788-7616. *1967*

PROSPECTS DIRECTORY.
C S U (Publications) Ltd. Armstrong House, Oxford Rd., Manchester M1 7ED, England. TEL 0161-236-9816. FAX 0161-236-8541. *5272*

PSYCHIATRIC GENETICS.
Rapid Science Publishers, The Old Malthouse, Paradise St., Oxford OX1 1LD, England. TEL 44-1865-790447. FAX 44-1865-244012. *749*

PSYCHOLOGICAL ABSTRACTS.
American Psychological Association, 750 First St., N.E., Washington, DC 20002-4242. TEL 202-336-5600. FAX 202-336-5568.
Producer(s): American Psychological Assn., NISC (PsycLIT), SilverPlatter Information, Inc. (PsycLIT). *5889*

PSYCHOLOGY TODAY
Sussex Publishers Inc., 49 E. 21st St., 11th Fl., New York, NY 10010. TEL 212-260-7210. FAX 212-260-7445.
Producer(s): University Microfilms International. *5876*

PSYCHOPATHOLOGIE AFRICAINE.
Societe de Psychopathologie et d'Hygiene Mentale de Dakar, B.P. 5097, Dakar-Fann, Senegal. *4864*

PUBLIC HEALTH.
Landesinstitut fuer den Oeffentlichen Gesundheitsdienst des Landes Nordrhein-Westfalen, Westerfeldstr. 35-37, 33611 Bielefeld, Germany. TEL 49-521-8007264. FAX 49-521-8007200. *4573*

PUBLIC UTILITIES REPORTS.
Public Utilities Reports, Inc., 8229 Boone Blvd., Ste. 401, Vienna, VA 22182. TEL 703-847-7720. FAX 703-917-6964 *2556*

PUBLICATIONS IN EDUCATION AND THE SOCIAL SCIENCES IN ISRAEL.
Henrietta Szold Institute, 9 Columbia St, Kiryat Menachem, Jerusalem 96583, Israel. TEL 972-2-419191. FAX 972-2-437698.
Available only on CD-ROM. *6442*

PUBLICUS.
Schwabe und Co. AG, Steinentorstr. 13, CH-4010 Basel, Switzerland. TEL 41-61-2725523. FAX 41-61-2725573. *5918*

PUBLISHERS, DISTRIBUTORS & WHOLESALERS OF THE UNITED STATES.
R.R. Bowker, A Division of Reed Elsevier Inc., 121 Chanlon Rd., New Providence, NJ 07974. TEL 908-464-6800. FAX 908-665-3502.
Producer(s): Bowker Electronic Publishing. *1635*

PUBLISHERS' INTERNATIONAL I S B N DIRECTORY (YEAR).
K.G. Saur Verlag KG, A member of the Reed Elsevier plc group, Ortlerstr. 8, 81373 Munich, Germany. TEL 49-89-76902-0. FAX 49-89-76902150.
Producer(s): K.G. Saur Verlag. *6015*

PUBLISHING MARKET PLACE REFERENCE PLUS.
R.R. Bowker, A Division of Reed Elsevier plc group, 121 Chanlon Rd., New Providence, NJ 07974. TEL 908-665-2866. FAX 908-665-3528.
Available only on CD-ROM. Producer(s): Bowker Electronic Publishing. *4021*

PUERTO RICO HEALTH SCIENCES JOURNAL.
University of Puerto Rico, Office of the Dean for Academic Affairs, Medical Sciences Campus, Box 365067, San Juan, PR 00936-5067. TEL 809-758-2525. FAX 809-764-2470. *4520*

PUNCH IN INTERNATIONAL TRAVEL AND ENTERTAINMENT MAGAZINE.
Enterprises Publishing, 400 E. 59th St., Ste. 9F, New York, NY 10022. TEL 212-755-4363. FAX 212-755-4365. *6908*

Q E X : A R R L EXPERIMENTERS' EXCHANGE.
American Radio Relay League, Inc., 225 Main St., Newington, CT 06111. TEL 860-594-0200. FAX 860-594-0303. *1938*

QST.
American Radio Relay League, Inc., 225 Main St., Newington, CT 06111. TEL 860-594-0200. FAX 860-584-0239. *1938*

QUALITY ASSURANCE IN EDUCATION.
M C B University Press Ltd., 60-62 Toller Ln., Bradford, W. Yorks BC8 9BY, England. TEL 44-1274-777700. FAX 44-1274-785200. *2365*

QUALITY OF LIFE RESEARCH.
Rapid Science Publishers, The Old Malthouse, Paradise St., Oxford OX1 1LD, England. TEL 44-1865-790447. FAX 44-1865-244012. *4521*

QUANTUM ELECTRONICS.
Turpin Distribution Services Ltd., Blackhorse Rd., Letchworth, Herts. SG6 1HN, England. TEL 44-1462-672555. FAX 44-1462-489047. *2717*

QUARTERLY FINANCIAL INSTITUTION RATINGS.
L A C E Financial Corp., 118 N. Court St., Frederick, MD 21701. TEL 301-662-1011. *1117*

QUEBEC (PROVINCE). SERVICES DOCUMENTAIRES MULTIMEDIA. CHOIX: DOCUMENTATION AUDIOVISUELLE.
Services Documentaires Multimedia Inc., 75 Port-Royal E., No. 300, Montreal, PQ H3L 3T1, Canada. TEL 514-382-0895. FAX 514-334-9139. *544*

QUEBEC (PROVINCE). SERVICES DOCUMENTAIRES MULTIMEDIA. CHOIX: DOCUMENTATION IMPRIMEE.
Services Documentaires Multimedia Inc., 75 Port-Royal E., No. 300, Montreal, PQ H3L 3T1, Canada. TEL 514-382-0895. FAX 514-334-9139. *544*

QUEBEC (PROVINCE). SERVICES DOCUMENTATION MULTIMEDIA. CHOIX JEUNESSE: DOCUMENTATION IMPRIMEE.
Services Documentaires Multimedia Inc., 75 Port-Royal E., No. 300, Montreal, PQ H3L 3T1, Canada. TEL 514-382-0895. FAX 514-384-9139. *544*

QUFU SHIFAN DAXUE XUEBAO.
Qufu Shifan Daxue, Xuebao Bianji bu, Qufu, Shandong 273165, People's Republic of China. TEL 86-537-4411831. *5339*

QUILL (GREENCASTLE).
Society of Professional Journalists, Box 77, Greencastle, IN 46135-0077. TEL 317-653-3333. FAX 317-653-4631. *3710*

R A M.
Televak Uitgeverij N.V., Postbus 75985, 1070 AZ Amsterdam, Netherlands. TEL 31-20-6659220. FAX 31-20-6657316. *1538*

R A P R A ABSTRACTS.
R A P R A Technology Ltd. Shawbury, Shrewsbury, Shrops. SY4 4NR, England TEL 44-1939-250383. FAX 44-1939-251118. *5220*

R A P R A ABSTRACTS - C D - R O M.
R A P R A Technology Ltd., Shawbury, Shrewsbury, Shrops. SY4 4NR, England TEL 44-1939-250383. FAX 44-1939-251118.
Available only on CD-ROM *6220*

R & D FOCUS.
IMSWORLD Publications Ltd., 7 Harewood Ave., London NW1 6JB, England TEL 0171-393-5000. FAX 0171-393-5900. *5211*

R I A TAX GUIDE.
Research Institute of America, Inc., 90 Fifth Ave., New York, NY 10011. TEL 212-645-4800. FAX 212-337-4279. *1560*

R I B A PRODUCT SELECTOR.
R I B A Information Services, Finsbury Mission, 39 Moreland St., London EC1V 8BB, England. TEL 44-171-250-4050. FAX 44-171-490-4434. *403*

R I L M ABSTRACTS OF MUSIC LITERATURE.
R I L M Abstracts, City University of New York, 33 W. 42nd St., New York, NY 10036. TEL 212-642-2709. FAX 212-642-1973
Producer(s): NISC (MUSE, Music Search). *5209*

R T E C S.
U.S. National Institute for Occupational Safety and Health 4676 Columbia Pkwy., Cincinnati, OH 45226.
Producer(s): SilverPlatter Information, Inc.. *5257*

RAPPORTI SOCIALI.
Edizioni Rapporti Sociali, Via Bruschetti 11, 20125 Milan, Italy. TEL 39-2-670-1306. *5702*

RAW MATERIALS REPORT.
Raavarugruppen Ekonomisk Foerening, P.O. Box 44062, S-100 73 Stockholm, Sweden. TEL 46-8-7440065. FAX 46-8-7440066. *313*

RAWAL MEDICAL JOURNAL.
Pakistan Medical Association, Rawalpindi-Islamabad Branch Rawalpindi, Pakistan. *4522*

RAWLINSONS NEW ZEALAND CONSTRUCTION HANDBOOK.
Rawlinsons New Zealand Construction Handbook Ltd., Rawlinson House, 4th Fl., 25-27 Broadway, Newmarket, Auckland, New Zealand. TEL 64-9-5290061. FAX 64-9-5244577. *1636*

CD-ROM

REACTIONS WEEKLY.
Adis International Limited, Private Bag 65901, Mairangi Bay, Auckland 10, New Zealand. TEL 64-9-479-8100. FAX 64-9-479-8145.
Producer(s): SilverPlatter Information, Inc.. *5451*

READERS' GUIDE ABSTRACTS.
H.W. Wilson Co., 950 University Ave., Bronx, NY 10452-9978. TEL 718-588-8400. FAX 718-590-1617.
Producer(s): SilverPlatter Information, Inc., H.W. Wilson (WILSONDISC). *23*

READERS' GUIDE TO PERIODICAL LITERATURE.
H.W. Wilson Co., 950 University Ave., Bronx, NY 10452-9978. TEL 718-588-8400. FAX 718-590-1617.
Producer(s): SilverPlatter Information, Inc., H.W. Wilson (WILSONDISC). *23*

LA RECHERCHE.
Societe d'Editions Scientifiques, 57 rue de Seine, 75280 Paris Cedex 06, France. TEL 43-54-32-84. FAX 46-34-75-08.
Producer(s): Chadwyck-Healey Inc.. *6274*

REFERATEDIENST ZUR LITERATURWISSENSCHAFT.
Geisteswissenschaftliche Zentren Berlin e.V., Zentrum fuer Literaturforschung, Jaegerstr. 10-11, 10117 Berlin, Germany. TEL 49-30-20192169. FAX 49-30-20192154. *4256*

REFERENCE AND RESEARCH BOOK NEWS.
Book News, Inc. (Portland), 5600 N.E. Hassalo St., Portland, OR 97213. TEL 503-281-9230. FAX 503-287-4485. *544*

RELIGION INDEX ONE: PERIODICALS.
American Theological Library Association, 820 Church St., Ste. 300, Evanston, IL 60201-5613. TEL 847-869-7788. FAX 847-869-8513. *6108*

RELIGION INDEX TWO: MULTI-AUTHOR WORKS.
American Theological Library Association, 820 Church St., Ste. 300, Evanston, IL 60201-5613. TEL 847-869-7788. FAX 847-869-8513. *6108*

RELIGION INDEXES: THESAURUS.
American Theological Library Association, 820 Church St., Ste. 300, Evanston, IL 60201-5613. TEL 847-869-7788. FAX 847-869-8513. *6087*

RELIGIOUS & THEOLOGICAL ABSTRACTS.
Religious & Theological Abstracts Inc., 100 W. Park, Box 215, Myerstown, PA 17067. TEL 717-866-6734. FAX 717-866-9280. *6108*

RENT REVIEW AND LEASE RENEWAL.
M C B University Press Ltd., 60-62 Toller Ln., Bradford, W. Yorks BD8 9BY, England. TEL 44-1274-777700. FAX 44-1274-785200. *6036*

REPERTORIO CRONOLOGICO DE LEGISLACION.
Editorial Aranzadi, S.A., Avda. Carlos III, 34, Apdo. 111, 31080 Pamplona, Spain. TEL 34-48-331212. FAX 34-48-330919. *3840*

REPERTORIO DE JURISPRUDENCIA.
Editorial Aranzadi, S.A., Avda. Carlos III, 34, Apdo. 111, 31080 Pamplona, Spain. TEL 34-48-331212. FAX 34-48-330919. *3840*

REPERTORIO DEL FORO ITALIANO.
Zanichelli Editore, Via Irnerio 34, 40126 Bologna, Italy. TEL 39-51-293111. FAX 39-51-249782. *3840*

REPERTORIUM.
Dutch Association of the Innovative Pharmaceutical Industry (NEFARMA), Postbus 9193, 3506 GD Utrecht, Netherlands. FAX 31-30-2631830. *4523*

REPINDEX.
Organizacion Panamericana de la Salud, Centro Panamericano de Ingenieria Sanitaria y Ciencias del Ambiente, Los Pinos 259, Urb. Camacho, Casilla Postal 4337, Lima 100, Peru. TEL 51-14-371077. FAX 51-14-378289. *2831*

RESEARCH IN MINISTRY.
American Theological Library Association, 820 Church St., Ste. 300, Evanston, IL 60201-5613. TEL 847-869-7788. FAX 847-869-8513. *6108*

RESEARCH MANUAL OF INDUSTRIAL LAW.
C C H Australia Ltd., P.O. Box 230, North Ryde, N.S.W. 2113, Australia. TEL 61-1-300300224. FAX 61-1-330306224. *3878*

RESOURCES IN EDUCATION.
E R I C Facility, 1301 Piccard Dr., Ste. 100, Rockville, MD 20850. TEL 301-258-5500. FAX 301-948-3695.
Producer(s): Knight-Ridder, Inc. (ERIC), NISC (ERIC on CD-ROM), OCLC (ERIC), SilverPlatter Information, Inc. (ERIC). *2392*

RESOURCES IN EDUCATION ANNUAL CUMULATION.
Oryx Press, 4041 N. Central Ave., No. 700, Phoenix, AZ 85012-3397. TEL 602-265-2651. FAX 602-265-6250.
Producer(s): NISC (ERIC). *2393*

RETAIL INTELLIGENCE.
Mintel International Group Ltd., 18-19 Long Ln., London EC1A 9HE, England. TEL 44-171-606-4533. FAX 44-171-606-5932. *1484*

REVIEW (WASHINGTON).
Heldref Publications, 1319 Eighteenth St., N.W., Washington, DC 20036-1802. TEL 202-296-6267.
Producer(s): University Microfilms International. *3322*

REVISTA BRASILEIRA DE PATOLOGIA.
Sociedade Brasileira de Patologia Clinica, Rua Sampaio Viana, 92, 20261-040 Rio de Janeiro, RJ, Brazil. TEL 55-21-2933848. FAX 55-21-2932041. *4523*

REVISTA COSTARRICENSE DE CIENCIAS MEDICAS.
Caja Costarricense de Seguro Social, Apdo. 10105, San Jose, Costa Rica. FAX 506-2338359. *4524*

REVISTA DE GASTROENTEROLOGIA DE MEXICO.
Obsidiana Editores, S.A., Czda. de Tlalpan 2365, Col. Ciudad Jardin, 04370 Mexico DF, Mexico. TEL 6899133. *4696*

REVISTA DE INVESTIGACION CLINICA.
Instituto Nacional de la Nutricion "Salvador Zubiran", Av. San Fernando y Viaducto Tlalpan, Mexico 22, D.F., Mexico. TEL 915-573-1200. FAX 915-655-1076. *4524*

REVISTA DE INVESTIGACION CONTABLE (TEUKEN).
Universidad Nacional de la Patagonia San Juan Bosca, Facultad de Ciencias Economicas, Sarmiento 553 Casilla de Correo 172, 9000 C. Rivadavia, Argentina. TEL 0967-24463. FAX 54-96724463. *1054*

REVISTA MEDICA DE MOCAMBIQUE.
Ministerio da Saude, Instituto Nacional de Saude, Universidade Eduardo Mondlane, Faculdade de Medicina, C.P. 264, Maputo, Mozambique. TEL 427131. FAX 258-1-423-726. *5974*

RHODE ISLAND BUSINESS DIRECTORY.
American Business Directories 5711 S. 86th Circle, Box 27347, Omaha, NE 68127. TEL 402-593-4600. FAX 402-331-5481. *1637*

RISK ABSTRACTS.
Cambridge Scientific Abstracts, 7200 Wisconsin Ave., 6th Fl., Bethesda, MD 20814. TEL 301-961-6700. FAX 301-961-6720.
Producer(s): Knight-Ridder, Inc. (Environmental Management), NISC (Health & Safety - Risk Abstracts). *2831*

RISK MANAGEMENT.
Risk Management Society Publishing, Inc., 655 Third Ave., 2nd Fl., New York, NY 10017-5617. TEL 212-286-9364. FAX 212-986-9716. *3664*

ROCKS AND MINERALS.
Heldref Publications, 1319 Eighteenth St., N.W., Washington, DC 20036-1802. TEL 202-296-6267. FAX 202-296-5149.
Producer(s): University Microfilms International. *5077*

ROCZNIKI NAUKOWE ZOOTECHNIKI.
Instytut Zootechniki, Ul. Sarego 2, 31-047 Krakow, Poland. TEL 48-12-227333. FAX 48-12-228065. *282*

ROLLING STONE.
Wenner Media, Inc., 1290 Ave. of Americas, New York, NY 10104. TEL 212-484-1616. FAX 212-759-2966.
Producer(s): University Microfilms International. *5194*

ROMULUS.
Canada Institute for Scientific and Technical Information, Information Resource Management, Ottawa, ON K1A 0S2, Canada. TEL 613-993-3449. *6303*

ROUGE ET NOIR.
V I P News Verlag GmbH, Taubstummengasse 13-4, A-1040 Vienna, Austria. TEL 01-5050801-0. FAX 01-505080121. *6478*

ROYAL ANTHROPOLOGICAL INSTITUTE. JOURNAL.
Royal Anthropological Institute of Great Britain and Ireland, 50 Fitzroy St., London W1P 5HS, England. TEL 44-171-3870455. FAX 44-171-3834235. *321*

RUBBER WORLD.
Lippincott & Peto, Inc., 1867 W. Market St., Akron, OH 44313. TEL 216-864-2122. *6219*

RURAL TECHNOLOGY GUIDE.
Natural Resources Institute, Central Ave., Chatham Maritime, Kent ME4 4TB, England. TEL 44-1634-880088. FAX 44-1634-880066. *149*

RUSSIAN ACADEMY OF SCIENCE. IZVESTIYA. MATHEMATICS.
Turpin Distribution Services Ltd., Blackhorse Rd., Letchworth, Herts. SG6 1HN, England. TEL 44-1462-672555. FAX 44-1462-480947. *4392*

RUSSIAN BOOKS IN PRINT ON C D - R O M.
Bowker - Saur Ltd., A member of the Reed Elsevier plc group, Maypole House, Maypole Rd., E. Grinstead, W. Sussex RH19 1HU, England. TEL 44-1342-330100. FAX 44-1342-330191.
Available only on CD-ROM. Producer(s): Bowker - Saur Ltd.. *545*

S I A - SURFACE AND INTERFACE ANALYSIS.
John Wiley & Sons Ltd., Journals, Baffins Ln., Chichester, W. Sussex PO19 1UD, England. TEL 44-1243-779777. FAX 44-1243-843232. *1720*

THE S I G C A T FOUNDATION COMPENDIUM OF C D - R O MS.
Special Interest Group on C D - R O M Applications & Technology, 11343 Sunset Hills Rd., Reston, VA 22090. TEL 202-512-1265. FAX 703-435-5553.
Available only on CD-ROM. *545*

S I R S GOVERNMENT REPORTER ON C D - R O M.
Social Issues Resources Series, Box 2348, Boca Raton, FL 33427-2348. TEL 407-994-0079. FAX 407-994-4704.
Available only on CD-ROM. *25*

S I R S INDEX-ONLY C D - R O M.
Social Issues Resources Series, Box 2348, Boca Raton, FL 33427-2348. TEL 407-994-0079. FAX 407-994-4704.
Available only on CD-ROM. *25*

S I R S RESEARCHER C D - R O M.
Social Issues Resources Series, Box 2348, Boca Raton, FL 33427-2348. TEL 407-994-0079. FAX 407-994-4704.
Available only on CD-ROM. *25*

SADO MARINE BIOLOGICAL STATION. REPORT.
Niigata Daigaku, Rigakubu Fuzoku Sado Rinkai Jikkenjo, 2-8050 Igarashi, Niigata 950-21, Japan. TEL 0259-75-2012. FAX 0259-75-2012. *605*

SAFETY AND HEALTH AT WORK.
International Labour Office, International Occupational Safety and Health Information Centre, CH-1211 Geneva 22, Switzerland. TEL 41-22-799-67-40. FAX 41-22-798-6253.
Producer(s): SilverPlatter Information, Inc.. *5261*

SALUD MENTAL.
Instituto Mexicana de Psiquiatria, Calz. Mexico-Xochimilco, No. 101, Col. San L. Huipulco, Del. Tlalpan, 14370 Mexico DF, Mexico. TEL 525-6552811 ext. 144. FAX 525-6550411. *4867*

SALUD PUBLICA DE MEXICO.
Instituto Nacional de Salud Publica, Secretaria de Salud, Av. Universidad, 665, Planta Baja, Col. Santa Maria Ahuacatitlad, 62508 Cuernavaca, Morelos, Mexico. TEL 52-73-110111. FAX 52-73-175745. *5975*

SAN FRANCISCO COUNTY COMMERCE AND INDUSTRY DIRECTORY.
Database Publishing Company, 1590 S. Lewis St., Anaheim, CA 92805-6423. TEL 714-778-6400. FAX 714-778-6811. *1638*

SAN MATEO COUNTY COMMERCE AND INDUSTRY DIRECTORY.
Database Publishing Company, 1590 S. Lewis St., Anaheim, CA 92805-6423. TEL 714-778-6400. FAX 714-778-6811. *1638*

SANTO TOMAS JOURNAL OF MEDICINE.
Santo Tomas University Press, Espana St., Manila 1008, Philippines. TEL 02-731-3101. FAX 632-731-3126. *4528*

SARDIUS.
Juta & Co. Ltd., P.O. Box 14373, Kenwyn 7790, South Africa. TEL 27-21-7975101. FAX 27-21-7615010.
Available only on CD-ROM. *5723*

SAUDI HEART JOURNAL.
King Abdul Aziz University Hospital, P.O. Box 6615, Jeddah 21452, Saudi Arabia. TEL 966-2-6697043. FAX 966-2-6697043. *4609*

SAUDI MEDICAL JOURNAL.
Saudi Arabian Armed Forces Ministry of Defence and Aviation, Medical Services Department, P.O. Box 7897, Riyadh 11159, Saudi Arabia. TEL 966-1-4777714. FAX 966-1-4777194. *4528*

SCANDINAVIAN JOURNAL OF DEVELOPMENT ALTERNATIVES AND AREA STUDIES.
Bethany Books, Sweden, P.O. Box 7444, S-103 91 Stockholm, Sweden. *6343*

SCANDINAVIAN STUDIES (PROVO).
Society for the Advancement of Scandinavian Study, c/o Office of Sec. Treas., 3003 JKHB, Brigham Young University, Provo, UT 84602-6118. TEL 801-378-5598. FAX 801-378-4649. *4263*

SCHOLASTIC UPDATE.
Scholastic Inc., 555 Broadway, New York, NY 10012-3999. TEL 212-343-6100.
Producer(s): University Microfilms International. *1805*

SCHWEIZERISCHE ZEITSCHRIFT FUER VOLKSWIRTSCHAFT UND STATISTIK.
Helbing und Lichtenhahn Verlag AG, Freie Str. 84, CH-4051 Basel, Switzerland. TEL 41-61-2721116. FAX 41-61-2721150.
Producer(s): SilverPlatter Information, Inc.. *959*

SCIENCE ACTIVITIES.
Heldref Publications, 1319 Eighteenth St., N.W., Washington, DC 20036-1802. TEL 202-296-6267. FAX 202-296-5149.
Producer(s): University Microfilms International. *2371*

SCIENCE CITATION INDEX.
Institute for Scientific Information, 3501 Market St., Philadelphia, PA 19104. TEL 215-386-0100. FAX 215-386-2991.
Producer(s): Institute for Scientific Information (SCI CDE). *6304*

SCIENCE NEWS.
Science Service, Inc., 1719 N St., N.W., Washington, DC 20036. TEL 202-785-2255. FAX 202-659-0365.
Producer(s): University Microfilms International. *6281*

SCITECH BOOK NEWS.
Book News, Inc. (Portland), 5600 N.E. Hassalo St., Portland, OR 97213. TEL 503-281-9230. FAX 503-287-4485. *545*

SCITECH REFERENCE PLUS.
R.R. Bowker, A Division of Reed Elsevier Inc., 121 Chanlon Rd., New Providence, NJ 07974. TEL 908-665-2866. FAX 908-665-3528.
Available only on CD-ROM. Producer(s): Bowker Electronic Publishing. *6304*

SCULPTURE REVIEW.
National Sculpture Society, 1177 Ave. of the Americas, New York, NY 10036. TEL 212-764-5645. FAX 212-764-5651. *451*

SEA GRANT ABSTRACTS.
Woods Hole Data Base, Inc., Box 712, Woods Hole, MA 02543. TEL 508-548-2743.
Producer(s): NISC (Oceanographic & Marine Resources). *2221*

SEARCHING DIALOG: THE COMPLETE GUIDE.
Dialog Information Services, Inc. (Palo Alto), 3460 Hillview Ave., Palo Alto, CA 94304. TEL 415-858-3785. FAX 415-858-7069. *4026*

SECURITE ET SANTE AU TRAVAIL.
International Labour Office, International Occupational Safety and Health Information Centre, CH-1211 Geneva 22, Switzerland. TEL 41-22-799-6740. FAX 41-22-798-6253.
Producer(s): SilverPlatter Information, Inc.. *5261*

SEIBT INDUSTRIEKATALOG.
Seibt Verlag GmbH, Leopoldstr. 208, 80804 Munich, Germany. TEL 49-89-360903-0. FAX 49-89-364317. *1639*

SEIBT MEDIZINISCHE TECHNIK.
Seibt Verlag GmbH, Leopoldstr. 208, 80804 Munich, Germany. TEL 49-89-360903-0. FAX 49-89-364317. *4529*

SEIBT OBERFLAECHENTECHNIK.
Seibt Verlag GmbH, Leopoldstr. 208, 80804 Munich, Germany. TEL 49-89-360903-0. FAX 49-89-364317. *5591*

SEIBT UMWELT TECHNIK.
Seibt Verlag GmbH, Leopoldstr. 208, 80804 Munich, Germany. TEL 49-89-360903-0. FAX 49-89-364317. *2819*

SERIALS DIRECTORY.
EBSCO Industries, Inc., Title Information Department, 5724 Hwy. 280 East, Birmingham, AL 35242. TEL 205-991-5600. FAX 205-995-1582. *546*

SESAME BULLETIN.
Centre de Cooperation Internationale en Recherche Agronomique pour le Developpement (CIRAD), B.P. 5035, 34032 Montpellier Cedex 1, France. TEL 67-61-58-00. FAX 67-61-58-20. *150*

SEVENTEEN.
K-III Communications Corp., 745 Fifth Ave., New York, NY 10151. TEL 212-745-0100.
Producer(s): University Microfilms International. *7006*

SHAREDEBATE INTERNATIONAL.
Applied Foresight, Inc., Box 20607, Bloomington, MN 55420. FAX 612-933-3092. *6343*

SHENGLI KEXUE JINZHAN.
Zhongguo Shengli Xuehui, 38 Xueyuan Rd., Beijing Medical University, Beijing 100083, People's Republic of China. TEL 861-209-1150. FAX 861-202-9252. *794*

SHOPPING CENTER DIRECTORY.
National Research Bureau, Inc. (Chicago), 150 N. Wacker Dr., Ste. 2222, Chicago, IL 60606-1608. TEL 312-541-0100 FAX 312-541-1492. *1639*

SICHUAN HUANJING.
Sichuan Huanjing Bianjibu, 18 Renmin Nanlu 4 Duan (Section 4), Chengdu, Sichuan 610041, People's Republic of China. TEL 028-5580473. *2819*

SIDE EFFECTS OF DRUGS ANNUAL.
Elsevier Science B.V.. Books Division, P.O. Box 211, 1000 AE Amsterdam, Netherlands. TEL 31-20-4853911. FAX 31-20-4853705.
Producer(s): SilverPlatter Information, Inc. (SEDBASE). *5443*

SINGAPORE JOURNAL OF OBSTETRICS & GYNAECOLOGY.
Obstetrical and Gynaecological Society of Singapore, c/o National University Hospital Dept. of O & G, Lower Kent Ridge Road, Singapore 0511, Singapore. TEL 7724267. FAX 779-4753. *4745*

SINGAPORE MEDICAL JOURNAL.
Singapore Medical Association, Level 2, Alumni Medical Centre, 2 College Rd., Singapore 0316, Singapore. TEL 2231264. FAX 2247827. *4531*

SINGAPORE MONTHLY TRADE STATISTICS: IMPORTS & EXPORTS.
Trade Statistics, 303 Upper Serangoon Rd., P.O. Box 485, Singapore 1334, Singapore. *1025*

SINGAPORE NATIONAL BIBLIOGRAPHY.
National Library Board, 91 Stamford Rd., Singapore 178896, Singapore. TEL 65-332-3683. FAX 65-332-3684. *3368*

SINGAPORE PERIODICALS INDEX.
National Library Board, 91 Stamford Rd., Singapore 1778896, Singapore. TEL 65-332-3683. FAX 65-332-3684. *26*

SINGAPORE TRADE CONNECTION.
Singapore Trade Development Board, 1 Maritime Square No. 10-40, World Trade Centre, Telok Blangah Rd., Singapore 0409, Singapore. TEL 279-0426. FAX 278-7023.
Available only on CD-ROM. *1254*

SMALL PRESS RECORD OF BOOKS IN PRINT.
Dustbooks, Box 100, Paradise, CA 95967. TEL 916-877-6110. FAX 916-877-0222.
Available only on CD-ROM. *546*

SOCIAL PLANNING - POLICY & DEVELOPMENT ABSTRACTS.
Sociological Abstracts, Inc., Box 22206, San Diego, CA 92192-0206. TEL 619-695-8803. FAX 619-695-0416.
Producer(s): NISC (SocioFile), SilverPlatter Information, Inc. (SocioFile). *6402*

SOCIAL POLICY.
Union Institute, 25 W. 43rd St., Rm. 620, New York, NY 10036. TEL 212-642-2929. FAX 212-642-1956.
Producer(s): H.W. Wilson *6431*

SOCIAL SCIENCES CITATION INDEX.
Institute for Scientific Information, 3501 Market St., Philadelphia, PA 19104. TEL 215-386-0100. FAX 215-386-2991.
Producer(s): Institute for Scientific Information (SSCI). *6358*

SOCIAL SCIENCES INDEX.
H.W. Wilson Co., 950 University Ave., Bronx, NY 10452. TEL 718-588-8400. FAX 718-590-1617.
Producer(s): SilverPlatter Information, Inc., H.W. Wilson. *6358*

SOCIAL WORK ABSTRACTS.
N A S W Press, 750 First St., N.E., Ste. 700, Washington, DC 20002-4241. TEL 202-408-8600. FAX 202-336-8312.
Producer(s): SilverPlatter Information, Inc. (SWAB-PLUS). *6402*

SOCIETY.
Transaction Publishers, Transaction Periodicals Consortium, Department E092, Rutgers University, New Brunswick, NJ 08903. TEL 908-445-2280. FAX 908-445-3138. *6347*

SOCIO-ECONOMIC SERIES.
Natural Resources Institute, Central Ave., Chatham Maritime, Kent ME4 4TB, England. TEL 44-1634-880088. FAX 44-1634-830066. *152*

SOCIOLOGICA.
Universidad Autonoma Metropolitana, Departamento de Sociologia, Av. San Pablo 18C, Azcapotzalco, 02200 Mexico, D.F., Mexico. TEL 525-724-4339. FAX 525-394-8093. *6422*

SOCIOLOGICAL ABSTRACTS.
Sociological Abstracts, Inc. Box 22206, San Diego, CA 92192-0206. TEL 619-695-3803. FAX 619-695-0416.
Producer(s): NISC (Sociofile), SilverPlatter Information, Inc. (Sociofile). *6442*

SOFTWARE ABSTRACTS FOR ENGINEERS.
C I T I S Ltd., 2 Rosemount Terrace, Blackrock, Dublin, Ireland. TEL 353-1-2886227. FAX 353-1-885971. *2003*

THE SOFTWARE USERS YEAR BOOK.
V N U Business Publications BV, 32-34 Broadwick St., London W1A 2HG, England. TEL 071-439-4242. FAX 071-437-7906. *2116*

SOLAR-GEOPHYSICAL DATA. PART 1 - PROMPT REPORTS.
U.S. National Geophysical Data Center, 325 Broadway, Boulder, CO 80303-3328. TEL 303-497-6836. FAX 303-497-6513. *486*

SOLAR-GEOPHYSICAL DATA: PART 2 - COMPREHENSIVE REPORTS.
U.S. National Geophysical Data Center, 325 Broadway, Boulder, CO 80303-3328. TEL 303-497-6836. FAX 303-497-6513. *486*

IL SOLE 24 ORE.
Editrice Il Sole - 24 Ore, S.p.A., Via Lomazzo 52, 20154 Milan, Italy. TEL 02-31031. FAX 02-312055.
Producer(s): Chadwyck-Healey Inc.. *3186*

IL SOLE 24 ORE SU C D - R O M.
Chadwyck-Healey Ltd., The Quorum, Barnwell Rd., Cambridge CB5 8SW, England. TEL 44-1223-215512. FAX 44-1223-215514.
Available only on CD-ROM. Producer(s): Chadwyck-Healey Inc.. *3186*

SOLEIL.
Soleil, 925 chemin St.-Louis, C.P. 1547 Terminus, Quebec, PQ G1K 7J6, Canada. TEL 418-686-3233. FAX 418-686-3260. *3125*

SORKINS DIRECTORY OF BUSINESS & GOVERNMENT (CHICAGO EDITION).
Sorkins Directories, Inc., 1001 Craig Rd., Ste. 260, St. Louis, MO 63146. TEL 314-872-2101. FAX 314-872-2102. *1531*

SOURCEMEX.
University of New Mexico, Latin American Institute, 801 Yale N.E., Albuquerque, NM 87131-1016. TEL 505-277-6839. FAX 505-277-5989.
Producer(s): NISC (Latin American Studies - Vol.2). *1240*

SOUTH AFRICAN CRIMINAL LAW REPORTS.
Juta & Co. Ltd., P.O. Box 14373, Kenwyn 7790, South Africa. TEL 27-21-7975101. FAX 27-21-7970121. *3913*

SOUTH AFRICAN LABOUR LIBRARY.
Juta & Co. Ltd., P.O. Box 14373, Kenwyn 7790, South Africa. TEL 27-21-7975101. FAX 27-21-7970121.
Available only on CD-ROM. *1395*

SOUTH AFRICAN LAW REPORTS.
Juta & Co. Ltd., P.O. Box 14373, Kenwyn 7790, South Africa. TEL 27-21-7975101. FAX 27-21-7970121. *3850*

SOUTH AFRICAN STATUTES.
Juta & Co. Ltd., P.O. Box 14373, Kenwyn 7790, South Africa. TEL 27-21-7975101. FAX 27-21-7970121.
Available only on CD-ROM. *3850*

SOUTH ASIAN SURVEY.
Sage Publications India Pvt. Ltd., P.O. Box 4215, New Delhi 110 048, India. TEL 91-11-644-4958. FAX 91-11-647-2426.
Producer(s): SilverPlatter Information, Inc.. *3384*

SOUTH CAROLINA BUSINESS DIRECTORY.
American Business Directories 5711 S. 86th Circle, Box 27347, Omaha, NE 68127. TEL 402-593-4600. FAX 402-331-5481. *1640*

SOUTH CAROLINA MANUFACTURERS REGISTER.
Manufacturers' News, Inc., 1633 Central St., Evanston, IL 60201-1569. TEL 847-864-7000. FAX 847-332-1100. *1640*

SOUTH DAKOTA BUSINESS DIRECTORY.
American Business Directories 5711 S. 86th Circle, Box 27347, Omaha, NE 68127. TEL 402-593-4600. FAX 402-331-5481. *1640*

SOUTHEAST ASIAN JOURNAL OF TROPICAL MEDICINE AND PUBLIC HEALTH.
Southeast Asian Ministers of Education Organisation (SEAMEO), Regional Tropical Medicine & Public Health Network (TROPMED), 420-6 Rajvithi Rd., Bangkok 10400, Thailand. TEL 66-2-2457193. FAX 66-2-2477721. *4628*

SOUTHEAST POWER REPORT.
McGraw-Hill Companies, 1221 Ave. of the Americas, New York, NY 10020. TEL 212-512-2000.
Producer(s): SilverPlatter Information, Inc. (McGraw-Hill Energy Library). *2558*

SOUTHERN AFRICAN BOOKS IN PRINT.
Books in Print Information Services, P.O. Box 15129, Vlaeberg 8018, South Africa. FAX 27-21-4615467. *547*

SOUTHERN CALIFORNIA BUSINESS DIRECTORY.
American Business Directories 5711 S. 86th Circle, Box 27347, Omaha, NE 68127. TEL 402-593-4600. FAX 402-331-5481. *1640*

SOUTHERN CALIFORNIA BUSINESS DIRECTORY AND BUYERS GUIDE.
Database Publishing Company, 1590 S. Lewis St., Anaheim, CA 92805-6423. TEL 714-778-6400. FAX 714-778-6811. *1640*

THE SOUTHERN REVIEW.
Louisiana State University, 43 Allen Hall, Baton Rouge, LA 70803-5005. TEL 504-388-5108. FAX 504-388-5098. *4269*

SPECIAL EDUCATION LAW AND LITIGATION TREATISE.
L R P Publications 747 Dresher Rd., Box 980, Horsham, PA 19044-0980. TEL 215-784-0941. FAX 215-784-9639. *2475*

SPECIALIST.
Doctor Publications (Pvt) Ltd., P.O. Box 8766, Raja Ghazanfar Ali Rd., Saddar, Karachi, Pakistan. TEL 92-21-5688791. FAX 92-21-5689860. *4533*

SPECIFICATION.
E M A P - Architecture, 33-39 Bowling Green Ln., London EC1R 0DA, England. TEL 44-171-837-1212. FAX 44-171-833-8072. *874*

SPEEDNEWS.
Speednews, Inc., 1801 Ave. of the Stars, Ste. 210, Los Angeles, CA 90067-5904. TEL 310-203-9603. FAX 310-203-9352. *6765*

SPORTSEARCH.
Sport Information Resource Centre (SIRC), 1600 James Naismith Drive, Gloucester, ON K1B 5N4, Canada. TEL 613-748-5658. FAX 613-748-5701.
Producer(s): SilverPlatter Information, Inc.. *6495*

STANDARD & POOR'S CORPORATE REGISTERED BOND INTEREST RECORD.
Standard & Poor's Corporation 25 Broadway, New York, NY 10004. TEL 212-208-8000. *1352*

STANDARD & POOR'S CORPORATION RECORDS.
Standard & Poor's 25 Broadway, New York, NY 10004. TEL 212-208-8000. FAX 212-412-0459. *1353*

STANDARD & POOR'S CORPORATION RECORDS. DAILY NEWS SECTION.
Standard & Poor's 25 Broadway, New York, NY 10004. TEL 212-208-8000. *962*

STANDARD & POOR'S REGISTER OF CORPORATIONS, DIRECTORS AND EXECUTIVES.
Standard & Poor's 25 Broadway, New York, NY 10004. TEL 212-208-8000. *1446*

STANDARD & POOR'S STOCK REPORTS. AMERICAN STOCK EXCHANGE.
Standard & Poor's 25 Broadway, New York, NY 10004. TEL 212-208-8000. *1353*

STANDARD & POOR'S STOCK REPORTS. N A S D A Q AND REGIONAL EXCHANGES.
Standard & Poor's 25 Broadway, New York, NY 10004. TEL 212-208-8000. *1353*

STANDARD & POOR'S STOCK REPORTS. NEW YORK STOCK EXCHANGE.
Standard & Poor's 25 Broadway, New York, NY 10004. TEL 212-208-8000. *1353*

STANDARD DIRECTORY OF ADVERTISERS (GEOGRAPHIC EDITION).
National Register Publishing, A Division of Reed Elsevier Inc., 121 Chanlon Rd., New Providence, NJ 07974. TEL 908-464-6800. FAX 908-464-3553.
Producer(s): Bowker Electronic Publishing. *1641*

STANDARD DIRECTORY OF ADVERTISING AGENCIES.
National Register Publishing, A Division of Reed Elsevier Inc., 121 Chanlon Rd., New Providence, NJ 07974. TEL 908-464-6800. FAX 908-464-3500.
Producer(s): Bowker Electronic Publishing. *1641*

STANDARD DIRECTORY OF INTERNATIONAL ADVERTISERS AND AGENCIES.
National Register Publishing, A Division of Reed Elsevier Inc., 121 Chanlon Rd., New Providence, NJ 07974. TEL 908-464-6800. FAX 908-665-6688.
Producer(s): Bowker Electronic Publishing. *1641*

STANDARD FEDERAL TAX REPORTS.
Commerce Clearing House, Inc., 2700 Lake Cook Rd., Riverwoods, IL 60015. TEL 847-267-7000. FAX 800-224-8299. *1562*

STANDARD PERIODICAL DIRECTORY.
Oxbridge Communications, Inc., 150 Fifth Ave., New York, NY 10011. TEL 212-741-0231. FAX 212-633-2938. *547*

STAPLES' GUIDE TO NEW ZEALAND INCOME TAX PRACTICE.
Brooker's Limited, Level 1 - Telecom Networks House, 68-86 Jervois Quay, Wellington, New Zealand. TEL 64-4-4998178. FAX 64-4-4998173. *1562*

STATE ACADEMIES OF SCIENCE ABSTRACTS.
AcadSci, Inc., Box 4157, Huntington, WV 25729. TEL 304-696-6742. FAX 304-525-5669. Available only on CD-ROM. *6304*

STATE ADMINISTRATIVE OFFICIALS.
The Council of State Governments, 3560 Iron Works Pike, Box 11910, Lexington, KY 40578-1910. TEL 606-244-8000. FAX 606-244-8001. *5921*

STATE TAX GUIDE.
Commerce Clearing House, Inc., 2700 Lake Cook Rd., Riverwoods, IL 60015. TEL 847-267-7000. FAX 800-224-8299. *1562*

STATE TAX NOTES.
Tax Analysts, 6830 N. Fairfax Dr., Arlington, VA 22213. TEL 703-533-4400. FAX 703-533-4444. *1562*

STATE TAX REPORTS.
Commerce Clearing House, Inc., 2700 Lake Cook Rd., Riverwoods, IL 60015. TEL 847-267-7000. FAX 800-224-8299. *1562*

STATE YELLOW BOOK.
Leadership Directories, Inc., 104 Fifth Ave., 2nd Fl., New York, NY 10011. TEL 212-627-4140. FAX 212-645-0931.
Producer(s): Chadwyck-Healey Inc.. *5924*

STATISTICAL REFERENCE INDEX.
Congressional Information Service, Inc., A member of the LEXIS-NEXIS family, 4520 East-West Hwy., Bethesda, MD 20814-3389. TEL 301-654-1550. FAX 301-654-4033. *6635*

STATISTIK UDEN GRAENSER.
Danmarks Statistik, Sejroegade 11, DK-2100 Copenhagen Oe, Denmark. TEL 45-31-17-31-50. FAX 45-31-18-48-01.
Available only on CD-ROM. *6636*

STATISTISCHES JAHRBUCH FUER DIE BUNDESREPUBLIK DEUTSCHLAND.
Statistisches Bundesamt, 65180 Wiesbaden, Germany. TEL 49-611-75-1. FAX 49-611-724000. *6637*

STEELS ALERT.
Cambridge Scientific Abstracts, 7200 Wisconsin Ave., Bethesda, MD 20814. TEL 301-961-6750. FAX 301-961-6720.
Producer(s): Knight-Ridder, Inc.. *4985*

STEVENS ENVIRONMENTAL SOURCEBOOK.
Stevens Publishing Corporation, 3700 J.H. Kultgen Frwy., Waco, TX 76706. TEL 817-776-9000. FAX 817-776-9018. *2820*

STOCKS IN THE S & P 500. OFFICIAL SERIES.
Standard & Poor's 25 Broadway, New York, NY 10004. TEL 212-208-8000. *1354*

STRUCTURAL SURVEY.
M C B University Press Ltd., 60-62 Toller Ln., Bradford, W. Yorks BD8 9BY, England. TEL 44-1274-777700. FAX 44-1274-785200. *875*

STRUCTURE.
Current Biology Ltd., 400 Market St., Ste. 700, Philadelphia, PA 19106. FAX 215-574-2270. *609*

STRUCTURIST.
Eli Bornstein, Ed. & Pub., Box 378, RPO University, University of Saskatchewan, Saskatoon, SK S7N 4J8, Canada. TEL 306-966-4198. FAX 306-966-8670. *453*

STUDIES IN INFORMATICS AND CONTROL.
Research Institute for Informatics, 8-10 Averescu Ave., 71316 Bucharest 1, Rumania. TEL 40-1-2223778. FAX 40-1-3128539. *4047*

STYLE (EDITION FRANCAISE).
N.V. Trends Magazines Bd. Louis Schmidt 97, 1040 Brussels, Belgium. TEL 32-2-7321860. FAX 32-2-7344018. *3115*

STYLE (NEDERLANDSE EDITIE).
N.V. Trends Magazines Bd. Louis Schmidt 97, 1040 Brussels, Belgium. TEL 32-2-7321860. FAX 32-2-7344018. *3115*

SUBJECT GUIDE TO BOOKS IN PRINT.
R.R. Bowker, A Division of Reed Elsevier Inc., 121 Chanlon Rd., New Providence, NJ 07974. TEL 908-464-6800. FAX 908-665-3502.
Producer(s): Bowker Electronic Publishing (Books In Print PLUS). *547*

SUBJECT GUIDE TO CHILDREN'S BOOKS IN PRINT.
R.R. Bowker, A Division of Reed Elsevier Inc., 121 Chanlon Rd., New Providence, NJ 07974. TEL 908-464-6800. FAX 908-665-3502.
Producer(s): Bowker Electronic Publishing. *547*

SUDAN MEDICAL JOURNAL.
Khartoum University Press, P.O. Box 321, Khartoum, Sudan. *4534*

SUNDAY TELEGRAPH.
Telegraph plc., 1 Canada Sq., Canary Wharf, London E14 5DT, England. TEL 44-171-538-5000. FAX 44-171-538-6242.
Producer(s): Chadwyck-Healey Inc.. *3160*

THE SUNDAY TIMES.
Times Newspapers Ltd., Virginia St., London E1 9XT, England. TEL 44-171-782-7000.
Producer(s): Chadwyck-Healey Inc.. *3160*

SUOMEN KIRJALLISUUS.
Helsingin Yliopiston Kirjasto, Unioninkatu 36, FIN-00014 Helsinki, University of Helsinki, Finland. FAX 358-0-70844341. *548*

SUPERCOMPUTING PROCEEDINGS.
I E E E Computer Society Press, 10662 Los Vaqueros Circle, Los Alamitos, CA 90720-1264. TEL 714-821-8380. FAX 714-821-4641. *2059*

SURFACE-MOUNTED DISCRETES D.A.T.A. DIGEST.
D.A.T.A. Business Publishing 15 Inverness Way E., Box 6510, Englewood, CO 80155-6510. FAX 303-799-4082. *2720*

SURFACE-MOUNTED INTEGRATED CIRCUITS D.A.T.A. DIGEST.
D.A.T.A. Business Publishing 15 Inverness Way E., Box 6510, Englewood, CO 80155-6510. FAX 303-799-4082. *2720*

SURFACE TREATMENT TECHNOLOGY ABSTRACTS.
Finishing Publications Ltd., 105 Whitney Dr., Stevenage, Herts. SG1 4DF, England. TEL 01438-745115. FAX 01438-364536. *4985*

SURGICAL PRODUCT COMPARISON SYSTEM.
E C R I, 5200 Butler Pike, Plymouth Meeting, PA 19462. TEL 610-825-6000. FAX 610-834-1275.
Producer(s): Knight-Ridder, Inc.. *4921*

SWISS FINANCIAL YEAR BOOK.
Elvetica Edizioni S.A., Via Vela 6, Casella Postale 134, CH-6834 Morbio, Switzerland. TEL 091-435056. FAX 091-437605. *1243*

SYNOPSIS OF BOILER & PRESSURE VESSEL LAWS, RULES AND REGULATIONS.
Uniform Boiler & Pressure Vessel Laws Society, Inc., 308 N. Evergreen Rd., Ste. 240, Louisville, KY 40243-1076. TEL 502-244-6029. *2770*

SYNTHESIS - REGENERATION: A MAGAZINE OF GREEN SOCIAL THOUGHT.
W D Press, Box 24115, St. Louis, MO 63130. TEL 314-727-5393 *5502*

SYSTEM UBW.
Ahriman Verlag GmbH, Stuebeweg 60, 79108 Freiburg, Germany. TEL 49-761-502303. FAX 49-761-502247. *5884*

T O M.
Information Access Company 362 Lakeside Dr., Foster City, CA 94404. TEL 415-378-5200. FAX 415-378-5369. *27*

T R I S ELECTRONIC BIBLIOGRAPHIC DATA BASE.
U.S. National Research Council, Transportation Research Board, 2101 Constitution Ave., N.W., Washington, DC 20418. TEL 202-334-3250. FAX 202-334-3495.
Producer(s): SilverPlatter Information, Inc.. *6746*

DIE TAGESZEITUNG.
T A Z Verlagsgenossenschaft e.G., Kochstr. 18, 10969 Berlin, Germany. TEL 030-25902-0. FAX 030-2518095. *3150*

TAIWAN BICYCLES & PARTS GUIDE (YEAR).
Trade Winds, Inc., No. 7, Lane 75, Yungkang St., P.O. Box 7-179 Taipei, Taiwan 10602, Republic of China. TEL 02-393-2718. FAX 02-396-4022. *1642*

TAIWAN YELLOW PAGES.
Taiwan Yellow Pages Corp., Chouwoo House 2F, P.O. Box 84-84, 57 Tunhwa S. Rd., Sec. 1, Taipei, Taiwan, Republic of China. TEL 886-2-570-9966. FAX 886-2-578-2739. *1642*

TAX ANALYST MICROFICHE DATABASE.
Tax Analysts, 6830 Fairfax Dr., Arlington, VA 22213. TEL 703-533-4400. FAX 703-533-4444. *1564*

TAX ANALYSTS LETTER RULING SERVICE.
Tax Analysts, 6830 N Fairfax Dr., Arlington, VA 22213. TEL 703-553-4400. FAX 703-533-4444. *1564*

THE TAX DIRECTORY.
Tax Analysts, 6830 N. Fairfax Dr., Arlington, VA 22213. TEL 703-553-4400. FAX 703-533-4444. *1564*

THE TAX EXECUTIVE.
Tax Executives Institute, Inc., 1001 Pennsylvania Ave., N.W., No. 320, Washington, DC 20004-2505. TEL 202-638-5601. FAX 202-638-5607. *1564*

TAX LIBRARY.
Juta & Co. Ltd., P.O. Box 14373, Kenwyn 7790, South Africa. TEL 27-21-7975101. FAX 27-21-7970121.
Available only on CD-ROM. *1565*

TAX MANAGEMENT COUNTRY PORTFOLIOS.
Tax Management, Inc. Heron House, 10 Dean Farrar St., London SW1H 0DX England. TEL 0171-222-8831. FAX 0171-222-0294. *1565*

TAX NOTES.
Tax Analysts, 6830 N. Fairfax Dr., Arlington, VA 22213. TEL 703-533-4400. FAX 703-533-4444. *1566*

TAX NOTES INTERNATIONAL.
Tax Analysts, 6830 N. Fairfax Dr., Arlington, VA 22213. TEL 703-533-4400. FAX 703-533-4444. *1566*

TAX TREATIES (RIVERWOODS).
Commerce Clearing House, Inc., 2700 Lake Cook Rd., Riverwoods, IL 60015. TEL 847-267-7000. FAX 800-224-8299. *1567*

TAX TREATIES DATA BASE ON C D - R O M.
I B F D Publications B.V., P.O. Box 20237, 1000 HE Amsterdam, Netherlands. TEL 31-20-6267726. FAX 31-20-6228658. *1567*

TAXATION IN LATIN AMERICA.
I B F D Publications B.V., P.O. Box 20237, 1000 HE Amsterdam, Netherlands. TEL 31-20-6267726. FAX 31-20-6228658. *1568*

TEACHING PRE K-8.
Early Years, Inc. 40 Richards Ave., Norwalk, CT 06854-2309. TEL 203-855-2650. FAX 203-855-2656. *2504*

TECH - EUROPE.
Europe Information Service, Rue de Geneve, 6, 1140 Brussels, Belgium. TEL 32-2-242-6020. FAX 32-2-242-9410. *1929*

TECHNICAL ANALYSIS OF STOCKS & COMMODITIES.
Technical Analysis, Inc., 4757 California Ave., S.W., Seattle, WA 98116-4499. TEL 206-938-0570. FAX 206-938-1307. *1355*

TECHNICAL GUIDE BOOK.
Screenprinting & Graphic Imaging Association International, 10015 Main St., Fairfax, VA 22031. TEL 703-385-1335. *5879*

TECHNIQUES.
American Vocational Association, 1410 King St., Alexandria, VA 22314. TEL 703-683-3111. FAX 703-683-7424.
Producer(s): University Microfilms International. *2402*

TELECOM SOURCES.
Asian Sources Media Group, G.P.O. Box 12367, Hong Kong. TEL 852-2555-4777 *1917*

TELEFACTS.
Datapro Research Group, McGraw-Hill House, Shoppenhangers Rd., Maidenhead, Berks. SL6 2QL, England. TEL 01628-773277. *1952*

TELEFAXBUCH DER DEUTSCHEN TELEKOM AG.
Deutsche Telekom Medien GmbH, Wiesenhuettenstr. 18, 60329 Frankfurt a.M., Germany. TEL 069-2682-0. FAX 069-26821101. *1933*

THE TELEGRAPH ON C D - R O M.
Chadwyck-Healey Ltd., The Quorum, Barnwell Rd., Cambridge CB5 8SW, England. TEL 44-1223-215512. FAX 44-1223-215514.
Available only on CD-ROM. Producer(s): Chadwyck-Healey Inc.. *3160*

TENNESSEE BUSINESS DIRECTORY.
American Business Directories 5711 S. 86th Circle, Box 27347, Omaha, NE 68127. TEL 402-593-4600. FAX 402-331-5481 *1642*

TENNESSEE RULES OF COURT, STATE AND FEDERAL.
West Publishing Corp., 620 Opperman Dr., Eagan, MN 55123. TEL 612-687-8000. FAX 612-687-7302. *3954*

TESTZENTRALE TESTKATALOG.
Hogrefe Verlag fuer Psychologie, Rohnsweg 25, 37085 Goettingen, Germany. TEL 49-551-49609-0. FAX 49-551-4960988. *5890*

TEXAS BUSINESS DIRECTORY.
American Business Directories 5711 S. 86th Circle, Box 27347, Omaha, NE 68127. TEL 402-593-4600. FAX 402-331-5481. *1643*

DIE TEXTIL-INDUSTRIE UND IHRE HELFER.
Industrieschau-Verlagsgesellschaft mbH, Postfach 100262, 64202 Darmstadt, Germany. TEL 49-6151-3892-0. FAX 49-615--33164. *6686*

TEXTILE TECHNOLOGY DIGEST.
Institute of Textile Technology, 2551 Ivy Rd, Charlottesville, VA 22903. TEL 804-296-5511. FAX 804-977-5400. *6690*

THEOLOGY.
Society for Promoting Christian Knowledge, Holy Trinity Church, Marylebone Rd., London NW1 4DU, England. TEL 44-171-387-5232. FAX 44-171-388-2352. *6099*

CD-ROM

THEORETICAL CHEMICAL ENGINEERING.
The Royal Society of Chemistry, Thomas Graham House, Science Park, Milton Rd., Cambridge CB4 4WF, England. TEL 44-1223-420066. FAX 44-1223-423429.
Producer(s): Knight-Ridder, Inc.. *2630*

THESAURUS OF E R I C DESCRIPTORS.
Oryx Press, 4041 N. Central Ave., No. 700, Phoenix, AZ 85012-3397. TEL 602-265-2651. FAX 602-265-6250.
Producer(s): NISC (ERIC). *2394*

THOMAS REGISTER OF AMERICAN MANUFACTURERS AND THOMAS REGISTER CATALOG FILE.
Thomas Publishing Company, Five Penn Plaza, 9th Fl., New York, NY 10001. TEL 212-290-7277. FAX 212-290-7365.
Producer(s): Knight-Ridder, Inc.. *1488*

THOM'S COMMERCIAL DIRECTORY.
Thom's Directories Ltd., 38 Merrion Sq., Dublin 2, Ireland. TEL 353-1-6767481. FAX 353-1-6762620. *1643*

THOM'S DUBLIN & COUNTY STREET DIRECTORY.
Thom's Directories Ltd., 38 Merrion Sq., Dublin 2, Ireland. TEL 353-1-6767481. FAX 353-1-6762620. *3275*

THORPE - R O M.
D.W. Thorpe, A member of the Reed Elsevier plc group, 18 Salmon St., Port Melbourne, Vic. 3207, Australia. TEL 03-9245-7370. FAX 03-9245-7395.
Available only on CD-ROM. *548*

THYRISTOR D.A.T.A. DIGEST.
D.A.T.A. Business Publishing 15 Inverness Way E., Box 6510, Englewood, CO 80155-6510. FAX 303-799-4082. *2721*

TIME.
Time Inc. Time & Life Bldg., Rockefeller Center, 1271 Ave. of the Americas, New York, NY 10020-1393. TEL 212-522-1212. FAX 212-522-0003.
Producer(s): University Microfilms International. *3240*

THE TIMES.
Times Newspapers Ltd., Virginia St., London E1 9XT, England. TEL 44-171-782-7000.
Producer(s): Chadwyck-Healey Inc.. *3160*

THE TIMES AND THE SUNDAY TIMES COMPACT DISC EDITION.
Chadwyck-Healey Ltd., The Quorum, Barnwell Rd., Cambridge CB5 8SW, England. TEL 44-1223-215512. FAX 44-1223-215514.
Available only on CD-ROM. Producer(s): Chadwyck-Healey Inc.. *3160*

TIMES EDUCATIONAL SUPPLEMENT.
Times Supplements Ltd., Admiral House, 66-68 E. Smithfield, London E1 9XY, England. TEL 44-171-782-3000. FAX 44-171-782-3200.
Producer(s): Chadwyck-Healey Inc.. *2378*

TIMES HIGHER EDUCATION SUPPLEMENT.
Times Supplements Ltd., Admiral House, 66-68 E. Smithfield, London E1 9XY, England. TEL 44-171-782-3000. FAX 44-171-782-3300.
Producer(s): Chadwyck-Healey Inc.. *2444*

TIMES INDEX.
Primary Source Media, P.O. Box 45, Reading RG1 8HF, England. TEL 44-1734-583247. FAX 44-1734-5912325. *3716*

THE TIMES LITERARY SUPPLEMENT INDEX.
Primary Source Media, P.O. Box 45, Reading RG1 8HF, England. TEL 44-1734-583247. FAX 44-1734-591325. *4295*

TOHKAI SEIKEI GEKA GAISHO KENKYU KAISHI.
Tohkai Seikei Geka Gaisho Kenkyukai, Gifu Kenritsu Tajimi Byoin Seikei Geka, 5-161, Maebatacho, Tajimi-shi, Gifu-ken 507, Japan. TEL 0572-22-5311. FAX 0572-25-1246. *4792*

TOHKAI SEKITSUI GEKA.
Tohkai Sekitsui Geka Konwakai, Gifu Kenritsu Tajimi Byoin, 5-161, Maebbatacho, Tajimi-shi, Gifuken 507, Japan. TEL 0572-22-5311. FAX 0572-25-1246. *4792*

TOKAI JOURNAL OF EXPERIMENTAL AND CLINICAL MEDICINE.
Tokai Daigaku Shuppansha - Tokai University Press (Kanagawa), Boseidai, Isehara, Kanagawa 259-11, Japan. FAX 0463-91-3328. *4538*

TONGJI MEDICAL UNIVERSITY. JOURNAL.
Tongji Medical University, c/o Prof. Liu Xunfang, Wuhan, Hubei 430030, People's Republic of China. TEL 01-506-6688. FAX 01-506-3101. *4538*

TOP MANAGEMENT BELGIUM - LUXEMBURG.
Alain Renier & Co. S.P.R.L., Ave. des Casernes 41A, 1040 Brussels, Belgium. TEL 32-2-6462740. FAX 32-2-6462017. *1448*

TOXICOLOGY ABSTRACTS.
Cambridge Scientific Abstracts, 7200 Wisconsin Ave., 6th Fl., Bethesda, MD 20814. TEL 301-961-6750. FAX 301-961-6720.
Producer(s): Knight-Ridder, Inc. (Toxicology & Pharmacology), SilverPlatter Information, Inc. (POLTOX1). *5451*

TRAINING FOR QUALITY.
M C B University Press Ltd., 60-62 Toller Ln., Bradford, W. Yorks BD8 9BY, England. TEL 44-1274-777700. FAX 44-1274-785200. *1513*

TRANSISTOR D.A.T.A. DIGEST.
D.A.T.A. Business Publishing 15 Inverness Way E., Box 6510, Englewood, CO 80155-6510. FAX 303-799-4082. *2721*

TRANSPORT EUROPE.
Europe Information Service, Rue de Geneve, 6, 1140 Brussels, Belgium. TEL 32-2-242-6020. FAX 32-2-242-9410. *6730*

TRENDS.
N.V. Trends Magazines Bd. Louis Schmidt 97, 1040 Brussels, Belgium. TEL 32-2-7321860. FAX 32-2-7344018. *3115*

TRENDS - TENDANCES.
N.V. Trends Magazines Bd. Louis Schmidt 97, 1040 Brussels, Belgium. TEL 32-2-7321860. FAX 32-2-7344018. *3115*

TRIBUNALI AMMINISTRATIVI REGIONALI.
Casa Editrice Italedi, Piazza Cavour 19, 00193 Rome, Italy. TEL 39-6-3210803. *3859*

TULANE TAX INSTITUTE.
Totaltape Publishing, 9417 Princess Palm Ave., Ste. 400, Tampa, FL 33619. FAX 800-345-8273. *1569*

LA TUNISIE MEDICALE.
Societe Tunisienne des Sciences Medicales, 16 Rue Touraine, 1002 Tunis - Belvedere, Tunisia. TEL 790-924. *4539*

TUTTODOLCE.
Essepiesse s.r.l., Via G. Galilei 14, 20124 Milan, Italy. FAX 39-2-654119. *3002*

U C DAVIS LAW REVIEW.
University of California at Davis, School of Law, Martin Luther King, Jr. Hall, Davis, CA 95616. TEL 916-752-2551. FAX 916-752-4704. *3859*

U K O P.
Chadwyck-Healey Ltd., The Quorum, Barnwell Rd., Cambridge CB5 8SW, England. TEL 44-1223-215512. FAX 44-1223-215514.
Available only on CD-ROM. Producer(s): Chadwyck-Healey Inc.. *5925*

U N B I S PLUS ON C D - R O M.
Chadwyck-Healey Inc., 1101 King Rd., Alexandria, VA 22314. TEL 703-683-4890. FAX 703-683-7589.
Available only on CD-ROM. Producer(s): Chadwyck-Healey Inc.. *5723*

U S A TODAY INDEX.
U M I Company 300 N. Zeeb Rd., Ann Arbor, MI 48106-1346. TEL 313-761-4700. FAX 800-864-0019. *3716*

U S GOVERNMENT PERIODICALS INDEX.
Congressional Information Service, Part of the Reed Elsevier group, 4520 East-West Hwy., Bethesda, MD 20814-3389. TEL 301-654-1550. FAX 301-654-4033. *27*

U S NEWS & WORLD REPORT.
U S News & World Report Inc., 1290 Ave. of the Americas, Ste. 600, New York, NY 10104. TEL 212-830-1500.
Producer(s): University Microfilms International. *3240*

ULRICH'S INTERNATIONAL PERIODICALS DIRECTORY.
R.R. Bowker, A Division of Reed Elsevier Inc., 121 Chanlon Rd., New Providence, NJ 07974. TEL 908-665-2847. FAX 908-771-7725.
Producer(s): Bowker Electronic Publishing (Ulrich's PLUS). *549*

ULRICH'S PLUS.
R.R. Bowker Electronic Publishing, 121 Chanlon Rd., New Providence, NJ 07974. FAX 908-665-3528.
Available only on CD-ROM. Producer(s): Bowker Electronic Publishing (Ulrich's PLUS). *549*

ULRICH'S UPDATE.
R.R. Bowker, A Division of Reed Elsevier Inc., 121 Chanlon Rd., New Providence, NJ 07974. TEL 908-665-2847. FAX 908-771-7725.
Producer(s): Bowker Electronic Publishing (Ulrich's PLUS). *549*

ULSTER MEDICAL JOURNAL.
Ulster Medical Society, c/o Queens University Medical Library, Institute of Clinical Science, Grosvenor Rd., Belfast BT12 6BA, Northern Ireland. TEL 44-1232-322043. FAX 44-1232-247068.
Producer(s): SilverPlatter Information, Inc. (MEDLINE). *4540*

UNIFORM COMMERCIAL CODE FILING GUIDE.
U C C Guide Inc., Rte. 9W, Southgate Plaza, Box 338, Ravena, NY 12143-1338. TEL 518-156-3366. FAX 800-822-0703. *3907*

UNITED NATIONS. STATISTICAL YEARBOOK.
United Nations Publications, Room DC2-853, New York, NY 10017. TEL 212-963-3802. FAX 212-963-3489. *6641*

UNITED NATIONS DOCUMENTS AND PUBLICATIONS.
NewsBank, Inc., 58 Pine St., New Canaan, CT 06840-5426. TEL 800-752-4650. FAX 203-966-6254. *549*

U.S. BUREAU OF LABOR STATISTICS. C P I DETAILED REPORT.
U.S. Bureau of Labor Statistics, 2 Massachusetts Ave., N.E., Washington, DC 20212. TEL 202-655-4000. *1244*

U.S. BUREAU OF MINES MINERALS AND MATERIALS INFORMATION ON C D - R O M.
U.S. Bureau of Mines, Office of Public Information, 810 Seventh St., N.W., MS-1040, Washington, DC 20241-0001. TEL 202-501-9649. FAX 202-219-2493.
Available only on CD-ROM. *5091*

U.S. CONGRESS. CONGRESSIONAL RECORD.
U.S. Congress, Washington, DC 20515. TEL 202-275-2051. FAX 202-275-0019. *5714*

U.S. DEPARTMENT OF JUSTICE. BUREAU OF JUSTICE STATISTICS. CRIME AND JUSTICE DATA.
Inter-University Consortium for Political and Social Research, National Archive of Criminal Justice Data, Box 1248, Ann Arbor, MI 48106-1248. TEL 313-764-2570. FAX 313-764-8041. *2180*

U.S. LIBRARY OF CONGRESS. CATALOGER'S DESKTOP.
U.S. Library of Congress, Cataloging Distribution Service, Washington, DC 20541-5017. TEL 202-707-6100. FAX 202-707-1334.
Available only on CD-ROM. *550*

U.S. LIBRARY OF CONGRESS. MUSIC CATALOG ON C D - R O M.
U.S. Library of Congress, Cataloging Distribution Service, Washington, DC 20541-5017. TEL 202-707-6100. FAX 202-707-1334.
Available only on CD-ROM. *551*

U.S. LIBRARY OF CONGRESS. MUSIC CATALOG ON MICROFICHE.
Advanced Library Systems, Inc., 100 Brickstone Sq., Box 246, Andover, MA 01810-0005. TEL 508-470-0610. FAX 508-475-1072.
Producer(s): NISC (Muse). *5209*

U.S. LIBRARY OF CONGRESS. NEW SERIAL TITLES.
U.S. Library of Congress, Cataloging Distribution Service, Washington, DC 20541-5017. TEL 202-707-6100. FAX 202-707-1334. *551*

U.S. OCCUPATIONAL SAFETY AND HEALTH REVIEW COMMISSION. ADMINISTRATIVE LAW JUDGE AND COMMISSION DECISIONS.
U.S. Occupational Safety and Health Review Commission, 1 Lafayette Ctr., 1120 20th St., N.W. 9th Fl., Washington, DC 20036-3419. TEL 202-606-5100. *5259*

U.S. PATENT AND TRADEMARK OFFICE. OFFICIAL GAZETTE. PATENTS.
U.S. Patent and Trademark Office, General Information Services Division, Crystal City Plaza 3, Rm. 2C02, Washington, DC 20231. TEL 703-308-4357. FAX 703-305-7786. *5345*

U.S. PATENT AND TRADEMARK OFFICE. OFFICIAL GAZETTE. TRADEMARKS.
U.S. Patent and Trademark Office, General Information Services Division, Crystal Plaza 3, Rm. 2C02, Washington, DC 20231. TEL 703-308-4357. FAX 703-305-7786. *5345*

UNITED STATES CODE UNANNOTATED.
Gould Publications, 1333 N. U.S. Hwy. 17-92, Longwood, FL 32750-3724. TEL 407-695-9500. FAX 407-695-9500. *3861*

UNIVERSITY OF ALEXANDRIA. FACULTY OF MEDICINE. BULLETIN.
University of Alexandria, Faculty of Medicine, 22 Sharia al-Gaish, Al-Shatby, Alexandria, Egypt. *4541*

UNIVERSITY OF COLORADO LAW REVIEW.
University of Colorado Law Review, Inc., 290 Fleming Law Bldg., Campus Box 401, Boulder, CO 80309-0401. TEL 303-492-6145. FAX 303-492-1200. *3862*

UNIVERSITY OF KUWAIT. JOURNAL (SCIENCE).
University of Kuwait, Faculty of Science, P.O. Box 5969, Kuwait. *6293*

UNIVERSITY OF PENNSYLVANIA LAW REVIEW.
University of Pennsylvania Law Review, 3400 Chestnut St., Philadelphia, PA 19104-6204. TEL 215-898-7060. FAX 215-573-2005. *3863*

UPSTATE NEW YORK BUSINESS DIRECTORY.
American Business Directories 5711 S. 86th Circle, Box 27347, Omaha, NE 68127. TEL 402-593-4600. FAX 402-331-5481. *1647*

URBADISC CD-ROM.
London Research Centre, Research Library, 81 Black Prince Rd., London SE1 7SZ, England. TEL 44-171-627-9661. FAX 44-171-627-8674. Available only on CD-ROM. *3603*

URBAN ABSTRACTS.
London Research Centre, Research Library, 81 Black Prince Rd., London SE1 7SZ, England. TEL 44-171-627-9666. FAX 44-171-627-9674. *5935*

UTAH BUSINESS DIRECTORY.
American Business Directories 5711 S. 86th Circle, Box 27347, Omaha, NE 68127. TEL 402-593-4600. FAX 402-331-5481. *1647*

UTILITY ENVIRONMENT REPORT.
McGraw-Hill, Inc., Energy & Business Newsletters, 1221 Ave. of the Americas, 36th Fl., New York, NY 10020. TEL 212-512-6410. Producer(s): SilverPlatter Information, Inc. (McGraw-Hill Energy Library). *2722*

V L M - VERZEICHNIS LIEFERBARER MUSIKALIEN C D - R O M.
Buchhaendler-Vereinigung GmbH, Postfach 100442, 60004 Frankfurt a.M., Germany. TEL 49-69-13060. FAX 49-69-1306201. Available only on CD-ROM. *5209*

V M R STANDARD USED CAR PRICES.
V M R International, Inc., 41 N. Main St., N. Grafton, MA 01536. TEL 508-839-6707. FAX 508-839-6266. *6805*

V O, VIE OUVRIERE.
Revue Vie Ouvriere Inc., 1215 Visitation, Ste. 101, Montreal, PQ H2L 3B5, Canada. TEL 514-523-5998. FAX 514-527-3403. *3126*

V R S.
Erich Schmidt Verlag GmbH & Co. (Berlin), Genthiner Str. 30G, 10785 Berlin, Germany. TEL 49-30-2500850. FAX 49-30-25008521. *3879*

V V B - VERZEICHNIS VERGRIFFENER BUECHER C D - R O M.
Buchhaendler-Vereinigung GmbH, Postfach 100442, 60004 Frankfurt a.M., Germany. TEL 49-69-1306-0. FAX 49-69-1306201. Available only on CD-ROM. *552*

VAARD I NORDEN.
Sygeplejerskerners Samarbejde i Norden, P.O. Box 2681, St. Hanshaugen, N-131 Oslo 1, Norway. TEL 47-22-38-20-00. FAX 47-22-38-54-47. Producer(s): SilverPlatter Information, Inc.. *4729*

VADEMECUM DEUTSCHER LEHR- UND FORSCHUNGSSTAETTEN. STAETTEN DER FORSCHUNG.
Raabe Fachverlag fuer Wissenschaftsinformation, Koenigswintererstr. 418, 53227 Bonn, Germany. TEL 49-228-9702025. FAX 49-228-9702036. *6294*

VADEMECUM VOOR HET VERZEKERINGSWEZEN.
Nijgh Periodieken B.V., Postbus 122, 3100 AC Schiedam, Netherlands. TEL 31-10-4274100. FAX 31-10-4739911. *3668*

VANDERBILT RUBBER HANDBOOK.
R.T. Vanderbilt Co., Inc., 30 Winfield St., Norwalk, CT 06855. TEL 203-353-1400. FAX 203-853-1452. *6220*

VARIETY'S VIDEO DIRECTORY PLUS.
R.R. Bowker, A Division of Reed Elsevier Inc., 121 Chanlon Rd., New Providence, NJ 07974. TEL 908-665-2866. FAX 908-665-3528. Available only on CD-ROM. Producer(s): Bowker Electronic Publishing. *5114*

VARTA - FUEHRER.
VARTA Aktiengesellschaft, Postfach 540, 30405 Hannover, Germany. TEL 49-511-3401310. *3573*

VATRA.
Uniunea Scriitorilor din Romania, Inspectoratul pentru Cultura al Judecului Mures, Str. Primariei, Nr. 1, 4300 Tirgu-Mures, Rumania. TEL 40-65-165008. *4171*

VENDOR CATALOG SERVICES INDEX.
Information Handling Services, 15 Inverness Way E., Englewood, CO 80150. TEL 303-790-0600. FAX 303-799-4085. *1647*

VERBAENDE, BEHOERDEN, ORGANISATIONEN DER WIRTSCHAFT.
Verlag Hoppenstedt GmbH, Havelstr. 9, 64295 Darmstadt, Germany. TEL 49-6151-380-0. FAX 49-6151-380-360. *1245*

VERFAHRENSTECHNISCHE BERICHTE.
Verlag Hoppenstedt GmbH, Havelstr. 9, 64295 Darmstadt, Germany. TEL 49-6151-380-0. FAX 49-6151-380360. *2631*

VERMONT BUSINESS DIRECTORY.
American Business Directories 5711 S. 86th Circle, Box 27347, Omaha, NE 68127. TEL 402-593-4600. FAX 402-331-5481. *1647*

VERZEICHNIS AUSLAENDISCHER ZEITSCHRIFTEN IN SCHWEIZERISCHEN BIBLIOTHEKEN.
Schweizerische Landesbibliothek, Hallwylstr. 15, CH-3003 Bern, Switzerland. TEL 41-31-3228911. FAX 41-31-3228463. *552*

VERZEICHNIS LIEFERBARER BUECHER.
K.G. Saur Verlag KG, A member of the Reed Elsevier plc group, Ortlerstr. 8, 81373 Munich, Germany. TEL 49-89-76902-0. FAX 49-89-76902150. Producer(s): K.G. Saur Verlag. *552*

VERZEICHNIS LIEFERBARER BUECHER - C D - R O M.
K.G. Saur Verlag KG, A member of the Reed Elsevier plc group, Ortlerstr. 8, 81373 Munich, Germany. TEL 49-89-76902-0. FAX 49-89-76901250. Available only on CD-ROM. Producer(s): K.G. Saur Verlag. *552*

VICTORIAN STATUTES CUMULATIVE SUPPLEMENT.
L B C Information Services, 50 Waterloo Rd., N. Ryde, N.S.W. 2113, Australia. TEL 61-2-99366444. FAX 61-2-8589706. *3893*

VIDEOLOG.
Trade Service Information Ltd., Cherryholt Rd., Stamford, Lincs. PE9 2HT, England. TEL 44-1780-64331. FAX 44-1780-482067. *1980*

VIE ET SANTE.
Editions Vie et Sante, 60 av. Emile Zola, 77192 Dammarie les Lys Cedex, France. FAX 64-87-00-66. *5537*

VIGILE URBANO.
Maggioli Editore, Viale Vespucci 12-n, Casella Postale 290, 47037 Rimini, Italy. TEL 0541-626777. FAX 0541-622220. *2178*

VIRGINIA BUSINESS DIRECTORY.
American Business Directories 5711 S. 86th Circle, Box 27347, Omaha, NE 68127. TEL 402-593-4600. FAX 402-331-5481. *1647*

VIRGINIA COURT RULES AND PROCEDURE, STATE AND FEDERAL.
West Publishing Corp., 620 Opperman Dr., Eagan, MN 55123. TEL 612-687-7302. FAX 612-687-7302. *3955*

VIRGINIA INDUSTRIAL DIRECTORY.
Virginia Chamber of Commerce, 9 S. Fifth St., Richmond, VA 23219. TEL 800-477-7682. FAX 804-783-6112. *1647*

VIROLOGY.
Academic Press, Inc., Journal Division, 525 B St., Ste. 1900, San Diego, CA 92101-4495. TEL 619-230-1340. FAX 619-688-6800. *767*

VIROLOGY AND AIDS ABSTRACTS.
Cambridge Scientific Abstracts, 7200 Wisconsin Ave., 6th Fl., Bethesda, MD 20814. TEL 301-961-6750. FAX 301-961-6720. Producer(s): SilverPlatter Information, Inc.. *4576*

VISUALISATION OF ENGINEERING RESEARCH.
John Wiley & Sons Ltd., Journals, Baffins Ln., Chichester, W. Sussex PO19 1UD, England. TEL 44-1243-779777. FAX 44-1243-843232. Available only on CD-ROM. *2681*

DE VOLKSKRANT.
De Volkskrant, P.O. Box 1002, 1000 BA Amsterdam, Netherlands. TEL 31-20-5629222. FAX 31-20-5626289. *3196*

THE WALL STREET JOURNAL INDEX.
U M I Company 300 N. Zeeb Rd., Ann Arbor, MI 48106. TEL 313-761-4700. FAX 800-864-0019. *1126*

WALL STREET LETTER.
Institutional Investor Newsletters, 477 Madison Ave., New York, NY 10022. TEL 212-224-3233. FAX 212-224-3353. *1358*

WANG IN THE NEWS.
Publications & Communications, Inc. 12416 Hymeadow, Austin, TX 78750-1849. TEL 512-250-9023. FAX 512-331-3900. *2033*

WARTA DEMOGRAFI.
University of Indonesia, Faculty of Economics, Demographic Institute, Jalan Salemba Raya 4, Jakarta 10430, Indonesia. TEL 06221-336434. FAX 06221-3102457. *5793*

WASHINGTON BUSINESS DIRECTORY.
American Business Directories 5711 S. 86th Circle, Box 27347, Omaha, NE 68127. TEL 402-593-4600. FAX 402-331-5481. *1648*

WASHINGTON COURT RULES, STATE AND FEDERAL.
West Publishing Corp., 620 Opperman Dr., Eagan, MN 55123. TEL 621-687-8000. FAX 612-687-7302. *3955*

WASHINGTON, DC AREA BUSINESS DIRECTORY.
American Business Directories 5711 S. 86th Circle, Box 27347, Omaha, NE 68127. TEL 402-593-4600. FAX 402-331-5481. *1548*

CD-ROM

WASHINGTON MANUFACTURERS REGISTER.
Database Publishing Company, 1590 S. Lewis St., Anaheim, CA 92805-6423. TEL 714-778-6400. FAX 714-778-6811. *1648*

THE WASHINGTON POST INDEX.
U M I Company 300 N. Zeeb Rd., Ann Arbor, MI 48106. TEL 313-761-4700. FAX 800-864-0019. *3716*

WATER RESOURCES ABSTRACTS (BETHESDA).
Cambridge Scientific Abstracts, 7200 Wisconsin Ave., 6th Fl., Bethesda, MD 20814. TEL 301-961-6750. FAX 301-961-6720.
Producer(s): NISC, SilverPlatter Information, Inc.. *6983*

WATER RESOURCES ABSTRACTS (C D - R O M).
National Information Services Corporation (NISC), Wyman Towers, Ste. 6, 3100 St. Paul St., Baltimore, MD 21218. TEL 410-243-0797. FAX 410-243-0982.
Available only on CD-ROM. Producer(s): NISC. *6983*

WATER RESOURCES WORLDWIDE.
National Information Services Corporation (NISC), Ste. 6, Wyman Towers, 3100 St. Paul St., Baltimore, MD 21218. TEL 410-243-0797. FAX 410-243-0982.
Available only on CD-ROM. Producer(s): NISC. *6983*

WEATHERWISE.
Heldref Publications, 1319 Eighteenth St., N.W., Washington, DC 20036-1802. TEL 202-296-6267. FAX 202-296-5149.
Producer(s): University Microfilms International. *5008*

WEEKEND KNACK.
N.V. R M G Bd. Louis Schmidt 97, 1040 Brussels, Belgium. TEL 32-2-7361175. FAX 32-2-73444018. *3116*

WEEKLY LAW REPORTS.
Incorporated Council of Law Reporting for England and Wales, 3 Stone Bldgs., Lincoln's Inn, London WC2A 3XN, England. TEL 44-171-242-6471. FAX 44-171-831-5247. *3868*

WER BAUT MASCHINEN IN DEUTSCHLAND.
Verlag Hoppenstedt GmbH, Havelstr. 9, 64295 Darmstadt, Germany. TEL 49-6151-380-0. FAX 49-6151-380-360. *2773*

WER LIEFERT WAS?
Wer Liefert Was? GmbH, Normannenweg 16-20, 20537 Hamburg, Germany. TEL 49-40-25440-0. FAX 49-40-25440100. *1648*

WER LIEFERT WAS? LIGHT.
Wer Liefert Was? GmbH, Normannenweg 16-20, 20537 Hamburg, Germany. TEL 49-40-25440-0. FAX 49-40-25440100.
Available only on CD-ROM. *1648*

WEST EUROPEAN POLITICS.
Frank Cass, Newbury House, 890-900 Eastern Ave., Newbury Park, Ilford, Essex 1G2 7HH. TEL 44-181-599-8866. FAX 44-181-599-0954. *5778*

WEST VIRGINIA BUSINESS DIRECTORY.
American Business Directories 5711 S. 86th Circle, Box 27347, Omaha, NE 68127. TEL 402-593-4600. FAX 402-331-5481. *1648*

WEST'S ALASKA REPORTER.
West Publishing Corp., 620 Opperman Dr., Eagan, MN 55123. TEL 312-387-8000. FAX 612-387-7302. *3868*

WEST'S CALIFORNIA REPORTER.
West Publishing Corp., 620 Opperman Dr., Eagan, MN 55123. TEL 612-687-8000. FAX 612-687-7302. *3868*

WEST'S FEDERAL REPORTER.
West Publishing Corp., 620 Opperman Dr., Eagan, MN 55123. TEL 612-687-8000. FAX 612-687-7302. *3888*

WEST'S FEDERAL RULES DECISIONS.
West Publishing Corp., 620 Opperman Dr., Eagan, MN 55213. TEL 612-687-8000. FAX 612-687-7302. *3868*

WEST'S LOUISIANA RULES OF COURT, STATE.
West Publishing Corp., 620 Opperman Dr., Eagan, MN 55123. TEL 612-687-8000. FAX 612-687-7302. *3955*

WETTBEWERBSRECHT VOLLTEXT C D - R O M.
C.H. Beck'sche Verlagsbuchhandlung, Wilhelmstr. 9, 80801 Munich, Germany. TEL 49-89-38189338. FAX 49-89-38189398.
Available only on CD-ROM. *5346*

WHAT'S ON SATELLITE.
Design Publishers, 800 Siesta Way, Sonoma, CA 95476-4413. TEL 707-939-9306. *1920*

WHICH DEGREE. WHICH UNIVERSITY: UNIVERSITIES - COLLEGES.
Hobsons Publishing plc., Bateman St., Cambridge CB2 1LZ, England. TEL 44-1223-460366. FAX 44-1223-301506.
Available only on CD-ROM. *2448*

WHITAKER'S BOOKS IN PRINT.
J. Whitaker & Sons Ltd., 12 Dyott St., London WC1A 1DF, England. TEL 071-836-8911. FAX 071-836-2909.
Producer(s): Bowker Electronic Publishing. *553*

WHO WAS WHO IN AMERICA.
Marquis Who's Who, A Division of Reed Elsevier Inc., 121 Chanlon Rd., New Providence, NJ 07974. TEL 908-464-6800. FAX 908-665-6688.
Producer(s): Bowker Electronic Publishing. *560*

WHO'S WHO IN AMERICA.
Marquis Who's Who, A Division of Reed Elsevier Inc., 121 Chanlon Rd., New Providence, NJ 07974. TEL 908-464-6800. FAX 908-665-6688.
Producer(s): Bowker Electronic Publishing. *560*

WHO'S WHO IN AMERICAN EDUCATION.
Marquis Who's Who, A Division of Reed Elsevier Inc., 121 Chanlon Rd., New Providence, NJ 07974. TEL 908-464-6800. FAX 908-665-6688.
Producer(s): Bowker Electronic Publishing. *560*

WHO'S WHO IN AMERICAN LAW.
Marquis Who's Who, A Division of Reed Elsevier Inc., 121 Chanlon Rd., New Providence, NJ 07974. TEL 908-464-6800. FAX 908-665-6688.
Producer(s): Bowker Electronic Publishing. *3869*

WHO'S WHO IN AMERICAN NURSING.
Marquis Who's Who, A Division of Reed Elsevier Inc., 121 Chanlon Rd., New Providence, NJ 07974. TEL 908-464-6800. FAX 908-665-6688.
Producer(s): Bowker Electronic Publishing. *4730*

WHO'S WHO IN FINANCE AND INDUSTRY.
Marquis Who's Who, A Division of Reed Elsevier Inc., 121 Chanlon Rd., New Providence, NJ 07974. TEL 908-464-6800. FAX 908-665-6688.
Producer(s): Bowker Electronic Publishing. *561*

WHO'S WHO IN SCIENCE AND ENGINEERING.
Marquis Who's Who, A Division of Reed Elsevier Inc., 121 Chanlon Rd., New Providence, NJ 07974. TEL 908-464-6800. FAX 908-665-6688.
Producer(s): Bowker Electronic Publishing. *562*

WHO'S WHO IN THE EAST.
Marquis Who's Who, A Division of Reed Elsevier Inc., 121 Chanlon Rd., New Providence, NJ 07974. TEL 908-464-6800. FAX 908-665-6688.
Producer(s): Bowker Electronic Publishing. *562*

WHO'S WHO IN THE MIDWEST.
Marquis Who's Who, A Division of Reed Elsevier Inc., 121 Chanlon Rd., New Providence, NJ 07974. TEL 908-464-6800. FAX 908-665-6688.
Producer(s): Bowker Electronic Publishing. *562*

WHO'S WHO IN THE SOUTH AND SOUTHWEST.
Marquis Who's Who, A Division of Reed Elsevier Inc., 121 Chanlon Rd., New Providence, NJ 07974. TEL 908-464-6800. FAX 908-665-6688.
Producer(s): Bowker Electronic Publishing. *562*

WHO'S WHO IN THE WEST.
Marquis Who's Who, A Division of Reed Elsevier Inc., 121 Chanlon Rd., New Providence, NJ 07974. TEL 908-464-6800. FAX 908-665-6688.
Producer(s): Bowker Electronic Publishing. *562*

WHO'S WHO IN THE WORLD.
Marquis Who's Who, A Division of Reed Elsevier Inc., 121 Chanlon Rd., New Providence, NJ 07974. TEL 800-521-8110. FAX 908-665-6688.
Producer(s): Bowker Electronic Publishing. *562*

WHO'S WHO OF AMERICAN WOMEN.
Marquis Who's Who, A Division of Reed Elsevier Inc., 121 Chanlon Rd., New Providence, NJ 07974. TEL 908-464-6800. FAX 908-665-6688.
Producer(s): Bowker Electronic Publishing. *562*

WICKS SUBJECT INDEX OF COMMONWEALTH LEGISLATION.
Law Book Co. Ltd., 44-50 Waterloo Rd., North Ryde, N.S.W. 2113, Australia. TEL 61-2-99366444. FAX 61-2-8887240. *3880*

WILDLIFE REVIEW (FORT COLLINS).
U.S. National Biological Service, Information Transfer Center, 1201 Oak Ridge Dr., No. 200, Ft. Collins, CO 80525-5562. TEL 970-226-9401. FAX 970-226-9455.
Producer(s): NISC (Wildlife Worldwide). *2148*

WILDLIFE WORLDWIDE.
National Information Services Corporation (NISC), Ste. 6, Wyman Towers, 3100 St. Paul St., Baltimore, MD 21218. TEL 410-243-0797. FAX 410-243-0982.
Available only on CD-ROM. Producer(s): NISC. *625*

WILEY EMPLOYMENT LAW UPDATE ON C D - R O M.
John Wiley & Sons, Inc., Law Publications, 605 Third Ave., New York, NY 10158. TEL 212-850-6645. FAX 212-850-6021.
Available only on CD-ROM. *3869*

WILSON APPLIED SCIENCE & TECHNOLOGY ABSTRACTS.
H.W. Wilson Co., 950 University Ave., Bronx, NY 10452. TEL 718-588-8400. FAX 718-590-1617.
Producer(s): SilverPlatter Information, Inc., H.W. Wilson. *2631*

WILSON ART ABSTRACTS.
H.W. Wilson Co., 950 University Ave., Bronx, NY 10452. TEL 718-588-8400. FAX 718-590-1617.
Producer(s): SilverPlatter Information, Inc., H.W. Wilson (WILSONDISC). *463*

WILSON BUSINESS ABSTRACTS.
H.W. Wilson Co., 950 University Ave., Bronx, NY 10452. TEL 718-588-8400. FAX 718-590-1617.
Producer(s): SilverPlatter Information, Inc., H.W. Wilson (WILSONDISC). *1035*

WILSON EDUCATION ABSTRACTS.
H.W. Wilson Co., 950 University Ave., Bronx, NY 10452. TEL 718-588-8400. FAX 718-590-1617.
Producer(s): SilverPlatter Information, Inc., H.W. Wilson (WILSONDISC). *2395*

WILSON GENERAL SCIENCE ABSTRACTS.
H.W. Wilson Co., 950 University Ave., Bronx, NY 10452. TEL 718-588-8400. FAX 718-590-1617.
Producer(s): SilverPlatter Information, Inc., H.W. Wilson (WILSONDISC). *6304*

WILSON HUMANITIES ABSTRACTS.
H.W. Wilson Co., 950 University Ave., Bronx, NY 10452. TEL 718-588-8400. FAX 718-590-1617.
Producer(s): H.W. Wilson (WILSONDISC). *3632*

WILSON SOCIAL SCIENCES ABSTRACTS.
H.W. Wilson Co., 950 University Ave., Bronx, NY 10452. TEL 718-588-8400. FAX 718-590-1617.
Producer(s): SilverPlatter Information, Inc., H.W. Wilson. *6358*

WINE ON LINE.
Enterprises Publishing, 400 E. 59th St., Ste. 9F, New York, NY 10022. TEL 212-755-4363. FAX 212-755-4365. *513*

WIRTSCHAFTS UND STEUER HEFTE.
D I E Verlag H. Schaefer GmbH, Postfach 2243, 61292 Bad Homburg, Germany. TEL 49-6172-9583-0. FAX 49-6172-71288. *971*

WISCONSIN BUSINESS DIRECTORY.
American Business Directories 5711 S. 86th Circle, Box 27347, Omaha, NE 68127. TEL 402-593-4600. FAX 402-331-5481. *1649*

CD-ROM

WISCONSIN BUSINESS SERVICE DIRECTORY.
W M C Service Corporation, 501 E. Washington
Ave., Box 352, Madison, WI 53701-0352.
TEL 608-258-3400. FAX 608-258-3413. *1649*

**WISCONSIN COURT RULES AND PROCEDURE,
STATE AND FEDERAL.**
West Publishing Corp., 620 Opperman Dr., Eagan,
MN 55123. TEL 612-687-8000. FAX 612-687-
7302. *3955*

WOMEN IN MANAGEMENT REVIEW & ABSTRACTS.
M C B University Press Ltd., 60-62 Toller Ln.,
Bradford, W. Yorks BD8 9BY, England. TEL 44-
1274-777700. FAX 44-1274-785200. *1450*

WOMEN STUDIES ABSTRACTS.
Transaction Publishers, Transaction Periodicals
Consortium, Department 3092, Rutgers University,
New Brunswick, NJ 08903. TEL 908-445-2280.
FAX 908-445-3138.
Producer(s): NISC (Women's Resources
International). *7022*

WOMEN'S REVIEW OF BOOKS.
Wellesley College, Center for Research on Women,
Wellesley, MA 02181. TEL 617-283-2087.
FAX 617-283-3645. *4173*

WOMEN'S SPORTS AND FITNESS.
2025 Pearl St., Boulder, CO 80302. TEL 303-440-
5111. FAX 303-440-3313.
Producer(s): University Microfilms International.
6492

WORDPERFECT FOR WINDOWS MAGAZINE.
Ivy International Communications, Inc., 270 W.
Center St., Orem, UT 84057. TEL 801-228-9626.
FAX 801-227-3478. *2118*

WORDPERFECT MAGAZINE.
Ivy International Communications, Inc., 270 W.
Center St., Orem, UT 84057. TEL 801-228-9626.
FAX 801-227-3478. *2118*

WORK STUDY.
M C B University Press Ltd., 60-62 Toller Ln.,
Bradford, W. Yorks BD8 9BY, England. TEL 44-
1274-777700. FAX 44-1274-785200. *1450*

WORKGROUP COMPUTING REPORT.
Patricia Seybold Group, 148 State St., 7th Fl.,
Boston, MA 02109. TEL 617-742-5200. FAX 617-
742-1028. *2077*

WORLD AROMATICS AND DERIVATIVES.
S R I Consulting, World Petrochemicals Program,
Chemical Business Research Center, Menlo Park,
CA 94025. TEL 415-859-5211. FAX 415-859-
2182. *1696*

WORLD AVIATION DIRECTORY.
McGraw-Hill Companies, Aviation Week Group (New
York), 1221 Ave. of the Americas, New York, NY
10020. TEL 215-237-4112. FAX 215-586-3232.
81

WORLD C4 HYDROCARBONS AND DERIVATIVES.
S R I Consulting, World Petrochemicals Program,
Chemical Business Research Center, Menlo Park,
CA 94025. TEL 415-859-5211. FAX 415-859-
2182. *1696*

WORLD DATA (YEAR).
World Bank, 1818 H. St., N.W., Washington, DC
20433.
Available only on CD-ROM. *1246*

WORLD DEBT TABLES.
World Bank, 1818 H St., N.W., Washington, DC
20433. TEL 202-473-1155. FAX 202-522-2627.
1317

**WORLD DIRECTORY OF HUMAN RIGHTS RESEARCH
AND TRAINING INSTITUTIONS.**
Unesco Publishing, 7 Place de Fontenoy, 75352
Paris 07SP, France. *1649*

WORLD DRUG MARKET MANUAL.
IMSWORLD Publications Ltd., 7 Harewoood Ave.,
London NW1 6JB, England. TEL 0171-393-5000.
FAX 0171-393-5900. *5447*

WORLD ENERGY AND NUCLEAR DIRECTORY (YEAR).
Longman Group UK Ltd., Westgate House, 6th Fl.,
The High, Harlow, Essex CM20 1YR, England.
TEL 44-1279-442601. FAX 44-1279-444501.
2585

WORLD ETHYLENE AND DERIVATIVES.
S R I Consulting, World Petrochemicals Program,
Chemical Business Research Center, Menlo Park,
CA 94025. TEL 415-859-5211. FAX 415-859-
2182. *1696*

WORLD FACTBOOK.
U.S. National Technical Information Service, 5285
Port Royal Rd., Springfield, VA 22161. TEL 703-
482-0623. *5778*

WORLD FEEDSTOCKS.
S R I Consulting, World Petrochemicals Program,
Chemical Business Research Center, Menlo Park,
CA 94025. TEL 415-859-5211. FAX 415-859-
2182. *1696*

WORLD GUIDE TO LIBRARIES.
K.G. Saur Verlag KG, A member of the Reed
Elsevier plc group, Ortlerstr. 8, 81373 Munich,
Germany. TEL 49-89-76902-0. FAX 49-89-
76902150.
Producer(s): Bowker Electronic Publishing
(Publishing Market Place Reference PLUS). *4035*

WORLD HEALTH.
World Health Organization, Distribution and Sales,
CH-1211 Geneva 27, Switzerland. TEL 41-22-791-
2111. FAX 41-22-791-4857.
Producer(s): University Microfilms International.
5979

**WORLD JOURNAL OF MICROBIOLOGY AND
BIOTECHNOLOGY.**
Rapid Science Publishers, The Old Malthouse,
Paradise St., Oxford OX1 1LD, England. TEL 44-
1865-790447. FAX 44-1865-244012. *768*

WORLD JOURNAL OF SURGERY.
Springer-Verlag, Medical Journals, 175 Fifth Ave.,
New York, NY 10010. TEL 212-460-1500.
FAX 212-473-6272. *4923*

WORLD LITERATURE TODAY.
110 Monnet Hall, University of Oklahoma, Norman,
OK 73019-0375. TEL 405-325-4531. FAX 405-
325-7495. *4297*

WORLD METHANOL AND DERIVATIVES.
S R I Consulting, World Petrochemicals Program,
Chemical Business Research Center, Menlo Park,
CA 94025. TEL 415-859-5211. FAX 415-859-
2182. *1696*

WORLD PRESS REVIEW.
Stanley Foundation (New York), 200 Madison Ave.,
Ste. 2104, New York, NY 10016. TEL 212-889-
5155. FAX 212-389-5634.
Producer(s): University Microfilms International.
4174

WORLD PROPYLENE AND DERIVATIVES.
S R I Consulting, World Petrochemicals Program,
Chemical Business Research Center, Menlo Park,
CA 94025. TEL 415-859-5211. FAX 415-859-
2182. *1696*

WORLD PUBLISHING MONITOR.
Pira International, Rancalls Rd., Leatherhead,
Surrey KT22 7RL, England. TEL 44-1372-802050.
FAX 44-1372-802239.
Producer(s): Knight-Ridder, Inc.. *2004*

**WORLDWIDE DIRECTORY OF DEFENSE
AUTHORITIES.**
Worldwide Government Directories, Inc., 7979 Old
Georgetown Rd., Ste. 900, Bethesda, MD 20814.
TEL 301-718-8770. FAX 301-718-8494. *5054*

WORLDWIDE GOVERNMENT DIRECTORY.
Worldwide Government Directories, Inc., 7979 Old
Georgetown Rd., Ste. 900, Bethesda, MD 20814.
TEL 301-718-8770. FAX 301-718-8494.
Producer(s): Knight-Ridder, Inc.. *1650*

WORLDWIDE TAX TREATIES ON CD-ROM.
Tax Analysts, 6830 N. Fairfax Dr., Arlington, VA
22213. FAX 703-533-4444.
Available only on CD-ROM. *1571*

THE WRITER.
Writer, Inc., 120 Boylston St., Boston, MA 02116.
TEL 617-423-3157.
Producer(s): University Microfilms International.
4287

WULIN.
Guangdong Kexue Puji Chubanshe, 3 Xingping Li,
Dahua Jie, Yingyuan Lu, Guangzhou, Guangdong
510047, People's Republic of China. *6493*

WYOMING BUSINESS DIRECTORY.
American Business Directories 5711 S. 86th Circle,
Box 27347, Omaha, NE 68127. TEL 402-593-
4600. FAX 402-331-5451. *1650*

XIBU TANKUANG GONGCHENG.
Xibu Tankuang Gongcheng Bianjibu, 16 Youhao
Beilu, Urumqi, Xinjiang 830000 People's Republic
of China. TEL 86-991-4818457. FAX 86-991-
4841517. *5082*

YAHOO! INTERNET LIFE.
Ziff-Davis Publishing Co., One Park Ave., New York,
NY 10016. TEL 212-503-4804 FAX 212-503-
5699. *2042*

YANTU GONGCHENG XUEBAO.
Zhongguo Tumu Gongcheng Xuehui, 34 Hujuguan,
Nanjing, Jiangsu 210024, People's Republic of
China. TEL 86-25-6633662. FAX 86-25-3310321.
Available only on CD-ROM. *2676*

**YEAR BOOK OF ANESTHESIOLOGY AND PAIN
MANAGEMENT.**
Mosby - Year Book, Inc., Continuity Division, 200 N.
LaSalle, Chicago, IL 60601. TEL 312-726-9733.
FAX 312-726-6075. *4534*

YEAR BOOK OF CARDIOLOGY.
Mosby - Year Book, Inc., Continuity Division, 200 N.
LaSalle, Chicago, IL 60601. TEL 312-726-9733.
FAX 312-726-6075.
Producer(s): SilverPlatter Information, Inc. (ClinMED-
CD). *4611*

YEAR BOOK OF CRITICAL CARE MEDICINE.
Mosby - Year Book, Inc., Continuity Division, 200 N.
LaSalle, Chicago, IL 60601. TEL 312-726-9733.
Producer(s): SilverPlatter Information, Inc. (ClinMED-
CD). *4545*

YEAR BOOK OF DENTISTRY.
Mosby - Year Book, Inc., Continuity Division, 200 N.
LaSalle, Chicago, IL 60601. TEL 312-726-9733.
FAX 312-726-6075. *4657*

YEAR BOOK OF ENDOCRINOLOGY.
Mosby - Year Book, Inc., Continuity Division, 200 N.
LaSalle, Chicago, IL 60601. TEL 312-726-9733.
FAX 312-726-6075.
Producer(s): SilverPlatter Information, Inc.. *4676*

YEARBOOK OF INTERNATIONAL ORGANIZATIONS.
K.G. Saur Verlag KG, A member of the Reed Elsivier
plc group, Ortlerstr. 8, 81373 Munich, Germany.
TEL 49-89-76902-0. FAX 49-89-75902150.
Producer(s): K.G. Saur Verlag. *5779*

YEAR BOOK OF ONCOLOGY.
Mosby - Year Book, Inc., Continuity Division, 200 N.
LaSalle, Chicago, IL 60601. TEL 312-726-9733.
FAX 312-726-6075.
Producer(s): SilverPlatter Information, Inc.. *4765*

YOD.
Institut National des Langues et Civilisations
Orientales, 2 rue de Lille, 75343 Paris Cedex 07,
France. TEL 49-26-42-74. FAX 49-26-42-99.
6131

YUNNAN ZHONGYI ZAZHI.
Yunnan Sheng Zhongyi Zhongyao Yanjiusuo,
Lianhua Chi, Kunming, Yunnan 650223, People's
Republic of China. TEL 5154-94. *293*

Z D.
Deutsches Bibliotheksinstitut, Abt. 1 - Publikationen,
Alt-Moabit 101A, 10559 Berlin, Germany. TEL 49-
30-39077-0. FAX 49-30-39077100. *553*

**Z V E I ELEKTRO UND ELEKTRONIK -
EINKAUFSFUEHRER.**
Verlag W. Sachon, Schloss Mindelburg, 87714
Mindelheim, Germany. TEL 49-8261-999-0.
FAX 49-8261-999-180. *2651*

ZASSHI KIJI SAKUIN. JINBUN SHAKAI HEN.
National Diet Library, 1-10-1 Nagata-cho, Chiyoda-ku, Tokyo 100, Japan. TEL 03-3581-2331. FAX 03-3597-9104. *3632*

ZEITSCHRIFT FUER VERMOEGENS- UND INVESTITIONSRECHT.
C.H. Beck'sche Verlagsbuchhandlung, Wilhelmstr. 9, 80801 Munich, Germany. TEL 089-38189338. FAX 089-38189398. *1572*

ZEITSCHRIFTEN - DATENBANK (Z D B).
Deutsches Bibliotheksinstitut, Abt. 1 - Publikationen, Alt-Moabit 101A, 10559 Berlin, Germany. TEL 49-30-39077-0. FAX 49-30-39077100. *4036*

ZENTRALBLATT FUER MATHEMATIK UND IHRE GRENZGEBIETE.
Springer-Verlag, Heidelberger Platz 3, 14197 Berlin, Germany. TEL 49-30-8207-0. FAX 49-30-8214091. *4406*

ZHEJIANG ZHONGYI ZAZHI.
Zhejiang Sheng Zhongyiyao Yanjiusuo, 26 Tianmushan Lu, Hangzhou, Zhejiang 310007, People's Republic of China. *293*

ZHONGGUO DAODAN YU HANGTIAN WENZHAI.
Hangtian Gongye Zong Gongsi, Keji Qingbao-suo, P.O. Box 1408, 1 Binhe Lu, Hepingli, Beijing 100013, People's Republic of China. TEL 86-10-837-2847. FAX 86-10-422-7606. *83*

ZHONGGUO YAOXUE ZAZHI.
Zhongguo Yaoxuehui, 42 Dongsi Xidajie, Beijing 100710, People's Republic of China. TEL 01-5133311. FAX 01-8354609. *5448*

ZHONGGUO YIXUE KEXUEYUAN XUEBAO.
Chinese Academy of Medical Sciences (CAMS), 9 Dong Dan San Tiao, Beijing 100730, People's Republic of China. TEL 86-10-5133074. *4547*

ZHONGGUO ZHONGLIU LINCHUANG.
Tianjin Zhongliu Yanjiusuo, Zhongguo Kang-Ai Xiehui, Huan-hu-xi Lu, Tiyuanbei, Hexi Qu, Tianjin 300060, People's Republic of China. TEL 86-22-374477. *4765*

ZHONGHUA CHUANRANBING ZAZHI.
Zhonghua Yixuehui, Shanghai Fenhui, 1623 Beijing Xilu, Shanghai 200040, People's Republic of China. TEL 86-21-62531885. FAX 86-21-62550842. *4547*

ZHONGHUA ERKE ZAZHI.
Guoji Shudian, Qikan Bu, Chegongzhuang Xilu 21, P.O. Box 399, Beijing, People's Republic of China. *4815*

ZHONGHUA FU-CHANKE ZAZHI.
Guoji Shudian, Qikan Bu, Chegongzhuang Xilu 21, P.O. Box 399, Beijing 100044, People's Republic of China. *4747*

ZHONGHUA GUKE ZAZHI.
Zhonghua Guke Zazhi Bianjibu, Tianjin Yiyuan, Jiefang Nanlu, Weiti Daokou, Tianjin 300211, People's Republic of China. TEL 86-22-2384734. *4793*

ZHONGHUA LAONIAN YIXUE ZAZHI.
Zhonghua Yixuehui, Beijing Yiyuan (Beijing Hospital), 1 Dahua Lu, Beijing 100730, People's Republic of China. TEL 5126611. *3298*

ZHONGHUA LILIAO ZAZHI.
Zhonghua Yixuehui, Tang Gang Zi, Anshan, Liaoning 114048, People's Republic of China. *4820*

ZHONGHUA LIUXINGBINGXUE ZAZHI.
Zhonghua Yufang Yixuehui, 16, Hepingli Zhongjie, Beijing 100013, People's Republic of China. TEL 4218457. *4547*

ZHONGHUA MAZUIXUE ZAZHI.
Guoji Shudian, Qikan Bu, Chegongzhuang Xilu 21, P.O. Box 399, Beijing 100044, People's Republic of China. *4594*

ZHONGHUA NEIFENMI DAIXIE ZAZHI.
Shanghai Institute of Endocrinology, 197 Ruijin Lu Sec. 2, Shanghai, People's Republic of China. TEL 8610-8232343. FAX 8610-8211656. *4676*

ZHONGHUA NEIKE ZAZHI.
Guoji Shudian, Qikan Bu, Chegongzhuang Xilu 21, P.O. Box 399, Beijing 100044, People's Republic of China. *4708*

ZHONGHUA SHENJING-JINGSHENKE ZAZHI.
Chinese Medical Association, P.O. Box 2258, 42 Dongsi Xidajie, Beijing 100710, People's Republic of China. TEL 1-550394. *4872*

ZHONGHUA SHENJING WAIKE ZAZHI.
Beijing Neurosurgical Institute, No.6, Tiantan Xili, Beijing 100050, People's Republic of China. TEL 86-10-5113169. FAX 86-10-7018349. *4872*

ZHONGHUA WAIKE ZAZHI.
Guoji Shudian, Qikan Bu, Chegongzhuang Xilu 21, P.O. Box 399, Beijing 100044, People's Republic of China. *4924*

ZHONGHUA WULI YIXUE ZAZHI.
Hebei Yixue Yuan, 5 Chang'an Xilu, Shijiazhuang, Hebei 050017, People's Republic of China. TEL 44121. *4820*

ZHONGHUA XIAOHUA ZAZHI.
Zhonghua Yixuehui, Shanghai Fenhui, 1623 Beijing Xilu, Shanghai 200040, People's Republic of China. TEL 86-21-62531885. FAX 86-21-62550842. *4697*

ZHONGHUA XIN-XUEGUANBING ZAZHI.
Chinese Medical Association, P.O. Box 2258, 42 Dongsi Xidajie, Beijing 100710, People's Republic of China. TEL 1-550394. *4611*

ZHONGHUA XUEYEXUE ZAZHI.
Zhongguo Yixue Kexueyuan, Xueye Yanjiusuo, 288 Nanjing Lu, Tianjin 300020, People's Republic of China. TEL 86-22-730-4167. FAX 86-22-7306542. *4703*

ZHONGHUA YISHI ZAZHI.
Guoji Shudian, Qikan Bu, Chegongzhuang Xilu 21, P.O. Box 399, Beijing 100044, People's Republic of China. *4547*

ZHONGHUA YUFANG YIXUE ZAZHI.
Zhonghua Yufang Yixuehui, 16, Hepingli Zhongjie, Beijing 100013, People's Republic of China. *4547*

ZHONGHUA ZHENGXING SHAOSHANG WAIKE ZAZHI.
Chinese Academy of Medical Sciences (CAMS), Plastic Surgery Hospital, Badachu Rd., Beijing 100041, People's Republic of China. TEL 86-1-8862233. FAX 86-1-8864137. *4924*

ZHONGHUA ZHONGLIU ZAZHI.
Zhonghua Zhongliu Zazhi Bianjibu, No. 1 Panjiayuan, Zuo'anmen Wai, Beijing 100021, People's Republic of China. TEL 86-10-7781331. *4765*

ZHONGXIAOXUE GUANLI.
Zhongxiaoxue Guanli Zazhishe, A-24 Huangsi Dajie, Dewai, Beijing 100011, People's Republic of China. TEL 2018316. *2465*

ZHUZAO JISHU.
Xi'an Zhuzao Xuehui, P.O. Box 608, Xi'an Ligong Daxue, Jinhua Nanlu, Xi'an, Shaanxi 710048, People's Republic of China. TEL 86-29-3239700. FAX 86-29-3235545. *4980*

ZIMPEL. SOFTWARE: Z DATA.
Verlag Dieter Zimpel, Angererstr. 36, 80796 Munich, Germany. TEL 49-89-3073445. FAX 49-89-302409. *2118*

ZOOLOGICAL RECORD.
BIOSIS, 2100 Arch St., Philadelphia, PA 19103-1399. TEL 215-587-4847. FAX 215-587-2016. Producer(s): SilverPlatter Information, Inc.. *625*

Producer Listing/
Serials on CD-ROM

AMERICAN PSYCHOLOGICAL ASSN.
750 First St., NE, Washington, DC 20002-4242.
Psychological Abstracts.

BOWKER ELECTRONIC PUBLISHING
(Division of Reed Elsevier Inc.)
121 Chanlon Rd., New Providence, NJ 07974. Tel:
908-464-6800 Telex: 138755
Fax: 908-665-3528.
A to Zoo. (Children's Reference PLUS)
Advertiser & Agency Red Books Plus.
American Book Trade Directory.
American Library Directory.
American Men and Women of Science.
America's Corporate Finance Directory.
Best Books for Children.
Books in Print. (Books in Print PLUS)
Books in Print Plus. (Books in Print PLUS)
Books in Print Supplement. (Books in Print
PLUS)
Books in Print with Book Reviews Plus. (Books in
Print PLUS)
Books Out-of-Print. (Books Out-of-Print PLUS)
Books Out-of-Print Plus. (Books Out-of-Print
PLUS)
Books Out-of-Print with Book Reviews Plus.
(Books Out-of-Print with Book Reviews PLUS)
The Bowker Annual Library and Book Trade
Almanac.
Bowker - Whitaker Global Books in Print Plus.
(Books In Print PLUS)
Bowker's Complete Video Directory.
Children's Books in Print. (Books in Print PLUS)
Children's Reference Plus.
Complete Directory of Large Print Books and
Serials.
Corporate Affiliations Plus.
Directory of American Research and Technology.
Directory of Corporate Affiliations.
El-Hi Textbooks and Serials in Print.
Forthcoming Books. (Books in Print PLUS)
Ingram - Books in Print Plus. (Books In Print
PLUS)
Ingram - Books in Print Plus with Book Reviews
Plus. (Books In Print PLUS)
International Literary Market Place.
Libros en Venta en Hispanoamerica y Espana
Plus.
Literary Market Place.
Martindale-Hubbell Law Directory.
Martindale-Hubbell Law Directory on C D - R O M.
Official A B M S Directory of Board Certified
Medical Specialists.
Paperbound Books in Print.
Publishers, Distributors & Wholesalers of the
United States.
Publishing Market Place Reference Plus.
SciTech Reference Plus.

Standard Directory of Advertisers (Geographic
Edition).
Standard Directory of Advertising Agencies.
Standard Directory of International Advertisers
and Agencies.
Subject Guide to Books in Print. (Books In Print
PLUS)
Subject Guide to Children's Books in Print.
Ulrich's International Periodicals Directory.
(Ulrich's PLUS)
Ulrich's Plus. (Ulrich's PLUS)
Ulrich's Update. (Ulrich's PLUS)
Variety's Video Directory Plus.
Whitaker's Books in Print.
Who Was Who in America.
Who's Who in America.
Who's Who in American Education.
Who's Who in American Law.
Who's Who in American Nursing.
Who's Who in Finance and Industry.
Who's Who in Science and Engineering.
Who's Who in the East.
Who's Who in the Midwest.
Who's Who in the South and Southwest.
Who's Who in the West.
Who's Who in the World.
Who's Who of American Women.
World Guide to Libraries. (Publishing Market
Place Reference PLUS)

BOWKER - SAUR LTD. (A Member of the
Reed Elsevier plc group)
Maypole House, Maypole Rd., East Grinstead, W.
Sussex RH19 1HH, United Kingdom Tel: 44-1342-
330-100
Fax: 44-1342-330-191.
A S S I A: Applied Social Sciences Index &
Abstracts.
A S S I A Plus.
B H I Plus.
British Humanities Index.
C T I Plus.
Catchword and Trade Name Index. (CTI Plus)
Current Research in Library & Information
Science.
Current Technology Index.
Institute of Management International Databases
Plus.
L I S A: Library & Information Science Abstracts.
L I S A Plus.
New Scientist.
Russian Books in Print on C D - R O M.

C I N A H L
P.O. Box 871, Glendale, CA 91209-0871.
1509 Wilson Terr., Glendale, CA 91209. Tel: 818-
409-8005 Fax: 818-546-5679.
Cumulative Index to Nursing & Allied Health
Literature.

CAMBRIDGE SCIENTIFIC ABSTRACTS (Subsidiary of:
Div. of Cambridge Information Group)
7200 Wisconsin Ave., Suite 601, Bethesda, MD
20814. Tel: 301-961-6750 Telex: 89-8452
Fax: 301-961-6720.
Index Medicus. (Compact Cambridge MEDLINE)
Index to Dental Literature. (Compact Cambridge
MEDLINE)
International Nursing Index. (Compact Cambridge
MEDLINE)

CHADWYCK-HEALEY INC.
1101 King St., Alexandria, VA 22314. Tel: 703-
683-4890
Fax: 703-683-7589.
A F P - Doc sur C D - R O M.
A F P Sciences.
A F P Sciences sur C D - R O M
Actualidad Economica.
Actualidad Economica en C D - R O M.
Associations Yellow Book.
Autoridades de la Biblioteca Nacional de Espana
en C D - R O M.
B N B on C D - R O M.
Bibliografia Espanola desde 1976 en C D - R O
M.
Bibliografia Nacional Portuguesa em C D - R O
M.
Bibliografia Nazionale Italiana.
Bibliographie Nationale Francaise. Livres.
Bibliographie Nationale Francaise. Publications en
Serie.
Bibliographie Nationale Francaise. Publications
Officielles.
Catalogue of British Official Publications Not
Published by H.M.S.O.
Congressional Yellow Book.
Corporate Yellow Book.
Daily Mail.
Daily Telegraph.
Deutsche Nationalbibliographie (C D - R O M
Aktuell).
The Economist.
Economist. Annual Index.
The Economist on C D - R O M.
Eurocat.
Expansion.
Expansion en C D - R O M.
Federal Regional Yellow Book.
Federal Yellow Book.

Film Index International.
Financial Times (Frankfurt Edition).
Financial Times (London, 1888).
Financial Times (North American Edition).
Financial Times on C D - R O M.
Financial Yellow Book.
Government Affairs Yellow Book.
Great Britain. House of Commons. Parliamentary
   Debates.
Great Britain. House of Commons. Parliamentary
   Debates (C D - R O M Edition).
Great Britain. House of Lords. Parliamentary
   Debates.
Great Britain. House of Lords. Parliamentary
   Debates (C D - R O M Edition).
The Guardian (Manchester).
The Guardian on C D - R O M.
The Independent.
The Independent on C D - R O M.
The Independent on Sunday.
Index to House of Commons Parliamentary
   Papers.
Intlec C D - R O M.
Judicial Yellow Book.
Law Firms Yellow Book.
Leadership Directories on C D - R O M.
The Mail on C D - R O M.
The Mail on Sunday.
Municipal Yellow Book.
News Media Yellow Book.
Nineteenth Century Bibliographic Records.
O J C D.
The Observer.
Official Journal of the European Communities. C
   Series: Information and Notices (English
   Edition).
Official Journal of the European Communities. L
   & C: Legislation and Competition.
La Recherche.
Il Sole 24 Ore.
Il Sole 24 Ore su C D - R O M.
State Yellow Book.
Sunday Telegraph.
The Sunday Times.
The Telegraph on C D - R O M.
The Times.
The Times and The Sunday Times Compact Disc
   Edition.
Times Educational Supplement.
Times Higher Education Supplement.
U K O P.
U N B I S Plus on C D - R O M.

DUN & BRADSTREET INFORMATION SERVICES
(Subsidiary of: Dun & Bradstreet Corp.)
899 Eaton Ave., Bethlehem, PA 18025. Tel: 610-
882-7000
Fax: 610-882-7269.
   Million Dollar Directory.

INSTITUTE FOR SCIENTIFIC INFORMATION
3501 Market St., Philadelphia, PA 19104.
Tel: 215-386-0100 Telex: 845305
Fax: 215-386-6362.
   Arts & Humanities Citation Index. (A&HCI/CDE)
   Index to Scientific & Technical Proceedings.
   Index to Social Sciences & Humanities
      Proceedings.
   Science Citation Index. (SCI CDE)
   Social Sciences Citation Index. (SSCI)

KNIGHT-RIDDER INFORMATION, INC.
2440 El Camino Real, Mountain View, CA 94040.
Tel: 415-254-7000
Fax: 415-254-8000.
   A S F A Marine Biotechnology Abstracts.
   Agricultural & Environmental Biotechnology
      Abstracts.
   Alloys Index.
   Aquatic Sciences & Fisheries Abstracts. Part 3:
      Aquatic Pollution and Environmental Quality.
      (Environmental Management)
   BioEngineering Abstracts. (Biotechnology &
      Bioengineering)
   Canadian Index.
   Chemical Hazards in Industry.
   Clinical Laboratory Product Comparison System.
   Country Report. Bolivia.
   Country Report. Bulgaria, Albania.
   Country Report. Peru.
   Current Biotechnology.
   C2C Abstracts: Japan - Analytical Chemistry.
   C2C Abstracts: Japan - Ceramics.
   C2C Abstracts: Japan - Chemical Engineering.
   C2C Abstracts: Japan - Crystallography.

C2C Abstracts: Japan - Hydrocarbons.
C2C Abstracts: Japan - Inorganic Chemistry.
C2C Abstracts: Japan - Materials Science.
C2C Abstracts: Japan - Metals.
C2C Abstracts: Japan - Organic Chemistry.
C2C Abstracts: Japan - Physical Chemistry.
C2C Abstracts: Japan - Plastics.
C2C Abstracts: Japan - Polymer Chemistry.
C2C Abstracts: Japan - Surface Chemistry.
C2C Abstracts: Japan - Textiles.
C2C Currents: Japan - Chemistry.
C2C Currents: Japan - Computers.
C2C Currents: Japan - Electronics.
C2C Currents: Japan - Materials.
Diagnostic Imaging & Radiology Product
   Comparison System.
Directory of Research Grants.
E I S.
Engineered Materials Abstracts.
Engineering Index Annual. (COMPENDEX PLUS
   CD-ROM)
Engineering Index Monthly. (COMPENDEX PLUS
   CD-ROM)
Health and Safety Science Abstracts. (Toxicology
   & Pharmacology)
Hospital Product Comparison System.
Index Medicus. (DIALOG OnDisc MEDLINE)
Index to Dental Literature. (DIALOG OnDisc
   MEDLINE)
International Aerospace Abstracts. (OnDisc
   Aerospace Database)
International Nursing Index. (DIALOG OnDisc
   MEDLINE)
International Packaging Abstracts.
Key Abstracts - Business Automation.
Laboratory Hazards Bulletin.
Medical & Pharmaceutical Biotechnology
   Abstracts. (Biotechnology & Bioengineering)
Metals Abstracts.
Metals Abstracts Index.
Music Index.
N T I S Bibliographic Data Base.
New England Water Works Association. Journal.
Nonferrous Metals Alert.
Nonwovens Abstracts.
Paperbase Abstracts.
Petroleum Abstracts.
Pollution Abstracts. (Environmental Management)
Polymers, Ceramics, Composites Alert.
Process and Chemical Engineering.
Resources in Education. (ERIC)
Risk Abstracts. (Environmental Management)
Steels Alert.
Surgical Product Comparison System.
Theoretical Chemical Engineering.
Thomas Register of American Manufacturers and
   Thomas Register Catalog File.
Toxicology Abstracts. (Toxicology &
   Pharmacology)
World Publishing Monitor.
Worldwide Government Directory.

NISC
3100 St. Paul St. Wyaman Towers, Suite 6,
Baltimore, MD 21218. Tel: 410-243-0797
Fax: 410-243-0982.
   A S F A Aquaculture Abstracts.
   A S F A Marine Biotechnology Abstracts.
   Agricultural & Environmental Biotechnology
      Abstracts.
   Alternative Press Index.
   Animal Behavior Abstracts.
   Antarctic Bibliography. (Arctic & Antarctic
      Regions)
   Aquatic Biology, Aquaculture & Fisheries
      Resources.
   Aquatic Sciences & Fisheries Abstracts. Part 1:
      Biological Sciences and Living Resources.
   Aquatic Sciences & Fisheries Abstracts. Part 2:
      Ocean Technology, Policy and Non-living
      Resources.
   Aquatic Sciences & Fisheries Abstracts. Part 3:
      Aquatic Pollution and Environmental Quality.
   Arctic & Antarctic Regions (Cold Regions).
   Bibliography of Economic Geology. (Geosearch)
   Bibliography on Cold Regions Science &
      Technology. (Arctic & Antarctic Regions)
   Ceramic Abstracts.
   Ceramic Abstracts (C D - R O M).
   Child Abuse & Neglect C D - R O M.
   Chronicle of Latin American Economic Affairs.
      (Latin American Studies - Vol.2)
   Consumer Health and Nutrition Index.
      (Consumers Reference Disc)
   Consumers Index. (Consumers Reference Disc)
   Consumers Reference Disc.

Current Index to Journals in Education. (ERIC on
   CD-ROM)
E I S.
E R I C on C D - R O M.
Earthquake Engineering Abstracts Database.
   (Earthquakes and the Built Environment Index)
Ecology Abstracts.
Entomology Abstracts.
Environmental Periodicals Bibliography.
Environmental Periodicals Bibliography (C D - R O
   M).
Essential Ecology, Zoology & Plant Science
   Abstracts.
Essential Fisheries Abstracts.
Essential Forestry & Wildfire Abstracts.
Essential Ornithological Abstracts.
Essential Wildlife & Conservation Biology
   Abstracts.
Estuaries and Coastal Waters of the British Isles.
   (Oceanographic & Marine Resources)
Family Relations.
Family Studies Database.
Fish & Fisheries Worldwide.
Fisheries Review. (Fish & Fisheries Worldwide)
GeoROM.
Geoscience Documentation. (Geosearch)
Geosources. (Geosearch)
Geotitles. (Geosearch)
Handbook of Latin American Studies: A Selected
   and Annotated Guide to Recent Publications.
   (Latin American Studies - Vol.1)
Health and Safety Science Abstracts. (Health &
   Safety - Risk Abstracts)
Hispanic American Periodicals Index. (Latin
   American Studies - Vol.1)
Hydrotitles. (HydroROM)
Journal of Marriage and the Family.
Latin American Studies. Volume 1.
Latin American Studies. Volume 2.
Linguistics and Language Behavior Abstracts.
Marine Pollution Research Titles. (Oceanographic
   & Marine Resources)
A Matter of Fact: Statements Containing Statistics
   on Current Social, Economic and Political
   Issues.
Microbiology Abstracts: Section A. Industrial &
   Applied Microbiology.
Microbiology Abstracts: Section C. Algology,
   Mycology and Protozoology.
Muse, Music Search.
N E L M Index Series.
Notimex on C D - R O M.
NotiSur. (Latin American Studies - Vol.2)
Oceanic Abstracts.
Oceanographic & Marine Resources.
Oceanographic Literature Review. (Oceanographic
   & Marine Resources)
Pollution Abstracts.
Psychological Abstracts. (PsycLIT)
R I L M Abstracts of Music Literature. (MUSE,
   Music Search)
Resources in Education. (ERIC on CD-ROM)
Resources in Education Annual Cumulation.
   (ERIC)
Risk Abstracts. (Health & Safety - Risk Abstracts)
Sea Grant Abstracts. (Oceanographic & Marine
   Resources)
Social Planning - Policy & Development
   Abstracts. (Sociofile)
Sociological Abstracts. (Sociofile)
SourceMex. (Latin American Studies - Vol.2)
Thesaurus of E R I C Descriptors. (ERIC)
U.S. Library of Congress. Music Catalog on
   Microfiche. (Muse)
Water Resources Abstracts (Bethesda).
Water Resources Abstracts (C D - R O M).
Water Resources Worldwide.
Wildlife Review (Fort Collins). (Wildlife Worldwide)
Wildlife Worldwide.
Women Studies Abstracts. (Women's Resources
   International)

OCLC ONLINE COMPUTER LIBRARY CTR., INC.
6565 Frantz Rd., Dublin, OH 43017-0702.
Tel: 614-764-6000 Telex: 810-339-2026
Fax: 614-764-6096.
   Current Index to Journals in Education.
   N T I S Bibliographic Data Base.
   Resources in Education. (ERIC)

PUBLIC AFFAIRS INFORMATION SERVICE, INC.
521 W. 43rd St., New York, NY 10036-4396.
Tel: 212-736-6629 Telex: 4909991777
Fax: 212-643-2848.
   P A I S International in Print. (PAIS ON CD-ROM)
   P A I S Select.

K. G. SAUR VERLAG (A Member of the Reed Elsevier plc group)
Ortlerstr. 8, 81373 Munich, Germany Tel: 089-76902 Telex: 5212067-SAUR-D
Fax: 089-76902150.
Book Review Digest.
Catalogo dei Libri in Commercio - C D - R O M.
International Books in Print.
International Books in Print Plus.
Libros en Venta en Hispanoamerica y Espana.
Publishers' International I S B N Directory (Year).
Verzeichnis Lieferbarer Buecher.
Verzeichnis Lieferbarer Buecher - C D - R O M.
Yearbook of International Organizations.

SILVERPLATTER INFORMATION, INC.
100 River Ridge Dr., Norwood, MA 02062.
Tel: 617-769-2599
Fax: 617-769-8763.
A H F S Drug Information.
A S F A Aquaculture Abstracts.
A S F A Marine Biotechnology Abstracts.
Access: The Supplementary Index to Periodicals.
Agricultural & Environmental Biotechnology Abstracts.
Agriculture and Environment for Developing Countries.
American Journal of Critical Care.
Analytical Abstracts.
Animal Behavior Abstracts.
Applied Science & Technology Index.
Aquatic Sciences & Fisheries Abstracts. Part 1: Biological Sciences and Living Resources.
Aquatic Sciences & Fisheries Abstracts. Part 2: Ocean Technology, Policy and Non-living Resources.
Aquatic Sciences & Fisheries Abstracts. Part 3: Aquatic Pollution and Environmental Quality.
Art Index.
Bibliography and Index of Geology. (GeoRef)
Bibliography of Agriculture.
Bibliography of Bioethics.
Biography Index.
Biological Abstracts.
Biological & Agricultural Index.
Biomedical and Environmental Sciences.
Business Periodicals Index.
C S A Neurosciences Abstracts.
Calcium and Calcified Tissue Abstracts.
Canadian Index.
Chemoreception Abstracts.
Choice (Middletown).
Choices: A Core Collection for Young Reluctant Readers.
Coal Week. (McGraw-Hill Energy Library)
Coal Week International. (McGraw-Hill Energy Library)
Country Report. Bolivia.
Country Report. Bulgaria, Albania.
Country Report. Peru.
Criminal Justice Abstracts.
Cumulative Book Index.
Cumulative Index to Nursing & Allied Health Literature.
Current Index to Journals in Education. (ERIC)
Current Mathematical Publications. (MathDisc)
E I S.
Ecology Abstracts.
Education Index.
Electric Utility Week. (McGraw-Hill Energy Library)
Electric Utility Week's Demand-Side Report. (McGraw-Hill Energy Library)
Entomology Abstracts.
Essay and General Literature Index.
Exceptional Child Education Resources.
Excerpta Medica Abstract Journals. (Excerpta Medica Library Service)
Excerpta Medica. Section 1: Anatomy, Anthropology, Embryology & Histology.
Excerpta Medica. Section 2: Physiology.
Excerpta Medica. Section 3: Endocrinology.
Excerpta Medica. Section 4: Microbiology: Bacteriology, Mycology, Parasitology and Virology.
Excerpta Medica. Section 5: General Pathology and Pathological Anatomy.
Excerpta Medica. Section 6: Internal Medicine.
Excerpta Medica. Section 7: Pediatrics and Pediatric Surgery.
Excerpta Medica. Section 8: Neurology and Neurosurgery.
Excerpta Medica. Section 9: Surgery.
Excerpta Medica. Section 10: Obstetrics and Gynecology.
Excerpta Medica. Section 11: Otorhinolaryngology.
Excerpta Medica. Section 12: Ophthalmology.

Excerpta Medica. Section 13: Dermatology and Venereology.
Excerpta Medica. Section 14: Radiology.
Excerpta Medica. Section 15: Chest Diseases, Thoracic Surgery and Tuberculosis.
Excerpta Medica. Section 16: Cancer.
Excerpta Medica. Section 17: Public Health, Social Medicine and Epidemiology.
Excerpta Medica. Section 18: Cardiovascular Diseases and Cardiovascular Surgery.
Excerpta Medica. Section 19: Rehabilitation and Physical Medicine.
Excerpta Medica. Section 20: Gerontology and Geriatrics.
Excerpta Medica. Section 21: Developmental Biology and Teratology.
Excerpta Medica. Section 22: Human Genetics.
Excerpta Medica. Section 23: Nuclear Medicine.
Excerpta Medica. Section 24: Anesthesiology.
Excerpta Medica. Section 25: Hematology.
Excerpta Medica. Section 26: Immunology, Serology and Transplantation.
Excerpta Medica. Section 27: Biophysics, Bio-Engineering and Medical Instrumentation.
Excerpta Medica. Section 28: Urology and Nephrology.
Excerpta Medica. Section 29: Clinical and Experimental Biochemistry.
Excerpta Medica. Section 30: Clinical and Experimental Pharmacology.
Excerpta Medica. Section 31: Arthritis and Rheumatism.
Excerpta Medica. Section 32: Psychiatry.
Excerpta Medica. Section 33: Orthopedic Surgery.
Excerpta Medica. Section 35: Occupational Health and Industrial Medicine.
Excerpta Medica. Section 36: Health Policy, Economics and Management.
Excerpta Medica. Section 38: Adverse Reactions Titles.
Excerpta Medica. Section 40: Drug Dependence, Alcohol Abuse and Alcoholism.
Excerpta Medica. Section 46: Environmental Health and Pollution Control.
Excerpta Medica. Section 48: Gastroenterology.
Excerpta Medica. Section 49: Forensic Science Abstracts.
Excerpta Medica. Section 50: Epilepsy Abstracts.
Excerpta Medica. Section 52: Toxicology.
Federal Technology Report. (McGraw-Hill Energy Library)
Film & Video Finder.
Findex (Year).
Food Science and Technology Abstracts. (COMPU-INFO)
General Science Index.
Genetics Abstracts.
Hazardous Waste Business. (McGraw-Hill Energy Library)
Health and Safety Science Abstracts. (PolTox1)
I N I S Atomindex. (INIS)
Immunology Abstracts.
Independent Power Report. (McGraw-Hill Energy Library)
Index Medicus. (MEDLINE)
Index to Dental Literature. (MEDLINE)
Index to Foreign Legal Periodicals.
Index to Legal Periodicals & Books.
Industrial Energy Bulletin. (McGraw-Hill Energy Library)
Inpharma Weekly.
Inside Energy with Federal Lands. (McGraw-Hill Energy Library)
Inside F E R C. (McGraw-Hill Energy Library)
Inside F E R C's Gas Market Report. (McGraw-Hill Energy Library)
Inside N R C. (McGraw-Hill Energy Library)
Integrated Waste Management. (McGraw-Hill Energy Library)
International Journal of Punjab Studies.
International Nursing Index. (MEDLINE)
International Pharmaceutical Abstracts.
Journal of Economic Literature.
Kompass Italia.
Library Literature.
Linguistics and Language Behavior Abstracts.
M L A International Bibliography of Books and Articles on the Modern Languages and Literatures.
Mathematical Reviews. (MathDisc)
A Matter of Fact: Statements Containing Statistics on Current Social, Economic and Political Issues.
Mechanical Engineering Abstracts.
Medical & Pharmaceutical Biotechnology Abstracts.
Meyler's Side Effects of Drugs. (SEDBASE)

Microbiology Abstracts: Section A. Industrial & Applied Microbiology.
Microbiology Abstracts: Section B. Bacteriology.
Microbiology Abstracts: Section C. Algology, Mycology and Protozoology.
Microcomputer Abstracts.
Monthly Catalog of United States Government Publications.
N T I S Bibliographic Data Base.
Northeast Power Report. (McGraw-Hill Energy Library)
NuclearFuel. (McGraw-Hill Energy Library)
Nucleic Acids Abstracts.
Nucleonics Week. (McGraw-Hill Energy Library)
Oncogenes and Growth Factors Abstracts.
P A I S International in Print. (PAIS INTERNATIONAL ON SILVERPLATTER)
Peterson's Guide to Graduate and Professional Programs: An Overview (Year) (Book 1). (PETERSON'S GRADLINE)
Peterson's Guide to Graduate Programs in Business, Education, Health, and Law (Year) (Book 6). (PETERSON'S GRADLINE)
Peterson's Guide to Graduate Programs in Engineering and Applied Sciences (Year) (Book 5). (PETERSON'S GRADLINE)
Peterson's Guide to Graduate Programs in the Biological and Agricultural Sciences (Year) (Book 3). (PETERSON'S GRADLINE)
Peterson's Guide to Graduate Programs in the Humanities and Social Sciences (Year) (Book 2). (PETERSON'S GRADLINE)
Peterson's Guide to Graduate Programs in the Physical Sciences and Mathematics (Year) (Book 4). (PETERSON'S GRADLINE)
Pollution Abstracts. (PolTox1)
Population Index.
Psychological Abstracts. (PsycLIT)
R T E C S.
Reactions Weekly.
Reader's Guide Abstracts.
Readers' Guide Abstracts.
Readers' Guide to Periodical Literature.
Resources in Education. (ERIC)
Safety and Health at Work.
Schweizerische Zeitschrift fuer Volkswirtschaft und Statistik.
Securite et Sante au Travail.
Side Effects of Drugs Annual. (SEDBASE)
Social Planning - Policy & Development Abstracts. (SocioFile)
Social Sciences Index.
Social Work Abstracts. (SWAB-PLUS)
Sociological Abstracts. (Sociofile)
South Asian Survey.
Southeast Power Report. (McGraw-Hill Energy Library)
SportSearch.
T R I S Electronic Bibliographic Data Base.
Toxicology Abstracts. (PolTox1)
Ulster Medical Journal. (MEDLINE)
Utility Environment Report. (McGraw-Hill Energy Library)
Vaard i Norden.
Virology and AIDS Abstracts.
Water Resources Abstracts (Bethesda).
Wilson Applied Science & Technology Abstracts.
Wilson Art Abstracts.
Wilson Business Abstracts.
Wilson Education Abstracts.
Wilson General Science Abstracts.
Wilson Social Sciences Abstracts.
Year Book of Cardiology. (ClinMED-CD)
Year Book of Critical Care Medicine. (ClinMED-CD)
Year Book of Endocrinology.
Year Book of Oncology.
Zoological Record.

UNIVERSITY MICROFILMS INTERNATIONAL
300 N. Zeeb Rd., Ann Arbor, MI 48106. Tel: 313-761-4700
Fax: 313-761-1203.
A B I - INFORM.
Acquisition of Greater Dayton.
America.
American Craft.
American Doctoral Dissertations.
American Journal of International Law.
Archives of Environmental Health.
Arts Education Policy Review.
Asian Affairs: An American Review.
The Atlantic Monthly.
Audubon.
Behavioral Medicine.
Bulletin of the Atomic Scientists.
Business Journal (Sacramento).

Producer

Business Mexico.
Change (Washington).
Christian Century.
The Clearing House.
College Teaching.
Commonweal.
Computer & Control Abstracts.
Consumer's Research Magazine.
Corporate Report Minnesota.
Critique: Studies in Modern Fiction.
Current (Washington, 1960).
Current Health 2.
Dayton Business Reporter.
Defense Counsel Journal.
Dissertation Abstracts International. Section A:
    Humanities and Social Sciences.
Dissertation Abstracts International. Section B:
    Physical Sciences and Engineering.
Dissertation Abstracts International. Section C:
    Worldwide.
Dissertation Abstracts on Disc.
Ebony.
The Education Digest.
Environment (Washington).
Environmental Action.
The Explicator.
Film Comment.
Foreign Affairs.
Fortune Magazine.
Genetic, Social, and General Psychology
    Monographs.
The Geographical Journal.
Germanic Review.
Harper's Magazine.
The Hemingway Review.
Historical Methods.
History and Theory.
History: Reviews of New Books.
History Today.
Hospital Topics.
I E E Review.
Jet.
Journal of American College Health.
Journal of Arts Management, Law, and Society.
The Journal of Economic Education.
Journal of Education for Business.
The Journal of Educational Research.

The Journal of Environmental Education.
Journal of Experimental Education.
The Journal of General Psychology.
The Journal of Genetic Psychology.
Journal of Group Psychotherapy, Psychodrama &
    Sociometry.
Journal of Higher Education.
Journal of Money, Credit & Banking.
Journal of Motor Behavior.
Journal of Popular Film and Television.
Journal of Sport Behavior.
Kiplinger's Personal Finance Magazine.
Life (New York).
Maclean's.
Masters Abstracts International.
Money (New York).
Mother Jones.
Motor Trend.
Multinational Business Review.
The Nation.
National Civic Review.
National Review.
Nation's Business.
Natural History.
The New Republic.
The New York Times.
Nieman Reports.
Outdoor Life.
Parents.
Perspectives on Political Science.
Physics Abstracts.
Ploughshares.
Popular Mechanics.
Popular Science.
Power Engineering Journal.
Preventing School Failure.
Psychology Today.
Review (Washington).
Rocks and Minerals.
Rolling Stone.
Scholastic Update.
Science Activities.
Science News.
Seventeen.
Techniques.
Time.
U S News & World Report.

Weatherwise.
Women's Sports and Fitness.
World Health.
World Press Review.
The Writer.

H. W. WILSON
  950 University Ave., Bronx, NY 10452. Tel: 718-
  588-8400 Cable: WILSONDEX
  Fax: 718-590-1617.
    Applied Science & Technology Index.
    Art Index. *(WILSONDISC)*
    Biography Index. *(WILSONDISC)*
    Biological & Agricultural Index. *(WILSONDISC)*
    Book Review Digest. *(WILSONDISC)*
    Business Periodicals Index. *(WILSONDISC)*
    Canadian Journal of History.
    Cumulative Book Index.
    Current Biography Yearbook. *(WILSONDISC)*
    Education Index. *(WILSONDISC)*
    Essay and General Literature Index.
        (WILSONDISC)
    General Science Index. *(WILSONDISC)*
    History and Theory.
    Humanities Index. *(WILSONDISC)*
    Index to Legal Periodicals & Books.
        (WILSONDISC)
    Library Literature. *(WILSONDISC)*
    Life (New York).
    Monthly Catalog of United States Government
        Publications.
    Ploughshares.
    Readers' Guide Abstracts. *(WILSONDISC)*
    Readers' Guide to Periodical Literature.
        (WILSONDISC)
    Social Policy.
    Social Sciences Index.
    Wilson Applied Science & Technology Abstracts.
    Wilson Art Abstracts. *(WILSONDISC)*
    Wilson Business Abstracts. *(WILSONDISC)*
    Wilson Education Abstracts. *(WILSONDISC)*
    Wilson General Science Abstracts. *(WILSONDISC)*
    Wilson Humanities Abstracts. *(WILSONDISC)*
    Wilson Social Sciences Abstracts.

Serials Available Online

This index contains abbreviated entries for all serials known to be available online. Vendor names are given if known, plus file names or numbers in parentheses. For full bibliographic information on these titles, please refer to the complete entry on the page indicated in italics.

A A B'S BIBLIOGRAPHY OF RARE & OUT-OF-PRINT TITLES FOR SALE.
A A B British Book Search Services (Oxford), Editorial Research Centre, P.O. Box 342, Oxford OX1 1NN, England. TEL 01865-792610. FAX 01865-792611. *6012*

A A B'S GUIDE TO PRIVATE ENGLISH LANGUAGE SCHOOLS IN THE U.K. FOR OVERSEAS STUDENTS.
A A B British Book Search Services (Oxford), Editorial Research Centre, P.O. Box 342, Oxford OX1 1NN, England. TEL 44-1865-792610. FAX 44-1865-792611. *2408*

A A B'S REGISTER OF WANTED PUBLICATIONS.
A A B British Book Search Services (Oxford), Editorial Research Centre, P.O. Box 342, Oxford OX1 1NN, England. TEL 44-1865-792610. FAX 44-1865-792611. *6012*

A A MAGAZINE.
V N U Business Publications BV, VNU House, 32-34 Broadwick St., London W1A 2HG, England. TEL 44-171-439-4242. FAX 44-171-437-7001. *1036*

A B A BANK COMPLIANCE.
American Bankers Association, 1120 Connecticut Ave., N.W., Washington, DC 20036. TEL 202-663-5497. FAX 202-663-7543.
Vendor(s): University Microfilms International. *1056*

A B A BANKING JOURNAL.
Simmons - Boardman Publishing Corp., 345 Hudson St., New York, NY 10014-4502. TEL 212-620-7200. FAX 212-633-1165.
Vendor(s): Dow Jones News Retrieval, Information Access Co., Knight-Ridder Information, Inc. (File no.648), Lexis-Nexis, Ovid Technologies, Inc. (TSAP), University Microfilms International. *1057*

A B A JOURNAL.
American Bar Association, 750 N. Lake Shore Dr., Chicago, IL 60611. TEL 312-988-5000. FAX 312-988-6014.
Vendor(s): Lexis-Nexis, University Microfilms International, West Services, Inc.. *3733*

A B A WASHINGTON LETTER.
American Bar Association, Governmental Affairs Office, 740 15th St., Washington, DC 20005-1009. TEL 202-662-1017. *3733*

A B B REVIEW.
A B B Corporate Communications Ltd., Ruetistr. 6, CH-5401 Baden, Switzerland. TEL 41-56-2054836. FAX 41-56-2212274.
Vendor(s): Data-Star, Knight-Ridder Information, Inc.. *2681*

A B C BELGE POUR LE COMMERCE ET L'INDUSTRIE.
A B C Belge pour le Commerce et l'Industrie B.V., Ave. de l'Heliport 21, 1000 Brussels, Belgium. TEL 32-2-2015414. FAX 32-2-2015471. *1582*

A B C DER DEUTSCHEN WIRTSCHAFT - QUELLENWERK FUR EINKAUF-VERKAUF.
A B C Publishing Group, Postfach 100262, 64202 Darmstadt, Germany. TEL 49-6151-3892-0. FAX 49-6151-33164.
Vendor(s): Data-Star, FIZ Technik. *1582*

A B C EUROP PRODUCTION.
A B C Publishing Group, Postfach 100262, 64202 Darmstadt, Germany. TEL 49-6151-3892-0. FAX 49-6151-33164.
Vendor(s): Data-Star, FIZ Technik. *1263*

A B C LUXEMBOURGEOIS POUR LE COMMERCE ET L'INDUSTRIE.
A B C Belge pour le Commerce et l'Industrie B.V., Ave. de l'Heliport 21, 1000 Brussels, Belgium. TEL 32-2-2015414. FAX 32-2-2015271. *1582*

A B E C O R COUNTRY REPORTS.
Barclays Bank plc., Economics Department, P.O. Box 12, Barclays House, 1 Wimborne Rd., Poole, Dorset BH15 2BB, England. TEL 01202-344023. FAX 01202-402303.
Vendor(s): Data-Star, Knight-Ridder Information, Inc.. *1172*

A B I - INFORM.
U M I Company 300 N. Zeeb Rd., Ann Arbor, MI 48106. TEL 313-761-4700. FAX 800-864-0019.
Vendor(s): Data-Star (INFO), European Space Agency (File no.30), Knight-Ridder Information, Inc. (File no.15), Lexis-Nexis (ABI), Orbit Search Service (INFO), Ovid Technologies, Inc. (INFO), STN International (STN), University Microfilms International. *973*

A B I X: AUSTRALASIAN BUSINESS INTELLIGENCE.
Business Intelligence Australia, McConnell Dowell House, 627 Chapel St., S. Yarra, Vic. 3141, Australia. TEL 61-3-98279088. FAX 61-3-98279099.
Vendor(s): AUSINET, Kiwinet. *973*

A C A JOURNAL.
American Compensation Association, 14040 N. Northsight Blvd., Scottsdale, AZ 85260. TEL 605-951-9191.
Vendor(s): University Microfilms International. *1498*

A C A NEWS.
American Compensation Association, 14040 N. Northsight Blvd., Scottsdale, AZ 85260. TEL 602-951-9191. FAX 602-483-8352.
Vendor(s): University Microfilms International. *1498*

A C M GUIDE TO COMPUTING LITERATURE.
Association for Computing Machinery, 1515 Broadway, 17th Fl., New York, NY 10036-5701. TEL 212-869-7440. FAX 212-869-0481.
Vendor(s): Knight-Ridder Information, Inc.. *2000*

A D C NEWS.
Automatic Identification Manufacturers U.S.A., 634 Alpha Dr., Pittsburgh, PA 15238-2802. TEL 412-963-8588. FAX 412-963-8753. *2011*

A F L - C I O NEWS.
American Federation of Labor - Congress of Industrial Organizations, 815 16th St., N.W., Washington, DC 20006. TEL 202-637-5010. FAX 202-637-5058.
Vendor(s): Knight-Ridder Information, Inc.. *3716*

A G A GAS ENERGY REVIEW.
American Gas Association, 515 Wilson Blvd., Arlington, VA 22209. TEL 703-841-8400. FAX 703-841-8406.
Vendor(s): University Microfilms International. *5348*

A G A R D REPORTS.
U.S. National Aeronautics and Space Administration, National Technology Transfer Center, c/o Wheeling Jesuit University, 316 Washington Ave., Wheeling, WV 26003. TEL 304-243-2440. FAX 304-243-4390.
Available only online. *51*

A H F S DRUG INFORMATION.
American Society of Health-System Pharmacists, 7272 Wisconsin Ave., Bethesda, MD 20814. TEL 301-657-3000. FAX 301-657-1641.
Vendor(s): Data-Star (DIFT), Knight-Ridder Information, Inc. (File no.229), Lexis-Nexis, Ovid Technologies, Inc. (DIFT). *5196*

A I-MAGAZINE.
American Association for Artificial Intelligence, 445 Burgess Dr., Menlo Park, CA 94025. TEL 415-328-3123. FAX 415-321-4457. *2004*

A I T REVIEW.
Asian Institute of Technology, Media and Information Services Office, P.O. Box 2754, Bangkok 10501, Thailand. TEL 66-2-516-0110. FAX 66-2-516-2126. *2588*

A J R.
American Roentgen Ray Society, Attn.: Leigh Myzk, 1891 Preston White Dr., VA 22091. TEL 703-648-8992. FAX 703-264-8863. *4872*

A L A W O N.
American Library Association, Washington Office, 1301 Pennsylvania Ave, N.W., Ste. 403, Washington, DC 20004. TEL 202-628-8410. FAX 202-628-8419. Available only online. *3969*

A L C T S NETWORK NEWS.
American Library Association, Association for Library Collections & Technical Services, 50 E. Huron St., Chicago, IL 60611-2759. TEL 312-280-5035. FAX 312-280-3257. Available only online. *4042*

A L M D ADVANCE.
Law Book Co. Ltd., 44-50 Waterloo Rd., North Ryde, N.S.W. 2113, Australia. TEL 61-2-9366444. FAX 61-2-8889706. *3734*

A M P S METER WEEKLY REPORTS.
S A Advertising Research Foundation, P.O. Box 98874, 2152 Sloane Park, South Africa. TEL 27-11-463-5340. FAX 27-11-463-5010. *48*

A M P S RADIO DIARY.
S A Advertising Research Foundation, P.O. Box 98874, 2152 Sloane Park, South Africa. TEL 27-11-463-5340. FAX 27-11-463-5010. *1922*

A M R E P DATABASE BULLETIN.
Australian Mineral Resource Politics Pty. Ltd., 10 Hampstead Hill Rd., Aldgate, S.A. 5154, Australia. TEL 8 339 2960. *5055*

A M S NEWSLETTER (BOSTON).
American Meteorological Society, 45 Beacon St., Boston, MA 02108-3693. TEL 617-227-2425. FAX 617-742-8718. Available only online. *4989*

A. MAGAZINE: THE ASIAN AMERICAN QUARTERLY.
Metro East Publications, Inc., 270 Lafayette St., Ste. 400, New York, NY 10012. TEL 212-925-2123. FAX 212-925-2896. *2859*

A N Q: A QUARTERLY JOURNAL OF SHORT ARTICLES, NOTES AND REVIEWS.
Heldref Publications, 1319 Eighteenth St., N.W., Washington, DC 20036-1802. TEL 202-296-6267. FAX 202-296-5149. Vendor(s): Information Access Co.. *4176*

A O A C INTERNATIONAL JOURNAL.
A O A C International, 481 N. Frederick Ave., Ste. 500, Gaithersburg, MD 20877-2417. TEL 703-522-3032. FAX 703-522-5468. Vendor(s): STN International (CJAOAC). *1712*

A P A I S: AUSTRALIAN PUBLIC AFFAIRS INFORMATION SERVICE.
National Library of Australia, Publications Section, Cultural and Educational Services Division, Canberra, A.C.T. 2600, Australia. TEL 61-6-262-1365. FAX 61-6-273-4493. *5929*

A P F REPORTER.
Alicia Patterson Foundation, 1730 Pennsylvania Ave., N.W., Ste. 850, Washington, DC 20006. TEL 202-393-5995. FAX 301-951-8512. *3700*

A P I S.
University of Florida, Institute of Food and Agricultural Sciences, Dept. of Entomology and Nematology, Bldg. 970, Gainesville, FL 32611-0620. TEL 904-392-1801. FAX 904-392-0190. *84*

A P S NEWS SERVICE.
Arab Press Service, A P S House, P.O. Box 3896, Nicosia, Cyprus. TEL 357-2-351778. FAX 357-2-350265. Vendor(s): Information Access Co.. *2540*

A S D A NEWS.
American Sleep Disorders Association, 1610 14th St., N.W., Ste. 300, Rochester, MN 55901. TEL 507-287-6006. FAX 507-287-6008. *4821*

A S F A AQUACULTURE ABSTRACTS.
Cambridge Scientific Abstracts, 7200 Wisconsin Ave., 6th Fl., Bethesda, MD 20814. TEL 301-961-6750. FAX 301-961-6720. Vendor(s): DIMDI, European Space Agency, Knight-Ridder Information, Inc. (File no.44), STN International (AQUASCI). *2946*

A S F A MARINE BIOTECHNOLOGY ABSTRACTS.
Cambridge Scientific Abstracts, 7200 Wisconsin Ave., 6th Fl., Bethesda, MD 20814. TEL 301-961-6750. FAX 301-961-6720. Vendor(s): European Space Agency, Knight-Ridder Information, Inc. (File nos.44 and 76), STN International. *615*

A S S I A: APPLIED SOCIAL SCIENCES INDEX & ABSTRACTS.
Bowker - Saur Ltd., A member of the Reed Elsevier plc group, Maypole House, Maypole Rd., E. Grinstead, W. Sussex RH19 1HU, England. TEL 44-1342-330100. FAX 44-1342-330191. Vendor(s): Data-Star (ASSI). *6355*

A S T I S BIBLIOGRAPHY.
Arctic Science & Technology Information System, Arctic Institute of North America, University of Calgary, 2500 University Dr. N.W., Calgary, AB T2N 1N4, Canada. TEL 403-220-4036. Vendor(s): QL Systems Ltd.. *2217*

A S T I S CURRENT AWARENESS BULLETIN.
Arctic Science & Technology Information System, Arctic Institute of North America, University of Calgary, 2500 University Dr. N.W., Calgary, AB T2N 1N4, Canada. TEL 403-284-7515. FAX 403-282-4609. Vendor(s): QL Systems Ltd.. *6671*

A S T I S OCCASIONAL PUBLICATIONS.
Arctic Science & Technology Information System, University of Calgary, 2500 University Dr. N.W., Calgary, AB T2N 1N4, Canada. TEL 403-220-4036. FAX 403-282-4609. Vendor(s): QL Systems Ltd.. *6221*

A S U RESEARCH MAGAZINE.
Arizona State University, A S U Research Magazine, Box 878206, Tempe, AZ 85387-8206. TEL 602-965-1266. FAX 602-965-9684. *6221*

A S U TRAVEL GUIDE.
A S U Travel Guide, Inc., 1525 Francisco Blvd., E., San Rafael, CA 94901. TEL 415-459-0300. FAX 415-459-0494. *6864*

A V VIDEO.
Knowledge Industry Publications, Inc., 01332077xxxster Ave., White Plains, NY 10604. TEL 914-328-9157. *1975*

ABILITY NETWORK MAGAZINE.
Ability Network Publishing Inc., 19 Mount Pleasant Ave., Dartmouth, NS B3A 3T3, Canada. TEL 902-461-9009. FAX 902-461-9484. *3303*

ABOUT MARKETING TO WOMEN.
About Women, Inc., 33 Broad St., Boston, MA 02109. TEL 617-723-4337. FAX 617-723-7107. Vendor(s): Information Access Co.. *1452*

ABSATZWIRTSCHAFT.
Verlagsgruppe Handelsblatt GmbH, Kasernenstr. 67, 40213 Duesseldorf, Germany. TEL 49-211-8870. FAX 49-211-329954. *1452*

ABSTRACTS AND REVIEWS FROM ZENTRALBLATT FUER MATHEMATIK.
Fachinformationszentrum Karlsruhe, Gesellschaft fuer wissenschaftlich-technische Information mbH, 76344 Eggenstein-Leopoldshafen, Germany. TEL 07247-808333. FAX 07247-808666. *4405*

ABSTRACTS IN BIOCOMMERCE.
BioCommerce Data Ltd., Prudential Bldgs., 95 High St., Slough, Berks. SL1 1DH, England. TEL 44-1753-511777. FAX 44-1753-512239. Vendor(s): Data-Star (CELL), Knight-Ridder Information, Inc. (file no.286). *615*

ABSTRACTS OF BULGARIAN SCIENTIFIC MEDICAL LITERATURE.
Tsentar za Informatsiia po Meditsina, 1, Sv. Georgi Sofiiski St., 1431 Sofia, Bulgaria. TEL 359-2-523171. *4548*

ABSTRACTS OF WORKING PAPERS IN ECONOMICS.
Cambridge University Press, Edinburgh Bldg., Shaftesbury Rd., Cambridge CB2 2RU, England. TEL 44-1223-312393. FAX 44-1223-315052. *973*

ABSTRACTS ON HYGIENE AND COMMUNICABLE DISEASES.
CAB International, Wallingford, Oxon. OX10 8DE, England. TEL 44-1491-832111. FAX 44-1491-833508. Vendor(s): DIMDI, Data-Star. *4548*

ABYA YALA NEWS.
South and Meso American Indian Rights Center, Box 28703, Oakland, CA 94604-8703. TEL 510-834-4263. FAX 510-834-4264. Vendor(s): Lexis-Nexis. *2860*

ACADEMIA.
Baker & Taylor, Inc., Box 734, Somerville, NJ 08876. TEL 908-218-0400. FAX 908-218-3980. Available only online. *5985*

ACADEMIC ABSTRACTS C D - R O M.
EBSCO Publishing 10 Estes St., Box 682, Ipswich, MA 01938. TEL 508-356-6500. FAX 508-356-6565. Vendor(s): Ovid Technologies, Inc.. *2*

ACADEMIC FILE INTERNATIONAL NEWS & PHOTO SYNDICATION.
Eastern Art Publishing, Acre House, 69-76 Long Acre, Covent Garden, London WC2E 9JH, England. TEL 44-81-392-1122. FAX 44-81-392-1422. Available only online. *408*

ACADEMIC INDEX.
Information Access Company 362 Lakeside Dr., Foster City, CA 94404. TEL 415-378-5200. FAX 415-378-5369. Vendor(s): Ovid Technologies, Inc. (ACAD), Knight-Ridder Information, Inc. (File no.88), Information Access Co.. *3631*

ACADEMY OF MANAGEMENT. JOURNAL.
Academy of Management, Box 3020, Briarcliff Manor, NY 10510-8020. TEL 914-923-2607. FAX 914-923-2615. Vendor(s): Information Access Co., University Microfilms International. *1404*

ACADEMY OF MANAGEMENT EXECUTIVE.
Academy of Management, Box 3020, Briarcliff Manor, NY 10510-8020. TEL 914-923-2607. FAX 914-923-2615. Vendor(s): Information Access Co., University Microfilms International. *1404*

ACADEMY OF MANAGEMENT REVIEW.
Academy of Management, Box 3020, Briarcliff Manor, NY 10510. TEL 914-923-2607. FAX 914-923-2615. Vendor(s): Information Access Co., University Microfilms International. *1404*

ACADEMY OF MARKETING SCIENCE. JOURNAL.
Sage Publications, Inc., 2455 Teller Rd., Thousand Oaks, CA 91320. TEL 805-499-0721. FAX 805-499-0871. Vendor(s): Knight-Ridder Information, Inc.. *1452*

ACADEMY OF MEDICINE, SINGAPORE. ANNALS.
Academy of Medicine, Singapore, 16 College Road, 01-01 College of Medicine Bldg., Singapore 0316, Singapore. TEL 2245166. FAX 2255155. Vendor(s): National Library of Medicine. *4417*

ACCENT ON LIVING.
Cheever Publishing, Inc., Box 700, Bloomington, IL 61702. TEL 309-378-2961. FAX 309-378-4420. Vendor(s): Information Access Co., University Microfilms International. *3315*

ACCESS E P A.
U.S. Environmental Protection Agency, Enterprise Management Division, 401 M St., S.W., Rm. 2003, 3404, Washington, DC 20460. *2773*

ACCESS REPORTS - FREEDOM OF INFORMATION.
Access Reports, Inc., 1624 Dogwood Lane, Lynchburg, VA 24503. TEL 804-384-5334. FAX 804-384-8272.
Vendor(s): NewsNet (GT10). *5724*

ACCESS: THE SUPPLEMENTARY INDEX TO PERIODICALS.
John Gordon Burke Publisher, Inc., Box 1492, Evanston, IL 60204-1492. TEL 847-866-8625. FAX 847-866-6639. *2*

ACCOUNT LIST FILE.
Data Management Services Group Ltd., Ramillies House, 1-2 Ramillies St., London W1V 1DF, England. TEL 44-171-287-0030. FAX 44-171-437-4505. *29*

ACCOUNTANCY.
Institute of Chartered Accountants in England and Wales, P.O. Box 433, Moorgate Pl., London EC2P 2BJ, England. TEL 44-171-833-3291.
Vendor(s): University Microfilms International. *1037*

ACCOUNTING AND FINANCE.
Accounting Association of Australia and New Zealand, University of Melbourne, Department of Accounting and Finance, Parkville, Vic. 3052, Australia. TEL 03-344-7658. FAX 03-344-6681.
Vendor(s): Information Access Co., University Microfilms International. *1038*

ACCOUNTING AND TAX INDEX.
U M I Company 300 N. Zeeb Rd., Ann Arbor, MI 48106. TEL 313-761-4700. FAX 800-864-0019.
Vendor(s): Knight-Ridder Information, Inc. (File no. 485). *973*

ACCOUNTING EDUCATION.
Chapman & Hall, Journals Department 2-6 Boundary Row, London SE1 8HN, England. TEL 44-171-8650066. FAX 44-171-8659623. *1038*

ACCOUNTING EDUCATION NEWS.
American Accounting Association, Paul F. Gerhardt Bldg., 5717 Bessie Dr., Sarasota, FL 34233-2399. TEL 941-921-7747. FAX 941-923-4093.
Vendor(s): University Microfilms International. *1038*

ACCOUNTING HISTORIANS JOURNAL.
Academy of Accounting Historians, c/o William D. Samson, Culverhouse School of Accountancy, University of Alabama, Tuscaloosa, AL 35487. TEL 205-348-2903.
Vendor(s): University Microfilms International. *1039*

ACCOUNTING HORIZONS.
American Accounting Association, Paul F. Gerhardt Bldg., 5717 Bessie Dr., Sarasota, FL 34233. TEL 941-921-7747. FAX 941-923-4093.
Vendor(s): University Microfilms International. *1039*

ACCOUNTING TECHNOLOGY.
Faulkner & Gray, Inc. (New York), 11 Penn Plaza, 17th Fl., New York, NY 10001. TEL 212-967-7000. FAX 212-967-7155.
Vendor(s): University Microfilms International. *1039*

ACCOUNTING TODAY.
Faulkner and Gray, Inc. (New York), 11 Penn Plaza, 17th Fl., New York, NY 10001. TEL 212-967-7000. FAX 212-967-7155.
Vendor(s): Information Access Co., University Microfilms International. *1040*

ACCOUNTS OF CHEMICAL RESEARCH.
American Chemical Society, 1155 16th St., N.W., Washington, DC 20036. TEL 202-872-4363. FAX 614-447-3671.
Vendor(s): STN International (CJACS). *1662*

ACKNOWLEDGE THE WINDOW LETTER.
Mendham Technology Group, 144 Talmadge Rd., Box 11, Mendham, NJ 07945. TEL 201-543-2273. FAX 201-543-6033.
Vendor(s): Information Access Co.. *2084*

ACQUISITION OF GREATER DAYTON.
Hannover Publishing Co., Inc., 6356 Far Hills Ave., Dayton, OH 45459-2782. TEL 513-291-1100. FAX 513-436-3426. *6018*

ACROSS THE BOARD.
Conference Board, Inc., 845 Third Ave., New York, NY 10022. TEL 212-759-0900. FAX 212-980-7014.
Vendor(s): Information Access Co., University Microfilms International. *1404*

ACTA PHARMACEUTICA.
Croatian Pharmaceutical Society, Masarykova 2-II, HR-41000 Zagreb, Croatia. TEL 041-427944. FAX 041-431301. *5396*

ACTA PHARMACEUTICA HUNGARICA.
Magyar Gyogyszereszeti Tarsasag, Gyomroi ut 19-21, P.O.B. 27, 1475 Budapest, Hungary. FAX 36-1-2605604. *5396*

ACTUALIDAD COLOMBIANA.
Instituto Latinoamericano de Servicios Legales Alternativos, Apdo. Aereo 077844, Bogota, Colombia. TEL 57-1-245-5955. FAX 57-1-2884854. *3735*

ACTUALIDAD ECONOMICA.
Recoletos 1, 7o, 28001 Madrid, Spain. TEL 34-1-3373220. FAX 34-1-5768150. *1172*

ACTUALITES PHARMACEUTIQUES.
S.U.T.I.P., 175 rue du Faubourg Poissonniere, 75009 Paris, France. FAX 42-82-98-00. *5397*

ADCOM NET.
Publitech, Inc., Box 840, Sherborn, MA 01770. TEL 508-651-3932.
Available only online. *29*

ADDICTION.
Carfax Publishing Co., P.O. Box 25, Abingdon, Oxon. OX14 3UE, England. TEL 44-1235-401000. FAX 44-1325-401550. *2192*

THE ADDICTION LETTER.
Manisses Communications Group, Inc., Box 9758, Providence, RI 02940-9758. TEL 401-831-6020. FAX 401-861-6370.
Vendor(s): Information Access Co.. *2192*

ADDRESS LIST, REGIONAL AND SUBREGIONAL LIBRARIES FOR THE BLIND AND PHYSICALLY HANDICAPPED.
U.S. Library of Congress, National Library Service for the Blind and Physically Handicapped, Washington, DC 20542. TEL 202-707-5100. FAX 202-707-0712. *3317*

ADHESION COMMUNICATIONS.
Gordon & Breach Science Publishers, c/o International Publishers Distributor, Box 3054, Langhorne, PA 19047-3054. TEL 215-750-2642. FAX 215-750-6343. *5628*

ADHESIVES ABSTRACTS.
R A P R A Technology Ltd., Shawbury, Shrewsbury, Shrops. SY4 4NR, England. TEL 44-1939-250383. FAX 44-1939-251118.
Vendor(s): Data-Star, Knight-Ridder Information, Inc., Orbit Search Service, STN International. *1697*

ADHESIVES AGE.
Intertec Publishing Corp. (Atlanta), 6151 Powers Ferry Rd., N.W., Atlanta, GA 30339-2941. TEL 770-955-2500. FAX 770-955-0400.
Vendor(s): Information Access Co., University Microfilms International. *2632*

ADMAP.
N T C Publications Ltd., Farm Rd., Henley-on-Thames, Oxfordshire RG9 1EJ, England. TEL 01491-411000. FAX 01491-571188. *30*

ADMINISTRATION & SOCIETY.
Sage Publications, Inc., 2455 Teller Rd., Thousand Oaks, CA 91320. TEL 805-499-0721. FAX 805-499-0871.
Vendor(s): Information Access Co.. *5890*

ADMINISTRATIVE SCIENCE QUARTERLY.
Cornell University Johnson Graduate School of Management, 20 Thornwood Dr., Ste. 100, Ithaca, NY 14850-1265. TEL 607-254-7143. FAX 607-254-7100.
Vendor(s): Dow Jones News Retrieval, Information Access Co., Knight-Ridder Information, Inc., Ovid Technologies, Inc., University Microfilms International. *5890*

ADOLESCENCE.
Libra Publishers, Inc., 3089C Clairemont Dr., Ste. 383, San Diego, CA 92117. TEL 619-571-1414.
Vendor(s): Information Access Co., University Microfilms International. *1759*

ADVANCED CERAMICS REPORT.
Elsevier Science Ltd., P.O. Box 800, Kidlington, Oxford OX5 1DX, England. TEL 44-1865-843000. FAX 44-1865-843010.
Vendor(s): Data-Star (PTEN), Information Access Co., Knight-Ridder Information, Inc. (File no.636). *1651*

ADVANCED COMPOSITES BULLETIN.
Elsevier Science Ltd., P.C. Box 800, Kidlington, Oxford OX5 1DX, England. TEL 44-1865-843000. FAX 44-1865-843010.
Vendor(s): Data-Star (PTEN), Information Access Co., Knight-Ridder Information, Inc. (File no.636). *5617*

ADVANCED IMAGING.
P T N Publishing Corp., 445 Broad Hollow Rd., Ste. 21, Melville, NY 11747-4722. TEL 516-845-2700. FAX 516-845-2797.
Vendor(s): Information Access Co.. *1926*

ADVANCED INTELLIGENT NETWORK NEWS.
Phillips Business Information, Inc., 1201 Seven Locks Rd., Potomac, MD 20854. TEL 301-424-3338. FAX 301-309-3847.
Vendor(s): Information Access Co., NewsNet (TE15). *2035*

ADVANCED MANAGEMENT JOURNAL.
Society for Advancement of Management, Box 889, Vinton, VA 24179. TEL 703-342-5563.
Vendor(s): Information Access Co., University Microfilms International. *1404*

ADVANCED MATERIALS & PROCESSES.
A S M International, Materials Information, Materials Park, OH 44073-0002. TEL 216-338-5151. FAX 216-338-4634.
Vendor(s): Information Access Co.. *2723*

ADVANCES (KALAMAZOO).
Fetzer Institute, 9292 West KL Ave., Kalamazoo, MI 49009-9398. TEL 616-375-2000. FAX 616-372-2163. *4420*

ADVANCES IN PHARMACEUTICAL SCIENCES.
Academic Press, Inc., 525 B St., Ste. 1900, San Diego, CA 92101-4495. TEL 619-231-0926. FAX 619-699-6715. *539*

ADVERTISING AGE.
Crain Communications, Inc (Chicago), 740 Rush St., Chicago, IL 60611. TEL 312-649-5286. FAX 312-280-3174.
Vendor(s): Information Access Co., Lexis-Nexis (ADAGE). *30*

ADWEEK (LOS ANGELES).
BPI Communications, Inc., 5055 Wilshire Blvd., Ste. 600, Los Angeles, CA 90036. TEL 213-525-2270. FAX 213-525-2391.
Vendor(s): Knight-Ridder Information, Inc. (File no.648), Ovid Technologies, Inc. (TSAP). *31*

ADWEEK (NEW YORK).
B P I Communications, Inc. (New York), 1515 Broadway, New York, NY 10036. TEL 212-536-5336. FAX 212-536-1416
Vendor(s): Information Access Co., Knight-Ridder Information, Inc. (File no.64E), Lexis-Nexis, Ovid Technologies, Inc. (TSAP). *31*

ADWEEK: MIDWEST.
A S M Communications, Inc. (Chicago), 222 Merchandise Mart Plaza, Ste 936, Chicago, IL 60654-1102. TEL 312-467-6500. FAX 312-321-0039.
Vendor(s): Information Access Co.. *31*

ADWEEK: SOUTHEAST.
A S M Communications, Inc. Atlanta), 5 Piedmont Center, Ste. 507, Atlanta, GA 30305. TEL 404-841-3333. FAX 404-841-3332.
Vendor(s): Information Access Co., Lexis-Nexis. *31*

ADWEEK: SOUTHWEST.
B P I, 3102 Maple Ave., Ste. 120, Dallas, TX 75201-1233. TEL 214-871-3550.
Vendor(s): Information Access Co.. *31*

Online

AERA.
Asahi Shimbun Publishing Co., 3-2 Tsukiji 5-chome, Chuo-ku, Tokyo 104-11, Japan. *3187*

AERONAUTICAL ENGINEERING: A CONTINUING BIOGRAPHY WITH INDEXES.
U.S. National Aeronautics and Space Administration, National Technology Transfer Center, c/o Wheeling Jesuit University, 316 Washington Ave., Wheeling, WV 26003. TEL 304-243-2440. FAX 301-243-4390.
Available only online. *82*

AEROSPACE AMERICA.
American Institute of Aeronautics and Astronautics, Inc., 370 L'Enfant Promenade, S.W., Washington, DC 20024. TEL 202-646-7471. FAX 202-646-7508.
Vendor(s): Lexis-Nexis (AEROAM). *53*

AEROSPACE DAILY.
McGraw-Hill Companies, Aviation Week Group (Washington), 1200 G St., N.W., Ste. 200, Washington, DC 20005. TEL 202-383-2350.
Vendor(s): Dow Jones News Retrieval, European Space Agency (File no.72/AEROSPACE DAILY), Knight-Ridder Information, Inc. (File nos.624,648), Lexis-Nexis (AIRDLY), NewsNet (AE29), Ovid Technologies, Inc. (TSAP). *53*

AEROSPACE ENGINEERING MAGAZINE.
Society of Automotive Engineers, 400 Commonwealth Dr., Warrendale, PA 15096-0001. TEL 412-772-7114. FAX 412-776-4026.
Vendor(s): Orbit Search Service. *53*

AEROSPACE MEDICINE AND BIOLOGY.
U.S. National Aeronautics and Space Administration, National Technology Transfer Center, c/o Wheeling Jesuit University, 316 Washington Ave., Wheeling, WV 26003. TEL 304-243-2440. FAX 304-243-4390.
Available only online. *4548*

AEROSPACE PROPULSION.
McGraw-Hill Companies, Aviation Week Group (Washington), 1200 G. St., N.W., Ste. 200, Washington, DC 20005. TEL 202-383-2350.
Vendor(s): Dow Jones News Retrieval (ASR), Knight-Ridder Information, Inc. (ASP), Lexis-Nexis (AERPRO), NewsNet (AE34). *54*

LES AFFAIRES.
Publications Transcontinental Inc., 1100 boul. Rene Levesque W., 24th Fl., Montreal, PQ H3B 4X9, Canada. TEL 514-392-9000. FAX 514-392-4723.
Vendor(s): Southam Electronic Publishing. *1057*

AFFIRMATIVE ACTION - E E O PERSONNEL UPDATE.
Nyper Publications, Box 662, Latham, NY 12110. TEL 518-786-1654. FAX 518-456-8582.
Vendor(s): Lexis-Nexis, NewsNet. *3737*

AFRICA ANALYSIS.
Africa Analysis Ltd., Ludgate House, 107-111 Fleet St., London EC4A 2AB, England. TEL 44-171-353-1117. FAX 44-171-353-1516. *1172*

AFRICA ECONOMIC DIGEST.
Concord Press of Nigeria, 26-32 Whistler St., London N5 1NJ, England. TEL 071-359-5335. FAX 071-359-9173. *1172*

AFRICA NEWS ONLINE.
Africa News Service, Inc., Box 3851, Durham, NC 27702. TEL 919-286-0747. FAX 919-286-2614. Available only online. Vendor(s): NewsNet. *5630*

AFRICA REPORT.
African-American Institute, 833 United Nations Plaza, New York, NY 10017. TEL 212-949-5666. FAX 212-682-6174.
Vendor(s): Information Access Co., University Microfilms International. *5740*

AFRICA TODAY.
Lynne Rienner Publishers, 1800 30th St., Ste. 314, Boulder, CO 80301. TEL 303-444-6684. FAX 303-444-0824.
Vendor(s): Information Access Co., University Microfilms International. *5631*

AFRICAN AFFAIRS.
Oxford University Press, Oxford Journals, Walton St., Oxford OX2 6DP, England. TEL 01865-56767. FAX 01865-56646.
Vendor(s): Information Access Co.. *5631*

AFRICAN AMERICAN REVIEW.
Indiana State University, Department of English, Terre Haute, IN 47809. TEL 812-237-2968. FAX 812-237-3156.
Vendor(s): Information Access Co., University Microfilms International. *2860*

AFRICAN ARTS.
University of California at Los Angeles, James S. Coleman African Studies Center, Los Angeles, CA 90024. TEL 310-825-1218.
Vendor(s): University Microfilms International. *409*

AFRICAN BUSINESS.
I.C. Publications Ltd., 7 Coldbath Sq., London EC1R 4LQ, England. TEL 44-171-713-7711. FAX 44-171-713-7898. *1301*

AFTERIMAGE.
Visual Studies Workshop, 31 Prince St., Rochester, NY 14607. TEL 716-442-8676.
Vendor(s): Information Access Co.. *5508*

AFTERMARKET BUSINESS.
Advanstar Communications, Inc., 7500 Old Oak Blvd., Cleveland, OH 44130. TEL 216-891-2604. FAX 216-891-2574.
Vendor(s): Information Access Co., Knight-Ridder Information, Inc.. *6768*

AGE AND AGEING.
Oxford University Press, Oxford Journals, Walton St., Oxford OX2 6DP, England. TEL 01865-267907. FAX 01865-267773.
Vendor(s): Information Access Co., Ovid Technologies, Inc.. *3282*

AGENCY SALES.
Manufacturers' Agents National Association, 23016 Mill Creek Rd., Box 3467, Laguna Hills, CA 92654-3467. TEL 714-859-4040.
Vendor(s): Information Access Co., University Microfilms International. *1452*

AGEXPORTER.
U.S. Department of Agriculture, Foreign Agricultural Service, Information Division, Rm. 4638-S, Washington, DC 20250-1000. TEL 202-720-9437. FAX 202-720-3229.
Vendor(s): Information Access Co.. *185*

AGGRESSIVE BEHAVIOR.
John Wiley & Sons, Inc., Journals, 605 Third Ave., New York, NY 10158. TEL 212-850-6645. FAX 212-850-6021. *5824*

AGING.
S U B I S, Mansion House, 19 Kingfield Rd., Sheffield S11 9AS, England. TEL 44-114-2554433. FAX 44-114-2554626.
Vendor(s): Information Access Co.. *3282*

AGING RESEARCH & TRAINING NEWS.
Business Publishers, Inc., 951 Pershing Dr., Silver Spring, MD 20910-4464. TEL 301-587-6300. FAX 301-585-9075.
Vendor(s): NewsNet. *3283*

AGRA EUROPE.
Agra Europe (London) Ltd., 25 Frant Rd., Tunbridge Wells, Kent TN2 5JT, England. TEL 44-1892-533813. FAX 44-1892-544895.
Vendor(s): Information Access Co.. *185*

AGRI FINANCE.
Century Communications Corp., 6201 W. Howard St., Niles, IL 60714-3435. TEL 708-647-1200. FAX 708-647-7055.
Vendor(s): University Microfilms International. *185*

AGRI MARKETING.
Doane Information Service, 11701 Borman Dr., St. Louis, MO 63146. TEL 314-569-2700. FAX 314-564-1083.
Vendor(s): University Microfilms International. *185*

AGRICULTURAL & ENVIRONMENTAL BIOTECHNOLOGY ABSTRACTS.
Cambridge Scientific Abstracts, 7200 Wisconsin Ave., 6th Fl., Bethesda, MD 20814. TEL 301-961-6700. FAX 301-961-6720.
Vendor(s): Knight-Ridder Information, Inc. (File no. 76/Life Sciences Collection), STN International (LIFESCI). *166*

AGRICULTURAL ENGINEERING.
American Society of Agricultural Engineers, 2950 Niles Rd., St. Joseph, MI 49085-9659. TEL 616-429-0300. FAX 616-429-3852.
Vendor(s): Information Access Co.. *209*

AGRICULTURAL ENGINEERING ABSTRACTS.
CAB International, Wallingford, Oxon. OX10 8DE, England. TEL 44-1491-832111. FAX 44-1491-835508.
Vendor(s): DIMDI, European Space Agency (File nos.16 & 124/CAB), Knight-Ridder Information, Inc., STN International. *166*

AGRICULTURAL HISTORY.
University of California Press, Journals Division, 2120 Berkeley Way, No. 5812, Berkeley, CA 94720-5812. TEL 510-643-7154. FAX 510-642-9917.
Vendor(s): Information Access Co.. *89*

AGRICULTURAL RESEARCH.
U.S. Department of Agriculture, Agriculture Research Service, Rm. 408, 6303 Ivy Ln., Greenbelt, MD 20770. TEL 301-344-2514. FAX 301-344-2325.
Vendor(s): Information Access Co., University Microfilms International. *90*

AGRICULTURAL RESEARCH DEPARTMENT. WINAND STARING CENTRE FOR INTEGRATED LAND, SOIL AND WATER RESEARCH. REPORTS.
Dienst Landbouwkundig Onderzoek, P.O. Box 125, 6700 AC Wageningen, Netherlands. TEL 31-8370-74200. FAX 31-8370-24812. *209*

AGRICULTURAL STATISTICS SERIES NO.2: ANIMAL PRODUCTION.
Statistical Office of the European Communities, Rue Alcide de Gasperi, 2920 Luxembourg, Luxembourg. TEL 43011. *166*

AGRICULTURAL SUPPLY INDUSTRY.
P J B Publications Ltd., 18-20 Hill Rise, Richmond, Surrey TW10 6UA, England. TEL 44-181-948-3262. FAX 44-181-332-8998.
Vendor(s): Knight-Ridder Information, Inc. (File no.648), Ovid Technologies, Inc. (TSAP). *91*

AGRICULTURE AND ENVIRONMENT FOR DEVELOPING COUNTRIES.
Koninklijk Instituut voor de Tropen, Mauritskade 63, 1092 AD Amsterdam, Netherlands. TEL 31-20-5688298. FAX 31-20-6654423.
Vendor(s): Orbit Search Service (TROPAG). *166*

AGRINDEX.
Food and Agriculture Organization of the United Nations (Rome), Via delle Terme de Caracalla, 00100 Rome, Italy. TEL 57974350. FAX 57975155.
Vendor(s): DIMDI, Knight-Ridder Information, Inc. (File no.203), European Space Agency (File no.29/AGRIS). *92*

AGROFORESTRY ABSTRACTS.
CAB International, Wallingford, Oxon. OX10 8DE, England. TEL 01491-832111. FAX 01491-833508.
Vendor(s): DIMDI, Data-Star, European Space Agency, Knight-Ridder Information, Inc., Ovid Technologies, Inc., STN International. *3030*

AGROW.
P J B Publications Ltd., 18-20 Hill Rise, Richmond, Surrey TW10 6UA, England. TEL 44-181-948-3262. FAX 44-181-332-8998.
Vendor(s): Data-Star, Knight-Ridder Information, Inc., Ovid Technologies, Inc. (PHIN,PHIC,PHID). *95*

AIDS BOOK REVIEW JOURNAL.
University of Illinois at Chicago, Library, Box 8198, Chicago, IL 60680-8198. TEL 312-996-2730. FAX 312-413-0424.
Available only online. *4615*

AIDS CARE.
Carfax Publishing Co., P.O. Box 25, Abingdon, Oxon. OX14 3UE, England. TEL 44-1235-401000. FAX 44-1235-401550. *4616*

AIDS NEWSLETTER.
CAB International, Wallingford, Oxon. OX10 8DE, England. TEL 44-1491-832111. FAX 44-1491-833508.
Vendor(s): DIMDI. *4616*

AIDS POLICY AND LAW.
L R P Publications 747 Dresher Rd., Box 980, Horsham, PA 19044-0980. TEL 215-784-0941. FAX 215-784-9639.
Vendor(s): Human Resources Information Network (CDD, HDD). *3737*

AIDS WEEKLY.
Charles W. Henderson, Ed. & Pub., Box 5528, Atlanta, GA 31107-0528. TEL 404-377-8895. FAX 205-991-1479.
Vendor(s): Data-Star (PTS NEWSLETTER DATABASE), Information Access Co., Knight-Ridder Information, Inc. (File no.636), NewsNet (HH14). *4617*

AIKIDO JOURNAL.
K.K. Aiki News, Lions Mansion No. 204, Tamagawa Gakuen 5-11-25, Machida-shi, Tokyo 194, Japan. TEL 81-427-24-8675. FAX 81-427-24-9119. *6449*

AIR CARGO REPORT.
Phillips Business Information, Inc., 1201 Seven Locks Rd., Potomac, MD 20854. TEL 301-424-3338. FAX 301-309-3847.
Vendor(s): Information Access Co., NewsNet. *6749*

AIR CARGO WORLD.
Intertec Publishshing Corp. (Atlanta), 6151 Powers Ferry Rd., N.W., Atlanta, GA 30339-2941. TEL 770-955-2500. FAX 770-955-0400.
Vendor(s): Information Access Co.. *6749*

AIR CONDITIONING, HEATING & REFRIGERATION NEWS.
Business News Publishing Company, 755 W. Big Beaver Rd., Ste. 1000, Troy, MI 48084. TEL 810-362-3700. FAX 810-362-0317.
Vendor(s): Dow Jones News Retrieval, Information Access Co., Knight-Ridder Information, Inc. (File no.648), Ovid Technologies, Inc. (TSAP). *3325*

AIR FRESHENERS AND INSECTICIDES: THE INTERNATIONAL MARKET.
Euromonitor, 60-61 Britton St., London EC1M 5NA, England. TEL 44-171-251-8024. FAX 44-171-608-3149.
Vendor(s): Data-Star, Knight-Ridder Information, Inc.. *1827*

AIR SAFETY WEEK.
Phillips Business Information, Inc., 1201 Seven Locks Rd., Potomac, MD 20854. TEL 301-424-3338. FAX 301-309-3847.
Vendor(s): Data-Star, Information Access Co., Knight-Ridder Information, Inc., NewsNet (AE16). *55*

AIR TRANSPORT WORLD.
Penton Publishing Co. (Stamford) 600 Summer St., Box 1361, Stamford, CT 06904. TEL 203-348-7531. FAX 203-348-4023.
Vendor(s): Information Access Co., Knight-Ridder Information, Inc., University Microfilms International. *55*

AIR - WATER POLLUTION REPORT.
Business Publishers, Inc., 951 Pershing Dr., Silver Spring, MD 20910-4464. TEL 301-587-6300. FAX 301-585-9075.
Vendor(s): Data-Star, Information Access Co., Knight-Ridder Information, Inc., NewsNet (EV10). *2774*

AIRCRAFT VALUE NEWSLETTER.
Phillips Business Information, Inc., 1201 Seven Locks Rd., Potomac, MD 20854. TEL 301-424-3338. FAX 301-309-3847.
Vendor(s): Information Access Co., NewsNet. *6750*

AIRFINANCE JOURNAL.
Euromoney Aviation Group, Playhouse Yard, Nestor House, London EC4V 5EX, England. TEL 44-171-779-8866. FAX 44-171-779-8867.
Vendor(s): University Microfilms International. *6750*

AIRLINE BUSINESS.
Reed Business Publishing Ltd. Quadrant House, The Quadrant, Sutton, Surrey SM2 5AS, England. TEL 0181-652-4996. FAX 0181-652-8914.
Vendor(s): Data-Star, Information Access Co., Reuters, Ltd.. *6750*

AIRLINE FINANCIAL NEWS.
Phillips Business Information, Inc., 1201 Seven Locks Rd., Potomac, MD 20854. TEL 301-424-3338. FAX 301-309-3847.
Vendor(s): Data-Star, Information Access Co., Knight-Ridder Information, Inc., NewsNet (AE25). *6750*

AIRLINE MARKETING NEWS.
Phillips Business Information, Inc., 1201 Seven Locks Rd., Potomac, MD 20854. TEL 301-424-3338. FAX 301-309-3847.
Vendor(s): Information Access Co.. *6751*

AIRMAN.
U.S. Air Force, Air Force News Agency, Kelly AFB, TX 78241-6105. TEL 210-925-7757. FAX 210-925-7219. *5020*

AIRPORTS.
McGraw-Hill Companies, Aviation Week Group (Washington), 1200 G St., N.W., Ste. 200, Washington, DC 20005. TEL 202-383-2350.
Vendor(s): Dow Jones News Retrieval, Knight-Ridder Information, Inc. (File no.624/McGRAW-HILL PUBLICATIONS ONLINE), Lexis-Nexis, NewsNet (AE21). *6752*

AIRPORTS INTERNATIONAL MAGAZINE.
E M A P, 151 Roseberry Ave., London EC1R 4QX, England.
Vendor(s): Information Access Co.. *56*

ALABAMA BUSINESS DIRECTORY.
American Business Directories 5711 S. 86th Cir., Box 27347, Omaha, NE 68127. TEL 402-593-4600. FAX 401-331-5481. *1583*

ALABAMA LAW REVIEW.
University of Alabama, School of Law, Box 870382, University, AL 35487-0382. TEL 205-348-7191.
Vendor(s): West Services, Inc.. *3738*

ALABAMA LAWYER.
State Bar of Alabama, Lock Box 4156, Montgomery, AL 36101. TEL 205-269-1515.
Vendor(s): West Services, Inc.. *3738*

ALASKA BUSINESS DIRECTORY.
American Business Directories 5711 S. 86th Cir., Box 27347, Omaha, NE 68127. TEL 402-593-4600. FAX 402-331-5481. *1583*

ALASKA BUSINESS MONTHLY.
Alaska Business Publishing Co., Box 241288, Anchorage, AK 99524-1288. TEL 907-276-4373. FAX 907-279-2900.
Vendor(s): Information Access Co., Knight-Ridder Information, Inc., Lexis-Nexis. *892*

ALASKA JOURNAL OF COMMERCE & PACIFIC RIM REPORTER.
Pacific Rim Publishing Co., Box 201894, Anchorage, AK 99520-1894. TEL 907-272-7500. FAX 907-279-1037.
Vendor(s): Knight-Ridder Information, Inc., University Microfilms International. *1162*

ALASKA SNOW SURVEY REPORT.
U.S. Natural Resources Conservation Service (Anchorage), 949 E. 35th Ave., Ste. 400, Anchorage, AK 99508-4362. TEL 907-271-2424. FAX 907-271-3951. *6962*

ALBANY LAW REVIEW.
Albany Law School, 80 New Scotland Ave., Albany, NY 12208. TEL 518-445-2372. FAX 518-472-5857.
Vendor(s): Lexis-Nexis, West Services, Inc., Wilsonline. *3738*

ALBERTA BUSINESS.
Sunrise Publishing Ltd., 2213-C Hanselman Ct., Saskatoon, SK S7L 6A8, Canada. TEL 306-244-5668. FAX 306-244-5679.
Vendor(s): Information Access Co.. *892*

ALBERTA DECISIONS. CIVIL AND CRIMINAL CASES.
Western Legal Publications, 301-1 Alexander St., Vancouver, BC V6A 1B2, Canada. TEL 604-687-5671. FAX 604-687-2796. *3738*

ALBERTA REPORTS.
Maritime Law Book Ltd., Box 302, Fredericton, NB E3B 4Y9, Canada. TEL 506-453-9921. FAX 506-453-9525.
Vendor(s): QL Systems Ltd.. *3739*

ALCOHOL HEALTH & RESEARCH WORLD.
U.S. National Institute on Alcohol Abuse and Alcoholism, 6000 Executive Blvd., Bethesda, MD 20892-7003. TEL 301-443-3850. FAX 301-480-1725.
Vendor(s): Information Access Co., University Microfilms International. *2194*

ALCOHOL OUTLOOK.
Information Resources, Inc., 1925 N. Lynn St., Ste. 1000, Arlington, VA 22204-1717. TEL 703-528-2500. FAX 703-528-1483.
Vendor(s): Information Access Co.. *5349*

ALCOHOLISM & DRUG ABUSE WEEKLY.
Manisses Communications Group, Inc., Box 9758, Providence, RI 02940-9758. TEL 401-861-6370. FAX 401-861-6370.
Vendor(s): Data-Star, Information Access Co., Knight-Ridder Information Inc., Ovid Technologies, Inc.. *2194*

ALL CANADA WEEKLY SUMMARIES - NATIONAL.
Canada Law Book Inc., 240 Edward St., Aurora, ON L4G 3S9, Canada. TEL 905-841-6472. FAX 905-841-5085. *3739*

ALL ENGLAND LAW REPORTS.
Butterworth & Co. (Publishers) Ltd., Part of the Reed Elsevier group, Halsbury House, 35 Chancery Ln., London WC2A 1EL, England. TEL 071-400-2500 FAX 071-400-2842.
Vendor(s): Lexis-Nexis. *3945*

ALL MEDIA & PRODUCT SURVEY.
S A Advertising Research Foundation, P.O. Box 98874, 2152 Sloane Park, South Africa. TEL 27-11-463-5340. FAX 27-11-463-5010. *48*

ALLOYS INDEX.
Cambridge Scientific Abstracts, 7200 Wisconsin Ave., 6th fl., Bethesda, MD 20814. TEL 301-961-6750. FAX 301-961-6720
Vendor(s): CEDOCAR, CIST, Data-Star (META), European Space Agency (File no.3), FIZ Technik (META), Knight-Ridder Information, Inc. (File no.32/METADEX), Orbit Search Service (MDEX), STN International. *4980*

ALMANAC OF FAMOUS PEOPLE.
Gale Research Inc., 835 Penobscot Bldg., Detroit, MI 48226. TEL 313-961-2242. FAX 313-961-6083.
Vendor(s): Lexis-Nexis. *554*

ALPHABETIC SUBJECT INDEX TO PETROLEUM ABSTRACTS.
University of Tulsa, Information Services Division, 600 S. College Ave., Tulsa, OK 74104-3189. TEL 913-631-2297. FAX 918-599-9361.
Vendor(s): Knight-Ridder Information, Inc. (File no.87,987), Orbit Search Service (TULSA). *5381*

ALTERNATIVE PRESS INDEX.
Alternative Press Center, Inc. Box 33109, Baltimore, MD 21218. TEL 410-243-2471. FAX 410-235-5325. *4175*

ALTERNATIVES JOURNAL.
University of Waterloo, Faculty of Environmental Studies, Waterloo, ON N2L 3G1, Canada. TEL 519-885-1221 ext. 6783. FAX 519-746-0292.
Vendor(s): Information Access Co.. *2775*

ALTERNATIVES TO THE HIGH COST OF LITIGATION.
C P R Institute for Dispute Resolution, 366 Madison Ave., New York, NY 10017-3122. TEL 212-949-6490. FAX 212-949-3859.
Vendor(s): Lexis-Nexis, West Services, Inc.. *3739*

ALUMINIUM INDUSTRY ABSTRACTS.
Aluminum Association, Inc., Materials Park, OH 44073. TEL 216-338-5151 FAX 216-338-4634.
Vendor(s): European Space Agency (File no.9/ALUMINUM), Knight-Ridder Information, Inc. (File no.33). *4980*

ALUMINIUM TODAY.
Argus Business Media Ltd., Fuel and Metals Journals Queensway House, 2 Queensway, Redhill, Surrey RH1 1QS, England. TEL 44-1737-768611. FAX 44-1737-761685.
Vendor(s): Information Access Co.. *4949*

AMERICA.
America Press Inc., 106 W. 56th St., New York, NY 10019. TEL 212-581-4640. FAX 212-399-3596.
Vendor(s): Information Access Co., University Microfilms International. *6167*

AMERICA: HISTORY AND LIFE. ARTICLE ABSTRACTS AND CITATIONS OF REVIEWS AND DISSERTATIONS COVERING THE UNITED STATES AND CANADA.
A B C-Clio, 130 Cremona, Box 1911, Santa Barbara, CA 93116-1911. TEL 805-968-1911. FAX 805-685-9685.
Vendor(s): Knight-Ridder Information, Inc. (File no.38). *3364*

AMERICAN ACADEMY OF CHILD AND ADOLESCENT PSYCHIATRY. JOURNAL.
Williams & Wilkins, 351 W. Camden St., Baltimore, MD 21201. TEL 410-528-4000. FAX 410-528-4312.
Vendor(s): Information Access Co.. *4823*

AMERICAN ADVERTISING.
American Advertising Federation, 1101 Vermont Ave., N.W., Ste. 500, Washington, DC 20005. TEL 202-898-0089. FAX 202-898-0159.
Vendor(s): University Microfilms International. *31*

AMERICAN AGENT AND BROKER.
Commerce Publishing Co., 330 N. Fourth St., St. Louis, MO 63102-2036. TEL 314-421-5445.
Vendor(s): University Microfilms International. *3640*

AMERICAN ALMANAC.
Reference Press Inc., Box 140375, Austin, TX 78714-0375. TEL 512-454-7778. FAX 512-454-9401. *2535*

AMERICAN ANTIQUITY.
Society for American Archaeology, 900 Second St., N.W., No. 12, Washington, DC 20002-3557. TEL 202-789-8200. FAX 202-789-0284.
Vendor(s): Information Access Co.. *338*

AMERICAN ARTIST.
B P I Communications, Inc. (New York), 1515 Broadway, 11th Fl., New York, NY 10036. TEL 212-764-7300. FAX 212-536-5351.
Vendor(s): Information Access Co.. *409*

AMERICAN ASSOCIATION OF STRATIGRAPHIC PALYNOLOGISTS. NEWSLETTER.
American Association of Stratigraphic Palynologists Foundation, Inc., c/o Vaughn M. Bryant, Jr., Palynology Laboratory, Texas A & M Univ., College Station, TX 77843-4352. TEL 409-845-5242. FAX 409-845-4070. *2224*

AMERICAN BANKER.
American Banker - Bond Buyer, Newsletter Division One State St. Plaza, New York, NY 10004-1549. FAX 212-843-9600.
Vendor(s): Data-Star (BANK), Information Access Co., Knight-Ridder Information, Inc. (File no.625), Lexis-Nexis, NewsNet (FI10), Ovid Technologies, Inc.. *1058*

AMERICAN BANKER INDEX.
U M I Company 300 N. Zeeb Rd., Ann Arbor, MI 48106. TEL 313-761-4700. FAX 800-864-0019.
Vendor(s): Knight-Ridder Information, Inc.. *974*

AMERICAN BANKER'S WASHINGTON WATCH.
American Banker - Bond Buyer, Newsletter Division One State St. Plaza, New York, NY 10004-1549. TEL 800-733-4371. FAX 212-943-2224.
Vendor(s): Information Access Co., Knight-Ridder Information, Inc., Lexis-Nexis, NewsNet (FI05). *1058*

AMERICAN BEHAVIORAL SCIENTIST.
Sage Publications, Inc., 2455 Teller Rd., Thousand Oaks, CA 91320. TEL 805-499-0721. FAX 805-499-0871.
Vendor(s): Information Access Co.. *6314*

AMERICAN BIBLIOGRAPHY OF SLAVIC AND EAST EUROPEAN STUDIES.
American Association for the Advancement of Slavic Studies, c/o Russian Research Bldg., 1737 Cambridge St., Cambridge, MA 02138. TEL 415-723-9668. *3364*

AMERICAN BIG BUSINESSES DIRECTORY.
American Business Directories 5711 S. 86th Circle, Box 27347, Omaha, NE 68127. TEL 402-593-4600. FAX 402-331-5481. *1583*

AMERICAN BUSINESS LAW JOURNAL.
Academy of Legal Studies in Business, c/o Daniel J. Herron, Dept. of Finance, 120 Upham Hall, Miami University, Oxford, OH 45056. TEL 513-529-2945. FAX 513-529-6992.
Vendor(s): Information Access Co.. *3893*

AMERICAN CHEMICAL SOCIETY. DIRECTORY OF GRADUATE RESEARCH.
American Chemical Society, 1155 16th St., N.W., Washington, DC 20036. TEL 800-227-5558. FAX 202-872-4615. *2409*

AMERICAN CHEMICAL SOCIETY. JOURNAL.
American Chemical Society, 1155 16th St., N.W., Washington, DC 20036.
Vendor(s): STN International (CJACS). *1664*

AMERICAN CITY & COUNTY.
Intertec Publishing Corp. (Atlanta), 6151 Powers Ferry Rd., N.W., Atlanta, GA 30339-2941. TEL 770-955-2500. FAX 770-955-0400.
Vendor(s): Information Access Co., LOGIN Information Services, University Microfilms International. *5937*

AMERICAN COLLEGE OF CARDIOLOGY. JOURNAL.
Elsevier Science Inc., Box 945, New York, NY 10159-0945. TEL 212-633-3730. FAX 212-633-3680.
Vendor(s): Ovid Technologies, Inc.. *4594*

AMERICAN COLLEGE OF SURGEONS. JOURNAL.
American College of Surgeons, Publishing Department, 54 E. Erie St., Chicago, IL 60611-2798. TEL 312-787-9282. FAX 312-440-7026.
Vendor(s): Lexis-Nexis. *4902*

AMERICAN CRAFT.
American Craft Council, 72 Spring St., New York, NY 10012. TEL 212-274-0630. FAX 212-274-0650.
Vendor(s): University Microfilms International. *464*

AMERICAN CRIMINAL LAW REVIEW.
Georgetown University Law Center, 600 New Jersey Ave., N.W., Washington, DC 20001. TEL 202-662-9468.
Vendor(s): Information Access Co., West Services, Inc. (ACRIMLREV).. *2157*

AMERICAN DEMOGRAPHICS.
American Demographics, Inc., Box 68, Ithaca, NY 14851-0068. TEL 607-273-6343. FAX 607-273-3196.
Vendor(s): Dow Jones News Retrieval, Information Access Co., Lexis-Nexis, University Microfilms International. *5780*

AMERICAN DIETETIC ASSOCIATION. JOURNAL.
American Dietetic Association, 216 W. Jackson Blvd., Ste. 800, Chicago, IL 60606-6995. TEL 312-899-0040. FAX 312-899-1757.
Vendor(s): Information Access Co., University Microfilms International. *5228*

AMERICAN DOCTORAL DISSERTATIONS.
U M I Company 300 N. Zeeb Rd., Ann Arbor, MI 48106. TEL 313-761-4700. FAX 800-864-0019.
Vendor(s): Data-Star, Knight-Ridder Information, Inc. (File no. 35), OCLC (EPIC), Ovid Technologies, Inc., STN International. *2419*

AMERICAN DRUGGIST.
Hearst Business Publishing, American Druggist, 1790 Broadway, Ste. 6, New York, NY 10019-1412. TEL 212-969-7508. FAX 212-969-7557.
Vendor(s): Information Access Co.. *5398*

AMERICAN ECONOMIST.
Omicron Delta Epsilon Fraternity, c/o Michael Szenberg, Ed., Graduate School of Business, Dept. of Economics, Pace University, New York, NY 10038. TEL 212-346-1921. FAX 212-346-1573.
Vendor(s): Information Access Co., University Microfilms International. *1173*

AMERICAN ENTERPRISE.
American Enterprise Institute for Public Policy Research, 1150 17th St., N.W., Washington, DC 20036. TEL 202-862-5800. FAX 202-862-7178.
Vendor(s): University Microfilms International. *5632*

AMERICAN FAMILY PHYSICIAN.
American Academy of Family Physicians, 8880 Ward Pkwy., Kansas City, MO 64114. TEL 816-333-9700. FAX 816-333-0303.
Vendor(s): Information Access Co., Lexis-Nexis, Ovid Technologies, Inc.. *4423*

AMERICAN FITNESS.
Aerobics and Fitness Association of America, 15250 Ventura Blvd., Ste. 310, Sherman Oaks, CA 91403. TEL 818-905-0040.
Vendor(s): Information Access Co., Knight-Ridder Information, Inc. (File no.149), University Microfilms International. *5524*

AMERICAN FORESTS.
American Forests, Box 2000, Washington, DC 20013. TEL 202-667-3300. FAX 202-667-7751.
Vendor(s): Information Access Co., University Microfilms International. *3010*

AMERICAN GAS.
American Gas Association, 1515 Wilson Blvd., Arlington, VA 22209. TEL 703-841-8400. FAX 703-841-8406.
Vendor(s): University Microfilms International. *5349*

AMERICAN GERIATRICS SOCIETY. JOURNAL.
Williams & Wilkins, 351 W. Camden St., Baltimore, MD 21201. TEL 410-528-4000. FAX 410-528-4312. *3283*

AMERICAN HEALTH.
Reader's Digest Association, Inc. (New York), 28 West 23rd St., New York, NY 10010. TEL 212-366-8900. FAX 212-366-8760.
Vendor(s): Information Access Co.. *5524*

AMERICAN HEALTH CARE ASSOCIATION. PROVIDER.
American Health Care Association, 1201 L St., N.W., Washington, DC 20005. TEL 202-842-4444. FAX 202-842-3860. *6360*

AMERICAN HEART JOURNAL.
Mosby - Year Book, Inc. 11830 Westline Industrial Dr., St. Louis, MO 63146-3318. TEL 314-872-8370. FAX 314-432-1380.
Vendor(s): Ovid Technologies, Inc.. *4595*

AMERICAN HERITAGE.
American Heritage 60 Fifth Ave., New York, NY 10011. TEL 212-206-5500. FAX 212-620-2332.
Vendor(s): Information Access Co., Knight-Ridder Information, Inc.. *3458*

AMERICAN HISTORICAL REVIEW.
American Historical Association, 400 A St., S.E., Washington, DC 20003-3889. TEL 202-544-2422. FAX 202-544-8307.
Vendor(s): University Microfilms International. *3336*

AMERICAN IMAGO.
Johns Hopkins University Press, Journals Publishing Division, 2715 N. Charles St., Baltimore, MD 21218. TEL 410-516-6980. FAX 410-516-6968.
Vendor(s): Information Access Co.. *4824*

AMERICAN INDIAN LAW REVIEW.
University of Oklahoma, College of Law, 300 Timberdell Rd., Norman, OK 73019. TEL 405-325-2840.
Vendor(s): West Services, Inc.. *3740*

AMERICAN INDIAN QUARTERLY.
University of Nebraska Press, 312 N. 14th St., Box 880484, Lincoln, NE 68588-0484. TEL 402-472-3581. FAX 402-472-6214.
Vendor(s): Information Access Co.. *300*

AMERICAN INSTITUTE OF PHYSICS. CENTER FOR HISTORY OF PHYSICS. NEWSLETTER.
American Institute of Physics, Center for History of Physics, One Physics Ellipse, College Park, MD 20740. TEL 301-209-3165. FAX 301-209-0882. *5541*

AMERICAN JEWISH HISTORY.
Johns Hopkins University Press, Journals Publishing Division, 2715 N. Charles St., Baltimore, MD 21218-4310. TEL 410-516-6980. FAX 410-516-6968. *2863*

AMERICAN JOURNAL OF AGRICULTURAL ECONOMICS.
American Agricultural Economics Association, 1110 Buckeye Ave., Ames, IA 50010-8063. TEL 515-233-3202. FAX 515-233-3101.
Vendor(s): Information Access Co., University Microfilms International. *187*

AMERICAN JOURNAL OF ANTHROPOMORPHICS.
Med Systems Co., Box 580009, Flushing, NY 11358-0009. TEL 718-359-5741. FAX 718-359-2768. *410*

AMERICAN JOURNAL OF CARDIOLOGY.
Excerpta Medica, Inc. 105 Raider Blvd., Belle Mead, NJ 08502. TEL 908-874-8550. FAX 908-874-8419.
Vendor(s): Lexis-Nexis, Ovid Technologies, Inc.. *4595*

AMERICAN JOURNAL OF CLINICAL NUTRITION.
American Society for Clinical Nutrition, Inc., 9650 Rockville Pike, Rm. 2310, Bethesda, MD 20814-3998. TEL 301-530-7026. FAX 301-530-7001.
Vendor(s): University Microfilms International. *5229*

AMERICAN JOURNAL OF COMMUNITY PSYCHOLOGY.
Plenum Publishing Corp., 233 Spring St., New York, NY 10013-1578. TEL 212-620-8000. FAX 212-463-0742.
Vendor(s): Information Access Co.. *6404*

AMERICAN JOURNAL OF DRUG AND ALCOHOL ABUSE.
Marcel Dekker Journals, 270 Madison Ave., New York, NY 10016. TEL 212-696-9000. FAX 212-685-4540.
Vendor(s): Information Access Co.. *2194*

AMERICAN JOURNAL OF ECONOMICS AND SOCIOLOGY.
American Journal of Economics & Sociology, Inc., 41 E. 72nd St., New York, NY 10021-0310. TEL 212-988-1680. FAX 212-399-6465.
Vendor(s): Information Access Co., University Microfilms International. *892*

AMERICAN JOURNAL OF INDUSTRIAL MEDICINE.
John Wiley & Sons, Inc., Journals, 605 Third Ave., New York, NY 10158. TEL 212-850-6645. FAX 212-850-6021. *5244*

AMERICAN JOURNAL OF INTERNATIONAL LAW.
American Society of International Law, 2223 Massachusetts Ave., N.W., Washington, DC 20008-2864. TEL 202-939-6000. FAX 202-797-7133.
Vendor(s): Lexis-Nexis. *3922*

AMERICAN JOURNAL OF KIDNEY DISEASES.
W.B. Saunders Co. Curtis Center, 3rd Fl., Independence Sq. W., Philadelphia, PA 19106-3399. TEL 215-238-7800. FAX 215-238-6445. *4924*

AMERICAN JOURNAL OF LAW & MEDICINE.
American Society of Law, Medicine & Ethics, 765 Commonwealth Ave., Ste. 1634, Boston, MA 02215. TEL 617-262-4990. FAX 617-437-7596.
Vendor(s): Information Access Co., Lexis-Nexis, West Services, Inc.. *3740*

AMERICAN JOURNAL OF LEGAL HISTORY.
Temple University, School of Law, Philadelphia, PA 19122. TEL 215-787-1256. FAX 215-787-1785.
Vendor(s): West Services, Inc.. *3740*

AMERICAN JOURNAL OF MATHEMATICS.
Johns Hopkins University Press, Journals Publishing Division, 2715 N. Charles St., Baltimore, MD 21218. TEL 410-516-6987. FAX 410-516-6968.
Vendor(s): Information Access Co.. *4352*

AMERICAN JOURNAL OF MEDICAL GENETICS.
John Wiley & Sons, Inc., Journals, 605 Third Ave., New York, NY 10158. TEL 212-850-6645. FAX 212-850-6021. *737*

THE AMERICAN JOURNAL OF MEDICINE.
Excerpta Medica, Inc. 105 Raider Blvd., Belle Mead, NJ 08502. TEL 908-874-8550. FAX 908-874-8419.
Vendor(s): Lexis-Nexis, Ovid Technologies, Inc.. *4424*

AMERICAN JOURNAL OF NURSING.
American Journal of Nursing Co., 555 W. 57th St., New York, NY 10019. TEL 212-582-8820. FAX 212-586-5462.
Vendor(s): University Microfilms International. *4709*

AMERICAN JOURNAL OF OBSTETRICS AND GYNECOLOGY.
Mosby - Year Book, Inc. 11830 Westline Industrial Dr., St. Louis, MO 63146-3318. TEL 314-872-8370. FAX 314-432-1380.
Vendor(s): Ovid Technologies, Inc.. *4731*

AMERICAN JOURNAL OF OPHTHALMOLOGY.
Ophthalmic Publishing Co., 77 W. Wacker Dr., Ste. 660, Chicago, IL 60601-1632. TEL 312-629-1690. FAX 312-629-1744.
Vendor(s): Information Access Co.. *4766*

AMERICAN JOURNAL OF PHARMACEUTICAL EDUCATION.
American Association of Colleges of Pharmacy, 1426 Prince St., Alexandria, VA 22314-2815. TEL 703-739-2330. *5398*

AMERICAN JOURNAL OF PHARMACY.
Philadelphia College of Pharmacy and Science, 600 S. 43rd St., Philadelphia, PA 19104-4495. TEL 215-596-8800. *5398*

AMERICAN JOURNAL OF PHILOLOGY.
Johns Hopkins University Press, Journals Publishing Division, 2715 N. Charles St., Baltimore, MD 21218. TEL 410-516-6987. FAX 410-516-6968.
Vendor(s): Information Access Co.. *4051*

AMERICAN JOURNAL OF PRIMATOLOGY.
John Wiley & Sons, Inc., Journals, 605 Third Ave., New York, NY 10108. TEL 212-850-6645. FAX 212-850-6021. *568*

AMERICAN JOURNAL OF PSYCHIATRY.
American Psychiatric Association, 1400 K St., N.W., Washington, DC 20005. TEL 202-682-6020. FAX 202-682-6016.
Vendor(s): Ovid Technologies, Inc., University Microfilms International. *4824*

AMERICAN JOURNAL OF PSYCHOLOGY.
University of Illinois Press, 1325 S. Oak St., Champaign, IL 61820. TEL 217-333-0950. FAX 217-244-8082.
Vendor(s): Information Access Co.. *5825*

AMERICAN JOURNAL OF PSYCHOTHERAPY.
Association for the Advancement of Psychotherapy, Belfer Education Center, 1300 Morris Park Ave., Rm. 402, Bronx, NY 10461-1602. TEL 718-430-3503. FAX 718-430-8907.
Vendor(s): University Microfilms International. *4824*

AMERICAN JOURNAL OF PUBLIC HEALTH.
American Public Health Association, 1015 15th St., N.W., Washington, DC 20005. TEL 202-789-5600.
Vendor(s): Ovid Technologies, Inc., University Microfilms International. *5954*

AMERICAN JOURNAL OF SPORTS MEDICINE.
American Orthopaedic Society for Sports Medicine, 230 Calvary St., Waltham, MA 02154. TEL 617-736-0707. FAX 617-736-0607.
Vendor(s): Information Access Co., University Microfilms International. *4897*

AMERICAN JOURNAL OF SURGERY.
Excerpta Medica, Inc. 105 Raider Blvd., Belle Mead, NJ 08502. TEL 908-874-8550. FAX 908-874-8419.
Vendor(s): Lexis-Nexis, Ovid Technologies, Inc.. *4903*

AMERICAN JOURNAL OF TAX POLICY.
American College of Tax Counsel, Box 870382, Tuscaloosa, AL 35487-0382. TEL 205-348-7372. FAX 205-348-3917.
Vendor(s): Lexis-Nexis, West Services, Inc.. *1534*

AMERICAN JOURNAL OF THERAPEUTICS.
Chapman & Hall, Journals Department 2-6 Boundary Row, London SE1 8HN, England. TEL 44-171-8560066. FAX 44-171-5229623. *4425*

AMERICAN JOURNALISM REVIEW.
American Journalism Review, 8701 Adelphi Rd., Adelphi, MD 20783. TEL 301-431-4771. FAX 301-431-0097.
Vendor(s): Information Access Co.. *3700*

THE AMERICAN LAWYER.
American Lawyer Media, L.P. (New York), 600 Third Ave., 2nd Fl., New York, NY 10016. TEL 212-973-2800. FAX 212-972-6253.
Vendor(s): Lexis-Nexis. *3740*

AMERICAN LEGION MAGAZINE.
Daniel S. Wheeler, Ed. & Pub., Box 1055, Indianapolis, IN 46206. TEL 317-630-1200. FAX 317-630-1280.
Vendor(s): University Microfilms International. *1847*

AMERICAN LIBRARIES.
American Library Association, 50 E. Huron St., Chicago, IL 60611-2795. TEL 800-545-2433. FAX 312-440-0901.
Vendor(s): Information Access Co., Knight-Ridder Information, Inc.. *3972*

AMERICAN LIBRARY DIRECTORY.
R.R. Bowker, A Division of Reed Elsevier Inc., 121 Chanlon Rd., New Providence, NJ 07974. TEL 908-464-6800. FAX 908-665-6688.
Vendor(s): Knight-Ridder Information, Inc. (File no.460). *3972*

AMERICAN MANUFACTURERS DIRECTORY.
American Business Directories 5711 S. 86th Circle, Box 27347, Omaha, NE 68127. TEL 402-593-4600. FAX 402-331-5481. *1584*

AMERICAN MARITIME CASES.
American Maritime Cases, Inc., 28 E. 21st St., Baltimore, MD 21218. TEL 410-752-2939. FAX 410-625-1174.
Vendor(s): Lexis-Nexis. *3956*

AMERICAN MARKETPLACE.
Business Publishers, Inc., 951 Pershing Dr., Silver Spring, MD 20910-4464. TEL 301-587-6300. FAX 301-585-9075.
Vendor(s): Information Access Co., NewsNet (AD13). *5780*

AMERICAN MATHEMATICAL SOCIETY. BULLETIN. NEW SERIES.
American Mathematical Society, Box 6248, Providence, RI 02940-6248. TEL 401-455-4000. *4353*

AMERICAN MEDICAL NEWS.
American Medical Association, 515 N. State St., Chicago, IL 60610. TEL 312-464-5000. FAX 312-464-5831.
Vendor(s): Information Access Co.. *4425*

AMERICAN MEN AND WOMEN OF SCIENCE.
R.R. Bowker, A Division of Reed Elsevier Inc., 121 Chanlon Rd., New Providence, NJ 07974. TEL 908-464-6800. FAX 908-665-6688.
Vendor(s): Knight-Ridder Information, Inc. (File no.236) *554*

AMERICAN METAL MARKET.
Capital Cities - A B C, Inc., Diversified Publishing Group, 825 Seventh Ave., New York, NY 10019. TEL 212-887-8560. FAX 212-887-8493.
Vendor(s): Information Access Co., Knight-Ridder Information, Inc.. *1453*

AMERICAN MIDLAND NATURALIST.
University of Notre Dame, Department of Biological Sciences, Box 369, Notre Dame, IN 46556. TEL 219-631-7481.
Vendor(s): Information Access Co.. *6225*

AMERICAN MUSIC.
University of Illinois Press, 1325 S. Oak St., Champaign, IL 61820. TEL 217-333-0950. FAX 217-244-8082.
Vendor(s): Information Access Co.. *5138*

AMERICAN MUSIC TEACHER.
Music Teachers National Association, Inc., Carew Tower, 441 Vine St., Ste. 505, Cincinnati, OH 45202-2314. TEL 513-421-1420. FAX 513-421-2503.
Vendor(s) University Microfilms International. *5138*

Online

AMERICAN ORIENTAL SOCIETY. JOURNAL.
American Oriental Society, Harlan Hatcher Graduate Library, University of Michigan, Ann Arbor, MI 48109-1205. TEL 313-747-4760.
Vendor(s): Information Access Co., University Microfilms International. *5277*

AMERICAN PAINT & COATINGS JOURNAL.
American Paint Journal Co., 2911 Washington Ave., St. Louis, MO 63103. TEL 314-530-0301.
Vendor(s): Information Access Co.. *5305*

AMERICAN PAPERMAKER.
Maclean Hunter Ltd., 777 Bay St., Toronto, ON M5W 1A7, Canada. TEL 416-596-5897. FAX 416-593-3170.
Vendor(s): Information Access Co., Lexis-Nexis. *5320*

AMERICAN PETROLEUM INSTITUTE. DIVISION OF STATISTICS. WEEKLY STATISTICAL BULLETIN.
American Petroleum Institute, Publications Section, 1220 L St., N.W., Washington, DC 20005. TEL 202-682-8378.
Vendor(s): PetroScan. *5381*

AMERICAN PHARMACEUTICAL ASSOCIATION. JOURNAL.
American Pharmaceutical Association, 2215 Constitution Ave., N.W., Washington, DC 20037. TEL 202-628-4410. *5398*

AMERICAN PHILOSOPHICAL QUARTERLY.
North American Philosophical Publications, Inc., 1012 Cathedral, University of Pittsburgh, Pittsburgh, PA 15260. TEL 412-624-5704. FAX 412-624-5377.
Vendor(s): Information Access Co. *5466*

AMERICAN PHOTO.
Hachette Filipacchi Magazines, Inc., 1633 Broadway, 45th Fl., New York, NY 10019. TEL 212-767-6000.
Vendor(s): Information Access Co.. *5508*

AMERICAN PLANNING ASSOCIATION. JOURNAL.
American Planning Association, 122 S. Michigan Ave., Ste. 1600, Chicago, IL 60603-6107. TEL 312-431-9100. FAX 312-431-9985.
Vendor(s): Information Access Co., University Microfilms International. *3575*

AMERICAN PODIATRIC MEDICAL ASSOCIATION. JOURNAL.
American Podiatric Medical Association, 9312 Old Georgetown Rd., Bethesda, MD 20814-1698. TEL 301-571-9200. FAX 301-530-2752.
Vendor(s): National Library of Medicine. *4780*

AMERICAN POETRY REVIEW.
World Poetry, Inc., 1721 Walnut St., Philadelphia, PA 19103. TEL 215-496-0439.
Vendor(s): Information Access Co., University Microfilms International. *4300*

AMERICAN POLITICAL SCIENCE REVIEW.
American Political Science Association, 1527 New Hampshire Ave., N.W., Washington, DC 20036. TEL 202-483-2512. FAX 202-483-2657.
Vendor(s): Information Access Co., University Microfilms International. *5633*

AMERICAN PRINTER.
Intertec Publishing Corp. (Overland Park), 9800 Metcalf Ave., Overland Park, KS 66202. TEL 910-341-1300.
Vendor(s): Information Access Co., University Microfilms International. *5808*

AMERICAN QUARTERLY.
Johns Hopkins University Press, Journals Publishing Division, 2715 N. Charles St., Baltimore, MD 21218. TEL 410-516-6987. FAX 410-516-6968. *3606*

AMERICAN RECORD GUIDE.
Record Guide Productions, 4412 Braddock St., Cincinnati, OH 45204. TEL 513-941-1116. FAX 513-941-1112.
Vendor(s): Information Access Co., University Microfilms International. *5139*

AMERICAN REHABILITATION.
U.S. Department of Education, Mary E. Switzer Bldg., Rm. 3127, 330 C St., S.W., Washington, DC 20202. TEL 202-732-1296.
Vendor(s): Information Access Co., University Microfilms International. *6361*

AMERICAN RENAISSANCE.
New Century Foundation, Box 1674, Louisville, KY 40201. TEL 502-637-3242. FAX 502-637-9324. *6404*

AMERICAN REVIEW OF PUBLIC ADMINISTRATION.
Georgia State University, School of Public Administration and Urban Studies, University Plaza, Atlanta, GA 30303-3083. TEL 404-651-4591. FAX 404-651-1378.
Vendor(s): Information Access Co., Knight-Ridder Information, Inc., University Microfilms International. *5891*

AMERICAN RIFLEMAN.
N R A Publications, 11250 Waples Mill Rd., Fairfax, VA 22030. TEL 703-267-1379. FAX 703-267-3971.
Vendor(s): University Microfilms International. *6450*

AMERICAN SALESMAN.
National Research Bureau, Box 1, Burlington, IA 52601-0001. TEL 319-752-5415. FAX 319-752-3421.
Vendor(s): Information Access Co., Knight-Ridder Information, Inc., Lexis-Nexis, University Microfilms International. *1453*

AMERICAN SCHOOL & UNIVERSITY.
Intertec Publishing Corp., 9800 Metcalf, Overland Park, KS 66212-2215. TEL 913-341-1300.
Vendor(s): Information Access Co.. *2454*

AMERICAN SCIENTIST.
Sigma Xi, Scientific Research Society, Box 13975, 99 Alexander Dr., Research Triangle Park, NC 27709. TEL 919-549-0097. FAX 919-549-0090.
Vendor(s): Information Access Co.. *6225*

AMERICAN SHIPPER.
Howard Publications, Inc., 33 S. Hogan St., Ste. 230, Box 4728, Jacksonville, FL 32201-4728. TEL 904-355-2601. FAX 904-791-8836.
Vendor(s): Information Access Co.. *6829*

AMERICAN SOCIETY FOR INFORMATION SCIENCE. BULLETIN.
American Society for Information Science, 8720 Georgia Ave, Ste. 501, Silver Spring, MD 20910. TEL 301-495-0900. FAX 301-495-0810.
Vendor(s): University Microfilms International. *3972*

AMERICAN SOCIETY OF C L U & CH F C. JOURNAL.
American Society of C L U & Ch F C, 270 Bryn Mawr Ave., Bryn Mawr, PA 19010. TEL 215-526-2500. FAX 215-526-2538.
Vendor(s): University Microfilms International. *3640*

AMERICAN SOCIETY OF MECHANICAL ENGINEERS. TRANSACTIONS.
American Society of Mechanical Engineers, 22 Law Dr., Fairfield, NJ 07007-2300. FAX 201-882-8113.
Vendor(s): Knight-Ridder Information, Inc.. *2750*

AMERICAN SOCIOLOGICAL REVIEW.
American Sociological Association, 1722 N St., N.W., Washington, DC 20036. TEL 202-833-3410. FAX 202-785-0146.
Vendor(s): University Microfilms International. *6405*

AMERICAN SPECTATOR.
2020 N. 14th St., Ste. 750, Box 549, Arlington, VA 22201. TEL 703-243-3733. FAX 703-243-6814.
Vendor(s): Information Access Co.. *4131*

AMERICAN STATISTICIAN.
American Statistical Association, 1429 Duke St., Alexandria, VA 22314-3402. TEL 703-684-1221. FAX 703-684-2037.
Vendor(s): Information Access Co.. *6584*

AMERICAN STATISTICS INDEX.
Congressional Information Service, Inc., A member of the LEXIS NEXIS family, 4520 East-West Hwy., Bethesda, MD 20814-3389. TEL 301-654-1550. FAX 301-654-4033.
Vendor(s): Knight-Ridder Information, Inc. (File no.102). *6585*

AMERICAN TAXATION ASSOCIATION. JOURNAL.
American Accounting Association, Paul F. Gerhardt Bldg., 5717 Bessie Dr., Sarasota, FL 34233. TEL 941-921-7747. FAX 941-923-4093.
Vendor(s): University Microfilms International. *1534*

AMERICAN THEATRE.
Theatre Communications Group, Inc., 355 Lexington Ave., New York, NY 10017. TEL 212-697-5230. FAX 212-983-4847.
Vendor(s): Information Access Co., University Microfilms International. *6691*

AMERICAN UNIVERSITY LAW REVIEW.
American University, Washington College of Law, 4400 Massachusetts Ave., N.W., Washington, DC 20016. TEL 202-274-4433.
Vendor(s): Lexis-Nexis, West Services, Inc.. *3740*

AMERICAN VISIONS.
Dialogue Diaspora, Inc., 1156 15th St. N.W., Ste. 615, Washington, DC 20005. TEL 202-496-9593.
Vendor(s): Information Access Co., University Microfilms International. *2864*

AMERICAN WINE ON THE WEB.
Box 5068, Lake Gregory, CA 92325. TEL 909-338-9776. FAX 909-338-4956.
Available only online. *499*

AMERICANS WITH DISABILITIES ACT UPDATE.
Nyper Publications, Box 370, Latham, NY 12112-0370. TEL 518-786-1654. FAX 518-456-8582.
Vendor(s): Lexis-Nexis, NewsNet. *3303*

AMERICANS WITH DISABILITIES CASES.
The Bureau of National Affairs, Inc., 1231 25th St., N.W., Washington, DC 20037. TEL 202-452-4200. FAX 202-822-8092.
Vendor(s): West Services, Inc. (FLB-CS, MLRR-CS). *3740*

AMERICAS.
Americas Magazine, 19th St. & Constitution Ave., N.W., Ste. 300, Washington, DC 20006. TEL 202-458-3278. FAX 202-458-6217.
Vendor(s): Information Access Co., University Microfilms International. *3607*

AMERICA'S COMMUNITY BANKER.
America's Community Bankers, 900 19th St., N.W., Ste. 400, Washington, DC 20006. TEL 202-857-3100. FAX 202-857-5581.
Vendor(s): Information Access Co., University Microfilms International. *1059*

AMERICA'S FUTURE.
Americas Future, Inc., 7800 Bahomme Ave., St. Louis, MO 63105. TEL 314-725-6003. FAX 314-721-3373. *5633*

AMERICA'S NETWORK.
Advanstar Communications, Inc., 7500 Old Oak Blvd., Cleveland, OH 44130. TEL 216-826-2839. FAX 216-891-2726.
Vendor(s): Information Access Co., Knight-Ridder Information, Inc.. *1942*

AMERICA'S NETWORK DIRECTORY.
Advanstar Communications, Inc., 7500 Old Oak Blvd., Cleveland, OH 44130. TEL 216-826-2839. FAX 216-891-2726.
Vendor(s): Knight-Ridder Information, Inc.. *1943*

AMICUS JOURNAL.
Natural Resources Defense Council Inc., 40 W. 20th St., New York, NY 10011. TEL 212-727-2700. FAX 212-727-1773.
Vendor(s): Information Access Co., University Microfilms International. *2776*

AMUSEMENT BUSINESS.
B P I Communications, Amusement Business Division, Box 24970, Nashville, TN 37202. TEL 615-321-4250. FAX 615-327-1575.
Vendor(s): Information Access Co., Knight-Ridder Information, Inc.. *6691*

ANALGESICS: THE INTERNATIONAL MARKET.
Euromonitor, 60-61 Britton St., London EC1M 5NA, England. TEL 44-171-251-8024. FAX 44-171-608-3149.
Vendor(s): Data-Star, Knight-Ridder Information, Inc.. *5398*

ANALYSE.
Nederlandse Vereniging van BioMedische Laboratoriummedewerkers, Wilhelminapark 52, 3581 NM Utrecht, Netherlands. TEL 31-30-2522881. FAX 31-30-2541814. *4676*

THE ANALYST.
The Royal Society of Chemistry, Thomas Graham House, Science Park, Milton Rd., Cambridge CB4 4WF, England. TEL 44-1223-420066. FAX 44-1223-423429.
Vendor(s): STN International (CJRSC). *1712*

ANALYTICA CHIMICA ACTA.
Elsevier Science B.V., P.O. Box 211, 1000 AE Amsterdam, Netherlands. TEL 31-20-4853911. FAX 31-20-4853598.
Vendor(s): STN International. *1713*

ANALYTICAL ABSTRACTS.
The Royal Society of Chemistry, Thomas Graham House, Science Park, Milton Rd., Cambridge CB4 4WF, England. TEL 44-1223-420066. FAX 44-1223-423429.
Vendor(s): Data-Star (ANAB), Knight-Ridder Information, Inc. (File no.305), Orbit Search Service (ANAB), STN International (ANABSTR). *1697*

ANALYTICAL CHEMISTRY.
American Chemical Society, 1155 16th St., N.W., Washington, DC 20036. TEL 800-333-9511. FAX 614-447-3671.
Vendor(s): STN International (CJACS). *1713*

ANALYTICAL COMMUNICATIONS.
The Royal Society of Chemistry, Thomas Graham House, Science Park, Milton Rd., Cambridge CB4 4WF, England. TEL 44-1223-420066. FAX 44-1223-423429. *1713*

ANALYTICAL INSTRUMENT INDUSTRY REPORT.
A I I Report, P.O. Box 78, E. Grinstead, W. Sussex RH19 2YW, England. TEL 44-1342-835935. FAX 44-1342-833488. *3633*

ANATOLIAN STUDIES.
British Institute of Archaeology at Ankara, 31-34 Gordon Sq., London WC1H 0PY, England. TEL 0171-388-2361. *339*

THE ANATOMICAL RECORD.
John Wiley & Sons, Inc., Journals, 605 Third Ave., New York, NY 10158. TEL 212-850-6645. FAX 212-850-6021. *568*

ANCIENT HISTORY BULLETIN.
c/o Dept. of Greek, Latin and Ancient History, University of Calgary, 2500 University Dr., N.W., Calgary AB T2N 1N4, Canada. *3336*

ANDREW SEYBOLD'S OUTLOOK ON COMMUNICATIONS & COMPUTING.
Pinecrest Press, Inc., Box 917, Brookdale, CA 95007. TEL 408-338-7701. FAX 408-338-7806. *2030*

ANESTHESIA AND ANALGESIA.
Williams & Wilkins, 351 W. Camden St., Baltimore, MD 21201. TEL 410-528-4000. FAX 410-528-4312.
Vendor(s): Ovid Technologies, Inc.. *4590*

ANESTHESIOLOGY.
Lippincott - Raven Publishers 227 E. Washington Sq., Philadelphia, PA 19106. TEL 215-238-4200.
Vendor(s): Ovid Technologies, Inc.. *4590*

ANGEWANDTE CHEMIE.
V C H Verlagsgesellschaft mbH, Postfach 101161, 69451 Weinheim, Germany. TEL 06201-606-0. FAX 06201-606328.
Vendor(s): STN International (CJVCH). *1664*

ANGEWANDTE CHEMIE: INTERNATIONAL EDITION.
V C H Verlagsgesellschaft mbH, Postfach 101161, 69451 Weinheim, Germany. TEL 49-6201-606-0. FAX 49-6201-606-328. *1665*

ANIMAL BEHAVIOR ABSTRACTS.
Cambridge Scientific Abstracts, 7200 Wisconsin Ave., 6th Fl., Bethesda, MD 20814. TEL 301-961-6750. FAX 301-961-6720.
Vendor(s): Knight-Ridder Information, Inc. (File no.76/LIFE SCIENCES COLLECTION), STN International (LIFESCI). *615*

ANIMAL BREEDING ABSTRACTS.
CAB International, Wallingford, Oxon. OX10 8DE, England. TEL 44-1491-832111. FAX 44-1491-833508.
Vendor(s): DIMDI, European Space Agency, Knight-Ridder Information, Inc.. *615*

ANIMAL DISEASE OCCURRENCE.
CAB International, Wallingford, Oxon. OX10 8DE, England. TEL 44-1491-832111. FAX 44-1491-833508.
Vendor(s): DIMDI, European Space Agency, Knight-Ridder Information, Inc.. *6961*

ANIMAL PHARM.
P J B Publications Ltd., 18-20 Hill Rise, Richmond, Surrey TW10 6UA, England. TEL 44-181-948-3262. FAX 44-181-332-8998.
Vendor(s): Data-Star, Knight-Ridder Information, Inc., Ovid Technologies, Inc. (PJIN,PHIC,PHID). *6941*

ANIMAL WELFARE INFORMATION CENTER BULLETIN.
U.S. Animal Welfare Information Center, National Agricultural Library 10301 Baltimore Blvd., 5th Fl., Beltsville, MD 20705-2351. TEL 301-504-6212. FAX 301-504-7125. *295*

ANIMALS.
Massachusetts Society for the Prevention of Cruelty to Animals, 350 S. Huntington Ave., Boston, MA 02130. TEL 617-541-5065. FAX 617-522-4885. *295*

ANNALES ACADEMIAE SCIENTIARUM FENNICAE MATHEMATICA.
Suomalainen Tiedeakatemia, Mariankatu 5, FIN-00170 Helsinki, Finland. *4353*

ANNALES DE PHYSIQUE.
Editions de Physique, Z.I. de Courtaboeuf, B.P. 112, 91944 Les Ulis Cedex, France. TEL 33-1-69-07-36-88. FAX 33-1-69-28-84-91. *5542*

ANNALS OF INTERNAL MEDICINE.
American College of Physicians, Independence Mall W., Sixth St. at Race, Philadelphia, PA 19106-1572. TEL 215-351-2400. FAX 215-351-2644.
Vendor(s): Ovid Technologies, Inc.. *4705*

ANNALS OF NEUROLOGY.
Little, Brown and Company, Medical Journals, 34 Beacon St., Boston, MA 02108. TEL 617-859-5500. FAX 617-859-0629.
Vendor(s): Lexis-Nexis, Ovid Technologies, Inc.. *4825*

THE ANNALS OF PHARMACOTHERAPY.
Harvey Whitney Books Company, Box 42696, Cincinnati, OH 45242. TEL 513-793-3555. FAX 513-793-3600. *5398*

ANNALS OF PLASTIC SURGERY.
Little, Brown and Company, Medical Journals, 34 Beacon St., Boston, MA 02108. TEL 617-859-5500. FAX 617-267-3507.
Vendor(s): Lexis-Nexis. *4903*

ANNALS OF SURGERY.
Lippincott - Raven Publishers 227 E. Washington Sq., Philadelphia, PA 19106. TEL 215-238-4200.
Vendor(s): Lexis-Nexis, Ovid Technologies, Inc.. *4903*

ANNALS OF THE RHEUMATIC DISEASES.
B M J Publishing Group, B.M.A. House, Tavistock Sq., London WC1H 9JR, England. TEL 44-171-383-6270. FAX 44-171-333-6402.
Vendor(s): Ovid Technologies, Inc.. *4892*

ANNALS OF THORACIC SURGERY.
Elsevier Science Inc., Box 945, New York, NY 10159-0945. TEL 212-633-3730. FAX 212-633-3680.
Vendor(s): Lexis-Nexis. *4904*

ANNALS OF TROPICAL MEDICINE AND PARASITOLOGY.
Carfax Publishing Co., P.O. Box 25, Abingdon, Oxon OX14 3UE, England. TEL 44-1235-401000. FAX 44-1235-401550. *4617*

ANNUAIRE TELEXPORT.
Chambre de Commerce et d'Industrie de Paris (CEDIP), 2 place de la Bourse, 75002 Paris, France.
Vendor(s): Data-Star. *1131*

ANNUAL BIBLIOGRAPHY OF ENGLISH LANGUAGE AND LITERATURE.
W.S. Maney & Son Ltd., Hudson St., Leeds LS9 7DL, England. TEL 01532-457481. FAX 01532-486983. *4291*

ANNUAL FORUM REPORTS.
Professional Education International, Inc., 303 E. Wacker Dr., Ste. 740, Chicago, IL 60601. TEL 312-938-3500. FAX 312-938-8787. *1895*

ANNUAL REVIEW OF COMMUNICATIONS.
Professional Education International, Inc., 303 E. Wacker Dr., Ste. 740, Chicago, IL 60601. TEL 312-938-3500. FAX 312-938-8787. *1895*

ANNUAL REVIEW OF GENETICS.
Annual Reviews Inc., 4139 El Camino Way, Box 10139, Palo Alto, CA 94303-0139. TEL 415-493-4400. FAX 415-424-0910.
Vendor(s): Information Access Co.. *737*

ANNUAL REVIEW OF MICROBIOLOGY.
Annual Reviews Inc., 4139 El Camino Way, Box 10139, Palo Alto, CA 94303-0139. TEL 415-493-4400. FAX 415-424-0910.
Vendor(s): Information Access Co.. *753*

ANNUAL REVIEW OF PSYCHOLOGY.
Annual Reviews Inc., 4139 El Camino Way, Box 10139, Palo Alto, CA 94303-0139. TEL 415-493-4400. FAX 415-424-0910.
Vendor(s): Information Access Co., University Microfilms International. *5826*

ANNUAL REVIEW OF SOCIOLOGY.
Annual Reviews Inc., 4139 El Camino Way, Box 10139, Palo Alto, CA 94303-0139. TEL 415-493-4400.
Vendor(s): Information Access Co., University Microfilms International. *5405*

ANNUAL SURVEY OF MANUFACTURES.
U.S. Bureau of the Census, Customer Services, Washington, DC 20233. TEL 301-457-4100. FAX 301-457-4714.
Vendor(s): CompuServe, Inc., Knight-Ridder Information, Inc.. *974*

ANSIBLE.
94 London Rd., Reading, Berks. RG1 5AU, England. FAX 44-118-966-9914 *4324*

ANTARCTIC BIBLIOGRAPHY.
U.S. Library of Congress, Washington, DC 20540. TEL 202-707-1181.
Vendor(s): Orbit Search Service (COLD). *6299*

ANTHROPOLOGICAL LITERATURE.
Harvard University, Tozzer Library, 21 Divinity Ave., Cambridge, MA 02138. TEL 617-495-2253. FAX 617-496-2741.
Vendor(s): Research Libraries Group Information Network. *327*

ANTI-CENSORSHIP NEWSLETTER.
The Parent S I G, 1640 Via Pacifica, Ste.F-105, Corona, CA 91720. *6406*

ANTIOCH REVIEW.
Antioch Review, Inc., Box 148, Yellow Springs, OH 45387. TEL 513-767-6389.
Vendor(s): Information Access Co., University Microfilms International. *4132*

ANTIQUITY.
Oxford University Press, Oxford Journals, Walton St., Oxford OX2 6DP, England. TEL 01865-267907. FAX 01865-267773.
Vendor(s): Information Access Co.. *340*

ANTITRUST.
American Bar Association, Antitrust Law Section, 750 N. Lake Shore Dr., Chicago, IL 60611. TEL 312-988-5605.
Vendor(s): West Services, Inc. (ANTITR). *3893*

ANTITRUST & TRADE REGULATION REPORT.
The Bureau of National Affairs, Inc. 1231 25th St., N.W., Washington, DC 20037. TEL 202-452-4200. FAX 202-822-8092.
Vendor(s): Lexis-Nexis (TRAGRG), West Services, Inc. (BNA-ATRR). *1514*

ANTITRUST BULLETIN.
Federal Legal Publications, Inc., 157 Chambers St., New York, NY 10007. TEL 212-619-4949.
Vendor(s): Information Access Co.. *3893*

Online

Online

ANTITRUST FREEDOM OF INFORMATION LOG.
Washington Regulatory Reporting Associates, Box 356, Basye, VA 22810. TEL 703-856-2216. FAX 703-856-8331.
Vendor(s): Information Access Co.. *1264*

ANTITRUST LAW JOURNAL.
American Bar Association, Antitrust Law Section, 750 N. Lake Shore Dr., Chicago, IL 60611. TEL 312-988-5606.
Vendor(s): Information Access Co., Lexis-Nexis, West Services, Inc. (ANTITRLJ). *3894*

ANTITRUST LITIGATION REPORTER.
Andrews Publications, 1646 West Chester Pike, Box 1000, Westtown, PA 19395. TEL 610-399-6600. FAX 610-399-6610.
Vendor(s): NewsNet. *1059*

ANTIVIRAL AGENTS BULLETIN.
Biotechnology Information Institute, 1700 Rockville Pike, Ste. 400, Rockville, MD 20852. TEL 301-424-0255. FAX 301-424-0257..
Vendor(s): Information Access Co.. *5399*

ANUARIO ESTATISTICO DOS TRANSPORTES.
Empresa Brasileira de Planejamento de Transportes, G E I P O T, SAN Quadra 3 Blocos N-O, 70040-920 Brasilia DF, Brazil. FAX 061-224-8642. *6713*

APICULTURAL ABSTRACTS.
International Bee Research Association, 18 North Rd., Cardiff CF1 3DY, Wales. TEL 44-1222-372409. FAX 44-1222-665522.
Vendor(s): European Space Agency (File nos.16 & 124/CAB), Knight-Ridder Information, Inc.. *167*

APOTHECARY.
Health Care Marketing Services, H C M S Inc., Box AP, Los Altos, CA 94023-0179. TEL 415-941-3955. FAX 415-941-2303. *5399*

APPAREL INDUSTRY MAGAZINE.
Shore-Varrone, Inc., 6255 Barfield Rd. N.E., Ste. 200, Atlanta, GA 30328-4300. TEL 404-252-8831. FAX 404-252-4436.
Vendor(s): Information Access Co., Knight-Ridder Information, Inc., University Microfilms International. *1830*

APPLIANCE.
Dana Chase Publications, Inc., 1110 Jorie Blvd., CS-9019, Oak Brook, IL 60522-9019. TEL 708-990-3484. FAX 708-990-0078.
Vendor(s): Information Access Co.. *2683*

APPLIANCE MANUFACTURER.
Business News Publishing Company, 755 W. Big Beaver, Ste. 1000, Troy, MI 48084. TEL 810-362-3700. FAX 810-362-0317.
Vendor(s): Information Access Co., Knight-Ridder Information, Inc., University Microfilms International. *2683*

APPLICATION DEVELOPMENT TRENDS.
Software Productivity Group, Inc., 180 Turnpike Rd., Westborough, MA 01581-2806. TEL 508-393-7100. FAX 508-393-3388. *2064*

APPLIED CATALYSIS A: GENERAL.
Elsevier Science B.V., P.O. Box 211, 1000 AE Amsterdam, Netherlands. TEL 31-20-4853911. FAX 31-20-4853598.
Vendor(s): STN International. *2633*

APPLIED ECONOMICS.
Chapman & Hall, Journals Department 2-6 Boundary Row, London SE1 8HN, England. TEL 44-171-8650066. FAX 44-171-5229623.
Vendor(s): Information Access Co.. *893*

APPLIED ECONOMICS LETTERS.
Chapman & Hall, Journals Department 2-6 Boundary Row, London SE1 8HN, England. TEL 44-171-8650066. FAX 44-171-5229623. *893*

APPLIED FINANCIAL ECONOMICS.
Chapman & Hall, Journals Department 2-6 Boundary Row, London SE1 8HN, England. TEL 44-171-8650066. FAX 44-171-5229623. *1174*

APPLIED GENETICS NEWS.
Business Communications Co., Inc. (Norwalk), 25 Van Zant St., Ste. 13, Norwalk, CT 06855. TEL 203-853-4266. FAX 203-853-0348.
Vendor(s): Data-Star, Information Access Co., Knight-Ridder Information, Inc., NewsNet (BT03). *738*

APPLIED MATHEMATICAL FINANCE.
Chapman & Hall, Journals Department 2-6 Boundary Row, London SE1 8HN, England. TEL 44-171-8650066. FAX 44-171-5229623. *4355*

APPLIED PHYSICS LETTERS.
American Institute of Physics, One Physics Ellipse, College Park, MD 20740-3843. TEL 301-209-3000.
Vendor(s): OCLC. *5542*

APPLIED SCIENCE & TECHNOLOGY INDEX.
H.W. Wilson Co., 950 University Ave., Bronx, NY 10452. TEL 718-588-8400. FAX 718-590-1617.
Vendor(s): OCLC, Wilsonline (AST). *2624*

APPRAISAL JOURNAL.
Appraisal Institute, 875 N. Michigan Ave., Ste. 2400, Chicago, IL 60611-1980. TEL 312-335-4100. FAX 312-353-4400.
Vendor(s): Information Access Co., University Microfilms International. *6018*

AQUACULTURE INTERNATIONAL.
Chapman & Hall, Journals Department 2-6 Boundary Row, London SE1 8HN, England. TEL 44-171-8650066. FAX 44-171-8659623. *2926*

AQUALINE ABSTRACTS.
W R C plc, P.O. Box 85, Frankland Rd., Blagrove, Swindon, Wilts SN5 8YF, England.
Vendor(s): European Space Agency, Orbit Search Service (AQUA). *6982*

AQUARIUM SCIENCES AND CONSERVATION.
Chapman & Hall, Journals Department 2-6 Boundary Row, London SE1 8HN, England. TEL 44-171-8650066. FAX 44-171-5229623. *2926*

AQUATIC SCIENCES & FISHERIES ABSTRACTS. PART 1: BIOLOGICAL SCIENCES AND LIVING RESOURCES.
Cambridge Scientific Abstracts, 7200 Wisconsin Ave., 6th Fl., Bethesda, MD 20814. TEL 301-961-6750. FAX 301-961-6720.
Vendor(s): DIMDI, European Space Agency, Knight-Ridder Information, Inc. (File no.44), STN International (AQUASCI). *6982*

AQUATIC SCIENCES & FISHERIES ABSTRACTS. PART 2: OCEAN TECHNOLOGY, POLICY AND NON-LIVING RESOURCES.
Cambridge Scientific Abstracts, 7200 Wisconsin Ave., 6th Fl., Bethesda, MD 20814. TEL 301-961-6750. FAX 301-961-6720.
Vendor(s): DIMDI, European Space Agency, Knight-Ridder Information, Inc. (File no.44), STN International (AQUASCI). *6983*

AQUATIC SCIENCES & FISHERIES ABSTRACTS. PART 3: AQUATIC POLLUTION AND ENVIRONMENTAL QUALITY.
Cambridge Scientific Abstracts, 7200 Wisconsin Ave., 6th Fl., Bethesda, MD 20814. TEL 301-961-6700. FAX 301-961-6720.
Vendor(s): DIMDI, European Space Agency, Knight-Ridder Information, Inc. (File no.44), STN International (AQUASCI). *2946*

ARAB STUDIES QUARTERLY.
Association of Arab-American University Graduates, Inc., 2121 Wisconsin Ave., N.W., Ste. 310, Washington, DC 20007-2258. TEL 202-337-7717. FAX 202-337-3302.
Vendor(s): Information Access Co., University Microfilms International. *2864*

ARCHAEOLOGY ON KAUA'I.
Anthropology Club of Kaua'i, 3-1901 Kaumualii Hwy., Lihue, HI 96766. TEL 808-245-8311. FAX 808-245-8220. *342*

ARCHITECTURAL PUBLICATIONS INDEX.
R I B A Publications, Finsbury Mission, 39 Moreland St., London EC1V 8BB, England. TEL 44-171-251-0791. FAX 44-171-608-2375.
Vendor(s): Knight-Ridder Information, Inc. (File no.179). *407*

ARCHITECTURAL RECORD.
McGraw-Hill Companies, 1221 Ave. of the Americas, New York, NY 10020. TEL 212-512-2000. FAX 212-512-4256.
Vendor(s): Dow Jones News Retrieval (ARCH), Knight-Ridder Information, Inc. (AR), NewsNet (BC13). *383*

ARCHITECTURAL REVIEW.
E M A P - Architecture, 33-39 Bowling Green Ln., London EC1R 0DA, England. TEL 0171-837-1212. FAX 0171-278-4003.
Vendor(s): University Microfilms International. *383*

ARCHITECTURE.
B P I Communications, Inc., 1130 Connecticut Ave., N.W., Ste. 625, Washington, DC 20036. TEL 202-828-0993. FAX 202-828-0825.
Vendor(s): Information Access Co.. *384*

ARCHITECTURE ON LINE.
Princeton Architectural Press, 37 E. Seventh St., New York, NY 10003. TEL 212-995-9620. FAX 212-995-9454.
Available only online. *384*

ARCHIV DER MATHEMATIK.
Birkhaeuser Verlag, P.O. Box 133, CH-4010 Basel, Switzerland. TEL 41-61-2050730. FAX 41-61-2050791. *4356*

ARCHIVES OF DERMATOLOGY.
American Medical Association, 515 N. State St., Chicago, IL 60610. TEL 312-464-5000. FAX 617-667-4948.
Vendor(s): Information Access Co., Knight-Ridder Information, Inc.. *4658*

ARCHIVES OF DISEASE IN CHILDHOOD.
B M J Publishing Group, B.M.A. House, Tavistock Sq., London WC1H 9JR, England. TEL 44-171-383-6270. FAX 44-171-383-6402.
Vendor(s): Ovid Technologies, Inc.. *4802*

ARCHIVES OF DISEASE IN CHILDHOOD. FETAL AND NEONATAL EDITION.
B M J Publishing Group, B.M.A. House, Tavistock Sq., London WC1H 9JR, England. TEL 44-171-387-4499. FAX 44-171-383-6661.
Vendor(s): Ovid Technologies, Inc.. *4731*

ARCHIVES OF ENVIRONMENTAL HEALTH.
Heldref Publications, 1319 Eighteenth St., N.W., Washington, DC 20036-1802. TEL 202-296-6267. FAX 202-296-5149.
Vendor(s): Information Access Co.. *4428*

ARCHIVES OF FAMILY MEDICINE.
American Medical Association, 515 N. State St., Chicago, IL 60610. TEL 312-464-5000. FAX 312-464-5831.
Vendor(s): Information Access Co., Knight-Ridder Information, Inc.. *4428*

ARCHIVES OF GENERAL PSYCHIATRY.
American Medical Association, 515 N. State St., Chicago, IL 60610. TEL 312-464-5000. FAX 312-464-5831.
Vendor(s): Information Access Co., Knight-Ridder Information, Inc.. *4826*

ARCHIVES OF INTERNAL MEDICINE.
American Medical Association, 515 N. State St., Chicago, IL 60610. TEL 312-464-5000. FAX 312-464-5831.
Vendor(s): Information Access Co., Knight-Ridder Information, Inc.. *4705*

ARCHIVES OF NEUROLOGY.
American Medical Association, 515 N. State St., Chicago, IL 60610. TEL 312-464-5000. FAX 312-464-5831.
Vendor(s): Information Access Co., Knight-Ridder Information, Inc.. *4826*

ARCHIVES OF OPHTHALMOLOGY.
American Medical Association, 515 N. State St., Chicago, IL 60610. TEL 312-464-5000. FAX 312-464-5831.
Vendor(s): Information Access Co., Knight-Ridder Information, Inc.. *4767*

ARCHIVES OF OTOLARYNGOLOGY - HEAD & NECK SURGERY.
American Medical Association, 515 N. State St., Chicago, IL 60610. TEL 312-464-5000. FAX 312-464-5831.
Vendor(s): Information Access Co., Knight-Ridder Information, Inc.. *4795*

ARCHIVES OF PATHOLOGY & LABORATORY MEDICINE.
College of American Pathologists, 325 Waukegan Rd., Northfield, IL 60093-2750. TEL 708-446-8800. FAX 708-446-3563.
Vendor(s): Lexis-Nexis. *4428*

ARCHIVES OF PEDIATRICS & ADOLESCENT MEDICINE.
American Medical Association, 515 N. State St., Chicago, IL 60610. TEL 312-464-5000. FAX 312-464-4181.
Vendor(s): Information Access Co., Knight-Ridder Information, Inc.. *4802*

ARCHIVES OF PHYSIOLOGY AND BIOCHEMISTRY.
Swets & Zeitlinger bv, P.O. Box 825, 2160 SZ Lisse, Netherlands. TEL 31-252-435111. FAX 31-252-415888. *785*

ARCHIVES OF SEXUAL BEHAVIOR.
Plenum Publishing Corp., 233 Spring St., New York, NY 10013-1578. TEL 212-620-8000. FAX 212-463-0742.
Vendor(s): Information Access Co.. *4428*

ARCHIVES OF SURGERY.
American Medical Association, 515 N. State St., Chicago, IL 60610. TEL 312-464-5000. FAX 312-464-5831.
Vendor(s): Information Access Co., Knight-Ridder Information, Inc.. *4904*

ARCHIVUM MATHEMATICUM.
Masarykova Universita, Janackovo Nam. 2a, 662 95 Brno, Czech Republic. TEL 42-5-41321251. FAX 42-5-41210337. *4356*

THE ARCHWAY (SMITHFIELD).
Bryant College, Box 7, 1150 Douglas Pike, Smithfield, RI 02917-1284. TEL 401-232-6028. FAX 401-232-6319. *1857*

AREA MAGAZINE.
Area Arts, 615 Mt. Pleasant Rd., Ste. 205, Toronto, ON M4S 3C5, Canada. TEL 416-368-9401. FAX 416-359-0755. *411*

ARETHUSA.
Johns Hopkins University Press, Journals Publishing Division, 2715 N. Charles St., Baltimore, MD 21218-4319. TEL 410-516-6987. FAX 410-516-6968. *1818*

ARGUMENTATION & ADVOCACY.
American Forensic Association, Box 256, River Falls, WI 54022-0256. FAX 715-425-9533.
Vendor(s): Information Access Co., University Microfilms International. *1896*

ARHIV ZA FARMACIJU.
Farmaceutsko Drustvo Srbije, Vojvode Stepe 450, Box 664, 11000 Belgrade, Yugoslavia. *5400*

ARID LANDS NEWSLETTER.
University of Arizona, Office of Arid Lands Studies, 1955 E. Sixth St., Tucson, AZ 85719. TEL 520-621-8584. FAX 520-621-3816.
Available only online. *2776*

ARIZONA BUSINESS DIRECTORY.
American Business Directories 5711 S. 86th Circle, Box 27347, Omaha, NE 68127. TEL 402-593-4600. FAX 402-331-5481. *1585*

ARIZONA BUSINESS GAZETTE.
Phoenix Newspapers, Inc., Box 1950, Phoenix, AZ 85001. TEL 602-271-7373. FAX 602-271-7363.
Vendor(s): Dow Jones News Retrieval, Knight-Ridder Information, Inc., Lexis-Nexis, VU/TEXT Information Services, Inc.. *894*

ARIZONA LEGISLATIVE REPORT.
Arizona News Service, 14 N. 18th Ave., Phoenix, AZ 85007. TEL 602-258-7026. FAX 602-258-2504. *3890*

ARIZONA STATE LAW JOURNAL.
Arizona State University, College of Law, Tempe, AZ 85287. TEL 602-965-6287. FAX 602-965-2427.
Vendor(s): West Services, Inc.. *3743*

ARKANSAS BUSINESS AND ECONOMIC REVIEW.
University of Arkansas, College of Business Administration, Fayetteville, AR 72701. TEL 501-575-4151. FAX 501-575-7687.
Vendor(s): Information Access Co., Knight-Ridder Information, Inc., University Microfilms International. *894*

ARKANSAS BUSINESS DIRECTORY.
American Business Directories 5711 S. 86th Circle, Box 27347, Omaha, NE 68127. TEL 402-593-4600. FAX 402-331-5481. *1585*

ARKANSAS HISTORICAL QUARTERLY.
Arkansas Historical Association, University of Arkansas, Department of History, Old Main 416, Fayetteville, AR 72701. TEL 501-575-5884. FAX 501-575-2642. *3460*

ARMED FORCES AND SOCIETY.
Transaction Publishers, Transaction Periodicals Consortium, Department 3092, Rutgers University, New Brunswick, NJ 08903. TEL 908-445-2280. FAX 908-445-3133.
Vendor(s): Information Access Co., University Microfilms International. *5021*

ARMED FORCES COMPTROLLER.
American Society of Military Comptrollers, 225 Reinekers Ln., Ste. 250, Alexandria, VA 22314-2875. TEL 703-549-0360. FAX 703-549-3181.
Vendor(s): University Microfilms International. *5021*

ARMS CONTROL TODAY.
Arms Control Association, 1726 M St., N.W., Ste. 201, Washington, DC 20036-4504. TEL 202-463-8270. FAX 202-463-8273.
Vendor(s): University Microfilms International. *5635*

ARMY LAWYER.
U.S. Army, Judge Advocate General's School, Charlottesville, VA 22903-1781. TEL 804-972-6393.
Vendor(s): West Services, Inc.. *3958*

ARS ORIENTALIS.
Department of History of Art, Tappan Hall, University of Michigan, Ann Arbor, MI 48109-1357. TEL 313-747-3307. FAX 313-763-8976. *5278*

ARS PHARMACEUTICA.
Universidad de Granada, Servicio de Publicaciones, Antiguo Colegio Maximo, Campus de Cartuja, 18071 Granada, Spain. TEL 34-58-243930. FAX 34-58-242827. *5400*

ART BULLETIN.
College Art Association, 275 Seventh Ave., New York, NY 10001. TEL 212-691-1051. FAX 212-627-2381.
Vendor(s): Information Access Co., University Microfilms International. *413*

ART CELLAR EXCHANGE.
Token Art Corporation, 2171 India St., Ste. H, San Diego, CA 92101. TEL 619-338-0797. FAX 619-338-0826.
Available only online. *413*

ART COM: CONTEMPORARY ART COMMUNICATIONS.
Contemporary Arts Press, Box 3123, Rincon Annex, San Francisco, CA 94119. TEL 415-431-7524. FAX 415-431-7841.
Available only online. *413*

ART IN AMERICA.
Brant Publications, Inc., 575 Broadway, 5th Fl., New York, NY 10021. TEL 212-941-2800. FAX 212-941-2819.
Vendor(s): Information Access Co., University Microfilms International. *414*

ART INDEX.
H.W. Wilson Co., 950 University Ave., Bronx, NY 10452. TEL 718-588-8400. FAX 718-590-1617.
Vendor(s): OCLC, Ovid Technologies, Inc., Wilsonline (File ART). *462*

ART JOURNAL (YEAR).
College Art Association, 275 Seventh Ave., New York, NY 10001. TEL 212-691-1051. FAX 212-627-2381.
Vendor(s): Information Access Co., University Microfilms International. *414*

ART SALES INDEX: OIL PAINTINGS, DRAWINGS, WATER COLOURS AND SCULPTURE.
Art Sales Index Ltd., 1 Thames St., Weybridge, Surrey KT13 8JG, England. TEL 44-1932-856426. FAX 44-1932-842482. *415*

ARTBIBLIOGRAPHIES MODERN.
A B C - Clio Ltd., 35A Great Clarendon St., Oxford OX2 6AT, England. TEL 44-1865-311350. FAX 44-1865-311358.
Vendor(s): Knight-Ridder Information, Inc. (File no.56). *462*

ARTFORUM.
Artforum International Magazine, Inc., 65 Bleecker St., New York, NY 10012. TEL 212-475-4000. FAX 212-529-1257.
Vendor(s): Information Access Co.. *416*

ARTHRITIS AND RHEUMATISM.
Lippincott - Raven Publishers 227 E. Washington Sq., Philadelphia, PA 19106. TEL 215-238-4200.
Vendor(s): Lexis-Nexis, Ovid Technologies, Inc.. *4892*

ARTHRITIS TODAY.
Arthritis Foundation, 1314 Spring St., N.W., Atlanta, GA 30309. TEL 404-872-7100. FAX 404-872-9559.
Vendor(s): Information Access Co.. *4893*

ARTHURIANA.
International Arthurian Society, North American Branch, Southern Methodist University, Dallas, TX 75275-0432. TEL 214-768-2959. FAX 214-768-4129. *3395*

ARTNET MAGAZINE.
ArtNet, 145 E. 57th St., 9th Fl., New York, NY 10022. TEL 212-497-9700. FAX 212-497-9707.
Available only online. *417*

ARTS & HUMANITIES CITATION INDEX.
Institute for Scientific Information, 3501 Market St., Philadelphia, PA 19104. TEL 215-386-0100. FAX 215-386-2991.
Vendor(s): Knight-Ridder Information, Inc. (File no.439), Ovid Technologies, Inc. (AHCI). *462*

ARTS EDUCATION POLICY REVIEW.
Heldref Publications, 1319 Eighteenth St., N.W., Washington, DC 20036-1802. TEL 202-296-6267. FAX 202-296-5149.
Vendor(s): Information Access Co., University Microfilms International. *418*

ARTSPEAK.
Art Liaison, Inc., 245 Eighth Ave. Ste. 285, New York, NY 10011. TEL 212-924-6531. *418*

ARZNEIMITTEL-FORSCHUNG.
Editio Cantor, Postfach 1255, 88322 Aulendorf, Germany. TEL 49-7525-940135. FAX 49-7525-940180. *5400*

ASAHI SHIMBUN SHUKUSATSUBAN.
Asahi Shimbun Publishing Co., 3-2 Tsukiji 5-chome, Chuo-ku, Tokyo 104-11, Japan. *3187*

ASBESTOS & LEAD ABATEMENT REPORT.
Business Publishers, Inc., 951 Pershing Dr., Silver Spring, MD 20910-4464. TEL 301-587-6300. FAX 301-587-1081.
Vendor(s): Data-Star, Human Resources Information Network, Information Access Co., Knight-Ridder Information, Inc., NewsNet [EV27]. *2776*

ASIA INC.
Intercontinental Marketing Corp., I.P.O. Box 5056, Tokyo 100-31, Japan. TEL 81-3-3661-7458. FAX 81-03-3667-9646. *1572*

ASIA - PACIFIC JOURNAL OF MANAGEMENT.
National University of Singapore, Faculty of Business Administration, 10 Kent Ridge Crescent, Singapore 0511, Singapore. TEL 7725395. FAX 7765641.
Vendor(s): University Microfilms International. *1406*

ASIA - PACIFIC POPULATION & POLICY.
East - West Center, 1777 East-West Rd., Honolulu, HI 96848. TEL 808-944-7480. FAX 808-944-7490. *5781*

ASIA - PACIFIC POPULATION RESEARCH ABSTRACTS.
East - West Center, 1777 East-West Rd., Honolulu, HI 96848. TEL 808-944-7480. FAX 808-944-7490. *5794*

ASIAMONEY.
Euromoney Publications plc, 20th Fl., Trust Tower, 68 Johnston Road, Wanchai, Hong Kong. TEL 852-529-5009. FAX 852-866-9046.
Vendor(s): University Microfilms International. *1060*

Online

ASIAN AVIATION NEWS.
Phillips Business Information, Inc., 1201 Seven Locks Rd., Potomac, MD 20854. TEL 301-424-3338. FAX 301-309-3847.
Vendor(s): Information Access Co. *6752*

ASIAN BUSINESS.
Far East Trade Press Ltd., Kai Tak Commercial Bldg., 2nd Fl., 317 Des Voeux Rd., Central, Hong Kong. TEL 545-7200. FAX 544-6979.
Vendor(s): University Microfilms International. *1514*

ASIAN FOLKLORE STUDIES.
Nanzan University, 18, Yamazato-cho, Showa-ku, Nagoya 466, Japan. TEL 052-832-3111. FAX 052-833-6157.
Vendor(s): Information Access Co. *2949*

ASIAN JOURNAL OF SURGERY.
Asian Surgical Association, Queen Mary Hospital, Hong Kong. TEL 852-2855-4080. FAX 852-2855-9950.
Vendor(s): Lexis-Nexis. *4904*

ASIAN MANUFACTURERS JOURNAL.
G.P.O. Box 6217, Hong Kong. TEL 852-2558-8131. FAX 852-2897-5087. *1514*

ASIAN STUDIES CENTER BACKGROUNDER.
Heritage Foundation, 214 Massachusetts Ave., N.E., Washington, DC 20002. TEL 202-546-4400. FAX 202-543-9647.
Vendor(s): Lexis-Nexis. *5742*

ASIAN SURVEY.
University of California Press, Journals Division, 2120 Berkeley Way, No. 5812, Berkeley, CA 94720-5812. TEL 510-643-7154. FAX 510-642-9917.
Vendor(s): Information Access Co., University Microfilms International. *5635*

ASIANWEEK.
Pan Asia Venture Capital Corporation, 809 Sacramento St., San Francisco, CA 94108. TEL 415-397-0220. FAX 415-397-7258.
Vendor(s): Lexis-Nexis (Ethnic Newswatch). *2865*

ASOCIACION DE DEMOGRAFIA HISTORICA. BOLETIN.
Asociacion de Demografia Historica, Centre d'Estudis Demografics, Edifici E2, Universitat Autonoma de Barcelona, 08193 Bellaterra, Spain. TEL 34-3-5813060. FAX 34-3-5813061. *5781*

ASSEMBLY (CAROL STREAM).
Hitchcock Publishing 191 S. Gary Ave., Carol Stream, IL 60188. TEL 708-665-1000. FAX 708-462-2225.
Vendor(s): Information Access Co.. *2590*

ASSET FINANCE AND LEASING DIGEST.
Euromoney Publications plc., Nestor House, Playhouse Yard, London EC4V 5EX, England. TEL 44-171-779-8935. FAX 44-171-779-8541.
Vendor(s): University Microfilms International. *1319*

ASSET SALES REPORT.
American Banker - Bond Buyer, Newsletter Division 1 State St. Plaza, New York, NY 10004-1549. TEL 800-733-4371. FAX 212-943-2224.
Vendor(s): Data-Star, Information Access Co., Knight-Ridder Information, Inc., Lexis-Nexis, NewsNet (FI33). *1319*

ASSOCIATION FOR COMPUTING MACHINERY. COMMUNICATIONS.
Association for Computing Machinery, 1515 Broadway, 17th Fl., New York, NY 10036-5701. TEL 212-869-7440. FAX 212-944-1318.
Vendor(s): Information Access Co., University Microfilms International. *2067*

ASSOCIATION MANAGEMENT.
American Society of Association Executives, 1575 Eye St., N.W., Washington, DC 20005-1168. TEL 202-626-2735. FAX 202-408-9635.
Vendor(s): Information Access Co., University Microfilms International. *1406*

THE ASTRONOMER.
16 Westminster Close, Basingstoke, Hants. RG22 4PP, England. TEL 44-1256-471074. FAX 44-1256-471074. *475*

ASTRONOMY.
Kalmbach Publishing Co., 210272 Crossroads Cir., Waukesha, WI 53187. TEL 414-796-8776. FAX 414-796-1142.
Vendor(s): Information Access Co., University Microfilms International. *477*

ASTRONOMY AND ASTROPHYSICS SUPPLEMENT SERIES.
Editions de Physique, 7 av.du Hoggar, B.P. 112, Z.I. de Courtaboeuf, 91944 Les Ulis cedex A, France. TEL 33-1-69-07-36-88. FAX 33-1-69-28-84-91. *477*

AT THE PARK.
Yellow Dot Publishing, Box 597783, Chicago, IL 60659-7783. TEL 312-465-4880. FAX 312-465-0084. *3962*

ATLANTA BUSINESS CHRONICLE.
Scripps Howard Business Publications (Atlanta), 1801 Peachtree St., No. 150, Atlanta, GA 30339-1859.
Vendor(s): Information Access Co., Knight-Ridder Information, Inc.. *1175*

THE ATLANTA CONSTITUTION AND JOURNAL INDEX.
U M I Company 300 N. Zeeb Rd., Ann Arbor, MI 48106-1346. TEL 313-761-4700. FAX 800-864-0019. *3714*

ATLANTIC ECONOMIC JOURNAL.
Atlantic Economic Society, c/o John M. Virgo, Ed., Box 1101, Southern Illinois University, Edwardsville, IL 62026-1101. TEL 618-692-2291. FAX 618-692-3400.
Vendor(s): Information Access Co., Knight-Ridder Information, Inc.. *895*

THE ATLANTIC MONTHLY.
Atlantic Monthly Co., 745 Boylston St., Boston, MA 02116. TEL 617-536-9500.
Vendor(s): Information Access Co.. *4133*

ATLANTIC TRADE REPORT & GLOBAL DEFENSE INDUSTRY.
Bergerac International Ltd., Rt. One, Box 309, Gainesville, VA 20065. TEL 703-349-2922. FAX 703-349-2922.
Vendor(s): Information Access Co.. *1264*

ATTENDERINGSBULLETIN BIBLIOTHEEK STARING-GEBOUW: LAND, BODEM, WATER.
International Institute for Land Reclamation and Improvement, Library - Staring Building, P.O. Box 45, 6700 AA Wageningen, Netherlands. TEL 31-873074733. FAX 31-8730-24812. *2827*

ATTORNEY - C P A.
American Association of Attorney-Certified Public Accountants, Inc., 24196 Alicia Pkwy., Ste. K, Mission Viejo, CA 92691. TEL 714-768-0336.
Vendor(s): University Microfilms International. *3894*

AUDIO (NEW YORK).
Hachette Filipacchi Magazines, Inc., 1633 Broadway, New York, NY 10019. TEL 212-767-6000. FAX 212-767-5619.
Vendor(s): Information Access Co.. *5140*

AUDIO: THE INTERNATIONAL MARKET.
Euromonitor, 60-61 Britton St., London EC1M 5NA, England. TEL 44-171-251-8024. FAX 44-171-608-3149.
Vendor(s): Data-Star, Knight-Ridder Information, Inc.. *2508*

AUDIO WEEK.
Warren Publishing, Inc., 2115 Ward Ct., N.W., Washington, DC 20037. TEL 212-686-5410. FAX 212-889-5097.
Vendor(s): Data-Star, Information Access Co., Knight-Ridder Information, Inc., NewsNet (EC93). *6444*

AUDIOCASSETTE & C D FINDER.
Plexus Publishing, Inc., 143 Old Marlton Pike, Medford, NJ 08055-8750. TEL 609-654-4888. FAX 609-654-4309.
Vendor(s): Knight-Ridder Information, Inc. (File no.46). *2385*

AUDIOTEX UPDATE.
Worldwide Videotex, Box 3273, Boynton Beach, FL 33424-3273. TEL 407-738-2276.
Vendor(s): Data-Star, Information Access Co., Knight-Ridder Information, Inc., NewsNet (TE16). *1926*

AUDIOVISUAL LIBRARIAN.
Aslib, Association for Information Management, c/o Anthony Hugh Thompson, Ed., Coach House Frongog, Llanbadarn Fawr, Aberystwyth SY23 3HN, Wales. TEL 44-1970-617322. FAX 44-1970-617322. *4042*

AUDITING.
American Accounting Association, Paul F. Gerhardt Bldg., 5717 Bessie Dr., Sarasota, FL 34233. TEL 941-921-7747. FAX 941-923-4093.
Vendor(s): University Microfilms International. *1041*

AUDUBON.
National Audubon Society, 700 Broadway, New York, NY 10003. TEL 212-979-3126. FAX 212-477-9069.
Vendor(s): Information Access Co., University Microfilms International. *2120*

AUSTIN BUSINESS JOURNAL.
American City Business Journals, Inc., 1301 Capital of Texas Hwy., Ste. B-224, Austin, TX 78746. TEL 512-328-0180. FAX 512-328-7304.
Vendor(s): University Microfilms International. *895*

AUSTRALIAN ACCOUNTANT.
Australian Society of Certified Practising Accountants, 170 Queen St., Melbourne, Vic. 3000, Australia. TEL 61-3-606-9606. FAX 61-3-670-8901.
Vendor(s): University Microfilms International. *1041*

AUSTRALIAN AND NEW ZEALAND JOURNAL OF MEDICINE.
Adis International Pty. Ltd., 9 Rodborough Rd., Frenchs Forest, N.S.W. 2089, Australia. TEL 61-2-9759100. FAX 61-2-9759199. *4431*

AUSTRALIAN ARCHITECTURAL PERIODICALS INDEX.
Stanton Library, Reader Services Department, P.O. Box 12, N. Sydney, N.S.W. 2059, Australia. TEL 61-2-99368400. FAX 61-2-99368440. *407*

AUSTRALIAN CORPORATE NEWS.
C C H Australia Ltd., P.O. Box 230, North Ryde, N.S.W. 2113, Australia. TEL 61-1-300300224. FAX 61-1-300306224. *3894*

AUSTRALIAN ECONOMIC REVIEW.
Blackwell Publishers Ltd., 108 Cowley Rd., Oxford OX4 1JF, England. TEL 44-1865-791100. FAX 44-1865-791347.
Vendor(s): University Microfilms International. *895*

AUSTRALIAN EDUCATION INDEX.
Australian Council for Educational Research, Private Bag 55, Camberwell, Vic. 3124, Australia. TEL 61-3-92775555. FAX 61-3-92775500.
Vendor(s): AUSINET. *2385*

AUSTRALIAN FAMILY AND SOCIETY ABSTRACTS.
Australian Institute of Family Studies, 300 Queen St., Melbourne, Vic. 3000, Australia. TEL 61-3-2147888. FAX 61-3-2147839. *6441*

AUSTRALIAN GOVERNMENT PUBLICATIONS.
National Library of Australia, Publications Section, Cultural and Educational Services Division, Canberra, A.C.T. 2600, Australia. TEL 61-6-262-1365. FAX 61-6-273-4493. *516*

AUSTRALIAN JOURNAL OF DAIRY TECHNOLOGY.
Dairy Industry Association of Australia, P.O. Box 8000, Glen Iris, Vic. 3146, Australia, Australia. FAX 61-3-92526555.
Vendor(s): Knight-Ridder Information, Inc. (File nos.50 & 53). *247*

AUSTRALIAN JOURNAL OF MANAGEMENT.
Australian Graduate School of Management, University of New South Wales, P.O. Box 1, Kensington, N.S.W. 2033, Australia. TEL 61-2-931-9259. FAX 61-2-662-7621. *1406*

AUSTRALIAN ROAD RESEARCH.
A R R B Transport Research Ltd., 500 Burwood Hwy., Vermont S., Vic. 3133, Australia. TEL 61-3-98811555. FAX 61-3-98878104. Available only online. *2624*

AUSTRALIAN SECURITIES COMMISSION RELEASES.
C C H Australia Ltd., P.O. Box 230, North Ryde, N.S.W. 2113, Australia. TEL 61-1-300300224. FAX 61-1-300306224. *3895*

AUSTRIA KULTUR.
Austrian Cultural Institute, 950 Third Ave., Fl. 20th, New York, NY 10022-2705. TEL 212-759-5165. *3112*

AUSTRIAN INFORMATION.
Austrian Press and Information Service, 3524 International Ct., N.W., Washington, DC 20008-3035. TEL 202-895-6775. FAX 202-895-6772. *5742*

AUSZUEGE AUS DEN EUROPAEISCHEN PATENTANMELDUNGEN. TEIL 1A. CHEMIE UND HUETTENWESEN.
Wila Verlag Wilhelm Lampl GmbH, Landsberger Str. 191A, 80687 Munich, Germany. TEL 089-54756-0. FAX 089-54756309. *5335*

AUSZUEGE AUS DEN EUROPAEISCHEN PATENTANMELDUNGEN. TEIL 2A. PHYSIK, OPTIK, AKUSTIK, FEINMECHANIK.
Wila Verlag Wilhelm Lampl GmbH, Landsberger Str. 191A, 80687 Munich, Germany. TEL 089-54756-0. FAX 089-54756309. *5335*

AUSZUEGE AUS DEN EUROPAEISCHEN PATENTANMELDUNGEN. TEIL 3A. UEBRIGE VERARBEITUNGSINDUSTRIE UND ARBEITSVERFAHREN, FAHRZEUGBAU, ERNAEHRUNG, LANDWIRTSCHAFT.
Wila Verlag Wilhelm Lampl GmbH, Landsberger Str. 191A, 80687 Munich, Germany. TEL 089-54756-0. FAX 089-54756309. *5335*

AUSZUEGE AUS DEN EUROPAEISCHEN PATENTSCHRIFTEN. TEIL 1. GRUND- UND ROHSTOFFINDUSTRIE, CHEMIE UND HUETTEN-WESEN, BAUWESEN UND BERGBAU.
Wila Verlag Wilhelm Lampl GmbH, Landsberger Str. 191A, 80687 Munich, Germany. TEL 089-54756-0. FAX 089-54756309. *5335*

AUSZUEGE AUS DEN GEBRAUCHSMUSTERN.
Wila Verlag Wilhelm Lampl GmbH, Landsberger Str. 191A, 80687 Munich, Germany. TEL 089-54756-0. FAX 089-54756309. *5335*

AUSZUEGE AUS DEN OFFENLEGUNGSSCHRIFTEN. TEIL 1. GRUND- UND ROHSTOFFINDUSTRIE, CHEMIE UND HUETTEN-WESEN, BAUWESEN UND BERGBAU.
Wila Verlag Wilhelm Lampl GmbH, Landsberger Str. 191A, 80687 Munich, Germany. TEL 089-54756-0. FAX 089-54756309. *5335*

AUSZUEGE AUS DEN OFFENLEGUNGSSCHRIFTEN. TEIL 2. ELEKTROTECHNIK, PHYSIK, FEINMECHANIK UND OPTIK, AKUSTIK.
Wila Verlag Wilhelm Lampl GmbH, Landsberger Str. 191A, 80687 Munich, Germany. TEL 089-54756-0. FAX 089-54756309. *5335*

AUSZUEGE AUS DEN OFFENLEGUNGSSCHRIFTEN. TEIL 3. UEBRIGE VERARBEITUNGSINDUSTRIE UND ARBEITSVERFAHREN, MASCHINEN- UND FAHRZEUGBAU, ERNAEHRUNG, LANDWIRTSCHAFT.
Wila Verlag Wilhelm Lampl GmbH, Landsberger Str. 191A, 80687 Munich, Germany. TEL 089-54756-0. FAX 089-54756309. *5335*

AUSZUEGE AUS DEN PATENTSCHRIFTEN.
Wila Verlag Wilhelm Lampl GmbH, Landsberger Str. 191A, 80687 Munich, Germany. TEL 089-54756-0. FAX 089-54756309. *5335*

AUTO PARTS REPORT.
International Trade Services, Box 5950, Bethesda, MD 20824-5950. TEL 301-229-2077. FAX 301-229-3995. *6771*

AUTOMATIC I D NEWS.
Advanstar Communications, Inc., 7500 Old Oak Blvd., Cleveland, OH 44130. TEL 216-826-2839. FAX 216-891-2726. Vendor(s): Information Access Co.. *2012*

AUTOMATIC MERCHANDISER.
Johnson Hill Press, Inc. 1233 Janesville Ave., Ft. Atkinson, WI 53538. TEL 414-563-6388. FAX 414-563-1702. Vendor(s): Information Access Co.. *1454*

AUTOMOBILE (NEW YORK).
K-III Communications Corp., 745 Fifth Ave., New York, NY 10151. TEL 212-745-0100. Vendor(s): Information Access Co.. *6773*

AUTOMOTIVE ENGINEERING MAGAZINE.
Society of Automotive Engineers, 400 Commonwealth Dr., Warrendale, PA 15096-0001. TEL 412-772-7114. FAX 412-776-4026. Vendor(s): Information Access Co., Orbit Search Service. *6774*

AUTOMOTIVE INDUSTRIES.
Chilton Co., 2600 Fisher Bldg., 3011 W. Grand Blvd., Detroit, MI 48202. TEL 313-875-2090. FAX 313-875-8148. Vendor(s): Information Access Co., Knight-Ridder Information, Inc., Lexis-Nexis. *6774*

AUTOMOTIVE NEWS.
Crain Communications Inc., (Detroit), Automotive News, 1400 Woodbridge Ave., Detroit, MI 48207-3187. TEL 313-446-6000. FAX 313-446-0383. Vendor(s): Information Access Co.. *6775*

AUTOMOTIVE NEWS MARKET DATA BOOK.
Crain Communications, Inc. (Detroit), Automotive News, 1400 Woodbridge Ave., Detroit, MI 48207. TEL 313-446-6000. FAX 313-446-0383. Vendor(s): Information Access Co.. *6775*

AUTOMOTIVE PRODUCTION.
Gardner Publications Inc., 6600 Clough Pike, Cincinnati, OH 45244-4090. TEL 513-231-8020. FAX 513-231-2818. Vendor(s): University Microfilms International. *1515*

AUTOMOTIVES: THE INTERNATIONAL MARKET.
Euromonitor, 60-61 Britton St., London EC1M 5NA, England. TEL 44-171-251-8024. FAX 44-171-608-3149. Vendor(s): Data-Star, Knight-Ridder Information, Inc.. *6775*

AUTOPARTS REPORT.
International Trade Services, Box 5950, Bethesda, MD 20824-5950. TEL 301-229-2077. FAX 301-229-3995. Vendor(s): Data-Star, Information Access Co., Knight-Ridder Information, Inc., NewsNet (AU09). *6775*

AUTOWEEK.
Crain Communications, Inc. (Detroit), 1400 Woodridge Ave., Detroit, MI 48207-3187. TEL 313-446-6000. FAX 313-446-1650. Vendor(s): Information Access Co., Lexis-Nexis. *6776*

AVERY INDEX TO ARCHITECTURAL PERIODICALS.
G.K. Hall & Co., c/o MacMillan Publishing USA, 1633 Broadway, 5th Fl., New York, NY 10019. TEL 212-654-8452. Vendor(s): Knight-Ridder Information, Inc., Research Libraries Group Information Network. *407*

AVIATION DAILY.
McGraw-Hill Companies, Aviation Week Group (Washington), 1200 G St., N.W., Ste. 200, Washington, DC 20005. TEL 202-383-2350. Vendor(s): Dow Jones News Retrieval, Knight-Ridder Information, Inc. (File no.624/McGRAW-HILL PUBLICATIONS ONLINE), Lexis-Nexis (AVDLY), NewsNet (AE28). *58*

AVIATION EUROPE.
McGraw-Hill Companies, Aviation Week Group (Washington), 1200 G St., N.W., Ste. 200, Washington, DC 20005. TEL 202-383-2350. Vendor(s): Dow Jones News Retrieval (AE), Knight-Ridder Information, Inc. (AE), Lexis-Nexis (AVEUR), NewsNet (AE35). *6752*

AVIATION WEEK & SPACE TECHNOLOGY.
McGraw-Hill Companies, Aviation Week Group (New York), 1221 Ave. of the Americas, New York, NY 10020. TEL 212-512-2000. FAX 212-512-4225. Vendor(s): Dow Jones News Retrieval, Knight-Ridder Information, Inc. (File no.624/McGRAW-HILL PUBLICATIONS ONLINE), Lexis-Nexis, NewsNet (AE30). *58*

AZ B - ARIZONA BUSINESS.
Arizona State University Center for Business Research, College of Business, Box 874406, Tempe, AZ 85287-4406. TEL 602-965-3961. FAX 602-965-5458. Vendor(s): Information Access Co., University Microfilms International. *896*

B B A - REVIEWS ON CANCER.
Elsevier Science B.V., P.O. Box 211, 1000 AE Amsterdam, Netherlands. TEL 31-20-4853911. FAX 31-20-4853598. *4748*

THE B B I NEWSLETTER.
Biomedical Business International 2 Park Plz., Ste. 900, Irvine, CA 92714-8519. TEL 714-755-5757. FAX 714-755-5724. Vendor(s): Information Access Co., Knight-Ridder Information, Inc.. *4432*

B C BUSINESS.
Canada Wide Magazines Ltd. (Toronto), 2 Carlton St., Ste. 801, Toronto, Oh M5B 1J3, Canada. TEL 416-595-5007. FAX 416-924-6308. Vendor(s): Information Access Co., Knight-Ridder Information, Inc.. *896*

B D I DEUTSCHLAND LIEFERT.
Verlag W. Sachon, Schloss Mindelburg, 87714 Mindelheim, Germany. TEL 49-8261-999-0. FAX 49-8261-999180. Vendor(s): Data-Star, FIZ Technik. *1265*

B H A.
Centre National de la Recherche Scientifique, Institut de l'Information Scientifique et Technique, 2 allee du Parc de Brabois, 54514 Vandoeuvre-Les-Nancy Cedex, France. TEL 33-50-46-00. FAX 83-50-46-50. Vendor(s): Knight-Ridder Information, Inc. (File no.191, Art Literature International), Telesystemes - Questel. *462*

B I R D.
Centre International de l'Enfance, Chateau de Longchamp, Bois de Boulogne, 75016 Paris, France. TEL 1-45-20-79-92. FAX 1-45-25-73-67. *1782*

B L A S T.
American Bar Association, Science and Technology Section, 750 N. Lake Shore Dr., Chicago, IL 60611. TEL 312-988-6067. FAX 312-988-6281. Vendor(s): Ovid Technologies, Inc., Knight-Ridder Information, Inc., Lexis-Nexis, West Services, Inc.. *3746*

B M D MONITOR.
Pasha Publications Inc., 1616 N. Ft. Myer Dr., Ste. 1000, Arlington, VA 22209-3107. TEL 703-528-1244. FAX 703-528-1253. Vendor(s): Information Access Co., NewsNet (DE05). *5024*

B M J.
B M J Publishing Group, B.M.A. House, Tavistock Sq., London WC1H 9JR, England. TEL 44-171-387-4499. FAX 44-171-383-6661. Vendor(s): Information Access Co., Ovid Technologies, Inc., University Microfilms International. *4432*

B M T ABSTRACTS.
B M T Ltd., Northumbria House, Dewy Bank, Wallsend. Tyne and Wear NE28 6UY, England. FAX 44-191-262-8754. *6736*

B N A PENSION & BENEFITS REPORTER.
The Bureau of National Affairs, Inc., 1231 25th St., N.W., Washington, DC 20037. TEL 202-452-4200. FAX 202-822-8092. Vendor(s): Human Resources Information Network (CDD, HDD), Lexis-Nexis (PENSN), West Services, Inc. (BNA-PEN). *1364*

B N A POLICY AND PRACTICE SERIES.
The Bureau of National Affairs, Inc., 1231 25th St., N.W., Washington, DC 20037. TEL 202-452-4200. FAX 202-822-8092. Vendor(s): Human Resources Information Network (BPP). *1498*

B N A POLICY AND PRACTICE SERIES. COMPENSATION.
The Bureau of National Affairs, Inc., 1231 25th St., N.W., Washington, DC 20037. TEL 202-452-4200. FAX 202-822-8092.
Vendor(s): Human Resources Information Network. *1364*

B N A POLICY AND PRACTICE SERIES. FAIR EMPLOYMENT PRACTICES.
The Bureau of National Affairs, Inc., 1231 25th St., N.W., Washington, DC 20037. TEL 202-452-4200. FAX 202-822-8092.
Vendor(s): Human Resources Information Network, Knight-Ridder Information, Inc.. *1364*

B N A POLICY AND PRACTICE SERIES. LABOR RELATIONS.
The Bureau of National Affairs, Inc., 1231 25th St., N.W., Washington, DC 20037. TEL 202-452-4200. FAX 202-822-8092.
Vendor(s): Human Resources Information Network. *1364*

B N A POLICY AND PRACTICE SERIES. PERSONNEL MANAGEMENT.
The Bureau of National Affairs, Inc., 1231 25th St., N.W., Washington, DC 20037. TEL 202-452-4200. FAX 202-822-8092.
Vendor(s): Human Resources Information Network. *1498*

B N A'S AMERICANS WITH DISABILITIES ACT MANUAL AND CASES.
The Bureau of National Affairs, Inc., 1231 25th St., N.W., Washington, DC 20037. TEL 202-452-4200. FAX 202-822-8092.
Vendor(s): Human Resources Information Network (ADAM), West Services, Inc. (FLB-CS, MLRR-CS). *3956*

B N A'S BANKING REPORT.
The Bureau of National Affairs, Inc., 1231 25th St., N.W., Washington, DC 20037. TEL 202-452-4200. FAX 202-822-8092.
Vendor(s): Bureau of National Affairs, Human Resources Information Network (CDD,HDD), Lexis-Nexis (BNABNK), West Services, Inc. (BNA-BNK). *3747*

B N A'S EMPLOYEE RELATIONS WEEKLY.
The Bureau of National Affairs, Inc., 1231 25th St., N.W., Washington, DC 20037. TEL 202-452-4200. FAX 202-822-8092.
Vendor(s): Human Resources Information Network (Files CDD, HDD). *1364*

B N A'S MEDICARE REPORT.
The Bureau of National Affairs, Inc., 1231 25th St., N.W., Washington, DC 20037. TEL 202-452-4200. FAX 202-822-8092.
Vendor(s): Human Resources Information Network (File DD). *4432*

B N A'S PATENT, TRADEMARK & COPYRIGHT JOURNAL.
Bureau of National Affairs, 1231 25th St., N.W., Washington, DC 20037. TEL 202-452-4200. FAX 202-833-8092.
Vendor(s): Lexis-Nexis, West Services, Inc. (BNA-PTCJ). *5335*

B N A'S WORKERS' COMPENSATION REPORT.
The Bureau of National Affairs, Inc., 1231 25th St., N.W., Washington, DC 20037. TEL 202-452-4200. FAX 202-822-8092.
Vendor(s): Human Resources Information Network (File DD). *1364*

B T TECHNOLOGY JOURNAL.
Chapman & Hall, Journals Department 2-6 Boundary Row, London SE1 8HN, England. TEL 44-171-8650066. FAX 44-171-5229623. *1896*

B T TODAY.
British Telecommunications plc., 81 Newgate St., Rm. A236, London EC14 7AJ, England. TEL 44-171-356-5307.
Vendor(s): Data-Star, Knight-Ridder Information, Inc., NewsNet (TE40). *1943*

BABY CARE PRODUCTS: THE INTERNATIONAL MARKET.
Euromonitor, 60-61 Britton St., London EC1M 5NA, England. TEL 44-171-251-8024. FAX 44-171-608-3149.
Vendor(s): Data-Star, Knight-Ridder Information, Inc.. *489*

BABY FOODS: THE INTERNATIONAL MARKET.
Euromonitor, 60-61 Britton St., London EC1M 5NA, England. TEL 44-171-251-8024. FAX 44-171-608-3149.
Vendor(s): Data-Star, Knight-Ridder Information, Inc.. *2961*

THE BACK LETTER.
Lippincott - Raven Publishers 227 E. Washington Sq., Philadelphia, PA 19106-3780. TEL 215-238-4200.
Vendor(s): Information Access Co.. *4781*

BACK STAGE.
B P I Communications, Inc. (New York), 1515 Broadway, 14th Fl., New York, NY 10036. TEL 212-764-7300. FAX 212-536-5318.
Vendor(s): Information Access Co.. *6693*

BACKGROUNDER.
Heritage Foundation, 214 Massachusetts Ave., N.E., Washington, DC 20002. TEL 202-546-4400. FAX 202-543-9647.
Vendor(s): Lexis-Nexis. *5742*

BACKGROUNDER UPDATE.
Heritage Foundation, 214 Massachusetts Ave., N.E., Washington, DC 20002. TEL 202-546-4400. FAX 202-543-9647.
Vendor(s): Lexis-Nexis. *5892*

BACKPACKER.
Rodale Press, Inc., 33 E. Minor St., Emmaus, PA 18049. TEL 610-967-5171. FAX 610-967-7725.
Vendor(s): Information Access Co., University Microfilms International. *6557*

BAKERY PRODUCTION AND MARKETING.
Cahners Publishing Company (Des Plaines), Division of Reed Elsevier Inc., 1350 E. Touhy Ave., Box 5080, Des Plaines, IL 60018-5080. TEL 847-635-8800. FAX 847-299-2445.
Vendor(s): Information Access Co., Knight-Ridder Information, Inc., Lexis-Nexis. *2998*

BAKERY PRODUCTS: THE INTERNATIONAL MARKET.
Euromonitor, 60-61 Britton St., London EC1M 5NA, England. TEL 44-171-251-8024. FAX 44-171-608-3149.
Vendor(s): Data-Star, Knight-Ridder Information, Inc.. *2998*

BALTIMORE BUSINESS JOURNAL.
American City Business Journals, Inc. (Baltimore), 117 Water St., 9th Fl., Baltimore, MD 21202. TEL 410-576-1161. FAX 410-752-3112.
Vendor(s): Information Access Co., Knight-Ridder Information, Inc.. *896*

BALTIMORE'S CHILD.
11 Dutton Ct., Baltimore, MD 21228. TEL 410-367-5883. FAX 410-719-9342. *1760*

BANGLADESH JOURNAL OF PUBLIC ADMINISTRATION.
Bangladesh Public Administration Training Centre, Attn: Asst. Publication Officer, Molla Mosharraf Hossain, Savar, Dhaka 1343, Bangladesh. TEL 831711-20-251. *5893*

BANGLADESH PHARMACEUTICAL JOURNAL.
Bangladesh Pharmaceutical Society, University of Dhaka, Ramna, Dhaka 2, Bangladesh. *5401*

BANGOR THEOLOGICAL SEMINARY. GENERAL THEOLOGICAL LIBRARY. BULLETIN.
Bangor Theological Seminary, 159 State St., Portland, ME 04101. TEL 207-874-2214. *6107*

BANK AUTOMATION NEWS.
Phillips Business Information, Inc., 1201 Seven Locks Rd., Potomac, MD 20854. TEL 301-424-3338. FAX 301-309-3847.
Vendor(s): Data-Star, Information Access Co., Knight-Ridder Information, Inc., NewsNet. *1128*

BANK LOAN REPORT.
Investment Dealers' Digest, 2 World Trade Center, 18th Fl., New York, NY 10048-0638. TEL 212-227-1200. FAX 212-321-2336.
Vendor(s): Information Access Co., University Microfilms International. *1065*

BANK MANAGEMENT.
Bank Administration Institute, 1 N. Franklin St., Chicago, IL 60606. TEL 312-683-2248. FAX 312-683-2373.
Vendor(s): Information Access Co., Lexis-Nexis, University Microfilms International. *1065*

BANK MARKETING.
Bank Marketing Association, 1120 Connecticut Ave., N.W., Washington, DC 20036-3902. TEL 202-663-5268. FAX 202-828-4540.
Vendor(s): Information Access Co., University Microfilms International. *1065*

BANK MERGERS & ACQUISITIONS.
S N L Securities, LP, 410 E. Main St., Box 2124, Charlottesville, VA 22902. TEL 804-977-1600. FAX 804-977-4466.
Vendor(s): NewsNet (FI59). *1065*

BANK MUTUAL FUND REPORT.
American Banker Newsletters, One State Street Plaza, 26th Fl., New York, NY 10004-1505. TEL 212-803-8300. FAX 212-843-9620.
Vendor(s): Data-Star, Knight-Ridder Information, Inc., Lexis-Nexis, NewsNet. *1065*

BANK NETWORK NEWS.
Faulkner & Gray, Inc., 118 S. Clinton, Ste. 450, Chicago, IL 60606. TEL 312-648-0261.
Vendor(s): Information Access Co., NewsNet (FI71). *1128*

BANK NEWS.
Bank News, Inc., 912 Baltimore Ave., Ste. 900, Kansas City, MO 64105. TEL 816-421-7941.
Vendor(s): University Microfilms International. *1066*

BANK OF CANADA. REVIEW.
Bank of Canada, Secretary's Dept., 234 Wellington St., Ottawa, On K1A 0G9, Canada. TEL 613-782-8248.
Vendor(s): University Microfilms International. *1066*

BANK OF HAWAII BUSINESS TRENDS.
Bank of Hawaii, Economics Department, Box 2900, Honolulu, HI 96846. TEL 808-537-8307. FAX 808-536-9433. *1177*

BANK OPERATIONS BULLETIN.
American Bankers Association, 1120 Connecticut Ave. N.W., Washington, DC 20036. TEL 202-663-5430. FAX 302-834-8405.
Vendor(s): University Microfilms International. *1128*

BANK PERSONNEL NEWS.
American Bankers Association, 1120 Connecticut Ave., N.W., Washington, DC 20036. TEL 202-663-5090. FAX 301-828-4540.
Vendor(s): University Microfilms International. *1067*

BANK SYSTEMS & TECHNOLOGY.
Miller Freeman Inc. (New York) One Penn Plaza, New York, NY 10119. TEL 212-714-1300. FAX 212-302-6273.
Vendor(s): University Microfilms International. *1067*

BANK TECHNOLOGY NEWS.
Faulkner & Gray, Inc. (New York), Eleven Penn Plaza, New York, NY 10001. TEL 212-967-7000.
Vendor(s): Information Access Co., NewsNet (FI70), University Microfilms International. *1067*

THE BANKER.
Financial Times Business Information, Magazines 2 Greystoke Pl., Fetter Ln., London EC4A 1ND, England. TEL 0171-405-6969. FAX 0171-405-5276.
Vendor(s): University Microfilms International. *1068*

BANKERS RESEARCH.
Bankers Research, Inc., Box 431, Westport, CT 06881-0431. TEL 203-227-1237.
Vendor(s): University Microfilms International. *1068*

BANKING POLICY REPORT.
Law and Business, Inc. 270 Sylvan Ave., Englewood Cliffs, NJ 07632. TEL 201-894-8484. FAX 201-894-8666.
Vendor(s): Lexis-Nexis. *1069*

BANKING TECHNOLOGY.
I B C Publishing, Gilmoora House, 57-61 Mortimer St., London W1N 7TD, England. TEL 0171-637-4383. FAX 0171-636-6414.
Vendor(s): University Microfilms International. *1069*

BANXQUOTE ONLINE.
Masterfund Inc., 45 Essex St., Millburn, NJ 07041-1606. TEL 800-666-2000. FAX 302-529-2211. Available only online. *1320*

BARCLAYS COUNTRY REPORTS.
Barclays Bank plc., Economics Department, P.O. Box 12, Barclays House, 1 Wimborne Rd., Poole, Dorset BH15 2BB, England. TEL 01202-344023. FAX 01202-402303.
Vendor(s): Data-Star, Knight-Ridder Information, Inc. *1178*

BARCLAYS ECONOMIC REVIEW.
Barclays Bank plc., Economics Department, P.O. Box 12, Barclays House, 1 Wimborne Rd., Poole, Dorset BH15 2BB, England. TEL 01202-344023. FAX 01202-402303.
Vendor(s): Data-Star, Knight-Ridder Information, Inc., University Microfilms International. *1071*

BARRON'S.
Dow Jones & Co., Inc., 200 Liberty St., New York, NY 10281. TEL 212-416-2700. FAX 212-416-2829.
Vendor(s): Dow Jones News Retrieval. *1321*

BATH AND SHOWER PRODUCTS: THE INTERNATIONAL MARKET.
Euromonitor, 60-61 Britton St., London EC1M 5NA, England. TEL 44-171-251-8024. FAX 44-171-608-3149.
Vendor(s): Data-Star, Knight-Ridder Information, Inc. *489*

BATTERY & E V TECHNOLOGY NEWS.
Business Communications Co., Inc. (Norwalk), 25 Van Zant St., Ste. 13, Norwalk, CT 06855. TEL 203-853-4266. FAX 203-853-0348.
Vendor(s): Data-Star, Information Access Co., Knight-Ridder Information, Inc., NewsNet (RD30). *2684*

BEAUTY COUNTER.
Miller Freeman Publishers Ltd. Sovereign Way, Tonbridge, Kent TN9 1RW, England. TEL 44-1732-364422. FAX 44-1732-361534.
Vendor(s): Information Access Co.. *494*

BEER: THE INTERNATIONAL MARKET.
Euromonitor, 60-61 Britton St., London EC1M 5NA, England. TEL 44-171-251-8024. FAX 44-171-908-3149.
Vendor(s): Data-Star, Knight-Ridder Information, Inc.. *500*

BEHAVIORAL HEALTH MANAGEMENT.
Medquest Communications Inc., 629 Euclid Ave., Ste. 500, Cleveland, OH 44114-3003. TEL 216-522-9700. FAX 216-522-9707.
Vendor(s): Information Access Co., University Microfilms International. *2195*

BEILSTEINS HANDBUCH DER ORGANISCHEN CHEMIE. SUPPLEMENT.
Springer-Verlag, 175 Fifth Ave., New York, NY 10010. TEL 212-460-1500. FAX 212-473-6272.
Vendor(s): Knight-Ridder Information, Inc. (File no.390). *1735*

DIE BEKLEIDUNGS- UND WAESCHE-INDUSTRIE UND IHRE HELFER.
Industrieschau-Verlagsgesellschaft mbH, Postfach 100262, 64202 Darmstadt, Germany. TEL 49-6151-38920. FAX 49-6151-33164. *1831*

BELLES LETTRES (NORTH POTOMAC).
2208 Spinnaker Ct., Reston, VA 22091-4704. TEL 301-294-0278. FAX 301-294-0023.
Vendor(s): Information Access Co.. *4186*

BENCHMARKS.
University of North Texas, Computing Center, Box 13495, Denton, TX 76203-6495. TEL 817-565-2324. FAX 817-565-4060. *1983*

BENEFITS QUARTERLY.
International Society of Certified Employee Benefit Specialists, Inc., Box 209, Brookfield, WI 53008-0209. TEL 414-786-8771. FAX 414-786-8650.
Vendor(s): University Microfilms International. *1499*

BERKELEY JOURNAL OF EMPLOYMENT AND LABOR LAW.
University of California Press, Journals Division, 2120 Berkeley Way, No. 5812, Berkeley, CA 94720-5812. TEL 510-643-7154. FAX 510-642-9917.
Vendor(s): Information Access Co.. *1365*

THE BERMUDA SUN.
Bermuda Sun Ltd., P.O. Box HM 1241, Hamilton HMDX, Bermuda. TEL 441-295-3902. FAX 441-292-5597. *3116*

BERNOULLI.
Chapman & Hall, Journals Department 2-6 Boundary Row, London SE1 8HN, England. TEL 44-171-8650066. FAX 44-171-5229623. *4357*

BEST'S REVIEW. LIFE - HEALTH INSURANCE EDITION.
A.M. Best Co., Ambest Rd., Oldwick, NJ 08858. TEL 908-439-2200. FAX 908-439-3296.
Vendor(s): Information Access Co., Knight-Ridder Information, Inc., University Microfilms International. *3642*

BEST'S REVIEW. PROPERTY - CASUALTY INSURANCE EDITION.
A.M. Best Co., Ambest Rd., Oldwick, NJ 08858. TEL 908-439-2200. FAX 908-439-3296.
Vendor(s): Information Access Co., Knight-Ridder Information, Inc., University Microfilms International. *3642*

BEST'S UNDERWRITING GUIDE.
A.M. Best Co., Ambest Rd., Oldwick, NJ 08858. TEL 908-439-2200. FAX 908-439-3296. *3643*

BEST'S UNDERWRITING NEWSLETTER.
A.M. Best Co., Ambest Rd., Oldwick, NJ 08858. TEL 908-439-2200 FAX 908-439-3296. *3643*

BETTER HOMES AND GARDENS.
Meredith Corporation, 1716 Locust St., Des Moines, IA 50309-3023. TEL 515-284-3048. FAX 515-284-3023.
Vendor(s): Information Access Co., University Microfilms International. *3674*

BETTER NUTRITION.
Intertec Publishing Corp. (Atlanta), 6151 Powers Ferry Rd., N.W. Atlanta, GA 30339-2941. TEL 770-955-2500. FAX 770-955-0400.
Vendor(s): Information Access Co., University Microfilms International. *5230*

BEVERAGE INDUSTRY.
Stagnito Publishing Company, 1935 Shermer Rd., Ste. 100, Northbrook, IL 60062. TEL 847-205-5660. FAX 847-205-5680.
Vendor(s): Information Access Co.. *501*

BEVERAGE WORLD (ENGLISH EDITION).
Strategic Business Communications, 226 W. 26th St., New York, NY 10011. TEL 212-822-5930. FAX 212-822-5931.
Vendor(s): Information Access Co., Knight-Ridder Information, Inc., Lexis-Nexis, University Microfilms International. *501*

BEVERLY HILLS BAR ASSOCIATION JOURNAL.
Beverly Hills Bar Association, 300 S. Beverly Dr., Ste. 201, Beverly Hills, CA 90212. TEL 213-553-6644. FAX 213-284-8290.
Vendor(s): West Services, Inc.. *3750*

BIBLIOGRAFIA BRASILEIRA.
Biblioteca Nacional de Brasil, Av. Rio Branco, 219, 20042 Rio de Janeiro, Brazil. TEL 021-262-8255. FAX 021-220-4173. *4037*

BIBLIOGRAFIA BRASILEIRA DE ENERGIA NUCLEAR.
Comissao Nacional de Energia Nuclear, Centro de Informacoes Nucleares, Rua General Severiano 90, Botafogo, 22294-900 Rio de Janeiro RJ, Brazil. TEL 55-21-5462440. FAX 55-21-5462447. *2561*

BIBLIOGRAFIA BRASILEIRA DE ODONTOLOGIA.
Universidade de Sao Paulo, Faculdade de Odontologia, Av. Prof. Lineu Prestes, 2227, Caixa Postal 8216, 05508-900 Sao Paulo SP, Brazil. TEL 55-11-8187861. FAX 55-11-8187413. *4549*

BIBLIOGRAFIA LATINOAMERICANA: PART I.
Universidad Nacional Autonoma de Mexico, Centro de Informacion Cientifica y Humanistica, Apdo. Postal 70-392, C.P. 04510 Mexico, D.F., Mexico. TEL 525-6223958. FAX 525-6162557. *518*

BIBLIOGRAFIA LATINOAMERICANA: PART II.
Universidad Nacional Autonoma de Mexico, Centro de Informacion Cientifica y Humanistica, Apdo. Postal 70-392, C.P. 04510 Mexico, D.F., Mexico. TEL 525-6223958. FAX 525-6162557. *518*

BIBLIOGRAFIA NAZIONALE ITALIANA.
Istituto Centrale per il Catalogo Unico delle Biblioteche Italiane e per le Informazioni Bibliografiche, Viale del Castro Pretorio, 105, Rome, Italy. *519*

BIBLIOGRAFIA VENEZOLANA.
Instituto Autonomo Biblioteca Nacional, Oficina de Information, Apdo. 80593, Pracos del Este, Caracas 1080-A, Venezuela. TEL 943-1361. FAX 941-5219. *3978*

BIBLIOGRAFIE NEDERLANDSE SOCIALE WETENSCHAPPEN.
Universiteit Utrecht, Bureau Bibliografie Nederlandse Sociale Wetenschappen, Trompenburggracht 11, 3512 CA Utrecht, Netherlands. TEL 31-30-2537272. FAX 31-30-2536560. *6356*

BIBLIOGRAFIE VAN DE NEDERLANDSE TAAL- EN LITERATUUR WETENSCHAP.
Stichting Bibliographica Neerlandica, Postbus 90751, 2509 LT The Hague, Netherlands. *4127*

BIBLIOGRAFIJA JUGOSLAVIJE. CLANCI I PRILOZI U SERIJSKIM PUBLIKACIJAMA. SERIJA A: DRUSTVENE NAUKE.
Jugoslovenski Bibliografsko-Informacijski Institut (YUBIN), Terazije 26, Belgrade, Yugoslavia. FAX 11-687-760. *6356*

BIBLIOGRAFIJA JUGOSLAVIJE. CLANCI I PRILOZI U SERIJSKIM PUBLIKACIJAMA. SERIJA B: PRIRODNE, PRIMENJENE MEDICINSKE I TEHNICKE NAUKE.
Jugoslovenski Bibliografsko-Informacijski Institut (YUBIN), Terazije 26, Belgrade, Yugoslavia. FAX 11-687-760. *6299*

BIBLIOGRAFIJA JUGOSLAVIJE. CLANCI I PRILOZI U SERIJSKIM PUBLIKACIJAMA. SERIJA C: UMETNOST, SPORT, FILOLOGIJA, KNJIZEVNOST.
Jugoslovenski Bibliografsko-Informacijski Institut (YUBIN), Terazije 26, Belgrade, Yugoslavia. FAX 11-687-760. *519*

BIBLIOGRAFIJA JUGOSLAVIJE. KNJIGE, BROSURE I MUZIKALIJE.
Jugoslovenski Bibliografsko-Informacijski Institut (YUBIN), Terazije 26, Belgrade, Yugoslavia. FAX 11-687-760. *519*

BIBLIOGRAFIJA PREVODA U S F R J.
Jugoslovenski Bibliografsko-Informacijski Institut (YUBIN), Terazije 26, Belgrade, Yugoslavia. FAX 11-687-760. *519*

BIBLIOGRAPHIA MEDICA CECHOSLOVACA.
Narodni Lekarska Knihovne, Sokolska 31, 121 32 Prague 2, Czech Republic. TEL 42-2-24915775. FAX 42-2-24924625. *4519*

BIBLIOGRAPHIC INDEX.
H.W. Wilson Co., 950 University Ave., Bronx, NY 10452. TEL 718-588-8400. FAX 718-590-1617.
Vendor(s): Wilsonline (BIB). *520*

BIBLIOGRAPHY AND INDEX OF GEOLOGY.
American Geological Institute, 4220 King St., Alexandria, VA 22302-1502. TEL 703-379-2480. FAX 703-379-7563.
Vendor(s): CISTI, Knight-Ridder Information, Inc., OCLC (EPIC and First Search), Orbit Search Service (GEOR), STN International (GeoRe). *2218*

BIBLIOGRAPHY OF AGRICULTURE.
Oryx Press, 4041 N. Central Ave., No. 700, Phoenix, AZ 85012-3397. TEL 602-265-2651. FAX 602-265-6250.
Vendor(s): CISTI. *169*

Online

BIBLIOGRAPHY OF BIOETHICS.
Kennedy Institute of Ethics, National Reference Center for Bioethics Literature, Georgetown University, Box 571212, Washington, DC 20057-1212. TEL 202-687-6738. FAX 202-687-6770. Vendor(s): Knight-Ridder Information, Inc., National Library of Medicine, Telesystemes - Questel (BIOETHICS). *4549*

BIBLIOGRAPHY OF ECONOMIC GEOLOGY.
Geosystems, P.O. Box 40, Didcot, Oxon. OX11 9BX, England. TEL 44-1235-813913. Vendor(s): Knight-Ridder Information, Inc. (File no.58). *2218*

BIBLIOGRAPHY OF EDUCATION THESES IN AUSTRALIA.
Australian Council for Educational Research, Private Bag 55, Camberwell, Vic. 3124, Australia. TEL 61-3-92775555. FAX 61-3-92775500. *2386*

BIBLIOGRAPHY OF THE HISTORY OF MEDICINE.
U.S. National Library of Medicine, 8600 Rockville Pike, Bethesda, MD 20894. Vendor(s): National Library of Medicine. *4550*

BIBLIOGRAPHY ON COLD REGIONS SCIENCE & TECHNOLOGY.
U.S. Army, Cold Regions Research and Engineering Laboratory, 72 Lyme Rd., Hanover, NH 03755-1290. TEL 603-646-4221. FAX 603-646-4712. Vendor(s): Orbit Search Service (COLD). *2625*

BIBLIOTHEEK VOOR HEDENDAAGSE DOKUMENTATIE. BULLETIN.
Biblioteek voor Hedendaagse Dokumentatie, Parklaan 2, B-9100 St. Niklaas Waas, Belgium. TEL 32-3-776-5063. FAX 32-3-778-0785. *4042*

BIBLIOTHEQUE AFRICAINE. LISTE DES ACQUISITIONS.
Bibliotheque Africaine, 65 rue Belliard, 1040 Brussels, Belgium. FAX 32-2-2382669. Vendor(s): BELINDIS (AFLI). *522*

BICYCLING.
Rodale Press, Inc., 33 E. Minor St., Emmaus, PA 18046. TEL 610-967-5171. FAX 610-967-8960. Vendor(s): Information Access Co., University Microfilms International. *6521*

BILDUNGSFORSCHUNG UND BILDUNGSPRAXIS.
Universitaetsverlag Freiburg, Perolles 42, CH-1700 Freiburg, Switzerland. TEL 41-37-864311. FAX 41-37-864300. *2316*

BILINGUAL REVIEW.
Bilingual Review Press, Hispanic Research Center, Arizona State University, Tempe, AZ 85287-2702. TEL 602-965-3867. FAX 602-965-8309. *4057*

BILLBOARD (NEW YORK).
B P I Communications, Inc. (New York), 1515 Broadway, New York, NY 10036. TEL 212-764-7300. FAX 212-536-5358. Vendor(s): Information Access Co., Knight-Ridder Information, Inc.. *5143*

BIOCHEMICAL JOURNAL.
Portland Press Ltd., 59 Portland Place, London W1N 3AJ, England. TEL 44-171-580-5530. FAX 44-171-323-1136. *632*

BIOCHEMISTRY.
American Chemical Society, 1155 16th St., N.W., Washington, DC 20036. TEL 800-335-9511. FAX 614-447-3671. Vendor(s): STN International (CJACS). *632*

BIOCOMMERCE FINANCIAL ABSTRACTS.
BioCommerce Data Ltd., Prudential Bldgs., 95 High St., Slough, Berks. SL1 1DH, England. TEL 44-1753-511777. FAX 44-1753-512239. Vendor(s): Data-Star (CELL), Knight-Ridder Information, Inc. (File no.286). *616*

BIOCONTROL NEWS AND INFORMATION.
CAB International, Wallingford, Oxon. OX10 8DE, England. TEL 44-1491-832111. FAX 44-1491-833508. Vendor(s): DIMDI, European Space Agency, Knight-Ridder Information, Inc., STN International. *571*

BIOCONTROL SCIENCE AND TECHNOLOGY.
Carfax Publishing Co., P.O. Box 25, Abingdon, Oxon. OX14 3UE, England. TEL 44-1235-401000. FAX 44-1235-401550. *213*

BIOCYCLE.
J G Press, Inc., 419 State Ave., Emmaus, PA 18049. TEL 610-967-4135. Vendor(s): University Microfilms International. *2850*

BIODETERIORATION ABSTRACTS.
CAB International, Wallingford, Oxon. OX10 3DE, England. TEL 44-1491-832111. FAX 44-1491-833508. Vendor(s): Data-Star, European Space Agency, Knight-Ridder Information, Inc., STN International. *616*

BIODIVERSITY AND CONSERVATION.
Chapman & Hall, Journals Department 2-6 Boundary Row, London SE1 8HN, England. TEL 44-171-8650066. FAX 44-171-5229623. *2121*

BIOELECTROMAGNETICS.
John Wiley & Sons, Inc., Journals, 605 Third Ave., New York, NY 10158. TEL 212-850-6645. FAX 212-850-6021. *652*

BIOGRAPHY AND GENEALOGY MASTER INDEX.
Gale Research Inc., 835 Penobscot Bldg., Detroit, MI 48226. TEL 313-961-2242. FAX 313-961-6083. Vendor(s): Knight-Ridder Information, Inc. (File nos.287,288). *563*

BIOGRAPHY INDEX.
H.W. Wilson Co., 950 University Ave., Bronx, NY 10452. TEL 718-588-8400. FAX 718-590-1617. Vendor(s): Wilsonline (File BIO). *563*

BIOIMAGING.
I O P Publishing Ltd., Techno House, Redcliffe Way, Bristol, Avon BS1 6NX, England. TEL 44-117-929-7481. FAX 44-117-929-4318. *5543*

BIOLOGICAL ABSTRACTS.
BIOSIS, 2100 Arch St., Philadelphia, PA 19103-1399. TEL 215-587-4847. FAX 215-587-2016. Vendor(s): CISTI, Central Institute for Scientific & Technical Information, DIMDI, Data-Star, European Space Agency, Knight-Ridder Information, Inc. (File nos.5 & 55), Ovid Technologies, Inc. (BIOL), STN International (BIOSIS). *616*

BIOLOGICAL ABSTRACTS - R R M.
BIOSIS, 2100 Arch St., Philadelphia, PA 19103-1399. TEL 215-587-4847. FAX 215-587-2016. Vendor(s): CISTI, Central Institute for Scientific & Technical Information, DIMDI, Data-Star, European Space Agency (File no.7/BIOSIS), Knight-Ridder Information, Inc. (File nos.5 & 55), Ovid Technologies, Inc. (BIOL), STN International (BIOSIS). *616*

BIOLOGICAL & AGRICULTURAL INDEX.
H.W. Wilson Co., 950 University Ave., Bronx, NY 10452. TEL 718-588-8400. FAX 718-590-1617. Vendor(s): OCLC, Wilsonline. *616*

BIOLOGICAL BULLETIN.
Marine Biological Laboratory, Woods Hole, MA 02543. TEL 508-289-7428. FAX 508-457-1924. Vendor(s): Information Access Co., University Microfilms International. *572*

BIOLOGICAL RHYTHM RESEARCH.
Swets & Zeitlinger bv, P.O. Box 825, 2160 SZ Lisse, Netherlands. TEL 31-252-435111. FAX 31-252-415888. *572*

BIOLOGICAL SCIENCE REPORT.
U.S. National Biological Service, Information Transfer Center, 1201 Oak Ridge Dr., Ste. 200, Ft. Collins, CO 80525-5589. TEL 970-226-9401. FAX 970-226-9455. *573*

BIOLOGY DIGEST.
Plexus Publishing, Inc., 143 Old Marlton Pike, Medford, NJ 08055. TEL 609-654-6500. FAX 609-654-4309. Vendor(s): OCLC. *616*

BIOMEDICAL MARKET NEWSLETTER.
David G. Anast, Ed.& Pub., 3237 Idaho Pl., Costa Mesa, CA 92626-2207. TEL 714-434-9500. FAX 714-434-9755. Vendor(s): CompuServe, Inc., Data-Star, Dow Jones News Retrieval, Information Access Co., Knight-Ridder Information, Inc., Lexis-Nexis. *1454*

BIOMEDICAL MATERIALS.
Elsevier Science Ltd., P.O. Box 800, Kidlington, Oxford OX5 1DX, England. TEL 44-1865-843000. FAX 44-1865-843010. Vendor(s): Data-Star, Information Access Co., Knight-Ridder Information, Inc.. *4435*

BIOMETALS.
Rapid Science Publishers, 2-6 Boundary Row, London SE1 8HN, England. TEL 44-171-865-0198. FAX 44-171-410-6600. *634*

BIOPHARM.
Advanstar Communications, Inc., 859 Willamette St., Eugene, OR 97401. TEL 503-343-5020. FAX 503-344-3514. Vendor(s): Information Access Co.. *5402*

BIOPOLYMERS.
John Wiley & Sons, Inc., Journals, 605 Third Ave., New York, NY 10158. TEL 212-692-6645. FAX 212-850-6021. Vendor(s): STN International (CJWILEY). *1735*

BIOS.
Beta Beta Beta, Box 670, Madison, NJ 07940-0670. TEL 201-377-8407. *574*

BIOSAFETY.
Science Reviews Ltd., P.O. Box 81, Northwood, Middlesex HA6 3DY, England. TEL 44-1923-823586. FAX 44-1923-825006. Available only online. *574*

BIOSCAN.
Oryx Press, 4041 N. Central Ave., No. 700, Phoenix, AZ 85012-3397. TEL 602-265-2651. FAX 602-265-6250. *657*

BIOSCIENCE.
American Institute of Biological Sciences, 1444 Eye St., N.W., Ste. 200, Washington, DC 20005. TEL 202-628-1500. FAX 202-628-1509. Vendor(s): Information Access Co., University Microfilms International. *574*

BIOTECH BUSINESS.
Worldwide Videotex, Box 3273, Boynton Beach, FL 33424-3273. TEL 407-738-2276. Vendor(s): Data-Star, Information Access Co., Knight-Ridder Information, Inc., NewsNet (BT06). *738*

BIOTECH DAILY.
Washington Business Information, Inc., c/o. Karen Harrington, 1117 North 19th St., Ste. 200, Arlington, VA 22269-1798. TEL 703-247-3434. Vendor(s): Lexis-Nexis. *658*

BIOTECHNOLOGY ABSTRACTS.
Derwent Publications Ltd., Derwent House, 14 Great Queen St., London WC2B 5DF, England. TEL 44-171-3442800. Vendor(s): Knight-Ridder Information, Inc. (File no.357), Orbit Search Service (BIOT). *617*

BIOTECHNOLOGY BUSINESS NEWS.
Financial Times Pharmaceuticals and Healthcare Publishing Maple House, 149 Tottenham Court Rd., London W1P 9LL, England. TEL 44-171-896-2204. FAX 44-171-896-2213. Vendor(s): Information Access Co.. *659*

BIOVENTURE VIEW.
BioVenture Publishing, 2555 Flores St., Ste. 555, San Mateo, CA 94403-2342. TEL 415-574-7128. FAX 415-574-8319. Vendor(s): CompuServe, Inc., Data-Star, Dow Jones News Retrieval, European Space Agency, Information Access Co., Knight-Ridder Information, Inc. (File no.636). *660*

BIRMINGHAM BUSINESS.
Birmingham Area Chamber of Commerce, 2027 First Ave. N., Birmingham, AL 35203. TEL 205-323-5461. FAX 205-250-7669. Vendor(s): University Microfilms International. *1133*

THE BLACK COLLEGIAN.
140 Carondelet St., New Orleans, LA 70130-2526. TEL 504-523-0154. FAX 504-523-0271. Vendor(s): Information Access Co., University Microfilms International. *1859*

BLACK ENTERPRISE.
Earl G. Graves Publishing Co., Inc., 130 Fifth Ave.,
New York, NY 10011. TEL 212-242-8000.
FAX 212-886-9610.
Vendor(s): Information Access Co., University
Microfilms International. *897*

BLACK NEWSPAPER INDEX.
U M I Company 300 N. Zeeb Rd., Ann Arbor, MI
48106. TEL 313-761-4700. FAX 800-864-0019.
Vendor(s): Knight-Ridder Information, Inc.. *2917*

BLACK SCHOLAR.
Black World Foundation, Box 2869, Oakland, CA
94609. TEL 510-547-6633.
Vendor(s): University Microfilms International.
2868

BLAETTERTEIG.
Media Austria, Postfach 95, A-1013 Vienna,
Austria. TEL 43-1-3665512. *3701*

BLOOD.
W.B. Saunders Co. Curtis Center, 3rd Fl.,
Independence Sq. W., Philadelphia, PA 19106-
3399. TEL 215-238-7800. FAX 215-238-6445.
Vendor(s): Lexis-Nexis, Ovid Technologies, Inc..
4698

BLOOD & APHORISMS.
Box 702, Sta. P, Toronto, ON M5S 2Y4, Canada.
TEL 416-535-1233. *4187*

BLOOD CELLS, MOLECULES, AND DISEASES.
Academic Press, Inc., Journal Division, 525 B St.,
Ste. 1900, San Diego, CA 92101. TEL 619-230-
1840. FAX 619-699-6800. *4698*

BLOOD WEEKLY.
Charles W. Henderson, Ed. & Pub., Box 5528,
Atlanta, GA 31107-0528. TEL 404-377-8895.
FAX 404-378-5411.
Vendor(s): CompuServe, Inc., Data-Star, Dow Jones
News Retrieval, Information Access Co., Knight-
Ridder Information, Inc., NewsNet, Ovid
Technologies, Inc.. *4698*

BLOODLINES.
United Kennel Club, Inc., 100 E. Kilgore Rd.,
Kalamazoo, MI 49001. TEL 616-343-9020.
FAX 616-343-7037. *5387*

BLOOMBERG PETROFLASH.
Bloomberg Financial Markets, 100 Business Park
Dr., Box 888, Princeton, NJ 08542-0888.
TEL 609-279-3000. FAX 609-683-7523.
Available only online. *5351*

**BLUE LIST OF CURRENT MUNICIPAL AND
CORPORATE OFFERINGS.**
Standard & Poors Corporation 25 Broadway, New
York, NY 10004. TEL 212-208-8000. *1321*

BLUES ACCESS.
Cary Wolfson, Ed. & Pub., 1455 Chestnut Pl.,
Boulder, CO 80304-3153. TEL 303-443-7245.
FAX 303-939-9729. *5144*

**BOARD OF TRADE OF METRO TORONTO BUSINESS
JOURNAL.**
Board of Trade of Metropolitan Toronto, P.O. Box
60, 1 First Canadian Place, Toronto, ON M5X 1C1,
Canada. TEL 416-366-6811. FAX 416-366-5620.
Vendor(s): Knight-Ridder Information, Inc.. *1162*

BOARDWATCH MAGAZINE.
8500 W. Bowler Ave., Ste. 210, Littleton, CO
80123. TEL 303-973-6038. FAX 303-973-3731.
2064

BOATING.
Hachette Filipacchi Magazines, Inc., 1633 Broadway,
43rd Fl., New York, NY 10009. TEL 212-767-
5574. FAX 212-767-5618.
Vendor(s): Information Access Co., Knight-Ridder
Information, Inc., University Microfilms International.
6532

BOATING INDUSTRY.
Intertec Publishing Corp. (Atlanta), 6151 Powers
Ferry Rd., N.W., Atlanta, GA 30339-2941.
TEL 770-955-2500. FAX 770-955-0400.
Vendor(s): Information Access Co.. *6533*

BOBBIN.
Bobbin Blenheim Media, 1110 Shop Rd., Box
1986, Columbia, SC 29202. TEL 803-771-7500.
FAX 803-799-1461.
Vendor(s): Information Access Co., University
Microfilms International. *1831*

BOCOEX INDEX.
Boston Computer Exchange Index, 55 Temple Pl.,
Boston, MA C2111. TEL 617-542-4414. FAX 617-
542-8849. *2030*

**BOERNEBIBLIOTEKSKATALOG. BOEGER &
TIDSSKRIFTER. EMNEKATALOG.**
Dansk BiblioteksCenter as, Tempovej 7-11, DK-
2750 Ballerup, Denmark. TEL 45-44-867777.
FAX 45-44-867892. *522*

**BOERNEBIBLIOTEKSKATALOG. BOEGER &
TIDSSKRIFTER. FORFATTERKATALOG.**
Dansk BiblioteksCenter as, Tempovej 7-11, DK-
2750 Ballerup, Denmark. TEL 45-44-867777.
FAX 45-44-867892. *522*

**BOERNEBIBLIOTEKSKATALOG. BOEGER &
TIDSSKRIFTER. TITELKATALOG.**
Dansk BiblioteksCenter as, Tempovej 7-11, DK-
2750 Ballerup, Denmark. TEL 45-44-867777.
FAX 45-44-867892. *522*

**BOERNEBIBLIOTEKSKATALOG.
GRAMMOFONPLADER, KASSETTEBAAND.**
Dansk BiblioteksCenter as, Tempovej 7-11, DK-
2750 Ballerup, Denmark. TEL 45-44-867777.
FAX 45-44-867892. *5207*

**BOERNEBIBLIOTEKSKATALOG. LYDBOEGER, BOG &
BAAND.**
Dansk BiblioteksCenter as, Tempovej 7-11, DK-
2750 Ballerup, Denmark. TEL 45-44-867777.
FAX 45-44-867892. *1782*

**BOLETIN OFICIAL DE LA PROPIEDAD INDUSTRIAL.
1: MARCAS Y OTROS SIGNOS DISTINTIVOS.**
Ministerio de Industria y Energia, Oficina Espanola
de Patentes y Marcas, Panama, 1, 28071 Madrid,
Spain. TEL 34-1-3495300.
Vendor(s): Oficina Espanola de Patentes y Marcas.
5336

**BOLETIN OFICIAL DE LA PROPIEDAD INDUSTRIAL.
2: PATENTES Y MODELOS DE UTILIDAD.**
Ministerio de Industria y Energia, Oficina Espanola
de Patentes y Marcas, Panama, 1, 28071 Madrid,
Spain. TEL 34-1-3495300.
Vendor(s): Oficina Espanola de Patentes y Marcas.
5336

**BOLETIN OFICIAL DE LA PROPIEDAD INDUSTRIAL.
3: MODELOS Y DIBUJOS INDUSTRIALES Y
ARTISTICOS.**
Ministerio de Industria y Energia, Oficina Espanola
de Patentes y Marcas, Panama, 1, 28071 Madrid,
Spain. TEL 34-1-3495300.
Vendor(s): Oficina Espanola de Patentes y Marcas.
5336

**BOLETIN OFICIAL DE LA PROPIEDAD INDUSTRIAL.
4: RESUMENES DE PATENTES.**
Ministerio de Industria y Energia, Oficina Espanola
de Patentes y Marcas, Panama, 1, 28071 Madrid,
Spain. TEL 34-1-3495300. FAX 34-1-4572586.
Vendor(s): Oficina Espanola de Patentes y Marcas.
5336

BOLETIN OFICIAL DEL ESTADO.
Boletin Oficial del Estado, Trafalgar, 27, 28071
Madrid, Spain. TEL 34-1-5382297. FAX 34-1-
5382275. *5894*

THE BOND BUYER.
American Banker - Bond Buyer, Newsletter Division
One State St. Plaza, New York, NY 10004-1549.
FAX 212-943-2224.
Vendor(s): Information Access Co., Knight-Ridder
Information, Inc. (File no.626), Lexis-Nexis, NewsNet
(FI08). *1322*

BOOK PUBLISHING REPORT.
SIMBA Information Inc. 11 Riverbend Dr. S., Box
4234, Stamford, CT 06907-0234. TEL 203-358-
9900. FAX 203-358-5824.
Vendor(s): Knight-Ridder Information, Inc., NewsNet
(PB19). *5989*

BOOK REVIEW DIGEST.
H.W. Wilson Co., 950 University Ave., Bronx, NY
10452. TEL 718-588-8400. FAX 718-590-1617.
Vendor(s): OCLC, Wilsonline (File BRD). *4134*

BOOK REVIEW INDEX.
Gale Research Inc., 835 Penobscot Bldg., Detroit,
MI 48226. TEL 313-961-2242. FAX 313-961-
6083.
Vendor(s): Knight-Ridder Information, Inc. (File
no.137). *6013*

BOOK WORLD.
Washington Post Co., 1150 15th St., N.W.,
Washington, DC 20071. TEL 202-334-6000.
FAX 202-334-5059.
Vendor(s): Knight-Ridder Information, Inc.. *5990*

BOOKS IN PRINT.
R.R. Bowker, A Division of Reed Elsevier Inc., 121
Chanlon Rd., New Providence, NJ 07974. TEL 908-
464-6800. FAX 908-665-3502.
Vendor(s): Knight-Ridder Information, Inc. (File
no.470), Ovid Technologies, Inc (BBIP). *523*

BOOKS IN PRINT SUPPLEMENT.
R.R. Bowker, A Division of Reed Elsevier Inc., 121
Chanlon Rd., New Providence, NJ 07974. TEL 908-
464-6800. FAX 908-665-3502.
Vendor(s): Knight-Ridder Information, Inc. (File
no.470), Ovid Technologies, Inc. (BBIP). *523*

BOOKS OUT-OF-PRINT.
R.R. Bowker, A Division of Reed Elsevier Inc., 121
Chanlon Rd., New Providence, NJ 07974. TEL 908-
464-6800. FAX 908-665-3502.
Vendor(s): Knight-Ridder Information, Inc. (File
no.470), Ovid Technologies, Inc. (BBIP). *523*

BOOKS OUT-OF-PRINT PLUS.
R.R. Bowker, A Division of Reed Elsevier Inc., 121
Chanlon Rd., New Providence, NJ 07974. TEL 908-
665-2866. FAX 908-665-3528 *523*

BOOKS OUT-OF-PRINT WITH BOOK REVIEWS PLUS.
R.R. Bowker, A Division of Reed Elsevier Inc., 121
Chanlon Rd., New Providence, NJ 07974. TEL 908-
665-2866. FAX 908-665-3528 *523*

BOOKS: THE INTERNATIONAL MARKET.
Euromonitor, 60-61 Britton St., London EC1M 5NA,
England. TEL 44-171-251-8024. FAX 44-171-608-
3149.
Vendor(s): Data-Star, Knight-Ridder Information, Inc..
5990

BOOT COVE ECONOMIC FORECAST.
Voight Industries, Inc., Box 200, Lubec, ME 04652.
TEL 207-733-5593.
Vendor(s): NewsNet (IV29). *1179*

BORDER CROSSINGS.
Arts Manitoba Publications Inc., Y300-393 Portage
Ave., Winnipeg, MB R3B 3H6, Canada. TEL 204-
942-5778. FAX 204-949-0793. *420*

BOSTON BUSINESS JOURNAL.
City Media, Inc., 821 Marquette Ave., Ste. 2000
Minneapolis, MN 55402-2922. TEL 617-330-
1000. FAX 617-330-1015.
Vendor(s): CompuServe, Inc., Data-Star, Dow Jones
News Retrieval, Knight-Ridder Information, Inc.,
National Data Corp., University Microfilms
International. *898*

**BOSTON COLLEGE ENVIRONMENTAL AFFAIRS LAW
REVIEW.**
Boston College, School of Law, 885 Centre St.,
Newton, MA 02159. TEL 617-552-4354. *2778*

BOSTON COLLEGE LAW REVIEW.
Boston College, School of Law, 885 Centre St.,
Newton, MA 02159. TEL 617-552-8575.
Vendor(s): West Services, Inc.. *3751*

THE BOSTON GLOBE INDEX.
U M I Company 300 N. Zeeb Rd., Ann Arbor, MI
48106. TEL 313-761-4700. FAX 800-864-0019.
Vendor(s): Knight-Ridder Information, Inc. (File no.
484). *3714*

BOSTON REVIEW.
Boston Critic, Inc., c/o MIT 77 Massachusetts Ave.,
No. E53-407, Cambridge, MA 02139-4307.
TEL 617-253-3642. FAX 617-252-1549. *4134*

BOSTON UNIVERSITY INTERNATIONAL LAW JOURNAL.
Boston University, School of Law, International Law Journal, 765 Commonwealth Ave., Boston, MA 02215. TEL 617-353-3157. FAX 617-353-7400. Vendor(s): West Services, Inc.. *3924*

BOSTON UNIVERSITY LAW REVIEW.
Boston University, School of Law, Law Review, 765 Commonwealth Ave., Boston, MA 02215. TEL 617-353-3118. FAX 617-353-6767. Vendor(s): Lexis-Nexis, West Services, Inc.. *3751*

THE BOTANICAL REVIEW.
New York Botanical Garden, Scientific Publications Department, Bronx, NY 10458-5126. TEL 718-817-8721. FAX 718-817-8842. Vendor(s): Information Access Co.. *674*

BOTTIN ENTREPRISES.
Bottin S A, 4 rue Andre Boulle, 94961 Cretil Cedex 9, France. TEL 49-81-56-56. FAX 49-81-56-76. *1587*

THE BOWKER ANNUAL LIBRARY AND BOOK TRADE ALMANAC.
R.R. Bowker, A Division of Reed Elsevier Inc., 121 Chanlon Rd., New Providence, NJ 07974. TEL 908-464-6800. FAX 908-665-6688. Vendor(s): European Space Agency, Knight-Ridder Information, Inc., Orbit Search Service, Ovid Technologies, Inc. (BBIP). *3981*

BOWKER - WHITAKER GLOBAL BOOKS IN PRINT PLUS.
R.R. Bowker, A Division of Reed Elsevier Inc., 121 Chanlon Rd., New Providence, NJ 07974. TEL 908-665-2866. FAX 908-665-3528. *524*

BOWNE DIGEST FOR CORPORATE & SECURITIES LAWYERS.
Brumberg Publications, Inc., 124 Harvard St., Brookline, MA 02146. TEL 617-734-1979. FAX 617-734-1989. Vendor(s): NewsNet (LA11). *3874*

BOXOFFICE.
R L D Communications, 6640 Sunset Blvd., Ste. 100, Hollywood, CA 90028. TEL 213-465-1186. FAX 213-465-5049. *5094*

BOYS' LIFE (INKPRINT EDITION).
Boy Scouts of America, Box 152079, Irving, TX 75015-2079. TEL 214-580-2000. Vendor(s): Information Access Co.. *1786*

BRAILLE BOOKS (LARGE PRINT EDITION).
U.S. Library of Congress, National Library Service for the Blind and Physically Handicapped, Washington, DC 20542. TEL 202-707-5100. FAX 202-707-0712. *3308*

BRAILLE FORUM.
American Council of the Blind, 1155 15th St. N.W., Ste. 720, Washington, DC 20005. TEL 202-467-5081. FAX 202-467-5085. *3317*

BRAILLE MONITOR (INKPRINT EDITION).
National Federation of the Blind, 1800 Johnson St., Baltimore, MD 21230. TEL 410-659-9314. FAX 410-685-5653. *3318*

BRAIN AND NERVE.
Igaku-Shoin Ltd., 5-24-3 Hongo, Bunkyo-ku, Tokyo 113-91, Japan. TEL 03-817-5701. Vendor(s): JICST. *4828*

BRANDS AND THEIR COMPANIES.
Gale Research Inc., 835 Penobscot Bldg., Detroit, MI 48226. TEL 313-961-2242. FAX 313-961-6083. Vendor(s): Knight-Ridder Information, Inc.. *5336*

BRANDWEEK.
B P I Communications, Inc. (New York), 1515 Broadway, New York, NY 10036. TEL 212-764-7300. FAX 212-944-1719. Vendor(s): Information Access Co., Knight-Ridder Information, Inc. (File no.648), Ovid Technologies, Inc. (TSAP). *32*

BRAZIL REPORT.
Lettres (U.K.) Ltd., 61 Old St., London EC1V 9HX, England. TEL 44-171-251-0012. FAX 44-171-253-8193. Vendor(s): Lexis-Nexis. *1179*

BRAZIL WATCH.
Orbis Publications, LLC, 3201 New Mexico Ave., N.W., Ste. 249, Washington, DC 20016. TEL 202-237-0155. FAX 202-237-0596. *1179*

BREAKFAST CEREALS: THE INTERNATIONAL MARKET.
Euromonitor, 60-61 Britton St., London EC1M 5NA, England. TEL 44-171-251-8024. FAX 44-171-608-3149. Vendor(s): Data-Star, Knight-Ridder Information, Inc.. *2961*

BREW-INFO.
European Brewery Convention, P.O. Box 510, 2380 BB Zoeterwoude, Netherlands. TEL 31-71-456047. FAX 31-71-410013. *502*

BRIGHAM YOUNG UNIVERSITY LAW REVIEW.
Brigham Young University, J. Reuben Clark Law School, 453 JRCB, Provo, UT 84602. TEL 801-378-5678. FAX 801-378-3595. Vendor(s): West Services, Inc.. *3751*

BRIGHT LIGHTS.
Box 420987, San Francisco, CA 94142-0987. TEL 513-641-4048. FAX 513-641-2049. Available only online. *5094*

BRITANNICA BOOK OF THE YEAR.
Encyclopaedia Britannica, Inc., 310 S. Michigan Ave., Chicago, IL 60604. TEL 312-347-7000. FAX 312-347-7914. *2536*

BRITISH CATALOGUE OF MUSIC.
Bowker - Saur Ltd., A member of the Reed Elsevier plc group, Maypole House, Maypole Rd., E. Grinstead, W. Sussex Rh19 1HU, England. TEL 44-01342-330100. FAX 44-1342-330191. *5145*

BRITISH COLUMBIA DECISIONS - CIVIL CASES.
Western Legal Publications, 301-1 Alexander St., Vancouver, BC V6A 1B2, Canada. TEL 604-681-5671. FAX 604-687-2796. *3880*

BRITISH COLUMBIA DECISIONS - CRIMINAL CONVICTION AND SENTENCE CASES.
Western Legal Publications, 301-1 Alexander St., Vancouver, BC V6A 1B2, Canada. TEL 604-687-5671. FAX 604-687-2796. *3908*

BRITISH COLUMBIA DECISIONS - FAMILY LAW CASES.
Western Legal Publications, 301-1 Alexander St., Vancouver, BC V6A 1B2, Canada. TEL 604-687-5671. FAX 604-687-2796. *3917*

BRITISH COLUMBIA DECISIONS - INSURANCE LAW CASES.
Western Legal Publications, 301-1 Alexander St., Vancouver, BC V6A 1B2, Canada. TEL 604-687-5671. FAX 604-687-2796. *3751*

BRITISH COLUMBIA DECISIONS - LABOUR ARBITRATION.
Western Legal Publications, 301 One Alexander St., Vancouver, BC V6A 1B2, Canada. TEL 604-687-5671. FAX 604-687-2796. *1365*

BRITISH COLUMBIA DECISIONS - LABOUR RELATIONS BOARD DIGESTS.
Western Legal Publications, 301-1 Alexander St., Vancouver, BC V6A 1B2, Canada. TEL 604-687-5671. FAX 604-687-2796. *1365*

BRITISH COLUMBIA DECISIONS - MUNICIPAL LAW CASES.
Western Legal Publications, 301-1 Alexander St., Vancouver, BC V6A 1B2, Canada. TEL 604-687-5671. FAX 604-687-2796. *3751*

BRITISH EDUCATION INDEX.
British Education Index, Brotherton Library, University of Leeds, Leeds LS2 9JT, England. TEL 44-113-233-5525. FAX 44-113-233-5524. Vendor(s): Knight-Ridder Information, Inc. (File no.121). *2386*

BRITISH EXPORTS.
Kompass Part of the Reed Elsevier group, Windsor Ct., E. Grinstead House, E. Grinstead, W. Sussex RH19 1XD, England. TEL 01342-326972. FAX 01342-335992. Vendor(s): Reed Information Services Ltd.. *1589*

THE BRITISH JOURNAL FOR THE PHILOSOPHY OF SCIENCE.
Oxford University Press, Oxford Journals, Walton St., Oxford OX2 6DP, England. TEL 44-1865-267907. FAX 44-1865-267773. Vendor(s): Information Access Co.. *6231*

THE BRITISH JOURNAL OF AESTHETICS.
Oxford University Press, Oxford Journals, Walton St., Oxford OX2 6DP, England. TEL 44-1865-267907. FAX 44-1865-267773. Vendor(s): Information Access Co.. *421*

BRITISH JOURNAL OF CLINICAL PHARMACOLOGY.
Blackwell Science Ltd., Osney Mead, Oxford OX2 OEL, England. TEL 44-1865-206206. FAX 44-1865-721205. *5402*

BRITISH JOURNAL OF CLINICAL PRACTICE.
Medicom (UK) Ltd., The Quadrant, 118 London Rd., Kingston-upon-Thames, Surrey KT2 6QJ, England. TEL 44-181-541-5666. FAX 44-181-541-4746. *4437*

THE BRITISH JOURNAL OF CRIMINOLOGY.
Oxford University Press, Oxford Journals, Walton St., Oxford OX2 6DP, England. TEL 44-1865-267907. FAX 44-1865-267773. Vendor(s): Information Access Co.. *2159*

BRITISH JOURNAL OF DERMATOLOGY.
Blackwell Science Ltd., Osney Mead, Oxford OX2 OEL, England. TEL 44-1865-206206. FAX 44-1865-721205. *4659*

BRITISH JOURNAL OF NEUROSURGERY.
Carfax Publishing Co., P.O. Box 25, Abingdon, Oxon. OX14 3UE, England. TEL 44-1235-401000. FAX 44-1235-401550. *4905*

BRITISH JOURNAL OF OBSTETRICS & GYNAECOLOGY.
Blackwell Science Ltd., Osney Mead, Oxford OX2 OEL, England. TEL 44-1865-206206. FAX 44-1865-721205. Vendor(s): Ovid Technologies, Inc.. *4733*

BRITISH JOURNAL OF PHARMACOLOGY.
Stockton Press Houndmills, Basingstoke, Hampshire RG21 2XS, England. TEL 01256-817245. FAX 01256-28339. *5402*

BRITISH JOURNAL OF POLITICAL SCIENCE.
Cambridge University Press, Edinburgh Bldg., Shaftesbury Rd., Cambridge CB2 2RU, England. TEL 44-1223-312393. FAX 44-1223-315052. Vendor(s): Information Access Co.. *5637*

BRITISH JOURNAL OF PSYCHOLOGY.
British Psychological Society, St. Andrew's House, 48 Princess Rd. E., Leicester LE1 7DR, England. TEL 44-166-254-9568. FAX 44-166-247-0787. Vendor(s): Information Access Co., University Microfilms International. *5832*

BRITISH JOURNAL OF RHEUMATOLOGY.
Oxford University Press, Oxford Journals, Walton St., Oxford OX2 6DP, England. TEL 01865-267907. FAX 01865-267773. Vendor(s): Ovid Technologies, Inc.. *4893*

BRITISH JOURNAL OF SURGERY.
Blackwell Science Ltd., Osney Mead, Oxford OX2 OEL, England. TEL 44-1865-206206. FAX 44-1865-721205. Vendor(s): Lexis-Nexis, Ovid Technologies, Inc.. *4905*

BRITISH JOURNAL OF UROLOGY.
Blackwell Science Ltd., Osney Mead, Oxford OX2 OEL, England. TEL 44-1865-206206. FAX 44-1865-721205. Vendor(s): Ovid Technologies, Inc.. *4925*

BRITISH LIBRARY. DOCUMENT SUPPLY CENTRE. INDEX OF CONFERENCE PROCEEDINGS.
British Library, Document Supply Centre, Boston Spa, Wetherby, W. Yorks. LS23 7BQ, England. TEL 44-1937-546080. FAX 44-1937-546286. *4938*

BRITISH NATIONAL BIBLIOGRAPHY.
British Library, National Bibliographic Service, Boston Spa, Wetherby, W. Yorks. LS23 7BQ, England. TEL 44-1937-546613. FAX 44-1937-546586. *524*

BRITISH PLASTICS AND RUBBER MAGAZINE.
M C M Publishing Ltd., 37 Nelson Rd., Caterham, Surrey CR3 5PP, England.
Vendor(s): Information Access Co.. *5618*

BRITISH RATE AND DATA.
E M A P Media 33-39 Bowling Green Ln., London EC1R 0DA, England. TEL 44-171-505-8265. FAX 44-171-505-8264. *524*

BROADBAND NETWORKING NEWS.
Phillips Business Information, Inc., 1201 Seven Locks Rd., Potomac, MD 20854. TEL 301-424-3338. FAX 301-309-3847.
Vendor(s): Information Access Co., NewsNet (TE51). *2067*

BROADCAST WEEK.
Globe and Mail Publishing, 444 Front St. W., Toronto, ON M5V 2S9, Canada. TEL 416-585-5045. *1897*

BROADCASTING & CABLE.
Cahners Publishing Company (Washington), Entertainment Division, Division of Reed Elsevier Inc., 1705 DeSales St., N.W., Washington, DC 20036. TEL 202-659-2340. FAX 202-429-0651.
Vendor(s): Information Access Co., Knight-Ridder Information, Inc., Lexis-Nexis. *1955*

BROADCASTING IN THE U K.
Key Note Ltd., Field House, 72 Oldfield Rd., Hampton, Middlesex TW12 2HQ, England. TEL 44-181-783-0755. FAX 44-181-783-1940. *1934*

BROKERS' MONTHLY & INSURANCE ADVISER.
Insurance Publishing & Printing Co., 7 Stourbridge Rd., Lye, Stourbridge, W. Midlands DY9 7DG, England.
Vendor(s): University Microfilms International. *3643*

BROOKINGS REVIEW.
Brookings Institution, 1775 Massachusetts Ave., N.W., Washington, DC 20036-2188. TEL 202-797-6243. FAX 202-797-6195.
Vendor(s): Information Access Co., University Microfilms International. *898*

BROOKLYN JOURNAL OF INTERNATIONAL LAW.
Brooklyn Law School, 250 Joralemon, Brooklyn, NY 11201. TEL 718-780-7971. FAX 718-780-0353.
Vendor(s): National Data Corp., West Services, Inc.. *3924*

BROOKLYN LAW REVIEW.
Brooklyn Law School, 250 Joralemon St., Brooklyn, NY 11201. TEL 718-780-7968.
Vendor(s): Lexis-Nexis. *3752*

BROWN UNIVERSITY CHILD AND ADOLESCENT BEHAVIOR LETTER.
Manisses Communications Group, Inc., Box 9758, Providence, RI 02940-9758. TEL 401-831-6020. FAX 401-861-6370.
Vendor(s): Information Access Co.. *1762*

BROWN UNIVERSITY DIGEST OF ADDICTION THEORY & APPLICATION DATA.
Manisses Communications Group, Inc., Box 9758, Providence, RI 02940-9758. TEL 401-831-6020. FAX 401-861-6370.
Vendor(s): Information Access Co.. *2195*

BROWN UNIVERSITY LONG-TERM CARE QUALITY LETTER.
Manisses Communications Group, Inc., Box 9758, Providence, RI 02940-9758. TEL 401-861-6370. FAX 401-861-6370.
Vendor(s): Information Access Co.. *3541*

BRUNSWICK BUSINESS JOURNAL.
A B J Publishing Inc., 599 Main St., Ste. 203, Moncton, NB E1C 1C8, Canada. TEL 506-857-9696. FAX 506-859-7395.
Vendor(s): University Microfilms International. *898*

BRYN MAWR CLASSICAL REVIEW.
Bryn Mawr Commentaries, Inc., Bryn Mawr College, Thomas Library, Bryn Mawr, PA 19010. TEL 215-526-5384. FAX 215-526-7475. *1819*

BRYN MAWR MEDIEVAL REVIEW.
Bryn Mawr Commentaries, Inc., Bryn Mawr College, Thomas Library, Bryn Mawr, PA 19010. TEL 215-526-5384.
Available only online. *3400*

BRYN MAWR REVIEWS.
Bryn Mawr Commentaries, Inc., Bryn Mawr College, Thomas Library, Bryn Mawr, PA 19010. TEL 215-526-5384.
Available only online. *3400*

BUFFALO LAW REVIEW.
State University of New York at Buffalo, Buffalo Law Review, 605 John Lord O'Brian Hall, Amherst Campus, Amherst, NY 14260. TEL 716-645-2059. FAX 716-645-2064.
Vendor(s): West Services, Inc.. *3752*

BUFFER.
National Energy Research Supercomputer Center, Lawrence Livermore National Laboratory, Box 5509, L-560, Livermore, CA 94551. *2566*

BUILDING RESEARCH AND INFORMATION.
Chapman & Hall, Journals Department 2-6 Boundary Row, London SE1 8HN, England. TEL 44-171-8650066. FAX 44-171-5229623. *841*

BUILDING SUPPLY BUSINESS.
Cahners Publishing Company (Des Plaines), Division of Reed Elsevier Inc., 1350 E. Touhy Ave., Box 5080, Des Plaines, IL 60018-5080. TEL 847-635-8800. FAX 847-635-9950.
Vendor(s): Dow Jones News Retrieval, Information Access Co., Knight-Ridder Information, Inc.. *841*

BUILDINGS.
Stamats Communications, Inc., Box 1888, Cedar Rapids, IA 52406-1888. TEL 319-364-6167. FAX 319-364-4278.
Vendor(s): Information Access Co., Knight-Ridder Information, Inc., University Microfilms International. *841*

BUKKYO DAIGAKU SHINRIGAKU KENKYUJO KIYO.
Bukkyo Daigaku, Shinrigaku Kenkyujo, Kitahananobocho, Murasakino, Kita-ku, Kyoto 603, Japan.
Vendor(s): University Microfilms International. *5832*

BULLETIN OF ECONOMIC RESEARCH.
Blackwell Publishers Ltd., 108 Cowley Rd., Oxford OX4 1JF, England. TEL 44-1865-791100. FAX 44-1865-791347.
Vendor(s): Information Access Co.. *899*

BULLETIN OF ENTOMOLOGICAL RESEARCH.
CAB International, Wallingford, Oxon. OX10 8DE, England. TEL 44-1491-832111. FAX 44-1491-833508.
Vendor(s): DIMDI, European Space Agency, Knight-Ridder Information, Inc.. *722*

BULLETIN OF NORTHERN IRELAND LAW.
S L S Legal Publications, School of Law, Queens University of Belfast, Belfast BT7 1NN, N. Ireland. TEL 44-1232-335224. FAX 44-1232-325590.
Vendor(s): Context Ltd.. *3753*

BULLETIN OF THE ATOMIC SCIENTISTS.
Educational Foundation for Nuclear Science, 6042 S. Kimbark Ave., Chicago, IL 60637. TEL 312-702-2555. FAX 312-702-0725.
Vendor(s): Information Access Co., University Microfilms International. *5743*

BULLETIN OF THE HISTORY OF MEDICINE.
Johns Hopkins University Press, Journals Publishing Division, 2715 N. Charles St., Baltimore, MD 21218. TEL 410-516-6987. FAX 410-516-6968. *4437*

BULLETIN ON NARCOTICS.
United Nations Publications, Room DC2-853, New York, NY 10017. TEL 212-963-8302. FAX 212-963-3489. *2195*

BULLETIN ON THE RHEUMATIC DISEASES.
Arthritis Foundation, 1314 Spring St., N.W., Atlanta, GA 30309. TEL 404-872-7100. FAX 404-872-9559.
Vendor(s): Lexis-Nexis. *4893*

BULLETIN SIGNALETIQUE DES TELECOMMUNICATIONS.
Centre National d'Etudes des Telecommunications, Service des Abonnements, 38-40 rue du General Leclerc, 92131 Issy-les-Moulineaux Cedex, France. TEL 45-29-51-08.
Vendor(s): Telesystemes - Questel. *1897*

BULLETIN TO MANAGEMENT.
The Bureau of National Affairs, Inc., 1231 25th St., N.W., Washington, DC 20037. TEL 202-452-4200. FAX 202-822-8092.
Vendor(s): Human Resources Information Network (CDD, HDD). *1499*

THE BULLETIN WITH NEWSWEEK.
A C P Publishing Pty. Ltd., 54-58 Park St., Sydney, N.S.W. 2000, Australia. TEL 61 2-2828302. FAX 61-2-2674359. *3110*

DIE BURGER.
P.O. Box 692, Cape Town 8000, South Africa. TEL 27-21-4062222. FAX 27-21-4062913. *3212*

BURTON GROUP NEWS ANALYSIS.
Burton Group, Box 3448, Salt Lake City, UT 84110-3448. TEL 801-943-1566. FAX 801-943-2425. *1983*

BURTON GROUP REPORT
Burton Group, Box 3448, Salt Lake City, UT 84110-3448. TEL 801-943-1566. FAX 801-943-2425. *1983*

BUSINESS AMERICA.
U.S. Department of Commerce, 14th St. between Constitution Ave. and Pennsylvania Ave., N.W., Washington, DC 20230. TEL 202-482-3251. FAX 202-482-5819.
Vendor(s): Dow Jones News Retrieval, Information Access Co., Knight-Ridder Information, Inc., University Microfilms International. *1266*

BUSINESS AND COMMERCIAL AVIATION.
McGraw-Hill Companies (Port Chester), Four International Dr., Port Chester, NY 10573. TEL 914-939-0300. FAX 914-939-1184.
Vendor(s): Information Access Co., Knight-Ridder Information, Inc.. *59*

BUSINESS AND HEALTH.
Medical Economics Publishing Co., Inc., 5 Paragon Dr., Montvale, NJ 07645. TEL 201-358-7208. FAX 201-573-1045.
Vendor(s): Information Access Co.. *3643*

BUSINESS AND SOCIETY.
Sage Publications, Inc., 2455 Teller Rd., Thousand Oaks, CA 91320. TEL 805-499-0721. FAX 805-499-0871.
Vendor(s): Information Access Co.. *899*

BUSINESS AND SOCIETY REVIEW.
Business and Society Review, c/o Hanover Publishers, 200 W. 57th St., New York, NY 10019. TEL 212-399-1088. FAX 212-245-1973.
Vendor(s): Information Access Co.. *899*

BUSINESS AND THE ENVIRONMENT.
Cutter Information Corp. 37 Broadway, Arlington, MA 02174-5552. TEL 617-648-8700. FAX 617-648-1950.
Vendor(s): Information Access Co.. *2778*

BUSINESS ASIA.
Economist Intelligence Unit, 111 W. 57th St., New York, NY 10019. TEL 212-554-0600. FAX 212-586-1182.
Vendor(s): Knight-Ridder Information, Inc.. *899*

BUSINESS CHINA.
Economist Intelligence Unit, 111 W. 57th St., New York, NY 10019. TEL 212-554-0600. FAX 212-586-1182.
Vendor(s): Lexis-Nexis. *1180*

BUSINESS COMMUNICATION QUARTERLY.
Association for Business Communication, c/o Dr. Robert J. Myers, Dept. of Speech Communication, Baruch College, 17 Lexington Ave., New York, NY 10010. TEL 817-565-4423.
Vendor(s): Information Access Co.. *1408*

BUSINESS COMMUNICATIONS REVIEW.
B C R Enterprises, Inc., 950 York Rd., Hinsdale, IL 60521-2939. TEL 312-586-1432.
Vendor(s): Information Access Co.. *1943*

BUSINESS COMPUTER DIGEST.
Association of Computer Users, Box 2189, Berkeley, CA 94702-0139. TEL 303-241-0125.
Vendor(s): NewsNet. *1152*

Online

BUSINESS COMPUTING BRIEF.
Financial Times Telecoms & Media Publishing Maple House, 149 Tottenham Court Rd., London W1P 9LL, England. TEL 44-171-896-2234. FAX 44-171-896-2256.
Vendor(s): Data-Star, Information Access Co., Lexis-Nexis. *1152*

BUSINESS CREDIT.
National Association of Credit Management, 8815 Centre Park Dr., Ste. 200, Columbia, MD 21045. TEL 410-740-5560. FAX 410-740-5574.
Vendor(s): Information Access Co., University Microfilms International. *1072*

BUSINESS DATELINE.
U M I Comapny (Louisville), 620 S. Third St., Louisville, KY 40202-2475.
Vendor(s): Knight-Ridder Information, Inc., Dow Jones News Retrieval, Human Resources Information Network, Lexis-Nexis. *900*

BUSINESS DAY.
Times Media Ltd., 11 Diagonal St., Johannesburg 2000, South Africa. TEL 27-11-4972711. FAX 27-11-8360805. *900*

BUSINESS DIGEST OF DELAWARE VALLEY.
Business Digest of Philadelphia Inc., 2449 Golf Rd., Philadelphia, PA 19131. TEL 215-477-8620.
Vendor(s): Knight-Ridder Information, Inc.. *1573*

BUSINESS EAST MIDLANDS.
Business Magazine Group, Briarwood House, St. John St., Mansfield, Notts NG18 1QH, England. TEL 0623-422522. FAX 0623-27479. *900*

BUSINESS EASTERN EUROPE.
Economist Intelligence Unit, 111 W. 57th St., New York, NY 10019. TEL 212-554-0600. FAX 212-586-1182.
Vendor(s): Knight-Ridder Information, Inc., Lexis-Nexis. *1180*

BUSINESS ECONOMICS.
National Association of Business Economists, 1233 20th St., N.W., Ste. 505, Washington, DC 20036-2304. TEL 202-463-6223. FAX 202-463-6239.
Vendor(s): Information Access Co., University Microfilms International. *900*

BUSINESS - EDUCATION INSIDER.
Heritage Foundation, 214 Massachusetts Ave., N.E., Washington, DC 20002. TEL 202-546-4400. FAX 202-543-9647.
Vendor(s): Lexis-Nexis. *1180*

BUSINESS EUROPA.
Central European Business Ltd. 2 Market St., Saffron Walden, Essex CB10 1H2, England. TEL 44-1799-521150. FAX 44-1799-524805.
Vendor(s): Information Access Co.. *901*

BUSINESS EUROPE.
Economist Intelligence Unit, 111 W. 57th St., New York, NY 10019. TEL 212-554-0600. FAX 212-586-1182.
Vendor(s): Knight-Ridder Information, Inc., Lexis-Nexis. *1266*

BUSINESS FIRST (BUFFALO).
Business First of New York, Inc., 472 Delaware Ave., Buffalo, NY 14202. TEL 716-882-6200. FAX 716-882-3020.
Vendor(s): Information Access Co., Knight-Ridder Information, Inc., Lexis-Nexis. *901*

BUSINESS FORUM (LOS ANGELES).
California State University, Los Angeles, School of Business & Economics, 5151 State University Dr., Los Angeles, CA 90032-8120. TEL 213-343-2806. FAX 213-343-2813.
Vendor(s): Information Access Co., University Microfilms International. *901*

BUSINESS FOUNDATION BOOK. GENERAL TRADE INDEX & BUSINESS GUIDE.
Business Foundation Co. Ltd., Ul. Krucza 38-42, 00-512 Warsaw, Poland. TEL 48-22-219993. FAX 48-22-219761. *1589*

BUSINESS HISTORY.
Frank Cass, Newbury House, 890-900 Eastern Ave., Newbury Park, Ilford, Essex IG2 7HH, England. TEL 44-181-599-8866. FAX 44-181-599-0984.
Vendor(s): Information Access Co.. *901*

BUSINESS HISTORY REVIEW.
Harvard Business School Publishing, 60 Harvard Way, Boston, MA 02163. TEL 617-496-5985. FAX 617-496-8066.
Vendor(s): Information Access Co., Knight-Ridder Information, Inc., University Microfilms International. *901*

BUSINESS IN BROWARD.
Lauderdale Publishing, 2455 E. Sunrise, P.O. Box 7375, Ft. Lauderdale, FL 33308-7375. TEL 954-563-8805. FAX 954-563-8853.
Vendor(s): Lexis-Nexis, University Microfilms International. *1573*

BUSINESS INDEX.
Information Access Company 362 Lakeside Dr., Foster City, CA 94404. TEL 415-378-5200. FAX 415-378-5369.
Vendor(s): Ovid Technologies, Inc., Knight-Ridder Information, Inc. (File no.148), Lexis-Nexis. *984*

BUSINESS INSURANCE.
Crain Communications, Inc. (Chicago), 740 Rush St., Chicago, IL 60611. TEL 312-649-5398. FAX 312-280-3174.
Vendor(s): Information Access Co., Lexis-Nexis. *3644*

THE BUSINESS JOURNAL (LIMA).
Box 388, Lima, OH 45802-0388. TEL 419-999-4762. FAX 419-991-6839.
Vendor(s): Information Access Co.. *1162*

BUSINESS JOURNAL (PHOENIX).
Phoenix Business Journal, Inc., 2910 N. Central Ave., Phoenix, AZ 85012. TEL 602-230-8400. FAX 602-230-0955.
Vendor(s): Information Access Co., Knight-Ridder Information, Inc.. *902*

BUSINESS JOURNAL (PORTLAND).
American City Business Journals, Inc. (Portland), Box 14490, Portland, OR 97214. TEL 503-274-8733. FAX 503-227-2650.
Vendor(s): Information Access Co.. *1180*

BUSINESS JOURNAL (SACRAMENTO).
City Media, Inc., 821 Marquette Ave., Ste. 2000, Minneapolis, MN 55402.
Vendor(s): CompuServe, Inc., Data-Star, Dow Jones News Retrieval, Information Access Co., Knight-Ridder Information, Inc., Lexis-Nexis. *902*

BUSINESS JOURNAL OF UPPER EAST TENNESSEE AND SOUTHWEST VIRGINIA.
Business Publishers Company, Box 643, Tri-Port Complex, 2333-D Hwy. 75, Blountville, TN 37617. TEL 615-323-7111. FAX 615-323-1479.
Vendor(s): University Microfilms International. *902*

BUSINESS JOURNAL SERVING GREATER MILWAUKEE.
Business Journal of Milwaukee Inc., 600 W. Virginia St., Ste. 500, Milwaukee, WI 53204-1551. TEL 414-278-7788. FAX 414-278-7028.
Vendor(s): Information Access Co., Knight-Ridder Information, Inc., University Microfilms International. *902*

BUSINESS LATIN AMERICA.
Economist Intelligence Unit, 111 W. 57th St., New York, NY 10019. TEL 212-554-0600. FAX 212-586-1182.
Vendor(s): Knight-Ridder Information, Inc., Lexis-Nexis. *1180*

BUSINESS LAW EUROPE.
Financial Times Professional Publishing Maple House, 149 Tottenham Court Rd., London W1P 9LL, England. TEL 44-171-896-2222. FAX 44-171-896-2276.
Vendor(s): Data-Star, Information Access Co., Lexis-Nexis. *3896*

BUSINESS LAWYER.
American Bar Association, Business Law Section, 750 N. Lake Shore Dr., Chicago, IL 60611. TEL 312-988-5588.
Vendor(s): Information Access Co., Lexis-Nexis (BUSLAW), West Services, Inc. (BUSLAW). *3897*

BUSINESS MAILERS REVIEW.
Pash Publications Inc., 1616 N. Ft. Myer Dr., Ste. 1000, Arlington, VA 22209-3107. TEL 703-816-8640. FAX 703-528-4926.
Vendor(s): Information Access Co.. *1931*

BUSINESS MARKETING.
Crain Communications, Inc. (Chicago), 740 Rush St., Chicago, IL 60611-2590. TEL 312-649-5260. FAX 312-649-5228.
Vendor(s): Information Access Co.. *1455*

BUSINESS MEXICO.
American Chamber of Commerce of Mexico, A.C., Lucerna 78, Col. Juarez, Del. Cuauhtemoc, 0600 Mexico DF, Mexico. TEL 724-3800. FAX 703-2911.
Vendor(s): Lexis-Nexis, University Microfilms International. *1134*

BUSINESS NORTH CAROLINA.
News and Observer Publishing Co., 5435 77 Center Dr., Ste. 50, Charlotte, NC 28217-0711. TEL 704-523-6987. FAX 704-523-4211.
Vendor(s): Information Access Co., Knight-Ridder Information, Inc., Lexis-Nexis, University Microfilms International. *1573*

BUSINESS NORTH EAST.
Business Magazine Group, Briarwood House, St. John St., Mansfield, Notts NG18 1QH, England. TEL 0642-232882. FAX 0623-232899. *903*

BUSINESS OPPORTUNITIES HANDBOOK.
Enterprise Magazines, Inc., 1020 N. Broadway, Ste. 111, Milwaukee, WI 53202. TEL 414-272-9977. FAX 414-272-9973. *1573*

BUSINESS ORGANIZATIONS, AGENCIES, AND PUBLICATIONS DIRECTORY.
Gale Research Inc., 835 Penobscot Bldg., Detroit, MI 48226. TEL 313-961-2242. FAX 313-961-6083. *1590*

BUSINESS PEOPLE MAGAZINE.
McCaine Davies Communications Ltd., 232 Henderson Hwy., Winnipeg, MB R2L 1L9, Canada. TEL 204-982-4000. FAX 204-982-4001.
Vendor(s): University Microfilms International. *1163*

BUSINESS PERIODICALS INDEX.
H.W. Wilson Co., 950 University Ave., Bronx, NY 10452. TEL 718-588-8400. FAX 718-590-1617.
Vendor(s): OCLC, Wilsonline (File BPI). *985*

BUSINESS PERSPECTIVES.
Memphis State University, Bureau of Business & Economic Research, Memphis, TN 38152. TEL 901-678-2281.
Vendor(s): Information Access Co.. *903*

BUSINESS QUARTERLY.
University of Western Ontario, Western Business School, c/o Angela Smith, London, ON N6A 3K7, Canada. TEL 519-661-3309. FAX 519-661-3838.
Vendor(s): Information Access Co., Knight-Ridder Information, Inc., University Microfilms International. *1409*

BUSINESS RECORD (DES MOINES).
Business Publications Corporation, The Depot at Fourth, 100 Fourth St., Des Moines, IA 50309. TEL 515-288-3336. FAX 515-288-0309.
Vendor(s): Knight-Ridder Information, Inc., Lexis-Nexis, University Microfilms International. *903*

BUSINESS TIMES.
Business Times, Inc., 315 Peck St., Box 580, New Haven, CT 06513-0580. TEL 203-782-1420. *1181*

BUSINESS TRAVEL NEWS.
Miller Freeman Inc. (New York) One Penn Plaza, New York, NY 10119. FAX 847-647-5972.
Vendor(s): Data-Star, Information Access Co., Knight-Ridder Information, Inc., NewsNet (TR08). *6871*

BUSINESS WEEK.
McGraw-Hill Companies, 1221 Ave. of the Americas, 39th Fl., New York, NY 10020. TEL 212-512-2000.
Vendor(s): Dow Jones News Retrieval, Knight-Ridder Information, Inc. (File no.624/McGRAW-HILL PUBLICATIONS ONLINE), Lexis-Nexis, NewsNet (GB55). *905*

BUSINESS WEST MIDLANDS.
Business Magazine Group, Briarwood House, St. John St., Mansfield, Notts NG18 1QH, England. TEL 021-308-0077. FAX 021-308-0385. *905*

THE BUSINESS WHO'S WHO OF AUSTRALIA.
Dun & Bradstreet Marketing Pty. Ltd., 19 Havilah St., Chatswood, N.S.W. 2067, Australia. TEL 61-2-9352700. FAX 61-2-9352777.
Vendor(s): AUSINET. *1590*

BUYOUTS NEWSLETTER.
Securities Data Publishing, 40 W. 57th St., 11th Fl., New York, NY 10019. TEL 212-765-5311. FAX 212-765-6123.
Vendor(s): Data-Star, Information Access Co., Knight-Ridder Information, Inc.. *905*

BUZZ (LOS ANGELES).
Buzz, Inc., 11835 W. Olympic Blvd., Ste. 450, Los Angeles, CA 90064. TEL 310-473-2721. FAX 310-473-2876. *4135*

BYTE.
McGraw-Hill Companies, Byte Publications, One Phoenix Mill Ln., Peterborough, NH 03458. TEL 603-924-9281. FAX 603-924-2550.
Vendor(s): Dow Jones News Retrieval, Knight-Ridder Information, Inc. (File no.624/McGRAW-HILL PUBLICATIONS ONLINE), Lexis-Nexis, NewsNet (EC34). *2054*

C A D - C A M UPDATE.
Worldwide Videotex, Box 3273, Boynton Beach, FL 33424-3273. TEL 407-738-2276.
Vendor(s): Information Access Co., NewsNet (MG15). *2025*

C B A RECORD.
Chicago Bar Association, 321 S. Plymouth Ct., Chicago, IL 60604-3907. TEL 312-554-2000.
Vendor(s): West Services, Inc.. *3754*

C - C PLUS PLUS USERS JOURNAL.
R & D Publications, Inc. 1601 W. 23rd St., Ste. 200, Lawrence, KS 66046. TEL 913-841-1631. FAX 913-841-2624.
Vendor(s): Information Access Co.. *2043*

C D A INVESTNET INSIDERS' CHRONICLE.
C D A Investment Technologies, Inc., 1355 Piccard Dr., Rockville, MD 20850. FAX 301-590-1329.
Vendor(s): Information Access Co.. *1324*

C D COMPUTING NEWS.
Worldwide Videotex, Box 3273, Boynton Beach, FL 33424-3273. TEL 407-738-2276.
Vendor(s): Information Access Co., Knight-Ridder Information, Inc., NewsNet (EC67). *2031*

C D - R O M DATABASES.
Worldwide Videotex, Box 3273, Boynton Beach, FL 33424-3273. TEL 407-738-2276.
Vendor(s): Information Access Co., Knight-Ridder Information, Inc., NewsNet (EC71). *4042*

C D - R O M PROFESSIONAL.
Online, Inc., 462 Danbury Rd., Wilton, CT 06897. TEL 203-761-1466. FAX 203-761-1444.
Vendor(s): Information Access Co., University Microfilms International. *4042*

C D - R O M WORLD.
P C World Communications, Inc., 501 Second St., Ste. 600, San Francisco, CA 94107. TEL 415-243-0500. FAX 415-442-1891.
Vendor(s): Knight-Ridder Information, Inc., NewsNet. *3983*

C E C COMMUNICATIONS.
Gordon & Breach Science Publishers, c/o International Publishers Distributor, Box 3054, Langhorne, PA 19047-3054. TEL 215-750-2642. FAX 215-750-6353. *2625*

C E R F NET NEWS.
California Education and Research Federation Network, Box 85608, San Diego, CA 92186-9784. TEL 619-534-5087. *2035*

C F O.
C F O Publishing Corporation 253 Summer St., Boston, MA 02210. TEL 617-345-9700. FAX 617-951-4090.
Vendor(s): University Microfilms International. *906*

C F O ALERT (WEEKLY).
American Banker Newsletters, One State Street Plaza, 26th Fl., New York, NY 10004-1505. TEL 212-803-8300. FAX 212-843-9620.
Vendor(s): Data-Star, Knight-Ridder Information, Inc., Lexis-Nexis, NewsNet. *1073*

C I N D A.
International Atomic Energy Agency, Wagramerstr. 5, P.O. Box 100, A-1400 Vienna, Austria. TEL 43-1-2060-22529. FAX 43-1-2060-29302. *5578*

C I S INDEX TO PUBLICATIONS OF THE UNITED STATES CONGRESS.
Congressional Information Service, Inc., A member of the LEXIS-NEXIS family, 4520 East-West Hwy., Bethesda, MD 20814. TEL 301-654-1550. FAX 301-654-4033.
Vendor(s): Knight-Ridder Information, Inc. (File no.101). *5930*

C L A S E.
Universidad Nacional Autonoma de Mexico, Centro de Informacion Cientifica y Humanistica, Apdo. Postal 70-392, C.P. 04510 Mexico, D.F., Mexico. TEL 525-6223958. FAX 525-6162557. *6356*

C M A.
Society of Management Accountants of Canada, 120 King St. W., Box 176 M.P.O., Hamilton, ON L8N 3C3, Canada. TEL 905-525-4100. FAX 905-525-4533.
Vendor(s): Information Access Co.. *1043*

C M A J.
Canadian Medical Association, P.O. Box 8650, Ottawa, ON K1G 0G8, Canada. TEL 613-731-9331. FAX 613-523-0937.
Available only online. Vendor(s): Ovid Technologies, Inc.. *4438*

C O M S A T TECHNICAL REVIEW.
COMSAT Corporation, 22300 COMSAT Dr., Clarksburg, MD 20871-9471. TEL 301-428-4512. FAX 301-428-7747. *1897*

C O N S E R MICROFICHE.
National Library of Canada, Canadiana Editorial Division, 395 Wellington St., Ottawa, ON K1A 0N4, Canada. TEL 819-994-6912. FAX 819-953-0291. *525*

C P A CLIENT BULLETIN.
American Institute of Certified Public Accountants, Harborside Financial Ctr., 201 Plaza Three, Jersey City, NJ 07311-3881 TEL 201-938-3201. FAX 201-938-3329.
Vendor(s): University Microfilms International. *1043*

C P A LETTER.
American Institute of Certified Public Accountants, 1211 Ave. of the Americas, New York, NY 10036. TEL 212-596-6200.
Vendor(s): University Microfilms International. *1043*

C Q RESEARCHER.
Congressional Quarterly Inc., 1414 22nd St., N.W., Washington, DC 20037. FAX 202-728-1863.
Vendor(s): Information Access Co.. *5638*

C Q'S WASHINGTON ALERT.
Congressional Quarterly Inc., 1414 22nd St., N.W., Washington, DC 20037. FAX 202-728-1863. *5938*

C S A NEUROSCIENCES ABSTRACTS.
Cambridge Scientific Abstracts, 7200 Wisconsin Ave., 6th Fl., Bethesda, MD 20814. TEL 301-961-6750. FAX 301-961-6720.
Vendor(s): Knight-Ridder Information, Inc. (File no.76/LIFE SCIENCES COLLECTION), STN International (LIFESCI). *4551*

C S E L T INFOTEL.
C S E L T - Centro Studi e Laboratori Telecomunicazioni S.p.A., Via Reiss Romoli, 274, 10148 Turin, Italy. TEL 39-11-2285111. FAX 39-11-2285095. *1922*

C S T COMMUNICATIONS.
Gordon & Breach Science Publishers, c/o International Publishers Distributor, Box 3054, Langhorne, PA 19047-3054. TEL 215-750-2642. FAX 215-750-6343. *1706*

C T D NEWS.
Center for Workplace Health, 410 Lancaster Ave., Ste. 15, Haverford, PA 19041. TEL 610-896-2770. FAX 610-896-2762.
Vendor(s): Information Access Co.. *5246*

C THEORY.
Concordia University, 1455 de Maisonneuve West, Montreal, PQ H3G 1M8, Canada. TEL 514-282-9298. FAX 514-987-9724. *5638*

C 4 I NEWS.
Phillips Business Information, Inc., 1201 Seven Locks Rd., Potomac, MD 20854. TEL 301-424-3338. FAX 301-309-3847.
Vendor(s): Information Access Co.. *5025*

CA - A CANCER JOURNAL FOR CLINICIANS.
Lippincott - Raven Publishers 227 E. Washington Sq., Philadelphia, PA 19106. TEL 215-238-4200.
Vendor(s): Information Access Co.. *4749*

CAB INTERNATIONAL. BUREAU OF NUTRITION. ANNOTATED BIBLIOGRAPHIES.
CAB International, Bureau of Nutrition, Wallingford, Oxon. OX10 8DE, England. TEL 44-1491-832111. FAX 44-1491-833508.
Vendor(s): CISTI, DIMDI, European Space Agency, Knight-Ridder Information, Inc., Ovid Technologies, Inc.. *5243*

CAB INTERNATIONAL. BUREAU OF SOILS. ANNOTATED BIBLIOGRAPHIES.
CAB International, Bureau of Soils. Wallingford, Oxon. OX10 8DE, England. TEL 44-491-832111. FAX 44-491-833508.
Vendor(s): Ovid Technologies, Inc. CISTI, DIMDI, Knight-Ridder Information, Inc., European Space Agency. *169*

CABLE - TELCO REPORT.
Business Research Publications, Inc., 1333 H St., N.W., Ste. 220 - W., Washington, DC 20005. FAX 202-842-3023.
Vendor(s): Information Access Co., NewsNet (TE106). *1957*

CABLEFAX.
Phillips Business Information, Inc., 1201 Seven Locks Rd., Potomac, MD 20854-1053. TEL 301-424-3338. FAX 301-309-3347.
Vendor(s): Information Access Co.. *1957*

CADALYST.
Advanstar Communications, Inc., CADalyst, 859 Willamette St., Eugene, OR 97401. TEL 503-343-1200. FAX 503-686-5732.
Vendor(s): Information Access Co.. *2026*

CADENCE UNIVERSE PERFORMANCE REPORT.
C D A - Cadence, 1355 Piccard Dr. Rockville, MD 20850. TEL 301-975-9600 FAX 301-590-1350. *1324*

CAHIERS D'ONCOLOGIE.
Springer-Verlag France, 26 rue des Carmes, 75005 Paris, France. TEL 33-1-44-41-15-80. FAX 33-1-43-54-49-08. *4749*

CALCIUM AND CALCIFIED TISSUE ABSTRACTS.
Cambridge Scientific Abstracts, 7200 Wisconsin Ave., 6th Fl., Bethesda, MD 20814. TEL 301-961-6750. FAX 301-961-6720.
Vendor(s): Knight-Ridder Information, Inc. (File no.76/LIFE SCIENCES COLLECTION) STN International (LIFESCI). *618*

CALGARY CITYSCOPE MAGAZINE.
I E Publication, Inc., 1324 11th Ave. S.W., No. 300, Calgary, Alta. T3C 0M6, Canada. TEL 403-228-7020. FAX 403-228-7193. *5094*

CALGARY HERALD.
215 16th St. S.E., Calgary, AB T2P 0W8, Canada. TEL 403-235-7400. FAX 403-235-7379.
Vendor(s): Lexis-Nexis, Southam Electronic Publishing. *3119*

CALIFORNIA BUSINESS.
1777 Rollins Rd., Burlingame, CA 95010. TEL 415-776-1472. FAX 415-776-9933.
Vendor(s): Information Access Co., Knight-Ridder Information, Inc.. *1182*

CALIFORNIA BUSINESS DIRECTORY.
American Business Directories 5711 S. 86th Circle, Box 27347, Omaha, NE 68127. TEL 402-593-4600. FAX 402-331-5481. *1590*

Online

CALIFORNIA LAW REVIEW.
University of California Press, Journals Division, 2120 Berkeley Way, No. 5812, Berkeley, CA 94720-5812. TEL 510-643-7154. FAX 510-642-9917.
Vendor(s): Information Access Co.. *3755*

CALIFORNIA MANAGEMENT REVIEW.
University of California at Berkeley, S549 Haas School of Business, Ste. 1900, Berkeley, CA 94720-1900. TEL 510-642-7159. FAX 510-642-1318.
Vendor(s): Information Access Co., University Microfilms International. *1410*

CALIFORNIA PLANNING AND DEVELOPMENT REPORT.
Torf Fulton Associates, 1275 Sunnycrest Ave., Ventura, CA 93003-1212. TEL 805-642-7838.
Vendor(s): Information Access Co., NewsNet (EV23). *5895*

CALIFORNIA PUBLIC FINANCE.
American Banker - Bond Buyer, Newsletter Division One State St. Plaza, New York, NY 10004-1549. TEL 800-733-4371. FAX 212-943-2224.
Vendor(s): Information Access Co., NewsNet (FI65). *1537*

CALIFORNIA STATE CONTRACTS REGISTER.
Department of General Services, Office of Small and Minority Business, 1531 I St., 2nd Fl., Sacramento, CA 95814-2016. TEL 916-323-5478. FAX 916-442-7855. *906*

CALLALOO.
Johns Hopkins University Press, Journals Publishing Division, 2715 N. Charles St., Baltimore, MD 21218. TEL 410-515-6987. FAX 410-516-6968.
Vendor(s): Information Access Co.. *4191*

CAMPAIGN.
Haymarket Campaign Magazines Ltd., 22 Lancaster Gate, London W2 3LY, England.
Vendor(s): Information Access Co., VU/TEXT Information Services, Inc.. *33*

CAMPAIGNS AND ELECTIONS.
Campaigns and Elections, 1511 K St., N.W., Ste. 1020, Washington, DC 20005. TEL 202-638-7788.
Vendor(s): Information Access Co., University Microfilms International. *5639*

CAMPBELL LAW REVIEW.
Campbell University, Box 1165, Buies Creek, NC 27506. TEL 919-893-4111.
Vendor(s): West Services, Inc.. *3756*

CAMPING MAGAZINE.
American Camping Association, Inc., 5000 State Rd. 67 N., Martinsville, IN 46151-7902. TEL 317-342-8456.
Vendor(s): Information Access Co.. *1762*

CAMPUS CRIME.
Business Publishers, Inc., 951 Pershing Dr., Silver Spring, MD 20910-4464. TEL 301-587-6300. FAX 301-585-9075.
Vendor(s): NewsNet. *2181*

CAMPUS LIFE.
Christianity Today, Inc., 465 Gundersen Dr., Carol Stream, IL 60188. TEL 708-260-6200. FAX 708-260-0114. *1860*

CAMPUS REPORT.
Accuracy in Academia, Inc., 4455 Connecticut Ave., N.W., Ste. 330, Washington, DC 20008. TEL 202-364-4401. FAX 202-364-4098. *2422*

CANADA STOCKWATCH. EASTERN EDITION.
Canjex Publishing, 700 W. Georgia St., Box 10371, Vancouver, BC V7Y 1J6, Canada. TEL 604-687-1500. FAX 604-687-2304. *1324*

CANADA STOCKWATCH. WESTERN EDITION.
Canjex Publishing, 700 W. Georgia St., Box 10371, Vancouver, BC V7Y 1J6, Canada. TEL 604-687-1500. FAX 604-687-2304. *1324*

CANADA - UNITED STATES LAW JOURNAL.
Case Western Reserve University, School of Law, 11075 East Blvd., Cleveland, OH 44106-7148. TEL 216-368-3304. FAX 216-368-3310.
Vendor(s): Lexis-Nexis. *3925*

CANADIAN BANKER.
Canadian Bankers Association, P.O. Box 348, Commerce Ct. W., Ste. 3000, 199 Bay St., Toronto, ON M5L 1G2, Canada. TEL 416-362-6092. FAX 416-362-5658.
Vendor(s): Information Access Co., University Microfilms International. *1074*

CANADIAN BUSINESS.
Canadian Business Media, 777 Bay St., 5th Fl., Toronto, ON M5W 1A7, Canada. TEL 416-596-5151. FAX 416-596-5152.
Vendor(s): Information Access Co.. *906*

CANADIAN BUSINESS REVIEW.
Conference Board of Canada, 255 Smyth Rd. , Ste. 100, Ottawa, ON K1H 8M7, Canada. TEL 613-526-3280. FAX 613-526-4857.
Vendor(s): Information Access Co., Knight-Ridder Information, Inc., University Microfilms International. *906*

CANADIAN CHEMICAL NEWS.
Chemcan Publishers Limited, 130 Slater St., Ste. 550, Ottawa, ON K1P 6E2, Canada. TEL 613-232-6252. FAX 613-232-5862.
Vendor(s): Information Access Co.. *1666*

CANADIAN CRIMINAL CASES.
Canada Law Book Inc., 240 Edward St., Aurora, ON L4G 3S9, Canada. TEL 905-841-6472. FAX 905-841-6472. *3908*

CANADIAN DIMENSION.
Dimension Publishing Inc., 228 Notre Dame Ave., Ste. 401, Winnipeg, MB R3B 1N7, Canada. TEL 204-957-1519. FAX 204-943-4617.
Vendor(s): Information Access Co.. *5639*

CANADIAN EDUCATION INDEX.
Micromedia Ltd., 20 Victoria St., Toronto, ON M5C 2N8, Canada. TEL 416-362-5211. FAX 416-362-6161. *2387*

CANADIAN FEDERAL GOVERNMENT HANDBOOK.
Globe Information Services, 444 Front St. W., Toronto, ON M5V 2S9, Canada. TEL 416-585-5250. FAX 416-585-5249. *555*

CANADIAN FOREIGN RELATIONS.
Department of External Affairs, Domestic Information Division, 125 Sussex Dr., Ottawa, ON K1A 0G2, Canada. TEL 613-996-9134.
Vendor(s): QL Systems Ltd.. *5744*

CANADIAN FOREST INDUSTRIES.
J C F T Forest Communications, 1 rue Pacifique, Ste-Anne-de-Bellevue, PQ H9X 1C5, Canada. TEL 514-457-2211.
Vendor(s): Southam Electronic Publishing. *3033*

CANADIAN GEOGRAPHIC.
Royal Canadian Geographical Society, 39 McArthur Ave., Vanier, ON K1L 8L7, Canada. TEL 613-745-4629. FAX 613-744-0947.
Vendor(s): Information Access Co., University Microfilms International. *3119*

CANADIAN HISTORICAL REVIEW.
University of Toronto Press, Journals Department, 5201 Dufferin St., Downsview, ON M3H 5T8, Canada. TEL 416-667-7781. FAX 416-667-7881.
Vendor(s): Information Access Co.. *3339*

CANADIAN INDEX.
Micromedia Ltd., 20 Victoria St., Toronto, ON M5C 2N8, Canada. TEL 416-362-5211. FAX 416-362-6161.
Vendor(s): Data-Star, IST-INFORMATHEQUE, Inc., Knight-Ridder Information, Inc. (File no.262), QL Systems Ltd.. *987*

CANADIAN JOURNAL OF ADMINISTRATIVE SCIENCES.
Administrative Sciences Association of Canada, Faculty of Commerce and Administration, Concordia University, 1455 de Maisonneuve Blvd. W., Montreal, PQ H3G 1M8, Canada. TEL 514-848-2719. FAX 514-848-2839.
Vendor(s): University Microfilms International. *906*

CANADIAN JOURNAL OF CRIMINOLOGY.
Canadian Criminal Justice Association, 383 Parkdale Ave., Ste. 304, Ottawa, ON K1Y 4R4, Canada. TEL 613-725-3715. FAX 613-725-3720.
Vendor(s): Information Access Co., University Microfilms International. *2160*

CANADIAN JOURNAL OF HISTORY.
University of Saskatchewan, 707 Arts Bldg., 9 Campus Dr., Saskatoon, SK S7N 5A5, Canada. TEL 306-966-5792. FAX 306-966-5852.
Vendor(s): Information Access Co., University Microfilms International. *3339*

CANADIAN JOURNAL OF HOSPITAL PHARMACY.
Canadian Society of Hospital Pharmacists, 1145 Hunt Club Rd., Ste. 350, Ottawa, ON K1V 0Y3, Canada. TEL 613-736-9733. FAX 613-736-5660. *5403*

CANADIAN JOURNAL OF PEDIATRICS.
Rodar Publishing Inc., 8102 Trans Canada Hwy., St. Laurent, PQ H4S 1Z4, Canada. TEL 514-333-5350. FAX 514-457-2679. *4803*

CANADIAN LITERATURE.
University of British Columbia, 167-1855 West Mall, Vancouver, BC V6T 1Z2, Canada. TEL 604-822-2780. FAX 604-822-9452.
Vendor(s): University Microfilms International. *4192*

CANADIAN MACHINERY & METALWORKING.
Maclean Hunter Ltd., Business Publication Division, Maclean-Hunter Bldg., 777 Bay St., Toronto, ON M5W 1A7, Canada. TEL 416-596-5720.
Vendor(s): Information Access Co.. *4336*

CANADIAN MANAGER.
Taylor Enterprises Ltd., 2175 Sheppard Ave. E., Ste. 310, Willowdale, ON M2J 1W8, Canada. TEL 416-493-0155. FAX 416-491-1670.
Vendor(s): Information Access Co., University Microfilms International. *1410*

CANADIAN MINING JOURNAL.
Southam Magazine Group, 1450 Don Mills Rd., Don Mills, ON M3B 2X7, Canada. TEL 416-445-6641. FAX 416-442-2272.
Vendor(s): Information Access Co., Southam Electronic Publishing. *5059*

CANADIAN OCCUPATIONAL HEALTH & SAFETY NEWS.
Southam Information and Technology Group, 1450 Don Mills Rd., Don Mills, ON M3B 2X7, Canada. TEL 416-445-6641. FAX 416-442-2200.
Vendor(s): Information Access Co.. *5247*

CANADIAN OUTLOOK.
Conference Board of Canada, 255 Smyth Rd., Ste. 100, Ottawa, ON K1H 8M7, Canada. TEL 613-526-3280. FAX 613-526-4857. *1182*

CANADIAN PACKAGING.
Maclean-Hunter Ltd., Business Publication Division, Maclean-Hunter Bldg., 777 Bay St., Toronto, ON M5W 1A7, Canada. TEL 416-596-6016.
Vendor(s): Information Access Co.. *5298*

CANADIAN PAPERMAKER.
Maclean Hunter Ltd., Business Publication Division, Maclean Hunter Bldg., 777 Bay St., Toronto, ON M5W 1A7, Canada. TEL 416-596-5518.
Vendor(s): Information Access Co., Lexis-Nexis. *5320*

CANADIAN PATENT REPORTER.
Canada Law Book Inc., 240 Edward St., Aurora, ON L4G 3S9, Canada. TEL 905-841-6472. FAX 905-841-5085. *3758*

CANADIAN PERIODICAL INDEX.
Gale Research Inc., 835 Penobscot Bldg., Detroit, MI 48226. TEL 313-961-2242. FAX 313-961-7086. *8*

CANADIAN PHARMACEUTICAL JOURNAL.
Keith Healthcare Communications, 21 Concourse Gate, No. 13, Nepean, ON K2E 7S4, Canada. TEL 613-727-1364. FAX 613-727-3757. *5403*

CANADIAN PLASTICS.
Southam Magazine and Information Group, 1450 Don Mills Rd., Don Mills, ON M3B 2X7, Canada. TEL 416-445-6641. FAX 416-442-2213.
Vendor(s): Information Access Co.. *5618*

CANADIAN PUBLIC ADMINISTRATION.
Institute of Public Administration of Canada, 150 Eglinton Ave. E., No. 305, Toronto, ON M4P 1E8, Canada. TEL 416-932-3666. FAX 416-932-3667.
Vendor(s): Information Access Co.. *5895*

CANADIAN RESEARCH INDEX, MICROLOG.
Micromedia Ltd., 20 Victoria St., Toronto, ON M5C 2N8, Canada. TEL 416-362-5211. FAX 416-362-6161. *8*

THE CANADIAN REVIEW OF SOCIOLOGY AND ANTHROPOLOGY.
Canadian Sociology and Anthropology Association, Concordia University, 1455 bd. de Maisonneuve W., Montreal, PQ H3G 1M8, Canada. TEL 514-848-8780. FAX 514-848-4539.
Vendor(s): Information Access Co.. *6408*

CANADIAN SHAREOWNER.
1090 University Ave. W., P.O. Box 7337, Windsor, ON N9C 4E9, Canada. TEL 519-252-9965. FAX 519-252-9570.
Vendor(s): University Microfilms International. *1325*

CANADIAN SPEECHES: ISSUES OF THE DAY.
Canadian Speeches, Box 250, Woodville, ON K0M 2T0, Canada. TEL 705-439-2580.
Vendor(s): Knight-Ridder Information, Inc.. *907*

CANADIAN THESES.
National Library of Canada, 395 Wellington St., Ottawa, ON K1A 0N4, Canada. TEL 819-994-6912. FAX 819-953-0291.
Vendor(s): CISTI. *526*

CANADIAN TREASURY MANAGEMENT REVIEW.
Royal Bank of Canada, S. Tower, 9th Fl., Royal Bank Plaza, Toronto, ON M5J 2J5, Canada. TEL 416-974-2274. FAX 416-974-0365.
Vendor(s): University Microfilms International. *1074*

CANADIAN UNDERWRITER.
Southam Magazine Group, 1450 Don Mills Rd., Don Mills, ON M3B 2X7, Canada. TEL 416-445-6641.
Vendor(s): Southam Electronic Publishing, University Microfilms International. *3645*

CANADIAN WHO'S WHO.
University of Toronto Press, 5201 Dufferin St., Downsview, ON M3H 5T8, Canada. TEL 416-667-7791. FAX 416-667-7832. *555*

CANADIANA.
National Library of Canada, 395 Wellington St., Ottawa, ON K1A 0N4, Canada. TEL 819-956-4800. FAX 819-994-1498. *526*

CANADIANA ON MICROFICHE.
National Library of Canada, 395 Wellington St., Ottawa, ON K1A 0N4, Canada. TEL 819-994-6912, 819-994-6912. FAX 819-953-0291.
Vendor(s): CISTI. *526*

CANADIANA PRE-1901.
National Library of Canada, 395 Wellington St., Ottawa, ON K1A 0N4, Canada. TEL 819-994-6912. FAX 819-996-0291.
Vendor(s): CISTI. *526*

CANCER CONTROL.
Moffitt Cancer Center, 12902 Magnolia Dr., Tampa, FL 33612. TEL 813-632-1349. FAX 813-632-1380. *4750*

CANCER GENE THERAPY.
Appleton & Lange, Journal Division Box 120041, Stamford, CT 06912-0041. TEL 203-406-4500. *4751*

THE CANCER JOURNAL FROM SCIENTIFIC AMERICAN.
Scientific American, Inc., 415 Madison Ave., New York, NY 10017-1111. TEL 212-754-0550. FAX 212-980-3062. *4751*

CANCER RESEARCHER WEEKLY.
Charles W. Henderson, Ed. & Pub., Box 5528, Atlanta, GA 31107-0528. TEL 404-377-8895. FAX 404-378-5411.
Vendor(s): CompuServe, Inc., Data-Star, Dow Jones News Retrieval, Information Access Co., Knight-Ridder Information, Inc., NewsNet (HH15), Ovid Technologies, Inc.. *4752*

CANDY INDUSTRY.
Advanstar Communications, Inc., 7500 Old Oak Blvd., Cleveland, OH 44130. TEL 216-826-2839. FAX 216-819-2651.
Vendor(s): Information Access Co., Knight-Ridder Information, Inc.. *2999*

CANNED FOODS: THE INTERNATIONAL MARKET.
Euromonitor, 60-61 Britton St., London EC1M 5NA, England. TEL 44-171-251-8024. FAX 44-171-608-3149.
Vendor(s): Data-Star, Knight-Ridder Information, Inc.. *2962*

CAPACITY MANAGEMENT REVIEW.
Institute for Computer Capacity Management, 1020 8th Ave. S., Ste. 6, Naples, FL 33940. TEL 941-261-8945. FAX 941-261-5456.
Vendor(s): University Microfilms International. *2071*

CAPITAL DISTRICT BUSINESS REVIEW.
Albany Business Journal, Inc., Box 15081, Albany, NY 12212-5081. TEL 518-432-1091.
Vendor(s): Knight-Ridder Information, Inc.. *1182*

CAPITAL UNIVERSITY LAW REVIEW.
Capital University, Law School, 665 S. High St., Columbus, OH 43215. TEL 614-445-8836. FAX 614-445-7125
Vendor(s): National Data Corp., West Services, Inc.. *2160*

CAR AFTERMARKET: THE INTERNATIONAL MARKET.
Euromonitor, 60-61 Britton St., London EC1M 5NA, England. TEL 44-171-251-8024. FAX 44-171-608-3149.
Vendor(s): Data-Star, Knight-Ridder Information, Inc.. *6779*

CAR AND DRIVER.
Hachette Filipacchi Magazines, Inc. (Ann Arbor), 2002 Hogback Rd., Ann Arbor, MI 48105. TEL 313-971-3500. FAX 313-971-9188.
Vendor(s): Information Access Co., Knight-Ridder Information, Inc., University Microfilms International. *6779*

CAR RENTAL: THE INTERNATIONAL MARKET.
Euromonitor, 60-61 Britton St., London EC1M 5NA, England. TEL 44-171-251-8024. FAX 44-171-608-3149.
Vendor(s): Data-Star, Knight-Ridder Information, Inc.. *6780*

CARBOHYDRATE RESEARCH.
Elsevier Science Ltd., P.O. Box 800, Kidlington, Oxford OX5 1DX, England. TEL 44-1865-843000. FAX 44-1865-843010.
Vendor(s): STN International. *1736*

CARD FAX.
Faulkner & Gray, Inc. (New York), 11 Penn Plaza, 17th Fl., New York, NY 10001. TEL 212-967-7000. FAX 212-967-7155.
Vendor(s): Information Access Co., NewsNet (FI67). *1074*

CARD NEWS.
Phillips Business Information, Inc., 1201 Seven Locks Rd., Potomac, MD 20854. TEL 301-424-3338. FAX 301-309-3847.
Vendor(s): Data-Star, Information Access Co., Knight-Ridder Information, Inc., NewsNet (FI24). *1074*

CARDIOLOGY CLINICS.
W.B. Saunders Co. Curtis Center, 3rd Fl., Independence Sq. W., Philadelphia, PA 19106-3399. TEL 215-238-7800. FAX 215-238-6445.
Vendor(s): Ovid Technologies, Inc.. *4598*

CARDIOVASCULAR AND INTERVENTIONAL RADIOLOGY.
Springer-Verlag, Medical Journals, 175 Fifth Ave., New York, NY 10010. TEL 212-460-1500. FAX 212-473-6272.
Vendor(s): FIZ Technik. *4874*

CAREER DEVELOPMENT QUARTERLY.
American Counseling Association, 5999 Stevenson Ave., Alexandria, VA 22304-3300. TEL 703-823-9800. FAX 703-823-0252.
Vendor(s): University Microfilms International. *5263*

CAREERS & MAJORS.
Oxendine Publishing, Inc. Box 14081, Gainesville, FL 32604-2081. TEL 904-373-6907. FAX 904-373-8120. *5264*

CARIBBEAN & CENTRAL AMERICA REPORT.
Lettres (U.K.) Ltd., 61 Old St., London EC1V 9HX, England. TEL 44-171-251-0012. FAX 44-171-253-8193.
Vendor(s): Lexis-Nexis. *182*

CARIBBEAN UPDATE.
Kal Wagenheim, Ed. & Pub., 52 Maple Ave., Maplewood, NJ 07040. TEL 201-762-1565. FAX 201-762-9585.
Vendor(s): Information Access Co.. *1268*

CAROLINA TIPS.
Carolina Biological Supply Co., 2700 York Rd., Burlington, NC 27215. TEL 910-584-0381. FAX 910-584-3399. *577*

CARPET & FLOORCOVERINGS REVIEW.
Miller Freeman Publishers Ltd. Sovereign Way, Tonbridge, Kent TN9 1RW, England. TEL 44-1732-364422. FAX 44-1732-351534.
Vendor(s): Information Access Co.. *3685*

CASE WESTERN RESERVE JOURNAL OF INTERNATIONAL LAW.
Case Western Reserve University, School of Law, 11075 East Blvd., Cleveland, OH 44106-7148. TEL 216-368-3304. FAX 216-368-3310.
Vendor(s): Lexis-Nexis. *3525*

CASE WESTERN RESERVE LAW REVIEW.
Case Western Reserve University, School of Law, 11075 East Blvd., Cleveland, OH 44106-7148. TEL 216-368-3304. FAX 216-369-3310.
Vendor(s): Lexis-Nexis. *3758*

CATALOG AGE.
Cowles Business Media, 11 River Bend Dr., S., Box 4949, Stamford, CT 06907-0949. TEL 203-358-9900. FAX 203-358-5811.
Vendor(s): Information Access Co., University Microfilms International. *53*

CATALOGO COLETIVO DE ANAIS DE EVENTOS.
Comissao Nacional de Energia Nuclear, Centro de Informacoes Nucleares, Rua General Severiano, 90 Botafogo, 22294-900 Rio de Janeiro RJ, Brazil. TEL 55-21-5462467. FAX 55-21-5462447. *6300*

CATALOGUE AFNOR (NORMES FRANCAISES).
Association Francaise de Normalisation, Tour Europe 92049 Paris La Defense, Cedex, France. TEL 42-91-55-55. FAX 42-31-56-56.
Vendor(s): Telesystemes - Questel. *5012*

THE CATALYST (WESTMINSTER).
National Council on Community Services & Continuing Education, c/o Sue Hartman, Professional Development Program, Front Range Community College, 3645 W. 112th Ave., Westminster, CO 80030. *2397*

CATHOLIC UNIVERSITY LAW REVIEW.
Catholic University of America, Columbus School of Law, 3600 John McCormack Rd., NE, Washington, DC 20064. TEL 202-319-5159. FAX 202-319-4459.
Vendor(s): Lexis-Nexis. *3759*

CATO JOURNAL.
Cato Institute, 1000 Massachusetts Ave., N.W., Washington, DC 20001-5403. TEL 202-842-0200. FAX 202-842-3490.
Vendor(s): University Microfilms International. *5640*

CAUSE. PROCEEDINGS OF NATIONAL CONFERENCE.
C A U S E, 4840 Pearl E. Circle, Ste. 302E, Boulder, CO 80301. TEL 303-939-0308. FAX 303-440-0461. *2404*

CAUSE - EFFECT MAGAZINE.
C A U S E, 4830 Pearl E. Cir. Ste. 302E, Boulder, CO 80301. TEL 303-449-4430. FAX 303-440-0461. *2404*

THE CAVALIER DAILY.
Cavalier Daily, Inc., Newcomb Hall, Charlottesville, VA 22903. TEL 804-924-1036. FAX 804-924-7290. *1861*

CELL MOTILITY AND THE CYTOSKELETON.
John Wiley & Sons, Inc., Journals, 605 Third Ave., New York, NY 10158. TEL 212-850-5645. FAX 212-350-6021. *713*

CELLULAR AND MOLECULAR LIFE SCIENCES.
Birkhaeuser Verlag, P.O. Box 133, CH-4010 Basel, Switzerland. TEL 41-61-2050730. FAX 41-61-2050791. *577*

CELLULAR BUSINESS.
Intertec Publishing Corp., 9800 Metcalf, Overland Park, KS 66212-2215. TEL 913-341-1300. FAX 913-967-1898.
Vendor(s): University Microfilms International. *1944*

CELLULAR SALES & MARKETING.
Creative Communications Inc. (Herndon), Box 1519-BKC, Herndon, VA 22070-1519. TEL 703-742-9696.
Vendor(s): NewsNet (TE72). *1944*

CELLULOSE.
Chapman & Hall, Journals Departmen, 2-6 Boundary Row, London SE1 8HN, England. TEL 44-171-8650066. FAX 44-171-5229623. *676*

CENSUS AND YOU.
U.S. Bureau of the Census, Customer Services, Washington, DC 20233. TEL 301-457-1584. FAX 301-457-4714.
Vendor(s): CompuServe, Inc., Knight-Ridder Information, Inc.. *6598*

CENSUS OF AGRICULTURE: FINAL REPORTS.
U.S. Bureau of the Census, Customer Services, Washington, DC 20233. TEL 301-457-4100. FAX 301-457-4714.
Vendor(s): CompuServe, Inc., Knight-Ridder Information, Inc.. *170*

CENSUS OF CONSTRUCTION INDUSTRIES: FINAL REPORTS.
U.S. Bureau of the Census, Customer Services, Washington, DC 20233. TEL 301-457-4100. FAX 301-457-4714.
Vendor(s): CompuServe, Inc., Knight-Ridder Information, Inc.. *844*

CENSUS OF GOVERNMENTS (FINAL REPORTS).
U.S. Bureau of the Census, Customer Services, Washington, DC 20233. TEL 301-457-4100. FAX 301-457-4714.
Vendor(s): CompuServe, Inc., Knight-Ridder Information, Inc.. *5930*

CENSUS OF MANUFACTURES: FINAL REPORTS.
U.S. Bureau of the Census, Customer Services, Washington, DC 20233. TEL 301-457-4100. FAX 301-457-4714.
Vendor(s): CompuServe, Inc., Knight-Ridder Information, Inc.. *988*

CENSUS OF RETAIL TRADE: FINAL REPORTS.
U.S. Bureau of the Census, Customer Services, Washington, DC 20233. TEL 301-457-4100. FAX 301-457-4714.
Vendor(s): CompuServe, Inc., Knight-Ridder Information, Inc.. *988*

CENSUS OF SERVICE INDUSTRIES: FINAL REPORTS.
U.S. Bureau of the Census, Customer Services, Washington, DC 20233. TEL 301-457-4100. FAX 301-457-4714.
Vendor(s): CompuServe, Inc., Knight-Ridder Information, Inc.. *988*

CENSUS OF WHOLESALE TRADE: FINAL REPORTS.
U.S. Bureau of the Census, Customer Services, Washington, DC 20233. TEL 301-457-4100. FAX 301-457-4714.
Vendor(s): CompuServe, Inc., Knight-Ridder Information, Inc.. *988*

CENTRAL EUROPEAN.
Euromoney Publications plc., Nestor House, Playhouse Yard, London EC4V 5EX, England. TEL 44-171-779-8935. FAX 44-171-779-8541.
Vendor(s): University Microfilms International. *1076*

CENTRAL NEW YORK BUSINESS JOURNAL.
C N Y Business Journal, 231 Walton St., Syracuse, NY 13202-1226. TEL 315-472-3104. FAX 315-472-3644.
Vendor(s): Knight-Ridder Information, Inc., University Microfilms International. *1183*

CENTRAL PENN BUSINESS JOURNAL.
C P N C Inc., 409 S. Second St., Ste. 3D, Harrisburg, PA 17104-1612. TEL 717-236-4300. FAX 717-236-6803.
Vendor(s): University Microfilms International. *908*

CERAMIC ABSTRACTS.
American Ceramic Society, 735 Ceramic Pl., Westerville, OH 43081. TEL 614-890-6136. FAX 614-899-6109.
Vendor(s): Knight-Ridder Information, Inc. (File no.335), Orbit Search Service (CERM), STN International. *1661*

CERAMIC INDUSTRY.
Business News Publishing Company, 755 W. Big Beaver Rd., Ste. 1000, Troy, MI 48084. TEL 810-362-3700. FAX 810-362-0317.
Vendor(s): Information Access Co.. *1653*

CERAMICS MONTHLY.
American Ceramic Society, 735 Ceramic Pl., Box 6102, Westerville, OH 43086-6102. TEL 614-523-1660. FAX 614-891-8960.
Vendor(s): Information Access Co., University Microfilms International. *1654*

CESKA A SLOVENSKA FARMACIE.
Nakladatelske Stredisko C L S J.E. Purkyne, Sokolska 31, 120 26 Prague 2, Czech Republic. FAX 42-0-202788. *5404*

CESKA NARODNI BIBLIOGRAFIE. KNIHY.
Narodni Knihovna Ceske Republiky, Klementinum 190, 110 01 Prague 1, Czech Republic. TEL 42-2-24229500. FAX 42-2-24227796. *527*

CHAIN STORE AGE.
Lebhar-Friedman, Inc., 425 Park Ave., New York, NY 10022. TEL 212-756-5000.
Vendor(s): Information Access Co., University Microfilms International. *1458*

CHAMBER JOBWATCH.
American Chamber of Commerce Executives, 4232 King St., Alexandria, VA 22302-9950. TEL 703-998-0072. FAX 703-931-5624. *1136*

CHANGE (WASHINGTON).
Heldref Publications, 1319 18th St., N.W., Washington, DC 20036-1802. TEL 202-296-6267. FAX 202-296-5149.
Vendor(s): Information Access Co.. *2423*

CHARTERED PROPERTY AND CASUALTY UNDERWRITERS SOCIETY. JOURNAL.
Chartered Property & Casualty Underwriters Society, Box 3009, 720 Providence Rd., Malvern, PA 19355. TEL 610-251-2743.
Vendor(s): University Microfilms International. *3645*

CHATELAINE (ENGLISH EDITION).
Maclean Hunter Ltd., Maclean Hunter Bldg., 777 Bay St., Toronto, ON M5W 1A7, Canada. TEL 416-596-5425. FAX 416-593-3197.
Vendor(s): Information Access Co.. *6989*

THE CHATTAHOOCHEE REVIEW.
DeKalb College, 2101 Womack Rd., Dunwoody, GA 30338. TEL 770-551-3166. FAX 770-604-3795. *4194*

CHEM-FACTS: ETHYLENE & PROPYLENE.
Chem-Intell, Reed Information Services Windsor Ct., East Grinstead House, E. Ginstead, W. Sussex RH19 1XA, England. TEL 44-1342-335831. FAX 44-1342-335612.
Vendor(s): Data-Star, Knight-Ridder Information, Inc.. *1736*

CHEM-FACTS: EUROPEAN REVIEW.
Chem-Intell, Reed Information Services Windsor Ct., East Grinstead House, E. Grinstead, W. Sussex RH19 1XA, England. TEL 44-1342-335831. FAX 44-1342-335612.
Vendor(s): Data-Star, Knight-Ridder Information, Inc.. *1667*

CHEM-FACTS: FRANCE.
Chem-Intell, Reed Information Services Windsor Ct., East Grinstead House, E. Grinstead, W. Sussex RH19 1XA, England. TEL 44-1342-335831. FAX 44-1342-335612.
Vendor(s): Data-Star, Knight-Ridder Information, Inc.. *1667*

CHEM-FACTS: GERMANY.
Chem-Intell, Reed Information Services Windsor Ct., East Grinstead House, E. Grinstead, W. Sussex RH19 1XA, England. TEL 44-1342-335831. FAX 44-1342-335612.
Vendor(s): Data-Star, Knight-Ridder Information, Inc.. *1667*

CHEM-FACTS: P V C.
Chem-Intell, Reed Information Services Windsor Ct., East Grinstead House, E. Grinstead, W. Sussex RH19 1XA, England. TEL 44-1342-335831. FAX 44-1342-335612.
Vendor(s): Data-Star, Knight-Ridder Information, Inc.. *1736*

CHEM-FACTS: POLYETHYLENE.
Chem-Intell, Reed Information Services Windsor Ct., East Grinstead House, E. Grinstead, W. Sussex RH19 1XA, England. TEL 44-1342-335831. FAX 44-1342-335612.
Vendor(s): Data-Star, Orbit Search Service. *1736*

CHEM-FACTS: POLYPROPYLENE.
Chem-Intell, Reed Information Services Windsor Ct., East Grinstead House, E. Grinstead, W. Sussex RH19 1XA, England. TEL 44-1342-335831. FAX 44-1342-335612.
Vendor(s): Data-Star, Knight-Ridder Information, Inc., Orbit Search Service. *1736*

CHEM-FACTS: STYRENICS.
Chem-Intell, Reed Information Services Windsor Ct., East Grinstead House, E. Grinstead, W. Sussex RH19 1XA, England. TEL 44-1342-335831. FAX 44-1342-335612.
Vendor(s): Data-Star, Knight-Ridder Information, Inc.. *1736*

CHEM-FACTS: UNITED KINGDOM.
Chem-Intell, Reed Information Services Windsor Ct., East Grinstead House, E. Grinstead, W. Sussex RH19 1XA, England. TEL 44-1342-335831. FAX 44-1342-335612.
Vendor(s): Data-Star, Knight-Ridder Information, Inc.. *1667*

CHEM SOURCES INTERNATIONAL.
Chemical Sources International, Inc., Box 1824, Clemson, SC 29633. TEL 803-646-7840. FAX 803-646-9938.
Vendor(s): STN International. *1592*

CHEM SOURCES U S A.
Chemical Sources International, Inc., Box 1824, Clemson, SC 29633-1824. TEL 803-646-7840. FAX 803-646-9938.
Vendor(s): STN International. *1592*

CHEMICAL ABSTRACTS.
Chemical Abstracts Service 2540 Olentangy River Rd., Box 3012, Columbus, OH 43210-0012. TEL 614-447-3600. FAX 614-447-3713.
Vendor(s): STN International. *1706*

CHEMICAL ABSTRACTS - APPLIED CHEMISTRY AND CHEMICAL ENGINEERING SECTIONS.
Chemical Abstracts Service 2540 Olentangy River Rd., Box 3012, Columbus, OH 43210-0012. TEL 614-447-3663. FAX 614-447-3713.
Vendor(s): STN International (CA). *1706*

CHEMICAL ABSTRACTS - BIOCHEMISTRY SECTIONS.
Chemical Abstracts Service 2540 Olentangy River Rd., Box 3012, Columbus, OH 43210-0012. TEL 614-447-3600. FAX 614-447-3713.
Vendor(s): STN International (CA). *1706*

CHEMICAL ABSTRACTS - MACROMOLECULAR SECTIONS.
Chemical Abstracts Service 2540 Olentangy River Rd., Box 3012, Columbus, OH 43210-0012. TEL 614-447-3600. FAX 614-447-3713.
Vendor(s): STN International (CA). *1706*

CHEMICAL ABSTRACTS - ORGANIC CHEMISTRY SECTIONS.
Chemical Abstracts Service 2540 Olentangy River Rd., Box 3012, Columbus, OH 43210-0012. TEL 614-447-3600. FAX 614-447-3713.
Vendor(s): STN International (CA). *1706*

CHEMICAL ABSTRACTS - PHYSICAL, INORGANIC AND ANALYTICAL CHEMISTRY SECTIONS.
Chemical Abstracts Service 2540 Olentangy River Rd., Box 3012, Columbus, OH 43210-0012. TEL 614-447-3600. FAX 614-447-3713.
Vendor(s): STN International (CA). *1707*

CHEMICAL ABSTRACTS SERVICE SOURCE INDEX.
Chemical Abstracts Service 2540 Olentangy River Rd., Columbus, OH 43210-0012. TEL 614-447-3600. FAX 614-447-3713. *1707*

CHEMICAL & PHARMACEUTICAL BULLETIN.
Pharmaceutical Society of Japan, 12-15, Shibuya 2-chome, Shibuya-ku, Tokyo 150, Japan. *1667*

CHEMICAL COMMUNICATIONS.
Royal Society of Chemistry, Thomas Graham House, Science Park, Milton Rd., Cambridge CB4 4WF, England. TEL 44-1223-420066. FAX 44-1223-423429.
Vendor(s): STN International (CJRSC). *1668*

CHEMICAL EDUCATOR.
Springer-Verlag, 175 Fifth Ave., New York, NY 10010. TEL 212-460-1500. FAX 212-473-6272. Available only online. *1668*

CHEMICAL ENGINEERING.
McGraw-Hill Companies, 1221 Ave. of the Americas, New York, NY 10020. TEL 212-512-2197.
Vendor(s): Dow Jones News Retrieval (CE), Knight-Ridder Information, Inc. (File no.624/McGRAW-HILL PUBLICATIONS ONLINE), Lexis-Nexis (CHEMEN), NewsNet (CH19). *2635*

CHEMICAL HAZARDS IN INDUSTRY.
The Royal Society of Chemistry, Thomas Graham House, Science Park, Milton Rd., Cambridge CB4 4WF, England. TEL 44-1223-420066. FAX 44-1223-423429.
Vendor(s): Data-Star (CSNB), Knight-Ridder Information, Inc. (File no.317), STN International (CSNB). *5247*

CHEMICAL INDUSTRY NOTES.
Chemical Abstracts Service 2540 Olentangy River Rd., Box 3012, Columbus, OH 43210-0012. TEL 614-447-3600. FAX 614-447-3713. *1707*

CHEMICAL MARKETING REPORTER.
Schnell Publishing Co., Inc., 80 Broad St., New York, NY 10004-2203. TEL 212-248-4177. FAX 212-248-4903.
Vendor(s): Information Access Co., Knight-Ridder Information, Inc., University Microfilms International. *1668*

CHEMICAL MONITOR.
Desktop Publishing, Box 314, Lindenhurst, NY 11757-0314. TEL 516-669-8147.
Vendor(s): Data-Star, Information Access Co., Knight-Ridder Information, Inc., NewsNet (CH15). *1714*

CHEMICAL PLANT FILE.
Chem-Intell, Reed Information Services Windsor Ct., East Grinstead House, E. Grinstead, W. Sussex RH19 1XA, England. TEL 44-1342-335831. FAX 44-1342-335612.
Vendor(s): Data-Star, Knight-Ridder Information, Inc., Reed Information Services Ltd.. *1668*

CHEMICAL REGULATION REPORTER.
The Bureau of National Affairs, Inc., 1231 25th St., N.W., Washington, DC 20037. TEL 202-452-4200. FAX 202-822-8092.
Vendor(s): Human Resources Information Network (File DD), Lexis-Nexis (BNA-CHEM), West Services, Inc.. *2780*

CHEMICAL RESEARCH IN TOXICOLOGY.
American Chemical Society, 1155 16th St., N.W., Washington, DC 20036. TEL 800-333-9511. FAX 614-447-3671.
Vendor(s): STN International. *2843*

CHEMICAL REVIEWS.
American Chemical Society, 1155 16th St., N.W., Washington, DC 20036. TEL 800-333-9511. FAX 614-447-3671.
Vendor(s): STN International (CJACS). *1669*

CHEMICAL SUBSTANCES CONTROL.
The Bureau of National Affairs, Inc., 1231 25th St., N.W., Washington, DC 20037. TEL 202-452-4200. FAX 202-822-8092.
Vendor(s): Human Resources Information Network (CDD, HDD). *1669*

CHEMICAL TITLES.
Chemical Abstracts Service 2540 Olentangy River Rd., Columbus, OH 43210-0012. TEL 614-447-3600. FAX 614-447-3713. *1707*

CHEMICAL WEEK.
Chemical Week Associates, 888 Seventh Ave., New York, NY 10106. TEL 212-621-4900. FAX 212-621-4949.
Vendor(s): Information Access Co., Lexis-Nexis. *2637*

CHEMISCHE INDUSTRIE.
Verlagsgruppe Handelsblatt GmbH, Kasernenstr. 67, 40213 Duesseldorf, Germany. TEL 49-211-8870. FAX 49-211-65531 *2638*

DIE CHEMISCHE INDUSTRIE UND IHRE HELFER.
Industrie-Verlagsgesellschaft mbH, Berliner Allee 8, 64295 Darmstadt, Germany. TEL 06151-38920. FAX 06151-33164. *2638*

CHEMIST & DRUGGIST.
Miller Freeman Publishers Ltd. Sovereign Way, Tonbridge, Kent TN9 1RW, England. TEL 44-1732-364422. FAX 44-1732-361534.
Vendor(s): Information Access Co.. *5404*

CHEMISTRY & BIOLOGY.
Current Biology Ltd., 400 Market St., Ste. 700, Philadelphia, PA 19106. FAX 215-574-2270. *660*

CHEMISTRY AND INDUSTRY.
Society of Chemical Industry, 14 Belgrave Sq., London SW1X 8PS, England. TEL 44-171-235-3681. FAX 44-171-235-9410.
Vendor(s): Information Access Co.. *1671*

CHEMORECEPTION ABSTRACTS.
Cambridge Scientific Abstracts, 7200 Wisconsin Ave., 6th Fl., Bethesda, MD 20814. TEL 301-961-6750. FAX 301-961-6720.
Vendor(s): Knight-Ridder Information, Inc. (File no.76/LIFE SCIENCES COLLECTION), STN International (LIFESCI). *1707*

CHEMSCOPE.
Chemscope, Inc..
Available only online. *4441*

CHEST.
American College of Chest Physicians, 3300 Dundee Rd., Northbrook, IL 60062. TEL 847-498-1400. FAX 849-498-5460.
Vendor(s): Information Access Co.. *4887*

CHIAROSCURO.
Reporter Publishing, Via Manzoni 31, 50018 Scandicci, Italy. TEL 39-55-2578346. FAX 39-55-250868. *4061*

CHICAGO (YEAR).
Harper Collins Publishers, Birnbaum Travel Guides, 10 E. 53rd St., New York, NY 10022-5299. TEL 212-207-7542.
Vendor(s): Information Access Co.. *6874*

CHICAGO AREA BUSINESS DIRECTORY.
American Business Directories 5711 S. 86th Circle, Box 27347, Omaha, NE 68127. TEL 402-593-4600. FAX 402-331-5481. *1592*

CHICAGO ARTISTS' NEWS.
Chicago Artists' Coalition, 11 E. Hubbard St., 7th Fl., Chicago, IL 60611. TEL 312-670-2060. FAX 312-670-2521. *423*

CHICAGO ENTERPRISE.
Commercial Club of Chicago, One First National Plaza, No. 2700, Chicago, IL 60603. TEL 312-853-1203. FAX 312-853-1209.
Vendor(s): Lexis-Nexis. *908*

CHICAGO JOURNAL OF THEORETICAL COMPUTER SCIENCE.
M I T Press, 55 Hayward St., Cambridge, MA 02142-1399. TEL 617-253-2889. FAX 617-258-6779.
Available only online. *1983*

CHICAGO - KENT LAW REVIEW.
Chicago - Kent College of Law, 565 W. Adams St., Chicago, IL 60661-3691. TEL 312-906-5190. FAX 312-906-5280.
Vendor(s): West Services, Inc.. *3759*

CHICAGO REVIEW.
Chicago Review, 5801 S. Kenwood, Chicago, IL 60637. TEL 312-702-0887. FAX 312-702-0887.
Vendor(s): Information Access Co.. *4195*

THE CHICAGO TRIBUNE INDEX.
U M I Company 300 N. Zeeb Rd., Ann Arbor, MI 48106-1346. TEL 313-751-4700. FAX 800-864-0019. *3714*

CHICANO - LATINO LAW REVIEW.
University of California at Los Angeles, School of Law, 405 Hilgard Ave., Los Angeles, CA 90024. TEL 310-825-2894.
Vendor(s): West Services, Inc.. *3759*

CHIEF EXECUTIVE MAGAZINE.
Chief Executive Group, Inc., 733 Third Ave., 21st Fl., New York, NY 10017. TEL 212-687-8288. FAX 212-687-8456.
Vendor(s): Information Access Co.. *1410*

CHIEF EXECUTIVE OFFICERS NEWSLETTER.
Center for Entrepreneurial Management, Inc., 180 Varick St., Penthouse, New York, NY 10014. TEL 212-633-0060. FAX 212-633-0063.
Vendor(s): NewsNet. *1410*

CHILD ABUSE & NEGLECT.
Elsevier Science Ltd., Pergamon, P.O. Box 800, Kidlington, Oxford OX5 1DX, England. TEL 44-1865-843000. FAX 44-1865-843010. *1762*

CHILD HEALTH ALERT.
Box 338, Newton Highlands, MA 02161.
Vendor(s): Information Access Co. *4804*

CHILD PROTECTION REPORT.
Business Publishers, Inc., 951 Pershing Dr., Silver Spring, MD 20910-4432. TEL 301-587-6300. FAX 301-585-9075.
Vendor(s): NewsNet. *1763*

CHILDHOOD EDUCATION.
Association for Childhood Education International, 11501 Georgia Ave., Ste. 315, Wheaton, MD 20902. TEL 301-942-2443.
Vendor(s): Information Access Co., University Microfilms International. *2819*

CHILDREN TODAY.
U.S. Department of Health and Human Services, Administration for Children and Families, Office of Public Affairs, 370 L'Enfant Promenade, S.W., 7th Fl., Washington, DC 20447. TEL 202-401-9215.
Vendor(s): Information Access Co., Knight-Ridder Information, Inc., University Microfilms International. *1764*

CHILDREN'S BOOKS IN PRINT.
R.R. Bowker, A Division of Reed Elsevier Inc., 121 Chanlon Rd., New Providence, NJ C7974. TEL 908-464-6800. FAX 908-665-6688.
Vendor(s): Knight-Ridder Information, Inc. (File no.470), Ovid Technologies Inc. (B3IP). *527*

CHILDREN'S BUSINESS.
Fairchild Fashion & Merchandising Group 7 W. 34th St., New York, NY 10001. TEL 212-630-4199. FAX 212-630-4201.
Vendor(s): Information Access Co.. *1839*

CHILLED FOODS, DELICATESSEN FOODS AND READY MEALS: THE INTERNATIONAL MARKET.
Euromonitor, 60-61 Britton St., London EC1M 5NA, England. TEL 44-171-251-8024. FAX 44-171-608-3149.
Vendor(s): Data-Star, Knight Ridder Information, Inc.. *2963*

CHILTON'S AUTOMOTIVE MARKETING.
Chilton Co. Chilton Way, Radnor, PA 19089. TEL 610-964-4000. FAX 610-964-4981.
Vendor(s): Information Access Co., Knight-Ridder Information, Inc., Lexis-Nexis *6780*

CHILTON'S DISTRIBUTION.
Chilton Co., Chilton Way, Radnor, PA 19089. TEL 215-964-4379.
Vendor(s): Information Access Co., Knight-Ridder Information, Inc., Lexis-Nexis. *6715*

CHILTON'S FOOD ENGINEERING.
Chilton Co., One Chilton Way Radnor, PA 19089. TEL 610-964-4455.
Vendor(s): Information Access Co., Knight-Ridder Information, Inc., Lexis-Nexis. *2963*

CHILTON'S FOOD ENGINEERING INTERNATIONAL.
Chilton Co., Chilton Way, Radnor, PA 19089.
TEL 610-964-4440.
Vendor(s): Information Access Co., Knight-Ridder Information, Inc.. *2963*

CHILTON'S HARDWARE AGE.
Chilton Co., Chilton Way, Radnor, PA 19089.
TEL 610-964-4282.
Vendor(s): Knight-Ridder Information, Inc.. *888*

CHILTON'S JEWELERS' CIRCULAR-KEYSTONE.
Chilton Co., Chilton Way, Radnor, PA 19089.
TEL 215-964-4474. FAX 215-964-4481.
Vendor(s): Knight-Ridder Information, Inc.. *3694*

CHILTON'S MOTOR AGE.
Chilton Co., One Chilton Way, Radnor, PA 19089.
TEL 610-964-4390. FAX 610-964-4251.
Vendor(s): Information Access Co., Knight-Ridder Information, Inc., Lexis-Nexis. *6781*

CHINA AEROSPACE ABSTRACTS.
Hangkong Gongye Chubanshe, 14 Xiaoguan Dongli, Anwai, Beijing 100029, People's Republic of China. TEL 8610-4918404. FAX 8610-4221696. *82*

CHINA AVIATION & AIRPORTS.
Euromoney Aviation Group, Playhouse Yard, Nestor House, London EC4V 5EX, England. TEL 44-171-779-8866. FAX 44-171-779-8867. *6753*

CHINA BUSINESS REVIEW.
China Business Council, 1818 N St., N.W., Ste. 200, Washington, DC 20036. TEL 202-429-0340. FAX 202-775-2476.
Vendor(s): Information Access Co., Knight-Ridder Information, Inc., University Microfilms International, Wilsonline. *1268*

CHINA HAND.
Economist Intelligence Unit, 111 W. 57th St., New York, NY 10019. TEL 212-554-0600. FAX 212-586-1182. *908*

CHINA QUARTERLY.
Oxford University Press, Oxford Journals, Walton St., Oxford OX2 6DP, England. TEL 01865-267907. FAX 01865-267773.
Vendor(s): University Microfilms International. *5281*

CHINA TODAY.
Jinri Zhongguo Zazhishe, 24 Baiwanzhuang Lu, Beijing 100037, People's Republic of China. TEL 8326037. FAX 8328338.
Vendor(s): Knight-Ridder Information, Inc.. *3129*

CHINESE MEDICAL JOURNAL.
Chinese Medical Association, P.O. Box 2258, 42 Dongsi Xidajie, Beijing 100710, People's Republic of China. TEL 5133311. *4441*

CHING FENG.
Christian Study Centre on Chinese Religion & Culture, 6-F Kiu Kin Mansion, 566 Nathan Rd., Kowloon, Hong Kong. TEL 7703310.
FAX 7826869.
Vendor(s): Knight-Ridder Information, Inc., Ovid Technologies, Inc.. *6051*

CHIROPRACTIC HISTORY.
Association for the History of Chiropractic, 1000 Brady St., Davenport, IA 52803. TEL 319-326-9894. FAX 319-326-9897.
Vendor(s): National Library of Medicine. *4612*

CHIRURGIA MAXILLOFACIALIS ET PLASTICA.
Hrvatski Lijecnicki Zbor, Drustvo za Maksilofacijalnu i Plasticnu Kirurgiju, Subiceva 9, Zagreb. TEL 385-41-420-470. FAX 385-41-425-629. *4906*

CHOICE (MIDDLETOWN).
Choice, 100 Riverview Ctr., Middletown, CT 06457.
TEL 203-347-6933. FAX 203-346-8586. *6013*

CHOICES (NEW YORK).
Choice in Dying, Inc., 200 Varick St., New York, NY 10014. TEL 212-366-5540. FAX 212-366-5337. *2149*

CHOICES: A CORE COLLECTION FOR YOUNG RELUCTANT READERS.
John Gordon Burke Publisher, Inc., Box 1492, Evanston, IL 60204-1492. TEL 847-866-8625.
FAX 847-866-6639. *1787*

CHRISTIAN CENTURY.
Christian Century Foundation, 407 S. Dearborn St., Chicago, IL 60605. TEL 312-427-5380.
Vendor(s): Information Access Co., University Microfilms International. *6051*

CHRISTIAN SCIENCE MONITOR.
Christian Science Publishing Society, One Norway St., Boston, MA 02115-3195, TEL 617-450-2000.
Vendor(s): Knight-Ridder Information, Inc.. *3226*

CHRISTIAN SCIENCE MONITOR INDEX.
U M I Company 300 N. Zeeb Rd., Ann Arbor, MI 48106-1346. TEL 313-761-4700. FAX 800-864-0019.
Vendor(s): Knight-Ridder Information, Inc.. *3714*

CHRISTIANITY TODAY.
Christianity Today, Inc., 465 Gunderson Dr., Carol Stream, IL 60188. TEL 708-260-6200. FAX 708-261-0114.
Vendor(s): Information Access Co., University Microfilms International. *6053*

THE CHRONICLE OF HIGHER EDUCATION.
Chronicle of Higher Education, Inc., 1255 23rd St., N.W., Ste. 700, Washington, DC 20037. TEL 202-466-1000. FAX 202-296-2691.
Vendor(s): University Microfilms International. *2423*

CHRONICLE OF LATIN AMERICAN ECONOMIC AFFAIRS.
University of Latin America, Latin American Institute, 801 Yale N.E., Albuquerque, NM 87131-1016.
TEL 505-277-6839. FAX 505-277-5989.
Vendor(s): Information Access Co., Knight-Ridder Information, Inc., Lexis-Nexis, NewsNet (IT43). *1183*

CHURCH HISTORY.
American Society of Church History, Box 8517, Red Bank, NJ 07701-8517.
Vendor(s): University Microfilms International. *6053*

CINCINNATI BUSINESS COURIER.
A C B J Business Publications Inc., 35 E. 7th St., Ste. 700, Cincinnati, OH 45202-2411. TEL 513-621-6665. FAX 513-621-2462.
Vendor(s): Information Access Co.. *909*

CINCINNATI LAW REVIEW.
University of Cincinnati, College of Law, Rm. 300, Cincinnati, OH 45221-0040. TEL 513-556-5101.
FAX 513-556-6265.
Vendor(s): West Services, Inc.. *3760*

CINEASTE.
Cineaste Publishers, Inc., 200 Park Ave. S., Ste. 1601, New York, NY 10003. TEL 212-982-1241.
FAX 212-982-1241.
Vendor(s): Information Access Co., University Microfilms International. *5096*

CINEMA REVUE.
Independent Publisher's Group, Box 40611, Memphis, TN 38174. TEL 901-272-7462. *5097*

CINFOLINK CANADIAN DATA BASE DIRECTORY.
Cinfolink Services, 85 Roe Ave., Toronto, ON M5M 2H6, Canada. TEL 416-485-8063. *2033*

CIRCULATION (DALLAS).
American Heart Association, 7272 Greenville Ave., Dallas, TX 75231-4596. TEL 214-706-1310.
FAX 214-691-6342.
Vendor(s): Ovid Technologies, Inc. (JWAT). *4599*

CIRCULATION RESEARCH.
American Heart Association, 7272 Greenville Ave., Dallas, TX 75231-4596. TEL 214-706-1310.
FAX 214-691-6342.
Vendor(s): Ovid Technologies, Inc.. *4599*

CITATIONS FOR SERIAL LITERATURE.
MIT Libraries, Rm. 14E-210A, Massachusetts Institute of Technology, Cambridge, MA 02139-4307.
Available only online. *4038*

CIVICA SCUOLA DI MUSICA. QUADERNI.
Civica Scuola di Musica, Via Stilicone 36, 20142 Milan, Italy. TEL 02-313334. FAX 02-3315697. *5149*

CLASSICAL AND QUANTUM GRAVITY.
I O P Publishing Ltd., Techno House, Redcliffe Way, Bristol, Avon BS1 6NX, England. TEL 44-117-929-7481. FAX 44-117-929-4318. *5544*

CLASSICAL ANTIQUITY.
University of California Press, Journals Division, 2120 Berkeley Way, No. 5812, Berkeley, CA 94720-5812. TEL 510-643-7154. FAX 510-642-9917.
Vendor(s): Information Access Co.. *1820*

CLASSICAL QUARTERLY.
Oxford University Press, Oxford Journals, Walton St., Oxford OX2 6DP, England. TEL 44-1865-267907. FAX 44-1865-267773.
Vendor(s): Information Access Co.. *1820*

CLEANING APPLIANCES: THE INTERNATIONAL MARKET.
Euromonitor, 60-61 Britton St., London EC1M 5NA, England. TEL 44-171-251-8024. FAX 44-171-608-3149.
Vendor(s): Data-Star, Knight-Ridder Information, Inc.. *2509*

THE CLEARING HOUSE.
Heldref Publications, 1319 Eighteenth St., N.W., Washington, DC 20036-1802. TEL 202-296-6267.
FAX 202-296-5149.
Vendor(s): Information Access Co.. *2320*

CLEVELAND STATE LAW REVIEW.
Cleveland State University, Cleveland-Marshall College of Law, 1983 E. 24th St., Cleveland, OH 44115. TEL 216-687-2336.
Vendor(s): West Services, Inc.. *3760*

CLINICA.
P J B Publications Ltd., 18-20 Hill Rise, Richmond, Surrey TW10 6UA, England. TEL 44-181-948-3262. FAX 44-181-332-8998.
Vendor(s): Data-Star, Knight-Ridder Information, Inc., Ovid Technologies, Inc. (PHIN,PHIC,PHID). *4442*

CLINICAL DIABETES.
American Diabetes Association, 1660 Duke St., Alexandria, VA 22314. TEL 703-549-1500.
FAX 703-836-7439.
Vendor(s): Information Access Co., Ovid Technologies, Inc.. *4666*

CLINICAL DYSMORPHOLOGY.
Chapman & Hall, Journals Department 2-6 Boundary Row, London SE1 8HN, England. TEL 44-171-8650066. FAX 44-171-5229623. *787*

CLINICAL LABORATORY.
Verlag Klinisches Labor, Im Breitspiel 15, 69126 Heidelberg, Germany. TEL 49-6221-3432133.
FAX 49-6221-300291. *4678*

CLINICAL LASER MONTHLY.
American Health Consultants, Inc., 3525 Piedmont Rd., N.E., Bldg. 6, Ste. 400, Atlanta, GA 30305.
TEL 800-688-2421. FAX 800-284-3291.
Vendor(s): Lexis-Nexis. *4906*

CLINICAL MOLECULAR PATHOLOGY.
B M J Publishing Group, B.M.A. House, Tavistock Sq., London WC1H 9JR, England. TEL 44-171-387-4499. FAX 44-171-383-6661.
Vendor(s): Ovid Technologies, Inc.. *4678*

CLINICAL ORTHOPAEDICS AND RELATED RESEARCH.
Lippincott - Raven Publishers 227 E. Washington Sq., Philadelphia, PA 19106. TEL 215-238-4200.
Vendor(s): Lexis-Nexis, Ovid Technologies, Inc.. *4782*

CLINICAL PEDIATRICS.
Westminster Publications Inc., 708 Glen Cove Ave., Glen Head, NY 11545. TEL 516-759-0025.
FAX 516-759-5524.
Vendor(s): Lexis-Nexis, Ovid Technologies, Inc.. *4804*

CLINICAL PHARMACOLOGY & THERAPEUTICS.
Mosby - Year Book, Inc. 11830 Westline Industrial Dr., St. Louis, MO 63146-3318. TEL 314-872-8370. FAX 314-432-1380.
Vendor(s): Ovid Technologies, Inc.. *5405*

CLIONET.
James Cook University of North Queensland, Department of History and Politics, P.O., Townsville, 4811 Qld., Australia. TEL 61-77-814170. FAX 61-77-814487.
Available only online. *3340*

CLUB MANAGEMENT.
Finan Publishing, 8730 Big Bend Blvd., St. Louis, MO 63119. TEL 314-961-6644. FAX 314-961-4809.
Vendor(s): University Microfilms International. *1848*

COAL.
Intertec Publishing Corp., 29 N. Wacker Dr., Chicago, IL 60606. TEL 312-726-2802. FAX 312-726-4103.
Vendor(s): Lexis-Nexis. *5060*

COAL & SYNFUELS TECHNOLOGY.
Pasha Publications Inc., 1616 N. Ft. Myer Dr., Ste. 1000, Arlington, VA 22209-3107. TEL 703-528-1244. FAX 703-528-1253.
Vendor(s): Information Access Co., NewsNet (EY49). *2541*

COAL HIGHLIGHTS.
I E A Coal Research, Gemini House, 10-18 Putney Hill, London SW15 6AA, England. TEL 44-181-780-0111. FAX 44-181-780-1746.
Vendor(s): QL Systems Ltd.. *2542*

COAL OUTLOOK.
Pasha Publications Inc., 1616 N. Ft. Myer Dr., Ste. 1000, Arlington, VA 22209-3107. TEL 703-528-1244. FAX 703-528-1253.
Vendor(s): Information Access Co., NewsNet (EY30). *5060*

COAL TECH INTERNATIONAL.
McGraw-Hill Companies, Energy & Business Newsletters, 1221 Ave. of the Americas, 36th Fl., New York, NY 10020.
Vendor(s): Dow Jones News Retrieval (CSL), Knight-Ridder Information, Inc. (File no.624/McGRAW-HILL PUBLICATIONS ONLINE), Lexis-Nexis (SYNFLS), NewsNet (EY76). *2542*

COAL U.K.
Financial Times Energy Publishing Maple House, 149 Tottenham Court Rd., London W1P 9LL, England. TEL 0171-896-2241. FAX 0171-896-2275.
Vendor(s): Data-Star, Knight-Ridder Information, Inc., Lexis-Nexis. *2542*

COAL WEEK.
McGraw-Hill Companies, Energy & Business Newsletters, 1221 Ave. of the Americas, 36th Fl., New York, NY 10020. TEL 212-512-6410.
Vendor(s): Dow Jones News Retrieval (COW), Knight-Ridder Information, Inc. (File no.624/McGRAW-HILL PUBLICATIONS ONLINE), Lexis-Nexis (COALWK), NewsNet (EY77). *5061*

COAL WEEK INTERNATIONAL.
McGraw-Hill Companies, Energy & Business Newsletters, 1221 Ave. of the Americas, 36th Fl., New York, NY 10020. TEL 212-512-6410.
Vendor(s): Dow Jones News Retrieval (CWI), Knight-Ridder Information, Inc. (File no.624/McGRAW-HILL PUBLICATIONS ONLINE), Lexis-Nexis (COALIN), NewsNet (EY78). *5061*

COAST BUSINESS.
Coast Magazine Corp., Box 1209, Gulfport, MS 39502-1209. TEL 601-868-1182. FAX 601-867-2986.
Vendor(s): University Microfilms International. *909*

COATINGS.
Kay Publishing Company Ltd., 406 N. Service Rd., E., Ste. 1, Oakville, ON L6H 5R2, Canada. TEL 905-844-9773. FAX 905-844-5672.
Vendor(s): Information Access Co.. *5306*

COLEGIO OFICIAL DE FARMACEUTICO. CIRCULAR FARMACEUTICA.
Colegio Oficial de Farmaceuticos de la Provincia de Barcelona, Pau Claris, 94, 08010 Barcelona, Spain. *5405*

COLLABORATIVE COMPUTING.
Chapman & Hall, Journals Department 2-6 Boundary Row, London SE1 8HN, England. TEL 44-171-8650066. FAX 44-171-5229623. *2035*

COLLECTIVE BARGAINING NEGOTIATIONS & CONTRACTS.
The Bureau of National Affairs, Inc., 1231 25th St., N.W., Washington, DC 20037. TEL 202-452-4200. FAX 202-822-8092.
Vendor(s): Human Resources Information Network, West Services, Inc.. *1367*

COLLEGAMENTO.
Utet Periodici Scientifici s.r.l., Via P. Giuria 20, 10125 Turin, Italy. TEL 39-2-29003555. FAX 39-2-6599049. *5405*

COLLEGE ENGLISH.
National Council of Teachers of English, 1111 W. Kenyon Rd., Urbana, IL 61801-1096. TEL 217-328-3870. FAX 217-328-0977.
Vendor(s): University Microfilms International. *2483*

COLLEGE HEIGHTS HERALD.
Western Kentucky University, 109 Garrett Center, Bowling Green, KY 42101. TEL 502-745-2653. FAX 502-745-2697. *1862*

COLLEGE LITERATURE.
West Chester University, 554 New Main, West Chester, PA 19383. TEL 610-436-2901. FAX 610-436-3150.
Vendor(s): Information Access Co.. *4197*

COLLEGE PRESS SERVICE.
Tribune Media Services, 435 N. Michigan Ave., Ste. 1417, Chicago, IL 60611-4008. *2424*

COLONIAL HOMES.
Hearst Magazines, Colonial Homes, 959 Eighth Ave., New York, NY 10019. TEL 212-262-5700. FAX 212-586-3455.
Vendor(s): Information Access Co.. *389*

COLORADO BUSINESS.
Wiesner Publishing, Inc., 7009 S. Potomac St., Englewood, CO 80112. TEL 303-397-7600. FAX 303-397-7619.
Vendor(s): Information Access Co., Knight-Ridder Information, Inc., Lexis-Nexis. *1184*

COLORADO BUSINESS DIRECTORY.
American Business Directories 5711 S. 86th Circle, Box 27347, Omaha, NE 68127. TEL 402-593-4600. FAX 402-331-5481. *1593*

COLORADO SPRINGS BUSINESS JOURNAL.
31 E. Platte Ave., Ste. 300, Box 1541, Colorado Springs, CO 80901. TEL 719-634-5905. FAX 719-634-5157.
Vendor(s): University Microfilms International. *909*

COLUMBIA JOURNAL OF LAW AND SOCIAL PROBLEMS.
Darby Publishing, 435 W. 116th St., New York, NY 10027. TEL 212-663-8708. FAX 212-866-9714.
Vendor(s): West Services, Inc.. *3761*

COLUMBIA JOURNAL OF TRANSNATIONAL LAW.
Columbia Journal of Transnational Law Association, Columbia University, 435 W. 116th St., Box D25, New York, NY 10027. TEL 212-663-8709.
Vendor(s): West Services, Inc.. *3926*

COLUMBIA JOURNAL OF WORLD BUSINESS.
J A I Press Inc., 55 Old Post Rd., No. 2, Box 1678, Greenwich, CT 06836-1678. TEL 203-661-7602. FAX 203-661-0792.
Vendor(s): Information Access Co.. *1269*

COLUMBIA JOURNALISM REVIEW.
Columbia University, Graduate School of Journalism, 700 Journalism Bldg., New York, NY 10027. TEL 212-854-1881. FAX 212-854-8580.
Vendor(s): Information Access Co., University Microfilms International. *3702*

COLUMBIA LAW REVIEW.
Columbia Law Review Association, 435 W. 116th St., New York, NY 10027. TEL 212-854-4398.
Vendor(s): Lexis-Nexis, West Services, Inc.. *3761*

COLUMBUS BUSINESS JOURNAL.
110 N. High St., Gahanna, OH 43230-9069.
Vendor(s): Knight-Ridder Information, Inc.. *909*

COLUMBUS FREE PRESS.
Columbus Institute for Contemporary Journalism, 1240 Bruden Rd., Columbus, OH 43205. TEL 614-258-3334.
Available only online. *4137*

COMBUSTION THEORY AND MODELLING.
I O P Publishing Ltd., Technoc House, Redcliffe Way, Bristol, Avon BS1 6NX, England. TEL 44-117-9297481. FAX 44-117-9294318. *5583*

COMERCIO EXTERIOR.
Banco Nacional de Comercio Exterior, S.A., Gerencia de la Revista Comercio Exterior, Camino a Santa Teresa 1679, Col. Jardires del Pedregal, 01900 Mexico D.F., Mexico. TEL 525-3276220. FAX 525-3275214. *1269*

COMMENTARII MATHEMATICI HELVETICI.
Birkhaeuser Verlag, P.O. Box 133, CH-4010 Basel, Switzerland. TEL 41-61-2050733. FAX 41-61-2050791. *4360*

COMMENTARY.
American Jewish Committee, 165 E. 56th St., New York, NY 10022. TEL 212-751-4000. FAX 212-751-1174.
Vendor(s): Information Access Co.. *4137*

COMMENTS ON MONEY AND CREDIT.
D R I - McGraw-Hill, 24 Hartwell Ave., Lexington, MA 02173. TEL 617-863-5100. FAX 617-860-6332. *1077*

COMMERCE BUSINESS DAILY.
U.S. International Trade Administration, U.S. Department of Commerce, Herber. C. Hoover Bldg., Rm. 3850, 14th St. & Constitution Ave., Washington, DC 20230. TEL 202-482-2867.
Vendor(s): Knight-Ridder Information, Inc. (File nos.194 & 195), NewsNet, Unitec Communications Group (CBD OnLine). *145*

COMMERCIAL NEWS U S A.
U.S. Department of Commerce, International Trade Administration, Rm. 1310, Washington, DC 20230. TEL 202-482-4918. FAX 202-482-5362. *1269*

COMMON CAUSE MAGAZINE.
Common Cause, 2030 M St., N.W. Washington, DC 20036. TEL 202-833-1200. FAX 202-659-3716.
Vendor(s): Information Access Co., Lexis-Nexis, University Microfilms International. *5643*

COMMONWEAL.
Commonweal Foundation, 15 Dutch St., New York, NY 10038. TEL 212-732-0600.
Vendor(s): Information Access Co., University Microfilms International. *4137*

COMMONWEALTH GOVERNMENT DIRECTORY.
Australian Government Publishing Service, G.P.O. Box 84, Canberra, A.C.T. 2601, Australia. TEL 61-6-295-4411. FAX 61-6-295-4455. *5897*

COMMONWEALTH LAW REPORTS.
L B C Information Services, 50 Waterloo Rd., N. Ryde, N.S.W. 2113, Australia. TEL 61-2-99366444. FAX 61-2-8889706. *3946*

COMMUNICATION EDUCATION.
Speech Communication Association, 5105 Backlick Rd., Bldg. E., Annandale, VA 22003. TEL 703-750-0533. FAX 703-914-9471.
Vendor(s): University Microfilms International. *2483*

COMMUNICATION MONOGRAPHS.
Speech Communication Association, 5105 Backlick Rd., Bldg. E., Annandale, VA 22003. TEL 703-750-0533. FAX 703-914-9471.
Vendor(s) University Microfilms International. *2320*

COMMUNICATION QUARTERLY.
Eastern Communication Association, c/o Kathleen M. Long, Exec. Sec., Department of Communication & Marketing, West Virginia Wesleyan College, 59 College Ave., Buckhannon, WV 26201-2997. TEL 304-473-8234.
Vendor(s): University Microfilms International. *2320*

COMMUNICATION STUDIES.
Boylor University, Waco, TX 76798. TEL 405-332-8000. FAX 405-332-1623.
Vendor(s): University Microfilms International. *1899*

COMMUNICATION WORLD.
International Association of Business Communicators, One Hallidie Plaza, Ste. 600, San Francisco, CA 94102. TEL 415-433-3400. FAX 415-362-8762.
Vendor(s): Information Access Co., Knight-Ridder Information, Inc., Lexis-Nexis, University Microfilms International. *1411*

COMMUNICATIONS AND THE LAW.
Fred B. Rothman & Co., 10368 W. Centennial Rd., Littleton, CO 80127. TEL 303-979-5657. FAX 303-978-1457.
Vendor(s): University Microfilms International. *1899*

COMMUNICATIONS BUSINESS & FINANCE.
Business Research Publications, Inc., 1333 H St., N.W., Ste. 200-W., Washington, DC 20005. FAX 202-842-3023.
Vendor(s): Information Access Co.. *1899*

COMMUNICATIONS DAILY.
Warren Publishing, Inc., 2115 Ward Ct., N.W., Washington, DC 20037. TEL 202-872-9200. FAX 202-293-3435.
Vendor(s): Data-Star, Information Access Co., Knight-Ridder Information, Inc., Lexis-Nexis, NewsNet (TE01). *1958*

COMMUNICATIONS INTERNATIONAL.
E M A P Business & Computer Publications Ltd., 33-39 Bowling Green Ln., London EC1R 0DA, England. TEL 44-171-837-1212. FAX 44-171-278-4003.
Vendor(s): Information Access Co., Lexis-Nexis, University Microfilms International. *1899*

COMMUNICATIONS NEWS.
Nelson Publishing Co., 2504 N. Tamiami Trail, Nokomis, FL 34275. TEL 813-966-9521. FAX 813-966-2590.
Vendor(s): Information Access Co., Knight-Ridder Information, Inc.. *1900*

COMMUNICATIONS STANDARDS NEWS.
Omnicom P B I, Rosemount House, Rosemount Ave., W. Byfleet, Surrey KT14 6NP, England. TEL 44-1932-355515. FAX 44-1932-355962.
Vendor(s): Information Access Co.. *2067*

COMMUNICATIONSWEEK.
C M P Publications, Inc., 600 Community Dr., Manhasset, NY 11030. TEL 516-562-5000. FAX 516-562-5718.
Vendor(s): Information Access Co., NewsNet (TE23). *1900*

COMMUNICATIONSWEEK INTERNATIONAL.
C M P Publications, Inc., 600 Community Dr., Manhasset, NY 11030. TEL 516-562-5000. FAX 516-562-5474.
Vendor(s): Data-Star, Information Access Co., Knight-Ridder Information, Inc., Lexis-Nexis, NewsNet (TE28). *1900*

COMMUNITY AND WORKER RIGHT-TO-KNOW NEWS.
Thompson Publishing Company, 1725 K St., N.W., Ste. 700, Washington, DC 20006. TEL 202-872-4000.
Vendor(s): Information Access Co.. *5247*

COMMUNITY PHARMACIST.
E L F Publications, 5285 W. Louisiana Ave., Ste. 122, Lakewood, CO 80232-5976. TEL 303-975-0075. FAX 303-975-0132. *5405*

COMMUNITY PHARMACY.
Miller Freeman Publishers Ltd. Sovereign Way, Tonbridge, Kent TN9 1RW, England. TEL 44-1732-364422. FAX 44-1732-361534.
Vendor(s): Information Access Co.. *5405*

COMMUTER - REGIONAL AIRLINE NEWS.
Phillips Business Information, Inc., 1201 Seven Locks Rd., Potomac, MD 20854. TEL 301-424-3338. FAX 301-309-3487.
Vendor(s): Data-Star, Information Access Co., Knight-Ridder Information, Inc., NewsNet (AE25). *6754*

COMMUTER REGIONAL AIRLINE NEWS INTERNATIONAL.
Phillips Business Information, Inc., 120 Seven Locks Rd., Potomac, MD 20854. TEL 301-424-3338. FAX 301-309-3847.
Vendor(s): Information Access Co., NewsNet (AE26). *6754*

COMPANIES AND THEIR BRANDS.
Gale Research Inc., 835 Penobscot Bldg., Detroit, MI 48226. TEL 313-961-2242. FAX 313-961-6083.
Vendor(s): Knight-Ridder Information, Inc.. *1593*

COMPARATIVE DRAMA.
Western Michigan University, Department of English, Kalamazoo, MI 49008-3851. TEL 616-387-2576. FAX 616-387-8750.
Vendor(s): University Microfilms International. *4197*

COMPARATIVE ECONOMIC STUDIES.
Association for Comparative Economic Studies, c/o Susan J. Linz, Ed., Department of Economics, Michigan State University, E. Lansing, MI 48824-1038. TEL 517-353-7280. FAX 517-336-1068.
Vendor(s): University Microfilms International. *1249*

COMPARATIVE EDUCATION.
Carfax Publishing Co., P.O. Box 25, Abingdon, Oxon. OX14 3UE, England. TEL 44-1235-401000. FAX 44-1235-401550. *2321*

COMPARATIVE LITERATURE.
University of Oregon, Comparative Literature, 1223 Friendly Hall, Eugene, OR 97403-1233. TEL 503-346-4022. FAX 503-346-4030.
Vendor(s): University Microfilms International. *4198*

COMPENSATION AND BENEFITS REVIEW.
American Management Association, 135 W. 50th St., New York, NY 10020. TEL 212-903-8069. FAX 212-903-8168.
Vendor(s): Information Access Co., Knight-Ridder Information, Inc., University Microfilms International. *1368*

COMPENSATION & BENEFITS SOFTWARE CENSUS.
Advanced Personnel Systems, 801 Riverside Ave., Box 1438, Roseville, CA 95678. TEL 916-781-2900. FAX 916-781-2901.
Vendor(s): Human Resources Information Network. *1152*

COMPLEMENTARY MEDICINE INDEX.
British Library, Medical Information Centre, Boston Spa, Wetherby, W. Yorks. LS23 7BQ, England. TEL 44-1937-546039. FAX 44-1937-546458. *3693*

COMPLETE DIRECTORY OF LARGE PRINT BOOKS AND SERIALS.
R.R. Bowker, A Division of Reed Elsevier Inc., 121 Chanlon Rd., New Providence, NJ 07974. TEL 908-464-6800. FAX 908-655-3502. *3309*

COMPLEXITY INTERNATIONAL.
c/o School of Information Techonology, Charles Sturt University, Panorama Ave., Bathurst, N.S.W. 2795, Australia. TEL 61-63-384272. FAX 61-63-384649.
Available only online. *2054*

THE COMPOSITES AND ADHESIVES NEWSLETTER.
T - C Press Box 36006, Los Angeles, CA 90036-0006. TEL 213-938-6923. FAX 213-938-6923.
Vendor(s): Data-Star, Information Access Co., Knight-Ridder Information, Inc.. *5619*

COMPOSITES INDUSTRY MONTHLY.
Composite Market Reports, 1345 E. Mian St., Ste. 100, Mesa, AZ 85203-8950. TEL 602-461-9445. FAX 602-461-8177.
Vendor(s): Dow Jones News Retrieval, Information Access Co., Knight-Ridder Information, Inc., NewsNet. *2729*

COMPOSITES NEWS: INFRASTRUCTURE.
Composites News International, 991 Lomas Santa Fe Dr., C469, Solana Beach, CA 92075-7010. TEL 619-755-1372. FAX 619-755-5271.
Vendor(s): Information Access Co.. *6648*

COMPREHENSIVE PSYCHIATRY.
W.B. Saunders Co. Curtis Center, 3rd Fl., Independence Sq. W., Philadelphia, PA 19106-3399. TEL 215-238-7800. FAX 215-238-6445. *4832*

COMPUMATH CITATION INDEX.
Institute for Scientific Information, 3501 Market St., Philadelphia, PA 19104. TEL 215-386-0100. FAX 215-386-2991.
Vendor(s): Ovid Technologies, Inc.. *4405*

COMPUSERVE MAGAZINE.
CompuServe Inc., 5000 Arlington Centre Blvd., Columbus, OH 43220. TEL 614-457-8600. FAX 614-538-1004.
Vendor(s): CompuServe, Inc.. *2094*

COMPUTER AIDED DESIGN REPORT.
C A D - C A M Publishing, Inc., 1010 Turquoise St., Ste. 320, San Diego, CA 92109-1268. TEL 619-488-0533. FAX 619-488-6052.
Vendor(s): Information Access Co.. *2026*

COMPUTER-AIDED ENGINEERING (CLEVELAND).
Penton Publishing Co. 1100 Superior Ave., Cleveland, OH 44114-2543. TEL 216-696-7000. FAX 216-696-8765.
Vendor(s): Information Access Co., Knight-Ridder Information, Inc.. *2677*

COMPUTER & CONTROL ABSTRACTS.
INSPEC, I.E.E., Michael Faraday House, Six Hills Way, Stevenage, Herts. SG1 2AY, England. TEL 44-1438-313311. FAX 44-1438-742840.
Vendor(s): CEDOCAR, Data-Star, European Space Agency (File no.8/INSPEC), FIZ Technik, Knight-Ridder Information, Inc., Orbit Search Service, STN International. *2001*

COMPUTER AND INFORMATION SYSTEMS ABSTRACTS JOURNAL.
Cambridge Scientific Abstracts, 7200 Wisconsin Ave., 6th Fl., Bethesda, MD 20814. TEL 301-961-6750. FAX 301-961-6720.
Vendor(s): STN International. *2001*

COMPUTER AUDIT UPDATE.
Elsevier Science Ltd., P.O. Box 800, Kidlington, Oxford OX5 1DX, England. TEL 44-1865-843000. FAX 44-1865-843010.
Vendor(s): Information Access Co.. *2049*

COMPUTER BOOK REVIEW.
Computer Book Review, 735 Ekekela Place, Honolulu, HI 96817.
Vendor(s): Knight-Ridder Information, Inc.. *1984*

COMPUTER BUSINESS REVIEW.
A P T Data Services Ltd., 12 Sutton Row, London W1V 5FH, England. TEL 44-171-208-4200. FAX 44-171-439-1105.
Vendor(s): Information Access Co.. *2031*

COMPUTER COUNSEL.
Computer Counsel, Inc., Box 819, Avon, CT 06001-0819. TEL 312-207-6900. FAX 312-207-1045.
Vendor(s): West Services, Inc.. *1984*

COMPUTER DATABASE.
Information Access Company 362 Lakeside Dr., Foster City, CA 94404. TEL 415-378-5200. FAX 415-378-5369.
Available only online. Vendor(s): Ovid Technologies, Inc. (CMPT), Data-Star (CMPT), Knight-Ridder Information, Inc. (File no.275). *2001*

COMPUTER DEALER NEWS.
Plesman Publications Ltd., 2005 Sheppard Ave. E., 4th Fl., Willowdale, ON M2J 5B1, Canada. TEL 416-497-9562. FAX 416-497-9427.
Vendor(s): Information Access Co.. *2048*

COMPUTER DEALER NEWS SOURCE GUIDE.
Plesman Publications Ltd., 2005 Sheppard Ave. E., 4th Fl., Willowdale, ON M2J 5B1, Canada. TEL 416-497-9562. FAX 416-497-9427. *2033*

COMPUTER DESIGN.
PennWell Publishing Co. (Nashua), Advanced Technology Group, 10 Tara Blvd., 5th Fl., Nashua, NH 03062-2801. TEL 603-891-9111. FAX 603-891-0514.
Vendor(s): Knight-Ridder Information, Inc.. *2026*

COMPUTER FRAUD AND SECURITY.
Elsevier Science Ltd., P.O. Box 800, Kidlington, Oxford OX5 1DX, England. TEL 44-1865-843000. FAX 44-1865-843010.
Vendor(s): Data-Star, Information Access Co., Knight-Ridder Information, Inc.. *2049*

COMPUTER GAMING WORLD.
Ziff-Davis Publishing Co. (San Francisco), 135 Main St., San Francisco, CA 94105. TEL 415-357-4900. FAX 415-357-4977.
Vendor(s): Information Access Co.. *2023*

COMPUTER GRAPHICS WORLD.
PennWell Publishing Co. (Nashua), Advanced Technology Group, 10 Tara Blvd., 5th Fl., Nashua, NH 03062-2801. TEL 603-891-0123. FAX 603-891-0539.
Vendor(s): Information Access Co., Knight-Ridder Information, Inc.. *2026*

COMPUTER INDUSTRY DAILY.
Computer Economics, Inc., 5841 Edison Pl., Carlsbad, CA 92008. TEL 619-438-8100. FAX 619-431-1126. *2031*

COMPUTER INDUSTRY FORECASTS.
Data Analysis Group, 5100 Cherry Creek Rd., Box 128, Cloverdale, CA 95425. TEL 707-539-3009. FAX 707-486-5618.
Vendor(s): Lexis-Nexis. *2001*

COMPUTER INDUSTRY REPORT.
International Data Corporation, 77 Franklin St., Boston, MA 02110. TEL 617-482-8785. FAX 617-338-0164.
Vendor(s): Information Access Co.. *2072*

COMPUTER LAWYER.
Aspen Law & Business 270 Sylvan Ave., Englewood Cliffs, NJ 07632-2513. FAX 201-894-8666.
Vendor(s): Lexis-Nexis, West Services, Inc.. *1985*

COMPUTER PROTOCOLS.
Worldwide Videotex, Box 3273, Boynton Beach, FL 33424-3273. TEL 407-738-2276.
Vendor(s): Data-Star, Information Access Co., Knight-Ridder Information, Inc., NewsNet (EC74). *1985*

COMPUTER PUBLISHING & ADVERTISING REPORT.
SIMBA Information Inc. 11 Riverbend Dr. S., Box 4234, Stamford, CT 06907-0234. TEL 203-358-9900. FAX 203-358-5824.
Vendor(s): Information Access Co.. *6016*

COMPUTER RESELLER NEWS.
C M P Publications, Inc., 600 Community Dr., Manhasset, NY 11030. TEL 516-562-5000. FAX 516-733-6916.
Vendor(s): Information Access Co., NewsNet (EC07). *2048*

COMPUTER RETAIL WEEK.
C M P Publications, Inc., 600 Community Dr., Manhasset, NY 11030. TEL 516-562-5000. FAX 516-562-5464.
Vendor(s): Information Access Co.. *2048*

COMPUTER SECURITY JOURNAL.
Computer Security Institute (San Francisco), 600 Harrison St., San Francisco, CA 94107. TEL 415-905-2370. FAX 415-905-2234.
Vendor(s): University Microfilms International. *2050*

COMPUTER SHOPPER.
Coastal Associates Publishing, L.P., Computer Publications Division One Park Ave., New York, NY 10016. FAX 212-503-3999.
Vendor(s): Information Access Co.. *2048*

COMPUTER TECHNOLOGY REVIEW.
West World Productions, Inc., 924 Westwood Blvd., Ste. 650, Los Angeles, CA 90024. TEL 310-208-1335. FAX 310-208-1054.
Vendor(s): University Microfilms International. *1986*

COMPUTER USER'S SURVIVAL MAGAZINE.
Enterprises Publishing, 400 E. 59th St., Ste. 9F, New York, NY 10022. TEL 212-755-4363. FAX 212-755-4365. *2094*

COMPUTER WEEKLY.
Reed Business Publishing Group Quadrant House, The Quadrant, Sutton, Surrey SM2 5AS, England. TEL 44-181-661-8642. FAX 44-181-661-8979.
Vendor(s): Information Access Co.. *1986*

COMPUTER WORKSTATIONS.
Worldwide Videotex, Box 3273, Boynton Beach, FL 33424-3273. TEL 407-738-2276.
Vendor(s): Information Access Co.. *2077*

COMPUTERGRAM INTERNATIONAL.
A P T Data Group plc., 12 Sutton Row, 4th Fl., London W1V 5FH, England. TEL 44-171-208-4200. FAX 44-171-439-1105.
Vendor(s): Information Access Co., NewsNet (EC72). *1986*

COMPUTERS IN LIBRARIES.
Information Today, Inc., 143 Old Marlton Pike, Medford, NJ 08055-8750. TEL 609-654-6266. FAX 609-654-4309.
Vendor(s): Information Access Co., NewsNet, University Microfilms International. *2085*

COMPUTERWORLD.
Computerworld, Inc 551 Old Connecticut Path, Box 9171, Framingham, MA 01701-9171. TEL 508-879-0700. FAX 508-875-8931.
Vendor(s): Knight-Ridder Information, Inc. (File no.674), Lexis-Nexis. *1987*

COMPUTERWORLD HONG KONG.
I D G Communications (HK) Ltd., Mount Parker House, Ste. 1011-15, 1111 King's Rd., Quarry Bay, Hong Kong. TEL 852-2861-3238. FAX 852-2861-0953. *2031*

COMPUTING CANADA.
Plesman Publications Ltd., 2005 Sheppard Ave. E., 4th Fl., Willowdale, ON M2J 5B1, Canada. TEL 416-497-9562. FAX 416-497-9427.
Vendor(s): Information Access Co.. *2108*

COMPUTING RESEARCH NEWS.
Computing Research Association, 1875 Connecticut Ave., N.W., Ste. 718, Washington, DC 20009. TEL 202-234-2111. FAX 202-667-1066. *4043*

COMPUTING REVIEWS.
Association for Computing Machinery, 1515 Broadway, 17th Fl., New York, NY 10036-5701. TEL 212-869-7440. FAX 212-944-1318.
Vendor(s): Knight-Ridder Information, Inc.. *2002*

COMPUTING TIMES.
Triad Publications, Box 14018, Tulsa, OK 74159-1018. TEL 918-585-8564. *2085*

CONCRETE PRODUCTS.
Intertec Publishing Corp., 29 N. Wacker Dr., Chicago, IL 60606. TEL 312-726-2802. FAX 312-726-2574.
Vendor(s): Information Access Co.. *846*

CONFECTIONERY: THE INTERNATIONAL MARKET.
Euromonitor, 60-61 Britton St., London EC1M 5NA, England. TEL 44-171-251-8024. FAX 44-171-608-3149.
Vendor(s): Data-Star, Knight-Ridder Information, Inc.. *2999*

CONFERENCE PAPERS ANNUAL INDEX.
Cambridge Scientific Abstracts, 7200 Wisconsin Ave., 6th Fl., Bethesda, MD 20814. TEL 301-961-6750. FAX 301-961-6720.
Vendor(s): Knight-Ridder Information, Inc. (File no. 77), STN International (CONFSCI). *4938*

CONFERENCE PAPERS INDEX.
Cambridge Scientific Abstracts, 7200 Wisconsin Ave., 6th Fl., Bethesda, MD 20814. TEL 301-961-6750. FAX 301-961-6720.
Vendor(s): Knight-Ridder Information, Inc. (File no.77), STN International (CONFSCI). *4938*

CONFIGURATIONS.
Johns Hopkins University Press, Journals Publishing Division, 2715 Charles St., Baltimore, MD 21218-4319. TEL 410-516-6987. FAX 410-516-6968. *4198*

CONFLICT RESOLUTION NOTES.
Conflict Resolution Center International, Inc., 2205 E. Carson St., Pittsburgh, PA 15203-2107. TEL 412-481-5559. FAX 412-481-5559. *3763*

CONGRESS IN PRINT.
Congressional Quarterly Inc., 1414 22 St., N.W., Washington, DC 20037. FAX 202-728-1863. *5644*

CONGRESSIONAL ACTIVITIES.
Oliphant Washington Service, Box 9808, Friendship Sta., Washington, DC 20016. TEL 202-298-7226. FAX 202-333-5005.
Vendor(s): NewsNet (GT20). *5897*

CONGRESSIONAL MONITOR.
Congressional Quarterly Inc., 1414 22nd St., N.W., Washington, DC 20037. FAX 202-728-1863. *5644*

CONGRESSIONAL QUARTERLY SERVICE. WEEKLY REPORT.
Congressional Quarterly Inc., 1414 22nd St., N.W., Washington, DC 20037. FAX 202-728-1863.
Vendor(s): Information Access Co.. *5644*

CONGRESSIONAL RECORD SCANNER.
Congressional Quarterly Inc., 1414 22nd St., N.W., Washington, DC 20037. FAX 202-728-1863. *5720*

CONGRESSIONAL RESEARCH REPORT.
Penny Hill Press, 6440 Wiscasset Rd., Bethesda, MD 20816. TEL 301-229-8229. FAX 301-229-6988.
Vendor(s): Information Access Co.. *527*

CONNECTICUT BUSINESS DIRECTORY.
American Business Directories 5711 S. 86th Cir., Box 27347, Omaha, NE 68127 TEL 402-593-4600. FAX 402-331-5481. *1593*

CONNECTICUT LAW REVIEW.
Connecticut Law Review Association, 65 Elizabeth St., Hartford, CT 06105-2290. TEL 203-241-4607. FAX 203-241-7665.
Vendor(s): West Services, Inc.. *3763*

CONNECTION SCIENCE.
Carfax Publishing Co., P.O. Box 25, Abingdon, Oxon. OX14 3UE, England. TEL 44-1235-401000. FAX 44-1235-401550. *2006*

CONNECTIONS (LOS GATOS).
Mactivity, Inc., 20 N. Santa Cruz Ave., Los Gatos, CA 95030. TEL 408-354-2500. FAX 408-354-2571. *2036*

CONNECTIONS NEWSLETTER (MEMPHIS).
Southern States Communication Association, c/o Dr. Richard R. Ranta, Exec. Dir. College of Communication & Fine Arts University of Memphis, Memphis, TN 38152. TEL 901-678-2350. FAX 901-678-5118. *190*

CONSCIOUS CONSUMER.
New Consumer Institute, Inc., Box 51, Wauconda, IL 60084. TEL 708-526-0522. FAX 708-885-1878.
Available only online. *2145*

CONSERLINE.
U.S. Library of Congress, Serial Record Division, 101 Independence Ave., S.E., Washington, DC 20540-4160. TEL 202-707-5947. FAX 202-707-6333.
Available only online. *3987*

CONSOLIDATED FEDERAL FUNDS REPORT.
U.S. Bureau of the Census, Customer Services, Washington, DC 20233. TEL 301-457-4100. FAX 301-457-4714.
Vendor(s): CompuServe, Inc. Knight-Ridder Information, Inc.. *5898*

CONSTITUTIONAL COMMENTARY.
Constitutional Commentary Inc., 229 19th Ave. S., Minneapolis, MN 55455. TEL 612-625-4819. FAX 612-625-2011.
Vendor(s): West Services, Inc.. *5726*

CONSTRUCTION BULLETIN (ATLANTA).
Construction Market Data, Inc., Attn Dorothy A. De Gennaro, 4126 Pleasantdale Rd., Ste. A8, Atlanta, GA 30340. FAX 770-613-5578. *847*

CONSTRUCTION CLAIMS CITATOR.
Select Press, Construction Industry Press, Box 9838, San Rafael, CA 94912 TEL 415-924-1612.
Vendor(s): NewsNet (BC12). *847*

CONSTRUCTION CLAIMS MONTHLY.
Business Publishers, Inc., 951 Pershing Dr., Silver Spring, MD 20910-4464. TEL 301-587-6300. FAX 301-585-9075.
Vendor(s): NewsNet. *847*

CONSTRUCTION CLAIMS TRAINING GUIDE.
Business Publishers, Inc., 951 Pershing Dr., Silver Spring, MD 20910-4464. TEL 301-587-6300. FAX 301-585-9075.
Vendor(s): NewsNet. *847*

CONSTRUCTION EQUIPMENT.
Cahners Publishing Company (Des Plaines), Division of Reed Elsevier Inc., 1350 E. Touhy Ave., Box 5080, Des Plaines, IL 60018-5080. TEL 847-635-8800. FAX 847-390-2690. *548*

Online

CONSTRUCTION INJURY LIABILITY MONTHLY.
Business Publishers, Inc., 951 Pershing Dr., Silver Spring, MD 20910-4464. TEL 301-587-6300. FAX 301-587-1081.
Vendor(s): NewsNet. *3764*

CONSTRUCTION LABOR REPORT.
The Bureau of National Affairs, Inc., 1231 25th St., N.W., Washington, DC 20037. TEL 202-452-4200. FAX 202-822-8092.
Vendor(s): Human Resources Information Network (File DD). *1368*

CONSTRUCTION MANAGEMENT AND ECONOMICS.
Chapman & Hall, Journals Department 2-6 Boundary Row, London SE1 8HN, England. TEL 44-171-8650066. FAX 44-171-5229623. *849*

CONSTRUCTION REVIEW.
U.S. International Trade Administration, Basic Industries Division, Department of Commerce, Herbert C. Hoover Bldg., ITA Rm. H4039, 14th St. and Constitution Ave., Washington, DC 20230. TEL 202-482-0132. FAX 202-482-0382.
Vendor(s): Information Access Co., Knight-Ridder Information, Inc., University Microfilms International. *882*

CONSULTANTS AND CONSULTING ORGANIZATIONS DIRECTORY.
Gale Research Inc., 835 Penobscot Bldg., Detroit, MI 48226. TEL 313-961-2242. FAX 313-961-6083.
Vendor(s): Human Resources Information Network (CCOD). *1411*

CONSULTANTS NEWS.
Kennedy Publications, Templeton Rd., Fitzwilliam, NH 03447. TEL 603-585-6544. FAX 603-585-9555.
Vendor(s): University Microfilms International. *1411*

CONSUMER CATERING: THE INTERNATIONAL MARKET.
Euromonitor, 60-61 Britton St., London EC1M 5NA, England. TEL 44-171-251-8024. FAX 44-171-608-3149.
Vendor(s): Data-Star, Knight-Ridder Information, Inc.. *2964*

CONSUMER INFORMATION APPLIANCE.
Jupiter Communications, 627 Broadway, New York, NY 10012. TEL 212-780-6060. FAX 212-780-6075.
Vendor(s): Information Access Co., NewsNet. *1944*

CONSUMER INFORMATION CATALOG.
U.S. General Services Administration, Consumer Information Center, 18th and F Sts., N.W., Rm. G-142, Washington, DC 20405. TEL 202-501-1794. FAX 202-501-4281. *528*

CONSUMER POLICY REVIEW.
Which? Ltd., 2 Marylebone Rd., London NW1 4DF, England. TEL 44-171-830-6000. FAX 44-171-830-6220.
Vendor(s): University Microfilms International. *2150*

CONSUMER REPORTS.
Consumers Union of the United States, Inc., 101 Truman Ave., Yonkers, NY 10703-1057. TEL 914-378-2000. FAX 914-378-2900.
Vendor(s): Information Access Co., Knight-Ridder Information, Inc. (File no.646), Lexis-Nexis. *2150*

CONSUMER REPORTS ON HEALTH.
Consumers Union of the United States, Inc., 101 Truman Ave., Yonkers, NY 10703-1057. TEL 914-378-2000. FAX 914-378-2906.
Vendor(s): Information Access Co., Knight-Ridder Information, Inc. (File no.646). *5526*

CONSUMER REPORTS TRAVEL LETTER.
Consumers Union of the United States, Inc., 101 Truman Ave., Yonkers, NY 10703-1057. TEL 914-378-2000. FAX 914-378-2906.
Vendor(s): Information Access Co., Knight-Ridder Information, Inc. (File no.646). *6875*

CONSUMERS DIGEST.
Consumers Digest, Inc., 5705 N. Lincoln Ave., Chicago, IL 60659. TEL 312-275-3590. FAX 312-275-7273.
Vendor(s): Information Access Co.. *2150*

CONSUMERS INDEX.
Pierian Press, Box 1808, Ann Arbor, MI 48106. TEL 313-434-5530. FAX 313-434-6409.
Vendor(s): OCLC. *2156*

CONSUMER'S RESEARCH MAGAZINE.
Consumers' Research, Inc., 800 Maryland Ave., N.E., Washington, DC 20002. TEL 202-546-1713. FAX 202-546-1638.
Vendor(s): Information Access Co., University Microfilms International. *2151*

CONTEMPORARY DRUG PROBLEMS.
Federal Legal Publications, Inc., 157 Chambers St., New York, NY 10007. TEL 212-619-4949.
Vendor(s): Information Access Co.. *2195*

CONTEMPORARY ECONOMIC POLICY.
Western Economic Association International, 7400 Center Ave., Ste. 109, Huntington Beach, CA 92647-3039. TEL 714-898-3222.
Vendor(s): Information Access Co.. *911*

CONTEMPORARY LITERATURE.
University of Wisconsin Press, Journal Division, 114 N. Murray St., Madison, WI 53715. TEL 608-262-4952. FAX 608-262-7560.
Vendor(s): Information Access Co., University Microfilms International. *4199*

CONTEMPORARY MUSICIANS.
Gale Research Inc., 835 Penobscot Bldg., Detroit, MI 48226. TEL 313-961-2242. FAX 313-961-6083.
Vendor(s): Lexis-Nexis. *5151*

THE CONTEMPORARY REVIEW.
Contemporary Review Co. Ltd., Cheam Business Centre, 14 Upper Mulgrave Rd., Cheam, Surrey SM2 7AZ, England. TEL 44-181-643-4846. FAX 44-181-241-7507.
Vendor(s): Information Access Co.. *4138*

CONTEMPORARY SOCIOLOGY.
American Sociological Association, 1722 N St., N.W., Washington, DC 20036. TEL 202-833-3410. FAX 202-785-0146.
Vendor(s): University Microfilms International. *6441*

CONTENTSDIRECT.
Elsevier Science Ltd., P.O. Box 800, Kidlington, Oxford OX2 5DK, England. TEL 44-1865-843000. FAX 44-1865-843010.
Available only online. *6300*

CONTRACEPTIVE TECHNOLOGY UPDATE.
American Health Consultants, 3525 Piedmont Rd., N.E., Bldg. 6, Ste. 400, Atlanta, GA 30305. TEL 404-262-7436. FAX 800-284-3291.
Vendor(s): Lexis-Nexis. *826*

CONTRACTING BUSINESS.
Penton Publishing Co. 1100 Superior Ave., Cleveland, OH 44114-2543. TEL 216-696-7000. FAX 216-696-7932.
Vendor(s): Information Access Co.. *3326*

THE CONTRARIAN'S VIEW.
132 Moreland St., Worcester, MA 01609. TEL 508-757-2881. *1326*

CONTROL AND INSTRUMENTATION.
Miller Freeman Technical Ltd. Miller Freeman House, 30 Calderwood St., London SE18 6QH, England. TEL 44-181-855-7777. FAX 44-181-316-3422.
Vendor(s): Information Access Co.. *2014*

CONTROLLER'S COST REPORT.
Warren, Gorham & Lamont, One Penn Plaza, New York, NY 10119. TEL 212-971-5000. FAX 212-971-5113.
Vendor(s): Information Access Co.. *911*

CONTROLLERS UPDATE.
Institute of Management Accountants, 10 Paragon Dr., Montvale, NJ 07645-1760. TEL 201-573-9000. FAX 201-573-8185.
Vendor(s): University Microfilms International. *1045*

CONVENIENCE STORE NEWS.
Macfadden Publishing, Macfadden Trade Publications, 233 Park Ave. S., 6th Fl., New York, NY 10003. TEL 212-780-2300. FAX 212-228-3142.
Vendor(s): Information Access Co.. *3003*

CONVERGENCE: INTERNATIONAL CONGRESS ON TRANSPORTATION ELECTRONICS. PROCEEDINGS.
Society of Automotive Engineers, 400 Commonwealth Dr., Warrendale, PA 15096-0001. TEL 412-776-4841. FAX 412-776-3036.
Vendor(s): European Space Agency, FIZ Technik, Orbit Search Service. *6782*

COOK POLITICAL REPORT.
Cook and Company, 900 Second St., N.E., Ste. 107, Washington, DC 20002. TEL 202-289-1625. FAX 202-289-0454. *5645*

COOK'S INDEX.
John Gordon Burke Publisher, Inc., Box 1492, Evanston, IL 60204-1492. TEL 847-866-8625. FAX 847-866-6639. *3528*

CO-OPSERVATIONS.
Co-operative Housing Federation of Canada, 225 Metcalfe St., Ste. 311, Ottawa, ON K2P 1P9, Canada. TEL 613-230-2201. FAX 613-230-2231. *3580*

COPY IMAGING AND REPRODUCTION.
P T N Publishing Corp., 445 Broad Hollow Rd., Ste. 21, Melville, NY 11747-4722. FAX 516-249-5774. *5809*

CORDELL CONSTRUCTION REPORTS.
Cordell Building Information Services P.O. Box 124, St. Leonards, N.S.W. 2065, Australia. TEL 61-2-934-5555. *850*

THE CORNELL HOTEL & RESTAURANT ADMINISTRATION QUARTERLY.
Elsevier Science Inc., Box 945, New York, NY 10159-0945. TEL 212-633-3730. FAX 212-633-3680.
Vendor(s): Information Access Co., University Microfilms International. *3560*

CORNELL INTERNATIONAL LAW JOURNAL.
Cornell University, Cornell Law School, Myron Taylor Hall, Ithaca, NY 14853. TEL 607-255-9666. FAX 607-255-7193.
Vendor(s): West Services, Inc.. *3927*

CORNELL JOURNAL OF LAW AND PUBLIC POLICY.
Cornell University, Cornell Law School, Myron Taylor Hall, Ithaca, NY 14853. TEL 607-255-0526. FAX 607-255-7193.
Vendor(s): West Services, Inc.. *3765*

CORNELL LAW REVIEW.
Cornell University, Cornell Law School, Myron Taylor Hall, Ithaca, NY 14853. TEL 607-255-3387. FAX 607-255-7193.
Vendor(s): Lexis-Nexis, West Services, Inc.. *3765*

CORNELL MAGAZINE.
Cornell Alumni Federation, 55 Brown Rd., Ithaca, NY 14850. FAX 607-257-1782. *1864*

CORNELL SCIENCE & TECHNOLOGY MAGAZINE.
C U M E, Inc, Cornell University, 217 Carpenter Hall, Ithaca, NY 14853. TEL 607-255-3312. FAX 607-255-9606. *2593*

CORPORATE BOARD.
Vanguard Publications, Inc., 6604 W. Saginaw Hwy., Lansing, MI 48917. TEL 517-321-0667.
Vendor(s): Information Access Co.. *1412*

CORPORATE CASHFLOW.
Intertec Publishing Corp. (Atlanta), 6151 Powers Ferry Rd., N.W., Atlanta, GA 30339-2941. TEL 770-955-2500. FAX 770-955-0400.
Vendor(s): Information Access Co., University Microfilms International. *1078*

CORPORATE DETROIT MAGAZINE.
Corporate Detroit, Inc., 3031 W. Grand Blvd., Ste. 624, Detroit, MI 48202-3019. TEL 313-872-6000. FAX 313-872-6009.
Vendor(s): Knight-Ridder Information, Inc., University Microfilms International. *911*

CORPORATE E F T REPORT.
Phillips Business Information, Inc., 1201 Seven Locks Rd., Potomac, MD 20854. TEL 301-424-3338. FAX 301-424-4297.
Vendor(s): Information Access Co., Knight-Ridder Information, Inc., Lexis-Nexis, NewsNet (FI12). *1078*

CORPORATE GIVING WATCH.
Taft Group 835 Penobscot Bldg., Detroit, MI 48226. TEL 313-961-2242. FAX 313-961-6083. Vendor(s): NewsNet (GB49). *6368*

CORPORATE GROWTH REPORT.
Quality Services Company, 5290 Overpass Rd., Ste. 126, Santa Barbara, CA 93111-9950. TEL 805-964-7841. FAX 805-964-1073. Vendor(s): University Microfilms International. *1326*

CORPORATE JOBS OUTLOOK!
Plunkett Research, Ltd., P.O. Box 8270, Galveston, TX 77553-8270. TEL 409-765-8530. FAX 409-765-8571. Vendor(s): Human Resources Information Network. *5265*

CORPORATE LEGAL TIMES.
Giant Steps Media, 3 E. Huron, Chicago, IL 60611. TEL 312-654-3500. FAX 312-654-3525. Vendor(s): Lexis-Nexis. *3899*

CORPORATE LOCATION.
Euromoney Publications plc., Nestor House, Playhouse Yard, London EC4 5EX, England. TEL 44-171-779-8368. FAX 44-171-779-8369. Vendor(s): University Microfilms International. *1304*

CORPORATE MONEY.
Centaur Communications Ltd., St. Giles House, 50 Poland St., London W1V 4AX, England. TEL 44-171-287-9800. FAX 44-171-439-1480. Vendor(s): Information Access Co.. *1079*

CORPORATE REPORT MINNESOTA.
City Media, Inc., 821 Marquette Ave., Ste. 2000, Minneapolis, MN 55402-2000. TEL 612-359-2100. FAX 612-359-2110. Vendor(s): CompuServe, Inc., Data-Star, Dow Jones News Retrieval, Information Access Co., Knight-Ridder Information, Inc., Lexis-Nexis, University Microfilms International. *1412*

CORPORATE REPORT VENTURES.
City Media Inc., 821 Marquette Ave., Ste. 2000, Minneapolis, MN 55402-2922. TEL 612-338-4288. FAX 612-373-0195. Vendor(s): University Microfilms International. *1574*

CORPORATE REPORT WISCONSIN.
Brady Co., Inc., N80 W12878 Fond du Lac Ave., Box 878, Menomonee Falls, WI 53052-0878. TEL 414-255-9077. FAX 414-255-3388. Vendor(s): University Microfilms International. *911*

CORPORATE SECURITY.
Business Research Publications, Inc., 65 Bleecker St., 5th Fl., New York, NY 10012-2450. TEL 212-673-4700. FAX 212-475-1790. Vendor(s): Information Access Co.. *2182*

CORPORATE VENTURING QUARTERLY.
Venture Economics, Inc., 40 W. 57th St., Ste. 802, New York, NY 10019. Vendor(s): Data-Star, Knight-Ridder Information, Inc.. *1326*

THE CORPS REPORT.
Pasha Publications Inc., 1616 N. Ft. Myer Dr., Ste. 1000, Arlington, VA 22209-3107. TEL 703-528-1244. FAX 703-528-1253. Vendor(s): Information Access Co.. *5026*

CORPTECH DIRECTORY OF TECHNOLOGY COMPANIES.
Corporate Technology Information Services Inc., 12 Alfred St., Ste. 200, Woburn, MA 01801. TEL 617-932-3939. FAX 617-932-6335. Vendor(s): Orbit Search Service (CORP). *1594*

CORRECTIONS TODAY.
American Correctional Association, 4380 Forbes Blvd., Lanham, MD 20706-4322. TEL 301-918-1800. Vendor(s): Information Access Co., University Microfilms International. *2161*

COSMETIC INSIDER'S REPORT.
Advanstar Communications, Inc., 7500 Old Oak Blvd., Cleveland, OH 44130. TEL 216-826-2839. FAX 216-891-2726. Vendor(s): Data-Star, Information Access Co., Knight-Ridder Information, Inc.. *495*

COSMETIC WORLD NEWS.
World News Publications, 130 Wigmore St., London W1H OAT, England. FAX 44-171-487-5436. Vendor(s): Information Access Co.. *495*

COSMETICS AND TOILETRIES.
Allured Publishing, 362 S. Schmale Rd., Carol Stream, IL 60188-2787. TEL 708-653-2155. FAX 708-653-2192. Vendor(s): Information Access Co.. *495*

COSMETICS INTERNATIONAL.
Cosmetics Communications Ltd., 335 Linen Hall, 162-168 Regent St., London W1R 5TB, England. TEL 44-171-434-1530. FAX 44-171-437-0915. Vendor(s): Information Access Co., Lexis-Nexis. *495*

COSMOPOLITAN.
Hearst Corporation, Cosmopolitan, 224 W. 57th St., New York, NY 10019. TEL 212-649-2000. FAX 212-956-3263. Vendor(s): Information Access Co.. *6990*

COST ENGINEERING (MORGANTOWN).
A A C E International, 209 Prairie Ave., Ste. 100, Morgantown, WV 25505. TEL 304-296-8444. FAX 304-291-5728. Vendor(s): University Microfilms International. *2594*

COST MANAGEMENT UPDATE.
Institute of Management Accountants, 10 Paragon Dr., Montvale, NJ 07645-1760. TEL 201-573-9000. Vendor(s): University Microfilms International. *1540*

COTTON. PART 1: BI-MONTHLY REVIEW OF THE WORLD SITUATION.
International Cotton Advisory Committee, 1629 K St. N.W., Ste. 702, Washington, DC 20006. TEL 202-463-6660. FAX 202-463-6950. Vendor(s): Information Access Co.. *6675*

COTTON AND TROPICAL FIBRES.
CAB International, Wallingford, Oxon. OX10 8DE, England. TEL 44-1491-832111. FAX 44-1491-833508. Vendor(s): DIMDI, European Space Agency (File nos.16 & 124/CAB', Knight-Ridder Information, Inc.. *171*

COUGH AND COLD REMEDIES: THE INTERNATIONAL MARKET.
Euromonitor, 60-61 Britton St., London EC1M 5NA, England. TEL 44-171-251-8024. FAX 44-171-608-3149. Vendor(s): Data-Star, Knight-Ridder Information, Inc.. *5406*

COUNTRY FORECAST. ALGERIA.
Economist Intelligence Unit, 111 W. 57th St., New York, NY 10019. TEL 212-554-0600. FAX 212-586-1182. Vendor(s): Information Access Co., Knight-Ridder Information, Inc., Lexis-Nexis. *5645*

COUNTRY FORECAST. ARGENTINA.
Economist Intelligence Unit, 111 W. 57th St., New York, NY 10019. TEL 212-554-0600. FAX 212-586-1182. Vendor(s): Information Access Co., Knight-Ridder Information, Inc., Lexis-Nexis. *5645*

COUNTRY FORECAST. ASIA - PACIFIC.
Economist Intelligence Unit, 111 W. 57th St., New York, NY 10019. TEL 212-554-0600. FAX 212-586-1182. Vendor(s): Information Access Co., Knight-Ridder Information, Inc., Lexis-Nexis. *5646*

COUNTRY FORECAST. AUSTRALIA.
Economist Intelligence Unit, 111 W. 57th St., New York, NY 10019. TEL 212-554-0600. FAX 212-586-1182. Vendor(s): Information Access Co., Knight-Ridder Information, Inc., Lexis-Nexis. *5646*

COUNTRY FORECAST. AUSTRIA.
Economist Intelligence Unit, 111 W. 57th St., New York, NY 10019. TEL 212-554-0600. FAX 212-586-1182. Vendor(s): Information Access Co., Knight-Ridder Information, Inc., Lexis-Nexis. *5646*

COUNTRY FORECAST. BELGIUM.
Economist Intelligence Unit, 111 W. 57th St., New York, NY 10019. TEL 212-554-0600. FAX 212-586-1182. Vendor(s): Information Access Co., Knight-Ridder Information, Inc., Lexis-Nexis. *5646*

COUNTRY FORECAST. BRAZIL.
Economist Intelligence Unit, 111 W. 57th St., New York, NY 10019. TEL 212-554-0600. FAX 212-586-1182. Vendor(s): Information Access Co., Knight-Ridder Information, Inc., Lexis-Nexis. *5646*

COUNTRY FORECAST. BULGARIA.
Economist Intelligence Unit, 111 W. 57th St., New York, NY 10019. TEL 212-554-0600. FAX 212-586-1182. Vendor(s): Information Access Co., Knight-Ridder Information, Inc., Lexis-Nexis. *5646*

COUNTRY FORECAST. CANADA.
Economist Intelligence Unit, 111 W. 57th St., New York, NY 10019. TEL 212-554-0600. FAX 212-586-1182. Vendor(s): Information Access Co., Knight-Ridder Information, Inc., Lexis-Nexis. *5646*

COUNTRY FORECAST. CHILE.
Economist Intelligence Unit, 111 W. 57th St., New York, NY 10019. TEL 212-554-0600. FAX 212-586-1182. Vendor(s): Information Access Co., Knight-Ridder Information, Inc., Lexis-Nexis. *5546*

COUNTRY FORECAST. CHINA.
Economist Intelligence Unit, 111 W. 57th St., New York, NY 10019. TEL 212-554-0600. FAX 212-586-1182. Vendor(s): Information Access Co., Knight-Ridder Information, Inc., Lexis-Nexis. *5646*

COUNTRY FORECAST. COLOMBIA.
Economist Intelligence Unit, 111 W. 57th St., New York NY 10019. TEL 212-554-0600. FAX 212-586-1182. Vendor(s): Information Access Co., Knight-Ridder Information, Inc., Lexis-Nexis. *5646*

COUNTRY FORECAST. CZECH REPUBLIC.
Economist Intelligence Unit, 111 W. 57th St., New York, NY 10019. TEL 212-554-0600. FAX 212-586-1182. Vendor(s): Information Access Co., Knight-Ridder Information, Inc., Lexis-Nexis. *5646*

COUNTRY FORECAST. DENMARK.
Economist Intelligence Unit, 111 W. 57th St., New York, NY 10019. TEL 212-554-0600. FAX 212-586-1182. Vendor(s): Information Access Co., Knight-Ridder Information, Inc., Lexis-Nexis. *5646*

COUNTRY FORECAST. EASTERN EUROPE AND THE FORMER SOVIET UNION.
Economist Intelligence Unit 111 W. 57th St., New York, NY 10019. TEL 212-554-0600. FAX 212-486-1182. Vendor(s): Information Access Co., Knight-Ridder Information, Inc., Lexis-Nexis. *5646*

COUNTRY FORECAST. ECUADOR.
Economist Intelligence Unit 111 W. 57th St., New York, NY 10019. TEL 212-554-0600. FAX 212-586-1182. Vendor(s): Information Access Co. Knight-Ridder Information, Inc., Lexis-Nexis. *5646*

COUNTRY FORECAST. EGYPT.
Economist Intelligence Unit, 111 W. 57th St., New York, NY 10019. TEL 212-554-0300. FAX 212-586-1182. Vendor(s): Information Access Co., Knight-Ridder Information, Inc., Lexis-Nexis. *5646*

COUNTRY FORECAST. EUROPE.
Economist Intelligence Unit, 111 W. 57th St., New York, NY 10019. TEL 212-554-0600. FAX 212-586-1182. Vendor(s): Information Access Co., Knight-Ridder Information, Inc., Lexis-Nexis. *5647*

COUNTRY FORECAST. FINLAND.
Economist Intelligence Unit 111 W. 57th St., New York, NY 10019. TEL 212-554-0600. FAX 212-586-1182. Vendor(s): Information Access Co., Knight-Ridder Information, Inc., Lexis-Nexis. *5647*

COUNTRY FORECAST. FRANCE.
Economist Intelligence Unit, 111 W. 57th St., New York, NY 10019. TEL 212-554-0600. FAX 212-586-1182.
Vendor(s): Information Access Co., Knight-Ridder Information, Inc., Lexis-Nexis. *5647*

COUNTRY FORECAST. GERMANY.
Economist Intelligence Unit, 111 W. 57th St., New York, NY 10019. TEL 212-554-0600. FAX 212-586-1182.
Vendor(s): Information Access Co., Knight-Ridder Information, Inc., Lexis-Nexis. *5647*

COUNTRY FORECAST. GLOBAL OUTLOOK.
Economist Intelligence Unit, 111 W. 57th St., New York, NY 10019. TEL 212-554-0600. FAX 212-586-1182.
Vendor(s): Information Access Co., Knight-Ridder Information, Inc., Lexis-Nexis. *5647*

COUNTRY FORECAST. GREECE.
Economist Intelligence Unit, 111 W. 57th St., New York, NY 10019. TEL 212-554-0600. FAX 212-586-1182.
Vendor(s): Information Access Co., Knight-Ridder Information, Inc., Lexis-Nexis. *5647*

COUNTRY FORECAST. HONG KONG.
Economist Intelligence Unit, 111 W. 57th St., New York, NY 10019. TEL 212-554-0600. FAX 212-586-1182.
Vendor(s): Information Access Co., Knight-Ridder Information, Inc., Lexis-Nexis. *5647*

COUNTRY FORECAST. HUNGARY.
Economist Intelligence Unit, 111 W. 57th St., New York, NY 10019. TEL 212-554-0600. FAX 212-586-1182.
Vendor(s): Information Access Co., Knight-Ridder Information, Inc., Lexis-Nexis. *5647*

COUNTRY FORECAST. INDIA.
Economist Intelligence Unit, 111 W. 57th St., New York, NY 10019. TEL 212-554-0600. FAX 212-586-1182.
Vendor(s): Information Access Co., Knight-Ridder Information, Inc., Lexis-Nexis. *5647*

COUNTRY FORECAST. INDONESIA.
Economist Intelligence Unit, 111 W. 57th St., New York, NY 10019. TEL 212-554-0600. FAX 212-586-1182.
Vendor(s): Information Access Co., Knight-Ridder Information, Inc., Lexis-Nexis. *5647*

COUNTRY FORECAST. IRAN.
Economist Intelligence Unit, 111 W. 57th St., New York, NY 10019. TEL 212-554-0600. FAX 212-486-1182.
Vendor(s): Information Access Co., Knight-Ridder Information, Inc., Lexis-Nexis. *5647*

COUNTRY FORECAST. IRAQ.
Economist Intelligence Unit, 111 W. 57th St., New York, NY 10019. TEL 212-554-0600. FAX 212-586-1182.
Vendor(s): Information Access Co., Knight-Ridder Information, Inc., Lexis-Nexis. *5647*

COUNTRY FORECAST. IRELAND.
Economist Intelligence Unit, 111 W. 57th St., New York, NY 10019. TEL 212-554-0600. FAX 212-586-1182.
Vendor(s): Information Access Co., Knight-Ridder Information, Inc., Lexis-Nexis. *5647*

COUNTRY FORECAST. ISRAEL.
Economist Intelligence Unit, 111 W. 57th St., New York, NY 10019. TEL 212-554-0600. FAX 212-586-1182.
Vendor(s): Information Access Co., Knight-Ridder Information, Inc., Lexis-Nexis. *5647*

COUNTRY FORECAST. ITALY.
Economist Intelligence Unit, 111 W. 57th St., New York, NY 10019. TEL 212-554-0600. FAX 212-586-1182.
Vendor(s): Information Access Co., Knight-Ridder Information, Inc., Lexis-Nexis. *5647*

COUNTRY FORECAST. JAPAN.
Economist Intelligence Unit, 111 W. 57th St., New York, NY 10019. TEL 212-554-0600. FAX 212-586-1182.
Vendor(s): Information Access Co., Knight-Ridder Information, Inc., Lexis-Nexis. *5647*

COUNTRY FORECAST. LATIN AMERICA.
Economist Intelligence Unit, 111 W. 57th St., New York, NY 10019. TEL 212-554-0600. FAX 212-586-1182.
Vendor(s): Information Access Co., Knight-Ridder Information, Inc., Lexis-Nexis. *5648*

COUNTRY FORECAST. MALAYSIA.
Economist Intelligence Unit, 111 W. 57th St., New York, NY 10019. TEL 212-554-0600. FAX 212-586-1182.
Vendor(s): Information Access Co., Knight-Ridder Information, Inc., Lexis-Nexis. *5648*

COUNTRY FORECAST. MEXICO.
Economist Intelligence Unit, 111 W. 57th St., New York, NY 10019. TEL 212-554-0600. FAX 212-586-1182.
Vendor(s): Information Access Co., Knight-Ridder Information, Inc., Lexis-Nexis. *5648*

COUNTRY FORECAST. MIDDLE EAST AND NORTH AFRICA.
Economist Intelligence Unit, 111 W. 57th St., New York, NY 10019. TEL 212-554-0600. FAX 212-586-1182.
Vendor(s): Information Access Co., Knight-Ridder Information, Inc., Lexis-Nexis. *5648*

COUNTRY FORECAST. NETHERLANDS.
Economist Intelligence Unit, 111 W. 57th St., New York, NY 10019. TEL 212-544-0600. FAX 212-586-1182.
Vendor(s): Information Access Co., Knight-Ridder Information, Inc., Lexis-Nexis. *5648*

COUNTRY FORECAST. NEW ZEALAND.
Economist Intelligence Unit, 111 W. 57th St., New York, NY 10019. TEL 212-554-0600. FAX 212-586-1182.
Vendor(s): Information Access Co., Knight-Ridder Information, Inc., Lexis-Nexis. *5648*

COUNTRY FORECAST. NIGERIA.
Economist Intelligence Unit, 111 W. 57th St., New York, NY 10019. TEL 212-554-0600. FAX 212-586-1182.
Vendor(s): Information Access Co., Knight-Ridder Information, Inc., Lexis-Nexis. *5648*

COUNTRY FORECAST. NORWAY.
Economist Intelligence Unit, 111 W. 57th St., New York, NY 10019. TEL 212-544-0600. FAX 212-586-1182.
Vendor(s): Information Access Co., Knight-Ridder Information, Inc., Lexis-Nexis. *5648*

COUNTRY FORECAST. PAKISTAN.
Economist Intelligence Unit, 111 W. 57th St., New York, NY 10019. TEL 212-554-0600. FAX 212-586-1182.
Vendor(s): Information Access Co., Knight-Ridder Information, Inc., Lexis-Nexis. *5648*

COUNTRY FORECAST. PERU.
Economist Intelligence Unit, 111 W. 57th St., New York, NY 10019. TEL 212-554-0600. FAX 212-586-1182.
Vendor(s): Information Access Co., Knight-Ridder Information, Inc., Lexis-Nexis. *5648*

COUNTRY FORECAST. PHILIPPINES.
Economist Intelligence Unit, 111 W. 57th St., New York, NY 10019. TEL 212-554-0600. FAX 212-586-1182.
Vendor(s): Information Access Co., Knight-Ridder Information, Inc., Lexis-Nexis. *5648*

COUNTRY FORECAST. POLAND.
Economist Intelligence Unit, 111 W. 57th St., New York, NY 10019. TEL 212-554-0600. FAX 212-586-1182.
Vendor(s): Information Access Co., Knight-Ridder Information, Inc., Lexis-Nexis. *5648*

COUNTRY FORECAST. PORTUGAL.
Economist Intelligence Unit, 111 W. 57th St., New York, NY 10019. TEL 212-554-0600. FAX 212-586-1182.
Vendor(s): Information Access Co., Knight-Ridder Information, Inc., Lexis-Nexis. *5648*

COUNTRY FORECAST. ROMANIA.
Economist Intelligence Unit, 111 W. 57th St., New York, NY 10019. TEL 212-554-0600. FAX 212-586-1182.
Vendor(s): Information Access Co., Knight-Ridder Information, Inc., Lexis-Nexis. *5648*

COUNTRY FORECAST. RUSSIA.
Economist Intelligence Unit, 111 W. 57th St., New York, NY 10019. TEL 212-554-0600. FAX 212-586-1182.
Vendor(s): Information Access Co., Knight-Ridder Information, Inc., Lexis-Nexis. *5648*

COUNTRY FORECAST. SAUDI ARABIA.
Economist Intelligence Unit, 111 W. 57th St., New York, NY 10019. TEL 212-554-0600. FAX 212-586-1182.
Vendor(s): Information Access Co., Knight-Ridder Information, Inc., Lexis-Nexis. *5649*

COUNTRY FORECAST. SINGAPORE.
Economist Intelligence Unit, 111 W. 57th St., New York, NY 10019. TEL 212-554-0600. FAX 212-586-1182.
Vendor(s): Information Access Co., Knight-Ridder Information, Inc., Lexis-Nexis. *5649*

COUNTRY FORECAST. SLOVAKIA.
Economist Intelligence Unit, 111 W. 57th St., New York, NY 10019. TEL 212-554-0600. FAX 212-586-1182.
Vendor(s): Information Access Co., Knight-Ridder Information, Inc., Lexis-Nexis. *5649*

COUNTRY FORECAST. SOUTH AFRICA.
Economist Intelligence Unit, 111 W. 57th St., New York, NY 10019. TEL 212-554-0600. FAX 212-586-1182.
Vendor(s): Information Access Co., Knight-Ridder Information, Inc., Lexis-Nexis. *5649*

COUNTRY FORECAST. SOUTH KOREA.
Economist Intelligence Unit, 111 W. 57th St., New York, NY 10019. TEL 212-554-0600. FAX 212-586-1182.
Vendor(s): Information Access Co., Knight-Ridder Information, Inc., Lexis-Nexis. *5649*

COUNTRY FORECAST. SPAIN.
Economist Intelligence Unit, 111 W. 57th St., New York, NY 10019. TEL 212-554-0600. FAX 212-586-1182.
Vendor(s): Information Access Co., Knight-Ridder Information, Inc., Lexis-Nexis. *5649*

COUNTRY FORECAST. SRI LANKA.
Economist Intelligence Unit, 111 W. 57th St., New York, NY 10019. TEL 212-554-0600. FAX 212-586-1182.
Vendor(s): Information Access Co., Knight-Ridder Information, Inc., Lexis-Nexis. *5649*

COUNTRY FORECAST. SUB-SAHARAN AFRICA.
Economist Intelligence Unit, 111 W. 57th St., New York, NY 10019. TEL 212-554-0600. FAX 212-486-1182.
Vendor(s): Information Access Co., Knight-Ridder Information, Inc., Lexis-Nexis. *5649*

COUNTRY FORECAST. SWEDEN.
Economist Intelligence Unit, 111 W. 57th St., New York, NY 10019. TEL 212-554-0600. FAX 212-586-1182.
Vendor(s): Information Access Co., Knight-Ridder Information, Inc., Lexis-Nexis. *5649*

COUNTRY FORECAST. SWITZERLAND.
Economist Intelligence Unit, 111 W. 57th St., New York, NY 10019. TEL 212-554-0600. FAX 212-586-1182.
Vendor(s): Information Access Co., Knight-Ridder Information, Inc., Lexis-Nexis. *5649*

COUNTRY FORECAST. TAIWAN.
Economist Intelligence Unit, 111 W. 57th St., New York, NY 10019. TEL 212-554-0600. FAX 212-586-1182.
Vendor(s): Information Access Co., Knight-Ridder Information, Inc., Lexis-Nexis. *5649*

COUNTRY FORECAST. THAILAND.
Economist Intelligence Unit, 111 W. 57th St., New York, NY 10019. TEL 212-554-0600. FAX 212-586-1182.
Vendor(s): Information Access Co., Knight-Ridder Information, Inc., Lexis-Nexis. *5649*

COUNTRY FORECAST. TURKEY.
Economist Intelligence Unit, 111 W. 57th St., New York, NY 10019. TEL 212-554-0600. FAX 212-586-1182.
Vendor(s): Information Access Co., Knight-Ridder Information, Inc., Lexis-Nexis. *5649*

COUNTRY FORECAST. UNITED KINGDOM.
Economist Intelligence Unit, 111 W. 57th St., New York, NY 10019. TEL 212-554-0600. FAX 212-586-1182.
Vendor(s): Information Access Co., Knight-Ridder Information, Inc., Lexis-Nexis. *5649*

COUNTRY FORECAST. UNITED STATES OF AMERICA.
Economist Intelligence Unit, 111 W. 57th St., New York, NY 10019. TEL 212-554-0600. FAX 212-586-1182.
Vendor(s): Information Access Co., Knight-Ridder Information, Inc., Lexis-Nexis. *5649*

COUNTRY FORECAST. VENEZUELA.
Economist Intelligence Unit, 111 W. 57th St., New York, NY 10019. TEL 212-554-0600. FAX 212-586-1182.
Vendor(s): Information Access Co., Knight-Ridder Information, Inc., Lexis-Nexis. *5650*

COUNTRY FORECAST. VIETNAM.
Economist Intelligence Unit, 111 W. 57th St., New York, NY 10019. TEL 212-554-0600. FAX 212-586-1182.
Vendor(s): Information Access Co., Knight-Ridder Information, Inc., Lexis-Nexis. *5650*

COUNTRY FORECASTS (NEW YORK).
Economist Intelligence Unit, 111 W. 57th St., New York, NY 10019. TEL 212-554-0600. FAX 212-586-1182.
Vendor(s): Knight-Ridder Information, Inc., Lexis-Nexis. *5650*

COUNTRY FORECASTS (SYRACUSE).
Political Risk Services, Box 248, E. Syracuse, NY 13057-0248. TEL 315-431-0511. FAX 315-431-0200.
Vendor(s): Data-Star (FSRI), Knight-Ridder Information, Inc., Information Access Co., NewsNet (IT933). *5650*

COUNTRY JOURNAL.
Cowles Business Media, 11 River Bend Dr., S., Box 4949, Stamford, CT 06907-0949. TEL 203-321-1778. FAX 203-358-5811.
Vendor(s): Information Access Co.. *3227*

COUNTRY MUSIC.
Silver Eagle Publishers, 329 Riverside Ave., Westport, CT 06880. TEL 203-221-4950. FAX 203-221-4948.
Vendor(s): Information Access Co.. *5152*

COUNTRY PROFILE. ALGERIA.
Economist Intelligence Unit, 111 W. 57th St., New York, NY 10019. TEL 212-554-0600. FAX 212-586-1182.
Vendor(s): Knight-Ridder Information, Inc., Lexis-Nexis. *5650*

COUNTRY PROFILE. ANGOLA.
Economist Intelligence Unit, 111 W. 57th St., New York, NY 10019. TEL 212-554-0600. FAX 212-586-1182.
Vendor(s): Knight-Ridder Information, Inc., Lexis-Nexis. *5650*

COUNTRY PROFILE. ARGENTINA.
Economist Intelligence Unit, 111 W. 57th St., New York, NY 10019. TEL 212-554-0600. FAX 212-586-1182.
Vendor(s): Knight-Ridder Information, Inc., Lexis-Nexis. *5650*

COUNTRY PROFILE. AUSTRALIA.
Economist Intelligence Unit, 111 W. 57th St., New York, NY 10019. TEL 212-554-0600. FAX 212-586-1182.
Vendor(s): Knight-Ridder Information, Inc., Lexis-Nexis. *5650*

COUNTRY PROFILE. AUSTRIA.
Economist Intelligence Unit, 111 W. 57th St., New York, NY 10019. TEL 212-554-0600. FAX 212-586-1182.
Vendor(s): Knight-Ridder Information, Inc., Lexis-Nexis. *5650*

COUNTRY PROFILE. BAHRAIN, QATAR.
Economist Intelligence Unit, 111 W. 57th St., New York, NY 10019. TEL 212-554-0600. FAX 212-586-1182.
Vendor(s): Knight-Ridder Information, Inc., Lexis-Nexis. *5650*

COUNTRY PROFILE. BALTIC REPUBLICS: LITHUANIA, LATVIA, ESTONIA.
Economist Intelligence Unit, 111 W. 57th St., New York, NY 10019. TEL 212-554-0600. FAX 212-586-1182.
Vendor(s): Knight-Ridder Information, Inc., Lexis-Nexis. *5650*

COUNTRY PROFILE. BANGLADESH.
Economist Intelligence Unit, 111 W. 57th St., New York, NY 10019. TEL 212-554-0600. FAX 212-586-1182.
Vendor(s): Knight-Ridder Information, Inc., Lexis-Nexis. *5650*

COUNTRY PROFILE. BELGIUM, LUXEMBOURG.
Economist Intelligence Unit, 111 W. 57th St., New York, NY 10019. TEL 212-554-0600. FAX 212-586-1182.
Vendor(s): Knight-Ridder Information, Inc., Lexis-Nexis. *5650*

COUNTRY PROFILE. BELIZE, BAHAMAS, BERMUDA.
Economist Intelligence Unit, 111 W. 57th St., New York, NY 10019. TEL 212-554-0600. FAX 212-586-1182.
Vendor(s): Knight-Ridder Information, Inc., Lexis-Nexis. *5650*

COUNTRY PROFILE. BOLIVIA.
Economist Intelligence Unit, 111 W. 57th St., New York, NY 10019. TEL 212-554-0600. FAX 212-586-1181.
Vendor(s): Knight-Ridder Information, Inc., Lexis-Nexis. *5651*

COUNTRY PROFILE. BOSNIA-HERCEGOVINA, CROATIA, SLOVENIA.
Economist Intelligence Unit, 111 W. 57th St., New York, NY 10019. TEL 212-554-0600. FAX 212-586-1182.
Vendor(s): Knight-Ridder Information, Inc., Lexis-Nexis. *5651*

COUNTRY PROFILE. BOTSWANA, LESOTHO.
Economist Intelligence Unit, 111 W. 57th St., New York, NY 10019. TEL 212-554-0600. FAX 212-586-1182.
Vendor(s): Knight-Ridder Information, Inc., Lexis-Nexis. *5651*

COUNTRY PROFILE. BRAZIL.
Economist Intelligence Unit, 111 W. 57th St., New York, NY 10019. TEL 212-554-0600. FAX 212-586-1182.
Vendor(s): Knight-Ridder Information, Inc., Lexis-Nexis. *5651*

COUNTRY PROFILE. BULGARIA, ALBANIA.
Economist Intelligence Unit, 111 W. 57th St., New York, NY 10019. TEL 212-554-0600. FAX 212-586-1182.
Vendor(s): Knight-Ridder Information, Inc., Lexis-Nexis. *5651*

COUNTRY PROFILE. CAMBODIA, LAOS, MYANMAR.
Economist Intelligence Unit, 111 W. 57th St., New York, NY 10019. TEL 212-554-0600. FAX 212-586-1182.
Vendor(s): Knight-Ridder Information, Inc., Lexis-Nexis. *5651*

COUNTRY PROFILE. CAMEROON, CENTRAL AFRICAN REPUBLIC, CHAD.
Economist Intelligence Unit, 111 W. 57th St., New York, NY 10019. TEL 212-554-0600. FAX 212-586-1182.
Vendor(s): Knight-Ridder Information, Inc., Lexis-Nexis. *5651*

COUNTRY PROFILE. CANADA.
Economist Intelligence Unit, 111 W. 57th St., New York, NY 10019. TEL 212-554-0600. FAX 212-586-1182.
Vendor(s): Knight-Ridder Information, Inc., Lexis-Nexis. *5651*

COUNTRY PROFILE. CHILE.
Economist Intelligence Unit, 111 W. 57th St., New York, NY 10019. TEL 212-554-0600. FAX 212-586-1182.
Vendor(s): Knight-Ridder Information, Inc., Lexis-Nexis. *5651*

COUNTRY PROFILE. CHINA, MONGOLIA.
Economist Intelligence Unit, 111 W. 57th St., New York, NY 10019. TEL 212-554-0600. FAX 212-586-1182.
Vendor(s): Knight-Ridder Information, Inc., Lexis-Nexis. *5651*

COUNTRY PROFILE. COLOMBIA.
Economist Intelligence Unit, 111 W. 57th St., New York, NY 10019. TEL 212-554-0600. FAX 212-586-1182.
Vendor(s): Knight-Ridder Information, Inc., Lexis-Nexis. *5651*

COUNTRY PROFILE. CONGO, SAO TOME AND PRINCIPE, GUINEA-BISSAU, CAPE VERDE.
Economist Intelligence Unit, 111 W. 57th St., New York, NY 10019. TEL 212-554-0600. FAX 212-586-1182.
Vendor(s): Knight-Ridder Information, Inc., Lexis-Nexis. *5651*

COUNTRY PROFILE. COSTA RICA, PANAMA.
Economist Intelligence Unit, 111 W. 57th St., New York, NY 10019. TEL 212-554-0600. FAX 212-586-1182.
Vendor(s): Knight-Ridder Information, Inc., Lexis-Nexis. *5651*

COUNTRY PROFILE. COTE DIVOIRE, MALI.
Economist Intelligence Unit, 111 W. 57th St., New York, NY 10019. TEL 212-554-0600. FAX 212-586-1182.
Vendor(s): Knight-Ridder Information, Inc., Lexis-Nexis. *5651*

COUNTRY PROFILE. CUBA.
Economist Intelligence Unit, 111 W. 57th St., New York, NY 10019. TEL 212-554-0600. FAX 212-586-1182.
Vendor(s): Knight-Ridder Information, Inc., Lexis-Nexis. *5652*

COUNTRY PROFILE. CYPRUS, MALTA.
Economist Intelligence Unit, 111 W. 57th St., New York, NY 10019. TEL 212-554-0500. FAX 212-9586-1182.
Vendor(s): Knight-Ridder Information, Inc., Lexis-Nexis. *5652*

COUNTRY PROFILE. CZECH REPUBLIC AND SLOVAKIA.
Economist Intelligence Unit, 111 W. 57th St., New York, NY 10019. TEL 212-554-0600. FAX 212-586-1182.
Vendor(s): Knight-Ridder Information, Inc., Lexis-Nexis. *5652*

COUNTRY PROFILE. DENMARK, ICELAND.
Economist Intelligence Unit, 111 W. 57th St., New York, NY 10019. TEL 212-554-0600. FAX 212-586-1182.
Vendor(s): Knight-Ridder Information, Inc., Lexis-Nexis. *5652*

COUNTRY PROFILE. DOMINICAN REPUBLIC, HAITI, PUERTO RICO.
Economist Intelligence Unit, 111 W. 57th St., New York, NY 10019. TEL 212-554-0600. FAX 212-586-1182.
Vendor(s): Knight-Ridder Information, Inc., Lexis-Nexis. *5652*

COUNTRY PROFILE. ECUADOR.
Economist Intelligence Unit, 111 W. 57th St., New York, NY 10019. TEL 212-554-0600. FAX 212-586-1182.
Vendor(s): Knight-Ridder Information, Inc., Lexis-Nexis. *5652*

COUNTRY PROFILE. EGYPT.
Economist Intelligence Unit, 111 W. 57th St., New York, NY 10019. TEL 212-554-0600. FAX 212-586-1182.
Vendor(s): Knight-Ridder Information, Inc., Lexis-Nexis. *5652*

COUNTRY PROFILE. ETHIOPIA, ERITREA, SOMALIA, DJIBOUTI.
Economist Intelligence Unit, 111 W. 57th St., New York, NY 10019. TEL 212-554-0600. FAX 212-586-1182.
Vendor(s): Knight-Ridder Information, Inc., Lexis-Nexis. *5652*

COUNTRY PROFILE. FINLAND.
Economist Intelligence Unit, 111 W. 57th St., New York, NY 10019. TEL 212-554-0600. FAX 212-586-1182.
Vendor(s): Knight-Ridder Information, Inc., Lexis-Nexis. *5652*

COUNTRY PROFILE. FRANCE.
Economist Intelligence Unit, 111 W. 57th St., New York, NY 10019. TEL 212-554-0600. FAX 212-586-1182.
Vendor(s): Knight-Ridder Information, Inc., Lexis-Nexis. *5652*

COUNTRY PROFILE. GABON, EQUATORIAL GUINEA.
Economist Intelligence Unit, 111 W. 57th St., New York, NY 10019. TEL 212-554-0600. FAX 212-586-1182.
Vendor(s): Knight-Ridder Information, Inc., Lexis-Nexis. *5652*

COUNTRY PROFILE. GEORGIA, ARMENIA, AZERBAIJAN.
Economist Intelligence Unit, 111 W. 57th St., New York, NY 10019. TEL 212-554-0600. FAX 212-586-1182.
Vendor(s): Knight-Ridder Information, Inc., Lexis-Nexis. *5652*

COUNTRY PROFILE. GERMANY.
Economist Intelligence Unit, 111 W. 57th St., New York, NY 10019. TEL 212-554-0600. FAX 212-586-1182.
Vendor(s): Knight-Ridder Information, Inc., Lexis-Nexis. *5652*

COUNTRY PROFILE. GHANA.
Economist Intelligence Unit, 111 W. 57th St., New York, NY 10019. TEL 212-554-0600. FAX 212-586-1182.
Vendor(s): Knight-Ridder Information, Inc., Lexis-Nexis. *5652*

COUNTRY PROFILE. GREECE.
Economist Intelligence Unit, 111 W. 57th St., New York, NY 10019. TEL 212-554-0600. FAX 212-586-1182.
Vendor(s): Knight-Ridder Information, Inc., Lexis-Nexis. *5652*

COUNTRY PROFILE. GUATEMALA, EL SALVADOR.
Economist Intelligence Unit, 111 W. 57th St., New York, NY 10019. TEL 212-554-0600. FAX 212-586-1182.
Vendor(s): Knight-Ridder Information, Inc., Lexis-Nexis. *5653*

COUNTRY PROFILE. GUINEA, SIERRA LEONE, LIBERIA.
Economist Intelligence Unit, 111 W. 57th St., New York, NY 10019. TEL 212-554-0600. FAX 212-586-1182.
Vendor(s): Knight-Ridder Information, Inc., Lexis-Nexis. *5653*

COUNTRY PROFILE. GUYANA, WINDWARD AND LEEWARD ISLANDS.
Economist Intelligence Unit, 111 W. 57th St., New York, NY 10019. TEL 212-554-0600. FAX 212-586-1182.
Vendor(s): Knight-Ridder Information, Inc., Lexis-Nexis. *5653*

COUNTRY PROFILE. HONG KONG, MACAU.
Economist Intelligence Unit, 111 W. 57th St., New York, NY 10019. TEL 212-554-0600. FAX 212-586-1182.
Vendor(s): Knight-Ridder Information, Inc., Lexis-Nexis. *5653*

COUNTRY PROFILE. HUNGARY.
Economist Intelligence Unit, 111 W. 57th St., New York, NY 10019. TEL 212-554-0600. FAX 212-586-1182.
Vendor(s): Knight-Ridder Information, Inc., Lexis-Nexis. *5653*

COUNTRY PROFILE. INDIA, NEPAL.
Economist Intelligence Unit, 111 W. 57th St., New York, NY 10019. TEL 212-554-0600. FAX 212-586-1182.
Vendor(s): Knight-Ridder Information, Inc., Lexis-Nexis. *5653*

COUNTRY PROFILE. INDONESIA.
Economist Intelligence Unit, 111 W. 57th St., New York, NY 10019. TEL 212-554-0600. FAX 212-586-1182.
Vendor(s): Knight-Ridder Information, Inc., Lexis-Nexis. *5653*

COUNTRY PROFILE. IRAN.
Economist Intelligence Unit, 111 W. 57th St., New York, NY 10019. TEL 212-554-0600. FAX 212-586-1182.
Vendor(s): Knight-Ridder Information, Inc., Lexis-Nexis. *5653*

COUNTRY PROFILE. IRAQ.
Economist Intelligence Unit, 111 W. 57th St., New York, NY 10019. TEL 212-554-0600. FAX 212-586-1182.
Vendor(s): Knight-Ridder Information, Inc., Lexis-Nexis. *5653*

COUNTRY PROFILE. IRELAND.
Economist Intelligence Unit, 111 W. 57th St., New York, NY 10019. TEL 212-554-0600. FAX 212-586-1182.
Vendor(s): Knight-Ridder Information, Inc., Lexis-Nexis. *5653*

COUNTRY PROFILE. ISRAEL, THE OCCUPIED TERRITORIES.
Economist Intelligence Unit, 111 W. 57th St., New York, NY 10019. TEL 212-554-0600. FAX 212-586-1182.
Vendor(s): Knight-Ridder Information, Inc., Lexis-Nexis. *5653*

COUNTRY PROFILE. ITALY.
Economist Intelligence Unit, 111 W. 57th St., New York, NY 10019. TEL 212-554-0600. FAX 212-586-1182.
Vendor(s): Knight-Ridder Information, Inc., Lexis-Nexis. *5653*

COUNTRY PROFILE. JAMAICA, BARBADOS.
Economist Intelligence Unit, 111 W. 57th St., New York, NY 10019. TEL 212-554-0600. FAX 212-586-1182.
Vendor(s): Knight-Ridder Information, Inc., Lexis-Nexis. *5653*

COUNTRY PROFILE. JAPAN.
Economist Intelligence Unit, 111 W. 57th St., New York, NY 10019. TEL 212-554-0600. FAX 212-586-1182.
Vendor(s): Knight-Ridder Information, Inc., Lexis-Nexis. *5653*

COUNTRY PROFILE. JORDAN.
Economist Intelligence Unit, 111 W. 57th St., New York, NY 10019. TEL 212-554-0600. FAX 212-586-1182.
Vendor(s): Knight-Ridder Information, Inc., Lexis-Nexis. *5653*

COUNTRY PROFILE. KENYA.
Economist Intelligence Unit, 111 W. 57th St., New York, NY 10019. TEL 212-554-0600. FAX 212-586-1192.
Vendor(s): Knight-Ridder Information, Inc., Lexis-Nexis. *5653*

COUNTRY PROFILE. KUWAIT.
Economist Intelligence Unit, 111 W. 57th St., New York, NY 10019. TEL 212-554-0600. FAX 212-586-1182.
Vendor(s): Knight-Ridder Information, Inc., Lexis-Nexis. *5654*

COUNTRY PROFILE. LEBANON.
Economist Intelligence Unit, 111 W. 57th St., New York, NY 10019. TEL 212-554-0600. FAX 212-586-1182.
Vendor(s): Knight-Ridder Information, Inc., Lexis-Nexis. *5654*

COUNTRY PROFILE. LIBYA.
Economist Intelligence Unit, 111 W. 57th St., New York, NY 10019. TEL 212-554-0600. FAX 212-586-1182.
Vendor(s): Knight-Ridder Information, Inc., Lexis-Nexis. *5654*

COUNTRY PROFILE. MACEDONIA, SERBIA-MONTENEGRO.
Economist Intelligence Unit, 111 W. 57th St., New York, NY 10019. TEL 212-554-0600. FAX 212-586-1182.
Vendor(s): Knight-Ridder Information, Inc., Lexis-Nexis. *5654*

COUNTRY PROFILE. MADAGASCAR.
Economist Intelligence Unit, 111 W. 57th St., New York, NY 10019. TEL 212-554-0600. FAX 212-586-1182.
Vendor(s): Knight-Ridder Information, Inc., Lexis-Nexis. *5654*

COUNTRY PROFILE. MALAWI.
Economist Intelligence Unit, 111 W. 57th St., New York, NY 10019. TEL 212-554-0600. FAX 212-586-1182.
Vendor(s): Knight-Ridder Information, Inc., Lexis-Nexis. *5654*

COUNTRY PROFILE. MALAYSIA, BRUNEI.
Economist Intelligence Unit, 111 W. 57th St., New York, NY 10019. TEL 212-554-0600. FAX 212-586-1182.
Vendor(s): Knight-Ridder Information, Inc., Lexis-Nexis. *5654*

COUNTRY PROFILE. MAURITIUS, SEYCHELLES.
Economist Intelligence Unit, 111 W. 57th St., New York, NY 10019. TEL 212-544-0600. FAX 212-586-1182.
Vendor(s): Knight-Ridder Information, Inc., Lexis-Nexis. *5654*

COUNTRY PROFILE. MEXICO.
Economist Intelligence Unit, 111 W. 57th St., New York, NY 10019. TEL 212-554-0600. FAX 212-586-1182.
Vendor(s): Knight-Ridder Information, Inc., Lexis-Nexis. *5654*

COUNTRY PROFILE. MOROCCO.
Economist Intelligence Unit, 111 W. 57th St., New York, NY 10019. TEL 212-554-0600. FAX 212-586-1182.
Vendor(s): Knight-Ridder Information, Inc., Lexis-Nexis. *5654*

COUNTRY PROFILE. MOZAMBIQUE.
Economist Intelligence Unit, 111 W. 57th St., New York, NY 10019. TEL 212-554-0600. FAX 212-586-1182.
Vendor(s): Knight-Ridder Information, Inc., Lexis-Nexis. *5654*

COUNTRY PROFILE. NAMIBIA, SWAZILAND.
Economist Intelligence Unit, 111 W. 57th St., New York, NY 10019. TEL 212-554-0600. FAX 212-586-1182.
Vendor(s): Knight-Ridder Information, Inc., Lexis-Nexis. *5654*

COUNTRY PROFILE. NETHERLANDS.
Economist Intelligence Unit, 111 W. 57th St., New York, NY 10019. TEL 212-554-0600. FAX 212-586-1182.
Vendor(s): Knight-Ridder Information, Inc., Lexis-Nexis. *5654*

COUNTRY PROFILE. NEW ZEALAND.
Economist Intelligence Unit, 111 W. 57th St., New York, NY 10019. TEL 212-554-0600. FAX 212-586-1182.
Vendor(s): Knight-Ridder Information, Inc., Lexis-Nexis. *5654*

COUNTRY PROFILE. NICARAGUA, HONDURAS.
Economist Intelligence Unit, 111 W. 57th St., New York, NY 10019. TEL 212-554-0600. FAX 212-586-1182.
Vendor(s): Knight-Ridder Information, Inc., Lexis-Nexis. *5654*

COUNTRY PROFILE. NIGER, BURKINA FASO.
Economist Intelligence Unit, 111 W. 57th St., New York, NY 10019. TEL 212-554-0600. FAX 212-586-1182.
Vendor(s): Knight-Ridder Information, Inc., Lexis-Nexis. *5655*

COUNTRY PROFILE. NIGERIA.
Economist Intelligence Unit, 111 W. 57th St., New York, NY 10019. TEL 212-554-0600. FAX 212-586-1182.
Vendor(s): Knight-Ridder Information, Inc., Lexis-Nexis. *5655*

COUNTRY PROFILE. NORWAY.
Economist Intelligence Unit, 111 W. 57th St., New York, NY 10019. TEL 212-554-0600. FAX 212-586-1182.
Vendor(s): Knight-Ridder Information, Inc., Lexis-Nexis. *5655*

COUNTRY PROFILE. OMAN, YEMEN.
Economist Intelligence Unit, 111 W. 57th St., New York, NY 10019. TEL 212-554-0600. FAX 212-586-1182.
Vendor(s): Knight-Ridder Information, Inc., Lexis-Nexis. *5655*

COUNTRY PROFILE. PACIFIC ISLANDS: FIJI, SOLOMON ISLANDS, WESTERN SAMOA, VANUATU, TONGA.
Economist Intelligence Unit, 111 W. 57th St., New York, NY 10019. TEL 212-554-0600. FAX 212-586-1182.
Vendor(s): Knight-Ridder Information, Inc., Lexis-Nexis. *5655*

COUNTRY PROFILE. PAKISTAN, AFGHANISTAN.
Economist Intelligence Unit, 111 W. 57th St., New York, NY 10019. TEL 212-554-0600. FAX 212-586-1182.
Vendor(s): Knight-Ridder Information, Inc., Lexis-Nexis. *5655*

COUNTRY PROFILE. PAPUA NEW GUINEA.
Economist Intelligence Unit, 111 W. 57th St., New York, NY 10019. TEL 212-554-0600. FAX 212-586-1182.
Vendor(s): Knight-Ridder Information, Inc., Lexis-Nexis. *5655*

COUNTRY PROFILE. PERU.
Economist Intelligence Unit, 111 W. 57th St., New York, NY 10019. TEL 212-554-0600. FAX 212-586-1182.
Vendor(s): Knight-Ridder Information, Inc., Lexis-Nexis. *5655*

COUNTRY PROFILE. PHILIPPINES.
Economist Intelligence Unit, 111 W. 57th St., New York, NY 10019. TEL 212-554-0600. FAX 212-586-1182.
Vendor(s): Knight-Ridder Information, Inc., Lexis-Nexis. *5655*

COUNTRY PROFILE. POLAND.
Economist Intelligence Unit, 111 W. 57th St., New York, NY 10019. TEL 212-554-0600. FAX 212-586-1182.
Vendor(s): Knight-Ridder Information, Inc., Lexis-Nexis. *5655*

COUNTRY PROFILE. PORTUGAL.
Economist Intelligence Unit, 111 W. 57th St., New York, NY 10019. TEL 212-554-0600. FAX 212-586-1182.
Vendor(s): Knight-Ridder Information, Inc., Lexis-Nexis. *5655*

COUNTRY PROFILE. ROMANIA.
Economist Intelligence Unit, 111 W. 57th St., New York, NY 10003-1658. TEL 212-554-0600. FAX 212-596-1182.
Vendor(s): Knight-Ridder Information, Inc., Lexis-Nexis. *5655*

COUNTRY PROFILE. RUSSIA.
Economist Intelligence Unit, 111 W. 57th St., New York, NY 10019. TEL 212-554-0600. FAX 212-586-1182.
Vendor(s): Knight-Ridder Information, Inc., Lexis-Nexis. *5655*

COUNTRY PROFILE. RWANDA, BURUNDI.
Economist Intelligence Unit, 111 W. 57th St., New York, NY 10019. TEL 212-554-0600. FAX 212-586-1182.
Vendor(s): Knight-Ridder Information, Inc., Lexis-Nexis. *5655*

COUNTRY PROFILE. SAUDI ARABIA.
Economist Intelligence Unit, 111 W. 57th St., New York, NY 10019. TEL 212-544-0600. FAX 212-586-1182.
Vendor(s): Knight-Ridder Information, Inc., Lexis-Nexis. *5655*

COUNTRY PROFILE. SENEGAL.
Economist Intelligence Unit, 111 W. 57th St., New York, NY 10019. TEL 212-554-0600. FAX 212-586-1182.
Vendor(s): Knight-Ridder Information, Inc., Lexis-Nexis. *5655*

COUNTRY PROFILE. SINGAPORE.
Economist Intelligence Unit, 111 W. 57th St., New York, NY 10019. TEL 212-544-0600. FAX 212-586-1182.
Vendor(s): Knight-Ridder Information, Inc., Lexis-Nexis. *5655*

COUNTRY PROFILE. SOUTH AFRICA.
Economist Intelligence Unit, 111 W. 57th St., New York, NY 10019. TEL 212-554-0600. FAX 212-586-1182.
Vendor(s): Knight-Ridder Information, Inc., Lexis-Nexis. *5656*

COUNTRY PROFILE. SOUTH KOREA, NORTH KOREA.
Economist Intelligence Unit, 111 W. 57th St., New York, NY 10019. TEL 212-554-0600. FAX 212-586-1182.
Vendor(s): Knight-Ridder Information, Inc., Lexis-Nexis. *5656*

COUNTRY PROFILE. SPAIN.
Economist Intelligence Unit, 111 W. 57th St., New York, NY 10019. TEL 212-554-0600. FAX 212-586-1182.
Vendor(s): Knight-Ridder Information, Inc., Lexis-Nexis. *5656*

COUNTRY PROFILE. SRI LANKA.
Economist Intelligence Unit, 111 W. 57th St., New York, NY 10019. TEL 212-554-0600. FAX 212-586-1182.
Vendor(s): Knight-Ridder Information, Inc., Lexis-Nexis. *5656*

COUNTRY PROFILE. SUDAN.
Economist Intelligence Unit, 111 W. 57th St., New York, NY 10019. TEL 212-554-0600. FAX 212-586-1182.
Vendor(s): Knight-Ridder Information, Inc., Lexis-Nexis. *5656*

COUNTRY PROFILE. SWEDEN.
Economist Intelligence Unit, 111 W. 57th St., New York, NY 10019. TEL 212-554-0600. FAX 212-586-1182.
Vendor(s): Knight-Ridder Information, Inc., Lexis-Nexis. *5656*

COUNTRY PROFILE. SWITZERLAND.
Economist Intelligence Unit, 111 W. 57th St., New York, NY 10019. TEL 212-554-0600. FAX 212-9586-1182.
Vendor(s): Knight-Ridder Information, Inc., Lexis-Nexis. *5656*

COUNTRY PROFILE. SYRIA.
Economist Intelligence Unit, 111 W. 57th St., New York, NY 10019. TEL 212-554-0600. FAX 212-586-1182.
Vendor(s): Knight-Ridder Information, Inc., Lexis-Nexis. *5656*

COUNTRY PROFILE. TAIWAN.
Economist Intelligence Unit, 111 W. 57th St., New York, NY 10019. TEL 212-554-0600. FAX 212-586-1182.
Vendor(s): Knight-Ridder Information, Inc., Lexis-Nexis. *5656*

COUNTRY PROFILE. TANZANIA, COMOROS.
Economist Intelligence Unit, 111 W. 57th St., New York, NY 10019. TEL 212-554-0600. FAX 212-586-1182.
Vendor(s): Knight-Ridder Information, Inc., Lexis-Nexis. *5656*

COUNTRY PROFILE. THAILAND.
Economist Intelligence Unit, 111 W. 57th St., New York, NY 10019. TEL 212-554-0600. FAX 212-586-1192.
Vendor(s): Knight-Ridder Information, Inc., Lexis-Nexis. *5656*

COUNTRY PROFILE. THE GAMBIA, MAURITANIA.
Economist Intelligence Unit, 111 W. 57th St., New York, NY 10019. TEL 212-554-0600. FAX 212-586-1182.
Vendor(s): Knight-Ridder Information, Inc., Lexis-Nexis. *5656*

COUNTRY PROFILE. TOGO, BENIN.
Economist Intelligence Unit, 111 W. 57th St., New York, NY 10019. TEL 212-554-0600. FAX 212-586-1182.
Vendor(s): Knight-Ridder Information, Inc., Lexis-Nexis. *5656*

COUNTRY PROFILE. TRINIDAD AND TOBAGO, SURINAME, NETHERLANDS ANTILLES, ARUBA.
Economist Intelligence Unit, 111 W. 57th St., New York, NY 10019. TEL 212-554-0600. FAX 212-586-1182.
Vendor(s): Knight-Ridder Information, Inc., Lexis-Nexis. *5656*

COUNTRY PROFILE. TUNISIA.
Economist Intelligence Unit, 111 W. 57th St., New York, NY 10019. TEL 212-554-0600. FAX 212-586-1182.
Vendor(s): Knight-Ridder Information, Inc., Lexis-Nexis. *5656*

COUNTRY PROFILE. TURKEY.
Economist Intelligence Unit, 111 W. 57th St., New York, NY 10019. TEL 212-554-0600. FAX 212-586-1182.
Vendor(s): Knight-Ridder Information, Inc., Lexis-Nexis. *5657*

COUNTRY PROFILE. UGANDA.
Economist Intelligence Unit, 111 W. 57th St., New York, NY 10019. TEL 212-554-0600. FAX 212-586-1182.
Vendor(s): Knight-Ridder Information, Inc., Lexis-Nexis. *5657*

COUNTRY PROFILE. UKRAINE.
Economist Intelligence Unit, 111 W. 57th St., New York, NY 10019. TEL 212-554-0600. FAX 212-586-1182.
Vendor(s): Knight-Ridder Information, Inc., Lexis-Nexis. *5657*

COUNTRY PROFILE. UNITED ARAB EMIRATES.
Economist Intelligence Unit, 111 W. 57th St., New York, NY 10019. TEL 212-554-0600. FAX 212-586-1182.
Vendor(s): Knight-Ridder Information, Inc., Lexis-Nexis. *5657*

COUNTRY PROFILE. UNITED KINGDOM.
Economist Intelligence Unit, 111 W. 57th St., New York, NY 10019. TEL 212-554-0600. FAX 212-586-1182.
Vendor(s): Knight-Ridder Information, Inc., Lexis-Nexis. *5657*

COUNTRY PROFILE. UNITED STATES OF AMERICA.
Economist Intelligence Unit, 111 W. 57th St., New York, NY 10019. TEL 212-554-0600. FAX 212-586-1182.
Vendor(s): Knight-Ridder Information, Inc., Lexis-Nexis. *5657*

COUNTRY PROFILE. URUGUAY, PARAGUAY.
Economist Intelligence Unit, 111 W. 57th St., New York, NY 10019. TEL 212-554-0600. FAX 212-586-1182.
Vendor(s): Knight-Ridder Information, Inc., Lexis-Nexis. *5657*

COUNTRY PROFILE. VENEZUELA.
Economist Intelligence Unit, 111 W. 57th St., New York, NY 10003-1658. TEL 212-554-0600. FAX 212-586-1182.
Vendor(s): Knight-Ridder Information, Inc., Lexis-Nexis. *5657*

COUNTRY PROFILE. ZAIRE.
Economist Intelligence Unit, 111 W. 57th St., New York, NY 10019. TEL 212-554-0600. FAX 212-586-1182.
Vendor(s): Knight-Ridder Information, Inc., Lexis-Nexis. *5657*

COUNTRY PROFILE. ZAMBIA.
Economist Intelligence Unit, 111 W. 57th St., New York, NY 10019. TEL 212-554-0600. FAX 212-586-1182.
Vendor(s): Knight-Ridder Information, Inc., Lexis-Nexis. *5557*

COUNTRY PROFILE. ZIMBABWE.
Economist Intelligence Unit, 111 W. 57th St., New York, NY 10019. TEL 212-554-0600. FAX 212-586-1182.
Vendor(s): Knight-Ridder Information, Inc., Lexis-Nexis. *5657*

Online

COUNTRY PROFILES.
Economist Intelligence Unit, 111 W. 57th St., New York, NY 10019. TEL 212-554-0600. FAX 212-586-1182.
Vendor(s): Knight-Ridder Information, Inc., Lexis-Nexis. *5657*

COUNTRY REPORT. ALGERIA.
Economist Intelligence Unit, 111 W. 57th St., New York, NY 10019. TEL 212-554-0600. FAX 212-586-1182.
Vendor(s): Knight-Ridder Information, Inc., Lexis-Nexis. *1187*

COUNTRY REPORT. ANGOLA.
Economist Intelligence Unit, 111 W. 57th St., New York, NY 10019. TEL 212-554-0600. FAX 212-938-1182.
Vendor(s): Knight-Ridder Information, Inc., Lexis-Nexis. *1187*

COUNTRY REPORT. ARGENTINA.
Economist Intelligence Unit, 111 W. 57th St., New York, NY 10019. TEL 212-554-0600. FAX 212-586-1182.
Vendor(s): Knight-Ridder Information, Inc., Lexis-Nexis. *1187*

COUNTRY REPORT. AUSTRALIA.
Economist Intelligence Unit, 111 W. 57th St., New York, NY 10019. TEL 212-554-0600. FAX 212-586-1182.
Vendor(s): Knight-Ridder Information, Inc., Lexis-Nexis. *1187*

COUNTRY REPORT. AUSTRIA.
Economist Intelligence Unit, 111 W. 57th St., New York, NY 10019. TEL 212-554-0600. FAX 212-586-1182.
Vendor(s): Knight-Ridder Information, Inc., Lexis-Nexis. *1188*

COUNTRY REPORT. BAHRAIN, QATAR.
Economist Intelligence Unit, 111 W. 57th St., New York, NY 10019. TEL 212-554-0600. FAX 212-586-1182.
Vendor(s): Knight-Ridder Information, Inc., Lexis-Nexis. *1188*

COUNTRY REPORT. BALTIC REPUBLICS: LITHUANIA, LATVIA, ESTONIA.
Economist Intelligence Unit, 111 W. 57th St., New York, NY 10019. TEL 212-554-0600. FAX 212-586-1182.
Vendor(s): Knight-Ridder Information, Inc., Lexis-Nexis. *1188*

COUNTRY REPORT. BANGLADESH.
Economist Intelligence Unit, 111 W. 57th St., New York, NY 10019. TEL 212-554-0600. FAX 212-586-1182.
Vendor(s): Knight-Ridder Information, Inc., Lexis-Nexis. *1188*

COUNTRY REPORT. BELGIUM, LUXEMBOURG.
Economist Intelligence Unit, 111 W. 57th St., New York, NY 10019. TEL 212-554-0600. FAX 212-586-1182.
Vendor(s): Knight-Ridder Information, Inc., Lexis-Nexis. *1188*

COUNTRY REPORT. BOLIVIA.
Economist Intelligence Unit, 111 W. 57th St., New York, NY 10019. TEL 212-554-0600. FAX 212-586-1182.
Vendor(s): Knight-Ridder Information, Inc., Lexis-Nexis. *1188*

COUNTRY REPORT. BOSNIA-HERCEGOVINA, CROATIA.
Economist Intelligence Unit, 111 W. 57th St., New York, NY 10019. TEL 212-554-0600. FAX 212-586-1182.
Vendor(s): Knight-Ridder Information, Inc., Lexis-Nexis. *1188*

COUNTRY REPORT. BRAZIL.
Economist Intelligence Unit, 111 W. 57th St., New York, NY 10019. TEL 212-554-0600. FAX 212-586-1182.
Vendor(s): Knight-Ridder Information, Inc., Lexis-Nexis. *1188*

COUNTRY REPORT. BULGARIA, ALBANIA.
Economist Intelligence Unit, 111 W. 57th St., New York, NY 10019. TEL 212-554-0600. FAX 212-586-1182.
Vendor(s): Knight-Ridder Information, Inc., Lexis-Nexis. *1188*

COUNTRY REPORT. CAMBODIA, LAOS.
Economist Intelligence Unit, 111 W. 57th St., New York, NY 10019. TEL 212-554-0600. FAX 212-586-1182.
Vendor(s): Knight-Ridder Information, Inc., Lexis-Nexis. *1189*

COUNTRY REPORT. CAMEROON, C.A.R., CHAD.
Economist Intelligence Unit, 111 W. 57th St., New York, NY 10019. TEL 212-554-0600. FAX 212-586-1182.
Vendor(s): Knight-Ridder Information, Inc., Lexis-Nexis. *1189*

COUNTRY REPORT. CANADA.
Economist Intelligence Unit, 111 W. 57th St., New York, NY 10019. TEL 212-554-0600. FAX 212-586-1182.
Vendor(s): Knight-Ridder Information, Inc., Lexis-Nexis. *1189*

COUNTRY REPORT. CHILE.
Economist Intelligence Unit, 111 W. 57th St., New York, NY 10019. TEL 212-554-0600. FAX 212-586-1182.
Vendor(s): Knight-Ridder Information, Inc., Lexis-Nexis. *1189*

COUNTRY REPORT. CHINA, MONGOLIA.
Economist Intelligence Unit, 111 W. 57th St., New York, NY 10019. TEL 212-554-0600. FAX 212-586-1182.
Vendor(s): Knight-Ridder Information, Inc., Lexis-Nexis. *1189*

COUNTRY REPORT. COLOMBIA.
Economist Intelligence Unit, 111 W. 57th St., New York, NY 10019. TEL 212-554-0600. FAX 212-586-1182.
Vendor(s): Knight-Ridder Information, Inc., Lexis-Nexis. *1189*

COUNTRY REPORT. CONGO, SAO TOME AND PRINCIPE, GUINEA-BISSAU, CAPE VERDE.
Economist Intelligence Unit, 111 W. 57th St., New York, NY 10019. TEL 212-554-0600. FAX 212-586-1182.
Vendor(s): Knight-Ridder Information, Inc., Lexis-Nexis. *1189*

COUNTRY REPORT. COSTA RICA, PANAMA.
Economist Intelligence Unit, 111 W. 57th St., New York, NY 10019. TEL 212-554-0600. FAX 212-586-1182.
Vendor(s): Knight-Ridder Information, Inc., Lexis-Nexis. *1189*

COUNTRY REPORT. COTE D'IVOIRE, MALI.
Economist Intelligence Unit, 111 W. 57th St., New York, NY 10019. TEL 212-554-0600. FAX 212-586-1182.
Vendor(s): Knight-Ridder Information, Inc., Lexis-Nexis. *1189*

COUNTRY REPORT. CUBA, DOMINICAN REPUBLIC, HAITI, PUERTO RICO.
Economist Intelligence Unit, 111 W. 57th St., New York, NY 10019. TEL 212-554-0600. FAX 212-586-1182.
Vendor(s): Knight-Ridder Information, Inc., Lexis-Nexis. *1189*

COUNTRY REPORT. CYPRUS, MALTA.
Economist Intelligence Unit, 111 W. 57th St., New York, NY 10019. TEL 212-554-0600. FAX 212-586-1182.
Vendor(s): Knight-Ridder Information, Inc., Lexis-Nexis. *1189*

COUNTRY REPORT. CZECH REPUBLIC, SLOVAKIA.
Economist Intelligence Unit, 111 W. 57th St., New York, NY 10019. TEL 212-554-0600. FAX 212-586-1182.
Vendor(s): Knight-Ridder Information, Inc., Lexis-Nexis. *1190*

COUNTRY REPORT. DENMARK, ICELAND.
Economist Intelligence Unit, 111 W. 57th St., New York, NY 10019. TEL 212-554-0600. FAX 212-586-1182.
Vendor(s): Knight-Ridder Information, Inc., Lexis-Nexis. *1190*

COUNTRY REPORT. ECUADOR.
Economist Intelligence Unit, 111 W. 57th St., New York, NY 10019. TEL 212-554-0600. FAX 212-586-1182.
Vendor(s): Knight-Ridder Information, Inc., Lexis-Nexis. *1190*

COUNTRY REPORT. EGYPT.
Economist Intelligence Unit, 111 W. 57th St., New York, NY 10019. TEL 212-554-0600. FAX 212-586-1182.
Vendor(s): Knight-Ridder Information, Inc., Lexis-Nexis. *1190*

COUNTRY REPORT. ETHIOPIA, ERITREA, SOMALIA, DJIBOUTI.
Economist Intelligence Unit, 111 W. 57th St., New York, NY 10019. TEL 212-554-0600. FAX 212-586-1182.
Vendor(s): Knight-Ridder Information, Inc., Lexis-Nexis. *1190*

COUNTRY REPORT. FINLAND.
Economist Intelligence Unit, 111 W. 57th St., New York, NY 10019. TEL 212-554-0600. FAX 212-586-1182.
Vendor(s): Knight-Ridder Information, Inc., Lexis-Nexis. *1190*

COUNTRY REPORT. FRANCE.
Economist Intelligence Unit, 111 W. 57th St., New York, NY 10019. TEL 212-554-0600. FAX 212-586-1182.
Vendor(s): Knight-Ridder Information, Inc., Lexis-Nexis. *1190*

COUNTRY REPORT. GABON, EQUATORIAL GUINEA.
Economist Intelligence Unit, 111 W. 57th St., New York, NY 10019. TEL 212-554-0600. FAX 212-586-1182.
Vendor(s): Knight-Ridder Information, Inc., Lexis-Nexis. *1190*

COUNTRY REPORT. GERMANY.
Economist Intelligence Unit, 111 W. 57th St., New York, NY 10019. TEL 212-554-0600. FAX 212-586-1182.
Vendor(s): Knight-Ridder Information, Inc., Lexis-Nexis. *1190*

COUNTRY REPORT. GHANA.
Economist Intelligence Unit, 111 W. 57th St., New York, NY 10019. TEL 212-554-0600. FAX 212-586-1182.
Vendor(s): Knight-Ridder Information, Inc., Lexis-Nexis. *1190*

COUNTRY REPORT. GREECE.
Economist Intelligence Unit, 111 W. 57th St., New York, NY 10019. TEL 212-554-0600. FAX 212-586-1182.
Vendor(s): Knight-Ridder Information, Inc., Lexis-Nexis. *1190*

COUNTRY REPORT. GUATEMALA, EL SALVADOR.
Economist Intelligence Unit, 111 W. 57th St., New York, NY 10019. TEL 212-554-0600. FAX 212-586-1182.
Vendor(s): Knight-Ridder Information, Inc., Lexis-Nexis. *1191*

COUNTRY REPORT. GUINEA, SIERRA LEONE, LIBERIA.
Economist Intelligence Unit, 111 W. 57th St., New York, NY 10019. TEL 212-554-0600. FAX 212-586-1182.
Vendor(s): Knight-Ridder Information, Inc., Lexis-Nexis. *1191*

COUNTRY REPORT. HONG KONG, MACAU.
Economist Intelligence Unit, 111 W. 57th St., New York, NY 10019. TEL 212-554-0600. FAX 212-586-1182.
Vendor(s): Knight-Ridder Information, Inc., Lexis-Nexis. *1191*

COUNTRY REPORT. HUNGARY.
Economist Intelligence Unit, 111 W. 57th St., New York, NY 10019. TEL 212-554-0600. FAX 212-586-1182.
Vendor(s): Knight-Ridder Information, Inc., Lexis-Nexis. *1191*

COUNTRY REPORT. INDIA, NEPAL.
Economist Intelligence Unit, 111 W. 57th St., New York, NY 10019. TEL 212-554-0600. FAX 212-586-1182.
Vendor(s): Knight-Ridder Information, Inc., Lexis-Nexis. *1191*

COUNTRY REPORT. INDONESIA.
Economist Intelligence Unit, 111 W. 57th St., New York, NY 10019. TEL 212-554-0600. FAX 212-586-4685.
Vendor(s): Knight-Ridder Information, Inc., Lexis-Nexis. *1191*

COUNTRY REPORT. IRAN.
Economist Intelligence Unit, 111 W. 57th St., New York, NY 10019. TEL 212-554-0600. FAX 212-586-1182.
Vendor(s): Knight-Ridder Information, Inc., Lexis-Nexis. *1191*

COUNTRY REPORT. IRAQ.
Economist Intelligence Unit, 111 W. 57th St., New York, NY 10019. TEL 212-554-0600. FAX 212-586-1182.
Vendor(s): Knight-Ridder Information, Inc., Lexis-Nexis. *1191*

COUNTRY REPORT. IRELAND.
Economist Intelligence Unit, 111 W. 57th St., New York, NY 10019. TEL 212-554-0600. FAX 212-586-1182.
Vendor(s): Knight-Ridder Information, Inc., Lexis-Nexis. *1191*

COUNTRY REPORT. ISRAEL, THE OCCUPIED TERRITORIES.
Economist Intelligence Unit, 111 W. 57th St., New York, NY 10019. TEL 212-554-0600. FAX 212-586-1182.
Vendor(s): Knight-Ridder Information, Inc., Lexis-Nexis. *1191*

COUNTRY REPORT. ITALY.
Economist Intelligence Unit, 111 W. 57th St., New York, NY 10019. TEL 212-554-0600. FAX 212-586-1182.
Vendor(s): Knight-Ridder Information, Inc., Lexis-Nexis. *1191*

COUNTRY REPORT. JAMAICA, BELIZE, BAHAMAS, BERMUDA, BARBADOS.
Economist Intelligence Unit, 111 W. 57th St., New York, NY 10019. TEL 212-554-0600. FAX 212-586-1182.
Vendor(s): Knight-Ridder Information, Inc., Lexis-Nexis. *1191*

COUNTRY REPORT. JAPAN.
Economist Intelligence Unit, 111 W. 57th St., New York, NY 10019. TEL 212-554-0600. FAX 212-586-1182.
Vendor(s): Knight-Ridder Information, Inc., Lexis-Nexis. *1192*

COUNTRY REPORT. JORDAN.
Economist Intelligence Unit, 111 W. 57th St., New York, NY 10019. TEL 212-554-0600. FAX 212-586-1182.
Vendor(s): Knight-Ridder Information, Inc., Lexis-Nexis. *1192*

COUNTRY REPORT. KAZAKHSTAN.
Economist Intelligence Unit, 111 W. 57th St., New York, NY 10019. TEL 212-554-0600. FAX 212-586-1182.
Vendor(s): Knight-Ridder Information, Inc., Lexis-Nexis. *1192*

COUNTRY REPORT. KENYA.
Economist Intelligence Unit, 111 W. 57th St., New York, NY 10019. TEL 212-554-0600. FAX 212-586-1182.
Vendor(s): Knight-Ridder Information, Inc., Lexis-Nexis. *1192*

COUNTRY REPORT. KUWAIT.
Economist Intelligence Unit, 111 W. 57th St., New York, NY 10019. TEL 212-554-0600. FAX 212-586-1182.
Vendor(s): Knight-Ridder Information, Inc., Lexis-Nexis. *1192*

COUNTRY REPORT. LEBANON.
Economist Intelligence Unit, 111 W. 57th St., New York, NY 10019. TEL 212-554-0600. FAX 212-586-1182.
Vendor(s): Knight-Ridder Information, Inc., Lexis-Nexis. *1192*

COUNTRY REPORT. LIBYA.
Economist Intelligence Unit, 111 W. 57th St., New York, NY 10019. TEL 212-554-0600. FAX 212-586-1182.
Vendor(s): Knight-Ridder Information, Inc., Lexis-Nexis. *1192*

COUNTRY REPORT. MALAYSIA, BRUNEI.
Economist Intelligence Unit, 111 W. 57th St., New York, NY 10019. TEL 212-554-0600. FAX 212-586-1182.
Vendor(s): Knight-Ridder Information, Inc., Lexis-Nexis. *1192*

COUNTRY REPORT. MAURITIUS, MADAGASCAR, SEYCHELLES.
Economist Intelligence Unit, 111 W. 57th St., New York, NY 10019. TEL 212-554-0600. FAX 212-586-1182.
Vendor(s): Knight-Ridder Information, Inc., Lexis-Nexis. *1192*

COUNTRY REPORT. MEXICO.
Economist Intelligence Unit, 111 W. 57th St., New York, NY 10019. TEL 212-554-0600. FAX 212-586-1182.
Vendor(s): Knight-Ridder Information, Inc., Lexis-Nexis. *1192*

COUNTRY REPORT. MOROCCO.
Economist Intelligence Unit, 111 W. 57th St., New York, NY 10019. TEL 212-554-0600. FAX 212-586-1182.
Vendor(s): Knight-Ridder Information, Inc., Lexis-Nexis. *1193*

COUNTRY REPORT. MOZAMBIQUE, MALAWI.
Economist Intelligence Unit, 111 W. 57th St., New York, NY 10019. TEL 212-554-0600. FAX 212-586-1182.
Vendor(s): Knight-Ridder Information, Inc., Lexis-Nexis. *1193*

COUNTRY REPORT. NETHERLANDS.
Economist Intelligence Unit, 111 W. 57th St., New York, NY 10019. TEL 212-554-0600. FAX 212-586-1182.
Vendor(s): Knight-Ridder Information, Inc., Lexis-Nexis. *1193*

COUNTRY REPORT. NEW ZEALAND.
Economist Intelligence Unit, 111 W. 57th St., New York, NY 10019. TEL 212-554-0600. FAX 212-586-1182.
Vendor(s): Knight-Fidder Information, Inc., Lexis-Nexis. *1193*

COUNTRY REPORT. NICARAGUA, HONDURAS.
Economist Intelligence Unit, 111 W. 57th St., New York, NY 10019. TEL 212-554-0600. FAX 212-586-1182.
Vendor(s): Knight-Ridder Information, Inc., Lexis-Nexis. *1193*

COUNTRY REPORT. NIGERIA.
Economist Intelligence Unit, 111 W. 57th St., New York, NY 10019. TEL 212-554-0600. FAX 212-586-1182.
Vendor(s): Knight-Ridder Information, Inc., Lexis-Nexis. *1193*

COUNTRY REPORT. NORWAY.
Economist Intelligence Unit, 111 W. 57th St., New York, NY 10019. TEL 212-554-0600. FAX 212-586-1182.
Vendor(s): Knight-Ridder Information, Inc., Lexis-Nexis. *1193*

COUNTRY REPORT. OMAN, YEMEN.
Economist Intelligence Unit, 111 W. 57th St., New York, NY 10019. TEL 212-554-0600. FAX 212-586-1182.
Vendor(s): Knight-Ridder Information, Inc., Lexis-Nexis. *1193*

COUNTRY REPORT. PACIFIC ISLANDS: PAPUA NEW GUINEA, FIJI, SOLOMON ISLANDS, WESTERN SAMOA, VANUATU, TONGA.
Economist Intelligence Unit, 111 W. 57th St., New York, NY 10019. TEL 212-554-0600. FAX 212-586-1327.
Vendor(s): Knight-Ridder Information, Inc., Lexis-Nexis. *1194*

COUNTRY REPORT. PAKISTAN, AFGHANISTAN.
Economist Intelligence Unit, 111 W. 57th St., New York, NY 10019. TEL 212-554-0600. FAX 212-586-1182.
Vendor(s): Knight-Ridder Information, Inc., Lexis-Nexis. *1194*

COUNTRY REPORT. PERU.
Economist Intelligence Unit, 111 W. 57th St., New York, NY 10019. TEL 212-554-0600. FAX 212-586-1182.
Vendor(s): Knight-Ridder Information, Inc., Lexis-Nexis. *1194*

COUNTRY REPORT. PHILIPPINES.
Economist Intelligence Unit, 111 W. 57th St., New York, NY 10019. TEL 212-554-0600. FAX 212-586-1182.
Vendor(s): Knight-Ridder Information, Inc., Lexis-Nexis. *1194*

COUNTRY REPORT. POLAND.
Economist Intelligence Unit, 111 W. 57th St., New York, NY 10019. TEL 212-554-0600. FAX 212-938-4685.
Vendor(s): Knight-Ridder Information, Inc., Lexis-Nexis. *1194*

COUNTRY REPORT. PORTUGAL.
Economist Intelligence Unit, 111 W. 57th St., New York, NY 10019. TEL 212-554-0600. FAX 212-586-1132.
Vendor(s): Knight-Ridder Information, Inc., Lexis-Nexis. *1194*

COUNTRY REPORT. ROMANIA.
Economist Intelligence Unit, 111 W. 57th St., New York, NY 10019. TEL 212-554-0600. FAX 212-586-1182.
Vendor(s): Knight-Ridder Information, Inc., Lexis-Nexis. *1194*

COUNTRY REPORT. RUSSIA.
Economist Intelligence Unit, 111 W. 57th St., New York, NY 10019. TEL 212-554-0600. FAX 212-586-1182.
Vendor(s): Knight-Ridder Information, Inc., Lexis-Nexis. *1194*

COUNTRY REPORT. SAUDI ARABIA.
Economist Intelligence Unit, 111 W. 57th St., New York, NY 10019. TEL 212-554-0600. FAX 212-586-1182.
Vendor(s): Knight-Ridder Information, Inc., Lexis-Nexis. *1194*

COUNTRY REPORT. SENEGAL, THE GAMBIA, MAURITANIA.
Economist Intelligence Unit, 111 W. 57th St., New York, NY 10019. TEL 212-554-0600. FAX 212-586-1182.
Vendor(s): Knight-Ridder Information, Inc., Lexis-Nexis. *1194*

COUNTRY REPORT. SINGAPORE.
Economist Intelligence Unit, 111 W. 57th St., New York, NY 10019. TEL 212-554-0600. FAX 212-586-1182.
Vendor(s): Knight-Ridder Information, Inc., Lexis-Nexis. *1194*

COUNTRY REPORT. SOUTH AFRICA.
Economist Intelligence Unit, 111 W. 57th St., New York, NY 10019. TEL 212-554-0600. FAX 212-586-1182.
Vendor(s): Knight-Ridder Information, Inc., Lexis-Nexis. *1194*

COUNTRY REPORT. SOUTH KOREA, NORTH KOREA.
Economist Intelligence Unit, 111 W. 57th St., New York, NY 10019. TEL 212-554-0600. FAX 212-586-1182.
Vendor(s): Knight-Ridder Information, Inc., Lexis-Nexis. *1195*

COUNTRY REPORT. SPAIN.
Economist Intelligence Unit, 111 W. 57th St., New York, NY 10019. TEL 212-554-0600. FAX 212-586-1182.
Vendor(s): Knight-Ridder Information, Inc., Lexis-Nexis. *1195*

COUNTRY REPORT. SRI LANKA.
Economist Intelligence Unit, 111 W. 57th St., New York, NY 10019. TEL 212-554-0600. FAX 212-586-1182.
Vendor(s): Knight-Ridder Information, Inc., Lexis-Nexis. *1195*

COUNTRY REPORT. SUDAN.
Economist Intelligence Unit, 111 W. 57th St., New York, NY 10019. TEL 212-554-0600. FAX 212-586-1182.
Vendor(s): Knight-Ridder Information, Inc., Lexis-Nexis. *1195*

COUNTRY REPORT. SWEDEN.
Economist Intelligence Unit, 111 W. 57th St., New York, NY 10019. TEL 212-554-0600. FAX 212-586-1182.
Vendor(s): Knight-Ridder Information, Inc., Lexis-Nexis. *1195*

COUNTRY REPORT. SWITZERLAND.
Economist Intelligence Unit, 111 W. 57th St., New York, NY 10019. TEL 212-554-0600. FAX 212-586-1182.
Vendor(s): Knight-Ridder Information, Inc., Lexis-Nexis. *1195*

COUNTRY REPORT. SYRIA.
Economist Intelligence Unit, 111 W. 57th St., New York, NY 10019. TEL 212-554-0600. FAX 212-586-1182.
Vendor(s): Knight-Ridder Information, Inc., Lexis-Nexis. *1195*

COUNTRY REPORT. TAIWAN.
Economist Intelligence Unit, 111 W. 57th St., New York, NY 10019. TEL 212-554-0600. FAX 212-586-1182.
Vendor(s): Knight-Ridder Information, Inc., Lexis-Nexis. *1195*

COUNTRY REPORT. TANZANIA, COMOROS.
Economist Intelligence Unit, 111 W. 57th St., New York, NY 10019. TEL 212-554-0600. FAX 212-586-1182.
Vendor(s): Knight-Ridder Information, Inc., Lexis-Nexis. *1195*

COUNTRY REPORT. THAILAND.
Economist Intelligence Unit, 111 W. 57th St., New York, NY 10019. TEL 212-554-0600. FAX 212-586-1182.
Vendor(s): Knight-Ridder Information, Inc., Lexis-Nexis. *1195*

COUNTRY REPORT. TOGO, NIGER, BENIN, BURKINA FASO.
Economist Intelligence Unit, 111 W. 57th St., New York, NY 10019. TEL 212-554-0600. FAX 212-586-1182.
Vendor(s): Knight-Ridder Information, Inc., Lexis-Nexis. *1195*

COUNTRY REPORT. TRINIDAD & TOBAGO, GUYANA, WINDWARD & LEEWARD ISLANDS, SURINAME, NETHERLANDS ANTILLES, ARUBA.
Economist Intelligence Unit, 111 W. 57th St., New York, NY 10019. TEL 212-554-0600. FAX 212-586-1182.
Vendor(s): Knight-Ridder Information, Inc., Lexis-Nexis. *1196*

COUNTRY REPORT. TUNISIA.
Economist Intelligence Unit, 111 W. 57th St., New York, NY 10019. TEL 212-554-0600. FAX 212-586-1182.
Vendor(s): Knight-Ridder Information, Inc., Lexis-Nexis. *1196*

COUNTRY REPORT. TURKEY.
Economist Intelligence Unit, 111 W. 57th St., New York, NY 10019. TEL 212-554-0600. FAX 212-586-1182.
Vendor(s): Knight-Ridder Information, Inc., Lexis-Nexis. *1196*

COUNTRY REPORT. UGANDA, RWANDA, BURUNDI.
Economist Intelligence Unit, 111 W. 57th St., New York, NY 10019. TEL 212-554-0600. FAX 212-586-1182.
Vendor(s): Knight-Ridder Information, Inc., Lexis-Nexis. *1196*

COUNTRY REPORT. UKRAINE.
Economist Intelligence Unit, 111 W. 57th St., New York, NY 10019. TEL 212-554-0600. FAX 212-586-1182.
Vendor(s): Knight-Ridder Information, Inc., Lexis-Nexis. *1196*

COUNTRY REPORT. UNITED ARAB EMIRATES.
Economist Intelligence Unit, 111 W. 57th St., New York, NY 10019. TEL 212-554-0600. FAX 212-586-1182.
Vendor(s): Knight-Ridder Information, Inc., Lexis-Nexis. *1196*

COUNTRY REPORT. UNITED KINGDOM.
Economist Intelligence Unit, 111 W. 57th St., New York, NY 10019. TEL 212-554-0600. FAX 212-586-1182.
Vendor(s): Knight-Ridder Information, Inc., Lexis-Nexis. *1196*

COUNTRY REPORT. UNITED STATES OF AMERICA.
Economist Intelligence Unit, 111 W. 57th St., New York, NY 10019. TEL 212-554-0600. FAX 212-586-1182.
Vendor(s): Knight-Ridder Information, Inc., Lexis-Nexis. *1196*

COUNTRY REPORT. URUGUAY, PARAGUAY.
Economist Intelligence Unit, 111 W. 57th St., New York, NY 10019. TEL 212-554-0600. FAX 212-586-1182.
Vendor(s): Knight-Ridder Information, Inc., Lexis-Nexis. *1196*

COUNTRY REPORT. VENEZUELA.
Economist Intelligence Unit, 111 W. 57th St., New York, NY 10019. TEL 212-554-0600. FAX 212-586-1182.
Vendor(s): Knight-Ridder Information, Inc., Lexis-Nexis. *1196*

COUNTRY REPORT. ZAMBIA, ZAIRE.
Economist Intelligence Unit, 111 W. 57th St., New York, NY 10019. TEL 212-554-0600. FAX 212-586-1182.
Vendor(s): Knight-Ridder Information, Inc., Lexis-Nexis. *1197*

COUNTRY REPORT. ZIMBABWE.
Economist Intelligence Unit, 111 W. 57th St., New York, NY 10019. TEL 212-554-0600. FAX 212-586-1182.
Vendor(s): Knight-Ridder Information, Inc., Lexis-Nexis. *1197*

COUNTRY REPORTS.
Economist Intelligence Unit, 111 W. 57th St., New York, NY 10019. TEL 212-554-0600. FAX 212-586-1182.
Vendor(s): Knight-Ridder Information, Inc., Lexis-Nexis. *1197*

COUNTRY RISK SERVICE.
Economist Intelligence Unit, 111 W. 57th St., New York, NY 10019. TEL 212-554-0600. FAX 212-586-1182.
Vendor(s): Lexis-Nexis. *1197*

COUNTRY RISK SERVICE. ALGERIA.
Economist Intelligence Unit, 111 w. 57th St., New York, NY 10019. TEL 212-554-0600. FAX 212-586-1182.
Vendor(s): Lexis-Nexis. *1197*

COUNTRY RISK SERVICE. ANGOLA.
Economist Intelligence Unit, 111 W. 57th St., New York, NY 10019. TEL 212-554-0600. FAX 212-586-1182.
Vendor(s): Lexis-Nexis. *1197*

COUNTRY RISK SERVICE. ARGENTINA.
Economist Intelligence Unit, 111 W. 57th St., New York, NY 10019. TEL 212-554-0600. FAX 212-586-1182.
Vendor(s): Lexis-Nexis. *1197*

COUNTRY RISK SERVICE. AUSTRALIA.
Economist Intelligence Unit, 111 W. 57th St., New York, NY 10019. TEL 212-554-0600. FAX 212-586-1182.
Vendor(s): Lexis-Nexis. *1197*

COUNTRY RISK SERVICE. BALTIC REPUBLICS.
Economist Intelligence Unit, 111 W. 57th St., New York, NY 10019. TEL 212-554-0600. FAX 212-586-1182.
Vendor(s): Lexis-Nexis. *1197*

COUNTRY RISK SERVICE. BANGLADESH.
Economist Intelligence Unit, 111 W. 57th St., New York, NY 10019. TEL 212-554-0600. FAX 212-586-1182.
Vendor(s): Lexis-Nexis. *1197*

COUNTRY RISK SERVICE. BOLIVIA.
Economist Intelligence Unit, 111 W. 57th St., New York, NY 10019. TEL 212-554-0600. FAX 212-586-1182.
Vendor(s): Lexis-Nexis. *1197*

COUNTRY RISK SERVICE. BRAZIL.
Economist Intelligence Unit, 111 W. 57th St., New York, NY 10019. TEL 212-554-0600. FAX 212-586-1182.
Vendor(s): Lexis-Nexis. *1197*

COUNTRY RISK SERVICE. BULGARIA.
Economist Intelligence Unit, 111 W. 57th St., New York, NY 10019. TEL 212-554-0600. FAX 212-586-1182.
Vendor(s): Lexis-Nexis. *1197*

COUNTRY RISK SERVICE. CAMEROON.
Economist Intelligence Unit, 111 W. 57th St., New York, NY 10019. TEL 212-554-0600. FAX 212-586-1182.
Vendor(s): Lexis-Nexis. *1197*

COUNTRY RISK SERVICE. CHILE.
Economist Intelligence Unit, 111 W. 57th St., New York, NY 10019. TEL 212-554-0600. FAX 212-586-1182.
Vendor(s): Lexis-Nexis. *1198*

COUNTRY RISK SERVICE. CHINA.
Economist Intelligence Unit, 111 W. 57th St., New York, NY 10019. TEL 212-554-0600. FAX 212-586-1182.
Vendor(s): Lexis-Nexis. *1198*

COUNTRY RISK SERVICE. COLOMBIA.
Economist Intelligence Unit, 111 W. 57th St., New York, NY 10019. TEL 212-554-0600. FAX 212-586-1182.
Vendor(s): Lexis-Nexis. *1198*

COUNTRY RISK SERVICE. CONGO.
Economist Intelligence Unit, 111 W. 57th St., New York, NY 10019. TEL 212-554-0600. FAX 212-586-1182.
Vendor(s): Lexis-Nexis. *1198*

COUNTRY RISK SERVICE. COSTA RICA.
Economist Intelligence Unit, 111 W. 57th St., New York, NY 10019. TEL 212-554-0600. FAX 212-586-1182.
Vendor(s): Lexis-Nexis. *1198*

COUNTRY RISK SERVICE. COTE D'IVOIRE.
Economist Intelligence Unit, 111 W. 57th St., New York, NY 10019. TEL 212-554-0600. FAX 212-586-1182.
Vendor(s): Lexis-Nexis. *1198*

COUNTRY RISK SERVICE. CYPRUS.
Economist Intelligence Unit, 111 W. 57th St., New York, NY 10019. TEL 212-554-0600. FAX 212-586-1182.
Vendor(s): Lexis-Nexis. *1198*

COUNTRY RISK SERVICE. CZECH REPUBLIC.
Economist Intelligence Unit, 111 W. 57th St., New York, NY 10019. TEL 212-554-0600. FAX 212-586-1182.
Vendor(s): Lexis-Nexis. *1198*

COUNTRY RISK SERVICE. DOMINICAN REPUBLIC.
Economist Intelligence Unit, 111 W. 57th St., New York, NY 10019. TEL 212-554-0600. FAX 212-586-1182.
Vendor(s): Lexis-Nexis. *1198*

COUNTRY RISK SERVICE. ECUADOR.
Economist Intelligence Unit, 111 W. 57th St., New York, NY 10019. TEL 212-554-0600. FAX 212-586-1182.
Vendor(s): Lexis-Nexis. *1198*

COUNTRY RISK SERVICE. EGYPT.
Economist Intelligence Unit, 111 W. 57th St., New York, NY 10019. TEL 212-554-0600. FAX 212-586-1182.
Vendor(s): Lexis-Nexis. *1198*

COUNTRY RISK SERVICE. EL SALVADOR.
Economist Intelligence Unit, 111 W. 57th St., New York, NY 10019. TEL 212-554-0600. FAX 212-586-1182.
Vendor(s): Lexis-Nexis. *1198*

COUNTRY RISK SERVICE. FORMER YUGOSLAV REPUBLICS.
Economist Intelligence Unit, 111 W. 57th St., New York, NY 10019. TEL 212-554-0600. FAX 212-586-1182.
Vendor(s): Lexis-Nexis. *1198*

COUNTRY RISK SERVICE. GABON.
Economist Intelligence Unit, 111 W. 57th St., New York, NY 10019. TEL 212-554-0600. FAX 212-538-1182.
Vendor(s): Lexis-Nexis. *1198*

COUNTRY RISK SERVICE. GHANA.
Economist Intelligence Unit, 111 W. 57th St., New York, NY 10019. TEL 212-554-0600. FAX 212-586-1182.
Vendor(s): Lexis-Nexis. *1198*

COUNTRY RISK SERVICE. GREECE.
Economist Intelligence Unit, 111 W. 57th St., New York, NY 10019. TEL 212-554-0600. FAX 212-586-1182.
Vendor(s): Lexis-Nexis. *1198*

COUNTRY RISK SERVICE. GUATEMALA.
Economist Intelligence Unit, 111 W. 57th St., New York, NY 10019. TEL 212-554-0600. FAX 212-586-1182.
Vendor(s): Lexis-Nexis. *1198*

COUNTRY RISK SERVICE. HONDURAS.
Economist Intelligence Unit, 111 W. 57th St., New York, NY 10019. TEL 212-554-0600. FAX 212-586-1182.
Vendor(s): Lexis-Nexis. *1198*

COUNTRY RISK SERVICE. HONG KONG.
Economist Intelligence Unit, 111 W. 57th St., New York, NY 10019. TEL 212-554-0600. FAX 212-586-1182.
Vendor(s): Lexis-Nexis. *1199*

COUNTRY RISK SERVICE. HUNGARY.
Economist Intelligence Unit, 111 W. 57th St., New York, NY 10019. TEL 212-554-0600. FAX 212-586-1182.
Vendor(s): Lexis-Nexis. *1199*

COUNTRY RISK SERVICE. INDIA.
Economist Intelligence Unit, 111 W. 57th St., New York, NY 10019. TEL 212-554-0600. FAX 212-586-1182.
Vendor(s): Lexis-Nexis. *1199*

COUNTRY RISK SERVICE. INDONESIA.
Economist Intelligence Unit, 111 W. 57th St., New York, NY 10019. TEL 212-554-0600. FAX 212-586-1182.
Vendor(s): Lexis-Nexis. *1199*

COUNTRY RISK SERVICE. IRAN.
Economist Intelligence Unit, 111 W. 57th St., New York, NY 10019. TEL 212-554-0600. FAX 212-586-1182.
Vendor(s): Lexis-Nexis. *1199*

COUNTRY RISK SERVICE. IRAQ.
Economist Intelligence Unit, 111 W. 57th St., New York, NY 10019. TEL 212-554-0600. FAX 212-586-1182.
Vendor(s): Lexis-Nexis. *1199*

COUNTRY RISK SERVICE. ISRAEL.
Economist Intelligence Unit, 111 W. 57th St., New York, NY 10019. TEL 212-554-0600. FAX 212-586-1182.
Vendor(s): Lexis-Nexis. *1199*

COUNTRY RISK SERVICE. JAMAICA.
Economist Intelligence Unit, 111 W. 57th St., New York, NY 10019. TEL 212-554-0600. FAX 212-586-1182.
Vendor(s): Lexis-Nexis. *1199*

COUNTRY RISK SERVICE. JORDAN.
Economist Intelligence Unit, 111 W. 57th St., New York, NY 10019. TEL 212-554-0600. FAX 212-586-1182.
Vendor(s): Lexis-Nexis. *1199*

COUNTRY RISK SERVICE. KAZAKHSTAN.
Economist Intelligence Unit, 111 W. 57th St., New York, NY 10019. TEL 212-554-0600. FAX 212-586-1182.
Vendor(s): Lexis-Nexis. *1199*

COUNTRY RISK SERVICE. KENYA.
Economist Intelligence Unit, 111 W. 57th St., New York, NY 10019. TEL 212-554-0600. FAX 212-586-1182.
Vendor(s): Lexis-Nexis. *1199*

COUNTRY RISK SERVICE. KUWAIT.
Economist Intelligence Unit, 111 W. 57th St., New York, NY 10019. TEL 212-554-0600. FAX 212-586-1182.
Vendor(s): Lexis-Nexis. *1199*

COUNTRY RISK SERVICE. LIBYA.
Economist Intelligence Unit, 111 W. 57th St., New York, NY 10019. TEL 212-554-0600. FAX 212-586-1182.
Vendor(s): Lexis-Nexis. *1199*

COUNTRY RISK SERVICE. MALAWI.
Economist Intelligence Unit, 111 W. 57th St., New York, NY 10019. TEL 212-554-0600. FAX 212-586-1182.
Vendor(s): Lexis-Nexis. *1199*

COUNTRY RISK SERVICE. MALAYSIA.
Economist Intelligence Unit, 111 W. 57th St., New York, NY 10019. TEL 212-554-0600. FAX 212-586-1182.
Vendor(s): Lexis-Nexis. *1199*

COUNTRY RISK SERVICE. MEXICO.
Economist Intelligence Unit, 111 W. 57th St., New York, NY 10019. TEL 212-554-0600. FAX 212-586-1182.
Vendor(s): Lexis-Nexis. *1199*

COUNTRY RISK SERVICE. MOROCCO.
Economist Intelligence Unit, 111 W. 57th St., New York, NY 10019. TEL 212-554-0600. FAX 212-586-1182.
Vendor(s): Lexis-Nexis. *1199*

COUNTRY RISK SERVICE. NAMIBIA.
Economist Intelligence Unit, 111 W. 57th St., New York, NY 10019. TEL 212-586-0600. FAX 212-586-1182.
Vendor(s): Lexis-Nexis. *1199*

COUNTRY RISK SERVICE. NEW ZEALAND.
Economist Intelligence Unit, 111 W. 57th St., New York, NY 10019. TEL 212-554-0600. FAX 212-586-1182.
Vendor(s): Lexis-Nexis. *1200*

COUNTRY RISK SERVICE. NICARAGUA.
Economist Intelligence Unit, 111 W. 57th St., New York, NY 10019. TEL 212-554-0600. FAX 212-586-1182.
Vendor(s): Lexis-Nexis. *1200*

COUNTRY RISK SERVICE. NIGERIA.
Economist Intelligence Unit, 111 W. 57th St., New York, NY 10019. TEL 212-554-0600. FAX 212-586-1182.
Vendor(s): Lexis-Nexis. *1200*

COUNTRY RISK SERVICE. PAKISTAN.
Economist Intelligence Unit, 111 W. 57th St., New York, NY 10019. TEL 212-554-0600. FAX 212-586-1182.
Vendor(s): Lexis-Nexis. *1200*

COUNTRY RISK SERVICE. PANAMA.
Economist Intelligence Unit, 111 W. 57th St., New York, NY 10019. TEL 212-554-0600. FAX 212-586-1182.
Vendor(s): Lexis-Nexis. *1200*

COUNTRY RISK SERVICE. PAPUA NEW GUINEA.
Economist Intelligence Unit, 111 W. 57th St., New York, NY 10019. TEL 212-554-0600. FAX 212-586-1182.
Vendor(s): Lexis-Nexis. *1200*

COUNTRY RISK SERVICE. PARAGUAY.
Economist Intelligence Unit, 111 W. 57th St., New York, NY 10019. TEL 212-554-0600. FAX 212-586-1182.
Vendor(s): Lexis-Nexis. *1200*

COUNTRY RISK SERVICE. PERU.
Economist Intelligence Unit, 111 W. 57th St., New York, NY 10019. TEL 212-554-0600. FAX 212-586-1182.
Vendor(s): Lexis-Nexis. *1200*

COUNTRY RISK SERVICE. PHILIPPINES.
Economist Intelligence Unit, 111 W. 57th St., New York, NY 10019. TEL 212-554-0600. FAX 212-8586-1182.
Vendor(s): Lexis-Nexis. *1200*

COUNTRY RISK SERVICE. POLAND.
Economist Intelligence Unit, 111 W. 57th St., New York, NY 10019. TEL 212-554-0600. FAX 212-586-1182.
Vendor(s): Lexis-Nexis. *1200*

COUNTRY RISK SERVICE. PORTUGAL.
Economist Intelligence Unit, 111 W. 57th St., New York, NY 10019. TEL 212-554-0600. FAX 212-586-1182.
Vendor(s): Lexis-Nexis. *1200*

COUNTRY RISK SERVICE. ROMANIA.
Economist Intelligence Unit, 111 W. 57th St., New York, NY 10019. TEL 212-554-0600. FAX 212-586-1182.
Vendor(s): Lexis-Nexis. *1200*

COUNTRY RISK SERVICE. RUSSIA.
Economist Intelligence Unit, 111 W. 57th St., New York, NY 10019. TEL 212-554-0600. FAX 212-586-1182.
Vendor(s): Lexis-Nexis. *1200*

COUNTRY RISK SERVICE. SAUDI ARABIA.
Economist Intelligence Unit, 111 W. 57th St., New York, NY 10019. TEL 212-554-0600. FAX 212-586-1182.
Vendor(s): Lexis-Nexis. *1200*

COUNTRY RISK SERVICE. SENEGAL.
Economist Intelligence Unit, 111 W. 57th St., New York, NY 10019. TEL 212-554-0600. FAX 212-586-1182.
Vendor(s): Lexis-Nexis. *1201*

COUNTRY RISK SERVICE. SINGAPORE.
Economist Intelligence Unit, 111 W. 57th St., New York, NY 10019. TEL 212-554-0600. FAX 212-586-1182.
Vendor(s): Lexis-Nexis. *1201*

COUNTRY RISK SERVICE. SLOVENIA.
Economist Intelligence Unit, 111 W. 57th St., New York, NY 10019. TEL 212-554-0600. FAX 212-586-1182.
Vendor(s): Lexis-Nexis. *1200*

COUNTRY RISK SERVICE. SOUTH AFRICA.
Economist Intelligence Unit, 111 W. 57th St., New York, NY 10019. TEL 212-554-0600. FAX 212-586-1182.
Vendor(s): Lexis-Nexis. *1200*

COUNTRY RISK SERVICE. SOUTH KOREA.
Economist Intelligence Unit, 111 W. 57th St., New York, NY 10019. TEL 212-554-0600. FAX 212-586-1182.
Vendor(s): Lexis-Nexis. *1201*

COUNTRY RISK SERVICE. SPAIN.
Economist Intelligence Unit, 111 W. 57th St., New York, NY 10019. TEL 212-554-0600. FAX 212-938-4685.
Vendor(s): Lexis-Nexis. *1201*

COUNTRY RISK SERVICE. SRI LANKA.
Economist Intelligence Unit, 111 W. 57th St., New York, NY 10019. TEL 212-554-0600. FAX 212-586-1182.
Vendor(s): Lexis-Nexis. *1201*

COUNTRY RISK SERVICE. SUDAN.
Economist Intelligence Unit, 111 W. 57th St., New York, NY 10019. TEL 212-554-0600. FAX 212-586-1182.
Vendor(s): Lexis-Nexis. *1201*

COUNTRY RISK SERVICE. SYRIA.
Economist Intelligence Unit, 111 W. 57th St., New York, NY 10019. TEL 212-554-0600. FAX 212-586-1182.
Vendor(s): Lexis-Nexis. *1201*

COUNTRY RISK SERVICE. TAIWAN.
Economist Intelligence Unit, 111 W. 57th St., New York, NY 10019. TEL 212-554-0600. FAX 212-586-1182.
Vendor(s): Lexis-Nexis. *1201*

COUNTRY RISK SERVICE. THAILAND.
Economist Intelligence Unit, 111 W. 57th St., New York, NY 10019. TEL 212-554-0600. FAX 212-586-1182.
Vendor(s): Lexis-Nexis. *1201*

COUNTRY RISK SERVICE. TRINIDAD AND TOBAGO.
Economist Intelligence Unit, 111 W. 57th St., New York, NY 10019. TEL 212-554-0600. FAX 212-586-1182.
Vendor(s): Lexis-Nexis. *1201*

COUNTRY RISK SERVICE. TUNISIA.
Economist Intelligence Unit, 111 W. 57th St., New York, NY 10019. TEL 212-554-0600. FAX 212-586-1182.
Vendor(s): Lexis-Nexis. *1201*

COUNTRY RISK SERVICE. TURKEY.
Economist Intelligence Unit, 111 W. 57th St., New York, NY 10019. TEL 212-554-0600. FAX 212-586-1182.
Vendor(s): Lexis-Nexis. *1201*

COUNTRY RISK SERVICE. UKRAINE.
Economist Intelligence Unit, 111 W. 57th St., New York, NY 10019. TEL 212-554-0600. FAX 212-586-1182.
Vendor(s): Lexis-Nexis. *1201*

COUNTRY RISK SERVICE. UNITED ARAB EMIRATES.
Economist Intelligence Unit, 111 W. 57th St., New York, NY 10019. TEL 212-554-0600. FAX 212-586-1182.
Vendor(s): Lexis-Nexis. *1201*

COUNTRY RISK SERVICE. URUGUAY.
Economist Intelligence Unit, 111 W. 57th St., New York, NY 10019. TEL 212-554-0600. FAX 212-586-1182.
Vendor(s): Lexis-Nexis. *1201*

COUNTRY RISK SERVICE. VENEZUELA.
Economist Intelligence Unit, 111 W. 57th St., New York, NY 10019. TEL 212-554-0600. FAX 212-586-1182.
Vendor(s): Lexis-Nexis. *1201*

COUNTRY RISK SERVICE. YEMEN.
Economist Intelligence Unit, 111 W. 57th St., New York, NY 10019. TEL 212-554-0600. FAX 212-586-1182.
Vendor(s): Lexis-Nexis. *1201*

COUNTRY RISK SERVICE. ZAIRE.
Economist Intelligence Unit, 111 W. 57th St., New York, NY 10019. TEL 212-554-0600. FAX 212-586-1182.
Vendor(s): Lexis-Nexis. *1201*

COUNTRY RISK SERVICE. ZAMBIA.
Economist Intelligence Unit, 111 W. 57th St., New York, NY 10019. TEL 212-554-0600. FAX 212-586-1182.
Vendor(s): Lexis-Nexis. *1201*

COUNTRY RISK SERVICE. ZIMBABWE.
Economist Intelligence Unit, 111 W. 57th St., New York, NY 10019. TEL 212-554-0600. FAX 212-586-1182.
Vendor(s): Lexis-Nexis. *1202*

COUNTRYSIDE AND SMALL STOCK JOURNAL.
Countryside Publications, Ltd., N2601 Winter Sports Rd., Withee, WI 54498-9317. TEL 715-785-7979. FAX 715-785-7414.
Vendor(s): Information Access Co.. *3227*

COUNTY AND CITY DATA BOOK.
U.S. Bureau of the Census, Customer Services, Washington, DC 20233. TEL 301-457-4100. FAX 301-457-4714.
Vendor(s): CompuServe, Inc., Knight-Ridder Information, Inc.. *6601*

COUNTY BUSINESS PATTERNS.
U.S. Bureau of the Census, Customer Services, Washington, DC 20233. TEL 301-457-4100. FAX 301-457-4714.
Vendor(s): CompuServe, Inc., Knight-Ridder Information, Inc.. *991*

THE COURIER.
Union Society, King's Walk, Newcastle-upon-Tyne NE1 8QB, England. TEL 44-191-232-4050. FAX 44-191-222-1876. *1864*

COURIER (PARIS).
Unesco, 7-9 pl. de Fontenoy, 75700 Paris, France. TEL 33-1-45-77-16-10.
Vendor(s): Information Access Co., Knight-Ridder Information, Inc.. *5746*

COVER.
Arts New York, Box 1215, Cooper Sta., New York, NY 10276. TEL 212-673-1152. FAX 212-505-7139. *3610*

COWLES - SIMBA MEDIA DAILY.
SIMBA Information Inc. 11 Riverbend Dr. S., Box 4234, Stamford, CT 06907-0234. TEL 203-358-9900. FAX 203-358-5824.
Vendor(s): CompuServe, Inc., Information Access Co., NewsNet. *1901*

CRAFTS 'N THINGS.
Clapper Communications Companies, 2400 E. Devon Ave., Ste. 375, Des Plaines, IL 60018-4618. TEL 847-635-5800. FAX 847-635-6311. *466*

CRAIN'S CHICAGO BUSINESS.
Crain Communications, Inc. (Chicago), 740 N. Rush St., Chicago, IL 60611-2525. TEL 312-649-5270. FAX 312-649-5228.
Vendor(s): Information Access Co., Knight-Ridder Information, Inc., Lexis-Nexis (CHIBUS). *912*

CRAIN'S CLEVELAND BUSINESS.
Crain Communications, Inc. (Detroit), 1400 Woodbridge Ave., Detroit, MI 48207-3187. TEL 800-678-9595. FAX 216-694-4264.
Vendor(s): Information Access Co., Knight-Ridder Information, Inc., Lexis-Nexis. *1202*

CRAIN'S DETROIT BUSINESS.
Crain Communications, Inc. (Detroit), 1400 Woodbridge Ave., Detroit, MI 48207-3187. TEL 313-446-0426. FAX 313-446-1650.
Vendor(s): Information Access Co., Knight-Ridder Information, Inc., Lexis-Nexis. *912*

CRAIN'S NEW YORK BUSINESS.
Crain Communications, Inc. (New York), 220 E. 42nd St., Ste. 1306, New York, NY 10017. TEL 212-210-0277. FAX 212-210-0799.
Vendor(s): Information Access Co., Knight-Ridder Information, Inc., Lexis-Nexis (NYBUS). *912*

CRANBERRIES.
Box 858, S. Carver, MA 02366. TEL 508-866-5055. FAX 508-866-9291.
Vendor(s): Knight-Ridder Information, Inc.. *2965*

CREATIVE NONFICTION.
Box 81536, Pittsburgh, PA 15217-0336. TEL 412-422-8404. FAX 412-422-8405. *4199*

CREATIVITY.
Advertising Trade Publications, Inc., c/o Dan Barron, Ed., 456 Glenbrook Rd., Stamford, CT 06906-1800. TEL 212-889-6500. FAX 212-889-6504.
Vendor(s): Information Access Co.. *35*

CREDIT AND CHARGE CARDS: THE INTERNATIONAL MARKET.
Euromonitor, 60-61 Britton St., London EC1M 5NA, England. TEL 44-171-251-8024. FAX 44-171-608-3149.
Vendor(s): Data-Star, Knight-Ridder Information, Inc.. *1080*

CREDIT CARD MANAGEMENT.
Faulkner & Gray, Inc., 300 S. Wacker Dr., 18th Fl., Chicago, IL 60606. TEL 312-913-1334.
Vendor(s): Information Access Co., Lexis-Nexis, NewsNet, University Microfilms International. *1080*

CREDIT CARD NEWS.
Faulkner & Gray, Inc. (New York), 11 Penn Plaza, 17th Fl., New York, NY 10001. TEL 212-967-7000. FAX 212-967-7155.
Vendor(s): Information Access Co., University Microfilms International. *1080*

CREDIT CONTROL.
House of Words Ltd., 7 Greding Walk, Hutton, Brentwood, Essex CM13 2UF, England. TEL 44-1277-225402. FAX 44-1277-201554.
Vendor(s): University Microfilms International. *1080*

CREDIT RISK MANAGEMENT.
Phillips Business Information, Inc., 1201 Seven Locks Rd., Potomac, MD 20854. TEL 301-424-3338. FAX 301-309-3847.
Vendor(s): NewsNet (FI57). *1081*

CREDIT UNION ACCOUNTANT.
American Banker - Bond Buyer, Newsletter Division One State St. Plaza, New York, NY 10004-1549. TEL 800-733-4371. FAX 212-943-2224.
Vendor(s): Information Access Co.. *1081*

CREDIT UNION EXECUTIVE.
C U N A Publications, Box 431, Madison, WI 53701. TEL 608-231-4000. FAX 608-231-4370.
Vendor(s): Information Access Co.. *1081*

CREDIT UNION MANAGEMENT.
Credit Union Executives Society, Box 14167, Madison, WI 53714-0167. TEL 608-271-2664. FAX 608-271-2303.
Vendor(s): University Microfilms International. *1081*

CREDIT WORLD.
International Credit Association, 243 N. Lindbergh Blvd., Box 419057, St. Louis, MO 63141-1757. TEL 314-991-3030. FAX 314-991-3029.
Vendor(s): University Microfilms International. *1081*

CREIGHTON LAW REVIEW.
Creighton University, Creighton Law School, 2133 California St., Omaha, NE 68178. TEL 402-280-2980.
Vendor(s): West Services, Inc.. *3766*

CRIME & DELINQUENCY.
Sage Publications, Inc., 2455 Teller Rd., Thousand Oaks, CA 91320. TEL 805-499-0721. FAX 805-499-0871.
Vendor(s): University Microfilms International. *2161*

CRIMINAL APPEAL REPORTS.
Sweet & Maxwell, South Quay Plaza, 7th Fl., 183 Marsh Wall, London E14 9FT, England. TEL 071-538-8686. FAX 071-538-9508.
Vendor(s): Lexis-Nexis. *2161*

CRIMINAL JUSTICE ABSTRACTS.
Willow Tree Press, Inc., 124 Willow Tree Rd., Monsey, NY 10952. TEL 914-354-9139. FAX 914-362-8376.
Vendor(s): West Services, Inc.. *2179*

CRIMINAL JUSTICE ETHICS.
Institute for Criminal Justice Ethics, John Jay College, 899 10th Ave., New York, NY 10019. TEL 212-237-8033. FAX 212-237-8901.
Vendor(s): Information Access Co.. *5471*

CRIMINAL JUSTICE PERIODICAL INDEX.
U M I Company 300 N. Zeeb Rd., Ann Arbor, MI 48106. TEL 313-761-4700. FAX 800-864-0019.
Vendor(s): Knight-Ridder Information, Inc. (File no. 171). *2179*

CRIMINOLOGY.
American Society of Criminology, 1314 Kinnear Rd., Columbus, OH 43212. TEL 614-292-9207.
Vendor(s): University Microfilms International. *2162*

CRITICAL ISSUES.
Heritage Foundation, 214 Massachusetts Ave., N.E., Washington, DC 20002. TEL 202-546-4400. FAX 202-543-9647.
Vendor(s): Lexis-Nexis. *5659*

CRITICAL STUDIES IN MASS COMMUNICATION.
Speech Communication Association, 5105 Backlick
Rd., Bldg. E., Annandale, VA 22003. TEL 703-750-
0533. FAX 703-914-9471.
Vendor(s): University Microfilms International.
1959

CRITICISM.
Wayne State University Press, 4809 Woodward
Ave., Detroit, MI 48201-1309. TEL 313-577-6120.
FAX 313-577-6131.
Vendor(s): Information Access Co., University
Microfilms International. *4200*

CRITIQUE: STUDIES IN MODERN FICTION.
Heldref Publications, 1319 Eighteenth St., N.W.,
Washington, DC 20036-1802. TEL 202-296-6267.
FAX 202-296-5149.
Vendor(s): Information Access Co., University
Microfilms International. *4200*

CROP PHYSIOLOGY ABSTRACTS.
CAB International, Wallingford, Oxon. OX10 8DE,
England. TEL 44-1491-832111. FAX 44-1491-
833508.
Vendor(s): DIMDI, European Space Agency, Knight-
Ridder Information, Inc., STN International. *171*

CROSS CURRENTS (NEW ROCHELLE).
Association for Religion and Intellectual Life, College
of New Rochelle, New Rochelle, NY 10805-2339.
TEL 914-654-5425. FAX 914-654-5925. *6056*

CROSS-STITCHER.
Clapper Communications Companies, 2400 E.
Devon Ave., Ste. 375, Des Plaines, IL 60018-4618.
TEL 847-635-5800. FAX 847-635-6311. *5211*

CRUISING WORLD.
Sailing Company, Box 3400, Newport, RI 02840-
0992. TEL 401-847-1588. FAX 401-848-5048.
Vendor(s): Information Access Co.. *6534*

CULTIVOS TROPICALES.
Instituto Nacional de Ciencias Agricolas, Gaveta
Postal No. 1, San Jose de las Lajas, Havana
32700, Cuba. TEL 064-63290. FAX 53-7-333295.
218

CUMBERLAND LAW REVIEW.
Samford University, Cumberland School of Law, 800
Lakeshore Dr., ROBBH 315, Birmingham, AL
35229. TEL 205-870-2757. FAX 205-870-2673.
Vendor(s): West Services, Inc.. *3766*

CUMULATIVE BOOK INDEX.
H.W. Wilson Co., 950 University Ave., Bronx, NY
10452. TEL 718-588-8400. FAX 718-590-1617.
Vendor(s): Ovid Technologies, Inc., Wilsonline (File
CBI). *528*

**CUMULATIVE INDEX TO NURSING & ALLIED
HEALTH LITERATURE.**
C I N A H L Information Systems, 1509 Wilson
Terrace, Box 871, Glendale, CA 91209-0871.
TEL 818-409-8005. FAX 818-546-5679.
Vendor(s): Data-Star (NAHL), Ovid Technologies, Inc.
(NAHL). *4553*

**CURRENT ADVANCES IN APPLIED MICROBIOLOGY &
BIOTECHNOLOGY.**
Elsevier Science Ltd., Pergamon, P.O. Box 800,
Kidlington, Oxford OX5 1DX, England. TEL 44-1865-
843000. FAX 44-1865-843010.
Vendor(s): Ovid Technologies, Inc. (CABS). *618*

CURRENT ADVANCES IN CANCER RESEARCH.
Elsevier Science Ltd., Pergamon, P.O. Box 800,
Kidlington, Oxford OX5 1DX, England. TEL 44-1865-
843000. FAX 44-1865-843010.
Vendor(s): Ovid Technologies, Inc. (CABS). *4553*

**CURRENT ADVANCES IN CELL & DEVELOPMENTAL
BIOLOGY.**
Elsevier Science Ltd., Pergamon, P.O. Box 800,
Kidlington, Oxford OX5 1DX, England. TEL 44-1865-
843000. FAX 44-1865-843010.
Vendor(s): Ovid Technologies, Inc. (CABS). *618*

CURRENT ADVANCES IN CLINICAL CHEMISTRY.
Elsevier Science Ltd., Pergamon, P.O. Box 800,
Kidlington, Oxford OX5 1DX, England. TEL 44-1865-
843000. FAX 44-1865-843010.
Vendor(s): Ovid Technologies, Inc. (CABS). *1707*

**CURRENT ADVANCES IN ECOLOGICAL AND
ENVIRONMENTAL SCIENCES.**
Elsevier Science Ltd., Pergamon, The Boulevard,
Langford Ln., Kidlington, Oxford OX5 1GB, England.
TEL 44-1865-843000. FAX 44-1865-843010.
Vendor(s): Ovid Technologies, Inc. (CABS). *2828*

**CURRENT ADVANCES IN ENDOCRINOLOGY &
METABOLISM.**
Elsevier Science Ltd., Pergamon, P.O. Box 800,
Kidlington, Oxford OX5 1DX, England. TEL 44-1865-
843000. FAX 44-1865-843010.
Vendor(s): Ovid Technologies, Inc. (CABS). *4553*

**CURRENT ADVANCES IN GENETICS AND
MOLECULAR BIOLOGY.**
Elsevier Science Ltd., Pergamon, P.O. Box 800,
Kidlington, Oxford OX5 1DX, England. TEL 44-1865-
843000. FAX 44-1865-843010.
Vendor(s): Ovid Technologies, Inc. (CABS). *619*

**CURRENT ADVANCES IN IMMUNOLOGY &
INFECTIOUS DISEASES.**
Elsevier Science Ltd., Pergamon, P.O. Box 800,
Kidlington, Oxford OX5 1DX, England. TEL 44-1865-
843000. FAX 44-1865-843010.
Vendor(s): Ovid Technologies, Inc. (CABS). *4553*

CURRENT ADVANCES IN NEUROSCIENCE.
Elsevier Science Ltd., Pergamon, P.O. Box 800,
Kidlington, Oxford OX5 1DX, England. TEL 44-1865-
843000. FAX 44-1865-843010.
Vendor(s): Ovid Technologies, Inc. (CABS). *4553*

CURRENT ADVANCES IN PLANT SCIENCE.
Elsevier Science Ltd., Pergamon, P.O. Box 800,
Kidlington, Oxford OX5 1DX, England. TEL 44-1865-
843000. FAX 44-1865-843010.
Vendor(s): Ovid Technologies, Inc. (CABS). *619*

CURRENT ADVANCES IN PROTEIN BIOCHEMISTRY.
Elsevier Science Ltd., Pergamon, P.O. Box 800,
Kidlington, Oxford OX5 1DX, England. TEL 44-1865-
843000. FAX 44-1865-843010.
Vendor(s): Ovid Technologies, Inc. (CABS). *619*

CURRENT ADVANCES IN TOXICOLOGY.
Elsevier Science Ltd., Pergamon, P.O. Box 800,
Kidlington, Oxford OX5 1DX, England. TEL 44-1865-
843000. FAX 44-1865-843010.
Vendor(s): Ovid Technologies, Inc. (CABS). *2828*

CURRENT AWARENESS IN BIOLOGICAL SCIENCES.
Elsevier Science Ltd., Pergamon, P.O. Box 800,
Kidlington, Oxford OX5 1DX, England. TEL 44-1865-
843000. FAX 44-1865-843010.
Vendor(s): Ovid Technologies, Inc. (CABS). *619*

CURRENT AWARENESS IN HEALTH EDUCATION.
U.S. Bureau of Health Education, Department of
Health and Human Services, Washington, DC
20201. TEL 202-655-4000.
Vendor(s): Ovid Technologies, Inc.. *5526*

**CURRENT BIBLIOGRAPHY ON SCIENCE AND
TECHNOLOGY: CHEMISTRY AND CHEMICAL
ENGINEERING (FOREIGN).**
Japan Information Center of Science and
Technology, 5-3 Yonbancho, Chiyoda-ku, Tokyo
102, Japan. TEL 03-3214-8413. FAX 03-5214-
8410.
Vendor(s): JICST. *1707*

**CURRENT BIBLIOGRAPHY ON SCIENCE AND
TECHNOLOGY: CHEMISTRY AND CHEMICAL
ENGINEERING (JAPANESE).**
Japan Information Center of Science and
Technology, 5-3 Yonbancho, Chiyoda-ku, Tokyo
102, Japan. TEL 03-5214-8413. FAX 03-5214-
8410.
Vendor(s): JICST. *1708*

**CURRENT BIBLIOGRAPHY ON SCIENCE AND
TECHNOLOGY: CIVIL ENGINEERING AND
ARCHITECTURE.**
Japan Information Center of Science and
Technology, 5-3, Yonbancho, Chiyoda-ku, Tokyo
102, Japan. TEL 03-5214-8413. FAX 03-5214-
8410.
Vendor(s): JICST. *2626*

**CURRENT BIBLIOGRAPHY ON SCIENCE AND
TECHNOLOGY: EARTH SCIENCE, MINING AND
METALLURGY.**
Japan Information Center of Science and
Technology, 5-3, Yonbancho, Chiyoda-ku, Tokyo 102,
Japan. TEL 03-5214-8413. FAX 03-5214-8410.
Vendor(s): JICST. *2218*

**CURRENT BIBLIOGRAPHY ON SCIENCE AND
TECHNOLOGY: ELECTRONICS AND ELECTRICAL
ENGINEERING.**
Japan Information Center of Science and
Technology, 5-3, Yonbancho, Chiyoda-ku, Tokyo
102, Japan. TEL 03-5214-8413. FAX 03-5214-
8410.
Vendor(s): JICST. *2626*

**CURRENT BIBLIOGRAPHY ON SCIENCE AND
TECHNOLOGY: ENERGY.**
Japan Information Center of Science and
Technology, 5-3, Yonbancho, Chiyoda-ku, Tokyo
102, Japan. TEL 03-5214-8413. FAX 03-5214-
8410.
Vendor(s): JICST. *2562*

**CURRENT BIBLIOGRAPHY ON SCIENCE AND
TECHNOLOGY: ENVIRONMENTAL POLLUTION.**
Japan Information Center of Science and
Technology, 5-3, Yonbancho, Chiyoda-ku, Tokyo 102,
Japan. TEL 03-5214-8413. FAX 03-3581-6446.
Vendor(s): JICST. *2828*

**CURRENT BIBLIOGRAPHY ON SCIENCE AND
TECHNOLOGY: LIFE SCIENCES.**
Japan Information Center of Science and
Technology, 5-3, Yonbancho, Chiyoda-ku, Tokyo
102, Japan. TEL 03-5214-8413. FAX 03-5214-
8410.
Vendor(s): JICST. *619*

**CURRENT BIBLIOGRAPHY ON SCIENCE AND
TECHNOLOGY: MANAGEMENT SCIENCE AND
SYSTEMS ENGINEERING.**
Japan Information Center of Science and
Technology, 5-3, Yonbancho, Chiyoca-ku, Tokyo
102, Japan. TEL 03-5214-8413. FAX 03-5214-
8410.
Vendor(s): JICST. *991*

**CURRENT BIBLIOGRAPHY ON SCIENCE AND
TECHNOLOGY: MECHANICAL ENGINEERING.**
Japan Information Center of Science and
Technology, 5-3, Yonbancho, Chiyoda-ku, Tokyo
102, Japan. TEL 03-5214-8413. FAX 03-5214-
8410.
Vendor(s): JICST. *2626*

**CURRENT BIBLIOGRAPHY ON SCIENCE AND
TECHNOLOGY: NUCLEAR ENGINEERING.**
Japan Information Center of Science and
Technology, 5-3, Yonbancho, Chiyoda-ku, Tokyo
102, Japan. TEL 03-5214-8413. FAX 03-5214-
8410.
Vendor(s): JICST. *2626*

**CURRENT BIBLIOGRAPHY ON SCIENCE AND
TECHNOLOGY: PURE AND APPLIED PHYSICS.**
Japan Information Center of Science and
Technology, 5-3, Yonbancho, Chiyoda-ku, Tokyo
102, Japan. TEL 03-5214-8413. FAX 03-5214-
8410.
Vendor(s): JICST. *5578*

CURRENT BIOTECHNOLOGY.
The Royal Society of Chemistry, Thomas Graham
House, Science Park, Milton Rd., Cambridge CB4
4WF, England. TEL 44-1223-420066. FAX 44-
1223-423429.
Vendor(s): Data-Star (CUBI), Knight-Ridder
Information, Inc. (File no.358). *619*

**CURRENT BUSINESS REPORTS: MONTHLY RETAIL
TRADE: SALES AND INVENTORIES.**
U.S. Bureau of the Census, Customer Services,
Washington, DC 20233. TEL 301-457-4100.
FAX 301-457-4714.
Vendor(s): CompuServe, Inc., Knight-Fidder
Information, Inc.. *991*

**CURRENT BUSINESS REPORTS: MONTHLY
WHOLESALE TRADE, SALES AND INVENTORIES.**
U.S. Bureau of the Census, Customer Services,
Washington, DC 20233. TEL 301-457-4100.
FAX 301-457-4714.
Vendor(s): CompuServe, Inc., Knight-Ridder
Information, Inc.. *1164*

**CURRENT CONSTRUCTION REPORTS: HOUSING
COMPLETIONS.**
U.S. Bureau of the Census, Customer Services,
Washington, DC 20233. TEL 301-457-4100.
FAX 301-457-4714. *3580*

CURRENT CONSTRUCTION REPORTS: HOUSING STARTS.
U.S. Bureau of the Census, Customer Services, Washington, DC 20233. TEL 310-457-4100. FAX 301-457-4714.
Vendor(s): CompuServe, Inc., Knight-Ridder Information, Inc.. *3580*

CURRENT CONSTRUCTION REPORTS: HOUSING UNITS AUTHORIZED BY BUILDING PERMITS.
U.S. Bureau of the Census, Customer Services, Washington, DC 20233. TEL 301-457-4100. FAX 301-457-4714.
Vendor(s): CompuServe, Inc., Knight-Ridder Information, Inc.. *3580*

CURRENT CONSTRUCTION REPORTS: NEW ONE-FAMILY HOUSES SOLD.
U.S. Bureau of the Census, Customer Services, Washington, DC 20233. TEL 301-457-4100. FAX 301-457-4714.
Vendor(s): CompuServe, Inc., Knight-Ridder Information, Inc.. *3580*

CURRENT CONSTRUCTION REPORTS: NEW RESIDENTIAL CONSTRUCTION IN SELECTED METROPOLITAN AREAS.
U.S. Bureau of the Census, Customer Services, Washington, DC 20233. TEL 301-457-4100. FAX 301-457-4714.
Vendor(s): CompuServe, Inc., Knight-Ridder Information, Inc.. *3580*

CURRENT CONSTRUCTION REPORTS: VALUE OF NEW CONSTRUCTION PUT IN PLACE.
U.S. Bureau of the Census, Customer Services, Washington, DC 20233. TEL 301-457-4100. FAX 301-457-4714.
Vendor(s): CompuServe, Inc., Knight-Ridder Information, Inc.. *3580*

CURRENT CONTENTS: AGRICULTURE, BIOLOGY & ENVIRONMENTAL SCIENCES.
Institute for Scientific Information, 3501 Market St., Philadelphia, PA 19104. TEL 215-386-0100. FAX 215-386-2991.
Vendor(s): Knight-Ridder Information, Inc. (File no.440), Ovid Technologies, Inc. (CTOC,CBIB,AGRI). *171*

CURRENT CONTENTS: ARTS & HUMANITIES.
Institute for Scientific Information, 3501 Market St., Philadelphia, PA 19104. TEL 215-386-0100. FAX 215-386-2991.
Vendor(s): Knight-Ridder Information, Inc. (File no.440), Ovid Technologies, Inc. (CTOC,CBIB,ARTS). *3632*

CURRENT CONTENTS: CLINICAL MEDICINE.
Institute for Scientific Information, 3501 Market St., Philadelphia, PA 19104. TEL 215-386-0100. FAX 215-386-2991.
Vendor(s): Knight-Ridder Information, Inc. (File no.440), Ovid Technologies, Inc. (CTOC,CBIB,CLIN). *4554*

CURRENT CONTENTS: ENGINEERING, COMPUTING & TECHNOLOGY.
Institute for Scientific Information, 3501 Market St., Philadelphia, PA 19104. TEL 215-386-0100. FAX 215-386-2991.
Vendor(s): Knight-Ridder Information, Inc. (File no.440), Ovid Technologies, Inc. (CTOC,CBIB,ENGI). *2626*

CURRENT CONTENTS: LIFE SCIENCES.
Institute for Scientific Information, 3501 Market St., Philadelphia, PA 19104. TEL 215-386-0100. FAX 215-386-2291.
Vendor(s): Knight-Ridder Information, Inc. (File no.440), Ovid Technologies, Inc. (CTOC,CBIB,LIFE). *619*

CURRENT CONTENTS: PHYSICAL, CHEMICAL & EARTH SCIENCES.
Institute for Scientific Information, 3501 Market St., Philadelphia, PA 19104. TEL 215-386-0100. FAX 215-386-2291.
Vendor(s): Knight-Ridder Information, Inc. (File no.440), Ovid Technologies, Inc. (CTOC,CBIB,PHYS). *1708*

CURRENT CONTENTS: SOCIAL & BEHAVIORAL SCIENCES.
Institute for Scientific Information, 3501 Market St., Philadelphia, PA 19104. TEL 215-386-0100. FAX 215-386-2291.
Vendor(s): Knight-Ridder Information, Inc. (File no.440), Ovid Technologies, Inc. (CTOC,CBIB,BEHA). *6441*

CURRENT DIGEST OF THE POST-SOVIET PRESS.
Current Digest of the Soviet Press, 3857 N. High St., Columbus, OH 43214-3747. TEL 614-292-4234. FAX 614-267-6310.
Vendor(s): Lexis-Nexis. *5721*

CURRENT GOVERNMENTS REPORTS.
U.S. Bureau of the Census, Governments Division, Washington, DC 20233. TEL 301-457-1523.
Available only online. *5898*

CURRENT GOVERNMENTS REPORTS: CITY EMPLOYMENT.
U.S. Bureau of the Census, Governments Division, Washington, DC 20233. TEL 301-457-1523.
Available only online. Vendor(s): CompuServe, Inc., Knight-Ridder Information, Inc.. *991*

CURRENT GOVERNMENTS REPORTS: CITY GOVERNMENT FINANCES.
U.S. Bureau of the Census, Governments Division, Washington, DC 20233. TEL 301-457-1523.
Available only online. *1540*

CURRENT GOVERNMENTS REPORTS: COUNTY GOVERNMENT EMPLOYMENT.
U.S. Bureau of the Census, Governments Division, Washington, DC 20233. TEL 301-457-1523.
Available only online. Vendor(s): CompuServe, Inc., Knight-Ridder Information, Inc.. *5898*

CURRENT GOVERNMENTS REPORTS: COUNTY GOVERNMENT FINANCES.
U.S. Bureau of the Census, Governments Division, Washington, DC 20233. TEL 202-457-1523.
Available only online. *1540*

CURRENT GOVERNMENTS REPORTS: FINANCES OF EMPLOYEE RETIREMENT SYSTEMS OF STATE AND LOCAL GOVERNMENTS.
U.S. Bureau of the Census, Governments Division, Washington, DC 20233. TEL 202-457-1523.
Available only online. *1541*

CURRENT GOVERNMENTS REPORTS: GOVERNMENT FINANCES.
U.S. Bureau of the Census, Governments Division, Washington, DC 20233. TEL 301-457-1523. FAX 301-457-4714.
Available only online. Vendor(s): CompuServe, Inc., Knight-Ridder Information, Inc.. *1541*

CURRENT GOVERNMENTS REPORTS: PUBLIC EMPLOYMENT.
U.S. Bureau of the Census, Governments Division, Washington, DC 20233. TEL 301-457-1523. FAX 301-457-4714.
Vendor(s): CompuServe, Inc., Knight-Ridder Information, Inc.. *1368*

CURRENT GOVERNMENTS REPORTS: STATE GOVERNMENT FINANCES.
U.S. Bureau of the Census, Governments Division, Washington, DC 20233. TEL 202-457-1586.
Available only online. *991*

CURRENT GOVERNMENTS REPORTS: STATE GOVERNMENT TAX COLLECTIONS.
U.S. Bureau of the Census, Customer Services, Washington, DC 20233. TEL 202-457-4100.
Vendor(s): CompuServe, Inc., Knight-Ridder Information, Inc.. *1541*

CURRENT HEALTH 2.
Weekly Reader Corporation, 245 Long Hill Rd., Box 2791, Middletown, CT 06457-9291. FAX 609-786-3360.
Vendor(s): Information Access Co., University Microfilms International. *5526*

CURRENT HISTORY.
Current History, Inc., 4225 Main St., Philadelphia, PA 19127. TEL 215-482-4464. FAX 215-482-9197.
Vendor(s): Knight-Ridder Information, Inc., Ovid Technologies, Inc.. *5660*

CURRENT HOUSING REPORTS: HOUSING VACANCIES AND HOME OWNERSHIP.
U.S. Bureau of the Census, Customer Services, Washington, DC 20233. TEL 301-457-4100. FAX 301-457-4714.
Vendor(s): CompuServe, Inc., Knight-Ridder Information, Inc.. *3581*

CURRENT INDEX TO JOURNALS IN EDUCATION.
Oryx Press, 4041 N. Central Ave., No. 700, Phoenix, AZ 85012-3397. TEL 602-265-2651. FAX 602-265-6250.
Vendor(s): CISTI, Knight-Ridder Information, Inc. (File no.1/ERIC), Orbit Search Service (ERIC), Ovid Technologies, Inc.. *2387*

CURRENT INDEX TO STATISTICS.
American Statistical Association, 1429 Duke St., Alexandria, VA 22314-3402. TEL 703-684-1221. FAX 703-684-2037.
Vendor(s): European Space Agency, Knight-Ridder Information, Inc., Ovid Technologies, Inc. (MATH). *4405*

CURRENT INDUSTRIAL REPORTS.
U.S. Bureau of the Census, Customer Services, Washington, DC 20233. TEL 301-457-4100. FAX 301-457-4714.
Available only online. Vendor(s): CompuServe, Inc., Knight-Ridder Information, Inc.. *1517*

CURRENT INDUSTRIAL REPORTS: BROADWOVEN FABRICS (GRAY).
U.S. Bureau of the Census, Customer Services, Washington, DC 20233. TEL 301-457-4100. FAX 301-457-4714.
Available only online. Vendor(s): CompuServe, Inc., Knight-Ridder Information, Inc.. *6690*

CURRENT INDUSTRIAL REPORTS: FATS AND OILS. OILSEED CRUSHINGS.
U.S. Bureau of the Census, Customer Services, Washington, DC 20233. TEL 301-457-4100. FAX 301-457-4714.
Available only online. Vendor(s): CompuServe, Inc., Knight-Ridder Information, Inc.. *2995*

CURRENT INDUSTRIAL REPORTS: FATS AND OILS. PRODUCTION, CONSUMPTION, AND STOCKS.
U.S. Bureau of the Census, Customer Services, Washington, DC 20233. TEL 301-457-4100. FAX 301-457-4714.
Available only online. Vendor(s): CompuServe, Inc., Knight-Ridder Information, Inc.. *2995*

CURRENT INDUSTRIAL REPORTS: NONFERROUS CASTINGS.
U.S. Bureau of the Census, Customer Services, Washington, DC 20233. TEL 301-457-4100. *4981*

CURRENT LAW INDEX.
Information Access Company, 362 Lakeside Dr., Foster City, CA 94404. TEL 415-378-5200. FAX 415-378-5369.
Vendor(s): Ovid Technologies, Inc., Knight-Ridder Information, Inc., Lexis-Nexis, West Services, Inc.. *3874*

CURRENT MATHEMATICAL PUBLICATIONS.
American Mathematical Society, Box 6248, Providence, RI 02940-6248. TEL 401-455-4000.
Vendor(s): European Space Agency, Knight-Ridder Information, Inc., Ovid Technologies, Inc.. *4405*

CURRENT OPINION IN ANAESTHESIOLOGY.
Rapid Science Publishers, 2-6 Boundary Row, London SE1 8HN, England. TEL 44-171-865-0198. FAX 44-171-410-6600.
Vendor(s): OCLC. *4556*

CURRENT OPINION IN BIOTECHNOLOGY.
Current Biology Ltd., 400 Market St., Ste. 700, Philadelphia, PA 19106. TEL 800-552-5866. FAX 215-574-2270.
Vendor(s): OCLC. *660*

CURRENT OPINION IN CARDIOLOGY.
Rapid Science Publishers, 2-6 Boundary Row, London SE1 8HN, England. TEL 44-171-865-0198. FAX 44-171-410-6600.
Vendor(s): OCLC. *4556*

CURRENT OPINION IN CELL BIOLOGY.
Current Biology Ltd., 400 Market St., Ste. 700, Philadelphia, PA 19106. FAX 215-574-2270.
Vendor(s): OCLC. *619*

CURRENT OPINION IN CRITICAL CARE.
Rapid Science Publishers, 2-6 Boundary Row,
London SE1 8HN, England. TEL 44-171-865-0198.
FAX 44-171-865-0198.
Vendor(s): OCLC. *4782*

CURRENT OPINION IN DERMATOLOGY.
Rapid Science Publishers, 2-6 Boundary Row,
London SE1 8HN, England. TEL 44-171-865-0198.
FAX 44-171-410-6600.
Vendor(s): OCLC. *4660*

**CURRENT OPINION IN ENDOCRINOLOGY &
DIABETES.**
Rapid Science Publishers, 2-6 Boundary Row,
London SE1 8HN, England. TEL 44-171-865-0198.
FAX 44-171-410-6600.
Vendor(s): OCLC. *4667*

CURRENT OPINION IN GASTROENTEROLOGY.
Rapid Science Publishers, 2-6 Boundary Row,
London SE1 8HN, England. TEL 44-171-865-0198.
FAX 44-171-410-6600.
Vendor(s): OCLC. *4557*

CURRENT OPINION IN GENETICS & DEVELOPMENT.
Current Biology Ltd., 400 Market St., Ste. 700,
Philadelphia, PA 19106. TEL 800-552-5866.
FAX 215-574-2270.
Vendor(s): OCLC. *620*

CURRENT OPINION IN HEMATOLOGY.
Rapid Science Publishers, 2-6 Boundary Row,
London SE1 8HN, England. TEL 44-171-865-0198.
FAX 44-171-410-6600.
Vendor(s): OCLC. *4699*

CURRENT OPINION IN IMMUNOLOGY.
Current Biology Ltd., 400 Market St., Ste. 700,
Philadelphia, PA 19106. FAX 215-574-2270.
Vendor(s): OCLC. *4557*

CURRENT OPINION IN INFECTIOUS DISEASES.
Rapid Science Publishers, 2-6 Boundary Row,
London SE1 8HN, England. TEL 44-171-865-0198.
FAX 44-171-410-6600.
Vendor(s): OCLC. *4557*

CURRENT OPINION IN LIPIDOLOGY.
Rapid Science Publishers, 2-6 Boundary Row,
London SE1 8HN, England. TEL 44-171-410-6600.
FAX 44-171-410-6600.
Vendor(s): OCLC. *4557*

**CURRENT OPINION IN NEPHROLOGY &
HYPERTENSION.**
Rapid Science Publishers, 2-6 Boundary Row,
London SE1 8HN, England. TEL 44-171-865-0198.
FAX 44-171-865-0198.
Vendor(s): OCLC. *4557*

CURRENT OPINION IN NEUROBIOLOGY.
Current Biology, Ltd., 400 Market St., Ste. 700,
Philadelphia, PA 19106. TEL 800-552-5866.
FAX 215-574-2270.
Vendor(s): OCLC. *620*

CURRENT OPINION IN NEUROLOGY.
Rapid Science Publishers, 2-6 Boundary Row,
London SE1 8HN, England. TEL 44-171-865-0198.
FAX 44-171-410-6600.
Vendor(s): OCLC. *4557*

**CURRENT OPINION IN OBSTETRICS &
GYNECOLOGY.**
Rapid Science Publishers, 2-6 Boundary Row,
London SE1 8HN, England. TEL 44-171-865-0198.
FAX 44-171-410-6600.
Vendor(s): OCLC. *4557*

CURRENT OPINION IN ONCOLOGY.
Rapid Science Publishers, 2-6 Boundary Row,
London SE1 8HN, England. TEL 44-171-865-0198.
FAX 44-171-410-6600.
Vendor(s): OCLC. *4557*

CURRENT OPINION IN OPHTHALMOLOGY.
Rapid Science Publishers, 2-6 Boundary Row,
London SE1 8HN, England. TEL 44-171-865-0198.
FAX 44-171-410-6600.
Vendor(s): OCLC. *4558*

CURRENT OPINION IN ORTHOPEDICS.
Rapid Science Publishers, 2-6 Boundary Row,
London SE1 8HN, England. TEL 44-171-865-0198.
FAX 44-171-410-6600.
Vendor(s): OCLC. *4558*

**CURRENT OPINION IN OTOLARYNGOLOGY & HEAD
AND NECK SURGERY.**
Rapid Science Publishers, 2-6 Boundary Row,
London SE1 8HN, England. TEL 44-171-865-0198.
FAX 44-171-410-6600.
Vendor(s): OCLC. *4796*

CURRENT OPINION IN PEDIATRICS.
Rapid Science Publishers, 2-6 Boundary Row,
London SE1 8HN, England. TEL 44-171-865-0198.
FAX 44-171-410-6600.
Vendor(s): OCLC. *4558*

CURRENT OPINION IN PERIODONTOLOGY.
Rapid Science Publishers, 2-6 Boundary Row,
London SE1 8HN, England. TEL 44-171-865-0198.
FAX 44-171-410-6600.
Vendor(s): OCLC. *4558*

CURRENT OPINION IN PSYCHIATRY.
Rapid Science Publishers, 2-6 Boundary Row,
London SE1 8HN, England. TEL 44-171-865-0198.
FAX 44-171-410-6600.
Vendor(s): OCLC. *4558*

CURRENT OPINION IN PULMONARY MEDICINE.
Rapid Science Publishers, 2-6 Boundary Row,
London SE1 8HN, England. TEL 44-171-865-0198.
FAX 44-171-410-6600.
Vendor(s): OCLC. *4837*

CURRENT OPINION IN RHEUMATOLOGY.
Rapid Science Publishers, 2-6 Boundary Row,
London SE1 8HN, England. TEL 44-171-865-0198.
FAX 44-171-410-6600.
Vendor(s): OCLC. *4558*

CURRENT OPINION IN STRUCTURAL BIOLOGY.
Current Biology Ltd., 400 Market St., Ste. 700,
Philadelphia, PA 19106. TEL 800-552-5866.
FAX 215-574-2270.
Vendor(s): OCLC. *620*

CURRENT OPINION IN SURGICAL INFECTIONS.
Rapid Science Publishers, 2-6 Boundary Row,
London SE1 8HN, England. TEL 44-171-865-0198.
FAX 44-171-410-6600.
Vendor(s): OCLC. *4907*

CURRENT OPINION IN UROLOGY.
Rapid Science Publishers, 2-6 Boundary Row,
London SE1 8HN, England. TEL 44-171-865-0198.
FAX 44-171-410-6600.
Vendor(s): OCLC. *4558*

CURRENT PHYSICS INDEX.
American Institute of Physics, One Physics Ellipse,
College Park, MD 20740-3843. TEL 301-209-
3000. *5578*

**CURRENT POPULATION REPORTS: CONSUMER
INCOME. MONEY INCOME OF HOUSEHOLDS,
FAMILIES AND PERSONS IN THE UNITED STATES
(YEAR).**
U.S. Bureau of the Census, Customer Services,
Washington, DC 20233. TEL 301-457-4100.
FAX 301-457-4714.
Vendor(s): CompuServe, Inc., Knight-Ridder
Information, Inc.. *5797*

**CURRENT POPULATION REPORTS: POPULATION
CHARACTERISTICS. GEOGRAPHICAL MOBILITY.**
U.S. Bureau of the Census, Customer Services,
Washington, DC 20233. TEL 301-457-4100.
FAX 301-457-4714.
Vendor(s): CompuServe, Inc., Knight-Ridder
Information, Inc.. *5797*

**CURRENT POPULATION REPORTS: POPULATION
CHARACTERISTICS. MARITAL STATUS AND
LIVING ARRANGEMENTS.**
U.S. Bureau of the Census, Customer Services,
Washington, DC 20233. TEL 301-457-4100.
FAX 301-457-4714.
Vendor(s): CompuServe, Inc., Knight-Ridder
Information, Inc.. *5797*

**CURRENT POPULATION REPORTS: POPULATION
CHARACTERISTICS. SCHOOL ENROLLMENT:
SOCIAL AND ECONOMIC CHARACTERISTICS OF
STUDENTS.**
U.S. Bureau of the Census, Customer Services,
Washington, DC 20233. TEL 301-457-4100.
FAX 301-457-4714.
Vendor(s): CompuServe, Inc., Knight-Ridder
Information, Inc.. *5797*

**CURRENT POPULATION REPORTS: POPULATION
ESTIMATES AND PROJECTIONS. UNITED STATES
POPULATION ESTIMATES BY AGE, SEX, RACE
AND HISPANIC ORIGIN.**
U.S. Bureau of the Census, Customer Services,
Washington, DC 20233. TEL 301-457-4100.
FAX 301-457-4714.
Vendor(s): CompuServe, Inc., Knight-Ridder
Information, Inc.. *5797*

**CURRENT POPULATION REPORTS: SERIES P-25.
POPULATION ESTIMATES AND PROJECTIONS.**
U.S. Bureau of the Census, Customer Services,
Washington, DC 20233. TEL 301-457-4100.
FAX 301-457-4714.
Vendor(s): CompuServe, Inc., Knight-Ridder
Information, Inc.. *5797*

**CURRENT POPULATION REPORTS: SERIES P-70.
HOUSEHOLD ECONOMIC STUDIES.**
U.S. Bureau of the Census, Customer Services,
Washington, DC 20402. TEL 301-457-4100.
FAX 301-457-4714.
Vendor(s): CompuServe, Inc., Knight-Ridder
Information, Inc.. *5798*

**CURRENT RESEARCH IN BRITAIN. BIOLOGICAL
SCIENCES.**
Longman Cartermill Ltd., Technology Centre, St.
Andrews, Fife KY16 9EA, Scotland. TEL 44-1937-
843434. FAX 44-1937-546333.
Vendor(s): Orbit Search Service (CRIB). *620*

CURRENT RESEARCH IN BRITAIN. HUMANITIES.
Longman Cartermill Ltd., Technology Centre, St.
Andrews, Fife KY16 9EA, Scotland. TEL 0937-
843434. FAX 0937-546333.
Vendor(s): Orbit Search Service (CRIB). *3632*

**CURRENT RESEARCH IN BRITAIN. PHYSICAL
SCIENCES.**
Longman Cartermill Ltd., Technology Centre, St.
Andrews, Fife KY16 9EA, Scotland. TEL 44-1937-
843434. FAX 44-1937-546333.
Vendor(s): Orbit Search Service (CFIB). *6301*

**CURRENT RESEARCH IN LIBRARY & INFORMATION
SCIENCE.**
Bowker - Saur Ltd., A member of the Reed Elsevier
plc group, Maypole House, Maypole Rd., E.
Grinstead, W. Sussex RH19 1HU, England. TEL 44-
1342-330100. FAX 44-1342-330191.
Vendor(s): Knight-Ridder Information, Inc. (File
no.61), Ovid Technologies, Inc. (LISA). *3987*

**CURRENT SCIENCE AND TECHNOLOGY RESEARCH
IN JAPAN.**
Japan Information Center of Science and
Technology, 5-3, Yonbancho, Chiyoda-ku, Tokyo
102, Japan. TEL 03-5214-8413. FAX 03-5214-
8410.
Vendor(s): JICST. *6301*

CURRENT TECHNOLOGY INDEX.
Bowker - Saur Ltd., A member of the Reed Elsevier
plc group, Maypole House, Maypole Rd., E.
Grinstead, W. Sussex RH19 1HU, England. TEL 44-
1342-330100. FAX 44-1342-330191.
Vendor(s): Knight-Ridder Information, Inc. (File
no.142). *6671*

CURSUS.
Universite de Montreal, Ecole de Bibliotheconomie et
des Sciences de l'Information C.P. 6128, succ.
Centre Ville, Montreal PQ H3C 3J7, Canada.
Available only online. *3987*

CUSTOM BUILDER.
Gruner & Jahr U.S.A. Publishing, 110 Fifth Ave.,
New York, NY 10011-5601. TEL 207-828-4470.
FAX 207-828-4478.
Vendor(s): Information Access Co.. *851*

CYCLE WORLD.
Hachette Filipacchi Magazines, Inc., 1633 Broadway,
New York, NY 10019. TEL 212-767-6000.
FAX 212-767-5619.
Vendor(s): Information Access Co., University
Microfilms International. *6522*

CYPRUS. OFFICIAL GAZETTE.
Government Printing Office, Nicosia, Cyprus.
TEL 357-2-302202. FAX 357-2-303175. *3132*

THE CYPRUS REVIEW.
Intercollege - Research and Development Center, P.O. Box 4005, 1700 Nicosia, Cyprus. TEL 357-2-357962. FAX 357-2-357964.
Vendor(s): Data-Star, Knight-Ridder Information, Inc., Ovid Technologies, Inc.. *6320*

C2C ABSTRACTS: JAPAN - ANALYTICAL CHEMISTRY.
Scan C2C, 1001 Pennsylvania Ave., N.W., No. 1300, Washington, DC 20024-2505. TEL 800-525-3865. FAX 202-863-3855.
Vendor(s): Data-Star (JPTC), European Space Agency (File no.241), Knight-Ridder Information, Inc. (File no.582), Orbit Search Service (JTEC). *1708*

C2C ABSTRACTS: JAPAN - CERAMICS.
Scan C2C, 1001 Pennsylvania Ave., N.W., No.1300, Washington, DC 20024-2505. TEL 800-525-3865. FAX 202-863-3855.
Vendor(s): Data-Star (JPTC), Knight-Ridder Information, Inc. (File no.582), European Space Agency (File no.241), Orbit Search Service (JTEC). *1661*

C2C ABSTRACTS: JAPAN - CHEMICAL ENGINEERING.
Scan C2C, 1001 Pennsylvania Ave., N.W., No. 1300, Washington, DC 20024-2505. TEL 800-525-3865. FAX 202-863-3855.
Vendor(s): Data-Star (JPTC), European Space Agency (File no.241), Knight-Ridder Information, Inc. (File no.582), Orbit Search Service (JTEC). *2626*

C2C ABSTRACTS: JAPAN - CRYSTALLOGRAPHY.
Scan C2C, 1001 Pennsylvania Ave., N.W., No. 1300, Washington, DC 20024-2505. TEL 800-525-3865. FAX 202-863-3855.
Vendor(s): Data-Star (JPTC), European Space Agency (File no.241), Knight-Ridder Information, Inc. (File no.582), Orbit Search Service (JTEC). *1708*

C2C ABSTRACTS: JAPAN - HYDROCARBONS.
Scan C2C, 1001 Pennsylvania Ave., N.W., No. 1300, Washington, DC 20024-2505. TEL 800-525-3865. FAX 202-863-3855.
Vendor(s): Data-Star (JPTC), European Space Agency (File no.241), Knight-Ridder Information, Inc. (File no.582), Orbit Search Service (JTEC). *1708*

C2C ABSTRACTS: JAPAN - INORGANIC CHEMISTRY.
Scan C2C, 1001 Pennsylvania Ave., N.W., No. 1300, Washington, DC 20024-2505. TEL 800-525-3865. FAX 202-863-3855.
Vendor(s): Data-Star (JPTC), European Space Agency (File no.241), Knight-Ridder Information, Inc. (File no.582), Orbit Search Service (JTEC). *1708*

C2C ABSTRACTS: JAPAN - MATERIALS SCIENCE.
Scan C2C, 1001 Pennsylvania Ave., N.W., No. 1300, Washington, DC 20024-2505. TEL 800-525-3865. FAX 202-863-3855.
Vendor(s): Data-Star (JPTC), European Space Agency (File no.241), Knight-Ridder Information, Inc. (File no.582), Orbit Search Service (JTEC). *2626*

C2C ABSTRACTS: JAPAN - METALS.
Scan C2C, 1001 Pennsylvania Ave., N.W., No. 1300, Washington, DC 20024-2505. TEL 800-525-3865. FAX 202-863-3855.
Vendor(s): Data-Star (JPTC), European Space Agency (File no.241), Knight-Ridder Information, Inc. (File no.582), Orbit Search Service (JTEC). *4981*

C2C ABSTRACTS: JAPAN - ORGANIC CHEMISTRY.
Scan C2C, 1001 Pennsylvania Ave., N.W., No. 1300, Washington, DC 20024-2505. TEL 800-525-3865. FAX 202-863-3855.
Vendor(s): Data-Star (JPTC), European Space Agency (File no.241), Knight-Ridder Information, Inc. (File no.582), Orbit Search Service (JTEC). *1708*

C2C ABSTRACTS: JAPAN - PHYSICAL CHEMISTRY.
Scan C2C, 1001 Pennsylvania Ave., N.W., No. 1300, Washington, DC 20024-2505. TEL 800-525-3865. FAX 202-863-3855.
Vendor(s): Data-Star (JPTC), European Space Agency (File no.241), Knight-Ridder Information, Inc. (File no.582), Orbit Search Service (JTEC). *1708*

C2C ABSTRACTS: JAPAN - PLASTICS.
Scan C2C, 1001 Pennsylvania Ave., N.W., No. 1300, Washington, DC 20024-2505. TEL 800-525-3865. FAX 202-863-3855.
Vendor(s): Data-Star (JPTC), European Space Agency (File no.241), Knight-Ridder Information, Inc. (File no.582), Orbit Search Service (JTEC). *5628*

C2C ABSTRACTS: JAPAN - POLYMER CHEMISTRY.
Scan C2C, 1001 Pennsylvania Ave., N.W., No. 1300, Washington, DC 20024-2505. TEL 800-525-3865. FAX 202-863-3855.
Vendor(s): Data-Star (JPTC), European Space Agency (File no.241), Knight-Ridder Information, Inc. (File no.582), Orbit Search Service (JTEC). *1708*

C2C ABSTRACTS: JAPAN - SURFACE CHEMISTRY.
Scan C2C, 1001 Pennsylvania Ave., N.W., No. 1300, Washington, DC 20024-2505. TEL 800-525-3865. FAX 202-863-3855.
Vendor(s): Data-Star (JPTC), European Space Agency (File no.241), Knight-Ridder Information, Inc. (File no.582), Orbit Search Service (JTEC). *1708*

C2C ABSTRACTS: JAPAN - TEXTILES.
Scan C2C, 1001 Pennsylvania Ave., N.W., No. 1300, Washington, DC 20024-2025. TEL 800-525-3865. FAX 202-863-3855.
Vendor(s): Data-Star (JPTC), European Space Agency (File no.241), Knight-Ridder Information, Inc. (File no.582), Orbit Search Service (JTEC). *6690*

C2C CURRENTS: JAPAN - CHEMISTRY.
Scan C2C, 1001 Pennsylvania Ave., N.W., No. 1300, Washington, DC 20024-2025. TEL 800-525-3865. FAX 202-863-3855.
Vendor(s): Data-Star (JPTC), European Space Agency (File no.241), Knight-Ridder Information, Inc. (File no.582), Orbit Search Service (JTEC). *1709*

C2C CURRENTS: JAPAN - COMPUTERS.
Scan C2C, 1001 Pennsylvania Ave., N.W., No. 1300, Washington, DC 20024-2025. TEL 800-525-3865. FAX 202-863-3855.
Vendor(s): Data-Star (JPTC), European Space Agency (File no.241), Knight-Ridder Information, Inc. (File no.582), Orbit Search Service (JTEC). *2002*

C2C CURRENTS: JAPAN - ELECTRONICS.
Scan C2C, 1001 Pennsylvania Ave., N.W., No. 1300, Washington, DC 20024-2505. TEL 800-525-3865. FAX 202-863-3855.
Vendor(s): Data-Star (JPTC), European Space Agency (File no.241), Knight-Ridder Information, Inc. (File no.582), Orbit Search Service (JTEC). *2510*

C2C CURRENTS: JAPAN - MATERIALS.
Scan C2C, 1001 Pennsylvania Ave., N.W., No. 1300, Washington, DC 20024-2505. TEL 800-525-3865. FAX 202-863-3855.
Vendor(s): Data-Star (JPTC), European Space Agency (File no.241), Knight-Ridder Information, Inc. (File no.582), Orbit Search Service (JTEC). *2626*

D A N B I B.
Dansk BiblioteksCenter as, Tempovej 7-11, DK-2750 Ballerup, Denmark. TEL 45-44-86-77-77. FAX 45-44-97-14-85.
Available only online. *528*

D B.
Diablo Publications, 2520 Camino Diablo, Walnut Creek, CA 94596. TEL 510-943-1111. FAX 510-943-1045.
Vendor(s): Lexis-Nexis, University Microfilms International. *1164*

D B M S.
Miller Freeman Inc. 411 Borel Ave. Ste. 100, San Mateo, CA 74402. TEL 415-358-9500. FAX 415-358-9855.
Vendor(s): Information Access Co.. *2108*

D E C U S MAGAZINE.
Digital Equipment Computer Users Society, Communications Organization, 334 South St., SHR3-1 - T25, Shrewsbury, MA 01545. TEL 508-841-3584. FAX 508-841-3357. *1988*

D I Y: THE INTERNATIONAL MARKET.
Euromonitor, 60-61 Britton St., London EC1M 5NA, England. TEL 44-171-251-8024. FAX 44-171-608-3149.
Vendor(s): Data-Star, Knight-Ridder Information, Inc.. *3685*

D I Y WEEK.
Miller Freeman Publishers Ltd. Sovereign Way, Tonbridge, Kent TN9 1RW, England. TEL 44-1732-364422. FAX 44-1732-361534.
Vendor(s): Information Access Co. *3603*

D K I LITERATUR-SCHNELLDIENST KUNSTSTOFFE KAUTSCHUK FASERN.
Deutsches Kunststoff-Institut, Schlossgartenstr. 6, 64289 Darmstadt, Germany. TEL 49-6151-162106. FAX 49-6151-292855.
Vendor(s): FIZ Technik, STN International. *5628*

D L A BULLETIN.
University of California, Division of Library Automation, 300 Lakeside Dr., 8th Fl., Oakland, CA 94612-3550. TEL 510-987-0564. *4043*

D M NEWS.
D M News Corp. 19 W. 21st St., New York, NY 10010. TEL 212-741-2095. FAX 212-633-9367.
Vendor(s): Lexis-Nexis. *1461*

D N R.
Fairchild Fashion Publication, Seven W. 34th St., New York, NY 10001. TEL 212-630-3600. FAX 212-630-2602.
Vendor(s): Information Access Co., Knight-Ridder Information, Inc.. *6676*

D R I - MCGRAW-HILL U S FORECAST SUMMARY.
D R I - McGraw-Hill, 24 Hartwell Ave., Lexington, MA 02173. TEL 617-863-5100. FAX 617-860-6332. *1203*

D V D AND FUTURE C D.
TechMedia, 52 Foundling Ct., London WC1N 1AN, England. TEL 44-171-837-0815. FAX 44-171-278-9917. *1976*

DAEDALUS.
American Academy of Arts and Sciences, Norton's Woods, 136 Irving St., Cambridge, MA 02138. TEL 617-492-8800.
Vendor(s): Information Access Co.. *3611*

DAILY BULLETIN - M T I.
Magyar Tavirati Iroda, Pl. Naphegy ter. 8, 1016 Budapest, Hungary. TEL 361-175-6722. FAX 361-118-8297. *3163*

DAILY CAMPUS (DALLAS).
Student Media Company, Inc., 3140 Dyer St., Dallas, TX 75275. TEL 214-768-4555. FAX 214-768-4573. *1864*

DAILY LABOR REPORT.
The Bureau of National Affairs, Inc., 1231 25th St., N.W., Washington, DC 20037. TEL 202-452-4200. FAX 202-822-8092.
Vendor(s): Bureau of National Affairs, Human Resources Information Network (CDD, HDD), Lexis-Nexis (DLABRT), West Services, Inc. (BNA-DLR). *1369*

DAILY OIL BULLETIN.
Southam Magazine & Information Group (Calgary), 999 Eighth St. S.W., Ste. 300, Calgary, AB T2R 1N7, Canada. TEL 403-244-6111. FAX 403-245-8666.
Vendor(s): Information Access Co., Southam Electronic Publishing. *5353*

DAILY REPORT FOR EXECUTIVES.
The Bureau of National Affairs, Inc., 1231 25th St., N.W., Washington, DC 20037. TEL 202-452-4200. FAX 202-822-8092.
Vendor(s): Human Resources Information Network (CDD, HDD), Lexis-Nexis (DREXEC), NewsNet, West Services, Inc. (BNA-DER). *1413*

DAILY TAX REPORT.
The Bureau of National Affairs, Inc., 1231 25th St., N.W., Washington, DC 20037. TEL 202-452-4200. FAX 202-822-8092.
Vendor(s): Bureau of National Affairs, Lexis-Nexis (BNADTR), NewsNet, West Services, Inc. (BNA-DTR). *1541*

DAILY TEXAN.
Texas Student Publications, Box D, Austin, TX 78713-9804. TEL 512-471-4591. FAX 512-471-1576. *1865*

DAIRY FOODS.
Cahners Publishing Company (Des Plaines), Division of Reed Elsevier Inc., 1350 E. Touhy Ave., Box 5080, Des Plaines, IL 60018-5080. TEL 847-635-8800. FAX 847-390-2445.
Vendor(s): Information Access Co., Knight-Ridder Information, Inc., Lexis-Nexis. *2965*

DAIRY MARKETS WEEKLY.
Agra Europe (London) Ltd., 25 Frant Rd., Tunbridge Wells, Kent TN2 5JT, England. TEL 44-1892-533813. FAX 44-1892-544895.
Vendor(s): Information Access Co.. *249*

DAIRY PRODUCTS: THE INTERNATIONAL MARKET.
Euromonitor, 60-61 Britton St., London EC1M 5NA, England. TEL 44-171-251-8024. FAX 44-171-608-3149.
Vendor(s): Data-Star, Knight-Ridder Information, Inc.. *249*

DAIRY SCIENCE ABSTRACTS.
CAB International, Wallingford, Oxon. OX10 8DE, England. TEL 44-1491-832111. FAX 44-1491-833508.
Vendor(s): DIMDI, European Space Agency, Knight-Ridder Information, Inc.. *171*

DALLAS BUSINESS JOURNAL.
Dallas Business Journal, Inc., 4131 N. Ctrl. Expwy., Ste. 310, Dallas, TX 75204. TEL 214-520-1010. FAX 214-522-5606. *913*

DALTON TRANSACTIONS.
The Royal Society of Chemistry, Thomas Graham House, Science Park, Milton Rd., Cambridge CB4 4WF, England. TEL 44-1223-420066. FAX 44-1223-423623.
Vendor(s): STN International (CJRSC). *1731*

DANCE MAGAZINE.
Dance Magazine, Inc., 33 W. 60th St., New York, NY 10023. TEL 212-245-9050. FAX 212-956-6487.
Vendor(s): Information Access Co., University Microfilms International. *2188*

DANSK ARTIKELINDEKS: AVISER OG TIDSSKRIFTER.
Dansk BiblioteksCenter as, Tempovej 7-11, DK-2750 Ballerup, Denmark. TEL 45-44-867777. FAX 45-44-867892. *3714*

DANSK LYDFORTEGNELSE.
Dansk BiblioteksCenter as, Tempovej 7-11, DK-2750 Ballerup, Denmark. TEL 45-44-867777. FAX 45-44-867892. *5208*

DATA BASED ADVISOR.
Advisor Publications Inc., 4010 Morena Blvd., San Diego, CA 92117. TEL 619-483-6400. FAX 619-483-9851. *2108*

DATA BROADCASTING NEWS.
M2 Communications Ltd., Reptile House, 20 Heathfield Rd., Coventry CV5 8BT, England. TEL 44-1203-717417. FAX 44-1203-717418.
Vendor(s): Information Access Co.. *2036*

DATA COMMUNICATIONS.
McGraw-Hill Companies, 1221 Ave. of the Americas, New York, NY 10020. TEL 212-512-2000.
Vendor(s): Dow Jones News Retrieval, Knight-Ridder Information, Inc. (File no.624/McGRAW-HILL PUBLICATIONS ONLINE), Lexis-Nexis, NewsNet (TE37). *2068*

DATA STORAGE REPORT.
Jonas Press Publishing Company, 53 Park Belmont Pl., San Jose, CA 95136-2506. TEL 408-629-8249. FAX 408-629-8249.
Vendor(s): Information Access Co., Knight-Ridder Information, Inc.. *2077*

DATABASE (WILTON).
Online, Inc., 462 Danbury Rd., Wilton, CT 06897. TEL 203-761-1466.
Vendor(s): Information Access Co., University Microfilms International. *2065*

DATABASE ALERT.
Knowledge Industry Publications, Inc., 701 Westchester Ave., White Plains, NY 10604. TEL 914-328-9157. FAX 914-328-9093. *2033*

DATABASE DIRECTORY.
Knowledge Industry Publications, Inc., 701 Westchester Ave., White Plains, NY 10604. TEL 914-328-9157. FAX 914-328-9093. *2033*

DATAMATION.
Cahners Publishing Company (Newton), Division of Reed Elsevier Inc., 275 Washington St., Newton, MA 02158-1630. TEL 617-964-3030. FAX 617-558-4506.
Vendor(s): Information Access Co., Knight-Ridder Information, Inc.. *2072*

DATAPRO DIRECTORY OF MICROCOMPUTER SOFTWARE.
Datapro Information Services Group 600 Delran Pkwy., Delran, NJ 08075. TEL 609-764-0100. FAX 609-764-2814.
Vendor(s): Knight-Ridder Information, Inc.. *2033*

DATAPRO DIRECTORY OF SOFTWARE.
Datapro Information Services Group 600 Delran Pkwy., Delran, NJ 08075. TEL 609-764-0100. FAX 609-764-2814.
Vendor(s): Knight-Ridder Information, Inc.. *2108*

DATATRENDS REPORT ON D E C.
DataTrends Publications, Inc., Box 4460, Leesburg, VA 20175. TEL 703-779-0574. FAX 703-779-2267.
Vendor(s): Information Access Co., NewsNet (ECO3). *2032*

DATENSCHUTZ UND INFORMATIONSRECHT.
Oesterreichische Gesellschaft fuer Datenschutz, Sautergasse 20, A-1170 Vienna, Austria. TEL 43-1-4897893. FAX 43-1-4897899310. *2050*

DAYTON BUSINESS REPORTER.
Hannover Publishing Co., Inc., 6356 Far Hills Ave., Dayton, OH 45459-2782. TEL 513-291-1100. FAX 513-436-3426.
Vendor(s): University Microfilms International. *913*

DE PAUL BUSINESS LAW JOURNAL.
DePaul University, College of Law, 25 E. Jackson Blvd., Chicago, IL 60504. TEL 312-362-8553. FAX 312-362-5931.
Vendor(s): West Services, Inc.. *3767*

DEALER BUSINESS.
M H West, Inc. 5743 Corsa Ave., Ste. 220, Westlake Village, CA 91362-4027. TEL 818-997-0644. FAX 818-997-1058.
Vendor(s): Information Access Co.. *6782*

DEALERNEWS.
Advanstar Communications, Inc., 7500 Old Oak Blvd., Cleveland, OH 44130. TEL 216-826-2839. FAX 216-891-2726.
Vendor(s): Information Access Co.. *6523*

DEALERSCOPE CONSUMER ELECTRONICS MARKETPLACE.
North American Publishing Co., 401 N. Broad St., Philadelphia, PA 19108. TEL 215-238-5300. FAX 215-238-5457.
Vendor(s): Knight-Ridder Information, Inc.. *2510*

DEALING WITH TECHNOLOGY.
Waters Information Services, Inc., Box 2248, Binghamton, NY 13902-2248. TEL 607-770-9242. FAX 607-770-9435.
Vendor(s): Data-Star, Knight-Ridder Information, Inc., NewsNet (FI53). *1129*

DECORATIVE ARTS PAINTING.
Clapper Communications Companies, 2400 E. Devon Ave., Ste. 375, Des Plaines, IL 60018-4618. TEL 847-635-5800. FAX 847-635-6311. *466*

DEFAULTED BONDS NEWSLETTER.
Bond Investors Association, Inc., 6175 N.W. 153rd St., Ste. 221, Miami Lakes, FL 33014-2435. TEL 305-557-1832. *1327*

DEFENSE & FOREIGN AFFAIRS STRATEGIC POLICY.
International Media Corporation Ltd., 175 Piccadilly, Ste. 1A, London W1V 9DB, England. TEL 071-491-2044. FAX 071-409-1923.
Vendor(s): Lexis-Nexis. *5661*

DEFENSE CLEANUP.
Pasha Publications Inc., 1616 N. Ft. Myer Dr., Ste. 1000, Arlington, VA 22209-3107. TEL 703-528-1244. FAX 703-528-1253.
Vendor(s): Information Access Co., NewsNet. *2851*

DEFENSE COUNSEL JOURNAL.
International Association of Defense Counsel, 1 N. Franklin St., Ste. 2400, Chicago, IL 60606-3401. TEL 312-368-1494. FAX 312-368-1854.
Vendor(s): Information Access Co., West Services, Inc.. *3882*

DEFENSE DAILY.
Phillips Business Information, Inc., 120 Seven Locks Rd., Potomac, MD 20854 TEL 301-424-3338. FAX 301-309-3847.
Vendor(s): Information Access Co., Knight-Ridder Information, Inc., NewsNet (DE01). *62*

DEFENSE ELECTRONICS.
Intertec Publishing Corp. (Atlanta), 6151 Powers Ferry Rd., N.W., Atlanta, GA 30339-2491. TEL 770-955-2500. FAX 770-955-0400.
Vendor(s): Information Access Co., Knight-Ridder Information, Inc., Lexis-Nexis. *2510*

DEFENSE WEEK.
King Publishing Group, Inc. 627 National Press Bldg., Washington, DC 20045. TEL 202-638-4260. FAX 202-662-9744.
Vendor(s): Information Access Co., Lexis-Nexis, NewsNet (DE16). *5029*

DELANEY REPORT.
149 Fifth Ave., New York, NY 10010. TEL 212-979-7881. FAX 212-979-0691.
Vendor(s): Information Access Co.. *35*

DELAWARE BUSINESS DIRECTORY
American Business Directories 5711 S. 86th Circle, Box 27347, Omaha, NE 63127. TEL 402-593-4600. FAX 402-331-5481. *1595*

DELAWARE BUSINESS REVIEW.
Independent Newspapers, Inc., Box 737, Dover, DE 19903. TEL 302-998-9550. FAX 302-998-1276.
Vendor(s): University Microfilms International. *913*

DELAWARE JOURNAL OF CORPORATE LAW.
Widerer University, School of Law, Box 7286, Wilmington, DE 19803. TEL 302-477-2145. FAX 302-477-2042.
Vendor(s): Lexis-Nexis, West Services, Inc.. *3900*

DELAWARE VALLEY RAIL PASSENGER.
Delaware Valley Association of Railroad Passengers, Box 7505, Philadelphia, PA 19010-7505. TEL 215-673-6445. FAX 215-885-7448. *6810*

DENDRON NEWS.
454 Willamette St., Ste. 216, Box 11284, Eugene, OR 97440-3484. TEL 503-341-0100. *4833*

DENTAL ECONOMICS.
PennWell Publishing Co., Dental Economics Division, Box 3408, Tulsa, OK 74101. TEL 918-835-3161. FAX 918-831-9804.
Vendor(s): University Microfilms International. *4638*

THE DENVER BUSINESS JOURNAL.
American City Business Journals (Denver), 1700 Broadway, No. 515, Denver, CO 80290. TEL 303-837-3500. FAX 303-837-3535.
Vendor(s): Information Access Co.. *914*

DENVER JOURNAL OF INTERNATIONAL LAW AND POLICY.
University of Denver, College of Law, 7039 E. 18th Ave., Ste. 235, Denver, CO 80220. TEL 303-871-6170.
Vendor(s): West Services, Inc.. *3928*

DENVER POST INDEX.
U M I Company 300 N. Zeeb Rd., Ann Arbor, MI 48106-1346. TEL 313-761-4700. FAX 800-864-0019.
Vendor(s): Knight-Ridder Information, Inc.. *3714*

DENVER UNIVERSITY LAW REVIEW.
University of Denver, College of Law, Porter Adm. Bldg., 7039 E. 18th Ave. Denver, CO 80220-1826. TEL 303-871-6172.
Vendor(s): Lexis-Nexis, West Services, Inc.. *3768*

DEODORANTS: THE INTERNATIONAL MARKET.
Euromonitor, 60-61 Britton St., London EC1M 5QU, England. TEL 44-171-251-8024. FAX 44-171-608-3149.
Vendor(s): Data-Star, Knight-Ridder Information, Inc.. *490*

DERMATOLOGY TIMES.
Advanstar Communications, Inc., 7500 Old Oak Blvd., Cleveland, OH 44130. TEL 216-826-2839. FAX 216-891-2726.
Vendor(s): Information Access Co., Knight-Ridder Information, Inc.. *4661*

DESIGN EXCHANGE.
Global Village Institute, Box 90, Summertown, TN 38483. TEL 615-964-3992. *2782*

DESIGN QUARTERLY.
M I T Press, 55 Hayward St., Cambridge, MA 02142. TEL 617-253-2889. FAX 617-577-1545.
Vendor(s): Information Access Co.. *391*

DETROIT NEWS INDEX.
U M I Company 300 N. Zeeb Rd., Ann Arbor, MI 48106-1346. TEL 313-731-4700. FAX 800-864-0019.
Vendor(s): Knight-Ridder Information, Inc.. *3714*

DETROITER.
Greater Detroit Chamber Communications Inc., 600 W. Lafayette, Box 33840, Detroit, MI 48232-0840. TEL 313-596-0352. FAX 313-964-0531.
Vendor(s): University Microfilms International. *1139*

DER DEUTSCHE APOTHEKER.
Verlag "Der Deutsche Apotheker", Hans-Thoma-Str. 1, 61440 Oberursel, Germany. TEL 49-6171-55012. FAX 49-6171-55142. *5406*

DEUTSCHE APOTHEKER ZEITUNG.
Deutscher Apotheker Verlag, Postfach 101061, 70009 Stuttgart, Germany. TEL 49-711-2582-0. FAX 49-711-2582290. *5406*

DEVELOPMENTAL DYNAMICS.
John Wiley & Sons, Inc., Journals, 605 Third Ave., New York, NY 10158. TEL 212-850-6645. FAX 212-850-6021. *580*

DEVELOPNET NEWS.
Volunteers in Technical Assistance, Inc., 1600 Wilson Blvd., Ste. 500, Arlington, VA 22209. TEL 703-276-1800. FAX 703-243-1865.
Available only online. *6649*

DEVICES & DIAGNOSTICS LETTER.
Washington Business Information, Inc., c/o Karen Harrington, 1117 N. 19th St., Ste. 200, Arlington, VA 22209. TEL 703-247-3434. FAX 703-247-3421.
Vendor(s): Ovid Technologies, Inc. (DIOG), Data-Star, Knight-Ridder Information, Inc.. *4448*

DEVOIR.
2050 rue de Bleury, 9e etage, Montreal, PQ H3A 3M9, Canada. TEL 514-985-3333.
Vendor(s): Southam Electronic Publishing. *3120*

DIABETES.
American Diabetes Association, 1660 Duke St., Alexandria, VA 22314. TEL 703-549-1500. FAX 703-836-7439.
Vendor(s): Information Access Co., Ovid Technologies, Inc.. *4667*

DIABETES CARE.
American Diabetes Association, 1660 Duke St., Alexandria, VA 22314. TEL 703-549-1500. FAX 703-836-7439.
Vendor(s): Ovid Technologies, Inc.. *4667*

DIABETES FORECAST.
American Diabetes Association, 1660 Duke St., Alexandria, VA 22314. TEL 703-549-1500. FAX 703-836-7439.
Vendor(s): Information Access Co.. *4668*

DIACRITICS.
Johns Hopkins University Press, Journals Publishing Division, 2715 N. Charles St., Baltimore, MD 21218. TEL 410-516-6987. FAX 410-516-6968. *4202*

DIAL ELECTRICAL - ELECTRONICS.
Dial Industry Publications Windsor Ct., Grinstead House, E. Grinstead, W. Sussex RH19 1XA, England. TEL 44-1342-326972. FAX 44-1342-335247.
Vendor(s): Reed Information Services Ltd.. *2511*

DIAL ENGINEERING.
Dial Industry Publications Windsor Ct., East Grinstead House, E. Grinstead, W. Sussex RH19 1XA, England. TEL 44-1342-326972. FAX 44-1342-335747.
Vendor(s): Reed Information Services Ltd.. *2730*

DIARIO CATARINESE.
R. Desembargador Pedro Silva 2958, 80080-900 Florianopolis, Santa Catarina, Brazil. TEL 55-482-494546. *3117*

DICKINSON JOURNAL OF INTERNATIONAL LAW.
Dickinson School of Law, 150 S. College St., Carlisle, PA 17013. TEL 717-243-4611. FAX 717-243-4443.
Vendor(s): West Services, Inc.. *3928*

DICKINSON LAW REVIEW.
Dickinson School of Law, 150 S. College St., Carlisle, PA 17013. TEL 717-240-5203. FAX 717-243-4443.
Vendor(s): Lexis-Nexis, West Services, Inc.. *3768*

DICTIONARY OF CONTEMPORARY QUOTATIONS.
John Gordon Burke Publisher, Inc., Box 1492, Evanston, IL 60204-1492. TEL 847-866-8625. *4203*

DIDASKALIA.
University of Tasmania, Department of Classics, Hobart, Tasmania 7001, Australia. TEL 61-02-202-294. FAX 61-02-202-288.
Available only online. *1821*

DIENST LANDBOUWKUNDIG ONDERZOEK. STARING CENTRUM, INSTITUUT VOOR ONDERZOEK VAN HET LANDELIJK GEBIED. JAARVERSLAG.
Dienst Landbouwkundig Onderzoek, Staring Centrum, Instituut voor Onderzoek van het Landelijk Gebied, P.O. Box 125, 6700 AC Wageningen, Netherlands. TEL 31-317-474200. FAX 31-317-424812. *2782*

DIENST LANDBOUWKUNDIG ONDERZOEK. STARING CENTRUM, INSTITUUT VOOR ONDERZOEK VAN HET LANDELIJK GEBIED. RAPPORT.
Dienst Landbouwkundig Onderzoek, Staring Centrum, Instituut voor Onderzoek van het Landelijk Gebied, P.O. Box 125, 6700 AC Wageningen, Netherlands. TEL 31-317-474200. FAX 31-317-424812. *2782*

DIESEL PROGRESS ENGINES & DRIVES.
Diesel & Gas Turbine Publications, 13555 Bishop's Ct., Brookfield, WI 53005-6286. TEL 414-784-9177. FAX 414-784-8133.
Vendor(s): Information Access Co.. *2753*

DIFFERENCES.
Indiana University Press, Journals Division, 601 N. Morton St., Bloomington, IN 47404. TEL 812-855-9449. FAX 812-855-8507.
Vendor(s): Information Access Co.. *7015*

DIFFUSION EXPRESS.
Electricite de France, Direction des Etudes et Recherches, Departement Systemes d'Information et de Documentation, 1, av. du General de Gaulle, 92141 Clamart, France. TEL 47-65-41-58. FAX 47-65-31-24.
Vendor(s): European Space Agency (File no.27), Telesystemes - Questel (Base EDF.DOC). *2626*

DIGEST OF ACTIVITIES OF CONGRESS.
Oliphant Washington Service, Box 9808, Friendship Sta., Washington, DC 20016. TEL 202-298-7226. FAX 202-333-5006.
Vendor(s): NewsNet. *5899*

DIGESTIVE REMEDIES: THE INTERNATIONAL MARKET.
Euromonitor, 60-61 Britton St., London EC1M 5NA, England. TEL 44-171-251-8024. FAX 44-171-608-3149.
Vendor(s): Data-Star, Knight-Ridder Information, Inc.. *5407*

DIGITAL AGE.
Cardinal Business Media, Inc., 1300 Virginia Dr., Ste. 400, Ft. Washington, PA 19034-3225. TEL 215-643-8000. FAX 215-643-3901.
Vendor(s): Information Access Co.. *1989*

DIGITAL MEDIA: A SEYBOLD REPORT.
Seybold Publications, 528 E. Baltimore Ave., Box 644, Media, PA 19063. TEL 610-565-2480. FAX 610-565-1858.
Vendor(s): Information Access Co.. *2086*

DIGITAL NEWS & REVIEW.
Cahners Publishing Company (Newton), Division of Reed Elsevier Inc., 275 Washington St., Newton, MA 02158-1630. TEL 617-964-3030. FAX 617-558-4759.
Vendor(s): Information Access Co., Knight-Ridder Information, Inc.. *2086*

DIGITAL SYSTEMS REPORT.
Computer Economics, Inc., 5841 Edison Pl., Carlsbad, CA 92008. TEL 619-438-8100. FAX 619-431-1126.
Vendor(s): Information Access Co.. *1989*

DIOGENES (ENGLISH EDITION).
Berghahn Books Inc., 165 Taber Ave., Providence, RI 02906. TEL 401-861-9330. FAX 401-521-0046.
Vendor(s): University Microfilms International. *6411*

DIRECT MARKETING.
Hoke Communications, 224 Seventh St., Garden City, Long Island, NY 11530. TEL 516-746-6700. FAX 516-294-8141.
Vendor(s): Information Access Co., Lexis-Nexis, University Microfilms International. *1462*

DIRECTION OF TRADE STATISTICS.
International Monetary Fund, Publication Services, 700 19th St., N.W., Ste. C-100, Washington, DC 20431. TEL 202-623-7430. FAX 202-623-7201. *993*

DIRECTORIES IN PRINT.
Gale Research Inc., 835 Penobscot Bldg., Detroit, MI 48226. TEL 313-961-2242. FAX 313-961-6083.
Vendor(s): Knight-Ridder Information, Inc.. *529*

DIRECTORS & BOARDS.
229 S. 18th St., 3rd Fl., Philadelphia, PA 19103. TEL 215-790-7000. FAX 215-790-7005.
Vendor(s): Information Access Co., University Microfilms International. *1414*

DIRECTORY OF ASSOCIATIONS IN CANADA.
Micromedia Ltd., 20 Victoria St., Toronto, ON M5C 2N8, Canada. TEL 416-362-5211. FAX 416-362-6161. *1597*

DIRECTORY OF BIOMEDICAL AND HEALTH CARE GRANTS.
Oryx Press, 4041 N. Central Ave., No. 700, Phoenix, AZ 85012-3397. TEL 602-265-2651. FAX 602-265-6250.
Vendor(s): Knight-Ridder Information, Inc.. *2387*

DIRECTORY OF COMMUNITY LEGISLATION IN FORCE.
Office for Official Publications of the European Communities, L-2985 Luxembourg, Luxembourg.
Vendor(s): Commission of the European Communities. *3769*

DIRECTORY OF CORPORATE AFFILIATIONS.
National Register Publishing, A Division of Reed Elsevier Inc., 121 Chanlon Rd., New Providence, NJ 07974. TEL 908-464-6800. FAX 908-771-7704.
Vendor(s): Knight-Ridder Information, Inc. (File no.513, Corporate Affiliations), Lexis-Nexis. *1598*

DIRECTORY OF DIRECTORS.
Reed Information Services Windsor Court, E. Grinstead House, E. Grinstead, W. Sussex RH19 1XA, England. TEL 01342-335832. FAX 01342-335948.
Vendor(s): Reed Information Services Ltd.. *1414*

DIRECTORY OF ELECTRONIC JOURNALS, NEWSLETTERS AND ACADEMIC DISCUSSION LISTS.
Association of Research Libraries, 21 Dupont Circle, Ste. 800, Washington, DC 20036. TEL 202-296-2296. FAX 202-872-0884. *529*

DIRECTORY OF GRANTS IN THE HUMANITIES.
Oryx Press, 4041 N. Central Ave., No. 700, Phoenix, AZ 85012-3397. TEL 602-265-2651. FAX 602-265-6250.
Vendor(s): Knight-Ridder Information, Inc.. *2387*

DIRECTORY OF HISTORICAL ORGANIZATIONS IN THE UNITED STATES AND CANADA.
American Association for State and Local History, 530 Church St., Ste. 600, Nashville, TN 37219-2325. TEL 615-255-2971. *3466*

DIRECTORY OF LIBRARIES IN CANADA.
Micromedia Ltd., 20 Victoria St., Toronto, ON M5C 2N8, Canada. TEL 416-362-5211. FAX 416-362-6161. *3989*

DIRECTORY OF OBSOLETE SECURITIES.
Financial Information Incorporated, 30 Montgomery St., Jersey City, NJ 07302. TEL 201-332-5400. FAX 201-432-9779. *1328*

DIRECTORY OF RESEARCH GRANTS.
Oryx Press, 4041 N. Central Ave., No. 700, Phoenix, AZ 85012-3397. TEL 602-265-2651. FAX 602-265-6250.
Vendor(s): Knight-Ridder Information, Inc.. *2427*

DISABILITY & SOCIETY.
Carfax Publishing Co., P.O. Box 25, Abingdon, Oxon. OX14 3UE, England. TEL 44-1235-401000. FAX 44-1235-401550. *3316*

DISABILITY ISSUES.
Information Center for Individuals with Disabilities, Box 256, Boston, MA 02117-0256. TEL 617-727-5540. FAX 617-345-5318. *3304*

DISABILITY STUDIES QUARTERLY.
c/o David Pfeiffer, Suffolk University, Dept. of Public Management, 8 Ashburton Place, Boxton, MA 02108-2770. TEL 617-523-3429. *3304*

DISCLOSURE (CHICAGO).
National Training and Information Center, 810 N. Milwaukee, Chicago, IL 60622. TEL 312-243-3035. FAX 312-243-7044.
Vendor(s): University Microfilms International. *2151*

DISCOUNT STORE NEWS.
Lebhar-Friedman, Inc., 425 Park Ave., New York, NY 10022. TEL 212-756-5000.
Vendor(s): Information Access Co., Knight-Ridder Information, Inc., Lexis-Nexis. *1462*

DISCOVER (BURBANK).
Walt Disney Magazine Publishing Group, 500 S. Buena Vista, Burbank, CA 91521-6012. TEL 818-973-4320.
Vendor(s): Knight-Ridder Information, Inc., Lexis-Nexis, VU/TEXT Information Services, Inc.. *6237*

DISCRETE AND CONTINUOUS DYNAMICAL SYSTEMS.
Department of Mathematics, Southwest Missouri State University, Springfield, MO 65804. TEL 417-836-5112. FAX 417-836-5610. *4362*

DISEASES OF THE COLON AND RECTUM.
Williams & Wilkins, 351 W. Camden St., Baltimore, MD 21201. TEL 410-528-4000. FAX 410-528-4312.
Vendor(s): Lexis-Nexis. *4908*

DISPLAY.
I N F O S C A N, Sigurdsgade 41, DK-2200 Copenhagen N, Denmark. TEL 45-31-81-66-66. FAX 45-35-82-16-55. *2036*

DISPOSABLE PAPER PRODUCTS: THE INTERNATIONAL MARKET.
Euromonitor, 60-61 Britton St., London EC1M 5NA, England. TEL 44-171-251-8024. FAX 44-171-608-3149.
Vendor(s): Data-Star, Knight-Ridder Information, Inc.. *5321*

DISSERTATION ABSTRACTS INTERNATIONAL. SECTION A: HUMANITIES AND SOCIAL SCIENCES.
U M I Company 300 N. Zeeb Rd., Ann Arbor, MI 48106. TEL 313-761-4700. FAX 800-864-0019. Vendor(s): Data-Star, Knight-Ridder Information, Inc. (File no.35), OCLC (EPIC), Ovid Technologies, Inc. (DISS), STN International. *3632*

DISSERTATION ABSTRACTS INTERNATIONAL. SECTION B: PHYSICAL SCIENCES AND ENGINEERING.
U M I Company 300 N. Zeeb Rd., Ann Arbor, MI 48106. TEL 313-761-4700. FAX 800-864-0019. Vendor(s): Data-Star, Knight-Ridder Information, Inc. (File no.35), OCLC (EPIC), Ovid Technologies, Inc. (DISS), STN International. *6301*

DISSERTATION ABSTRACTS INTERNATIONAL. SECTION C: WORLDWIDE.
U M I Company 300 N. Zeeb Rd., Ann Arbor, MI 48106. TEL 313-761-4700. FAX 800-864-0019. Vendor(s): Data-Star, Knight-Ridder Information, Inc. (File no.35), OCLC (EPIC), Ovid Technologies, Inc. (DISS), STN International. *3632*

DISSERTATION ABSTRACTS ON DISC.
U M I Company 300 N. Zeeb Rd., Ann Arbor, MI 48016-1304. TEL 313-761-4700. FAX 800-864-0019.
Vendor(s): Data-Star, Knight-Ridder Information, Inc., OCLC (ERIC), Ovid Technologies, Inc. (DISS), STN International. *3632*

DISTRIBUTED COMPUTING MONITOR.
Patricia Seybold Group, 148 State St., 7th Fl., Boston, MA 02109. TEL 617-742-5200. FAX 617-742-1028. *2055*

DISTRIBUTED SYSTEMS ENGINEERING.
I O P Publishing Ltd., Techno House, Redcliffe Way, Bristol, Avon BS1 6NS, England. TEL 44-117-929-7481. FAX 44-117-929-4318. *5546*

DISTRIBUTION.
Vereinigte Fachverlage GmbH, Lise-Meitner-Str. 2, 55129 Mainz, Germany. TEL 49-6131-992-150. FAX 49-6131-992-100.
Vendor(s): Knight-Ridder Information, Inc.. *1462*

DO-IT-YOURSELF RETAILING.
National Retail Hardware Association, 5822 W. 74th St., Indianapolis, IN 46278. TEL 317-297-1190. FAX 317-328-4354.
Vendor(s): Information Access Co.. *3603*

DOCUMENT IMAGING REPORT.
Phillips Business Information, Inc., 1201 Seven Locks Rd., Potomac, MD 20854. TEL 301-424-3338. FAX 301-309-3847.
Vendor(s): Information Access Co., NewsNet (ECO2). *2068*

DOING BUSINESS WITH EASTERN EUROPE.
Ecomomist Intelligence Unit, 111 W. 57th St., New York, NY 10019-2211. TEL 212-460-0600. FAX 212-955-3837.
Vendor(s): Lexis-Nexis. *1271*

DOLLARS & SENSE.
Economic Affairs Bureau, Inc., 1 Summer St., Somerville, MA 02143. TEL 617-628-8411. FAX 617-628-2025.
Vendor(s): Information Access Co.. *1203*

DOMINION LAW REPORTS.
Canada Law Book Inc., 240 Edward St., Aurora, ON L4G 3S9, Canada. TEL 905-841-6472. FAX 905-841-5085. *3771*

DOORS AND HARDWARE.
Door and Hardware Institute, 14170 Newbrook Dr., Chantilly, VA 22021. TEL 703-222-2010. FAX 703-222-2410.
Vendor(s): Information Access Co.. *888*

DOWN BEAT.
Maher Publications, Inc., 102 N. Haven Rd., Elmhurst, IL 60126. TEL 708-941-2030. FAX 708-941-3210.
Vendor(s): Information Access Co., University Microfilms International. *5154*

DOWNSTATE ILLINOIS BUSINESS DIRECTORY.
American Business Directories 5711 S. 86th Circle, Box 27347, Omaha, NE 68127. TEL 402-593-4600. FAX 402-331-5481. *1603*

DOWNSTREAM TRENDS.
Arab Press Service. A P S House, P.O. Box 3896, Nicosia, Cyprus. TEL 357-2-351778. FAX 357-2-350265.
Vendor(s): Information Access Co.. *2542*

DR. DOBB'S JOURNAL.
Miller Freeman, Inc., 600 Harrison St., San Francisco, CA 94107. TEL 415-905-2200. FAX 415-905-2232.
Vendor(s): Information Access Co.. *2086*

DRAGOCO REPORT.
Dragoco Gerberding & Co. AG, Dragocostr., 37601 Holzminden, Germany. TEL 05531-97-0. FAX 05531-971391. *495*

DRAKE LAW REVIEW.
Drake University, Law School, Cartwright Hall, Des Moines, IA 50311. TEL 515-271-2930.
Vendor(s): West Services, Inc.. *3771*

DRUG ABUSE.
Swedish Council for Information on Alcohol and other Drugs (CAN), Information and Documentation Center, P.O. Box 27302, S 102 54 Stockholm, Sweden. FAX 46-8-661-64-84. *2196*

DRUG AND CHEMICAL TOXICOLOGY.
Marcel Dekker Journals, 270 Madison Ave., New York, NY 10016. TEL 212-696-9000. FAX 212-685-4540. *5407*

DRUG AND COSMETIC INDUSTRY.
Advanstar Communications Inc., 7500 Old Oak Blvd., Cleveland, OH 44130. TEL 216-826-2839. FAX 216-891-2726.
Vendor(s): Information Access Co., Knight-Ridder Information, Inc., University Microfilms International. *495*

DRUG DATA REPORT.
J.R. Prous, S.A. International Publishers, Apdo. de Correos 540, 08080 Barcelona, Spain. TEL 343-459-2220. FAX 343-458-1535.
Vendor(s): Knight-Ridder Information, Inc.. *5408*

DRUG DETECTION REPORT
Pace Publications, 443 Park Ave. S., New York, NY 10016. TEL 212-685-5450. FAX 212-679-4701.
Vendor(s): Information Access Co.. *1501*

DRUG DEVELOPMENT AND INDUSTRIAL PHARMACY.
Marcel Dekker Journals, 270 Madison Ave., New York, NY 10016. TEL 212-696-9000. FAX 212-685-4540. *5408*

DRUG FACTS AND COMPARISONS.
Facts and Comparisons, 111 W. Port Plaza, Ste. 300, St. Louis, MO 63146-3098. FAX 314-878-5563. *5408*

DRUG INFORMATION JOURNAL.
Drug Information Association, Box 3113, Maple Glen, PA 19002. TEL 215-628-2288. FAX 215-641-1229. *5408*

DRUG NEWS & PERSPECTIVES.
J.R. Prous, S.A. International Publishers, Apdo. de Correos 540, 08080 Barcelona, Spain. TEL 343-459-2220. FAX 343-458-1535.
Vendor(s): Knight-Ridder Information, Inc.. *5409*

DRUG RESISTANCE WEEKLY.
Charles W. Henderson, Ed. & Pub., Box 5528, Atlanta, GA 31107-0523. TEL 404-377-8895. FAX 404-378-5411.
Vendor(s): Information Access Co.. *5409*

DRUG STORE NEWS.
Lebhar-Friedman, Inc., 425 Park Ave., New York, NY 10022. TEL 212-756-5000.
Vendor(s): Information Access Co., Lexis-Nexis. *1463*

DRUG THERAPY.
Excerpta Medica, Inc., Core Publishing Division 105 Raider Blvd., Belle Mead, NJ 08052. TEL 908-874-8550. FAX 908-874-0707. *5409*

DRUG TOPICS.
Medical Economics Publishing Co., Inc., 5 Paragon Dr., Montvale, NJ 07645. TEL 201-358-7200. FAX 201-573-1045.
Vendor(s): Information Access Co., University Microfilms International. *5409*

DRUGS MADE IN GERMANY.
Editio Cantor, Postfach 1255, 88322 Aulendorf, Germany. TEL 49-7525-940135. FAX 49-7525-940180. *5410*

DUKE LAW JOURNAL.
Duke University, School of Law, Box 90364, Durham, NC 27708-0364. TEL 919-613-7101. FAX 919-613-7231.
Vendor(s): Lexis-Nexis, West Services, Inc.. *3771*

DULUTHIAN.
Duluth Area Chamber of Commerce, 118 E. Superior St., Duluth, MN 55802. TEL 218-722-5501.
Vendor(s): University Microfilms International. *1139*

DUQUESNE LAW REVIEW.
Duquesne University, Duquesne School of Law, 900 Locust St., Pittsburgh, PA 15282. TEL 412-396-6297. FAX 412-396-6294.
Vendor(s): West Services, Inc.. *3772*

DUTCHESS COUNTY HISTORICAL SOCIETY. YEARBOOK.
Dutchess County Historical Society, Box 88, Poughkeepsie, NY 12602.
Vendor(s): Knight-Ridder Information, Inc.. *3467*

DYNAMIC BUSINESS.
S M C Business Councils, 1400 S. Braddock Ave., Pittsburgh, PA 15218-1264. TEL 412-371-1500. FAX 412-371-0460. *1574*

E A: THE JOURNAL OF THE NATIONAL ASSOCIATION OF ENROLLED AGENTS.
National Association of Enrolled Agents, 200 Orchard Ridge Dr., Ste. 302, Gaithersburg, MD 20878-1978. TEL 301-212-9608. FAX 301-990-1611. *1542*

E & P ENVIRONMENT.
J & E Communications, Inc., 6804 Hwy. 6 S., Ste. 394, Houston, TX 77083. TEL 713-879-7828.
Vendor(s): Information Access Co., NewsNet. *5353*

E B QUARTERLY.
American Bankers Association, 1120 Connecticut Ave., N.W., Washington, DC 20036. TEL 202-663-5087. FAX 202-663-7543.
Vendor(s): University Microfilms International. *1084*

E C ENERGY MONTHLY.
Financial Times Energy Publishing Maple House, 149 Tottenham Court Rd., London W1P 9LL, England. TEL 44-171-896-2241. FAX 44-171-896-2275.
Vendor(s): Data-Star, Information Access Co., Knight-Ridder Information, Inc., Lexis-Nexis. *2543*

E D I NEWS.
Phillips Business Information, Inc., 1201 Seven Locks Rd., Potomac, MD 20854. TEL 301-424-3338. FAX 301-309-3847.
Vendor(s): Information Access Co., NewsNet (TE80). *2069*

E D N MAGAZINE.
Cahners Publishing Company (Newton), Division of Reed Elsevier Inc., 275 Washington St., Newton, MA 02158-1630. TEL 617-964-3030. FAX 617-558-4470.
Vendor(s): Information Access Co., Knight-Ridder Information, Inc.. *2512*

E D P WEEKLY.
Computer Age & E D P News Services 714 Church St., Alexandria, VA 22314-4202. TEL 703-739-8500. FAX 703-739-8505.
Vendor(s): Information Access Co.. *2073*

E D U Q.
Services Documentaires Multimedia Inc., 75 Port-Royal E., No. 300, Montreal, PQ H3L 3T1, Canada. TEL 514-382-0895. FAX 514-384-9139. *2387*

E E I ENVIRONMENTAL DIRECTORY OF U.S. POWER PLANTS.
Utility Data Institute 1200 G St., N.W., Ste. 250, Washington, DC 20005. TEL 202-942-8788. FAX 202-942-8789. *2690*

E F T REPORT.
Phillips Business Information, Inc., 1201 Seven Locks Rd., Potomac, MD 20854. TEL 301-424-3338. FAX 301-309-3847.
Vendor(s): Information Access Co., Knight-Ridder Information, Inc., Lexis-Nexis, NewsNet (FI11). *1129*

E L H.
Johns Hopkins University Press, Journals Publishing Division, 2715 N. Charles St., Baltimore, MD 21218. TEL 410-516-6987. FAX 410-516-6968.
Vendor(s): Information Access Co.. *4204*

E LAW.
Murdoch University, School of Law, Perth, W.A. 6150, Australia. FAX 61-9-3106671.
Available only online. *3772*

E-LETTER ON SYSTEMS, CONTROL, & SIGNAL PROCESSING.
Eindhoven University of Technology, Department of Mathematics & Computing Science, P.O. Box 513, 5600 MB Eindhoven, Netherlands. TEL 31-10-472378. FAX 31-40-465995.
Available only online. *2055*

E M F KEEPTRACK.
Center for Energy Information, One Grandview Place, Winthrop, ME 04364.
Vendor(s): NewsNet. *2543*

E M M S.
Telecommunications Reports, 1333 H St., N.W., 11th Fl.-W., Washington, DC 20005. TEL 202-842-3022. FAX 202-842-1875.
Vendor(s): Information Access Co., NewsNet (EC32). *1902*

E-MED NEWS.
P J B Publications Ltd., 18-20 Hill Rise, Richmond, Surrey TW10 6UA, England. TEL 44-181-332-8934. FAX 44-181-332-8940.
Vendor(s): Knight-Ridder Information, Inc., Ovid Technologies, Inc. (PHIN,PHIC,PHID), STN International. *4630*

E N A.
Austrian Press and Information Service, 3524 International Ct., N.W., Washington, DC 20008-3035. TEL 202-895-6775. FAX 202-895-6772. *1204*

E - N F A I S NOTES.
National Federation of Abstracting and Information Services, 1518 Walnut St., Ste. 307, Philadelphia, PA 19102. TEL 215-893-1561. FAX 215-893-1564.
Available only online. *11*

E N R.
McGraw-Hill Companies, 1221 Ave. of the Americas, New York, NY 10020. TEL 212-512-2000. FAX 212-512-2565.
Vendor(s): Dow Jones News Retrieval (ENR), Information Access Co., Knight-Ridder Information, Inc. (File no.624/McGRAW-HILL PUBLICATIONS ONLINE), Lexis-Nexis (ENR), NewsNet (BC06). *2658*

E P A JOURNAL.
U.S. Environmental Protection Agency, Office of Communication, Education, and Public Affairs, Waterside Mall, 401 M St., S.W., Washington, DC 20460. TEL 202-260-6643.
Vendor(s): Information Access Co., University Microfilms International. *2783*

E P S L ONLINE.
Elsevier Science B.V., P.O. Box 211, 1000 AE Amsterdam, Netherlands. TEL 31-20-4853911. FAX 31-20-4853705.
Available only online. *2207*

E R I C CLEARINGHOUSE ON URBAN EDUCATION. DIGEST.
E R I C Clearinghouse on Urban Education, Box 40, Teachers College, Columbia University, New York, NY 10027. TEL 212-678-3433. FAX 212-678-4012.
Vendor(s): The Source. *2325*

E U D I S E D - EUROPEAN EDUCATIONAL RESEARCH YEARBOOK.
K.G. Saur Verlag KG, A member of the Reed Elsevier plc group, Ortlerstr. 8, 81373 Munich, Germany. TEL 49-89-76902-0. FAX 49-89-76902150.
Vendor(s): European Space Agency (File no.24/EUDISED R&D). *2388*

EARLY AMERICAN HOMES.
Cowles Enthusiast Media, History Group, 6405 Flank Dr., Box 8200, Harrisburg, PA 17105-8200. TEL 717-657-9555. FAX 717-657-9526.
Vendor(s): Information Access Co.. *3686*

EARLY AMERICAN LITERATURE.
University of North Carolina Press, Box 2288, Chapel Hill, NC 27515-2288. TEL 919-966-3561. FAX 800-272-6817.
Vendor(s): University Microfilms International. *4204*

EARLY MUSIC.
Oxford University Press, Oxford Journals, Walton St., Oxford OX2 6DP, England. TEL 44-1865-267773. FAX 44-1865-267773.
Vendor(s): Information Access Co.. *5155*

EARNINGS GUIDE ON P C.
Box 1, Horsham, W. Sussex RH12 3YY, England. TEL 0403-791155. FAX 0403-701152. *1084*

EARTH AND PLANETARY SCIENCE LETTERS.
Elsevier Science B.V., P.O. Box 211, 1000 AE Amsterdam, Netherlands. TEL 31-20-4853911. FAX 31-20-4853598. *2207*

EARTH ISLAND JOURNAL.
Earth Island Institute, 300 Broadway, Ste. 28, San Francisco, CA 94133-3312. TEL 415-788-3666. FAX 415-788-7324.
Vendor(s): University Microfilms International. *2783*

EARTH OBSERVER.
U.S. National Aeronautics and Space Administration, Earth Observing System Project, Goddard Space Flight Center, Greenbelt, MD 20771. TEL 301-286-3411. FAX 301-286-1738. *63*

EARTHQUAKE ENGINEERING ABSTRACTS DATABASE.
University of California at Berkeley, Earthquake Engineering Research Center, 1301 S. 46th St., Richmond, CA 94804-4698. TEL 510-231-9401. FAX 510-231-9461. *2627*

EAST ASIAN EXECUTIVE REPORTS.
International Executive Reports, Ltd., 717 D St., N.W., Ste. 300, Washington, DC 20004-2807. TEL 202-628-6900. FAX 202-628-6618.
Vendor(s): Lexis-Nexis, University Microfilms International. *1204*

EAST EUROPE AGRICULTURE & FOOD.
Agra Europe (London) Ltd., 25 Frant Rd., Tunbridge Wells, Kent TN2 5JT, England. TEL 44-1892-533813. FAX 44-1892-544895.
Vendor(s): Information Access Co.. *1606*

EAST EUROPE & THE REPUBLICS: A POLITICAL RISK ANNUAL.
Political Risk Services, Box 248, E. Syracuse, NY 13057-0248. TEL 315-431-0511. FAX 315-431-0200.
Vendor(s): Data-Star (FSRI), Lexis-Nexis (IBCRPT). *1204*

EAST EUROPEAN ENERGY REPORT.
Financial Times Energy Publishing Maple House, 149 Tottenham Court Rd., London W1P 9LL, England. TEL 0171-896-2241. FAX 0171-896-2275.
Vendor(s): Data-Star, Knight-Ridder Information, Inc., Lexis-Nexis. *2543*

EAST EUROPEAN INSURANCE REPORT.
Financial Times Financial Publishing Maple House, 149 Tottenham Court Rd., London W1P 9LL, England. TEL 44-171-896-2314. FAX 44-171-896-2319.
Vendor(s): Information Access Co.. *3647*

EAST EUROPEAN MARKETS.
Pearson Professional Ltd., Financial Times Newsletters and Management Reports Maple House, 149 Tottenham Court Rd., London W1P 9LL, England. TEL 44-171-896-2325. FAX 44-171-896-2333.
Vendor(s): Data-Star, Information Access Co., Lexis-Nexis. *1463*

EAST EUROPEAN POLITICS & SOCIETIES.
University of California Press, Journals Division, 2120 Berkeley Way, No. 5812, Berkeley, CA 94720-5812. TEL 510-643-7154. FAX 510-642-9917.
Vendor(s): Information Access Co.. *5663*

EAST EUROPEAN QUARTERLY.
East European Quarterly, University of Colorado, Box 29, Regent Hall, Boulder, CO 80309. TEL 941-753-4782.
Vendor(s): Information Access Co., University Microfilms International. *6321*

EASTERN ECONOMIC JOURNAL.
Eastern Economic Association, Iona College, New Rochelle, RI 10801. TEL 610-559-8050. FAX 610-250-8961.
Vendor(s): University Microfilms International. *915*

EBONY.
Johnson Publishing Co., Inc., 820 S. Michigan Ave., Chicago, IL 60605. TEL 312-322-9200. FAX 312-322-9375.
Vendor(s): Information Access Co., University Microfilms International. *2876*

ECO-LOG WEEK.
Southam Information and Technology Group, 1450 Don Mills Rd., Don Mills, ON M3B 2X7, Canada. TEL 416-445-6641. FAX 416-442-2200.
Vendor(s): Information Access Co., Southam Electronic Publishing. *2828*

ECOLOGICAL ABSTRACTS.
Elsevier - Geo Abstracts Regency House, 34 Duke St., Norwich NR3 3AP, England. TEL 44-603-626327. FAX 44-603-667934.
Vendor(s): Knight-Ridder Information, Inc. (File no.292), Orbit Search Service (GEOB). *2828*

ECOLOGICAL MONOGRAPHS.
Ecological Society of America, 2010 Massachusetts Ave., N.W., Ste. 400, Washington, DC 20036. TEL 202-833-8773. FAX 202-833-8775.
Vendor(s): Information Access Co., University Microfilms International. *2784*

THE ECOLOGIST.
Ecosystems Ltd., Agriculture House, Bath Rd., Sturminster Newton, Dorset DT10 1DU, England. TEL 01258-473476. FAX 01258-473748.
Vendor(s): Information Access Co.. *2785*

ECOLOGY.
Ecological Society of America, 2010 Massachusetts Ave., N.W., Ste. 400, Washington, DC 20036. TEL 202-833-8773. FAX 202-833-8775.
Vendor(s): Information Access Co., University Microfilms International. *2785*

ECOLOGY ABSTRACTS.
Cambridge Scientific Abstracts, 7200 Wisconsin Ave., 6th Fl., Bethesda, MD 20814. TEL 301-961-6750. FAX 301-961-6720.
Vendor(s): Knight-Ridder Information, Inc. (File no.76/LIFE SCIENCES COLLECTION), STN International. *2828*

ECONEWS.
Northcoast Environmental Center, Inc., 879 Ninth St., Arcata, CA 95521. TEL 707-822-6918. FAX 707-822-0827.
Vendor(s): CompuServe, Inc.. *2785*

ECONOMIC COMMENTARY.
Federal Reserve Bank of Cleveland, Box 6387, Cleveland, OH 44101. TEL 216-579-3079. FAX 216-579-2477.
Vendor(s): Information Access Co., University Microfilms International. *917*

ECONOMIC DEVELOPMENT REVIEW.
American Economic Development Council, 9801 W. Higgins Rd., Ste. 540, Rosemont, IL 60018-4726. TEL 847-692-9944. FAX 847-696-2990.
Vendor(s): University Microfilms International. *1518*

ECONOMIC GEOGRAPHY.
Clark University, 950 Main St., Worcester, MA 01610-1477. TEL 508-793-7311. FAX 508-794-8881.
Vendor(s): Information Access Co., University Microfilms International. *3253*

ECONOMIC INDICATORS (WASHINGTON).
U.S. Executive Office of the President, Council of Economic Advisers, Executive Office Bldg., Washington, DC 20500. TEL 202-395-5062.
Vendor(s): Information Access Co., Knight-Ridder Information, Inc.. *1206*

ECONOMIC INQUIRY.
Western Economic Association International, 7400 Center Ave., Ste. 109, Huntington Beach, CA 92647. TEL 714-898-3222.
Vendor(s): Information Access Co., Knight-Ridder Information, Inc.. *913*

ECONOMIC JOURNAL.
Blackwell Publishers Ltd., 108 Cowley Rd., Oxford OX4 1JF, England. TEL 44-1865-791100. FAX 44-1865-791347.
Vendor(s): Information Access Co.. *918*

ECONOMIC OPPORTUNITY REPORT.
Business Publishers, Inc., 951 Pershing Dr., Silver Spring, MD 20910-4464. TEL 301-587-6300. FAX 301-585-9075.
Vendor(s): NewsNet. *6370*

ECONOMIC PERSPECTIVES (CHICAGO).
Federal Reserve Bank of Chicago, Public Information Center, Box 834, Chicago, IL 60690. TEL 312-322-5112.
Vendor(s): Information Access Co., University Microfilms International. *1206*

ECONOMIC RECORD.
Economic Society of Australia, c/o R.A. Williams, Ed., Dept. of Economics, Melbourne University, Melbourne, Vic. 3052, Australia. TEL 61-3-93447426. FAX 61-3-93446899.
Vendor(s): Information Access Co., University Microfilms International. *918*

ECONOMIC REPORT OF THE PRESIDENT.
U.S. Executive Office of the President, Council of Economic Advisers, Washington, DC 20500. TEL 202-395-7332. *1206*

ECONOMIC REVIEW.
Economic and Industrial Publications, Al-Masiha, 47 Abdullah Haroon Rd. P.O. Box 7843, Karachi 74400, Pakistan.
Vendor(s): Information Access Co.. *918*

ECONOMIC REVIEW.
Federal Reserve Bank of Cleveland, Box 6387, Cleveland, OH 44101. TEL 216-579-3079. FAX 216-579-2477
Vendor(s): University Microfilms International. *1084*

ECONOMIC TRENDS (CLEVELAND).
Federal Reserve Bank of Cleveland, Box 6387, Cleveland, OH 44101. TEL 216-579-3079. FAX 216-579-2477 *1207*

ECONOMIC WEEK.
Citibank - G F N A, 55 Water St., 43rd Fl., New York, NY 10043. TEL 212-825-5026.
Vendor(s): Lexis-Nexis. *1084*

ECONOMISCH-STATISTISCHE BERICHTEN.
Nederlands Economisch Instituut, P.O. Box 4224, 3006 AE Rotterdam, Netherlands. TEL 31-10-4538743. FAX 31-10-4525840. *1207*

ECONOMIST.
Mainichi Newspapers, 1-1-1 Hitotsubashi, Chiyoda-ku, Tokyo 100-51, Japan. TEL 03-3212-0321. FAX 03-3211-0895.
Vendor(s): University Microfilms International. *1207*

THE ECONOMIST.
Economist Newspaper Ltd., 25 St. James's St., London SW1A 1HG, England. TEL 44-171-830-7000. FAX 44-171-839-2968.
Vendor(s): Information Access Co., Lexis-Nexis, VU/TEXT Information Services, Inc.. *1207*

ECOTOXICOLOGY.
Chapman & Hall, Journals Department 2-6 Boundary Row London SE1 8HN, England. TEL 44-171-8650066. FAX 44-171-5229623. *2844*

ECQUID NOVI.
Institute for Communication Research, Potchefstroom University, Potchefstroom 2520, South Africa. TEL 27-148-2991648. FAX 27-148-2991651. *3703*

ECUMENICAL REVIEW.
World Council of Churches, 150 route de Ferney, P.O. Box 2100, CH-1211 Geneva 2, Switzerland. TEL 41-22-791-6111. FAX 41-22-791-0361.
Vendor(s): Information Access Co., University Microfilms International. *6059*

EDITOR & PUBLISHER INTERNATIONAL YEAR BOOK.
Editor & Publisher Co., Inc. 11 W 19th St., New York, NY 10011. TEL 212-675-4380. FAX 212-929-1259. *1902*

EDITOR & PUBLISHER MARKET GUIDE.
Editor & Publisher Co., Inc. 11 W 19th St., New York, NY 10011. TEL 212-675-4380. FAX 212-929-1259. *1463*

EDITOR & PUBLISHER - THE FOURTH ESTATE.
Editor & Publisher Co., Inc. 11 W 19th St., New York, NY 10011. TEL 212-675-4380. FAX 212-929-1259.
Vendor(s): Information Access Co.. *3703*

EDITORS ONLY.
Editors Only Publications, Box 17108, Fountain Hills, AZ 85269. TEL 602-337-6492. FAX 602-837-6872.
Vendor(s): NewsNet (PB130). *3703*

EDMONTON CHAMBER OF COMMERCE. COMMERCE NEWS.
Edmonton Chamber of Commerce, Suite 600, 10123-99 St., Edmonton Alta. T5J 3G9, Canada. TEL 403-424-7946. FAX 403-424-7946.
Vendor(s): University Microfilms International. *1140*

THE EDMONTON JOURNAL
P.O. Box 2421, Edmonton AB T5J 2S6, Canada. TEL 403-429-5100. FAX 403-429-5500. *3120*

EDUCATION AUTHORITIES' DIRECTORY AND ANNUAL.
School Government Publishing Co. Ltd., Darby House, Bletchingley Rd., Nerstham, Redhill, Surrey RH1 3DN, England. TEL 01737-642223. FAX 01737-644283. *2327*

EDUCATION DAILY.
Capitol Publications Inc., 1101 King St., Ste. 444, Alexandria, VA 22314. TEL 703-683-4100. FAX 703-739-6501.
Vendor(s): NewsNet (ED0E). *2327*

THE EDUCATION DIGEST.
Prakken Publications, Inc. Box 8623, Ann Arbor, MI 48107. TEL 313-769-1211. FAX 313-769-8383.
Vendor(s): University Microfilms International. *2328*

EDUCATION INDEX.
H.W. Wilson Co., 950 University Ave., Bronx, NY 10452. TEL 718-590-8400. FAX 718-590-1617.
Vendor(s): OCLC, Wilsonline (File EDI). *2388*

EDUCATION TECHNOLOGY NEWS.
Business Publishers, Inc., 951 Pershing Dr., Silver Spring, MD 20910-4464. TEL 301-587-6300. FAX 301-585-9075.
Vendor(s): Information Access Co., NewsNet. *2019*

EDUCATION WEEK.
Editorial Projects in Education, Inc., 4301 Connecticut Ave., N.W., Ste. 432 Washington, DC 20008. TEL 202-364-4114. *2329*

EDUCATIONAL LEADERSHIP.
Association for Supervision and Curriculum Development, 1250 N. Pitt St., Alexandria, VA 22314-1453. TEL 703-549-9110. FAX 703-549-3891.
Vendor(s): Information Access Co., University Microfilms International. *2485*

EDUCATIONAL MARKETER.
SIMBA Information Inc. 11 Riverbend Dr. S., Box 4234, Stamford, CT 06907-0234. TEL 203-358-9900. FAX 203-358-5834.
Vendor(s): Information Access Co., Knight-Ridder Information, Inc., NewsNet (PB20). *2485*

EDUCATIONAL RECORD.
American Council on Education, One Dupont Circle, N.W., Washington, DC 20036-1193. TEL 202-939-9380. FAX 202-833-4760.
Vendor(s): University Microfilms International. *2331*

EDUCOM REVIEW.
Turnkey Publishing, Box 200549, Austin, TX 78720. TEL 512-335-2286. FAX 512-335-3083. *2405*

EGYPTIAN JOURNAL OF PHARMACEUTICAL SCIENCES.
National Information and Documentation Centre (NIDOC), Tahrir St., Dokki, Awqaf P.O., Cairo, Egypt. TEL 20-2-701696. *5410*

EIGHTEENTH CENTURY LIFE.
Johns Hopkins University Press, Journals Publishing Division, 2715 N. Charles St., Baltimore, MD 21218. TEL 410-516-6987. FAX 410-516-6968. *3408*

EIGHTEENTH-CENTURY STUDIES.
Johns Hopkins University Press, Journals Publishing Division, 2715 N. Charles St., Baltimore, MD 21218-4319. TEL 410-516-6987. FAX 410-516-6968. *3341*

EINKAUFS 1X1 DER DEUTSCHEN INDUSTRIE.
Deutscher Adressbuch Verlag, Arheilger Weg 17, 64380 Rossdorf, Germany. TEL 06154-699500. FAX 06154-6995490.
Vendor(s): Data-Star, FIZ Technik. *1607*

DIE EISEN, BLECH UND METALL VERARBEITENDE INDUSTRIE, STAHLVERFORMUNG UND IHRE HELFER.
Industrieschau-Verlagsgesellschaft mbH, Postfach 100262, 64202 Darmstadt, Germany. TEL 49-6151-38920. FAX 49-6151-33164. *4954*

DIE EISEN-, STAHL- UND N E METALL-INDUSTRIE UND IHRE HELFER.
Industrieschau-Verlagsgesellschaft mbH, Postfach 100262, 64202 Darmstadt, Germany. TEL 49-6151-38920. FAX 49-6151-33164. *4954*

EKISTICS.
Athens Technological Organization, Athens Center of Ekistics, 24 Strat. Syndemou, 106-73 Athens, Greece. TEL 30-1-3623-216. FAX 30-1-3633-395. Vendor(s): University Microfilms International. *3582*

ELDERCARE FORUM.
ElderCare Financial Management, Inc., 170 Elaine Dr., Roswell, GA 30075. TEL 770-518-2767. *1085*

ELECTRIC LIGHT AND POWER.
PennWell Publishing Co., Box 1260, Tulsa, OK 74101. TEL 918-835-3161. FAX 918-831-9497. Vendor(s): Information Access Co.. *2691*

ELECTRIC PERSPECTIVES.
Edison Electric Institute, 701 Pennsylvania Ave., N.W., Washington, DC 20004-2696. TEL 202-508-5000. FAX 202-508-5030.
Vendor(s): University Microfilms International. *2691*

ELECTRIC UTILITY WEEK.
McGraw-Hill, Inc., 1221 Ave. of the Americas, New York, NY 10020. TEL 212-512-6410.
Vendor(s): Knight-Ridder Information, Inc. (File no.624/McGRAW-HILL PUBLICATIONS ONLINE), Dow Jones News Retrieval (EUW), Lexis-Nexis (ELUTL), NewsNet (EY65). *2691*

ELECTRIC UTILITY WEEK'S DEMAND-SIDE REPORT.
McGraw-Hill, Inc., 1221 Ave. of the Americas, New York, NY 10020. TEL 212-512-6410.
Vendor(s): Knight-Ridder Information, Inc. (DSR), Dow Jones News Retrieval (DSR), NewsNet (EY87). *2568*

ELECTRICAL & ELECTRONICS ABSTRACTS.
INSPEC, I.E.E., Michael Faraday House, Six Hill Way, Stevenage, Herts. SG1 2AY, England. TEL 44-1438-313311. FAX 44-1438-742840.
Vendor(s): CEDOCAR, Data-Star, European Space Agency, FIZ Technik, Knight-Ridder Information, Inc., Orbit Search Service, STN International. *2627*

ELECTRICAL CONSTRUCTION & MAINTENANCE.
Intertec Publishing Corp., 9800 Metcalf Ave., Overland Park, KS 66212-2215. TEL 913-341-1300. FAX 913-967-1898.
Vendor(s): Information Access Co.. *2692*

ELECTRICAL WORLD.
McGraw-Hill Companies, 1221 Ave. of the Americas, New York, NY 10020. TEL 212-512-2000.
Vendor(s): Dow Jones News Retrieval (EWL), Knight-Ridder Information, Inc. (EW), Lexis-Nexis (ELECWD), NewsNet (EY03). *2693*

THE ELECTRICITY JOURNAL.
1501 Western Ave., Ste. 100, Seattle, WA 98101-1570. TEL 206-382-0195.
Vendor(s): University Microfilms International. *2568*

ELECTRO MANUFACTURING.
Worldwide Videotex, Box 3273, Boynton Beach, FL 33424-3273. TEL 407-738-2276.
Vendor(s): Information Access Co., NewsNet. *2679*

ELECTRONIC ANTIQUITY.
University of Tasmania, Department of Classics, Hobart, Tasmania 7001, Australia. TEL 61-02-202-294. FAX 61-02-202-288.
Available only online. *1821*

ELECTRONIC BUSINESS TODAY.
Cahners Publishing Company (Newton), Division of Reed Elsevier Inc., 275 Washington St., Newton, MA 02158-1630. TEL 617-964-3030. FAX 617-558-4470.
Vendor(s): Information Access Co., Knight-Ridder Information, Inc.. *2513*

ELECTRONIC BUYERS' NEWS.
C M P Publications, Inc., 600 Community Dr., Manhasset, NY 11030. TEL 516-562-5000. FAX 516-562-5123.
Vendor(s): Information Access Co., NewsNet (EC12). *2513*

ELECTRONIC CHEMICALS NEWS.
Chemical Week Associates, 888 Seventh Ave., New York, NY 10106. TEL 212-621-4900. FAX 212-621-4949.
Vendor(s): Information Access Co.. *2513*

ELECTRONIC DESIGN.
Penton Publishing (Hasbrouck Heights) 611 Rte. 46 W., Hasbrouck Heights, NJ 07604. TEL 201-393-6228.
Vendor(s): Information Access Co., Knight-Ridder Information, Inc., Lexis-Nexis. *2514*

ELECTRONIC ENGINEERING TIMES.
C M P Publications, Inc., 600 Community Dr., Manhasset, NY 11030. TEL 516-562-5000. FAX 516-562-5325.
Vendor(s): Information Access Co., NewsNet (EC14). *2514*

ELECTRONIC GREEN JOURNAL.
University of Idaho Library, University of Idaho Library, Moscow, ID 83844. TEL 208-885-6631. FAX 208-885-6817.
Available only online. *2786*

ELECTRONIC INFORMATION REPORT.
SIMBA Information Inc. 11 Riverbend Dr. S., Box 4234, Stamford, CT 06907-0234. TEL 203-358-9900. FAX 203-358-5824.
Vendor(s): Information Access Co., Knight-Ridder Information, Inc., NewsNet (PB22). *2065*

ELECTRONIC JOURNAL OF SOCIOLOGY.
University of Alberta, Department of Sociology, Edmonton, AB T6G 2H4, Canada.
Available only online. *6411*

ELECTRONIC JOURNAL OF STRATEGIC INFORMATION SYSTEMS.
University of Sheffield, Information Studies Department, 211 Portobello St., Regents Court, Rm. 315, Sheffield S10 2UH, England. TEL 44-742-768555. FAX 44-742-780300.
Available only online. *2080*

ELECTRONIC JOURNAL OF THEORETICAL CHEMISTRY.
John Wiley & Sons Ltd., Journals, Baffins Ln., Chichester, W. Sussex PO19 1UD, England. TEL 44-1243-779777. FAX 44-1243-843232. *1715*

ELECTRONIC LEARNING.
Scholastic Inc., 555 Broadway, New York, NY 10012-3999. TEL 212-343-6100.
Vendor(s): Information Access Co., Knight-Ridder Information, Inc., University Microfilms International. *2405*

ELECTRONIC MARKETPLACE REPORT.
SIMBA Information Inc. 11 Riverbend Dr. S., Box 4234, Stamford, CT 06907-0234. TEL 203-358-9900. FAX 203-358-5824.
Vendor(s): Information Access Co.. *1902*

ELECTRONIC MATERIALS AND PACKAGING.
Research Information Ltd., 222 Maylands Ave., Hemel Hempstead, Herts. HP2 7TD, England. TEL 44-1442-213222. FAX 44-1442-259395. Vendor(s): Information Access Co.. *2514*

ELECTRONIC MATERIALS TECHNOLOGY NEWS.
Business Communications Co., Inc. (Norwalk), 25 Van Zant St., Ste. 13, Norwalk, CT 06855. TEL 203-853-4266. FAX 203-853-0348.
Vendor(s): Information Access Co., NewsNet (ML04) . *2514*

ELECTRONIC MEDIA.
Crain Communications, Inc. (Chicago), 740 N. Rush St., Chicago, IL 60611-2590. TEL 312-649-5200. FAX 312-649-5465.
Vendor(s): Information Access Co., Lexis-Nexis. *1960*

ELECTRONIC MESSAGING NEWS.
Phillips Business Information, Inc., 1201 Seven Locks Rd., Potomac, MD 20854. TEL 301-424-3338. FAX 301-309-3847.
Vendor(s): NewsNet (TE05). *1927*

ELECTRONIC NEWS.
International Publishing Corporation (New York), 302 Fifth Ave., New York, NY 10001. TEL 212-736-3900. FAX 212-736-5125.
Vendor(s): Information Access Co., Knight-Ridder Information, Inc.. *2515*

ELECTRONIC WORLD NEWS.
C M P Publications, Inc., 600 Community Dr., Manhasset, NY 11030. TEL 516-562-5000.
Vendor(s): NewsNet (EC13). *2515*

ELECTRONICS AND COMMUNICATIONS ABSTRACTS JOURNAL.
Cambridge Scientific Abstracts, 7200 Wisconsin Ave., 6th Fl., Bethesda, MD 20814. TEL 301-961-6750. FAX 301-961-6720.
Vendor(s): STN International (ELCOM). *1923*

ELECTRONICS LETTERS.
I.E.E., Michael Faraday House, Six Hills Way, Stevenage, Herts. SG1 2AY, England. TEL 44-1438-313311. FAX 44-1438-742840.
Vendor(s): OCLC. *2516*

ELECTRONICS LETTERS ONLINE.
I.E.E., Michael Faraday House, Six Hills Way, Stevenage, Herts. SG1 2AY, England. TEL 44-1438-313311. FAX 44-1438-742840.
Available only online. Vendor(s): OCLC. *2516*

ELECTRONICS NOW.
Gernsback Publications, Inc., 500 Bi-County Blvd., Farmingdale, NY 11735. TEL 516-293-3000. FAX 516-293-3115.
Vendor(s): Information Access Co.. *2517*

ELECTRONICS TIMES.
Morgan-Grampian Technical Press Ltd. Morgan-Grampian House, 30 Calderwood St., London SE18 6QH, England. TEL 44-181-855-7777. FAX 44-181-854-1793.
Vendor(s): Information Access Co.. *2517*

ELECTRONICS WEEKLY.
Reed Business Publishing Ltd. Quadrant House, The Quadrant, Sutton, Surrey SM2 5AS, England. TEL 44-181-652-3142. FAX 44-181-652-8956.
Vendor(s): Information Access Co.. *2517*

DIE ELEKTRO-INDUSTRIE, ELEKTRONIK UND IHRE HELFER.
Industrieschau-Verlagsgesellschaft mbH, Postfach 100262, 64202 Darmstadt, Germany. TEL 49-6151-3892-0. FAX 49-6151-33164. *2518*

ELEKTRON.
Smena Publishing House, Prazska 11, 812 84 Bratislava, Slovakia. TEL 406-06. *6238*

ELSEVIER SCIENCE. CATALOGUE - BOOKS.
Elsevier Science B.V., P.O. Box 211, 1000 AE Amsterdam, Netherlands. TEL 31-20-4853911. FAX 31-20-4853598. *6238*

ELSEVIER SCIENCE. CATALOGUE - JOURNALS.
Elsevier Science B.V., P.O. Box 211, 1000 AE Amsterdam, Netherlands. TEL 31-20-4853911. FAX 31-20-4853598. *6238*

EM ABERTO.
Instituto Nacional de Estudos e Pesquisas Educacionais, Campus da UnB, Acesso Sul, 70910-900 Brasilia, DF, Brazil. TEL 061-347-8970. FAX 061-273-3233. *2332*

EMERGENCY MEDICINE REPORTS.
American Health Consultants, Inc., 3525 Piedmont Rd., N.E., Bldg. 6, Ste. 400, Atlanta, GA 30305. TEL 404-262-7436. FAX 404-262-7837. Vendor(s): Ovid Technologies, Inc.. *4451*

EMERGENCY PREPAREDNESS NEWS.
Business Publishers, Inc., 951 Pershing Dr., Silver Spring, MD 20910-4464. TEL 301-587-6300. FAX 301-585-9075. Vendor(s): NewsNet (GT34). *1816*

EMERGING & SPECIAL SITUATIONS.
Standard & Poor's Corporation 25 Broadway, New York, NY 10004. TEL 212-208-8000. Vendor(s): Knight-Ridder Information, Inc. (ESS), Dow Jones News Retrieval (ESS), NewsNet (FI16). *1329*

EMERGING INFECTIOUS DISEASES.
U.S. National Center for Infectious Diseases, 1600 Clifton Rd., Mailstop C-12, Atlanta, GA 30333. TEL 404-639-3967. FAX 404-639-3039. *5958*

EMORY INTERNATIONAL LAW REVIEW.
Emory University, School of Law, Gambrell Hall, Atlanta, GA 30322. TEL 404-727-6830. FAX 404-727-6820. Vendor(s): West Services, Inc.. *3929*

EMORY LAW JOURNAL.
Emory University, School of Law, Gambrell Hall, Atlanta, GA 30322. TEL 404-727-6830. FAX 404-727-6820. Vendor(s): West Services, Inc.. *3773*

EMPLOYEE BENEFIT CASES.
The Bureau of National Affairs, Inc., 1231 25th St., N.W., Washington, DC 20037. TEL 202-452-4200. FAX 202-822-8092. *1370*

EMPLOYEE BENEFIT PLAN REVIEW.
Charles D. Spencer & Associates, Inc., 250 S. Wacker Dr., Ste. 600, Chicago, IL 60606-5834. TEL 312-993-7900. Vendor(s): University Microfilms International. *1370*

EMPLOYEE HEALTH AND FITNESS.
American Health Consultants, Inc., 3525 Piedmont Rd., N.E., Bldg. 6, Ste. 400, Atlanta, GA 30305. TEL 404-262-7436. FAX 800-284-3291. Vendor(s): Lexis-Nexis. *5526*

EMPLOYEE RELATIONS.
M C B University Press Ltd., 60-62 Toller Ln., Bradford, W. Yorks BD8 9BY, England. TEL 44-1274-777700. FAX 44-1274-785200. Vendor(s): Information Access Co.. *1371*

EMPLOYEE RELATIONS LAW JOURNAL.
John Wiley & Sons, Inc., Journals, 605 Third Ave., New York, NY 10158. TEL 212-850-6645. FAX 212-850-6021. Vendor(s): Information Access Co., Knight-Ridder Information, Inc.. *3773*

EMPLOYMENT GUIDE.
The Bureau of National Affairs, Inc., 1231 25th St., N.W., Washington, DC 20037. TEL 202-452-4200. FAX 202-822-8092. Vendor(s): Human Resources Information Network (EMPG, CDD, HDD). *1501*

EMPLOYMENT INFORMATION IN THE MATHEMATICAL SCIENCES.
American Mathematical Society, Box 6248, Providence, RI 02940-6248. TEL 401-455-4000. Vendor(s): Human Resources Information Network. *4364*

EMPLOYMENT OPPORTUNITIES (ENGLEWOOD).
National Guild of Community Schools of the Arts, Box 8018, Englewood, NJ 07631. TEL 201-871-3337. Vendor(s): NewsNet. *5266*

EN ROUTE TECHNOLOGY.
Telecom Publishing Group, 1011 King St., Box 1455, VA 22313-2055. FAX 703-739-6940. Vendor(s): Information Access Co., NewsNet (TE33). *6808*

ENCYCLOPEDIA OF ASSOCIATIONS.
Gale Research Inc., 835 Penobscot Bldg., Detroit, MI 48226. TEL 313-961-2242. FAX 313-961-6083. Vendor(s): Knight-Ridder Information, Inc. (File no.114). *253E*

ENDLESS VACATION.
Endless Vacation Publications, Box 80260, Indianapolis, IN 46280-0260. TEL 317-871-9504. FAX 317-871-9507. Vendor(s): Information Access Co.. *6879*

ENERGIA: BIBLIOGRAFIA SELETIVA.
Comissao Nacional de Energia Nuclear, Centro de Informacoes Nucleares, Rua General Severiano, 90, Botafogo, 22294-900 Rio de Janeiro RJ, Brazil. TEL 55-21-5462440. FAX 55-21-5462447. Available only online. *2562*

ENERGY & ENVIRONMENT.
Multi-Science Publishing Co. Ltd., 107 High St., Brentwood, Essex CM14 4RX, England. TEL 44-1277-224632. FAX 44-1277-223453. Vendor(s): Information Access Co.. *2545*

ENERGY & FUELS.
American Chemical Society, 1155 16th St., N.W., Washington, DC 20036. TEL 800-333-9511. FAX 614-447-3671. Vendor(s): STN International (CJACS). *2545*

ENERGY BUSINESS REVIEW.
Arab Press Service, P.O. Box 3896, Nicosia, Cyprus. FAX 357-2-350265. Vendor(s): Information Access Co.. *2545*

ENERGY CONSERVATION NEWS.
Business Communications Co., Inc. (Norwalk), 25 Van Zant St., Ste. 13 Norwalk, CT 06855. TEL 203-853-4266. FAX 203-853-0348. Vendor(s): Data-Star, Information Access Co., Knight-Ridder Information, Inc., NewsNet (EY59). *2545*

ENERGY DAILY.
King Publishing Group, Inc., 627 National Press Bldg., Washington, DC 20045. TEL 202-638-4260. FAX 202-662-9744. Vendor(s): Data-Star, Information Access Co., Knight-Ridder Information, Inc., Lexis-Nexis, NewsNet (EY57). *2546*

ENERGY DATA BASE.
U.S. National Technical Information Service, 5285 Port Royal Rd., Springfield, VA 22161. TEL 703-487-4630. Available only online. Vendor(s): Knight-Ridder Information, Inc., STN International. *2546*

ENERGY DESIGN UPDATE.
Cutter Information Corp., 37 Broadway, Arlington, MA 02174. TEL 617-648-8700. FAX 617-648-1950. Vendor(s): NewsNet (BC08). *854*

ENERGY ECONOMIST.
Financial Times Energy Publishing Maple House, 149 Tottenham Court Rd. London W1P 9LL, England. TEL 0171-896-2241. FAX 0171-896-2275. Vendor(s): Data-Star, Knight-Ridder Information, Inc., Lexis-Nexis. *2546*

ENERGY JOURNAL.
International Association for Energy Economics, 28790 Chagrin Blvd., Ste. 210, Cleveland, OH 44122. TEL 216-464-5365. Vendor(s): Information Access Co.. *2547*

ENERGY LAW JOURNAL.
Federal Energy Bar Association, 1350 Connecticut Ave., N.W., Ste. 300, Washington, DC 20036. TEL 202-223-5625. FAX 202-833-5566. Vendor(s): West Services, Inc.. *3774*

ENERGY REPORT.
Pasha Publications Inc., 1616 N. Fort Myer Dr., Ste. 1000, Arlington, VA 22209-3107. TEL 703-528-1244. FAX 703-528-1253. Vendor(s): Data-Star, Information Access Co., Knight-Ridder Information, Inc., Lexis-Nexis, NewsNet (EY5C). *2547*

ENERGY REPORT.
Springfield Information Services, P.O. Box 31, Peterborough, Cambs. PE1 1SD, England. TEL 44-1733-267272. Vendor(s): Information Access Co. *2547*

ENERGY RESEARCH ABSTRACTS.
U.S. Department of Energy, Office of Scientific and Technical Information, Box 62, Oak Ridge, TN 37831. TEL 615-576-9362. Vendor(s): Knight-Ridder Information, Inc., STN International (ENERGY). *2363*

ENERGY USER NEWS.
Chilton Co. Chilton Way, Radnor, PA 19089. TEL 215-964-4028. Vendor(s): Information Access Co. Knight-Ridder Information, Inc., Lexis-Nexis. *2548*

THE ENGINEER.
Miller Freeman Technical Ltd. Miller Freeman House, 30 Calderwood St., London SE18 6QH, England. TEL 44-181-855-7777. FAX 44-181-854-7476. Vendor(s): Information Access Co. *2596*

ENGINEERED MATERIALS ABSTRACTS.
Cambridge Scientific Abstracts, 7200 Wisconsin Ave., Bethesda, MD 20814. TEL 301-961-6750. FAX 301-961-6720. Vendor(s): European Space Agency (File no.134), Knight-Ridder Information, Inc. (File no.293), Orbit Search Service (EMAB), STN International (EMA). *2627*

ENGINEERING & MINING JOURNAL.
Intertec Publishing Corp., 29 N. Wacker Dr., Chicago, IL 60606. TEL 312-726-2802. FAX 312-726-4103. Vendor(s): Information Access Co. Lexis-Nexis. *5062*

ENGINEERING DIMENSIONS.
Association of Professional Engineers of Ontario, 25 Sheppard Ave. W., Ste. 1000, North York, ON M2N 6S9, Canada. TEL 416-224-1100. FAX 416-224-8168 *2596*

ENGINEERING ECONOMIST.
Institute of Industrial Engineers, 25 Technology Park-Atlanta, Norcross, GA 30092. TEL 404-449-0460 FAX 404-263-8532. Vendor(s): Information Access Co. University Microfilms International. *2596*

ENGINEERING INDEX ANNUAL.
Engineering Information, Inc., Castle Point on the Hudson, Hoboken, NJ 07030. TEL 201-216-8500. FAX 201-216-8532. Vendor(s): Ovid Technologies, Inc. (COMP), CEDOCAR, Data-Star, Knight-Ridder Information, Inc. (File no.8), European Space Agency, Orbit Search Service, STN International. *2627*

ENGINEERING INDEX MONTHLY.
Engineering Information Inc., Castle Point on the Hudson, Hoboken, NJ 07030. TEL 201-216-8500. FAX 201-216-8532. Vendor(s): CEDOCAR, CISTI, Data-Star, European Space Agency, Knight-Ridder Information, Inc. (File no.8), Orbit Search Service Ovid Technologies, Inc. (COMP), STN International (COMFENDEX). *2627*

ENGLISH HISTORICAL REVIEW.
Longman Group UK Ltd., Longman House, Burnt Mill, Harlow, Essex CM20 2JE, England. TEL 44-1279-426721. FAX 44-1279-431059. Vendor(s): Information Access Co. *3408*

ENGLISH JOURNAL.
National Council of Teachers of English, 1111 W. Kenyon Rd., Urbana, IL 61801-1096. TEL 217-328-3870. FAX 217-328-0977. Vendor(s): University Microfilms International. *2332*

ENGLISH LANGUAGE NOTES.
University of Colorado, English Language Notes, CB 226, Boulder, CO 80309. TEL 303-492-7176. FAX 303-492-3521. Vendor(s): Information Access Co. *4206*

ENHANCED ENERGY RECOVERY NEWS.
Business Communications Co., Inc. (Norwalk), 25 Van Zant St., Ste. 13, Norwalk, CT 06855. TEL 203-853-4266. FAX 203-853-0348. Vendor(s): Information Access Co. NewsNet (EY60). *2548*

Online

ENTERPRISE (NEW YORK).
Equitable Life Assurance Society of the U.S., 787 Seventh Ave., Area 37K, New York, NY 10019. TEL 212-554-4738.
Vendor(s): University Microfilms International. *3648*

ENTERPRISE SOLUTIONS FOR MANAGERS OF WINDOWS NT.
Cardinal Business Media, Inc., 1300 Virginia Dr., Ste. 400, Fort Washington, PA 19034. TEL 215-643-8000. FAX 215-643-8099. *2036*

ENTERPRISE SYSTEMS JOURNAL.
Cardinal Business Media, Inc., 12225 Greenville Ave., Ste. 700, Dallas, TX 75243-9338. TEL 214-669-9000. FAX 214-669-9909.
Vendor(s): Information Access Co.. *2073*

ENTERTAINMENT & SPORTS LAW REVIEW.
University of Miami, School of Law, Box 248087, Coral Gables, FL 33124-8087. TEL 305-284-6886.
Vendor(s): West Services, Inc.. *3774*

THE ENTERTAINMENT MAGAZINE ON-LINE.
S W Alternatives, Inc., Box 3355, Tucson, AZ 85722. TEL 520-623-3733.
Available only online. *5156*

ENTERTAINMENT MARKETING LETTER.
E P M Communications, 160 Mercer St., 3rd Fl., New York, NY 10012-3212. TEL 212-941-0099. FAX 212-941-1622.
Vendor(s): Information Access Co.. *1464*

ENTERTAINMENT SOFTWARE: THE INTERNATIONAL MARKET.
Euromonitor, 60-61 Britton St., London EC1M 5NA, England. TEL 44-171-251-8024. FAX 44-171-608-3149.
Vendor(s): Data-Star, Knight-Ridder Information, Inc.. *3963*

ENTERTAINMENT WEEKLY.
Entertainment Weekly Inc. 1675 Broadway, New York, NY 10019. TEL 212-522-5600. FAX 212-522-0074.
Vendor(s): Information Access Co., VU/TEXT Information Services, Inc.. *3228*

ENTOMOLOGY ABSTRACTS.
Cambridge Scientific Abstracts, 7200 Wisconsin Ave., 6th Fl., Bethesda, MD 20814. TEL 301-961-6750. FAX 301-961-6720.
Vendor(s): Knight-Ridder Information, Inc. (File no.76/LIFE SCIENCES COLLECTION), STN International (LIFESCI). *620*

ENTREPRENEURSHIP: THEORY AND PRACTICE.
Baylor University, Hankamer School of Business, John F. Baugh Center for Entrepreneurship, BU Box 98011, Waco, TX 76798-8011. TEL 817-755-2265. FAX 817-755-2271.
Vendor(s): Information Access Co., University Microfilms International. *1575*

ENTREZ DOCUMENT RETRIEVAL SYSTEM.
U.S. National Center for Biotechnology Information, National Library of Medicine, Bldg. 38A, Rm. 8N-803, 8600 Rockville Pike, Bethesda, MD 20894. TEL 301-496-2475. FAX 301-480-9241.
Available only online. *4559*

ENVIRONMENT (WASHINGTON).
Heldref Publications, 1319 Eighteenth St., N.W., Washington, DC 20036-1802. TEL 202-296-6267. FAX 202-296-5149.
Vendor(s): Information Access Co., University Microfilms International. *2787*

ENVIRONMENT ABSTRACTS.
Congressional Information Service, Inc., A member of the LEXIS NEXIS family, 4520 East-West Hwy., Bethesda, MD 20814-3389. TEL 301-654-1550. FAX 301-654-4033.
Vendor(s): Data-Star (ENVN/Environline), European Space Agency (File no.11/ENVIROLINE and File no.109/Acid Rain Abstracts), FIZ Technik (ENVIROLINE), Knight-Ridder Information, Inc. (File no.40), Orbit Search Service (ENVIRONLINE). *2829*

ENVIRONMENT ABSTRACTS ANNUAL.
Congressional Information Service, Inc., A member of the LEXIS-NEXIS family, 4520 East-West Hwy., Ste. 800, Bethesda, MD 20814-3389. TEL 301-654-1550. FAX 301-654-4033.
Vendor(s): Data-Star (ENVN/Enviroline), European Space Agency (File no.11/ENVIROLINE and File no.109/Acid Rain Abstracts), Knight-Ridder Information, Inc. (File no.40), Orbit Search Service (Enviroline). *2829*

ENVIRONMENT AND SAFETY BRIEFING.
Barbour Index, New Lodge Drift Rd., Windsor, Berks. SL4 4RQ, England. TEL 01344-884121. FAX 01483-884112. *2787*

ENVIRONMENT BUSINESS.
Information for Industry Ltd., 18-20 Ridgway, London SW19 4QN, England. TEL 44-181-944-2930. FAX 44-181-944-1982.
Vendor(s): Information Access Co.. *2787*

ENVIRONMENT INDEX.
Asian Institute of Technology, Environmental Systems Information Center (ENSIC), P.O. Box 2754, Bangkok 10501, Thailand. FAX 66-2-5245870. *2787*

ENVIRONMENT REPORTER.
The Bureau of National Affairs, Inc., 1231 25th St., N.W., Washington, DC 20037. TEL 202-452-4200. FAX 202-822-8092.
Vendor(s): Human Resources Information Network, Lexis-Nexis (ENVREP), West Services, Inc. (BNA-ER). *2788*

ENVIRONMENT WATCH: LATIN AMERICA.
Cutter Information Corp., 37 Broadway, Arlington, MA 02174-5552. FAX 617-648-1950.
Vendor(s): Information Access Co., NewsNet (EV44). *2788*

ENVIRONMENT WATCH: WEST EUROPE.
Cutter Information Corp., 37 Broadway, Arlington, MA 02174-5552. TEL 617-648-8700. FAX 617-648-1950.
Vendor(s): Information Access Co.. *2788*

ENVIRONMENT WEEK.
King Publishing Group, Inc., 627 National Press Bldg., Washington, DC 20045. TEL 202-638-4260. FAX 202-662-9744.
Vendor(s): Data-Star, Information Access Co., Knight-Ridder Information, Inc., Lexis-Nexis, NewsNet (EV25). *2788*

ENVIRONMENTAL ACTION.
Environmental Action Foundation, 6930 Carroll Ave., Ste. 600, Takoma Park, MD 20912. TEL 301-891-1106. FAX 301-891-2218.
Vendor(s): Information Access Co., University Microfilms International. *2788*

ENVIRONMENTAL AND ECOLOGICAL STATISTICS.
Chapman & Hall, Journals Department 2-6 Boundary Row, London SE1 8HN, England. TEL 44-171-8650066. FAX 44-171-5229623. *2829*

ENVIRONMENTAL AND MOLECULAR MUTAGENESIS.
John Wiley & Sons, Inc., Journals, 605 Third Ave., New York, NY 10158. TEL 212-850-6645. FAX 212-850-6021. *740*

ENVIRONMENTAL BUSINESS JOURNAL.
Environmental Business International Inc., 4452 Park Blvd., Ste. 306, San Diego, CA 92116-4039. TEL 619-295-7685. FAX 619-295-5743.
Vendor(s): Information Access Co.. *2789*

ENVIRONMENTAL GEOCHEMISTRY AND HEALTH.
Chapman & Hall, Journals Department 2-6 Boundary Row, London SE1 8HN, England. TEL 44-171-8560066. FAX 44-171-5229623. *2790*

ENVIRONMENTAL HEALTH LETTER.
Business Publishers, Inc., 951 Pershing Dr., Silver Spring, MD 20910-4464. TEL 301-587-6300. FAX 301-585-9075.
Vendor(s): NewsNet. *4451*

ENVIRONMENTAL HEALTH PERSPECTIVES.
U.S. Department of Health and Human Services, National Institute of Environmental Health Sciences, Box 12233, Research Triangle Park, NC 27709. TEL 919-541-3406. FAX 919-541-0273. *2790*

ENVIRONMENTAL HYDROLOGY REPORT.
International Association for Environmental Hydrology, Box 35324, San Antonio, TX 78235-5324. TEL 210-344-5418. FAX 210-344-9941.
Available only online. *2285*

ENVIRONMENTAL LAW (PORTLAND).
Northwestern School of Law, Lewis and Clark College, 10015 S.W. Terwilliger Blvd., Portland, OR 97219. TEL 503-768-6700. FAX 503-768-6671.
Vendor(s): Information Access Co., Lexis-Nexis, West Services, Inc.. *2791*

ENVIRONMENTAL LAW REPORTER.
Environmental Law Institute, 1616 P St., S.W., Ste. 200, Washington, DC 20036. TEL 202-328-5150.
Vendor(s): Lexis-Nexis, West Services, Inc.. *2791*

ENVIRONMENTAL MANAGEMENT BRIEFING.
Barbour Index, New Lodge Drift Rd., Windsor, Berks. SL4 4RQ, England. TEL 01344-884121. FAX 01344-884112. *2851*

ENVIRONMENTAL MANAGEMENT TODAY.
Enterprise Communications Inc., 1483 Chain Bridge Rd., Ste. 202, McLean, VA 22101. TEL 703-448-0336. FAX 703-448-0270.
Vendor(s): University Microfilms International. *2792*

ENVIRONMENTAL NUTRITION.
Environmental Nutrition, Inc., 52 Riverside Dr., Ste. 15A, New York, NY 10024-6599. TEL 212-362-0424. FAX 212-362-2066.
Vendor(s): Information Access Co. *5232*

ENVIRONMENTAL PERIODICALS BIBLIOGRAPHY.
International Academy at Santa Barbara, 800 Garden St., Ste. D, Santa Barbara, CA 93101-1552. TEL 805-965-5010. FAX 805-965-6071.
Vendor(s): Knight-Ridder Information, Inc. (File no.68). *2829*

ENVIRONMENTAL PROBLEMS & REMEDIATION.
Merton Allen Associates, InfoTeam Inc., Box 15640, Plantation, FL 33318-5640. TEL 954-473-9560. FAX 954-473-0544.
Vendor(s): Data-Star, Information Access Co., NewsNet. *2792*

ENVIRONMENTAL REMEDIATION TECHNOLOGY.
Business Publishers, Inc., 951 Pershing Dr., Silver Spring, MD 20910-4464. TEL 301-587-6300. FAX 301-589-5103.
Vendor(s): Information Access Co.. *2793*

ENVIRONMENTAL SCIENCE & TECHNOLOGY (WASHINGTON).
American Chemical Society, 1155 16th St., N.W., Washington, DC 20036. TEL 800-333-9511. FAX 614-447-3671.
Vendor(s): STN International (CJACS). *2794*

ENVIRONMENTAL SENSORS.
I O P Publishing Ltd., Techno House, Redcliffe Way, Bristol, Avon BS1 6NX, England. TEL 44-117-929-7481. FAX 44-117-929-4318. *2794*

ENVIRONMENTAL SOLUTIONS.
Advanstar Communications, Inc., 7500 Old Oak Blvd., Cleveland, OH 44130. TEL 216-826-2839. FAX 216-891-2726.
Vendor(s): Information Access Co.. *2851*

THE ENVIRONMENTALIST.
Chapman & Hall, Journals Department 2-6 Boundary Row, London SE1 8HN, England. TEL 44-171-8560066. FAX 44-171-5229623. *2795*

EPIPHANY JOURNAL.
Epiphany Press, 1516 N. Delaware St., Indianapolis, IN 46202-2419.
Vendor(s): Knight-Ridder Information, Inc., Ovid Technologies, Inc.. *6060*

EQUAL OPPORTUNITIES REVIEW.
Eclipse Group Ltd., Industrial Relations Services, 18-20 Highbury Pl., London N5 1QP, England. TEL 44-171-354-5858. FAX 44-171-354-8106.
Vendor(s): University Microfilms International. *1373*

EQUIPMENT AND MATERIALS UPDATE.
Merton Allen Associates, InfoTeam Inc., Box 15640, Plantation, FL 33318-5640. TEL 954-473-9560. FAX 954-473-0544.
Vendor(s): Information Access Co.. *6239*

EQUIPMENT LEASING TODAY.
Equipment Leasing Association, 1300 N. 17th St., Ste. 1010, Arlington, VA 22209. TEL 703-527-8655. FAX 703-527-2649.
Vendor(s): University Microfilms International. *4337*

ESQUIRE.
Hearst Corporation, Esquire, 250 W. 55th St., New York, NY 10019. TEL 212-649-2040. FAX 212-977-3158.
Vendor(s): Information Access Co.. *4940*

ESSAY AND GENERAL LITERATURE INDEX.
H.W. Wilson Co., 950 University Ave., Bronx, NY 10452. TEL 718-588-8400. FAX 718-590-1617.
Vendor(s): Wilsonline (File EGL). *4293*

ESSAYS IN LITERATURE.
Western Illinois University, Department of English, 114 Simpkins Hall, Macomb, IL 61455-1396. TEL 309-298-2212. FAX 309-298-2212.
Vendor(s): Information Access Co., University Microfilms International. *4207*

ESSENCE (NEW YORK).
Essence Communications Inc., 1500 Broadway, New York, NY 10036-4015. TEL 212-642-0600. FAX 212-921-5173.
Vendor(s): Information Access Co. *6993*

ESSOR.
Union Francaise d'Annuaires Professionnels, 13 av. Hennequin, B.P. 36, 78192 Trappes Cedex, France. TEL 1-30-50-61-48. FAX 1-30-50-48-27. *1272*

ESTATE PLANNER'S ALERT.
Research Institute of America, Inc., 90 Fifth Ave., New York, NY 10011. TEL 212-645-4800. FAX 212-337-4279.
Vendor(s): Lexis-Nexis. *3914*

ESTATE PLANNING (NEW YORK).
Warren, Gorham & Lamont, One Penn Plaza, New York, NY 10119. TEL 212-971-5000. FAX 212-971-5113.
Vendor(s): Lexis-Nexis (TAXRIA-Library), West Services, Inc. (WGL-ESTPLN). *3914*

ESTATES GAZETTE.
Estates Gazette Ltd. 151 Wardour St., London W1V 4BN, England. TEL 44-171-437-0141. FAX 44-171-437-2432. *6024*

ESTUDIOS PUBLICOS.
Centro de Estudios Publicos, Monsenor Sotero Sanz No. 175, Providencia, Santiago 9, Chile. TEL 56-2-2315324. FAX 56-2-2335253. *6322*

ESTUDIOS RURALES LATINOAMERICANOS.
Fundacion Estudios Rurales Latinoamericanos, Apdo. Aereo 11386, Bogota, Colombia. TEL 2837771. *1209*

ETC.
International Society for General Semantics, Box 728, Concord, CA 94522. TEL 510-798-0311.
Vendor(s): Information Access Co., University Microfilms International. *4067*

ETHNOLOGY.
University of Pittsburgh, Department of Anthropology, Pittsburgh, PA 15260. TEL 412-648-7503. FAX 412-648-5911.
Vendor(s): Information Access Co., University Microfilms International. *308*

EURO-EAST.
Europe Information Service, Rue de Geneve, 6, 1140 Brussels, Belgium. TEL 32-2-242-6020. FAX 32-2-242-9410.
Vendor(s): Lexis-Nexis. *5749*

EUROBIOLOGISTE.
Centre National des Biologistes, 80 Av. du Maine, 75014 Paris, France. TEL 43-22-97-70. FAX 43-21-73-12. *638*

EUROFOOD.
Agra Europe (London) Ltd., 25 Frant Rd., Tunbridge Wells, Kent TN2 5JT, England. TEL 44-1892-533813. FAX 44-1892-544895.
Vendor(s): Information Access Co.. *2966*

EUROFOOD MONITOR.
Agra Europe (London) Ltd., 25 Frant Rd., Tunbridge Wells, Kent TN2 5JT, England. TEL 44-1892-533813. FAX 44-1892-544895. *2966*

EUROMARKETING.
Crain Communications Inc., New Garden House, 78 Hatton Garden, London EC1N 8JQ, England. TEL 44-171-457-1400. FAX 44-171-457-1440.
Vendor(s): Information Access Co.. *36*

EUROMONEY.
Euromoney Publications plc., Nestor House, Playhouse Yard, London EC4V 5EX, England. TEL 44-171-779-8935. FAX 44-171-779-8541.
Vendor(s): Information Access Co., Knight-Ridder Information, Inc., University Microfilms International. *1086*

THE EUROMONITOR BOOK REPORT (YEAR).
Euromonitor, 60-61 Britton St., London EC1M 5NA, England. TEL 44-171-251-8024. FAX 44-171-608-3149. *5995*

EURONOMICS.
International Business Consortium Alphen, P.O. Box 1154, 2400 BD Alphen aan den Rijn, Netherlands. TEL 31-1720-25529. FAX 31-1720-26099. *921*

EUROPA CHEMIE.
Verlagsgruppe Handelsblatt GmbH, Kasernenstr. 67, 40213 Duesseldorf, Germany. TEL 49-211-8870. FAX 49-211-329954. *2640*

EUROPA VAN MORGEN.
European Commission Office in the Netherlands, Postbus 30465, 2500 GL The Hague, Netherlands. TEL 31-70-3469326. FAX 31-70-3646619. *5749*

EUROPAGES.
Euredit s.a., 9, Avenue de Friedland, 75008 Paris, France. TEL 1-53-77-54-00. FAX 42-89-34-73. *1608*

EUROPE.
Office for Official Publications of the European Communities, L-2985 Luxembourg, Luxembourg. Vendor(s): Information Access Co. *1210*

EUROPE - ASIA STUDIES.
Carfax Publishing Co., P.O. Box 25, Abingdon, Oxon. OX14 3UE, England. TEL 44-1235-401000. FAX 44-1235-401550.
Vendor(s): Information Access Co.. *922*

EUROPE ENERGY.
Europe Information Service, Rue de Geneve, 6, 1140 Brussels, Belgium. TEL 32-2-242-6020. FAX 32-2-242-9410.
Vendor(s): Information Access Co., Lexis-Nexis. *2548*

EUROPE ENVIRONMENT.
Europe Information Service, Rue de Geneve, 6, 1140 Brussels, Belgium. TEL 32-2-242-6020. FAX 32-2-242-9410.
Vendor(s): Information Access Co., Lexis-Nexis. *2796*

THE EUROPEAN.
The European Ltd., 200 Gray's Inn Rd., London WC1X 8NE, England. TEL 44-171-418-7777. FAX 44-171-713-1840. *3136*

EUROPEAN ADHESIVES & SEALANTS.
Argus Business Media Ltd., Fuel and Metals Journals Queensway House, 2 Queensway, Redhill, Surrey RH1 1QS, England. TEL 44-1737-768611. FAX 44-1737-761685.
Vendor(s): Information Access Co.. *4954*

THE EUROPEAN BUSINESS JOURNAL.
Whurr Publishers Ltd., 19b Compton Terrace, London N1 2UN, England. TEL 44-171-359-5979. FAX 44-171-226-5290.
Vendor(s): University Microfilms International. *922*

EUROPEAN CHEMICAL NEWS.
Reed Business Publishing Group Quadrant House, The Quadrant, Sutton, Surrey SM2 5AS, England. TEL 0181-652-3187. FAX 0181-652-3357. *2640*

EUROPEAN COSMETIC MARKETS.
Nicholas Hall & Company, 35 Alexandra St., Southend-on-Sea, Essex SS1 1BW, England. TEL 44-1702-220200. FAX 44-1702-430787.
Vendor(s): Information Access Co.. *496*

EUROPEAN ENERGY REPORT.
Financial Times Energy Publishing Maple House, 149 Tottenham Court Rd., London W1P 9LL, England. TEL 44-171-896-2241. FAX 44-171-896-2275.
Vendor(s): Data-Star, Information Access Co., Knight-Ridder Information, Inc., Lexis-Nexis. *2549*

EUROPEAN INDUSTRIAL RELATIONS REVIEW.
Eclipse Group Ltd., Industrial Relations Services, 18-20 Highbury Pl., London N5 1QP, England. TEL 44-171-354-5858. FAX 44-171-354-8106.
Vendor(s): University Microfilms International. *1373*

EUROPEAN INSIGHT.
Europe Information Service Rue de Geneve, 6, 1140 Brussels, Belgium. TEL 32-2-242-6020. FAX 32-2-242-9410.
Vendor(s): Lexis-Nexis. *5749*

EUROPEAN JOURNAL OF DRUG METABOLISM AND PHARMACOKINETICS.
Editions Medecine et Hygiene, Case Postale 456, CH-1211 Geneva 4, Switzerland. TEL 41-22-7029311. FAX 41-22-7029355. *5411*

EUROPEAN JOURNAL OF EMERGENCY MEDICINE.
Chapman & Hall, Journals Department 2-6 Boundary Row, London SE1 8HN, England. TEL 44-171-8650066. FAX 44-171-5229623. *4783*

THE EUROPEAN JOURNAL OF FINANCE.
Chapman & Hall, Journals Department 2-6 Boundary Row, London SE1 8HN, England. TEL 44-171-8650066. FAX 44-171-5229623. *1086*

EUROPEAN JOURNAL OF MORPHOLOGY.
Swets & Zeitlinger bv, P.O. Box 825, 2160 SZ Lisse, Netherlands. TEL 31-252-435111. FAX 31-252-415888. *787*

EUROPEAN JOURNAL OF ORTHOPAEDIC SURGERY & TRAUMATOLOGY.
Springer-Verlag France, 26 rue des Carmes, 75005 Paris, France. TEL 33-1-43-41-15-80. FAX 33-1-43-54-49-08. *4783*

EUROPEAN JOURNAL OF PHARMACEUTICS AND BIOPHARMACEUTICS.
Elsevier Science B.V., P.O. Box 211, 1000 AE Amsterdam, Netherlands. TEL 31 20-4853757. FAX 31-20-4853432. *5411*

EUROPEAN JOURNAL OF PHYSICS.
I O P Publishing Ltd., Techno House, Redcliffe Way, Bristol, Avon BS1 6NX, England. TEL 44-117-929-7481. FAX 44-117-929-4318. *5547*

EUROPEAN MEDIA ART FESTIVAL.
International Experimenta Film Workshop, Postfach 1861, 49008 Osnabrued, Germany. TEL 49-541-21658. FAX 49-541-28327. *5700*

EUROPEAN MEDIA BUSINESS & FINANCE.
Phillips Business Information, Inc. 1201 Seven Locks Rd., Potomac, MD 20854. TEL 301-424-3338. FAX 301-309-3847.
Vendor(s): Information Access Co.. *1086*

EUROPEAN POLYMERS PAINT COLOUR JOURNAL.
Argus Business Media Ltd. Fuel and Metals Journals Queensway House, 2 Queensway Redhill, Surrey RH1 1QS, England. TEL 44-1737-768611. FAX 44-1737-761685.
Vendor(s): Information Access Co.. *5307*

EUROPEAN POWER NEWS.
Argus Business Media Ltd. Fuel and Metals Journals Queensway House, 2 Queensway Redhill, Surrey RH1 1QS, England. TEL 44-1737-768611. FAX 44-1737-761685.
Vendor(s): Information Access Co.. *2698*

EUROPEAN REPORT.
Europe Information Service, Rue de Geneve, 6, 1140 Brussels, Belgium. TEL 32-2-242-6020. FAX 32-2-242-9410.
Vendor(s): Information Access Co., Lexis-Nexis. *1087*

EUROPEAN RUBBER JOURNAL.
Crain Communications Inc., New Garden House, 78 Hatton Garden, London EC1N 8JQ, England. TEL 44-171-457-1400. FAX 44-171-457-1440.
Vendor(s): Information Access Co.. *6216*

Online

EUROPEAN SOCIAL POLICY.
Europe Information Service, Rue de Geneve, 6, 1140 Brussels, Belgium. TEL 32-2-242-6020. FAX 32-2-242-9410.
Vendor(s): Information Access Co., Lexis-Nexis. *5749*

EUROPHYSICS LETTERS.
Editions de Physique, Zone Industrielle ᴊe Courtaboeuf, B.P. 112, 91944 Les Ulis Cedex, France. TEL 33-1-69-07-36-88. FAX 33-1-69-28-84-91. *5547*

EUROSTATISTICS DATA FOR SHORT TERM ECONOMIC ANALYSIS.
Office for Official Publications of the European Communities, Rue Alcide de Gasperi, 2920 Luxembourg, Luxembourg.
Vendor(s): Commission of the European Communities. *996*

EUROWEEK.
Euromoney Publications plc., Nestor House, Playhouse Yard, London EC4V 5EX, England. TEL 44-171-779-8935. FAX 44-171-779-8541.
Vendor(s): University Microfilms International. *1087*

EVALUATION COMMENT.
University of California at Los Angeles, Center for the Study of Evaluation, 405 Hilgard Ave., 1320 Moore Hall, Los Angeles, CA 90095-1522. TEL 310-206-1532. *2486*

EVALUATION OF DRUG INTERACTIONS.
Professional Drug Systems, Inc., 530 Maryville Centre Dr., Ste. 250, St. Louis, MO 63141. TEL 314-275-8848. FAX 314-275-8819. *5412*

EVANS-NOVAK POLITICAL REPORT.
Eagle Publishing, A Phillips Publishing International Company, 422 First St., S.E., Washington, DC 20003. TEL 202-546-5005. FAX 202-546-8759.
Vendor(s): Information Access Co.. *5665*

EVANSVILLE BUSINESS JOURNAL.
Evansville Business Journal, Inc., Box 3275, Evansville, IN 47731-3275. TEL 812-425-2210. FAX 812-422-4984.
Vendor(s): University Microfilms International. *922*

EVENTLINE.
Elsevier Science B.V., P.O. Box 521, 1000 AM Amsterdam, Netherlands. TEL 31-20-4853911. FAX 31-20-4853598.
Vendor(s): Data-Star, European Space Agency, Knight-Ridder Information, Inc.. *1609*

EVOLUTION.
Allen Press, Inc., 1041 New Hampshire Ave., Box 1897, Lawrence, KS 66044-8897. FAX 913-843-1274.
Vendor(s): Information Access Co.. *740*

EVOLUTIONARY ECOLOGY.
Chapman & Hall, Journals Department 2-6 Boundary Row, London SE1 8HN, England. TEL 44-171-8650066. FAX 44-171-5229623. *2796*

EXCEPTIONAL CHILDREN.
Council for Exceptional Children, 1920 Association Dr., Reston, VA 22091. TEL 703-620-3660. FAX 703-264-9494.
Vendor(s): Information Access Co., University Microfilms International. *1767*

EXCEPTIONAL HUMAN EXPERIENCE.
Exceptional Human Experience Network, Inc., 414 Rockledge Rd., New Bern, NC 28562. TEL 919-636-8734. FAX 919-636-8371. *5334*

EXCEPTIONAL PARENT.
Psy-Ed. Corp., 120 State St., Hackensack, NJ 07601-5421. TEL 201-489-0871. FAX 201-489-1240.
Vendor(s): Information Access Co., University Microfilms International. *1767*

EXCERPTA MEDICA ABSTRACT JOURNALS.
Excerpta Medica P.O. Box 548, 1000 AM Amsterdam, Netherlands. TEL 31-20-4853507. FAX 31-20-4853222.
Vendor(s): DIMDI, Data-Star, JICST, Knight-Ridder Information, Inc., Ovid Technologies, Inc.. *4559*

EXCERPTA MEDICA. SECTION 1: ANATOMY, ANTHROPOLOGY, EMBRYOLOGY & HISTOLOGY.
Excerpta Medica P.O. Box 548, 1000 AM Amsterdam, Netherlands. TEL 31-20-4853507. FAX 31-20-4853222.
Vendor(s): DIMDI, Data-Star, JICST, Knight-Ridder Information, Inc., Ovid Technologies, Inc.. *4559*

EXCERPTA MEDICA. SECTION 2: PHYSIOLOGY.
Excerpta Medica P.O. Box 548, 1000 AM Amsterdam, Netherlands. TEL 31-20-4853507. FAX 31-20-4853222.
Vendor(s): DIMDI, Data-Star, JICST, Knight-Ridder Information, Inc., Ovid Technologies, Inc.. *4560*

EXCERPTA MEDICA. SECTION 3: ENDOCRINOLOGY.
Excerpta Medica P.O. Box 548, 1000 AM Amsterdam, Netherlands. TEL 31-20-4853507. FAX 31-20-4853222.
Vendor(s): DIMDI, Data-Star, JICST, Knight-Ridder Information, Inc., Ovid Technologies, Inc.. *4560*

EXCERPTA MEDICA. SECTION 4: MICROBIOLOGY: BACTERIOLOGY, MYCOLOGY, PARASITOLOGY AND VIROLOGY.
Excerpta Medica P.O. Box 548, 1000 AM Amsterdam, Netherlands. TEL 31-20-4853507. FAX 31-20-4853222.
Vendor(s): DIMDI, Data-Star, JICST, Knight-Ridder Information, Inc., Ovid Technologies, Inc.. *4560*

EXCERPTA MEDICA. SECTION 5: GENERAL PATHOLOGY AND PATHOLOGICAL ANATOMY.
Excerpta Medica P.O. Box 548, 1000 AM Amsterdam, Netherlands. TEL 31-20-4853507. FAX 31-20-4853222.
Vendor(s): DIMDI, Data-Star, JICST, Knight-Ridder Information, Inc., Ovid Technologies, Inc.. *4560*

EXCERPTA MEDICA. SECTION 6: INTERNAL MEDICINE.
Excerpta Medica P.O. Box 548, 1000 AM Amsterdam, Netherlands. TEL 31-20-4853507. FAX 31-20-4853222.
Vendor(s): DIMDI, Data-Star, JICST, Knight-Ridder Information, Inc., Ovid Technologies, Inc.. *4560*

EXCERPTA MEDICA. SECTION 7: PEDIATRICS AND PEDIATRIC SURGERY.
Excerpta Medica P.O. Box 548, 1000 AM Amsterdam, Netherlands. TEL 31-20-4853507. FAX 31-20-4853222.
Vendor(s): DIMDI, Data-Star, JICST, Knight-Ridder Information, Inc., Ovid Technologies, Inc.. *4560*

EXCERPTA MEDICA. SECTION 8: NEUROLOGY AND NEUROSURGERY.
Excerpta Medica P.O. Box 548, 1000 AM Amsterdam, Netherlands. TEL 31-20-4853507. FAX 31-20-4853222.
Vendor(s): DIMDI, Data-Star, JICST, Knight-Ridder Information, Inc., Ovid Technologies, Inc.. *4560*

EXCERPTA MEDICA. SECTION 9: SURGERY.
Excerpta Medica P.O. Box 548, 1000 AM Amsterdam, Netherlands. TEL 31-20-4853507. FAX 31-20-4853222.
Vendor(s): DIMDI, Data-Star, JICST, Knight-Ridder Information, Inc., Ovid Technologies, Inc.. *4561*

EXCERPTA MEDICA. SECTION 10: OBSTETRICS AND GYNECOLOGY.
Excerpta Medica P.O. Box 548, 1000 AM Amsterdam, Netherlands. TEL 31-20-4853507. FAX 31-20-4853222.
Vendor(s): DIMDI, Data-Star, JICST, Knight-Ridder Information, Inc., Ovid Technologies, Inc.. *4561*

EXCERPTA MEDICA. SECTION 11: OTORHINOLARYNGOLOGY.
Excerpta Medica P.O. Box 548, 1000 AM Amsterdam, Netherlands. TEL 31-20-4853507. FAX 31-20-4853222.
Vendor(s): DIMDI, Data-Star, JICST, Knight-Ridder Information, Inc., Ovid Technologies, Inc.. *4561*

EXCERPTA MEDICA. SECTION 12: OPHTHALMOLOGY.
Excerpta Medica P.O. Box 548, 1000 AM Amsterdam, Netherlands. TEL 31-20-4853507. FAX 31-20-4853222.
Vendor(s): DIMDI, Data-Star, JICST, Knight-Ridder Information, Inc., Ovid Technologies, Inc.. *4561*

EXCERPTA MEDICA. SECTION 13: DERMATOLOGY AND VENEREOLOGY.
Excerpta Medica P.O. Box 548, 1000 AM Amsterdam, Netherlands. TEL 31-20-4853507. FAX 31-20-4853222.
Vendor(s): DIMDI, Data-Star, JICST, Knight-Ridder Information, Inc., Ovid Technologies, Inc.. *4561*

EXCERPTA MEDICA. SECTION 14: RADIOLOGY.
Excerpta Medica P.O. Box 548, 1000 AM Amsterdam, Netherlands. TEL 31-20-4853507. FAX 31-20-4853222.
Vendor(s): DIMDI, Data-Star, JICST, Knight-Ridder Information, Inc., Ovid Technologies, Inc.. *4561*

EXCERPTA MEDICA. SECTION 15: CHEST DISEASES, THORACIC SURGERY AND TUBERCULOSIS.
Excerpta Medica P.O. Box 548, 1000 AM Amsterdam, Netherlands. TEL 31-20-4853507. FAX 31-20-4853222.
Vendor(s): DIMDI, Data-Star, JICST, Knight-Ridder Information, Inc., Ovid Technologies, Inc.. *4561*

EXCERPTA MEDICA. SECTION 16: CANCER.
Excerpta Medica P.O. Box 548, 1000 AM Amsterdam, Netherlands. TEL 31-20-4853507. FAX 31-20-4853222.
Vendor(s): DIMDI, Data-Star, JICST, Knight-Ridder Information, Inc., Ovid Technologies, Inc.. *4562*

EXCERPTA MEDICA. SECTION 17: PUBLIC HEALTH, SOCIAL MEDICINE AND EPIDEMIOLOGY.
Excerpta Medica P.O. Box 548, 1000 AM Amsterdam, Netherlands. TEL 31-20-4853507. FAX 31-20-4853222.
Vendor(s): DIMDI, Data-Star, JICST, Knight-Ridder Information, Inc., Ovid Technologies, Inc.. *5982*

EXCERPTA MEDICA. SECTION 18: CARDIOVASCULAR DISEASES AND CARDIOVASCULAR SURGERY.
Excerpta Medica P.O. Box 548, 1000 AM Amsterdam, Netherlands. TEL 31-20-4853507. FAX 31-20-4853222.
Vendor(s): DIMDI, Data-Star, JICST, Knight-Ridder Information, Inc., Ovid Technologies, Inc.. *4562*

EXCERPTA MEDICA. SECTION 19: REHABILITATION AND PHYSICAL MEDICINE.
Excerpta Medica P.O. Box 548, 1000 AM Amsterdam, Netherlands. TEL 31-20-4853507. FAX 31-20-4853222.
Vendor(s): DIMDI, Data-Star, JICST, Knight-Ridder Information, Inc., Ovid Technologies, Inc.. *4562*

EXCERPTA MEDICA. SECTION 20: GERONTOLOGY AND GERIATRICS.
Excerpta Medica P.O. Box 548, 1000 AM Amsterdam, Netherlands. TEL 31-20-4853507. FAX 31-20-4853222.
Vendor(s): DIMDI, Data-Star, JICST, Knight-Ridder Information, Inc., Ovid Technologies, Inc.. *3299*

EXCERPTA MEDICA. SECTION 21: DEVELOPMENTAL BIOLOGY AND TERATOLOGY.
Excerpta Medica P.O. Box 548, 1000 AM Amsterdam, Netherlands. TEL 31-20-4853507. FAX 31-20-4853222.
Vendor(s): DIMDI, Data-Star, JICST, Knight-Ridder Information, Inc., Ovid Technologies, Inc.. *4562*

EXCERPTA MEDICA. SECTION 22: HUMAN GENETICS.
Excerpta Medica P.O. Box 548, 1000 AM Amsterdam, Netherlands. TEL 31-20-4853507. FAX 31-20-4853222.
Vendor(s): DIMDI, Data-Star, JICST, Knight-Ridder Information, Inc., Ovid Technologies, Inc.. *621*

EXCERPTA MEDICA. SECTION 23: NUCLEAR MEDICINE.
Excerpta Medica P.O. Box 548, 1000 AM Amsterdam, Netherlands. TEL 31-20-4853507. FAX 31-20-4853222.
Vendor(s): DIMDI, Data-Star, JICST, Knight-Ridder Information, Inc., Ovid Technologies, Inc.. *4562*

EXCERPTA MEDICA. SECTION 24: ANESTHESIOLOGY.
Excerpta Medica P.O. Box 548, 1000 AM Amsterdam, Netherlands. TEL 31-20-4853507. FAX 31-20-4853222.
Vendor(s): DIMDI, Data-Star, JICST, Knight-Ridder Information, Inc., Ovid Technologies, Inc.. *4562*

EXCERPTA MEDICA. SECTION 25: HEMATOLOGY.
Excerpta Medica P.O. Box 548, 1000 AM
Amsterdam, Netherlands. TEL 31-20-4853507.
FAX 31-20-4853222.
Vendor(s): DIMDI, Data-Star, JICST, Knight-Ridder
Information, Inc., Ovid Technologies, Inc.. *4562*

EXCERPTA MEDICA. SECTION 26: IMMUNOLOGY, SEROLOGY AND TRANSPLANTATION.
Excerpta Medica P.O. Box 548, 1000 AM
Amsterdam, Netherlands. TEL 31-20-4853507.
FAX 31-20-4853222.
Vendor(s): DIMDI, Data-Star, JICST, Knight-Ridder
Information, Inc., Ovid Technologies, Inc.. *4563*

EXCERPTA MEDICA. SECTION 27: BIOPHYSICS, BIO-ENGINEERING AND MEDICAL INSTRUMENTATION.
Excerpta Medica P.O. Box 548, 1000 AM
Amsterdam, Netherlands. TEL 31-20-4853507.
FAX 31-20-4853222.
Vendor(s): DIMDI, Data-Star, JICST, Knight-Ridder
Information, Inc., Ovid Technologies, Inc.. *4563*

EXCERPTA MEDICA. SECTION 28: UROLOGY AND NEPHROLOGY.
Excerpta Medica P.O. Box 548, 1000 AM
Amsterdam, Netherlands. TEL 31-20-4853507.
FAX 31-20-4853222.
Vendor(s): DIMDI, Data-Star, JICST, Knight-Ridder
Information, Inc., Ovid Technologies, Inc.. *4563*

EXCERPTA MEDICA. SECTION 29: CLINICAL AND EXPERIMENTAL BIOCHEMISTRY.
Excerpta Medica P.O. Box 548, 1000 AM
Amsterdam, Netherlands. TEL 31-20-4853507.
FAX 31-20-4853222.
Vendor(s): DIMDI, Data-Star, JICST, Knight-Ridder
Information, Inc., Ovid Technologies, Inc.. *4563*

EXCERPTA MEDICA. SECTION 30: CLINICAL AND EXPERIMENTAL PHARMACOLOGY.
Excerpta Medica P.O. Box 548, 1000 AM
Amsterdam, Netherlands. TEL 31-20-4853507.
FAX 31-20-4853222.
Vendor(s): DIMDI, Data-Star, JICST, Knight-Ridder
Information, Inc., Ovid Technologies, Inc.. *5450*

EXCERPTA MEDICA. SECTION 31: ARTHRITIS AND RHEUMATISM.
Excerpta Medica P.O. Box 548, 1000 AM
Amsterdam, Netherlands. TEL 31-20-4853507.
FAX 31-20-4853222.
Vendor(s): DIMDI, Data-Star, JICST, Knight-Ridder
Information, Inc., Ovid Technologies, Inc.. *4563*

EXCERPTA MEDICA. SECTION 32: PSYCHIATRY.
Excerpta Medica P.O. Box 548, 1000 AM
Amsterdam, Netherlands. TEL 31-20-4853507.
FAX 31-20-4853222.
Vendor(s): DIMDI, Data-Star, JICST, Knight-Ridder
Information, Inc., Ovid Technologies, Inc.. *4563*

EXCERPTA MEDICA. SECTION 33: ORTHOPEDIC SURGERY.
Excerpta Medica P.O. Box 548, 1000 AM
Amsterdam, Netherlands. TEL 31-20-4853507.
FAX 31-20-4853222.
Vendor(s): DIMDI, Data-Star, JICST, Knight-Ridder
Information, Inc., Ovid Technologies, Inc.. *4563*

EXCERPTA MEDICA. SECTION 35: OCCUPATIONAL HEALTH AND INDUSTRIAL MEDICINE.
Excerpta Medica P.O. Box 548, 1000 AM
Amsterdam, Netherlands. TEL 31-20-4853507.
FAX 31-20-4853222.
Vendor(s): DIMDI, Data-Star, JICST, Knight-Ridder
Information, Inc., Ovid Technologies, Inc.. *4563*

EXCERPTA MEDICA. SECTION 36: HEALTH POLICY, ECONOMICS AND MANAGEMENT.
Excerpta Medica P.O. Box 548, 1000 AM
Amsterdam, Netherlands. TEL 31-20-4853507.
FAX 31-20-4853222.
Vendor(s): DIMDI, Data-Star, JICST, Knight-Ridder
Information, Inc., Ovid Technologies, Inc.. *3557*

EXCERPTA MEDICA. SECTION 38: ADVERSE REACTIONS TITLES.
Excerpta Medica P.O. Box 548, 1000 AM
Amsterdam, Netherlands. TEL 31-20-4853507.
FAX 31-20-4853222.
Vendor(s): DIMDI, Data-Star, JICST, Knight-Ridder
Information, Inc., Ovid Technologies, Inc.. *4564*

EXCERPTA MEDICA. SECTION 40: DRUG DEPENDENCE, ALCOHOL ABUSE AND ALCOHOLISM.
Excerpta Medica P.O. Box 548, 1000 AM
Amsterdam, Netherlands. TEL 31-20-4853507.
FAX 31-20-4853222.
Vendor(s): DIMDI, Data-Star, JICST, Knight-Ridder
Information, Inc., Ovid Technologies, Inc.. *2202*

EXCERPTA MEDICA. SECTION 46: ENVIRONMENTAL HEALTH AND POLLUTION CONTROL.
Excerpta Medica P.O. Box 548, 1000 AM
Amsterdam, Netherlands. TEL 31-20-4853507.
FAX 31-20-4853222.
Vendor(s): DIMDI, Data-Star, JICST, Knight-Ridder
Information, Inc., Ovid Technologies, Inc.. *2829*

EXCERPTA MEDICA. SECTION 48: GASTROENTEROLOGY.
Excerpta Medica P.O. Box 548, 1000 AM
Amsterdam, Netherlands. TEL 31-20-4853507.
FAX 31-20-4853222.
Vendor(s): DIMDI, Data-Star, JICST, Knight-Ridder
Information, Inc., Ovid Technologies, Inc.. *4564*

EXCERPTA MEDICA. SECTION 49: FORENSIC SCIENCE ABSTRACTS.
Excerpta Medica P.O. Box 548, 1000 AM
Amsterdam, Netherlands. TEL 31-20-4853507.
FAX 31-20-4853222.
Vendor(s): DIMDI, Data-Star, JICST, Knight-Ridder
Information, Inc., Ovid Technologies, Inc.. *4564*

EXCERPTA MEDICA. SECTION 50: EPILEPSY ABSTRACTS.
Excerpta Medica P.O. Box 548, 1000 AM
Amsterdam, Netherlands. TEL 31-20-4853507.
FAX 31-20-4853222.
Vendor(s): DIMDI, Data-Star, JICST, Knight-Ridder
Information, Inc., Ovid Technologies, Inc.. *4564*

EXCERPTA MEDICA. SECTION 52: TOXICOLOGY.
Excerpta Medica P.O. Box 548, 1000 AM
Amsterdam, Netherlands. TEL 31-20-4853507.
FAX 31-20-4853222.
Vendor(s): DIMDI, Data-Star, JICST, Knight-Ridder
Information, Inc., Ovid Technologies, Inc.. *2830*

EXECUTIVE ACCOUNTANT.
Institute of Cost and Executive Accountants, 141-149 Fonthill Rd., London N4 3HF, England. TEL 44-171-272-3925. FAX 44-171-281-5723.
Vendor(s): University Microfilms International. *1046*

EXECUTIVE BRIEF.
Society for Information Management, 401 N.
Michigan Ave., Chicago, IL 60611-4267. TEL 312-644-6610. FAX 312-245-1083. *2080*

EXECUTIVE EXCELLENCE.
Institute for Principle-Centered Leadership, 1344 E.
1120 S., Provo, UT 84606. TEL 801-375-4014.
FAX 801-377-5960.
Vendor(s): University Microfilms International. *1502*

EXECUTIVE FEMALE.
National Association for Female Executives, 30
Irving Pl., 5th Fl., New York, NY 10003. TEL 212-477-2200.
Vendor(s): Information Access Co.. *6993*

EXECUTIVE HEALTH'S GOOD HEALTH REPORT.
Executive Health, 383 Route 46 W., Fairfield, NJ
07004-2402. TEL 201-575-3507.
Vendor(s): Information Access Co.. *5527*

EXECUTIVE MEMORANDUM.
Heritage Foundation, 214 Massachusetts Ave., N.E.,
Washington, DC 20002. TEL 202-546-4400.
FAX 202-543-9647.
Vendor(s): Lexis-Nexis. *5750*

EXECUTIVE REPORT.
Riverview Publications, Inc., 3 Gateway Center, 5th
Fl., Pittsburgh, PA 15222-1004. TEL 412-471-4585. FAX 412-644-3006.
Vendor(s): Knight-Ridder Information, Inc., Lexis-Nexis, University Microfilms International. *1575*

EXECUTIVE SPEAKER.
Executive Speaker Co., Box 292437, Dayton, OH
45429. TEL 513-294-8493. FAX 513-294-6044.
Vendor(s): Lexis-Nexis. *36*

EXECUTIVE SPEECHES.
Executive Speaker Co., Box 292437, Dayton, OH
45429. TEL 513-294-8493. FAX 513-294-6044.
Vendor(s): University Microfilms International. *923*

EXPERIMENTAL & APPLIED ACAROLOGY.
Chapman & Hall, Journals Department 2-6
Boundary Row, London SE1 8HN, England. TEL 44-171-8560066. FAX 44-171-5229623. *582*

THE EXPERT AND THE LAW.
National Forensic Center, 17 Temple Terr.,
Lawrenceville, NJ 08648. TEL 609-883-0550.
Vendor(s): Lexis-Nexis. *3777*

EXPERTS CONTACT DIRECTORY.
Gale Research Inc., 835 Penobscot Bldg., Detroit,
MI 48226. TEL 313-961-2242. FAX 313-961-6083. *1867*

THE EXPLICATOR.
Heldref Publications, 1319 Eighteenth St., N.W.,
Washington, DC 20036-1802. TEL 202-296-6267.
FAX 202-296-5149.
Vendor(s): Information Access Co., University
Microfilms International. *4209*

THE EXPORTER.
Trade Data Reports, Inc., 34 W. 37th St., New York,
NY 10018. TEL 212-563-2772. FAX 212-563-2798.
Vendor(s): NewsNet (IT04). *1274*

L'EXPRESS.
Case Postale 561, CH-2001 Neuchatel,
Switzerland. TEL 038-256501. FAX 038-247736.
3219

EXTRAPOLATION.
Kent State University Press, Box 5190, Kent, OH
44242-0001. TEL 330-672-7913. FAX 330-672-3104.
Vendor(s): Information Access Co.. *4326*

EYE.
Box 303, New York, NY 10009. TEL 910-370-1702. FAX 910-370-1603. *3223*

EYEWEAR: THE INTERNATIONAL MARKET.
Euromonitor, 60-61 Britton Rd., London EC1 5NA,
England. TEL 44-171-251-8024. FAX 44-171-608-3149.
Vendor(s): Data-Star, Knight-Ridder Information, Inc..
4783

F B I LAW ENFORCEMENT BULLETIN.
U.S. Federal Bureau of Investigation, F B I Academy,
Madison Bldg., Rm. 209, Quantico, VA 22135.
TEL 703-640-8666. FAX 703-640-1474.
Vendor(s): Information Access Co.. University
Microfilms International. *2163*

F C C REPORT.
Capitol Publications Inc., Telecom Publishing Group,
1101 King St., Ste. 444, Box 1455, Alexandria, VA
22313-2055. TEL 800-327-7203. FAX 703-739-6490.
Vendor(s): Information Access Co., Knight-Ridder
Information, Inc., NewsNet (TE52). *1903*

F D A CONSUMER.
U.S. Food and Drug Administration, Office of Public
Affairs, 5600 Fishers Ln., Rockville, MD 20857.
TEL 301-443-3220.
Vendor(s): Information Access Co., Knight-Ridder
Information, Inc., University Microfilms International.
2151

F D A ENFORCEMENT REPORT.
U.S. Food and Drug Administration, Office of Public
Affairs, Rm. 15A-11, Parklawn Bldg., 5600 Fishers
Ln., Rockville, MD 20857. TEL 301-443-3285.
Vendor(s): Information Access Co., Ovid
Technologies, Inc. (DIOG). *2163*

F D A MEDICAL BULLETIN.
U.S. Food and Drug Administration, Office of Public
Affairs, 5600 Fisher's Ln., Rockville, MD 20857.
TEL 301-443-3220.
Vendor(s): Data-Star, Information Access Co.,
Knight-Ridder Information, Inc., Ovid Technologies,
Inc. (DIOG). *5412*

F I I ANNUAL GUIDE TO BONDS.
Financial Information Incorporated 30 Montgomery
St., Jersey City, NJ 07302. TEL 201-332-5400.
FAX 201-432-9779. *1323*

F I I ANNUAL GUIDE TO STOCKS.
Financial Information Incorporated, 30 Montgomery St., Jersey City, NJ 07302. TEL 201-332-5400. FAX 201-432-9779. *1329*

F O I A UPDATE.
U.S. Department of Justice, Office of Information and Privacy, Constitution Ave. & Tenth Sts., N.W., Washington, DC 20530. TEL 202-514-5105. FAX 202-514-1009. *3703*

F R A N C I S. 519: PHILOSOPHIE.
Centre National de la Recherche Scientifique, Institut de l'Information Scientifique et Technique, 2 allee du Parc de Brabois, 54514 Vandoeuvre-les-Nancy Cedex, France. TEL 83-50-46-00. FAX 83-50-46-50.
Vendor(s): Telesystemes - Questel. *5507*

F R A N C I S. 520: SCIENCES DE L'EDUCATION.
Centre National de la Recherche Scientifique, Institut de l'Information Scientifique et Technique, 2 allee du Parc de Brabois, 54514 Vandoeuvre-les-Nancy Cedex, France. TEL 83-50-46-00. FAX 83-50-46-50.
Vendor(s): Telesystemes - Questel. *2389*

F R A N C I S. 521: SOCIOLOGIE.
Centre National de la Recherche Scientifique, Institut de l'Information Scientifique et Technique, 2 allee du Parc de Brabois, 54514 Vandoeuvre-les-Nancy Cedex, France. TEL 83-50-46-00. FAX 83-50-46-50.
Vendor(s): Telesystemes - Questel. *6441*

F R A N C I S. 522: HISTOIRE DES SCIENCES ET DE TECHNIQUES.
Centre National de la Recherche Scientifique, Institut de l'Information Scientifique et Technique, 2 allee du Parc de Brabois, 54514 Vandoeuvre-les-Nancy Cedex, France. TEL 83-50-46-00. FAX 83-50-46-50.
Vendor(s): European Space Agency, Telesystemes - Questel. *3366*

F R A N C I S. 523: HISTOIRE ET SCIENCES DE LA LITTERATURE.
Centre National de la Recherche Scientifique, Institut de l'Information Scientifique et Technique, 2 allee du Parc de Brabois, 54514 Vandoeuvre-les-Nancy Cedex, France. TEL 83-50-46-00. FAX 83-50-46-50.
Vendor(s): Telesystemes - Questel. *4293*

F R A N C I S. 524: SCIENCES DU LANGAGE.
Centre National de la Recherche Scientifique, Institut de l'Information Scientifique et Technique, 2 allee du Parc de Brabois, 54514 Vandoeuvre-les-Nancy Cedex, France. TEL 83-50-46-00. FAX 83-50-46-50.
Vendor(s): Telesystemes - Questel. *4127*

F R A N C I S. 525: PREHISTOIRE ET PROTOHISTOIRE.
Centre National de la Recherche Scientifique, Institut de l'Information Scientifique et Technique, 2 allee du Parc de Brabois, 54514 Vandoeuvre-les-Nancy Cedex, France. TEL 83-50-46-00. FAX 83-50-46-50.
Vendor(s): Telesystemes - Questel. *380*

F R A N C I S. 526: ART ET ARCHEOLOGIE.
Centre National de la Recherche Scientifique, Institut de l'Information Scientifique et Technique, 2 allee du Parc de Brabois, 54514 Vandoeuvre-les-Nancy Cedex, France. TEL 83-50-46-00. FAX 83-50-46-50.
Vendor(s): Telesystemes - Questel. *462*

F R A N C I S. 527: HISTOIRE ET SCIENCES DES RELIGIONS.
Centre National de la Recherche Scientifique, Institut de l'Information Scientifique et Technique, 2 allee du Parc de Brabois, 54514 Vandoeuvre-les-Nancy Cedex, France. TEL 83-50-46-00. FAX 83-50-46-50.
Vendor(s): Telesystemes - Questel. *6107*

F R A N C I S. 528: BIBLIOGRAPHIE INTERNATIONALE DE SCIENCE ADMINISTRATIVE.
Centre National de la Recherche Scientifique, Institut de l'Information Scientifique et Technique, 2 allee du Parc de Brabois, 54514 Vandoeuvre-les-Nancy Cedex, France. TEL 83-50-46-00. FAX 83-50-46-50.
Vendor(s): Telesystemes - Questel. *997*

F R A N C I S. 529: ETHNOLOGIE.
Centre National de la Recherche Scientifique, Institut de l'Information Scientifique et Technique, 2 allee du Parc de Brabois, 54514 Vandoeuvre-les-Nancy Cedex, France. TEL 83-50-46-00. FAX 83-50-46-50.
Vendor(s): Telesystemes - Questel. *328*

F R A N C I S. 531: BIBLIOGRAPHIE GEOGRAPHIQUE INTERNATIONALE.
Centre National de la Recherche Scientifique, Institut de l'Information Scientifique et Technique, 2 allee du Parc de Brabois, 54514 Vandoeuvre-les-Nancy Cedex, France. TEL 83-50-46-00. FAX 83-50-46-50.
Vendor(s): Telesystemes - Questel. *3279*

F R A N C I S. 603: INFORMATIQUE ET SCIENCES JURIDIQUES.
Centre National de la Recherche Scientifique, Institut de l'Information Scientifique et Technique, 2 allee du Parc de Brabois, 54514 Vandoeuvre-les-Nancy Cedex, France. TEL 83-50-46-00. FAX 83-50-46-50.
Vendor(s): Telesystemes - Questel. *3889*

F R A N C I S. 617: E C O D O C.
Centre National de la Recherche Scientifique, Institut de l'Information Scientifique et Technique, 2 allee du Parc de Brabois, 54514 Vandoeuvre-les-Nancy Cedex, France. TEL 83-50-46-00. FAX 83-50-46-50.
Vendor(s): Telesystemes - Questel. *997*

F R A N C I S. 731: ECONOMIE DE L'ENERGIE.
Centre National de la Recherche Scientifique, Institut de l'Information Scientifique et Technique, 2 allee du Parc de Brabois, 54514 Vandoeuvre-les-Nancy Cedex, France. TEL 83-50-46-00. FAX 83-50-46-50.
Vendor(s): Telesystemes - Questel. *2563*

F T C FREEDOM OF INFORMATION LOG.
Washington Regulatory Reporting Associates, Box 356, Basye, VA 22810. TEL 703-856-2216. FAX 703-856-8331.
Vendor(s): Information Access Co.. *1275*

F T C WATCH.
Washington Regulatory Reporting Associates, Box 356, Basye, VA 22810. TEL 703-856-2216.
Vendor(s): Information Access Co., Lexis-Nexis, NewsNet (GT17). *1275*

F X WEEK.
Waters Information Services, Inc., Box 2248, Binghamton, NY 13902-2248. TEL 607-770-9242. FAX 607-770-9435.
Vendor(s): Data-Star, Knight-Ridder Information, Inc., NewsNet (FI54). *1275*

FACILITIES DESIGN AND MANAGEMENT.
Miller Freeman Inc. (New York) One Penn Plaza, New York, NY 10119. TEL 212-714-1300. FAX 212-714-1313.
Vendor(s): University Microfilms International. *1418*

FACTS ON FILE WORLD NEWS DIGEST WITH INDEX.
Facts on File, Inc., 460 Park Ave. S., New York, NY 10016. TEL 212-683-2244.
Vendor(s): Information Access Co., Knight-Ridder Information, Inc. (File no.264), Lexis-Nexis. *3342*

FAIR EMPLOYMENT PRACTICES SUMMARY OF LATEST DEVELOPMENTS.
The Bureau of National Affairs, Inc., 1231 25th St., N.W., Washington, DC 20037. TEL 202-452-4200. FAX 202-822-8092.
Vendor(s): Human Resources Information Network (CDD, HDD). *1373*

FAIR EMPLOYMENT REPORT.
Business Publishers, Inc., 951 Pershing Dr., Silver Spring, MD 20910-4464. TEL 301-587-6300. FAX 301-585-9075.
Vendor(s): NewsNet. *1373*

FAIRFIELD COUNTY BUSINESS JOURNAL.
Westfair Communications, Inc., 108 Corporate Park Dr., Ste. 105, White Plains, NY 10604-3805. TEL 914-694-3600. FAX 914-694-3699.
Vendor(s): University Microfilms International. *1211*

FAMILIES IN SOCIETY.
Families International, Inc., 11700 W. Lake Park Dr., Milwaukee, WI 53224. TEL 414-359-1040. FAX 414-359-1074.
Vendor(s): University Microfilms International. *6371*

FAMILY ADVOCATE.
American Bar Association, Family Law Section, 750 N. Lake Shore Dr., Chicago, IL 60611. TEL 708-675-2864.
Vendor(s): West Services, Inc. (FAMADVO). *3918*

FAMILY CIRCLE.
Family Circle, Inc. 110 Fifth Ave., New York, NY 10011. TEL 212-463-1000. FAX 212-463-1808.
Vendor(s): Information Access Co.. *3522*

THE FAMILY HANDYMAN.
Home Service Publications, Inc. 7900 International Dr., Ste. 950, Minneapolis, MN 55425. TEL 612-854-3000. FAX 612-854-8009.
Vendor(s): Information Access Co., University Microfilms International. *3603*

FAMILY LAW QUARTERLY.
American Bar Association, Family Law Section, 750 N. Lake Shore Dr., Chicago, IL 60611. TEL 312-988-6068.
Vendor(s): West Services, Inc. (FAMLQ). *3918*

FAMILY LAW REPORTS.
Jordan Publishing Ltd., 21 St. Thomas St., Bristol BS1 6JS, England. TEL 0117-923-0600. FAX 0117-923-0063.
Vendor(s): Lexis-Nexis. *3919*

FAMILY PLANNING PERSPECTIVES.
Alan Guttmacher Institute, 120 Wall St., New York, NY 10005. TEL 212-248-1111. FAX 212-248-1951.
Vendor(s): University Microfilms International. *4735*

FAMILY RELATIONS.
National Council on Family Relations, 3989 Central Ave., N.E., Ste. 550, Minneapolis, MN 55421-3921. TEL 612-781-9331. FAX 612-781-9348.
Vendor(s): Knight-Ridder Information, Inc., Ovid Technologies, Inc., University Microfilms International. *6413*

FAR EASTERN ECONOMIC REVIEW.
Review Publishing Co. Ltd., G.P.O. Box 160, Hong Kong. TEL 852-2508-4300. FAX 852-2503-1549.
Vendor(s): Dow Jones News Retrieval. *1211*

FARADAY DISCUSSIONS.
The Royal Society of Chemistry, Thomas Graham House, Science Park, Milton Rd., Cambridge CB4 4WF, England. TEL 44-1223-420066. FAX 44-1223-423429.
Vendor(s): STN International (CJRSC). *1750*

FARADAY TRANSACTIONS.
The Royal Society of Chemistry, Thomas Graham House, Science Park, Milton Rd., Cambridge CB4 4WF, England. TEL 44-1223-420066. FAX 44-1223-423623.
Vendor(s): STN International (CJRSC). *1751*

FARM AND FOOD.
Teagasc, 19 Sandymount Ave., Dublin 4, Ireland. TEL 353-1-6688188. FAX 353-1-6688023. *114*

FARMACEUTEN.
Dansk Farmaceutforening, Toldbbodgade 36, 1253 Copenhagen K, Denmark. *5412*

FARMACEUTICKY OBZOR.
Ministerstvo Zdravotnictva, Institut pre Dalsie Vzdelavanie Pracovnikov, Limbova 12, 833 39 Bratislava, Slovakia. *5412*

FARMACEUTSKI GLASNIK.
Hrvatsko Farmaceutsko Drustvo, Masarykova 2, 41000 Zagreb, Croatia. TEL 41-427944. FAX 41-431301. *5412*

FARMACEVTISK REVY.
Sveriges Farmacevtfoerbund, Vasagatan 48, Box 3215, S-103 64 Stockholm, Sweden. *5412*

FARMACEVTSKI VESTNIK.
Slovensko Farmacevtsko Drustvo, P.O. Box 311, Masera Spasica 10, 61001 Ljubljana, Slovenia. TEL 061-221-078. *5413*

FARMACI.
Danmarks Apotekerforening, Bredgade 54, 1260 Copenhagen K, Denmark. TEL 45-33-76-76-00. FAX 45-33-76-76-99. *5413*

FARMACIA.
Uniunea Societatilor de Stiinte Medicale din Romania, Str. Progresului 8, 70754 Bucharest, Rumania. *5413*

FARMACJA POLSKA.
Polskie Towarzystwo Farmaceutyczne, Dluga 16, 00-238 Warsaw, Poland. TEL 48-22-310241. FAX 48-22-310243. *5413*

FAST FOOD: THE INTERNATIONAL MARKET.
Euromonitor, 60-61 Britton St., London EC1M 5NA, England. TEL 44-171-251-8024. FAX 44-171-608-3149.
Vendor(s): Data-Star, Knight-Ridder Information, Inc.. *2967*

FATE.
Llewellyn Worldwide, 84 S. Wabasha St., Box 64383, St. Paul, MN 55164-0383. TEL 612-291-1970. FAX 612-291-1908. *5330*

THE FATE OF THE ARABIAN PENINSULA.
Arab Press Service, A P S House, P.O. Box 3896, Ncosia, Cyprus. TEL 357-2-351778. FAX 357-2-350265.
Vendor(s): Information Access Co.. *2549*

FAULKNER AND GRAY'S MEDICINE AND HEALTH.
Faulkner & Gray, Healthcare Information Center 1133 15th St., N.W., Ste. 450, Washington, DC 20005. TEL 202-828-4148.
Vendor(s): Information Access Co., NewsNet (HH21). *4454*

FEDERAL & STATE INSURANCE WEEK.
J R Publishing, Box 6654, McLean, VA 22106. TEL 703-532-2235.
Vendor(s): Information Access Co., NewsNet (IN04). *3648*

FEDERAL APPLIED TECHNOLOGY DATABASE.
U.S. National Technical Information Service, 5285 Port Royal Rd., Springfield, VA 22161. TEL 703-487-4630.
Available only online. Vendor(s): Ovid Technologies, Inc.. *6651*

FEDERAL BENEFITS FOR VETERANS AND DEPENDENTS, IS-1 FACT SHEET.
U.S. Department of Veterans Affairs, 810 Vermont Ave., N.W., Washington, DC 20420. TEL 202-233-3557. *5030*

FEDERAL CAREER OPPORTUNITIES.
Federal Research Service, Inc., 243 Church St., N.W., Box 1059, Vienna, VA 22183-1059. TEL 703-281-0200. FAX 703-281-7639. *5266*

FEDERAL COMPUTER MARKET REPORT.
Computer Age & E D P News Services 714 Church St., Alexandria, VA 22314-4202. TEL 703-739-8500. FAX 703-739-8505.
Vendor(s): Information Access Co.. *2055*

FEDERAL CONTRACT DISPUTES.
Business Publishers, Inc., 951 Pershing Dr., Silver Spring, MD 20910-4464. TEL 301-587-6300. FAX 301-585-9075.
Vendor(s): NewsNet. *3901*

FEDERAL CONTRACTS REPORT.
The Bureau of National Affairs, Inc., 1231 25th St., N.W., Washington, DC 20037. TEL 202-452-4200. FAX 202-822-8092.
Vendor(s): Lexis-Nexis (FDCONT), West Services, Inc.. *1519*

FEDERAL COURT OF APPEAL DECISIONS.
Western Legal Publications, 301-1 Alexander St., Vancouver, BC V6A 1B2, Canada. TEL 604-687-5671. FAX 604-687-2796. *3947*

FEDERAL GRANTS & CONTRACTS WEEKLY.
Capitol Publications Inc., 1101 King St., Ste. 444, Alexandria, VA 22314. TEL 703-683-4100. FAX 703-739-6501.
Vendor(s): NewsNet (GT37). *5901*

FEDERAL LAWYER.
Federal Bar Association, 1815 H St., N.W., Ste. 408, Washington, DC 20006-3697. TEL 202-638-0252. FAX 202-775-0295.
Vendor(s): West Services, Inc.. *3778*

FEDERAL PROBATION.
U.S. Administrative Office of the United States Courts, Federal Corrections and Supervision Division, Washington, DC 20402-9371. TEL 202-273-1627. FAX 202-273-1603
Vendor(s): Information Access Co.. *2164*

FEDERAL REGISTER.
U.S. Office of the Federal Register, National Archives and Records Administration, Washington, DC 20408. TEL 202-523-5230.
Vendor(s): Knight-Ridder Information, Inc. (File no.669), Lexis Nexis, Ovid Technologies, Inc. (DIOG), West Services, Inc.. *5901*

FEDERAL RESEARCH IN PROGRESS DATABASE.
U.S. National Technical Information Service, 5285 Port Royal Rd., Springfield, VA 22161. TEL 703-487-4630.
Available only online. Vendor(s): Knight-Ridder Information, Inc. (File nos.265,266). *2599*

FEDERAL RESEARCH REPORT.
Business Publishers, Inc., 951 Pershing Dr., Silver Spring, MD 20910-4464. TEL 301-587-6300. FAX 301-585-9075.
Vendor(s): NewsNet (RD10). *2334*

FEDERAL RESERVE BANK OF CLEVELAND. WORKING PAPER.
Federal Reserve Bank of Cleveland, Box 6387, Cleveland, OH 44101. TEL 216-579-2380. FAX 216-579-3050.
Available only online. *1088*

FEDERAL RESERVE BANK OF MINNEAPOLIS. QUARTERLY REVIEW.
Federal Reserve Bank of Minneapolis, 250 Marquette Ave., Minneapolis, MN 55401-2171. TEL 612-340-2341. FAX 612-340-2366.
Vendor(s): University Microfilms International. *1088*

FEDERAL RESERVE BANK OF NEW YORK. ECONOMIC POLICY REVIEW.
Federal Reserve Bank of New York, Public Information, 33 Liberty St., New York, NY 10045-0001. TEL 212-720-6150.
Vendor(s): Knight-Ridder Information, Inc., University Microfilms International. *1211*

FEDERAL RESERVE BANK OF PHILADELPHIA. BUSINESS REVIEW.
Federal Reserve Bank of Philadelphia, Box 66, Philadelphia, PA 19105. TEL 215-574-6540. FAX 215-574-4364.
Vendor(s): University Microfilms International. *1211*

FEDERAL RESERVE BANK OF RICHMOND. ECONOMIC QUARTERLY.
Federal Reserve Bank of Richmond, Research Department, 701 E. Byrd St., Richmond, VA 23219. TEL 804-697-8000.
Vendor(s): Information Access Co.. *1211*

FEDERAL RESERVE BANK OF ST. LOUIS. REVIEW.
Federal Reserve Bank of St. Louis, Box 442, St. Louis, MO 63166. TEL 314-444-8444.
Vendor(s): Information Access Co., University Microfilms International. *1212*

FEDERAL RESERVE BANK OF SAN FRANCISCO. ECONOMIC LETTER.
Federal Reserve Bank of San Francisco, Box 7702, San Francisco, CA 94120. TEL 415-974-3230. FAX 415-974-3341. *1212*

FEDERAL RESERVE BANK OF SAN FRANCISCO. ECONOMIC REVIEW.
Federal Reserve Bank of San Francisco, Box 7702, San Francisco, CA 94120. TEL 415-974-3230. FAX 415-974-3341.
Vendor(s): University Microfilms International. *1212*

FEDERAL RESERVE BULLETIN.
U.S. Federal Reserve System, Board of Governors, Publications Services, Rm MS-138, Washington, DC 20551. TEL 202-452-3244. FAX 202-728-5886.
Vendor(s): Information Access Co., Knight-Ridder Information, Inc., Lexis-Nexis, University Microfilms International. *1088*

FEDERAL SENTENCING REPORTER.
University of California Press, Journals Division, 2120 Berkeley Way, No. B812, Berkeley, CA 94720-5812. TEL 510-643-7154. FAX 510-642-9917.
Vendor(s): Lexis-Nexis, West Services, Inc.. *2164*

FEDERAL TAX COORDINATOR 2D.
Research Institute of America, Inc., 90 Fifth Ave., New York, NY 10011. TEL 212-645-4800. FAX 212-337-4279.
Vendor(s): Lexis-Nexis. *1544*

FEDERAL TAX REGULATIONS.
Research Institute of America, Inc., 90 Fifth Ave., New York, NY 10011. TEL 212-645-4800.
Vendor(s): Research Institute of America. *1544*

FEDERAL TECHNOLOGY REPORT.
McGraw-Hill Companies, Energy & Business Newsletters, 1221 Ave. of the Americas, 36th Fl., New York, NY 10020. TEL 212-512-6410.
Vendor(s): Dow Jones News Retrieval (TTR), Knight-Ridder Information, Inc. (TR), Lexis-Nexis (FEDTEC), NewsNet (RD46). *2543*

FEDGAZETTE: FEDERAL RESERVE BANK OF MINNEAPOLIS REGIONAL BUSINESS & ECONOMICS NEWSPAPER.
Federal Reserve Bank of Minneapolis, Box 291, Minneapolis, MN 55480-0291. TEL 612-340-2446. FAX 612-335-2855.
Vendor(s): University Microfilms International. *1212*

FEMINIST STUDIES.
Feminist Studies, Inc., c/o Department of Women's Studies, University of Maryland, College Park, MD 20742. TEL 301-405-7415. FAX 301-314-9190.
Vendor(s): Information Access Co., University Microfilms International. *7016*

FERROELECTRICS COMMUNICATIONS.
Gordon & Breach Science Publishers, c/o International Publishers Distributor, Box 3054, Langhorne, PA 19047-3054. TEL 215-750-2642. FAX 215-750-6343. *5578*

FERTILIZER INTERNATIONAL.
British Sulphur Publishing 31 Mount Pleasant, London WC1X 0AD, England. TEL 44-171-837-5600. FAX 44-171-837-1292.
Vendor(s): Information Access Co.. *221*

FIBER OPTICS NEWS.
Phillips Business Information, Inc, 1201 Seven Locks Rd., Potomac, MD 20854. TEL 301-424-3338. FAX 301-424-4297.
Vendor(s): Information Access Co., Knight-Ridder Information, Inc., NewsNet (TE29). *1904*

FIBER OPTICS WEEKLY UPDATE.
Information Gatekeepers, Inc., 214 Harvard Ave., Boston, MA 02134. TEL 617-232-3111. FAX 617-734-8562.
Vendor(s): NewsNet. *1904*

FICTION DIGEST.
Amcam Inc., 187 Vanderbilt Ave., Apt. 3, Brooklyn, NY 11205-3305. TEL 718-643-2988. FAX 718-797-9403. *3992*

FIDO NEWS.
Fido Software, 55 Rodel Pl., San Francisco, CA 94103-3406.
Available only online. *2037*

FIELD & STREAM.
Times Mirror Magazines, Inc., 2 Park Ave., New York, NY 10016. TEL 212-779-5000. FAX 212-725-3836.
Vendor(s): Information Access Co., University Microfilms International. *5562*

FIELD CROP ABSTRACTS.
CAB International, Wallingford, Oxon. OX10 8DE, England. TEL 44-1491-832111 FAX 44-1491-833508.
Vendor(s): DIMDI, European Space Agency, Knight-Ridder Information, Inc., STN International. *172*

FILIERA CARNE.
Essepiesse s.r.l., Via G. Galilei 14, 21024 Milan, Italy. TEL 39-2-29003814. *2968*

FILM & VIDEO FINDER.
Plexus Publishing, Inc., 143 Old Marlton Pike, Medford, NJ 08055-8750. TEL 609-654-4888. FAX 609-654-4309.
Vendor(s): Knight-Ridder Information, Inc. (File no.46). *2389*

FILM COMMENT.
Film Society of Lincoln Center, 70 Lincoln Center Plaza, New York, NY 10023-6595. TEL 212-875-5610. FAX 212-875-5636.
Vendor(s): Information Access Co., University Microfilms International. *5101*

FILM QUARTERLY.
University of California Press, Journals Division, 2120 Berkeley Way, No. 5812, Berkeley, CA 94720-5812. TEL 510-643-7154. FAX 510-642-9917.
Vendor(s): Information Access Co.. *5102*

FILMSTRIP AND SLIDE SET FINDER.
Plexus Publishing, Inc., 143 Old Marlton Pike, Medford, NJ 08055-8750. TEL 609-654-6500. FAX 609-654-4309. *2389*

THE FINAL CALL.
Final Call Newspaper, 734 W. 79th St., Chicago, IL 60620. TEL 312-602-1230. *6117*

FINANCE AND DEVELOPMENT.
International Monetary Fund, Publication Services, 700 19th St., N.W., Washington, DC 20431. TEL 202-623-7430. FAX 202-623-7201.
Vendor(s): Information Access Co., University Microfilms International. *1089*

FINANCE EAST EUROPE.
Financial Times Business Information, Newsletters 126 Jermyn St., London SW1Y 4UJ, England. TEL 44-171-411-4414. FAX 44-171-411-4415.
Vendor(s): Information Access Co.. *1089*

FINANCIAL ANALYSTS JOURNAL.
Association for Investment Management and Research, Box 3668, Charlottesville, VA 22903. TEL 804-980-3668. FAX 804-980-9755.
Vendor(s): University Microfilms International. *1330*

FINANCIAL EXECUTIVE.
Financial Executives Institute, 10 Madison Ave., Box 1938, Morristown, NJ 07962-1938. TEL 201-898-4621. FAX 201-267-4031.
Vendor(s): Information Access Co., Knight-Ridder Information, Inc., University Microfilms International. *1418*

FINANCIAL MANAGEMENT.
Financial Management Association, University of South Florida, College of Business, Tampa, FL 33620. TEL 813-974-2084. FAX 813-974-3318.
Vendor(s): Information Access Co., University Microfilms International. *1418*

FINANCIAL MARKET TRENDS.
Organization for Economic Cooperation and Development, 2 rue Andre-Pascal, 75775 Paris Cedex 16, France.
Vendor(s): Information Access Co., University Microfilms International. *1090*

FINANCIAL MARKETING UPDATE.
I B C Publishing, c/o Helen Cruickshank, Gilmoora House, 57-61 Mortimer St., London W1N 7TD, England. TEL 0171-637-4383. FAX 0171-636-6414.
Vendor(s): University Microfilms International. *1465*

FINANCIAL MARKETS, INSTITUTIONS AND INSTRUMENTS.
Blackwell Publishers, 238 Main St., Cambridge, MA 02142. TEL 617-547-7110. FAX 617-547-0789.
Vendor(s): University Microfilms International. *1090*

FINANCIAL PLANNING (NEW YORK).
Securities Data Publishing, 40 W. 57th St., 11th Fl., New York, NY 10019. TEL 212-765-5311. FAX 212-765-6123.
Vendor(s): Information Access Co.. *1418*

FINANCIAL POST.
Financial Post Co., Ltd., 333 King St. E., Toronto, ON M5A 4N2, Canada. TEL 416-350-6300. FAX 416-350-6601.
Vendor(s): Information Access Co., Southam Electronic Publishing. *1091*

FINANCIAL POST DIRECTORY OF DIRECTORS.
Financial Post Co., Ltd., 333 King St. E., Toronto, ON M5A 4N2, Canada. TEL 416-350-6116. FAX 416-350-6501.
Vendor(s): Southam Electronic Publishing. *1418*

FINANCIAL POST MAGAZINE.
Financial Post Co., Ltd., 333 King St. E., Toronto, ON M5A 4N2, Canada. TEL 416-350-6516. FAX 416-350-6501. *1091*

FINANCIAL REGULATION REPORT.
Financial Times Business Information, Newsletters 126 Jermyn St., London SW1Y 4UJ, England. TEL 0171-441-4414. FAX 0171-441-4415.
Vendor(s): Data-Star, Lexis-Nexis. *1091*

FINANCIAL REVIEW (STATESBORO).
Eastern Finance Association, c/o Univ. of Tennessee, 426 Stokley Management Ctr., Knoxville, TN 37996-0540. TEL 423-974-1713. FAX 423-974-1716.
Vendor(s): Information Access Co.. *1091*

FINANCIAL SERVICES REPORT.
Phillips Business Information, Inc., 1201 Seven Locks Rd., Potomac, MD 20854. TEL 301-424-3338. FAX 301-424-4297.
Vendor(s): Information Access Co., NewsNet (FI18). *1091*

FINANCIAL TECHNOLOGY INSIGHT.
Elsevier Science Ltd., P.O. Box 800, Kidlington, Oxford OX5 1DX, England. TEL 44-1865-843000. FAX 44-1865-843010.
Vendor(s): Data-Star, Information Access Co., Knight-Ridder Information, Inc.. *1154*

FINANCIAL TECHNOLOGY INTERNATIONAL BULLETIN.
I B C Publishing, c/o Helen Cruickshank, Gilmoora House, 57-61 Mortimer St., London W1N 7TD, England. TEL 0171-637-4383. FAX 0171-636-6414.
Vendor(s): University Microfilms International. *1091*

FINANCIAL TIMES WORLD TAX REPORT.
Financial Times Professional Publishing Maple House, 149 Tottenham Court Rd., London W1P 9LL, England. TEL 44-171-896-2222. FAX 44-171-896-2276.
Vendor(s): Information Access Co., Knight-Ridder Information, Inc., Lexis-Nexis. *1544*

FINANCIAL WORLD.
Financial World Partners, 1328 Broadway, New York, NY 10001. TEL 212-594-5030. FAX 212-629-0021.
Vendor(s): Data-Star, Information Access Co., Knight-Ridder Information, Inc., Lexis-Nexis, University Microfilms International. *1092*

DE FINANCIEEL EKONOMISCHE TIJD.
Uitgeversbedrijf Tijd n.v., Franklin Building, Posthoflei 3, 2600 Berchem (Antwerp), Belgium. TEL 32-3-2860211. FAX 32-3-2860310. *924*

HET FINANCIEELE DAGBLAD.
Het Financieele Dagblad B.V., P.O. Box 216, 1000 AE Amsterdam, Netherlands. TEL 31-20-5928800. FAX 31-20-5928600. *924*

EL FINANCIERO INTERNATIONAL EDITION.
El Financiero International, Inc., Lago Bolsena 176, Col. Anahuac, 11320 Mexico DF, Mexico. TEL 525-227-7600. FAX 525-227-7634. *1091*

FINANCING FOREIGN OPERATIONS. AMERICAS.
Economist Intelligence Unit, 111 W. 57th St., New York, NY 10019. TEL 212-554-0600. FAX 212-586-1181.
Vendor(s): Knight-Ridder Information, Inc., Lexis-Nexis. *1092*

FINANCING FOREIGN OPERATIONS. ARGENTINA.
Economist Intelligence Unit, 111 W. 57th St., New York, NY 10019. TEL 212-554-0600. FAX 212-586-1181.
Vendor(s): Knight-Ridder Information, Inc., Lexis-Nexis. *1092*

FINANCING FOREIGN OPERATIONS. ASIA.
Economist Intelligence Unit, 111 W. 57th St., New York, NY 10019. TEL 212-554-0600. FAX 212-586-1181.
Vendor(s): Knight-Ridder Information, Inc., Lexis-Nexis. *1092*

FINANCING FOREIGN OPERATIONS. AUSTRALIA.
Economist Intelligence Unit, 111 W. 57th St., New York, NY 10019. TEL 212-554-0600. FAX 212-586-1181.
Vendor(s): Knight-Ridder Information, Inc., Lexis-Nexis. *1093*

FINANCING FOREIGN OPERATIONS. BELGIUM.
Economist Intelligence Unit, 111 W. 57th St., New York, NY 10019. TEL 212-554-0600. FAX 212-586-1181.
Vendor(s): Knight-Ridder Information, Inc., Lexis-Nexis. *1093*

FINANCING FOREIGN OPERATIONS. BRAZIL.
Economist Intelligence Unit, 111 W. 57th St., New York, NY 10019. TEL 212-554-0600. FAX 212-586-1181.
Vendor(s): Knight-Ridder Information, Inc., Lexis-Nexis. *1093*

FINANCING FOREIGN OPERATIONS. CANADA.
Economist Intelligence Unit, 111 W. 57th St., New York, NY 10019. TEL 212-554-0600. FAX 212-586-1181.
Vendor(s): Knight-Ridder Information, Inc., Lexis-Nexis. *1093*

FINANCING FOREIGN OPERATIONS. CENTRAL AMERICA: COSTA RICA, EL SALVADOR, GUATEMALA, HONDURAS, NICARAGUA.
Economist Intelligence Unit, 111 W. 57th St., New York, NY 10019. TEL 212-554-0600. FAX 212-586-1181.
Vendor(s): Knight-Ridder Information, Inc., Lexis-Nexis. *1093*

FINANCING FOREIGN OPERATIONS. CHILE.
Economist Intelligence Unit, 111 W. 57th St., New York, NY 10019. TEL 212-554-0600. FAX 212-586-1181.
Vendor(s): Knight-Ridder Information, Inc., Lexis-Nexis. *1093*

FINANCING FOREIGN OPERATIONS. COLOMBIA.
Economist Intelligence Unit, 111 W. 57th St., New York, NY 10019. TEL 212-554-0600. FAX 212-586-1181.
Vendor(s): Knight-Ridder Information, Inc., Lexis-Nexis. *1093*

FINANCING FOREIGN OPERATIONS. CZECH REPUBLIC.
Economist Intelligence Unit, 111 W. 57th St., New York, NY 10019. TEL 212-554-0600. FAX 212-586-1181.
Vendor(s): Knight-Ridder Information, Inc., Lexis-Nexis. *1093*

FINANCING FOREIGN OPERATIONS. FRANCE.
Economist Intelligence Unit, 111 W. 57th St., New York, NY 10019. TEL 212-554-0600. FAX 212-586-1181.
Vendor(s): Knight-Ridder Information, Inc., Lexis-Nexis. *1093*

FINANCING FOREIGN OPERATIONS. GERMANY.
Economist Intelligence Unit, 111 W. 57th St., New York, NY 10019. TEL 212-554-0600. FAX 212-586-1181.
Vendor(s): Knight-Ridder Information, Inc., Lexis-Nexis. *1093*

FINANCING FOREIGN OPERATIONS. GLOBAL EDITION.
Economist Intelligence Unit, 111 W. 57th St., New York, NY 10019. TEL 212-554-0600. FAX 212-586-1181.
Vendor(s): Knight-Ridder Information, Inc., Lexis-Nexis. *1093*

FINANCING FOREIGN OPERATIONS. GREECE.
Economist Intelligence Unit, 111 W. 57th St., New York, NY 10019. TEL 212-554-0600. FAX 212-586-1181.
Vendor(s): Knight-Ridder Information, Inc., Lexis-Nexis. *1093*

FINANCING FOREIGN OPERATIONS. HONG KONG.
Economist Intelligence Unit, 111 W. 57th St., New York, NY 10019. TEL 212-554-0600. FAX 212-586-1181.
Vendor(s): Knight-Ridder Information, Inc., Lexis-Nexis. *1093*

FINANCING FOREIGN OPERATIONS. HUNGARY.
Economist Intelligence Unit, 111 W. 57th St., New York, NY 10019. TEL 212-554-0600. FAX 212-586-1181.
Vendor(s): Knight-Ridder Information, Inc., Lexis-Nexis. *1093*

FINANCING FOREIGN OPERATIONS. INDIA.
Economist Intelligence Unit, 111 W. 57th St., New York, NY 10019. TEL 212-554-0600. FAX 212-586-1181.
Vendor(s): Knight-Ridder Information, Inc., Lexis-Nexis. *1094*

FINANCING FOREIGN OPERATIONS. ITALY.
Economist Intelligence Unit, 111 W. 57th St., New York, NY 10019. TEL 212-554-0600. FAX 212-586-1181.
Vendor(s): Knight-Ridder Information, Inc., Lexis-Nexis. *1094*

FINANCING FOREIGN OPERATIONS. JAPAN.
Economist Intelligence Unit, 111 W. 57th St., New York, NY 10019. TEL 212-554-0600. FAX 212-586-1182.
Vendor(s): Knight-Ridder Information, Inc., Lexis-Nexis. *1094*

FINANCING FOREIGN OPERATIONS. MALAYSIA.
Economist Intelligence Unit, 111 W. 57th St., New York, NY 10019. TEL 212-554-0600. FAX 212-586-1181.
Vendor(s): Knight-Ridder Information, Inc., Lexis-Nexis. *1094*

FINANCING FOREIGN OPERATIONS. MEXICO.
Economist Intelligence Unit, 111 W. 57th St., New York, NY 10019. TEL 212-554-0600. FAX 212-586-1181.
Vendor(s): Knight-Ridder Information, Inc., Lexis-Nexis. *1094*

FINANCING FOREIGN OPERATIONS. MIDDLE EAST - AFRICA.
Economist Intelligence Unit, 111 W. 57th St., New York, NY 10019. TEL 212-554-0600. FAX 212-586-1181.
Vendor(s): Knight-Ridder Information, Inc., Lexis-Nexis. *1094*

FINANCING FOREIGN OPERATIONS. NETHERLANDS.
Economist Intelligence Unit, 111 W. 57th St., New York, NY 10019. TEL 212-554-0600. FAX 212-586-1181.
Vendor(s): Knight-Ridder Information, Inc., Lexis-Nexis. *1094*

FINANCING FOREIGN OPERATIONS. NIGERIA.
Economist Intelligence Unit, 111 W. 57th St., New York, NY 10019. TEL 212-554-0600. FAX 212-586-1181.
Vendor(s): Knight-Ridder Information, Inc., Lexis-Nexis. *1094*

FINANCING FOREIGN OPERATIONS. NORWAY.
Economist Intelligence Unit, 111 W. 57th St., New York, NY 10019. TEL 212-554-0600. FAX 212-586-1181.
Vendor(s): Knight-Ridder Information, Inc., Lexis-Nexis. *1094*

FINANCING FOREIGN OPERATIONS. PANAMA.
Economist Intelligence Unit, 111 W. 57th St., New York, NY 10019. TEL 212-554-0600. FAX 212-586-1181.
Vendor(s): Knight-Ridder Information, Inc., Lexis-Nexis. *1094*

FINANCING FOREIGN OPERATIONS. PHILIPPINES.
Economist Intelligence Unit, 111 W. 57th St., New York, NY 10019. TEL 212-554-0600. FAX 212-586-1181.
Vendor(s): Knight-Ridder Information, Inc., Lexis-Nexis. *1094*

FINANCING FOREIGN OPERATIONS. POLAND.
Economist Intelligence Unit, 111 W. 57th St., New York, NY 10019. TEL 212-554-0600. FAX 212-586-1181.
Vendor(s): Knight-Ridder Information, Inc., Lexis-Nexis. *1094*

FINANCING FOREIGN OPERATIONS. RUSSIA.
Economist Intelligence Unit, 111 W. 57th St., New York, NY 10019. TEL 212-554-0600. FAX 212-586-1181.
Vendor(s): Knight-Ridder Information, Inc., Lexis-Nexis. *1095*

FINANCING FOREIGN OPERATIONS. SAUDI ARABIA.
Economist Intelligence Unit, 111 W. 57th St., New York, NY 10019. TEL 212-554-0600. FAX 212-586-1181.
Vendor(s): Knight-Ridder Information, Inc., Lexis-Nexis. *1095*

FINANCING FOREIGN OPERATIONS. SINGAPORE.
Economist Intelligence Unit, 111 W. 57th St., New York, NY 10019. TEL 212-554-0600. FAX 212-586-1181.
Vendor(s): Knight-Ridder Information, Inc., Lexis-Nexis. *1095*

FINANCING FOREIGN OPERATIONS. SOUTH AFRICA.
Economist Intelligence Unit, 111 W. 57th St., New York, NY 10019. TEL 212-554-0600. FAX 212-586-1181.
Vendor(s): Knight-Ridder Information, Inc., Lexis-Nexis. *1095*

FINANCING FOREIGN OPERATIONS. SOUTH KOREA.
Economist Intelligence Unit, 111 W. 57th St., New York, NY 10019. TEL 212-554-0600. FAX 212-586-1181.
Vendor(s): Knight-Ridder Information, Inc., Lexis-Nexis. *1095*

FINANCING FOREIGN OPERATIONS. SPAIN.
Economist Intelligence Unit, 111 W. 57th St., New York, NY 10019. TEL 212-554-0600. FAX 212-586-1181.
Vendor(s): Knight-Ridder Information, Inc., Lexis-Nexis. *1095*

FINANCING FOREIGN OPERATIONS. SWEDEN.
Economist Intelligence Unit, 111 W. 57th St., New York, NY 10019. TEL 212-554-0600. FAX 212-586-1181.
Vendor(s): Knight-Ridder Information, Inc., Lexis-Nexis. *1095*

FINANCING FOREIGN OPERATIONS. SWITZERLAND.
Economist Intelligence Unit, 111 W. 57th St., New York, NY 10019. TEL 212-554-0600. FAX 212-586-1181.
Vendor(s): Knight-Ridder Information, Inc., Lexis-Nexis. *1095*

FINANCING FOREIGN OPERATIONS. TAIWAN.
Economist Intelligence Unit, 111 W. 57th St., New York, NY 10019. TEL 212-554-0600. FAX 212-586-1181.
Vendor(s): Knight-Ridder Information, Inc., Lexis-Nexis. *1095*

FINANCING FOREIGN OPERATIONS. THAILAND.
Economist Intelligence Unit, 111 W. 57th St., New York, NY 10019. TEL 212-554-0600. FAX 212-586-1181.
Vendor(s): Knight-Ridder Information, Inc., Lexis-Nexis. *1095*

FINANCING FOREIGN OPERATIONS. UNITED KINGDOM.
Economist Intelligence Unit, 111 W. 57th St., New York, NY 10019. TEL 212-554-0600. FAX 212-586-1181.
Vendor(s): Knight-Ridder Information, Inc., Lexis-Nexis. *1095*

FINANCING FOREIGN OPERATIONS. UNITED STATES OF AMERICA.
Economist Intelligence Unit, 111 W. 57th St., New York, NY 10019. TEL 212-554-0600. FAX 212-586-1181.
Vendor(s): Knight-Ridder Information, Inc., Lexis-Nexis. *1095*

FINANCING FOREIGN OPERATIONS. VENEZUELA.
Economist Intelligence Unit, 111 W. 57th St., New York, NY 10019. TEL 212-554-0600. FAX 212-586-1181.
Vendor(s): Knight-Ridder Information, Inc., Lexis-Nexis. *1095*

FINDEX (YEAR).
Euromonitor, 60-61 Britton St., London EC1M 5NA, England. TEL 44-171-251-8024. FAX 44-171-608-3149.
Vendor(s): Knight-Ridder Information, Inc. (File no.196). *998*

FIRMEN DER NEUEN BUNDESLAENDER.
Verlag Hoppenstedt Gmb~, Havestr. 9, 64295 Darmstadt, Germany. TEL 49-6151-380-0. FAX 49-6151-380-360.
Vendor(s): Data-Star, Knight-Ridder Information, Inc.. *1520*

FIRST MONDAY.
Munksgaard International Publishers Ltd., Noerre Soegade 35, P.O. Box 2148, DK 1016 Copenhagen, Denmark. TEL 45-33-127030. *2037*

FIRST THINGS.
Institute on Religion & Public Life 156 Fifth Ave., Ste. 400, New York, NY 10010. TEL 212-627-2288. FAX 212-627-2184. *6052*

FISCAL STUDIES.
Institute of Fiscal Studies, 7 Ridgmount St., London WC1E 7AE, England. TEL 44-171-636-3784. FAX 44-171-323-4780.
Vendor(s): University Microfilms International. *1545*

FISH AND GAME FINDER.
Fish and Game Finder Magazines 41 W. Michigan, Orlando, FL 32806. TEL 407-425-0045. FAX 407-425-1529. *6563*

FISHERIES MARKET NEWS REPORT.
Urner Barry Publications, Inc., Box 389, Toms River, NJ 08754. TEL 908-240-5330. FAX 908-341-0891. *2947*

FITOTERAPIA.
IdB Holding, Viale Ortles 12, 20139 Milan, Italy. TEL 39-2-57496442. FAX 39-2-57496443. *680*

FIVE PERCENT OWNERSHIP PORTFOLIOS.
C D A Investment Technologies, Inc., 1355 Piccard Dr., Rockville, MD 20850. FAX 301-590-1350. *1330*

FIVE-YEAR INFORMATION RESOURCES MANAGEMENT PROGRAM.
U.S. Department of Veterans Affairs, 810 Vermont Ave., N.W. (008B3), Washington, DC 20420. TEL 202-233-3557. *3993*

FLAME RETARDANCY NEWS
Business Communications Co., Inc. (Norwalk), 25 Van Zant St., Ste. 13, Norwalk, CT 06855. TEL 203-853-4266. FAX 203-853-0348.
Vendor(s): Information Access Co. NewsNet (RD40). *6651*

FLEET EQUIPMENT.
Maple Publishing, 134 W. Slade St., Palatine, IL 60067. TEL 847-359-6100. FAX 847-359-6420.
Vendor(s): University Microfilms International. *6857*

FLETCHER FORUM OF WORLD AFFAIRS.
Fletcher School of Law and Diplomacy, Tufts University, Medford, MA 02155. TEL 617-623-3610 FAX 617-627-3973.
Vendor(s): West Services, Inc.. *5750*

FLIGHT INTERNATIONAL.
Reed Business Publishing Group Quadrant House, The Quadrant, Sutton, Surrey SM2 5AS, England. TEL 44-181-652-3882. FAX 44-181-652-3840.
Vendor(s): Data-Star, Information Access Co., Lexis-Nexis. *64*

FLOORING.
Douglas Publications, Inc., 2609 Gayton Rd., Ste. 100, Richmond, VA 23233 TEL 804-741-6704. FAX 804-750-2399.
Vendor(s): Information Access Co.. *3687*

FLORIDA BAR JOURNAL.
Florida Bar, 650 Apalachee Pkwy., Tallahassee, FL 32399-2300. TEL 904-561-5680. FAX 904-681-3859.
Vendor(s): West Services, Inc.. *3779*

Online

FLORIDA BUSINESS DIRECTORY.
American Business Directories 5711 S. 86th Circle, Box 27347, Omaha, NE 68127. TEL 402-593-4600. FAX 402-331-5481. *1610*

FLORIDA LAW REVIEW.
University of Florida, College of Law, Gainesville, FL 32611. TEL 904-392-2148.
Vendor(s): West Services, Inc.. *3780*

FLORIDA LEADER.
Oxendine Publishing, Inc., Box 14081, Gainesville, FL 32604-2081. TEL 904-373-6907. FAX 904-373-8120. *1868*

FLORIDA STATE UNIVERSITY LAW REVIEW.
Florida State University, College of Law, Tallahassee, FL 32306. TEL 904-644-2045.
Vendor(s): West Services, Inc.. *3780*

FLORIDA TREND.
Florida Trend Inc., Box 611, St. Petersburg, FL 33731. TEL 813-821-5800. FAX 813-822-5083.
Vendor(s): Information Access Co., Knight-Ridder Information, Inc., Lexis-Nexis, University Microfilms International. *1212*

FLOWER AND GARDEN.
K C Publishing Inc., 700 47th St., Ste. 310, Kansas City, MO 64112. TEL 816-531-5730. FAX 816-531-3873.
Vendor(s): Information Access Co., Knight-Ridder Information, Inc., University Microfilms International. *3050*

FLOWER & GARDEN CRAFTS EDITION.
K C Publishing Inc., 700 W. 47th St., Ste. 310, Kansas City, MO 64112. TEL 816-531-5730. FAX 816-531-3873.
Vendor(s): Knight-Ridder Information, Inc.. *5212*

FLUID ABSTRACTS: CIVIL ENGINEERING.
Elsevier Science Ltd., P.O. Box 800, Kidlington, Oxford OX5 1DX, England. TEL 44-1865-843000. FAX 44-1865-843010.
Vendor(s): European Space Agency (File no.48/FLUIDEX), Knight-Ridder Information, Inc. (File no.96/FLUIDEX). *2627*

FLUID ABSTRACTS: PROCESS ENGINEERING.
Elsevier Science Ltd., P.O. Box 800, Kidlington, Oxford OX5 1DX, England. TEL 44-1865-843000. FAX 44-1865-843010.
Vendor(s): European Space Agency (File no.48/FLUIDEX), Knight-Ridder Information, Inc. (File no.96/FLUIDEX). *2628*

FLY MAGAZINE.
University of Plymouth, Student Union, Drake Circus, Plymouth, Devon OL4 8AA, England. TEL 44-1752-663337. FAX 44-1752-251669. *1868*

FLYING.
Hachette Filipacchi Magazines, Inc., 1633 Broadway, New York, NY 10019. TEL 212-767-6953.
Vendor(s): Information Access Co., Knight-Ridder Information, Inc., University Microfilms International. *64*

FOCUS (MADISON).
University of Wisconsin at Madison, Institute for Research on Poverty, 3412 Social Science Bldg., 1180 Observatory Dr., Madison, WI 53706. TEL 608-262-6358. FAX 608-265-3119. *6372*

FOCUS (NEW YORK, 1950).
American Geographical Society, 156 Fifth Ave., Ste. 600, New York, NY 10010-7002. TEL 212-242-0214.
Vendor(s): University Microfilms International. *3254*

FOCUS JAPAN.
Japan External Trade Organization, 2-5 Toranomon 2-chome, Minato-ku, Tokyo 105, Japan. TEL 03-3582-5521. FAX 03-3582-0504. *1276*

FOCUS ON EXCEPTIONAL CHILDREN.
Love Publishing Co., Box 22353, Denver, CO 80222. TEL 303-757-2579. FAX 303-782-5683. *2468*

FOLIA PHARMACOLOGICA JAPONICA.
Japanese Pharmacological Society, Editorial Office, Kantohya Bldg., Gokomachi-Ebisugawa, Nakagyo-ku, Kyoto 604, Japan. TEL 075-252-4641. FAX 075-252-4618. *5414*

FOLIO (STAMFORD).
Cowles Business Media 11 River Bend Dr., S., Box 4949, Stamford, CT 06907-0949. TEL 203-358-9900. FAX 203-349-3848.
Vendor(s): Information Access Co., Knight-Ridder Information, Inc., University Microfilms International. *5996*

FOLKLIFE CENTER NEWS.
U.S. Library of Congress, American Folklife Center, Washington, DC 20540-4610. TEL 202-707-6590. FAX 202-707-2076. *2951*

FOOD & BEVERAGE MARKETING.
Charleson Publishing Co., 105 College Rd. E., Princeton, NJ 08540-6622. TEL 609-243-9500. FAX 609-243-9415.
Vendor(s): Information Access Co., Lexis-Nexis. *2968*

FOOD & DRINK DAILY.
King Publishing Group, Inc., 627 National Press Bldg., Washington, DC 20045. TEL 202-638-4260. FAX 202-662-9744.
Vendor(s): Information Access Co., Lexis-Nexis, NewsNet (FB03). *2969*

FOOD AND DRUG LETTER.
Washington Business Information, Inc., c/o Karen Harrington, 1117 N. 19th St., Ste. 200, Arlington, VA 22209. TEL 703-247-3434. FAX 703-247-3421.
Vendor(s): Ovid Technologies, Inc. (DIOG), Data-Star, Knight-Ridder Information, Inc.. *1520*

FOOD & DRUG PACKAGING.
Independent Publishing Company, 210 S. Fifth St., Ste. 202, St. Charles, IL 60174. TEL 630-377-0100. FAX 630-377-1678.
Vendor(s): Information Access Co.. *5299*

FOOD CHEMICAL NEWS.
Food Chemical News, Inc., 1101 Pennsylvania Ave., S.E., Washington, DC 20003. TEL 202-544-1980. FAX 202-546-3890.
Vendor(s): Data-Star, Information Access Co., Knight-Ridder Information, Inc., NewsNet (FB07). *2969*

FOOD, COSMETICS AND DRUGS PACKAGING.
Elsevier Science Ltd., P.O. Box 800, Kidlington, Oxford OX5 1DX, England. TEL 44-1865-843000. FAX 44-1865-843010.
Vendor(s): Information Access Co., Knight-Ridder Information, Inc.. *5299*

FOOD IN CANADA.
Maclean Hunter Ltd., Business Publication Division, Maclean Hunter Bldg., 777 Bay St., Toronto, ON M5W 1A7, Canada. TEL 416-596-5884. FAX 416-596-5526.
Vendor(s): Information Access Co., Lexis-Nexis. *2970*

FOOD INGREDIENT NEWS.
Business Communications Co., Inc. (Norwalk), 25 Van Zant St., Ste. 13, Norwalk, CT 06855. TEL 203-853-4266. FAX 203-853-0348.
Vendor(s): Information Access Co.. *2970*

THE FOOD INSTITUTE REPORT.
Food Institute, 28-12 Broadway, Fair Lawn, NJ 07410. TEL 201-791-5570. FAX 201-791-5222.
Vendor(s): Information Access Co.. *2970*

FOOD LABELING AND NUTRITION NEWS.
Food Chemical News, Inc., 1101 Pennsylvania Ave., S.E., Washington, DC 20003. TEL 202-544-1980. FAX 202-546-3890.
Vendor(s): Information Access Co.. *2970*

FOOD MANUFACTURE INTERNATIONAL.
Miller Freeman Technical Ltd. Miller Freeman House, 30 Calderwood St., London SE18 6QH, England. TEL 44-181-855-7777. FAX 44-181-316-3206.
Vendor(s): Information Access Co., Lexis-Nexis. *2971*

FOOD NUTRITION AND AGRICULTURE.
Food and Agriculture Organization of the United Nations, Sales & Distribution Section, Via delle Terme di Caracalla, 00100 Rome, Italy. TEL 57971. FAX 6799563.
Vendor(s): Information Access Co.. *5232*

FOOD PROCESSING (TONBRIDGE).
I M L Group plc, Blair House, High St., Tonbridge, Kent TN9 1BQ, England. TEL 44-1732-359990. FAX 44-1732-770049.
Vendor(s): Information Access Co.. *2971*

FOOD RETAILERS: THE INTERNATIONAL MARKET.
Euromonitor, 60-61 Turnmill St., London EC1M 5QU, England. TEL 44-171-251-8024. FAX 44-171-608-3149.
Vendor(s): Data-Star, Knight-Ridder Information, Inc.. *3004*

FOOD SAFETY BRIEFING.
Barbour Index, New Lodge Drift Rd., Windsor, Berks. SL4 4RQ, England. TEL 01344-884121. FAX 01344-884112. *5249*

FOOD SCIENCE AND TECHNOLOGY ABSTRACTS.
International Food Information Service (I F I S Publishing), Lane End House, Shinfield, Reading, Berks. RG2 9BB, England. TEL 01734-883895. FAX 01734-885065.
Vendor(s): CISTI, DIMDI, Data-Star (FSTA), Knight-Ridder Information, Inc. (File no.51), Orbit Search Service (FSTA), STN International. *2996*

FOOD TRADE REVIEW.
Food Trade Press Ltd., Station House, Hortons Way, Westerham, Kent TN16 1BZ, England. TEL 44-1959-563944. FAX 44-1959-561285.
Vendor(s): Information Access Co., Lexis-Nexis. *2973*

FOODS ADLIBRA.
Foods Adlibra Publications, 9000 Plymouth Ave. N., Minneapolis, MN 55427. TEL 612-540-2720. FAX 612-540-3166.
Vendor(s): Knight-Ridder Information, Inc. (File no.79). *2996*

FOODS ADLIBRA BEVERAGE EDITION.
Foods Adlibra Publications, 9000 Plymouth Ave., N., Minneapolis, MN 55427. TEL 612-540-2720. FAX 612-540-3166.
Vendor(s): Knight-Ridder Information, Inc. (File no.79). *514*

FOODS ADLIBRA FOODSERVICE EDITION.
Foods Adlibra Publications, 9000 Plymouth Ave., N., Minneapolis, MN 55427. TEL 612-540-2720. FAX 612-540-3166.
Vendor(s): Knight-Ridder Information, Inc. (File no.79). *2996*

FOODS ADLIBRA SEAFOOD EDITION.
Foods Adlibra Publications, 9000 Plymouth Ave., N., Minneapolis, MN 55427. TEL 612-540-2720. FAX 612-540-3166.
Vendor(s): Knight-Ridder Information, Inc. (File no.79). *2996*

FOODS ADLIBRA SNACK & CONFECTIONS EDITION.
Foods Adlibra Publications, 9000 Plymouth Ave., N., Minneapolis, MN 55427. TEL 612-540-2720. FAX 612-540-3166.
Vendor(s): Knight-Ridder Information, Inc. (File no.79). *2996*

THE FOODSERVICE DISTRIBUTOR.
Penton Publishing Co. 1100 Superior Ave., Cleveland, OH 44114-2543. TEL 216-696-7000. FAX 216-696-8765.
Vendor(s): Information Access Co.. *2973*

FOOTWEAR NEWS.
Fairchild Fashion & Merchandising Group 7 W. 34th St., New York, NY 10001. TEL 212-630-4199. FAX 212-630-4201.
Vendor(s): Information Access Co., Knight-Ridder Information, Inc., Lexis-Nexis. *6307*

FOR YOUR EYES ONLY.
Tiger Publications, Box 8759, Amarillo, TX 79114-8759. TEL 806-655-2009.
Vendor(s): NewsNet (DE15). *5031*

FORBES.
Forbes, Inc., 60 Fifth Ave., New York, NY 10011. TEL 212-620-2200.
Vendor(s): Dow Jones News Retrieval, Information Access Co., Knight-Ridder Information, Inc., Lexis-Nexis. *1419*

FORD INVESTMENT MANAGEMENT REPORT.
Ford Investor Services, 11722 Sorrento Valley Rd., Ste. 1, San Diego, CA 92121. TEL 619-755-1327. *1330*

FORD VALUE REPORT.
Ford Investor Services, 11722 Sorrento Valley Rd., Ste. 1, San Diego, CA 92121. TEL 619-755-1327. *1330*

FORDHAM INTELLECTUAL PROPERTY, MEDIA & ENTERTAINMENT LAW JOURNAL.
Lincoln Center, 140 W. 62nd St., New York, NY 10023. TEL 212-636-6948. FAX 212-636-6582. Vendor(s): West Services, Inc.. *3781*

FORDHAM INTERNATIONAL LAW JOURNAL.
Fordham University, School of Law, 140 W. 62nd St., Rm. 015, New York, NY 10023-7477. TEL 212-636-6931. FAX 212-636-6932. Vendor(s): West Services, Inc.. *3930*

FORDHAM LAW REVIEW.
Fordham University, School of Law, Lincoln Center, 140 W. 62nd St., Rm. 04, New York, NY 10023. TEL 212-636-6876. FAX 212-636-6965. Vendor(s): Lexis-Nexis, West Services, Inc.. *3781*

FORDHAM URBAN LAW JOURNAL.
Fordham University, School of Law, Lincoln Center, 140 W. 62nd St., New York, NY 10023. TEL 212-636-6881. Vendor(s): West Services, Inc.. *3781*

FOREIGN AFFAIRS.
Council on Foreign Relations, Inc., 58 E. 68th St., New York, NY 10021. TEL 212-734-0400. Vendor(s): Information Access Co., Lexis-Nexis, University Microfilms International. *5750*

FOREIGN POLICY (WASHINGTON).
Carnegie Endowment for International Peace, 2400 N St., N.W., Ste. 700, Washington, DC 20037. TEL 202-862-7940. Vendor(s): Information Access Co., University Microfilms International. *5750*

FOREIGN POLICY BULLETIN.
Kluwer Law International Postbus 85889, 2508 CN The Hague, NE. TEL 31-70-3081500. FAX 31-70-3081515. Vendor(s): Data-Star, Knight-Ridder Information, Inc., Ovid Technologies, Inc.. *5751*

FOREIGN SERVICE JOURNAL.
American Foreign Service Association, 2101 E St., N.W., Washington, DC 20037. TEL 202-338-4045. FAX 202-338-8244. *5751*

FOREIGN TRADE REPORTS. U.S. EXPORT AND IMPORT MERCHANDISE TRADE AND SUPPLEMENT.
U.S. Bureau of the Census, Foreign Trade Division, Washington, DC 20233. TEL 301-763-5140. Vendor(s): CompuServe, Inc., Knight-Ridder Information, Inc.. *1276*

FORENSIC SERVICES DIRECTORY.
National Forensic Center, 17 Temple Terr., Lawrenceville, NJ 08648. TEL 609-883-0550. Vendor(s): Lexis-Nexis, West Services, Inc.. *3781*

FOREST PRODUCTS ABSTRACTS.
CAB International, Wallingford, Oxon. OX10 8DE, England. TEL 44-1491-832111. FAX 44-1491-826090. Vendor(s): CISTI, DIMDI, European Space Agency (File nos.16 & 124/CAB), Knight-Ridder Information, Inc., Ovid Technologies, Inc. (CABA). *3031*

FOREST PRODUCTS JOURNAL.
Forest Products Society, 2801 Marshall Ct., Madison, WI 53705. TEL 608-231-1361. FAX 608-231-2152. Vendor(s): University Microfilms International. *3034*

FORESTRY.
Oxford University Press, Oxford Journals, Walton St., Oxford OX2 6DP, England. TEL 44-1865-267907. FAX 44-1865-267773. Vendor(s): European Space Agency (File nos.16 & 124/CAB). *3016*

FORESTRY ABSTRACTS.
CAB International, Wallingford, Oxon. OX10 8DE, England. TEL 44-1491-832111. FAX 44-1491-826090. Vendor(s): CISTI, DIMDI, European Space Agency, Knight-Ridder Information, Inc., Ovid Technologies, Inc. (CABA). *3031*

FORESTRY ABSTRACTS. LEADING ARTICLE REPRINT SERIES.
CAB International, Wallingford, Oxon. OX10 8DE, England. TEL 44-1491-832111. FAX 44-1491-833508. Vendor(s): DIMDI, European Space Agency, Knight-Ridder Information, Inc., STN International. *3031*

FORLAGSSERIEKATALOG FOR BOERNE- OG SKOLEBIBLIOTEKER.
Dansk BiblioteksCenter as, Tempovej 7-11, DK-2750 Ballerup, Denmark. TEL 45-44-867777. FAX 45-44-867892. *2389*

FORMULARY.
Advanstar Communications, Inc., 7500 Old Oak Blvd., Cleveland, OH 44130. TEL 216-826-2839. FAX 216-891-2726. *5414*

FORTHCOMING BOOKS.
R.R. Bowker, A Division of Reed Elsevier Inc., 121 Chanlon Rd., New Providence, NJ 07974. TEL 908-464-6800. FAX 908-665-3502. Vendor(s): Knight-Ridder Information, Inc. (File no.470), Ovid Technologies, Inc. (BBIP). *531*

FORTSCHRITTE DER ARZNEIMITTELFORSCHUNG.
Birkhaeuser Verlag, P.O. Box 133, CH-4010 Basel, Switzerland. TEL 41-2050730. FAX 41-61-2050791. *5414*

FORTUNE INTERNATIONAL.
Time Warner Publishing BV Ottho Heldring Straat 5, 1066 AZ Amsterdam, Netherlands. TEL 31-20-5104911. FAX 31-20-6175077. *925*

FORTUNE MAGAZINE.
Time Inc. Time & Life Bldg., Rockefeller Center, New York, NY 10020-1393. TEL 212-522-1212. Vendor(s): CompuServe, Inc., Information Access Co., University Microfilms International, VU/TEXT Information Services, Inc.. *1419*

FORWARD (NEW YORK).
Forward Association, 45 E. 33rd St., New York, NY 10016. TEL 212-889-8200. FAX 212-447-6406. *2879*

FORWARD MOTION.
Forward Motion, Box 150311, Brooklyn, NY 11215-0311. TEL 718-789-2551. *5667*

FOSTER NATURAL GAS REPORT.
Foster Associates, 1015 15th St., N.W., Washington, DC 20005-2605. TEL 202-408-7710. FAX 202-408-7723. Vendor(s): Lexis-Nexis. *5355*

FOUNDATION DIRECTORY.
Foundation Center, 79 Fifth Ave., New York, NY 10003. TEL 212-620-4230. FAX 212-807-3677. Vendor(s): Knight-Ridder Information, Inc.. *6400*

FOUNDATION GIVING WATCH.
Taft Group 835 Penobscot Bldg., Detroit, MI 48226. TEL 313-961-2242. FAX 313-961-6083. Vendor(s): NewsNet (GB50). *6373*

FOUNDATION GRANTS INDEX.
Foundation Center, 79 Fifth Ave., New York, NY 10003. TEL 212-620-4230. FAX 212-807-3677. Vendor(s): Knight-Ridder Information, Inc.. *6401*

FOUNDATION GRANTS INDEX QUARTERLY.
Foundation Center, 79 Fifth Ave., New York, NY 10003. TEL 212-620-4230. FAX 212-807-3677. Vendor(s): Knight-Ridder Information, Inc.. *6401*

FOUNDATION NEWS AND COMMENTARY.
Council on Foundations, Inc., 1828 L St., N.W., Ste. 300, Washington, DC 20036. TEL 202-466-6512. FAX 202-785-3926. Vendor(s): University Microfilms International. *6373*

FOUNDRY MANAGEMENT & TECHNOLOGY.
Penton Publishing Co. 1100 Superior Ave., Cleveland, OH 44114-2543. TEL 216-696-7000. FAX 216-696-8765. Vendor(s): Information Access Co. Knight-Ridder Information, Inc.. *4955*

FRANCE. CONSEIL NATIONAL DU CREDIT. STATISTIQUES MENSUELLES.
Banque de France, Service de l'Information, 48, rue Croix des Petits Champs, 75001 Paris, France. TEL 1-42-92-39-08. FAX 1-42-92-39-40. Vendor(s): GSI-ECO. *999*

FRANCE. CONSEIL NATIONAL DU CREDIT. STATISTIQUES TRIMESTRIELLES.
Banque de France, Service de l'Information, 48, Croix des Petits Champs, 75001 Paris, France. TEL 1-42-92-39-08. FAX 1-42-92-39-40. Vendor(s): GSI-ECO. *999*

THE FRANCHISE HANDBOOK.
Enterprise Magazines, Inc. 1020 N. Broadway, Ste. 111, Milwaukee, WI 53202. TEL 414-272-9977. FAX 414-272-9973. *1575*

FRANCHISING WORLD.
International Franchise Association, 1350 New York Ave., N.W., Ste. 900, Washington, DC 20005. TEL 202-628-8000. FAX 202-628-0812. Vendor(s): University Microfilms International. *1466*

FREE CHOICE.
Freedom Organisation for the Right to Enjoy Smoking Tobacco (F O R E S T), 2 Grosvenor Gardens, London SW1W 0DH, England. TEL 44-171-823-6550. FAX 44-171-823-4534. *5728*

FREE INQUIRY.
Council for Secular Humanism, Box 664, Buffalo, NY 14226. TEL 716-636-7425. FAX 716-636-1733. Vendor(s): Information Access Co. University Microfilms International. *5176*

FREE OR FAIR TRADE?
Instituto Latinoamericano de Servicios Legales Alternativos, Apdo. Aereo 077844, Bogota, Colombia. TEL 57-1-245-5355. FAX 57-1-2884354. *3901*

FREEDOM REVIEW.
Transaction Publishers, Transaction Periodicals Consortium, Department 3092, Rutgers University, New Brunswick, NJ 08903. TEL 908-445-2280. FAX 908-445-3138. *5723*

FREEMAN.
Foundation for Economic Education, Inc., 30 S. Broadway, Irvington-on-Hudson, NY 10533. TEL 914-591-7230. FAX 914-591-8910. *5668*

FRENCH HISTORICAL STUDIES.
Duke University Press, Box 90660, Durham, NC 27708-0660. TEL 919-687-3600. FAX 919-688-4574. Vendor(s): University Microfilms International. *3411*

FREQUENT FLYER.
Reed Travel Group (Oak Brook), Part of the Reed Elsevier group 2000 Clearwater Dr., Oak Brook, IL 60521. TEL 708-574-6000. FAX 708-574-6222. *6756*

FRESHWATER FISHERIES LABORATORY PITLOCHRY. ANNUAL REVIEW.
Scottish Office, Agriculture and Fisheries Department, Faskally, Pitlochry, Perthshire PH16 5LB, Scotland. TEL 0796-472060. FAX 0796-473523. Vendor(s): Knight-Ridder Information, Inc.. *2933*

FRIDAY MEMO.
Information Industry Association, 1625 Massachusetts Ave., N.W., Ste. 700, Washington, DC 20036-2212. TEL 202-639-8262. FAX 202-638-4403. Vendor(s): NewsNet (PB15). *1990*

FROHLINGER'S MARKETING REPORT.
Marketing Strategist Communications, Ltd., 7 Coppel Dr., Tenafly, NJ 07670-2903. TEL 201-567-4447. FAX 201-568-3538. Vendor(s): Information Access Co. *1466*

FRONTIERS.
Mercury Capital, Inc., 7985 Santa Monica Blvd., Ste. 109, W. Hollywood, CA 90046. TEL 213-848-2222. FAX 213-656-8784.
Vendor(s): Information Access Co.. *3531*

FRONTIERS: A JOURNAL OF WOMEN STUDIES.
Frontiers Editorial Collective, Wilson 12, Washington State University, Pullman, WA 99164-4007. TEL 509-335-7268. FAX 509-335-4377.
Vendor(s): University Microfilms International. *7016*

FRONTIERS OF HEALTH SERVICES MANAGEMENT.
Health Administration Press, 1 N. Franklin St., Ste. 1700, Chicago, IL 60606-3421. TEL 312-424-2800. FAX 312-424-0014.
Vendor(s): University Microfilms International. *3544*

FROZEN AND CHILLED FOODS.
Argus Business Media Ltd., Fuel and Metals Journals Queensway House, 2 Queensway, Redhill, Surrey RH1 1QS, England. TEL 44-1737-768611. FAX 44-1737-761685.
Vendor(s): Information Access Co.. *2974*

FROZEN FOOD AGE.
Progressive Grocer Associates, 263 Tresser Blvd., Stamford, CT 06901-3202. TEL 203-325-3500. FAX 203-325-4377.
Vendor(s): Information Access Co., University Microfilms International. *2974*

FROZEN FOOD DIGEST.
Frozen Food Digest, Inc., 271 Madison Ave., New York, NY 10016. TEL 212-557-8600. FAX 212-986-9868.
Vendor(s): Information Access Co.. *2974*

FROZEN FOODS: THE INTERNATIONAL MARKET.
Euromonitor, 87-88 Turnmill St., London EC1M 5QU, England. TEL 44-171-251-8024. FAX 44-171-608-3149.
Vendor(s): Data-Star, Knight-Ridder Information, Inc.. *2974*

FRUIT AND VEGETABLES: THE INTERNATIONAL MARKET.
Euromonitor, 60-61 Britton St., London EC1M 5NA, England. TEL 44-171-251-8024. FAX 44-171-608-3149.
Vendor(s): Data-Star, Knight-Ridder Information, Inc.. *2974*

FRUIT JUICES: THE INTERNATIONAL MARKET.
Euromonitor, 60-61 Brotton St., London EC1M 5NA, England. TEL 44-171-251-8024. FAX 44-171-608-3149.
Vendor(s): Data-Star, Knight-Ridder Information, Inc.. *505*

FULLTEXT SOURCES ONLINE.
BiblioData, Box 61, Needham Heights, MA 02194. TEL 617-444-1154. FAX 617-449-4584.
Vendor(s): Data-Star. *531*

FUND RAISING MANAGEMENT.
Hoke Communications, Inc., 224 Seventh St., Garden City, NY 11530. TEL 516-746-6700. FAX 516-294-8141.
Vendor(s): Information Access Co., Knight-Ridder Information, Inc., University Microfilms International. *1097*

FUNDS TRANSFER REPORT.
Bankers Research, Inc., Box 431, Westport, CT 06881-0431. TEL 203-227-1237.
Vendor(s): University Microfilms International. *1097*

FUSION POWER REPORT.
Business Publishers, Inc., 951 Pershing Dr., Silver Spring, MD 20910-4464. TEL 301-587-6300. FAX 301-585-9075.
Vendor(s): Information Access Co., Knight-Ridder Information, Inc., NewsNet (EY46). *2576*

THE FUTURE OF CHILDREN.
David and Lucile Packard Foundation, Center for the Future of Children, 300 Second St., Ste. 102, Los Altos, CA 94022. TEL 415-948-3696. FAX 415-948-6498. *1768*

FUTURES (CEDAR FALLS).
Oster Communications, Inc., 219 Parkade, Cedar Falls, IA 50613. TEL 319-277-1271. FAX 319-277-5803.
Vendor(s): Information Access Co.. *1331*

FUTURES MARKET SERVICE.
Knight-Ridder Financial, 30 S. Wacker Dr., Ste. 1810, Chicago, IL 60606. TEL 312-454-1801. FAX 312-454-0239. *1331*

FUTURES WORLD NEWS.
Oster Communications, Inc., 219 Parkade, Cedar Falls, IA 50613. TEL 319-277-1271. FAX 319-277-5803.
Available only online. *1331*

FUTURESCOPE.
Decision Resources, Inc., 1100 Winter St., Waltham, MA 02154-1238. TEL 617-487-3737. FAX 617-487-5750.
Vendor(s): Knight-Ridder Information, Inc. (File no. 192). *1331*

THE FUTURIST.
World Future Society, 7910 Woodmont Ave., Ste. 450, Bethesda, MD 20814. TEL 301-656-8274.
Vendor(s): Information Access Co., Knight-Ridder Information, Inc., University Microfilms International. *6241*

THE G M P LETTER.
Washington Business Information, Inc., c/o Karen Harrington, 1117 N. 19th St., Ste. 200, Arlington, VA 22209. TEL 703-247-3434. FAX 703-247-3421.
Vendor(s): Ovid Technologies, Inc. (DIOG), Data-Star, Knight-Ridder Information, Inc.. *3634*

G N N MAGAZINE.
Global Network Navigator 2855 Telegraph Ave., Ste. 503, Berkeley, CA 94705. TEL 510-883-7220.
Available only online. *2037*

G N N NEWS.
Global Network Navigator 2855 Telegraph Ave., Ste. 503, Berkeley, CA 94705. TEL 510-883-7220.
Available only online. *2037*

G P.
Haymarket Medical Ltd., 30 Lancaster Gate, London W2 3LP, England. TEL 0171-413-4095.
Vendor(s): Data-Star (GPGP). *4457*

G R I D.
Gas Research Institute, Member Relations and Communications, 8600 W. Bryn Mawr Ave., Chicago, IL 60631. TEL 312-399-8100. FAX 312-399-8170.
Vendor(s): Information Access Co.. *5355*

G S A TODAY.
Geological Society of America, 3300 Penrose Pl., Box 9140, Boulder, CO 80301. TEL 303-447-2020. FAX 303-447-1133. *2233*

G U I PROGRAM NEWS.
Worldwide Videotex, Box 3273, Boynton Beach, FL 33424-3273. TEL 407-738-2276.
Vendor(s): Information Access Co.. *2110*

GAJOOB.
Box 3201, Salt Lake City, UT 84110. TEL 801-364-5110. *5159*

GALE DIRECTORY OF DATABASES.
Gale Research Inc., 835 Penobscot Bldg., Detroit, MI 48226. TEL 313-961-2242. FAX 313-961-6038.
Vendor(s): Data-Star, Orbit Search Service, Telesystemes - Questel. *2066*

GALE DIRECTORY OF PUBLICATIONS AND BROADCAST MEDIA.
Gale Research Inc., 835 Penobscot Bldg., Detroit, MI 48226. TEL 313-961-2242. FAX 313-961-6083.
Vendor(s): Knight-Ridder Information, Inc.. *531*

GALLUP POLL MONTHLY.
Gallup Poll News Service, 47 Hulfish St., Box 628, Princeton, NJ 08542. TEL 609-924-9600. FAX 609-683-9256. *5668*

GARDENING: THE INTERNATIONAL MARKET.
Euromonitor, 60-61 Britton St., London EC1M 5NA, England. TEL 44-171-251-8024. FAX 44-171-608-3149.
Vendor(s): Data-Star, Knight-Ridder Information, Inc.. *3052*

GAS ABSTRACTS.
Institute of Gas Technology, 1700 S. Mount Prospect Rd., Des Plaines, IL 60018-1804. TEL 847-768-0673. FAX 847-768-0669. *5382*

GAS DAILY.
Pasha Publications Inc., 1616 N. Ft. Myer Dr., Ste. 1000, Arlington, VA 22209-3107. TEL 703-528-1244. FAX 703-528-1253.
Vendor(s): Data-Star, Information Access Co., Knight-Ridder Information, Inc.. *5356*

GAS MARKET TRENDS.
Arab Press Service, A P S House, P.O. Box 3896, Nicosia, Cyprus. TEL 357-2-351778. FAX 357-2-350265.
Vendor(s): Information Access Co.. *2549*

GASSHO.
Dharmanet International, Box 4951, Berkeley, CA 94704-4951. TEL 510-620-0936. *6110*

GASTROENTEROLOGY.
W.B. Saunders Co. Curtis Center, 3rd Fl., Independence Sq. W., Philadelphia, PA 19106-3399. TEL 215-238-7800. FAX 215-238-6445.
Vendor(s): Ovid Technologies, Inc.. *4692*

GAY SCOTLAND.
58A Broughton St., Edinburgh EH1 3SA, Scotland. TEL 0131-557-2625. FAX 0131-333-1949. *3532*

GAZETTE.
250 rue St-Antoine O., Montreal, PQ H2Y 3R7, Canada.
Vendor(s): Southam Electronic Publishing. *3121*

GEBORENER DEUTSCHER.
William L. Gage, Ed. & Pub., 805 Alvarado Dr. N.E., Albuquerque, NM 87108-1648. TEL 505-268-1310. *3084*

GENDER AND DEVELOPMENT.
Carfax Publishing Co., P.O. Box 25, Abingdon, Oxon OX14 3UE, England. TEL 44-1235-401000. FAX 44-1235-401550. *7016*

GENDER AND EDUCATION.
Carfax Publishing Co., P.O. Box 25, Abingdon, Oxon. OX14 3UE, England. TEL 44-1235-401000. FAX 44-1235-401550. *2336*

GENDER, PLACE AND CULTURE.
Carfax Publishing Co., P.O. Box 25, Abingdon, Oxon. OX14 3UE, England. TEL 44-1235-401000. FAX 44-1235-401550. *7016*

GENE.
Elsevier Science B.V., P.O. Box 211, 1000 AE Amsterdam, Netherlands. TEL 31-20-4853911. FAX 31-20-4853598. *741*

THE GENE EXCHANGE.
Union of Concerned Scientists (Washington), 1616 P St., N.W., Washington, DC 20036. TEL 202-332-0900. FAX 202-332-0905. *741*

GENERAL SCIENCE INDEX.
H.W. Wilson Co., 950 University Ave., Bronx, NY 10452. TEL 718-588-8400. FAX 718-590-1617.
Vendor(s): OCLC, Wilsonline (File GSI). *6301*

GENESIS REPORT - DX.
Genesis Group Associates, Inc., 29 Park St., Montclair, NJ 07042. TEL 201-509-7735. FAX 201-509-7745.
Vendor(s): Data-Star, Dow Jones News Retrieval, Information Access Co., Knight-Ridder Information, Inc., Lexis-Nexis. *4459*

GENESIS REPORT - RX.
Genesis Group Associates, Inc., 29 Park St., Montclair, NJ 07042. TEL 201-509-7735. FAX 201-509-7745.
Vendor(s): Data-Star, Dow Jones News Retrieval, Information Access Co., Knight-Ridder Information, Inc., Lexis-Nexis. *5415*

GENETIC EPIDEMIOLOGY.
John Wiley & Sons, Inc., Journals, 605 Third Ave., New York, NY 10158. TEL 212-850-6645. FAX 212-850-6021. *742*

GENETICS ABSTRACTS.
Cambridge Scientific Abstracts, 7200 Wisconsin Ave., 6th Fl., Bethesda, MD 20814. TEL 301-961-6750. FAX 301-961-6720. Vendor(s): Knight-Ridder Information, Inc. (File no.76/LIFE SCIENCES COLLECTION), STN International (LIFESCI). *621*

GENGO TO KYOIKU NO KENKYU.
Saitama Daigaku Kyoiku Gakubu, Kyoiku Gakubu, Takenaga Laboratory, 255, Shimo Okubo, Urawa-shi 338, Japan. TEL 048-858-3175. FAX 048-858-3690. *2488*

GENITOURINARY MEDICINE.
B M J Publishing Group, B.M.A. House, Tavistock Sq., London WC1H 9JR, England. TEL 44-171-387-4499. FAX 44-171-383-6402. Vendor(s): Ovid Technologies, Inc.. *4661*

GENRE MAGAZINE.
7080 Hollywood Blvd., Ste. 1104, Hollywood, CA 90028. TEL 213-467-8300. FAX 213-467-8365. *4941*

GEO INFO SYSTEMS.
Advanstar Communications, Inc., 7500 Old Oak Blvd., Cleveland, OH 44130. TEL 216-826-2839. FAX 216-891-2726. Vendor(s): Information Access Co.. *3281*

GEOGRAPHICAL ABSTRACTS: HUMAN GEOGRAPHY.
Elsevier - Geo Abstracts Regency House, 34 Duke St., Norwich NR3 3AP, England. TEL 44-603-626327. FAX 44-603-667934. Vendor(s): Knight-Ridder Information, Inc. (File no.292), Orbit Search Service (GEOB). *3280*

GEOGRAPHICAL ABSTRACTS: PHYSICAL GEOGRAPHY.
Elsevier - Geo Abstracts Regency House, 34 Duke St., Norwich NR3 3AP, England. TEL 44-603-626327. FAX 44-603-667934. Vendor(s): Knight-Ridder Information, Inc. (File no.292), Orbit Search Service (GEOB). *3280*

THE GEOGRAPHICAL JOURNAL.
Royal Geographical Society, 1 Kensington Gore, London SW7 2AR, England. TEL 44-171-589-5466. FAX 44-171-584-4447. Vendor(s): Information Access Co., University Microfilms International. *3257*

GEOGRAPHICAL MAGAZINE.
World Publications Ltd., B B C Enterprises, Rm. A1040, 80 Wood Ln., Woodlands, London W12 0TT, England. TEL 44-181-576-2000. FAX 44-181-576-2931. Vendor(s): Information Access Co.. *3257*

GEOGRAPHICAL REVIEW.
American Geographical Society, 156 Fifth Ave., New York, NY 10010-7002. TEL 212-242-0214. Vendor(s): Information Access Co., University Microfilms International. *3258*

GEOLOGICAL ABSTRACTS.
Elsevier - Geo Abstracts Regency House, 34 Duke St., Norwich NR3 3AP, England. TEL 44-603-626327. FAX 44-603-667934. Vendor(s): Knight-Ridder Information, Inc. (File no.292), Orbit Search Service (GEOB). *2218*

GEOLOGICAL SOCIETY OF INDIA. JOURNAL.
Geological Society of India, Post Box 1922, Gavipuram, Bangalore 560 019, India. TEL 080-6613352. Vendor(s): Knight-Ridder Information, Inc. (File no.89). *2237*

GEOMETRIC AND FUNCTIONAL ANALYSIS.
Birkhaeuser Verlag, P.O. Box 133, CH-4010 Basel, Switzerland. TEL 41-61-2050730. FAX 41-61-2050791. *4366*

GEORGE MASON LAW REVIEW.
George Mason Law Journal Association, 3401 N. Fairfax Dr., Arlington, VA 22201. TEL 703-993-8161. FAX 703-993-8088. Vendor(s): Lexis-Nexis, West Services, Inc.. *3783*

GEORGE WASHINGTON JOURNAL OF INTERNATIONAL LAW AND ECONOMICS.
George Washington University, National Law Center, 2008 G St., N.W., Washington, DC 20052. TEL 202-676-3847. FAX 202-676-3876. Vendor(s): Lexis-Nexis, West Services, Inc.. *3931*

GEORGE WASHINGTON LAW REVIEW.
George Washington University, G W Law Review, 2008 G St., N.W., Washington, DC 20052. TEL 202-676-3868. FAX 202-676-3876. Vendor(s): Lexis-Nexis, West Services, Inc.. *3783*

GEORGE WELLS' WASHINGTON BEVERAGE INSIGHT.
George Wells & Associates, 2942 S. Columbus St., Ste. A-2, Arlington, VA 22206. TEL 703-671-8140. Vendor(s): Information Access Co., NewsNet. *505*

GEORGETOWN IMMIGRATION LAW JOURNAL.
Georgetown University Law Center, 600 New Jersey Ave., N.W., Washington, DC 20001. TEL 202-662-9468. Vendor(s): West Services, Inc.. *3783*

GEORGETOWN INTERNATIONAL ENVIRONMENTAL LAW REVIEW.
Georgetown University Law Center, 600 New Jersey Ave., N.W., Washington, DC 20001. TEL 202-662-9468. Vendor(s): West Services, Inc.. *2798*

GEORGETOWN LAW JOURNAL.
Georgetown University Law Center, 600 New Jersey Ave., N.W., Washington, DC 20001. TEL 202-662-9468. Vendor(s): Lexis-Nexis, West Services, Inc.. *3783*

GEORGETOWN REVIEW.
Georgetown College, Box 6309, Southern Sta., Hattiesburg, MS 39406-6309. TEL 601-583-6940. FAX 601-583-6940. *4213*

GEORGIA BUSINESS DIRECTORY.
American Business Directories 5711 S. 86th Circle, Box 27347, Omaha, NE 68127. TEL 402-593-4600. FAX 402-331-5481. *1612*

GEORGIA JOURNAL OF INTERNATIONAL AND COMPARATIVE LAW.
Georgia Journal of International and Comparative Law, Inc., University of Georgia, School of Law, Athens, GA 30602. TEL 706-542-5205. Vendor(s): Lexis-Nexis, West Services, Inc.. *3931*

GEORGIA LAW REVIEW.
University of Georgia, School of Law, Athens, GA 30602. TEL 706-542-7286. FAX 706-542-5556. Vendor(s): West Services, Inc.. *3783*

GEORGIA TREND.
Grimes Publications, Inc., Box 1266, Athens, GA 30603. TEL 404-354-0463. FAX 404-354-6824. Vendor(s): Information Access Co., Knight-Ridder Information, Inc., Lexis-Nexis, University Microfilms International. *1097*

GEOSCIENCE DOCUMENTATION.
Geosystems, P.O. Box 40, Didcot, Oxon. OX11 9BX, England. TEL 44-1235-813913. Vendor(s): Knight-Ridder Information, Inc. (File no.58). *2219*

GEOTECHNICAL AND GEOLOGICAL ENGINEERING.
Chapman & Hall, Journals Department 2-6 Boundary Row, London SE1 8HN, England. TEL 44-171-8650066. FAX 44-171-522-9623. *5063*

GEOTHERMAL RESOURCES COUNCIL. BULLETIN.
Geothermal Resources Council, Box 1350, Davis, CA 95617-1350. TEL 916-758-2360. FAX 916-758-2839. *2572*

GEOTITLES.
Geosystems, P.O. Box 40, Didcot, Oxon. OX11 9BX, England. TEL 44-1235-813913. Vendor(s): Knight-Ridder Information, Inc. (File no.58). *2219*

GERIATRIC NURSING.
Mosby Year - Book, Inc. 11830 Westline Industrial Dr., St. Louis, MO 63146-3318. TEL 314-872-8370. FAX 314-432-1380. *3287*

GERIATRICS.
Advanstar Communications, Inc., 7500 Old Oak Blvd., Cleveland, OH 44130. TEL 216-826-2839. FAX 216-891-2726. Vendor(s): Information Access Co., University Microfilms International. *3287*

GERMAN BRIEF.
Frankfurter Allgemeine Zeitung GmbH, Information Services, Hellerhofstr. 2-4, 60327 Frankfurt a.M., Germany. TEL 49-69-759-2219. FAX 49-69-75912188. *926*

GERMAN LIFE.
Zeitgeist Publishing, 1 Corporate Dr., Grantsville, MD 21536. TEL 301-895-3859. FAX 301-895-5029. Vendor(s): Lexis-Nexis. *3144*

GERMANIC REVIEW.
Heldref Publications, 1319 Eighteenth St., N.W., Washington, DC 20036-1802. TEL 202-296-6267. FAX 202-296-5149. Vendor(s): University Microfilms International. *4071*

GERMANY'S TOP 500.
Frankfurter Allgemeine Zeitung GmbH, Information Services, Hellerhofstr. 2-4, 60327 Frankfurt a.M., Germany. TEL 49-69-759-2219. FAX 49-69-75912188. *1612*

GERONTOLOGIST.
Gerontological Society of America, 1275 K St., N.W., Ste. 350, Washington, DC 20005-4006. TEL 202-842-1275. FAX 202-842-1150. Vendor(s): University Microfilms International. *3288*

GETTING RESULTS...FOR THE HANDS-ON MANAGER.
American Management Association, Periodical Division, 1601 Broadway, New York, NY 10019. TEL 212-586-8100. FAX 212-903-8083. Vendor(s): Information Access Co., University Microfilms International. *1419*

DIE GIESSEREI-INDUSTRIE UND IHRE HELFER.
Industrieschau-Verlagsgesellschaft mbH, Postfach 100262, 64202 Darmstadt, Germany. TEL 49-6151-38920. FAX 49-6151-33164. *4956*

GIFTS & DECORATIVE ACCESSORIES.
Geyer-McAllister Publications, Inc., 51 Madison Ave., New York, NY 10010. TEL 212-689-4411. Vendor(s): Information Access Co., Knight-Ridder Information, Inc.. *3300*

GIORNALE DI MEDICINA MILITARE.
Direzione Generale della Sanita Militare, Via S. Stefano Rotondo, n.4, 00184 Rome, Italy. TEL 39-4735-7939. *4459*

GIRLJOCK.
Rox-A-Tronic Publishing, Box 882723, San Francisco, CA 94188. TEL 415-282-6833. FAX 415-282-6833. *3552*

GLACIAL GEOLOGY AND GEOMORPHOLOGY.
John Wiley & Sons Ltd., Journals, Baffins Ln., Chichester, W. Sussex PO19 1UD, England. TEL 44-1243-779777. FAX 44-1243-843232. Available only online. *2219*

GLASS (REDHILL).
Argus Business Media Ltd. Fuel and Metals Journals Queensway House, 2 Queensway Redhill, Surrey RH1 1QS, England. TEL 44-1737-768611. FAX 44-1737-761685. Vendor(s): Information Access Co.. *1656*

GLASS INTERNATIONAL.
Argus Business Media Ltd. Fuel and Metals Journals Queensway House, 2 Queensway Redhill, Surrey RH1 1QS, England. TEL 44-1737-768611. FAX 44-1737-761685. Vendor(s): Information Access Co.. *1656*

GLOBAL COMPANY HANDBOOK.
C I F A R Publications, Inc. 3490 US Hwy 1, BL012, Princeton, NJ 08540-5920. TEL 609-520-9333. FAX 609-520-0905. Vendor(s): Lexis-Nexis. *1277*

GLOBAL ENVIRONMENTAL CHANGE.
Butterworth - Heinemann, Part of the Reed Elsevier group, Linacre House, Jordan Hill, Oxford OX2 8DP, England. TEL 44-1865-310366. FAX 44-1865-310898.
Vendor(s): Data-Star, Knight-Ridder Information, Inc., NewsNet. *2798*

GLOBAL ENVIRONMENTAL CHANGE REPORT.
Cutter Information Corp., 37 Broadway, Arlington, MA 02174. TEL 617-648-8700. FAX 617-648-1950.
Vendor(s): Information Access Co.. *2798*

GLOBAL INVESTOR.
Euromoney Publications plc., Nestor House, Playhouse Yard, London EC4V 5EX, England. TEL 44-171-779-8935. FAX 44-171-779-8541.
Vendor(s): University Microfilms International. *1098*

GLOBAL PESTICIDE CAMPAIGNER.
Pesticide Action Network, North America Regional Center, 116 New Montgomery St., No. 810, San Francisco, CA 94105-3607. TEL 415-541-9140. FAX 415-541-9253. *2845*

GLOBAL POSITIONING & NAVIGATION NEWS.
Phillips Business Information, Inc., 1201 Seven Locks Rd., Potomac, MD 20854. TEL 301-424-3338. FAX 301-309-3847.
Vendor(s): Information Access Co., NewsNet (DE24). *1945*

GLOBAL PRIVATE POWER.
Financial Times Energy Publishing Maple House, 149 Tottenham Court Rd., London W1P 9LL, England. TEL 0171-896-2241. FAX 0171-896-2275.
Vendor(s): Data-Star, Knight-Ridder Information, Inc., Lexis-Nexis. *2569*

GLOBE AND MAIL REPORT ON BUSINESS.
Globe and Mail Publishing, 444 Front St. W., Toronto, ON M5V 2S9, Canada. TEL 416-585-5000. *1214*

GLYCOCONJUGATE JOURNAL.
Chapman & Hall, Journals Department 2-6 Boundary Row, London SE1 8HN, England. TEL 44-171-8650066. FAX 44-171-5229623. *639*

GOING PUBLIC - THE I P O REPORTER.
Investment Dealers' Digest, 2 World Trade Ctr., 18th Fl., New York, NY 10048. TEL 212-432-0045.
Vendor(s): Data-Star, Information Access Co., Knight-Ridder Information, Inc., University Microfilms International. *1098*

GOLDEN GATE UNIVERSITY LAW REVIEW.
Golden Gate University, School of Law, 536 Mission St., San Francisco, CA 94105. TEL 415-442-6691.
Vendor(s): West Services, Inc.. *3784*

GOLF MAGAZINE (NEW YORK).
Times Mirror Magazines, Inc., 2 Park Ave., New York, NY 10016. TEL 212-779-5000.
Vendor(s): Information Access Co.. *6504*

GOLOB'S OIL POLLUTION BULLETIN.
World Information Systems, Box 535, Harvard Sq. Sta., Cambridge, MA 02238. FAX 617-491-5100.
Vendor(s): NewsNet (EV05). *2852*

GOOD HOUSEKEEPING.
Hearst Corporation, Good Housekeeping, 959 Eighth Ave., New York, NY 10019. TEL 212-649-2200. FAX 212-265-3307.
Vendor(s): Information Access Co.. *3523*

GOVERNING.
2300 N St., N.W., Ste. 760, Washington, DC 20037. TEL 202-862-8802. FAX 202-862-0032.
Vendor(s): Lexis-Nexis, LOGIN Information Services. *5942*

GOVERNMENT COMPUTER NEWS.
Cahners Publishing Company (Silver Spring), Division of Reed Elsevier Inc., 8601 Georgia Ave., Ste. 300, Silver Spring, MD 20910. TEL 301-650-2000. FAX 301-650-2111.
Vendor(s): Information Access Co., Knight-Ridder Information, Inc.. *5935*

GOVERNMENT EMPLOYEE RELATIONS REPORT.
The Bureau of National Affairs, Inc., 1231 25th St., N.W., Washington, DC 20037. TEL 202-452-4200. FAX 202-822-8092.
Vendor(s): Human Resources Information Network (CDD, HDD), Lexis-Nexis (GOVEMP), West Services, Inc.. *1375*

GOVERNMENT EXECUTIVE.
National Journal, Inc. 1501 M St., N.W., Ste. 300, Washington, DC 20005. TEL 202-739-8400. FAX 202-833-8069.
Vendor(s): University Microfilms International. *5903*

GOVERNMENT FINANCE REVIEW.
Government Finance Officers Association, 180 N. Michigan Ave., Ste. 800, Chicago, IL 60601. TEL 312-977-9700. FAX 312-977-4806.
Vendor(s): Information Access Co.. *1546*

GOVERNMENT PRODUCT NEWS.
Penton Publishing Co. 1100 Superior Ave., Cleveland, OH 44114-2543. TEL 216-696-7000. FAX 216-696-7658.
Vendor(s): Knight-Ridder Information, Inc.. *5903*

GOVERNMENT REPORTS ANNOUNCEMENTS & INDEX.
U.S. National Technical Information Service, 5285 Port Royal Rd., Springfield, VA 22161. TEL 703-487-4630. FAX 703-321-8547.
Vendor(s): CEDOCAR, CISTI, Data-Star, European Space Agency, JICST, Knight-Ridder Information, Inc. (File no.6), Orbit Search Service (NTIS), Ovid Technologies, Inc., STN International (NTIS). *5931*

GOVERNMENT RESEARCH DIRECTORY.
Gale Research Inc., 835 Penobscot Bldg., Detroit, MI 48226. TEL 313-961-2242. FAX 313-961-6083.
Vendor(s): Knight-Ridder Information, Inc.. *6651*

GOWER FEDERAL SERVICE - MINING.
Rocky Mountain Mineral Law Foundation, Porter Administration Bldg., 7039 E. 18th Ave., Denver, CO 80220. TEL 303-321-8100. FAX 303-321-7657.
Vendor(s): West Services, Inc. (Gower Federal Service). *5064*

GOWER FEDERAL SERVICE - MISCELLANEOUS LAND DECISIONS.
Rocky Mountain Mineral Law Foundation, Porter Administration Bldg., 7039 E. 18th Ave., Denver, CO 80220. TEL 303-321-8100. FAX 303-321-7657.
Vendor(s): West Services, Inc. (Gower Federal Service). *5064*

GOWER FEDERAL SERVICE - OIL AND GAS.
Rocky Mountain Mineral Law Foundation, Porter Administration Bldg., 7039 E. 18th Ave., Denver, CO 80220. TEL 303-321-8100. FAX 303-321-7657.
Vendor(s): West Services, Inc. (Gower Federal Service). *5357*

GOWER FEDERAL SERVICE - OUTER CONTINENTAL SHELF.
Rocky Mountain Mineral Law Foundation, Porter Administration Bldg., 7039 E. 18th Ave., Denver, CO 80220. TEL 303-321-8100. FAX 303-321-7657.
Vendor(s): West Services, Inc. (Gower Federal Service). *5357*

THE GRAMOPHONE CLASSICAL CATALOGUE.
Retail Establishment Data Publishing Ltd., Paulton House, 8 Shepherdess Walk, London N1 7LR, England. TEL 0171-490-0049. FAX 0171-253-1308. *5160*

GRAND RAPIDS BUSINESS JOURNAL.
Gemini Publications, 549 Ottawa Ave. N.W., Grand Rapids, MI 49503-1444. TEL 616-459-4545. FAX 616-459-4800.
Vendor(s): Knight-Ridder Information, Inc., University Microfilms International. *1165*

GRAND TIMES.
Grand Times Publishing, Inc., 403 Village Dr., El Cerrito, CA 94530-3355. TEL 510-527-4337. *3288*

GRAPEVINE (NORMAL).
c/o Dr. Edward R. Hines, Ed., Educational Administration and Foundations Dept., Illinois State University, Campus Box 5900, Normal, IL 61761. TEL 309-438-5405. FAX 309-438-8683.
Available only online. *2430*

GRAPEVINE (RED BANK).
Reunions U S A, Box 124, Red Bank, NJ 07701. TEL 908-530-2065. *3086*

GRAPHIC ARTS MONTHLY.
Cahners Publishing Company (New York), Division of Reed Elsevier Inc., 245 W. 17th St., New York, NY 10011. TEL 212-463-6834. FAX 212-463-6530.
Vendor(s): Information Access Co., Knight-Ridder Information, Inc., Lexis-Nexis. *5812*

GRASSLANDS AND FORAGE ABSTRACTS.
CAB International, Wallingford, Oxon. OX10 8DE, England. TEL 44-1491-832111. FAX 44-1491-833508.
Vendor(s): DIMDI, European Space Agency, Knight-Ridder Information, Inc., Ovid Technologies, Inc., STN International. *173*

GREAT BRITAIN. H.M.S.O. ANNUAL CATALOGUE.
H.M.S.O. Books, 51 Nine Elms Ln., London SW8 5DT, England. TEL 071-873-8499.
Vendor(s): Knight-Ridder Information, Inc.. *532*

GREAT BRITAIN. H.M.S.O. BOOKS IN PRINT.
H.M.S.O. Books, 51 Nine Elms Ln., London SW8 5DR, England. TEL 44-171-873-0011. FAX 44-171-873-8247.
Vendor(s): Knight-Ridder Information, Inc.. *532*

GREAT BRITAIN. H.M.S.O. DAILY LIST.
H.M.S.O. Books, 51 Nine Elms Ln., London SW8 5DR, England. TEL 44-171-873-0011.
Vendor(s): Knight-Ridder Information, Inc.. *532*

GREAT BRITAIN. H.M.S.O. GOVERNMENT PUBLICATIONS SECTIONAL LISTS.
H.M.S.O. Books, 51 Nine Elms Ln., London SW8 5DT, England.
Vendor(s): Knight-Ridder Information, Inc.. *532*

GREAT BRITAIN. H.M.S.O. MONTHLY CATALOGUE.
H.M.S.O. Books, 51 Nine Elms Ln., London SW8 5DR, England. TEL 44-171-873-0011. FAX 44-171-873-8247.
Vendor(s): Knight-Ridder Information, Inc.. *532*

GREAT BRITAIN. H.M.S.O. PUBLICATIONS CATALOGUE.
H.M.S.O. Books, 51 Nine Elms Ln., London SW8 5DR, England. TEL 44-171-873-0011. FAX 44-171-873-8247.
Vendor(s): Knight-Ridder Information, Inc.. *532*

GREAT BRITAIN. H.M.S.O. STATUTORY INSTRUMENTS LIST.
H.M.S.O. Books, 51 Nine Elms Ln., London SW8 5DR, England. TEL 44-171-873-0011. FAX 44-171-873-8247.
Vendor(s): Knight-Ridder Information, Inc.. *532*

GREAT BRITAIN. NATURAL RESOURCES INSTITUTE. BULLETIN.
Natural Resources Institute, Central Ave., Chatham Maritime, Kent ME4 4TB, England. TEL 44-1634-880088. FAX 44-1634-880066. *120*

GREAT BRITIAN. H.M.S.O. COMMITTEE REPORTS INDEX.
H.M.S.O. Books, Subscriptions, 51 Nine Elms Ln., London SW8 5DR, England. TEL 071-873-8499.
Vendor(s): Knight-Ridder Information, Inc.. *532*

GREECE AND ROME.
Oxford University Press, Oxford Journals, Walton St., Oxford OX2 6DP, England. TEL 44-1865-267907. FAX 44-1865-267773.
Vendor(s): Information Access Co.. *1822*

GREEK, ROMAN AND BYZANTINE STUDIES.
Duke University, Department of Classical Studies, Box 90199, Durham, NC 27708-0199. TEL 919-684-6456.
Vendor(s): University Microfilms International. *1822*

GREEN MARKETS.
Pike & Fischer, Inc., 4600 East-West Hwy., Ste. 200, Bethesda, MD 20814. TEL 301-654-6262. FAX 301-654-6297. *120*

GRIFFITHIANA.
Cineteca del Friuli, Via Osoppo 26, 33014 Gemona, Italy. TEL 39-432-980458. FAX 39-432-970542. *5104*

GRIST ON-LINE.
Box 20805, Columbus Circle Sta., New York, NY 18023. TEL 212-787-2861. *4307*

GROCER.
William Reed Publishing Ltd., Broadfield Park, Crawley, W. Sussex RH11 9RT, England. TEL 44-1293-613400. FAX 44-1293-610340. *3005*

GROCERY MARKETING.
Trend Publishing Inc., 625 N. Michigan Ave., Ste. 2500, Chicago, IL 60611. TEL 312-222-2000. FAX 312-222-2026.
Vendor(s): Information Access Co., Lexis-Nexis. *3005*

GROUND WATER.
Ground Water Publishing Co., 2600 Ground Water Way, Columbus, OH 43219. TEL 614-337-8229.
Vendor(s): Information Access Co., University Microfilms International. *2285*

GROUND WATER MONITOR.
Business Publishers, Inc., 951 Pershing Dr., Silver Spring, MD 20910-4464. TEL 301-587-6300. FAX 301-585-9075.
Vendor(s): Data-Star (PTBN), Information Access Co., Knight-Ridder Information, Inc., NewsNet (EV18). *6969*

GROUP & ORGANIZATION MANAGEMENT.
Sage Publications, Inc., 2455 Teller Rd., Thousand Oaks, CA 91320. TEL 805-499-0721. FAX 805-499-0871.
Vendor(s): Information Access Co.. *1502*

GROWING EDGE MAGAZINE.
New Moon Publishing, Inc., 215 S.W. Second St., Box 1027, Corvallis, OR 97339-1027. TEL 507-757-0027. FAX 503-757-0028. *3054*

GROWTH AND CHANGE.
Blackwell Publishers, 238 Main St., Cambridge, MA 02141. TEL 617-547-7110. FAX 617-547-0789.
Vendor(s): Information Access Co., University Microfilms International. *1521*

GROWTH REGULATION.
Churchill Livingstone Robert Stevenson House, 1-3 Baxter's Pl., Leith Walk, Edinburgh EH1 3AF, Scotland. TEL 44-131-5562424. FAX 44-131-5351704.
Available only online. *4671*

GUARANTOR (NEW YORK).
American Banker - Bond Buyer, Newsletter Division One State St. Plaza, New York, NY 10004-1549. FAX 212-943-2224.
Vendor(s): Information Access Co.. *1098*

THE GUARDIAN (MANCHESTER).
Guardian Newspapers Ltd. 164 Deansgate, Manchester M60 2RR, England. TEL 44-161-832-7200. FAX 44-161-876-5362. *3155*

GUARDIAN WEEKLY.
Guardian Publications Ltd., 75 Farringdon Rd., London EC1M 3HQ, England. TEL 44-171-713-4400. FAX 44-171-242-0985.
Vendor(s): Lexis-Nexis. *3156*

GUIDE TO THE CANADIAN FINANCIAL SERVICES INDUSTRY.
Globe Information Services, 444 Front St. W., Toronto, ON M5V 2S9, Canada. TEL 416-585-5250. FAX 416-585-5249. *1613*

GUITAR PLAYER.
Miller Freeman Inc. (San Mateo) 411 Borel Ave., Ste. 100, San Mateo, CA 94402. TEL 415-358-9500. FAX 415-358-9216.
Vendor(s): Information Access Co.. *5161*

GUNS & AMMO.
Petersen Publishing Co., 6420 Wilshire Blvd., Los Angeles, CA 90048. TEL 213-782-2000.
Vendor(s): Knight-Ridder Information, Inc.. *6565*

GUT.
B M J Publishing Group, B.M.A. House, Tavistock Sq., London WC1H 9JR, England. TEL 44-171-387-4499. FAX 44-171-383-6661.
Vendor(s): Ovid Technologies, Inc.. *4693*

H D T V REPORT.
Phillips Business Information, Inc., 1201 Seven Locks Rd., Potomac, MD 20854. TEL 301-424-3338. FAX 301-309-3847.
Vendor(s): Information Access Co., NewsNet (PB31). *1961*

H F N.
Fairchild Publications, Fairchild Fashion & Merchandising Group 7 W. 34th St., New York, NY 10001. TEL 212-630-4000. FAX 212-630-3675.
Vendor(s): Information Access Co., Knight-Ridder Information, Inc., Lexis-Nexis. *3688*

H P PROFESSIONAL.
Cardinal Business Media, Inc., 1300 Virginia Dr., Ste. 400, Fort Washington, PA 19034-3225. TEL 215-643-3000. FAX 215-643-4827.
Vendor(s): Information Access Co.. *2087*

H R FOCUS.
American Management Association, 135 W. 50th St., New York, NY 10020. TEL 212-586-8100.
Vendor(s): Information Access Co., University Microfilms International. *1503*

H R MAGAZINE.
Society for Human Resource Management, 606 N. Washington St., Alexandria, VA 22314-1914. TEL 703-548-344C. FAX 703-836-0367.
Vendor(s): Human Resources Information Network, Information Access Co., University Microfilms International. *1503*

H T F S DIGEST.
A.E.A. Technology, Harwell Bldg. 392.7, Didcot, Oxon OX11 0RA, England. TEL 44-1235-432862. FAX 44-1235-831981.
Vendor(s): European Space Agency (File no.138/HEATFLO). *2641*

HAIR CARE PRODUCTS: THE INTERNATIONAL MARKET.
Euromonitor, 60-61 Britton St., London EC1M 5NA, England. TEL 44-171-251-8024. FAX 44-171-608-3149.
Vendor(s): Data-Star, Knight-Ridder Information, Inc.. *491*

HAMLINE LAW REVIEW.
Hamline University School of Law, Hamline Law Review, 1536 Hewitt Ave., St. Paul, MN 55104-1284. TEL 612-641-2350. FAX 612-641-2435.
Vendor(s): West Services, Inc. *3785*

HANDBOOK ON INJECTABLE DRUGS.
American Society of Health-System Pharmacists, 7272 Wisconsin Ave., Bethesda, MD 20814. TEL 301-657-3000. FAX 301-657-8817.
Vendor(s): Knight-Ridder Information, Inc. (File no.229), Ovid Technologies, Inc. (DIFT) *5415*

HANDBUCH DER GROSSUNTERNEHMEN.
Verlag Hoppenstedt GmbH, Havelstr. 9, 64295 Darmstadt, Germany. TEL 49-6151-380-0. FAX 49-6151-380-360.
Vendor(s): Data-Star, GBI, Knight-Ridder Information, Inc.. *1521*

HANDELSBLATT.
Verlagsgruppe Handelsblatt GmbH, Kasernenstr. 67, 40213 Duesseldorf, Germany. TEL 49-211-8870. FAX 49-211-329954. *1165*

HANGZHOU DAXUE XUEBAO (ZIRAN KEXUE BAN).
Hangzhou Daxue, 34 Tianmushan Lu, Hangzhou, Zhejiang 310028, People's Republic of China.
Vendor(s): Knight-Ridder Information, Inc.. *6243*

HARFORD BUSINESS LEDGER.
Harford Business Ledger, Inc., Box 40, Aberdeen, MD 21001-0075. TEL 410-893-9191. FAX 410-272-4208.
Vendor(s): University Microfilms International. *927*

HARPER'S BAZAAR.
Hearst Corp., Harper's Bazaar, 959 Eighth Ave., New York, NY 10019. TEL 212-935-5900.
Vendor(s): Information Access Co.. *1841*

HARPER'S MAGAZINE.
Harpers Magazine Foundation, 666 Broadway, New York, NY 10012-2317. TEL 212-614-6500. FAX 212-228-5889.
Vendor(s): Information Access Co., University Microfilms International. *4145*

HARVARD BUSINESS REVIEW.
Harvard Business School Publishing Corporation, 60 Harvard Way, Boston, MA 02163. TEL 617-495-6800. FAX 617-495-9933.
Vendor(s): Data-Star (HBRO), Human Resources Information Network, Knight-Ridder Information, Inc. (File no.122), Lexis-Nexis, Ovid Technologies, Inc. (HBRO). *927*

HARVARD CIVIL RIGHTS - CIVIL LIBERTIES LAW REVIEW.
Harvard University, Law School, Publications Center, Hastings Hall, Cambridge, MA 02138. TEL 617-495-3694.
Vendor(s): West Services Inc.. *3883*

HARVARD EDUCATIONAL REVIEW.
Harvard University, Graduate School of Education, Gutman Library, Ste. 349 6 Appian Way, Cambridge, MA 02138. TEL 617-495-3432.
Vendor(s): University Microfilms International. *2338*

HARVARD ENVIRONMENTAL LAW REVIEW.
Harvard University, Law School, Publications Center, Hastings Hall, Cambridge. MA 02138. TEL 617-495-3694.
Vendor(s): West Services. Inc.. *3786*

HARVARD HEALTH LETTER.
Harvard Health Publications Group, 164 Longwood Ave. Boston, MA 02115. TEL 617-432-1485. FAX 617-432-1506.
Vendor(s): Information Access Co.. *5528*

HARVARD HEART LETTER
Harvard Health Publications Group, 164 Longwood Ave., Boston, MA 02115. TEL 800-829-9171. FAX 617-432-1506.
Vendor(s): Information Access Co.. *4602*

HARVARD INTERNATIONAL LAW JOURNAL.
Harvard University, Law School, Publications Center, Hastings Hall, Cambridge MA 02138. TEL 617-495-3694.
Vendor(s): West Services, Inc.. *3931*

HARVARD JOURNAL OF LAW AND PUBLIC POLICY.
Harvard Society for Law and Public Policy, Inc., Harvard Law School, Cambridge MA 02138. TEL 617-495-3105. FAX 617-495-1110.
Vendor(s): University Microfilms International, West Services, Inc.. *3786*

HARVARD JOURNAL ON LEGISLATION.
Harvard University, Law School, Publications Center, Hastings Hall, Cambridge, MA 02138. TEL 617-495-3694.
Vendor(s): West Services Inc.. *3786*

HARVARD LAW REVIEW.
Harvard Law Review Association, Gannett House, Cambridge, MA 02138. TEL 617-495-4650.
Vendor(s): Lexis-Nexis (Lexis), West Services, Inc.. *3786*

HARVARD MENTAL HEALTH LETTER.
Harvard Health Publications Group, 164 Longwood Ave., Boston, MA 02115. FAX 617-432-1506.
Vendor(s): Information Access Co.. *4839*

HARVARD THEOLOGICAL REVIEW.
Harvard Divinity School, 45 Francis Ave., Cambridge, MA 02138. TEL 617-495-5786. FAX 617-495-9489.
Vendor(s): Information Access Co.. *6065*

HARVARD WOMEN'S HEALTH WATCH.
Harvard Health Publications Group, 164 Longwood Ave., Boston, MA 02115. FAX 617-432-1506.
Vendor(s): Information Access Co.. *6984*

HARVARD WOMEN'S LAW JOURNAL.
Harvard University, Law School (Women's Law Journal), Publications Center, Hastings Hall, Cambridge, MA 02138. TEL 617-495-3726. FAX 617-495-1110.
Vendor(s): Lexis-Nexis, West Services, Inc.. *3786*

HASTINGS CENTER REPORT.
Hastings Center, 255 Elm Rd., Briarcliff Manor, NY 10510. TEL 914-762-8500. FAX 914-762-2124. Vendor(s): Information Access Co., University Microfilms International. *4462*

HASTINGS COMMUNICATIONS AND ENTERTAINMENT LAW JOURNAL (COMM - ENT).
University of California at San Francisco, Hastings College of the Law, 200 McAllister St., San Francisco, CA 94102-4978. TEL 415-565-4731. FAX 415-565-4814. Vendor(s): West Services, Inc.. *3786*

HASTINGS CONSTITUTIONAL LAW QUARTERLY.
University of California at San Francisco, Hastings College of the Law, 200 McAllister St., San Francisco, CA 94102-4978. TEL 415-565-4726. FAX 415-565-4814. Vendor(s): West Services, Inc.. *3891*

HASTINGS INTERNATIONAL AND COMPARATIVE LAW REVIEW.
University of California at San Francisco, Hastings College of the Law, 200 McAllister St., San Francisco, CA 94102-4978. TEL 415-565-4730. FAX 415-565-4814. Vendor(s): West Services, Inc.. *3931*

HASTINGS LAW JOURNAL.
University of California at San Francisco, Hastings College of the Law, 200 McAllister St., San Francisco, CA 94102-4978. TEL 415-565-4727. FAX 415-565-4814. Vendor(s): Lexis-Nexis, West Services, Inc.. *3786*

HASTINGS WOMEN'S LAW JOURNAL.
University of California at San Francisco, Hastings College of the Law, 200 McAllister St., San Francisco, CA 94102. TEL 415-565-4870. FAX 415-464-4814. Vendor(s): West Services, Inc.. *3786*

HAWAII BUSINESS.
Hawaii Business Publishing Corp., Box 913, Honolulu, HI 96808. TEL 808-946-3978. Vendor(s): Information Access Co., Knight-Ridder Information, Inc., Lexis-Nexis, University Microfilms International. *1214*

HAWAII BUSINESS DIRECTORY.
American Business Directories 5711 S. 86th Circle, Box 27347, Omaha, NE 68127. TEL 402-593-4600. FAX 402-331-5481. *1614*

HAZARDOUS MATERIALS INTELLIGENCE REPORT.
World Information Systems, Box 535, Harvard Sq. Sta., Cambridge, MA 02238. TEL 617-491-5100. FAX 617-492-3312. Vendor(s): NewsNet. *2852*

HAZARDOUS MATERIALS TRANSPORTATION.
The Bureau of National Affairs, Inc., 1231 25th St., N.W., Washington, DC 20037. TEL 202-452-4200. FAX 202-822-8092. Vendor(s): NewsNet (EV35). *6718*

HAZARDOUS WASTE BUSINESS.
McGraw-Hill Companies, Energy & Business Newsletters, 1221 Ave. of the Americas, 36th Fl., New York, NY 10020. TEL 212-521-6410. Vendor(s): Dow Jones News Retrieval (HWB), Knight-Ridder Information, Inc. (HWB), Lexis-Nexis (HWB), NewsNet (EV41). *2852*

HAZARDOUS WASTE NEWS.
Business Publishers, Inc., 951 Pershing Dr., Silver Spring, MD 20910-4464. TEL 301-587-6300. FAX 301-585-9075. Vendor(s): Information Access Co., Knight-Ridder Information, Inc., NewsNet (CH10). *2853*

HAZMAT TRANSPORT NEWS.
Business Publishers, Inc., 951 Pershing Dr., Silver Spring, MD 20910-4464. TEL 301-587-6300. FAX 301-585-9075. Vendor(s): Information Access Co., NewsNet (CH14). *2853*

HAZNEWS.
Profitastral Ltd., Park House, 140 Battersea Park Rd., London SW11 4NB, England. TEL 44-171-498-2511. FAX 44-171-498-2343. Vendor(s): Data-Star (PTBN,PTSP), Information Access Co., Knight-Ridder Information, Inc. (File nos.636 & 16). *2853*

HEADWAY.
Richberg Communications, Inc., 13555 Bammel N. Houston, Ste. 227, Houston, TX 77066. TEL 713-444-4265. FAX 713-583-9534. Vendor(s): NewsNet (PO05). *5671*

HEALTH (SAN FRANCISCO).
Health Publishing Group 301 Howard St., 18th Fl., San Francisco, CA 94105. TEL 415-512-9100. Vendor(s): Information Access Co., University Microfilms International. *5528*

HEALTH AFFAIRS.
Project Hope, 7500 Old Georgetown Rd., No. 600, Bethesda, MD 20814-6133. TEL 301-656-7401. FAX 301-654-2845. Vendor(s): University Microfilms International. *5961*

HEALTH ALLIANCE ALERT.
Faulkner & Gray, Healthcare Information Center 1133 15th St., N.W., Ste. 450, Washington, DC 20005. TEL 202-828-4148. Vendor(s): Information Access Co., Knight-Ridder Information, Inc., NewsNet (HH23). *4462*

HEALTH AND SAFETY SCIENCE ABSTRACTS.
Cambridge Scientific Abstracts, 7200 Wisconsin Ave., 6th Fl., Bethesda, MD 20814. TEL 301-961-6750. FAX 301-961-6720. Vendor(s): Orbit Search Service (ORBIT). *5982*

HEALTH & SOCIAL WORK.
N A S W Press, 750 First St., N.E., Ste. 700, Washington, DC 20002-4241. TEL 202-408-8600. FAX 202-336-8312. Vendor(s): Information Access Co., University Microfilms International. *6375*

HEALTH CARE FINANCING REVIEW.
Health Care Financing Administration, Office of Research and Demonstrations, 7500 Security Blvd., C-3-11-07, Baltimore, MD 21244-1850. TEL 410-786-6577. FAX 410-786-5768. Vendor(s): Information Access Co., University Microfilms International. *4463*

HEALTH CARE MANAGEMENT REVIEW.
Aspen Publishers, Inc., 200 Orchard Ridge Dr., Gaithersburg, MD 20878. FAX 301-417-7550. Vendor(s): Information Access Co., University Microfilms International. *3545*

HEALTH CARE STRATEGIC MANAGEMENT.
Business Word Inc., 5350 S. Roslyn St., Ste. 400, Englewood, CO 80111-2145. TEL 303-290-8500. FAX 303-290-9025. Vendor(s): University Microfilms International. *3545*

HEALTH CARE SUPERVISOR.
Aspen Publishers, Inc., 200 Orchard Ridge Dr., Gaithersburg, MD 20878. FAX 301-417-7550. Vendor(s): University Microfilms International. *4714*

HEALTH DEVICES ALERTS.
E C R I, 5200 Butler Pike, Plymouth Meeting, PA 19462. TEL 610-825-6000. FAX 610-834-1275. Vendor(s): Knight-Ridder Information, Inc. (File no.198). *4565*

HEALTH DEVICES SOURCEBOOK.
E C R I, 5200 Butler Pike, Plymouth Meeting, PA 19462. TEL 610-825-6000. FAX 610-834-1275. Vendor(s): Knight-Ridder Information, Inc. (File no.188). *4463*

HEALTH GRANTS & CONTRACTS WEEKLY.
Capitol Publications Inc., 1101 King St., Ste. 444, Alexandria, VA 22314. TEL 703-683-4100. FAX 703-739-6501. Vendor(s): NewsNet (HH10). *5905*

HEALTH INDEX.
Information Access Company 362 Lakeside Dr., Foster City, CA 94404. TEL 415-378-5200. FAX 415-378-5369. Vendor(s): Data-Star (HLTH), Knight-Ridder Information, Inc. (File no.149), Ovid Technologies, Inc. (HEAL). *4565*

HEALTH INDUSTRY TODAY.
Business Word Inc., 5350 S. Roslyn St., Ste. 400, Englewood, CO 80111-2145. TEL 303-290-8500. FAX 303-290-9025. Vendor(s): Information Access Co., University Microfilms International. *4463*

HEALTH LEGISLATION.
Faulkner & Gray, Healthcare Information Center 1133 15th St., N.W., Ste. 450, Washington, DC 20005. TEL 202-828-4148. Vendor(s): Information Access Co., NewsNet (HH22). *4464*

HEALTH MANAGEMENT TECHNOLOGY.
Intertec Publishing Corp. (Atlanta), 6151 Powers Ferry Rd., N.W., Atlanta, GA 30339-2491. TEL 770-955-2500. FAX 770-955-0400. Vendor(s): Information Access Co., Knight-Ridder Information, Inc., University Microfilms International. *4631*

HEALTH MATRIX: JOURNAL OF LAW-MEDICINE.
Case Western Reserve University, School of Law, 11075 East Blvd., Cleveland, OH 44106-7148. TEL 216-368-3304. FAX 216-368-3310. Vendor(s): Lexis-Nexis. *3787*

HEALTH NEWS DAILY.
F-D-C Reports, Inc., 5550 Friendship Blvd., Ste. One, Chevy Chase, MD 20815. FAX 301-664-7238. Vendor(s): Data-Star (HNDO), Knight-Ridder Information, Inc. (File no.43), NewsNet (HH01). *4464*

HEALTH POLICY & BIOMEDICAL RESEARCH: THE BLUE SHEET.
F-D-C Reports, Inc., 5550 Friendship Blvd., Ste. One, Chevy Chase, MD 20815. FAX 301-664-7238. Vendor(s): Data-Star (FDCR), Knight-Ridder Information, Inc. (File no.187), Lexis-Nexis, Ovid Technologies, Inc. (FDCR). *4464*

HEALTH PROGRESS.
Catholic Health Association of the United States, 4455 Woodson Rd., St. Louis, MO 63134-3797. TEL 314-427-2500. FAX 314-427-0029. *3545*

HEALTH SCIENCES SERIALS.
U.S. National Library of Medicine, 8600 Rockville Pike, Bethesda, MD 20894. Vendor(s): National Library of Medicine. *4565*

HEALTH SERVICE ABSTRACTS.
Department of Health, Library and Information Services, Rm. 5C07, Quarry House, Quarry Hill, Leeds LS2 7UE, England. TEL 0113-254-5072. FAX 0113-254-5084. Vendor(s): Data-Star. *4565*

HEALTH SERVICES RESEARCH.
Health Administration Press, 1 North Franklin St., Ste. 1700, Chicago, IL 60606. TEL 312-424-2800. FAX 312-424-0014. Vendor(s): Information Access Co., University Microfilms International. *3545*

HEALTH, SLIMMING AND DIETETIC FOODS: THE INTERNATIONAL MARKET.
Euromonitor, 60-61 Britton St., London EC1M 5NA, England. TEL 44-171-251-8024. FAX 44-171-608-3149. Vendor(s): Data-Star, Knight-Ridder Information, Inc.. *2975*

HEALTH SYSTEMS REVIEW.
F A H S Review, Inc., 1405 N. Pierce St., Ste. 308, Little Rock, AR 72207. TEL 501-661-9555. FAX 501-663-4903. Vendor(s): University Microfilms International. *3546*

HEALTH WHICH?
Which? Ltd., 2 Marylebone Rd., London NW1 4DF, England. TEL 44-171-830-6000. FAX 44-171-830-7664. *5529*

HEALTHCARE EXECUTIVE.
American College of Healthcare Executives, One N. Franklin St., Ste. 1700, Chicago, IL 60606-3491. TEL 312-424-3800. FAX 312-424-0023. Vendor(s): University Microfilms International. *3546*

HEALTHCARE FINANCIAL MANAGEMENT.
Healthcare Financial Management Association, Two Westbrook Corporate Center, Ste. 700, Westchester, IL 60154. TEL 708-531-9600. FAX 708-531-0032. Vendor(s): Information Access Co., Knight-Ridder Information, Inc., University Microfilms International. *3546*

HEALTHCARE FORUM JOURNAL.
Healthcare Forum, 425 Market St., San Francisco, CA 94105. TEL 415-436-4300.
Vendor(s): University Microfilms International. *3546*

HEALTHCARE P R & MARKETING NEWS.
Phillips Business Information, Inc., 1201 Seven Locks Rd., Potomac, MD 20854. TEL 301-424-3338. FAX 301-309-3847.
Vendor(s): Information Access Co.. *4465*

HEALTHCARE SYSTEMS STRATEGY REPORT.
Capitol Publications Inc., 1101 King St., Ste. 444, Alexandria, VA 22314. TEL 703-683-4100. FAX 703-739-6501.
Vendor(s): Information Access Co., NewsNet (HH11). *3546*

HEALTHCARE TECHNOLOGY & BUSINESS OPPORTUNITIES.
Biomedical Business International 2 Park Plz, Ste. 900, Irvine, CA 92714-8519. TEL 714-755-5757. FAX 714-755-5724.
Vendor(s): Information Access Co., Knight-Ridder Information, Inc.. *4465*

HEALTHFACTS.
Center for Medical Consumers, 237 Thompson St., New York, NY 10012. TEL 212-674-7105. FAX 212-674-7100.
Vendor(s): Information Access Co.. *4465*

HEALTHSPAN.
Prentice Hall Law & Business, Inc., 270 Sylvan Ave., Englewood Cliffs, NJ 07632. TEL 800-223-0231. *1421*

HEART.
B M J Publishing Group, B.M.A. House, Tavistock Sq., London WC1H 9JR, England. TEL 0171-383-6270. FAX 0171-383-6402.
Vendor(s): Ovid Technologies, Inc.. *4602*

HEART & LUNG.
Mosby - Year Book, Inc. 11830 Westline Industrial Dr., St. Louis, MO 63146-3318. TEL 314-872-8370. FAX 314-432-1380.
Vendor(s): Ovid Technologies, Inc.. *4714*

HEAT ENGINEERING.
Foster Wheeler Corp., Perryville Corporate Park, Clinton, NJ 08809-4000. TEL 908-730-4000. FAX 908-730-5315. *2600*

HEATING - PIPING - AIR CONDITIONING.
Penton Publishing Co. 1100 Superior Ave., Cleveland, OH 44114-2543. TEL 216-969-7000. FAX 216-696-8765.
Vendor(s): Information Access Co.. *3328*

L'HEBDO.
Pont Bessieres 3, CH-1005 Lausanne, Switzerland. TEL 41-21-3203611. FAX 41-21-3203617. *3219*

HECATE.
Hecate Press, c/o English Dept., Univ. of Queensland, St. Lucia, Qld. 4067, Australia. TEL 61-7-365-3146. FAX 61-7-365-2799.
Vendor(s): Information Access Co., University Microfilms International. *7017*

HELICOPTER NEWS.
Phillips Business Information, Inc., 1201 Seven Locks Rd., Potomac, MD 20854. TEL 301-424-3338. FAX 301-309-3847.
Vendor(s): Data-Star, Information Access Co., Knight-Ridder Information, Inc., NewsNet (AE12). *66*

HELLER REPORT ON EDUCATION TECHNOLOGY AND TELECOMMUNICATIONS MARKETS.
Nelson B. Heller & Associates, 1910 1st St. Ste 303, Highland Park, IL 60035-3146. TEL 847-441-2920. FAX 847-926-0202.
Vendor(s): NewsNet (ED11). *1467*

HELMINTHOLOGICAL ABSTRACTS.
CAB International, Wallingford, Oxon. OX10 8DE, England. TEL 44-1491-832111. FAX 44-1491-833508.
Vendor(s): CISTI, DIMDI, European Space Agency (File nos.16 & 124/CAB), Knight-Ridder Information, Inc., Ovid Technologies, Inc. (VETR). *174*

HEMATOLOGY AND CELL THERAPY.
Springer-Verlag France, 26, rue des Carmes, 75005 Paris. TEL 331-44-41-15-80. FAX 33-1-43544908. *4701*

THE HEMINGWAY REVIEW.
University of Idaho Press, c/o Susan F. Beegel, Ed., 180 Polpis Rd., Nantucket, MA 02554. TEL 508-325-7157.
Vendor(s): Information Access Co.. *4217*

THE HENRY JAMES REVIEW.
Johns Hopkins University Press, Journals Publishing Division, 2715 N. Charles St., Baltimore, MD 21218. TEL 410-516-6987. FAX 410-516-6968. *4217*

HERALD.
Montgomery County Genealogical & Historical Society, Inc., Box 867, Conroe, TX 77305-0867. TEL 409-756-8625
Vendor(s): University Microfilms International. *3087*

HERALD EXPRESS.
Herald Express Publications Ltd., Barton Hill Rd., Torquay, Devon TQ2 8JN, England. TEL 44-1803-676000. FAX 44-1803-676299. *3156*

HERALDO DE SAN LUIS POTOSI.
Villerias 305, 78000 San Luis Potosi, Mexico. TEL 48-12-33-12. FAX 48-12-20-81. *3192*

HERBA POLONICA.
Instytut Roslin i Przetworow Zielarskich, Libelta 27, 61-707 Poznan, Poland. TEL 48-61-525616. FAX 48-61-527463. *684*

HERITAGE (AUSTIN).
Texas Historical Foundation, Box 50314, Austin, TX 78763. TEL 512-453-2154. FAX 512-451-3323. *3470*

HERITAGE (CARSON).
Heritage Publishers 20218 Tajauta Ave., Carson, CA 90746-2566. FAX 310-763-8296. *2881*

HERITAGE FOUNDATION. ISSUE BULLETINS.
Heritage Foundation, 214 Massachusetts Ave., N.E., Washington, DC 20002. TEL 202-546-4400. FAX 202-543-9647.
Vendor(s): Lexis-Nexis. *5671*

HERITAGE LECTURES.
Heritage Foundation, 214 Massachusetts Ave., N.E., Washington, DC 20002. TEL 202-546-4400. FAX 202-543-9647.
Vendor(s): Lexis-Nexis. *5905*

HERMENAUT.
Shapely Mind Press, 3010 Hennepin Ave. S., No. 165, Minneapolis, MN 55408. *5477*

HESSISCHE BIBLIOGRAPHIE.
K.G. Saur Verlag KG, A member of the Reed Elsevier plc group, Ortlerstr. 8, 81373 Munich, Germany. TEL 49-89-76902-0. FAX 49-89-76902150. *533*

HEWLETT-PACKARD JOURNAL.
Hewlett Packard Co. (Palo Alto), 3000 Hanover St., Palo Alto, CA 94304. TEL 415-857-2387. FAX 415-857-2157.
Vendor(s): Information Access Co., Knight-Ridder Information, Inc.. *2087*

HIGH PERFORMANCE PLASTICS.
Elsevier Science Ltd., P.O. Box 800, Kidlington, Oxford OX5 1DX, England. TEL 44-1865-843000. FAX 44-1865-843010.
Vendor(s): Data-Star, Information Access Co., Knight-Ridder Information, Inc.. *5620*

HIGH PERFORMANCE POLYMERS.
I O P Publishing Ltd., Techno House, Redcliffe Way, Bristol, Avon BS1 6NX, England. TEL 44-117-929-7481. FAX 44-117-929-4318. *1738*

HIGH PERFORMANCE TEXTILES.
Elsevier Science Ltd., P.O. Box 800, Kidlington, Oxford OX5 1DX, England. TEL 44-1865-843000. FAX 44-1865-843010.
Vendor(s): Information Access Co., Knight-Ridder Information, Inc.. *6677*

HIGH - TC UPDATE.
Iowa State University, Ames Laboratory, A219 Physics, Ames, IA 50011-3020. TEL 515-294-3877. FAX 515-294-1134. *5549*

HIGH TECH CERAMICS NEWS.
Business Communications Co., Inc. (Norwalk), 25 Van Zant St., Ste. 13, Norwalk, CT 06855. TEL 203-853-4266. FAX 203-853-0348.
Vendor(s): Data-Star, Information Access Co., Knight-Ridder Information Inc., NewsNet (ML05). *1657*

HIGH TECH SEPARATIONS NEWS.
Business Communications Co., Inc. (Norwalk), 25 Van Zant St., Ste. 13, Norwalk, CT 06855. TEL 203-853-4266. FAX 203-853-0348.
Vendor(s): Data-Star, Information Access Co., Knight-Ridder Information, Inc., NewsNet (BT04). *1716*

HIGH TECHNOLOGY CAREERS.
High Technology Careers 4701 Patrick Henry Dr., Ste. 1901, Santa Clara, CA 95054. TEL 408-970-8800. FAX 408-980-5103. *5257*

HIGH YIELD REPORT.
American Banker - Bond Buyer, Newsletter Division One State St. Plaza, New York, NY 10004-1549. TEL 800-733-4371. FAX 212-943-2224.
Vendor(s): Information Access Co., Knight-Ridder Information, Inc., Lexis-Nexis, NewsNet. *1099*

HIGHWAY SAFETY - ANNUAL REPORT.
U.S. Federal Highway Administration, Office of Highway Information Management, Department of Transportation, 400 Seventh St. S.W., Washington, DC 20590. TEL 202-366-0180. FAX 202-366-7742. *6740*

HIGHWAY SAFETY PERFORMANCE. FATAL AND INJURY ACCIDENT RATES ON PUBLIC ROADS IN THE UNITED STATES.
U.S. Federal Highway Administration, Office of Highway Information Management, Department of Transportation, 400 Seventh St. S.W., Washington, DC 20590. TEL 202-366-0180. FAX 202-366-7742. *6740*

HILVERSUMMARY.
Nederlandse Omroep Stichting, Postbus 26444, 1202 JJ Hilversum, Netherlands. TEL 31-35-6773197. FAX 31-35-6773585. *1936*

HIPPOCRATES.
Heath Publishing Group 301 Howard St., 18th Fl., San Francisco, CA 94105-2252. TEL 415-512-9100. *4466*

HISPANIC.
Hispanic Publishing Corp., 98 San Jacinto Blvd., Ste. 1150, Austin, TX 78701-4039.
Vendor(s): Information Access Co.. *2882*

HISPANIC AMERICAN PERIODICALS INDEX.
Latin American Studies Center Publications, University of California, Los Angeles, Box 951447, 10347 Bunche Hall, Los Angeles, CA 90095-1447. TEL 310-825-0810. FAX 310-206-2634. *3366*

HISPANIC REVIEW.
University of Pennsylvania, Romance Languages Department, Philadelphia, PA 19104-6305. TEL 215-898-7420. FAX 215-898-0933.
Vendor(s): University Microfilms International. *4073*

THE HISTOCHEMICAL JOURNAL.
Chapman & Hall, Journals Department 2-6 Boundary Row, London SE1 8HN, England. TEL 44-171-8650066. FAX 44-171-5229623. *715*

THE HISTORIAN (EAST LANSING).
Michigan State University Press, Manly Miles Bldg., Ste. 25, 1405 S. Harrison Rd., East Lansing, MI 48823-5202. TEL 517-432-9543. FAX 517-336-2611.
Vendor(s): Information Access Co., University Microfilms International *3345*

HISTORICAL ABSTRACTS. PART A: MODERN HISTORY ABSTRACTS, 1450-1914.
A B C-Clio, 130 Cremona, Box 1911, Santa Barbara, CA 93116-1911. TEL 805-968-1911. FAX 805-685-9685.
Vendor(s): Knight-Ridder Information, Inc. (File no.39). *3366*

HISTORICAL ABSTRACTS. PART B: TWENTIETH CENTURY ABSTRACTS, 1914 TO THE PRESENT.
A B C-Clio, 130 Cremona, Box 1911, Santa Barbara, CA 93116-1911. TEL 805-968-1911. FAX 805-685-9685.
Vendor(s): Knight-Ridder Information, Inc. (File no.39). *3366*

HISTORICAL ABSTRACTS. PART B: TWENTIETH CENTURY ABSTRACTS, 1914 TO THE PRESENT. ANNUAL INDEX.
A B C-Clio, 130 Cremona, Box 1911, Santa Barbara, CA 93116-1911. TEL 805-968-1911. FAX 805-685-9685.
Vendor(s): Knight-Ridder Information, Inc. (File no.39). *3367*

HISTORICAL JOURNAL OF FILM, RADIO AND TELEVISION.
Carfax Publishing Co., P.O. Box 25, Abingdon, Oxon. OX14 3UE, England. TEL 44-1235-401000. FAX 44-1235-401550.
Vendor(s): Information Access Co.. *3345*

HISTORY AND THEORY.
Blackwell Publishers, 238 Main St., Cambridge, MA 02142. TEL 617-547-7110. FAX 617-547-0789.
Vendor(s): Information Access Co., University Microfilms International. *3346*

HISTORY TODAY.
History Today Ltd., 20 Old Compton St., London W1V 5PE, England. TEL 44-171-439-8315.
Vendor(s): Information Access Co., University Microfilms International. *3347*

HOCKEY PLAYER MAGAZINE.
Hockey Player Magazine L.P., Box 312, Okemos, MI 48805-0312. *6463*

HOFSTRA LABOR LAW JOURNAL.
Hofstra School of Law, Hempstead, NY 11550. TEL 516-463-5006. FAX 516-565-0074.
Vendor(s): West Services, Inc.. *3788*

HOFSTRA LAW REVIEW.
Hofstra University, Hofstra Law Review, Hempstead, NY 11550. TEL 516-463-5910. FAX 516-463-5092.
Vendor(s): Lexis-Nexis, West Services, Inc.. *3788*

HOLLAND EXPORTS.
A B C voor Handel en Industrie C.V., P.O. Box 190, 2000 AD Haarlem, Netherlands. TEL 31-23-5319031. FAX 31-23-5327033.
Vendor(s): Data-Star. *1278*

HOLLYWOOD REPORTER.
Hollywood Reporter, 5055 Wilshire Blvd., Los Angeles, CA 90036-4396. TEL 213-525-2000. FAX 213-525-2372.
Vendor(s): Information Access Co., Lexis-Nexis. *5104*

HOME FASHIONS MAGAZINE.
Fairchild Fashion & Merchandising Group 7 W. 34th St., New York, NY 10001. TEL 212-630-4199. FAX 212-630-4201.
Vendor(s): Information Access Co.. *3688*

HOME MECHANIX.
Times Mirror Magazines, Inc., 2 Park Ave., New York, NY 10016-5601. TEL 212-779-5000. FAX 212-779-5468.
Vendor(s): Information Access Co., University Microfilms International. *3603*

HOME OFFICE COMPUTING.
Scholastic Inc., 555 Broadway, New York, NY 10012-3999. TEL 212-505-3000.
Vendor(s): Information Access Co., University Microfilms International. *2095*

HONGKONGIANA.
Hong Kong Polytechnic Library, Hung Hom, Kowloon, Hong Kong. TEL 852-7666857. FAX 852-7658274.
Available only online. *14*

HOOSIER BANKER.
Indiana Bankers Association, One N. Capitol, Ste. 315, Indianapolis, IN 46204. TEL 317-236-0750. FAX 317-236-0754.
Vendor(s): University Microfilms International. *1099*

HOOVER'S DIRECTORY OF HUMAN RESOURCES EXECUTIVES.
Reference Press, Inc., Box 140375, Austin, TX 78714-0375. TEL 512-454-7778. FAX 512-454-9401. *1615*

HOOVER'S GUIDE TO COMPUTER COMPANIES.
Reference Press, Inc., Box 140375, Austin, TX 78714-0375. TEL 512-454-7778. FAX 512-454-9401. *2034*

HOOVER'S GUIDE TO PRIVATE COMPANIES.
Reference Press, Inc., Box 140375, Austin, TX 78714-0375. TEL 512-454-7778. FAX 512-454-9401. *1615*

HOOVER'S GUIDE TO THE BOOK BUSINESS.
Reference Press, Inc., Box 140375, Austin, TX 78714-0375. TEL 512-454-7778. FAX 512-454-9401. *1615*

HOOVER'S GUIDE TO THE TOP CHICAGO COMPANIES.
Reference Press, Inc., Box 140375, Austin, TX 78714-0375. TEL 512-454-7778. FAX 512-454-9401. *1615*

HOOVER'S GUIDE TO THE TOP NEW YORK COMPANIES.
Reference Press, Inc., Box 140375, Austin, TX 78714-0375. TEL 512-454-7778. FAX 512-454-9401. *1615*

HOOVER'S GUIDE TO THE TOP SOUTHERN CALIFORNIA COMPANIES.
Reference Press, Inc., Box 140375, Austin, TX 78714-0375. TEL 512-454-7778. FAX 512-454-9401. *1615*

HOOVER'S GUIDE TO THE TOP TEXAS COMPANIES.
Reference Press, Inc., Box 140375, Austin, TX 78714-0375. TEL 512-454-7778. FAX 512-454-9401. *1615*

HOOVER'S HANDBOOK OF AMERICAN BUSINESS.
Reference Press Inc., Box 140375, Austin, TX 78714-0375. TEL 512-454-7778. FAX 512-454-9401. *1615*

HOOVER'S HANDBOOK OF EMERGING COMPANIES.
Reference Press, Inc., Box 140375, Austin, TX 78714-0375. TEL 512-454-7778. FAX 512-454-9401. *1615*

HOOVER'S HANDBOOK OF WORLD BUSINESS.
Reference Press Inc., Box 140375, Austin, TX 78714-0375. TEL 512-454-7778. FAX 512-454-9401. *1615*

HOOVER'S MASTERLIST OF MAJOR LATIN AMERICAN COMPANIES.
Reference Press, Inc., Box 140375, Austin, TX 78714-0375. TEL 512-454-7778. *1615*

HOOVER'S MASTERLIST OF MAJOR U S COMPANIES (YEAR).
Reference Press, Inc., Box 140375, Austin, TX 78714-0375. TEL 512-454-7778. FAX 512-454-9401. *1615*

HORN BOOK MAGAZINE.
Horn Book, Inc., 11 Beacon St., Ste. 1000, Boston, MA 02108-3017. TEL 617-227-1555. FAX 617-523-0299.
Vendor(s): Information Access Co.. *5998*

HORTICULTURAL ABSTRACTS.
CAB International, Wallingford, Oxon. OX10 8DE, England. TEL 44-1491-832111. FAX 44-1491-833508.
Vendor(s): DIMDI, European Space Agency, Knight-Ridder Information, Inc., STN International. *3070*

HORTICULTURE.
Horticulture Inc., 98 N. Washington St., Boston, MA 02114-1913. TEL 617-742-5600. FAX 617-367-6364.
Vendor(s): Information Access Co., University Microfilms International. *3056*

HOSPITAL ADMITTING MONTHLY.
American Health Consultants, Inc., 3525 Piedmont Rd., N.E., Bldg. 6, Ste. 400, Atlanta, GA 30305. TEL 404-262-7436. FAX 800-284-3291.
Vendor(s): Lexis-Nexis. *3547*

HOSPITAL & HEALTH SERVICES ADMINISTRATION.
Health Administration Press, 1 North Franklin St., Ste. 1700, Chicago, IL 60606. TEL 312-424-2800. FAX 312-424-0014.
Vendor(s): Information Access Co., University Microfilms International. *3547*

HOSPITAL EMPLOYEE HEALTH.
American Health Consultants, Inc., 3525 Piedmont Rd., N.E., Bldg. 6, Ste. 400, Atlanta, GA 30305. TEL 404-262-7436.
Vendor(s): Lexis-Nexis. *3548*

HOSPITAL INFECTION CONTROL.
American Health Consultants, Inc., 3525 Piedmont Rd., N.E., Bldg. 6, Ste. 400, Atlanta, GA 30305. TEL 404-262-7436. FAX 800-284-3291.
Vendor(s): Lexis-Nexis. *3548*

HOSPITAL LITERATURE INDEX.
American Hospital Association, One North Franklin, Chicago, IL 60606. TEL 312-422-2000. FAX 312-422-4700.
Vendor(s): DIMDI, National Library of Medicine. *3557*

HOSPITAL MATERIALS MANAGEMENT.
Business Word Inc., 5350 S. Roslyn St., Ste. 400, Englewood, CO 80111-2145. TEL 303-290-8500. FAX 303-290-9025.
Vendor(s): Information Access Co., University Microfilms International. *3549*

HOSPITAL MATERIEL MANAGEMENT QUARTERLY.
Aspen Publishers, Inc., 200 Orchard Ridge Dr., Gaithersburg, MD 20878. FAX 301-417-7550.
Vendor(s): University Microfilms International. *3549*

HOSPITAL PAYMENT AND INFORMATION MANAGEMENT.
American Health Consultants, Inc., 3525 Piedmont Rd., N.E., Bldg. 6, Ste. 400, Atlanta, GA 30305. TEL 404-262-7436. FAX 800-284-3291.
Vendor(s): Lexis-Nexis, NewsNet. *3549*

HOSPITAL PEER REVIEW.
American Health Consultants, Inc., 3525 Piedmont Rd., N.E., Bldg. 6, Ste. 400, Atlanta, GA 30305. TEL 404-262-7436. FAX 800-284-3291.
Vendor(s): Lexis-Nexis. *3549*

HOSPITAL PRACTICE.
McGraw-Hill Companies (Minneapolis), 4530 W. 77th St., Minneapolis, MN 55434. TEL 612-835-3222. FAX 612-835-3460. *4467*

HOSPITAL RISK CONTROL.
E C R I, 5200 Butler Pike, Plymouth Meeting, PA 19462. TEL 610-825-6000. FAX 610-834-1275. *3549*

HOSPITAL RISK MANAGEMENT.
American Health Consultants, Inc., 3525 Piedmont Rd., N.E., Bldg. 6, Ste. 400, Atlanta, GA 30305. TEL 404-262-7436. FAX 800-284-3291.
Vendor(s): Lexis-Nexis. *3549*

HOSPITAL TOPICS.
Heldref Publications, 1319 Eighteenth St., N.W., Washington, DC 20036. TEL 202-296-6267. FAX 202-296-5149. *3549*

HOSPITALIS.
Hospitalis Verlag AG, Hermetschloostr. 75, Postfach 1632, CH-8048 Zurich, Switzerland. TEL 41-1-4330080. FAX 41-1-4330242.
Vendor(s): Knight-Ridder Information, Inc.. *3550*

HOSPITALITY DESIGN.
Bill Communications, Inc., 355 Park Ave. S., 3rd Fl., New York, NY 10010-1706. TEL 212-592-6200.
Vendor(s): Information Access Co.. *3678*

HOSPITALS AND HEALTH NETWORKS.
American Hospital Publishing, Inc. 737 N. Michigan Ave., Ste. 700, Chicago, IL 60611. TEL 312-440-6800. FAX 312-951-8491.
Vendor(s): Information Access Co., Knight-Ridder Information, Inc., Lexis-Nexis, University Microfilms International. *3550*

HOT ROD.
Petersen Publishing Co., 6420 Wilshire Blvd., Los Angeles, CA 90048. TEL 213-782-2000. FAX 213-782-2865.
Vendor(s): Information Access Co., Knight-Ridder Information, Inc.. *6788*

HOTEL AND MOTEL MANAGEMENT.
Advanstar Communications, Inc., 7500 Old Oak Blvd., Cleveland, OH 44130. TEL 216-826-2839. FAX 216-891-2675.
Vendor(s): Information Access Co., Knight-Ridder Information, Inc. *3563*

HOTLINE (FALLS CHURCH).
American Political Network, Inc., 3129 Mount Vernon Ave., Alexandria, VA 22305-2640. TEL 703-237-5130.
Vendor(s): NewsNet (PO01). *5671*

HOTWIRED.
Wired Ventures Ltd., 520 Third St., 4th Fl., San Francisco, CA 94107. TEL 415-222-6200. FAX 415-222-6369.
Available only online. *1991*

HOUSE BEAUTIFUL.
Hearst Magazines, House Beautiful, 1700 Broadway, New York, NY 10019-5970. TEL 212-903-5000. FAX 212-765-8292.
Vendor(s): Information Access Co.. *3678*

HOUSEHOLD CLEANING AGENTS: THE INTERNATIONAL MARKET.
Euromonitor, 60-61 Britton St., London EC1M 5QU, England. TEL 44-171-251-8024. FAX 44-171-608-3149.
Vendor(s): Data-Star, Knight-Ridder Information, Inc.. *1828*

HOUSEWARES.
Miller Freeman Publishers Ltd. Sovereign Way, Tonbridge, Kent TN9 1RW, England. TEL 44-1732-364422. FAX 44-1732-361534.
Vendor(s): Information Access Co.. *3689*

HOUSEWARES: THE INTERNATIONAL MARKET.
Euromonitor, 60-61 Britton St., London EC1M 5NA, England. TEL 44-171-251-8024. FAX 44-171-608-3146.
Vendor(s): Data-Star, Knight-Ridder Information, Inc.. *3689*

HOUSTON BUSINESS JOURNAL.
American City Business Journals, Inc. (Houston), One West Loop S., Ste. 650, Houston, TX 77027. TEL 713-688-8811. FAX 713-963-0482.
Vendor(s): Knight-Ridder Information, Inc., Lexis-Nexis. *1215*

HOUSTON JOURNAL OF INTERNATIONAL LAW.
University of Houston, Law Center, 4800 Calhoun Rd., BLB, Ste. 29, Houston, TX 77004-6370. TEL 713-749-3774.
Vendor(s): West Services, Inc.. *3788*

HOUSTON LAW REVIEW.
Houston Law Review Inc., University of Houston Law Center-University Park, Houston, TX 77004. TEL 713-749-3195. FAX 713-749-4661.
Vendor(s): West Services, Inc.. *3788*

HOUSTON POST INDEX.
U M I Company 300 N. Zeeb Rd., Ann Arbor, MI 48106-1346. TEL 313-761-4700. FAX 800-864-0019.
Vendor(s): Knight-Ridder Information, Inc.. *3715*

HOWARD LAW JOURNAL.
Howard University, School of Law, 2900 Van Ness St., N.W., Washington, DC 20008. TEL 202-806-8084. FAX 202-806-8098.
Vendor(s): Lexis-Nexis, West Services, Inc.. *3788*

HUADONG LIGONG DAXUE XUEBAO.
Huadong Ligong Daxue, Xuebao Bianjibu, 130 Meilong Rd., Shanghai 200237, People's Republic of China. TEL 4756027. FAX 86-21-6477-5678.
Vendor(s): Knight-Ridder Information, Inc.. *2641*

HUMAN BIOLOGY (DETROIT).
Wayne State University Press, 4809 Woodward Ave., Detroit, MI 48201-1309. TEL 313-577-6120. FAX 313-577-6131.
Vendor(s): Information Access Co., University Microfilms International. *585*

HUMAN ECOLOGY (NEW YORK).
Plenum Publishing Corp., 233 Spring St., New York, NY 10013-1578. TEL 212-620-8000. FAX 212-463-0742.
Vendor(s): Information Access Co.. *311*

HUMAN ECOLOGY FORUM.
New York State College of Human Ecology, 1150 Comstock Hall, Cornell University, Ithaca, NY 14850-0998.
Vendor(s): Information Access Co.. *6326*

HUMAN FACTORS.
Human Factors and Ergonomics Society, Box 1369, Santa Monica, CA 90406-1369. TEL 310-394-1811. FAX 310-394-2410.
Vendor(s): Information Access Co.. *2601*

HUMAN GENOME PROGRAM REPORT.
U.S. Department of Energy, Human Genome Program, Office of Health and Environmental Research, ER-72 GTN, Washington, DC 20585. TEL 301-903-6488. FAX 301-903-5051. *744*

HUMAN LIFE REVIEW.
Human Life Foundation, Inc., 150 E. 35th St., New York, NY 10016. TEL 212-685-5210. FAX 212-725-9793.
Vendor(s): Information Access Co.. *6415*

HUMAN MOLECULAR GENETICS.
Oxford University Press, Oxford Journals, Walton St., Oxford OX2 6DP, England. TEL 44-1865-267907. FAX 44-1865-267435. *744*

HUMAN RELATIONS.
Plenum Publishing Corp., 233 Spring St., New York, NY 10013-1578. TEL 212-260-8000. FAX 212-463-0742.
Vendor(s): Information Access Co., University Microfilms International. *6326*

HUMAN RESOURCE EXECUTIVE.
Axon Group, 747 Dresher Rd., Ste. 500, Box 980, Horsham, PA 19044. TEL 215-784-0860. FAX 215-784-0870
Vendor(s): Human Resources Information Network. *1503*

HUMAN RESOURCE PLANNING.
Human Resource Planning Society, 41 E. 42nd St., Ste. 1509, New York, NY 10017-5200. TEL 212-490-6387. FAX 212-682-6851.
Vendor(s): Information Access Co., University Microfilms International. *1504*

HUMAN RIGHTS.
American Bar Association, Individual Rights and Responsibilities Section, 750 N. Lake Shore Dr., Chicago, IL 60611. TEL 312-988-5990. FAX 312-988-6281.
Vendor(s): West Services, Inc. (HUMRT). *5728*

HUMAN RIGHTS QUARTERLY.
Johns Hopkins University Press, Journals Publishing Division, 2715 N. Charles St., Baltimore, MD 21218. TEL 410-516-6987. FAX 410-516-6968.
Vendor(s): Information Access Co.. *6415*

HUMAN SYSTEMS MANAGEMENT.
I O S Press, Van Diemenstraat 94, 1013 CN Amsterdam, Netherlands. TEL 31-20-6382189. FAX 31-20-6203419.
Vendor(s): University Microfilms International. *1421*

THE HUMANIST.
American Humanist Association, 7 Harwood Dr., Box 1188, Amherst, NY 14226-7188. TEL 716-839-5080. FAX 716-839-5079.
Vendor(s): Information Access Co., University Microfilms International. *5478*

HUMANITIES INDEX.
H.W. Wilson Co., 950 University Ave., Bronx, NY 10452. TEL 718-588-8400. FAX 718-590-1617.
Vendor(s): OCLC, Ovid Technologies, Inc. (WHUM), Wilsonline (File HUM). *3632*

HYDRAULICS & PNEUMATICS.
Penton Publishing Co. 1100 Superior Ave., Cleveland, OH 44114-2543. TEL 216-696-7000. FAX 216-696-8765.
Vendor(s): Information Access Co., Knight-Ridder Information, Inc.. *2743*

HYDROCARBON PROCESSING.
Gulf Publishing Co., Box 2608, Houston, TX 77252-2608. TEL 713-529-4301. FAX 713-520-4433.
Vendor(s): Information Access Co.. *5359*

HYDROTITLES.
Geosystems, P.O. Box 40, Didcot, Oxon. OX11 9BX, England. TEL 44-1235-813913.
Vendor(s): Knight-Ridder Information, Inc. (File no.58). *2219*

HYPATIA.
Indiana University Press, Journals Division, 601 N. Morton St., Bloomington, IN 47404. TEL 812-855-9449. FAX 812-855-8507.
Vendor(s): Information Access Co., Knight-Ridder Information, Inc. (File no.57), University Microfilms International. *7017*

HYPERMARKETS AND SUPERSTORES: THE INTERNATIONAL MARKET.
Euromonitor, 60-61 Britton St., London EC1M 5NA, England. TEL 44-171-251-8024. FAX 44-171-608-3149.
Vendor(s): Data-Star, Knight-Ridder Information, Inc.. *3006*

I A F C ON SCENE.
International Association of Fire Chiefs, 4025 Fair Ridge Dr., Fairfax, VA 22033-2868. TEL 703-273-0911. FAX 703-273-9363. *2921*

I & T MAGAZINE.
European Commission, Directorate-General for Telecommunications, Information Industries and Innovation (DG XIII), Rue de la Loi, 200, B-1049 Brussels, Belgium. *1905*

I B J MONTHLY REPORT.
Industrial Bank of Japan, 1-3-3 Marunouchi, Chiyoda-ku, Tokyo, Japan. *1215*

I B T.
International Business Communications (IBC) Ltd., P.O. Box 145, Tel Aviv 61001, Israel. TEL 972-3-6397194. FAX 972-3-6397195.
Vendor(s): Information Access Co., NewsNet (IT92). *1165*

I D C JAPAN REPORT.
International Data Corporation, 77 Franklin St., Boston, MA 02110. TEL 617-482-8785. FAX 617-338-0164.
Vendor(s): Information Access Co.. *2032*

I D R C REPORTS.
International Development Research Centre, Box 8500, Ottawa, ON K1G 3H9, Canada. TEL 613-236-6163. FAX 613-563-2476.
Available only online. *1508*

I E E E JOURNAL OF TECHNOLOGY COMPUTER AIDED DESIGN.
Institute of Electrical and Electronics Engineers, Inc., 345 E. 47th St., New York, NY 10017-2394.
Available only online. *2028*

I E E PROCEEDINGS - CIRCUITS, DEVICES AND SYSTEMS.
I.E.E., Michael Faraday House, Six Hills Way, Stevenage, Herts. SG1 2AY, England. TEL 44-1438-313311. FAX 44-1438-742840. *2705*

I E E PROCEEDINGS - COMMUNICATIONS.
I.E.E., Michael Faraday House, Six Hills Way, Stevenage, Herts. SG1 2AY, England. TEL 44-1438-313311. FAX 44-1438-742840. *2706*

I E E PROCEEDINGS - COMPUTERS AND DIGITAL TECHNIQUES.
I.E.E., Michael Faraday House, Six Hills Way, Stevenage, Herts. SG1 2AY, England. TEL 44-1438-313311. FAX 44-1438-742840. *2078*

I E E PROCEEDINGS - CONTROL THEORY AND APPLICATIONS.
I.E.E., Michael Faraday House, Six Hills Way, Stevenage, Herts. SG1 2AY, England. TEL 44-1438-313311. FAX 44-1438-742840. *2706*

I E E PROCEEDINGS - ELECTRIC POWER APPLICATIONS.
I.E.E., Michael Faraday House, Six Hills Way, Stevenage, Herts. SG1 2AY, England. TEL 44-1438-313311. FAX 44-1438-742840. *2706*

I E E PROCEEDINGS - GENERATION, TRANSMISSION AND DISTRIBUTION.
I.E.E., Michael Faraday House, Six Hills Way, Stevenage, Herts. SG1 2AY, England. TEL 44-1438-313311. FAX 44-1438-742840. *2706*

I E E PROCEEDINGS - MICROWAVES, ANTENNAS & PROPAGATION.
I.E.E., Michael Faraday House, Six Hills Way, Stevenage, Herts. SG1 2AY, England. TEL 44-1438-313311. FAX 44-1438-742840. *2706*

I E E PROCEEDINGS - OPTOELECTRONICS.
I.E.E., Michael Faraday House, Six Hills Way, Stevenage, Herts. SG1 2AY, England. TEL 44-1438-313311. FAX 44-1438-742840. *5603*

I E E PROCEEDINGS - RADAR, SONAR AND NAVIGATION.
I.E.E., Michael Faraday House, Six Hills Way, Stevenage, Herts. SG1 2AY, England. TEL 44-1438-313311. FAX 44-1438-742840. *2706*

I E E PROCEEDINGS - SCIENCE, MEASUREMENT AND TECHNOLOGY.
I.E.E, Michael Faraday House, Six Hills Way, Stevenage, Herts. SG1 2AY, England. TEL 44-1438-313311. FAX 44-1438-742840. *2706*

I E E PROCEEDINGS - VISION, IMAGE & SIGNAL PROCESSING.
I.E.E., Michael Faraday House, Six Hills Way, Stevenage, Herts. SG1 2AY, England. TEL 44-1438-313311. FAX 44-1438-742840. *2706*

I G C C NEWSLETTER.
Institute on Global Conflict and Cooperation, University of California, San Diego, 9500 Gilman Dr., Dept. 0518, La Jolla, CA 92093-0518. TEL 619-534-1979. FAX 619-534-7655. *5753*

I I C S QUARTERLY.
International Interactive Communications Society, 14657 S.W. Teal Blvd., Ste. 119, Beaverton, OR 97007. TEL 503-579-4427. FAX 503-579-6272. *1927*

I I E SOLUTIONS.
Institute of Industrial Engineers, Norcross, GA 30092. TEL 404-449-0460.
Vendor(s): Knight-Ridder Information, Inc., University Microfilms International. *2747*

I I E TRANSACTIONS.
Chapman & Hall, Journals Department 2-6 Boundary Row, London SE1 8HN, England. TEL 44-171-8560066. FAX 44-171-5229623. *2747*

I J O NEWSLETTER.
International Juridicial Organization for Environment and Development, Via Barberini 3, 00187 Rome, Italy. TEL 39-6-4742117. FAX 39-6-4745779. *2801*

I M M ABSTRACTS AND INDEX.
Institution of Mining and Metallurgy, 44 Portland Pl., London W1N 4BR, England. TEL 0171-580-3802. FAX 0171-436-5388.
Vendor(s): European Space Agency (IMMAGE). *5084*

I N F O R JOURNAL.
University of Toronto Press, Journals Department, 5201 Dufferin St., Downsview, ON M3H 5T8, Canada. TEL 416-667-7781. FAX 416-667-7881.
Vendor(s): University Microfilms International. *2074*

I N I S ATOMINDEX.
International Atomic Energy Agency, Wagramerstrasse 5, Box 100, A-1400 Vienna, Austria. TEL 43-1-2060-22529. FAX 43-1-2060-29302.
Vendor(s): BELINDIS, CISTI, European Space Agency (File no.28/INIS), STN International (ENERGY). *5579*

I P A REVIEW.
Institute of Public Affairs, 128-36 Jolimont Rd., Jolimont, Vic. 3002, Australia. TEL 61-3-96547499. FAX 61-3-96507627.
Vendor(s): University Microfilms International. *930*

I R S PUBLICATIONS.
Commerce Clearing House, Inc., 2700 Lake Cook Rd., Riverwoods, IL 60015. TEL 847-267-7000. FAX 800-224-8299.
Vendor(s): Wilsonline. *1548*

I S D N NEWS.
Phillips Business Information, Inc., 1201 Seven Locks Rd., Potomac, MD 20854. TEL 301-424-3338. FAX 301-309-3847.
Vendor(s): Data-Star, Information Access Co., Knight-Ridder Information, Inc., NewsNet (TE90). *1927*

I S T E UPDATE.
International Society for Technology in Education, 1787 Agate St., Eugene, OR 97403-1923. TEL 541-346-4414. FAX 541-346-5890. *2340*

I TO CHO.
Igaku-Shoin Ltd., 5-24-3 Hongo, Bunkyo-ku, Tokyo 113-91, Japan. TEL 03-817-5714.
Vendor(s): JICST. *4693*

IBERLEX.
Boletin Oficial del Estado, Trafalgar, 27, 28071 Madrid, Spain. TEL 34-1-5382297. FAX 34-1-5382275. *3891*

ICE CREAM REPORTER.
F I N D - S V P, Inc., 625 Avenue of the Americas, New York, NY 10011-2002. TEL 212-645-4500. FAX 212-645-7681.
Vendor(s): NewsNet (FB04). *3000*

ICE CREAM, YOGHURTS AND CHILLED DESSERTS: THE INTERNATIONAL MARKET.
Euromonitor, 60-61 Britton St., London EC1M 5NA, England. TEL 44-171-251-8024. FAX 44-171-608-3149.
Vendor(s): Data-Star, Knight-Ridder Information, Inc.. *2976*

ICELANDIC FISHING NEWS.
Midlun hf., Fjoelmidlavaktin, Aegisgata 7, P.O. Box 155, IS-121 Reykjavik, Iceland. TEL 354-562-2288. FAX 354-552-6994. *2935*

IDAHO BUSINESS DIRECTORY.
American Business Directories 5711 S. 86th Circle, Box 27347, Omaha, NE 68127. TEL 402-593-4600. FAX 402-331-5481. *1615*

IDAHO GOVERNMENT DIGEST.
Ridenbaugh Press, Box 2276, Boise, ID 83701. TEL 208-344-9700. FAX 208-338-9769. *3948*

IDAHO LAW REVIEW.
University of Idaho, College of Law, Moscow, ID 83843. TEL 208-885-7241.
Vendor(s): West Services, Inc.. *3789*

IGAKU CHUO ZASSHI.
Igaku Chuo Zasshi Kankokai, 5-18, Takaido Higashi 2-chome, Suginami-ku, Tokyo 168, Japan. *4469*

ILLINOIS BUSINESS DIRECTORY.
American Business Directories 5711 S. 86th Circle, Box 27347, Omaha, NE 68127. TEL 402-593-4600. FAX 402-331-5481. *1616*

ILLINOIS BUSINESS REVIEW.
University of Illinois at Urbana-Champaign, Bureau of Economic and Business Research, 428 Commerce Bldg., W., 1206 S. Sixth St., Champaign, IL 61820. TEL 217-333-2331. FAX 217-233-7410.
Vendor(s): Information Access Co., Knight-Ridder Information, Inc., University Microfilms International. *930*

ILLINOIS LEGAL TIMES.
Giant Steps Publishing Corporation, 3 E. Huron St., Chicago, IL 60611. TEL 312-644-4378. FAX 312-644-0765.
Vendor(s): Lexis-Nexis, West Services, Inc.. *3789*

ILLUSTRATED CASE REPORTS IN GASTROENTEROLOGY.
Chapman & Hall, Journals Department 2-6 Boundary Row, London SE1 8HN, England. TEL 44-171-8650066. FAX 44-171-5229323. *4693*

IMAGING ABSTRACTS.
Pira International, Randalls Rd., Leatherhead, Surrey KT22 7RU, England. TEL 44-1372-802050. FAX 44-1372-802239.
Vendor(s): Data-Star (PIRA), FIZ Technik, Knight-Ridder Information, Inc. (F248), Orbit Search Service (PIRA/IMAB), STN International (PIRA). *5523*

IMAGING UPDATE.
Worldwide Videotex, Box 3273, Boynton Beach, FL 33424-3273. TEL 407-738-2276.
Vendor(s): Data-Star, Information Access Co., Knight-Ridder Information, Inc., NewsNet (EC05). *2028*

IMAGING WORLD.
Cardinal Business Media, Inc., 1300 Virginia Dr., Ste. 400, Fort Washington, PA 19034. TEL 215-643-8000. FAX 215-643-8099. *2028*

IMMUNOLOGY ABSTRACTS.
Cambridge Scientific Abstracts, 7200 Wisconsin Ave., 6th Fl., Bethesda, MD 20814. TEL 301-961-6750. FAX 301-961-6720.
Vendor(s): Knight-Ridder Information, Inc. (File no.76/LIFE SCIENCES COLLECTION), STN International (LIFESCI). *4566*

IMMUNOLOGY TODAY.
Elsevier Science Ltd., P.O. Box 800, Kidlington, Oxford OX5 1DX, England. TEL 44-1865-843000. FAX 44-1865-843010.
Vendor(s): OCLC. *4583*

IMPLEMENT & TRACTOR.
Freiberg Publishing Company, Inc., 2302 W. First St., Box 7, Cedar Falls, IA 50613. TEL 319-277-3599. FAX 319-277-3783.
Vendor(s): Information Access Co.. *204*

IMPRESA & STATO.
Camera di Commercio, Industria, Artiganato e Agricoltura di Milano, Via Meravigli 9-B, 20123 Milan, Italy. TEL 39-2-85154206. *1143*

IMPROVED RECOVERY WEEK.
F. Jay Schempf, Ed. & Pub., Box 2607, Bellaire, TX 77402-2607. TEL 713-680-0914. FAX 713-680-9343.
Vendor(s): Data-Star, Information Access Co., Knight-Ridder Information, Inc., Lexis-Nexis. *2550*

IN-CAR ENTERTAINMENT: THE INTERNATIONAL MARKET.
Euromonitor, 60-61 Britton St., London EC1M 5NA, England. TEL 44-171-251-8024. FAX 44-171-608-3149.
Vendor(s): Data-Star, Knight-Ridder Information, Inc.. *2523*

IN HAND.
31 Randolph Dr., Southwood, Farnborough, Hants. GU14 0QQ, England. TEL 01252-518960. FAX 01252-518960. *2078*

IN VIVO.
Windhover Information, Inc., 50 Washington St., 5th Fl., South Norwalk, CT 06864. TEL 203-838-4401. FAX 203-838-3214.
Vendor(s): Information Access Co.. *4470*

INC.
Goldhirsh Group, Inc., 38 Commercial Wharf, Boston, MA 02110. TEL 617-248-8000. FAX 617-248-8040.
Vendor(s): Information Access Co., Knight-Ridder Information, Inc., Lexis-Nexis. *1576*

INCENTIVE (AKRON).
Bill Communications, Inc., 355 Park Ave. S., 5th Fl., New York, NY 10010-1789. TEL 212-592-6200. FAX 212-592-6339.
Vendor(s): University Microfilms International. *1468*

INCOME OPPORTUNITIES.
Essence Communications Inc., 1500 Broadway, Ste. 600, New York, NY 10036-4015. TEL 212-642-0600. FAX 212-302-8269. *1576*

INCOME SECURITIES ADVISOR.
Bond Investors Association, Inc., 617 N.W. 153rd St., Ste. 221, Miami Lakes, FL 33014-2435. TEL 305-557-1832. *1333*

INDEPENDENT BANKER.
Independent Bankers Association of America, Box 267, Sauk Centre, MN 56378. TEL 612-352-6546.
Vendor(s): University Microfilms International. *1100*

INDEPENDENT ENERGY.
PennWell Publishing Company (Milaca), 620 Central Ave., N., Milaca, MN 56363-1788. TEL 612-983-6892. FAX 612-983-6893. Vendor(s): University Microfilms International. *2551*

INDEPENDENT POWER REPORT.
McGraw-Hill Companies, Energy & Business Newsletters, 1221 Ave. of the Americas, 36th Fl., New York, NY 10020. TEL 212-512-6410. Vendor(s): Dow Jones News Retrieval (COG), Knight-Ridder Information, Inc. (File no.624/McGRAW-HILL PUBLICATIONS ONLINE), Lexis-Nexis (IPR), NewsNet (EY67). *2551*

INDEPENDENT SMALL PRESS REVIEW.
Independent Small Press Review (I.S.P.R.), No. 91336 Victoria Court, Santa Barbara, CA 93190-1336. TEL 805-687-4087. FAX 805-964-3337. *5998*

INDEX ANALYTIQUE SIGNALETIQUE BIBLIOGRAPHIQUE.
Ministere de la Population, Centre National de Documentation, Charii Hadj Ahmed Cherkaoui - Haut Agdal, B.P. 826 - 10004, Rabat, Morocco. TEL 212-7-7749-44. FAX 212-7-7731-34. *1005*

INDEX MEDICUS.
U.S. National Library of Medicine, 8600 Rockville Pike, Bethesda, MD 20894. Vendor(s): Knight-Ridder Information, Inc. (File nos.154 & 155/MEDLINE), National Library of Medicine, Ovid Technologies, Inc. (MESH, MESZ), STN International (MEDLINE). *4566*

INDEX NEW ZEALAND.
National Library of New Zealand, P.O. Box 1467, Wellington, New Zealand. TEL 64-4-4743098. FAX 64-4-4753124. Vendor(s): Kiwinet. *15*

INDEX OF ARTICLES ON JEWISH STUDIES.
Jewish National and University Library, P.O. Box 34165, Jerusalem 91341, Israel. TEL 972-2-585039. FAX 972-2-511771. *2917*

INDEX OF CURRENT RESEARCH ON PIGS.
CAB International, Wallingford, Oxon., England. TEL 44-1491-832111. FAX 44-1491-833508. Vendor(s): DIMDI, European Space Agency, Knight-Ridder Information, Inc., STN International. *174*

INDEX OF ECONOMIC ARTICLES IN JOURNALS AND COLLECTIVE VOLUMES.
American Economic Association, 2014 Broadway, Ste. 305, Nashville, TN 37203. TEL 615-322-2595. Vendor(s): Knight-Ridder Information, Inc. (File no.139). *1005*

INDEX OF FUNGI.
CAB International, Wallingford, Oxon. OX10 8DE, England. TEL 44-1491-432111. FAX 44-1491-833508. Vendor(s): DIMDI, European Space Agency, Knight-Ridder Information, Inc., STN International. *621*

INDEX TO CURRENT URBAN DOCUMENTS.
Greenwood Press, Inc., Subscription Publications 88 Post Rd. W., Box 5007, Westport, CT 06881-5007. TEL 203-226-3571. FAX 203-222-1502. *3602*

INDEX TO DENTAL LITERATURE.
American Dental Association, 211 E. Chicago Ave., Chicago, IL 60611. TEL 312-440-2500. FAX 312-440-2550. Vendor(s): Ovid Technologies, Inc. (MESH, MESZ), Knight-Ridder Information, Inc. (File nos.154 & 155/MEDLINE), National Library of Medicine, STN International (MEDLINE). *4566*

INDEX TO HEBREW PERIODICALS.
Centre for Public Libraries, P.O. Box 242, Jerusalem 91002, Israel. TEL 972-2-252949. Available only online. *534*

INDEX TO LEGAL PERIODICALS & BOOKS.
H.W. Wilson Co., 950 University Ave., Bronx, NY 10452. TEL 718-588-8400. FAX 718-590-1617. Vendor(s): Lexis-Nexis, OCLC, Ovid Technologies, Inc., West Services, Inc., Wilsonline (File ILP). *3876*

INDEX TO SCIENTIFIC & TECHNICAL PROCEEDINGS.
Institute for Scientific Information, 3501 Market St., Philadelphia, PA 19104. TEL 215-386-0100. FAX 215-386-2991. Vendor(s): Orbit Search Service. *6302*

INDEX TO SCIENTIFIC BOOK CONTENTS.
Institute for Scientific Information, 3501 Market St., Philadelphia, PA 19104. TEL 215-386-0100. FAX 215-386-2291. Vendor(s): DIMDI (ISTP&B Search). *6302*

INDEX TO SOUTH AFRICAN PERIODICALS.
State Library, P.O. Box 397, Pretoria 0001, South Africa. TEL 27-12-21-8931. FAX 27-12-325-5984. *6014*

INDEX TO THE SPORTING NEWS.
John Gordon Burke Publisher, Inc., Box 1492, Evanston, IL 60204-1492. TEL 847-866-8625. *6494*

INDEX VETERINARIUS.
CAB International, Wallingford, Oxon. OX10 8DE, England. TEL 44-1491-832111. FAX 44-1491-833508. Vendor(s): DIMDI, European Space Agency, Knight-Ridder Information, Inc., STN International. *6961*

INDIAN CONCRETE JOURNAL.
Associated Cement Companies, Ltd., C R S Complex, L.B. Shastri Marg., Thane 400 604, India. TEL 5323631. FAX 91-22-5320962. *2662*

INDIAN JOURNAL OF HOSPITAL PHARMACY.
Indian Hospital Pharmacists' Association, R-566 New Rajinder Nagar, New Delhi 110 060, India. TEL 5754344. *5417*

INDIAN JOURNAL OF PHARMACEUTICAL SCIENCES.
Indian Pharmaceutical Association, Kalina Santacruz East, Bombay 400098, India. *5417*

INDIANA BUSINESS DIRECTORY.
American Business Directories 5711 S. 86th Circle, Box 27347, Omaha, NE 68127. TEL 402-593-4600. FAX 402-331-5481. *1616*

INDIANA BUSINESS MAGAZINE.
Curtis Magazine Group, 1200 Waterway Blvd., Indianapolis, IN 46202-2157. TEL 317-692-1200. FAX 317-692-4250. Vendor(s): Information Access Co., Knight-Ridder Information, Inc., Lexis-Nexis, University Microfilms International. *1215*

INDIANA BUSINESS REVIEW.
Indiana University, School of Business, Bloomington, IN 47405. TEL 812-855-5507. Vendor(s): University Microfilms International. *931*

INDIANA LAW JOURNAL.
Indiana University, School of Law, Law Building, Bloomington, IN 47405. TEL 812-855-5175. FAX 812-855-0555. Vendor(s): Lexis-Nexis, West Services, Inc.. *3790*

INDIANA LAW REVIEW.
Indiana University, Indianapolis School of Law, 735 W. New York St., Indianpolis, IN 46202. TEL 317-274-4039. FAX 317-274-8825. Vendor(s): West Services, Inc.. *3790*

INDIANA LEGISLATIVE INSIGHT.
Edward D. Feigenbaum, Ed. & Pub., Box 383, Noblesville, IN 46060. TEL 317-773-8715. FAX 317-773-9998. *5906*

INDIANAPOLIS BUSINESS JOURNAL.
I B J Corp., 431 N. Pennsylvania, Indianapolis, IN 46204-1806. TEL 317-634-6200. FAX 317-263-5060. Vendor(s): Information Access Co., University Microfilms International. *1166*

INDIAWORLD.
Ravi Database Consultants Pvt. Ltd., 304 Tulsiani Chambers, 212 Nariman Point, Bombay 400 021, India. TEL 91-22-2842959. FAX 91-22-2023904. Available only online. *3170*

INDICE ESPANOL DE CIENCIA Y TECNOLOGIA.
Centro de Informacion y Documentacion Cientifica (Cindoc), Joaquin Costa 22, 28002 Madrid, Spain. TEL 34-1-5635482. FAX 34-1-5642644. *6302*

INDICE ESPANOL DE CIENCIAS SOCIALES. SERIES A: PSYCHOLOGY AND EDUCATIONAL SCIENCES.
Centro de Informacion y Documentacion Cientifica (Cindoc), Pinar, 25, 28006 Madrid, Spain. TEL 34-1-4111098. FAX 34-1-5645059. *5889*

INDICE ESPANOL DE CIENCIAS SOCIALES. SERIES B: ECONOMICS, SOCIOLOGY AND POLITICAL SCIENCE.
Centro de Informacion y Documentacion Cientifica (Cindoc), Pinar, 25, 3, 28006 Madrid, Spain. TEL 34-1-4111098. FAX 34-1-5645069. *1005*

INDICE ESPANOL DE CIENCIAS SOCIALES. SERIES C: LAW.
Centro de Informacion y Documentacion Cientifica (Cindoc), Pinar, 25, 3, 28006 Madrid, Spain. TEL 34-1-4111098. FAX 34-1-5645069. *3876*

INDICE ESPANOL DE CIENCIAS SOCIALES. SERIES D: SCIENCE AND SCIENTIFIC INFORMATION.
Centro de Informacion y Documentacion Cientifica (Cindoc), Pinar, 25, 3, 28006 Madrid, Spain. TEL 34-1-4111098. FAX 34-1-5645069. *6302*

INDICE ESPANOL DE CIENCIAS SOCIALES. SERIES E: URBAN PLANNING.
Centro de Informacion y Documentacion Cientifica (Cindoc), Pinar, 25, 3, 28006 Madrid, Spain. TEL 34-1-4111098. FAX 34-1-5645069. *3602*

INDICE ESPANOL DE HUMANIDADES. SERIES A: ART.
Centro de Informacion y Documentacion Cientifica (Cindoc), Pinar, 25, 3, 28006 Madrid, Spain. TEL 34-3-4111098. FAX 34-1-5645069. *463*

INDICE ESPANOL DE HUMANIDADES. SERIES B: HISTORICAL SCIENCES.
Centro de Informacion y Documentacion Cientifica (Cindoc), Pinar 25, 3, 28006 Madrid, Spain. TEL 34-1-4111098. FAX 34-1-5645069. *3367*

INDICE ESPANOL DE HUMANIDADES. SERIES C: LINGUISTICS AND LITERATURE.
Centro de Informacion y Documentacion Cientifica (Cindoc), Pinar 25, 3, 28006 Madrid, Spain. TEL 34-1-4111098. FAX 34-1-5645069. *4127*

INDICE ESPANOL DE HUMANIDADES. SERIES D: PHILOSOPHY.
Centro de Informacion y Documentacion Cientifica (Cindoc), Pinar, 25, 3, 28006 Madrid, Spain. TEL 34-1-4111098. FAX 34-1-5645069. *5507*

INDICE MEDICO ESPANOL.
Generalitat Valenciana Conselleria de Sanitat i Consum, Avda. Blasco Ibanez - 17, 46010 Valencia, Spain. TEL 96-361-06-54. FAX 96-3613975. *4566*

INDIVIDUAL EMPLOYMENT RIGHTS.
The Bureau of National Affairs, Inc., 1231 25th St., N.W., Washington, DC 20037 TEL 202-452-4200. FAX 202-822-8092. Vendor(s): Human Resources Information Network (CDD, HDD), West Services, Inc. (File FLB-CS, LRR-IERN). *1378*

INDIVIDUALS WITH DISABILITIES EDUCATION LAW REPORTER.
L R P Publications 747 Dresher Rd., Box 980, Horsham, PA 19044-0980. TEL 215-784-0941. FAX 215-784-9639. *2469*

INDOOR AIR QUALITY UPDATE.
Cutter Information Corp., 37 Broadway, Arlington, MA 02174. TEL 617-648-8700. FAX 617-648-1950. *395*

INDUSTRIAL & ENGINEERING CHEMISTRY RESEARCH.
American Chemical Society, 1155 16th St. N.W., Washington, DC 20036. TEL 300-333-9511. FAX 614-447-3671. Vendor(s): STN International (CJACS). *2642*

INDUSTRIAL AND LABOR RELATIONS REVIEW.
Cornell University, New York State School of Industrial and Labor Relations, Ithaca, NY 14853-3901. TEL 607-255-2732. FAX 607-255-8016. Vendor(s): Information Access Co., Knight-Ridder Information, Inc.. *1373*

INDUSTRIAL CASES REPORTS.
Incorporated Council of Law Reporting for England
and Wales, 3 Stone Bldgs., Lincoln's Inn, London
WC2A 3XN, England. TEL 44-171-242-6471.
FAX 44-171-831-5247.
Vendor(s): Lexis-Nexis. *3902*

INDUSTRIAL DISTRIBUTION.
Cahners Publishing Company (Newton), Division of
Reed Elsevier Inc., 275 Washington St., Newton, MA
02158-1630. TEL 617-558-4564. FAX 617-558-
4327.
Vendor(s): Information Access Co., Knight-Ridder
Information, Inc.. *1468*

INDUSTRIAL ENERGY BULLETIN.
McGraw-Hill Companies, Energy & Business
Newsletters, 1221 Ave. of the Americas, 36th Fl.,
New York, NY 10020. TEL 212-512-2000.
Vendor(s): Dow Jones News Retrieval, Knight-Ridder
Information, Inc. (File no.624/McGRAW-HILL
PUBLICATIONS ONLINE), Lexis-Nexis, NewsNet
(EY68). *2551*

INDUSTRIAL ENVIRONMENT.
Worldwide Videotex, Box 3273, Boynton Beach, FL
33424-3273. TEL 407-738-2276.
Vendor(s): Information Access Co.. *2801*

INDUSTRIAL HEALTH.
National Institute of Industrial Health, 21-1 Nagao
6-chome, Tama-ku, Kawasaki-shi, Kanagawa-ken
214, Japan. TEL 81-044-865-6111. FAX 81-044-
865-6116.
Vendor(s): JICST, Knight-Ridder Information, Inc..
5250

INDUSTRIAL HEALTH & HAZARDS UPDATE.
Merton Allen Associates, InfoTeam Inc., Box 15640,
Plantation, FL 33318-5640. TEL 954-473-9560.
FAX 954-473-0544.
Vendor(s): Data-Star, Human Resources Information
Network, Information Access Co., NewsNet (LA04).
5250

INDUSTRIAL MANAGEMENT.
Institute of Industrial Engineers, 25 Technology
Park-Atlanta, Norcross, GA 30092. TEL 404-449-
0460.
Vendor(s): Information Access Co., University
Microfilms International. *1422*

INDUSTRIAL PAINT & POWDER.
Hitchcock Publishing 191 S. Gary Ave., Carol
Stream, IL 60188. TEL 708-665-1000. FAX 708-
462-2225.
Vendor(s): Information Access Co., Knight-Ridder
Information, Inc.. *5308*

INDUSTRIAL RELATIONS JOURNAL.
Blackwell Publishers Ltd., 108 Cowley Rd., Oxford
OX4 1JF, England. TEL 44-1865-791100. FAX 44-
1865-791347.
Vendor(s): Information Access Co.. *1378*

INDUSTRIAL RELATIONS LAW REPORTS.
Eclipse Group Ltd., Industrial Relations Services, 18-
20 Highbury Pl., London N5 1QP, England. TEL 44-
171-354-5858. FAX 44-171-354-8106.
Vendor(s): Lexis-Nexis. *1378*

INDUSTRIAL REPORTS.
L B C Information Services, 50 Waterloo Rd., N.
Ryde, N.S.W. 2113, Australia. TEL 61-2-
99366444. FAX 61-2-8889706.
Vendor(s): Info-One International Pty Ltd.. *3902*

INDUSTRIAL RESEARCHER.
Pranava Industrial Services Pvt. Ltd., 18, Sagar
Tarang, Bhulabhai Desai Rd., Bombay 400 036,
India. TEL 3633236.
Vendor(s): Knight-Ridder Information, Inc.. *931*

INDUSTRIAL SPECIALTIES NEWS.
Blendon Information Services, 68 Longmore St.,
Willowdale, ON M2N 6T8, Canada. TEL 416-223-
5397. FAX 416-223-8532.
Vendor(s): Data-Star, Dow Jones News Retrieval,
Information Access Co., Knight-Ridder Information,
Inc.. *5065*

INDUSTRIES IN TRANSITION.
Business Communications Co., Inc. (Norwalk), 25
Van Zant St., Norwalk, CT 06855. TEL 203-853-
4266. FAX 203-853-0348.
Vendor(s): Data-Star, Information Access Co.,
Knight-Ridder Information, Inc., NewsNet (GB46).
1523

INDUSTRY GROUP MARKET VALUES.
Standard & Poor's 25 Broadway, New York, NY
10004. TEL 212-208-8000. *1334*

INDUSTRY WEEK.
Penton Publishing Co. 1100 Superior Ave.,
Cleveland, OH 44114-2543. TEL 216-696-7000.
FAX 216-969-7670.
Vendor(s): Information Access Co., Knight-Ridder
Information, Inc., Lexis-Nexis, University Microfilms
International. *1422*

INFECTION CONTROL WEEKLY.
Charles W. Henderson, Ed. & Pub., Box 5528,
Atlanta, GA 31107-0528. TEL 404-377-8895.
FAX 404-378-5411.
Vendor(s): Information Access Co.. *4621*

INFERTILITY.
c/o Dr. Louis A. Mucelli, Ed., 614 2nd Ave., Ste. H,
New York, NY 10016. TEL 212-684-4242.
FAX 212-684-4290. *4738*

INFERTILITY HELPER.
Helper Publishing, 36 Norwood Rd., Toronto, ON
M4E 2S2, Canada. TEL 416-690-9593. FAX 416-
690-9593. *4738*

INFLAMMATION RESEARCH.
Birkhaeuser Verlag, P.O. Box 133, CH-4010 Basel,
Switzerland. TEL 41-61-2050730. FAX 41-61-
2050791. *5417*

INFORMATIK - FORSCHUNG UND ENTWICKLUNG.
Springer-Verlag, Heidelberger Platz 3, 14197
Berlin, Germany. TEL 49-30-8207-0. FAX 49-30-
8214091. *2081*

THE INFORMATION ADVISOR.
Find SUP, 625 Avenue of Americas, New York, NY
10010.
Vendor(s): Information Access Co. (Trade & Industry
Index). *4044*

INFORMATION & INTERACTIVE SERVICES REPORT.
Telecommunications Reports 1333 H St., N.W., 2nd
Fl.-W., Washington, DC 20005. TEL 202-842-1875.
FAX 202-842-3047.
Vendor(s): Information Access Co., NewsNet (TE41).
6017

INFORMATION EAUX.
Office International de l'Eau, Direction de la
Documentation et des Donnees, Rue Edouard
Chamberland, 87065 Limoges Cedex, France.
TEL 55-11-47-80. FAX 55-77-71-15.
Vendor(s): European Space Agency (File no.73/
AFEE). *6970*

THE INFORMATION FREEWAY REPORT.
Washington Researchers, Ltd., Box 19005, 20th St.
Sta., Washington, DC 20036-9005. TEL 202-333-
3499. FAX 202-625-0656.
Vendor(s): NewsNet. *2037*

INFORMATION LAW ALERT.
Voorhees Reports, 411 First St., Brooklyn, NY
11215-2507.
Vendor(s): Information Access Co.. *5340*

INFORMATION MANAGEMENT REPORT.
Elsevier Science Ltd., P.O. Box 800, Kidlington,
Oxford OX5 1DX, England. TEL 44-1865-843000.
FAX 44-1865-843010.
Vendor(s): Data-Star (PTBN), Knight-Ridder
Information, Inc. (File no.636). *4044*

INFORMATION NETWORKS.
Capitol Publications Inc., Telecom Publishing Group,
1101 King St., Ste. 444, Box 1455, Alexandria, VA
22313-2055. FAX 703-739-6490.
Vendor(s): Information Access Co., Knight-Ridder
Information, Inc., NewsNet (TE81). *1946*

THE INFORMATION REPORT.
Washington Researchers, Ltd., Box 19005, 20th St.
Sta., Washington, DC 20036-9005. TEL 202-333-
3499. FAX 202-625-0656.
Vendor(s): NewsNet (IT08). *535*

INFORMATION SCIENCE ABSTRACTS.
I F I - Plenum 233 Spring St., New York, NY
10013. TEL 212-620-8000. FAX 212-463-0742.
Vendor(s): Knight-Ridder Information, Inc. (File
no.202). *4039*

INFORMATION TECHNOLOGY AND LIBRARIES.
American Library Association, 50 E. Huron St,
Chicago, IL 60611-2795. TEL 312-944-6780.
FAX 312-440-9374.
Vendor(s): Information Access Co., University
Microfilms International. *4044*

INFORMATION TECHNOLOGY DIGEST.
University of Michigan, Information Technology
Division, 535 W. William Argus Bldg., Ann Arbor, MI
48103. TEL 313-763-8980. FAX 313-763-8937.
1992

INFORMATION TODAY.
Information Today, Inc., 143 Old Marlton Pike,
Medford, NJ 08055. TEL 609-654-6266. FAX 609-
654-4309.
Vendor(s): Information Access Co., Lexis-Nexis,
University Microfilms International. *4045*

INFORMATION WEEK.
C M P Publications, Inc., 600 Community Dr.,
Manhasset, NY 11030. TEL 516-562-5000.
FAX 516-562-7013.
Vendor(s): Information Access Co., NewsNet (TE34).
2066

**INFORMATIONS RECENTES SUR LES COMPTES
NATIONAUX DES PAYS EN DEVELOPPEMENT.**
Organization for Economic Cooperation and
Development, 2 rue Andre-Pascal, 75775 Paris
Cedex 16, France. *1309*

INFORMATIONSDIENST KRANKENHAUSWESEN.
Technische Universitaet Berlin, Institut fuer
Gesundheitswesen, Str. des 17. Juni 135, 10623
Berlin, Germany. TEL 49-30-31423980. FAX 49-
30-31424743.
Vendor(s): DIMDI. *3550*

INFORMAZIONE FILOSOFICA.
Ediform - Informazione e Cultura, Viale Monte Nero
68, 20135 Milan, Italy. TEL 39-2-55190714.
FAX 39-2-55015245. *5479*

INFOSYS.
Massey University, Information Systems
Department, Albany, New Zealand. TEL 64-9-
4439612. FAX 64-9-4439640.
Available only online. *2082*

INFOWORLD.
InfoWorld Publishing 155 Bovet Rd., Ste. 800, San
Mateo, CA 94402. TEL 415-572-7341. FAX 415-
358-1269.
Vendor(s): Information Access Co., Lexis-Nexis,
University Microfilms International. *2087*

INGRAM'S MAGAZINE.
Ingram Investment Co., 306 E. 12th St., Ste. 1014,
Kansas City, MO 64106. TEL 816-842-9994.
FAX 816-474-1111.
Vendor(s): Information Access Co., Knight-Ridder
Information, Inc.. *932*

INJURY PREVENTION.
B M J Publishing Group, B.M.A. House, Tavistock
Sq., London WC1H 9JR, England. TEL 44-171-387-
4499. FAX 44-171-383-6661.
Vendor(s): Ovid Technologies, Inc.. *4806*

INK & PRINT INTERNATIONAL.
Batiste Publications Ltd., Pembroke House,
Campsbourne Rd., Hornsey, London N8 7PE,
England. TEL 44-181-340-3291. FAX 44-181-341-
4840.
Vendor(s): Information Access Co.. *5814*

INKLINGS.
Inkspot, Toronto, ON, Canada.
Available only online. *2037*

INLINE.
Sports & Fitness Publishing, 2025 Pearl St.,
Boulder, CO 80302-4429. TEL 303-440-5111.
FAX 303-440-3313. *6566*

INNOVATION (ST. ANDREWS).
Longman Cartermill Ltd., Technology Centre, St.
Andrews, Fife KY16 9EA, Scotland. TEL 44-1334-
77660. *6247*

INNOVATOR'S DIGEST.
Merton Allen Associates, InfoTeam Inc., Box 15640,
Plantation, FL 33318-5640. TEL 954-473-9560.
FAX 954-473-0544.
Vendor(s): Data-Star, Information Access Co.,
NewsNet (RD09). *6247*

INORGANIC CHEMISTRY.
American Chemical Society, 1155 16th St., N.W., Washington, DC 20036. TEL 800-333-9511. FAX 614-447-3671.
Vendor(s): STN International (CJACS). *1731*

INPHARMA WEEKLY.
Adis International Limited, Private Bag 65901, Mairangi Bay, Auckland 10, New Zealand. TEL 64-9-479-8100. FAX 64-9-479-8145.
Vendor(s): Knight-Ridder Information, Inc. (PHD, IPHC,IPHA,IPZZ). *5450*

INSIDE D O T & TRANSPORTATION WEEK.
King Publishing Group, Inc., 627 National Press Bldg., Washington, DC 20045. TEL 202-638-4260. FAX 202-662-9744.
Vendor(s): Information Access Co., Lexis-Nexis, NewsNet (GT41). *6719*

INSIDE ENERGY WITH FEDERAL LANDS.
McGraw-Hill Companies, Energy & Business Newsletters, 1221 Ave. of the Americas, 36th Fl., New York, NY 10020. TEL 212-512-6410.
Vendor(s): Dow Jones News Retrieval (IE), Knight-Ridder Information, Inc. (File no.624/McGRAW-HILL PUBLICATIONS ONLINE), Lexis-Nexis (INERGY), NewsNet (EY69). *2551*

INSIDE EQUINE.
Equine Research Centre, University of Guelph, Guelph, ON N1G 2W1, Canada. TEL 519-837-0061. FAX 519-767-1081. *6947*

INSIDE F E R C.
McGraw-Hill Companies, 1221 Ave. of the Americas, New York, NY 10020.
Vendor(s): Dow Jones News Retrieval (FERC), Knight-Ridder Information, Inc. (File no.624/McGRAW-HILL PUBLICATIONS ONLINE), Lexis-Nexis (INFERC), NewsNet (EY70). *2551*

INSIDE F E R C'S GAS MARKET REPORT.
McGraw-Hill Companies, Energy & Business Newsletters, 1221 Ave. of the Americas, 36th Fl., New York, NY 10020. TEL 212-512-6410.
Vendor(s): Dow Jones News Retrieval (GSMR), Knight-Ridder Information, Inc. (File no.624/McGRAW-HILL PUBLICATIONS ONLINE), Lexis-Nexis (GASMKT), NewsNet (EY66). *5360*

INSIDE I V H S.
Waters Information Services, Inc., Box 2248, Binghamton, NY 13902-2248. TEL 607-770-9242. FAX 607-770-9435.
Vendor(s): Information Access Co., NewsNet (TS01). *6740*

INSIDE INDIANA.
Hoosier Publications Inc., P.O. Box 1231, 4615 E. Morningside Dr., Bloomington, IN 47408. TEL 812-334-9722. FAX 812-334-9756. *6506*

INSIDE M S.
National Multiple Sclerosis Society, 733 Third Ave., New York, NY 10017-3288. TEL 212-986-3240. FAX 212-986-7981.
Vendor(s): Information Access Co. *4841*

INSIDE MARKET DATA.
Waters Information Services, Inc., Box 2248, Binghamton, NY 13902-2248. TEL 607-770-9242. FAX 607-770-9435.
Vendor(s): Data-Star, Information Access Co., Knight-Ridder Information, Inc., NewsNet (PB37). *1129*

INSIDE MEDIA.
Cowles Business Media, 11 River Bend Dr., S., Box 4949, Stamford, CT 06907-0949. TEL 203-358-9900. FAX 203-358-5811.
Vendor(s): Information Access Co. *38*

INSIDE N R C.
McGraw-Hill Companies, Energy and Business Newsletters, 1221 Ave. of the Americas, 36th Fl., New York, NY 10020.
Vendor(s): Dow Jones News Retrieval (NRC), Knight-Ridder Information, Inc. (File no.624/McGRAW-HILL PUBLICATIONS ONLINE), Lexis-Nexis (INNRC), NewsNet (EY71). *2577*

INSIDE THE NEW COMPUTER INDUSTRY.
25420 Via Cicindela, Carmel, CA 93923-8412. TEL 408-726-1232. FAX 408-726-1233.
Vendor(s): Data-Star, Knight-Ridder Information, Inc.. *1993*

INSIDER HOLDINGS.
C D A Investment Technologies, Inc., 1355 Piccard Dr., Rockville, MD 20850. FAX 301-590-1329. *1334*

INSIDERS SKI LETTER.
Skiletter, Inc., 115 Lilly Pond Ln., Katonah, NY 10536. TEL 914-232-5094. *6566*

INSIGHT ON THE NEWS.
Washington Times Corporation, 3600 New York Ave., N.E., Washington, DC 20002. TEL 202-636-8800. FAX 202-529-2484.
Vendor(s): Information Access Co.. *3230*

INSTITUTE OF ASIAN STUDIES. JOURNAL.
Institute of Asian Studies, 377, 10th East St., Thiruvanmiyur, Madras 600 041, India. TEL 91-44-416728. FAX 91-44-419866. *6416*

INSTITUTE OF ELECTRICAL AND ELECTRONICS ENGINEERS. PROCEEDINGS.
Institute of Electrical and Electronics Engineers, Inc., 345 E. 47th St., New York, NY 10017-2394. TEL 908-981-0060. FAX 908-981-9667.
Vendor(s): OCLC. *2708*

INSTITUTE OF PAPER SCIENCE AND TECHNOLOGY. ABSTRACT BULLETIN.
Institute of Paper Science and Technology, 500 10th St., N.W., Atlanta, GA 30318. TEL 404-894-5700. FAX 404-894-4778.
Vendor(s): Knight-Ridder Information, Inc. (File nos.240 & 84C/PAPERCHEM). *5328*

INSTITUTE OF PHYSICS CONFERENCE SERIES.
I O P Publishing Ltd., Techno House, Redcliffe Way, Bristol, Avon BS1 6NX, England. TEL 44-117-929-7481. FAX 44-117-929-4318. *5551*

INSTITUTIONAL DISTRIBUTION.
Bill Communications, Inc., 355 Park Ave. S., 5th Fl., New York, NY 10010-1789. TEL 212-592-6200. FAX 212-592-6339.
Vendor(s): Information Access Co., Knight-Ridder Information, Inc., Lexis-Nexis. *2977*

INSTITUTIONAL INVESTOR.
Institutional Investor, Inc., 488 Madison Ave., New York, NY 10022. TEL 212-224-3570. FAX 212-224-3592.
Vendor(s): Information Access Co.. *1334*

INSTRUCTOR.
Scholastic Inc., 555 Broadway, New York, NY 10012-3999. TEL 212-643-6100.
Vendor(s): Information Access Co. *2342*

INSTRUMENTATION AND CONTROL SYSTEMS.
Chilton Co., One Chilton Way, Radnor, PA 19089. TEL 610-964-4417. FAX 610-964-2919.
Vendor(s): Knight-Ridder Information, Inc.. *3635*

INSURANCE ACCOUNTANT.
American Banker - Bond Buyer, Newsletter Division One State St. Plaza, New York, NY 10004-1549. TEL 800-733-4371. FAX 212-943-2224.
Vendor(s): Information Access Co.. *3652*

INSURANCE AND TECHNOLOGY.
Miller Freeman Inc. (New York) One Penn Plaza, New York, NY 10119. TEL 212-714-1300. FAX 212-302-6273.
Vendor(s): University Microfilms International. *3672*

INSURANCE PERIODICALS INDEX.
N I L S Publishing Company, 21625 Prairie St., Box 2507, Chatsworth, CA 91311. TEL 818-998-8830. FAX 818-718-8482.
Vendor(s): Knight-Ridder Information, Inc. (File no.169), Lexis-Nexis, West Services, Inc.. *3671*

INSURANCE REGULATOR.
American Banker - Bond Buyer, Newsletter Division One State St. Plaza, New York, NY 10004-1549. TEL 800-733-4371. FAX 212-943-2224.
Vendor(s): Information Access Co.. *3653*

INSURANCE SYSTEMS BULLETIN.
I B C Publishing, c/o Helen Cruickshank, Gilmoora House, 57-61 Mortimer St., London W1N 7TD. TEL 0171-637-4383. FAX 0171-636-6414.
Vendor(s): University Microfilms International. *3672*

INTEGRATED CIRCUITS INTERNATIONAL.
Elsevier Science Ltd., P.O. Box 800, Kidlington, Oxford OX5 1DX, England. TEL 44-1865-843000. FAX 44-1865-843010.
Vendor(s): Data-Star, Information Access Co., Knight-Ridder Information Inc.. *2018*

INTEGRATED PEST MANAGEMENT REVIEWS.
Chapman & Hall, Journals Department 2-6 Boundary Row, London SE1 8HN, England. TEL 44-171-8650066. FAX 44-171-5229623. *226*

INTEGRATED WASTE MANAGEMENT.
McGraw-Hill Companies, Energy & Business Newsletters, 1221 Ave. of the Americas, 36th Fl., New York, NY 10020. TEL 212-512-6410.
Vendor(s): Dow Jones News Retrieval, Knight-Ridder Information, Inc. (File no. 624/McGRAW-HILL PUBLICATIONS ONLINE), Lexis-Nexis, NewsNet (EV40). *2853*

INTELLIGENT MANUFACTURING.
Lionheart Publishing, Inc., 2555 Cumberland Pkwy., Ste. 299, Atlanta, GA 30339. TEL 770-431-0867. FAX 770-432-6969. *1523*

INTELLIGENT SOFTWARE STRATEGIES.
Cutter Information Corp., 37 Broadway, Arlington, MA 02174. TEL 617-648-8700. FAX 617-648-1950. *2007*

INTERACTIVE CONTENT.
Jupiter Communications, 627 Broadway, New York, NY 10012. TEL 212-780-6060. FAX 212-780-6075
Vendor(s): Information Access Co. *2038*

INTERACTIVE P R.
Phillips Business Information, Inc., 1201 Seven Locks Rd., Potomac, MD 20854. TEL 301-424-3338. FAX 301-309-3847. *38*

INTERACTIVE VIDEO NEWS.
Phillips Business Information, Inc., 1201 Seven Locks Rd., Potomac, MD 20854. TEL 301-424-3338. FAX 301-309-3847.
Vendor(s): Information Access Co., NewsNet (AD07). *1469*

INTER-AMERICAN LAW REVIEW.
University of Miami, School of Law, Box 248087, Coral Gables, FL 33124. TEL 305-284-5562.
Vendor(s): West Services, Inc.. *3933*

INTER-AMERICAN TRADE AND INVESTMENT LAW.
National Law Center for Inter-American Free Trade, 111 S. Church Ave., Ste. 200, Tucson, AZ 85701-1602. TEL 602-622-1200. FAX 602-622-0957. *3933*

INTER-CORPORATE OWNERSHIP.
Statistics Canada, Publications Division, Ottawa, ON K1A 0T6, Canada. TEL 613-951-7277. FAX 613-951-1584.
Vendor(s): Southam Electronic Publishing. *1166*

INTEREST GROUP IN PURE AND APPLIED LOGICS. BULLETIN.
Interest Group in Pure and Applied Logics, c/o Max-Planck-Institut fuer Informatik Im Stadtwald, 66123 Saarbruecken, Germany. *5430*

INTERFACE (BOSTON SPA).
British Library, National Bibliographic Service, Boston Spa, Wetherby, W. Yorks. LS23 7BQ England. TEL 44-9137-546585. FAX 44-1935-546586. *4045*

INTERIOR DESIGN.
Cahners Publishing Company (New York), Design Division, Division of Reed Elsevier Inc., 245 W. 17th St., New York, NY 10011. TEL 212-645-0067. FAX 212-463-6667.
Vendor(s): Information Access Co.. *3679*

INTERIORS: FOR THE CONTRACT DESIGN PROFESSIONAL.
B P I Communications, Inc. (New York), 1515 Broadway, 11th Fl., New York, NY 10036. TEL 212-536-5141. FAX 212-536-5357.
Vendor(s): Information Access Co.. *3579*

INTERNAL AUDITOR.
Institute of Internal Auditors, Inc., 249 Maitland Ave., Altamonte Springs, FL 32701-4201. TEL 407-830-7600. FAX 407-831-5171.
Vendor(s): Information Access Co., University Microfilms International. *1048*

Online

INTERNATIONAL AEROSPACE ABSTRACTS.
American Institute of Aeronautics and Astronautics, 3370 L'Enfant Promedade, S.W., Washington, DC 20024. TEL 202-646-7400. FAX 202-646-7508. Vendor(s): Knight-Ridder Information, Inc. (File no.108). *82*

INTERNATIONAL ASTRONOMICAL UNION. CENTRAL BUREAU FOR ASTRONOMICAL TELEGRAMS. CIRCULAR.
Smithsonian Institution Astrophysical Observatory, 60 Garden St., Cambridge, MA 02138. TEL 617-495-7244. *481*

INTERNATIONAL ASTRONOMICAL UNION. MINOR PLANET CENTER. MINOR PLANET CIRCULARS - MINOR PLANETS AND COMETS.
Smithsonian Institution Astrophysical Observatory, 60 Garden St., Cambridge, MA 02138. TEL 617-495-7244. *481*

INTERNATIONAL BANKING REGULATOR.
American Banker - Bond Buyer, Newsletter Division One State St. Plaza, New York, NY 10004-1549. TEL 800-733-4371. FAX 212-943-2224. Vendor(s): Information Access Co., NewsNet (IT36). *1101*

INTERNATIONAL BIBLIOGRAPHY OF THE SOCIAL SCIENCES. ECONOMICS.
Routledge, 11 New Fetter Lane, London EC4P 4EE, England. TEL 071-583-9855. FAX 071-583-0701. Vendor(s): QL Systems Ltd.. *1006*

INTERNATIONAL BIBLIOGRAPHY OF THE SOCIAL SCIENCES. SOCIAL AND CULTURAL ANTHROPOLOGY.
Routledge, 11 New Fetter Lane, London EC4P 4EE, England. TEL 071-583-9855. FAX 071-583-0701. Vendor(s): QL Systems Ltd.. *328*

INTERNATIONAL BIODETERIORATION & BIODEGRADATION.
Elsevier Science Ltd., P.O. Box 800, Kidlington, Oxford OX5 1DX, England. TEL 44-1865-843000. FAX 44-1865-843010. Vendor(s): CISTI, DIMDI, European Space Agency (File nos.16 & 124/CAB), Knight-Ridder Information, Inc., Ovid Technologies, Inc.. *662*

INTERNATIONAL BRANDS AND THEIR COMPANIES.
Gale Research Inc., 835 Penobscot Bldg., Detroit, MI 48226-4094. TEL 800-877-GALE. FAX 313-961-6083. Vendor(s): Knight-Ridder Information, Inc.. *5340*

INTERNATIONAL BUILDING SERVICES ABSTRACTS.
Building Services Research and Information Association, Old Bracknell Ln. W., Bracknell, Berks. RG12 7AH, England. TEL 44-1344-426511. FAX 44-1344-487575. *3335*

INTERNATIONAL BULLETIN OF MISSIONARY RESEARCH.
Overseas Ministries Study Center, 490 Prospect St., New Haven, CT 06511-2196. TEL 203-624-6672. Vendor(s): Information Access Co., University Microfilms International. *6148*

INTERNATIONAL BULLETIN ON ATOMIC AND MOLECULAR DATA FOR FUSION.
International Atomic Energy Agency, Wagramerstr. 5, P.O. Box 100, A-1400 Vienna, Austria. TEL 43-1-20600. FAX 43-1-20607. *2577*

INTERNATIONAL BUSINESS.
International Business & Trade Magazines, 9 E. 40th St., 10 Fl., New York, NY 10016. TEL 212-683-2426. Vendor(s): University Microfilms International. *1280*

INTERNATIONAL COAL REPORT.
Financial Times Energy Publishing Maple House, 149 Tottenham Court Rd., London W1P 9LL, England. TEL 44-171-896-2241. FAX 44-171-896-2275. Vendor(s): Data-Star, Information Access Co., Knight-Ridder Information, Inc., Lexis-Nexis. *5066*

INTERNATIONAL COMMERCIAL LITIGATION.
Euromoney Publications plc., Nestor House, Playhouse Yard, London EC4V 5EX, England. TEL 44-171-779-8935. FAX 44-171-779-8541. Vendor(s): University Microfilms International. *3903*

INTERNATIONAL COUNTERTERRORISM & SECURITY.
Counterterrorism & Security, Inc., Box 10265, Arlington, VA 22210. TEL 703-243-0993. FAX 703-243-1197. Vendor(s): NewsNet. *2182*

INTERNATIONAL COUNTRY RISK GUIDE.
Political Risk Services, Box 248, E. Syracuse, NY 13057-0248. TEL 315-431-0511. FAX 315-431-0200. Vendor(s): Data-Star, Information Access Co., Knight-Ridder Information, Inc., Lexis-Nexis. *1217*

INTERNATIONAL DEFENSE REVIEW.
Jane's Information Group, Sentinel House, 163 Brighton Rd., Coulsdon, Surrey CR5 2NH, England. TEL 44-181-700-3700. FAX 44-181-700-3700. Vendor(s): Knight-Ridder Information, Inc., Lexis-Nexis. *5034*

INTERNATIONAL DEVELOPMENT ABSTRACTS.
Elsevier - Geo Abstracts Regency House, 34 Duke St., Norwich NR3 3AP, England. TEL 44-603-626327. FAX 44-603-667934. Vendor(s): Knight-Ridder Information, Inc. (File no.292), Orbit Search Service. *3280*

INTERNATIONAL DEVELOPMENT RESEARCH CENTRE. ANNUAL REPORT.
International Development Research Centre, Box 8500, Ottawa, ON K1G 3H9, Canada. TEL 613-236-6163. FAX 613-563-2476. Available only online. *932*

INTERNATIONAL DIRECTORY OF DESIGN.
Penrose Press, Box 470925, San Francisco, CA 94147. TEL 415-567-4157. FAX 415-567-4165. *435*

INTERNATIONAL ENERGY ANNUAL.
U.S. Energy Information Administration, National Energy Information Center, EI-231, James Forrestal Bldg., Rm. 1F-048, 1000 Independence Ave., S.W., Washington, DC 20585. TEL 202-586-8800. *2552*

INTERNATIONAL ENVIRONMENT REPORTER.
The Bureau of National Affairs, Inc., 1231 25th St., N.W., Washington, DC 20037. TEL 202-452-4200. FAX 202-822-8092. Vendor(s): Lexis-Nexis. *2803*

INTERNATIONAL EXAMINER.
622 S. Washington, Seattle, WA 98104. *2884*

INTERNATIONAL FINANCIAL LAW REVIEW.
Euromoney Publications plc., Nestor House, Playhouse Yard, London EC4V 5EX, England. TEL 44-171-779-8935. FAX 44-171-779-8541. Vendor(s): University Microfilms International. *3935*

INTERNATIONAL FINANCIAL STATISTICS.
International Monetary Fund, Publications Unit, 700 19th St., N.W., Washington, DC 20431. TEL 202-623-7430. FAX 202-623-7201. Vendor(s): National Data Corp.. *1006*

INTERNATIONAL FOOD MANUFACTURE.
Miller Freeman Technical Ltd. Miller Freeman House, 30 Calderwood St., London SE18 6QH, England. TEL 44-181-855-7777. FAX 44-181-316-3206. Vendor(s): Information Access Co.. *2978*

INTERNATIONAL GAMING & WAGERING BUSINESS.
B M T Communications, Inc., 7 Penn Plaza, New York, NY 10001-3900. TEL 212-594-4120. FAX 212-714-0514. Vendor(s): Information Access Co.. *6465*

INTERNATIONAL GAS REPORT.
Financial Times Energy Publishing Maple House, 149 Tottenham Court Rd., London W1P 9LL, England. TEL 44-171-896-2241. FAX 44-171-896-2275. Vendor(s): Data-Star, Information Access Co., Knight-Ridder Information, Inc., Lexis-Nexis. *5360*

INTERNATIONAL GAS TECHNOLOGY HIGHLIGHTS.
Institute of Gas Technology, 1700 S. Mt. Prospect Rd., Des Plaines, IL 60018. TEL 708-768-0512. FAX 708-768-0516. Available only online. *5360*

THE INTERNATIONAL INFORMATION REPORT.
Washington Researchers, Ltd., Box 19005, 20th St. Sta., Washington, DC 20036-9005. TEL 202-333-3499. FAX 202-625-0656. Vendor(s): NewsNet (IT75). *536*

INTERNATIONAL INSURANCE MONITOR.
International Insurance Monitor, Box 9001, Mt. Vernon, NY 10552. TEL 914-699-2020. Vendor(s): University Microfilms International. *3654*

INTERNATIONAL JOURNAL OF ADVERTISING.
Blackwell Publishers Ltd., 108 Cowley Rd., Oxford OX4 1JF, England. TEL 44-1865-791100. FAX 44-1865-791347. Vendor(s): Information Access Co.. *38*

INTERNATIONAL JOURNAL OF COMPARATIVE SOCIOLOGY.
E.J. Brill, P.O. Box 9000, 2300 PA Leiden, Netherlands. TEL 31-71-5353500. FAX 31-71-5317532. Vendor(s): Information Access Co.. *6417*

INTERNATIONAL JOURNAL OF COMPUTER INTEGRATED MANUFACTURING.
Taylor & Francis Ltd., 1 Gunpowder Sq., London EC4A 3DE, England. TEL 44-171-583-0490. FAX 44-171-583-0585. *1155*

INTERNATIONAL JOURNAL OF COSMETIC SCIENCE.
Chapman & Hall, Journals Department 2-6 Boundary Row, London SE1 8HN, England. TEL 44-171-8650066. FAX 44-171-5229623. *496*

INTERNATIONAL JOURNAL OF GOVERNMENT AUDITING.
International Organization of Supreme Audit Institutions, c/o U.S. General Accounting Office, 441 G St., N.W., Rm.7806, Washington, DC 20548. TEL 202-512-4707. FAX 1-202-512-4021. Vendor(s): University Microfilms International. *5907*

INTERNATIONAL JOURNAL OF HEALTH SERVICES.
Baywood Publishing Co., Inc., 26 Austin Ave., Box 337, Amityville, NY 11701. TEL 516-691-1270. FAX 516-691-1770. *5965*

INTERNATIONAL JOURNAL OF MANPOWER.
M C B University Press Ltd., 60-62 Toller Ln., Bradford, W. Yorks BD8 9BY, England. TEL 44-1274-777700. FAX 44-1274-785200. Vendor(s): Information Access Co.. *1379*

INTERNATIONAL JOURNAL OF OPERATIONS AND PRODUCTION MANAGEMENT.
M C B University Press Ltd., 60-62 Toller Ln., Bradford, W. Yorks BD8 9BY, England. TEL 44-1274-777700. FAX 44-1274-785200. Vendor(s): Information Access Co.. *1424*

INTERNATIONAL JOURNAL OF PHARMACEUTICS.
Elsevier Science B.V., P.O. Box 211, 1000 AE Amsterdam, Netherlands. TEL 31-20-4853911. FAX 31-20-4853598. *5418*

INTERNATIONAL JOURNAL OF PHARMACOGNOSY.
Swets & Zeitlinger bv, P.O. Box 825, 2160 SZ Lisse, Netherlands. TEL 31-252-435111. FAX 31-252-415888. *5419*

INTERNATIONAL JOURNAL OF PHYSICAL DISTRIBUTION & LOGISTICS MANAGEMENT.
M C B University Press Ltd., 60-62 Toller Ln., Bradford, W. Yorks BD8 9BY, England. TEL 44-1274-777700. FAX 44-1274-785200. Vendor(s): Information Access Co.. *6858*

INTERNATIONAL JOURNAL OF PUBLIC ADMINISTRATION.
Marcel Dekker Journals, 270 Madison Ave., New York, NY 10016. TEL 212-696-9000. FAX 212-685-4540. Vendor(s): Information Access Co.. *5907*

INTERNATIONAL JOURNAL OF PUNJAB STUDIES.
Sage Publications India Pvt. Ltd., Box 4215, New Delhi 110 048, India. TEL 91-11-644-4958. FAX 91-11-647-2426. *6329*

INTERNATIONAL JOURNAL OF PURCHASING & MATERIALS MANAGEMENT.
National Association of Purchasing Management, 2055 E. Centennial Circle, Box 22160, Tempe, AZ 85285-2160. TEL 602-752-6276. FAX 602-752-7890.
Vendor(s): Information Access Co., Knight-Ridder Information, Inc., University Microfilms International. *1469*

INTERNATIONAL JOURNAL OF QUALITY & RELIABILITY MANAGEMENT.
M C B University Press Ltd., 60-62 Toller Ln., Bradford, W. Yorks BD8 9BY, England. TEL 44-1274-777700. FAX 44-1274-785200.
Vendor(s): Information Access Co. *1424*

INTERNATIONAL JOURNAL OF QUALITY SCIENCE.
M C B University Press Ltd., 60-62 Toller Ln., Bradford, W. Yorks BD8 9BY, England. TEL 44-1274-777700. FAX 44-1274-785200. *1425*

INTERNATIONAL JOURNAL OF REHABILITATION RESEARCH.
Chapman & Hall, Journals Department 2-6 Boundary Row, London SE1, England. TEL 44-171-8650066. FAX 44-171-5229623. *3305*

INTERNATIONAL JOURNAL OF RETAIL & DISTRIBUTION MANAGEMENT.
M C B University Press Ltd., 60-62 Toller Ln., Bradford, W. Yorks BD8 9BY, England. TEL 44-1274-777700. FAX 44-1274-785200.
Vendor(s): Information Access Co.. *1469*

INTERNATIONAL JOURNAL OF ROCK MECHANICS & MINING SCIENCES.
Elsevier Science Ltd., Pergamon, P.O. Box 800, Kidlington, Oxford OX5 1DX, England. TEL 44-1865-843000. FAX 44-1865-843010.
Vendor(s): Orbit Search Service (GEOM). *5066*

INTERNATIONAL JOURNAL OF SOCIAL PSYCHIATRY.
Avenue Publishing Co., 55 Woodstock Ave., London NW11 9RG, England. TEL 44-181-455-2940.
Vendor(s): University Microfilms International. *4842*

INTERNATIONAL JOURNAL OF SUPERCOMPUTER APPLICATIONS AND HIGH-PERFORMANCE COMPUTING.
Sage Publications, Inc., Sage Science Press, 2455 Teller Rd., Thousand Oaks, CA 91320. TEL 805-499-0721. FAX 805-499-0871.
Vendor(s): Knight-Ridder Information, Inc.. *2111*

INTERNATIONAL JOURNAL OF WATER RESOURCES DEVELOPMENT.
Carfax Publishing Co., P.O. Box 25, Abingdon, Oxon. OX14 3UE, England. TEL 44-1235-401000. FAX 44-1235-401550. *6971*

INTERNATIONAL LABOUR DOCUMENTATION.
I L O Publications, CH-1211 Geneva 22, Switzerland. TEL 022-799-6111. FAX 022-798-6358.
Vendor(s): European Space Agency (File no.53/LABORDOC), Human Resources Information Network, Orbit Search Service (LDOC). *1006*

INTERNATIONAL LABOUR REVIEW.
I L O Publications, CH-1211 Geneva 22, Switzerland. TEL 41-22-799-6111. FAX 41-22-798-6358.
Vendor(s): Information Access Co., University Microfilms International. *1380*

INTERNATIONAL LAWYER.
American Bar Association, International Law and Practice Section, 750 N. Lake Shore Dr., Chicago, IL 60611. TEL 312-988-6067.
Vendor(s): Lexis-Nexis, West Services, Inc.. *3936*

INTERNATIONAL LEGAL MATERIALS.
American Society of International Law, 2223 Massachusetts Ave., N.W., Washington, DC 20008-2864. TEL 202-939-6000. FAX 202-797-7133.
Vendor(s): Lexis-Nexis. *3936*

INTERNATIONAL MARKET ALERT.
International Reports, Inc. 11300 Rockville Pike, Ste. 1100, Rockville, MD 20852-3035.
Vendor(s): Lexis-Nexis, NewsNet (FI58). *1334*

INTERNATIONAL MATHEMATICS RESEARCH NOTICES.
Duke University Press, Box 90660, Durham, NC 27708-0660. TEL 919-687-3600. FAX 919-688-4574. *4370*

INTERNATIONAL MEDICAL JOURNAL.
Japan International Cultural Exchange Foundation, 2-15-5-207 Shoto, Shibuya-ku, Tokyo 150, Japan. TEL 81-3-3424-9090. FAX 81-3-3424-9119. *4474*

INTERNATIONAL MIGRATION REVIEW.
Center for Migration Studies, 209 Flagg Pl., Staten Island, NY 10304-1199. TEL 718-351-8800. FAX 718-667-4598.
Vendor(s): Information Access Co., University Microfilms International. *5786*

INTERNATIONAL MONETARY FUND. BALANCE OF PAYMENTS STATISTICS YEARBOOK.
International Monetary Fund, Publication Services, 700 19th St., N.W., Washington, DC 20431. TEL 202-623-7430. FAX 020-623-7201. *1007*

INTERNATIONAL MONETARY FUND. STAFF PAPERS.
International Monetary Fund, Publication Services, 700 19th St., N.W., Ste. C-100, Washington, DC 20431. TEL 202-623-7430. FAX 202-623-7201.
Vendor(s): Information Access Co., University Microfilms International. *1102*

INTERNATIONAL NURSING INDEX.
American Journal of Nursing Co., 555 W. 57th St., New York, NY 10019. TEL 212-582-8820.
Vendor(s): Knight-Ridder Information, Inc. (File nos.154 & 155/MEDLINE), National Library of Medicine, Ovid Technologies, Inc., STN International (MEDLINE). *4556*

INTERNATIONAL ORGANIZATION.
M I T Press, 55 Hayward St., Cambridge, MA 02142. TEL 617-253-2889. FAX 617-577-1545.
Vendor(s): Information Access Co.. *5755*

INTERNATIONAL PACKAGING ABSTRACTS.
Pira International, Randalls Rd., Leatherhead, Surrey KT22 7RJ, England. TEL 44-1372-802050. FAX 44-1372-802239.
Vendor(s): Data-Star, FIZ Technik, Knight-Ridder Information, Inc., Orbit Search Service (PIRA), STN International. *5305*

INTERNATIONAL PETROLEUM ABSTRACTS.
John Wiley & Sons Ltd., Journals, Baffins Ln., Chichester, W. Sussex PO19 1UD, England. TEL 44-1243-779777. FAX 44-1243-843232.
Vendor(s): Orbit Search Service (IPAB). *5383*

INTERNATIONAL PHARMACEUTICAL ABSTRACTS.
American Society of Health-System Pharmacists, 7272 Wisconsin Ave., Bethesda, MD 20814. TEL 301-657-3000. FAX 301-657-1641.
Vendor(s): DIMDI, Data-Star (IPAB), Knight-Ridder Information, Inc. (File no.74), National Library of Medicine, Ovid Technologies, Inc. (IPAB). *5450*

INTERNATIONAL PLAY JOURNAL.
Chapman & Hall, Journals Department 2-6 Boundary Row, London SE1 8HN, England. TEL 44-171-8650066. FAX 44-171-5229623. *5850*

INTERNATIONAL POPULATION DATA.
U.S. Bureau of the Census, Customer Services, Washington, DC 20233. TEL 301-457-4100. FAX 301-457-4714.
Vendor(s): CompuServe, Inc., Knight-Ridder Information, Inc.. *5799*

INTERNATIONAL PRODUCT ALERT.
Marketing Intelligence Service Ltd., 6473D State Rt. 64, Naples, NY 14512-9726. TEL 716-374-6326. FAX 716-374-5217.
Vendor(s): CompuServe, Inc., Data-Star, Dow Jones News Retrieval, Information Access Co., Knight-Ridder Information, Inc. (File no. 9), NewsNet (AD25). *1469*

INTERNATIONAL RESEARCH CENTERS DIRECTORY.
Gale Research Inc., 835 Penobscot Bldg., Detroit, MI 48226. TEL 313-961-2242. FAX 313-961-6083.
Vendor(s): Knight-Ridder Information, Inc.. *2343*

INTERNATIONAL REVIEW OF MISSION.
World Council of Churches, 150 route de Ferney, P.O. Box 2100, CH-121. Geneva 2, Switzerland. TEL 41-22-791-6111. FAX 41-22-791-0361.
Vendor(s): Information Access Co., University Microfilms International. *6068*

INTERNATIONAL ROAD HAULAGE BY UNITED KINGDOM REGISTERED VEHICLES.
H.M.S.O., 51 Nine Elms Ln., London SW8 5DR, England. TEL 44-171-973-0011. FAX 44-171-873-8247. *6858*

INTERNATIONAL SATELLITE DIRECTORY.
Design Publishers, 800 Siesta Way, Sonoma, CA 95476-4413. *69*

INTERNATIONAL SECURITIES REGULATION REPORT.
L R P Publications, 747 Dresher Rd., Box 980, Horsham, PA 19044-0980. TEL 215-784-0941. FAX 215-784-9639.
Vendor(s): Lexis-Nexis. *1335*

INTERNATIONAL SECURITY.
M I T Press, 55 Hayward St., Cambridge, MA 02142. TEL 617-253-2889. FAX 617-577-1545.
Vendor(s): Information Access Co.. *5756*

INTERNATIONAL SMALL BUSINESS JOURNAL.
Woodcock Publications Ltd., P.O. Box 1, Macclesfield, Cheshire SK10 4YQ England. TEL 44-1625-528516. FAX 44-1625-532644.
Vendor(s): Information Access Co., University Microfilms International. *1576*

INTERNATIONAL SOLAR ENERGY INTELLIGENCE REPORT.
Business Publishers, Inc., 951 Pershing Dr., Silver Spring, MD 20910-4464. TEL 301-587-6300. FAX 301-585-9075.
Vendor(s): Data-Star, Information Access Co., Knight-Ridder Information, Inc., NewsNet. *2585*

INTERNATIONAL STUDIES OF MANAGEMENT AND ORGANIZATION.
M.E. Sharpe, Inc., 80 Business Park Dr., Armonk, NY 10504. TEL 914-273-1800. FAX 914-273-2106.
Vendor(s): Information Access Co., University Microfilms International. *1425*

INTERNATIONAL TAX DIGEST.
I B C Publishing, Gilmoora House, 57-61 Mortimer St., London W1N 7TD, England. TEL 0171-637-4383. FAX 0171-636-6414.
Vendor(s): University Microfilms International. *1549*

INTERNATIONAL TAX REPORT.
I B C Publishing, Gilmoora House, 57-61 Mortimer St., London W1N 7TD, England. TEL 0171-637-4383. FAX 0171-636-6414.
Vendor(s): Data-Star, Lexis-Nexis, University Microfilms International. *1550*

INTERNATIONAL TAX REVIEW.
Euromoney Publications plc., Nestor House, Playhouse Yard, London EC4V 5EX, England. TEL 44-171-779-8935. FAX 44-171-779-8541.
Vendor(s): University Microfilms International. *1281*

INTERNATIONAL TOURISM REPORTS.
Economist Intelligence Unit, 111 W. 57th St., New York, NY 10019. TEL 212-554-0600. FAX 212-586-1181. *6893*

INTERNATIONAL TRADE FINANCE.
Financial Times Business Information Newsletters 126 Jermyn St., London SW1Y 4UJ, England. TEL 44-171-411-4414. FAX 44-171-441-4415.
Vendor(s): Information Access Co.. *1103*

INTERNATIONAL TRADE FORUM.
International Trade Centre, Palais des Nations, CH-1211 Geneva 10, Switzerland. FAX 41-22-733-4439.
Vendor(s): Information Access Co., University Microfilms International. *1281*

INTERNATIONAL TRADE REPORTER.
The Bureau of National Affairs, Inc., 1231 25th St., N.W., Washington, DC 20037. TEL 202-452-4200. FAX 202-822-8092.
Vendor(s): Lexis-Nexis (INTRAD), West Services, Inc. (BNA-ITR). *1281*

INTERNATIONAL TRAVEL NEWS.
Martin Publications Inc., 2120 28th St., Sacramento, CA 95818. TEL 916-457-3643. Vendor(s): Information Access Co.. *6894*

INTERNATIONAL WILDLIFE.
National Wildlife Federation, 1400 16th St., N.W., Washington, DC 20036-2266. TEL 202-797-6800. Vendor(s): Information Access Co.. *2131*

INTERNATIONALE BIBLIOGRAPHIE DER REZENSIONEN WISSENSCHAFTLICHER LITERATUR.
Zeller Verlag GmbH, Postfach 1949, 49009 Osnabrueck, Germany. TEL 49-541-4045914. FAX 49-541-41255. *6302*

INTERNATIONALE BIBLIOGRAPHIE DER ZEITSCHRIFTENLITERATUR AUS ALLEN GEBIETEN DES WISSENS.
Zeller Verlag GmbH, Postfach 1949, 49009 Osnabrueck, Germany. TEL 49-541-4045914. FAX 49-541-41255. *536*

INTERNET BUSINESS EUROPE.
TechMedia, 52 Foundling Ct., London WC1N 1AN, England. TEL 44-171-837-0815. FAX 44-171-278-9917. *1946*

INTERNET WEEK.
Phillips Business Information, Inc., 1201 Seven Locks Rd., Potomac, MD 20854. TEL 301-424-3338. FAX 301-309-3847. *2038*

INTERNETWORK.
Cardinal Business Media, Inc., 1300 Virginia Dr., Ste. 400, Fort Washington, PA 19034. TEL 215-643-8000. FAX 215-643-3901. Vendor(s): Information Access Co.. *2038*

INTERPRETER (NASHVILLE).
United Methodist Communications, 810 12th Ave. S., Nashville, TN 37203-4744. TEL 615-742-5400. FAX 615-742-5460. Vendor(s): University Microfilms International. *6148*

INTER-UNIVERSITY CONSORTIUM FOR POLITICAL AND SOCIAL RESEARCH. GUIDE TO RESOURCES AND SERVICES.
Inter-University Consortium for Political and Social Research, Box 1248, Ann Arbor, MI 48106-1248. TEL 313-764-2570. FAX 313-764-8041. *6330*

INTERVIEW (NEW YORK).
Brant Publications, Inc., 575 Broadway, 5th Fl., New York, NY 10012. TEL 212-941-2800. Vendor(s): Information Access Co.. *3230*

INVERSE PROBLEMS.
I O P Publishing Ltd., Techno House, Redcliffe Way, Bristol, Avon BS1 6NX, England. TEL 44-117-929-7481. FAX 44-117-929-4318. *4410*

INVESTIGACION BIBLIOTECOLOGICA.
Universidad Nacional Autonoma de Mexico, Centro Universitario de Investigaciones Bibliotecologicas, Torre II de Humanidades, pisos 12 y 13, Ciudad Universitaria, 04510 Mexico, D.F., Mexico. TEL 525-6230352. FAX 525-5507461. *4001*

INVESTING, LICENSING AND TRADING CONDITIONS ABROAD. AMERICAS.
Economist Intelligence Unit, 111 W. 57th St., New York, NY 10019. TEL 212-554-0600. FAX 212-586-1181. Vendor(s): Knight-Ridder Information, Inc., Lexis-Nexis. *1282*

INVESTING, LICENSING AND TRADING CONDITIONS ABROAD. ARGENTINA.
Economist Intelligence Unit, 111 W. 57th St., New York, NY 10019. TEL 212-554-0600. FAX 212-586-1181. Vendor(s): Knight-Ridder Information, Inc., Lexis-Nexis. *1282*

INVESTING, LICENSING AND TRADING CONDITIONS ABROAD. ASIA.
Economist Intelligence Unit, 111 W. 57th St., New York, NY 10019. TEL 212-554-0600. FAX 212-586-1181. Vendor(s): Knight-Ridder Information, Inc., Lexis-Nexis. *1282*

INVESTING, LICENSING AND TRADING CONDITIONS ABROAD. AUSTRALIA.
Economist Intelligence Unit, 111 W. 57th St., New York, NY 10019. TEL 212-554-0600. FAX 212-596-1181. Vendor(s): Knight-Ridder Information, Inc., Lexis-Nexis. *1282*

INVESTING, LICENSING AND TRADING CONDITIONS ABROAD. AUSTRIA.
Economist Intelligence Unit, 111 W. 57th St., New York, NY 10019. TEL 212-554-0600. FAX 212-586-1181. Vendor(s): Knight-Ridder Information, Inc., Lexis-Nexis. *1282*

INVESTING, LICENSING AND TRADING CONDITIONS ABROAD. BELGIUM.
Economist Intelligence Unit, 111 W. 57th St., New York, NY 10019. TEL 212-554-0600. FAX 212-586-1181. Vendor(s): Knight-Ridder Information, Inc., Lexis-Nexis. *1282*

INVESTING, LICENSING AND TRADING CONDITIONS ABROAD. BRAZIL.
Economist Intelligence Unit, 111 W. 57th St., New York, NY 10019. TEL 212-554-0600. FAX 212-586-1181. Vendor(s): Knight-Ridder Information, Inc., Lexis-Nexis. *1282*

INVESTING, LICENSING AND TRADING CONDITIONS ABROAD. BRITAIN.
Economist Intelligence Unit, 111 W. 57th St., New York, NY 10019. TEL 212-554-0600. FAX 212-586-1181. Vendor(s): Knight-Ridder Information, Inc., Lexis-Nexis. *1283*

INVESTING, LICENSING AND TRADING CONDITIONS ABROAD. CANADA.
Economist Intelligence Unit, 111 W. 57th St., New York, NY 10019. TEL 212-554-0600. FAX 212-586-1181. Vendor(s): Knight-Ridder Information, Inc., Lexis-Nexis. *1283*

INVESTING, LICENSING AND TRADING CONDITIONS ABROAD. CENTRAL AMERICA.
Economist Intelligence Unit, 111 W. 57th St., New York, NY 10019. TEL 212-554-0600. FAX 212-586-1181. Vendor(s): Knight-Ridder Information, Inc., Lexis-Nexis. *1283*

INVESTING, LICENSING AND TRADING CONDITIONS ABROAD. CHILE.
Economist Intelligence Unit, 111 W. 57th St., New York, NY 10019. TEL 212-554-0600. FAX 212-586-1181. Vendor(s): Knight-Ridder Information, Inc., Lexis-Nexis. *1283*

INVESTING, LICENSING AND TRADING CONDITIONS ABROAD. CHINA.
Economist Intelligence Unit, 111 W. 57th St., New York, NY 10019. TEL 212-554-0600. FAX 212-586-1181. Vendor(s): Knight-Ridder Information, Inc., Lexis-Nexis. *1283*

INVESTING, LICENSING AND TRADING CONDITIONS ABROAD. COLOMBIA.
Economist Intelligence Unit, 111 W. 57th St., New York, NY 10019. TEL 212-554-0600. FAX 212-586-1181. Vendor(s): Knight-Ridder Information, Inc., Lexis-Nexis. *1283*

INVESTING, LICENSING AND TRADING CONDITIONS ABROAD. CZECH REPUBLIC AND SLOVAKIA.
Economist Intelligence Unit, 111 W. 57th St., New York, NY 10019. TEL 212-554-0600. FAX 212-586-1181. Vendor(s): Knight-Ridder Information, Inc., Lexis-Nexis. *1283*

INVESTING, LICENSING AND TRADING CONDITIONS ABROAD. DENMARK.
Economist Intelligence Unit, 111 W. 57th St., New York, NY 10019. TEL 212-554-0600. FAX 212-586-1181. Vendor(s): Knight-Ridder Information, Inc., Lexis-Nexis. *1283*

INVESTING, LICENSING AND TRADING CONDITIONS ABROAD. ECUADOR.
Economist Intelligence Unit, 111 W. 57th St., New York, NY 10019. TEL 212-554-0600. FAX 212-586-1181. Vendor(s): Knight-Ridder Information, Inc., Lexis-Nexis. *1283*

INVESTING, LICENSING AND TRADING CONDITIONS ABROAD. EGYPT.
Economist Intelligence Unit, 111 W. 57th St., New York, NY 10019. TEL 212-554-0600. FAX 212-586-1181. Vendor(s): Knight-Ridder Information, Inc., Lexis-Nexis. *1283*

INVESTING, LICENSING AND TRADING CONDITIONS ABROAD. FINLAND.
Economist Intelligence Unit, 111 W. 57th St., New York, NY 10019. TEL 212-554-0600. FAX 212-586-1181. Vendor(s): Knight-Ridder Information, Inc., Lexis-Nexis. *1283*

INVESTING, LICENSING AND TRADING CONDITIONS ABROAD. FRANCE.
Economist Intelligence Unit, 111 W. 57th St., New York, NY 10019. TEL 212-554-0600. FAX 212-586-1181. Vendor(s): Knight-Ridder Information, Inc., Lexis-Nexis. *1283*

INVESTING, LICENSING AND TRADING CONDITIONS ABROAD. GERMANY.
Economist Intelligence Unit, 111 W. 57th St., New York, NY 10019. TEL 212-554-0600. FAX 212-586-1181. Vendor(s): Knight-Ridder Information, Inc., Lexis-Nexis. *1283*

INVESTING, LICENSING AND TRADING CONDITIONS ABROAD. GLOBAL EDITION.
Economist Intelligence Unit, 111 W. 57th St., New York, NY 10019. TEL 212-554-0600. FAX 212-586-1181. Vendor(s): Knight-Ridder Information, Inc., Lexis-Nexis. *1284*

INVESTING, LICENSING AND TRADING CONDITIONS ABROAD. GREECE.
Economist Intelligence Unit, 111 W. 57th St., New York, NY 10019. TEL 212-554-0600. FAX 212-586-1181. Vendor(s): Knight-Ridder Information, Inc., Lexis-Nexis. *1284*

INVESTING, LICENSING AND TRADING CONDITIONS ABROAD. HONG KONG.
Economist Intelligence Unit, 111 W. 57th St., New York, NY 10019. TEL 212-554-0600. FAX 212-586-1181. Vendor(s): Knight-Ridder Information, Inc., Lexis-Nexis. *1284*

INVESTING, LICENSING AND TRADING CONDITIONS ABROAD. HUNGARY.
Economist Intelligence Unit, 215 Park Ave. S., New York, NY 10003-1658. TEL 212-554-0600. FAX 212-586-1182. Vendor(s): Knight-Ridder Information, Inc., Lexis-Nexis. *1284*

INVESTING, LICENSING AND TRADING CONDITIONS ABROAD. INDIA.
Economist Intelligence Unit, 111 W. 57th St., New York, NY 10019. TEL 212-554-0600. FAX 212-586-1181. Vendor(s): Knight-Ridder Information, Inc., Lexis-Nexis. *1284*

INVESTING, LICENSING AND TRADING CONDITIONS ABROAD. INDONESIA.
Economist Intelligence Unit, 111 W. 57th St., New York, NY 10019. TEL 212-554-0600. FAX 212-586-1181. Vendor(s): Knight-Ridder Information, Inc., Lexis-Nexis. *1284*

INVESTING, LICENSING AND TRADING CONDITIONS ABROAD. IRELAND.
Economist Intelligence Unit, 111 W. 57th St., New York, NY 10019. TEL 212-554-0600. FAX 212-586-1181. Vendor(s): Knight-Ridder Information, Inc., Lexis-Nexis. *1284*

INVESTING, LICENSING AND TRADING CONDITIONS ABROAD. ISRAEL.
Economist Intelligence Unit, 111 W. 57th St., New York, NY 10019. TEL 212-554-0600. FAX 212-586-1181.
Vendor(s): Knight-Ridder Information, Inc., Lexis-Nexis. *1284*

INVESTING, LICENSING AND TRADING CONDITIONS ABROAD. ITALY.
Economist Intelligence Unit, 111 W. 57th St., New York, NY 10019. TEL 212-554-0600. FAX 212-586-1181.
Vendor(s): Knight-Ridder Information, Inc., Lexis-Nexis. *1284*

INVESTING, LICENSING AND TRADING CONDITIONS ABROAD. JAPAN.
Economist Intelligence Unit, 111 W. 57th St., New York, NY 10019. TEL 212-554-0600. FAX 212-586-1181.
Vendor(s): Knight-Ridder Information, Inc., Lexis-Nexis. *1284*

INVESTING, LICENSING AND TRADING CONDITIONS ABROAD. KENYA.
Economist Intelligence Unit, 111 W. 57th St., New York, NY 10019. TEL 212-554-0600. FAX 212-586-1181.
Vendor(s): Knight-Ridder Information, Inc., Lexis-Nexis. *1284*

INVESTING, LICENSING AND TRADING CONDITIONS ABROAD. LUXEMBOURG.
Economist Intelligence Unit, 111 W. 57th St., New York, NY 10019. TEL 212-554-0600. FAX 212-586-1181.
Vendor(s): Knight-Ridder Information, Inc., Lexis-Nexis. *1284*

INVESTING, LICENSING AND TRADING CONDITIONS ABROAD. MALAYSIA.
Economist Intelligence Unit, 111 W. 57th St., New York, NY 10019. TEL 212-554-0600. FAX 212-586-1181.
Vendor(s): Knight-Ridder Information, Inc., Lexis-Nexis. *1284*

INVESTING, LICENSING AND TRADING CONDITIONS ABROAD. MEXICO.
Economist Intelligence Unit, 111 W. 57th St., New York, NY 10019. TEL 212-554-0600. FAX 212-586-1181.
Vendor(s): Knight-Ridder Information, Inc., Lexis-Nexis. *1284*

INVESTING, LICENSING AND TRADING CONDITIONS ABROAD. MIDDLE EAST - AFRICA.
Economist Intelligence Unit, 111 W. 57th St., New York, NY 10019. TEL 212-554-0600. FAX 212-586-1181.
Vendor(s): Knight-Ridder Information, Inc., Lexis-Nexis. *1284*

INVESTING, LICENSING AND TRADING CONDITIONS ABROAD. NETHERLANDS.
Economist Intelligence Unit, 111 W. 57th St., New York, NY 10019. TEL 212-554-0600. FAX 212-586-1181.
Vendor(s): Knight-Ridder Information, Inc., Lexis-Nexis. *1285*

INVESTING, LICENSING AND TRADING CONDITIONS ABROAD. NEW ZEALAND.
Economist Intelligence Unit, 111 W. 57th St., New York, NY 10019. TEL 212-554-0600. FAX 212-586-1181.
Vendor(s): Knight-Ridder Information, Inc., Lexis-Nexis. *1285*

INVESTING, LICENSING AND TRADING CONDITIONS ABROAD. NIGERIA.
Economist Intelligence Unit, 111 W. 57th St., New York, NY 10019. TEL 212-554-0600. FAX 212-586-1181.
Vendor(s): Knight-Ridder Information, Inc., Lexis-Nexis. *1285*

INVESTING, LICENSING AND TRADING CONDITIONS ABROAD. NORWAY.
Economist Intelligence Unit, 111 W. 57th St., New York, NY 10019. TEL 212-554-0600. FAX 212-586-1181.
Vendor(s): Knight-Ridder Information, Inc., Lexis-Nexis. *1285*

INVESTING, LICENSING AND TRADING CONDITIONS ABROAD. PAKISTAN.
Economist Intelligence Unit, 111 W. 57th St., New York, NY 10019. TEL 212-554-0600. FAX 212-586-1181.
Vendor(s): Knight-Ridder Information, Inc., Lexis-Nexis. *1285*

INVESTING, LICENSING AND TRADING CONDITIONS ABROAD. PANAMA.
Economist Intelligence Unit, 111 W. 57th St., New York, NY 10019. TEL 212-554-0600. FAX 212-586-1181.
Vendor(s): Knight-Ridder Information, Inc., Lexis-Nexis. *1285*

INVESTING, LICENSING AND TRADING CONDITIONS ABROAD. PERU.
Economist Intelligence Unit, 111 W. 57th St., New York, NY 10019. TEL 212-554-0600. FAX 212-586-1181.
Vendor(s): Knight-Ridder Information, Inc., Lexis-Nexis. *1285*

INVESTING, LICENSING AND TRADING CONDITIONS ABROAD. PHILIPPINES.
Economist Intelligence Unit, 111 W. 57th St., New York, NY 10019. TEL 212-554-0600. FAX 212-586-1181.
Vendor(s): Knight-Ridder Information, Inc., Lexis-Nexis. *1285*

INVESTING, LICENSING AND TRADING CONDITIONS ABROAD. POLAND.
Economist Intelligence Unit, 111 W. 57th St., New York, NY 10019. TEL 212-554-0600. FAX 212-586-1181.
Vendor(s): Knight-Ridder Information, Inc., Lexis-Nexis. *1285*

INVESTING, LICENSING AND TRADING CONDITIONS ABROAD. PORTUGAL.
Economist Intelligence Unit, 111 W. 57th St., New York, NY 10019. TEL 212-554-0600. FAX 212-586-1181.
Vendor(s): Knight-Ridder Information, Inc., Lexis-Nexis. *1285*

INVESTING, LICENSING AND TRADING CONDITIONS ABROAD. PUERTO RICO.
Economist Intelligence Unit, 111 W. 57th St., New York, NY 10019. TEL 212-554-0600. FAX 212-586-1181.
Vendor(s): Knight-Ridder Information, Inc., Lexis-Nexis. *1285*

INVESTING, LICENSING AND TRADING CONDITIONS ABROAD. RUSSIA.
Economist Intelligence Unit, 111 W. 57th St., New York, NY 10019. TEL 212-554-0600. FAX 212-586-1181.
Vendor(s): Knight-Ridder Information, Inc., Lexis-Nexis. *1285*

INVESTING, LICENSING AND TRADING CONDITIONS ABROAD. SAUDI ARABIA.
Economist Intelligence Unit, 111 W. 57th St., New York, NY 10019. TEL 212-554-0600. FAX 212-586-1181.
Vendor(s): Knight-Ridder Information, Inc., Lexis-Nexis. *1285*

INVESTING, LICENSING AND TRADING CONDITIONS ABROAD. SINGAPORE.
Economist Intelligence Unit, 111 W. 57th St., New York, NY 10019. TEL 212-554-0600. FAX 212-586-1181.
Vendor(s): Knight-Ridder Information, Inc., Lexis-Nexis. *1285*

INVESTING, LICENSING AND TRADING CONDITIONS ABROAD. SOUTH AFRICA.
Economist Intelligence Unit, 111 W. 57th St., New York, NY 10019. TEL 212-554-0600. FAX 212-586-1181.
Vendor(s): Knight-Ridder Information, Inc., Lexis-Nexis. *1285*

INVESTING, LICENSING AND TRADING CONDITIONS ABROAD. SOUTH KOREA.
Economist Intelligence Unit, 111 W. 57th St., New York, NY 10019. TEL 212-554-0600. FAX 212-586-1181.
Vendor(s): Knight Ridder Information, Inc., Lexis-Nexis. *1286*

INVESTING, LICENSING AND TRADING CONDITIONS ABROAD. SPAIN.
Economist Intelligence Unit, 111 W. 57th St., New York, NY 10019. TEL 212-554-0600. FAX 212-585-1181.
Vendor(s): Knight-Ridder Information, Inc., Lexis-Nexis. *1286*

INVESTING, LICENSING AND TRADING CONDITIONS ABROAD. SWEDEN.
Economist Intelligence Unit, 111 W. 57th St., New York, NY 10019. TEL 212-544-0600. FAX 212-586-1181.
Vendor(s): Knight-Ridder Information, Inc., Lexis-Nexis. *1286*

INVESTING, LICENSING AND TRADING CONDITIONS ABROAD. SWITZERLAND.
Economist Intelligence Unit, 111 W. 57th St., New York, NY 10019. TEL 212-554-0600. FAX 212-586-1181.
Vendor(s): Knight-Ridder Information, Inc., Lexis-Nexis. *1286*

INVESTING, LICENSING AND TRADING CONDITIONS ABROAD. TAIWAN.
Economist Intelligence Unit, 111 W. 57th St., New York, NY 10019. TEL 212-554-0600. FAX 212-586-1181.
Vendor(s): Knight-Ridder Information, Inc., Lexis-Nexis. *1286*

INVESTING, LICENSING AND TRADING CONDITIONS ABROAD. THAILAND.
Economist Intelligence Unit, 111 W. 57th St., New York, NY 10019. TEL 212-554-0600. FAX 212-586-1181.
Vendor(s): Knight-Ridder Information, Inc., Lexis-Nexis. *1286*

INVESTING, LICENSING AND TRADING CONDITIONS ABROAD. TURKEY.
Economist Intelligence Unit, 111 W. 57th St., New York, NY 10019. TEL 212-554-0600. FAX 212-586-1181.
Vendor(s): Knight-Ridder Information, Inc., Lexis-Nexis. *1286*

INVESTING, LICENSING AND TRADING CONDITIONS ABROAD. UNITED STATES OF AMERICA.
Economist Intelligence Unit, 111 W. 57th St., New York, NY 10019. TEL 212-554-0600. FAX 212-586-1181.
Vendor(s): Knight-Ridder Information, Inc., Lexis-Nexis. *1286*

INVESTING, LICENSING AND TRADING CONDITIONS ABROAD. URUGUAY.
Economist Intelligence Unit, 111 W. 57th St., New York, NY 10019. TEL 212-554-0500. FAX 212-586-1181.
Vendor(s): Knight-Ridder Information, Inc., Lexis-Nexis. *1286*

INVESTING, LICENSING AND TRADING CONDITIONS ABROAD. VENEZUELA.
Economist Intelligence Unit, 111 W. 57th St., New York, NY 10019. TEL 212-554-0600. FAX 212-586-1181.
Vendor(s): Knight-Ridder Information, Inc., Lexis-Nexis. *1286*

INVESTING, LICENSING AND TRADING CONDITIONS ABROAD. VIETNAM.
Economist Intelligence Unit, 111 W. 57th St., New York, NY 10019. TEL 212-554-0600. FAX 212-586-1181.
Vendor(s): Knight-Ridder Information, Inc., Lexis-Nexis. *1286*

INVESTMENT ADVISORS EQUITY CHARACTERISTICS.
C D A - Cadence, 1355 Piccard Dr., Rockville, MD 20850. TEL 301-975-9600. FAX 301-590-1350. *1335*

INVESTMENT COMPANY PORTFOLIOS.
C D A Investment Technologies, Inc., 1355 Piccard Dr., Rockville, MD 20850. FAX 301-590-1329. *1335*

INVESTMENT COMPANY STOCK HOLDINGS.
C D A Investment Technologies, Inc. 1355 Piccard Dr., Rockville, MD 20850. FAX 301-590-1329. *1335*

INVESTMENT DEALERS' DIGEST.
Investment Dealers' Digest, 2 World Trade Ctr., 18th Fl., New York, NY 10048. TEL 212-432-0045. Vendor(s): Information Access Co., University Microfilms International. *1336*

INVESTMENT QUALITY TRENDS.
Value Trend Analysis, 7440 Girard Ave., Ste. 4, La Jolla, CA 92037. TEL 619-459-3818. FAX 619-459-3819. *1336*

THE INVESTMENT REPORTER.
Share Holder Communication Systems, 4600 Campus Dr., Ste. 205, Newport Beach, CA 92660-1801. TEL 714-724-0444. Vendor(s): Information Access Co.. *1336*

INVESTOR'S DAILY.
Box 66370, Los Angeles, CA 90066-0370. Vendor(s): Lexis-Nexis. *1336*

INVESTOR'S DIGEST OF CANADA.
M P L Communications Inc., 133 Richmond St. W., Ste. 700, Toronto, ON M5H 3M8, Canada. TEL 416-869-1177. FAX 416-869-0456. Vendor(s): Orbit Search Service, QL Systems Ltd.. *1337*

IOWA BUSINESS DIRECTORY.
American Business Directories 5711 S. 86th Circle, Box 27347, Omaha, NE 68127. TEL 402-593-4600. FAX 402-331-5481. *1618*

IOWA LAW REVIEW.
University of Iowa, College of Law, 190 Boyd Law Bldg., Iowa City, IA 52242-1113. TEL 319-335-9132. FAX 319-335-9019. Vendor(s): Lexis-Nexis, West Services, Inc.. *3793*

IOWA LEGISLATIVE NEWS SERVICE BULLETIN.
Iowa Legislative News Service, Box 8370, Des Moines, IA 50301-8370. TEL 515-266-6066. FAX 515-266-6626. *5907*

IRISH AMERICAN POST.
Irish American Post Ltd., 301 N. Water St., 3rd Floor, Milwaukee, WI 53202-5713. TEL 414-273-8132. FAX 414-273-8196. *2885*

IRISH GEOGRAPHY.
Geographical Society of Ireland, Department of Geography, St. Patrick's College, Maynooth, County Kildare, Ireland. TEL 01-7083684. FAX 01-6289063. *3263*

IRISH JOURNAL OF AGRICULTURAL AND FOOD RESEARCH.
Teagasc, 19 Sandymount Ave., Dublin 4, Ireland. TEL 353-1-6688188. FAX 353-1-6688023. *127*

IRRIGATION AND DRAINAGE ABSTRACTS.
CAB International, Wallingford, Oxon. OX10 8DE, England. TEL 44-1491-832111. FAX 44-1491-833508. Vendor(s): DIMDI, European Space Agency, Knight-Ridder Information, Inc., STN International. *175*

ISLAND TRAVEL TRADER.
Island Publications Ltd, 26 St. Ursula St., Valletta VLT 06, Malta. TEL 356-431864. FAX 356-431864. *6894*

ISRAEL PHARMACEUTICAL JOURNAL.
Pharmaceutical Association of Israel, P.O. Box 566, Tel Aviv 65 112, Israel. *5419*

ISSUES IN ACCOUNTING EDUCATION.
American Accounting Association, Paul F. Gerhardt Bldg., 5717 Bessie Dr., Sarasota, FL 33583-2399. TEL 941-921-7747. FAX 941-923-4093. Vendor(s): University Microfilms International. *1048*

ISSUES IN LAW AND MEDICINE.
National Legal Center for the Medically Dependent and Disabled, Inc., Box 1586, Terre Haute, IN 47808-1586. TEL 812-232-0103. Vendor(s): Information Access Co., National Library of Medicine, West Services, Inc.. *4475*

ISSUES IN SCIENCE AND TECHNOLOGY.
John Wiley & Sons, Inc., Journals, 605 Third Ave., New York, NY 10158. TEL 212-850-6645. FAX 212-850-6021. Vendor(s): Information Access Co., University Microfilms International. *6249*

ITEM PROCESSING REPORT.
Phillips Business Information, Inc., 1201 Seven Locks Rd., Potomac, MD 20854. TEL 301-424-3338. FAX 301-309-3847. Vendor(s): Data-Star, Information Access Co., Knight-Ridder Information, Inc., NewsNet (EC19). *2075*

IWATE MEDICAL UNIVERSITY SCHOOL OF LIBERAL ARTS & SCIENCES. ANNUAL REPORT.
Iwate Ika Daigaku Kyoyobu, 16-1, 3-chome, Honcho-dori, Morioka-shi, Iwate-ken 020, Japan. TEL 0196-51-5111. FAX 0196-25-5816. Vendor(s): JICST (JOIS-III). *6250*

J A M A: THE JOURNAL OF THE AMERICAN MEDICAL ASSOCIATION.
American Medical Association, 515 N. State St., Chicago, IL 60610. TEL 312-464-5000. FAX 312-464-4184. Vendor(s): Information Access Co., Knight-Ridder Information, Inc., Ovid Technologies, Inc. (JWAR). *4476*

J A S A.
American Statistical Association, 1429 Duke St., Alexandria, VA 22314-3402. TEL 703-684-1221. FAX 703-684-2037. Vendor(s): Information Access Co.. *6613*

J A S T.
American Studies Association of Turkey, c/o Dr. Irem Balkir, Dept. of English, Bilkent Universitesi, 06553 Ankara, Turkey. FAX 90-312-2664934. *3473*

J C T: JOURNAL OF COATINGS TECHNOLOGY.
Federation of Societies for Coatings Technology, 492 Norristown Rd., Blue Bell, PA 19422-2350. TEL 215-940-0777. FAX 215-940-0292. Vendor(s): Information Access Co.. *5308*

J E I.
Association for Evolutionary Economics, 1101 McClung Tower, University of Tennessee, Knoxville, TN 37996-0411. TEL 615-974-1689. FAX 615-974-3915. Vendor(s): Information Access Co., University Microfilms International. *1256*

J E I REPORT.
Japan Economic Institute, 1000 Connecticut Ave., N.W., Washington, DC 20036. TEL 202-296-5633. FAX 202-296-8333. Vendor(s): Information Access Co.. *1287*

J I C S T ONLINE INFORMATION SYSTEM.
U.S. National Technical Information Service, 5285 Port Royal Rd., Springfield, VA 22161. TEL 703-487-4630. Available only online. Vendor(s): JICST. *6305*

JACK O'DWYER'S NEWSLETTER.
J.R. O'Dwyer Co., Inc., 271 Madison Ave., New York, NY 10016. TEL 212-679-2471. FAX 212-683-2750. Vendor(s): Lexis-Nexis. *38*

JANE'S DEFENCE WEEKLY.
Jane's Information Group, Sentinel House, 163 Brighton Rd., Coulsdon, Surrey CR5 2NH, England. TEL 44-181-700-3700. FAX 44-181-763-1007. Vendor(s): Knight-Ridder Information, Inc.. *5034*

JANE'S INTELLIGENCE REVIEW.
Jane's Information Group, Sentinel House, 163 Brighton Rd., Coulsdon, Surrey CR5 2NH, England. TEL 44-181-700-3700. FAX 44-181-700-3788. Vendor(s): Knight-Ridder Information, Inc.. *5035*

JAPAN ECONOMIC ALMANAC.
Nihon Keizai Shimbun, Inc., 1-9-5 Otemachi, Chiyoda-ku, Tokyo 100-66, Japan. TEL 03-3270-0251. *1523*

JAPAN QUARTERLY.
Asahi Shimbun Publishing Co., 3-2, Tsukiji 5-chome, Chuo-ku, Tokyo 104-11, Japan. TEL 03-3545-0131. FAX 03-3544-1428. Vendor(s): University Microfilms International. *4149*

JAPAN SOCIETY FOR SIMULATION TECHNOLOGY. JOURNAL.
Japan Technical Information Service, Sogo Kojimachi No. 3 Bldg., 6th Fl., 1-6 Koji-machi, Chiyoda-ku, Tokyo 102, Japan. TEL 03-3239-4711. FAX 03-3239-4714. Vendor(s): JICST (JOIS). *2052*

JAPAN - U S BUSINESS REPORT.
Japan Economic Institute, 1000 Connecticut Ave., N.W., Washington, DC 20036. TEL 202-296-5633. FAX 202-296-8333. Vendor(s): Information Access Co.. *1287*

JAPANESE JOURNAL OF CLINICAL ONCOLOGY.
Foundation for Promotion of Cancer Research, c/o National Cancer Center Hospital, 1-1, Tsukiji 5-chome, Chuo-ku, Tokyo 104, Japan. TEL 03-3542-2511. FAX 03-3545-3567. Vendor(s): JICST. *4758*

JAPANESE JOURNAL OF OPHTHALMOLOGY.
University of Tokyo, School of Medicine, Department of Ophthalmology, 7-3-1 Hongo, Bunkyo-ku, Tokyo 113, Japan. TEL 81-3-3815-5411. FAX 81-3-3817-0798. Vendor(s): CompuServe, Inc., DataArkiv A.B., JICST. *4771*

JAPANESE JOURNAL OF PHARMACOLOGY.
Japanese Pharmacological Society, Editorial Office, Kantohya Bld., Gokomachi-Ebisugawa, Nakagyo-ku, Kyoto 604, Japan. TEL 075-252-4641. FAX 075-252-4618. *5420*

THE JERUSALEM POST.
Jerusalem Post, P.O. Box 81, Jerusalem 91000, Israel. TEL 972-2-315666. FAX 972-2-389017. Vendor(s): Lexis-Nexis. *3182*

THE JERUSALEM POST (EDITION FRANCAISE).
Jerusalem Post, P.O. Box 81, Jerusalem 91000, Israel. TEL 972-2-315666. FAX 972-2-389017. Vendor(s): Lexis-Nexis. *3182*

THE JERUSALEM POST (INTERNATIONAL EDITION).
Jerusalem Post, P.O. Box 81, Jerusalem 91000, Israel. TEL 972-2-315666. FAX 972-2-389017. Vendor(s): Lexis-Nexis. *3182*

JET.
Johnson Publishing Co., Inc., 820 S. Michigan Ave., Chicago, IL 60605-2190. TEL 312-322-9200. Vendor(s): Information Access Co., University Microfilms International. *3230*

JEWELERS' CIRCULAR - KEYSTONE.
Chilton Co., Jewelers' Circular - Keystone, One Chilton Way, Radnor, PA 19089. TEL 610-964-4000. FAX 610-964-4481. Vendor(s): Information Access Co.. *3696*

JIBI INKOKA, TOKEIBU GEKA.
Igaku-Shoin Ltd., 5-24-3 Hongo, Bunkyo-ku, Tokyo 113-91, Japan. TEL 03-817-5710. Vendor(s): JICST. *4797*

JOB PRATIQUE MAGAZINE.
23 rue des Appenins, 75017 Paris, France. TEL 42-28-59-00. FAX 42-28-24-58. *5269*

JOB SAFETY & HEALTH (WASHINGTON).
The Bureau of National Affairs, Inc., 1231 25th St., N.W., Washington, DC 20037. TEL 202-452-4200. FAX 202-822-8092. Vendor(s): Human Resources Information Network (CDD, HDD). *5251*

JOHN MARSHALL LAW REVIEW.
Christensen Inc. (Chicago), 315 S. Plymouth Ct., Chicago, IL 60604. TEL 312-987-1415. FAX 312-427-8307. Vendor(s): Lexis-Nexis, West Services, Inc.. *3795*

JOINT COMMISSION PERSPECTIVES.
Mosby-Yearbook, Inc., 11830 Westline Dr., St. Louis, MO 63146-3318. TEL 800-453-4351. FAX 314-432-1380. Vendor(s): Lexis-Nexis. *5966*

THE JOURNAL (COLUMBUS).
Ohio State University, Department of English, 421 Denney Hall, 164 W. 17th Ave., Columbus, OH 43210. TEL 614-292-4076. Vendor(s): University Microfilms International. *4223*

JOURNAL DE MEDECINE LEGALE DROIT MEDICAL.
Editions E S K A, 27 rue Dunois, 75013 Paris, France. TEL 44-06-80-42. FAX 44-24-06-94. *4687*

JOURNAL DE PHYSIQUE I.
Editions de Physique, 7 av. du Hoggar, Z.I. de Courtaboeuf, B.P. 112, 91944 Les Ulis Cedex A, France. TEL 33-1-69-07-36-88. FAX 33-1-69-28-84-91. *5553*

JOURNAL DE PHYSIQUE II.
Editions de Physique, 7 av. du Hoggar, Z.I. de Courtaboeuf, B.P. 112, 91944 Les Ulis Cedex A, France. TEL 33-1-69-07-36-88. FAX 33-1-69-28-84-91. *5553*

JOURNAL DE PHYSIQUE III.
Editions de Physique, 7 av. du Hoggar, Z.I. de Courtaboeuf, B.P 112, 91944 Les Ulis Cedex A, France. TEL 33-1-69-07-36-88. FAX 33-1-69-28-84-91. *5553*

JOURNAL FOR QUALITY AND PARTICIPATION.
Association for Quality and Participation, 801-B W. 8th St., Ste. 501, Cincinnati, OH 45203. TEL 513-381-1959. FAX 513-381-0070.
Vendor(s): University Microfilms International. *1506*

JOURNAL FOR THE SCIENTIFIC STUDY OF RELIGION.
Society for the Scientific Study of Religion, c/o Ralph Hood, Department of Psychology, University of Tennessee, Chattanooga, TN 37403. TEL 423-755-4262.
Vendor(s): Information Access Co., University Microfilms International. *6070*

JOURNAL FOR UNIVERSAL COMPUTER SCIENCE.
Springer-Verlag, Heidelberger Platz 3, 14197 Berlin, Germany. TEL 49-30-8207-0. FAX 49-30-8214091. *1994*

JOURNAL OF ABNORMAL CHILD PSYCHOLOGY.
Plenum Publishing Corp., 233 Spring St., New York, NY 10013-1578. TEL 212-620-8000. FAX 212-463-0742.
Vendor(s): Information Access Co. *5851*

JOURNAL OF ACCOUNTANCY.
American Institute of Certified Public Accountants, 1211 Ave. of the Americas, New York, NY 10036. TEL 212-596-6200.
Vendor(s): Information Access Co., University Microfilms International. *1049*

JOURNAL OF ACCOUNTING LITERATURE.
University of Florida, Accounting Research Center, Fisher School of Accounting-267 BUS, College of Business Administration, Gainsville, FL 32611. TEL 904-392-0155.
Vendor(s): University Microfilms International. *1049*

JOURNAL OF ADVERTISING.
American Academy of Advertising, Clemson University, College of Commerce & Industry, 245 Sirrine Hall, Clemson, SC 29634-1325.
Vendor(s): Information Access Co., Lexis-Nexis, University Microfilms International. *38*

JOURNAL OF ADVERTISING RESEARCH.
Advertising Research Foundation, 641 Lexington Ave., 11th Fl., New York, NY 10022. TEL 212-751-5656. FAX 212-319-5265.
Vendor(s): Information Access Co., University Microfilms International. *38*

JOURNAL OF AFRICAN HISTORY.
Cambridge University Press, Edinburgh Bldg., Shaftesbury Rd., Cambridge CB2 2RU, England. TEL 44-1223-312393. FAX 44-1223-315052.
Vendor(s): Information Access Co.. *3373*

JOURNAL OF AGRICULTURAL AND FOOD CHEMISTRY.
American Chemical Society, 1155 16th St., N.W., Washington, DC 20036. TEL 800-333-9511. FAX 614-447-3671.
Vendor(s): STN International (CJACS). *228*

JOURNAL OF AGRICULTURAL LENDING.
American Bankers Association, 1120 Connecticut Ave., N.W., Washington, DC 20036. TEL 202-663-5378. FAX 202-828-4540.
Vendor(s): University Microfilms International. *1103*

JOURNAL OF AIR LAW AND COMMERCE.
S M U Law Review Association, Southern Methodist University, School of Law, Dallas, TX 75275. TEL 214-768-8250. FAX 214-768-3946.
Vendor(s): West Services, Inc.. *3796*

THE JOURNAL OF ALLERGY AND CLINICAL IMMUNOLOGY.
Mosby - Year Book, Inc. 11830 Westline Industrial Dr., St. Louis, MO 63146-3318. TEL 314-872-8370. FAX 314-872-9164.
Vendor(s): Ovid Technologies, Inc.. *4584*

JOURNAL OF AMERICAN CULTURE.
Popular Press, Bowling Green State University, Bowling Green, OH 43403. TEL 419-372-2981.
Vendor(s): University Microfilms International. *3616*

JOURNAL OF AMERICAN ETHNIC HISTORY.
Transaction Publishers, Transaction Periodicals Consortium, Department 3092, Rutgers University, New Brunswick, NJ 08903. TEL 908-445-2280. FAX 908-445-3138.
Vendor(s): Information Access Co.. *2889*

JOURNAL OF AMERICAN HISTORY.
Organization of American Historians, 112 N Bryan St., Bloomington, IN 47408. TEL 812-855-7311.
Vendor(s): University Microfilms International. *3474*

JOURNAL OF ANALYTICAL ATOMIC SPECTROMETRY.
The Royal Society of Chemistry, Thomas Graham House, Science Park, Milton Rd., Cambridge CB4 4WF, England. TEL 44-1223-420066. FAX 44-1223-423429.
Vendor(s): STN International (CJRSC). *1716*

JOURNAL OF APPLIED ELECTROCHEMISTRY.
Chapman & Hall, Journals Department 2-6 Boundary Row, London SE1 8HN, England. TEL 44-171-8650066. FAX 44-171-5229623. *1729*

JOURNAL OF APPLIED PHYSICS.
American Institute of Physics, One Physics Ellipse, College Park, MD 20740-3843. TEL 301-209-3000. *5553*

JOURNAL OF APPLIED PHYSIOLOGY.
American Physiological Society, 9650 Rockville Pike, Bethesda, MD 20814. TEL 301-530-7164. FAX 301-571-8313.
Vendor(s): OCLC. *789*

JOURNAL OF APPLIED POLYMER SCIENCE.
John Wiley & Sons, Inc., Journals, 605 Third Ave., New York, NY 10158. TEL 212-850-6645. FAX 212-850-6021.
Vendor(s): STN International (CJWILEY). *2643*

JOURNAL OF APPLIED STATISTICS.
Carfax Publishing Co., P.O. Box 25, Abingdon, Oxon. OX14 3UE, England. TEL 44-1235-401000. FAX 44-1235-401550. *6614*

JOURNAL OF AQUARICULTURE AND AQUATIC SCIENCES.
The Written Word, 7601 E. Forest Lake Dr., N.W., Parkville, MO 64152. TEL 816-842-5936. FAX 816-474-5597.
Vendor(s): CompuServe, Inc.. *589*

JOURNAL OF ARCHITECTURE.
Chapman & Hall, 2-6 Boundary Row, London SE1 8HN, England. TEL 44-171-8650066. FAX 44-171-5229623. *396*

JOURNAL OF ART & ENTERTAINMENT LAW.
Depaul University, College of Law, 25 E. Jackson Blvd., Chicago, IL 60604. TEL 312-362-5635. *3796*

JOURNAL OF ASIAN AND AFRICAN STUDIES.
E.J. Brill, P.O. Box 900C, 2300 PA Leiden, Netherlands. TEL 31-71-5353500. FAX 31-71-5317532.
Vendor(s): Information Access Co.. *6419*

JOURNAL OF ASIAN STUDIES.
Association for Asian Studies, Inc., 1 Lane Hall, University of Michigan, Ann Arbor, MI 48109. TEL 313-665-2490.
Vendor(s): University Microfilms International. *5287*

JOURNAL OF BANK COST & MANAGEMENT ACCOUNTING.
National Association of Bank Cost and Management Accounting, 2385 Castilian Cir., Box 458, Northbrook, IL 60062-7514. TEL 847-272-4233. FAX 847-272-6445.
Vendor(s): University Microfilms International. *1104*

JOURNAL OF BIOLOGICAL CHEMISTRY.
American Society for Biochemistry and Molecular Biology, Inc., Box 630591, Baltimore, MD 21263. *641*

JOURNAL OF BLACKS IN HIGHER EDUCATION.
CH I Publishers, Inc., 200 W. 57th St., New York, NY 10019. TEL 212-399-1084. FAX 212-245-1973.
Vendor(s): Lexis-Nexis. *3889*

JOURNAL OF BONE AND JOINT SURGERY: AMERICAN VOLUME.
Journal of Bone and Joint Surgery, Inc., 20 Pickering St., Needham, MA 02192-3157. TEL 617-449-9738.
Vendor(s): Ovid Technologies, Inc.. *4785*

JOURNAL OF BROADCASTING AND ELECTRONIC MEDIA.
Broadcast Education Association, 1771 N St., N.W., Washington, DC 20036. TEL 202-429-5354.
Vendor(s): University Microfilms International. *1963*

JOURNAL OF BUDDHIST ETHICS.
University of London, Goldsmiths, London SE14, England. TEL 44-171-919 7497. FAX 44-171-919-7398.
Available only online. *6110*

THE JOURNAL OF BUSINESS (CHICAGO).
University of Chicago Press, Journals Division, Box 37005, Chicago, IL 60637. TEL 312-753-3347. FAX 312-753-0811.
Vendor(s): Information Access Co. *935*

JOURNAL OF BUSINESS (SPOKANE).
Northwest Business Press, Inc., 112 E. First Ave., Spokane, WA 99202. TEL 509-456-5257.
Vendor(s): University Microfilms International. *1104*

JOURNAL OF BUSINESS ADMINISTRATION.
University of British Columbia, Faculty of Commerce and Business Administration, Vancouver, BC V6T 1Z2, Canada. TEL 604-822 9434. FAX 604-822-8489.
Vendor(s): Information Access Co.. *1426*

JOURNAL OF BUSINESS COMMUNICATION.
Association for Business Communication, c/o Dr. Rovert J. Myers, Dept. of Speech Communication, Baruch College, 17 Lexington Ave., New York, NY 10010. TEL 817-565-4423.
Vendor(s): Information Access Co., University Microfilms International. *1426*

JOURNAL OF BUSINESS ETHICS.
Kluwer Academic Publishers Postbus 17, 3300 AA Dordrecht, Netherlands. TEL 31-78-5392392. FAX 31-78-6392254.
Vendor(s): Information Access Co., University Microfilms International. *935*

JOURNAL OF BUSINESS FORECASTING METHODS AND SYSTEMS.
Graceway Publishing Co., Box 670159, Flushing, NY 11367-0159. TEL 718-453-3914. FAX 718-544-9086.
Vendor(s): University Microfilms International. *935*

JOURNAL OF BUSINESS LOGISTICS.
Council of Logistics Management, 2803 Butterfield, Oak Brook, IL 60521. TEL 708-574 0985. FAX 708-574-0989.
Vendor(s): University Microfilms International. *1470*

JOURNAL OF BUSINESS STRATEGY.
Faulkner & Gray, Inc. (New York), 11 Penn Plaza, 17th Fl., New York, NY 10001. TEL 212-967-7000. FAX 212-967-7155.
Vendor(s): Information Access Co., University Microfilms International. *1426*

JOURNAL OF CAREER PLANNING & EMPLOYMENT.
National Association of Colleges and Employers, 62 Highland Ave., Bethlehem, PA 18017. TEL 610-868-1421. FAX 610-868-0208.
Vendor(s): University Microfilms International. *5270*

JOURNAL OF CELLULAR BIOCHEMISTRY.
John Wiley & Sons, Inc., Journals, 605 Third Ave., New York, NY 10158. TEL 212-850-6645. FAX 212-850-6021. *716*

JOURNAL OF CELLULAR PHYSIOLOGY.
John Wiley & Sons, Inc., Journals, 605 Third Ave., New York, NY 10158. TEL 212-850-6645. FAX 212-850-6021. *789*

JOURNAL OF CHEMICAL AND ENGINEERING DATA.
American Chemical Society, 1155 16th St. N.W., Washington, DC 20036. TEL 800-333-9511. FAX 614-447-3671.
Vendor(s): STN International (CJACS). *1680*

JOURNAL OF CHEMICAL EDUCATION.
American Chemical Society, c/o Dept. of Chemistry, Montana State University, Bozeman, MT 59717-0340. TEL 406-994-5393. FAX 406-994-5407.
Vendor(s): University Microfilms International. *1680*

JOURNAL OF CHEMICAL INFORMATION AND COMPUTER SCIENCES.
American Chemical Society, 1155 16th St. N.W., Washington, DC 20036. TEL 800-333-9511. FAX 614-447-3671.
Vendor(s): STN International (CJACS). *1724*

JOURNAL OF CHEMICAL PHYSICS.
American Institute of Physics, One Physics Ellipse, College park, MD 20740-3843. TEL 301-209-3000. FAX 516-349-9704. *5553*

JOURNAL OF CHEMICAL RESEARCH.
The Royal Society of Chemistry, Thomas Graham House, Science Park, Milton Rd., Cambridge CB4 4WF, England. TEL 44-1223-420066. FAX 44-1223-423429.
Vendor(s): STN International (CJRSC). *1681*

JOURNAL OF CLINICAL EPIDEMIOLOGY.
Elsevier Science Inc., Box 945, New York, NY 10159-0945. TEL 212-633-3730. FAX 212-633-3680. *4480*

JOURNAL OF CLINICAL INVESTIGATION.
Rockefeller University Press, 222 E. 70th St., New York, NY 10021. TEL 212-327-8572. FAX 212-327-7944.
Vendor(s): Ovid Technologies, Inc.. *4480*

JOURNAL OF CLINICAL ONCOLOGY.
W.B. Saunders Co. Curtis Center, 3rd Fl., Independence Sq. W., Philadelphia, PA 19106-3399. TEL 215-238-7800. FAX 215-238-6445. *4758*

JOURNAL OF CLINICAL PATHOLOGY.
B M J Publishing Group, B.M.A. House, Tavistock Sq., London WC1H 9JR, England. TEL 44-171-383-6270. FAX 44-171-383-6402.
Vendor(s): Ovid Technologies, Inc.. *4480*

JOURNAL OF CLINICAL PHARMACOLOGY.
Lippincott - Raven Publishers 227 E. Washington Sq., Philadelphia, PA 19106. TEL 215-238-4200. *5421*

JOURNAL OF CLINICAL PSYCHOLOGY.
John Wiley & Sons, Inc., Journals, 605 Third Ave., New York, NY 10158-0012. TEL 212-850-6645. FAX 212-850-6021.
Vendor(s): University Microfilms International. *5854*

JOURNAL OF COGNITIVE NEUROSCIENCE.
M I T Press, 55 Hayward St., Cambridge, MA 02142. TEL 617-253-2889. FAX 617-577-1545.
Vendor(s): Information Access Co.. *4844*

JOURNAL OF COMMERCE AND COMMERCIAL.
Journal of Commerce, Inc. 2 World Trade Center, 27th Fl., New York, NY 10048-0203. TEL 212-837-7000. FAX 212-837-7035.
Vendor(s): Knight-Ridder Information, Inc., VU/TEXT Information Services, Inc.. *1166*

JOURNAL OF COMMON MARKET STUDIES.
Blackwell Publishers Ltd., 108 Cowley Rd., Oxford OX4 1JF, England. TEL 44-1865-791100. FAX 44-1865-791347.
Vendor(s): Information Access Co.. *5676*

JOURNAL OF COMMUNICATION.
Oxford University Press, Journals, 2001 Evans Rd., Cary, NC 27513. TEL 919-677-0977. FAX 919-677-1714.
Vendor(s): University Microfilms International. *1908*

JOURNAL OF COMMUNITY HEALTH.
Human Sciences Press, Inc. 233 Spring St., New York, NY 10013-1578. TEL 212-620-8000. FAX 212-463-0742.
Vendor(s): Information Access Co.. *4480*

JOURNAL OF COMPARATIVE FAMILY STUDIES.
University of Calgary, Department of Sociology, 2500 University Dr. N.W., Calgary, AB T2N 1N4, Canada. TEL 403-220-7317. FAX 403-282-9298.
Vendor(s): Information Access Co., University Microfilms International. *6419*

JOURNAL OF COMPARATIVE RELIGION.
Universal Publications (a division of S T C), P.O. Box 7305, Ottawa, ON K1L 8E4, Canada. TEL 613-831-1052. FAX 613-831-8452. *6070*

JOURNAL OF CONSUMER AFFAIRS.
American Council on Consumer Interests, 240 Stanley Hall, University of Missouri, Columbia, MO 65211. TEL 573-882-3817. FAX 573-884-6571.
Vendor(s): Information Access Co., Knight-Ridder Information, Inc., University Microfilms International. *2153*

JOURNAL OF CONSUMER POLICY.
Kluwer Academic Publishers, Postbus 17, 3300 AA Dordrecht, Netherlands. TEL 31-78-6392392. FAX 31-78-6392254.
Vendor(s): Information Access Co.. *2153*

JOURNAL OF CONSUMER RESEARCH.
University of Chicago Press, Journals Division, Box 37005, Chicago, IL 60637. TEL 312-753-3347. FAX 312-753-0811.
Vendor(s): Information Access Co., Knight-Ridder Information, Inc., Lexis-Nexis. *1470*

JOURNAL OF CONTEMPORARY NEUROLOGY.
M I T Press, 55 Hayward St., Cambridge, MA 02142. TEL 617-253-2889. FAX 617-258-6779.
Available only online. *4845*

JOURNAL OF CORPORATION LAW.
University of Iowa, College of Law, 190 Boyd Law Bldg., Iowa City, IA 52242-1113. TEL 319-335-9061. FAX 319-335-9019.
Vendor(s): West Services, Inc.. *3903*

JOURNAL OF COUNSELING & DEVELOPMENT.
American Counseling Association, 5999 Stevenson Ave., Alexandria, VA 22304-3300. TEL 703-823-9800. FAX 703-823-0252.
Vendor(s): University Microfilms International. *5855*

THE JOURNAL OF CREDIT & RISK MANAGEMENT.
Robert Morris Associates, One Liberty Place, Ste. 2300, 1650 Market St., Philadelphia, PA 19107. TEL 215-851-9100.
Vendor(s): Information Access Co., University Microfilms International. *1104*

JOURNAL OF CRIMINAL JUSTICE AND POPULAR CULTURE.
State University of New York at Albany, School of Criminal Justice, 135 Western Ave., Albany, NY 12222. TEL 518-442-5210.
Available only online. *3911*

JOURNAL OF CRIMINAL LAW & CRIMINOLOGY.
Northwestern University, School of Law - Office of Legal Publications, 357 E. Chicago Ave., Chicago, IL 60611. TEL 312-503-8467.
Vendor(s): Information Access Co., University Microfilms International, West Services, Inc.. *2167*

JOURNAL OF DEMOCRACY.
Johns Hopkins University Press, Journals Publishing Division, 2715 N. Charles St., Baltimore, MD 21218. TEL 410-516-6987. FAX 410-516-6968. *5676*

THE JOURNAL OF DEVELOPMENT STUDIES.
Frank Cass, Newbury House, 890-900 Eastern Ave., Newbury Park, Ilford, Essex 1G2 7HH, England. TEL 44-181-599-8866. FAX 44-181-599-0984.
Vendor(s): Information Access Co., University Microfilms International. *1310*

JOURNAL OF DRUG EDUCATION.
Baywood Publishing Co., Inc., 26 Austin Ave., Box 337, Amityville, NY 11701. TEL 516-691-1270. FAX 516-691-1770. *2198*

JOURNAL OF DRUG ISSUES.
Journal of Drug Issues Inc., Box 4021, Leon Sta., Tallahassee, FL 32315. TEL 904-668-6669. *2198*

JOURNAL OF DRUG RESEARCH OF EGYPT.
National Organisation for Drug Control and Research, Drug Research and Control Center, 6, Abou-Hazem St., Pyramids Ave., Box 29, Cairo, Egypt. *5421*

JOURNAL OF EARLY CHRISTIAN STUDIES.
Johns Hopkins University Press, Journals Publishing Division, 2715 N. Charles St., Ste. 750, Baltimore, MD 21218-4319. TEL 410-516-6987. FAX 410-516-6968. *6071*

JOURNAL OF ECONOMIC LITERATURE.
American Economic Association, 2014 Broadway, Ste. 305, Nashville, TN 37203. TEL 615-322-2595.
Vendor(s): Knight-Ridder Information, Inc. (Economic Literature Index File no. 139). *1010*

JOURNAL OF EDUCATION FOR BUSINESS.
Heldref Publications, 1319 18th St., N.W., Washington, DC 20036-1802. TEL 202-296-6267. FAX 202-296-5149.
Vendor(s): University Microfilms International. *937*

JOURNAL OF EDUCATION FOR TEACHING.
Carfax Publishing Co., P.O. Box 25, Abingdon, Oxon. OX14 3UE, England. TEL 44-1235-401000. FAX 44-1235-401550. *2434*

JOURNAL OF ELECTRONIC DEFENSE.
Horizon - House - Publications, Inc., 685 Canton St., Norwood, MA 02062. TEL 617-769-9750. FAX 617-762-9230.
Vendor(s): Information Access Co.. *5036*

JOURNAL OF ENERGY, NATURAL RESOURCES AND ENVIRONMENTAL LAW.
University of Utah, College of Law, Salt Lake City, UT 84112. TEL 801-581-6833.
Vendor(s): West Services, Inc.. *2553*

JOURNAL OF ENGLISH AND GERMANIC PHILOLOGY.
University of Illinois Press, 1325 S. Oak St., Champaign, IL 61820. TEL 217-333-0950. FAX 217-244-8082.
Vendor(s): Information Access Co.. *4078*

JOURNAL OF ENVIRONMENTAL HEALTH.
National Environmental Health Association, 720 S. Colorado Blvd., No. 970 S. Tower, Denver, CO 80222-1925. TEL 303-756-9090. FAX 303-691-9490.
Vendor(s): Information Access Co., University Microfilms International. *2805*

JOURNAL OF ENVIRONMENTAL HYDROLOGY.
International Association for Environmental Hydrology, Box 35324, San Antonio, TX 78235-5324. TEL 703-683-9768. FAX 703-683-6137.
Available only online. *2287*

JOURNAL OF ENVIRONMENTAL PLANNING AND MANAGEMENT.
Carfax Publishing Co., P.O. Box 25, Abingdon, Oxon. OX14 3UE, England. TEL 44-1235-401000. FAX 44-1235-401550. *3586*

JOURNAL OF EUROPEAN INDUSTRIAL TRAINING.
M C B University Press Ltd., 60-62 Toller Ln., Bradford, W. Yorks BD8 9BY, England. TEL 44-1274-777700. FAX 44-1274-785200.
Vendor(s): Information Access Co.. *1427*

JOURNAL OF EUROPEAN STUDIES.
Alpha Academic Halfpenny Furze, Mill Ln., Chalfont St. Giles, Bucks. HP8 4NR, England. TEL 44-1494-872509.
Vendor(s): Information Access Co., University Microfilms International. *3421*

JOURNAL OF EVOLUTIONARY BIOLOGY.
Birkhaeuser Verlag, P.O. Box 133, CH-4010 Basel,
Switzerland. TEL 41-61-2050730. FAX 41-61-
2050791. *745*

**JOURNAL OF EXPERIMENTAL AND THEORETICAL
PHYSICS.**
American Institute of Physics, One Physics Ellipse,
College Park, MD 20740-3843. TEL 301-209-
3000. *5554*

**JOURNAL OF EXPERIMENTAL PSYCHOLOGY:
GENERAL.**
American Psychological Association, 750 First St.,
N.E., Washington, DC 20002-4242. TEL 202-336-
5600. FAX 202-336-5568.
Vendor(s): Information Access Co. *5856*

JOURNAL OF EXPERIMENTAL ZOOLOGY.
John Wiley & Sons, Inc., Journals, 605 Third Ave.,
New York, NY 10158. TEL 212-850-6645.
FAX 212-850-6021. *810*

JOURNAL OF EXTENSION (ASCII EDITION).
Virginia Tech, 233 Smyth Hall, Blacksburg, VA
24061-0452. TEL 703-231-7880.
Available only online. *2346*

JOURNAL OF FAMILY HISTORY.
Sage Publications, Inc., 2455 Teller Rd., Thousand
Oaks, CA 91320. TEL 805-499-0721. FAX 805-
499-0871.
Vendor(s): Information Access Co., Ovid
Technologies, Inc. *6419*

JOURNAL OF FAMILY ISSUES.
Sage Publications, Inc., 2455 Teller Rd., Thousand
Oaks, CA 91320. TEL 805-499-0721. FAX 805-
499-0871.
Vendor(s): Ovid Technologies, Inc. *6419*

JOURNAL OF FAMILY PRACTICE.
Appleton & Lange, Journal Division Box 120041,
Stamford, CT 06912-0041. TEL 203-406-4500.
Vendor(s): Information Access Co. *4481*

JOURNAL OF FINANCE.
American Finance Association, c/o W. Michael
Keenan, Stern School of Business, New York
University, 44 W. 4th St., Ste. 9-190, New York, NY
10012. TEL 212-998-0355.
Vendor(s): Information Access Co. *1104*

**JOURNAL OF FINANCIAL MANAGEMENT AND
ANALYSIS.**
Om Sai Ram Centre for Financial Management
Research, 15 Prakash Co-operative Housing
Society, Relief Rd., Santacruz (W.), Bombay 400
054, India. TEL 91-22-6121715. *1105*

JOURNAL OF FINANCIAL PLANNING TODAY.
New Directions Publications, Inc., Box 6097, W.
Palm Beach, FL 33405. TEL 407-434-0100.
FAX 407-641-4801.
Vendor(s): University Microfilms International.
1105

JOURNAL OF FINANCIAL RESEARCH.
Virginia Polytechnic Institute and State University,
College of Business, Department of Finance, 1016
Pamplin Hall, Blacksburg, VA 24061-0221.
TEL 540-231-7699. FAX 540-231-4706.
Vendor(s): Information Access Co. *937*

**JOURNAL OF FUNCTIONAL AND LOGIC
PROGRAMMING.**
M I T Press, 55 Hayward St., Cambridge, MA
02142-1399. TEL 617-253-2889. FAX 617-258-
6779.
Available only online. *2045*

THE JOURNAL OF GENERAL PSYCHOLOGY.
Heldref Publications, 1319 Eighteenth St., N.W.,
Washington, DC 20036. TEL 202-296-6267.
FAX 202-296-5149.
Vendor(s): Information Access Co., University
Microfilms International. *5857*

THE JOURNAL OF GENETIC PSYCHOLOGY.
Heldref Publications, 1319 Eighteenth St., N.W.,
Washington, DC 20036-1802. TEL 202-296-6267.
FAX 202-296-5149.
Vendor(s): Information Access Co., University
Microfilms International. *5857*

JOURNAL OF GERONTOLOGICAL NURSING.
Slack, Inc., 6900 Grove Rd., Thorofare, NJ 08086-
9447. TEL 609-848-1000. FAX 609-853-5991.
3290

JOURNAL OF HARD MATERIALS.
I O P Publishing Ltd., Techno House, Redcliffe Way,
Bristol, Avon BS1 6NX, England. TEL 44-117-929-
7481. FAX 44-117-929-4318. *2734*

JOURNAL OF HEALTH AND SOCIAL BEHAVIOR.
American Sociological Association, 1722 N St.,
N.W., Washington, DC 20036. TEL 202-833-3410.
FAX 202-785-0146.
Vendor(s): University Microfilms International.
6419

JOURNAL OF HEALTH CARE FINANCE.
Aspen Publishers, Inc., 200 Orchard Ridge Dr.,
Gaithersburg, MD 20878. FAX 301-417-7550.
Vendor(s): Information Access Co., University
Microfilms International. *3551*

JOURNAL OF HEALTH CARE MARKETING.
American Marketing Association, 250 S. Wacker Dr.,
Ste. 200, Chicago, IL 60606. TEL 312-648-0536.
FAX 312-993-7542.
Vendor(s): Information Access Co., University
Microfilms International. *1471*

JOURNAL OF HEALTH COMMUNICATION.
Taylor & Francis Inc., 1900 Frost Rd., Ste. 101,
Bristol, PA 19007-1598. TEL 215-785-5800.
FAX 215-785-5515. *4481*

JOURNAL OF HIGHER EDUCATION.
Ohio State University Press, 1070 Carmack Rd.,
Columbus, OH 43210. TEL 614-292-6930.
Vendor(s): Information Access Co., University
Microfilms International. *2434*

JOURNAL OF HUMAN RESOURCES.
University of Wisconsin Press, Social Science Bldg.,
1180 Observatory Dr., Madison, WI 53706.
TEL 608-262-4952. FAX 608-262-7560.
Vendor(s): Information Access Co., University
Microfilms International. *1506*

JOURNAL OF IMAGE GUIDED SURGERY.
John Wiley & Sons, Inc., Journals, 605 Third Ave.,
New York, NY 10158-0012. TEL 212-850-6645.
FAX 212-850-6021. *4912*

JOURNAL OF INDIGENOUS STUDIES.
Gabriel Dumont Institute of Native Studies and
Applied Research, 505 - 23rd St., E., Saskatoon, SK
S7K 4K7, Canada. TEL 306-934-4941. FAX 306-
244-0252. *314*

JOURNAL OF INDUSTRIAL ECONOMICS.
Blackwell Publishers Ltd., 108 Cowley Rd., Oxford
OX4 1JF, England. TEL 44-1865-791100. FAX 44-
1865-791347.
Vendor(s): Information Access Co. *937*

JOURNAL OF INFECTION.
W.B. Saunders Ltd. 24-28 Oval Rd., London, NW1
7DX, England. TEL 0171-267-4466. FAX 0171-
482-2293. *4624*

JOURNAL OF INFECTIOUS DISEASES.
University of Chicago Press, Journals Division, Box
37005, Chicago, IL 60637. TEL 312-753-3347.
FAX 312-753-0811.
Vendor(s): Ovid Technologies, Inc. (JWAT). *4624*

JOURNAL OF INFLAMMATION.
John Wiley & Sons, Inc., Journals, 605 Third Ave.,
New York, NY 10158. TEL 212-850-6645.
FAX 212-850-6021. *4606*

JOURNAL OF INFORMATION TECHNOLOGY.
Chapman & Hall, Journals Department 2-6
Boundary Row, London SE1 8HN, England. TEL 44-
171-8650066. FAX 44-171-5229623. *4002*

JOURNAL OF INSURANCE REGULATION.
National Association of Insurance Commissioners,
120 W. 12th St., Kansas City, MO 64105.
TEL 816-374-7259.
Vendor(s): University Microfilms International.
3655

JOURNAL OF INTELLIGENT MANUFACTURING.
Chapman & Hall, Journals Department 2-6
Boundary Row, London SE1 8HN, England. TEL 44-
171-8650066. FAX 44-171-5229624. *2016*

**JOURNAL OF INTERAMERICAN STUDIES AND
WORLD AFFAIRS.**
University of Miami, North - South Center
Publications, Box 248205, Coral Gables, FL
33124-3027. TEL 305-284-8914. FAX 305-284-
5083.
Vendor(s): Information Access Co., University
Microfilms International. *5759*

JOURNAL OF INTERDISCIPLINARY HISTORY.
M I T Press, 55 Hayward St., Cambridge, MA
02142. TEL 617-253-2889. FAX 617-577-1545.
Vendor(s): Information Access Co. *3349*

JOURNAL OF INTERDISCIPLINARY STUDIES.
Institute for Interdisciplinary Research, 2828 Third
St., Ste. 11, Santa Monica, CA 90405-4150.
TEL 310-396-0517. *367*

JOURNAL OF INTERNATIONAL AFFAIRS.
Columbia University, Journal of International Affairs,
420 W. 118th St., Box 4, International Affairs Bldg.,
New York, NY 10027. TEL 212-854-4775.
FAX 212-662-0398.
Vendor(s): Information Access Co., University
Microfilms International. *5759*

JOURNAL OF INTERNATIONAL BUSINESS STUDIES.
University of Western Ontario, Western Business
School, London, ON N6A 3K7, Canada. TEL 519-
661-4031. FAX 519-661-3700.
Vendor(s): Information Access Co., University
Microfilms International. *937*

JOURNAL OF INTERNATIONAL TAXATION.
Warren, Gorham & Lamont, One Penn Plaza, New
York, NY 10119. TEL 212-971-5000. FAX 212-
971-5113.
Vendor(s): Lexis-Nexis. *1551*

JOURNAL OF INVESTIGATIVE DERMATOLOGY.
Blackwell Science Inc., 238 Main St., Cambridge
MA 02142. TEL 617-876-7022 FAX 617-492-
5263. *4663*

**THE JOURNAL OF LABORATORY AND CLINICAL
MEDICINE.**
Mosby - Year Book, Inc. 11830 Westline Industrial
Dr., St. Louis, MO 63146. TEL 314-872-8370.
FAX 314-432-1380.
Vendor(s): Ovid Technologies, Inc. *4681*

JOURNAL OF LASER APPLICATIONS.
Chapman & Hall, Journals Department 2-6
Boundary Row, London SE1 8HN England. TEL 44-
171-8650066. FAX 44-171-5229623. *5605*

JOURNAL OF LATIN AMERICAN STUDIES.
Cambridge University Press, Edinburgh Bldg.,
Shaftesbury Rd., Cambridge CB2 2RU, England.
TEL 44-1223-312393. FAX 44-1223-315052.
Vendor(s): Information Access Co. *3474*

JOURNAL OF LAW & COMMERCE.
University of Pittsburgh, School of Law, 3900
Forbes Ave., Pittsburgh, PA 15260. TEL 412-648-
1361. FAX 412-648-2649.
Vendor(s): Lexis-Nexis, West Services, Inc. *3903*

JOURNAL OF LEGAL ECONOMICS.
American Academy of Economic and Financial
Experts, University of North Alabama, Box 5077,
Florence, AL 35632. TEL 205-760-4144. FAX 205-
760-4170. *1258*

JOURNAL OF LEISURE RESEARCH.
National Recreation and Park Association, 2775 S.
Quincy St., No. 300, Arlington, VA 22206. TEL 703-
820-4940. FAX 703-671-6772.
Vendor(s): Information Access Co., University
Microfilms International. *3964*

JOURNAL OF LEUKOCYTE BIOLOGY.
Federation of American Societies for Experimental
Biology, 9650 Rockville Pike, Bethesda, MD
20814. TEL 301-530-7000. FAX 301-571-1855.
4482

JOURNAL OF MACROMARKETING.
University of Colorado, Business Research Division,
Campus Box 420, Boulder, CO 80309-0420.
TEL 303-492-8227. FAX 303-492-3620.
Vendor(s): University Microfilms International.
1471

JOURNAL OF MAGNETIC RESONANCE IMAGING.
Williams & Wilkins, 351 W. Camden St., Baltimore, MD 21201-2436. TEL 410-528-4000. FAX 410-528-4312.
Vendor(s): National Library of Medicine. *4878*

JOURNAL OF MANAGEMENT.
J A I Press Inc., 55 Old Post Rd., No. 2, Box 1678, Greenwich, CT 06836-1678. TEL 203-661-7602. FAX 203-661-0792.
Vendor(s): Information Access Co. *1428*

JOURNAL OF MANAGEMENT ACCOUNTING RESEARCH.
American Accounting Association, Paul F. Gerhardt Bldg., 5717 Bessie Dr., Sarasota, FL 34233. TEL 941-921-7747. FAX 941-923-4093.
Vendor(s): University Microfilms International. *1050*

JOURNAL OF MANAGEMENT CONSULTING.
858 Longview Rd., Burlingame, CA 94010-6974. TEL 415-342-1954. FAX 415-344-5005.
Vendor(s): University Microfilms International. *1428*

JOURNAL OF MANAGEMENT INFORMATION SYSTEMS.
M.E. Sharpe, Inc., 80 Business Park Dr., Armonk, NY 10504. TEL 914-273-1800. FAX 914-273-2106.
Vendor(s): University Microfilms International. *2083*

JOURNAL OF MANAGEMENT STUDIES.
Blackwell Publishers Ltd., 108 Cowley Rd., Oxford OX4 1JF, England. TEL 44-1865-791100. FAX 44-1865-791347.
Vendor(s): Information Access Co. *1428*

JOURNAL OF MANAGERIAL ISSUES.
Pittsburg State University, Department of Economics, Finance & Banking, 1701 S. Broadway, Pittsburg, KS 66762-7533. TEL 316-235-4547. FAX 316-235-4578.
Vendor(s): Information Access Co. *1428*

JOURNAL OF MANAGERIAL PSYCHOLOGY.
M C B University Press Ltd., 60-62 Toller Ln., Bradford, W. Yorks BD8 9BY, England. TEL 44-1274-777700. FAX 44-1274-785200.
Vendor(s): Information Access Co. *1428*

JOURNAL OF MANUFACTURING SYSTEMS.
Elsevier Science Ltd., P.O. Box 800, Kidlington, Oxford OX5 1DX, England. TEL 44-1865-843000. FAX 44-1865-843010.
Vendor(s): University Microfilms International. *2056*

JOURNAL OF MARITAL AND FAMILY THERAPY.
American Association for Marriage and Family Therapy, 1133 15th St., N.W., Ste. 300, Washington, DC 20005.
Vendor(s): University Microfilms International. *5858*

JOURNAL OF MARKETING.
American Marketing Association, 250 S. Wacker Dr., Ste. 200, Chicago, IL 60606. TEL 312-648-0536. FAX 312-993-7542.
Vendor(s): Information Access Co., Lexis-Nexis, University Microfilms International. *1471*

JOURNAL OF MARKETING COMMUNICATIONS.
Chapman & Hall, Journals Department 2-6 Boundary Row, London SE1 8HN, England. TEL 44-171-8650066. FAX 44-171-5229623. *1472*

JOURNAL OF MARKETING RESEARCH.
American Marketing Association, 250 S. Wacker Dr., Ste. 200, Chicago, IL 60606. TEL 312-648-0536. FAX 312-993-7542.
Vendor(s): Information Access Co., Lexis-Nexis. *1472*

JOURNAL OF MARRIAGE AND THE FAMILY.
National Council on Family Relations, 3989 Central Ave., N.E., Ste. 550, Minneapolis, MN 55421-3921. TEL 612-781-9331. FAX 612-781-9348.
Vendor(s): Knight-Ridder Information, Inc., Ovid Technologies, Inc., University Microfilms International. *6420*

JOURNAL OF MATERIALS SCIENCE.
Chapman & Hall, Journals Department 2-6 Boundary Row, London SE1 8HN, England. TEL 44-171-8650066. FAX 44-171-5229623. *2735*

JOURNAL OF MATERIALS SCIENCE LETTERS.
Chapman & Hall, Journals Department 2-6 Boundary Row, London SE1 8HN, England. TEL 44-171-8650066. FAX 44-171-5229623. *2735*

JOURNAL OF MATERIALS SCIENCE: MATERIALS IN ELECTRONICS.
Chapman & Hall, Journals Department 2-6 Boundary Row, London SE1 8HN, England. TEL 44-171-8650066. FAX 44-171-5229623. *2735*

JOURNAL OF MATERIALS SCIENCE: MATERIALS IN MEDICINE.
Chapman & Hall, Journals Department 2-6 Boundary Row, London SE1 8HN, England. TEL 44-171-8650066. FAX 44-171-5229623. *2735*

JOURNAL OF MATHEMATICAL PHYSICS.
American Institute of Physics, One Physics Ellipse, College Park, MD 20740-3843. TEL 301-209-3000. *5554*

JOURNAL OF MEDICAL AND PHARMACEUTICAL MARKETING.
Fred Atoki Publishing Co. Ltd., Plot 25 Kekere-Ekun St., Orile-Iganmu, Box 7313, Lagos, Nigeria. *1472*

JOURNAL OF MEDICAL ETHICS.
B M J Publishing Group, B.M.A. House, Tavistock Sq., London WC1H 9JR, England. TEL 44-171-383-6270. FAX 44-171-383-6402.
Vendor(s): University Microfilms International. *4483*

JOURNAL OF MEDICAL MICROBIOLOGY.
Chapman & Hall, Journals Department, 2-6 Boundary Row, London SE1 8HN, England. TEL 44-171-8650066. FAX 44-171-5229623. *4483*

JOURNAL OF MEDICAL VIROLOGY.
John Wiley & Sons, Inc., Journals, 605 Third Ave., New York, NY 10158. TEL 212-850-6645. FAX 212-850-6021. *4483*

JOURNAL OF MEDICINAL CHEMISTRY.
American Chemical Society, 1155 16th St., N.W., Washington, DC 20036. TEL 800-333-9511. FAX 614-447-3671.
Vendor(s): STN International (CJACS). *5422*

JOURNAL OF MENTAL HEALTH.
Carfax Publishing Co., P.O. Box 25, Abingdon, Oxon. OX14 3UE, England. TEL 44-1235-401000. FAX 44-1235-401550. *4846*

JOURNAL OF MICROMECHANICS AND MICROENGINEERING.
I O P Publishing Ltd., Techno House, Redcliffe Way, Bristol, Avon BS1 6NX, England. TEL 44-117-929-7481. FAX 44-117-929-4318. *2760*

JOURNAL OF MILITARY HISTORY.
Society for Military History, c/o Virginia Military Institute, Lexington, VA 24450. TEL 540-464-7468. FAX 540-464-5229.
Vendor(s): University Microfilms International. *5036*

JOURNAL OF MOLECULAR BIOLOGY.
Academic Press Ltd. 24-28 Oval Rd., London NW1 7DX, England. TEL 44-171-2674466. FAX 44-171-4822293. *716*

JOURNAL OF MONEY, CREDIT & BANKING.
Ohio State University Press, 1070 Carmack Rd., Columbus, OH 43210. TEL 614-292-6930.
Vendor(s): Information Access Co. *1105*

JOURNAL OF MORMON HISTORY.
Mormon History Association, 2470 N. 1000 W., Layton, UT 84041-1236. FAX 801-378-4048.
Vendor(s): Knight-Ridder Information, Inc. (File nos.38,39). *6208*

JOURNAL OF MUSCLE RESEARCH AND CELL MOTILITY.
Chapman & Hall, Journals Department 2-6 Boundary Row, London SE1 8HN, England. TEL 44-171-8650066. FAX 44-171-5229623. *4484*

JOURNAL OF MUSICOLOGY.
University of California Press, Journals Division, 2120 Berkeley Way, No. 5812, Berkeley, CA 94720-5812. TEL 510-643-7154. FAX 510-642-9917.
Vendor(s): Information Access Co.. *5168*

JOURNAL OF NATURAL PRODUCTS.
American Society of Pharmacognosy, Dept. L-0011, Columbus, OH 43268-0011. TEL 614-447-3776. FAX 614-447-3671. *5422*

JOURNAL OF NEAR EASTERN STUDIES.
University of Chicago Press, Journals Division, Box 37005, Chicago, IL 60637. TEL 312-753-3347. FAX 312-753-0811.
Vendor(s): Knight-Ridder Information, Inc.. *360*

JOURNAL OF NEGRO EDUCATION.
Howard University Press, Marketing Department, 2600 Sixth St., N.W., Washington, DC 20059. TEL 202-806-8120. FAX 202-806-8434.
Vendor(s): Information Access Co., University Microfilms International. *2347*

JOURNAL OF NEGRO HISTORY.
Association for the Study of Afro-American Life and History, Inc., c/o Alton Hornsby, Jr., Ed., Dept. of History, Morehouse College, Atlanta, GA 30314. TEL 404-215-2620. FAX 404-215-2715.
Vendor(s): Information Access Co.. *2890*

JOURNAL OF NEUROCYTOLOGY.
Chapman & Hall, Journals Department 2-6 Boundary Row, London SE1 8HN, England. TEL 44-171-8650066. FAX 44-171-5229623. *716*

JOURNAL OF NEUROLOGY, NEUROSURGERY AND PSYCHIATRY.
B M J Publishing Group, B.M.A. House, Tavistock Sq., London WC1H 9JR, England. TEL 44-171-383-6270. FAX 44-171-383-6402.
Vendor(s): Ovid Technologies, Inc.. *4847*

JOURNAL OF OCCUPATIONAL AND ORGANIZATIONAL PSYCHOLOGY.
British Psychological Society, St. Andrew's House, 48 Princess Rd. E., Leicester LE1 7DR, England. TEL 44-116-254-9568. FAX 44-116-247-0787.
Vendor(s): Information Access Co. *5859*

JOURNAL OF ORGANIC CHEMISTRY (WASHINGTON)
.
American Chemical Society, 1155 16th St., N.W., Washington, DC 20036. TEL 800-333-9511. FAX 614-447-3671.
Vendor(s): STN International (CJACS). *1739*

JOURNAL OF ORGANOMETALLIC CHEMISTRY.
Elsevier Science S.A., P.O. Box 564, CH-1001 Lausanne 1, Switzerland. TEL 41-21-3207381. FAX 41-21-3235444.
Vendor(s): STN International. *1740*

JOURNAL OF PALESTINE STUDIES.
University of California Press, Journals Division, 2120 Berkeley Way, No. 5812, Berkeley, CA 94720-5812. TEL 510-643-7154. FAX 510-642-9917.
Vendor(s): Information Access Co.. *3497*

JOURNAL OF PARAPSYCHOLOGY.
Parapsychology Press, 402 N. Buchanan Blvd., Durham, NC 27701-1728. TEL 919-688-8241. FAX 919-683-4338.
Vendor(s): Information Access Co., University Microfilms International. *5331*

JOURNAL OF PARENTERAL AND ENTERAL NUTRITION.
American Society for Parenteral and Enteral Nutrition, 8630 Fenton St., Ste. 412, Silver Spring, MD 20910-3805. TEL 301-587-6315. FAX 301-587-3323. *5236*

JOURNAL OF PARTNERSHIP TAXATION.
Warren, Gorham & Lamont, One Penn Plaza, New York, NY 10119. TEL 212-971-5000. FAX 212-971-5113.
Vendor(s): Lexis-Nexis (TAXRIA-Library), West Services, Inc. (WGL JPTAX). *1552*

JOURNAL OF PEDIATRIC SURGERY.
W.B. Saunders Co, Curtis Center, Independence Sq. W., Philadelphia, PA 19106-3399. TEL 215-238-7800. FAX 215-238-6445.
Vendor(s): Lexis-Nexis. *4913*

JOURNAL OF PEDIATRICS.
Mosby - Year Book, Inc. 11830 Westline Industrial Dr., St. Louis, MO 63146-3318. TEL 314-872-8370. FAX 314-432-1380.
Vendor(s): Ovid Technologies, Inc.. *4807*

JOURNAL OF PHARMACEUTICAL SCIENCES.
American Pharmaceutical Association, 2215 Constitution Ave., N.W., Washington, DC 20037. TEL 202-628-4410. FAX 202-638-3783. *5423*

JOURNAL OF PHARMACOLOGY AND EXPERIMENTAL THERAPEUTICS.
Williams & Wilkins, 351 W. Camden St., Baltimore, MD 21201. TEL 410-528-4000. FAX 410-528-4312. *5423*

JOURNAL OF PHYSICAL CHEMISTRY.
American Chemical Society, 1155 16th St., N.W., Washington, DC 20036. TEL 800-333-9511. FAX 614-447-3671.
Vendor(s): STN International (CJACS). *1754*

JOURNAL OF PHYSICAL EDUCATION, RECREATION AND DANCE.
American Alliance for Health, Physical Education, Recreation, and Dance, 1900 Association Dr., Reston, VA 22091. TEL 703-476-3400. FAX 703-476-9527.
Vendor(s): Information Access Co., University Microfilms International. *2492*

JOURNAL OF PHYSICS A: MATHEMATICAL AND GENERAL.
I O P Publishing Ltd., Techno House, Redcliffe Way, Bristol, Avon BS1 6NX, England. TEL 44-117-929-7481. FAX 44-117-929-4318. *5555*

JOURNAL OF PHYSICS B: ATOMIC, MOLECULAR AND OPTICAL PHYSICS.
I O P Publishing Ltd., Techno House, Redcliffe Way, Bristol, Avon BS1 6NX, England. TEL 44-117-929-7481. FAX 44-117-929-4318. *5555*

JOURNAL OF PHYSICS: CONDENSED MATTER.
I O P Publishing Ltd., Techno House, Redcliffe Way, Bristol, Avon BS1 6NX, England. TEL 44-117-929-7481. FAX 44-117-929-4318. *5555*

JOURNAL OF PHYSICS D: APPLIED PHYSICS.
I O P Publishing Ltd., Techno House, Redcliffe Way, Bristol, Avon BS1 6NX, England. TEL 44-117-929-7481. FAX 44-117-929-4318. *5555*

JOURNAL OF PHYSICS G: NUCLEAR AND PARTICLE PHYSICS.
I O P Publishing Ltd., Techno House, Redcliffe Way, Bristol, Avon BS1 6NX, England. TEL 44-117-929-7481. FAX 44-117-929-4318. *5595*

JOURNAL OF PLANNING AND ENVIRONMENT LAW.
Sweet & Maxwell, South Quay Plaza, 7th Fl., 183 Marsh Wall, London E14 9FT, England. TEL 0171-538-8686. FAX 0171-538-9508. *3798*

JOURNAL OF POLYMER SCIENCE. PART A: POLYMER CHEMISTRY.
John Wiley & Sons, Inc., Journals, 605 Third Ave., New York, NY 10158. TEL 212-850-6645. FAX 212-850-6021.
Vendor(s): STN International (CJWILEY). *1740*

JOURNAL OF POLYMER SCIENCE. PART B: POLYMER PHYSICS.
John Wiley & Sons, Inc., Journals, 605 Third Ave., New York, NY 10158. TEL 212-850-6645. FAX 212-850-6021.
Vendor(s): STN International (CJWILEY). *1740*

JOURNAL OF POLYMER SCIENCE. SYMPOSIA PROCEEDINGS.
John Wiley & Sons, Inc., Journals, 605 Third Ave., New York, NY 10158-0012. TEL 212-850-6000. FAX 212-850-6088.
Vendor(s): STN International. *1740*

JOURNAL OF POPULAR CULTURE.
Popular Press, Bowling Green State University, Bowling Green, OH 43403. TEL 419-372-7866.
Vendor(s): University Microfilms International. *4224*

JOURNAL OF POPULAR FILM AND TELEVISION.
Heldref Publications, 1319 Eighteenth St., N.W., Washington, DC 20036-1802. TEL 202-296-6267. FAX 202-296-5149.
Vendor(s): Information Access Co., University Microfilms International. *5106*

JOURNAL OF PORTFOLIO MANAGEMENT.
Institutional Investor Journals, 488 Madison Ave., New York, NY 10022. TEL 212-224-3185. FAX 212-224-3527.
Vendor(s): Information Access Co., Lexis-Nexis. *1338*

JOURNAL OF POST KEYNESIAN ECONOMICS.
M.E. Sharpe, Inc., 80 Business Park Dr., Armonk, NY 10504. TEL 914-273-1800. FAX 914-273-2106.
Vendor(s): Information Access Co., University Microfilms International. *1258*

JOURNAL OF PROGRAMMING LANGUAGES.
Chapman & Hall, Journals Department 2-6 Boundary Row, London SE1 8HN, England. TEL 44-171-8650066. FAX 44-171-5229623. *2045*

JOURNAL OF PROPERTY MANAGEMENT.
Institute of Real Estate Management, 430 N. Michigan Ave., Chicago, IL 60611. TEL 312-329-6073. FAX 312-661-0217.
Vendor(s): Information Access Co., University Microfilms International. *6028*

JOURNAL OF PROPERTY RESEARCH.
Chapman & Hall, Journals Department 2-6 Boundary Row, London SE1 8HN, England. TEL 44-171-8650066. FAX 44-171-5229623. *3587*

JOURNAL OF PSYCHOLOGY AND THEOLOGY.
Biola University, Rosemead School of Psychology, 13800 Biola Ave., La Mirada, CA 90639-0001. TEL 310-903-4727. FAX 310-903-4786.
Vendor(s): Knight-Ridder Information, Inc., Ovid Technologies, Inc.. *5861*

JOURNAL OF PSYCHOLOGY: INTERDISCIPLINARY & APPLIED.
Heldref Publications, 1319 Eighteenth St., N.W., Washington, DC 20036-1802. TEL 202-296-6267. FAX 202-296-5149.
Vendor(s): Information Access Co. *5861*

JOURNAL OF PUBLIC POLICY & MARKETING.
American Marketing Association, 250 S. Wacker Dr., Chicago, IL 60606-5819. TEL 312-648-0536.
Vendor(s): Information Access Co., University Microfilms International. *1472*

JOURNAL OF RADIOLOGICAL PROTECTION.
I O P Publishing Ltd., Techno House, Redcliffe Way, Bristol, Avon BS1 6NX, England. TEL 44-117-929-7481. FAX 44-117-929-4318. *2578*

JOURNAL OF REGIONAL AND LOCAL STUDIES.
c/o Univeristy of Humberside, Inglemire Ave., Hull HU6 7LU, England. FAX 01482-449624. *3422*

JOURNAL OF REHABILITATION.
National Rehabilitation Association, 633 S. Washington St., Alexandria, VA 22314-4109. TEL 703-836-0850. FAX 703-836-0848.
Vendor(s): Information Access Co., University Microfilms International. *6379*

JOURNAL OF REHABILITATION RESEARCH AND DEVELOPMENT.
Department of Veterans Affairs, Office of Technology Transfer, 103 S. Gay St., Baltimore, MD 21202. TEL 410-962-1800. FAX 410-962-9670.
Vendor(s): University Microfilms International. *4787*

JOURNAL OF RELIGIOUS THOUGHT.
Howard University Press, 1240 Randolph St., N.E., Washington, DC 20017. TEL 202-806-4935. FAX 202-806-4946.
Vendor(s): University Microfilms International. *6072*

JOURNAL OF RETAIL BANKING.
American Banker - Bond Buyer, Newsletter Division One State St. Plaza, New York, NY 10004-1549. TEL 212-943-5908.
Vendor(s): Information Access Co.. *1105*

JOURNAL OF RETAILING.
J A I Press Inc., 55 Old Post Rd., No. 2, Box 1678, Greenwich, CT 06836. TEL 203-661-7602. FAX 203-661-0792.
Vendor(s): Information Access Co., Knight-Ridder Information, Inc.. *1473*

JOURNAL OF RISK AND INSURANCE.
American Risk and Insurance Association, c/o Chase Communications, Stephen H. Acunto, Exec. Dir., Box 9001, Mt. Vernon, NY 10552. TEL 914-699-2020. FAX 914-699-2025
Vendor(s): Information Access Co., Knight-Ridder Information, Inc.. *3655*

JOURNAL OF SCHOOL HEALTH.
American School Health Association, Box 708, Kent, OH 44240. TEL 216-678-1601 FAX 216-678-4526.
Vendor(s): Information Access Co., University Microfilms International. *5967*

JOURNAL OF SEX RESEARCH.
Society for the Scientific Study of Sex, Box 208, Mt. Vernon, IA 52314. TEL 319-895-8407. FAX 319-895-6203.
Vendor(s): University Microfilms International. *5862*

JOURNAL OF SMALL BUSINESS MANAGEMENT.
West Virginia University, Bureau of Business Research, Box 6025, Morgantown, WV 26506-6025. TEL 304-293-7534.
Vendor(s): Information Access Co., University Microfilms International. *1577*

JOURNAL OF SOCIAL HISTORY.
Carnegie - Mellon University Press, Schenley Park, Pittsburgh, PA 15213. TEL 412-268-2884. FAX 412-268-5288.
Vendor(s): Information Access Co., University Microfilms International. *5421*

JOURNAL OF SOCIAL ISSUES.
Blackwell Publishers, 238 Main St., Cambridge, MA 02142. TEL 617-547-7110. FAX 617-547-0789.
Vendor(s): Information Access Co., University Microfilms International. *5862*

JOURNAL OF SOCIAL, POLITICAL AND ECONOMIC STUDIES.
Council for Social and Economic Studies, Box 34070, N.W., Washington, DC 20043. TEL 202-371-2700. FAX 202-371-1523.
Vendor(s): University Microfilms International. *5677*

THE JOURNAL OF SOCIAL PSYCHOLOGY.
Heldref Publications, 1319 Eighteenth St., N.W., Washington, DC 20036-1802. TEL 202-296-6267. FAX 202-296-5149.
Vendor(s): Information Access Co., University Microfilms International. *5862*

THE JOURNAL OF SOCIO-ECONOMICS.
J A I Press Inc., 55 Old Post Rd., No. 2, Greenwich, CT 06836-1678. TEL 203-661-7602. FAX 203-661-0792.
Vendor(s): Information Access Co. *1258*

JOURNAL OF SOCIOLOGY AND SOCIAL WELFARE.
Western Michigan University, School of Social Work, c/o Gary Mathews, Manag. Ed., Kalamazoo, MI 49008-5034. TEL 616-387-3198. FAX 616-387-3217. *6421*

JOURNAL OF SOIL AND WATER CONSERVATION.
Soil and Water Conservation Society, 7515 N.E. Ankeny Rd., Ankeny, IA 50021. TEL 515-289-2331 FAX 515-289-1227.
Vendor(s): Information Access Co. University Microfilms International. *229*

JOURNAL OF SOUTHEAST ASIAN STUDIES.
Singapore University Press, 10 Kent Ridge Crescent, Singapore 119260, Singapore. TEL 7761148. FAX 7740252.
Vendor(s): Information Access Co. *3381*

JOURNAL OF SPORT BEHAVIOR.
University of South Alabama, Department of Health, Physical Education and Leisure Services, Mobile, AL 36688. TEL 334-460-7131. FAX 334-460-7252.
Vendor(s): Information Access Co. University Microfilms International. *6466*

JOURNAL OF SPORTS SCIENCES.
Chapman & Hall, Journals Department 2-6 Boundary Row, London SE1 8HN, England. TEL 44-171-8650066. FAX 44-171-5229623. *6466*

JOURNAL OF STRATEGIC MARKETING.
Chapman & Hall, Journals Department 2-6 Boundary Row, London SE1 8HN, England. TEL 44-171-8650066. FAX 44-171-5229623. *1473*

JOURNAL OF SURGICAL ONCOLOGY.
John Wiley & Sons, Inc., Journals, 605 Third Ave., New York, NY 10158. TEL 212-850-6645. FAX 212-850-6021. *4913*

JOURNAL OF SURGICAL PATHOLOGY.
Chapman & Hall, Journals Department 2-6 Boundary Row, London SE1 8HN, England. TEL 44-171-8650066. FAX 44-171-5229623. *4485*

JOURNAL OF SYSTEMS MANAGEMENT.
Association for Systems Management, Box 38370, Cleveland, OH 44138. TEL 216-243-6900. Vendor(s): Information Access Co., Knight-Ridder Information, Inc., University Microfilms International. *1429*

THE JOURNAL OF TAXATION.
Warren, Gorham & Lamont, One Penn Plaza, New York, NY 10119. TEL 212-971-5185. FAX 212-971-5113.
Vendor(s): Lexis-Nexis (TAXRIA-Library), West Services, Inc. (WGL-JTAX). *1552*

JOURNAL OF TECHNOLOGY EDUCATION.
Virginia Polytechnic Institute, Technology Education Program, c/o Mark Sanders, Ed., 144 Smyth Hall, Blacksburg, VA 24061-0432. FAX 703-231-4188. *2492*

JOURNAL OF TECHNOLOGY TRANSFER.
Technology Transfer Society, 55 S. State Ave., Ste. 3-F2, Indianapolis, IN 46201-7876.
Vendor(s): Knight-Ridder Information, Inc., Ovid Technologies, Inc.. *6655*

JOURNAL OF THE HISTORY OF IDEAS.
Johns Hopkins University Press, Journals Publishing Division, 2715 N. Charles St., Baltimore, MD 21218-4319. TEL 410-516-6987. FAX 410-516-6968. *3617*

JOURNAL OF THEOLOGICAL STUDIES.
Oxford University Press, Oxford Journals, Walton St., Oxford OX2 6DP, England. TEL 44-1865-267907. FAX 44-1865-267773.
Vendor(s): Information Access Co.. *6072*

JOURNAL OF TOXICOLOGY. CLINICAL TOXICOLOGY.
Marcel Dekker Journals, 270 Madison Ave., New York, NY 10016. TEL 212-696-9000. FAX 212-685-4540. *2847*

JOURNAL OF TRAVEL RESEARCH.
University of Colorado, Business Research Division, Campus Box 420, Boulder, CO 80309-0420. TEL 303-492-8227. FAX 303-492-3620.
Vendor(s): University Microfilms International. *6895*

JOURNAL OF WOMEN'S HISTORY.
Indiana University Press, Journals Division, 601 N. Morton St., Bloomington, IN 47404. TEL 812-855-9449. FAX 812-855-8507.
Vendor(s): University Microfilms International. *7018*

JOURNAL OF YOUTH AND ADOLESCENCE.
Plenum Publishing Corp., 233 Spring St., New York, NY 10013-1578. TEL 212-620-8000. FAX 212-463-0742.
Vendor(s): Information Access Co., University Microfilms International. *1770*

JOURNAL RECORD.
Dolan Media, Box 26370, Oklahoma City, OK 73126-0370. TEL 405-235-3100. FAX 405-278-6918. *938*

JOURNALISM AND MASS COMMUNICATION EDUCATOR.
Association for Education in Journalism and Mass Communications, 1621 College St., University of South Carolina, Columbia, SC 29208-0251. TEL 830-777-2005. FAX 803-777-4728.
Vendor(s): University Microfilms International. *3706*

JOURNALISM HISTORY.
Greenspun School of Communication, University of Nevada, Las Vegas, NV 89154-5007. TEL 702-895-3964. FAX 702-895-4805.
Vendor(s): University Microfilms International. *3706*

JOURNALS OF GERONTOLOGY. SERIES A: BIOLOGICAL SCIENCES & MEDICAL SCIENCES.
Gerontological Society of America, 1275 K St., N.W., Ste. 250, Washington, DC 20005-4006. TEL 202-842-1275. FAX 202-842-1150.
Vendor(s): University Microfilms International. *3291*

JOURNALS OF GERONTOLOGY. SERIES B: PSYCHOLOGICAL SCIENCES & SOCIAL SCIENCES.
Gerontological Society of America, 1275 K St., N.W., Ste. 250, Washington, DC 20005-4006. TEL 202-842-1275. FAX 202-842-1150.
Vendor(s): University Microfilms International. *3291*

JUDAISM.
American Jewish Congress, 15 E. 84th St., New York, NY 10028. TEL 212-879-4500.
Vendor(s): Information Access Co., University Microfilms International. *6126*

JUDICATURE.
American Judicature Society, 180 N. Michigan Ave., Ste. 600, Chicago, IL 60601-7401.
Vendor(s): West Services, Inc.. *3949*

JUDICIAL CONDUCT REPORTER.
American Judicature Society, Center for Judicial Conduct Organizations, 180 N. Michigan, Ste. 600, Chicago, IL 60601. TEL 312-558-6900. FAX 312-558-9175.
Vendor(s): West Services, Inc.. *3949*

JUXTA.
977 Seminole Trail, No. 331, Charlottesville, VA 22901. *4225*

K G B.
K G B Media Inc., 133 Bowery, New York, NY 10002. TEL 212-343-1512. *3231*

KAIJO HOANCHO. SUIROBU KANSOKU HOKOKU. KAIYO HEN.
Kaijo Hoancho, Suirobu, 3-1, Tsukiji 5-chome, Chuo-ku, Tokyo 104, Japan. FAX 81-3-3545-2885. *2287*

KALAMAZOO COLLEGE QUARTERLY.
Kalamazoo College, 1200 Academy St., Kalamazoo, MI 49006-3295. TEL 616-377-7304. FAX 616-337-7305. *1873*

KANE'S BEVERAGE WEEK.
Whitaker Newsletters Inc., 313 South Ave., Box 192, Fanwood, NJ 07023. TEL 908-889-6336. FAX 908-889-6339.
Vendor(s): NewsNet (FB06). *507*

KANSAS BUSINESS DIRECTORY.
American Business Directories 5711 S. 86th Circle, Box 27347, Omaha, NE 68127. TEL 402-593-4600. FAX 402-331-5481. *1619*

KANSAS CITY BOARD OF TRADE REVIEW.
Kansas City Board of Trade, 4800 Main St., No.303, Kansas City, MO 64112. TEL 816-753-7500. FAX 816-753-3944. *259*

THE KANSAS CITY BUSINESS JOURNAL.
American City Business Journals, Inc. (Kansas City), 1101 Walnut St., Ste. 800, Kansas City, MO 64106-2122. TEL 816-421-5900. FAX 816-472-4010.
Vendor(s): Information Access Co.. *1219*

KARMA LAPEL.
Fifth Man Press, Box 5467, Evanston, IL 60204-5467. TEL 312-573-1700 ext. 23. FAX 312-573-0520. *4149*

KASPAH RASTER.
Box 8831, Portland, OR 97207.
Available only online. *4149*

KATALOG FOR SKOLEBIBLIOTEKER. SKOLEBIBLIOTEKARENS.
Dansk BiblioteksCenter as, Tempovej 7-11, DK-2750 Ballerup, Denmark. TEL 45-44-867777. FAX 45-44-867892. *537*

KATALOG FOR SKOLEBIBLIOTEKER. TITELKATALOG.
Dansk BiblioteksCenter as, Tempovej 7-11, DK-2750 Ballerup, Denmark. TEL 45-44-867777. FAX 45-44-867892. *537*

KAUPPALEHTI.
Kustannus oy Kauppalehti, P.O. Box 189, SF-00101, Vetotie no.3, 01610 Vantaa, Finland. TEL 90 50781.
Vendor(s): Helsinki School of Economics. *938*

KEESING'S RECORD OF WORLD EVENTS.
Longman Group UK Ltd., Westgate House, 6th Fl., The High, Harlow, Essex CM20 1YR, England. TEL 44-1279-442601. FAX 44-1279-444501. *5722*

KEJI GUANLI YANJIU.
Science & Technology Management Research Periodicals House, No. 100, Xianlie Zhonglu, Guangzhou, Guangdong 510070, People's Republic of China. TEL 86-20-8766-8145. FAX 86-20-8777-5791. *6253*

KELLY'S DIRECTORY.
Kelly's Directories Part of the Reed Elsevier group, Windsor Court, E. Grinstead House, E. Grinstead, W. Sussex RH19 1XB, England. TEL 01342-326972. FAX 01342-335747.
Vendor(s): Reed Information Services Ltd.. *1619*

KELLY'S LINK.
Kelly's Directories Part of the Reed Elsevier group, Windsor Court, E. Grinstead House, E. Grinstead, W. Sussex RH19 1XB, England. TEL 01342-326972. FAX 01342-335747.
Vendor(s): Reed Information Services Ltd.. *1619*

KELLY'S OIL & GAS DIRECTORY.
Kelly's Directories Part of the Reed Elsevier group, Windsor Court, E. Grinstead House, E. Grinstead, W. Sussex RH19 1XB, England. TEL 01342-326972. FAX 01342-335747.
Vendor(s): Reed Information Services Ltd.. *1619*

KENNEDY INSTITUTE OF ETHICS JOURNAL.
Johns Hopkins University Press, Journals Publishing Division, 2715 N. Charles St., Baltimore, MD 21218. TEL 410-516-6987. FAX 410-516-6968. *4486*

KENTUCKY BANKER.
Kentucky Bankers Association, Ste. 1000, Waterfront Plaza, 325 W. Main St., Louisville, KY 40202. TEL 502-582-2453. FAX 502-584-6390.
Vendor(s): University Microfilms International. *1106*

KENTUCKY BUSINESS DIRECTORY.
American Business Directories 5711 S. 86th Circle, Box 27347, Omaha, NE 68127. TEL 402-593-4600. FAX 402-331-5481. *1619*

KENTUCKY BUSINESS LEDGER.
Kentucky Communications, Inc., Box 470867, Charlotte, NC 28247.
Vendor(s): Knight-Ridder Information, Inc.. *938*

KENTUCKY LAW JOURNAL.
University of Kentucky, College of Law, Lexington, KY 40506. TEL 606-257-4747. FAX 606-323-1061.
Vendor(s): West Services, Inc.. *3801*

THE KENTUCKY MANUFACTURER.
Industrial Marketing, Inc., PO Box 4310, Lexington, KY 40544-4310. TEL 606-266-3303. FAX 606-266-3230.
Vendor(s): University Microfilms International. *938*

KERMIT NEWS.
Columbia University Academic Information Systems, Kermit Development and Distribution, 612 W. 115th St., New York, NY 10025. TEL 212-854-3703. FAX 212-663-8202. *2045*

KEXUE (SHANGHAI).
Shanghai Keji Chubanshe, 450 Ruijin 2 Lu, Shanghai 200020, People's Republic of China. TEL 86-21-473465. FAX 86-21-4730679.
Vendor(s): University Microfilms International. *6253*

KEY ABSTRACTS - BUSINESS AUTOMATION.
INSPEC, I.E.E., Michael Faraday House, Six Hill Way, Stevenage, Herts. SG1 2AY, England. TEL 44-1438-313311. FAX 44-1438-742840.
Vendor(s): CEDOCAR, Data-Star, European Space Agency, FIZ Technik, Knight-Ridder Information, Inc., Orbit Search Service, STN International. *2002*

KEY BRITISH ENTERPRISES.
Dun & Bradstreet Ltd., Holmers Farm Way, High Wycombe, Bucks. HP12 4UL, England. TEL 44-1494-422000. FAX 44-1494-422260. *939*

KEY NOTE MARKET REPORT: ACCOUNTANCY.
Key Note Ltd., Field House, 72 Oldfield Rd., Hampton, Middlesex TW12 2HQ, England. TEL 44-181-783-0755. FAX 44-181-783-1940. *1050*

KEY NOTE MARKET REPORT: ADHESIVES.
Key Note Ltd., Field House, 72 Oldfield Rd., Hampton, Middlesex TW12 2HQ, England. TEL 44-181-783-0755. FAX 44-181-783-1940. *2644*

KEY NOTE MARKET REPORT: ADVERTISING AGENCIES.
Key Note Ltd., Field House, 72 Oldfield Rd., Hampton, Middlesex TW12 2HQ, England. TEL 44-181-783-0755. FAX 44-181-783-1940. *39*

KEY NOTE MARKET REPORT: AEROSPACE.
Key Note Ltd., Field House, 72 Oldfield Rd., Hampton, Middlesex TW12 2HQ, England. TEL 44-181-783-0755. FAX 44-181-783-1940. *71*

KEY NOTE MARKET REPORT: AFTER DINNER DRINKS.
Key Note Ltd., Field House, 72 Oldfield Rd., Hampton, Middlesex TW12 2HQ, England. TEL 44-181-783-0755. FAX 44-181-783-1940. *507*

KEY NOTE MARKET REPORT: AGRICULTURAL MACHINERY.
Key Note Ltd., Field House, 72 Oldfield Rd., Hampton, Middlesex TW12 2HQ, England. TEL 44-181-783-0755. FAX 44-181-783-1940. *205*

KEY NOTE MARKET REPORT: AGROCHEMICALS & FERTILIZERS.
Key Note Ltd., Field House, 72 Oldfield Rd., Hampton, Middlesex TW12 2HQ, England. TEL 44-181-783-0755. FAX 44-181-783-1940. *229*

KEY NOTE MARKET REPORT: AIRLINES.
Key Note Ltd., Field House, 72 Oldfield Rd., Hampton, Middlesex TW12 2HQ, England. TEL 44-181-783-0755. FAX 44-181-783-1940. *6761*

KEY NOTE MARKET REPORT: AIRPORTS.
Key Note Ltd., Field House, 72 Oldfield Rd., Hampton, Middlesex TW12 2HQ, England. TEL 44-181-783-0755. FAX 44-181-783-1940. *6761*

KEY NOTE MARKET REPORT: ANIMAL FEEDSTUFFS.
Key Note Ltd., Field House, 72 Oldfield Rd., Hampton, Middlesex TW12 2HQ, England. TEL 44-181-783-0755. FAX 44-181-783-1940. *259*

KEY NOTE MARKET REPORT: AUTOMATIC VENDING.
Key Note Ltd., Field House, 72 Oldfield Rd., Hampton, Middlesex TW12 2HQ, England. TEL 44-181-783-0755. FAX 44-181-783-1940. *1473*

KEY NOTE MARKET REPORT: AUTOPARTS.
Key Note Ltd., Field House, 72 Oldfield Rd., Hampton, Middlesex TW12 2HQ, England. TEL 44-181-783-0755. FAX 44-181-783-1940. *6790*

KEY NOTE MARKET REPORT: BABY PRODUCTS.
Key Note Ltd., Field House, 72 Oldfield Rd., Hampton, Middlesex TW12 2HQ, England. TEL 44-181-783-0755. FAX 44-181-783-1940. *1771*

KEY NOTE MARKET REPORT: BATHS & SANITARYWARE.
Key Note Ltd., Field House, 72 Oldfield Rd., Hampton, Middlesex TW12 2HQ, England. TEL 44-181-783-0755. FAX 44-181-783-1940. *492*

KEY NOTE MARKET REPORT: BETTING & GAMING.
Key Note Ltd., Field House, 72 Oldfield Rd., Hampton, Middlesex TW12 2HQ, England. TEL 44-181-783-0755. FAX 44-181-783-1940. *6467*

KEY NOTE MARKET REPORT: BICYCLES.
Key Note Ltd., Field House, 72 Oldfield Rd., Hampton, Middlesex TW12 2HQ, England. TEL 44-181-783-0755. FAX 44-181-783-1940. *6524*

KEY NOTE MARKET REPORT: BISCUITS & CAKES.
Key Note Ltd., Field House, 72 Oldfield Rd., Hampton, Middlesex TW12 2HQ, England. TEL 44-181-783-0755. FAX 44-181-783-1940. *3000*

KEY NOTE MARKET REPORT: BOOK PUBLISHING.
Key Note Ltd., Field House, 72 Oldfield Rd., Hampton, Middlesex TW12 2HQ, England. TEL 44-181-783-0755. FAX 44-181-783-1940. *6000*

KEY NOTE MARKET REPORT: BOOKSELLING.
Key Note Ltd., Field House, 72 Oldfield Rd., Hampton, Middlesex TW12 2HQ, England. TEL 44-181-783-0755. FAX 44-181-783-1940. *6000*

KEY NOTE MARKET REPORT: BOTTLED WATERS.
Key Note Ltd., Field House, 72 Oldfield Rd., Hampton, Middlesex TW12 2HQ, England. TEL 44-181-783-0755. FAX 44-181-783-1940. *507*

KEY NOTE MARKET REPORT: BREAD BAKERS.
Key Note Ltd., Field House, 72 Oldfield Rd., Hampton, Middlesex TW12 2HQ, England. TEL 44-181-783-0755. FAX 44-181-783-1940. *3000*

KEY NOTE MARKET REPORT: BREAKFAST CEREALS.
Key Note Ltd., Field House, 72 Oldfield Rd., Hampton, Middlesex TW12 2HQ, England. TEL 44-181-783-0755. FAX 44-181-783-1940. *2981*

KEY NOTE MARKET REPORT: BREWERIES & THE BEER MARKET.
Key Note Ltd., Field House, 72 Oldfield Rd., Hampton, Middlesex TW12 2HQ, England. TEL 44-181-783-0755. FAX 44-181-783-1940. *507*

KEY NOTE MARKET REPORT: BRICKS & TILES.
Key Note Ltd., Field House, 72 Oldfield Rd., Hampton, Middlesex TW12 2HQ, England. TEL 44-181-783-0755. FAX 44-181-783-1940. *862*

KEY NOTE MARKET REPORT: BROWN GOODS.
Key Note Ltd., Field House, 72 Oldfield Rd., Hampton, Middlesex TW12 2HQ, England. TEL 44-181-783-0755. FAX 44-181-783-1940. *2526*

KEY NOTE MARKET REPORT: BUILDING CONTRACTING.
Key Note Ltd., Field House, 72 Oldfield Rd., Hampton, Middlesex TW12 2HQ, England. TEL 44-181-783-0755. FAX 44-181-783-1940. *862*

KEY NOTE MARKET REPORT: BUILDING MATERIALS.
Key Note Ltd., Field House, 72 Oldfield Rd., Hampton, Middlesex TW12 2HQ, England. TEL 44-181-783-0755. FAX 44-181-783-1940. *862*

KEY NOTE MARKET REPORT: BUILDING SOCIETIES.
Key Note Ltd., Field House, 72 Oldfield Rd., Hampton, Middlesex TW12 2HQ, England. TEL 44-181-783-0755. FAX 44-181-783-1940. *862*

KEY NOTE MARKET REPORT: BUS & COACH OPERATORS.
Key Note Ltd., Field House, 72 Oldfield Rd., Hampton, Middlesex TW12 2HQ, England. TEL 44-181-783-0755. FAX 44-181-783-1940. *6721*

KEY NOTE MARKET REPORT: BUSINESS PRESS.
Key Note Ltd., Field House, 72 Oldfield Rd., Hampton, Middlesex TW12 2HQ, England. TEL 44-181-783-0755. FAX 44-181-783-1940. *939*

KEY NOTE MARKET REPORT: BUSINESS TRAVEL.
Key Note Ltd., Field House, 72 Oldfield Rd., Hampton, Middlesex TW12 2HQ, England. TEL 44-181-783-0755. FAX 44-181-783-1940. *6896*

KEY NOTE MARKET REPORT: C D - R O M.
Key Note Ltd., Field House, 72 Oldfield Rd., Hampton, Middlesex TW12 2HQ, England. TEL 44-181-783-0755. FAX 44-181-783-1940. *1928*

KEY NOTE MARKET REPORT: C T N'S.
Key Note Ltd., Field House, 72 Oldfield Rd., Hampton, Middlesex TW12 2HQ, England. TEL 44-181-783-0755. FAX 44-181-783-1940. *1106*

KEY NOTE MARKET REPORT: CABLE AND SATELLITE T V.
Key Note Ltd., Field House, 72 Oldfield Rd., Hampton, Middlesex TW12 2HQ, England. TEL 44-181-783-0755. FAX 44-181-783-1940. *1963*

KEY NOTE MARKET REPORT: CAMERAS & CAMCORDERS.
Key Note Ltd., Field House, 72 Oldfield Rd., Hampton, Middlesex TW12 2HQ, England. TEL 44-181-783-0755. FAX 44-181-783-1940. *5514*

KEY NOTE MARKET REPORT: CAMPING & CARAVANNING.
Key Note Ltd., Field House, 72 Oldfield Rd., Hampton, Middlesex TW12 2HQ, England. TEL 44-181-783-0755. FAX 44-181-783-1940. *3964*

KEY NOTE MARKET REPORT: CANNED FOODS.
Key Note Ltd., Field House, 72 Oldfield Rd., Hampton, Middlesex TW12 2HQ, England. TEL 44-181-783-0755. FAX 44-181-783-1940. *2981*

KEY NOTE MARKET REPORT: CAR DEALERS.
Key Note Ltd., Field House, 72 Oldfield Rd., Hampton, Middlesex TW12 2HQ, England. TEL 44-181-783-0755. FAX 44-181-783-1940. *6790*

KEY NOTE MARKET REPORT: CARPETS & FLOORCOVERINGS.
Key Note Ltd., Field House, 72 Oldfield Rd., Hampton, Middlesex TW12 2HQ, England. TEL 44-181-783-0755. FAX 44-181-783-1940. *3689*

KEY NOTE MARKET REPORT: CASH & CARRY OUTLETS.
Key Note Ltd., Field House, 72 Oldfield Rd., Hampton, Middlesex TW12 2HQ, England. TEL 44-181-783-0755. FAX 44-181-783-1940. *1473*

KEY NOTE MARKET REPORT: CHARITIES.
Key Note Ltd., Field House, 72 Oldfield Rd., Hampton, Middlesex TW12 2HQ, England. TEL 44-181-783-0755. FAX 44-181-783-1940. *6380*

KEY NOTE MARKET REPORT: CHEMICAL INDUSTRY.
Key Note Ltd., Field House, 72 Oldfield Rd., Hampton, Middlesex TW12 2HQ, England. TEL 44-181-783-0755. FAX 44-181-783-1940. *2644*

KEY NOTE MARKET REPORT: CHILDRENSWEAR.
Key Note Ltd., Field House, 72 Oldfield Rd., Hampton, Middlesex TW12 2HQ, England. TEL 44-181-783-0755. FAX 44-181-783-1940. *1834*

KEY NOTE MARKET REPORT: CHILLED FOODS.
Key Note Ltd., Field House, 72 Oldfield Rd., Hampton, Middlesex TW12 2HQ, England. TEL 44-181-783-0755. FAX 44-181-783-1940. *2981*

KEY NOTE MARKET REPORT: CHINA & EARTHENWARE.
Key Note Ltd., Field House, 72 Oldfield Rd., Hampton, Middlesex TW12 2HQ, England. TEL 44-181-783-0755. FAX 44-181-783-1940. *1658*

KEY NOTE MARKET REPORT: CIDER.
Key Note Ltd., Field House, 72 Oldfield Rd., Hampton, Middlesex TW12 2HQ, England. TEL 44-181-783-0755. FAX 44-181-783-1940. *508*

KEY NOTE MARKET REPORT: CIGARETTES & TOBACCO.
Key Note Ltd., Field House, 72 Oldfield Rd., Hampton, Middlesex TW12 2HQ, England. TEL 44-181-783-0755. FAX 44-181-783-1940. *6709*

KEY NOTE MARKET REPORT: CIVIL ENGINEERING.
Key Note Ltd., Field House, 72 Oldfield Rd., Hampton, Middlesex TW12 2HQ, England. TEL 44-181-783-0755. FAX 44-181-783-1940. *2667*

KEY NOTE MARKET REPORT: CLOTHING MANUFACTURING.
Key Note Ltd., Field House, 72 Oldfield Rd., Hampton, Middlesex TW12 2HQ, England. TEL 44-181-783-0755. FAX 44-181-783-1940. *1834*

KEY NOTE MARKET REPORT: CLOTHING RETAILING.
Key Note Ltd., Field House, 72 Oldfield Rd., Hampton, Middlesex TW12 2HQ, England. TEL 44-181-783-0755. FAX 44-181-783-1940. *1834*

KEY NOTE MARKET REPORT: COMMERCIAL RADIO.
Key Note Ltd., Field House, 72 Oldfield Rd., Hampton, Middlesex TW12 2HQ, England. TEL 44-181-783-0755. FAX 44-181-783-1940. *1937*

KEY NOTE MARKET REPORT: COMMERCIAL T V.
Key Note Ltd., Field House, 72 Oldfield Rd., Hampton, Middlesex TW12 2HQ, England. TEL 44-181-783-0755. FAX 44-181-783-1940. *1963*

Online

KEY NOTE MARKET REPORT: COMMERCIAL VEHICLES.
Key Note Ltd., Field House, 72 Oldfield Rd., Hampton, Middlesex TW12 2HQ, England. TEL 44-181-783-0755. FAX 44-181-783-1940. *6790*

KEY NOTE MARKET REPORT: COMPUTER SERVICES.
Key Note Ltd., Field House, 72 Oldfield Rd., Hampton, Middlesex TW12 2HQ, England. TEL 44-181-783-0755. FAX 44-181-783-1940. *2032*

KEY NOTE MARKET REPORT: COMPUTER SOFTWARE.
Key Note Ltd., Field House, 72 Oldfield Rd., Hampton, Middlesex TW12 2HQ, England. TEL 44-181-783-0755. FAX 44-181-783-1940. *2112*

KEY NOTE MARKET REPORT: CONFECTIONERY.
Key Note Ltd., Field House, 72 Oldfield Rd., Hampton, Middlesex TW12 2HQ, England. TEL 44-181-783-0755. FAX 44-181-783-1940. *3000*

KEY NOTE MARKET REPORT: CONSUMER MAGAZINES.
Key Note Ltd., Field House, 72 Oldfield Rd., Hampton, Middlesex TW12 2HQ, England. TEL 44-181-783-0755. FAX 44-181-783-1940. *6000*

KEY NOTE MARKET REPORT: CONTRACEPTIVES.
Key Note Ltd., Field House, 72 Oldfield Rd., Hampton, Middlesex TW12 2HQ, England. TEL 44-181-783-0755. FAX 44-181-783-1940. *827*

KEY NOTE MARKET REPORT: CONTRACT CATERING.
Key Note Ltd., Field House, 72 Oldfield Rd., Hampton, Middlesex TW12 2HQ, England. TEL 44-181-783-0755. FAX 44-171-783-1940. *3566*

KEY NOTE MARKET REPORT: CONTRACT CLEANING.
Key Note Ltd., Field House, 72 Oldfield Rd., Hampton, Middlesex TW12 2HQ, England. TEL 44-181-783-0755. FAX 44-181-783-1940. *1828*

KEY NOTE MARKET REPORT: CONVENIENCE RETAILING.
Key Note Ltd., Field House, 72 Oldfield Rd., Hampton, Middlesex TW12 2HQ, England. TEL 44-181-783-0755. FAX 44-181-783-1940. *1473*

KEY NOTE MARKET REPORT: COSMETICS & FRAGRANCES.
Key Note Ltd., Field House, 72 Oldfield Rd., Hampton, Middlesex TW12 2HQ, England. TEL 44-181-783-0755. FAX 44-181-783-1940. *496*

KEY NOTE MARKET REPORT: COURIER & EXPRESS SERVICES.
Key Note Ltd., Field House, 72 Oldfield Rd., Hampton, Middlesex TW12 2HQ, England. TEL 44-181-783-0755. FAX 44-181-783-1940. *1931*

KEY NOTE MARKET REPORT: CREDIT & OTHER FINANCE CARDS.
Key Note Ltd., Field House, 72 Oldfield Rd., Hampton, Middlesex TW12 2HQ, England. TEL 44-181-783-0755. FAX 44-181-783-1940. *1106*

KEY NOTE MARKET REPORT: DEBT MANAGEMENT & FACTORING.
Key Note Ltd., Field House, 72 Oldfield Rd., Hampton, Middlesex TW12 2HQ, England. TEL 44-181-783-0755. FAX 44-181-783-1940. *1106*

KEY NOTE MARKET REPORT: DEFENCE EQUIPMENT.
Key Note Ltd., Field House, 72 Oldfield Rd., Hampton, Middlesex TW12 2HQ, England. TEL 44-181-783-0755. FAX 44-181-783-1940. *5037*

KEY NOTE MARKET REPORT: DIRECT MARKETING.
Key Note Ltd., Field House, 72 Oldfield Rd., Hampton, Middlesex TW12 2HQ, England. TEL 44-181-783-0755. FAX 44-181-783-1940. *1473*

KEY NOTE MARKET REPORT: DISPOSABLE PAPER PRODUCTS.
Key Note Ltd., Field House, 72 Oldfield Rd., Hampton, Middlesex TW12 2HQ, England. TEL 44-181-783-0755. FAX 44-181-783-1940. *5323*

KEY NOTE MARKET REPORT: DISTILLERS (WHISKY).
Key Note Ltd., Field House, 72 Oldfield Rd., Hampton, Middlesex TW12 2HQ, England. TEL 44-181-783-0755. FAX 44-181-783-1940. *508*

KEY NOTE MARKET REPORT: DOMESTIC HEATING.
Key Note Ltd., Field House, 72 Oldfield Rd., Hampton, Middlesex TW12 2HQ, England. TEL 44-181-783-0755. FAX 44-181-783-1940. *3330*

KEY NOTE MARKET REPORT: DRY BATTERIES.
Key Note Ltd., Field House, 72 Oldfield Rd., Hampton, Middlesex TW12 2HQ, England. TEL 44-181-783-0755. FAX 44-181-783-1940. *5582*

KEY NOTE MARKET REPORT: ELECTRICAL CONTRACTING.
Key Note Ltd., Field House, 72 Oldfield Rd., Hampton, Middlesex TW12 2HQ, England. TEL 44-181-783-0755. FAX 44-181-783-1940. *2711*

KEY NOTE MARKET REPORT: ELECTRONIC COMPONENT DISTRIBUTION.
Key Note Ltd., Field House, 72 Oldfield Rd., Hampton, Middlesex TW12 2HQ, England. TEL 44-181-783-0755. FAX 44-181-783-1940. *2526*

KEY NOTE MARKET REPORT: ELECTRONIC COMPONENT MANUFACTURERS.
Key Note Ltd., Field House, 72 Oldfield Rd., Hampton, Middlesex TW12 2HQ, England. TEL 44-181-783-0755. FAX 44-181-783-1940. *2526*

KEY NOTE MARKET REPORT: ELECTRONIC GAMES.
Key Note Ltd., Field House, 72 Oldfield Rd., Hampton, Middlesex TW12 2HQ, England. TEL 44-181-783-0755. FAX 44-181-783-1940. *2024*

KEY NOTE MARKET REPORT: EMPLOYMENT AGENCIES.
Key Note Ltd., Field House, 72 Oldfield Rd., Hampton, Middlesex TW12 2HQ, England. TEL 44-181-783-0755. FAX 44-181-783-1940. *5270*

KEY NOTE MARKET REPORT: EQUIPMENT LEASING.
Key Note Ltd., Field House, 72 Oldfield Rd., Hampton, Middlesex TW12 2HQ, England. TEL 44-181-783-0755. FAX 44-181-783-1940. *1577*

KEY NOTE MARKET REPORT: ESTATE AGENTS.
Key Note Ltd., Field House, 72 Oldfield Rd., Hampton, Middlesex TW12 2HQ, England. TEL 44-181-783-0755. FAX 44-181-783-1940. *3915*

KEY NOTE MARKET REPORT: ETHNIC FOODS.
Key Note Ltd., Field House, 72 Oldfield Rd., Hampton, Middlesex TW12 2HQ, England. TEL 44-181-783-0755. FAX 44-181-783-1940. *2981*

KEY NOTE MARKET REPORT: EXHIBITIONS AND CONFERENCE ORGANISERS.
Key Note Ltd., Field House, 72 Oldfield Rd., Hampton, Middlesex TW12 2HQ, England. TEL 44-181-783-0755. FAX 44-181-783-1940. *4935*

KEY NOTE MARKET REPORT: FAST FOOD AND HOME DELIVERY OUTLETS.
Key Note Ltd., Field House, 72 Oldfield Rd., Hampton, Middlesex TW12 2HQ, England. TEL 44-181-783-0755. FAX 44-181-783-1940. *2981*

KEY NOTE MARKET REPORT: FIBRES.
Key Note Ltd., Field House, 72 Oldfield Rd., Hampton, Middlesex TW12 2HQ, England. TEL 44-181-783-0755. FAX 44-181-783-1940. *6681*

KEY NOTE MARKET REPORT: FINANCE HOUSES.
Key Note Ltd., Field House, 72 Oldfield Rd., Hampton, Middlesex TW12 2HQ, England. TEL 44-181-783-0755. FAX 44-181-783-1940. *1106*

KEY NOTE MARKET REPORT: FIRE PROTECTION EQUIPMENT.
Key Note Ltd., Field House, 72 Oldfield Rd., Hampton, Middlesex TW12 2HQ, England. TEL 44-181-783-0755. FAX 44-181-783-1940. *2921*

KEY NOTE MARKET REPORT: FOOD FLAVOURINGS & INGREDIENTS.
Key Note Ltd., Field House, 72 Oldfield Rd., Hampton, Middlesex TW12 2HQ, England. TEL 44-181-783-0755. FAX 44-181-783-1940. *2981*

KEY NOTE MARKET REPORT: FOOTWEAR.
Key Note Ltd., Field House, 72 Oldfield Rd., Hampton, Middlesex TW12 2HQ, England. TEL 44-181-783-0755. FAX 44-181-783-1940. *6307*

KEY NOTE MARKET REPORT: FREIGHT FORWARDING.
Key Note Ltd., Field House, 72 Oldfield Rd., Hampton, Middlesex TW12 2HQ, England. TEL 44-181-783-0755. FAX 44-181-783-1940. *6721*

KEY NOTE MARKET REPORT: FROZEN FOODS.
Key Note Ltd., Field House, 72 Oldfield Rd., Hampton, Middlesex TW12 2HQ, England. TEL 44-181-783-0755. FAX 44-181-783-1940. *2981*

KEY NOTE MARKET REPORT: FRUIT & VEGETABLES.
Key Note Ltd., Field House, 72 Oldfield Rd., Hampton, Middlesex TW12 2HQ, England. TEL 44-181-783-0755. FAX 44-181-783-1940. *3006*

KEY NOTE MARKET REPORT: FRUIT JUICES & HEALTH DRINKS.
Key Note Ltd., Field House, 72 Oldfield Rd., Hampton, Middlesex TW12 2HQ, England. TEL 44-181-783-0755. FAX 44-181-783-1940. *508*

KEY NOTE MARKET REPORT: GARDEN EQUIPMENT.
Key Note Ltd., Field House, 72 Oldfield Rd., Hampton, Middlesex TW12 2HQ, England. TEL 44-181-783-0755. FAX 44-181-783-1940. *3059*

KEY NOTE MARKET REPORT: GIFTWARE.
Key Note Ltd., Field House, 72 Oldfield Rd., Hampton, Middlesex TW12 2HQ, England. TEL 44-181-783-0755. FAX 44-181-783-1940. *3301*

KEY NOTE MARKET REPORT: GLASSWARE.
Key Note Ltd., Field House, 72 Oldfield Rd., Hampton, Middlesex TW12 2HQ, England. TEL 44-181-783-0755. FAX 44-181-783-1940. *1658*

KEY NOTE MARKET REPORT: GREETINGS CARDS.
Key Note Ltd., Field House, 72 Oldfield Rd., Hampton, Middlesex TW12 2HQ, England. TEL 44-181-783-0755. FAX 44-181-783-1940. *3301*

KEY NOTE MARKET REPORT: HAND LUGGAGE & LEATHER GOODS.
Key Note Ltd., Field House, 72 Oldfield Rd., Hampton, Middlesex TW12 2HQ, England. TEL 44-181-783-0755. FAX 44-181-783-1940. *3960*

KEY NOTE MARKET REPORT: HEALTH CLUBS AND LEISURE CENTRES.
Key Note Ltd., Field House, 72 Oldfield Rd., Hampton, Middlesex TW12 2HQ, England. TEL 44-181-783-0755. FAX 44-181-783-1940. *6467*

KEY NOTE MARKET REPORT: HEALTH FOODS.
Key Note Ltd., Field House, 72 Oldfield Rd., Hampton, Middlesex TW12 2HQ, England. TEL 44-181-783-0755. FAX 44-181-783-1940. *2981*

KEY NOTE MARKET REPORT: HEATING, VENTILATING & AIR CONDITIONING.
Key Note Ltd., Field House, 72 Oldfield Rd., Hampton, Middlesex TW12 2HQ, England. TEL 44-181-783-0755. FAX 44-181-783-1940. *3330*

KEY NOTE MARKET REPORT: HOME FURNISHINGS.
Key Note Ltd., Field House, 72 Oldfield Rd., Hampton, Middlesex TW12 2HQ, England. TEL 44-181-783-0755. FAX 44-181-783-1940. *3689*

KEY NOTE MARKET REPORT: HOME LEISURE.
Key Note Ltd., Field House, 72 Oldfield Rd., Hampton, Middlesex TW12 2HQ, England. TEL 44-181-783-0755. FAX 44-181-783-1940. *3964*

KEY NOTE MARKET REPORT: HOME SHOPPING.
Key Note Ltd., Field House, 72 Oldfield Rd., Hampton, Middlesex TW12 2HQ, England. TEL 44-181-783-0755. FAX 44-181-783-1940. *1473*

KEY NOTE MARKET REPORT: HORTICULTURAL RETAILING.
Key Note Ltd., Field House, 72 Oldfield Rd., Hampton, Middlesex TW12 2HQ, England. TEL 44-181-783-0755. FAX 44-181-783-1940. *3059*

KEY NOTE MARKET REPORT: HOT DRINKS.
Key Note Ltd., Field House, 72 Oldfield Rd., Hampton, Middlesex TW12 2HQ, England. TEL 44-181-783-0755. FAX 44-181-783-1940. *508*

KEY NOTE MARKET REPORT: HOTELS.
Key Note Ltd., Field House, 72 Oldfield Rd., Hampton, Middlesex TW12 2HQ, England. TEL 44-181-783-0755. FAX 44-181-783-1940. *3566*

KEY NOTE MARKET REPORT: HOUSEBUILDING.
Key Note Ltd., Field House, 72 Oldfield Rd.,
Hampton, Middlesex TW12 2HQ, England. TEL 44-
181-783-0755. FAX 44-181-783-1940. *862*

KEY NOTE MARKET REPORT: HOUSEHOLD
APPLIANCES (WHITE GOODS).
Key Note Ltd., Field House, 72 Oldfield Rd.,
Hampton, Middlesex TW12 2HQ, England. TEL 44-
181-783-0755. FAX 44-181-783-1940. *3690*

KEY NOTE MARKET REPORT: HOUSEHOLD
FURNITURE.
Key Note Ltd., Field House, 72 Oldfield Rd.,
Hampton, Middlesex TW12 2HQ, England. TEL 44-
181-783-0755. FAX 44-181-783-1940. *3690*

KEY NOTE MARKET REPORT: ICE-CREAMS &
FROZEN DESSERTS.
Key Note Ltd., Field House, 72 Oldfield Rd.,
Hampton, Middlesex TW12 2HQ, England. TEL 44-
181-783-0755. FAX 44-181-783-1940. *2981*

KEY NOTE MARKET REPORT: INDUSTRIAL
FASTENERS.
Key Note Ltd., Field House, 72 Oldfield Rd.,
Hampton, Middlesex TW12 2HQ, England. TEL 44-
181-783-0755. FAX 44-181-783-1940. *2736*

KEY NOTE MARKET REPORT: INDUSTRIAL PUMPS.
Key Note Ltd., Field House, 72 Oldfield Rd.,
Hampton, Middlesex TW12 2HQ, England. TEL 44-
181-783-0755. FAX 44-181-783-1940. *2744*

KEY NOTE MARKET REPORT: INDUSTRIAL VALVES.
Key Note Ltd., Field House, 72 Oldfield Rd.,
Hampton, Middlesex TW12 2HQ, England. TEL 44-
181-783-0755. FAX 44-181-783-1940. *2748*

KEY NOTE MARKET REPORT: INSULATION
PRODUCTS.
Key Note Ltd., Field House, 72 Oldfield Rd.,
Hampton, Middlesex TW12 2HQ, England. TEL 44-
181-783-0755. FAX 44-181-783-1940. *862*

KEY NOTE MARKET REPORT: JEWELLERY, WATCHES
& FASHION ACCESSORIES.
Key Note Ltd., Field House, 72 Oldfield Rd.,
Hampton, Middlesex TW12 2HQ, England. TEL 44-
181-783-0755. FAX 44-181-783-1940. *3697*

KEY NOTE MARKET REPORT: KITCHENWARE.
Key Note Ltd., Field House, 72 Oldfield Rd.,
Hampton, Middlesex TW12 2HQ, England. TEL 44-
181-783-0755. FAX 44-181-783-1940. *3690*

KEY NOTE MARKET REPORT: LIGHTING
EQUIPMENT.
Key Note Ltd., Field House, 72 Oldfield Rd.,
Hampton, Middlesex TW12 2HQ, England. TEL 44-
181-783-0755. FAX 44-181-783-1940. *3690*

KEY NOTE MARKET REPORT: LINGERIE.
Key Note Ltd., Field House, 72 Oldfield Rd.,
Hampton, Middlesex TW12 2HQ, England. TEL 44-
181-783-0755. FAX 44-181-783-1940. *1834*

KEY NOTE MARKET REPORT: LOW ALCOHOL
DRINKS.
Key Note Ltd., Field House, 72 Oldfield Rd.,
Hampton, Middlesex TW12 2HQ, England. TEL 44-
181-783-0755. FAX 44-181-783-1940. *508*

KEY NOTE MARKET REPORT: MACHINE TOOLS.
Key Note Ltd., Field House, 72 Oldfield Rd.,
Hampton, Middlesex TW12 2HQ, England. TEL 44-
181-783-0755. FAX 44-181-783-1940. *2749*

KEY NOTE MARKET REPORT: MANAGEMENT
CONSULTANTS.
Key Note Ltd., Field House, 72 Oldfield Rd.,
Hampton, Middlesex TW12 2HQ, England. TEL 44-
181-783-0755. FAX 44-181-783-1940. *1429*

KEY NOTE MARKET REPORT: MEAT & MEAT
PRODUCTS.
Key Note Ltd., Field House, 72 Oldfield Rd.,
Hampton, Middlesex TW12 2HQ, England. TEL 44-
181-783-0755. FAX 44-181-783-1940. *2981*

KEY NOTE MARKET REPORT: MECHANICAL
HANDLING.
Key Note Ltd., Field House, 72 Oldfield Rd.,
Hampton, Middlesex TW12 2HQ, England. TEL 44-
181-783-0755. FAX 44-181-783-1940. *2761*

KEY NOTE MARKET REPORT: MEDICAL EQUIPMENT.
Key Note Ltd., Field House, 72 Oldfield Rd.,
Hampton, Middlesex TW12 2HQ, England. TEL 44-
181-783-0755. FAX 44-181-783-1940. *4486*

KEY NOTE MARKET REPORT: MILK & DAIRY
PRODUCTS.
Key Note Ltd., Field House, 72 Oldfield Rd.,
Hampton, Middlesex TW12 2HQ, England. TEL 44-
181-783-0755. FAX 44-181-783-1940. *251*

KEY NOTE MARKET REPORT: MORTGAGE FINANCE.
Key Note Ltd., Field House, 72 Oldfield Rd.,
Hampton, Middlesex TW12 2HQ, England. TEL 44-
181-783-0755. FAX 44-181-783-1940. *1106*

KEY NOTE MARKET REPORT: NEWSPAPERS.
Key Note Ltd., Field House, 72 Oldfield Rd.,
Hampton, Middlesex TW12 2HQ, England. TEL 44-
181-783-0755. FAX 44-181-783-1940. *3707*

KEY NOTE MARKET REPORT: O T C
PHARMACEUTICALS.
Key Note Ltd., Field House, 72 Oldfield Rd.,
Hampton, Middlesex TW12 2HQ, England. TEL 44-
181-783-1940. FAX 44-181-783-1940. *5425*

KEY NOTE MARKET REPORT: OFF-LICENSE TRADE.
Key Note Ltd., Field House, 72 Oldfield Rd.,
Hampton, Middlesex TW12 2HQ, England. TEL 44-
181-783-0755. FAX 44-181-783-1940. *1524*

KEY NOTE MARKET REPORT: OFFICE FURNITURE.
Key Note Ltd., Field House, 72 Oldfield Rd.,
Hampton, Middlesex TW12 2HQ, England. TEL 44-
181-783-0755. FAX 44-181-783-1940. *1494*

KEY NOTE MARKET REPORT: OPHTHALMIC GOODS
& SERVICES.
Key Note Ltd., Field House, 72 Oldfield Rd.,
Hampton, Middlesex TW12 2HQ, England. TEL 44-
181-783-0755. FAX 44-181-783-1940. *4772*

KEY NOTE MARKET REPORT: OWN BRANDS.
Key Note Ltd., Field House, 72 Oldfield Rd.,
Hampton, Middlesex TW12 2HQ, England. TEL 44-
181-783-0755. FAX 44-181-783-1940. *1474*

KEY NOTE MARKET REPORT: PACKAGING (GLASS).
Key Note Ltd., Field House, 72 Oldfield Rd.,
Hampton, Middlesex TW12 2HQ, England. TEL 44-
181-783-0755. FAX 44-181-783-1940. *5301*

KEY NOTE MARKET REPORT: PACKAGING (METALS
& AEROSOLS).
Key Note Ltd., Field House, 72 Oldfield Rd.,
Hampton, Middlesex TW12 2HQ, England. TEL 44-
181-783-0755. FAX 44-181-783-1940. *5301*

KEY NOTE MARKET REPORT: PACKAGING (PAPER &
BOARD).
Key Note Ltd., Field House, 72 Oldfield Rd.,
Hampton, Middlesex TW12 2HQ, England. TEL 44-
181-783-0755. FAX 44-181-783-1940. *5301*

KEY NOTE MARKET REPORT: PACKAGING
(PLASTICS).
Key Note Ltd., Field House, 72 Oldfield Rd.,
Hampton, Middlesex TW12 2HQ, England. TEL 44-
181-783-0755. FAX 44-181-783-1940. *5301*

KEY NOTE MARKET REPORT: PAINTS & VARNISHES.
Key Note Ltd., Field House, 72 Oldfield Rd.,
Hampton, Middlesex TW12 2HQ, England. TEL 44-
181-783-0755. FAX 44-181-783-1940. *5308*

KEY NOTE MARKET REPORT: PASSENGER
SHIPPING.
Key Note Ltd., Field House, 72 Oldfield Rd.,
Hampton, Middlesex TW12 2HQ, England. TEL 44-
181-783-0755. FAX 44-181-783-1940. *6838*

KEY NOTE MARKET REPORT: PERISHABLE FAST-
MOVING CONSUMER GOODS.
Key Note Ltd., Field House, 72 Oldfield Rd.,
Hampton, Middlesex TW12 2HQ, England. TEL 44-
181-783-0755. FAX 44-181-783-1940. *2981*

KEY NOTE MARKET REPORT: PET FOODS.
Key Note Ltd., Field House, 72 Oldfield Rd.,
Hampton, Middlesex TW12 2HQ, England. TEL 44-
181-783-0755. FAX 44-181-783-1940. *5391*

KEY NOTE MARKET REPORT: PHOTOCOPIERS & FAX
MACHINES.
Key Note Ltd., Field House, 72 Oldfield Rd.,
Hampton, Middlesex TW12 2HQ, England. TEL 44-
181-783-1940. *1494*

KEY NOTE MARKET REPORT: PHOTOGRAPHIC
SERVICES.
Key Note Ltd., Field House, 72 Oldfield Rd.,
Hampton, Middlesex TW12 2HQ, England. TEL 44-
181-783-1940. *5514*

KEY NOTE MARKET REPORT: PLANT HIRE.
Key Note Ltd., Field House, 72 Oldfield Rd.,
Hampton, Middlesex TW12 2HQ, England. TEL 44-
181-783-1940. *1219*

KEY NOTE MARKET REPORT: PLASTICS
PROCESSING.
Key Note Ltd., Field House, 72 Oldfield Rd.,
Hampton, Middlesex TW12 2HQ, England. TEL 44-
181-783-0755. FAX 44-181-783-1940. *5621*

KEY NOTE MARKET REPORT: PREMIUM LAGERS,
BEERS AND CIDERS.
Key Note Ltd., Field House, 72 Oldfield Rd.,
Hampton, Middlesex TW12 2HQ, England. TEL 44-
181-783-0755. FAX 44-181-783-1940. *508*

KEY NOTE MARKET REPORT: PRESCRIBED
PHARMACEUTICALS.
Key Note Ltd., Field House, 72 Oldfield Rd.,
Hampton, Middlesex TW12 2HQ, England. TEL 44-
181-783-0755. FAX 44-181-783-1940. *5425*

KEY NOTE MARKET REPORT: PRINTED CIRCUITS.
Key Note Ltd., Field House, 72 Oldfield Rd.,
Hampton, Middlesex TW12 2HQ, England. TEL 44-
181-783-0755. FAX 44-181-783-1940. *2018*

KEY NOTE MARKET REPORT: PRINTING.
Key Note Ltd., Field House, 72 Oldfield Rd.,
Hampton, Middlesex TW12 2HQ, England. TEL 44-
181-783-0755. FAX 44-181-783-1940. *5814*

KEY NOTE MARKET REPORT: PRISON SERVICES.
Key Note Ltd., Field House, 72 Oldfield Rd.,
Hampton, Middlesex TW12 2HQ, England. TEL 44-
181-783-0755. FAX 44-181-783-1940. *2183*

KEY NOTE MARKET REPORT: PRIVATE
HEALTHCARE.
Key Note Ltd., Field House, 72 Oldfield Rd.,
Hampton, Middlesex TW12 2HQ, England. TEL 44-
181-783-0755. FAX 44-181-783-1940. *4486*

KEY NOTE MARKET REPORT: PROCESS PLANT.
Key Note Ltd., Field House, 72 Oldfield Rd.,
Hampton, Middlesex TW12 2HQ, England. TEL 44-
181-783-0755. FAX 44-181-783-1940. *1524*

KEY NOTE MARKET REPORT: PUBLIC HOUSES.
Key Note Ltd., Field House, 72 Oldfield Rd.,
Hampton, Middlesex TW12 2HQ, England. TEL 44-
181-783-0755. FAX 44-181-783-1940. *3567*

KEY NOTE MARKET REPORT: READY MEALS.
Key Note Ltd., Field House, 72 Oldfield Rd.,
Hampton, Middlesex TW12 2HQ, England. TEL 44-
181-783-0755. FAX 44-181-783-1940. *2981*

KEY NOTE MARKET REPORT: RESTAURANTS.
Key Note Ltd., Field House, 72 Oldfield Rd.,
Hampton, Middlesex TW12 2HQ, England. TEL 44-
181-783-0755. FAX 44-181-783-1940. *3567*

KEY NOTE MARKET REPORT: RETAIL BRANCH
BANKING.
Key Note Ltd., Field House, 72 Oldfield Rd.,
Hampton, Middlesex TW12 2HQ, England. TEL 44-
181-783-0755. FAX 44-181-783-1940. *1106*

KEY NOTE MARKET REPORT: RETAIL CHEMISTS &
DRUG STORES.
Key Note Ltd., Field House, 72 Oldfield Rd.,
Hampton, Middlesex TW12 2HQ, England. TEL 44-
181-783-0755. FAX 44-181-783-1940. *5425*

KEY NOTE MARKET REPORT: ROAD HAULAGE.
Key Note Ltd., Field House, 72 Oldfield Rd.,
Hampton, Middlesex TW12 2HQ, England. TEL 44-
181-783-0755. FAX 44-181-783-1940. *6858*

Online

KEY NOTE MARKET REPORT: RUBBER MANUFACTURING & PROCESSING.
Key Note Ltd., Field House, 72 Oldfield Rd., Hampton, Middlesex TW12 2HQ, England. TEL 44-181-783-0755. FAX 44-181-783-1940. *6217*

KEY NOTE MARKET REPORT: SAUCES AND SPREADS.
Key Note Ltd., Field House, 72 Oldfield Rd., Hampton, Middlesex TW12 2HQ, England. TEL 44-181-783-0755. FAX 44-181-783-1940. *2981*

KEY NOTE MARKET REPORT: SCIENTIFIC INSTRUMENTS.
Key Note Ltd., Field House, 72 Oldfield Rd., Hampton, Middlesex TW12 2HQ, England. TEL 44-181-783-0755. FAX 44-181-783-1940. *3636*

KEY NOTE MARKET REPORT: SCRAP METAL PROCESSING.
Key Note Ltd., Field House, 72 Oldfield Rd., Hampton, Middlesex TW12 2HQ, England. TEL 44-181-783-0755. FAX 44-181-783-1940. *4962*

KEY NOTE MARKET REPORT: SELF-ASSEMBLY FURNITURE.
Key Note Ltd., Field House, 72 Oldfield Rd., Hampton, Middlesex TW12 2HQ, England. TEL 44-181-783-0755. FAX 44-181-783-1940. *3690*

KEY NOTE MARKET REPORT: SHOP FITTING.
Key Note Ltd., Field House, 72 Oldfield Rd., Hampton, Middlesex TW12 2HQ, England. TEL 44-181-783-0755. FAX 44-181-783-1940. *1474*

KEY NOTE MARKET REPORT: SHOWERS & SHOWER ACCESSORIES.
Key Note Ltd., Field House, 72 Oldfield Rd., Hampton, Middlesex TW12 2HQ, England. TEL 44-181-783-0755. FAX 44-181-783-1940. *3690*

KEY NOTE MARKET REPORT: SLIMMING MARKET.
Key Note Ltd., Field House, 72 Oldfield Rd., Hampton, Middlesex TW12 2HQ, England. TEL 44-181-783-0755. FAX 44-181-783-1940. *1524*

KEY NOTE MARKET REPORT: SMALL DOMESTIC ELECTRICAL APPLIANCES.
Key Note Ltd., Field House, 72 Oldfield Rd., Hampton, Middlesex TW12 2HQ, England. TEL 44-181-783-0755. FAX 44-181-783-1940. *2526*

KEY NOTE MARKET REPORT: SNACK FOODS.
Key Note Ltd., Field House, 72 Oldfield Rd., Hampton, Middlesex TW12 2HQ, England. TEL 44-181-783-0755. FAX 44-181-783-1940. *2981*

KEY NOTE MARKET REPORT: SOAPS & DETERGENTS.
Key Note Ltd., Field House, 72 Oldfield Rd., Hampton, Middlesex TW12 2HQ, England. TEL 44-181-783-0755. FAX 44-181-783-1940. *1828*

KEY NOTE MARKET REPORT: SOFT DRINKS (CARBONATES & CONCENTRATES).
Key Note Ltd., Field House, 72 Oldfield Rd., Hampton, Middlesex TW12 2HQ, England. TEL 44-181-783-0755. FAX 44-181-783-1940. *508*

KEY NOTE MARKET REPORT: SPORTS CLOTHING AND FOOTWEAR.
Key Note Ltd., Field House, 72 Oldfield Rd., Hampton, Middlesex TW12 2HQ, England. TEL 44-181-783-0755. FAX 44-181-783-1940. *1834*

KEY NOTE MARKET REPORT: SPORTS EQUIPMENT.
Key Note Ltd., Field House, 72 Oldfield Rd., Hampton, Middlesex TW12 2HQ, England. TEL 44-181-783-0755. FAX 44-181-783-1940. *6467*

KEY NOTE MARKET REPORT: STATIONERY (PERSONAL & OFFICE).
Key Note Ltd., Field House, 72 Oldfield Rd., Hampton, Middlesex TW12 2HQ, England. TEL 44-181-783-0755. FAX 44-181-783-1940. *1494*

KEY NOTE MARKET REPORT: STEEL STOCKHOLDING.
Key Note Ltd., Field House, 72 Oldfield Rd., Hampton, Middlesex TW12 2HQ, England. TEL 44-181-783-0755. FAX 44-181-783-1940. *1338*

KEY NOTE MARKET REPORT: SUPERMARKETS & SUPERSTORES.
Key Note Ltd., Field House, 72 Oldfield Rd., Hampton, Middlesex TW12 2HQ, England. TEL 44-181-783-0755. FAX 44-181-783-1940. *2981*

KEY NOTE MARKET REPORT: T V & VIDEO RENTAL.
Key Note Ltd., Field House, 72 Oldfield Rd., Hampton, Middlesex TW12 2HQ, England. TEL 44-181-783-0755. FAX 44-181-783-1940. *2526*

KEY NOTE MARKET REPORT: TELECOMMUNICATIONS.
Key Note Ltd., Field House, 72 Oldfield Rd., Hampton, Middlesex TW12 2HQ, England. TEL 44-181-783-0755. FAX 44-181-783-1940. *1909*

KEY NOTE MARKET REPORT: TIMBER & JOINERY.
Key Note Ltd., Field House, 72 Oldfield Rd., Hampton, Middlesex TW12 2HQ, England. TEL 44-181-783-0755. FAX 44-181-783-1940. *3035*

KEY NOTE MARKET REPORT: TOILETRIES.
Key Note Ltd., Field House, 72 Oldfield Rd., Hampton, Middlesex TW12 2HQ, England. TEL 44-181-783-0755. FAX 44-181-783-1940. *492*

KEY NOTE MARKET REPORT: TOURIST ATTRACTIONS.
Key Note Ltd., Field House, 72 Oldfield Rd., Hampton, Middlesex TW12 2HQ, England. TEL 44-181-783-0755. FAX 44-181-783-1940. *6896*

KEY NOTE MARKET REPORT: TOYS & GAMES.
Key Note Ltd., Field House, 72 Oldfield Rd., Hampton, Middlesex TW12 2HQ, England. TEL 44-181-783-0755. FAX 44-181-783-1940. *3301*

KEY NOTE MARKET REPORT: TRAINING.
Key Note Ltd., Field House, 72 Oldfield Rd., Hampton, Middlesex TW12 2HQ, England. TEL 44-181-783-0755. FAX 44-181-783-1940. *2400*

KEY NOTE MARKET REPORT: TRAVEL AGENTS & OVERSEAS TOUR OPERATORS.
Key Note Ltd., Field House, 72 Oldfield Rd., Hampton, Middlesex TW12 2HQ, England. TEL 44-181-783-0755. FAX 44-181-783-1940. *6896*

KEY NOTE MARKET REPORT: VEHICLE LEASING & HIRE.
Key Note Ltd., Field House, 72 Oldfield Rd., Hampton, Middlesex TW12 2HQ, England. TEL 44-181-783-0755. FAX 44-181-783-1940. *6790*

KEY NOTE MARKET REPORT: VEHICLE SECURITY.
Key Note Ltd., Field House, 72 Oldfield Rd., Hampton, Middlesex TW12 2HQ, England. TEL 44-181-783-0755. FAX 44-181-783-1940. *6790*

KEY NOTE MARKET REPORT: VIDEO RETAIL & HIRE.
Key Note Ltd., Field House, 72 Oldfield Rd., Hampton, Middlesex TW12 2HQ, England. TEL 44-181-783-0755. FAX 44-181-783-1940. *1977*

KEY NOTE MARKET REPORT: WALLCOVERINGS.
Key Note Ltd., Field House, 72 Oldfield Rd., Hampton, Middlesex TW12 2HQ, England. TEL 44-181-783-0755. FAX 44-181-783-1940. *3679*

KEY NOTE MARKET REPORT: WASTE MANAGEMENT.
Key Note Ltd., Field House, 72 Oldfield Rd., Hampton, Middlesex TW12 2HQ, England. TEL 44-181-783-0755. FAX 44-181-783-1940. *2854*

KEY NOTE MARKET REPORT: WATER UTILITIES.
Key Note Ltd., Field House, 72 Oldfield Rd., Hampton, Middlesex TW12 2HQ, England. TEL 44-181-783-0755. FAX 44-181-783-1940. *6971*

KEY NOTE MARKET REPORT: WINDOWS & DOORS.
Key Note Ltd., Field House, 72 Oldfield Rd., Hampton, Middlesex TW12 2HQ, England. TEL 44-181-783-0755. FAX 44-181-783-1940. *3690*

KEY NOTE MARKET REPORT: WINE.
Key Note Ltd., Field House, 72 Oldfield Rd., Hampton, Middlesex TW12 2HQ, England. TEL 44-181-783-0755. FAX 44-181-783-1940. *508*

KEY NOTE MARKET REPORT: WOMEN'S MAGAZINES.
Key Note Ltd., Field House, 72 Oldfield Rd., Hampton, Middlesex TW12 2HQ, England. TEL 44-181-783-0755. FAX 44-181-783-1940. *6998*

KEY NOTE MARKET REVIEW: CORPORATE SERVICES IN THE U K.
Key Note Ltd., Field House, 72 Oldfield Rd., Hampton, Middlesex TW12 2HQ, England. TEL 44-181-783-0755. FAX 44-181-783-1940. *1619*

KEY NOTE MARKET REVIEW: D I Y & HOME IMPROVEMENTS.
Key Note Ltd., Field House, 72 Oldfield Rd., Hampton, Middlesex TW12 2HQ, England. TEL 44-181-783-0755. FAX 44-181-783-1940. *3679*

KEY NOTE MARKET REVIEW: ENERGY INDUSTRY IN THE U K.
Key Note Ltd., Field House, 72 Oldfield Rd., Hampton, Middlesex TW12 2HQ, England. TEL 44-181-783-0755. FAX 44-181-783-1940. *2553*

KEY NOTE MARKET REVIEW: GREY MARKET IN THE U K.
Key Note Ltd., Field House, 72 Oldfield Rd., Hampton, Middlesex TW12 2HQ, England. TEL 44-181-783-0755. FAX 44-181-783-1940. *1474*

KEY NOTE MARKET REVIEW: MULTIMEDIA IN U K.
Key Note Ltd., Field House, 72 Oldfield Rd., Hampton, Middlesex TW12 2HQ, England. TEL 44-181-783-0755. FAX 44-181-783-1940. *1928*

KEY NOTE MARKET REVIEW: PASSENGER TRAVEL IN U K.
Key Note Ltd., Field House, 72 Oldfield Rd., Hampton, Middlesex TW12 2HQ, England. TEL 44-181-783-0755. FAX 44-181-783-1940. *6896*

KEY NOTE MARKET REVIEW: PERSONAL FINANCE IN THE U K.
Key Note Ltd., Field House, 72 Oldfield Rd., Hampton, Middlesex TW12 2HQ, England. TEL 44-181-783-0755. FAX 44-181-783-1940. *1106*

KEY NOTE MARKET REVIEW: RETAILING IN THE U K.
Key Note Ltd., Field House, 72 Oldfield Rd., Hampton, Middlesex TW12 2HQ, England. TEL 44-181-783-0755. FAX 44-181-783-1940. *1474*

KEY NOTE MARKET REVIEW: U K CATERING MARKET.
Key Note Ltd., Field House, 72 Oldfield Rd., Hampton, Middlesex TW12 2HQ, England. TEL 44-181-783-0755. FAX 44-181-783-1940. *3567*

KEY NOTE MARKET REVIEW: U K CHEMICAL INDUSTRY.
Key Note Ltd., Field House, 72 Oldfield Rd., Hampton, Middlesex TW12 2HQ, England. TEL 44-181-783-0755. FAX 44-181-783-1940. *1683*

KEY NOTE MARKET REVIEW: U K CLOTHING & FOOTWEAR.
Key Note Ltd., Field House, 72 Oldfield Rd., Hampton, Middlesex TW12 2HQ, England. TEL 44-181-783-0755. FAX 44-181-783-1940. *1834*

KEY NOTE MARKET REVIEW: U K COMPUTER MARKET.
Key Note Ltd., Field House, 72 Oldfield Rd., Hampton, Middlesex TW12 2HQ, England. TEL 44-181-783-0755. FAX 44-181-783-1940. *2032*

KEY NOTE MARKET REVIEW: U K CONSTRUCTION INDUSTRY.
Key Note Ltd., Field House, 72 Oldfield Rd., Hampton, Middlesex TW12 2HQ, England. TEL 44-181-783-0755. FAX 44-181-783-1940. *862*

KEY NOTE MARKET REVIEW: U K DEFENCE INDUSTRY.
Key Note Ltd., Field House, 72 Oldfield Rd., Hampton, Middlesex TW12 2HQ, England. TEL 44-181-783-0755. FAX 44-181-783-1940. *5037*

KEY NOTE MARKET REVIEW: U K DISTRIBUTION.
Key Note Ltd., Field House, 72 Oldfield Rd., Hampton, Middlesex TW12 2HQ, England. TEL 44-181-783-0755. FAX 44-181-783-1940. *1524*

KEY NOTE MARKET REVIEW: U K DRINKS MARKET.
Key Note Ltd., Field House, 72 Oldfield Rd., Hampton, Middlesex TW12 2HQ, England. TEL 44-181-783-0755. FAX 44-181-783-1940. *508*

KEY NOTE MARKET REVIEW: U K EDUCATION INDUSTRY.
Key Note Ltd., Field House, 72 Oldfield Rd., Hampton, Middlesex TW12 2HQ, England. TEL 44-181-783-0755. FAX 44-181-783-1940. *2459*

KEY NOTE MARKET REVIEW: U K FOOD MARKET.
Key Note Ltd., Field House, 72 Oldfield Rd., Hampton, Middlesex TW12 2HQ, England. TEL 44-181-783-0755. FAX 44-181-783-1940. *2981*

KEY NOTE MARKET REVIEW: U K HEALTHCARE.
Key Note Ltd., Field House, 72 Oldfield Rd., Hampton, Middlesex TW12 2HQ, England. TEL 44-181-783-0755. FAX 44-181-783-1940. *4486*

KEY NOTE MARKET REVIEW: U K HOUSEHOLD MARKET - FURNITURE, FITTINGS & DECOR.
Key Note Ltd., Field House, 72 Oldfield Rd., Hampton, Middlesex TW12 2HQ, England. TEL 44-181-783-0755. FAX 44-181-783-1940. *3690*

KEY NOTE MARKET REVIEW: U K HOUSEHOLD MARKET - HOUSEHOLD APPLIANCES AND HOUSEWARES.
Key Note Ltd., Field House, 72 Oldfield Rd., Hampton, Middlesex TW12 2HQ, England. TEL 44-181-783-0755. FAX 44-181-783-1940. *3690*

KEY NOTE MARKET REVIEW: U K INSURANCE MARKET.
Key Note Ltd., Field House, 72 Oldfield Rd., Hampton, Middlesex TW12 2HQ, England. TEL 44-181-783-0755. FAX 44-181-783-1940. *3655*

KEY NOTE MARKET REVIEW: U K LEISURE AND RECREATION.
Key Note Ltd., Field House, 72 Oldfield Rd., Hampton, Middlesex TW12 2HQ, England. TEL 44-181-783-0755. FAX 44-181-783-1940. *3964*

KEY NOTE MARKET REVIEW: U K MOTOR INDUSTRY.
Key Note Ltd., Field House, 72 Oldfield Rd., Hampton, Middlesex TW12 2HQ, England. TEL 44-181-783-0755. FAX 44-181-783-1940. *6790*

KEY NOTE MARKET REVIEW: U K OFFICE EQUIPMENT.
Key Note Ltd., Field House, 72 Oldfield Rd., Hampton, Middlesex TW12 2HQ, England. TEL 44-181-783-0755. FAX 44-181-783-1940. *1494*

KEY NOTE MARKET REVIEW: U K PACKAGING INDUSTRY.
Key Note Ltd., Field House, 72 Oldfield Rd., Hampton, Middlesex TW12 2HQ, England. TEL 44-181-783-0755. FAX 44-181-783-1940. *5301*

KEY NOTE MARKET REVIEW: U K PET MARKET.
Key Note Ltd., Field House, 72 Oldfield Rd., Hampton, Middlesex TW12 2HQ, England. TEL 44-181-783-0755. FAX 44-181-783-1940. *1474*

KEY NOTE MARKET REVIEW: U K PHARMACEUTICAL INDUSTRY.
Key Note Ltd., Field House, 72 Oldfield Rd., Hampton, Middlesex TW12 2HQ, England. TEL 44-181-783-0755. FAX 44-181-783-1940. *5425*

KEY NOTE MARKET REVIEW: U K PUBLISHING.
Key Note Ltd., Field House, 72 Oldfield Rd., Hampton, Middlesex TW12 2HQ, England. TEL 44-181-783-0755. FAX 44-181-783-1940. *6000*

KEY NOTE MARKET REVIEW: U K SECURITY MARKET.
Key Note Ltd., Field House, 72 Oldfield Rd., Hampton, Middlesex TW12 2HQ, England. TEL 44-181-783-0755. FAX 44-181-783-1940. *2183*

KEY NOTE MARKET REVIEW: U K SOFT DRINKS.
Key Note Ltd., Field House, 72 Oldfield Rd., Hampton, Middlesex TW12 2HQ, England. TEL 44-181-783-0755. FAX 44-181-783-1940. *508*

KEY NOTE MARKET REVIEW: U K SPORTS MARKET.
Key Note Ltd., Field House, 72 Oldfield Rd., Hampton, Middlesex TW12 2HQ, England. TEL 44-181-783-0755. FAX 44-181-783-1940. *6467*

KEY NOTE MARKET REVIEW: U K TELECOMMUNICATIONS.
Key Note Ltd., Field House, 72 Oldfield Rd., Hampton, Middlesex TW12 2HQ, England. TEL 44-181-783-0755. FAX 44-181-783-1940. *1909*

KEY NOTE MARKET REVIEW: U K TOILETRIES & COSMETICS MARKET.
Key Note Ltd., Field House, 72 Oldfield Rd., Hampton, Middlesex TW12 2HQ, England. TEL 44-181-783-0755. FAX 44-181-783-1940. *497*

KEY NOTE MARKET REVIEW: U K TRAVEL & TOURISM.
Key Note Ltd., Field House, 72 Oldfield Rd., Hampton, Middlesex TW12 2HQ, England. TEL 44-181-783-0755. FAX 44-181-783-1940. *6896*

KEY NOTE MARKET REVIEW: U K WEDDING MARKET.
Key Note Ltd., Field House, 72 Oldfield Rd., Hampton, Middlesex TW12 2HQ, England. TEL 44-181-783-0755. FAX 44-181-783-1940. *4414*

KEY NOTE MARKET REVIEW: WHOLESALING IN THE U K.
Key Note Ltd., Field House, 72 Oldfield Rd., Hampton, Middlesex TW12 2HQ, England. TEL 44-181-783-0755. FAX 44-181-783-1940. *1474*

KEY NOTE MARKET REVIEW: YOUTH MARKET IN THE U.K.
Key Note Ltd., Field House, 72 Oldfield Rd., Hampton, Middlesex TW12 2HQ, England. TEL 44-181-783-0755. FAX 44-181-783-1940. *39*

KEY NOTE REPORT: FURNITURE.
Key Note Publications Ltd., Field House, 72 Oldfield Rd., Hampton, Middlesex TW12 2HQ, England. TEL 0181-783-0755. FAX 0181-783-1720. *3690*

KEY NOTE REPORT: PRINTING INKS.
Key Note Publications Ltd., Field House, 72 Oldfield Rd., Hampton, Middlesex TW12 2HQ, England. TEL 0181-783-0755. FAX 0181-783-1720. *5814*

KICK IT OVER.
Kick it Over Collective, P.O. Box 5811, Sta. A, Toronto, ON M5W 1P2, Canada. *5678*

KIDTECH NEWS.
KidTECH-BG Associates, Box 200, New York, NY 10044. TEL 212-935-7873. FAX 212-935-7873. *2349*

KIPLINGER'S PERSONAL FINANCE MAGAZINE.
Kiplinger Washington Editors, Inc., 1729 H St., N.W., Washington, DC 20006. TEL 202-887-6400. FAX 202-331-1206.
Vendor(s): Information Access Co., Knight-Ridder Information, Inc., University Microfilms International. *1106*

KNIGHT EXAMINER.
Jersey City State College, 2039 Kennedy Blvd., Jersey City, NJ 07305-1597. TEL 201-200-3575. FAX 201-200-3238. *1874*

KOKYU TO JUNKAN.
Igaku Shoin Ltd , 5-24-3 Hongo, Bunkyo-ku, Tokyo 113-91, Japan. TEL 03-817-5703.
Vendor(s): JICS. *4888*

KOMPASS AUSTRALIA.
Peter Isaacson Publications Pty. Ltd., 46-50 Porter St., Prahran, Vic. 3181, Australia. TEL 61-3-2457777. FAX 61-3-2457840. *1620*

KOMPASS BELGIUM.
Editus Belgium S.A., Av. Moliere 256, 1060 Brussels, Belgium. TEL 32-2-3459070. FAX 32-2-3473340. *1620*

KOMPASS ELECTRONIC AND ELECTRICAL PRODUCTS.
Peter Isaacson Publications Pty. Ltd., 46-50 Porter St., Prahran, Vic 3181, Australia. TEL 61-3-2457777. FAX 61-3-2457840. *1620*

KOMPASS FOOD & BEVERAGE.
Peter Isaacson Publications Pty. Ltd., 46-50 Porter St., Prahran, Vic. 3181, Australia. TEL 61-3-2457777. FAX 61-3-2457840. *1620*

KOMPASS PLASTIC, RUBBER AND CHEMICAL PRODUCTS.
Peter Isaacson Publications Pty. Ltd., 46-50 Porter St., Prahran, Vic. 3181, Australia. TEL 61-3-2457777. FAX 61-3-2457840. *1620*

KOMPASS SOUTH AFRICA.
SAFTO, Publishing Division, P.O. Box 782706, Sandton 2146, South Africa. TEL 27-11-883-3737. FAX 27-11-883-6569 *1621*

KOMPASS SVERIGE.
Kompass Sverige AB, Torsgatan 21, S-113 90 Stockholm, Sweden, Sweden. FAX 46-8-7363022.
Vendor(s): Knight-Ridder Information, Inc.. *1621*

KOMPASS UNITED KINGDOM.
Kompass Part of the Reed Elsevier group, Windsor Ct., E. Grinstead House, E. Grinstead, W. Sussex RH19 1XD, England. TEL 01342-326972. FAX 01342-335992.
Vendor(s): Reed Information Services Ltd.. *1621*

KONZERNE IN SCHAUBILDERN.
Verlag Hoppenstedt GmbH, Havelstr. 9, 64295 Darmstadt, Germany. TEL 49-6151-380-0. FAX 49-6151-380360.
Vendor(s): Lexis-Nexis. *1521*

KOREAN JOURNAL OF PARASITOLOGY.
Korean Society for Parasitology, c/o Dept. of Parasitology, College of Medicine, Seoul National University, Seoul 110 799, S. Korea. TEL 82-2-740-8348. FAX 82-2-765-6142. *4625*

KUKA KUKIN ON.
Kustannusosakeyhtio Otava, Uudenmaankatu 7R 8-12, SF-00120 Helsinki, Finland. TEL 358-0-19961. FAX 358-0-643086. *558*

DIE KUNSTSTOFF-INDUSTRIE UND IHRE HELFER.
Industrieschau-Verlagsgesellschaft mbH, Postfach 100262, 64202 Darmstadt, Germany. TEL 49-6151-3892-0. FAX 49-6151-33164. *5622*

KYKLOS.
Blackwell Publishers Ltd., 108 Cowley Rd., Oxford OX4 1JF, England. TEL 44-1865-791100. FAX 44-1865-791347.
Vendor(s): University Microfilms International. *1220*

L A N PRODUCT NEWS.
Worldwide Videotex, Box 3273, Boynton Beach, FL 33424-3273. TEL 407-738-2276.
Vendor(s): Data-Star, Information Access Co., Knight-Ridder Information, Inc., NewsNet (EC99). *2039*

L A N TIMES.
McGraw-Hill Companies, 1221 Ave. of the Americas, New York, NY 10020. TEL 212-512-2000.
Vendor(s): Dow Jones News Retrieval (LNTM), Knight-Ridder Information, Inc. (LAN), Lexis-Nexis (LANTME), NewsNet (EC42). *2096*

L D C DEBT REPORT.
American Banker - Bond Buyer, Newsletter Division One State St. Plaza, New York, NY 10004-1549. TEL 800-733-4371. FAX 212-943-2224.
Vendor(s): Information Access Co. Knight-Ridder Information, Inc., Lexis-Nexis, NewsNet (FI42). *1107*

L I M R A'S MARKETFACTS.
LIMRA International, Inc., Box 208 Hartford, CT 06141-0208. TEL 203-287-7725.
Vendor(s): University Microfilms International. *3656*

L I S A: LIBRARY & INFORMATION SCIENCE ABSTRACTS.
Bowker - Saur Ltd., A member of the Reed Elsevier plc group, Maypole House, Maypole Rd., E. Grinstead, W. Sussex RH19 1HU, England. TEL 44-1342-330100. FAX 44-1342-330191.
Vendor(s): Knight-Ridder Information, Inc. (File no.61/LISA), Orbit Search Service (LISA), Ovid Technologies, Inc. (LISA). *2039*

L N G OBSERVER.
Institute of Gas Technology, 1700 S. Mount Prospect Rd., Des Plaines, IL 60018-1804. TEL 847-768-0512. FAX 847-768-0516. *5362*

L P I TECHNICAL REPORT.
Lunar and Planetary Institute, 3600 Bay Area Blvd., Houston, TX 77058-1113. TEL 713-486-2143. FAX 713-486-2125. *483*

LABOR - MANAGEMENT RELATIONS ANALYSIS - NEWS AND BACKGROUND INFORMATION.
The Bureau of National Affairs, Inc. 1231 25th St., N.W., Washington, DC 20037. TEL 202-452-4200. FAX 202-822-8092.
Vendor(s): Human Resources Information Network (File DD), West Services, Inc. (File LR-NEWS). *1383*

LABOR RELATIONS REFERENCE MANUAL.
The Bureau of National Affairs, Inc., 1231 25th St., N.W., Washington, DC 20037. TEL 202-452-4200. FAX 202-822-8092.
Vendor(s): Human Resources Information Network (Files BOARDS, COURTS), West Services, Inc. (File FLB-CS). *1383*

Online

LABOR RELATIONS REPORTER.
The Bureau of National Affairs, Inc., 1231 25th St., N.W., Washington, DC 20037. TEL 202-452-4200. FAX 202-822-8092.
Vendor(s): Knight-Ridder Information, Inc. (File no. 244, Laborlaw), West Services, Inc.. *1383*

LABOR RELATIONS REPORTER. FAIR EMPLOYMENT PRACTICES.
The Bureau of National Affairs, Inc., 1231 25th St., N.W., Washington, DC 20037. TEL 202-452-4200. FAX 202-822-8092.
Vendor(s): Knight-Ridder Information, Inc., West Services, Inc.. *1384*

LABOR RELATIONS REPORTER. LABOR ARBITRATION AND DISPUTE SETTLEMENTS.
The Bureau of National Affairs, Inc., 1231 25th St., N.W., Washington, DC 20037. TEL 202-452-4200. FAX 202-822-8092.
Vendor(s): Human Resources Information Network (File LAR), Knight-Ridder Information, Inc. (Files 243, 244), Lexis-Nexis, West Services, Inc. (File LRR-LA). *1384*

LABOR RELATIONS REPORTER. WAGES AND HOURS.
The Bureau of National Affairs, Inc., 1231 25th St., N.W., Washington, DC 20037. TEL 202-452-4200. FAX 202-822-8092.
Vendor(s): Knight-Ridder Information, Inc., West Services, Inc.. *1384*

LABOR RELATIONS WEEK.
The Bureau of National Affairs, Inc., 1231 25th St., N.W., Washington, DC 20037. TEL 202-452-4200. FAX 202-822-8092.
Vendor(s): Human Resources Information Network (CDD, HDD). *1384*

LABOR STUDIES JOURNAL.
Transaction Publishers, Transaction Periodicals Consortium, Department 3092, Rutgers University, New Brunswick, NJ 08903. TEL 908-445-2280. FAX 908-445-3138.
Vendor(s): Information Access Co.. *1384*

LABOR TRENDS.
Business Research Publications, Inc., 65 Bleecker St., New York, NY 10012-2450. TEL 212-673-4700. FAX 212-475-1790.
Vendor(s): Information Access Co.. *1384*

LABORATORY HAZARDS BULLETIN.
The Royal Society of Chemistry, Thomas Graham House, Science Park, Milton Rd., Cambridge CB4 4WF, England. TEL 44-1223-420066. FAX 44-1223-423429.
Vendor(s): Data-Star (CSNB), Knight-Ridder Information, Inc. (File no.317), STN International (CSNB). *5252*

LABOUR ARBITRATION CASES.
Canada Law Book Inc., 240 Edward St., Aurora, ON L4G 3S9, Canada. TEL 905-841-6472. FAX 905-841-5085. *1385*

LACROSSETALK.
All England Women's Lacrosse Association, 4 Western Ct., Bromley St., Digbeth, Birmingham 9, England. TEL 44-121-773-4422. *6507*

LADIES HOME JOURNAL (INKPRINT EDITION).
Meredith Corporation, 1716 Locust St., Des Moines, IA 50336. TEL 515-284-3000.
Vendor(s): Information Access Co., Knight-Ridder Information, Inc.. *6999*

LAFAYETTE BUSINESS DIGEST.
Laurendeau Communications, Box 587, Lafayette, IN 47902. TEL 317-742-6918. FAX 317-423-8133.
Vendor(s): University Microfilms International. *1220*

LAGNIAPPE LETTER.
Latin American Information Services, Inc., 159 W. 53rd St., 28th fl., New York, NY 10019. TEL 212-765-5520. FAX 212-765-2927.
Vendor(s): Information Access Co., Knight-Ridder Information, Inc., Lexis-Nexis. *1288*

LAGNIAPPE QUARTERLY MONITOR.
Latin American Information Services, Inc., 159 W. 53rd St., 28th fl., New York, NY 10019. TEL 212-765-5520. FAX 212-765-2927.
Vendor(s): Information Access Co.. *1311*

LAKEWOOD REPORT ON POSITIVE EMPLOYEE PRACTICES.
Lakewood Publications, Inc., 50 S. Ninth St., Minneapolis, MN 55402. TEL 612-333-0471. FAX 612-333-6526.
Vendor(s): University Microfilms International. *1430*

LAKEWOOD REPORT ON TECHNOLOGY FOR LEARNING NEWSLETTER.
Lakewood Publications, Inc., 50 S. Ninth St., Minneapolis, MN 55402. TEL 612-333-0471. FAX 612-333-6526. *2350*

LAMBDA BOOK REPORT.
Lambda Rising, Inc., 1625 Connecticut Ave., N.W., Washington, DC 20009-1013. TEL 202-462-7924. FAX 202-462-7257.
Vendor(s): Information Access Co., University Microfilms International. *3534*

LANCASTER COUNTY HISTORICAL SOCIETY. JOURNAL.
Lancaster County Historical Society, 230 NE. President Ave., Lancaster, PA 17603-3125. TEL 717-392-4633. *3475*

THE LANCET.
The Lancet Ltd. 42 Bedford Sq., London WC1B 3SL, England. TEL 44-171-4364981. FAX 44-171-4367570.
Vendor(s): Information Access Co., Ovid Technologies, Inc., University Microfilms International. *4489*

LAND ECONOMICS.
University of Wisconsin Press, Journal Division, 114 N. Murray St., Madison, WI 53715. TEL 608-262-4952. FAX 608-262-7560.
Vendor(s): Information Access Co.. *194*

LAND MOBILE RADIO NEWS.
Phillips Business Information, Inc., 1201 Seven Locks Rd., Potomac, MD 20854. TEL 301-424-3338. FAX 301-424-4297.
Vendor(s): Information Access Co., Knight-Ridder Information, Inc., NewsNet (TE13). *1947*

LAND USE LAW REPORT.
Business Publishers, Inc., 951 Pershing Dr., Silver Spring, MD 20910-4464. TEL 301-587-6300. FAX 301-585-9075.
Vendor(s): NewsNet (EV02). *3588*

LANE REPORT.
Lane Communications Group, 269 W. Main St., Lexington, KY 40507. TEL 606-244-3522. FAX 606-244-3544.
Vendor(s): University Microfilms International. *940*

LANGMUIR.
American Chemical Society, 1155 16th St., N.W., Washington, DC 20036. TEL 800-333-9511. FAX 614-447-3671.
Vendor(s): STN International (CJACS). *1755*

LANGUAGE ARTS.
National Council of Teachers of English, 1111 W. Kenyon Rd., Urbana, IL 61801-1096. TEL 217-328-3870. FAX 217-328-0977.
Vendor(s): University Microfilms International. *2350*

LARGE KITCHEN APPLIANCES: THE INTERNATIONAL MARKET.
Euromonitor, 60-61 Britton St., London EC1M 5NA, England. TEL 44-171-251-8024. FAX 44-171-608-3149.
Vendor(s): Data-Star, Knight-Ridder Information, Inc.. *2526*

LARGE MIXED RETAILERS: THE INTERNATIONAL MARKET.
Euromonitor, 60-61 Britton St., London EC1M 5NA, England. TEL 44-171-251-8024. FAX 44-171-608-3149.
Vendor(s): Data-Star, Knight-Ridder Information, Inc.. *1474*

LAS VEGAS BUSINESS PRESS.
Business Communications, Box 27409, Las Vegas, NV 89126-1409. TEL 702-871-6780. FAX 702-871-3470.
Vendor(s): Lexis-Nexis, University Microfilms International. *941*

LATE IMPERIAL CHINA.
Johns Hopkins University Press, Journals Publishing Division, 2715 N. Charles St., MD 21218-4319. TEL 410-516-6987. FAX 410-740-6968. *3382*

LATIN AMERICAN INFORMES ESPECIALES.
Lettres (U.K.) Ltd., 61 Old St., London EC1V 9HX, England. TEL 44-171-251-0012. FAX 44-171-253-8193.
Vendor(s): Lexis-Nexis. *1339*

LATIN AMERICAN REGIONAL REPORTS - ANDEAN GROUP.
Latin American Newsletters, 61 Old St., London EC1V 9HX, England. TEL 44-171-251-0012. FAX 44-171-253-8193.
Vendor(s): Lexis-Nexis. *1220*

LATIN AMERICAN RESEARCH REVIEW.
Latin American Studies Association (Albuquerque), c/o University of New Mexico, 801 Yale N.E., Albuquerque, NM 87131-1016. TEL 505-277-5985. FAX 505-277-5989.
Vendor(s): Information Access Co., University Microfilms International. *6333*

LATIN AMERICAN TRAVEL ADVISOR.
Latin American Travel Consultants, Box 17-17-908, Quito, Ecuador. FAX 593-2-562-566. *6896*

LATIN AMERICAN WEEKLY REPORT.
Latin American Newsletters, 61 Old St., London EC1V 9HX, England. TEL 44-171-251-0012. FAX 44-171-253-8193.
Vendor(s): Lexis-Nexis. *1220*

LATINFINANCE.
Latin American Financial Publications, Inc., 2121 Ponce de Leon Blvd., Ste. 1020, Coral Gables, FL 33134. TEL 305-448-6593. FAX 305-448-0718.
Vendor(s): Information Access Co.. *1107*

LAW & BUSINESS DIRECTORY OF CORPORATE COUNSEL.
Law & Business, Inc. 270 Sylvan Ave., Englewood Cliffs, NJ 07632. TEL 201-894-8484.
Vendor(s): West Services, Inc.. *3904*

LAW AND ORDER.
Hendon, Inc., 1000 Skokie Blvd., Wilmette, IL 60091. TEL 708-256-8555. FAX 708-256-8574.
Vendor(s): CompuServe, Inc.. *2168*

LAW AND POLICY IN INTERNATIONAL BUSINESS.
Georgetown University Law Center, 600 New Jersey Ave., N.W., Washington, DC 20001. TEL 202-662-9468.
Vendor(s): Information Access Co., West Services, Inc.. *3937*

LAW OFFICE TECHNOLOGY REVIEW.
2640 W. 183 St., Box 2577, Homewood, IL 60430. TEL 708-957-3322. FAX 708-957-3337.
Vendor(s): Information Access Co., Knight-Ridder Information, Inc., NewsNet (LA15), West Services, Inc.. *3889*

LAW PRACTICE MANAGEMENT.
American Bar Association, Law Practice Management Section, 750 N. Lake Shore Dr., Chicago, IL 60611. TEL 312-988-5000.
Vendor(s): Lexis-Nexis, West Services, Inc.. *3805*

LAWYERS' LIABILITY REVIEW.
Timeline Publishing Co., Inc., Box 1435, Bellevue, WA 98009. TEL 206-462-7714. FAX 206-462-0411. *3806*

LAWYERS' MICRO USERS GROUP NEWSLETTER.
Paul Bernstein, Ed. & Pub. (Chicago), 333 E. Ontario St., Ste. 2102-B, Chicago, IL 60611. TEL 312-951-8451.
Available only online. Vendor(s): NewsNet (LA05). *3890*

LEAD AND ZINC STATISTICS.
International Lead and Zinc Study Group, Metro House, 58 St. James's St., London SW1A 1LD, England. TEL 44-171-499-9373. FAX 44-171-493-3725. *4983*

LEADERSHIP IN HEALTH SERVICES.
Canadian Healthcare Association, 17 York St., Ottawa, ON K1N 9J6, Canada. TEL 613-241-8005. FAX 613-241-5055. *3552*

LEADS FROM L A M A.
American Library Association, Library Administration and Management Association, 50 E. Huron St., Chicago, IL 60611-2795. TEL 312-944-6780. FAX 312-440-9374.
Available only online. *4005*

LEATHER.
Miller Freeman Publishers Ltd. Sovereign Way, Tonbridge, Kent TN9 1RW, England. TEL 44-1732-364422. FAX 44-1732-361534.
Vendor(s): Information Access Co.. *3960*

LEGAL ASSISTANT TODAY.
James Publishing Group, Inc., 3520 Cadillac Ave., Ste. E, Costa Mesa, CA 92626-1419. TEL 714-755-5450.
Vendor(s): University Microfilms International. *3807*

LEGAL ONLINE.
1617 JFK Blvd., Ste. 960, Philadelphia, PA 19103. TEL 215-557-2300. FAX 215-557-2301. *3808*

LEGAL PUBLISHER.
J K Publishing, Box 71020, Milwaukee, WI 53211. TEL 414-332-1625. FAX 414-964-0843.
Vendor(s): Information Access Co., NewsNet. *3808*

LEGAL TIMES.
American Lawyer Media, L.P., 1730 M St., N.W., Ste. 802, Washington, DC 20036. TEL 202-457-0686. FAX 202-457-0718.
Vendor(s): Lexis-Nexis. *3809*

LEGALTRAC.
Information Access Company, 362 Lakeside Dr., Foster City, CA 94404. TEL 415-378-5200. FAX 415-378-5369.
Vendor(s): Ovid Technologies, Inc. (LAWS), Knight-Ridder Information, Inc. (File no.150), Lexis-Nexis (LGLIND), West Services, Inc. (LRI). *3877*

LEGISLATIVE NETWORK FOR NURSES.
Business Publishers, Inc., 951 Pershing Dr., Silver Spring, MD 20910-4464. TEL 301-587-6300. FAX 301-585-9075.
Vendor(s): NewsNet. *4720*

LEISURE INTELLIGENCE.
Mintel International Group Ltd., 18-19 Long Ln., London EC1A 9HE, England. TEL 44-171-606-4533. FAX 44-171-606-5932. *3965*

LEISURE, RECREATION AND TOURISM ABSTRACTS.
CAB International, Wallingford, Oxon. OX10 8DE, England. TEL 44-1491-832111. FAX 44-1491-833508.
Vendor(s): DIMDI, European Space Agency, Knight-Ridder Information, Inc., STN International. *6930*

LEISURE STUDIES.
Chapman & Hall, Journals Department 2-6 Boundary Row, London SE1 8HN, England. TEL 171-8650066. FAX 171-5229623. *3965*

LETTER TO LIBRARIES ONLINE.
Oregon State Library, Salem, OR 97310-0640. TEL 503-378-2112. FAX 503-588-7119.
Available only online. *4045*

LETTRE MENSUEL DE FRANCE PHARMACIE LABORATOIRES.
41 rue Gambetta, 92100 Boulogne Billancourt, France. TEL 46-04-52-46. FAX 46-05-65-47. *5426*

LIABILITY WEEK.
J R Publishing Inc., Box 6654, McLean, VA 22106. TEL 703-532-2235. FAX 703-532-2236.
Vendor(s): Information Access Co., NewsNet. *3656*

LIBRARY LITERATURE.
H.W. Wilson Co., 950 University Ave., Bronx, NY 10452. TEL 718-588-8400. FAX 718-590-1617.
Vendor(s): OCLC, Wilsonline (File LIB). *4040*

LIBRARY RESOURCES FOR THE BLIND AND PHYSICALLY HANDICAPPED.
U.S. Library of Congress, National Library Service for the Blind and Physically Handicapped, Washington, DC 20542. TEL 202-707-5100. FAX 202-707-0712. *4009*

LIBRARY SOFTWARE REVIEW.
Sage Publications, Inc., 2455 Teller Rd., Thousand Oaks, CA 91320. TEL 805-499-0721. FAX 805-499-0871.
Vendor(s): Information Access Co.. *2112*

LIBRARY TECHNOLOGY REPORTS.
American Library Association, 50 E. Huron St., Chicago, IL 60611-2795. TEL 800-545-2433. FAX 312-440-9374.
Vendor(s): Information Access Co.. *4009*

LIBRARY TRENDS.
University of Illinois at Urbana-Champaign, Graduate School of Library and Information Science, 501 E. Daniel St., Champaign, IL 61820-6211. TEL 217-333-1359. FAX 217-244-7329.
Vendor(s): Information Access Co.. *4009*

LIBRES: LIBRARY AND INFORMATION SCIENCE RESEARCH ELECTRONIC JOURNAL.
R&D Librarian, Curtin University of Technology, GPO Box U1987, Perth, WA 6001, Australia. TEL 61-9-3513212. FAX 61-9-3512424.
Available only online. *4009*

LIBROS ESPANOLES EN VENTA.
Ministerio de Cultura, Centro del Libro y de la Lectura, C. Santiago Rusinol, 8, 28040 Madrid, Spain. TEL 536-88-30. FAX 553-99-90. *538*

LICENSED PRACTICAL NURSE.
McClain Publishing Co., Box 10619, Charlotte, NC 28212-5677. *4720*

LICENSING LETTER.
E P M Communications, 160 Mercer St., 3rd Fl., New York, NY 10012-3212. TEL 212-941-0099. FAX 212-941-1622.
Vendor(s): Information Access Co.. *5341*

LIDOVE NOVINY.
Narodni 11, 111 21 Prague 1, Czech Republic. *3133*

LIFE (NEW YORK).
Time Inc. Time & Life Bldg., Rockefeller Center, 1271 Ave. of the Americas, New York, NY 10020. TEL 212-522-1212. FAX 212-522-1863.
Vendor(s): Information Access Co., Knight-Ridder Information, Inc., Lexis-Nexis, University Microfilms International. *3231*

THE LIGHTHOUSE ELECTRONIC MAGAZINE.
Polarized Publications, 256 E. College Ave., Ste. 302, State College, PA 16801. TEL 814-238-6730. FAX 814-238-6730.
Available only online. *5208*

LIMITED PARTNERSHIP INVESTMENT REVIEW.
Limited Partnership Investment Review, Inc., 55 Morris Ave., Springfield, NJ 07081. TEL 201-467-8700. FAX 201-467-0368.
Vendor(s): NewsNet. *1553*

LINGUISTICS AND LANGUAGE BEHAVIOR ABSTRACTS.
Sociological Abstracts, Inc., Box 22206, San Diego, CA 92192-0206. TEL 619-695-8803. FAX 619-695-0416.
Vendor(s): Knight-Ridder Information, Inc. (File no.36). *4128*

LINK-UP.
Information Today, Inc., 143 Old Marlton Pike, Medford, NJ 08055. TEL 609-654-6266. FAX 609-654-4309.
Vendor(s): Lexis-Nexis University Microfilms International. *2070*

LINK-UP.
National Library of Australia, Cultural and Educations Services, Canberra, A.C.T. 2600, Australia. TEL 61-6-2621207. FAX 61-6-2734493. *3306*

LINKS.
Southern Links Magazine Publishing Associates, 1040 William Hilton Pkwy., Ste. 200, Hilton Head Island, SC 29938. TEL 803-842-6200. FAX 803-842-6233. *6507*

LINX DATABASE.
Auckland District Law Society, P.O. Box 58, Auckland, New Zealand. TEL 64-9-3031040. FAX 64-9-3033359.
Available only online. Vendor(s): Kiwinet. *3877*

THE LION AND THE UNICORN.
Johns Hopkins University Press, Journals Publishing Division, 2715 N. Charles St., Baltimore, MD 21218. TEL 410-516-6937. FAX 410-516-6968. *4230*

LIST OF SCIENTIFIC AND TECHNICAL LITERATURE RELATING TO THAILAND.
Thailand Institute of Scientific and Technological Research, 196 Phahonyothin Rd. Chatuchak, Bangkok 10900, Thailand. TEL 579-8594. FAX 662-579-8594. *6302*

LIST OF SERIALS INDEXED FOR ONLINE USERS.
U.S. National Library of Medicine 8600 Rockville Pike, Bethesda, MD 20894.
Vendor(s): National Library of Medicine. *4567*

LITERARY REVIEW.
Fairleigh Dickinson University, Literary Review, 285 Madison Ave., Madison, NJ 07940. TEL 201-443-8564.
Vendor(s): Information Access Co., University Microfilms International. *4231*

LITERATURE & MEDICINE.
Johns Hopkins University Press, Journals Publishing Division, 2715 N. Charles St., Baltimore, MD 21218. TEL 410-565-6967. FAX 410-565-6968. *4232*

LITERATURINFORMATIONEN ZUR BERUFLICHEN BILDUNG.
W. Bertelsmann Verlag, Postfach 100633, 33506 Bielefeld, Germany. TEL 0521-91101-0. FAX 0521-9110179. *5270*

LITIGATION.
American Bar Association, Litigation Section, 750 N. Lake Shore Dr., Chicago, IL 60611. TEL 312-988-5555.
Vendor(s): West Services, Inc.. *3810*

LITTERATUR PAA INDVANDRERSPROG I DANSKE FOLKEBIBLIOTEKER.
Dansk BiblioteksCenter as, Tempovej 7-11, 2750 Ballerup, Denmark. TEL 45-44-867777. FAX 45-44-867892. *4294*

LIVESTOCK, DAIRY AND POULTRY SITUATION & OUTLOOK.
U.S. Department of Agriculture, Economic Research Service, c/o Debbie Haugar, Rm. 110, 1301 New York Ave., N.W., Washington, DC 20005-4788. TEL 202-219-4060.
Vendor(s): Information Access Co., Knight-Ridder Information, Inc.. *276*

LLOYDS BANK ANNUAL REVIEW.
Lloyds Bank plc., Economics Department, P.O. Box 19, Hays Lane House, 1 Hays Ln., London SE1 2HA, England. TEL 44-171-407-1300. FAX 44-171-357-4378.
Vendor(s): Information Access Co.. *1107*

LOCAL COMPETITION REPORT.
Capitol Publications Inc., Telecom Publishing Group, 1101 King St., Ste. 444, Box 1455, Alexandria, VA 22313-2055. TEL 800-327-7205. FAX 703-739-6490.
Vendor(s): Information Access Co.. *1947*

LOCAL GOVERNMENT AND ENVIRONMENTAL REPORTS OF AUSTRALIA.
L B C Information Services, 50 Waterloo Rd., N. Ryde, N.S.W. 2113, Australia. TEL 61-2-99366444. FAX 61-2-8882229.
Vendor(s): Info-One International Pty Ltd.. *3949*

LOCAL GOVERNMENT CHRONICLE.
E M A P - Business Publishing Ltd., 33-39 Bowling Green Ln., London EC1R 0DA, England. TEL 44-171-505-8400. FAX 44-171-278-9509. *5945*

LOCAL TELECOM COMPETITION NEWS.
Capitol Publications Inc., Telecom Publishing Group, 1101 King St., Ste. 444, Box 1455, Alexandria, VA 22313-2055. FAX 703-739-6490.
Vendor(s): Information Access Co.. *1910*

LODGING HOSPITALITY.
Penton Publishing Co. 1100 Superior Ave., Cleveland, OH 44114-2543. TEL 216-696-7000. FAX 216-696-8765.
Vendor(s): Information Access Co., Knight-Ridder Information, Inc., University Microfilms International. *3567*

Online

LOGIBASE.
Services Documentaires Multimedia Inc., 75 Port-Royal E., No. 300, Montreal, PQ H3L 3T1, Canada. TEL 514-382-0895. FAX 514-384-9139. *2113*

LOGISTICS AND TRANSPORTATION REVIEW.
University of British Columbia, Centre for Transportation Studies, Vancouver, BC V6T 1Z2, Canada. TEL 604-822-4510. FAX 604-822-8521. Vendor(s): Information Access Co., University Microfilms International. *6722*

LOGISTICS MANAGEMENT.
Cahners Publishing Company (Newton), Division of Reed Elsevier Inc., 275 Washington St., Newton, MA 02158-1630. TEL 617-558-4473. FAX 617-558-4327. Vendor(s): Information Access Co.. *6722*

LONDON BUSINESS MONTHLY MAGAZINE.
Bowes Publishers Ltd., P.O. Box 7400 Sta. E, London, ON N5Y 4X3, Canada. TEL 519-472-7601. FAX 519-473-2256. Vendor(s): Knight-Ridder Information, Inc.. *941*

LONDON MAGAZINE.
Blackburn Magazine Group, 231 Dundas St., Ste. 203, London, ON N6A 1H1, Canada. TEL 519-679-4901. FAX 519-434-7842. *3123*

LONG ISLAND BUSINESS NEWS.
Long Island Commercial Review, Inc., 2150 Smithtown Ave., Ronkonkoma, NY 11779-7327. TEL 516-737-1700. FAX 516-737-1890. Vendor(s): Information Access Co.. *942*

LONGEVITY.
Longevity International, Ltd. 277 Park Ave., 4th Fl., New York, NY 10172. TEL 212-702-6000. FAX 212-702-6282. Available only online. *3292*

LOOKOUT - FOODS.
Marketing Intelligence Service Ltd., 6473D Route 64, Naples, NY 14512-9726. TEL 716-374-6326. FAX 716-374-5217. Vendor(s): Data-Star, Knight-Ridder Information, Inc. (File no. 16 & 570). *2983*

LOOKOUT - NONFOODS.
Marketing Intelligence Service Ltd., 6473D Route 64, Naples, NY 14512-9726. TEL 716-374-6326. FAX 716-374-5217. Vendor(s): Data-Star, Knight-Ridder Information, Inc. (File no. 16 & 570). *497*

LOS ANGELES.
11100 Santa Monica Blvd., 7th Fl., Los Angeles, CA 90025. TEL 310-996-6870. Vendor(s): Information Access Co., Lexis-Nexis, University Microfilms International. *3231*

LOS ANGELES BUSINESS JOURNAL.
Scripps Howard Business Publications (Los Angeles), 5700 Wilshire Blvd., Ste. 1701, Los Angeles, CA 90010. Vendor(s): Information Access Co.. *1220*

LOS ANGELES READER.
Burnside Group, Inc., 5550 Wilshire Blvd., No. 301, Los Angeles, CA 90036. TEL 213-965-7430. FAX 213-933-0281. *3231*

THE LOS ANGELES TIMES INDEX.
U M I Company 300 N. Zeeb Rd., Ann Arbor, MI 48106-1346. TEL 313-761-4700. FAX 800-864-0019. Vendor(s): Knight-Ridder Information, Inc.. *3715*

LOTERIA.
Loteria Nacional de Beneficencia, Departamento de Beneficencia Cultural, Apdo. 21, Panama 1, Panama. TEL 507-27-2202. FAX 507-27-3710. *3204*

LOUISIANA BUSINESS DIRECTORY.
American Business Directories 5711 S. 86th Circle, Box 27347, Omaha, NE 68127. TEL 402-593-4600. FAX 402-331-5481. *1623*

LOUISIANA LAW REVIEW.
Louisiana State University, Law Center, Baton Rouge, LA 70803. TEL 504-388-1683. FAX 504-388-1685. Vendor(s): Lexis-Nexis, West Services, Inc.. *3811*

LOUISVILLE MAGAZINE.
Louisville Magazine, Inc., 137 W. Muhammed Ali, Louisville, KY 40202. TEL 502-625-0100. FAX 502-625-0109. Vendor(s): Knight-Ridder Information, Inc., Lexis-Nexis, University Microfilms International. *3231*

LOUNGE LOS ANGELES.
Box 39532, Los Angeles, CA 90039. TEL 213-243-9671. *3567*

LOVTIDENDE A FOR KONGERIGET DANMARK.
Justisministeriet, Sekretariatet for Retsinformation, Axeltorv 6, 5. sal, D-1609 Copenhagen V, Denmark. TEL 45-33-32-52-22. FAX 45-33-91-28-01. *3812*

LOVTIDENDE C FOR KONGERIGET DANMARK.
Justitsministeriet, Sekretariatet for Retsinformation, Axeltorv 6, 5. sal, D-1609 Copenhagen V, Denmark. TEL 45-33-32-52-22. FAX 45-33-91-28-01. *3938*

LOW TEMPERATURE PHYSICS.
American Institute of Physics, One Physics Ellipse, College Park, MD 20740-3843. TEL 301-209-3000. *5585*

LOYOLA LAW REVIEW.
Loyola University, School of Law, 7214 St. Charles, New Orleans, LA 70118. TEL 504-861-5558. Vendor(s): West Services, Inc.. *3812*

LOYOLA OF LOS ANGELES INTERNATIONAL AND COMPARATIVE LAW JOURNAL.
Loyola of Los Angeles Law School, 919 South Albany St., Los Angeles, CA 90015-0019. TEL 213-736-1405. FAX 213-385-6247. Vendor(s): West Services, Inc.. *3812*

LOYOLA UNIVERSITY CHICAGO LAW JOURNAL.
Loyola University Chicago, Law School, One E. Pearson St., Chicago, IL 60611. TEL 312-915-7183. FAX 312-915-7201. *3812*

LUNAR AND PLANETARY INFORMATION BULLETIN.
Lunar and Planetary Institute, 3600 Bay Area Blvd., Houston, TX 77058-1113. TEL 713-486-2175. FAX 713-486-2125. *483*

M.
M2 Communications Ltd., Reptile House, 20 Heathfield Rd., Coventry CV5 8BT, England. TEL 44-1203-717417. FAX 44-1203-717418. *1947*

M C L C COMMUNICATIONS.
Gordon & Breach Science Publishers, c/o International Publishers Distributor, P.o. Box 3054, Langhorne, PA 19047-3054. TEL 215-750-2642. FAX 215-750-6343. *1710*

M C N: AMERICAN JOURNAL OF MATERNAL CHILD NURSING.
American Journal of Nursing Co., 555 W. 57th St., New York, NY 10019. TEL 212-582-8820. *4720*

M E L U S.
Society for the Study of the Multi-Ethnic Literature of the United States, 272 Bartlett Hall, Department of English, University of Massachusetts, Amherst, MA 01003. TEL 413-545-3166. FAX 413-545-3880. Vendor(s): Information Access Co., University Microfilms International. *4234*

M.E.N. MAGAZINE.
Seattle M.E.N., 7552 31st Ave., N.E., Seattle, WA 98115. TEL 206-522-9701. *4947*

M I R A AUTOMOBILE ABSTRACTS.
Motor Industry Research Association, Watling St., Nuneaton, Warwickshire CV10 0TU, England. FAX 44-1203-343772. Vendor(s): Data-Star, European Space Agency. *6742*

M I R A AUTOMOTIVE BUSINESS NEWS.
Motor Industry Research Association, Watling St., Nuneaton, Warwickshire CV10 0TU, England. FAX 44-1203-343772. Vendor(s): European Space Agency. *1013*

M I S QUARTERLY.
M I S Research Center, University of Minnesota, Carlson School of Management, 271 19th Ave. S, Minneapolis, MN 55455. TEL 612-624-2035. FAX 612-624-2056. Vendor(s): Information Access Co., University Microfilms International. *1431*

M L A INTERNATIONAL BIBLIOGRAPHY OF BOOKS AND ARTICLES ON THE MODERN LANGUAGES AND LITERATURES.
Modern Language Association of America, 10 Astor Place, New York, NY 10003. TEL 212-475-9500. FAX 212-477-9863. *4294*

M L N.
Johns Hopkins University Press, Journals Publishing Division, 2715 N. Charles St., Baltimore, MD 21218. TEL 410-516-6987. FAX 410-516-6968. Vendor(s): Information Access Co.. *4090*

M L O.
Medical Economics Publishing Co., Inc., 5 Paragon Dr., Montvale, NJ 07645. TEL 201-358-7200. FAX 201-573-0344. Vendor(s): Information Access Co.. *4683*

M P T REVIEW.
Navellier and Associates, Inc., Box 10012, Incline Village, NV 89450-1012. FAX 702-832-4909. Vendor(s): NewsNet (IV48). *1340*

M T I ECONEWS.
Magyar Tavirati Iroda, Pl. Naphegy ter. 8, 1016 Budapest, Hungary. TEL 36-1-1188204. FAX 36-1-2012690. *1167*

M UND A - MESSEPLANER INTERNATIONAL.
M und A Verlag fuer Messen, Ausstellungen und Kongresse GmbH Postfach 101528, 60015 Frankfurt a.M., Germany. TEL 49-69-759502. FAX 49-69-75951280. *1623*

MAANEDSBLADET PRESS.
Maanedsbladet Press, Studiestraede 24, 1, DK-1455 Copenhagen K, Denmark. TEL 45-33-11-58-11. FAX 45-33-11-68-66. *3134*

THE MACCABEAN.
Freeman Center for Strategic Studies, Box 35709-395, Houston, TX 77235-5709. TEL 713-723-6016. *5682*

MCCALL'S.
McCall's Magazine 110 Fifth Ave., New York, NY 10011. TEL 212-463-1000. Vendor(s): Information Access Co.. *7000*

MCGILL LAW JOURNAL.
Chancellor Day Hall, 3644 Peel St., Montreal, PQ H3A 1W9, Canada. TEL 514-874-9038. FAX 514-398-7397. *3812*

MCGRAW-HILL'S BIOTECHNOLOGY NEWSWATCH.
McGraw-Hill Companies, Energy & Business Newsletters, 1221 Ave. of the Americas, 36th Fl., New York, NY 10020. TEL 212-512-6410. Vendor(s): Dow Jones News Retrieval (BIO), Knight-Ridder Information, Inc. (File no.624/McGRAW-HILL PUBLICATIONS ONLINE), Lexis-Nexis (BIOTEC), NewsNet (BT08). *663*

MACHINE DESIGN.
Penton Publishing Co. 1100 Superior Ave., Cleveland, OH 44114-2543. TEL 216-696-7000. FAX 216-696-8765. Vendor(s): Information Access Co., Knight-Ridder Information, Inc., University Microfilms International. *2762*

MACHINE LEARNING.
Kluwer Academic Publishers Boston, Box 358, Accord Sta., Hingham, MA 02018-0358. TEL 617-871-6300. FAX 617-871-6528. *1995*

MACHINE LEARNING ONLINE.
Kluwer Academic Publishers Boston, Box 358, Accord Sta., Hingham, MA 02018-0358. TEL 617-871-6600. FAX 617-871-6528. Available only online. *-1995*

MACINTOSH PRODUCT REGISTRY.
Redgate Communications Corp., 660 Beachland Blvd., Vero Beach, FL 32963. TEL 407-231-6904. FAX 407-231-7872. *2097*

MACINTOSH TIPS & TRICKS.
Giles Road Press, Box 212, Harrington Park, NJ 07640-0212. TEL 201-767-7001. FAX 201-767-7457. *2097*

THE MCKINSEY QUARTERLY.
McKinsey & Co. Inc., 55 E. 52nd St., New York, NY 10022. TEL 212-446-7000. Vendor(s): Information Access Co., University Microfilms International. *1432*

MACLEAN'S.
Maclean Hunter Ltd., Maclean Hunter Bldg., 777 Bay St., Toronto, ON M5W 1A7, Canada. TEL 416-596-5386. FAX 416-596-7730.
Vendor(s): Information Access Co., Lexis-Nexis, Southam Electronic Publishing, University Microfilms International. *3123*

MACROMOLECULES.
American Chemical Society, 1155 16th St., N.W., Washington, DC 20036. TEL 800-333-9511. FAX 614-447-3671.
Vendor(s): STN International (CJACS). *1741*

MCTRANS: CENTER FOR MICROCOMPUTERS IN TRANSPORTATION. NEWSLETTER.
University of Florida, Transportation Research Center, 512 Weil Hall, Gainesville, FL 32611-2083. TEL 904-392-0378. FAX 904-392-3224. *6722*

MACUSER.
Ziff-Davis Publishing Co. (Foster City), 950 Tower Ln., Foster City, CA 94404. TEL 415-378-5600.
Vendor(s): Information Access Co.. *2097*

MACWEEK.
Coastal Associates Publishing, L.P. One Park Ave., New York, NY 10016. TEL 212-503-3500.
Vendor(s): Information Access Co., Lexis-Nexis. *2097*

MACWORLD.
Macworld Communications, 501 Second St., Ste. 500, San Francisco, CA 94107. TEL 415-243-0505.
Vendor(s): Information Access Co., University Microfilms International. *2097*

THE MAGAZINE ANTIQUES.
Brant Publications, Inc., 575 Broadway, 5th Fl., New York, NY 10012. TEL 212-941-2800.
Vendor(s): Information Access Co.. *333*

MAGAZINE ARTICLE SUMMARIES.
EBSCO Publishing 10 Estes St., Box 682, Ipswich, MA 01938. TEL 508-356-6500. FAX 508-356-6565.
Vendor(s): Ovid Technologies, Inc. (PMRO). *18*

MAGAZINE INDEX.
Information Access Company 362 Lakeside Dr., Foster City, CA 94404. TEL 415-378-5200. FAX 415-378-5369.
Vendor(s): Ovid Technologies, Inc. (MAGS), Knight-Ridder Information, Inc. (File no.47), Lexis-Nexis. *6015*

MAGAZINE WORLD.
International Federation of the Periodical Press, Queen's House, 55-56 Lincolns Inn Fields, London WC2A 3LJ, England. TEL 44-171-404-4169. FAX 44-171-404-4170. *6002*

MAGAZINES IN SPECIAL MEDIA.
U.S. Library of Congress, National Library Service for the Blind and Physically Handicapped, Washington, DC 20542. TEL 202-707-5100. FAX 202-707-0712. *3309*

MAGICAL BLEND.
Magical Blend Publishers, 133 1/2 Broadway, Chico, CA 95928. TEL 916-893-9037. FAX 916-894-9076. *5218*

MAGILL'S CINEMA ANNUAL.
Gale Research Inc., 835 Penobscot Bldg., Detroit, MI 48226. FAX 313-961-6241.
Vendor(s): Knight-Ridder Information, Inc.. *5107*

MAGNETIC RESONANCE MATERIALS IN PHYSICS, BIOLOGY AND MEDICINE.
Chapman & Hall, Journals Department 2-6 Boundary Row, London SE1 8HN, England. TEL 44-171-8560066. FAX 44-171-5229623. *5596*

MAGYAR ELEKTRONIKUS TOZSDE.
Pf. 311, Budapest 1536, Hungary. TEL 361-252-6697.
Available only online. *1340*

MAIL & GUARDIAN.
M & G Media Ltd., P.O. Box 32362, Braamfontein 2017, South Africa. TEL 27-11-4037111. FAX 27-11-4031025. *3213*

MAIL ORDER AND HOME SHOPPING: THE INTERNATIONAL MARKET.
Euromonitor, 60-61 Britton St., London EC1M 5NA, England. TEL 44-171-251-8024. FAX 44-171-608-3149.
Vendor(s): Data-Star, Knight-Ridder Information, Inc.. *1475*

MAIN GROUP CHEMISTRY NEWS COMMUNICATIONS.
Gordon & Breach Science Publishers, c/o International Publishers Distributor, P.O. Box 3054, Langhorne, PA 19047-3054. TEL 215-750-2642. FAX 215-750-6343. *1710*

MAINE BUSINESS DIRECTORY.
American Business Directories 5711 S. 86th Circle, Box 27347, Omaha, NE 68127. TEL 402-593-4600. FAX 402-331-5481. *1623*

MAINE LAW REVIEW.
University of Maine, School of Law, 246 Deering Ave., Portland, ME 04102. TEL 207-780-4357.
Vendor(s): Lexis-Nexis, West Services, Inc.. *3813*

MAINE TIMES.
Maine Times, Inc., 561 Congress St., Portland, ME 04101-3308. FAX 207-828-5432.
Vendor(s): University Microfilms International. *2809*

MAINFRAME COMPUTING.
Worldwide Videotex, Box 3273, Boynton Beach, FL 33424-3273. TEL 407-738-2276.
Vendor(s): Data-Star, Information Access Co., Knight-Ridder Information, Inc., NewsNet (EC87). *2078*

MAIZE ABSTRACTS.
CAB International, Wallingford, Oxon. OX10 8DE, England. TEL 44-1491-832111. FAX 44-1491-833508.
Vendor(s): DIMDI, European Space Agency, Knight-Ridder Information, Inc., STN International. *176*

MAJOR 20TH-CENTURY WRITERS.
Gale Research Inc., 835 Penobscot Bldg., Detroit, MI 48226-4094. TEL 313-961-2242. FAX 313-961-6083.
Vendor(s): Lexis-Nexis (GALBIO). *4235*

MAKE-UP AND COLOUR COSMETICS: THE INTERNATIONAL MARKET.
Euromonitor, 60-61 Britton St., London EC1M 5NA, England. TEL 44-171-251-8024. FAX 44-171-608-3149.
Vendor(s): Data-Star, Knight-Ridder Information, Inc.. *492*

MAKING THE ROUNDS IN HEALTH, FAITH AND ETHICS.
Park Ridge Center, 211 E. Ontario St., Ste. 800, Chicago, IL 60611-3219. TEL 312-266-2222. FAX 312-266-6086.
Vendor(s): Information Access Co.. *4491*

MANAGE.
National Management Association, 2210 Arbor Blvd., Dayton, OH 45439. TEL 513-294-0421.
Vendor(s): Information Access Co., University Microfilms International. *1432*

MANAGED CARE LAW OUTLOOK.
Capitol Publications Inc., 1101 King St., Ste. 444, Alexandria, VA 22314. TEL 703-683-4100. FAX 703-739-6501.
Vendor(s): Information Access Co., NewsNet (HH16). *3552*

MANAGED CARE OUTLOOK.
Capitol Publications Inc., 1101 King St., Ste. 444, Alexandria, VA 22314. TEL 703-683-4100. FAX 703-739-6501.
Vendor(s): Information Access Co., NewsNet (HH12). *3552*

MANAGED CARE WEEK.
Atlantic Information Services, Inc., 1050 17th St., N.W., Ste. 480, Washington, DC 20036-5500. TEL 202-775-9008. FAX 202-331-9542.
Vendor(s): Information Access Co.. *4491*

MANAGED HEALTHCARE NEWS.
Quadrant HealthCom, 105 Raider Blvd., Belle Mead, NJ 08502-1510. TEL 908-874-0707. FAX 908-874-5611.
Vendor(s): Information Access Co.. *4492*

MANAGEMENT ACCOUNTING.
Chartered Institute of Management Accountants, c/o Management Accounting, 63 Portland Pl., London W1N 4AB. TEL 44-171-637-2311. FAX 44-171-495-6098.
Vendor(s): University Microfilms International. *1050*

MANAGEMENT ACCOUNTING.
Institute of Management Accountants, 10 Paragon Dr., Montvale, NJ 07645 1760. TEL 201-573-9000. FAX 201-573-0639.
Vendor(s): Information Access Co., University Microfilms International. *1051*

MANAGEMENT AND MARKETING ABSTRACTS.
Pira International, Randals Rd., Leatherhead, Surrey KT22 7RU, England. TEL 44-1372-802050. FAX 44-1372-802239.
Vendor(s): Data-Star. *1015*

MANAGEMENT CONTENTS.
Information Access Company 362 Lakeside Dr., Foster City, CA 94409. TEL 415-378-5200. FAX 415-378-5369.
Available only online. Vendor(s): Ovid Technologies, Inc. (MGMT), Data-Star (MGMT), Knight-Ridder Information, Inc. (File no.75). *1015*

MANAGEMENT DECISION.
M C B University Press Ltd., 60-62 Toller Ln., Bradford, W. Yorks BD8 9BY, England. TEL 44-1274-777700. FAX 44-1274-785200.
Vendor(s): Information Access Co.. *1432*

MANAGEMENT INTERNATIONAL REVIEW.
Betriebswirtschaftlicher Verlag Dr. Th. Gabler GmbH, Taunusstr. 54, 65183 Wiesbaden, Germany. TEL 49-611-534-0. FAX 49-611-534430.
Vendor(s): Information Access Co., University Microfilms International. *1433*

MANAGEMENT MATTERS.
Marton Allen Associates, InfoTeam Inc., Box 15640, Plantation, FL 33318-5640. TEL 954-473-9560. FAX 954-473-0544.
Vendor(s): Data-Star, Human Resources Information Network, Information Access Co., NewsNet (MT11). *1433*

MANAGEMENT QUARTERLY.
National Rural Electric Cooperative Association, 4301 Wilson Blvd., Arlington, VA 22203-1860. TEL 703-907-5500.
Vendor(s): Information Access Co., University Microfilms International. *1433*

MANAGEMENT REVIEW.
American Management Association, 135 W. 50th St., New York, NY 10020-1201. TEL 212-586-8100. FAX 212-903-8168.
Vendor(s): Information Access Co., University Microfilms International. *1433*

MANAGEMENT SERVICES.
Institute of Management Services, 1 Cecil Ct., London Rd., Enfield, Mddx., England. TEL 44-181-366-1260. FAX 44-181-367-8149.
Vendor(s): University Microfilms International. *1434*

MANAGEMENT TODAY.
Institute of Management Foundation, 2 Savoy Ct., 3rd. Fl. Strand, England. TEL 44-171-497-0580. FAX 44-171-497-0463.
Vendor(s): University Microfilms International. *1434*

MANAGERIAL LAW.
Barmarck Publications, Enholmes Hall, Patrington, N. Humber HU12 0PR, England. TEL 44-1964-630033. FAX 44-1274-547143.
Vendor(s): Lexis-Nexis. *1387*

MANAGER'S MAGAZINE.
LIMRA International, Inc., Box 208, Hartford, CT 06141-0208. TEL 203-298-3952.
Vendor(s): Information Access Co., University Microfilms International. *3657*

MANAGING INTELLECTUAL PROPERTY.
Euromoney Publications plc., Nestor House, Playhouse Yard, London EC4V 5EX, England. TEL 44-171-779-8686. FAX 44-171-779-8500.
Vendor(s): University Microfilms International. *5342*

MANAGING OFFICE TECHNOLOGY.
Penton Publishing Co. 1100 Superior Ave., Cleveland, OH 44114-2543. TEL 216-696-7000. FAX 216-696-7648.
Vendor(s): Information Access Co., Knight-Ridder Information, Inc., University Microfilms International. *1494*

MANITOBA BUSINESS MAGAZINE.
Canada Wide Magazines Ltd. (Toronto), 2 Carlton St., Ste. 801, Toronto, ON M5B 1J3, Canada. TEL 416-595-5007. FAX 416-924-6308.
Vendor(s): Information Access Co., Lexis-Nexis. *1435*

MANITOBA DECISIONS - CIVIL AND CRIMINAL CASES.
Western Legal Publications, 301-1 Alexander St., Vancouver, BC V6A 1B2, Canada. TEL 604-687-5671. FAX 604-687-2796. *3950*

MANITOBA REPORTS.
Maritime Law Book Ltd., Box 302, Fredericton, NB E3B 4Y9, Canada. TEL 506-453-9921. FAX 506-453-9525.
Vendor(s): QL Systems Ltd.. *3813*

MANUFACTURING AUTOMATION.
Vital Information Publications, 754 Caravel Ln., Foster City, CA 94404. TEL 415-345-7018. FAX 415-345-7018.
Vendor(s): Data-Star, Information Access Co., Knight-Ridder Information, Inc., NewsNet (MG17). *1475*

MANUFACTURING CHEMIST.
Miller Freeman Technical Ltd. Miller Freeman House, 30 Calderwood St., London SE18 6QH, England. TEL 44-181-855-7777. FAX 44-181-316-3206.
Vendor(s): Information Access Co. *2645*

MANUFACTURING ENGINEERING.
Society of Manufacturing Engineers, One SME Dr., Box 930, Dearborn, MI 48121-0930. TEL 313-271-1500. FAX 313-271-2861.
Vendor(s): University Microfilms International. *2609*

MANUFACTURING NEWS.
Publishers & Producers, Box 36, Annandale, VA 22003. TEL 703-750-2664. FAX 703-750-0064.
Vendor(s): Information Access Co. *1526*

MAPLE ORCHARD.
Loyal Ontario Group Interested in Computers Inc. (LOGIC), P.O. Box 958, Thornhill, ON L3T 4A5, Canada. TEL 416-323-0828. *2097*

MARINE FISHERIES REVIEW.
U.S. National Marine Fisheries Service, Scientific Publications Office, 7600 Sandpoint Way, N.E., Bin C15700, Seattle, WA 98115. TEL 206-526-6107. FAX 206-526-6426.
Vendor(s): Information Access Co. *2938*

MARINE LOG.
Simmons - Boardman Publishing Corp., 345 Hudson St., New York, NY 10014-4502. TEL 212-620-7200.
Vendor(s): Lexis-Nexis. *6841*

MARINEFACTS.
Running End Ltd., Box 257, Crownsville, MD 21032-0257. TEL 410-923-1325. *6536*

MARITIME INFORMATION REVIEW.
Maritime Information Centre, Bibliotheek T U Delft, P.O. Box 98, 2600 MG Delft, Netherlands. TEL 31-15-2786663. FAX 31-15-2786855.
Vendor(s): European Space Agency. *6742*

MARKET: ASIA PACIFIC.
Market: newsletters, 202 The Commons, Ste. 401, Ithaca, NY 14850. TEL 607-277-0934. FAX 607-277-0935.
Vendor(s): Data-Star, Information Access Co., Knight-Ridder Information, Inc.. *1290*

MARKET DIRECTION REPORTS.
Euromonitor, 60-61 Britton St., London EC1M 5NA, England. TEL 44-171-251-8024. FAX 44-171-608-3149.
Vendor(s): Data-Star, Knight-Ridder Information, Inc.. *1475*

MARKET: EUROPE.
Market: newletters, 202 The Commons, Ste. 401, Ithaca, NY 14850. TEL 607-277-0934. FAX 607-277-0935.
Vendor(s): CompuServe, Inc., Data-Star, Information Access Co., Knight-Ridder Information, Inc., NewsNet. *1290*

MARKET INTELLIGENCE.
Mintel International Group Ltd., 18-19 Long Ln., London EC1A 9HE, England. TEL 44-171-606-4533. FAX 44-171-606-5932. *1475*

MARKET: LATIN AMERICA.
Market: newsletters, 202 The Commons, Ste. 401, Ithaca, NY 14850. TEL 607-277-0934. FAX 607-277-0935.
Vendor(s): CompuServe, Inc., Data-Star, Information Access Co., Knight-Ridder Information, Inc.. *1290*

MARKET RESEARCH ABSTRACTS.
Market Research Society, 15 Northburgh St., London EC1V 0AH, England. TEL 44-171-490-4911. FAX 44-171-490-0608.
Vendor(s): Data-Star, Knight-Ridder Information, Inc.. *1015*

MARKET RESEARCH EUROPE.
Euromonitor, 60-61 Britton St., London EC1M 5NA, England. TEL 44-171-251-8024. FAX 44-171-608-3149.
Vendor(s): Lexis-Nexis. *1475*

MARKET RESEARCH SOCIETY. JOURNAL.
Market Research Society, 15 Northburgh St., London EC1V 0AH, England. TEL 44-171-490-4911. FAX 44-171-490-0608.
Vendor(s): Information Access Co. *1476*

MARKET SCREEN.
Market Guide Inc., 49 Glen Head Rd., Glen Head, NY 11545. TEL 516-759-1253. FAX 516-676-9240. *1340*

MARKETING.
Haymarket Marketing Publications Ltd., 174 Hammersmith Rd., London W6 7JP, England. TEL 44-171-413-4307. FAX 44-171-413-4509.
Vendor(s): Information Access Co., VU/TEXT Information Services, Inc.. *1476*

MARKETING COMPUTERS.
B P I Communications, Inc. (New York), 1515 Broadway, New York, NY 10036. TEL 212-764-7300.
Vendor(s): Information Access Co.. *2032*

MARKETING MANAGEMENT.
American Marketing Association, 250 S. Wacker Dr., Chicago, IL 60606-5819. TEL 312-648-0536. FAX 312-993-7542.
Vendor(s): University Microfilms International. *1477*

MARKETING NEWS.
American Marketing Association, 250 S. Wacker Dr., Ste. 200, Chicago, IL 60606. TEL 312-648-0536. FAX 312-993-7542.
Vendor(s): Information Access Co., Lexis-Nexis, University Microfilms International. *1477*

MARKETING RESEARCH.
American Marketing Association, 250 S. Wacker Dr., Ste. 200, Chicago, IL 60606. TEL 312-648-0536. FAX 312-993-7542.
Vendor(s): University Microfilms International. *1478*

MARKETING SERIES.
Natural Resources Institute, Central Ave., Chatham Maritime, Kent ME4 4TB, England. TEL 44-1634-880088. FAX 44-1634-880066. *1478*

MARKETING WEEK.
Centaur Communications Ltd., 50 Poland St., London W1V 4AX, England. TEL 44-171-287-9800. FAX 44-171-439-1480.
Vendor(s): University Microfilms International. *1478*

MARKETPLACE MAGAZINE.
A D D Inc., 211 N. Lynndale Dr., Ste. 8, Appleton, WI 54913-1897. TEL 414-735-5969. FAX 414-735-5970.
Vendor(s): University Microfilms International. *943*

MARKT & WIRTSCHAFT.
Industrie- und Handelskammer Koeln, Unter Sachsenhausen 10-26, 50667 Cologne, Germany. TEL 0221-1640-0. FAX 0221-1640123. *1145*

MARQUETTE LAW REVIEW.
Marquette University, Law School, 1103 W. Wisconsin Ave., Milwaukee, WI 53233. TEL 414-288-5143.
Vendor(s): West Services, Inc.. *3813*

MARTINDALE-HUBBELL LAW DIRECTORY.
Martindale-Hubbell, A Division of Reed Elsevier Inc., 121 Chanlon Rd., New Providence, NJ 07974. FAX 908-464-3553.
Vendor(s): Lexis-Nexis. *3814*

MARTINDALE: THE EXTRA PHARMACOPOEIA.
Royal Pharmaceutical Society of Great Britain, 1 Lambeth High St., London SE1 7JN, England. TEL 071-735-9141. FAX 071-735-7629.
Vendor(s): Data-Star, Knight-Ridder Information, Inc. (File no.141). *5427*

MARYLAND. POLICE AND CORRECTIONAL TRAINING COMMISSIONS. ANNUAL REPORT.
Police and Correctional Training Commission, 3085 Hernwood Rd., Rm. 16, Woodstock, MD 21163. TEL 410-442-2700. FAX 410-442-5852.
Vendor(s): Knight-Ridder Information, Inc.. *2169*

MARYLAND BUSINESS & LIVING.
Philos Publications Inc., c/o D.N. Kuryk, 5 Light St., Ste. 950, Baltimore, MD 21202.
Vendor(s): Knight-Ridder Information, Inc.. *943*

MARYLAND BUSINESS DIRECTORY.
American Business Directories 5711 S. 86th Circle, Box 27347, Omaha, NE 68127. TEL 402-593-4600. FAX 402-331-5481. *1625*

MARYLAND LAW REVIEW.
University of Maryland, School of Law, 500 W. Baltimore St., Baltimore, MD 21201. TEL 410-706-7414.
Vendor(s): West Services, Inc.. *3814*

MASS HIGH TECH.
Mass Tech Communications, 200 High St., 4th Fl., Boston, MA 02110-3036. TEL 617-478-0430. FAX 617-478-0438. *6657*

MASSACHUSETTS BUSINESS DIRECTORY.
American Business Directories 5711 S. 86th Circle, Omaha, NE 68127. TEL 402-593-4600. FAX 402-331-5481. *1625*

MASSACHUSETTS C P A REVIEW.
Massachusetts Society of Certified Public Accountants, Inc., 105 Chauncy St., 10th Fl., Boston, MA 02111-1742. TEL 617-556-4000. FAX 617-556-4126.
Vendor(s): University Microfilms International. *1051*

MASSACHUSETTS LAWYER WEEKLY.
Lawyers Weekly Publications, 41 West St., Boston, MA 02111. TEL 617-451-7700. FAX 617-451-7324.
Vendor(s): Lexis-Nexis. *3815*

MASSACHUSETTS REVIEW.
Massachusetts Review, Inc., Memorial Hall, University of Massachusetts, Amherst, MA 01003. TEL 413-545-2689.
Vendor(s): University Microfilms International. *4154*

MASTERS ABSTRACTS INTERNATIONAL.
U M I Company 300 N. Zeeb Rd., Ann Arbor, MI 48106. TEL 313-761-4700. FAX 800-864-0019.
Vendor(s): Knight-Ridder Information, Inc. (File no.35), OCLC (EPIC), Ovid Technologies, Inc., STN International. *2391*

THE MASTHEAD.
National Conference of Editorial Writers, 6223 Executive Blvd., Rockville, MD 20852. TEL 301-984-3015. FAX 301-231-0026.
Vendor(s): Information Access Co.. *3707*

MATERIAL HANDLING ENGINEERING.
Penton Publishing Co. 1100 Superior Ave., Cleveland, OH 44114-2543. TEL 216-696-7000. FAX 216-696-8765.
Vendor(s): Information Access Co., University Microfilms International. *4342*

MATERIALS BUSINESS INFORMATION.
Institute of Materials, 1 Carlton House Terrace, London SW1Y 5DB, England. TEL 44-171-839-4071. FAX 44-171-839-2078.
Vendor(s): Knight-Ridder Information, Inc. (File no.269). *4984*

MATERIALS INFORMATION TRANSLATIONS SERVICE.
Institute of Materials, 1 Carlton House Terr., London SW1Y 5DB, England. TEL 44-171-839-4071. FAX 44-171-839-2289.
Vendor(s): Knight-Ridder Information, Inc. *4964*

MATHEMATICA IN EDUCATION AND RESEARCH.
Telos: The Electronic Library of Science 3600 Pruneridge Ave., Ste. 200, Santa Clara, CA 95051. TEL 408-249-9314. FAX 408-777-4643. *4379*

MATHEMATICAL REVIEWS.
American Mathematical Society, Box 6248, Providence, RI 02940-6248. TEL 401-455-4000.
Vendor(s): European Space Agency (File no.80/MATHSCI), Knight-Ridder Information, Inc., Ovid Technologies, Inc. (MATH). *4406*

A MATTER OF FACT: STATEMENTS CONTAINING STATISTICS ON CURRENT SOCIAL, ECONOMIC AND POLITICAL ISSUES.
Pierian Press, Box 1808, Ann Arbor, MI 48106. TEL 313-434-5530. FAX 313-434-6409.
Vendor(s): OCLC. *3352*

MEALEY'S EMERGING INSURANCE DISPUTES.
Mealey's Publications, Inc., Box 446, Wayne, PA 19087-0446. TEL 610-688-6566. FAX 610-688-7552.
Vendor(s): Lexis-Nexis (MEALEY), West Services, Inc. *3658*

MEALEY'S EMERGING TOXIC TORTS.
Mealey Publications, Inc., Box 446, Wayne, PA 19087. TEL 610-688-6566. FAX 610-688-7552.
Vendor(s): Lexis-Nexis (MEALEY), West Services, Inc.. *3884*

MEALEY'S INSURANCE SUPPLEMENT.
Mealey Publications, Inc., Box 446, Wayne, PA 19087. TEL 610-688-6566.
Vendor(s): Lexis-Nexis (MEALEY), West Services, Inc.. *3658*

MEALEY'S INTERNATIONAL ARBITRATION REPORT.
Mealey Publications, Inc., Box 446, Wayne, PA 19087. TEL 610-688-6566. FAX 610-688-7552.
Vendor(s): Lexis-Nexis (MEALEY), West Services, Inc.. *3938*

MEALEY'S LITIGATION REPORT: ASBESTOS.
Mealey Publications, Inc., Box 446, Wayne, PA 19087. TEL 610-688-6566. FAX 610-688-7552.
Vendor(s): Lexis-Nexis (MEALEY), West Services, Inc.. *3884*

MEALEY'S LITIGATION REPORT: BAD FAITH.
Mealey Publications, Inc., Box 446, Wayne, PA 19087. TEL 610-688-6566. FAX 610-688-7552.
Vendor(s): Lexis-Nexis (MEALEY), West Services, Inc.. *3885*

MEALEY'S LITIGATION REPORT: BREAST IMPLANTS.
Mealey Publications, Inc., Box 446, Wayne, PA 19807. TEL 610-688-6566. FAX 610-688-7552.
Vendor(s): Lexis-Nexis (MEALEY), West Services, Inc.. *3885*

MEALEY'S LITIGATION REPORT: DRUGS AND MEDICAL DEVICES.
Mealey Publications, Inc., Box 446, Wayne, PA 19087. TEL 215-688-6566. FAX 215-688-7552.
Vendor(s): Lexis-Nexis (MEALEY), West Services, Inc.. *3904*

MEALEY'S LITIGATION REPORT: INSURANCE.
Mealey Publications, Inc., Box 446, Wayne, PA 19087. TEL 610-688-6566. FAX 610-688-7552.
Vendor(s): Lexis-Nexis (MEALEY), West Services, Inc.. *3885*

MEALEY'S LITIGATION REPORT: INSURANCE FRAUD.
Mealey Publications, Inc., Box 446, Wayne, PA 19087. TEL 610-688-6566. FAX 610-688-7552.
Vendor(s): Lexis-Nexis (MEALEY), West Services, Inc.. *3885*

MEALEY'S LITIGATION REPORT: INSURANCE INSOLVENCY.
Mealey Publications, Inc., Box 446, Wayne, PA 19087. TEL 610-688-6566. FAX 610-688-7552.
Vendor(s): Lexis-Nexis (MEALEY), West Services, Inc.. *3885*

MEALEY'S LITIGATION REPORT: INTELLECTUAL PROPERTY.
Mealey Publications, Inc., Box 446, Wayne, PA 19087-0446. TEL 610-688-6566. FAX 610-688-7552.
Vendor(s): Lexis-Nexis (MEALEY), West Services, Inc.. *5342*

MEALEY'S LITIGATION REPORT: LEAD.
Mealey Publications, Inc., Box 446, Wayne, PA 19087. TEL 610-688-6566. FAX 610-688-7552.
Vendor(s): Lexis-Nexis (MEALEY), West Services, Inc.. *3885*

MEALEY'S LITIGATION REPORT: PATENTS.
Mealey Publications, Inc., P.O. Box 446, Wayne, PA 19087-0446. TEL 610-688-6566. FAX 610-688-7552.
Vendor(s): Lexis-Nexis (MEALEY), West Services, Inc.. *5342*

MEALEY'S LITIGATION REPORT: PEDICLE SCREWS.
Mealey Publications, Inc., Box 446, Wayne, PA 19087. TEL 215-688-6566. FAX 215-688-7552.
Vendor(s): Lexis-Nexis (MEALEY), West Services, Inc.. *3904*

MEALEY'S LITIGATION REPORT: REINSURANCE.
Mealey Publications, Inc., Box 446, Wayne, PA 19087. TEL 610-688-6566. FAX 610-688-7552.
Vendor(s): Lexis-Nexis (MEALEY), West Services, Inc.. *3885*

MEALEY'S LITIGATION REPORT: SUPERFUND.
Mealey Publications, Inc., Box 446, Wayne, PA 19087. TEL 610-688-6566. FAX 610-688-7552.
Vendor(s): Lexis-Nexis (MEALEY), West Services, Inc.. *3885*

MEALEY'S LITIGATION REPORT: TOBACCO.
Mealey Publications, Inc., Box 446, Wayne, PA 19087. TEL 215-688-6566. FAX 215-688-7552.
Vendor(s): Lexis-Nexis (MEALEY), West Services, Inc.. *3885*

MEASUREMENT SCIENCE AND TECHNOLOGY.
I O P Publishing Ltd., Techno House, Redcliffe Way, Bristol, Avon BS1 6NX, England. TEL 44-117-929-7481. FAX 44-117-929-4318. *3636*

MEAT AND POULTRY: THE INTERNATIONAL MARKET.
Euromonitor, 60-61 Britton St., London EC1M 5QU, England. TEL 44-171-251-8024. FAX 44-171-608-3149.
Vendor(s): Data-Star, Knight-Ridder Information, Inc.. *2983*

MECHANICAL ENGINEERING.
American Society of Mechanical Engineers, 22 Law Dr., Fairfield, NJ 07007-2300.
Vendor(s): Information Access Co., Lexis-Nexis, University Microfilms International. *2763*

MECHANICAL ENGINEERING ABSTRACTS.
Cambridge Scientific Abstracts, 7200 Wisconsin Ave., 6th Fl., Bethesda, MD 20814. TEL 301-961-6700. FAX 301-961-6720.
Vendor(s): European Space Agency (File no.10/ISMEC), Knight-Ridder Information, Inc. (File no.14), STN International (ISMEC). *2629*

MED AD NEWS.
Engel Publishing Partners, 820 Bear Tavern Rd., W. Trenton, NJ 08628. TEL 609-530-0044. FAX 609-530-0207.
Vendor(s): Information Access Co.. *1479*

MEDECONOMICS.
Haymarket Medical Ltd., 30 Lancaster Gate, London W2 3LP, England. TEL 0171-413-4402.
Vendor(s): Data-Star. *4493*

MEDIA INDUSTRY NEWSLETTER.
Phillips Business Information, Inc., 1201 Seven Locks Rd., Potomac, MD 20854. TEL 301-424-3338. FAX 301-309-3847.
Vendor(s): Information Access Co., NewsNet (PB14). *41*

MEDIA MONITOR.
Financial Times Telecoms & Media Publishing Maple House, 149 Tottenham Court Rd., London W1P 9LL, England. TEL 0171-896-2234. FAX 0171-896-2256.
Vendor(s): Data-Star. *1911*

MEDIA WEEK.
E M A P Media 33-39 Bowling Green Ln., London EC1R 0DA, England. TEL 44-171-505-8341. FAX 44-171-505-8363. *41*

MEDIAWEEK.
B P I Communications, Inc. (New York), 1515 Broadway, New York, NY 10036. TEL 212-536-5336. FAX 212-536-5353.
Vendor(s): Information Access Co., Knight-Ridder Information, Inc., Lexis-Nexis, University Microfilms International. *41*

MEDICAL AND HEALTH CARE BOOKS AND SERIALS IN PRINT.
R.R. Bowker, A Division of Reed Elsevier Inc., 121 Chanlon Rd., New Providence, NJ 07974. TEL 908-464-6800. FAX 908-665-3502.
Vendor(s): Knight-Ridder Information, Inc., Ovid Technologies, Inc. (BBIP,ULRI). *4568*

MEDICAL AND PEDIATRIC ONCOLOGY.
John Wiley & Sons, Inc., Journals, 605 Third Ave., New York, NY 10158. TEL 212-850-6645. FAX 212-850-6021. *4760*

MEDICAL & PHARMACEUTICAL BIOTECHNOLOGY ABSTRACTS.
Cambridge Scientific Abstracts, 7200 Wisconsin Ave., 6th Fl., Bethesda, MD 20814. TEL 301-961-6700. FAX 301-961-6720.
Vendor(s): Knight-Ridder Information, Inc. (File no.76/LIFE SCIENCES COLLECTION), STN International (LIFESCI). *4568*

MEDICAL DEVICE APPROVAL LETTER.
Washington Information Source, 6506 Old Stage Rd., Ste. 100, Rockville, MD 20852-4326. TEL 301-770-5553.
Vendor(s): Information Access Co.. *4683*

MEDICAL DEVICES, DIAGNOSTICS & INSTRUMENTATION REPORTS: THE GRAY SHEET.
F-D-C Reports, Inc., 5550 Friendship Blvd., Ste. One, Chevy Chase, MD 20815. FAX 301-664-7238.
Vendor(s): Data-Star (FDCF), Knight-Ridder Information, Inc. (File no.187), Lexis-Nexis, Ovid Technologies, Inc. (FDCR). *4494*

MEDICAL ECONOMICS.
Medical Economics Publishing Co., Inc., 5 Paragon Dr., Montvale, NJ 07645. TEL 201-358-7200. FAX 201-573-1045.
Vendor(s): Information Access Co., Knight-Ridder Information, Inc.. *4494*

MEDICAL JOURNAL OF AUSTRALIA.
Australasian Medical Publishing Co., Private Bag 901, N. Sydney, N.S.W. 2059, Australia. TEL 61-2-99543666. FAX 61-2-99567644. *4495*

MEDICAL LETTER ON DRUGS AND THERAPEUTICS (ENGLISH EDITION).
Medical Letter, Inc., 1000 Main St., New Rochelle, NY 10801. TEL 914-235-0500. FAX 914-632-1733.
Vendor(s): University Microfilms International. *5427*

MEDICAL MARKETING & MEDIA.
C P S Communications, Inc., 7200 W. Camino Real, Ste. 215, Boca Raton, FL 33433. TEL 407-368-9301. FAX 407-368-7870
Vendor(s): Information Access Co., Lexis-Nexis, University Microfilms International. *5427*

MEDICAL ONCOLOGY.
Chapman & Hall, Journals Department 2-6 Boundary Row, London SE1 8HN, England. TEL 44-171-8560066. FAX 44-171-5229623. *4760*

MEDICAL OUTCOMES AND GUIDELINES ALERT.
Faulkner & Gray, Healthcare Information Center 11 Penn Plaza, 17th Fl., New York, NY 10001. TEL 212-967-7000.
Vendor(s): Information Access Co., Knight-Ridder Information, Inc., NewsNet. *4496*

Online

MEDICAL SCIENCE RESEARCH.
Chapman & Hall, Journals Department 2-6 Boundary Row, London SE1 8HN, England. TEL 44-171-8560066. FAX 44-171-5229623.
Vendor(s): DIMDI, Data-Star, Ovid Technologies, Inc.. *4497*

MEDICAL TEXTILES.
Elsevier Science Ltd., P.O. Box 800, Kidlington, Oxford OX5 1DX, England. TEL 44-1865-843000. FAX 44-1865-843010.
Vendor(s): Data-Star, Information Access Co., Knight-Ridder Information, Inc.. *4498*

MEDICAL UPDATE.
Benjamin Franklin Literary and Medical Society, Inc., Medical Education and Research Foundation, Box 567, 1100 Waterway Blvd., Indianapolis, IN 46202. FAX 317-684-8094.
Vendor(s): Information Access Co.. *5532*

MEDICAL UTILIZATION MANAGEMENT.
Faulkner & Gray, Healthcare Information Center 11 Penn Plaza, 17th Fl., New York, NY 10001. TEL 212-967-7000.
Vendor(s): Information Access Co., Knight-Ridder Information, Inc., NewsNet. *4498*

MEDICAL WASTE NEWS.
Business Publishers, Inc., 951 Pershing Dr., Silver Spring, MD 20910-4432. TEL 301-587-6300. FAX 301-585-9075.
Vendor(s): Data-Star, Information Access Co., Knight-Ridder Information, Inc., NewsNet (EV30). *2854*

MEDICATED SKINCARE: THE INTERNATIONAL MARKET.
Euromonitor, 60-61 Britton St., London EC1M 5NA, England. TEL 44-171-251-8024. FAX 44-171-608-3149.
Vendor(s): Data-Star, Knight-Ridder Information, Inc.. *5427*

MEDICINAL AND AROMATIC PLANTS ABSTRACTS.
Council of Scientific and Industrial Research, Publications & Information Directorate, Hillside Rd., New Delhi 110 012, India. TEL 11-5726014. FAX 11-5787062. *4568*

MEDICINE (BALTIMORE).
Williams & Wilkins, 351 W. Camden St., Baltimore, MD 21201. TEL 410-528-4000. FAX 410-528-4312.
Vendor(s): Information Access Co.. *4499*

MEDIO AMBIENTE.
Universidad Austral de Chile, Instituto de Ecologia y Evolucion, Facultad de Ciencias, Casilla 567, Valdivia, Chile. FAX 56-63-221344. *2809*

MEDIUM AEVUM.
Society for the Study of Mediaeval Languages and Literature, c/o Dr. D.G. Pattison, Hon. Treas., Magdalen College, Oxford OX1 4AU, England. TEL 44-1865-276087.
Vendor(s): Information Access Co., University Microfilms International. *4236*

MEETINGS AND CONVENTIONS.
Reed Travel Group, Part of the Reed Elsevier group 500 Plaza Dr., Secaucus, NJ 07096. TEL 201-902-1700. FAX 201-319-1796.
Vendor(s): Information Access Co.. *4936*

MEMBRANE & SEPARATION TECHNOLOGY NEWS.
Business Communications Co., Inc. (Norwalk), 25 Van Zant St., Norwalk, CT 06855. TEL 203-853-4266. FAX 203-853-0348.
Vendor(s): Data-Star, Information Access Co., Knight-Ridder Information, Inc., NewsNet (BT05). *663*

MEMPHIS BUSINESS JOURNAL.
Mid-South Communications, Inc., 88 Union, Ste. 102, Memphis, TN 38103-5195. TEL 901-523-1000. FAX 901-526-5240.
Vendor(s): Information Access Co., Knight-Ridder Information, Inc., Lexis-Nexis, University Microfilms International. *943*

MENDELEEV COMMUNICATIONS.
The Royal Society of Chemistry, Thomas Graham House, Science Park, Milton Rd., Cambridge CB4 4WF, England. TEL 44-1223-420066. FAX 44-1223-423429. *1686*

MENOPAUSE NEWS.
Menopause News, 2074 Union St., San Francisco, CA 94123. FAX 415-567-2368.
Vendor(s): Information Access Co.. *6985*

MEN'S HEALTH.
Rodale Press, Inc., 33 E. Minor St., Emmaus, PA 18049. TEL 610-967-5171. FAX 610-967-7725.
Vendor(s): Information Access Co., University Microfilms International. *4939*

MEN'S TOILETRIES: THE INTERNATIONAL MARKET.
Euromonitor, 60-61 Britton St., London EC1M 5NA, England. TEL 44-171-251-8024. FAX 44-171-608-3149.
Vendor(s): Data-Star, Knight-Ridder Information, Inc.. *492*

MENTAL HEALTH LAW REPORTER.
Business Publishers, Inc., 951 Pershing Dr., Silver Spring, MD 20910-4464. TEL 301-587-6300. FAX 301-585-9075.
Vendor(s): NewsNet. *3886*

MENTAL HEALTH REPORT.
Business Publishers, Inc., 951 Pershing Dr., Silver Spring, MD 20910-4464. TEL 301-587-6300. FAX 301-585-9075.
Vendor(s): NewsNet. *6382*

MENTAL HEALTH WEEKLY.
Manisses Communications Group, Inc., Box 9758, Providence, RI 02906-9758. TEL 401-861-6020. FAX 401-861-6370. *5865*

MERCER BUSINESS MAGAZINE.
Mercer County Chamber of Commerce, 2550 Kuser Rd., Box 8307, Trenton, NJ 08650. TEL 609-586-2056. FAX 609-586-8052.
Vendor(s): Knight-Ridder Information, Inc., University Microfilms International. *1145*

MERCER LAW REVIEW.
Mercer University, Walter F. George School of Law, Macon, GA 31207. TEL 912-752-2622.
Vendor(s): West Services, Inc.. *3815*

MERCK INDEX: AN ENCYCLOPEDIA OF CHEMICALS AND DRUGS.
Merck Publishing Co., Box 2000, Rg 7-220, Rahway, NJ 07065. TEL 908-594-4600.
Vendor(s): CISTI, Knight-Ridder Information, Inc., Ovid Technologies, Inc. (MRCK), STN International, Telesystemes - Questel. *5451*

MERGERS & ACQUISITIONS.
Investment Dealers' Digest, 2 World Trade Center, 18th Fl., New York, NY 10048. TEL 212-227-1200. FAX 212-321-2336.
Vendor(s): Information Access Co., University Microfilms International. *944*

MERGERS & ACQUISITIONS REPORT.
Investment Dealers' Digest, 2 World Trade Center, 18th Fl., New York, NY 10048-0638. TEL 212-432-0045. FAX 212-321-2336.
Vendor(s): Information Access Co., University Microfilms International. *944*

MERGERS AND RESTRUCTURINGS.
Securities Data Publishing, 40 W. 57th St., 11th Fl., New York, NY 10019. TEL 212-765-5311. FAX 212-765-6123.
Vendor(s): Information Access Co., NewsNet. *944*

METABOLISM: CLINICAL AND EXPERIMENTAL.
W.B. Saunders Co. Curtis Center, 3rd Fl., Independence Sq. W., Philadelphia, PA 19106-3399. TEL 215-238-7800. FAX 215-238-6445. *4673*

METAL CENTER NEWS.
Hitchcock Publishing 191 S. Gary Ave., Carol Stream, IL 60188. TEL 708-665-1000. FAX 708-462-2225.
Vendor(s): Information Access Co.. *4965*

METAL HEAT TREATING.
Penton Publishing Co., 1100 Superior Ave., Cleveland, OH 44114-2543. TEL 216-696-7000.
Vendor(s): Information Access Co.. *4965*

METAL INDUSTRY INDICATORS.
U.S. Bureau of Mines, Office of Public Information, 810 Seventh St., N.W., MS-1040, Washington, DC 20241-0001. TEL 202-501-9649. FAX 202-219-2493. *5069*

METALLURGIA: THE JOURNAL OF METALS TECHNOLOGY, METAL FORMING AND THERMAL PROCESSING.
Argus Business Publications Ltd. Queensway House, 2 Queensway, Redhill, Surrey RH1 1QS, England. TEL 44-1737-768611. FAX 44-1737-761685.
Vendor(s): Information Access Co.. *4967*

METALS ABSTRACTS.
Cambridge Scientific Abtracts, 7200 Wisconsin Ave., Bethesda, MD 20814. TEL 301-961-6750. FAX 301-961-6720.
Vendor(s): CEDOCAR, CISTI, Data-Star (META), European Space Agency (File no.3/METADEX), FIZ Technik (META), Knight-Ridder Information, Inc. (File no.32/METADEX), Orbit Search Service (MDEX), STN International (METADEX). *4984*

METALS ABSTRACTS INDEX.
Cambridge Scientific Abstracts, 7200 Wisconsin Ave., Bethesda, MD 20814. TEL 301-961-6750. FAX 301-961-6720.
Vendor(s): CEDOCAR, CISTI, Data-Star (META), European Space Agency (File no.3/METADEX), FIZ Technik (META), Knight-Ridder Information, Inc. (File no.32/METADEX), Orbit Search Service (MDEX), STN International (METADEX). *4984*

METALS INDUSTRY NEWS.
Argus Business Media Ltd., Fuel and Metals Journals Queensway House, 2 Queensway, Redhill, Surrey RH1 1QS, England. TEL 44-1737-768611. FAX 44-1737-761685.
Vendor(s): Information Access Co.. *4967*

METALS WEEK.
McGraw-Hill Companies, Commodity Services Group, 1221 Avenue of the Americas, 42nd Fl., New York, NY 10020. TEL 212-512-2000.
Vendor(s): Dow Jones News Retrieval (MW), Knight-Ridder Information, Inc. (File no.624/McGRAW-HILL PUBLICATIONS ONLINE), Lexis-Nexis (METLWK), NewsNet (ML01). *5069*

METEOROLOGICAL AND GEOASTROPHYSICAL ABSTRACTS.
American Meteorological Society, c/o Inforonics, Inc., 550 Newtown Rd., Littleton, MA 01460. TEL 508-486-8976. FAX 508-486-0027.
Vendor(s): Knight-Ridder Information, Inc. (File no.29). *5011*

METROPOLITAN HOME.
Hachette Filipacchi Magazines, Inc., 1633 Broadway, 41st Fl., New York, NY 10019. TEL 212-767-6000. FAX 212-767-5636.
Vendor(s): Information Access Co., University Microfilms International. *3680*

METROPOLITAN LIFE INSURANCE COMPANY. STATISTICAL BULLETIN S B.
Metropolitan Life Insurance Company, 1 Madison Ave., New York, NY 10010. TEL 212-578-5014. FAX 212-213-0577.
Vendor(s): Information Access Co.. *6619*

MEXICAN STUDIES.
University of California Press, Journals Division, 2120 Berkeley Way, No. 5812, Berkeley, CA 94720-5812. TEL 510-643-7154. FAX 510-642-9917.
Vendor(s): Information Access Co.. *3619*

MEXICO & N A F T A REPORT.
Lettres (U.K.) Ltd., 61 Old St., London EC1V 9HX, England. TEL 44-171-251-0012. FAX 44-171-253-8193.
Vendor(s): Lexis-Nexis. *1222*

MEXICO BUSINESS MONTHLY.
Kal Wagenheim, Ed. & Pub., 52 Maple Ave., Maplewood, NJ 07040. TEL 201-762-1565. FAX 201-762-9585.
Vendor(s): Information Access Co.. *1290*

MEXICO CONSENSUS ECONOMIC FORECAST.
Arizona State University, Economic Outlook Center, Box 874406, Tempe, AZ 85287-4406. TEL 602-965-5543. FAX 602-964-5458. *1222*

MEXICO SERVICE.
International Reports, Inc., 11300 Rockville Pike, Ste. 1100, Rockville, MD 20852-3035. TEL 301-816-8950. FAX 301-816-8945. *1341*

MEYLER'S SIDE EFFECTS OF DRUGS.
Elsevier Science B.V., Books Division, P.O. Box 211, 1000 AE Amsterdam, Netherlands. TEL 31-20-4853911. FAX 31-20-4853705.
Vendor(s): Data-Star (SEDB), Knight-Ridder Information, Inc. (File no.70/SEDBASE), Ovid Technologies, Inc.. *5428*

MICHIGAN BAR JOURNAL.
State Bar of Michigan, 306 Townsend, Lansing, MI 48933. TEL 517-372-9030.
Vendor(s): West Services, Inc.. *3815*

MICHIGAN BUSINESS DIRECTORY.
American Business Directories 5711 S. 86th Circle, Box 27347, Omaha, NE 68127. TEL 402-593-4600. FAX 402-331-5481. *1626*

MICHIGAN C P A.
Michigan Association of C P A, Box 9054, 28116 Orchard Lake Rd., Farmington Hills, MI 48333. TEL 313-855-2288. FAX 313-855-9122.
Vendor(s): Information Access Co., University Microfilms International. *1051*

MICHIGAN CITIZEN.
Newday Publishing, 12541 Second, Box 03560, Highland Park, MI 48203. TEL 313-869-0033. FAX 313-869-0430.
Vendor(s): Lexis-Nexis (ETHNIC NEWSWATCH). *2894*

MICHIGAN JOURNAL OF POLITICAL SCIENCE.
University of Michigan, Michigan Journal of Political Science, 5620 Haven Hall, Ann Arbor, MI 48109-1045. TEL 313-764-6386. *5683*

MICHIGAN LAW REVIEW.
Michigan Law Review Association, Ann Arbor, MI 48109-1215. TEL 313-763-5870. FAX 313-764-8309.
Vendor(s): Information Access Co., Lexis-Nexis, West Services, Inc.. *3816*

MICHIGAN LAWYERS WEEKLY.
Michigan Lawyers Weekly, 333 S. Washington Sq., No.300, Lansing, MI 48933. TEL 517-374-6200. FAX 517-374-6222.
Vendor(s): Lexis-Nexis. *3816*

MICHNET NEWS.
Merit Network, Inc., c/o Patricia O. McGregor, Ed., 4251 Plymouth Rd., Ann Arbor, MI 48105-2785. TEL 313-764-9430. FAX 313-747-3185. *2039*

MICROBIOLOGY ABSTRACTS: SECTION A. INDUSTRIAL & APPLIED MICROBIOLOGY.
Cambridge Scientific Abstracts, 7200 Wisconsin Ave., 6th Fl., Bethesda, MD 20814. TEL 301-961-6750. FAX 301-961-6720.
Vendor(s): Knight-Ridder Information, Inc. (File no.76/LIFE SCIENCES COLLECTION), STN International (LIFESCI). *621*

MICROBIOLOGY ABSTRACTS: SECTION B. BACTERIOLOGY.
Cambridge Scientific Abstracts, 7200 Wisconsin Ave., 6th Fl., Bethesda, MD 20814. TEL 301-961-6750. FAX 301-961-6720.
Vendor(s): Knight-Ridder Information, Inc. (File no.76/LIFE SCIENCES COLLECTION), STN International (LIFESCI). *621*

MICROBIOLOGY ABSTRACTS: SECTION C. ALGOLOGY, MYCOLOGY AND PROTOZOOLOGY.
Cambridge Scientific Abstracts, 7200 Wisconsin Ave., 6th Fl., Bethesda, MD 20814. TEL 301-961-6750. FAX 301-961-6720.
Vendor(s): Knight-Ridder Information, Inc. (File no.76/LIFE SCIENCES COLLECTION), STN International (LIFESCI). *622*

MICROCIRCULATION (LONDON).
Chapman & Hall 2-6 Boundary Row, London SE1 8HN, England. TEL 44-171-8650066. FAX 44-171-5229623. *4502*

MICROCOMPUTER ABSTRACTS.
Information Today, Inc., 143 Old Marlton Pike, Medford, NJ 08055. TEL 609-654-6266. FAX 609-654-4309.
Vendor(s): Knight-Ridder Information, Inc. (File no.233). *2003*

MICROPROCESSOR REPORT.
874 Gravenstein Hwy., Ste.14, Sebastopol, CA 95472. TEL 707-824-4004. FAX 707-823-0504.
Vendor(s): Information Access Co.. *2089*

MICROSCOPY MICROANALYSIS MICROSTRUCTURES.
Societe Française de Microscopie Electronique, Case 243, Universite Paris VI, 4 place Jussieu, 75252 Paris Cedex 05, France. TEL 30-1-46-70-28-44. FAX 30-1-46 70-83-46. *5607*

MICROSOFT SYSTEMS JOURNAL.
Miller Freeman, 411 Bord Ave., San Mateo, CA 94402. TEL 415-358-9500. FAX 415-358-9865.
Vendor(s): Information Access Co.. *2046*

MICROSTATION MANAGER.
MicroManagement, Inc., Box 1536, Santa Fe, NM 87501. TEL 505-982-5181. FAX 505-986-3816. *407*

MICROWAVE JOURNAL (INTERNATIONAL EDITION).
Horizon - House - Publications, Inc., 685 Canton St., Norwood, MA 02062. TEL 617-769-9750. FAX 617-762-9230.
Vendor(s): Information Access Co.. *2713*

MID-AMERICA COMMERCE & INDUSTRY.
M A C I Inc., 1824 Cheyenne Rd., Topeka, KS 66604. TEL 913-272-5280.
Vendor(s): University Microfilms International. *1222*

MID-AMERICAN JOURNAL OF BUSINESS.
Ball State University, Bureau of Business Research, Muncie, IN 47306. TEL 317-285-5926. FAX 317-285-8024.
Vendor(s): University Microfilms International. *944*

THE MIDDLE EAST.
I.C. Publications Ltd., 7 Coldbath Sq., London EC1R 4LQ, England. TEL 44-171-713-7711. FAX 44-171-713-7898.
Vendor(s): Information Access Co.. *4154*

MIDDLE EAST: ABSTRACTS AND INDEX.
Aristarchus Publications, Box 1020, Aberdeen, WA 98520. TEL 800-435-8221.
Vendor(s): Knight-Ridder Information, Inc. (File no.248). *18*

MIDDLE EAST ECONOMIC DIGEST.
E M A P - Business Information, 21 John St., London WC1N 2BP, England. TEL 44-171-404-5513. FAX 44-171-430-0337.
Vendor(s): Information Access Co.. *1222*

MIDDLE EAST EXECUTIVE REPORTS.
International Executive Reports, Ltd., 717 D St., N.W., Ste. 300, Washington, DC 20004-2807. TEL 202-628-6900. FAX 202-628-6618.
Vendor(s): Lexis-Nexis, University Microfilms International. *1290*

MIDDLE EAST JOURNAL.
Middle East Institute, 1761 N St., N.W., Washington, DC 20036. TEL 202-785-0191.
Vendor(s): University Microfilms International. *5761*

MIDDLE EASTERN STUDIES.
Frank Cass, Newbury House, 890-900 Eastern Ave., Newbury Park, Ilford, Essex 1G2 7HH, England. TEL 44-181-599-8836. FAX 44-181-599-0984.
Vendor(s): Information Access Co., University Microfilms International. *3498*

MIDDLESEX MAGAZINE.
Chronicle Communications, 615 Main St., Cromwell, CT 06416. TEL 209-635-1819. FAX 203-632-7203.
Vendor(s): University Microfilms International. *944*

MIDRANGE SYSTEMS.
Cardinal Business Media, Inc., 1300 Virginia Dr., Ste. 400, Fort Washington, PA 19034-3225. TEL 215-643-8000. FAX 215-643-3901.
Vendor(s): Information Access Co.. *2092*

MIDWEST QUARTERLY.
Pittsburg State University, Midwest Quarterly, Pittsburg, KS 66762. TEL 316-235-4317. FAX 316-232-7515.
Vendor(s): Information Access Co., University Microfilms International. *3619*

MIGRATION WORLD.
Center for Migration Studies, 209 Flagg Pl., Staten Island, NY 10304-1199. TEL 718-351-8800. FAX 718-667-4598.
Vendor(s): Information Access Co., University Microfilms International. *5788*

THE MILBANK QUARTERLY.
Blackwell Publishers, 238 Main St., Cambridge, MA 02142. TEL 617-547-7110. FAX 617-547-0789.
Vendor(s): Information Access Co.. *5684*

MILITARY & COMMERCIAL FIBER BUSINESS.
Phillips Publishing, Inc., Defense - Aviation Group, 1111 19th St., N., Ste. 503, Arlington, VA 22209-1704. TEL 703-522-8333. FAX 703-522-6448.
Vendor(s): Data-Star, Knight-Ridder Information, Inc., NewsNet (DE06). *5039*

MILITARY LAW REVIEW.
U.S. Army, Judge Advocate General's School, Charlottesville, VA 22903-1781. TEL 804-972-6395.
Vendor(s): Lexis-Nexis, West Services, Inc.. *3958*

MILITARY ROBOTICS NEWSLETTER.
L & B Limited, 19 Rock Creek Church Rd., N.W., Washington, DC 20011-6005. TEL 202-723-1600. FAX 202-726-2979.
Vendor(s): Information Access Co., Knight-Ridder Information, Inc. (NL0650), NewsNet (DE14). *2105*

MILITARY SPACE.
Pasha Publications Inc., 1616 N. Ft. Myer Dr., Ste. 1000, Arlington, VA 22209-3107. TEL 703-528-1244. FAX 703-528-1253.
Vendor(s): Information Access Co., NewsNet (DE04). *5040*

MILITARY SPECIFICATIONS AND STANDARDS SERVICES NUMERIC INDEX.
Information Handling Services, 15 Inverness Way East, Englewood, CO 80150. TEL 303-790-0600. FAX 303-799-4085.
Vendor(s): Knight-Ridder Information, Inc.. *5040*

MILLIENNIAL PROPHECY REPORT.
Millennium Watch Institute, Box 34021, Philadelphia, PA 19101-4021. *5078*

MILLING & BAKING NEWS.
Sosland Publishing Company, 4800 Main St., Ste. 100, Kansas City, MO 64112. TEL 816-756-1000. FAX 816-756-0494.
Vendor(s): Information Access Co.. *3001*

MILLION DOLLAR DIRECTORY.
Dun and Bradstreet Information Services 3 Sylvan Way, Parsippany, NJ 07054-3896. TEL 201-605-6000.
Vendor(s): Knight-Ridder Information, Inc. (File no.517), Orbit Search Service. *1526*

MIND.
Oxford University Press, Oxford Journals, Walton St., Oxford OX2 6DP, England. TEL 44-1865-267907. FAX 44-1865-267773.
Vendor(s): Information Access Co.. *5486*

MINDSPARKS.
Molecudyne Research, Box 1302, Laurel, MD 20725-1302. *4329*

MINE REGULATION REPORTER.
Pasha Publications Inc., 1616 N. Ft. Myer Dr., Ste. 1000, Arlington, VA 22209-3107. TEL 703-528-1244. FAX 703-528-1253.
Vendor(s): Information Access Co.. *5069*

MINERAL INDUSTRY SURVEYS.
U.S. Bureau of Mines, Office of Public Information, 810 Seventh St., N.W., MS-1040, Washington, DC 20241-0001. TEL 202-501-9649. FAX 202-219-2493. *5084*

MINERAL WATER: THE INTERNATIONAL MARKET.
Euromonitor, 60-61 Brittor St., London EC1M 5NA, England. TEL 44-171-251-8024. FAX 44-171-608-3149.
Vendor(s): Data-Star, Knight-Ridder Information, Inc.. *509*

THE MINERALOGICAL RECORD.
Mineralogical Record, Inc., 4531 Paseo Tubutama, Tucson, AZ 85740. FAX 520-544-0815.
Vendor(s): Information Access Co., University Microfilms International. *3510*

MINERALS YEARBOOK.
U.S. Bureau of Mines, Office of Public Information, 810 Seventh St., N.W., MS-1040, Washington, DC 20241-0001. TEL 202-501-9649. FAX 202-219-2493. *5071*

THE MINI-ANNALS OF IMPROBABLE RESEARCH.
Annals of Improbable Research, Box 380853, Cambridge, MA 02238. TEL 617-491-4437. FAX 617-661-0927.
Available only online. *6259*

MINING ANNUAL REVIEW.
Mining Journal Ltd., 60 Worship St., London EC2A 2HD, England. TEL 44-171-216-6060. FAX 44-171-216-6050.
Vendor(s): Lexis-Nexis. *5072*

MINING MAGAZINE.
Mining Journal Ltd., 60 Worship St., London EC2A 2HD, England. TEL 44-171-216-6060. FAX 44-171-216-6050.
Vendor(s): Information Access Co., Lexis-Nexis. *5072*

MINISTERIALTIDENDE FOR KONGERIGET DANMARK.
Justisministeriet, Sekretariatet for Retsinformation, Axeltorv 6, 5. sal, DK-1609 Copenhagen V, Denmark. TEL 45-33-32-52-22. FAX 45-33-91-28-01. *5911*

MINNEAPOLIS - ST. PAUL CITYBUSINESS.
City Media, Inc., 821 Marquette Ave., Ste. 2000, Minneapolis, MN 55402-2922. TEL 612-288-2141. FAX 612-288-2121.
Vendor(s): CompuServe, Inc., Data-Star, Dow Jones News Retrieval, Knight-Ridder Information, Inc., Lexis-Nexis. *944*

MINNESOTA BUSINESS DIRECTORY.
American Business Directories 5711 S. 86th Circle, Box 27347, Omaha, NE 68127. TEL 402-593-4600. FAX 402-331-5481. *1627*

MINNESOTA LAW REVIEW.
University of Minnesota, Law School, 229 19th Ave. S., Minneapolis, MN 55455. TEL 612-625-8034. Vendor(s): Lexis-Nexis, West Services, Inc.. *3816*

MINNESOTA MEDICINE.
Minnesota Medical Association, 3433 Broadway St., N.E., Ste. 300, Minneapolis, MN 55413-1761. TEL 612-378-1875. FAX 612-378-3875. *4503*

MINORITY MARKETS ALERT.
E P M Communications, 160 Mercer St., 3rd. Fl., New York, NY 10012-3212. TEL 212-941-0099. FAX 212-941-1622.
Vendor(s): Information Access Co., Knight-Ridder Information, Inc., Lexis-Nexis. *1479*

MISSISSIPPI BUSINESS DIRECTORY.
American Business Directories 5711 S. 86th Circle, Box 27347, Omaha, NE 68127. TEL 402-593-4600. FAX 402-331-5481. *1627*

MISSISSIPPI COLLEGE LAW REVIEW.
Mississippi College Law Review, 151 E. Griffith St., Jackson, MS 39201. TEL 601-925-7167. FAX 601-925-7113.
Vendor(s): West Services, Inc.. *3816*

MISSISSIPPI LAW JOURNAL.
Mississippi Law Journal, Box 849, University, MS 38677. TEL 601-232-7361. FAX 601-232-7731. Vendor(s): West Services, Inc.. *3816*

THE MISSISSIPPI QUARTERLY.
Mississippi State University, College of Arts and Sciences, Box 5272, Mississippi State, MS 39762. TEL 601-325-3069. FAX 601-325-3299. Vendor(s): Information Access Co., University Microfilms International. *4154*

MISSOURI BUSINESS DIRECTORY.
American Business Directories 5711 S. 86th Circle, Box 27347, Omaha, NE 68127. TEL 402-593-4600. FAX 402-331-5481. *1627*

MISSOURI LAW REVIEW.
University of Missouri at Columbia, School of Law, Box 203, Hulston Hall, Columbia, MO 65211. TEL 573-882-7055. FAX 573-882-9676. Vendor(s): West Services, Inc.. *3817*

MITTELSTAENDISCHE UNTERNEHMEN.
Verlag Hoppenstedt GmbH, Havelstr. 9, 64295 Darmstadt, Germany. TEL 49-6151-380-0. FAX 49-6151-380-360.
Vendor(s): Data-Star, GBI, Knight-Ridder Information, Inc.. *1526*

MOBILE COMMUNICATIONS.
Financial Times Telecoms & Media Publishing Maple House, 149 Tottenham Court Rd., London W1P 9LL, England. TEL 44-171-896-2234. FAX 44-171-896-2256.
Vendor(s): Information Access Co.. *1911*

MOBILE DATA REPORT.
Capitol Publications Inc., Telecom Publishing Group, 1101 King St., Ste. 444, Box 1455, Alexandria, VA 22313-2055. TEL 800-327-7205. FAX 703-739-6490.
Vendor(s): Information Access Co.. *1928*

MOBILE PHONE NEWS.
Phillips Business Information, Inc., 1201 Seven Locks Rd., Potomac, MD 20854. TEL 301-424-3338. FAX 301-309-3847.
Vendor(s): Information Access Co., NewsNet (TE25). *1947*

MOBILE SATELLITE NEWS (POTOMAC).
Phillips Business Information, Inc., 1201 Seven Locks Rd., Potomac, MD 20854. TEL 301-424-3338. FAX 301-309-3847.
Vendor(s): Information Access Co., NewsNet (TE27). *1947*

MOBILE SATELLITE REPORTS.
Warren Publishing, Inc., 2115 Ward Court, N.W., Washington, DC 20037. TEL 202-872-9200. FAX 202-293-3435.
Vendor(s): Data-Star, Information Access Co., Knight-Ridder Information, Inc., NewsNet (TE32). *1911*

MODEL RAILROADER.
Kalmbach Publishing Co., 21027 Crossroads Cir., Waukesha, WI 53187. TEL 414-796-8776. FAX 414-796-0126.
Vendor(s): Information Access Co.. *3511*

MODEM USER NEWS.
Worldwide Videotex, Box 3273, Boynton Beach, FL 33424-3273. TEL 407-738-2276.
Vendor(s): Data-Star, Information Access Co., Knight-Ridder Information, Inc., NewsNet (EC97). *2079*

MODERN AGING RESEARCH.
John Wiley & Sons, Inc., Journals, 605 Third Ave., New York, NY 10158. TEL 212-475-7700. *3293*

MODERN BREWERY AGE.
Business Journals, 50 Day St., Box 5550, Norwalk, CT 06856. TEL 203-853-6015.
Vendor(s): Information Access Co., Lexis-Nexis. *509*

MODERN BRIDE.
K-III Communications Corp., 745 Fifth Ave., New York, NY 10151. TEL 212-745-0100.
Vendor(s): Knight-Ridder Information, Inc.. *4414*

MODERN CASTING.
American Foundrymen's Society, Inc., 505 State St., Des Plaines, IL 60016. TEL 708-824-0181.
Vendor(s): Information Access Co.. *4968*

MODERN DRAMA.
University of Toronto Press, Journals Department, 5201 Dufferin St., Downsview, ON M3H 5T8, Canada. TEL 416-667-7781. FAX 416-667-7881.
Vendor(s): University Microfilms International. *4238*

MODERN FICTION STUDIES.
Johns Hopkins University Press, Journals Publishing Division, 2715 N. Charles St., Baltimore, MD 21218-4319. TEL 410-516-6900. FAX 410-516-6968. *4238*

MODERN HEALTHCARE (YEAR).
Crain Communications, Inc. (Chicago), 740 N. Rush St., Chicago, IL 60611-2590. TEL 312-649-5341. FAX 312-280-3189.
Vendor(s): Information Access Co.. *3553*

MODERN JUDAISM.
Johns Hopkins University Press, Journals Publishing Division, 2715 N. Charles St., Baltimore, MD 21218. TEL 410-516-6987. FAX 410-516-6968. *2895*

MODERN LANGUAGE QUARTERLY.
Duke University Press, Box 90660, Durham, NC 27708-0660. TEL 919-687-3600. FAX 919-688-4574.
Vendor(s): Information Access Co.. *4238*

MODERN MACHINE SHOP.
Gardner Publications, Inc., 6600 Clough Pike, Cincinnati, OH 45244-4090. TEL 513-231-8020. FAX 513-231-2818.
Vendor(s): Information Access Co.. *4343*

MODERN MATERIALS HANDLING.
Cahners Publishing Company (Newton), Division of Reed Elsevier Inc., 275 Washington St., Newton, MA 02158-1630. TEL 617-964-3030. FAX 617-558-4402.
Vendor(s): Information Access Co.. *4343*

MODERN MATURITY.
American Association of Retired Persons, 601 E St., N.W., Washington, DC 20049. TEL 202-728-4700.
Vendor(s): Information Access Co., University Microfilms International. *3293*

MODERN PAINT AND COATINGS.
Intertec Publishing Corp. (Atlanta), 6151 Powers Ferry Rd., N.W., Atlanta, GA 30339-2941. TEL 770-955-2500. FAX 770-955-0400.
Vendor(s): Information Access Co., University Microfilms International. *5309*

MODERN PLASTICS.
McGraw-Hill Companies, 1221 Ave. of the Americas, New York, NY 10020. TEL 212-512-6245. FAX 212-512-6111.
Vendor(s): Dow Jones News Retrieval (MP), Knight-Ridder Information, Inc. (MP), Lexis-Nexis (MODPLA), NewsNet (CH23). *5623*

MODERN POWER SYSTEMS.
Wilmington Publishing, Wilmington House, Church Hill, Dartford, Kent UA1 7EF, England. TEL 44-1322-277788. FAX 44-1322-276476.
Vendor(s): Information Access Co.. *2553*

MODERN TIRE DEALER.
Bill Communications, Inc. (Akron), 341 White Pond Dr., Box 3599, Akron, OH 44309-3599. TEL 330-867-4401. FAX 330-867-0019.
Vendor(s): Information Access Co., Knight-Ridder Information, Inc.. *6217*

MODERNISM - MODERNITY.
Johns Hopkins University Press, Journals Publishing Division, 2715 N. Charles St., Baltimore, MD 21218. TEL 410-516-6987. FAX 410-516-6968. *3353*

DIE MOEBEL-INDUSTRIE UND IHRE HELFER.
Industrieschau-Verlagsgesellschaft mbH, Postfach 100262, 64202 Darmstadt, Germany. TEL 49-6151-3892-0. FAX 49-6151-33164. *3691*

MOLECULES.
Springer-Verlag, Heidelberger Platz 3, 14197 Berlin, Germany. TEL 49-30-8207-0. *1742*

LE MONDE.
Le Monde S.A., 21 rue Claude Bernard, 75005 Paris, France. TEL 42-17-2000. FAX 42-17-2121.
Vendor(s): Telesystemes - Questel. *3139*

MONEY (NEW YORK).
Time Inc. Time & Life Bldg., Rockefeller Center, 1271 Ave. of the Americas, New York, NY 10020. TEL 212-522-1212.
Vendor(s): Information Access Co., Knight-Ridder Information, Inc., Lexis-Nexis, University Microfilms International, VU/TEXT Information Services, Inc.. *2153*

MONEY FUND REPORT.
I B C - Donoghue, Inc., 290 Eliot St., Ashland, MA 01721. TEL 508-881-2800. FAX 508-881-0982. *1341*

MONEY LAUNDERING ALERT.
Alert Publications Partners, Box 11390, Miami, FL 33101. TEL 305-530-0500. FAX 305-530-9434.
Vendor(s): Data-Star, Dow Jones News Retrieval, Information Access Co., Knight-Ridder Information, Inc., Lexis-Nexis, NewsNet. *2169*

MONEY MARKET INSIGHT.
IBC - Donoghue, Inc., 290 Eliot St., Ashland, MA 01721. TEL 508-881-2800. FAX 508-881-0982. *1341*

MONEYLETTER (ASHLAND).
IBC - Donoghue, Inc., Box 9104, Ashland, MA 01721-9104. TEL 508-881-2800. FAX 508-881-0982. *1342*

MONITOR DE LA FARMACIA Y DE LA TERAPEUTICA.
Centros Farmaceuticos Nacional S.A., Julian Camarillo, 37, 28037 Madrid, Spain. TEL 17754-43-84. FAX 1-754-56-59. *5429*

MONTANA BUSINESS DIRECTORY.
American Business Directories 5711 S. 86th Circle, Box 27347, Omaha, NE 68127. TEL 402-593-4600. FAX 402-331-5481. *1627*

MONTANA BUSINESS QUARTERLY.
University of Montana, Bureau of Business and Economic Research, Missoula, MT 59812. TEL 406-243-5113. FAX 406-243-2086. Vendor(s): Information Access Co., University Microfilms International. *945*

MONTHLY CATALOG OF UNITED STATES GOVERNMENT PUBLICATIONS.
U.S. Government Printing Office, Superintendent of Documents, Washington, DC 20402-9341. Vendor(s): Knight-Ridder Information, Inc. (File no.66), Ovid Technologies, Inc.. *5932*

MONTHLY LABOR REVIEW.
U.S. Bureau of Labor Statistics, 2 Massachusetts Ave., N.E., Washington, DC 20212. TEL 202-606-5902. Vendor(s): Information Access Co., Knight-Ridder Information, Inc., University Microfilms International. *1223*

MONTHLY PLANET.
Nuclear Weapons Freeze of Santa Cruz County, 320 Cedar St., Ste. G., Santa Cruz, CA 95060-4362. TEL 408-429-8755. *5762*

MONTHLY PRODUCT ANNOUNCEMENT.
U.S. Bureau of the Census, Customer Services, Washington, DC 20233. TEL 301-457-4100. FAX 301-457-4714. Vendor(s): CompuServe, Inc., Knight-Ridder Information, Inc.. *5788*

MONTHLY REVIEW.
Monthly Review, 122 W. 27th St., 10th fl., New York, NY 10001. TEL 212-691-2555. FAX 212-727-3676. Vendor(s): Information Access Co., University Microfilms International. *5685*

MORE LIGHT UPDATE.
Presbyterians for Lesbian & Gay Concerns, Inc., Box 38, New Brunswick, NJ 08903-0038. TEL 908-249-1016. *3535*

MORTGAGE-BACKED SECURITIES LETTER.
Investment Dealers' Digest, 2 World Trade Center, 18th Fl., New York, NY 10048-0638. TEL 212-432-0045. FAX 212-321-2336. Vendor(s): Information Access Co., University Microfilms International. *1343*

MORTGAGE BANKING.
Mortgage Bankers Association of America, 1125 15th St., N.W., Washington, DC 20005-2766. TEL 202-861-1930. FAX 202-861-1930. Vendor(s): Information Access Co.. *1110*

THE MORTGAGE MARKETPLACE.
American Banker - Bond Buyer, Newsletter Division One State St. Plaza, New York, NY 10004-1549. TEL 800-733-4371. FAX 212-943-2224. Vendor(s): Information Access Co.. *1343*

MOSAIC (WINNIPEG, 1967).
University of Manitoba, 208 Tier Bldg., Winnipeg, MB R3T 2N2, Canada. TEL 204-474-9763. FAX 204-261-9086. Vendor(s): Information Access Co.. *4239*

MOSCOW NEWS.
16-2 Tverckaya ul., Moscow, Russia. TEL 7095-209-1984. FAX 7095-209-0267. Vendor(s): Knight-Ridder Information, Inc., GBI. *3209*

MOTHER EARTH NEWS.
Sussex Publishers Inc., 49 E. 21st St., 11th Fl., New York, NY 10010. TEL 212-260-7210. FAX 212-260-7445. Vendor(s): Information Access Co., University Microfilms International. *3233*

MOTHER JONES.
Foundation for National Progress, 731 Market St., Ste. 600, San Francisco, CA 94103. TEL 415-665-6637. FAX 415-665-6696. Vendor(s): CompuServe, Inc., Information Access Co., Knight-Ridder Information, Inc.. *4155*

MOTHERING.
Mothering Magazine, Box 1690, Santa Fe, NM 87504. FAX 505-986-8335. Vendor(s): Information Access Co.. *6985*

MOTOR BOATING & SAILING.
Hearst Magazines, Motor Boating & Sailing, 959 Eighth Ave., New York, NY 10019. TEL 212-649-4092. FAX 212-489-9258. Vendor(s): Information Access Co.. *6537*

MOTOR BUSINESS EUROPE.
Economist Intelligence Unit, 111 W. 57th St., New York, NY 10019. TEL 212-554-0600. FAX 212-586-1182. *6793*

MOTOR BUSINESS INTERNATIONAL.
Economist Intelligence Unit, 111 W. 57th St., New York, NY 10019. TEL 212-554-0600. FAX 212-586-1182. *6793*

MOTOR BUSINESS JAPAN.
Economist Intelligence Unit, 111 W. 57th St., New York, NY 10019. TEL 212-554-0600. FAX 212-586-1182. *6793*

MOTOR TREND.
Petersen Publishing Co., 6420 Wilshire Blvd., Los Angeles, CA 90048. TEL 213-782-2220. FAX 213-782-2866. Vendor(s): Information Access Co., Knight-Ridder Information, Inc.. *6794*

MOTORCYCLE SHOPPER.
Payne Corp., 1353 Herndon Ave., Deltona, FL 32725-9046. TEL 407-860-1989. FAX 407-574-1014. *6526*

MOUNT SINAI JOURNAL OF MEDICINE.
Mount Sinai Hospital Committee on Medical Education and Publications, 50 E. 98th St., Box 1094, New York, NY 10029. TEL 212-241-6108. FAX 212-722-6386. Vendor(s): Knight-Ridder Information, Inc.. *4504*

MOUNTAIN XPRESS.
Mountain Xpress, Inc., Box 144, Asheville, NC 28802. TEL 704-251-1333. FAX 704-251-1311. *3233*

MPLS. - ST. PAUL MAGAZINE.
M S P Communications, Pillsbury Ctr., S. Tower, 220 S. Sixth St., Ste. 500, Minneapolis, MN 55402. TEL 612-339-7571. Vendor(s): Information Access Co., University Microfilms International. *3233*

MULTICHANNEL NEWS.
Capital Cities - A B C, Inc., Diversified Publishing Group, 825 Seventh Ave., New York, NY 10019. TEL 212-887-8400. Vendor(s): Information Access Co.. *1965*

MULTIMEDIA.
HighText Verlag, Seitzstr. 9, 80538 Munich, Germany. TEL 49-89-29160088. FAX 49-89-2904398. *1928*

MULTIMEDIA BUSINESS REPORT.
SIMBA Information Inc. 11 Riverbend Dr. S., Box 4234, Stamford, CT 06907-0234. TEL 203-358-9900. FAX 203-358-5824. Vendor(s): Information Access Co.. *1911*

MULTIMEDIA COMPUTING & PRESENTATIONS.
Multimedia Computing Corporation, P.O. Box 60369, Sunnyvale, CA 94088-0369. TEL 408-737-7575. FAX 408-739-8019. *2113*

MULTIMEDIA MONITOR.
Future Systems Inc., Box 26, Falls Church, VA 22040. TEL 703-241-1799. FAX 703-532-0529. Vendor(s): Information Access Co., Knight-Ridder Information, Inc., NewsNet (EC70). *2057*

MULTIMEDIA PUBLISHER.
Worldwide Videotex, Box 3273, Boynton Beach, FL 33424-3273. TEL 407-738-2276. Vendor(s): Information Access Co.. *1928*

MULTIMEDIA SCHOOLS.
Online Inc., 462 Danbury Rd., Wilton, CT 06897-2126. TEL 203-761-1466. FAX 203-761-1444. *2407*

MULTIMEDIA WEEK.
Phillips Business Information, Inc., 1201 Seven Locks Rd., Potomac, MD 20854. TEL 301-424-3338. FAX 301-309-3847. Vendor(s): Information Access Co.. *2029*

MULTINATIONAL BUSINESS REVIEW.
University of Detroit Mercy, College of Business Administration, Box 199C0, Detroit, MI 48219-0900. TEL 313-993-1264. FAX 313-993-1052. Vendor(s): University Microfilms International. *1290*

MULTINATIONAL MONITOR.
Essential Information, Box 19405, Washington, DC 20036. TEL 202-387-8034. FAX 202-234-5176. Vendor(s): Information Access Co.. *1290*

MULTINATIONAL SERVICE.
Europe Information Service, Rue de Geneve, 6, 1140 Brussels, Belgium. TEL 32-2-242-6020. FAX 32-2-242-9410. Vendor(s): Information Access Co., Lexis-Nexis. *1290*

MUNICIPAL AND INDUSTRIAL WATER AND POLLUTION CONTROL.
Zanny Publications Ltd., 1C 966 Woodbine Ave., Gormley, ON L0H 1G0, Canada. TEL 905-887-5048. FAX 905-479-4839. Vendor(s): Information Access Co.. *2838*

MUSIC ACCESS.
Music Access, Inc., 90 Fifth Ave., Brooklyn, NY 11217. TEL 718-398-2146. FAX 718-230-5539. *5175*

MUSIC AND LETTERS.
Oxford University Press, Oxford Journals, Walton St., Oxford OX2 6DP, England. TEL 44-1865-267907. FAX 44-1865-267773. Vendor(s): Information Access Co.. *5175*

MUSIC & MEDIA.
B P I Communications, Rijnsburgstraat 11, 1059 AT Amsterdam, Netherlands. TEL 31-20-6691961. FAX 31-20-6691941. Vendor(s): Information Access Co.. *5175*

MUSIC TRADES.
Music Trades Corporation, c/o Paul A. Majeski, Ed., Box 432, 80 West St., Englewood, NJ 07631. TEL 201-871-1965. Vendor(s): Information Access Co.. *5177*

MUSIC WEEK.
Spotlight Publications Ltd. Ludgate House, 245 Blackfriars Rd., London SE1 9UR, England. TEL 44-171-620-3636. FAX 44-171-407-8036. Vendor(s): Information Access Co.. *5177*

MUSICOPYRIGHT INTELLIGENCE.
E.S. Proteus, 1657 The Farway, Ste. 123, Jenkintown, PA 19046. TEL 215-885-3154. Vendor(s): CompuServe, Inc. (71553,3665). *5342*

N A B E OUTLOOK & POLICY SURVEY.
National Association of Business Economists, 1233 20th St., N.W., Ste. 505, Washington, DC 20036-2304. TEL 202-463-6223. FAX 202-463-6239. Vendor(s): Information Access Co.. *1223*

N A B P NEWSLETTER.
National Association of Boards of Pharmacy, 700 Busse Hwy., Park Ridge, IL 60068-2402. TEL 708-698-6227. *5429*

N A C L A REPORT ON THE AMERICAS.
North American Congress on Latin America, Inc., 475 Riverside Dr., Rm. 454, New York, NY 10115. TEL 212-870-3146. FAX 212-870-3305. Vendor(s): Information Access Co.. *5762*

Online

N A S A PATENT ABSTRACTS BIBLIOGRAPHY: A CONTINUING BIBLIOGRAPHY. SECTION 2. INDEXES.
U.S. National Aeronautics and Space Administration, National Technology Transfer Center, c/o Wheeling Jesuit University, 316 Washington Ave., Wheeling, WV 26003. TEL 304-243-2440. FAX 304-243-4390.
Available only online. *5347*

N A S A THESAURUS SUPPLEMENT. PART 1. HEIRARCHICAL LISTING.
U.S. National Aeronautics and Space Administration, National Technology Transfer Center, c/o Wheeling Jesuit University, 316 Washington Ave., Wheeling, WV 26003. TEL 304-243-2440. FAX 304-243-4390. *82*

N A S A THESAURUS SUPPLEMENT. PART 2. ACCESS VOCABULARY.
U.S. National Aeronautics and Space Administration, National Technology Transfer Center, c/o Wheeling Jesuit University, 316 Washington Ave., Wheeling, WV 26003. TEL 304-243-2440. FAX 304-243-4390. *82*

N A S A THESAURUS SUPPLEMENT. PART 3. DEFINITIONS.
U.S. National Aeronautics and Space Administration, National Technology Transfer Center, c/o Wheeling Jesuit University, 316 Washington Ave., Wheeling, WV 26003. TEL 304-243-2440. FAX 304-243-4390. *83*

N A S F A A NEWSLETTER.
National Association of Student Financial Aid Administrators, 1920 L St., N.W., Ste. 200, Washington, DC 20036-5020. TEL 202-785-0453. FAX 202-785-1487. *2436*

N A S I G NEWSLETTER.
North American Serials Interest Group, Northern Arizona Univ., Cline Library, Bibliographic Services, Flagstaff, AZ 86011. TEL 520-523-6779. FAX 520-523-3770. *4013*

N A T O ADVANCED SCIENCE INSTITUTES SERIES A: LIFE SCIENCES.
Plenum Publishing Corp., 233 Spring St., New York, NY 10013-1578. TEL 212-620-8000. FAX 212-463-0742.
Vendor(s): European Space Agency (File no.128). *596*

N A T O ADVANCED SCIENCE INSTITUTES SERIES B: PHYSICS.
Plenum Publishing Corp., 233 Spring St., New York, NY 10013-1578. TEL 212-620-8000. FAX 212-463-0742.
Vendor(s): European Space Agency (File no.128). *5560*

N A T O ADVANCED SCIENCE INSTITUTES SERIES C: MATHEMATICAL AND PHYSICAL SCIENCES.
Kluwer Academic Publishers, Postbus 17, 3300 AA Dordrecht, Netherlands. TEL 31-78-6392392. FAX 31-78-6392254.
Vendor(s): European Space Agency (File no.128). *4384*

N A T O ADVANCED SCIENCE INSTITUTES SERIES D: BEHAVIOURAL AND SOCIAL SCIENCES.
Kluwer Academic Publishers, Postbus 17, 3300 AA Dordrecht, Netherlands. TEL 31-78-6392392. FAX 31-78-6392254.
Vendor(s): European Space Agency (File no.128). *5866*

N A T O ADVANCED SCIENCE INSTITUTES SERIES E: APPLIED SCIENCES.
Kluwer Academic Publishers, Postbus 17, 3300 AA Dordrecht, Netherlands. TEL 31-78-6392392. FAX 31-78-6392254.
Vendor(s): European Space Agency (File no.128). *6658*

N A T O ADVANCED SCIENCE INSTITUTES SERIES F: COMPUTER AND SYSTEMS SCIENCES.
Kluwer Academic Publishers, Postbus 17, 3300 AA Dordrecht, Netherlands. TEL 31-78-6392392. FAX 31-78-6392254.
Vendor(s): European Space Agency (File no.128). *2057*

N A T O ADVANCED SCIENCE INSTITUTES SERIES G: ECOLOGICAL SCIENCES.
Kluwer Academic Publishers, Postbus 17, 3300 AA Dordrecht, Netherlands. TEL 31-78-6392392. FAX 31-78-6392254.
Vendor(s): European Space Agency (File no.128). *2811*

N A T O ADVANCED SCIENCE INSTITUTES SERIES H: CELL BIOLOGY.
Kluwer Academic Publishers, Postbus 17, 3300 AA Dordrecht, Netherlands. TEL 31-78-6392392. FAX 31-78-6392254.
Vendor(s): European Space Agency (File no.128). *717*

N A T O DATA.
North Atlantic Treaty Organization, Integrated Data Service, Leopold III Laan, Brussels 1110, Belgium. TEL 32-2-7284599. FAX 32-2-7285229.
Available only online. *5040*

N A T O SCIENTIFIC PUBLICATIONS. NEWSLETTER.
N A T O Publication Coordination Office, Elcerlyclaan 2, B-3090 Overijse, Belgium. TEL 32-2-6876636. *6260*

N B A INSIDE STUFF.
Quarton Group Publishers, Inc., 888 W. Big Beaver Rd., Ste. 600, Troy, MI 48084. TEL 810-362-7400. *6508*

N C A H F NEWSLETTER.
National Council Against Health Fraud, Inc., Box 1276, Loma Linda, CA 92354. TEL 909-824-4690. FAX 909-824-4838.
Vendor(s): Information Access Co., University Microfilms International. *5970*

N C J R S DOCUMENT RETRIEVAL INDEX.
U.S. National Institute of Justice, National Criminal Justice Reference Service, Box 6000, Department F, Rockville, MD 20850. TEL 301-251-5500. FAX 301-251-5212.
Vendor(s): Knight-Ridder Information, Inc.. *2180*

N D A PIPELINE.
F-D-C Reports, Inc., 5550 Friendship Blvd., Ste. 1, Chevy Chase, MD 20815. FAX 301-664-7238.
Vendor(s): Data-Star (NDAP). *5429*

N E A TODAY.
National Education Association of the United States, 1201 16th St., N.W., Washington, DC 20036. TEL 202-822-7207. FAX 202-822-7206.
Vendor(s): Information Access Co., University Microfilms International. *2355*

N I O S H T I C DATABASE.
U.S. National Technical Information Service, 5285 Port Royal Rd., Springfield, VA 22161. TEL 703-487-4630.
Vendor(s): Knight-Ridder Information, Inc., Orbit Search Service. *5253*

N P NEWS.
Springhouse Corporation 1111 Bethlehem Pike, Box 908, Springhouse, PA 19477. TEL 215-646-8700.
Vendor(s): University Microfilms International. *4721*

N S F BULLETIN.
U.S. National Science Foundation, 4201 Wilson Blvd., Ste. 245, Arlington, VA 22230. *6260*

N T I S ALERTS: FOREIGN TECHNOLOGY.
U.S. National Technical Information Service, 5285 Port Royal Rd., Springfield, VA 22161. TEL 703-487-4630. FAX 703-321-8547.
Vendor(s): Information Access Co.. *6672*

N T I S BIBLIOGRAPHIC DATA BASE.
U.S. National Technical Information Service, 5285 Port Royal Rd., Springfield, VA 22161. TEL 703-487-4630.
Vendor(s): Data-Star, Knight-Ridder Information, Inc., Orbit Search Service, Ovid Technologies, Inc., STN International. *6017*

N T T TOPICS.
Ruder, Finn & Rotman, N T T Information Desk, 301 E. 57th St., New York, NY 10022.
Vendor(s): Information Access Co.. *1948*

N U C O M 6.
National Library of Australia, Publications Section, Cultural and Educational Services Division, Canberra, A.C.T. 2600, Australia. TEL 61-6-262-1365. FAX 61-6-273-4493. *540*

AN NAHAR.
An Nahar S.C.P.A., Banque du Liban St., P.O. Box 11-0226, Beirut, Lebanon. TEL 961-1-340960. FAX 961-1-340960. *3190*

DIE NAHRUNGS- UND GENUSSMITTEL-INDUSTRIE UND IHRE HELFER.
Industrieschau-Verlagsgesellschaft mbH, Postfach 100262, 64202 Darmstadt, Germany. TEL 49-6151-38920. FAX 49-6151-33164. *2985*

NAMIBIA TRADE DIRECTORY.
Namibia Trade Directory CC, P.O. Box 21593, Windhoek, Namibia. TEL 264-61-225665. FAX 264-61-220410. *1628*

NANJING HUAGONG XUEYUAN XUEBAO.
Nanjing Huagong Xueyuan, 5 Xinmofan Malu, Nanjing, Jiangsu 210009, People's Republic of China. TEL 316755. FAX 307716.
Vendor(s): Knight-Ridder Information, Inc.. *2645*

NANOTECHNOLOGY.
I O P Publishing Ltd., Techno House, Redcliffe Way, Bristol, Avon BS1 6NX, England. TEL 44-117-929-7481. FAX 44-117-929-4318. *5560*

NASHVILLE BUSINESS JOURNAL.
Mid-South Communications, Box 23229, Nashville, TN 37202. TEL 615-248-2222. FAX 615-248-6246.
Vendor(s): Lexis-Nexis, University Microfilms International. *946*

THE NATION.
The Nation Company, L.P., 72 Fifth Ave., New York, NY 10011. TEL 212-242-8400. FAX 212-463-9712.
Vendor(s): Information Access Co.. *4155*

NATIONAL AGRICULTURAL STATISTICS SERVICE. CATTLE ON FEED.
U.S. Department of Agriculture, National Agricultural Statistics Service, Independence Ave., between 12th & 14th Sts., S.W., South Bldg., Rm. 4117, Washington, DC 20250. TEL 202-655-4000.
Vendor(s): Knight-Ridder Information, Inc.. *177*

NATIONAL ASSOCIATION OF BOARDS OF PHARMACY. PROCEEDINGS.
National Association of Boards of Pharmacy, 700 Busse Hwy., Park Ridge, IL 60068-2402. TEL 708-698-6227. *5429*

NATIONAL ASSOCIATION OF INSURANCE COMMISSIONERS. PROCEEDINGS.
National Association of Insurance Commissioners, 120 W. 12th St., Kansas City, MO 64105. TEL 816-374-7259.
Vendor(s): Lexis-Nexis. *3659*

NATIONAL BIBLIOGRAPHY OF BARBADOS.
National Library Service, Culloden Farm, Culloden Rd., St. Michael, Barbados, W.I. TEL 809-429-5716. FAX 809-436-1501. *540*

THE NATIONAL BOOK OF BUSINESS LISTS.
Reference Press, Inc., Box 140375, Austin, TX 78714-0375. TEL 512-454-7778. FAX 512-454-9401. *1628*

NATIONAL BUSINESS REVIEW.
Fourth Estate Holdings Ltd., P.O. Box 1734, Auckland, New Zealand. TEL 64-9-307-1629. FAX 64-9-373-3997.
Vendor(s): Kiwinet. *1224*

NATIONAL CANCER INSTITUTE. JOURNAL.
Oxford University Press, Oxford Journals, Walton St., Oxford OX2 6DP, England. TEL 44-1865-267907. FAX 44-1865-267485.
Vendor(s): Lexis-Nexis, Ovid Technologies, Inc.. *4760*

NATIONAL CATHOLIC REPORTER.
National Catholic Reporter Publishing Company, Inc., 115 E. Armour Blvd., Box 419281, Kansas City, MO 64141. TEL 816-531-0538. FAX 816-968-2280.
Vendor(s): Information Access Co.. *6189*

NATIONAL CIVIC REVIEW.
National Civic League, Inc., 1445 Market St., Ste. 300, Denver, CO 80202-1728. TEL 303-571-4343.
Vendor(s): Information Access Co., University Microfilms International. *5947*

NATIONAL CONTRACT MANAGEMENT JOURNAL.
National Contract Management Association, 1912 Woodford Rd., Vienna, VA 22182-3728.
Vendor(s): University Microfilms International. *1436*

NATIONAL COUNCIL ON FAMILY RELATIONS. REPORT.
National Council on Family Relations, 3989 Central Ave., N.E., Ste. 550, Minneapolis, MN 55421-3921. TEL 612-781-9331. FAX 612-781-9348. *6423*

NATIONAL DIRECTORY OF LAW ENFORCEMENT ADMINISTRATORS AND CORRECTIONAL INSTITUTIONS.
National Police Chiefs & Sheriffs Information Bureau, Box 365, Stevens Point, WI 54481. TEL 800-647-7579. FAX 715-345-7288.
Vendor(s): Lexis-Nexis. *2170*

NATIONAL FISHERMAN.
Journal Publications (Rockland), Box 7238, Portland, ME 04112-7438. TEL 207-842-5608. FAX 207-842-5609.
Vendor(s): Information Access Co.. *2939*

NATIONAL FORUM (AUBURN).
Honor Society of Phi Kappa Phi (Auburn), c/o Dr. James P. Kaetz, Ed., 129 Quad Center, Mell St., Auburn, AL 36849-5306. TEL 334-844-5200. FAX 334-844-5994.
Vendor(s): Information Access Co., University Microfilms International. *1878*

NATIONAL HOME CENTER NEWS.
Lebhar-Friedman, Inc., 425 Park Ave., New York, NY 10022. TEL 212-756-5000.
Vendor(s): Information Access Co.. *867*

NATIONAL INSTITUTE ECONOMIC REVIEW.
National Institute of Economic and Social Research, 2 Dean Trench St., Smith Sq., London SW1P 3HE, England. TEL 44-171-222-7665. FAX 44-171-222-1435.
Vendor(s): Information Access Co., University Microfilms International. *946*

THE NATIONAL INTEREST.
National Affairs, Inc., 1112 16th St., N.W., Ste. 540., Washington, DC 20036. TEL 202-467-4884. FAX 202-467-0006.
Vendor(s): Information Access Co.. *5763*

NATIONAL JEWELER.
Miller Freeman Inc. (New York) One Penn Plaza, New York, NY 10119. TEL 212-714-1300. FAX 212-279-3960. *3697*

NATIONAL JOURNAL.
National Journal, Inc. 1501 M St., N.W., Ste. 300, Washington, DC 20005. TEL 202-739-8400. FAX 202-833-8069.
Vendor(s): University Microfilms International. *5685*

NATIONAL LAW JOURNAL.
New York Law Publishing Co., 345 Park Ave. S., New York, NY 10010. TEL 212-779-9200.
Vendor(s): Lexis-Nexis. *3820*

NATIONAL MEDICAL ASSOCIATION. JOURNAL.
Slack, Inc., 6900 Grove Rd., Thorofare, NJ 08086-9447. TEL 609-848-1000. FAX 609-853-5991. *4506*

NATIONAL MORTGAGE NEWS.
Faulkner & Gray, 22nd Fl., 11 Penn Plaza, New York, NY 10001. TEL 212-967-7000. FAX 212-564-8879.
Vendor(s): University Microfilms International. *1111*

NATIONAL NEWSPAPER INDEX.
Information Access Company 362 Lakeside Dr., Foster City, CA 94404. TEL 415-378-5200. FAX 415-378-5369.
Vendor(s): Knight-Ridder Information, Inc. (File no.111), Lexis-Nexis, Ovid Technologies, Inc. (NOOZ). *3715*

NATIONAL PARKS.
National Parks and Conservation Association, 1776 Massachusetts Ave., N.W., Washington, DC 20036. TEL 202-223-6722 FAX 202-659-0650.
Vendor(s): Information Access Co., University Microfilms International. *3966*

NATIONAL PETROLEUM NEWS.
Hunter Publishing Limited Partnership, 2101 S. Arlington Heights, Arlington Heights, IL 60005. TEL 708-427-9512 FAX 708-427-2006.
Vendor(s): Information Access Co., Knight-Ridder Information, Inc.. *5364*

NATIONAL PHARMACEUTICAL ASSOCIATION. JOURNAL.
National Pharmaceutical Association, Inc., c/o Texas Southern University, College of Pharmacy, 3100 Cleburne, Houston, TX 77004. TEL 713-527-7164. FAX 713-639-1091. *5429*

NATIONAL POLICY WATCH.
National Center for Public Policy Research, 300 Eye St., N.E., Ste. 3, Washington, DC 20002. TEL 202-543-1286. FAX 202-543-4779. *5686*

NATIONAL PRODUCTIVITY REVIEW.
John Wiley & Sons, Inc., Journals, 605 Third Ave., New York, NY 10158. TEL 212-850-6645. FAX 212-850-6021.
Vendor(s): Information Access Co.. *1437*

NATIONAL PUBLIC ACCOUNTANT.
National Society of Public Accountants, 1010 N. Fairfax St., Alexandria, VA 22314. TEL 703-549-6400.
Vendor(s): University Microfilms International. *1051*

NATIONAL REAL ESTATE INVESTOR.
Intertec Publishing Corp. (Atlanta), 6151 Powers Ferry Rd., N.W., Atlanta, GA 30339-2941. TEL 770-955-2500. FAX 770-955-0400.
Vendor(s): Information Access Co., University Microfilms International. *6031*

NATIONAL REPORT ON COMPUTERS AND HEALTH.
United Communications Group, 11300 Rockville Pike, Ste. 1100, Rockville, MD 20852-3030. TEL 301-816-8950. FAX 301-816-8945.
Vendor(s): Data-Star, Information Access Co., Knight-Ridder Information, Inc.. *4632*

NATIONAL REPORT ON SUBSTANCE ABUSE.
L R P Publications 747 Dresher Rd., Box 908, Horsham, PA 19044-0980. TEL 215-784-0941. FAX 215-784-9639.
Vendor(s): Human Resources Information Network (CDD, HDD). *2199*

NATIONAL REPORT ON WORK & FAMILY.
Business Publishers, Inc., 951 Pershing Dr., Silver Spring, MD 20910-4464. TEL 301-587-6300. FAX 301-585-9075.
Vendor(s): Human Resources Information Network. *5271*

NATIONAL REPORTER.
Maritime Law Book Ltd., Box 302, Fredericton, NB E3B 4Y9, Canada. TEL 506-453-9921. FAX 506-453-9525.
Vendor(s): QL Systems Ltd.. *3820*

NATIONAL REVIEW.
National Review, Inc., 150 E. 35th St., New York, NY 10016. TEL 212-679-7330. FAX 212-696-0309.
Vendor(s): Information Access Co., Knight-Ridder Information, Inc.. *5686*

NATIONAL SCIENCE FOUNDATION. DIRECTORATE FOR ENGINEERING. ENGINEERING NEWS.
National Science Foundation, Directorate for Engineering, 4201 Wilson Blvd., Rm 505, Arlington, VA 22230. TEL 703-306-1300. *2611*

NATIONAL TAX JOURNAL.
National Tax Association - Tax Institute of America, 5310 E. Main St., Ste. 104, Columbus, OH 43213. TEL 614-864-1221. FAX 614-864-1375.
Vendor(s): Information Access Co.. *1555*

NATIONAL UNDERWRITER. LIFE AND HEALTH - HEALTH & FINANCIAL SERVICES EDITION.
National Underwriter Co., 505 Gest St., Cincinnati, OH 45203-1716. TEL 513-721-2140. FAX 513-721-0126.
Vendor(s): Information Access Co., University Microfilms International. *3660*

NATIONAL UNDERWRITER. PROPERTY & CASUALTY - RISK & BENEFITS MANAGEMENT EDITION.
National Underwriter Co., 505 Gest St., Cincinnati, OH 45203. TEL 513-721-2140 FAX 513-721-0126.
Vendor(s): Information Access Co., University Microfilms International. *3660*

NATIONAL WATER RIGHTS DIGEST.
Ridenbaugh Press, Box 2276, Boise, ID 83701. TEL 208-338-9700. FAX 208-338-9769. *6973*

NATIONAL WILDLIFE.
National Wildlife Federation, 1400 16th St., N.W., Washington, DC 20036-2266. TEL 202-797-6800.
Vendor(s): Information Access Co.. *2135*

NATIONAL WRITING PROJECT. CENTER FOR THE STUDY OF WRITING. QUARTERLY.
National Writing Project, Center for the Study of Writing, Tolman Hall, University of California, Berkeley, CA 94720. TEL 510-642-0976. *2496*

NATION'S BUSINESS.
U.S. Chamber of Commerce, 1615 H St., N.W., Washington, DC 20062-2000. TEL 202-463-5650. FAX 202-887-3437.
Vencor(s): Information Access Co., University Microfilms International. *1146*

NATION'S CITIES WEEKLY.
National League of Cities, 1301 Pennsylvania Ave., N.W., Washington, DC 20004. TEL 202-626-3040.
Vendor(s): Information Access Co.. *5947*

NATION'S RESTAURANT NEWS.
Lebhar-Friedman, Inc., 425 Park Ave., New York, NY 10022. TEL 212-756-5000. FAX 212-838-9487.
Vendor(s): Information Access Co., University Microfilms International. *3568*

NATURAL HEALTH.
Natural Health L.P., 17 Station St., Box 1200, Brookline, MA 02147. TEL 617-232-1000. FAX 617-232-1572.
Vendor(s): Information Access Co.. *292*

NATURAL HISTORY.
American Museum of Natural History, Central Park W. at 79th St., New York, NY 10024-5192. TEL 212-769-5500. FAX 212-769-5511.
Vendor(s): Information Access Co., Knight-Ridder Information, Inc., University Microfilms International. *6263*

NATURAL RESOURCES & ENVIRONMENT.
American Bar Association Natural Resources, Energy, and Environmental Law Section, 750 N. Lake Shore Dr., Chicago IL 60611. TEL 312-988-5000.
Vendor(s): West Services, Inc.. *2135*

NATURE CONSERVANCY MAGAZINE.
Nature Conservancy, 1815 N. Lynn St., Arlington, VA 22209. TEL 703-841-5300. *2136*

NAVY NEWS & UNDERSEA TECHNOLOGY.
Pasha Publications Inc., 1616 N. Ft. Myer Dr., Ste. 1000, Arlington, VA 22209-3107. TEL 703-528-1244. FAX 703-528-1253.
Vendor(s): Information Access Co., NewsNet (DE18). *5042*

NEBRASKA BUSINESS DIRECTORY.
American Business Directories 5711 S. 86th Circle, Box 27347, Omaha, NE 68127. TEL 402-593-4600. FAX 402-331-5431. *1629*

NEBRASKA LAW REVIEW.
University of Nebraska at Lincoln, College of Law, Lincoln, NE 68583-0902. TEL 402-472-1267.
Vendor(s): Lexis-Nexis, West Services, Inc.. *3821*

NEBRASKA LIBRARIES: A DIRECTORY.
Nebraska Library Commission, 1200 N St., Nc. 120, Lincoln, NE 68508-2023 TEL 402-471-2045.
Available only online. *4015*

NEDERLANDS A B C DIENSTVERLENERS.
A B C voor Handel en Industrie C.V., P.O. Box 190, 2000 AD Haarlem, Netherlands. TEL 31-23-5319031. FAX 31-23-5327033.
Vendor(s): Data-Star. *1629*

NEDERLANDS A B C VOOR HANDEL EN INDUSTRIE.
A B C voor Handel en Industrie C.V., P.O. Box 190, 2000 AD Haarlem, Netherlands. TEL 31-23-5319031. FAX 31-23-5327033.
Vendor(s): Data-Star. *1629*

NEEDLE TIPS AND THE HEPATITIS B COALITION NEWS.
Immunization Action Coalition, 1573 Selby Ave., Ste. 229, St. Paul, MN 55104. TEL 612-647-9009. FAX 612-647-9131. *4586*

NEMATOLOGICAL ABSTRACTS.
CAB International, Wallingford, Oxon. OX10 8DE, England. TEL 44-1491-832111. FAX 44-1491-833508.
Vendor(s): CISTI, DIMDI, European Space Agency (File nos.16 & 124/CAB), Knight-Ridder Information, Inc., Ovid Technologies, Inc. (CABA). *177*

THE NETHERLANDER.
Het Financieele Dagblad B.V., P.O. Box 216, 1000 AE Amsterdam, Netherlands. TEL 31-20-5928888. FAX 31-20-5928600. *946*

NETWORK BRIEFING.
A P T Data Group plc., 12 Sutton Row, 4th Fl., London W1V 5FH, England. TEL 44-171-208-4200. FAX 44-171-439-1105.
Vendor(s): Information Access Co.. *1948*

NETWORK: COMPUTATION IN NEURAL SYSTEMS.
I O P Publishing Ltd., Techno House, Redcliffe Way, Bristol, Avon BS1 6NX, England. TEL 44-117-929-7481. FAX 44-117-929-4318. *6306*

NETWORK COMPUTING (MANHASSET).
C M P Publications, Inc., 600 Community Dr., Manhasset, NY 11030. TEL 516-562-5000. FAX 516-365-4601.
Vendor(s): Information Access Co.. *2040*

NETWORK V A R.
Miller Freeman, Inc. 600 Harrison St., San Francisco, CA 94107. TEL 415-905-2200. FAX 415-905-2232.
Vendor(s): Information Access Co.. *2040*

NETWORK WORLD.
Network World Inc., 161 Worcester Rd., 5th Fl., Framingham, MA 01701. TEL 508-875-6400. FAX 508-879-3167.
Vendor(s): Knight-Ridder Information, Inc. (File no.674), Lexis-Nexis, University Microfilms International. *2040*

NETWORKS UPDATE.
Worldwide Videotex, Box 3273, Boynton Beach, FL 33424-3273. TEL 407-738-2276.
Vendor(s): Data-Star, Information Access Co., Knight-Ridder Information, Inc., NewsNet (EC95). *2040*

NEUROLOGICAL SURGERY.
Igaku Shoin Ltd., 24-3 Hongo 5-chome, Bunkyo-ku, Tokyo 113-91, Japan. TEL 03-817-5702.
Vendor(s): JICST. *4915*

NEUROSCIENCE COMMUNICATIONS.
Gordon & Breach Science Publishers, c/o International Publishers Distributor, P.O. Box 3054, Langhorne, PA 19047-3054. TEL 215-750-2642. FAX 215-750-6343. *4569*

NEVADA BUSINESS DIRECTORY.
American Business Directories 5711 S. 86th Circle, Box 27347, Omaha, NE 68127. TEL 402-593-4600. FAX 402-331-5481. *1630*

NEVADA LAWYER.
State Bar of Nevada, 1325 Airmotive Way, Ste. 140, Reno, NV 89502-3239. TEL 702-329-4100. FAX 702-329-0522.
Vendor(s): Lexis-Nexis, West Services, Inc.. *3821*

NEVADA WAGE SURVEY.
Employment, Training and Rehabilitation Department, Employment Security Division, 500 E. Third St., Carson City, NV 89713. TEL 702-687-4550. *1389*

NEW ACCOUNTANT.
Real Estate News Corp., 3525 W. Petersen Ave., Chicago, IL 60659.
Vendor(s): University Microfilms International. *1052*

NEW AFRICAN.
I.C. Publications Ltd., 7 Coldbath Sq., London EC1R 4LQ, England. TEL 44-171-713-7711. FAX 44-171-713-7898. *1311*

NEW ASTRONOMY.
Elsevier Science B.V., P.O. Box 211, 1000 AE Amsterdam, Netherlands. TEL 31-20-4853911. FAX 31-20-4853705. *484*

NEW BRUNSWICK REPORTS.
Maritime Law Book Ltd., Box 302, Fredericton, NB E3B 4Y9, Canada. TEL 506-453-9921. FAX 506-453-9525.
Vendor(s): QL Systems Ltd.. *3822*

NEW ENGLAND ECONOMIC INDICATORS.
Federal Reserve Bank of Boston, Research Department, 600 Atlantic Ave., Boston, MA 02106. TEL 617-973-3397. FAX 617-973-4292. *1224*

NEW ENGLAND ECONOMIC REVIEW.
Federal Reserve Bank of Boston, Research Department, Research Library D, Box 2076, Boston, MA 02106-2076. TEL 617-973-3397. FAX 617-973-4292.
Vendor(s): Information Access Co.. *1224*

NEW ENGLAND JOURNAL OF MEDICINE.
Massachusetts Medical Society, 10 Shattuck St., Boston, MA 02115. TEL 617-734-9800. FAX 617-893-8103.
Vendor(s): Ovid Technologies, Inc. (NEJM). *4507*

NEW ENGLAND LAW REVIEW.
New England School of Law, New England Law Review, 154 Stuart St., Boston, MA 02116. TEL 617-422-7294. FAX 617-422-7451.
Vendor(s): Lexis-Nexis, West Services, Inc.. *3822*

NEW FRONTIER.
New Frontier Education Society, 41 White Oak Rd., Arden, NC 28704-9557. TEL 704-251-0109. FAX 704-251-0727. *5219*

NEW GERMAN REVIEW.
University of California at Los Angeles, Department of Germanic Languages, 302 Royce Hall, Los Angeles, CA 90034. TEL 310-825-3955. FAX 310-825-7954. *4242*

NEW HAMPSHIRE BUSINESS DIRECTORY.
American Business Directories 5711 S. 86th Circle, Box 27347, Omaha, NE 68127. TEL 402-593-4600. FAX 402-331-5481. *1630*

NEW HAMPSHIRE BUSINESS REVIEW.
Business Publications, Inc. (Manchester), 150 Dow St., Manchester, NH 03101-1227. TEL 603-624-1442. FAX 603-624-1310.
Vendor(s): Knight-Ridder Information, Inc., University Microfilms International. *1168*

NEW JERSEY BUSINESS.
New Jersey Business Magazine, 310 Passaic Ave., Fairfield, NJ 07004. TEL 201-882-5004.
Vendor(s): Lexis-Nexis, University Microfilms International. *1527*

NEW JERSEY BUSINESS DIRECTORY.
American Business Directories 5711 S. 86th Circle, Box 27347, Omaha, NE 68127. TEL 402-593-4600. FAX 402-331-5481. *1630*

NEW JERSEY INDUSTRY ENVIRONMENTAL ALERT.
Business & Legal Reports, Inc., Attn: Carin Roaldset, 39 Academy St., Madison, CT 06443. TEL 203-245-7448. FAX 203-245-2559.
Vendor(s): Information Access Co.. *2812*

NEW JERSEY LAW JOURNAL.
American Lawyer Media, L.P. (Newark), 238 Mulberry St., Box 20081, Newark, NJ 07101-6081. TEL 201-642-0075. FAX 201-642-0920.
Vendor(s): Lexis-Nexis. *3822*

NEW JERSEY LAWYER (NEW BRUNSWICK).
New Jersey State Bar Association, 1 Constitution Sq., New Brunswick, NJ 08901. TEL 908-249-5000.
Vendor(s): West Services, Inc.. *3822*

NEW LAW JOURNAL.
Butterworth & Co. (Publishers) Ltd., Part of the Reed Elsevier group, Halsbury House, 35 Chancery Ln., London WC2A 1EL, England. TEL 071-400-2500. FAX 071-400-2842.
Vendor(s): Lexis-Nexis. *3822*

THE NEW LEADER.
American Labor Conference on International Affairs, Inc., 275 Seventh Ave., New York, NY 10001. TEL 212-807-8240. FAX 212-727-2229.
Vendor(s): Information Access Co., Knight-Ridder Information, Inc.. *3233*

NEW LITERARY HISTORY.
Johns Hopkins University Press, Journals Publishing Division, 2715 N. Charles St., Baltimore, MD 21218. TEL 410-516-6987. FAX 410-516-6968.
Vendor(s): Information Access Co.. *4242*

NEW MANUFACTURING PROCESSES AND MATERIALS SERIES.
Chapman & Hall 2-6 Boundary Row, London SE1 8HN, England. TEL 44-171-8560066. FAX 44-171-5229623. *2740*

NEW MATERIALS - JAPAN.
International Newsletters, P.O. Box 133, Witney, Oxon OX8 6ZH, England.
Vendor(s): Data-Star, Information Access Co., Knight-Ridder Information, Inc.. *6659*

NEW MEDIA MARKETS.
Financial Times Telecoms & Media Publishing Maple House, 149 Tottenham Court Rd., London W1P 9LL, England. TEL 0171-896-2234. FAX 0171-896-2256.
Vendor(s): Information Access Co.. *1966*

NEW MEXICO BUSINESS DIRECTORY.
American Business Directories 5711 S. 86th Circle, Box 27347, Omaha, NE 68127. TEL 402-593-4600. FAX 402-331-5481. *1630*

NEW MEXICO BUSINESS JOURNAL.
Sierra Publishing Group, Inc., Box 30550, Albuquerque, NM 87190-0550. TEL 505-889-2911. FAX 505-889-0822.
Vendor(s): Information Access Co., Knight-Ridder Information, Inc., University Microfilms International. *947*

NEW MEXICO LAW REVIEW.
University of New Mexico, School of Law, 1117 Stanford, N.E., Albuquerque, NM 87131. TEL 505-277-8659.
Vendor(s): Lexis-Nexis, West Services, Inc.. *3823*

NEW ORLEANS CITYBUSINESS.
New Orleans City Business, 111 Veterans Blvd., Ste. 1830, Metairie, LA 70005. TEL 504-834-9292. FAX 504-837-2258.
Vendor(s): Knight-Ridder Information, Inc., Lexis-Nexis, University Microfilms International. *1578*

NEW ORLEANS MAGAZINE.
New Orleans Publishing Group, 111 Veterans Blvd., Ste. 1810, Metairie, LA 70005. TEL 504-831-3731. FAX 504-837-2258.
Vendor(s): Information Access Co., University Microfilms International. *3234*

NEW PERSPECTIVES QUARTERLY.
Blackwell Publishers, 238 Main St., Cambridge, MA 02142. TEL 617-547-7110. FAX 617-547-0789.
Vendor(s): Information Access Co., University Microfilms International. *5687*

NEW POLITICAL SCIENCE.
Caucus for a New Political Science, c/o John C. Berg, Treas., Department of Government, Suffolk University, Boston, MA 02108-2770. TEL 617-573-8126. FAX 617-367-4623. *5687*

NEW PRODUCT LAUNCH LETTER.
IMSWORLD Publications Ltd., 7 Harewood Ave., London NW1 6JB, England. TEL 0171-393-5000. FAX 0171-393-5900.
Vendor(s): Data-Star. *5430*

NEW PRODUCT NEWS.
Trend Publishing Inc., 625 N. Michigan Ave., Ste. 2500, Chicago, IL 60611-3109. TEL 312-654-2300. FAX 312-654-2323.
Vendor(s): Information Access Co., Lexis-Nexis. *2985*

THE NEW REPUBLIC.
1220 19th St., N.W., Washington, DC 20036.
TEL 202-331-7494. FAX 202-331-0275.
Vendor(s): Information Access Co., Knight-Ridder
Information, Inc., University Microfilms International.
4156

NEW SCIENTIST.
I P C Magazines, Specialist Magazine Group King's
Reach Tower, Stamford St., London SE1 9LS,
England. TEL 44-171-261-5000. FAX 44-1444-
445599.
Vendor(s): Information Access Co., VU/TEXT
Information Services, Inc.. *6266*

NEW SOUTH WALES LAW REPORTS.
L B C Information Services, 50 Waterloo Rd., N.
Ryde, N.S.W. 2113, Australia. TEL 61-2-
99366444. FAX 61-2-8889706.
Vendor(s): Info-One International Pty Ltd.. *3951*

NEW STATESMAN.
New Statesman Ltd., 7th Fl., Victoria Station House,
191 Victoria St., London SW9E 5NE, England.
TEL 44-171-828-1232. FAX 44-171-828-1881.
Vendor(s): Information Access Co., University
Microfilms International. *4157*

NEW STEEL.
Hitchcock Publishing 191 S. Gary Ave., Carol
Stream, IL 60188. TEL 708-462-4641. FAX 708-
462-2205.
Vendor(s): Information Access Co., Knight-Ridder
Information, Inc.. *4969*

NEW TECHNOLOGY WEEK.
King Publishing Group, Inc., 627 National Press
Bldg., Washington, DC 20045. TEL 202-638-4260.
FAX 202-662-9744.
Vendor(s): Data-Star, Information Access Co.,
Knight-Ridder Information, Inc., Lexis-Nexis,
NewsNet (RD23). *6659*

NEW WAVES (COLLEGE STATION).
Texas Water Resources Institute, c/o Texas A & M
Univ., Texas Agricultural Experiment Sta., College
Station, TX 77843-2118. TEL 409-845-8571.
FAX 409-845-8554. *6973*

NEW YORK BUSINESS DIRECTORY.
American Business Directories 5711 S. 86th Circle,
Box 27347, Omaha, NE 68127. TEL 402-593-
4600. FAX 402-331-5481. *1630*

NEW YORK LAW JOURNAL.
New York Law Publishing Co., 345 Park Ave. S.,
New York, NY 10010. TEL 212-779-9200.
Vendor(s): Lexis-Nexis, Wilsonline. *3823*

NEW YORK MAGAZINE.
K-III Communications Corp., 745 Fifth Ave., New
York, NY 10151. TEL 212-745-0100.
Vendor(s): Information Access Co.. *3234*

NEW YORK METRO BUSINESS DIRECTORY.
American Business Directories 5711 S. 86th Circle,
Box 27347, Omaha, NE 68127. TEL 402-593-
4600. FAX 402-331-5481. *1630*

NEW YORK REVIEW OF BOOKS.
N Y R E V, Inc., 250 W. 57th St., New York, NY
10107. TEL 212-757-8070. FAX 212-333-5374.
Vendor(s): University Microfilms International.
4157

NEW YORK STATE BAR JOURNAL.
New York State Bar Association, One Marine
Midland Plaza, Binghamton, NY 13902. FAX 607-
772-6093.
Vendor(s): West Services, Inc. (NYSTBJ). *3824*

NEW YORK STATE CONSERVATIONIST.
Department of Environmental Conservation, 50 Wolf
Rd., Albany, NY 12233. TEL 518-457-5547.
FAX 518-457-0858.
Vendor(s): University Microfilms International.
2136

THE NEW YORK TIMES.
New York Times Company, 229 W. 43rd St., New
York, NY 10036, TEL 212-556-1234. FAX 212-
556-4603.
Vendor(s): Lexis-Nexis, University Microfilms
International. *3234*

THE NEW YORK TIMES INDEX.
U M I Company 300 N. Zeeb Rd., Ann Arbor, MI
48106. TEL 313-751-4700. FAX 800-864-0019.
3715

NEW YORK UNIVERSITY LAW REVIEW.
New York University Law Review, 110 W. Third St.,
New York, NY 10012. TEL 212-998-6350.
FAX 212-995-4032.
Vendor(s): Lexis-Nexis, West Services, Inc.. *3824*

**NEW ZEALAND MANUFACTURER (WELLINGTON,
1992).**
New Zealand Manufacturers Federation, 3 Church
St., P.O. Box 11-543, Wellington 1, New Zealand.
TEL 64-4-4733-000. FAX 64-4-4733-004.
Vendor(s): University Microfilms International. *947*

NEW ZEALAND NATIONAL BIBLIOGRAPHY.
National Library of New Zealand, P.O. Box 1467,
Wellington, New Zealand. TEL 64-4-4743067.
FAX 64-4-4743124. *541*

NEW ZEALAND SERIALS.
National Library of New Zealand, P.O. Box 1467,
Wellington, New Zealand. TEL 64-4-7473067.
FAX 64-4-4743124. *541*

**NEWFOUNDLAND & PRINCE EDWARD ISLAND
REPORTS.**
Maritime Law Book Ltd., Box 302, Fredericton, NB
E3B 4Y9, Canada. TEL 506-453-9921. FAX 506-
453-9525.
Vendor(s): QL Systems Ltd.. *3825*

NEWS I S.
Xephon, 1301 W. Hwy. 407, Ste. 201-450,
Lewisville, TX 75067. TEL 817-455-7050.
FAX 817-455-2492.
Available only online. *2089*

NEWS INC.
SIMBA Information Inc. 11 Riverbend Dr. S., Box
4234, Stamford, CT 06907-0234. TEL 203-358-
9900. FAX 203-358-5824.
Vendor(s): Information Access Co.. *6003*

NEWS LIBRARY NEWS.
Special Libraries Association, News Division, c/o
Providence Journal, 75 Fountain St., Providence, RI
02902.
Vendor(s): VU/TEXT Information Services, Inc..
4016

NEWS OF NORWAY.
Royal Norwegian Embassy, 2720-34th St., N.W.,
Washington, DC 20008. TEL 202-333-6000.
FAX 202-337-0870. *2899*

NEWS PHOTOGRAPHER.
National Press Photographers Association, Inc.,
1446 Conneaut Ave., Bowling Green, OH 43402-
2145. TEL 419-352-8175. FAX 419-354-5435.
Vendor(s): Information Access Co., University
Microfilms International. *5515*

NEWS 3X-400.
Duke Communications International, 221 E. 29th
St., Ste. 242, Loveland, CO 80538. TEL 970-663-
4700. FAX 970-669-3016. *2079*

NEWSBRIEFNEWS.
TransAtlantic, Koniginneweg 201, 1075 CR
Amsterdam, Netherlands. TEL 31-20-6711818.
FAX 31-20-6711818. *4016*

NEWSCOPE.
United Methodist Publishing House, 201 Eighth
Ave. S., Box 801, Nashville, TN 37202. TEL 615-
749-6732. FAX 615-749-6079. *6154*

NEWSLETTER ON SERIALS PRICING ISSUES.
Marcia Tuttle, Ed. & Pub., Serials Department, C.B.
3938, Davis Library, University of North Carolina at
Chapel Hill, Chapel Hill, NC 27514-8890. TEL 919-
962-1067. FAX 919-962-4450.
Available only online. *4016*

**NEWSLETTER - THE INTERNATIONAL
COMMUNICATION PROJECT.**
AStA Universitaet Hannover, Foundation for
International Communication, Welfengarten 1,
30167 Hannover, Germany. TEL 49-511-
7625063. FAX 49-511-717441. *1311*

NEWSLETTERS IN PRINT.
Gale Research Inc., 835 Penobscot Bldg., Detroit,
MI 48226-9948. TEL 313-961 2242. FAX 313-
961-6083.
Vendor(s): Human Resources Information Network
(NIP), Knight-Ridder Information Inc.. *542*

NEWSMAKERS.
Gale Research Inc., 835 Penobscot Bldg., Detroit,
MI 48226. TEL 319-96 2242 FAX 313-221-
7086.
Vendor(s): Lexis-Nexis. *558*

NEWSNET ACTION LETTER.
NewsNet, Inc., 945 Haverford Rd., Bryn Mawr, PA
19010. TEL 610-527-8230. FAX 610-527-0338.
Vendor(s): NewsNet (PB99). *1929*

NEWSPAPER ABSTRACTS.
U M I Company (Louisville) 620 S. Third St.,
Louisville, KY 40202-2475.
Vendor(s): Knight-Ridder Information, Inc.. *3715*

NEWSPAPER RESEARCH JOURNAL.
Association for Education in Journalism and Mass
Communication, 1621 College St., University of
South Carolina, Columbia SC 29208-0251.
TEL 803-777-2005.
Vendor(s): University Microfilms International.
3708

NEWSWEEK.
Newsweek, Inc. 251 W. 57th St., New York, NY
10019. TEL 212-445-4300.
Vendor(s): Lexis-Nexis. *3234*

NEXTNET.
Telecommunications Reports, 1333 H. St., N.W.,
2nd Fl.-W., Washington, DC 20005. TEL 202-842-
3022. FAX 202-842-1875.
Vendor(s): Information Access Co., NewsNet (TE30).
1966

NEXUS NEW TIMES.
P.O. Box 30, Mapleton, Qid. 4650, Australia.
TEL 51-74-42-9543. FAX 61-74-42-9381. *5331*

NIEMAN REPORTS.
Nieman Foundation, Harvard University, 1 Francis
Ave. Cambridge, MA 02138. TEL 617-495-2237.
FAX 617-495-8976.
Vendor(s): Information Access Co., University
Microfilms International. *3709*

NIGRIZIA.
Missionari Comboniani, Vicolo Pozzo 1, 37129
Verona, Italy. *6081*

NIHON KONCHU GAKKAI TAIKAI KOEN YOSHI.
Entomological Society of Japan, Kokuritsu Kagaku
Hakubutsukan Dobutsu Kenkyubu, 23-1
Hyakunincho 3-chome, Shinjuku-ku, Tokyo 160,
Japan. TEL 03-3364-7129. FAX 03-3364-7104.
622

THE NIKKEI WEEKLY.
Nihon Keizai Shimbun, Inc., 1-9-5 Otemachi,
Chiyoda-ku, Tokyo 100, Japan. TEL 03-3270-0251.
FAX 03-5255-2661.
Vendor(s): Lexis-Nexis. *548*

NINETEENTH-CENTURY LITERATURE (BERKELEY).
University of California Press, Journals Division,
2120 Berkeley Way, No. 5812, Berkeley, CA
94720-5812. TEL 510-643-7154. FAX 510-642-
9917.
Vendor(s): Information Access Co.. *4243*

19TH-CENTURY MUSIC.
University of California Press, Journals Division,
2120 Berkeley Way, No. 5812, Berkeley, CA
94720-5812. TEL 510-643-7154. FAX 510-642-
9917.
Vendor(s): Information Access Co.. *5183*

**NIPPON JUI CHIKUSAN DAIGAKU KENKYU
HOKOKU.**
Nippon Jui Chikusan Daigaku, 1-7-1 Kyonan-cho,
Musashino-shi, Tokyo 180, Japan. TEL 422-31-
4151. FAX 422-33-2035. *6951*

NIPPON MEDICAL SCHOOL JOURNAL.
Nippon Medical School, Medical Association, 1-1-5
Sencagi, Bunkyo-ku, Tokyo 113, Japan. TEL 81-3-
3822-2131. FAX 81-3-3822-3759.
Vencor(s): JICST. *4508*

Online

NITROGEN.
British Sulphur Publishing 31 Mount Pleasant, London WC1X 0AD, England. TEL 44-171-837-5600. FAX 44-171-837-0292.
Vendor(s): Information Access Co.. *232*

NOISE AND VIBRATION WORLDWIDE.
I O P Publishing Ltd., Techno House, Redcliffe Way, Bristol, Avon BS1 6NX, England. TEL 44-117-929-7481. FAX 44-117-929-4318. *5615*

NOISE REGULATION REPORT.
Business Publishers, Inc., 951 Pershing Dr., Silver Spring, MD 20910-4464. TEL 301-587-6300. FAX 301-585-9075.
Vendor(s): NewsNet (EV19). *2839*

NON-FOODS MERCHANDISING.
Cardinal Business Media, Inc., 200 Connecticut Ave., Ste. 5-D, Norwalk, CT 06854. TEL 203-838-9100. FAX 203-838-2550.
Vendor(s): Information Access Co. *1481*

NONFERROUS METALS ALERT.
Cambridge Scientific Abstracts, 7200 Wisconsin Ave., Bethesda, MD 20814. TEL 301-961-6750. FAX 301-961-6720.
Vendor(s): CEDOCAR, CISTI, Data-Star (MBUS), European Space Agency (File no.111), Knight-Ridder Information, Inc. (File no.269), Orbit Search Service (MABU), STN International (MATBUS). *4984*

NONLINEAR SCIENCE TODAY.
Springer-Verlag, Science Journals, 175 Fifth Ave., New York, NY 10010. TEL 212-460-1500. FAX 212-473-6272.
Available only online. *4385*

NONPRESCRIPTION PHARMACEUTICALS AND NUTRITIONALS: THE TAN SHEET.
F-D-C Reports, Inc., 5550 Friendship Blvd., Ste. 1, Chevy Chase, MD 20815. FAX 301-664-7238.
Vendor(s): Data-Star (FDCR), Knight-Ridder Information, Inc. (File no.187), Lexis-Nexis. *5430*

NONPROFIT WORLD.
Society for Nonprofit Organizations, 6314 Odana Rd., Ste. 1, Madison, WI 53719. TEL 608-274-9777. FAX 608-274-9978.
Vendor(s): University Microfilms International. *6385*

NONWOVENS ABSTRACTS.
Pira International, Randalls Rd., Leatherhead, Surrey KT22 7RU, England. TEL 44-1372-802050. FAX 44-1372-802239.
Vendor(s): Data-Star, FIZ Technik, Knight-Ridder Information, Inc., Orbit Search Service, STN International. *5629*

NONWOVENS INDUSTRY.
Rodman Publications, Inc., 17 S. Franklin Tpk., Box 555, Ramsey, NJ 07446. TEL 201-825-2552. FAX 201-825-0553.
Vendor(s): Information Access Co.. *6682*

NORDIC JOURNAL OF PHILOSOPHICAL LOGIC.
Scandinavian University Press, P.O. Box 2959 Toeyen, N-0608 Oslo, Norway. TEL 47-22-575400. FAX 47-22-575353. *5488*

NORDIC LINGUISTIC BULLETIN.
Nordic Linguistic Bulletin, Harald Haarfagersgt. 31, N-5007 Bergen, Norway. TEL 47-55-58-29-54. FAX 47-55-58-94-70.
Available only online. *4095*

NORDICOM.
Nordic Documentation Center for Mass Communication Research, Statsbiblioteket, Universitetsparken, DK-8000 Aarhus C, Denmark. TEL 45-86-12-20-22. FAX 45-86-13-27-04. *1925*

NORTH AMERICAN FAUNA.
U.S. National Biological Service, Information Transfer Center, c/o Managing Editor, 1201 Oak Ridge Dr., Ste. 200, CO 80525-5589. TEL 970-226-9401. FAX 970-226-9455. *816*

THE NORTH AMERICAN REVIEW.
c/o Robley Wilson, Ed., University of Northern Iowa, Cedar Falls, IA 50614-0516. TEL 319-273-6455. FAX 319-273-6455.
Vendor(s): Information Access Co., University Microfilms International. *4157*

NORTH CAROLINA BUSINESS DIRECTORY.
American Business Directories 5711 S. 86th Circle, Box 27347, Omaha, NE 68127. TEL 402-593-4600. FAX 402-331-5481. *1631*

NORTH CAROLINA JOURNAL OF INTERNATIONAL LAW AND COMMERCIAL REGULATION.
University of North Carolina at Chapel Hill, School of Law, No. 3380, Chapel Hill, NC 27599-3380. TEL 910-962-4402. FAX 910-962-4713.
Vendor(s): Lexis-Nexis, West Services, Inc.. *3940*

NORTH CAROLINA LAW REVIEW.
North Carolina Law Review Association, Univ. of N. Carolina at Chapel Hill, School of Law, Van Hecke-Wettach Hall, Chapel Hill, NC 27599-3380. TEL 919-962-3926.
Vendor(s): Lexis-Nexis, West Services, Inc.. *3826*

NORTH DAKOTA BUSINESS DIRECTORY.
American Business Directories 5711 S. 86th Circle, Box 27347, Omaha, NE 68127. TEL 402-593-4600. FAX 402-331-5481. *1631*

NORTH DAKOTA LAW REVIEW.
University of North Dakota, School of Law, Box 9003, Grand Forks, ND 58201. TEL 701-777-2941. FAX 701-777-2217.
Vendor(s): West Services, Inc.. *3826*

NORTH SEA LETTER.
Financial Times Energy Publishing Maple House, 149 Tottenham Court Rd., London W1P 9LL, England. TEL 44-171-896-2241. FAX 44-171-896-2275.
Vendor(s): Data-Star, Information Access Co., Knight-Ridder Information, Inc., Lexis-Nexis. *5366*

NORTH SEA RIG FORECAST.
Financial Times Energy Publications Maple House, 149 Tottenham Court Rd., London W1P 9LL, England. TEL 44-171-896-2241. FAX 44-171-896-2275.
Vendor(s): Data-Star, Information Access Co., Knight-Ridder Information, Inc., Lexis-Nexis. *2554*

NORTHEAST POWER REPORT.
McGraw-Hill Companies, Energy & Business Newsletters, 1221 Ave. of the Americas, 36th Fl., New York, NY 10020. TEL 212-512-6410. FAX 212-512-2723.
Vendor(s): Dow Jones News Retrieval (NEPR), Knight-Ridder Information, Inc. (NPR), NewsNet (EY88). *2570*

NORTHERN CALIFORNIA BUSINESS DIRECTORY.
American Business Directories 5711 S. 86th Circle, Box 27347, Omaha, NE 68127. TEL 402-593-4600. FAX 402-331-5481. *1631*

NORTHERN HOUSE PAMPHLET POETS.
Northern House, 12 Queens Terrace, Newcastle-upon-Tyne NE2 2PJ, England. TEL 44-191-281-2614. *4312*

NORTHERN IRELAND NEWS SERVICE.
Box 57, Albany, NY 12211-0057. TEL 518-329-3003.
Vendor(s): NewsNet (IT74). *5688*

NORTHERN KENTUCKY LAW REVIEW.
Northern Kentucky University, Salmon P. Chase College of Law, Highland Heights, KY 41076. TEL 606-572-5444.
Vendor(s): West Services, Inc.. *3826*

THE NORTHERN MINER.
Southam Magazine Group, 1450 Don Mills Rd., Don Mills, ON M3B 2X7, Canada. TEL 416-445-6641. FAX 416-442-2272.
Vendor(s): Information Access Co., Southam Electronic Publishing. *5074*

NORTHERN ONTARIO BUSINESS.
Laurentian Publishing Co., 158 Elgin St., Sudbury, ON P3E 3N5, Canada. TEL 705-673-5705. FAX 705-673-9542.
Vendor(s): Lexis-Nexis, University Microfilms International. *948*

NORTHWESTERN JOURNAL OF INTERNATIONAL LAW & BUSINESS.
Northwestern University, School of Law - Office of Legal Publications, 357 E. Chicago Ave., Chicago, IL 60611. TEL 312-503-8467.
Vendor(s): West Services, Inc.. *3940*

NORTHWESTERN UNIVERSITY LAW REVIEW.
Northwestern University, School of Law - Office of Legal Publications, 357 E. Chicago Ave., Chicago, IL 60611. TEL 312-503-8467.
Vendor(s): Lexis-Nexis, West Services, Inc.. *3826*

NORWAVES.
NorWaves - N K I, P.O. Box 111, 1341 Bekkestua, Norway.
Available only online. *3201*

NOTES AND QUERIES.
Oxford University Press, Oxford Journals, Walton St., Oxford OX2 6DP, England. TEL 44-1865-267907. FAX 44-1865-267773.
Vendor(s): Information Access Co.. *4244*

NOTISUR.
University of New Mexico, Latin American Institute, 801 Yale N.E., Albuquerque, NM 87131-1016. TEL 505-277-6839. FAX 505-277-5989.
Vendor(s): Information Access Co., Knight-Ridder Information, Inc., Lexis-Nexis, NewsNet. *5689*

NOTIZIARIO CHIMICO E FARMACEUTICO.
Societa Editoriale Farmaceutica s.r.l., Via Ausonio, 12, 20123 Milan, Italy. TEL 02-89404545. FAX 02-89401168. *5430*

NOTRE DAME LAW REVIEW.
University of Notre Dame, School of Law, Box 988, Notre Dame, IN 46556. TEL 219-631-7097. FAX 219-631-6371.
Vendor(s): West Services, Inc.. *3826*

NOVA ASTRONAUTICA.
Associazione Sviluppo Propulsione Spaziale, Via N. Martoglio 22, 00137 Rome, Italy. TEL 39-6-87131068. *74*

NOVA LAW REVIEW.
Nova Law Review, 3305 College Ave., Fort Lauderdale, FL 33314. TEL 954-452-6195.
Vendor(s): West Services, Inc.. *3827*

NOVA SCOTIA REPORTS.
Maritime Law Book Ltd., P.O. Box 302, Fredericton, NB E3B 4Y9, Canada. TEL 506-453-9921. FAX 506-453-9525.
Vendor(s): QL Systems Ltd.. *3827*

NOVEL: A FORUM ON FICTION.
Brown University, Department of Literature, Box 1984, Providence, RI 02912. TEL 414-863-3756.
Vendor(s): University Microfilms International. *4245*

NOW AND THEN.
East Tennessee State University, Center for Appalachian Studies and Services, Box 70556, Johnson City, TN 37614-0556. TEL 423-929-5348. FAX 423-929-6340. *4245*

NUCLEAR AWARENESS NEWS.
Nuclear Awareness Project, P.O. Box 104, Uxbridge ON L9P 1M6, Canada. TEL 905-852-0571. *2580*

NUCLEAR DATA NEWSLETTER.
International Atomic Energy Agency, Wagramerstr. 5, P.O. Box 100, A-1400 Vienna, Austria. TEL 43-1-20600. FAX 43-1-20607. *2580*

NUCLEAR DATA SHEETS.
Academic Press, Inc., Journal Division, 525 B St., Ste. 1900, San Diego, CA 92101-4495. TEL 619-230-1840. FAX 619-699-6800. *2580*

NUCLEAR MEDICINE COMMUNICATIONS.
Chapman & Hall, Journals Department 2-6 Boundary Row, London SE1 8HN, England. TEL 44-171-8650066. FAX 44-171-522-9623. *4881*

NUCLEAR NEWS.
American Nuclear Society, 555 N. Kensington Ave., La Grange Park, IL 60525. TEL 708-352-6611.
Vendor(s): Lexis-Nexis. *2581*

NUCLEAR WASTE NEWS.
Business Publishers, Inc., 951 Pershing Dr., Silver Spring, MD 20910-4464. TEL 301-587-6300. FAX 301-585-9075.
Vendor(s): Information Access Co., NewsNet (EV03). *2855*

NUCLEARFUEL.
McGraw-Hill Companies, 1221 Ave. of the Americas, New York, NY 10020. Vendor(s): Dow Jones News Retrieval (NUF), Knight-Ridder Information, Inc. (File no.624/McGRAW-HILL PUBLICATIONS ONLINE), Lexis-Nexis (NUFUEL), NewsNet (EY72). *2581*

NUCLEIC ACIDS ABSTRACTS.
Cambridge Scientific Abstracts, 7200 Wisconsin Ave., 6th Fl., Bethesda, MD 20814. TEL 301-961-6750. FAX 301-961-6720. Vendor(s): Knight-Ridder Information, Inc. (File no.76/LIFE SCIENCES COLLECTION), STN International (LIFESCI). *622*

NUCLEIC ACIDS RESEARCH.
Oxford University Press, Oxford Journals, Walton St., Oxford OX2 6DP, England. TEL 44-1865-267907. FAX 44-1865-267485. *646*

NUCLEONICS WEEK.
McGraw-Hill Companies, Energy & Business Newsletters, 1221 Ave. of the Americas, 36th Fl., New York, NY 10020. TEL 212-512-6410. Vendor(s): Dow Jones News Retrieval (NUC), Knight-Ridder Information, Inc. (File no.624/McGRAW-HILL PUBLICATIONS ONLINE), Lexis-Nexis (NUWEEK), NewsNet (EY73). *2554*

NUCLEOTECNICA.
Comision Chilena de Energia Nuclear, Amunategui 95, Casilla 188-D, Santiago, Chile. TEL 56-2-6990070. FAX 56-2-6991618. *2581*

NUMERISCHE MATHEMATIK.
Springer-Verlag, Heidelberger Platz 3, 14197 Berlin, Germany. TEL 49-30-8207-0. FAX 49-30-8214091. *4412*

THE NURSE PRACTITIONER.
Springhouse Corporation 1111 Bethlehem Pike, Box 908, Springhouse, PA 19477. TEL 215-646-8700. *4722*

NURSING HOMES.
Medquest Communications, Inc., 629 Euclid Ave., Ste. 500, Cleveland, OH 44114-3003. TEL 216-522-9700. FAX 216-522-9707. Vendor(s): Information Access Co., Knight-Ridder Information, Inc., University Microfilms International. *4723*

NURSING OUTLOOK.
Mosby Year - Book, Inc. 11830 Westline Industrial Dr., St. Louis, MO 63146-3318. TEL 314-872-8370. FAX 314-432-1380. *4724*

NURSING RESEARCH.
American Journal of Nursing Co., 555 W. 57th St., New York, NY 10019. TEL 212-582-8820. *4724*

THE NUTMEG POINT DISTRICT MAIL.
Box 43072, Upper Montclair, NJ 07043-0072. Available only online. *4329*

NUTRITION ABSTRACTS AND REVIEWS. SERIES A: HUMAN AND EXPERIMENTAL.
CAB International, Wallingford, Oxon. OX10 8DE, England. TEL 44-1491-832111. FAX 44-1491-833508. Vendor(s): DIMDI, European Space Agency, Knight-Ridder Information, Inc., STN International. *5244*

NUTRITION ABSTRACTS AND REVIEWS. SERIES B: LIVESTOCK FEEDS AND FEEDING.
CAB International, Wallingford, Oxon. OX10 8DE, England. TEL 01491-832111. FAX 01491-833508. Vendor(s): CISTI, DIMDI, European Space Agency (File nos.16 & 124/CAB), Knight-Ridder Information, Inc., Ovid Technologies, Inc. (VETR). *177*

NUTRITION ACTION HEALTHLETTER.
Center for Science in the Public Interest, 1875 Connecticut Ave., N.W., Ste. 300, Washington, DC 20009-5728. TEL 202-332-9110. FAX 202-265-4954. Vendor(s): Information Access Co., University Microfilms International. *5238*

NUTRITION FORUM.
Prometheus Books Incorporated, 59 John Glenn Dr., Amherst, NY 14228. TEL 716-691-0133. FAX 716-564-2711. Vendor(s): Information Access Co. *5239*

NUTRITION HEALTH REVIEW.
Vegetus Publications, Box 406, Haverford, PA 19041. TEL 610-896-1853. FAX 610-896-1857. Vendor(s): Information Access Co.. *5239*

NUTRITION RESEARCH NEWSLETTER.
Lyda Associates, Inc., Box 700, Palisades, NY 10964. TEL 914-359-8282. FAX 914-359-1229. Vendor(s): Information Access Co.. *5239*

NUTRITION REVIEWS.
Allen Press, Inc., Box 1897, Lawrence, KS 66044. TEL 913-843-1234. FAX 913-843-1274. Vendor(s): University Microfilms International. *5239*

NUTRITION TODAY.
Williams and Wilkins, 351 W. Camden St., Baltimore, MD 21201. TEL 410-528-4000. FAX 410-528-4312. Vendor(s): Information Access Co. *5240*

NY LITTERATUR OM KVINNOR.
Goeteborgs Universitet, Universitetsbibliotek, Centralbiblioteket, F.O. Box 5096, S-402 22 Goeteborg, Sweden. *7022*

NYERE DANSK FAGLITTERATUR.
Dansk BiblioteksCenter as, Tempovej 7-11, DK-2750 Ballerup, Denmark. TEL 45-44-867777. FAX 45-44-867892. *542*

NYTT JURIDISKT ARKIV. AVD. 1 - RAETTSFALL FRAAN HOEGSTA DOMSTOLEN.
Fritzes Foerlag AB, Norstedts Juridik, P.O. Box 6472, S-113 82 Stockholm, Sweden. TEL 46-8-690-91-90. FAX 46-8-690-90-70. Vendor(s): DAFA Data AB. *3827*

O C L C ANNUAL REPORT.
Online Computer Library Center, Inc., 6565 Frantz Rd., Dublin, OH 43017. TEL 614-764-6000. FAX 614-764-6096. *4017*

O C L C NEWSLETTER.
Online Computer Library Center, Inc., 6565 Frantz Rd., Dublin, OH 43017. TEL 614-764-6000. *4017*

O E C D ECONOMIC OUTLOOK.
Organization for Economic Cooperation and Development, 2 rue Andre-Pascal, 75775 Paris Cedex 16, France. TEL 33-1-45-24-82-00. FAX 33-1-45-24-85-00. Vendor(s): Information Access Co., University Microfilms International. *1225*

O E C D ECONOMIC STUDIES.
Organization for Economic Cooperation and Development, 2 rue Andre-Pascal, 75775 Paris Cedex 16, France. TEL 33-1-45-24-82-00. FAX 33-1-45-24-85-00. Vendor(s): Information Access Co.. *1225*

O E C D ECONOMIC SURVEYS: AUSTRIA.
Organization for Economic Cooperation and Development, 2 rue Andre-Pascal, 75775 Paris 16, France. TEL 33-1-45-24-82-00. FAX 333-1-45-24-85-00. Vendor(s): Information Access Co.. *1225*

O E C D ECONOMIC SURVEYS: CANADA.
Organization for Economic Cooperation and Development 2 rue Andre-Pascal, 75775 Paris Cedex 16, France. TEL 33-1-45-24-82-00. FAX 33-1-45-24-85-00. Vendor(s): Information Access Co.. *1226*

O E C D ECONOMIC SURVEYS: DENMARK.
Organization for Economic Cooperation and Development, 2 rue Andre-Pascal, 75775 Paris Cedex 16, France. TEL 33-1-45-24-82-00. FAX 33-1-45-24-80-00. Vendor(s): Information Access Co.. *1226*

O E C D ECONOMIC SURVEYS: ICELAND.
Organization for Economic Cooperation and Development, 2 rue Andre-Pascal, 75775 Paris Cedex 16, France. TEL 33-1-45-24-82-00. FAX 33-1-45-24-58-00. Vendor(s): Information Access Co.. *1226*

O E C D ECONOMIC SURVEYS: SPAIN.
Organization for Economic Cooperation and Development, 2 rue Andre-Pascal, 75775 Paris Cedex 16, France. TEL 33-1-45-24-82-00. FAX 33-1-45-24-85-00. Vendor(s): Information Access Co.. *1226*

O E C D ECONOMIC SURVEYS: UNITED STATES.
Organization for Economic Cooperation and Development, 2 rue Andre-Pascal, 75775 Paris Cedex 16, France. TEL 33-1-45-24-82-00. FAX 33-1-45-24-85-00. Vendor(s): Information Access Co.. *1227*

O E C D OBSERVER.
Organization for Economic Cooperation and Development, 2 rue Andre-Pascal, 75775 Paris Cedex 16, France. TEL 33-1-45-24-82-00. FAX 33-1-45-24-85-00. Vendor(s): Information Access Co., University Microfilms International. *1227*

O E C D QUARTERLY OIL STATISTICS AND ENERGY BALANCES.
Organization for Economic Cooperation and Development, 2 rue Andre-Pascal, 75775 Paris Cedex 16, France. *5384*

O E REPORTS.
International Society for Optical Engineering (SPIE), 1000 20th St., Box 10, Bellingham, WA 98227-0010. TEL 360-676-3230. FAX 360-647-1445. *5608*

O M R I DAILY DIGEST.
Open Media Research Institute, Motokov Bldg., Na Strzi 63, 14062 Prague 4, Czech Republic. TEL 42-2-61142114. FAX 42-2-61143184. Available only online. *5755*

O S H BRIEFING.
Babour Index plc., New Lodge Drift Rd., Windsor, Berks. SL4 4RQ, England. TEL 44-1344-884121. FAX 44-1344-884112. *5254*

O S S C BULLETIN.
University of Oregon College of Education, Oregon School Study Council, 1737 Agate St., Eugene, OR 97403-5207. TEL 503-346-5043. FAX 503-346-2334. *2359*

OBJECT CURRENTS.
Sigs Publications, Inc., 71 W. 23rd St., New York, NY 10010. TEL 212-242-7447. FAX 212-242-7574. Available only online. *2046*

OBJECT-ORIENTED STRATEGIES.
Cutter Information Corp., 37 Broadway, Arlington, MA 02174. TEL 617-643-8700. FAX 617-648-1950. *2076*

OBJECT-ORIENTED SYSTEMS.
Chapman & Hall, Journals Department 2-6 Boundary Row, London SE1 8HN, England. TEL 44-171-8650066. FAX 44-171-5229623. *2046*

OBSTETRICS AND GYNECOLOGY.
Elsevier Science Inc., Box 945, New York, NY 10159-0945. TEL 212-633-3730. FAX 212-633-3680. Vendor(s): Ovid Technologies, Inc.. *4743*

OCCUPATIONAL ERGONOMICS.
Chapman & Hall, Journals Department 2-6 Boundary Row, London SE1 8HN, England. TEL 44-171-8650066. FAX 44-171-5229623. *5254*

OCCUPATIONAL HAZARDS.
Perton Publishing Co. 1.00 Superior Ave., Cleveland, OH 44114-2543. TEL 216-696-7000. FAX 216-696-8765. Vendor(s): Information Access Co., University Microfilms International. *5254*

OCCUPATIONAL HEALTH & SAFETY.
Stevens Publishing Corporation 3700 J.H. Kultgen Frwy., Waco, TX 76706. TEL 817-776-9000. FAX 817-776-9018. Vendor(s): University Microfilms International. *5255*

OCCUPATIONAL HEALTH & SAFETY LETTER.
Business Publishers, Inc. 951 Pershing Dr., Silver Spring, MD 20910-4464. TEL 301-587-6300. FAX 301-585-9075. Vendor(s): Information Access Co., NewsNet. *5255*

OCCUPATIONAL OUTLOOK QUARTERLY.
U.S. Bureau of Labor Statistics, 2 Massachusetts Ave., N.E., Washington, DC 20212. TEL 202-606-5701. Vendor(s): Information Access Co., University Microfilms International. *5272*

OCCUPATIONAL SAFETY & HEALTH REPORTER.
The Bureau of National Affairs, Inc., 1231 25th St., N.W., Washington, DC 20037. TEL 202-452-4200. FAX 202-822-8092.
Vendor(s): Human Resources Information Network (CDD, HDD), Knight-Ridder Information, Inc. (Laborlaw, File no.244). *5255*

OCCUPATIONAL THERAPY INDEX.
British Library, Medical Information Centre, Boston Spa, Wetherby, W. Yorks. LS23 7BQ, England. TEL 01937-546039. FAX 01937-546458. *4570*

OCEAN OIL WEEKLY REPORT.
PennWell Publishing Co. (Houston), Box 1941, Houston, TX 77251. TEL 713-621-9720. FAX 713-963-6285. *5367*

OCEANIA.
University of Sydney, Sydney, N.S.W. 2006, Australia. TEL 61-2-692-2666. FAX 61-2-692-2666.
Vendor(s): Information Access Co., University Microfilms International. *318*

OCEANIC ABSTRACTS.
Cambridge Scientific Abstracts, 7200 Wisconsin Ave., 6th Fl., Bethesda, MD 20814. TEL 301-961-6750. FAX 301-961-6720.
Vendor(s): European Space Agency (File no.17/OCEANIC), Knight-Ridder Information, Inc. (File no.28), STN International (OCEAN). *2220*

OCEANUS.
Woods Hole Oceanographic Institution, Research Library MS 26, 360 Woods Hole Rd., Woods Hole, MA 02543-1541. TEL 508-457-2000. FAX 508-289-2156.
Vendor(s): Information Access Co. *2303*

OCTANE WEEK.
Information Resources, Inc., 1925 N. Lynn St., Ste. 1000, Arlington, VA 22204-1707. TEL 703-528-2500. FAX 703-528-1483.
Vendor(s): Data-Star, Dow Jones News Retrieval, Information Access Co., Knight-Ridder Information, Inc. *5367*

O'DWYER'S P R SERVICES REPORT.
J.R. O'Dwyer Co., Inc., 271 Madison Ave., New York, NY 10016. TEL 212-679-2471. FAX 212-683-2750.
Vendor(s): Lexis-Nexis. *42*

OFF-HIGHWAY ENGINEERING.
Society of Automotive Engineers, 400 Commonwealth Dr., Warrendale, PA 15096-0001. TEL 412-772-7114. FAX 412-776-4026.
Vendor(s): Orbit Search Service. *6797*

OFF ROAD.
Argus Publishers Corporation, 774 S. Placentia Ave., Placentia, CA 92670-6832. TEL 310-820-3601. FAX 310-207-9388.
Vendor(s): Information Access Co. *6797*

OFFSHORE (TULSA).
PennWell Publishing Co., Box 1260, Tulsa, OK 74101. TEL 918-835-3161. FAX 918-832-9295.
Vendor(s): Information Access Co., Lexis-Nexis. *5367*

OFFSHORE FIELD DEVELOPMENT INTERNATIONAL.
Offshore Data Services, Inc., Box 19909, Houston, TX 77224-1909. TEL 713-781-2713. FAX 713-781-9594. *5367*

OFFSHORE RIG LOCATOR.
Offshore Data Services, Inc., Box 19909, Houston, TX 77224-1909. TEL 713-781-2713. FAX 713-781-9594. *5368*

OHIO BUSINESS DIRECTORY.
American Business Directories 5711 S. 86th Circle, Box 27347, Omaha, NE 68127. TEL 402-593-4600. FAX 402-331-5481. *1632*

THE OHIO C P A JOURNAL.
Ohio Society of Certified Public Accountants, 535 Metro Place S., Box 1810, Dublin, OH 43017-7810. TEL 614-764-2727. FAX 614-764-5880.
Vendor(s): Information Access Co., University Microfilms International. *1052*

OHIO STATE JOURNAL ON DISPUTE RESOLUTION.
Ohio State University, College of Law, 55 W. 1th Ave., Columbus, OH 43210-1391. TEL 614-292-7170.
Vendor(s): West Services, Inc., Wilsonline. *3828*

OHIO STATE LANTERN.
Ohio State University, School of Journalism, c/o Lee Becker, 242 W. 18th Ave., Columbus, OH 43210. TEL 614-292-2031. FAX 614-292-3722. *1879*

OHIO STATE LAW JOURNAL.
Ohio State University, College of Law, 55 W. 12th Ave., Columbus, OH 43210-1391. TEL 614-292-6829.
Vendor(s): Lexis-Nexis, West Services, Inc., Wilsonline. *3828*

OIL & GAS INTERESTS NEWSLETTER.
Hart Publications, Inc. (Denver) 4545 Post Oak Pl., Ste. 210, Houston, TX 77027. TEL 713-993-9320.
Vendor(s): Information Access Co. *5368*

OIL AND GAS INVESTOR.
Hart Publications, Inc. (Houston) 4545 Post Oak Place, Ste. 210, Houston, TX 77027. TEL 713-993-9320.
Vendor(s): University Microfilms International. *5368*

OIL & GAS JOURNAL.
PennWell Publishing Co., Box 1260, Tulsa, OK 74101. TEL 918-835-3161. FAX 918-832-9295.
Vendor(s): Information Access Co., Lexis-Nexis, University Microfilms International. *5368*

OIL DAILY.
Oil Daily Co., 1401 New York Ave., N.W., Ste. 500, Washington, DC 20005. TEL 202-662-0700. FAX 202-783-8320.
Vendor(s): Knight-Ridder Information, Inc. *5369*

OIL MARKET REPORT.
Financial Times Energy Publishing Maple House, 149 Tottenham Court Rd., London W1P 9LL, England. TEL 0171-896-2241. FAX 0171-896-2275.
Vendor(s): Data-Star, Knight-Ridder Information, Inc., Lexis-Nexis. *2555*

OIL MARKET TRENDS.
Arab Press Service, A P S House, P.O. Box 3896, Nicosia, Cyprus. TEL 357-2-351778. FAX 357-2-350265.
Vendor(s): Information Access Co. *2555*

OIL PRICE INFORMATION SERVICE.
United Communications Group, 11300 Rockville Pike, Ste. 1100, Rockville, MD 20852-3030. TEL 301-816-8950.
Vendor(s): NewsNet (EY02), United Communications Group (PETROSCAN). *5369*

OIL SPILL INTELLIGENCE REPORT.
Cutter Information Corp., 37 Broadway, Arlington, MA 02174. TEL 617-648-8700. FAX 617-648-1950.
Vendor(s): Information Access Co. *5369*

OIL SPILL U S LAW REPORT.
Cutter Information Corp., 37 Broadway, Arlington, MA 02174. TEL 617-648-8700. FAX 617-648-8707.
Vendor(s): NewsNet (EV06). *3829*

OILS AND FATS: THE INTERNATIONAL MARKET.
Euromonitor, 60-61 Britton St., London EC1M 5NA, England. TEL 44-171-251-8024. FAX 44-171-608-3149.
Vendor(s): Data-Star, Knight-Ridder Information, Inc. *2986*

OILWEEK.
Maclean-Hunter Ltd. (Calgary), Ste. 2450, 101-6th Ave. S.W., Calgary, AB T2P 3P4, Canada. TEL 403-266-8700. FAX 403-266-6634.
Vendor(s): Information Access Co. *5370*

OKLAHOMA BUSINESS DIRECTORY.
American Business Directories 5711 S. 86th Circle, Box 27347, Omaha, NE 68127. TEL 402-593-4600. FAX 402-331-5481. *1632*

OKLAHOMA CITY UNIVERSITY LAW REVIEW.
Oklahoma City University, School of Law, 2501 N. Blackwelder, Oklahoma City, OK 73106. TEL 405-521-5280. FAX 405-521-5172.
Vendor(s): West Services, Inc. *3829*

OKLAHOMA LAW REVIEW.
University of Oklahoma, College of Law, 300 Timberdell Rd., Norman, OK 73019. TEL 405-325-5191.
Vendor(s): West Services, Inc. *3829*

OLDER AMERICANS REPORT.
Business Publishers, Inc., 951 Pershing Dr., Silver Spring, MD 20910-4464. TEL 301-587-6300. FAX 301-585-9075.
Vendor(s): NewsNet. *6386*

OMNI.
Omni International, Ltd. 277 Park Ave., 4th Fl., New York, NY 10172. TEL 212-702-6000. FAX 212-702-6282.
Available only online. Vendor(s): Information Access Co. *6269*

ONCOGENES AND GROWTH FACTORS ABSTRACTS.
Cambridge Scientific Abstracts, 7200 Wisconsin Ave., 6th Fl., Bethesda, MD 20814. TEL 301-961-6750. FAX 301-961-6720.
Vendor(s): Knight-Ridder Information, Inc. (File no.76), STN International (LIFESCI). *4570*

ONE TO ONE (FRESNO).
CreeYadio Services, Box 9787, Fresno, CA 93794. TEL 209-448-0700. FAX 209-448-0761.
Vendor(s): CompuServe, Inc. *1938*

ONGOING CURRENT BIBLIOGRAPHY OF PLASTIC & RECONSTRUCTIVE SURGERY.
Creative Products, Inc., 23 Pinewood Farm Ct., Owings Mills, MD 21117. TEL 410-252-4022. FAX 410-252-3142.
Vendor(s): National Library of Medicine. *4570*

ONKRUID.
Stichting Onkruid, West 32, 1633 JC Avenhorn, Netherlands. TEL 31-2295-42800. FAX 31-2295-42315. *5219*

ONLINE (WILTON).
Online, Inc., 462 Danbury Rd., Wilton, CT 06897. TEL 203-761-1466. FAX 203-761-1444.
Vendor(s): Information Access Co. *2041*

THE ONLINE JOURNAL OF CURRENT CLINICAL TRIALS.
Chapman & Hall, Journals Department 2-6 Boundary Row, London SE1 8HN, England. TEL 44-171-8650066. FAX 44-171-5229623.
Vendor(s): OCLC. *4511*

ONLINE JOURNAL OF KNOWLEDGE SYNTHESIS FOR NURSING.
Sigma Theta Tau International Honor Society of Nursing, 550 W. North St., Indianapolis, IN 46202. TEL 317-634-8171. FAX 317-634-8188.
Available only online. Vendor(s): OCLC. *4725*

ONLINE LIBRARIES AND MICROCOMPUTERS.
Information Intelligence, Inc., Box 31098, Phoenix, AZ 85046. TEL 602-996-2283.
Vendor(s): Data-Star, Dow Jones News Retrieval, European Space Agency, Information Access Co., Knight-Ridder Information, Inc., NewsNet (PB42). *4046*

ONLINE NEWSLETTER.
Information Intelligence Inc., Box 31098, Phoenix, AZ 85046. TEL 602-996-2283.
Vendor(s): Data-Star, Dow Jones News Retrieval, European Space Agency, Information Access Co., Knight-Ridder Information, Inc., NewsNet (PB41). *2041*

ONLINE PRODUCT NEWS.
Worldwide Videotex, Box 3273, Boynton Beach, FL 33424-3273. TEL 407-738-2276.
Vendor(s): Information Access Co., NewsNet (TE27). *2067*

ONTARIO. LABOUR RELATIONS BOARD. REPORTS. A MONTHLY SERIES OF DECISIONS.
Labour Relations Board, 400 University Ave., Toronto, ON M7A 1V4, Canada. TEL 416-326-7500. FAX 416-326-7531.
Vendor(s): QL Systems Ltd. *1391*

ONTARIO APPEAL CASES.
Maritime Law Book Ltd., Box 302, Fredericton, NB E3B 4Y9, Canada. TEL 506-453-9921. FAX 506-453-9525.
Vendor(s): QL Systems Ltd. *3829*

ONTARIO REPORTS.
Butterworths Canada Ltd., Part of the Reed Elsevier group, 75 Clegg Rd., Markham, ON L6G 1A1, Canada. TEL 905-479-2665. FAX 905-479-2826. Vendor(s): QL Systems Ltd.. *3830*

OPEN INFORMATION SYSTEMS.
Patricia Seybold Group, 148 State St., 7th Fl., Boston, MA 02109. TEL 617-742-5200. FAX 617-742-1028. *2057*

OPERA NEWS.
Metropolitan Opera Guild, Inc., 70 Lincoln Center Plaza, New York, NY 10023. TEL 212-769-7080. FAX 212-769-7007. Vendor(s): Information Access Co., University Microfilms International. *5185*

OPERATIONS IN OIL DIPLOMACY.
Arab Press Service, A P S House, P.O. Box 3896, Nicosia, Cyprus. TEL 357-2-351778. FAX 357-2-350265. Vendor(s): Information Access Co.. *5765*

OPHTHALMOLOGY TIMES.
Advanstar Communications, Inc., 7500 Old Oak Blvd., Cleveland, OH 44130. TEL 216-826-2839. FAX 216-891-2726. Vendor(s): Information Access Co., Knight-Ridder Information, Inc.. *4775*

OPTICAL AND QUANTUM ELECTRONICS.
Chapman & Hall, Journals Department 2-6 Boundary Row, London SE1 8HN, England. TEL 44-171-8650066. FAX 44-171-5229623. *2529*

OPTICAL MATERIALS AND ENGINEERING NEWS.
Business Communications Co., Inc. (Norwalk), 25 Van Zant St., Norwalk, CT 06855. TEL 203-853-4266. FAX 203-853-0348. Vendor(s): Data-Star, Information Access Co., Knight-Ridder Information, Inc., NewsNet (RD37). *5609*

OPTICAL MEMORY NEWS.
Phillips Business Information, Inc., 1201 Seven Locks Rd., Potomac, MD 20854. TEL 301-424-3338. FAX 301-309-3847. Vendor(s): Information Access Co., NewsNet (EC50). *2079*

OPTIMUM.
Canada Communication Group, Publishing Division, Ottawa, ON K1A 0S9, Canada. TEL 819-956-4802. Vendor(s): Information Access Co.. *1438*

OPTIONS.
International Institute for Applied Systems Analysis, A-2361 Laxenburg, Austria. TEL 43-2236-807-0. FAX 43-2236-73149. *2083*

OPTO & LASER EUROPE.
I O P Publishing Ltd., Techno House, Redcliffe Way, Bristol, Avon BS1 6NX, England. TEL 44-117-929-7481. FAX 44-117-929-4318. *5610*

OPTOMETRY CLINICS.
Appleton & Lange, Journal Division Box 120041, Stamford, CT 06912-0041. TEL 203-406-4500. *4776*

ORAL HYGIENE PRODUCTS: THE INTERNATIONAL MARKET.
Euromonitor, 60-61 Britton St., London EC1M 5NA, England. TEL 44-171-251-8024. FAX 44-171-608-3149. Vendor(s): Data-Star, Knight-Ridder Information, Inc.. *492*

ORANGE COUNTY BUSINESS JOURNAL.
Orange County Business Journal, 4590 MacArthur Blvd., Ste. 100, Newport Beach, CA 92660. TEL 714-833-8373. FAX 714-833-8751. Vendor(s): Knight-Ridder Information, Inc., University Microfilms International. *1228*

ORBIS.
J A I Press Inc., 55 Old Post Rd., No. 2, Box 1678, Greenwich, CT 06836-1678. TEL 203-661-7602. FAX 203-661-0792. Vendor(s): Information Access Co.. *5765*

OREGON BUSINESS DIRECTORY.
American Business Directories 5711 S. 86th Circle, Box 27347, Omaha, NE 68127. TEL 402-593-4600. FAX 402-331-5481. *1633*

OREGON BUSINESS MAGAZINE.
Oregon Business Media, 610 S.W. Broadway, No. 200, Portland OR 97205-3431. TEL 503-223-0304. FAX 503-221-6544. Vendor(s): Information Access Co.. *949*

OREGON LAW REVIEW.
University of Oregon, School of Law, Eugene, OR 97403-1221. TEL 541-346-3844. FAX 541-346-3844. Vendor(s): Lexis-Nexis, West Services, Inc.. *3830*

ORGANIC GARDENING.
Rodale Press, Inc., 33 E. Minor St., Emmaus, PA 18049. TEL 610-967-5171. FAX 610-967-7725. Vendor(s): Information Access Co., University Microfilms International. *3063*

ORGANIC GARDENING.
Wardnest Ltd., P.O. Box 4, Wivelscombe, Taunton, Somerset TA4 2QY, England. TEL 44-1984-623998. FAX 44-1984-623998. Vendor(s): Information Access Co.. *3063*

ORGANIZATION STUDIES.
Walter de Gruyter und Co., Genthiner Str. 13, 10785 Berlin, Germany. TEL 49-30-26005-0. FAX 49-30-26005251. Vendor(s): Information Access Co., University Microfilms International. *6337*

ORGANIZATIONAL DYNAMICS.
American Management Association, 135 W. 50 St., New York, NY 10020. TEL 212-586-8100. Vendor(s): Information Access Co., University Microfilms International. *1439*

ORGANOMETALLICS.
American Chemical Society, 1155 16th St., N.W., Washington, DC 20036. TEL 800-333-9511. FAX 614-447-3671. Vendor(s): STN International (CJACS). *1743*

ORIGINATION NEWS.
Faulkner & Gray, 22nd Fl., 11 Penn Plaza, New York, NY 10001. TEL 212-967-7000. Vendor(s): University Microfilms International. *1114*

ORIGINS, C N S DOCUMENTARY SERVICE.
Catholic News Service, 3211 4th St., N.E., Washington, DC 20017. TEL 202-541-3290. FAX 202-541-3255. Vendor(s): NewsNet (CN03). *6191*

ORION (CHICO).
California State University, Chico, College of Communication, Department of Journalism, Chico, CA 95929-0600. TEL 916-898-5625. FAX 916-898-4839. *1380*

ORLANDO BUSINESS JOURNAL.
American City Business Journals (Orlando), 315 E. Robinson St., Ste. 250, Orlando, FL 32801-1949. TEL 407-649-3470 FAX 407-649-8469. Vendor(s): Information Access Co.. *949*

ORNAMENTAL HORTICULTURE.
CAB International, Wallingford, Oxon. OX10 8DE, England. TEL 44-1491-832111. FAX 44-1491-833508. Vendor(s): DIMDI, European Space Agency, Knight-Ridder Information, Inc., STN International. *3070*

ORPHAN DISEASE UPDATE.
National Organization for Rare Disorders, Inc. (NORD), Box 8923, New Fairfield, CT 06812-8923. TEL 203-746-6518. FAX 203-746-6481. *4511*

ORTHOPEDICS TODAY.
Slack, Inc., 6900 Grove Rd., Thorofare, NJ 08086-9447. TEL 609-848-1000. FAX 609-853-5991. *4789*

OSTOMY QUARTERLY.
United Ostomy Association, Inc., 36 Executive Park, Ste. 120, Irvine, CA 92714-6744. TEL 714-660-8624. FAX 714-660-9262. Vendor(s): Information Access Co.. *4512*

OTTAWA WEEKLY UPDATE.
Publinet, P.O. Box 828, Sta. B, Ottawa, Ont. K1P 5P9, Canada. TEL 613-238-4831. FAX 613-238-7698. *5914*

OUTDOOR LIFE.
Times Mirror Magazines, Inc., 2 Park Ave., New York, NY 10016. TEL 212-779-5000. FAX 212-686-6877. Vendor(s): Information Access Co., Knight-Ridder Information, Inc., University Microfilms International. *6572*

OUTLOOK.
Canadian Jewish Outlook Society, 6184 Ash St., Ste. 3, Vancouver, BC V5Z 3G9, Canada. TEL 604-324-5101. FAX 604-325-2470. Vendor(s): University Microfilms International. *2901*

OUTLOOK (REDWOOD CITY).
California Society of Certified Public Accountants, 275 Shoreline Dr., Redwood City, CA 94065. TEL 415-802-2427. FAX 415-802-2300. Vendor(s): Information Access Co.. *1052*

OUTLOOK (YEAR) PROCEEDINGS.
U.S. Department of Agriculture, World Agricultural Outlook Board, 14th St. and Independence Ave., S.W., Rm. 5143-S, Washington, DC 20250-3900. TEL 202-447-5447. Vendor(s): Ovid Technologies, Inc., Knight-Ridder Information, Inc.. *197*

OUTSTATE BUSINESS.
Harbor House Publishers Inc., 221 Water St., Boyne City, MI 49712. TEL 616 582-2814. FAX 616-582-3392. Vendor(s): University Microfilms International. *1228*

OVERSEAS DEVELOPMENT INSTITUTE. BRIEFING PAPER.
Overseas Development Institute, Regent's College, Inner Circle, Regent's Park, London NW1 4NS, England. TEL 0171-487-7413. FAX 0171-487-7590. *1312*

OXBRIDGE DIRECTORY OF NEWSLETTERS.
Oxbridge Communications Inc., 150 Fifth Ave., New York. NY 10011. TEL 212-741-0231. FAX 212-633-2938. *543*

OXFORD BULLETIN OF ECONOMICS AND STATISTICS.
Blackwell Publishers Ltd., 108 Cowley Rd., Oxford OX4 1JF, England. TEL 44-1865-791100. FAX 44-1865-791347. Vendor(s): Information Access Co.. *950*

OXFORD ECONOMIC PAPERS.
Oxford University Press, Oxford Journals, Walton St., Oxford OX2 6DP, England. TEL 44-1865-267907. FAX 44-1865-267773. Vendor(s): Information Access Co.. *950*

OXY-FUEL NEWS.
Information Resources, Inc., 1925 N. Lynn St., Ste. 1000, Arlington, VA 22204-1707. TEL 703-528-2500. FAX 703-528-1483. Vendor(s): Information Access Co., NewsNet. *2555*

P A COMMUNICATIONS.
Gordon & Breach Science Publishers, c/o International Publishers Distributor, P.O. Box 3054, Langhorne, PA 19047-3054. TEL 215-750-2642. FAX 215-750-6343. *5579*

P A I S INTERNATIONAL IN PRINT.
Public Affairs Information Service Inc., 521 W. 43rd St., 5th Fl., New York, NY 10036-4396. TEL 212-736-6629. FAX 212-643 2848. Vendor(s): Data-Star (PAIS), Knight-Ridder Information, Inc. (File no.49/PAIS), OCLC, Research Libraries Group Information Network. *1020*

P A S C A L E 11: PHYSIQUE ATOMIQUE ET MOLECULAIRE. PLASMAS.
Centre National de la Recherche Scientifique, Institut de l'Information Scientifique et Technique, 2 allee du Parc de Brabois, 54514 Vandoeuvre-Les-Nancy Cedex, France. TEL 83-50-46-00. FAX 83-50-46-50. Vendor(s): European Space Agency (File no.14), Knight-Ridder Information Inc. (File no.144), Telesystemes - Questel. *5579*

P A S C A L. E 12: ETAT CONDENSE.
Centre National de la Recherche Scientifique, Institut de l'Information Scientifique et Technique, 2 allee du Parc de Brabois, 54514 Vandoeuvre-Les-Nancy Cedex, France. TEL 83-50-46-00. FAX 83-50-46-50.
Vendor(s): European Space Agency (File no.14), Knight-Ridder Information, Inc. (File no.144), Telesystemes - Questel. *5579*

P A S C A L. E 13: STRUCTURE DES LIQUIDES ET DES SOLIDES - CRISTALLOGRAPHIE.
Centre National de la Recherche Scientifique, Institut de l'Information Scientifique et Technique, 2 allee du Parc de Brabois, 54514 Vandoeuvre-les-Nancy Cedex, France. TEL 83-50-46-00. FAX 83-50-46-50.
Vendor(s): European Space Agency (File no.14), Knight-Ridder Information, Inc. (File no.144), Telesystemes - Questel. *1710*

P A S C A L. E 18: CHROMATOGRAPHIE.
Centre National de la Recherche Scientifique, Institut de l'Information Scientifique et Technique, 2 allee du Parc de Brabois, 54514 Vandoeuvre-les-Nancy Cedex, France. TEL 83-50-46-00. FAX 83-50-46-50.
Vendor(s): European Space Agency (File no.14), Knight-Ridder Information, Inc. (File no.144), Telesystemes - Questel. *1710*

P A S C A L. E 20: ELECTRONIQUE ET TELECOMMUNICATIONS.
Centre National de la Recherche Scientifique, Institut de l'Information Scientifique et Technique, 2 allee du Parc de Brabois, 54514 Vandoeuvre-les-Nancy Cedex, France. TEL 83-50-46-00. FAX 83-50-46-50.
Vendor(s): European Space Agency (File no.14), Knight-Ridder Information, Inc. (File no.144), Telesystemes - Questel. *2529*

P A S C A L. E 27: METHODES DE FORMATION ET TRAITEMENT DES IMAGES.
Centre National de la Recherche Scientifique, Institut de l'Information Scientifique et Technique, 2 allee du Parc de Brabois, 54514 Vandoeuvre-les-Nancy Cedex, France. TEL 83-50-46-00. FAX 83-50-46-50.
Vendor(s): European Space Agency (File no.14), Knight-Ridder Information, Inc. (File no.144), Telesystemes - Questel. *5579*

P A S C A L. E 30: MICROSCOPIE ELECTRONIQUE ET DIFFRACTION ELECTRONIQUE.
Centre National de la Recherche Scientifique, Institut de l'Information Scientifique et Technique, 2 allee du Parc de Brabois, 54514 Vandoeuvre-Les-Nancy Cedex, France. TEL 83-50-46-00. FAX 83-50-46-50.
Vendor(s): European Space Agency (File no.14), Knight-Ridder Information, Inc. (File no.144), Telesystemes - Questel. *622*

P A S C A L. E 32: METROLOGIE ET APPAREILLAGE EN PHYSIQUE ET PHYSICOCHIMIE.
Centre National de la Recherche Scientifique, Institut de l'Information Scientifique et Technique, 2 allee du Parc de Brabois, 54514 Vandoeuvre-Les-Nancy Cedex, France. TEL 83-50-46-00. FAX 83-50-46-50.
Vendor(s): European Space Agency (File no.14), Knight-Ridder Information, Inc. (File no.144), Telesystemes - Questel. *5019*

P A S C A L. E 33. INFORMATIQUE.
Centre National de la Recherche Scientifique, Institut de l'Information Scientifique et Technique, 2 allee du Parc de Brabois, 54514 Vandoeuvre-Les-Nancy Cedex, France. TEL 83-50-46-00. FAX 83-50-46-50.
Vendor(s): European Space Agency, Knight-Ridder Information, Inc., Telesystemes - Questel. *2003*

P A S C A L. E 34. ROBOTIQUE, AUTOMATIQUE ET AUTOMATISATION DES PROCESSUS INDUSTRIELS.
Centre National de la Recherche Scientifique, Institut de l'Information Scientifique et Technique, 2 allee du Parc de Brabois, 54514 Vandoeuvre-Les-Nancy Cedex, France. TEL 83-50-46-00. FAX 83-50-46-50.
Vendor(s): European Space Agency (File no.14), Knight-Ridder Information, Inc. (File no.144), Telesystemes - Questel. *2003*

P A S C A L. E 36: POLLUTION DE L'EAU, DE L'AIR ET DU SOL - DECHETS - BRUIT.
Centre National de la Recherche Scientifique, Institut de l'Information Scientifique et Technique, 2 allee du Parc de Brabois, 54514 Vandoeuvre-Les-Nancy, France. TEL 83-50-46-00. FAX 83-50-46-50.
Vendor(s): European Space Agency (File no.14), Knight-Ridder Information, Inc. (File no.144), Telesystemes - Questel. *2830*

P A S C A L. E 48: ENVIRONNEMENT COSMIQUE TERRESTRE, ASTRONOMIE ET GEOLOGIE EXTRATERRESTRE.
Centre National de la Recherche Scientifique, Institut de l'Information Scientifique et Technique, 2 allee du Parc de Brabois, 54514 Vandoeuvre-Les-Nancy, France. TEL 83-50-46-00. FAX 83-50-46-50.
Vendor(s): European Space Agency (File no.14), Knight-Ridder Information, Inc. (File no.144), Telesystemes - Questel. *2220*

P A S C A L. E 49: METEOROLOGIE, GLACIOLOGIE, PHYSIQUE DES OCEANS.
Centre National de la Recherche Scientifique, Institut de l'Information Scientifique et Technique, 2 allee du Parc de Brabois, 54514 Vandoeuvre-Les-Nancy Cedex, France. TEL 83-50-46-00. FAX 83-50-46-50.
Vendor(s): European Space Agency (File no.14), Knight-Ridder Information, Inc. (File no.144), Telesystemes - Questel. *5011*

P A S C A L. E 58: GENETIQUE.
Centre National de la Recherche Scientifique, Institut de l'Information Scientifique et Technique, 2 allee du Parc de Brabois, 54514 Vandoeuvre-Les-Nancy Cedex, France. TEL 83-50-46-00. FAX 83-50-46-50.
Vendor(s): European Space Agency (File no.14), Knight-Ridder Information, Inc. (File no.144), Telesystemes - Questel. *623*

P A S C A L. E 61: MICROBIOLOGIE: BACTERIOLOGIE, VIROLOGIE, MYCOLOGIE, PROTOZOAIRES PATHOGENES.
Centre National de la Recherche Scientifique, Institut de l'Information Scientifique et Technique, 2 allee du Parc de Brabois, 54514 Vandoeuvre-Les-Nancy Cedex, France. TEL 83-50-46-00. FAX 83-50-46-50.
Vendor(s): European Space Agency (File no.14), Knight-Ridder Information, Inc. (File no. 144), Telesystemes - Questel. *623*

P A S C A L. E 62: IMMUNOLOGIE.
Centre National de la Recherche Scientifique, Institut de l'Information Scientifique et Technique, 2 allee du Parc de Brabois, 54514 Vandoeuvre-Les-Nancy Cedex, France. TEL 83-50-46-00. FAX 83-50-46-50.
Vendor(s): European Space Agency (File no.14), Knight-Ridder Information, Inc. (File no.144), Telesystemes - Questel. *623*

P A S C A L. E 63: TOXICOLOGIE.
Centre National de la Recherche Scientifique, Institut de l'Information Scientifique et Technique, 2 allee du Parc de Brabois, 54514 Vandoeuvre-Les-Nancy Cedex, France. TEL 83-50-46-00. FAX 83-50-46-50.
Vendor(s): European Space Agency (File no.14), Knight-Ridder Information, Inc. (File no.144), Telesystemes - Questel. *2831*

P A S C A L. E 64: ENDOCRINOLOGIE HUMAINE ET EXPERIMENTALE. ENDOCRINOPATHIES.
Centre National de la Recherche Scientifique, Institut de l'Information Scientifique et Technique, 2 allee du Parc de Brabois, 54514 Vandoeuvre-Les-Nancy Cedex, France. TEL 83-50-46-00. FAX 83-50-46-50.
Vendor(s): European Space Agency (File no.14), Knight-Ridder Information, Inc. (File no.144), Telesystemes - Questel. *4570*

P A S C A L. E 65: PSYCHOLOGIE, PSYCHOPATHOLOGIE, PSYCHIATRIE.
Centre National de la Recherche Scientifique, Institut de l'Information Scientifique et Technique, 2 allee du Parc de Brabois, 54514 Vandoeuvre-Les-Nancy Cedex, France. TEL 83-50-46-00. FAX 83-50-46-50.
Vendor(s): European Space Agency (File no.14), Knight-Ridder Information, Inc. (File no.144), Telesystemes - Questel. *4570*

P A S C A L. E 68: GENETIQUE HUMAINE.
Centre National de la Recherche Scientifique, Institut de l'Information Scientifique et Technique, 2 allee du Parc de Brabois, 54514 Vandoeuvre-les-Nancy Cedex, France. TEL 83-50-46-00. FAX 83-50-46-50.
Vendor(s): European Space Agency, Knight-Ridder Information, Inc., Telesystemes - Questel. *623*

P A S C A L. E 71: OPHTALMOLOGIE.
Centre National de la Recherche Scientifique, Institut de l'Information Scientifique et Technique, 2 allee du Parc de Brabois, 54514 Vandoeuvre-Les-Nancy Cedex, France. TEL 83-50-46-00. FAX 83-50-46-50.
Vendor(s): European Space Agency (File no.14), Knight-Ridder Information, Inc. (File no. 144), Telesystemes - Questel. *4570*

P A S C A L. E 72: OTORHINOLARYNGOLOGIE. STOMATOLOGIE. PATHOLOGIE CERVICOFACIALE.
Centre National de la Recherche Scientifique, Institut de l'Information Scientifique et Technique, 2 allee du Parc de Brabois, 54514 Vandoeuvre-Les-Nancy, France. TEL 83-50-46-00. FAX 83-50-46-50.
Vendor(s): European Space Agency (File no.14), Knight-Ridder Information, Inc. (File no.144), Telesystemes - Questel. *4571*

P A S C A L. E 73: DERMATOLOGIE. MALADIES SEXUELLEMENT TRANSMISSIBLES.
Centre National de la Recherche Scientifique, Institut de l'Information Scientifique et Technique, 2 allee du Parc de Brabois, 54514 Vandoeuvre-Les-Nancy, France. TEL 83-50-46-00. FAX 83-50-46-50.
Vendor(s): European Space Agency (File no.14), Knight-Ridder Information, Inc. (File no.144), Telesystemes - Questel. *4571*

P A S C A L. E 74: PNEUMOLOGIE.
Centre National de la Recherche Scientifique, Institut de l'Information Scientifique et Technique, 2 allee du Parc de Brabois, 54514 Vandoeuvre-Les-Nancy Cedex, France. TEL 83-50-46-00. FAX 83-50-46-50.
Vendor(s): European Space Agency (File no.14), Knight-Ridder Information, Inc. (File no.144), Telesystemes - Questel. *4571*

P A S C A L. E 75: CARDIOLOGIE ET APPAREIL CIRCULATOIRE.
Centre National de la Recherche Scientifique, Institut de l'Information Scientifique et Technique, 2 allee du Parc de Brabois, 54514 Vandoeuvre-Les-Nancy Cedex, France. TEL 83-50-46-00. FAX 83-50-46-50.
Vendor(s): European Space Agency (File no.14), Knight-Ridder Information, Inc. (File no.144), Telesystemes - Questel. *4571*

P A S C A L. E 76: GASTROENTEROLOGIE, FOIE, PANCREAS, ABDOMEN.
Centre National de la Recherche Scientifique, Institut de l'Information Scientifique et Technique, 2 allee du Parc de Brabois, 54514 Vandoeuvre-Les-Nancy Cedex, France. TEL 83-50-46-00. FAX 83-50-46-50.
Vendor(s): European Space Agency (File no.14), Knight-Ridder Information, Inc. (File no.144), Telesystemes - Questel. *4571*

P A S C A L. E 77: NEPHROLOGIE. VOIES URINAIRES.
Centre National de la Recherche Scientifique, Institut de l'Information Scientifique et Technique, 2 allee du Parc de Brabois, 54514 Vandoeuvre-Les-Nancy Cedex, France. TEL 83-50-46-00. FAX 83-50-46-50.
Vendor(s): European Space Agency (File no.14), Knight-Ridder Information, Inc. (File no.144), Telesystemes - Questel. *4571*

P A S C A L. E 78: NEUROLOGIE.
Centre National de la Recherche Scientifique, Institut de l'Information Scientifique et Technique, 2 allee du Parc de Brabois, 54514 Vandoeuvre-Les-Nancy Cedex, France. TEL 83-50-46-00. FAX 83-50-46-50.
Vendor(s): European Space Agency (File no.14), Knight-Ridder Information, Inc. (File no.144), Telesystemes - Questel. *4571*

P A S C A L. E 79: PATHOLOGIE ET PHYSIOLOGIE OSTEOARTICULAIRES.
Centre National de la Recherche Scientifique, Institut de l'Information Scientifique et Technique, 2 allee du Parc de Brabois, 54514 Vandoeuvre-Les-Nancy Cedex, France. TEL 83-50-46-00. FAX 83-50-46-50.
Vendor(s): European Space Agency (File no.14), Knight-Ridder Information, Inc. (File no.144), Telesystemes - Questel. *4571*

P A S C A L. E 80: HEMATOLOGIE.
Centre National de la Recherche Scientifique, Institut de l'Information Scientifique et Technique, 2 allee du Parc de Brabois, 54514 Vandoeuvre-Les-Nancy Cedex, France. TEL 83-50-46-00. FAX 83-50-46-50.
Vendor(s): European Space Agency (File no.14), Knight-Ridder Information, Inc. (File no.144), Telesystemes - Questel. *4571*

P A S C A L. E 82: GYNECOLOGIE, OBSTETRIQUE, ANDROLOGIE.
Centre National de la Recherche Scientifique, Institut de l'Information Scientifique et Technique, 2 allee du Parc de Brabois, 54514 Vandoeuvre-Les-Nancy Cedex, France. TEL 83-50-46-00. FAX 83-50-46-50.
Vendor(s): European Space Agency (File no.14), Knight-Ridder Information, Inc. (File no.144), Telesystemes - Questel. *4571*

P A S C A L. E 83: ANESTHESIE ET REANIMATION.
Centre National de la Recherche Scientifique, Institut de l'Information Scientifique et Technique, 2 allee du Parc de Brabois, 54514 Vandoeuvre-Les-Nancy Cedex, France. TEL 83-50-46-00. FAX 83-50-46-50.
Vendor(s): European Space Agency (File no.14), Knight-Ridder Information, Inc. (File no.144), Telesystemes - Questel. *4571*

P A S C A L. E 84: GENIE BIOMEDICAL. INFORMATIQUE BIOMEDICALE.
Centre National de la Recherche Scientifique, Institut de l'Information Scientifique et Technique, 2 allee du Parc de Brabois, 54514 Vandoeuvre-Les-Nancy Cedex, France. TEL 83-50-46-00. FAX 83-50-46-50.
Vendor(s): European Space Agency (File no.14), Knight-Ridder Information, Inc. (File no.144), Telesystemes - Questel. *4572*

P A S C A L. E 89: CANCER.
Centre National de la Recherche Scientifique, Institut de l'Information Scientifique et Technique, 2 allee du Parc de Brabois, 54514 Vandoeuvre-les-Nancy Cedex, France. TEL 83-50-46-00. FAX 83-50-46-50.
Vendor(s): European Space Agency (File no.14), Knight-Ridder Information, Inc. (File no.144), Telesystemes - Questel. *4572*

P A S C A L. F 10: MECANIQUE, ACOUSTIQUE ET TRANSFERT DE CHALEUR.
Centre National de la Recherche Scientifique, Institut de l'Information Scientifique et Technique, 2 allee du Parc de Brabois, 54514 Vandoeuvre-Les-Nancy Cedex, France. TEL 83-50-46-00. FAX 83-50-46-50.
Vendor(s): European Space Agency (File no.14), Knight-Ridder Information, Inc. (File no.144), Telesystemes - Questel. *5580*

P A S C A L. F 16: CHIMIE ANALYTIQUE, MINERALE ET ORGANIQUE.
Centre National de la Recherche Scientifique, Institut de l'Information Scientifique et Technique, 2 allee du Parc de Brabois, 54514 Vandoeuvre-Les-Nancy Cedex, France. TEL 83-50-46-00. FAX 83-50-46-50.
Vendor(s): European Space Agency (File no.14), Knight-Ridder Information, Inc. (File no.144), Telesystemes - Questel. *1710*

P A S C A L. F 17: CHIMIE GENERALE, MINERALE ET ORGANIQUE.
Centre National de la Recherche Scientifique, Institut de l'Information Scientifique et Technique, 2 allee du Parc de Brabois, 54514 Vandoeuvre-Les-Nancy Cedex, France. TEL 83-50-46-00. FAX 83-50-46-50.
Vendor(s): European Space Agency (File no.14), Knight-Ridder Information, Inc. (File no.144), Telesystemes - Questel. *1710*

P A S C A L. F 23: GENIE CHIMIQUE. INDUSTRIES CHIMIQUE ET PARACHIMIQUE.
Centre National de la Recherche Scientifique, Institut de l'Information Scientifique et Technique, 2 allee du Parc de Brabois, 54514 Vandoeuvre-Les-Nancy Cedex, France. TEL 83-50-46-00. FAX 83-50-46-50.
Vendor(s): European Space Agency (File no.14), Knight-Ridder Information, Inc. (File no.144), Telesystemes - Questel. *1710*

P A S C A L. F 24: POLYMERES - PEINTURES - BOIS.
Centre National de la Recherche Scientifique, Institut de l'Information Scientifique et Technique, 2 allee du Parc de Brabois, 54514 Vandoeuvre-Les-Nancy Cedex, France. TEL 83-50-46-00. FAX 83-50-46-50.
Vendor(s): European Space Agency (File no.14), Knight-Ridder Information, Inc. (File no.144), Telesystemes - Questel. *1711*

P A S C A L. F 40: MINERALOGIE. GEOCHIMIE. GEOLOGIE EXTRATERRESTRE.
Centre National de la Recherche Scientifique, Institut de l'Information Scientifique et Technique, 2 allee du Parc de Brabois, 54514 Vandoeuvre-Les-Nancy Cedex, France. TEL 83-50-46-00. FAX 83-50-46-50.
Vendor(s): European Space Agency (File no.14), Knight-Ridder Information, Inc. (File no.144), Telesystemes - Questel. *2220*

P A S C A L. F 41: GISEMENTS METALLIQUES ET NON METALLIQUES.
Centre National de la Recherche Scientifique, Institut de l'Information Scientifique et Technique, 2 allee du Parc de Brabois, 54514 Vandoeuvre-Les-Nancy Cedex, France. TEL 83-50-46-00. FAX 83-50-46-50.
Vendor(s): European Space Agency (File no.14), Knight-Ridder Information, Inc. (File no.144), Telesystemes - Questel. *5084*

P A S C A L. F 42: ROCHES CRISTALLINES.
Centre National de la Recherche Scientifique, Institut de l'Information Scientifique et Technique, 2 allee du Parc de Brabois, 54514 Vandoeuvre-Les-Nancy Cedex, France. TEL 83-50-46-00. FAX 83-50-46-50.
Vendor(s): European Space Agency (File no.14), Knight-Ridder Information, Inc. (File no.144), Telesystemes - Questel. *2220*

P A S C A L. F 43: ROCHES SEDIMENTAIRES. GEOLOGIE MARINE.
Centre National de la Recherche Scientifique, Institut de l'Information Scientifique et Technique, 2 allee du Parc de Brabois, 54514 Vandoeuvre-Les-Nancy Cedex, France. TEL 83-50-46-00. FAX 83-50-46-50.
Vendor(s): European Space Agency (File no.14), Knight-Ridder Information, Inc. (File no.144), Telesystemes - Questel. *2220*

P A S C A L. F 44: STRATIGRAPHIE, GEOLOGIE REGIONALE, GEOLOGIE GENERALE.
Centre National de la Recherche Scientifique, Institut de l'Information Scientifique et Technique, 2 allee du Parc de Brabois, 54514 Vandoeuvre-Les-Nancy Cedex, France. TEL 83-50-46-00. FAX 83-50-46-50.
Vendor(s): European Space Agency (File no.14), Knight-Ridder Information, Inc. (File no.144), Telesystemes - Questel. *2220*

P A S C A L. F 45: TECTONIQUE, GEOPHYSIQUE INTERNE.
Centre National de la Recherche Scientifique, Institut de l'Information Scientifique et Technique, 2 allee du Parc de Brabois, 54514 Vandoeuvre-Les-Nancy Cedex, France. TEL 83-50-46-00. FAX 83-50-46-50.
Vendor(s): European Space Agency (File no.14), Knight-Ridder Information, Inc. (File no.144), Telesystemes - Questel. *2220*

P A S C A L. F 46: HYDROLOGIE. GEOLOGIE DE L'INGENIEUR. FORMATIONS SUPERFICIELLES.
Centre National de la Recherche Scientifique, Institut de l'Information Scientifique et Technique, 2 allee du Parc de Brabois, 54514 Vandoeuvre-Les-Nancy Cedex, France. TEL 83-50-46-00. FAX 83-50-46-50.
Vendor(s): European Space Agency (File no.14), Knight-Ridder Information, Inc. (File no.144), Telesystemes - Questel. *2221*

P A S C A L. F 47: PALEONTOLOGIE.
Centre National de la Recherche Scientifique, Institut de l'Information Scientifique et Technique, 2 allee du Parc de Brabois, 54514 Vandoeuvre-Les-Nancy Cedex, France. TEL 83-50-46-00. FAX 83-50-46-50.
Vendor(s): European Space Agency (File no.14), Knight-Ridder Information, Inc. (File no.144), Telesystemes - Questel. *5319*

P A S C A L. F 52: BIOCHIMIE - BIOPHYSIQUE - MOLECULAIRE - BIOLOGIE MOLECULAIRE ET CELLULAIRE.
Centre National de la Recherche Scientifique, Institut de l'Information Scientifique et Technique, 2 allee du Parc de Brabois, 54514 Vandoeuvre-Les-Nancy Cedex, France. TEL 83-50-46-00. FAX 83-50-46-50.
Vendor(s): European Space Agency (File no.14), Knight-Ridder Information, Inc. (File no.144), Telesystemes - Questel. *523*

P A S C A L. F 53: ANATOMIE ET PHYSIOLOGIE DES VERTEBRES.
Centre National de la Recherche Scientifique, Institut de l'Information Scientifique et Technique, 2 allee du Parc de Brabois, 54514 Vandoeuvre-Les-Nancy Cedex, France. TEL 83-50-46-00. FAX 83-50-46-50.
Vendor(s): European Space Agency (File no.14), Knight-Ridder Information, Inc. (File no.144), Telesystemes - Questel. *623*

P A S C A L. F 54: REPRODUCTION DES VERTEBRES, EMBRYOLOGIE DES VERTEBRES ET DES INVERTEBRES.
Centre National de la Recherche Scientifique, Institut de l'Information Scientifique et Technique, 2 allee du Parc de Brabois, 54514 Vandoeuvre-Les-Nancy Cedex, France. TEL 83-50-46-00. FAX 83-50-46-50.
Vendor(s): European Space Agency (File no.14), Knight-Ridder Information, Inc. (File no.144), Telesystemes - Questel. *4572*

P A S C A L. F 55: BIOLOGIE VEGETALE.
Centre National de la Recherche Scientifique, Institut de l'Information Scientifique et Technique, 2 allee du Parc de Brabois, 54514 Vandoeuvre-Les-Nancy Cedex, France. TEL 83-50-46-00. FAX 83-50-46-50.
Vendor(s): European Space Agency (File no.14), Knight-Ridder Information, Inc. (File no.144), Telesystemes - Questel. *523*

P A S C A L. F 56: ECOLOGIE ANIMALE, VEGETALE ET MICROBIENNE. ETHOLOGIE ANIMALE.
Centre National de la Recherche Scientifique, Institut de l'Information Scientifique et Technique, 2 allee du Parc de Brabois, 54514 Vandoeuvre-Les-Nancy Cedex, France. TEL 83-50-46-00. FAX 83-50-46-50.
Vendor(s): European Space Agency (File no.14), Knight-Ridder Information, Inc. (File no.144), Telesystemes - Questel. *623*

P A S C A L. F 70: PHARMACOLOGIE. TRAITEMENTS MEDICAMENTEUX.
Centre National de la Recherche Scientifique, Institut de l'Information Scientifique et Technique, 2 allee du Parc de Brabois, 54514 Vandoeuvre-Les-Nancy Cedex, France. TEL 83-50-46-00. FAX 83-50-46-50.
Vendor(s): European Space Agency (File no.14), Knight-Ridder Information, Inc. (File no.144), Telesystemes - Questel. *5451*

P A S C A L. T 205: SCIENCES DE L'INFORMATION. DOCUMENTATION.
Centre National de la Recherche Scientifique, Institut de l'Information Scientifique et Technique, 2 allee du Parc de Brabois, 54514 Vandoeuvre-les-Nancy Cedex, France. TEL 83-50-46-00. FAX 83-50-46-50.
Vendor(s): European Space Agency (File no.14), Knight-Ridder Information, Inc. (File no.144), Telesystemes - Questel. *4040*

P A S C A L. T 215: BIOTECHNOLOGIES.
Centre National de la Recherche Scientifique, Institut de l'Information Scientifique et Technique, 2 allee du Parc de Brabois, 54514 Vandoeuvre-les-Nancy Cedex, France. TEL 83-50-46-00. FAX 83-50-46-50.
Vendor(s): European Space Agency (File no.14), Knight-Ridder Information, Inc. (File no.144), Telesystemes - Questel. *4572*

P A S C A L. T 230: ENERGIE.
Centre National de la Recherche Scientifique, Institut de l'Information Scientifique et Technique, 2 allee du Parc de Brabois, 54514 Vandoeuvre-Les-Nancy Cedex, France. TEL 83-50-46-00. FAX 83-50-46-50.
Vendor(s): European Space Agency (File no.14), Knight-Ridder Information, Inc. (File no.144), Telesystemes - Questel. *5580*

P A S C A L. T 235: MEDECINE TROPICALE.
Centre National de la Recherche Scientifique, Institut de l'Information Scientifique et Technique, 2 allee du Parc de Brabois, 54514 Vandoeuvre-Les-Nancy Cedex, France. TEL 83-50-46-00. FAX 83-50-46-50.
Vendor(s): European Space Agency (File no.14), Knight-Ridder Information, Inc. (File no.144), Telesystemes - Questel. *4572*

P A S C A L. T 240: METAUX - METALLURGIE.
Centre National de la Recherche Scientifique, Institut de l'Information Scientifique et Technique, 2 allee du Parc de Brabois, 54514 Vandoeuvre-Les-Nancy Cedex, France. TEL 83-50-46-00. FAX 83-50-46-50.
Vendor(s): European Space Agency (File no.14), Knight-Ridder Information, Inc. (File no.144), Telesystemes - Questel. *4984*

P A S C A L. T 260: ZOOLOGIE FONDAMENTALE ET APPLIQUEE DES INVERTEBRES.
Centre National de la Recherche Scientifique, Institut de l'Information Scientifique et Technique, 2 allee du Parc de Brabois, 54514 Vandoeuvre-Les-Nancy Cedex, France. TEL 83-50-46-00. FAX 83-50-46-50.
Vendor(s): European Space Agency (File no.14), Knight-Ridder Information, Inc. (File no.144), Telesystemes - Questel. *623*

P A S C A L. T 280: SCIENCES AGRONOMIQUES ET FORESTIERES: PRODUCTIONS VEGETALES.
Centre National de la Recherche Scientifique, Institut de l'Information Scientifique et Technique, 2 allee du Parc de Brabois, 54514 Vandoeuvre-Les-Nancy Cedex, France. TEL 83-50-46-00. FAX 83-50-46-50.
Vendor(s): European Space Agency (File no.14), Knight-Ridder Information, Inc. (File no.144), Telesystemes - Questel. *178*

P A S C A L. T 295: BATIMENT. TRAVAUX PUBLICS.
Centre National de la Recherche Scientifique, Institut de l'Information Scientifique et Technique, 2 allee du Parc de Brabois, 54514 Vandoeuvre-les-Nancy Cedex, France. TEL 83-50-46-00. FAX 83-50-46-50.
Vendor(s): European Space Agency (File no.14), Knight-Ridder Information, Inc. (File no.144), Telesystemes - Questel. *2629*

P A S C A L V.4 SCIENCES DE LA TERRE.
Centre National de la Recherche Scientifique, Institut de l'Information Scientifique et Technique, 2 allee du Parc de Brabois, 54514 Vandoeuvre-les-Nancy Cedex, France. TEL 83-50-46-00. FAX 83-50-46-50.
Vendor(s): European Space Agency (File no.14), Knight-Ridder Information, Inc. (File no.144), Telesystemes - Questel. *2221*

P & S JOURNAL.
Columbia University, College of Physicians and Surgeons, 630 W. 168 St., New York, NY 10032. TEL 212-305-3877. FAX 212-928-5799. *4512*

P & T.
Quadrant HealthCom, 105 Raider Blvd., Belle Mead, NJ 08052-1510. TEL 908-874-0707. FAX 908-874-5611. *5431*

P C BUSINESS PRODUCTS.
Worldwide Videotex, Box 3273, Bounton Beach, FL 33424-3273. TEL 508-477-8979.
Vendor(s): Data-Star, Information Access Co., Knight-Ridder Information, Inc., NewsNet (EC94). *1130*

P C - COMPUTING.
Ziff-Davis Publishing Co. (Foster City), Computer Publications Division, 950 Tower Ln., Foster City, CA 94404. TEL 415-578-7000. FAX 415-578-7059.
Vendor(s): Information Access Co.. *2099*

P C GAMES.
Computec Verlag, Isarstr. 32-34, 90451 Nuernberg, Germany. TEL 49-911-96832-0. FAX 49-911-6426333. *2024*

P C MAGAZIN.
Markt und Technik Verlag AG, Hans-Pinsel-Str. 2, 85540 Haar, Germany. TEL 089-4613-0. FAX 089-4613-774.
Vendor(s): Knight-Ridder Information, Inc.. *2099*

P C MAGAZINE (U.K.).
Ziff-Davis UK Ltd., Cottons Centre, Hay's Ln., London SE1 2QT, England. TEL 44-171-378-6800. FAX 44-171-403-0668.
Vendor(s): Information Access Co.. *2099*

P C NETTER NEWSLETTER.
Architecture Technology Corporation, Box 24344, Minneapolis, MN 55424. TEL 612-935-2035. FAX 612-829-5871.
Vendor(s): Information Access Co.. *2100*

P C PRESENTATIONS PRODUCTIONS.
Pisces Publishing Group, Inc., 417 Bridgeport Ave., Devon, CT 06460-4105. TEL 203-877-1927. FAX 203-877-1927.
Available only online. *2100*

P C PRICE TRACKING SERVICE.
Computer Economics, Inc., 5841 Edison Pl., Carlsbad, CA 92008. TEL 619-438-8100. FAX 619-431-1126. *2048*

P C S WEEK.
Phillips Business Information, Inc., 1201 Seven Locks Rd., Potomac, MD 20854. TEL 301-424-3338. FAX 301-309-3847.
Vendor(s): Information Access Co., NewsNet (TE12). *1913*

P C T GAZETTE.
World Intellectual Property Organization (WIPO), Publications Sales and Distribution Unit, 34 chemin des Colombettes, CH-1211 Geneva 20, Switzerland. TEL 41-22-730-9111. FAX 41-22-733-5428. *5347*

P C USER.
E M A P Business & Computer Publications Ltd., 33-39 Bowling Green Ln., London EC1R 0DA, England. TEL 44-171-837-1212. FAX 44-171-278-4008.
Vendor(s): Information Access Co.. *2090*

P C WEEK.
Ziff-Davis Publishing Co. (Medford), One Park Ave., New York, NY 10016-5146. TEL 212-503-5100.
Vendor(s): CompuServe, Inc., Information Access Co.. *2101*

P C WORLD.
D J Communications, Inc., One Exeter Plaza, Boston, MA 02116. TEL 617-534-1200.
Vendor(s): CompuServe, Inc. (GO PWOFORUM), Information Access Co.. *2101*

P C WORLD MALAYSIA.
Communication Resources Pte. Ltd., Blk. 1008, Toa Payoh North, No. 07-01, Singapore 318996, Singapore. TEL 65-256-6201. FAX 65-251-0348. *2101*

P C WORLD SINGAPORE.
Communication Resources Pte. Ltd., Blk. 1008, Toa Payoh North, No. 07-01, Singapore 318996, Singapore. TEL 65-2566201. FAX 65-251-0348. *2102*

P D A JOURNAL OF PHARMACEUTICAL SCIENCE AND TECHNOLOGY.
Parenteral Drug Association, Inc., 7500 Old Georgetown Rd., Ste. 620, Bethesda, MD 20814-6133. TEL 301-986-0293. FAX 301-986-0296. *5431*

P L E R U S.
Universidad de Puerto Rico, Escuela Graduada de Planificacion, P.O. Box 23354, UPR Sta., San Juan, PR 00931-3354. TEL 809-763-7590. FAX 809-763-5375. *3590*

P M L A.
Modern Language Association of America, 10 Astor Pl., New York, NY 10003. TEL 212-475-9500. FAX 212-477-9863.
Vendor(s): University Microfilms International. *4247*

P N I.
U M I Company 300 N. Zeeb Rd., Ann Arbor, MI 48106-1346. TEL 313-761-4700. FAX 800-864-0019.
Vendor(s): Knight-Ridder Information, Inc. (File no.42), Orbit Search Service, Ovid Technologies, Inc. (PNII), STN International. *5451*

P O S NEWS.
Faulkner & Gray, Inc., 118 S. Clinton St., Ste. 450, Chicago, IL 60606. TEL 312-648-0264.
Vendor(s): Information Access Co., University Microfilms International. *1114*

P P O LETTER.
Capitol Publications Inc., 1101 King St., Ste. 444, Box 1455, Alexandria, VA 22314. TEL 703-683-4100. FAX 703-739-6517.
Vendor(s): NewsNet. *950*

P S A JOURNAL.
Photographic Society of America, Inc., 3000 United Founders Blvd., No. 103, Oklahoma City, OK 73112-3940. TEL 405-843-1437. FAX 405-843-1438.
Vendor(s): Information Access Co.. *5516*

P S P BULLETIN.
Association of American Publishers, Inc., Professional & Scholarly Publishing Division, 71 Fifth Ave., New York, NY 10003-3004. TEL 212-255-0200. FAX 212-255-7007. *6004*

P S: POLITICAL SCIENCE & POLITICS.
American Political Science Association, 1527 New Hampshire Ave., N.W., Washington, DC 20036. TEL 202-483-2512. FAX 202-483-2657.
Vendor(s): Information Access Co.. *5690*

P T N.
P T N Publishing Corp., 445 Broad Hollow Rd., Ste. 21, Melville, NY 11747-4722. TEL 516-845-2700. FAX 516-845-7109.
Vendor(s): Information Access Co.. *5516*

PACIFIC AFFAIRS.
Pacific Affairs, University of British Columbia, 2029 West Mall, Vancouver, BC V6T 1Z2, Canada. TEL 604-822-6508. FAX 604-822-9452.
Vendor(s): Information Access Co., University Microfilms International. *5690*

PACIFIC BUSINESS NEWS.
American City Business Journals, Inc., 128 Tregon St., Ste. 2000, Charlotte, NC 28202. TEL 704-375-7404.
Vendor(s): Knight-Ridder Information, Inc., Lexis-Nexis. *950*

PACIFIC HISTORICAL REVIEW.
University of California Press, Journals Division, 2120 Berkeley Way, No. 5812, Berkeley, CA 94720-5812. TEL 510-643-7154. FAX 510-642-9917.
Vendor(s): Information Access Co.. *3482*

PACIFIC LAW JOURNAL.
Western Newspaper Publishing, Co., 3200 Fifth Ave., Sacramento, CA 95817. TEL 916-739-7171. FAX 916-739-7111.
Vendor(s): Lexis-Nexis, West Services, Inc.. *3831*

PACK-O-FUN.
Clapper Communications Companies, 2400 E. Devon Ave., Ste. 375, Des Plaines, IL 60018-4618. TEL 847-635-5800. FAX 847-635-6311. *469*

PACKAGING DIGEST.
Cahners Publishing Company (Des Plaines), Division of Reed Elsevier Inc., 1350 E. Touhy Ave., Box 5080, Des Plaines, IL 60018-5080. TEL 847-635-8800. FAX 847-390-2460.
Vendor(s): Information Access Co.. *5302*

PACKAGING SCIENCE AND TECHNOLOGY ABSTRACTS.
Fraunhofer Institut fuer Lebensmitteltechnologie und Verpackung, Schragenhofstr. .35, 80992 Munich, Germany. TEL 49-89-149009-0. FAX 49-89-14900980.
Vendor(s): DIMDI, Data-Star, FIZ Technik, Knight-Ridder Information, Inc. (File no.252), Orbit Search Service, STN International. *5305*

PACKAGING TECHNOLOGY AND ENGINEERING.
North American Publishing Co., 401 N. Broad St., Philadelphia, PA 19108. TEL 215-238-5300. FAX 215-238-5457.
Vendor(s): Information Access Co.. *5303*

PACKAGING WEEK.
Miller Freeman Publishers Ltd. Sovereign Way, Tonbridge, Kent TN9 1RW, England. TEL 44-1732-364422. FAX 44-1732-353328.
Vendor(s): Information Access Co.. *5303*

PAINT AND INK INTERNATIONAL.
Argus Business Media Ltd., Fuel and Metals Journals Queensway House, 2 Queensway, Redhill, Surrey RH1 1QS, England. TEL 44-1737-768611. FAX 44-1737-761685.
Vendor(s): Information Access Co.. *5309*

PALAESTRA.
Challenge Publications, Ltd., Circulation Department, 1948 Riverview Dr., Box 508, Macomb, IL 61455-1277. TEL 309-833-1902. FAX 309-833-1902.
Vendor(s): Information Access Co.. *3307*

PAPER & PULP EUROPE.
Miller Freeman, Inc., 123 A chaussee de Charleroi, Bte. 5, 1060 Brussels, Belgium. TEL 32-2-5386040. FAX 32-2-5375626.
Vendor(s): Information Access Co.. *5323*

PAPER, FILM AND FOIL CONVERTER.
Intertec Publishing Corp., 29 N. Wacker Dr., Chicago, IL 60606. TEL 312-726-2802. FAX 312-726-2574.
Vendor(s): Information Access Co.. *5304*

PAPERBASE ABSTRACTS.
Pira International, Randalls Rd., Leatherhead, Surrey KT22 7RU, England. TEL 44-1372-802050. FAX 44-1372-802239.
Vendor(s): Data-Star, FIZ Technik, Knight-Ridder Information, Inc., Orbit Search Service (PIRA), STN International. *5329*

PAPERBOARD PACKAGING.
Advanstar Communications, Inc., 7500 Old Oak Blvd., Cleveland, OH 44130. TEL 216-826-2839. FAX 216-891-2726.
Vendor(s): Information Access Co., Knight-Ridder Information, Inc.. *5304*

PAPERBOUND BOOKS IN PRINT.
R.R. Bowker, A Division of Reed Elsevier Inc., 121 Chanlon Rd., New Providence, NJ 07974. TEL 908-464-6800. FAX 908-665-3502.
Vendor(s): Knight-Ridder Information, Inc. (File no.470), Ovid Technologies, Inc. (BBIP). *543*

PAPERPLATES.
19 Kenwood Ave., Toronto, ON M6C 2R8, Canada. TEL 416-651-2551. *4249*

PAPERS ON LANGUAGE AND LITERATURE.
Southern Illinois University at Edwardsville, Edwardsville, IL 62026. TEL 618-692-2119. FAX 618-692-3509.
Vendor(s): Information Access Co., University Microfilms International. *4249*

PARABOLA.
Society for the Study of Myth and Tradition, 656 Broadway, New York, NY 10012-2317. TEL 212-505-6200. FAX 212-979-7325.
Vendor(s): Information Access Co.. *2955*

PARAPLEGIA NEWS.
P V A Publications, 2111 E. Highland Ave., Ste. 180, Phoenix, AZ 85016-4702. TEL 602-224-0500. FAX 602-224-0507.
Vendor(s): Information Access Co.. *3316*

PARENTS.
Gruner & Jahr U.S.A. Publishing, 110 Fifth Ave., New York, NY 10011. TEL 212-463-1600.
Vendor(s): Information Access Co.. *1775*

PARIS-ANGLOPHONE.
Anglophone S A, 32 rue Edouard Vaillant, 93100 Montreuil, France. TEL 33-1-48-59-66-58. FAX 33-1-48-59-66-68. *1633*

PARIS REVIEW.
Paris Review, Inc., 541 E. 72nd St., New York, NY 10021. TEL 212-861-0016. FAX 212-861-0282.
Vendor(s): University Microfilms International. *4249*

PARKS AND RECREATION.
National Recreation and Park Association, 2775 S. Quincy St., No. 300 Arlington, VA 22206. TEL 703-820-4940. FAX 703-671-6772.
Vendor(s): Information Access Co., University Microfilms International. *3966*

PARLIAMENTARY AFFAIRS.
Oxford University Press, Oxford Journals, Walton St., Oxford OX2 6DP, England. TEL 44-1865-267907. FAX 44-1865-267773.
Vendor(s): Information Access Co.. *5691*

PARTY & PAPER RETAILER.
4Ward Corporation, 70 New Canaan Ave., Norwalk, CT 06850-2600. TEL 203-845-8020. FAX 203-845-8022.
Vendor(s): Information Access Co.. *3966*

PASTA PRODUCTS: THE INTERNATIONAL MARKET.
Euromonitor, 60-61 Britton St., London EC1M 5NA, England. TEL 44-171-251-8024. FAX 44-171-608-3149.
Vendor(s): Data-Star Knight-Ridder Information, Inc.. *2986*

PATENTS ABSTRACTS.
American Petroleum Institute, Central Abstracting & Information Services. 275 Seventh Ave., New York, NY 10001-6708. TEL 212-366-4040. FAX 212-366-4298.
Vendor(s): Orbit Search Service, STN International. *5384*

PATIENT CARE.
Medical Economics Publishing Co., Inc., 5 Paragon Dr., Montvale, NJ 07645. TEL 201-358-7200. FAX 201-573-4625.
Vendor(s): Information Access Co., University Microfilms International. *4514*

PATIENT EDUCATION AND COUNSELING.
Elsevier Science Ireland Ltd., P.O. Box 85, Limerick, Ireland. TEL 353-61-471944. FAX 353-61-472144. *5972*

PATIENTS' RIGHTS REPORTER.
Cox Publications, Box 20316, Billings, MT 59104-0316. TEL 406-256-8822.
Available only online. *3554*

PAX.
Svenska Freds- och Skiljedomsforeningen, Brannkyrkagatan 76 P.O. Box 17515, 118 91 Stockholm, Sweden. TEL 46-0-8-658-21-80. FAX 46-0-8-663-18-70. *5691*

PAYMENT SYSTEMS REPORT.
National Automated Clearing House Association, 607 Herndon Pkwy., Herndon, VA 20170. TEL 703-742-9190. FAX 703-787-0996.
Vendor(s): University Microfilms International. *1130*

PAYMENT SYSTEMS WORLDWIDE.
F.I.A. Financial Publishing Co., 582 Oakwood Ave., Ste. 203, Lake Forest, IL 60045. TEL 708-615-0405. FAX 708-615-0416.
Vendor(s): University Microfilms International. *1114*

PAYROLL ADMINISTRATION GUIDE.
The Bureau of National Affairs, Inc., 1231 25th St., N.W., Washington, DC 20037. TEL 202-452-4200. FAX 202-822-8092.
Vendor(s): Human Resources Information Network (File DD). *1391*

PAYROLL ADMINISTRATION GUIDE NEWSLETTER.
The Bureau of National Affairs, Inc., 1231 25th St., N.W., Washington, DC 20037. TEL 202-452-4200. FAX 202-822-8092.
Vendor(s): Human Resources Information Network (File DD). *1391*

PEACE NEWS.
Peace News Ltd., 5 Caledonian Rd., London N1 9DX, England. TEL 0-71-278-3344. FAX 0171-278-0444. *5691*

PEACE NEWSLETTER.
Syracuse Peace Council, 924 Burnet Ave., Syracuse, NY 13203. TEL 315-472-5478. *5691*

PEACEKEEPING & INTERNATIONAL RELATIONS.
Canadian PeaceKeeping Press, Pearson Peacekeeping Centre Cornwallis Park, P.O. Box 100, Clementsport, NS B0S 1E0, Canada. TEL 902-638-8808. FAX 902-638-8888.
Vendor(s): University Microfilms International. *5767*

PEDIATRICS (ENGLISH EDITION).
American Academy of Pediatrics, 141 Northwest Point Blvd., Box 927, Elk Grove Village, IL 60009-0927. TEL 847-228-5005. FAX 847-228-5097.
Vendor(s): Lexis-Nexis, Ovid Technologies, Inc.. *4812*

PEDIATRICS FOR PARENTS.
Pediatrics for Parents, Inc. Box 1069, Bangor, ME 04402-1069. TEL 207-942-6212.
Vendor(s): Information Access Co.. *4812*

PENNSYLVANIA ACADEMY OF SCIENCE. JOURNAL.
Pennsylvania Academy of Science, c/o Dr. S.K. Majumdar, Ed., Dept. of Biology, Lafayette College, Easton, PA 18042. TEL 6-10-250-5464. FAX 610-250-5557. *6271*

PENNSYLVANIA BUSINESS AND TECHNOLOGY.
Pittsburgh High Technology Council, 4516 Henry St., Pittsburgh, PA 15213 9916. TEL 412-687-2700. FAX 412-687-2795.
Vendor(s): University Microfilms International. *6660*

PENNSYLVANIA BUSINESS DIRECTORY.
American Business Directories 5711 S. 86th Circle, Box 27347, Omaha, NE 68127. TEL 402-593-4600. FAX 402-331-5481. *1633*

PENNSYLVANIA C P A JOURNAL.
Pennsylvania Institute of Certified Public Accountants, 1608 Walnut St., 3rd Fl., Philadelphia, PA 19103. TEL 215-735-2635. FAX 215-735-3694.
Vendor(s): University Microfilms International. *1053*

PENNSYLVANIA STATE UNIVERSITY. ENVIRONMENTAL RESOURCES RESEARCH INSTITUTE. NEWSLETTER
Pennsylvania State University, Environmental Resources Research Institute, 125 Land and Water Research Bldg., University Park, PA 16802-4900. TEL 814-863-0291. FAX 814-865-3378. *2139*

PENSION MANAGEMENT.
Intertec Publishing Corp. (Atlanta), 6151 Powers Ferry Rd., N.W., Atlanta, GA 30339-2941. TEL 770-955-2500. FAX 770-955-0400.
Vendor(s): Information Access Co.. *1115*

PENSIONS & INVESTMENTS.
Crain Communications, Inc. (New York), 220 E. 42nd St., New York, NY 10017-5806. TEL 212-210-0100. FAX 212-210-0799.
Vendor(s): Information Access Co., Lexis-Nexis (PENINV). *1346*

PENTHOUSE.
Penthouse International, Ltd. 277 Park Ave., 4th Fl., New York, NY 10172. TEL 212-702-6000. FAX 212-702-6282. *4944*

PEOPLE WEEKLY.
Time Inc. Time & Life Bldg., Rockefeller Center, 1271 Ave. of the Americas, New York, NY 10020-1393. TEL 212-522-1212.
Vendor(s): Information Access Co., Lexis-Nexis, University Microfilms International VU/TEXT Information Services, Inc.. *3236*

PEOPLE'S MEDICAL SOCIETY NEWSLETTER.
People's Medical Society, 462 Walnut St., Allentown, PA 18102-5488. TEL 610-770-1670. FAX 610-770-0607.
Vendor(s): Information Access Co.. *2154*

PEPPERDINE LAW REVIEW.
Pepperdine University, School of Law, 24255 Pacific Coast Hwy., Malibu, CA 90263-4694. TEL 310-456-4694. FAX 310-317-7283.
Vendor(s): West Services, Inc.. *3832*

PEPSY. PEDAGOGISK LITTERATUR I NORDEN.
Nordisk Arbetsgrupp foer Pedagogi och Psykologi, Jyvaskylae University Library, Seminaarink. 15, SF-40100 Jyvaeskylae, Finland.
Available only online. *2362*

PERFORMING ARTS AND ENTERTAINMENT IN CANADA.
Canadian Stage and Art Publications, 104 Glenrose Ave., Toronto, ON M4T 1K8, Canada. TEL 416-484-4534. FAX 416-484-6214.
Vendor(s): Information Access Co., University Microfilms International. *6700*

PERFORMING ARTS JOURNAL.
Johns Hopkins University Press, Journals Publishing Division, 2715 N. Charles St., Baltimore, MD 21218. TEL 410-516-6988. FAX 410-516-6968.
Vendor(s): Information Access Co.. *6700*

PERFUMER & FLAVORIST.
Allured Publishing, 362 S. Schmale Rd., Carol Stream, IL 60188-2787. TEL 708-653-2155. FAX 708-653-2192. *497*

PERFUMES AND FRAGRANCES: THE INTERNATIONAL MARKET.
Euromonitor, 60-61 Britton St., London EC1M 5NA, England. TEL 44-171-251-8024. FAX 44-171-608-3149.
Vendor(s): Data-Star, Knight-Ridder Information, Inc.. *493*

PERIODICA. INDICE DE REVISTAS LATINOAMERICANAS EN CIENCIAS.
Universidad Nacional Autonoma de Mexico, Centro de Informacion Cientifica y Humanistica, Apdo. Postal 70-392, C.P. 04510 Mexico, D.F., Mexico. TEL 525-6223958. FAX 525-6162557. *6303*

PERIODICAL ABSTRACTS.
U M I Company 300 N. Zeeb Rd., Ann Arbor, MI 48106. TEL 313-761-4700. FAX 800-864-0019.
Vendor(s): Knight-Ridder Information, Inc., University Microfilms International. *22*

PERIODICALS IN SOUTHERN AFRICAN LIBRARIES.
State Library, P.O. Box 397, Pretoria 0001, South Africa. TEL 27-12-21-8931. FAX 27-12-325-5984. *543*

PERISCOPE (GREAT NECK).
Keller International Publishing Corporation, 150 Great Neck Rd., Great Neck, NY 11201. TEL 516-829-9210. FAX 516-829-7265.
Vendor(s): Information Access Co.. *510*

PERSONAL CARE APPLIANCES: THE INTERNATIONAL MARKET.
Euromonitor, 60-61 Britton St., London EC1M 5NA, England. TEL 44-171-251-8024. FAX 44-171-608-3149.
Vendor(s): Data-Star, Knight-Ridder Information, Inc.. *2529*

PERSONAL COMPUTER MARKETS.
Blackwell Publishers Ltd., 108 Cowley Rd., Oxford OX4 1JF, England. TEL 44-1865-791100. FAX 44-1865-791347.
Vendor(s): Data-Star, Information Access Co.. *1481*

PERSONAL FINANCE INTELLIGENCE.
Mintel International Group Ltd., 18-19 Long Ln., London EC1A 9HE, England. TEL 44-171-606-4533. FAX 44-171-606-5932. *1115*

PERSONALIST FORUM.
Mercer University Press, 6316 Peake Rd., Macon, GA 31210. TEL 912-752-2880. FAX 912-752-2264.
Vendor(s): Knight-Ridder Information, Inc.. *5489*

PERSONNEL JOURNAL.
A C C Communications, Inc., Box 2440, Costa Mesa, CA 92628. TEL 714-751-1883. FAX 714-751-4106.
Vendor(s): Information Access Co., University Microfilms International. *1509*

PERSONNEL PSYCHOLOGY.
Personnel Psychology, Inc., 745 Haskins Rd., Ste. A, Bowling Green, OH 43402-1600. TEL 419-352-1562. FAX 419-352-2645.
Vendor(s): Information Access Co., University Microfilms International. *5870*

PERSONNEL REVIEW.
M C B University Press Ltd., 60-62 Toller Ln., Bradford, W. Yorks BD8 9BY, England. TEL 44-1274-777700. FAX 44-1274-785200.
Vendor(s): Information Access Co.. *1509*

PERSONNEL SOFTWARE CENSUS.
Advanced Personnel Systems, Box 1438, Roseville, CA 95678. TEL 916-781-2900. FAX 916-781-2901.
Vendor(s): Human Resources Information Network. *1509*

PERSPECTIVES (TORONTO).
Gerontological Nursing Association, P.O. Box 368, Station "K", Toronto, ON M4P 2G7, Canada. TEL 416-767-4454. FAX 416-591-6812. *3294*

PERSPECTIVES OF NEW MUSIC.
Perspectives of New Music, Inc., University of Washington, Music, Box 353450, Seattle, WA 98195-3450. TEL 206-543-0196. FAX 206-543-9285.
Vendor(s): Information Access Co.. *5188*

PEST CONTROL.
Advanstar Communications, Inc., 7500 Old Oak Blvd., Cleveland, OH 44130. TEL 216-243-8100. FAX 216-891-2675.
Vendor(s): Information Access Co.. *234*

PESTICIDE & TOXIC CHEMICAL NEWS.
Food Chemical News, Inc., 1101 Pennsylvania Ave., S.E., Washington, DC 20003. TEL 202-544-1980. FAX 202-546-3890.
Vendor(s): Data-Star, Information Access Co., Knight-Ridder Information, Inc., NewsNet (CH18). *2987*

THE PESTICIDE MANUAL.
The Royal Society of Chemistry, Thomas Graham House, Science Park, Milton Rd., Cambridge CB4 4WF, England. TEL 01223-420066. FAX 01223-423429.
Vendor(s): Data-Star, Knight-Ridder Information, Inc. (File no.306). *144*

PET FOODS AND PRODUCTS: THE INTERNATIONAL MARKET.
Euromonitor, 60-61 Britton St., London EC1M 5NA, England. TEL 44-171-251-8024. FAX 44-171-608-3149.
Vendor(s): Data-Star, Knight-Ridder Information, Inc.. *2987*

PET PRODUCT NEWS.
Fancy Publications, Box 6040, Mission Viejo, CA 92690. TEL 714-855-8822. FAX 714-855-3045.
Vendor(s): Information Access Co.. *5393*

PETERSEN'S PHOTOGRAPHIC.
Petersen Publishing Co., 6420 Wilshire Blvd., Los Angeles, CA 90048. TEL 213-782-2000. FAX 213-782-2465.
Vendor(s): Information Access Co., Knight-Ridder Information, Inc.. *5516*

PETERSON'S GUIDE TO FOUR-YEAR COLLEGES (YEAR).
Peterson's Guides, Inc., 202 Carnegie Center, Box 2123, Princeton, NJ 08543-2123. TEL 609-243-9111. FAX 609-243-9150.
Vendor(s): CompuServe, Inc. (PCG), Dow Jones News Retrieval (SCHOOL), Knight-Ridder Information, Inc. (File no.214), Ovid Technologies, Inc. (PETE). *2415*

PETERSON'S GUIDE TO GRADUATE AND PROFESSIONAL PROGRAMS: AN OVERVIEW (YEAR) (BOOK 1).
Peterson's Guides, Inc., 202 Carnegie Center, Box 2123, Princeton, NJ 08543-2123. TEL 609-243-9111. FAX 609-243-9150.
Vendor(s): Knight-Ridder Information, Inc. (File no.273). *2415*

PETERSON'S GUIDE TO GRADUATE PROGRAMS IN BUSINESS, EDUCATION, HEALTH, AND LAW (YEAR) (BOOK 6).
Peterson's Guides, Inc., 202 Carnegie Center, Box 2123, Princeton, NJ 08543-2123. TEL 609-243-9111. FAX 609-243-9150.
Vendor(s): Knight-Ridder Information, Inc. (File no.273). *2415*

PETERSON'S GUIDE TO GRADUATE PROGRAMS IN ENGINEERING AND APPLIED SCIENCES (YEAR) (BOOK 5).
Peterson's Guides, Inc., 202 Carnegie Center, Box 2123, Princeton, NJ 08543-2123. TEL 609-243-9111. FAX 609-243-9150.
Vendor(s): Knight-Ridder Information, Inc. (File no.273). *2415*

PETERSON'S GUIDE TO GRADUATE PROGRAMS IN THE BIOLOGICAL AND AGRICULTURAL SCIENCES (YEAR) (BOOK 3).
Peterson's Guides, Inc., 202 Carnegie Center, Box 2123, Princeton, NJ 08543-2123. TEL 609-243-9111. FAX 609-243-9150.
Vendor(s): Knight-Ridder Information, Inc. (File no.273). *2415*

PETERSON'S GUIDE TO GRADUATE PROGRAMS IN THE HUMANITIES AND SOCIAL SCIENCES (YEAR) (BOOK 2).
Peterson's Guides, Inc., 202 Carnegie Center, Box 2123, Princeton, NJ 08543-2123. TEL 609-243-9111. FAX 609-243-9150.
Vendor(s): Knight-Ridder Information, Inc. (File no.273). *2415*

PETERSON'S GUIDE TO GRADUATE PROGRAMS IN THE PHYSICAL SCIENCES AND MATHEMATICS (YEAR) (BOOK 4).
Peterson's Guides, Inc., 202 Carnegie Center, Box 2123, NJ 08543-2123. TEL 609-243-9111. FAX 609-243-9150.
Vendor(s): Knight-Ridder Information, Inc. (File no.273). *2415*

PETERSON'S GUIDE TO TWO-YEAR COLLEGES (YEAR).
Peterson's Guides, Inc., 202 Carnegie Center, Box 2123, Princeton, NJ 08543-2123. TEL 609-243-9111. FAX 609-243-9150.
Vendor(s): CompuServe, Inc. (PCG), Dow Jones News Retrieval (SCHOOL), Knight-Ridder Information, Inc. (File no.214), Ovid Technologies, Inc. (PETE). *2415*

PETROLEUM ABSTRACTS.
University of Tulsa, Information Services Division, 600 S. College Ave., Tulsa, OK 74104-3189. TEL 918-631-2297. FAX 918-599-9361.
Vendor(s): Knight-Ridder Information, Inc. (File no. 87,987), Orbit Search Service (TULSA). *5384*

PETROLEUM ECONOMIST.
Euromoney Publications plc., Nestor House, Playhouse Yard, London EC4V 5EX, England. TEL 44-171-779-8935. FAX 44-171-779-8541.
Vendor(s): Information Access Co.. *5371*

PETROLEUM - ENERGY BUSINESS NEWS INDEX.
American Petroleum Institute, Central Abstracting & Information Services, 275 Seventh Ave., New York, NY 10001-6708. TEL 212-366-4040. FAX 212-366-4298.
Vendor(s): Knight-Ridder Information, Inc., Orbit Search Service (ABIZ), Telesystemes - Questel. *5384*

PETROLEUM INDEPENDENT.
Petroleum Independent Publishers, Inc., 1101 16th St., N.W., Washington, DC 20036. TEL 202-857-4774. FAX 202-857-4799.
Vendor(s): Information Access Co.. *5372*

PETS MAGAZINE.
Moorshead Magazines Ltd., 10 Gateway Blvd., Ste. 490, North York, ON M3C 3T4, Canada. TEL 416-696-5488. FAX 416-696-7395. *5393*

PHARMA MARKETLETTER.
Marketletter (Publications) Ltd., 54-55 Wilton Rd., London SW1V 1DE, England. TEL 44-171-828-7272. FAX 44-171-828-0415.
Vendor(s): Data-Star, Information Access Co.. *5432*

PHARMA TIMES.
Indian Pharmaceutical Association, Kalina Santacruz East, Bombay 400098, India. *5433*

PHARMACEUTICA ACTA HELVETIAE.
Elsevier Science B.V., P.O. Box 211, 1000 AE Amsterdam, Netherlands. TEL 31-20-4853911. FAX 31-20-4853598. *5433*

PHARMACEUTICAL APPROVALS MONTHLY.
F-D-C Reports, Inc., 5550 Friendship Blvd., Ste. One, Chevy Chase, MD 20815. FAX 301-664-7238.
Vendor(s): Data-Star (FDCR), Knight-Ridder Information, Inc. (File no.187), Lexis-Nexis, Ovid Technologies, Inc. (FDCR). *5433*

PHARMACEUTICAL BUSINESS NEWS.
Financial Times Pharmaceuticals and Healthcare Publishing Maple House, 149 Tottenham Court Rd., London W1P 9LL, England. TEL 44-171-896-2204. FAX 44-171-896-2213.
Vendor(s): Information Access Co.. *5433*

PHARMACEUTICAL COMPANY PROFILES.
IMSWORLD Publications Ltd., 7 Harewood Ave., London NW1 6JB, England. TEL 0171-393-5000. FAX 0171-393-5900. *5433*

PHARMACEUTICAL EXECUTIVE.
Advanstar Communications, Inc. (Eugene), 859 Willamette St., Eugene, OR 97401-6806. TEL 541-343-1200. FAX 541-344-3514.
Vendor(s): Information Access Co., University Microfilms International. *5434*

PHARMACEUTICAL MANUFACTURING REVIEW.
Argus Business Media Ltd., Fuel and Metals Journals Queensway House, 2 Queensway, Redhill, Surrey RH1 1QS, England. TEL 44-1737-768611. FAX 44-1737-761685.
Vendor(s): Information Access Co.. *5434*

PHARMACEUTICAL SOCIETY OF JAPAN. JOURNAL.
Pharmaceutical Society of Japan, 12-15, Shibuya 2-chome, Shibuya-ku, Tokyo 150, Japan. *5435*

PHARMACEUTICALS MONTHLY.
Yakugyo Jiho Co. Ltd., 2-36 Kanda Jimbo-cho, Chiyoda-ku, Tokyo 101, Japan. *5435*

PHARMACIEN DE FRANCE.
Federation des Syndicats Pharmaceutiques de France, 13 rue Ballu, 75009 Paris, France. TEL 42-81-15-96. *5435*

PHARMACIEN RURAL.
Association de Pharmacie Rural, 24 rue Vintimille, 75009 Paris, France. TEL 48-74-64-26. FAX 45-26-13-37. *5435*

PHARMACIES AND DRUGSTORES: THE INTERNATIONAL MARKET.
Euromonitor, 60-61 Britton St., London EC1M 5NA, England. TEL 44-171-251-8024. FAX 44-171-608-3149.
Vendor(s): Data-Star, Knight-Ridder Information, Inc.. *5435*

PHARMACIST NEWS.
Maclean-Hunter Ltd., Business Publication Division, Maclean-Hunter Bldg., 777 Bay St., Toronto, ON M5W 1A7, Canada. TEL 416-596-5950. *5435*

PHARMACOECONOMICS AND OUTCOMES NEWS.
Adis International Limited, Private Bag 65901, Mairangi Bay, Auckland 10, New Zealand. TEL 64-9-479-8100. FAX 64-9-479-8145.
Vendor(s): Knight-Ridder Information, Inc.. *5436*

PHARMACOGENETICS.
Chapman & Hall, Journals Department 2-6 Boundary Row, London SE1 8HN, England. TEL 44-171-8650066. FAX 44-171-5229623. *749*

PHARMACY IN HISTORY.
American Institute of the History of Pharmacy, Pharmacy Bldg., Madison, WI 53706. TEL 608-262-5378. *5437*

PHARMACY PRACTICE NEWS.
McMahon Group, 148 W. 24th St., 8th Fl., New York, NY 10011-1916. TEL 212-620-4600. FAX 212-620-5928. *5437*

PHARMACY TIMES.
Romaine Pierson Publishing Co., 80 Shore Rd., Port Washington, NY 11050. TEL 516-883-6350. FAX 516-883-6609. *5438*

DIE PHARMAZEUTISCHE INDUSTRIE.
Editio Cantor, Postfach 1255, 88322 Aulendorf, Germany. TEL 49-7525-940135. FAX 49-7525-940180. *5438*

DIE PHARMAZIE.
Govi Pharmazeutischer Verlag GmbH, Ginnheimerstr. 26, 65760 Eschborn, Germany. TEL 49-6196-928262. FAX 49-6196-928203. *5438*

PHI DELTA KAPPAN.
Phi Delta Kappa, Inc., Box 789, Bloomington, IN 47402-0789. TEL 812-339-1156. FAX 812-339-0018.
Vendor(s): Information Access Co., University Microfilms International. *2362*

PHILADELPHIA BUSINESS JOURNAL.
City Media Inc., 821 Marquette Ave., Ste. 2000, Minneapolis, MN 55402.
Vendor(s): CompuServe, Inc., Data-Star, Dow Jones News Retrieval Information Access Co., Knight-Ridder Information, Inc., Lexis-Nexis, University Microfilms International. *1229*

PHILOLOGICAL QUARTERLY.
University of Iowa, Iowa City, IA 52242. TEL 319-335-0435.
Vendor(s): Information Access Co.. *4098*

PHILOSOPHER'S INDEX.
Philosopher's Information Center, 1616 E. Wooster St., Box P, Bowling Green, OH 43402. TEL 419-353-8830. FAX 419-353-8784.
Vendor(s): Knight-Ridder Information, Inc. (File no.57). *5507*

PHILOSOPHICAL FORUM.
Philosophical Forum, Inc., c/o Baruch College, Box 239, 17 Lexington Ave., NY 10010. TEL 212-387-1682.
Vendor(s): Ovid Technologies, Inc.. *5491*

PHILOSOPHY AND LITERATURE.
Johns Hopkins University Press, Journals Publishing Division, 2715 N. Charles St., Baltimore, MD 21218. TEL 410-516-6987. FAX 410-516-6968. *5492*

PHILOSOPHY AND PUBLIC AFFAIRS.
Princeton University Press, 41 William St., Princeton, NJ 08540. TEL 609-258-4900. FAX 609-258-6305
Vendor(s): University Microfilms International. *5693*

PHILOSOPHY EAST AND WEST.
University of Hawaii Press, Journals Department, 2840 Kolowalu St., Honolulu, HI 96822. TEL 808-956-8833. FAX 808-988-6052.
Vendor(s): Information Access Co.. *5493*

PHILOSOPHY, PSYCHIATRY & PSYCHOLOGY.
Johns Hopkins University Press, Journals Publishing Division, 2715 N. Charles St., Baltimore, MD 21218. TEL 410-516-6980. FAX 410-516-6968. *5493*

PHILOTELIA.
Hellenic Philatelic Society, 57 Akademias St., 106 79 Athens, Greece. TEL 30-1-3621-125. *5461*

PHOTOBULLETIN.
PhotoSource International, Pine Lake Farm, Osceola, WI 54020. TEL 715-248-3800. FAX 715-248-7394.
Vendor(s): NewsNet (PB26). *5517*

PHOTOBULLETIN DAILY.
PhotoSource International, Pine Lake Farm, Osceola, WI 54020. TEL 715-248-3800. FAX 715-248-7394.
Vendor(s): NewsNet. *5517*

PHOTOGRAPHY: THE INTERNATIONAL MARKET.
Euromonitor, 60-61 Britton St., London EC1M 5NA, England. TEL 44-171-251-8024. FAX 44-171-608-3149.
Vendor(s): Data-Star, Knight-Ridder Information, Inc.. *5519*

PHOTOMARKET.
PhotoSource International, Pine Lake Farm, Osceola, WI 54020. TEL 715-248-3800. FAX 715-248-7394.
Vendor(s): NewsNet (PB17). *5519*

PHOTON.
Icon Publications Ltd., Maxwell Ln., Kelso, Roxburghshire TD5 7BB, England. TEL 01573-226032. FAX 01573-226000. *5519*

PHOTONICS SPECTRA.
Laurin Publishing Co., Inc., Box 4949, Berkshire Common, Pittsfield, MA 01202-4949. TEL 413-499-0514. FAX 413-442-3180.
Vendor(s): Information Access Co.. *5611*

PHOTOSTOCKNOTES.
PhotoSource International, Pine Lake Farm, 1910 35th Rd., Osceola, WI 54020. TEL 715-248-3800. FAX 715-248-7394.
Vendor(s): NewsNet (PB12). *5519*

PHYSICAL EDUCATION INDEX.
Benoak Publishing Company, Box 474, Cape Girardeau, MO 63702-0474. TEL 573-334-8789. FAX 573-334-7996. *5539*

PHYSICAL REVIEW LETTERS.
American Physical Society, One Physics Ellipse, College Park, MD 20740-3844. TEL 301-209-3202.
Vendor(s): OCLC. *5563*

PHYSICAL THERAPY.
American Physical Therapy Association, 1111 N. Fairfax St., Alexandria, VA 22314-1488. TEL 703-684-2782. FAX 703-684-7343.
Vendor(s): Central Institute for Scientific & Technical Information, Information Access Co., Ovid Technologies, Inc.. *4819*

THE PHYSICIAN AND SPORTSMEDICINE.
McGraw-Hill Companies (Minneapolis), 4530 W. 77th St., Minneapolis, MN 55435. TEL 612-835-3222.
Vendor(s): Dow Jones News Retrieval, Information Access Co., Knight-Ridder Information, Inc., NewsNet (ME05). *4899*

PHYSICIAN EXECUTIVE.
American College of Physician Executives, Two Urban Centre, Ste. 200, 4890 W. Kennedy Blvd., Tampa, FL 33609. TEL 813-287-2000. FAX 813-287-8993.
Vendor(s): Information Access Co.. *3554*

PHYSICIAN MANAGER.
Atlantic Information Services, Inc. 1050 17th St., N.W., Ste. 480, Washington, DC 20036. TEL 202-775-9008. FAX 202-331-9542.
Vendor(s): Information Access Co.. *4515*

PHYSICIANS' DESK REFERENCE.
Medical Economics Publishing Co., Inc., 5 Paragon Dr., Montvale, NJ 07645. TEL 201-357-7200. FAX 201-573-1045. *4516*

PHYSICIANS' DESK REFERENCE FOR NONPRESCRIPTION DRUGS.
Medical Economics Publishing Co., Inc., 5 Paragon Dr., Montvale, NJ 07645. TEL 201-358-7200. FAX 201-573-1045. *4516*

PHYSICIANS' DESK REFERENCE FOR OPHTHALMOLOGY.
Medical Economics Publishing Co., Inc., 5 Paragon Dr., Montvale, NJ 07645. TEL 201-358-7246. FAX 201-573-0344. *4776*

PHYSICS ABSTRACTS.
INSPEC, I.E.E., Michael Faraday House, Six Hills Way, Stevenage, Herts. SG1 2AY, England. TEL 44-1438-313311. FAX 44-1438-742840.
Vendor(s): CEDOCAR, Data-Star, European Space Agency, FIZ Technik, Knight-Ridder Information, Inc., Orbit Search Service, STN International. *5580*

PHYSICS EDUCATION.
I O P Publishing Ltd., Techno House, Redcliffe Way, Bristol, Avon BS1 6NX, England. TEL 44-117-929-7481. FAX 44-117-929-4318. *5564*

PHYSICS IN MEDICINE AND BIOLOGY.
I O P Publishing Ltd., Techno House, Redcliffe Way, Bristol, Avon BS1 6NX, England. TEL 44-117-929-7481. FAX 44-117-929-4318. *4516*

PHYSICS OF FLUIDS.
American Institute of Physics, One Physics Ellipse, College Park, MD 20740-3843. TEL 301-209-3000. *5564*

PHYSICS OF PARTICLES AND NUCLEI.
American Institute of Physics, One Physics Ellipse, College Park, MD 20740-3843. TEL 301-209-3000. *5599*

PHYSICS OF PLASMAS.
American Institute of Physics, One Physics Ellipse, College Park, MD 20740-3843. TEL 301-209-3000. *5564*

PHYSICS OF THE SOLID STATE.
American Institute of Physics, One Physics Ellipse, College Park, MD 20740-3843. TEL 301-209-3000. *5564*

Online

PHYSICS WORLD.
I O P Publishing Ltd., Techno House, Redcliffe Way, Bristol, Avon BS1 6NX, England. TEL 44-117-929-7481. FAX 44-117-929-4318. *5565*

PHYSIOLOGICAL MEASUREMENT.
I O P Publishing Ltd., Techno House, Redcliffe Way, Bristol, Avon BS1 6NX, England. TEL 44-117-929-7481. FAX 44-117-929-4318. *4516*

PHYSIOLOGICAL REVIEWS.
American Physiological Society, 9650 Rockville Pike, Bethesda, MD 20814. TEL 301-530-7164. FAX 301-571-8313.
Vendor(s): Information Access Co.. *792*

PHYSIOTHERAPY INDEX.
British Library, Medical Information Centre, Boston Spa, Wetherby, W. Yorks. LS23 7BQ, England. TEL 01937-546039. FAX 01937-546458. *4573*

PIG NEWS & INFORMATION.
CAB International, Wallingford, Oxon. OX10 8DE, England. TEL 44-1491-832111. FAX 44-1491-833508.
Vendor(s): DIMDI, European Space Agency, Knight-Ridder Information, Inc., STN International. *280*

PIPELINE & GAS JOURNAL.
Oildom Publishing Co. of Texas, Inc., Box 219368, Houston, TX 77218-9368. TEL 713-558-6930. FAX 712-558-7029.
Vendor(s): Information Access Co.. *5373*

PIPELINE & UTILITIES CONSTRUCTION.
Oildom Publishing Co. of Texas, Inc., Box 219368, Houston, TX 77218-9368. TEL 713-558-6930. FAX 713-558-7029.
Vendor(s): Information Access Co.. *5373*

PIPELINE INDUSTRY (TULSA).
Midwest Publishing Company, Box 50350, Tulsa, OK 74150-0350. TEL 918-582-2000. FAX 918-587-9349.
Vendor(s): Information Access Co.. *5373*

PIRRADAZISH: BULLETIN OF ACHAEMENIAN STUDIES.
University of Chicago, Oriental Institute, 1155 E. 58th St., Chicago, IL 60637-1569. TEL 312-702-9508. FAX 312-702-9853. *3499*

PIT & QUARRY.
Advanstar Communications, Inc., 7500 Old Oak Blvd., Cleveland, OH 44130. TEL 216-826-2839. FAX 216-891-2726.
Vendor(s): Information Access Co.. *5075*

PITTSBURGH BUSINESS TIMES - JOURNAL.
Pittsburgh Business Times, 2313 E. Carson St., Ste. 200, Pittsburgh, PA 15203-2109. TEL 412-481-6397. FAX 412-481-9956.
Vendor(s): Information Access Co., University Microfilms International. *951*

PLADEANMELDELSER, RYTMISK MUSIK.
Dansk BiblioteksCenter as, Tempovej 7-11, 2750 Ballerup, Denmark. TEL 5-44-867777. FAX 45-44-867892.
Available only online. *5188*

PLAGUE WATCH.
DeMigalt Media Group, Box 6, Bucyrus, MO 65444-0006. TEL 713-863-0244. FAX 713-864-2607. *4161*

PLANETARY REPORT.
Planetary Society, 65 N. Catalina, Pasadena, CA 91106-2301. TEL 818-793-5100. FAX 818-793-5528. *485*

PLANNING COMMISSIONERS JOURNAL.
Champlain Planning Press, Box 4295, Burlington, VT 05406-4295. TEL 802-864-9083. FAX 802-862-1882. *3591*

PLANNING PERSPECTIVES.
Chapman & Hall, Journals Department 2-6 Boundary Row, London SE1 8HN, England. TEL 44-171-8650066. FAX 44-171-5229623. *3355*

PLANNING PRACTICE AND RESEARCH.
Carfax Publishing Co., P.O. Box 25, Abingdon, Oxon. OX14 3UE, England. TEL 44-1235-401000. FAX 44-1235-401550. *3591*

PLANNING REVIEW.
The Planning Forum, 435 N. Michigan Ave., Ste. 1717, Chicago, OH 60611-4008. TEL 312-644-0829. FAX 312-644-8557.
Vendor(s): Information Access Co.. *1440*

PLANT BREEDING ABSTRACTS.
CAB International, Wallingford, Oxon. OX10 8DE, England. TEL 44-1491-832111. FAX 44-1491-833508.
Vendor(s): DIMDI, European Space Agency, Knight-Ridder Information, Inc., STN International. *3070*

PLANT ENGINEERING.
Cahners Publishing Company (Newton), Division of Reed Elsevier Inc., 275 Washington St., Newton, MA 02158-1630. TEL 617-964-3030.
Vendor(s): Information Access Co., Knight-Ridder Information, Inc.. *2614*

PLANT GENETIC RESOURCES ABSTRACTS.
CAB International, Wallingford, Oxon OX10 8DE, England. TEL 44-1491-832111. FAX 44-1491-826090. *623*

PLANT GROWTH REGULATOR ABSTRACTS.
CAB International, Wallingford, Oxon. OX10 8DE, England. TEL 44-1491-832111. FAX 44-1491-833508.
Vendor(s): DIMDI, European Space Agency, Knight-Ridder Information, Inc., STN International. *179*

PLANTA MEDICA.
Georg Thieme Verlag, Ruedigerstr. 14, 70469 Stuttgart, Germany. TEL 0711-8931-0. FAX 0711-8931298. *5439*

PLANT'S REVIEW OF BOOKS.
3635 S.E. Alder, Portland, OR 97214. TEL 503-234-4036. FAX 503-234-4036.
Available only online. *6005*

PLANTS, SITES & PARKS.
B P I Communications, 1801 West End Ave., Ste. 400, Nashville, TN 37203. TEL 615-329-4940. FAX 615-329-4733.
Vendor(s): Information Access Co.. *1528*

PLASMA PHYSICS AND CONTROLLED FUSION.
I O P Publishing Ltd., Techno House, Redcliffe Way, Bristol, Avon BS1 6NX, England. TEL 44-117-929-7481. FAX 44-117-929-4318. *5566*

PLASMA SOURCES SCIENCE AND TECHNOLOGY.
I O P Publishing Ltd., Techno House, Redcliffe Way, Bristol, Avon BS1 6NX, England. TEL 44-117-929-7481. FAX 44-117-929-4318. *5566*

PLASTICS BUSINESS NEWS.
Market Search, Inc., 2727 Holland Sylvania Rd., Ste. A, Toledo, OH 43615. TEL 419-535-7899. FAX 419-535-1243.
Vendor(s): NewsNet (CH17). *5624*

PLASTICS ENGINEERING.
Society of Plastics Engineers, Inc., 14 Fairfield Dr., Box 403, Brookfield, CT 06804-0403. TEL 203-775-0471. FAX 203-775-8490.
Vendor(s): Information Access Co.. *5624*

PLASTICS NEWS.
Crain Communications Inc. (Akron), 1725 Merriman Rd., Akron, OH 44313-3185. TEL 216-836-9180. FAX 216-836-2365.
Vendor(s): Information Access Co.. *5625*

PLASTICS TECHNOLOGY.
Bill Communications, Inc., 355 Park Ave. S., 5th Fl., New York, NY 10010-1789. TEL 212-592-6200. FAX 212-592-6339.
Vendor(s): Information Access Co.. *5625*

PLASTICS WORLD.
P T N Publishing Corp., 445 Broad Hollow Rd., Ste. 21, Melville, NY 11747-4722. TEL 516-845-2700.
Vendor(s): Information Access Co.. *5625*

PLATT'S INTERNATIONAL PETROCHEMICAL REPORT.
McGraw-Hill Companies, 1221 Ave. of the Americas, New York, NY 10020.
Vendor(s): Dow Jones News Retrieval, Knight-Ridder Information, Inc. (File no.624/McGRAW-HILL PUBLICATIONS ONLINE), Lexis-Nexis, NewsNet (CH20). *5373*

PLATT'S OILGRAM NEWS.
McGraw-Hill Companies, Commodity Services Group, 1221 Ave. of the Americas, 42nd Fl., New York, NY 10020. TEL 212-512-2000.
Vendor(s): Dow Jones News Retrieval (PON), Knight-Ridder Information, Inc. (File no.624/McGRAW-HILL PUBLICATIONS ONLINE), Lexis-Nexis (PONEWS), NewsNet (EY74). *5373*

PLATT'S OILGRAM PRICE REPORT.
McGraw-Hill Companies, Commodity Services Group, 1221 Ave. of the Americas, 42nd Fl., New York, NY 10020.
Vendor(s): Dow Jones News Retrieval (POP), Knight-Ridder Information, Inc. (File no.624/McGRAW-HILL PUBLICATIONS ONLINE), Lexis-Nexis (PPRICE), NewsNet (EY75). *5373*

PLAYBOY.
Playboy Enterprises, Inc., 680 N. Lake Shore Dr., Chicago, IL 60611. TEL 312-751-8000. FAX 312-751-2818.
Vendor(s): Information Access Co.. *4944*

PLAYTHINGS.
Geyer-McAllister Publications, Inc., 51 Madison Ave., New York, NY 10010. TEL 212-689-4411.
Vendor(s): Information Access Co., Knight-Ridder Information, Inc.. *3301*

PLOUGHSHARES.
Ploughshares, Inc., Emerson College, 100 Beacon St., Boston, MA 02116. TEL 617-824-8753.
Vendor(s): Information Access Co., University Microfilms International. *4251*

PLUMBING AND MECHANICAL DIRECTORY.
Business News Publishing Company, 55 W. Big Beaver Rd., Ste. 1000, Troy, MI 48084. TEL 810-362-3700. FAX 810-362-0317. *1634*

PLYMOUTH COUNTY BUSINESS REVIEW.
Plymouth County Development Council, Box 1620, Pembroke, MA 02359. TEL 617-826-3136. FAX 617-826-0444.
Vendor(s): University Microfilms International. *1168*

POETRY (CHICAGO).
Modern Poetry Association, 60 W. Walton St., Chicago, IL 60610. TEL 312-255-3703.
Vendor(s): Information Access Co.. *4315*

POINT DE REPERE.
Services Documentaires Multimedia Inc., 75 Port Royal E., No. 300, Montreal, PQ H3L 3T1, Canada. TEL 514-382-0895. FAX 514-384-9139.
Vendor(s): IST-INFORMATHEQUE, Inc.. *22*

POLAR AND GLACIOLOGICAL ABSTRACTS.
Cambridge University Press, Edinburgh Bldg., Shaftesbury Rd., Cambridge CB2 2RU, England. TEL 44-1223-312393. FAX 44-1223-315052.
Vendor(s): QL Systems Ltd.. *2221*

POLAR RESEARCH.
Norwegian Polar Institute, Middelthuns gate 29, P.O. Box 5072 Majorstua, N-0301 Oslo, Norway. TEL 47-22-95-95-00. FAX 47-22-95-95-01. *6272*

POLICY REVIEW.
Heritage Foundation, 214 Massachusetts Ave., N.E., Washington, DC 20002. TEL 202-546-4400. FAX 202-546-8328.
Vendor(s): Information Access Co., Lexis-Nexis. *5693*

POLICY STUDIES JOURNAL.
Policy Studies Organization, University of Illinois at Urbana-Champaign, 361 Lincoln Hall, Urbana, IL 61801. TEL 217-359-8541.
Vendor(s): Information Access Co., University Microfilms International. *5693*

POLISH JOURNAL OF PHARMACOLOGY.
Polska Akademia Nauk, Instytut Farmakologii, Ul. Smetna 12, 31-343 Krakow, Poland. TEL 48-12-374022. FAX 48-12-374500. *5439*

POLISH MUSIC.
Agencja Autorska, Ul. Hipoteczna 2, P.O. Box 133, 00-950 Warsaw, Poland. TEL 22-27-83-96. FAX 22-27-58-82.
Available only online. *5189*

POLITICAL FINANCE & LOBBY REPORTER.
Amward Publications, Inc., 2030 Clarendon Blvd.,
Ste. 401, Arlington, VA 22201. TEL 703-525-
7227. FAX 703-525-3536.
Vendor(s): Lexis-Nexis, NewsNet (POO2). *5695*

POLITICAL RISK LETTER.
Political Risk Services, Box 248, E. Syracuse, NY
13057-0248. TEL 315-431-0511. FAX 315-431-
0200.
Vendor(s): Information Access Co., NewsNet (IT29).
1293

**POLITICAL RISK SERVICES. COUNTRY REPORTS:
WORLD SERVICE.**
Political Risk Services, Box 248, E. Syracuse, NY
13057-0248. TEL 315-431-0511. FAX 315-431-
0200.
Vendor(s): Data-Star (FSRI), Lexis-Nexis (IBCRPT).
1229

**POLITICAL RISK SERVICES. COUNTRY REPORTS:
ALGERIA.**
Political Risk Services, Box 248, E. Syracuse, NY
13057-0248. TEL 315-431-0511. FAX 315-431-
0200.
Vendor(s): Data-Star, Lexis-Nexis. *1229*

**POLITICAL RISK SERVICES. COUNTRY REPORTS:
ARGENTINA.**
Political Risk Services, Box 248, E. Syracuse, NY
13057-0248. TEL 315-431-0511. FAX 315-431-
0200.
Vendor(s): Data-Star, Lexis-Nexis. *1229*

**POLITICAL RISK SERVICES. COUNTRY REPORTS:
BOLIVIA.**
Political Risk Services, Box 248, E. Syracuse, NY
13057-0248. TEL 315-431-0511. FAX 315-431-
0200.
Vendor(s): Data-Star, Lexis-Nexis. *1229*

**POLITICAL RISK SERVICES. COUNTRY REPORTS:
BRAZIL.**
Political Risk Services, Box 248, E. Syracuse, NY
13057-0248. TEL 315-431-0511. FAX 315-431-
0200.
Vendor(s): Data-Star, Lexis-Nexis. *1229*

**POLITICAL RISK SERVICES. COUNTRY REPORTS:
BULGARIA.**
Political Risk Services, Box 248, E. Syracuse, NY
13057-0248. TEL 315-431-0511. FAX 315-431-
0200.
Vendor(s): Data-Star, Lexis-Nexis. *1229*

**POLITICAL RISK SERVICES. COUNTRY REPORTS:
CAMEROON.**
Political Risk Services, Box 248, E. Syracuse, NY
13057-0248. TEL 315-431-0511. FAX 315-431-
0200.
Vendor(s): Data-Star, Lexis-Nexis. *1229*

**POLITICAL RISK SERVICES. COUNTRY REPORTS:
CHILE.**
Political Risk Services, Box 248, E. Syracuse, NY
13057-0248. TEL 315-431-0511. FAX 315-431-
0200.
Vendor(s): Data-Star, Lexis-Nexis. *1229*

**POLITICAL RISK SERVICES. COUNTRY REPORTS:
CHINA.**
Political Risk Services, Box 248, E. Syracuse, NY
13057-0248. TEL 315-431-0511. FAX 315-431-
0200.
Vendor(s): Data-Star, Lexis-Nexis. *1229*

**POLITICAL RISK SERVICES. COUNTRY REPORTS:
COLOMBIA.**
Political Risk Services, Box 248, E. Syracuse, NY
13057-0248. TEL 315-431-0511. FAX 315-431-
0200.
Vendor(s): Data-Star, Lexis-Nexis. *1229*

**POLITICAL RISK SERVICES. COUNTRY REPORTS:
COSTA RICA.**
Political Risk Services, Box 248, E. Syracuse, NY
13057-0248. TEL 315-431-0511. FAX 315-431-
0200.
Vendor(s): Data-Star, Lexis-Nexis. *1229*

**POLITICAL RISK SERVICES. COUNTRY REPORTS:
COTE D'IVOIRE.**
Political Risk Services, Box 248, E. Syracuse, NY
13057-0248. TEL 315-431-0511. FAX 315-431-
0200.
Vendor(s): Data-Star, Lexis-Nexis. *1229*

**POLITICAL RISK SERVICES. COUNTRY REPORTS:
CZECH REPUBLIC.**
Political Risk Services, Box 248, E. Syracuse, NY
13057-0248. TEL 315-431-0511. FAX 315-431-
0200.
Vendor(s): Data-Star, Lexis-Nexis. *1229*

**POLITICAL RISK SERVICES. COUNTRY REPORTS:
DOMINICAN REPUBLIC.**
Political Risk Services, Box 248, E. Syracuse, NY
13057-0248. TEL 315-431-0511. FAX 315-431-
0200.
Vendor(s): Data-Star, Lexis-Nexis. *1229*

**POLITICAL RISK SERVICES. COUNTRY REPORTS:
ECUADOR.**
Political Risk Services, Box 248, E. Syracuse, NY
13057-0248. TEL 315-431-0511. FAX 315-431-
0200.
Vendor(s): Data-Star, Lexis-Nexis. *1230*

**POLITICAL RISK SERVICES. COUNTRY REPORTS:
EGYPT.**
Political Risk Services, Box 248, E. Syracuse, NY
13057-0248. TEL 315-431-0511. FAX 315-431-
0200.
Vendor(s): Data-Star, Lexis-Nexis. *1230*

**POLITICAL RISK SERVICES. COUNTRY REPORTS: EL
SALVADOR.**
Political Risk Services, Box 248, E. Syracuse, NY
13057-0248. TEL 315-431-0511. FAX 315-431-
0200.
Vendor(s): Data-Star, Lexis-Nexis. *1230*

**POLITICAL RISK SERVICES. COUNTRY REPORTS:
GABON.**
Political Risk Services, Box 248, E. Syracuse, NY
13057-0248. TEL 315-431-0511. FAX 315-431-
0200.
Vendor(s): Data-Star, Lexis-Nexis. *1230*

**POLITICAL RISK SERVICES. COUNTRY REPORTS:
GUATEMALA.**
Political Risk Services, Box 248, E. Syracuse, NY
13057-0248. TEL 315-431-0511. FAX 315-431-
0200.
Vendor(s): Data-Star, Lexis-Nexis. *1230*

**POLITICAL RISK SERVICES. COUNTRY REPORTS:
GUINEA.**
Political Risk Services, Box 248, E. Syracuse, NY
13057-0248. TEL 315-431-0511. FAX 315-431-
0200.
Vendor(s): Data-Star, Lexis-Nexis. *1230*

**POLITICAL RISK SERVICES. COUNTRY REPORTS:
HAITI.**
Political Risk Services, Box 248, E. Syracuse, NY
13057-0248. TEL 315-431-0511. FAX 315-431-
0200.
Vendor(s): Data-Star, Lexis-Nexis. *1230*

**POLITICAL RISK SERVICES. COUNTRY REPORTS:
HONDURAS.**
Political Risk Services, Box 248, E. Syracuse, NY
13057-0248. TEL 315-431-0511. FAX 315-431-
0200.
Vendor(s): Data-Star, Lexis-Nexis. *1230*

**POLITICAL RISK SERVICES. COUNTRY REPORTS:
HONG KONG.**
Political Risk Services, Box 248, E. Syracuse, NY
13057-0248. TEL 315-431-0511. FAX 315-431-
0200.
Vendor(s): Data-Star, Lexis-Nexis. *1230*

**POLITICAL RISK SERVICES. COUNTRY REPORTS:
HUNGARY.**
Political Risk Services, Box 248, E. Syracuse, NY
13057-0243. TEL 315-431-0511. FAX 315-431-
0200.
Vendor(s): Data-Star, Lexis-Nexis. *1230*

**POLITICAL RISK SERVICES. COUNTRY REPORTS:
INDIA.**
Political Risk Services, Box 248, E. Syracuse, NY
13057-0243. TEL 315-431-0511. FAX 315-431-
0200.
Vendor(s): Data-Star, Lexis-Nexis. *1230*

**POLITICAL RISK SERVICES. COUNTRY REPORTS:
INDONESIA.**
Political Risk Services, Box 248, E. Syracuse, NY
13057-0248. TEL 315-431-0511. FAX 315-431-
0200.
Vendor(s): Data-Star, Lexis-Nexis. *1230*

**POLITICAL RISK SERVICES. COUNTRY REPORTS:
IRAN.**
Political Risk Services, Box 248, E. Syracuse, NY
13057-0248. TEL 315-431-0511. FAX 315-431-
0200.
Vendor(s): Data-Star, Lexis-Nexis *1230*

**POLITICAL RISK SERVICES. COUNTRY REPORTS:
IRAQ.**
Political Risk Services, Box 248, E. Syracuse, NY
13057-0248. TEL 315-431-0511. FAX 315-431-
0200.
Vendor(s): Data-Star, Lexis-Nexis *1230*

**POLITICAL RISK SERVICES. COUNTRY REPORTS:
ISRAEL.**
Political Risk Services, Box 248, E. Syracuse, NY
13057-0248. TEL 315-431-0511. FAX 315-431-
0200.
Vendor(s): Data-Star, Lexis-Nexis *1230*

**POLITICAL RISK SERVICES. COUNTRY REPORTS:
JAMAICA.**
Political Risk Services, Box 248, E. Syracuse, NY
13057-0248. TEL 315-431-0511. FAX 315-431-
0200.
Vendor(s): Data-Star, Lexis-Nexis *1230*

**POLITICAL RISK SERVICES. COUNTRY REPORTS:
KENYA.**
Political Risk Services, Box 248, E. Syracuse, NY
13057-0248. TEL 315-431-0511. FAX 315-431-
0200.
Vendor(s): Data-Star, Lexis-Nexis *1230*

**POLITICAL RISK SERVICES. COUNTRY REPORTS:
KUWAIT.**
Political Risk Services, Box 248, E. Syracuse, NY
13057-0248. TEL 315-431-0511. FAX 315-431-
0200.
Vendor(s): Data-Star, Lexis-Nexis *1230*

**POLITICAL RISK SERVICES. COUNTRY REPORTS:
LIBYA.**
Political Risk Services, Box 248, E. Syracuse, NY
13057-0248. TEL 315-431-0511. FAX 315-431-
0200.
Vendor(s): Data-Star, Lexis-Nexis. *1230*

**POLITICAL RISK SERVICES. COUNTRY REPORTS:
MALAYSIA.**
Political Risk Services, Box 248, E. Syracuse, NY
13057-0248. TEL 315-431-0511. FAX 315-431-
0200.
Vendor(s): Data-Star, Lexis-Nexis. *1230*

**POLITICAL RISK SERVICES. COUNTRY REPORTS:
MEXICO.**
Political Risk Services, Box 248, E. Syracuse, NY
13057-0248. TEL 315-431-0511. FAX 315-431-
0200.
Vendor(s): Data-Star, Lexis-Nexis. *1230*

**POLITICAL RISK SERVICES. COUNTRY REPORTS:
MOROCCO.**
Political Risk Services, Box 248, E. Syracuse, NY
13057-0248. TEL 315-431-0511. FAX 315-431-
0200.
Vendor(s): Data-Star, Lexis-Nexis. *1230*

**POLITICAL RISK SERVICES. COUNTRY REPORTS:
NICARAGUA.**
Political Risk Services, Box 248, E. Syracuse, NY
13057-0248. TEL 315-431-0511. FAX 315-431-
0200.
Vendor(s): Data-Star, Lexis-Nexis. *1230*

**POLITICAL RISK SERVICES. COUNTRY REPORTS:
NIGERIA.**
Political Risk Services, Box 248, E. Syracuse, NY
13057-0248. TEL 315-431-0511. FAX 315-431-
0200.
Vendor(s): Data-Star, Lexis-Nexis. *1230*

**POLITICAL RISK SERVICES. COUNTRY REPORTS:
OMAN.**
Political Risk Services, Box 248, E. Syracuse, NY
13057-0248. TEL 315-431-0511. FAX 315-431-
0200.
Vendor(s): Data-Star, Lexis-Nexis. *1231*

**POLITICAL RISK SERVICES. COUNTRY REPORTS:
PAKISTAN.**
Political Risk Services, Box 248, E. Syracuse, NY
13057-0248. TEL 315-431-0511. FAX 315-431-
0200.
Vendor(s): Data-Star, Lexis-Nexis. *1231*

POLITICAL RISK SERVICES. COUNTRY REPORTS: PANAMA.
Political Risk Services, Box 248, E. Syracuse, NY 13057-0248. TEL 315-431-0511. FAX 315-431-0200.
Vendor(s): Data-Star, Lexis-Nexis. *1231*

POLITICAL RISK SERVICES. COUNTRY REPORTS: PERU.
Political Risk Services, Box 248, E. Syracuse, NY 13057-0248. TEL 315-431-0511. FAX 315-431-0200.
Vendor(s): Data-Star, Lexis-Nexis. *1231*

POLITICAL RISK SERVICES. COUNTRY REPORTS: PHILIPPINES.
Political Risk Services, Box 248, E. Syracuse, NY 13057-0248. TEL 315-431-0511. FAX 315-431-0200.
Vendor(s): Data-Star, Lexis-Nexis. *1231*

POLITICAL RISK SERVICES. COUNTRY REPORTS: POLAND.
Political Risk Services, Box 248, E. Syracuse, NY 13057-0248. TEL 315-431-0511. FAX 315-431-0200.
Vendor(s): Data-Star, Lexis-Nexis. *1231*

POLITICAL RISK SERVICES. COUNTRY REPORTS: ROMANIA.
Political Risk Services, Box 248, E. Syracuse, NY 13057-0248. TEL 315-431-0511. FAX 315-431-0200.
Vendor(s): Data-Star, Lexis-Nexis. *1231*

POLITICAL RISK SERVICES. COUNTRY REPORTS: RUSSIA.
Political Risk Services, Box 248, E. Syracuse, NY 13057-0248. TEL 315-431-0511. FAX 315-431-0200.
Vendor(s): Data-Star, Lexis-Nexis. *1231*

POLITICAL RISK SERVICES. COUNTRY REPORTS: SAUDI ARABIA.
Political Risk Services, Box 248, E. Syracuse, NY 13057-0248. TEL 315-431-0511. FAX 315-431-0200.
Vendor(s): Data-Star, Lexis-Nexis. *1231*

POLITICAL RISK SERVICES. COUNTRY REPORTS: SINGAPORE.
Political Risk Services, Box 248, E. Syracuse, NY 13057-0248. TEL 315-431-0511. FAX 315-431-0200.
Vendor(s): Data-Star, Lexis-Nexis. *1231*

POLITICAL RISK SERVICES. COUNTRY REPORTS: SOUTH AFRICA.
Political Risk Services, Box 248, E. Syracuse, NY 13057-0248. TEL 315-431-0511. FAX 315-431-0200.
Vendor(s): Data-Star, Lexis-Nexis. *1231*

POLITICAL RISK SERVICES. COUNTRY REPORTS: SOUTH KOREA.
Political Risk Services, Box 248, E. Syracuse, NY 13057-0248. TEL 315-431-0511. FAX 315-431-0200.
Vendor(s): Data-Star, Lexis-Nexis. *1231*

POLITICAL RISK SERVICES. COUNTRY REPORTS: SRI LANKA.
Political Risk Services, Box 248, E. Syracuse, NY 13057-0248. TEL 315-431-0511. FAX 315-431-0200.
Vendor(s): Data-Star, Lexis-Nexis. *1231*

POLITICAL RISK SERVICES. COUNTRY REPORTS: SUDAN.
Political Risk Services, Box 248, E. Syracuse, NY 13057-0248. TEL 315-431-0511. FAX 315-431-0200.
Vendor(s): Data-Star, Lexis-Nexis. *1231*

POLITICAL RISK SERVICES. COUNTRY REPORTS: SYRIA.
Political Risk Services, Box 248, E. Syracuse, NY 13057-0248. TEL 315-431-0511. FAX 315-431-0200.
Vendor(s): Data-Star, Lexis-Nexis. *1231*

POLITICAL RISK SERVICES. COUNTRY REPORTS: TAIWAN.
Political Risk Services, Box 248, E. Syracuse, NY 13057-0248. TEL 315-431-0511. FAX 315-431-0200.
Vendor(s): Data-Star, Lexis-Nexis. *1231*

POLITICAL RISK SERVICES. COUNTRY REPORTS: TUNISIA.
Political Risk Services, Box 248, E. Syracuse, NY 13057-0248. TEL 315-431-0511. FAX 315-431-0200.
Vendor(s): Data-Star, Lexis-Nexis. *1231*

POLITICAL RISK SERVICES. COUNTRY REPORTS: TURKEY.
Political Risk Services, Box 248, E. Syracuse, NY 13057-0248. TEL 315-431-0511. FAX 315-431-0200.
Vendor(s): Data-Star, Lexis-Nexis. *1231*

POLITICAL RISK SERVICES. COUNTRY REPORTS: UKRAINE.
Political Risk Services, Box 248, E. Syracuse, NY 13057-0248. TEL 315-431-0511. FAX 315-431-0200.
Vendor(s): Data-Star, Lexis-Nexis. *1231*

POLITICAL RISK SERVICES. COUNTRY REPORTS: UNITED ARAB EMIRATES.
Political Risk Services, Box 248, E. Syracuse, NY 13057-0248. TEL 315-431-0511. FAX 315-431-0200.
Vendor(s): Data-Star, Lexis-Nexis. *1231*

POLITICAL RISK SERVICES. COUNTRY REPORTS: URUGUAY.
Political Risk Services, Box 248, E. Syracuse, NY 13057-0248. TEL 315-431-0511. FAX 315-431-0200.
Vendor(s): Data-Star, Lexis-Nexis. *1231*

POLITICAL RISK SERVICES. COUNTRY REPORTS: VENEZUELA.
Political Risk Services, Box 248, E. Syracuse, NY 13057-0248. TEL 315-431-0511. FAX 315-431-0200.
Vendor(s): Data-Star, Lexis-Nexis. *1231*

POLITICAL RISK SERVICES. COUNTRY REPORTS: VIETNAM.
Political Risk Services, Box 248, E. Syracuse, NY 13057-0248. TEL 315-431-0511. FAX 315-431-0200.
Vendor(s): Data-Star, Lexis-Nexis. *1231*

POLITICAL RISK SERVICES. COUNTRY REPORTS: ZAIRE.
Political Risk Services, Box 248, E. Syracuse, NY 13057-0248. TEL 315-431-0511. FAX 315-431-0200.
Vendor(s): Data-Star, Lexis-Nexis. *1231*

POLITICAL RISK SERVICES. COUNTRY REPORTS: ZAMBIA.
Political Risk Services, Box 248, E. Syracuse, NY 13057-0248. TEL 315-431-0511. FAX 315-431-0200.
Vendor(s): Data-Star, Lexis-Nexis. *1232*

POLITICAL RISK SERVICES. COUNTRY REPORTS: ZIMBABWE.
Political Risk Services, Box 248, E. Syracuse, NY 13057-0248. TEL 315-431-0511. FAX 315-431-0200.
Vendor(s): Data-Star, Lexis-Nexis. *1232*

POLITICAL RISK SERVICES. EXECUTIVE REPORTS: AUSTRALIA.
Political Risk Services, Box 248, E. Syracuse, NY 13057-0248. TEL 315-431-0511. FAX 315-431-0200.
Vendor(s): Data-Star, Lexis-Nexis. *1232*

POLITICAL RISK SERVICES. EXECUTIVE REPORTS: AUSTRIA.
Political Risk Services, Box 248, E. Syracuse, NY 13057-0248. TEL 315-431-0511. FAX 315-431-0200.
Vendor(s): Data-Star, Lexis-Nexis. *1232*

POLITICAL RISK SERVICES. EXECUTIVE REPORTS: BELGIUM.
Political Risk Services, Box 248, E. Syracuse, NY 13057-0248. TEL 315-431-0511. FAX 315-431-0200.
Vendor(s): Data-Star, Lexis-Nexis. *1232*

POLITICAL RISK SERVICES. EXECUTIVE REPORTS: CANADA.
Political Risk Services, Box 248, E. Syracuse, NY 13057-0248. TEL 315-431-0511. FAX 315-431-0200.
Vendor(s): Data-Star, Lexis-Nexis. *1232*

POLITICAL RISK SERVICES. EXECUTIVE REPORTS: DENMARK.
Political Risk Services, Box 248, E. Syracuse, NY 13057-0248. TEL 315-431-0511. FAX 315-431-0200.
Vendor(s): Data-Star, Lexis-Nexis. *1232*

POLITICAL RISK SERVICES. EXECUTIVE REPORTS: FINLAND.
Political Risk Services, Box 248, E. Syracuse, NY 13057-0248. TEL 315-431-0511. FAX 315-431-0200.
Vendor(s): Data-Star, Lexis-Nexis. *1232*

POLITICAL RISK SERVICES. EXECUTIVE REPORTS: FRANCE.
Political Risk Services, Box 248, E. Syracuse, NY 13057-0248. TEL 315-431-0511. FAX 315-431-0200.
Vendor(s): Data-Star, Lexis-Nexis. *1232*

POLITICAL RISK SERVICES. EXECUTIVE REPORTS: GERMANY.
Political Risk Services, Box 248, E. Syracuse, NY 13057-0248. TEL 315-431-0511. FAX 315-431-0200.
Vendor(s): Data-Star, Lexis-Nexis. *1232*

POLITICAL RISK SERVICES. EXECUTIVE REPORTS: GREECE.
Political Risk Services, Box 248, E. Syracuse, NY 13057-0248. TEL 315-431-0511. FAX 315-431-0200.
Vendor(s): Data-Star, Lexis-Nexis. *1232*

POLITICAL RISK SERVICES. EXECUTIVE REPORTS: IRELAND.
Political Risk Services, Box 248, E. Syracuse, NY 13057-0248. TEL 315-431-0511. FAX 315-431-0200.
Vendor(s): Data-Star, Lexis-Nexis. *1232*

POLITICAL RISK SERVICES. EXECUTIVE REPORTS: ITALY.
Political Risk Services, Box 248, E. Syracuse, NY 13057-0248. TEL 315-431-0511. FAX 315-431-0200.
Vendor(s): Data-Star, Lexis-Nexis. *1232*

POLITICAL RISK SERVICES. EXECUTIVE REPORTS: JAPAN.
Political Risk Services, Box 248, E. Syracuse, NY 13057-0248. TEL 315-431-0511. FAX 315-431-0200.
Vendor(s): Data-Star, Lexis-Nexis. *1232*

POLITICAL RISK SERVICES. EXECUTIVE REPORTS: NETHERLANDS.
Political Risk Services, Box 248, E. Syracuse, NY 13057-0248. TEL 315-431-0511. FAX 315-431-0200.
Vendor(s): Data-Star, Lexis-Nexis. *1232*

POLITICAL RISK SERVICES. EXECUTIVE REPORTS: NEW ZEALAND.
Political Risk Services, Box 248, E. Syracuse, NY 13057-0248. TEL 315-431-0511. FAX 315-431-0200.
Vendor(s): Data-Star, Lexis-Nexis. *1233*

POLITICAL RISK SERVICES. EXECUTIVE REPORTS: NORWAY.
Political Risk Services, Box 248, E. Syracuse, NY 13057-0248. TEL 315-431-0511. FAX 315-431-0200.
Vendor(s): Data-Star, Lexis-Nexis. *1233*

POLITICAL RISK SERVICES. EXECUTIVE REPORTS: PORTUGAL.
Political Risk Services, Box 248, E. Syracuse, NY 13057-0248. TEL 315-431-0511. FAX 315-431-0200.
Vendor(s): Data-Star, Lexis-Nexis. *1233*

POLITICAL RISK SERVICES. EXECUTIVE REPORTS: PUERTO RICO.
Political Risk Services, Box 248, E. Syracuse, NY 13057-0248. TEL 315-431-0511. FAX 315-431-0200.
Vendor(s): Data-Star, Lexis-Nexis. *1233*

POLITICAL RISK SERVICES. EXECUTIVE REPORTS: SPAIN.
Political Risk Services, Box 248, E. Syracuse, NY 13057-0248. TEL 315-431-0511. FAX 315-431-0200.
Vendor(s): Data-Star, Lexis-Nexis. *1233*

POLITICAL RISK SERVICES. EXECUTIVE REPORTS: SWEDEN.
Political Risk Services, Box 248, E. Syracuse, NY 13057-0248. TEL 315-431-0511. FAX 315-431-0200.
Vendor(s): Data-Star, Lexis-Nexis. *1233*

POLITICAL RISK SERVICES. EXECUTIVE REPORTS: THAILAND.
Political Risk Services, Box 248, E. Syracuse, NY 13057-0248. TEL 315-431-0511. FAX 315-431-0200.
Vendor(s): Data-Star, Lexis-Nexis. *1233*

POLITICAL RISK SERVICES. EXECUTIVE REPORTS: UNITED KINGDOM.
Political Risk Services, Box 248, E. Syracuse, NY 13057-0248. TEL 315-431-0511. FAX 315-431-0200.
Vendor(s): Data-Star, Lexis-Nexis. *1233*

POLITICAL RISK SERVICES. EXECUTIVE REPORTS: UNITED STATES.
Political Risk Services, Box 248, E. Syracuse, NY 13057-0248. TEL 315-431-0511. FAX 315-431-0200.
Vendor(s): Data-Star, Lexis-Nexis. *1233*

POLITICAL RISK YEARBOOK.
Political Risk Services, Box 248, E. Syracuse, NY 13057-0248. TEL 315-431-0511. FAX 315-431-0200.
Vendor(s): Data-Star (FSRI), Lexis-Nexis. *1115*

POLITICAL RISK YEARBOOK. VOLUME 1: NORTH & CENTRAL AMERICA.
Political Risk Services, Box 248, E. Syracuse, NY 13057-0248. TEL 315-431-0511. FAX 315-431-0200.
Vendor(s): Data-Star (FSRI), Lexis-Nexis. *1115*

POLITICAL RISK YEARBOOK. VOLUME 2: MIDDLE EAST & NORTH AFRICA.
Political Risk Services, Box 248, E. Syracuse, NY 13057-0248. TEL 315-431-0511. FAX 315-431-0200.
Vendor(s): Data-Star (FSRI), Lexis-Nexis. *1115*

POLITICAL RISK YEARBOOK. VOLUME 3: SOUTH AMERICA.
Political Risk Services, Box 248, E. Syracuse, NY 13057-0248. TEL 315-431-0511. FAX 315-431-0200.
Vendor(s): Data-Star (FSRI), Lexis-Nexis. *1115*

POLITICAL RISK YEARBOOK. VOLUME 4: SUB-SAHARAN AFRICA.
Political Risk Services, Box 248, E. Syracuse, NY 13057-0248. TEL 315-431-0511. FAX 315-431-0200.
Vendor(s): Data-Star (FSRI), Lexis-Nexis. *1115*

POLITICAL RISK YEARBOOK. VOLUME 5: ASIA & THE PACIFIC.
Political Risk Services, Box 248, E. Syracuse, NY 13057-0248. TEL 315-431-0511. FAX 315-431-0200.
Vendor(s): Data-Star (FSRI), Lexis-Nexis. *1115*

POLITICAL RISK YEARBOOK. VOLUME 6: EUROPE - COUNTRIES OF THE EUROPEAN UNION.
Political Risk Services, Box 248, E. Syracuse, NY 13057-0248. TEL 315-431-0511. FAX 315-431-0200.
Vendor(s): Data-Star (FSRI), Lexis-Nexis. *1115*

POLITICAL RISK YEARBOOK. VOLUME 7: EUROPE - OUTSIDE THE EUROPEAN UNION.
Political Risk Services, Box 248, E. Syracuse, NY 13057-0248. TEL 315-431-0511. FAX 315-431-0200.
Vendor(s): Data-Star (FSRI), Lexis-Nexis. *1116*

POLITICAL SCIENCE QUARTERLY.
Academy of Political Science, 475 Riverside Dr., Ste. 1274, New York, NY 10115-1274. TEL 212-870-2500. FAX 212-870-2202.
Vendor(s): University Microfilms International. *5697*

POLITICAL WOMAN HOTLINE.
Political Woman, Inc., 276 Chatterton Pkwy., White Plains, NY 10606. TEL 914-285-9761.
Available only online. *5697*

POLITICS IN AMERICA.
Congressional Quarterly Inc., 1414 22nd St., N.W., Washington, DC 20037. TEL 202-887-8500. FAX 202-887-8706 *5697*

POLLUTION ABSTRACTS.
Cambridge Scientific Abstracts, 7200 Wisconsin Ave., 6th Fl., Bethesda, MD 20814. TEL 301-961-6750. FAX 301-961-6720.
Vendor(s): Data-Star (POLL), European Space Agency (File no.18/POLLUTION), Knight-Ridder Information, Inc. (File no.41), STN International (POLLUAB). *2331*

POLYMER ENGINEERING AND SCIENCE.
Society of Plastics Engineers, Inc., 14 Fairfield Dr., Box 403, Brookfield, CT 06804-0403. TEL 203-775-0471. FAX 203-775-8490.
Vendor(s): Information Access Co.. *2647*

POLYMERS AND RUBBER ASIA.
S K C Communications Ltd., Southfields, South View Rd., Wadhurst, E. Sussex TN5 6TP, England. TEL 44-1892-784099. FAX 44-1892-784089.
Vendor(s): Information Access Co.. *5627*

POLYMERS, CERAMICS, COMPOSITES ALERT.
Cambridge Scientific Abstracts, 7200 Wisconsin Ave., Bethesda, MD 20814. TEL 301-961-6750. FAX 301-961-6720.
Vendor(s): CEDOCAR, CISTI, Data-Star (MBUS), European Space Agency (File no.111), Knight-Ridder Information, Inc. (File no.269), Orbit Search Service (MABU), STN International (MATBUS). *5629*

POPULAR MECHANICS.
Hearst Corp., Popular Mechanics, 959 Eighth Ave., New York, NY 10019. TEL 212-649-2100.
Vendor(s): Information Access Co.. *6661*

POPULAR PHOTOGRAPHY.
Hachette Filipacchi Magazines, Inc., 1633 Broadway, New York, NY 10019. TEL 212-767-6000.
Vendor(s): Information Access Co., Knight-Ridder Information, Inc., University Microfilms International. *5519*

POPULAR SCIENCE.
Times Mirror Magazines, Inc., 2 Park Ave., New York, NY 10016. TEL 212-779-5000.
Vendor(s): Information Access Co., Knight-Ridder Information, Inc., University Microfilms International. *6661*

POPULATION AND DEVELOPMENT REVIEW.
Population Council, 1 Dag Hammarskjold Plaza, New York, NY 10017. TEL 212-339-0500. FAX 212-755-6052.
Vendor(s): Information Access Co.. *5789*

POPULATION INDEX.
Princeton University, Office of Population Research, 21 Prospect Ave., Princeton, NJ 08544-2091. TEL 609-258-4949. FAX 609-258-1039.
Vendor(s): National Library of Medicine. *5803*

PORTAVOZ.
Instituto Latinoamericano de Servicios Legales Alternativos, Apdo. Aereo 077844, Bogota, Colombia. TEL 57-1-2455955. FAX 57-1-2884854. *3833*

POSTGRADUATE MEDICAL JOURNAL.
B M J Publishing Group, B.M.A. House, Tavistock Sq., London WC1H 9JR, England. TEL 44-171-383-6270. FAX 44-171-383-6402. *4518*

POSTGRADUATE MEDICINE.
McGraw-Hill Companies (Minneapolis), 4530 W. 77th St., Minneapolis, 609-426-7070, MN 55435. TEL 612-835-3222.
Vendor(s): Dow Jones News Retrieval (PGM), Information Access Co., Knight-Ridder Information, Inc. (PGM), NewsNet (ME06). *4518*

POSTMODERN CULTURE.
Oxford University Press, Journals, 2001 Evans Rd., Cary, NC 27513. TEL 919-677-0977. FAX 919-677-1714. *4252*

POTATO ABSTRACTS.
CAB International, Wallingford, Oxon. OX10 8DE, England. TEL 44-1491-832111. FAX 44-1491-833508.
Vendor(s): DIMDI, European Space Agency, Knight-Ridder Information, Inc., STN International. *179*

POTATO NEWSLETTER.
Department of Agriculture, Plant Industry Branch, Box 6000, Fredericton, NE E3B 5H1, Canada. TEL 506-457-7244. FAX 506-457-7267. *236*

POTENTIALS IN MARKETING.
Lakewood Publications, Inc., 50 S. Ninth St., Minneapolis, MN 55402. TEL 612-333-0471. FAX 612-333-6526.
Vendor(s): Information Access Co.. *1482*

POULTRY ABSTRACTS.
CAB International, Wallingford, Oxon. OX10 8DE, England. TEL 44-1491-832111. FAX 44-1491-833508.
Vendor(s): DIMDI, European Space Agency, Knight-Ridder Information, Inc., STN International. *179*

POWER (NEW YORK).
McGraw-Hill Companies, 1221 Ave. of the Americas, New York, NY 10020. TEL 212-512-2000.
Vendor(s): Dow Jones News Retrieval (PWR), Knight-Ridder Information Inc. (PDW), Lexis-Nexis (POWER), NewsNet (EY84). *2767*

POWER ENGINEERING.
PennWell Publishing Co., Box 1260, Tulsa, OK 74101. TEL 918-835-3161. FAX 918-832-9295.
Vendor(s): Information Access Co.. *2716*

POWER IN ASIA.
Financial Times Energy Publishing Maple House, 149 Tottenham Court Rd., London W1P 9LL, England. TEL 44-171-896 2241. FAX 44-171-896-2275.
Vendor(s): Data-Star, Information Access Co., Knight-Ridder Information, Inc., Lexis-Nexis. *2717*

POWER IN EUROPE.
Financial Times Energy Publishing Maple House, 149 Tottenham Court Rd., London W1P 9LL, England. TEL 44-171-896 2241. FAX 44-171-896-2275.
Vendor(s): Data-Star, Information Access Co., Knight-Ridder Information, Inc., Lexis-Nexis. *2570*

POWER IN LATIN AMERICA.
Financial Times Energy Publishing Maple House, 149 Tottenham Court Rd., London W1P 9LL, England. TEL 0171-896-2241. FAX 0171-896-2275.
Vendor(s): Data-Star, Knight-Ridder Information, Inc., Lexis-Nexis. *2570*

POWER U K.
Financial Times Energy Publishing Maple House, 149 Tottenham Court Rd., London W1P 9LL, England. TEL 0171-896-2241. FAX 0171-896-2275.
Vendor(s): Data-Star, Knight-Ridder Information, Inc., Lexis-Nexis. *2570*

THE PRACTICAL ACCOUNTANT.
Faulkner and Gray, Inc. (New York), 11 Penn Plaza, 17th Fl., New York, NY 10001. TEL 212-967-7000. FAX 212-967-7155.
Vendor(s): Information Access Co., University Microfilms International. *1053*

PRACTICAL ANARCHY.
Spunk Press, P.O. Box 721, Madison, WI 53701-0721. TEL 608-251-4307. *5723*

THE PRACTICAL LAWYER.
American Law Institute - American Bar Association, Committee on Continuing Professional Education, 4025 Chestnut St., Philadelphia, PA 19104. TEL 215-243-1604. FAX 215-243-1664.
Vendor(s): University Microfilms International. *3833*

THE PRACTICAL LITIGATOR.
American Law Institute - American Bar Association, Committee on Continuing Professional Education, 4025 Chestnut St., Philadelphia, PA 19104. TEL 215-243-1604. FAX 215-243-1664.
Vendor(s): University Microfilms International. *3833*

THE PRACTICAL REAL ESTATE LAWYER.
American Law Institute - American Bar Association, Committee on Continuing Professional Education, 4025 Chestnut St., Philadelphia, PA 19104. TEL 215-243-1604. FAX 215-243-1664.
Vendor(s): University Microfilms International. *3834*

THE PRACTICAL TAX LAWYER.
American Law Institute - American Bar Association, Committee on Continuing Professional Education, 4025 Chestnut St., Philadelphia, PA 19104. TEL 215-243-1604. FAX 215-243-1664. Vendor(s): University Microfilms International. *3834*

PRACTICING C P A.
American Institute of Certified Public Accountants, 1211 Ave. of the Americas, New York, NY 10036. TEL 212-596-6200. Vendor(s): University Microfilms International. *1053*

PRECISION TOOLMAKER.
Argus Business Media Ltd., International Trade Publications Queensway House, 2 Queensway, Redhill, Surrey RH1 1QS, England. TEL 44-1737-768611. FAX 44-1737-773993. Vendor(s): Information Access Co.. *4971*

PREDICASTS BASEBOOK.
Information Access Company 362 Lakeside Dr., Foster City, CA 94404. TEL 415-378-5200. FAX 415-358-4759. Vendor(s): Data-Star, Knight-Ridder Information, Inc.. *1022*

PREDICASTS F & S INDEX EUROPE.
Information Access Company 362 Lakeside Dr., Foster City, CA 94404. TEL 415-378-5200. FAX 415-358-4759. Vendor(s): Ovid Technologies, Inc. (PTSI), Data-Star, Knight-Ridder Information, Inc.. *1022*

PREDICASTS F & S INDEX INTERNATIONAL.
Information Access Company 362 Lakeside Dr., Foster City, CA 94404. TEL 415-378-5200. FAX 415-378-5369. Vendor(s): Ovid Technologies, Inc. (PTSI), Data-Star, Knight-Ridder Information, Inc.. *1022*

PREDICASTS F & S INDEX OF CORPORATE CHANGE.
Information Access Company 362 Lakeside Dr., Foster City, CA 94404. TEL 415-378-5200. FAX 415-358-4759. Vendor(s): Ovid Technologies, Inc. (PTSI), Knight-Ridder Information, Inc.. *1022*

PREDICASTS F & S INDEX UNITED STATES.
Information Access Company 362 Lakeside Dr., Foster City, CA 94404. TEL 415-378-5200. FAX 415-378-5369. Vendor(s): Ovid Technologies, Inc. (PTSI), Data-Star, Knight-Ridder Information, Inc.. *1022*

PREDICASTS FORECASTS.
Information Access Company 362 Lakeside Dr., Foster City, CA 94404. TEL 415-378-5200. FAX 415-358-4759. Vendor(s): Data-Star (PTFC), Knight-Ridder Information, Inc.. *1023*

PREDICASTS OVERVIEW OF MARKETS AND TECHNOLOGY.
Information Access Company 362 Lakeside Dr., Foster City, CA 94404. TEL 415-978-5200. FAX 415-358-4759. Vendor(s): Data-Star, Knight-Ridder Information, Inc., Ovid Technologies, Inc. (PTSP). *2629*

PREDIKANT EN SAMENLEVING.
Bond van Nederlandse Predikanten, Cornelis Houtmanstraat 2, 3572 LV Utrecht, Netherlands. TEL 31-30-716133. FAX 31-30-733429. *6156*

PREMIERE (NEW YORK).
Hachette Filipacchi Magazines, Inc. 1633 Broadway, 45th Fl., New York, NY 10019. TEL 212-767-6000. FAX 212-767-5450. Vendor(s): Information Access Co.. *5110*

PREPARED FOODS.
Cahners Publishing Company (Des Plaines), Division of Reed Elsevier Inc., 1350 E. Touhy Ave., Box 5080, Des Plaines, IL 60018-5080. TEL 847-635-8800. FAX 847-390-2445. Vendor(s): Information Access Co., Lexis-Nexis. *2988*

PREPARED SOUPS: THE INTERNATIONAL MARKET.
Euromonitor, 60-61 Britton St., London EC1M 5NA, England. TEL 44-171-251-8024. FAX 44-171-608-3149. Vendor(s): Data-Star, Knight-Ridder Information, Inc.. *2988*

PREPRESS COMMENTARY.
Pira International, Randalls Rd., Leatherhead, Surrey KT22 7RU, England. TEL 44-1372-802080. FAX 44-1372-802239. Vendor(s): Information Access Co.. *6017*

PRESCRIBERS' JOURNAL.
H.M.S.O., 51 Nine Elms Ln., London SW8 5DR, England. TEL 44-171-873-0011. FAX 44-171-873-8463. *5439*

PRESCRIPTION PHARMACEUTICALS AND BIOTECHNOLOGY: THE PINK SHEET.
F-D-C Reports, Inc., 5550 Friendship Blvd., Ste. 1, Chevy Chase, MD 20815. FAX 301-664-7238. Vendor(s): Data-Star (FDCR), Knight-Ridder Information, Inc. (File no.187), Lexis-Nexis, Ovid Technologies, Inc. (FDCR). *5440*

PRESENCE MAGAZINE.
Presence Magazine Inc., 2715 Cote Ste-Catherine, Montreal, PQ H3T 1B6, Canada. TEL 514-739-9797. FAX 514-739-1664. *6085*

PRESIDENTIAL STUDIES QUARTERLY.
Center for the Study of the Presidency, 208 E. 75th St., New York, NY 10021. TEL 212-249-1200. FAX 212-628-9503. Vendor(s): University Microfilms International. *5699*

PREVENTION.
Rodale Press, Inc., 33 E. Minor St., Emmaus, PA 18049. TEL 610-967-5171. FAX 610-967-7725. Vendor(s): Information Access Co., University Microfilms International. *5534*

PREVIEW OF UNITED STATES SUPREME COURT CASES.
American Bar Association, Public Education Division, 750 N. Lake Shore Dr., Chicago, IL 60611. TEL 312-988-5728. FAX 312-988-5494. Vendor(s): West Services, Inc.. *3952*

PRIMARY EDUCATION DIRECTORY.
School Government Publishing Co. Ltd., Darby House, Bletchingley Rd., Merstham, Redhill, Surrey RH1 3DN, England. TEL 01737-642223. FAX 01737-644283. *2415*

PRINCIPIA CYBERNETICA NEWSLETTER.
Principia Cybernetica Project, c/o Free University of Brussels, Pleinlaan 2, 1050 Brussels, Belgium. TEL 32-2-6412525. FAX 32-2-6412489. Available only online. *2063*

PRINT.
R C Publications, Inc., 104 Fifth Ave., 19th Fl., New York, NY 10011. TEL 212-463-0600. FAX 212-989-9891. Vendor(s): Information Access Co.. *2030*

PRINT BUSINESS REGISTER.
P T N Publishing (Chicago), 20 E. Jackson Blvd., Ste. 700, Chicago, IL 60604-2203. TEL 312-922-5402. FAX 312-922-0856. *5816*

PRINTED CIRCUIT DESIGN.
Miller Freeman, Inc. 600 Harrison St., San Francisco, CA 94107. TEL 415-905-2200. FAX 415-905-2232. Vendor(s): University Microfilms International. *2530*

PRINTER PRICE TRACKING SERVICE.
Computer Economics, Inc., 5841 Edison Pl., Carlsbad, CA 92008. TEL 619-438-8100. FAX 619-431-1126. *2048*

PRINTING ABSTRACTS.
Pira International, Randalls Rd., Leatherhead, Surrey KT22 7RU, England. TEL 44-1372-802050. FAX 44-1372-802239. Vendor(s): Data-Star, FIZ Technik, Knight-Ridder Information, Inc., Orbit Search Service (PIRA), STN International. *5820*

PRINTING IMPRESSIONS.
North American Publishing Co., 401 N. Broad St., Philadelphia, PA 19108. TEL 215-238-5300. FAX 215-238-5457. Vendor(s): Information Access Co.. *5817*

PRINTING NEWS - EAST.
P T N Publishing Corp., 445 Broad Hollow Rd., Melville, NY 11474-4722. TEL 516-845-2700. FAX 516-845-7109. Vendor(s): Information Access Co.. *5817*

THE PRISON JOURNAL.
Sage Publications, Inc., 2455 Teller Rd., Thousand Oaks, CA 91320. TEL 805-499-0721. FAX 805-499-0871. Vendor(s): Information Access Co.. *2174*

PRIVACY JOURNAL.
Robert Ellis Smith, Ed. & Pub., Box 28577, Providence, RI 02908. TEL 401-274-7861. Vendor(s): NewsNet. *5734*

PRIVATE LABEL.
E.W. Williams Publications Co., 2125 Center Ave., Ste. 305, Fort Lee, NJ 07024-5859. TEL 201-592-7007. FAX 201-592-7171. Vendor(s): Information Access Co.. *1529*

PRIVATE LINE (CARMICHAEL).
Tom Farley, Ed. & Pub., Box 1059, Isleton, CA 95641. TEL 916-777-4420. *1949*

PRIVATE PLACEMENT REPORTER.
American Banker - Bond Buyer, Newsletter Division One State St. Plaza, New York, NY 10004-1549. TEL 800-733-4371. FAX 212-943-2224. Vendor(s): Information Access Co., Knight-Ridder Information, Inc., Lexis-Nexis, NewsNet (FI61). *1116*

PRIVATISATION INTERNATIONAL.
Privatisation International Ltd., Butlers Wharf Business Centre, Ste. 404, 45 Curlew St., London SE1 2ND, England. TEL 44-171-378-1620. FAX 44-171-403-7876. Vendor(s): Information Access Co.. *952*

PRIVREDNA IZGRADNJA.
Savez Ekonomista Vojvodine, Zmaj Jovine 26, 21000 Novi Sad, Yugoslavia. TEL 021 24-971. *952*

PRO SOUND NEWS EUROPE.
Spotlight Publications Ltd., Ludgate House, 245 Blackfriars Rd., London SE1 9UR, England. TEL 44-171-620-3636. FAX 44-171-401-8036. Vendor(s): Information Access Co.. *6446*

PROARBEIT.
Bundesanstalt fuer Arbeit, Institut fuer Arbeitsmarkt- und Berufsforschung, Regensburgerstr. 104, 90327 Nuernberg, Germany. TEL 49-911-1793011. FAX 49-911-1791147. *1023*

PROBATE & PROPERTY.
American Bar Association, Real Property, Probate and Trust Law Section, 750 N. Lake Shore Dr., Chicago, IL 60611. TEL 312-988-5591. Vendor(s): West Services, Inc.. *3916*

PROBE (BELTSVILLE).
U.S. National Agricultural Library, 10301 Baltimore Ave., 4th Fl., Beltsville, MD 20705-2351. TEL 301-504-6613. FAX 301-504-7098. *749*

PROCESS AND CHEMICAL ENGINEERING.
The Royal Society of Chemistry, Thomas Graham House, Science Park, Milton Rd., Cambridge CB4 4WF, England. TEL 44-1223-420066. FAX 44-1223-423429. Vendor(s): Data-Star (CEAB), Knight-Ridder Information, Inc. (File no.315), Orbit Search Service (CEABA). *2630*

PROCESS ENGINEERING.
Miller Freeman Technical Ltd. Miller Freeman House, 30 Calderwood St., London SE18 6QH, England. TEL 44-181-855-7777. FAX 44-181-316-3206. Vendor(s): Information Access Co.. *2648*

PRODUCER PRICE INDEXES.
U.S. Bureau of Labor Statistics, 2 Massachusetts Ave., N.E., Washington, DC 20212. TEL 202-655-4000. *1236*

PRODUCT ALERT.
Marketing Intelligence Service Ltd., 6473D Route 64, Naples, NY 14512-9726. TEL 716-374-6326. FAX 716-374-5217. Vendor(s): CompuServe, Inc., Data-Star, Dow Jones News Retrieval, Information Access Co., Knight-Ridder Information, Inc. (File no. 636), NewsNet (AD24). *2988*

PRODUCT SAFETY LETTER.
Washington Business Information, Inc., c/o Karen Harrington, 1117 N. 19th St., Ste. 200, Arlington, VA 22209. TEL 703-247-3434. FAX 703-247-3421.
Vendor(s): NewsNet (GB52). *5973*

PRODUCTION AND INVENTORY MANAGEMENT JOURNAL.
American Production & Inventory Control Society, 500 W. Annandale Rd., Falls Church, VA 22046-4274. TEL 703-237-8344.
Vendor(s): University Microfilms International. *1441*

PRODUCTIVITY SOFTWARE.
Worldwide Videotex, Box 3273, Boynton Beach, FL 33424-3273. TEL 407-738-2276.
Vendor(s): Data-Star, Information Access Co., Knight-Ridder Information, Inc., NewsNet (EC80). *2114*

PRODUCTS LIABILITY REPORTER.
Commerce Clearing House, Inc., 2700 Lake Cook Rd., Riverwoods, IL 60015. TEL 847-267-7000. FAX 800-224-8299. *3835*

PROFESSIONAL BUILDER.
Cahners Publishing Company (Des Plaines), Division of Reed Elsevier Inc., 1350 E. Touhy Ave., Box 5080, Des Plaines, IL 60018-5080. TEL 847-635-8800. FAX 847-635-9950.
Vendor(s): Information Access Co.. *870*

PROFESSIONAL ETHICS REPORT.
American Association for the Advancement of Science, 1200 New York Ave., N.W., Washington, DC 20005. TEL 202-326-6600. FAX 202-289-4950. *5494*

PROFESSIONAL SAFETY.
American Society of Safety Engineers, 1800 E. Oakton St., Des Plaines, IL 60018-2187. TEL 708-692-4121. FAX 708-296-3769.
Vendor(s): University Microfilms International. *5256*

PROFESSIONAL UPDATE.
Association of Professional Engineers, Scientists and Managers, Australia, 163 Eastern Rd., S. Melbourne, Vic. 3205, Australia. TEL 61-3-96958800. FAX 61-3-96969312.
Vendor(s): Knight-Ridder Information, Inc., Orbit Search Service. *2616*

PROGRES TECHNIQUE.
Association Nationale de la Recherche Technique, 101 av. Raymond Poincare, 75016 Paris, France. TEL 33-1-44-05-04-40. FAX 33-1-47-04-25-20. *6661*

PROGRESS IN CARDIOVASCULAR DISEASES.
W.B. Saunders Co. Curtis Center, 3rd Fl., Independence Sq. W., Philadelphia, PA 19106-3399. TEL 215-238-7800. FAX 215-238-6445.
Vendor(s): Lexis-Nexis. *4608*

PROGRESSIVE (MADISON).
Progressive, Inc., 409 E. Main St., Madison, WI 53703. TEL 608-257-4626. FAX 608-257-3373.
Vendor(s): Information Access Co., University Microfilms International. *5700*

PROGRESSIVE FARMER.
Southern Progressive Co., 2100 Lakeshore Dr., Birmingham, AL 35209. TEL 205-877-6000. FAX 205-877-6700. *146*

PROGRESSIVE GROCER.
Progressive Grocer Associates, LLC, 263 Tresser Blvd., 6th Fl., Stamford, CT 06901. TEL 203-325-3500. FAX 203-977-7645.
Vendor(s): Information Access Co., Knight-Ridder Information, Inc., Lexis-Nexis, University Microfilms International. *3007*

PROMAX INTERNATIONAL.
Promotion & Marketing Executives in the Electronic Media, 2029 Century Pk. E., Ste. 555, Los Angeles, CA 90067-2906. TEL 310-788-7600. FAX 310-788-7616. *1967*

PROMO.
SIMBA Information Inc. 11 Riverbend Dr. S., Box 4234, Stamford, CT 06907-0234. TEL 203-358-9900. FAX 203-358-5824.
Vendor(s): Information Access Co.. *1482*

PROMPT.
Pasadena I B M User Group, 2303 Glen Canyon Rd., Altadena, CA 91001-3539. TEL 818-791-1600. FAX 818-791-1600. *1997*

PROOFTEXTS.
Johns Hopkins University Press, Journals Publishing Division, 2715 N. Charles St., Baltimore, MD 21218. TEL 410-516-6987. FAX 410-516-6968. *6128*

PROPERTY, PLANNING AND COMPENSATION REPORTS.
Sweet & Maxwell, South Quay Plaza, 7th Fl., 183 Marsh Wall, London E14 9FT, England. TEL 071-538-8686. FAX 071-538-9508.
Vendor(s): Lexis-Nexis. *3835*

THE PROSTATE.
John Wiley & Sons, Inc., Journals, 605 Third Ave., New York, NY 10158. TEL 212-850-6645. FAX 212-850-6021 *4520*

PROSUS.
Scandinavian University Press, P.O. Box 2959 Toeyen, N-0608 Oslo, Norway. TEL 47-22-57-53-00. FAX 47-22-57-53-53. *6339*

PROTECT.
Tennessee Environmental Council, 1700 Hayes St., Ste.101, Nashville, TN 37203-2921. TEL 615-321-5075. *2816*

PROTEIN SCIENCE.
Cambridge University Press, Edinburgh Bldg., Shaftesbury Rd., Cambridge CB2 2RU, England. TEL 44-1223-312393. FAX 44-1223-315052. *648*

PROTOZOOLOGICAL ABSTRACTS.
CAB International, Wallingford, Oxon. OX10 8DE, England. TEL 44-1491-832111. FAX 44-1491-833508.
Vendor(s): DIMDI, European Space Agency, Knight-Ridder Information, Inc., STN International. *4573*

PROVINCIAL OUTLOOK.
Conference Board of Canada, 255 Smyth Rd., Ste. 100, Ottawa, ON K1H 8M7, Canada. TEL 613-526-3280. FAX 613-526-4857. *1236*

PSYCHE.
Monash University, Department of Computer Science, Clayton Vic. 3168, Australia. TEL 61-3-94271242. FAX 61-3-99055146. *5872*

PSYCHOLOGICAL ABSTRACTS.
American Psychological Association, 750 First St., N.E., Washington, DC 20002-4242. TEL 202-336-5600. FAX 202-336-5568.
Vendor(s): DIMDI, Data-Star (PSYC), Knight-Ridder Information, Inc. (File no.11/PsycINFO), Orbit Search Service, Ovid Technologies, Inc.. *5889*

THE PSYCHOLOGICAL RECORD.
Kenyon College, Gambier, OH 43022-9623. TEL 614-427-5377. FAX 614-427-4950.
Vendor(s): Information Access Co., University Microfilms International. *5874*

PSYCHOLOGY GRADUATE STUDENT JOURNAL.
c/o School of Psychology, University of Ottawa, 145 Jean Jacques Lussier, Ottawa ON K1N 6N5, Canada.
Available only online. *5876*

PSYCHOLOGY TODAY.
Sussex Publishers Inc., 49 E. 21st St., 11th Fl., New York, NY 10010. TEL 212-260-7210. FAX 212-260-7445.
Vendor(s): Information Access Co., Knight-Ridder Information, Inc., University Microfilms International. *5876*

PSYCHOPHARMACOLOGY BULLETIN.
U.S. Public Health Service, 5600 Fishers Ln., Rockville, MD 20857. TEL 301-496-4000.
Vendor(s): National Library of Medicine. *5440*

PSYCOLOQUY.
c/o Cognitive Sciences Centre, Dept. of Psychology, Univ. of Southampton, Highfield, Southampton SO17 1BJ, England.
Available only online. *5877*

PUBLIC ACCESS COMPUTER SYSTEMS NEWS.
University of Houston Libraries, Houston, TX 77204-2091. TEL 713-743-98C8. FAX 713-743-9811. *4046*

PUBLIC ADMINISTRATION.
Blackwell Publishers Ltd., 108 Cowley Rd., Oxford OX4 1JF, England. TEL 44-1865-791100. FAX 44-1865-791347.
Vendor(s): Information Access Co. *5916*

PUBLIC ADMINISTRATION QUARTERLY.
Southern Public Administration Education Foundation, c/o Dr. Jack Rabin, Pennsylvania State University at Harrisburg, Division of Public Affairs, Middletown, PA 17057. TEL 717-948-6363. FAX 717-540-1383.
Vendor(s): University Microfilms International. *5916*

PUBLIC ADMINISTRATION REVIEW.
American Society for Public Administration, 1120 G St., N.W., Ste. 700, Washington, DC 20005. TEL 202-393-7878. FAX 202-638-4952.
Vendor(s): Information Access Co., University Microfilms International. *5916*

PUBLIC BROADCASTING REPORT.
Warren Publishing, Inc., 2115 Ward Ct., N.W., Washington, DC 20037. TEL 202-872-9200. FAX 202-293-3435.
Vendor(s): Information Access Co., NewsNet (PB04) . *1967*

PUBLIC BUDGETING AND FINANCE.
Transaction Publishers, Transaction Periodicals Consortium, Department 3092, Rutgers University, New Brunswick, NJ 08903. TEL 908-445-2280. FAX 908-445-3138.
Vendor(s): University Microfilms International. *1559*

PUBLIC CONTRACT LAW JOURNAL.
American Bar Association, Public Contract Law Section, 750 N. Lake Shore Dr., Chicago, IL 60611. TEL 312-988-5000.
Vendor(s): West Services Inc.. *3836*

PUBLIC FINANCE QUARTERLY.
Sage Publications, Inc., 2455 Teller Rd., Thousand Oaks, CA 91320. TEL 805-499-0721. FAX 805-499-0871.
Vendor(s): Information Access Co.. *1559*

PUBLIC HEALTH REPORTS.
U.S. Public Health Service Department of Health and Human Services, J.F.K. Federal Bldg., Rm. 1826, Boston, MA 02203. TEL 617-565-1442. FAX 617-565-4260.
Vendor(s): Information Access Co., Lexis-Nexis, University Microfilms International. *5973*

PUBLIC INTEREST.
National Affairs, Inc., 1112 16th St., N.W., Ste. 530, Washington, DC 20036. TEL 202-785-8555. FAX 202-467-0006.
Vendor(s): Information Access Co., University Microfilms International. *5339*

PUBLIC MANAGEMENT.
International City - County Management Association, 777 North Capitol, N.E., Ste. 500, Washington, DC 20002-4201. TEL 202-962-3619. FAX 202-962-3500.
Vendor(s): Information Access Co., University Microfilms International. *5949*

THE PUBLIC MANAGER.
Bureaucrat, Inc., 12007 Titian Way, Potomac, MD 20854. TEL 301-279-9445. FAX 301-251-5872.
Vendor(s): Information Access Co.. *5917*

PUBLIC PERSONNEL MANAGEMENT.
International Personnel Management Association, 1617 Duke St., Alexandria, VA 22314. TEL 703-549-7100. FAX 703-684-0948.
Vendor(s): Information Access Co.. *1510*

PUBLIC PERSPECTIVE.
Roper Center for Public Opinion Research, Box 440, Storrs, CT 06269. TEL 203-486-4440. FAX 203-486-6308.
Vendor(s): Lexis-Nexis (PUBPER). *5701*

Online

PUBLIC PRODUCTIVITY AND MANAGEMENT REVIEW.
Sage Publications, Inc., 2455 Teller Rd., Thousand Oaks, CA 91320. TEL 805-499-0721. FAX 805-499-0871.
Vendor(s): University Microfilms International. *5917*

PUBLIC PULSE.
Roper Starch Worldwide, 205 E. 42nd St., New York, NY 10017. TEL 212-599-0700. FAX 212-867-7008.
Vendor(s): Lexis-Nexis. *1483*

PUBLIC RELATIONS NEWS.
Phillips Business Information, Inc., 1201 Seven Locks Rd., Potomac, MD 20854. TEL 301-424-3338. FAX 301-309-3847.
Vendor(s): Information Access Co.. *44*

PUBLIC RELATIONS QUARTERLY.
44 W. Market St., Box 311, Rhinebeck, NY 12572. TEL 914-876-2081. FAX 914-876-2561.
Vendor(s): Information Access Co., University Microfilms International. *44*

PUBLIC RELATIONS REVIEW.
J A I Press Inc., 55 Old Post Rd., No.2, Box 1678, Greenwich, CT 06836-1678. TEL 203-661-7602. FAX 203-661-0792.
Vendor(s): Information Access Co.. *44*

PUBLIC ROADS.
U.S. Federal Highway Administration, Office of Highway Information Management, Department of Transportation, 400 Seventh St., S.W., Washington, DC 20590. TEL 703-285-2443. FAX 703-285-2379.
Vendor(s): Information Access Co., University Microfilms International. *2671*

PUBLIC TREASURER.
L G C Communications, 33-39 Bowling Green Ln., London EC1R 0DA, England. TEL 44-171-505-8400. FAX 44-171-837-2725. *1559*

PUBLIC UNDERSTANDING OF SCIENCE.
I O P Publishing Ltd., Techno House, Redcliffe Way, Bristol, Avon BS1 6NX, England. TEL 44-117-929-7481. FAX 44-117-929-4318. *6273*

PUBLIC UTILITIES FORTNIGHTLY.
Public Utilities Reports, Inc., 8229 Boone Blvd., Ste. 401, Vienna, VA 22182. TEL 703-847-7720. FAX 703-917-6964.
Vendor(s): Information Access Co., Lexis-Nexis, University Microfilms International, West Services, Inc.. *1441*

PUBLIC UTILITIES REPORTS.
Public Utilities Reports, Inc., 8229 Boone Blvd., Ste. 401, Vienna, VA 22182. TEL 703-847-7720. FAX 703-917-6964.
Vendor(s): Lexis-Nexis, West Services, Inc.. *2556*

PUBLIC WELFARE.
American Public Welfare Association, c/o Publication Services, 810 First St., N.E., Ste. 500, Washington, DC 20002-4267. TEL 202-682-0100. FAX 202-289-6555.
Vendor(s): Information Access Co., University Microfilms International. *6388*

PUBLIC WORKS.
Public Works Journal Corporation, 200 S. Broad St., Ridgewood, NJ 07451. TEL 201-445-5800. FAX 201-445-5170.
Vendor(s): Information Access Co.. *5949*

PUBLISHERS DIRECTORY.
Gale Research Inc., 835 Penobscot Bldg., Detroit, MI 48226. TEL 313-961-2242. FAX 313-961-6083.
Vendor(s): Knight-Ridder Information, Inc.. *6006*

PUBLISHERS, DISTRIBUTORS & WHOLESALERS OF THE UNITED STATES.
R.R. Bowker, A Division of Reed Elsevier Inc., 121 Chanlon Rd., New Providence, NJ 07974. TEL 908-464-6800. FAX 908-665-3502.
Vendor(s): Knight-Ridder Information, Inc. (File no.450). *1635*

PUBLISHERS WEEKLY.
Cahners Publishing Company (New York), Printing and Publishing Division, Division of Reed Elsevier Inc., 249 W. 17th St., New York, NY 10011. TEL 212-645-0067. FAX 212-242-7216.
Vendor(s): Information Access Co.. *6006*

PUBLISHING TECHNOLOGY REVIEW.
Pira International, Randalls Rd., Leatherhead, Surrey KT22 7RU, England. TEL 44-1372-802050. FAX 44-1372-802239.
Vendor(s): Information Access Co.. *6006*

PUBLIUS.
Meyner Center for the Study of State and Local Government, Kirby Hall of Civil Rights, Lafayette College, Easton, PA 18042-1785. TEL 610-250-5598. FAX 610-559-4048.
Vendor(s): Information Access Co.. *5701*

PUEBLO BUSINESS JOURNAL.
201 W. 8th St., Ste. 408, Box 1544, Pueblo, CO 81002. TEL 719-542-3616. FAX 719-542-4506.
Vendor(s): University Microfilms International. *1236*

PUGET SOUND BUSINESS JOURNAL.
Scripps Howard Business Publications (Seattle), 720 Third Ave., Ste. 800, Seattle, WA 98104. TEL 206-583-0701.
Vendor(s): Information Access Co., Knight-Ridder Information, Inc.. *953*

PULP AND PAPER.
Miller Freeman, Inc., 600 Harrison St., San Francisco, CA 94107. TEL 415-905-2200. FAX 415-905-2232.
Vendor(s): Information Access Co., Lexis-Nexis, University Microfilms International. *5325*

PULP & PAPER CANADA.
Southam Magazine Group (St. Laurent), 3300 Cote Vertu, Ste. 410, St. Laurent, PQ H4R 2B7, Canada. TEL 514-339-1399. FAX 514-339-1396.
Vendor(s): Information Access Co., Southam Electronic Publishing. *5326*

PULP & PAPER CANADA'S ANNUAL & DIRECTORY.
Southam Magazine Group (St. Laurent), 3300 Cote Vertu, Ste. 410, St. Laurent, PQ H4R 2B7, Canada. TEL 514-339-1399. FAX 514-339-1396. *5326*

PULP & PAPER INTERNATIONAL.
Miller Freeman, Inc. 600 Harrison St., San Francisco, CA 94107. TEL 415-905-2200. FAX 415-905-2232.
Vendor(s): Information Access Co., Lexis-Nexis. *5326*

PUNCH IN INTERNATIONAL TRAVEL AND ENTERTAINMENT MAGAZINE.
Enterprises Publishing, 400 E. 59th St., Ste. 9F, New York, NY 10022. TEL 212-755-4363. FAX 212-755-4365. *6908*

PURCHASING (NEWTON).
Cahners Publishing Company (Newton), Division of Reed Elsevier Inc., 275 Washington St., Newton, MA 02158-1630. TEL 617-946-3030. FAX 617-558-4327.
Vendor(s): Information Access Co.. *1483*

PURDUE UNIVERSITY. INDIANA WATER RESOURCES RESEARCH CENTER. ANNUAL REPORT.
Purdue University, Indiana Water Resources Research Center, 1284 School of Civil Engineering, W. Lafayette, IN 47907-1284. TEL 317-494-8041. FAX 317-494-2720.
Available only online. *6974*

PURE AND APPLIED OPTICS.
I O P Publishing Ltd., Techno House, Redcliffe Way, Bristol, Avon BS1 6NX, England. TEL 44-117-929-7481. FAX 44-117-929-4318. *5611*

QUALITY PROGRESS.
American Society for Quality Control, 611 E. Wisconsin Ave., Box 3005, Milwaukee, WI 53201-3005. TEL 414-272-8575. FAX 414-272-1734.
Vendor(s): University Microfilms International. *2616*

QUARTERLY JOURNAL OF BUSINESS AND ECONOMICS.
University of Nebraska at Lincoln, College of Business Administration, CBA Bldg., Lincoln, NE 68588-0407. TEL 402-472-3309. FAX 402-472-9777.
Vendor(s): Information Access Co.. *953*

QUARTERLY JOURNAL OF ECONOMICS.
M I T Press, 55 Hayward St., Cambridge, MA 02142. TEL 617-253-2889. FAX 617-577-1545.
Vendor(s): Information Access Co.. *1260*

QUARTERLY JOURNAL OF MEDICINE.
Oxford University Press, Oxford Journals, Walton St., Oxford OX2 6DP, England. TEL 01865-267907. FAX 01865-267773.
Vendor(s): Ovid Technologies, Inc.. *4521*

THE QUARTERLY REVIEW OF ECONOMICS AND FINANCE.
J A I Press Inc., 55 Old Post Rd., No. 2, Box 1678, Greenwich, CT 06836-1678. TEL 203-661-7602. FAX 203-661-0792.
Vendor(s): Information Access Co.. *954*

QUEBEC (PROVINCE). SERVICES DOCUMENTAIRES MULTIMEDIA. CHOIX: DOCUMENTATION AUDIOVISUELLE.
Services Documentaires Multimedia Inc., 75 Port-Royal E., No. 300, Montreal, PQ H3L 3T1, Canada. TEL 514-382-0895. FAX 514-384-9139. *544*

QUEBEC (PROVINCE). SERVICES DOCUMENTAIRES MULTIMEDIA. CHOIX: DOCUMENTATION IMPRIMEE.
Services Documentaires Multimedia Inc., 75 Port-Royal E., No. 300, Montreal, PQ H3L 3T1, Canada. TEL 514-382-0895. FAX 514-384-9139. *544*

QUEBEC (PROVINCE). SERVICES DOCUMENTATION MULTIMEDIA. CHOIX JEUNESSE: DOCUMENTATION IMPRIMEE.
Services Documentaires Multimedia Inc., 75 Port-Royal E., No. 300, Montreal, PQ H3L 3T1, Canada. TEL 514-382-0895. FAX 514-384-9139. *544*

QUERY (SUNNYVALE).
Syllabus Press, 1307 S. Mary Ave., No. 211, Sunnyvake, CA 94087. TEL 408-746-2000. FAX 408-746-2711. *2407*

QUICK FROZEN FOODS INTERNATIONAL.
E.W. Williams Publications Co., 2125 Center Ave., Ste. 305, Fort Lee, NJ 07024-5859. TEL 201-592-7007. FAX 201-592-7171.
Vendor(s): Information Access Co.. *2989*

QUILL (GREENCASTLE).
Society of Professional Journalists, Box 77, Greencastle, IN 46135-0077. TEL 317-653-3333. FAX 317-653-4631.
Vendor(s): Information Access Co., Knight-Ridder Information, Inc.. *3710*

QUINNIPIAC LAW REVIEW.
Quinnipiac Law School, 275 Mt. Carmel Ave., Hamden, CT 06518-1950.
Vendor(s): West Services, Inc.. *3837*

R A D!
Conspiracy M.E.D.I.A., 826 Old Charlotte Pike E., Franklin, TN 37064. TEL 615-791-1624. *5190*

R A P R A ABSTRACTS.
R A P R A Technology Ltd., Shawbury, Shrewsbury, Shrops. SY4 4NR, England. TEL 44-1939-250383. FAX 44-1939-251118.
Vendor(s): Data-Star, European Space Agency, Knight-Ridder Information, Inc., Orbit Search Service (RAPRA), Telesystemes - Questel. *6220*

R A P R A NEW TRADE NAMES IN THE RUBBER AND PLASTICS INDUSTRIES.
R A P R A Technology Ltd., Shawbury, Shrewsbury, Shrops. SY4 4NR, England. TEL 44-1939-250383. FAX 44-1939-251118.
Vendor(s): Data-Star, European Space Agency, Knight-Ridder Information, Inc., Orbit Search Service (RAPRA), STN International. *6218*

R & D FOCUS.
IMSWORLD Publications Ltd., 7 Harewood Ave., London NW1 6JB, England. TEL 0171-393-5000. FAX 0171-393-5900.
Vendor(s): Data-Star, Knight-Ridder Information, Inc.. *5441*

R & D MANAGEMENT.
Blackwell Publishers Ltd., 108 Cowley Rd., Oxford OX4 1JF, England. TEL 44-1865-791100. FAX 44-1865-791347.
Vendor(s): Information Access Co.. *1442*

R B O C UPDATE.
Worldwide Videotex, Box 3273, Boynton Beach, FL 33424-3273. TEL 407-738-2276.
Vendor(s): Information Access Co.. *1949*

R I C NEWS.
Rare-earth Information Center, Institute for Physical Research and Technology, Iowa State University, 255 Spedding Hall, Ames, IA 50011-3020. TEL 515-294-2272. FAX 515-294-3709. *4972*

R I L M ABSTRACTS OF MUSIC LITERATURE.
R I L M Abstracts, City University of New York, 33 W. 42nd St., New York, NY 10036. TEL 212-642-2709. FAX 212-642-1973.
Vendor(s): OCLC. *5209*

R N.
Medical Economics Publishing Co., Inc., 5 Paragon Dr., Montvale, NJ 07645. TEL 201-358-7200. FAX 201-573-8979.
Vendor(s): Information Access Co., University Microfilms International. *4727*

R Q.
American Library Association, 50 E. Huron St., Chicago, IL 60611-2795. TEL 800-545-2433. FAX 312-440-9374.
Vendor(s): Information Access Co.. *4021*

R R.
Domstolsverket, Organisationsenheten, S-551 81 Joenkoeping, Sweden. *3837*

R T C WATCH.
Thomson Financial Services, One State St. Plaza, New York, NY 10004. TEL 800-733-4371. FAX 301-654-1678.
Vendor(s): NewsNet (FI03). *1117*

R T E C S.
U.S. National Institute for Occupational Safety and Health, 4676 Columbia Pkwy., Cincinnati, OH 45226.
Vendor(s): Canadian Centre for Occupational Health & Safety, Chemical Information Systems, Data-Star, Knight-Ridder Information, Inc. (File no.336), National Library of Medicine, STN International. *5257*

R V BUSINESS.
T L Enterprises, Inc., 3601 Calle Tecate, Camarillo, CA 93012. TEL 805-389-0300. FAX 805-389-0484.
Vendor(s): Information Access Co.. *6494*

RACHEL'S ENVIRONMENT & HEALTH WEEKLY.
Environmental Research Foundation, Box 5036, Annapolis, MD 21403-7036. TEL 410-263-1584. FAX 410-263-8944. *2816*

DER RADIOLOGE.
Springer-Verlag, Heidelberger Platz 3, 14197 Berlin, Germany. TEL 49-30-8207-0. FAX 49-30-8214091.
Vendor(s): FIZ Technik. *4882*

RADIOLOGIC CLINICS OF NORTH AMERICA.
W.B. Saunders Co. Curtis Center, 3rd Fl., Independence Sq. W., Philadelphia, PA 19106-3399. TEL 215-238-7800. FAX 215-238-6445.
Vendor(s): Ovid Technologies, Inc.. *4883*

RADIOLOGICAL HEALTH BULLETIN.
U.S. Food and Drug Administration, Center for Devices and Radiological Health, 5600 Fishers Ln., Rockville, MD 20857. TEL 301-443-5860. FAX 301-227-6834. *4883*

RADIOLOGY.
Radiological Society of North America, Inc., 2021 Spring Rd., Ste. 600, Oak Brook, IL 60521-1860. TEL 708-571-2670. FAX 708-571-7837. *4883*

RAETTSFALL FRAAN FOERSAEKRINGSOEVERDOMSTOLEN.
Domstolsverket, S-551 81 Joenkoeping, Sweden. *3663*

RAFT.
c/o John A.C. Greppin, Ed., Cleveland State University, Cleveland OH 44115. TEL 216-687-3967. FAX 216-687-9214. *4318*

RAILWAY AGE.
Simmons - Boardman Publishing Corp., 345 Hudson St., New York, NY 10014-4502. TEL 212-620-7200.
Vendor(s): Information Access Co., University Microfilms International. *6816*

RANDOM LENGTHS.
Random Lengths Publications, Inc., Box 867, Eugene, OR 97440-0867. TEL 541-686-9925. FAX 800-874-7979. *3037*

RANDOM LENGTHS MIDWEEK MARKET REPORT.
Random Lengths Publications, Inc., Box 867, Eugene, OR 97440. TEL 541-686-9629. FAX 541-686-9629. *3037*

RAPAPORT DIAMOND REPORT.
Rapaport Corp. 15 W. 47th St., Ste. 700, New York, NY 10036. TEL 212-354-0575. FAX 212-840-0243. *3698*

RAPID PROTOTYPING REPORT.
C A D - C A M Publishing, Inc., 1010 Turquoise St., Ste. 320, San Diego, CA 92109-1268. TEL 619-488-0533. FAX 619-488-6052.
Vendor(s): Information Access Co.. *2030*

RATEGRAM.
Bradshaw Group, Limited, Box 3517, San Rafael, CA 94912-3517. TEL 415-479-3815.
Vendor(s): NewsNet (IV61). *1117*

RE-DRAWING THE ISLAMIC MAP.
Arab Press Service, A P S House, P.O. Box 3896, Nicosia, Cyprus. TEL 357-2-351778. FAX 357-2-350265.
Vendor(s): Information Access Co.. *5768*

REACTIONS WEEKLY.
Adis International Limited, Private Bag 65901, Mairangi Bay, Auckland 10, New Zealand. TEL 64-9-479-8100. FAX 64-9-479-8145.
Vendor(s): Knight-Ridder Information, Inc. (READ, REAC,REAA,REZZ). *5451*

READERS' GUIDE ABSTRACTS.
H.W. Wilson Co., 950 University Ave., Bronx, NY 10452-9978. TEL 718-588-8400. FAX 718-590-1617.
Vendor(s): OCLC, Wilsonline (File RDG). *23*

READERS' GUIDE TO PERIODICAL LITERATURE.
H.W. Wilson Co., 950 University Ave., Bronx, NY 10452-9978. TEL 718-588-8400. FAX 718-590-1617.
Vendor(s): OCLC, Wilsonline (File RDG). *23*

REAL ESTATE ECONOMICS.
Edward Bros., 2500 S. State St., Ann Arbor, MI 48106. TEL 313-769-1004. FAX 313-769-7653.
Vendor(s): Information Access Co.. *6034*

REAL ESTATE FINANCE.
Insitutional Investor Journals, 488 Madison Ave., New York, NY 10022. TEL 212-224-3185. FAX 212-224-3527.
Vendor(s): University Microfilms International. *6034*

REAL ESTATE FINANCE TODAY.
Mortgage Bankers Association of America, 1125 15th St., N.W., Washington, DC 20005-2766. TEL 202-861-6555. FAX 202-861-1930.
Vendor(s): University Microfilms International. *6034*

REAL ESTATE ISSUES.
Counselors of Real Estate, 430 N. Michigan Ave., Chicago, IL 60611. TEL 312-329-8427. FAX 312-329-8881.
Vendor(s): University Microfilms International. *6034*

REAL ESTATE TODAY.
National Association of Realtors (Chicago), 430 N. Michigan Ave., Chicago, IL 60611. TEL 312-329-8458. FAX 312-329-5978.
Vendor(s): Information Access Co.. *6035*

REAL ESTATE WEEKLY.
Hagedorn Communications Corp., One Madison Ave., 35th Fl., New York, NY 10010. TEL 212-679-1234.
Vendor(s): Information Access Co.. *6035*

REAL PROPERTY, PROBATE AND TRUST JOURNAL.
American Bar Association, Real Property, Probate and Trust Law Section, 750 N. Lake Shore Dr., Chicago, IL 60611. TEL 312-988-6083.
Vendor(s): University Microfilms International, West Services, Inc.. *3916*

REAL TIMES.
Michael Redman, Ed. & Pub., Box 1686, Bloomington, IN 47402. TEL 812-332-3498. *3236*

REALITIES.
Realities Library, 2745 Monterey Hwy. No. 76, San Jose, CA 95111.
Available only online. *4319*

REASON.
Reason Foundation, 3415 S. Sepulveda Blvd., Ste. 400, Los Angeles, CA 90034-6060. TEL 310-391-2245. FAX 310-391-4395.
Vendor(s): Information Access Co.. *4163*

RECALL NEWSLETTER.
C T I Modern Languages, University of Hull, School of European Languages & Cultures, Cottingham Rd., Hull HU6 7RX, England. TEL 44-1482-466373. FAX 44-1482-473816. *4130*

RECHERCHE EN MATIERE D'ECONOMIE DES TRANSPORTS.
Organization for Economic Cooperation and Development, European Conference of Ministers of Transport, 2 rue Andre Pascal, 75775 Paris Cedex 16, France. TEL 33-1-45-24-82-00. FAX 33-1-49-10-42-76.
Vendor(s): European Space Agency (File no.74/TRANSDOC Subfile: RESEARCH). *6726*

RECHERCHES UNIVERSITAIRES SUR L'INTEGRATION EUROPEENNE.
Commission of the European Communities, Rue de la Loi 200, B-1049 Brussels, Belgium. *5723*

RECORDS MANAGEMENT QUARTERLY.
Association of Records Managers and Administrators, 4200 Somerset Dr., Ste. 215, Prairie Village, KS 66208. TEL 913-341-3808.
Vendor(s): Information Access Co., University Microfilms International. *4022*

RECUEIL DES BREVETS D'INVENTION.
Ministry of Economic Affairs, Office de la Propriete Industrielle, 154 Bd. E. Jacqmain 1210 Brussels, Belgium. TEL 32-2-2064111. FAX 32-2-2065750.
Vendor(s): BELINDIS. *5343*

RED POLITICS.
R P Publishing, 2-77 Holden St. N., Fitzroy, Vic. 3068, Australia.
Available only online. *5702*

REDBOOK.
Hearst Corporation, Redbook, 224 W. 57th St., New York, NY 10019. TEL 212-649-2000.
Vendor(s): Information Access Co.. *7006*

REEVES JOURNAL.
Business News Publishing Company, 755 W. Big Beaver Rd., Ste. 1000, Troy, MI 48084. TEL 810-362-3700. FAX 810-362-0317. *3332*

REFERATE: MESSEN MECHENISCHER GROESSEN.
F I Z Technik e.V., Ostbahnhofstr. 13, 60314 Frankfurt a.M., Germany. *2630*

REFERATE: SCHWEISSEN UND VERWANDTE VERFAHREN.
Bundesanstalt fuer Materialforschung und -pruefung, Unter den Eichen 87, 12205 Berlin, Germany. TEL 49-30-81041555. FAX 49-81041557. *4984*

Online

REFERATE ZERSTOERUNGSFREIE PRUEFUNG.
Bundesanstalt fuer Materialforschung und -pruefung, Unter den Eichen 87, 12205 Berlin, Germany. TEL 49-30-81043638. FAX 49-30-81045089. *2630*

REFERENCE AND RESEARCH BOOK NEWS.
Book News, Inc. (Portland), 5600 N.E. Hassalo St., Portland, OR 97213. TEL 503-281-9230. FAX 503-287-4485. *544*

REFERENCE BOOK OF CORPORATE MANAGEMENTS.
Dun's Marketing Services 3 Sylvan Way, Parsippany, NJ 07054-3896. TEL 201-455-0900. Vendor(s): Orbit Search Service (RBCM). *1442*

REFLECTOR NEWSLETTER.
Astronomical League, 5027 W. Stanford, Dallas, TX 75209-3319. TEL 214-357-2744. Vendor(s): CompuServe, Inc.. *485*

REFRIGERATION SERVICE AND CONTRACTING.
Business News Publishing Company, 755 W. Big Beaver Rd., Ste. 1000, Troy, MI 48084. TEL 810-362-3700. FAX 810-362-0317. *3332*

REGENT ONLINE JOURNAL OF COMMUNICATION.
Regent University, College of Communication and the Arts, School of Communication Studies, Virginia Beach, VA 23464-9800. TEL 804-523-7943. FAX 804-424-7051. Available only online. *5111*

REGIONAL STUDIES.
Carfax Publishing Co., P.O. Box 25, Abingdon, Oxon. OX14 3UE, England. TEL 44-1235-401000. FAX 44-1235-401550. Vendor(s): Information Access Co.. *3593*

REGULATORY COMPLIANCE WATCH.
American Banker - Bond Buyer, Newsletter Division One State St. Plaza, New York, NY 10004-1549. TEL 800-733-4371. FAX 212-943-2224. Vendor(s): Information Access Co., NewsNet (FI04). *1118*

REGULATORY UPDATE.
Lewis B. Weisfeld, Ed. & Pub., 1 Franklin Town Blvd., Ste. 1204, Philadelphia, PA 19103. TEL 215-567-7235. FAX 215-567-7235. *5627*

REHABILITATION INDEX.
British Library, Medical Information Centre, Boston Spa, Wetherby, W. Yorks. LS23 7BQ, England. TEL 01937-546520. FAX 01937-546458. *4574*

RELEASE 1.0.
EDventure Holdings, 104 Fifth Ave., New York, NY 10011-6987. TEL 212-924-8800. FAX 212-924-0240. Vendor(s): Information Access Co. *2034*

RELIGION IN EASTERN EUROPE.
Christian Association for Relationships with Eastern Europe, c/o Rosemont College, Rosemont, PA 19010. TEL 215-527-0200. FAX 215-696-8970. Vendor(s): Knight-Ridder Information, Inc., Ovid Technologies, Inc.. *6087*

RELIGIOUS LEADERS OF AMERICA.
Gale Research Inc., 835 Penobscot Bldg., Detroit, MI 48226. TEL 800-877-4253. FAX 313-961-6083. Vendor(s): Lexis-Nexis. *6088*

RELIGIOUS STUDIES.
Cambridge University Press, Edinburgh Bldg., Shaftesbury Rd., Cambridge CB2 2RU, England. TEL 44-1223-312393. FAX 44-1223-315052. Vendor(s): Information Access Co.. *6088*

RENAISSANCE QUARTERLY.
Renaissance Society of America, 24 W. 12th St., New York, NY 10011-8604. TEL 212-998-3797. FAX 212-995-4205. Vendor(s): Information Access Co., University Microfilms International. *4257*

RENEW NEWSLETTER.
Network for Alternative Technology and Technology Assessment, c/o Energy and Environment Research Unit, Faculty of Technology, Open University, Walton Hall, Milton Keynes, Bucks. MK7 6AA, England. TEL 44-1908-654638. FAX 44-1908-653744. *2557*

RENEWABLE ENERGY REPORT.
Financial Times Energy Publishing Maple House, 149 Tottenham Court Rd., London W1P 9LL, England. TEL 0171-896-2241. FAX 0171-896-2275. Vendor(s): Data-Star, Knight-Ridder Information, Inc., Lexis-Nexis. *2557*

REPERTOIRE DES BANQUES DE DONNEES TELETEL POUR L'ENTREPRISE.
Editions F L A Consultants, 27 rue de la Vistule, 75013 Paris, France. TEL 45-82-75-75. FAX 45-82-46-04. *1929*

REPORT ON A T & T.
Capitol Publications Inc., Telecom Publishing Group, 1101 King St., Ste. 444, Box 1455, Alexandria, VA 22313-2055. TEL 800-327-7205. FAX 703-739-6490. Vendor(s): Information Access Co., NewsNet (TE50). *1929*

REPORT ON CORPORATE EDUCATIONAL SUPPORT.
Business Publishers, Inc., 951 Pershing Dr., Silver Spring, MD 20910-4464. TEL 301-587-6300. FAX 301-585-9075. Vendor(s): NewsNet. *2462*

REPORT ON DEFENSE PLANT WASTE.
Business Publishers, Inc., 951 Pershing Dr., Silver Spring, MD 20910-4464. TEL 301-587-6300. FAX 301-585-9075. Vendor(s): Information Access Co., NewsNet (EV28). *2856*

REPORT ON DISABILITY PROGRAMS.
Business Publishers, Inc., 951 Pershing Dr., Silver Spring, MD 20910-4464. TEL 301-587-6300. FAX 301-585-9075. Vendor(s): NewsNet. *6389*

REPORT ON EDUCATION OF THE DISADVANTAGED.
Business Publishers, Inc., 951 Pershing Dr., Silver Spring, MD 20910-4464. TEL 301-587-6300. FAX 301-585-9075. Vendor(s): NewsNet. *2474*

REPORT ON HEALTHCARE MANAGEMENT SOLUTIONS.
Business Publishers, Inc., 951 Pershing Dr., Silver Spring, MD 20910-4464. TEL 301-587-6300. FAX 301-585-9075. Vendor(s): NewsNet. *3555*

REPORT ON I B M.
DataTrends Publications, Inc., Box 4460, Leesburg, VA 20175. TEL 703-779-0574. FAX 703-779-2267. Vendor(s): Information Access Co., NewsNet (EC45). *2079*

REPORT ON LITERACY PROGRAM.
Business Publishers, Inc., 951 Pershing Dr., Silver Spring, MD 20910-4464. TEL 301-587-6300. FAX 301-585-9075. Vendor(s): NewsNet (ED10). *2366*

REPORT ON MICROSOFT.
DataTrends Publications, Inc., Box 4460, Leesburg, VA 20175. TEL 703-779-0574. FAX 703-779-2267. Vendor(s): Information Access Co.. *2032*

REPORT ON PRESCHOOL PROGRAMS.
Business Publishers, Inc., 951 Pershing Dr., Silver Spring, MD 20910-4464. TEL 301-587-6300. FAX 301-585-9075. Vendor(s): NewsNet. *2366*

REPORT ON SCHOOL-AGE CHILD CARE.
Business Publishers, Inc., 951 Pershing Dr., Silver Spring, MD 20910-4464. TEL 301-587-6300. FAX 301-585-9075. Vendor(s): NewsNet. *1776*

REPORTS ON PROGRESS IN PHYSICS.
I O P Publishing Ltd., Techno House, Redcliffe Way, Bristol, Avon BS1 6NX, England. TEL 44-117-929-7481. FAX 44-117-929-4318. *5568*

REPRODUCTIVE RIGHTS UPDATE.
American Civil Liberties Union, Reproductive Freedom Project, 132 W. 43rd St., New York, NY 10036. TEL 212-944-9800. FAX 212-869-4314. *5735*

RESEARCH ALERT (NEW YORK).
E P M Communications, 160 Mercer St., 3rd Fl., New York, NY 10012-3212. TEL 212-941-0099. FAX 212-941-1622. Vendor(s): Information Access Co., Knight-Ridder Information, Inc., Lexis-Nexis. *1483*

RESEARCH & DEVELOPMENT.
Cahners Publishing Company (Des Plaines), Division of Reed Elsevier Inc., 1350 E. Touhy Ave., Box 5080, Des Plaines, IL 60018-5080. TEL 847-635-8800. FAX 847-390-2618. Vendor(s): Information Access Co., Knight-Ridder Information, Inc.. *6662*

RESEARCH CENTERS DIRECTORY.
Gale Research Inc., 835 Penobscot Bldg., Detroit, MI 48226. TEL 313-961-2242. FAX 313-961-6083. Vendor(s): Knight-Ridder Information, Inc.. *6275*

RESEARCH HORIZONS.
Georgia Institute of Technology, Research Communications Office, 223 Centennial Research Bldg., Atlanta, GA 30332-0828. TEL 404-894-4259. FAX 404-894-6983. *2616*

RESEARCH IN AFRICAN LITERATURES.
Indiana University Press, 601 N. Morton St., Bloomington, IN 47404. TEL 812-855-9449. FAX 812-855-8507. Vendor(s): Information Access Co., University Microfilms International. *4257*

RESEARCH QUARTERLY FOR EXERCISE AND SPORT.
American Alliance for Health, Physical Education, Recreation, and Dance, 1900 Association Dr., Reston, VA 22091. TEL 703-476-3400. FAX 703-476-9527. Vendor(s): Information Access Co., University Microfilms International. *5534*

RESEARCH SERVICES DIRECTORY.
Gale Research Inc., 835 Penobscot Bldg., Detroit, MI 48226. TEL 313-961-2242. FAX 313-961-6083. Vendor(s): Knight-Ridder Information, Inc.. *1637*

RESILOG.
Environment Canada, Transboundary Movement Division, Ottawa, ON K1A 0H3, Canada. TEL 819-997-3377. FAX 819-997-3068. *2856*

RESOURCES IN EDUCATION.
E R I C Facility, 1301 Piccard Dr., Ste. 100, Rockville, MD 20850. TEL 301-258-5500. FAX 301-948-3695. Vendor(s): Knight-Ridder Information, Inc., Ovid Technologies, Inc.. *2392*

RESPIRATORY MEDICINE.
W.B. Saunders Co. Ltd. 24-28 Oval Rd., London NW1 7DX, England. TEL 0171-267-4466. FAX 0171-482-2293. Vendor(s): Ovid Technologies, Inc.. *4891*

RESPONSE T V.
Advanstar Communications, Inc., 7500 Old Oak Blvd., Cleveland, OH 44130. TEL 216-826-2839. FAX 216-891-2726. Vendor(s): Information Access Co.. *1968*

RESTAURANT BUSINESS.
Bill Communications, Inc., 355 Park Ave. S., 5th Fl., New York, NY 10010-1789. TEL 212-592-6200. FAX 212-592-6339. Vendor(s): Information Access Co., University Microfilms International. *3569*

RESTAURANT HOSPITALITY.
Penton Publishing Co. 1100 Superior Ave., Cleveland, OH 44114-2543. TEL 216-696-7000. FAX 216-696-8765. Vendor(s): Information Access Co., University Microfilms International. *3570*

RESTAURANTS AND INSTITUTIONS.
Cahners Publishing Company (Des Plaines), Division of Reed Elsevier Inc., 1350 E. Touhy Ave., Box 5080, Des Plaines, IL 60018-5080. TEL 847-635-8800. FAX 847-390-2080. Vendor(s): Information Access Co.. *3570*

RETAIL BUSINESS: MARKET REPORTS.
Corporate Intelligence on Retailing, 51 Doughty St., London WC1 N2LS, England. TEL 44-171-696-9006. *1484*

RETAIL INTELLIGENCE.
Mintel International Group Ltd., 18-19 Long Ln., London EC1A 9HE, England. TEL 44-171-606-4533. FAX 44-171-606-5932. *1484*

RETAIL STATIONERY: THE INTERNATIONAL MARKET.
Euromonitor, 60-61 Britton St., London EC1M 5NA, England. TEL 44-171-251-8024. FAX 44-171-608-3149.
Vendor(s): Data-Star, Knight-Ridder Information, Inc.. *1496*

RETAIL STORE IMAGE.
Intertec Publishing Corp. (Atlanta), 6151 Powers Ferry Rd., N.W., Atlanta, GA 30339-2941. TEL 770-955-2500. FAX 770-9550-0400.
Vendor(s): Information Access Co.. *3681*

RETAIL TRADE INTERNATIONAL.
Euromonitor, 60-61 Britton St., London EC1M 5NA, England. TEL 44-171-251-8024. FAX 44-171-608-3149. *1484*

REVIEW OF AGRICULTURAL ENTOMOLOGY.
CAB International, Wallingford, Oxon. OX10 8DE, England. TEL 44-1491-832111. FAX 44-1491-833508.
Vendor(s): DIMDI, European Space Agency, Knight-Ridder Information, Inc., STN International. *180*

REVIEW OF AROMATIC AND MEDICINAL PLANTS.
CAB International, Wallingford, Oxon. OX10 8DE, England. TEL 44-1491-832111. FAX 44-1491-826090. *4574*

THE REVIEW OF BANKING AND FINANCIAL SERVICES.
Standard & Poor's Corporation 25 Broadway, New York, NY 10004. TEL 212-208-8000.
Vendor(s): Dow Jones News Retrieval (RBFS), Knight-Ridder Information, Inc. (BFS), Lexis-Nexis (RBFS), NewsNet (FI17). *1119*

REVIEW OF BLACK POLITICAL ECONOMY.
Transaction Publishers, Transaction Periodicals Consortium, Department 3092, Rutgers University, New Brunswick, NJ 08903. TEL 908-445-2280. FAX 908-445-3138.
Vendor(s): Information Access Co., University Microfilms International. *955*

REVIEW OF BUSINESS.
St. John's University, College of Business Administration, Bent Hall, 8000 Utopia Pkwy., NY 11439. TEL 718-990-6768. FAX 718-990-1868.
Vendor(s): Information Access Co., University Microfilms International. *955*

THE REVIEW OF CONTEMPORARY FICTION.
Review of Contemporary Fiction, Inc., 4241 Illinois State University, Normal, IL 61790-4241. TEL 309-438-7555. FAX 309-437-7422.
Vendor(s): Information Access Co., University Microfilms International. *4258*

REVIEW OF EDUCATIONAL RESEARCH.
American Educational Research Association, 1230 17th St., N.W., Washington, DC 20036-3078. TEL 202-223-9485. FAX 202-775-1824.
Vendor(s): University Microfilms International. *2367*

REVIEW OF ENGLISH STUDIES.
Oxford University Press, Oxford Journals, Walton St., Oxford OX2 6DP, England. TEL 44-1865-267907. FAX 44-1865-267773.
Vendor(s): Information Access Co.. *4258*

REVIEW OF FINANCIAL ECONOMICS.
J A I Press Inc., Box 1678, 55 Old Post Rd., No. 2, Greenwich, CT 06836-1678. TEL 203-661-7602. FAX 203-661-0792.
Vendor(s): Information Access Co.. *955*

REVIEW OF MEDICAL AND VETERINARY ENTOMOLOGY.
CAB International, Wallingford, Oxon. OX10 8DE, England. TEL 44-1491-832111. FAX 44-1491-833508.
Vendor(s): DIMDI, European Space Agency, Knight-Ridder Information, Inc., STN International. *6961*

REVIEW OF MEDICAL AND VETERINARY MYCOLOGY.
CAB International, Wallingford, Oxon. OX10 8DE, England. TEL 44-1491-832111. FAX 44-1491-833508.
Vendor(s): DIMDI, European Space Agency, Knight-Ridder Information, Inc., STN International. *624*

THE REVIEW OF METAPHYSICS.
Philosophy Education Society, Inc., Catholic University of America, Washington, DC 20064. TEL 202-635-8778 FAX 202-319-4481.
Vendor(s): Information Access Co.. *5495*

REVIEW OF PLANT PATHOLOGY.
CAB International, Wallingford, Oxon. OX10 8DE, England. TEL 44-1491-832111. FAX 44-1491-833508.
Vendor(s): DIMDI, European Space Agency, Knight-Ridder Information, Inc., STN International. *624*

REVIEW OF PUBLIC PERSONNEL ADMINISTRATION.
University of South Carolina, Institute of Public Affairs, Columbia, SC 29208. TEL 803-777-8157.
Vendor(s): University Microfilms International. *5919*

REVIEW OF SCIENTIFIC INSTRUMENTS.
American Institute of Physics, One Physics Ellipse, College Park, MD 20740-3843. TEL 301-209-3000. *3637*

THE REVIEW OF SECURITIES & COMMODITIES REGULATION.
Standard & Poor's 25 Broadway, New York, NY 10004. TEL 212-208-8650. FAX 212-412-0240.
Vendor(s): Dow Jones News Retrieval (RSCR), Knight-Ridder Information, Inc. (SCR), Lexis-Nexis (RSCR), NewsNet (FI20). *1349*

REVIEW OF SOCIAL ECONOMY.
Routledge, 11 New Fetter Ln., London EC4P 4EE, England. TEL 44-171-583-9855. FAX 44-171-842-2298.
Vendor(s): Information Access Co.. *956*

REVIEWS IN AMERICAN HISTORY.
Johns Hopkins University Press, Journals Publishing Division, 2715 N. Charles St., Baltimore, MD 21218. TEL 410-516-6987. FAX 410-516-6968.
Vendor(s): Information Access Co.. *3485*

REVIEWS IN FISH BIOLOGY AND FISHERIES.
Chapman & Hall, Journals Department 2-6 Boundary Row, London SE1 8HN, England. TEL 44-171-8650066. FAX 44-171-5229623. *819*

REVIEWS IN MEDICAL MICROBIOLOGY.
Chapman & Hall, Journals Department Boundary Row, London SE1 8HN, England. TEL 44-171-8650066. FAX 44-171-5229323. *766*

REVISTA CANARIA DE ESTUDIOS INGLESES.
Universidad de La Laguna, Secretariado de Publicaciones, San Agustin, 30, 38201 La Laguna-Tenerife, Islas Canarias, Spain. TEL 922-25-81-27. *4102*

REVISTA COLOMBIANA DE CIENCIAS QUIMICO FARMACEUTICAS.
Universidad Nacional de Colombia, Departamento de Farmacia, Apdo. Aereo 14490, Bogota, Colombia. *5442*

REVISTA CUBANA DE FARMACIA.
Ministerio de Salud Publica, Centro Nacional de Informacion de Ciencias Medicas, Calle E No. 452, e-19 y 21, Plaza de la Revolucion, Apdo. 6520, Havana, Cuba. TEL 809-32-5338. *5442*

REVISTA CUBANA DE MEDICINA GENERAL INTEGRAL.
Ministerio de Salud Publica, Centro Nacional de Informacion de Ciencias Medicas, Calle E No. 452, e-19 y 21, Plaza de la Revolucion, Apdo. 6520, Havana, Cuba. TEL 809-32-5338. *4524*

REVISTA DE ESTUDIOS EXTREMENOS.
Centro de Estudios Extremenos, Servicio de Publicaciones, Felipe Checa 15, 06071 Badajoz, Spain. *3216*

REVISTA DE MICROBIOLOGIA.
Sociedade Brasileira de Microbiologia, c/o Luiz Rachid Trabulsi, Ed., Depto. de Microbiologia, Instituto de Ciencias Biomedicas USP, Av. Prof. Lineu Prestes, 1374, 05208-900 Sao Paulo, SP, Brazil. TEL 55-11-81396-7. FAX 55-11-81396747. *766*

REVISTA ECONOMIA.
Universidad de Los Andes, Facultad de Economia, IIES, La Hechicera, Edf. B 1r, Merida 5101, Venezuela. TEL 074-401281. FAX 074-401120. *956*

REVISTA FARMACEUTICA.
Academia Argentina de Farmacia y Bioquimica, Junin 956, Buenos Aires 1113, Argentina. *5442*

REVISTA PORTUGUESA DE FARMACIA.
Ordem de Farmaceuticos, Rua da Sociedade Farmaceutica, No. 18, 1150 Lisbon, Portugal. TEL 351-1-3151104. FAX 351-1-3524480. *5442*

RHODE ISLAND BUSINESS DIRECTORY.
American Business Directories 5711 S. 86th Circle, Box 27347, Omaha, NE 68127. TEL 402-593-4600. FAX 402-331-548. *1637*

RICE ABSTRACTS.
CAB International, Wallingford, Oxon. OX10 8DE, England. TEL 44-1491-832111. FAX 44-1491-833508.
Vendor(s): DIMDI, European Space Agency, Knight-Ridder Information, Inc., STN International. *180*

RICE THRESHER.
Rice University, Student Publications, 6100 Main St., Houston, TX 77005. TEL 713-527-4801. FAX 713-285-5238. *1834*

RIDE ON!
Washington Bicycling Association, 818 Connecticut Ave., N.W., Washington, DC 20006. TEL 202-872-9830. FAX 202-862-9762. *2140*

RIGAKU RYOHO JANARU.
Igaku-Shoin Ltd., 5-24-3 Hongo, Bunkyo-ku, Tokyo 113-91, Japan. TEL 03-3317-5703.
Vendor(s): JICST. *4820*

RIGHT-TO-KNOW PLANNING GUIDE (SERIES).
The Bureau of National Affairs, Inc., 1231 25th St., N.W., Washington, DC 20037. TEL 202-452-4200. FAX 202-822-8092.
Vendor(s): Human Resources Information Network (File DD). *6389*

RIGHT-TO-KNOW PLANNING GUIDE NEWSLETTER.
The Bureau of National Affairs, Inc., 1231 25th St., N.W., Washington, DC 20037. TEL 202-452-4200. FAX 202-822-8092.
Vendor(s): Human Resources Information Network (File DD). *6389*

RIHABIRITESHON IGAKU.
Japanese Association of Rehabilitation Medicine, 1-1-17 Komone, Itabashi-ku, Tokyo, Japan. TEL 81-3-5966-2031. FAX 81-3-5966-2033.
Vendor(s): JICST. *4820*

RISK, DECISION AND POLICY.
Chapman & Hall, Journals Department 2-6 Boundary Row, London SE1 8HN, England. TEL 44-171-8650066. FAX 44-171-5229623. *1444*

RISK: HEALTH, SAFETY & ENVIRONMENT.
Franklin Pierce Law Center, 2 White St., Concord, NH 03301. TEL 603-228-1541. FAX 603-224-3342.
Vendor(s): West Services, Inc.. *5975*

RISK MANAGEMENT.
Risk Management Society Publishing, Inc., 655 Third Ave., 2nd Fl., New York, NY 10017-5617. TEL 212-286-9364. FAX 212-986-9716.
Vendor(s): Information Access Co., University Microfilms International. *3664*

ROAD & TRACK.
Hachette Filipacchi Magazines, Inc. (Newport Beach), Road & Track, 1499 Monrovia Ave., Newport Beach, CA 92663. TEL 714-720-5300. FAX 714-631-2757.
Vendor(s): Information Access Co., University Microfilms International. *6500*

ROAD TRAFFIC REPORTS.
Kenneth Mason Publications Ltd., 12 North St., Emsworth, Hants. PO10 7DQ, England. TEL 0243-377977. FAX 0243-379136.
Vendor(s): Lexis-Nexis. *6825*

ROBOTRONICS AGE NEWSLETTER.
Twenty-First Century Media Communications, Inc., 548 Cardero St., Vancouver, B.C. V6N 2K3, Canada. TEL 604-261-5712.
Vendor(s): NewsNet (EC16). *2010*

ROCHESTER BUSINESS JOURNAL.
55 St. Paul St., Rochester, NY 14604-1343. TEL 716-546-8303. FAX 716-546-3398. *1238*

ROCKEFELLER ARCHIVE CENTER NEWSLETTER.
Rockefeller University, Rockefeller Archive Center, Pocantico Hills, 15 Dayton Ave., N. Tarrytown, NY 10591-1598. TEL 914-631-4505. FAX 914-631-6017. *3357*

ROCZNIKI NAUKOWE ZOOTECHNIKI.
Instytut Zootechniki, Ul. Sarego 2, 31-047 Krakow, Poland. TEL 48-12-227333. FAX 48-12-228065. *282*

ROLL CALL.
Roll Call, Inc. 900 Second St., N.E., Ste. 107, Washington, DC 20002. TEL 202-289-4900. FAX 202-289-2205.
Vendor(s): Lexis-Nexis. *5704*

ROMANCE PHILOLOGY.
University of California Press, Journals Division, 2120 Berkeley Way, No. 5812, Berkeley, CA 94720-5812. TEL 510-643-7154. FAX 510-642-9117.
Vendor(s): Information Access Co.. *4104*

ROMANIC REVIEW.
Columbia University, c/o Prof. Michael Riffaterre, Ed., 518 Philosophy Hall, Columbia University, New York, NY 10027. TEL 212-854-2500.
Vendor(s): Information Access Co.. *4261*

ROMULUS.
Canada Institute for Scientific and Technical Information, Information Resource Management, Ottawa, ON K1A 0S2, Canada. TEL 613-993-3449.
Vendor(s): CISTI. *6303*

ROUGH NOTES.
Rough Notes Co., Inc., Box 1990, Carmel, IN 46032-4990. TEL 317-582-1600. FAX 317-816-1003.
Vendor(s): University Microfilms International. *3664*

ROYAL ANTHROPOLOGICAL INSTITUTE. JOURNAL.
Royal Anthropological Institute of Great Britain and Ireland, 50 Fitzroy St., London W1P 5HS, England. TEL 44-171-3870455. FAX 44-171-3834235.
Vendor(s): University Microfilms International. *321*

ROYAL SOCIETY OF CHEMISTRY. JOURNAL: PERKIN TRANSACTIONS 1.
The Royal Society of Chemistry, Thomas Graham House, Science Park, Milton Rd., Cambridge CB4 4WF, England. TEL 44-1223-420066. FAX 44-1223-423623.
Vendor(s): STN International (CJRSC). *1746*

ROYAL SOCIETY OF CHEMISTRY. JOURNAL: PERKIN TRANSACTIONS 2.
The Royal Society of Chemistry, Thomas Graham House, Science Park, Milton Rd., Cambridge CB4 4WF, England. TEL 44-1223-420066. FAX 44-1223-423623.
Vendor(s): STN International (CJRSC). *1757*

ROYAL SOCIETY OF MEDICINE. JOURNAL.
Royal Society of Medicine Press Ltd., 1 Wimpole St., London W1M 8AE, England. TEL 0171-290-2900. FAX 0171-290-2929. *4527*

RUBBER & PLASTICS NEWS.
Crain Communications Inc. (Akron), 1725 Merriman Rd., Ste. 300, Akron, OH 44313-5251. TEL 330-836-9180. FAX 330-836-1005.
Vendor(s): Information Access Co.. *6218*

RUBBER & PLASTICS NEWS II.
Crain Communications Inc. (Akron), 1725 Merriman Rd., Ste. 300, Akron, OH 44313-5251. TEL 330-836-9180. FAX 330-836-1005.
Vendor(s): Information Access Co.. *6218*

RUBBER TRENDS.
Economist Intelligence Unit, 111 W. 57th St., New York, NY 10019. TEL 212-554-0600. FAX 212-586-1182.
Vendor(s): Information Access Co.. *6219*

RUBBER WORLD.
Lippincott & Peto, Inc., 1867 W. Market St., Akron, OH 44313. TEL 216-864-2122.
Vendor(s): Information Access Co.. *6219*

RUNNER'S WORLD.
Rodale Press, Inc., 33 E. Minor St., Emmaus, PA 18049. TEL 610-967-5171. FAX 610-967-7725.
Vendor(s): Information Access Co., University Microfilms International. *6478*

RURAL DEVELOPMENT ABSTRACTS.
CAB International, Wallingford, Oxon. OX10 8DE, England. TEL 44-1491-832111. FAX 44-1491-833508.
Vendor(s): DIMDI, European Space Agency, Knight-Ridder Information, Inc., STN International. *5933*

RURAL LIBRARIES.
Center for the Study of Rural Librarianship, Clarion University of Pennsylvania, Clarion, PA 16214. TEL 814-226-2383.
Vendor(s): Knight-Ridder Information, Inc., Wilsonline. *4023*

RURAL TECHNOLOGY GUIDE.
Natural Resources Institute, Central Ave., Chatham Maritime, Kent ME4 4TB, England. TEL 44-1634-880088. FAX 44-1634-880066. *149*

RURAL TELECOMMUNICATIONS.
National Telephone Cooperative Association, 2626 Pennsylvania Ave., N.W., Washington, DC 20037. TEL 202-298-2300. FAX 202-298-2320.
Vendor(s): University Microfilms International. *1949*

RUSSIA.
Russian Information Novosti, 4 Zubovsky Blvd., Moscow 116021, Russia. FAX 7-95-2017299.
Vendor(s): Information Access Co.. *3209*

RUSSIA AND COMMONWEALTH BUSINESS LAW REPORT.
L R P Publications, 747 Dresher Rd., Box 980, Horsham, PA 19044-0980. TEL 215-784-0941. FAX 215-784-9639.
Vendor(s): Lexis-Nexis. *3844*

RUSSIA BRIEFING.
E E N Ltd., 70 Bassein Park Rd., London W12 9RZ, England. TEL 0181-743-2829. FAX 0181-743-8637. *5705*

RUSSIAN AND EAST EUROPEAN FINANCE AND TRADE.
M.E. Sharpe, Inc., 80 Business Park Dr., Armonk, NY 10504. TEL 914-273-1800. FAX 914-273-2106.
Vendor(s): University Microfilms International. *1294*

RUSSIAN DEFENSE BUSINESS DIRECTORY (YEAR).
U.S. Department of Commerce, U.S.-Russia Defense Conversion Subcommittee, 14th St. between Constitution & E Sts., N.W., Washington, DC 20230. TEL 202-482-4695. *1314*

THE RUSSIAN REVIEW.
Ohio State University Press, 1070 Carmack Rd., Columbus, OH 43210. TEL 617-292-6930. FAX 617-292-2065.
Vendor(s): Information Access Co., University Microfilms International. *3441*

RUSSIAN SOCIAL SCIENCE REVIEW.
M.E. Sharpe, Inc., 80 Business Park Dr., Armonk, NY 10504. TEL 914-273-1800. FAX 914-273-2106.
Vendor(s): University Microfilms International. *5705*

S A A O NEWSLETTER.
South Africa Astronomical Observatory, P.O. Box 9, Observatory 7935, South Africa. TEL 27-21-470025. FAX 27-21-473639. *486*

S A C NEWSMONTHLY.
S A C, Inc., Box 159, Bogalusa, LA 70429-0159. TEL 504-732-2322. FAX 504-732-3744. *470*

S A E HANDBOOK.
Society of Automotive Engineers, 400 Commonwealth Dr., Warrendale, PA 15096-0001. TEL 412-776-4841. FAX 412-776-3036.
Vendor(s): Orbit Search Service. *6800*

S A E TECHNICAL LITERATURE ABSTRACTS.
Society of Automotive Engineers, 400 Commonwealth Dr., Warrendale, PA 15096-0001. TEL 412-776-4841. FAX 412-776-3036.
Vendor(s): Orbit Search Service. *6744*

S A E TECHNICAL PAPERS.
Society of Automotive Engineers, 400 Commonwealth Dr., Warrendale, PA 15096-0001. TEL 412-776-4841. FAX 412-776-3036.
Vendor(s): European Space Agency, FIZ Technik, Orbit Search Service. *6800*

S A I S REVIEW.
Johns Hopkins University Press, Journals Publishing Division, 2715 N. Charles St., Baltimore, Washington, MD 21218. TEL 410-516-6980. FAX 410-516-6968. *5770*

S C A D BULLETIN.
Commission of the European Communities, 200 rue de la Loi, B-1049 Brussels, Belgium.
Vendor(s): Commission of the European Communities. *3879*

S C A N.
U.S. National Aeronautics and Space Administration, National Technology Transfer Center, c/o Wheeling Jesuit University, 316 Washington Ave., Wheeling, WV 26003. TEL 304-243-2440. FAX 304-243-4390. *83*

S E C DOCKET.
U.S. Securities and Exchange Commission, 450 Fifth St., N.W., MISC-11, Washington, DC 20549. TEL 202-272-7460. FAX 202-272-7050.
Vendor(s): West Services, Inc.. *1350*

S E C NEWS DIGEST.
U.S. Securities and Exchange Commission, 450 Fifth St., N.W., MISC-11, Washington, DC 20549. TEL 202-272-7460. FAX 202-272-7050.
Vendor(s): Bureau of National Affairs, NewsNet (EV96), West Services, Inc.. *1350*

S E R EN EL 2000.
Hipolito Yrigoyen 1994, 2do. 4, 1089 Buenos Aires, Argentina. TEL 54-1-9510712. *5046*

S I M NETWORK.
Society for Information Management, 401 N. Michigan Ave., Chicago, IL 60611-4267. TEL 312-644-6610. FAX 312-245-1083. *2084*

S I R O W NEWSLETTER.
Southwest Institute for Research on Women, c/o Women's Studies, 102 Douglass Bldg., University of Arizona, Tucson, AZ 85721. TEL 521-621-7338. FAX 521-621-1533. *7019*

S M R COMMODITY CHARTS.
Security Market Research, Box 7476, Boulder, CO 80306-7476. TEL 303-494-8035. FAX 303-494-5474. *1350*

S M R STOCK CHARTS.
Security Market Research, Box 7476, Boulder, CO 80306-7476. TEL 303-494-8035. FAX 303-494-5474. *1350*

S M T TRENDS.
New Insights, 3033 Vallejo St., Crockett, CA 94525. TEL 510-787-2273.
Vendor(s): Data-Star, Information Access Co., Knight-Ridder Information, Inc., NewsNet (MG18). *2531*

S O C M A NEWSLETTER.
Synthetic Organic Chemical Manufacturers Association, 1100 New York Ave., Ste. 1090, Washington, DC 20007. TEL 202-414-4100. FAX 202-289-8584. *1692*

S S D A YEDION - NEWSLETTER.
Hebrew University, Faculty of Social Sciences, Mount Scopus, Jerusalem 91905, Israel. TEL 972-2-883007. FAX 972-2-883004. *6342*

S T A R.
U.S. National Aeronautics and Space Administration, National Technology Transfer Center, c/o Wheeling Jesuit University, 316 Washington Ave., Wheeling, WV 26003. TEL 304-243-2440. FAX 304-243-4390.
Available only online. Vendor(s): European Space Agency, Knight-Ridder Information, Inc. (File no.108). *83*

S T N.
Times Mirror Magazines, Inc., 2 Park Ave., New York, NY 10016. TEL 212-779-5465.
Vendor(s): Information Access Co., Knight-Ridder Information, Inc.. *6575*

S T P PHARMA SCIENCES.
Editions de Sante, 5 rue Las Cases, 75007 Paris, France. TEL 33-1-45519494. *5442*

SADO MARINE BIOLOGICAL STATION. REPORT.
Niigata Daigaku, Rigakubu Fuzoku Sado Rinkai Jikkenjo, 2-8050 Igarashi, Niigata 950-21, Japan. TEL 0259-75-2012. FAX 0259-75-2012. *605*

SAFETY AND HEALTH AT WORK.
International Labour Office, International Occupational Safety and Health Information Centre, CH-1211 Geneva 22, Switzerland. TEL 41-22-799-67-40. FAX 41-22-798-6253.
Vendor(s): European Space Agency (File no.40/CISDOC), IST-INFORMATHEQUE, Inc., Orbit Search Service, Telesystemes - Questel. *5261*

ST. LOUIS BUSINESS JOURNAL.
St. Louis Business Journal Corp. 1 Metropolitan Sq., Ste. 2170, St. Louis, MO 63102-2733. TEL 314-421-6200.
Vendor(s): Knight-Ridder Information, Inc.. *958*

ST. LOUIS COMMERCE.
Commerce Magazine, Inc., 100 S. Fourth St., Ste. 500, St. Louis, MO 63102. TEL 314-231-5555. FAX 314-444-1122.
Vendor(s): Lexis-Nexis, University Microfilms International. *1148*

ST. LOUIS JOURNALISM REVIEW.
Charles L. Klotzer, Ed. & Pub., 8380 Olive Blvd., St. Louis, MO 63132. TEL 314-991-1698. FAX 314-997-1898.
Vendor(s): Information Access Co.. *3711*

SAINT LOUIS UNIVERSITY LAW JOURNAL.
Saint Louis University, School of Law, 3700 Lindell Blvd., St. Louis, MO 63108. TEL 314-977-3933.
Vendor(s): West Services, Inc.. *3845*

ST. THOMAS LAW REVIEW.
St. Thomas University, School of Law, 16400 N.W. 32nd Ave., Miami, FL 33054. TEL 305-623-2373. FAX 305-623-2390.
Vendor(s): Lexis-Nexis, West Services, Inc.. *3845*

SALES & MARKETING MANAGEMENT.
Bill Communications, Inc., 355 Park Ave. S., 5th Fl., New York, NY 10010-1789. TEL 212-592-6200. FAX 212-592-6339.
Vendor(s): Information Access Co., University Microfilms International. *1485*

SALES AND MARKETING MANAGEMENT.
I S M Publishing Ltd., Nat West House, 31 Upper George St., Luton, Beds. LU1 2RD, England. FAX 44-1582-454945.
Vendor(s): Knight-Ridder Information, Inc., University Microfilms International. *1485*

SALES AUTOMATION SUCCESS.
Denali Group, Inc., 2815 N.W. Pine Cone Dr., Ste. 100, Issaquah, WA 98027-8698. TEL 206-392-3514. FAX 206-391-7982. *1485*

SALESDOCTORS.
SeaBird Associates, Inc., 5455 N. Federal Hwy., Ste. Q, Boca Raton, FL 33487. TEL 407-997-9345. FAX 407-997-9375.
Available only online. *1485*

SALMAGUNDI.
Skidmore College, Saratoga Springs, NY 12866. TEL 518-581-7400. FAX 518-581-7400.
Vendor(s): Information Access Co., University Microfilms International. *3624*

SALUD PUBLICA DE MEXICO.
Instituto Nacional de Salud Publica, Secretaria de Salud, Av. Universidad, 665, Planta Baja, Col. Santa Maria Ahuacatitlad, 62508 Cuernavaca, Morelos, Mexico. TEL 52-73-110111. FAX 52-73-175745.
Vendor(s): DIMDI, Data-Star, Knight-Ridder Information, Inc., Ovid Technologies, Inc.. *5975*

SAME-DAY SURGERY.
American Health Consultants, Inc., 3525 Piedmont Rd., N.E., Bldg. 6, Ste. 400, Atlanta, GA 30305. TEL 404-262-7436. FAX 800-284-3291.
Vendor(s): Lexis-Nexis. *4919*

SAN ANTONIO BUSINESS JOURNAL.
American City Business Journals, Inc. (San Antonio), 8200 W. Interstate Hwy. 10, Ste. 300, San Antonio, TX 78230-3877. TEL 512-341-3202. FAX 512-341-3031.
Vendor(s): Information Access Co.. *958*

SAN DIEGO BUSINESS JOURNAL.
San Diego Business Journal, Inc., 4909 Murphy Canyon Rd., No. 20C, San Diego, CA 92123. TEL 619-277-6359. FAX 619-571-3628.
Vendor(s): Information Access Co., Knight-Ridder Information, Inc., University Microfilms International. *958*

SAN DIEGO DAILY TRANSCRIPT.
Transcript Publishing Co., 2131 Third Ave., San Diego, CA 92101-2095. TEL 619-232-4381. FAX 619-236-8126.
Vendor(s): Lexis-Nexis. *3846*

SAN FRANCISCO BUSINESS TIMES.
San Francisco Business Times, 275 Battery St., Ste. 940, San Francisco, CA 94111. TEL 415-989-2522. FAX 415-398-2494.
Vendor(s): Information Access Co.. *1169*

SANTA CLARA COMPUTER AND HIGH-TECHNOLOGY LAW JOURNAL.
Santa Clara University, School of Law, Santa Clara, CA 95053. TEL 408-554-4197. FAX 408-554-4191. *3846*

SANTA CLARA LAW REVIEW.
Santa Clara University, School of Law, Santa Clara, CA 95053. TEL 408-554-4074.
Vendor(s): West Services, Inc.. *3846*

SARASOTA MAGAZINE.
Clubhouse Publishing, Inc., 601 S. Osprey Ave., Sarasota, FL 34236. TEL 813-366-8225. FAX 813-365-7272.
Vendor(s): Information Access Co., Lexis-Nexis. *3238*

SARKO.
D.I.H. Press, P.O. Box 1010, Shatin, N.T., Hong Kong. TEL 852-605-7212. FAX 852-605-7238. *4263*

SASKATCHEWAN BUSINESS.
Sunrise Publishing Ltd., 2213-C Hanselman Ct., Saskatoon, SK S7L 6A8, Canada. TEL 306-244-5668. FAX 306-244-5679.
Vendor(s): Information Access Co.. *958*

SASKATCHEWAN DECISIONS, CIVIL AND CRIMINAL CASES.
Western Legal Publications, 301-1 Alexander St., Vancouver, BC V6A 1B2, Canada. TEL 604-687-5671. FAX 604-687-2796. *3846*

SASKATCHEWAN REPORTS.
Maritime Law Book Ltd., Box 302, Fredericton, NB E3B 4Y9, Canada. TEL 506-453-9921. FAX 506-453-9525.
Vendor(s): QL Systems Ltd.. *3846*

SATELLITE COMMUNICATIONS.
Intertec Publishing Corp. (Atlanta), 6151 Powers Ferry Rd., N.W., Atlanta, GA 30339-2491. TEL 770-955-2500. FAX 770-955-0400.
Vendor(s): Information Access Co., University Microfilms International. *1915*

SATELLITE INDUSTRY DIRECTORY.
Phillips Business Information, Inc., 1201 Seven Locks Rd., Potomac, MD 20854. TEL 301-424-3338. FAX 301-309-3847.
Vendor(s): NewSNet (TE83E). *1638*

SATELLITE NEWS.
Phillips Business Information, Inc., 1201 Seven Locks Rd., Potomac, MD 20854. TEL 301-424-3338. FAX 301-309-3847.
Vendor(s): Information Access Co., NewSNet (TE03). *1915*

SATELLITE WEEK.
Warren Publishing, Inc., 2115 Ward Ct., N.W., Washington, DC 20037. TEL 202-872-9200. FAX 202-293-3435.
Vendor(s): Information Access Co., NewSNet (AE01). *1968*

SATURDAY EVENING POST.
Benjamin Franklin Literary & Medical Society, Box 1144, 1100 Waterway Blvd., Indianapolis, IN 46202. TEL 317-636-8881.
Vendor(s): Information Access Co., Knight-Ridder Information, Inc., University Microfilms International. *3238*

SATURDAY NIGHT.
Saturday Night, 184 Front St., E., Ste. 400, Toronto, ON M5A 4N3, Canada. TEL 416-368-7237. FAX 416-368-5112.
Vendor(s): Information Access Co., University Microfilms International. *3125*

SAVANNAH BUSINESS JOURNAL.
Blum Publishing Co., 6203 Abercorn, Ste. 103E, Savannah, GA 31405. TEL 912-354-5553. FAX 912-354-5558.
Vendor(s): University Microfilms International. *958*

SAVOURY SNACKS: THE INTERNATIONAL MARKET.
Euromonitor, 60-61 Brittor St., London EC1M 5NA, England. TEL 44-171-251-8024. FAX 44-171-608-3149.
Vendor(s): Data-Star, Knight-Ridder Information, Inc.. *2990*

SCANDINAVIAN JOURNAL OF NUTRITION.
Swedish Nutrition Foundation, Ideon, S-223 70 Lund, Sweden. TEL 46-(0)-46-18-22-80. FAX 46-0-46-18-22-81. *5241*

SCANDINAVIAN STUDIES (PROVO)
Society for the Advancement of Scandinavian Study, c/o Office of Sec. Treas., 3003 JKHB, Brigham Young University, Provo, UT 84602-6118. TEL 801-378-5598. FAX 801-373-4649.
Vendor(s): Information Access Co.. *4263*

SCANP.
Helsinki School of Economics, Runeberginkatu 22-24, FIN-00100 Helsinki, Finland. Vendor(s): Helsinki School of Economics. *1025*

SCHIZOPHRENIA BULLETIN.
U.S. Public Health Service, National Institute of Mental Health, 5600 Fishers Ln., Rockville, MD 20857. TEL 301-443-9772. *4867*

SCHOLASTIC CHOICES.
Scholastic Inc., 555 Broadway, New York, NY 10012-3999. TEL 212-343-6100.
Vendor(s): Knight-Ridder Information, Inc.. *1804*

SCHOLASTIC COACH.
Scholastic Inc., 555 Broadway, New York, NY 10012-3999. TEL 212-343-6100.
Vendor(s): Information Access Co.. *5535*

SCHOLASTIC UPDATE.
Scholastic Inc., 555 Broadway, New York, NY 10012-3999. TEL 212-343-6100.
Vendor(s): Information Access Co., Knight-Ridder Information, Inc., University Microfilms International. *1805*

SCHOOL ARTS.
Davis Publications, Inc. (Worcester), 50 Portland St., Printers Bldg., Worcester, MA 01608. TEL 508-754-7201. FAX 508-753-3834.
Vendor(s): Information Access Co.. *2501*

SCHOOL LEADERSHIP & MANAGEMENT.
Carfax Publishing Co., P.O. Box 25, Abingdon, Oxon OX14 3UE, England. TEL 44-1235-401000. FAX 44-1235-401550. *2463*

SCHOOL PLANNING AND MANAGEMENT.
Peter Li, Inc., 330 Progress Rd., Dayton, OH 45449. TEL 573-847-5900. FAX 513-847-5910.
Vendor(s): Information Access Co., Knight-Ridder Information, Inc.. *2370*

Online

SCHRIFTTUMS FUER DEN BEREICH HAUSHALT UND VERBAUCH. BIBLIOGRAPHIE.
Bundesforschungsanstalt fuer Ernaehrung, Institut fuer Ernaehrungsoekonomie und -soziologie, Garbenstr. 13, 70599 Stuttgart, Germany. TEL 0711-455063. FAX 0711-4569355. Vendor(s): DIMDI. *3526*

SCHWEIZERISCHE ZEITSCHRIFT FUER VOLKSWIRTSCHAFT UND STATISTIK.
Helbing und Lichtenhahn Verlag AG, Freie Str. 84, CH-4051 Basel, Switzerland. TEL 41-61-2721116. FAX 41-61-2721150. Vendor(s): Knight-Ridder Information, Inc.. *959*

SCIENCE.
American Association for the Advancement of Science, 1200 New York Ave., N.W., Washington, DC 20005. TEL 202-326-6417. Vendor(s): Information Access Co., Ovid Technologies, Inc. (SCIE), University Microfilms International. *6279*

SCIENCE & SOCIETY.
Guilford Publications, Inc., 72 Spring St., 4th Fl., New York, NY 10012. TEL 212-431-9800. FAX 212-966-6708. Vendor(s): University Microfilms International. *5706*

SCIENCE & TECHNOLOGY REVIEW.
Lawrence Livermore National Laboratory, c/o National Technical Information Service, 5285 Port Royal Rd., Springfield, VA 22161. *6280*

SCIENCE CITATION INDEX.
Institute for Scientific Information, 3501 Market St., Philadelphia, PA 19104. TEL 215-386-0100. FAX 215-386-2991. Vendor(s): DIMDI, Data-Star, Knight-Ridder Information, Inc. (Files nos.34,432,433,434/ SCISEARCH), Orbit Search Service. *6304*

SCIENCE NEWS.
Science Service, Inc., 1719 N St., N.W., Washington, DC 20036. TEL 202-785-2255. FAX 202-659-0365. Vendor(s): Information Access Co., University Microfilms International. *6281*

SCIENCE WORLD.
Scholastic Inc., 555 Broadway, New York, NY 10012-3999. TEL 212-343-6100. Vendor(s): Information Access Co.. *6282*

THE SCIENCES.
New York Academy of Sciences, 2 E. 63rd St., New York, NY 10021. Vendor(s): Information Access Co., University Microfilms International. *6283*

SCIENTIA PHARMACEUTICA.
Oesterreichische Apotheker-Verlagsgesellschaft mbH, Spitalgasse 31, A-1094 Vienna, Austria. TEL 01-4023588. FAX 01-4085355. *5443*

SCIENTIFIC AMERICAN.
Scientific American, Inc., 415 Madison Ave., New York, NY 10017-1111. TEL 212-754-0550. FAX 212-754-1138. Vendor(s): Information Access Co., Ovid Technologies, Inc. (SAMM). *6283*

SCIENTIFIC AMERICAN MEDICINE.
Scientific American, Inc., 415 Madison Ave., New York, NY 10017-1111. TEL 212-754-0550. FAX 212-754-1138. Vendor(s): Ovid Technologies, Inc. (SAMM). *4529*

SCIENTIFIC COMPUTING WORLD.
I O P Publishing Ltd., Techno House, Redcliffe Way, Bristol, Avon BS1 6NX, England. TEL 44-117-929-7481. FAX 44-117-927-4318. *1998*

SCIENTIFIC SERIALS IN THAI LIBRARIES.
Thailand Institute of Scientific and Technological Research, 196 Phahonyothin Rd., Chatuchak, Bangkok 10900, Thailand. TEL 579-8594. FAX 662-579-8594. *6304*

THE SCIENTIST.
The Scientist, Inc., 3600 Market St., Philadelphia, PA 19104-2645. TEL 215-386-9601. FAX 215-387-7542. Vendor(s): CompuServe, Inc. (71764.2561). *6283*

SCITECH BOOK NEWS.
Book News, Inc. (Portland), 5600 N.E. Hassalo St., Portland, OR 97213. TEL 503-281-9230. FAX 503-287-4485. *545*

SCOUTING.
Scout Association, Baden-Powell House, Queen's Gate, London SW7 5JS, England. FAX 071-581-9953. Vendor(s): Knight-Ridder Information, Inc.. *1805*

SCREEN DIGEST.
Screen Digest Ltd., 37 Gower St., London WC1E 6HH, England. TEL 44-171-580-2842. FAX 44-171-580-0060. Vendor(s): CompuServe, Inc., Data-Star, Information Access Co.. *1969*

SCREEN FINANCE.
Financial Times Telecoms & Media Publishing Maple House, 149 Tottenham Court Rd., London W1P 9LL, England. TEL 44-171-896-2234. FAX 44-171-896-2256. Vendor(s): Information Access Co., Lexis-Nexis. *5112*

THE SCRIBE.
University of Bridgeport, Student Center, 244 University Ave., Bridgeport, CT 06601. TEL 203-576-4382. FAX 203-576-4941. *1885*

SCRIBES JOURNAL OF LEGAL WRITING.
American Society of Writers on Legal Subjects, Wake Forest University, School of Law, Box 7206, Winston-Salem, NC 27109. TEL 910-759-5440. FAX 910-759-6077. Vendor(s): West Services, Inc.. *3847*

SCRIP - WORLD PHARMACEUTICAL NEWS.
P J B Publications Ltd., 18-20 Hill Rise, Richmond, Surrey TW10 6UA, England. TEL 44-181-948-3262. FAX 44-181-332-8998. Vendor(s): Data-Star (PHIND), Knight-Ridder Information, Inc., Ovid Technologies, Inc. (PHIN, PHIC,PHID). *5443*

SCROLL OF PHI DELTA THETA.
Phi Delta Theta Fraternity, 2 So. Campus, Oxford, OH 45056. TEL 513-523-6345. FAX 513-523-9200. *1885*

SEA FRONTIERS.
400 S.E. Second Ave., 4th Fl., Knight Centre, Miami, FL 33131. TEL 305-375-8498. Vendor(s): Information Access Co., University Microfilms International. *2305*

SEARCHABLE PHYSICS INFORMATION NOTICES.
American Institute of Physics, One Physics Ellipse, College Park, MD 20740-3843. TEL 301-209-3000. Vendor(s): Knight-Ridder Information, Inc. (File no.62/SPIN). *5581*

SEARCHING DIALOG: THE COMPLETE GUIDE.
Dialog Information Services, Inc. (Palo Alto), 3460 Hillview Ave., Palo Alto, CA 94304. TEL 415-858-3785. FAX 415-858-7069. *4026*

SEATTLE UNIVERSITY LAW REVIEW.
Seattle University, School of Law, 950 Broadway Plaza, Tacoma, WA 98402. TEL 206-591-2995. FAX 206-591-6313. Vendor(s): Lexis-Nexis, West Services, Inc.. *3847*

SECURED LENDER.
Commercial Finance Association, 225 W. 34th St., Rm. 1815, New York, NY 10122-0008. TEL 212-594-3480. Vendor(s): University Microfilms International. *1120*

SECURITE ET SANTE AU TRAVAIL.
International Labour Office, International Occupational Safety and Health Information Centre, CH-1211 Geneva 22, Switzerland. TEL 41-22-799-6740. FAX 41-22-798-6253. Vendor(s): European Space Agency, IST-INFORMATHEQUE, Inc., Orbit Search Service, Telesystemes - Questel. *5261*

SECURITIES EXCHANGE OF THAILAND. HANDBOOK.
Securities Exchange of Thailand, Sinthom Bldg., 2nd Fl., 132 Wireless Rd., Bangkok 10500, Thailand. *1351*

SECURITIES REGULATION & LAW REPORT.
The Bureau of National Affairs, Inc., 1231 25th St., N.W., Washington, DC 20037. TEL 202-452-4200. FAX 202-822-8092. Vendor(s): Bureau of National Affairs, Lexis-Nexis (SECREG), West Services, Inc. (BNA-SRLR). *3847*

SECURITIES WEEK.
McGraw-Hill Companies, 1221 Ave. of the Americas, New York, NY 10020. TEL 212-512-4214. Vendor(s): Dow Jones News Retrieval (SW), Knight-Ridder Information, Inc. (File no.624/McGRAW-HILL PUBLICATIONS ONLINE), Lexis-Nexis.(SECWK), NewsNet (FI27). *1351*

SECURITY INTELLIGENCE.
Interests, Ltd., 8512 Cedar St., Silver Spring, MD 20910-4322. TEL 301-588-7916. FAX 301-588-2085. Vendor(s): NewsNet (IT64). *5706*

SECURITY MANAGEMENT.
American Society for Industrial Security, 1655 N. Fort Myer Dr., Ste. 1200, Arlington, VA 22209-3198. TEL 703-522-5800. FAX 703-522-5226. Vendor(s): Information Access Co., University Microfilms International. *1444*

SEE FLORIDA MAGAZINES.
Miles Media Group, Inc., 3675 Clark Rd., Sarasota, FL 34233-2358. TEL 941-922-3575. FAX 941-923-6309. *6912*

SEED ABSTRACTS.
CAB International, Wallingford, Oxon. OX10 8DE, England. TEL 44-1491-832111. FAX 44-1491-833508. Vendor(s): DIMDI, European Space Agency, Knight-Ridder Information, Inc., STN International. *180*

SEED PATHOLOGY AND MICROBIOLOGY.
CAB International, Wallingford, Oxon. OX10 8DE, England. TEL 44-1491-832111. FAX 44-1491-833508. *180*

SEIBT INDUSTRIEKATALOG.
Seibt Verlag GmbH, Leopoldstr. 208, 80804 Munich, Germany. TEL 49-89-360903-0. FAX 49-89-364317. Vendor(s): GBI. *1639*

SEIBT MEDIZINISCHE TECHNIK.
Seibt Verlag GmbH, Leopoldstr. 208, 80804 Munich, Germany. TEL 49-89-360903-0. FAX 49-89-364317. Vendor(s): GBI. *4529*

SEIBT OBERFLAECHENTECHNIK.
Seibt Verlag GmbH, Leopoldstr. 208, 80804 Munich, Germany. TEL 49-89-360903-0. FAX 49-89-364317. Vendor(s): GBI. *5591*

SEIBT UMWELT TECHNIK.
Seibt Verlag GmbH, Leopoldstr. 208, 80804 Munich, Germany. TEL 49-89-360903-0. FAX 49-89-364317. *2819*

SEICHO.
Aichi-Gakuin University, Department of Anatomy, 1-100 Kusumoto-cho, Chikusaku-ku, Nagoya 464, Japan. TEL 052-751-2561. FAX 052-752-5988. Vendor(s): JICST. *606*

SEISHIN IGAKU.
Igaku-Shoin Ltd., 5-24-3 Hongo, Bunkyo-ku, Tokyo 113-91, Japan. TEL 03-817-5711. Vendor(s): JICST. *4868*

SELECTA MATHEMATICA.
Birkhaeuser Verlag, P.O. Box 133, CH-4010 Basel, Switzerland. TEL 41-61-2050730. FAX 41-61-2050791. *4394*

SEMICONDUCTOR INDUSTRY & BUSINESS SURVEY NEWSLETTER.
H T E Research, Inc., 400 Oyster Point Blvd., Ste. 220, S. San Francisco, CA 94080. TEL 415-871-4377. FAX 415-871-0513. Vendor(s): Information Access Co., NewsNet (EC35). *2532*

SEMICONDUCTOR SCIENCE AND TECHNOLOGY.
I O P Publishing Ltd., Techno House, Redcliffe Way, Bristol, Avon BS1 6NX, England. TEL 44-117-929-7481. FAX 44-117-929-4318. *2532*

SEMICONDUCTORS.
American Institute of Physics, One Physics Ellipse, College Park, MD 20740-3843. TEL 301-209-3000. *5570*

SEMINARS IN ANESTHESIA.
W.B. Saunders Co. Curtis Center, 3rd Fl., Independence Sq. W., Philadelphia, PA 19106-3399. TEL 215-238-7800. FAX 215-238-6445. *4593*

SEMINARS IN DERMATOLOGY.
W.B. Saunders Co. Curtis Center, 3rd Fl., Independence Sq. W., Philadelphia, PA 19106-3399. TEL 215-238-7800. FAX 215-238-6445. *4664*

SEMINARS IN DIAGNOSTIC PATHOLOGY.
W.B. Saunders Co. Curtis Center, 3rd Fl., Independence Sq. W., Philadelphia, PA 19106-3399. TEL 215-238-7800. FAX 215-238-6445. *4530*

SEMINARS IN HEMATOLOGY.
W.B. Saunders Co. Curtis Center, 3rd Fl., Independence Sq. W., Philadelphia, PA 19106-3399. TEL 215-238-7800. FAX 215-238-6445. Vendor(s): Lexis-Nexis. *4702*

SEMINARS IN NEPHROLOGY.
W.B. Saunders Co. Curtis Center, 3rd Fl., Independence Sq. W., Philadelphia, PA 19106-3399. TEL 215-238-7800. FAX 215-238-6445. *4930*

SEMINARS IN NEUROLOGY.
Thieme, 381 Park Ave. S., Ste. 1501, New York, NY 10016. TEL 212-683-5088. FAX 212-779-9020.
Vendor(s): Ovid Technologies, Inc.. *4868*

SEMINARS IN RESPIRATORY AND CRITICAL CARE MEDICINE.
Thieme, 381 Park Ave. S., Ste. 1501, New York, NY 10016. TEL 212-683-5088. FAX 212-779-9020.
Vendor(s): Ovid Technologies, Inc.. *4891*

SEMINARS IN ROENTGENOLOGY.
W.B. Saunders Co. Curtis Center, 3rd Fl., Independence Sq. W., Philadelphia, PA 19106-3399. TEL 215-238-7800. FAX 215-238-6445. *4884*

SEMINARS IN ULTRASOUND, C T AND M R.
W.B. Saunders Co. Curtis Center, 3rd Fl., Independence Sq. W., Philadelphia, PA 19106-3399. TEL 215-238-7800. FAX 215-238-6445. *4884*

SENSOR BUSINESS DIGEST.
Vital Information Publications, 754 Caravel Ln., Foster City, CA 94404. TEL 415-345-7018. FAX 415-345-7018.
Vendor(s): Data-Star, Information Access Co., Knight-Ridder Information, Inc., NewsNet (MG16). *1486*

SENSOR REVIEW.
M C B University Press Ltd., 60-62 Toller Ln., Bradford, W. Yorks BD8 9BY, England. TEL 44-1274-777700. FAX 44-1274-785200.
Vendor(s): Data-Star, Knight-Ridder Information, Inc.. *4346*

SERVICE COMMUNICATIONS.
M2 Communications Ltd., Reptile House, 20 Heathfield Rd., Coventry CV5 8BT, England. TEL 44-1203-717417. FAX 44-1203-717418. *1915*

THE SERVICE INDUSTRIES JOURNAL.
Frank Cass, Newbury House, 890-900 Eastern Ave., Newbury Park, Ilford, Essex IG2 7HH, England. TEL 44-181-599-8866. FAX 44-181-599-0984.
Vendor(s): University Microfilms International. *959*

SERVICE STATIONS: THE INTERNATIONAL MARKET.
Euromonitor, 60-61 Britton St., London EC1M 5NA, England. TEL 44-171-251-8024. FAX 44-171-608-3149.
Vendor(s): Data-Star, Knight-Ridder Information, Inc.. *6801*

SERVICE TECHNICIAN.
G.I.E., Inc. Publishers, 4012 Bridge Ave., Cleveland, OH 44113. TEL 216-961-4130. FAX 216-961-0364. *2650*

SET-ASIDE ALERT.
Pasha Publications Inc., 1616 N. Ft. Myer Dr., Ste. 1000, Arlington, VA 22209-3107. TEL 703-528-1244. FAX 703-528-1253.
Vendor(s): Information Access Co. *5920*

SETON HALL LEGISLATIVE JOURNAL.
Seton Hall University, Seton Hall Legislative Bureau, Newark, NJ 07102. TEL 201-642-8261. FAX 201-642-8734.
Vendor(s): West Services, Inc.. *3848*

SETTOP & SERVER BULLETIN.
TechMedia, 52 Foundling Ct., London WC1N 1AN, England. TEL 44-171-837-0815. FAX 44-171-278-9917. *1969*

SEVENTEEN.
K-III Communications Corp., 745 Fifth Ave., New York, NY 10151. TEL 212-745-0100.
Vendor(s): Information Access Co. *7006*

SEWANEE REVIEW.
University of the South, Sewanee Review, Sewanee, TN 37383-1000. TEL 615-598-1246. FAX 615-598-1145. *4264*

SEX ROLES.
Plenum Publishing Corp., 233 Spring St., New York, NY 10013-1578. TEL 212-620-8000. FAX 212-463-0742.
Vendor(s): Information Access Co.. *5882*

SEXUALLY TRANSMITTED DISEASES.
Lippincott - Raven Publishers 227 E. Washington Sq., Philadelphia PA 19106. TEL 215-238-4200.
Vendor(s): Lexis-Nexis, Ovid Technologies, Inc.. *4664*

SEYBOLD REPORT ON DESKTOP PUBLISHING.
Seybold Publications, 428 E. Baltimore Ave., Box 644, Media, PA 19063. TEL 610-565-2480. FAX 610-565-1858.
Vendor(s): Information Access Co.. *2091*

SEYBOLD REPORT ON PUBLISHING SYSTEMS.
Seybold Publications, 428 E. Baltimore Ave., Box 644, Media, PA 19063. TEL 610-565-2480. FAX 610-656-1858.
Vendor(s): Information Access Co.. *6017*

SHAKESPEARE QUARTERLY.
Folger Shakespeare Library, 201 E. Capitol St., S.E., Washington, DC 20003-1094. TEL 202-675-0351. FAX 202-544-4623.
Vendor(s): University Microfilms International. *4265*

SHAREDEBATE INTERNATIONAL.
Applied Foresight, Inc., Box 20607, Bloomington, MN 55420. FAX 612-933-3092. *6343*

SHINSHIN-IGAKU.
Igaku-Shoin Ltd., 5-24-3 Hongo, Bunkyo-ku, Tokyo 113-91, Japan. TEL 03-817-5711.
Vendor(s): JICST. *4863*

THE SHOCK AND VIBRATION DIGEST.
Vibration Institute, 6262 S. Kingery Hwy., Ste. 212, Willowbrook, IL 60514. TEL 708-654-2254. FAX 708-654-2271. *2741*

SHONIKA.
Kanehara & Co., Ltd., 31-14 Yushima 2-chome, Bunkyo-ku, Tokyo 113, Japan.
Vendor(s): Ovid Technologies, Inc.. *4814*

SHOOT.
B P I Communications, Inc. (New York), 1515 Broadway, New York, NY 10036. TEL 212-764-7300. FAX 212-536-5321.
Vendor(s): Information Access Co.. *5113*

SHOOTING INDUSTRY.
Publishers' Development Corp., 591 Camino de la Reina, Ste. 200, San Diego, CA 92108. TEL 619-297-5350. FAX 619-297-5353.
Vendor(s): Information Access Co.. *6480*

SHOPPER REPORT.
Consumer Network. Inc, 3624 Market St., Philadelphia, PA 19104. TEL 215-561-2921. FAX 215-557-7692.
Vendor(s): Data-Star, Information Access Co., Knight-Ridder Information, Inc.. *1486*

SHOPPING CENTER WORLD.
Intertec Publishing Corp. (Atlanta), 6151 Powers Ferry Rd., N.W., Atlanta, GA 30339-2941. TEL 770-955-2500. FAX 770-955-0400.
Vendor(s): Information Access Co.. *1486*

SICKNESS AND WELLNESS PUBLICATIONS.
John Gordon Burke Publisher, Inc., Box 1492, Evanston, IL 60204-1492. TEL 847-866-8625. *4574*

SIDE EFFECTS OF DRUGS ANNUAL.
Elsevier Science B.V., Books Division, P.O. Box 211, 1000 AE Amsterdam, Netherlands. TEL 31-20-4853911. FAX 31-20-4853705
Vendor(s): Data-Star (SEDE), Knight-Ridder Information, Inc. (File no.70/SEDEASE), Ovid Technologies, Inc.. *5443*

SIERRA.
Sierra Club, 730 Polk St., San Francisco, CA 94109. TEL 415-776-2211.
Vendor(s): Information Access Co. University Microfilms International. *2141*

SIGLO XXI CIENCIA AND TECNOLOGIA.
El Mercurio S.A.P., Av. Santa Maria 5542, Apdo. Postal 13 D, Las Condes, Chile. TEL 562-3301461. FAX 562-2421128. *6285*

THE SIMBA REPORT ON DIRECTORY PUBLISHING.
SIMBA Information Inc. 11 Riverbend Dr. S., Box 4234, Stamford, CT 06907-0234. TEL 203-358-9900. FAX 203-358-5824.
Vendor(s): Information Access Co., Knight-Ridder Information, Inc. (File no.636), NewsNet (PB30). *6009*

SIMMONS STUDY OF MEDIA & MARKETS (YEAR).
Simmons Market Research Bureau, Inc., 309 W. 49th St., New York, NY 10019. TEL 212-373-8900. FAX 212-373-8918. *1925*

SINCERE SINGLES.
Adrienne Schiff, Ed. & Pub. Box 1719, Ann Arbor, MI 48106-1719. TEL 810-476-6110. FAX 810-476-6110. *6310*

SINGLE SCENE - ARIZONA.
Box 10159, Scottsdale, AZ 85271. TEL 602-945-6746. FAX 602-945-3766. *6311*

SITUATION & OUTLOOK REPORT. AGRICULTURAL EXPORTS.
U.S. Department of Agriculture, Economic Research Service, c/o Debbie Haugan, Rm. 110, 1301 New York Ave., N.W., Washington, DC 20005. TEL 202-219-0515.
Vendor(s): Information Access Co.. *199*

SITUATION & OUTLOOK REPORT. AGRICULTURAL INCOME & FINANCE.
U.S. Department of Agriculture, Economic Research Service, c/o Debbie Haugan, Rm. 110, 1301 New York Ave., N.W., Washington, DC 20005-4788. TEL 202-219-0515.
Vendor(s): Knight-Ridder Information, Inc.. *199*

SITUATION & OUTLOOK REPORT. FRUIT & TREE NUTS.
U.S. Department of Agriculture, Economic Research Service, c/o Debbie Haugan, Rm. 110, 1301 New York Ave., N.W., DC 20005-4788. TEL 202-219-0515.
Vendor(s): Information Access Co., Knight-Ridder Information, Inc.. *240*

SITUATION & OUTLOOK REPORT. SUGAR & SWEETENER.
U.S. Department of Agriculture, Economic Research Service, c/o Debbie Haugan, Rm. 110, 1301 New York Ave., N.W., Washington, DC 20005-4788. TEL 202-219-0515.
Vendor(s): Information Access Co., Knight-Ridder Information, Inc.. *199*

SITUATION & OUTLOOK REPORT. TOBACCO.
U.S. Department of Agriculture Economic Research Service, c/o Debbie Haugan, Rm. 110, 1301 New York Ave. N.W., DC 20005-4789. TEL 202-219-4060.
Vendor(s) Information Access Co., Knight-Ridder Information, Inc.. *199*

SITUATION & OUTLOOK REPORT. VEGETABLES & SPECIALTIES.
U.S. Department of Agriculture, Economic Research Service, c/o Debbie Haugan, Rm. 110, 1301 New York Ave., N.W., Washington, DC 20005-4788. TEL 202-219-0515.
Vendor(s): Information Access Co., Knight-Ridder Information, Inc. *200*

SKEPTICAL INQUIRER.
Committee for the Scientific Investigation of Claims of the Paranormal, Box 703, Buffalo, NY 14226-0703. TEL 716-636-1425. FAX 716-636-1733.
Vendor(s): Information Access Co. *5333*

SKIING.
Times Mirror Magazines, Inc., 2 Park Ave., New York, NY 10016. TEL 212-779-5000.
Vendor(s): Information Access Co., University Microfilms International. *6576*

SKIN CARE: THE INTERNATIONAL MARKET.
Euromonitor, 87-88 Turnmill St., London EC1M 5QU, England. TEL 44-171-251-8024. FAX 44-171-608-3149.
Vendor(s): Data-Star, Knight-Ridder Information, Inc.. *493*

SKIN DIVER MAGAZINE.
Petersen Publishing Co., 6420 Wilshire Blvd., Los Angeles, CA 90048. TEL 213-782-2000.
Vendor(s): Information Access Co., Knight-Ridder Information, Inc.. *6481*

SKY AND TELESCOPE.
Sky Publishing Corp., 49 Bay State Rd., Cambridge, MA 02138. TEL 617-864-7360. FAX 617-864-6117.
Vendor(s): Information Access Co., University Microfilms International. *486*

SLATE.
Microsoft Corp., 1 Microsoft Way, Redmond, WA 98052. TEL 206-882-8080. *4166*

THE SLAVE RIVER JOURNAL.
P.O. Box 990, Fort Smith, NT X0E 0P0, Canada. TEL 403-872-2784. FAX 403-872-2754. *3125*

SLOAN MANAGEMENT REVIEW.
Massachusetts Institute of Technology, Sloan School of Management, 292 Main St., E38-120, Cambridge, MA 02139. TEL 617-253-7170. FAX 617-253-5584.
Vendor(s): University Microfilms International. *1445*

SLUDGE NEWSLETTER.
Business Publishers, Inc., 951 Pershing Dr., Silver Spring, MD 20910-4464. TEL 301-587-6300. FAX 301-585-9075.
Vendor(s): Information Access Co., NewsNet (CH13). *2857*

SMALL ANIMALS.
CAB International, Wallingford, Oxon. OX10 8DE, England. TEL 44-1491-832111. FAX 44-1491-833508.
Vendor(s): DIMDI, European Space Agency, Knight-Ridder Information, Inc., STN International. *6961*

SMALL BUSINESS NEWS - AKRON.
Small Business News, Inc., 14725 Detroit Ave., Ste. 300, Cleveland, OH 44107-4103. TEL 216-228-6397. FAX 216-529-8924.
Vendor(s): University Microfilms International. *1579*

SMALL BUSINESS NEWS - CLEVELAND.
Small Business News, Inc., 14725 Detroit Ave., Ste. 300, Cleveland, OH 44107-4103. TEL 216-228-6397. FAX 216-529-8924.
Vendor(s): University Microfilms International. *1580*

SMALL BUSINESS TAX REVIEW.
A-N Group, Inc., Box 895, Melville, NY 11747-0895. TEL 516-549-4090.
Vendor(s): NewsNet (TX15). *1561*

SMALL KITCHEN APPLIANCES: THE INTERNATIONAL MARKET.
Euromonitor, 60-61 Britton St., London EC1M 5NA, England. TEL 44-171-251-8024. FAX 44-171-608-3149.
Vendor(s): Data-Star, Knight-Ridder Information, Inc.. *2532*

SMALL PRESS BOOK REVIEW.
Greenfield Press, Box 176, Southport, CT 06490. TEL 203-332-7629.
Available only online. *6009*

SMART MATERIALS AND STRUCTURES.
I O P Publishing Ltd., Techno House, Redcliffe Way, Bristol, Avon BS1 6NX, England. TEL 44-117-929-7481. FAX 44-117-929-4318. *5616*

SMART'S CALIFORNIA WORKERS' COMP BULLETIN.
Smart's Publishing Group, 1 Waters Park Dr., Ste. 104, San Mateo, CA 94403-1137. TEL 415-341-2432. FAX 415-341-3304. *3665*

SMART'S INSURANCE BULLETIN.
Smart's Publishing Group, 1 Waters Park Dr., Ste. 104, San Mateo, CA 94403-1137. TEL 415-982-1480. FAX 415-982-3504. *3665*

SMITHSONIAN.
Smithsonian Institution, Arts & Industries Bldg., 900 Jefferson Dr., S.W., Washington, DC 20560. TEL 202-357-2888. FAX 202-786-2564.
Vendor(s): Information Access Co., Knight-Ridder Information, Inc.. *6344*

SNAKE RIVER BASIN ADJUDICATION DIGEST.
Ridenbaugh Press, Box 2276, Boise, ID 83701. TEL 208-338-9700. FAX 208-338-9769. *3849*

SNOW LION NEWSLETTER & CATALOG.
Snow Lion Publications, Box 6483, Ithaca, NY 14851. TEL 607-273-8519. FAX 607-273-8508. *6111*

SOAP, COSMETICS, CHEMICAL SPECIALTIES.
P T N Publishing Corp., 445 Broadhollow Rd., Melville, NY 11747-3601.
Vendor(s): Information Access Co., Lexis-Nexis. *498*

SOAP, PERFUMERY & COSMETICS.
Wilmington Publishing, Wilmington House, Church Hill, Dartford, Kent UA2 7EF, England. TEL 44-1322-277788. FAX 44-1322-276474.
Vendor(s): Information Access Co.. *498*

SOCIAL FORCES.
University of North Carolina Press, Box 2288, Chapel Hill, NC 27515-2288. TEL 919-966-3561. FAX 919-966-3829.
Vendor(s): Information Access Co., University Microfilms International. *6430*

SOCIAL INVENTIONS.
Institute for Social Inventions, 20 Heber Rd., London NW2 6AA, England. TEL 44-181-208-2853. FAX 44-181-452-6434. *6430*

SOCIAL JUSTICE.
Global Options, Box 40601, San Francisco, CA 94140. TEL 415-550-1703.
Vendor(s): Information Access Co.. *5771*

SOCIAL PATHOLOGY.
Harrow and Heston Publishers, 1830 Western Ave., Albany, NY 12203. TEL 518-456-4894. FAX 518-456-4894. *6431*

SOCIAL PLANNING - POLICY & DEVELOPMENT ABSTRACTS.
Sociological Abstracts, Inc., Box 22206, San Diego, CA 92192-0206. TEL 619-695-8803. FAX 619-695-0416.
Vendor(s): DIMDI (SA63), Data-Star (SOCA), Knight-Ridder Information, Inc. (File No.37), OCLC, Ovid Technologies, Inc. (SOCA). *6402*

SOCIAL POLICY.
Union Institute, 25 W. 43rd St., Rm. 620, New York, NY 10036. TEL 212-642-2929. FAX 212-642-1956.
Vendor(s): Information Access Co., University Microfilms International. *6431*

SOCIAL PROBLEMS.
University of California Press, Journals Division, 2120 Berkeley Way, Berkeley, CA 94720. TEL 510-643-7154. FAX 510-642-9917.
Vendor(s): Information Access Co., University Microfilms International. *6431*

SOCIAL RESEARCH.
New School for Social Research, 66 W. Twelfth St., New York, NY 10003. TEL 212-229-5776. FAX 212-229-5476.
Vendor(s): Information Access Co., University Microfilms International. *6345*

SOCIAL SCIENCE & MEDICINE.
Elsevier Science Ltd., Pergamon, P.O. Box 800, Kidlington, Oxford OX5 1DX, England. TEL 44-1865-843000. FAX 44-1865-843010. *4532*

THE SOCIAL SCIENCE JOURNAL.
J A I Press Inc., 55 Old Post Rd., No. 2, Box 1678, Greenwich, CT 06836-1678. TEL 203-661-7602. FAX 203-661-0792.
Vendor(s): Information Access Co.. *6346*

SOCIAL SCIENCES CITATION INDEX.
Institute for Scientific Information, 3501 Market St., Philadelphia, PA 19104. TEL 215-386-0100. FAX 215-386-2991.
Vendor(s): DIMDI, Data-Star, Knight-Ridder Information, Inc. (File no.7/SOCIAL SCISEARCH), Ovid Technologies, Inc. (SSCI). *6358*

SOCIAL SCIENCES INDEX.
H.W. Wilson Co., 950 University Ave., Bronx, NY 10452. TEL 718-588-8400. FAX 718-590-1617.
Vendor(s): OCLC, University Microfilms International (PROQUEST), Wilsonline (File SSI). *6358*

SOCIAL SECURITY BULLETIN.
U.S. Social Security Administration, Office of Research, Evaluation, and Statistics, Publications Staff, Van Ness Center, Rm. 209, 4301 Connecticut Ave., N.W., Washington, DC 20008. TEL 202-282-7138. FAX 202-282-7219.
Vendor(s): Information Access Co., University Microfilms International. *3665*

THE SOCIAL STUDIES.
Heldref Publications, 1319 Eighteenth St., N.W., Washington, DC 20036-1802. TEL 202-296-6267. FAX 202-296-5149.
Vendor(s): Information Access Co., University Microfilms International. *2373*

SOCIAL WORK.
N A S W Press, 750 First St., N.E., Ste. 700, Washington, DC 20002-4241. TEL 202-408-8600. FAX 202-336-8312.
Vendor(s): Information Access Co., University Microfilms International. *6393*

SOCIAL WORK ABSTRACTS.
N A S W Press, 750 First St., N.E., Ste. 700, Washington, DC 20002-4241. TEL 202-408-8600. FAX 202-336-8312.
Vendor(s): Ovid Technologies, Inc. (SWAB). *6402*

SOCIETE FRANCAISE DE CARDIOLOGIE. BULLETIN D'INFORMATIONS.
Grou-Radenez-Joly, 19 rue des Saints Peres, 75006 Paris, France. *4609*

SOCIETY.
Transaction Publishers, Transaction Periodicals Consortium, Department 3092, Rutgers University, New Brunswick, NJ 08903. TEL 908-445-2280. FAX 908-445-3138.
Vendor(s): Information Access Co.. *6347*

SOCIETY FOR ROMANIAN STUDIES NEWSLETTER.
Huntington College Society, Dept. of History, Huntington College, Huntington, IN 46750. TEL 219-356-6000. FAX 219-356-9448. *3444*

SOCIETY OF RESEARCH ADMINISTRATORS. JOURNAL.
Society of Research Administrators, Inc., 1200 19th St., N.W., Washington, DC 20002. TEL 312-661-1700. FAX 312-661-0769.
Vendor(s): Information Access Co., University Microfilms International. *1445*

SOCIO-ECONOMIC SERIES.
Natural Resources Institute, Central Ave., Chatham Maritime, Kent ME4 4TB, England. TEL 44-1634-880088. FAX 44-1634-880066. *152*

SOCIOLOGICAL ABSTRACTS.
Sociological Abstracts, Inc., Box 22206, San Diego, CA 92192-0206. TEL 619-695-8803. FAX 619-695-0416.
Vendor(s): DIMDI (SA63), Data-Star (SOCA), Knight-Ridder Information, Inc. (File no.37), OCLC, Ovid Technologies, Inc. (SOCA). *6442*

SOCIOLOGICAL PERSPECTIVES.
J A I Press Inc., 55 Old Post Rd., No. 2, Box 1678, Greenwich, CT 06836-1678. TEL 203-661-7602. FAX 203-661-0792.
Vendor(s): Information Access Co. *6433*

SOCIOLOGICAL RESEARCH ONLINE.
Sage Publications Ltd., 6 Bonhill St., London EC2 4PU, England. TEL 44-171-374-0645. FAX 44-171-374-8741.
Available only online. *6433*

SOCIOLOGY.
Cambridge University Press, Edinburgh Bldg., Shaftesbury Rd., Cambridge CB2 2RU, England. TEL 44-1223-312393. FAX 44-1223-315052.
Vendor(s): Information Access Co., University Microfilms International. *6434*

SOCIOLOGY OF EDUCATION.
American Sociological Association, 1722 N St., N.W., Washington, DC 20036. TEL 202-833-3410. FAX 202-785-0146.
Vendor(s): University Microfilms International. *6434*

SOCIOLOGY OF RELIGION.
Association for the Sociology of Religion, 401 N. Ridge, Cambridge, IL 61238-1154. TEL 309-937-5696.
Vendor(s): Information Access Co., University Microfilms International. *6435*

SOFT DRINKS: THE INTERNATIONAL MARKET.
Euromonitor, 60-61 Britton St., London EC1M 5NA, England. TEL 44-171-251-8024. FAX 44-171-608-3149.
Vendor(s): Data-Star, Knight-Ridder Information, Inc.. *511*

SOFT.LETTER.
Mercury Group, Inc., 17 Main St., Watertown, MA 02172-4491. TEL 617-924-3944. FAX 617-924-7288.
Vendor(s): Information Access Co.. *2115*

SOFTWARE CATALOG: MICROCOMPUTERS.
Elsevier Science Inc., Box 945, New York, NY 10159-0945. TEL 212-633-3730. FAX 212-633-3680.
Vendor(s): CompuServe, Inc., Knight-Ridder Information, Inc.. *2091*

SOFTWARE ENCYCLOPEDIA.
R.R. Bowker, A Division of Reed Elsevier Inc., 121 Chanlon Rd., New Providence, NJ 07974. TEL 908-464-6800. FAX 908-665-3502.
Vendor(s): Knight-Ridder Information, Inc. (File no.278). *2115*

SOFTWARE FUTURES.
A P T Data Group plc., 12 Sutton Row, 4th Fl., London W1V 5FH, England. TEL 44-171-528-7083. FAX 44-171-439-1105.
Vendor(s): Information Access Co.. *2115*

SOFTWARE INDUSTRY REPORT.
Computer Age & E D P News Services 714 Church St., Alexandria, VA 22314-4202. TEL 703-739-8500. FAX 703-739-8505.
Vendor(s): Information Access Co.. *2116*

SOFTWARE MAGAZINE.
Sentry Publishing Company, Inc., 1 Research Dr., Ste. 400B, Westborough, MA 01581-3907. TEL 508-366-2031. FAX 508-836-4732.
Vendor(s): Information Access Co., University Microfilms International. *2116*

SOFTWARE QUALITY JOURNAL.
Chapman & Hall, Journals Department 2-6 Boundary Row, London SE1 8HN, England. TEL 44-171-8650066. FAX 44-171-5229623. *2116*

SOILS AND FERTILIZERS.
CAB International, Wallingford, Oxon. OX10 8DE, England. TEL 44-1491-832111. FAX 44-1491-833508.
Vendor(s): DIMDI. *181*

SOLID STATE AND SUPERCONDUCTIVITY ABSTRACTS.
Cambridge Scientific Abstracts, 7200 Wisconsin Ave., 6th Fl., Bethesda, MD 20814. TEL 301-961-6750. FAX 301-961-6720.
Vendor(s): STN International (SOLIDSTATE). *5581*

SOLID STATE TECHNOLOGY.
PennWell Publishing Co. (Nashua), 10 Tara Blvd., 5th Fl., Nashua, NH 03062-2801. TEL 603-891-0123. FAX 609-891-0597.
Vendor(s): Information Access Co.. *2533*

SOLID WASTE REPORT.
Business Publishers, Inc , 951 Pershing Dr., Silver Spring, MD 20910-4464. TEL 301-587-6300. FAX 301-585-9075.
Vendor(s): Information Access Co., NewsNet (EV20). *2819*

SOLSTICE: AN ELECTRONIC JOURNAL OF GEOGRAPHY AND MATHEMATICS.
Institute of Mathematical Geography, 2790 Briarcliff, Ann Arbor, MI 48105-1429. TEL 313-761-1231. *4396*

SOLUCIONES AVANZADAS.
Xview, S.A. de C.V. Tuxpan 2, Desp. 603, Col. Roma Sur, 06760 Mexico DF, Mexico. TEL 574-5316. FAX 574-5318. *1156*

SOLUTIONS FOR BETTER HEALTH.
Haymarket Group Ltd., 45 W. 34th St., New York, NY 10001 TEL 212-239-0855. *3297*

SOMALIA NEWS UPDATE.
Somalia News Update, c/o Dept. of Cultural Anthropology, University of Uppsala, Traedgaardsgatan 18, S-753 09 Uppsala, Sweden. FAX 46-18-151160.
Available only online. *3211*

SORGHUM AND MILLETS.
CAB International, Wallingford, Oxon. OX10 8DE, England. TEL 44-1419-832111. FAX 44-1491-833508.
Vendor(s): DIMDI, European Space Agency, Knight-Ridder Information, Inc., STN International. *181*

SOUND & HI FI.
Technical Press S.A., 31 Praxitelous St., 167 77 Athens, Greece. TEL 30-1-9961-861. FAX 30-1-9961-864. *5198*

SOUND & VISION.
Sound & Vision, 99 Atlantic Ave., Ste. 302, Toronto, ON M6K 3J8, Canada. TEL 416-535-7611. FAX 416-535-6325. *2533*

SOURCEMEX.
University of New Mexico, Latin American Institute, 801 Yale N.E., Albuquerque, NM 87131-1016. TEL 505-277-6839. FAX 505-277-5989.
Vendor(s): Information Access Co., Knight-Ridder Information, Inc., Lexis-Nexis, NewsNet (IT99). *1240*

SOURCES.
Barrie Zwicker, Ed. & Pub., 4 Phipps St., Ste. 109, Toronto, ON M4Y 1J5, Canada. TEL 416-964-7799. FAX 416-964-8763. *1640*

SOUTH AFRICAN FOOD & BEVERAGE MANUFACTURING REVIEW.
National Publishing (Pty) Ltd., P.O. Box 2271, Clareinch 7740, South Africa. TEL 27-21-611140. FAX 27-21-611389
Vendor(s): Information Access Co., University Microfilms International. *2991*

SOUTH AFRICAN JOURNAL OF ECONOMIC HISTORY.
Economic History Society of Southern Africa, University of South Africa, Economics Department, P.O. Box 392, Pretoria 0C01. TEL 27-12-4294502. FAX 27-12-4293433. *1261*

SOUTH AFRICAN PHARMACEUTICAL JOURNAL.
Pharmaceutical Society of South Africa, P.O. Box 31360, Braamfontein, Johannesburg 2017, South Africa. TEL 27-11-339-1752. FAX 27-11-403-1309. *5444*

SOUTH ASIAN SURVEY.
Sage Publications Incia Pvt. Ltd., P.O. Box 4215, New Delhi 110 048, India. TEL 91-11-644-4958. FAX 91-11-647-2425. *3384*

SOUTH AUSTRALIAN STATE REPORTS.
L B C Information Services 50 Waterloo Rd., N. Ryde, N.S.W. 2113, Australia. TEL 61-2-00366444. FAX 61-2-8889706.
Vendor(s): Info-One International Pty Ltd.. *3850*

SOUTH CAROLINA BUSINESS DIRECTORY.
American Business Directories 5711 S. 86th Circle, Box 27347, Omaha, NE 68127. TEL 402-593-4600. FAX 402-331-5481. *1640*

SOUTH CAROLINA LAW REVIEW.
University of South Carolina, School of Law, Columbia, SC 29208. TEL 803-777 5874. FAX 803-777-2368.
Vendor(s): Lexis-Nexis, West Services, Inc.. *3850*

SOUTH DAKOTA BUSINESS DIRECTORY.
American Business Directories 5711 S. 86th Circle, Box 27347, Omaha, NE 68127. TEL 402-593-4600. FAX 402-331-5481. *1640*

SOUTH DAKOTA BUSINESS REVIEW.
University of South Dakota, School of Business, 414 E. Clark St., Vermillion, SD 57069-2390. TEL 605-677-5287. FAX 605-677-5427.
Vendor(s): Information Access Co., University Microfilms International. *961*

SOUTH DAKOTA LAW REVIEW.
University of South Dakota, School of Law, 414 E. Clark St., Vermilion, SD 57069-2390. TEL 605-677-5646. FAX 605-677-5417.
Vendor(s): West Services, Inc. *3850*

SOUTH FLORIDA BUSINESS JOURNAL.
American City Business Journals, Inc. (Miami), 1050 Lee Wagener Blvd., Ste 302, Ft. Lauderdale, FL 33315-3500. FAX 305-591-1892.
Vendor(s): Information Access Co.. *961*

SOUTH TEXAS LAW REVIEW.
South Texas Law Review, Inc., 1303 San Jacinto St., Houston, TX 77002.
Vendor(s): West Services, Inc.. *3850*

SOUTHEAST POWER REPORT.
McGraw-Hill Companies, 1221 Ave. of the Americas, New York, NY 10020. TEL 212-512-2000.
Vendor(s) Dow Jones News Retrieval (SEPR), Knight-Ridder Information, Inc. SPR), NewsNet (EY89). *2558*

SOUTHEAST REAL ESTATE NEWS.
Intertec Publishing Corp. (Atlanta), 6151 Powers Ferry Rd., N.W., Atlanta, GA 30339-2941. TEL 770-955-2500. FAX 770-955-0400. *6037*

SOUTHERN CALIFORNIA BUSINESS.
Los Angeles Area Chamber of Commerce, 350 S. Bixel St., Los Angeles, CA 90017. TEL 213-580-7571. FAX 213-580-7586.
Vendor(s): Information Access Co., University Microfilms International. *1149*

SOUTHERN CALIFORNIA BUSINESS DIRECTORY.
American Business Directories 5711 S. 86th Circle, Box 27347, Omaha, NE 68127. TEL 402-593-4600. FAX 402-331-5481. *1640*

SOUTHERN CONE REPORT.
Lettres (U.K.) Ltd., 61 Old St., London EC1V 9HX, England. TEL 44-171-251-0012. FAX 44-171-253-8193.
Vendor(s): Lexis-Nexis. *1240*

SOUTHERN ECONOMIC JOURNAL.
University of North Carolina at Chapel Hill, Southern Economic Association, 300 Hanes Hall CB 3540, Chapel Hill NC 27514. TEL 919-966-5261. FAX 919-932-5469.
Vendor(s): Information Access Co.. *961*

SOUTHERN ILLINOIS UNIVERSITY LAW JOURNAL.
Southern Illinois University at Carbondale, School of Law, Lesar Law Bldg., Carbondale, IL 62901. TEL 618-453-8721. FAX 618-453-8759.
Vendor(s): Lexis-Nexis, West Services, Inc.. *3850*

SOUTHERN LIVING.
Southern Progress Corp. c/o H. Johnson, V.P. Circulation, 2100 Lakeshore Dr., Birmingham, AL 35209. TEL 205-877-6000. FAX 205 877-6422. *3238*

THE SOUTHERN REVIEW.
Louisiana State University, 43 Allen Hall, Baton Rouge, LA 70803-5005. TEL 504-388-5108. FAX 504-388-5098.
Vendor(s): Information Access Co., University Microfilms International. *4269*

SOUTHERN SOCIAL STUDIES JOURNAL.
Kentucky Council for the Social Studies, Morehead State University, U.P.O 738, Morehead, KY 40351. TEL 606-783-2765. FAX 606-783-2678. Vendor(s): Knight-Ridder Information, Inc., Ovid Technologies, Inc.. *6347*

SOUTHSCAN.
SouthScan Ltd., P.O. Box 724, London N16 5RZ, England. TEL 44-171-923-1467. FAX 44-171-923-2545. *5709*

SOUTHWEST JOURNAL OF BUSINESS AND ECONOMICS.
University of Texas at El Paso, Texas Centers, El Paso, TX 79968. Vendor(s): Information Access Co.. *961*

SOUTHWEST REAL ESTATE NEWS.
Intertec Publishing Corp. (Atlanta), 6151 Powers Ferry Rd., N.W., Atlanta, GA 30339-2941. TEL 770-955-2500. FAX 770-955-0400. *6037*

SOUTHWEST REVIEW.
Southern Methodist University, 307 Fondren Library W., Box 374, Dallas, TX 75275. TEL 214-768-1037. FAX 214-768-1408. Vendor(s): Information Access Co., Information Intelligence Inc., University Microfilms International. *4167*

SOUTHWESTERN LAW JOURNAL.
S M U Law Review Association, Southern Methodist University, School of Law, Dallas, TX 75275. TEL 214-768-2594. FAX 214-768-3946. Vendor(s): West Services, Inc.. *3851*

SOWITIMES.
Studenteninformationsverein Public Media, Stifterstr. 20, A-4100 Ottensheim, Austria. TEL 04234-4547. *2442*

SOYABEAN ABSTRACTS.
CAB International, Wallingford, Oxon. OX10 8DE, England. TEL 44-1491-832111. FAX 44-1491-833508. Vendor(s): DIMDI, European Space Agency, Knight-Ridder Information, Inc., STN International. *181*

SPACE BUSINESS NEWS.
Phillips Business Information, Inc., 1201 Seven Locks Rd., Potomac, MD 20854. TEL 301-424-3338. FAX 301-309-3847. Vendor(s): Data-Star, Information Access Co., Knight-Ridder Information, Inc., NewsNet (AE11). *77*

SPACE CALENDAR.
Space Age Publishing Company, 75-5751 Kuakini Hwy., Ste. 209, Kaulua-Kona, HI 96740. TEL 808-326-2014. FAX 808-326-1825. Vendor(s): NewsNet (AE04). *77*

SPACE FAX DAILY.
Space Age Publishing Company, 75-5751 Kuakini Hwy., Ste. 209, Kaulua-Kona, HI 96740. TEL 808-326-2014. FAX 808-326-1825. Vendor(s): NewsNet (AE07). *78*

SPACE R & D ALERT.
Aerospace Communications, c/o Jeffrey K. Manber, Ed., 519 N. Alfred St., Alexandria, VA 22314-2226. Vendor(s): NewsNet. *78*

SPAIN. REGISTRO MERCANTIL. BOLETIN OFICIAL.
Boletin Oficial del Estado, Trafalgar, 27, 28071 Madrid, Spain. TEL 34-1-5382297. FAX 34-1-5382275. *961*

SPECIAL DELIVERY.
Association of Labor Assistants & Childbirth Educators, Box 382724, Cambridge, MA 02238. TEL 617-441-2500. FAX 617-441-3167. Vendor(s): Information Access Co.. *4746*

THE SPECIAL EDUCATOR.
L R P Publications 747 Dresher Rd., Horsham, PA 19044. TEL 215-784-0941. FAX 215-784-9639. *2475*

SPECIAL LIBRARIES.
Special Libraries Association, 1700 18th St., N.W., Washington, DC 20009. TEL 202-234-4700. FAX 202-265-9317. Vendor(s): Information Access Co.. *4028*

SPECIALITY CHEMICALS.
Argus Business Media Ltd., Fuel and Metals Journals Queensway House, 2 Queensway, Redhill, Surrey RH1 1QS, England. TEL 44-1737-768611. FAX 44-1737-761685. Vendor(s): Information Access Co.. *2650*

SPECTRUM (LEXINGTON).
Council of State Governments, 3560 Iron Works Pike, Box 11910, Lexington, KY 40578-1910. TEL 606-244-8000. FAX 606-244-8001. Vendor(s): Information Access Co., University Microfilms International. *5921*

SPECTRUM CONVERTIBLES.
C D A Investment Technologies, Inc., 1355 Piccard Dr., Rockville, MD 20850. FAX 301-590-1329. *1352*

SPECTRUM INTERNATIONAL.
C D A Investment Technologies, Inc., 1355 Piccard Dr., Rockville, MD 20850. FAX 301-590-1329. *1352*

SPEEDNEWS.
Speednews, Inc., 1801 Ave. of the Stars, Ste. 210, Los Angeles, CA 90067-5904. TEL 310-203-9603. FAX 310-203-9352. Vendor(s): NewsNet (AE15). *6765*

SPIRITS: THE INTERNATIONAL MARKET.
Euromonitor, 60-61 Britton St., London EC1M 5NA, England. TEL 44-171-251-8024. FAX 44-171-608-3146. Vendor(s): Data-Star, Knight-Ridder Information, Inc.. *511*

SPORT.
Petersen Publishing Co., 6420 Wilshire Blvd., Los Angeles, CA 90048. TEL 213-782-2000. Vendor(s): Information Access Co.. *6482*

SPORT THESAURUS.
Sport Information Resource Centre (SIRC), 1600 James Naismith Dr., Gloucester, ON K1B 5N4, Canada. TEL 613-748-5658. FAX 613-748-5701. Vendor(s): Data-Star, Knight-Ridder Information, Inc., Ovid Technologies, Inc.. *6495*

SPORTING GOODS BUSINESS.
Miller Freeman Inc. (New York) One Penn Plaza, New York, NY 10119. TEL 212-714-1300. FAX 212-714-1313. Vendor(s): Information Access Co., University Microfilms International. *6484*

THE SPORTING NEWS.
Sporting News Publishing Co. 1212 N. Lindbergh Blvd., St. Louis, MO 63132. TEL 314-997-7111. FAX 314-993-7726. Vendor(s): Information Access Co., Lexis-Nexis, University Microfilms International. *6484*

SPORTS AFIELD.
Hearst Magazines, Sports Afield, 250 W. 55th St., New York, NY 10019. TEL 212-649-4000. Vendor(s): Information Access Co.. *6578*

SPORTS ILLUSTRATED.
Time Inc. Time & Life Bldg., Rockefeller Center, 1271 Ave. of the Americas, New York, NY 10020-1393. TEL 212-522-1212. Vendor(s): CompuServe, Inc., Information Access Co., Knight-Ridder Information, Inc., Lexis-Nexis, University Microfilms International, VU/TEXT Information Services, Inc.. *6485*

SPORTSEARCH.
Sport Information Resource Centre (SIRC), 1600 James Naismith Drive, Gloucester, ON K1B 5N4, Canada. TEL 613-748-5658. FAX 613-748-5701. Vendor(s): Data-Star, Knight-Ridder Information, Inc., Ovid Technologies, Inc. (SFDB). *6495*

SPORTSTYLE.
Fairchild Fashion & Merchandising Group 7 W. 34th St., New York, NY 10001. TEL 212-630-4870. FAX 212-630-4879. Vendor(s): Information Access Co., Knight-Ridder Information, Inc.. *6486*

SPRAY TECHNOLOGY & MARKETING.
Industry Publications, Inc. (Fairfield), 389 Passaic Ave., Fairfield, NJ 07006. TEL 201-227-5151. FAX 201-227-9219. *5304*

SPRINGFIELD BUSINESS JOURNAL.
313 Park Central, W., Springfield, MO 65806-1244. TEL 471-831-3238. FAX 417-831-5478. Vendor(s): University Microfilms International. *961*

STAMPS.
American Publishing Company of New York 85 Canisteo St., Hornell, NY 14843. TEL 607-324-2212. FAX 607-324-1753. Vendor(s): Information Access Co., University Microfilms International. *5463*

STANDARD & POOR'S CORPORATION RECORDS.
Standard & Poor's 25 Broadway, New York, NY 10004. TEL 212-208-8000. FAX 212-412-0459. Vendor(s): Knight-Ridder Information, Inc. (File no.133/Corporate Descriptions), Lexis-Nexis, NewsNet. *1353*

STANDARD & POOR'S CORPORATION RECORDS. DAILY NEWS SECTION.
Standard & Poor's 25 Broadway, New York, NY 10004. TEL 212-208-8000. Vendor(s): Knight-Ridder Information, Inc. (File no.133). *962*

STANDARD & POOR'S DIVIDEND RECORD (DAILY).
Standard & Poor's Corporation 25 Broadway, New York, NY 10004. TEL 212-208-8000. *1353*

STANDARD & POOR'S REGISTER OF CORPORATIONS, DIRECTORS AND EXECUTIVES.
Standard & Poor's 25 Broadway, New York, NY 10004. TEL 212-208-8000. *1446*

STANDARD DIRECTORY OF ADVERTISERS (BUSINESS CLASSIFICATIONS EDITION).
National Register Publishing, A Division of Reed Elsevier Inc., 121 Chanlon Rd., New Providence, NJ 07974. TEL 908-464-6800. FAX 908-464-3553. Vendor(s): Lexis-Nexis. *1641*

STANDARD FEDERAL TAX REPORTS.
Commerce Clearing House, Inc., 2700 Lake Cook Rd., Riverwoods, IL 60015. TEL 847-267-7000. FAX 800-224-8299. Vendor(s): University Microfilms International. *1562*

STANFORD JOURNAL OF INTERNATIONAL LAW.
Stanford University, Stanford Law School, Crown Quadrangle, Stanford, CA 94305-8610. TEL 415-723-1375. Vendor(s): West Services, Inc.. *3942*

STANFORD LAW & POLICY REVIEW.
Stanford Law School, Crown Quadrangle, Stanford, CA 94305-8610. TEL 415-725-7297. FAX 415-723-0501. Vendor(s): West Services, Inc.. *3852*

STANFORD LAW REVIEW.
Stanford University, Stanford Law School, Crown Quadrangle, Stanford, CA 94305-8610. Vendor(s): Lexis-Nexis, West Services, Inc.. *3852*

STANFORD UNIVERSITY LIBRARIES. NEWS NOTES.
Stanford University Libraries, Green Library, Stanford, CA 94305. TEL 415-723-2018. Available only online. *4029*

STAPP CAR CRASH CONFERENCE. PROCEEDINGS.
Society of Automotive Engineers, 400 Commonwealth Dr., Warrendale, PA 15096-0001. TEL 412-776-4841. FAX 412-776-3036. Vendor(s): European Space Agency, FIZ Technik, Orbit Search Service. *6802*

STATE & LOCAL COMMUNICATIONS REPORT.
Business Research Publications, Inc., 1333 H St., N.W., Ste. 200-W., Washington, DC 20005. FAX 212-842-3023. Vendor(s): NewsNet (TE59). *1916*

STATE AND METROPOLITAN AREA DATA BOOK.
U.S. Bureau of the Census, Customer Services, Washington, DC 20233. TEL 301-457-4100. FAX 301-457-4714. Vendor(s): CompuServe, Inc., Knight-Ridder Information, Inc.. *6634*

STATE CAPITALS. CIVIL RIGHTS.
Wakeman-Walworth, Inc., 300 N. Washington St., Alexandria, VA 22314. TEL 703-549-8606. FAX 703-549-1372. Vendor(s): West Services, Inc.. *5921*

STATE CAPITALS. ENVIRONMENTAL REGULATION.
Wakeman-Walworth, Inc., 300 N. Washington St., Alexandria, VA 22314. TEL 703-549-8606. FAX 703-549-1372.
Vendor(s): West Services, Inc.. *5922*

STATE CAPITALS. INSURANCE REGULATION.
Wakeman-Walworth, Inc., 300 N. Washington St., Alexandria, VA 22314. TEL 703-549-8606. FAX 703-549-1372.
Vendor(s): West Services, Inc.. *5922*

STATE CAPITALS. PUBLIC UTILITIES.
Wakeman-Walworth, Inc., 300 N. Washington St., Alexandria, VA 22314. TEL 703-549-8606. FAX 703-549-1372.
Vendor(s): West Services, Inc.. *5923*

STATE CAPITALS. TAXATION AND REVENUE POLICIES.
Wakeman-Walworth, Inc., 300 N. Washington St., Alexandria, VA 22314. TEL 703-549-8606. FAX 703-549-1372.
Vendor(s): West Services, Inc.. *5923*

STATE CAPITALS. TAXES - PROPERTY.
Wakeman-Walworth, Inc., 300 N. Washington St., Alexandria, VA 22314. TEL 703-549-8606. FAX 703-549-1372.
Vendor(s): West Services, Inc.. *5923*

STATE CAPITOLS REPORT.
State Net, 2101 K St., Sacramento, CA 95816. TEL 916-444-0840. FAX 916-446-5369. *5923*

THE STATE JOURNAL.
State Journal Corp., 904 Virginia St. E., Charleston, WV 25301-2815. TEL 304-344-1630. FAX 304-345-2721.
Vendor(s): University Microfilms International. *962*

STATE LEGISLATURES.
National Conference of State Legislatures, 1560 Broadway, Ste. 700, Denver, CO 80202-5140. TEL 303-830-2200. FAX 303-863-8003.
Vendor(s): Information Access Co.. *5710*

STATE TAX NOTES.
Tax Analysts, 6830 N. Fairfax Dr., Arlington, VA 22213. TEL 703-533-4400. FAX 703-533-4444.
Vendor(s): Knight-Ridder Information, Inc., Lexis-Nexis. *1562*

STATE TAX REVIEW.
Commerce Clearing House, Inc., 2700 Lake Cook Rd., Riverwoods, IL 60015. TEL 847-267-7000. FAX 800-224-8299.
Vendor(s): NewsNet, University Microfilms International. *1562*

STATE TELEPHONE REGULATION REPORT.
Capitol Publications Inc., Telecom Publishing Group, 1101 King St., Ste. 444, Box 1455, Alexandria, VA 22313-2055. TEL 800-327-7205. FAX 703-739-6490.
Vendor(s): Information Access Co., NewsNet (TE47). *1950*

STATISTICAL ABSTRACT OF THE UNITED STATES (YEAR).
U.S. Bureau of the Census, Customer Services, Washington, DC 20233. TEL 301-457-4100. FAX 301-457-4714.
Vendor(s): CompuServe, Inc., Knight-Ridder Information, Inc.. *6634*

STATISTICAL OFFICE OF THE EUROPEAN COMMUNITIES. ENERGY STATISTICS MONTHLY BULLETIN.
Statistical Office of the European Communities, Rue de Gasperi, 2920 Luxembourg, Luxembourg.
Vendor(s): GSI-ECO. *2565*

STATISTICS AND COMPUTING.
Chapman & Hall, Journals Department 2-6 Boundary Row, London SE1 8HN, England. TEL 44-171-8650066. FAX 44-171-5229623. *6636*

STEELS ALERT.
Cambridge Scientific Abstracts, 7200 Wisconsin Ave., Bethesda, MD 20814. TEL 301-961-6750. FAX 301-961-6720.
Vendor(s): CISTI, CREDOC, Data-Star (MBUS), European Space Agency (File no.111), Knight-Ridder Information, Inc. (File no.269), Orbit Search Service (MABU), STN International (MATBUS). *4985*

STEREO REVIEW.
Hachette Filipacchi Magazines, Inc., 1633 Broadway, New York, NY 10019. TEL 212-767-6000.
Vendor(s): Information Access Co., Knight-Ridder Information, Inc., University Microfilms International. *6447*

STETSON LAW REVIEW.
Stetson University, College of Law, 1401 61 St. S., St. Petersburg, FL 33707. TEL 813-345-1300. FAX 813-345-8973.
Vendor(s): West Services, Inc.. *3853*

STOCKS, BONDS, BILLS AND INFLATION (YEAR) YEARBOOK.
Ibbotson Associates, 225 N. Michigan Ave., Ste. 700, Chicago, IL 60601. TEL 312-616-1620. FAX 312-616-0404. *1354*

STOCKS IN THE S & P 500. OFFICIAL SERIES.
Standard & Poor's 25 Broadway, New York, NY 10004. TEL 212-208-8000. *1354*

STONE WORLD.
Business News Publishing Company, 755 W. Big Beaver, Ste. 100C, Troy, MI 48084. TEL 810-362-3700. FAX 810-362-0317. *1660*

STORES.
N R F Enterprises, Inc., 325 7th St., N.W., Ste. 1000, Washington, DC 20004-2802. TEL 202-626-8101. FAX 202-626-8191.
Vendor(s): Information Access Co., Lexis-Nexis, University Microfilms International. *1446*

STRATEGIC BALANCE IN THE MIDDLE EAST.
Arab Press Service, A P S House, P.O. Box 3896, Nicosia, Cyprus. FAX 357-2-350265.
Vendor(s): Information Access Co.. *5772*

STRESSFORSKNINGSRAPPORTER.
Karolinska Institutet, Institutionen foer Klinisk Neurovetenskap, P.O. Box 230, S-171 77 Stockholm, Sweden. TEL 46-08-7286400. FAX 46-08-344143. *5883*

STROKE.
American Heart Association, 7272 Greenville Ave., Dallas, TX 75231-4596. TEL 214-706-1310. FAX 214-691-6342.
Vendor(s): Ovid Technologies, Inc.. *4609*

STRUCTURE.
Current Biology Ltd., 400 Market St., Ste. 700, Philadelphia, PA 19106. FAX 215-574-2270. *609*

STRUCTURIST.
Eli Bornstein, Ed. & Pub. Box 378, RPO University, University of Saskatchewan, Saskatoon, SK S7N 4J8, Canada. TEL 306-966-4198. FAX 306-966-8670. *453*

STUDIES IN AMERICAN FICTION.
Northeastern University, Department of English, Boston, MA 02115. TEL 617-437-3687.
Vendor(s): Information Access Co.. *4272*

STUDIES IN BIBLIOGRAPHY.
University Press of Virginia, Box 3608, University Sta., Charlottesville, VA 22903. TEL 804-924-3468. FAX 804-982-2655. *547*

STUDIES IN ENGLISH LITERATURE 1500-1900.
Rice University, SEL-MS 46, 6100 Main St., Houston, TX 77005-1892. TEL 713-527-4697. FAX 713-285-5207.
Vendor(s): Information Access Co., University Microfilms International. *4272*

STUDIES IN FAMILY PLANNING.
Population Council, 1 Dag Hammarskjold Plaza, New York, NY 10017. TEL 212-339-0500. FAX 212-755-6052.
Vendor(s): Information Access Co.. *5792*

STUDIES IN NONLINEAR DYNAMICS AND ECONOMETRICS.
M I T Press, 55 Hayward St., Cambridge, MA 02142-1399. TEL 617-253-2889. FAX 617-258-6779.
Available only online. *4338*

STUDIES IN PHILOLOGY.
University of North Carolina Press, Box 2288, Chapel Hill, NC 27515-2288. TEL 919-966-3561. FAX 800-272-6817.
Vendor(s): University Microfilms International. *4114*

STUDIES IN SHORT FICTION.
Newberry College, 2100 College St., Newberry, SC 29108. TEL 803-321-5195. FAX 803-321-5232.
Vendor(s): Information Access Co., University Microfilms International. *4273*

STUDIES IN THE NOVEL.
University of North Texas, English Department, Denton, TX 76203. TEL 817-565-2025. FAX 807-565-4355.
Vendor(s): Information Access Co., University Microfilms International. *4273*

STUDIES ON NEOTROPICAL FAUNA AND ENVIRONMENT.
Swets & Zeitlinger bv, P.O. Box 825, 2160 SZ Lisse, Netherlands. TEL 31-252-435111. FAX 31-252-415888. *821*

THE STUTE.
Stevens Institute of Technology, CastlePoint on the Hudson, Hoboken, NJ 07030. TEL 201-659-3404. *1887*

STYLE (DEKALB).
Northern Illinois University, Department of English, DeKalb, IL 60115. TEL 815-753-0611. FAX 815-753-1824.
Vendor(s): Information Access Co., University Microfilms International. *4274*

SUBJECT GUIDE TO BOOKS IN PRINT.
R.R. Bowker, A Division of Reed Elsevier Inc., 121 Chanlon Rd., New Providence, NJ 07974. TEL 908-464-6800. FAX 908-665-3502.
Vendor(s): Knight-Ridder Information Inc. (File no.470), Ovid Technologies, Inc. (BBP). *547*

SUBJECT GUIDE TO CHILDREN'S BOOKS IN PRINT.
R.R. Bowker, A Division of Reed Elsevier Inc., 121 Chanlon Rd., New Providence, NJ 07974. TEL 908-464-6800. FAX 908-665-3502. *547*

SUBSTANCE ABUSE REPORT.
Business Research Publications, Inc., 65 Bleecker St., 5th Fl., New York, NY 10012-2450. TEL 212-673-4700. FAX 212-475-1790.
Vendor(s): Information Access Co.. *2201*

SUCCESS MAGAZINE.
Lang Communications, Inc., 230 Park Ave., 7th Fl., New York, NY 10169-0014. TEL 212-551-9500. FAX 212-922-2919.
Vendor(s): Information Access Co.. *5274*

SUCCESSFUL FARMING.
Meredith Corporation, 1716 Locust St., Des Moines, IA 50309-3023. TEL 515-284-3000. FAX 515-284-3563.
Vendor(s): Information Access Co., University Microfilms International. *154*

SUCCESSFUL MEETINGS.
Bill Communications, Inc., 355 Park Ave. S., 5th Fl., New York, NY 10010-1789. TEL 212-592-6200. FAX 212-592-6339.
Vendor(s): University Microfilms International. *1487*

SUEDDEUTSCHE ZEITUNG.
Sueddeutscher Verlag GmbH, Sendlingerstr. 8, 80331 Munich, Germany. TEL 49-89-2183-0. FAX 49-89-2183787. *3149*

SUFFOLK TRANSNATIONAL LAW REVIEW.
Suffolk University Law School, Suffolk Transnational Law Review, 41 Temple St., Boston, MA 02114-4280. TEL 617-573-8610.
Vendor(s): Lexis-Nexis, West Services, Inc.. *3854*

SUFFOLK UNIVERSITY LAW REVIEW.
Joe Christensen, Inc. (Boston), Beacon Hill, 41 Temple St., Boston, MA 02114. TEL 617-573-8180. FAX 617-723-5847.
Vendor(s): West Services, Inc.. *3854*

SUICIDE AND LIFE-THREATENING BEHAVIOR.
Guilford Publications, Inc., 72 Spring St., 4th Fl., New York, NY 10012. TEL 212-431-9800. FAX 212-966-6708.
Vendor(s): University Microfilms International. *5884*

SULPHUR.
British Sulphur Publishing 31 Mount Peasant, London WC1X 0AD, England. TEL 44-171-837-5600. FAX 44-171-837-0292.
Vendor(s): Information Access Co.. *181*

SUMMARY OF WORLD BROADCASTS. PART 1: FORMER U S S R (DAILY).
B B C Monitoring, Caversham Park, Reading, Berks. RG4 8TZ, England. TEL 01734-469289. FAX 01734-463823.
Vendor(s): Data-Star, Lexis-Nexis, Reuters, Ltd.. *1242*

SUMMARY OF WORLD BROADCASTS. PART 1: FORMER U S S R (WEEKLY ECONOMIC REPORT).
B B C Monitoring, Caversham Park, Reading, Berks. RG4 8TZ, England. TEL 01734-469289. FAX 01734-463823.
Vendor(s): Data-Star, Lexis-Nexis, Reuters, Ltd.. *1242*

SUMMARY OF WORLD BROADCASTS. PART 2: CENTRAL EUROPE, THE BALKANS (DAILY).
B B C Monitoring, Caversham Park, Reading, Berks. RG4 8TZ, England. TEL 01734-469289. FAX 01734-463823.
Vendor(s): Data-Star, Lexis-Nexis, Reuters, Ltd.. *1242*

SUMMARY OF WORLD BROADCASTS. PART 2: CENTRAL EUROPE, THE BALKANS (WEEKLY ECONOMIC REPORT).
B B C Monitoring, Caversham Park, Reading, Berks. RG4 8TZ, England. TEL 01734-469289. FAX 01734-463823.
Vendor(s): Data-Star, Lexis-Nexis, Reuters, Ltd.. *1242*

SUMMARY OF WORLD BROADCASTS. PART 3: ASIA - PACIFIC (DAILY).
B B C Monitoring, Caversham Park, Reading, Berks. RG4 8TZ, England. TEL 01734-469289. FAX 01734-463823.
Vendor(s): Data-Star, Lexis-Nexis, Reuters, Ltd.. *1242*

SUMMARY OF WORLD BROADCASTS. PART 3: ASIA - PACIFIC (WEEKLY ECONOMIC REPORT).
B B C Monitoring, Caversham Park, Reading, Berks. RG4 8TZ, England. TEL 01734-469289. FAX 01734-463823.
Vendor(s): Data-Star, Lexis-Nexis, Reuters, Ltd.. *1242*

SUMMARY OF WORLD BROADCASTS. PART 4: MIDDLE EAST (DAILY).
B B C Monitoring, Caversham Park, Reading, Berks. RG4 8TZ, England. TEL 01734-469289. FAX 01734-463823.
Vendor(s): Data-Star, Lexis-Nexis, Reuters, Ltd.. *1242*

SUMMARY OF WORLD BROADCASTS. PART 4: MIDDLE EAST (WEEKLY ECONOMIC REPORT).
B B C Monitoring, Caversham Park, Reading, Berks. RG4 8TZ, England. TEL 01734-469289. FAX 01734-463823.
Vendor(s): Data-Star, Lexis-Nexis, Reuters, Ltd.. *1242*

SUMMARY OF WORLD BROADCASTS. PART 5: AFRICA, LATIN AMERICA AND THE CARIBBEAN (DAILY).
B B C Monitoring, Caversham Park, Reading, Berks. RG4 8TZ, England. TEL 01734-469289. FAX 01734-463823.
Vendor(s): Data-Star, Lexis-Nexis, Reuters, Ltd.. *1242*

SUMMARY OF WORLD BROADCASTS. PART 5: AFRICA, LATIN AMERICA AND THE CARIBBEAN (WEEKLY ECONOMIC REPORT).
B B C Monitoring, Caversham Park, Reading, Berks. RG4 8TZ, England. TEL 01734-469289. FAX 01734-463823.
Vendor(s): Data-Star, Lexis-Nexis, Reuters, Ltd.. *1242*

SUN CARE: THE INTERNATIONAL MARKET.
Euromonitor, 60-61 Britton St., London EC1M 5NA, England. TEL 44-171-251-8024. FAX 44-171-608-3149.
Vendor(s): Data-Star, Knight-Ridder Information, Inc.. *493*

SUNDAY MAIL.
Queensland Newspapers Pty. Ltd., Campbell St., Bowen Hills, Brisbane, Qld., Australia. TEL 61-7-2526001. FAX 61-7-2526692. *3112*

SUNSET.
Sunset Publishing Corp., 80 Willow Rd., Menlo Park, CA 94025-3691. TEL 415-321-3600. FAX 415-321-0551.
Vendor(s): Information Access Co., Knight-Ridder Information, Inc.. *3239*

SUPER MARKETING.
Reed Business Publishing Group Quadrant House, The Quadrant, Sutton, Surrey SM2 5AS, England. TEL 44-181-652-8275. FAX 44-181-652-3958. *3008*

SUPERCONDUCTOR SCIENCE & TECHNOLOGY.
I O P Publishing Ltd., Techno House, Redcliffe Way, Bristol, Avon BS1 6NX, England. TEL 44-117-929-7481. FAX 44-117-929-4318. *5572*

SUPERCONDUCTOR WEEK.
Atlantic Information Services, Inc., 1050 17th St., N.W., Ste. 480, Washington, DC 20036. TEL 202-775-9008. FAX 202-331-9542.
Vendor(s): Data-Star, Information Access Co., Knight-Ridder Information, Inc., NewsNet. *5572*

SUPERFUND WEEK.
Pasha Publications Inc., 1616 N. Ft. Myer Dr., Ste. 1000, Arlington, VA 22209-3107. TEL 703-528-1244. FAX 703-528-1253.
Vendor(s): Information Access Co., NewsNet (EV22). *2821*

SUPERMARKET BUSINESS.
Howfrey Communications, 1086 Teaneck Rd., Teaneck, NJ 07666-4838. TEL 201-833-1900. FAX 201-833-1273.
Vendor(s): Information Access Co., Lexis-Nexis. *3008*

SUPERMARKET NEWS.
Fairchild Publications 7 W. 34th St., New York, NY 10001. TEL 212-630-4199. FAX 212-630-4201.
Vendor(s): Information Access Co., Knight-Ridder Information, Inc., Lexis-Nexis. *3008*

SUPERMARKET STRATEGIC ALERT.
Pollack Associates, 140 E. 81st St., Ste. 5E, New York, NY 10028. TEL 212-734-0753. FAX 212-988-9394. *3008*

SUPERVISION.
National Research Bureau, Box 1, Burlington, IA 52601-0001. TEL 319-752-5415. FAX 319-752-3421.
Vendor(s): Information Access Co., University Microfilms International. *1395*

SUPREME COURT OF CANADA DECISIONS.
Western Legal Publications, 301-1 Alexander St., Vancouver, BC V6A 1B2, Canada. TEL 604-687-5671. FAX 604-687-2796. *3954*

SURPLUS RECORD.
Surplus Record, Inc., 20 N. Wacker Dr., Chicago, IL 60606. TEL 312-372-9077. FAX 312-372-6537. *4346*

SURVEY OF BUSINESS.
University of Tennessee at Knoxville, Center for Business and Economic Research, Knoxville, TN 37996-4170. TEL 615-974-5441. FAX 615-974-3100.
Vendor(s): University Microfilms International. *963*

SURVEY OF CURRENT BUSINESS.
U.S. Bureau of Economic Analysis, U.S. Department of Commerce, Washington, DC 20230. TEL 202-606-9900.
Vendor(s): Information Access Co., Knight-Ridder Information, Inc., University Microfilms International. *1243*

SUSSEX PAST AND PRESENT.
Sussex Archaeological Society, Bull House, 92 High St., Lewes, Sussex BN7 1XH, England. TEL 44-1273-486260. FAX 44-1273-486990.
Vendor(s): Information Access Co.. *376*

SVENSK FARMACEVTISK TIDSKRIFT.
Swedish Pharmaceutical Press, P.O. Box 1136, S-111 81 Stockholm, Sweden. TEL 46-8-723-50-00. FAX 46-8-14-95-80. *5444*

SWEDEN. SOCIALSTYRELSEN. FOERFATTNINGSSAMLING: MEDICAL.
Socialstyrelsen, S-106 30 Stockholm, Sweden. FAX 48-8-783-30-06. *4535*

SWEDEN. SOCIALSTYRELSEN. FOERFATTNINGSSAMLING: SOCIAL.
Socialstyrelsen, 106 30 Stockholm, Sweden. *6396*

THE SWEDISH ECONOMY.
Fritzes AB, S-106 47 Stockholm, Sweden. TEL 46-468-690-9090. FAX 46-468-205021.
Vendor(s): Information Access Co.. *963*

SWEDISH EXAMPLE.
Nordic News Network, P.O. Box 1181, S-181 23 Lidingoe, Sweden. TEL 46-8-731-92-00. FAX 46-8-731-92-00.
Available only online. *5711*

SWEET & SAVOURY BISCUITS: THE INTERNATIONAL MARKET.
Euromonitor, 60-61 Britton St., London EC1M 5NA, England. TEL 44-171-251-8024. FAX 44-171-608-3149.
Vendor(s): Data-Star, Knight-Ridder Information, Inc.. *3002*

SWISS BUSINESS.
S H Z Fachverlag AG, Seestr. 37, CH-8027 Zurich, Switzerland. TEL 41-1-2022046. FAX 41-1-2811970.
Vendor(s): Information Access Co.. *1355*

SYLLABUS (SUNNYVALE).
Syllabus Press, 1307 S. Mary Ave., No. 211, Sunnyvale, CA 94087. TEL 408-746-2000. FAX 408-746-2711. *2408*

SYMPOSIUM.
Heldref Publications, 1319 Eighteenth St., N.W., Washington, DC 20036-1802. TEL 202-296-6267. FAX 202-296-5149.
Vendor(s): Information Access Co.. *4275*

SYNAGOGEN RUNDSCHAU.
Arthur-Custos-Gedaechtnis-Archiv, Tinnagel 5, 47608 Geldern, Germany. TEL 49-2831-2759. FAX 49-2831-98537. *6130*

SYNTHETIC METHODS OF ORGANIC CHEMISTRY.
S. Karger AG, Allschwilerstr. 10, P.O. Box, CH-4009 Basel, Switzerland. TEL 061-3061111. FAX 061-3061234.
Vendor(s): Orbit Search Service. *1746*

SYRACUSE JOURNAL OF INTERNATIONAL LAW & COMMERCE.
Joe Christensen, Inc. (Syracuse), E I White Hall, Ste. 0041, Syracuse, NY 13244-1030. TEL 315-443-2056.
Vendor(s): West Services, Inc.. *3943*

SYSTEMS & NETWORK MANAGEMENT REPORT.
DataTrends Publications, Inc., Box 4460, Leesburg, VA 20177. TEL 703-779-0574. FAX 703-779-2267.
Vendor(s): Information Access Co.. *2117*

T A J A.
Anthropological Society of New South Wales, c/o Dept. of Anthropology, Univ. of Sydney, Sydney, N.S.W. 2006, Australia. TEL 61-2-3515489. FAX 61-2-3515489.
Vendor(s): Information Access Co.. *323*

T A M BULLETIN.
Travelling Art Mail, c/o T A M, Postbus 10388, 5000 JJ Tilburg, Netherlands. TEL 31-13-5366103. *455*

T B WEEKLY.
Charles W. Henderson, Ed. & Pub., Box 5528, Atlanta, GA 31107-0528. TEL 404-377-8895. FAX 404-378-5411.
Vendor(s): CompuServe, Inc., Data-Star, Dow Jones News Retrieval, Information Access Co., Knight-Ridder Information, Inc., NewsNet, Ovid Technologies, Inc.. *4628*

T C I.
Theatre Crafts International, 32 W. 18th St., New York, NY 10011-4612. TEL 212-229-2965. FAX 212-229-2084.
Vendor(s): Information Access Co., University Microfilms International. *6703*

T D R.
M I T Press, 55 Hayward St., Cambridge, MA 02142. TEL 617-253-2889. FAX 617-577-1545.
Vendor(s): Information Access Co.. *6704*

T H E JOURNAL.
Ed Warnshius Ltd., 150 El Camino Real, Ste. 112, Tustin, CA 92680-3670. TEL 714-730-4011. FAX 714-730-3739.
Vendor(s): Information Access Co.. *2408*

T M A EXECUTIVE SUMMARY.
Tobacco Merchants Association of the United States, Inc., 231 Clarksville Rd., Ste. 6, Box 8019, Princeton, NJ 08543-8019. TEL 609-275-4900. FAX 609-275-8379. *6710*

T M A LEGISLATIVE BULLETIN.
Tobacco Merchants Association of the United States, Inc., 231 Clarksville Rd., Ste. 6, Box 8019, Princeton, NJ 08543-8019. TEL 609-275-4900. FAX 609-275-8379. *6710*

T M A TOBACCO BAROMETER: SMOKING, CHEWING, SNUFF.
Tobacco Merchants Association of the United States, Inc., 231 Clarksville Rd., Ste. 6, Box 8019, Princeton, NJ 08543-8019. TEL 609-275-4900. FAX 609-275-8379. *6710*

T M A TRADEMARK REPORT.
Tobacco Merchants Association of the United States, Inc., 231 Clarksville Rd., Ste. 6, Box 8019, Princeton, NJ 08543-8019. TEL 609-275-4900. FAX 609-275-8379. *6710*

T M A WORLD ALERT.
Tobacco Merchants Association of the United States, Inc., 231 Clarksville Rd., Ste. 6, Box 8019, Princeton, NJ 08543-8019. TEL 609-275-4900. FAX 609-275-8379. *6710*

T R I S ELECTRONIC BIBLIOGRAPHIC DATA BASE.
U.S. National Research Council, Transportation Research Board, 2101 Constitution Ave., N.W., Washington, DC 20418. TEL 202-334-3250. FAX 202-334-3495.
Vendor(s): Knight-Ridder Information, Inc. (File no. 63). *6746*

T R WIRELESS NEWS.
Business Research Publications, Inc., 1333 H St., N.W., Ste. 200-W., Washington, DC 20005. FAX 202-842-3023.
Vendor(s): Information Access Co., NewsNet (TE45). *1916*

T V SPORTSFILE.
Gould Media Services, Box 446, York, ME 03909. TEL 207-363-6037. FAX 207-363-7824. *6488*

TACTICAL TECHNOLOGY.
Phillips Business Information, Inc., 1201 Seven Locks Rd., Potomac, MD 20854. TEL 301-424-3338. FAX 301-309-3847.
Vendor(s): Information Access Co., NewsNet (GT45). *5049*

DIE TAGESZEITUNG.
T A Z Verlagsgenossenschaft e.G., Kochstr. 18, 10969 Berlin, Germany. TEL 030-25902-0. FAX 030-2518095. *3150*

TALKING POINTS.
Heritage Foundation, 214 Massachusetts Ave., N.E., Washington, DC 20002. TEL 202-546-4400. FAX 202-543-9647.
Vendor(s): Lexis-Nexis. *5773*

TAMPA BAY BUSINESS JOURNAL.
Hoerner Publications of Tampa Bay, Inc., Box 24185, Tampa, FL 33623. TEL 813-877-6627.
Vendor(s): Information Access Co. *1243*

TAPE - DISC BUSINESS.
Knowledge Industry Publications, Inc., 701 Westchester Ave., White Plains, NY 10604-3002. TEL 914-328-9157. FAX 914-328-9093.
Vendor(s): Information Access Co. *1532*

TARGET MARKETING.
North American Publishing Co., 401 N. Broad St., Philadelphia, PA 19108. TEL 215-238-5300. FAX 215-238-5457.
Vendor(s): Information Access Co. *1488*

TAROT NEWS.
Tarot Special Interest Group of American Mensa, Tarot Special-Interest Group, Box 561, Quincy, IL 62306-0561. TEL 217-222-9082. *5333*

TASMANIAN REPORTS.
L B C Information Services, 50 Waterloo Rd., N. Ryde, N.S.W. 2113, Australia. TEL 61-2-99366444. FAX 51-2-8889706.
Vendor(s): Info-One International Pty Ltd.. *3954*

THE TAX ADVISER.
American Institute of Certified Public Accountants, 1211 Ave. of the Americas, New York, NY 10036. TEL 212-596-6200.
Vendor(s): Information Access Co., University Microfilms International *1564*

THE TAX DIRECTORY.
Tax Analysts, 6830 N. Fairfax Dr., Arlington, VA 22213. TEL 703-553-4400. FAX 703-533-4444.
Vendor(s): Knight-Ridder Information, Inc., Lexis-Nexis. *1564*

THE TAX EXECUTIVE.
Tax Executives Institute, Inc., 1001 Pennsylvania Ave., N.W. No. 320, Washington, DC 20004-2505. TEL 202-638-56C1. FAX 202-638-5607.
Vendor(s): Information Access Co., University Microfilms International. *1564*

TAX LAWYER.
American Bar Association, Taxation Section, 470 15th St., N.W., Washington, DC 20005-1009. TEL 202-331-2656. FAX 202-331-2220.
Vendor(s): Lexis-Nexis, West Services, Inc.. *3855*

TAX MANAGEMENT COMPENSATION PLANNING.
Tax Management, Inc. 1250 23rd St., N.W., Washington, DC 20037-1166. TEL 202-833-7240. FAX 202-833-7297.
Vendor(s): West Services, Inc. (File TM-CP, TM-CP-OLD, TM-CPJ). *1565*

TAX MANAGEMENT COMPENSATION PLANNING JOURNAL.
Tax Management, Inc. 1250 23rd St., N.W., Washington, DC 20037-1166. TEL 202-833-7240. FAX 202-833-7297.
Vendor(s): University Microfilms International, West Services, Inc. (File TM-CPJ). *1447*

TAX MANAGEMENT ESTATES, GIFTS AND TRUSTS.
Tax Management, Inc. 1250 23rd St., N.W., Washington, DC 20037-1166. TEL 202-833-7240. FAX 202-833-7297.
Vendor(s): West Services, Inc. (Files TM-EGT, TM-EGT-OLD, TM-EGTJ). *1565*

TAX MANAGEMENT ESTATES, GIFTS AND TRUSTS JOURNAL.
Tax Management, Inc. 1250 23rd St., N.W., Washington, DC 20037-1166. TEL 202-452-4200. FAX 202-822-8092.
Vendor(s): Knight-Ridder Information, Inc. (Files 15, 485), University Microfilms International, West Services, Inc. (File TM-EGTJ). *1355*

TAX MANAGEMENT FINANCIAL PLANNING JOURNAL.
Tax Management, Inc. 1250 23rd St., N.W., Washington, DC 20037. TEL 202-833-7240. FAX 202-833-7297.
Vendor(s): University Microfilms International. *1123*

TAX MANAGEMENT FOREIGN INCOME PORTFOLIOS.
Tax Management, Inc. 1250 23rd St., N.W., Washington, DC 20037-1166. TEL 202-833-7240. FAX 202-833-7297.
Vendor(s): West Services, Inc. (File TM-FOR). *1565*

TAX MANAGEMENT INTERNATIONAL JOURNAL.
Tax Management, Inc. 1250 23rd St., N.W., Washington, DC 20037-1166. TEL 202-833-7240. FAX 202-833-7297.
Vendor(s): Knight-Ridder Information, Inc. (Files 15, 485), University Microfilms International. *1565*

TAX MANAGEMENT MEMORANDUM.
Tax Management, Inc. 1231 23rd St., N.W., Washington, DC 20037-1166. TEL 202-833-7240. FAX 202-833-7297
Vendor(s): University Microfilms International, West Services, Inc (File TM-TMM). *1565*

TAX MANAGEMENT REAL ESTATE.
Tax Management, Inc. 1250 23rd St., N.W., Washington, DC 20037-1166. TEL 202-833-7240. FAX 202-833-7297
Vendor(s): West Services, Inc. (Files TM-RE, TM-RE-OLD, TM-REJ). *6037*

TAX MANAGEMENT REAL ESTATE JOURNAL.
Tax Management, Inc. 1250 23rd St., N.W., Washington, DC 20037-1166. TEL 202-833-7240. FAX 202-833-7297.
Vendor(s): University Microfilms International, West Services, Inc. (File TM-REJ). *5037*

TAX MANAGEMENT U S INCOME.
Tax Management, Inc. 1250 23rd St., N.W., Washington, DC 20037-1166. TEL 202-833-7240. FAX 202-833-7297.
Vendor(s): West Services, Inc. (Files TM-US, TM-US-OLD, TM-TMWR). *1566*

TAX MANAGEMENT WEEKLY REPORT.
Tax Management, Inc. 1250 23rd St., N.W., Washington, DC 20037-1166. TEL 202-833-7240. FAX 202-833-7297.
Vendor(s): Human Resources Information Network (File DD), NewsNet (File TMWEEK), West Services, Inc. (File TM-TMWR). *1566*

TAX NEWS SERVICE.
I B F D Publications B.V., P.O. Box 20237, 1000 HE Amsterdam, Netherlands. TEL 31-20-6267726. FAX 31-20-6228658.
Vendor(s): I B F D Pubns. BV Lexis-Nexis. *1566*

TAX NOTES.
Tax Analysts, 6830 N. Fairfax Dr., Arlington, VA 22213. TEL 703-533-4400. FAX 703-533-4444.
Vendor(s): Knight-Ridder Information, Inc., Lexis-Nexis. *1566*

TAX NOTES INTERNATIONAL.
Tax Analysts, 6830 N. Fairfax Dr., Arlington, VA 22213. TEL 703-533-4400. FAX 703-533-4444.
Vendor(s): Knight-Ridder Information, Inc., Lexis-Nexis. *1566*

TAX PROFILE.
C C H Canadian Ltd., 6 Garamond Ct., North York, ON M3C 1Z5, Canada. TEL 416-441-2992. FAX 416-444-9011.
Vendor(s): QL Systems Ltd.. *1567*

TAX TREATIES DATA BASE ON C D - F O M.
I B F D Publications B.V., P.O. Box 20237, 1000 HE Amsterdam, Netherlands. TEL 31-20-6267726. FAX 31-20-6228658.
Vendor(s): I B F D Pubns. BV, Lexis-Nexis. *1567*

TAX WEEK.
C C H Australia Ltd., P.O. Box 230, North Ryde, N.S.W. 2113, Australia. TEL 61-1-300300224. FAX 61-1-300306224. *1567*

TAXATION FOR ACCOUNTANTS.
Warren, Gorham & Lamont, One Penn Plaza, New York, NY 10119. TEL 212-971-5000. FAX 212-971-5113.
Vendor(s) Lexis-Nexis. *1567*

TAXATION FOR LAWYERS.
Warren, Gorham & Lamont, One Penn Plaza, New York, NY 10119. TEL 212-971-5000. FAX 212-971-5240.
Vendor(s): Lexis-Nexis. *1568*

TAXES (RIVERWOODS).
Commerce Clearing House, Inc. 2700 Lake Cook Rd., Riverwoods, IL 60015. TEL 847-267-7000. FAX 800-224-8299.
Vendor(s): University Microfilms International. *1568*

TEA AND COFFEE TRADE JOURNAL.
Lockwood Trade Journal Co., Inc., 130 W. 42nd St., New York, NY 10036-7802. TEL 212-391-2060. FAX 212-827-0945.
Vendor(s): Information Access Co., Lexis-Nexis. *2992*

TEACHER.
Editorial Projects in Education, Inc., 4301 Connecticut Ave., N.W., Ste. 432, Washington, DC 20008. TEL 202-364-4114. *2503*

TEACHERS COLLEGE RECORD.
Columbia University, Teachers College Record Office, 525 W. 120th St., New York, NY 10027. TEL 212-678-3719. FAX 212-678-4048.
Vendor(s): University Microfilms International. *2376*

Online

TEACHING CHILDREN MATHEMATICS.
National Council of Teachers of Mathematics, 1906 Association Dr., Reston, VA 22091-1593. TEL 703-620-9840. FAX 703-476-2970.
Vendor(s): Information Access Co.. *4399*

TEACHING EDUCATION.
University of South Carolina, College of Education, Columbia, SC 29208. TEL 803-777-6301. FAX 803-777-3090. *2376*

TECH - EUROPE.
Europe Information Service, Rue de Geneve, 6, 1140 Brussels, Belgium. TEL 32-2-242-6020. FAX 32-2-242-9410.
Vendor(s): Information Access Co., Lexis-Nexis. *1929*

TECHNICAL ANALYSIS OF STOCKS & COMMODITIES.
Technical Analysis, Inc., 4757 California Ave., S.W., Seattle, WA 98116-4499. TEL 206-938-0570. FAX 206-938-1307. *1355*

TECHNICAL COMMUNICATION.
Society for Technical Communication, 901 N. Stuart St., Ste. 904, Arlington, VA 22203-1822. TEL 703-522-4114.
Vendor(s): Information Access Co., University Microfilms International. *1916*

TECHNICAL LITERATURE ABSTRACTS.
American Petroleum Institute, Central Abstracting & Information Services, 275 Seventh Ave., New York, NY 10001-6708. TEL 212-366-4040. FAX 212-366-4298.
Vendor(s): Knight-Ridder Information, Inc., Orbit Search Service (APILIT), STN International (APILIT), Telesystemes - Questel. *5385*

TECHNICAL LITERATURE ABSTRACTS: CATALYSTS - ZEOLITES.
American Petroleum Institute, Central Abstracting & Information Services, 275 Seventh Ave., New York, NY 10001-6708. TEL 212-366-4040. FAX 212-366-4298.
Vendor(s): Knight-Ridder Information, Inc., Orbit Search Service (APILIT), STN International, Telesystemes - Questel. *1711*

TECHNICAL LITERATURE ABSTRACTS: FUEL REFORMULATION.
American Petroleum Institute, Central Abstracting & Information Services, 275 Seventh Ave., New York, NY 10001-6708. TEL 212-366-4040. FAX 212-366-4298.
Vendor(s): Knight-Ridder Information, Inc., Orbit Search Service (APILIT), STN International (APILIT), Telesystemes - Questel. *1711*

TECHNICAL LITERATURE ABSTRACTS: OILFIELD CHEMICALS.
American Petroleum Institute, Central Abstracting & Information Services, 275 Seventh Ave., New York, NY 10001-6708. TEL 212-366-4040. FAX 212-366-4298.
Vendor(s): Knight-Ridder Information, Inc., Orbit Search Service (APILIT), STN International (APILIT), Telesystemes - Questel. *5385*

TECHNICAL LITERATURE ABSTRACTS: TRIBOLOGY.
American Petroleum Institute, Central Abstracting & Information Services, 275 Seventh Ave., New York, NY 10001-6708. TEL 212-366-4040. FAX 212-366-4298.
Vendor(s): Knight-Ridder Information, Inc., Orbit Search Service (APILIT), STN International (APILIT), Telesystemes - Questel. *1711*

TECHNICAL PHYSICS.
American Institute of Physics, One Physics Ellipse, College Park, MD 20740-3843. TEL 301-209-3000. *5573*

TECHNICAL PHYSICS LETTERS.
American Institute of Physics, One Physics Ellipse, College Park, MD 20740-3843. TEL 301-209-3000. *5573*

TECHNOLOGY ACCESS REPORT.
University R & D Opportunities, Inc., 8 Digital Dr., Ste. 250, Novato, CA 94949-5759. TEL 415-883-7600. FAX 415-883-6421.
Vendor(s): DataArkiv A.B., Knight-Ridder Information, Inc., NewsNet (RD38). *6666*

TECHNOLOGY ALERT.
Merton Allen Associates, InfoTeam Inc., Box 15640, Plantation, FL 33318-5640. TEL 954-473-9560. FAX 954-473-0544.
Vendor(s): Data-Star, Information Access Co., NewsNet (RD09). *6667*

TECHNOLOGY AND LEARNING.
Peter Li, Inc., 330 Progress Rd., Dayton, OH 45449. TEL 513-847-5900.
Vendor(s): Information Access Co., Knight-Ridder Information, Inc., University Microfilms International. *2408*

TECHNOLOGY MANAGEMENT ACTION.
Technology News Center, 6810 Butler Valley Rd., Korbel, CA 95550. TEL 707-668-4027. FAX 707-668-4055. *1296*

TECHNOLOGY REVIEW.
Massachusetts Institute of Technology, W59-200, Cambridge, MA 02139. TEL 617-253-8250.
Vendor(s): Knight-Ridder Information, Inc., University Microfilms International. *6290*

TECHNOLOGY STUDIES.
Walter de Gruyter und Co., Genthiner Str. 13, 10785 Berlin, Germany. TEL 49-30-26005-0. FAX 49-30-26005251. *6349*

TECHNOLOGY TRANSFER HIGHLIGHTS.
Argonne National Laboratory, Industrial Technology Development Center, 9700 S. Cass Ave., Bldg. 900, Argonne, IL 60439. TEL 708-252-6393. FAX 708-252-5230. *6668*

TECHNOLOGY TRANSFER WEEK.
Phillips Business Information, Inc., 1201 Seven Locks Rd., Potomac, MD 20854. TEL 301-424-3338. FAX 301-309-3847.
Vendor(s): Data-Star, Information Access Co., Knight-Ridder Information, Inc., NewsNet (DE17). *5049*

TECHNOLOGY WATCH.
Technology Watch, Inc., Box 2206, Springfield, VA 22152. *2030*

TEEN.
Petersen Publishing Co., 6420 Wilshire Blvd., Los Angeles, CA 90048. TEL 213-782-2000.
Vendor(s): Information Access Co., Knight-Ridder Information, Inc.. *1808*

TEIRESIAS.
Department of Classics, McGill University, 855 Sherbrooke St. W., Montreal, PQ H3A 2T7, Canada. TEL 514-392-5335. *1826*

TEKSTILEC.
Urednistvo Tekstilec, Snezniska 5, p.p. 311, 61000 Ljubljana, Slovenia. TEL 61 224-417.
Vendor(s): Knight-Ridder Information, Inc.. *6685*

TELCO BUSINESS REPORT.
Capitol Publications Inc., Telecom Publishing Group, 1101 King St., Ste. 444, Box 1455, Alexandria, VA 22313-2055. TEL 800-327-7205. FAX 703-739-6490.
Vendor(s): Information Access Co., Knight-Ridder Information, Inc., NewsNet (TE49). *1950*

TELCO COMPETITION REPORT.
Business Research Publications, Inc., 1333 H St., N.W., Ste. 200-W., Washington, DC 20005. FAX 202-842-3023.
Vendor(s): Information Access Co., NewsNet (TE62). *1925*

TELE-SERVICE NEWS.
Worldwide Videotex, Box 3273, Boynton Beach, FL 33424-3273. TEL 407-738-2276.
Vendor(s): Data-Star, Information Access Co., Knight-Ridder Information, Inc., NewsNet (TE21). *1950*

TELECOM ADVERTISING REPORT.
SIMBA Information Inc. 11 Riverbend Dr. S., Box 4234, Stamford, CT 06907-0234. TEL 203-358-9900. FAX 203-358-5824.
Vendor(s): Information Access Co. *46*

TELECOM & NETWORK SECURITY REVIEW.
Pasha Publications Inc., 1616 N. Ft. Myer Dr., Ste. 1000, Arlington, VA 22209-3107. TEL 703-528-1244. FAX 703-528-1253.
Vendor(s): Information Access Co.. *1950*

TELECOM CALENDAR.
Information Gatekeepers, Inc., 214 Harvard Ave., Boston, MA 02134. TEL 617-232-3111. FAX 617-734-8562.
Vendor(s): NewsNet (TE65). *1916*

TELECOM DATA NETWORKS.
Capitol Publications Inc., Telecom Publishing Group, 1101 King St., Ste. 444, Box 1455, Alexandria, VA 22313-2055. TEL 703-739-6490. FAX 703-739-6490.
Vendor(s): Data-Star, Knight-Ridder Information, Inc., NewsNet (TE94). *1916*

TELECOM MARKETS.
Financial Times Telecoms & Media Publishing Maple House, 149 Tottenham Court Rd., London W1P 9LL, England. TEL 44-171-896-2234. FAX 44-171-896-2256.
Vendor(s): Data-Star, Information Access Co., Lexis-Nexis. *1532*

TELECOMEUROPA'S DEVELOPING WORLD TELECOMMUNICATIONS.
Telecomeuropa News Bureau Publications, 3 Princes Bldgs., George St., Bath, Avon BA1 2ED, England. TEL 44-1225-445283. FAX 44-1225-445283. *1917*

TELECOMEUROPA'S INTERACTIVE VIDEO NEWSLETTER.
Telecomeuropa News Bureau Publications, 3 Princes Bldgs., George St., Bath, Avon BA1 2ED, England. TEL 44-1225-445282. FAX 44-1225-445283. *1978*

TELECOMEUROPA'S INTERNATIONAL REGULATORY UPDATE.
Telecomeuropa News Bureau Publications, 3 Princes Bldgs., George St., Bath, Avon BA1 2ED, England. TEL 44-1225-445282. FAX 44-1225-445283. *1917*

TELECOMEUROPA'S MESSAGING NEWSLETTER.
Telecomeuropa News Bureau Publications, 3 Princes Bldgs., George St., Bath, Avon BA1 2ED, England. TEL 44-1225-445282. FAX 44-1225-445283. *1930*

TELECOMEUROPA'S MOBILE PHONE MONITOR.
Telecomeuropa News Bureau Publications, 3 Princes Bldgs., George St., Bath, Avon BA1 2ED, England. TEL 44-1225-445282. FAX 44-1225-445283. *1951*

TELECOMEUROPA'S SATELLITE COMMUNICATIONS NEWSLETTER.
Telecomeuropa News Bureau Publications, 3 Princes Bldgs., George St., Bath, Avon BA1 2ED, England. TEL 44-1225-445282. FAX 44-1225-445283. *1917*

TELECOMEUROPA'S TELECOMS STANDARDS MONITOR.
Telecomeuropa News Bureau Publications, 3 Princes Bldgs., George St., Bath, Avon BA1 2ED, England. TEL 44-1225-445282. FAX 44-1225-445283. *1917*

TELECOMEUROPA'S TELECOMS TARIFFS INNOVATION.
Telecomeuropa News Bureau Publications, 3 Princes Bldgs., George St., Bath, Avon BA1 2ED, England. TEL 44-1225-445282. FAX 44-1225-445283. *1917*

TELECOMMUNICATIONS (NORTH AMERICAN EDITION).
Horizon House Publications, Inc., 685 Canton St., Norwood, MA 02062. TEL 617-769-9750. FAX 617-762-9230.
Vendor(s): Information Access Co., University Microfilms International. *1917*

TELECOMMUNICATIONS ALERT.
C C M I, 11300 Rockville Pike, Ste. 1100, Rockville, MD 20852-3030. TEL 301-816-8945. FAX 301-816-8945.
Vendor(s): Information Access Co., NewsNet (TE75). *1925*

TELECOMMUNICATIONS AMERICAS.
Portland House, Stag Pl., London SW1E 5XT, England. TEL 44-171-957-0030. FAX 44-171-957-0031.
Vendor(s): University Microfilms International. *1951*

TELECOMMUNICATIONS INTERNATIONAL.
Portland House, Stag Pl., London SW1E 5XT, England. TEL 071-957-0030. FAX 071-957-0031. Vendor(s): University Microfilms International. *1951*

TELECOMMUNICATIONS REPORTS.
Business Research Publications, Inc., 1333 H St., N.W., Ste. 200-W., Washington, DC 20005. FAX 202-842-3023. Vendor(s): Information Access Co., NewsNet (TE11). *1918*

TELECOMMUNICATIONS REPORTS INTERNATIONAL.
Business Research Publications, Inc., 1333 H St., N.W., Ste.200-W., Washington, DC 20005. FAX 202-842-3023. Vendor(s): Information Access Co., NewsNet (TE14). *1918*

TELECOMMUTING REVIEW.
Gil Gordon Associates, 10 Donner Ct., Monmouth Junction, NJ 08852. TEL 908-329-2266. Vendor(s): Information Access Co. *1512*

TELECONNECT.
Gerald A. Friesen, Inc., 12 W. 21st St., New York, NY 10010. TEL 212-691-8215. Vendor(s): Information Access Co. *1951*

TELEFAXBUCH DER DEUTSCHEN TELEKOM AG.
Deutsche Telekom Medien GmbH, Wiesenhuettenstr. 18, 60329 Frankfurt a.M., Germany. TEL 069-2682-0. FAX 069-26821101. *1933*

TELEMARKETING.
Technology Marketing Corporation, One Technology Plaza, Norwalk, CT 06854. TEL 203-852-6800. FAX 203-853-2845. Vendor(s): Information Access Co. *1918*

TELEPHONE I P NEWS.
Worldwide Videotex, Box 3273, Boynton Beach, FL 33424-3273. TEL 407-738-2276. Vendor(s): Information Access Co. *1918*

TELEPHONE INDUSTRY DIRECTORY.
Phillips Business Information, Inc., 1201 Seven Locks Rd., Potomac, MD 20854. TEL 301-424-3338. FAX 301-309-3847. Vendor(s): NewsNet (TE83E). *1642*

TELEPHONY.
Telephony Publishing One I B M Plaza, Chicago, IL 60611. TEL 312-595-1080. Vendor(s): Information Access Co., University Microfilms International. *1952*

TELESIS (OTTAWA).
Bell-Northern Research Ltd., 3500 Carling Ave., Ottawa, ON K1Y 4H7, Canada. TEL 613-765-2520. FAX 613-763-2008. Vendor(s): University Microfilms International. *1952*

TELEVISION AND VIDEO: THE INTERNATIONAL MARKET.
Euromonitor, 60-61 Britton St., London EC1M 5NA, England. TEL 44-171-251-8024. FAX 44-171-608-3149. Vendor(s): Data-Star, Knight-Ridder Information, Inc. *2534*

TELEVISION DIGEST WITH CONSUMER ELECTRONICS.
Warren Publishing, Inc., 2115 Ward Ct., N.W., Washington, DC 20037. TEL 202-872-9200. FAX 202-293-3435. Vendor(s): Information Access Co., NewsNet (PB01). *1973*

TELEVISION NEWS INDEX AND ABSTRACTS.
Vanderbilt University, Vanderbilt Television News Archive, 110 21st Ave. S., Ste. 704, Nashville, TN 37240-0007. TEL 615-322-2927. FAX 615-343-8250. *1925*

TEMPLE LAW REVIEW.
Temple University School of Law, Philadelphia, PA 19122. TEL 215-204-4528. Vendor(s): West Services, Inc. *3855*

THE TEMPTATION OF SAINT ANTHONY.
Martin Bormann's Cranial Splints, Box 8166, Philadelphia, PA 19101-8166. TEL 215-627-9846. *4276*

TENNESSEE BAR JOURNAL.
Tennessee Bar Association, c/o Mary M. Tucker, 3622 West End Ave., Nashville, TN 37205-2403. Vendor(s): West Services, Inc. *3855*

TENNESSEE BUSINESS DIRECTORY.
American Business Directories 5711 S. 86th Circle, Box 27347, Omaha, NE 68127. TEL 402-593-4600. FAX 402-331-5481. *1642*

TENNESSEE LAW REVIEW.
Tennessee Law Review Association, Inc., College Law - Dunyard Hall, 915 Volunteer Blvd., Knoxville, TN 37996-4070. TEL 423-974-4464. Vendor(s): West Services, Inc. *3856*

TERATOGENESIS, CARCINOGENESIS, AND MUTAGENESIS.
John Wiley & Sons, Inc., Journals, 605 Third Ave., New York, NY 10158. TEL 212-850-6645. FAX 212-850-6021. *4536*

TERATOLOGY.
John Wiley & Sons, Inc. Journals, 605 Third Ave., New York, NY 10158. TEL 212-850-6645. FAX 212-850-6021. *610*

TERRY FAMILY HISTORIAN.
c/o Robert M. Terry, Ed., 1518 Skyline Cir., Sapulpa, OK 74066. *3103*

TETRAHEDRON ALERT.
Elsevier Science Ltd., Pergamon, P.O. Box 800, Kidlington, Oxford OX5 1DX, England. TEL 44-1865-843000. FAX 44-1865-843100. Available only online. *1594*

TEXAS BANKING.
912 Baltimore, Ste. 900, Kansas City, MO 64105. TEL 512-472-8388. FAX 512-473-2560. Vendor(s): University Microfilms International. *1124*

TEXAS BUSINESS DIRECTORY.
American Business Directories 5711 S. 86th Circle, Box 27347, Omaha, NE 68127. TEL 402-593-4600. FAX 402-331-5481. *1643*

TEXAS BUSINESS REVIEW.
University of Texas at Austin, Bureau of Business Research, Box 7459, Austin, TX 78713. TEL 512-471-1616. FAX 512-471-1063. Vendor(s): Information Access Co. *964*

TEXAS HEART INSTITUTE JOURNAL.
Texas Heart Institute, Publications & Communications, MC 1-194, Box 20345, Houston, TX 77225-0345. TEL 713-794-6630. FAX 713-791-3714. *4610*

TEXAS INDUSTRIAL EXPANSION.
University of Texas at Austin, Bureau of Business Research, Box 7459, Austin, TX 78713. TEL 512-471-1616. FAX 512-471-1063. *1532*

TEXAS JOURNAL OF WOMEN AND THE LAW.
727 E. 26th St., Austin, TX 78705. TEL 512-471-3227. FAX 512-475-6741. Vendor(s): West Services, Inc. *3856*

TEXAS LABOR MARKET REVIEW.
Texas Workforce Commission, Economic Research and Analysis Department 15th and Congress, Rm. 252T, Austin, TX 78778. TEL 512-463-2841. FAX 512-475-1241. *1396*

TEXAS LAW REVIEW.
University of Texas at Austin, School of Law Publications, Box 149084, Austin, TX 78714-9084. TEL 512-471-3164. FAX 512-471-6988. Vendor(s): Lexis-Nexis. *3856*

TEXAS LAWYER.
American Lawyer Media, L.P. (New York), 600 Third Ave., 3rd Fl., New York, NY 10016. TEL 212-973-2800. FAX 214-741-2325. Vendor(s): Lexis-Nexis. *3856*

TEXAS MONTHLY.
Texas Monthly, Inc., Box 1569, Austin, TX 78767. TEL 512-320-6900. FAX 512-476-9007. Vendor(s): University Microfilms International. *3240*

TEXAS ON-SITE INSIGHTS.
Texas Water Resources Institute, c/o Texas A & M Univ., College Station, TX 77343-2118. TEL 409-845-8571. FAX 409-845-8554. *6975*

TEXAS REGISTER.
Secretary of State, Texas Register Division, Box 13824, TX 78711-3824. TEL 512-463-5561. FAX 512-463-5569. *5924*

TEXAS TECH LAW REVIEW.
Texas Tech University, School of Law, Lubbock, TX 79409-0004. TEL 806-742-3789. FAX 806-742-1629. Vendor(s): West Services, Inc. *3857*

TEXAS TRANSPORTATION RESEARCHER.
Texas Transportation Institute, Texas A & M Univ. System, College Station, TX 77843-3135. TEL 409-845-1734. FAX 409-845-7575. Vendor(s): Knight-Ridder Information, Inc. (File no.63). *6728*

TEXAS WATER RESOURCES.
Texas Water Resources Institute, c/c Texas A & M University, College Station, TX 77843-2118. TEL 409-845-8571. FAX 409-845-8554. *6975*

TEXAS WATER RESOURCES INSTITUTE. TECHNICAL REPORT.
Texas Water Resources Institute, c/o Texas A & M University, College Station, TX 77843-2118. TEL 409-845-8571. FAX 409-845-8554. *6975*

DIE TEXTIL-INDUSTRIE UND IHRE HELFER.
Industrieschau-Verlagsgesellschaft mbH, Postfach 100262, 64202 Darmstadt, Germany. TEL 49-6151-3892-0. FAX 49-6151-33164. *6686*

TEXTILE AND FABRIC WASHING PRODUCTS: THE INTERNATIONAL MARKET.
Euromonitor, 60-61 Britton St., London EC1M 5QU, England. TEL 44-171-251-8024. FAX 44-171-608-3149. Vendor(s): Data-Star, Knight-Ridder Information, Inc. *1829*

TEXTILE RENTAL.
Textile Rental Services Association of America, Box 1283, Hallandale, FL 33008 TEL 954-457-7555. FAX 954-457-3890. *1829*

TEXTILE TECHNOLOGY DIGEST.
Institute of Textile Technology, 2551 Ivy Rd, Charlottesville, VA 22903. TEL 804-296-5511. FAX 804-977-5400. Vendor(s): Knight-Ridder Information, Inc. (File no.119). *6690*

TEXTILE WORLD.
Intertec Publishing Corp., Textile Publications, P.O. Box 12901, Overland Park, KS 66282-2901. Vendor(s): Information Access Co., University Microfilms International. *6688*

THAI ABSTRACTS, SERIES A. SCIENCE AND TECHNOLOGY.
Thailand Institute of Scientific and Technological Research, 196 Phahonyothin Rd., Chatuchak, Bangkok 10900, Thailand. TEL 579-8594. FAX 662-579-8594. *6304*

THAT'S MY BABY.
That's My Baby, Inc., Box 1156, Lake Oswego, OR 97035. TEL 503-620-9132. FAX 503-620-3800. *1779*

THEATRE JOURNAL (BALTIMORE).
Johns Hopkins University Press, Journals Publishing Division, 2715 N. Charles St., Baltimore, MD 21218. TEL 410-516-6987. FAX 410-516-6968. Vendor(s): Information Access Co. *6706*

THEATRE RESEARCH INTERNATIONAL.
Oxford University Press, Oxford Journals, Walton St., Oxford OX2 6DP, England. TEL 44-1865-267907. FAX 44-1865-267773. Vendor(s): Information Access Co. *6706*

THEATRE TOPICS.
Johns Hopkins University Press, Journals Publishing Division, 2715 N. Charles St., Baltimore, MD 21218. TEL 410-516-6987. FAX 410-516-6968. *6706*

Online

THEOLOGICAL STUDIES.
Theological Studies, Inc., Georgetown University, 37th and O Sts., N.W., Washington, DC 20057. TEL 202-338-0754. FAX 202-687-7679. Vendor(s): Information Access Co., University Microfilms International. *6098*

THEOLOGY.
Society for Promoting Christian Knowledge, Holy Trinity Church, Marylebone Rd., London NW1 4DU, England. TEL 44-171-387-5282. FAX 44-171-388-2352. Vendor(s): Knight-Ridder Information, Inc.. *6099*

THEORETICAL CHEMICAL ENGINEERING.
The Royal Society of Chemistry, Thomas Graham House, Science Park, Milton Rd., Cambridge CB4 4WF, England. TEL 44-1223-420066. FAX 44-1223-423429. Vendor(s): Data-Star, Knight-Ridder Information, Inc., Orbit Search Service. *2630*

THIRD WORLD QUARTERLY.
Carfax Publishing Co., P.O. Box 25, Abingdon, Oxon. OX14 3UE, England. TEL 44-1235-401000. FAX 44-1235-401550. *1315*

THOMAS REGISTER OF AMERICAN MANUFACTURERS AND THOMAS REGISTER CATALOG FILE.
Thomas Publishing Company, Five Penn Plaza, 9th Fl., New York, NY 10001. TEL 212-290-7277. FAX 212-290-7365. Vendor(s): Knight-Ridder Information, Inc. (File no.535). *1488*

THORA-ZINE MAGAZINE.
Brent Comiskey, Ed. & Pub., Box 4930, Austin, TX 78765. TEL 512-453-6747. *5202*

THORAX.
B M J Publishing Group, B.M.A. House, Tavistock Sq., London WC1H 9JR, England. TEL 44-171-383-6270. FAX 44-171-383-6402. Vendor(s): Ovid Technologies, Inc.. *4537*

THURGOOD MARSHALL LAW REVIEW.
Texas Southern University, Thurgood Marshall School of Law, 3100 Cleburne, Houston, TX 77004. TEL 713-527-7246. FAX 713-639-1049. Vendor(s): West Services, Inc.. *3857*

TIDINGS (CAMDEN).
National Marine Representatives Association, Box 660, 2742 Old Natchez Trace Trail, Camden, TN 38320-0660. TEL 901-584-0203. FAX 901-584-0420. *1170*

TIDSSKRIFTINDEKS FOR SKOLEBIBLIOTEKER.
Dansk BiblioteksCenter as, Tempovej 7-11, DK-2750 Ballerup, Denmark. TEL 45-44-867777. FAX 45-44-867892. *548*

TIKKUN MAGAZINE.
Institute for Labor & Mental Health, 5100 Leona St., Oakland, CA 94619. TEL 510-482-0805. FAX 510-482-3379. Vendor(s): Information Access Co.. *2911*

TIME.
Time Inc. Time & Life Bldg., Rockefeller Center, 1271 Ave. of the Americas, New York, NY 10020-1393. TEL 212-522-1212. FAX 212-522-0003. Vendor(s): Dow Jones News Retrieval, Information Access Co., Lexis-Nexis, University Microfilms International, VU/TEXT Information Services, Inc.. *3240*

TIME PILOT.
New Legends Group, 203 W. Holly St., Ste. 325, Bellingham, WA 98225-4329. TEL 206-733-7306. *4333*

TIMES (BETHLEHEM).
Council on Tall Buildings and Urban Habitat, Lehigh University, 13 E. Packer Ave., Bethlehem, PA 18015. TEL 610-758-3515. FAX 610-758-4522. Vendor(s): University Microfilms International. *3596*

TIMES: IN HARNESS.
Times: standard inc., 8125 Jonestown Rd., Harrisburg, PA 17112. TEL 717-469-2000. FAX 717-469-2005. *6552*

TIMES LAW REPORTS.
T & T Clark Ltd., 59 George St., Edinburgh EH2 2LQ, Scotland. TEL 44-131-225-4703. FAX 44-131-220-4260. Vendor(s): Context Ltd.. *3858*

TIN INTERNATIONAL.
M I I D A Ltd., P.O. Box 2137, London NW10 6TN, England. TEL 0181-961-7407. FAX 0181-961-7487. Vendor(s): Knight-Ridder Information, Inc.. *4977*

TIRE BUSINESS.
Crain Communications Inc. (Akron), 1725 Merriman Rd., Ste. 300, Akron, OH 44313-5251. TEL 330-836-9180. FAX 330-836-1005. Vendor(s): Information Access Co.. *6219*

TOBACCO INDUSTRY LITIGATION REPORTER.
Andrews Publications, 1646 West Chester Pike, Box 1000, Westtown, PA 19395. TEL 610-399-6600. FAX 610-399-6610. Vendor(s): NewsNet. *3858*

TODAY'S TRAVELER.
Bluestone Group, Inc., 68 E. Wacker Pl., Ste. 800, Chicago, IL 60601. TEL 312-853-4775. FAX 312-782-7367. *6916*

TOHKAI SEIKEI GEKA GAISHO KENKYU KAISHI.
Tohkai Seikei Geka Gaisho Kenkyukai, Gifu Kenritsu Tajimi Byoin Seikei Geka, 5-161, Maebatacho, Tajimi-shi, Gifu-ken 507, Japan. TEL 0572-22-5311. FAX 0572-25-1246. *4792*

TOHKAI SEKITSUI GEKA.
Tohkai Sekitsui Geka Konwakai, Gifu Kenritsu Tajimi Byoin, 5-161, Maebbatacho, Tajimi-shi, Gifuken 507, Japan. TEL 0572-22-5311. FAX 0572-25-1246. *4792*

TOHO UNIVERSITY MEDICAL SOCIETY. JOURNAL.
Toho University Medical Society, c/o Library, School of Medicine, 5-21-16 Omori Nishi, Ota-ku, Tokyo 143, Japan. FAX 764-1642. *4538*

TOILETRIES, FRAGRANCES AND SKIN CARE: THE ROSE SHEET.
F-D-C Reports, Inc., 5550 Friendship Blvd., Ste. 1, Chevy Chase, MD 20815. FAX 301-664-7238. Vendor(s): Data-Star (FDCR), Knight-Ridder Information, Inc. (File no.187), Lexis-Nexis, Ovid Technologies, Inc. (FDCR). *498*

TOKELAU NATIONAL BIBLIOGRAPHY.
National Library of New Zealand, P.O. Box 1467, Wellington, New Zealand. TEL 64-4-4743067. FAX 64-4-4743124. *548*

TOKYO FINANCIAL REVIEW.
Bank of Tokyo, Ltd., 3-26 Kanda Nishikicho, Chiyoda-ku, Toyko 101, Japan. *1124*

TOLEDO BUSINESS JOURNAL.
Telex Communications, Inc., 27 Broadway St., Toledo, OH 43602-1701. TEL 419-244-8200. FAX 419-244-5773. Vendor(s): University Microfilms International. *965*

TOOLING & PRODUCTION.
Huebcore Communications, Inc., 29100 Aurora Rd., Ste. 200, Solon, OH 44139. TEL 216-248-1125. FAX 612-686-0214. Vendor(s): Information Access Co., Knight-Ridder Information, Inc.. *4347*

TORT & INSURANCE LAW JOURNAL.
American Bar Association, Tort and Insurance Practice Section, 750 N. Lake Shore Dr., Chicago, IL 60611. TEL 312-988-5000. Vendor(s): Lexis-Nexis, West Services, Inc.. *3888*

TOTAL HEALTH.
Total Health Communications, Inc., 165 N. 100 St. E., Ste. 2, Saint George, UT 84770-2505. TEL 801-673-1789. FAX 801-634-9336. Vendor(s): Information Access Co., University Microfilms International. *5242*

TOTAL QUALITY MANAGEMENT.
Carfax Publishing Co., P.O. Box 25, Abingdon, Oxon. OX14 3UE, England. TEL 44-1235-401000. FAX 44-1235-401550. *1449*

TOUR & TRAVEL NEWS - T T G NORTH AMERICA.
Miller Freeman, Inc. (New York) One Penn Plaza, New York, NY 10119. TEL 212-714-1300. FAX 212-714-1313. Vendor(s): Data-Star, Information Access Co., Knight-Ridder Information, Inc., NewsNet (TR09). *6916*

TOWN AND COUNTRY.
Hearst Magazines, Town and Country, 1700 Broadway, New York, NY 10019. TEL 212-903-5000. FAX 212-765-8308. Vendor(s): Information Access Co.. *3240*

TOXICOLOGY ABSTRACTS.
Cambridge Scientific Abstracts, 7200 Wisconsin Ave., 6th Fl., Bethesda, MD 20814. TEL 301-961-6750. FAX 301-961-6720. Vendor(s): Knight-Ridder Information, Inc. (File no.76/LIFE SCIENCES COLLECTION), STN International (LIFESCI). *5451*

TOXICOLOGY AND APPLIED PHARMACOLOGY.
Academic Press, Inc., Journal Division, 525 B St., Ste. 1900, San Diego, CA 92101-4495. TEL 619-230-1840. FAX 619-699-6800. *2849*

TOXICOLOGY LETTERS.
Elsevier Science Ireland Ltd., P.O. Box 85, Limerick, Ireland. TEL 353-61-471944. FAX 353-61-472144. *2849*

TOXICS LAW REPORTER.
The Bureau of National Affairs, Inc., 1231 25th St. N.W., Washington, DC 20037. TEL 202-452-4200. FAX 202-822-8092. Vendor(s): Human Resources Information Network (CDD, HDD). *2858*

TOYS AND GAMES: THE INTERNATIONAL MARKET.
Euromonitor, 60-61 Britton St., London EC1M 5NA, England. TEL 0171-251-8024. FAX 0171-608-3149. Vendor(s): Data-Star, Knight-Ridder Information, Inc.. *3302*

TRADE & INDUSTRY INDEX.
Information Access Company 362 Lakeside Dr., Foster City, CA 94404. TEL 415-378-5200. FAX 415-358-4759. Available only online. Vendor(s): Ovid Technologies, Inc. (TSAP), Knight-Ridder Information, Inc. (File no.148). *1032*

TRADEMARK REGISTER OF THE UNITED STATES.
Trademark Register, National Press Bldg., 1297, Washington, DC 20045. TEL 202-662-1233. FAX 202-347-4408. *5345*

TRADESCOPE.
Japan External Trade Organization, 2-5 Toranomon 2-chome, Minato-ku, Tokyo 104, Japan. TEL 03-3582-5521. FAX 03-3582-0504. *1644*

TRADING SYSTEMS TECHNOLOGY.
Waters Information Services, Inc., Box 2248, Binghamton, NY 13902-2248. TEL 607-770-9242. FAX 607-770-9435. Vendor(s): Data-Star, Information Access Co., Knight-Ridder Information, Inc., NewsNet (FI39). *1130*

TRAFFIC REPORT.
Department of Economic Development and Tourism, P.O. Box 6000, Fredericton, NB E3B 5H1, Canada. TEL 506-457-7340. *5936*

TRAFFIC WORLD.
Journal of Commerce, Inc. (Washington), 741 National Press Bldg., Washington, DC 20045. TEL 202-383-6140. FAX 202-737-3349. Vendor(s): Information Access Co.. *6729*

TRAILER BOATS.
Poole Publications, Inc., 20700 Belshaw Ave., Carson, CA 90746. TEL 310-537-6322. FAX 310-537-8735. Vendor(s): Information Access Co., University Microfilms International. *6541*

TRAILER LIFE.
A G I, 2575 Vista Del Mar, Ventura, CA 93001. TEL 805-667-4300. FAX 805-667-4213. Vendor(s): Information Access Co.. *6580*

TRAINING.
Lakewood Publications, Inc., 50 S. Ninth St., Minneapolis, MN 55402. TEL 612-333-0471. FAX 612-333-6526.
Vendor(s): Human Resources Information Network, Information Access Co., University Microfilms International. *1449*

TRAINING & DEVELOPMENT.
American Society for Training and Development, 1640 King St., Box 1443, Alexandria, VA 22313. TEL 703-683-8100. FAX 703-683-8103.
Vendor(s): Information Access Co. *1513*

TRAINING AND DEVELOPMENT ORGANIZATIONS DIRECTORY.
Gale Research Inc., 835 Penobscot Bldg., Detroit, MI 48226. TEL 313-961-2242. FAX 313-961-6083.
Vendor(s): Human Resources Information Network (TDOD). *1449*

TRAINS.
Kalmbach Publishing Co., 21027 Crossroads Cir., Waukesha, WI 53187. TEL 414-796-8776. FAX 414-796-0126.
Vendor(s): Information Access Co.. *6819*

TRANS.
Passim Inc., 109 W. 17th St., New York, NY 10011. *456*

TRANSGENIC RESEARCH.
Chapman & Hall, Journals Department 2-6 Boundary Row, London SE1 8HN, England. TEL 44-171-8650066. FAX 44-171-5229623. *750*

TRANSIT RESEARCH ABSTRACTS.
U.S. National Research Council, Transportation Research Board, 2101 Constitution Ave., N.W., Washington, DC 20418. TEL 202-334-3213. FAX 202-334-2519.
Vendor(s): Knight-Ridder Information, Inc. (File no.63). *6746*

TRANSITION METAL CHEMISTRY.
Chapman & Hall, Journals Department 2-6 Boundary Row, London SE1 8HN, England. TEL 44-171-8650066. FAX 44-171-5229623. *4978*

TRANSMISSION AND DISTRIBUTION.
Intertec Publishing Corp., 9800 Metcalf, Overland Park, KS 66212-2215. TEL 913-341-1300. FAX 913-967-1904.
Vendor(s): University Microfilms International. *2721*

TRANSPACIFIC.
Transpacific Media Inc., 23715 W. Malibu Rd., No.390, Malibu, CA 90265-5000. TEL 310-456-0790. FAX 310-456-3724.
Vendor(s): Information Access Co.. *2911*

TRANSPLANTATION PROCEEDINGS.
Appleton & Lange, Journal Division Box 120041, Stamford, CT 06912-0041. TEL 203-406-4500. *4922*

TRANSPLANTATION 2006.
R.G. Landes Company, Medical Intelligence Unit, Box 4858, Austin, TX 78765. TEL 512-863-7762. FAX 512-863-0081. *4922*

TRANSPORT EUROPE.
Europe Information Service, Rue de Geneve, 6, 1140 Brussels, Belgium. TEL 32-2-242-6020. FAX 32-2-242-9410.
Vendor(s): Information Access Co., Lexis-Nexis. *6730*

TRANSPORTATION & DISTRIBUTION.
Penton Publishing Co. 1100 Superior Ave., Cleveland, OH 44114-2543. TEL 216-696-7000. FAX 216-696-8765.
Vendor(s): Information Access Co., Knight-Ridder Information, Inc., University Microfilms International. *6731*

TRANSPORTATION JOURNAL.
American Society of Transportation and Logistics, Inc., 216 E. Church St., Lock Haven, PA 17745-2010. TEL 717-748-8515.
Vendor(s): Information Access Co., University Microfilms International. *6731*

TRANSPORTATION LAW JOURNAL.
University of Denver, College of Law, 7039 E. 18th Ave., Denver, CO 30220. TEL 303-871-6162. FAX 303-871-6165.
Vendor(s): West Services, Inc.. *3859*

TRAVAIL ET EMPLOI.
Documentation Francaise, 29 quai Voltaire, 75344 Paris Cedex 07, France TEL 40-15-70-00. FAX 40-15-72-30.
Vendor(s): Telesystemes - Questel. *1396*

TRAVEL AGENT.
Universal Media, Inc., 801 Second Ave., New York, NY 10017. TEL 212-370-5050. FAX 212-370-4491.
Vendor(s): Information Access Co.. *6919*

TRAVEL ALERT BULLETIN.
Nationwide Intelligence, Box 1922, Saginaw, MI 48605. TEL 517-752-6123. FAX 517-752-1605. *6919*

TRAVEL & LEISURE.
American Express Publishing Corp. (New York), 1120 Ave. of the Americas, New York, NY 10036. TEL 212-382-5600. FAX 212-768-1568. *6919*

TRAVEL & TOURISM ANALYST.
Corporate Intelligence or Retailing, 51 Doughty St., London WC1 N2LS, England. TEL 44-171-696-9006.
Vendor(s): Lexis-Nexis. *5919*

TRAVEL AND TOURISM: THE INTERNATIONAL MARKET.
Euromonitor, 60-6 Britton St., London EC1M 5NA, England. TEL 44-171-251-8024. FAX 44-171-608-3149.
Vendor(s): Data-Star, Knight-Ridder Information, Inc.. *6920*

TRAVEL BOOKS WORLDWIDE.
Travel Keys, Box 162266, Sacramento, CA 95816-2266. TEL 916-452-5200. *6920*

TRAVEL HOLIDAY.
Hachette Filipacchi Magazines, Inc., 1633 Broadway, New York, NY 100_9. TEL 212-767-6000.
Vendor(s): Information Access Co.. *6920*

TRAVEL MANAGEMENT DAILY.
Reed Travel Group, Part of the Reed Elsevier group 500 Plaza Dr., Secaucus, NJ 07096. TEL 201-902-1700. FAX 201-902-1967. *6920*

TRAVEL TRADE GAZETTE EUROPA.
Miller Freeman Technical Ltd. Miller Freeman House, 30 Calderwood St., London SE18 6QH, England. TEL 44-181-855-7777. FAX 44-181-316-3354.
Vendor(s): Information Access Co.. *6921*

TRAVEL TRADE GAZETTE U K & IRELAND.
Miller Freeman Technical Ltd. Miller Freeman House, 30 Calderwood St., London SE18 6QH, England. TEL 44-181-855-7777. FAX 44-181-316-3354.
Vendor(s): Information Access Co.. *6921*

TRAVEL WEEKLY.
Reed Travel Group, Part of the Reed Elsevier group 500 Plaza Dr., Secaucus, NJ 07096. TEL 201-902-2000. FAX 201-317-1755.
Vendor(s): Information Access Co.. *6921*

TRAX D J MUSIC GUIDE.
Trax Entertainment, 111 N. La Cienega Blvd., Beverly Hills, CA 90211-2206. TEL 310-659-7852. FAX 310-659-7855. *5202*

TREASURY MANAGER'S REPORT.
Phillips Business Information, Inc., 1201 Seven Locks Rd., Potomac, MD 20854. TEL 301-424-3338. FAX 301-309-3847.
Vendor(s): Information Access Co.. *1124*

TREE PHYSIOLOGY.
Heron Publishing, 202-3994 Shelbourne St., Victoria, BC V8N 3E2, Canada. TEL 604-721-9921. FAX 604-721-9924.
Vendor(s): Knight-Ridder Information, Inc.. *706*

TRI-CITY COMPUTING MAGAZINE.
A J A Consulting, 141 S. Lake Ave., Albany, NY 12208. TEL 518-446-1944. *1999*

TRIAL.
Association of Trial Lawyers of America, 1050 31st St., N.W., Washington, DC 20007. TEL 202-965-3500. FAX 202-965-0030.
Vendor(s): Information Access Co.. *3954*

TRIANGLE BUSINESS JOURNAL.
American City Business Journals, Inc., 3125 Poplarwood Ct., Ste. 304, Raleigh, NC 27604. TEL 919-878-0010. FAX 919-790-6885.
Vendor(s): Lexis-Nexis. *965*

TRIBUNA FARMACEUTICA.
Universidade Federal do Parana, Faculdade de Farmacie, Rua Coronel Dulcicio 638, Caixa Postal 888, 80000 Curitiba, Parana Brazil. FAX 041-2642243. *5445*

TRIBUNE DESFOSSES.
42 rue Notre Dame des Victoires, 75002 Paris, France. TEL 1-42-33-21-30. FAX 1-42-33-12-36. *965*

TRIQUARTERLY.
Northwestern University, 2020 Ridge Ave., Evanston, IL 60208-4302. TEL 847-491-3490. FAX 847-467-2096.
Vendor(s): Information Access Co., University Microfilms International. *4170*

TROPICAL DISEASES BULLETIN.
CAB International, Wallingford Oxon. OX10 8DE, England. TEL 44-1491-832111. FAX 44-1491-833508.
Vendor(s): DIMDI. *4575*

TROPICAL OIL SEEDS.
CAB International, Wallingford Oxon. OX10 8DE, England. TEL 44-1491-832111. FAX 44-1491-833508.
Vendor(s): DIMDI, European Space Agency, Knight-Ridder Information, Inc., STN International. *182*

TRUST LETTER.
American Bankers Association Trust and Private Banking Center, 1120 Connecticut Ave., N.W., Washington, DC 20036. TEL 202-663-5087. FAX 202-663-7543.
Vendor(s) University Microfilms International. *1124*

TRUSTEE.
American Hospital Publishing, Inc. 737 N. Michigan Ave., Ste. 700, Chicago, IL 60611. TEL 312-440-6800. FAX 312-951-8491.
Vendor(s): University Microfilms International. *3556*

TRUSTS AND ESTATES.
Intertec Publishing Corp. (Atlanta), 6151 Powers Ferry Rd., N.W., Atlanta, GA 30339-2941. TEL 770-955-2500. FAX 770-955-0400.
Vendor(s): Information Access Co., University Microfilms International. *1356*

TRUTH SEEKER.
Truth Seeker Co., Inc., 16935 W. Bernardo Dr., Ste. 103, San Diego, CA 92117. TEL 619-676-0430. FAX 619-676-0433. *5503*

TUFTS UNIVERSITY DIET AND NUTRITION LETTER.
53 Park Pl., 8th Fl., New York, NY 10007. TEL 212-608-6515. FAX 212-308-5317.
Vendor(s): Information Access Co., University Microfilms International. *5242*

TUIJIN JISHU.
Zhongguo Hangtian Gongye Zongongsi, Di 3 Yanjiuyuan 31 Yanjiusho, P.O. Box 7208-26, Beijing 100074, People's Republic of China. TEL 86-10-6837-6141. FAX 86-10-6837-4052. *79*

TULANE ENVIRONMENTAL LAW JOURNAL.
Tulane University, School of Law 6329 Freret St., Joseph Merrick Jones Hall, New Orleans, LA 70118. TEL 504-865-5939. FAX 504-855-6748.
Vendor(s): Lexis-Nexis, West Services, Inc.. *2822*

TULANE LAW REVIEW.
Tulane University, School of Law, 6329 Freret St., New Orleans, LA 70118. TEL 504-865-5939. FAX 504-865-6748.
Vendor(s): Lexis-Nexis, West Services, Inc.. *3859*

TULANE MARITIME LAW JOURNAL.
Tulane University, School of Law, 6329 Freret St., New Orleans, LA 70118. TEL 504-865-5939. FAX 504-865-6748.
Vendor(s): Lexis-Nexis, West Services, Inc.. *3958*

TULSA LAW JOURNAL.
University of Tulsa, College of Law, 3120 E. Fourth Pl., Tulsa, OK 74104. TEL 918-631-2408. FAX 918-631-3556.
Vendor(s): West Services, Inc.. *3859*

TUMOR TARGETING.
Chapman & Hall, Journals Department 2-6 Boundary Row, London SE1 8HN, England. TEL 44-171-8650066. FAX 44-171-5229623. *4765*

TURING INSTITUTE ABSTRACTS IN ARTIFICIAL INTELLIGENCE.
Springer-Verlag London Ltd., Sweetapple House, Catteshall Rd., Godalming, Surrey GU7 3DJ, England. TEL 44-1483-418800. FAX 44-1483-415144.
Vendor(s): Data-Star. *2004*

TUTTODOLCE.
Essepiesse s.r.l., Via G. Galilei 14, 20124 Milan, Italy. FAX 39-2-654119. *3002*

TWENTIETH CENTURY LITERATURE.
Hofstra University, 203 Student Center, Hempstead, NY 11550. TEL 516-463-5460.
Vendor(s): Information Access Co., University Microfilms International. *4280*

TWILIGHT WORLD.
P.O. Box 67, 3500 AB Utrecht, Netherlands. TEL 31-30-7891429.
Available only online. *4333*

TWIN CITIES READER.
City Media, Inc., 821 Marquette Ave., Ste. 2000, Minneapolis, MN 55402. FAX 612-321-7333.
Vendor(s): CompuServe, Inc., Data-Star, Dow Jones News Retrieval, Knight-Ridder Information, Inc., Lexis-Nexis. *3240*

U C A R QUARTERLY.
University Corporation for Atmospheric Research, Box 3000, Boulder, CO 80307. TEL 303-497-8611. FAX 303-497-8610. *5008*

U C DAVIS LAW REVIEW.
University of California at Davis, School of Law, Martin Luther King, Jr. Hall, Davis, CA 95616. TEL 916-752-2551. FAX 916-752-4704.
Vendor(s): Lexis-Nexis, West Services, Inc.. *3859*

U C L A LAW REVIEW.
University of California at Los Angeles, School of Law, Attn: Sherry Taylor, Box 951476, CA 90095-1476. TEL 213-825-4929. FAX 310-206-6489.
Vendor(s): Lexis-Nexis. *3860*

U K GAS REPORT.
Financial Times Energy Publishing Maple House, 149 Tottenham Court Rd., London W1P 9LL, England. TEL 0171-896-2241. FAX 0171-896-2275.
Vendor(s): Data-Star, Knight-Ridder Information, Inc., Lexis-Nexis. *2559*

U K INDUSTRIAL TRADE NAMES.
Kompass Part of the Reed Elsevier group, Windsor Ct., E. Grinstead House, E. Grinstead, W. Sussex RH19 1XD, England. TEL 01342-326972. FAX 01342-335992.
Vendor(s): Reed Information Services Ltd.. *1645*

U K VENTURE CAPITAL JOURNAL.
Venture Capital The Quadrangle, 180 Wardour, London W1A 4YG, England. TEL 44-171-434-0411. FAX 44-171-434-3918.
Vendor(s): Information Access Co.. *1356*

U N CHRONICLE.
United Nations Publications, Room DC2-853, New York, NY 10017. TEL 212-963-8302. FAX 212-963-3489.
Vendor(s): Information Access Co., University Microfilms International. *5774*

U P NEWSLETTER.
University of the Philippines, Information Office, 1st Fl. Mezzanine, Quezon Hall, U.P. Diliman, Quezon City, Philippines. FAX 96-15-72. *1889*

U S A GYMNASTICS.
U S A Gymnastics, 201 S. Capitol Ave., Ste. 300, Pan American Plaza, Indianapolis, IN 46225. TEL 317-237-5050. FAX 317-237-5069. *6490*

U S A TODAY.
Society for the Advancement of Education, 99 W. Hawthorne Ave., Ste. 518, Valley Stream, NY 11580-6101. TEL 516-568-9191.
Vendor(s): Information Access Co., Knight-Ridder Information, Inc., Lexis-Nexis, University Microfilms International, VU/TEXT Information Services, Inc.. *2378*

U S A TODAY INDEX.
U M I Company 300 N. Zeeb Rd., Ann Arbor, MI 48106-1346. TEL 313-761-4700. FAX 800-864-0019. *3716*

U S BANKER.
Faulkner & Gray, Inc. (New York), 11 Penn Plaza, 17th Fl., New York, NY 10001. TEL 212-967-7000. FAX 212-967-7155.
Vendor(s): Information Access Co., Lexis-Nexis, University Microfilms International. *1356*

U S CATHOLIC.
Claretian Publications, 205 W. Monroe St., Chicago, IL 60606. TEL 312-236-7782. FAX 312-236-8207.
Vendor(s): Information Access Co.. *6199*

U S NEWS & WORLD REPORT.
U S News & World Report Inc., 1290 Ave. of the Americas, Ste. 600, New York, NY 10104. TEL 212-830-1500.
Vendor(s): Information Access Co., Knight-Ridder Information, Inc., Lexis-Nexis, University Microfilms International. *3240*

U S OIL WEEK.
Capitol Publications Inc., 1101 King St., Ste. 444, Alexandria, VA 22314. TEL 703-683-4100. FAX 703-739-6517.
Vendor(s): Information Access Co., Knight-Ridder Information, Inc., NewsNet (EY55). *5378*

U S PHARMACIST.
Jobson Publishing, Inc., 100 Ave. of the Americas, New York, NY 10013-1678. TEL 212-274-7000. FAX 212-431-0500. *5446*

U S RAIL NEWS.
Business Publishers, Inc., 951 Pershing Dr., Silver Spring, MD 20910-4464. TEL 301-587-6300. FAX 301-585-9075.
Vendor(s): Information Access Co., NewsNet (TS11). *6819*

ULAM QUARTERLY.
Gordon and Breach Science Publishers, c/o International Publishers Distributor, P.O. Box 3054, Langhorne, PA 19047-3054. TEL 215-750-2642. FAX 215-750-6343. *4401*

ULRICH'S INTERNATIONAL PERIODICALS DIRECTORY.
R.R. Bowker, A Division of Reed Elsevier Inc., 121 Chanlon Rd., New Providence, NJ 07974. TEL 908-665-2847. FAX 908-771-7725.
Vendor(s): Knight-Ridder Information, Inc. (File no.480), Ovid Technologies, Inc. (ULRI). *549*

ULRICH'S UPDATE.
R.R. Bowker, A Division of Reed Elsevier Inc., 121 Chanlon Rd., New Providence, NJ 07974. TEL 908-665-2847. FAX 908-771-7725.
Vendor(s): Knight-Ridder Information, Inc. (File no.480), Ovid Technologies, Inc. (ULRI). *549*

UNDERGROUND.
Scarborough College Student Press, 1265 Military Trail, West Hill, Ont. M1C 1A4, Canada. TEL 416-978-2011. *4170*

UNIGRAM.X.
G-2 Computer Intelligence Inc., 3 Maple Place, P.O. Box 7, Glen Head, NY 11545-0007. TEL 516-759-7025. FAX 516-759-7028. *2117*

UNION LABOR REPORT.
The Bureau of National Affairs, Inc., 1231 25th St., N.W., Washington, DC 20037. TEL 202-452-4200. FAX 202-822-8092.
Vendor(s): Human Resources Information Network. *1397*

UNION LABOR REPORT WEEKLY NEWSLETTER.
The Bureau of National Affairs, Inc., 1231 25th St., N.W., Washington, DC 20037. TEL 202-452-4200. FAX 202-822-8092.
Vendor(s): Human Resources Information Network (CDD, HDD). *1397*

UNION LIST OF SERIALS IN ISRAEL LIBRARIES.
Jewish National and University Library, P.O.Box 34165, Jerusalem 91341, Israel. TEL 972-2-585028. FAX 972-511771.
Available only online. *549*

UNIONE MATEMATICA ITALIANA. NOTIZIARIO.
Unione Matematica Italiana, Piazza Porta San Donato 5, 40126 Bologna, Italy. TEL 39-51-243190. FAX 39-51-243190. *4402*

UNITAS.
Union Bank of Finland, FIN-00020 UBF, Finland. FAX 358-0-6572898.
Vendor(s): University Microfilms International. *1244*

UNITED NATIONS. NATIONAL ACCOUNTS STATISTICS. MAIN AGGREGATES AND DETAILED TABLES.
United Nations Publications, Room DC2-0853, New York, NY 10017. TEL 212-963-8302. FAX 212-963-3489. *1034*

U.S. BUREAU OF LABOR STATISTICS. C P I DETAILED REPORT.
U.S. Bureau of Labor Statistics, 2 Massachusetts Ave., N.E., Washington, DC 20212. TEL 202-655-4000. *1244*

U.S. BUREAU OF LABOR STATISTICS. NATIONAL OFFICE NEWS RELEASES.
U.S. Bureau of Labor Statistics, 2 Massachusetts Ave., N.E., Washington, DC 20212. TEL 202-655-4000. *1244*

U.S. BUREAU OF MINES. ANNUAL RESEARCH REPORT.
U.S. Bureau of Mines, Office of Public Information, 810 Seventh St., N.W., MS-1040, Washington, DC 20241-0001. TEL 202-501-9649. FAX 202-219-2493. *5080*

U.S. BUREAU OF MINES. MINERAL INDUSTRY SURVEYS: ALABAMA.
U.S. Bureau of Mines, Office of Public Information, 810 Seventh St., N.W., MS-1040, Washington, DC 20241-0001. TEL 202-501-9649. FAX 202-219-2493. *5085*

U.S. BUREAU OF MINES. MINERAL INDUSTRY SURVEYS: ALASKA.
U.S. Bureau of Mines, Office of Public Information, 810 Seventh St., N.W., MS-1040, Washington, DC 20241-0001. TEL 202-501-9649. FAX 202-219-2493. *5085*

U.S. BUREAU OF MINES. MINERAL INDUSTRY SURVEYS: ARKANSAS.
U.S. Bureau of Mines, Office of Public Information, 810 Seventh St., N.W., MS-1040, Washington, DC 20241-0001. TEL 202-501-9649. FAX 202-219-2493. *5085*

U.S. BUREAU OF MINES. MINERAL INDUSTRY SURVEYS: CALIFORNIA.
U.S. Bureau of Mines, Office of Public Information, 810 Seventh St., N.W., MS-1040, Washington, DC 20241-0001. TEL 202-501-9649. FAX 202-219-2493. *5085*

U.S. BUREAU OF MINES. MINERAL INDUSTRY SURVEYS: COLORADO.
U.S. Bureau of Mines, Office of Public Information, 810 Seventh St., N.W., MS-1040, Washington, DC 20241-0001. TEL 202-501-9619. FAX 202-219-2493. *5085*

U.S. BUREAU OF MINES. MINERAL INDUSTRY SURVEYS - COMMODITIES: ANTIMONY.
U.S. Bureau of Mines, Office of Public Information, 810 Seventh St., N.W., MS-1040, Washington, DC 20241-0001. TEL 202-501-9649. FAX 202-219-2493. *5085*

U.S. BUREAU OF MINES. MINERAL INDUSTRY SURVEYS - COMMODITIES: ALUMINUM, BAUXITE, AND ALUMINA.
U.S. Bureau of Mines, Office of Public Information, 810 Seventh St., N.W., MS-1040, Washington, DC 20241-0001. TEL 202-501-9649. FAX 202-219-2493. *5086*

U.S. BUREAU OF MINES. MINERAL INDUSTRY SURVEYS - COMMODITIES: ABRASIVE MATERIALS.
U.S. Bureau of Mines, Office of Public Information, 810 Seventh St., N.W., MS-1040, Washington, DC 20241-0001. TEL 202-501-9649. FAX 202-219-2493. *5086*

U.S. BUREAU OF MINES. MINERAL INDUSTRY SURVEYS - COMMODITIES: BISMUTH.
U.S. Bureau of Mines, Office of Public Information, 810 Seventh St., N.W., MS-1040, Washington, DC 20241-0001. TEL 202-501-6949. FAX 202-219-2493. *5086*

U.S. BUREAU OF MINES. MINERAL INDUSTRY SURVEYS - COMMODITIES: BROMINE.
U.S. Bureau of Mines, Office of Public Information, 810 Seventh St., N.W., MS-1040, Washington, DC 20241. TEL 202-501-9649. FAX 202-219-2493. *5086*

U.S. BUREAU OF MINES. MINERAL INDUSTRY SURVEYS - COMMODITIES: CADMIUM.
U.S. Bureau of Mines, Office of Public Information, 810 Seventh St., N.W., MS-1040, Washington, DC 20241-0001. TEL 202-501-9649. FAX 202-2109-2493. *5086*

U.S. BUREAU OF MINES. MINERAL INDUSTRY SURVEYS - COMMODITIES: CHROMIUM.
U.S. Bureau of Mines, Office of Public Information, 810 Seventh St., N.W., MS-1040, Washington, DC 20241-0001. TEL 202-501-9469. FAX 202-219-2493. *5086*

U.S. BUREAU OF MINES. MINERAL INDUSTRY SURVEYS - COMMODITIES: COLUMBIUM (NIOBIUM) AND TANTALUM.
U.S. Bureau of Mines, Office of Public Information, 810 Seventh St., N.W., MS-1040, Washington, DC 20241-0001. TEL 202-501-9649. FAX 202-219-2493. *5086*

U.S. BUREAU OF MINES. MINERAL INDUSTRY SURVEYS - COMMODITIES: CRUSHED STONE.
U.S. Bureau of Mines, Office of Public Information, 810 Seventh St., N.W., MS-1040, Washington, DC 20241-0001. TEL 202-501-9649. FAX 202-219-2493. *5086*

U.S. BUREAU OF MINES. MINERAL INDUSTRY SURVEYS - COMMODITIES: CONSTRUCTION SAND AND GRAVEL.
U.S. Bureau of Mines, Office of Public Information, 810 Seventh St., N.W., MS-1040, Washington, DC 20241. TEL 202-501-9649. FAX 202-219-2493. *5086*

U.S. BUREAU OF MINES. MINERAL INDUSTRY SURVEYS - COMMODITIES: DIMENSION STONE.
U.S. Bureau of Mines, Office of Public Information, 810 Seventh St., N.W., MS-1040, Washington, DC 20241-0001. TEL 202-501-9649. FAX 202-219-2493. *5086*

U.S. BUREAU OF MINES. MINERAL INDUSTRY SURVEYS - COMMODITIES: FELDSPAR.
U.S. Bureau of Mines, Office of Public Information, 810 Seventh St., N.W., MS-1040, Washington, DC 20241-0001. TEL 202-501-9649. FAX 202-219-2493. *5086*

U.S. BUREAU OF MINES. MINERAL INDUSTRY SURVEYS - COMMODITIES: FLUORSPAR.
U.S. Bureau of Mines, Office of Public Information, 810 Seventh St., N.W., MS-1040, Washington, DC 20241-0001. TEL 202-501-9649. FAX 202-219-2493. *5086*

U.S. BUREAU OF MINES. MINERAL INDUSTRY SURVEYS - COMMODITIES: GEMSTONES.
U.S. Bureau of Mines, Office of Public Information, 810 Seventh St., N.W., MS-1040, Washington, DC 20241-0001. TEL 202-501-9649. FAX 202-219-2493. *5086*

U.S. BUREAU OF MINES. MINERAL INDUSTRY SURVEYS - COMMODITIES: GRAPHITE.
U.S. Bureau of Mines, Office of Public Information, 810 Seventh St., N.W., MS-1040, Washington, DC 20241-0001. TEL 202-501-9649. FAX 202-219-2493. *5086*

U.S. BUREAU OF MINES. MINERAL INDUSTRY SURVEYS - COMMODITIES: IRON AND STEEL.
U.S. Bureau of Mines, Office of Public Information, 810 Seventh St., N.W., MS-1040, Washington, DC 20241-0001. TEL 202-501-9649. FAX 202-219-2493. *5086*

U.S. BUREAU OF MINES. MINERAL INDUSTRY SURVEYS - COMMODITIES: INDUSTRIAL EXPLOSIVES AND BLASTING AGENTS.
U.S. Bureau of Mines, Office of Public Information, 810 Seventh St., N.W., MS-1040, Washington, DC 20241-0001. TEL 202-501-9649. FAX 202-219-2493. *5087*

U.S. BUREAU OF MINES. MINERAL INDUSTRY SURVEYS - COMMODITIES: BARITE.
U.S. Bureau of Mines, Office of Public Information, 810 Seventh St., N.W., MS-1040, Washington, DC 20241-0001. TEL 202-501-9649. FAX 202-219-2493. *5087*

U.S. BUREAU OF MINES. MINERAL INDUSTRY SURVEYS - COMMODITIES: BORON.
U.S. Bureau of Mines, Office of Public Information, 810 Seventh St., N.W., MS-1040, Washington, DC 20241-0001. TEL 202-501-9649. FAX 202-219-2493. *5087*

U.S. BUREAU OF MINES. MINERAL INDUSTRY SURVEYS - COMMODITIES: CEMENT.
U.S. Bureau of Mines, Office of Public Information, 810 Seventh St., N.W., MS-1040, Washington, DC 20241-0001. TEL 202-501-9649. FAX 202-219-2493. *5087*

U.S. BUREAU OF MINES. MINERAL INDUSTRY SURVEYS - COMMODITIES: CLAYS.
U.S. Bureau of Mines, Office of Public Information, 810 Seventh St., N.W., MS-1040, Washington, DC 20241-0001. TEL 202-501-9649. FAX 202-219-2493. *5087*

U.S. BUREAU OF MINES. MINERAL INDUSTRY SURVEYS - COMMODITIES: COBALT.
U.S. Bureau of Mines, Office of Public Information, 810 Seventh St., N.W., MS-1040, Washington, DC 20241-0001. TEL 202-501-6349. FAX 202-219-2493. *5087*

U.S. BUREAU OF MINES. MINERAL INDUSTRY SURVEYS - COMMODITIES: GOLD.
U.S. Bureau of Mines, Office of Public Information, 810 Seventh St., N.W., MS-1040, Washington, DC 20241-0001. TEL 202-501-9649. FAX 202-219-2493. *5087*

U.S. BUREAU OF MINES. MINERAL INDUSTRY SURVEYS - COMMODITIES: GYPSUM.
U.S. Bureau of Mines, Office of Public Information, 810 Seventh St., N.W., MS-1040, Washngton, DC 20241-0001. TEL 202-501-9649. FAX 202-219-2493. *5087*

U.S. BUREAU OF MINES. MINERAL INDUSTRY SURVEYS - COMMODITIES: HELIUM.
U.S. Bureau of Mines, Office of Public Information, 810 Seventh St., N.W., MS-1040, Washington, DC 20241-0001. TEL 202-501-9649. FAX 202-219-2493. *5087*

U.S. BUREAU OF MINES. MINERAL INDUSTRY SURVEYS - COMMODITIES: IODINE.
U.S. Bureau of Mines, Office of Public Information, 810 Seventh St., N.W., MS-1040, Washington, DC 20241-0001. TEL 202-501-9649. FAX 202-219-2493. *5087*

U.S. BUREAU OF MINES. MINERAL INDUSTRY SURVEYS - COMMODITIES: LEAD.
U.S. Bureau of Mines, Office of Public Information, 810 Seventh St., N.W., MS-1040, Washington, DC 20241-0001. TEL 202-501-9649. FAX 202-219-2493. *5087*

U.S. BUREAU OF MINES. MINERAL INDUSTRY SURVEYS - COMMODITIES: LIME.
U.S. Bureau of Mines, Office of Public Information, 810 Seventh St., N.W., MS-1040, Washington, DC 20241-0001. TEL 202-501-9649. FAX 202-219-2493. *5087*

U.S. BUREAU OF MINES. MINERAL INDUSTRY SURVEYS - COMMODITIES: MICA.
U.S. Bureau of Mines, Office of Public Information, 810 Seventh St., N.W., MS-1040, Washington, DC 20241-0001. TEL 202-501-9649. FAX 202-219-2493. *5087*

U.S. BUREAU OF MINES. MINERAL INDUSTRY SURVEYS - COMMODITIES: NICKEL.
U.S. Bureau of Mines, Office of Public Information, 810 Seventh St., N.W., MS-1040, Washington, DC 20241-0001. TEL 202-501-9649. FAX 202-219-2493. *5087*

U.S. BUREAU OF MINES. MINERAL INDUSTRY SURVEYS - COMMODITIES: PEAT.
U.S. Bureau of Mines, Office of Public Information, 810 Seventh St., N.W., MS-1040, Washington, DC 20241-0001. TEL 202-501-9649. FAX 202-219-2493. *5087*

U.S. BUREAU OF MINES. MINERAL INDUSTRY SURVEYS - COMMODITIES: POTASH.
U.S. Bureau of Mines, Office of Public Information, 810 Seventh St., N.W., MS-1040, Washington, DC 20241-0001. TEL 202-501-9649. FAX 202-219-2493. *5087*

U.S. BUREAU OF MINES. MINERAL INDUSTRY SURVEYS - COMMODITIES: SALT.
U.S. Bureau of Mines, Office of Public Information, 810 Seventh St., N.W., MS-C800, Washington, DC 20241-0001. TEL 202-501-9649. FAX 202-219-2493. *5087*

U.S. BUREAU OF MINES. MINERAL INDUSTRY SURVEYS - COMMODITIES: SILVER.
U.S. Bureau of Mines, Office of Public Information, 810 Seventh St., N.W., MS-1040, Washington, DC 20241-0001. TEL 202-501-9649. FAX 202-219-2493. *5088*

U.S. BUREAU OF MINES. MINERAL INDUSTRY SURVEYS - COMMODITIES: SULFUR.
U.S. Bureau of Mines, Office of Public Information, 810 Seventh St., N.W., MS-1400, Washington, DC 20241-0001. TEL 202-501-9649. FAX 202-219-2493. *5088*

U.S. BUREAU OF MINES. MINERAL INDUSTRY SURVEYS - COMMODITIES: TIN.
U.S. Bureau of Mines, Office of Public Information, 810 Seventh St., N.W., MS-1040, Washington, DC 20241-0001. TEL 202-501-9649. FAX 202-219-2493. *5088*

U.S. BUREAU OF MINES. MINERAL INDUSTRY SURVEYS - COMMODITIES: ZINC.
U.S. Bureau of Mines, Office of Public Information, 810 Seventh St., N.W., MS-1040, Washington, DC 20241-0001. TEL 202-501-9649. FAX 202-219-2493. *5088*

U.S. BUREAU OF MINES. MINERAL INDUSTRY SURVEYS - COMMODITIES: IRON ORE.
U.S. Bureau of Mines, Office of Public Information, 810 Seventh St., N.W., MS-1040, Washington, DC 20241. TEL 202-501-9649. FAX 202-219-2493. *5088*

U.S. BUREAU OF MINES. MINERAL INDUSTRY SURVEYS - COMMODITIES: INDUSTRIAL SAND AND GRAVEL.
U.S. Bureau of Mines, Office of Public Information, 810 Seventh St., N.W., MS-1040, Washington, DC 20241-0001. TEL 202-501-9649. FAX 202-219-2493. *5088*

U.S. BUREAU OF MINES. MINERAL INDUSTRY SURVEYS - COMMODITIES: KYANITE AND RELATED MINERALS.
U.S. Bureau of Mines, Office of Public Information, 810 Seventh St., N.W., MS-1040, Washington, DC 20241-0001. TEL 202-501-9649. FAX 202-219-2493. *5088*

U.S. BUREAU OF MINES. MINERAL INDUSTRY SURVEYS - COMMODITIES: LITHIUM.
U.S. Bureau of Mines, Office of Public Information, 810 Seventh St., N.W., MS-1040, Washington, DC 20241-0001. TEL 202-501-9649. FAX 202-219-2493. *5088*

U.S. BUREAU OF MINES. MINERAL INDUSTRY SURVEYS - COMMODITIES - MANGANESE.
U.S. Bureau of Mines, Office of Public Information, 810 Seventh St., N.W., MS-1400, Washington, DC 20241. TEL 202-501-9649. FAX 202-219-2493. *5088*

U.S. BUREAU OF MINES. MINERAL INDUSTRY SURVEYS - COMMODITIES: MERCURY.
U.S. Bureau of Mines, Office of Public Information, 810 Seventh St., N.W., MS-1040, Washington, DC 20241-0001. TEL 202-501-9649. FAX 202-219-2493. *5088*

U.S. BUREAU OF MINES. MINERAL INDUSTRY SURVEYS - COMMODITIES: MOLYBDENUM.
U.S. Bureau of Mines, Office of Public Information, 810 Seventh St., N.W., MS-1040, Washington, DC 20241-0001. TEL 202-512-9649. FAX 202-219-2493. *5088*

U.S. BUREAU OF MINES. MINERAL INDUSTRY SURVEYS - COMMODITIES: MAGNESIUM AND MAGNESIUM COMPOUNDS.
U.S. Bureau of Mines, Office of Public Information, 810 Seventh St., N.W., MS-1040, Washington, DC 20241-0001. TEL 202-501-9649. FAX 202-219-2493. *5088*

U.S. BUREAU OF MINES. MINERAL INDUSTRY SURVEYS - COMMODITIES: NITROGEN.
U.S. Bureau of Mines, Office of Public Information, 810 Seventh St., N.W., MS-1040, Washington, DC 20241-0001. TEL 202-501-9649. FAX 202-219-2493. *5088*

U.S. BUREAU OF MINES. MINERAL INDUSTRY SURVEYS - COMMODITIES: NONRENEWABLE ORGANIC MATERIALS.
U.S. Bureau of Mines, Office of Public Information, 810 Seventh St., N.W., MS-1040, Washington, DC 20241-0001. TEL 202-501-9649. FAX 202-219-2493. *5088*

U.S. BUREAU OF MINES. MINERAL INDUSTRY SURVEYS - COMMODITIES: PLATINUM-GROUP METALS.
U.S. Bureau of Mines, Office of Public Information, 810 Seventh St., N.W., MS-1400, Washington, DC 20241-0001. TEL 202-501-9649. FAX 202-219-2493. *5088*

U.S. BUREAU OF MINES. MINERAL INDUSTRY SURVEYS - COMMODITIES: PHOSPHATE ROCK.
U.S. Bureau of Mines, Office of Public Information, 810 Seventh St., N.W., MS-1040, Washington, DC 20241-0001. TEL 202-501-9649. FAX 202-219-2493. *5089*

U.S. BUREAU OF MINES. MINERAL INDUSTRY SURVEYS - COMMODITIES: RARE EARTHS - THE LANTHANIDES, YTTRIUM, AND SCANDIUM.
U.S. Bureau of Mines, Office of Public Information, 810 Seventh St., N.W., MS-1040, Washington, DC 20241-0001. TEL 202-501-9649. FAX 202-219-2493. *5089*

U.S. BUREAU OF MINES. MINERAL INDUSTRY SURVEYS - COMMODITIES: RECYCLING IRON AND STEEL SCRAP.
U.S. Bureau of Mines, Office of Public Information, 810 Seventh St., N.W., MS-1040, Washington, DC 20241-0001. TEL 202-501-9649. FAX 202-219-2493. *5089*

U.S. BUREAU OF MINES. MINERAL INDUSTRY SURVEYS - COMMODITIES: SILICON.
U.S. Bureau of Mines, Office of Public Information, 810 Seventh St., N.W., MS-1040, Washington, DC 20241-0001. TEL 202-501-9649. *5089*

U.S. BUREAU OF MINES. MINERAL INDUSTRY SURVEYS - COMMODITIES: SODA ASH.
U.S. Bureau of Mines, Office of Public Information, 810 Seventh St., S.W., MS-1040, Washington, DC 20241-0001. TEL 202-501-9649. FAX 202-219-2493. *5089*

U.S. BUREAU OF MINES. MINERAL INDUSTRY SURVEYS - COMMODITIES: SLAG - IRON AND STEEL.
U.S. Bureau of Mines, Office of Public Information, 810 Seventh St., N.W., MS-1040, Washington, DC 20241-0001. TEL 202-501-9649. FAX 202-219-2493. *5089*

U.S. BUREAU OF MINES. MINERAL INDUSTRY SURVEYS - COMMODITIES: SODIUM SULFATE.
U.S. Bureau of Mines, Office of Public Information, 810 Seventh St., N.W., MS-1040, Washington, DC 20241-0001. TEL 202-501-9649. FAX 202-219-2493. *5089*

U.S. BUREAU OF MINES. MINERAL INDUSTRY SURVEYS - COMMODITIES: TITANIUM.
U.S. Bureau of Mines, Office of Public Information, 810 Seventh St., N.W., MS-1040, Washington, DC 20241-0001. TEL 202-501-9649. FAX 202-219-2493. *5089*

U.S. BUREAU OF MINES. MINERAL INDUSTRY SURVEYS - COMMODITIES: TUNGSTEN.
U.S. Bureau of Mines, Office of Public Information, 810 Seventh St., N.W., MS-1040, Washington, DC 20241-0001. TEL 202-501-9649. FAX 202-219-2493. *5089*

U.S. BUREAU OF MINES. MINERAL INDUSTRY SURVEYS - COMMODITIES: VANADIUM.
U.S. Bureau of Mines, Office of Public Information, 810 Seventh St., N.W., MS-1040, Washington, DC 20241-0001. TEL 202-501-9649. FAX 202-219-2493. *5089*

U.S. BUREAU OF MINES. MINERAL INDUSTRY SURVEYS - COMMODITIES: ZIRCONIUM AND HAFNIUM.
U.S. Bureau of Mines, Office of Public Information, 810 Seventh St., N.W., MS-1040, Washington, DC 20241-0001. TEL 202-501-9649. FAX 202-219-2493. *5089*

U.S. BUREAU OF MINES. MINERAL INDUSTRY SURVEYS: CONNECTICUT.
U.S. Bureau of Mines, Office of Public Information, 810 Seventh St., N.W., MS-1040, Washington, DC 20241-0001. TEL 202-501-9649. FAX 202-219-2493. *5089*

U.S. BUREAU OF MINES. MINERAL INDUSTRY SURVEYS: DELAWARE.
U.S. Bureau of Mines, Office of Public Information, 810 Seventh St., N.W., MS-1040, Washington, DC 20241-0001. TEL 202-501-9649. FAX 202-219-2493. *5089*

U.S. BUREAU OF MINES. MINERAL INDUSTRY SURVEYS: FLORIDA.
U.S. Bureau of Mines, Office of Public Information, 810 Seventh St., N.W., MS-1040, Washington, DC 20241-0001. TEL 202-501-9649. FAX 202-219-2493. *5089*

U.S. BUREAU OF MINES. MINERAL INDUSTRY SURVEYS: GEORGIA.
U.S. Bureau of Mines, Office of Public Information, 810 Seventh St., N.W., MS-1040, Washington, DC 20241-0001. TEL 202-501-9649. FAX 202-219-2493. *5089*

U.S. BUREAU OF MINES. MINERAL INDUSTRY SURVEYS: HAWAII.
U.S. Bureau of Mines, Office of Public Information, 810 Seventh St., N.W., MS-1040, Washington, DC 20241-0001. TEL 202-501-9649. FAX 202-219-2493. *5089*

U.S. BUREAU OF MINES. MINERAL INDUSTRY SURVEYS: IDAHO.
U.S. Bureau of Mines, Office of Public Information, 810 Seventh St., N.W., MS-1040, Washington, DC 20241-0001. TEL 202-501-9649. FAX 202-219-2493. *5089*

U.S. BUREAU OF MINES. MINERAL INDUSTRY SURVEYS: ILLINOIS.
U.S. Bureau of Mines, Office of Public Information, 810 Seventh St., N.W., MS-1040, Washington, DC 20241-0001. TEL 202-501-9649. FAX 202-219-2493. *5089*

U.S. BUREAU OF MINES. MINERAL INDUSTRY SURVEYS: INDIANA.
U.S. Bureau of Mines, Office of Public Information, 810 Seventh St., N.W., MS-1040, Washington, DC 20241-0001. TEL 202-501-9649. FAX 202-219-2493. *5090*

U.S. BUREAU OF MINES. MINERAL INDUSTRY SURVEYS: IOWA.
U.S. Bureau of Mines, Office of Public Information, 810 Seventh St., N.W., MS-1040, Washington, DC 20241-0001. TEL 202-501-9649. FAX 202-219-2493. *5090*

U.S. BUREAU OF MINES. MINERAL INDUSTRY SURVEYS: KANSAS.
U.S. Bureau of Mines, Office of Public Information, 810 Seventh St., N.W., MS-1040, Washington, DC 20241-0001. TEL 202-501-9649. FAX 202-219-2493. *5090*

U.S. BUREAU OF MINES. MINERAL INDUSTRY SURVEYS: KENTUCKY.
U.S. Bureau of Mines, Office of Public Information, 810 Seventh St., N.W., MS-1040, Washington, DC 20241-0001. TEL 202-501-9649. FAX 202-219-2493. *5090*

U.S. BUREAU OF MINES. MINERAL INDUSTRY SURVEYS: LOUISIANA.
U.S. Bureau of Mines, Office of Public Information, 810 Seventh St., N.W., MS-1040, Washington, DC 20241-0001. TEL 202-501-9649. FAX 202-219-2493. *5090*

U.S. BUREAU OF MINES. MINERAL INDUSTRY SURVEYS: MAINE.
U.S. Bureau of Mines, Office of Public Information, 810 Seventh St., N.W., MS-1040, Washington, DC 20241-0001. TEL 202-501-9649. FAX 202-219-2493. *5090*

U.S. BUREAU OF MINES. MINERAL INDUSTRY SURVEYS: MARYLAND.
U.S. Bureau of Mines, Office of Public Information, 810 Seventh St., N.W., MS-1040, Washington, DC 20241-0001. TEL 202-501-9649. FAX 202-219-2493. *5090*

U.S. BUREAU OF MINES. MINERAL INDUSTRY SURVEYS: MASSACHUSETTS.
U.S. Bureau of Mines, Office of Public Information, 810 Seventh St., N.W., MS-1040, Washington, DC 20241-0001. TEL 202-501-9649. FAX 202-219-2493. *5090*

U.S. BUREAU OF MINES. MINERAL INDUSTRY SURVEYS: MICHIGAN.
U.S. Bureau of Mines, Office of Public Information, 810 Seventh St., N.W., MS-1040, Washington, DC 20241-0001. TEL 202-501-9649. FAX 202-219-2493. *5090*

U.S. BUREAU OF MINES. MINERAL INDUSTRY SURVEYS: MINNESOTA.
U.S. Bureau of Mines, Office of Public Information, 810 Seventh St., N.W., MS-1040, Washington, DC 20241-0001. TEL 202-501-9649. FAX 202-219-2493. *5090*

U.S. BUREAU OF MINES. MINERAL INDUSTRY SURVEYS: MISSISSIPPI.
U.S. Bureau of Mines, Office of Public Information, 810 Seventh St., N.W., MS-1040, Washington, DC 20241-0001. TEL 202-510-9649. FAX 202-219-2493. *5090*

U.S. BUREAU OF MINES. MINERAL INDUSTRY SURVEYS: MISSOURI.
U.S. Bureau of Mines, Office of Public Information, 810 Seventh St., N.W., MS-1040, Washington, DC 20241-0001. TEL 202-501-9649. FAX 202-219-2493. *5090*

U.S. BUREAU OF MINES. MINERAL INDUSTRY SURVEYS: MONTANA.
U.S. Bureau of Mines, Office of Public Information, 810 Seventh St., N.W., MS-1040, Washington, DC 20241-0001. TEL 202-501-9649. FAX 202-219-2493. *5090*

U.S. BUREAU OF MINES. MINERAL INDUSTRY SURVEYS: NEBRASKA.
U.S. Bureau of Mines, Office of Public Information, 810 Seventh St., N.W., MS-1040, Washington, DC 20241-0001. TEL 202-501-9649. FAX 202-219-2493. *5090*

U.S. BUREAU OF MINES. MINERAL INDUSTRY SURVEYS: NEVADA.
U.S. Bureau of Mines, Office of Public Information, 810 Seventh St., N.W., MS-1040, Washington, DC 20241-0001. TEL 202-501-9649. FAX 202-501-2493. *5090*

U.S. BUREAU OF MINES. MINERAL INDUSTRY SURVEYS: NEW HAMPSHIRE.
U.S. Bureau of Mines, Office of Public Information, 810 Seventh St., N.W., MS-1040, Washington, DC 20241-0001. TEL 202-501-9649. FAX 202-219-2493. *5090*

U.S. BUREAU OF MINES. MINERAL INDUSTRY SURVEYS: NEW JERSEY.
U.S. Bureau of Mines, Office of Public Information, 810 Seventh St., N.W., MS-1040, Washington, DC 20241-0001. TEL 202-501-9649. FAX 202-219-2493. *5090*

U.S. BUREAU OF MINES. MINERAL INDUSTRY SURVEYS: NEW MEXICO.
U.S. Bureau of Mines, Office of Public Information, 810 Seventh St., N.W., MS-1040, Washington, DC 20241-0001. TEL 202-501-9649. FAX 202-219-2493. *5090*

U.S. BUREAU OF MINES. MINERAL INDUSTRY SURVEYS: NEW YORK.
U.S. Bureau of Mines, Office of Public Information, 810 Seventh St., N.W., MS-1040, Washington, DC 20241-0001. TEL 202-501-9649. FAX 202-219-2493. *5090*

U.S. BUREAU OF MINES. MINERAL INDUSTRY SURVEYS: NORTH CAROLINA.
U.S. Bureau of Mines, Office of Public Information, 810 Seventh St., N.W., MS-1040, Washington, DC 20241-0001. TEL 202-501-9649. FAX 202-219-2493. *5090*

U.S. BUREAU OF MINES. MINERAL INDUSTRY SURVEYS: NORTH DAKOTA.
U.S. Bureau of Mines, Office of Public Information, 810 Seventh St., N.W., MS-1040, Washington, DC 20241-0001. TEL 202-501-9649. FAX 202-219-2493. *5090*

U.S. BUREAU OF MINES. MINERAL INDUSTRY SURVEYS: OHIO.
U.S. Bureau of Mines, Office of Public Information, 810 Seventh St., N.W., MS-1040, Washington, DC 20241-0001. TEL 202-501-9649. FAX 202-219-2493. *5091*

U.S. BUREAU OF MINES. MINERAL INDUSTRY SURVEYS: OKLAHOMA.
U.S. Bureau of Mines, Office of Public Information, 810 Seventh St., N.W., MS-1040, Washington, DC 20241-0001. TEL 202-501-9649. FAX 202-219-2493. *5091*

U.S. BUREAU OF MINES. MINERAL INDUSTRY SURVEYS: OREGON.
U.S. Bureau of Mines, Office of Public Information, 810 Seventh St., N.W., MS-1040, Washington, DC 20241-0001. TEL 202-501-9649. FAX 202-219-2493. *5091*

U.S. BUREAU OF MINES. MINERAL INDUSTRY SURVEYS: PENNSYLVANIA.
U.S. Bureau of Mines, Office of Public Information, 810 Seventh St., N.W., MS-1040, Washington, DC 20241-0001. TEL 202-501-9649. FAX 202-219-2493. *5091*

U.S. BUREAU OF MINES. MINERAL INDUSTRY SURVEYS: PUERTO RICO.
U.S. Bureau of Mines, Office of Public Information, 810 Seventh St., N.W., MS-1040, Washington, DC 20241-0001. TEL 202-501-9649. FAX 202-219-2493. *5091*

U.S. BUREAU OF MINES. MINERAL INDUSTRY SURVEYS: RHODE ISLAND.
U.S. Bureau of Mines, Office of Public Information, 810 Seventh St., N.W., MS-1040, Washington, DC 20241-0001. TEL 202-501-9649. FAX 202-219-2493. *5091*

U.S. BUREAU OF MINES. MINERAL INDUSTRY SURVEYS: SOUTH CAROLINA.
U.S. Bureau of Mines, Office of Public Information, 810 Seventh St., N.W., MS-1040, Washington, DC 20041-0001. TEL 202-501-9649. FAX 202-219-2493. *5091*

U.S. BUREAU OF MINES. MINERAL INDUSTRY SURVEYS: SOUTH DAKOTA.
U.S. Bureau of Mines, Office of Public Information, 810 Seventh St., N.W., MS-1040, Washington, DC 20041-0001. TEL 202-501-9649. FAX 202-219-2493. *5091*

U.S. BUREAU OF MINES. MINERAL INDUSTRY SURVEYS: TENNESSEE.
U.S. Bureau of Mines, Office of Public Information, 810 Seventh St., N.W., MS-1040, Washington, DC 20241-0001. TEL 202-501-9649. FAX 202-219-2493. *5091*

U.S. BUREAU OF MINES. MINERAL INDUSTRY SURVEYS: TEXAS.
U.S. Bureau of Mines, Office of Public Information, 810 Seventh St., N.W., MS-1040, Washington, DC 20041-0001. TEL 202-501-9649. FAX 202-219-2493. *5091*

U.S. BUREAU OF MINES. MINERAL INDUSTRY SURVEYS: UTAH.
U.S. Bureau of Mines, Office of Public Information, 810 Seventh St., N.W., MS-1040, Washington, DC 20241-0001. TEL 202-501-9649. FAX 202-219-2493. *5091*

U.S. BUREAU OF MINES. MINERAL INDUSTRY SURVEYS: VERMONT.
U.S. Bureau of Mines, Office of Public Information, 810 Seventh St., N.W., MS-1040, Washington, DC 20241-0001. TEL 202-501-9649. FAX 202-219-2493. *5091*

U.S. BUREAU OF MINES. MINERAL INDUSTRY SURVEYS: VIRGINIA.
U.S. Bureau of Mines, Office of Public Information, 810 Seventh St., N.W., MS-1040, Washington, DC 20241-0001. TEL 202-501-9649. FAX 202-219-2493. *5091*

U.S. BUREAU OF MINES. MINERAL INDUSTRY SURVEYS: WASHINGTON.
U.S. Bureau of Mines, Office of Public Information, 810 Seventh St., N.W., MS-1040, Washington, DC 20241-0001. TEL 202-501-9649. FAX 202-219-2493. *5091*

U.S. BUREAU OF MINES. MINERAL INDUSTRY SURVEYS: WEST VIRGINIA.
U.S. Bureau of Mines, Office of Public Information, 810 Seventh St., N.W., MS-1040, Washington, DC 20241-0001. TEL 202-501-9649. FAX 202-219-2493. *5091*

U.S. BUREAU OF MINES. MINERAL INDUSTRY SURVEYS: WISCONSIN.
U.S. Bureau of Mines, Office of Public Information, 810 Seventh St., N.W., MS-1040, Washington, DC 20241-0001. TEL 202-501-9649. FAX 202-219-2493. *5091*

U.S. BUREAU OF MINES. MINERAL INDUSTRY SURVEYS: WYOMING.
U.S. Bureau of Mines, Office of Public Information, 810 Seventh St., N.W., MS-1040, Washington, DC 20241-0001. TEL 202-501-9649. FAX 202-219-2493. *5091*

U.S. CENTERS FOR DISEASE CONTROL. MORBIDITY AND MORTALITY WEEKLY REPORT.
U.S. Department of Health and Human Services, Centers for Disease Control (MS: A28), Epidemiology Program Office, 1600 Clifton Rd. N.E., Atlanta, GA 30333. TEL 800-843-6356. Vendor(s): Information Access Co., NewsNet, Ovid Technologies, Inc.. *5978*

U.S. CONGRESS. CONGRESSIONAL RECORD.
U.S. Congress, Washington, DC 20515. TEL 202-275-2051. FAX 202-275-0019. *5714*

U.S. DEPARTMENT OF AGRICULTURE. AGRICULTURAL OUTLOOK.
U.S. Department of Agriculture, Economic Research Service, c/o Debbie Haugan, Rm. 110, 1301 New York Ave., N.W., Washington, DC 20005-4788. TEL 202-219-0515. Vendor(s): Knight-Ridder Information, Inc.. *200*

U.S. DEPARTMENT OF AGRICULTURE. AGRICULTURAL STATISTICS BOARD REPORT: AGRICULTURAL PRICES.
U.S. Department of Agriculture, Agricultural Statistics Board, Publications South Bldg., Rm. 5829, Washington, DC 20250. TEL 202-655-4000.
Vendor(s): Knight-Ridder Information, Inc.. *182*

U.S. DEPARTMENT OF AGRICULTURE. AGRICULTURAL STATISTICS BOARD REPORT: CROP PRODUCTION.
U.S. Department of Agriculture, Agricultural Statistics Board, Publications Rm. 5829, South Bldg., Washington, DC 20250. TEL 202-655-4000. Vendor(s): Knight-Ridder Information, Inc.. *182*

U.S. DEPARTMENT OF AGRICULTURE. ECONOMIC RESEARCH SERVICE. FOOD REVIEW.
U.S. Department of Agriculture, Economic Research Service, c/o Debbie Haugan Rm. 110, 1301 New York Ave., N.W., Washington, DC 20005-4788. TEL 202-219-0515.
Vendor(s): Lexis-Nexis. *200*

U.S. DEPARTMENT OF AGRICULTURE. SITUATION & OUTLOOK REPORT. AGRICULTURE AND TRADE: FORMER U S S R.
U.S. Department of Agriculture, Economic Research Service, c/o Debbie Haugan, Rm. 110, 1301 New York Ave., N.W., Washington, DC 20005-4788. TEL 202-219-0515.
Vendor(s): Information Access Co., Knight-Ridder Information, Inc.. *201*

U.S. DEPARTMENT OF STATE. KEY OFFICERS OF FOREIGN SERVICE POSTS.
U.S. Department of State, Office of Information Services, Washington, DC 20520. TEL 202-655-4000.
Vendor(s): Knight-Ridder Information, Inc.. *5776*

U.S. DEPARTMENT OF STATE DISPATCH.
U.S. Department of State, Bureau of Public Affairs, 2201 C St., N.W., Washington, DC 20502. TEL 202-647-6265.
Vendor(s): Information Access Co., Knight-Ridder Information, Inc.. *5776*

U.S. ENERGY INFORMATION ADMINISTRATION. ANNUAL ENERGY REVIEW.
U.S. Energy Information Administration, National Energy Information Center, EI-231, James Forrestal Bldg., Rm. 1F-048, 1000 Independence Ave., S.W., Washington, DC 20585. TEL 202-586-8800. *2559*

U.S. ENERGY INFORMATION ADMINISTRATION. QUARTERLY COAL REPORT.
U.S. Energy Information Administration, National Energy Information Center, EI-231, c/o Paulette Young, Coal Division, 1000 Independence Ave., S.W., EI-522, DC 20585. TEL 202-586-8800. FAX 202-586-0727.
Vendor(s): Knight-Ridder Information Inc.. *2559*

U.S. ENERGY INFORMATION ADMINISTRATION. WEEKLY PETROLEUM STATUS REPORT.
U.S. Energy Information Administration, National Energy Information Center, EI-231, James Forrestal Bldg., Rm. 1F-048, 1000 Independence Ave., S.W., Washington, DC 20585. TEL 202-586-8800.
Vendor(s): PetroScan. *5379*

U.S. FEDERAL HIGHWAY ADMINISTRATION. HIGHWAY STATISTICS.
U.S. Federal Highway Administration, Office of Highway Information Management, Department of Transportation, 400 Seventh St., S.W., Washington, DC 20590. TEL 202-366-0180. FAX 202-366-7742. *6747*

U.S. GENERAL SERVICES ADMINISTRATION. CATALOG OF FEDERAL DOMESTIC ASSISTANCE.
U.S. General Services Administration, Publications, 18th and F Sts., N.W., DC 20405. TEL 202-501-1794. FAX 202-501-4281. *5925*

U.S. NATIONAL AERONAUTICS AND SPACE ADMINISTRATION. VIDEO CATALOG.
U.S. National Aeronautics and Space Administration, National Technology Transfer Center, c/o Wheeling Jesuit University, 316 Washington Ave., Wheeling, WV 26003. TEL 304-243-2440. FAX 301-243-4390. *83*

U.S. NATIONAL COMMITTEE FOR MAN AND THE BIOSPHERE PROGRAM. BULLETIN.
U.S. National Committee for Man and the Biosphere Program, Man and the Biosphere Secretariat, U.S. Department of State, SA-44C, 1st Fl., Washington, DC 20522-4401. TEL 202-466-1934. FAX 202-466-2106. *2144*

U.S. OFFICE OF THE FEDERAL REGISTER. WEEKLY COMPILATION OF PRESIDENTIAL DOCUMENTS.
U.S. Office of the Federal Register, National Archives and Records Administration, Eighth St. and Pennsylvania Ave., N.W., Washington, DC 20408. TEL 202-523-5230.
Vendor(s): Information Access Co.. *5926*

UNITED STATES DISTRIBUTION JOURNAL.
B M T Communications, Inc., 7 Penn Plaza, New York, NY 10001-3900. TEL 212-594-4120. FAX 212-714-0514.
Vendor(s): Information Access Co.. *6712*

UNITED STATES LAW WEEK.
The Bureau of National Affairs, Inc., 1231 25th St., N.W., Washington, DC 20037. TEL 202-452-4200. FAX 202-822-8092.
Vendor(s): Lexis-Nexis (USLW), West Services, Inc.. *3861*

UNITED STATES PATENTS QUARTERLY.
The Bureau of National Affairs, Inc., 1231 25th St., N.W., Washington, DC 20037. TEL 202-452-4200. FAX 202-822-8092.
Vendor(s): Knight-Ridder Information, Inc. (Patlaw, File 243), Orbit Search Service. *5346*

UNITED STATES POLITICAL SCIENCE DOCUMENTS.
University of Pittsburgh, Mid-Atlantic Technology Applications Center (MTAC), 823 William Pitt Union, Pittsburgh, PA 15260. TEL 412-648-7000. FAX 412-648-7003.
Vendor(s): Knight-Ridder Information, Inc. (File no.93). *5724*

UNITED STATES TAX COURT REPORTS.
U.S. Tax Court, 400 Second St., N.W., Washington, DC 20217. TEL 202-783-3238. FAX 202-606-8704.
Vendor(s): West Services, Inc.. *1570*

UNITS.
National Apartment Association, 201 N. Union St., No. 200, Alexandria, VA 22314. TEL 703-518-6141. FAX 703-518-6191.
Vendor(s): Information Access Co.. *3597*

UNIVERSIDAD DE ZULIA. FACULTAD DE INGENIERIA. REVISTA TECNICA.
Universidad del Zulia, Facultad de Ingenieria, Apdo. 10-482, Correo Bella Vista, Maracaibo, Venezuela. TEL 58-61-525732. FAX 58-61-525732. *2622*

UNIVERSIDADE DE SAO PAULO. REVISTA DE FARMACIA E BIOQUIMICA.
Universidade de Sao Paulo, Faculdade de Ciencias Farmaceuticas, C.P. 66083, 05389-970 Sao Paulo, Brazil. TEL 55-11-8137251. FAX 55-11-2128194. *5446*

UNIVERSITAET DES SAARLANDES. JAHRESBIBLIOGRAPHIE.
Universitaet des Saarlandes, Universitaetsbibliothek, 66123 Saarbruecken, Germany. TEL 49-681-3023010. FAX 49-681-3022796. *552*

UNIVERSITAS COMENIANA. ACTA MATHEMATICA.
Univerzita Komenskeho, Matematicko-fizikalna Fakulta, Mlynska dlina, 842 15 Bratislava, Slovakia. TEL 42-7-725741. FAX 42-7-725882. *4402*

UNIVERSITE DE BORDEAUX III. CENTRE DE RECHERCHES SUR L'AMERIQUE ANGLOPHONE. ANNALES.
Maison des Sciences de l'Homme d'Aquitaine, Esplanade des Antilles, Domaine Universitaire, 33405 Talence Cedex, France. TEL 56-84-68-00. FAX 56-84-68-10. *4281*

UNIVERSITY OF BALTIMORE LAW REVIEW.
University of Baltimore School of Law, Business Editor, 1420 N. Charles St., Baltimore, MD 21201. TEL 410-837-4490.
Vendor(s): West Services, Inc.. *3862*

UNIVERSITY OF CALGARY GAZETTE.
University of Calgary, Public Affairs, 2500 University Dr., N.W., Calgary, Alta. T2N 1N4, Canada. TEL 403-220-3500. FAX 403-282-8413. *1891*

UNIVERSITY OF CALIFORNIA. DIVISION OF LIBRARY AUTOMATION. TECHNICAL REPORTS.
University of California, Division of Library Automation, 300 Lakeside Dr., 8th Fl., Oakland, CA 94612-3550. TEL 510-987-0564. *4047*

UNIVERSITY OF CALIFORNIA AT BERKELEY WELLNESS LETTER.
Health Letter Associates, Box 412, Prince St. Sta., New York, NY 10012. TEL 212-505-2255. FAX 212-505-5462.
Vendor(s): Information Access Co., University Microfilms International. *5537*

UNIVERSITY OF CHICAGO LAW REVIEW.
University of Chicago, Law School, 1111 E. 60th St., Chicago, IL 60637. TEL 312-702-9832. FAX 312-702-0730.
Vendor(s): Lexis-Nexis. *3862*

UNIVERSITY OF CHICAGO LEGAL FORUM.
University of Chicago, Law School, 1111 E. 60th St., Chicago, IL 60637. TEL 312-702-9832. FAX 312-702-0730.
Vendor(s): West Services, Inc.. *3862*

UNIVERSITY OF COLORADO LAW REVIEW.
University of Colorado Law Review, Inc., 290 Fleming Law Bldg., Campus Box 401, Boulder, CO 80309-0401. TEL 303-492-6145. FAX 303-492-1200.
Vendor(s): Lexis-Nexis, West Services, Inc.. *3862*

UNIVERSITY OF DAYTON LAW REVIEW.
University of Dayton, Law School, 300 College Park, Dayton, OH 45469-1350. TEL 513-229-3642.
Vendor(s): Lexis-Nexis, West Services, Inc.. *3862*

UNIVERSITY OF ILLINOIS LAW REVIEW.
University of Illinois at Urbana-Champaign, College of Law, Champaign, IL 61820. TEL 217-333-3156.
Vendor(s): West Services, Inc.. *3862*

UNIVERSITY OF IOWA. LIBRARIES. NEWSLETTER.
University of Iowa Libraries, Iowa City, IA 52242. TEL 319-335-5871. *4033*

UNIVERSITY OF KANSAS LAW REVIEW.
University of Kansas, School of Law, Rm. 510, Green Hall, Lawrence, KS 66045. TEL 913-864-3463. FAX 913-864-3680.
Vendor(s): Lexis-Nexis, West Services, Inc.. *3862*

UNIVERSITY OF MANCHESTER. DEPARTMENT OF COMPUTER SCIENCE. TECHNICAL REPORT SERIES.
University of Manchester, Department of Computer Science, Oxford Rd., Manchester M13 9PL, England. TEL 44-161-275-6130. FAX 44-161-275-6236. *2059*

UNIVERSITY OF NEW BRUNSWICK LAW JOURNAL.
University of New Brunswick, Faculty of Law, P.O. Box 4400, Fredericton, NB E3B 5A3, Canada. TEL 506-453-4657. FAX 506-453-5186.
Vendor(s): West Services, Inc.. *3863*

UNIVERSITY OF PENNSYLVANIA JOURNAL OF INTERNATIONAL ECONOMIC LAW.
University of Pennsylvania, Law School, 3400 Chestnut St., Philadelphia, PA 19104-6204. TEL 215-898-6869. FAX 215-573-2025.
Vendor(s): Lexis-Nexis, West Services, Inc.. *3944*

UNIVERSITY OF PENNSYLVANIA LAW REVIEW.
University of Pennsylvania Law Review, 3400 Chestnut St., Philadelphia, PA 19104-6204. TEL 215-898-7060. FAX 215-573-2005.
Vendor(s): Lexis-Nexis. *3863*

UNIVERSITY OF PITTSBURGH LAW REVIEW.
University of Pittsburgh, School of Law, Pittsburgh, PA 15260. TEL 412-648-1354.
Vendor(s): Lexis-Nexis, West Services, Inc.. *3863*

UNIVERSITY OF RICHMOND LAW REVIEW.
University of Richmond, T.C. Williams School of Law, Richmond, VA 23173. TEL 804-289-8216. FAX 804-289-8683.
Vendor(s): West Services, Inc.. *3863*

UNIVERSITY OF SAN FRANCISCO LAW REVIEW.
University of San Francisco, School of Law, Kendrick Hall, 2130 Fulton St., San Francisco, CA 94117. TEL 415-666-6154. FAX 415-666-6433.
Vendor(s): Lexis-Nexis, West Services, Inc.. *3863*

UNIVERSITY OF TORONTO BULLETIN.
University of Toronto, Department of Public Affairs, 21 King's College Circle, Toronto, ON M5S 1A1, Canada. TEL 416-978-7016. FAX 416-978-7430. *1891*

UNIX NEWS.
12 Sutton Row, 4th Fl., London W1V 5FH, England. TEL 44-171-867-9880.
Vendor(s): Information Access Co.. *2060*

UNIX REVIEW.
Miller Freeman, Inc. 600 Harrison St., San Francisco, CA 94107. TEL 415-905-2200. FAX 415-905-2232.
Vendor(s): Information Access Co., University Microfilms International. *2047*

UNIX UPDATE.
Worldwide Videotex, Box 3273, Boynton Beach, FL 33424-3273. TEL 407-738-2276.
Vendor(s): Information Access Co.. *2117*

UNO MAS MAGAZINE.
Jim Saah, Ed. & Pub., Box 1832, Silver Spring, MD 20915. TEL 301-946-5232. FAX 301-770-3250. *4171*

UPSIDE.
Upside Publishing Company, 2015 Pioneer Ct., San Mateo, CA 94403-1736. TEL 415-377-0950. FAX 415-377-1961.
Vendor(s): University Microfilms International. *1357*

UPSTATE NEW YORK BUSINESS DIRECTORY.
American Business Directories 5711 S. 86th Circle, Box 27347, Omaha, NE 68127. TEL 402-593-4600. FAX 402-331-5481. *1647*

URBAN ABSTRACTS.
London Research Centre, Research Library, 81 Black Prince Rd., London SE1 7SZ, England. TEL 44-171-627-9666. FAX 44-171-627-9674.
Vendor(s): European Space Agency. *5935*

URBAN DESIGN INTERNATIONAL.
Chapman & Hall, Journals Department 2-6 Boundary Row, London SE1 8HN, England. TEL 44-171-8650066. FAX 44-171-5229623. *3597*

URBAN STUDIES.
Carfax Publishing Co., P.O. Box 25, Abingdon, Oxon OX14 3UE, England. TEL 44-1235-401000. FAX 44-1235-401550.
Vendor(s): Information Access Co.. *3598*

URBAN TRANSPORT NEWS.
Business Publishers, Inc., 951 Pershing Dr., Silver Spring, MD 20910-4464. TEL 301-587-6300. FAX 301-585-9075.
Vendor(s): Information Access Co., NewsNet (TS10). *6733*

URETHANES TECHNOLOGY.
Crain Communications Ltd., Cowcross Ct., 2nd Fl., 75-77 Cowcross St., London EC1M 6BP, England. TEL 44-171-608-1116. FAX 44-171-608-1173.
Vendor(s): Information Access Co.. *6220*

UROLOGY TIMES.
Advanstar Communications, Inc., 7500 Old Oak Blvd., Cleveland, OH 44130. TEL 216-826-2839. FAX 216-891-2726.
Vendor(s): Information Access Co., Knight-Ridder Information, Inc.. *4932*

USED EQUIPMENT DIRECTORY.
Penton Publishing Co. (Hasbrouck Heights) 611 Rte. 46 W., Hasbrouck Heights, NJ 07604. TEL 201-393-9558. FAX 201-393-9553. *4347*

USPEKHI FIZICHESKIKH NAUK.
Uspekhi Fizicheskikh Nauk, Leninskii prospekt, 15, 117071 Moscow, Russia. TEL 7-095-1904244. FAX 7-095-1358860. *5575*

UTAH BUSINESS DIRECTORY.
American Business Directories 5711 S. 86th Circle, Box 27347, Omaha, NE 68127. TEL 402-593-4600. FAX 402-331-5481. *1647*

UTAH LAW REVIEW.
University of Utah, College of Law, Salt Lake City,
UT 84112. TEL 801-581-6833.
Vendor(s): West Services, Inc.. *3864*

UTAH STATE DIGEST.
Division of Administrative Rules, Box 141007, Salt
Lake City, UT 84114-1007. TEL 801-538-3218.
FAX 801-538-3844. *5952*

UTILITY ENVIRONMENT REPORT.
McGraw-Hill, Inc., Energy & Business Newsletters,
1221 Ave. of the Americas, 36th Fl., New York, NY
10020. TEL 212-512-6410.
Vendor(s): Knight-Ridder Information, Inc. (UER),
Dow Jones News Retrieval (UER), Lexis-Nexis (UER)
, NewsNet (EV42). *2722*

UTILITY REPORTER - FUELS ENERGY & POWER.
Merton Allen Associates, InfoTeam Inc., Box 15640,
Plantation, FL 33318-5640. TEL 954-473-9560.
FAX 954-473-0544.
Vendor(s): Data-Star, Information Access Co.,
NewsNet (EY12). *2560*

UTNE LENS.
Lens Publishing Co., Inc., 1624 Harmon Pl., Ste.
330, Minneapolis, MN 55403. TEL 612-338-5040.
Available only online. *4171*

V A R BUSINESS.
C M P Publications, Inc., 600 Community Dr.,
Manhasset, NY 11030-3847. TEL 516-562-6700.
FAX 516-562-8585.
Vendor(s): Information Access Co.. *2000*

V H L FAMILY FORUM.
V H L Family Alliance, 171 Clinton Rd., Brookline,
MA 02146. TEL 617-232-5946. FAX 617-734-
8233. *4871*

THE V L D B JOURNAL.
Springer-Verlag, Heidelberger Platz 3, Berlin
14197, Germany. TEL 49-30-82070. FAX 49-30-
8207448. *2067*

VAARD I NORDEN.
Sygeplejerskerners Samarbejde i Norden, P.O. Box
2681, St. Hanshaugen, N-131 Oslo 1, Norway.
TEL 47-22-38-20-00. FAX 47-22-38-54-47.
Vendor(s): Ovid Technologies, Inc., Data-Star, Knight-
Ridder Information, Inc.. *4729*

VACCINE.
Elsevier Science Ltd., Oxford Fulfilment Centre, P.O.
Box 800, Kidlington, Oxford OX5 1DX, England.
TEL 44-1865-843000. FAX 44-1865-843010.
4587

VACCINE WEEKLY.
Charles W. Henderson, Ed. & Pub., Box 5528,
Atlanta, GA 31107-0528. TEL 404-377-8895.
FAX 404-378-4511.
Vendor(s): Information Access Co.. *5446*

**VADEMECUM DEUTSCHER LEHR- UND
FORSCHUNGSSTAETTEN. STAETTEN DER
FORSCHUNG.**
Raabe Fachverlag fuer Wissenschaftsinformation,
Koenigswintererstr. 418, 53227 Bonn, Germany.
TEL 49-228-9702025. FAX 49-228-9702036.
Vendor(s): STN International. *6294*

VAESTRA SVERIGES AFFAERER & FOERETAG.
Vaestra Sveriges Affaerer & Foeretag, P.O. Box 411,
S-401 26 Goeteborg, Sweden. TEL 46-031-
624060. FAX 46-031-624066. *1489*

VALPARAISO UNIVERSITY LAW REVIEW.
Valparaiso University, School of Law, Valparaiso, IN
46383. TEL 219-465-7807. FAX 219-465-7872.
Vendor(s): West Services, Inc.. *3864*

VANDERBILT JOURNAL OF TRANSNATIONAL LAW.
Vanderbilt University, School of Law, Nashville, TN
37240. TEL 615-322-2284. FAX 615-343-6023.
Vendor(s): West Services, Inc.. *3944*

VANDERBILT LAW REVIEW.
Vanderbilt University, School of Law, Nashville, TN
37240. TEL 615-322-4766. FAX 615-343-6023.
Vendor(s): Lexis-Nexis, West Services, Inc.. *3864*

THE VEGAN NEWS.
Vegan Action, Box 4353, Berkeley, CA 94704.
TEL 510-654-6297. FAX 510-595-7569. *5242*

VEGETARIAN TIMES.
Cowles Enthusiast Media, Healthy Lifestyles Group,
4 High Ridge Park, Stamford, CT 06905. TEL 203-
321-1755. FAX 203-322-1966.
Vendor(s): Information Access Co.. *5242*

VENDING: THE INTERNATIONAL MARKET.
Euromonitor, 60-61 Britton St., London EC1M 5NA,
England. TEL 44-171-251-8024. FAX 44-171-608-
3149.
Vendor(s): Data-Star, Knight-Ridder Information, Inc..
1490

VENTURE CAPITAL JOURNAL.
Securities Data Publishing, 40 W. 57th St., 11th Fl.,
New York, NY 10019. TEL 212-765-5311.
FAX 212-765-6123.
Vendor(s): Information Access Co.. *1358*

**VERBAENDE, BEHCERDEN, ORGANISATIONEN DER
WIRTSCHAFT.**
Verlag Hoppenstedt GmbH, Havelstr. 9, 64295
Darmstadt, Germany. TEL 49-6151-380-0. FAX 49-
6151-380-360.
Vendor(s): GBI. *245*

VERMONT BUSINESS DIRECTORY.
American Business Directories 5711 S. 86th Circle,
Box 27347, Omaha, NE 68127. TEL 402-593-
4600. FAX 402-331-5481. *1647*

VERMONT BUSINESS MAGAZINE.
Lake Iroquois Publishing, Inc., 2 Church St.,
Burlington, VT 05401. TEL 802-863-8038.
FAX 802-363-8059.
Vendor(s) Knight Ridder Information, Inc., University
Microfilms International. *968*

**VERONIS, SUHLER & ASSOCIATES
COMMUNICATIONS INDUSTRY REPORT.**
Veronis, Suhler & Associates Inc., 350 Park Ave.,
New York, NY 10022. TEL 212-935-4990.
Vendor(s) Information Access Co.. *968*

VERSICHERUNGSRECHT.
Verlag Versicherungswirtschaft e.V., Klosestr. 20-24,
76137 Karlsruhe Germany. TEL 49-721-
3509126. FAX 49-721-31833. *3668*

VERTICAL FILE INDEX.
H.W. Wilson Co., 950 University Ave., Bronx, NY
10452. TEL 718-588-8400. FAX 718-590-1617.
Vendor(s): Wilsonline (File VFI). *27*

**VERZEICHNIS AUSLAENDISCHER ZEITSCHRIFTEN IN
SCHWEIZERISCHEN BIBLIOTHEKEN.**
Schweizerische Landesbibliothek, Hallwylstr. 15, CH-
3003 Bern, Switzerland. TEL 41-31-3228911.
FAX 41-31-3228463. *552*

VETERINARY BIOTECHNOLOGY NEWSLETTER.
Office International des Epizooties, 12 rue de Prony,
75017 Paris, France. TEL 33-1-44-15-18-88.
FAX 33-1-42-67-09-87.
Available only online. *6957*

VETERINARY BULLETIN.
CAB International, Wallingford, Oxon. OX10 8DE,
England. TEL 44-1491-832111. FAX 44-1491-
833508.
Vendor(s): DIMDI, European Space Agency, Knight-
Ridder Information, Inc., STN International. *6961*

VIBRANT LIFE.
Review and Herald Publishing Association, 55 W.
Oak Ridge Dr., Hagerstown, MD 21740. TEL 301-
791-7000.
Vendor(s): Information Access Co.. *5537*

VICTORIAN REPORTS.
Butterworths, Division of Reed International Books
Australia Pty. Ltd. 271-273 Lane Cove Rd., North
Ryde, N.S.W. 2113, Australia. TEL 61-2-3354444.
FAX 61-2-3354678.
Vendor(s): Info-One International Pty Ltd.. *3865*

VICTORIAN STUDIES.
Indiana University Press 601 N. Morton,
Bloomington, IN 47404. TEL 812-855-9449.
FAX 812-855-8507.
Vendor(s): Information Access Co., University
Microfilms International. *3630*

VIDEO MAGAZINE.
Hachette Filipacchi Magazines, Inc., 1633 Broadway,
43rd. Fl., New York, NY 10019. TEL 212-767-
6000. FAX 212-767-5619.
Vendor(s): Information Access Co.. *1979*

VIDEO REVIEW.
Media Works Group Inc., P.C. Box 2047,
Larchmont, NY 10538-8247. TEL 914-576-8800.
FAX 914-576-8841.
Vendor(s): Information Access Co., University
Microfilms International. *5115*

VIDEO STORE.
Advanstar Communications, Inc., 7500 Old Oak
Blvd., Cleveland, OH 44130. TEL 216-243-8100.
Vendor(s): Information Access Co., Knight-Ridder
Information, Inc.. *1979*

VIDEO TECHNOLOGY NEWS.
Phillips Business Information Inc., 1201 Seven
Locks Rd., Potomac, MD 20854. TEL 301-424-
3338. FAX 301-309-3847.
Vendor(s): Data-Star, Information Access Co.,
Knight-Ridder Information, Inc., NewsNet (PB39).
1979

VIDEO WEEK.
Warren Publishing, Inc., 2115 Ward Ct., N.W.,
Washington, DC 20037. TEL 202-872-9200.
FAX 202-293-3435.
Vendor(s): Information Access Co., NewsNet (EL01).
1980

VIDEOLOG.
Trade Service Corporation, 10996 Torreyana Rd.,
San Diego, CA 92121. TEL 619-457-5920.
FAX 619-457-1320. *1926*

VIDEOMAKER.
Videomaker Inc., Box 4591, Chico, CA 95927.
TEL 916-891-8410. FAX 916-891-8443.
Vendor(s): CompuServe, Inc. (71161,1722). *1980*

VIDEOS FOR BUSINESS AND TRAINING.
Gale Research Inc., 835 Penobscot Bldg., Detroit,
MI 48226-4094. TEL 313-961-2242. FAX 313-
961-6083.
Vendor(s): Human Resources Information Network
(Video). *1980*

VILLAGE VOICE.
V V Publishing Corporation, 36 Cooper Sq., New
York, NY 10003. TEL 212-475-3300. FAX 212-
475-8944.
Vendor(s): Dow Jones News Retrieval, Lexis-Nexis.
3241

VILLANOVA LAW REVIEW.
Villanova University Law School, 229 N. Spring Mill
Rd., Villanova, PA 19085. TEL 215-545-7053.
Vendor(s): West Services, Inc. *3865*

VIRGIN MEAT.
Steve Blum, Ed. & Pub., 2325 West Ave., K-15,
Lancaster, CA 93536. TEL 805-722-1758.
Vendor(s): CompuServe, Inc.. *4283*

VIRGINIA BUSINESS DIRECTORY.
American Business Directories 5711 S. 86th Circle,
Box 27347, Omaha, NE 68127. TEL 402-593-
4600. FAX 402-331-5481. *1647*

VIRGINIA ENVIRONMENTAL LAW JOURNAL.
Virginia Environmental Law Journal, University of
Virginia, School of Law, Charottesville, VA 22901.
TEL 804-924-3683. FAX 804-924-7536.
Vendor(s): West Services, Inc. *3866*

VIRGINIA JOURNAL OF INTERNATIONAL LAW.
Virginia Journal of International Law Association,
University of Virginia, School of Law, 580 Massie
Rd., Charlottesville, VA 22901. TEL 804-924-
3415. FAX 804-924-7536.
Vendor(s): Lexis-Nexis, West Services, Inc.. *3944*

VIRGINIA LAW REVIEW.
Virginia Law Review Association, University of
Virginia, School of Law, 580 Massie Rd., VA
22903-1789. TEL 804-924-3079. FAX 804-982-
2818.
Vendor(s): National Data Corp., West Services, Inc..
3866

VIRGINIA MAGAZINE OF HISTORY AND BIOGRAPHY.
Virginia Historical Society, Box 7311 Richmond, VA
23221. TEL 804-358-4901. FAX 804-355-2399.
Vendor(s): University Microfilms International.
3492

VIRGINIA TAX REVIEW.
Virginia Tax Review Association, University of
Virginia, School of Law, Charlottesville, VA 22901.
TEL 804-924-4726. FAX 804-924-7536.
Vendor(s): West Services, Inc.. *1570*

VIROLOGY AND AIDS ABSTRACTS.
Cambridge Scientific Abstracts, 7200 Wisconsin
Ave., 6th Fl., Bethesda, MD 20814. TEL 301-961-
6750. FAX 301-961-6720.
Vendor(s): Knight-Ridder Information, Inc. (File
no.76/LIFE SCIENCES COLLECTION), STN
International (LIFESCI). *4576*

VIRTUAL PROTOTYPING JOURNAL.
M C B University Press Ltd., 60-62 Toller Ln.,
Bradford, W. Yorks BD8 9BY, England. TEL 44-
1274-777700. FAX 44-1274-785200. *2681*

VISION QUEST.
Visionary Publishing, 25 Walbridge St., Apt. 3,
Allston, MA 02134-3802. TEL 516-626-3500.
Available only online. *2957*

VITAL SPEECHES OF THE DAY.
City News Publishing Co. Inc., Box 1247, Mt.
Pleasant, SC 29465-1247. TEL 803-881-8733.
FAX 803-881-4007.
Vendor(s): Information Access Co., University
Microfilms International. *3712*

**VITAMINS AND DIETARY SUPPLEMENTS: THE
INTERNATIONAL MARKET.**
Euromonitor, 60-61 Britton St., London EC1M 5NA,
England. TEL 44-171-251-8024. FAX 44-171-608-
3149.
Vendor(s): Data-Star, Knight-Ridder Information, Inc..
5447

VITIS.
Bundesanstalt fuer Zeuchtungsforschung an
Kulturpflanzen, Institut fuer Rebenzuechtung
Geilweilerhof, 76833 Siebeldingen, Germany.
TEL 44-6345-410. FAX 44-6345-41177.
Vendor(s): DIMDI, Knight-Ridder Information, Inc.,
STN International. *515*

VITIS - VITICULTURE AND OENOLOGY ABSTRACTS.
Bundesanstalt fuer Zeuchtungsforschung an
Kulturpflanzen, 76833 Siebeldingen-Pflaz,
Germany. TEL 49-63-45410. FAX 49-63-
4541177.
Vendor(s): DIMDI, Knight-Ridder Information, Inc.,
STN International. *183*

VODOHOSPODARSKY CASOPIS.
Slovenska Akademia Vied, Ustav Hydrologie,
Racianska 75, P.O. Box 94, 830 08 Bratislava,
Slovakia. TEL 42-7-253000. FAX 42-7-259404.
2289

VOICE TECHNOLOGY & SERVICES NEWS.
Phillips Business Information, Inc., 1201 Seven
Locks Rd., Potomac, MD 20854. TEL 301-424-
3338. FAX 301-309-3847.
Vendor(s): Data-Star, Information Access Co.,
Knight-Ridder Information, Inc., NewsNet. *1920*

**VOTING RECORD: SENATE NATIONAL SECURITY
INDEX.**
Council for a Livable World, 110 Maryland Ave.,
N.E., Washington, DC 20002. TEL 202-543-4100.
5716

W A A C NEWSLETTER.
Western Association for Art Conservation, 5905
Wilshire Blvd., Los Angeles, CA 90036. TEL 602-
433-0461. *459*

W C E L NEWS.
West Coast Environmental Law Research
Foundation, 1001-207 W. Hastings, Vancouver, BC
V6B 1H7, Canada. TEL 604-684-7378. FAX 604-
684-1312. *2825*

W I N NEWS.
Women's International Network, 187 Grant St.,
Lexington, MA 02173-2140. TEL 617-862-9431.
Vendor(s): Information Access Co., University
Microfilms International. *7020*

W R R I NEWS.
University of North Carolina, Water Resources
Research Institute, Box 7912, Raleigh, NC 27695-
7912. TEL 919-515-2815. FAX 919-515-7802.
Vendor(s): VU/TEXT Information Services, Inc..
6977

WALL STREET & TECHNOLOGY.
United News & Media, One Penn Plaza, New York,
NY 10119. TEL 212-869-1300.
Vendor(s): Information Access Co., University
Microfilms International. *1130*

WALL STREET JOURNAL (EASTERN EDITION).
Dow Jones & Co., Inc., 200 Liberty St., New York,
NY 10281. TEL 212-416-2000.
Vendor(s): Dow Jones News Retrieval. *1126*

THE WALL STREET JOURNAL INDEX.
U M I Company 300 N. Zeeb Rd., Ann Arbor, MI
48106. TEL 313-761-4700. FAX 800-864-0019.
1126

WALL STREET TRANSCRIPT.
Wall Street Transcript Corp., 100 Wall St., New
York, NY 10005. TEL 212-747-9500.
Vendor(s): Information Access Co., VU/TEXT
Information Services, Inc.. *1358*

WALT DISNEY WORLD (YEAR).
Hearst Corporation, Walt Disney World, 250 W.
55th St., 11th Fl., New York, NY 10019. TEL 212-
903-5190. *6925*

WARD'S AUTO WORLD.
Ward's Communications 3000 Town Center, Ste.
2750, Southfield, MI 48075-1212. TEL 810-357-
0800. FAX 810-357-0810.
Vendor(s): Information Access Co., University
Microfilms International. *6806*

WARFIELD'S BUSINESS RECORD.
11 E. Saratoga St., Baltimore, MD 21202.
TEL 410-752-3849. FAX 410-332-0698.
Vendor(s): Lexis-Nexis, University Microfilms
International. *1245*

WARNING LETTER BULLETIN.
Washington Information Source, 6506 Old Stage
Rd., Ste. 100, Rockville, MD 20852-4326.
TEL 301-770-5553.
Vendor(s): Information Access Co.. *4543*

WARREN'S CABLE REGULATION MONITOR.
Warren Publishing, Inc., 2115 Ward Ct., N.W.,
Washington, DC 20037. TEL 202-872-9200.
FAX 202-293-3435. *1974*

WARSAW VOICE.
Warsaw Voice S.A., Ksiecia Janusza 64, 01-452
Warsaw, Poland. TEL 48-22-366377. FAX 48-22-
371995.
Vendor(s): Lexis-Nexis. *3207*

WASHINGTON AND LEE LAW REVIEW.
Washington and Lee University, School of Law, Lewis
Hall, Lexington, VA 24450-1799. TEL 703-463-
8566. FAX 703-463-8488.
Vendor(s): Lexis-Nexis, University Microfilms
International, West Services, Inc.. *3867*

WASHINGTON BUSINESS DIRECTORY.
American Business Directories 5711 S. 86th Circle,
Box 27347, Omaha, NE 68127. TEL 402-593-
4600. FAX 402-331-5481. *1648*

WASHINGTON BUSINESS JOURNAL.
American City Business Journals, Inc. (Arlington),
2000 14th St., N. Ste. 500, Arlington, VA 22201.
TEL 703-875-2200. FAX 703-875-2231. *969*

WASHINGTON C E O.
Fivash Publishing Group, 2505 Second Ave., Ste.
602, Seattle, WA 98121. TEL 206-441-8415.
FAX 206-441-8325. *1450*

WASHINGTON, DC AREA BUSINESS DIRECTORY.
American Business Directories 5711 S. 86th Circle,
Box 27347, Omaha, NE 68127. TEL 402-593-
4600. FAX 402-331-5481. *1648*

WASHINGTON DRUG LETTER (WASHINGTON, 1979)
Washington Business Information, Inc., c/o Karen
Harrington, 1117 N. 19th St., Arlington, VA 22209.
TEL 703-247-3434. FAX 703-247-3421.
Vendor(s): Ovid Technologies, Inc. (DIOG), Data-Star.
5447

WASHINGTON INTERNATIONAL BUSINESS REPORT.
International Business-Government Counsellors Inc.,
818 Connecticut Ave. N.W., 12th Fl., Washington,
DC 20006-2702. TEL 202-872-8181. FAX 202-
872-8696. *1299*

WASHINGTON LAW REVIEW.
Washington Law Review Association, University of
Washington, School of Law, Condon Hall, JB-20,
1100 N.E. Campus Pkwy., Seattle, WA 98105.
TEL 206-543-4069. FAX 206-543-5671.
Vendor(s): Lexis-Nexis, West Services, Inc.. *3867*

THE WASHINGTON MONTHLY.
Washington Monthly Co., 1611 Connecticut Ave.,
N.W., Washington, DC 20009. TEL 202-462-0128.
FAX 202-332-8413.
Vendor(s): Information Access Co., Knight-Ridder
Information, Inc., University Microfilms International.
5716

THE WASHINGTON POST INDEX.
U M I Company 300 N. Zeeb Rd., Ann Arbor, MI
48106. TEL 313-761-4700. FAX 800-864-0019.
3716

WASHINGTON QUARTERLY.
M I T Press, 55 Hayward St., Cambridge, MA
02142. TEL 617-253-2889. FAX 617-577-1545.
Vendor(s): Information Access Co., Lexis-Nexis.
5777

WASHINGTON REMOTE SENSING LETTER.
Washington Federal Science Newsletter, Inc., 1057-
B National Press Bldg., Washington, DC 20045.
TEL 202-393-3640. FAX 301-428-0557.
Vendor(s): NewsNet. *80*

WASHINGTON TELECOM NEWS.
Phillips Business Information, Inc., 1201 Seven
Locks Rd., Potomac, MD 20854. TEL 301-424-
3338. FAX 301-309-3847.
Vendor(s): Information Access Co., NewsNet (TE04).
1953

THE WASHINGTON TIMES INDEX.
U M I Company 300 N. Zeeb Rd., Ann Arbor, MI
48106. TEL 313-761-4700. FAX 800-864-0019.
3716

WASHINGTON TRADE DAILY.
Trade Reports International Group, 2104 National
Press Bldg., Washington, DC 20045. TEL 301-946-
0817. FAX 301-946-2631.
Vendor(s): NewsNet. *1299*

WASHINGTON UNIVERSITY LAW QUARTERLY.
Washington University, School of Law, St. Louis, MO
63130. TEL 314-935-6498. FAX 314-935-6493.
Vendor(s): Lexis-Nexis, West Services, Inc.. *3867*

WASHINGTONIAN.
Washington Magazine Inc., 1828 L St., N.W., Ste.
200, Washington, DC 20036. TEL 202-296-3600.
Vendor(s): Lexis-Nexis. *3242*

WASTE TREATMENT TECHNOLOGY NEWS.
Business Communications Co., Inc. (Norwalk), 25
Van Zant St., Norwalk, CT 06855. TEL 203-853-
4266. FAX 203-853-0348.
Vendor(s): Information Access Co., NewsNet (EV26).
2859

WATER ENGINEERING AND MANAGEMENT.
Scranton Gillette Communications, Inc., 380 E.
Northwest Hwy., Des Plaines, IL 60016-2282.
TEL 708-298-6622. FAX 708-390-0408.
Vendor(s): University Microfilms International.
6978

WATER QUALITY INTERNATIONAL.
Elsevier Science Ltd., Pergamon, P.O. Box 800,
Kidlington, Oxford OX5 1DX, England. TEL 44-1865-
843000. FAX 44-1865-843010. *2841*

**WATER RESEARCH IN AUSTRALIA: CURRENT
PROJECTS.**
Department of Primary Industries and Energy,
G.P.O. Box 858, Canberra, A.C.T. 2601, Australia.
FAX 062-724526. *6980*

WATER RESOURCES ABSTRACTS (BETHESDA).
Cambridge Scientific Abstracts, 7200 Wisconsin
Ave., 6th Fl., Bethesda, MD 20814. TEL 301-961-
6750. FAX 301-961-6720.
Vendor(s): Knight-Ridder Information, Inc. (File
no.117). *6983*

WATER TECHNOLOGY NEWS.
Business Communications Co., Inc. (Norwalk), 25
Van Zant St., Norwalk, CT 06855. TEL 203-853-
4266. FAX 203-853-0348.
Vendor(s): Information Access Co.. *2859*

WATERMARKS.
University of Texas at Austin, Center for Research in Water Resources, J.J. Pickle Campus, Austin, TX 78712. TEL 512-471-3131.
Available only online. *6981*

WAVES IN RANDOM MEDIA.
I O P Publishing Ltd., Techno House, Redcliffe Way, Bristol, Avon BS1 6NX, England. TEL 44-117-929-7481. FAX 44-117-929-4318. *5576*

WAYNE LAW REVIEW.
Wayne State University Law School, 468 W. Ferry, Detroit, MI 48202. TEL 313-577-3939. FAX 313-577-5498.
Vendor(s): Lexis-Nexis, West Services, Inc.. *3868*

WEATHERWISE.
Heldref Publications, 1319 Eighteenth St., N.W., Washington, DC 20036-1802. TEL 202-296-6267. FAX 202-296-5149.
Vendor(s): Information Access Co., University Microfilms International. *5008*

WEB FINANCE.
Investment Dealers' Digest,
Available only online. *1127*

WEED ABSTRACTS.
CAB International, Wallingford, Oxon OX10 8DE, England. TEL 44-1491-832111. FAX 44-1491-833508.
Vendor(s): DIMDI, European Space Agency, Knight-Ridder Information, Inc., STN International. *184*

THE WEEK IN GERMANY.
German Information Center, 950 Third Ave., New York, NY 10022. TEL 212-888-9840. FAX 212-752-6691.
Vendor(s): Information Access Co., Lexis-Nexis, NewsNet (IT65). *3150*

WEEKLY CONGRESSIONAL MONITOR.
Congressional Quarterly Inc., 1414 22nd St., N.W., Washington, DC 20037. TEL 800-432-2250. FAX 202-728-1863. *5717*

WEEKLY CRIMINAL BULLETIN.
Canada Law Book Inc., 240 Edward St., Aurora, ON L4G 3S9, Canada. TEL 905-841-6472. FAX 905-941-5085. *3914*

WEEKLY LAW REPORTS.
Incorporated Council of Law Reporting for England and Wales, 3 Stone Bldgs., Lincoln's Inn, London WC2A 3XN, England. TEL 44-171-242-6471. FAX 44-171-831-5247.
Vendor(s): Lexis-Nexis. *3868*

WEEKLY NEWS UPDATE ON THE AMERICAS.
Nicaragua Solidarity Network, 339 Lafayette St., New York, NY 10012. TEL 212-674-9499. FAX 212-674-9139. *3128*

WEEKLY OF BUSINESS AVIATION.
McGraw-Hill Companies, Aviation Week Group (Washington), 1200 G St., N.W., Ste. 200, Washington, DC 20005. TEL 202-383-2350.
Vendor(s): Dow Jones News Retrieval (BA), Knight-Ridder Information, Inc. (File no.624/McGRAW-HILL PUBLICATIONS ONLINE), Lexis-Nexis (WBA), NewsNet (AE20). *6766*

WEEKLY PHARMACY REPORTS: THE GREEN SHEET.
F-D-C Reports, Inc., 5550 Friendship Blvd., Ste. One, Chevy Chase, MD 20815. FAX 301-664-7238.
Vendor(s): Lexis-Nexis. *5447*

WEEKLY REVIEW.
Louisiana News Bureau, Inc., Box 44212, Baton Rouge, LA 70804. TEL 504-342-1240.
Available only online. *5927*

WEIGHT WATCHERS MAGAZINE.
Weight Watchers-Twenty-First Corporation, 360 Lexington Ave., New York, NY 10017. TEL 212-370-0644. FAX 212-687-4398.
Vendor(s): Information Access Co.. *5243*

WELARA JOURNAL.
Welara Pony Society, Box 401, Yucca Valley, CA 92286. TEL 619-364-2048. FAX 619-364-2048. *6553*

WELDING ABSTRACTS.
T W I - The Welding Institute, Abington Hall, Abington, Cambridge CB1 6AL. TEL 44-1223-891162. FAX 44-1223-894588.
Vendor(s): FIZ Technik Search Service, Telesystemes - Questel. *1985*

WELDING REVIEW INTERNATIONAL.
Argus Business Media Ltd., International Trade Publications Queensway House, 2 Queensway, Redhill, Surrey RH1 1QS, England. TEL 44-1737-768611. FAX 44-1737-761989.
Vendor(s): Information Access Co. *4989*

WENATCHEE BUSINESS JOURNAL.
Wenatchee Business Journal Inc., 304 S. Mission St., Wenatchee, WA 98801-3044. TEL 509-663-6730.
Vendor(s): University Microfilms International. *970*

WER BAUT MASCHINEN IN DEUTSCHLAND.
Verlag Hoppenstedt GmbH, Havelstr. 9, 64295 Darmstadt, Germany. TEL 49-6151-380-0. FAX 49-6151-380-360. *2773*

WER LIEFERT WAS?
Wer Liefert Was? GmbH, Normannenweg 16-20, 20537 Hamburg, Germany. TEL 49-40-25440-0. FAX 49-40-2544010.
Vendor(s): FIZ Technik, Knight-Ridder Information, Inc., Lexis-Nexis. *1648*

WEST EUROPEAN POLITICS.
Frank Cass, Newbury House, 890-900 Eastern Ave., Newbury Park, Ilford, Essex IG2 7HH. TEL 44-181-599-8866. FAX 44-181-599-0954.
Vendor(s): Information Access Co.. *5778*

WEST VIRGINIA BUSINESS DIRECTORY.
American Business Directories 5711 S. 86th Circle, Box 27347, Omaha, NE 68127. TEL 402-593-4600. FAX 402-331-5481. *1648*

WESTCHESTER COUNTY BUSINESS JOURNAL.
Westfair Communications, Inc., 108 Corporate Park Dr., Ste. 105, White Plains, NY 10604-3805. TEL 914-694-3600 FAX 914-694-3699.
Vendor(s): Lexis-Nexis, University Microfilms International. *1246*

WESTERN AUSTRALIA REPORTS.
L B C Information Services, 50 Waterloo Rd., N. Ryde, N.S.W. 2113, Australia. TEL 61-2-99366444. FAX 61-2-8889706.
Vendor(s): Info-One International Pty Ltd.. *3955*

WESTERN ECONOMIC DEVELOPMENTS.
Federal Reserve Bank of San Francisco, Box 7702, San Francisco CA 94120. TEL 415-974-3230. FAX 415-974-3341. *1246*

WESTERN GROWER AND SHIPPER.
Western Grower and Shipper Publishing Co., Box 2130, Newport Beach, CA 92658. TEL 714-863-1000. FAX 714-863-9028.
Vendor(s): Knight-Ridder Information, Inc.. *245*

WESTERN JOURNAL OF COMMUNICATION.
Western States Communication Association, c/o Dennis Alexander, Department of Communication, University of Utah, Salt Lake City, UT 84112. TEL 801-581-6526. FAX 801-585-6255.
Vendor(s): University Microfilms International. *4123*

WESTERN JOURNAL OF MEDICINE.
California Medical Association, Box 7690, 221 Main St., San Francisco, CA 94105. TEL 415-882-5179. FAX 415-882-5116.
Vendor(s): Information Access Co.. *4543*

WESTERN WEEKLY REPORTS.
Carswell, One Corporate Plaza, 2075 Kennedy Rd., Scarborough, ON M1T 3V4, Canada. TEL 416-609-8000. FAX 416-298-5094.
Vendor(s): QL Systems Ltd.. *3868*

WESTPREUSSEN - JAHRBUCH.
Westpreussen-Verlag Muenster, Norbertstr. 29, 48151 Muenster, Germany. TEL 0251-523424. FAX 0251-533830. *3455*

WHAT'S ON SATELLITE.
Design Publishers, 800 Siesta Way, Sonoma, CA 95476-4413. TEL 707-939-9306. *1920*

WHEAT, BARLEY AND TRITICALE ABSTRACTS.
CAB International, Wallingford, Oxon OX10 8DE, England. TEL 44-1491-832111. FAX 44-1491-833508.
Vendor(s): DIMDI, European Space Agency, Knight-Ridder Information, Inc., STN International. *184*

WHITAKER'S BOOKS IN PRINT.
J. Whitaker & Sons Ltd., 12 Dyott St., London WC1A 1DF, England. TEL 071-836-8911. FAX 071-836-2909.
Vendor(s): Knight-Ridder Information, Inc. (File no.430). *553*

WHITE COUNTY HERITAGE.
White County Historical Society, Box 537, Searcy, AR 72145. TEL 501-268-8726. *3492*

WHO OWNS WHOM. AUSTRALASIA AND FAR EAST.
Dun & Bradstreet Ltd., Holmers Farm Way, High Wycombe, Bucks. HP12 4UL, England. TEL 44-1494-422000. FAX 44-1494-422260. *1649*

WHO OWNS WHOM. CONTINENTAL EUROPE.
Dun & Bradstreet Ltd., Holmers Farm Way, High Wycombe, Bucks. HP12 4UL, England. TEL 44-1494-422000. FAX 44-1494-422260. *1450*

WHO OWNS WHOM. NORTH AMERICA.
Dun & Bradstreet Ltd., Holmers Farm Way, High Wycombe, Bucks. HP12 4UL, England. TEL 44-1494-422000. FAX 44-1494-422260. *1490*

WHO OWNS WHOM. UNITED KINGDOM AND REPUBLIC OF IRELAND.
Dun & Bradstreet Ltd., Holmers Farm Way, High Wycombe, Bucks. HP12 4UL, England. TEL 44-1494-422000. FAX 44-1494-422260. *1649*

WHOLE EARTH REVIEW.
Point Foundation, 27 Gate Five Rd., Sausalito, CA 94965. TEL 415-332-1716. FAX 415-332-3110.
Vendor(s): Information Access Co., Knight-Ridder Information, Inc., Lexis-Nexis, Ovid Technologies, Inc., University Microfilms International. *5222*

THE WHOLE INTERNET CATALOGUE.
Global Network Navigator 2855 Telegraph Ave., Ste. 503, Berkeley, CA 94705. TEL 510-883-7220.
Available only online. *2022*

WHO'S WHO AMONG BLACK AMERICANS.
Gale Research Inc., 835 Penobscot Bldg., Detroit, MI 48226. TEL 313-961-2242. FAX 313-961-6083.
Vendor(s): Lexis-Nexis. *560*

WHO'S WHO AMONG HISPANIC AMERICANS.
Gale Research Inc., 835 Penobscot Bldg., Detroit, MI 48226. TEL 800-877-4253 FAX 313-961-6083.
Vendor(s): Lexis-Nexis. *560*

WHO'S WHO IN AMERICA.
Marquis Who's Who, A Division of Reed Elsevier Inc., 121 Chanlon Rd., New Providence, NJ 07974. TEL 908-464-6800. FAX 908-665-6688.
Vendor(s): Knight-Ridder Information, Inc. (File no.234). *560*

WHO'S WHO IN AMERICAN ART.
R.R. Bowker, A Division of Reed Elsevier Inc., 121 Chanlon Rd., New Providence, NJ 07974. TEL 908-464-6800. FAX 908-665-6683.
Vendor(s): Knight-Ridder Information, Inc. (File no.236). *560*

WHO'S WHO IN AMERICAN POLITICS.
R.R. Bowker, A Division of Reed Elsevier Inc., 121 Chanlon Rd., New Providence, NJ 07974. TEL 908-464-6800. FAX 908-665-6688.
Vendor(s): Knight-Ridder Information, Inc. (File no.236). *560*

WHO'S WHO IN TECHNOLOGY.
Gale Research Inc., Dept. 77748, Detroit, MI 48226. TEL 313-961-2242. FAX 313-961-6083.
Vendor(s): Lexis-Nexis, Orbit Search Service (WHOTECH). *562*

WICHITA BUSINESS JOURNAL.
American City Business Journals, Inc. (Wichita), 110 S. Main St., Ste. 200, Wichita, KS 67202-3745. TEL 316-267-6406. FAX 316-267-8570.
Vendor(s): Lexis-Nexis. *970*

WIDE ANGLE.
Johns Hopkins University Press, Journals Publishing Division, 2715 N. Charles St., Baltimore, MD 21218. TEL 410-516-6987. FAX 410-516-6968. *5115*

WILDERNESS.
Wilderness Society, 900 17th St., N.W., Washington, DC 20006-2596. TEL 202-833-2300. FAX 202-842-8756.
Vendor(s): Information Access Co., University Microfilms International. *2146*

WILDERNESS AND ENVIRONMENTAL MEDICINE.
Chapman & Hall, Journals Department 2-6 Boundary Row, London SE1 8HN, England. TEL 44-171-8650066. FAX 44-171-5229623. *4901*

WILDERNESS RECORD.
California Wilderness Coalition, 2655 Portage Bay E., Ste. 5, Davis, CA 95616. TEL 916-758-0380. FAX 916-758-0382. *2146*

WILLIAM MITCHELL LAW REVIEW.
William Mitchell College of Law, 875 Summit Ave., St. Paul, MN 55105. TEL 612-290-6450. FAX 612-290-6450.
Vendor(s): Lexis-Nexis, West Services, Inc.. *3869*

WILSON APPLIED SCIENCE & TECHNOLOGY ABSTRACTS.
H.W. Wilson Co., 950 University Ave., Bronx, NY 10452. TEL 718-588-8400. FAX 718-590-1617.
Vendor(s): OCLC, Wilsonline (AST). *2631*

WILSON ART ABSTRACTS.
H.W. Wilson Co., 950 University Ave., Bronx, NY 10452. TEL 718-588-8400. FAX 718-590-1617.
Vendor(s): OCLC, Ovid Technologies, Inc., Wilsonline (File ART). *463*

WILSON BULLETIN.
Wilson Ornithological Society, c/o Charles R. Blem, Ed., Department of Biology, Virginia Commonwealth University, Richmond, VA 23289-2012. TEL 804-367-1562. FAX 804-367-0503.
Vendor(s): Information Access Co.. *783*

WILSON BUSINESS ABSTRACTS.
H.W. Wilson Co., 950 University Ave., Bronx, NY 10452. TEL 718-588-8400. FAX 718-590-1617.
Vendor(s): OCLC, Wilsonline (File BPI). *1035*

WILSON EDUCATION ABSTRACTS.
H.W. Wilson Co., 950 University Ave., Bronx, NY 10452. TEL 718-588-8400. FAX 718-590-1617.
Vendor(s): OCLC, Wilsonline (File EDI). *2395*

WILSON GENERAL SCIENCE ABSTRACTS.
H.W. Wilson Co., 950 University Ave., Bronx, NY 10452. TEL 718-588-8400. FAX 718-590-1617.
Vendor(s): OCLC, Wilsonline (File GSI). *6304*

WILSON HUMANITIES ABSTRACTS.
H.W. Wilson Co., 950 University Ave., Bronx, NY 10452. TEL 718-588-8400. FAX 718-590-1617.
Vendor(s): OCLC, Ovid Technologies, Inc. (WHUM), Wilsonline (File HUM). *3632*

WILSON LIBRARY BULLETIN.
H.W. Wilson Co., 950 University Ave., Bronx, NY 10452. TEL 718-588-8400. FAX 718-590-1617.
Available only online. *4035*

WILSON QUARTERLY.
Woodrow Wilson International Center for Scholars, 901 D St., S.W., Ste. 704, Washington, DC 20024-2518.
Vendor(s): Information Access Co., University Microfilms International. *4173*

WILSON SOCIAL SCIENCES ABSTRACTS.
H.W. Wilson Co., 950 University Ave., Bronx, NY 10452. TEL 718-588-8400. FAX 718-590-1617.
Vendor(s): OCLC, University Microfilms International (PROQUEST), Wilsonline (File SSI). *6358*

WINDOW (RESEDA).
Armenian Church Research & Analysis Group, c/o Armenian National Commission, 104 N. Belmont St., Ste. 208, Glendale, CA 91206-4492. TEL 818-881-5734. *6215*

WINDOWS DEVELOPER'S JOURNAL.
R & D Publications, Inc. 1601 W. 23rd St., Ste. 200, Lawrence, KS 66046. TEL 913-841-1631. FAX 913-841-2624.
Vendor(s): Information Access Co.. *2047*

WINDOWS JOURNAL.
Wugnet Publications 7, Media, PA 19063. TEL 215-56 215-565-7106.
Vendor(s): CompuSer 0

WINDOWS SOURCES.
Ziff-Davis Publishing Co. Ave., New York, NY 10016. TEL 212-50 FAX 212-503-4141.
Vendor(s): Information Acc o.. *2000*

WINE ON LINE.
Enterprises Publishing, 400 E. 59th St., Ste. 9F, New York, NY 10022. TEL 212-755-4363. FAX 212-755-4365. *513*

WINE: THE INTERNATIONAL MARKET.
Euromonitor, 87-88 Turnmill St., London EC1M 5NA, England. TEL 44-171-251-8024. FAX 44-171-608-3149.
Vendor(s): Data-Star, Knight-Ridder Information, Inc.. *514*

WINES AND VINES.
Hiaring Co., 1800 Lincoln Ave., San Rafael, CA 94901-1298. TEL 415-453-9700. FAX 415-453-2517.
Vendor(s): Information Access Co.. *514*

WING.
Koku Shinbunsha, Kanda Kitamura Bldg., 30 Kanda Higashi-Konya-cho, Chiyoda-ku, Tokyo 101, Japan. TEL 03-3258-0880. FAX 03-3258-5004.
Vendor(s): NewsNet (AE06). *81*

WING NEWSLETTER.
Koku Shinbunsha, Kanda Kitamura Bldg., 30 Kanda Higashi-Konya-cho, Chiyoda-ku, Tokyo 101, Japan. TEL 03-3258-0880. FAX 03-3258-5004.
Vendor(s): Data-Star, Knight-Ridder Information, Inc., NewsNet. *81*

WIRELESS BUSINESS & FINANCE.
Phillips Business Information, Inc., 1201 Seven Locks Rd., Potomac, MD 20854. TEL 301-424-3338. FAX 301-309-3847.
Vendor(s): Information Access Co.. *1920*

WIRELESS DATA NEWS.
Phillips Business Information, Inc., 1201 Seven Locks Rd., Potomac, MD 20854. TEL 301-424-3338. FAX 301-309-3847.
Vendor(s): Information Access Co.. *2070*

WIRTSCHAFTSWOCHE.
Wirtschafts-Trend Zeitschriftenverlagsgesellschaft mbH, Marc-Aurel-Str. 10-12, A-1010 Vienna, Austria. TEL 01-53470-0. FAX 01-53470349. *971*

WIRTSCHAFTSWOCHE.
Verlagsgruppe Handelsblatt GmbH, Kasernenstr. 67, 40213 Duesseldorf, Germany. TEL 49-211-887-0. FAX 49-211-374955. *1246*

WISCONSIN BUSINESS DIRECTORY.
American Business Directories 5711 S. 86th Circle, Box 27347, Omaha, NE 68127. TEL 402-593-4600. FAX 402-331-5481. *1649*

WISCONSIN JEWISH CHRONICLE.
Milwaukee Jewish Federation, Inc., 1360 N. Prospect Ave., Milwaukee, WI 53202. TEL 414-271-2992. FAX 414-271-0487. *2915*

WISCONSIN LAW REVIEW.
University of Wisconsin at Madison, Law School, 975 Bascom Mall, Madison, WI 53706-1399. TEL 608-262-5815. FAX 608-262-5485.
Vendor(s): Lexis-Nexis, West Services, Inc.. *3869*

DIE WOCHE.
Die Woche Zeitungsverlag GmbH, Van-der-Smissen-Str. 3, 22767 Hamburg, Germany. TEL 49-40-3803503. FAX 49-40-38035339.
Vendor(s): Lexis-Nexis. *3151*

WOMAN'S DAY.
Hachette Filipacchi Magazines, Inc., 1633 Broadway, 42nd Fl., New York, NY 10009. TEL 212-767-6000.
Vendor(s): Information Access Co., University Microfilms International. *3527*

WOMEN AND ENVIRONMENTS.
Weed Foundation, 736 Bathurst St., Toronto, ON M5S 2R4, Canada. TEL 416-516-2379. FAX 416-531-6214.
Vendor(s): University Microfilms International. *7020*

WOMEN AND LANGUAGE.
George Mason University, Communication Department, 4400 University Dr., Fairfax, VA 22030-4444. TEL 703-993-1099. FAX 703-993-1096.
Vendor(s): Information Access Co.. *4123*

WOMEN STUDIES ABSTRACTS.
Transaction Publishers, Transaction Periodicals Consortium, Department 3092, Rutgers University, New Brunswick, NJ 08903. TEL 908-445-2280. FAX 908-445-3138. *7022*

WOMEN'S ENVIRONMENT AND DEVELOPMENT ORGANIZATION NEWS & VIEWS.
Women's Environment and Development Organization (WEDO), 845 Third Ave., 15th Fl., New York, NY 10022. TEL 212-759-7982. FAX 212-759-8647. *7012*

WOMEN'S REVIEW OF BOOKS.
Wellesley College, Center for Research on Women, Wellesley, MA 02181. TEL 617-283-2087. FAX 617-283-3645.
Vendor(s): University Microfilms International. *4173*

WOMEN'S SPORTS AND FITNESS.
2025 Pearl St., Boulder, CO 80302. TEL 303-440-5111. FAX 303-440-3313.
Vendor(s): Information Access Co., University Microfilms International. *6492*

WOMEN'S STUDIES (NEW YORK).
Gordon and Breach Science Publishers, c/o International Publishers Distributor, P.O. Box 3054, Langhorne, PA 19047-3054. TEL 215-750-2642. FAX 215-750-6343.
Vendor(s): Information Access Co.. *7021*

WOMEN'S WEAR DAILY.
Fairchild Publications, Fashion & Merchandising Group 7 W. 34th St., New York, NY 10001. TEL 212-630-4000. FAX 212-630-3566.
Vendor(s): Information Access Co., Knight-Ridder Information, Inc., Lexis-Nexis. *1837*

WOOD & WOOD PRODUCTS.
Vance Publishing Corporation (Lincolnshire), Box 1414, Lincolnshire, IL 60069-1414. TEL 708-634-2600. FAX 708-634-4379.
Vendor(s): Information Access Co.. *3039*

WOOD BASED PANELS INTERNATIONAL.
Miller Freeman Publishers Ltd. Sovereign Way, Tonbridge, Kent TN9 1RW, England. TEL 44-1732-364422. FAX 44-1732-361534.
Vendor(s): Information Access Co.. *3039*

WOOD TECHNOLOGY.
Miller Freeman, Inc. 600 Harrison St., San Francisco, CA 94107. TEL 415-905-2200. FAX 415-905-2232.
Vendor(s): Knight-Ridder Information, Inc., University Microfilms International. *3040*

WORDPERFECT FOR WINDOWS MAGAZINE.
Ivy International Communications, Inc., 270 W. Center St., Orem, UT 84057. TEL 801-228-9626. FAX 801-227-3478.
Vendor(s): CompuServe, Inc.. *2118*

WORDPERFECT MAGAZINE.
Ivy International Communications, Inc., 270 W. Center St., Orem, UT 84057. TEL 801-228-9626. FAX 801-227-3478. *2118*

WORK ALERT.
C C H Australia Ltd., P.O. Box 230, North Ryde, N.S.W. 2113, Australia. TEL 61-1-300300224. FAX 61-1-300306224. *1399*

WORK AND OCCUPATIONS.
Sage Publications, Inc., 2455 Teller Rd., Thousand Oaks, CA 91320. TEL 805-499-0721. FAX 805-499-0871.
Vendor(s): University Microfilms International. *6440*

WORKBENCH.
K C Publishing Inc., 700 W. 74th St., Ste. 310, Kansas City, MO 64112. TEL 816-531-5730. FAX 816-531-3873.
Vendor(s): Information Access Co., Knight-Ridder Information, Inc., University Microfilms International. *3604*

WORKGROUP COMPUTING REPORT.
Patricia Seybold Group, 148 State St., 7th Fl., Boston, MA 02109. TEL 617-742-5200. FAX 617-742-1028.
Vendor(s): Information Access Co., NewsNet. *2077*

WORKING WOMAN.
Lang Communications, Inc., 230 Park Ave., New York, NY 10169. TEL 212-551-9500.
Vendor(s): Information Access Co., Knight-Ridder Information, Inc.. *7013*

WORKLIFE REPORT.
I R Research Services, P.O. Box 1092, Kingston, ON K7L 4Y5, Canada. TEL 613-542-5596.
Vendor(s): University Microfilms International. *1400*

WORLD ACCOUNTING REPORT.
Financial Times Professional Publishing, Newsletters Maple House, 149 Tottenham Court Rd., London W1P 9LL, England. TEL 44-171-896-2222. FAX 44-171-896-2276.
Vendor(s): Data-Star, Information Access Co., Lexis-Nexis (WAR). *1056*

WORLD AFFAIRS (WASHINGTON).
Heldref Publications, 1319 Eighteenth St., N.W., Washington, DC 20036-1802. TEL 202-296-6267. FAX 202-296-5149.
Vendor(s): Information Access Co., University Microfilms International. *5778*

WORLD AFFAIRS REPORT.
California Institute of International Studies, Hoover Institution, Stanford, CA 94305-6010. TEL 415-322-2026. FAX 415-723-1687.
Available only online. *5778*

WORLD AGRICULTURAL ECONOMICS AND RURAL SOCIOLOGY ABSTRACTS.
CAB International, Wallingford, Oxon. OX10 8DE, England. TEL 44-1491-832111. FAX 44-1491-833508.
Vendor(s): DIMDI, European Space Agency, Knight-Ridder Information, Inc., STN International. *184*

WORLD AGRICULTURAL PRODUCTION.
U.S. Department of Agriculture, Foreign Agricultural Service, Information Division, Rm. 5920-S, Washington, DC 20250-1000. TEL 202-720-7937.
Vendor(s): Information Access Co.. *163*

WORLD AGRICULTURAL SUPPLY AND DEMAND ESTIMATES.
U.S. Department of Agriculture, World Agricultural Outlook Board, 14th St. and Independence Ave., S.W., Rm. 5143-S, Washington, DC 20250-3800. TEL 202-250-3800.
Vendor(s): Knight-Ridder Information, Inc.. *202*

WORLD AIRLINE NEWS.
Phillips Business Information, Inc., 1201 Seven Locks Rd., Potomac, MD 20854. TEL 301-424-3338. FAX 301-309-3847.
Vendor(s): Information Access Co., NewsNet (AE31). *6766*

WORLD AIRPORT WEEK.
Phillips Business Information, Inc., 1201 Seven Locks Rd., Potomac, MD 20854. TEL 301-424-3338. FAX 301-309-3847.
Vendor(s): Information Access Co., NewsNet. *6766*

WORLD BANK ANNUAL CONFERENCE ON DEVELOPMENT ECONOMICS. PROCEEDINGS.
World Bank, International Bank for Reconstruction and Development, 1818 H St., N.W., Washington, DC 20433. TEL 202-473-1155. FAX 202-522-2627.
Vendor(s): Knight-Ridder Information, Inc.. *971*

WORLD BANK RESEARCH OBSERVER.
World Bank, 1818 H St., N.W., Washington, DC 20433. TEL 202-473-1155. FAX 202-522-2627.
Vendor(s): Knight-Ridder Information, Inc., University Microfilms International. *1127*

WORLD CERAMICS ABSTRACTS.
Ceram Research Ltd., Queens Rd., Penkhull, Stoke-on-Trent, Staffs. ST4 7LQ, England.
Vendor(s): Orbit Search Service. *1662*

WORLD COTTON SITUATION.
U.S. Department of Agriculture, Foreign Agricultural Service, Information Division, Rm. 5920-S, Washington, DC 20250-1000. TEL 202-720-7937.
Vendor(s): Information Access Co.. *246*

WORLD DEBT TABLES.
World Bank, 1818 H St., N.W., Washington, DC 20433. TEL 202-473-1155. FAX 202-522-2627.
Vendor(s): GSI-ECO. *1317*

WORLD DIRECTORY OF HUMAN RIGHTS RESEARCH AND TRAINING INSTITUTIONS.
Unesco Publishing, 7 Place de Fontenoy, 75352 Paris 07SP, France. *1649*

WORLD DRUG MARKET MANUAL.
IMSWORLD Publications Ltd., 7 Harewood Ave., London NW1 6JB, England. TEL 0171-393-5000. FAX 0171-393-5900. *5447*

WORLD ECONOMIC OUTLOOK.
International Monetary Fund, Publication Services, 700 19th St., N.W., Washington, DC 20431. TEL 202-623-7430. FAX 202-623-7201.
Vendor(s): Information Access Co.. *1247*

WORLD FACTBOOK.
U.S. National Technical Information Service, 5285 Port Royal Rd., Springfield, VA 22161. TEL 703-482-0623.
Vendor(s): Lexis-Nexis. *5778*

WORLD HEALTH.
World Health Organization, Distribution and Sales, CH-1211 Geneva 27, Switzerland. TEL 41-22-791-2111. FAX 41-22-791-4857.
Vendor(s): Information Access Co., Knight-Ridder Information, Inc., University Microfilms International. *5979*

WORLD HEALTH ORGANIZATION. BULLETIN.
World Health Organization, Distribution and Sales, CH-1211 Geneva 27, Switzerland. TEL 41-22-791-2476. FAX 41-22-791-4857.
Vendor(s): Information Access Co.. *4544*

WORLD HOSPITALS AND HEALTH SERVICES.
International Hospital Federation, 4 Abbots Pl., London NW6 4NP, England. TEL 0171-372-7181. FAX 0171-328-7433. *3556*

WORLD INSURANCE REPORT.
Financial Times Financial Publishing Maple House, 149 Tottenham Ct. Rd., London W1P 9LL, England. TEL 44-171-896-2314. FAX 44-171-896-2319.
Vendor(s): Information Access Co.. *3669*

WORLD LITERATURE TODAY.
110 Monnet Hall, University of Oklahoma, Norman, OK 73019-0375. TEL 405-325-4531. FAX 405-325-7495.
Vendor(s): Information Access Co., University Microfilms International. *4287*

WORLD MEDIA. BROADCASTING NEWS.
B B C Monitoring, Caversham Park, Reading, Berks. RG4 8TZ, England. TEL 44-1734-469289. FAX 44-1734-463823.
Vendor(s): Data-Star, Lexis-Nexis. *1942*

WORLD MEDIA. BROADCASTING SCHEDULES.
B B C Monitoring, Caversham Park, Reading, Berks. RG4 8TZ, England. TEL 44-1734-469289. FAX 44-1734-463823. *1942*

WORLD NUCLEAR PERFORMANCE.
McGraw-Hill Companies, Energy & Business Newsletters, 1221 Ave. of the Americas, 36th Fl., New York, NY 10020. TEL 212-512-6410. *2585*

WORLD OIL.
Gulf Publishing Co., Box 2608, Houston, TX 77252-2608. TEL 713-529-4301. FAX 713-520-4433.
Vendor(s): Information Access Co.. *5380*

WORLD POLICY GUIDE.
Financial Times Financial Publishing Maple House, 149 Tottenham Court Rd., London W1P 9LL, England. TEL 44-171-896-2314. FAX 44-171-896-2319. *3670*

WORLD POLICY JOURNAL.
World Policy Institute, 65 Fifth Ave., Ste. 413, New York, NY 10003-3003. TEL 212-229-5808. FAX 212-229-5579.
Vendor(s): Information Access Co., University Microfilms International. *5779*

WORLD POLITICS (BALTIMORE).
Johns Hopkins University Press, Journals Publishing Division, 2715 N. Charles St., Baltimore, MD 21218-4319. TEL 410-516-6987. FAX 410-516-6968.
Vendor(s): Information Access Co.. *5779*

WORLD POWER SYSTEMS INTELLIGENCE.
Forecast International Inc. - DMS, 22 Commerce Rd., Newtown, CT 06470-1643. TEL 203-426-0800. FAX 203-426-0233.
Vendor(s): Knight-Ridder Information, Inc.. *2560*

WORLD PRESS REVIEW.
Stanley Foundation (New York), 200 Madison Ave., Ste. 2104, New York, NY 10016. TEL 212-889-5155. FAX 212-889-5634.
Vendor(s): Information Access Co., University Microfilms International. *4174*

WORLD PUBLISHING MONITOR.
Pira International, Randalls Rd., Leatherhead, Surrey KT22 7RU, England. TEL 44-1372-802050. FAX 44-1372-802239.
Vendor(s): Data-Star, FIZ Technik, Knight-Ridder Information, Inc., Orbit Search Service, STN International. *2004*

WORLD RIG FORECAST.
Financial Times Energy Publishing Maple House, 149 Tottenham Court Rd., London W1P 9LL, England. TEL 0171-896-2241. FAX 0171-896-2275.
Vendor(s): Data-Star, Knight-Ridder Information, Inc., Lexis-Nexis. *2561*

WORLD SURFACE COATING ABSTRACTS.
Paint Research Association, 8 Waldegrave Rd., Teddington, Middlesex TW11 8LD, England. TEL 44-181-977-4427. FAX 44-181-943-4705.
Vendor(s): Orbit Search Service (WSCA). *5312*

WORLD TEXTILE ABSTRACTS.
Elsevier Science Ltd., P.O. Box 300, Kidlington, Oxford OX5 1DX, England. TEL 44-1865-843000. FAX 44-1365-843010.
Vendor(s): Knight-Ridder Information, Inc. (File no.67), Orbit Search Service (WTA). *5691*

WORLD TRADE.
Freedom Magazines, Inc., 17702 Cowan, Ste. 100, Irvine, CA 92714-6035. TEL 714-793-3500.
Vendor(s) University Microfilms International. *1300*

WORLD TRANSLATIONS INDEX.
International Translations Centre (ITC), Schuttersveld 2, 2611 WE Delft, Netherlands. TEL 31-15-2142242. FAX 31-15-2158535.
Vendor(s): European Space Agency (File no.33/WTI), Knight-Ridder Information, Inc. (File no.295). *6305*

WORLD TUNNELLING.
Mining Journal Ltd., 60 Worship St., London EC2A 2HD, England. TEL 44-171-216-6060. FAX 44-171-216-5050.
Vendor(s): Information Access Co.. *2676*

WORLD WASTES.
Intertec Publishing Corp. (Atlanta), 6151 Powers Ferry Rd., N.W., Atlanta, GA 30339-2941. TEL 770-955-2500. FAX 770-955-0400.
Vendor(s): Information Access Co., University Microfilms International. *2859*

WORLD WATCH.
Worldwatch Institute, 1776 Massachusetts Ave., N.W., Washington, DC 20036. TEL 202-452-1999. FAX 202-296-7365.
Vendor(s): Information Access Co., University Microfilms International. *2826*

WORLDCASTS: PRODUCT EDITION.
Information Access Company 362 Lakeside Dr., Foster City, CA 94404. TEL 415-378-5200. FAX 415-358-4759.
Vendor(s): Data-Star, Knight-Ridder Information, Inc.. *1036*

WORLDCASTS: REGIONAL EDITION.
Information Access Company 362 Lakeside Dr., Foster City, CA 94404. TEL 415-378-5200. FAX 415-358-4759.
Vendor(s): Data-Star, Knight-Ridder Information, Inc.. *1036*

THE WORLDPAPER.
World Times, Inc., 210 World Trade Center, Boston, MA 02210. TEL 617-439-5400. FAX 617-439-5415.
Vendor(s): Lexis-Nexis. *5779*

WORLDSCOPE COMPANY DATABASE.
Worldscope-Disclosure Partners, 1000 Lafayette Blvd., Bridgeport, CT 06604. TEL 203-330-5000. FAX 203-330-5001.
Vendor(s): Dow Jones News Retrieval, Lexis-Nexis, OCLC. *1360*

WORLDVIEWS.
Third World Resources, 464 19th St., Oakland, CA 94612-2297. TEL 510-835-4692. FAX 510-835-3017.
Vendor(s): Knight-Ridder Information, Inc.. *1318*

WORLDWIDE BIOTECH.
Worldwide Videotex, Box 3273, Boynton Beach, FL 33424-3273. TEL 407-738-2276.
Vendor(s): Data-Star, Information Access Co., Knight-Ridder Information, Inc.. *666*

WORLDWIDE DATABASES.
Worldwide Videotex, Box 3273, Boynton Beach, FL 33424-3273. TEL 407-738-2276.
Vendor(s): Data-Star, Information Access Co., Knight-Ridder Information, Inc., NewsNet (PB44). *2067*

WORLDWIDE ENERGY.
Worldwide Videotex, Box 3273, Boynton Beach, FL 33424-3273. TEL 407-738-2276.
Vendor(s): Information Access Co., NewsNet (EY63). *2561*

WORLDWIDE TELECOM.
Worldwide Videotex, Box 3273, Boynton Beach, FL 33424-3273. TEL 407-738-2276.
Vendor(s): Data-Star, Information Access Co., Knight-Ridder Information, Inc., NewsNet (TE19). *1953*

WORLDWIDE VIDEOTEX UPDATE.
Worldwide Videotex, Box 3273, Boynton Beach, FL 33424-3273. TEL 407-738-2276.
Vendor(s): Data-Star, Information Access Co., Knight-Ridder Information, Inc., NewsNet (PB08). *1930*

THE WRITER.
Writer, Inc., 120 Boylston St., Boston, MA 02116. TEL 617-423-3157.
Vendor(s): Information Access Co., University Microfilms International. *4287*

WRITER'S DIGEST.
F & W Publications, Inc., 1507 Dana Ave., Cincinnati, OH 45207. TEL 513-531-2222.
Vendor(s): Information Access Co., University Microfilms International. *3713*

WYOMING BUSINESS DIRECTORY.
American Business Directories 5711 S. 86th Circle, Box 27347, Omaha, NE 68127. TEL 402-593-4600. FAX 402-331-5481. *1650*

WYOMING LABOR FORCE TRENDS.
Wyoming Department of Employment, Research & Planning Division, Box 2760, Casper, WY 82602. TEL 307-438-3808. *1400*

X MAGAZINE.
Jeff Hansen, Ed. & Pub., Box 1077, Royal Oak, MI 48068-1077. *5206*

YACHTING.
Times Mirror Magazines, Inc. (Greenwich), 20 Elm St., Greenwich, CT 06830. TEL 203-625-4480. FAX 203-625-4481.
Vendor(s): Information Access Co.. *6542*

YAHOO! INTERNET LIFE.
Ziff-Davis Publishing Co., One Park Ave., New York, NY 10016. TEL 212-503-4804. FAX 212-503-5699. *2042*

YALE JOURNAL OF CRITICISM.
Johns Hopkins University Press, Journals Publishing Division, 2715 N. Charles St., Baltimore, MD 21218-4319. TEL 410-516-6987. FAX 410-516-6968. *4289*

YALE JOURNAL OF INTERNATIONAL LAW.
Yale Journal of International Law, Inc., Yale Law School, Box 208215, New Haven, CT 06520-8215. TEL 203-432-4884. FAX 203-432-2592. *3945*

YALE JOURNAL ON REGULATION.
Yale University, School of Law, Box 208215, New Haven, CT 06520. TEL 203-432-7652. FAX 203-432-2592.
Vendor(s): West Services, Inc.. *3870*

YALE LAW JOURNAL.
Yale University, School of Law, Box 208215, New Haven, CT 06520. TEL 203-432-1666. FAX 203-432-4863.
Vendor(s): Information Access Co., Lexis-Nexis. *3871*

YEAR BOOK OF ANESTHESIOLOGY AND PAIN MANAGEMENT.
Mosby - Year Book, Inc., Continuity Division, 200 N. LaSalle, Chicago, IL 60601. TEL 312-726-9733. FAX 312-726-6075.
Vendor(s): Ovid Technologies, Inc.. *4594*

YEAR BOOK OF CARDIOLOGY.
Mosby - Year Book, Inc., Continuity Division, 200 N. LaSalle, Chicago, IL 60601. TEL 312-726-9733. FAX 312-726-6075.
Vendor(s): Ovid Technologies, Inc.. *4611*

YEAR BOOK OF DENTISTRY.
Mosby - Year Book, Inc., Continuity Division, 200 N. LaSalle, Chicago, IL 60601. TEL 312-726-9733. FAX 312-726-6075.
Vendor(s): Ovid Technologies, Inc.. *4657*

YEAR BOOK OF DERMATOLOGIC SURGERY.
Mosby - Year Book, Inc. (Chicago) 200 N. LaSalle St., Chicago, IL 60601. TEL 312-726-9733.
Vendor(s): Ovid Technologies, Inc.. *4665*

YEAR BOOK OF DERMATOLOGY.
Mosby - Year Book, Inc., Continuity Division, 200 N. LaSalle, Chicago, IL 60601. TEL 312-726-9733. FAX 312-726-6075.
Vendor(s): Ovid Technologies, Inc.. *4665*

YEAR BOOK OF DIAGNOSTIC RADIOLOGY.
Mosby - Year Book, Inc., Continuity Division, 200 N. LaSalle, Chicago, IL 60601. TEL 312-726-9733. FAX 312-726-6075.
Vendor(s): Ovid Technologies, Inc.. *4885*

YEAR BOOK OF DIGESTIVE DISEASES.
Mosby - Year Book, Inc., Continuity Division, 200 N. LaSalle, Chicago, IL 60601. TEL 312-726-9746. FAX 312-726-6933.
Vendor(s): Ovid Technologies, Inc.. *4697*

YEAR BOOK OF DRUG THERAPY.
Mosby - Year Book, Inc., Continuity Division, 200 N. LaSalle, Chicago, IL 60601. TEL 312-726-9733.
Vendor(s): Ovid Technologies, Inc.. *5448*

YEAR BOOK OF EMERGENCY MEDICINE.
Mosby - Year Book, Inc., Continuity Division, 200 N. LaSalle, Chicago, IL 60601. TEL 312-726-9733. FAX 312-726-6075.
Vendor(s): Ovid Technologies, Inc.. *4793*

YEAR BOOK OF FAMILY PRACTICE.
Mosby - Year Book, Inc., Continuity Division, 200 N. LaSalle, Chicago, IL 60601. TEL 312-726-9733. FAX 312-726-6075.
Vendor(s): Ovid Technologies, Inc.. *4545*

YEAR BOOK OF GERIATRICS AND GERONTOLOGY.
Mosby - Year Book, Inc. (Chicago) 200 N. LaSalle St., Chicago, IL 60601-1080. TEL 312-726-9733. FAX 312-726-6075.
Vendor(s): Ovid Technologies, Inc.. *3298*

YEAR BOOK OF HAND SURGERY.
Mosby - Year Book, Inc., Continuity Division, 200 N. LaSalle St., Chicago, IL 60601-1080. TEL 312-726-9733. FAX 312-726-6075.
Vendor(s): Ovid Technologies, Inc.. *4923*

YEAR BOOK OF HEMATOLOGY.
Mosby - Year Book, Inc., Continuity Division, 200 N. LaSalle, Chicago, IL 60601. TEL 312-726-9733. FAX 312-726-6075.
Vendor(s): Ovid Technologies, Inc.. *4703*

YEAR BOOK OF INFECTIOUS DISEASES.
Mosby - Year Book, Inc. (Chicago) 200 N. LaSalle St., Chicago, IL 60601-1080. TEL 312-726-9733. FAX 312-726-6075.
Vendor(s): Ovid Technologies, Inc.. *4629*

YEAR BOOK OF MEDICINE.
Mosby - Year Book, Inc., Continuity Division, 200 N. LaSalle, Chicago, IL 60601. TEL 312-726-9733. FAX 312-726-6075.
Vendor(s): Ovid Technologies, Inc.. *4545*

THE YEAR BOOK OF NEONATAL AND PERINATAL MEDICINE.
Mosby - Year Book, Inc., Continuity Division, 200 N. LaSalle, Chicago, IL 60601. TEL 312-726-9746. FAX 312-726-6075.
Vendor(s): Ovid Technologies, Inc.. *4746*

YEAR BOOK OF NEPHROLOGY.
Mosby - Year Book, Inc. (Chicago) 200 N. LaSalle St., Chicago, IL 60601-1080. TEL 312-726-9733. FAX 312-726-6075.
Vendor(s): Ovid Technologies, Inc.. *4932*

YEAR BOOK OF NEUROLOGY & NEUROSURGERY.
Mosby - Year Book, Inc., Continuity Division, 200 N. LaSalle, Chicago, IL 60601. TEL 312-726-9733. FAX 312-726-6075.
Vendor(s): Ovid Technologies, Inc.. *4871*

YEAR BOOK OF NEURORADIOLOGY.
Mosby - Year Book, Inc. (Chicago) 200 N. LaSalle St., Chicago, IL 60601. TEL 312-726-9733.
Vendor(s): Ovid Technologies, Inc.. *4885*

YEAR BOOK OF NUCLEAR MEDICINE.
Mosby - Year Book, Inc., Continuity Division, 200 N. LaSalle, Chicago, IL 60601. TEL 312-726-9733. FAX 312-726-6075.
Vendor(s): Ovid Technologies, Inc.. *4885*

YEAR BOOK OF OBSTETRICS AND GYNECOLOGY.
Mosby - Year Book, Inc., Continuity Division, 200 N. LaSalle, Chicago, IL 60601. TEL 312-726-9733. FAX 312-726-6075.
Vendor(s): Ovid Technologies, Inc.. *4746*

YEAR BOOK OF OCCUPATIONAL AND ENVIRONMENTAL MEDICINE.
Mosby - Year Book, Inc. (Chicago) 200 N. LaSalle St., Chicago, IL 60601-1080. TEL 312-726-9733. FAX 312-726-6075.
Vendor(s): Ovid Technologies, Inc.. *4545*

YEAR BOOK OF ONCOLOGY.
Mosby - Year Book, Inc., Continuity Division, 200 N. LaSalle, Chicago, IL 60601. TEL 312-726-9733. FAX 312-726-6075.
Vendor(s): Ovid Technologies, Inc.. *4765*

YEAR BOOK OF OPHTHALMOLOGY.
Mosby - Year Book, Inc., Continuity Division, 200 N. LaSalle, Chicago, IL 60601. TEL 312-726-9733. FAX 312-726-6075.
Vendor(s): Ovid Technologies, Inc.. *4779*

YEAR BOOK OF ORTHOPEDICS.
Mosby - Year Book, Inc., Continuity Division, 200 N. LaSalle, Chicago, IL 60601. TEL 312-726-9733. FAX 312-726-6075.
Vendor(s): Ovid Technologies, Inc.. *4793*

YEAR BOOK OF PATHOLOGY AND LABORATORY MEDICINE.
Mosby - Year Book, Inc., Continuity Division, 200 N. LaSalle, Chicago, IL 60601. TEL 312-726-9733. FAX 312-726-6075.
Vendor(s): Ovid Technologies, Inc.. *4545*

YEAR BOOK OF PEDIATRICS.
Mosby - Year Book, Inc., Continuity Division, 200 N. LaSalle, Chicago, IL 60601. TEL 312-726-9733. FAX 312-726-6075.
Vendor(s): Ovid Technologies, Inc.. *4815*

YEAR BOOK OF PLASTIC, RECONSTRUCTIVE, AND AESTHETIC SURGERY.
Mosby - Year Book, Inc., Continuity Division, 200 N. LaSalle, Chicago, IL 60601. TEL 312-726-9733. FAX 312-726-6075.
Vendor(s): Ovid Technologies, Inc.. *4923*

Online

YEAR BOOK OF PSYCHIATRY AND APPLIED MENTAL HEALTH.
Mosby - Year Book, Inc., Continuity Division, 200 N. LaSalle, Chicago, IL 60601. TEL 312-726-9733. FAX 312-726-6075.
Vendor(s): Ovid Technologies, Inc.. *4871*

YEAR BOOK OF PULMONARY DISEASE.
Mosby - Year Book, Inc., Continuity Division, 200 N. LaSalle, Chicago, IL 60601. TEL 312-726-9746. FAX 312-726-6075.
Vendor(s): Ovid Technologies, Inc.. *4892*

YEAR BOOK OF SURGERY.
Mosby - Year Book, Inc., Continuity Division, 200 N. LaSalle, Chicago, IL 60601. TEL 312-726-9733. FAX 312-726-6075.
Vendor(s): Ovid Technologies, Inc.. *4923*

YEAR BOOK OF TRANSPLANTATION.
Mosby - Year Book, Inc. (Chicago) 200 LaSalle St., Chicago, IL 60601. TEL 312-726-9733.
Vendor(s): Ovid Technologies, Inc.. *4923*

YEAR BOOK OF ULTRASOUND.
Mosby - Year Book, Inc. (Chicago) 200 N. LaSalle St., Chicago, IL 60601-1080. TEL 312-726-9733. FAX 312-726-6075.
Vendor(s): Ovid Technologies, Inc.. *4885*

YEAR BOOK OF UROLOGY.
Mosby - Year Book, Inc., Continuity Division, 200 N. LaSalle, Chicago, IL 60601. TEL 312-726-9733. FAX 312-726-6075.
Vendor(s): Ovid Technologies, Inc.. *4932*

YEAR BOOK OF VASCULAR SURGERY.
Mosby - Year Book, Inc., Continuity Division, 200 N. LaSalle, Chicago, IL 60601. TEL 312-726-9733. FAX 312-726-6075.
Vendor(s): Ovid Technologies, Inc.. *4611*

YELLOW PAGES & DIRECTORY REPORT.
SIMBA Information Inc. 11 Riverbend Dr. S., Box 4324, Stamford, CT 06907-0234. TEL 203-358-9900. FAX 203-358-5824.
Vendor(s): Information Access Co.. *1650*

YINGSHI WENXUE.
Shandong Sheng Yingshi Zhizuo Zhongxin, No. 55, Wenhua Donglu, Jinan, Shandong 250014, People's Republic of China. TEL 86-0531-657715. *4289*

YOUTH MARKETS ALERT.
E P M Communications, 160 Mercer St., 3rd Fl., New York, NY 10012-3212. TEL 212-941-0099. FAX 212-941-1622.
Vendor(s): Information Access Co., Knight-Ridder Information, Inc., Lexis-Nexis (AD12). *1491*

Z V E I ELEKTRO UND ELEKTRONIK - EINKAUFSFUEHRER.
Verlag W. Sachon, Schloss Mindelburg, 87714 Mindelheim, Germany. TEL 49-8261-999-0. FAX 49-8261-999-180.
Vendor(s): Data-Star, FIZ Technik. *2681*

ZEITSCHRIFT FUER ANGEWANDTE MATHEMATIK UND PHYSIK.
Birkhaeuser Verlag, P.O. Box 133, CH-4010 Basel, Switzerland. TEL 41-61-2050730. FAX 41-61-2050791. *4405*

ZEITSCHRIFTEN - DATENBANK (Z D B).
Deutsches Bibliotheksinstitut, Abt. 1 - Publikationen, Alt-Moabit 101A, 10559 Berlin, Germany. TEL 49-30-39077-0. FAX 49-30-39077100. *4036*

ZENTRALBLATT FUER DIDAKTIK DER MATHEMATIK.
Fachinformationszentrum Karlsruhe, Gesellschaft fuer wissenschaftlich-technische Information mbH, 76344 Eggenstein-Leopoldshafen, Germany. TEL 07247-808-333. FAX 07247-808-135.
Vendor(s): STN International. *4405*

ZENTRALBLATT FUER MATHEMATIK UND IHRE GRENZGEBIETE.
Springer-Verlag, Heidelberger Platz 3, 14197 Berlin, Germany. TEL 49-30-8207-0. FAX 49-30-8214091.
Vendor(s): STN International (MATH). *4406*

ZERO HORA.
Zero Hora Editora Jornalistica S.A., Av. Ipiranga 1075, 90169-900 Porto Alegre, RS, Brazil. TEL 55-51-2184400. FAX 55-51-2184580. *3118*

ZHONGGUO FALU NIANJIAN.
Zhongguo Faxuehui, Zhongguo Falu Nianjian Bianjibu, No. 6 Nandajie, Xizhimen, Beijing 100035, People's Republic of China. TEL 010-6038971. FAX 010-6032251.
Available only online. *3872*

ZHONGGUO SHENGWUXUE WENZHAI.
Zhongguo Kexueyuan, Shanghai Wenxian Qingbao Zhongxin, 319 Yueyang Lu, Shanghai 200031, People's Republic of China. TEL 0086-021-4336650. FAX 0086-021-4718906. *625*

ZHONGGUO XINLI WEISHENG ZAZH .
Beijing Yike Daxue, Jingshen Weisheng Yanjiusuo, 38 Huayuan Beilu, Beijing 100083, People's Republic of China. TEL 861-2010890. FAX 861-2027314.
Vendor(s): Knight-Ridder Information, Inc.. *5888*

ZHONGGUO YANGFENG.
Zhongguo Nongye Kexueyuan, Yangfeng Yanjiusuo, Xiangshan, Beijing 100093, People's Republic of China. TEL 81-10-6259-1473. FAX 86-10-6259-1620.
Vendor(s): Knight-Ridder Information, Inc.. *165*

ZOO BIOLOGY.
John Wiley & Sons, Inc., Journals, 605 Third Ave., New York, NY 10158. TEL 212-850-6645. FAX 212-850-6021. *824*

ZOOLOGICAL RECORD.
BIOSIS, 2100 Arch St., Philadelphia PA 19103-1399. TEL 215-587-4847. FAX 215-587-2016.
Vendor(s): Knight-Ridder Information, Inc. (File no.185). *625*

ZUZU'S PETALS QUARTERLY ONLINE.
Zeitgeist Publishing (Whitehall), Box 156, Whitehall, PA 18052. TEL 610-821-1324. *4291*

4 1 1 NEWSLETTER.
C C M I, 11300 Rockville Pike, Ste. 1100, Rockville, MD 20852-3030. TEL 301-816-8950. FAX 301-816-8945.
Vendor(s): Data-Star (PTBN) Knight-Ridder Information, Inc. (File no.636), NewsNet (TE95). *1953*

13(F) INSTITUTIONAL PORTFOLIOS.
C D A Investment Technologies, Inc., 1355 Piccard Dr., Rockville, MD 20850. FAX 301-590-1329. *1360*

13(F) INSTITUTIONAL STOCK HOLDINGS.
C D A Investment Technologies, Inc., 1355 Piccard Dr., Rockville, MD 20850. FAX 301-590-1329. *1360*

360 DEGREES: ART & LITERARY REVIEW.
360 Degree Exchange, Inc., 980 Bush St., Ste. 200, San Francisco, CA 94109. TEL 202-628-1836. FAX 202-628-1843. *1815*

4080 HIP HOP MAGAZINE.
4080 Publishing, 2550 Shattuck, Ste. 107, Berkeley, CA 94704. TEL 510-848-4080. FAX 510-848-2499. *3242*

Vendor Listing/Serials Online

AUSINET
Information Management Group, 310 Ferntree Gully
Rd., Clayton, Vic. 3168, Australia Tel: 554 8433
A B I X: Australasian Business Intelligence.
Australian Education Index.
The Business Who's Who of Australia.

BELINDIS (Subsidiary of: Belgian Ministry of
Economic Affairs)
Data Processing Centre, 30 rue de Mot, 1040
Brussels, Belgium Tel: 32-22336737 Telex:
23509 energi B
Fax: 32-22304619.
Bibliotheque Africaine. Liste des Acquisitions.
(AFLI)
I N I S Atomindex.
Recueil des Brevets d'Invention.

BUREAU OF NATIONAL AFFAIRS
Book Div., 1250 23rd St., NW, Washington, DC
20037. Tel: 202-452-4132 Telex: 892692
Fax: 202-452-4062.
B N A's Banking Report.
Daily Labor Report.
Daily Tax Report.
S E C News Digest.
Securities Regulation & Law Report.

CEDOCAR
26 Bd. Victor, 75996 Paris Armees, France
Tel: 33-145523456 Telex: 202778 F
Fax: 33-145524993.
Alloys Index.
Computer & Control Abstracts.
Electrical & Electronics Abstracts.
Engineering Index Annual.
Engineering Index Monthly.
Government Reports Announcements & Index.
Key Abstracts - Business Automation.
Metals Abstracts.
Metals Abstracts Index.
Nonferrous Metals Alert.
Physics Abstracts.
Polymers, Ceramics, Composites Alert.

CISTI (Subsidiary of: National Research
Council of Canada)
Montreal Rd., Bldg. M55, Ottawa, Ont. K1A 0S2,
Canada Tel: 613-993-1210 Telex: 0533115
Fax: 613-952-8244.
Alloys Index.
Bibliography and Index of Geology.
Bibliography of Agriculture.
Biological Abstracts.
Biological Abstracts - R R M.

CAB International. Bureau of Nutrition. Annotated
Bibliographies.
CAB International. Bureau of Soils. Annotated
Bibliographies.
Canadian Theses.
Canadiana on Microfiche.
Canadiana Pre-1901.
Current Index to Journals in Education.
Engineering Index Monthly.
Food Science and Technology Abstracts.
Forest Products Abstracts.
Forestry Abstracts.
Government Reports Announcements & Index.
Helminthological Abstracts.
I N I S Atomindex.
International Biodeterioration & Biodegradation.
Merck Index: An Encyclopedia of Chemicals and
Drugs.
Metals Abstracts.
Metals Abstracts Index.
Nematological Abstracts.
Nonferrous Metals Alert.
Nutrition Abstracts and Reviews. Series B:
Livestock Feeds and Feeding.
Polymers, Ceramics, Composites Alert.
Romulus.
Steels Alert.

CREDOC
34 rue de la Montagne, BP 11, 1000 Brussels,
Belgium Tel: 33 (2) 513 9213 Telex: 63129
CREDOC B
Fax: 32-25130911.
Steels Alert.

**CANADIAN CENTRE FOR OCCUPATIONAL HEALTH
AND SAFETY**
250 Main St., Hamilton, Ont. L8N 1H6, Canada
Tel: 416-525-2981
R T E C S.

**CENTRAL INSTITUTE FOR SCIENTIFIC AND
TECHNICAL INFORMATION**
52 A.G. Nasser, Sofia 1C40, Bulgaria Tel: 71-91-
91 Telex: 22404
Biological Abstracts.
Biological Abstracts - R R M.
Physical Therapy.

CHEMICAL INFORMATION SYSTEMS (Subsidiary of:
Div. of Fein-Marquart Assocs., Inc.)
7215 York Rd., Baltimore, MD 21212. Tel: 410-
321-8440 Telex: 9103801738
Fax: 301-296-0712.
R T E C S.

COMMISSION OF THE EUROPEAN COMMUNITIES
Rue de la Loi 200, 1049 Brussels, Belgium
Tel: 322-235-00-01
Fax: 322-2360624.
Directory of Community Legislation in Force.
Eurostatistics Data for Short Term Economic
Analysis.
S C A D Bulletin.

COMPUSERVE, INC.
5000 Arlington Centre Blvd., Columbus, OH 43220
Tel: 614-457-0802
Fax: 614-457-0348.
Annual Survey of Manufactures.
Biomedical Market Newsletter.
BioVenture View.
Blood Weekly.
Boston Business Journal.
Business Journal (Sacramento).
Cancer Researcher Weekly.
Census and You.
Census of Agriculture: Final Reports.
Census of Construction Industries: Final Reports.
Census of Governments (Final Reports).
Census of Manufactures: Final Reports.
Census of Retail Trade: Final Reports.
Census of Service Industries: Final Reports.
Census of Wholesale Trade: Final Reports.
CompuServe Magazine.
Consolidated Federal Funds Report.
Corporate Report Minnesota.
County and City Data Book.
County Business Patterns.
Cowles - SIMBA Media Daily.
Current Business Reports: Monthly Retail Trade:
Sales and Inventories.
Current Business Reports: Monthly Wholesale
Trade, Sales and Inventories.
Current Construction Reports: Housing Starts.
Current Construction Reports: Housing Units
Authorized by Building Permits.
Current Construction Reports: New One-Family
Houses Sold.
Current Construction Reports: New Residential
Construction in Selected Metropolitan Areas.
Current Construction Reports: Value of New
Construction Put in Place.
Current Governments Reports: City Employment.
Current Governments Reports: County
Government Employment.
Current Governments Reports: Government
Finances.
Current Governments Reports: Public
Employment.
Current Governments Reports: State Government
Tax Collections.
Current Housing Reports: Housing Vacancies and
Home Ownership.

Vendor

Current Industrial Reports.
Current Industrial Reports: Broadwoven Fabrics (Gray).
Current Industrial Reports: Fats and Oils. Oilseed Crushings.
Current Industrial Reports: Fats and Oils. Production, Consumption, and Stocks.
Current Population Reports: Consumer Income. Money Income of Households, Families and Persons in the United States (Year).
Current Population Reports: Population Characteristics. Geographical Mobility.
Current Population Reports: Population Characteristics. Marital Status and Living Arrangements.
Current Population Reports: Population Characteristics. School Enrollment: Social and Economic Characteristics of Students.
Current Population Reports: Population Estimates and Projections. United States Population Estimates by Age, Sex, Race and Hispanic Origin.
Current Population Reports: Series P-25. Population Estimates and Projections.
Current Population Reports: Series P-70. Household Economic Studies.
Econews.
Foreign Trade Reports. U.S. Export and Import Merchandise Trade and Supplement.
Fortune Magazine.
International Population Data.
International Product Alert.
Japanese Journal of Ophthalmology.
Journal of Aquariculture and Aquatic Sciences.
Law and Order.
Market: Europe.
Market: Latin America.
Minneapolis - St. Paul CityBusiness.
Monthly Product Announcement.
Mother Jones.
MusiCopyright Intelligence. *(71553,3665)*
One to One (Fresno).
P C Week.
P C World. *(GO PWOFORUM)*
Peterson's Guide to Four-Year Colleges (Year). *(PCG)*
Peterson's Guide to Two-Year Colleges (Year). *(PCG)*
Philadelphia Business Journal.
Product Alert.
Reflector Newsletter.
The Scientist. *(71764.2561)*
Screen Digest.
Software Catalog: Microcomputers.
Sports Illustrated.
State and Metropolitan Area Data Book.
Statistical Abstract of the United States (Year).
T B Weekly.
Twin Cities Reader.
Videomaker. *(71161,1722)*
Virgin Meat.
Windows Journal.
WordPerfect for Windows Magazine.

CONTEXT LTD.
Tranley Hse., Tranley Mews, Fleet Rd., London NW2 2QW, United Kingdom Tel: 44-171-267-7055 Fax: 44-171-267-2745.
Bulletin of Northern Ireland Law.
Times Law Reports.

DAFA DATA AB
Box 34101, 100 26 Stockholm, Sweden Tel: 46-8-738-4480
Nytt Juridiskt Arkiv. Avd. 1 - Raettsfall fraan Hoegsta Domstolen.

D I M D I (Subsidiary of: Deutsches Institut fuer Medizinische Dokumentation und Information)
Box 42 05 60, Weisshausstrasse 27, D-5000 Cologne, Germany Tel: (49) 221-4721-1 Telex: 88 81 364 dim D Fax: (49) 221411429.
A S F A Aquaculture Abstracts.
Abstracts on Hygiene and Communicable Diseases.
Agricultural Engineering Abstracts.
Agrindex.
Agroforestry Abstracts.
AIDS Newsletter.
Animal Breeding Abstracts.
Animal Disease Occurrence.
Aquatic Sciences & Fisheries Abstracts. Part 1: Biological Sciences and Living Resources.

Aquatic Sciences & Fisheries Abstracts. Part 2: Ocean Technology, Policy and Non-living Resources.
Aquatic Sciences & Fisheries Abstracts. Part 3: Aquatic Pollution and Environmental Quality.
Biocontrol News and Information.
Biological Abstracts.
Biological Abstracts - R R M.
Bulletin of Entomological Research.
CAB International. Bureau of Nutrition. Annotated Bibliographies.
CAB International. Bureau of Soils. Annotated Bibliographies.
Cotton and Tropical Fibres.
Crop Physiology Abstracts.
Dairy Science Abstracts.
Excerpta Medica Abstract Journals.
Excerpta Medica. Section 1: Anatomy, Anthropology, Embryology & Histology.
Excerpta Medica. Section 2: Physiology.
Excerpta Medica. Section 3: Endocrinology.
Excerpta Medica. Section 4: Microbiology: Bacteriology, Mycology, Parasitology and Virology.
Excerpta Medica. Section 5: General Pathology and Pathological Anatomy.
Excerpta Medica. Section 6: Internal Medicine.
Excerpta Medica. Section 7: Pediatrics and Pediatric Surgery.
Excerpta Medica. Section 8: Neurology and Neurosurgery.
Excerpta Medica. Section 9: Surgery.
Excerpta Medica. Section 10: Obstetrics and Gynecology.
Excerpta Medica. Section 11: Otorhinolaryngology.
Excerpta Medica. Section 12: Ophthalmology.
Excerpta Medica. Section 13: Dermatology and Venereology.
Excerpta Medica. Section 14: Radiology.
Excerpta Medica. Section 15: Chest Diseases, Thoracic Surgery and Tuberculosis.
Excerpta Medica. Section 16: Cancer.
Excerpta Medica. Section 17: Public Health, Social Medicine and Epidemiology.
Excerpta Medica. Section 18: Cardiovascular Diseases and Cardiovascular Surgery.
Excerpta Medica. Section 19: Rehabilitation and Physical Medicine.
Excerpta Medica. Section 20: Gerontology and Geriatrics.
Excerpta Medica. Section 21: Developmental Biology and Teratology.
Excerpta Medica. Section 22: Human Genetics.
Excerpta Medica. Section 23: Nuclear Medicine.
Excerpta Medica. Section 24: Anesthesiology.
Excerpta Medica. Section 25: Hematology.
Excerpta Medica. Section 26: Immunology, Serology and Transplantation.
Excerpta Medica. Section 27: Biophysics, Bio-Engineering and Medical Instrumentation.
Excerpta Medica. Section 28: Urology and Nephrology.
Excerpta Medica. Section 29: Clinical and Experimental Biochemistry.
Excerpta Medica. Section 30: Clinical and Experimental Pharmacology.
Excerpta Medica. Section 31: Arthritis and Rheumatism.
Excerpta Medica. Section 32: Psychiatry.
Excerpta Medica. Section 33: Orthopedic Surgery.
Excerpta Medica. Section 35: Occupational Health and Industrial Medicine.
Excerpta Medica. Section 36: Health Policy, Economics and Management.
Excerpta Medica. Section 38: Adverse Reactions Titles.
Excerpta Medica. Section 40: Drug Dependence, Alcohol Abuse and Alcoholism.
Excerpta Medica. Section 46: Environmental Health and Pollution Control.
Excerpta Medica. Section 48: Gastroenterology.
Excerpta Medica. Section 49: Forensic Science Abstracts.
Excerpta Medica. Section 50: Epilepsy Abstracts.
Excerpta Medica. Section 52: Toxicology.
Field Crop Abstracts.
Food Science and Technology Abstracts.
Forest Products Abstracts.
Forestry Abstracts.
Forestry Abstracts. Leading Article Reprint Series.
Grasslands and Forage Abstracts.
Helminthological Abstracts.
Horticultural Abstracts.
Hospital Literature Index.
Index of Current Research on Pigs.
Index of Fungi.

Index to Scientific Book Contents. *(ISTP&B Search)*
Index Veterinarius.
Informationsdienst Krankenhauswesen.
International Biodeterioration & Biodegradation.
International Pharmaceutical Abstracts.
Irrigation and Drainage Abstracts.
Leisure, Recreation and Tourism Abstracts.
Maize Abstracts.
Medical Science Research.
Nematological Abstracts.
Nutrition Abstracts and Reviews. Series A: Human and Experimental.
Nutrition Abstracts and Reviews. Series B: Livestock Feeds and Feeding.
Ornamental Horticulture.
Packaging Science and Technology Abstracts.
Pig News & Information.
Plant Breeding Abstracts.
Plant Growth Regulator Abstracts.
Potato Abstracts.
Poultry Abstracts.
Protozoological Abstracts.
Psychological Abstracts.
Review of Agricultural Entomology.
Review of Medical and Veterinary Entomology.
Review of Medical and Veterinary Mycology.
Review of Plant Pathology.
Rice Abstracts.
Rural Development Abstracts.
Salud Publica de Mexico.
Schrifttums fuer den Bereich Haushalt und Verbauch. Bibliographie.
Science Citation Index.
Seed Abstracts.
Small Animals.
Social Planning - Policy & Development Abstracts. *(SA63)*
Social Sciences Citation Index.
Sociological Abstracts. *(SA63)*
Soils and Fertilizers.
Sorghum and Millets.
Soyabean Abstracts.
Tropical Diseases Bulletin.
Tropical Oil Seeds.
Veterinary Bulletin.
Vitis.
Vitis - Viticulture and Oenology Abstracts.
Weed Abstracts.
Wheat, Barley and Triticale Abstracts.
World Agricultural Economics and Rural Sociology Abstracts.

DATA ARKIV AB
PO Box 12079, 102 22 Stockholm, Sweden Tel: 46 (8) 16 52 20
Japanese Journal of Ophthalmology.
Technology Access Report.

DATA-STAR
114 Jermyn St., Plaza Suite, London SW1Y 6HJ, United Kingdom Tel: 44-71-930-5503, 44-71-930-2581
Radio Suisse AG, Laupenstr. 18A, CH-3008 Berne, Switzerland Tel: 41-31-509500 Fax: 41-31-509675.
A B B Review.
A B C der Deutschen Wirtschaft - Quellenwerk fur Einkauf-verkauf.
A B C Europ Production.
A B E C O R Country Reports.
A B I - INFORM. *(INFO)*
A H F S Drug Information. *(DIFT)*
A S S I A: Applied Social Sciences Index & Abstracts. *(ASSI)*
Abstracts in BioCommerce. *(CELL)*
Abstracts on Hygiene and Communicable Diseases.
Adhesives Abstracts.
Advanced Ceramics Report. *(PTBN)*
Advanced Composites Bulletin. *(PTBN)*
Agroforestry Abstracts.
Agrow.
AIDS Weekly. *(PTS NEWSLETTER DATABASE)*
Air Fresheners and Insecticides: The International Market.
Air Safety Week.
Air - Water Pollution Report.
Airline Business.
Airline Financial News.
Alcoholism & Drug Abuse Weekly.
Alloys Index. *(META)*
American Banker. *(BANK)*
American Doctoral Dissertations.
Analgesics: The International Market.
Analytical Abstracts. *(ANAB)*

Animal Pharm.
Annuaire Telexport.
Applied Genetics News.
Asbestos & Lead Abatement Report.
Asset Sales Report.
Audio: The International Market.
Audio Week.
Audiotex Update.
Automotives: The International Market.
Autoparts Report.
B D I Deutschland Liefert.
B T Today.
Baby Care Products: The International Market.
Baby Foods: The International Market.
Bakery Products: The International Market.
Bank Automation News.
Bank Mutual Fund Report.
Barclays Country Reports.
Barclays Economic Review.
Bath and Shower Products: The International Market.
Battery & E V Technology News.
Beer: The International Market.
BioCommerce Financial Abstracts. (CELL)
Biodeterioration Abstracts.
Biological Abstracts.
Biological Abstracts - R R M.
Biomedical Market Newsletter.
Biomedical Materials.
Biotech Business.
BioVenture View.
Blood Weekly.
Books: The International Market.
Boston Business Journal.
Breakfast Cereals: The International Market.
Business Computing Brief.
Business Journal (Sacramento).
Business Law Europe.
Business Travel News.
Buyouts Newsletter.
C F O Alert (Weekly).
Canadian Index.
Cancer Researcher Weekly.
Canned Foods: The International Market.
Car Aftermarket: The International Market.
Car Rental: The International Market.
Card News.
Chem-Facts: Ethylene & Propylene.
Chem-Facts: European Review.
Chem-Facts: France.
Chem-Facts: Germany.
Chem-Facts: P V C.
Chem-Facts: Polyethylene.
Chem-Facts: Polypropylene.
Chem-Facts: Styrenics.
Chem-Facts: United Kingdom.
Chemical Hazards in Industry. (CSNB)
Chemical Monitor.
Chemical Plant File.
Chilled Foods, Delicatessen Foods and Ready Meals: The International Market.
Cleaning Appliances: The International Market.
Clinica.
Coal U.K.
Communications Daily.
CommunicationsWeek International.
Commuter - Regional Airline News.
The Composites and Adhesives Newsletter.
Computer & Control Abstracts.
Computer Database. (CMPT)
Computer Fraud and Security.
Computer Protocols.
Confectionery: The International Market.
Consumer Catering: The International Market.
Corporate Report Minnesota.
Corporate Venturing Quarterly.
Cosmetic Insider's Report.
Cough and Cold Remedies: The International Market.
Country Forecasts (Syracuse). (FSRI)
Credit and Charge Cards: The International Market.
Cumulative Index to Nursing & Allied Health Literature. (NAHL)
Current Biotechnology. (CUBI)
The Cyprus Review.
C2C Abstracts: Japan - Analytical Chemistry. (JPTC)
C2C Abstracts: Japan - Ceramics. (JPTC)
C2C Abstracts: Japan - Chemical Engineering. (JPTC)
C2C Abstracts: Japan - Crystallography. (JPTC)
C2C Abstracts: Japan - Hydrocarbons. (JPTC)
C2C Abstracts: Japan - Inorganic Chemistry. (JPTC)
C2C Abstracts: Japan - Materials Science. (JPTC)
C2C Abstracts: Japan - Metals. (JPTC)

C2C Abstracts: Japan - Organic Chemistry. (JPTC)
C2C Abstracts: Japan - Physical Chemistry. (JPTC)
C2C Abstracts: Japan - Plastics. (JPTC)
C2C Abstracts: Japan - Polymer Chemistry. (JPTC)
C2C Abstracts: Japan - Surface Chemistry. (JPTC)
C2C Abstracts: Japan - Textiles. (JPTC)
C2C Currents: Japan - Chemistry. (JPTC)
C2C Currents: Japan - Computers. (JPTC)
C2C Currents: Japan - Electronics. (JPTC)
C2C Currents: Japan - Materials. (JPTC)
D I Y: The International Market.
Dairy Products: The International Market.
Dealing with Technology.
Deodorants: The International Market.
Devices & Diagnostics Letter.
Digestive Remedies: The International Market.
Disposable Paper Products: The International Market.
Dissertation Abstracts International. Section A: Humanities and Social Sciences.
Dissertation Abstracts International. Section B: Physical Sciences and Engineering.
Dissertation Abstracts International. Section C: Worldwide.
Dissertation Abstracts on Disc.
E C Energy Monthly.
East Europe & the Republics: A Political Risk Annual. (FSRI)
East European Energy Report.
East European Markets.
Einkaufs 1x1 der Deutschen Industrie.
Electrical & Electronics Abstracts.
Energy Conservation News.
Energy Daily.
Energy Economist.
Energy Report.
Engineering Index Annual.
Engineering Index Monthly.
Entertainment Software: The International Market.
Environment Abstracts. (ENVN/Environline)
Environment Abstracts Annual. (ENVN/Environline)
Environment Week.
Environmental Problems & Remediation.
European Energy Report.
Eventline.
Excerpta Medica Abstract Journals.
Excerpta Medica. Section 1: Anatomy, Anthropology, Embryology & Histology.
Excerpta Medica. Section 2: Physiology.
Excerpta Medica. Section 3: Endocrinology.
Excerpta Medica. Section 4: Microbiology: Bacteriology, Mycology, Parasitology and Virology.
Excerpta Medica. Section 5: General Pathology and Pathological Anatomy.
Excerpta Medica. Section 6: Internal Medicine.
Excerpta Medica. Section 7: Pediatrics and Pediatric Surgery.
Excerpta Medica. Section 8: Neurology and Neurosurgery.
Excerpta Medica. Section 9: Surgery.
Excerpta Medica. Section 10: Obstetrics and Gynecology.
Excerpta Medica. Section 11: Otorhinolaryngology.
Excerpta Medica. Section 12: Ophthalmology.
Excerpta Medica. Section 13: Dermatology and Venereology.
Excerpta Medica. Section 14: Radiology.
Excerpta Medica. Section 15: Chest Diseases, Thoracic Surgery and Tuberculosis.
Excerpta Medica. Section 16: Cancer.
Excerpta Medica. Section 17: Public Health, Social Medicine and Epidemiology.
Excerpta Medica. Section 18: Cardiovascular Diseases and Cardiovascular Surgery.
Excerpta Medica. Section 19: Rehabilitation and Physical Medicine.
Excerpta Medica. Section 20: Gerontology and Geriatrics.
Excerpta Medica. Section 21: Developmental Biology and Teratology.
Excerpta Medica. Section 22: Human Genetics.
Excerpta Medica. Section 23: Nuclear Medicine.
Excerpta Medica. Section 24: Anesthesiology.
Excerpta Medica. Section 25: Hematology.
Excerpta Medica. Section 26: Immunology, Serology and Transplantation.
Excerpta Medica. Section 27: Biophysics, Bio-Engineering and Medical Instrumentation.
Excerpta Medica. Section 28: Urology and Nephrology.
Excerpta Medica. Section 29: Clinical and Experimental Biochemistry.

Excerpta Medica. Section 30: Clinical and Experimental Pharmacology.
Excerpta Medica. Section 31: Arthritis and Rheumatism.
Excerpta Medica. Section 32: Psychiatry.
Excerpta Medica. Section 33: Orthopedic Surgery.
Excerpta Medica. Section 35: Occupational Health and Industrial Medicine.
Excerpta Medica. Section 36: Health Policy, Economics and Management.
Excerpta Medica. Section 38: Adverse Reactions Titles.
Excerpta Medica. Section 40: Drug Dependence, Alcohol Abuse and Alcoholism.
Excerpta Medica. Section 46: Environmental Health and Pollution Control.
Excerpta Medica. Section 48: Gastroenterology.
Excerpta Medica. Section 49: Forensic Science Abstracts.
Excerpta Medica. Section 50: Epilepsy Abstracts.
Excerpta Medica. Section 52: Toxicology.
Eyewear: The International Market.
F D A Medical Bulletin.
F X Week.
Fast Food: The International Market.
Financial Regulation Report.
Financial Technology Insight.
Financial World.
Firmen der Neuen Bundeslaender.
Flight International.
Food and Drug Letter.
Food Chemical News.
Food Retailers: The International Market.
Food Science and Technology Abstracts. (FSTA)
Foreign Policy Bulletin.
Frozen Foods: The International Market.
Fruit and Vegetables: The International Market.
Fruit Juices: The International Market.
Fulltext Sources Online.
The G M P Letter.
G P (GPGP)
Gale Directory of Databases.
Gardening: The International Market.
Gas Daily.
Genesis Report - Dx.
Genesis Report - Rx.
Global Environmental Change.
Global Private Power.
Going Public - The I P O Reporter.
Government Reports Announcements & Index.
Ground Water Monitor. (PTBN)
Hair Care Products: The International Market.
Handbuch der Grossunternehmen.
Harvard Business Review (HBRO)
Haznews. (PTBN,PTSP)
Health Index. (HLTH)
Health News Daily. (HNDO)
Health Policy & Biomedical Research: The Blue Sheet. (FDCR)
Health Service Abstracts.
Health, Slimming and Dietetic Foods: The International Market.
Helicopter News.
High Performance Plastics.
High Tech Ceramics News.
High Tech Separations News.
Holland Exports.
Household Cleaning Agents: The International Market.
Housewares: The International Market.
Hypermarkets and Superstores: The International Market.
I S D N News.
Ice Cream, Yoghurts and Chilled Desserts: The International Market.
Imaging Abstracts. (PIRA)
Imaging Update.
Improved Recovery Week.
In-Car Entertainment: The International Market.
Industrial Health & Hazards Update.
Industrial Specialties News.
Industries in Transition.
Information Management Report. (PTBN)
Innovator's Digest.
Inside Market Data.
Inside the New Computer Industry.
Integrated Circuits International.
International Coal Report.
International Country Risk Guide.
International Gas Report.
International Packaging Abstracts.
International Pharmaceutical Abstracts. (IPAB)
International Product Alert.
International Solar Energy Intelligence Report.
International Tax Report.
Item Processing Report.
Key Abstracts - Business Automation.
L A N Product News.

Vendor

Laboratory Hazards Bulletin. (CSNB)
Large Kitchen Appliances: The International Market.
Large Mixed Retailers: The International Market.
Lookout - Foods.
Lookout - Nonfoods.
M I R A Automobile Abstracts.
Mail Order and Home Shopping: The International Market.
Mainframe Computing.
Make-Up and Colour Cosmetics: The International Market.
Management and Marketing Abstracts.
Management Contents. (MGMT)
Management Matters.
Manufacturing Automation.
Market: Asia Pacific.
Market Direction Reports.
Market: Europe.
Market: Latin America.
Market Research Abstracts.
Martindale: the Extra Pharmacopoeia.
Meat and Poultry: The International Market.
Medeconomics.
Media Monitor.
Medical Devices, Diagnostics & Instrumentation Reports: The Gray Sheet. (FDCR)
Medical Science Research.
Medical Textiles.
Medical Waste News.
Medicated Skincare: The International Market.
Membrane & Separation Technology News.
Men's Toiletries: The International Market.
Metals Abstracts. (META)
Metals Abstracts Index. (META)
Meyler's Side Effects of Drugs. (SEDB)
Military & Commercial Fiber Business.
Mineral Water: The International Market.
Minneapolis - St. Paul CityBusiness.
Mittelstaendische Unternehmen.
Mobile Satellite Reports.
Modem User News.
Money Laundering Alert.
N D A Pipeline. (NDAP)
N T I S Bibliographic Data Base.
National Report on Computers and Health.
Nederlands A B C Dienstverleners.
Nederlands A B C voor Handel en Industrie.
Networks Update.
New Materials - Japan.
New Product Launch Letter.
New Technology Week.
Nonferrous Metals Alert. (MBUS)
Nonprescription Pharmaceuticals and Nutritionals: The Tan Sheet. (FDCR)
Nonwovens Abstracts.
North Sea Letter.
North Sea Rig Forecast.
Octane Week.
Oil Market Report.
Oils and Fats: The International Market.
Online Libraries and Microcomputers.
Online Newsletter.
Optical Materials and Engineering News.
Oral Hygiene Products: The International Market.
P A I S International in Print. (PAIS)
P C Business Products.
Packaging Science and Technology Abstracts.
Paperbase Abstracts.
Pasta Products: The International Market.
Perfumes and Fragrances: The International Market.
Personal Care Appliances: The International Market.
Personal Computer Markets.
Pesticide & Toxic Chemical News.
The Pesticide Manual.
Pet Foods and Products: The International Market.
Pharma Marketletter.
Pharmaceutical Approvals Monthly. (FDCR)
Pharmacies and Drugstores: The International Market.
Philadelphia Business Journal.
Photography: The International Market.
Physics Abstracts.
Political Risk Services. Country Reports: World Service. (FSRI)
Political Risk Services. Country Reports: Algeria.
Political Risk Services. Country Reports: Argentina.
Political Risk Services. Country Reports: Bolivia.
Political Risk Services. Country Reports: Brazil.
Political Risk Services. Country Reports: Bulgaria.
Political Risk Services. Country Reports: Cameroon.
Political Risk Services. Country Reports: Chile.
Political Risk Services. Country Reports: China.

Political Risk Services. Country Reports: Colombia.
Political Risk Services. Country Reports: Costa Rica.
Political Risk Services. Country Reports: Cote d'Ivoire.
Political Risk Services. Country Reports: Czech Republic.
Political Risk Services. Country Reports: Dominican Republic.
Political Risk Services. Country Reports: Ecuador.
Political Risk Services. Country Reports: Egypt.
Political Risk Services. Country Reports: El Salvador.
Political Risk Services. Country Reports: Gabon.
Political Risk Services. Country Reports: Guatemala.
Political Risk Services. Country Reports: Guinea.
Political Risk Services. Country Reports: Haiti.
Political Risk Services. Country Reports: Honduras.
Political Risk Services. Country Reports: Hong Kong.
Political Risk Services. Country Reports: Hungary.
Political Risk Services. Country Reports: India.
Political Risk Services. Country Reports: Indonesia.
Political Risk Services. Country Reports: Iran.
Political Risk Services. Country Reports: Iraq.
Political Risk Services. Country Reports: Israel.
Political Risk Services. Country Reports: Jamaica.
Political Risk Services. Country Reports: Kenya.
Political Risk Services. Country Reports: Kuwait.
Political Risk Services. Country Reports: Libya.
Political Risk Services. Country Reports: Malaysia.
Political Risk Services. Country Reports: Mexico.
Political Risk Services. Country Reports: Morocco.
Political Risk Services. Country Reports: Nicaragua.
Political Risk Services. Country Reports: Nigeria.
Political Risk Services. Country Reports: Oman.
Political Risk Services. Country Reports: Pakistan.
Political Risk Services. Country Reports: Panama.
Political Risk Services. Country Reports: Peru.
Political Risk Services. Country Reports: Philippines.
Political Risk Services. Country Reports: Poland.
Political Risk Services. Country Reports: Romania.
Political Risk Services. Country Reports: Russia.
Political Risk Services. Country Reports: Saudi Arabia.
Political Risk Services. Country Reports: Singapore.
Political Risk Services. Country Reports: South Africa.
Political Risk Services. Country Reports: South Korea.
Political Risk Services. Country Reports: Sri Lanka.
Political Risk Services. Country Reports: Sudan.
Political Risk Services. Country Reports: Syria.
Political Risk Services. Country Reports: Taiwan.
Political Risk Services. Country Reports: Tunisia.
Political Risk Services. Country Reports: Turkey.
Political Risk Services. Country Reports: Ukraine.
Political Risk Services. Country Reports: United Arab Emirates.
Political Risk Services. Country Reports: Uruguay.
Political Risk Services. Country Reports: Venezuela.
Political Risk Services. Country Reports: Vietnam.
Political Risk Services. Country Reports: Zaire.
Political Risk Services. Country Reports: Zambia.
Political Risk Services. Country Reports: Zimbabwe.
Political Risk Services. Executive Reports: Australia.
Political Risk Services. Executive Reports: Austria.
Political Risk Services. Executive Reports: Belgium.
Political Risk Services. Executive Reports: Canada.
Political Risk Services. Executive Reports: Denmark.
Political Risk Services. Executive Reports: Finland.
Political Risk Services. Executive Reports: France.
Political Risk Services. Executive Reports: Germany.
Political Risk Services. Executive Reports: Greece.
Political Risk Services. Executive Reports: Ireland.
Political Risk Services. Executive Reports: Italy.
Political Risk Services. Executive Reports: Japan.
Political Risk Services. Executive Reports: Netherlands.

Political Risk Services. Executive Reports: New Zealand.
Political Risk Services. Executive Reports: Norway.
Political Risk Services. Executive Reports: Portugal.
Political Risk Services. Executive Reports: Puerto Rico.
Political Risk Services. Executive Reports: Spain.
Political Risk Services. Executive Reports: Sweden.
Political Risk Services. Executive Reports: Thailand.
Political Risk Services. Executive Reports: United Kingdom.
Political Risk Services. Executive Reports: United States.
Political Risk Yearbook. (FSRI)
Political Risk Yearbook. Volume 1: North & Central America. (FSRI)
Political Risk Yearbook. Volume 2: Middle East & North Africa. (FSRI)
Political Risk Yearbook. Volume 3: South America. (FSRI)
Political Risk Yearbook. Volume 4: Sub-Saharan Africa. (FSRI)
Political Risk Yearbook. Volume 5: Asia & the Pacific. (FSRI)
Political Risk Yearbook. Volume 6: Europe - Countries of the European Union. (FSRI)
Political Risk Yearbook. Volume 7: Europe - Outside the European Union. (FSRI)
Pollution Abstracts. (POLL)
Polymers, Ceramics, Composites Alert. (MBUS)
Power in Asia.
Power in Europe.
Power in Latin America.
Power U K.
Predicasts Basebook.
Predicasts F & S Index Europe.
Predicasts F & S Index International.
Predicasts F & S Index United States.
Predicasts Forecasts. (PTFC)
Predicasts Overview of Markets and Technology.
Prepared Soups: The International Market.
Prescription Pharmaceuticals and Biotechnology: The Pink Sheet. (FDCR)
Printing Abstracts.
Process and Chemical Engineering. (CEAB)
Product Alert.
Productivity Software.
Psychological Abstracts. (PSYC)
R A P R A Abstracts.
R A P R A New Trade Names in the Rubber and Plastics Industries.
R & D Focus.
R T E C S.
Renewable Energy Report.
Retail Stationery: The International Market.
S M T Trends.
Salud Publica de Mexico.
Savoury Snacks: The International Market.
Science Citation Index.
Screen Digest.
Scrip - World Pharmaceutical News. (PHIND)
Sensor Business Digest.
Sensor Review.
Service Stations: The International Market.
Shopper Report.
Side Effects of Drugs Annual. (SEDB)
Skin Care: The International Market.
Small Kitchen Appliances: The International Market.
Social Planning - Policy & Development Abstracts. (SOCA)
Social Sciences Citation Index.
Sociological Abstracts. (SOCA)
Soft Drinks: The International Market.
Space Business News.
Spirits: The International Market.
Sport Thesaurus.
SportSearch.
Steels Alert. (MBUS)
Summary of World Broadcasts. Part 1: Former U S S R (Daily).
Summary of World Broadcasts. Part 1: Former U S S R (Weekly Economic Report).
Summary of World Broadcasts. Part 2: Central Europe, the Balkans (Daily).
Summary of World Broadcasts. Part 2: Central Europe, the Balkans (Weekly Economic Report)
Summary of World Broadcasts. Part 3: Asia - Pacific (Daily).
Summary of World Broadcasts. Part 3: Asia - Pacific (Weekly Economic Report).
Summary of World Broadcasts. Part 4: Middle East (Daily).

Summary of World Broadcasts. Part 4: Middle
    East (Weekly Economic Report).
Summary of World Broadcasts. Part 5: Africa,
    Latin America and the Caribbean (Daily).
Summary of World Broadcasts. Part 5: Africa,
    Latin America and the Caribbean (Weekly
    Economic Report).
Sun Care: The International Market.
Superconductor Week.
Sweet & Savoury Biscuits: The International
    Market.
T B Weekly.
Technology Alert.
Technology Transfer Week.
Tele-Service News.
Telecom Data Networks.
Telecom Markets.
Television and Video: The International Market.
Textile and Fabric Washing Products: The
    International Market.
Theoretical Chemical Engineering.
Toiletries, Fragrances and Skin Care: The Rose
    Sheet. (FDCR)
Tour & Travel News - T T G North America.
Toys and Games: The International Market.
Trading Systems Technology.
Travel and Tourism: The International Market.
Turing Institute Abstracts in Artificial Intelligence.
Twin Cities Reader.
U K Gas Report.
Utility Reporter - Fuels Energy & Power.
Vaard i Norden.
Vending: The International Market.
Video Technology News.
Vitamins and Dietary Supplements: The
    International Market.
Voice Technology & Services News.
Washington Drug Letter (Washington, 1979).
Wine: The International Market.
Wing Newsletter.
World Accounting Report.
World Media. Broadcasting News.
World Publishing Monitor.
World Rig Forecast.
Worldcasts: Product Edition.
Worldcasts: Regional Edition.
Worldwide Biotech.
Worldwide Databases.
Worldwide Telecom.
Worldwide Videotex Update.
Z V E I Elektro und Elektronik - Einkaufsfuehrer.
4 1 1 Newsletter. (PTBN)

DOW JONES NEWS RETRIEVAL
PO Box 300, Princeton, NJ 08540. Tel: 609-452-
1511
Fax: 609-520-4775.
    A B A Banking Journal.
    Administrative Science Quarterly.
    Aerospace Daily.
    Aerospace Propulsion. (ASR)
    Air Conditioning, Heating & Refrigeration News.
    Airports.
    American Demographics.
    Architectural Record. (ARCH)
    Arizona Business Gazette.
    Aviation Daily.
    Aviation Europe. (AE)
    Aviation Week & Space Technology.
    Barron's.
    Biomedical Market Newsletter.
    BioVenture View.
    Blood Weekly.
    Boston Business Journal.
    Building Supply Business.
    Business America.
    Business Dateline.
    Business Journal (Sacramento).
    Business Week.
    Byte.
    Cancer Researcher Weekly.
    Chemical Engineering. (CE)
    Coal Tech International. (CSL)
    Coal Week. (COW)
    Coal Week International. (CWI)
    Composites Industry Monthly.
    Corporate Report Minnesota.
    Data Communications.
    E N R. (ENR)
    Electric Utility Week. (EUW)
    Electric Utility Week's Demand-Side Report.
        (DSR)
    Electrical World. (EWL)
    Emerging & Special Situations. (ESS)
    Far Eastern Economic Review.
    Federal Technology Report. (TTR)
    Forbes.

Genesis Report - Dx.
Genesis Report - Rx.
Hazardous Waste Business. (HWB)
Independent Power Report. (COG)
Industrial Energy Bulletin.
Industrial Specialties News.
Inside Energy with Federal Lands. (IE)
Inside F E R C. (FEPC)
Inside F E R C's Gas Market Report. (GSMR)
Inside N R C. (NRC)
Integrated Waste Management.
International Product Alert.
L A N Times. (LNTM)
McGraw-Hill's Biotechnology Newswatch. (BIO)
Metals Week. (MW)
Minneapolis - St. Paul CityBusiness.
Modern Plastics. (MP)
Money Laundering Alert.
Northeast Power Report. (NEPR)
NuclearFuel. (NUF)
Nucleonics Week. (NUC)
Octane Week.
Online Libraries and Microcomputers.
Online Newsletter.
Peterson's Guide to Four-Year Colleges (Year).
    (SCHOOL)
Peterson's Guide to Two-Year Colleges (Year).
    (SCHOOL)
Philadelphia Business Journal.
The Physician and Sportsmedicine.
Platt's International Petrochemical Report.
Platt's Oilgram News. (PON)
Platt's Oilgram Price Report. (POP)
Postgraduate Medicine. (PGM)
Power (New York). (PWR)
Product Alert.
The Review of Banking and Financial Services.
    (REFS)
The Review of Securities & Commodities
    Regulation. (RSCR)
Securities Week. (SW)
Southeast Power Report. (SEPR)
T B Weekly.
Time.
Twin Cities Reader.
Utility Environment Report. (UER)
Village Voice.
Wall Street Journal (Eastern Edition).
Weekly of Business Aviation. (BA)
Worldscope Company Database.

EUROPEAN SPACE AGENCY
Via Galileo Galilei, I-00044 Frascati (Rome), Italy
Tel: 39-6-941801 Telex: 610637 ESRIN1
    A B I - INFORM. (File no.30)
    A S F A Aquaculture Abstracts.
    A S F A Marine Biotechnology Abstracts.
    Aerospace Daily. (File no.72/AEROSPACE DAILY)
    Agricultural Engineering Abstracts. (File nos.16 &
        124/CAB)
    Agrindex. (File no.29/AGRIS)
    Agroforestry Abstracts.
    Alloys Index. (File no.3)
    Aluminium Industry Abstracts. (File no.9/
        ALUMINUM)
    Animal Breeding Abstracts.
    Animal Disease Occurrence.
    Apicultural Abstracts. (File nos.16 & 124/CAB)
    Aqualine Abstracts.
    Aquatic Sciences & Fisheries Abstracts. Part 1:
        Biological Sciences and Living Resources.
    Aquatic Sciences & Fisheries Abstracts. Part 2:
        Ocean Technology, Policy and Non-living
        Resources.
    Aquatic Sciences & Fisheries Abstracts. Part 3:
        Aquatic Pollution and Environmental Quality.
    Biocontrol News and Information.
    Biodeterioration Abstracts.
    Biological Abstracts.
    Biological Abstracts - R R M. (File no.7/BIOSIS)
    BioVenture View.
    The Bowker Annual Library and Book Trade
        Almanac.
    Bulletin of Entomological Research.
    CAB International. Bureau of Nutrition. Annotated
        Bibliographies.
    CAB International. Bureau of Soils. Annotated
        Bibliographies.
    Computer & Control Abstracts. (File no.8/
        INSPEC)
    Convergence: International Congress on
        Transportation Electronics. Proceedings.
    Cotton and Tropical Fibres. (File nos.16 & 124/
        CAB)
    Crop Physiology Abstracts.
    Current Index to Statistics.
    Current Mathematical Publications.

C2C Abstracts: Japan - Analytical Chemistry. (File
    no.241)
C2C Abstracts: Japan - Ceramics. (File no.241)
C2C Abstracts: Japan - Chemical Engineering.
    (File no.241)
C2C Abstracts: Japan - Crystallography. (File
    no.241)
C2C Abstracts: Japan - Hydrocarbons. (File
    no.241)
C2C Abstracts: Japan - Inorganic Chemistry. (File
    no.241)
C2C Abstracts: Japan - Materials Science. (File
    no.241)
C2C Abstracts: Japan - Metals. (File no.241)
C2C Abstracts: Japan - Organic Chemistry. (File
    no.241)
C2C Abstracts: Japan - Physical Chemistry. (File
    no.241)
C2C Abstracts: Japan - Plastics. (File no.241)
C2C Abstracts: Japan - Polymer Chemistry. (File
    no.241)
C2C Abstracts: Japan - Surface Chemistry. (File
    no.241)
C2C Abstracts: Japan - Textiles. (File no.241)
C2C Currents: Japan - Chemistry. (File no.241)
C2C Currents: Japan - Computers. (File no.241)
C2C Currents: Japan - Electronics. (File no.241)
C2C Currents: Japan - Materials. (File no.241)
Dairy Science Abstracts.
Diffusion Express. (File no.27)
E U D I S E D - European Educational Research
    Yearbook. (File no.24/EUDISED R&D)
Electrical & Electronics Abstracts.
Engineered Materials Abstracts. (File no.134)
Engineering Index Annual.
Engineering Index Monthly.
Environment Abstracts. (File no.11/ENVIROLINE
    and File no.109/Acid Rain Abstracts)
Environment Abstracts Annual. (File no.11/
    ENVIROLINE and File no.109/Acid Rain
    Abstracts)
Eventline.
F R A N C I S. 522: Histoire des Sciences et de
    Techniques.
Field Crop Abstracts.
Fluid Abstracts: Civil Engineering. (File no.48/
    FLUIDEX)
Fluid Abstracts: Process Engineering. (File no.43/
    FLUIDEX)
Forest Products Abstracts. (File nos.16 & 124/
    CAB)
Forestry. (File nos.16 & 124/CAB)
Forestry Abstracts.
Forestry Abstracts. Leading Article Reprint Series.
Government Reports Announcements & Index.
Grasslands and Forage Abstracts.
H T F S Digest. (File no.138/HEATFLO)
Helminthological Abstracts. (File nos.16 & 124/
    CAB)
Horticultural Abstracts.
I M M Abstracts and Index. (IMMAGE)
I N I S Atomindex. (File no.28/INIS)
Index of Current Research on Pigs.
Index of Fungi.
Index Veterinarius.
Information Eaux. (File no.73/AFEE)
International Biodeterioration & Biodegradation.
    (File nos.16 & 124/CAB)
International Labour Documentation. (File no.53/
    LABORDOC)
Irrigation and Drainage Abstracts.
Key Abstracts - Business Automation.
Leisure, Recreation and Tourism Abstracts.
M I R A Automobile Abstracts.
M I R A Automotive Business News.
Maize Abstracts.
Maritime Information Review.
Mathematical Reviews. (File no.30/MATHSCI)
Mechanical Engineering Abstracts. (File no.10/
    ISMEC)
Metals Abstracts. (File no.3/METADEX)
Metals Abstracts Index. (File no 3/METADEX)
N A T O Advanced Science Institutes Series A:
    Life Sciences. (File no.128)
N A T O Advanced Science Institutes Series B:
    Physics. (File no.128)
N A T O Advanced Science Institutes Series C:
    Mathematical and Physical Sciences. (File
    no.128)
N A T O Advanced Science Institutes Series D:
    Behavioural and Social Sciences. (File no.123)
N A T O Advanced Science Institutes Series E:
    Applied Sciences. (File no.128)
N A T O Advanced Science Institutes Series F:
    Computer and Systems Sciences. (File no.128)
N A T O Advanced Science Institutes Series G:
    Ecological Sciences. (File no.128)

N A T O Advanced Science Institutes Series H:
Cell Biology. *(File no.128)*
Nematological Abstracts. *(File nos.16 & 124/CAB)*
Nonferrous Metals Alert. *(File no.111)*
Nutrition Abstracts and Reviews. Series A: Human
and Experimental.
Nutrition Abstracts and Reviews. Series B:
Livestock Feeds and Feeding. *(File nos.16 & 124/CAB)*
Oceanic Abstracts. *(File no.17/OCEANIC)*
Online Libraries and Microcomputers.
Online Newsletter.
Ornamental Horticulture.
P A S C A L. E 11: Physique Atomique et
Moleculaire. Plasmas. *(File no.14)*
P A S C A L. E 12: Etat Condense. *(File no.14)*
P A S C A L. E 13: Structure des Liquides et des
Solides - Cristallographie. *(File no.14)*
P A S C A L. E 18: Chromatographie. *(File no.14)*
P A S C A L. E 20: Electronique et
Telecommunications. *(File no.14)*
P A S C A L. E 27: Methodes de Formation et
Traitement des Images. *(File no.14)*
P A S C A L. E 30: Microscopie Electronique et
Diffraction Electronique. *(File no.14)*
P A S C A L. E 32: Metrologie et Appareillage en
Physique et Physicochimie. *(File no.14)*
P A S C A L. E 33. Informatique.
P A S C A L. E 34. Robotique, Automatique et
Automatisation des Processus Industriels. *(File no.14)*
P A S C A L. E 36: Pollution de l'Eau, de l'Air et
du Sol - Dechets - Bruit. *(File no.14)*
P A S C A L. E 48: Environnement Cosmique
Terrestre, Astronomie et Geologie
Extraterrestre. *(File no.14)*
P A S C A L. E 49: Meteorologie, Glaciologie,
Physique des Oceans. *(File no.14)*
P A S C A L. E 58: Genetique. *(File no.14)*
P A S C A L. E 61: Microbiologie: Bacteriologie,
Virologie, Mycologie, Protozoaires Pathogenes.
(File no.14)
P A S C A L. E 62: Immunologie. *(File no.14)*
P A S C A L. E 63: Toxicologie. *(File no.14)*
P A S C A L. E 64: Endocrinologie Humaine et
Experimentale. Endocrinopathies. *(File no.14)*
P A S C A L. E 65: Psychologie,
Psychopathologie, Psychiatrie. *(File no.14)*
P A S C A L. E 68: Genetique Humaine.
P A S C A L. E 71: Ophtalmologie. *(File no.14)*
P A S C A L. E 72: Otorhinolaryngologie.
Stomatologie. Pathologie Cervicofaciale. *(File no.14)*
P A S C A L. E 73: Dermatologie. Maladies
Sexuellement Transmissibles. *(File no.14)*
P A S C A L. E 74: Pneumologie. *(File no.14)*
P A S C A L. E 75: Cardiologie et Appareil
Circulatoire. *(File no.14)*
P A S C A L. E 76: Gastroenterologie, Foie,
Pancreas, Abdomen. *(File no.14)*
P A S C A L. E 77: Nephrologie. Voies Urinaires.
(File no.14)
P A S C A L. E 78: Neurologie. *(File no.14)*
P A S C A L. E 79: Pathologie et Physiologie
Osteoarticulaires. *(File no.14)*
P A S C A L. E 80: Hematologie. *(File no.14)*
P A S C A L. E 82: Gynecologie, Obstetrique,
Andrologie. *(File no.14)*
P A S C A L. E 83: Anesthesie et Reanimation.
(File no.14)
P A S C A L. E 84: Genie Biomedical.
Informatique Biomedicale. *(File no.14)*
P A S C A L. E 89: Cancer. *(File no.14)*
P A S C A L. F 10: Mecanique, Acoustique et
Transfert de Chaleur. *(File no.14)*
P A S C A L. F 16: Chimie Analytique, Minerale
et Organique. *(File no.14)*
P A S C A L. F 17: Chimie Generale, Minerale et
Organique. *(File no.14)*
P A S C A L. F 23: Genie Chimique. Industries
Chimique et Parachimique. *(File no.14)*
P A S C A L. F 24: Polymeres - Peintures - Bois.
(File no.14)
P A S C A L. F 40: Mineralogie. Geochimie.
Geologie Extraterrestre. *(File no.14)*
P A S C A L. F 41: Gisements Metalliques et Non
Metalliques. *(File no.14)*
P A S C A L. F 42: Roches Cristallines. *(File no.14)*
P A S C A L. F 43: Roches Sedimentaires.
Geologie Marine. *(File no.14)*
P A S C A L. F 44: Stratigraphie, Geologie
Regionale, Geologie Generale. *(File no.14)*
P A S C A L. F 45: Tectonique, Geophysique
Interne. *(File no.14)*

P A S C A L. F 46: Hydrologie. Geologie de
l'Ingenieur. Formations Superficielles. *(File no.14)*
P A S C A L. F 47: Paleontologie. *(File no.14)*
P A S C A L. F 52: Biochimie - Biophysique -
Moleculaire - Biologie Moleculaire et Cellulaire.
(File no.14)
P A S C A L. F 53: Anatomie et Physiologie des
Vertebres. *(File no.14)*
P A S C A L. F 54: Reproduction des Vertebres,
Embryologie des Vertebres et des Invertebres.
(File no.14)
P A S C A L. F 55: Biologie Vegetale. *(File no.14)*
P A S C A L. F 56: Ecologie Animale, Vegetale et
Microbienne. Ethologie Animale. *(File no.14)*
P A S C A L. F 70: Pharmacologie. Traitements
Medicamenteux. *(File no.14)*
P A S C A L. T 205: Sciences de l'Information.
Documentation. *(File no.14)*
P A S C A L. T 215: Biotechnologies. *(File no.14)*
P A S C A L. T 230: Energie. *(File no.14)*
P A S C A L. T 235: Medecine Tropicale. *(File no.14)*
P A S C A L. T 240: Metaux - Metallurgie. *(File no.14)*
P A S C A L. T 260: Zoologie Fondamentale et
Appliquee des Invertebres. *(File no.14)*
P A S C A L. T 280: Sciences Agronomiques et
Forestieres: Productions Vegetales. *(File no.14)*
P A S C A L. T 295: Batiment. Travaux Publics.
(File no.14)
P A S C A L V.4 Sciences de la Terre. *(File no.14)*
Physics Abstracts.
Pig News & Information.
Plant Breeding Abstracts.
Plant Growth Regulator Abstracts.
Pollution Abstracts. *(File no.18/POLLUTION)*
Polymers, Ceramics, Composites Alert. *(File no.111)*
Potato Abstracts.
Poultry Abstracts.
Protozoological Abstracts.
R A P R A Abstracts.
R A P R A New Trade Names in the Rubber and
Plastics Industries.
Recherche en Matiere d'Economie des
Transports. *(File no.74/TRANSDOC Subfile: RESEARCH)*
Review of Agricultural Entomology.
Review of Medical and Veterinary Entomology.
Review of Medical and Veterinary Mycology.
Review of Plant Pathology.
Rice Abstracts.
Rural Development Abstracts.
S A E Technical Papers.
S T A R.
Safety and Health at Work. *(File no.40/CISDOC)*
Securite et Sante au Travail.
Seed Abstracts.
Small Animals.
Sorghum and Millets.
Soyabean Abstracts.
Stapp Car Crash Conference. Proceedings.
Steels Alert. *(File no.111)*
Tropical Oil Seeds.
Urban Abstracts.
Veterinary Bulletin.
Weed Abstracts.
Wheat, Barley and Triticale Abstracts.
World Agricultural Economics and Rural Sociology
Abstracts.
World Translations Index. *(File no.33/WTI)*

F I Z TECHNIK
Ostbahnhofstrasse 13, D-6000 Frankfurt 60,
Germany Tel: (069) 4308-1
Fax: 49-494308200.
A B C der Deutschen Wirtschaft - Quellenwerk fur
Einkauf-verkauf.
A B C Europ Production.
Alloys Index. *(META)*
B D I Deutschland Liefert.
Cardiovascular and Interventional Radiology.
Computer & Control Abstracts.
Convergence: International Congress on
Transportation Electronics. Proceedings.
D K I Literatur-Schnelldienst Kunststoffe
Kautschuk Fasern.
Einkaufs 1x1 der Deutschen Industrie.
Electrical & Electronics Abstracts.
Environment Abstracts. *(ENVIROLINE)*
Imaging Abstracts.
International Packaging Abstracts.
Key Abstracts - Business Automation.
Metals Abstracts. *(META)*
Metals Abstracts Index. *(META)*

Nonwovens Abstracts.
Packaging Science and Technology Abstracts.
Paperbase Abstracts.
Physics Abstracts.
Printing Abstracts.
Der Radiologe.
S A E Technical Papers.
Stapp Car Crash Conference. Proceedings.
Welding Abstracts.
Wer Liefert Was?
World Publishing Monitor.
Z V E I Elektro und Elektronik - Einkaufsfuehrer.

**G B I (GESELLSCHAFT FUER
BETRIEBSWIRTSCHAFTLICHE INFORMATION
MBH)**
Freischuetzstrasse 96, 81927 Munich, Germany
Tel: 089-9570064
Fax: 089-954229.
Handbuch der Grossunternehmen.
Mittelstaendische Unternehmen.
Moscow News.
Seibt Industriekatalog.
Seibt Medizinische Technik.
Seibt Oberflaechentechnik.
Verbaende, Behoerden, Organisationen der
Wirtschaft.

GSI-ECO
45 rue de la Procession, 75015 Paris, France
Tel: 45-66-78-89 Telex: 250 682 F
Fax: 47-34-46-92.
France. Conseil National du Credit. Statistiques
Mensuelles.
France. Conseil National du Credit. Statistiques
Trimestrielles.
Statistical Office of the European Communities.
Energy Statistics Monthly Bulletin.
World Debt Tables.

HELSINKI SCHOOL OF ECONOMICS
Runeberginkatu 22-24, SF-00100 Helsinki, Finland
Tel: 358-0-43131 Telex: 122220 econ sf
Fax: 358-0-4313539.
Kauppalehti.
Scanp.

HUMAN RESOURCE INFORMATION NETWORK
(Subsidiary of: Executive Telecom System,
Inc.)
9585 Valparaiso Ct., College Park N., Indianapolis,
IN 46268. Tel: 317-872-2045
Fax: 317-872-2059.
AIDS Policy and Law. *(CDD, HDD)*
Asbestos & Lead Abatement Report.
B N A Pension & Benefits Reporter. *(CDD, HDD)*
B N A Policy and Practice Series. *(BPP)*
B N A Policy and Practice Series. Compensation.
B N A Policy and Practice Series. Fair
Employment Practices.
B N A Policy and Practice Series. Labor
Relations.
B N A Policy and Practice Series. Personnel
Management.
B N A's Americans with Disabilities Act Manual
and Cases. *(ADAM)*
B N A's Banking Report. *(CDD,HDD)*
B N A's Employee Relations Weekly. *(Files CDD, HDD)*
B N A's Medicare Report. *(File DD)*
B N A's Workers' Compensation Report. *(File DD)*
Bulletin to Management. *(CDD, HDD)*
Business Dateline.
Chemical Regulation Reporter. *(File DD)*
Chemical Substances Control. *(CDD, HDD)*
Collective Bargaining Negotiations & Contracts.
Compensation & Benefits Software Census.
Construction Labor Report. *(File DD)*
Consultants and Consulting Organizations
Directory. *(CCOD)*
Corporate Jobs Outlook!
Daily Labor Report. *(CDD, HDD)*
Daily Report for Executives. *(CDD, HDD)*
Employment Guide. *(EMPG, CDD, HDD)*
Employment Information in the Mathematical
Sciences.
Environment Reporter.
Fair Employment Practices Summary of Latest
Developments. *(CDD, HDD)*
Government Employee Relations Report. *(CDD, HDD)*
H R Magazine.
Harvard Business Review.
Human Resource Executive.

Individual Employment Rights. *(CDD, HDD)*
Industrial Health & Hazards Update.
International Labour Documentation.
Job Safety & Health (Washington). *(CDD, HDD)*
Labor - Management Relations Analysis - News
 and Background Information. *(File DD)*
Labor Relations Reference Manual. *(Files
 BOARDS, COURTS)*
Labor Relations Reporter. Labor Arbitration and
 Dispute Settlements. *(File LAR)*
Labor Relations Week. *(CDD, HDD)*
Management Matters.
National Report on Substance Abuse. *(CDD, HDD)*
National Report on Work & Family.
Newsletters in Print. *(NIP)*
Occupational Safety & Health Reporter. *(CDD,
 HDD)*
Payroll Administration Guide. *(File DD)*
Payroll Administration Guide Newsletter. *(File DD)*
Personnel Software Census.
Right-to-Know Planning Guide (Series). *(File DD)*
Right-to-Know Planning Guide Newsletter. *(File
 DD)*
Tax Management Weekly Report. *(File DD)*
Toxics Law Reporter. *(CDD, HDD)*
Training.
Training and Development Organizations
 Directory. *(TDOD)*
Union Labor Report.
Union Labor Report Weekly Newsletter. *(CDD,
 HDD)*
Videos for Business and Training. *(Video)*

IBFD PUBNS. BV
 Sarphattistraat 602, P.O. Box 20237, 1000 HE
 Amsterdam, Netherlands Tel: 31-0-20-6467726
 Telex: 13217 intax nl
 Fax: 31-0-20-6228658.
  Tax News Service.
  Tax Treaties Data Base on C D - R O M.

IST-INFORMATHEQUE, INC.
 1611 Cremazie Blvd., E., Montreal, PQ H2M 2P2,
 Canada Tel: 514-383-1611
 Fax: 514-383-7233.
  Canadian Index.
  Point de Repere.
  Safety and Health at Work.
  Securite et Sante au Travail.

INFO-ONE INTERNATIONAL PTY LTD.
 Level 3, 2 Elizabeth Plaza, North Sydney, NSW
 2060, Australia Tel: 02-959-5075
 Fax: 02-929-5127.
  Industrial Reports.
  Local Government and Environmental Reports of
   Australia.
  New South Wales Law Reports.
  South Australian State Reports.
  Tasmanian Reports.
  Victorian Reports.
  Western Australia Reports.

INFORMATION ACCESS CO. (Subsidiary of: The
 Thomson Corp.)
 362 Lakeside Dr., Foster City, CA 94404.
 Tel: 415-378-5000
 Fax: 800-676-2345.
  A B A Banking Journal.
  A N Q: A Quarterly Journal of Short Articles,
   Notes and Reviews.
  A P S News Service.
  About Marketing to Women.
  Academic Index.
  Academy of Management. Journal.
  Academy of Management Executive.
  Academy of Management Review.
  Accent on Living.
  Accounting and Finance.
  Accounting Today.
  Acknowledge the Window Letter.
  Across the Board.
  The Addiction Letter.
  Adhesives Age.
  Administration & Society.
  Administrative Science Quarterly.
  Adolescence.
  Advanced Ceramics Report.
  Advanced Composites Bulletin.
  Advanced Imaging.
  Advanced Intelligent Network News.
  Advanced Management Journal.
  Advanced Materials & Processes.
  Advertising Age.

Adweek (New York).
Adweek: Midwest.
Adweek: Southeast.
Adweek: Southwest.
Africa Report.
Africa Today.
African Affairs.
African American Review.
Afterimage.
Aftermarket Business.
Age and Ageing.
Agency Sales.
AgExporter.
Aging
Agra Europe.
Agricultural Engineering.
Agricultural History
Agricultural Research.
AIDS Weekly.
Air Cargo Report.
Air Cargo World.
Air Conditioning, Heating & Refrigeration News.
Air Safety Week.
Air Transport World.
Air - Water Pollution Report.
Aircraft Value Newsletter.
Airline Business.
Airline Financial News.
Airline Marketing News.
Airports International Magazine.
Alaska Business Monthly.
Alberta Business.
Alcohol Health & Research World.
Alcohol Outlook.
Alcoholism & Drug Abuse Weekly.
Alternatives Journal.
Aluminium Today.
America.
American Academy of Child and Adolescent
 Psychiatry. Journal.
American Antiquity.
American Artist.
American Banker.
American Banker's Washington Watch.
American Behavioral Scientist.
American Business Law Journal.
American City & County.
American Criminal Law Review.
American Demographics.
American Dietetic Association. Journal.
American Druggist.
American Economist.
American Family Physician.
American Fitness.
American Forests.
American Health.
American Heritage.
American Imago.
American Indian Quarterly.
American Journal of Agricultural Economics.
American Journal of Community Psychology.
American Journal of Drug and Alcohol Abuse.
American Journal of Economics and Sociology.
American Journal of Law & Medicine.
American Journal of Mathematics.
American Journal of Ophthalmology.
American Journal of Philology.
American Journal of Psychology.
American Journal of Sports Medicine.
American Journalism Review.
American Libraries.
American Marketplace.
American Medical News.
American Metal Market.
American Midland Naturalist.
American Music.
American Oriental Society. Journal.
American Paint & Coatings Journal.
American Papermaker.
American Philosophical Quarterly.
American Photo.
American Planning Association. Journal.
American Poetry Review.
American Political Science Review.
American Printer.
American Record Guide.
American Rehabilitation.
American Review of Public Administration.
American Salesman.
American School & University.
American Scientist.
American Shipper.
American Spectator.
American Statistician.
American Theatre.
American Visions.
Americas.
America's Community Banker.

America's Network.
Amicus Journal.
Amusement Business.
Annual Review of Genetics.
Annual Review of Microbiology.
Annual Review of Psychology.
Annual Review of Sociology.
Antioch Review.
Antiquity.
Antitrust Bulletin.
Antitrust Freedom of Information Log.
Antitrust Law Journal.
Antiviral Agents Bulletin.
Apparel Industry Magazine.
Appliance.
Appliance Manufacturer.
Applied Economics.
Applied Genetics News.
Appraisal Journal.
Arab Studies Quarterly.
Architecture.
Archives of Dermatology
Archives of Environmental Health.
Archives of Family Medicine.
Archives of General Psychiatry.
Archives of Internal Medicine.
Archives of Neurology.
Archives of Ophthalmology.
Archives of Otolaryngology - Head & Neck
 Surgery.
Archives of Pediatrics & Adolescent Medicine.
Archives of Sexual Behavior.
Archives of Surgery.
Argumentation & Advocacy.
Arkansas Business and Economic Review.
Armed Forces and Society.
Art Bulletin.
Art in America.
Art Journal (Year).
Artforum.
Arthritis Today.
Arts Education Policy Review.
Asbestos & Lead Abatement Report.
Asian Aviation News.
Asian Folklore Studies.
Asian Survey.
Assembly (Carol Stream).
Asset Sales Report.
Association for Computing Machinery.
 Communications.
Association Management.
Astronomy.
Atlanta Business Chronicle.
Atlantic Economic Journal.
The Atlantic Monthly.
Atlantic Trade Report & Global Defense Industry.
Audio (New York).
Audio Week.
Audiotex Update.
Audubon.
Automatic I D News.
Automatic Merchandiser.
Automobile (New York).
Automotive Engineering Magazine.
Automotive Industries.
Automotive News.
Automotive News Market Data Book.
Autoparts Report.
AutoWeek.
AZ B - Arizona Business.
The B B I Newsletter.
B C Business.
B M D Monitor.
B M J.
The Back Letter.
Back Stage.
Backpacker.
Bakery Production and Marketing.
Baltimore Business Journal.
Bank Automation News.
Bank Loan Report.
Bank Management.
Bank Marketing.
Bank Network News.
Bank Technology News.
Battery & E V Technology News.
Beauty Counter.
Behavioral Health Management.
Belles Lettres (North Potomac).
Berkeley Journal of Employment and Labor Law.
Best's Review. Life - Health Insurance Edition.
Best's Review. Property - Casualty Insurance
 Edition.
Better Homes and Gardens.
Better Nutrition.
Beverage Industry.
Beverage World (English Edition).
Bicycling.

Billboard (New York).
Biological Bulletin.
Biomedical Market Newsletter.
Biomedical Materials.
BioPharm.
BioScience.
Biotech Business.
Biotechnology Business News.
BioVenture View.
The Black Collegian.
Black Enterprise.
Blood Weekly.
Boating.
Boating Industry.
Bobbin.
The Bond Buyer.
The Botanical Review.
Boys' Life (Inkprint Edition).
Brandweek.
The British Journal for the Philosophy of Science.
The British Journal of Aesthetics.
The British Journal of Criminology.
British Journal of Political Science.
British Journal of Psychology.
British Plastics and Rubber Magazine.
Broadband Networking News.
Broadcasting & Cable.
Brookings Review.
Brown University Child and Adolescent Behavior
    Letter.
Brown University Digest of Addiction Theory &
    Application Data.
Brown University Long-Term Care Quality Letter.
Building Supply Business.
Buildings.
Bulletin of Economic Research.
Bulletin of the Atomic Scientists.
Business America.
Business and Commercial Aviation.
Business and Health.
Business and Society.
Business and Society Review.
Business and the Environment.
Business Communication Quarterly.
Business Communications Review.
Business Computing Brief.
Business Credit.
Business Economics.
Business Europa.
Business First (Buffalo).
Business Forum (Los Angeles).
Business History.
Business History Review.
Business Insurance.
The Business Journal (Lima).
Business Journal (Phoenix).
Business Journal (Portland).
Business Journal (Sacramento).
Business Journal Serving Greater Milwaukee.
Business Law Europe.
Business Lawyer.
Business Mailers Review.
Business Marketing.
Business North Carolina.
Business Perspectives.
Business Quarterly.
Business Travel News.
Buyouts Newsletter.
C A D - C A M Update.
C - C Plus Plus Users Journal.
C D A Investnet Insiders' Chronicle.
C D Computing News.
C D - R O M Databases.
C D - R O M Professional.
C M A.
C Q Researcher.
C T D News.
C 4 I News.
Ca - A Cancer Journal for Clinicians.
Cable - Telco Report.
Cablefax.
CADALYST.
California Business.
California Law Review.
California Management Review.
California Planning and Development Report.
California Public Finance.
Callaloo.
Campaign.
Campaigns and Elections.
Camping Magazine.
Canadian Banker.
Canadian Business.
Canadian Business Review.
Canadian Chemical News.
Canadian Dimension.
Canadian Geographic.
Canadian Historical Review.

Canadian Journal of Criminology.
Canadian Journal of History.
Canadian Machinery & Metalworking.
Canadian Manager.
Canadian Mining Journal.
Canadian Occupational Health & Safety News.
Canadian Packaging.
Canadian Papermaker.
Canadian Plastics.
Canadian Public Administration.
The Canadian Review of Sociology and
    Anthropology.
Cancer Researcher Weekly.
Candy Industry.
Car and Driver.
Card Fax.
Card News.
Caribbean Update.
Carpet & Floorcoverings Review.
Catalog Age.
Ceramic Industry.
Ceramics Monthly.
Chain Store Age.
Change (Washington).
Chatelaine (English Edition).
Chemical Marketing Reporter.
Chemical Monitor.
Chemical Week.
Chemist & Druggist.
Chemistry and Industry.
Chest.
Chicago (Year).
Chicago Review.
Chief Executive Magazine.
Child Health Alert.
Childhood Education.
Children Today.
Children's Business.
Chilton's Automotive Marketing.
Chilton's Distribution.
Chilton's Food Engineering.
Chilton's Food Engineering International.
Chilton's Motor Age.
China Business Review.
Christian Century.
Christianity Today.
Chronicle of Latin American Economic Affairs.
Cincinnati Business Courier.
Cineaste.
Classical Antiquity.
Classical Quarterly.
The Clearing House.
Clinical Diabetes.
Coal & Synfuels Technology.
Coal Outlook.
Coatings.
College Literature.
Colonial Homes.
Colorado Business.
Columbia Journal of World Business.
Columbia Journalism Review.
Commentary.
Common Cause Magazine.
Commonweal.
Communication World.
Communications Business & Finance.
Communications Daily.
Communications International.
Communications News.
Communications Standards News.
CommunicationsWeek.
CommunicationsWeek International.
Community and Worker Right-to-Know News.
Community Pharmacy.
Commuter - Regional Airline News.
Commuter Regional Airline News International.
Compensation and Benefits Review.
The Composites and Adhesives Newsletter.
Composites Industry Monthly.
Composites News: InfraStructure.
Computer Aided Design Report.
Computer-Aided Engineering (Cleveland).
Computer Audit Update.
Computer Business Review.
Computer Dealer News.
Computer Fraud and Security.
Computer Gaming World.
Computer Graphics World.
Computer Industry Report.
Computer Protocols.
Computer Publishing & Advertising Report.
Computer Reseller News.
Computer Retail Week.
Computer Shopper.
Computer Weekly.
Computer Workstations.
Computergram International.
Computers in Libraries.

Computing Canada.
Concrete Products.
Congressional Quarterly Service. Weekly Report.
Congressional Research Report.
Construction Review.
Consumer Information Appliance.
Consumer Reports.
Consumer Reports on Health.
Consumer Reports Travel Letter.
Consumers Digest.
Consumer's Research Magazine.
Contemporary Drug Problems.
Contemporary Economic Policy.
Contemporary Literature.
The Contemporary Review.
Contracting Business.
Control and Instrumentation.
Controller's Cost Report.
Convenience Store News.
The Cornell Hotel & Restaurant Administration
    Quarterly.
Corporate Board.
Corporate Cashflow.
Corporate E F T Report.
Corporate Money.
Corporate Report Minnesota.
Corporate Security.
The Corps Report.
Corrections Today.
Cosmetic Insider's Report.
Cosmetic World News.
Cosmetics and Toiletries.
Cosmetics International.
Cosmopolitan.
Cotton. Part 1: Bi-monthly Review of the World
    Situation.
Country Forecast. Algeria.
Country Forecast. Argentina.
Country Forecast. Asia - Pacific.
Country Forecast. Australia.
Country Forecast. Austria.
Country Forecast. Belgium.
Country Forecast. Brazil.
Country Forecast. Bulgaria.
Country Forecast. Canada.
Country Forecast. Chile.
Country Forecast. China.
Country Forecast. Colombia.
Country Forecast. Czech Republic.
Country Forecast. Denmark.
Country Forecast. Eastern Europe and the Former
    Soviet Union.
Country Forecast. Ecuador.
Country Forecast. Egypt.
Country Forecast. Europe.
Country Forecast. Finland.
Country Forecast. France.
Country Forecast. Germany.
Country Forecast. Global Outlook.
Country Forecast. Greece.
Country Forecast. Hong Kong.
Country Forecast. Hungary.
Country Forecast. India.
Country Forecast. Indonesia.
Country Forecast. Iran.
Country Forecast. Iraq.
Country Forecast. Ireland.
Country Forecast. Israel.
Country Forecast. Italy.
Country Forecast. Japan.
Country Forecast. Latin America.
Country Forecast. Malaysia.
Country Forecast. Mexico.
Country Forecast. Middle East and North Africa.
Country Forecast. Netherlands.
Country Forecast. New Zealand.
Country Forecast. Nigeria.
Country Forecast. Norway.
Country Forecast. Pakistan.
Country Forecast. Peru.
Country Forecast. Philippines.
Country Forecast. Poland.
Country Forecast. Portugal.
Country Forecast. Romania.
Country Forecast. Russia.
Country Forecast. Saudi Arabia.
Country Forecast. Singapore.
Country Forecast. Slovakia.
Country Forecast. South Africa.
Country Forecast. South Korea.
Country Forecast. Spain.
Country Forecast. Sri Lanka.
Country Forecast. Sub-Saharan Africa.
Country Forecast. Sweden.
Country Forecast. Switzerland.
Country Forecast. Taiwan.
Country Forecast. Thailand.
Country Forecast. Turkey.

Country Forecast. United Kingdom.
Country Forecast. United States of America.
Country Forecast. Venezuela.
Country Forecast. Vietnam.
Country Forecasts (Syracuse).
Country Journal.
Country Music.
Countryside and Small Stock Journal.
Courier (Paris).
Cowles - SIMBA Media Daily.
Crain's Chicago Business.
Crain's Cleveland Business.
Crain's Detroit Business.
Crain's New York Business.
Creativity.
Credit Card Management.
Credit Card News.
Credit Union Accountant.
Credit Union Executive.
Criminal Justice Ethics.
Criticism.
Critique: Studies in Modern Fiction.
Cruising World.
Current Health 2.
Custom Builder.
Cycle World.
D B M S.
D I Y Week.
D N R.
Daedalus.
Daily Oil Bulletin.
Dairy Foods.
Dairy Markets Weekly.
Dance Magazine.
Data Broadcasting News.
Data Storage Report.
Database (Wilton).
Datamation.
DataTrends Report on D E C.
Dealer Business.
DealerNews.
Defense Cleanup.
Defense Counsel Journal.
Defense Daily.
Defense Electronics.
Defense Week.
Delaney Report.
The Denver Business Journal.
Dermatology Times.
Design Quarterly.
Diabetes.
Diabetes Forecast.
Diesel Progress Engines & Drives.
Differences.
Digital Age.
Digital Media: A Seybold Report.
Digital News & Review.
Digital Systems Report.
Direct Marketing.
Directors & Boards.
Discount Store News.
Do-It-Yourself Retailing.
Document Imaging Report.
Dollars & Sense.
Doors and Hardware.
Down Beat.
Downstream Trends.
Dr. Dobb's Journal.
Drug and Cosmetic Industry.
Drug Detection Report.
Drug Resistance Weekly.
Drug Store News.
Drug Topics.
E & P Environment.
E C Energy Monthly.
E D I News.
E D N Magazine.
E D P Weekly.
E F T Report.
E L H.
E M M S.
E N R.
E P A Journal.
Early American Homes.
Early Music.
East Europe Agriculture & Food.
East European Insurance Report.
East European Markets.
East European Politics & Societies.
East European Quarterly.
Ebony.
Eco-Log Week.
Ecological Monographs.
The Ecologist.
Ecology.
Economic Commentary.
Economic Geography.
Economic Indicators (Washington).

Economic Inquiry.
Economic Journal.
Economic Perspectives (Chicago).
Economic Record.
Economic Review.
The Economist.
Ecumenical Review.
Editor & Publisher - the Fourth Estate.
Education Technology News.
Educational Leadership.
Educational Marketer.
Electric Light and Power.
Electrical Construction & Maintenance.
Electro Manufacturing.
Electronic Business Today.
Electronic Buyers' News.
Electronic Chemicals News.
Electronic Design.
Electronic Engineering Times.
Electronic Information Report.
Electronic Learning.
Electronic Marketplace Report.
Electronic Materials and Packaging.
Electronic Materials Technology News.
Electronic Media.
Electronic News.
Electronics Now.
Electronics Times.
Electronics Weekly.
Employee Relations.
Employee Relations Law Journal.
En Route Technology.
Endless Vacation.
Energy & Environment.
Energy Business Review.
Energy Conservation News.
Energy Daily.
Energy Journal.
Energy Report
Energy Report
Energy User News.
The Engineer.
Engineering & Mining Journal.
Engineering Economist.
English Historical Review.
English Language Notes.
Enhanced Energy Recovery News.
Enterprise Systems Journal.
Entertainment Marketing Letter.
Entertainment Weekly.
Entrepreneurship: Theory and Practice.
Environment (Washington).
Environment Business.
Environment Watch: Latin America.
Environment Watch: West Europe.
Environment Week.
Environmental Action.
Environmental Business Journal.
Environmental Law (Portland).
Environmental Nutrition.
Environmental Problems & Remediation.
Environmental Remediation Technology.
Environmental Solutions.
Equipment and Materials Update.
Esquire.
Essays in Literature.
Essence (New York).
ETC.
Ethnology.
Eurofood.
Euromarketing.
Euromoney.
Europe.
Europe - Asia Studies.
Europe Energy.
Europe Environment.
European Adhesives & Sealants.
European Cosmetic Markets.
European Energy Report.
European Media Business & Finance.
European Polymers Paint Colour Journal.
European Power News.
European Report.
European Rubber Journal.
European Social Policy.
Evans-Novak Political Report.
Evolution.
Exceptional Children.
Exceptional Parent.
Executive Female.
Executive Health's Good Health Report.
The Explicator.
Extrapolation.
F B I Law Enforcement Bulletin.
F C C Report.
F D A Consumer.
F D A Enforcement Report.
F D A Medical Bulletin.

F T C Freedom of Information Log.
F T C Watch.
Facts on File World News Digest with Index.
Family Circle.
The Family Handyman.
The Fate of the Arabian Peninsula.
Faulkner and Gray's Medicine and Health.
Federal & State Insurance Week.
Federal Computer Market Report.
Federal Probation.
Federal Reserve Bank of Richmond. Economic
    Quarterly.
Federal Reserve Bank of St. Louis. Review.
Federal Reserve Bulletin.
Feminist Studies.
Fertilizer International.
Fiber Optics News.
Field & Stream.
Film Comment.
Film Quarterly.
Finance and Development.
Finance East Europe.
Financial Executive.
Financial Management.
Financial Market Trends.
Financial Planning (New York).
Financial Post.
Financial Review (Statesboro).
Financial Services Report.
Financial Technology Insight.
Financial Times World Tax Report.
Financial World.
Flame Retardancy News.
Flight International.
Flooring.
Florida Trend.
Flower and Garden.
Flying.
Folio (Stamford).
Food & Beverage Marketing.
Food & Drink Daily.
Food & Drug Packaging.
Food Chemical News.
Food, Cosmetics and Drugs Packaging.
Food in Canada.
Food Ingredient News.
The Food Institute Report.
Food Labeling and Nutrition News.
Food Manufacture International.
Food Nutrition and Agriculture.
Food Processing (Tonbridge).
Food Trade Review.
The Foodservice Distributor.
Footwear News.
Forbes.
Foreign Affairs.
Foreign Policy (Washington).
Fortune Magazine.
Foundry Management & Technology.
Free Inquiry.
Frohinger's Marketing Report.
Frontiers.
Frozen and Chilled Foods.
Frozen Food Age.
Frozen Food Digest.
Fund Raising Management.
Fusion Power Report.
Futures (Cedar Falls).
The Futurist.
G R I D.
G U I Program News.
Gas Daily.
Gas Market Trends.
Genesis Report - Dx.
Genesis Report - Rx.
Geo Info Systems.
The Geographical Journal.
Geographical Magazine.
Geographical Review.
George Wells' Washington Beverage Insight.
Georgia Trend.
Geriatrics.
Getting Results...for the Hands-On Manager.
Gifts & Decorative Accessories.
Glass (Redhill).
Glass International.
Global Environmental Change Report.
Global Positioning & Navigation News.
Going Public - The I P O Reporter.
Golf Magazine (New York).
Good Housekeeping.
Government Computer News.
Government Finance Review.
Graphic Arts Monthly.
Greece and Rome.
Grocery Marketing.
Ground Water.
Ground Water Monitor.

Group & Organization Management.
Growth and Change.
Guarantor (New York).
Guitar Player.
H D T V Report.
H F N.
H P Professional.
H R Focus.
H R Magazine.
Harper's Bazaar.
Harper's Magazine.
Harvard Health Letter.
Harvard Heart Letter.
Harvard Mental Health Letter.
Harvard Theological Review.
Harvard Women's Health Watch.
Hastings Center Report.
Hawaii Business.
Hazardous Waste News.
HazMat Transport News.
Haznews.
Health (San Francisco).
Health Alliance Alert.
Health & Social Work.
Health Care Financing Review.
Health Care Management Review.
Health Industry Today.
Health Legislation.
Health Management Technology.
Health Services Research.
Healthcare Financial Management.
Healthcare P R & Marketing News.
Healthcare Systems Strategy Report.
Healthcare Technology & Business Opportunities.
HealthFacts.
Heating - Piping - Air Conditioning.
Hecate.
Helicopter News.
The Hemingway Review.
Hewlett-Packard Journal.
High Performance Plastics.
High Performance Textiles.
High Tech Ceramics News.
High Tech Separations News.
High Yield Report.
Hispanic.
The Historian (East Lansing).
Historical Journal of Film, Radio and Television.
History and Theory.
History Today.
Hollywood Reporter.
Home Fashions Magazine.
Home Mechanix.
Home Office Computing.
Horn Book Magazine.
Horticulture.
Hospital & Health Services Administration.
Hospital Materials Management.
Hospitality Design.
Hospitals and Health Networks.
Hot Rod.
Hotel and Motel Management.
House Beautiful.
Housewares.
Human Biology (Detroit).
Human Ecology (New York).
Human Ecology Forum.
Human Factors.
Human Life Review.
Human Relations.
Human Resource Planning.
Human Rights Quarterly.
The Humanist.
Hydraulics & Pneumatics.
Hydrocarbon Processing.
Hypatia.
I B T.
I D C Japan Report.
I S D N News.
Illinois Business Review.
Imaging Update.
Implement & Tractor.
Improved Recovery Week.
In Vivo.
Inc.
Indiana Business Magazine.
Indianapolis Business Journal.
Industrial and Labor Relations Review.
Industrial Distribution.
Industrial Environment.
Industrial Health & Hazards Update.
Industrial Management.
Industrial Paint & Powder.
Industrial Relations Journal.
Industrial Specialties News.
Industries in Transition.
Industry Week.
Infection Control Weekly.

The Information Advisor. *(Trade & Industry Index)*
Information & Interactive Services Report.
Information Law Alert.
Information Networks.
Information Technology and Libraries.
Information Today.
Information Week.
InfoWorld.
Ingram's Magazine.
Ink & Print International.
Innovator's Digest.
Inside D O T & Transportation Week.
Inside I V H S.
Inside M S.
Inside Market Data.
Inside Media.
Insight on the News.
Institutional Distribution.
Institutional Investor.
Instructor.
Insurance Accountant.
Insurance Regulator.
Integrated Circuits International.
Interactive Content.
Interactive Video News.
Interior Design.
Interiors: For the Contract Design Professional.
Internal Auditor.
International Banking Regulator.
International Bulletin of Missionary Research.
International Coal Report.
International Country Risk Guide.
International Food Manufacture.
International Gaming & Wagering Business.
International Gas Report.
International Journal of Advertising.
International Journal of Comparative Sociology.
International Journal of Manpower.
International Journal of Operations and
    Production Management.
International Journal of Physical Distribution &
    Logistics Management.
International Journal of Public Administration.
International Journal of Purchasing & Materials
    Management.
International Journal of Quality & Reliability
    Management.
International Journal of Retail & Distribution
    Management.
International Labour Review.
International Migration Review.
International Monetary Fund. Staff Papers.
International Organization.
International Product Alert.
International Review of Mission.
International Security.
International Small Business Journal.
International Solar Energy Intelligence Report.
International Studies of Management and
    Organization.
International Trade Finance.
International Trade Forum.
International Travel News.
International Wildlife.
Internetwork.
Interview (New York).
Investment Dealers' Digest.
The Investment Reporter.
Issues in Law and Medicine.
Issues in Science and Technology.
Item Processing Report.
J A M A: The Journal of the American Medical
    Association.
J A S A.
J C T: Journal of Coatings Technology.
J E I.
J E I Report.
Japan - U S Business Report.
Jet.
Jewelers' Circular - Keystone.
Journal for the Scientific Study of Religion.
Journal of Abnormal Child Psychology.
Journal of Accountancy.
Journal of Advertising.
Journal of Advertising Research.
Journal of African History.
Journal of American Ethnic History.
Journal of Asian and African Studies.
The Journal of Business (Chicago).
Journal of Business Administration.
Journal of Business Communication.
Journal of Business Ethics.
Journal of Business Strategy.
Journal of Cognitive Neuroscience.
Journal of Common Market Studies.
Journal of Community Health.
Journal of Comparative Family Studies.
Journal of Consumer Affairs.

Journal of Consumer Policy.
Journal of Consumer Research.
The Journal of Credit & Risk Management.
Journal of Criminal Law & Criminology.
The Journal of Development Studies.
Journal of Electronic Defense.
Journal of English and Germanic Philology.
Journal of Environmental Health.
Journal of European Industrial Training.
Journal of European Studies.
Journal of Experimental Psychology: General.
Journal of Family History.
Journal of Family Practice.
Journal of Finance.
Journal of Financial Research.
The Journal of General Psychology.
The Journal of Genetic Psychology.
Journal of Health Care Finance.
Journal of Health Care Marketing.
Journal of Higher Education.
Journal of Human Resources.
Journal of Industrial Economics.
Journal of Interamerican Studies and World
    Affairs.
Journal of Interdisciplinary History.
Journal of International Affairs.
Journal of International Business Studies.
Journal of Latin American Studies.
Journal of Leisure Research.
Journal of Management.
Journal of Management Studies.
Journal of Managerial Issues.
Journal of Managerial Psychology.
Journal of Marketing.
Journal of Marketing Research.
Journal of Money, Credit & Banking.
Journal of Musicology.
Journal of Negro Education.
Journal of Negro History.
Journal of Occupational and Organizational
    Psychology.
Journal of Palestine Studies.
Journal of Parapsychology.
Journal of Physical Education, Recreation and
    Dance.
Journal of Popular Film and Television.
Journal of Portfolio Management.
Journal of Post Keynesian Economics.
Journal of Property Management.
Journal of Psychology: Interdisciplinary & Applied.
Journal of Public Policy & Marketing.
Journal of Rehabilitation.
Journal of Retail Banking.
Journal of Retailing.
Journal of Risk and Insurance.
Journal of School Health.
Journal of Small Business Management.
Journal of Social History.
Journal of Social Issues.
The Journal of Social Psychology.
The Journal of Socio-Economics.
Journal of Soil and Water Conservation.
Journal of Southeast Asian Studies.
Journal of Sport Behavior.
Journal of Systems Management.
Journal of Theological Studies.
Journal of Youth and Adolescence.
Judaism.
The Kansas City Business Journal.
Kiplinger's Personal Finance Magazine.
L A N Product News.
L D C Debt Report.
Labor Studies Journal.
Labor Trends.
Ladies Home Journal (Inkprint Edition).
Lagniappe Letter.
Lagniappe Quarterly Monitor.
Lambda Book Report.
The Lancet.
Land Economics.
Land Mobile Radio News.
Latin American Research Review.
LatinFinance.
Law and Policy in International Business.
Law Office Technology Review.
Leather.
Legal Publisher.
Liability Week.
Library Software Review.
Library Technology Reports.
Library Trends.
Licensing Letter.
Life (New York).
Literary Review.
Livestock, Dairy and Poultry Situation & Outlook.
Lloyds Bank Annual Review.
Local Competition Report.
Local Telecom Competition News.

Lodging Hospitality.
Logistics and Transportation Review.
Logistics Management.
Long Island Business News.
Los Angeles.
Los Angeles Business Journal.
M E L U S.
M I S Quarterly.
M L N.
M L O.
McCall's.
Machine Design.
The McKinsey Quarterly.
Maclean's.
MacUser.
MacWEEK.
MacWorld.
The Magazine Antiques.
Mainframe Computing.
Making the Rounds in Health, Faith and Ethics.
Manage.
Managed Care Law Outlook.
Managed Care Outlook.
Managed Care Week.
Managed Healthcare News.
Management Accounting.
Management Decision.
Management International Review.
Management Matters.
Management Quarterly.
Management Review.
Manager's Magazine.
Managing Office Technology.
Manitoba Business Magazine.
Manufacturing Automation.
Manufacturing Chemist.
Manufacturing News.
Marine Fisheries Review.
Market: Asia Pacific.
Market: Europe.
Market: Latin America.
Market Research Society. Journal.
Marketing.
Marketing Computers.
Marketing News.
The Masthead.
Material Handling Engineering.
Mechanical Engineering.
Med Ad News.
Media Industry Newsletter.
MediaWeek.
Medical Device Approval Letter.
Medical Economics.
Medical Marketing & Media.
Medical Outcomes and Guidelines Alert.
Medical Textiles.
Medical Update.
Medical Utilization Management.
Medical Waste News.
Medicine (Baltimore).
Medium Aevum.
Meetings and Conventions.
Membrane & Separation Technology News.
Memphis Business Journal.
Menopause News.
Men's Health.
Mergers & Acquisitions.
Mergers & Acquisitions Report.
Mergers and Restructurings.
Metal Center News.
Metal Heat Treating.
Metallurgia: The Journal of Metals Technology,
    Metal Forming and Thermal Processing.
Metals Industry News.
Metropolitan Home.
Metropolitan Life Insurance Company. Statistical
    Bulletin S B.
Mexican Studies.
Mexico Business Monthly.
Michigan C P A.
Michigan Law Review.
Microprocessor Report.
Microsoft Systems Journal.
Microwave Journal (International Edition).
The Middle East.
Middle East Economic Digest.
Middle Eastern Studies.
Midrange Systems.
Midwest Quarterly.
Migration World.
The Milbank Quarterly.
Military Robotics Newsletter.
Military Space.
Milling & Baking News.
Mind.
Mine Regulation Reporter.
The Mineralogical Record.
Mining Magazine.

Minority Markets Alert.
The Mississippi Quarterly.
Mobile Communications.
Mobile Data Report.
Mobile Phone News.
Mobile Satellite News (Potomac).
Mobile Satellite Reports.
Model Railroader.
Modem User News.
Modern Brewery Age.
Modern Casting.
Modern Healthcare (Year).
Modern Language Quarterly.
Modern Machine Shop.
Modern Materials Handling.
Modern Maturity.
Modern Paint and Coatings.
Modern Power Systems.
Modern Tire Dealer.
Money (New York).
Money Laundering Alert.
Montana Business Quarterly.
Monthly Labor Review.
Monthly Review.
Mortgage-Backed Securities Letter.
Mortgage Banking.
The Mortgage Marketplace.
Mosaic (Winnipeg, 1967).
Mother Earth News.
Mother Jones.
Mothering.
Motor Boating & Sailing.
Motor Trend.
Mpls. - St. Paul Magazine.
Multichannel News.
Multimedia Business Report.
Multimedia Monitor.
Multimedia Publisher.
Multimedia Week.
Multinational Monitor.
Multinational Service.
Municipal and Industrial Water and Pollution
    Control.
Music and Letters.
Music & Media.
Music Trades.
Music Week.
N A B E Outlook & Policy Survey.
N A C L A Report on the Americas.
N C A H F Newsletter.
N E A Today.
N T I S Alerts: Foreign Technology.
N T T Topics.
The Nation.
National Catholic Reporter.
National Civic Review.
National Fisherman.
National Forum (Auburn).
National Home Center News.
National Institute Economic Review.
The National Interest.
National Parks.
National Petroleum News.
National Productivity Review.
National Real Estate Investor.
National Report on Computers and Health.
National Review.
National Tax Journal.
National Underwriter. Life and Health - Health &
    Financial Services Edition.
National Underwriter. Property & Casualty - Risk
    & Benefits Management Edition.
National Wildlife.
Nation's Business.
Nation's Cities Weekly.
Nation's Restaurant News.
Natural Health.
Natural History.
Navy News & Undersea Technology.
Network Briefing.
Network Computing (Manhasset).
Network V A R.
Networks Update.
New England Economic Review.
New Jersey Industry Environmental Alert.
The New Leader.
New Literary History.
New Materials - Japan.
New Media Markets.
New Mexico Business Journal.
New Orleans Magazine.
New Perspectives Quarterly.
New Product News.
The New Republic.
New Scientist.
New Statesman.
New Steel.
New Technology Week.

New York Magazine.
News Inc.
News Photographer.
NextNet.
Nieman Reports.
Nineteenth-Century Literature (Berkeley).
19th-Century Music.
Nitrogen.
Non-Foods Merchandising.
Nonwovens Industry.
The North American Review.
North Sea Letter.
North Sea Rig Forecast.
The Northern Miner.
Notes and Queries.
NotiSur.
Nuclear Waste News.
Nursing Homes.
Nutrition Action Healthletter.
Nutrition Forum.
Nutrition Health Review.
Nutrition Research Newsletter.
Nutrition Today.
O E C D Economic Outlook.
O E C D Economic Studies.
O E C D Economic Surveys: Austria.
O E C D Economic Surveys: Canada.
O E C D Economic Surveys: Denmark.
O E C D Economic Surveys: Iceland.
O E C D Economic Surveys: Spain.
O E C D Economic Surveys: United States.
O E C D Observer.
Occupational Hazards.
Occupational Health & Safety Letter.
Occupational Outlook Quarterly.
Oceania.
Oceanus.
Octane Week.
Off Road.
Offshore (Tulsa).
The Ohio C P A Journal.
Oil & Gas Interests Newsletter.
Oil & Gas Journal.
Oil Market Trends.
Oil Spill Intelligence Report.
Oilweek.
Omni.
Online (Wilton).
Online Libraries and Microcomputers.
Online Newsletter.
Online Product News.
Opera News.
Operations in Oil Diplomacy.
Ophthalmology Times.
Optical Materials and Engineering News.
Optical Memory News.
Optimum.
Orbis
Oregon Business Magazine
Organic Gardening.
Organic Gardening.
Organization Studies.
Organizational Dynamics.
Orlando Business Journal.
Ostomy Quarterly.
Outdoor Life.
Outlook (Redwood City).
Oxford Bulletin of Economics and Statistics.
Oxford Economic Papers.
Oxy-Fuel News.
P C Business Products.
P C - Computing.
P C Magazine (U.K.).
P C Netter Newsletter.
P C S Week.
P C User.
P C Week.
P C World.
P O S News.
P S A Journal.
P S: Political Science & Politics.
P T N.
Pacific Affairs.
Pacific Historical Review.
Packaging Digest.
Packaging Technology and Engineering.
Packaging Week.
Paint and Ink International.
Palaestra.
Paper & Pulp Europe.
Paper, Film and Foil Converter.
Paperboard Packaging.
Papers on Language and Literature.
Parabola.
Paraplegia News.
Parents.
Parks and Recreation.
Parliamentary Affairs.

Party & Paper Retailer.
Patient Care.
Pediatrics for Parents.
Pension Management.
Pensions & Investments.
People Weekly.
People's Medical Society Newsletter.
Performing Arts and Entertainment in Canada.
Performing Arts Journal.
Periscope (Great Neck).
Personal Computer Markets.
Personnel Journal.
Personnel Psychology.
Personnel Review.
Perspectives of New Music.
Pest Control.
Pesticide & Toxic Chemical News.
Pet Product News.
Petersen's Photographic.
Petroleum Economist.
Petroleum Independent.
Pharma Marketletter.
Pharmaceutical Business News.
Pharmaceutical Executive.
Pharmaceutical Manufacturing Review.
Phi Delta Kappan.
Philadelphia Business Journal.
Philological Quarterly.
Philosophy East and West.
Photonics Spectra.
Physical Therapy.
The Physician and Sportsmedicine.
Physician Executive.
Physician Manager.
Physiological Reviews.
Pipeline & Gas Journal.
Pipeline & Utilities Construction.
Pipeline Industry (Tulsa).
Pit & Quarry.
Pittsburgh Business Times - Journal.
Planning Review.
Plant Engineering.
Plants, Sites & Parks.
Plastics Engineering.
Plastics News.
Plastics Technology.
Plastics World.
Playboy.
Playthings.
Ploughshares.
Poetry (Chicago).
Policy Review.
Policy Studies Journal.
Political Risk Letter.
Polymer Engineering and Science.
Polymers and Rubber Asia.
Popular Mechanics.
Popular Photography.
Popular Science.
Population and Development Review.
Postgraduate Medicine.
Potentials in Marketing.
Power Engineering.
Power in Asia.
Power in Europe.
The Practical Accountant.
Precision Toolmaker.
Premiere (New York).
Prepared Foods.
Prepress Commentary.
Prevention.
Print.
Printing Impressions.
Printing News - East.
The Prison Journal.
Private Label.
Private Placement Reporter.
Privatisation International.
Pro Sound News Europe.
Process Engineering.
Product Alert.
Productivity Software.
Professional Builder.
Progressive (Madison).
Progressive Grocer.
Promo.
The Psychological Record.
Psychology Today.
Public Administration.
Public Administration Review.
Public Broadcasting Report.
Public Finance Quarterly.
Public Health Reports.
Public Interest.
Public Management.
The Public Manager.
Public Personnel Management.
Public Relations News.

Public Relations Quarterly.
Public Relations Review.
Public Roads.
Public Utilities Fortnightly.
Public Welfare.
Public Works.
Publishers Weekly.
Publishing Technology Review.
Publius.
Puget Sound Business Journal.
Pulp and Paper.
Pulp & Paper Canada.
Pulp & Paper International.
Purchasing (Newton).
Quarterly Journal of Business and Economics.
Quarterly Journal of Economics.
The Quarterly Review of Economics and Finance.
Quick Frozen Foods International.
Quill (Greencastle).
R & D Management.
R B O C Update.
R N.
R Q.
R V Business.
Railway Age.
Rapid Prototyping Report.
Re-Drawing the Islamic Map.
Real Estate Economics.
Real Estate Today.
Real Estate Weekly.
Reason.
Records Management Quarterly.
Redbook.
Regional Studies.
Regulatory Compliance Watch.
Release 1.0.
Religious Studies.
Renaissance Quarterly.
Report on A T & T.
Report on Defense Plant Waste.
Report on I B M.
Report on Microsoft.
Research Alert (New York).
Research & Development.
Research in African Literatures.
Research Quarterly for Exercise and Sport.
Response T V.
Restaurant Business.
Restaurant Hospitality.
Restaurants and Institutions.
Retail Store Image.
Review of Black Political Economy.
Review of Business.
The Review of Contemporary Fiction.
Review of English Studies.
Review of Financial Economics.
The Review of Metaphysics.
Review of Social Economy.
Reviews in American History.
Risk Management.
Road & Track.
Romance Philology.
Romanic Review.
Rubber & Plastics News.
Rubber & Plastics News II.
Rubber Trends.
Rubber World.
Runner's World.
Russia.
The Russian Review.
S M T Trends.
S T N.
St. Louis Journalism Review.
Sales & Marketing Management.
Salmagundi.
San Antonio Business Journal.
San Diego Business Journal.
San Francisco Business Times.
Sarasota Magazine.
Saskatchewan Business.
Satellite Communications.
Satellite News.
Satellite Week.
Saturday Evening Post.
Saturday Night.
Scandinavian Studies (Provo).
Scholastic Coach.
Scholastic Update.
School Arts.
School Planning and Management.
Science.
Science News.
Science World.
The Sciences.
Scientific American.
Screen Digest.
Screen Finance.
Sea Frontiers.

Security Management.
Semiconductor Industry & Business Survey Newsletter.
Sensor Business Digest.
Set-Aside Alert.
Seventeen.
Sex Roles.
Seybold Report on Desktop Publishing.
Seybold Report on Publishing Systems.
Shoot.
Shooting Industry.
Shopper Report.
Shopping Center World.
Sierra.
The SIMBA Report on Directory Publishing.
Situation & Outlook Report. Agricultural Exports.
Situation & Outlook Report. Fruit & Tree Nuts.
Situation & Outlook Report. Sugar & Sweetener.
Situation & Outlook Report. Tobacco.
Situation & Outlook Report. Vegetables & Specialties.
Skeptical Inquirer.
Skiing.
Skin Diver Magazine.
Sky and Telescope.
Sludge Newsletter.
Smithsonian.
Soap, Cosmetics, Chemical Specialties.
Soap, Perfumery & Cosmetics.
Social Forces.
Social Justice.
Social Policy.
Social Problems.
Social Research.
The Social Science Journal.
Social Security Bulletin.
The Social Studies.
Social Work.
Society.
Society of Research Administrators. Journal.
Sociological Perspectives.
Sociology.
Sociology of Religion.
Soft.letter.
Software Futures.
Software Industry Report.
Software Magazine.
Solid State Technology.
Solid Waste Report.
SourceMex.
South African Food & Beverage Manufacturing Review.
South Dakota Business Review.
South Florida Business Journal.
Southern California Business.
Southern Economic Journal.
The Southern Review.
Southwest Journal of Business and Economics.
Southwest Review.
Space Business News.
Special Delivery.
Special Libraries.
Speciality Chemicals.
Spectrum (Lexington).
Sport.
Sporting Goods Business.
The Sporting News.
Sports Afield.
Sports Illustrated.
SportStyle.
Stamps.
State Legislatures.
State Telephone Regulation Report.
Stereo Review.
Stores.
Strategic Balance in the Middle East.
Studies in American Fiction.
Studies in English Literature 1500-1900.
Studies in Family Planning.
Studies in Short Fiction.
Studies in the Novel.
Style (DeKalb).
Substance Abuse Report.
Success Magazine.
Successful Farming.
Sulphur.
Sunset.
Superconductor Week.
Superfund Week.
Supermarket Business.
Supermarket News.
Supervision.
Survey of Current Business.
Sussex Past and Present.
The Swedish Economy.
Swiss Business.
Symposium.
Systems & Network Management Report.

T A J A.
T B Weekly.
T C I.
T D R.
T H E Journal.
T R Wireless News.
Tactical Technology.
Tampa Bay Business Journal.
Tape - Disc Business.
Target Marketing.
The Tax Adviser.
The Tax Executive.
Tea and Coffee Trade Journal.
Teaching Children Mathematics.
Tech - Europe.
Technical Communication.
Technology Alert.
Technology and Learning.
Technology Transfer Week.
Teen.
Telco Business Report.
Telco Competition Report.
Tele-Service News.
Telecom Advertising Report.
Telecom & Network Security Review.
Telecom Markets.
Telecommunications (North American Edition).
Telecommunications Alert.
Telecommunications Reports.
Telecommunications Reports International.
Telecommuting Review.
Teleconnect.
Telemarketing.
Telephone I P News.
Telephony.
Television Digest with Consumer Electronics.
Texas Business Review.
Textile World.
Theatre Journal (Baltimore).
Theatre Research International.
Theological Studies.
Tikkun Magazine.
Time.
Tire Business.
Tooling & Production.
Total Health.
Tour & Travel News - T T G North America.
Town and Country.
Trading Systems Technology.
Traffic World.
Trailer Boats.
Trailer Life.
Training.
Training & Development.
Trains.
Transpacific.
Transport Europe.
Transportation & Distribution.
Transportation Journal.
Travel Agent.
Travel Holiday.
Travel Trade Gazette Europa.
Travel Trade Gazette U K & Ireland.
Travel Weekly.
Treasury Manager's Report.
Trial.
TriQuarterly.
Trusts and Estates.
Tufts University Diet and Nutrition Letter.
Twentieth Century Literature.
U K Venture Capital Journal.
U N Chronicle.
U S A Today.
U S Banker.
U S Catholic.
U S News & World Report.
U S Oil Week.
U S Rail News.
U.S. Centers for Disease Control. Morbidity and
    Mortality Weekly Report.
U.S. Department of Agriculture. Situation &
    Outlook Report. Agriculture and Trade: Former
    U S S R.
U.S. Department of State Dispatch.
U.S. Office of the Federal Register. Weekly
    Compilation of Presidential Documents.
United States Distribution Journal.
Units.
University of California at Berkeley Wellness
    Letter.
UNIX News.
UNIX Review.
UNIX Update.
Urban Studies.
Urban Transport News.
Urethanes Technology.
Urology Times.
Utility Reporter - Fuels Energy & Power.

V A R Business.
Vaccine Weekly.
Vegetarian Times.
Venture Capital Journal.
Veronis, Suhler & Associates Communications
    Industry Report.
Vibrant Life.
Victorian Studies.
Video Magazine.
Video Review.
Video Store.
Video Technology News.
Video Week.
Vital Speeches of the Day.
Voice Technology & Services News.
W I N News.
Wall Street & Technology.
Wall Street Transcript.
Ward's Auto World.
Warning Letter Bulletin.
The Washington Monthly.
Washington Quarterly.
Washington Telecom News.
Waste Treatment Technology News.
Water Technology News.
Weatherwise.
The Week in Germany.
Weight Watchers Magazine.
Welding Review International.
West European Politics.
Western Journal of Medicine.
Whole Earth Review
Wilderness.
Wilson Bulletin.
Wilson Quarterly.
Windows Developer's Journal.
Windows Sources.
Wines and Vines.
Wireless Business & Finance.
Wireless Data News.
Woman's Day.
Women and Language.
Women's Sports and Fitness.
Women's Studies (New York).
Women's Wear Daily.
Wood & Wood Products.
Wood Based Panels International.
Workbench.
Workgroup Computing Report.
Working Woman.
World Accounting Report.
World Affairs (Washington).
World Agricultural Production.
World Airline News.
World Airport Week.
World Cotton Situation.
World Economic Outlook.
World Health.
World Health Organization. Bulletin.
World Insurance Report.
World Literature Today.
World Oil.
World Policy Journal.
World Politics (Baltimore).
World Press Review.
World Tunnelling.
World Wastes.
World Watch.
Worldwide Biotech.
Worldwide Databases
Worldwide Energy.
Worldwide Telecom.
Worldwide Videotex Update.
The Writer.
Writer's Digest.
Yachting.
Yale Law Journal.
Yellow Pages & Directory Report.
Youth Markets Alert.

INFORMATION INTELLIGENCE, INC.
    P.O. Box 31098, Phoenix, AZ 85046. Tel: 602-
    996-2283
        Southwest Review.

J I C S T
c/o U S A C O Corp., Tsutsumi Bldg., 13-12
Shimbashi 1-chome, Minato-ku, Tokyo 105, Japan
Shirobu-Shushuka, 5-2 Nagatacho 2-chome,
Chiyoda-ku, Tokyo 100, Japan Tel: 813-581-6411
Telex: 02223604 J
    Brain and Nerve.
    Current Bibliography on Science and Technology:
        Chemistry and Chemical Engineering (Foreign).

Current Bibliography on Science and Technology:
    Chemistry and Chemical Engineering
    (Japanese).
Current Bibliography on Science and Technology:
    Civil Engineering and Architecture.
Current Bibliography on Science and Technology:
    Earth Science, Mining and Metallurgy.
Current Bibliography on Science and Technology:
    Electronics and Electrical Engineering.
Current Bibliography on Science and Technology:
    Energy.
Current Bibliography on Science and Technology:
    Environmental Pollution.
Current Bibliography on Science and Technology:
    Life Sciences.
Current Bibliography on Science and Technology:
    Management Science and Systems
    Engineering.
Current Bibliography on Science and Technology:
    Mechanical Engineering.
Current Bibliography on Science and Technology:
    Nuclear Engineering.
Current Bibliography on Science and Technology:
    Pure and Applied Physics.
Current Science and Technology Research in
    Japan.
Excerpta Medica Abstract Journals.
Excerpta Medica. Section 1: Anatomy,
    Anthropology, Embryology & Histology.
Excerpta Medica. Section 2: Physiology.
Excerpta Medica. Section 3: Endocrinology.
Excerpta Medica. Section 4: Microbiology:
    Bacteriology, Mycology, Parasitology and
    Virology.
Excerpta Medica. Section 5: General Pathology
    and Pathological Anatomy.
Excerpta Medica. Section 6: Internal Medicine.
Excerpta Medica. Section 7: Pediatrics and
    Pediatric Surgery.
Excerpta Medica. Section 8: Neurology and
    Neurosurgery.
Excerpta Medica. Section 9: Surgery.
Excerpta Medica. Section 10: Obstetrics and
    Gynecology.
Excerpta Medica. Section 11:
    Otorhinolaryngology.
Excerpta Medica. Section 12: Ophthalmology.
Excerpta Medica. Section 13: Dermatology and
    Venereology.
Excerpta Medica. Section 14: Radiology.
Excerpta Medica. Section 15: Chest Diseases,
    Thoracic Surgery and Tuberculosis.
Excerpta Medica. Section 16: Cancer.
Excerpta Medica. Section 17: Public Health,
    Social Medicine and Epidemiology.
Excerpta Medica. Section 18: Cardiovascular
    Diseases and Cardiovascular Surgery.
Excerpta Medica. Section 19: Rehabilitation and
    Physical Medicine.
Excerpta Medica. Section 20: Gerontology and
    Geriatrics.
Excerpta Medica. Section 21: Developmental
    Biology and Teratology.
Excerpta Medica. Section 22: Human Genetics.
Excerpta Medica. Section 23: Nuclear Medicine.
Excerpta Medica. Section 24: Anesthesiology.
Excerpta Medica. Section 25: Hematology.
Excerpta Medica. Section 26: Immunology,
    Serology and Transplantation.
Excerpta Medica. Section 27: Biophysics, Bio-
    Engineering and Medical Instrumentation.
Excerpta Medica. Section 28: Urology and
    Nephrology.
Excerpta Medica. Section 29: Clinical and
    Experimental Biochemistry.
Excerpta Medica. Section 30: Clinical and
    Experimental Pharmacology.
Excerpta Medica. Section 31: Arthritis and
    Rheumatism.
Excerpta Medica. Section 32: Psychiatry.
Excerpta Medica. Section 33: Orthopedic Surgery.
Excerpta Medica. Section 35: Occupational Health
    and Industrial Medicine.
Excerpta Medica. Section 36: Health Policy,
    Economics and Management.
Excerpta Medica. Section 38: Adverse Reactions
    Titles.
Excerpta Medica. Section 40: Drug Dependence,
    Alcohol Abuse and Alcoholism.
Excerpta Medica. Section 46: Environmental
    Health and Pollution Control.
Excerpta Medica. Section 48: Gastroenterology.
Excerpta Medica. Section 49: Forensic Science
    Abstracts.
Excerpta Medica. Section 52: Epilepsy Abstracts.
Excerpta Medica. Section 52: Toxicology.
Government Reports Announcements & Index.
I to Cho.

Industrial Health.
Iwate Medical University School of Liberal Arts & Sciences. Annual Report. *(JOIS-III)*
J I C S T Online Information System.
Japan Society for Simulation Technology. Journal. *(JOIS)*
Japanese Journal of Clinical Oncology.
Japanese Journal of Ophthalmology.
Jibi Inkoka, Tokeibu Geka.
Kokyu to Junkan.
Neurological Surgery.
Nippon Medical School. Journal.
Rigaku Ryoho Janaru.
Rihabiriteshon Igaku.
Seicho.
Seishin Igaku.
Shinshin-Igaku.

KIWINET
P.O. Box 12-264, Wellington, New Zealand Tel: 64-4-474-3182
Fax: 64-4-474-3042.
A B I X: Australasian Business Intelligence.
Index New Zealand.
LINX Database.
National Business Review.

KNIGHT-RIDDER INFORMATION, INC.
2440 El Camino Real, Mountain View, CA 94040.
Tel: 415-254-7000
Fax: 415-254-8000.
A B A Banking Journal. *(File no.648)*
A B B Review.
A B E C O R Country Reports.
A B I - INFORM. *(File no.15)*
A C M Guide to Computing Literature.
A F L - C I O News.
A H F S Drug Information. *(File no.229)*
A S F A Aquaculture Abstracts. *(File no.44)*
A S F A Marine Biotechnology Abstracts. *(File nos.44 and 76)*
Abstracts in BioCommerce. *(file no.286)*
Academic Index. *(File no.88)*
Academy of Marketing Science. Journal.
Accounting and Tax Index. *(File no. 485)*
Adhesives Abstracts.
Administrative Science Quarterly.
Advanced Ceramics Report. *(File no.636)*
Advanced Composites Bulletin. *(File no.636)*
Adweek (Los Angeles). *(File no.648)*
Adweek (New York). *(File no.648)*
Aerospace Daily. *(File nos.624,648)*
Aerospace Propulsion. *(ASP)*
Aftermarket Business.
Agricultural & Environmental Biotechnology Abstracts. *(File no. 76/Life Sciences Collection)*
Agricultural Engineering Abstracts.
Agricultural Supply Industry. *(File no.648)*
Agrindex. *(File no.203)*
Agroforestry Abstracts.
Agrow.
AIDS Weekly. *(File no.636)*
Air Conditioning, Heating & Refrigeration News. *(File no.648)*
Air Fresheners and Insecticides: The International Market.
Air Safety Week.
Air Transport World.
Air - Water Pollution Report.
Airline Financial News.
Airports. *(File no.624/McGRAW-HILL PUBLICATIONS ONLINE)*
Alaska Business Monthly.
Alaska Journal of Commerce & Pacific Rim Reporter.
Alcoholism & Drug Abuse Weekly.
Alloys Index. *(File no.32/METADEX)*
Alphabetic Subject Index to Petroleum Abstracts. *(File no.87,987)*
Aluminium Industry Abstracts. *(File no.33)*
America: History and Life. Article Abstracts and Citations of Reviews and Dissertations Covering the United States and Canada. *(File no.38)*
American Banker. *(File no.625)*
American Banker Index.
American Banker's Washington Watch.
American Doctoral Dissertations. *(File no. 35)*
American Fitness. *(File no.149)*
American Heritage.
American Libraries.
American Library Directory. *(File no.460)*
American Men and Women of Science. *(File no.236)*
American Metal Market.
American Review of Public Administration.

American Salesman.
American Society of Mechanical Engineers. Transactions.
American Statistics Index. *(File no.102)*
America's Network.
America's Network Directory.
Amusement Business.
Analgesics: The International Market.
Analytical Abstracts. *(File no.305)*
Animal Behavior Abstracts. *(File no.76/LIFE SCIENCES COLLECTION)*
Animal Breeding Abstracts.
Animal Disease Occurrence.
Animal Pharm.
Annual Survey of Manufactures.
Apicultural Abstracts.
Apparel Industry Magazine.
Appliance Manufacturer.
Applied Genetics News.
Aquatic Sciences & Fisheries Abstracts. Part 1: Biological Sciences and Living Resources. *(File no.44)*
Aquatic Sciences & Fisheries Abstracts. Part 2: Ocean Technology, Policy and Non-living Resources. *(File no.44)*
Aquatic Sciences & Fisheries Abstracts. Part 3: Aquatic Pollution and Environmental Quality. *(File no.44)*
Architectural Publications Index. *(File no.179)*
Architectural Record. *(AR)*
Archives of Dermatology.
Archives of Family Medicine.
Archives of General Psychiatry.
Archives of Internal Medicine.
Archives of Neurology.
Archives of Ophthalmology.
Archives of Otolaryngology - Head & Neck Surgery.
Archives of Pediatrics & Adolescent Medicine.
Archives of Surgery.
Arizona Business Gazette.
Arkansas Business and Economic Review.
Artbibliographies Modern. *(File no.56)*
Arts & Humanities Citation Index. *(File no.439)*
Asbestos & Lead Abatement Report.
Asset Sales Report.
Atlanta Business Chronicle.
Atlantic Economic Journal.
Audio: The International Market.
Audio Week.
Audiocassette & C D Finder. *(File no.46)*
Audiotex Update.
Australian Journal of Dairy Technology. *(File nos.50 & 53)*
Automotive Industries.
Automotives: The International Market.
Autoparts Report.
Avery Index to Architectural Periodicals.
Aviation Daily. *(File no.624/McGRAW-HILL PUBLICATIONS ONLINE)*
Aviation Europe. *(AE)*
Aviation Week & Space Technology. *(File no.624/McGRAW-HILL PUBLICATIONS ONLINE)*
The B B I Newsletter.
B C Business.
B H A. *(File no.191, Art Literature International)*
B L A S T.
B N A Policy and Practice Series. Fair Employment Practices.
B T Today.
Baby Care Products: The International Market.
Baby Foods: The International Market.
Bakery Production and Marketing.
Bakery Products: The International Market.
Baltimore Business Journal.
Bank Automation News.
Bank Mutual Fund Report.
Barclays Country Reports.
Barclays Economic Review.
Bath and Shower Products: The International Market.
Battery & E V Technology News.
Beer: The International Market.
Beilsteins Handbuch der Organischen Chemie. Supplement. *(File no.390)*
Best's Review. Life - Health Insurance Edition.
Best's Review. Property - Casualty Insurance Edition.
Beverage World (English Edition).
Bibliography and Index of Geology.
Bibliography of Bioethics.
Bibliography of Economic Geology. *(File no.58)*
Billboard (New York).
BioCommerce Financial Abstracts. *(File no.286)*
Biocontrol News and Information.
Biodeterioration Abstracts.
Biography and Genealogy Master Index. *(File nos.287,288)*

Biological Abstracts. *(File nos.5 & 55)*
Biological Abstracts - R R M. *(File nos.5 & 55)*
Biomedical Market Newsletter.
Biomedical Materials.
Biotech Business.
Biotechnology Abstracts. *(File no.357)*
BioVenture View. *(File no.636)*
Black Newspaper Index.
Blood Weekly.
Board of Trade of Metro Toronto Business Journal.
Boating.
The Bond Buyer. *(File no.626)*
Book Publishing Report.
Book Review Index. *(File no.137)*
Book World.
Books in Print. *(File no.470)*
Books in Print Supplement. *(File no.470)*
Books Out-of-Print. *(File no.470)*
Books: The International Market.
Boston Business Journal.
The Boston Globe Index. *(File no. 484)*
The Bowker Annual Library and Book Trade Almanac.
Brands and Their Companies.
Brandweek. *(File no.648)*
Breakfast Cereals: The International Market.
British Education Index. *(File no.121)*
Broadcasting & Cable.
Building Supply Business.
Buildings.
Bulletin of Entomological Research.
Business America.
Business and Commercial Aviation.
Business Asia.
Business Dateline.
Business Digest of Delaware Valley.
Business Eastern Europe.
Business Europe.
Business First (Buffalo).
Business History Review.
Business Index. *(File no.148)*
Business Journal (Phoenix).
Business Journal (Sacramento).
Business Journal Serving Greater Milwaukee.
Business Latin America.
Business North Carolina.
Business Quarterly.
Business Record (Des Moines).
Business Travel News.
Business Week. *(File no.624/McGRAW-HILL PUBLICATIONS ONLINE)*
Buyouts Newsletter.
Byte. *(File no.624/McGRAW-HILL PUBLICATIONS ONLINE)*
C D Computing News.
C D - R O M Databases.
C D - R O M World.
C F O Alert (Weekly).
C I S Index to Publications of the United States Congress. *(File no.101)*
C S A Neurosciences Abstracts. *(File no.76/LIFE SCIENCES COLLECTION)*
CAB International. Bureau of Nutrition. Annotated Bibliographies.
CAB International. Bureau of Soils. Annotated Bibliographies.
Calcium and Calcified Tissue Abstracts. *(File no.76/LIFE SCIENCES COLLECTION)*
California Business.
Canadian Business Review.
Canadian Index. *(File no.262)*
Canadian Speeches: Issues of the Day.
Cancer Researcher Weekly.
Candy Industry.
Canned Foods: The International Market.
Capital District Business Review.
Car Aftermarket: The International Market.
Car and Driver.
Car Rental: The International Market.
Card News.
Census and You.
Census of Agriculture: Final Reports.
Census of Construction Industries: Final Reports.
Census of Governments (Final Reports).
Census of Manufactures: Final Reports.
Census of Retail Trade: Final Reports.
Census of Service Industries: Final Reports.
Census of Wholesale Trade: Final Reports.
Central New York Business Journal.
Ceramic Abstracts. *(File no.335)*
Chem-Facts: Ethylene & Propylene.
Chem-Facts: European Review.
Chem-Facts: France.
Chem-Facts: Germany.
Chem-Facts: P V C.
Chem-Facts: Polypropylene.
Chem-Facts: Styrenics.

Chem-Facts: United Kingdom.
Chemical Engineering. (File no.624/McGRAW-
    HILL PUBLICATIONS ONLINE)
Chemical Hazards in Industry. (File no.317)
Chemical Marketing Reporter.
Chemical Monitor.
Chemical Plant File.
Chemoreception Abstracts. (File no.76/LIFE
    SCIENCES COLLECTION)
Children Today.
Children's Books in Print. (File no.470)
Chilled Foods, Delicatessen Foods and Ready
    Meals: The International Market.
Chilton's Automotive Marketing.
Chilton's Distribution.
Chilton's Food Engineering.
Chilton's Food Engineering International.
Chilton's Hardware Age.
Chilton's Jewelers' Circular-Keystone.
Chilton's Motor Age.
China Business Review.
China Today.
Ching Feng.
Christian Science Monitor.
Christian Science Monitor Index.
Chronicle of Latin American Economic Affairs.
Cleaning Appliances: The International Market.
Clinica.
Coal Tech International. (File no.624/McGRAW-
    HILL PUBLICATIONS ONLINE)
Coal U.K.
Coal Week. (File no.624/McGRAW-HILL
    PUBLICATIONS ONLINE)
Coal Week International. (File no.624/McGRAW-
    HILL PUBLICATIONS ONLINE)
Colorado Business.
Columbus Business Journal.
Commerce Business Daily. (File nos.194 & 195)
Communication World.
Communications Daily.
Communications News.
CommunicationsWeek International.
Commuter - Regional Airline News.
Companies and Their Brands.
Compensation and Benefits Review.
The Composites and Adhesives Newsletter.
Composites Industry Monthly.
Computer-Aided Engineering (Cleveland).
Computer & Control Abstracts.
Computer Book Review.
Computer Database. (File no.275)
Computer Design.
Computer Fraud and Security.
Computer Graphics World.
Computer Protocols.
Computerworld. (File no.674)
Computing Reviews.
Confectionery: The International Market.
Conference Papers Annual Index. (File no. 77)
Conference Papers Index. (File no.77)
Consolidated Federal Funds Report.
Construction Review.
Consumer Catering: The International Market.
Consumer Reports. (File no.646)
Consumer Reports on Health. (File no.646)
Consumer Reports Travel Letter. (File no.646)
Corporate Detroit Magazine.
Corporate E F T Report.
Corporate Report Minnesota.
Corporate Venturing Quarterly.
Cosmetic Insider's Report.
Cotton and Tropical Fibres.
Cough and Cold Remedies: The International
    Market.
Country Forecast. Algeria.
Country Forecast. Argentina.
Country Forecast. Asia - Pacific.
Country Forecast. Australia.
Country Forecast. Austria.
Country Forecast. Belgium.
Country Forecast. Brazil.
Country Forecast. Bulgaria.
Country Forecast. Canada.
Country Forecast. Chile.
Country Forecast. China.
Country Forecast. Colombia.
Country Forecast. Czech Republic.
Country Forecast. Denmark.
Country Forecast. Eastern Europe and the Former
    Soviet Union.
Country Forecast. Ecuador.
Country Forecast. Egypt.
Country Forecast. Europe.
Country Forecast. Finland.
Country Forecast. France.
Country Forecast. Germany.
Country Forecast. Global Outlook.
Country Forecast. Greece.

Country Forecast. Hong Kong.
Country Forecast. Hungary.
Country Forecast. India.
Country Forecast. Indonesia.
Country Forecast. Iran.
Country Forecast. Iraq.
Country Forecast. Ireland.
Country Forecast. Israel.
Country Forecast. Italy.
Country Forecast. Japan.
Country Forecast. Latin America.
Country Forecast. Malaysia.
Country Forecast. Mexico.
Country Forecast. Middle East and North Africa.
Country Forecast. Netherlands.
Country Forecast. New Zealand.
Country Forecast. Nigeria.
Country Forecast. Norway.
Country Forecast. Pakistan.
Country Forecast. Peru.
Country Forecast. Philippines.
Country Forecast. Poland.
Country Forecast. Portugal.
Country Forecast. Romania.
Country Forecast. Russia.
Country Forecast. Saudi Arabia.
Country Forecast. Singapore.
Country Forecast. Slovakia.
Country Forecast. South Africa.
Country Forecast. South Korea.
Country Forecast. Spain.
Country Forecast. Sri Lanka.
Country Forecast. Sub-Saharan Africa.
Country Forecast. Sweden.
Country Forecast. Switzerland.
Country Forecast. Taiwan.
Country Forecast. Thailand.
Country Forecast. Turkey.
Country Forecast. United Kingdom.
Country Forecast. United States of America.
Country Forecast. Venezuela.
Country Forecast. Vietnam.
Country Forecasts (New York).
Country Forecasts (Syracuse).
Country Profile. Algeria.
Country Profile. Angola.
Country Profile. Argentina.
Country Profile. Australia.
Country Profile. Austria.
Country Profile. Bahrain, Qatar.
Country Profile. Baltic Republics: Lithuania,
    Latvia, Estonia.
Country Profile. Bangladesh.
Country Profile. Belgium, Luxembourg.
Country Profile. Belize, Bahamas, Bermuda.
Country Profile. Bolivia.
Country Profile. Bosnia-Hercegovina, Croatia,
    Slovenia.
Country Profile. Botswana, Lesotho.
Country Profile. Brazil.
Country Profile. Bulgaria, Albania.
Country Profile. Cambodia, Laos, Myanmar.
Country Profile. Cameroon, Central African
    Republic, Chad.
Country Profile. Canada.
Country Profile. Chile.
Country Profile. China, Mongolia.
Country Profile. Colombia.
Country Profile. Congo, Sao Tome and Principe,
    Guinea-Bissau, Cape Verde.
Country Profile. Costa Rica, Panama.
Country Profile. Cote d'Ivoire, Mali.
Country Profile. Cuba.
Country Profile. Cyprus, Malta.
Country Profile. Czech Republic and Slovakia.
Country Profile. Denmark, Iceland.
Country Profile. Dominican Republic, Haiti, Puerto
    Rico.
Country Profile. Ecuador.
Country Profile. Egypt.
Country Profile. Ethiopia, Eritrea, Somalia,
    Djibouti.
Country Profile. Finland.
Country Profile. France.
Country Profile. Gabon, Equatorial Guinea.
Country Profile. Georgia, Armenia, Azerbaijan.
Country Profile. Germany.
Country Profile. Ghana.
Country Profile. Greece.
Country Profile. Guatemala, El Salvador.
Country Profile. Guinea, Sierra Leone, Liberia.
Country Profile. Guyana, Windward and Leeward
    Islands.
Country Profile. Hong Kong, Macau.
Country Profile. Hungary.
Country Profile. India, Nepal.
Country Profile. Indonesia.
Country Profile. Iran.

Country Profile. Iraq.
Country Profile. Ireland.
Country Profile. Israel, the Occupied Territories.
Country Profile. Italy.
Country Profile. Jamaica, Barbados.
Country Profile. Japan.
Country Profile. Jordan.
Country Profile. Kenya.
Country Profile. Kuwait.
Country Profile. Lebanon.
Country Profile. Libya.
Country Profile. Macedonia, Serbia-Montenegro
Country Profile. Madagascar.
Country Profile. Malawi.
Country Profile. Malaysia, Brunei.
Country Profile. Mauritius, Seychelles.
Country Profile. Mexico.
Country Profile. Morocco.
Country Profile. Mozambique.
Country Profile. Namibia, Swaziland.
Country Profile. Netherlands.
Country Profile. New Zealand.
Country Profile. Nicaragua, Honduras.
Country Profile. Niger, Burkina Faso.
Country Profile. Nigeria.
Country Profile. Norway.
Country Profile. Oman, Yemen.
Country Profile. Pacific Islands: Fiji, Solomon
    Islands, Western Samoa, Vanuatu, Tonga.
Country Profile. Pakistan, Afghanistan.
Country Profile. Papua New Guinea.
Country Profile. Peru.
Country Profile. Philippines.
Country Profile. Poland.
Country Profile. Portugal.
Country Profile. Romania.
Country Profile. Russia.
Country Profile. Rwanda, Burundi
Country Profile. Saudi Arabia.
Country Profile. Senegal.
Country Profile. Singapore
Country Profile. South Africa.
Country Profile. South Korea, North Korea.
Country Profile. Spain.
Country Profile. Sri Lanka
Country Profile. Sudan.
Country Profile. Sweden.
Country Profile. Switzerland.
Country Profile. Syria.
Country Profile. Taiwan.
Country Profile. Tanzania, Comoros.
Country Profile. Thailand.
Country Profile. The Gambia, Mauritania.
Country Profile. Togo, Benin.
Country Profile. Trinidad and Tobago, Suriname,
    Netherlands Antilles, Aruba.
Country Profile. Tunisia.
Country Profile. Turkey.
Country Profile. Uganda.
Country Profile. Ukraine.
Country Profile. United Arab Emirates.
Country Profile. United Kingdom.
Country Profile. United States of America.
Country Profile. Uruguay, Paraguay.
Country Profile. Venezuela.
Country Profile. Zaire.
Country Profile. Zambia.
Country Profile. Zimbabwe.
Country Profiles.
Country Report. Algeria.
Country Report. Angola.
Country Report. Argentina.
Country Report. Australia.
Country Report. Austria.
Country Report. Bahrain, Qatar.
Country Report. Baltic Republics: Lithuania,
    Latvia, Estonia.
Country Report. Bangladesh.
Country Report. Belgium, Luxembourg.
Country Report. Bolivia.
Country Report. Bosnia-Hercegovina, Croatia.
Country Report. Brazil.
Country Report. Bulgaria, Albania.
Country Report. Cambodia, Laos.
Country Report. Cameroon, C.A.R., Chad.
Country Report. Canada.
Country Report. Chile.
Country Report. China, Mongolia.
Country Report. Colombia.
Country Report. Congo, Sao Tome and Principe,
    Guinea-Bissau, Cape Verde.
Country Report. Costa Rica, Panama.
Country Report. Cote d'Ivoire, Mali.
Country Report. Cuba, Dominican Republic, Haiti,
    Puerto Rico.
Country Report. Cyprus, Malta.
Country Report. Czech Republic, Slovakia.
Country Report. Denmark, Iceland.

Country Report. Ecuador.
Country Report. Egypt.
Country Report. Ethiopia, Eritrea, Somalia, Djibouti.
Country Report. Finland.
Country Report. France.
Country Report. Gabon, Equatorial Guinea.
Country Report. Germany.
Country Report. Ghana.
Country Report. Greece.
Country Report. Guatemala, El Salvador.
Country Report. Guinea, Sierra Leone, Liberia.
Country Report. Hong Kong, Macau.
Country Report. Hungary.
Country Report. India, Nepal.
Country Report. Indonesia.
Country Report. Iran.
Country Report. Iraq.
Country Report. Ireland.
Country Report. Israel, the Occupied Territories.
Country Report. Italy.
Country Report. Jamaica, Belize, Bahamas, Bermuda, Barbados.
Country Report. Japan.
Country Report. Jordan.
Country Report. Kazakhstan.
Country Report. Kenya.
Country Report. Kuwait.
Country Report. Lebanon.
Country Report. Libya.
Country Report. Malaysia, Brunei.
Country Report. Mauritius, Madagascar, Seychelles.
Country Report. Mexico.
Country Report. Morocco.
Country Report. Mozambique, Malawi.
Country Report. Netherlands.
Country Report. New Zealand.
Country Report. Nicaragua, Honduras.
Country Report. Nigeria.
Country Report. Norway.
Country Report. Oman, Yemen.
Country Report. Pacific Islands: Papua New Guinea, Fiji, Solomon Islands, Western Samoa, Vanuatu, Tonga.
Country Report. Pakistan, Afghanistan.
Country Report. Peru.
Country Report. Philippines.
Country Report. Poland.
Country Report. Portugal.
Country Report. Romania.
Country Report. Russia.
Country Report. Saudi Arabia.
Country Report. Senegal, The Gambia, Mauritania.
Country Report. Singapore.
Country Report. South Africa.
Country Report. South Korea, North Korea.
Country Report. Spain.
Country Report. Sri Lanka.
Country Report. Sudan.
Country Report. Sweden.
Country Report. Switzerland.
Country Report. Syria.
Country Report. Taiwan.
Country Report. Tanzania, Comoros.
Country Report. Thailand.
Country Report. Togo, Niger, Benin, Burkina Faso.
Country Report. Trinidad & Tobago, Guyana, Windward & Leeward Islands, Suriname, Netherlands Antilles, Aruba.
Country Report. Tunisia.
Country Report. Turkey.
Country Report. Uganda, Rwanda, Burundi.
Country Report. Ukraine.
Country Report. United Arab Emirates.
Country Report. United Kingdom.
Country Report. United States of America.
Country Report. Uruguay, Paraguay.
Country Report. Venezuela.
Country Report. Zambia, Zaire.
Country Report. Zimbabwe.
Country Reports.
County and City Data Book.
County Business Patterns.
Courier (Paris).
Crain's Chicago Business.
Crain's Cleveland Business.
Crain's Detroit Business.
Crain's New York Business.
Cranberries.
Credit and Charge Cards: The International Market.
Criminal Justice Periodical Index. *(File no. 171)*
Crop Physiology Abstracts.
Current Biotechnology. *(File no.358)*
Current Business Reports: Monthly Retail Trade: Sales and Inventories.

Current Business Reports: Monthly Wholesale Trade, Sales and Inventories.
Current Construction Reports: Housing Starts.
Current Construction Reports: Housing Units Authorized by Building Permits.
Current Construction Reports: New One-Family Houses Sold.
Current Construction Reports: New Residential Construction in Selected Metropolitan Areas.
Current Construction Reports: Value of New Construction Put in Place.
Current Contents: Agriculture, Biology & Environmental Sciences. *(File no.440)*
Current Contents: Arts & Humanities. *(File no.440)*
Current Contents: Clinical Medicine. *(File no.440)*
Current Contents: Engineering, Computing & Technology. *(File no.440)*
Current Contents: Life Sciences. *(File no.440)*
Current Contents: Physical, Chemical & Earth Sciences. *(File no.440)*
Current Contents: Social & Behavioral Sciences. *(File no.440)*
Current Governments Reports: City Employment.
Current Governments Reports: County Government Employment.
Current Governments Reports: Government Finances.
Current Governments Reports: Public Employment.
Current Governments Reports: State Government Tax Collections.
Current History.
Current Housing Reports: Housing Vacancies and Home Ownership.
Current Index to Journals in Education. *(File no.1/ERIC)*
Current Index to Statistics.
Current Industrial Reports.
Current Industrial Reports: Broadwoven Fabrics (Gray).
Current Industrial Reports: Fats and Oils. Oilseed Crushings.
Current Industrial Reports: Fats and Oils. Production, Consumption, and Stocks.
Current Law Index.
Current Mathematical Publications.
Current Population Reports: Consumer Income. Money Income of Households, Families and Persons in the United States (Year).
Current Population Reports: Population Characteristics. Geographical Mobility.
Current Population Reports: Population Characteristics. Marital Status and Living Arrangements.
Current Population Reports: Population Characteristics. School Enrollment: Social and Economic Characteristics of Students.
Current Population Reports: Population Estimates and Projections. United States Population Estimates by Age, Sex, Race and Hispanic Origin.
Current Population Reports: Series P-25. Population Estimates and Projections.
Current Population Reports: Series P-70. Household Economic Studies.
Current Research in Library & Information Science. *(File no.61)*
Current Technology Index. *(File no.142)*
The Cyprus Review.
C2C Abstracts: Japan - Analytical Chemistry. *(File no.582)*
C2C Abstracts: Japan - Ceramics. *(File no.582)*
C2C Abstracts: Japan - Chemical Engineering. *(File no.582)*
C2C Abstracts: Japan - Crystallography. *(File no.582)*
C2C Abstracts: Japan - Hydrocarbons. *(File no.582)*
C2C Abstracts: Japan - Inorganic Chemistry. *(File no.582)*
C2C Abstracts: Japan - Materials Science. *(File no.582)*
C2C Abstracts: Japan - Metals. *(File no.582)*
C2C Abstracts: Japan - Organic Chemistry. *(File no.582)*
C2C Abstracts: Japan - Physical Chemistry. *(File no.582)*
C2C Abstracts: Japan - Plastics. *(File no.582)*
C2C Abstracts: Japan - Polymer Chemistry. *(File no.582)*
C2C Abstracts: Japan - Surface Chemistry. *(File no.582)*
C2C Abstracts: Japan - Textiles. *(File no.582)*
C2C Currents: Japan - Chemistry. *(File no.582)*
C2C Currents: Japan - Computers. *(File no.582)*
C2C Currents: Japan - Electronics. *(File no.582)*
C2C Currents: Japan - Materials. *(File no.582)*

D I Y: The International Market.
D N R.
Dairy Foods.
Dairy Products: The International Market.
Dairy Science Abstracts.
Data Communications. *(File no.624/McGRAW-HILL PUBLICATIONS ONLINE)*
Data Storage Report.
Datamation.
Datapro Directory of Microcomputer Software.
Datapro Directory of Software.
Dealerscope Consumer Electronics Marketplace.
Dealing with Technology.
Defense Daily.
Defense Electronics.
Denver Post Index.
Deodorants: The International Market.
Dermatology Times.
Detroit News Index.
Devices & Diagnostics Letter.
Digestive Remedies: The International Market.
Digital News & Review.
Directories in Print.
Directory of Biomedical and Health Care Grants.
Directory of Corporate Affiliations. *(File no.513, Corporate Affiliations)*
Directory of Grants in the Humanities.
Directory of Research Grants.
Discount Store News.
Discover (Burbank).
Disposable Paper Products: The International Market.
Dissertation Abstracts International. Section A: Humanities and Social Sciences. *(File no.35)*
Dissertation Abstracts International. Section B: Physical Sciences and Engineering. *(File no.35)*
Dissertation Abstracts International. Section C: Worldwide. *(File no.35)*
Dissertation Abstracts on Disc.
Distribution.
Drug and Cosmetic Industry.
Drug Data Report.
Drug News & Perspectives.
Dutchess County Historical Society. Yearbook.
E C Energy Monthly.
E D N Magazine.
E F T Report.
E-Med News.
E N R. *(File no.624/McGRAW-HILL PUBLICATIONS ONLINE)*
East European Energy Report.
Ecological Abstracts. *(File no.292)*
Ecology Abstracts. *(File no.76/LIFE SCIENCES COLLECTION)*
Economic Indicators (Washington).
Economic Inquiry.
Educational Marketer.
Electric Utility Week. *(File no.624/McGRAW-HILL PUBLICATIONS ONLINE)*
Electric Utility Week's Demand-Side Report. *(DSR)*
Electrical & Electronics Abstracts.
Electrical World. *(EW)*
Electronic Business Today.
Electronic Design.
Electronic Information Report.
Electronic Learning.
Electronic News.
Emerging & Special Situations. *(ESS)*
Employee Relations Law Journal.
Encyclopedia of Associations. *(File no.114)*
Energy Conservation News.
Energy Daily.
Energy Data Base.
Energy Economist.
Energy Report.
Energy Research Abstracts.
Energy User News.
Engineered Materials Abstracts. *(File no.293)*
Engineering Index Annual. *(File no.8)*
Engineering Index Monthly. *(File no.8)*
Entertainment Software: The International Market.
Entomology Abstracts. *(File no.76/LIFE SCIENCES COLLECTION)*
Environment Abstracts. *(File no.40)*
Environment Abstracts Annual. *(File no.40)*
Environment Week.
Environmental Periodicals Bibliography. *(File no.68)*
Epiphany Journal.
Euromoney.
European Energy Report.
Eventline.
Excerpta Medica Abstract Journals.
Excerpta Medica. Section 1: Anatomy, Anthropology, Embryology & Histology.
Excerpta Medica. Section 2: Physiology.
Excerpta Medica. Section 3: Endocrinology.

Excerpta Medica. Section 4: Microbiology: Bacteriology, Mycology, Parasitology and Virology.
Excerpta Medica. Section 5: General Pathology and Pathological Anatomy.
Excerpta Medica. Section 6: Internal Medicine.
Excerpta Medica. Section 7: Pediatrics and Pediatric Surgery.
Excerpta Medica. Section 8: Neurology and Neurosurgery.
Excerpta Medica. Section 9: Surgery.
Excerpta Medica. Section 10: Obstetrics and Gynecology.
Excerpta Medica. Section 11: Otorhinolaryngology.
Excerpta Medica. Section 12: Ophthalmology.
Excerpta Medica. Section 13: Dermatology and Venereology.
Excerpta Medica. Section 14: Radiology.
Excerpta Medica. Section 15: Chest Diseases, Thoracic Surgery and Tuberculosis.
Excerpta Medica. Section 16: Cancer.
Excerpta Medica. Section 17: Public Health, Social Medicine and Epidemiology.
Excerpta Medica. Section 18: Cardiovascular Diseases and Cardiovascular Surgery.
Excerpta Medica. Section 19: Rehabilitation and Physical Medicine.
Excerpta Medica. Section 20: Gerontology and Geriatrics.
Excerpta Medica. Section 21: Developmental Biology and Teratology.
Excerpta Medica. Section 22: Human Genetics.
Excerpta Medica. Section 23: Nuclear Medicine.
Excerpta Medica. Section 24: Anesthesiology.
Excerpta Medica. Section 25: Hematology.
Excerpta Medica. Section 26: Immunology, Serology and Transplantation.
Excerpta Medica. Section 27: Biophysics, Bio-Engineering and Medical Instrumentation.
Excerpta Medica. Section 28: Urology and Nephrology.
Excerpta Medica. Section 29: Clinical and Experimental Biochemistry.
Excerpta Medica. Section 30: Clinical and Experimental Pharmacology.
Excerpta Medica. Section 31: Arthritis and Rheumatism.
Excerpta Medica. Section 32: Psychiatry.
Excerpta Medica. Section 33: Orthopedic Surgery.
Excerpta Medica. Section 35: Occupational Health and Industrial Medicine.
Excerpta Medica. Section 36: Health Policy, Economics and Management.
Excerpta Medica. Section 38: Adverse Reactions Titles.
Excerpta Medica. Section 40: Drug Dependence, Alcohol Abuse and Alcoholism.
Excerpta Medica. Section 46: Environmental Health and Pollution Control.
Excerpta Medica. Section 48: Gastroenterology.
Excerpta Medica. Section 49: Forensic Science Abstracts.
Excerpta Medica. Section 50: Epilepsy Abstracts.
Excerpta Medica. Section 52: Toxicology.
Executive Report.
Eyewear: The International Market.
F C C Report.
F D A Consumer.
F D A Medical Bulletin.
F X Week.
Facts on File World News Digest with Index. (File no.264)
Family Relations.
Fast Food: The International Market.
Federal Register. (File no.669)
Federal Research in Progress Database. (File nos.265,266)
Federal Reserve Bank of New York. Economic Policy Review.
Federal Reserve Bulletin.
Federal Technology Report. (TTR)
Fiber Optics News.
Field Crop Abstracts.
Film & Video Finder. (File no.46)
Financial Executive.
Financial Technology Insight.
Financial Times World Tax Report.
Financial World.
Financing Foreign Operations. Americas.
Financing Foreign Operations. Argentina.
Financing Foreign Operations. Asia.
Financing Foreign Operations. Australia.
Financing Foreign Operations. Belgium.
Financing Foreign Operations. Brazil.
Financing Foreign Operations. Canada.

Financing Foreign Operations. Central America: Costa Rica. El Salvador, Guatemala, Honduras, Nicaragua.
Financing Foreign Operations. Chile.
Financing Foreign Operations. Colombia.
Financing Foreign Operations. Czech Republic.
Financing Foreign Operations. France.
Financing Foreign Operations. Germany.
Financing Foreign Operations. Global Edition.
Financing Foreign Operations. Greece.
Financing Foreign Operations. Hong Kong.
Financing Foreign Operations. Hungary.
Financing Foreign Operations. India.
Financing Foreign Operations. Italy.
Financing Foreign Operations. Japan.
Financing Foreign Operations. Malaysia.
Financing Foreign Operations. Mexico.
Financing Foreign Operations. Middle East - Africa.
Financing Foreign Operations. Netherlands.
Financing Foreign Operations. Nigeria.
Financing Foreign Operations. Norway.
Financing Foreign Operations. Panama.
Financing Foreign Operations. Philippines.
Financing Foreign Operations. Poland.
Financing Foreign Operations. Russia.
Financing Foreign Operations. Saudi Arabia.
Financing Foreign Operations. Singapore.
Financing Foreign Operations. South Africa.
Financing Foreign Operations. South Korea.
Financing Foreign Operations. Spain.
Financing Foreign Operations. Sweden.
Financing Foreign Operations. Switzerland.
Financing Foreign Operations. Taiwan.
Financing Foreign Operations. Thailand.
Financing Foreign Operations. United Kingdom.
Financing Foreign Operations. United States of America.
Financing Foreign Operations. Venezuela.
Findex (Year). (File no.196)
Firmen der Neuen Bundeslaender.
Florida Trend.
Flower and Garden.
Flower & Garden Crafts Edition.
Fluid Abstracts: Civil Engineering. (File no.96/FLUIDEX)
Fluid Abstracts: Process Engineering. (File no.96/FLUIDEX)
Flying.
Folio (Stamford).
Food and Drug Letter.
Food Chemical News.
Food, Cosmetics and Drugs Packaging.
Food Retailers: The International Market.
Food Science and Technology Abstracts. (File no.51)
Foods Adlibra. (File no.79)
Foods Adlibra Beverage Edition. (File no.79)
Foods Adlibra Foodservice Edition. (File no.79)
Foods Adlibra Seafood Edition. (File no.79)
Foods Adlibra Snack & Confections Edition. (File no.79)
Footwear News.
Forbes.
Foreign Policy Bulletin.
Foreign Trade Reports. U.S. Export and Import Merchandise Trade and Supplement.
Forest Products Abstracts.
Forestry Abstracts.
Forestry Abstracts. Leading Article Reprint Series.
Forthcoming Books. (File no.470)
Foundation Directory.
Foundation Grants Index.
Foundation Grants Index Quarterly.
Foundry Management & Technology.
Freshwater Fisheries Laboratory Pitlochry. Annual Review.
Frozen Foods: The International Market.
Fruit and Vegetables: The International Market.
Fruit Juices: The International Market.
Fund Raising Management.
Fusion Power Report.
Futurescope. (File no. 192)
The Futurist.
The G M P Letter.
Gale Directory of Publications and Broadcast Media.
Gardening: The International Market.
Gas Daily.
Genesis Report - Dx.
Genesis Report - Rx.
Genetics Abstracts. (File no.76/LIFE SCIENCES COLLECTION)
Geographical Abstracts: Human Geography. (File no.292)
Geographical Abstracts: Physical Geography. (File no.292)
Geological Abstracts. (File no.292)
Geological Society of India. Journal. (File no.89)

Georgia Trend.
Geoscience Documentation. (File no.58)
Geotitles. (File no.58)
Gifts & Decorative Accessories.
Global Environmental Change.
Global Private Power.
Going Public - The I P O Reporter.
Government Computer News.
Government Product News.
Government Reports Announcements & Index. (File no.6)
Government Research Directory.
Grand Rapids Business Journal.
Graphic Arts Monthly.
Grasslands and Forage Abstracts.
Great Britain. H.M.S.O. Annual Catalogue.
Great Britain. H.M.S.O. Books in Print.
Great Britain. H.M.S.O. Daily List.
Great Britain. H.M.S.O. Government Publications Sectional Lists.
Great Britain. H.M.S.O. Monthly Catalogue.
Great Britain. H.M.S.O. Publications Catalogue.
Great Britain. H.M.S.O. Statutory Instruments List.
Great Britain. H.M.S.O. Committee Reports Index.
Ground Water Monitor.
Guns & Ammo.
H F N.
Hair Care Products: The International Market.
Hancbook on Injectable Drugs. (File no.229)
Handbuch der Grossunternehmen.
Hangzhou Daxue Xuebao (Ziran Kexue Ban).
Harvard Business Review. (File no.122)
Hawaii Business.
Hazardous Waste Business. (HWB)
Hazardous Waste News.
Haznews. (File nos.636 & 16)
Health Alliance Alert.
Health Devices Alerts. (File no.198)
Health Devices Sourcebook. (File no.188)
Health Index. (File no.149)
Health Management Technology.
Health News Daily. (File no.43)
Health Policy & Biomedical Research: The Blue Sheet. (File no.187)
Health, Slimming and Dietetic Foods: The International Market.
Healthcare Financial Management.
Healthcare Technology & Business Opportunities.
Helicopter News.
Helminthological Abstracts.
Hewlett-Packard Journal.
High Performance Plastics.
High Performance Textiles.
High Tech Ceramics News.
High Tech Separations News.
High Yield Report.
Historical Abstracts. Part A: Modern History Abstracts, 1450-1914. (File no.39)
Historical Abstracts. Part B: Twentieth Century Abstracts, 1914 to the Present. (File no.39)
Historical Abstracts. Part B: Twentieth Century Abstracts, 1914 to the Present Annual Index. (File no.39)
Horticultural Abstracts.
Hospitals.
Hospitals and Health Networks.
Hot Rod.
Hotel and Motel Management.
Household Cleaning Agents: The International Market.
Housewares: The International Market.
Houston Business Journal.
Houston Post Index.
Huadong Ligong Daxue Xuebao.
Hydraulics & Pneumatics.
Hydrotitles. (File no.58)
Hypatia. (File no.57)
Hypermarkets and Superstores: The International Market.
I I E Solutions.
I S D N News.
Ice Cream, Yoghurts and Chilled Desserts: The International Market.
Illinois Business Review.
Imaging Abstracts. (F248)
Imaging Update.
Immunology Abstracts. (File no.76/LIFE SCIENCES COLLECTION)
Improved Recovery Week.
In-Car Entertainment: The International Market.
Inc.
Independent Power Report. (File no.624/McGRAW-HILL PUBLICATIONS ONLINE)
Index Medicus. (File nos.154 & 155/MEDLINE)
Index of Current Research or Pigs.
Index of Economic Articles in Journals and Collective Volumes. (File no.139)
Index of Fungi.

Index to Dental Literature. (File nos.154 & 155/MEDLINE)
Index Veterinarius.
Indiana Business Magazine.
Industrial and Labor Relations Review.
Industrial Distribution.
Industrial Energy Bulletin. (File no.624/McGRAW-HILL PUBLICATIONS ONLINE)
Industrial Health.
Industrial Paint & Powder.
Industrial Researcher.
Industrial Specialties News.
Industries in Transition.
Industry Week.
Information Management Report. (File no.636)
Information Networks.
Information Science Abstracts. (File no.202)
Ingram's Magazine.
Inpharma Weekly. (PHD,IPHC,IPHA,IPZZ)
Inside Energy with Federal Lands. (File no.624/McGRAW-HILL PUBLICATIONS ONLINE)
Inside F E R C. (File no.624/McGRAW-HILL PUBLICATIONS ONLINE)
Inside F E R C's Gas Market Report. (File no.624/McGRAW-HILL PUBLICATIONS ONLINE)
Inside Market Data.
Inside N R C. (File no.624/McGRAW-HILL PUBLICATIONS ONLINE)
Inside the New Computer Industry.
Institute of Paper Science and Technology. Abstract Bulletin. (File nos.240 & 840/PAPERCHEM)
Institutional Distribution.
Instrumentation and Control Systems.
Insurance Periodicals Index. (File no.169)
Integrated Circuits International.
Integrated Waste Management. (File no. 624/McGRAW-HILL PUBLICATIONS ONLINE)
International Aerospace Abstracts. (File no.108)
International Biodeterioration & Biodegradation.
International Brands and Their Companies.
International Coal Report.
International Country Risk Guide.
International Defense Review.
International Development Abstracts. (File no.292)
International Gas Report.
International Journal of Purchasing & Materials Management.
International Journal of Supercomputer Applications and High-Performance Computing.
International Nursing Index. (File nos.154 & 155/MEDLINE)
International Packaging Abstracts.
International Pharmaceutical Abstracts. (File no.74)
International Population Data.
International Product Alert. (File no. 9)
International Research Centers Directory.
International Solar Energy Intelligence Report.
Investing, Licensing and Trading Conditions Abroad. Americas.
Investing, Licensing and Trading Conditions Abroad. Argentina.
Investing, Licensing and Trading Conditions Abroad. Asia.
Investing, Licensing and Trading Conditions Abroad. Australia.
Investing, Licensing and Trading Conditions Abroad. Austria.
Investing, Licensing and Trading Conditions Abroad. Belgium.
Investing, Licensing and Trading Conditions Abroad. Brazil.
Investing, Licensing and Trading Conditions Abroad. Britain.
Investing, Licensing and Trading Conditions Abroad. Canada.
Investing, Licensing and Trading Conditions Abroad. Central America.
Investing, Licensing and Trading Conditions Abroad. Chile.
Investing, Licensing and Trading Conditions Abroad. China.
Investing, Licensing and Trading Conditions Abroad. Colombia.
Investing, Licensing and Trading Conditions Abroad. Czech Republic and Slovakia.
Investing, Licensing and Trading Conditions Abroad. Denmark.
Investing, Licensing and Trading Conditions Abroad. Ecuador.
Investing, Licensing and Trading Conditions Abroad. Egypt.
Investing, Licensing and Trading Conditions Abroad. Finland.

Investing, Licensing and Trading Conditions Abroad. France.
Investing, Licensing and Trading Conditions Abroad. Germany.
Investing, Licensing and Trading Conditions Abroad. Global Edition.
Investing, Licensing and Trading Conditions Abroad. Greece.
Investing, Licensing and Trading Conditions Abroad. Hong Kong.
Investing, Licensing and Trading Conditions Abroad. Hungary.
Investing, Licensing and Trading Conditions Abroad. India.
Investing, Licensing and Trading Conditions Abroad. Indonesia.
Investing, Licensing and Trading Conditions Abroad. Ireland.
Investing, Licensing and Trading Conditions Abroad. Israel.
Investing, Licensing and Trading Conditions Abroad. Italy.
Investing, Licensing and Trading Conditions Abroad. Japan.
Investing, Licensing and Trading Conditions Abroad. Kenya.
Investing, Licensing and Trading Conditions Abroad. Luxembourg.
Investing, Licensing and Trading Conditions Abroad. Malaysia.
Investing, Licensing and Trading Conditions Abroad. Mexico.
Investing, Licensing and Trading Conditions Abroad. Middle East - Africa.
Investing, Licensing and Trading Conditions Abroad. Netherlands.
Investing, Licensing and Trading Conditions Abroad. New Zealand.
Investing, Licensing and Trading Conditions Abroad. Nigeria.
Investing, Licensing and Trading Conditions Abroad. Norway.
Investing, Licensing and Trading Conditions Abroad. Pakistan.
Investing, Licensing and Trading Conditions Abroad. Panama.
Investing, Licensing and Trading Conditions Abroad. Peru.
Investing, Licensing and Trading Conditions Abroad. Philippines.
Investing, Licensing and Trading Conditions Abroad. Poland.
Investing, Licensing and Trading Conditions Abroad. Portugal.
Investing, Licensing and Trading Conditions Abroad. Puerto Rico.
Investing, Licensing and Trading Conditions Abroad. Russia.
Investing, Licensing and Trading Conditions Abroad. Saudi Arabia.
Investing, Licensing and Trading Conditions Abroad. Singapore.
Investing, Licensing and Trading Conditions Abroad. South Africa.
Investing, Licensing and Trading Conditions Abroad. South Korea.
Investing, Licensing and Trading Conditions Abroad. Spain.
Investing, Licensing and Trading Conditions Abroad. Sweden.
Investing, Licensing and Trading Conditions Abroad. Switzerland.
Investing, Licensing and Trading Conditions Abroad. Taiwan.
Investing, Licensing and Trading Conditions Abroad. Thailand.
Investing, Licensing and Trading Conditions Abroad. Turkey.
Investing, Licensing and Trading Conditions Abroad. United States of America.
Investing, Licensing and Trading Conditions Abroad. Uruguay.
Investing, Licensing and Trading Conditions Abroad. Venezuela.
Investing, Licensing and Trading Conditions Abroad. Vietnam.
Irrigation and Drainage Abstracts.
Item Processing Report.
J A M A: The Journal of the American Medical Association.
Jane's Defence Weekly.
Jane's Intelligence Review.
Journal of Commerce and Commercial.
Journal of Consumer Affairs.
Journal of Consumer Research.
Journal of Economic Literature. (Economic Literature Index File no. 139)
Journal of Marriage and the Family.

Journal of Mormon History. (File nos.38,39)
Journal of Near Eastern Studies.
Journal of Psychology and Theology.
Journal of Retailing.
Journal of Risk and Insurance.
Journal of Systems Management.
Journal of Technology Transfer.
Kentucky Business Ledger.
Key Abstracts - Business Automation.
Kiplinger's Personal Finance Magazine.
Kompass Sverige.
L A N Product News.
L A N Times. (LAN)
L D C Debt Report.
L I S A: Library & Information Science Abstracts. (File no.61/LISA)
Labor Relations Reporter. (File no. 244, Laborlaw)
Labor Relations Reporter. Fair Employment Practices.
Labor Relations Reporter. Labor Arbitration and Dispute Settlements. (Files 243, 244)
Labor Relations Reporter. Wages and Hours.
Laboratory Hazards Bulletin. (File no.317)
Ladies Home Journal (Inkprint Edition).
Lagniappe Letter.
Land Mobile Radio News.
Large Kitchen Appliances: The International Market.
Large Mixed Retailers: The International Market.
Law Office Technology Review.
LegalTrac. (File no.150)
Leisure, Recreation and Tourism Abstracts.
Life (New York).
Linguistics and Language Behavior Abstracts. (File no.36)
Livestock, Dairy and Poultry Situation & Outlook.
Lodging Hospitality.
London Business Monthly Magazine.
Lookout - Foods. (File no. 16 & 570)
Lookout - Nonfoods. (File no. 16 & 570)
The Los Angeles Times Index.
Louisville Magazine.
McGraw-Hill's Biotechnology Newswatch. (File no.624/McGRAW-HILL PUBLICATIONS ONLINE)
Machine Design.
Magazine Index. (File no.47)
Magill's Cinema Annual.
Mail Order and Home Shopping: The International Market.
Mainframe Computing.
Maize Abstracts.
Make-Up and Colour Cosmetics: The International Market.
Management Contents. (File no.75)
Managing Office Technology.
Manufacturing Automation.
Market: Asia Pacific.
Market Direction Reports.
Market: Europe.
Market: Latin America.
Market Research Abstracts.
Martindale: the Extra Pharmacopoeia. (File no.141)
Maryland. Police and Correctional Training Commissions. Annual Report.
Maryland Business & Living.
Masters Abstracts International. (File no.35)
Materials Business Information. (File no.269)
Materials Information Translations Service.
Mathematical Reviews.
Meat and Poultry: The International Market.
Mechanical Engineering Abstracts. (File no.14)
MediaWeek.
Medical and Health Care Books and Serials in Print.
Medical & Pharmaceutical Biotechnology Abstracts. (File no.76/LIFE SCIENCES COLLECTION)
Medical Devices, Diagnostics & Instrumentation Reports: The Gray Sheet. (File no.187)
Medical Economics.
Medical Outcomes and Guidelines Alert.
Medical Textiles.
Medical Utilization Management.
Medical Waste News.
Medicated Skincare: The International Market.
Membrane & Separation Technology News.
Memphis Business Journal.
Men's Toiletries: The International Market.
Mercer Business Magazine.
Merck Index: An Encyclopedia of Chemicals and Drugs.
Metals Abstracts. (File no.32/METADEX)
Metals Abstracts Index. (File no.32/METADEX)
Metals Week. (File no.624/McGRAW-HILL PUBLICATIONS ONLINE)

Meteorological and Geoastrophysical Abstracts. *(File no.29)*
Meyler's Side Effects of Drugs. *(File no.70/ SEDBASE)*
Microbiology Abstracts: Section A. Industrial & Applied Microbiology. *(File no.76/LIFE SCIENCES COLLECTION)*
Microbiology Abstracts: Section B. Bacteriology. *(File no.76/LIFE SCIENCES COLLECTION)*
Microbiology Abstracts: Section C. Algology, Mycology and Protozoology. *(File no.76/LIFE SCIENCES COLLECTION)*
Microcomputer Abstracts. *(File no.233)*
Middle East: Abstracts and Index. *(File no.248)*
Military & Commercial Fiber Business.
Military Robotics Newsletter. *(NL0650)*
Military Specifications and Standards Services Numeric Index.
Million Dollar Directory. *(File no.517)*
Mineral Water: The International Market.
Minneapolis - St. Paul CityBusiness.
Minority Markets Alert.
Mittelstaendische Unternehmen.
Mobile Satellite Reports.
Modem User News.
Modern Bride.
Modern Plastics. *(MP)*
Modern Tire Dealer.
Money (New York).
Money Laundering Alert.
Monthly Catalog of United States Government Publications. *(File no.66)*
Monthly Labor Review.
Monthly Product Announcement.
Moscow News.
Mother Jones.
Motor Trend.
Mount Sinai Journal of Medicine.
Multimedia Monitor.
N C J R S Document Retrieval Index.
N I O S H T I C Database.
N T I S Bibliographic Data Base.
Nanjing Huagong Xueyuan Xuebao.
National Agricultural Statistics Service. Cattle on Feed.
National Newspaper Index. *(File no.111)*
National Petroleum News.
National Report on Computers and Health.
National Review.
Natural History.
Nematological Abstracts.
Network World. *(File no.674)*
Networks Update.
New Hampshire Business Review.
The New Leader.
New Materials - Japan.
New Mexico Business Journal.
New Orleans CityBusiness.
The New Republic.
New Steel.
New Technology Week.
Newsletters in Print.
Newspaper Abstracts.
Nonferrous Metals Alert. *(File no.269)*
Nonprescription Pharmaceuticals and Nutritionals: The Tan Sheet. *(File no.187)*
Nonwovens Abstracts.
North Sea Letter.
North Sea Rig Forecast.
Northeast Power Report. *(NPR)*
NotiSur.
NuclearFuel. *(File no.624/McGRAW-HILL PUBLICATIONS ONLINE)*
Nucleic Acids Abstracts. *(File no.76/LIFE SCIENCES COLLECTION)*
Nucleonics Week. *(File no.624/McGRAW-HILL PUBLICATIONS ONLINE)*
Nursing Homes.
Nutrition Abstracts and Reviews. Series A: Human and Experimental.
Nutrition Abstracts and Reviews. Series B: Livestock Feeds and Feeding.
Occupational Safety & Health Reporter. *(Laborlaw, File no.244)*
Oceanic Abstracts. *(File no.28)*
Octane Week.
Oil Daily.
Oil Market Report.
Oils and Fats: The International Market.
Oncogenes and Growth Factors Abstracts. *(File no.76)*
Online Libraries and Microcomputers.
Online Newsletter.
Ophthalmology Times.
Optical Materials and Engineering News.
Oral Hygiene Products: The International Market.
Orange County Business Journal.
Ornamental Horticulture.

Outdoor Life.
Outlook (Year) Proceedings.
P A I S International in Print. *(File no.49/PAIS)*
P A S C A L. E 11: Physique Atomique et Moleculaire. Plasmas. *(File no.144)*
P A S C A L. E 12: Etat Condense. *(File no.144)*
P A S C A L. E 13: Structure des Liquides et des Solides - Cristallographie. *(File no.144)*
P A S C A L. E 18: Chromatographie. *(File no.144)*
P A S C A L. E 20: Electronique et Telecommunications. *(File no.144)*
P A S C A L. E 27: Methodes de Formation et Traitement des Images. *(File no.144)*
P A S C A L. E 30: Microscopie Electronique et Diffraction Electronique. *(File no.144)*
P A S C A L. E 32: Metrologie et Appareillage en Physique et Physicochimie. *(File no.144)*
P A S C A L. E 33: Informatique.
P A S C A L. E 34: Robotique, Automatique et Automatisation des Processus Industriels. *(File no.144)*
P A S C A L. E 36: Pollution de l'Eau, de l'Air et du Sol - Dechets - Bruit. *(File no.144)*
P A S C A L. E 48: Environnement Cosmique Terrestre, Astronomie et Geologie Extraterrestre. *(File no.144)*
P A S C A L. E 49: Meteorologie, Glaciologie, Physique des Oceans. *(File no.144)*
P A S C A L. E 58: Genetique. *(File no.144)*
P A S C A L. E 61: Microbiologie: Bacteriologie, Virologie, Mycologie, Protozoaires Pathogenes. *(File no. 144)*
P A S C A L. E 62: Immunologie. *(File no.144)*
P A S C A L. E 63: Toxicologie. *(File no.144)*
P A S C A L. E 64: Endocrinologie Humaine et Experimentale. Endocrinopathies. *(File no.144)*
P A S C A L. E 65: Psychologie, Psychopathologie, Psychiatrie. *(File no.144)*
P A S C A L. E 68: Genetique Humaine.
P A S C A L. E 71: Ophtalmologie. *(File no. 144)*
P A S C A L. E 72: Otorhinolaryngologie. Stomatologie. Pathologie Cervicofaciale. *(File no.144)*
P A S C A L. E 73: Dermatologie. Maladies Sexuellement Transmissibles. *(File no.144)*
P A S C A L. E 74: Pneumologie. *(File no.144)*
P A S C A L. E 75: Cardiologie et Appareil Circulatoire. *(File no.144)*
P A S C A L. E 76: Gastroenterologie, Foie, Pancreas, Abdomen. *(File no.144)*
P A S C A L. E 77: Nephrologie. Voies Urinaires. *(File no.144)*
P A S C A L. E 78: Neurologie. *(File no.144)*
P A S C A L. E 79: Pathologie et Physiologie Osteoarticulaires. *(File no.144)*
P A S C A L. E 80: Hematologie. *(File no.144)*
P A S C A L. E 82: Gynecologie, Obstetrique, Andrologie. *(File no.144)*
P A S C A L. E 83: Anesthesie et Reanimation. *(File no.144)*
P A S C A L. E 84: Genie Biomedical. Informatique Biomedicale. *(File no.144)*
P A S C A L. E 89: Cancer. *(File no.144)*
P A S C A L. F 10: Mecanique, Acoustique et Transfert de Chaleur. *(File no.144)*
P A S C A L. F 16: Chimie Analytique, Minerale et Organique. *(File no.144)*
P A S C A L. F 17: Chimie Generale, Minerale et Organique. *(File no.144)*
P A S C A L. F 23: Genie Chimique. Industries Chimique et Parachimique. *(File no.144)*
P A S C A L. F 24: Polymeres - Peintures - Bois. *(File no.144)*
P A S C A L. F 40: Mineralogie. Geochimie. Geologie Extraterrestre. *(File no.144)*
P A S C A L. F 41: Gisements Metalliques et Non Metalliques. *(File no.144)*
P A S C A L. F 42: Roches Cristallines. *(File no.144)*
P A S C A L. F 43: Roches Sedimentaires. Geologie Marine. *(File no.144)*
P A S C A L. F 44: Stratigraphie, Geologie Regionale, Geologie Generale. *(File no.144)*
P A S C A L. F 45: Tectonique, Geophysique Interne. *(File no.144)*
P A S C A L. F 46: Hydrologie. Geologie de l'Ingenieur. Formations Superficielles. *(File no.144)*
P A S C A L. F 47: Paleontologie. *(File no.144)*
P A S C A L. F 52: Biochimie - Biophysique - Moleculaire - Biologie Moleculaire et Cellulaire. *(File no.144)*
P A S C A L. F 53: Anatomie et Physiologie des Vertebres. *(File no.144)*
P A S C A L. F 54: Reproduction des Vertebres, Embryologie des Vertebres et des Invertebres. *(File no.144)*

P A S C A L. F 55: Biologie Vegetale. *(File no.144)*
P A S C A L. F 56: Ecologie Animale, Vegetale et Microbienne. Ethologie Animale. *(File no.144)*
P A S C A L. F 70: Pharmacologie. Traitements Medicamenteux. *(File no.144)*
P A S C A L. T 205: Sciences de l'Information. Documentation. *(File no.144)*
P A S C A L. T 215: Biotechnologies. *(File no.144)*
P A S C A L. T 230: Energie. *(File no.144)*
P A S C A L. T 235: Medecine Tropicale. *(File no.144)*
P A S C A L. T 240: Metaux - Metallurgie. *(File no.144)*
P A S C A L. T 260: Zoologie Fondamentale et Appliquee des Invertebres. *(File no.144)*
P A S C A L. T 280: Sciences Agronomiques et Forestieres: Productions Vegetales. *(File no.144)*
P A S C A L. T 295: Batiment. Travaux Publics. *(File no.144)*
P A S C A L V.4 Sciences de la Terre. *(File no.144)*
P C Business Products.
P C Magazin.
P N I. *(File no.42)*
Pacific Business News.
Packaging Science and Technology Abstracts. *(File no.252)*
Paperbase Abstracts.
Paperboard Packaging.
Paperbound Books in Print. *(File no.470)*
Pasta Products: The International Market.
Perfumes and Fragrances: The International Market.
Periodical Abstracts.
Personal Care Appliances: The International Market.
Personalist Forum.
Pesticide & Toxic Chemical News.
The Pesticide Manual. *(File no.306)*
Pet Foods and Products: The International Market.
Petersen's Photographic.
Peterson's Guide to Four-Year Colleges (Year). *(File no.214)*
Peterson's Guide to Graduate and Professional Programs: An Overview (Year) (Book 1). *(File no.273)*
Peterson's Guide to Graduate Programs in Business, Education, Health, and Law (Year) (Book 6). *(File no.273)*
Peterson's Guide to Graduate Programs in Engineering and Applied Sciences (Year) (Book 5). *(File no.273)*
Peterson's Guide to Graduate Programs in the Biological and Agricultural Sciences (Year) (Book 3). *(File no.273)*
Peterson's Guide to Graduate Programs in the Humanities and Social Sciences (Year) (Book 2). *(File no.273)*
Peterson's Guide to Graduate Programs in the Physical Sciences and Mathematics (Year) (Book 4). *(File no.273)*
Peterson's Guide to Two-Year Colleges (Year). *(File no.214)*
Petroleum Abstracts. *(File no. 87,987)*
Petroleum - Energy Business News Index.
Pharmaceutical Approvals Monthly. *(File no.187)*
Pharmacies and Drugstores: The International Market.
Pharmacoeconomics and Outcomes News.
Philadelphia Business Journal.
Philosopher's Index. *(File no.57)*
Photography: The International Market.
The Physician and Sportsmedicine.
Physics Abstracts.
Pig News & Information.
Plant Breeding Abstracts.
Plant Engineering.
Plant Growth Regulator Abstracts.
Platt's International Petrochemical Report. *(File no.624/McGRAW-HILL PUBLICATIONS ONLINE)*
Platt's Oilgram News. *(File no.624/McGRAW-HILL PUBLICATIONS ONLINE)*
Platt's Oilgram Price Report. *(File no.624/ McGRAW-HILL PUBLICATIONS ONLINE)*
Playthings.
Pollution Abstracts. *(File no.41)*
Polymers, Ceramics, Composites Alert. *(File no.269)*
Popular Photography.
Popular Science.
Postgraduate Medicine. *(PGM)*
Potato Abstracts.
Poultry Abstracts.

Vendor

Power (New York). *(POW)*
Power in Asia.
Power in Europe.
Power in Latin America.
Power U K.
Predicasts Basebook.
Predicasts F & S Index Europe.
Predicasts F & S Index International.
Predicasts F & S Index of Corporate Change.
Predicasts F & S Index United States.
Predicasts Forecasts.
Predicasts Overview of Markets and Technology.
Prepared Soups: The International Market.
Prescription Pharmaceuticals and Biotechnology:
    The Pink Sheet. *(File no.187)*
Printing Abstracts.
Private Placement Reporter.
Process and Chemical Engineering. *(File no.315)*
Product Alert. *(File no. 636)*
Productivity Software.
Professional Update.
Progressive Grocer.
Protozoological Abstracts.
Psychological Abstracts. *(File no.11/PsycINFO)*
Psychology Today.
Publishers Directory.
Publishers, Distributors & Wholesalers of the
    United States. *(File no.450)*
Puget Sound Business Journal.
Quill (Greencastle).
R A P R A Abstracts.
R A P R A New Trade Names in the Rubber and
    Plastics Industries.
R & D Focus.
R T E C S. *(File no.336)*
Reactions Weekly. *(READ,REAC,REAA,REZZ)*
Religion in Eastern Europe.
Renewable Energy Report.
Research Alert (New York).
Research & Development.
Research Centers Directory.
Research Services Directory.
Resources in Education.
Retail Stationery: The International Market.
Review of Agricultural Entomology.
The Review of Banking and Financial Services.
    (BFS)
Review of Medical and Veterinary Entomology.
Review of Medical and Veterinary Mycology.
Review of Plant Pathology.
The Review of Securities & Commodities
    Regulation. *(SCR)*
Rice Abstracts.
Rural Development Abstracts.
Rural Libraries.
S M T Trends.
S T A R. *(File no.108)*
S T N.
St. Louis Business Journal.
Sales and Marketing Management.
Salud Publica de Mexico.
San Diego Business Journal.
Saturday Evening Post.
Savoury Snacks: The International Market.
Scholastic Choices.
Scholastic Update.
School Planning and Management.
Schweizerische Zeitschrift fuer Volkswirtschaft
    und Statistik.
Science Citation Index. *(Files
    nos.34,432,433,434/SCISEARCH)*
Scouting.
Scrip - World Pharmaceutical News.
Searchable Physics Information Notices. *(File
    no.62/SPIN)*
Securities Week. *(File no.624/McGRAW-HILL
    PUBLICATIONS ONLINE)*
Seed Abstracts.
Sensor Business Digest.
Sensor Review.
Service Stations: The International Market.
Shopper Report.
Side Effects of Drugs Annual. *(File no.70/
    SEDBASE)*
The SIMBA Report on Directory Publishing. *(File
    no.636)*
Situation & Outlook Report. Agricultural Income &
    Finance.
Situation & Outlook Report. Fruit & Tree Nuts.
Situation & Outlook Report. Sugar & Sweetener.
Situation & Outlook Report. Tobacco.
Situation & Outlook Report. Vegetables &
    Specialties.
Skin Care: The International Market.
Skin Diver Magazine.
Small Animals.
Small Kitchen Appliances: The International
    Market.

Smithsonian.
Social Planning - Policy & Development
    Abstracts. *(File No.37)*
Social Sciences Citation Index. *(File no.7/SOCIAL
    SCISEARCH)*
Sociological Abstracts. *(File no.37)*
Soft Drinks: The International Market.
Software Catalog: Microcomputers.
Software Encyclopedia. *(File no.278)*
Sorghum and Millets.
SourceMex.
Southeast Power Report. *(SPR)*
Southern Social Studies Journal.
Soyabean Abstracts.
Space Business News.
Spirits: The International Market.
Sport Thesaurus.
Sports Illustrated.
SportSearch.
SportStyle.
Standard & Poor's Corporation Records. *(File
    no.133/Corporate Descriptions)*
Standard & Poor's Corporation Records. Daily
    News Section. *(File no.133)*
State and Metropolitan Area Data Book.
State Tax Notes.
Statistical Abstract of the United States (Year).
Steels Alert. *(File no.269)*
Stereo Review.
Subject Guide to Books in Print. *(File no.470)*
Sun Care: The International Market.
Sunset.
Superconductor Week.
Supermarket News.
Survey of Current Business.
Sweet & Savoury Biscuits: The International
    Market.
T B Weekly.
T R I S Electronic Bibliographic Data Base. *(File
    no. 63)*
The Tax Directory.
Tax Management Estates, Gifts and Trusts
    Journal. *(Files 15, 485)*
Tax Management International Journal. *(Files 15,
    485)*
Tax Notes.
Tax Notes International.
Technical Literature Abstracts.
Technical Literature Abstracts: Catalysts -
    Zeolites.
Technical Literature Abstracts: Fuel
    Reformulation.
Technical Literature Abstracts: Oilfield Chemicals.
Technical Literature Abstracts: Tribology.
Technology Access Report.
Technology and Learning.
Technology Review.
Technology Transfer Week.
Teen.
Tekstilec.
Telco Business Report.
Tele-Service News.
Telecom Data Networks.
Television and Video: The International Market.
Texas Transportation Researcher. *(File no.63)*
Textile and Fabric Washing Products: The
    International Market.
Textile Technology Digest. *(File no.119)*
Theology.
Theoretical Chemical Engineering.
Thomas Register of American Manufacturers and
    Thomas Register Catalog File. *(File no.535)*
Tin International.
Toiletries, Fragrances and Skin Care: The Rose
    Sheet. *(File no.187)*
Tooling & Production.
Tour & Travel News - T T G North America.
Toxicology Abstracts. *(File no.76/LIFE SCIENCES
    COLLECTION)*
Toys and Games: The International Market.
Trade & Industry Index. *(File no.148)*
Trading Systems Technology.
Transit Research Abstracts. *(File no.63)*
Transportation & Distribution.
Travel and Tourism: The International Market.
Tree Physiology.
Tropical Oil Seeds.
Twin Cities Reader.
U K Gas Report.
U S A Today.
U S News & World Report.
U S Oil Week.
Ulrich's International Periodicals Directory. *(File
    no.480)*
Ulrich's Update. *(File no.480)*
U.S. Department of Agriculture. Agricultural
    Outlook.

U.S. Department of Agriculture. Agricultural
    Statistics Board Report: Agricultural Prices.
U.S. Department of Agriculture. Agricultural
    Statistics Board Report: Crop Production.
U.S. Department of Agriculture. Situation &
    Outlook Report. Agriculture and Trade: Former
    U S S R.
U.S. Department of State. Key Officers of Foreign
    Service Posts.
U.S. Department of State Dispatch.
U.S. Energy Information Administration. Quarterly
    Coal Report.
United States Patents Quarterly. *(Patlaw, File
    243)*
United States Political Science Documents. *(File
    no.93)*
Urology Times.
Utility Environment Report. *(UER)*
Vaard i Norden.
Vending: The International Market.
Vermont Business Magazine.
Veterinary Bulletin.
Video Store.
Video Technology News.
Virology and AIDS Abstracts. *(File no.76/LIFE
    SCIENCES COLLECTION)*
Vitamins and Dietary Supplements: The
    International Market.
Vitis.
Vitis - Viticulture and Oenology Abstracts.
Voice Technology & Services News.
The Washington Monthly.
Water Resources Abstracts (Bethesda). *(File
    no.117)*
Weed Abstracts.
Weekly of Business Aviation. *(File no.624/
    McGRAW-HILL PUBLICATIONS ONLINE)*
Wer Liefert Was?
Western Grower and Shipper.
Wheat, Barley and Triticale Abstracts.
Whitaker's Books in Print. *(File no.430)*
Whole Earth Review.
Who's Who in America. *(File no.234)*
Who's Who in American Art. *(File no.236)*
Who's Who in American Politics. *(File no.236)*
Wine: The International Market.
Wing Newsletter.
Women's Wear Daily.
Wood Technology.
Workbench.
Working Woman.
World Agricultural Economics and Rural Sociology
    Abstracts.
World Agricultural Supply and Demand Estimates.
World Bank Annual Conference on Development
    Economics. Proceedings.
World Bank Research Observer.
World Health.
World Power Systems Intelligence.
World Publishing Monitor.
World Rig Forecast.
World Textile Abstracts. *(File no.67)*
World Translations Index. *(File no.295)*
Worldcasts: Product Edition.
Worldcasts: Regional Edition.
WorldViews.
Worldwide Biotech.
Worldwide Databases.
Worldwide Telecom.
Worldwide Videotex Update.
Youth Markets Alert.
Zhongguo Xinli Weisheng Zazhi.
Zhongguo Yangfeng.
Zoological Record. *(File no.185)*
4 1 1 Newsletter. *(File no.636)*

LEXIS-NEXIS (A Member of the Reed
Elsevier plc group)
9443 Springboro Pike, Miamisburg, OH 45342.
Fax: 513-865-1211.
A B A Banking Journal.
A B A Journal.
A B I - INFORM. *(ABI)*
A H F S Drug Information.
Abya Yala News.
Advertising Age. *(ADAGE)*
Adweek (New York).
Adweek: Southeast.
Aerospace America. *(AEROAM)*
Aerospace Daily. *(AIRDLY)*
Aerospace Propulsion. *(AERPRO)*
Affirmative Action - E E O Personnel Update.
Airports.
Alaska Business Monthly.
Albany Law Review.
All England Law Reports.
Almanac of Famous People.

Alternatives to the High Cost of Litigation.
American Banker.
American Banker's Washington Watch.
American College of Surgeons. Journal.
American Demographics.
American Family Physician.
American Journal of Cardiology.
American Journal of International Law.
American Journal of Law & Medicine.
The American Journal of Medicine.
American Journal of Surgery.
American Journal of Tax Policy.
The American Lawyer.
American Maritime Cases.
American Papermaker.
American Salesman.
American University Law Review.
Americans with Disabilities Act Update.
Annals of Neurology.
Annals of Plastic Surgery.
Annals of Surgery.
Annals of Thoracic Surgery.
Antitrust & Trade Regulation Report. (TRADRG)
Antitrust Law Journal.
Archives of Pathology & Laboratory Medicine.
Arizona Business Gazette.
Arthritis and Rheumatism.
Asian Journal of Surgery.
Asian Studies Center Backgrounder.
AsianWeek. (Ethnic Newswatch)
Asset Sales Report.
Automotive Industries.
AutoWeek.
Aviation Daily. (AVDLY)
Aviation Europe. (AVEUR)
Aviation Week & Space Technology.
B L A S T.
B N A Pension & Benefits Reporter. (PENSN)
B N A's Banking Report. (BNABNK)
B N A's Patent, Trademark & Copyright Journal.
Backgrounder.
Backgrounder Update.
Bakery Production and Marketing.
Bank Management.
Bank Mutual Fund Report.
Banking Policy Report.
Beverage World (English Edition).
Biomedical Market Newsletter.
Biotech Daily.
Blood.
The Bond Buyer.
Boston University Law Review.
Brazil Report.
British Journal of Surgery.
Broadcasting & Cable.
Brooklyn Law Review.
Bulletin on the Rheumatic Diseases.
Business China.
Business Computing Brief.
Business Dateline.
Business Eastern Europe.
Business - Education Insider.
Business Europe.
Business First (Buffalo).
Business in Broward.
Business Index.
Business Insurance.
Business Journal (Sacramento).
Business Latin America.
Business Law Europe.
Business Lawyer. (BUSLAW)
Business Mexico.
Business North Carolina.
Business Record (Des Moines).
Business Week.
Byte.
C F O Alert (Weekly).
Calgary Herald.
Canada - United States Law Journal.
Canadian Papermaker.
Caribbean & Central America Report.
Case Western Reserve Journal of International
  Law.
Case Western Reserve Law Review.
Catholic University Law Review.
Chemical Engineering. (CHEMEN)
Chemical Regulation Reporter. (BNA-CHEM)
Chemical Week.
Chicago Enterprise.
Chilton's Automotive Marketing.
Chilton's Distribution.
Chilton's Food Engineering.
Chilton's Motor Age.
Chronicle of Latin American Economic Affairs.
Clinical Laser Monthly.
Clinical Orthopaedics and Related Research.
Clinical Pediatrics.
Coal.

Coal Tech International. (SYNFLS)
Coal U.K.
Coal Week. (COALWK)
Coal Week International. (COALIN)
Colorado Business.
Columbia Law Review.
Common Cause Magazine.
Communication World.
Communications Daily.
Communications International.
CommunicationsWeek International.
Computer Industry Forecasts.
Computer Lawyer.
Computerworld.
Consumer Reports.
Contemporary Musicians.
Contraceptive Technology Update.
Cornell Law Review.
Corporate E F T Report.
Corporate Legal Times.
Corporate Report Minnesota.
Cosmetics International.
Country Forecast. Algeria.
Country Forecast. Argentina.
Country Forecast. Asia - Pacific.
Country Forecast. Australia.
Country Forecast. Austria.
Country Forecast. Belgium.
Country Forecast. Brazil.
Country Forecast. Bulgaria.
Country Forecast. Canada.
Country Forecast. Chile.
Country Forecast. China.
Country Forecast. Colombia.
Country Forecast. Czech Republic.
Country Forecast. Denmark.
Country Forecast. Eastern Europe and the Former
  Soviet Union.
Country Forecast. Ecuador.
Country Forecast. Egypt.
Country Forecast. Europe.
Country Forecast. Finland.
Country Forecast. France.
Country Forecast. Germany.
Country Forecast. Global Outlook.
Country Forecast. Greece.
Country Forecast. Hong Kong.
Country Forecast. Hungary.
Country Forecast. India.
Country Forecast. Indonesia.
Country Forecast. Iran.
Country Forecast. Iraq.
Country Forecast. Ireland.
Country Forecast. Israel.
Country Forecast. Italy.
Country Forecast. Japan.
Country Forecast. Latin America.
Country Forecast. Malaysia.
Country Forecast. Mexico.
Country Forecast. Middle East and North Africa.
Country Forecast. Netherlands.
Country Forecast. New Zealand.
Country Forecast. Nigeria.
Country Forecast. Norway.
Country Forecast. Pakistan.
Country Forecast. Peru.
Country Forecast. Philippines.
Country Forecast. Poland.
Country Forecast. Portugal.
Country Forecast. Romania.
Country Forecast. Russia.
Country Forecast. Saudi Arabia.
Country Forecast. Singapore.
Country Forecast. Slovakia.
Country Forecast. South Africa.
Country Forecast. South Korea.
Country Forecast. Spain.
Country Forecast. Sri Lanka.
Country Forecast. Sub-Saharan Africa.
Country Forecast. Sweden.
Country Forecast. Switzerland.
Country Forecast. Taiwan.
Country Forecast. Thailand.
Country Forecast. Turkey.
Country Forecast. United Kingdom.
Country Forecast. United States of America.
Country Forecast. Venezuela.
Country Forecast. Vietnam.
Country Forecasts (New York).
Country Profile. Algeria.
Country Profile. Angola.
Country Profile. Argentina.
Country Profile. Australia.
Country Profile. Bahrain, Qatar.
Country Profile. Baltic Republics: Lithuania,
  Latvia, Estonia.
Country Profile. Bangladesh.

Country Profile. Belgium, Luxembourg.
Country Profile. Belize, Bahamas, Bermuda.
Country Profile. Bolivia.
Country Profile. Bosnia-Hercegovina, Croatia,
  Slovenia.
Country Profile. Botswana, Lesotho.
Country Profile. Brazil.
Country Profile. Bulgaria, Albania.
Country Profile. Cambocia, Laos, Myanmar.
Country Profile. Cameroon, Central African
  Republic, Chad.
Country Profile. Canada.
Country Profile. Chile.
Country Profile. China, Mongolia.
Country Profile. Colombia.
Country Profile. Congo, Sao Tome and Principe,
  Guinea-Bissau, Cape Verde.
Country Profile. Costa Rica, Panama.
Country Profile. Cote d'Ivoire, Mali.
Country Profile. Cuba.
Country Profile. Cyprus, Malta.
Country Profile. Czech Republic and Slovakia.
Country Profile. Denmark, Iceland.
Country Profile. Dominican Republic, Haiti, Puerto
  Rico.
Country Profile. Ecuador.
Country Profile. Egypt.
Country Profile. Ethiopia, Eritrea, Somalia,
  Dibouti.
Country Profile. Finland.
Country Profile. France.
Country Profile. Gabon, Equatorial Guinea.
Country Profile. Georgia, Armenia, Azerbaijan.
Country Profile. Germany.
Country Profile. Ghana.
Country Profile. Greece.
Country Profile. Guatemala, El Salvador.
Country Profile. Guinea, Sierra Leone, Liberia.
Country Profile. Guyana, Windward and Leeward
  Islands.
Country Profile. Hong Kong, Macau.
Country Profile. Hungary.
Country Profile. India, Nepal.
Country Profile. Indonesia.
Country Profile. Iran.
Country Profile. Iraq.
Country Profile. Ireland.
Country Profile. Israel, the Occupied Territories.
Country Profile. Italy.
Country Profile. Jamaica, Barbados.
Country Profile. Japan.
Country Profile. Jordan.
Country Profile. Kenya.
Country Profile. Kuwait.
Country Profile. Lebanon.
Country Profile. Libya.
Country Profile. Macedonia, Serbia-Montenegro.
Country Profile. Madagascar.
Country Profile. Malawi.
Country Profile. Malaysia, Brunei.
Country Profile. Mauritius, Seychelles.
Country Profile. Mexico.
Country Profile. Morocco.
Country Profile. Mozambique.
Country Profile. Namibia, Swaziland.
Country Profile. Netherlands.
Country Profile. New Zealand.
Country Profile. Nicaragua, Honduras.
Country Profile. Niger, Burkina Faso.
Country Profile. Nigeria.
Country Profile. Norway.
Country Profile. Oman, Yemen.
Country Profile. Pacific Islands: Fiji, Solomon
  Islands, Western Samoa, Vanuatu, Tonga.
Country Profile. Pakistan, Afghanistan.
Country Profile. Papua New Guinea.
Country Profile. Peru.
Country Profile. Philippines.
Country Profile. Poland.
Country Profile. Portugal.
Country Profile. Romania.
Country Profile. Russia.
Country Profile. Rwanda, Burundi.
Country Profile. Saudi Arabia.
Country Profile. Senegal.
Country Profile. Singapore.
Country Profile. South Africa.
Country Profile. South Korea, North Korea.
Country Profile. Spain.
Country Profile. Sri Lanka.
Country Profile. Sudan.
Country Profile. Sweden.
Country Profile. Switzerland.
Country Profile. Syria.
Country Profile. Taiwan.
Country Profile. Tanzania, Comoros.
Country Profile. Thailand.
Country Profile. The Gambia, Mauritania.

Vendor

Country Profile. Togo, Benin.
Country Profile. Trinidad and Tobago, Suriname, Netherlands Antilles, Aruba.
Country Profile. Tunisia.
Country Profile. Turkey.
Country Profile. Uganda.
Country Profile. Ukraine.
Country Profile. United Arab Emirates.
Country Profile. United Kingdom.
Country Profile. United States of America.
Country Profile. Uruguay, Paraguay.
Country Profile. Venezuela.
Country Profile. Zaire.
Country Profile. Zambia.
Country Profile. Zimbabwe.
Country Profiles.
Country Report. Algeria.
Country Report. Angola.
Country Report. Argentina.
Country Report. Australia.
Country Report. Austria.
Country Report. Bahrain, Qatar.
Country Report. Baltic Republics: Lithuania, Latvia, Estonia.
Country Report. Bangladesh.
Country Report. Belgium, Luxembourg.
Country Report. Bolivia.
Country Report. Bosnia-Hercegovina, Croatia.
Country Report. Brazil.
Country Report. Bulgaria, Albania.
Country Report. Cambodia, Laos.
Country Report. Cameroon, C.A.R., Chad.
Country Report. Canada.
Country Report. Chile.
Country Report. China, Mongolia.
Country Report. Colombia.
Country Report. Congo, Sao Tome and Principe, Guinea-Bissau, Cape Verde.
Country Report. Costa Rica, Panama.
Country Report. Cote d'Ivoire, Mali.
Country Report. Cuba, Dominican Republic, Haiti, Puerto Rico.
Country Report. Cyprus, Malta.
Country Report. Czech Republic, Slovakia.
Country Report. Denmark, Iceland.
Country Report. Ecuador.
Country Report. Egypt.
Country Report. Ethiopia, Eritrea, Somalia, Djibouti.
Country Report. Finland.
Country Report. France.
Country Report. Gabon, Equatorial Guinea.
Country Report. Germany.
Country Report. Ghana.
Country Report. Greece.
Country Report. Guatemala, El Salvador.
Country Report. Guinea, Sierra Leone, Liberia.
Country Report. Hong Kong, Macau.
Country Report. Hungary.
Country Report. India, Nepal.
Country Report. Indonesia.
Country Report. Iran.
Country Report. Iraq.
Country Report. Ireland.
Country Report. Israel, the Occupied Territories.
Country Report. Italy.
Country Report. Jamaica, Belize, Bahamas, Bermuda, Barbados.
Country Report. Japan.
Country Report. Jordan.
Country Report. Kazakhstan.
Country Report. Kenya.
Country Report. Kuwait.
Country Report. Lebanon.
Country Report. Libya.
Country Report. Malaysia, Brunei.
Country Report. Mauritius, Madagascar, Seychelles.
Country Report. Mexico.
Country Report. Morocco.
Country Report. Mozambique, Malawi.
Country Report. Netherlands.
Country Report. New Zealand.
Country Report. Nicaragua, Honduras.
Country Report. Nigeria.
Country Report. Norway.
Country Report. Oman, Yemen.
Country Report. Pacific Islands: Papua New Guinea, Fiji, Solomon Islands, Western Samoa, Vanuatu, Tonga.
Country Report. Pakistan, Afghanistan.
Country Report. Peru.
Country Report. Philippines.
Country Report. Poland.
Country Report. Portugal.
Country Report. Romania.
Country Report. Russia.
Country Report. Saudi Arabia.

Country Report. Senegal, The Gambia, Mauritania.
Country Report. Singapore.
Country Report. South Africa.
Country Report. South Korea, North Korea.
Country Report. Spain.
Country Report. Sri Lanka.
Country Report. Sudan.
Country Report. Sweden.
Country Report. Switzerland.
Country Report. Syria.
Country Report. Taiwan.
Country Report. Tanzania, Comoros.
Country Report. Thailand.
Country Report. Togo, Niger, Benin, Burkina Faso.
Country Report. Trinidad & Tobago, Guyana, Windward & Leeward Islands, Suriname, Netherlands Antilles, Aruba.
Country Report. Tunisia.
Country Report. Turkey.
Country Report. Uganda, Rwanda, Burundi.
Country Report. Ukraine.
Country Report. United Arab Emirates.
Country Report. United Kingdom.
Country Report. United States of America.
Country Report. Uruguay, Paraguay.
Country Report. Venezuela.
Country Report. Zambia, Zaire.
Country Report. Zimbabwe.
Country Reports.
Country Risk Service.
Country Risk Service. Algeria.
Country Risk Service. Angola.
Country Risk Service. Argentina.
Country Risk Service. Australia.
Country Risk Service. Baltic Republics.
Country Risk Service. Bangladesh.
Country Risk Service. Bolivia.
Country Risk Service. Brazil.
Country Risk Service. Bulgaria.
Country Risk Service. Cameroon.
Country Risk Service. Chile.
Country Risk Service. China.
Country Risk Service. Colombia.
Country Risk Service. Congo.
Country Risk Service. Costa Rica.
Country Risk Service. Cote d'Ivoire.
Country Risk Service. Cyprus.
Country Risk Service. Czech Republic.
Country Risk Service. Dominican Republic.
Country Risk Service. Ecuador.
Country Risk Service. Egypt.
Country Risk Service. El Salvador.
Country Risk Service. Former Yugoslav Republics.
Country Risk Service. Gabon.
Country Risk Service. Ghana.
Country Risk Service. Greece.
Country Risk Service. Guatemala.
Country Risk Service. Honduras.
Country Risk Service. Hong Kong.
Country Risk Service. Hungary.
Country Risk Service. India.
Country Risk Service. Indonesia.
Country Risk Service. Iran.
Country Risk Service. Iraq.
Country Risk Service. Israel.
Country Risk Service. Jamaica.
Country Risk Service. Jordan.
Country Risk Service. Kazakhstan.
Country Risk Service. Kenya.
Country Risk Service. Kuwait.
Country Risk Service. Libya.
Country Risk Service. Malawi.
Country Risk Service. Malaysia.
Country Risk Service. Mexico.
Country Risk Service. Morocco.
Country Risk Service. Namibia.
Country Risk Service. New Zealand.
Country Risk Service. Nicaragua.
Country Risk Service. Nigeria.
Country Risk Service. Pakistan.
Country Risk Service. Panama.
Country Risk Service. Papua New Guinea.
Country Risk Service. Paraguay.
Country Risk Service. Peru.
Country Risk Service. Philippines.
Country Risk Service. Poland.
Country Risk Service. Portugal.
Country Risk Service. Romania.
Country Risk Service. Russia.
Country Risk Service. Saudi Arabia.
Country Risk Service. Senegal.
Country Risk Service. Singapore.
Country Risk Service. Slovenia.
Country Risk Service. South Africa.
Country Risk Service. South Korea.
Country Risk Service. Spain.
Country Risk Service. Sri Lanka.

Country Risk Service. Sudan.
Country Risk Service. Syria.
Country Risk Service. Taiwan.
Country Risk Service. Thailand.
Country Risk Service. Trinidad and Tobago.
Country Risk Service. Tunisia.
Country Risk Service. Turkey.
Country Risk Service. Ukraine.
Country Risk Service. United Arab Emirates.
Country Risk Service. Uruguay.
Country Risk Service. Venezuela.
Country Risk Service. Yemen.
Country Risk Service. Zaire.
Country Risk Service. Zambia.
Country Risk Service. Zimbabwe.
Crain's Chicago Business. *(CHIBUS)*
Crain's Cleveland Business.
Crain's Detroit Business.
Crain's New York Business. *(NYBUS)*
Credit Card Management.
Criminal Appeal Reports.
Critical Issues.
Current Digest of the Post-Soviet Press.
Current Law Index.
D B.
D M News.
Daily Labor Report. *(DLABRT)*
Daily Report for Executives. *(DREXEC)*
Daily Tax Report. *(BNADTR)*
Dairy Foods.
Data Communications.
Defense & Foreign Affairs Strategic Policy.
Defense Electronics.
Defense Week.
Delaware Journal of Corporate Law.
Denver University Law Review.
Dickinson Law Review.
Direct Marketing.
Directory of Corporate Affiliations.
Discount Store News.
Discover (Burbank).
Diseases of the Colon and Rectum.
Doing Business with Eastern Europe.
Drug Store News.
Duke Law Journal.
E C Energy Monthly.
E F T Report.
E N R. *(ENR)*
East Asian Executive Reports.
East Europe & the Republics: A Political Risk Annual. *(IBCRPT)*
East European Energy Report.
East European Markets.
Economic Week.
The Economist.
Electric Utility Week. *(ELUTL)*
Electrical World. *(ELECWD)*
Electronic Design.
Electronic Media.
Employee Health and Fitness.
Energy Daily.
Energy Economist.
Energy Report.
Energy User News.
Engineering & Mining Journal.
Environment Reporter. *(ENVREP)*
Environment Week.
Environmental Law (Portland).
Environmental Law Reporter.
Estate Planner's Alert.
Estate Planning (New York). *(TAXRIA-Library)*
Euro-East.
Europe Energy.
Europe Environment.
European Energy Report.
European Insight.
European Report.
European Social Policy.
Executive Memorandum.
Executive Report.
Executive Speaker.
The Expert and the Law.
F T C Watch.
Facts on File World News Digest with Index.
Family Law Reports.
Federal Contracts Report. *(FDCONT)*
Federal Register.
Federal Reserve Bulletin.
Federal Sentencing Reporter.
Federal Tax Coordinator 2d.
Federal Technology Report. *(FEDTEC)*
Financial Regulation Report.
Financial Times World Tax Report.
Financial World.
Financing Foreign Operations. Americas.
Financing Foreign Operations. Argentina.
Financing Foreign Operations. Asia.
Financing Foreign Operations. Australia.

Financing Foreign Operations. Belgium.
Financing Foreign Operations. Brazil.
Financing Foreign Operations. Canada.
Financing Foreign Operations. Central America:
    Costa Rica, El Salvador, Guatemala, Honduras,
    Nicaragua.
Financing Foreign Operations. Chile.
Financing Foreign Operations. Colombia.
Financing Foreign Operations. Czech Republic.
Financing Foreign Operations. France.
Financing Foreign Operations. Germany.
Financing Foreign Operations. Global Edition.
Financing Foreign Operations. Greece.
Financing Foreign Operations. Hong Kong.
Financing Foreign Operations. Hungary.
Financing Foreign Operations. India.
Financing Foreign Operations. Italy.
Financing Foreign Operations. Japan.
Financing Foreign Operations. Malaysia.
Financing Foreign Operations. Mexico.
Financing Foreign Operations. Middle East - Africa.
Financing Foreign Operations. Netherlands.
Financing Foreign Operations. Nigeria.
Financing Foreign Operations. Norway.
Financing Foreign Operations. Panama.
Financing Foreign Operations. Philippines.
Financing Foreign Operations. Poland.
Financing Foreign Operations. Russia.
Financing Foreign Operations. Saudi Arabia.
Financing Foreign Operations. Singapore.
Financing Foreign Operations. South Africa.
Financing Foreign Operations. South Korea.
Financing Foreign Operations. Spain.
Financing Foreign Operations. Sweden.
Financing Foreign Operations. Switzerland.
Financing Foreign Operations. Taiwan.
Financing Foreign Operations. Thailand.
Financing Foreign Operations. United Kingdom.
Financing Foreign Operations. United States of
    America.
Financing Foreign Operations. Venezuela.
Flight International.
Florida Trend.
Food & Beverage Marketing.
Food & Drink Daily.
Food in Canada.
Food Manufacture International.
Food Trade Review.
Footwear News.
Forbes.
Fordham Law Review.
Foreign Affairs.
Forensic Services Directory.
Foster Natural Gas Report.
Genesis Report - Dx.
Genesis Report - Rx.
George Mason Law Review.
George Washington Journal of International Law
    and Economics.
George Washington Law Review.
Georgetown Law Journal.
Georgia Journal of International and Comparative
    Law.
Georgia Trend.
German Life.
Global Company Handbook.
Global Private Power.
Governing.
Government Employee Relations Report.
    (GOVEMP)
Graphic Arts Monthly.
Grocery Marketing.
Guardian Weekly.
H F N.
Harvard Business Review.
Harvard Law Review. (Lexis)
Harvard Women's Law Journal.
Hastings Law Journal.
Hawaii Business.
Hazardous Waste Business. (HWB)
Health Matrix: Journal of Law-Medicine.
Health Policy & Biomedical Research: The Blue
    Sheet.
Heritage Foundation. Issue Bulletins.
Heritage Lectures.
High Yield Report.
Hofstra Law Review.
Hollywood Reporter.
Hospital Admitting Monthly.
Hospital Employee Health.
Hospital Infection Control.
Hospital Payment and Information Management.
Hospital Peer Review.
Hospital Risk Management.
Hospitals and Health Networks.
Houston Business Journal.
Howard Law Journal.
Illinois Legal Times.

Improved Recovery Week.
Inc.
Independent Power Report. (IPR)
Index to Legal Periodicals & Books.
Indiana Business Magazine.
Indiana Law Journal.
Industrial Cases Reports.
Industrial Energy Bulletin.
Industrial Relations Law Reports.
Industry Week.
Information Today.
InfoWorld.
Inside D O T & Transportation Week.
Inside Energy with Federal Lands. (INERGY)
Inside F E R C. (INFERC)
Inside F E R C's Gas Market Report. (GASMKT)
Inside N R C. (INNRC)
Institutional Distribution.
Insurance Periodicals Index.
Integrated Waste Management.
International Coal Report.
International Country Risk Guide.
International Defense Review.
International Environment Reporter.
International Gas Report.
International Lawyer.
International Legal Materials.
International Market Alert.
International Securities Regulation Report.
International Tax Report.
International Trade Reporter. (INTRAD)
Investing, Licensing and Trading Conditions
    Abroad. Americas.
Investing, Licensing and Trading Conditions
    Abroad. Argentina.
Investing, Licensing and Trading Conditions
    Abroad. Asia.
Investing, Licensing and Trading Conditions
    Abroad. Australia.
Investing, Licensing and Trading Conditions
    Abroad. Austria.
Investing, Licensing and Trading Conditions
    Abroad. Belgium.
Investing, Licensing and Trading Conditions
    Abroad. Brazil.
Investing, Licensing and Trading Conditions
    Abroad. Britain.
Investing, Licensing and Trading Conditions
    Abroad. Canada.
Investing, Licensing and Trading Conditions
    Abroad. Central America.
Investing, Licensing and Trading Conditions
    Abroad. Chile.
Investing, Licensing and Trading Conditions
    Abroad. China.
Investing, Licensing and Trading Conditions
    Abroad. Colombia.
Investing, Licensing and Trading Conditions
    Abroad. Czech Republic and Slovakia.
Investing, Licensing and Trading Conditions
    Abroad. Denmark.
Investing, Licensing and Trading Conditions
    Abroad. Ecuador.
Investing, Licensing and Trading Conditions
    Abroad. Egypt.
Investing, Licensing and Trading Conditions
    Abroad. Finland.
Investing, Licensing and Trading Conditions
    Abroad. France.
Investing, Licensing and Trading Conditions
    Abroad. Germany.
Investing, Licensing and Trading Conditions
    Abroad. Global Edition.
Investing, Licensing and Trading Conditions
    Abroad. Greece.
Investing, Licensing and Trading Conditions
    Abroad. Hong Kong.
Investing, Licensing and Trading Conditions
    Abroad. Hungary.
Investing, Licensing and Trading Conditions
    Abroad. India.
Investing, Licensing and Trading Conditions
    Abroad. Indonesia.
Investing, Licensing and Trading Conditions
    Abroad. Ireland.
Investing, Licensing and Trading Conditions
    Abroad. Israel.
Investing, Licensing and Trading Conditions
    Abroad. Italy.
Investing, Licensing and Trading Conditions
    Abroad. Japan.
Investing, Licensing and Trading Conditions
    Abroad. Kenya.
Investing, Licensing and Trading Conditions
    Abroad. Luxembourg.
Investing, Licensing and Trading Conditions
    Abroad. Malaysia.

Investing, Licensing and Trading Conditions
    Abroad. Mexico.
Investing, Licensing and Trading Conditions
    Abroad. Middle East - Africa.
Investing, Licensing and Trading Conditions
    Abroad. Netherlands.
Investing, Licensing and Trading Conditions
    Abroad. New Zealand
Investing, Licensing and Trading Conditions
    Abroad. Nigeria.
Investing, Licensing and Trading Conditions
    Abroad. Norway.
Investing, Licensing and Trading Conditions
    Abroad. Pakistan.
Investing, Licensing and Trading Conditions
    Abroad. Panama.
Investing, Licensing and Trading Conditions
    Abroad. Peru.
Investing, Licensing and Trading Conditions
    Abroad. Philippines.
Investing, Licensing and Trading Conditions
    Abroad. Poland.
Investing, Licensing and Trading Conditions
    Abroad. Portugal.
Investing, Licensing and Trading Conditions
    Abroad. Puerto Rico.
Investing, Licensing and Trading Conditions
    Abroad. Russia.
Investing, Licensing and Trading Conditions
    Abroad. Saudi Arabia.
Investing, Licensing and Trading Conditions
    Abroad. Singapore.
Investing, Licensing and Trading Conditions
    Abroad. South Africa.
Investing, Licensing and Trading Conditions
    Abroad. South Korea.
Investing, Licensing and Trading Conditions
    Abroad. Spain.
Investing, Licensing and Trading Conditions
    Abroad. Sweden.
Investing, Licensing and Trading Conditions
    Abroad. Switzerland.
Investing, Licensing and Trading Conditions
    Abroad. Taiwan.
Investing, Licensing and Trading Conditions
    Abroad. Thailand.
Investing, Licensing and Trading Conditions
    Abroad. Turkey.
Investing, Licensing and Trading Conditions
    Abroad. United States of America.
Investing, Licensing and Trading Conditions
    Abroad. Uruguay.
Investing, Licensing and Trading Conditions
    Abroad. Venezuela.
Investing, Licensing and Trading Conditions
    Abroad. Vietnam.
Investor's Daily.
Iowa Law Review.
Jack O'Dwyer's Newsletter.
The Jerusalem Post.
The Jerusalem Post (Edition Française).
The Jerusalem Post (International Edition).
John Marshall Law Review.
Joint Commission Perspectives.
Journal of Advertising.
Journal of Blacks in Higher Education.
Journal of Consumer Research.
Journal of International Taxation.
Journal of Law & Commerce.
Journal of Marketing.
Journal of Marketing Research.
Journal of Partnership Taxation. (TAXRIA-Library)
Journal of Pediatric Surgery.
Journal of Portfolio Management.
The Journal of Taxation. (TAXRIA-Library)
Konzerne in Schaubildern.
L A N Times. (LANTME)
L D C Debt Report.
Labor Relations Reporter. Labor Arbitration and
    Dispute Settlements.
Lagniappe Letter.
Las Vegas Business Press.
Latin American Informes Especiales.
Latin American Regional Reports - Andean
    Group.
Latin American Weekly Report.
Law Practice Management.
Legal Times.
LegalTrac. (LGLIND)
Life (New York).
Link-Up.
Los Angeles.
Louisiana Law Review.
Louisville Magazine.
McGraw-Hill's Biotechnology Newswatch. (BIOTEC)
Maclean's.
MacWEEK.
Magazine Index.

Maine Law Review.
Major 20th-Century Writers. *(GALBIO)*
Managerial Law.
Manitoba Business Magazine.
Marine Log.
Market Research Europe.
Marketing News.
Martindale-Hubbell Law Directory.
Massachusetts Lawyer Weekly.
Mealey's Emerging Insurance Disputes. *(MEALEY)*
Mealey's Emerging Toxic Torts. *(MEALEY)*
Mealey's Insurance Supplement. *(MEALEY)*
Mealey's International Arbitration Report.
   (MEALEY)
Mealey's Litigation Report: Asbestos. *(MEALEY)*
Mealey's Litigation Report: Bad Faith. *(MEALEY)*
Mealey's Litigation Report: Breast Implants.
   (MEALEY)
Mealey's Litigation Report: Drugs and Medical
   Devices. *(MEALEY)*
Mealey's Litigation Report: Insurance. *(MEALEY)*
Mealey's Litigation Report: Insurance Fraud.
   (MEALEY)
Mealey's Litigation Report: Insurance Insolvency.
   (MEALEY)
Mealey's Litigation Report: Intellectual Property.
   (MEALEY)
Mealey's Litigation Report: Lead. *(MEALEY)*
Mealey's Litigation Report: Patents. *(MEALEY)*
Mealey's Litigation Report: Pedicle Screws.
   (MEALEY)
Mealey's Litigation Report: Reinsurance.
   (MEALEY)
Mealey's Litigation Report: Superfund. *(MEALEY)*
Mealey's Litigation Report: Tobacco. *(MEALEY)*
Mechanical Engineering.
MediaWeek.
Medical Devices, Diagnostics & Instrumentation
   Reports: The Gray Sheet.
Medical Marketing & Media.
Memphis Business Journal.
Metals Week. *(METLWK)*
Mexico & N A F T A Report.
Michigan Citizen. *(ETHNIC NEWSWATCH)*
Michigan Law Review.
Michigan Lawyers Weekly.
Middle East Executive Reports.
Military Law Review.
Mining Annual Review.
Mining Magazine.
Minneapolis - St. Paul CityBusiness.
Minnesota Law Review.
Minority Markets Alert.
Modern Brewery Age.
Modern Plastics. *(MODPLA)*
Money (New York).
Money Laundering Alert.
Multinational Service.
Nashville Business Journal.
National Association of Insurance Commissioners.
   Proceedings.
National Cancer Institute. Journal.
National Directory of Law Enforcement
   Administrators and Correctional Institutions.
National Law Journal.
National Newspaper Index.
Nebraska Law Review.
Network World.
Nevada Lawyer.
New England Law Review.
New Jersey Business.
New Jersey Law Journal.
New Law Journal.
New Mexico Law Review.
New Orleans CityBusiness.
New Product News.
New Technology Week.
New York Law Journal.
The New York Times.
New York University Law Review.
Newsmakers.
Newsweek.
The Nikkei Weekly.
Nonprescription Pharmaceuticals and Nutritionals:
   The Tan Sheet.
North Carolina Journal of International Law and
   Commercial Regulation.
North Carolina Law Review.
North Sea Letter.
North Sea Rig Forecast.
Northern Ontario Business.
Northwestern University Law Review.
NotiSur.
Nuclear News.
NuclearFuel. *(NUFUEL)*
Nucleonics Week. *(NUWEEK)*
O'Dwyer's P R Services Report.
Offshore (Tulsa).

Ohio State Law Journal.
Oil & Gas Journal.
Oil Market Report.
Oregon Law Review.
Pacific Business News.
Pacific Law Journal.
Pediatrics (English Edition).
Pensions & Investments. *(PENINV)*
People Weekly.
Pharmaceutical Approvals Monthly.
Philadelphia Business Journal.
Platt's International Petrochemical Report.
Platt's Oilgram News. *(PONEWS)*
Platt's Oilgram Price Report. *(PPRICE)*
Policy Review.
Political Finance & Lobby Reporter.
Political Risk Services. Country Reports: World
   Service. *(IBCRPT)*
Political Risk Services. Country Reports: Algeria.
Political Risk Services. Country Reports:
   Argentina.
Political Risk Services. Country Reports: Bolivia.
Political Risk Services. Country Reports: Brazil.
Political Risk Services. Country Reports: Bulgaria.
Political Risk Services. Country Reports:
   Cameroon.
Political Risk Services. Country Reports: Chile.
Political Risk Services. Country Reports: China.
Political Risk Services. Country Reports:
   Colombia.
Political Risk Services. Country Reports: Costa
   Rica.
Political Risk Services. Country Reports: Cote
   d'Ivoire.
Political Risk Services. Country Reports: Czech
   Republic.
Political Risk Services. Country Reports:
   Dominican Republic.
Political Risk Services. Country Reports: Ecuador.
Political Risk Services. Country Reports: Egypt.
Political Risk Services. Country Reports: El
   Salvador.
Political Risk Services. Country Reports: Gabon.
Political Risk Services. Country Reports:
   Guatemala.
Political Risk Services. Country Reports: Guinea.
Political Risk Services. Country Reports: Haiti.
Political Risk Services. Country Reports:
   Honduras.
Political Risk Services. Country Reports: Hong
   Kong.
Political Risk Services. Country Reports: Hungary.
Political Risk Services. Country Reports: India.
Political Risk Services. Country Reports:
   Indonesia.
Political Risk Services. Country Reports: Iran.
Political Risk Services. Country Reports: Iraq.
Political Risk Services. Country Reports: Israel.
Political Risk Services. Country Reports: Jamaica.
Political Risk Services. Country Reports: Kenya.
Political Risk Services. Country Reports: Kuwait.
Political Risk Services. Country Reports: Libya.
Political Risk Services. Country Reports:
   Malaysia.
Political Risk Services. Country Reports: Mexico.
Political Risk Services. Country Reports: Morocco.
Political Risk Services. Country Reports:
   Nicaragua.
Political Risk Services. Country Reports: Nigeria.
Political Risk Services. Country Reports: Oman.
Political Risk Services. Country Reports:
   Pakistan.
Political Risk Services. Country Reports: Panama.
Political Risk Services. Country Reports: Peru.
Political Risk Services. Country Reports:
   Philippines.
Political Risk Services. Country Reports: Poland.
Political Risk Services. Country Reports:
   Romania.
Political Risk Services. Country Reports: Russia.
Political Risk Services. Country Reports: Saudi
   Arabia.
Political Risk Services. Country Reports:
   Singapore.
Political Risk Services. Country Reports: South
   Africa.
Political Risk Services. Country Reports: South
   Korea.
Political Risk Services. Country Reports: Sri
   Lanka.
Political Risk Services. Country Reports: Sudan.
Political Risk Services. Country Reports: Syria.
Political Risk Services. Country Reports: Taiwan.
Political Risk Services. Country Reports: Tunisia.
Political Risk Services. Country Reports: Turkey.
Political Risk Services. Country Reports: Ukraine.
Political Risk Services. Country Reports: United
   Arab Emirates.

Political Risk Services. Country Reports: Uruguay.
Political Risk Services. Country Reports:
   Venezuela.
Political Risk Services. Country Reports: Vietnam.
Political Risk Services. Country Reports: Zaire.
Political Risk Services. Country Reports: Zambia.
Political Risk Services. Country Reports:
   Zimbabwe.
Political Risk Services. Executive Reports:
   Australia.
Political Risk Services. Executive Reports: Austria.
Political Risk Services. Executive Reports:
   Belgium.
Political Risk Services. Executive Reports:
   Canada.
Political Risk Services. Executive Reports:
   Denmark.
Political Risk Services. Executive Reports:
   Finland.
Political Risk Services. Executive Reports: France.
Political Risk Services. Executive Reports:
   Germany.
Political Risk Services. Executive Reports: Greece.
Political Risk Services. Executive Reports: Ireland.
Political Risk Services. Executive Reports: Italy.
Political Risk Services. Executive Reports: Japan.
Political Risk Services. Executive Reports:
   Netherlands.
Political Risk Services. Executive Reports: New
   Zealand.
Political Risk Services. Executive Reports:
   Norway.
Political Risk Services. Executive Reports:
   Portugal.
Political Risk Services. Executive Reports: Puerto
   Rico.
Political Risk Services. Executive Reports: Spain.
Political Risk Services. Executive Reports:
   Sweden.
Political Risk Services. Executive Reports:
   Thailand.
Political Risk Services. Executive Reports: United
   Kingdom.
Political Risk Services. Executive Reports: United
   States.
Political Risk Yearbook.
Political Risk Yearbook. Volume 1: North &
   Central America.
Political Risk Yearbook. Volume 2: Middle East &
   North Africa.
Political Risk Yearbook. Volume 3: South
   America.
Political Risk Yearbook. Volume 4: Sub-Saharan
   Africa.
Political Risk Yearbook. Volume 5: Asia & the
   Pacific.
Political Risk Yearbook. Volume 6: Europe -
   Countries of the European Union.
Political Risk Yearbook. Volume 7: Europe -
   Outside the European Union.
Power (New York). *(POWER)*
Power in Asia.
Power in Europe.
Power in Latin America.
Power U K.
Prepared Foods.
Prescription Pharmaceuticals and Biotechnology:
   The Pink Sheet.
Private Placement Reporter.
Progress in Cardiovascular Diseases.
Progressive Grocer.
Property, Planning and Compensation Reports.
Public Health Reports.
Public Perspective. *(PUBPER)*
Public Pulse.
Public Utilities Fortnightly.
Public Utilities Reports.
Pulp and Paper.
Pulp & Paper International.
Religious Leaders of America.
Renewable Energy Report.
Research Alert (New York).
The Review of Banking and Financial Services.
   (RBFS)
The Review of Securities & Commodities
   Regulation. *(RSCR)*
Road Traffic Reports.
Roll Call.
Russia and Commonwealth Business Law Report.
St. Louis Commerce.
St. Thomas Law Review.
Same-Day Surgery.
San Diego Daily Transcript.
Sarasota Magazine.
Screen Finance.
Seattle University Law Review.
Securities Regulation & Law Report. *(SECREG)*
Securities Week. *(SECWK)*

Seminars in Hematology.
Sexually Transmitted Diseases.
Soap, Cosmetics, Chemical Specialties.
SourceMex.
South Carolina Law Review.
Southern Cone Report.
Southern Illinois University Law Journal.
The Sporting News.
Sports Illustrated.
Standard & Poor's Corporation Records.
Standard Directory of Advertisers (Business Classifications Edition).
Stanford Law Review.
State Tax Notes.
Stores.
Suffolk Transnational Law Review.
Summary of World Broadcasts. Part 1: Former U S S R (Daily).
Summary of World Broadcasts. Part 1: Former U S S R (Weekly Economic Report).
Summary of World Broadcasts. Part 2: Central Europe, the Balkans (Daily).
Summary of World Broadcasts. Part 2: Central Europe, the Balkans (Weekly Economic Report).
Summary of World Broadcasts. Part 3: Asia - Pacific (Daily).
Summary of World Broadcasts. Part 3: Asia - Pacific (Weekly Economic Report).
Summary of World Broadcasts. Part 4: Middle East (Daily).
Summary of World Broadcasts. Part 4: Middle East (Weekly Economic Report).
Summary of World Broadcasts. Part 5: Africa, Latin America and the Caribbean (Daily).
Summary of World Broadcasts. Part 5: Africa, Latin America and the Caribbean (Weekly Economic Report).
Supermarket Business.
Supermarket News.
Talking Points.
The Tax Directory.
Tax Lawyer.
Tax News Service.
Tax Notes.
Tax Notes International.
Tax Treaties Data Base on C D - R O M.
Taxation for Accountants.
Taxation for Lawyers.
Tea and Coffee Trade Journal.
Tech - Europe.
Telecom Markets.
Texas Law Review.
Texas Lawyer.
Time.
Toiletries, Fragrances and Skin Care: The Rose Sheet.
Tort & Insurance Law Journal.
Transport Europe.
Travel & Tourism Analyst.
Triangle Business Journal.
Tulane Environmental Law Journal.
Tulane Law Review.
Tulane Maritime Law Journal.
Twin Cities Reader.
U C Davis Law Review.
U C L A Law Review.
U K Gas Report.
U S A Today.
U S Banker.
U S News & World Report.
U.S. Department of Agriculture. Economic Research Service. Food Review.
United States Law Week. (USLW)
University of Chicago Law Review.
University of Colorado Law Review.
University of Dayton Law Review.
University of Kansas Law Review.
University of Pennsylvania Journal of International Economic Law.
University of Pennsylvania Law Review.
University of Pittsburgh Law Review.
University of San Francisco Law Review.
Utility Environment Report. (UER)
Vanderbilt Law Review.
Village Voice.
Virginia Journal of International Law.
Warfield's Business Record.
Warsaw Voice.
Washington and Lee Law Review.
Washington Law Review.
Washington Quarterly.
Washington University Law Quarterly.
Washingtonian.
Wayne Law Review.
The Week in Germany.
Weekly Law Reports.
Weekly of Business Aviation. (WBA)

Weekly Pharmacy Reports: The Green Sheet.
Wer Liefert Was?
Westchester County Business Journal.
Whole Earth Review.
Who's Who Among Black Americans.
Who's Who Among Hispanic Americans.
Who's Who in Technology.
Wichita Business Journal.
William Mitchell Law Review.
Wisconsin Law Review.
Die Woche.
Women's Wear Daily.
World Accounting Report. (WAR)
World Factbook.
World Media. Broadcasting News.
World Rig Forecast.
The WorldPaper.
Worldscope Company Database.
Yale Law Journal.
Youth Markets Alert. (AD12)

LOGIN INFORMATION SERVICES
245 E. Sixth St., Suite 809, Saint Paul, MN 55101-9006.
Fax: 612-225-1133.
American City & County.
Governing.

NATIONAL DATA CORP.
2 National Data Plaza, Corporate Sq., Atlanta, GA 30329. Tel: 404-728-2000
Fax: 609-667-5030.
Boston Business Journal.
Brooklyn Journal of International Law.
Capital University Law Review.
International Financial Statistics.
Virginia Law Review.

NATIONAL LIBRARY OF MEDICINE
8600 Rockville Pike, Bethesda, MD 20209.
Tel: 301-496-6193
Fax: 301-496-4000.
Academy of Medicine, Singapore. Annals.
American Podiatric Medical Association. Journal.
Bibliography of Bioethics.
Bibliography of the History of Medicine.
Chiropractic History.
Health Sciences Serials.
Hospital Literature Index.
Index Medicus.
Index to Dental Literature.
International Nursing Index.
International Pharmaceutical Abstracts.
Issues in Law and Medicine.
Journal of Magnetic Resonance Imaging.
List of Serials Indexed for Online Users.
Ongoing Current Bibliography of Plastic & Reconstructive Surgery.
Population Index.
Psychopharmacology Bulletin.
R T E C S.

NEWSNET (Subsidiary of: Independent Pubns.)
945 Haverford Rd., Bryn Mawr, PA 19010.
Tel: 610-527-8030
Fax: 610-527-0338.
Access Reports - Freedom of Information. (GT10)
Advanced Intelligent Network News. (TE15)
Aerospace Daily. (AE29)
Aerospace Propulsion. (AE34)
Affirmative Action - E E O Personnel Update.
Africa News Online.
Aging Research & Training News.
AIDS Weekly. (HH14)
Air Cargo Report.
Air Safety Week. (AE16)
Air - Water Pollution Report. (EV10)
Aircraft Value Newsletter.
Airline Financial News. (AE25)
Airports. (AE21)
American Banker. (FI10)
American Banker's Washington Watch. (FI05)
American Marketplace. (AD13)
Americans with Disabilities Act Update.
Antitrust Litigation Reporter.
Applied Genetics News. (BT03)
Architectural Record. (BC13)
Asbestos & Lead Abatement Report. (EV27)
Asset Sales Report. (FI33)
Audio Week. (EC93)
Audiotex Update. (TE16)
Autoparts Report. (4UOS)
Aviation Daily. (AE28)

Aviation Europe. (AE35)
Aviation Week & Space Technology. (AE30)
B M D Monitor. (DE05)
B T Today. (TE40)
Bank Automation News
Bank Mergers & Acquisitions. (FI59)
Bank Mutual Fund Report.
Bank Network News. (FI71)
Bank Technology News. (FI70)
Battery & E V Technology News. (RD30)
Biotech Business. (BT06)
Blood Weekly.
The Bond Buyer. (FI08)
Book Publishing Report. (PB19)
Boot Cove Economic Forecast. (IV29)
Bowne Digest for Corporate & Securities Lawyers. (LA11)
Broadband Networking News. (TE51)
Business Computer Digest.
Business Travel News. (TR08)
Business Week. (GB55)
Byte. (EC34)
C A D - C A M Update. (MG15)
C D Computing News. (EC67)
C D - R O M Databases. (EC71)
C D - R O M World.
C F O Alert (Weekly).
Cable - Telco Report. (TE106)
California Planning and Development Report. (EV23)
California Public Finance. (FI65)
Campus Crime.
Cancer Researcher Weekly. (HH15)
Card Fax. (FI67)
Card News. (FI24)
Cellular Sales & Marketing. (TE72)
Chemical Engineering. (CH19)
Chemical Monitor. (CH15)
Chief Executive Officers Newsletter.
Child Protection Report.
Chronicle of Latin American Economic Affairs. (IT43)
Coal & Synfuels Technology. (EY49)
Coal Outlook. (EY30)
Coal Tech International. (EY76)
Coal Week. (EY77)
Coal Week International. (EY78)
Commerce Business Daily.
Communications Daily. (TE01)
CommunicationsWeek. (TE23)
CommunicationsWeek International. (TE28)
Commuter - Regional Airline News (AE25)
Commuter Regional Airline News International. (AE26)
Composites Industry Monthly.
Computer Protocols. (EC74)
Computer Reseller News. (EC07)
Computergram International. (EC72)
Computers in Libraries.
Congressional Activities. (GT20)
Construction Claims Citator. (BC12)
Construction Claims Monthly.
Construction Claims Training Guide.
Construction Injury Liability Monthly.
Consumer Information Appliance.
Corporate E F T Report. (FI12)
Corporate Giving Watch. (GS49)
Country Forecasts (Syracuse). (IT933)
Cowles - SIMBA Media Daily.
Credit Card Management.
Credit Risk Management. (FI57)
Daily Report for Executives.
Daily Tax Report.
Data Communications. (TE37)
DataTrends Report on D E C. (EC03)
Dealing with Technology. (FI53)
Defense Cleanup.
Defense Daily. (DE01)
Defense Week. (DE16)
Digest of Activities of Congress.
Document Imaging Report. (EC02)
E & P Environment.
E D I News. (TE80)
E F T Report. (FI11)
E M F Keeptrack.
E M M S. (EC32)
E N R. (BC06)
Economic Opportunity Report.
Editors Only. (PB13)
Education Daily. (ED08)
Education Technology News.
Educational Marketer. (PB20)
Electric Utility Week. (EY65)
Electric Utility Week's Demand Side Report. (EY87)
Electrical World. (EY03)
Electro Manufacturing.
Electronic Buyers' News. (EC12)

Electronic Engineering Times. *(EC14)*
Electronic Information Report. *(PB22)*
Electronic Materials Technology News. *(ML04)*
Electronic Messaging News. *(TE05)*
Electronic World News. *(EC13)*
Emergency Preparedness News. *(GT34)*
Emerging & Special Situations. *(FI16)*
Employment Opportunities (Englewood).
En Route Technology. *(TE33)*
Energy Conservation News. *(EY59)*
Energy Daily. *(EY57)*
Energy Design Update. *(BC08)*
Energy Report. *(EY50)*
Enhanced Energy Recovery News. *(EY60)*
Environment Watch: Latin America. *(EV44)*
Environment Week. *(EV25)*
Environmental Health Letter.
Environmental Problems & Remediation.
The Exporter. *(IT04)*
F C C Report. *(TE52)*
F T C Watch. *(GT17)*
F X Week. *(FI54)*
Fair Employment Report.
Faulkner and Gray's Medicine and Health.
    (HH21)
Federal & State Insurance Week. *(IN04)*
Federal Contract Disputes.
Federal Grants & Contracts Weekly. *(GT37)*
Federal Research Report. *(RD10)*
Federal Technology Report. *(RD46)*
Fiber Optics News. *(TE29)*
Fiber Optics Weekly Update.
Financial Services Report. *(FI18)*
Flame Retardancy News. *(RD40)*
Food & Drink Daily. *(FB03)*
Food Chemical News. *(FB07)*
For Your Eyes Only. *(DE15)*
Foundation Giving Watch. *(GB50)*
Friday Memo. *(PB15)*
Fusion Power Report. *(EY46)*
George Wells' Washington Beverage Insight.
Global Environmental Change.
Global Positioning & Navigation News. *(DE24)*
Golob's Oil Pollution Bulletin. *(EV05)*
Ground Water Monitor. *(EV18)*
H D T V Report. *(PB31)*
Hazardous Materials Intelligence Report.
Hazardous Materials Transportation. *(EV35)*
Hazardous Waste Business. *(EV41)*
Hazardous Waste News. *(CH10)*
HazMat Transport News. *(CH14)*
Headway. *(POO5)*
Health Alliance Alert. *(HH23)*
Health Grants & Contracts Weekly. *(HH10)*
Health Legislation. *(HH22)*
Health News Daily. *(HH01)*
Healthcare Systems Strategy Report. *(HH11)*
Helicopter News. *(AE12)*
Heller Report on Education Technology and
    Telecommunications Markets. *(ED11)*
High Tech Ceramics News. *(ML05)*
High Tech Separations News. *(BT04)*
High Yield Report.
Hospital Payment and Information Management.
Hotline (Falls Church). *(POO1)*
I B T. *(IT92)*
I S D N News. *(TE90)*
Ice Cream Reporter. *(FB04)*
Imaging Update. *(EC05)*
Independent Power Report. *(EY67)*
Industrial Energy Bulletin. *(EY68)*
Industrial Health & Hazards Update. *(LA04)*
Industries in Transition. *(GB46)*
Information & Interactive Services Report. *(TE41)*
The Information Freeway Report.
Information Networks. *(TE81)*
The Information Report. *(ITO8)*
Information Week. *(TE34)*
Innovator's Digest. *(RD09)*
Inside D O T & Transportation Week. *(GT41)*
Inside Energy with Federal Lands. *(EY69)*
Inside F E R C. *(EY70)*
Inside F E R C's Gas Market Report. *(EY66)*
Inside I V H S. *(TS01)*
Inside Market Data. *(PB37)*
Inside N R C. *(EY71)*
Integrated Waste Management. *(EV40)*
Interactive Video News. *(AD07)*
International Banking Regulator. *(IT36)*
International Counterterrorism & Security.
The International Information Report. *(IT75)*
International Market Alert. *(FI58)*
International Product Alert. *(AD25)*
International Solar Energy Intelligence Report.
Item Processing Report. *(EC19)*
Kane's Beverage Week. *(FB06)*
L A N Product News. *(EC99)*
L A N Times. *(EC42)*

L D C Debt Report. *(FI42)*
Land Mobile Radio News. *(TE13)*
Land Use Law Report. *(EV02)*
Law Office Technology Review. *(LA15)*
Lawyers' Micro Users Group Newsletter. *(LA05)*
Legal Publisher.
Legislative Network for Nurses.
Liability Week.
Limited Partnership Investment Review.
M P T Review. *(IV48)*
McGraw-Hill's Biotechnology Newswatch. *(BT08)*
Mainframe Computing. *(EC87)*
Managed Care Law Outlook. *(HH16)*
Managed Care Outlook. *(HH12)*
Management Matters. *(MT11)*
Manufacturing Automation. *(MG17)*
Market: Europe.
Media Industry Newsletter. *(PB14)*
Medical Outcomes and Guidelines Alert.
Medical Utilization Management.
Medical Waste News. *(EV30)*
Membrane & Separation Technology News.
    (BT05)
Mental Health Law Reporter.
Mental Health Report.
Mergers and Restructurings.
Metals Week. *(ML01)*
Military & Commercial Fiber Business. *(DE06)*
Military Robotics Newsletter. *(DE14)*
Military Space. *(DE04)*
Mobile Phone News. *(TE25)*
Mobile Satellite News (Potomac). *(TE27)*
Mobile Satellite Reports. *(TE32)*
Modem User News. *(EC97)*
Modern Plastics. *(CH23)*
Money Laundering Alert.
Multimedia Monitor. *(EC70)*
Navy News & Undersea Technology. *(DE18)*
Networks Update. *(EC95)*
New Technology Week. *(RD23)*
NewsNet Action Letter. *(PB99)*
NextNet. *(TE30)*
Noise Regulation Report. *(EV19)*
Northeast Power Report. *(EY88)*
Northern Ireland News Service. *(IT74)*
NotiSur.
Nuclear Waste News. *(EV03)*
NuclearFuel. *(EY72)*
Nucleonics Week. *(EY73)*
Occupational Health & Safety Letter.
Oil Price Information Service. *(EY02)*
Oil Spill U S Law Report. *(EV06)*
Older Americans Report.
Online Libraries and Microcomputers. *(PB42)*
Online Newsletter. *(PB41)*
Online Product News. *(TE27)*
Optical Materials and Engineering News. *(RD37)*
Optical Memory News. *(EC50)*
Origins, C N S Documentary Service. *(CN03)*
Oxy-Fuel News.
P C Business Products. *(EC94)*
P C S Week. *(TE12)*
P P O Letter.
Pesticide & Toxic Chemical News. *(CH18)*
Photobulletin. *(PB26)*
Photobulletin Daily.
Photomarket. *(PB17)*
PhotoStockNotes. *(PB12)*
The Physician and Sportsmedicine. *(ME05)*
Plastics Business News. *(CH17)*
Platt's International Petrochemical Report.
    (CH20)
Platt's Oilgram News. *(EY74)*
Platt's Oilgram Price Report. *(EY75)*
Political Finance & Lobby Reporter. *(POO2)*
Political Risk Letter. *(IT29)*
Postgraduate Medicine. *(ME06)*
Power (New York). *(EY84)*
Privacy Journal.
Private Placement Reporter. *(FI61)*
Product Alert. *(AD24)*
Product Safety News. *(GB52)*
Productivity Software. *(EC80)*
Public Broadcasting Report. *(PB04)*
R T C Watch. *(FI03)*
RateGram. *(IV61)*
Regulatory Compliance Watch. *(FI04)*
Report on A T & T. *(TE50)*
Report on Corporate Educational Support.
Report on Defense Plant Waste. *(EV28)*
Report on Disability Programs.
Report on Education of the Disadvantaged.
Report on Healthcare Management Solutions.
Report on I B M. *(EC45)*
Report on Literacy Program. *(ED10)*
Report on Preschool Programs.
Report on School-Age Child Care.

The Review of Banking and Financial Services.
    (FI17)
The Review of Securities & Commodities
    Regulation. *(FI20)*
Robotronics Age Newsletter. *(EC16)*
S E C News Digest. *(EV96)*
S M T Trends. *(MG18)*
Satellite Industry Directory. *(TE83E)*
Satellite News. *(TE03)*
Satellite Week. *(AE01)*
Securities Week. *(FI27)*
Security Intelligence. *(IT64)*
Semiconductor Industry & Business Survey
    Newsletter. *(EC35)*
Sensor Business Digest. *(MG16)*
The SIMBA Report on Directory Publishing.
    (PB30)
Sludge Newsletter. *(CH13)*
Small Business Tax Review. *(TX15)*
Solid Waste Report. *(EV20)*
SourceMex. *(IT99)*
Southeast Power Report. *(EY89)*
Space Business News. *(AE11)*
Space Calendar. *(AE04)*
Space Fax Daily. *(AE07)*
Space R & D Alert.
Speednews. *(AE15)*
Standard & Poor's Corporation Records.
State & Local Communications Report. *(TE59)*
State Tax Review.
State Telephone Regulation Report. *(TE47)*
Superconductor Week.
Superfund Week. *(EV22)*
T B Weekly.
T R Wireless News. *(TE45)*
Tactical Technology. *(GT45)*
Tax Management Weekly Report. *(File TMWEEK)*
Technology Access Report. *(RD38)*
Technology Alert. *(RDO9)*
Technology Transfer Week. *(DE17)*
Telco Business Report. *(TE49)*
Telco Competition Report. *(TE62)*
Tele-Service News. *(TE21)*
Telecom Calendar. *(TE65)*
Telecom Data Networks. *(TE94)*
Telecommunications Alert. *(TE75)*
Telecommunications Reports. *(TE11)*
Telecommunications Reports International.
    (TE14)
Telephone Industry Directory. *(TE83E)*
Television Digest with Consumer Electronics.
    (PB01)
Tobacco Industry Litigation Reporter.
Tour & Travel News - T T G North America.
    (TR09)
Trading Systems Technology. *(FI39)*
U S Oil Week. *(EY55)*
U S Rail News. *(TS11)*
U.S. Centers for Disease Control. Morbidity and
    Mortality Weekly Report.
Urban Transport News. *(TS10)*
Utility Environment Report. *(EV42)*
Utility Reporter - Fuels Energy & Power. *(EY12)*
Video Technology News. *(PB39)*
Video Week. *(EL01)*
Voice Technology & Services News.
Washington Remote Sensing Letter.
Washington Telecom News. *(TE04)*
Washington Trade Daily.
Waste Treatment Technology News. *(EV26)*
The Week in Germany. *(IT65)*
Weekly of Business Aviation. *(AE20)*
Wing. *(AE06)*
Wing Newsletter.
Workgroup Computing Report.
World Airline News. *(AE31)*
World Airport Week.
Worldwide Databases. *(PB44)*
Worldwide Energy. *(EY63)*
Worldwide Telecom. *(TE19)*
Worldwide Videotex Update. *(PB08)*
4 1 1 Newsletter. *(TE95)*

OCLC ONLINE COMPUTER LIBRARY CTR., INC.
6565 Frantz Rd., Dublin, OH 43017-0702.
Tel: 614-764-6000 Telex: 810-339-2026
Fax: 614-764-6096.
    American Doctoral Dissertations. *(EPIC)*
    Applied Physics Letters.
    Applied Science & Technology Index.
    Art Index.
    Bibliography and Index of Geology. *(EPIC and
        First Search)*
    Biological & Agricultural Index.
    Biology Digest.
    Book Review Digest.
    Business Periodicals Index.

Consumers Index.
Current Opinion in Anaesthesiology.
Current Opinion in Biotechnology.
Current Opinion in Cardiology.
Current Opinion in Cell Biology.
Current Opinion in Critical Care.
Current Opinion in Dermatology.
Current Opinion in Endocrinology & Diabetes.
Current Opinion in Gastroenterology.
Current Opinion in Genetics & Development.
Current Opinion in Hematology.
Current Opinion in Immunology.
Current Opinion in Infectious Diseases.
Current Opinion in Lipidology.
Current Opinion in Nephrology & Hypertension.
Current Opinion in Neurobiology.
Current Opinion in Neurology.
Current Opinion in Obstetrics & Gynecology.
Current Opinion in Oncology.
Current Opinion in Ophthalmology.
Current Opinion in Orthopedics.
Current Opinion in Otolaryngology & Head and
  Neck Surgery.
Current Opinion in Pediatrics.
Current Opinion in Periodontology.
Current Opinion in Psychiatry.
Current Opinion in Pulmonary Medicine.
Current Opinion in Rheumatology.
Current Opinion in Structural Biology.
Current Opinion in Surgical Infections.
Current Opinion in Urology.
Dissertation Abstracts International. Section A:
  Humanities and Social Sciences. (EPIC)
Dissertation Abstracts International. Section B:
  Physical Sciences and Engineering. (EPIC)
Dissertation Abstracts International. Section C:
  Worldwide. (EPIC)
Dissertation Abstracts on Disc. (ERIC)
Education Index.
Electronics Letters.
Electronics Letters Online.
General Science Index.
Humanities Index.
Immunology Today.
Index to Legal Periodicals & Books.
Institute of Electrical and Electronics Engineers.
  Proceedings.
Journal of Applied Physiology.
Library Literature.
Masters Abstracts International. (EPIC)
A Matter of Fact: Statements Containing Statistics
  on Current Social, Economic and Political
  Issues.
The Online Journal of Current Clinical Trials.
Online Journal of Knowledge Synthesis for
  Nursing.
P A I S International in Print.
Physical Review Letters.
R I L M Abstracts of Music Literature.
Reader's Guide Abstracts.
Readers' Guide Abstracts.
Readers' Guide to Periodical Literature.
Social Planning - Policy & Development
  Abstracts.
Social Sciences Index.
Sociological Abstracts.
Wilson Applied Science & Technology Abstracts.
Wilson Art Abstracts.
Wilson Business Abstracts.
Wilson Education Abstracts.
Wilson General Science Abstracts.
Wilson Humanities Abstracts.
Wilson Social Sciences Abstracts.
Worldscope Company Database.

OFICINA ESPANOLA DE PATENTES Y MARCAS
Panama 1, 28071 Madrid, Spain Tel: 349-53-00
Telex: 47020 RPI-E
Fax: 457-22-80.
  Boletin Oficial de la Propiedad Industrial. 1:
    Marcas y Otros Signos Distintivos.
  Boletin Oficial de la Propiedad Industrial. 2:
    Patentes y Modelos de Utilidad.
  Boletin Oficial de la Propiedad Industrial. 3:
    Modelos y Dibujos Industriales y Artisticos.
  Boletin Oficial de la Propiedad Industrial. 4:
    Resumenes de Patentes.

ORBIT SEARCH SERVICE
8000 Westpark Dr., McLean, VA 22102. Tel: 703-
442-0900
Tel: 44-81-992-3456Fax: 703-983-4632.
  A B I - INFORM. (INFO)
  Adhesives Abstracts.
  Aerospace Engineering Magazine.

Agriculture and Environment for Developing
  Countries. (TROPAG)
Alloys Index. (MDEX)
Alphabetic Subject Index to Petroleum Abstracts.
  (TULSA)
Analytical Abstracts. (ANAB)
Antarctic Bibliography. (COLD)
Aqualine Abstracts. (AQUA)
Automotive Engineering Magazine.
Bibliography and Index of Geology. (GEOR)
Bibliography on Cold Regions Science &
  Technology (COLD)
Biotechnology Abstracts. (BIOT)
The Bowker Annual Library and Book Trade
  Almanac.
Ceramic Abstracts. (CERM)
Chem-Facts: Polyethylene.
Chem-Facts: Polypropylene.
Computer & Control Abstracts.
Convergence: International Congress on
  Transportation Electronics. Proceedings.
Corptech Directory of Technology Companies.
  (CORP)
Current Index to Journals in Education. (ERIC)
Current Research in Britain. Biological Sciences.
  (CRIB)
Current Research in Britain. Humanities. (CRIB)
Current Research in Britain. Physical Sciences.
  (CRIB)
C2C Abstracts: Japan - Analytical Chemistry.
  (JTEC)
C2C Abstracts: Japan - Ceramics. (JTEC)
C2C Abstracts: Japan - Chemical Engineering.
  (JTEC)
C2C Abstracts: Japan - Crystallography. (JTEC)
C2C Abstracts: Japan - Hydrocarbons. (JTEC)
C2C Abstracts: Japan - Inorganic Chemistry.
  (JTEC)
C2C Abstracts: Japan - Materials Science. (JTEC)
C2C Abstracts: Japan - Metals. (JTEC)
C2C Abstracts: Japan - Organic Chemistry.
  (JTEC)
C2C Abstracts: Japan - Physical Chemistry.
  (JTEC)
C2C Abstracts: Japan - Plastics. (JTEC)
C2C Abstracts: Japan - Polymer Chemistry.
  (JTEC)
C2C Abstracts: Japan - Surface Chemistry.
  (JTEC)
C2C Abstracts: Japan - Textiles. (JTEC)
C2C Currents: Japan - Chemistry. (JTEC)
C2C Currents: Japan - Computers. (JTEC)
C2C Currents: Japan - Electronics. (JTEC)
C2C Currents: Japan - Materials. (JTEC)
Ecological Abstracts. (GEOB)
Electrical & Electronics Abstracts.
Engineered Materials Abstracts. (EMAB)
Engineering Index Annual.
Engineering Index Monthly.
Environment Abstracts. (ENVIRONLINE)
Environment Abstracts Annual. (Enviroline)
Food Science and Technology Abstracts. (FSTA)
Gale Directory of Databases.
Geographical Abstracts: Human Geography.
  (GEOB)
Geographical Abstracts: Physical Geography.
  (GEOB)
Geological Abstracts. (GEOB)
Government Reports Announcements & Index.
  (NTIS)
Health and Safety Science Abstracts. (ORBIT)
Imaging Abstracts. (PIRA/IMAB)
Index to Scientific & Technical Proceedings.
International Development Abstracts.
International Journal of Rock Mechanics & Mining
  Sciences. (GEOM)
International Labour Documentation. (LDOC)
International Packaging Abstracts. (PIRA)
International Petroleum Abstracts. (IPAB)
Investor's Digest of Canada.
Key Abstracts - Business Automation.
L I S A: Library & Information Science Abstracts.
  (LISA)
Metals Abstracts. (MDEX)
Metals Abstracts Index. (MDEX)
Million Dollar Directory.
N I O S H T I C Database.
N T I S Bibliographic Data Base.
Nonferrous Metals Alert. (MABU)
Nonwovens Abstracts.
Off-Highway Engineering
P N I.
Packaging Science and Technology Abstracts.
Paperbase Abstracts. (PIRA)
Patents Abstracts.
Petroleum Abstracts. (TULSA)
Petroleum - Energy Business News Index. (ABIZ)
Physics Abstracts.

Polymers, Ceramics, Composites Alert. (MABU)
Printing Abstracts. (PIRA)
Process and Chemical Engineering. (CEABA)
Professional Update.
Psychological Abstracts.
R A P R A Abstracts. (RAPRA)
R A P R A New Trade Names in the Rubber and
  Plastics Industries. (RAPRA)
Reference Book of Corporate Managements.
  (RBCM)
S A E Handbook.
S A E Technical Literature Abstracts.
S A E Technical Papers.
Safety and Health at Work.
Science Citation Index.
Securite et Sante au Travail.
Stapp Car Crash Conference. Proceedings.
Steels Alert. (MABU)
Synthetic Methods of Organic Chemistry.
Technical Literature Abstracts. (APILIT)
Technical Literature Abstracts: Catalysts -
  Zeolites. (APILIT)
Technical Literature Abstracts: Fuel
  Reformulation. (APILIT)
Technical Literature Abstracts: Oilfield Chemicals.
  (APILIT)
Technical Literature Abstracts: Tribology. (APILIT)
Theoretical Chemical Engineering
United States Patents Quarterly.
Welding Abstracts.
Who's Who in Technology. (WHOTECH)
World Ceramics Abstracts
World Publishing Monitor.
World Surface Coating Abstracts. (WSCA)
World Textile Abstracts. (WTA)

OVID TECHNOLOGIES, INC.
333 Seventh Ave., New York, NY 10001.
Tel: 212-563-3006
Fax: 212-563-3784.
  A B A Banking Journal. (TSAP)
  A B I - INFORM. (INFO)
  A H F S Drug Information. (DIFT)
  Academic Abstracts C D - R O M.
  Academic Index. (ACAD)
  Administrative Science Quarterly.
  Adweek (Los Angeles). (TSAP)
  Adweek (New York). (TSAP)
  Aerospace Daily. (TSAP)
  Age and Ageing.
  Agricultural Supply Industry. (TSAP)
  Agroforestry Abstracts.
  Agrow. (PHIN,PHIC,PHID)
  Air Conditioning, Heating & Refrigeration News.
    (TSAP)
  Alcoholism & Drug Abuse Weekly.
  American Banker.
  American College of Cardiology. Journal.
  American Doctoral Dissertations.
  American Family Physician.
  American Heart Journal.
  American Journal of Cardiology.
  The American Journal of Medicine.
  American Journal of Obstetrics and Gynecology.
  American Journal of Psychiatry.
  American Journal of Public Health.
  American Journal of Surgery.
  Anesthesia and Analgesia.
  Anesthesiology.
  Animal Pharm. (PJIN,PHIC,PHID)
  Annals of Internal Medicine.
  Annals of Neurology.
  Annals of Surgery.
  Annals of the Rheumatic Diseases.
  Archives of Disease in Childhood.
  Archives of Disease in Childhood. Fetal and
    Neonatal Edition.
  Art Index.
  Arthritis and Rheumatism.
  Arts & Humanities Citation Index. (AHCI)
  B L A S T.
  B M J.
  Biological Abstracts. (BIOL)
  Biological Abstracts - R R M. (BIOL)
  Blood.
  Blood Weekly.
  Books in Print. (BBIP)
  Books in Print Supplement. (BBIP)
  Books Out-of-Print. (BBIP)
  The Bowker Annual Library and Book Trade
    Almanac. (BBIP)
  Brandweek. (TSAP)
  British Journal of Obstetrics & Gynaecology.
  British Journal of Rheumatology.
  British Journal of Surgery.
  British Journal of Urology.
  Business Index.

Vendor

C M A J.
CAB International. Bureau of Nutrition. Annotated Bibliographies.
CAB International. Bureau of Soils. Annotated Bibliographies.
Cancer Researcher Weekly.
Cardiology Clinics.
Children's Books in Print. *(BBIP)*
Ching Feng.
Circulation (Dallas). *(JWAT)*
Circulation Research.
Clinica. *(PHIN,PHIC,PHID)*
Clinical Diabetes.
Clinical Molecular Pathology.
Clinical Orthopaedics and Related Research.
Clinical Pediatrics.
Clinical Pharmacology & Therapeutics.
Compumath Citation Index.
Computer Database. *(CMPT)*
Cumulative Book Index.
Cumulative Index to Nursing & Allied Health Literature. *(NAHL)*
Current Advances in Applied Microbiology & Biotechnology. *(CABS)*
Current Advances in Cancer Research. *(CABS)*
Current Advances in Cell & Developmental Biology. *(CABS)*
Current Advances in Clinical Chemistry. *(CABS)*
Current Advances in Ecological and Environmental Sciences. *(CABS)*
Current Advances in Endocrinology & Metabolism. *(CABS)*
Current Advances in Genetics and Molecular Biology. *(CABS)*
Current Advances in Immunology & Infectious Diseases. *(CABS)*
Current Advances in Neuroscience. *(CABS)*
Current Advances in Plant Science. *(CABS)*
Current Advances in Protein Biochemistry. *(CABS)*
Current Advances in Toxicology. *(CABS)*
Current Awareness in Biological Sciences. *(CABS)*
Current Awareness in Health Education.
Current Contents: Agriculture, Biology & Environmental Sciences. *(CTOC,CBIB,AGRI)*
Current Contents: Arts & Humanities. *(CTOC,CBIB,ARTS)*
Current Contents: Clinical Medicine. *(CTOC,CBIB,CLIN)*
Current Contents: Engineering, Computing & Technology. *(CTOC,CBIB,ENGI)*
Current Contents: Life Sciences. *(CTOC,CBIB,LIFE)*
Current Contents: Physical, Chemical & Earth Sciences. *(CTOC,CBIB,PHYS)*
Current Contents: Social & Behavioral Sciences. *(CTOC,CBIB,BEHA)*
Current History.
Current Index to Journals in Education.
Current Index to Statistics. *(MATH)*
Current Law Index.
Current Mathematical Publications.
Current Research in Library & Information Science. *(LISA)*
The Cyprus Review.
Devices & Diagnostics Letter. *(DIOG)*
Diabetes.
Diabetes Care.
Dissertation Abstracts International. Section A: Humanities and Social Sciences. *(DISS)*
Dissertation Abstracts International. Section B: Physical Sciences and Engineering. *(DISS)*
Dissertation Abstracts International. Section C: Worldwide. *(DISS)*
Dissertation Abstracts on Disc. *(DISS)*
E-Med News. *(PHIN,PHIC,PHID)*
Emergency Medicine Reports.
Engineering Index Annual. *(COMP)*
Engineering Index Monthly. *(COMP)*
Epiphany Journal.
Excerpta Medica Abstract Journals.
Excerpta Medica. Section 1: Anatomy, Anthropology, Embryology & Histology.
Excerpta Medica. Section 2: Physiology.
Excerpta Medica. Section 3: Endocrinology.
Excerpta Medica. Section 4: Microbiology: Bacteriology, Mycology, Parasitology and Virology.
Excerpta Medica. Section 5: General Pathology and Pathological Anatomy.
Excerpta Medica. Section 6: Internal Medicine.
Excerpta Medica. Section 7: Pediatrics and Pediatric Surgery.
Excerpta Medica. Section 8: Neurology and Neurosurgery.
Excerpta Medica. Section 9: Surgery.
Excerpta Medica. Section 10: Obstetrics and Gynecology.
Excerpta Medica. Section 11: Otorhinolaryngology.

Excerpta Medica. Section 12: Ophthalmology.
Excerpta Medica. Section 13: Dermatology and Venereology.
Excerpta Medica. Section 14: Radiology.
Excerpta Medica. Section 15: Chest Diseases, Thoracic Surgery and Tuberculosis.
Excerpta Medica. Section 16: Cancer.
Excerpta Medica. Section 17: Public Health, Social Medicine and Epidemiology.
Excerpta Medica. Section 18: Cardiovascular Diseases and Cardiovascular Surgery.
Excerpta Medica. Section 19: Rehabilitation and Physical Medicine.
Excerpta Medica. Section 20: Gerontology and Geriatrics.
Excerpta Medica. Section 21: Developmental Biology and Teratology.
Excerpta Medica. Section 22: Human Genetics.
Excerpta Medica. Section 23: Nuclear Medicine.
Excerpta Medica. Section 24: Anesthesiology.
Excerpta Medica. Section 25: Hematology.
Excerpta Medica. Section 26: Immunology, Serology and Transplantation.
Excerpta Medica. Section 27: Biophysics, Bio-Engineering and Medical Instrumentation.
Excerpta Medica. Section 28: Urology and Nephrology.
Excerpta Medica. Section 29: Clinical and Experimental Biochemistry.
Excerpta Medica. Section 30: Clinical and Experimental Pharmacology.
Excerpta Medica. Section 31: Arthritis and Rheumatism.
Excerpta Medica. Section 32: Psychiatry.
Excerpta Medica. Section 33: Orthopedic Surgery.
Excerpta Medica. Section 35: Occupational Health and Industrial Medicine.
Excerpta Medica. Section 36: Health Policy, Economics and Management.
Excerpta Medica. Section 38: Adverse Reactions Titles.
Excerpta Medica. Section 40: Drug Dependence, Alcohol Abuse and Alcoholism.
Excerpta Medica. Section 46: Environmental Health and Pollution Control.
Excerpta Medica. Section 48: Gastroenterology.
Excerpta Medica. Section 49: Forensic Science Abstracts.
Excerpta Medica. Section 50: Epilepsy Abstracts.
Excerpta Medica. Section 52: Toxicology.
F D A Enforcement Report. *(DIOG)*
F D A Medical Bulletin. *(DIOG)*
Family Relations.
Federal Applied Technology Database.
Federal Register. *(DIOG)*
Food and Drug Letter. *(DIOG)*
Foreign Policy Bulletin.
Forest Products Abstracts. *(CABA)*
Forestry Abstracts. *(CABA)*
Forthcoming Books. *(BBIP)*
The G M P Letter. *(DIOG)*
Gastroenterology.
Genitourinary Medicine.
Government Reports Announcements & Index.
Grasslands and Forage Abstracts.
Gut.
Handbook on Injectable Drugs. *(DIFT)*
Harvard Business Review. *(HBRO)*
Health Index. *(HEAL)*
Health Policy & Biomedical Research: The Blue Sheet. *(FDCR)*
Heart.
Heart & Lung.
Helminthological Abstracts. *(VETR)*
Humanities Index. *(WHUM)*
Index Medicus. *(MESH, MESZ)*
Index to Dental Literature. *(MESH, MESZ)*
Index to Legal Periodicals & Books.
Injury Prevention.
International Biodeterioration & Biodegradation.
International Nursing Index.
International Pharmaceutical Abstracts. *(IPAB)*
J A M A: The Journal of the American Medical Association. *(JWAR)*
The Journal of Allergy and Clinical Immunology.
Journal of Bone and Joint Surgery: American Volume.
Journal of Clinical Investigation.
Journal of Clinical Pathology.
Journal of Family History.
Journal of Family Issues.
Journal of Infectious Diseases. *(JWAT)*
The Journal of Laboratory and Clinical Medicine.
Journal of Marriage and the Family.
Journal of Neurology, Neurosurgery and Psychiatry.
Journal of Pediatrics.
Journal of Psychology and Theology.

Journal of Technology Transfer.
L I S A: Library & Information Science Abstracts. *(LISA)*
The Lancet.
LegalTrac. *(LAWS)*
Magazine Article Summaries. *(PMRO)*
Magazine Index. *(MAGS)*
Management Contents. *(MGMT)*
Masters Abstracts International.
Mathematical Reviews. *(MATH)*
Medical and Health Care Books and Serials in Print. *(BBIP,ULRI)*
Medical Devices, Diagnostics & Instrumentation Reports: The Gray Sheet. *(FDCR)*
Medical Science Research.
Merck Index: An Encyclopedia of Chemicals and Drugs. *(MRCK)*
Meyler's Side Effects of Drugs.
Monthly Catalog of United States Government Publications.
N T I S Bibliographic Data Base.
National Cancer Institute. Journal.
National Newspaper Index. *(NOOZ)*
Nematological Abstracts. *(CABA)*
New England Journal of Medicine. *(NEJM)*
Nutrition Abstracts and Reviews. Series B: Livestock Feeds and Feeding. *(VETR)*
Obstetrics and Gynecology.
Outlook (Year) Proceedings.
P N I. *(PNII)*
Paperbound Books in Print. *(BBIP)*
Pediatrics (English Edition).
Peterson's Guide to Four-Year Colleges (Year). *(PETE)*
Peterson's Guide to Two-Year Colleges (Year). *(PETE)*
Pharmaceutical Approvals Monthly. *(FDCR)*
Philosophical Forum.
Physical Therapy.
Predicasts F & S Index Europe. *(PTSI)*
Predicasts F & S Index International. *(PTSI)*
Predicasts F & S Index of Corporate Change. *(PTSI)*
Predicasts F & S Index United States. *(PTSI)*
Predicasts Overview of Markets and Technology. *(PTSP)*
Prescription Pharmaceuticals and Biotechnology: The Pink Sheet. *(FDCR)*
Psychological Abstracts.
Quarterly Journal of Medicine.
Radiologic Clinics of North America.
Religion in Eastern Europe.
Resources in Education.
Respiratory Medicine.
Salud Publica de Mexico.
Science. *(SCIE)*
Scientific American. *(SAMM)*
Scientific American Medicine. *(SAMM)*
Scrip - World Pharmaceutical News. *(PHIN,PHIC,PHID)*
Seminars in Neurology.
Seminars in Respiratory and Critical Care Medicine.
Sexually Transmitted Diseases.
Shonika.
Side Effects of Drugs Annual.
Social Planning - Policy & Development Abstracts. *(SOCA)*
Social Sciences Citation Index. *(SSCI)*
Social Work Abstracts. *(SWAB)*
Sociological Abstracts. *(SOCA)*
Southern Social Studies Journal.
Sport Thesaurus.
SportSearch. *(SFDB)*
Stroke.
Subject Guide to Books in Print. *(BBIP)*
T B Weekly.
Thorax.
Toiletries, Fragrances and Skin Care: The Rose Sheet. *(FDCR)*
Trade & Industry Index. *(TSAP)*
Ulrich's International Periodicals Directory. *(ULRI)*
Ulrich's Update. *(ULRI)*
U.S. Centers for Disease Control. Morbidity and Mortality Weekly Report.
Vaard i Norden.
Washington Drug Letter (Washington, 1979). *(DIOG)*
Whole Earth Review.
Wilson Art Abstracts.
Wilson Humanities Abstracts. *(WHUM)*
Year Book of Anesthesiology and Pain Management.
Year Book of Cardiology.
Year Book of Dentistry.
Year Book of Dermatologic Surgery.
Year Book of Dermatology.
Year Book of Diagnostic Radiology.

Year Book of Digestive Diseases.
Year Book of Drug Therapy.
Year Book of Emergency Medicine.
Year Book of Family Practice.
Year Book of Geriatrics and Gerontology.
Year Book of Hand Surgery.
Year Book of Hematology.
Year Book of Infectious Diseases.
Year Book of Medicine.
The Year Book of Neonatal and Perinatal
    Medicine.
Year Book of Nephrology.
Year Book of Neurology & Neurosurgery.
Year Book of Neuroradiology.
Year Book of Nuclear Medicine.
Year Book of Obstetrics and Gynecology.
Year Book of Occupational and Environmental
    Medicine.
Year Book of Oncology.
Year Book of Ophthalmology.
Year Book of Orthopedics.
Year Book of Pathology and Laboratory Medicine.
Year Book of Pediatrics.
Year Book of Plastic, Reconstructive, and
    Aesthetic Surgery.
Year Book of Psychiatry and Applied Mental
    Health.
Year Book of Pulmonary Disease.
Year Book of Surgery.
Year Book of Transplantation.
Year Book of Ultrasound.
Year Book of Urology.
Year Book of Vascular Surgery.

PETROSCAN (Subsidiary of: United
    Communications Group)
One Central Plaza, 11300 Rockville Pike, Suite
1100, Rockville, MD 20852. Tel: 301-816-8950
Fax: 301-816-8945.
    American Petroleum Institute. Division of
        Statistics. Weekly Statistical Bulletin.
    U.S. Energy Information Administration. Weekly
        Petroleum Status Report.

QL SYSTEMS, LTD.
1819 Granville St., Halifax, Nova Scotia B3, Canada
275 Sparks St., Ste. 901, St. Andrews Tower,
Ottawa, ON KlR7X9, Tel: 613-238-3499
    A S T I S Bibliography.
    A S T I S Current Awareness Bulletin.
    A S T I S Occasional Publications.
    Alberta Reports.
    Canadian Foreign Relations.
    Canadian Index.
    Coal Highlights.
    International Bibliography of the Social Sciences.
        Economics.
    International Bibliography of the Social Sciences.
        Social and Cultural Anthropology.
    Investor's Digest of Canada.
    Manitoba Reports.
    National Reporter.
    New Brunswick Reports.
    Newfoundland & Prince Edward Island Reports.
    Nova Scotia Reports.
    Ontario. Labour Relations Board. Reports. A
        Monthly Series of Decisions.
    Ontario Appeal Cases.
    Ontario Reports.
    Polar and Glaciological Abstracts.
    Saskatchewan Reports.
    Tax Profile.
    Western Weekly Reports.

REED INFORMATION SERVICES LTD.
    (A Member of the Reed Elsevier plc group)
Windsor Ct., East Grinstead Hse., East Grinstead,
West Sussex RH19 1XA, United Kingdom
Tel: 44-1342-326972 Telex: 95127 INFSER G
Fax: 44-1342-335612.
    British Exports.
    Chemical Plant File.
    Dial Electrical - Electronics.
    Dial Engineering.
    Directory of Directors.
    Kelly's Directory.
    Kelly's Link.
    Kelly's Oil & Gas Directory.
    Kompass United Kingdom.
    U K Industrial Trade Names.

RESEARCH INSTITUTE OF AMERICA (Subsidiary of:
    International Thomson Organization, Inc.)
90 Fifth Ave., New York, NY 10011. Tel: 212-
645-4800
Fax: 201-816-3581.
    Federal Tax Regulations.

**RESEARCH LIBRARIES GROUP INFORMATION
NETWORK**
1200 Villa St., Mountain View, CA 94041-1100.
Tel: 415-691-2211
Fax: 415-964-0943.
    Anthropological Literature.
    Avery Index to Architectural Periodicals.
    P A I S International in Print.

REUTERS, LTD.
85 Fleet St., London EC4P 4AJ, United Kingdom
Tel: 44-171-250-1122
Fax: 44-171-510-6227.
    Airline Business.
    Summary of World Broadcasts. Part 1: Former U
        S S R (Daily).
    Summary of World Broadcasts. Part 1: Former U
        S S R (Weekly Economic Report).
    Summary of World Broadcasts. Part 2: Central
        Europe, the Balkans (Daily).
    Summary of World Broadcasts. Part 2: Central
        Europe, the Balkans (Weekly Economic Report).
    Summary of World Broadcasts. Part 3: Asia -
        Pacific (Daily).
    Summary of World Broadcasts. Part 3: Asia -
        Pacific (Weekly Economic Report).
    Summary of World Broadcasts. Part 4: Middle
        East (Daily).
    Summary of World Broadcasts. Part 4: Middle
        East (Weekly Economic Report).
    Summary of World Broadcasts. Part 5: Africa,
        Latin America and the Caribbean (Daily).
    Summary of World Broadcasts. Part 5: Africa,
        Latin America and the Caribbean (Weekly
        Economic Report).

S T N INTERNATIONAL
c/o Chemical Abstracts Service, 2540 Olentengy
River Rd., Box 3012, Columbus, OH 43210.
Tel: 614-421-3600, 800-848-6533 Telex: 6842086
CHMAB
    A B I - INFORM. (STN)
    A O A C International Journal. (CJAOAC)
    A S F A Aquaculture Abstracts. (AQUASCI)
    A S F A Marine Biotechnology Abstracts.
    Accounts of Chemical Research. (CJACS)
    Adhesives Abstracts.
    Agricultural & Environmental Biotechnology
        Abstracts. (LIFESCI)
    Agricultural Engineering Abstracts.
    Agroforestry Abstracts.
    Alloys Index.
    American Chemical Society. Journal. (CJACS)
    American Doctoral Dissertations.
    The Analyst. (CJPSC)
    Analytica Chimica Acta.
    Analytical Abstracts. (ANABSTR)
    Analytical Chemistry. (CJACS)
    Angewandte Chemie. (CJVCH)
    Animal Behavior Abstracts. (LIFESCI)
    Applied Catalysis A: General.
    Aquatic Sciences & Fisheries Abstracts. Part 1:
        Biological Sciences and Living Resources.
        (AQUASCI)
    Aquatic Sciences & Fisheries Abstracts. Part 2:
        Ocean Technology, Policy and Non-living
        Resources. (AQUASCI)
    Aquatic Sciences & Fisheries Abstracts. Part 3:
        Aquatic Pollution and Environmental Quality.
        (AQUASCI)
    Bibliography and Index of Geology. (GeoRef)
    Biochemistry. (CJACS)
    Biocontrol News and Information.
    Biodeterioration Abstracts.
    Biological Abstracts. (BIOSIS)
    Biological Abstracts - R R M. (BIOSIS)
    Biopolymers. (CJWILEY)
    C S A Neurosciences Abstracts. (LIFESCI)
    Calcium and Calcified Tissue Abstracts. (LIFESCI)
    Carbohydrate Research.
    Ceramic Abstracts.
    Chem Sources International.
    Chem Sources U S A.
    Chemical Abstracts.
    Chemical Abstracts - Applied Chemistry and
        Chemical Engineering Sections. (CA)
    Chemical Abstracts - Biochemistry Sections. (CA)

Chemical Abstracts - Macromolecular Sections.
    (CA)
Chemical Abstracts - Organic Chemistry Sections.
    (CA)
Chemical Abstracts - Physical, Inorganic and
    Analytical Chemistry Sections. (CA)
Chemical Communications. (CJRSC)
Chemical Hazards in Industry. (CSNB)
Chemical Research in Toxicology.
Chemical Reviews. (CJACS)
Chemoreception Abstracts. (LIFESCI)
Computer & Control Abstracts.
Computer and Information Systems Abstracts
    Journal.
Conference Papers Annual Index. (CONFSCI)
Conference Papers Index. (CONFSCI)
Crop Physiology Abstracts.
D K I Literatur-Schnelldienst Kunststoffe
    Kautschuk Fasern.
Dalton Transactions. (CJRSC)
Dissertation Abstracts International. Section A:
    Humanities and Social Sciences.
Dissertation Abstracts International. Section B:
    Physical Sciences and Engineering.
Dissertation Abstracts International. Section C:
    Worldwide.
Dissertation Abstracts on Disc.
E-Med News.
Ecology Abstracts.
Electrical & Electronics Abstracts.
Electronics and Communications Abstracts
    Journal. (ELCOM)
Energy & Fuels. (CJACS)
Energy Data Base.
Energy Research Abstracts. (ENERGY)
Engineered Materials Abstracts. (EMA)
Engineering Index Annual.
Engineering Index Monthly. (COMPENDEX)
Entomology Abstracts. (LIFESCI)
Environmental Science & Technology
    (Washington). (CJACS)
Faraday Discussions. (CJRSC)
Faraday Transactions. (CJRSC)
Field Crop Abstracts.
Food Science and Technology Abstracts.
Forestry Abstracts. Leading Article Reprint Series.
Genetics Abstracts. (LIFESCI)
Government Reports Announcements & Index.
    (NTIS)
Grasslands and Forage Abstracts.
Horticultural Abstracts.
I N I S Atomindex. (ENERGY)
Imaging Abstracts. (PIRA)
Immunology Abstracts. (LIFESCI)
Index Medicus. (MEDLINE)
Index of Current Research on Pigs.
Index of Fungi.
Index to Dental Literature. (MEDLINE)
Index Veterinarius.
Industrial & Engineering Chemistry Research.
    (CJACS)
Inorganic Chemistry. (CJACS)
International Nursing Index. (MEDLINE)
International Packaging Abstracts.
Irrigation and Drainage Abstracts.
Journal of Agricultural and Food Chemistry.
    (CJACS)
Journal of Analytical Atomic Spectrometry.
    (CJRSC)
Journal of Applied Polymer Science. (CJWILEY)
Journal of Chemical and Engineering Data.
    (CJACS)
Journal of Chemical Information and Computer
    Sciences. (CJACS)
Journal of Chemical Research. (CJRSC)
Journal of Medicinal Chemistry. (CJACS)
Journal of Organic Chemistry (Washington).
    (CJACS)
Journal of Organometallic Chemistry.
Journal of Physical Chemistry. (CJACS)
Journal of Polymer Science. Part A: Polymer
    Chemistry. (CJWILEY)
Journal of Polymer Science. Part B: Polymer
    Physics. (CJWILEY)
Journal of Polymer Science. Symposia
    Proceedings.
Key Abstracts - Business Automation.
Laboratory Hazards Bulletin. (CSNB)
Langmuir. (CJACS)
Leisure, Recreation and Tourism Abstracts.
Macromolecules. (CJACS)
Maize Abstracts.
Masters Abstracts International.
Mechanical Engineering Abstracts. (ISMEC)
Medical & Pharmaceutical Biotechnology
    Abstracts. (LIFESCI)
Merck Index: An Encyclopedia of Chemicals and
    Drugs.

Metals Abstracts. *(METADEX)*
Metals Abstracts Index. *(METADEX)*
Microbiology Abstracts: Section A. Industrial &
    Applied Microbiology. *(LIFESCI)*
Microbiology Abstracts: Section B. Bacteriology.
    (LIFESCI)
Microbiology Abstracts: Section C. Algology,
    Mycology and Protozoology. *(LIFESCI)*
N T I S Bibliographic Data Base.
Nonferrous Metals Alert. *(MATBUS)*
Nonwovens Abstracts.
Nucleic Acids Abstracts. *(LIFESCI)*
Nutrition Abstracts and Reviews. Series A: Human
    and Experimental.
Oceanic Abstracts. *(OCEAN)*
Oncogenes and Growth Factors Abstracts.
    (LIFESCI)
Organometallics. *(CJACS)*
Ornamental Horticulture.
P N I.
Packaging Science and Technology Abstracts.
Paperbase Abstracts.
Patents Abstracts.
Physics Abstracts.
Pig News & Information.
Plant Breeding Abstracts.
Plant Growth Regulator Abstracts.
Pollution Abstracts. *(POLLUAB)*
Polymers, Ceramics, Composites Alert. *(MATBUS)*
Potato Abstracts.
Poultry Abstracts.
Printing Abstracts.
Protozoological Abstracts.
R A P R A New Trade Names in the Rubber and
    Plastics Industries.
R T E C S.
Review of Agricultural Entomology.
Review of Medical and Veterinary Entomology.
Review of Medical and Veterinary Mycology.
Review of Plant Pathology.
Rice Abstracts.
Royal Society of Chemistry. Journal: Perkin
    Transactions 1. *(CJRSC)*
Royal Society of Chemistry. Journal: Perkin
    Transactions 2. *(CJRSC)*
Rural Development Abstracts.
Seed Abstracts.
Small Animals.
Solid State and Superconductivity Abstracts.
    (SOLIDSTATE)
Sorghum and Millets.
Soyabean Abstracts.
Steels Alert. *(MATBUS)*
Technical Literature Abstracts. *(APILIT)*
Technical Literature Abstracts: Catalysts -
    Zeolites.
Technical Literature Abstracts: Fuel
    Reformulation. *(APILIT)*
Technical Literature Abstracts: Oilfield Chemicals.
    (APILIT)
Technical Literature Abstracts: Tribology. *(APILIT)*
Toxicology Abstracts. *(LIFESCI)*
Tropical Oil Seeds.
Vademecum Deutscher Lehr- und
    Forschungsstaetten. Staetten der Forschung.
Veterinary Bulletin.
Virology and AIDS Abstracts. *(LIFESCI)*
Vitis.
Vitis - Viticulture and Oenology Abstracts.
Weed Abstracts.
Wheat, Barley and Triticale Abstracts.
World Agricultural Economics and Rural Sociology
    Abstracts.
World Publishing Monitor.
Zentralblatt fuer Didaktik der Mathematik.
Zentralblatt fuer Mathematik und Ihre
    Grenzgebiete. *(MATH)*

SOURCE TELECOMPUTING CORP.
1616 Anderson Rd., McLean, VA 22102.
    E R I C Clearinghouse on Urban Education.
    Digest.

SOUTHAM ELECTRONIC PUBLISHING
1450 Don Mills Rd., Don Mills, ON M3B 2X7,
Canada Tel: 416-442-2198
Fax: 416-445-3508.
    Les Affaires.
    Calgary Herald.
    Canadian Forest Industries.
    Canadian Mining Journal.
    Canadian Underwriter.
    Daily Oil Bulletin.
    Devoir.
    Eco-Log Week.
    Financial Post.

Financial Post Directory of Directors.
Gazette.
Inter-Corporate Ownership.
Maclean's.
The Northern Miner.
Pulp & Paper Canada.

TELESYSTEMES-QUESTEL
83-85 blvd. Vincent Auriol, Paris 75013, France
Tel: 33-144236464 Telex: 204594 TELQUES F
Fax: 33-144236465.
    B H A.
    Bibliography of Bioethics. *(BIOETHICS)*
    Bulletin Signaletique des Telecommunications.
    Catalogue Afnor (Normes Francaises).
    Diffusion Express. *(Base EDF.DOC)*
    F R A N C I S. 519: Philosophie.
    F R A N C I S. 520: Sciences de l'Education.
    F R A N C I S. 521: Sociologie.
    F R A N C I S. 522: Histoire des Sciences et de
        Techniques.
    F R A N C I S. 523: Histoire et Sciences de la
        Litterature.
    F R A N C I S. 524: Sciences du Langage.
    F R A N C I S. 525: Prehistoire et Protohistoire.
    F R A N C I S. 526: Art et Archeologie.
    F R A N C I S. 527: Histoire et Sciences des
        Religions.
    F R A N C I S. 528: Bibliographie Internationale
        de Science Administrative.
    F R A N C I S. 529: Ethnologie.
    F R A N C I S. 531: Bibliographie Geographique
        Internationale.
    F R A N C I S. 603: Informatique et Sciences
        Juridiques.
    F R A N C I S. 617: E C O D O C.
    F R A N C I S. 731: Economie de l'Energie.
    Gale Directory of Databases.
    Merck Index: An Encyclopedia of Chemicals and
        Drugs.
    Le Monde.
    P A S C A L. E 11: Physique Atomique et
        Moleculaire. Plasmas.
    P A S C A L. E 12: Etat Condense.
    P A S C A L. E 13: Structure des Liquides et des
        Solides - Cristallographie.
    P A S C A L. E 18: Chromatographie.
    P A S C A L. E 20: Electronique et
        Telecommunications.
    P A S C A L. E 27: Methodes de Formation et
        Traitement des Images.
    P A S C A L. E 30: Microscopie Electronique et
        Diffraction Electronique.
    P A S C A L. E 32: Metrologie et Appareillage en
        Physique et Physicochimie.
    P A S C A L. E 33. Informatique.
    P A S C A L. E 34. Robotique, Automatique et
        Automatisation des Processus Industriels.
    P A S C A L. E 36: Pollution de l'Eau, de l'Air et
        du Sol - Dechets - Bruit.
    P A S C A L. E 48: Environnement Cosmique
        Terrestre, Astronomie et Geologie
        Extraterrestre.
    P A S C A L. E 49: Meteorologie, Glaciologie,
        Physique des Oceans.
    P A S C A L. E 58: Genetique.
    P A S C A L. E 61: Microbiologie: Bacteriologie,
        Virologie, Mycologie, Protozoaires Pathogenes.
    P A S C A L. E 62: Immunologie.
    P A S C A L. E 63: Toxicologie.
    P A S C A L. E 64: Endocrinologie Humaine et
        Experimentale. Endocrinopathies.
    P A S C A L. E 65: Psychologie,
        Psychopathologie, Psychiatrie.
    P A S C A L. E 68: Genetique Humaine.
    P A S C A L. E 71: Ophtalmologie.
    P A S C A L. E 72: Otorhinolaryngologie.
        Stomatologie. Pathologie Cervicofaciale.
    P A S C A L. E 73: Dermatologie. Maladies
        Sexuellement Transmissibles.
    P A S C A L. E 74: Pneumologie.
    P A S C A L. E 75: Cardiologie et Appareil
        Circulatoire.
    P A S C A L. E 76: Gastroenterologie, Foie,
        Pancreas, Abdomen.
    P A S C A L. E 77: Nephrologie. Voies Urinaires.
    P A S C A L. E 78: Neurologie.
    P A S C A L. E 79: Pathologie et Physiologie
        Osteoarticulaires.
    P A S C A L. E 80: Hematologie.
    P A S C A L. E 82: Gynecologie, Obstetrique,
        Andrologie.
    P A S C A L. E 83: Anesthesie et Reanimation.
    P A S C A L. E 84: Genie Biomedical.
        Informatique Biomedicale.
    P A S C A L. E 89: Cancer.

P A S C A L. F 10: Mecanique, Acoustique et
    Transfert de Chaleur.
P A S C A L. F 16: Chimie Analytique, Minerale
    et Organique.
P A S C A L. F 17: Chimie Generale, Minerale et
    Organique.
P A S C A L. F 23: Genie Chimique. Industries
    Chimique et Parachimique.
P A S C A L. F 24: Polymeres - Peintures - Bois.
P A S C A L. F 40: Mineralogie. Geochimie.
    Geologie Extraterrestre.
P A S C A L. F 41: Gisements Metalliques et Non
    Metalliques.
P A S C A L. F 42: Roches Cristallines.
P A S C A L. F 43: Roches Sedimentaires.
    Geologie Marine.
P A S C A L. F 44: Stratigraphie, Geologie
    Regionale, Geologie Generale.
P A S C A L. F 45: Tectonique, Geophysique
    Interne.
P A S C A L. F 46: Hydrologie. Geologie de
    l'Ingenieur. Formations Superficielles.
P A S C A L. F 47: Paleontologie.
P A S C A L. F 52: Biochimie - Biophysique -
    Moleculaire - Biologie Moleculaire et Cellulaire.
P A S C A L. F 53: Anatomie et Physiologie des
    Vertebres.
P A S C A L. F 54: Reproduction des Vertebres,
    Embryologie des Vertebres et des Invertebres.
P A S C A L. F 55: Biologie Vegetale.
P A S C A L. F 56: Ecologie Animale, Vegetale et
    Microbienne. Ethologie Animale.
P A S C A L. F 70: Pharmacologie. Traitements
    Medicamenteux.
P A S C A L. T 205: Sciences de l'Information.
    Documentation.
P A S C A L. T 215: Biotechnologies.
P A S C A L. T 230: Energie.
P A S C A L. T 235: Medecine Tropicale.
P A S C A L. T 240: Metaux - Metallurgie.
P A S C A L. T 260: Zoologie Fondamentale et
    Appliquee des Invertebres.
P A S C A L. T 280: Sciences Agronomiques et
    Forestieres: Productions Vegetales.
P A S C A L. T 295: Batiment. Travaux Publics.
P A S C A L. V.4 Sciences de la Terre.
Petroleum - Energy Business News Index.
R A P R A Abstracts.
Safety and Health at Work.
Securite et Sante au Travail.
Technical Literature Abstracts.
Technical Literature Abstracts: Catalysts -
    Zeolites.
Technical Literature Abstracts: Fuel
    Reformulation.
Technical Literature Abstracts: Oilfield Chemicals.
Technical Literature Abstracts: Tribology.
Travail et Emploi.
Welding Abstracts.

UNITED COMMUNICATIONS GROUP
11300 Rockville Pike, Ste. 1100, Rockville, MD
20852. Tel: 301-816-8950
Fax: 301-816-8945.
    Commerce Business Daily. *(CBD OnLine)*
    Oil Price Information Service. *(PETROSCAN)*

UNIVERSITY MICROFILMS INTERNATIONAL
300 N. Zeeb Rd., Ann Arbor, MI 48106. Tel: 313-
761-4700
Fax: 313-761-1203.
    A B A Bank Compliance.
    A B A Banking Journal.
    A B A Journal.
    A B I - INFORM.
    A C A Journal.
    A C A News.
    A G A Gas Energy Review.
    Academy of Management. Journal.
    Academy of Management Executive.
    Academy of Management Review.
    Accent on Living.
    Accountancy.
    Accounting and Finance.
    Accounting Education News.
    Accounting Historians Journal.
    Accounting Horizons.
    Accounting Technology.
    Accounting Today.
    Across the Board.
    Adhesives Age.
    Administrative Science Quarterly.
    Adolescence.
    Advanced Management Journal.
    Africa Report.
    Africa Today.

African American Review.
African Arts.
Agency Sales.
Agri Finance.
Agri Marketing.
Agricultural Research.
Air Transport World.
Airfinance Journal.
Alaska Journal of Commerce & Pacific Rim
  Reporter.
Alcohol Health & Research World.
America.
American Advertising.
American Agent and Broker.
American City & County.
American Craft.
American Demographics.
American Dietetic Association. Journal.
American Economist.
American Enterprise.
American Fitness.
American Forests.
American Gas.
American Historical Review.
American Journal of Agricultural Economics.
American Journal of Clinical Nutrition.
American Journal of Economics and Sociology.
American Journal of Nursing.
American Journal of Psychiatry.
American Journal of Psychotherapy.
American Journal of Public Health.
American Journal of Sports Medicine.
American Legion Magazine.
American Music Teacher.
American Oriental Society. Journal.
American Planning Association. Journal.
American Poetry Review.
American Political Science Review.
American Printer.
American Record Guide.
American Rehabilitation.
American Review of Public Administration.
American Rifleman.
American Salesman.
American Society for Information Science.
  Bulletin.
American Society of C L U & Ch F C. Journal.
American Sociological Review.
American Taxation Association. Journal.
American Theatre.
American Visions.
Americas.
America's Community Banker.
Amicus Journal.
Annual Review of Psychology.
Annual Review of Sociology.
Antioch Review.
Apparel Industry Magazine.
Appliance Manufacturer.
Appraisal Journal.
Arab Studies Quarterly.
Architectural Review.
Argumentation & Advocacy.
Arkansas Business and Economic Review.
Armed Forces and Society.
Armed Forces Comptroller.
Arms Control Today.
Art Bulletin.
Art in America.
Art Journal (Year).
Arts Education Policy Review.
Asia - Pacific Journal of Management.
Asiamoney.
Asian Business.
Asian Survey.
Asset Finance and Leasing Digest.
Association for Computing Machinery.
  Communications.
Association Management.
Astronomy.
Attorney - C P A.
Auditing.
Audubon.
Austin Business Journal.
Australian Accountant.
Australian Economic Review.
Automotive Production.
AZ B - Arizona Business.
B M J.
Backpacker.
Bank Loan Report.
Bank Management.
Bank Marketing.
Bank News.
Bank of Canada. Review.
Bank Operations Bulletin.
Bank Personnel News.
Bank Systems & Technology.

Bank Technology News.
The Banker.
Bankers Research.
Banking Technology.
Barclays Economic Review.
Behavioral Health Management.
Benefits Quarterly.
Best's Review. Life - Health Insurance Edition.
Best's Review. Property - Casualty Insurance
  Edition.
Better Homes and Gardens.
Better Nutrition.
Beverage World (English Edition).
Bicycling.
BioCycle.
Biological Bulletin.
BioScience.
Birmingham Business.
The Black Collegian.
Black Enterprise.
Black Scholar.
Boating.
Bobbin.
Boston Business Journal.
British Journal of Psychology.
Brokers' Monthly & Insurance Adviser.
Brookings Review.
Brunswick Business Journal.
Buildings.
Bukkyo Daigaku Shinrigaku Kenkyujo Kiyo.
Bulletin of the Atomic Scientists.
Business America.
Business Credit.
Business Economics.
Business Forum (Los Angeles).
Business History Review.
Business in Broward.
Business Journal of Upper East Tennessee and
  Southwest Virginia.
Business Journal Serving Greater Milwaukee.
Business Mexico.
Business North Carolina.
Business People Magazine.
Business Quarterly.
Business Record (Des Moines).
C D - R O M Professional.
C F O.
C P A Client Bulletin.
C P A Letter.
California Management Review.
Campaigns and Elections.
Canadian Banker.
Canadian Business Review.
Canadian Geographic.
Canadian Journal of Administrative Sciences.
Canadian Journal of Criminology.
Canadian Journal of History.
Canadian Literature.
Canadian Manager.
Canadian Shareowner.
Canadian Treasury Management Review.
Canadian Underwriter.
Capacity Management Review.
Car and Driver.
Career Development Quarterly.
Catalog Age.
Cato Journal.
Cellular Business.
Central European
Central New York Business Journal.
Central Penn Business Journal.
Ceramics Monthly.
Chain Store Age.
Chartered Property and Casualty Underwriters
  Society Journal.
Chemical Marketing Reporter.
Childhood Education.
Children Today.
China Business Review.
China Quarterly.
Christian Century.
Christianity Today
The Chronicle of Higher Education.
Church History.
Cineaste.
Club Management
Coast Business.
College English.
Colorado Springs Business Journal.
Columbia Journalism Review.
Common Cause Magazine.
Commonweal.
Communication Education.
Communication Monographs.
Communication Quarterly.
Communication Studies.
Communication World.
Communications and the Law.

Communications International.
Comparative Drama.
Comparative Economic Studies.
Comparative Literature.
Compensation and Benefits Review.
Computer Security Journal.
Computer Technology Review.
Computers in Libraries.
Construction Review.
Consultants News.
Consumer Policy Review.
Consumer's Research Magazine.
Contemporary Literature.
Contemporary Sociology.
Controllers Update.
The Cornell Hotel & Restaurant Administration
  Quarterly.
Corporate Cashflow.
Corporate Detroit Magazine.
Corporate Growth Report.
Corporate Location.
Corporate Report Minnesota.
Corporate Report Ventures
Corporate Report Wisconsin.
Corrections Today.
Cost Engineering (Morgantown).
Cost Management Update.
Credit Card Management.
Credit Card News.
Credit Control.
Credit Union Management.
Credit World.
Crime & Delinquency.
Criminology.
Critical Studies in Mass Communication.
Criticism.
Critique: Studies in Modern Fiction.
Current Health 2.
Cycle World.
D B.
Dance Magazine.
Database (Wilton).
Dayton Business Reporter.
Delaware Business Review.
Dental Economics.
Detroiter.
Diogenes (English Edition).
Direct Marketing.
Directors & Boards.
Disclosure (Chicago).
Down Beat.
Drug and Cosmetic Industry
Drug Topics.
Duluthian.
E B Quarterly.
E P A Journal.
Early American Literature.
Earth Island Journal.
East Asian Executive Reports.
East European Quarterly.
Eastern Economic Journal.
Ebony.
Ecological Monographs.
Ecology.
Economic Commentary.
Economic Development Review.
Economic Geography.
Economic Perspectives (Chicago).
Economic Record.
Economic Review.
Economist.
Ecumenical Review.
Edmonton Chamber of Commerce. Commerce
  News.
The Education Digest.
Educational Leadership.
Educational Record.
Ekistics.
Electric Perspectives.
The Electricity Journal.
Electronic Learning.
Employee Benefit Plan Review.
Engineering Economist.
English Journal.
Enterprise (New York).
Entrepreneurship: Theory and Practice.
Environment (Washington).
Environmental Action.
Environmental Management Today.
Equal Opportunities Review.
Equipment Leasing Today.
Essays in Literature.
ETC.
Ethnology.
Euromoney.
The European Business Journal.
European Industrial Relations Review.
Euroweek.

Evansville Business Journal.
Exceptional Children.
Exceptional Parent.
Executive Accountant.
Executive Excellence.
Executive Report.
Executive Speeches.
The Explicator.
F B I Law Enforcement Bulletin.
F D A Consumer.
Facilities Design and Management.
Fairfield County Business Journal.
Families in Society.
The Family Handyman.
Family Planning Perspectives.
Family Relations.
Federal Reserve Bank of Minneapolis. Quarterly
    Review.
Federal Reserve Bank of New York. Economic
    Policy Review.
Federal Reserve Bank of Philadelphia. Business
    Review.
Federal Reserve Bank of St. Louis. Review.
Federal Reserve Bank of San Francisco. Economic
    Review.
Federal Reserve Bulletin.
Fedgazette: Federal Reserve Bank of Minneapolis
    Regional Business & Economics Newspaper.
Feminist Studies.
Field & Stream.
Film Comment.
Finance and Development.
Financial Analysts Journal.
Financial Executive.
Financial Management.
Financial Market Trends.
Financial Marketing Update.
Financial Markets, Institutions and Instruments.
Financial Technology International Bulletin.
Financial World.
Fiscal Studies.
Fleet Equipment.
Florida Trend.
Flower and Garden.
Flying.
Focus (New York, 1950).
Folio (Stamford).
Foreign Affairs.
Foreign Policy (Washington).
Forest Products Journal.
Fortune Magazine.
Foundation News and Commentary.
Franchising World.
Free Inquiry.
French Historical Studies.
Frontiers: a Journal of Women Studies.
Frontiers of Health Services Management.
Frozen Food Age.
Fund Raising Management.
Funds Transfer Report.
The Futurist.
The Geographical Journal.
Geographical Review.
Georgia Trend.
Geriatrics.
Germanic Review.
Gerontologist.
Getting Results...for the Hands-On Manager.
Global Investor.
Going Public - The I P O Reporter.
Government Executive.
Grand Rapids Business Journal.
Greek, Roman and Byzantine Studies.
Ground Water.
Growth and Change.
H R Focus.
H R Magazine.
Harford Business Ledger.
Harper's Magazine.
Harvard Educational Review.
Harvard Journal of Law and Public Policy.
Hastings Center Report.
Hawaii Business.
Health (San Francisco).
Health Affairs.
Health & Social Work.
Health Care Financing Review.
Health Care Management Review.
Health Care Strategic Management.
Health Care Supervisor.
Health Industry Today.
Health Management Technology.
Health Services Research.
Health Systems Review.
Healthcare Executive.
Healthcare Financial Management.
Healthcare Forum Journal.
Hecate.

Herald.
Hispanic Review.
The Historian (East Lansing).
History and Theory.
History Today.
Home Mechanix.
Home Office Computing.
Hoosier Banker.
Horticulture.
Hospital & Health Services Administration.
Hospital Materials Management.
Hospital Materiel Management Quarterly.
Hospitals and Health Networks.
Human Biology (Detroit).
Human Relations.
Human Resource Planning.
Human Systems Management.
The Humanist.
Hypatia.
I I E Solutions.
I N F O R Journal.
I P A Review.
Illinois Business Review.
Incentive (Akron).
Independent Banker.
Independent Energy.
Indiana Business Magazine.
Indiana Business Review.
Indianapolis Business Journal.
Industrial Management.
Industry Week.
Information Technology and Libraries.
Information Today.
InfoWorld.
Insurance and Technology.
Insurance Systems Bulletin.
Internal Auditor.
International Bulletin of Missionary Research.
International Business.
International Commercial Litigation.
International Financial Law Review.
International Insurance Monitor.
International Journal of Government Auditing.
International Journal of Purchasing & Materials
    Management.
International Journal of Social Psychiatry.
International Labour Review.
International Migration Review.
International Monetary Fund. Staff Papers.
International Review of Mission.
International Small Business Journal.
International Studies of Management and
    Organization.
International Tax Digest.
International Tax Report.
International Tax Review.
International Trade Forum.
Interpreter (Nashville).
Investment Dealers' Digest.
Issues in Accounting Education.
Issues in Science and Technology.
J E I.
Japan Quarterly.
Jet.
The Journal (Columbus).
Journal for Quality and Participation.
Journal for the Scientific Study of Religion.
Journal of Accountancy.
Journal of Accounting Literature.
Journal of Advertising.
Journal of Advertising Research.
Journal of Agricultural Lending.
Journal of American Culture.
Journal of American History.
Journal of Asian Studies.
Journal of Bank Cost & Management Accounting.
Journal of Broadcasting and Electronic Media.
Journal of Business (Spokane).
Journal of Business Communication.
Journal of Business Ethics.
Journal of Business Forecasting Methods and
    Systems.
Journal of Business Logistics.
Journal of Business Strategy.
Journal of Career Planning & Employment.
Journal of Chemical Education.
Journal of Clinical Psychology.
Journal of Communication.
Journal of Comparative Family Studies.
Journal of Consumer Affairs.
Journal of Counseling & Development.
The Journal of Credit & Risk Management.
Journal of Criminal Law & Criminology.
The Journal of Development Studies.
Journal of Education for Business.
Journal of Environmental Health.
Journal of European Studies.
Journal of Financial Planning Today.

The Journal of General Psychology.
The Journal of Genetic Psychology.
Journal of Health and Social Behavior.
Journal of Health Care Finance.
Journal of Health Care Marketing.
Journal of Higher Education.
Journal of Human Resources.
Journal of Insurance Regulation.
Journal of Interamerican Studies and World
    Affairs.
Journal of International Affairs.
Journal of International Business Studies.
Journal of Leisure Research.
Journal of Macromarketing.
Journal of Management Accounting Research.
Journal of Management Consulting.
Journal of Management Information Systems.
Journal of Manufacturing Systems.
Journal of Marital and Family Therapy.
Journal of Marketing.
Journal of Marriage and the Family.
Journal of Medical Ethics.
Journal of Military History.
Journal of Negro Education.
Journal of Parapsychology.
Journal of Physical Education, Recreation and
    Dance.
Journal of Popular Culture.
Journal of Popular Film and Television.
Journal of Post Keynesian Economics.
Journal of Property Management.
Journal of Public Policy & Marketing.
Journal of Rehabilitation.
Journal of Rehabilitation Research and
    Development.
Journal of Religious Thought.
Journal of School Health.
Journal of Sex Research.
Journal of Small Business Management.
Journal of Social History.
Journal of Social Issues.
Journal of Social, Political and Economic Studies.
The Journal of Social Psychology.
Journal of Soil and Water Conservation.
Journal of Sport Behavior.
Journal of Systems Management.
Journal of Travel Research.
Journal of Women's History.
Journal of Youth and Adolescence.
Journalism and Mass Communication Educator.
Journalism History.
Journals of Gerontology. Series A: Biological
    Sciences & Medical Sciences.
Journals of Gerontology. Series B: Psychological
    Sciences & Social Sciences.
Judaism.
Kentucky Banker.
The Kentucky Manufacturer.
Kexue (Shanghai).
Kiplinger's Personal Finance Magazine.
Kyklos.
L I M R A's MarketFacts.
Lafayette Business Digest.
Lakewood Report on Positive Employee Practices.
Lambda Book Report.
The Lancet.
Lane Report.
Language Arts.
Las Vegas Business Press.
Latin American Research Review.
Legal Assistant Today.
Life (New York).
Link-Up.
Literary Review.
Lodging Hospitality.
Logistics and Transportation Review.
Los Angeles.
Louisville Magazine.
M E L U S.
M I S Quarterly.
Machine Design.
The McKinsey Quarterly.
Maclean's.
MacWorld.
Maine Times.
Manage.
Management Accounting.
Management Accounting.
Management International Review.
Management Quarterly.
Management Review.
Management Services.
Management Today.
Manager's Magazine.
Managing Intellectual Property.
Managing Office Technology.
Manufacturing Engineering.
Marketing Management.

Marketing News.
Marketing Research.
Marketing Week.
Marketplace Magazine.
Massachusetts C P A Review.
Massachusetts Review.
Material Handling Engineering.
Mechanical Engineering.
MediaWeek.
Medical Letter on Drugs and Therapeutics
    (English Edition).
Medical Marketing & Media.
Medium Aevum.
Memphis Business Journal.
Men's Health.
Mercer Business Magazine.
Mergers & Acquisitions.
Mergers & Acquisitions Report.
Metropolitan Home.
Michigan C P A.
Mid-America Commerce & Industry.
Mid-American Journal of Business.
Middle East Executive Reports.
Middle East Journal.
Middle Eastern Studies.
Middlesex Magazine.
Midwest Quarterly.
Migration World.
The Mineralogical Record.
The Mississippi Quarterly.
Modern Drama.
Modern Maturity.
Modern Paint and Coatings.
Money (New York).
Montana Business Quarterly.
Monthly Labor Review.
Monthly Review.
Mortgage-Backed Securities Letter.
Mother Earth News.
Mpls. - St. Paul Magazine.
Multinational Business Review.
N C A H F Newsletter.
N E A Today.
N P News.
Nashville Business Journal.
National Civic Review.
National Contract Management Journal.
National Forum (Auburn).
National Institute Economic Review.
National Journal.
National Mortgage News.
National Parks.
National Public Accountant.
National Real Estate Investor.
National Underwriter. Life and Health - Health &
    Financial Services Edition.
National Underwriter. Property & Casualty - Risk
    & Benefits Management Edition.
Nation's Business.
Nation's Restaurant News.
Natural History.
Network World.
New Accountant.
New Hampshire Business Review.
New Jersey Business.
New Mexico Business Journal.
New Orleans CityBusiness.
New Orleans Magazine.
New Perspectives Quarterly.
The New Republic.
New Statesman.
New York Review of Books.
New York State Conservationist.
The New York Times.
New Zealand Manufacturer (Wellington, 1992).
News Photographer.
Newspaper Research Journal.
Nieman Reports.
Nonprofit World.
The North American Review.
Northern Ontario Business.
Novel: A Forum on Fiction.
Nursing Homes.
Nutrition Action Healthletter.
Nutrition Reviews.
O E C D Economic Outlook.
O E C D Observer.
Occupational Hazards.
Occupational Health & Safety.
Occupational Outlook Quarterly.
Oceania.
The Ohio C P A Journal.
Oil and Gas Investor.
Oil & Gas Journal.
Opera News.
Orange County Business Journal.
Organic Gardening.
Organization Studies.

Organizationa Dynamics.
Origination News.
Outdoor Life.
Outlook.
Outstate Business.
P M L A.
P O S News.
Pacific Affairs.
Papers on Language and Literature.
Paris Review.
Parks and Recreation.
Patient Care.
Payment Systems Report.
Payment Systems Worldwide.
Peacekeeping & International Relations.
Pennsylvania Business and Technology.
Pennsylvania C P A Journal.
People Weekly.
Performing Arts and Entertainment in Canada.
Periodical Abstracts.
Personnel Journal.
Personnel Psychology.
Pharmaceutical Executive.
Phi Delta Kappan.
Philadelphia Business Journal.
Philosophy and Public Affairs.
Pittsburgh Business Times - Journal.
Ploughshares.
Plymouth County Business Review.
Policy Studies Journal.
Political Science Quarterly.
Popular Photography.
Popular Science.
The Practical Accountant.
The Practical Lawyer.
The Practical Litigator.
The Practical Real Estate Lawyer.
The Practical Tax Lawyer.
Practicing C P A.
Presidential Studies Quarterly.
Prevention.
Printed Circuit Design.
Production and Inventory Management Journal.
Professional Safety.
Progressive (Madison).
Progressive Grocer.
The Psychological Record.
Psychology Today.
Public Administration Quarterly.
Public Administration Review.
Public Budgeting and Finance.
Public Health Reports.
Public Interest.
Public Management.
Public Productivity and Management Review.
Public Relations Quarterly.
Public Roads.
Public Utilities Fortnightly.
Public Welfare.
Pueblo Business Journal.
Pulp and Paper.
Quality Progress.
R N.
Railway Age.
Real Estate Finance.
Real Estate Finance Today.
Real Estate Issues.
Real Property, Probate and Trust Journal.
Records Management Quarterly.
Renaissance Quarterly.
Research in African Literatures.
Research Quarterly for Exercise and Sport.
Restaurant Business.
Restaurant Hospitality.
Review of Black Political Economy.
Review of Business.
The Review of Contemporary Fiction.
Review of Educational Research.
Review of Public Personnel Administration.
Risk Management.
Road & Track.
Rough Notes.
Royal Anthropological Institute. Journal.
Runner's World.
Rural Telecommunications.
Russian and East European Finance and Trade.
The Russian Review.
Russian Social Science Review.
St. Louis Commerce.
Sales & Marketing Management.
Sales and Marketing Management.
Salmagundi.
San Diego Business Journal.
Satellite Communications.
Saturday Evening Post.
Saturday Night.
Savannah Business Journal.
Scholastic Update.

Science.
Science & Society.
Science News.
The Sciences.
Sea Frontiers.
Secured Lender.
Security Management.
The Service Industries Journal.
Shakespeare Quarterly.
Sierra.
Skiing.
Sky and Telescope.
Sloan Management Review.
Small Business News - Akron.
Small Business News - Cleveland.
Social Forces.
Social Policy.
Social Problems.
Social Research.
Social Sciences Index. *(PROQUEST)*
Social Security Bulletin.
The Social Studies.
Social Work.
Society of Research Administrators. Journal.
Sociology.
Sociology of Education.
Sociology of Religion.
Software Magazine.
South African Food & Beverage Manufacturing
    Review.
South Dakota Business Review.
Southern California Business.
The Southern Review.
Southwest Review.
Spectrum (Lexington).
Sporting Goods Business.
The Sporting News.
Sports Illustrated.
Springfield Business Journal.
Stamps.
Standard Federal Tax Reports.
The State Journal.
State Tax Review.
Stereo Review.
Stores.
Studies in English Literature 1500-1900.
Studies in Philology.
Studies in Short Fiction.
Studies in the Novel.
Style (DeKalb).
Successful Farming.
Successful Meetings.
Suicide and Life-Threatening Behavior.
Supervision.
Survey of Business.
Survey of Current Business.
T C I.
The Tax Adviser.
The Tax Executive.
Tax Management Compensation Planning
    Journal.
Tax Management Estates, Gifts and Trusts
    Journal.
Tax Management Financial Planning Journal.
Tax Management International Journal.
Tax Management Memorandum.
Tax Management Real Estate Journal.
Taxes (Riverwoods).
Teachers College Record.
Technical Communication.
Technology and Learning.
Technology Review.
Telecommunications (North American Edition).
Telecommunications Americas.
Telecommunications International.
Telephony.
Telesis (Ottawa).
Texas Banking.
Texas Monthly.
Textile World.
Theological Studies.
Time.
Times (Bethlehem).
Toledo Business Journal.
Total Health.
Trailer Boats.
Training.
Transmission and Distribution.
Transportation & Distribution.
Transportation Journal.
TriQuarterly.
Trust Letter.
Trustee.
Trusts and Estates.
Tufts University Diet and Nutrition Letter.
Twentieth Century Literature.
U N Chronicle.
U S A Today.

U S Banker.
U S News & World Report.
Unitas.
University of California at Berkeley Wellness
  Letter.
UNIX Review.
Upside.
Vermont Business Magazine.
Victorian Studies.
Video Review.
Virginia Magazine of History and Biography.
Vital Speeches of the Day.
W I N News.
Wall Street & Technology.
Ward's Auto World.
Warfield's Business Record.
Washington and Lee Law Review.
The Washington Monthly.
Water Engineering and Management.
Weatherwise.
Wenatchee Business Journal.
Westchester County Business Journal.
Western Journal of Communication.
Whole Earth Review.
Wilderness.
Wilson Quarterly.
Wilson Social Sciences Abstracts. *(PROQUEST)*
Woman's Day.
Women and Environments.
Women's Review of Books.
Women's Sports and Fitness.
Wood Technology.
Work and Occupations.
Workbench.
Worklife Report.
World Affairs (Washington).
World Bank Research Observer.
World Health.
World Literature Today.
World Policy Journal.
World Press Review.
World Trade.
World Wastes.
World Watch.
The Writer.
Writer's Digest.

VU/TEXT INFORMATION SERVICES, INC. (Subsidiary
of: Knight-Ridder, Inc.)
325 Chestnut St., Suite 1300, Philadelphia, PA
19106. Tel: 215-574-4400
2852 Bluebill Dr., Virginia Beach, VA 23456. Tel:
215-665-3300Fax: 215-627-0195.
  Arizona Business Gazette.
  Campaign.
  Discover (Burbank).
  The Economist.
  Entertainment Weekly.
  Fortune Magazine.
  Journal of Commerce and Commercial.
  Marketing.
  Money (New York).
  New Scientist.
  News Library News.
  People Weekly.
  Sports Illustrated.
  Time.
  U S A Today.
  W R R I News.
  Wall Street Transcript.

WEST SERVICES, INC. (Subsidiary of: West
Publishing Co.)
620 Opperman Dr., Eagan, MN 55123. Tel: 612-
687-5604
  A B A Journal.
  Alabama Law Review.
  Alabama Lawyer.
  Albany Law Review.
  Alternatives to the High Cost of Litigation.
  American Criminal Law Review. *(ACRIMLREV)*
  American Indian Law Review.
  American Journal of Law & Medicine.
  American Journal of Legal History.
  American Journal of Tax Policy.
  American University Law Review.
  Americans with Disabilities Cases. *(FLB-CS,
    MLRR-CS)*
  Antitrust. *(ANTITR)*
  Antitrust & Trade Regulation Report. *(BNA-
    ATRR)*
  Antitrust Law Journal. *(ANTITRLJ)*
  Arizona State Law Journal.
  Army Lawyer.
  B L A S T.
  B N A Pension & Benefits Reporter. *(BNA-PEN)*

B N A's Americans with Disabilities Act Manual
  and Cases. *(FLB-CS, MLRR-CS)*
B N A's Banking Report. *(BNA-BNK)*
B N A's Patent, Trademark & Copyright Journal.
  (BNA-PTCJ)
Beverly Hills Bar Association Journal.
Boston College Law Review.
Boston University International Law Journal.
Boston University Law Review.
Brigham Young University Law Review.
Brooklyn Journal of International Law.
Buffalo Law Review.
Business Lawyer. *(BUSLAW)*
C B A Record.
Campbell Law Review.
Capital University Law Review.
Chemical Regulation Reporter.
Chicago - Kent Law Review.
Chicano - Latino Law Review.
Cincinnati Law Review.
Cleveland State Law Review.
Collective Bargaining Negotiations & Contracts.
Columbia Journal of Law and Social Problems.
Columbia Journal of Transnational Law.
Columbia Law Review.
Computer Counsel.
Computer Lawyer.
Connecticut Law Review.
Constitutional Commentary.
Cornell International Law Journal.
Cornell Journal of Law and Public Policy.
Cornell Law Review.
Creighton Law Review.
Criminal Justice Abstracts.
Cumberland Law Review.
Current Law Index.
Daily Labor Report. *(BNA-DLR)*
Daily Report for Executives. *(BNA-DER)*
Daily Tax Report. *(BNA-DTR)*
De Paul Business Law Journal.
Defense Counsel Journal.
Delaware Journal of Corporate Law.
Denver Journal of International Law and Policy.
Denver University Law Review.
Dickinson Journal of International Law.
Dickinson Law Review.
Drake Law Review.
Duke Law Journal.
Duquesne Law Review.
Emory International Law Review.
Emory Law Journal.
Energy Law Journal.
Entertainment & Sports Law Review.
Environment Reporter. *(BNA-ER)*
Environmental Law (Portland).
Environmental Law Reporter.
Estate Planning (New York). *(WGL-ESTPLN)*
Family Advocate. *(FAMADVO)*
Family Law Quarterly. *(FAMLQ)*
Federal Contracts Report.
Federal Lawyer.
Federal Register.
Federal Sentencing Reporter.
Fletcher Forum of World Affairs.
Florida Bar Journal.
Florida Law Review.
Florida State University Law Review.
Fordham Intellectual Property, Media &
  Entertainment Law Journal.
Fordham International Law Journal.
Fordham Law Review.
Fordham Urban Law Journal.
Forensic Services Directory.
George Mason Law Review.
George Washington Journal of International Law
  and Economics.
George Washington Law Review.
Georgetown Immigration Law Journal.
Georgetown International Environmental Law
  Review.
Georgetown Law Journal.
Georgia Journal of International and Comparative
  Law.
Georgia Law Review.
Golden Gate University Law Review.
Government Employee Relations Report.
Gower Federal Service - Mining. *(Gower Federal
  Service)*
Gower Federal Service - Miscellaneous Land
  Decisions. *(Gower Federal Service)*
Gower Federal Service - Oil and Gas. *(Gower
  Federal Service)*
Gower Federal Service - Outer Continental Shelf.
  (Gower Federal Service)
Hamline Law Review.
Harvard Civil Rights - Civil Liberties Law Review.
Harvard Environmental Law Review.
Harvard International Law Journal.

Harvard Journal of Law and Public Policy.
Harvard Journal on Legislation.
Harvard Law Review.
Harvard Women's Law Journal.
Hastings Communications and Entertainment Law
  Journal (Comm - Ent).
Hastings Constitutional Law Quarterly.
Hastings International and Comparative Law
  Review.
Hastings Law Journal.
Hastings Women's Law Journal.
Hofstra Labor Law Journal.
Hofstra Law Review.
Houston Journal of International Law.
Houston Law Review.
Howard Law Journal.
Human Rights. *(HUMRT)*
Idaho Law Review.
Illinois Legal Times.
Index to Legal Periodicals & Books.
Indiana Law Journal.
Indiana Law Review.
Individual Employment Rights. *(File FLB-CS, LRR-
  IERN)*
Insurance Periodicals Index.
Inter-American Law Review.
International Lawyer.
International Trade Reporter. *(BNA-ITR)*
Iowa Law Review.
Issues in Law and Medicine.
John Marshall Law Review.
Journal of Air Law and Commerce.
Journal of Corporation Law.
Journal of Criminal Law & Criminology.
Journal of Energy, Natural Resources and
  Environmental Law.
Journal of Law & Commerce.
Journal of Partnership Taxation. *(WGL JPTAX)*
The Journal of Taxation. *(WGL-JTAX)*
Judicature.
Judicial Conduct Reporter.
Kentucky Law Journal.
Labor - Management Relations Analysis - News
  and Background Information. *(File LLR-NEWS)*
Labor Relations Reference Manual. *(File FLB-CS)*
Labor Relations Reporter.
Labor Relations Reporter. Fair Employment
  Practices.
Labor Relations Reporter. Labor Arbitration and
  Dispute Settlements. *(File LRR-LA)*
Labor Relations Reporter. Wages and Hours.
Law & Business Directory of Corporate Counsel.
Law and Policy in International Business.
Law Office Technology Review.
Law Practice Management.
LegalTrac. *(LRI)*
Litigation.
Louisiana Law Review.
Loyola Law Review.
Loyola of Los Angeles International and
  Comparative Law Journal.
Maine Law Review.
Marquette Law Review.
Maryland Law Review.
Mealey's Emerging Insurance Disputes.
Mealey's Emerging Toxic Torts.
Mealey's Insurance Supplement.
Mealey's International Arbitration Report.
Mealey's Litigation Report: Asbestos.
Mealey's Litigation Report: Bad Faith.
Mealey's Litigation Report: Breast Implants.
Mealey's Litigation Report: Drugs and Medical
  Devices.
Mealey's Litigation Report: Insurance.
Mealey's Litigation Report: Insurance Fraud.
Mealey's Litigation Report: Insurance Insolvency.
Mealey's Litigation Report: Intellectual Property.
Mealey's Litigation Report: Lead.
Mealey's Litigation Report: Patents.
Mealey's Litigation Report: Pedicle Screws.
Mealey's Litigation Report: Reinsurance.
Mealey's Litigation Report: Superfund.
Mealey's Litigation Report: Tobacco.
Mercer Law Review.
Michigan Bar Journal.
Michigan Law Review.
Military Law Review.
Minnesota Law Review.
Mississippi College Law Review.
Mississippi Law Journal.
Missouri Law Review.
Natural Resources & Environment.
Nebraska Law Review.
Nevada Lawyer.
New England Law Review.
New Jersey Lawyer (New Brunswick).
New Mexico Law Review.
New York State Bar Journal. *(NYSTBJ)*

New York University Law Review.
North Carolina Journal of International Law and
  Commercial Regulation.
North Carolina Law Review.
North Dakota Law Review.
Northern Kentucky Law Review.
Northwestern Journal of International Law &
  Business.
Northwestern University Law Review.
Notre Dame Law Review.
Nova Law Review.
Ohio State Journal on Dispute Resolution.
Ohio State Law Journal.
Oklahoma City University Law Review.
Oklahoma Law Review.
Oregon Law Review.
Pacific Law Journal.
Pepperdine Law Review.
Preview of United States Supreme Court Cases.
Probate & Property.
Public Contract Law Journal.
Public Utilities Fortnightly.
Public Utilities Reports.
Quinnipiac Law Review.
Real Property, Probate and Trust Journal.
Risk: Health, Safety & Environment.
S E C Docket.
S E C News Digest.
Saint Louis University Law Journal.
St. Thomas Law Review.
Santa Clara Law Review.
Scribes Journal of Legal Writing.
Seattle University Law Review.
Securities Regulation & Law Report. (BNA-SRLR)
Seton Hall Legislative Journal.
South Carolina Law Review.
South Dakota Law Review.
South Texas Law Review.
Southern Illinois University Law Journal.
Southwestern Law Journal.
Stanford Journal of International Law.
Stanford Law & Policy Review.
Stanford Law Review.
State Capitals. Civil Rights.
State Capitals. Environmental Regulation.
State Capitals. Insurance Regulation.
State Capitals. Public Utilities.
State Capitals. Taxation and Revenue Policies.
State Capitals. Taxes - Property.
Stetson Law Review.
Suffolk Transnational Law Review.
Suffolk University Law Review.

Syracuse Journal of International Law &
  Commerce.
Tax Lawyer.
Tax Management Compensation Planning. (File
  TM-CP, TM-CP-OLD, TM-CPJ)
Tax Management Compensation Planning
  Journal. (File TM-CPJ)
Tax Management Estates, Gifts and Trusts. (Files
  TM-EGT, TM-EGT-OLD, TM-EGTJ)
Tax Management Estates, Gifts and Trusts
  Journal. (File TM-EGTJ)
Tax Management Foreign Income Portfolios. (File
  TM-FOR)
Tax Management Memorandum. (File TM-TMM)
Tax Management Real Estate. (Files TM-RE, TM-
  RE-OLD, TM-REJ)
Tax Management Real Estate Journal. (File TM-REJ)
Tax Management U S Income. (Files TM-US, TM-
  US-OLD, TM-TMWR)
Tax Management Weekly Report. (File TM-TMWR)
Temple Law Review.
Tennessee Bar Journal.
Tennessee Law Review.
Texas Journal of Women and the Law.
Texas Tech Law Review.
Thurgood Marshall Law Review.
Tort & Insurance Law Journal.
Transportation Law Journal.
Tulane Environmental Law Journal.
Tulane Law Review.
Tulane Maritime Law Journal.
Tulsa Law Journal.
U C Davis Law Review.
United States Law Week.
United States Tax Court Reports.
University of Baltimore Law Review.
University of Chicago Legal Forum.
University of Colorado Law Review.
University of Dayton Law Review.
University of Illinois Law Review.
University of Kansas Law Review.
University of New Brunswick Law Journal.
University of Pennsylvania Journal of International
  Economic Law.
University of Pittsburgh Law Review.
University of Richmond Law Review.
University of San Francisco Law Review.
Utah Law Review.
Valparaiso University Law Review.
Vanderbilt Journal of Transnational Law.
Vanderbilt Law Review.
Villanova Law Review.
Virginia Environmental Law Journal.

Virginia Journal of International Law.
Virginia Law Review.
Virginia Tax Review.
Washington and Lee Law Review.
Washington Law Review.
Washington University Law Quarterly.
Wayne Law Review.
William Mitchell Law Review.
Wisconsin Law Review.
Yale Journal on Regulation.

WILSONLINE (Subsidiary of: H W. Wilson
  Co.)
  950 University Ave., Bronx, NY 10452. Tel: 718-
  588-8400
  Fax: 718-538-2746.
  Albany Law Review.
  Applied Science & Technology Index. (AST)
  Art Index. (File ART)
  Bibliographic Index. (BIB)
  Biography Index. (File BIC)
  Biological & Agricultural Index.
  Book Review Digest. (File BRD)
  Business Periodicals Index. (File BPI)
  China Business Review.
  Cumulative Book Index. (File CBI)
  Education Index. (File EDI)
  Essay and General Literature Index. (File EGL)
  General Science Index. (File GSI)
  Humanities Index. (File HUM)
  I R S Publications.
  Index to Legal Periodicals & Books. (File ILP)
  Library Literature. (File LIB)
  New York Law Journal.
  Ohio State Journal on Dispute Resolution.
  Ohio State Law Journal.

  Readers' Guide Abstracts. (File RDG)
  Readers' Guide to Periodical Literature. (File
    RDG)
  Rural Libraries.
  Social Sciences Index. (File SSI)
  Vertical File Index. (File VF)
  Wilson Applied Science & Technology Abstracts.
    (AST)
  Wilson Art Abstracts. (File ART)
  Wilson Business Abstracts. (File BPI)
  Wilson Education Abstracts. (File EDI)
  Wilson General Science Abstracts. (File GSI)
  Wilson Humanities Abstracts. (File HUM)
  Wilson Social Sciences Abstracts. (File SSI)

Index to Publications of International Organizations

This index is divided into four sections: publications of international organizations, of international congresses, of the European Communities, and of the United Nations. Numbers refer to the page in the Classified List of Serials where the full entry appears.

INTERNATIONAL ORGANIZATIONS

A C A R T S O D Monograph Series. (African Centre for Applied Research and Training in Social Development) 1300

A C A R T S O D Newsletter. (African Centre for Applied Research and Training in Social Development) 1300

A D B Quarterly Review. (Asian Development Bank) 1300

A I L A Bulletin. (Association Internationale de Linguistique Appliquee) 4047

A P O Annual Report. (Asian Productivity Organization) 1513

A P O News. (Asian Productivity Organization) 1513

A S A I H L Seminar Reports. (Association of Southeast Asian Institutions of Higher Learning) 2418

A S E A N Economic Info View. (Association of South East Asian Nations) 1301

A S I F A News. (Association Internationale du Film d'Animation) 5092

A T A - I A T A Reservations Interline Message Procedures - Passenger. 6748

Academy of European Law. Collected Courses/ Academie de Droit Europeen. Recueil des Cours. 3921

Across the Oceans. 2290

Acta Astronautica. 51

Acta Colloquii Didactici Classici. 4048

Acta Crystallographica. Section A: Foundations of Crystallography. 1725

Acta Crystallographica. Section B: Structural Science. 1725

Acta Crystallographica. Section C: Crystal Structure Communications. 1725

Acta Crystallographica. Section D: Biological Crystallography. 1725

Acta Cytologica. 710

Acta Geneticae Medicae et Gemellologiae: Twin Research. 4418

Acta Haematologica. 4697

Acta Horticulturae. 3042

Acta Musicologica. 5137

Acta Oncologica. 4747

Acta Radiologica. 4872

The Adelphi Papers. 5740

Advances in Limnology/Ergebnisse der Limnologie. 2284

Advances in Space Research. 52

Aerospace U F O News. 54

Africa Media Monograph Series. 3700

Africa Media Review. 1895

African Development Bank. Report by the Board of Directors/Banque Africaine de Developpement. Rapport du Conseil d'Administration. 1301

African Development Fund. Annual Report/Fonds Africain de Developpement. Rapport Annuel. 1301

African Journal of Plant Protection/Revue Africaine de la Protection des Vegetaux. 208

African Livestock Research. 262

African News Sheet. 3639

African Tax Systems. 1534

Africom. 1895

Afro Asian Economic Review. 1301

Afro-Asian Publications. 3370

Agroforestry Systems. 93

Air Waybill Handbook. 6750

Airline Advertising Project. 31

Airline Coding Directory. 6750

Airline Economic Results and Prospects. 6750

Airport Handling Manual. 6751

Al-Akademiyyah al-Arabiyyah lil-Ulum wal-Teknologia. Majallah/Arab Academy for Science and Technology. Journal. 6225

Alcoholism. 2194

Allergy & Clinical Immunology International. 4578

Aluminium Industry Abstracts. 4980

America Cooperativa. 1157

Americas. 3607

Amnesty International Report. 5741

Amphibia Reptilia. 797

Anales Galdosianos. 4181

Analytical and Quantitative Cytology and Histology. 711

Analytical Cellular Pathology. 711

Anatomia, Histologia, Embryologia. 6941

Anciens Pays et Assemblees d'Etats. 5633

Andrologia. 4426

Anesthesia and Analgesia. 4590

Animals International. 295

Annals of Glaciology. 2224

Annals of Oncology. 4748

Annals of Public and Cooperative Economics. 1157

L'Annee Hippique. 6543

L'Annee Philologique. 1827

Annotated Bibliography of Literature on Cooperative Movements in South-East Asia. 516

Annuaire des Arachnologistes Mondiaux 720

Annuaire des Centres de Recherche Demographique/ Directory of Demographic Research Centers. 5780

Annuaire Economique des Pays Membres de l'Organisation de l'Unite Africaine/Economic Yearbook of Member States of the Organization of African Unity. 1174

Annual Bibliography of the History of the Printed Book and Library. 5820

Annual Report on International Statistics. 6585

Annual Report on the Results of Treatment in Gynecological Cancer. 4748

Anthos. 382

Antiviral Research. 753

Anuario Estadistico Centroamericano de Comercio Exterior. 974

Anuario Interamericano de Derechos Humanos/Inter-American Yearbook on Human Rights. 3922

Apiacta. 97

Applied Geochemistry. 2224

Applied Numerical Mathematics. 4407

Aqua. 6962

Aquatic Mammals. 798

Arab Journal of Language Studies/Al-Majallah al-'Arabiyyah lil-Dirasat al-Lughawiyyah. 4053

Arab League Educational, Scientific, and Cultural Organization. Information Newsletter. 2312

Arab Petroleum. 5349

Arab Struggle. 3494

Archiv fuer Rechts- und Sozialphilosophie/Archives de Philosophie du Droit et de Philosophie Sociale/Archives for Philosophy of Law and Social Philosophy. 5467

Archiv fuer Rechts- und Sozialphilosophie. Beihefte. 5467

Archiv fuer Religionspsychologie. 6044

Artificial Intelligence Communications. 2005

Asia - Pacific Scouting. 1760

Asia - Pacific Tax Bulletin. 1534

Asian and Pacific Council. Food and Fertilizer Technology Center. Extension - Technical Bulletin. 98

Asian and Pacific Labour. 3717

Asian Development Bank. Annual Report. 1060

Asian Development Bank. Board of Governors. Summary of Proceedings. 1302

Asian Development Bank. Key Indicators of Developing Asian and Pacific Countries. 1060

Asian Development Bank. Statistical Report Series. 975

Asian Institute of Technology. Annual Research and Activities Report. 6646

Asian News Sheet. 3640

Asian Peoples' Anti-Communist League. Charts About Chinese Communists on the Mainland. 3377

Asociacion. 1760

Asociacion Interamericana de Bibliotecarios, Documentalistas y Especialistas en Informacion Agricola. Boletin Especial. 99

Asociacion Interamericana de Bibliotecarios, Documentalistas y Especialistas en Informacion Agricola. Boletin Informativo. 3975

Association Internationale d'Etudes du Sud-Est Europeen. Bulletin. 3395

Association Internationale d'Etudes Patristiques. Bulletin d'Information et de Liaison. 6045

Association Internationale de Signalisation Maritime. Bulletin/I A L A Bulletin. 6829

Association Internationale pour l'Histoire du Verre. Bulletin. 1652

Association of Commonwealth Universities. Annual Report of the Council Together with the Accounts of the Association. 2420

Association of Institutes for European Studies. Annuaire. 3395

Association of Institutes for European Studies. Year-Book. 3395

Association of Southeast Asian Institutions of Higher Learning. Newsletter. 2420

Atherosclerosis. 4596

Atlantic Series. 5742

Audiology. 4795

Automatic Identification in the Airline Industry Handbook. 6752

Automatica. 2012

Automation in Construction. 2012

Aviation Regulatory Watch Group Reports. 6752

B I C - Code. (Bureau International des Containers) 5298

B I R D. (Base d'Information Robert-Debre) 1782

B S P Data Interchange Specifications Handbook. 1061

Babel. 4055

Bank for International Settlements. Annual Report. 1064

Bank Settlement Plan Quick Reference Handbook. 1067

Behavioral Ecology. 570

Benelux Economic Union. Conseil Central de l'Economie. Rapport du Secretaire sur l'Activite du Conseil. 1515

Benelux Publikatieblad/Bulletin Benelux. 5893

Bibliographie de la Philosophie/Bibliography of Philosophy. 5507

Bibliographie Internationale de l'Humanisme et de la Renaissance. 3631

Bibliography on Irrigation, Drainage, River Training and Flood Control/Bibliographie de la C I I D. Irrigation, Drainage et Maitrise des Crues. 6983

Bibliography on Soilless Culture. 169

Biochemical Education. 631

Biochemistry and Molecular Biology International. 633

Biofactors. 633

Biology and Fertility of Soils. 213

Biology International: I U B S Newsmagazine. (International Union of Biological Sciences) 574

Biorheology. 653

Blutalkohol. 2195

Boletim Tecnico Interamericano de Formacion Profesional. 2480

Boreas. 2225

Brahmavidya. 6203

Brain Pathology. 4828

Building and Wood. 3718

Building Research and Information. 841

Bulletin de Philosophie Medievale. 5470

Bulletin du Bibliophile. 5991

Bulletin Eucarpia. 675

Bulletin for International Fiscal Documentation. 1536

Bulletin G C I D. (Greek National Committee) 6963

Bulletin of Volcanology. 2271

Bureau International des Societes Gerant les Droits d'Enregistrement et de Reproduction Mecanique. Bulletin. 5809

C A R A P H I N News. (Caribbean Animal and Plant Health Information Network) 104

C C I A Background Information. (World Council of Churches, Commission of the Churches on International Affairs) 6049

C D - Info. (Christian Democrat International) 5638

C E R N Courier. 5593

C E R N - H E R A Reports. 5593

C E R N Reports. 5593

C E R N School of Computing. Proceedings. 6305

C E R N School of Physics. Proceedings. 5593

C I A T in Perspective. (Centro Internacional de Agricultura Tropical) 104

C.I.C.A.E. Bulletin d'Information. (Confederation Internationale des Cinemas d'Art et d'Essai) 5094

C I L E C T News. (Centre International de Liaison des Ecoles de Cinema et de Television) 1956

C I N T E R F O R Estudios y Monografias. (Centro Interamericano de Investigacion y Documentacion sobre Formacion Profesional) 2481

C I R A Bulletin. (Centre International de Recherches sur l'Anarchisme) 5638

C.I.R.P. Annals. 2751

C I S Steel Information. (Commonwealth of Independent States) 4951

C M A S Bulletin d'Information/C M A S Newsletter. (Confederation Mondiale des Activites) 2291

C M I News Letter. (Comite Maritime International) 6831

C M I Year Book. (Comite Maritime International) 6831

C O D E S R I A Book Series. (Council for the Development of Economic and Social Research in Africa (CODESRIA)) 5638

C O N C A W E Review. 2779

C O S P A R Information Bulletin. (Committee on Space Research) 60

CAB International. Abstract Journal. 3030

CAB International. Bureau of Nutrition. Annotated Bibliographies. 5243

Cahiers de Droit Fiscal International. 3925

Cahiers Ligures de Prehistoire et de Protohistoire. 348

Cardiovascular Drugs and Therapy. 4598

Cardiovascular Surgery. 4599

Cargo Agent's Handbook. 6753

Cargo Community Systems Directory and Guidelines. 6753

Cargo Interchange Message Procedures Manual. 6753

Cargo Services Conference Resolutions Manual. 6753

Cargo Tariff Coordinating Conferences Resolutions Manual. 6753

Cargo Today. 6738

Catalogo de Publicaciones Latinoamericanas sobre Formacion Profesional. 2482

Catalogus Musicus. 5147

Catalogus
Translationem et Commentatorium. 4292

Cellular Engineering. 626

Central and East European Tax Directory. 1539

Centre International de Documentation Arachnologique. Liste des Travaux Arachnologiques. 618

Centre International de l'Enfance. Paris. Travaux et Documents. 6408

Centro de Estudios Monetarios Latinoamericanos. Ensayos. 1076

Centro Interamericano de Investigacion y Documentacion sobre Formacion Profesional. Informes. 2482

Centro Interamericano de Investigacion y Documentacion sobre Formacion Profesional. Serie Bibliografica. 2482

Centro Latinoamericano de Economia Humana. Cuadernos. 6318

Chaine/Keten. 295

Chemical Geology. 2205

Chemistry International. 1671

Chemoreception Abstracts. 1707

Child Abuse & Neglect. 1762

Children in the Tropics. 1764

Child's Nervous System. 4831

Chronica Horticulturae. 3047

Chronicle of Parliamentary Elections and Developments. 5641

Chronobiologia. 578

Chronobiology International. 578

Ciencia Interamericana. 6234

Clinical Hemorheology. 4699

Coal Highlights. 2542

Coal Prospects and Policies in I E A Countries. 5060

Coastline. 2292

Colecciones Basicas C I N T E R F O R. 2482

Collection of Documents for the Study of International Non-Governmental Relations. 3925

Colombo Plan Bureau. The Colombo Plan Council Report. 1303

Colombo Plan for Co-operative Economic and Social Development in Asia and the Pacific. Consultative Committee. Proceedings and Conclusions. 1303

Colombo Plan for Co-operative Economic and Social Development in Asia and the Pacific. Development Perspectives. Country Issues Papers by Member Governments to the Consultative Committee. 1303

Colombo Plan Newsletter. 1303

Columbus Logbook. 61

Comite Consultatif pour la Masse et les Grandeurs Apparentees. 5012

Comite International de Cooperation dans les Recherches Nationales en Demographie. Actes des Seminaires. 5782

Comite International de Dachau. Bulletin. 3404

Comite International des Poids et Mesures. Comite Consultatif d'Electricite. (Rapport et Annexes). 5012

Comite International des Poids et Mesures. Comite Consultatif de Photometrie et Radiometrie. (Rapport et Annexes). 5012

Comite International des Poids et Mesures. Comite Consultatif de Thermometrie. Rapports et Annexes. 5012

Comite International des Poids et Mesures. Comite Consultatif des Unites (Rapport et Annexes). 5012

Comite International des Poids et Mesures. Comite Consultatif pour la Definition de la Seconde. (Rapport et Annexes). 5012

Comite International des Poids et Mesures. Comite Consultatif pour la Definition du Metre (Rapport et Annexes). 5012

Comite International des Poids et Mesures. Comite Consultatif pour les Etalons des Mesure des Rayonnements Ionisants (Rapport et Annexes). 5013

Comite International des Poids et Mesures. Proces-Verbaux des Seances. 5013

Comite International des Poids et Mesures. Systeme International d'Unites. 5013

Commission for the Geological Map of the World. Bulletin. 2229

Commonwealth Judicial Journal. 3926

Commonwealth Universities Yearbook. 2424

Communication World. 1411

Comparative History of Literatures in European Languages/Histoire Comparee des Litteratures en Langues Europeennes. 4197

Comparative Labor Law Journal. 1367

Compendium of Tourism Statistics. 6929

Competition Policy n O E C D Countries. 1303

Composers of the Americas/Compositores de America. 5150

CompStat Symposium. Proceedings. (Computational Statistics) 6600

Computational Mechanics Advances. 4408

Computers & Geosciences. 2222

Computers & Security. 2050

Confederacion Latinoamericana de Asociaciones Cristianas de Jovenes. Carta. 6055

Conference de la Haye de Droit International Prive. Actes et Documents/Hague Conference on Private International Law. Proceedings. 3927

Conference Generale des Poids et Mesures. Comptes Rendus des Seances. 5013

Conscience et Liberte. 5726

Consejo Superior Universitario Centroamericano. Actas de la Reunion Ordinaria. 2425

Consumer Policy in O E C D Countries. 1164

Contemporary Philosophy. 5471

The Controller. 61

Convenios Centroamericanos de Integration Economica. 1303

Convergence: International Congress on Transportation Electronics. Proceedings. 6782

Cooperative Press in South-East Asia. 3702

Cooperative Trade Directory for Southeast Asia. 1158

Coral Reefs. 2292

Corporate Air Travel Survey. 6754

Cotton. Part 1: Bi-monthly Review of the World Situation. 6675

Cotton. Part 2: World Statistics. 6690

Cross-Cultural Psychology Bulletin. 5838

Crude Steel Production. 4981

Current Dialogue. 6056

Dangerous Goods Training Programme. 6754

Deep Sea Fisheries Development Project Reports. 2929

Democratic Journalist. 3702

Dento-Maxillo-Facial Radiology. 4875

Dento-Maxillo-Facial Radiology. Supplement. 4875

Dermatologic Surgery. 4908

Desert Locust Control Organization for Eastern Africa. Annual Report. 218

Development, Genes and Evolution. 579

Developmental and Comparative Immunology. 4580

Diabetes Research and Clinical Practice. 4668

Dialogues et Cultures. 4064

Diamond World Review. 3696

Diarrhoeal Diseases/Maladies Diarrheiques. 4558

Directory of the National Productivity Organizations in A P O Member Countries. 1518

Disease Information. 6945

Division d'Aide et de Cooperation Francaise. Bulletin Trimestriel de Statistique. 993

Documenta Ophthalmologica. 4769

Documentacion de la Seguridad Social Americana. 3647

Documentation Bulletin for South-East Asia. 530

Droit Nucleaire. 2575

Drug and Alcohol Dependence. 2196

E B U Technical Review. (European Broadcasting Union) 1902

E C M T Statistical Report on Road Accidents. (European Council of Ministers of Transport) 6738

E C S L News. (European Centre for Space) 63

E F I L Latest Edition. (European Federation for Intercultural Learning) 2450

E I Monthly Monitor. (Education International) 2324

E P P O Bulletin. (European and Mediterranean Plant Protection Organization) 219

E S A Bulletin. (European Space Agency) 63

E S A - I R S News & Views. (European Space Agency) 4043

E S A Journal. (European Space Agency) 63

E S A R B I C A Journal. (International Council on Archives, Eastern and Southern Africa Regional Branch) 3991

E S O M A R Handbook/E S O M A R Annuaire/E S O M A R Handbuch. (European Society for Opinion and Marketing Research) 1463

Earth Observation Quarterly. 63

Earthquake Engineering and Structural Dynamics. 2659

Ecological Economics. 2784

Ecology and Farming. 112

Economics and Development Resource Center. Report Series. 1084

Economie Familiale/Home Economics. 3521

Ecumenical Letter on Evangelism. 6059

Ecumenical Refugee and Migration News. 5748

Ecumenical Review. 6059

Education in O E C D Countries: Compendium of Statistical Information. 2328

Education International Quarterly Magazine. 2328

Educational and Vocational Guidance - Bulletin A I O S P, I A E V G, I V S B B. (Association Internationale d'Orientation Scolaire et Professionnelle) 5266

Electrochimica Acta. 1729

Electroencephalography and Clinical Neurophysiology Including Evoked Potentials and Electromyography and Motor Control. 4835

Electroencephalography and Clinical Neurophysiology. Supplements. 4835

Electromyography and Motor Control. 4835

Elements de Bibliographie sur les Pays du Sahel/ Elements for a Bibliography on the Sahelian Countries. 530

Encyclopedia of World Problems and Human Potential. 5748

Energy Balances of O E C D Countries. 2545

Energy Policies of I E A Countries. 2547

Energy Statistics of O E C D Countries. 2563

Enfant en Milieu Tropical. 1766

Environment Newsletter. 2788

Environmental Monitor. 2792

Environmental Policy and Law. 2792

Environmental Policy and Law Papers. 2792

Environmental Review. 2793

Enzyme and Protein. 638

Epilepsia. 4835

Episodes (Nottingham). 2232

Erosion Control. 2126

Estadistica. 6603

Estadisticas Macroeconomicas de Centroamerica. 995

Estudios de la Seguridad Social. 3648

Europastimme. 5749

The European Accounting Review. 1046

European Archives of Oto-Rhino-Laryngology. 4796

European Association for Animal Production. Publications. 271

European Bibliography of Soviet, East European and Slavonic Studies/Bibliographie Europeene des Travaux sur l'URSS et l'Europe de l'Est/Europaeische Bibliographie der Sowjet- und Oesteuropastudien. 3366

European Centre for Medium-Range Weather Forecasts. Technical Report. 4994

European Child & Adolescent Psychiatry. 4836

European Community Shipowners' Associations. Annual Report. 6833

European Conference on Controlled Fusion and Plasma Physics. Proceedings. 5594

European Court of Human Rights. Publications. Series A: Judgments and Decisions/Cour Europeenne des Droits de l'Homme. Publications. Serie A: Arrets et Decisions. 5727

European Economic Review. 922

European Federation of Finance House Associations. Annual Report. 1086

European Federation of Finance House Associations. Newsletter. 1086

European Free Trade Association. Annual Report. 1273

European Geophysical Society Series on Hydrological Sciences. 2285

European Journal of Biochemistry. 638

European Journal of Cancer. 4755

European Journal of Cancer. Part B: Oral Oncology. 4755

European Journal of Clinical Investigation. 4452

European Journal of Clinical Investigation. Supplement. 4453

European Journal of Human Genetics. 740

European Journal of Implant and Refractive Surgery. 4769

European Journal of Obstetrics & Gynecology and Reproductive Biology. 4735

European Journal of Pharmaceutical Sciences. 5411

European Journal of Political Research. 5665

European Journal of Population/Revue Europeenne de Demographie. 5798

European Journal of Prosthodontics and Restorative Dentistry. 4641

European Journal of Radiology. 4875

European Journal of Surgical Oncology. 4755

European League for Economic Cooperation. Publications. 1306

European League for Economic Cooperation. Report of the Secretary General on the Activities of E.L.E.C. 1306

The European Legacy. 5475

European Materials Research Society. Monographs. 2731

European Neuropsychopharmacology. 4836

European Organisation for Civil Aviation Equipment. General Assembly. Annual Report. 63

European Organization for Nuclear Research. List of Scientific Publications/Conseil Europeen pour la Recherche Nucleaire. Liste des Publications Scientifiques. 5578

European Organization for Research on Treatment of Cancer. Monograph Series. 4755

European Quality. 6650

European Radiology. 4875

The European Respiratory Journal. 4887

European Southern Observatory. Annual Report. 480

European Space Agency. Scientific and Technical Memoranda. 63

European Space Agency. Scientific and Technical Reports. 63

European Tax Handbook. 1542

European Taxation. 1543

European Taxation Data Base on C D - R O M. 1543

European Water Pollution Control. 2836

Europhysics Conference Abstracts. 5578

EUROSIM - Simulation News Europe. 2052

Evoked Potentials. 4837

Expression. 6993

Extensions and Corrections to the U D C. 3992

Eye to Eye. 4769

F A N S Facts Sheet. (Future Air Navigation Systems) 63

F D I World Dental Press. Technical Reports. 4641

F E B S Letters. (Federation of European Biochemical Societies) 639

F E M S. Immunology and Medical Microbiology. (Federation of European Microbiological Societies) 757

F E M S. Microbiology. (Federation of European Microbiological Societies) 757

F E M S. Microbiology Ecology. (Federation of European Microbiological Societies) 757

F E M S. Microbiology Letters. (Federation of European Microbiological Societies) 757

F E M S. Microbiology Reviews. (Federation of European Microbiological Societies) 757

F I A F Classification Scheme for Literature on Film and Television. (International Federation of Film Archives (F I A F)) 5100

F I D Directory. (Federation Internationale d'Information et de Documentation) 3992

F I D News Bulletin. (Federation Internationale d'Information et de Documentation) 3992

F I F A Handbook. (Federation Internationale de Football Association) 6501

F I F A Magazine. 6501

F I F A News. 6501

F I F A Olympic Football Tournament. (Federation Internationale de Football Association) 6501

F I F A Technical Reports. (Federation Internationale de Football Association) 6501

F I F A U-17 World Championship. (Federation Internationale de Football Association) 6501

F I F A World Cup. 6501

F I F A World Youth Championship. 6501

F I O D S Revue. (Federation Internationale des Organisations de Donneurs de Sang Benevoles) 4602

F I S Bulletin. (International Ski Federation) 6562

Facts & Figures. 2549

Faith and Order Papers. 6061

Federacion Panamericana de Asociaciones de Facultades de Medicina. Boletin. 4454

Federation Internationale de Gymnastique. Bulletin. 6460

Federation Internationale de Rugby Amateur. Annuaire. 6501

Federation Internationale Motocycliste. Annuaire. 6523

Financial Market Trends. 1090

Financing and External Debt of Developing Countries. 1307

Fisheries Newsletter. 2931

Flash. 3721

Flashes from the Trade Unions. 3721

Fluoride. 4564

Folia Linguistica. 4069

Folia Phoniatrica et Logopaedica. 4796

Fontes Artis Musicae. 5208

Fred och Frihet. 5751

Free Labour World. 3721

Fundamenta Informaticae. 4409

Futuribles. 6414

Futurology. 6651

Fuzzy Sets and Systems. 4365

General Relativity and Gravitation. 5549

General Treaty for Central American Economic Integration. Permanent Secretariat. Newsletter. 1307

Genetic Counseling. 742

Geneva Papers on Risk and Insurance - Issues and Practice. 3649

Geneva Papers on Risk and Insurance Theory. 3649

Geographical Distribution of Financial Flows to Developing Countries. Disbursements - Commitments - Economic Indicators. 1307

Geophysical Prospecting. 2274

Geothermics. 2209

Giornale Storico della Lunigiana e del Territorio Lucense. 3413

The Global Tenant. 3583

Gold (Year). 5064

Gold Institute. International Conference on Gold & Silver in Medicine. Proceedings. 5064

Gold News/Nouvelles de l'Or. 5064

Greenhouse Issues. 2836

Grotiana. 3785

Guide to Health Services of the World. 3544

Guide to the European V A T Directives. 1546

Guides to European Taxation: Taxation & Investment in Central and East European Countries. 1547

Guides to European Taxation: Taxation of Companies in Europe. 1547

Guides to European Taxation: Taxation of Individuals in Europe. 1547

Guides to European Taxation: Taxation of Patent Royalties, Dividends, Interest in Europe. 1547

Guides to European Taxation: Taxation of Private Investment Income. 1547

Guides to European Taxation: Value Added Taxation in Europe. 1547

Gynecological Endocrinology. 4671

Haemophilia. 4700

Haemophilia. Supplement. 4700

Handbook on the 1989 Double Taxation Convention Between the Federal Republic of Germany and the United States of America. 1547

Health Policy. 5963

Hegel - Studien Beihefte. 5477

Higher Education Management. 2431

Higher Education Policy. 2431

Histopathology. 4756

History of European Ideas. 5478

Homeostasis. 4840

Horticultural Research International. 3056

Hospital Management International. 3549

Human Rights Bulletin (New York). 5729

Hydrographic Journal. 2210

Hydrographic Society. International Headquarters. Special Publications. 2210

Hydrological Sciences Journal/Journal des Sciences Hydrologiques. 2286

Hypertension in Pregnancy. 4603

I A B S E Report. (International Association for Bridge and Structural Engineering) 2661

I A G A News. (International Association of Geomagnetism and Aeronomy) 2275

I A J R C Journal. (International Association of Jazz Record Collectors) 5163

I A L News. (International Association of Laryngectomees) 2469

I A M C R Newsletter. (International Association for Mass Communications Research) 1905

I A S A Journal. (International Association of Sound Archives) 6445

I A S L Newsletter. (International Association of School Librarianship) 3996

I A T A Airport and En-Route Aviation Charges Manual. (International Air Transport Association) 6758

I A T A Annual Report. (International Air Transport Association) 6758

I A T A City Code Directory. (International Air Transport Association) 6758

I A T A - I A L Air Distances. (International Air Transport Association) 6759

I A T A List of Ticket and Airport Taxes and Fees. (International Air Transport Association) 6759

I A T A Review. (International Air Transport Association) 6759

I A W A Journal. (International Association of Wood Anatomists) 684

I B A Review. (International Bauxite Association) 5064

I B N S Journal. (International Bank Note Society) 5225

I C A A. International Institutes on the Prevention and Treatment of Alcoholism. Papers. (International Congress on Alcoholism and Addictions) 2197

I C A A News. (International Congress on Alcoholism and Addictions) 2197

I C A C Recorder. (International Cotton Advisory Committee) 6678

I C A Regional Bulletin. (International Cooperative Alliance) 1160

I C A S A L S Newsletter. (International Center for Arid and Semiarid Land Studies) 122

I C A S E - L A R C Interdisciplinary Series in Science. (Institute for Computer Applications in Science and Engineering, Langley Research Center) 6246

I C C O Annual Report. (International Cocoa Organization) 2976

I C C O Cocoa Newsletter. (International Cocoa Organization) 2976

I C C O Quarterly Bulletin of Cocoa Statistics. (International Cocoa Organization) 2976

I C C O World Cocoa Directory. (International Cocoa Organization) 2976

I C E L References. (International Council of Environmental Law) 2830

I C E M Review. (International Council for Educational Media) 2340

I C E S Cooperative Research Report/Rapport des Recherches Collectives. (International Council for the Exploration of the Sea) 2935

I C E S Fisheries Statistics/Bulletin Statistique des Peches Maritimes. 2947

I C E S Journal of Marine Science. (International Council for the Exploration of the Sea) 2295

I C E S Oceanographic Data Lists and Inventories. 2295

I C H S Information Bulletin. (International Council of Homehelp Services) 4714

I C I D Journal. (International Commission on Irrigation and Drainage) 122

I C J Review. (International Commission of Jurists) 3932

I C M A Newsletter. (International City - County Management Association) 5943

I C O M News. (International Council of Museums) 5123

I C S U Newsletter. (International Council of Scientific Unions) 5246

I D F Directory. (International Diabetes Federation) 4671

I D O C Internazionale. (International Documentation and Communication Center) 5357

I E A Coal Research. Newsletter. (International Energy Agency) 2550

I E A Coal Research. Perspectives. (International Energy Agency) 2550

I E A Coal Research. Profiles. (International Energy Agency) 2550

I E C Bulletin. (International Electrotechnical Commission) 2700

I E C Catalogue of Publications. (International Electrotechnical Commission) 2521

I E E E International Conference on Acoustics, Speech and Signal Processing. Proceedings. 2701

I E E E International Symposium on Electrical Insulation. I E E E Conference Record. 2701

I E S A Information. (International Society for Electrosleep and Electroanaesthesia) 4840

I F A P Newsletter. (International Federation of Agricultural Producers) 122

I F H O H Journal. (International Federation of the Hard of Hearing) 3313

I F J Information. (International Federation of Journalists) 3705

I F L A Directory. (International Federation of Library Associations and Institutions) 3996

I F L A Journal. (International Federation of Library Associations and Institutions) 3996

I F L A Publications. (International Federation of Library Associations and Institutions) 3996

I F L Nieuws. (International Friendship League) 1850

I G F - Journal. (International Graphical Federation) 5813

I H F Management Handbooks. (International Hospital Federation) 3550

I I A S A Annual Report. (International Institute for Applied Systems Analysis) 2081

I I C A in the Americas. (Inter-American Institute for Cooperation on Agriculture) 122

I I R A Bulletin. (International Industrial Relations Association) 1376

I L C A Annual Report and Programme Highlights. (International Livestock Centre for Africa) 272

I L C A Newsletter. 272

I L C A Proceedings. (International Livestock Centre for Africa) 272

I L C A Research Report. (International Livestock Centre for Africa) 272

I L G A Bulletin. (International Lesbian and Gay Association) 3533

I M C Journal. (International Information Management Congress) 4043

I M F News. (International Metalworkers Federation) 4957

I M U Canberra Circular. (International Mathematical Union) 4368

I O I News. (International Ocean Institute) 2296

I O J Newsletter. (International Organization of Journalists) 3705

I P D Cahier/P A I D Reports. (Institut Panafricain pour le Developpement) 1308

I P I Report. (International Press Institute) 3705

I P S F News Bulletin. (International Pharmaceutical Students Federation) 5416

I P T C Spectrum. (International Press Telecommunications Council) 1945

I R R I Program Report. (International Rice Research Institute) 259

I S B N Newsletter. (International Standard Book Number) 5998

I S M S Newsletter. (International Society for Mushroom Science) 684

I S O Bulletin (English Edition). (International Organization for Standardization) 5014

I S O Memento. (International Organization for Standardization) 5014

I S O News. (International Society of Organbuilders) 5163

I S P R S Journal of Photogrammetry and Remote Sensing. (International Society for Photogrammetry and Remote Sensing) 3261

I S S A. Committee on Provident Funds. Reports. (International Social Security Association) 3651

I S S A. Social Security Documentation. Caribbean Series. (International Social Security Association) 3651

I S T A News Bulletin. (International Seed Testing Association) 224

I S U Constitution. (International Skating Union) 6464

I S U Regulations. (International Skating Union) 6464

I T C Journal. 3261

I T M F Country Statements. (International Textile Manufacturers Federation) 6678

I T M F Directory. (International Textile Manufacturers Federation) 6678

I T U Review. (International Typographical Union) 3722

I U C N Bulletin. (International Union for Conservation of Nature and Natural Resources) 2129

I U G G Year Book. (International Union of Geodesy and Geophysics) 2275

I U O M A Magazine. (International Union of Mail Artists) 432

I U P I W Views. (International Union of Petroleum & Industrial Workers) 5359

I U S Newsletter. (International Union of Students) 2432

I U S S P Newsletter/U I E S P Bulletin de Liaison. (International Union for the Scientific Study of Population) 5785

I U S S P Papers/U I E S P Documents de l'Union. (International Union for the Scientific Study of Population) 5785

I U S Womens Newsletter. (International Union of Students) 6997

I W G I A Documents. (International Work Group for Indigenous Affairs) 312

Ice. 2243

Immunizations/Les Vaccinations/Vacunaciones. 4566

Immunology Letters. 4583

Index of African Social Science Periodical Articles. 6357

Index to Plant Chromosome Numbers. 685

Indigenous Affairs. (International Work Group for Indigenous Affairs) 312

Indologica Taurinensia. 5285

Industrial Policy in O E C D Countries. 1216

Inform Quarterly Newsletter. 4686

Information and Management. 2066

Information Bulletin for Catholic Rural Organizations. 124

Information, Computer and Communications Policy. 1906

Information Europe. 3998

Information Technology Catalogue. 6759

Information Technology Outlook/Perspectives des Technologies de l'Information. 4044

Informations Recentes sur les Comptes Nationaux des Pays en Developpement/Latest Information on National Accounts of Developing Countries. 1309

Ingenieria Sanitaria. 5965

Innovation and Employment. 5268

Inspel. 3999

Institut de Droit International. Annuaire. 3932

Institut International du Froid. Bulletin/International Institute of Refrigeration. Bulletin. 3329

Institut International du Froid. Comptes Rendus de Reunions de Commissions/International Institute of Refrigeration. Proceedings of Commision Meetings. 3329

Institut Panafricain pour le Developpement. Travaux d'Etudiants. Bulletin Analytique. 1309

Institut Panafricain pour le Developpement. Travaux Manuscrits. 193

Instituto Interamericano de Cooperacion para la Agricultura. Informe Anual. 125

Instituto Interamericano de Cooperacion para la Agricultura - O E A. Documentos Oficiales. 125

Instituto Interamericano del Nino. Boletin. 1769

Instituto Panamericano de Geografia e Historia. Boletin Aereo. 3262

Integrated Coastal Fisheries Management Project Technical Document. 2936

Intensive Care Medicine. 4472

Inter American Press Association. Freedom of the Press Annual Report. 5674

Inter-American Bar Association. Letter to Members. 3792

Inter-American Center of Tax Administrators. Informativo - Newsletter. 1548

Interamerican Children's Institute. Report of the General Director. 6377

Inter-American Commission of Women. News Bulletin. 6998

Inter-American Commission of Women. Noticiero. 6998

Inter-American Council for Education, Science, and Culture. Final Report. 2342

Inter-American Council of Commerce and Production. Uruguayan Section. Publicaciones. 1309

Inter-American Development Bank. Annual Report. 1101

Inter-American Development Bank. Institute for Latin American Integration. Annual Report. 1309

Inter-American Economic and Social Council. Final Report of the Annual Meeting at the Ministerial Level. 3473

Inter-American Institute for Cooperation on Agriculture. Executive Committee. Yearly Meeting Report. 125

Inter-American Institute for Cooperation on Agriculture. News. 125

Inter-American Review of Bibliography/Revista Interamericana de Bibliografia. 535

Inter-American Tropical Tuna Commission. Annual Report/Comision Interamericana del Atun Tropical. Informe Anual. 2936

Inter-American Tropical Tuna Commission. Bulletin/Comision Interamericana del Atun Tropical. Boletin. 2936

Inter-American Tropical Tuna Commission. Data Report. 2936

InterMedia. 1962

International Abstracts in Operations Research. 2002

International Academy of Legal Medicine and Social Medicine. Newsletter. 4686

International Air Transport Association. Annual General Meeting. Reports and Proceedings. 6759

International Air Transport Association. List of Operators at Each Airport. 6759

International Angiology. 4604

International Archery Federation. Bulletin Officiel. 6465

International Arthurian Society. Bibliographical Bulletin/Societe Internationale Arthurienne. Bulletin Bibliographique. 4293

International Association for Byzantine Studies. Bulletin d'Information et de Coordination. 3419

International Association for Educational and Vocational Information. Studies and Reports. 2342

International Association for Media and History. Newsletter. 5105

International Association for Shell and Spatial Structures. Journal. 2663

International Association for the Exchange of Students for Technical Experience. Annual Report. 2451

International Association for the Physical Science of the Ocean. Proces-Verbaux. 2296

International Association of Agricultural Information Specialists. Quarterly Bulletin. 4000

International Association of Engineering Geology. Bulletin. 2244

International Association of Geodesy. Central Bureau for Satellite Geodesy. Bibliography. 3280

International Association of Geodesy. Central Bureau for Satellite Geodesy. Information Bulletin. 3262

International Association of Geodesy. Commission Permanente des Marees Terrestres. Marees Terrestres Bulletin d'Information. 2275

International Association of Geodesy Symposia. 2275

International Association of Hydrogeologists. Memoires. 2286

International Association of Law Libraries. Directory. 4000

International Association of Liberal Religious Women. Newsletter. 6067

International Association of Literary Critics. Revue. 5999

International Association of Theoretical and Applied Limnology. Communications/Internationale Vereinigung fuer Theoretische und Angewandte Limnologie. Mitteilungen. 2286

International Association of Theoretical and Applied Limnology. Proceedings/Internationale Vereinigung fuer Theoretische und Angewandte Limnologie. Verhandlungen. 2286

International Astronomical Union. Transactions. 481

International Baccalaureate Organisation. Annual Report. 1873

International Badminton Federation. Annual Statute Book. 6465

International Bibliography of Historical Demography/Bibliographie Internationale de la Demographie Historique. 5799

International Bibliography of the Forensic Sciences. 4566

International Brain Research Organization Monograph Series. 4841

International Bureau of Fiscal Documentation. Annual Report. 1549

International Business Lawyer. 3933

International Cargo Handling - Buyers Guide to Manufacturers. 6836

International Cataloguing and Bibliographic Control. 4000

International Centre for Settlement of Investment Disputes. Annual Report. 1334

International Child Health: A Digest of Current Information. 4806

International Children's Centre. Paris. Report of the Director-General to the Executive Board. 6417

International Civil Defence Journal/Revue Internationale de Protection Civile/Revista Internacional de Proteccion Civil. 1816

International College of Dentists. European Section. Newsletter. 4643

International Commission for Uniform Methods of Sugar Analysis. Report of the Proceedings of the Session (Year). 2977

International Commission on Irrigation and Drainage. Congress Reports. 2744

International Commission on Irrigation and Drainage. Report. 6970

International Commission on Large Dams. Bulletin. 2663

International Commission on Radiological Protection. Annals. 4877

International Committee for Historical Science. Bulletin d'Information. 3348

International Committee of the Red Cross. Annual Report - Rapport d'Activite - Informe de Actividad. 6377

International Committee on Urgent Anthropological and Ethnological Research. Bulletin. 312

International Confederation of Free Trade Unions. World Congress Reports. 3722

International Confederation of Societies of Authors and Composers. 5340

International Conference on Data Processing in the Field of Social Security. Reports. 3654

International Congress on Combustion Engines. Proceedings. 2757

International Congress Science Series. 4935

International Consumer Directory. 2152

International Cooperative Alliance. Cooperative Series. 1160

International Cotton Industry Statistics. 6690

International Council of Scientific Unions. Year Book. 6248

International Customs Journal/Bulletin International des Douanes. 1549

International Dairy Federation. Bulletin/Federation Internationale de Laiterie. Bulletin. 251

International Dairy Federation. Catalogue of I D F Publications/Federation Internationale Laitiere. Catalogue des Publications. 174

International Dairy Federation. International Standard/Federation Internationale de Laiterie. Norme Internationale. 251

International Dental Journal. 4643

International Directory of Film and T V Documentation Collections. 5105

International Directory of Prisoners Aid Agencies. 2166

International Earth Rotation Service. Annual Report. 482

International Earth Rotation Service. Monthly Bulletin. 482

International Egg Commission. Broadsheet. 2978

International Egg Commission. Market Review Situation & Outlook Report. 2978

International Egg Commission. Monthly Chick Placement Bulletin. 2978

International Egg Commission. Monthly News Letter. 2978

International Electrotechnical Commission. Yearbook - Annuaire. 2708

International Energy Agency. Greenhouse Gas R & D Programme. Annual Report. 2837

International Energy Agency. Greenhouse Gas R & D Programme. Proceedings. 2837

International Energy Agency. Greenhouse R&D Programme. Public Summary Reports. 2837

International Federation for Housing and Planning. Directory. 3585

International Federation of Commercial Clerical, Professional and Technical Employees. Newsletter. 3723

International Federation of Journalists and Travel Writers. Official List/Repertoire Officiel. 6893

International Federation of Medical Students' Associations. Newsletter. 4472

International FilmArchive C D - R O M. 5116

International Fiscal Association. Yearbook. 3935

International Grains Council. Food Aid Shipments. 2978

International Grains Council. Grain Market Report. 194

International Grains Council. Ocean Freight Rates. 6837

International Grains Council. Report for Fiscal Year. 259

International Grains Council. World Grain Statistics (Year). 174

International Graphical Federation. Report of Activities. 3723

International Gravimetrique Bureau. Bulletin d'Information. 2275

International Guide to Mergers and Acquisitions. 1549

The International Guide to Partnerships. 1549

International Handbook of Universities and Other Institutions of Higher Education. 2433

International Handbook on Commercial Arbitration. 3935

International Hotel Guide. 3585

International Humanist News. 5480

International Hydrographic Bulletin. 2296

International Hydrographic Organization. Yearbook. 2297

International Hydrographic Review. 2297

International Index to Film Periodicals. 5116

International Institute for Land Reclamation and Improvement. Annual Report. 226

International Institute for Land Reclamation and Improvement. Bibliography. 174

International Institute for Land Reclamation and Improvement. Publication. 226

International Institute of Administrative Sciences Monographs. 5906

International Institute of Seismology and Earthquake Engineering. Bulletin. 2275

International Institute of Seismology and Earthquake Engineering. Individual Studies by Participants at I I S E E. 2275

International Institute of Seismology and Earthquake Engineering. Year Book. 2276

International Institute on the Prevention and Treatment of Addictions. Selected Papers. 2197

International Iron and Steel Institute. Report of Conference Proceedings. 4959

International Journal for Consumer Safety. 2152

International Journal for the Advancement of Counselling. 2342

International Journal of Angiology. 4604

International Journal of Biometeorology. 4999

International Journal of Cancer. 4757

International Journal of Continuing Engineering Education. 2604

International Journal of Dermatology. 4562

International Journal of Developmental Neuroscience. 4841

International Journal of Early Childhood. 1769

International Journal of Environment and Pollution. 2837

International Journal of Fertility and Menopausal Studies. 4473

International Journal of Food Microbiology. 759

International
Journal of Government Auditing. 5907

International Journal of Group Tensions. 5850

International Journal of Gynaecology and Obstetrics.
4738

International Journal of Hospitality Management.
3566

International Journal of Hydrogen Energy. 2552

International Journal of Industrial Ergonomics. 2605

International Journal of Legal Information. 4001

International Journal of Leprosy and Other
Mycobacterial Diseases. 4623

International Journal of Microcirculation: Clinical &
Experimental. 4473

International Journal of Occupational Medicine,
Immunology and Toxicology. 5251

International Journal of Oral & Maxillofacial Surgery.
4644

International Journal of Physical Education/
Internationale Zeitschrift fuer Sportpaedagogik. 2490

International Journal of Prosthodontics. 4644

International Journal of Psycho-Analysis. 5850

International Journal of Psychology/Journal
International de Psychologie. 5850

International Journal of Psychophysiology. 5850

International Journal of Speleology. 2245

International Journal of Sport Psychology. 4898

International Journal of Systematic Bacteriology. 759

International Journal of the Classical Tradition. 1823

International Journal of University Adult Education.
2400

The International Journal on Hydropower & Dams.
2572

International Linguistic Association. Monograph. 4076

International Linguistic Association. Special
Publications. 4076

International Narcotics Control Board. Report for
(Year). 5419

International Narcotics Control Board. Statistics on
Psychotropic Substances for (Year). 5450

International Naturist Guide/Internationaler FKK-
Reisefuehrer/Guide Naturiste Internationale. 6567

International Navigation Association. Proceedings of
Annual Meeting. 69

International Navigation Association Newsletter. 6760

International Newsletter on Chemical Education. 1678

International Nursing Review. 4716

International Ocean Institute. Occasional Papers.
2297

International Office of Cocoa, Chocolate and Sugar
Confectionery. Annual Statistical Bulletin. 3000

International Oil Scouts Association. Official Publication.
5360

International Organization. 5755

International Organization for Migration. Annual Report.
5786

International Orthopaedics. 4785

International Pacific Halibut Commission (U.S. and
Canada). Annual Report. 2936

International Pacific Halibut Commission (U.S. and
Canada). Scientific Reports. 2936

International Peace Research Newsletter. 5756

International Peace Update. 5756

International Peat Journal. 5066

International Peat Society. Bulletin/Internationale Moor-
und Torf-Gesellschaft. Mitteilungen. 5066

International Pediatric Association. Proceedings of
Congress. 4807

International Political Science Abstracts/Documentation
Politique Internationale. 5722

International Political Science Association. World
Congress. 5674

International Political Science Review/Revue
Internationale de Science Politique. 5756

International Population Conference. Proceedings.
5786

International Prisoners Aid Association. Newsletter.
6377

International Psychologist. 5850

International Railway Statistics. 6741

International Rayon and Synthetic Fibres Committee.
Statistical Yearbook. 6690

International Rehabilitation Review. 4474

International Rescue Committee Annual Report. 6377

International Review for Business Education/Revue
Internationale pour l'Enseignement Commercial/
Internationale Zeitschrift fuer Kaufmaennisches
Bildungswesen/Rivista Internazionale per la Cultura
Commerciale/Revista Internacional para la Ensenanza
Comercial. 933

International Review of Administrative Sciences. 5907

International Review of Mission. 6068

International Review of Social History. 3348

International Review of the Red Cross. 3936

International Rubber Digest. 6216

International Scheduled and Charter Freight Forecast.
6760

International Scheduled Passenger Forecast. 6760

International Seismological Centre. Bulletin. 2276

International Silk Association. Monthly Newsletter.
6680

International Skating Union. Ice Dancing Regulations.
6465

International Social Security Association. Studies and
Research. 3654

International Social Security Review. 3654

International Social Work. 6377

International Society for Labor Law and Social Security.
Bulletin. 1380

International Society for Mushroom Science. Symposia
Proceedings. 686

International Society for Respiratory Protection.
Journal. 4888

International Society of Criminology. Bulletin. 2166

International Society of Plant Morphologists. Yearbook.
686

International Society of Soil Science. Bulletin. 227

International Statistical Handbook of Urban Public
Transport/Recueil International de Statistiques des
Transports Publics Urbains/Internationales Statistik-
Handbuch fuer den Oeffentlichen Stadtverkehr. 6741

International Statistical Review. 6611

International Studies Notes. 5757

International Sugar Organization. Statistical Bulletin.
2996

International Surgery. 4911

International Symposium on Canine Heartworm
Disease. Proceedings. 6948

International Textile Machinery Shipment Statistics.
6690

International Textile Manufacturing. 6680

International Tin Research Institute. Annual Report.
4959

International Transactions in Operational Research.
1993

International U S Surgeon. 4911

International Union for Inland Navigation. Annual
Report. 6720

International Union for Vacuum Science, Technique and
Applications. News Bulletin. 5552

International Union of Alpine Associations. Bulletin/
Union Internationale des Associations d'Alpinisme.
Bulletin. 6894

International Union of Crystallography. Abstracts of the
Triennial Congress. 1726

International Union of Food, Agricultural, Hotel,
Restaurant, Catering, Tobacco and Allied Workers'
Associations. News Bulletin. 3723

International V A T Monitor. 1550

International Whaling Commission. Annual Report.
2936

International Women's News. 6998

Der Internationalen Gesellschaft fuer Geschichte der
Pharmazie. Veroeffentlichungen. Neue Folge. 5419

Internationale Gesellschaft fuer Urheberrecht.
Yearbook. 5340

Internationale Seilbahn-Rundschau/International Aerial
Lift Review. 6720

Internationale Stiftung Mozarteum. Mitteilungen.
5166

Internationaler Verband Forstlicher
Forschungsanstalten. Weltkongress Berichtswerk.
3019

Inter-Parliamentary Bulletin. 5757

Inter-Parliamentary Union. Series: "Reports and
Documents". 5674

Intervirology. 760

Inventaria Archaeologica Belgique. 358

Inventaria Archaeologica Ceskoslovensko. 358

Inventaria Archaeologica Denmark. 358

Inventaria Archaeologica Deutschland. 358

Inventaria Archaeologica Espana. 358

Inventaria Archaeologica France. 358

Inventaria Archaeologica Italia. 358

Inventaria Archaeologica Jugoslavija. 358

Inventaria Archaeologica Norway. 358

Inventaria Archaeologica Oesterreich. 358

Inventaria Archaeologica Pologne. 358

Inventaria Archaeologica Ungarn. 358

Invertebrate Reproduction and Development. 729

Iron Production. 4983

Islamic Academy of Sciences. Journal. 6249

Islamic Thought and Scientific Creativity. 6118

Isotope and
Radiation Research. 4877

J A R Amendment Service to Regulatory Documents.
6760

Jazzforschung/Jazz Research. 5167

Jazzmen's Reference Book. 5167

Joint Aviation Authorities. Certification Information -
Procedures. 6761

Joint Aviation Authorities. General Information -
Procedures. Information Leaflets. 6761

Joint Aviation Authorities. Maintenance Information -
Procedures. 6761

Joint Aviation Authorities. Notice of Proposed
Amendment Scheme. 6761

Joint Aviation Authorities. Regulatory Documents.
6761

Journal of Adolescent and Adult Literacy. 2345

Journal of Applied Crystallography. 1726

Journal of Applied Electrochemistry. 1729

Journal of Biomechanics. 4479

Journal of Bronchology. 4888

Journal of Cardiovascular Surgery. 4606

Journal of Cerebral Blood Flow and Metabolism. 4844

Journal of Coastal Conservation. 2297

Journal of Communication. 1908

Journal of Cranio-Maxillo-Facial Surgery. 4911

Journal of Cryptology. 4373

Journal of Energy and Natural Resources Law. 3796

Journal of Environmental Pathology, Toxicology and
Oncology. 2846

Journal of Film Preservation. 5106

Journal of Geochemical Exploration. 2211

Journal of Geodesy. 2277

Journal of Glaciology. 2246

The Journal of Heart and Lung Transplantation. 4912

Journal of Hepatology. 4694

Journal of Hydraulic Research. 2744

Journal of Hypertension. 4606

Journal of Hypertension. Supplement. 4606

Journal of Logic, Language and Information. 4079

Journal of Magnetism and Magnetic Materials. 5554

Journal of Marine Systems. 2298

Journal of Medical & Veterinary Mycology. 4624

Journal of Medical and Veterinary Mycology.
Supplement. 4624

Journal of Molecular and Cellular Cardiology. 4606

Journal of Near-Death Studies. 5858

Journal of Neurochemistry. 642

Journal of Neuroimmunology. 4846

Journal of Neurology/Zeitschrift fuer Neurologie.
4847

Journal of Oral Pathology & Medicine. 4646

Journal of Orofacial Pain. 4646

Journal of Psychosomatic Obstetrics and Gynaecology.
4740

Journal of Reproductive Immunology. 4585

Journal of Rural Cooperation. 1160

Journal of Sports Medicine and Physical Fitness.
4898

Journal of Structural Learning. 5862

Journal of Systems Architecture. 2088

Journal of Terramechanics. 6721

Journal of the Fantastic in the Arts. 4328

Journal of the Neurological Sciences. 4849

The Journal of Trace Elements in Experimental
Medicine. 4681

Journal of Traffic Medicine. 4787

Journal of Tropical Ecology. 2807

Journal of Wind Engineering and Industrial
Aerodynamics. 2761

Justice. 3800

Kidney International. 4928

Kidney International. Supplement. 4928

Knowledge Organization. 4004

Labor (Year). 1382

Labor Press and Information. 3724

Labour Market and Social Policy Occasional Papers.
1385

Leben und Umwelt. 2132

Leonardo: Art Science and Technology. 439

Leonardo Music Journal. 5171

Lethaia. 5315

Ligue Internationale Contre la Concurrence Deloyale.
Annuaire. 1288

Ligue Internationale Contre la Concurrence Deloyale.
Communication. 1525

Linguistic Bibliography/Bibliographie Linguistique.
4128

Livestock Production Science. 276

Log of the Star Class. 6536

Lotus. 4233

Lung Cancer. 4759

Lymphology. 4673

Marketing and Research Today. 1476

Materials Characterization. 4964

Mathematical and Computer Modelling. 4379

Mathematics and Computers in Simulation. 2052

Maturitas. 3293

Ma'yanot. 2894

Measurement. 5015

Meat Balances in O E C D Countries. 176

Mechanism and Machine Theory. 2764

Medailles. 3510

Media Development. 1910

Medical & Biological Engineering & Computing. 628

Medical and Pediatric Oncology. 4760

Medical and Pediatric Oncology. Supplement. 4760

The Messianic Jew (and Hebrew Christian). 6077

Metabolic, Pediatric and Systemic Ophthalmology.
4773

Metrologia. 5015

Microgravity News from E S A. 72

Microtables Imports - Exports of O E C D Countries.
1290

Microwave Power Symposium Proceedings. 2713

Migration News. 5788

Migration Today. 5788

Mileage Manual. 6762

The Military Balance. 5039

Milk and Milk Products Balances in O E C D Countries.
176

Ministerial Formation. 6078

Modern Gold Coinage (Year). 5225

Multilateral Interline Traffic Agreements Manual.
6762

Mushroom Science. 691

Music in the Media - I M Z Bulletin. 5176

Musikforum - Referate und Informationen des
Deutschen Musikrates. 5180

Muslim World. 5685

N A T O Advanced Science Institutes Series.
Partnership Sub-Series 3: High Technologies. 6658

N A T O Advanced Science Institutes Series.
Partnership Sub-Series 4: Science and Technology
Policy. 6260

N A T O Advanced Science Institutes Series A: Life
Sciences. (North Atlantic Treaty Organization) 596

N A T O Advanced Science Institutes Series B: Physics.
(North Atlantic Treaty Organization) 5560

N A T O Advanced Science Institutes Series C:
Mathematical and Physical Sciences. (North Atlantic
Treaty Organization) 4384

N A T O Advanced Science Institutes Series D:
Behavioural and Social Sciences. (North Atlantic Treaty
Organization) 5866

N A T O Advanced Science Institutes Series E: Applied
Sciences. 6658

N A T O Advanced Science Institutes Series F:
Computer and Systems Sciences. 2057

N A T O Advanced Science Institutes Series G:
Ecological Sciences. 2811

N A T O Advanced Science Institutes Series H: Cell
Biology. 717

N A T O Advanced Study Institutes Series. Partnership
Sub-Series 1: Disarmament Technologies. 5040

N A T O Basic Documents/O T A N Documents
Fondamentaux. 5762

N A T O Data. 5040

N A T O Final Communiques/O T A N Communiques
Finals. 5762

N A T O Handbook. 5762

N A T O Review. 5685

N A T O Scientific Publications. Newsletter. 6260

N E A Issue Brief. (Nuclear Energy Agency) 2579

N E A Newsletter. (Nuclear Energy Agency) 2579

Narcotic Drugs: Estimated World Requirements for
(Year). 5451

National Accounts of O E C D Countries. Volume 1
Main Aggregates. 1016

National Accounts of O E C D Countries. Volume 2 Detailed Tables. 1016

Natural Hazards. 2213

Naturism. 6902

Neohelicon. 4241

Nestor. 380

Neural Networks. 2010

Neuroendocrinology. 4673

Neuroscience. 4857

News from I C S I D. (International Centre for Settlement of Investment Disputes) 1345

News from O E C D. 1224

Nonrenewable Resources. 5074

Nonviolence Training in Africa. 5733

Nordisk Statistisk Aarsbok/Yearbook of Nordic Statistics. 6622

Nordisk Statistisk Skriftserie/Statistical Reports of the Nordic Countries. 6622

Nordisk Statutsamling. 3825

North Atlantic Report. 6762

North Atlantic Treaty Organization. Facts and Figures/ Alliance Atlantique. Structure, Faits et Chiffres. 5764

North Pacific Anadromous Fish Commission. Annual Report. 2940

Noticias de Galapagos. 6268

Nuclear Law Bulletin. 2580

Nuclear Waste Bulletin/Bulletin sur les Dechets Nucleaires. 2854

Numen. 6081

Numen Supplements. 6081

Nutricion en Salud Publica. 5983

Nutrition de Sante Publique. 5983

O A P E C Monthly Bulletin. (Organization of Arab Petroleum Exporting Countries) 5366

O A S. General Secretariat. Annual Report. (Organization of American States) 3481

O E C D Agricultural Policies, Markets and Trade. Monitoring Outlook. (Organization for Economic Cooperation and Development) 1557

O E C D Catalogue of Publications. (Organization for Economic Cooperation and Development) 542

O E C D Coal Information. (Organization for Economic Cooperation and Development) 5074

O E C D Code of Liberalization of Capital Movements/O C D E Code de la Liberation des Mouvements de Capitaux. 1113

O E C D Development Centre Seminars. 1312

O E C D Development Centre Studies. 1312

O E C D Development Cooperation. 1312

O E C D Economic Outlook. 1225

O E C D Economic Outlook Historical Statistics. 1018

O E C D Economic Studies. 1225

O E C D Economic Surveys. 1225

O E C D Economic Surveys: Australia. 1225

O E C D Economic Surveys: Austria. 1225

O E C D Economic Surveys: Belgium - Luxembourg. 1226

O E C D Economic Surveys: Canada. 1226

O E C D Economic Surveys: Denmark. 1226

O E C D Economic Surveys: Finland. 1226

O E C D Economic Surveys: France. 1226

O E C D Economic Surveys: Germany. 1226

O E C D Economic Surveys: Greece. 1226

O E C D Economic Surveys: Hungary. 1226

O E C D Economic Surveys: Iceland. 1226

O E C D Economic Surveys: Ireland. 1226

O E C D Economic Surveys: Italy. 1226

O E C D Economic Surveys: Japan. 1226

O E C D Economic Surveys: Mexico. 1226

O E C D Economic Surveys: Netherlands. 1226

O E C D Economic Surveys: New Zealand. 1226

O E C D Economic Surveys: Norway. 1226

O E C D Economic Surveys: Poland. 1226

O E C D Economic Surveys: Portugal. 1226

O E C D Economic Surveys: Spain. 1226

O E C D Economic Surveys: Sweden. 1227

O E C D Economic Surveys: Switzerland. 1227

O E C D Economic Surveys: The Czech and Slovak Republics. 1227

O E C D Economic Surveys: Turkey. 1227

O E C D Economic Surveys: United Kingdom. 1227

O E C D Economic Surveys: United States. 1227

O E C D Employment Outlook. 1227

O E C D Environmental Data Compendium. 2830

O E C D External Debt Statistics. 1019

O E C D Financial Statistics/Statistiques Financieres de l'O C D E. 1019

O E C D Financial Statistics. Part 1: Monthly Financial Statistics. 1019

O E C D Financial Statistics. Part 2: Financial Accounts. 1019

O E C D Financial Statistics. Part 3: Non-Financial Enterprises Financial Statements. 1019

O E C D Food Consumption Statistics. 2996

O E C D Foreign Trade by Commodities. Series C. 1019

O E C D Indicators of Industrial Activity. 1019

O E C D Industrial Structure Statistics. 1019

O E C D Iron and Steel Industry. 4970

O E C D Labour Force Statistics/O C D E Statistiques de la Population Active. 1019

O E C D Liaison Bulletin Between Research and Training Institutes. 1528

O E C D Library Special Annotated Bibliography: Automation/O C D E Bibliotheque Bibliographie Speciale Analytique: Automation. 2003

O E C D Main Economic Indicators/O C D E Principaux Indicateurs Economiques. 1227

O E C D Main Economic Indicators. Historical Statistics/O C D E Principaux Indicateurs Economiques. Statistiques Retrospectives. 1019

O E C D Main Science and Technology Indicators/O C D E Principaux Indicateurs de la Science et de la Technologie. 6660

O E C D Maritime Transport Committee. Maritime Transport. 6844

O E C D Monthly Statistics of Foreign Trade Series A/O C D E Statistiques Mensuel du Commerce Exterieur. 1019

O E C D Nuclear Energy Agency. Nuclear Energy Data. 2582

O E C D Nuclear Energy Agency Activities in (Year). 2582

O E C D Observer. 1227

O E C D Oil and Gas Information/O C D E Donnees sur le Petrole et sur le Gaz. 5383

O E C D Oil Information. 5367

O E C D Oil Statistics. Supply and Disposal. 5383

O E C D Quarterly Labour Force Statistics/O C D E Statistiques Trimestrielles de la Population Active. 1390

O E C D Quarterly National Accounts/O C D E Bulletin des Comptes Nationaux Trimestriels. 1557

O E C D Quarterly Oil Statistics and Energy Balances. 5384

O E C D Social Policy Studies Series. 5913

O E C D Steel Market in (Year) and Outlook for (Year). 1019

O E C D World Energy Statistics. 2564

O I E Bulletin. (Office International des Epizooties) 6951

O I E C Bulletin. (Office International de l'Enseignement Catholique) 2359

O I E Revue Scientifique et Technique/O I E Scientific and Technical Review. (Office International des Epizooties) 6951

O I V Bulletin. (Office International de la Vigne et du Vin) 510

O I V Lettre. (Office International de la Vigne et du Vin) 510

O P E C Review. (Organization of the Petroleum Exporting Countries) 5367

Ocean Yearbook. 2303

Ocular Immunology and Inflammation. 4773

Odonto-Stomatologie Tropicale/Tropical Dental Journal. 4649

Oecologia. 599

Oekologie und Landbau. 141

Office International de la Vigne et du Vin. Reglements de la C E E. 510

Oil and Arab Cooperation. 5368

Olympic Review (Year). 6473

Onoma. 4096

Ophthalmic Genetics. 4774

Options Mediterraneennes. Serie A: Seminaires Mediterraneens. 142

Orbis. 4097

Orbis Geographicus. 3268

Orbit. 4776

Organization for Economic Cooperation and Development. Activities: Report by the Secretary General. 1312

Organization of African Unity. Scientific Technical and Research Commission. Publication. 6269

Organization of American States. Department of Cultural Affairs. Manuales del Bibliotecario. 4018

Organization of American States. Department of Scientific Affairs. Report of Activities. 6269

Organization of American States. Department of Scientific Affairs. Serie de Biologia: Monografias. 599

Organization of American States. Department of Scientific Affairs. Serie de Fisica: Monografias. 5561

Organization of American States. Department of Scientific Affairs. Serie de Matematica: Monografias. 4387

Organization of American States. Department of Scientific Affairs. Serie de Quimica: Monografias. 1687

Organization of American States. General Assembly. Actas y Documentos. 5765

Organization of American States. Official Records. Indice y Lista General. 3482

Organization of Arab Petroleum Exporting Countries. Secretary General's Annual Report. 5370

Organization of the Petroleum Exporting Countries. Annual Report. 5370

Organization of the Petroleum Exporting Countries. Annual Statistical Bulletin. 5384

Oriens. 5291

Origins of Life and Evolution of the Biosphere. 599

Osteoporosis International. 4511

P C R Information. (Programme to Combat Racism) 5733

P E B Exchange. (Programme on Educational Building) 2461

P T T I Studies. (Postal Telegraph and Telephone International) 1932

Pacific AIDS Alert Bulletin. 4626

Pacific Salmon Commission. Annual Report. 2940

Pain. 4860

Pan American Federation of Engineering Societies. Bulletin. 2614

Pan American Institute of Geography and History. Commission on Geophysics. Boletin. 2279

Paraplegia. 4860

Parlements et Francophonie. 4160

Participation. 5691

Passenger and Cargo Services News - Insight. 6763

Passenger Reservations Manual. 6763

Passenger Services Conference Resolutions Manual. 6763

Passenger Tariff Coordinating Conferences Resolutions Manual. 6763

Pathophysiology. 792

Pattern Recognition Letters. 2029

Patterns in Reconciliation. 5733

Peace and the Sciences. 5766

Peace Courier. 5767

Pediatric Allergy and Immunology. 4810

Pediatric Allergy and Immunology. Supplementum. 4810

Pediatric Nephrology. 4930

Pediatric Neurosurgery. 4860

Pedofauna. 234

People. 828

Permanent International Altaistic Conference (PIAC). Newsletter. 5291

Permanent International Association of Navigation Congresses. Bulletin. 6845

Personality and Individual Differences. 5869

Perspectives Economiques de l'O E C D. 951

Pest Advisory Leaflet. 234

Pharmacology and Therapeutics. 5436

Philosophical Problems Today/Problemes Philosophiques d'Aujourd'hui. 5491

Phlebology. 4608

Phonetica. 4098

Phycologia. 695

Physica A - Statistical and Theoretical Physics. 5562

Physica B - Physics of Condensed Matter. 5562

Physica C - Superconductivity. 5562

Physica D - Nonlinear Phenomena. 5563

Physics and Chemistry of Minerals. 5075

Phytochemistry. 696

Phytomorphology. 696

Phytopathological Papers. 696

Planetary and Space Science. 485

Plant Molecular Biology. 501

Plant Tissue Culture and Biotechnology. 699

Police Chief. 2172

Politique du Tourisme et Tourisme International dans les Pays Membres de l'O C D E. 6907

Precambrian Research. 2257

Prehospital and Disaster Medicine. 4518

Preparing for the Future: E S A Technology Quarterly. 75

Principles of Cargo Handling and Perishable Cargo Handling Guide. 6764

Promotion et Education. 5973

Prospect. 3592

Prosthetics and Orthotics International. 4790

Psychiatric Rehabilitation Journal. 5872

Psychoneuroendocrinology. 4864

Psychotherapy and Psychosomatics. 4865

Public Health Nutrition. 5983

Public Transport International. 6725

Pulp and Paper Industry in O E C D Member Countries/Industrie des Pates et Papiers dans les Pays Membres de l'O C D E. 5326

Purchasing Power Parities and Real Expenditures/Parites de Pouvoir d'Achat et Depenses Reelles. 1236

Pure and Applied Chemistry. 1689

Quarantine Advisory Leaflet. 237

Quarterly Bulletin on Solar Activity. 489

Quaternary International. 2257

Quaternary Perspective. 2257

R I. 5734

R I L M Abstracts of Music Literature. (Repertoire International de Litterature Musicale) 5209

The Radio Science Bulletin. 1940

Radiotherapy and Oncology. 4883

Rail International/Schienen der Welt. 6815

Reaching for the Skies. 75

The Reading Professor. 2443

Reading Research Quarterly. 2366

Reading Teacher. 2499

Recherche en Matiere d'Economie des Transports/Research on Transport Economics. 6726

Reformation Review. 6086

Reformed World. 6158

Regards sur l'Etain. 4972

Regional Tuna Bulletin. 2941

Regnum Vegetabile. 700

Regulatory Affairs Review. 6764

Rejuvenation. 3295

Reliability Engineering and System Safety. 2616

Repertoire International des Medievistes. 3437

Repertorium Plantarum Succulentarum. 700

Report on the Situation on Human Rights in the Republic of Guatemala. 5734

Resuscitation. 4891

Revenue Accounting Manual. 6765

Revenue Statistics of O E C D Member Countries. 1024

Review of Fisheries in O E C D Member Countries. 2942

Review of Income and Wealth. 1402

Review of International Cooperation. 5769

Review of Population Reviews. 5791

Reviews of Manpower and Social Policies. 1393

Reviews of National Policies for Education. 2462

Reviews of National Science and Technology Policy. 6662

Revista Geofisica. 2280

Revista Geografica. 3271

Revista Interamericana de Planificacion. 1530

Revista Latinoamericana de Quimica. 1690

Revue de Bio-Mathematique/Biomathematics. 4391

Revue Informatique et Statistique dans les Sciences Humaines. 1998

Revue Internationale de Police Criminelle. 2175

Risk Book Series. 6090

Rivista di Studi Liguri/Revue d'Etudes Ligures. 3439

The Rotarian. 1853

Rubber Statistical Bulletin. 6220

S A B R A C Journal. (Society for the Advancement of Breeding Researches in Asia and Oceania) 149

S P R E P Environmental Case Studies. (South Pacific Regional Environment Programme) 2818

S P R E P Fact Sheet. (South Pacific Regional Environment Programme) 2818

S P R E P Meeting Reports. (South Pacific Regional Environment Programme) 2818

S P R E P Occasional Papers. 2818

S P R E P Topic Review. 2818

S P R E P Training Reports. 2818

S T I Review. (Science Technology Industry) 6663

Salar. 2942

Scandinavian Cardiovascular Journal. 4919

Scandinavian Cardiovascular Journal. Supplementum. 4919

Scandinavian Journal of History. 3358

Scandinavian Journal of Rheumatology. 4896

Scandinavian Journal of Rheumatology. Supplement. 4896

Scandinavian Journal of Social Medicine. 4528

Scandinavian Journal of Social Medicine. Supplement. 4528

Scientia Horticulturae. 3066

Screening. 4745

Secondary Aluminium. 5078

Secretaria Permanente del Tratado General de Integracion Economica Centroamericana. Boletin Estadistico. 5706

Secretaria Permanente del Tratado General de Integracion Economica Centroamericana. Boletin Informativo. 1314

Secretaria Permanente del Tratado General de Integracion Economica Centroamericana. Cuadernos. 1294

Security Dialogue. 5706

Sedimentology. 2260

Seed Science and Technology. 702

Sennacieca Revuo. 5771

Series Estadisticas Seleccionadas de Centroamerica y Panama. 1025

Share International. 5220

Shock. 4531

Short-Term Economic Indicators Central and Eastern Europe. 1240

Signal Processing. 2046

Signal Processing: Image Communication. 2070

Simulation Practice and Theory. 2053

Situation et Statistiques Mondiales du Secteur Viticole. 515

Skeletal Radiology. 4884

Small Ruminant Research. 284

Social Anthropology. 322

Social Networks. 6345

Societe Francaise de Psycho-Prophylaxie Obstetricale. Bulletin Officiel. 4745

Socio-Economic Differential Mortality in Industrialized Societies. 5792

Sociologia Ruralis. 6432

Soil and Tillage Research. 152

Solar Energy. 2586

Sols Africains/African Soils. 241

Solubility Data Series. 1693

Sources of Contemporary Jewish Thought/Mekevot. 4167

South Pacific Commission. Agricultural News. 153

South Pacific Commission. Annual Report. 5772

South Pacific Commission. Handbook. 1314

South Pacific Commission. Information Circular. 5976

South Pacific Commission. Information Document. 1314

South Pacific Commission. Report of Meetings. 1240

South Pacific Commission. Statistical Bulletin. 6633

South Pacific Commission. Technical Paper. 6664

South Pacific Conference. Report. 5772

South Pacific Economies: Statistical Summary. 1028

South Pacific Foods Leaflet. 2991

Southeast Asian Archives. 3385

Speakers' Papers: Speeches from the Gold and Silver Institutes' (Year) Annual Meeting. 5079

Species. 2141

Speech Communication. 4110

Speleological Abstracts/Bulletin Bibliographique Speleologique. 2221

Sport International. 6483

Standard Schedules Information Manual. 6765

Statistical Theory and Method Abstracts. 4406

Statistical Trends in Transport. 6745

Statistics on Insurance. 3672

Steel Statistical Yearbook (Year). 4985

Steel Statistics of Developing Countries. 4985

Stereotactic and Functional Neurosurgery. 4920

Stochastic Processes and Their Applications. 4397

Strategic Survey. 5772

Structure Reports. Section A: Metals and Inorganic Compounds. 1727

Structure Reports. Section B: Organic Compounds. 1727

Studi Genuensi. 374

Studies in Conservation. 454

Studies in Social History. 6348

Summary of Airport Capacities. 6765

Supplementary Service to European Taxation. 1563

Survey of Remittances of Foreign Balances. 6765

Surveys in Geophysics. 2282

Systems Research. 2059

T U I A F P W Information. (Trade Union International of Agricultural, Forestry and Plantation Workers) 3729

Tax - Benefit Position of Production Workers/Situation des Ouvriers au Regard de l'Impot et des Transferts Sociaux. 1564

Tax News Service. 1566

Tax Treaties Data Base on C D - R O M. 1567

Tax Treatment of Cross-Border Donations. 1567

Tax Treatment of Transfer Pricing. 1567

Taxation and Investment in Canada. 1567

Taxation & Investment in Mexico. 1567

Taxation & Investment in South Africa. 1567

Taxation and Investment in the Caribbean. 1567

Taxation and Investment in the People's Republic of China. 1567

Taxation in Latin America. 1568

Taxation Laws of Indonesia. 1568

Taxes and Investment in Asia and the Pacific. 1568

Taxon. 705

Teachers of the World. 2376

Technology and Health Care. 4536

Terminologies Nouvelles. 4117

Terra et Aqua. 6851

Terra Nova. 2216

Terra Una. 6098

Textes et Etudes du Moyen Age. 3450

Theatre en Pologne/Theatre in Poland. 6705

Theosophist. 5502

Thrombosis and Haemostasis. 4610

Ticketing Handbook. 6765

Torah Education. 6130

Tourism Policy and International Tourism in O E C D Member Countries. 6918

Toxicon. 5445

Trade Unions International of Agricultural, Forestry and Plantation Workers. Bulletin. 3027

Trade Unions International of Workers in Commerce. Bulletin. 3730

Trade Unions International of Workers in Commerce. News. 3730

Translatio. 4118

Transnational Associations/Associations Transnationales. 5774

Transport Museums. 6730

Transport Workers of the World. 3730

Travel Agent's Handbook. 6919

Travel and Tourism Barometer. 6932

Trends in Biochemical Sciences. 650

Trends in Biochemical Sciences (Reference Edition). 650

Trends in Pharmacological Sciences. 5445

Trends in Pharmacological Sciences (Reference Edition). 5445

Tropical Ecology. 706

Tubercle and Lung Disease. 4892

Tuna and Billfish Assessment Programme Technical Report. 2945

Tunnelling and Underground Space Technology. 2621

Typographical Journal. 3730

U I A Newsletter. (Union Internationale des Architectes) 405

U I C C International Calendar of Meetings on Cancer. (Union Internationale Contre le Cancer) 4937

U I C C International Directory of Cancer Institutes and Organizations. (Union Internationale Contre le Cancer) 4765

U I S Bulletin. (Union Internationale de Speleologie) 2265

U I T B B Bulletin. (Trade Unions International of Workers of the Building, Wood and Building Materials Industries) 3730

U I T Journal. (Union International de Tir) 6490

U I T P Biblio-Express. (International Union of Public Transport) 6747

U L D Control Manual. 6765

U L D Technical Manual. (Unit Load Devices) 6765

Uganda Freshwater Fisheries Research Organization. Annual Report. 2945

Ultrasound in Medicine & Biology. 611

Ultrasound in Obstetrics & Gynecology. 4746

Uniform Law Review/Revue de Droit Uniforme. 3943

Union Mondiale des Organisations Syndicales sur Bases Economique et Sociale Liberales. Conferences: Rapport. 3731

Union of European Football Associations. Handbook of U E F A. 6518

United States Board on Books for Young People. Newsletter. 6011

United Towns News Newsletter. 5952

University and College Entrance: The Official Guide. 2446

Uranium: Resources, Production and Demand/ Uranium: Ressources, Production et Demande. 5081

Veterinary Biotechnology Newsletter. 6957

Veterinary Dermatology. 6957

Vetus Testamentum. 6101

Voice of Silence Newsletter. 3315

Volunteer. 2914

Vox Sanguinis. 4588

Vsemirnoe Profsoyuznoe Dvizhenie. 3731

W A Y Forum. (World Assembly of Youth) 1811

W F D Y News. (World Federation of Democratic Youth) 1811

W I Z O Review (English Edition). (Women's International Zionist Organization) 7009

W T O News. (World Tourism Organization) 6925

Water Quality International. 2841

Water Research. 6979

Water Science and Technology. 6981

Welding in the World/Soudage dans le Monde. 4989

What is the I B A C. (International Business Aviation Council) 81

White Ribbon Bulletin. 2202

Who's Who in Cargo Handling. 6853

Women's News. 7012

Women's World. 7022

Wood Science and Technology. 3040

Work Accomplished by the Inter-American Juridical Committee during Its Meeting. 3870

Workshop of Peace/Muntada al-Salaam. 2453

World Advertising Expenditures. 47

World Air Transport Statistics. 6748

World Alliance of Y M C A's Directory. 1855

World Animal Health in (Year). 6960

World Bibliography of Social Security/Bibliographie Universelle de Securite Sociale. 1035

World Council of Churches. Office of Education. Education Newsletter. 6104

World Development Report. 1318

World Directory of Mathematicians. 4404

World Disasters Report. 5979

World Economic Outlook. 1247

World Farmers' Times. 163

World Federation of Teachers' Unions. Information Letter. 2383

World Highways/Routes du Monde. 6828

World Hockey. 6492

World Hospitals and Health Services. 3556

World Journal of Surgery. 4923

World List of Universities, Other Institutions of Higher Education and University Organisations/Liste Mondiale des Universites. 2417

World Methodist Historical Society. Historical Bulletin. 6165

World Mine Production of Gold. 5082

World Mining Congress. Report. 5082

The World of Music. 5206

World Press Freedom Review. 3713

World S F Newsletter. 4333

World Scout Organization Report. 1780

World Scouting News/Bulletin du Scoutisme Mondial. 1780

World Steel in Figures (Year). 4986

World Steel Statistics Monthly. 4986

World Student News. 2383

World Transport Data/Statistiques Mondiales de Transport. 6748

World Youth/Jeunesse du Monde/Juventud del Mundo. 1812

World Zionist Press Service. 3182

Y M C A World. (Young Men's Christian Association) 1780

Yearbook Commercial Arbitration. 3945

Yearbook for Traditional Music. 5206

Yearbook of International Organizations/Annuaire des Organisations Internationales. 5779

Yearbook of Tourism Statistics. 6933

Youthlink. 1814

Zahlentafeln der Physikalisch-Chemischen Untersuchungen des Rheinwassers/Tableaux Numeriques des Analyses Physico-Chimiques des Eaux du Rhin. 2841

Zeitschrift fuer Fremdenverkehr/Revue de Tourisme/ Tourist Review. 6928

Zeitschrift fuer Lebensmittel-Untersuchung und - Forschung. 2997

Zhenshchiny Mira. 7013

Zionist Literature. 6015

Zshurnalist. 3714

INTERNATIONAL CONGRESS PROCEEDINGS

Acoustica Imaging. 5613

Acta Endocrinologica Panamericana. 4665

Acta I M E K O. (International Measurement Confederation (IMEKO)) 5011

Acta Medica et Sociologica. 6403

Acta Medicinae Legalis et Socialis. 4685

Advances in Natural and Technological Hazards Research. 5953

Afro-Asian Peoples' Conference Proceedings. 3370

Afro-Asian Peoples' Solidarity Organization. Council. Documents of the Session. 3370

Allergologicum; Transactions of the Collegium Internationale. 4577

Applications of Fibonacci Numbers. 4355

Archivum. 3974

Asian Pacific Congress of Cardiology. Symposia. 4596

Assemblee de l'Union de l'Europe Occidentale. Lettre de l'Assemblee. 3923

Association Internationale pour l'Histoire du Verre. Annales des Congres. 1652

Baptist World Alliance. Congress Reports. 6135

Bayesian Statistics. 6594

Biometeorology. 4991

Brown Boveri Symposia. Proceedings. 2685

C I E S - The Food Business Forum. Annual Executive Summary. (Comite International des Entreprises a Succursales) 2962

Caribbean Congress of Labour. Report. 3718

Carnegie-Rochester Conference Series on Public Policy. 907

Carotenoids Other Than Vitamin A. 635

Chemistry of Natural Products. 1737

Clinical Neurosurgery: Proceedings. 4832

Colloques Internationaux d'Histoire Maritime. Travaux. 6832

Colloquium on the Law of Outer Space. Proceedings. 61

Colombo Plan for Co-operative Economic and Social Development in Asia and the Pacific. Consultative Committee. Proceedings and Conclusions. 1303

Commonwealth Magistrates' Conference. Report. 3762

Comparative Education Society in Europe. Proceedings of the General Meeting. 2321

Computational Acoustics. 5581

Computational Intelligence. 2005

Conference de la Haye de Droit International Prive. Actes et Documents/Hague Conference on Private International Law. Proceedings 3927

Conference Internationale sur les Phenomenes d'Ionisation dans les Gaz. Comptes Rendus. 1750

Conferencia de Facultades Latinoamericanas de Derecho. (Documentos Oficiales). 3763

Congres International d'Histoire des Sciences. Actes. 6235

Congreso Latinamericano de Siderurgia. Memoria Tecnica. 4952

Congresos Indigenistas Interamericanos. Actas. 306

Congress in Park and Recreation Administration. Programme. 4933

Congress in Park and Recreation Administration. Reports. 6560

Congress of Local and Regional Authorities of Europe. Official Reports of Debates. 5897

Congress of Local and Regional Authorities of Europe. Texts Adopted. 5897

Congresso Europeo di Storia Ospitaliera. Atti. 3542

Congresso Latinoamericano de Hidraulica (Papers). 6965

Coordination Chemistry. 1672

Council for the Social Sciences in East Africa. Social Science Conference. Proceedings. 6319

Council of American Building Officials. One and Two Family Dwelling Code. 851

Credit Communal de Belgique. Collection Histoire. Series in 8. 3405

Developments in Biological Standardization. 5013

Developments in Hematology and Immunology. 4699

E A P R Abstracts of Conference Papers. (European Association for Potato Research) 219

E S O M A R Marketing Research Congress. (European Society for Opinion and Marketing Research) 1463

Educator. 2468

Electra. 2691

Electrochemical Society. Proceedings. 1728

Etudes Historiques. 3342

European Association for Personnel Management. Congress Reports. 1502

European Association for Research on Plant Breeding. Report of the Congress. 679

European Brewery Convention. Proceedings of the International Congress. 504

European Civil Aviation Conference (Report of Session) 6755

European Congress of Anaesthesiology. Proceedings. 4591

European Congress of Cardiology. Proceedings. 4601

European Congress on Electron Microscopy. 769

European Grassland Federation. Proceedings of the General Meeting. 220

European League for Economic Cooperation. Reports of the International Congress. 1306

European Materials Research Society. Symposia Proceedings. 2731

European Ophthalmological Society. Congress Acta. 4769

European Organization for Quality. Conference Proceedings. 6650

F E M S Symposium. (Federation of European Microbiological Societies) 757

F I P Notes. 2659

Falk Symposium. 4454

Federation Internationale des Produceurs de Jus de Fruits. Compte-Rendu du Congres/International Federation of Fruit Juice Producers. Proceedings of Congress. 505

Federation Internationale des Producteurs de Jus de Fruits. Rapport Annuel d'Activite. 2967

Financial and Monetary Policy Studies. 1089

Fordham Corporate Law Institute (Proceedings). 3901

Hybrid Microelectronics Symposium. (Papers). 2521

I A B S E Congress Report. (International Association for Bridge and Structural Engineering) 2661

I A T A Annual Report. (International Air Transport Association) 6758

I B B Y Congress Proceedings. (International Board on Books for Young People) 5998

I C C A Congress Series. (International Council for Commercial Arbitration) 3902

I C E S Marine Science Symposia/Actes du Symposium. (International Council for the Exploration of the Sea) 2935

I C H P E R Congress Proceedings. (International Council on Health, Physical Education and Recreation) 5530

I E E E International Conference on Communications. Conference Record. 1905

I E E E International Conference on Systems, Man, and Cybernetics. Conference Proceedings. 2061

I E E E International Symposium on Circuits and Systems. Proceedings. 2522

I F A C Workshop Series. (International Federation of Automatic Control) 2755

I F A Congress Seminar Series. (International Fiscal Association) 1548

I F L A Annual. (International Federation of Library Associations and Institutions) 3996

I N S E R M Symposia. (Institut National de la Sante et de la Recherche Medicale) 4468

I S O S C Proceedings. (International Society for Soilless Culture) 3057

I S S X Proceedings. (International Society for the Study of Xenobiotics) 4468

Index to Malaysian Conferences/Indeks Persidangan Malaysia. 4938

Information Network and Data Communication. 2037

Inter-African Conference on Co-Operative Societies Meeting. Reunion. 1160

Inter-African Conference on Food and Nutrition. Programa e Informacoes. 5234

Inter-African Conference on Food and Nutrition. Report. 5234

Inter-African Conference on Industrial Commercial and Agricultural Education Meeting. 2451

Inter-African Conference on Medical Co-Operation. Meeting. 4472

Inter-African Conference on Social Science Meeting. 6329

Inter-African Conference on the Treatment of Offenders. Meetings. Reunion. 2165

Inter-African Forestry Conference. Conference Forestiere Interafricaine (Communications). 3019

Inter-African Labour Conference Reports, Recommendations and Conclusions. 1379

Inter-American Commission of Women. Special Assembly. Final Act/Comision Interamericana de Mujeres. Asamblea Extrarodinaria. Acta Final. 5730

Inter-American Development Bank. Board of Governors. Proceedings of the Meeting. 1101

International Academy of Legal Medicine and Social Medicine. Congress Reports. 4686

International Air Safety Seminar Proceedings. 68

International Anatomical Congress. Proceedings. 4472

International Association for Cereal Science and Technology. Congress Proceedings. 2977

International Association for Classical Archaeology. Proceedings of Congress. 357

International Association for Cross-Cultural Psychology. International Conference. Selected Papers. 5849

International Association for Dental Research. Abstracts of the General Meeting. 4566

International Association for Hydraulic Research. Congress Proceedings. 2744

International Association for Scientific Study of Mental Deficiency. Proceedings of International Congress. 4841

International Association of Hail Insurers. Congress Report. 3654

International Association of Logopedics and Phoniatrics. Reports of Congress. 4841

International Association of Meteorology and Atmospheric Physics. Report of Proceedings of General Assembly. 4998

International Association of Milk Control Agencies. Proceedings of Annual Meetings. 251

International Association of Museums of Arms and Military History. Congress Reports. 5123

International Association of Performing Arts Libraries and Museums. Congress Proceedings. 435

International Association of Physical Education and Sports for Girls and Women. Proceedings of the International Congress. 6465

International Association of Plant Breeders for the Protection of Plant Varieties. Congress Reports. 685

International Association of State Lotteries. (Reports of Congress). 1549

International Association of Workers for Troubled Children and Youth. Congress Reports. 2469

International Astronomical Union. General Assembly. Highlights. 481

International Astronomical Union. Proceedings of Symposia. 481

International Astronomical Union. Transactions. 481

International Basketball Federation. Official Report of the World Congress. 6506

International Beekeeping Congress. Reports. 126

International Biodeterioration Symposium. Proceedings. 662

International Biophysics Congress. Abstracts. 621

International Bridge Conference. Proceedings. 2663

International Ceramic Congress. Proceedings. 1658

International Commission of Sugar Technology. Proceedings of the General Assembly. 2978

International Commission on Irrigation and Drainage. Congress Reports. 2744

International Commission on Large Dams. Transactions. 2663

International Comparative Literature Association. Proceedings of the Congress. 4220

International Confederation for Agricultural Credit. Assembly and Congress Reports. 193

International Confederation of Free Trade Unions. World Congress Reports. 3722

International Confederation of Midwives. Congress Reports. 4738

International
  Conference of Agricultural Economists. Proceedings.
  193

International Conference of Building Officials. Analysis
  of Revisions to the (Year) Uniform Codes. 860

International Conference of Building Officials. Building
  Department Administration. 860

International Conference of Building Officials. Code
  Changes Committee. Annual Report. 860

International Conference of Building Officials. Dwelling
  Construction Under the Uniform Building Code.
  860

International Conference of Building Officials. Plan
  Review Manual. 860

International Conference of Building Officials. Uniform
  Code for the Abatement of Dangerous Buildings.
  860

International Conference of Building Officials. Uniform
  Fire Code. 860

International Conference of Building Officials. Uniform
  Housing Code. 860

International Conference of Building Officials. Uniform
  Mechanical Code. 860

International Conference of Ethiopian Studies.
  Proceedings. 3372

International Conference of Social Security Actuaries
  and Statisticians. Reports. 3654

International Conference of Social Work. Conference
  Proceedings. 6377

International Conference on Acoustics. Reports. 5614

International Conference on Asphalt Pavements.
  Proceedings. 6823

International Conference on Basement Tectonics.
  Proceedings. 2210

International Conference on Chemical Vapor
  Deposition. Proceedings. 1678

International Conference on Cloud Physics.
  Proceedings. 4999

International Conference on Computer
  Communications. (Proceedings). 2069

International Conference on Computing Fixed Points
  with Applications. Proceedings. 4369

International Conference on Cosmic Rays.
  (Proceedings). 5595

International Conference on Large High Voltage Electric
  Systems. Proceedings. 2708

International Conference on Lead. Proceedings. 4959

International Conference on Lighthouses and Other
  Aids to Navigation. Reports. 6836

International Conference on Liquefied Natural Gas.
  Papers. 5360

International Conference on Noise Control Engineering.
  Proceedings. 2837

International Conference on Piagetian Theory and the
  Helping Professions. Proceedings. 2342

International Conference on Port and Ocean
  Engineering under Arctic Conditions. Proceedings.
  2604

International Conference on Pressure Surges.
  Proceedings. 2757

International Conference on the Physics of Electronic
  and Atomic Collisions. Abstracts of Contributed
  Papers and Invited Papers. 5595

International Conference on Vehicle Structural
  Mechanics. Proceedings. 6789

International Conference on Wafer Scale Integration.
  2007

International Congress Calendar. 4935

International Congress for Analytical Psychology.
  Proceedings. 5849

International Congress for Byzantine Studies. Acts/
  Congres International des Etudes Byzantines. Actes.
  3419

International Congress for Cybernetics. Proceedings/
  Congres International de Cybernetique. Actes.
  2061

International Congress for Papyrology. Proceedings.
  357

International Congress for Stereology. Proceedings.
  2732

International Congress for the Study of Pre-Columbian
  Cultures of the Lesser Antilles. Proceedings. 312

International Congress of Angiology. Proceedings.
  4604

International Congress of Electroencephalography and
  Clinical Neurophysiology (Proceedings). 4841

International Congress of Entomology. 729

International Congress of Hematology. Proceedings.
  4701

International Congress of Histochemistry and
  Cytochemistry. Proceedings. 640

International Congress of Home Economics. Report.
  3524

International Congress of Libraries and Museums of
  the Performing Arts. Acts. 6697

International Congress of Linguists. Proceedings.
  4075

International Congress of Occupational Therapy.
  Proceedings. 5251

International Congress of Ophthalmology. Abstracts.
  4770

International Congress of Parasitology. Proceedings.
  808

International Congress of Pharmaceutical Sciences.
  Proceedings. 5418

International Congress of Primatology. Proceedings.
  312

International Congress of Psychology. Proceedings.
  5849

International Congress of Radiology. (Reports). 4877

International Congress of Sugarcane Technologists.
  Proceedings. 2978

International Congress of Verdi Studies. Proceedings.
  5165

International Congress on Alcoholism and Addictions.
  Proceedings. 2197

International Congress on Animal Reproduction.
  Proceedings. 6948

International Congress on Canned Foods. Texts of
  Papers Presented and Resolutions/Congres
  International de la Conserve. Textes des
  Communications. 2978

International Congress on Metallic Corrosion.
  (Proceedings). 4959

International Congress on Technology and Technology
  Exchange. Proceedings. 2604

International Congress on the History of Art.
  Proceedings. 435

International Congress Series. 6248

International Congresses on Tropical Medicine and
  Malaria. (Proceedings). 4622

International Council of Homehelp Services. Reports of
  Congress. 4715

International Council of Onomastic Sciences. Congress
  Proceedings. 4075

International Economic Association. Proceedings of the
  Conferences and Congresses. 932

International Electron Devices Meeting. I E D M
  Technical Digest. 2524

International Eucharist Congress. Proceedings. 6182

International Federation for Information and
  Documentation. Proceedings of Congress. 4000

International Federation for Psychotherapy. Congress
  Reports. 4841

International Federation of Agricultural Producers.
  General Conference Proceedings. 126

International Federation of Asian and Western Pacific
  Contractors' Associations. Proceedings of the Annual
  Convention. 4935

International Federation of Catholic Universities.
  General Assembly. Report. 2433

International Federation of Medical Students'
  Associations. Minutes and Reports of the General
  Assembly. 4472

International Federation of Operational Research
  Societies. Airline Group (A G I F O R S)
  Proceedings. 6760

International Federation of Prestressing. Congress
  Proceedings. 2663

International Federation of Prestressing.
  Recommendations. 2663

International Federation of Prestressing. Special
  Reports. 2663

International Forum on Traffic Records Systems
  Proceedings. 6823

International Foundry Congress. Papers and
  Communications. 4959

International Gas Union. Proceedings of World Gas
  Conferences. 5360

International Grassland Congress. Proceedings. 226

International Hop Growers Convention. Report of
  Congress. 259

International Horticultural Congress. Proceedings.
  3058

International Humanist and Ethical Union. Proceedings
  of the Congress. 5480

International Hydrographic Conference. Reports of
  Proceedings. 2297

International Institute for Beet Research. Congress
  Proceedings. 226

International Institute of Administrative Sciences.
  Reports of the International Congress. 5906

International Institute of Ibero-American Literature.
  Congress Proceedings. Memoria. 4220

International Institute of Philosophy. Actes. 5480

International Institute of Synthetic Rubber Producers.
  Annual Meeting Proceedings. 6216

International Joint Conference on Artificial Intelligence.
  Advance Papers of the Conference. 2007

International Joint Conference on Artificial Intelligence.
  Proceedings. 2008

International Journal of Psycho-Analysis. 5850

International Law Association. Reports of Conferences.
  3935

International Literary and Artistic Association.
  Proceedings and Reports of Congress. 3615

International Meeting of Animal Nutrition Experts.
  Proceedings. 274

International Metalworkers' Congress. Reports. 4959

International Mineralogical Association. Proceedings of Meetings. 5066

International Navigation Congress. Papers. 6837

International Navigation Congress. Proceedings. 6837

International Ocean Institute. Pacem in Maribus. Proceedings. 2297

International Office of Cocoa, Chocolate and Sugar Confectionery. Report of the General Assembly. 3000

International Olympic Academy. Report of the Sessions. 6465

International Organization for Cooperation in Health Care. General Assembly. Report. 4474

International Organization of Citrus Virologists. Proceedings of the Conference. 3058

International Ornithological Congress. Proceedings. 777

International Orthopaedics. 4785

International Pediatric Association. Proceedings of Congress. 4807

International Philatelic Federation. General Assembly. Proces-Verbal. 5457

International Political Science Association. World Congress. 5674

International Population Conference. Proceedings. 5786

International Potash Institute. Colloquium. Proceedings. 227

International Potash Institute. Congress Proceedings. 227

International Publishers Association. Proceedings of Congress. 5999

International Road Congresses. Proceedings. 6823

International Satellite Symposium on Acute Renal Failure. Proceedings. 4927

International School of Physics "Enrico Fermi". Proceedings. 5552

International Seaweed Symposium. Proceedings. 686

International Sedimentological Congress. Guidebook. 2245

International Skating Union. Minutes of Congress. 6465

International Social Security Association. Reports of the General Assemblies of the ISSA. 3654

International Society for Labour Law and Social Legislation. Proceedings of Congress. 3793

International Society for Mushroom Science. Symposia Proceedings. 686

International Society for Rock Mechanics. Congress. Proceedings. 2664

International Society for Soil Mechanics and Foundation Engineering. Proceedings. 2664

International Society for Terrain-Vehicle Systems. Proceedings of International Conference. 2664

International Society of Blood Transfusion. Proceedings of the Congress. 4701

International Society of Urology. Reports of Congress. 4927

International Society on Optics within Life Sciences. Series (Proceedings). 588

International Statistical Institute. Bulletin. Proceedings of the Biennial Sessions. 6611

International Studies. Nordic Seminar on Human Rights. Proceedings. 3793

International Sweetener Association. Conference Proceedings. 2979

International Symposium on Atherosclerosis. Proceedings. 4604

International Symposium on Canine Heartworm Disease. Proceedings. 6948

International Symposium on Chemical Reaction Engineering. Proceedings. 2643

International Symposium on Computer Hardware Description Languages. Proceedings. 2078

International Symposium on Concrete Roads. Reports. 2664

International Symposium on Crop Protection. Proceedings. 227

International Symposium on Fault-Tolerant Computing. Digest of Papers. 1993

International Symposium on Rarefied Gas Dynamics. Proceedings. 5552

International Symposium on Regional Development. Papers and Proceedings. 3586

International Symposium on Subscriber Loop and Services. Proceedings. 2710

International Symposium on the Aerodynamics and Ventilation of Vehicle Tunnels. Proceedings. 2664

International Symposium on the Chemistry of Cement. Proceedings. 1679

International Television Symposium and Technical Exhibition, Montreux. Symposium Record. 1963

International Thermal Spraying Conference. Preprint of Papers. 4987

International Trade Conference of Workers of the Building, Wood and Building Materials Industries. (Brochure). 860

International U V - E B Processing Conference and Exhibition. Proceedings. 1679

International Union against Cancer. Proceedings of Congress. 4757

International Union against Tuberculosis and Lung Disease. Conference Proceedings. 4888

International Union for Conservation of Nature and Natural Resources. Proceedings of the General Assembly. 2130

International Union of Anthropological and Ethnological Sciences Newsletter. 313

International Union of Biological Sciences. General Assemblies. Proceedings. 588

International Union of Crystallography. Abstracts of the Triennial Congress. 1726

International Union of Food, Agricultural, Hotel, Restaurant, Catering, Tobacco and Allied Workers' Associations. Meeting of the Executive Committee. I. Documents of the Secretariat. II. Summary Report. 3723

International Union of Geodesy and Geophysics. Proceedings of the General Assembly. 2276

International Union of Latin Notaries. Proceedings of Congress. 5907

International Union of Producers and Distributors of Electrical Energy. Congress Proceedings. 2710

International Union of Public Transport. Reports of the Congresses. 6720

International Union of Radio Science. Proceedings of General Assemblies. 1936

International Water Conference. Proceedings. 6971

International Workshop on H D T V. Proceedings. 1928

Internationaler Weltkongress der U F O-Forscher. Dokumentarbericht. 69

Inter-Parliamentary Union. Summary Records of the Inter-Parliamentary Conferences. 5757

Istituto Internazionale di Studi Liguri. Collezione di Monografie Preistoriche e Archeologiche. 359

Jet Cutting Technology. 2759

Journees Biochimiques Latines. Rapports. 643

Kongres ha-Tsiyoni. Hahlatot/World Zionist Organization. Zionist Congress. 5678

Kongresa Libro. 4935

Macromolecular Chemistry. 1741

Mathematics and Computers in Simulation. 2052

Medical Virology. 4625

Mikroelektronik. 2528

Mushroom Science. 691

N A D C A International Die Casting Congress. Transactions. (North American Die Casting Association) 2739

N A T O Annual Economic Colloquia. Proceedings. 1291

N A T O Challenges of Modern Society. 2811

Nobel Symposium Series. 3620

North Atlantic Treaty Organization. Expert Panel on Air Pollution Modeling. Proceedings. 2839

Open Door International for the Emancipation of the Woman Worker. Report of Congress. 1391

Organization of American States. Permanent Council. Decisions Taken at Meetings (Cumulated Edition). 3482

Pacific Science Association. Congress and Inter-Congress Proceedings. 6270

Pain Research and Clinical Management. 4512

Parapsychology Foundation. Proceedings of International Conferences. 5332

Perugia Quadrennial International Conferences on Cancer. Proceedings. 4762

Photochemistry. 1755

Program of Plenary Sessions and Advance Abstracts of Short Communications. 4573

Progress in Protozoology. 818

Rencontres de Philosophie Medievale. 5495

Rubber Research Institute of Malaysia. Rubber Growers' Conference - Proceedings. 6219

Scandinavian Conference on Artificial Intelligence. 2011

Societe d'Ergonomie de Langue Francaise. Actes du Congres. 5883

Soil & Environment. 2819

Studies in Logic and the Foundations of Mathematics. 4398

Surfactants in Solution. 2650

Symposia Foundation Merieux. 4535

Symposium (International) on Combustion. 1758

Teletraffic Science and Engineering. 1930

Trade Unions International of Chemical, Oil and Allied Workers. International Trade Conference. Documents. 3730

TropMed Seminars on Tropical Medicine. Proceedings. 4629

Unesco. Records of the General Conference. Proceedings. 5775

Unesco. Records of the General Conference. Resolutions. 5775

Union Academique Internationale. Compte Rendu de la Session Annuelle du Comite. 3628

Union Mondiale des Organisations Syndicales sur Bases Economique et Sociale Liberales. Conferences: Rapport. 3731

United Nations Issues Conference. Report. 5776

United Nations of the Next Decade Conference. Report. 5776

United Schools International. Documents of the Biennial Conference. 2453

Vetus Testamentum. Supplements. 6101

Water Supply. 6981

Wenner Gren Center International Symposium Series. 6295

World Association for Educational Research. Congress Reports. 2383

World Buiatrics Congress. 6960

World Conference on Animal Production. Proceedings. 287

World Congress of Psychiatry. Proceedings. 4871

World Congress of the W F D. Proceedings. (World Federation of the Deaf) 3315

World Congress on Fertility and Sterility. Proceedings. 614

World Congress on the Prevention of Occupational Accidents and Diseases. Proceedings. 5260

World Congresses on Information Processing. Proceedings. 4035

World Council of Churches. General Assembly. Assembly - Reports. 6104

World Council of Churches. Minutes and Reports of the Central Committee Meeting. 6104

World Council of Service Clubs. Minutes of the General Meeting. 6399

World Energy Conference. Plenary Conferences. Transactions. 2560

World Federation for Mental Health. Annual Report. 5887

World Movement of Mothers. Reports of Meetings. 6399

World Muslim Conference. Proceedings. 6122

World Union of Jewish Studies. 2915

World Zionist Organization. General Council. Addresses, Debates, Resolutions. 5718

World's Poultry Science Association. Proceedings of World's Poultry Congress. 287

World's Woman's Christian Temperance Union. Triennial Report. 2202

EUROPEAN COMMUNITIES

A C P - E E C Council of Ministers. Annual Report (Year). 1300

Agricultural Markets: Prices. 186

Agricultural Statistics Series No.1: Crop Production. 166

Agricultural Statistics Series No.2: Animal Production. 166

Basic Statistics of the European Union. 6593

Biblio Europe. 3978

Biomedical & Health Research. 4434

Biomedical and Health Research Series. 4434

Bulletin d'Information Sportive/Sports Information Bulletin. 6454

Bulletin of European Studies on Time. 6407

Bulletin of the European Communities and Supplements. 1180

Bulletin of the European Union. 1180

C E E International. Droit et Affaires. (Communaute Economique Europeenne) 3924

C O M Documents. 5743

Commission of the European Communities. Collection of Agreements. 1269

Commission of the European Communities. Community Law. 3926

Commission of the European Communities. Directorate of Taxation. Inventory of Taxes. 1540

Commission of the European Communities. Joint Research Centre, Ispra. Annual Report: Program Biology-Health Protection. 578

Commission of the European Communities. Operation of Nuclear Power Stations. 2574

Commission of the European Communities. Report on Competition Policy. 1517

Commission of the European Communities. Report on the Social Developments. 6319

Commission of the European Communities. Trade Union Information Bulletin. 3719

Community Report. 1184

Completing the Internal Market of the European Community: 1992 Legislation - Business. 3926

Completing the Internal Market of the European Community: 1992 Legislation - Financial Services and Capital Movements. 3926

Completing the Internal Market of the European Community: 1992 Legislation. 3926

Completing the Internal Market of the European Community: 1992 Legislation - Transport, Customs & Travel. 3927

Completing the Internal Market of the European Community: 1992 Legislation - Technical Standards. 3927

Completing the Internal Market of the European Community: 1992 Legislation - Veterinary & Phytosanitary Controls. 3927

Council of Europe. Centre Naturopa. Newsletter. 2124

Council of Europe. Committee of Independent Experts on the European Social Charter. Conclusions. 6368

Council of Europe. Documentation Section. Biblio Bulletin. Series: Crises. 5720

Council of Europe. Documentation Section. Biblio Bulletin. Series: East - West Relations. 5720

Council of Europe. Documentation Section. Biblio Bulletin. Series: Legal Affairs. 3874

Council of Europe. Documentation Section. Biblio Bulletin. Series: Political, Economic and Social Affairs. 5720

Council of Europe. European Treaty Series. 3927

Council of Europe. Parliamentary Assembly. Documents: Working Papers. 3927

Council of Europe. Parliamentary Assembly. Official Report of Debates. 3927

Council of Europe. Parliamentary Assembly. Orders of the Day, Minutes of Proceedings. 3927

Council of Europe. Parliamentary Assembly. Texts Adopted by the Assembly. 3927

Council of Europe. Standing Committee on the European Convention on Establishment (Individuals). Periodical Report. 5726

Council of Europe. Study Series: Local and Regional Authorities in Europe. 5940

Council of Europe. Symposium on Legal Processing. Proceedings. 3889

Council of Europe Forum. 5645

Council of the European Communities. Review of the Council's Work. 1185

Courier. Africa - Caribbean - Pacific - European Union. 1304

Cultural Policy. 5746

Current Topics in Veterinary Medicine and Animal Science. 6944

Debates of the European Parliament. 3927

Developments in Clinical Biochemistry. 637

Developments in Pharmacology. 5407

Developments in the European Communities. Report. 1203

Directory of Community Legislation in Force. 3769

Directory of European Community Trade and Professional Associations/Repertoire des Organisations Professionnelles de la Communaute Europeene/Verzeichnis der Verbaende in der Europaeischen Gemeinschaft. 1599

Dossier Europa. 5662

E C H O News. (European Community Humanitarian Office) 1305

E C S C Financial Report. (European Coal and Steel Community) 1542

E F News. (European Foundation for the Improvement of Living and Working Conditions) 6321

E G Magazin. (Europaeische Gemeinschaft) 5663

E I B - Information. (European Investment Bank) 1328

E L F. (European Labour Forum) 5747

E P News. (Spanish edition: Tribuna del Parlamento Europeo) 3928

E S R A Newsletter. (European Safety and Reliability Association) 5958

E U D I S E D - European Educational Research Yearbook. (European Documentation and Information System for Education) 2388

Earnings - Industry and Services. 994

Education and Culture. Section 1: Cultural Development. 2327

Education and Culture. Section 2: Higher Education and Research. 2327

Education in Europe. Cultural Development. 2328

Education in Europe. Section 1: Higher Education and Research. 2427

Energy in Europe. 2546

Environment Features. 2787

Environmental Research Newsletter. 2793

Erasmus Newsletter. 2428

Eur-Op News. 5749

Euro Abstracts.
6671

Euro Courses. Advanced Scientific Techniques.　6650

Euro Courses. Chemical and Environmental Sciences.
2795

Euro Courses. Computer and Information Science.
1989

Euro Courses. Environmental Impact Assessment.
2795

Euro Courses. Environmental Management.　2796

Euro Courses. Health Physics and Radiation
Protection.　2575

Euro Courses. Mechanical and Materials Science.
2731

Euro Courses. Nuclear Science and Technology.　2575

Euro Courses. Reliability and Risk Analysis.　6650

Euro Courses. Remote Sensing.　6650

Euro Courses. Technological Innovation.　6650

Euro - Who's Who.　556

Eurocat.　5901

Eurolink Age Bulletin.　3286

Europa Transport.　6717

Europa van Morgen.　5749

Europe.　1210

Europe Information Development.　1306

European Access.　922

European Art Exhibitions. Catalog.　428

European Aspects, Law Series.　3776

European Aspects, Social Studies Series.　6412

European Co-Operation.　3929

European Coal and Steel Community. Consultative
Committee. Yearbook.　1306

European Commission. Directory.　3929

European Commission. Tacis Programme. Contract
Information Update.　1306

European Commission of Human Rights. Decisions and
Reports.　5727

European Communities. Court of Justice and Court of
First Instance. Proceedings.　3947

European Communities. Court of Justice and Court of
First Instance. Reports of Cases before the Court.
3929

European Communities. Diario Oficial.　5901

European Communities. Economic and Social
Committee. Bulletin.　922

European Communities. Economic and Social
Committee. Commission Documents.　922

European Communities. Economic and Social
Consultative Assembly. Annual Report.　922

European Community Humanitarian Office. Annual
Report.　1306

European Convention on Human Rights. Yearbook.
5727

European Court of Human Rights. Publications. Series
B: Pleadings, Oral Arguments and Documents/Cour
Europeenne des Droits de l'Homme. Publications.
Serie B: Memoires, Plaidoiries et Documents.　5727

European Economy. Series A: Recent Economic
Trends.　1210

European Economy. Series B: Business and Consumer
Survey Results.　1210

European File.　1273

European Foundation for the Improvement of Living
and Working Conditions. Annual Report.　6412

European Investment Bank. Annual Report.　1086

European Parliament. Bulletin.　5749

European Parliament. Christian-Democratic Group.
Report on the Activities.　5665

European Participation Monitor.　6323

European Regional Planning Study Series.　5941

European Savings Bank. Report.　1087

European Yearbook/Annuaire Europeen.　3930

Eurostat. Rapid Reports. Environment.　2829

Eurostat. Rapid Reports. Services and Transports.
6738

Eurostat. Statistics in Focus. Agriculture, Forestry and
Fisheries.　172

Eurostat. Statistics in Focus. Economy and Finance.
995

Eurostat. Statistics in Focus. Energy and Industry.
995

Eurostat. Statistics in Focus. External Trade.　996

Eurostat. Statistics in Focus. Population and Social
Conditions.　996

Eurostat. Statistics in Focus. Regions.　996

Eurostat. Statistics in Focus. Research and
Development.　996

Eurostat. Statistik Kurzgefasst. Bevoelkerung und
Soziale Bedingungen.　996

Eurostat. Statistik Kurzgefasst. Energie und Industrie.
996

Eurostat. Statistik Kurzgefasst. Forschung und
Entwicklung.　996

Eurostat. Statistik Kurzgefasst. Land- und
Forstwirtschaft, Fischerei.　172

Eurostat. Statistik Kurzgefasst. Wirtschaft und
Finanzen.　996

Eurostat. Statistiques en Bref. Agriculture, Sylviculture
et Peche.　172

Eurostat. Statistiques en Bref. Economie et Finances.
996

Eurostat. Statistiques en Bref. Energie et Industrie.
996

Eurostat. Statistiques en Bref. Population et Conditions
Sociales.　996

Eurostat. Statistiques en Bref. Recherche et
Developpement.　996

Eurostat Catalogue.　5995

Eurostatistics Data for Short Term Economic Analysis.
996

Eurozoom.　1903

Evropa.　5750

External Trade: Nomenclature of Goods/Commerce
Exterieur: Nomenclature des Pays.　1274

Frontier-Free Europe.　1277

General Report on the Activities of the European
Communities.　1213

Green Europe.　120

I & T Magazine. (Industrie et Telecoms)　1905

I & T Magazine News Review.　1905

Industrial Trends.　1006

Info - C (English Edition).　2152

Info Phare.　1309

Information Service of the European Communities.
Newsletter on the Common Agricultural Policy.
193

Innovation and Technology Transfer.　3999

Ispra Courses on Energy Systems and Technology.
2578

Ispra Courses on Nuclear Engineering and Technology
Series.　2578

Janus.　1381

Joint Nuclear Research Center, Ispra, Italy. Annual
Report.　2578

Local and Regional Authorities in Europe. Study Series.
5944

Mines Safety and Health Commission. Report/Organe
Permanent pour la Securite dans les Mines de
Houille. Rapport.　5071

Nature and Environment Series.　2135

Naturopa.　2136

Nouvelles Universitaires Europeenes/European
University News.　2358

O J C D. (Official Journal of the European
Communities)　5765

O J Index. (Official Journal of the European
Communities)　5765

Official Journal of the European Communities. C Series:
Information and Notices (English Edition).　5765

Official Journal of the European Communities. L & C:
Legislation and Competition.　5765

Panorama of E U Industry.　1292

Perspectives.　1115

Practical Guide to the Use of the European
Communities' Scheme of Generalized Tariff
Preferences.　1293

Prison Information Bulletin.　2173

Progress in Coal Steel and Related Social Research.
5085

Recent Demographic Developments in Europe and
North America.　5790

Recent Publications on the European Union Received
by the Library/Publicaciones Recientes sobre la
Union Europea Recibidas por la Biblioteca/Nye
Publikationer om den Europaeiske Union Modtaget
af Biblioteket/Neuerscheinungen ueber die
Europaeische Union Eingegangen in der Bibliothek/
Publications Recentes sur l'Union Europeenne
Recues par la Bibliotheque/Pubblicazioni Recenti
sull'Unione Europea Recevute della Biblioteca.
5723

Recherches Universitaires sur l'Integration
Europeenne/University Research on European
Integration.　5723

Results of the Business Survey Carried Out Among
Managements in the Community.　1530

S C A D Bulletin. (Systeme Communautaire d'Acces a
la Documentation)　3879

Sardius.　5723

Sigma.　6628

Sigma.　6628

Social Europe.　6392

Statistical Office of the European Communities.
Agricultural Prices.　181

Statistical Office of the European Communities. Bulletin
of Energy Prices.　2565

Statistical Office of the European Communities. Energy Statistics. Yearbook. 2565

Statistical Office of the European Communities. Energy Statistics Monthly Bulletin. 2565

Statistical Office of the European Communities. National Accounts Yearbook. 1029

Statistical Office of the European Communities. Statistical Studies and Surveys. 1030

Statistical Office of the European Communities. Statistical Yearbook. Agriculture. 181

Statistical Office of the European Communities. Transport, Communications, Tourisme - Annuaire Statistique. 6745

Terminologie et Traduction. 4117

Vocational Training. 5274

Vocational Training Information Bulletin. 5274

World Patent Information. 5346

Yearbook of the European Communities and of the Other European Organizations/Annuaire des Communautes Europeennes et des Autres Organisations Europeennes/Jahrbuch der Europaeischen Gemeinschaften und der Anderen Europaeischen Organisationen. 5928

UNITED NATIONS

A B C Human Rights Teaching. 2449

A C E I D Newsletter. (Asian Centre of Educational Innovation for Development) 2449

A D I Quarterly News Letter. (Asian Development Institute) 1300

A F R O Technical Papers. 5953

A F R O Technical Report Series. 5953

Accident - Incident Reporting A D R E P. 6735

Adult Education Information Notes. 2395

Advances in Materials Technology: Monitor. 2724

Aeronautical Information Services Provided by States/Services d'Information Aeronautique Assures par les Etats/Aeronavigatsionnoe Informatsionnoe Obsluzhivanie, Predostavlyaemoe Gosudarstvami/Servicios de Informacion Aeronautica Suministrados por los Estados. 6748

African Journal of Science and Technology. Series A. Technology. 6645

African Journal of Science and Technology. Series B. Basic Sciences. 6224

African Journal of Science and Technology. Series C. General. 6224

African Population Newsletter (Bilingual Edition). 5780

Agricultural Review for Europe. 186

Agricultural Taxation Studies. 186

Agricultural Trade in Europe. 186

Agrindex. 92

Agro-Chemicals News in Brief. 209

AIDS - S T D Health Promotion Exchange. 4617

Aircraft Accident Digest. 55

Aircraft Characteristics Data Bank. Volume 1 - Summary and Explanation. 6750

Aircraft Type Designators/Indicatifs de Type d'Aeronef/Designadores de Tipos de Aeronave. 56

Airport Characteristics Data Bank. Volume 2 - Indian Ocean Region. 6751

Airport Characteristics Data Bank. Volume 3 - Carribbean and South American Regions. 6751

Airport Characteristics Data Bank. Volume 4 - European Region. 6751

Airport Characteristics Data Bank. Volume 5 - Middle East and Asia Regions. 6751

Airport Characteristics Data Bank. Volume 6 - North Atlantic, North American and Pacific Regions. 6751

Alpha - Current Research in Literacy. 2311

Animal Health Yearbook 6941

Animal Production and Health Newsletter. 4873

Annotated Accessions List of Studies and Reports in the Field of Science Statistics. 516

Annual Bulletin of Coal Statistics for Europe and North America. 5082

Annual Bulletin of Electric Energy Statistics for Europe. 2561

Annual Bulletin of Gas Statistics for Europe/Bulletin Annuel de Statistiques de Gaz pour l'Europe. 5381

Annual Bulletin of General Energy Statistics for Europe. 2561

Annual Bulletin of Housing and Building Statistics for Europe. 880

Annual Bulletin of Steel Statistics for Europe. 4981

Annual Bulletin of Trade in Chemical Products. 1514

Annual Bulletin of Transport Statistics for Europe. 6735

Annual Report on Development Assistance to Mauritius. 1301

Annual Review of Engineering Industries and Automation. 2728

Anuario Estadistico de America Latina y el Caribe/Statistical Yearbook for Latin America and the Caribbean. 6585

Anuario Hidrologico del Istmo Centroamericano. 2284

Art. 412

Asia - Pacific Development Journal. 1174

Asia - Pacific Fishery Commission. Report. 2927

Asia - Pacific in Figures. 6587

Asia - Pacific Population Journal. 5781

Asian Bibliography. 3365

Asian - Pacific Book Development. 5987

Asian - Pacific Cultural Centre for Unesco. Organization and Activities. 5279

Asian Pacific Culture. 5279

Atlas of Mineral Resources of the E S C A P Region. 5056

B F H I News. (Baby-Friendly Hospital Initiative) 6362

B I B E Quarterly Bulletin. 2385

Basic Facts about the United Nations. 5742

Bibliographical Services Throughout the World. 520

Bold. 3284

Boletin de Arte. 420

Bollettino per le Farmacodipendenze e l'Alcoolismo. 2195

Border Epidemiological Bulletin/Boletin Epidemiologico Fronterizo. 5956

Border Health/Salud Fronteriza. 5956

Bulletin of Labour Statistics. 984

Bulletin on Ageing. 3284

Bulletin on Narcotics. 2195

C C I V S News. (Coordinating Committee for International Voluntary Service) 6363

C E P A L Review. (Comision Economica para America Latina y el Caribe) 1181

C I F A Technical Papers. (Committee for Inland Fisheries of Africa) 2928

C I N D A. 5578

Caribbean Documentation Centre. Current Awareness Bulletin. 526

Catalogue of I L O Publications in Print. 988

Catalogue of Reproductions of Paintings, 1860-1979. 422

Catalonia Cultura. 3215

Census of Motor Traffic on Main International Traffic Arteries. 6821

Centro Latinoamericano de Demografia. Boletin Demografico. 5782

Centro Latinoamericano de Demografia. Notas de Poblacion. 5782

Centro Latinoamericano de Demografia. Serie A/Latin American Demographic Centre. Serie A. 5782

Centro Latinoamericano de Demografia. Serie C/Latin American Demographic Centre. Serie C. 5782

Centro Latinoamericano de Demografia. Serie D/Latin American Demographic Centre. Serie D. 5782

Centro Latinoamericano de Demografia. Serie OI: Publicaciones Conjuntas con Instituciones Nacionales de Paises de America Latina. 5782

Centro Pan-Americano de Febre Aftosa. Boletin. 5957

Cereal Policies Review. 256

Ceres. 107

Chemical Industry in (Year) - Annual Review. 1516

Children First! 6366

Civil Aviation Statistics of the World (Year). 6738

Codes and Abbreviations for the Use of the International Telecommunications Services. 1944

Comision Economica para America Latina y el Caribe. Desarrollo Productivo. 1303

Comision Economica para America Latina y el Caribe. Serie Financiamiento del Desarrollo. 1303

Comision Economica para America Latina y el Caribe. Serie INFOPLAN. 1303

Comision Economica para America Latina y el Caribe. Serie Reformas de Politica Publica. 1184

Commodity Trade Statistics. 950

Composition of the W M O. (World Meteorological Organization) 4993

Conditions of Work Digest. 1368

Confluence. 6965

Connaissance de l'Orient. Collection Unesco d'Oeuvres Representatives. 4198

Connect. 2781

Copyright Bulletin. 3765

Copyright Laws and Treaties of the World. 5337

Copyright Laws and Treaties of the World. Supplement. 5337

Corriere Unesco. 306

The Cost of Social Security. 6368

Courier (Paris). 5746

Cuadernos de la C E P A L. 1159

D O C P A L Resumenes sobre Poblacion en America Latina/D O C P A L Latin American Population Abstracts. 5798

Demographic Handbook for Africa/Guide Demographie de l'Afrique. 5783

Demographic Yearbook. 5783

Desertification Control Bulletin. 2206

Designators for Aircraft Operating Agencies, Aeronautical Authorities and Services. 62

Development Business. 1305

Development Forum. 1305

Development Information Abstracts/Bulletin Analytique sur le Developpement/Resumenes de Informacion sobre el Desarrollo. 993

Diogenes (English Edition). 6411

Direction of Trade Statistics. 993

Directory of On-Going Research in Cancer Epidemiology. 4754

Disarmament. 5029

Disarmament Newsletter. 5662

Disarmament Times. 5662

Disaster Preparedness and Mitigation in the Americas. 5958

Documentation, Libraries and Archives: Studies and Research. 3990

E D I Development Policy Case Series. (Economic Development Institute) 915

E S C A P Energy News. (United Nations Economic and Social Commission for Asia and the Pacific) 2543

E S C W A Population Bulletin. (Economic and Social Commission for Western Asia) 5783

Earth Sciences Series. 2207

East-West Investment News. 1328

Economic and Social Commission for Asia and the Pacific. Annual Report. 1305

Economic and Social Commission for Asia and the Pacific. Annual Report. Supplement. 1305

Economic and Social Survey of Asia and the Pacific. 1205

Economic Bulletin for Europe (Annual). 1205

Economic Commission for Europe. Annual Report. 917

Economic Survey of Europe. 1206

Economic Survey of Latin America and the Caribbean. 1206

Educacion Medica y Salud. 2411

Education in Asia and the Pacific: Reviews, Reports and Notes. 2328

Educational Building Digest. 854

Educational Innovation and Information. 2450

Educational Studies and Documents. 2331

Electric Power in Asia and the Pacific. 2691

Emergency Response Guidance for Aircraft Incidents Involving Dangerous Goods. 6754

Emerging Stock Markets Factbook. 1085

Energy Balances and Electricity Profiles. 2568

Energy Balances of Developing Countries. 2569

Energy Statistics Yearbook. 2563

Enfants du Monde. 6370

Environmentally Sustainable Development Proceedings Series. 1306

Epidemiological Surveillance of Rabies for the Americas. 6945

Estudios e Informes de la C E P A L/C E P A L Studies and Reports. 1306

European Civil Aviation Conference (Report of Session) 6755

Everyone's United Nations. 5750

F A O Agricultural Services Bulletin. (Food and Agriculture Organization of the United Nations) 190

F A O Animal Production and Health Papers. (Food and Agriculture Organization of the United Nations) 271

F A O Commodity Review and Outlook. (Food and Agriculture Organization of the United Nations) 190

F A O Documentation - Current Bibliography. 2947

F A O Economic and Social Development Paper. 923

F A O Fertilizer and Plant Nutrition Bulletin. (Food and Agriculture Organization of the United Nations) 190

F A O Fertilizer Yearbook. 220

F A O Fisheries Circulars. 2930

F A O Fisheries Reports. 2930

F A O Fisheries Series. 2930

F A O Fisheries Technical Paper. 2930

F A O Food and Nutrition Series. (Food and Agriculture Organization of the United Nations) 5232

F A O Irrigation and Drainage Papers. 6968

F A O Land and Development Series. 113

F A O Legislative Study. 114

F A O Plant Protection Bulletin (Multilingual Edition). 680

F A O Production Yearbook. (Food and Agriculture Organization of the United Nations) 190

F A O Quarterly Bulletin of Statistics/Bulletin Trimestriel F A O de Statistiques/Boletin Trimestral F A O de Estadisticas. 172

F A O Regional Conference for Africa. Report. 114

F A O Regional Conference for Asia and the Pacific. Report. 114

F A O Regional Conference for Europe. Report. 114

F A O Regional Conference for Latin America and the Caribbean. Report. 114

F A O Regional Conference for the Near East. Report. 114

F A O Soils Bulletin. (Food and Agriculture Organization of the United Nations) 220

F A Q Terminology Bulletin. 114

F A O Yearbook, Trade. 191

Farm Management Notes for Asia and the Far East. 191

Fertilizer Trade Information Monthly Bulletin. 221

Finance and Development. 1089

First Call for Children. 6372

Flora, Fauna y Areas Silvestres. 6240

Food and Agricultural Legislation. 3781

Food and Agriculture Organization of the United Nations. Asia and Pacific Plant Protection Commission. Quarterly Newsletter. 222

Food and Agriculture Organization of the United Nations. Asia and Pacific Plant Protection Commission. Technical Document. 222

Food and Agriculture Organization of the United Nations. Asia and the Pacific Commission on Agricultural Statistics. Periodic Report. 172

Food and Agriculture Organization of the United Nations. Basic Texts. 118

Food and Agriculture Organization of the United Nations. European Inland Fisheries Advisory Commission. Occasional Papers. 2933

Food and Agriculture Organization of the United Nations. European Inland Fisheries Advisory Commission. Technical Papers. 2933

Food and Agriculture Organization of the United Nations. World Soil Resources Reports. 222

Food and Agriculture Organization of the United Nations Conference. Report. 118

Food and Nutrition Bulletin. 5232

Food Irradiation Newsletter. 2970

Food Nutrition and Agriculture/Alimentation Nutrition et Agriculture/Alimentacion Nutricion y Agricultura. 5232

Foreign Trade Statistics of Africa. Series A: Direction of Trade. 999

Foreign Trade Statistics of Africa. Series C: Summary Tables/Statistiques Africaines du Commerce Exterieur. Serie C: Tableaux Recapitulatifs. 999

Foreign Trade Statistics of Asia and the Pacific. 999

Freshwater and Aquaculture Contents Tables. 2933

Fuentes Unesco. 6324

Fundamentals of Educational Planning. 2450

G A T T Activities. (General Agreement on Tariffs and Trade) 1277

G A T T Focus. (General Agreement on Tariffs and Trade) 1277

General Agreement on Tariffs and Trade. Basic Instruments and Selected Documents Series. Supplement. 1277

General Agreement on Tariffs and Trade. International Trade. 1277

General Fisheries Council for the Mediterranean. Reports of the Sessions. 2933

General Fisheries Council for the Mediterranean. Studies and Reviews. 2933

General Information Program - U N I S I S T Newsletter. 3994

Geological Correlation. 2236

Global Population Policy Database (Year). 5784

Guide to National Bibliographical Information Centres. 3994

Guide to Sources of International Population Assistance. 5784

Guide to U N C T A D Publications. 1003

Handbook of State Trading Organizations of Developing Countries/Repertoire des Organismes de Commerce d'Etat des Pays en Developpement/Repertorio de las Organizaciones Comerciales Estatales de Paises en Desarrollo/Dalil al-Hay'at at-Tiganiyya al-Hukumiyya fi al-Buldan an-Namiya. 1003

High Frequency Broadcasting Schedule. 1936

Higher Education in Europe. 2431

Human Factors Digest. 67

Human Rights Bulletin. 5729

Human Rights Newsletter. 5729

Human Settlements Basic Statistics/Statistiques de Base Etablissements Humains/Estadisticas Basicas de Asentamientos Humanos. 3602

I A E A Bulletin. (International Atomic Energy Agency) 2577

I A E A Library Film Catalog. (International Atomic Energy Agency) 2577

I A E A Technical Documents Series. (International Atomic Energy Agency) 2577

I A R C Biennial Report. (International Agency for Research on Cancer) 4756

I A R C Monographs on the Evaluation of Carcinogenic Risk of Chemicals to Humans. (International Agency for Research on Cancer) 4756

I A R C Scientific Publications. (International Agency for Research on Cancer) 4756

I A R C Technical Reports. (International Agency for Research on Cancer) 4756

I C A O Abbreviations and Codes. (International Civil Aviation Organization) 6759

I C A O Circulars. (International Civil Aviation Organization) 6759

The I C A O Financial Regulations. (International Civil Aviation Organization) 6759

I C A O Journal. (International Civil Aviation Organization) 67

I C A O Publications and Audio Visual Training Aids Catalogue. (International Civil Aviation Organization) 6740

I C A O Publications Regulations. (International Civil Aviation Organization) 6759

I C T P Series in Theoretical Physics. (International Centre for Theoretical Physics) 5550

I F A D Update. (International Fund for Agricultural Development) 1308

I F C Discussion Paper. (International Finance Corporation) 1308

I I E P Occasional Papers. (International Institute for Educational Planning) 2450

I I E P Research Reports. (International Institute for Educational Planning) 2450

I I E P Seminar Papers. (International Institute for Educational Planning) 2450

I L C A Proceedings. (International Livestock Centre for Africa) 272

I L O Judgements of the Administrative Tribunal. (International Labour Office) 3789

I L O Publications. (International Labour Office) 1004

I L P E S Cuadernos. (Instituto Latinamericano y del Caribe de Planificacion Economica y Social) 1401

I M F Survey. (International Monetary Fund) 1004

I M O News. (International Maritime Organization) 6836

I M S Newsletter. (International Marine Science) 2296

I N I S Atomindex. (International Atomic Energy Agency) 5579

I N I S Newsletter. 3996

I N I S Reference Series. 3996

I N S T R A W News. (International Research and Training Institute for the Advancement of Women) 6997

ILOLEX C D - R O M. (International Labour Office) 1377

Index Translationum. 4039

Indicators for the Telegram Retransmission System (TRS) - Telex Identification Codes. 1946

Industrial Development News for Asia and the Pacific. 1309

Industrial Property and Copyright. 5339

Industrial Property, Statistics B. Part 1 - Patents/Propriete Industrielle, Statistiques B. Partie 1 - Brevets. 5347

Industrial Property, Statistics B. Part 2 - Trademarks and Service Marks, Utility Models, Industrial Designs, Varieties of Plants, Microorganisms/Propriete Industrielle, Statistiques B. Partie 2 - Marques de Produits et des Services, Modeles d'Utilite, Dessins et Modeles Industriels, Obtentions Vegetales, Micro-organismes. 5347

Industry and Environment. 2802

Infoterra Programme Activity Centre. Exchange of Environmental Experience Series. 2802

Inpaz en las Americas. (Instituto Panamericano de Proteccion de Alimentos y Zoonosis) 6947

Insect and Pest Control Newsletter. 2642

Instituto de Nutricion de Centro America y Panama (INCAP). Informe Anual. 5234

Instituto Panamericano de Proteccion de Alimentos y Zoonosis. Publicacion Tecnica. 6948

Intergovernmental Oceanographic Commission. Technical Series. 2296

International Accounting and Reporting Issues. 1048

International Administration. 3933

International Atomic Energy Agency. Annual Report. 2577

International Atomic Energy Agency. Legal Series. 3792

International Atomic Energy Agency. Nuclear Power Reactors in the World. 2577

International Atomic Energy Agency. Panel Proceedings Series. 2577

International Atomic Energy Agency. Proceedings Series. 2577

International Atomic Energy Agency. Safety Series. 5965

International Atomic Energy Agency. Technical Directories. 2577

International Atomic Energy Agency. Technical Report Series. 2577

International Award for Literacy Research/Prix International de Recherche en Alphabetisation/Premio Internacional a la Investigacion en Alfabetizacion. 2342

International Bulletin on Atomic and Molecular Data for Fusion. 2577

International Catalogue of Occupational Safety and Health Films. 5261

International Centre for Theoretical Physics. Annual Report. 5551

International Civil Aviation Organization. Aeronautical Agreements and Arrangements. Annual Supplement. 6759

International Civil Aviation Organization. Aeronautical Chart Catalogue. 6759

International Civil Aviation Organization. Air Navigation Plan. Africa - Indian Ocean Region. 68

International Civil Aviation Organization. Air Navigation Plan. Caribbean and South American Regions. 68

International Civil Aviation Organization. Air Navigation Plan. Middle East and Asia Regions. 68

International Civil Aviation Organization. Air Navigation Plan. North Atlantic, North American and Pacific Regions. 68

International Civil Aviation Organization. Aircraft Operations. 6759

International Civil Aviation Organization. Annexes to the Convention on Civil Aviation. 6759

International Civil Aviation Organization. Assembly. Minutes of the Plenary Meetings. 6759

International Civil Aviation Organization. Assembly. Report and Minutes of the Administrative Commission. 6759

International Civil Aviation Organization. Assembly. Report and Minutes of the Economic Commission. 6759

International Civil Aviation Organization. Assembly. Report and Minutes of the Legal Commission. 6759

International Civil Aviation Organization. Assembly. Report of the Technical Commission. 68

International Civil Aviation Organization. Assembly. Reports and Minutes of the Executive Committee. 6760

International Civil Aviation Organization. Assembly. Resolutions. 6760

International Civil Aviation Organization. Committee on Aviation Environmental Protection. Report of the Meeting. 68

International Civil Aviation Organization. Conventions. 6760

International Civil Aviation Organization. Council. Annual Report. 6760

International Civil Aviation Organization. Council to Contracting States on Charges for Airports and Air Navigation Systems. Statements. 68

International Civil Aviation Organization. Digests of Statistics. Series AF. Airport and Route Facilities. Financial Data and Summary Traffic Data/Organisation de l'Aviation Civile. Recueil de Statistiques. Serie AF. Installations et Services d'Aeroport et de Route. Donnes Financieres et Statistiques de Traffic Sommaires/Mezhdunarodnaya Organizatsiya Grazhdanskoi Aviatsii. Statisticheski Sbornik. Seriya AF. Aeroportnoe i Marshrutnoe Oborudovanie. Finansovye Izlozheniya Dannykh po Perenozhkam/Organizacion de Aviacion Civil Internacional. Compendio Estadistico. Serie AF. Instalaciones y Servicios de Aeropuerto y en Ruta. Datos Financieros y Resumen de Datos de Trafico. 6740

International Civil Aviation Organization. Digests of Statistics. Series AT. Airport Traffic. 6741

International Civil Aviation Organization. Digests of Statistics. Series F. Financial Data - Commercial Air Carriers. 6741

International Civil Aviation Organization. Digests of Statistics. Series FP. Fleet - Personnel - Commercial Air Carriers. 6741

International Civil Aviation Organization. Digests of Statistics. Series OFOD. On-Flight Origin and Destination/Organisation de l'Aviation Civile Internationale. Receuil de Statistiques. Serie OFOD. Origine et Destination par Vol/Mezhdunarodnaya Organizatsiya Grazhdanskoi Aviatsii. Statisticeski Sbornik. Seriya OFOD. Nasalny i Konesny Punkty Poleta/Organizacion de Aviacion Civil Internacional. Compendio Estadistico. Serie OFOD. Origen y Destino por Vuelo. 6741

International Civil Aviation Organization. Digests of Statistics. Series R. Civil Aircraft on Register. 6741

International Civil Aviation Organization. Digests of Statistics. Series TF. Traffic by Flight Stage. 6741

International Civil Aviation Organization. Digests of Statistics. Series T. Traffic, Commercial Air Traffic. 6741

International Civil Aviation Organization. Legal Committee. Minutes and Documents (of Sessions). 6760

International Civil Aviation Organization. Location Indicators. 587

International Civil Aviation Organization. Protocols. 6760

International Civil Aviation Organization. Report of the Air Navigation Conference. 6760

International Civil Aviation Organization. Rules of the Air and Air Traffic Services. 6760

International Civil Aviation Organization. Special Committee for the Monitoring and Co-ordination of Development and Transition Planning for the Future Air Navigation System (FANS - Phase II). Report of the Meeting. 69

International Civil Aviation Organization. Visual Aids Panel. Report of the Meeting. 6760

International Conference on Education. Final Report/ Conference International de l'Education. Rapport Final. 2342

International Court of Justice. Bibliography/Cour Internationale de Justice. Bibliographie. (International Court of Justice) 3876

International Court of Justice. Yearbook. 3934

International Designs Bulletin. 5340

International Digest of Health Legislation. 5965

International Directory of New and Renewable Energy Information Sources and Research Centres. 2551

International Directory of Sources. Infoterra. 2803

International Energy Agency. Energy Prices and Taxes. 2552

International Finance Corporation. Report. 1102

International Financial Statistics. 1006

International Financial Statistics Yearbook. 1006

International Frequency List/Liste Internationale des Frequences/Lista Internacional de Frecuencias. 1963

International Frequency List. Preface. 1963

International Institute for Labour Studies. Research Series. 1379

International Journal of Global Energy Issues. 2552

International Labour Conference. Reports to the Conference and Record of Proceedings. 1380

International Labour Documentation. 1006

International Labour Office. Official Bulletin. Series A. 1380

International Labour Office. Official Bulletin. Series B. 1380

International Labour Review. 1380

International Maritime Organization. International Code for the Construction and Equipment of Ships Carrying Liquefied Gases in Bulk. 6837

International Maritime Organization. Testing and Evaluation of Life-Saving Appliances. 6837

International Markets for Meat. 274

International Monetary Fund. Annual Report of the Executive Board. 1102

International Monetary Fund. Annual Report on Exchange Arrangements and Exchange Restrictions. 1102

International Monetary Fund. Balance of Payments Statistics Yearbook. 1007

International Monetary Fund. Government Finance Statistics Yearbook. 1007

International Monetary Fund. Occasional Papers. 1102

International Monetary Fund. Pamphlet Series. 1102

International Monetary Fund. Selected Decisions of the International Monetary Fund and Selected Documents. 1102

International Monetary Fund. Staff Papers. 1102

International Monetary Fund. Summary Proceedings of the Annual Meeting of the Board of Governors. 1102

International Monetary Fund. World Economic and Financial Surveys. 1102

International Narcotics Control Board. Report for (Year). 5419

International Narcotics Control Board. Statistics on Psychotropic Substances for (Year). 5450

International Oceanographic Tables. 2297

International Radio Consultative Committee. Plenary Assembly. Proceedings. 1936

International Review for the Sociology of Sport. 6418

International Review of Criminal Policy. 2166

International Review of Education/Internationale Zeitschrift fuer Erziehungswissenschaft/Revue Internationale de Pedagogie. 2343

International Rice Commission. Newsletter. 227

International SafetyNet Manual. 1907

International Social Science Journal. 6330

International Telecommunication Union. Booklets. 1908

International Telecommunication Union. Central Library. List of Annuals/Union Internationale des Telecommunications. Bibliotheque Centrale. Listes des Publications Annuelles/Union Internacional de Telecomunicaciones. Biblioteca Central. Lista de Publicaciones Anuales. 1924

International Telecommunication Union. Central Library. List of Periodicals/Union Internationale des Telecommunications. Bibliotheque Centrale. Liste des Periodiques/Union Internacional de Telcomunicaciones. Biblioteca Central. Lista de Revistas. 1924

International Telecommunication Union. Central Library. List of Recent Acquisitions/Union Internationale des Telecommunications. Bibliotheque Centrale. Liste des Acquisitions Recentes/Union Internacional de Telecomunicaciones. Biblioteca Central. Lista de Adquisiciones Recientes. 1924

International Telecommunication Union. List of Telegraph Offices Open for International Service. 1946

International Telecommunication Union. Operational Bulletin. 1946

International Telecommunication Union. Report on the Activities. 1946

International Telecommunication Union. Seminars. 1908

International Telegraph and Telephone Consultative Committee. Plans. 1946

International Telegraph and Telephone Consultative Committee. Plenary Assembly. Proceedings. 1946

International Trade Forum. 1281

International Trade Statistics Yearbook. 1007

International Travel and Health: Vaccination Requirements and Health Advice. 5966

International Yearbook of Education. 2343

International Yearbook of Industrial Statistics. 1007

Inventory of Population Projects in Developing Countries Around the World. 5786

Joint F A O - W H O Codex Alimentarius Commission. Report of the Session. 5966

Journal of Development Planning. 1310

Korean Social Science Journal. 6332

L I L A C S - C D - R O M. (Literatura Latinoamericana y del Caribe en Ciencias de la Salud) 4567

Labour Education. 1385

Labour-Management Relations Series. 1385

Land Reform, Land Settlement and Cooperatives. 194

Lead and Zinc Statistics. 4983

Lifelong Education Network. 2351

List of Cables Forming the World Submarine Network. 1947

List of E C A Documents Issued/Liste des Documents Publies par la C E A. 1311

List of International Telephone Routes. 1947

Litani. 5037

Management Development Series. 1432

Manufacture of Narcotic Drugs and Psychotropic Substances under International Control. 2199

Marine Science Contents Tables. 621

Market Trends & Prospects for Chemical Products. 1685

MARPOL 73 - 78 Amendments. 2133

Marques Internationales. 5342

Meetings on Atomic Energy. 4936

Migrant Pest Newsletter. 231

Monitoring Information Summary. 1937

Monographs on Oceanographic Methodology. 2301

Museum International. 5127

Museums and Monuments Series. 5128

Mutation Breeding Newsletter. 231

N A T I S - News. (National Information System) 4013

N G O News on Human Settlements. (Non-Governmental Organization) 3589

Narcotic Drugs: Estimated World Requirements for (Year). 5451

Natural Resources Research. 2213

Nature and Resources (English Edition). 2135

Nature et Faune. 2136

Navtex Manual. 1912

New Acquisitions in the U N E C A Library. 541

New Trends in Biology Teaching. 597

New Trends in Chemistry Teaching. 1687

New Trends in Integrated Science Teaching. 2496

New Trends in Physics Teaching. 5560

New United Nations Publications. 5687

News from I C T P. (International Centre for Theoretical Physics) 5560

Nomenclature des Stations de Radiocommunications Spatiales et des Stations de Radioastronomie/List of Space Radiocommunication Stations and Radioastronomy Station/Nomenclator de las Estaciones de Radiocomunicacion Espacial y de las Estaciones de Radioastronomia. 1938

Nomenclature des Voies de Telecommunication Utilisees pour la Transmission des Telegrammes/List of Telecommunication Channels Used for the Transmission of Telegrams/Nomenclator de las Vias de Telecomunicacion Empleadas para la Transmision de Telegramas. 1948

Notas sobre la Economia y el Desarrollo. 1225

Nuclear Data Newsletter. 2580

Nuclear Fusion/Fusion Nucleaire. 5596

Objective: Justice. 5733

Occupational Safety and Health Series. 5256

Oficina Sanitaria Panamericana. Boletin. 5971

Operational Hydrology Report. 2288

Our Planet. 2814

P C T Gazette. (Patent Cooperation Treaty) 5347

Palestine Refugees Today. 6386

Pan American Health Organization. Bulletin. 5972

Periodicals of Asia and the Pacific. 3280

Permanent Missions to the United Nations. 5767

Personnel des Nations Unies et des Agences Specialisees en Republique de Rwanda. 1313

Perspectives. 2362

Pesticide Residues in Food. 5972

Plant Variety Protection. 236

Population Bulletin of the United Nations. 5789

Population Education in Asia and the Pacific Newsletter and Forum. 5789

Population Headliners. 5789

Population Studies. 5790

Populi. 5790

Prices of Agricultural Products and Selected Inputs in Europe and North America. 198

Professional Training Series. 5734

The Progress of Nations. 6387

La Propriete Industrielle et le Droit d'Auteur. 5343

Prospects. 2364

Rapport Annuel sur l'Assistance au Developpement: Rwanda. 1313

Rapport Annuel sur la Cooperation au Developpement - Burundi. 1313

Recommendations on the Safe Use of Pesticides in Ships. 2847

Refugee Survey Quarterly. 5803

Refugees Magazine. 5768

Regional Development Dialogue. 1313

Regional Development Studies. 1314

Regional Differences in Fares, Rates and Costs for International Air Transport (Year). 6764

Regional Information Support Service. 180

Repindex. 2831

Report on Development Assistance to Ethiopia. 1314

Report on Development Cooperation to the Democratic Republic of the Sudan. 1314

Report on the World Health Situation. 5974

Reports and Papers in the Social Sciences. 6340

Reports and Papers on Mass Communications. 1914

Review of Maritime Transport. 6846

Revista Internacional de Ciencias Sociales. 6341

Revista Internacional del Trabajo. 1393

Revue de Coree. 5292

Revue Internationale des Sciences Sociales. 6341

Revue Internationale du Travail. 1394

Rural Progress. 1314

Safety and Health at Work. 5261

Sample Surveys in the ESCAP Region. 1024

Science Policy Studies and Documents. 6281

Securite et Sante au Travail. 5261

Selective Inventory of Social Science Information and Documentation Services. 6343

Ship Safety and Pollution Prevention - Ship Management and Port State Control. 2848

Siren. 2305

Sister Communities Health Profiles of the U S - Mexico Border/Perfiles de Salud de las Comunidades Hermanas de la Frontera Mexico - Estados Unidos. 5984

Small Industry Bulletin for Asia and the Pacific. 1445

Social Development Newsletter. 6430

Social Indicators of Development (Year). 1314

Soils Newsletter. 241

Solas - International Convention for the Safety of Life at Sea. Amendments. 2848

State of Food and Agriculture. 153

The State of the World's Children. 6395

State of World Population. 5792

Statistical Indicators for Asia and the Pacific. 1029

Statistical Indicators of Short Term Economic Changes in E.C.E. Countries. 1241

Statistical Information Bulletin for Africa/Bulletin d'Information Statistique pour l'Afrique. 1029

Statistical Yearbook for Asia and the Pacific/Annuaire Statistique pour l'Asie et le Pacifique. 1030

Statistics of Road Traffic Accidents in Europe and North America. 6745

Statistics of World Trade in Steel. 4985

Steel Market. 4976

Studies and Reports in Hydrology Series. 2289

Studies in Mathematics Education. 2452

Studies in the Processing, Marketing and Distribution of Commodities. 1487

Study Abroad/Etudes a l'Etranger/Estudios en el Extranjero. 2452

Survey of Economic and Social Conditions in Africa. 1315

Surveys of International Air Transport Fares and Rates. 6765

Table of International Telex Relations and Traffic. 1950

Technical Instructions for the Safe Transport of Dangerous Goods by Air. 5765

Technical Papers in Hydrology Series. 2289

Telecommunication Journal. 1917

Tiger Paper. 2143

Timber Bulletin. 3038

Tots: Quaderns d'Educacio Ambiental. 2822

Trade and Development Report. 1296

Trade Policy Review. 1297

Transnational Corporations. 1297

Transnational Corporations and Transborder Data Flows. 1157

Transport & Communications Bulletin for Asia & the Pacific 6729

Trends in Developing Economies (Year). 1315

Tsetse and Trypanosomiasis Information Quarterly. 625

Tungsten Statistics. 4985

U I E Handbooks. (Unesco Institute for Education) 2378

U I E Studies in Education. (Unesco Institute for Education) 2378

U I P - Berichte/U I E Reports, Dossiers I U E. (Unesco Institut fuer Paedagogik) 2378

U N A New Z. (United Nations Association of New Zealand) 5713

U N B I S Plus on C D - R O M. (United Nations Bibliographic Information System) 5723

U N C H S (Habitat) Shelter Bulletin. (United Nations Centre for Human Settlements (Habitat)) 3596

U N C H S Habitat News. (United Nations Centre for Human Settlements (Habitat)) 3596

U N C R D Annual Report. (United Nations Centre for Regional Development) 1315

U N C R D Newsletter. 1315

U N C T A D Bulletin. (United Nations Conference on Trade and Development) 1297

U N C T A D Commodity Yearbook. (United Nations Conference on Trade and Development) 1033

U N C T A D Review. (United Nations Conference on Trade and Development) 1297

U N Chronicle. 5774

U N D O C: Current Index. (United Nations Documents) 5723

U N I C E F Policy Review Series. (United Nations Children's Fund) 6397

U N I D I R Newsletter/Lettre de l'U N I D I R. (United Nations Institute for Disarmament Research) 5774

U N I D O Links. (United Nations Industrial Development Organization) 1315

U N R I S D Social Development News. (United Nations Research Institute for Social Development) 6350

Unasylva. 3027

Unesco. Centro de Documentacion Cultural, Havana. Informaciones Trimestrales. 3528

Unesco. Comision Nacional Cubana. Boletin. 3628

Unesco. Principal Regional Office for Asia and Pacific. Abstract Bibliography Series on Population Education. 2394

Unesco. Principal Regional Office for Asia and the Pacific. Bulletin. 2379

Unesco. Records of the General Conference. Proceedings. 5775

Unesco. Records of the General Conference. Resolutions. 5775

Unesco. Regional Office for Science and Technology for Latin America and the Caribbean. Boletin. 6669

Unesco. Report of the Director-General on the Activities of the Organization. 5775

Unesco. Scientific Maps and Atlases and Other Related Publications. 549

Unesco. Studies on Books and Reading. 6010

Unesco Association - U S A Newsletter. 5775

Unesco Australia. 1316

Unesco General History of Africa. 3376

Unesco List of Documents and Publications. 2394

Unesco Nairobi Bulletin. 6292

Unesco Reports in Marine Science. 611

Unesco Statistical Reports and Studies. 6641

Unesco Statistical Yearbook. 6641

Union Postale. 1933

Union Postale Universelle. Actes. 1933

Union Postale Universelle. Statistique des Services Postaux. 1933

United Nations. Conference on Trade and Development. Trade and Development Board. Official Records. 1316

United Nations. Conference on Trade and Development. Trade and Development Board. Official Records. Supplements. 5775

United Nations. Department of International Economic and Social Affairs. Statistical Office. Construction Statistic Yearbook. 885

United Nations. Department of Public Information. Programme Update. 5775

United Nations. Development Programme. Compendium of Approved Projects. 1316

United Nations. Division of Narcotic Drugs. Information Letter. 2201

United Nations. Economic and Social Commission for Asia and the Pacific. Asian Population Studies Series. 5793

United Nations. Economic and Social Commission for Asia and the Pacific. Development Papers. 2143

United Nations. Economic and Social Commission for Asia and the Pacific. Mineral Resources Development Series. 5080

United Nations. Economic and Social Commission for Asia and the Pacific. Natural Resources - Water Series. 6975

United Nations. Economic and Social Commission for Asia and the Pacific. Water Resources Series. 6975

United Nations. Economic and Social Council. Annexes. 966

United Nations. Economic and Social Council. Index to Proceedings. 5723

United Nations. Economic and Social Council. Official Records. 5775

United Nations. Economic Commission for Asia and the Pacific. Energy Resources Development Series. 2559

United Nations. Economic Commission for Europe. Economic Studies. 1244

United Nations. Economic Commission for Europe. Statistical Journal. 6641

United Nations. General Assembly. Annexes. 966

United Nations. General Assembly. Index to Proceedings. 5723

United Nations. General Assembly. Official Records. 966

United Nations. General Assembly. Provisional Records. 966

United Nations. International Law Commission Yearbook. 3943

United Nations. Multilateral Treaties Deposited with the Secretary-General. 3943

United Nations. National Accounts Statistics. Analysis of Main Aggregates. 1034

United Nations. National Accounts Statistics. Government Accounts and Tables. 1034

United Nations. National Accounts Statistics. Main Aggregates and Detailed Tables. 1034

United Nations. Population and Vital Statistics Report. 5806

United Nations. Security Council. Index to Proceedings. 5724

United Nations. Security Council. Official Records. 5775

United Nations. Security Council. Official Records. Supplement. 5775

United Nations. Statistical Yearbook. 6641

United Nations. Treaty Series. 3943

United Nations. Treaty Series. Cumulative Index. 3879

United Nations. Trusteeship Council. Index to Proceedings. 5724

United Nations. Trusteeship Council. Official Records. 5775

United Nations. Trusteeship Council. Official Records. Annexes - Sessional Fascicle. 5775

United Nations. Trusteeship Council. Official Records. Resolutions. 5775

United Nations. Trusteeship Council. Official Records. Supplements. 5775

United Nations. Trusteeship Council. Official Records. Verbatim Records of Plenary Meetings. 5775

United Nations. Yearbook. 5775

United Nations Association of the Republic of China News Letter. 5775

The United Nations Blue Books Series. 5776

United Nations Children's Fund. Annual Report. 6397

United Nations Children's Fund. Programme Division. Staff Working Papers Series. 6397

United Nations Commission on International Trade Law. Report on the Work of Its Session. 3943

United Nations Commission on International Trade Law. Yearbook. 3943

United Nations Conference on the Standardization of Geographical Names. Report of the Conference. 3276

United Nations Conference on Trade and Development: Proceedings. 1298

United Nations Congress on the Prevention of Crime and the Treatment of Offenders. Report. 2177

United Nations Disarmament Yearbook. 5051

United Nations Economic and Social Commission for Asia and the Pacific. Social Development Division. Social Work Education and Development. 6397

United Nations Economic and Social Commission for Asia and the Pacific. Statistical Newsletter. 1034

United Nations Economic and Social Council. Disarmament Study Series. 5051

United Nations Economic and Social Council. Official Records. Supplements and Special Supplements. 966

United Nations Economic and Social Council. Resolutions and Decisions. 966

United Nations Economic and Social Council. Summary Records of Plenary Meetings. 966

United Nations Economic Commission for Africa. Annual Report. 1316

United Nations Economic Commission for Africa. Biennial Report of the Executive Secretary. 1316

United Nations Economic Commission for Africa. Statistical Newsletter. 1034

United Nations Economic Commission for Europe. Discussion Papers. 1244

United Nations Environment Programme. Environmental Data Report. 2823

United Nations Environment Programme. Governing Council. Report on the Work of its Session. 2823

United Nations Environment Programme. The State of the Environment; Report of the Executive Director. 2823

United Nations Interregional Crime and Justice Research Institute. Issues and Reports Series/ Institute Interregional de Recherche des Nations Unies sur la Criminalite et la Justice. Themes et Rapports Serie. 2177

United Nations Interregional Crime and Justice Research Institute. Publication. 2177

United Nations Juridical Yearbook. 3943

United Nations Law Report. 3943

United Nations Library. Monthly Bibliography. Part 1: Books, Official Documents, Serials. 5724

United Nations Library. Monthly Bibliography. Part 2: Selected Articles. 5724

United Nations Population Fund. Annual Report. 5793

United Nations Population Fund. Annual Review of Population Law. 5793

United Nations Regional Cartographic Conference for Asia and the Pacific. Report of the Conference. 3276

United Nations Regional Cartographic Conference for the Americas. Report of the Conference. 3276

United Nations Resolutions. Series 1. Resolutions Adopted by the General Assembly. 3944

United Nations Resolutions. Series 2. Resolutions and Decisions of the Security Council. 3944

United Nations Review. 5776

United Nations Statistical Office. Monthly Bulletin of Statistics. 6641

United Nations University. Work in Progress. 1316

Urban Age. 1316

Vigilancia Epidemiologica de la Rabia para las Americas. 6960

W E P Studies. (World Employment Programme) 1398

W H O AIDS Series. (World Health Organization) 4629

W H O Food Additives Series. (World Health Organization) 2994

W H O Technical Report Series. (World Health Organization) 4543

W M O Bulletin. (World Meteorological Organization) 5008

Waste Management Research Abstracts. 5985

Water Resources Journal. 6980

Weekly Epidemiological Record. 5979

World Animal Review. 287

World Bank. Annual Report. 1317

World Bank. E D I Development Study. (Economic Development Institute) 1317

World Bank. Global Environment Facility Paper. 1317

World Bank. Publications Update. 1317

The World Bank and the Environment. 1299

World Bank Annual Conference on Development Economics. Proceedings. 971

World Bank Atlas. 1317

World Bank Country Study. 1317

World Bank Discussion Paper. 1317

The World Bank Economic Review. 1246

World Bank Policy Paper. 1317

World Bank Policy Research Bulletin. 1317

World Bank Regional and Sectoral Studies. 1317

World Bank Research Observer. 1127

World Bank Research Program. 1035

World Bank Technical Paper. 1317

World Cartography. 3278

World Data (Year). 1246

World Debt Tables. 1317

World Directory of Human Rights Research and Training Institutions. 1649

World Economic Outlook. 1247

World Education Report. 2383

World Food Programme Journal. 5243

World Health. 5979

World Health Forum. 4544

World Health Organization. Bulletin. 4544

World Health Organization. Handbook of Resolutions and Decisions of the World Health Assembly and the Executive Board. 5979

World Health Organization. Regional Office for Africa. Report of the Regional Committee. 5979

World Health Organization. Regional Office for Africa. Report of the Regional Director. 5979

World Health Organization. Regional Office for the Eastern Mediterranean. Annual Report of the Regional Director. 5979

World Health Organization. Regional Office for the Western Pacific. Annual Report of the Regional Director to the Regional Committee for the Western Pacific. 5980

World Health Report. 5980

World Health Statistics Annual. 5985

World Health Statistics Quarterly/Rapport Trimestriel de Sanitares Mondiales. 5985

World Investment Report. 1360

World List of Social Science Periodicals. 6358

World Market for Dairy Products. 163

World Media Handbook. 1921

World Meteorological Congress. Proceedings. 5009

World Meteorological Organization. Abridged Final Reports of Sessions of Technical Commissions. 5009

World Meteorological Organization. Annual Report. 5009

World Meteorological Organization. Basic Documents. 5009

World Meteorological Organization. Commission for Aeronautical Meteorology. Abridged Final Report of the (No.) Session. 5009

World Meteorological Organization. Commission for Agricultural Meteorology. Abridged Final Report of the (No.) Session. 5009

World Meteorological Organization. Commission for Basic Systems. Abridged Final Report of the (No.) Session. 5009

World Meteorological Organization. Commission for Hydrology. Abridged Final Report of the (No.) Session. 5009

World Meteorological Organization. Commission for Instruments and Methods of Observation. Abridged Final Report of the (No.) Session. 5009

World Meteorological Organization. Commission for Marine Meteorology. Abridged Final Report of the (No.) Session. 5009

World Meteorological Organization. Congress. Abridged Report with Resolutions. 5010

World Meteorological Organization. Executive Council Session. Abridged Final Reports with Resolutions. 5010

World Meteorological Organization. Regional Association I (Africa). Abridged Final Report of the (No.) Session. 5010

World Meteorological Organization. Regional Association II (Asia). Abridged Final Report of the (No.) Session. 5010

World Meteorological Organization. Regional Association III (South America). Abridged Final Report of the (No.) Session. 5010

World Meteorological Organization. Regional Association IV (North America and Central America). Abridged Final Report of the (No.) Session. 5010

World Meteorological Organization. Regional Association V (South West Pacific). Abridged Final Report of the (No.) Session. 5010

World Meteorological Organization. Reports on Marine Science Affairs. 2308

World Meteorological Organization. Special Environmental Reports. 2826

World Meteorological Organization. Technical Notes. 5010

World Meteorological Organization. Weather Reporting. Volume A: Observing Stations. 5010

World Meteorological Organization. Weather Reporting. Volume B: Data Processing. 5010

World Meteorological Organization. Weather Reporting. Volume C2: Transmissions. 5010

World Meteorological Organization. Weather Reporting. Volume D: Information for Shipping. 5010

The World of Civil Aviation. 6756
World of Work. (International Labour Office) 1400

World Patent Information. 5345

World Population Projections. 3807

World Trade Annual. 1036

World Trade Annual Supplement. 1035

World Weather Watch Planning Reports. 5010

Yearbook of Common Carrier Telecommunication Statistics/Annuaire Statistique des Telecommunications du Secteur Public. 1921

Yearbook of Forest Products/Annuaire des Produits Forestiers/Anuario de Productos Forestales. 3040

Year Book of Labour Statistics. 1036

Yearbook on Human Rights. 5739

Your United Nations. 3364

Controlled Circulation Serials

A A A A S F NEWS.
American Association for Accreditation of
Ambulatory Surgery Facilities, 1202 Allanson Rd.,
Mundelein, IL 60060. TEL 708-949-6058.
circ. 500. *4901*

A A A TODAY MAGAZINE.
Automobile Club Publications, 1000 AAA Dr.,
Heathrow, FL 32746-5063. TEL 407-444-8200.
circ. 1,700,000. *6766*

A A A TRAVELER (FLORHAM PARK).
New Jersey Automobile Club, 1 Hanover Rd.,
Florham Park, NJ 07932. TEL 201-377-7200.
FAX 201-377-2979.
circ. 175,000. *6864*

A A B BULLETIN.
American Association of Bioanalysts, 818 Olive St.,
Ste. 918, St. Louis, MO 63101. TEL 314-241-
1445.
circ. 1,700. *4676*

A A C E BONUS BRIEFS.
American Association for Career Education, 2900
Amby Pl., Hermosa Beach, CA 90254-2216.
TEL 310-376-7318. FAX 310-374-1360.
circ. 500. *5261*

A A C E DISTINGUISHED MEMBER SERIES.
American Association for Career Education, 2900
Amby Pl., Hermosa Beach, CA 90254-2216.
TEL 310-376-7378. FAX 310-374-1360.
circ. 500. *5261*

A A G BIJDRAGEN.
Landbouwuniversiteit Wageningen, Vakgroep
Agrarische Geschiedenis, Hollandseweg 1, 6706 KN
Wageningen, Netherlands. TEL 31-8370-84027.
circ. 1,100. *3390*

A A I S VIEWPOINT.
American Association of Insurance Services, 1035
S. York Rd., Bensenville, IL 60106. TEL 708-595-
3225. FAX 708-595-4647.
circ. 1,500. *3639*

A A L C REPORTER.
African-American Labor Center, A F L - C I O, 1925
K St., Ste. 300, Washington, DC 20006. TEL 202-
778-4600. FAX 202-778-4601.
circ. 3,500. *3716*

A A MAGAZINE.
V N U Business Publications BV, VNU House, 32-34
Broadwick St., London W1A 2HG, England. TEL 44-
171-439-4242. FAX 44-171-437-7001.
circ. 62,202. *1036*

A A P A NEWS.
American Academy of Physician Assistants, 950 N.
Washington St., Alexandria, VA 22314-1552.
TEL 703-836-2272. FAX 703-684-1924.
circ. 22,000. *4416*

A A P S NEWSLETTER.
American Association of Pharmaceutical Scientists,
1650 King St., 2nd Fl., Alexandria, VA 22314-
2747. TEL 703-548-3000. FAX 703-684-7349.
circ. 7,000. *5396*

A.A.R.N. NEWSLETTER.
Alberta Association of Registered Nurses, 11620-
168 St., Edmonton, AB T5M 4A6, Canada.
TEL 403-451-0043. FAX 403-452-3276.
circ. 24,000. *4708*

A B C COLOR.
A B C Color, Yegros 745, CC 1241, Asuncion,
Paraguay. TEL 595-21-491-160. FAX 595-21-493-
059. *3205*

A B C DIALOGUE.
Association of Bridal Consultants, 200 Chestnutland
Rd., New Milford, CT 06776-2521. TEL 860-355-
0464. FAX 860-354-1404.
circ. 1,700. *4412*

A.B.D.
Air Service Directory, Inc. 105 Calvert St., Harrison,
NY 10528-3138. TEL 914-835-7200.
circ. 20,500. *50*

A B E S P BOLETIM.
Associacao Brasileira de Endodontia, Seccao Sao
Paulo, Praca Amadeu Amaral 47-8, Sao Paulo, SP,
Brazil.
circ. 2,500. *4632*

A B Q CORRESPONDENT.
A B Q Communications Corporation, Box 1432,
Corrales, NM 87048. TEL 505-897-0822.
FAX 505-898-6525.
circ. 100. *6645*

A C J S PROGRAM BOOK.
Academy of Criminal Justice Sciences, 402 Nunn
Hall, Northern Kentucky University, Highland
Heights, KY 41099-5998. TEL 606-572-5434.
FAX 606-572-6665.
circ. 2,000. *2417*

A C M S I G P L A N NOTICES.
Association for Computing Machinery, Special
Interest Group on Programming Languages, 1515
Broadway, 17th Fl., New York, NY 10036.
TEL 212-869-7440. FAX 212-302-5826.
circ. 11,600. *2042*

A C O G NEWSLETTER.
American College of Obstetricians and
Gynecologists, 409 12th St. S.W., Washington, DC
20024. TEL 202-863-2423. FAX 202-479-6826.
circ. 35,000. *4730*

A C S A NEWS.
Association of Collegiate Schools of Architecture,
Inc., 1735 New York Ave., N.W., Washington, DC
20006. TEL 202-785-2324 FAX 202-628-0448.
circ. 3,800. *380*

**A C U BULLETIN OF CURRENT DOCUMENTATION
(ABCD).**
Association of Commonwealth Universities, John
Foster House, 36 Gordon Sq. London WC1H 0PF,
England. TEL 44-171-387-8572. FAX 44-171-387-
2655. *2417*

A D L LAW ENFORCEMENT BULLETIN.
Anti-Defamation League, 823 United Nations Plaza,
New York, NY 10017. TEL 212-490-2525.
circ. 5,000. *3733*

A D N O C NEWS.
Abu Dhabi National Oil Company, Public Relations
Department, P.O. Box 898, Abu Dhabi, United Arab
Emirates. TEL 666000. FAX 655745
circ. 3,500. *5348*

A D R NEWS.
State Bar of Wisconsin, Alternative Dispute
Resolution Section, 402 W. Wilson St., Madison, WI
53703. TEL 608-257-3838. FAX 608-257-5502.
circ. 188. *3733*

A E A ADVOCATE.
Arizona Education Association, 100 W Clarendon,
Ste. 1600 Phoenix, AZ 85013 3511. TEL 602-
264-1774. FAX 602-240-6887.
circ. 30,000. *2309*

A E R REPORT.
Association for Education and Rehabilitation of the
Blind and Visually Impaired (AER), 206 N.
Washington St., Alexandria, VA 22314 TEL 703-
548-1884 *3316*

A F F I LETTER.
American Frozen Food Institute, 2000 Corporate
Ridge., Ste. 1000, McLean, VA 22102. TEL 703-
821-0770. FAX 703-821-1350
circ. 1,300 *2958*

A G E REFDEX.
Geotechnical Engineering International Resources Center, c/o Asian Institute of Technology, Box 2754, Bangkok 10501, Thailand. TEL 66-2-524-5862. FAX 66-2-516-2126.
circ. 300. *2217*

A G M A ZINE.
American Guild of Musical Artists, 1727 Broadway, New York, NY 10019-5284.
circ. 6,000. *5136*

A G NEWS.
Associated Grocers of Colorado Inc., 707 17th St., Ste. 2800, Denver, CO 80202-3428.
circ. 2,000. *3002*

A H & M A'S REGISTER (YEAR).
American Hotel & Motel Association, 1201 New York Ave., N.W., Washington, DC 20005-3931. TEL 202-289-3100. FAX 202-289-3199.
circ. 12,000. *3558*

A I A - D C NEWS.
American Institute of Architects, Washington Chapter, 1777 Church St., N.W., Washington, DC 20036. TEL 202-667-1798. FAX 202-667-4327.
circ. 1,500. *381*

A I ARCHITECT.
American Institute of Architects Press, 1735 New York Ave., N.W., Washington, DC 20006. TEL 202-626-7465.
circ. 56,000. *381*

A I C NEWS.
American Institute for Conservation of Historic and Artistic Works, 1717 K St., N.W., Ste. 301, Washington, DC 20006. TEL 202-452-9545. FAX 202-452-9328.
circ. 3,000. *408*

A I D - AUSLAENDER IN DEUTSCHLAND.
Isoplan Institut, Martin-Luther-Str. 20, 66111 Saarbruecken, Germany. TEL 49-681-936460. FAX 49-681-9364611.
circ. 33,000. *5780*

A I D RESEARCH AND DEVELOPMENT ABSTRACTS.
U.S. Agency for International Development, Policy Directorate, POL-CDIE-DI, Dept. of State, Washington, DC 20523-1802. TEL 202-875-4818. FAX 703-351-4039.
circ. 5,000. *973*

A I M C FORUM.
Association of International Management Consultants, 7960 Soquel Dr., Ste. B296, Aptos, CA 95003-3945. TEL 716-657-7878. FAX 716-657-4070.
circ. 500. *1403*

A I M INTERNATIONAL.
Africa Inland Mission International, Box 178, Pearl River, NY 10965. TEL 914-735-4014. FAX 914-735-1814.
circ. 30,000. *6041*

A I S NEWSLETTER.
American Indian Society of Washington D.C., Box 6431, Falls Church, VA 22040-6531. TEL 804-448-3707. FAX 804-448-2493.
circ. 500. *2859*

A L E B C I; BOLETIN INFORMATIVO.
Asociacion Latinoamericana de Escuelas de Bibliotecologia y Ciencias de la Informacion, Escuela de Bibliotecologia, Centro Regional de Veraguas, Santiago de Veraguas, Panama. FAX 984056.
circ. 500. *3969*

A L S A R.
Ediciones Anel, San Vicente Ferrer 13, Granada, Spain.
circ. 25,000. *83*

A L T A CAPITAL COMMENT.
American Land Title Association, 1828 L St. N.W., Washington, DC 20036-5182. TEL 202-296-3671.
circ. 4,300. *6018*

A M.
Editora Ave Maria Ltda, Rua Martins Francisco 646, Caixa Postal, 615, 01000 Sao Paulo, Brazil.
circ. 50,000. *6166*

A M A - AGRICULTURAL MECHANIZATION IN ASIA, AFRICA AND LATIN AMERICA.
Shin-Norinsha Co., Ltd., 7, 2-chome, Kanda Nishiki-cho, Chiyoda-ku, Tokyo 101, Japan. TEL 03-3291-3674. FAX 03-3291-5717.
circ. 15,000. *202*

A M A MANAGEMENT BRIEFINGS.
American Management Association, 135 W. 50th St., New York, NY 10020-1201. TEL 212-586-8100. *1403*

A M A VICTORIA BRANCH NEWS.
Australian Medical Association, Victoria Branch, 293 Royal Parade, Parkville, Vic. 3052, Australia. FAX 03-347-9871. *4417*

A M MAGAZINE.
Aston Martin Owners' Club Ltd., 22 Bank St., Braintree, Essex CM7 7UP, England. FAX 44-1376-551431.
circ. 4,000. *6767*

A M O A LOCATION.
Amusement and Music Operators Association, 401 N. Michigan Ave., Chicago, IL 60611. TEL 312-245-1021. FAX 312-321-6869.
circ. 2,000. *5136*

A N S A JOURNAL.
Association of Nurses in Substance Abuse, 18 St. Johns St., Bury St. Edmunds, Suffolk IP33 1SJ, England. TEL 0284-762377. FAX 0284-724374.
circ. 400. *4708*

A O.
Stichting I V I O, Postbus 37, 8200 AA Lelystad, Netherlands. TEL 31-3200-76411. FAX 31-3200-33756.
circ. 7,000. *3195*

A P C O BULLETIN.
Association of Public-Safety Communications Officials International, Inc., 2040 S. Ridgewood Ave., Daytona Beach, FL 32119-8437. TEL 904-322-2500. FAX 904-322-2501.
circ. 12,500. *5953*

A P F NEWS.
Association of Professional Foresters, 7-9 West St., Belford, Northumber. NE70 7QA, England. TEL 44-1668-213937. FAX 44-1668-213555.
circ. 1,300. *3009*

A P F REPORTER.
Alicia Patterson Foundation, 1730 Pennsylvania Ave., N.W., Ste. 850, Washington, DC 20006. TEL 202-393-5995. FAX 301-951-8512.
circ. 3,200. *3700*

A P N Y NEWSLETTER.
Advertising Photographers of New York, 27 W. 20th St., Rm. 601, New York, NY 10011. TEL 212-807-0399. FAX 212-727-8120.
circ. 1,000. *5508*

A P R O DIRECTORY.
B M I Publications Ltd., Suffolk House, George St., Croydon, Surrey CR9 1SR, England. TEL 44-181-649-7233. FAX 44-649-7234.
circ. 1,000. *6864*

A PLUS ARCHITECTURE.
Centre d'Information de l'Architecture, de l'Urbanisme et du Design, Chaussee de Ruisbroek 83, 1190 Brussels, Belgium. TEL 32-2-3322472. FAX 32-2-3322208.
circ. 13,200. *381*

A R D R I NEWS.
University of Fort Hare, Agricultural and Rural Development Research Institute, Private Bag X1314, Alice 5700, South Africa. TEL 0404-31154. FAX 0404-31730.
circ. 1,000. *84*

A S A EXPO GUIDE AND MEMBERSHIP DIRECTORY (YEARS).
American Sportfishing Association, 1033 N. Fairfax St., Ste. 200, Alexandria, VA 22314-1540. TEL 703-519-9691. FAX 703-519-1872.
circ. 10,000. *2924*

A S A NEWS.
American Supply Association, 222 Merchandise Mart Pl., Ste. 1360, Chicago, IL 60654. TEL 312-464-0090. FAX 312-464-0091.
circ. 17,000. *3325*

A S B A TODAY.
American Small Business Association, Box 3323, Oakton, VA 22124. TEL 800-235-3298.
circ. 112,000. *1572*

A S D A TODAY.
American Society for Dental Aesthetics, 635 Madison Ave., New York, NY 10022. TEL 212-371-4575.
circ. 3,000. *4633*

A S H R M FORUM.
American Hospital Association, One North Franklin, Chicago, IL 60606. TEL 312-422-3989. FAX 312-422-4580.
circ. 3,000. *3539*

A S I D REPORT.
American Society of Interior Designers, 608 Massachusetts Ave., N.E., Washington, DC 20002-6006. TEL 202-546-3480. FAX 202-546-3240.
circ. 35,000. *3672*

A S M A NEWS.
American Sports Medicine Association, Board of Certification, 660 W. Duarte Rd., Arcadia, CA 91007. TEL 818-445-1978.
circ. 3,500. *6448*

A S P A FLASH.
International Business Ventures Corp., Box 42450, Phoenix, AZ 85080-2450. TEL 602-272-2900. FAX 602-269-1843.
circ. 195. *6767*

A S T R NEWSLETTER.
American Society for Theatre Research, c/o P.T. Dircks, Ed., C.W. Post College, Dept. of English, Greenvale, NY 11548. TEL 516-299-2391.
circ. 600. *6691*

A S U NATIONAL.
Australian Services Union, National Executive, 2nd Fl., 116-124 Queensberry St., Carlton South, Vic. 3053, Australia. TEL 03-348-1788. FAX 03-349-1108.
circ. 190,000. *3716*

A S VORORT.
Verlag Glueckauf GmbH, Postfach 185620, 45206 Essen, Germany. TEL 49-2054-92412023. FAX 49-2054-924129. *5055*

A T.
Svenska Arkitekters Riksfoerbund (SAR), Norrlandsgatan 18, S-111 43 Stockholm, Sweden. TEL 46-8-679-27-60. FAX 46-8-611-49-30.
circ. 5,500. *381*

A T F ANNUAL REPORT.
Australian Teachers Union, c/o Australian Educators Union, 220 Clavendon St., E. Melbourne, Vic. 3002, Australia. TEL 03-254-1800. FAX 03-254-1805. *2309*

A T I P.
Association Technique de l'Industrie Papetiere, 154 bd. Haussmann, 75008 Paris, France. FAX 33-1-45-63-53-09.
circ. 1,850. *5320*

A T L REPORT.
Association of Teachers and Lecturers, 7 Northumberland St., London WC2N 5DA, England. TEL 44-171-930-6441. FAX 44-171-930-1359.
circ. 161,000. *2309*

A U T BULLETIN.
Association of University Teachers, United House, 9 Pembridge Rd., London W11 3JY, England. TEL 0171-221-4370. FAX 0171-727-6547.
circ. 35,000. *2418*

A U T UPDATE.
Association of University Teachers, United House, 9 Pembridge Rd., London W11 3JY, England. TEL 0171-221-4370. FAX 0171-727-6547.
circ. 35,000. *2418*

A U T WOMAN.
Association of University Teachers, United House, 9 Pembridge Rd., London W11 3JY, England. TEL 0171-221-4370. FAX 0171-727-6547.
circ. 35,000. *2418*

A W H P ACTION.
Association for Worksite Health Promotion, 60
Revere Dr., Ste. 500, Northbrook, IL 60062-1577.
TEL 708-480-9574. FAX 708-480-9282.
circ. 3,000. *5523*

A W S C P A. NEWSLETTER.
American Women's Society of Certified Public
Accountants, 401 N. Michigan Ave., Chicago, IL
60611. TEL 312-644-6610.
circ. 5,000. *1037*

AAKA SKIDOR.
Hummelgren & Almebaeck Foerlag AB, P.O. Box
8014, S-104 20 Stockholm, Sweden. TEL 46-8-
650-05-25. FAX 46-8-650-04-07.
circ. 56,000. *6554*

AANDRIJVEN & BESTUREN.
Samsom Bedrijfsinformatie B.V. Postbus 4, 2400
MA Alphen aan den Rijn, Netherlands. TEL 31-
1720-66359. FAX 31-172-440681.
circ. 7,500. *2652*

ABBEY.
White Urp Press, 5360 Fallriver Row Ct., Columbia,
MD 21044.
circ. 200. *4299*

ABERDEEN PETROLEUM REPORT.
Aberdeen Petroleum Publishing Ltd., 35 Huntly St.,
Aberdeen AB10 1TJ, Scotland. TEL 44-1224-
644725. FAX 44-1224-647574. *5348*

ABERDEEN'S CONCRETE JOURNAL.
Aberdeen Group, 426 S. Westgate St., Addison, IL
60101. TEL 708-543-0870. FAX 708-543-3112.
circ. 15,000. *830*

ABERDEEN'S CONCRETE SOURCEBOOK.
Aberdeen Group, 426 S. Westgate St., Addison, IL
60101. TEL 708-543-0870. FAX 708-543-3112.
circ. 30,000. *830*

ABERDEEN'S CONSTRUCTION MARKETING TODAY.
Aberdeen Group, 426 S. Westgate St., Addison, IL
60101. TEL 708-543-0870. FAX 708-543-3112.
circ. 4,600. *830*

ABOVE & BEYOND.
Box 2348, Yellow Knife, NT X1A 2P7, Canada.
TEL 403-873-2299. FAX 403-873-2295.
circ. 28,200. *2860*

ABSTRACT OF STATISTICS FOR TAMIL NADU.
Director of Statistics, Madras 600006, India. *6583*

**ABU DHABI. DA'IRAT AL-TAKHTIT. AL-NASHRAH AL-
SANAWIYYAH LI-AS'AR AL-TAJZI'AH.**
Planning Administration, Statistical Department, P.O.
Box 12, Abu Dhabi, United Arab Emirates.
TEL 727200.
circ. 500. *973*

**ABU DHABI. DA'IRAT AL-TAKHTIT. AL-NASHRAH AL-
SHAHRIYYAH LI-AS'AR AL-TAJZI'AH.**
Planning Administration, Statistical Department, P.O.
Box 12, Abu Dhabi, United Arab Emirates.
TEL 727200. *973*

ABU DHABI. FOREIGN TRADE STATISTICS.
Government of Abu Dhabi, P.O. Box 255, Abu
Dhabi, United Arab Emirates. TEL 720700. *973*

**ABU DHABI CHAMBER OF COMMERCE AND
INDUSTRY. ANNUAL REPORT.**
Abu Dhabi Chamber of Commerce and Industry,
P.O. Box 662, Abu Dhabi, United Arab Emirates.
TEL 2-214000. FAX 2-215867.
circ. 500. *1130*

ACADEMIA.
Oesterreichischer Cartell-Verband, Lerchenfelderstr.
14, A-1080 Vienna, Austria. FAX 0222-42162233.
circ. 20,000. *4130*

**ACADEMIA CAMPINENSE DE LETRAS.
PUBLICACOES.**
Academia Campinense de Letras, Rua Marechal
Deodoro, 525, 13020-000 Campinas SP, Brazil.
circ. 200. *4176*

**ACADEMIA DE CIENCIAS DE CUBA. INSTITUTO DE
GEOLOGIA. SERIE GEOLOGICA.**
Academia de Ciencias de Cuba, Instituto de
Geologia, Calzada no. 851, Esq. a Calle 4, Havana
4, Cuba. *2222*

**ACADEMIC FILE INTERNATIONAL NEWS & PHOTO
SYNDICATION.**
Eastern Art Publishing, Acre House, 69-76 Long
Acre, Covent Garden, London WC2E 9JH, England.
TEL 44-81-392-1122. FAX 44-81-392-1422. *408*

ACADEMIC TEXT REVIEW.
Kay Ward & Associates, 2666 Shrewsbury Rd.,
Columbus, OH 43221. TEL 614-325-5735.
FAX 614-459-9273.
circ. 5,000. *5986*

THE ACADEMY.
United States Sports Academy, One Academy Dr.,
Daphne, AL 36526. TEL 205-626-3303. FAX 205-
626-3874.
circ. 10,000. *6448*

ACADEMY OF MANAGEMENT NEWSLETTER.
Academy of Management (Monroe), c/o Lawrence
R. Jauch, Ed., Northeast Lousiana Univ., ADMN-3-
17, Monroe, LA 71209-8813. TEL 318-342-1210.
FAX 318-342-1209.
circ. 10,000. *1404*

ACADEMY REPORTER.
American Pharmaceutical Association, 2215
Constitution Ave., N.W., Washington, DC 20037.
TEL 202-628-4410.
circ. 23,000. *5396*

ACCENT.
I O G T - N T O, Birger Jarlsgatan 25, 11145
Stockholm, Sweden. TEL 46-8-789-49-50. FAX 46-
8-20-43-54.
circ. 50,271. *2192*

ACCESS (MELBOURNE).
Arts Access Society, Inc., 109-111 Sturt St., S.
Melbourne, Vic. 3205 Australia. TEL 61-3-
96998299. FAX 61-3-96998868.
circ. 1,500. *3303*

ACCOMMODATOR.
Motels Ontario, 347 Fido Rd., Unit 2, R.R. 6,
Peterborough, ON K9J 6X7, Canada. TEL 705-745-
4982. FAX 705-745-4983.
circ. 1,300. *3558*

ACCOUNTANCY S A.
South African Institute of Chartered Accountants,
P.O. Box 59875, Kengray 2100, South Africa.
TEL 27-11-622-6655. FAX 27-11-622-3321.
circ. 21,445. *1037*

THE ACCOUNTANT.
Institute of Certified Public Accountants of Kenya,
P.O. Box 59963, Nairobi, Kenya. TEL 254-2-
224629. FAX 254-2-211563.
circ. 14,000. *1037*

ACCOUNTING PROFESSIONALS PRODUCT NEWS.
Accounting Professional Product News, Inc., 4210
W. Vickery Blvd., Ft. Worth, TX 76107. TEL 817-
738-3371. FAX 817-731-9704.
circ. 40,000. *1039*

**ACCREDITATION COUNCIL FOR ACCOUNTANCY AND
TAXATION. ACTION LETTER.**
Accreditation Council for Accountancy and Taxation,
1010 N. Fairfax St., Alexandria, VA 22314-1574.
TEL 703-549-6400. FAX 703-549-2984.
circ. 6,000. *1040*

ACERVO.
Arquivo Nacional, Rua Azeredo Coutinho 77,
20230-170 Rio de Janeiro, Brazil.
circ. 2,000. *3457*

ACHETEURS.
Edipresse, 16 rue Guillaume Tell, 75017 Paris,
France. TEL 1-47 56 00 05. FAX 47-66-46-94.
circ. 4,478. *1452*

ACHIEVEMENT.
World Trade Magazines Ltd., World Trade House, 49
Dartford Rd., Sevenoaks, Kent TN13 3TE, England.
TEL 44-1732-458144. FAX 44-1732-456295.
circ. 10,220. *1263*

ACKNOWLEDGE.
Austin College, 900 N. Grand Ave., Ste. 6G,
Sherman, TX 75090-4440. TEL 903-813-2386.
FAX 903-813-2415.
circ. 13,500. *1855*

ACQUA ARIA.
Editrice Arti Poligrafiche Europee, Via Casella 16,
20156 Milan, Italy. TEL 39-2-392281. FAX 39-2-
39214341.
circ. 4,854. *2774*

ACQUISITION COLUMBUS.
Acquisition Columbus, 2910 Brockdown Dr.,
Columbus, OH 43235-2704. TEL 614-841-0085.
6018

ACROS ORGANICS ACTA.
Acros Organics Europe, Janssen Pharmaceuticalaan
3a, 2440 Geel, Belgium. TEL 32-14-575211.
FAX 32-14-593434.
circ. 100,000. *1734*

**ACTA ACADEMIAE AGRICULTURAE AC TECHNICAE
OLSTENENSIS. AEDIFICATIO ET MECHANICA.**
Wydawnictwo A R T Olsztyn, Blok 12, 10-957
Olsztyn-Kortowo, Poland. TEL 48-89-273310.
circ. 140. *2750*

**ACTA ACADEMIAE AGRICULTURAE AC TECHNICAE
OLSTENENSIS. AGRICULTURA.**
Wydawnictwo A R T Olsztyn, Blok 12, 10-957
Olsztyn-Kortowo, Poland. TEL 48-89-273310.
circ. 180. *208*

**ACTA ACADEMIAE AGRICULTURAE AC TECHNICAE
OLSTENENSIS. GEODAESIA ET RURIS REGULATIO.**
Wydawnictwo A R T Olsztyn, Blok 12, 10-957
Olsztyn-Kortowo, Poland. TEL 48-89-273310.
circ. 140. *85*

**ACTA ACADEMIAE AGRICULTURAE AC TECHNICAE
OLSTENENSIS. OECONOMICA.**
Wydawnictwo A R T Olsztyn, Blok 12, 10-957
Olsztyn-Kortowo, Poland. TEL 48-89-273310.
circ. 130. *185*

**ACTA ACADEMIAE AGRICULTURAE AC TECHNICAE
OLSTENENSIS. PROTECTIO AQUARUM ET
PISCATORIA.**
Wydawnictwo A R T Olsztyn, Blok 12, 10-957
Olsztyn-Kortowo, Poland. TEL 48-89-273310.
circ. 130. *6962*

**ACTA ACADEMIAE AGRICULTURAE AC TECHNICAE
OLSTENENSIS. TECHNOLOGIA ALIMENTORUM.**
Wydawnictwo A R T Olsztyn, Blok 12, 10-957
Olsztyn-Kortowo, Poland. TEL 48-89-273310.
circ. 130. *2958*

**ACTA ACADEMIAE AGRICULTURAE AC TECHNICAE
OLSTENENSIS. VETERINARIA.**
Wydawnictwo A R T Olsztyn Blok 12, 10-957
Olsztyn-Kortowo, Poland. TEL 48-89-273310.
circ. 130. *6939*

**ACTA ACADEMIAE AGRICULTURAE AC TECHNICAE
OLSTENENSIS. ZOOTECHNICA.**
Wydawnictwo A R T Olsztyn. Blok 12, 10-957
Olsztyn-Kortowo, Poland. TEL 48-89-273310.
circ. 130. *255*

ACTA BIOLOGICA VENEZUELICA.
Universidad Central de Venezuela, Instituto de
Zoologia Tropical, Facultad de Ciencias, Apdo.
47058, Caracas 1041-A, Venezuela. FAX 58-2-
6052136.
circ. 1,500. *565*

ACTA BIOQUIMICA CLINICA LATINOAMERICANA.
Federacion Bioquimica de la Provincia de Buenos
Aires, Calle 6, No. 1344, 1900 La Plata, Buenos
Aires, Argentina. TEL 021-38321-42797. FAX 54-
21-254224.
circ. 3,000. *628*

ACTA GEOLOGICA HISPANICA.
Universidad de Barcelona, Biblioteca Facultat de
Geologia, Marti Franques s-n 08028 Barcelona,
Spain. TEL 34-3-4021420. FAX 34-3-4021421.
circ. 600. *2222*

ACTA MEDICA ET BIOLOGICA.
Niigata Daigaku, Igakubu, Ichiban-cho, Asahimachi-
dori, Niigata 951, Japan.
circ. 600. *4419*

ACTA MEDICA OKAYAMA.
Okayama Daigaku, Igakubu, 2-5-1 Shikata-cho,
Okayama-shi, Okayama-ken 700, Japan. TEL 81-86-
223-7151. FAX 81-86-225-6295.
circ. 600. *4419*

ACTA OCEANOGRAFICA DEL PACIFICO.
Instituto Oceanografico de la Armada, Av. 25 de Julio, Via al Puerto Maritimo, P.O. Box 5940, Guayaquil, Ecuador. TEL 593-4-480033. FAX 593-4-484723.
circ. 3,000. *2290*

ACTA ORDINIS FRATRUM MINORUM.
Ordo Fratrum Minorum, Curia Generalis, Via S. Maria Mediatrice, 25, I-00165 Rome, Italy.
TEL (06) 632241. *6166*

ACTA PEDIATRICA ESPANOLA.
San Martin de Porres 26, 28035 Madrid, Spain. TEL 34-3-2090255. FAX 34-3-2020643.
circ. 8,000. *4801*

ACTUALITE CHIMIQUE.
Societe Francaise de Chimie, 250 rue Saint Jacques, 75005 Paris, France. TEL 43-25-20-78. FAX 43-25-87-63.
circ. 2,378. *1663*

AD FUNDUM.
Uitgeverij Lakerveld B.V., Mangaanstraat 86, Postbus 43250, 2504 AG The Hague, Netherlands. TEL 31-70-3218218. FAX 31-70-3298744.
circ. 5,000. *499*

AD MARGINEM.
Universitaet zu Koeln, Institut fuer Musikalische Volkskunde, Gronewaldstr. 2, 50931 Cologne, Germany. TEL 49-221-470-5269. *5137*

AD VERBUM.
Confederacion Argentina de Sordomudos, Av. Pedro Medrano 1352, Buenos Aires, Argentina.
circ. 5,000. *3310*

ADAM.
Foerster-Verlag, Schaefergasse 27, 60313 Frankfurt a.M., Germany. TEL 49-69-831022. FAX 49-69-845991.
circ. 31,000. *3528*

ADAY.
Mindanao State University, Mamitua Saber Research Center, P.O. Box 5594, Iligan City 9200, Philippines.
circ. 500. *4177*

ADDICTION RESEARCH FOUNDATION OF ONTARIO. ANNUAL REPORT.
Addiction Research Foundation of Ontario, Subscription - Public Affairs Department, 33 Russell St., Toronto, ON M5S 2S1, Canada. TEL 416-595-6054. FAX 416-593-4694.
circ. 2,000. *2193*

ADHESIVE TRENDS.
Adhesive Manufacturers Association, 401 N. Michigan Ave., Chicago, IL 60611-4267. TEL 312-644-6610. FAX 312-321-6869.
circ. 300. *6215*

ADLINE.
Adline Publishing Ltd., 361-363 Moseley Rd., Birmingham B12 9DE, England. TEL 0121-446-4466. FAX 0121-446-4462.
circ. 11,225. *30*

ADMARINE.
Compass Rose Ltd., 92 The Avenue, Sunbury-on-Thames, Middlesex TW16 5EX, England.
circ. 20,000. *6531*

ADOBE MAGAZINE.
Adobe Systems, 411 First Ave., S., Seattle, WA 98104. TEL 206-622-5500. FAX 206-343-3273.
circ. 23,361. *2107*

ADVANCE (LIBERTY).
Target Marketing, Inc., 5 Victory Ln., Ste. 101, Liberty, MO 64068. TEL 816-781-7557. FAX 816-792-3892.
circ. 250,000. *5262*

ADVANCE NEWS JOURNAL.
Advance Publishing Company, 1101 N. Cage, Twin Palm Plaza, Ste. C1, Pharr, TX 78577. TEL 210-783-0036.
circ. 3,500. *891*

ADVANCE - TITAN.
Advance - Titan, 800 Algoma Blvd., Oshkosh, WI 54901. TEL 414-424-3047. FAX 414-424-0866.
circ. 11,000. *1855*

ADVANCED COMPOSITES MANUFACTURING CENTRE NEWSLETTER.
Advanced Composites Manufacturing Centre, University of Plymouth, School of Manufacturing, Materials and Mechanical Engineering, Drake Circus, Plymouth, Devon PL4 8AA, England. TEL 44-1752-232650. FAX 44-1752-232638.
circ. 4,600. *5617*

ADVANCES IN PSYCHIATRIC TREATMENT.
Royal College of Psychiatrists, 17 Belgrave Sq., London SW1X 8PG, England. TEL 44-171-235-2351. FAX 44-171-245-1231.
circ. 1,200. *4823*

ADVANCES IN THERAPY.
Health Communications Inc., 20 Highland Ave., Metuchen, NJ 08840. TEL 908-548-9130. FAX 908-548-8555.
circ. 3,500. *5397*

ADVENTURE ANNUAL.
Mountain Travel - Sobek, 6420 Fairmount Ave., El Cerrito, CA 94530. TEL 510-527-8100. FAX 510-525-7710.
circ. 100,000. *6865*

ADVERTENTIEBLAD.
B. V. Rotadruk, Postbus 16, Axel, Netherlands. *30*

ADVERTISING AGE'S CREATIVITY.
Crain Communications, Inc. (New York), 220 E. 42nd St., New York, NY 10017-5806. TEL 212-210-0100. FAX 212-210-0111.
circ. 30,000. *34*

THE ADVISOR.
Carter Spencer Publishing Ltd., Chancery Ct., Lincoln Rd., High Wycombe, Bucks. HP12 3RE, England. TEL 44-1494-442424. FAX 44-1494-472790.
circ. 3,500. *208*

ADVOCATE (PANHANDLE).
Peace Farm, HCR2 Box 25, Panhandle, TX 79068. TEL 806-335-1715. FAX 806-335-1715.
circ. 400. *5630*

ADVOCATE (ST. PAUL).
Minnesota Education Association, 41 Sherburne Ave., St. Paul, MN 55103. TEL 612-227-9541. FAX 612-227-4868.
circ. 46,000. *2310*

ADVOKATEN.
Danske Advokatsamfund, Kronprinsessegade 28, 1306 Copenhagen K, Denmark. TEL 45-33-96-97-98. FAX 45-33-32-18-31.
circ. 5,800. *3737*

AEROGRAM.
Cranfield University, College of Aeronautics, Cranfield, Beds. MK43 0AL, England. FAX 44-1234-751181.
circ. 3,000. *52*

AEROLOGICAL DATA OF JAPAN.
Kishocho, 3-4, Otemachi 1-chome, Chiyoda-ku, Tokyo 100, Japan. *4990*

AEROMEXICO PREMIER.
Impresiones Aereas, S.A. de C.V., Arquimedes 5, Col. Polanco, 11560 Mexico DF, Mexico.
circ. 32,000. *6933*

AERONAUTICA AND AIR LABEL COLLECTOR.
Aeronautica & Air Label Collectors Club, Box 1239, Elgin, IL 60121-1239. TEL 708-468-0840. *5452*

AERONAUTICAL SATELLITE NEWS.
Inmarsat, 99 City Rd., London EC1Y 1AX, England. TEL 0171-728-1449. FAX 0171-728-1344.
circ. 13,000. *52*

AEROSPACE ASIA - PACIFIC.
Miller Freeman Pte. Ltd., 100 Beach Rd., 26-00 Shaw Towers, Singapore 0718, Singapore. TEL 294-3366. FAX 298-5534.
circ. 11,375. *53*

AEROSPACE NEWS.
Aerospace Industries Association of Canada, 60 Queen St., Ste. 1200, Ottawa, ON K1P 5Y7, Canada. TEL 613-232-4297. FAX 613-232-1142.
circ. 2,400. *54*

AEROSPACE PRODUCTS.
Phillips Publishing International Inc., 1201 Seven Locks Rd., Ste. 300, Potomac, MD 20854. TEL 301-340-1520. *54*

AEROSPACE REVIEW.
Smiths Industries Aerospace & Defence Systems Co., 765 Finchley Rd., London NW11 8DS, England. TEL 44-181-458-3232. FAX 44-181-209-0526.
circ. 6,500. *54*

AERSCEALA.
Aer Lingus, Communications Department, Dublin Airport PA6, Dublin, Ireland. TEL 01-7052326.
circ. 9,000. *54*

AERZTE ZEITUNG.
Aerzte Zeitung Verlagsgesellschaft mbH, Am Forsthaus Gravenbruch 5, 63263 Neu-isenburg, Germany. TEL 49-6102-5060. FAX 49-6102-58740.
circ. 65,000. *4421*

AERZTLICHER RATGEBER FUER WERDENDE UND JUNGE MUETTER.
Wort und Bild Verlag Konradshoehe GmbH, Konradshoehe, 82065 Baierbrunn, Germany. TEL 089-74433-0. FAX 089-74433155.
circ. 240,000. *4731*

AETNAIZER.
Aetna Life and Casualty, 151 Farmington Ave., RWAB, Hartford, CT 06156. TEL 203-273-7973.
circ. 18,000. *3639*

AFFILIATED WAREHOUSE COMPANIES DIRECTORY.
Affiliated Warehouse Companies, Inc., Box 295, Hazlet, NJ 07730. TEL 908-739-2323.
circ. 16,000. *1583*

AFFILIATES DIRECTORY.
C B I Employee Relocation Council, Centre Point, 103 New Oxford St., London WC1A 1DU, England. TEL 44-171-379-7400. FAX 44-171-836-1114.
circ. 2,000. *1498*

AFFIRMATIVE ACTION REGISTER.
Joyce R. Green, Ed. & Pub., 8356 Olive Blvd., St. Louis, MO 63132. TEL 314-991-1335. FAX 314-997-1788.
circ. 60,000. *5262*

AFINIDAD.
Instituto Quimico de Sarria, Asociacion de Quimicos, Via Augusta 390, 08017 Barcelona, Spain. TEL 34-3-2804276. FAX 34-3-2804276.
circ. 2,500. *1663*

AFRICA HEALTH.
F S G Communications Ltd., Vine House, Fair Green, Reach, Cambridge CB5 0JD, England. TEL 44-1638-743633. FAX 44-1638-743998.
circ. 5,000. *4421*

AFRICA LINK.
Africa Regional Secretariat, Planned Parenthood Federation, Madison Insurance House, Upper Mill, P.O. Box 30234, Nairobi, Kenya. TEL 254-2-720280. FAX 254-2-726596.
circ. 3,000. *826*

AFRICA PRODUCT DIGEST.
SAFTO, Publishing Division, P.O. Box 782706, Sandton 2146, South Africa. TEL 27-11-883-3737. FAX 27-11-883-6569.
circ. 6,000. *1263*

AFRICA TODAY.
Lynne Rienner Publishers, 1800 30th St., Ste. 314, Boulder, CO 80301. TEL 303-444-6684. FAX 303-444-0824.
circ. 1,627. *5631*

AFRICAN AMERICAN LITERARY REVIEW.
5381 La Paseo, No. 105, Ft. Worth, TX 76112. TEL 817-429-6150. FAX 817-336-7527.
circ. 900. *4177*

AFRICAN AMERICAN REVIEW.
Indiana State University, Department of English, Terre Haute, IN 47809. TEL 812-237-2968. FAX 812-237-3156.
circ. 298. *2860*

AFRICAN BOOK PUBLISHING RECORD.
Hans Zell Publishers P.O. Box 56, Oxford OX1 2SJ, England. TEL 44-1865-511428. FAX 44-1865-311534.
circ. 800. *6012*

AFRICAN BUSINESS.
African Business Publications (Pty) Ltd., Private Bag 2821, Cresta 2118, South Africa. TEL 27-11-886-8484. FAX 27-11-886-8484.
circ. 17,500. *1130*

AFRICAN BUSINESS SPOTLIGHT.
African Business Publications (Pty) Ltd., Private Bag 2821, Cresta 2118, South Africa. TEL 27-11-886-8484. FAX 27-11-886-8484.
circ. 18,500. *1130*

AFRICAN PRINTER.
Coast Graphix Inc., P.O. Box 751119, Gardenview 2047, South Africa. TEL 27-11-6224800. FAX 27-11-6222480.
circ. 8,000. *5808*

AFRICANA LIBRARIES NEWSLETTER.
c/o Joseph J. Lauer, Ed., Africana Bibliographer, Michigan State University Libraries, E. Lansing, MI 48824-1048. TEL 517-355-2366. FAX 517-336-1445.
circ. 600. *3971*

THE AFTERNOON DESPATCH & COURIER.
Courier Publications Pvt. Ltd., Afternoon House, 6, Nanabhai Lane, Fort, Bombay 400 001, India. TEL 2871616. FAX 2870371.
circ. 500. *3165*

AFTERNOON ON SUNDAY.
Courier Publications Pvt. Ltd., Afternoon House, 6 Nanabhai Lane, Fort, Bombay 400 001, India. TEL 2871616. FAX 2870371.
circ. 1,000. *3165*

AG RETAILER MAGAZINE.
Doane Agricultural Service Co., 11701 Borman Dr., Ste. 100, Saint Louis, MO 63146-4199. TEL 314-569-2700. FAX 314-569-1083.
circ. 21,966. *208*

AGENDA (NEW YORK, 1991).
Scholastic Inc., 555 Broadway, New York, NY 10012-3999. TEL 212-343-6100.
circ. 250,000. *2311*

AGENT ORANGE REVIEW.
U.S. Department of Veterans Affairs, Environmental Agents Service - 131, V.A. Headquarters, 810 Vermont Ave., N.W., Washington, DC 20420. TEL 202-565-4183. *3737*

AGFOCUS.
Cornell Cooperative Extension, 420 E. Main St., Batavia, NY 14020. TEL 716-343-3040. FAX 716-439-8455.
circ. 1,000. *85*

AGGIORNAMENTI DI TERAPIA OFTALMOLOGICA.
Farmigea S.p.A., Via Carmignani, 2, 56127 Pisa, Italy. TEL 39-50-544000. FAX 39-50-544304.
circ. 7,200. *4766*

AGORA.
Lakehead University, Student Union, Thunder Bay, ON P7B 5E1, Canada. TEL 807-343-8193. FAX 807-343-8192.
circ. 2,000. *1856*

AGRARTECHNIK (WUERZBURG).
B L V Verlagsgesellschaft mbH, Lothstr. 29, 80797 Munich, Germany. TEL 49-89-12705-0. FAX 49-89-12705354.
circ. 13,308. *86*

AGRI DERGISI.
Turk Algoloji Derneginin, Istanbul Tip Fakultesi, Agri Merkezi, Capa Klinikleri, 34390 Istanbul, Turkey. TEL 90-212-6350135. FAX 90-212-6310541.
circ. 500. *4823*

AGRICULTURA EM SAO PAULO.
Instituto de Economia Agricola, Av. Miguel Estefano, 3900, Caixa Postal 6802, 04301-903 Sao Paulo, Brazil. FAX 55-11-2764062. *185*

AGRICULTURA TECNICA EN MEXICO.
Instituto Nacional de Investigaciones Forestales y Agropecuarias, Vocalia Division Agricola, Apdo. Postal 6-882, 06600 Mexico, D.F., Mexico.
circ. 1,000. *89*

AGRICULTURAL EDUCATORS DIRECTORY.
Charles M. Henry Printing Co., Box 68, Greensburg, PA 15601. TEL 412-834-7600. FAX 412-836-7759.
circ. 12,000. *39*

AGRICULTURAL ENGINEERING IN SOUTH AFRICA.
South African Institute of Agricultural Engineers, P.O. Box 912 719, Silverton 0127, South Africa. TEL 27-12-8041540. FAX 27-12-8040753.
circ. 600. *202*

AGRICULTURAL FINANCE REVIEW.
Cornell University, Department of Agricultural Economics, 155 Warren Hall, Ithaca, NY 14853-7801. TEL 607-255-4534. FAX 607-255-9984.
circ. 1,200. *186*

AGRICULTURAL FINANCIAL STATISTICS.
Statistics Canada, Ottawa, ON K1A 0T6, Canada. TEL 613-951-7277. FAX 613-951-1584.
circ. 400. *166*

AGRICULTURAL STATISTICS OF SABAH.
Department of Agriculture, Statistics Unit, 88632 Kota Kinabalu, Sabah, Malaysia. TEL 088-55155. FAX 088-239046.
circ. 500. *166*

AGRO-NOUVELLES.
Order of Agrologists of Quebec, 1259 Berri St., Ste. 710, Montreal, PQ H2L 4C7, Canada. TEL 514-844-3833. FAX 514-844-7462. *93*

AGROBOREALIS.
University of Alaska at Fairbanks, Agricultural and Forestry Experiment Station, Fairbanks, AK 99775. TEL 907-474-7653.
circ. 4,000. *93*

AGROCIENCIA.
Colegio de Postgraduados, Instituto de Estudios, Investigaciones y Servicio Agripefor Chapingo S.C., Cerro del Vigilante 166, Col. Romero de Terrenos, 04310 Mexico DF, Mexico. TEL 915-5-541304.
circ. 1,500. *93*

AGROCIENCIA. MATEMATICAS APLICADAS, ESTADISTICA Y COMPUTACION.
Colegio de Postgraduados, Instituto de Estudios, Investigaciones y Servicio Agripefor Chapingo S.C., Cerro del Vigilante 166, Col. Romero de Terrenos, 04310 Mexico DF, Mexico. TEL 915-5-54-14-03.
circ. 1,500. *186*

AGROCIENCIA. PROTECCION VEGETAL.
Colegio de Postgraduados, Instituto de Estudios, Investigaciones y Servicio Agripefor Chapingo S.C., Cerro del Vigilante 166, Col. Romero de Terrenos, 04310 Mexico DF, Mexico. TEL 915-5-54-14-03.
circ. 1,500. *209*

AGROFORESTRY TODAY.
International Centre for Research in Agroforestry, P.O. Box 30677, Nairobi, Kenya. TEL 254-2-521450. FAX 254-2-521001.
circ. 6,000. *94*

AGWAY COOPERATOR.
Agway Inc., Box 4933, Syracuse, NY 13221. TEL 315-479-6117. FAX 315-449-6041.
circ. 61,000. *95*

AICHI MEDICAL UNIVERSITY ASSOCIATION. JOURNAL.
Aichi Medical University Association, 21, Yazakokarimata, Nagakutecho, Aichi-gun, Aichi-ken 480-11, Japan. TEL 81-561-62-3311. FAX 81-561-62-3348.
circ. 1,700. *4422*

AIR CADET.
Headquarters Air Cadets, R.A.F. Cranwell, Sleaford, Lincolnshire NG34 8HB, England. TEL 44-1400-261201. FAX 44-1400-261201.
circ. 38,000. *1783*

AIR CHINA.
Regie Club International, Cromwell House, 136 Cromwell Rd., London SW7 4HA, England. TEL 44-71-244-6565.
circ. 60,000. *6933*

AIR CONDITIONING & REFRIGERATION NEWS.
Faversham House Group Ltd., 232a Addington Rd., South Croydon, Surrey CR2 8LE, England. TEL 44-181-651-7100. FAX 44-181-651-7117.
circ. 10,249. *3325*

AIR MARKET NEWS.
General Publications, Inc., Box 480, Hatch, NM 87937-0480. TEL 505-267-1030. FAX 505-267-1920.
circ. 18,500. *55*

AIR QUALITY DATA FOR ARIZONA.
Department of Health Services, Bureau of Air Quality Control, 1740 W. Adams St., Phoenix, AZ 85007. TEL 602-255-1142. *2774*

AIR TRAFFIC MANAGEMENT.
Euromoney Aviation Group, Playhouse Yard, Nestor House, London EC4V 5EX England. TEL 44-171-779-8866. FAX 44-171-779-8867.
circ. 4,449. *6749*

AIR TRANSPORT WORLD.
Penton Publishing Co. (Stamford) 600 Summer St., Box 1361, Stamford, CT 06904. TEL 203-348-7531. FAX 203-348-4023.
circ. 40,100. *55*

AIR UNIVERSITY LIBRARY INDEX TO MILITARY PERIODICALS.
U.S. Air Force, Air University Library, Maxwell AFB, AL 36112-6424. TEL 334-953-2504. FAX 334-953-1192.
circ. 1,500. *5054*

AIRBORNE LOG.
Lockheed Martin, 542642 LOCKHEED MARA, 86 S. Cobb Dr., Marietta, GA 30063-0244. TEL 770-494-2406. FAX 770-494-4309.
circ. 30,000. *55*

AIRCRAFT ECONOMICS.
Euromoney Aviation Group, Playhouse Yard, Nestor House, London EC4V 5EX, England. TEL 44-171-779-8866. FAX 44-171-779-8867.
circ. 4,000. *6750*

AIRCRAFT MAINTENANCE TECHNOLOGY.
Johnson Hill Press, Inc. 1233 Janesville Ave., Fort Atkinson, WI 53538. TEL 414-563-6388. FAX 414-563-1701.
circ. 41,000. *6750*

AIRCRAFT TECHNOLOGY ENGINEERING & MAINTENANCE.
Aviation Industry Press, 31 Palace St., London SW1E 5HW, England. TEL 44-171-828-4376. FAX 44-171-828-9154.
circ. 10,000. *56*

AIRFINANCE JOURNAL.
Euromoney Aviation Group, Playhouse Yard, Nestor House, London EC4V 5EX, England. TEL 44-171-779-8866. FAX 44-171-779-8867.
circ. 900. *6750*

AIRLINE MAINTENANCE WORLD.
A M W Publishing Ltd., 40 Cromham Rd., Sunningdale, Berks. SI5 0DX, England. TEL 44-1344-784866. FAX 44-1344-874543.
circ. 12,708. *6751*

AIRPORT BUSINESS MANAGEMENT AND DEVELOPMENT.
Euromoney Aviation Group, Playhouse Yard, Nestor House, London EC4V 5EX. TEL 44-171-779-8866. FAX 44-171-779-8867.
circ. 7,686. *6751*

AIRPORT REPORT.
American Association of Airport Executives, 4212 King St., Alexandria, VA 22302. TEL 703-824-0504. FAX 703-820-1395. *6752*

AITIA MAGAZINE.
State University of New York at Farmingdale, Center for Philosophy, Law, Citizenship, Knapp Hall 15, Farmingdale, NY 11735. TEL 516-420-2050. FAX 516-420-2698.
circ. 3,000. *3606*

AJMAN.
Ajman Chamber of Commerce and Industry, P.O. Box 662, Ajman, United Arab Emirates. TEL 422177.
circ. 1,000. *1130*

AKADEMIA ROLNICZO-TECHNICZNA IM. M. OCZAPOWSKIEGO. HUMANISTYKA I PRZYRODOZNAWSTWO.
Wydawnictwo A R T Olsztyn, Blok 12, 10-957 Olsztyn-Kortowo, Poland. TEL 48-89-273310. circ. 200. *3606*

AL-AKADEMIYYAH AL-ARABIYYAH LIL-ULUM WAL-TEKNOLOGIA. MAJALLAH.
Arab Academy for Science and Technology, P.O. Box 1029, Alexandria, Egypt. TEL 20-3-5862325. FAX 20-3-5862325. circ. 3,000. *6225*

AKAROA MAIL.
Akaroa Mail and Banks Peninsula Advertiser, P.O. Box 9, Akaroa, New Zealand. TEL 64-3-3277-622. circ. 6,500. *3196*

AKHBAR AL-BUTRUL WAL-SINA'A.
Ministry of Petroleum and Mineral Wealth, P.O. Box 59, Abu Dhabi, United Arab Emirates. TEL 651810. FAX 663414. circ. 2,000. *5348*

AKKAS DAILY.
Akkas Daily, 1-1, Khetra Das Lane, West Bengal 700012, India. TEL 91-33-261187. FAX 91-33-269644. circ. 44,000. *3165*

AKRON.
University of Akron, Department of University Communications, Akron, OH 44325-0604. TEL 216-972-7820. FAX 216-972-6168. circ. 85,000. *1856*

AKTUEL ELEKTRONIK.
Teknisk Forlag A-S, Skelbaekgade 4, DK-1780 Copenhagen V, Denmark. TEL 45-31-21-68-01. FAX 45-31-21-04-01. circ. 19,820. *2682*

AKTUELLT MAALERI.
Maalarmaestarnas Riksoferening, P.O. Box 16286, S-103 25 Stockholm, Sweden. circ. 2,681. *5305*

ALABAMA CATTLEMAN.
Alabama Cattleman's Association, 201 S. Bainbridge St., Box 2499, Montgomery, AL 36102-2499. FAX 334-834-6326. circ. 17,000. *262*

ALABAMA'S TREASURED FORESTS.
Alabama Forestry Commission, Box 302550, Montgomery, AL 36130-2550. TEL 334-240-9355. FAX 334-240-9390. circ. 10,000. *3010*

ALASKA AIRLINES MAGAZINE.
Paradigm Communications Group, 2701 First Ave., Ste. 250, Seattle, WA 98121. TEL 206-441-5871. FAX 206-448-6939. circ. 50,000. *6934*

ALASKA HOUSING FINANCE CORPORATION. ANNUAL REPORT.
Alaska Housing Finance Corporation, 520 E. 34th Ave., Anchorage, AK 99503. TEL 907-561-1900. FAX 907-561-0364. circ. 2,500. *3575*

ALASKA LIBRARY DIRECTORY.
Alaska Library Association (Fairbanks), c/o AKLA Treas., Box 81084, Fairbanks, AK 99708. TEL 907-479-5196. *3971*

ALBA POMPEIA.
Comune di Alba, Museo Civico "Federico Eusebio", Via Paruzza 1-a, 12051 Alba, Italy. TEL 39-173-290092. FAX 39-173-362075. circ. 500. *338*

THE ALBANY REPORT.
Sawchuk, Brown Associates, 41 State St., Albany, NY 12207. TEL 518-462-0318. FAX 518-462-0688. circ. 1,200. *1173*

ALBERTA AGRICULTURE. ANNUAL REPORT.
Department of Agriculture, Publishing Branch, 7000 113th St., Edmonton, AB T6H 5T6, Canada. TEL 403-427-2121. FAX 403-427-2861. *96*

ALBERTA AGROLOGIST.
Alberta Institute of Agrologists, 8506 - 104 St., Edmonton, AB T6E 4G4, Canada. TEL 403-432-0663. FAX 403-439-8414. circ. 1,300. *96*

ALBERTA ASSOCIATION OF COLLEGE LIBRARIANS. NEWSLETTER.
Alberta Association of College Librarians, Canadian Union College Library, 50 Ramona Dr., College Heights, AB T4L 2B7, Canada. FAX 403-782-3977. circ. 100. *3971*

ALBERTA SWEETGRASS.
Aboriginal Multi-Media Society of Canada, 15001-112 Ave., N.W., Edmonton AB T5M 2V6, Canada. TEL 403-455-2945. FAX 403-455-7639. circ. 6,500. *2862*

ALBRIGHTIAN.
Albright College, Albrightian, Box 15234, Reading, PA 19612-5234. circ. 1,600. *1856*

ALDRICHIMICA ACTA.
Aldrich Chemical Company, Inc., 1001 W. St. Paul Ave., Milwaukee, WI 53233. FAX 414-273-4979. circ. 200,000. *1734*

ALE STREET NEWS.
Tuscarora Inc., Box 1125, Maywood, NJ 07607. TEL 201-368-9100. FAX 201-368-9101. circ. 100,000. *499*

ALERE FLAMMAM.
Comando Scuola di Guerra, 00053 Civitavecchia, Italy. TEL 0766-30051. FAX 0766-500680. circ. 900. *5020*

ALIMENTOS BALANCEADOS PARA ANIMALES.
Watt Publishing Co., 122 S. Wesley Ave., Mt. Morris, IL 61054. TEL 815-734-4171. FAX 815-734-4201. circ. 9,000. *255*

ALL ABOUT KIDS.
All About Kids, 1077 Celestial St., Ste. 101, Cincinnati, OH 45202. TEL 513-684-0501. FAX 513-684-0507. circ. 55,000. *1760*

I ALLAGHI.
E. Karelli & Co., Kazani Str. 4, Iraklion 71202, Crete, Greece. TEL 30-81-280022. FAX 30-81-243370. circ. 3,100. *3161*

ALLEGHENY COUNTY MEDICAL SOCIETY. BULLETIN.
Allegheny County Medical Society, 713 Ridge Ave., Pittsburgh, PA 15212. TEL 412-321-5030. FAX 412-321-5323. circ. 3,700. *4423*

ALLEGRO.
Associated Musicians of Greater New York, AFM, Local 802, 322 W. 48th St., 5th Fl., New York, NY 10036. TEL 212-245-4802. FAX 212-245-6255. circ. 15,000. *3717*

ALLGEMEINER HOCHSCHUL-ANZEIGER.
Frankfurter Allgemeine Zeitung GmbH, Hellerhofstr. 2-4, 60327 Frankfurt a.M., Germany. TEL 49-69-75912326. FAX 49-69-75912184. circ. 300,000. *5262*

ALLIANCE (OTTAWA).
Public Service Alliance of Canada, 233 Gilmour St., Ottawa, ON K2P 0P1, Canada. TEL 613-560-4200. FAX 613-236-1654. circ. 130,000. *3717*

ALLT OM HUSVAGN OCH CAMPING.
Caravan Press AB, P.O. Box 1263, S-171 24 Solna, Sweden. TEL 46-8-730-54-85. FAX 46-8-735-57-10. circ. 25,600. *6554*

ALLT OM M C.
Albinsson & Sjoeberg, P.O. Box 529, S-371 23 Karlskrona, Sweden. TEL 46-455-3353-30. FAX 46-455-311715. circ. 35,900. *6520*

ALLURE.
Target s.r.l., Via Bondi 23, 2, 40138 Bologna, Italy. TEL 39-51-342426. FAX 39-51-345554. circ. 35,000. *494*

ALPHA PSI OMEGA: PLAYBILL.
Alpha Psi Omega National Theatre Honorary, c/o Wabash College, Crawfordsville, IN 47933. TEL 317-361-6394. FAX 317-361-6341. circ. 7,000. *6691*

ALPINO.
Associazione Nazionale Alpini, Via Marsala 9, 20121 Milan, Italy. TEL 02-6552692. FAX 02-6592364. circ. 370,000. *3182*

ALT OM DATA.
Audio Media A-S, St. Kongensgade 72, DK-1264 Copenhagen K, Denmark. TEL 45-33-91-28-33. FAX 45-33-91-01-21. circ. 40,000. *2071*

ALUMINIUM NEWS.
Promech Publishing, P.O. Box 85502, Emmarentia 2029, South Africa. TEL 27-11-7811401. FAX 27-11-7811403. circ. 4,000. *4948*

ALUMNI COMPANION.
University of New Hampshire, Elliott Alumni Center, 9 Edgewood Rd., Durham, NH 03824. TEL 603-862-2040. FAX 603-862-4126. circ. 65,000. *1856*

ALUMNI NEWS (GREENSBORO).
University of North Carolina at Greensboro, Alumni Association, Greensboro, NC 27412-5001. TEL 910-334-5921. FAX 910-334-4055. circ. 4,000. *1856*

ALUMNI NEWS (ST. LOUIS).
School of the Art Institute of Chicago, 37 S. Wabash, Chicago, IL 60603. FAX 312-263-0141. circ. 12,000. *1856*

ALUMNI U B C CHRONICLE.
University of British Columbia, Alumni Association, Cecil Green Park, 6251 Cecil Green Park Rd., Vancouver, BC V6T 1Z1, Canada. TEL 604-882-3313. FAX 604-822-8928. circ. 95,000. *1856*

AMATEUR ATHLETE.
Eliot Wineberg, Ed. & Pub., 7840 N. Lincoln Ave., Skokie, IL 60077. TEL 847-675-0200. FAX 847-675-2903. circ. 55,000. *6449*

AMATEUR DANCERS.
United States Amateur Ballroom Dancers Association, Inc., 1427 Gibsonwood Rd., Baltimore, MD 21228. TEL 410-747-7855. FAX 410-747-7955. circ. 12,200. *2185*

AMATEUR THEATRE YEARBOOK.
Platform Publications Ltd., 83 George St., London W1H 5PL, England. TEL 44-171-486-1732. FAX 44-171-224-2215. circ. 2,000. *6691*

AMBULATORY PEDIATRIC ASSOCIATION NEWSLETTER.
Ambulatory Pediatric Association, Department of Pediatrics, c/o Dr. John M. Pascoe, Communications Dir., 600 Highland Ave., Madison, WI 53792. TEL 608-263-9405. FAX 608-263-0440. circ. 1,500. *4802*

AMERICA COOPERATIVA.
Organization of the Cooperatives of America, Carrera 11 No. 86-32 Ofc. 101, 241263 Bogota, D.E., Colombia. TEL 2181295. FAX 057-1-610-19-12. circ. 5,000. *1157*

AMERICAN.
American University, Office of University Publications, Washington, DC 20016-8121. TEL 202-885-5970. FAX 202-885-5949. circ. 65,000. *1856*

AMERICAN ACADEMY OF CLINICAL SEXOLOGISTS. BULLETIN.
American Academy of Clinical Sexologists, 1929 18th St., N.W., Ste. 1166, Washington, DC 20008. FAX 407-628-5293. circ. 1,000. *4823*

AMERICAN ACADEMY OF ORTHOPAEDIC SURGEONS. BULLETIN.
American Academy of Orthopaedic Surgeons, 6300 N. River Rd., Rosemont, IL 60018. TEL 847-384-4130. FAX 847-823-8033.
circ. 25,000. *4780*

AMERICAN ACADEMY OF OSTEOPATHY YEARBOOK.
American Academy of Osteopathy, 3500 DePauw Blvd., Ste. 1080, Indianapolis, IN 46268-1136. TEL 317-879-1881. FAX 317-879-0563.
circ. 1,600. *4611*

AMERICAN ASSOCIATION OF BIOANALYSTS. PROFICIENCY TESTING SERVICE. TEST OF THE MONTH.
American Association of Bioanalysts, 205 W. Levee, Brownsville, TX 78520. TEL 512-546-5313.
circ. 4,500. *4676*

AMERICAN ASSOCIATION OF DENTAL EDITORS. NEWSLETTER.
American Association of Dental Editors, 1100 Lake St., Ste. 240, Oak Park, IL 60301. TEL 708-445-0322. FAX 708-445-0321.
circ. 325. *3700*

AMERICAN ASSOCIATION OF DENTAL EXAMINERS. BOARD BULLETIN.
American Association of Dental Examiners, 211 E. Chicago Ave., Ste. 844, Chicago, IL 60611. TEL 312-440-7464. FAX 312-440-7494.
circ. 1,100. *4634*

AMERICAN ASSOCIATION OF STATE HIGHWAY AND TRANSPORTATION OFFICIALS. SUB-COMMITTEE ON COMPUTER TECHNOLOGY. NATIONAL CONFERENCE. PROCEEDINGS.
American Association of State Highway and Transportation Officials, 444 N. Capitol St., N.W., Ste. 225, Washington, DC 20001. TEL 202-624-5800. FAX 202-624-5806. *6808*

AMERICAN ASSOCIATION OF TISSUE BANKS NEWSLETTER.
American Association of Tissue Banks, 1350 Beverly Rd., Ste. 220A, McLean, VA 22101. TEL 703-827-9582. FAX 703-356-2198.
circ. 1,000. *4423*

AMERICAN ASSOCIATION OF WOMEN DENTISTS. CHRONICLE.
American Association of Women Dentists, 401 N. Michigan Ave., Chicago, IL 60611-4267. TEL 312-644-6610. FAX 312-527-6640.
circ. 2,200. *4634*

AMERICAN BIBLE SOCIETY RECORD.
American Bible Society, 1865 Broadway, New York, NY 10023. TEL 212-408-1480. FAX 212-408-1456.
circ. 270,000. *6043*

AMERICAN BICYCLIST.
Willow Publishing, 400 Skokie Blvd., Northbrook, IL 60062-2816. TEL 847-291-1117. FAX 847-559-4444.
circ. 12,500. *6520*

AMERICAN BIG TWIN DEALER.
Advanstar Communications, Inc. (Santa Ana), 201 Sandpointe Ave., Ste. 600, Santa Ana, CA 92707-5761. TEL 714-513-8400. FAX 714-513-8414.
circ. 6,000. *6520*

AMERICAN BIOTECHNOLOGY LABORATORY.
International Scientific Communications, Inc., 30 Controls Dr., Box 870, Shelton, CT 06484-0870. TEL 203-926-9300. FAX 203-926-9310.
circ. 70,016. *656*

AMERICAN BREWERIANA JOURNAL.
American Breweriana Association, Inc., Box 11157, Pueblo, CO 81001. TEL 719-544-9267.
circ. 3,300. *3501*

AMERICAN BRUSSELS GRIFFON ASSOCIATION. BULLETIN.
American Brussels Griffon Association, c/o Mr. Terry J. Smith, 221 E. Scott, Box 56, Grand Ledge, MI 48837.
circ. 80. *5386*

AMERICAN BUILDER MAGAZINE.
Transcontinental Publishing Inc., Box 45454, Phoenix, AZ 85064-5454. TEL 602-331-8900. FAX 602-331-8448. *831*

AMERICAN CLINICAL LABORATORY.
International Scientific Communications, Inc., 30 Controls Dr., Box 870, Shelton, CT 06484-0870. TEL 203-926-9300. FAX 203-926-9310.
circ. 62,050. *4676*

AMERICAN COLLEGE OF CARDIOLOGY SCIENTIFIC SESSION NEWS.
American College of Cardiology, 9111 Old Georgetown Rd., Bethesda, MD 20814. TEL 301-897-5400. FAX 301-897-9745.
circ. 41,000. *4595*

AMERICAN COLLEGE OF PHYSICIANS OBSERVER.
American College of Physicians, Independence Mall W., Sixth St. at Race Philadelphia, PA 19106-1572. TEL 215-351-2400.
circ. 67,468. *4423*

AMERICAN COLLEGE OF SURGEONS. BULLETIN.
American College of Surgeons, Communications Department, 55 E. Erie St., Chicago, IL 60611-2797. TEL 312-664-4050. FAX 312-440-7014.
circ. 67,257. *4902*

AMERICAN COMPOSERS ALLIANCE BULLETIN.
American Composers Alliance, 170 W. 74th St., New York, NY 10023. TEL 212-362-8900. FAX 212-362-8902. *5138*

AMERICAN CONTRACT BRIDGE LEAGUE. BULLETIN.
American Contract Bridge League, 2990 Airways Blvd., Memphis, TN 38116-3847. TEL 901-332-5586. FAX 901-398-7754.
circ. 147,000. *6449*

AMERICAN CONTRACTOR.
Transcontinental Publishing Inc., Box 45454, Phoenix, AZ 85064-5454. TEL 602-331-8900. FAX 602-331-8448. *831*

THE AMERICAN DREAM.
Yorktown Publishing, 125 Union Pl., Lynbrook, NY 11563-4116. TEL 914-962-2565.
circ. 11,350. *3683*

AMERICAN DROP-SHIPPERS DIRECTORY.
World Wide Trade Service, Box 283, Medina, WA 98039.
circ. 8,500. *1453*

AMERICAN ECONOMIC DEVELOPMENT COUNCIL. COUNCIL NEWS.
American Economic Development Council, 9801 W. Higgins, Ste. 540, Rosemont, IL 60018-4726. TEL 847-692-9944. FAX 847-696-2990.
circ. 2,700. *1173*

AMERICAN FAMILY PHYSICIAN.
American Academy of Family Physicians, 8880 Ward Pkwy., Kansas City, MO 64114. TEL 816-333-9700. FAX 816-333-0303.
circ. 150,000. *4423*

AMERICAN FIREARMS INDUSTRY.
A F I Communications Group Inc., 2455 E. Sunrise Blvd., 9th Fl., Ft. Lauderdale, FL 33304-3118. TEL 954-561-3505. FAX 954-561-4129.
circ. 32,000. *6449*

AMERICAN FOREIGN LAW ASSOCIATION NEWSLETTER.
American Foreign Law Association, c/o James R. Maxeiner, Ed., 11 White Plains Post Rd., Bronxville, NY 10708.
circ. 550. *3922*

AMERICAN FROZEN FOOD INSTITUTE. MEMBERSHIP DIRECTORY AND BUYER'S GUIDE.
American Frozen Food Institute, 2000 Corporate Ridge, Ste. 1000, McLean, VA 22102. TEL 703-821-0770. FAX 703-821-1350.
circ. 3,500. *2960*

AMERICAN INDIAN REPORT.
Falmouth Institute, Inc., 3918 Prosperity Ave., Ste. 302, Fairfax, VA 22031-3333. TEL 703-641-9100. FAX 703-641-1558.
circ. 7,000. *2863*

AMERICAN INSTITUTE FOR CANCER RESEARCH NEWSLETTER.
American Institute for Cancer Research (AICR), 1759 R St., N.W., Washington, DC 20009. TEL 202-328-7744. FAX 202-328-7226.
circ. 1,500,000. *4748*

THE AMERICAN JOURNAL OF ANESTHESIOLOGY.
Quadrant HealthCom, 105 Raider Blvd., Belle Mead, NJ 08502-1510. TEL 908-874-0707. FAX 903-874-5611.
circ. 18,045. *4589*

AMERICAN LABORATORY.
International Scientific Communications, Inc., 30 Controls Dr., Box 870, Shelton, CT 06484-0870. TEL 203-926-9300. FAX 203-926-9310.
circ. 135,000. *1712*

AMERICAN LEGACY.
American Heritage 60 Fifth Ave., New York, NY 10011. TEL 212-620-1833. FAX 212-620-2332.
circ. 515,000. *2863*

AMERICAN MACHINIST.
Penton Publishing Co. 1100 Superior Ave., Cleveland, OH 44114-2543. TEL 216-696-7000. FAX 216-696-0177.
circ. 82,000. *1514*

AMERICAN NOTARY.
American Society of Notaries, Box 7663, Tallhassee, FL 32314-7663. TEL 202-955-6162. FAX 202-785-3209.
circ. 22,000. *3740*

AMERICAN ORTHODONTIC SOCIETY. WIRELINE.
American Orthodontic Society, 11384 Greenville Ave., No. 112, Dallas, TX 75243-3537. TEL 214-343-0805. FAX 214-343-1628.
circ. 15,000. *4634*

AMERICAN PRINTER.
Intertec Publishing Corp. (Overland Park), 9800 Metcalf Ave., Overland Park, KS 66202. TEL 910-341-1300.
circ. 93,780. *5808*

AMERICAN RED ANGUS.
Red Angus Association of America, 4201 I-35 North, Denton, TX 76207. TEL 817-387-3502. FAX 817-383-4036.
circ. 6,000. *263*

AMERICAN ROMANIAN ACADEMY OF ARTS AND SCIENCES. JOURNAL.
A R A Publications, Department of French and Italian, University of California, Sproul Hall, Davis, CA 95616. TEL 916-758-7720.
circ. 400. *2419*

AMERICAN SMALL FARM.
Magnet Communications, Inc., 21822 Sherman Way, Ste. 200, Canoga Park, CA 91303-1942. TEL 818-727-2236. FAX 813-727-1358.
circ. 65,000. *97*

AMERICAN TOWMAN.
American Towman Network, 75 N. Maple Ave., Ridgewood, NJ 07450-3247. TEL 201-612-1300.
circ. 15,900. *6768*

AMERICAN TRUST FOR THE BRITISH LIBRARY. NEWSLETTER.
British Library, Humanities and Social Sciences, Great Russell St., London WC1B 3DG, England. TEL 44-171-412-7538. FAX 44-171-412-7563. *3973*

AMERON NEWS.
Ameron, 245 S. Los Robles Ave., Pasadena, CA 91101. FAX 818-683-4060.
circ. 10,000. *6646*

AMI DES JARDINS ET DE LA MAISON.
Ami des Jardins, S.A., 8-10 rue Pierre Brossolette, 92300 Levallois Perret, France.
circ. 200,000. *3044*

AMICI.
American Friends of the Vatican Library, 157 Lakeshore Rd., Grosse Pointe Farms, MI 48236. TEL 313-885-8855.
circ. 1,500. *6167*

AMITYVILLE HISTORICAL SOCIETY DISPATCH.
Amityville Historical Society, Box 764 Amityville, NY 11701. TEL 516-598-1486.
circ. 500. *3459*

AMOCO TRAVELER.
Amoco Enterprises, Inc., 200 E Randolph Dr., Chicago, IL 60601. TEL 212-303-6937. FAX 312-856-2379.
circ. 75,000. *6866*

AN PHOBLACHT.
58 Parnell Sq., Dublin 1, Ireland. TEL 01-8733839.
FAX 01-8733074.
circ. 30,000. *3180*

ANAIS HIDROGRAFICOS.
Ministerio da Marinha, Diretoria de Hidrografia e
Navegacao, Rio de Janeiro, Brazil. *6962*

**ANALECTA VATICANO-BELGICA. DEUXIEME SERIE.
SECTION A: NONCIATURE DE FLANDRE.**
N.V. Brepols, Steenweg op Tielen 68, 2300
Turnhout, Belgium. TEL 32-14-402500. FAX 32-14-
428919. *6168*

**ANALECTA VATICANO-BELGICA. DEUXIEME SERIE.
SECTION B: NONCIATURE DE COLOGNE.**
N.V. Brepols, Steenweg op Tielen 68, 2300
Turnhout, Belgium. TEL 32-14-402500. FAX 32-14-
428919. *6168*

**ANALECTA VATICANO-BELGICA. DEUXIEME SERIE.
SECTION C: NONCIATURE DE BRUXELLES.**
N.V. Brepols, Steenweg op Tielen 68, 2300
Turnhout, Belgium. TEL 32-14-402500. FAX 32-14-
428919. *6168*

**ANALECTA VATICANO-BELGICA. PREMIERE SERIE:
DOCUMENTS RELATIFS AUX ANCIENS DIOCESES
DE CAMBRAI, LIEGE, THEROUANNE ET TOURNAI.**
N.V. Brepols, Steenweg op Tielen 68, 2300
Turnhout, Belgium. TEL 32-14-402500. FAX 32-14-
428919. *6168*

ANALES DE LA LEGISLACION ARGENTINA.
Ediciones la Ley S.A., 1471 Tucuman, 1050
Buenos Aires, Argentina. TEL 541-495481.
FAX 541-4760953.
circ. 11,000. *3740*

ANALOG DIALOGUE.
Analog Devices, Inc., 1 Technology Way, Box 9106,
Norwood, MA 02062-9106. TEL 617-461-3392.
FAX 617-326-8703.
circ. 100,000. *2020*

ANALYSE.
Nederlandse Vereniging van BioMedische
Laboratoriummedewerkers, Wilhelminapark 52,
3581 NM Utrecht, Netherlands. TEL 31-30-
2522881. FAX 31-30-2541814.
circ. 3,500. *4676*

ANCASTER NEWS.
4 Cameron Dr., Ancaster, ON L9G 2L3, Canada.
TEL 905-648-4464. FAX 905-648-7458.
circ. 8,257. *3118*

ANDAR PER CERAMICHE NEL MONDO.
Via Statutaria 46-C, 42013 Casalgrande, Reggio
Emilia, Italy. TEL 0522-846239. FAX 0522-
841063.
circ. 8,000. *1651*

ANDEAN PAST.
Cornell University, Latin American Studies Program,
Ithaca, NY 14853. TEL 607-255-2245. FAX 607-
255-8919.
circ. 50. *339*

ANDERS LEBEN.
Big Ben Verlag GmbH, Hamburgerstr. 15, 28205
Bremen, Germany. TEL 0421-492784. FAX 0421-
4986387.
circ. 6,000. *3044*

ANGLIA FARMER AND CONTRACTOR.
B C Publications, 16C Market Pl., Diss, Norfolk
IP22 3AB, England. TEL 44-1379-644200.
FAX 44-1379-650480.
circ. 7,600. *97*

ANGLO-AMERICAN FORUM.
Peter Lang GmbH Europaeischer Verlag der
Wissenschaften, Eschborner Landstr. 42-50, 60489
Frankfurt a.M., Germany. TEL 49-69-7807050.
FAX 49-69-785893.
circ. 200. *4181*

ANGLO-NORDIC TIMES INTERNATIONAL.
Peregrine Publishing & Trojan Graphics Co. Ltd.,
Yorksville, 86A Kingsley Park Terrace, Kingsley
Park, Northampton, Northants NN2 7HJ, England.
TEL 44-1604-713777. FAX 44-1604-717999.
circ. 5,721. *1264*

**ANGOLA. SECRETARIA PROVINCIAL DE SAUDE,
TRABALHO. PREVIDENCIA E ASSISTENCIA.
SINTESE DA ACTIVIDADE DOS SERVICOS E
ORGANISMOS.**
Secretaria Provincial de Saude, Trabalho,
Previdencia e Assistencia, Luanda, Angola. *5954*

ANIMALDOM.
Pennsylvania S.P.C.A., 350 E. Erie Ave.,
Philadelphia, PA 19134. TEL 215-426-6300.
circ. 42,000. *5386*

ANIMALS' VOICE.
Ontario S P C A, 16640 Yonge St., Newmarket, ON
L3Y 4V8, Canada. TEL 905-898-7122. FAX 905-
853-8643.
circ. 50,000. *295*

**ANNALI ITALIANI DI DERMATOLOGIA CLINICA E
SPERIMENTALE.**
Pensiero Scientifico Editore s.r.l., Via Bradano 3-C,
00199 Rome, Italy. TEL 06-86207158. FAX 06-
86207160.
circ. 1,200. *4658*

ANNALS OF OPHTHALMOLOGY.
American Society of Contemporary Ophthalmology,
4711 Golf Rd., Ste. 408, Skokie, IL 60076-1242.
TEL 847-568-1500. FAX 847-568-1527.
circ. 2,565. *4766*

ANNALS OF SAUDI MEDICINE.
King Faisal Specialist Hospital and Research Centre,
P.O. Box 3354, Riyadh 11211, Saudi Arabia.
TEL 966-1-4647272. FAX 966-1-4427237.
circ. 19,500. *4427*

ANNUAIRE DE L'AFRIQUE DU NORD.
C N R S Editions, 20-22 rue St. Amand, 75015
Paris, France. TEL 45-33-16-00. FAX 45-33-92-13.
circ. 1,500. *6314*

**ANNUAIRE DE LEGISLATION FRANCAISE ET
ETRANGERE.**
C N R S Editions, 20-22 rue St. Amand, 75105
Paris, France. TEL 45-33-16-00. FAX 45-33-92-13.
circ. 1,250. *3741*

ANNUAIRE FRANCAIS DE DROIT INTERNATIONAL.
C N R S Editions, 20-22 rue St. Amand, 75015
Paris, France. TEL 45-33-16-00. FAX 45-33-92-13.
circ. 1,500. *3922*

ANNUAL AUSTRALIAN NOTICES TO MARINERS.
Hydrographic Office R A N, Locked Bag 8801,
Wollongong, N.S.W. 2521. FAX 61-42-218599.
circ. 3,200. *6829*

**ANNUAL EDUCATIONAL SUMMARY, NEW YORK
STATE.**
Education Department, Information, Reporting &
Technology Services, Education Bldg. Annex, Rm.
962, Albany, NY 12234. TEL 518-474-7082.
FAX 518-474-4351. *2312*

**ANNUAL NEW MEXICO WATER CONFERENCE.
PROCEEDINGS.**
New Mexico Water Resources Research Institute,
Box 30001, Dept. 3167, New Mexico State
University, Las Cruces, NM 88003-0001. TEL 505-
646-4337. FAX 505-646-6418.
circ. 500. *6962*

**ANNUAL SUMMARY OF PROGRESS IN GRAVITATION
SCIENCES.**
Minas Ensanian Corporation, Box 98, Eldred, PA
16731. TEL 814-225-3296.
circ. 100. *5542*

ANRITSU TECHNICAL BULLETIN.
Anritsu Corporation, 10-27, Minamiazabu 5-chome,
Minato-ku, Tokyo 106, Japan.
circ. 5,000. *2683*

ANTIK & AUKTION.
Aller Specialtidningar AB, Landskronavaegen 23, S-
251 85 Helsingborg, Sweden. TEL 46-42-173500.
FAX 46-42-173600.
circ. 50,600. *328*

ANTIOCH NEW ENGLAND NOTES.
Antioch New England Graduate School, 40 Avon St.,
Keene, NH 03431-3516. TEL 603-357-3122.
FAX 603-357-0718.
circ. 6,700. *2419*

ANTIQUES FOLIO.
Antiques & General Advertising, 24 Comely Bank,
Edinburgh EH14 1AL, Scotland. TEL 44-131-332-
4481.
circ. 5,000. *329*

ANTITRUST LAW NEWSLETTER.
Illinois State Bar Association, Illinois Bar Center,
Springfield, IL 62701. TEL 217-525-1760.
FAX 217-525-0712.
circ. 550. *3741*

ANUARIO INDIGENISTA.
Instituto Indigenista Interamericano, Apdo. Postal
20315, 01001 Mexico DF, Mexico. TEL 525-
5680819. FAX 525-6521274. *303*

AOMORIKEN KISHO GEPPO.
Kishocho, Aomori Chiho Kishodai, 255-14 Tsukuda,
Aomori-shi, Aomori-ken 030, Japan.
circ. 340. *4991*

AOMORIKEN NOGYO KISHO JUNPO.
Kishodai, Aomori Chiho Kishodai, 255-14 Tsukuda,
Aomori-shi, Aomori-ken 030, Japan.
circ. 180. *4991*

APARTMENT OWNER.
Apartment Association, 14550 Archwood St., Van
Nuys, CA 91405. TEL 818-374-3240. FAX 818-
781-6018.
circ. 3,000. *6018*

L'APICOLTORE MODERNO.
Universita di Torino, Osservatorio di Apicoltura, Via
Leonardo da Vinci 44, 10095 Grugliasco TO, Italy.
TEL 011-4033893. FAX 011-4033894.
circ. 2,000. *98*

APOGEE.
High Point College, High Point, NC 27262.
TEL 919-841-9000.
circ. 400. *4182*

APOTEKSASSISTENTEN.
Danske Apoteksteknikeres Forening, Skt. Peders Str.
36, DK-1453 Copenhagen K, Denmark. TEL 45-33-
12-06-00. FAX 45-33-14-06-66.
circ. 6,269. *5399*

APOTHECARY.
Health Care Marketing Services, H C M S Inc., Box
AP, Los Altos, CA 94023-0179. TEL 415-941-
3955. FAX 415-941-2303.
circ. 65,000. *5399*

APOTHEEKMANAGEMENT.
Mediselect B.V., Postbus 28091, 3828 ZH
Hoogland, Netherlands. TEL 31-33-4808020.
FAX 31-33-4805881.
circ. 2,600. *5399*

APPAREL INDUSTRY.
Yaffa Publishing Group, 17-21 Bellevue St., Surry
Hills, N.S.W. 2010, Australia. TEL 61-2-281-2333.
FAX 61-2-281-2750.
circ. 3,566. *1830*

APPAREL INDUSTRY MAGAZINE.
Shore-Varrone, Inc., 6255 Barfield Rd. N.E., Ste.
200, Atlanta, GA 30328-4300. TEL 404-252-
8831. FAX 404-252-4436.
circ. 18,600. *1830*

APPLELAND BULLETIN.
Genealogical Society of North Central Washington,
Box 5280, Wenatchee, WA 98807-5280. TEL 509-
664-5989.
circ. 212. *3074*

APPLICATOR.
Sealant, Waterproofing and Restoration Institute,
3101 Broadway, Ste. 585, Kansas City, MO
64111. TEL 816-561-8230. FAX 816-561-7765.
circ. 800. *831*

APPROACH.
Takenaka Corporation, 1-13, 4-chome, Hon-machi,
Chuo-ku, Osaka 541, Japan. TEL 06-252-1201.
FAX 06-271-0398.
circ. 10,000. *382*

APUNTES DE INGENIERIA.
Pontificia Universidad Catolica de Chile, Escuela de
Ingenieria, Casilla 306, Correo 22, Santiago, Chile.
TEL 562-552-2375. FAX 562-552-4054.
circ. 1,000. *2589*

AQUASPHERE.
New England Aquarium, Central Wharf, Boston, MA 02110. TEL 617-742-8830.
circ. 13,000. *2776*

AQUATICS INTERNATIONAL.
Intertec Publishing Corp. (Atlanta), 6151 Powers Ferry Rd., N.W., Atlanta, GA 30339-2941. TEL 770-955-2500. FAX 770-955-0400.
circ. 30,120. *6450*

AQUI.
Asociacion Aqui - Avance, Casilla 10937, La Paz, Bolivia. TEL 34-35-24. FAX 35-24-55.
circ. 5,000. *3116*

AQUI (PHOENIX).
Wilcox Graphics, c/o Owens and Associates, 6530 N. 16th St., Ste. 101, Phoenix, AZ 85016-1311. TEL 602-230-2424. FAX 602-274-5130.
circ. 10,000. *2864*

AQUILO. SERIE BOTANICA.
Societas Amicorum Naturae Ouluensis, Department of Botany, University of Oulu, Linnanmaa, FIN-90570 Oulu, Finland. FAX 981-553-1500.
circ. 305. *670*

L'AQUILON.
P.O. Box 1325, Yellowknife, NT X1A 2N9, Canada. TEL 403-873-6603. FAX 403-873-2158.
circ. 1,000. *3118*

ARAMCO WORLD.
Aramco Services Company, Box 2106, Houston, TX 77252-2106. TEL 713-423-4426. FAX 713-432-5536.
circ. 180,000. *2864*

ARBEJDSMARKEDSPOLITISK AGENDA.
Dansk Arbejdsgiverforening, 113 Vester Voldgade, DK-1790 Copenhagen V, Denmark. TEL 45-33-93-40-00. FAX 45-33-93-40-00.
circ. 4,500. *1363*

ARBETAREN.
Sveriges Arbetares Centralorganisation, P.O. Box 6507, S-113 83 Stockholm, Sweden. TEL 46-8-16-08-90. FAX 46-8-673-03-45.
circ. 3,000. *3217*

ARBETSLEDAREN.
Sveriges Arbetsledarefoerbund (SALF), P.O. Box 12069, 102 22 Stockholm 12, Sweden. FAX 08-539968.
circ. 93,000. *3717*

ARBITRO.
Federazione Italiana Giuoco Calcio, Via Gregorio Allegri 14, 00198 Rome, Italy.
circ. 20,000. *6496*

ARCHAEOLOGICAL REPORTS.
University of Durham, Department of Archaeology, South Rd., Durham DH1 3LE, England. FAX 44-191-374-3740.
circ. 200. *341*

ARCHAEOLOGICAL REVIEW FROM CAMBRIDGE.
c/o Department of Archaeology, Downing St., Cambridge CB2 3D2, England. TEL 44-1223-333520. FAX 44-1223-333503.
circ. 200. *341*

ARCHAEONAUTICA.
C N R S Editions, 20-22 rue St. Amand, 75105 Paris, France. TEL 45-33-16-00. FAX 45-33-92-13.
circ. 1,250. *343*

ARCHITECT, BUILDER, CONTRACTOR & DEVELOPER.
Ascent Publishing Ltd., 91-93 High St., Bromsgrove, Worcs. B61 8AQ, England. TEL 44-1527-836600. FAX 44-1527-574388.
circ. 24,344. *831*

ARCHITECTS CATALOG.
Architects Catalog, Inc., 1305 Post Rd., Ste. 305, Fairfield, CT 06430-6016. TEL 203-256-1600. FAX 203-254-8166.
circ. 40,000. *1584*

ARCHITECTS' GUIDE TO GLASS, METAL & GLAZING.
U S Glass Publications, Inc., Box 569, Garrisonville, VA 22463. TEL 540-720-5584. FAX 540-720-5687.
circ. 18,000. *383*

ARCHITECTURAL LIGHTING.
Miller Freeman Inc. (New York) One Penn Plaza, New York, NY 10119. TEL 212-714-1300. FAX 212-714-1313.
circ. 35,000. *383*

ARCHIV FUER STENOGRAFIE, TEXTVERARBEITUNG, MASCHINENSCHREIBEN, BUEROTECHNIK.
Forschungs- und Ausbildungsstaette fuer Kurzschrift und Maschinenschreiben in Bayreuth e.V., Berneckerstr. 11, 95448 Bayreuth, Germany. TEL 0921-23445. FAX 0921-23445.
circ. 400. *2478*

ARCHIVES OF HISTOLOGY AND CYTOLOGY.
Japan Society of Histological Documentation, c/o Department of Anatomy, Niigata University School of Medicine, Asahimachi, Niigata, Japan. FAX 025-224-1767.
circ. 700. *711*

ARCHIVES PARLEMENTAIRES DE 1787 A 1860.
C N R S Editions, 20-22 rue St. Amand, 75015 Paris, France. TEL 45-33-16-00. FAX 45-33-92-13.
circ. 1,500. *5634*

ARCHIVES SOCIETY OF ALBERTA. NEWSLETTER.
Archives Society of Alberta, P.O. Box 21080, Dominion Postal Outlet, Calgary, AB T2P 4H5, Canada.
circ. 300. *3974*

ARCHIVOS ARGENTINOS DE DERMATOLOGIA.
Paraguay 1307, 4 38, 1057 Buenos Aires, Argentina. TEL 541-01-813-4698.
circ. 1,600. *4659*

ARCTIC MEDICAL RESEARCH.
Nordic Council for Arctic Medical Research, Aapistie 1, FIN-90220 Oulu, Finland. TEL 358-81-537-6201. FAX 358-81-537-6203.
circ. 1,500. *4429*

ARENA (EDINBURGH).
Scottish Sports Council, Caledonia House, South Gyle, Edinburgh EH12 9DQ, Scotland. TEL 0131-317-7200. FAX 0131-317-7202.
circ. 2,000. *6450*

ARENA DI POLA.
Associazione Venezia Giulia e Dalmazia, Via Mazzini 7, 34170 Gorizia, Italy. TEL 39-481-533911.
circ. 3,500. *3183*

ARGUS (SAN FRANCISCO).
American Academy of Ophthalmology, Box 7424, San Francisco, CA 94120-7424. TEL 415-561-8500. FAX 415-561-8567.
circ. 21,000. *4767*

ARGUS DES METAUX.
Editions Montmartre, 142 rue Momtmartre, 75002 Paris, France. FAX 33-1-4039-9752.
circ. 300. *4950*

ARI.
Nihon Arirui Kenkyukai, c/o Shiraume Gakuen Tanki Daigaku, 1-830, Ogawa-cho, Kodaira-shi, Tokyo 187, Japan. TEL 81-423-42-2311.
circ. 140. *721*

ARID LANDS NEWSLETTER.
University of Arizona, Office of Arid Lands Studies, 1955 E. Sixth St., Tucson, AZ 85719. TEL 520-621-8584. FAX 520-621-3816.
circ. 2,500. *2776*

ARION.
Boston University, 10 Lenox St., Brookline, MA 02146. TEL 617-353-6430. FAX 617-353-5905.
circ. 800. *1819*

ARIZONA. DEPARTMENT OF HEALTH SERVICES. ANNUAL REPORT.
Department of Health Services, 1740 W. Adams St., Phoenix, AZ 85007. TEL 602-542-1001. FAX 602-542-1062.
circ. 500. *5955*

ARIZONA A A A HIGHROADS.
Arizona Automobile Association, Box 33119, 3144 N. 7th Ave., Phoenix, AZ 85013. TEL 602-274-1116. FAX 602-277-1194.
circ. 260,000. *6866*

ARIZONA GROCER.
Arizona Grocers Publishing Co., 120 E. Pierce, Phoenix, AZ 85004. TEL 602-252-9761. FAX 602-252-9021.
circ. 2,300. *3002*

ARIZONA STATE UNIVERSITY ANTHROPOLOGICAL RESEARCH PAPERS.
Arizona State University, Department of Anthropology, Tempe, AZ 85287-2402. TEL 602-965-7596. FAX 602-965-7671.
circ. 750. *303*

THE ARK.
Rare Breeds Survival Trust, National Agricultural Centre, Kenilworth, Warwickshire CV8 2LG, England. TEL 44-1203-696551. FAX 44-1203-696706.
circ. 10,000. *2120*

ARKANSAS. EMPLOYMENT SECURITY DEPARTMENT. ANNUAL REPORT.
Department of Labor, Employment Security Department, Box 2981, Little Rock, AR 72203. TEL 501-682-3119. *5262*

ARKANSAS EPISCOPALIAN.
Episcopal Diocese of Arkansas, Box 164668, Little Rock, AR 72216-4668. TEL 501-372-2168.
circ. 8,000. *6133*

ARKANSAS OIL AND GAS STATISTICAL BULLETIN.
Oil and Gas Commission, Box 1472, El Dorado, AR 71731-1472. TEL 501-862-4965. FAX 501-862-8823.
circ. 350. *5381*

ARKITEKTUR.
Arkitektur Foerlag AB, P.O. Box 1742, S-111 87 Stockholm, Sweden. TEL 46-3-679-61-05. FAX 46-8-611-52-70.
circ. 6,200. *386*

ARMY RESERVE MAGAZINE.
U.S. Army Reserve, 1815 N Ft. Myer Dr., Rm. 204, Arlington, VA 22209-1805. TEL 703-696-6212. FAX 703-696-5300.
circ. 665,000. *5023*

AROGYA.
Kasturba Medical College Trust, Maripal, Department of Clinical Biochemistry, Editor - Arogyal, Manipal - 576 119, India. TEL 20060.
circ. 1,000. *5524*

AROUND & ABOUT K S U.
Kentucky State University, Office of University Relations, Hume Hall, Frankfort, KY 40601. TEL 502-227-5927.
circ. 10,000. *1857*

ARQUIVOS DE GASTROENTEROLOGIA.
Instituto Brasileiro de Estudos e Pesquisas de Gastroenterologia, Rua Dr. Seng 320 01331-020 Sao Paulo SP, Brazil. TEL 55-11-2882119. FAX 55-11-2892768.
circ. 5,000. *4690*

ARROWHEAD.
Society of Archer-Antiquaries, c/o Doug Elmy, 61 Lambert Rd., Bridlington, Yorks YO16 5RD, England. TEL 44-1262-601604. *6450*

ARS DECORATIVA.
Iparmuveszeti Muzeum, Hopp Ferenc Keletazsiai Muveszeti Muzeum, Ulloi ut 33-37, 1091 Budapest 9, Hungary. TEL 36-1-2175222. FAX 36-1-2175588.
circ. 1,000. *5117*

ARS LYRICA: JOURNAL OF LYRICA.
Lyrica Society for Word-Music Relations, 90 Church St., Guilford, CT 06437. TEL 203-453-1503. FAX 203-432-2522.
circ. 250. *5140*

ART BUSINESS TODAY.
Fine Art Trade Guild, 16-18 Empress Pl., London SW6 1TT, England. TEL 0171-381-6616. FAX 0171-381-2596.
circ. 8,580. *413*

ART ISSUES.
Foundation for Advanced Critical Studies, Inc., 8721 Santa Monica Blvd., Ste. 6, W. Hollywood, CA 90069. TEL 213-876-4508. FAX 213-376-5061.
circ. 8,000. *414*

ART ON SCREEN.
Program for Art on Film, 2875 Broadway, 2nd Fl., New York, NY 10025-7805. TEL 212-854-9570. FAX 212-854-9577.
circ. 11,000. *5093*

ART WORKERS GUILD. ANNUAL REPORT.
Art Workers Guild, 6 Queen Sq., London WC1N 3AR, England.
circ. 400. *415*

ARTEFACT.
Archaeological and Anthropological Society of Victoria, G.P.O. 328C, Melbourne, Vic. 3001, Australia. TEL 61-3-95230549.
circ. 450. *345*

ARTS ALIVE!
Admar Associates - Theatrical Faces Inc., 548 N. New St., Bethlehem, PA 18018. TEL 215-758-8211. FAX 215-691-0234.
circ. 15,000. *6692*

ARTS & LEISURE TIMES.
Kevin Browne, Ed. & Pub., 2446 E. 65th St., Brooklyn, NY 11234. TEL 718-763-7034. FAX 718-763-7035.
circ. 212,000. *3962*

ARTS EN AUTO.
Wegener Tijdschriften Groep B.V., Postbus 1860, 1110 CD Diemen, Netherlands. TEL 31-20-6603300. FAX 31-20-6603303.
circ. 59,645. *6768*

ARTWORKER.
Queensland Artworkers Alliance Inc., 497 Adelaide St., Brisbane, Qld., 4000, Australia. TEL 61-7-38322230. FAX 61-7-38322231.
circ. 1,000. *418*

ARZTRECHT.
Verlag fuer Arztrecht, Schinnrainstr. 15, 76227 Karlshue, Germany. TEL 0721-402904. *4429*

ASAHI EVENING NEWS.
Asahi Shimbun Publishing Co., 5-3-2, Tsukiji, Chuo-ku, Tokyo 104-11, Japan. TEL 03-5540-7641. FAX 03-3542-6172.
circ. 38,800. *3187*

ASBESTOS WORKER.
International Association of Asbestos Workers, Machinists Bldg., 1776 Massachusetts Ave. N.W., Ste. 301, Washington, DC 20036. TEL 202-785-2388. *3717*

ASEGURADORES.
Colegios de Agentes y Corredores de Seguros, Consejo General, Nunez de Balboa 116, 28006 Madrid, Spain. FAX 2622702.
circ. 29,000. *3640*

ASEPSIS.
Ad-Com Inc. Publishing, 2003 E. Lamar Blvd., Arlington, TX 76006. FAX 817-261-1399.
circ. 30,000. *4430*

ASHEVILLE REPORT.
Asheville Area Chamber of Commerce, Box 1010, Asheville, NC 28802. TEL 704-258-6131. FAX 704-251-0926.
circ. 2,700. *1132*

ASIA PACIFIC CHEMICALS.
Reed Business Publishing Group Quadrant House, The Quadrant, Sutton, Surrey SM2 5AS, England. TEL 0181-652-8146. FAX 0181-652-8918.
circ. 7,514. *1665*

ASIA - PACIFIC FISHERY COMMISSION. REPORT.
Asia - Pacific Fishery Commission, c/o Secretary, F A O Regional Office for Asia and the Pacific, Maliwan Mansion, 39 Phra Athit Rd., Bangkok 10200, Thailand. FAX 662-2800-445.
circ. 1,000. *2927*

ASIA PACIFIC FOODSERVICE PRODUCT NEWS.
Young - Conway Publications, 1101 Richmond Ave., Ste. 201, Point Pleasant Beach, NJ 08742-3049.
circ. 41,152. *3558*

ASIA - PACIFIC I.T. TIMES.
R M Technology Media Pte. Ltd., 1 North Bridge Rd., 24-06 High St. Ctr., Singapore 0617, Singapore. TEL 65-3340393. FAX 65-3343097.
circ. 21,468. *2054*

ASIA - PACIFIC SATELLITE.
Icom Publications Ltd., Chancery House, St. Nicholas Way, Sutton, Surrey SM1 1JB, England. TEL 44-181-642-1117. FAX 44-181-642-1941.
circ. 7,503. *1954*

ASIA TRAVEL TRADE.
Interasia Publications, Ltd., No. 11-01 Fortune Centre, 190 Middle Rd., Singapore 0718, Singapore. TEL 339-7622. FAX 339-8521.
circ. 14,300. *6867*

ASIAN AND PACIFIC COUNCIL. FOOD AND FERTILIZER TECHNOLOGY CENTER. EXTENSION - TECHNICAL BULLETIN.
Asian and Pacific Council, Food and Fertilizer Technology Center, 14 Wenchow St., 5th Fl., Taipei, Taiwan, Republic of China. FAX 02-362-0478.
circ. 4,300. *98*

ASIAN ELECTRICITY.
Reed Business Publishing Group Quadrant House, The Quadrant, Sutton, Surrey SM2 5AS, England. TEL 0181-652-8773. FAX 0181-652-8986.
circ. 6,567. *2684*

ASIAN HOSPITAL.
Health Asia Communications, Ltd., G.P.O. Box 1099, Hong Kong. TEL 852-2869-4933. FAX 852-2525-6086.
circ. 38,361. *4430*

ASIAN JOURNAL OF SURGERY.
Asian Surgical Association, Queen Mary Hospital, Hong Kong. TEL 852-2855-4080. FAX 852-2855-9950.
circ. 1,800. *4904*

ASIAN PLASTICS NEWS.
E M A P Maclaren Ltd., 19 Scarbrook Rd., Croydon, Surrey CR9 1QH, England. TEL 0181-688-7788. FAX 0181-668-8375.
circ. 9,877. *5618*

ASIAN POWER.
Icom Publications Ltd., Chancery House, St. Nicholas Way, Sutton, Surrey SM1 1JB, England. TEL 44-181-642-1117. FAX 44-181-642-1941.
circ. 8,572. *2684*

ASIAN TRADER.
Asian Trade Publications Ltd., Garavi Gujarat House, 1-2 Silex St., London SE1 0DW, England. TEL 44-171-928-1234. FAX 44-171-261-0055.
circ. 45,713. *1585*

ASPHALT.
Asphalt Institute, Box 14052, Lexington, KY 40512-4052. FAX 606-288-4999.
circ. 16,000. *6821*

ASSISTANT LIBRARIAN.
Association of Assistant Librarians, c/o 7 Ridgmount St., London VC1E 7AE, England.
circ. 10,500. *3975*

ASSOCIACAO PAULISTA DE CIRURGIOES DENTISTAS. JOURNAL.
Associacao Paulista de Cirurgioes Dentistas, Rua Humaita 389, 01321 Sao Paulo, SP, Brazil.
circ. 23,500. *4635*

ASSOCIATED ACCOUNTING FIRMS INTERNATIONAL NEWSLETTER.
Associated Accounting Firms International, 1000 Connecticut Ave., N.W. , Ste. 1006, Washington, DC 20036-5302. TEL 202-463-7900. FAX 202-296-0741.
circ. 3,500. *1040*

ASSOCIATED SCIENTIFIC AND TECHNICAL SOCIETIES OF SOUTH AFRICA. ANNUAL PROCEEDINGS.
Associated Scientific and Technical Societies of South Africa, P.O. Box 93480, Yeoville 2143, South Africa. TEL 27-11-4871512. FAX 27-11-6481876. *6228*

ASSOCIATION FOR PSYCHOANALYTIC MEDICINE. BULLETIN.
Association for Psychoanalytic Medicine, 252 W. 85 St., New York, NY 10024.
circ. 1,500. *5828*

ASSOCIATION NATIONALE DES COMMUNAUTES EDUCATIVES. BULLETIN HEBDOMADAIRE D'INFORMATIONS.
Association Nationale des Communautes Educatives, 145 bd. de Magenta, 75010 Paris, France. TEL 66-63-51-15. FAX 42-85-56-14. *2313*

ASSOCIATION NATIONALE DES COMMUNAUTES EDUCATIVES. BULLETIN MENSUEL D'INFORMATIONS.
Association Nationale des Communautes Educatives, 145 bd. de Magenta, 75010 Paris, France. TEL 44-63-51-15. FAX 42-85-56-14. *2313*

ASSOCIATION OF AMERICAN LAW SCHOOLS. NEWSLETTER.
Association of American Law Schools, 1201 Connecticut Ave., N.W., Ste. 800, Washington, DC 20036. TEL 202-296-8851. *3744*

ASSOCIATION OF AMERICAN UNIVERSITY PRESSES DIRECTORY.
Association of American University Presses, Inc., 584 Broadway, Ste. 410, New York, NY 10012. TEL 212-941-6610. *5987*

ASSOCIATION OF CARIBBEAN UNIVERSITY RESEARCH AND INSTITUTIONAL LIBRARIES. CARTA INFORMATIVA DE A C U R I L.
Association of Caribbean University Research and Institutional Libraries, Box 23317, San Juan, PR 00931. TEL 809-764-0000. FAX 809-765-5685. *3976*

ASSOCIATION OF LIFE INSURANCE MEDICAL DIRECTORS OF AMERICA. TRANSACTIONS.
Association of Life Insurance Medical Directors of America, Southeastern Head Office, Metropolitan Plaza, Tampa, FL 33607.
circ. 1,000. *3640*

ASSOCIATION OF MENTAL HEALTH ADMINISTRATORS. NEWSLETTER.
Association of Mental Health Administrators, 60 Revere Dr., Ste. 500, Northbrook, IL 60062. TEL 708-480-9626.
circ. 1,800. *5955*

ASSOCIATION OF NEW BRUNSWICK LAND SURVEYORS. ANNUAL REPORT.
Association of New Brunswick Land Surveyors, 535 Beaverbrook Ct. No. 120, Fredericton, NB E3B 1X6, Canada. TEL 506-458-8266. FAX 506-458-8267.
circ. 250. *6019*

ASSOCIATION OF PAEDIATRIC CHARTERED PHYSIOTHERAPISTS. JOURNAL.
Association of Paediatric Chartered Physiotherapists, 14 Bedford Row, London WC1R 4ED, England. TEL 44-171-242-1941. FAX 44-171-831-4509.
circ. 1,300. *4816*

ASSOCIATION OF STEEL DISTRIBUTORS. NEWS AND VIEWS.
Association of Steel Distributors, 401 N. Michigan Ave., Chicago, IL 60611-4267. TEL 312-644-6610. FAX 312-321-6774.
circ. 300. *4950*

ASSOCIAZIONE LAICA.
Endas Regionale Lazio, 238 Via Cavour, 00184 Rome, Italy. TEL 39-6-4741057.
circ. 10,000. *3183*

ASSURANTIE MAGAZINE.
Samsom BedrijfsInformatie B.V. Postbus 4, 2400 MA Alphen aan den Rijn, Netherlands. TEL 31-172-466775. FAX 31-172-440681.
circ. 28,393. *3641*

ASSYRIAN STAR.
Assyrian-American National Federation, c/o Jatrum Zaia, Box 192, Turlock, CA 95380. TEL 408-723-1646.
circ. 1,500. *2865*

ASTROPHILE.
Space Topics Study Unit, Box 522579, Marathon Shores, FL 33052-2579. TEL 305-289-1847.
circ. 1,000. *5452*

ASU HYVIN.
Kauppiaitten Kustannus Oy, Kanavakatu 3.B, FIN-00160 Helsinki, Finland. TEL 358-0-228821.
circ. 29,414. *888*

Contr Circ

AT RANDOM.
Random House, 201 E. 50th St., New York, NY 10022. TEL 212-940-7315. FAX 212-572-4949. circ. 100,000. *5987*

AT THE PARK.
Yellow Dot Publishing, Box 597783, Chicago, IL 60659-7783. TEL 312-465-4880. FAX 312-465-0084. circ. 18,000. *3962*

ATENEA.
Universidad de Puerto Rico, Faculty of Arts and Sciences, Mayaguez Campus, Mayaguez, PR 00681. FAX 809-834-3031. circ. 800. *4133*

ATHLETIC BUSINESS.
Athletic Business Publications, Inc., 1846 Hoffman St., Madison, WI 53704. TEL 608-249-0186. FAX 608-249-1153. circ. 41,452. *6450*

ATHLETIC MANAGEMENT.
College Athletic Administrator, Inc., 438 W. State St., Ithaca, NY 14850-5220. TEL 607-272-0265. FAX 607-273-0701. circ. 30,000. *2454*

ATLANTA BABY.
4330 Georgetown Sq. II, No. 506, Atlanta, GA 30338-6217. TEL 770-454-7599. FAX 770-454-7699. circ. 30,000. *1760*

ATLANTA N O W NEWS.
National Organization for Women, Atlanta Chapter, Box 8556, Atlanta, GA 30306-0556. TEL 404-523-1227. FAX 404-688-0869. circ. 700. *6988*

ATLANTA PARENT.
Atlanta Parent, Inc., 4330 Georgetown Sq., Ste. 506, Atlanta, GA 30338. TEL 770-454-7599. FAX 770-454-7699. circ. 65,000. *1760*

ATLANTA SMALL BUSINESS MONTHLY.
Media 3 Publications, Inc., 4721 Chamblee Dunwoody Rd., 100-B, Atlanta, GA 30338-6000. TEL 404-394-2811. FAX 404-394-2719. circ. 25,000. *1572*

ATLANTIC BOOKS TODAY.
Atlantic Provinces Book Review Society, 2085 Maitland St., Halifax, NS B3K 2Z8, Canada. TEL 902-420-5716. circ. 30,000. *5987*

ATLANTIC BUSINESS REPORT.
A B J Publishing Inc., 599 Main St., Ste. 203, Moncton, NB E1C 1C8, Canada. TEL 506-857-9696. FAX 506-859-7395. circ. 14,000. *6829*

ATLANTIC INFLIGHT.
Hang Gliding Association of Newfoundland, 16 Woodbine Ave., Corner Brook, NF A2H 3N8, Canada. TEL 709-785-2697. circ. 35. *57*

ATLAS HISTORIQUE DES VILLES DE FRANCE.
C N R S Editions, 20-22 rue St. Amand, 75015 Paris, France. TEL 45-33-16-00. FAX 45-33-92-13. circ. 1,500. *3396*

ATMA JAYA RESEARCH CENTRE. SOCIO-RELIGIOUS RESEARCH REPORT.
Atma Jaya Research Centre, Jalan Jenderal Sudirman 51, P.O. Box 2639, Jakarta 10001, Indonesia. *6045*

ATOMIC DATA AND NUCLEAR DATA TABLES.
Academic Press, Inc., Journal Division, 525 B. St., Ste. 1900, San Diego, CA 92101-4495. TEL 619-230-1840. FAX 619-699-6800. *5593*

ATTUALITA ITALIA - AUSTRALIA.
Italian - Australian Chamber of Commerce, Via Barberini 86, 00187 Rome, Italy. TEL 39-6-4743565. FAX 39-6-4817813. circ. 80,000. *1132*

AUCTUS.
Medical University of South Carolina, Office of Development, 171 Ashley Ave., Charleston, SC 29425. TEL 803-792-4275. circ. 20,000. *1857*

AUDACITY.
Forbes, Inc., 60 Fifth Ave., New York, NY 10011. TEL 212-620-2200. circ. 100,000. *895*

AUDIO-DIGEST GASTROENTEROLOGY.
Audio-Digest Foundation 1577 E. Chevy Chase Dr., Glendale, CA 91206. TEL 213-245-8505. FAX 818-240-7379. *4690*

AUDIO-DIGEST INTERNAL MEDICINE.
Audio-Digest Foundation 1577 E. Chevy Chase Dr., Glendale, CA 91206. TEL 213-245-8505. FAX 818-240-7379. *4705*

AUDIO-DIGEST OBSTETRICS - GYNECOLOGY.
Audio-Digest Foundation 1577 E. Chevy Chase Dr., Glendale, CA 91206. TEL 213-245-8505. FAX 818-240-7379. *4732*

AUDIO-DIGEST OPHTHALMOLOGY.
Audio-Digest Foundation 1577 E. Chevy Chase Dr., Glendale, CA 91206. TEL 213-245-8505. FAX 818-240-7379. *4767*

AUDIO-DIGEST ORTHOPAEDICS.
Audio-Digest Foundation 1577 E. Chevy Chase Dr., Glendale, CA 91206. TEL 213-245-8505. FAX 818-240-7379. *4781*

AUDIO-DIGEST UROLOGY.
Audio-Digest Foundation 1577 E. Chevy Chase Dr., Glendale, CA 91206. TEL 213-245-8505. FAX 818-240-7379. *4925*

AUGSBURGER ALLGEMEINE.
Presse Druck- und Verlagsgesellschaft mbH, Curt-Frenzel-Str. 2, 86167 Augsburg, Germany. TEL 49-821-777-0. FAX 49-821-704471. circ. 368,649. *3141*

AURA WEALTH NEWSLETTER.
Aura Publishing Co., 441 Central Ave., Box 1367, Scarsdale, NY 10538. TEL 914-834-2322. FAX 914-833-0930. circ. 300. *1175*

AURORA.
Northern Lights Library System, Postal Bag 8, Elk Point, AB T0A 1A0, Canada. TEL 403-724-2596. FAX 403-724-2597. circ. 700. *3976*

DIE AUSLESE.
Dr. Krueger Verlag, Am Schiessberg 19, 35745 Herborn, Germany. TEL 49-2772-2427. FAX 49-2772-2420. circ. 26,000. *6045*

AUSTIN GREENSHEET.
Gordon Publications (Austin), Box 140721, Austin, TX 78714-0721. TEL 512-454-1003. FAX 512-454-2442. *2148*

AUSTIN HEALTH & FITNESS.
Metro Publishing, Box 2534, Cedar Park, TX 78630. TEL 512-918-8190. FAX 512-331-9271. circ. 50,000. *5525*

AUSTIN HOME FINDER.
Southeast Publishing Ventures, 528 East Blvd., Charlotte, NC 28203-5110. circ. 25,000. *6019*

AUSTIN HOMES & GARDENS.
Publications & Communications, Inc., 12416 Hymeadow, Austin, TX 78750-1896. TEL 512-250-9023. FAX 512-331-3900. circ. 25,000. *3673*

AUSTIN LAWYERS JOURNAL.
Travis County Bar Association, 700 Lavaca, Ste. 602, Austin TX 78701. TEL 512-472-0279. FAX 512-473-2720. circ. 3,200. *3744*

AUSTRALIAN ABORIGINAL STUDIES.
Australian Institute of Aboriginal and Torres Strait Islander Studies, P.O. Box 553, Canberra, A.C.T. 2601, Australia. TEL 61-6-2461111. FAX 61-6-2497310. *304*

AUSTRALIAN BALLET NEWS.
Australian Ballet Foundation, 2 Kavanagh St., Southbank, Vic. 3006, Australia. TEL 61-3-684-8600. FAX 61-3-686-7081. circ. 40,000. *2186*

AUSTRALIAN BUILDING NEWS.
Sydney Building Information Centre Ltd., 525 Elizabeth St., Surry Hills, N.S.W. 2010, Australia. TEL 02-318-2988. FAX 02-319-1890. circ. 17,656. *832*

AUSTRALIAN CITRUS NEWS.
Australian Citrus Growers Federation, Rm. 107, 10th Fl., 118 King William St., Adelaide. S.A. 5000, Australia. TEL 61-8-212-4245. FAX 61-8-2313413. circ. 3,000. *3044*

AUSTRALIAN DEFENCE FORCE JOURNAL.
Department of Defence, E-4-26, Canberra, A.C.T. 2600, Australia. FAX 61-6-2656972. circ. 17,500. *5023*

AUSTRALIAN HISTORICAL STUDIES.
University of Melbourne, Department of History, Parkville, Vic. 3052, Australia. TEL 61-3-9344-5963. FAX 61-3-9344-7894. circ. 1,500. *3338*

AUSTRALIAN JOURNAL OF PHYSIOTHERAPY.
Australian Physiotherapy Association, P.o. Box 6465 Melbourne, Vic. 3004, Australia. TEL 61-3-95349400. FAX 61-3-95349199. circ. 8,700. *4816*

AUSTRALIAN JUNIOR CHAMBER.
Australian Junior Chamber, 6 Thesiger Court, Deakin, A.C.T. 2600, Australia. TEL 61-6-281-1066. FAX 61-6-281-4701. circ. 3,000. *1847*

AUSTRALIAN LAWYER.
Law Institute of Victoria, 470 Bourke St., Melbourne, Vic. 3000, Australia. TEL 61-3-96079342. FAX 61-3-96079451. circ. 31,751. *3746*

AUSTRALIAN NINETEENTH CENTURY LITERATURE IN PRINT.
Mulini Press, P.O. Box 82, Jamison Centre, A.C.T. 2614, Australia. TEL 61-6-2512519. circ. 430. *4292*

AUSTRALIAN NUGGET JOURNAL.
Goldcorp Australia, 300 Hay St., E. Perth, W.A. 6004, Australia. TEL 61-9-421-7222. FAX 61-9-221-3812. circ. 3,500. *5057*

AUSTRALIAN PARKS & RECREATION.
Royal Australian Institute of Parks & Recreation, Bldg. E, National Exhibition Centre, Flemington Rd., Lyneham, A.C.T. 2602, Australia. TEL 06-241-4371. FAX 06-241-5817. circ. 1,800. *2120*

AUSTRALIAN PRESCRIBER.
Commonwealth Department of Human Services and Health, P.O. Box 100, Woden, A.C.T. 2606, Australia. TEL 61-6-289-7035. circ. 60,000. *5401*

AUSTRALIAN PRIVATE DOCTOR.
Private Doctors of Australia Ltd., 194 Derby St., Penrith, N.S.W. 2750, Australia. TEL 61-47-322977. FAX 61-47-323762. circ. 2,500. *4431*

AUSTRALIAN SCIENCE TEACHERS' JOURNAL.
Australian Science Teachers Association, G.P.O. Box 2682, Canberra, A.C.T. 2601 Australia. TEL 61-6-2489250. FAX 61-6-2489565. circ. 6,000. *2479*

AUSTRALIAN SERVICE STATION & CONVENIENCE STORE NEWS.
Berg Bennett & Associates Pty Ltd., 1-109 Lousa Rd., Birchgrove, N.S.W. 2041, Australia. TEL 61-2-5551355. FAX 61-2-5551434. circ. 10,458. *6769*

AUSTRALIAN STOCK HORSE JOURNAL.
P.O. Box 238, Scone, N.S.W. 2337, Australia. TEL 61-65-451122. FAX 61-65-452155. circ. 6,500. *6544*

AUSTRALIAN TRADER.
Exportad Pty. Ltd., 115-117 Cooper St. Surry Hills, N.S.W. 2010, Australia. circ. 5,500. *1265*

AUSTRALIAN WINE RESEARCH INSTITUTE TECHNICAL REVIEW.
Australian Wine Research Institute, P.O. Box 197, Glen Osmond, S.A. 5064, Australia. TEL 61-8-3036600. FAX 61-8-3036601.
circ. 600. *500*

AUSTRALIAN WOODWORKER.
Skills Book Publishing Pty. Ltd., 40-44 Red Lion St., Rozelle, N.S.W. 2039, Australia. TEL 61-2-810-6222. FAX 61-2-818-5675.
circ. 22,450. *885*

AUTO OG BOLIG MONTERING.
Sadelmager- og Tapetmestrelaget i Danmark, Fortunstraede 5, 1065 Copenhagen K, Denmark. TEL 45-33-13-80-38.
circ. 3,200. *3684*

AUTO C A D WORLD.
12416 Hymeadow Dr., Austin, TX 78750-1896. TEL 512-250-9023. FAX 512-331-3900.
circ. 29,000. *2035*

AUTO IMPACT.
Kempec Publications, Inc., 1275 Bloomfield Ave., No. 6-36, Fairfield, NJ 07004-2708. TEL 201-785-0764. FAX 201-785-0753.
circ. 3,830. *6770*

AUTO-JOURNAL.
Societe EDP, 8-10, rue Pierre Brossolette, 92300 Levallois Perret, France. FAX 40-87-42-37.
circ. 267,000. *6770*

AUTO MERCHANDISING NEWS.
Mortimer Communications, Inc., Box 1185, Fairfield, CT 06430. TEL 203-384-9323. FAX 203-375-1463.
circ. 23,224. *6770*

AUTO RENTAL NEWS.
Bobit Publishing Company, 2512 Artesia Blvd., Redondo Beach, CA 90278-3210. TEL 310-376-8788. FAX 310-376-9043.
circ. 16,500. *1454*

AUTO REVISTA.
Revista Communications, Inc., 14330 Midway Rd., Ste. 202, Dallas, TX 75244-3514. TEL 214-386-0040. FAX 214-386-4255.
circ. 41,000. *6771*

AUTO TREND.
Adsale Publishing Company, 4-F, Stanhope House, 734 King's Rd., North Point, Hong Kong. TEL 852-2811-8897. FAX 852-2516-5119.
circ. 22,000. *6771*

AUTOCCASION.
Maxipress S.A., 52 rue Broodcoorens, 1310 La Hulpe, Belgium. TEL 32-2-6520020. FAX 32-2-6521129.
circ. 35,000. *6772*

AUTOFACHMANN.
Vogel Verlag und Druck GmbH & Co. KG, Max-Planck-Str. 7-9, 97082 Wuerzburg, Germany. TEL 0931-418-2145. FAX 0931-4182640.
circ. 92,953. *6772*

AUTOMATISERING GIDS.
Ten Hagen & Stam b.v. Postbus 34, 2501 AG The Hague, Netherlands. TEL 31-70-3045700. FAX 31-70-3045812.
circ. 27,550. *1982*

AUTOMOBIL-INDUSTRIE.
Vogel Verlag und Druck GmbH & Co. KG, Max-Planck-Str. 7-9, 97082 Wuerzburg, Germany. TEL 0931-4182145. FAX 0931-4182640.
circ. 10,000. *6773*

AUTOMOBILES CLASSIQUES.
Excelsior Publications, 1 rue du colonel Pierre Avia, 75503 Paris Cedex 15, France. TEL 46-48-48-48. FAX 46-48-48-09.
circ. 25,383. *6773*

AUTOMOTIVE & TRANSPORTATION INTERIORS.
Shore-Varrone, Inc., 6255 Barfield Rd. N.E., Ste. 200, Atlanta, GA 30328-4300. TEL 404-252-8831. FAX 404-252-4436.
circ. 12,444. *6774*

AUTOMOTIVE BODY REPAIR NEWS.
Chilton Co., Chilton Way, Radnor, PA 19089. TEL 610-964-4000. FAX 610-964-4981.
circ. 60,000. *6774*

AUTOMOTIVE ENGINEER.
Institute of Automotive Mechanical Engineers (Inc.), 227 Great North Rd., Fivedock, N.S.W. 2046, Australia. TEL 61-2-7134711. FAX 61-2-7132671.
circ. 26,801. *6774*

AUTOMOTIVE FLEET.
Bobit Publishing Company, 2512 Artesia Blvd., Redondo Beach, CA 90278-3210. TEL 310-376-8788. FAX 310-376-9043.
circ. 22,000. *6774*

AUTOMOTIVE INTERNATIONAL.
Leading Edge Publishing, 2 Oxted Chambers, 185-187 Station St. E., Oxted, Surrey RH8 0QE, England. TEL 44-181-687-2340. FAX 44-181-646-7926.
circ. 17,500. *6775*

AUTOMOTIVE MANAGEMENT.
1 Oxted Chambers, 185-187 Station Rd. E., Oxted, Surrey RH8 0QE, England. TEL 44-1883-732000. FAX 44-1883-730933.
circ. 21,913. *6775*

AUTOMOTIVE MANAGEMENT INFORMATION SYSTEMS COUNCIL NEWSLETTER.
Automotive Management Information Systems Council, Box 13966, Durham, NC 27709-3966. TEL 201-569-8500.
circ. 150. *1491*

AUTOMOTIVE REBUILDER.
Babcox Publications, 11 S. Forge St., Box 1810, Akron, OH 44309-1810. TEL 216-535-6117. FAX 216-535-0874.
circ. 23,000. *6775*

AUTOMOVIL DE VENEZUELA.
Ortiz y Asociados, s.r.l., Av. Caurimare, Qta. Expo., Colinas de Bello Monte, Caracas, Venezuela. TEL 58-2-751-1355. FAX 58-2-751-11-22.
circ. 7,500. *6775*

AUTOPART.
M & M Publications, P.O. Box 8859, Johannesburg 2000, South Africa. TEL 27-11-880-5790. FAX 27-11-880-5789. *6775*

AUTOPISTA.
Luike - Motorpress, C. Ancora 40, 28045 Madrid, Spain. TEL 34-1-3470100. FAX 34-1-3470135.
circ. 90,000. *6776*

AUTOSPORT.
Medipress Sociedade Editora de Publicacoes, Lda., Av. Infante D. Henrique 334, 1800 Lisbon, Portugal. TEL 351-1-8520756. FAX 351-1-8518990.
circ. 75,000. *6776*

AVENTURA LIFESTYLES.
G S & J Publishing, Inc., 5212 N.W. 54th Ave., Pompano Beach, FL 33073-3755. TEL 305-977-5901.
circ. 15,000. *3224*

AVIATION DIGEST.
Aviation Digest Associates, 288 Christian St., No. 16, Oxford, CT 06478-1038. TEL 203-264-4333. FAX 203-264-4511.
circ. 25,000. *58*

AVIATION EQUIPMENT MAINTENANCE.
Phillips Business Information, Inc., 1201 Seven Locks Rd., Potomac, MD 20854. TEL 301-424-3338. FAX 301-309-3487.
circ. 37,488. *58*

AVICULTURA PROFESIONAL.
Avicultura Profesional, Inc., Box 84, Athens, GA 30603. TEL 706-549-4092. FAX 706-543-1854.
circ. 7,500. *265*

AVIFAUNISTISCHER INFORMATIONSDIENST BAYERN.
Ornithologische Gesellschaft in Bayern e.V., c/o Institut fuer Vogelkunde, Am Kreuzweiher 3, 91746 Weidenbach, Germany. TEL 49-9826-9730. FAX 49-9826-1610.
circ. 1,150. *772*

AVIONICS.
Phillips Business Information, Inc., 1201 Seven Locks Rd., Potomac, MD 20854. TEL 301-424-3338. FAX 301-309-3847. *59*

AYIN L'TZION.
Zionist Organization of America, 4 E. 34 St., New York, NY 10016. TEL 212-481-1500.
circ. 2,500. *2866*

AYLESFORD CARMELITE NEWSLETTER.
Lay Carmelite Office, 8501 Bailey Road, Darien, IL 60561. TEL 708-969-5050. FAX 708-969-5536.
circ. 12,000. *6169*

AZ B - ARIZONA BUSINESS.
Arizona State University, Center for Business Research, College of Business, Box 874406, Tempe, AZ 85287-4406. TEL 602-965-3961. FAX 602-965-5458.
circ. 630. *896*

AZIONE COOPERATIVA.
Comitato Regionale Lombardo delle Cooperative, Via Palmanova 22, 20132 Milan, Italy. TEL 2845-6208.
circ. 10,000. *6362*

B A A FLIGHT GUIDE.
Mediamark Publishing International Ltd., 35 Gresse St., Rathbone Pl., London W1P 1PN, England. TEL 44-171-580-3105. FAX 44-171-580-1695.
circ. 120,000. *6753*

B A P C O NEWS.
Bahrain Petroleum Co. B.S.C., P.O. Box 25149, Awali, Bahrain. TEL 755047. FAX 755999.
circ. 1,000. *5350*

B A R GIORNALE.
Agepe Gruppo Editoriale, Via Domenico Trentacoste, 9, 20134 Milan, Italy. TEL 02-215621. FAX 02-2640330.
circ. 246,244. *3559*

B & P A.
Murray State University, College of Business and Public Affairs, Murray, KY 42071. TEL 502-762-4181. FAX 502-762-3482.
circ. 1,000. *896*

B B B - BAUMASCHINE - BAUGERAET - BAUSTELLE.
Technopress Fachzeitschriften Verlagsgesellschaft mbH, Iglaseegasse 21-23, Postfach 176, A-1191 Vienna, Austria. TEL 43-1-322551. FAX 43-1-327427.
circ. 17,000. *833*

B C & T NEWS.
Bakery, Confectionery and Tobacco Workers International Union, 10401 Connecticut Ave., Kensington, MD 20895. TEL 301-933-8600. FAX 301-946-8452.
circ. 135,000. *3718*

B C DAIRY DIRECTORY.
DoMac Publications Ltd., 20316 56th Ave., Ste. 200, Langley, BC V3A 3Y7, Canada. TEL 604-532-8400. FAX 604-532-8401.
circ. 1,600. *1586*

B C L A REPORTER.
British Columbia Library Association, 6545 Bonsor Ave., Ste. 110, Burnaby, BC V5H 1H3, Canada. TEL 604-430-9633. FAX 604-430-8595.
circ. 810. *3977*

B C S JOURNAL.
Boston Computer Society, 101 1st Ave., No. 2, Waltham, MA 02154-1160. TEL 617-252-0600. FAX 617-577-9365.
circ. 15,000. *2084*

B C T C - C A M R A S O - FOCUS.
British Carpet Technical Centre, Cleaning & Maintenance Research & Services Organization, Wira House, West Park, Ring Rd., Leeds LS16 6QL, England. TEL 44-113-259-1999. FAX 44-113-278-0306.
circ. 300. *6674*

B F L R ARBEITSPAPIERE.
Bundesforschungsanstalt fuer Landeskunde und Raumordnung, Am Michaelshof 8, 53177 Bonn, Germany. TEL 49-288-826-0. FAX 49-228-826266.
circ. 200. *3577*

B G F BULLETIN.
Banana Growers Federation Co-operative Ltd., P.O.
Box 31, Murwillumbah, N.S.W. 2484, Australia.
TEL 066-722488. FAX 066-724868.
circ. 2,000. *212*

B.G. RUDOLPH LECTURES IN JUDAIC STUDIES.
Syracuse University, Jewish Studies Program,
Syracuse, NY 13244-1170. TEL 315-443-3861.
FAX 315-443-5390.
circ. 500. *6122*

B I F U REPORT.
Banking Insurance & Finance Union, Sheffield
House, 1B Amity Grove, Raynes Park, London
SW20 0LG, England. TEL 44-171-946-9151.
FAX 44-171-879-3728.
circ. 112,000. *1061*

B L E S M A G.
M & B (Felstead) Ltd., 185-187 High Rd., Chadwell
Heath, Essex RM6 6NA, England. TEL 44-181-590-
1124. FAX 44-181-599-2932.
circ. 10,000. *6362*

B L Z.
G E W - Gewerkschaft Erziehung und Wissenschaft,
Loeningstr. 35, 28195 Bremen, Germany. TEL 49-
421-33764-0. FAX 49-421-3376430.
circ. 4,500. *2479*

B M A NEWS REVIEW.
B M J Publishing Group, B.M.A. House, Tavistock
Sq., London WC1H 9JP, England. TEL 0171-387-
4499. FAX 0171-383-6566.
circ. 95,000. *4432*

B M MAGAZINE.
British Museum Society, Great Russell St., London
WC1B 3DG, England. TEL 44-171-323-8605.
FAX 44-171-323-8614.
circ. 10,000. *5119*

B M T NEWS.
British Maritime Technology Ltd., Orlando House, 1
Waldegrove Rd., Teddington, Mddx. TW11 8LZ,
England.
circ. 7,000. *6830*

B-MAX.
Blk Publishing Company, Box 83912, Los Angeles,
CA 90083-0912. TEL 310-410-0808. FAX 310-
410-9250.
circ. 42,000. *3529*

B N A C COMMUNICATOR.
B N A Communications, Inc. 9439 Key West Ave.,
Rockville, MD 20850-3396. TEL 301-948-0540.
FAX 301-948-2085.
circ. 200,000. *896*

B O M I NEWSLETTER.
Box Office Management International, Inc., 250 W.
57th St., Ste. 722, New York, NY 10107. TEL 212-
581-0600. FAX 212-581-0885.
circ. 1,300. *1454*

B P I STATISTICAL HANDBOOK.
British Phonographic Industry, 25 Savile Row,
London W1X 1AA, England. TEL 44-171-287-4422.
FAX 44-171-287-2252.
circ. 1,000. *5207*

**B P I - THE BUSINESS OF PHOTOGRAPHY &
IMAGING.**
Market Link House, Tye Green, Elsenham, Bishops
Stratford, Herts. CM22 6DY, England. TEL 0279-
647555. FAX 0279-815300.
circ. 6,500. *5509*

B S A A (YEAR) THAILAND SHIPPING HANDBOOK.
Cosmic Group of Companies, 4th Fl., Phyathai Bldg.,
31 Phyathai Rd., Rajthevi, Bangkok 10400,
Thailand. TEL 245-3850. FAX 246-4737.
circ. 5,000. *6830*

B T T G INDEPENDENT.
British Textile Technology Group, Wira House, West
Park Ring Rd., Leeds LS16 6QL, England. TEL 44-
113-259-1999. FAX 44-113-278-0306.
circ. 1,500. *6674*

B V A BULLETIN.
Blinded Veterans Association, National Board of
Directors, 477 H St. N.W., Washington, DC 20001.
TEL 202-371-8880. FAX 202-371-8258.
circ. 21,200. *3317*

BABSON BULLETIN.
Babson College, Babson Park, MA 02157-0310.
TEL 617-239-5256. FAX 617-239-5989.
circ. 31,000. *1857*

**BABY AND CHILD CARE QUICK REFERENCE
ENCYCLOPEDIA.**
Family Communications, Inc., 37 Hanna Ave.,
Toronto, ON M5K 1X1, Canada. TEL 416-537-
2604. FAX 416-538-1794.
circ. 100,000. *6988*

BABY MAGAZINE INFANT CARE GUIDE.
Baby Magazine 124 E. 40th St., Ste. 1101, New
York, NY 10016. TEL 212-986-1422.
circ. 3,800,000. *4803*

BABY SHOP.
Spindle Publishing Co., 4136 Library Rd.,
Pittsburgh, PA 15234-1300. TEL 412-531-9742.
FAX 412-531-2004.
circ. 10,000. *3299*

BADEN-WUERTTEMBERGISCHE BIOGRAPHIEN.
Kommission fuer Geschichtliche Landeskunde in
Baden-Wuerttemberg, Eugenstr. 7, 70182 Stuttgart,
Germany.
circ. 800. *554*

BAECKER-WERK.
Baecker - Innung Nuernberg, Ostendstr. 149-151,
90482 Nuernberg, Germany.
circ. 3,000. *2997*

BAEDER JOURNAL.
Oesterreichischer Baecerverband, Rosenhuegelstr.
198, A-1238 Vienna, Austria. TEL 43-1-3339-
7346. FAX 43-1-3339-7346.
circ. 200. *1407*

BAELDER.
Coxland Press, c/o 60 Elmhurst Rd., Reading,
Berks. RG1 5HY, England. TEL 01734-875509.
5215

BAENDER, BLECHE ROHRE.
Vogel Verlag und Druck GmbH & Co. KG, Max-
Planck-Str. 7-9, 97082 Wuerzburg, Germany.
TEL 0931-4182145. FAX 0931-4182640.
circ. 11,166. *4950*

DET BAESTA.
Reader's Digest AB, P.O. Box 25, 164 93 Kista,
Sweden. TEL 46-8-752-03-60. FAX 46-8-752-87-
01.
circ. 245,100. *3217*

**BAHAMAS. CHAMBER OF COMMERCE. ANNUAL
DIRECTORY.**
Chamber of Commerce, Attn: Executive Dir., P.O.
Box N665, Nassau, Bahamas. TEL 809-322-2145.
FAX 809-322-4649.
circ. 10,000. *1132*

BAHNENGOLFER.
Deutscher Bahnengolf-Verband, Bernkastelerstr.
33a, 54472 Braureberg, Germany. TEL 06534-
1279.
circ. 1,300. *6496*

BAIQIUEN YIKE DAXUE XUEBAO.
Baiqiu'en Yike Daxue, Xuebao Bianjibu, 86, Xinmin
Dajie, Changchun, Jilin 130021, People's Republic
of China. TEL 86-431-5645911. FAX 86-431-
644739.
circ. 1,000. *4433*

BAKING BUYER.
Sosland Publishing Company, 4800 Main St., Ste.
100, Kansas City, MO 64112. TEL 816-756-1000.
FAX 816-756-0494.
circ. 30,000. *2998*

BALAIR - C T A YELLOW WINGS.
Airpage AG, Haldenstr. 65, CH-8045 Zurich,
Switzerland. TEL 01-451-2920. FAX 01-451-2961.
circ. 150,000. *6934*

BALDE BRANCO.
Cooperativa Central de Laticinios do Estado de Sao
Paulo, Rua Gomes Cardim 532, 03050 Sao Paulo,
SP, Brazil.
circ. 30,000. *247*

BALNEOLOGIA POLSKA.
Polskie Towarzystwo Balneoklimatologii,
Bioklimatologii i Medycyny Fizykalnej, Ul.
Mickiewicza 16, 87-720 Ciechocinek, Poland.
TEL 48-54-833211. FAX 48-54-837220.
circ. 700. *4433*

BALTIMORE COUNTY MUSTER.
Sons of the American Revolution, Maryland Society,
10605 Lakespring Way, Hunt Valley, MD 21030-
2818. TEL 410-628-2490.
circ. 150. *3460*

BALTIMORE'S CHILD.
11 Dutton Ct., Baltimore, MD 21228. TEL 410-
367-5883. FAX 410-719-9342.
circ. 70,000. *1760*

BANCA Y COMERCIO.
Escue a Bancaria y Comercial, Paseo de la Reforma
202, Mexico 06600 D.F., Mexico. FAX 905-546-
0326.
circ. 6,500. *1062*

**BANCO DO BRASIL. BOLETIM DE INFORMACAO AO
PESSOAL.**
Banco do Brasil S.A., Departamento Geral de
Selecao e Desenvolvimento do Pessoal, Setor
Bancario Sul, Lote 23, Bloco C, C.P. 562, Brasilia,
D.F., Brazil.
circ. 100,000. *1063*

BANDARI.
Kenya Ports Authority, P.O. Box 95009, Mombasa,
Kenya. FAX 254-11-311867.
circ. 12,000. *6713*

BANDERSNATCH.
Lewis Carroll Society, 69 Ashby Rd, Woodville
Swadlincote, Derbyshire DE11 7BZ, England.
circ. 350. *4185*

BANGLADESH JOURNAL OF FOREST SCIENCE.
Bangladesh Forest Research Institute, Chittagong
4000, Bangladesh. TEL 880-31-212685. FAX 880-
31-210901.
circ. 1,000. *3011*

BANK CREDIT ANALYST.
B C A Publications Ltd., 1002 Sherbrooke St. W.
16th Fl. Montreal, PQ H3A 3L6, Canada. TEL 514-
499-9706. FAX 514-499-9709. *1320*

**BANK FOR INTERNATIONAL SETTLEMENTS.
ANNUAL REPORT.**
Bank for International Settlements, 7
Centralbahnstr., Case Postale 262, CH-4002 Basel,
Switzerland. *1064*

BANK INVESTMENT REPRESENTATIVE.
Quantum Communications, Inc., Box 4364, Logan,
UT 84321-4364. TEL 801-752-1173. FAX 801-
752-1193.
circ. 31,209. *1065*

BANK NEGARA MALAYSIA. ANNUAL REPORT.
Bank Negara Malaysia, P.O. Box 10922, Jalan
Dato'Onn. 50480 Kuala Lumpur, Malaysia.
TEL 2988044. FAX 2912990 *1177*

**BANK NEGARA MALAYSIA. BULLETIN EKONOMI
SUKU TAHUNAN.**
Bank Negara Malaysia, P.O. Box 10922, Jalan
Dato'Onn, 50480 Kuala Lumpur, Malaysia. TEL 03-
2988044. FAX 03-2912990 *1177*

BANK NEGARA MALAYSIA. STATISTICAL BULLETIN.
Bank Negara Malaysia, P.O. Box 10922, Jalan
Dato'onn, 50480 Kuala Lumpur, Malaysia.
TEL 2988044. FAX 2912990 *981*

BANK OF JAMAICA. ECONOMIC STATISTICS.
Bank of Jamaica, P.O. Box 621, King St., Kingston,
Jamaica, W.I. TEL 809-922-0750. FAX 809-967-
4265.
circ. 1,200. *981*

BANK SYSTEMS & TECHNOLOGY.
Miller Freeman Inc. (New York) One Penn Plaza,
New York, NY 10119. TEL 212-714-1300.
FAX 212-302-6273.
circ. 23,400. *1067*

BANKGESELLSCHAFT BERLIN. DEVISENBRIEF.
Bankgesellschaft Berlin AG, Alexanderplatz 2,
10178 Berlin, Germany. TEL 49-30-245500.
FAX 49-30-24566333.
circ. 4,600. *1178*

BANKGESELLSCHAFT BERLIN. UNTERNEHMERBRIEF.
Bankgesellschaft Berlin AG, Alexanderplatz 2, 10178 Berlin, Germany. TEL 49-30-245500. FAX 49-30-24566333.
circ. 1,500. *1178*

BAPTIST PROGRESS.
Baptist Missionary Association of Texas, Box 2085, Waxahachie, TX 75165. TEL 214-923-0756. FAX 214-923-2679.
circ. 12,000. *6135*

BAPTIST PUBLIC RELATIONS ASSOCIATION NEWSLETTER.
Baptist Public Relations Association, Box 270187, Nashville, TN 37227-0187. TEL 615-227-7836. *6135*

BAPTIST UNION OF WESTERN CANADA. YEARBOOK.
Baptist Union of Western Canada, 605, 999 8 St., S.W., Calgary, AB T2R 1J5, Canada. TEL 403-228-9559. FAX 403-228-9048.
circ. 700. *6135*

BARCHE E CATALOGO.
Gruppo Editoriale Commerciale, Via G. Galilei, 6, 20124 Milan, Italy. TEL 02-29097-1. FAX 02-29097-209.
circ. 26,000. *6532*

BARCLAYS PREMIER WORLD MAGAZINE.
The Publishing Team, Exmouth House, 3-11 Pine St., London EC1R 0JH, England. TEL 44-171-923-5400. FAX 44-171-923-5401.
circ. 70,000. *1071*

BARCOS.
Editorial Barcos S.R.L., Blanco Encalada 121, 1642 San Isidro, B.A., Argentina. TEL 54-1-7354404. FAX 54-1-7354404.
circ. 8,000. *6532*

BARNARDO NEWS.
Barnardo's, Tanners Ln., Barkingside, Ilford, Essex IG6 1QG, England. TEL 44-181-550-5522. FAX 44-181-550-0429.
circ. 6,400. *6362*

BARS AND STRIPES.
Detroit Police Lieutenants & Sergeants Association, 28 W. Adams St., No. 1308, Detroit, MI 48226.
circ. 2,900. *2158*

BARTENDER.
Foley Publishing Corp., Box 158, Liberty Corner, NJ 07938. TEL 908-766-6006. FAX 908-766-6607.
circ. 130,703. *500*

BARTER COMMUNIQUE.
Full Circle Marketing Corp., Box 2527, Sarasota, FL 33578. TEL 813-349-3300.
circ. 50,000. *1586*

BASEBALL HOBBY NEWS.
4540 Kearny Villa Rd., Ste. 215, San Diego, CA 92123. TEL 619-565-2848. FAX 619-565-6608.
circ. 91,000. *6497*

BASILICATA.
Basilicata Editrice, Via Ridola 20, Casella Postale 70, Matera 75100, Italy.
circ. 10,000. *5636*

BASSE NORMANDIE AUTOMOBILE.
Chambre Syndicale Nationale du Commerce et de la Reparation Automobile, Secteur Regional Basse-Normandie, 4 rue Pasteur, B.P. No. 7, 14011 Caen Cedex, France.
circ. 1,000. *6777*

BATTELLE TODAY.
Battelle Memorial Institute, Communications Office, Attn: Harriet A. Craig, Ed., 505 King Ave., Columbus, OH 43201. TEL 614-424-5336. FAX 614-424-3889.
circ. 36,000. *6646*

BATTLER COLUMNS.
Alderson-Broaddus College, Philippi, WV 26416. TEL 304-457-1700. FAX 304-457-1700.
circ. 1,200. *1858*

BAUEN.
Fachschriften Verlag GmbH, Hoehenstr. 17, 70736 Fellbach, Germany. TEL 0711-5206-256. FAX 0711-5281424.
circ. 76,253. *834*

DAS BAUZENTRUM.
Verlag das Beispiel GmbH, Spreestr. 9, 64295 Darmstadt, Germany. TEL 06151-33557. FAX 06151-313089.
circ. 40,000. *387*

BAY AREA BABY.
Bay Area Publishing Group Inc., 401 Alberto Way, Ste. A, Los Gatos, CA 95032-5404. TEL 408-358-1414. FAX 408-356-4903.
circ. 60,000. *1761*

BAY AREA REPORTER.
Benro Enterprises, Inc., 395 Ninth St., San Francisco, CA 94103-3831. TEL 415-861-5019.
circ. 37,500. *3529*

BAYER ALKALIZER.
Bayer Corp., 1884 Miles Ave., Elkhart, IN 46514. TEL 219-264-8111. FAX 219-262-7209.
circ. 6,500. *570*

BAYERISCH-SCHWAEBISCHE WIRTSCHAFT.
Industrie- und Handelskammer fuer Augsburg und Schwaben, Stettenstr. 1-3, 86150 Augsburg, Germany. TEL 49-821-3162-0. FAX 49-821-3162323.
circ. 87,500. *1132*

BAYERISCHES LANDESAMT FUER WASSERWIRTSCHAFT. INFORMATIONSBERICHTE.
Bayerisches Landesamt fuer Wasserwirtschaft, Lazarettstr. 67, 80636 Munich, Germany. TEL 49-89-12101203.
circ. 1,000. *6963*

BAYLOR DENTAL JOURNAL.
Baylor College of Dentistry, Office of Alumni and Public Affairs, 3302 Gaston Ave., Dallas, TX 75246. TEL 214-828-8214. FAX 214-828-8906.
circ. 7,000. *4635*

BAYOU BENGAL.
Louisiana State University at Eunice, Box 1129, Eunice, LA 70535. TEL 318-457-7311. FAX 318-546-6620.
circ. 1,000. *1858*

DE BAZUIN.
Stichting De Bazuin, Simon Stevinweg 17, 5223 AX 's Hertogenbosch, Netherlands.
circ. 5,000. *6045*

BEACON (GEORGIA).
Georgia Southern University, Department of Foreign Languages, Statesboro, GA 30460. TEL 912-681-5278.
circ. 1,000. *2315*

THE BEACON REVIEW.
Century Publications, Inc., 1805 S. Bellaire, Ste. 235, Denver, CO 80222. TEL 303-692-8940.
circ. 30,000. *3284*

BEAN PROGRAM ANNUAL REPORT.
Centro Internacional de Agricultura Tropical, Apdo. Aereo 6713, Cali, Colombia. TEL 57-23-4450000. FAX 57-23-4450273.
circ. 600. *100*

BEAUTY.
H.J. Pichler Verlagsgesellschaft, Muthgasse 109, Postfach 16, A-1195 Vienna, Austria. TEL 43-1-31851510. FAX 43-1-375736.
circ. 80,000. *489*

BEAUTY COUNTER.
Miller Freeman Publishers Ltd. Sovereign Way, Tonbridge, Kent TN9 1RW, England. TEL 44-1732-364422. FAX 44-1732-361534.
circ. 13,813. *494*

BEAUTY INC.
Beauty & Barber Supply Institute, Inc., 11811 N. Tatum Blvd., Ste. 1085, Phoenix, AZ 85028-1618. TEL 602-404-1800. FAX 602-404-8900.
circ. 5,000. *490*

BEAUTY MAGAZINE.
Cosmetics Communications Ltd., 335 Linen Hall, 162-168 Regent St., London W1R 5TB, England. TEL 44-171-434-1530. FAX 44-171-437-0915.
circ. 13,200. *494*

BEBIDAS MEXICANAS.
Alfa Editores Tecnicos S.A., Libertad No. 107-402, 03660 Mexico DF, Mexico. TEL 525-579-3333. FAX 525-532-9504.
circ. 5,000. *500*

BEDFORD INSTITUTE OF OCEANOGRAPHY. SCIENCE REVIEW.
Department of Fisheries and Oceans, Bedford Institute of Oceanography, Dartmouth, N.S. B2Y 4A2, Canada. TEL 902-426-4093. FAX 902-426-2256.
circ. 5,000. *2291*

BEER CANS & BREWERY COLLECTIBLES.
Beer Can Collectors of America, 747 Merus Ct., Fenton, MO 63026-2092. TEL 314-343-6486.
circ. 4,000. *3503*

BEERMAT MAGAZINE.
British Beer-mat Collectors Society (BBCS), c/o Tony Matthews, Hon. Sec., 69 Dunnington Ave., Kidderminster, Worcs. DY10 2YT, England.
circ. 500. *3503*

BEGEGNUNG (BONN).
Varus Verlag Birgit Laube, Koenigswintererstr. 552, 53227 Bonn, Germany. TEL 0228-440015. FAX 0228-440017.
circ. 12,000. *2450*

BEGONIAN.
American Begonia Society, Box 471651, San Francisco, CA 94147-1651. TEL 817-728-3485.
circ. 2,000. *3045*

BEIERSDORF JOURNAL.
Beiersdorf AG, Unnastr. 48, 20253 Hamburg, Germany. FAX 040-5693434. *1515*

BEITRAEGE ZUR ZEITGESCHICHTE OBEROESTERREICHS.
Oberoesterreichisches Landesarchiv, Anzengruberstr. 19, A-4020 Linz, Austria. TEL 43-732-6555230. FAX 43-732-655523-4619.
circ. 500. *3397*

HET BELANG VAN LIMBURG.
Concentra Uitgeversmaatschappij, Herckenrodesingel 10, 3500 Hasselt, Belgium. TEL 32-11-878111. FAX 32-11-878204.
circ. 110,688. *3114*

BELGIAN BUSINESS MAGAZINE.
Business & Industrie Meiboomlaan 33, 8800 Roeselare, Belgium.
circ. 31,500. *1515*

BELGIUM. RIJKSSTATION VOOR LANDBOUWTECHNIEK. MEDEDELINGEN.
Rijksstation voor Landbouwtechniek, Van Gansberghelaan 115, B-9820 Merelbeke, Belgium. TEL 32-9-252-521821. FAX 32-9-252-524234. *101*

BELOIT MAGAZINE.
Beloit College, 700 College St., Beloit, WI 53511. TEL 608-363-2828. FAX 608-363-2870.
circ. 20,000. *1858*

BELSER KUNST KATALOG.
Chr. Belser Verlag, Pfizerstr. 5-7, 70184 Stuttgart, Germany. TEL 49-711-2191410. FAX 49-711-2191413.
circ. 60,000. *5119*

BELSER KUNST QUARTAL.
Chr. Belser Verlag, Pfizerstr. 5-7, 70184 Stuttgart, Germany. TEL 49-711-2191410. FAX 49-711-2191413.
circ. 33,000. *5119*

BERGEN COUNTY DENTAL SOCIETY. NEWSLETTER.
Bergen County Dental Society, 1060 Main St., River Edge, NJ 07661.
circ. 700. *4636*

BERKELEY MONTHLY.
Klaber Publishing Corp., 1301 59th St., Emeryville, CA 94608-2115. TEL 510-658-9811. FAX 510-658-9902.
circ. 75,000. *4134*

BERLINER AERZTEBLATT.
CB Verlag Carl Boldt, Baseler Str. 80, 12205 Berlin, Germany. TEL 49-30-8337087. FAX 49-30-8339125.
circ. 18,500. *4434*

BERLINGSKE TIDENDE.
Berlingske Dagblade, Pilestraede 34, DK-1147 Copenhagen K, Denmark. TEL 45-33-75-75-00. FAX 45-33-75-20-72.
circ. 134,415. *3133*

BERMUDA SHORTS.
Bermuda Department of Tourism, 310 Madison Ave., Ste. 201, New York, NY 10017. TEL 212-818-9800.
circ. 6,000. *6869*

BERNAN GOVERNMENT PUBLICATIONS NEWS.
Bernan, 4611-F Assembly Dr., Lanham, MD 20706-5728. TEL 301-459-7666. FAX 301-459-0056.
circ. 7,000. *3977*

BESCHAFFUNGSDIENST GALABAU.
Rolf Soll Verlag GmbH, Postfach 650680, 22366 Hamburg, Germany. TEL 49-40-6068820. FAX 49-40-60688288.
circ. 8,500. *3045*

BEST READ GUIDE.
Box 1958, 77 Finlay Rd., Orleans, MA 02653. TEL 508-240-1212. FAX 508-240-2912. *6870*

BEST WISHES.
Family Communications, Inc., 37 Hanna Ave., Toronto, ON M6K 1X1, Canada.
circ. 170,000. *1761*

BETA PHI MU NEWSLETTER.
Beta Phi Mu, International Library and Information Science Honor Society, c/o School of Library and Information Studies, Florida State University, Tallahassee, FL 32306-2048. TEL 904-644-3907. FAX 904-644-3253.
circ. 20,000. *3978*

BETA THETA PI.
Beta Theta Pi Fraternity, Box 6277, Oxford, OH 45056-6277. TEL 513-523-7591. FAX 513-523-2381.
circ. 81,000. *1858*

BETHANY MAGAZINE.
Bethany College, 421 N. First, Lindsborg, KS 67456-1897. TEL 913-227-3311.
circ. 7,500. *1858*

BETHEL FOCUS.
Bethel College (St. Paul), 3900 Bethel Dr., St. Paul, MN 55112. TEL 612-638-6083. FAX 612-638-6003.
circ. 35,000. *1858*

BETON.
FeBe - Federation de l'Industrie du Beton, Bd. Aug. Reyers 207-209, 1030 Brussels, Belgium. TEL 32-2-7358015. FAX 32-2-7347794.
circ. 8,500. *836*

BETRIEBLICHE AUSBILDUNGSPRAXIS.
Verlag und Vertriebsgesellschaft mbH, Breite Str. 69, Postfach 8232, 40211 Duesseldorf, Germany.
circ. 1,800. *4950*

DER BETRIEBSLEITER.
Verlag fuer Technik und Wirtschaft GmbH & Co., Lise-Meitner-Str. 2, 55129 Mainz, Germany. TEL 49-6131-992-0. FAX 49-6131-992100.
circ. 17,000. *1407*

BETRIEBSSTATISTIK.
Bundesministerium fuer Wirtschaftliche Angelegenheiten, Bundeslastverteiler, Dienststelle Statistik, Am Hof 6a, A-1010 Vienna, Austria. TEL 43-1-531132004. FAX 43-1-531132092.
circ. 400. *2561*

BETTER ROADS.
William O. Dannhausen, Pub., Box 558, Park Ridge, IL 60068. TEL 312-693-7710. FAX 847-696-3445. *2653*

BETWEEN THE LEAVES.
Queensland Forest Service, G.P.O. Box 944, Brisbane, Qld. 4001, Australia. TEL 07-234-0157.
circ. 5,000. *3011*

BEVERAGE & FOOD DYNAMICS.
Adams Publishing Companies, 68-860 Perez Rd., Ste. J, Cathedral City, CA 92234. TEL 619-770-4370.
circ. 75,000. *501*

BEVERAGE WORLD EN ESPANOL.
Strategic Business Communications, 226 W. 26th St., New York, NY 10011. TEL 212-822-5930. FAX 212-822-5931.
circ. 10,600. *501*

BEYOND COMPUTING.
International Business Machines (IBM) Corporation, 590 Madison Ave., New York, NY 10022. TEL 212-745-6336. FAX 212-745-6058.
circ. 170,552. *1983*

BEYOND P E.
420 E. 54th St., Apt. 33-B, New York, NY 10022-5154. TEL 212-779-0294. FAX 212-779-1526.
circ. 80,000. *3525*

BEYOND WORDS.
Wycliffe Bible Translators Australia, Graham Rd., Kangaroo Ground, Vic. 3097, Australia. TEL 61-3-97122777. FAX 61-3-97122799.
circ. 9,500. *6046*

BHABHA ATOMIC RESEARCH CENTRE. NUCLEAR PHYSICS DIVISION. ANNUAL REPORT.
Bhabha Atomic Research Centre, Trombay, Bombay 400085, India. *5593*

BIBEL UND GEMEINDE.
Bibelbund e.V., Narzissenweg 11, 35447 Reiskirchen, Germany. TEL 0228-638784.
circ. 3,500. *6046*

BIBLIOEXPORT.
Association for the Export of Canadian Books, 504-1 Nicholas St., Ottawa, ON K1N 7B7, Canada. TEL 613-562-2324. FAX 613-562-2329.
circ. 920. *5988*

BIBLIOGRAFIA VENEZOLANA.
Instituto Autonomo Biblioteca Nacional, Oficina de Information, Apdo. 80593, Prados del Este, Caracas 1080-A, Venezuela. TEL 943-1361. FAX 941-5219.
circ. 1,500. *3978*

BIBLIOGRAPHIA SCIENTIAE NATURALIS HELVETICA.
Schweizerische Landesbibliothek, Hallwylstr. 15, CH-3003 Bern, Switzerland. TEL 41-31-3228911. FAX 41-31-3228463.
circ. 800. *6300*

BIBLIOGRAPHICAL SOCIETY OF CANADA. BULLETIN.
Bibliographical Society of Canada, P.O. Box 575, Sta. "P", Toronto, ON M5S 2T1, Canada.
circ. 400. *520*

BIBLIOGRAPHIE ANNUELLE DE L'HISTOIRE DE FRANCE.
C N R S Editions, 20-22 rue St. Amand, 75015 Paris, France. TEL 45-33-16-00. FAX 45-33-92-13.
circ. 1,500. *3365*

BIBLIOGRAPHIE ZUR GESCHICHTE OBEROESTERREICHS.
Oberoesterreichisches Landesarchiv, Anzengruberstr. 19, A-4020 Linz, Austria. TEL 43-732-6555230. FAX 43-732-655523-4519.
circ. 500. *3398*

BIBLIOGRAPHY ON SMOKING AND HEALTH.
U.S. Centers for Disease Control, National Center for Chronic Disease Prevention and Health Promotion, 4770 Buford Hwy. N.E., MS K-50, Atlanta, GA 30341-3724. TEL 404-488-5705. FAX 404-488-5939. *5538*

BIBLIOTECA "JOSE ARTIGAS". BOLETIN - JUNTA DE VECINOS.
Biblioteca "Jose Artigas", 25 de Mayo 609, Montevideo, Uruguay.
circ. 300. *522*

BIBLIOTEKSBLADET.
Sveriges Allmaenna Biblioteksfoerening, P.O. Box 3127, S-103 62 Stockholm, Sweden. TEL 46-8-723-00-82. FAX 46-8-723-00-83.
circ. 4,918. *3979*

BIBLIOTEKSPRESSEN
Bibliotek 70, Lindevangs Alle 2, DK-2000 Frederiksberg, Denmark. TEL 45-38-88-17-70. FAX 45-38-88-31-01.
circ. 5,970. *3979*

BICYCLE RETAILER AND INDUSTRY NEWS.
JayWalker Publication, 502 W. Cordova Rd., Santa Fe, NM 87501-4144. FAX 505-988-7224.
circ. 14,000. *6521*

BIENVENIDOS A MIAMI.
Welcome Publications, Inc. Box 630518, Miami, FL 33163. TEL 305-944-9444.
circ. 13,000. *6934*

BIG APPLE PARENTS' PAPER.
Family Communications, 35 E. 12th St., 4th Fl., New York, NY 10003-4634. TEL 212-533-2277. FAX 212-475-6186.
circ. 62,000. *1761*

BIJBEL EN WETENSCHAP.
Stichting Bijbel en Wetenschap, Postbus 957 3800 AZ Amersfoort, Netherlands. TEL 31-33-462-1732.
circ. 3,500. *6048*

BIJNOR TIMES.
Ram Ganga Prakashan, Bijnor Times Rd., Utta Pradesh 246701, India. TEL 01342-62602.
circ. 52,000. *3166*

DE BIJSTAANDER.
Sociale Dienst, Vlaardingenlaan 1E, 1062 HN Amsterdam, Netherlands. TEL 31-20-5160800. FAX 31-20-6141631.
circ. 2,900. *6363*

BILLINGTON'S STOCK FOCUS II.
Billington Securities Ltd., 1660 Benson Rd., Pt. Roberts, WA 98281. TEL 206-945-1491. FAX 206-945-1089.
circ. 62,500. *1321*

BILSPORT.
Albinsson & Sjoeberg, P.O. Box 529, S-371 23 Karlskrona, Sweden. TEL 46-455-3353-25. FAX 46-455-31-1715.
circ. 53,700. *6777*

BINDEN EN BOUWEN.
Sint-Bernardinuscollege, Akerstraat 95, Heerlen, Netherlands.
circ. 2,000. *1858*

BINGO NEWS & GAMING HI-LITES.
Bingo Hi-Lites Ltd., 101, 10171 Saskatchewan Dr., Box 106, Edmonton, AB T6E 4R5, Canada. TEL 403-986-5088. FAX 403-986-5089.
circ. 25,000. *2148*

BIOCELL.
Centro Regional de Investigaciones Cientificas y Tecnologicas, Casilla de Correo 131, 5500 Mendoza, Argentina. TEL 54-61-205020 ext. 2670. FAX 54-61-380232.
circ. 300. *768*

BIOCONNECTION.
Michigan Biotechnology Institute, 3900 Collins Rd., Box 27609, Lansing, MI 48909. TEL 517-337-3181. FAX 517-337-2122.
circ. 2,500. *657*

BIOLOGIA OGGI.
Associazione Nazionale Laureati in Scienze Biologiche, Via Guglielmo degl Ubertni, 64, 00176 Rome, Italy. TEL 39-6-21707494.
circ. 1,000. *572*

BIOLOGIA PESQUERA.
Universidad Catolica de la Santisima Concepcion Casilla 297, Concepcion, Chile. TEL 56-41-246175. FAX 56-41-245908. *2927*

BIOLOGISCHE ARBEITSSTOFF TOLERANZ WERTE UND EXPOSITIONSAEQUIVALENTE FUER KREBSERZEUGENDE ARBEITSSTOFFE.
V C H Verlagsgesellschaft mbH, Postfach 101161, 69451 Weinheim, Germany. TEL 06201-606-0. FAX 06201-606328.
circ. 600. *5246*

IL BIOLOGO.
Associazione Nazionale Laureati in Scienze Biologiche, Via Guglielmo degl Ubertini 64, 00176 Rome, Italy. TEL 39-6-21707494.
circ. 1,000. *573*

BIOMEDICAL TECHNOLOGY MANAGEMENT.
Second Source Publications, Inc., 10 Fisho Ave., East Providence, RI 02914-1215. TEL 401-434-1050. FAX 401-434-1090.
circ. 12,500. *4435*

BIOMETEOROLOGY BULLETIN.
International Society of Biometeorology, c/o N.N. Barthakur, Ed., Dept. of Natural Resource Science, Universite McGill-Campus MacDonald, 21,111 Lakeshore Rd., Ste. Anne de Bellevue, PQ H9X 3V9, Canada. *4991*

BIOTECH BUYER'S GUIDE.
American Chemical Society, 1155 16th St., N.W., Washington, DC 20036. TEL 800-227-5558. FAX 202-872-4615.
circ. 65,000. *658*

BIOTECH PRODUCTS INTERNATIONAL.
Pan European Publishing Co. Rue Verte 216, 1030 Brussels, Belgium. TEL 32-2-2402611. FAX 32-2-2427111.
circ. 30,020. *658*

BIRMINGHAM & WARWICKSHIRE ARCHAEOLOGICAL SOCIETY. TRANSACTIONS.
Birmingham & Warwickshire Archaeological Society, Birmingham & Midland Institute, Margaret Street, Birmingham B3 3BS, England.
circ. 350. *347*

BIRMINGHAM BAR ASSOCIATION. BULLETIN.
Birmingham Bar Association, 2021 Second Ave. N., Birmingham, AL 35203-3703. TEL 205-251-8006.
circ. 1,600. *3750*

BIZ (ST. LOUIS).
American City Business Journals, Inc. (St. Louis), 1 Metropolitan Sq., Ste. 2170, St. Louis, MO 63102. TEL 314-421-6200.
circ. 70,000. *3225*

BIZZ - MISSETS ZAKENBLAD.
Misset Postbus 4, 7000 BA Doetinchem, Netherlands. TEL 31-8340-49371. FAX 31-8340-63638.
circ. 250,210. *897*

BLACK EMPLOYMENT AND EDUCATION.
Hamdani, Inc., 2625 Piedmont Rd., Ste. 56-282, Atlanta, GA 30324. TEL 404-469-5891.
circ. 120,000. *2867*

BLACK SPOTS.
Black Spots Publishing, 1283 S. LaBrea Ave., Ste. 304, Los Angeles, CA 90019. TEL 213-938-0101.
circ. 10,000. *2868*

BLACKPOOL HOTEL & GUEST HOUSE ASSOCIATION. JOURNAL.
Blackpool Hotel and Guest House Association Ltd., 87a Coronation St., Blackpool FY1 4PD, Lancastershire, England. *3559*

BLAETTERTEIG.
Media Austria, Postfach 95, A-1013 Vienna, Austria. TEL 43-1-3665512.
circ. 2,000. *3701*

BLAKES REPORT ON INTELLECTUAL PROPERTY.
Blake, Cassels & Graydon, Box 25, Commerce Court West, Toronto, Ont. M5L 1A9, Canada. TEL 416-863-5840. FAX 416-863-2653.
circ. 5,500. *3750*

BLESK.
Na Florenci 19, 112 86 Prague 1, Czech Republic. TEL 42-2-282-2870. FAX 42-2-232-3630.
circ. 485,000. *3133*

BLICKPUNKT SCHULE.
Hessischer Philologenverband, Schlichterstr. 18, 65185 Wiesbaden, Germany. TEL 0611-307445. FAX 0611-376905.
circ. 6,000. *2316*

BLOCH-ALMANACH.
Ernst-Bloch-Archiv, Bismarckstr. 44-48, 67012 Ludwigshafen, Germany. TEL 0621-5042592. FAX 0621-5042450.
circ. 500. *4134*

BLOMSTER.
Blomster ApS, P.O. Box 100, Storegade 26, DK-4550 Asnaes, Denmark. TEL 45-53-45-10-24. FAX 45-53-45-08-17.
circ. 2,200. *3070*

BLOMSTER-BRANSCHEN.
Blomster-Branschen i Bromma AB, P.O. Box 808, S-161 24 Bromma, Sweden. TEL 46-8-25-97-31. FAX 46-8-26-96-06.
circ. 3,000. *3070*

BLUE GRASS ROOTS.
Kentucky Genealogical Society, Box 153, Frankfurt, KY 40602.
circ. 1,500. *3076*

BLUE PITCHER.
Unicorn Press, Inc., 200 E. Bessemer Ave, Greensboro, NC 27401-1416. TEL 919-852-0281.
circ. 1,000. *4302*

BLUELINE (POTSDAM).
Potsdam College, English Department, Potsdam, NY 13676. TEL 315-267-2005. FAX 315-267-3256.
circ. 400. *4188*

BLUEPRINT (NOTTINGHAM).
Boots Co., plc., 1 Thane Rd. W., Nottingham NG2 3AA, England. TEL 44-115-959-2365. FAX 44-115-959-5684.
circ. 63,000. *1499*

BLUEPRINT (WINFRITH).
Dorset Police, Force Headquarters, Winfrith, Nr. Dorchester DT2 8DZ, England. FAX 44-1929-463755.
circ. 4,000. *2159*

BLUES AT THE FOUNDATION.
Blues Foundation, 174 Beale St., Memphis, TN 38103. TEL 901-527-2583. FAX 901-529-4030.
circ. 3,000. *5144*

BOATING BUSINESS.
Rushton Marine Press Ltd., Woodside, Burnhams Rd., Little Bookham, Leatherhead, Surrey KT23 3BA, England. TEL 44-1372-453316. FAX 44-1372-459974.
circ. 8,500. *6532*

BODY POSITIVE.
Body Positive, New York, 19 Fulton St., Ste. 308B, New York, NY 10038. TEL 212-566-7333. FAX 212-566-4539.
circ. 10,000. *4618*

BODYSHOP BUSINESS.
Babcox Publications, 11 S. Forge St., Box 1810, Akron, OH 44309-1810. TEL 216-535-6117. FAX 216-535-0874.
circ. 58,057. *6777*

BODYSHOP MAGAZINE.
Juniper Court, Boxwell Rd., Berkhamsted, Herts. HP4 3ET, England. TEL 44-1442-876686. FAX 44-1442-870740.
circ. 14,000. *6777*

BOERN & UNGE.
Fagbladet Boern og Unge, Blegdamsvej 124, 4, DK-2100 Copenhagen Oe, Denmark. TEL 47-35-43-21-43. FAX 47-35-43-22-99.
circ. 53,218. *2316*

BOERNETEATERAVISEN.
Teatercentrum i Danmark, Frederiksborggade 20, DK-1360 Copenhagen K, Denmark. TEL 45-33-15-69-00. FAX 45-33-13-14-39.
circ. 14,000. *6693*

BOGAZICI JOURNAL: REVIEW OF SOCIAL, ECONOMIC AND ADMINISTRATIVE SCIENCES.
Bogazici Universitesi, Bebek, 80815 Istanbul, Turkey. TEL 90-212-2631500. FAX 90-212-2656479.
circ. 150. *6316*

BOGG.
Bogg Publications, 422 N. Cleveland St., Arlington, VA 22201. TEL 703-243-6019.
circ. 850. *4302*

BOLETIM U E R J.
Universidade do Estado do Rio de Janeiro, R. Sao Francisco Xavier, 524 sala T-01, CEP 20550 Maracana, Rio de Janeiro, Brazil.
circ. 2,000. *2316*

BOLETIN DE ARQUEOLOGIA MEDIEVAL.
Asociacion Espanola de Arqueologia Medieval, Apdo. Postal 50449, Breton de los Herreros 59, 30 Izq., 28003 Madrid, Spain.
circ. 613. *347*

BOLETIN DE SEGUROS.
Superintendencia de Bancos, Avda. 12 de Octubre 1561, Apdo. de Correos 17-17-770, Quito, Ecuador. FAX 563-652. *3643*

BOLETIN HIDROLOGICO.
Instituto Costarricense de Electricidad (ICE), Apdo. 10032, 1000 San Jose, Costa Rica. TEL 506-207720. *2284*

BOLETIN I I E.
Instituto de Investigaciones Electricas, Division de Informacion Tecnologica y Desarrollo Profesional, Liebnitz 14, 3 piso, Col. Anzures, Del. M. Hidalgo, 11590 Mexico, D.F., Mexico. FAX 73-189-854.
circ. 5,500. *2685*

BOLETIN OFICIAL ECLESIASTICO DEL ARZOBISPADO CASTRENSE DE ESPANA.
Arzobispado Castrense de Orpana, C. Nuncio 13, 28005 Madrid, Spain. TEL 34-1-366-8228. FAX 34-1-366-8225.
circ. 700. *6048*

BOLLETTINO BIBLIOGRAFICO E RASSEGNA ARCHIVISTICA E DI STUDI STORICI DELLA SARDEGNA.
C V E C Edizioni, Via Tocmino 33, Cagliari, Italy. TEL 39-70-276220.
circ. 1,000. *3365*

BOMBUS.
Verein fuer Naturwissenschaftliche Heimatforschung zu Hamburg e.V., Zoologisches Institut und Museum, Martin-Luther-King-Platz 3, 20146 Hamburg, Germany.
circ. 300. *722*

BOND.
Lutheran Brotherhood, 625 Fourth Ave. S., Minneapolis, MN 55415. TEL 612-340-7000.
circ. 540,000. *6136*

BONDINGS.
New Ways Ministry, 4012 29th St., Mt. Rainier, MD 20712. TEL 301-277-5674. FAX 301-864-6948.
circ. 3,200. *3529*

BONNER JAPANFORSCHUNGEN.
Bonner Verein zur Foerderung der Japanforschung, Regina-Pacis-Weg 7, 53113 Bonn, Germany. TEL 0228-737223. FAX 0228-737020.
circ. 500. *5280*

BONNER UMWELT ZEITUNG.
Oekozentrum Bonn e.V., Heerstr. 20a, 53111 Bonn, Germany. TEL 0228-692220. FAX 0228-631124.
circ. 10,000. *2778*

THE BOOK ARTS CLASSIFIED.
Box 77167, Washington, DC 20013. FAX 800-538-7549.
circ. 5,000. *5989*

BOOK OF BRITISH EXCELLENCE.
Custom Publishing Company Ltd., 45 Station Rd., Redhill, Surrey RH1 1QH, England. TEL 0737-767213. FAX 0737-771662.
circ. 150,000. *837*

BOOKENDS.
Friends of the Reading-Berks Public Libraries, Box 227, Wernersville, PA 19565. TEL 610-678-6480.
circ. 2,000. *3980*

BOOKMARK.
B.C. Teachers' Federation, 100-550 W. 6th Ave., Vancouver, BC V5Z 4P2, Canada. TEL 604-871-1848. FAX 604-871-2291.
circ. 1,000. *2316*

BOOKMARK (MOSCOW, IDAHO).
University of Idaho Library, Moscow, ID 83844. TEL 208-885-6584. FAX 208-885-6817.
circ. 1,100. *3981*

BOOKS AND LIBRARIES AT THE UNIVERSITY OF KANSAS.
University of Kansas Libraries, Lawrence, KS 66045. TEL 913-864-4334. *3981*

BOOSEY AND HAWKES NEWSLETTER.
Boosey and Hawkes, Inc., 24 E. 21st St., New York, NY 10010-7200. TEL 212-228-3300. FAX 212-473-5730.
circ. 10,000. *5144*

BOPUXUE ZAZHI.
Zhongguo Kexueyuan, Wuhan Wuli Yanjiusuo, P.O. Box 71010, Xiaohongshan, Wuchang-qu, Wuhan, Hubei 430071, People's Republic of China. TEL 86-27-786-7791. FAX 86-27-788-5291.
circ. 200. *5602*

BORAX PIONEER.
Borax Consolidated Ltd., 170 Priestley Rd., Guildford, Surrey GU2 5RQ, England. TEL 44-1483-734000. FAX 44-1483-4576764. circ. 6,000. *1666*

BORD IASCAIGH MHARA. TUARASCAIL AGUS CUNTAISI.
Irish Sea Fisheries Board, P.O. Box 12, Crofton Rd., Dun Laoghaire, Co. Dublin, Ireland. TEL 01-2841544. FAX 01-2841123. circ. 3,500. *2927*

BORDER - LINES.
P.O. Box 459, Station P, Toronto, ON M5S 2S9, Canada. TEL 416-921-6446. FAX 416-921-3984. circ. 500. *420*

BORTHWICK INSTITUTE OF HISTORICAL RESEARCH. BORTHWICK PAPERS.
St. Anthony's Press, St. Anthony's Hall, York YO1 2PW, England. TEL 44-1904-642315. circ. 350. *3399*

BOSCH TECHNISCHE BERICHTE.
Robert Bosch GmbH, Abteilung BFV21, Postfach 106050, 70049 Stuttgart, Germany. *2685*

BOSHI KAGAKU RYOHO.
Boshi Kagaku Ryoho Kenkyujo, 55-12, Ikebukuro 2-chome, Toshima-ku, Tokyo 171, Japan. TEL 03-3980-6139. circ. 250. *4803*

BOSO NO KONCHU.
Chibaken Konchu Danwakai, c/o Mr. Yasutoshi Matsui, 3-102, 427-5 Nedo, Kashiwa-shi, Chiba-ken 277, Japan. circ. 200. *722*

BOTANICA.
Delhi University Botanical Society, Department of Botany, University of Delhi, Delhi 110007, India. circ. 500. *673*

BOTANICAL SURVEY OF INDIA. BULLETIN.
Botanical Survey of India, c/o Ministry of the Environment and Forests, Paryavaran Bhavan, C G O Complex Phase II, Lodi Rd., New Delhi 110 002, India. TEL 436-3951. circ. 250. *674*

DE BOUWADVISEUR.
Samsom Bedrijfsinformatie B.V. Postbus 4, 2400 MA Alphen aan den Rijn, Netherlands. TEL 31-172-466775. FAX 31-172-440681. circ. 4,660. *837*

BOUWREVUE.
Misset Postbus 4, 7000 BA Doetinchem, Netherlands. TEL 31-8340-49911. FAX 31-8340-43839. circ. 14,000. *837*

BOWLING PROPRIETOR.
Bowling Proprietors' Association of America, Box 5802, Arlington, TX 76005. TEL 817-649-5105. FAX 817-633-2940. circ. 4,500. *6498*

BRACTON LAW JOURNAL.
University of Exeter, Faculty of Law, Amory Bldg., Exeter EX4 4RJ, England. TEL 44-1392-263371. circ. 600. *3751*

BRADEA.
Herbarium Bradeanum, C.P. 15005, 20031-040 Rio de Janeiro, RJ, Brazil. circ. 400. *674*

BRAILLE TECHNICAL TABLES BANK CATALOG.
National Braille Association, Inc., 3 Townline Cir., Rochester, NY 14623. TEL 716-427-8260. *3318*

BRAINSCAN.
Elsevier Science B.V., P.O. Box 211, 1000 AE Amsterdam, Netherlands. TEL 31-20-4853911. FAX 31-20-4853598. *4829*

BRANCHING OUT.
Baltimore County Public Library, 320 York Rd., Towson, MD 21204. TEL 301-296-8500. FAX 301-296-3139. circ. 1,000. *3981*

BRANCHLINE.
Bytown Railway Society, Box 141, Sta. A, Ottawa, ON K1N 8V1, Canada. TEL 613-745-1201. circ. 70. *6809*

BRANCHLINES.
Fine Gael Party, Fine Gael Press Rooms, Leinster House, Dublin 2, Ireland. TEL 353-1-6789030. FAX 353-1-6735806. circ. 17,000. *5637*

BRANDING IRON.
The Branding Iron, 12436 Landale St., Studio City, CA 91604. TEL 818-761-1415. circ. 400. *3461*

BRAVE NEW WORLD.
Metropolis Group, 5th Fl., Julco House, 26-28 Great Portland St., London W1N 6AS, England. TEL 44-181-559-2015. FAX 44-181-505-2267. circ. 30,000. *5094*

BRAZIL. DEPARTAMENTO NACIONAL DA PRODUCAO MINERAL. RELATORIO ANUAL DE ATIVIDADES E PROGRAMACAO.
Departamento Nacional da Producao Mineral, Setor Autarquia Norte, Quadra 1, Bloco B, 70040-200 Brasilia D.F., Brazil. TEL 55-61-224-2670. FAX 55-61-2258274. circ. 150. *5058*

BRAZIL. SERVICO NACIONAL DE APRENDIZAGEM COMERCIAL. BOLETIM TECNICO.
Servico Nacional de Aprendizagem Comercial, Rua Dona Mariana, 48, 7 andar, Botafogo, 22280 Rio de Janeiro RJ, Brazil. FAX 55-21-2860645. circ. 2,700. *2316*

THE BREEZE (MATHISTON).
Wood Junior College, Box 289, Mathiston, MO 39752. circ. 1,200. *1859*

BRENNSTOFFSTATISTIK.
Bundesministerium fuer Wirtschaftliche Angelegenheiten Bundeslastverteiler, Dienststelle Statistik, Am Hof 6a, A-1010 Vienna, Austria. TEL 43-1-531132004. FAX 43-1-531132092. circ. 400. *2561*

BRETHREN MISSIONARY HERALD.
Brethren Missionary Herald, Inc., Box 544, Winona Lake, IN 46590. TEL 219-267-7158. FAX 219-267-4745. circ. 1,600. *6203*

BREW-INFO.
European Brewery Convention, P.O. Box 510, 2380 BB Zoeterwoude, Netherlands. TEL 31-71-456047. FAX 31-71-410013. circ. 400. *502*

BREWING AND MALTING BARLEY RESEARCH INSTITUTE. ANNUAL REPORT.
Brewing and Malting Barley Research Institute, 206-167 Lombard Ave., Winnipeg, MB R3B 0T6, Canada. TEL 204-942-1407. circ. 700. *503*

THE BRIDGE (INDIANAPOLIS).
Indiana Historical Society, 315 W. Ohio St., Indianapolis, IN 46202. TEL 317-233-3156. FAX 317-233-3109. circ. 11,000. *3461*

BRIDGE S A.
South African Bridge Federation, P.O. Box 890347, Lyndhurst 2106, South Africa. TEL 27-11-3374030. FAX 27-11-4406435. circ. 2,500. *6454*

BRIEFING ON BRITAIN.
Invest in Britain Bureau 1 Victoria St., London SW1H 0ET, England. TEL 44-171-215-5638. FAX 44-171-215-5651. circ. 13,750. *1323*

BRITAIN THE PREFERRED LOCATION.
Invest in Britain Bureau, 1 Victoria St., London SW1H 0ET, England. TEL 44-171-215-5638. FAX 44-171-215-5651. circ. 11,500. *1323*

BRITISH AIRWAYS EXECUTIVE.
British Airways PLC., Box 10, Heathrow Airport, Middlesex TW6 2JA, England. circ. 110,000. *6753*

BRITISH ARACHNOLOGICAL SOCIETY. BULLETIN.
British Arachnological Society, c/o Dr. P. Merret, Ed., 5 Hillcrest, Swanage Dorset BH19 2HS, England. circ. 700. *801*

BRITISH CACTUS & SUCCULENT JOURNAL.
British Cactus & Succulent Society, 71 Lakes Ln., Newport Pagnell, Bucks. MK16 8HT, England. TEL 44-1908-611650. circ. 5,600. *674*

BRITISH COLUMBIA. LAW REFORM COMMISSION. ANNUAL REPORT.
Law Reform Commission, 126-800 Hornby St., Vancouver, BC V6Z 2C5, Canada. TEL 604-660-2366. FAX 604-660-2378. circ. 2,000. *3751*

BRITISH COLUMBIA. MINISTRY OF EDUCATION. ANNUAL REPORT.
Ministry of Education, Parliament Bldgs., Victoria, BC V8V 2M4, Canada. TEL 604-356-2500. FAX 604-356-5945. circ. 6,000. *2316*

BRITISH COLUMBIA AGRI DIGEST.
DoMac Publications Ltd., 20316 56th Ave., Ste. 200, Langley, BC V3A 3Y7, Canada. TEL 604-679-5362. FAX 604-679-5362. circ. 7,500. *103*

BRITISH COLUMBIA ORCHARDIST.
Box 423, Salmon Arm, BC V1E 4N6, Canada. TEL 604-833-0071. FAX 604-833-0622. circ. 2,728. *3046*

BRITISH ELECTROTECHNICAL APPROVALS BOARD. ANNUAL LIST OF APPROVED ELECTROTECHNICAL EQUIPMENT.
B E A B, Mark House, the Green, 9-11 Queen's Rd., Hersham, Walton-on-Thames, Surrey KT12 5NA, England. TEL 01932-244401. FAX 01932-226603. circ. 10,000. *6647*

BRITISH EXPORTS.
Kompass Part of the Reed Elsevier group, Windsor Ct., E. Grinstead House, E. Grinstead, W. Sussex RH19 1XD, England. TEL 01342-326972. FAX 01342-335992. circ. 40,000. *1589*

BRITISH-ISRAEL TRADE.
British-Israel Chamber of Commerce, 14-15 Rodmarton St., London W1H 3FW, England. TEL 071-486-2371. FAX 071-224-1783. circ. 2,300. *1133*

BRITISH JOURNAL OF INTENSIVE CARE.
Greycoat Publishing, 1 Harley St., London W1N 1DA, England. TEL 44-171-637-1828. FAX 44-171-631-3020. circ. 13,878. *4437*

BRITISH JOURNAL OF RUSSIAN PHILATELY.
Postbus 16636, 1001 RC Amsterdam, Netherlands. circ. 250. *5453*

BRITISH JOURNAL OF THEATRE NURSING.
National Association of Theatre Nurses, 22 Mount Parade, Harrogate HG1 1BX, England. TEL 44-1423-508079. FAX 44-1423-531613. circ. 8,000. *4710*

BRITISH LIBRARY. NEWSPAPER LIBRARY. NEWSLETTER.
British Library, Newspaper Library, Colindale Ave., London NW9 5HE, England. TEL 44-171-412-7353. FAX 44-171-412-7379. circ. 2,000. *3981*

BRITISH LIBRARY NEWS.
British Library, Document Supply Centre, Boston Spa, Wetherby, W. Yorks. LS23 7BQ, England. TEL 44-1937-546054. FAX 44-1937-546571. circ. 8,000. *3982*

BRITISH NATURISM.
Central Council for British Naturism, Assurance House, 30-32 Wycliffe Rd., Northampton NN1 5JF, England. TEL 01604-20361. FAX 01604-230176. circ. 11,000. *5525*

BRITISH RACING NEWS.
British Racing & Sports Car Club, Brands Hatch Circuit, Fawkham, Dartford, Kent DA3 8NH, England.
circ. 4,500. *6454*

BRNENSKY VECERNIK.
Brnensky Vecernik s.r.o., Jakubske Nam. 7, 664 83 Brno, Czech Republic. TEL 42-5-42321227. FAX 42-5-42215150.
circ. 15,000. *3133*

BROADCAST TECHNOLOGY.
Diversified Publications Ltd., 6 Farmer's Lane, Box 420, Bolton, ON L7E 5T3, Canada. TEL 905-857-6076. FAX 905-857-6045.
circ. 6,500. *1897*

BROADCASTING & CABLE INTERNATIONAL.
Cahners Publishing Company (New York), Division of Reed Elsevier Inc., 245 W 17th St., New York, NY 10011. TEL 212-337-6944. FAX 212-337-7028.
circ. 8,500. *1955*

BROKEN SPOKE.
Calgary Sports Car Club, P.O. Box 61143 Kensington Postal Stn., Calgary, AB T2N 4S6, Canada. TEL 403-285-1177. FAX 403-289-7256.
circ. 200. *6778*

BRONTE SOCIETY TRANSACTIONS.
Bronte Society, c/o Publications Secretary, Bronte Parsonage Museum, Haworth, Keighley, W. Yorks. BD22 8DR, England. TEL 44-1535-642323. FAX 44-1535-647131.
circ. 3,500. *4189*

BROTHERHOOD.
National Federation of Temple Brotherhoods, 838 Fifth Ave., New York, NY 10021. TEL 212-570-0707. FAX 212-570-0960.
circ. 60,000. *6123*

BROTS DE COLLCEROLA.
C.E.A. Aliga de Vallvidrera, Mont d'Orsa 17, 08017 Barcelona, Spain.
circ. 150. *1847*

BROWARD TIMES.
Broward Times, Inc., 1001 W. Cypress Creek Rd., Ste. 111, Fort Lauderdale, FL 33309-1947. TEL 305-351-9070. FAX 305-351-3099.
circ. 25,000. *2868*

BRUCE TRAIL NEWS.
Trail News Inc., 17 Marlborough Ave., Toronto, Ont. M5R 1X5, Canada. TEL 416-964-7281.
circ. 10,000. *6558*

BRUG.
Publicarto N.V., Langestraat 170, B-1150 Brussels, Belgium. TEL 32-2-7790000. FAX 32-2-7791616.
circ. 41,236. *2317*

BRUNSWICKAN.
University of New Brunswick, Student Union, P.O. Box 4400, Fredericton, NB E3B 5A3, Canada. TEL 506-453-4983. FAX 506-458-4958.
circ. 10,000. *1859*

BUCH UND BIBLIOTHEK.
Bock und Herchen Verlag, Postfach 1145, 53581 Bad Honnef, Germany. TEL 02224-5443. FAX 02224-78310.
circ. 7,200. *3982*

BUCHKULTUR.
Buchkultur Verlagsgesellschaft mbH, Waehringerstr. 104, A-1180 Vienna, Austria. TEL 01-4794642-0. FAX 01-479464210.
circ. 14,500. *4135*

BUDAPEST STUDIES IN ARABIC.
Eotvos Lorand University, Chair for Arabic Studies, Muzeum kit. 4-b, 1088 Budapest, Hungary.
circ. 600. *4057*

BUDAPESTI KOZGAZDASAGTUDOMANYI EGYETEM OKTATOINAK SZAKIRODALMI MUNKASSAGA.
Budapesti Kozgazdasagtudomanyi Egyetem, Fovam Ter 8, II-268, 1093 Budapest IX, Hungary. TEL 2179-377. FAX 2174-910.
circ. 300. *984*

BUDDHISTISCHE MONATSBLAETTER.
Buddhistische Gesellschaft e.V., Beisserstr. 23, 22337 Hamburg, Germany. TEL 49-40-6313696. FAX 49-40-6313690.
circ. 580. *6109*

BUEHNE.
Orac Zeitschriftenverlag GmbH, Schoenbrunnerstr. 59-61, A-1050 Vienna, Austria. TEL 43-1-54621-0. FAX 43-1-5462178.
circ. 103,800. *6693*

BUFFALO.
Girl Guides of Canada, Manitoba Council, 872 St. James St., Winnipeg, MB R3G 3J7, Canada. TEL 204-774-1939. FAX 204-774-9271.
circ. 1,500. *1762*

BUILD.
28 Lower Baggot St., Dublin 2, Ireland. TEL 766192. FAX 619781.
circ. 4,400. *838*

BUILDER (COLUMBUS).
Midland Mutual Life Insurance Company, 250 E. Broad St., Columbus, OH 43215. TEL 614-228-2001.
circ. 1,300. *3643*

BUILDER PROFILE.
Builder Profile Inc., Box 354, Bloomingdale, IL 60108. TEL 708-582-8888. FAX 708-582-8895.
circ. 7,500. *838*

BUILDERS' MERCHANT NEWS.
B & M Publications (London) Ltd., P.O. Box 13, Hereford House, Bridle Path, Croydon, Surrey CR9 4NL, England. TEL 44-181-680-4200. FAX 44-181-681-5049.
circ. 7,591. *838*

BUILDING & CONSTRUCTION NEWS.
Al Hilal Publishing & Marketing Group, P.O. Box 224, Manama, Bahrain. TEL 973-293131. FAX 973-293400.
circ. 7,175. *839*

BUILDING & REMODELING NEWS.
S R Sound Inc., 600C Lake St., Ramsey, NJ 07446-1245. TEL 201-327-1600. FAX 201-327-3185.
circ. 75,000. *839*

BUILDING CONSTRUCTION NEWS.
Builders Exchange, Inc., 981 Keynote Circle, Cleveland, OH 44131-1842. *839*

BUILDING FOR LEISURE.
Stable Publishing, 19-21 High St., Sutton, Surrey SM1 1DJ, England. TEL 081-770-1080. FAX 081-643-9846.
circ. 12,000. *840*

BUILDING INDUSTRIES FEDERATION. ANNUAL REPORT.
Building Industries Federation, Attn.: Information Services Manager, 14 Alexandra Ave., Halfway House 1685, South Africa. TEL 27-11-8051985. FAX 27-11-3151644.
circ. 6,000. *840*

BUILDING INSPECTORS' ASSOCIATION OF NOVA SCOTIA. REPORTER.
Building Inspectors' Association of Nova Scotia, 2543 Barrington St., Halifax, NS B3K 2X2, Canada.
circ. 250. *840*

BUILDING OKLAHOMA.
Oklahoma Retailer Publishing Co., Inc., 4500 N. Sewell, Ste. 12, Oklahoma City, OK 73118. TEL 405-528-0903.
circ. 3,000. *840*

BUILDING PRODUCTS.
Hanley-Wood Inc., One Thomas Circle, Ste. 600, Washington, DC 20006. TEL 202-736-3301. FAX 202-785-1974.
circ. 80,000. *840*

BUILDINGS.
Stamats Communications, Inc., Box 1888, Cedar Rapids, IA 52406-1888. TEL 319-364-6167. FAX 319-364-4278.
circ. 46,000. *841*

BULL & BEAR FINANCIAL NEWSPAPER.
Box 917179, Longwood, FL 32791. TEL 407-682-6170.
circ. 10,000. *1323*

THE BULL BULLETIN.
c/o Industrial Controls Consulting, Inc., 104 S. Main St., Ste. 320, Fond du Lac, WI 54935. TEL 414-929-6544. FAX 414-929-9344.
circ. 4,000. *2013*

THE BULLETIN.
Ackroyd Publications, 329 Av. Moliere, 1180 Brussels, Belgium. TEL 32-2-3439909. FAX 32-2-3439822.
circ. 16,000. *3115*

BULLETIN OF CONCERNED ASIAN SCHOLARS.
Bulletin of Concerned Asian Scholars, Inc., 3239 Ninth St., Boulder, CO 80304-2112. TEL 303-449-7439.
circ. 300. *5743*

BULLETIN OF TROPICAL MEDICINE AND INTERNATIONAL HEALTH.
Royal Society of Tropical Medicine and Hygiene, Manson House, 26 Portland Pl., London W1N 4EY, England. TEL 44-171-580-2127. FAX 44-171-436-1389.
circ. 3,600. *4618*

BULLETIN OF ZOO MANAGEMENT.
Royal Zoological Society of South Australia, Inc., Zoological Gardens, Frome Road, Adelaide, S.A. 5000, Australia.
circ. 250. *801*

BULLPEN.
Babe Ruth League, 1770 Brunswick Ave., Box 5000, Trenton, NJ 09638. TEL 609-695-1434. FAX 609-695-2505.
circ. 32,000. *6499*

THE BULLRUSH.
Innes Clan Society, 129 Ravenna Dr., Long Beach, CA 90803. TEL 310-438-6331.
circ. 300. *3077*

BUNDESGESETZBLATT FUER DIE REPUBLIK OESTERREICH.
Oesterreichische Staatsdruckerei, Rennweg 12a, A-1037 Vienna, Austria. TEL 01-79789307. FAX 01-79789419.
circ. 10,000. *3890*

BURRELLE'S CLIPPING ANALYST.
Burrelle's Press Clipping Service, 75 E. Northfield Rd., Livingston, NJ 07039. TEL 201-992-6600. FAX 201-992-5122.
circ. 5,000. *32*

BUS & COACH BUYER.
Bus & Coach Buyer Ltd., The Publishing Centre, 1 Woolram Wygate, Spalding, Lincs. PE11 1NU, England. TEL 44-1775-711777. FAX 44-1775-711737.
circ. 6,405. *6714*

BUS FAYRE.
Autobus Review Publications Ltd., 42 Coniston Ave., Queensbury, Bradford, W. Yorks. BD13 2JD, England. TEL 44-01274-881640.
circ. 2,000. *6714*

BUS TOURS MAGAZINE.
National Bus Trader, Inc., 9698 Judson Rd., Polo, IL 61064. TEL 815-946-2341. FAX 815-946-2347.
circ. 7,200. *6714*

BUSINESS AND HEALTH.
Medical Economics Publishing Co., Inc., 5 Paragon Dr., Montvale, NJ 07645. TEL 201-358-7208. FAX 201-573-1045.
circ. 38,000. *3643*

BUSINESS DIGEST OF CENTRAL MASSACHUSETTS.
Business Digest, 381 Main St., 200, Worcester, MA 01608-1710. TEL 508-755-4500. FAX 508-799-0256.
circ. 10,500. *1573*

BUSINESS DIGEST OF GREATER BURLINGTON.
Mill Publishing, Inc., 1233 Shelburne Rd., E-5, S. Burlington, VT 05403. TEL 802-862-4109. FAX 802-862-9322.
circ. 5,800. *900*

BUSINESS DIGEST OF GREATER DANBURY.
Drew Publishing, 118 Stony Hill Vlg., Brookfield, CT
06804-3959. TEL 203-798-7063.
circ. 6,000. *900*

BUSINESS DIGEST OF GREATER WATERBURY.
Four Stars Publishing Co., Inc., Box 9018, 197
Tranquility Rd., Middlebury, CT 06702-2230.
TEL 203-754-9922. FAX 203-754-5192.
circ. 6,300. *900*

BUSINESS DIRECTORY.
Mt. Diablo Peace Center, 65 Eckley Lane, Walnut
Creek, CA 94596. TEL 415-933-7850. FAX 284-
5357.
circ. 5,000. *1162*

BUSINESS EQUIPMENT HOTLINE.
Business Technology Association, 12411 Wornall
Rd., Kansas City, MO 64145. TEL 816-941-3100.
FAX 816-941-8034.
circ. 4,000. *1491*

BUSINESS EXECUTIVE.
Business Executive Inc., 466 Speers Rd., Ste. 220,
Oakville ON L6K 3W9, Canada. TEL 905-845-8300.
FAX 905-845-9086.
circ. 21,000. *1573*

BUSINESS FORUM (LOS ANGELES).
California State University, Los Angeles, School of
Business & Economics, 5151 State University Dr.,
Los Angeles, CA 90032-8120. TEL 213-343-2806.
FAX 213-343-2813.
circ. 1,000. *901*

**BUSINESS FOUNDATION. BUSINESS & PLEASURE. A
GENERAL GUIDE TO POLAND.**
Business Foundation Co. Ltd., Ul. Krucza 38-42, 00-
512 Warsaw, Poland. TEL 48-22-219993. FAX 48-
22-219761.
circ. 20,000. *6871*

**BUSINESS FOUNDATION. POLAND. INNOVATION,
RESEARCH & DEVELOPMENT.**
Business Foundation Co. Ltd., Ul. Krucza 38-42, 00-
512 Warsaw, Poland. TEL 48-22-219993. FAX 48-
22-219761.
circ. 4,000. *1589*

**BUSINESS FOUNDATION BOOK. GENERAL TRADE
INDEX & BUSINESS GUIDE.**
Business Foundation Co. Ltd., Ul. Krucza 38-42, 00-
512 Warsaw, Poland. TEL 48-22-219993. FAX 48-
22-219761.
circ. 20,000. *1589*

BUSINESS GAZETTE.
Datateam Publishing Ltd., Tovil Hill, Maidstone, Kent
ME15 6QS, England. TEL 01622-687031.
FAX 01622-757646.
circ. 15,000. *1408*

BUSINESS GEOGRAPHICS.
G I S World, Inc., 155 E. Boardwalk Dr., Ste. 250,
Ft. Collins, CO 80525. TEL 970-223-4848.
FAX 970-223-5700.
circ. 22,120. *3249*

BUSINESS INSIGHT (RICHLAND).
B C O Marketing Communications, Inc., Box 347,
Richland, MI 49083-0347. TEL 616-629-3131.
FAX 616-629-0803.
circ. 8,692. *1573*

BUSINESS JOURNAL (PORTLAND).
American City Business Journals, Inc. (Portland),
Box 14490, Portland, OR 97214. TEL 503-274-
8733. FAX 503-227-2650.
circ. 4,100. *1180*

THE BUSINESS JOURNAL (SAN JOSE).
American City Business Journals Inc., 96 N. 3rd St.,
Ste. 100, San Jose, CA 95112. TEL 408-295-
3800. FAX 408-295-5028.
circ. 2,800. *902*

BUSINESS MARKET NEWS.
Hemsing Advertising, 755 W. Big Beaver Rd., Ste.
416, Troy, MI 48084-4903. TEL 810-362-0448.
FAX 810-362-3884. *903*

BUSINESS MARKETING.
Crain Communications, Inc. (Chicago), 740 Rush
St., Chicago, IL 60611-2590. TEL 312-649-5260.
FAX 312-649-5228.
circ. 47,853. *1455*

BUSINESS MEMO FROM BELGIUM.
Embassy of Belgium, Investments Office, 3330
Garfield St. N.W., Washington, DC 20008. TEL 202-
625-5888. FAX 202-625-7567.
circ. 2,000. *1134*

BUSINESS NEWS (SOUTH WALES EDITION).
Euro Publications Ltd., Euro House, 14 Pearl St.,
Cardiff CF2 1HD, Wales.
circ. 5,000. *1180*

BUSINESS NEWS (WEST OF ENGLAND EDITION).
Euro Publications Ltd., Euro House, 14 Pearl St.,
Cardiff CF2 1HD, Wales.
circ. 5,000. *1181*

BUSINESS NEWS (WESTFORD).
U.S. Business Council for Southeast Europe, P.O.
Box 786, Westford, MA 01886-0024. TEL 508-
692-1530. FAX 508-692-1532.
circ. 300. *903*

BUSINESS OPPORTUNITIES JOURNAL.
Business Service Corporation, Box 60762, San
Diego, CA 92156. TEL 619-223-5661. FAX 619-
223-1705.
circ. 25,000. *1324*

BUSINESS PHILADELPHIA.
Penn Communications Group, Inc., 260 S. Broad
St., Philadelphia, PA 19102. TEL 215-735-6969.
FAX 215-735-6965.
circ. 29,000. *1134*

BUSINESS SPACE REGISTER.
Business Space Registers Ltd., The Foremans
Centre, High St., Headcorn, Kent TN27 9NE,
England. TEL 44-1622-891589. FAX 44-1622-
891590.
circ. 25,000. *6021*

BUSINESS SYSTEMS MAGAZINE.
Corry Publishing, 2820 W. 21st St., Erie, PA
16506-2970. TEL 814-838-0025. FAX 814-838-
0035.
circ. 30,000. *1492*

BUSINESS TO BUSINESS.
Bracebridge Examiner Ltd., 16 Manitoba St., Box
1049, Bracebridge, Ont. P0B 1C0, Canada.
TEL 705-645-8771. FAX 705-645-1718.
circ. 6,034. *904*

BUSINESS TRENDS ASIA REPORT: INDONESIA.
M P R C (Asia) Sdn. Berhad, P.O. Box 10706,
50722 Kuala Lumpur, Malaysia. TEL 60-3-
2217762. FAX 60-3-7564478. *1181*

BUSINESSMATTERS.
G M C Publications Ltd., 166 High St., Lewes, E.
Sussex BN7 1XU, England. TEL 01273-477374.
FAX 01273-486300.
circ. 30,000. *1409*

BUTLER ALUMNI QUARTERLY.
Butler University, 4600 Sunset Ave., Indianapolis, IN
46208. TEL 317-283-9426.
circ. 24,000. *1860*

BUTLER AVIATION'S ECHELON.
Halsey Publishing Co., 438 Main St., Buffalo, NY
14202-3207. TEL 305-893-1520. *6753*

BUTLER COLLEGIAN.
Butler University, Journalism Department, 4600
Sunset Blvd., Indianapolis, IN 46208-3485.
TEL 317-283-9358. FAX 317-283-9930.
circ. 3,000. *1860*

BUVISINDI.
Rannsoknastofnun Landbunadarins, Keldnaholti, IS-
112 Reykjavik, Iceland. TEL 354-587-3230.
FAX 354-587-4604.
circ. 600. *104*

BYG-TEK & BYGGERI.
Odsgaard ApS, Hovedvejen 182, DK-2600 Glostrup,
Denmark. TEL 45-43-45-34-91. FAX 45-43-43-13-
28.
circ. 26,000. *842*

BYGG & JAERNHANDELN.
Bygg och Jaernhandelns Foerlag, P.O. Box 14083,
S-104 40 Stockholm, Sweden. TEL 46-8-6636905.
FAX 46-8-6677148.
circ. 3,400. *1457*

BYGG & TEKNIK.
Foerlags AB Bygg & Teknik, P.O Box 19099, S-
104 32 Stockholm, Sweden. TEL 46-8-612-17-50.
FAX 46-8-612-54-81.
circ. 6,595. *842*

BYGGEINDUSTRIEN.
Teknisk Forlag A-S, Skelbaekkgade 4, DK-1780
Copenhagen V, Denmark. TEL 45-31-21-68-01.
FAX 45-31-21004-01.
circ. 2,793. *842*

BYGGFAKTA PROJEKTNYTT.
Byggfakta AB, S-827 81 Ljusdal, Sweden. TEL 46-
651-194-00.
circ. 18,000. *842*

BYWAYS (FAIRFAX).
National Motorcoach Network, Inc., Patriot Sq.,
10527-C Braddock Rd., Fairfax, VA 22032.
TEL 703-250-7897. FAX 703-250-1477.
circ. 48,000. *6871*

C A D - C A M & INDUSTRIAL SOFTWARE GUIDE.
Business & Management Editions Brussels s.p.r.l,
Rue Stephanie, 17, 1020 Brussels, Belgium.
TEL 32-2-4266115. FAX 32-2-4258226.
circ. 25,000. *2025*

C A D - C A M REPORT.
Dressler Verlag GmbH, Gaisbergsr. 55, 69115
Heidelberg, Germany. TEL 06221-91130.
FAX 06221-911321.
circ. 19,700. *2025*

C A - D E NEWS.
Council for Alcohol - Drug Education of N.J., Box
10130, Trenton, NJ 08650-3130. TEL 609-291-
0500.
circ. 16,000. *2195*

**C A M M A C SOUTHERN ONTARIO REGION
NEWSLETTER.**
Canadian Amateur Musicians, Southern Ontario
Region, 283 Bogert Ave., Toronto, ON M2N 1L4,
Canada. TEL 416-250-8527.
circ. 470. *5145*

C A M MAGAZINE.
Construction Association of Michigan, 1625 S.
Woodward Ave., Box 3204 Bloomfield Hill, MI
48302-3204. TEL 810-972-1000. FAX 810-972-
1001.
circ. 4,200. *843*

C A S BULLETIN.
Catholic Archives Society, c/o P. Bracken, 43
Garthland Dr., Glasgow G31 2RE, Scotland.
circ. 280. *6171*

C B REPORT.
Higher Education Coordinating Board, Box 12788,
Capitol Sta., Austin, TX 78711. TEL 512-483-
6111. FAX 512-483-6127
circ. 1,000. *2421*

C. BREWER TODAY.
C. Brewer & Co. Ltd., Box 1826, Honolulu, HI
96805 TEL 808-536-4461.
circ. 2,000. *1516*

C D N L A O NEWSLETTER.
National Diet Library, 1-10-1, Nagata-cho, Chiyoda-
ku, Tokyo 100, Japan. TEL 3-3581-2331.
FAX 03-3597-9104.
circ. 950. *3983*

C D SICHERHEITS-MANAGEMENT.
Richard Boorberg Verlag (Stuttgart), Scharrstr. 2,
70563 Stuttgart, Germany. TEL 0711-73850.
FAX 0711-7352244.
circ. 14.000. *2181*

C F A DIGEST.
Association for Investment Management and
Research, Box 3668, Charlottesville, VA 22903.
TEL 804-977-3668. FAX 804-980-9755.
circ. 19,000. *1073*

C - F A R NEWSLETTER.
Citizens for Foreign Aid Reform Inc., Box 332, Stn.
B, Etobicoke, Ont. M9W 5L3 Canada. TEL 905-
897-7221. FAX 905-277-3914.
circ. 1,500. *1302*

Contr Circ

C F B COMOX TOTEM TIMES.
C F B Comox Totem Times, Lazo, BC V0R 2K0,
Canada. TEL 604-339-2541. FAX 604-339-5209.
circ. 2,600. *5024*

C F E NEWS.
Association of Certified Fraud Examiners, 716 West
Ave., Austin, TX 78701. TEL 512-478-9297.
circ. 10,000. *2181*

C F P TODAY.
Institute of Certified Financial Planners, 3801 E.
Florida Ave., 708, Denver, CO 80210-2571.
TEL 303-751-7600. FAX 303-751-1037.
circ. 47,000. *1409*

C H A C INFO.
Catholic Health Association of Canada, 1247
Kilborn Pl., Ottawa, ON K1H 6K9, Canada. TEL 613-
731-7148. FAX 613-731-7797.
circ. 1,240. *3541*

C H I L D NEWSLETTER.
C H I L D, Inc., Box 2604, Sioux City, IA 51106.
TEL 712-948-3500. FAX 712-948-3500.
circ. 440. *1762*

C I A T IN PERSPECTIVE.
Centro Internacional de Agricultura Tropical, Apdo.
Aereo 6713, Cali, Colombia. TEL 57-2-4450000.
FAX 57-2-4450273.
circ. 3,500. *104*

C I L E C T NEWS.
Centre International de Liaison des Ecoles de
Cinema et de Television, CILECT Secretariat, Rue
Theresienne, 8, 1000 Brussels, Belgium. TEL 32-2-
5119839. FAX 32-2-5110035.
circ. 400. *1956*

C I M NOTES.
Cleveland Institute of Music, 11021 E. Boulevard,
Cleveland, OH 44106. TEL 216-791-5000.
FAX 216-791-3063.
circ. 12,000. *5146*

C I O CANADA.
Laurentian Technomedia Inc. 501 Oakdale Rd.,
North York ON M3N 1W7, Canada. TEL 416-746-
7360. FAX 416-746-1421.
circ. 7,600. *2031*

C I R I A REPORT.
Construction Industry Research and Information
Association, 6 Storey's Gate, Westminster, London
SW1P 3AU, England. TEL 44-171-222-8891.
FAX 44-171-222-1708.
circ. 500. *2654*

C I S NEWS.
Chemical Information Systems, Inc., 810 Glen
Eagles Ct., Ste. 300, Baltimore, MD 21286-2203.
TEL 410-321-8440. FAX 410-296-0712.
circ. 2,500. *1723*

C K OF A JOURNAL.
Catholic Knights of America, 1850 Dalton Ave.,
Cincinnati, OH 45214. TEL 513-721-0781.
FAX 513-721-0783.
circ. 9,600. *1847*

C L R.
Medical Economics Publishing Co., Inc., Five
Paragon Dr., Montvale, NJ 07645. TEL 201-358-
7200. FAX 201-573-0344.
circ. 59,000. *4678*

C M B E S - S C G B NEWSLETTER.
Canadian Medical and Biological Engineering Society
Inc., Rm. 393, Bldg. M-55, National Research
Council, Ottawa, ON K1A 0R8, Canada. TEL 613-
993-1686. FAX 613-954-2216. *4438*

C N C AND SOFTWARE GUIDE.
Gardner Publications, Inc., 6600 Clough Pike,
Cincinnati, OH 45244-4090. TEL 513-231-8020.
FAX 513-231-2818.
circ. 70,000. *4349*

C N N TRAVELLER.
Mediamark Publishing International Ltd., 35 Gresse
St., Rathbone Pl., London W1P 1PN, England.
TEL 44-171-580-3105. FAX 44-171-580-1695.
circ. 20,000. *1956*

C N S FOCUS.
Cargo Network Services, 300 Garden City Plaza,
Ste. 312, Garden City, NY 11530-3325. TEL 516-
747-3375. FAX 516-747-3312.
circ. 7,000. *6753*

C O M D A KEY.
Canadian Office Machine Dealers Association, 3464
Kingston Rd., Ste. 204, Scarborough, ON M1M
1R5, Canada. TEL 416-261-1607. FAX 416-261-
1679.
circ. 1,837. *1492*

C O P A CONVERSATION.
Canadian Office Products Association, 1243
Islington Ave., Ste. 911, Toronto, ON M8X 1Y9,
Canada. TEL 416-239-2737. FAX 416-239-1553.
circ. 4,900. *1492*

C P A C MONITOR.
Center for Process Analytical Chemistry, Box
351700, University of Washington, Seattle, WA
98195-1700. TEL 206-685-2326. FAX 206-543-
6506.
circ. 1,800. *1714*

C P D A NEWS.
Council for Periodical Distributors Associations, 60
E. 42nd St., Ste. 2122, New York, NY 10165.
TEL 212-818-0234. FAX 212-983-4699.
circ. 4,900. *5992*

C Q RADIO AMATEUR.
Cetisa - Boixareu S.A., Concepcion Arenal 5, 08027
Barcelona, Spain. TEL 34-3-3527061. FAX 34-3-
3492350.
circ. 11,500. *2685*

C R R I ROAD ABSTRACTS.
Central Road Research Institute, P.O. Central Road
Research Institute, New Delhi 110020, India.
TEL 6832274. *2625*

C S A JOURNAL.
Cicero-Berwyn Press, 2701 S. Harlem Ave., Berwyn,
IL 60402.
circ. 11,000. *2869*

C S A MAGAZIN.
C S A Europa e.V., Rhoenstr. 1, 61381
Friedrichsdorf, Germany. TEL 06007-661.
FAX 06007-7802.
circ. 5,000. *5216*

C S A NEWS.
Council of Supervisors and Administrators of the
City of New York, Local 1, American Federation of
School Administrators, AFL-CIO, 16 Court St., 4th
Fl., Brooklyn, NY 11241. TEL 718-852-3000.
FAX 718-403-0278.
circ. 11,000. *2455*

C S E A ANNUAL REPORT.
California Society of Enrolled Agents, 3200 Ramos
Circle, Sacramento, CA 95827. TEL 916-366-
6646. FAX 916-366-6674.
circ. 3,500. *1537*

C S S P NEWS.
Council of Scientific Society Presidents, 1155 16th
St., N.W., Washington, DC 20036. TEL 202-872-
4452. FAX 202-872-4079.
circ. 1,000. *6232*

C T A ACTION.
California Teachers Association, 1705 Murchison
Dr., Burlingame, CA 94010-4583. TEL 415-697-
1400. FAX 415-697-0786.
circ. 250,000. *2422*

C T E.
David Sheppard & Associates, 35 Picadilly, London
W1V 1PB, England. TEL 0171-734-6143.
FAX 0171-734-1737.
circ. 1,400. *1956*

C W A NEWS.
Communications Workers of America, 501 Third St.,
N.W., Washington, DC 20001. TEL 202-434-1100.
FAX 202-434-1482.
circ. 520,000. *3718*

**C W R U: THE MAGAZINE OF CASE WESTERN
RESERVE UNIVERSITY.**
Case Western Reserve University, 10900 Euclid
Ave., Cleveland, OH 44106. TEL 216-368-6265.
FAX 216-368-4835.
circ. 92,000. *1860*

CA - A CANCER JOURNAL FOR CLINICIANS.
Lippincott - Raven Publishers 227 E. Washington
Sq., Philadelphia, PA 19106. TEL 215-238-4200.
circ. 300,000. *4749*

CABLE WORLD.
Cowles Business Media (Denver) 1905 Sherman St.,
Denver, CO 80203. TEL 303-837-0900.
circ. 20,000. *1957*

CACHE CITIZEN.
Utah State University, Department of
Communications, Box 703, Logan, UT 84321.
TEL 801-750-3292.
circ. 18,000. *3225*

CADERNOS DO PATRIMONIO CULTURAL.
Secretaria Municipal de Cultura, Departamento
Geral do Patrimonio Cultural, Rua Afonso
Cavalcanti, 455, sala 207, 20211-110 Cidade
Nova, Rio de Janeiro RJ, Brazil. TEL 55-21-
2734095. FAX 55-21-5032158.
circ. 1,000. *6317*

CAFE REVIEW.
c/o Yes Books, 20 Danforth St., Portland, ME
04101.
circ. 250. *4190*

CAHIERS DE L'UNIVERSITE DE PERPIGNAN.
Universite de Perpignan, 52 av. de Villeneuve,
66860 Perpignan Cedex, France. TEL 68-66-20-
00. FAX 68-66-20-19.
circ. 300. *4190*

CAHIERS DE NUTRITION ET DE DIETETIQUE.
Masson - Periodiques, Villa Laromiguiere, 75005
Paris, France. TEL 1-40-46-62-00. FAX 1-40-46-
62-01.
circ. 3,500. *5230*

CAHIERS DE PALEOANTHROPOLOGIE.
C N R S Editions, 20-22 rue St. Amand, 75015
Paris, France. TEL 45-33-16-00. FAX 45-33-92-13.
circ. 1,250. *5313*

CAHIERS DE PALEONTOLOGIE.
C N R S Editions, 20-22 rue St. Amand, 75015
Paris, France. TEL 45-33-16-00. FAX 45-33-92-13.
circ. 1,500. *5313*

CAHIERS DE PALEONTOLOGIE EST-AFRICAINE.
C N R S Editions, 20-22 rue St. Amand, 75015
Paris, France. TEL 45-33-16-00. FAX 45-33-92-13.
circ. 1,500. *5313*

CAHIERS NEPALAIS.
C N R S Editions, 20-22 rue St. Amand, 75015
Paris, France. TEL 45-33-16-00. FAX 45-33-92-13.
circ. 1,500. *5638*

THE CAIRN.
Whyte Museum of the Canadian Rockies, 111 Bear
St., Box 160, Banff, AB T0L 0C0, Canada. TEL 403-
762-2291. FAX 403-762-8919.
circ. 2,500. *5119*

**CALIFORNIA. DEPARTMENT OF WATER RESOURCES.
BULLETIN.**
Department of Water Resources, Box 924836,
Sacramento, CA 94236-0001. TEL 916-445-9248.
6964

**CALIFORNIA. TEACHER'S RETIREMENT BOARD.
STATE TEACHER'S RETIREMENT SYSTEM;
ANNUAL REPORT TO THE GOVERNOR AND THE
LEGISLATURE.**
Teacher's Retirement Board, Box 15275,
Sacramento, CA 95851-0275. TEL 916-229-3700.
circ. 1,500. *2455*

**CALIFORNIA ACCOUNTANCY ACT WITH RULES AND
REGULATIONS.**
Department of Consumer Affairs, Board of
Accountancy, 2000 Evergreen St., Ste. 250,
Sacramento, CA 95815-3832. TEL 916-263-3680.
FAX 916-263-3975.
circ. 45,000. *1043*

**CALIFORNIA COOPERATIVE OCEANIC FISHERIES
INVESTIGATIONS REPORTS.**
California Cooperative Oceanic Fisheries
Investigations, Scripps Institution of Oceanography,
University of California, La Jolla, CA 92093-0227.
TEL 619-534-4236. FAX 619-534-6500.
circ. 1,200. *2928*

CALIFORNIA FAMILY PHYSICIAN.
California Academy of Family Physicians, 114 Sansome St., Ste. 1305, San Francisco, CA 94104-3824. TEL 415-394-9121. FAX 415-394-9119. circ. 6,900. *4439*

CALIFORNIA PARKS & RECREATION.
California Park & Recreation Society Inc., 3031 F St., Ste. 202, 7971 Freeport Blvd., Sacramento, CA 95832-9701. TEL 916-446-2777. circ. 4,000. *3962*

CALIFORNIA PRUNE NEWS.
California Prune Board, 5990 Stoneridge Dr., Ste. 101, Pleasanton, CA 94588-3234. TEL 510-734-0150. FAX 510-734-0525. circ. 1,750. *215*

CALIFORNIA SCHOOL EMPLOYEE.
California School Employees Association, Box 640, San Jose, CA 95106. TEL 408-263-8000. FAX 408-954-0948. circ. 106,000. *2455*

CALIFORNIA TEACHER.
California Federation of Teachers, One Kaiser Plaza, Ste. 1440, Oakland, CA 94612. TEL 510-832-8812. FAX 510-832-5044. circ. 45,000. *2318*

CALIFORNIA WATER ENVIRONMENT ASSOCIATION. BULLETIN.
California Water Environment Association, 7677 Oakport St., Ste. 525, Oakland, CA 94621-1935. FAX 510-382-7810. circ. 7,000. *6964*

CALL NUMBER.
University of North Texas, School of Library and Information Sciences, N.T. Box 13796, Denton, TX 76203. TEL 817-565-2445. FAX 817-565-3101. circ. 3,000. *3984*

CALL OF THE LOON.
Ontario Federation of Anglers & Hunters, P.O. Box 2800, Station Main, Peterborough, ON K9J 8L5, Canada. TEL 705-748-6324. FAX 705-748-9577. circ. 1,600. *2122*

CALL TO ACTION.
Board of Education, 5057 Woodward, Detroit, MI 48202. TEL 313-494-1000. circ. 22,000. *2318*

CALORIE CONTROL COMMENTARY.
Calorie Control Council, 5775 Peachtree-Dunwoody Rd., Ste. 500-G, Atlanta, GA 30342. TEL 404-252-3663. FAX 404-252-0774. circ. 12,000. *5230*

CAMARA ARGENTINA DE PRODUCTOS QUIMICOS. BOLETIN INFORMATIVO.
Camara Argentina del Libro, Ave. Belgrano 1580, 6 Piso, 1093 Buenos Aires, Argentina. circ. 250. *1666*

CAMARA DE COMERCIO HISPANO-SUECA DE MADRID. INFO.
Camara de Comercio Hispano-Sueca de Madrid, Caracas, 23, 28010 Madrid, Spain. circ. 500. *1135*

CAMARA DE COMERCIO URUGUAYO - BRITANICA. BOLETIN INFORMATIVO.
Camara de Comercio Uruguayo - Britanica, Av. Libertador Brig. Gral. Lavalleja, P. 2, Of. 201, 11000 Montevideo, Uruguay. TEL 5982-98-0349. FAX 5982-90-0936. circ. 150. *906*

CAMARA NACIONAL DE LA INDUSTRIA DE TRANSFORMACION. BOLETIN INFORMATIVO.
Camara Nacional de la Industria de Transformacion, Apdo. Postal 60-468, Av. San Antonio 256, 03849 Mexico, D.F., Mexico. TEL 5-563-3500. *1516*

CAMBRIDGE TIMES.
240 Holiday Inn Dr., Cambridge, ON, Canada. TEL 519-651-2390. FAX 519-651-2358. circ. 31,400. *3119*

CAMBRIDGE UNIVERSITY ALUMNI MAGAZINE.
Ashley House Ltd., 8 Nursery Rd., London SW9 8BP, England. TEL 44-171-738-7707. FAX 44-171-738-6908. circ. 136,000. *1860*

CAMPBELL'S LIST.
Campbell's List, Inc., Campbell Bldg., 100 E. Ventris Ave., Maitland FL 32751. TEL 407-644-8298. FAX 407-740-6494. circ. 10,000. *3756*

CAMPESINO.
Editora Dosmil, Carrera 39 A No 15-11, Bogota D.E., Colombia circ. 70,000. *3131*

CAMPGROUND MANAGEMENT.
Woodall Publishing Co., 13975 W. Polo Trail Dr., Lake Forest, IL 60045. TEL 708-362-6700. FAX 708-362-8776. circ. 14,000. *5558*

CAMPING AND R V MAGAZINE.
Box 458, Washburn, WI 54891-0458. TEL 715-373-5556. FAX 715-373-5003. circ. 4,000. *6559*

CAMPUS ACTIVITIES PROGRAMMING.
National Association for Campus Activities, 13 Harbison Way, Columbia, SC 29212-3401. TEL 803-732-6222. FAX 803-749-1047. circ. 6,500. *2422*

CAMPUS LE MAG.
Rayonnement 5, 4 rue Barthelemy, 92120 Montrouge, France. TEL 42-53-90-89. FAX 42-53-78-75. circ. 150,000. *1786*

CAMPUS LEADER.
University of Manila, 546 Dr. M.V. de los Santos St., Sampaloc, Manila D-403, Philippines. circ. 8,000. *2318*

CAMROSE BOOSTER.
Camrose Booster Ltd., 4925 48th St., Camrose, AB T4V 1L7, Canada. TEL 403-672-3142. FAX 403-672-2518. circ. 12,357. *3119*

CAN MAKERS REPORT.
Can Makers Information Service, 1 Chelsea Manor Gardens, London SW3 5PN, England. TEL 44-171-351-2400. FAX 44-171-352-6246. circ. 3,000. *503*

CAN TECHNOLOGY INTERNATIONAL.
Trend Publishing Inc., 625 N. Michigan Ave., Ste. 2500, Chicago, IL 60611-3109. TEL 312-654-2300. FAX 312-654-2323. circ. 5,500. *5298*

CANADA. GRAIN COMMISSION. CORPORATE SERVICES. EXPORTS OF CANADIAN GRAIN AND WHEAT FLOUR.
Grain Commission, Corporate Services, 747-303 Main St., Winnipeg, MB R3C 3G8, Canada. TEL 204-983-2759. circ. 250. *256*

CANADIAN ART.
Canadian Art Foundation, 6 Church St., 2nd Fl., Toronto, ON M5E 1M1, Canada. TEL 416-368-8854. FAX 416-594-3375. circ. 4,000. *422*

CANADIAN ASSOCIATION FOR ANATOMY, NEUROBIOLOGY AND CELL BIOLOGY. BULLETIN.
Canadian Association for Anatomy, Neurology and Cell Biology, c/o Dept. of Anatomy, University of Manitoba, Winnipeg, MB R3E 0W3, Canada. TEL 204-789-3796. *576*

CANADIAN ASSOCIATION FOR LABORATORY ANIMAL SCIENCE NEWSLETTER.
Canadian Association for Laboratory Animal Science (CALAS), c/o Dr. Donald G. McKay, Biosciences Animal Service, University of Alberta, Edmonton, AB T6G 2E9, Canada. circ. 1,000. *4678*

CANADIAN ASSOCIATION OF SLAVISTS NEWSLETTER.
Canadian Association of Slavists, c/o Gust Olson, University of Alberta, 347 Arts Building, Edmonton, AB T6G 2E6, Canada. TEL 403-492-2566. FAX 403-492-2715. circ. 400. *3609*

CANADIAN BIOTECH RESEARCH.
Canadian Biotechnology News Service, 20 Stone Park Lane, Nepean, ON K2H 9P4, Canada. TEL 613-726-0115. FAX 613-726-7344. circ. 3,000. *626*

CANADIAN ELECTRONICS.
Action Communications Inc., 135 Spy Court, Markham, ON L3R 5H6, Canada. TEL 905-477-3222. FAX 905-477-4320. circ. 22,000. *2685*

CANADIAN ELECTRONICS ENGINEERING ANNUAL BUYER'S GUIDE.
Action Communications Inc., 135 Spy Court, Markham, ON L3R 5H6, Canada. TEL 905-477-3222. FAX 905-477-4320. circ. 22,000. *2685*

CANADIAN ENVIRONMENTAL PROTECTION.
Baum Publications Ltd., 1225 Ingleton Ave., Burnaby, BC V5C 4L8, Canada. TEL 604-291-9900. FAX 604-291-1906. circ. 23,393. *2779*

CANADIAN EQUESTRIAN FEDERATION. BULLETIN.
Canadian Equestrian Federation, 1600 James Naismith Dr., Ottawa, ON K1B 4S8, Canada. TEL 613-748-5632. FAX 613-747-2920. circ. 10,000. *6545*

CANADIAN FACILITY MANAGEMENT & DESIGN.
C F M Communications, 62 Olsen Dr., Don Mills, ON M3A 3J3, Canada. TEL 416-447-3417. FAX 416-447-4410. circ. 6,000. *3674*

CANADIAN FRUITGROWER.
N C C Publishing, 222 Argyle Ave., Delhi, ON N4B 2Y2, Canada. TEL 519-582-2510. FAX 519-582-4040. circ. 4,000. *3047*

CANADIAN GUIDER.
Girl Guides of Canada, National Council, 50 Merton St., Toronto, ON M4S 1A3, Canada. TEL 416-487-5281. FAX 416-487-5570. circ. 50,000. *1786*

CANADIAN HOME ECONOMICS JOURNAL.
Canadian Home Economics Association, Burnside Bldg., Ste. 901, 901 - 151 Slater St., Ottawa, ON K1P 5H3, Canada. TEL 613-238-8817. FAX 613-238-1677. circ. 2,800. *3520*

CANADIAN INDEPENDENT ADJUSTER.
Journal Management, 55 Queen St. E., Toronto, ON M5C 1R6, Canada. circ. 3,400. *3644*

CANADIAN JOURNAL OF ALLERGY AND CLINICAL IMMUNOLOGY.
Medicopea International Inc., 3333 Cote Vertu Blvd., Ste. 300, St. Laurent, PQ H4R 2N1 Canada. TEL 514-333-4561. FAX 514-336-1129. circ. 3,600. *4579*

CANADIAN JOURNAL OF CARDIOLOGY.
Pulsus Group Inc., 2902 S. Sheridan Way, Oakville, ON L6J 7L6, Canada. TEL 905-829-4770. FAX 905-829-4799. circ. 16,000. *4597*

CANADIAN JOURNAL OF CLINICAL PHARMACOLOGY.
Pulsus Group Inc., 2902 S. Sheridan Way, Oakville, ON L6J 7L6, Canada. TEL 905-829-4770. FAX 905-829-4799. circ. 18,000. *5403*

CANADIAN JOURNAL OF DERMATOLOGY.
Rodar Publishing Inc., 8102 Trans Canada Hwy., St. Laurent, PQ H4S 1Z4, Canada. TEL 514-333-5350. circ. 9,640. *4659*

CANADIAN JOURNAL OF DIABETES CARE.
Canadian Diabetes Association 15 Toronto St., Ste. 1001, Toronto, ON M5C 2E3, Canada. TEL 416-363-3373. FAX 416-363-3393. circ. 1,500. *4666*

CANADIAN JOURNAL OF GASTROENTEROLOGY.
Pulsus Group Inc., 2902 S. Sheridan Way, Oakville, ON L6J 7L6, Canada. TEL 905-829-4770. FAX 905-329-4799. circ. 16,000. *4690*

CANADIAN JOURNAL OF INFECTION CONTROL.
Pulsus Group Inc., 2902 S. Sheridan Way, Oakville, ON L6J 7L6, Canada. TEL 905-829-4770. FAX 905-829-4799.
circ. 3,000. *4619*

CANADIAN JOURNAL OF NETHERLANDIC STUDIES.
Canadian Association for the Advancement of Netherlandic Studies, Department of French, University of Windsor, Windsor, ON N9B 3P4, Canada. TEL 519-253-4232. FAX 971-36487050.
circ. 300. *4192*

CANADIAN JOURNAL OF OB-GYN & WOMEN'S HEALTH CARE.
Rodar Publishing Inc., 8102 Trans Canada Hwy., St. Laurent, PQ H4S 1Z4, Canada. TEL 514-333-5350.
circ. 17,000. *4733*

CANADIAN JOURNAL OF OCCUPATIONAL THERAPY.
Canadian Association of Occupational Therapists, CTTC Ste. 3400, 1125 Colonel By-drive, Ottawa, ON K1S 5R1, Canada. TEL 613-523-2268. FAX 613-523-2552.
circ. 6,172. *5247*

CANADIAN JOURNAL OF PEDIATRICS.
Rodar Publishing Inc., 8102 Trans Canada Hwy., St. Laurent, PQ H4S 1Z4, Canada. TEL 514-333-5350. FAX 514-457-2679.
circ. 15,800. *4803*

CANADIAN LEATHERCRAFT.
Canadian Society of Creative Leathercraft, c/o Lois MacPherson, 1506 - 205 Queen Mary Dr., Oakville, ON L6K 3K8, Canada.
circ. 90. *465*

CANADIAN METEOROLOGICAL AND OCEANOGRAPHIC SOCIETY. ANNUAL CONGRESS.
Canadian Meteorological and Oceanographic Society, Ste. 903, 151 Slater St., Ottawa, ON K1P 5H3, Canada. TEL 613-237-3393. FAX 613-238-1677.
circ. 850. *4992*

CANADIAN MUSEUM OF FLIGHT & TRANSPORTATION. MUSEUM NEWSLETTER.
Canadian Museum of Flight & Transportation, Unit 200, 5333 216th St. Langley Airport, Langley, BC V3A 4R1, Canada. TEL 604-532-0035. FAX 604-532-0056.
circ. 2,000. *5120*

CANADIAN MUSIC TRADE.
Norris - Whitney Communications Inc., 23 Hannover Dr., No. 7, St. Catharines, ON L2W 1A3, Canada. TEL 905-641-3471. FAX 905-641-1648.
circ. 3,000. *5147*

CANADIAN MUSLIM.
Ottawa Muslim Association, P.O. Box 2952, Sta. D, Ottawa, Ont. 51P 5W9, Canada. TEL 613-725-0004.
circ. 2,000. *6116*

CANADIAN PHILATELIST.
Philaprint Ltd., Box 100, First Canadian Pl., Toronto, ON M5X 1B2, Canada. TEL 519-846-9954.
circ. 7,000. *5454*

CANADIAN PROCESS EQUIPMENT & CONTROL NEWS.
Canadian Process Equipment & Control News Ltd., 343 Eglinton Ave. E., Toronto, ON M4P 1L7, Canada. TEL 416-481-6483. FAX 416-481-6436.
circ. 25,118. *907*

CANADIAN PROFESSIONAL SALES ASSOCIATION. CONTACT.
Canadian Professional Sales Association, 145 Wellington St. W., Ste. 310, Toronto, ON M5J 1H8, Canada. TEL 416-408-2685. FAX 416-408-2684.
circ. 30,000. *1458*

CANADIAN PROPERTY MANAGEMENT.
MediaEdge Communications Inc., 33 Fraser Ave., Ste. 208, Toronto, ON M6K 3J9, Canada. TEL 416-588-6220. FAX 416-588-5217.
circ. 14,210. *6022*

CANADIAN PURCHASING JOURNAL.
Powershift Communications Inc., 245 Fairview Mall Dr., Ste. 308, North York, ON M2J 4T1, Canada. TEL 416-494-1066. FAX 905-946-8931.
circ. 14,000. *1458*

CANADIAN RAIL.
Canadian Railroad Historical Association, Box 22, Sta. B, Montreal, PQ H3B 3J5, Canada.
circ. 1,100. *6809*

CANADIAN REALTOR NEWS.
Canadian Real Estate Association, Place de Ville, Tower A, 320 Queen St., 21st Fl., Ottawa, ON K1R 5A3, Canada. TEL 613-237-7111. FAX 613-234-2567.
circ. 72,000. *6022*

CANADIAN SAILOR.
Seafarers International Union of Canada, 1333 rue St-Jacques, Montreal, Que. H3C 4K2, Canada. FAX 514-931-3667.
circ. 5,000. *5025*

CANADIAN SOCIETY FOR MECHANICAL ENGINEERING. TRANSACTIONS.
Canadian Society for Mechanical Engineering, Dept. of Mechanical Engineering, University of Alberta, Rm. 4-9 Mec.E. Bldg., Edmonton, AB T6G 2G8, Canada. TEL 403-492-9616. FAX 403-492-2200.
circ. 350. *2751*

CANADIAN SPORTSCARD COLLECTOR.
Trajan Publishing Corp., 103 Lakeshore Rd., Ste. 202, St. Catharines, ON L2N 2T6, Canada. TEL 905-646-7744. FAX 905-646-0995.
circ. 150. *3504*

CANADIAN TRAVEL PRESS.
Baxter Publishing Co., 310 Dupont St., Toronto, ON M5R 1V9, Canada. TEL 416-968-7252. FAX 416-968-2377.
circ. 13,000. *6872*

CANADIAN WOOD PRODUCTS.
J C F T Forest Communications, 1 rue Pacifique, Ste.-Anne-de-Bellevue, PQ H9X 1C5, Canada. TEL 514-457-2211.
circ. 7,000. *3033*

CANCER CONTROL.
Moffitt Cancer Center, 12902 Magnolia Dr., Tampa, FL 33612. TEL 813-632-1349. FAX 813-632-1380.
circ. 25,000. *4750*

CANCER RESEARCH CAMPAIGN. ANNUAL REVIEW.
Cancer Research Campaign, Cambridge House, 6-10 Cambridge Terr., Regent's Park, London NW1 4JL, England. TEL 071-224-1333. *4752*

CANINE COURIER.
United States Police Canine Association, Inc., Rte. 2, Box 221 J, Angier, NC 27501. TEL 919-639-0490. FAX 919-639-6091.
circ. 3,000. *5388*

CANOE FOCUS.
British Canoe Union, Adbolton Ln., W. Bridgford, Nottingham NG2 5AS, England. TEL 0115-9821100. FAX 0115-9821797.
circ. 23,000. *6534*

CANOMA.
Canadian Permanent Committee on Geographical Names, Secretariat CPCGN - Geographical Names, 650 - 615 Booth St., Ottawa, ON K1A 0E9, Canada. TEL 613-992-3892. FAX 613-943-8282.
circ. 500. *3250*

CANTERAS Y EXPLOTACIONES.
Pedeca Sociedad Cooperativa, Ltda., Maria Auxiliadora 5, 28040 Madrid, Spain. TEL 1-450-88-37. FAX 1-450-94-29.
circ. 10,273. *5059*

CAPE COD LIFE.
Cape Cod Life, Inc., Box 1385, Pocasset, MA 02559-1385. TEL 508-564-4466. FAX 508-564-4470.
circ. 3,694. *3225*

CAPITAL GAY.
Stonewall Press Ltd., 1 Tavistock Chambers, Bloomsbury Way, London WC1A 2SE, England. TEL 0171-242-2750. FAX 0171-242-3334.
circ. 21,586. *3529*

CAPITAL MAGAZINE.
Cappub, Inc., 300 Mill St., Vienna, VA 22180-4524. FAX 703-938-4562.
circ. 70,000. *6873*

CAPITAL NURSING.
District of Columbia Nurses Association, 5100 Wisconsin Ave., N.W., Ste. 306, Washington, DC 20016. TEL 202-244-2705. FAX 202-362-8285.
circ. 15,000. *4711*

CAPITAL REGION U S A.
Phoenix Publishing & Media Ltd., 18-20 Scrutton St., London EC2A 4RJ, England. TEL 44-171-247-0537. FAX 44-171-377-2741.
circ. 95,000. *6873*

CAPITAL SPORTS FOCUS.
Capital Sports Focus, Inc., 124 E. Diamond Ave., Ste. 7, Gaithersburg, MD 20877-3072. TEL 301-670-6717. FAX 301-670-9043.
circ. 100,000. *6455*

CAPTION.
National Captioning Institute, Inc., 1900 Gallows Rd., Ste. 3000, Vienna, VA 22182-3865. FAX 703-998-2450.
circ. 100,000. *1958*

CARD PLAYER.
3140 S. Polaris Ave., Las Vegas, NV 89102. TEL 702-871-1720. FAX 702-798-5577.
circ. 40,000. *6455*

CARDIOVASCULARIA.
M M V Medizin Verlag, Neumarkter Str. 18, 81673 Munich, Germany. TEL 49-89-43189647. FAX 49-89-43189633.
circ. 55,000. *4599*

CAREER SUCCESS.
Target Marketing, Inc., 5 Victory Ln., Ste. 101, Liberty, MO 64068. TEL 816-781-7557. FAX 816-792-3892.
circ. 400,000. *5264*

CAREERS & COLLEGES.
E.M. Guild, Inc., 989 Ave. of the Americas, 6th Fl., New York, NY 10018. TEL 212-563-4688. FAX 212-967-2531.
circ. 500,000. *5264*

CAREERS & MAJORS.
Oxendine Publishing, Inc., Box 14081, Gainesville, FL 32604-2081. TEL 904-373-6907. FAX 904-373-8120.
circ. 18,000. *5264*

CAREERS UNLIMITED.
Target Marketing, Inc., 5 Victory Ln., Ste. 101, Liberty, MO 64068. TEL 816-781-7557. FAX 816-792-3892.
circ. 200,000. *5025*

CARGO CLAN.
Emphasis HK Ltd., 505-508 Westlands Centre, 20 Westlands Rd., Quarry Bay, Hong Kong. TEL 25161000. FAX 25613306.
circ. 10,000. *6831*

CARGOVISION.
K L M Royal Dutch Airlines, Information and Documentation Department, Postbus 7700, 1117 ZL Schiphol, Netherlands. TEL 31-20-6494545. FAX 31-20-6439261.
circ. 40,000. *6753*

CARIBBEAN UPDATE.
Kal Wagenheim, Ed. & Pub., 52 Maple Ave., Maplewood, NJ 07040. TEL 201-762-1565. FAX 201-762-9585. *1268*

CARIBBEAN WEEK.
Caribbean Communications Inc., Lefferts Pl., River Rd., St. Michael, Barbados, W.I. TEL 809-436-1902.
circ. 26,400. *3243*

CARING TIMES.
Hawker Publications, 13 Park House, 140 Battersea Park Rd., London SW11 4NB, England. TEL 0171-720-2108. FAX 0171-498-3023.
circ. 16,500. *6364*

CARING TODAY.
1 Ewood Ct., Hebden Bridge, W. Yorks. HX7 5QX, England. TEL 44-1422-882467. FAX 44-1422-885160.
circ. 12,500. *6364*

CARNEGIE MUSEUM OF NATURAL HISTORY. BULLETIN.
Carnegie Museum of Natural History, Office of Scientific Publications, 4400 Forbes Ave., Pittsburgh, PA 15213-4080. TEL 412-622-3287. FAX 412-622-8837. *6232*

CARNETEC.
Marketing and Technology Group, Inc., 1415 N. Dayton St., Chicago, IL 60622. TEL 312-266-3311. FAX 312-266-3363.
circ. 4,400. *2962*

CAROLINA STYLE.
Carolina Style, Inc., Box 546, Wrightsville Beach, NC 28480-0546. TEL 919-341-3033.
circ. 100,000. *3226*

THE CARPENTER.
United Brotherhood of Carpenters and Joiners of America, 101 Constitution Ave., N.W., Washington, DC 20001. TEL 202-546-6206. FAX 202-543-5724.
circ. 500,000. *885*

CARROSSERIE.
Nederlandse Vereniging van Ondernemers in het Carrosseriebedrijf, Postbus 299, 2170 AG Sassenheim, Netherlands. TEL 31-252-265222. FAX 31-252-265255.
circ. 3,100. *6780*

CARSON - NEWMAN STUDIES.
Carson - Newman College, Jefferson City, TN 37760. TEL 423-471-3275. FAX 423-471-3502.
circ. 600. *2423*

CASA STILE.
Agenzia Gestione Periodici, Via D. Trentacoste 9, 20134 Milan, Italy. TEL 02-215621. FAX 02-2640330.
circ. 12,000. *3675*

CASE ALUMNUS.
Case Western Reserve University, Case Alumni Association, Crawford Hall, 10900 Euclid Ave., Cleveland, OH 44106-7073. TEL 216-231-4567. FAX 216-368-4714.
circ. 15,000. *1861*

THE CASE MANAGER.
Mosby - Year Book, Inc. 11830 Westline Industrial Dr., St. Louis, MO 63146-3318. TEL 314-872-8370. FAX 314-432-1380.
circ. 9,000. *4439*

CASHEW BULLETIN.
Cashew Export Promotion Council of India, Chittoor Rd., Cochin 682 016, India.
circ. 700. *2962*

CASSIOPEIA.
Canadian Astronomical Society, c/o Dept. of Mathematics, Physics & Engineering, Mount Royal College, 4825 Richard Rd., S.W., Calgary, AB T3E 6K6, Canada. TEL 403-240-6029. FAX 430-240-6664.
circ. 400. *478*

CASTING DESIGN & APPLICATION.
Penton Publishing Co. 1100 Superior Ave., Cleveland, OH 44114. TEL 216-696-7000.
circ. 22,000. *4951*

CASUALTY SIMULATION.
Casualties Union, 1 Grosvenor Crescent, London SW1X 7EE, England. TEL 44-171-2355366.
circ. 2,000. *5957*

CAT FANCIERS' ASSOCIATION. ANNUAL YEARBOOK.
Cat Fanciers' Association, Inc., 1805 Atlantic Ave., Box 1805, Manasquan, NJ 08736-1005. TEL 908-528-9797. FAX 908-528-7391.
circ. 7,500. *5388*

CATALOGO MOTORISTICO.
Azienda Cataloghi Italiani s.a.s., Via B. Crespi, 30-2, 20159 Milan, Italy. TEL 39-2-606052. FAX 39-2-606487.
circ. 35,000. *6780*

CATALYST (WASHINGTON).
National Crime Prevention Council, 1700 K St., N.W., 2nd Fl., Washington, DC 20006-3817. TEL 202-466-6272. FAX 202-296-1356.
circ. 15,000. *2160*

CATALYST: RESEARCH AT THE UNIVERSITY OF CALGARY.
University of Calgary, Research Services, Public Affairs, 2500 University Drive N.W., Calgary, AB T2N 1N4, Canada. TEL 403-220-3783. FAX 403-282-8413.
circ. 3,000. *5233*

CATERING BUTCHER.
9 Vermont Pl., Tongwell, Milton Keynes, Bucks. MK15 8JA. TEL 01908-613323. FAX 01908-210656.
circ. 16,065. *2962*

CATERVEG MAGAZINE.
Caterveg Association for Vegetarian Catering, Caterveg House, 15 The Old Stables, E. Langton, Leics. LE16 7TW, England. TEL 44-1858-545733. FAX 44-1858-545419.
circ. 40,000. *3559*

CATHEDRAL.
Cathedral Church of St. John the Divine, 1047 Amsterdam Ave. at 112th St., New York, NY 10025. TEL 212-316-7564. FAX 212-932-7348.
circ. 13,000. *3701*

THE CATHOLIC.
Incorporated Catholic Truth Society, 192 Vauxhall Bridge Rd., London SW1V 1PD, England. TEL 0171-834 4392. FAX 0171-630-1124.
circ. 25,000. *6172*

CATHOLIC ARCHDIOCESE OF LOUISVILLE. RECORD.
Catholic Archdiocese of Louisville, 1200 S. Shelby St., Louisville, KY 40203-2600. TEL 502-587-1327.
circ. 61,700. *5172*

CATHOLIC BOOK PUBLISHERS ASSOCIATION DIRECTORY.
Catholic Book Publishers Association, 333 Glen Head Rd., Old Brookville, NY 11545. TEL 516-671-9342. FAX 516-759-4227.
circ. 2,200. *5993*

CATHOLIC FORESTER.
Catholic Order of Foresters, 355 Shuman Blvd., Box 3012, Naperville, IL 60566-7012. TEL 708-983-4900. FAX 708-983-4057.
circ. 100,000. *3226*

CATHOLIC NEAR EAST MAGAZINE.
Catholic Near East Welfare Association, 1011 First Ave., New York, NY 10022-4195. TEL 212-826-1480. FAX 212-826-8979.
circ. 110,000. *6173*

CATHOLIC UNIVERSITY MEDICAL COLLEGE JOURNAL.
Catholic University, Graduate School, c/o Catholic Medical College, 505 Banpo-dong, Kangnam-gu, Seoul 135, S. Korea. TEL 02-593-5141. FAX 02-532-3112.
circ. 1,000. *4440*

CATHOLIC WORKMAN.
Box 47, New Prague, MN 56071. TEL 612-758-2229. FAX 612-758-6221.
circ. 8,500. *6175*

CATNAP.
Narcolepsy Association (U.K.), 1 Brook St., Stoke-on-Trent ST4 1JN, England. TEL 44-1782-416417. FAX 44-1782-416417.
circ. 500. *4830*

CATS.
Our Dogs Publishing Co. Ltd., 5 James Leigh St., Manchester M1 6EX, England. TEL 44-161-237-1272. FAX 44-161-236-5534.
circ. 7,000. *5388*

CAVALLO MAGAZINE.
Solitaire S.p.A., Via Enrco Mattei 106, 40138 Bologna, Italy. TEL 39-51-536496. FAX 39-51-536497.
circ. 26,322. *295*

CE B I T NEWS.
Portman Communications Ltd., 52 Foundling Ct., London WC1N 1AN, England. TEL 44-171-837-0815. FAX 44-171-273-9917.
circ. 50,000. *2031*

CENTENNIAL STATE LIBRARIES.
State Library, Department of Education, 201 E Colfax Ave., Rm. 309, Denver, CO 80203. TEL 303-866-6732. FAX 303-866-6940.
circ. 3,500. *3984*

CENTER NEWS.
Memorial Sloan-Kettering Cancer Center, Department of Public Affairs, 1275 York Ave., New York, NY 10021. TEL 212-639-3573. FAX 212-639-3576.
circ. 250,000. *4753*

CENTCOTTO A.
Gruppo Editoriale Faenza Editrice S.p.A., Via Pier. de Crescenzi 44, 48018 Faenza RA, Italy. TEL 39-546-663688. FAX 39-546-660440.
circ. 9,650. *1847*

CENTRAL BANK OF BARBADOS. BALANCE OF PAYMENTS.
Central Bank of Barbados Research Department, P.O. Box 1016, Spry St., Bridgetown, Barbados, W.I. TEL 809-436-6870. FAX 809-427-1431.
circ. 2,000. *988*

CENTRAL COUNCIL FOR EDUCATION AND TRAINING IN SOCIAL WORK. REPORT OF COUNCIL MEETING.
Central Council for Education and Training in Social Work, Derbyshire House, St. Chad's St., London WC1H 8AD, England. TEL 44-171-278-2455. FAX 44-171-278-2934. *5365*

CENTRAL FLORIDA FAMILY JOURNAL.
Family Journal Publications, Inc., Box 1100, Orlando, FL 32802-1100. TEL 407-774-9863. FAX 407-788-2099.
circ. 56,312. *1762*

CENTRAL PENN BUSINESS JOURNAL.
C P N C Inc., 409 S. Second St., Ste. 3D, Harrisburg, PA 17104-1632. TEL 717-236-4300. FAX 717-236-6803.
circ. 16,000. *908*

CENTRAL RAILWAY CHRONICLE.
Central Railway Club of Buffalo, 950 French St., Buffalo, NY 14227-3632. TEL 716-825-0248.
circ. 295. *6809*

CENTRAL ROAD RESEARCH INSTITUTE, NEW DELHI. ROAD RESEARCH PAPER.
Central Road Research Institute, P.O. Central Road Research Institute, New Delhi 110020, India. TEL 6832274. *6822*

CENTRAL SERICULTURAL RESEARCH AND TRAINING INSTITUTE. ANNUAL REPORT.
Central Sericultural Research and Training Institute, Manandavadi Rd., Srirampura, Mysore 570008, India. FAX 91-821-520845.
circ. 300. *106*

CENTRE FOR CONFLICT RESOLUTION. ANNUAL REPORT.
Centre for Conflict Resolution, c/o University of Cape Town, Rondebosch 7700, South Africa. TEL 27-21-6502503. FAX 27-21-6852142.
circ. 2,200. *6408*

CENTRE FOR PLANT BREEDING AND REPRODUCTION RESEARCH. ANNUAL REPORT.
C P R O - D L O, Postbus 16, 6700 AA Wageningen, Netherlands. TEL 31-317-477000. FAX 31-317-418094.
circ. 3,000. *215*

CENTRE NATIONAL DE DOCUMENTATION SCIENTIFIQUE ET TECHNIQUE. RAPPORT D'ACTIVITE.
Centre National de Documentation Scientifique et Technique, 4 Bd. de l'Empereur, B-1000 Brussels, Belgium.
circ. 1,000. *6647*

CENTRE NATIONAL DE LA RECHERCHE SCIENTIFIQUE. ANNUAIRE EUROPEEN D'ADMINISTRATION PUBLIQUE.
C N R S Editions, 20-22 rue St. Amand, 75015 Paris, France. TEL 45-33-16-00. FAX 45-33-92-13.
circ. 1,500. *5896*

CENTREPOINT.
Christian Centre Party, 157 Vicarage Rd., London E10 5DJ, England. TEL 44-181-539-3876. *5641*

CEREAL RUST BULLETIN.
U.S. Department of Agriculture, Agricultural
Research Service (St. Paul), 1551 Lindig St., St.
Paul, MN 55108. TEL 612-625-6299. FAX 612-
649-5054.
circ. 500. *215*

CERTIFICATION NEWS.
Institute for Certification of Computing
Professionals, 2200 E. Devon Ave., Ste. 247, Des
Plaines, IL 60018-4503. TEL 847-299-4227.
FAX 847-299-4280.
circ. 25,000. *2031*

CERTIFIED LETTER.
Institute of Certified Professional Managers, James
Madison University, Harrisonburg, VA 27807.
TEL 703-568-3247. FAX 703-568-3587.
circ. 5,300. *1410*

CERVEZA Y MALTA.
Asociacion Espanola de Tecnicos de Cerveza y
Malta, Ramirez de Prado, 8-1o F, 28045 Madrid,
Spain. TEL 34-1-5277255. FAX 34-1-5285507.
circ. 1,500. *503*

C'EST POUR QUAND.
Family Communications, Inc., 37 Hanna Ave.,
Toronto, ON M6K 1X1, Canada.
circ. 52,000. *1762*

CHAMBER NEWS.
Greater Hartsville Chamber of Commerce, Box 578,
Hartsville, SC 29551. TEL 803-332-6401.
FAX 803-332-8017.
circ. 600. *1136*

**CHAMBRE DE COMMERCE, D'AGRICULTURE,
D'INDUSTRIE ET D'ARTISANAT DU NIGER.
WEEKLY BULLETIN.**
Chambre de Commerce, d'Agriculture, d'Industrie et
d'Artisanat du Niger, B.P. 209, Niamey, Niger.
circ. 170. *1136*

CHAMPLAIN SOCIETY, TORONTO. REPORT.
Champlain Society, Box 592, Station "R", Toronto
ON M4G 4E1, Canada. TEL 416-482-9635.
FAX 416-482-9341.
circ. 930. *3340*

CHANCE.
Unicum Verlag GmbH, Willy-Brandt-Platz 5-7,
44787 Bochum, Germany. TEL 49-234-96151-0.
FAX 49-234-60256.
circ. 333,000. *1861*

CHANGES (DEERFIELD BEACH).
U S Journal Inc., Enterprise Center, 3201 S.W. 15th
St., Deerfield Beach, FL 33442-8190. TEL 305-
360-0909.
circ. 10,000. *5834*

CHANGING MEDICAL MARKETS.
Theta Corporation, Theta Bldg., Middlefield, CT
06455. TEL 203-349-1054. FAX 203-349-1227.
4440

CHANNEL (MADISON).
Department of Public Instruction, Division for Library
Services, 125 S. Webster St., 5th Fl., Box 7841,
Madison, WI 53707. TEL 608-266-9679. FAX 608-
267-1052.
circ. 3,600. *3985*

CHANNEL (SUNNYVALE).
Mathews & Clark Communications, 710 Lakeway,
Ste. 170, Sunnyvale, CA 94086. TEL 408-736-
1120. FAX 408-736-2523.
circ. 8,500. *2509*

THE CHANTICLEER.
Jacksonville State University, Communications
Board, Jacksonville, AL 36265. TEL 205-782-
5701. FAX 205-782-5445.
circ. 7,000. *1861*

CHAOS NETWORK.
People Technologies, 1801 Woodfield Dr., No.A,
Savoy, IL 61874-9505. TEL 217-328-0032.
circ. 500. *908*

CHAPLIN.
FilmhusFoerlaget AB, P.O. Box 27126, S-102 52
Stockholm, Sweden. TEL 46-8-665-1100. FAX 46-
8-663-8009.
circ. 5,200. *5095*

CHARAKTER.
Charakter Medien Verlag GmbH, Lotzestr. 29,
37083 Goettingen, Germany. TEL 0551-507510.
FAX 0551-73047.
circ. 14,700. *3143*

CHARETTE.
American Institute of Architecture Students, 1735
New York Ave., N.W., Washington, DC 20006.
TEL 202-626-7472. FAX 202-626-7414.
circ. 10,000. *2319*

CHARTER INDUSTRY.
Charter Industry Services, Inc., 43 Kindred St.,
Stuart, FL 34994. TEL 407-288-1066.
circ. 750. *6534*

CHARTERED BANKER.
Financial & Business Publications, 4 Cavendish Sq.,
London W1M 9HA, England. TEL 44-171-637-
1115. FAX 44-171-637-1117.
circ. 44,700. *1076*

CHARTERED BUILDING PROFESSIONAL.
Australian Institute of Building, 217 Northbourne
Ave., Turner, A.C.T. 2601, Australia. TEL 61-62-
477433. FAX 61-62-489030.
circ. 3,000. *845*

**CHARTERED INSTITUTE OF PUBLIC FINANCE AND
ACCOUNTANCY. CONFERENCE HANDBOOK.**
Chartered Institute of Public Finance and
Accountancy, 3 Robert St., London WC2N 6BH,
England. TEL 44-171-543-5600. FAX 44-171-543-
5700. *1044*

**CHARTERED INSURANCE INSTITUTE. SOCIETY OF
FELLOWS. JOURNAL.**
Chartered Insurance Institute, Society of Fellows, 20
Aldermanbury, London EC2V 7HY, England. TEL 44-
171-606-3835. FAX 44-171-726-0131.
circ. 18,000. *3645*

CHAT.
I P C Magazines, Weeklies Group King's Reach
Tower, Stamford St., London SE1 9LS, England.
TEL 44-171-261-5000. FAX 44-1444-445599.
6989

CHECKOUT.
Checkout Publications Ltd., 22 Crofton Rd.,
Dunlaoire, Co. Dublin, Ireland. TEL 353-1-2808415.
FAX 353-1-2808309.
circ. 5,500. *1458*

CHECKOUT FRESH.
Reed Business Publishing Group Quadrant House,
The Quadrant, Sutton, Surrey SM2 5AS, England.
TEL 0181-652-3258. FAX 0181-652-8925.
circ. 12,500. *3003*

CHEERS.
Adams Publishing Companies, 68-860 Perez Rd.,
Ste. J, Cathedral City, CA 92234. TEL 619-770-
4370.
circ. 92,000. *3559*

CHEMICAL DISTILLATIONS.
Cyrus J. Lawrence, Inc., 1290 Ave. of the Americas,
New York, NY 10104. TEL 212-468-5000. *1668*

CHEMICAL INDUSTRY MONITOR.
Cyrus J. Lawrence, Inc., 1290 Ave. of the Americas,
New York, NY 10104. TEL 212-468-5000. *1668*

CHEMICAL PROCESSING.
Putman Publishing Co., 301 E. Erie St., Chicago, IL
60611. TEL 312-644-2020. FAX 312-644-1131.
circ. 80,042. *2637*

CHEMICAL TECHNOLOGY EUROPE.
V C H Verlagsgesellschaft mbH, Postfach 101161,
69451 Weinheim, Germany. TEL 49-6201-
606147. FAX 49-6201-606117.
circ. 30,000. *2637*

**CHEMICALS, ADHESIVES AND PHARMACEUTICALS
(YEAR).**
SAFTO, Publishing Division, P.O. Box 782706,
Sandton 2146, South Africa. TEL 27-11-883-3737.
FAX 27-11-883-6569. *2637*

CHEMIE-ANLAGEN UND VERFAHREN.
Konradin Verlag Robert Kohlhammer GmbH, Ernst-
Mey-Str. 8, 70771 Leinfelden-Echterdingen,
Germany. TEL 49-711-7594-0. FAX 49-711-
7594390.
circ. 25,487. *2637*

CHEMISCHE RUNDSCHAU.
Vogt-Schild AG, Zuchwilerstr. 21, CH-4501
Solothurn, Switzerland. TEL 065-247247. FAX 065-
247235.
circ. 18,500. *1670*

CHEMIST & DRUGSTORE NEWS.
India Publications Co., Denabank House, 2nd Fl., 31
Hamam St., Bombay 1, India. *5404*

CHESHIRE SMILE INTERNATIONAL.
Leonard Cheshire Foundation, 26-29 Maunsel St.,
London SW1P 2QN, England. TEL 0171-828-1822.
FAX 0171-976-5704.
circ. 8,000. *3316*

**CHESTER DISTRICT GENEALOGICAL SOCIETY.
BULLETIN.**
Chester District Genealogical Society, Box 336,
Richburg, SC 29729.
circ. 150. *3078*

CHIANG MAI MEDICAL BULLETIN.
Chiang Mai University, Faculty of Medicine, 110
Intavaroros Street, Chiang Mai 50002, Thailand.
TEL 52-221122. FAX 53-217144.
circ. 1,000. *4441*

CHIBA DAIGAKU KOGAKUBU KENKYU HOKOKU.
Chiba Daigaku Kogakubu, 1-33 Yayoicho, Chiba
280, Japan. TEL 0472-51-1111. FAX 0472-51-
7337.
circ. 550. *2592*

CHICAGO GENEALOGIST.
Chicago Genealogical Society, Box 1160, Chicago,
IL 60690.
circ. 1,000. *3078*

CHICAGO JEWISH STAR.
Box 268, Skokie, IL 60076-0268. TEL 708-674-
7827. FAX 708-674-0014.
circ. 24,000. *2871*

CHICAGO MARKET.
Bolger Publications Inc., 3301 Como Ave., S.E.,
Minneapolis, MN 55414. TEL 612-645-6311.
FAX 612-645-1750.
circ. 26,000. *3300*

CHICAGO PARENT MAGAZINE.
Wednesday Journal Inc., 141 S. Oak Park Ave., Oak
Park, IL 60302-2901. TEL 708-386-5555.
FAX 708-524-0447.
circ. 85,000. *1762*

CHICAGO PURCHASOR.
Purchasing Management Association of Chicago,
201 N. Wells, Chicago, IL 60606. TEL 312-782-
1940. FAX 312-782-9732.
circ. 5,000. *1458*

CHIEF INFORMATION OFFICER JOURNAL.
Faulkner & Gray, Inc. (New York), 11 Penn Plaza,
17th Fl., New York, NY 10001. TEL 212-967-
7000. FAX 212-967-7155.
circ. 8,095. *2080*

CHIEFTAIN.
Black Hawk College, Quad Cities Campus, 6600
34th Ave., Moline, IL 61265. FAX 309-792-5976.
circ. 3,000. *1861*

CHILD MAGAZINE'S GUIDE TO BABY PRODUCTS.
New York Times Company, Magazine Group, 110
Fifth Ave., New York, NY 10011. TEL 212-463-
1600. FAX 212-463-1383.
circ. 600,000. *1763*

CHILD MAGAZINE'S GUIDE TO HAVING A BABY.
New York Times Company, Magazine Group, 110
Fifth Ave., New York, NY 10011. TEL 212-463-
1600. FAX 212-463-1553.
circ. 1,200,000. *1763*

CHILD SAFETY REVIEW.
Child Accident Prevention Trust, Clerks Ct., 4th Fl.,
18-20 Farringdon Ln., London EC1R 3AU, England.
TEL 44-171-636-3828.
circ. 500. *1763*

CHILDBIRTH INSTRUCTOR.
Cradle Publishing, Inc., 124 E. 40th St., Rm. 1101,
New York, NY 10016-1723. TEL 212-986-1422.
FAX 212-986-0816.
circ. 10,000. *4733*

CHILDREN'S HEALTH CARE.
Lawrence Erlbaum Associates, Inc., 10 Industrial Dr., Mahwah, NJ 07430-2262. TEL 201-236-9500. FAX 201-236-0072.
circ. 4,000. *6366*

CHILDREN'S MONITOR.
Child Welfare League of America, Inc., 440 First St., N.W., Ste. 310, Washington, DC 20001. TEL 202-638-2952. FAX 202-638-4004. *3918*

CHILE. SERVICIO NACIONAL DE PESCA. ANUARIO ESTADISTICO DE PESCA.
Servicio Nacional de Pesca, Departamento Sistemas de Informacion y Estadisticas Pesqueras, Yungay 1731 4o piso, Valparaiso, Chile. FAX 56-32-259564. *2929*

CHILEAN NEWS.
Anglo-Chilean Society, 12 Devonshire St., London W1N 2DS, England. TEL 44-171-580-1271.
circ. 600. *5744*

CHILTON'S MOTOR AGE.
Chilton Co., One Chilton Way, Radnor, PA 19089. TEL 610-964-4390. FAX 610-964-4251.
circ. 146,400. *6781*

CHILTON'S PRODUCT DESIGN AND DEVELOPMENT.
Chilton Co., One Chilton Way, Radnor, PA 19089. TEL 610-964-4351.
circ. 168,000. *2592*

THE CHIMES (LA MIRADA).
Biola University, 13800 Biola Ave., La Mirada, CA 90639. TEL 310-903-4879.
circ. 2,000. *1862*

CHINA EXCHANGE NEWS.
Committee on Scholarly Communication with China, 1112 16th St., N.W. Ste. 340, Washington, DC 20036. TEL 202-337-1250. FAX 202-337-3109.
circ. 2,500. *6233*

CHINAMAC JOURNAL.
Adsale Publishing Company, 4-F, Stanhope House, 734 King's Rd., North Point, Hong Kong. TEL 852-2811-8897. FAX 852-2516-5119.
circ. 22,000. *4337*

CHIP.
Vogel Verlag und Druck GmbH & Co. KG, Max-Planck-Str. 7-9, 97082 Wuerzburg, Germany. TEL 0931-4182335. FAX 0931-4182090.
circ. 215,172. *2085*

CHIPS FROM THE FORESTERS TREE.
Catholic Association of Foresters, 347 Commonwealth Ave., Boston, MA 02115. TEL 617-536-8221. FAX 617-536-2819.
circ. 5,500. *3012*

CHIPS-O-WOOD.
Wood Junior College, Alumni Development, Box 289, Mathiston, MS 39752. TEL 601-263-5352.
circ. 7,000. *1862*

THE CHIROPRACTIC JOURNAL.
2950 N. Dobson Rd., Ste. 1, Chandler, AZ 85224-1800. TEL 602-786-9235. FAX 602-732-9313.
circ. 60,000. *4612*

CHIROPRACTIC PRODUCTS.
Novicom, Inc., 20000 Mariner Ave., Ste. 480, Torrance, CA 90503. TEL 310-793-4141. FAX 310-793-4138.
circ. 35,059. *4612*

CHIZU.
Nihon Kokusai Chizu Gakkai, 9-6 Aobadai 4-chome, Meguro-ku, Tokyo 153, Japan. *3251*

CHIZU NO TOMO.
Japan Map Association, Shinsen Bldg., 8-2 Shinsen-cho, Shibuya, Tokyo 150, Japan. FAX 03-3461-0244. *3251*

CHLODNICTWO.
Wydawnictwo Czasopism i Ksiazek Technicznych SIGMA - NOT, Ul. Ratuszowa 11, P.O. Box 1004, 00-950 Warsaw, Poland. TEL 48-22-180918. FAX 48-22-192187.
circ. 1,050. *3326*

CHOCOLATE AND NUT WORLD.
Lott Publishing Co., Box 710, Santa Monica, CA 90406. TEL 310-397-4217.
circ. 3,000. *2999*

CHOICES IN CARDIOLOGY.
Choices Publishing Group, Inc., 129 Washington St., Hoboken, NJ 07030. TEL 201-792-1900. FAX 201-792-3955.
circ. 17,000. *4599*

CHONGQING HUANJING KEXUE.
Chongqing Huanjing Kexue Xuehui, 212 Renmin Lu, Chongqing, Sichuar 630015, People's Republic of China. TEL 86-811-3868871. FAX 86-811-3850021.
circ. 5,000. *2780*

CHRISTCHURCH MAIL.
1st Fl., Paxus House, Cnr. Tuam & High Sts., Christchurch, Canterbury, New Zealand. TEL 03-366-1622. FAX 03-365-6623.
circ. 124,000. *3196*

CHRISTIAN MEDICAL COLLEGE VELLORE ALUMNI JOURNAL.
Christian Medical College, Alumni Association, Vellore 632 002, Tamil Nadu, India. TEL 91-416-22603. FAX 91-416-32788.
circ. 2,000. *4441*

CHRISTIAN SCHOOL ADMINISTRATOR.
Great River Publishing, Inc., 4715 Spottswood Ave., Memphis, TN 38117-4818. TEL 901-762-0329. FAX 901-762-0718.
circ. 11,500. *2455*

CHRISTIANS IN CRISIS.
Christian Forum Research Foundation, 1111 Fairgrounds Rd., Grand Rapids, MN 55744. TEL 218-326-2688.
circ. 1,000. *6053*

CHRONICA DERMATOLOGICA.
Istituto Dermopatico dell'Immacolata, Via Monti di Creta, 104, 00167 Rome, Italy. FAX 39-6-66464437.
circ. 7,000. *4659*

CHRONICLE (GRAYSLAKE).
College of Lake County, 19351 W. Washington, Grayslake, IL 60030. TEL 708-223-3634. FAX 708-223-9371.
circ. 3,750. *1862*

CHRONICLE (HEMPSTEAD).
Hofstra University, 203 Student Center, Hempstead, NY 11550. TEL 516-463-6965.
circ. 11,000. *1862*

CHUGOKU ELECTRIC POWER CO. TECHNICAL LABORATORY. REPORT.
Chugoku Electric Power Co., Inc., Technical Research Center, 4-32, Ozu 4-chome, Hiroshima-shi, Hiroshima-ken 730, Japan. *2686*

CHUKI KEIZAI YOSOKU.
Japan Center for Economic Research, Nikkei Kayabacho Bldg., 6-1 Nihonbashi Kayaba-cho 2-chome, Chuo-ku, Tokyo 103, Japan. TEL 03-3639-2801. *1184*

CHURCH MUSIC QUARTERLY.
Royal School of Church Music, Cleveland Lodge, Westhumble, Dorking RH5 6BW, England. TEL 44-181-341-6408. FAX 44-181-340-0021.
circ. 13,700. *5149*

CHURCHES PURCHASING SCHEME.
Ecclesiastical Insurance Office, Desk Top Publishing Unit, Beaufort House, Brunswick Rd., Gloucester GL1 1JZ, England. TEL 0452-383080. FAX 0452-383621.
circ. 32,500. *908*

CIAO.
Ciao Publishing Co., 1081 Bas l'Assomption Nord, Ville de l'Assomption, Que. J0K 1G0, Canada. FAX 514-589-4485.
circ. 40,000. *2872*

CIENCIA BIOLOGICA: BIOLOGIA MOLECULAR E CELULAR.
Universidade de Coimbra, Departamento de Zoologia, Coimbra, Portugal. TEL 351-39-34729. FAX 351-39-26798.
circ. 600. *802*

CIENCIA MEDICA.
Alpe Editores, S.A., Pedro Rico, 27, 28029 Madrid, Spain. TEL 34-1-7338811. FAX 34-1-3159652.
circ. 8,000. *4442*

CIENCIA PHARMACEUTICA.
Alpe Editores, S.A., Pedro Rico, 27, 28029 Madrid, Spain. TEL 34-1-7338852. FAX 34-1-3159652.
circ. 6,000. *5404*

CIENCIA RURAL.
Universidade Federal de Santa Maria, Centro de Ciencias Rurais, Campus Universitario, 97119-900 Santa Maria, Rio Grande do Sul, Brazil. TEL 55-55-226-2347.
circ. 750. *107*

CINDERELLA PHILATELIST.
Cinderella Stamp Club, c/o L.N. Williams, 44 The Ridgeway, London NW11 8QS, England.
circ. 800. *5454*

CINE-OJA.
Sociedad Civil Cine al Dia, Apdo. 50446, Sabana Grande, Caracas, Venezuela.
circ. 2,500. *5096*

CINEMATOGRAPH.
San Francisco Cinematheque, 480 Potrero, San Francisco, CA 94110. TEL 415-558-8129. FAX 415-558-0455.
circ. 1,800. *5097*

CIRCLE (PORTLAND).
Circle Forum, Box 176, Portland, OR 97207. *4303*

CIRCUIT RIDER (NASHVILLE).
United Methodist Publishing House, 201 Eighth Ave. S., Box 801, Nashville, TN 37202. TEL 615-749-6319. FAX 615-749-5079.
circ. 40,000. *6139*

CIRCUITS ASSEMBLY.
Miller Freeman, Inc. 600 Harrison St., San Francisco, CA 94107. TEL 415-905-2200. FAX 415-905-2232.
circ. 40,000. *2509*

CIRCULATION MANAGEMENT.
Ganesa Corporation, 611 Broadway, Ste. 401, New York, NY 10012-2608. TEL 212-989-2133. FAX 212-620-0396.
circ. 10,000. *5993*

CIRUGIA DEL URUGUAY.
Sociedad de Cirugia del Uruguay, Casilla de Correos 10972, Montevideo, Uruguay.
circ. 1,000. *4906*

CITY & COUNTRY CLUB LIFE.
Club Publications, 665 La Villa Dr., Miami Springs, FL 33166. TEL 305-887-1701. FAX 305-885-1923.
circ. 26,000. *3226*

CITY CLUB GADFLY.
City Club of New York, 33 W. 42nd St., New York, NY 10036. TEL 212-921-9870.
circ. 2,500. *5939*

THE CITY JOURNAL.
Manhattan Institute, Inc., 52 Vanderbilt Ave., New York, NY 10017-3808. TEL 212-599-7000. FAX 212-599-3494.
circ. 2,000. *5642*

CITY LIMITS.
City Limits Community Information Service, Inc., 40 Prince St., New York, NY 10012. TEL 212-925-9820. FAX 212-966-3407
circ. 1,000. *3579*

CITY LINE NEWS.
City Line News, Box 569, Bala Cynwyd, PA 19004. TEL 610-667-6623. FAX 610-667-6624.
circ. 32,000. *1184*

CITY TREES.
Society of Municipal Arborists, Wellesley Park and Tree Division, 56 Woodlawn Ave., Wellesley Hills, MA 02181. TEL 617-235-7600. FAX 617-431-7569.
circ. 260. *3013*

CITYSIDE.
University of Regina, School of Journalism and Communications, Regina, SK S4S 0A2, Canada. TEL 306-584-5051. FAX 306-585-4867.
circ. 1,000. *1862*

CIUDADANO.
Fundacion Ciudadano, C. Atocha 26, 28012
Madrid, Spain. TEL 34-1-3691285. FAX 34-1-
3690827.
circ. 70,000. *2149*

CIVIL AVIATION TRAINING.
Monch UK Ltd., 84 Alexandra Rd., Farnborough,
Hants GU14 6DD, England. TEL 01252-517974.
FAX 01252-512714.
circ. 12,000. *6754*

CIVIL ENGINEERING CONTRACTOR.
Brooke Pattrick (Pty) Ltd., P.O. Box 422,
Bedfordview 2008, South Africa. TEL 27-11-
6224666. FAX 27-11-6167196.
circ. 4,500. *2655*

CIVIL LIBERTIES REPORTER.
American Civil Liberties Union of New Jersey, 2
Washington Place, Newark, NJ 07102. TEL 201-
642-2084.
circ. 6,600. *3881*

CIVIL SERVICE PENSIONER.
Civil Service Pensioners Alliance, 7 The Beeches,
Shaw Hill, Melksham, Wilts. SN12 8EW, England.
TEL 01225-702416.
circ. 59,000. *3285*

CIVITAN MAGAZINE.
Civitan International, Box 130744, Birmingham, AL
35213-0744. TEL 205-591-8910. FAX 205-592-
6307.
circ. 37,000. *1848*

CLAMAVI.
Stichting Mensen in Nood - Caritas Nederland,
Postbus 1041, 5200 BA 's-Hertogenbosch,
Netherlands. TEL 31-73-6456789. FAX 31-73-
6456700.
circ. 250,000. *6367*

CLAN MCLAREN SOCIETY, U S A. QUARTERLY.
Clan McLaren Society, U S A, 5843 Royalcrest,
Dallas, TX 75230.
circ. 145. *3078*

CLAN ROSS NEWSLETTER.
Clan Ross Association of the United States, Inc., Box
235, Montezuma, NC 28653-9999. TEL 912-727-
2560.
circ. 400. *2872*

CLARIN INTERNACIONAL.
Arte Grafico Editorial Argentino S.A., Piedras 1743,
Buenos Aires, Argentina. *3109*

CLARION ALUMNI NEWS.
Clarion University, 974 E. Wood St., Clarion, PA
16214. TEL 814-226-2334.
circ. 27,000. *1862*

CLARK UNIVERSITY NEWS.
Clark University, 950 Main St., Worcester, MA
01610. TEL 508-793-7441. FAX 508-794-7565.
circ. 25,000. *1862*

CLASS.
Class Editori, Via Burigozzo 5, 20122 Milan, Italy.
TEL 39-2-582191. FAX 39-2-58317429.
circ. 90,000. *1500*

CLASSICUM.
Classical Association of New South Wales, c/o H.
Tarrant, Ed., Dept. of Classics, University of
Newcastle, N.S.W. 2308, Australia. FAX 61-49-21-
6947.
circ. 300. *1820*

CLEANING MANAGEMENT.
National Trade Publications, Inc., 13 Century Hill,
Latham, NY 12110-2197. TEL 518-783-1281.
FAX 518-783-1386.
circ. 41,274. *845*

CLEANROOMS.
PennWell Publishing Co., Box 1260, Tulsa, OK
74101. TEL 918-835-3161. FAX 918-832-9295.
circ. 42,000. *2746*

CLEMATIS.
Bairnsdale Field Naturalists' Club, P.O. Box 563,
Bairnsdale, Vic. 3875, Australia. *2780*

**CLEMSON UNIVERSITY. DEPARTMENT OF FOREST
RESOURCES. FORESTRY BULLETIN.**
Clemson University, Department of Forest
Resources, Clemson, SC 29634-1003. TEL 803-
656-3302.
circ. 500. *3013*

**CLEMSON UNIVERSITY. WATER RESOURCES
RESEARCH INSTITUTE. REPORT.**
Clemson University, Water Resources Research
Institute, Strom Thurmond Institute, Clemson, SC
29634-5130. TEL 864-656-0225. FAX 864-656-
4780.
circ. 200. *6964*

CLEMSON WORLD.
Clemson University, Office of Publication &
Graphics, 103 Fike, Clemson, SC 29634-5608.
TEL 803-656-2467. FAX 803-656-5004.
circ. 68,000. *1862*

CLEVEDON PORTISHEAD NEALSEA ADMAG.
Admag Newspapers 11 Beacons Field Rd., Weston-
super-Mare, Avon BS23 1YE, England. TEL 44-
1934-417921. FAX 44-1934-635031.
circ. 80,000. *3153*

CLIENT DIRECTORY AND AGENCY LIST.
International Federation of Advertising Agencies,
1450 E. American Ln., Ste. 1400, Schaumburg, IL
60173-4973. TEL 847-330-6344. FAX 847-517-
4459.
circ. 100. *34*

CLIENT - SERVER COMPUTING.
Sentry Publishing Company, Inc., 1 Research Dr.,
Ste. 400B, Westborough, MA 01581-3907.
TEL 508-366-2031.
circ. 90,000. *1492*

CLINICA CARDIOVASCULAR.
Alpe Editores, S.A., Pedro Rico, 27, 28029 Madrid,
Spain. TEL 34-1-7338811. FAX 34-1-3159652.
circ. 6,500. *4600*

CLINICAL CONGRESS NEWS.
Cambridge Medical Publications Ltd., Wicker House,
High St., Worthing, W. Sussex BN11 1DJ, England.
TEL 01903-205884. FAX 01903-234862. *4443*

CLINICAL LABORATORY INTERNATIONAL.
Pan European Publishing Co. Rue Verte 216, 1030
Brussels, Belgium. TEL 32-2-2402611. FAX 32-2-
2427111.
circ. 30,002. *4678*

CLINICAL SYMPOSIA.
Ciba Geigy Corporation, 556 Morris Ave., Summit,
NJ 07901. TEL 908-277-4478. FAX 908-277-
4478.
circ. 161,000. *4443*

CLINICIAN REVIEWS.
Clinicians Publishing Group, 4 Brighton Rd., Clifton,
NJ 07012. TEL 201-916-1000. FAX 201-916-
0021.
circ. 52,000. *4444*

CLUB DIRECTOR.
National Club Association, 3050 K St., N.W., Ste.
330, Washington, DC 20007-5108. TEL 202-625-
2080. FAX 202-625-9044.
circ. 8,500. *1848*

CLUB LIVING.
Club Living, Inc., 16 Copper Beech Cir., White
Plains, NY 10605-4702.
circ. 51,000. *6456*

CLUB MANAGEMENT IN AUSTRALIA.
Club Managers' Association Australia, 2A Lord St.,
Botany, N.S.W. 2019, Australia. TEL 02-316-6788.
FAX 02-316-6244. *1411*

CLUB MIRROR.
Quantam Publishing Ltd., 29-31 Lower Coombe St.,
Croydon CR9 0LX, England. TEL 0181-681-2099.
FAX 0181-681-2389.
circ. 25,855. *1848*

COACH OPERATORS HANDBOOK.
E M A P - Response Publishing Ltd., Wentworth
House, Wentworth St., Peterborough, Cambs. PE1
2DS, England. TEL 01733-63100. FAX 01733-
62656.
circ. 4,500. *6715*

COAL.
Intertec Publishing Corp., 29 N. Wacker Dr.,
Chicago, IL 60606. TEL 312-726-2802. FAX 312-
726-4103.
circ. 18,623. *5060*

COASTGUARD.
Department of Transport, H.M. Coastguard, Rm.
S13-03 2, Marsham St., London SW1P 3EB,
England. TEL 0171-276-5082. FAX 0171-276-
6080.
circ. 16,000. *6832*

COCOA GROWERS BULLETIN.
Cadbury Ltd., Bournville, Birmingham B30 2LU,
England.
circ. 1,500. *216*

COFFEE MAZDOOR SAHAKARI.
All India Coffee Workers Cooperative Societies
Federation Ltd., 10 U.B. Bungalow Rd., Jawahar
Nagar, Delhi 7, India. *2964*

COGENERATION AND RESOURCE RECOVERY.
Cogeneration and Small Power, 3 Fairway Ln., Old
Tappan, NJ 07675-7017. TEL 703-759-5060.
FAX 703-759-0232.
circ. 1,500. *2567*

COIFFURE.
Samsom Bedrijfsinformatie B.V. Postbus 4, 2400
MA Alphen aan den Rijn, Netherlands. TEL 31-172-
466775. FAX 31-172-440681.
circ. 4,430. *490*

COLD FACTS.
Cryogenic Society of America, c/o Huget
Advertising, Inc., 1033 South Blvd., Ste. 13, Oak
Park, IL 60302. TEL 708-383-6220. FAX 708-
383-9337.
circ. 2,000. *5583*

**COLD SPRING HARBOR LABORATORY. ABSTRACTS
OF PAPERS PRESENTED AT MEETINGS.**
Cold Spring Harbor Laboratory Press, Publications
Department, Box 100, Cold Spring Harbor, NY
11724. TEL 800-843-4388. FAX 516-349-1946.
578

**COLD SPRING HARBOR LABORATORY. ANNUAL
REPORT.**
Cold Spring Harbor Laboratory Press, Publications
Department, Box 100, Cold Spring Harbor, NY
11724. TEL 800-843-4388. FAX 516-349-1946.
578

COLLEAGUE.
Michigan Judicial Institute, Box 30205, Lansing, MI
48909. TEL 517-334-7805. *3946*

THE COLLECTOR.
Barrington Publications, 54 Uxbridge Rd., London
W12 8LP, England.
circ. 18,500. *331*

**COLLEGE AND UNIVERSITY ADMISSIONS AND
ENROLLMENT, NEW YORK STATE.**
Education Department, Post-Secondary Policy
Analysis, Cultural Education Bldg., Rm. 5B44,
Albany, NY 12230. TEL 518-474-3874. *2423*

**COLLEGE AND UNIVERSITY DEGREES CONFERRED,
NEW YORK STATE.**
Education Department, Post Secondary Policy
Analysis, Cultural Education Bldg., Rm. 5B44,
Albany, NY 12230. TEL 518-474-3874. *2423*

**COLLEGE AND UNIVERSITY EMPLOYEES, NEW YORK
STATE.**
Education Department, Office of Post-Secondary
Policy Analysis, c/o James J. Brady, Chief, Bureau
of Post-Secondary Statistical Service, Rm. 5B44
CEC, Albany, NY 12230. TEL 518-474-3874.
2424

**COLLEGE OF PSYCHOLOGISTS OF ONTARIO.
BULLETIN.**
College of Psychologists of Ontario, 1246 Yonge
St., Ste. 201, Toronto, ON M4T 1W5, Canada.
TEL 416-961-8817. FAX 416-961-2635.
circ. 2,400. *5836*

COLLEGE OUTLOOK.
Townsend Outlook Publishing, 20 E. Gregory,
Kansas City, MO 64114. TEL 816-361-0616.
FAX 816-361-0616. *5265*

COLLEGE UNION & ON-CAMPUS HOSPITALITY.
Executive Business Media, Inc., 825 Old Country Rd., Box 1500, Westbury, NY 11590. TEL 516-334-3030.
circ. 11,000. *1863*

COLLEGIAN (ELYRIA).
Lorain County Community College, Student Activities Office, 1005 N. Abbe Rd., Elyria, OH 44035. TEL 216-365-5122. *1863*

COLLOQUIUM.
University of Alberta, c/o Dean of Engineering, 5-1 Mechanical Engineering Bldg., Edmonton, AB T6G 2H1, Canada. TEL 403-492-4514. FAX 403-492-0500.
circ. 11,600. *2751*

COLOMBO PLAN NEWSLETTER.
Colombo Plan Bureau, 12 Melbourne Ave., P.O. Box 596, Colombo 4, Sri Lanka. TEL 94-1-581813. FAX 94-1-581754.
circ. 2,500. *1303*

COLOR PUBLISHING.
PennWell Publishing Co. (Nashua), 10 Tara Blvd., 5th Fl., Nashua, NH 03062-2801. TEL 603-891-9168. FAX 603-891-0539.
circ. 24,000. *5993*

COLORADO MEDICINE.
Colorado Medical Society, 7800 E. Dorado Pl., Englewood, CO 80111. TEL 303-779-5455. FAX 303-771-8657.
circ. 5,500. *4444*

COLOUR.
Ulick Publishing Co., 150 Houston St., Ste. 308, Batavia, IL 60510-1953. TEL 708-406-8330.
circ. 80,000. *5993*

COLUMBAN MISSION.
Columban Fathers, St. Columbans, NE 68056. FAX 402-291-8693.
circ. 100,000. *6177*

COLUMBIA COLLEGE TODAY.
Columbia University, Columbia College, Office of Alumni Affairs, 475 Riverside Dr., Rm. 917, New York, NY 10115. TEL 212-870-2752. FAX 212-870-2747.
circ. 46,000. *1863*

COLUMBIA REVIEW.
Columbia University, Columbia Review, 101 Ferris Booth Hall, New York, NY 10027. TEL 212-854-3611.
circ. 500. *4197*

COLUMNS (SEATTLE).
University of Washington Alumni Association, 1415 N.E. 45th St., Seattle, WA 98105. TEL 206-543-0540. FAX 206-685-0611.
circ. 170,000. *1863*

COMBAT CREW.
U.S. Air Force Strategic Air Command, c/o Superintendent of Documents, Box 371954, Pittsburgh, PA 15250-7954. *5026*

COMBONI MISSIONS.
Comboni Missionaries of the Heart of Jesus, 8108 Beechmont Ave., Cincinnati, OH 45255. TEL 513-474-4997. FAX 513-474-0382.
circ. 25,000. *6177*

COMEDIA.
Commissariaat voor de Media, Postbus 1426, 1200 BK Hilversum, Netherlands. TEL 31-35-721721. FAX 31-35-721722. *1958*

COMERCIO HISPANO BRITANICO.
Spanish Chamber of Commerce in Great Britain, 5 Cavendish Sq., London WIM 0DP, England. TEL 071-637-9061. FAX 071-436-7188.
circ. 2,500. *1138*

COMERCIO Y PRODUCCION.
Chamber of Commerce of Puerto Rico, Box 3789, San Juan, PR 00904.
circ. 1,500. *1138*

COMICS RETAILER.
Krause Publications, Inc., 700 E. State St., Iola, WI 54990. TEL 715-445-2214. FAX 715-445-4087.
circ. 6,768. *1574*

COMISION ECONOMICA PARA AMERICA LATINA Y EL CARIBE. SERIE REFORMAS DE POLITICA PUBLICA.
Comision Economica para America Latina y el Caribe, Edificio Naciones Unidas, Av. Dag Hammarskjold, Casilla 197-D, Santiago, Chile. *1184*

COMMAND.
Officers' Christian Fellowship of the United States of America, Box 1177, Englewood, CO 80150-1177. TEL 303-761-1984. FAX 303-761-6226.
circ. 10,000. *5026*

THE COMMERCIAL IMAGE.
P T N Publishing Corp., 445 Broad Hollow Rd., Ste. 21, Melville, NY 11747-4722. TEL 516-845-2700. FAX 516-845-7109.
circ. 25,000. *5510*

COMMERCIAL INVESTMENT REAL ESTATE JOURNAL.
Commercial Investment Real Estate Institute, 430 N. Michigan Ave., Chicago, IL 60611-4092. TEL 312-321-4470. FAX 312-321-4530.
circ. 9,000. *6022*

COMMERCIAL NEWS U S A.
U.S. Department of Commerce, International Trade Administration, Rm. 1310, Washington, DC 20230. TEL 202-482-4918. FAX 202-482-5362. *1269*

COMMERCIAL PROPERTY NEWS.
Miller Freeman Inc. (New York) One Penn Plaza, New York, NY 10119. TEL 212-714-1300. FAX 212-714-1313.
circ. 35,521. *5022*

COMMERZBANK JOURNAL.
Commerzbank AG, Neue-Mainzer-Str. 32-36, 60311 Frankfurt a.M., Germany. TEL 49-69-1362-0. FAX 49-69-13629336.
circ. 260,000. *1077*

COMMISSION ON PRESERVATION AND ACCESS ANNUAL REPORT.
Commission on Preservation & Access, 1400 16th St., N.W., Ste. 740, Washington, DC 20036-2217. TEL 202-939-3400. FAX 202-939-3407.
circ. 2,500. *3986*

COMMISSION ON PRESERVATION AND ACCESS NEWSLETTER.
Commission on Preservation and Access, 1400 16th St., N.W., Ste. 740, Washington, DC 20036-2217. TEL 202-939-3400. FAX 202-939-3407.
circ. 2,000. *3986*

COMMON GROUND MAGAZINE.
356 Dupont St., Toronto, ON M5R 1V9, Canada. TEL 416-964-0528.
circ. 50,000. *5216*

COMMONWEALTH INSTITUTE, LONDON. ANNUAL REPORT.
Commonwealth Institute, Kensington High St., London W8 6NQ, England. TEL 44-171-603-4535. FAX 44-171-603-7374. *3251*

COMMONWEALTH LAW BULLETIN.
Commonwealth Secretariat, Publications Division, Marlborough House, Pall Mall, London S1Y 5HX, England. TEL 44-171-747-6389. FAX 44-171-930-0827.
circ. 1,700. *3881*

COMMUNICATE.
Economist Newspaper Ltd., 25 St. James's St., London SW1A 1HG, England. TEL 44-171-839-7000. FAX 44-171-839-2968.
circ. 15,500. *1944*

COMMUNICATIO.
Unisa Press, Periodicals, P.O. Box 392, Pretoria 0001, South Africa. TEL 27-12-4296565. FAX 27-12-4293346.
circ. 1,800. *1898*

COMMUNICATION RESEARCH TRENDS.
Centre for the Study of Communication and Culture, 321 N. Spring Ave., Box 56907, St. Louis, MO 63156-0907. TEL 314-977-7290. FAX 314-977-7296.
circ. 600. *1899*

COMMUNICATIONS INDUSTRIES REPORT.
International Communications Industries Association, 3150 Spring St., Fairfax, VA 22031-2399. TEL 703-273-7200. FAX 703-278-8082.
circ. 15,000. *1899*

COMMUNICATOR (LOS ANGELES).
The Librarians' Guild, AFSCME Local 2626, 234 Loma Dr., Los Angeles, CA 90026-5908.
circ. 400. *3986*

COMMUNIQUE (ITHACA).
Cornell University, Office of University Development, 55 Brown Rd., Ithaca, NY 14850-1266. TEL 607-254-7111. FAX 607-254-7167
circ. 17,000. *1863*

COMMUNITY NURSE.
Macmillan Magazines Ltd. Porters South, 4-6 Crinan St., London N1 9XW, England. TEL 44-171-833-4000. FAX 44-171-843-4640.
circ. 15,000. *4445*

COMMUNITY PHARMACY.
Miller Freeman Publishers Ltd. Sovereign Way, Tonbridge, Kent TN9 1RW England. TEL 44-1732-364422. FAX 44-1732-361534.
circ. 13,813. *5405*

COMMUNITY SERVICE NEWSLETTER.
Community Service, Inc., Box 243, Yellow Springs, OH 45387. TEL 513-767-2161.
circ. 350. *6409*

COMMUNITY TRANSPORTATION REPORTER.
Community Transportation Association of America, 1440 New York Ave., N.W., Ste. 440, Washington, DC 20005. TEL 202-628-1480. FAX 202-737-9197.
circ. 10,000. *6716*

COMPANY.
3441 N. Ashland Ave., Chicago, IL 60657. TEL 312-281-1534. FAX 312-281-2667.
circ. 115,000. *6177*

COMPANY CLOTHING.
Aquarius Publications, 578 Kingston Rd., Raynes Park, London SW20 8DR, England. TEL 081-544-9526. FAX 081-540-8388.
circ. 8,000. *1828*

COMPANY DIGEST.
Piton Publishing House Ltd. 79-81 High St., Godalming, Surrey GU7 1AW, England. TEL 44-1483-425454. FAX 44-1483-414262.
circ. 11,200. *909*

COMPASS (JACKSONVILLE).
Jacksonville University, 2800 University Blvd. N., Jacksonville, FL 32211. TEL 904-745-7045. FAX 904-775-7047.
circ. 17,000. *1863*

COMPASSION MAGAZINE (COLORADO SPRINGS).
Compassion International, Box 7000, Colorado Springs, CO 80933. TEL 719-594-9900. FAX 719-536-9618.
circ. 158,000. *6139*

COMPETITION ANGLER.
2160 Renwick Dr., Poland, OH 44514. TEL 216-757-8171.
circ. 500. *6560*

COMPILER.
Illinois Criminal Justice Information Authority, 120 S. Riverside Plaza, Rm. 1016, Chicago, IL 60606-3997. TEL 312-793-8550. FAX 312-793-8422.
circ. 9,000. *2160*

COMPLIANCE MAGAZINE.
I H S Publishing Group, Inc. 17730 W. Peterson Rd., Libertyville, IL 60048-C 59. TEL 847-362-8711. FAX 847-362-3484.
circ. 60,000. *5247*

COMPONENTS IN ELECTRONICS.
T A S Publishing Ltd., 80 Highgate Rd., London NW5 1PB, England. TEL 0171-267 9521. FAX 0171-485-9030.
circ. 18 292. *2509*

COMPOSANTS INSTRUMENTATION ELECTRONIQUES.
Elsevier - Thomas, 128 rue d'Aguesseau, 92100 Boulogne Billancourt, France. TEL 41-10-40-70. FAX 48-25-14-00.
circ. 25,000. *2509*

COMPRESSED AIR.
Compressed Air Magazine Co., 253 E. Washington Ave., Washington, NJ 07882. TEL 908-850-7818. FAX 908-689-5576.
circ. 140,000. *2752*

COMPUSERVE MAGAZINE.
CompuServe Inc., 5000 Arlington Centre Blvd., Columbus, OH 43220. TEL 614-457-8600. FAX 614-538-1004.
circ. 1,500,000. *2094*

COMPUTABLE.
V N U Business Publications B.V., Postbus 9194, 1006 CC Amsterdam, Netherlands. TEL 31-20-4875487. FAX 31-20-4875700.
circ. 69,870. *2071*

COMPUTER-AIDED ENGINEERING (CLEVELAND).
Penton Publishing Co. 1100 Superior Ave., Cleveland, OH 44114-2543. TEL 216-696-7000. FAX 216-696-8765.
circ. 60,000. *2677*

COMPUTER DESIGN.
PennWell Publishing Co. (Nashua), Advanced Technology Group, 10 Tara Blvd., 5th Fl., Nashua, NH 03062-2801. TEL 603-891-9111. FAX 603-891-0514.
circ. 106,000. *2026*

COMPUTER GRAPHICS.
Technews (Pty) Ltd., P.O. Box 626, Kloof 3640, South Africa. TEL 27-31-7640593. FAX 27-31-7640386.
circ. 4,595. *2026*

COMPUTER LAW ASSOCIATION BULLETIN.
Computer Law Association Inc., 3028 Javier Rd., Ste. 500 E, Fairfax, VA 22031. TEL 703-560-7747. FAX 703-207-7028.
circ. 1,300. *3889*

COMPUTER RESELLER NEWS.
C M P Publications, Inc., 600 Community Dr., Manhasset, NY 11030. TEL 516-562-5000. FAX 516-733-6916.
circ. 104,000. *2048*

COMPUTER SOURCES.
Asian Sources Media Group, 1038 Leigh Ave., Ste. 100, San Jose, CA 95126-4155. TEL 408-295-5900. FAX 408-295-4595.
circ. 30,000. *2033*

COMPUTEREPORT.
Virginia Commonwealth University, Academic Computing, 1015 Floyd Ave., Box 174, Richmond, VA 23284. TEL 804-786-4719. *1986*

COMPUTERLAND MAGAZINE.
ComputerLand Corporation, 5964 W. Las Positas, Pleasanton, CA 94588-8575. TEL 510-734-4087. FAX 510-734-4802.
circ. 270,000. *1153*

COMPUTERWORLD.
I D G Danmark A-S, Krumtappen 4, 2500 Valby, Denmark. TEL 36-44-28-00. FAX 36-44-20-33.
circ. 24,300. *1987*

COMPUTERWORLD HONG KONG.
I D G Communications (HK) Ltd., Mount Parker House, Ste. 1011-15, 1111 King's Rd., Quarry Bay, Hong Kong. TEL 852-2861-3238. FAX 852-2861-0953.
circ. 11,500. *2031*

COMPUTERWORLD SINGAPORE.
I D G Communications (S) Pte. Ltd., 80 Masire Pasade Rd., 13-09 Parkway Parade, Singapore 1544, Singapore. TEL 65-345-8383. FAX 65-345-7097.
circ. 24,793. *2031*

CONCATENATION.
5 Charlieville Rd., North Heath, Kent DA8 1HJ, England.
circ. 3,000. *4325*

CONCORDIA ALUMNI NEWS.
Concordia College, 901 S. Eighth St., Moorhead, MN 56562. TEL 218-299-4000. FAX 218-299-3646.
circ. 34,000. *1863*

CONCORDIA TORCH.
Concordia Mutual Life Association, 3041 Woodcreek Dr., Downers Grove, IL 60515. TEL 708-971-8000. FAX 708-971-9332.
circ. 17,000. *3646*

THE CONDENSER.
Tongaat-Hulett Group Ltd., P.O. Box 3, Tongaat 4400, Natal, South Africa. TEL 27-322-21000. FAX 27-322-21094.
circ. 14,000. *910*

CONFISERIE.
Editions de la Confiserie, 103 rue La Fayette, 75481 Paris Cedex 10, France. TEL 42-85-18-20. FAX 40-16-01-45.
circ. 4,000. *2999*

CONGRESOS CONVENCIONES E INCENTIVOS.
Princesa 1, Torre de Madrid, planta 13-2, 28008 Madrid, Spain. TEL 91-548-09-73. FAX 91-5479813.
circ. 6,000. *4933*

CONGRESSO.
Cura Enterprises Ltd., 10865 96th St., No. 11, Edmonton, AB T5H 2K2, Canada. TEL 403-424-3010.
circ. 5,000. *2873*

CONNECTICUT CONSTRUCTION HIGHLIGHTS OF THE WEEK.
Connecticut Construction Industries Association, Inc., 912 Silas Deane Hgwy., Wethersfield, CT 06109. TEL 860-529-6855. FAX 860-563-0616.
circ. 650. *846*

CONNECTICUT FAMILY.
New York Family Publications, Inc., 141 Halstead Ave., Ste. 3D, Mamaroneck, NY 10543-2652. TEL 914-381-7474.
circ. 30,000. *1765*

CONNECTICUT GOVERNMENT.
University of Connecticut, Institute of Public Service, Storrs, CT 06269-4014. TEL 203-486-2828.
5898

CONNECTICUT STATE DENTAL ASSOCIATION. JOURNAL.
Connecticut State Dental Association, 131 New London Tpke., Glastonburg, CT 06033. TEL 203-659-2623.
circ. 3,000. *4637*

CONNECTION (FALLS CHURCH).
National Association of Plumbing - Heating - Cooling Contractors, 180 S. Washington St., Falls Church, VA 22046-1148. TEL 703-237-8100. FAX 703-237-7442.
circ. 7,000. *3326*

CONNECTIONS.
Chartered Institute of Marketing, Moor Hall, Cookham, Maidenhead, Berkshire SL6 9QH, England. TEL 44-1628-427500. FAX 44-1628-427499.
circ. 25,000. *1459*

CONNECTIONS.
Muscular Dystrophy Association of Canada, 2345 Yonge St., 9th Fl., Toronto, ON M4P 2E5, Canada. TEL 416-488-0030. FAX 416-488-7523.
circ. 16,000. *4893*

CONNECTIVITY.
PC User Group, P.O. Box 360, 84-88 Pinner Rd., Harrow, Middx. HA1 4LQ, England. TEL 44-181-863-1191. FAX 44-181-863-6095.
circ. 10,000. *2094*

CONNSTRUCTION MAGAZINE.
McHugh Design, 62 LaSalle Rd., Ste. 211, W. Hartford, CT 06107. TEL 203-523-7518. FAX 203-231-8808.
circ. 7,000. *846*

CONSERVER.
British Trust for Conservation Volunteers, 36 St. Mary's St., Wallingford, Oxon. OX10 0EU, England. TEL 44-1491-839766. FAX 44-1491-839646.
circ. 20,000. *2124*

CONSTRUCTION ALBERTA NEWS.
Construction Alberta News Ltd., 10536 106th St., Edmonton, Alta. T5H 2X8, Canada. TEL 403-424-1146. FAX 403-425-5886.
circ. 3,962. *847*

CONSTRUCTION EQUIPMENT OPERATION AND MAINTENANCE.
Construction Publications, Inc., Box 1689, Cedar Rapids, IA 52406. TEL 319-366-1597. FAX 319-364-4853.
circ. 62,827. *848*

CONSULTING ENGINEERS OF BRITISH COLUMBIA. COMMENTARY.
Consulting Engineers of British Columbia, 514-409 Granville St., Vancouver, BC V6C 1T2, Canada. TEL 604-687-2811. FAX 604-688-7110.
circ. 2,000. *2593*

CONSUMER CHOICE.
Consumers Association of Ireland Ltd., 45 Upper Mount St., Dublin 2, Ireland. TEL 01-6686836. FAX 01-6612464.
circ. 10,000. *2150*

CONTACT (CRAWLEY).
Bowthorpe plc., Gatwick Rd., Crawley, W. Sussex RH10 2RZ, England. TEL 44-1293-528888. FAX 44-1293-541905.
circ. 7,000. *3153*

CONTACT (HANK).
E P S, P.O. Box 40, 4273 ZG Hank, Netherlands. TEL 31-162-403350. FAX 31-162-403802.
circ. 3,000. *4768*

CONTACT (QUEBEC).
Communications Services, Pavillon Alphonse Desjardins, Local 3577, Laval University, Quebec, PQ G1K 7P4, Canada. TEL 418-656-2571. FAX 418-656-2809.
circ. 90,000. *3119*

CONTACT MAGAZINE.
British Chiropractic Association, Gillets Farm House, Woodville, Stour Provost, Dorset SP8 5LX, England. TEL 44-1747-838553. FAX 44-1747-838039.
circ. 1,000. *4612*

CONTEMPORARY ORTHOPAEDICS.
Bobit Publishing Company, 2512 Artesia Blvd., Redondo Beach, CA 90278-3210. TEL 310-376-8788. FAX 310-376-9043.
circ. 30,000. *4782*

CONTEMPORARY SURGERY.
Bobit Publishing Company, 2512 Artesia Blvd., Redondo Beach, CA 90278-3210. TEL 310-376-8788. FAX 310-376-9043.
circ. 50,000. *4907*

CONTINGENCIES.
American Academy of Actuaries, 1100 17th St., N.W., 7 Fl., Washington, DC 20036. TEL 202-223-8196. FAX 202-872-1948.
circ. 22,000. *3646*

CONTRACT FURNISHING DIRECTORY.
British Contract Furnishing Association, Ste. 214, Business Design Centre, 52 Upper St., London N1 0QH, England. TEL 0171-226-6641. FAX 0171-228-6190.
circ. 3,000. *3685*

CONTRACTING BUSINESS.
Penton Publishing Co. 1100 Superior Ave., Cleveland, OH 44114-2543. TEL 216-696-7000. FAX 216-696-7932.
circ. 52,600. *3326*

CONTRACTOR'S GUIDE.
Century Communications Corp., 6201 W. Howard St., Niles, IL 60714-3435. TEL 708-647-1200. FAX 708-647-7055.
circ. 32,000. *850*

CONVENIENCE STORE DECISIONS.
Donohue - Meehan Publishing Company (Bensalem), 2 Greenwood Sq., Ste. 410, 3331 Street Rd., Bensalem, PA 19020-2023. TEL 215-245-4555. FAX 215-245-4060.
circ. 42,000. *3003*

CONVENIENCE STORE NEWS.
Macfadden Publishing, Macfadden Trade Publications, 233 Park Ave. S., 6th Fl., New York, NY 10003. TEL 212-780-2300. FAX 212-228-3142.
circ. 5,512. *3003*

CONVENIENT AUTOMOTIVE SERVICES RETAILER.
Graphic Concepts, Inc., 1801 Rockville Pike, Ste. 330, Rockville, MD 20852. TEL 301-984-4000. FAX 301-984-7340.
circ. 15,000. *6782*

CONVENTIONS & MEETINGS CANADA.
Effective Communications Ltd., 5762 Highway 7, Ste. 207, Markham, ON L3P 1A8, Canada. TEL 905-471-1550. FAX 905-471-1552.
circ. 10,416. *4934*

CONVENTIONSOUTH.
Covey Communications Corp., Box 2267, Gulf Shores, AL 36547. TEL 334-968-5300. FAX 334-968-4532.
circ. 10,000. *4934*

CONVERTER.
Faversham House Group Ltd., Faversham House, 232a Addington Rd., South Croydon, Surrey CR2 8LE, England. TEL 44-181-651-7100. FAX 44-181-651-7117.
circ. 3,780. *5321*

CONVERTING WORLD.
Maclean Hunter Ltd., Maclean Hunter House, Chalk Ln., Cockfosters Rd., Barnet, Herts EN4 0BU, England. TEL 081-975-9759. FAX 081-975-9764.
circ. 5,711. *5298*

COOP - ZEITUNG.
Coop Schweiz, Thiersteinerallee 12, Postfach 2550, CH-4002 Basel, Switzerland. TEL 41-61-3367118. FAX 41-61-3367072.
circ. 984,469. *1158*

COOPER HELLER RESEARCH. NEWSLETTER.
Cooper Heller Research, Inc., 622 S. 42nd St., Philadelphia, PA 19104. TEL 215-823-5490.
4043

COOPERATIVE FARMER.
Charles I. Batchelor, Ed. & Pub., Box 26234, Richmond, VA 23260. TEL 804-281-1317. FAX 804-281-1141.
circ. 178,262. *108*

COOPERAZIONE ITALIANA.
Editrice Cooperativa, Via G. Tomassetti 12, 00161 Rome, Italy. TEL 6-8844942. FAX 6-84439406.
circ. 20,000. *1159*

COPE.
Media America, Inc., Box 682268, Franklin, TN 37068-2268. TEL 615-790-2400. FAX 615-794-0179.
circ. 30,000. *4753*

COPPER TOPICS.
Copper Development Association Inc., 260 Madison Ave., New York, NY 10016-2401. TEL 212-251-7200. FAX 203-251-7234.
circ. 35,000. *4952*

COR ET VASA.
Praha Publishing Ltd., Anglicka 19, 120 00 Prague 2, Czech Republic. TEL 42-2-66312615. FAX 42-2-24247568. *4600*

COREL MAGAZINE.
Omray Inc., 9801 Anderson Mill Rd., Ste. 207, Austin, TX 78750. TEL 512-250-1700. FAX 512-219-3156.
circ. 7,000. *2027*

CORN FARMER.
Meredith Corporation, 1716 Locust St., Des Moines, IA 50336. TEL 515-284-2700.
circ. 68,000. *217*

CORNELL FOCUS.
Cornell University, Agricultural Experiment Station, 1150 Comstock Hall, College of Agriculture & Life Sciences, Ithaca, NY 14853. TEL 607-255-1876. FAX 607-255-9873.
circ. 5,000. *108*

CORNELL UNIVERSITY. NEW YORK STATE COLLEGE OF AGRICULTURE AND LIFE SCIENCES. BIOMETRICS UNIT. ANNUAL REPORT.
New York State College of Agriculture and Life Sciences, Department of Plant Breeding and Biometry, Cornell University, 337 Warren Hall, Ithaca, NY 14853. TEL 607-255-5488. FAX 607-255-4598. *618*

CORNHUSKER FAMILY PHYSICIAN.
Nebraska Academy of Family Physicians, 7101 Newport Ave., No. 201, Omaha, NE 68152-2158. TEL 402-572-3530. FAX 402-572-3532.
circ. 3,000. *4445*

CORNISH METHODIST HISTORICAL ASSOCIATION JOURNAL.
c/o Barrie S. May, Pelmear Villa, Carharrack, Redruth, Cornwall TR16 5RB, England. TEL 01209-820381.
circ. 300. *6140*

CORPORATE COMPUTING.
Ziff-Davis Publishing Co. (Foster City), 950 Tower Lane, Foster City, CA 94404. TEL 415-578-7600. FAX 415-578-7799.
circ. 155,000. *1153*

CORPORATE CRUISE NEWS.
Landry & Kling, Inc., 1390 S. Dixie Hwy., Ste. 1207, Coral Gables, FL 33146-2943. TEL 305-661-1880. *6875*

CORPORATE DETROIT MAGAZINE.
Corporate Detroit, Inc., 3031 W. Grand Blvd., Ste. 624, Detroit, MI 48202-3019. TEL 313-872-6000. FAX 313-872-6009.
circ. 27,000. *911*

CORPORATE EVENT SERVICES.
Showcase Publications Ltd., 38c The Broadway, London N8 9SU, England. TEL 44-181-348-2332. FAX 44-181-340-3750.
circ. 14,000. *4934*

CORPORATE REPORT MINNESOTA.
City Media, Inc., 821 Marquette Ave., Ste. 2000, Minneapolis, MN 55402-2000. TEL 612-359-2100. FAX 612-359-2110.
circ. 1,491. *1412*

CORPORATE UNIVERSITY REVIEW.
Enterprise Communications Inc., 1483 Chain Bridge Rd., Ste. 202, McLean, VA 22101. TEL 703-448-0336. FAX 703-448-0270.
circ. 17,000. *1500*

CORPORATION OF BRITISH COLUMBIA LAND SURVEYORS. REPORT OF PROCEEDINGS.
Corporation of British Columbia Land Surveyors, 895 Fort St., Ste. 306, Victoria, BC V8W 1H7, Canada. TEL 604-382-4323. FAX 604-382-5092.
circ. 500. *3251*

CORPUS CHRISTI BAY AREA BUSINESS.
Woolford Publishing 711 N. Carancahua St., Ste. 500, Corpus Christi, TX 78475-1301. TEL 512-883-8833. FAX 512-883-4329.
circ. 6,500. *911*

CORPUS CHRISTI MARINER NEWS.
Box 1960, Corpus, TX 78403. TEL 512-882-7262.
circ. 60. *6832*

CORPUS DES LUTHISTES FRANCAIS.
C N R S Editions, 20-22 rue St. Amand, 75015 Paris, France. TEL 45-33-16-00. FAX 45-33-92-13.
circ. 1,500. *5151*

CORPUS VITREARUM.
C N R S Editions, 20-22 rue St. Amand, 75015 Paris, France. TEL 45-33-16-00. FAX 45-33-92-13.
circ. 1,500. *424*

CORRECTIONS FORUM.
Corrections Forum, 320 Broadway, Bethpage, NY 11714. TEL 516-942-3601. FAX 516-942-3606.
circ. 14,600. *2161*

CORREIO AGRICOLA.
Bayer Portugal S A R L, Apdo. 3306, 1308 Lisbon, Portugal. TEL 417-21-21. FAX 417-20-64. *217*

CORREIO POPULAR.
Correio Popular S.A., Rua Conceicao, 124 (Centro), 13010-902 Campinas SP, Brazil. TEL 55-192-328588. FAX 55-192-318152.
circ. 1,000. *3117*

CORRESPONDENT (APPLETON).
Aid Association for Lutherans, 4321 N. Ballard Rd., Appleton, WI 54919. TEL 414-734-5721. FAX 414-730-3757.
circ. 920,000. *3646*

COSMETIC DERMATOLOGY.
Quadrant HealthCom, 105 Raider Blvd., Belle Mead, NJ 08502-1510. TEL 908-874-0707. FAX 908-874-5611.
circ. 13,403. *4659*

COSMETIC NEWS.
Seperm s.r.l., Via Giovanni Livragh 9, 20126 Milan, Italy. TEL 39-2-27001110. FAX 39-2-27000652.
circ. 3,000. *495*

THE COTTAGE GARDENER.
Cottage Garden Society, c/o Clive Lane, Sec., Hurstfield House, 244 Edleston Rd., Crewe, Ches CW2 7EJ, England. TEL 44-1270-250776. FAX 44-1270-250118.
circ. 5,500. *3048*

COTTAGE LIFE.
Quarto Communications, 111 Queen St. E., Ste. 408, Toronto, ON M5C 1S2, Canada. TEL 416-360-6880. FAX 416-360-6814.
circ. 14,000. *3120*

COUNCIL OF JEWISH THEATRES NEWSLETTER.
National Foundation for Jewish Culture, 330 Seventh Ave., 21st Fl., New York, NY 10001. TEL 212-629-0500. FAX 212-629-0508.
circ. 350. *6694*

COUNTERMAN.
Babcox Publications, 11 S. Forge St., Box 1810, Akron, OH 44309-1810. TEL 216-535-6617. FAX 216-535-0874.
circ. 50,500. *6782*

COUNTY NEWS.
National Association of Counties, 440 First St., N.W., Washington, DC 20001. TEL 202-393-6226. FAX 202-393-2630.
circ. 27,000. *5940*

THE COURIER.
Union Society, King's Walk, Newcastle-upon-Tyne NE1 8QB, England. TEL 44-191-232-4050. FAX 44-191-222-1876.
circ. 3,000. *1864*

COURIER (LEXINGTON).
National Tour Association, Inc., 546 E. Main St., Lexington, KY 40508-2342. TEL 606-253-1036. FAX 606-231-9837.
circ. 5,200. *6876*

COURT NEWS.
Judicial Council of California, Administrative Office of the California Courts, 303 Second St., S. Twr., San Francisco, CA 94107-1366. FAX 415-396-9349.
circ. 3,800. *3947*

COWARD FAMILY NEWSLETTER.
2140 Marion St., Birmingham AL 35226-3012. TEL 205-822-2446.
circ. 300. *3079*

CRESCENDO.
Toronto Musicians' Association 101 Thorncliffe Park Dr., Toronto, Ont. M4H 1M2, Canada. TEL 416-421-1020. FAX 416-421-7011.
circ. 5,600. *5152*

CRESCENDO (INTERLOCHEN).
Interlochen Center for the Arts, Interlochen Arts Camp, Interlochen, MI 49643. TEL 616-276-7200. FAX 616-276-6321.
circ. 58,000. *2322*

CRITERION (RIVERSIDE).
Riverside County Publishing Co., 7190 Jurupa Ave., Riverside, CA 92504-1016.
circ. 2,000. *1864*

CRITICA.
Universidad Nacional Autonoma de Mexico, Instituto de Investigaciones Filosoficas, Apdo. Postal 70-447, Mexico, D.F., Mexico.
circ. 800. *5472*

CROISSANCE PERSONNELLE.
Publications Neomag Inc., P.O. Box 339, Bellefeuille, PQ J0R 1A0, Canada. TEL 514-565-9256. FAX 514-565-2797.
circ. 21,000. *4938*

CROP PROTECTION COURIER (INTERNATIONAL).
Bayer AG, Abteilung Publikationen, 51368 Leverkusen, Germany. TEL 49-214-3062875. FAX 49-214-3071985.
circ. 33,500. *217*

CROSSROADS FOR MEETING PROFESSIONALS.
International Association of Convention and Visitor Bureaus, 2000 L St., N.W., Ste. 702, Washington, DC 20036-4990. TEL 202-296-7888. FAX 202-296-7889.
circ. 19,000. *4934*

CROSSTALK.
Zuerichsee Zeitschriftenverlag, Seestr. 86, CH-8712 Staefa, Switzerland. TEL 01-9285611. FAX 01-9285600.
circ. 70,000. *6934*

CROWN JOURNAL.
Higgs and Hill plc., Crown House, Kingston Rd., New Malden, Surrey KT3 3ST, England. TEL 44-181-942-8921. FAX 44-181-949-9280.
circ. 10,000. *851*

CROYDON AIRPORT SOCIETY JOURNAL.
Croydon Airport Society, 193 Commonside E., Mitcham, Surrey CR4 1HB, England. TEL 44-181-648-3906. FAX 44-181-770-4750.
circ. 800. *61*

CRUISE AND VACATION VIEWS.
Orban Communications, Inc., 25 Washington St., 4th Fl., Morristown, NJ 07960.
circ. 35,000. *6876*

CRUISE ENTERTAINMENT MAGAZINE.
Tony Rome Enterprises, Inc., 660 Livernois, Ferndale, MI 48220. TEL 810-545-9040. FAX 810-545-1073.
circ. 5,000. *3530*

CRUISING ASSOCIATION. HANDBOOK.
Cruising Association, C A House, 1 Northey St., Limestone Basin, London E14 8BT, England. TEL 44-171-537-2828. FAX 44-171-537-2266.
circ. 5,000. *6534*

CRUISING ASSOCIATION. MAGAZINE.
Cruising Association, C A House, 1 Northey St., Limestone Basin, London E14 8BT, England. TEL 44-171-537-2828. FAX 44-171-537-2266.
circ. 5,000. *6534*

CUADERNOS DE ECONOMIA.
Pontificia Universidad Catolica de Chile, Instituto de Economia, Casilla 76, Correo 17, Santiago, Chile. TEL 56-2-6864314. FAX 56-2-5521310. *912*

CUADERNOS DE SEGURIDAD.
Estudios Tecnicos, S.A., Xaudaro 9, 28034 Madrid, Spain. TEL 34-1-3580045. FAX 34-1-7293188.
circ. 3,833. *2182*

CUBA. OFICINA NACIONAL DE INVENCIONES, INFORMACION TECNICA Y MARCAS. BOLETIN OFICIAL.
Oficina Nacional de Invenciones, Informacion Tecnica y Marcas, Picota no. 15 c/o Luz y Acosta, Havana Vieja, C.P. 10100 Havana 1, Cuba. TEL 61-0185. FAX 537-338212.
circ. 200. *5337*

CUISINE ET VINS DE FRANCE.
Groupe Marie Claire, 11 bis., rue Boissy d'Anglas, 75008 Paris, France. TEL 1-42-66-88-88. FAX 47-42-89-16.
circ. 85,000. *2965*

CURRENT CANADIAN BOOKS.
John Coutts Library Services Ltd., 6900 Kinsmen, P.O. Box 1000, Niagara Falls, ON L2E 7E7, Canada. TEL 905-356-6382. FAX 905-356-5064.
circ. 100. *5994*

CURRENT SAUCE.
Northwestern State University of Louisiana, Student Publications, NSU Box 5306, Natchitoches, LA 71497. TEL 318-357-5213. FAX 318-357-6564.
circ. 3,500. *1864*

CURRENTS & EDDIES.
Connecticut River Watershed Council, Inc., 1 Ferry St., Easthampton, MA 01027-1244. TEL 413-529-9500. FAX 413-529-9501.
circ. 2,000. *2124*

CURTIS LINE.
Curtis Circulation Co., 2500 McClellan Ave., Pennsauken, NJ 08109-4660. TEL 609-488-5700. FAX 609-488-2219.
circ. 2,400. *5994*

CUSTOM BUILDER.
Gruner & Jahr U.S.A. Publishing, 110 Fifth Ave., New York, NY 10011-5601. TEL 207-828-4470. FAX 207-828-4478.
circ. 30,000. *851*

CUSTOM HOMES BOOK OF PLANS.
Custom Publishing Company Ltd. 45 Station Rd., Redhill, Surrey RH1 1QH, England. TEL 0737-767213. FAX 0737-771662.
circ. 40,000. *390*

CUSTOM TAILOR.
Custom Tailors and Designers Association of America, Inc., Box 53052, Washington, DC 20009-9052. TEL 212-661-1960.
circ. 1,000. *1832*

CUSTOM WOODWORKING BUSINESS.
Vance Publishing Corporation (Lincolnshire), Box 1414, Lincolnshire, IL 60069-1414. TEL 708-634-2600. FAX 708-634-4379.
circ. 60,000. *885*

CYSTISK FIBROSE.
Landsforeningen til Bekaempelse af Cystisk Fibrose, Hyrdebakken 246, DK-8800 Viborg, Denmark. TEL 45-86-67-44-22. FAX 45-86-67-66-66.
circ. 1,800. *4447*

D B M S.
Miller Freeman Inc. 411 Borel Ave. Ste. 100, San Mateo, CA 74402. TEL 415-358-9500. FAX 415-358-9855.
circ. 56,360. *2108*

D B Z.
Deutsche Briefmarkenzeitung GmbH & Co. KG, Postfach 1363, 56373 Nassau, Germany. TEL 02604-970144. FAX 02604-970151.
circ. 52,867. *5455*

D E C PROFESSIONNEL.
Presse Professionnelle SNC, 45 rue de Henri-de-Regnier, Versailles, France. TEL 39-53-95-26. FAX 39-02-39-71.
circ. 7,500. *1988*

D E R - DEPONIE ENTSORGUNG RECYCLING.
Verlag Binkert AG, Postfach 32, CH-5080 Laufenburg, Switzerland. TEL 41-62-8697272. FAX 41-62-8697333.
circ. 5,200. *2851*

D F W PEOPLE - THE AIRPORT NEWSPAPER.
Wood Publications, Inc., 400 Fuller-Wiser, Ste. 125, Euless, TX 76039. TEL 817-540-4666. FAX 817-685-7562.
circ. 13,000. *6754*

D G A A E NACHRICHTEN.
Deutsche Gesellschaft fuer Allgemeine und Angewandte Entomologie, Schwabenheimerstr. 101, 69221 Dossenheim, Germany. TEL 49-621-85238. FAX 49-621-861222.
circ. 800. *723*

D H LAWRENCE REVIEW.
Southwest Texas State University, Department of English, San Marcos, TX 78666. TEL 512-245-7682.
circ. 850. *4201*

D-I-Y RADIO.
Radio Society of Great Britain, Lambda House, Cranborne Rd., Potters Bar, Herts EN6 3JE, England. TEL 44-1707-659015. FAX 44-1707-645105.
circ. 10,000. *1935*

D I Y SUPERSTORE.
Faversham House Group Ltd., Faversham House, 232a Addington Rd., South Croydon, Surrey CR2 8LE, England. TEL 44-181-651-7100. FAX 44-181-651-7117.
circ. 4,631. *3603*

D J K - AKTIV.
Deutsche Jugendkraft e.V., Deutschhoeferstr. 17, 97422 Schweinfurt, Germany. TEL 09721-24163.
circ. 2,500. *6457*

D M E COMMUNICAZIONE.
Deus Editore s.r.l., Via Breno 1, 20139 Milan, Italy.
circ. 7,467. *1461*

D M NEWS.
D M News Corp. 19 W. 21st St., New York, NY 10010. TEL 212-741-2095. FAX 212-633-9367.
circ. 31,000. *1461*

D R C MISSISSIPPI NEWSLETTER.
Delta Resources Committee, Inc., 300 N. Edison St., Box 584, Greenville, MS 38702. TEL 601-335-3121. FAX 601-335-3123.
circ. 1,500. *6140*

D R D O NEWSLETTER.
Defence Research & Development Organization, Metcalfe House, New Delhi 110 054, India. TEL 011-2932252. FAX 011-2919151.
circ. 1,900. *5660*

D S S NEWSLETTER.
Department of Social Services, Public Information Office, 1510 Guilford Ave., Baltimore, MD 21202. TEL 301-361-2002. FAX 301-361-3150.
circ. 4,000. *6369*

D S W R.
C.H. Beck'sche Verlagsbuchhandlung, Wilhelmstr. 9, 80801 Munich, Germany. TEL 089-38189-338. FAX 089-38189-398.
circ. 35,900. *2072*

DAG OG TID.
Pilestredet 8, N-0180 Oslo, Norway. TEL 47-22-33-00-97. FAX 47-22-41-42-10.
circ. 6,011. *3199*

DAILY CAMPUS (DALLAS).
Student Media Company, Inc., 3140 Dyer St., Dallas, TX 75275. TEL 214-768-4555. FAX 214-768-4573.
circ. 4,500. *1864*

DAILY INQILAB.
Inqilab Enterprise & Publications Ltd., 2-1 R.K. Mission Rd., Dhaka 1203, Bangladesh. TEL 880-2-868440. FAX 880-2-833122.
circ. 5,000. *3114*

DAILY OTHER.
MacMurray College, Journalism Program, Jacksonville, IL 62650. TEL 217-479-7049.
circ. 700. *1865*

DAILY PURBANCHAL.
Purbanchal Publishers, 38 Iqbal Nagar, Khulna 9100, Bangladesh. TEL 880-41-22251. FAX 880-2-839209.
circ. 3,000. *3114*

DAILY TIMES.
Daily Times of Nigeria Ltd., Publications Division, New Isheri Rd., P.M.B. 21340, Agidingbi, Ikeja, Lagos State, Nigeria. TEL 234-1-4900840. FAX 234-1-6421333.
circ. 250,000. *3198*

DAILY TRADE NEWS.
Korea Foreign Trade Association, 159-1 Samsung-dong, Dang-nam-ku, Seoul 135-729, S. Korea. TEL 02-551-5441. FAX 02-551-5400.
circ. 20,000. *1270*

DAINIK MEILLAT.
Daily Meillat, 28 Toyenbee Circular Rd., Motijheel Commercial Area, Dhaka 1000, Bangladesh. TEL 880-2-240026. FAX 880-2-863797.
circ. 10,000. *3114*

DAIRY FIELD.
Stagnito Publishing Company, 1935 Shermer Rd., Ste. 100, Northbrook, IL 60062. TEL 847-205-5660. FAX 847-205-5680.
circ. 18,000. *248*

DAIRY WORLD.
Independent Buyers Association Inc., 27 Providence
Rd., Millbury, MA 01527. TEL 508-865-2507.
circ. 41,250. *249*

DALLAS - FORT WORTH HOME BUYER'S GUIDE.
Home Buyer's Guide (Dallas), 5501 LBJ Frwy., Ste.
300, Dallas, TX 75240-6202. TEL 214-239-2399.
circ. 75,000. *6023*

DANCE EAST.
B C Publications, 16C Market Pl., Diss, Norfolk
IP22 3AB, England. TEL 44-1379-644200.
FAX 44-1379-650480.
circ. 2,500. *2187*

DANCE INK.
Dance Ink, Inc., 145 Central Park W., New York, NY
10023. TEL 212-228-0540. FAX 212-228-0654.
circ. 2,000. *2188*

DANCE RESEARCH.
Oxford University Press, Oxford Journals, Walton St.,
Oxford OX2 6DP, England. TEL 01865-267907.
FAX 01865-267773.
circ. 650. *2188*

**DANGEROUS PROPERTIES OF INDUSTRIAL
MATERIALS REPORT.**
Van Nostrand Reinhold, 115 Fifth Ave., New York,
NY 10003. TEL 212-254-3232. FAX 212-673-
1239.
circ. 2,000. *5248*

DANSK LANDBRUG.
Vest Media A-S, Storegade 28, Skansen, 6800
Varde, Denmark. TEL 75 22 44 00. FAX 75-22-44-
77.
circ. 126,495. *110*

DANSK SMEDE-TIDENDE.
Danmarks Smedemesterforening, Magnoliavej 2,
DK-5250 Odense SV, Denmark. TEL 45-66-17-33-
12. FAX 45-66-17-36-12.
circ. 3,700. *4953*

DANSKE MALERMESTRE.
Danske Malermestre, Snaregade 12, DK-1205
Copenhagen K, Denmark. TEL 45-33-93-36-00.
FAX 45-33-93-42-10.
circ. 3,200. *5306*

DANSKE PIONEER.
Bertelsen Publishing Co., 1582 Glen Lake Rd.,
Hoffman Estates, IL 60195. TEL 847-882-2552.
FAX 847-882-7082.
circ. 3,400. *2874*

DANSKE VOGNMAEND.
Danske Vognmaend Hovedorganisationen,
Gammeltorv 18, 1457 Copenhagen K, Denmark.
TEL 33-13-88-00. FAX 33-32-57-07.
circ. 6,900. *6856*

DATA MANAGEMENT REVIEW.
Powell Publishing, Inc., 19380 Emerald Dr.,
Brookfield, WI 53045-3617. TEL 414-792-9696.
FAX 414-792-9777.
circ. 50,000. *2065*

DATA NEWS.
Diligentia Business Press N.V., 42 av. du Houx,
1170 Brussels, Belgium. TEL 32-2-6781611.
FAX 32-2-6603600.
circ. 23,400. *1926*

DATACOM.
E M A P Business Communications, E M A P
Computing, Greater London House, Hampstead Rd.,
London NW1 7QZ, England. TEL 0171-388-2430.
FAX 0171-388-2480.
circ. 21,000. *2036*

DATAPACK.
Quest Magazines Ltd., Publishing House, 652
Victoria Rd., South Ruislip, Mddx. HA4 0SX,
England. TEL 44-181-842-1010. FAX 44-181-841-
2557.
circ. 3,000. *1595*

DATATID.
Datatid AS, P.O. Box 2476 Solli, N-0202 Oslo,
Norway. TEL 47-22-94-76-00. FAX 47-22-94-76-
07.
circ. 22,000. *1988*

DATAWEEK.
Technews (Pty) Ltd., P.O. Box 626, Kloof 3640,
South Africa. TEL 27-31-7640593. FAX 27-31-
7640386.
circ. 3,482. *6648*

DATELINE WINNIPEG.
Better Business Bureau of Winnipeg & Manitoba,
301-365 Hargrave St., Winnipeg, MB R3B 2K3,
Canada. TEL 204-942-7166. FAX 204-943-1489.
circ. 2,000. *913*

DATENSCHUTZ NACHRICHTEN.
Deutsche Vereinigung fuer Datenschutz, Reuterstr.
44, 53113 Bonn, Germany. TEL 49-228-222498.
circ. 500. *2050*

DATENSCHUTZ UND INFORMATIONSRECHT.
Oesterreichische Gesellschaft fuer Datenschutz,
Sautergasse 20, A-1170 Vienna, Austria. TEL 43-1-
4897893. FAX 43-1-4897899310.
circ. 800. *2050*

**DAVID DAVIES MEMORIAL INSTITUTE OF
INTERNATIONAL STUDIES. OCCASIONAL PAPER.**
David Davies Memorial Institute of International
Studies, 2 Chadwick St., London SW1P 2EP,
England. TEL 44-171-222-4063. FAX 44-171-233-
2863.
circ. 1,000. *5746*

DAYTON BUSINESS REPORTER.
Hannover Publishing Co., Inc., 6356 Far Hills Ave.,
Dayton, OH 45459-2782. TEL 513-291-1100.
FAX 513-436-3426.
circ. 10,000. *913*

DE VERE HOTELS MAGAZINE.
Media Partners CPR, Northern Rock House, 20
Market Pl., Guisborough, Cleveland TS14 6HF,
England. TEL 44-1287-639111. FAX 44-1287-
637201.
circ. 30,000. *5560*

DEALER BUSINESS.
M H West, Inc. 5743 Corsa Ave., Ste. 220,
Westlake Village CA 91362-4027. TEL 818-997-
0644. FAX 818-997-1058.
circ. 33,501. *6782*

DEALERNEWS.
Advanstar Communications, Inc., 7500 Old Oak
Blvd., Cleveland, OH 44130. TEL 216-826-2839.
FAX 216-891-2726.
circ. 14,203. *6523*

DEALERS' CHOICE.
Texas Automobile Dealers Association, 1108 Lavaca
St., Box 1028, Austin, TX 78767-1028. TEL 512-
476-2686. FAX 512-476-2179.
circ. 1,800. *6732*

DEEPWATER.
Greater Baton Rouge Port Commission, Box 380,
Pt. Allen, LA 70767. TEL 504-342-1660. FAX 504-
342-1666.
circ. 1,000. *6832*

DEFENSE INDUSTRY & AEROSPACE REPORT.
Business Communications Group, P.O. Box 250,
Mawson, A.C.T. 2607, Australia. TEL 61-6-
2864605. FAX 61-6-2863441.
circ. 6,000. *5028*

DEFENSE TRANSPORTATION JOURNAL.
National Defense Transportation Association, 50
South Pickett St., No. 220, Alexandria, VA 22304-
3008. TEL 703-751-5011. FAX 703-823-8761.
circ. 8,500. *6716*

DEGREES NORTH.
University of Leeds, Alumni Office, 18 Blenheim
Terrace, Leeds LS2 9HD, England. TEL 44-113-
233-6023. FAX 44-113-233-6026.
circ. 55,000. *1856*

DEHI RAZAKAR.
National Farm Guide Council of Pakistan, c/o Dr. A.
Rahim Chaudhary. Chairman, 405 Ferozepur Rd.,
Lahore 54600, Pakistan. TEL 92-42-5864155.
FAX 92-42-5864155. *110*

DEKE QUARTERLY.
Delta Kappa Epsilon Fraternity, Inc., 35 McKinley
Place, Grosse Pte Farms, MI 48236. TEL 313-886-
2400. FAX 313-8362227.
circ. 25,000. *1848*

DEL CONDOMINIUM LIFE.
Del Property Management Inc., 4800 Dufferin St.,
Downsview, ON M3H 5S9, Canada. TEL 416-736-
2552. FAX 416-661-8923.
circ. 25,000. *3676*

DELAWARE BEVERAGE MONTHLY
Melton Communications Inc., 1518 N. Van Buren
St., Wilmington, DE 19806. TEL 302-655-2800.
FAX 302-655-2805.
circ. 1,800. *504*

DELEGATES.
Blenheim, Blenheim House, 630 Chiswick High Rd.,
London W4 5BG, England. TEL 44-181-742-2828.
FAX 44-181-742-0387.
circ. 17,307. *4934*

DELTA EPSILON SIGMA JOURNAL.
Delta Epsilon Sigma National Scholastic Honor
Society, c/o George Hernd., Ed., Belmont Abbey
College, Belmont, NC 28012. TEL 704-825-5026.
FAX 305-899-3026.
circ. 20,000. *1866*

DELTA OPTIMIST.
Today Publishing Ltd., 5435 48th Ave., Delta, BC
V4K 1X2, Canada. TEL 604-946-4451. FAX 604-
946-5680.
circ. 15,000. *3120*

DELUXE.
Maxwell Custom Publishing 1999 Shepard Rd., St.
Paul, MN 55116. TEL 612-690-7200. FAX 612-
690-7357. *1082*

DENKMALPFLEGE INFORMATIONEN.
Bayerisches Landesamt fuer Denkmalpflege,
Hofgraben 4, 80539 Munich, Germany. TEL 089-
2114-213. FAX 089-2114-300.
circ. 3,000. *5899*

DENTAL ASSISTANT JOURNAL.
American Dental Assistants Association, 203 N. La
Salle St., Ste. 1320, Chicago, IL 60601-1210.
TEL 312-541-1550. FAX 312-541-1496.
circ. 15,000. *4638*

DENTAL HEALTH.
British Dental Hygienists' Association, St. Luke,
Maywood Dr., Portsmouth Rd., Camberley, Surrey
GU15 1LH, England. TEL 44-1276-677156.
FAX 44-1276-671072.
circ. 2,200. *4638*

DENTAL PRODUCTS REPORT.
Medical Economics Publishing Co., Inc., 5 Paragon
Dr., Montvale, NJ 07645. TEL 201-358-7246.
FAX 201-573-0344.
circ. 147,801. *4639*

DENTISTRY IN SOUTH DAKOTA.
South Dakota Dental Association, 330 S. Poplar
Ave., Box 1194, Pierre, SD 57501 1194. TEL 605-
224-9133. FAX 605-224-9168.
circ. 500. *4640*

DENTISTRY TODAY.
Dentistry Today, Inc., 26 Park St., Montclair, NJ
07042. TEL 201-783-3190. FAX 201-783-6835.
circ. 140,000. *4640*

DENVER HOUSING GUIDE.
Baker Publications, 14406 E Evans Ave., Ste. 200,
Aurora, CO 80014-1479. TEL 303-695-8440.
FAX 303-695-8449.
circ. 70,000. *6023*

**DEPARTMENT STORE WORKERS' UNION. LOCAL 1-S
NEWS.**
Department Store Workers' Union, Local 1- S, Retail,
Wholesale and Dept. Store Union, A F L - C I O, 140
W. 31st St., New York, NY 10001.
circ. 10,000. *3720*

DESARROLLO NACIONAL.
Intercontinental Media, P.O. Box 3410, Milford, CT
06460. TEL 203-874-1401. FAX 203-222-8793.
circ. 22,000. *2657*

DESERT AIRMAN.
Territorial Newspapers, P.O. Box 27087, Tucson, AZ
85726-7087. TEL 602-297 107. FAX 602-297-
6253.
circ. 11,500. *5029*

DESERT MOBILE HOME NEWS.
Box 3386, Palm Desert, CA 92261. TEL 619-568-6633.
circ. 10,000. *3227*

DESIGN - BUILD BUSINESS.
McKellar Publications, Inc., 333 E. Glenoaks Blvd., Ste. 204, Glendale, CA 91207-2074. TEL 818-241-0250. FAX 818-241-4406.
circ. 57,000. *852*

DESIGN COST & DATA.
L M Rector Corporation, 8602 N. 40th St., Tampa, FL 33604. TEL 813-989-9300. FAX 813-980-3982.
circ. 12,500. *391*

DESIGN NEWS O E M - SUPPLIERS SPECIAL ISSUE.
Cahners Publishing Company (Newton), Division of Reed Elsevier Inc., 275 Washington St., Newton, MA 02158-1630. TEL 617-964-3030. FAX 617-558-4470. *4337*

DESIGN PRODUCT NEWS.
Action Communications Inc., 135 Spy Court, Markham, ON L3R 5H6, Canada. TEL 905-477-3222. FAX 905-477-4320.
circ. 19,020. *2594*

DESIGNS.
Association Communication Innovation Designs 4, 85 St. Paul St. W., Montreal, PQ H2Y 3V4, Canada. TEL 514-842-4436. FAX 514-848-9730.
circ. 13,900. *3676*

DESKTOP PUBLISHING TODAY.
Andrew Bond, Ed. & Pub., Vine House, East St., Harrietsham, Maidstone, Kent ME17 1HJ, England. TEL 01732-359990. FAX 01732-770049.
circ. 10,500. *6016*

DESTINATION CALGARY.
Calgary Convention & Visitors Bureau, 237 Eighth Ave., S.E., Calgary, AB T2G OK8, Canada. TEL 403-750-8510. FAX 403-262-3809.
circ. 1,100. *6877*

DEUCE.
University of Central England, Students' Union, Perry Barr, Birmingham B42 2SU, England. TEL 44-121-356-8164. FAX 44-121-344-3670.
circ. 4,000. *1866*

DEUTSCHE EINHEITSVERFAHREN ZUR WASSER-, ABWASSER- UND SCHLAMMUNTERSUCHUNG.
V C H Verlagsgesellschaft mbH, Postfach 101161, 69451 Weinheim, Germany. TEL 06201-606-0. FAX 06201-606328.
circ. 5,500. *2835*

DEUTSCHE MILCHWIRTSCHAFT.
Verlag Th. Mann, Nordring 10, 45894 Gelsenkirchen, Germany. TEL 49-209-9304184. FAX 49-209-9304185.
circ. 3,512. *249*

DEUTSCHER RAT FUER LANDESPFLEGE. SCHRIFTENREIHE.
Deutscher Rat fuer Landespflege, Konstantinstr. 110, 53179 Bonn, Germany. TEL 0228-331097. FAX 0228-334727.
circ. 2,000. *2782*

DEUTSCHES DISCOTHEKEN JAHRBUCH.
Verlag Disco Post GmbH, Oststr. 2, 56424 Staudt, Germany. TEL 49-2602-70044. FAX 49-2602-69939.
circ. 10,000. *1848*

DEUTSCHES INSTITUT FUER WIRTSCHAFTSFORSCHUNG. ECONOMIC BULLETIN.
Deutsches Institut fuer Wirtschaftsforschung, Koenigin-Luise-Str. 5, 14195 Berlin, Germany. TEL 49-30-897890. FAX 49-30-89789200.
circ. 400. *1203*

DEUTSCHES SOLDATENJAHRBUCH.
Schild-Verlag GmbH, Henschelstr. 7, 81249 Munich, Germany. TEL 49-89-8641189. FAX 49-89-8632310.
circ. 7,000. *5029*

DEUTSCHES STEUERRECHT.
C.H. Beck'sche Verlagsbuchhandlung, Wilhelmstr. 9, 80801 Munich, Germany. TEL 089-38189-338. FAX 089-38189-398.
circ. 25,135. *1541*

THE DEVELOPER.
Foundation for African Development, P.O. Box 16206, Kampala, Uganda. TEL 256-41-231824. FAX 256-41-251243.
circ. 2,000. *1304*

DIA CUATRO QUE FUERA...
Junta Central de Fiestas de Moros y Cristianos, Palacio Municipal, Villena, Alicante, Spain. *6458*

DIABETES.
Finnish Diabetes Association, Kirjoniementie 15, 33680 Tampere, Finland. TEL 358-31-28-60-111. FAX 358-31-3600-462.
circ. 50,000. *4667*

DIABETES PATH FINDER.
American Diabetes Association, Washington Affiliate, Inc., 557 Roy St., Lower Lever, Seattle, WA 98109. TEL 206-282-4616. FAX 206-282-4729.
circ. 15,000. *4668*

DIABETES SELF-MANAGEMENT.
R.A. Rapaport Publishing, Inc., 150 W. 22nd St., New York, NY 10011. TEL 212-989-0200. FAX 212-989-4786.
circ. 30,000. *4668*

DIABETES UND STOFFWECHSEL.
Verlag Kirchheim und Co. GmbH, Kaiserstr. 41, 55116 Mainz, Germany. TEL 49-6131-96070-0. FAX 49-6131-9607070.
circ. 13,000. *4668*

DIABLO.
Diablo Publications, 2520 Camino Diablo, Walnut Creek, CA 94596. TEL 510-943-1111. FAX 510-943-1045.
circ. 50,000. *3227*

DIAKONIESCHWESTER.
Ev. Diakonieverein e.V., Glockenstr. 8, 14163 Berlin, Germany. TEL 030-8018091. FAX 030-8022452.
circ. 3,500. *6057*

DIAL ELECTRICAL - ELECTRONICS.
Dial Industry Publications Windsor Ct., Grinstead House, E. Grinstead, W. Sussex RH19 1XA, England. TEL 44-1342-326972. FAX 44-1342-335247.
circ. 15,000. *2511*

DIAL ENGINEERING.
Dial Industry Publications Windsor Ct., East Grinstead House, E. Grinstead, W. Sussex RH19 1XA, England. TEL 44-1342-326972. FAX 44-1342-335747.
circ. 18,000. *2730*

DIALOGO SOCIAL.
Centro de Capacitacion Social, Apdo. 9a-192, Calle 66AE, Carasquilla, Panama. TEL 29-1542.
circ. 7,800. *6411*

DIANGONG JISHU XUEBAO.
China Machine Press, 1 Nanjie, Baiwanzhuang, Beijing 100037, People's Republic of China. TEL 8610-8326677. FAX 8610-8326337.
circ. 3,000. *2689*

DIANNAO KAIFA YU YINGYONG.
Beifang Zidong Kongzhi Jishu Yanjiusuo, P.O. Box 8, Qi Xian (County), Shanxi 030900, People's Republic of China. TEL 86-351-7043553. FAX 86-351-7042975.
circ. 500. *1989*

DIBEVO VAKBLAD.
Landelijke Organisatie DIBEVO, Postbus 94, 3800 AB Amersfoort, Netherlands. TEL 31-33-550433. FAX 31-33-552835.
circ. 5,770. *5389*

AL-DIBLOMASI.
Ministry of Foreign Affairs, Department of Legal Affairs and Studies, P.O. Box 1, Abu Dhabi, United Arab Emirates. TEL 652200. FAX 668015.
circ. 500. *5747*

DICKINSON COUNTY HERITAGE CENTER. GAZETTE.
Dickinson County Heritage Center, 412 S. Campbell St., Abilene, KS 67410-2905. TEL 913-263-2681.
circ. 600. *3466*

DICTUM.
New Jersey State Bar Association, One Constitution Sq., New Brunswick, NJ 08901-1500. TEL 908-249-5000. FAX 908-828-0034.
circ. 3,000. *3768*

DIENST LANDBOUWKUNDIG ONDERZOEK. STARING CENTRUM, INSTITUUT VOOR ONDERZOEK VAN HET LANDELIJK GEBIED. JAARVERSLAG.
Dienst Landbouwkundig Onderzoek, Staring Centrum, Instituut voor Onderzoek van het Landelijk Gebied, P.O. Box 125, 6700 AC Wageningen, Netherlands. TEL 31-317-474200. FAX 31-317-424812.
circ. 2,500. *2782*

DIER - EN - ARTS.
Transmondial B.V., Baron van Nagellstr. 27, 3781 AP Voorthuizen, Netherlands. TEL 31-342-473135. FAX 31-342-473154.
circ. 3,200. *6945*

DIESEL & GAS TURBINE WORLDWIDE.
Diesel & Gas Turbine Publications, 13555 Bishop's Court, Brookfield, WI 53005-6286. TEL 414-784-9177. FAX 414-784-8133.
circ. 21,000. *2752*

A DIFFERENT LIGHT REVIEW.
A Different Light Bookstores, 151 W. 19th St., New York, NY 10011. TEL 212-989-4850. FAX 212-989-2158.
circ. 60,000. *3530*

DIGEST OF LABOUR CASES.
V. Subramanian, Ed. & Pub., 337 Thambu Chetty St., Madras 600001, India.
circ. 280. *3769*

DIGGER.
Oregon Association of Nurserymen, 2780 S.E. Harrison, Ste. 102, Milwaukie, OR 97222. TEL 503-653-8733. FAX 503-653-1528.
circ. 4,710. *3049*

DIGITAL NEWS & REVIEW.
Cahners Publishing Company (Newton), Division of Reed Elsevier Inc., 275 Washington St., Newton, MA 02158-1630. TEL 617-964-3030. FAX 617-558-4759.
circ. 60,000. *2086*

DIGITAL TECHNICAL JOURNAL.
Digital Equipment Corporation, LJO2/D10, 30 Porter Rd., Littleton, MA 01460-1446. TEL 508-486-2538. FAX 508-486-2444.
circ. 18,000. *2020*

DIGNITY - U S A.
Dignity - U S A, 1500 Massachusetts Ave. N.W., Ste. 11, Washington, DC 20005. TEL 219-484-6492.
circ. 500. *3530*

DIMENSIONAL STONE MAGAZINE.
Dimensional Stone Institute, Inc., 6300 Variel Ave., Ste. I, Woodland Hills, CA 91367-2513. TEL 818-704-5555. FAX 818-704-6500.
circ. 15,000. *852*

DIPLOMAT.
Diplomatist Associates Ltd., 58 Theobalds Rd., London, England. TEL 0171-405-4878. FAX 0171-831-0667.
circ. 3,000. *5747*

DIPLOMATE.
American Board of Professional Psychology, 2100 E. Broadway, Ste. 313, Columbia, MO 65201-6082. TEL 573-875-1267. FAX 573-443-1199.
circ. 3,000. *5840*

DIPLOMATISCHER PRESSEDIENST.
Diplomatischer Pressedienst, Neustiftgasse 104, A-1070 Vienna, Austria. TEL 43-1-5268080. FAX 43-1-5261810.
circ. 5,000. *5747*

DIRASAT. HUMAN AND SOCIAL SCIENCES.
University of Jordan, Deanship of Academic Research, Amman, Jordan. TEL 962-6-843555. FAX 962-6-840263.
circ. 1,000. *3612*

DIRASAT. NATURAL AND ENGINEERING SCIENCES.
University of Jordan, Deanship of Academic
Research, Amman, Jordan. TEL 962-6-843555.
FAX 962-6-840263.
circ. 1,000. *6237*

DIRECT FROM MIDREX.
Midrex Direct Reduction Corporation, Charlotte
Plaza, Charlotte, NC 28244. TEL 704-373-1600.
FAX 704-373-1611.
circ. 2,000. *4953*

DIRECT MARKETING NEWS.
C D M N Publishing, 1200 Markham Rd., Ste. 301,
Scarborough, ON M1H 3C3, Canada. TEL 416-439-
4083. FAX 416-439-4086.
circ. 7,000. *1462*

DIRECT RESPONSE.
Brainstorm Publishing Co., 4 Market Pl., Hertford,
Herts. SG14 1EB, England. TEL 01992-501177.
FAX 01992-500387.
circ. 7,400. *1462*

DIRECTIONS.
New Zealand Automobile Association, 342 Lambton
Quay, P.O. Box 1, Wellington, New Zealand. TEL 64-
4-4738738. FAX 64-4-4712080.
circ. 520,747. *3196*

DIRECTIONS FOR UTAH LIBRARIES.
Department of Community and Economic
Development, State Library Division, 2150 S. 300
W., Ste. 16, Salt Lake City, UT 84115. TEL 801-
466-5888. FAX 801-533-4657.
circ. 1,900. *3988*

DIRECTOR.
N F D A Publications, Inc., 11121 W. Oklahoma
Ave., Box 27641, Milwaukee, WI 53227-0641.
TEL 414-541-2500. FAX 414-541-1909.
circ. 275. *3040*

**DIRECTOR OF SELECTIVE SERVICE. ANNUAL
REPORT.**
U.S. Selective Service System, 1515 Wilson Blvd.,
Arlington, VA 22209. TEL 703-235-2053. *5029*

DIRECTORIO DE LA INDUSTRIA CARNICA.
Alfa Editores Tecnicos S.A., Libertad No. 107-402,
03660 Mexico DF, Mexico. TEL 525-579-3333.
FAX 525-532-9504.
circ. 5,000. *1596*

**DIRECTORIO DE LA INDUSTRIA MEXICANA DE
BEBIDAS.**
Alfa Editores Tecnicos S.A., Libertad No. 107-402,
03660 Mexico DF, Mexico. TEL 525-579-3333.
FAX 525-532-9504.
circ. 5,000. *1596*

DIRECTORIO DE LACTEOS MEXICANOS.
Alfa Editores Tecnicos S.A., Libertad No. 107-402,
03660 Mexico DF, Mexico. TEL 525-579-3333.
FAX 525-532-9504.
circ. 5,000. *1596*

DIRECTORIO HISPANO.
685 S. Hwy. 427, Longwood, FL 32750-6403.
TEL 407-767-0070. FAX 407-767-5478.
circ. 50,000. *1596*

DIRECTORIO INDUSTRIAL Y COMERCIAL.
Legis S.A., Av. Eldorado 81-10, Apdo. Aereo
98888, Bogota, Colombia. TEL 91-263-2990.
FAX 91-410-0628.
circ. 50,000. *1596*

**DIRECTORIO INTERNACIONAL DE LA INDUSTRIA
PESQUERA Y LA AQUACULTURA.**
Alfa Editores Tecnicos S.A., Libertad No. 107-402,
03660 Mexico DF, Mexico. TEL 525-579-3333.
FAX 525-5329504.
circ. 5,000. *1596*

**DIRECTORY IN RUSSIAN OF BRITISH FIRMS
INTERESTED IN TRADE WITH THE F S U.**
Exact Communications Ltd., 90 Moorsom St.,
Birmingham B6 4NT, England. TEL 44-121-333-
4644. FAX 44-121-333-5823. *1271*

DIRECTORY OF FIRMS.
Structural Engineers Trading Organisation Ltd., 11
Upper Belgrave St., London SW1X 8BH, England.
TEL 44-171-235-4535. FAX 44-171-235-4294.
circ. 5,000. *1599*

DIRECTORY OF FLORIDA INDUSTRIES.
Harris InfoSource International, 2057 E. Aurora Rd.,
Twinsburg, OH 44087-1999. TEL 216-425-9000.
FAX 216-425-7150.
circ. 5,000. *1599*

DIRECTORY OF FULBRIGHT ALUMNI.
United States Educational Foundation in India,
Fulbright House, 12 Hailey Rd., New Delhi 110001,
India. *2426*

DIREKT-KONTAKT BETRIEBSBEDARF.
Konradin Verlag Robert Kohlhammer GmbH, Ernst-
Mey-Str. 8, 70771 Leinfelden-Echterdingen,
Germany. TEL 49-711-7594-0. FAX 49-711-
7594390.
circ. 25,000. *1462*

DISABILITY TIMES.
Disability Times Ltd., 27 Delancey St., Regent's
Park, London NW1 7RX, England. TEL 44-171-
380-0099. FAX 44-171-387-7575.
circ. 19,500. *3304*

DISASTER RECOVERY JOURNAL.
Systems Support, Inc., Box 510110, St. Louis, MO
63151. TEL 314-894-0276. FAX 314-894-7474.
circ. 30,000. *1493*

DISCO POST.
Verlag Disco Post GmbH, Oststr. 2, 56424 Staudt,
Germany. TEL 49-2602-70044. FAX 49-2602-
69939.
circ. 20,000. *1848*

DISCOVER F M A.
Fabricators and Manufacturers Association
International (FMA), 833 Featherstone Rd.,
Rockford, IL 61107. TEL 815-399-8775. FAX 815-
399-7679.
circ. 2,500. *4953*

**DISCOVER NORTH AMERICA TRAVEL TRADE
DIRECTORY.**
Phoenix Publishing & Media Ltd., 18-20 Scrutton
St., London EC2A 4RJ, England. TEL 44-171-247-
0537. FAX 44-171-377-2741.
circ. 15,000. *6877*

DISPATCHER (COLUMBUS).
Nebraska Public Power District, Box 499,
Columbus, NE 68602-0499. TEL 402-563-5811.
FAX 402-563-5166.
circ. 3,500. *2689*

DISPLAY & DESIGN IDEAS.
Shore-Varrone, Inc., 6255 Barfield Rd. N.E., Ste.
200, Atlanta, GA 30328-4300. TEL 404-252-
8831. FAX 404-252-4436.
circ. 18,039. *3676*

DISTRIBUTION.
Trinity Publishing Ltd., Times House, Station
Approach, Ruislip, Middx. HA4 8NB, England.
TEL 44-1895-677677. FAX 44-1895-676027.
circ. 12,000. *6716*

DISTRIBUTION BUSINESS.
Landor Industrial Services Publications Ltd. Quadrant
House, 250 Kennington Ln., London SE11 5RD,
England. TEL 44-171-735-4502. FAX 44-171-587-
0497.
circ. 11,500. *1414*

**DISTRIBUTION OF HIGH SCHOOL GRADUATES AND
COLLEGE GOING RATE, NEW YORK STATE.**
Education Department, Information, Reporting &
Technology Services, Education Bldg. Annex, Rm.
962, Albany, NY 12234. TEL 518-474-7082.
FAX 518-474-4351. *2387*

DIVERSION (NEW YORK).
Hearst Business Communications, 1790 Broadway,
Ste. 6, New York, NY 10019-1412. TEL 212-969-
7500. FAX 212-969-7557.
circ. 179,000. *3963*

DOBOKU GAKKAISHI.
Japan Society of Civil Engineers, Yotsuya 1-chome,
Shinjuku-ku, Tokyo 160, Japan. *2657*

DOCTOR JAZZ MAGAZINE.
Vijverweg 4, 5461 AL Veghel, Netherlands. TEL 31-
413-363542. FAX 31-413-363542.
circ. 850. *5154*

DOCTOR - PATIENT STUDIES.
University of Chicago, Center for Clinical Medical
Ethics, MC 6098, 5811 S. Maryland, Chicago, IL
60637. TEL 312-702-3742. FAX 312-702-0090.
circ. 600. *4449*

DOCTOR'S SHOPPER.
Marketing Communications, Inc., 1086 Remsen
Ave., Brooklyn, NY 11236. TEL 718-257-8484
FAX 718-257-8845.
circ. 208,000. *4449*

DOCUMENT PROCESSING TECHNOLOGY.
R B Publishing Company, 2701 E. Washington Ave.,
Madison, WI 53704. TEL 608-241-8777. FAX 608-
241-8666.
circ. 10,000. *5809*

DOCUMENTATIE REVUE.
Misset Postbus 4, 7000 BA Doetinchem,
Netherlands. TEL 31-8340-49911. FAX 31-8340-
43839.
circ. 15,000. *1463*

DOLLARSENSE.
E.F. Baumer & Company, 401 Shatto Pl., Ste. 105,
Los Angeles, CA 90020. TEL 213-386-2111.
FAX 213-386-6470.
circ. 800,000. *1084*

**DOMINICAN REPUBLIC. CENTRO NACIONAL DE
INVESTIGACIONES AGROPECUARIAS.
LABORATORIO DE SANIDAD VEGETAL. SANIDAD
VEGETAL.**
Centro Nacional de Investigaciones Agropecuarias,
Laboratorio de Sanidad Vegetal, San Cristobal,
Dominican Republic. *580*

THE DOOR.
Oxford Diocesan Publications Ltd. Diocesan Church
House, North Hinksey, Oxford OX2 0NB, England.
TEL 44-1865-244566. FAX 44-1865-790470.
circ. 53,000. *6142*

DOORKIJK.
Katholiek Vrouwengilde Nederland, Bisonspoor
1204, 3605 KZ Maarssen, Netherlands.
TEL 03465-73670.
circ. 500. *2595*

DOORS AND HARDWARE.
Door and Hardware Institute, 14170 Newbrook Dr.,
Chantilly, VA 22021. TEL 703-222-2010.
FAX 703-222-2410.
circ. 10,000. *888*

DOSSIER EUROPA.
Commissione Europea, Rappresentanza in Italia, Via
Poli 29, 00187 Rome, Italy. TEL 39-6-6991160
FAX 39-6-6793652.
circ. 5,000. *5662*

DOTS AND DASHES.
Morse Telegraph Club, Inc., 1101 Maplewood Dr.
Normal, IL 61761. TEL 309-454-2029.
circ. 2,500. *1945*

DOTS AND TAPS.
Canadian National Institute for the Blind, National
Office, 1929 Bayview Ave. Toronto, ON M4G 3E8,
Canada. TEL 416-480-7417. FAX 416-480-7699.
circ. 310. *3319*

DOWN THE ROAD.
Mike Eyrnes & Associates, 2025 N. Third St., Ste
155, Phoenix, AZ 85004. TEL 602-252-4868.
FAX 602-252-8120.
circ. 2,600. *5266*

DREAMIN'
Hood County News, Box 879, Granbury, TX 76048.
TEL 817-573-7066.
circ. 10,000. *3227*

DRILLING CONTRACTOR.
Drilling Contractor Publications, Inc., Box 4287,
Houston, TX 77210. TEL 713-578-7171. FAX 713-
578-0589.
circ. 36,000. *5353*

DROIT INTERNATIONAL PRIVE.
C N R S Editions, 20-22 rue St. Amand, 75015
Paris, France. TEL 45-33-15-00. FAX 45-33-92-13.
circ. 1,500. *3928*

DROVERS JOURNAL.
Vance Publishing Corporation (Lenexa), 10901 W. 84th Terr., Ste. 200, Lenexa, KS 66214-1631. TEL 913-438-8700. FAX 913-438-0695. circ. 79,271. *270*

DRUM! (SAN JOSE).
1275 Lincoln Ave., No. 13, San Jose, CA 95125. TEL 408-971-9794. FAX 408-971-0382. circ. 30,000. *5154*

DRURY MIRROR.
Drury College, 900 N. Benton, Springfield, MO 65802. TEL 417-865-8731. FAX 416-865-3138. circ. 1,000. *1866*

DUBAI EXTERNAL TRADE STATISTICS.
Central Accounting Administration, Statistics Section, P.O. Box 516, Dubai, United Arab Emirates. TEL 531074. FAX 531959. circ. 500. *994*

DUCA POST.
Duca Community Credit Union Ltd., Box 1100, Willowdale, ON M2N 5W5, Canada. TEL 416-223-8502. FAX 416-223-2575. circ. 13,000. *1084*

DUMBO.
Ehapa Verlag GmbH, Im Riedenberg 54, 70771 Leinfelden-Echterdingen, Germany. TEL 0711-79711. FAX 0711-7971239. circ. 120,000. *1790*

DURBAN MUSEUM NOVITATES.
Durban Natural Science Museum, P.O. Box 4085, Durban 4000, South Africa. TEL 27-31-3006211. FAX 27-31-3006302. circ. 280. *804*

DYNA.
Universidad Nacional de Colombia, Facultad Nacional de Minas, Apdo. Aereo 1027, Medellin, Colombia. TEL 2344503. FAX 2341002. circ. 1,500. *2595*

DYNAMIC BUSINESS.
S M C Business Councils, 1400 S. Braddock Ave., Pittsburgh, PA 15218-1264. TEL 412-371-1500. FAX 412-371-0460. circ. 10,000. *1574*

E A A REVIEW.
Edinburgh Architectural Association, 15 Rutland Sq., Edinburgh EH1 2BE, Scotland. FAX 031-228-2188. circ. 1,200. *392*

E.A.S.L. NEWSLETTER.
Florida Bar, 650 Apalachee Pkwy., Tallahassee, FL 32399-2300. TEL 904-561-5624. circ. 745. *3772*

E C S C FINANCIAL REPORT.
Commission of the European Communities, L-2985 Luxembourg, Luxembourg. *1542*

E D N MAGAZINE.
Cahners Publishing Company (Newton), Division of Reed Elsevier Inc., 275 Washington St., Newton, MA 02158-1630. TEL 617-964-3030. FAX 617-558-4470. circ. 161,500. *2512*

E D V UND KOMMUNIKATION FUER DAS HANDWERK.
Gruber und Fischer Verlagsgesellschaft mbH, Kapellenstr. 46, 76596 Forbach, Germany. TEL 49-7220-213. FAX 49-7220-215. circ. 40,000. *3603*

E I.
Huethig GmbH, Paul-Gerhardt-Allee 46, 81245 Munich, Germany. TEL 49-89-83948-0. FAX 49-89-8394848. circ. 16,991. *2512*

E N B NEWS.
English National Board for Nursing, Midwifery, and Health Visiting, Victory House, 170 Tottenham Ct. Rd., London W1P 0HA, England. TEL 0171-388-3131. FAX 0171-383-4031. circ. 20,000. *4713*

E O NEWS SETTIMANALE.
Gruppo Editoriale Jackson S.p.A., Via M. Gorki 69, 20092 Cinisello B. (MI), Italy. TEL 39-2-66034247. FAX 39-2-66034238. circ. 9,216. *2512*

E P & T.
Lakeview Publications Inc., 1200 Aerowood Dr., 27, Mississauga, ON L4W 2S7, Canada. TEL 905-624-8100. FAX 905-624-1760. circ. 24,002. *2512*

E P & T'S ELECTROSOURCE PRODUCT REFERENCE GUIDE & TELEPHONE DIRECTORY.
Lakeview Publications Inc., 1200 Aerowood Dr., 27, Mississauga, ON L4W 2S7, Canada. TEL 905-624-8100. FAX 905-624-1760. circ. 24,002. *2512*

E P E JOURNAL.
E P E Association, Secretariat S R B E, Av. de la Plaine 2, 1050 Brussels, Belgium. TEL 32-2-6292819. FAX 32-2-6293620. circ. 3,100. *2512*

E P MAGAZINE.
N Z C C A, P.O. Box 3278, Wellington, New Zealand. TEL 04-237-4753. circ. 250. *6459*

E-QUAD NEWS.
Princeton University, School of Engineering and Applied Science, C218 Engineering Quadrangle, Princeton, NJ 08544-5263. TEL 609-258-3617. FAX 609-258-6744. circ. 12,300. *2595*

E R A TECHNOLOGY NEWS.
E R A Technology Ltd., Cleeve Rd., Leatherhead, Surrey KT22 7SA, England. TEL 44-1372-367000. FAX 44-1372-367099. circ. 900. *1463*

E R S BULLETIN.
Educational Research Service, 2000 Clarendon Blvd., Arlington, VA 22201-2908. TEL 703-243-2100. FAX 703-243-8316. circ. 2,700. *2456*

E S E NOTES.
University of North Carolina at Chapel Hill, School of Public Health, CB 7400, Chapel Hill, NC 27599-7400. TEL 919-966-1024. FAX 919-966-2283. circ. 3,000. *2783*

E S F QUARTERLY.
State University of New York at Syracuse, College of Environmental Science and Forestry, Office of News and Publications, 122 Bray Hall, One Forestry Dr., Syracuse, NY 13210. TEL 315-470-6644. FAX 315-470-6897. circ. 18,000. *3013*

E S S EMPLOYMENT OPPORTUNITIES.
National Society of Fund Raising Executives, 1101 King St., Ste. 700, Alexandria, VA 22314. TEL 703-684-0410. FAX 703-684-0540. circ. 16,000. *5266*

E.T.N. REVUE DE L'ENTRETIEN DES TEXTILES ET NETTOYAGE.
Centre Technique de la Teinture et du Nettoyage (CTTN), Chemin des Mouilles, B.P. 41, 69131 Ecully Cedex, France. FAX 78-43-34-12. *6676*

EARLY CHILDHOOD TEACHER.
Scholastic Inc., 555 Broadway, New York, NY 10012-3999. TEL 212-343-6100. circ. 60,000. *2325*

EARLY CHINA.
University of California at Berkeley, Institute of East Asian Studies, 2223 Fulton St., Berkeley, CA 94720-2318. TEL 510-643-6325. FAX 510-643-7062. circ. 250. *3379*

EARLY INTERVENTION.
Illinois Public Health Association, 428 W. Jefferson, Springfield, IL 62702. TEL 217-522-5687. circ. 4,300. *2468*

EARTH (LOS ANGELES).
Shepherd Media Group, Box 6789, Los Angeles, CA 90022. TEL 310-463-4043. FAX 310-699-0491. circ. 5,200. *853*

EARTH AND MINERAL SCIENCES.
Pennsylvania State University, College of Earth & Mineral Sciences, 116 Deike Bldg., University Park, PA 16802. TEL 814-863-4667. circ. 18,000. *2207*

EAST BAY LABOR JOURNAL.
Alameda County Central Labor Council, 7992 Capwell Dr., Oakland, CA 94621. TEL 510-632-4242. FAX 510-632-3993. circ. 6,000. *3720*

EAST CAROLINIAN.
East Carolina University, Student Publications Bldg. - ECU, Greenville, NC 27858-4353. TEL 919-328-6366. FAX 919-328-6558. circ. 12,000. *1867*

EAST YORKSHIRE LOCAL HISTORY SOCIETY. BULLETIN.
East Yorkshire Local History Society, Beverley Library, Champney Rd., Beverley, N. Humber. HU17 9BQ, England. TEL 01482-864108. FAX 01482-881084. circ. 420. *3407*

EASTBOURNIAN.
Eastbourne College, Eastbourne, Sussex, England. circ. 1,200. *1867*

EASTERN AFTERMARKET JOURNAL.
Stan Hubsher, Ed. & Pub., Box 373, Cedarhurst, NY 11516. TEL 516-295-3680. FAX 516-569-5296. circ. 9,517. *6783*

EASTERN AIR EASTERN.
Regie Club International, Cromwell House, 136 Cromwell Rd., London SW7 4HA, England. TEL 44-71-244-6565. FAX 44-71-3670-3727. circ. 60,000. *6934*

EASTERN CHALLENGE.
International Missions, Inc., Box 14866, Reading, PA 19612-4866. TEL 610-375-0300. FAX 610-375-6862. circ. 22,000. *6142*

EASTERN MASSACHUSETTS REGIONAL LIBRARY SYSTEM. EASTERN REGION NEWS.
Eastern Massachusetts Regional Library System, Boston Public Library, Copley Square, Boston, MA 02117. TEL 617-536-4010. FAX 617-267-0364. circ. 2,400. *3991*

EASY LIVING MAGAZINE.
Eagle Promotions Ltd., Ste. 201, 20039 96th Ave., Langley, BC V1M 3C6, Canada. TEL 604-882-9380. FAX 604-882-9349. circ. 150,000. *3120*

ECHO (SKOKIE).
United Order True Sisters, Inc., c/o Mrs. Joanne F. Caldara, Ed., 212 Fifth Ave., New York, NY 10016. TEL 212-679-6790. circ. 12,000. *1848*

ECHO DE FRONTENAC.
5040 boul. Veterans, Lac Megantic, PQ G6B 2G5, Canada. TEL 819-583-1630. FAX 819-583-1124. circ. 4,394. *3120*

L'ECHO DU TRANSPORT.
Editions Bomart Ltee., 7493 TransCanada Hwy., Ste. 103, St. Laurent, PQ H4T 1T3, Canada. TEL 514-337-9043. FAX 514-337-1862. circ. 19,517. *6856*

ECO (MOUNT KISCO).
Eco, Inc., 420 Lexington Ave., New York, NY 10170-0002. TEL 914-242-0140. FAX 914-242-0046. circ. 80,000. *915*

ECO DEGLI ORATORI E DEI CIRCOLI GIOVANILI.
Fondazione Oratori Milanesi, Via S. Antonio 5, 20122 Milan, Italy. TEL 02-58304383. FAX 02-58304003. circ. 1,100. *1766*

ECOLOGY CENTER TERRAIN.
Ecology Center, 2530 San Pablo Ave., Berkeley, CA 94702. TEL 510-548-2220. circ. 7,500. *2785*

ECONEWS.
Northcoast Environmental Center, Inc., 879 Ninth St., Arcata, CA 95521. TEL 707-822-6918. FAX 707-822-0827. circ. 2,300. *2785*

ECONOMIA.
Yokohama Kokuritsu Daigaku, 156 Tokiwadai, Hodogaya-ku, Yokohama 240, Japan. circ. 1,800. *916*

ECONOMIA.
Italienische Handelskammer fuer Deutschland, Bockenheimer Landstr. 59, 60325 Frankfurt a.M., Germany. TEL 069-971452-0. FAX 069-97145299.
circ. 3,000. *1139*

ECONOMIA CAFETERA.
Federacion Nacional de Cafeteros de Colombia, Estudios y Proyectos Basicos Cafeteros, Calle 73 No. 8-13, piso 10 B, Bogota D.E., Colombia. TEL 57-1-3451088. FAX 57-1-2171021.
circ. 8,000. *190*

ECONOMIA GUIPUZCOANA.
Camara Oficial de Comercio, Industria y Navegacion de Guipuzcoa, Ramon Maria Lili, 6, San Sebastian, Spain. TEL 43-27-2100. FAX 43-29-3105.
circ. 12,000. *1139*

ECOS.
Editorial Sucre, Monzon a Barcenas No. 135, Caracas, Venezuela.
circ. 18,000. *6370*

ECOTROPICA. ECOSISTEMAS TROPICALES.
Universidad de Bogota Jorge Tadeo Lozano, Museo del Mar, Carrera 4, No. 22-61, Bogota, Colombia. TEL 57-1-3422961. FAX 57-1-2826197.
circ. 1,200. *2293*

EDINBURGH ACADEMY CHRONICLE.
Edinburgh Academy, Henderson Row, Edinburgh EH3 5BL, Scotland.
circ. 4,100. *2326*

EDISI CHUSUS BULLETIN KOPERASI.
Department of Cooperatives, Directorate General of the Institutional Promotion for Cooperatives - Direktorat Bina Penyuluhan Koperasi, Jalan H.R. Rasuna Said Kav. 3-5, Jakarta 12940, Indonesia. TEL 5204382.
circ. 7,500. *1208*

EDIT.
Edit Efau e.V., Kochstr. 132, 04277 Leipzig, Germany. TEL 0341-3080117. FAX 0341-3080113.
circ. 700. *4305*

EL EDITOR (LUBBOCK).
El Editor Newspapers, 1502 Ave. M, Lubbock, TX 79401. TEL 806-763-3841. FAX 806-741-1110.
circ. 15,000. *2876*

EDITORIAL PACE.
Derus Media Service, Inc., 500 N. Dearborn, Chicago, IL 60610. TEL 312-644-4360.
circ. 10,000. *3703*

EDMONTON CHAMBER OF COMMERCE. COMMERCE NEWS.
Edmonton Chamber of Commerce, Suite 600, 10123-99 St., Edmonton, Alta. T5J 3G9, Canada. TEL 403-424-7946. FAX 403-424-7946.
circ. 14,000. *1140*

EDNEWS.
Department of Education, Office of Communication Services, 1933 Capital Plaza Tower, Frankfort, KY 40601. TEL 502-564-3421. FAX 502-564-6771.
circ. 50,000. *2326*

EDPLAY.
Fahy - Williams Publishing, Inc., Box 1080, Geneva, NY 14456-8080. TEL 315-789-0458.
circ. 7,000. *3300*

EDUCATION.
S. Kumar and Associates, Mass Communications Division, 32 Sarojini Debi Ln., Maqboolganj, Lucknow 226 078, Uttar Pradesh, India. TEL 91-52-224-1010.
circ. 2,000. *2326*

EDUCATION AND HEALTH.
Schools Health Education Unit, University of Exeter, School of Education, Heavitree Rd., Exeter EX1 2LU, England. TEL 01392-264722. FAX 01392-264761.
circ. 6,000. *2456*

EDUCATION EQUIPMENT.
Bouverie Publishing Company Ltd., 147-151 Temple Chambers, Temple Ave., London EC4Y 0DT, England. TEL 0171-583-3030. FAX 0171-583-6481.
circ. 13,394. *2456*

EDUCATION FORUM.
Ontario Seconcary School Teachers' Federation, 60 Mobile Dr., Toronto, ON M4A 2P3, Canada. TEL 416-751-8300. FAX 416-751-3394.
circ. 46,000. *2328*

EDUCATION QUARTERLY.
University of the Philippines, College of Education, Diliman, Quezon City, Philippines. *2329*

EDUCATION REPORTER.
Education Writers Association, 1331 H St., N.W., Ste. 307, Washington, DC 20005. TEL 202-637-9700. FAX 202-637-9707.
circ. 850. *2329*

EDUCATION SAN DIEGO COUNTY.
Department of Education, Superintendent of Schools, 6401 Linda Vista Rd., San Diego, CA 92111. TEL 619-292-3500.
circ. 13,000. *2329*

EDUCATION STATISTICS, NEW YORK STATE.
Education Department, Information, Reporting & Technology Services, Education Bldg. Annex, Rm. 962, Albany, NY 12234. TEL 518-474-7082. FAX 518-474-4351 *2388*

EDUCATION TODAY.
Ontario Public School Board's Association, 439 University Ave. Ste. 1850, Toronto, ON M5G 1Y8, Canada. TEL 416-340-2540. FAX 416-340-7571.
circ. 500. *2457*

EDUCATIONAL DEALER.
Fahy - Williams Publishing, Inc., Box 1080, Geneva, NY 14456-8080. TEL 315-789-0458.
circ. 13,712. *1607*

EDUCATIONAL FACILITY PLANNER.
Council of Educational Facility Planners, 8687 E. Via de Ventura Ste. 311, Scottsdale, AZ 85258-3347. TEL 602-948-2337. *2330*

EFFEKTIVT LANDBRUG.
Teknisk Forlag A-S, Skelbaekgade 4, DK-1780 Copenhagen V, Denmark. TEL 45-31-21-68-01. FAX 45-31-21-04-01.
circ. 30,997. *112*

EIGEN AARD.
Publicarto N.V. Langestraat 170, B-1150 Brussels 15, Belgium. TEL 32-2-7790000. FAX 32-2-7791616.
circ. 156,273. *6992*

EILBOTE.
Eilbote Boomgaarden Verlag GmbH, Winsener Landstr. 7, OT Luhdorf, 21423 Winsen-Luhe, Germany. TEL 04171-76074. FAX 04171-74984.
circ. 8,500. *203*

EISENBAHN MODELLBAHN MAGAZIN.
Alba Publikationen Alf Teloeken, Roemerstr. 9, 40476 Duesseldorf, Germany. TEL 0211-469010. FAX 0211-484382.
circ. 61,556. *5810*

EL.
Svenska Elverksfoereningen, P.O. Box 3192, S-103 63 Stockholm, Sweden. TEL 08-791 69 00. *2691*

ELECTRIC CONSUMER.
Indiana Statewide Association of Rural Electric Cooperatives Inc., 720 N. High School Rd., Indianapolis, IN 46214. TEL 317-487-2220. FAX 317-247-5220.
circ. 172. *2567*

THE ELECTRICAL DISTRIBUTOR.
National Association of Electrical Distributors, 45 Danbury Rd., Wilton, CT 06897. TEL 203-761-4900. FAX 203-762-0324.
circ. 29,000. *2692*

ELECTRICAL EQUIPMENT REPRESENTATIVES ASSOCIATION. DIRECTORY.
Electrical Equipment Representatives Association, c/o John S. McDermott, Ed., 406 W. 34th St., Kansas City, MO 64111-2736. TEL 816-753-0210. FAX 816-753-1954.
circ. 1,000. *2692*

ELECTRICAL NEWS.
Box 660760, Arcadia, CA 91006. TEL 818-446-8652. FAX 818-447-6047.
circ. 30,000. *2693*

ELECTRICAL UNION WORLD.
International Brotherhood of Electrical Workers, A F L - C I O, Local Union No 3, 158-11 Harry Van Arsdale Jr. Ave., Flushing, NY 11365. TEL 718-591-4000. FAX 718-380 8998.
circ. 50,000. *3720*

ELECTRICAL WORLD DIRECTORY OF ELECTRIC UTILITIES IN CANADA.
McGraw-Hill Companies, 1221 Ave. of the Americas, New York, NY 10020. *2568*

ELECTRICITE DE FRANCE. STATISTIQUES DE LA PRODUCTION ET DE LA CONSOMMATION.
Electricite de France, Direction de la Production et du Transport, Departement Statistiques, 6 rue de Messine, 75008 Paris, France. *2627*

ELECTRICITY INTERNATIONAL.
Icom Publications Ltd., Chancery House, St. Nicholas Way, Sutton, Surrey SM1 1JB, England. TEL 44-181-642-1117. FAX 44-181-642-1941.
circ. 11,300. *2694*

ELECTRICITY TODAY.
Canadian Electricity Forum, 345 Kingston Rd., Ste. 101, Pickering, ON L1V 1A1, Canada. TEL 905-509-4448. FAX 905-509-4451.
circ. 11,566. *2694*

ELECTROCHEMISTRY AND INDUSTRIAL PHYSICAL CHEMISTRY.
Electrochemical Society of Japan, Shin-yurakucho Bldg. 1-12-1 Yuraku-cho Chiyoca-ku, Tokyo 100, Japan. TEL 81-3-3214-6001. FAX 81-3-3287-0037.
circ. 2,500. *1729*

ELECTRONIC BUSINESS ASIA.
Cahners Publishing Company (Newton), Division of Reed Elsevier Inc., 275 Washington St., Newton, MA 02158-1630. TEL 617-964-3030. FAX 617-558-4506.
circ. 31,075. *2513*

ELECTRONIC BUSINESS TODAY.
Cahners Publishing Company (Newton), Division of Reed Elsevier Inc., 275 Washington St., Newton, MA 02158-1630. TEL 617-964-3030. FAX 617-558-4470.
circ. 73,000. *2513*

ELECTRONIC DISTRIBUTION TODAY.
Custom Media, Inc., 7912 County Ln., Chagrin Falls, OH 44023. TEL 216-543-9451. FAX 216-543-9764.
circ. 6,982. *2514*

THE ELECTRONIC EDGE.
R.R. Bowker Electronic Publishing A Division of Reed Elsevier Inc., 121 Chanlon Rd., New Providence, NJ 07974. TEL 908-665-2810. FAX 908-665-3575.
circ. 12,000. *2109*

ELECTRONIC ENGINEERING TIMES.
C M P Publications, Inc., 600 Community Dr., Manhasset, NY 11030. TEL 516 562-5000. FAX 516-562-5325.
circ. 125,000. *2514*

ELECTRONIC EQUIPMENT NEWS - THE INDUSTRIAL BUYER.
Southam Magazine Group, 1450 Don Mills Rd., Don Mills ON M3B 2X7, Canada. TEL 416-445-6641. FAX 415-442-2261.
circ. 23,262. *2514*

ELECTRONIC GREEN JOURNAL.
University of Idaho Library, University of Idaho Library, Moscow, ID 83844. TEL 208-885-6631. FAX 208-885-6817.
circ. 2,000. *2786*

ELECTRONIC HOUSE.
E H Publishing, Inc., Box 339, Stillwater, OK 74076-0339. TEL 405-624-8015. FAX 405-743-3374.
circ. 4,500. *392*

ELECTRONIC PRODUCT DESIGN.
I M L Group plc, Blair House, High St., Tonbridge, Kent TN9 1BQ, England. TEL 01732-359990. FAX 01732-77049.
circ. 24,500. *2695*

ELECTRONIC PRODUCT NEWS.
Pan European Publishing Co. Rue Verte 216, 1030 Brussels, Belgium. TEL 32-2-2402611. FAX 32-2-2427111.
circ. 60,007. *2515*

ELECTRONIC PRODUCTION.
Angel Business Communications Ltd., Kingsland House, 361-373 City Rd., London EC1V 1LR, England. TEL 44-171-417-7400. FAX 44-171-417-7500.
circ. 13,000. *2515*

ELECTRONIC PRODUCTS.
Hearst Business Publishing UTP Division, 645 Stewart Ave., Garden City, NY 11530. TEL 516-227-1300. FAX 516-227-1444.
circ. 124,126. *2515*

ELECTRONIC PUBLISHING.
Pennwell Publishing Co. (Nashua), 10 Tara Blvd., 5th Fl., Nashua, NH 03062-2801. TEL 603-891-9159. FAX 603-891-0539.
circ. 52,500. *6016*

ELECTRONIC WORLD NEWS.
C M P Publications, Inc., 600 Community Dr., Manhasset, NY 11030. TEL 516-562-5000.
circ. 32,000. *2515*

ELECTRONICS COOLING.
Flomerics Ltd., 13 Uxbridge Rd., Kingston-upon-Thames, Surrey KT1 2LH, England. TEL 0181-547-3418. FAX 0181-547-3419.
circ. 10,000. *2516*

ELECTRONICS MANUFACTURING INTERNATIONAL.
Pan European Publishing Co. Rue Verte 216, 1030 Brussels, Belgium. TEL 32-2-2402611. FAX 32-2-2427111.
circ. 30,016. *2517*

ELECTRONIQUE INTERNATIONAL HEBDO.
Groupe Tests, Immeuble Europaris, 26 rue d'Oradour sur Glane, 75504 Paris Cedex 15, France. TEL 1-44-25-30-60. FAX 1-45-57-80-57.
circ. 15,202. *2517*

ELECTROSONIC WORLD.
Electrosonic Limited, Hawley Mill, Hawley Rd., Dartford, Kent DA2 7SY, England. TEL 44-1322-222211. FAX 44-1322-282282.
circ. 80,000. *1902*

ELEKTRIKERN.
Svenska Elektrikerfoerbundet, P.O. Box 1123, S-111 81 Stockholm, Sweden. TEL 46-8-402-14-00. FAX 46-8-402-14-02.
circ. 32,327. *2695*

ELEKTRISCHE ENERGIE TECHNIK.
Huethig GmbH, Postfach 102869, 69018 Heidelberg, Germany. TEL 49-6221-489-0. FAX 49-6221-489482.
circ. 8,974. *2695*

ELEKTRO RADIO HANDEL.
Erb Verlag GmbH, Eichenstr. 38, A-1120 Vienna, Austria.
circ. 9,000. *1935*

ELEKTROMARKT.
Vogel Verlag und Druck GmbH & Co. KG, Max-Planck-Str. 7-9, 97082 Wuerzburg, Germany. TEL 0931-4182145. FAX 0931-4182640.
circ. 18,950. *2518*

ELEKTRONICA REVUE.
Misset Postbus 4, 7000 BA Doetinchem, Netherlands. TEL 31-8340-49911. FAX 31-8340-43839. *2518*

ELEKTRONIK NYT.
Teknisk Forlag A - S, Skelbaekgade 4, DK-1717 Copenhagen V, Denmark. TEL 45-31-21-68-01. FAX 45-31-21-04-01.
circ. 14,288. *2518*

ELEKTRONIKA UMACHSHAVIM.
Tzavta Publishing, P.O. Box 18287, Tel Aviv 61181, Israel. TEL 03-5622076. FAX 3-5618549.
circ. 8,500. *1989*

ELEKTRONIKK BRANSJEN.
Elektronikk Forbundet, Brynsengvn. 2, P.O. Box 6322, Etterstad, N-0604 Oslo, Norway. TEL 47-22-72-21-40. FAX 47-22-72-21-21.
circ. 2,900. *2518*

ELEKTRONIKPRAXIS.
Vogel Verlag und Druck GmbH & Co. KG, Max-Planck-Str. 7-9, 97082 Wuerzburg, Germany. TEL 0931-4182145. FAX 0931-4182640.
circ. 36,000. *2518*

ELEKTRONIKSCHAU.
Erb Verlag GmbH, Eichenstr. 38, A-1120 Vienna, Austria.
circ. 16,000. *1960*

ELEKTROTECHNIK.
Vogel Verlag und Druck GmbH & Co. KG, Max-Planck-Str. 7-9, 97082 Wuerzburg, Germany. TEL 0931-4182145. FAX 0931-4182640.
circ. 17,000. *2696*

ELETTRONICA OGGI.
Gruppo Editoriale Jackson S.p.A., Via M. Corki 69, 20092 Cinisello B. (MI), Italy. TEL 39-2-660341. FAX 39-2-66034238.
circ. 81,546. *2519*

ELEVATOR CONSTRUCTOR.
International Union of Elevator Constructor Companies, Clark Bldg., Ste. 310, Columbia, MD 21044. TEL 410-997-9000. FAX 410-997-0243.
circ. 17,500. *854*

ELISABETHBUEHNE MAGAZIN.
Elisabethbuehne Salzburg, Im Petersbrunnhof, Erzabt-Klotz-Str. 22, A-5020 Salzburg, Austria. TEL 43-662-8580-0. FAX 43-662-858033.
circ. 22,000. *6695*

THE ELIZABETHAN REVIEW.
123-60 83rd Ave., Kew Gardens, NY 11415. TEL 718-575-9656.
circ. 500. *3408*

ELLIS COUSINS NEWSLETTER.
Ellis Publishers Inc., 1201 Maple St., Friona, TX 68935. TEL 806-247-3053.
circ. 700. *3081*

ELMHURST COLLEGE MAGAZINE.
Elmhurst College, 190 Prospect Ave., Elmhurst, IL 60126. TEL 708-617-3033. FAX 708-617-3282.
circ. 30,000. *1867*

ELRAD.
Verlag Heinz Heise GmbH und Co. KG, Helstorferstr. 7, 30625 Hannover, Germany. TEL 49-511-5352-0. FAX 49-511-5352-129.
circ. 21,359. *2697*

ELTEKNIK.
Teknisk Forlag A-S, Skelbaekgade 4, DK-1780 Copenhagen V, Denmark. TEL 31-216801. FAX 31-212396.
circ. 5,159. *2697*

EMAJL, KERAMIKA, STAKLO.
Udruzenje Emajliraca Jugoslavije, Srebrnjak 169, 41000 Zagreb, Croatia.
circ. 1,000. *1655*

EMERGENCY MEDICINE NEWS.
Lippincott - Raven Publishers 227 E. Washington Sq., Philadelphia, PA 19106. TEL 215-238-4200. *4451*

EMIGRATE.
Outbound Newspapers, 1 Commercial Rd., Eastbourne, E. Sussex BN21 3XQ, England. TEL 44-1323-412001. FAX 44-1323-649249.
circ. 1,000. *6879*

EMORY MAGAZINE.
Emory University, Office of University Periodicals, 1655 N. Decatur Rd., Atlanta, GA 30322. TEL 404-727-7872. FAX 404-727-0169.
circ. 78,000. *1867*

EMPIRE STATE FOOD SERVICE NEWS.
Wood Publishing, Box 89, Skaneateles, NY 13152-0089. TEL 315-685-3300.
circ. 15,000. *3560*

EMPIRE STATE MASON.
Grand Lodge Free and Accepted Masons of the State of New York, Committee on Publications, 37 Oliver St., Lockport, NY 14094-4615. TEL 716-434-4946. FAX 716-434-4946.
circ. 120,000. *1849*

EMPIRISCHE SOZIALFORSCHUNG.
Campus Verlag, Heerstr. 149, 60488 Frankfurt a.M., Germany. TEL 069-9765160. FAX 069-97651678.
circ. 800. *6322*

EMPLOI PLUS.
D G R Publication, 125 Principale N. St., Ste. 013, L'Annonciation, Quebec, PQ J0T 1T0, Canada. TEL 819-275-3293.
circ. 500. *4206*

EMPLOYMENT LAW REPORTS.
The Round Hall Press, Kill Ln., Blackrock, Co. Dublin, Ireland. TEL 2892922. FAX 2893072.
circ. 400. *3773*

EMPLOYMENT OUTLOOK SURVEY.
Manpower Temporary Services, International Headquarters, 5301 N. Ironwood Rd., Milwaukee, WI 53201. TEL 414-961-1000. FAX 414-332-0796.
circ. 40,000. *1372*

EMPURIES.
Departament de Cultura, Museu d'Arqueologia de Catalunya, Passeig de Santa Madrona, 39-41, Parque de Montjuich, 08038 Barcelona, Spain. *352*

ENCOUNTER (JOLIET).
College of St. Francis, Journalism - Communications Department, 500 N. Wilcox, Joliet, IL 60435. TEL 815-740-3461. FAX 815-740-4285.
circ. 1,200. *1867*

ENDUSTRI MUHENDISLIGI.
Chamber of Mechanical Engineers, Sumer Sokak, 36-1-A Demirtepe, 06440 Ankara, Turkey. TEL 4-2313164. FAX 4-2313165.
circ. 5,000. *2753*

ENERGIA Y MEDIO AMBIENTE.
Sociedad de la Energia y el Medio Ambiente de Madrid, Princesa 5, 28008 Madrid, Spain. TEL 34-1-5599179. FAX 34-1-5597344.
circ. 8,500. *2544*

ENERGIE UND CHARAKTER.
Gottschedstr. 2, 13357 Berlin, Germany. TEL 030-4653882. FAX 030-6223140.
circ. 1,000. *5842*

ENERGIEONDERZOEK CENTRUM NEDERLAND. JAARVERSLAG.
Energieonderzoek Centrum Nederland, Postbus 1, 1755 ZG Petten, Netherlands. TEL 331-224-564949. FAX 31-224-5464480.
circ. 4,000. *2544*

ENERGIEWENDE.
Oesterreichisches Oekologie Institut, Seidengasse 13, A-1070 Vienna, Austria. TEL 43-1-5236105-0. FAX 43-1-5235843.
circ. 1,700. *2544*

ENERGY NEWS EXCHANGE.
Kentucky Utilities Company, One Quality St., Lexington, KY 40507. TEL 606-255-2100. FAX 606-288-1165.
circ. 3,000. *2547*

ENERGYWISE.
Energy Publications, Livanos House, Granhams Rd., Great Shelford, Cambridgeshire CB2 5LQ, England. TEL 44-12223-844040. FAX 44-1223-843208.
circ. 12,600. *2548*

ENGINE REPAIR AND REMANUFACTURE.
R G O Exhibitions and Publications Ltd., Oakapple Cottage, Furnace Ln., Broad Oak Brede, Rye, E. Sussex TN31 6ES, England. TEL 44-1424-882702. FAX 44-1424-882702.
circ. 1,400. *6717*

ENGINEER - I.M.E. NEWS.
Institution of Mechanical Engineers (India), Janmabhoomi Chambers, 3rd Fl., 29 W. Hirachand Marg, Ballard Estate, Bombay 400 038, India. TEL 91-22-2612885. FAX 91-22-2614815.
circ. 22,000. *2753*

ENGINEERED SYSTEMS.
Business News Publishing Co.mpany, 755 W. Big Beaver Rd., Ste. 1000, Troy, MI 48084. TEL 810-362-3700. FAX 810-362-0317.
circ. 57,518. *3327*

ENGINEERING & MINING JOURNAL.
Intertec Publishing Corp., 29 N. Wacker Dr., Chicago, IL 60606. TEL 312-726-2802. FAX 312-726-4103.
circ. 22,892. *5062*

ENGINEERING CAPACITY.
Construction Publications Ltd., 2-6 Boundary Row, London SE1 8HN, England. TEL 0171-410-6611. FAX 0171-522-9646.
circ. 10,136. *2596*

ENGINEER'S DIGEST (SOLON).
Huebcore Communications, Inc., 29100 Aurora Rd., Ste. 200, Solon, OH 44139. TEL 216-248-1125. FAX 216-248-0187.
circ. 123,754. *2598*

ENGINEERS NEWS.
International Union of Operating Engineers, Local No. 3, 1620 S. Loop Rd., Alameda, CA 94502. TEL 510-748-7400. FAX 510-748-7401.
circ. 35,000. *3720*

ENGINEERS NEWS REPORT.
International Union of Operating Engineers, Local 428, 1426 N. First St., Phoenix, AZ 85004. TEL 602-254-5266. FAX 602-257-8674.
circ. 3,500. *2659*

ENJINIASU.
Union of Japanese Scientists and Engineers, 5-10-11 Sendagaya, Shibuya-ku, Tokyo 151, Japan. TEL 03-5379-1227. FAX 03-3225-1813.
circ. 11,000. *2598*

ENJOY.
Publishing People, Inc., Box 610, Alta Loma, CA 91701. FAX 800-692-3233.
circ. 143,000. *2151*

ENTERPRISE SYSTEMS JOURNAL.
Cardinal Business Media, Inc., 12225 Greenville Ave., Ste. 700, Dallas, TX 75243-9338. TEL 214-669-9000. FAX 214-669-9909.
circ. 83,500. *2073*

ENTERTAINMENT, ARTS & SPORTS LAW.
New York State Bar Association, Entertainment, Arts & Sports Law Section, 1 Elk St., Albany, NY 12207-1096. TEL 518-463-3200. FAX 518-463-8844.
circ. 1,450. *3774*

ENTERTAINMENT TODAY.
Best Publishing Inc., 801 S. Main St., Ste. L, Burbank, CA 91506. TEL 818-566-4030. FAX 818-566-4295.
circ. 205,000. *3227*

ENVIRON.
Wary Canary Press, Box 2204, Ft. Collins, CO 80522. TEL 303-224-0083.
circ. 2,000. *2786*

ENVIRONMENT NEWSLETTER.
South Pacific Regional Environment Programme, P.O. Box 240, Apia, Western Samoa. TEL 685-21929. FAX 685-20231.
circ. 1,000. *2788*

ENVIRONMENTAL AND URBAN ISSUES.
Florida Atlantic University - Florida International University, Joint Center for Environmental and Urban Problems, 220 S.E. Second Ave., Ste. 709, Ft. Lauderdale, FL 33301. TEL 305-355-5255. FAX 305-760-5666.
circ. 3,800. *2789*

ENVIRONMENTAL CAREERS BULLETIN.
11693 San Vicente Blvd., Ste. 327, Los Angeles, CA 90049. TEL 310-399-3533. FAX 310-399-8763.
circ. 30,000. *2789*

ENVIRONMENTAL CAREERS ORGANIZATION. CONNECTIONS.
Environmental Careers Organization, Inc., 286 Congress St., 3rd Fl., Boston, MA 02210-1009. TEL 617-426-4375. FAX 617-423-0998.
circ. 15,000. *2789*

ENVIRONMENTAL ENGINEER.
American Academy of Environmental Engineers, 130 Holiday Ct., Ste. 100, Annapolis, MD 21401. TEL 410-266-3311. FAX 410-266-7653. *2790*

ENVIRONMENTAL RESEARCH IN JAPAN.
Environment Agency, 1-2-2 Kasumigaseki, Chiyoda-ku, Tokyo 100, Japan. TEL 03-3580-1703. FAX 03-3580-3542.
circ. 320. *2793*

ENVIRONMENTAL RESEARCH NEWSLETTER.
Environment Institute, Joint Research Centre, 21020 Ispra, Italy. TEL 39-332-789981. FAX 39-332-785631.
circ. 4,000. *2793*

ENVIRONMENTAL TECHNOLOGY.
Adams - Green Industry Publishing, Inc., Adams Trade Press, 2100 Powers Ferry Rd., N.W., Ste. 405, Atlanta, GA 30339-5014. TEL 770-937-0222. FAX 770-937-0303.
circ. 64,000. *2795*

ENVIRONMENTAL TESTING AND ANALYSIS.
Target Group, 1907 W. Burbank Blvd., 2nd Fl., Burbank, CA 91506. TEL 818-842-4777. FAX 818-842-0578.
circ. 20,000. *2795*

EQUIPE DE ODONTOLOGIA SANITARIA. BOLETIM.
Departamento da Saude, Esplanada dos Ministerios, Bloco 11, 70058 Brasilia, D.F., Brazil.
circ. 1,000. *4640*

EQUIPMENT TODAY.
Johnson Hill Press, Inc. 1233 Janesville Ave., Ft. Atkinson, WI 53538. TEL 414-563-6388. FAX 414-563-1699.
circ. 82,000. *855*

EQUITY NEWS.
Dick Moore & Associates, Inc., Box 21216, Saint Paul, MN 55121-0216. TEL 212-719-9570.
circ. 36,500. *6696*

ERGOTHERAPIE.
Ergotherapeutinnen Verband Schweiz, Stauffacherstr. 96, CH-8026 Zurich, Switzerland. TEL 41-1-2425464. FAX 41-1-2915440.
circ. 5,000. *2468*

ERICH MARIA REMARQUE JAHRBUCH.
Erich Maria Remarque Archiv, Postfach 4469, 49034 Osnabrueck, Germany. TEL 0541-9694511. FAX 0541-9694774.
circ. 500. *4207*

EROSION CONTROL.
Forester Communications, Inc., 5638 Hollister Ave., Ste. 301, Goleta, CA 93117-3474. TEL 805-681-1300. FAX 805-681-1312.
circ. 20,000. *2126*

ERYTHROPOIESIS.
Adis International Ltd., Chowley Oak Ln., Tattenhall, Chester, Ches. CH3 9GA, England. TEL 44-1829-771155. FAX 44-1829-770330.
circ. 9,000. *4699*

ESCALPELO.
Universidad de Puerto Rico, School of Medicine, Office of the Dean of Students, San Juan, PR 00905.
circ. 500. *1867*

ESHER AND LEATHERHEAD COURIER.
Surrey Advertiser Group, 134 High St., Esher, Surrey KT10 9QJ, England. TEL 01372-463553. FAX 01372-469045.
circ. 34,000. *3154*

ESOTERIK HEUTE.
Gesellschaft zur Pflege, Verbreitung und Erforschung Esoterische Grenzwissenschaften, Wartholzstr. 12, A-2651 Reichenau, Austria. TEL 02666-2967. FAX 02666-29674.
circ. 13,500. *5330*

ESPACES TROPICAUX.
Centre de Recherches sur les Espaces Tropicaux, Universite Michel de Montaigne, Esplanade des Antilles, 33405 Talence Cedex, France. TEL 56-84-50-50. FAX 56-84-51-28.
circ. 400. *3253*

ESSEX FAMILY HISTORIAN.
Essex Society for Family History, The Old Granary, Justice Wood, Polstead, Suffolk CO6 5DH, England. TEL 44-1787-211361.
circ. 2,000. *3081*

ESTACION EXPERIMENTAL REGION AGROPECUARIA PERGAMINO. INFORME TECNICO.
Instituto Nacional de Tecnologia Agropecuaria, Estacion Experimental Regional Agropecuaria Pergamino, C.C.31, 2700 Pergamino, Argentina.
circ. 2,000. *113*

ESTATISTICA BRASILEIRA DE ENERGIA.
Conselho Mundial da Energia, Comite Nacional Brasileiro, Rua Real Grandeza, 219, 22283-900 Rio de Janeiro RJ, Brazil. TEL 55-21-246-8593. FAX 55-21-226-0508.
circ. 1,000. *2563*

ESTIA.
7 Anthimou Gazi, Athens 105 61, Greece. TEL 30-1-322-0481. FAX 30-1-324-3071.
circ. 5,000. *3162*

ESTRATEGIA FINANCIERA.
Grupo Especial Directivos, C. Orense 39 2o D, 28020 Madrid, Spain. TEL 34-1-5566411. FAX 34-1-5554118.
circ. 8,000. *1085*

ESTUDIOS OCEANOLOGICOS.
Universidad de Antofagasta, Facultad de Recursos del Mar, Casilla 170, Antofagasta, Chile. FAX 56-55-247542.
circ. 600. *2294*

ESTUDOS AFRO-ASIATICOS.
Sociedade Brasileira de Instrucao, Centro de Estudos Afro-Asiaticos, Rua da Assembleia, 10 Conj. 501, 20011-000 Rio de Janeiro, Brazil. TEL 55-21-5312636. FAX 55-21-5312155.
circ. 1,000. *6322*

ESTUDOS LEOPOLDENSES.
Unisinos, Av. Unisinos, 950, 93022-000 Sao Leopoldo RS, Brazil. TEL 55-51-5920333 ext. 1951. FAX 55-51-5921035.
circ. 1,400. *2795*

ETAT-KALKULATOR.
Creativ Collection Verlag GmbH, Basler Landstr. 51, 79111 Freiburg, Germany. TEL 49-761-42606. FAX 49-761-42608.
circ. 5,000. *36*

ETELA - POHJANMAA.
Ilkka Oy, PL 10, Koulukatu 10, FIN-60101 Seinajoki, Finland. TEL 964-4186711. FAX 964-4144905.
circ. 9,203. *3137*

ETHNICITY & DISEASE.
International Society on Hypertension in Blacks, 2045 Manchester St., N.E. Atlanta, GA 30324-4110. TEL 404-875-6263. FAX 404-875-6334.
circ. 150. *4452*

ETUDES CELTIQUES.
C N R S Editions, 20-22 rue St. Amand, 75015 Paris, France. TEL 45-33-15-00. FAX 45-33-92-13.
circ. 1,250. *4067*

ETUDES D'HISTOIRE DE L'ART.
N.V. Brepols, Steenweg op Tielen 68, 2300 Turnhout, Belgium. TEL 32-14-402500. FAX 32-14-428919. *428*

ETUDES D'HISTOIRE ECONOMIQUE ET SOCIALE.
N.V. Brepols, Steenweg op Tielen 68, 2300 Turnhout, Belgium. TEL 32-14-402500. FAX 32-14-428919. *1254*

ETUDES DE PHILOLOGIE, D'ARCHEOLOGIE ET D'HISTOIRE ANCIENNE.
N.V. Brepols, Steenweg op Tielen 68, 2300 Turnhout, Belgium. TEL 32-14-402500. FAX 32-14-428919. *4067*

EURO-JAPANESE ECONOMIC JOURNAL.
Anglo-Japanese Economic Institute, Moreley House, Rm. 1-5, 2nd Fl., 314-322 Regent St., London W1R 5AD, England. TEL 44-171-637-7872. FAX 44-171-636-3614. *1272*

EUROPEAN CLINICAL LABORATORY.
International Scientific Communications, Inc., 30 Controls Dr., Box 870, Shelton, CT 06484-0870. TEL 203-926-9300. FAX 203-926-9310.
circ. 32,801. *4679*

EUROPEAN COAL AND STEEL COMMUNITY. CONSULTATIVE COMMITTEE. YEARBOOK.
European Coal and Steel Community, Consultative Committee, Secretariat, B.P. 1907, L-2920 Luxembourg, Luxembourg. FAX 430134455.
circ. 1,170. *1306*

EUROPEAN COMMUNICATIONS.
Harrington Kilbridge plc, The Publishing House, Highbury Station Rd., Islington, London N1 1SE, England. TEL 44-171-226-2222. FAX 44-171-226-1255.
circ. 15,048. *1945*

EUROPEAN COMMUNITY MORTGAGE BULLETIN.
Council of Mortgage Lenders, 3 Savile Row, London W1X 1AF, England. TEL 44-171-437-0655. FAX 44-171-287-0109. *6025*

EUROPEAN CUTTING TOOLS.
Engineering Publicity Services, 1 Queens Dr., Newport, Shrops. TF10 7EU, England. TEL 0952-811444.
circ. 2,000. *4348*

EUROPEAN FEDERATION OF FINANCE HOUSE ASSOCIATIONS. ANNUAL REPORT.
European Federation of Finance House Associations, 267 av. de Tervuren, 1150 Brussels, Belgium. FAX 32-2-7780579. *1086*

EUROPEAN FEDERATION OF FINANCE HOUSE ASSOCIATIONS. NEWSLETTER.
European Federation of Finance House Associations, 267 av. de Tervuren, 1150 Brussels, Belgium. FAX 32-2-7780579. *1086*

EUROPEAN MEDIA ART FESTIVAL.
International Experimental Film Workshop, Postfach 1861, 49008 Osnabrueck, Germany. TEL 49-541-21658. FAX 49-541-28327.
circ. 1,000. *5100*

EUROPEAN PATTERN BOOK.
Weatherbys, Sanders Rd., Wellingborough, Northants. NN8 6UJ, England. TEL 44-1933-440077. FAX 44-1933-440807.
circ. 5,000. *6546*

EUROPEAN PLASTICS NEWS.
E M A P Maclaren Ltd., 19 Scarbrook Rd., Croydon, Surrey CR9 1HQ, England. TEL 0181-688-7788. FAX 0181-688-8375.
circ. 24,051. *5619*

EUROPEAN SEMICONDUCTOR.
Angel Business Communications Ltd., Kingsland House, 361-373 City Rd., London EC1V 1LR, England. TEL 44-171-417-7400. FAX 44-171-417-7500.
circ. 9,350. *2519*

EUROPETROLEUM.
Aberdeen Petroleum Publishing Ltd., 35 Huntly St., Aberdeen AB10 1TJ, Scotland. TEL 44-1224-644725. FAX 44-1224-647574. *5354*

EUROSUD.
Centro Studi Comunita Europee, c/o Eurocampus, Strata Prov. Bitonto, Km. 2.200, S. Spirito, 70032 Bitonto, Italy.
circ. 1,800. *5750*

L'EVENEMENT IMMOBILIER.
Groupe R. Dupuis, Rue de Stalle 70-82, 1180 Brussels, Belgium. TEL 32-2-3330700. FAX 32-2-3320598.
circ. 30,000. *922*

EVERY WEDNESDAY.
Afro-American Co. of Baltimore City, 2519 N. Charles St., Baltimore, MD 21218. TEL 410-554-8200. FAX 410-554-8213.
circ. 15,000. *2877*

EXCALIBUR.
Excalibur Publications Inc., 4700 Keele St., Downsview, ON M3J 1P3, Canada. TEL 416-736-5239. FAX 416-736-5841.
circ. 17,000. *1867*

EXCEPTIONAL PARENT.
Psy-Ed. Corp., 120 State St., Hackensack, NJ 07601-5421. TEL 201-489-0871. FAX 201-489-1240.
circ. 33,000. *1767*

EXCLAIMER.
University Outreach & Extension, 817 Clark Hall, Columbia, MO 65211. TEL 314-882-0604. FAX 314-884-4511.
circ. 10,000. *2428*

EXCURSIONS EN AUTOCAR.
Publicom Inc., C.P. 365, Place d'Armes, Montreal, PQ H2Y 3H1, Canada. TEL 514-274-0004. FAX 514-274-5884.
circ. 6,447. *6880*

EXECUTIVE ENGINEER.
Institution of Incorporated Executive Engineers, Wix Hill House, W. Housley, Surrey KT24 6DZ, England. TEL 44-1483-222383. FAX 44-1483-211109.
circ. 4,000. *2599*

EXECUTIVE LIVING.
Mid-Yorkshire Chamber of Commerce and Industry, Commerce House, Wakefield Rd., Huddersfield, W. Yorks. HD5 9AA, England. TEL 44-1484-426591. FAX 44-1484-51419.
circ. 19,000. *3676*

EXECUTIVE NORTH EAST.
Executive North East Magazine, 30 Queen St., Redcar, Cleveland TS10 1BD, England. TEL 0642-477155. FAX 0642-477143.
circ. 10,000. *1210*

EXECUTIVE TRAVEL.
Reed Travel Group (London), Part of the Reed Elsevier Group Church St., Dunstable, Beds LU5 4HB, England. TEL 44-1582-695498. FAX 44-1582-695095.
circ. 43,000. *6880*

EXETER BULLETIN.
Phillips Exeter Academy, 20 Main St., Exeter, NH 03833-2460. TEL 603-778-3450. FAX 603-778-4397.
circ. 26,500. *1867*

EXISTENZANALYSE.
Gesellschaft fuer Logotherapie und Existenzanalyse, Ed.-Suess-Gasse 10, A-1150 Vienna, Austria. TEL 0222-9859566. FAX 0222-9824845.
circ. 2,100. *4837*

EXPANSION MANAGEMENT.
New Hope Communications, Inc., 1301 Spruce St., Boulder, CO 80302-4832. TEL 303-939-8440. FAX 303-939-8640.
circ. 40,000. *1417*

EXPAT INVESTOR.
Tolley Publishing Co. Ltd., Tolley House, 2 Addiscombe Rd., Croydon, Surrey CR9 5AF, England. TEL 44-181-686-9141. FAX 44-181-760-0588.
circ. 30,000. *1087*

EXPECTATIONS.
Braille Institute of America, Inc., 741 N. Vermont Ave., Los Angeles, CA 90029. TEL 213-663-1111.
circ. 3,000. *3319*

EXPECTING.
Family Communications, Inc., 37 Hanna Ave., Toronto, ON M6K 1X1, Canada. TEL 416-537-2604. FAX 416-538-1794.
circ. 145,000. *1767*

EXPECTING.
Gruner & Jahr U.S.A. Publishing, 110 Fifth Ave., New York, NY 10011. TEL 212-463-1636.
circ. 1,300,000. *4735*

EXPEDITEUR.
Editions Bomart Ltee., 7493 TransCanada Hwy., Ste. 103, St. Laurent, PQ H4T 1T3, Canada. TEL 514-337-9043. FAX 514-337-1862.
circ. 10,828. *6717*

EXPERIENCED LIVING.
Worrell Enterprises, 119 Riverbend Dr., Box 4810, Sevierville, TN 37864.
circ. 10,000. *3286*

EXPLORER (NOTRE DAME).
Explorer Publications Co., Box 210, Notre Dame, IN 46556. TEL 219-277-3465.
circ. 50. *4209*

EXPLORER NEWS.
Barossa News Pty. Ltd., 27 Murray St., Tanunda, S.A. 5352, Australia. TEL 61-85-632041. FAX 61-85-633655.
circ. 30,000. *6880*

EXPO (KANSAS CITY).
Atwood Convention Publishing, 11600 College Blvd., Overland Park, KS 66210. TEL 913-469-1185. FAX 913-469-0806.
circ. 7,500. *1417*

EXPORT COURIER.
Stokes & Lindley-Jones Ltd., 36 Stonehills House, Welwyn Garden City, Herts AL8 6NA, England. TEL 44-1707-326688. FAX 44-1707-323447.
circ. 9,500. *1273*

EXPORT FINANCE & INSURANCE REVIEW.
Export Finance and Insurance Corporation, 22 Pitt St., Sydney, N.S.W. 2000, Australia. FAX 61-2-2012294.
circ. 5,000. *1273*

EXPORT - IMPORT NEWS.
India - International News Service, 12 India Exchange Place, Calcutta 700 001, India. *1274*

EXPRESS.
Mediamark Publishing International Ltd., 35 Gresse St., Rathbone Pl., London W1P 1PN, England. TEL 44-171-580-3105. FAX 44-171-580-1695.
circ. 50,000. *1903*

L'EXPRESS.
Case Postale 561, CH-2001 Neuchatel, Switzerland. TEL 038-256501. FAX 038-247736.
circ. 33,428. *3219*

EXPRESSION.
Redwood Publishing Ltd., 101 Bayham St., London NW1 0AG, England. TEL 0171-331-8000. FAX 0171-331-8001.
circ. 300,500. *3155*

EXTENSAO EM MINAS GERAIS.
Empresa de Assistencia Tecnica e Extensao Rural do Estado de Minas Gerais, Assessoria de Relacoes Publicas & Impresa, Av. Raja Gabaglia 1626, 1 andar, 30350-540 Belo Horizonte MG, Brazil. TEL 55-31-349-8000. FAX 55-31-349-8250.
circ. 4,500. *113*

EXTRA EQUITY FOR HOMEBUYERS.
Smart Marketing, Home & Land Publishing, Inc., RR 6 Box 284, Okatie, SC 29910-9806. TEL 203-225-0855. FAX 203-259-0724.
circ. 250,000. *6025*

EYELINE.
Queensland Artworkers Alliance Inc. (Red Hill), c/o Academy of the Arts - Visual Arts, Locked Bag 2, Red Hill, Qld. 4059, Australia. TEL 61-7-38545520. FAX 61-7-38643974.
circ. 2,000. *428*

F A P I G.
First Atomic Power Industry Group, Nissho-Iwai Bldg. 3rd Fl., 2-4-5 Akasaka, Minato-ku, Tokyo 107, Japan. TEL 03-3588-4231. FAX 03-3588-4232.
circ. 2,000. *2575*

F E B S LETTERS.
Elsevier Science B.V., P.O. Box 211, 1000 AE Amsterdam, Netherlands. TEL 31-20-4853911. FAX 31-20-4853598. *639*

F I Z CHEMIE AKTUELL.
Fachinformationszentrum Chemie, Franklinstr. 11, 10587 Berlin, Germany. TEL 030-39076233. FAX 030-39076334.
circ. 2,200. *1709*

F L I C C NEWSLETTER.
U.S. Library of Congress, Federal Library and Information Center Committee, Washington, DC 20540. TEL 202-707-4828. FAX 202-707-4818. *3992*

F M T.
Verlag fuer Technik und Handwerk GmbH, Robert-Bosch-Str. 4, 76532 Baden-Baden, Germany. TEL 49-7221-5087-0. FAX 49-7221-508752.
circ. 43,000. *3506*

F N V - MAGAZINE (WOERDEN).
F N V Dienstenbond, Postbus 550, 3440 AN
Woerden, Netherlands. TEL 31-3480-87788.
FAX 31-3480-31498.
circ. 92,000. *3720*

F P A NEWS.
Dorcom International Ltd., 700 Lawrence Ave. W.,
Ste. 435, Toronto, ON M6A 3B4, Canada.
circ. 400. *3703*

F P A P ANNUAL REPORT.
Family Planning Association of Pakistan, 3-A
Temple Rd., Lahore, Pakistan.
circ. 1,000. *826*

**F P S MEMBERSHIP DIRECTORY AND ANNUAL
REPORT.**
Fluid Power Society, 2433 N. Mayfair Rd., Ste.
111, Milwaukee, WI 53226. TEL 414-257-0910.
FAX 414-257-4092.
circ. 3,000. *5588*

F U: NACHRICHTEN.
Freie Universitaet Berlin, Kaiserswertherstr. 16-18,
14195 Berlin, Germany. TEL 030-83873180.
FAX 030-83873187.
circ. 20,000. *1868*

F W'S CORPORATE FINANCE.
Financial World Partners, 1328 Broadway, New
York, NY 10001. TEL 212-594-5030. FAX 212-
629-0026.
circ. 60,000. *1087*

F-5 TECHNICAL DIGEST.
Northrop Corporation, Northrop Aircraft Group, One
Northrop Ave., Hawthorne, CA 90250. TEL 213-
970-2000.
circ. 50,000. *63*

FAAGLAR I NORRKOEPINGSTRAKTEN.
Faagelfoereningen i Norrkoeping (FiNk), c/o Juhani
Vuorinen, ed., Bergslagsgatan 37, S-602 18
Norrkoeping, Sweden.
circ. 350. *775*

FABRICATION & GLAZING INDUSTRIES.
T B B Publications Ltd., 4 Simon Campion Ct., High
St., Epping, Essex CM16 4AU, England.
TEL 01992-560215. FAX 01992-560216.
circ. 8,329. *1655*

FABRICNEWS.
Arthur J. Imparato Associates, 80 Park Ave., New
York, NY 10016. TEL 213-274-6752.
circ. 9,500. *6676*

FACETS OF FRESHWATER.
Freshwater Foundation, 725 County Rd. 6,
Wayzata, MN 55391. TEL 612-449-0092.
FAX 617-449-0592. *6968*

**FACHBUCHVERZEICHNIS
WIRTSCHAFTSWISSENSCHAFTEN.**
Rossipaul Kommunikation GmbH, Menzingerstr. 37,
80638 Munich, Germany. TEL 49-89-179106-0.
FAX 49-89-17910622.
circ. 25,000. *997*

FACILITIES.
Bedrock Communications, Inc., 650 First Ave., 7th
Fl., New York, NY 10016-3240. TEL 212-532-
4150. FAX 212-213-6382.
circ. 29,137. *1418*

FACTS.
African Oxygen Ltd., Box 5404, Johannesburg
2000, South Africa. TEL 27-11-490-0400. FAX 27-
11-493-8828.
circ. 8,500. *2599*

FACTS & FIGURES.
Organization of the Petroleum Exporting Countries,
Information Department, Obere Donaustr. 93, A-
1020 Vienna, Austria. TEL 43-1-21112. FAX 43-1-
2149827.
circ. 6,000. *2549*

FAITH AND MISSION.
Southeastern Baptist Theological Seminary, Inc.,
Wake Forest, NC 27587. TEL 919-556-3101.
FAX 919-556-0998.
circ. 1,000. *6144*

FAITH FOR DAILY LIVING.
Faith for Daily Living Foundation, P.O. Box 3737,
Durban, Natal. South Africa.
circ. 120,000. *6205*

FAKTA.
Fakta Oy, Hitsaajankatu 7, FIN-00081 A-Lehdet,
Finland. TEL 358-0-75961. FAX 358-0-783526.
circ. 22,176. *924*

FAMILIEN.
Hjemmet Mortensens Forlag AS, Soerkedalsveien 10
A, N-0369 Oslo, Norway. TEL 47-2-961-500.
FAX 47-2-961-382.
circ. 152,778. *3200*

FAMILY BACKTRACKING.
Puget Sound Genealogical Society, Box 601,
Tracyton, WA 98393-0601. TEL 206-871-0202.
circ. 200. *3082*

FAMILY LAW REVIEW.
New York State Bar Association, Family Law Section,
1 Elk St., Albany, NY 12207-1096. TEL 518-463-
3200. FAX 518-463-8844.
circ. 3,850. *3919*

THE FAMILY MAGAZINE.
Family Assurance Friendly Society Ltd., 17 West St.,
Brighton, Sussex BN1 2RL, England. TEL 01273-
725272. FAX 01273-736958.
circ. 400,000. *3963*

FAMILY TIMES (WILMINGTON).
Family Times, Inc., 1900 Superfine Ln., No. 6,
Wilmington, DE 19802. TEL 302-575-0935.
FAX 302-575-0933.
circ. 50,000. *1767*

FAMILY TRAVELERS.
4709 Cumberland Ave., Chevy Chase, MD 20815-
5457. TEL 301-986-1227.
circ. 10,000. *6880*

FANLIGHT NEWS.
Fanlight Productions, 47 Halifax St., Boston, MA
02130. TEL 617-524-0980. FAX 617-524-8838.
circ. 15,000. *4454*

FARM BUREAU PRESS.
Arkansas Farm Bureau Federation, 10720 Kanis
Road, Little Rock, AR 72211. TEL 501-224-4400.
FAX 501-228-1557.
circ. 200,000. *115*

FARM EQUIPMENT.
Johnson Hill Press, Inc. 1233 Janesville Ave., Ft.
Atkinson, WI 53538. TEL 414-563-6388. FAX 414-
563-1701.
circ. 13,500. *203*

FARM INDUSTRY NEWS.
Intertec Publishing Corp., Webb Division, 7900
International Dr., Ste. 300, Minneapolis, MN
55425. TEL 612-851-4684. FAX 612-851-4601.
circ. 257,000. *115*

FARM SUPPLY RETAILING.
Quirk Enterprises, Box 23536, Minneapolis, MN
55423. TEL 612-861-8051. FAX 612-861-1836.
circ. 22,000. *257*

FARMERS AND CONSUMERS MARKET BULLETIN.
Department of Agriculture, 19 Martin Luther King
Jr., Rm. 226, Capitol Sq., Atlanta, GA 30334-
4250. TEL 404-656-3722. FAX 404-651-7957.
circ. 250,000. *116*

FARMING.
Farming Magazine, 43 So. Water St. E., Fort
Atkinson, WI 53508. TEL 414-563-9500.
circ. 600,000. *191*

FARMING AHEAD.
Kondinin Group, P.O. Box 913, Cloverdale, W.A.
6105, Australia. TEL 61-9-4783343. FAX 61-9-
4783353.
circ. 29,000. *116*

FARMING BUSINESS.
Genus Ltd., Westmere Dr., Crewe, Ches. CW1 1ZY,
England. TEL 44-1270-536536. FAX 44-1270-
536601.
circ. 40,000. *250*

FARMIS - REPTILEN.
Farmaceutiska Studentkaaren, P.O. Box 8036, S-
750 08 Uppsala, Sweden.
circ. 1,200. *5413*

EL FARO.
Associated Collectors of El Salvador, c/o Jeff Brasor,
Ed., Box 173, Coconut Creek, FL 33097.
circ. 100. *5456*

FARUMASHIA.
Pharmaceutical Society of Japan 12-15, Shibuya 2-
chome, Shibuya-ku, Tokyo 150, Japan.
circ. 22,000. *5413*

FASTENER TECHNOLOGY INTERNATIONAL.
Initial Publications Inc., 3869 Darrow Rd., Ste. 109,
Stow, OH 44224. TEL 216-686-9544. FAX 216-
686-9563.
circ. 13,000. *889*

FASTIGHET.
Vi i Villa, P.O. Box 12010 S-102 21 Stockholm.
TEL 08-105730. FAX 46-8-108215.
circ. 110,000. *855*

FATIMA FINDINGS.
Reparation Society of the Immaculate Heart of
Mary. Inc., Fatima House, 3006 Caliburn Ct.,
Pasadena, MD 21122-6478. TEL 410-685-7403.
circ. 4,000. *6205*

FAX PLUS.
Montreal Children's Hospital, 2300 Tupper St., Ste.
E-203, Montreal, PQ H3H 1P3, Canada. TEL 514-
934-4307.
circ. 1,200. *3543*

FEATURE.
Feature Publishing Ltd., Maison Astral, 2100 Rue
Ste-Catherine Ouest, Bureau 900 Montreal, PQ
H3H 2T3. TEL 514-939-5024. FAX 514-939-
1515.
circ. 290,000. *1960*

**FEDERAL CIVILIAN WORK FORCE STATISTICS. PAY
STRUCTURE OF THE FEDERAL CIVIL SERVICE.**
U.S. Office of Personnel Management, Personnel
Systems and Oversight Group, Office of Workforce
Information, Washington, DC 20415. TEL 703-487-
4650 FAX 202-606-1713.
circ. 900. *997*

**FEDERAL CIVILIAN WORK FORCE STATISTICS.
WORK YEARS AND PERSONNEL COSTS.
EXECUTIVE BRANCH, UNITED STATES
GOVERNMENT.**
U.S. Office of Personnel Management, Personnel
Systems and Oversight Group, Office of Workforce
Information, 1900 E St., N.W., Washington, DC
20415. TEL 703-487-4650.
circ. 400. *997*

**FEDERAL CIVILIAN WORKFORCE STATISTICS.
EMPLOYMENT AND TRENDS.**
U.S. Office of Personnel Management, Personnel
Systems and Oversight Group, Office of Workforce
Information, 1900 E St., N.W., Washington, DC
20415. TEL 202-606-1178.
circ. 950. *997*

FEDERAL PHYSICIAN.
Federal Physicians Association, Box 45150,
Washington, DC 20026. TEL 703-455-5947.
FAX 703-455-8282.
circ. 1,000. *5959*

FEDERATION.
Federation of Worker Writers & Community
Publishers, c/o 60 Upper Valley Rd., Sheffield S8
9HB, England. TEL 01782-322327.
circ. 1,500. *3703*

**FEDERATION INTERNATIONALE DE RUGBY
AMATEUR. ANNUAIRE.**
International Amateur Rugby Federation, 9 rue de
Liege, 75009 Paris, France FAX 45-26-19-19.
circ. 700. *6501*

FEDERATION JAZZ.
Federation of Jazz Societies 2787 Del Monte St.,
W. Sacramento, CA 95691. TEL 916-372-5277.
FAX 916-372-3479.
circ. 800. *5157*

Contr Circ

FEDERATION NEWS (WILTON).
Forefront Publishing Group, 5 River Rd., Ste. 113, Wilton, CT 06897-4069. TEL 203-834-0631. FAX 203-834-0940. circ. 10,750. *4909*

FEDERATION OF KENYA EMPLOYERS. NEWSLETTER.
Federation of Kenya Employers, P.O. Box 48311, Nairobi, Kenya. TEL 254-2-721929. FAX 254-2-721990. circ. 3,000. *1374*

FEED AND GRAIN.
Johnson Hill Press, Inc. 1233 Janesville Ave., Ft. Atkinson, WI 53538. TEL 414-563-6388. FAX 414-563-1702. circ. 19,000. *257*

FEED INTERNATIONAL.
Watt Publishing Co., 122 S. Wesley Ave., Mt. Morris, IL 61054. TEL 815-734-4171. FAX 815-734-4201. circ. 20,605. *257*

FEED LEGISLATION.
H G M Publications, Abney House, School Ln., Baslow, Bakewell, Derbyshire DE45 1RZ, England. TEL 44-1246-582470. FAX 44-1246-582425. circ. 600. *257*

FEED MANAGEMENT.
Watt Publishing Co., 122 S. Wesley Ave., Mt. Morris, IL 61054. TEL 815-734-4171. FAX 815-734-4201. circ. 20,182. *258*

FELIX LETTER.
Clara Felix, Ed. & Pub., Box 7094, Berkeley, CA 94707. TEL 510-526-6268. circ. 1,500. *5232*

FENESTRATION.
Ashlee Publishing Co., Inc., 18 E. 41st St., Phse., New York, NY 10017-6222. TEL 212-376-7722. FAX 212-376-7723. circ. 14,000. *855*

FERNSEH- UND KINO-TECHNIK.
Huethig GmbH, Postfach 102869, 69018 Heidelberg, Germany. TEL 49-6221-489411. FAX 49-6221-489323. circ. 3,000. *5100*

FERRETECNIC - F Y T.
Publitecnic S.A., Calle 4, no. 188, Apdo. Postal 74-290, 09070 Mexico DF, Mexico. TEL 685-28-19. FAX 6706318. circ. 10,000. *4954*

FERRUM MAGAZINE.
Ferrum College, Ferrum, VA 24088. TEL 540-365-4216. FAX 540-365-4203. circ. 14,000. *1868*

FIDELITY FOCUS.
Fidelity Investments, 82 Devonshire St., R20E, Boston, MA 02109. *1329*

FIFTH ESTATE.
Fifth Estate Newspaper, 4632 Second Ave., Detroit, MI 48201. TEL 313-831-6800. circ. 5,000. *4143*

FIJI. OFFICE OF THE OMBUDSMAN. ANNUAL REPORT OF THE OMBUDSMAN.
Office of the Ombudsman, Suva, Fiji. TEL 679-211652. FAX 679-314756. circ. 200. *3779*

FILM BILL.
Film Bill, Inc., 250 W. 54 St., New York, NY 10019. TEL 212-977-4140. FAX 212-977-4404. circ. 500,000. *5100*

FILM CLIPS.
San Jose Convention and Visitors Bureau, Film and Video Commission, 333 W. San Carlos St., Ste. 1000, San Jose, CA 95110-2720. TEL 408-295-9600. FAX 408-295-3937. circ. 3,975. *5101*

FILTRATION NEWS.
Eagle Publications, Inc., 42400 Nine Mile Rd., Ste. B, Novi, MI 48375. TEL 810-347-3490. FAX 810-347-3492. circ. 26,000. *2797*

FINANCIAL ADVISER (LONDON).
Financial Times Business Information, Magazines 2 Greystoke Pl., Fetter Ln., London EC4A 1ND, England. TEL 0171-405-6969. FAX 0171-405-5276. *1329*

FINANCIAL INSTITUTIONS DIRECTORY OF NEW ENGLAND.
Shawmut Bank, N.A., Correspondent Banking Group, One Federal St., Boston, MA 02211. TEL 617-292-3823. FAX 617-292-4417. *1090*

FINANSTIDNINGEN.
Sveriges Finansnyheter AB, P.O. Box 70347, S-107 23 Stockholm, Sweden. TEL 46-8-677-4500. FAX 46-8-14-99-30. circ. 250. *1096*

FINANZA MARKETING E PRODUZIONE.
E G E A s.p.a., Via Sarfatti 25, 20136 Milan, Italy. TEL 39-2-58363726. FAX 39-2-58363793. circ. 3,000. *1418*

DER FINANZBERATER.
Akademie fuer Finanz-Marketing, Postfach 102143, 40745 Langenfeld, Germany. TEL 02173-23048. FAX 02173-235754. circ. 18,000. *1096*

FINE ART TRADE GUILD. DIRECTORY.
Fine Art Trade Guild, 16-18 Empress Pl., London SW6 1TT, England. TEL 0171-381-6616. FAX 0171-381-2596. circ. 1,800. *428*

FINE FOODS.
Griffin Publishing Company, Inc., 1099 Hingham St., Rockland, MA 02370. TEL 617-878-5300. FAX 617-871-4721. circ. 14,500. *2968*

FIRE MARSHALS ASSOCIATION OF NORTH AMERICA. DIRECTORY.
Fire Marshals Association of North America, NFPA, Baterymarch Park, Quincy, MA 02269-9101. TEL 617-770-3000. circ. 1,400. *2920*

FIRE NEWS.
National Fire Protection Association, 1 Batterymarch Park, Quincy, MA 02269. TEL 617-770-3500. circ. 67,000. *2920*

FIRES & FIREPLACES.
Carter Spencer Publishing Ltd., Chancery Ct., Lincoln Rd., High Wycombe, Bucks. HP12 3RE, England. TEL 44-1494-442424. FAX 44-1494-472790. circ. 10,000. *3687*

FIRST CALL FOR CHILDREN.
United Nations Children's Fund (UNICEF), UNICEF House, 3 United Nations Plaza, New York, NY 10017. TEL 212-326-7787. FAX 212-326-7768. circ. 65,000. *6372*

FIRST-TIME PARENTS.
K-III Communications Corp., 745 Fifth Ave., New York, NY 10151. TEL 212-745-0100. circ. 500,000. *1767*

FIRUDO BAIOROJISUTO.
Gunma Yagai Seibutsu Gakkai, c/o Mr. S. Saito, Gunma Pref. Women's University, 1395 Kaminote, Tamamuramachi, Sawa-gun, Gunma-ken 370-11, Japan. TEL 0270-65-8511. FAX 0270-65-9538. circ. 500. *583*

FISH.
Institute of Fisheries Management, 22 Rushworth Ave., W. Bridgford, Notts. NG2 7LF, England. TEL 0115-982-2317. FAX 0115-982-6150. circ. 1,500. *2931*

FISH AND GAME FINDER.
Fish and Game Finder Magazines, 41 W. Michigan, Orlando, FL 32806. TEL 407-425-0045. FAX 407-425-1529. circ. 720,000. *6563*

FISHERMAN.
Fisherman Publishing Society, 111 Victoria Dr., No. 160, Vancouver, B.C. V5L 4C4, Canada. TEL 604-255-1366. FAX 604-255-3162. circ. 10,500. *2932*

FISHING BOAT WORLD.
Baird Publications Pty. Ltd., 10 Oxford St., South Yarra, Vic. 3141, Australia. TEL 61-3-98268741. FAX 61-3-98270704. circ. 4,000. *2932*

FISHING TACKLE TRADE NEWS.
Fishing Tackle Trade News, Inc., Div. Vickers Communications, Box 2669, Vancouver, WA 98668-2669. TEL 360-693-4721. FAX 360-693-3997. circ. 21,500. *6563*

FISKERITIDSKRIFT FOER FINLAND.
Kalatalouden Keskusliitto, Koydenpunojankatu 7 B 23, 00180 Helsinki 18, Finland. TEL 358-0-640126. FAX 358-0-608309. circ. 4,878. *2933*

FITECH INTERNATIONAL.
Argus Business Media Ltd., Fuel and Metals Journals Queensway House, 2 Queensway, Redhill, Surrey RH1 1QS, England. TEL 44-1737-768611. FAX 44-1737-761685. *2921*

FITOTERAPIA.
IdB Holding, Viale Ortles 12, 20139 Milan, Italy. TEL 39-2-57496442. FAX 39-2-57496443. circ. 5,000. *680*

FJARMALATIDINDI.
Sedlabanki Islands, Hagfraedideild, Kalkofnsvegur 1, IS-150 Reykjavik, Iceland. TEL 354-569-9600. FAX 354-562-1802. circ. 3,000. *1096*

FL A C S.
American Chemical Society, Florida Section, c/o Harold Van Wart, Department of Chemistry, Florida State University, Tallahassee, FL 32306. circ. 2,350. *1675*

FLASCHENPOST.
Lotharstr. 65, 47048 Duisburg, Germany. TEL 0203-3792397. FAX 0203-3793333. circ. 1,000. *1904*

FLASH POINT.
Tile Heritage Foundation, Box 1850, Healdsburg, CA 95448. TEL 707-431-8453. FAX 707-431-8455. *332*

FLATIRONS - THE BOULDER MAGAZINE.
Mac Media L L C, 5775 Flatiron Pkwy., Ste. 205, Boulder, CO 80301-5730. TEL 970-449-1847. FAX 970-440-5421. circ. 25,000. *3228*

FLAX CRAFT.
Virginia Handy, Ed. & Pub., 3503 Edwards Rd., Sodus, MI 49126. TEL 616-944-5719. FAX 616-944-5719. circ. 50. *467*

FLEET EQUIPMENT.
Maple Publishing, 134 W. Slade St., Palatine, IL 60067. TEL 847-359-6100. FAX 847-359-6420. circ. 63,000. *6857*

FLEET MANAGEMENT JOURNAL.
Powershift Communications Inc., 245 Fairview Mall Dr., Ste. 308, North York, ON M2J 4T1, Canada. TEL 416-494-2960. FAX 905-946-8931. circ. 13,000. *6785*

FLEET NORTH.
Tweedprint Ltd., 97 Heaton St., Standish, Wigan, Lancashire WN6 0DA, England. TEL 0257-427332. FAX 0257-422054. circ. 17,100. *6785*

FLEET OPERATORS HANDBOOK.
E M A P - Response Publishing Ltd., Wentworth House, Wentworth St., Peterborough, Cambs. PE1 1DS, England. TEL 01733-63100. FAX 01733-67367. circ. 10,000. *6785*

FLEET OWNER.
Intertec Publishing Corp. (White Plains), 707 Westchester Ave., Ste. 101, White Plains, NY 10604-3102. TEL 914-949-8500. FAX 914-287-6752. circ. 100,150. *6857*

FLEETLINE.
Historic Commercial Vehicle Association Co-Op, G.P.O. Box 1010, Sydney, N.S.W. 2001, Australia. FAX 61-2-8914947.
circ. 500. *6717*

FLEISCH UND FEINKOST.
Verband Schweizer Metzgermeister, Postfach 284, CH-8028 Zurich, Switzerland. TEL 01-2527766. FAX 01-262874.
circ. 4,938. *2968*

DIE FLEISCHMEHL-INDUSTRIE.
Wirtschaftsdienst der Fleischmehl-Industrie GmbH, Kaiserstr. 9, 53113 Bonn, Germany. TEL 49-228-212185. FAX 49-228-212198.
circ. 500. *2852*

FLIGHTPATH.
Kingsclere Publications Ltd., Furlongs House, Peasemore, Newbury, Berks RG16 0JE, England. TEL 0635-247770. FAX 0635-247272.
circ. 10,000. *6935*

FLIPPING FLIPPINS.
Nova A. Lemons, Ed. & Pub., 12206 Brisbane Ave., Dallas, TX 75234-6528. TEL 214-241-2739. FAX 214-620-1416.
circ. 65. *3083*

FLORACULTURE INTERNATIONAL.
International Horticulture Publications, Box 9, 335 N. River St., Batavia, IL 61510-0009. TEL 708-208-9080. FAX 708-208-9350.
circ. 11,200. *3050*

FLORIDA AND THE OTHER FORTY-NINE.
Department of Commerce, Bureau of Economic Analysis, 107 W. Gaines St., Tallahassee, FL 32399-2000. TEL 904-487-2971. *998*

FLORIDA CONSTRUCTOR.
Associated Publications Corporation, 495 E. Summerlin St., Box 89, Bartow, FL 33830. TEL 813-533-4835.
circ. 21,000. *855*

FLORIDA COUNTY COMPARISONS.
Department of Commerce, Bureau of Economic Analysis, 107 W. Gaines St., Tallahassee, FL 32399-2000. TEL 904-487-2971. *998*

FLORIDA COUNTY PROFILES.
Department of Commerce, Bureau of Economic Analysis, 107 W. Gaines St., Tallahassee, FL 32399-2000. TEL 904-487-2971. *1141*

FLORIDA FORUM.
F R S A, Drawer 4850, Winter Park, FL 32793. TEL 407-671-3772. FAX 407-679-0010.
circ. 9,200. *855*

FLORIDA GOLF REPORTER.
Golf Reporter Enterprises Inc., Box 951422, Lake Mary, FL 32795-1422. FAX 407-767-5748.
circ. 20,000. *6501*

FLORIDA INDEPENDENT ACCOUNTANT.
Florida Association of Independent Accountants, Box 13089, Tallahassee, FL 32317. TEL 904-878-3134. FAX 904-878-1291.
circ. 900. *1047*

FLORIDA LIBRARIES.
Florida Library Association, 1133 W. Morse Blvd., No. 201, Winter Park, FL 32789-3788. TEL 407-647-8839. FAX 407-629-2502.
circ. 1,300. *3993*

FLORIDA MARKET BULLETIN.
Department of Agriculture and Consumer Services, 545 E. Tennessee St., Tallahassee, FL 32308.
circ. 30,000. *117*

FLORIDA PUBLIC DOCUMENTS.
State Library, Documents Section, Tallahassee, FL 32399. TEL 904-487-2651. *5902*

FLORIDA RURAL ELECTRIC NEWS.
Florida Rural Electric Cooperatives Association, Box 590, Tallahassee, FL 32302. FAX 904-656-5485.
circ. 9,000. *2698*

FLORIDA SPECIFIER.
National Technical Communications Co., Inc., Box 2027, Winter Park, FL 32790. TEL 407-671-7777. FAX 407-671-7757.
circ. 16,500. *2797*

FLORIDA TRUCK NEWS.
Florida Trucking Association, Inc., 350 E. College Ave., Tallahassee, FL 32301. TEL 904-222-9900. FAX 904-222-9363.
circ. 2,300. *5857*

FLUE CURED TOBACCO FARMER.
Specialized Agricultural Publications, Inc., 3000 Highwoods Blvd., Raleigh, NC 27604-1029. TEL 919-872-5040. FAX 919-872-6531.
circ. 25,000. *6709*

FLUID POWER HANDBOOK & DIRECTORY.
Penton Publishing Co. 1100 Superior Ave., Cleveland, OH 44114-2543. TEL 216-696-7000. FAX 216-696-8765.
circ. 36,000. *2731*

FLYDOSCOPE.
Luxair, L-2987 Luxembourg, Luxembourg. TEL 4798-2221. FAX 43-63-44.
circ. 160,000. *6935*

FLYING DUTCHMAN.
Media Partners, P.O. Box 2215, 1180 EE Amstelveen, Netherlands. TEL 31-20-5473600. FAX 31-20-6475121.
circ. 100,000. *6935*

FLYNYTT.
Norsk Aero Klubb, P.O. Box 3869, Ullevaal Hageby, N-0805 Oslo 8, Norway.
circ. 10,000. *65*

FLYV.
Danish General Aviation ApS, Lufthavnsvej 28, DK-4000 Roskilde, Denmark. TEL 45-31-35-45-00. FAX 45-31-35-97-68.
circ. 8,500. *65*

FOCUS (NEW YORK, 1978).
State University of New York, Health Science Center at Brooklyn, 450 Clarkson Ave., Brooklyn, NY 11203. *4455*

FOCUS (WESTFIELD).
Westfield State College, Public Affairs Office, Western Ave., Westfield, MA 01086. TEL 413-572-5208. FAX 413-572-4843.
circ. 22,000. *1968*

FOCUS ON FOOD & BEVERAGE.
Food Processing Machinery and Supplies Association, 200 Daingerfield Rd., Alexandria, VA 22314. TEL 703-684-1080. FAX 703-548-6563.
circ. 3,000. *2968*

FOCUS ON H M A T.
National Asphalt Pavement Association, N.A.P.A. Bldg. 5100 Forbes Blvd., Lanham, MD 20706-4413. TEL 301-731-4748. FAX 301-731-4621.
circ. 20,000. *6822*

FOCUS ON MISSIONS.
Fellowship of Missions, Box 136, Middletown, DE 19709-0136. TEL 302-378-1525.
circ. 23,000. *6145*

FOCUS ON PAKISTAN.
Pakistan Tourism Development Corporation Ltd., House No. 2, Street 61, F-7-4, P.O. Box 1465, Islambad 44000, Pakistan. TEL 92-51-811001. FAX 92-51-824173.
circ. 5,000. *6881*

FOCUS ON THE FAMILY.
Focus on the Family, Inc., 8605 Explorer Dr., Colorado Springs, CO 80920-1051. TEL 719-531-3400. FAX 719-531-3499.
circ. 2,000,000. *6062*

FOCUS ON WOMEN.
Campbell Communications Inc., 1218 Langley St., 3rd Fl., Victoria, BC V8W 1W2, Canada. TEL 604-388-7231. FAX 604-383-1140.
circ. 35,000. *6994*

FOCUS PLUS.
Society of Teachers in Business Education, 28 Norlands Crescent, Chislehurst, Kent BR7 5RN, England.
circ. 1,800. *2487*

FOCUS WEST (PHOENIX).
Valley National Corporation, Communication Services (4-646), Box 71, Phoenix, AZ 85001. TEL 602-221-4840. FAX 602-221-4899.
circ. 9,500. *1096*

FOERDERUNGSDIENST.
Bundesministerium fuer Land- und Forstwirtschaft, Stubenring 1, A-1010 Vienna, Austria.
circ. 3,500. *118*

FOERSVARSFORSKNINGSREFERAT.
Foersvarets Forskningsanstalt (FOA), Centralkansliet, 172 90 Sundbyberg, Sweden.
circ. 950. *1817*

FOLK DANCE PROBLEM SOLVER.
Society of Folk Dance Historians, 2100 Rio Grande, Austin, TX 78705-5513. TEL 512-478-9676. FAX 512-478-8900.
circ. 350. *2189*

FOLK OG FRITID.
Folkeligt Oplysnings Forbund, Moellevej 9, DK-5683 Haarby, Denmark.
circ. 7,500. *2335*

FOLKEVIRKE.
Folkevirke, Niels Hemmingsensgade 10, 3. sal, DK-1153 Copenhagen K, Denmark. TEL 45-33-32-83-01. FAX 45-33-32-83-11.
circ. 2,000. *4143*

FOLKLIVSSTUDIER.
Svenska Litteratursaellskapet i Finland, Marieg. 8, 00170 Helsinki 17, Finland. FAX 358-0-632820. *310*

FOMRHI QUARTERLY.
Fellowship of Makers and Researchers of Historical Instruments, c/o Jeremy Montagu 171 Iffley Rd., Oxford OX4 1EL, England. FAX 01365-276128.
circ. 700. *5158*

FOOD AND AGRICULTURAL EXPORT DIRECTORY.
U.S. Department of Agriculture, Foreign Agricultural Service, Information Division, Rm. 5920-S, Washington, DC 20250-1000. TEL 202-720-7937.
circ. 10,000. *191*

FOOD AND AGRICULTURE ORGANIZATION OF THE UNITED NATIONS. ASIA AND PACIFIC PLANT PROTECTION COMMISSION. TECHNICAL DOCUMENT.
Food and Agriculture Organization of the United Nations, Regional Office for Asia and the Pacific, Maliwan Mansion, Phra Atit Rd., Bangkok 10200, Thailand.
circ. 500. *222*

FOOD & BEVERAGE MARKETING.
Charleson Publishing Co., 105 College Rd. E., Princeton, NJ 08540-6622. TEL 609-243-9500. FAX 609-243-9415.
circ. 20,219. *2968*

FOOD & BEVERAGE MONITOR.
Donaldson, Lufkin & Jenrette 140 Broadway, New York, NY 10005. TEL 212-504-4209. *1330*

FOOD & BEVERAGE SPOTLIGHT.
Donaldson, Lufkin & Jenrette 140 Broadway, New York, NY 10005. TEL 212-504-4209. *1330*

FOOD, DRUG, COSMETIC, AND MEDICAL DEVICE LAW DIGEST.
New York State Bar Association, Food, Drug and Cosmetic Law Section, One Elk St., Albany, NY 12207. TEL 518-463-3200. FAX 518-463-8844.
circ. 400. *3781*

FOOD PROCESSING (CHICAGO).
Putman Publishing Co., 301 E. Erie St., Chicago, IL 60611. TEL 312-644-2020
circ. 75,000. *2971*

FOOD SCIENCE AND TECHNOLOGY TODAY.
Institute of Food Science and Technology, 210 Shepherd's Bush Rd., London W6 7NJ, England. TEL 44-171-603-6317. FAX 44-171-602-9936.
circ. 3,500. *2972*

THE FOODSERVICE DISTRIBUTOR.
Penton Publishing Co. 1100 Superior Ave., Cleveland, OH 44114-2543. TEL 216-696-7000. FAX 216-696-8765.
circ. 38,946. *2973*

FOODSERVICE EAST.
Newbury Street Group, Inc., 75 Summer St., Boston, MA 02110. TEL 617-695-9030.
circ. 22,000. *2973*

FOODSERVICE PRODUCT NEWS.
Young - Conway Publications, 1101 Richmond Ave.,
Ste. 201, Point Pleasant Beach, NJ 08742-3049.
circ. 135,000. *3561*

FOODWATCH UPDATE.
Agriculture Council of America, 927 15th St., N.W.,
Ste. 800, Washington, DC 20005. TEL 202-682-
9200. FAX 202-289-6648.
circ. 10,000. *2151*

FOOTBALL REFEREE.
Referees' Association, 15 Penrith Ave., Whitefield,
Manchester M45 6UJ, England. TEL 44-161-773-
5917. FAX 44-161-773-5917.
circ. 8,000. *6502*

FOOTPRINTS (PLAINVIEW).
Wayland Baptist University, 1900 W. 7th St.,
Plainview, TX 79072. TEL 806-296-4844.
FAX 806-296-4580.
circ. 12,000. *1868*

FOOTWEAR BUSINESS INTERNATIONAL.
S A T R A Footwear Technology Centre, SATRA
House, Rockingham Rd., Kettering, Northants NN16
9JH, England. TEL 01536-410000. FAX 01536-
410626.
circ. 1,500. *6307*

FOOTWEAR PLUS.
Earnshaw Publications, Inc., 225 W. 34th St., Ste.
1212, New York, NY 10001. TEL 212-563-2742.
circ. 18,000. *6307*

FOR THE RECORD (VALLEY FORGE).
Great Valley Publishing, Box 2224, Valley Forge, PA
19482. TEL 610-917-9300. FAX 610-917-9186.
circ. 45,000. *4456*

FORBES A S A P.
Forbes, Inc., 60 Fifth Ave., New York, NY 10011.
TEL 212-620-2200.
circ. 760,000. *1154*

FORCES.
Societe d'Edition de la Revue Forces, 500 rue
Sherbrooke Oeust, Bur. 430, Montreal, Que. H3A
3C6, Canada. TEL 514-286-7600. *3121*

FORCES NEWS.
Mandrake Associates Ltd., 6 North Brink, Wisbech,
Cambs PE13 1JR, England. TEL 01945-65177.
FAX 01945-64712.
circ. 35,000. *1097*

FORD NEW HOLLAND NEWS.
Ford New Holland, Inc., 500 Diller Ave., New
Holland, PA 17557. TEL 717-354-1121.
circ. 420,000. *118*

FOREIGN SERVICE.
Diplomatist Associates Ltd., 58 Theobalds Rd.,
London WC1X 8SF, England. TEL 0171-405-4874.
FAX 0171-831-0667.
circ. 3,000. *5751*

FOREST RESEARCH BIENNIAL REPORT.
Forest Research Centre, P.O. Box 1407, 90008
Sandakan, Sabah, Malaysia. TEL 089-531522.
FAX 089-531068. *3015*

FORGING.
Penton Publishing Co. 1100 Superior Ave.,
Cleveland, OH 44114-2534. TEL 216-696-7000.
FAX 216-696-7658.
circ. 5,000. *4955*

FORM & FUNCTION.
U S G Corporation, 125 S. Franklin St., Chicago, IL
60606-4678. TEL 312-606-4181. FAX 312-606-
5566.
circ. 140,000. *393*

FORMACIO.
Editorial Interpress S.L., Benedicto Mateo 8-10
bajos, 08034 Barcelona, Spain. TEL 34-3-
2800522. FAX 34-3-2054620.
circ. 20,000. *855*

FORMAT.
Stilt Press, c/o Alan & Joan Tucker, The Bookshop,
Station Rd., Stroud GL5 3AP, England. TEL 44-
1453-764738. FAX 44-1453-766899.
circ. 150. *4306*

**FORSCHUNGSGEMEINSCHAFT
EISENHUETTENSCHLACKEN. SCHRIFTENREIHE.**
Forschungsgemeinschaft Eisenhuettenschlacken,
Bliersheimerstr. 62, 47229 Duisburg, Germany.
TEL 49-2065-9945-0. FAX 49-2065-994510.
circ. 2,000. *2852*

FORSIKRING.
Forlaget Forsikring, Amaliegade 10, DK-1256
Copenhagen K, Denmark. TEL 45-33-13 75 55.
FAX 45-33-33-02-71.
circ. 3,000. *3649*

FORTSCHRITTE DER MEDIZIN.
Urban und Vogel, Lindwurmstr. 95, 80337 Munich,
Germany. TEL 49-89-53292-0. FAX 49-89-53292-
100.
circ. 47,000. *4456*

FORUM.
Office of Court Administration, Vela St., Stop 35 1-
2, Hato Rey Station, P.O. Box 190917, San Juan,
PR 00919-0917.
circ. 600. *3781*

FORUM (SYRACUSE).
Independent Insurance Agents Association of New
York State, Inc., Box 9001, Mt. Vernon, NY 10552.
TEL 914-699-2020. FAX 914-664-1503.
circ. 3,000. *3649*

FORUM (VANCOUVER).
Association of British Columbia Professional
Foresters, 1201-1130 W. Pender St., Vancouver,
BC V6E 4A4, Canada. TEL 604-687-8027.
FAX 604-687-3264.
circ. 3,500. *3017*

FORUM DR. MED.
Medizinische Fachzeitschriften GmbH, A-2464
Goettlesbrunn 124, Austria. TEL 43-2162-8735.
FAX 43-2162-87354.
circ. 28,500. *4456*

FORUM FOR READING.
University of Pittsburgh, School of Education, 5T01
Forbes Quadrangle, Pittsburgh, PA 15260.
circ. 650. *2487*

FORVM.
Museumstr. 5, A-1070 Vienna, Austria.
FAX 938368.
circ. 25,000. *4143*

FOTBALL.
Hjemmet Mortensens Forlag AS, Soerkedalsveien 10
A, N-0369 Oslo, Norway. TEL 47-2-961-500.
FAX 47-2-961-382.
circ. 86,354. *6502*

FOTO - VENTAS.
Fopren S.L., Caspe 54 5o, 08010 Barcelona, Spain.
TEL 93-301-28-89. FAX 93-412-53-75.
circ. 5,000. *5511*

FOTO VIDEO AUDIO NEWS (DUTCH EDITION).
Mema N.V., Wielewaalstraat 20, 2610 Wilrijk,
Belgium. TEL 32-3-4480827. FAX 32-3-4480832.
circ. 6,000. *5511*

FOUNDERS HALL.
St. Michael's College, Winooski Park, Colchester, VT
05439. TEL 802-654-2535. FAX 802-654-2592.
circ. 17,000. *1868*

FOUNDRY DATABOOK & CATALOG FILE.
Penton Publishing Co. 1100 Superior Ave.,
Cleveland, OH 44114-2543. TEL 216-696-7000.
FAX 216-696-8765.
circ. 24,000. *4955*

FOUNDRY MANAGEMENT & TECHNOLOGY.
Penton Publishing Co. 1100 Superior Ave.,
Cleveland, OH 44114-2543. TEL 216-696-7000.
FAX 216-696-8765.
circ. 22,000. *4955*

FRACHT UND MATERIALFLUSS.
Konradin Verlag Robert Kohlhammer GmbH, Ernst-
Mey-Str. 8, 70771 Leinfelden-Echterdingen,
Germany. TEL 49-711-7594-0. FAX 49-711-7594-
390.
circ. 16,333. *6717*

FRAENKISCHES VOLKSBLATT.
Volksblatt Verlagsgesellschaft mbH,
Juliuspromenade 64, 97070 Wuerzburg, Germany.
TEL 0931-3091-0. FAX 0931-13270. *3143*

**FRANCE. COMMISSION CENTRALE POUR LA
NAVIGATION DU RHIN. RAPPORT ANNUEL.**
Commission Centrale pour la Navigation du Rhin,
Palais du Rhin, 67082 Strasbourg Cedex, France.
TEL 88-52-20-10. FAX 88-32-10-72.
circ. 500. *6834*

**FRANCE. CONSEIL NATIONAL DU CREDIT.
STATISTIQUES MENSUELLES.**
Banque de France, Service de l'Information, 48, rue
Croix des Petits Champs, 75001 Paris, France.
TEL 1-42-92-39-08. FAX 1-42-92-39-40. *999*

**FRANCE. CONSEIL NATIONAL DU CREDIT.
STATISTIQUES TRIMESTRIELLES.**
Banque de France, Service de l'Information, 48,
Croix des Petits Champs, 75001 Paris, France.
TEL 1-42-92-39-08. FAX 1-42-92-39-40. *999*

FRANCE AVIATION.
Societe d'Informations et d'Editions Aeronautiques,
25 bd de Vaugirard, 75757 Paris Cedex 15,
France. TEL 43-23-05-02. FAX 43-23-94-02.
circ. 65,000. *65*

FRANCE MAGAZINE.
Maison Francaise, 4101 Reservoir Rd., N.W.,
Washington, DC 20007. TEL 202-944-6069.
FAX 202-944-6072.
circ. 67,000. *3139*

FRANCE PAYS-BAS.
Nederlands - Franse Kamer van Koophandel,
Postbus 90852, 2509 LW The Hague, Netherlands.
TEL 31-70-3820551. FAX 31-70-3477975.
circ. 2,500. *1141*

FRANKLIN MINT ALMANAC.
Franklin Mint, Franklin Center, PA 19091. TEL 610-
459-6000. FAX 610-459-6880.
circ. 2,100. *5224*

FRAUENSOLIDARITAET.
Frauensolidaritaet, Weyrgasse 5, A-1030 Vienna,
Austria. TEL 43-1-713359480. FAX 43-1-
713359473.
circ. 1,500. *7016*

FREE STATE EDUCATIONAL NEWS.
Ficksburg Press (Pty) Ltd., P.O. Box 521,
Bloemfontein 9300, South Africa.
circ. 1,000. *2336*

FREEDOM TO READ FOUNDATION NEWS.
Freedom to Read Foundation, 50 E. Huron St.,
Chicago, IL 60611. TEL 312-280-4226. FAX 312-
280-4227. *3993*

FREEDOM WRITER.
Institute for First Amendment Studies, Inc., Box
589, Great Barrington, MA 01230. TEL 413-528-
3800. FAX 413-528-4466.
circ. 54,000. *5728*

FREETHOUGHT TODAY.
Freedom from Religion Foundation, Box 750,
Madison, WI 53701. TEL 608-256-5800. FAX 608-
256-1116.
circ. 700. *6063*

FREIE FAHRT.
Auto-, Motor- und Radfahrerbund Oesterreichs,
Mariahilferstr. 180, A-1150 Vienna, Austria.
TEL 43-1-89121257. FAX 43-1-89121227.
circ. 400,000. *6786*

FREIGHT.
Freight Transport Association Ltd., Hermes House,
St. John's Rd., Tunbridge Wells, Kent TN4 9UZ,
England. TEL 01892-26171. FAX 01892-34989.
circ. 14,989. *6718*

FREIGHT & TRADING WEEKLY.
Travel and Trade Publishing (Pty) Ltd., P.O. Box
662, Auckland Park 2006, South Africa. TEL 27-
11-7263036. FAX 27-11-7263994.
circ. 3,493. *925*

FREIGHT HANDLER.
K.A.V. Publicity (Glasgow) Ltd., Wheatsheaf House, Montgomery St., The Village, E. Kilbride G74 4JS, Scotland. TEL 44-13552-79077. FAX 44-13552-79088.
circ. 9,500. *6718*

FREIZEIT UND SPORT.
Otto Hoffmanns Verlag GmbH, Arnulfstr. 10, 80335 Munich, Germany. TEL 49-89-545845-0. FAX 49-89-54584520.
circ. 2,100,000. *3963*

FREMANTLE PORT NEWS.
Fremantle Port Authority, P.O. Box 95, Fremantle, W.A. 6160, Australia. TEL 61-9-430-3438. FAX 61-9-430-4112.
circ. 3,000. *6834*

FREMDSPRACHE DEUTSCH.
Klett Edition Deutsch, Kuehbachstr. 11, 81543 Munich, Germany. TEL 089-623084-0. FAX 089-650256.
circ. 6,500. *4070*

FRENCH - AMERICAN NEWS.
French - American Chamber of Commerce, 1350 Ave. of the Americas, 6th Fl., New York, NY 10019-4702. TEL 212-765-4460. FAX 212-765-4650.
circ. 650. *1141*

FRIENDLY EXCHANGE.
Aegis Group - Publishers 30400 Van Dyke Ave., Warren, MI 48093. TEL 810-574-9100. FAX 810-558-5897.
circ. 5,700,000. *3228*

FRIHET.
Sveriges Socialdemokratiska Ungdomsfoerbund (SSU), P.O. Box 11544, 100 61 Stockholm, Sweden. TEL 46-8-714-48-00.
circ. 32,500. *5668*

FRIT ERHVERV (COPENHAGEN, 1985).
Landsforeningen for Erhvervsinteresser. Grossist-Sammenslutningen af 1930, Vesterbrogade 12, DK-1620 Copenhagen V, Denmark.
circ. 110,736. *1520*

FROBBER.
FROBCO, c/o Embarcadero Venture, Box 2600, Menlo Park, CA 94026-2600.
circ. 200. *2087*

FRONTIERES.
Universite de Quebec a Montreal, Service des Publications, Centre d'Etudes sur la Mort, Box 8888, Succ. A, Montreal, PQ H3C 3P8, Canada. TEL 514-987-8537. FAX 514-987-0307.
circ. 1,500. *5844*

FRONTPAGE.
Newspaper Guild of New York, A F L - C I O, C L C, 133 W. 44th St., New York, NY 10036. TEL 212-575-1580.
circ. 4,800. *3721*

FRUIT PROCESSING.
Verlag Fluessiges Obst GmbH, Diezer Str. 5, 56370 Schoenborn, Germany. TEL 49-6486-8016. FAX 49-6486-6220.
circ. 3,758. *505*

FUELING INDIANA.
Indiana Oil Marketers Association, Inc., 101 W. Washington St., Ste. 1338, Indianapolis, IN 46204-3413. FAX 317-875-6721.
circ. 1,000. *5355*

FUER SIE PRIVAT.
V S R W Verlag, Annabergerstr. 283, 53175 Bonn, Germany. TEL 49-228-95124-0. FAX 49-228-9512490.
circ. 9,500. *1545*

FUJIAN LINXUEYUAN XUEBAO.
Fujian Linxueyuan, Xiqin, Nanping, Fujian 353001, People's Republic of China. TEL 0599-528080. FAX 0599-528085.
circ. 400. *3017*

FULCRUM.
University of the Witwatersrand, Johannesburg, Student Engineers Council, CM 1124-1125, P.O. Box WITS, Johannesburg 2050, South Africa. FAX 27-11-716-5467.
circ. 3,000. *2599*

FULCRUM.
Deep Foundations Institute, 120 Charlotte Pl., 3rd Fl., Englewood Cliffs, NJ 07632-2607. TEL 201-567-4232. FAX 201-567-4436.
circ. 1,000. *2660*

FUNE TO KISHO.
Nihon Kisho Kyokai Senpaku Bunkai, 9-2, Kanda Nishikicho 2-chome, Chiyoda-ku, Tokyo 102, Japan. TEL 81-3-3295-1525. FAX 81-3-3295-1097.
4995

FURNISHING.
Times House, Station Approach, Ruislip, Mddx. HA4 8NB, England. TEL 01895-677677. FAX 01895-676027.
circ. 10,552. *3687*

FUTURES (CEDAR FALLS).
Oster Communications, Inc., 219 Parkade, Cedar Falls, IA 50613. TEL 319-277-1271. FAX 319-277-5303.
circ. 62,000. *1331*

FUTURES (EAST LANSING).
Michigan State University, Agricultural Experiment Station, 310 Agriculture Hall, East Lansing, MI 48824-1039. TEL 517-432-1555. FAX 517-355-1804.
circ. 5,000. *119*

G A P P MAGAZIN.
Varus Verlag Birgit Laube, Koenigswintererstr. 552, 53227 Bonn, Germany. TEL 0228-440015. FAX 0228-440017.
circ. 4,000. *2450*

G E I C O DIRECT.
Maxwel Custom Publishing, 1999 Shepard Rd., St. Paul, MN 55666. TEL 612-690-7200. FAX 612-690-7357. *3649*

G E S. BOLETIN DE INFORMACION.
General Espanola de Seguros, S.A., Plaza de las Cortes, 2, Madrid 28014, Spain.
circ. 1,500. *3649*

G F A NEWS.
Georgia Forestry Association, Inc., 500 Pinnacle Way, Ste. 505, Norcross, GA 30071-3634. TEL 770-416-7521. FAX 770-840-8961.
circ. 4,800. *3017*

G F W C OF MINNESOTA NEWS.
General Federation of Women's Clubs of Minnesota, Inc., 5701 Normandale Rd., Ste. 345, Minneapolis, MN 55424. TEL 612-920-2057.
circ. 4,000. *1849*

G I S ASIA - PACIFIC.
Pearson Professional, 133 Cecil St., No. 12-01 Keck Seng Tower, Singapore 0106, Singapore. TEL 65-323-6373. FAX 65-323-4725.
circ. 6,000. *3281*

G I S NEWSLETTER.
Geoscience Information Society, c/o American Geological Institute, 4220 King St., Alexandria, VA 22302.
circ. 300. *2208*

G L A FACHBERICHTE.
Bayerisches Geologisches Landesamt, Hessstr. 128, 80797 Munich, Germany. TEL 089-12132600. FAX 089-12132547.
circ. 1,000. *2797*

G M I ALUMNI NEWS.
G M I Engineering & Management Institute, 1700 W. Third Ave., Flint, MI 48504-4898. TEL 313-762-9752. FAX 313-762-7435.
circ. 18,500. *1869*

G R I D.
Gas Research Institute, Member Relations and Communications, 8600 W. Bryn Mawr Ave., Chicago, IL 60631. TEL 312-399-8100. FAX 312-399-8170.
circ. 11,000. *5355*

G S B CHICAGO.
University of Chicago, Graduate School of Business, 5801 Ellis Ave., Chicago, IL 60637. TEL 312-702-1234.
circ. 35,000. *925*

G T E AUTOMATIC ELECTRIC WORLD-WIDE COMMUNICATIONS JOURNAL.
G T E Communications Systems, 400 N. Wolf Rd., Melrose Park, IL 60164
circ. 9,000. *1927*

GAAF GOED.
Uitgeverij Cobbenhage B.V., Treubstraat 1N, Postbus 1890, 2280 DW Rijswijk. TEL 31-70-3995108. FAX 31-70-3302488.
circ. 2,600. *3688*

GACETA MEDICA.
Asociacion Colombiana de Facultades de Medicina, Av. 68 No. 40-21 Sur, Bogota, Colombia. TEL 571-2303573.
circ. 12,000. *4457*

GALLIA. SUPPLEMENT.
C N R S Editions, 20-22 rue St. Amand, 75015 Paris, France. TEL 45-33-16-00. FAX 45-33-92-13.
circ. 1,500. *354*

GALLIA PREHISTOIRE. SUPPLEMENT.
C N R S Editions, 20-22 rue St. Amand, 75015 Paris, France. TEL 45-33-16-00. FAX 45-33-92-13.
circ. 1,500. *354*

GALWAY ADVERTISER.
Galway Advertiser Ltd., 2-3 Church Ln., Galway, Ireland. TEL 091-67077. FAX 091-67079.
circ. 33,000. *3181*

THE GANDER.
Wild Geese Association, 6 N. Water St., Greenwich, CT 06830. TEL 203-531-7755.
circ. 5,000. *3155*

GARAGE & SERVICE STATION NEWS.
Garage & Service Station News Publishing Co., No. 204, 260 Raymur Ave., Vancouver 6, B.C., Canada. *6786*

GARAGE TRADER.
Main Stream Publications, 139 Thomas St., Portadown, Co. Armagh B 52 3BE, N. Ireland. TEL 44-1762-334272. FAX 44-1762-351046.
circ. 10,214. *6786*

THE GARDEN DESIGN JOURNAL.
Society of Garden Designers, 6 Borough Rd., Kingston-upon-Thames, Surrey KT2 6BD, England. TEL 44-181-974-9483.
circ. 600. *3051*

GARDEN NEWSLETTER.
Friends of the Georgia State Botanical Garden, 2450 S. Milledge Ave., Athens, GA 30605. TEL 706-542-1244. FAX 706-542-3091.
circ. 1,900. *3051*

GARDEN PESKEM.
University of Queensland, Gatton College, Lawes (via Gatton), Qld. 4343, Australia. TEL 074-601-291. FAX 074-601-283.
circ. 300. *3051*

GARDEN SUPPLY RETAILER GREEN BOOK.
Chilton Co., 201 King of Prussia Rd., Radnor, PA 19089. TEL 610-964-4275.
circ. 27,000. *3051*

GARDEN TRADE NEWS.
Trade Promotion Services Ltd., Apex House, Oundle Rd., Peterborough PE2 9NF, England. TEL 44-1733-898100. FAX 44-1733-312025.
circ. 6,077. *3051*

GARRISON.
Land Force Central Area, P.O. Box 17, 5775 Yonge St., Toronto, ON M5R 2T1, Canada. TEL 416-733-4781. FAX 416-733-5315.
circ. 11,000. *5031*

GARTENKURIER.
Bernhard Thalacker Verlag GmbH, Postfach 3361, 38023 Braunschweig, Germany. TEL 49-531-380040. FAX 49-531-3800425.
circ. 129,662. *3052*

GARUDA MAGAZINE.
Aerospace Communications Pte. Ltd., 14 Shaw Rd., No. 04-03, BTC Bldg., Singapore 1336, Singapore. TEL 65-344-6465. FAX 65-345-9919.
circ. 75,000. *6935*

GAS APPLIANCES.
Carter Spencer Publishing Ltd., Chancery Ct., Lincoln Rd., High Wycombe, Bucks. HP12 3RE, England. TEL 44-1494-442424. FAX 44-1494-472790.
circ. 30,000. *5356*

GAS INDUSTRIES MAGAZINE.
Gas Industries Inc., Box 558, Park Ridge, IL 60068. TEL 312-693-3682. FAX 847-696-3445.
circ. 11,000. *5356*

GASNYTT.
Svenska Gasfoereningen, Sct. Eriksgatan 44, P.O. Box 49134, S-100 29 Stockholm, Sweden. TEL 46-8-692-1845. FAX 46-8-654-46-15.
circ. 2,500. *5357*

GATEWAY.
University of Alberta, Students Union, Students' Union Bldg., Edmonton, AB T6G 2J7, Canada. TEL 403-492-5168. FAX 403-492-4643.
circ. 13,000. *1869*

GAZETA DE TRANSILVANIA.
3 Mihail Sadoveanu St., 2200 Brasov, Romania. TEL 0040-68-142029. FAX 0040-68-152927.
circ. 10,000. *3208*

GAZETA KRAKOWSKA.
Wydawnictwo Gazeta Krakowska Spolka z o.o., Ul. Warnenczyka 14, 30-510 Krakow, Poland. TEL 48-12-563796. FAX 48-12-236557.
circ. 120. *3206*

GAZETTE DES COMMUNES, DES DEPARTEMENTS, DES REGIONS.
Publications du Moniteur, 17, Rue d'Uzes, 75002 Paris, France. TEL 1-40-13-30-30. FAX 1-40-26-20-94.
circ. 20,079. *1419*

GAZETTE DES FEMMES.
Conseil du Statut de la Femme, 8 rue Cook, 3e Etage, Bur. 300, Quebec, PQ G1R 5J7, Canada. TEL 418-643-4326. FAX 418-643-8926.
circ. 17,000. *6995*

GAZZETTINO AGRICOLO (PARMA).
Unione Provinciale Agricoltori di Parma, Piazzale A. Barezzi 3, 43100 Parma, Italy. TEL 22-546.
circ. 6,500. *119*

GEGENSCHEIN.
Gegenschein Press, 421 Hudson St., Ste. 220, New York, NY 10014. TEL 212-989-7845. FAX 212-627-1797.
circ. 100. *4212*

GEMS OF GENEALOGY.
Bay Area Genealogical Society, Inc., c/o Lisa Youngblood, Box 283, Green Bay, WI 54305-0283.
circ. 80. *3084*

THE GEN.
PowerGen plc, Westwood Business Park, Westwood Way, Coventry CV4 8LG, England. TEL 44-1203-424862. FAX 44-1203-425292.
circ. 16,000. *2569*

GENERAL-ANZEIGER.
Bonner Zeitungsdruckerei und Verlagsanstalt H. Neusser GmbH, Justus-von-Liebig-Str. 15, 53121 Bonn, Germany. TEL 0228-6688-0. FAX 0228-6688148.
circ. 93,250. *3144*

GENERATIONS (WAYZATA).
National Ataxia Foundation, 750 Twelve Oaks Center, 15500 Wayzata Blvd., Wayzata, MN 55391. TEL 612-473-7666. FAX 612-473-9289.
circ. 9,000. *4838*

GENETICS NEWSLETTER.
South African Genetic Society, c/o Department of Genetics, University of Stellenbosch, Stellenbosch, South Africa. *743*

GENEVE LE MENSUEL.
Promoedition SA, 2 rue Bovy-Lysberg, Case postale 5615, CH-1211 Geneva 11, Switzerland. TEL 41-22-8279100. FAX 41-22-3215513.
circ. 15,000. *3219*

GENGO TO KYOIKU NO KENKYU.
Saitama Daigaku Kyoiku Gakubu, Kyoiku Gakubu, Takenaga Laboratory, 255, Shimo Okubo, Urawa-shi 338, Japan. TEL 048-858-3175. FAX 048-858-3690. *2488*

GENRE MAGAZINE.
7080 Hollywood Blvd., Ste. 1104, Hollywood, CA 90028. TEL 213-467-8300. FAX 213-467-8365.
circ. 20,000. *4941*

IL-GENS.
Media Centre, National Rd., Blata L-Bajda HMR 02, Malta. TEL 356-246677. FAX 356-234057.
circ. 12,000. *3192*

GEOFISICA INTERNACIONAL.
Universidad Nacional Autonoma de Mexico, Instituto de Geofisica, Circuito Exterior, Ciudad Universitaria, Mexico 20, D.F., Mexico. TEL 525-622-4113. FAX 525-550-2486.
circ. 1,200. *2273*

GEOLOGIA COLOMBIANA.
Universidad Nacional de Colombia, Departamento de Geociencias, Apdo. Aereo 14490, Bogota D.C., Colombia. TEL 3681227. FAX 3681326.
circ. 1,000. *2235*

GEOMINAS.
Universidad de Oriente, Escuela de Ciencias de la Tierra, c/o Comision de Publicaciones, La Sabanita, Ciudad Bolivar, 8001, Venezuela. FAX 58-85-26678. *2209*

GEORGESON REPORT.
Georgeson & Company Inc., 88 Pine St., New York, NY 10005. FAX 212-440-9014.
circ. 8,000. *1331*

GEORGIA ADVOCATE.
University of Georgia Law School Association, University of Georgia School of Law, Athens, GA 30602. TEL 706-542-5172. FAX 706-542-5556.
circ. 7,500. *1869*

GEORGIA ALUMNI RECORD.
University of Georgia Alumni Society, Alumni House, Athens, GA 30602-4370. TEL 706-542-3354. FAX 706-542-9492.
circ. 25,000. *1869*

GEORGIA ANCHORAGE.
Georgia Ports Authority, Box 2406, Savannah, GA 31402. TEL 912-964-3811. FAX 912-964-3921.
circ. 13,000. *6834*

GEORGIA COURTS JOURNAL.
Administrative Office of the Courts, 244 Washington St., S.W., Ste. 550, Atlanta, GA 30334. TEL 404-656-5171. FAX 404-651-6449.
circ. 3,000. *3948*

GEORGIA DESCRIPTIONS IN DATA.
Operational Support and Development, Office of Planning and Budget, 254 Washington St., S.W., Rm. 640, Atlanta, GA 30334-8501. TEL 404-656-0911. FAX 404-656-3828.
circ. 1,000. *5799*

GEORGIA FORESTRY.
Forestry Commission, Forest Education Department, Box 819, Macon, GA 31298. TEL 912-751-3534. FAX 912-751-3465.
circ. 8,000. *3017*

GEORGIA HUMANITIES.
Georgia Humanities Council, 50 Hurt Plaza, S.E., Ste. 440, Atlanta, GA 30303-2915.
circ. 8,000. *3613*

GEORGIA JOURNAL - LIVING.
Grimes Publications, Inc., Box 1266, Athens, GA 30603. TEL 404-354-0463. FAX 404-354-6824.
circ. 14,000. *3228*

GEORGIA STATE UNIVERSITY SIGNAL.
Georgia State University, Box 1862, University Plaza, Atlanta, GA 30303. TEL 404-651-2242. FAX 404-651-1045.
circ. 15,000. *1869*

GEORGIA STRAIGHT.
Vancouver Free Press Publishing Corp., 1770 Burrard St., 2nd Fl., Vancouver, BC V6J 3G7, Canada. TEL 604-730-7000. FAX 604-730-7010.
circ. 97,000. *3121*

GEORGIA TREND.
Grimes Publications, Inc., Box 1266, Athens, GA 30603. TEL 404-354-0463. FAX 404-354-6824.
circ. 39,400. *1097*

GEORGIA VITAL STATISTICS REPORT.
Department of Human Resources, Division of Public Health, 2 Peachtree St., S.W., Ste. 3-522, Atlanta, GA 30303-3186. TEL 404-657-6321.
circ. 650. *5799*

GEOSUR.
Asociacion Sudamericana de Estudios Geopoliticos e Internacionales, Casilla de Correo 5006, 11200 Montevideo, Uruguay. TEL 598-2-692953. FAX 598-2-961923.
circ. 1,500. *5751*

GERIATRIC CONSULTANT.
Medical Publishing Enterprises, 15-22 Fair Lawn Ave., Fair Lawn, NJ 07410. TEL 201-796-6500.
circ. 97,500. *3287*

GERIATRIKA.
Alpe Editores, S.A., Pedro Rico, 27, 28029 Madrid, Spain. TEL 34-1-7338811. FAX 34-1-3159652.
circ. 7,000. *3287*

GESAMTSTATISTIK DER KRAFTFAHRTVERSICHERUNG.
Verband der Haftpflicht- , Unfall- und Kraftverkehrsversicherer e.V., Glockengiesserwall 1, 20095 Hamburg, Germany. *3671*

GESELLSCHAFT FUER BIBLIOTHEKSWESEN UND DOKUMENTATION DES LANDBAUES. MITTEILUNGEN.
Gesellschaft fuer Bibliothekswesen und Dokumentation des Landbaues, Engesserstr. 20, 76131 Karlsruhe, Germany. TEL 49-721-6625148. FAX 49-721-6625111.
circ. 150. *173*

GESELLSCHAFT FUER LOGOTHERAPIE UND EXISTENZANALYSE. TAGUNGSBERICHTE.
Gesellschaft fuer Logotherapie und Existenzanalyse, Ed.-Suess-Gasse 10, A-1150 Vienna, Austria. TEL 0222-9859566. FAX 0222-9824845.
circ. 1,000. *4838*

GESTION HOSPITALARIA.
Alpe Editores, S.A., Pedro Rico, 27, 28029 Madrid, Spain. TEL 34-1-7338811. FAX 34-1-3159652.
circ. 6,500. *3544*

GESUNDES TIROL.
Ablinger und Garber, Johannesfeldstr. 2, A-6111 Volders, Austria. TEL 05224-57367. FAX 05224-5736717.
circ. 80,000. *4459*

GET KINKY.
Contact Advertising, 2010 St. Lucie Blvd., Ft. Pierce, FL 34946. TEL 561-464-5447. FAX 561-466-7294.
circ. 30,000. *4941*

GETTING ABOUT BRITAIN.
Drumport Ltd., 21 Church Walk, Thames Ditton, Surrey KT7 0NP, England. TEL 44-81-398-8332. FAX 44-81-398-8322.
circ. 47,000. *6888*

GHANA. NATIONAL COUNCIL ON WOMEN AND DEVELOPMENT. ANNUAL REPORT.
National Council on Women and Development, Box M. 53, Accra, Ghana. TEL 233-21-229119.
circ. 3,000. *6995*

GHAQDA BIBLJOTEKARJI.
Library Association, c/o University Library, Msida MSD 06, Malta. TEL 356-32902412.
circ. 100. *3994*

GHOSTWRITER.
Children's Television Workshop, 1 Lincoln Plaza, New York, NY 10023. TEL 212-595-3456.
circ. 2,000,000. *1792*

GIFTWARE NEWS.
Giftware News, Box 5398, Deptford, NJ 08096. TEL 609-227-0798.
circ. 42,400. *3300*

GINTONG BUTIL.
National Food Authority, E. Rodriguez Sr. Ave., Quezon City, Philippines. FAX 7121364.
circ. 10,000. *258*

GIORNALE.
Europea di Edizioni S.p.A., Via G. Negri 4, 20123 Milan, Italy.
circ. 300,000. *3184*

GIORNALE DELLO SPETTACOLO.
Gestioni Editoriali A G I S, Via di Villa Patrizi 10, 00161 Rome, Italy. TEL 39-6-4402704. FAX 39-6-4404257.
circ. 13,000. *2189*

GIRL SCOUT LEADER.
Girl Scouts of the U.S.A., 420 Fifth Ave., New York, NY 10018-2702. TEL 212-852-8000. FAX 212-852-6511.
circ. 800,000. *1768*

GLASGOW UNIVERSITY STUDENTS' HANDBOOK.
Students Representative Council, John McIntyre Bldg., The University, Glasgow G12 8QQ, Scotland. TEL 041-339-8541. FAX 041-337-3557.
circ. 8,000. *2337*

GLASS & PORSELEN.
A-S Ursus Forlag og Pressbyraa, Odins gt. 26, 0266 Oslo, Norway. TEL 47-22-43-40-60. FAX 47-22-43-61-43.
circ. 3,000. *1656*

GLEN BURNIELAND.
9195-H Hitching Post Ln., Laurel, MD 20723. TEL 301-604-8236.
circ. 500. *4145*

GLENMARY CHALLENGE.
Glenmary Home Missioners, Box 465618, Cincinnati, OH 45246-5618. TEL 513-874-8900. FAX 513-874-1690.
circ. 100,000. *6063*

GLOBAL CHANGE NEWSLETTER.
Royal Swedish Academy of Science, International Geosphere-Biosphere Programme, P.O. Box 50005, S-104 05 Stockholm, Sweden. TEL 46-8-16-46-48. FAX 46-8-16-45-05.
circ. 9,000. *2241*

GLOBAL RISK MANAGER (YEAR).
Regent Publications Ltd., Hadleigh Business Centre, 351 London Rd., Hadleigh, Essex SS7 2BT, England. TEL 44-1702-551556. FAX 44-1702-551511.
circ. 18,000. *3650*

GLOBAL STAMP NEWS.
Brandewie Inc., 110 N. Ohio Ave., Box 97, Sidney, OH 45365. TEL 513-492-3183. FAX 513-492-6514.
circ. 20,000. *5456*

GLOBAL VILLAGE VOICE.
Canadian Catholic Organization for Development and Peace, 3028 Danforth Ave., Toronto, ON M4C 1N2, Canada. TEL 416-698-7770. FAX 416-698-8269.
circ. 48,950. *1307*

GO!
Shell South Africa (Pty) Ltd., P.O. Box 2231, Cape Town 8000, South Africa. TEL 021-408-4911. FAX 021-253807.
circ. 1,500. *6787*

GO WEST.
Motor Transport Publishers Inc., 11344 Coloma Rd., Ste. 445, Gold River, CA 95670. TEL 916-852-5700. FAX 916-852-5707.
circ. 36,144. *6857*

GOING PLACES.
Intercontinental Church Society, 175 Tower Bridge Rd., London SE1 2AQ, England. TEL 071-407-4588. FAX 071-378-0541.
circ. 5,000. *6064*

GOING PLACES (MINOT).
Box 1427, Minot, ND 58702-1427. TEL 701-839-0809. FAX 701-852-0408.
circ. 40,000. *6888*

GOLD BULLETIN.
World Gold Council, 1 rue de la Rotisserie, CH-1204 Geneva, Switzerland. TEL 022-3119666. FAX 022-3108160.
circ. 5,500. *4982*

GOLDA MEIR LIBRARY NEWSLETTER.
University of Wisconsin at Milwaukee, Golda Meir Library, 2311 E. Hartford Ave., Box 604, Milwaukee, WI 53201. TEL 414-229-4786. FAX 414-229-4380.
circ. 4,000. *3994*

GOLDEN CALIFORNIA (SACRAMENTO).
R H L - Golden State, 801 K St., Ste. 1600, Sacramento, CA 95314.
circ. 3,125,000. *6988*

GOLDEN GATER.
San Francisco State University, 1600 Holloway Ave., San Francisco, CA 94132. TEL 415-338-3123. FAX 415-338-3111.
circ. 10,000. *1870*

GOLF INDUSTRY.
Sterling Southeast, Inc., 3301 Ponce De Leon Blvd., No.300, Coral Gables, FL 33134-7273. TEL 305-893-8771. FAX 305-893-8783.
circ. 16,692. *6504*

GOLF MARKET TODAY.
National Golf Foundation, 1150 S. U.S. Hwy. One, Jupiter, FL 33477. TEL 407-744-6006. FAX 407-744-6107.
circ. 9,000. *6504*

GOLF VACATIONS.
Pacom Publications Pte. Ltd., 190 Middle Rd. 14-07, Fortune Centre, Singapore 0718, Singapore. TEL 65-3370255. FAX 65-3394857.
circ. 15,000. *6505*

GONGYE JIANZHU.
Yejin-bu, Jianzhu Yanjiu Zongyuan, 33 Xitucheng Lu, Haidian-qu, Beijing 100088, People's Republic of China. TEL 86-10-6201-5599. FAX 86-10-6201-1361.
circ. 8,000. *855*

GOOD MOTORING.
Good Motoring (Publishers) Ltd., c/o Guild of Experienced Motorists, Station Rd., Forest Row, E. Sussex RH18 5EN, England. TEL 44-1342-825676. FAX 44-1342-824847.
circ. 53,000. *6787*

GOOD NEWS (BIRMINGHAM).
Additional Curates Society for England and Wales, Gordon Browning House, 8 Spitfire Rd., Birmingham B24 9PB, England. TEL 44-121-382-5533. FAX 44-121-382-6999.
circ. 20,000. *6064*

THE GOOD NEWS LETTER (WASHINGTON, 1972).
National Institute for the Word of God, 487 Michigan Ave., N.E., Washington, DC 20017. TEL 202-529-0001. FAX 202-636-4460.
circ. 2,500. *6181*

GOPHER OVERSEA'R.
Veterans of Foreign Wars of the United States, Department of Minnesota, Veterans Service Bldg., St. Paul, MN 55155. TEL 612-291-1757. FAX 612-291-2753.
circ. 85,000. *5032*

THE GOSPEL HERALD AND SUNDAY SCHOOL TIMES.
Union Gospel Press, Box 6059, Cleveland, OH 44101. TEL 216-749-2100. FAX 216-459-1337.
circ. 50,000. *6064*

GOSPEL OUTREACH.
Concordia Gospel Outreach, Box 201, St. Louis, MO 63166-0201. TEL 314-268-1363. FAX 314-268-1329.
circ. 9,000. *6064*

GOSS AND CRESTED CHINA.
Milestone Publications, 62 Murray Rd., Horndean, Waterlooville, Hants PO8 9JL, England. TEL 44-1705-597440. FAX 44-1705-591975.
circ. 1,000. *332*

GOURMET RETAILER.
Sterling Southeast Inc., 3301 Ponce De Leon Blvd., No.300, Coral Gables, FL 33134-7273. TEL 305-893-8771.
circ. 17,389. *2975*

GOVERNMENT BUSINESS
Momentum Media Management 4040 Creditview Rd., Unit 11, Box 1800, Mississauga, ON L5C 3Y8, Canada. TEL 905-813-7100. FAX 905-813-7117.
circ. 23,000. *1466*

GOVERNMENT COMPUTING AND INFORMATION MANAGEMENT.
Government Group Publications, Southbank House, Black Prince Rd., London SE1 7SJ, England. TEL 0171-582-9191. FAX 0171-587-1810.
circ. 11,445. *5936*

GOVERNMENT INFORMATION AND IMAGING TECHNOLOGY.
1738 Elton Rd., Ste. 304, Silver Spring, MD 20903-1725. TEL 301-445-4405. FAX 301-445-5722.
circ. 34,000. *1976*

GOVERNMENT PRODUCT NEWS.
Penton Publishing Co. 1100 Superior Ave., Cleveland, OH 44114-2543. TEL 216-696-7000. FAX 216-696-7658.
circ. 85,000. *5903*

GOVERNMENT PURCHASING GUIDE.
Moorshead Magazines Ltd. 10 Gateway Blvd., Ste. 490, North York, ON M3C 3T4, Canada. TEL 416-696-5488. FAX 416-696-7395.
circ. 17,000. *5903*

GOVERNMENT TECHNOLOGY.
G T Publications, Inc., 9719 Lincoln Village Dr., No. 500, Sacramento, CA 95827-3303. TEL 916-363-5000. FAX 916-363-5197.
circ. 56,000. *5936*

GRACE TIDINGS.
Grace University, Ninth & William, Omaha, NE 68108-3600. TEL 402-449-2800. FAX 402-341-9587.
circ. 19,000. *1870*

GRAFISK FAKTORSTIDNING.
Grafiska Faktors- och Tjaerstemannafcerbundet, Sankt Eriksgatan 26 III, P.O. Box 12069, S-102 22 Stockholm, Sweden. TEL 46-8-6935597.
circ. 3,500. *5811*

GRAFISKT FORUM.
Grafiska Foeretagens Foerbund, P.O. Box 16383, Blasieholmsgatan 4 A, S-103 27 Stockholm, Sweden. TEL 468-762-6800. FAX 468-611-6102.
circ. 4,200. *5811*

GRAND TIMES.
Grand Times Publishing, Inc. 403 Village Dr., El Cerrito, CA 94530-3355. TEL 510 527-4337.
circ. 30,000. *3288*

GRANDE DISTRIBUZIONE E DISTRIBUZIONE ORGANIZZATA.
Agepe Gruppo Editoriale, Via D. Trentacoste 9, 20134 Milan, Italy. TEL 02-215621. FAX 02-2640330.
circ. 41,500. *926*

GRANDS NOTABLES DU PREMIER EMPIRE.
C N R S Editions, 20-22 rue St. Amand, 75015 Paris, France. TEL 45-33-16-00. FAX 45-33-92-13.
circ. 1,500. *556*

GRANITE STATE LIBRARIES.
New Hampshire State Library, Department of Cultural Affairs, 20 Park St., Concord, NH 03301-6314. TEL 603-271-2393. FAX 603-271-6826.
circ. 2,500. *3994*

GRAPHIC ARTS MONTHLY.
Cahners Publishing Company (New York), Division of Reed Elsevier Inc., 245 W. 17th St., New York, NY 10011. TEL 212-463-6834. FAX 212-463-6530.
circ. 94,000. *5812*

GRAPHIC DESIGN: U S A.
Kaye Publishing Corporation, 1556 3rd Ave. Ste. 405, New York, NY 10128-3106. TEL 212-534-5003. FAX 212-534-4415.
circ. 30,186. *5812*

GRAPHIC NEWS.
Printing Industry of Minnesota Inc., 450 North Syndicate Ste. 200, St. Paul, MN 55104. TEL 612-646-4826. FAX 612-646-8673.
circ. 5,000. *5812*

GRAPHICS UPDATE.
Printing Association of Florida, Inc., Box 170010, Hialeah, FL 33017-0010. TEL 305-558-4855. FAX 305-823-8965.
circ. 10,000. *5812*

GRAPHICUS.
Associazione Culturale Progresso Grafico, Via Morgari 36/B, 10125 Turin, Italy. TEL 39-11-6690577. FAX 39-11-6689200.
circ. 6,250. *5812*

GRAPHIX DIRECT RESPONSE.
Graphix Publications (Pty) Ltd., P.O. Box 751119, Gardenview 2047, South Africa. TEL 27-11-6224800. FAX 27-11-6222480.
circ. 3,300. *5812*

GRASSY KNOLL GAZETTE.
Cutler Designs, Box 1465, Manchester, MA 01944. TEL 508-526-1521.
circ. 250. *2164*

GRAVES FAMILY NEWSLETTER.
Graves Family Association, 261 South St., Wrentham, MA 02093-1504. TEL 508-384-8084.
circ. 90. *3086*

GRAVURE ENVIRONMENTAL NEWSLETTER.
Gravure Association of America, Inc., 1200A Scottsville Rd., Rochester, NY 14624-5703. TEL 716-436-2150. FAX 716-436-7689.
circ. 1,400. *5813*

GRAYBAR OUTLOOK.
Graybar Electric Co., Box 7231, St. Louis, MO 63177. TEL 314-512-9200. *2699*

GREAT BRITAIN. NATURAL ENVIRONMENT RESEARCH COUNCIL. BRITISH GEOLOGICAL SURVEY. UNITED KINGDOM OFFSHORE REGIONAL REPORTS.
Natural Environment Research Council, British Geological Survey, Kingsley Dunham Centre, Keyworth, Nottingham NG12 5GG, England. TEL 44-115-936-3100. FAX 44-115-936-3200.
circ. 1,000. *2242*

GREAT BRITAIN. OVERSEAS DEVELOPMENT ADMINISTRATION. REPORT ON RESEARCH AND DEVELOPMENT.
Overseas Development Administration, Abercrombie House, Library, Eaglesham Rd., E. Kilbride, Glasgow G75 8EA, Scotland. *1307*

GREAT LAKES GETAWAY.
Camden Publications, 331 E. Bell St., Box 8, Camden, MI 49232-0008. TEL 517-368-0365. FAX 517-368-5131.
circ. 130,000. *6889*

GREAT LAKES PILOT NEWS.
1219 Van Dusen, Ann Arbor, MI 48103. TEL 313-439-8847. FAX 313-769-6471.
circ. 13,000. *65*

GREAT LAKES SCIENCE ADVISORY BOARD. REPORT.
International Joint Commission, Great Lakes Regional Office, 100 Ouellette Ave., 8th Fl., Windsor, ON N9A 6T3, Canada. TEL 519-257-6700. FAX 519-257-6740.
circ. 8,000. *6969*

GREATER WASHINGTON BOARD OF TRADE NEWS.
Greater Washington Board of Trade, 1129 20th St., N.W., Washington, DC 20036. TEL 202-857-5900. FAX 202-223-2648.
circ. 5,875. *1165*

GREATER WASHINGTON BOARD OF TRADE PROGRESS REPORT.
Greater Washington Board of Trade, 1129 20th St., N.W., Ste. 200, Washington, DC 20036. TEL 202-857-5900. FAX 202-223-2648.
circ. 6,700. *1142*

THE GREEN BOOK: ENVIRONMENTAL RESOURCE DIRECTORY.
Green Book, Inc., Corporate Place, 100 Burh Rd., Andover, MA 01810. TEL 508-474-5000. FAX 508-474-5054.
circ. 120,000. *2799*

GREEN PAGES.
Murdoch, Walrath & Holmes, 1130 K St., Ste. 210, Sacramento, CA 95814. TEL 916-441-3883.
circ. 6,000. *1612*

GREENHOUSE PRODUCT NEWS.
Scranton Gillette Communications, Inc., 380 E. Northwest Hwy., Des Plaines, IL 60016-2282. TEL 708-298-6622. FAX 708-390-0408.
circ. 20,000. *3072*

GREYHOUND ADVISER.
Greyhound Racing Control Board (Victoria), 1 Queens Rd., Melbourne, Vic., Australia. TEL 61-3-98673377. FAX 61-3-98662494.
circ. 6,000. *5390*

GROCERS REPORT.
Supermarket Productions, Box 6124, San Rafael, CA 94903-0124. TEL 415-479-0211.
circ. 15,000. *3005*

GROCERY DISTRIBUTION.
Trend Publishing, Inc., 625 N. Michigan Ave., Ste. 2500, Chicago, IL 60611. TEL 312-654-2300. FAX 312-654-2323.
circ. 15,000. *3005*

GROENE MARKT.
M'Xpress vof, P.O. Box 66, 5258 ZH Berlicum, Netherlands. TEL 31-73-5034347. FAX 31-73-5034347.
circ. 2,500. *3054*

GROUND SUPPORT EQUIPMENT TODAY.
General Publications, Inc., Box 480, Hatch, NM 87937-0480. TEL 505-267-1030. FAX 505-267-1920.
circ. 14,000. *66*

GROUNDS MAINTENANCE.
Intertec Publishing Corp., 9800 Metcalf, Overland Park, KS 66212-2215. TEL 913-341-1300. FAX 913-967-1898.
circ. 45,521. *3054*

GROUNDSMAN.
Adam Publishing Ltd., 42 West End Ave., Pinner, Mddx. HA5 1BJ, England. TEL 44-181-868-3600. FAX 44-181-429-2374.
circ. 6,000. *6565*

GROUP CIRCLE.
American Group Psychotherapy Association, 25 E. 21st St., 6th Fl., New York, NY 10010. TEL 212-477-2677. FAX 212-979-6627.
circ. 4,000. *5845*

GROUP TRAVEL LEADER.
Group Travel Leader, Inc., 130 N. Broadway St., Lexington, KY 40507-1227. TEL 606-253-0455. FAX 606-253-0499.
circ. 30,000. *6889*

GROWTH AND CHANGE.
Blackwell Publishers, 238 Main St., Cambridge, MA 02141. TEL 617-547-7110. FAX 617-547-0789.
circ. 150. *1521*

GRUE MAGAZINE.
Hell's Kitchen Productions, Inc., Box 370, Times Sq. Sta., New York, NY 10108-0370. TEL 212-245-2329.
circ. 2,000. *4327*

GUIA AUTOMOTRIZ DE VENEZUELA.
Ortiz y Asociados, s.r.l., Av. Caurimare, Qta. Expo., Colinas de Bello Monte, Caracas, Venezuela. TEL 7511355. FAX 582-7511122.
circ. 8,000. *6787*

GUIA FAMILIAR.
Box 9090, Van Nuys, CA 91409. TEL 818-781-2605. FAX 818-781-2625.
circ. 229,644. *5104*

THE GUIDE (PEACHTREE CITY).
Print Graphics Services, Inc., Box 2752, Peachtree City, GA 30269. TEL 770-631-9159. FAX 770-631-8852.
circ. 40,000. *3229*

GUIDE DE L'INGENIERIE.
Genie Industriel Multimedia, 9 rue Denis Poisson, 75017 Paris, France. TEL 40-63-12-12. FAX 40-68-12-29. *2600*

GUIDE DES FUTURS EPOUX.
11 bis rue du Docteur Baudin, 28004 Chartres Cedex 92, France.
circ. 400,000. *6415*

GUIDE TO EATING ONTARIO SPORT FISH.
Ministry of Environment and Energy, Environmental Monitoring and Reporting Branch, 135 St. Clair Ave. W., Toronto, ON M4V 1P5, Canada. TEL 416-314-7886. FAX 416-314-7930. *2934*

GUIDELINES LETTER.
Guidelines, Box 456, Orinda, CA 94563. TEL 510-299-1323. FAX 510-299-0181.
circ. 3,000. *394*

GUILD NEWS.
Graphic Artists Guild, 11 W. 20th St., 8th Fl., New York, NY 10011-3704. TEL 212-463-7730. FAX 212-463-8779.
circ. 5,000. *431*

GULDSMEDEBLADET.
Guldsmedefagets Faellesraad, Ryvangs Alle 26, DK-2100 Copenhagen Oe, Denmark. TEL 45-39-29-52-11. FAX 45-39-27-08-11.
circ. 1,400. *3696*

GULDSMEDSTIDNINGEN.
Sveriges Juvelerare- och Guldsmedsfoerbund, Klostergatan 19, S-753 21 Uppsala, Sweden. TEL 46-18-132300. FAX 46-18-132324.
circ. 1,250. *3696*

GULF COAST GOLFER.
Golfer Magazines, Inc., 9182 Old Katy Rd., Ste. 212, Houston, TX 77055. TEL 713-464-0308. FAX 713-464-0129.
circ. 32,000. *6506*

GULF CONSTRUCTION & SAUDI ARABIA REVIEW.
Al Hilal Publishing & Marketing Group, P.O. Box 224, Manama, Bahrain. TEL 973-293131. FAX 973-293400.
circ. 10,200. *857*

GUNNERIA.
Norges Teknisk-Naturvitenskapelige Universitet, Vitenskapmuseet, N-7004 Trondheim, Norway. TEL 47-73-59-21-45. FAX 47-73-59-22-23.
circ. 250. *355*

GUYANA. NATIONAL INSURANCE BOARD. ANNUAL REPORT: GUYANA NATIONAL INSURANCE SCHEME.
National Insurance Board, Brickdam and Winter Place, Georgetown, Guyana. TEL 592-02-66797. FAX 592-02-52273.
circ. 300. *3671*

THE H E D U BULLETIN.
University of Botswana, Higher Education Development Unit, Private Bag 0022, Gaborone, Botswana. TEL 267-351151. FAX 267-356591.
circ. 800. *2430*

H I V O S MAGAZINE.
Humanistisch Instituut voor Ontwikkelingssamenwerking, Raamweg 16, 2596 HL The Hague, Netherlands. TEL 31-701-3636907. FAX 31-70-3617447.
circ. 10,000. *1307*

H M K KURIER - STIMME DER MAERTYRER.
Hilfsaktion Maertyrerkirche e.V., Postfach 1160, 88683 Uhldingen, Germany. TEL 49-7556-92110. FAX 49-7556-921130.
circ. 38,000. *6065*

H N O AKTUELL.
Dr. R. Kaden Verlag, Poststr. 24-26, 69115 Heidelberg, Germany. TEL 49-6221-10313. FAX 49-6221-29910.
circ. 4,000. *4797*

H P A C TECHLIT SELECTOR.
Penton Publishing Co. 1100 Superior Ave., Cleveland, OH 44114-2543. TEL 216-696-7000. FAX 216-696-8765.
circ. 52,000. *2755*

H R A I NEWS.
Heating, Refrigerating and Air Conditioning Institute of Canada, 5045 Orbitor Dr., Bldg. 11, Ste. 300, Mississauga, ON L4W 4Y4, Canada. TEL 905-602-4700. FAX 905-602-1197.
circ. 1,200. *3328*

H R D I ADVISORY.
Human Resources Development Institute, 815 16th St., N.W., Washington, DC 20006. TEL 202-638-3912.
circ. 2,700. *1375*

H S R C - R G N IN FOCUS.
Human Sciences Research Council, Private Bag
X41, Pretoria 0001, South Africa.
circ. 4,000. *6325*

HABIT.
Mentor Communications ab, P.O. Box 27817, S-
115 93 Stockholm, Sweden. TEL 46-8-6704128.
FAX 46-8-6616455.
circ. 8,049. *1841*

HABITAT (NEW YORK CITY EDITION).
Carol Group Ltd., 928 Broadway, New York, NY
10010. TEL 212-505-2030. FAX 212-254-6795.
circ. 10,000. *6026*

HABITAT (REGIONAL EDITION).
Carol Group Ltd., 928 Broadway, Ste. 1105, New
York, NY 10010. TEL 212-505-2030. FAX 212-
254-6795.
circ. 8,000. *6026*

HAFLINGERSPORT.
Reitclub St. Erhard, Haymogasse 19, A-1238
Vienna, Austria. TEL 01-8827224.
circ. 1,500. *6547*

HAFRANNSOKNIR.
Hafrannsoknastofnunin, Skulagata 4, P.O. Box
1390, 121 Reykjavik, Iceland. TEL 354-552-0240.
circ. 420. *2934*

AL-HAHOMA.
Hashomar Hatzair Israel, 7 Bezalel Yaffe St., Tel
Aviv 65204, Israel. TEL 972-3-291161. FAX 972-
3-202601.
circ. 5,000. *5671*

HAIYANG YUYE.
Zhongguo Shuichan Kexue Yanjiuyuan, Donghai
Shuichan Yanjiusuo, 300 Jungong Lu, Shanghai
200090, People's Republic of China. TEL 86-21-
5434690. FAX 86-21-5432926.
circ. 500. *2934*

HALLASCHKA.
Brueckenhofstr. 84, 34132 Kassel, Germany.
circ. 50. *4145*

HAMBURG AFRICAN STUDIES.
Institut fuer Afrika-Kunde, Neuer Jungfernstieg 21,
20354 Hamburg, Germany. TEL 49-40-3562523.
FAX 49-40-3562511.
circ. 300. *5671*

HAMILTON ALUMNI REVIEW.
Hamilton College, Trustees of Hamilton College,
198 College Hill Rd., Anderson-Connell Alumni
Center, Clinton, NY 13323. TEL 315-859-4680.
FAX 315-859-4648.
circ. 19,000. *1870*

HANDBUCH KULTURMANAGEMENT.
Dr. Josef Raabe Verlags GmbH, Schadowstr. 48-50,
40212 Duesseldorf, Germany. TEL 0211-16675-0.
FAX 0211-1667510.
circ. 2,500. *1420*

HANDELSBESTYREREN.
Handelsbestyrerforbundet, Arbeidersamfundets
Plass 1, 0181 Oslo, Norway. TEL 02-20-52-40.
FAX 47-2-113194.
circ. 1,450. *1420*

**HANDLING AND PACKAGING PRODUCT
INFORMATION CARDS.**
Trinity Publishing Ltd., Times House, Station
Approach, Ruislip, Middx. HA4 8NB, England.
TEL 44-1895-677677. FAX 44-1895-676027.
circ. 21,500. *5300*

AL-HARAKAH.
Islamic Party of Malaysia, 28A Jalan Pahang Barat,
Off Jalan Pahang, 53000 Kuala Lumpur, Malaysia.
TEL 603-4213343. FAX 603-4212422.
circ. 50,000. *5671*

HARDHAT (OKLAHOMA CITY).
National Marketing Center, Inc., Box 60150,
Oklahoma City, OK 73146. TEL 405-840-2135.
857

HARDWARE AGE "WHO MAKES IT" BUYERS' GUIDE.
Chilton Co., Chilton Way, Radnor, PA 19089.
TEL 215-964-4269. *1613*

HARDWARE AND GARDEN REVIEW.
Faversham House Group Ltd., Faversham House,
232a Addington Rd., South Croydon, Surrey CR2
8LE, England. TEL 44-181-651-7100. FAX 44-181-
651-7117.
circ. 14,970. *889*

HARDWARE TRADE.
Screened Porch Publishing Co., 10510 France Ave.
S., No. 225, Boomington, MN 55431-3538.
TEL 612-944-3172.
circ. 17,242. *889*

HARDWOOD FLOORS.
Athletic Business Publications, Inc., 1846 Hoffman
St., Madison, WI 53704. TEL 608-249-0186.
FAX 608-249-1153.
circ. 24,153. *886*

HARPA.
Internationales Harfen Zentrum, Dorneckstr. 105,
CH-4143 Dornach, Switzerland. TEL 41-61-
7018866. FAX 41-61-7018858.
circ. 1,500. *5162*

HARSTAD TIDENDE.
Harstad Tidende A-S, P.O. Box 85, Storgaten 11,
Harstad, N-9401 Troms, Norway. TEL 47-770-
18000. FAX 47-770-18005.
circ. 16,448. *3200*

HARTFORD DENTAL SOCIETY NEWSLETTER.
Hartford Dental Society, 230 Scarborough St.,
Hartford, CT 06105. TEL 203-523-8657. FAX 203-
523-8657.
circ. 600. *4642*

HARVARD DENTAL BULLETIN.
Harvard School of Dental Medicine, 188 Longwood
Ave., Boston, MA 02115. TEL 617-432-1533.
FAX 617-432-4266.
circ. 2,500. *4642*

**HARVARD UNIVERSITY. GRADUATE SCHOOL OF
EDUCATION. BULLETIN.**
Harvard University, Graduate School of Education,
Appian Way, Cambridge, MA 02138. TEL 617-495-
3615.
circ. 20,500. *2338*

HARYANA HEALTH JOURNAL.
State Health Education Bureau, Directorate of Health
Services, 36 Madhaya Marg, Sector 7C, Chandigarh,
Haryana, India. *5961*

HASSADEH.
G.K. Hassadeh Monthly Review Ltd., 8 Shaul
Hamelech St., P.O. Box 40044, 61400 Tel Aviv,
Israel. TEL 972-3-6929978. FAX 972-3-6929979.
circ. 8,000. *121*

HAUSAPOTHEKE.
Otto Hoffmanns Verlag GmbH, Arnulfstr. 10, 80335
Munich, Germany. TEL 49-89-545845-0. FAX 49-
89-54584520.
circ. 2,100,000. *5415*

HAUSARZT SACHSEN-ANHALT.
B M V - Berliner Medizinische Verlagsanstalt GmbH,
Lietzenburgerstr. 97, 10719 Berlin, Germany.
TEL 49-30-8823569. FAX 49-30-8812225.
circ. 2,000. *4462*

HAUSARZT SEMINAR.
B M V - Berliner Medizinische Verlagsanstalt GmbH,
Lietzenburgerstr. 97, 10719 Berlin, Germany.
TEL 49-30-8823569. FAX 49-30-8812225.
circ. 26,000. *4462*

DAS HAUSBAU MAGAZIN.
Fachschriften Verlag GmbH, Hoehenstr. 17, 70736
Fellbach, Germany. TEL 0711-5206-256.
FAX 0711-5281424.
circ. 74,062. *857*

HAUSMEISTER UND HAUSVERWALTUNG.
Rolf Soll Verlag GmbH, Postfach 650680, 22366
Hamburg, Germany. TEL 49-40-6068820. FAX 49-
40-60688288.
circ. 15,000. *3584*

HAUT DECOR.
Haut Decor, Inc., 180 N.E. 39th St., Ste. 221,
Miami, FL 33137-3650. TEL 305-576-1677.
FAX 305-576-1343.
circ. 15,000. *3577*

HAVEN.
Det Danske Haveselskab, Jaegersborgvej 47, DK-
2800 Lyngby, Denmark. TEL 45-93-60-00. FAX 45-
93-51-44.
circ. 74,000. *3055*

HAWAII. OFFICE OF THE OMBUDSMAN. REPORT.
Office of the Ombudsman, Kekuanaoa Bldg., 4th Fl.,
465 S. King St., Honolulu, HI 96813. TEL 808-
587-0770. FAX 808-587-0773 *5942*

HAWAII DENTAL JOURNAL.
Hawaii Dental Association, 1000 Bishop St., Ste.
805, Honolulu, HI 96813. TEL 808-536-2135.
FAX 808-536-2137.
circ. 950. *4642*

HAWAII HEALTH MESSENGER.
Department of Health, Communication Office, Box
3378, Honolulu, HI 96801. TEL 808-586-4442.
FAX 808-586-4444.
circ. 5,500. *5961*

HAWAII HOSPITALITY.
Rainbow Pacific Publishing Co., Ltd., 1188 Bishop
St., Ste. 1512, Honolulu, HI 96813. TEL 808-521-
8877. FAX 808-521-8875.
circ. 3,800. *3562*

HAWAIIAN ACQUISITION LIST.
University of Hawaii Library, Hawaiian Collection,
2550 the Mall, Honolulu, HI 96822. TEL 808-956-
7923. FAX 808-956-5963.
circ. 180. *533*

HAWAIIAN JOURNAL OF HISTORY.
Hawaiian Historical Society, 560 Kawaiahao St.,
Honolulu, HI 96813. TEL 808-537-6271.
circ. 2,000. *3388*

HAYNES ALLOYS DIGEST.
Haynes International, Inc., 1020 W. Park Ave., Box
9013, Kokomo, IN 46904-9013 TEL 317-456-
6000. FAX 317-456-6905.
circ. 11,000. *4986*

HAZELDEN VOICE.
Hazelden Foundation, Box 11, Center City, MN
55012-0011. TEL 612-213-4455. FAX 612-257-
1055.
circ. 60,000. *2197*

HE LINES.
Streamline Fashion Publishing Ltd., 6-8 Vestry St.,
2nd Fl., London N1 7RE, England. TEL 0171-490-
0745. FAX 0171-490-0739.
circ. 10,000. *1833*

HEADLINER.
Kempec Publications, Inc., 1275 Bloomfield Ave.,
No. 6-36, Fairfield, NJ 07004-2708. TEL 201-785-
0764 FAX 201-785-0447.
circ. 2,300. *6787*

HEADLINES.
J R Publishing, Inc. (Boston), 13432 Third Ave.,
N.E., Brandenton, FL 34202-2729.
circ. 135,000. *4642*

HEADLINES (LONDON).
Newspaper Society, Bloomsbury House, 74-77 Gt.
Russell St., London WC1B 3DA, England. TEL 44-
171-636-7014. FAX 44-171-631-5119.
circ. 8,000. *3704*

HEALTH AND PHYSICAL EDUCATION.
Taishukan Publishing Co. Ltd., 3-24 Kanda
Nishikicho, Chiyoda-ku, Tokyo 101, Japan. FAX 03-
3295-4108.
circ. 5,000. *2338*

HEALTH & SAFETY NEWSLINE.
Engineering Employers' Federation Broadway
House, Tothill St., London SW1H 9NQ, England.
TEL 0171-222-7777. FAX 0171-222-2782.
circ. 8,000. *5962*

HEALTH & SAFETY RESOURCE.
Ontario Natural Resources Safety Association, Box
2050, 690 McKeown Ave. North Bay, ON P1B
9P1, Canada. TEL 705-474-SAFE. FAX 705-472-
5800.
circ. 10,000. *5250*

HEALTH JOURNAL.
Madison Publishing, 263 Summer St., Boston, MA
02210. TEL 617-428-4600. FAX 617-428-4626.
circ. 1,108,229. *5529*

HEALTH LAW BULLETIN.
Institute of Government - North Carolina, UNC - Knapp Bldg. CB3330, Chapel Hill, NC 27599-3330. TEL 919-966-4119. FAX 919-962-2707. circ. 500. *5962*

HEALTH LAW REVIEW.
Health Law Institute, 457 Law Centre, University of Alberta, Edmonton, AB T6G 2H5, Canada. TEL 403-492-8343. FAX 403-492-4924. circ. 1,000. *3787*

HEALTH PROMOTION IN CANADA.
Health Canada, Ottawa, ON K1A 1B4, Canada. TEL 613-954-8842. FAX 613-990-7097. circ. 14,000. *5963*

HEALTH SYSTEMS REVIEW.
F A H S Review, Inc., 1405 N. Pierce St., Ste. 308, Little Rock, AR 72207. TEL 501-661-9555. FAX 501-663-4903. circ. 35,000. *3546*

HEALTHCARE NEW ORLEANS.
CityBusiness - New Orleans Publishing Group, 111 Veterans Blvd., Rm. 1810, Metairie, LA 70005. TEL 504-834-9292. FAX 504-837-2258. circ. 25,000. *5529*

HEARING CONCERN.
British Association of the Hard of Hearing, 7-11 Armstrong Rd., London W3 7JL, England. TEL 44-181-743-1110. FAX 44-181-742-9043. circ. 6,000. *3312*

HEARING JOURNAL.
Williams & Wilkins, 351 W. Camden St., Baltimore, MD 21201. TEL 410-528-4000. FAX 410-528-4312. circ. 22,000. *3312*

HEARTBEAT (NASHVILLE).
Free Will Baptist Foreign Missions, Box 5002, Antioch, TN 37011-5002. TEL 615-731-6812. FAX 615-731-5345. circ. 45,000. *6146*

HEARTH & HOME.
Village West Publishing, Box 2008, Laconia, NH 03247-2008. TEL 603-528-4285. FAX 603-524-0643. circ. 19,000. *2550*

HEARTLAND.
Susquehanna Radio Corp., 8120 Knue Rd., Indianapolis, IN 46250. TEL 317-842-9550. FAX 317-577-3361. circ. 108,872. *1936*

HEARTLAND RETAILER.
Podany Printing Co., 10310 Ellison Circle, Omaha, NE 68134. TEL 402-496-0717. FAX 402-496-0678. circ. 14,500. *3328*

HEARTLAND U S A.
U S T Publishing 1 Sound Shore Dr., Ste. 3, Greenwich, CT 06830-7251. TEL 203-622-3456. FAX 203-863-5393. circ. 750,000. *4942*

HEATHROW VILLAGER.
Town Crier Printing & Publisher, 260 Kingston Rd., Staines, Middlesex TW18 1PS, England. TEL 44-1784-453196. circ. 29,369. *3156*

HEATING AND VENTILATING REVIEW.
Faversham House Group Ltd., Faversham House, 232a Addington Rd., South Croydon, Surrey CR2 8LE, England. TEL 44-181-651-7100. FAX 44-181-651-7117. circ. 23,265. *3328*

HEATING - PIPING - AIR CONDITIONING.
Penton Publishing Co. 1100 Superior Ave., Cleveland, OH 44114-2543. TEL 216-969-7000. FAX 216-696-8765. circ. 52,000. *3328*

HEBEI CAIKUAI.
Hebei Sheng Caizheng Ting, Fu 9, Kangle Jie, Shijiazhuang, Hebei 050051, People's Republic of China. TEL 744621. *1047*

HEBEI FAXUE.
Hebei Sheng Zhengfa Ganbu Guanli Xueyuan, Wuqi Lu, Shijiazhuang, Hebei 050061, People's Republic of China. TEL 86-311-639286. circ. 5,000. *3787*

HEBREW UNIVERSITY OF JERUSALEM. AUTHORITY FOR RESEARCH AND DEVELOPMENT. CURRENT RESEARCH.
Hebrew University of Jerusalem, Authority for Research and Development, Jerusalem 91904, Israel. TEL 972-2-6586633. *6325*

HEILMITTEL AUS DER NATUR.
Otto Hoffmanns Verlag GmbH, Arnulfstr. 10, 80335 Munich, Germany. TEL 49-89-545845-0. FAX 49-89-54584520. circ. 2,100,000. *290*

HELICE.
Mexican Air Line Pilots Association, c/o Capt. J.J. Castillo A., Av. Palomas 110, Lomas de Sotelo, Mexico 10, D.F., Mexico. FAX 52-5-202-25-73. circ. 2,000. *66*

HELLENIC VETERINARY MEDICAL SOCIETY. BULLETIN.
Hellenic Veterinary Medical Society, P.O. Box 18281, 116 10 Athens, Greece. circ. 1,000. *6946*

HELLO ISRAEL.
Tourguide Ltd., P.O. Box 3656, Tel Aviv 61036, Israel. TEL 972-3-490930. FAX 972-3-497640. circ. 15,000. *6891*

HELSINGIN KAUPUNGIN TIETOKESKUKSEN NELJANNESVUOSIJULUAISU. KVARTTI.
Helsingin Kaupungin Tietokeskus, P.O. Box 303, SF-00171 Helsinki, Finland. FAX 358-0-169-3777. circ. 800. *6608*

HEMVAERNET.
Rikshemvaernsraadet (RiksHvr), S-107 87 Stockholm, Sweden. TEL 46-8-788-97-19. FAX 46-8-664-57-90. circ. 130,000. *5032*

HERALDO DE SALTILLO.
Cia. Editora de Coahuila, Abasolo 228, 25000 Saltillo, Coahuila, Mexico. TEL 52-84-142250. FAX 52-84-148874. circ. 5,000. *3192*

HERE AND NOW.
Institute of Psychological Research, Inc., 34 Fleury St. W., Montreal, PQ H3L 1S9, Canada. TEL 514-382-3000. FAX 514-382-3007. circ. 2,000. *5846*

HERON.
Technische Universititeit Delft, Faculty of Civil Engineering, c/o J.G.M van Mier, P.O. Box 5048, 2600 GA Delft, Netherlands. TEL 31-15-2784568. FAX 31-15-2786993. circ. 2,000. *2661*

HEWLETT-PACKARD JOURNAL.
Hewlett Packard Co. (Palo Alto), 3000 Hanover St., Palo Alto, CA 94304. TEL 415-857-2387. FAX 415-857-2157. circ. 130,000. *2087*

HI CLASS LIVING.
M N R Promotions, Inc., 111 Charlotte Pl., Englewood Cliffs, NJ 07632. TEL 201-871-2221. FAX 201-871-2223. circ. 15,000. *3229*

HIFI & VIDEO MARKT.
S Z V Spezial Zeitschriftengesellschaft mbH, Schmiedberg 4, 86415 Mering, Germany. TEL 49-8233-4117. FAX 49-8233-30206. circ. 13,896. *2521*

HIGH-PERFORMANCE COMPOSITES.
Ray Publishing, 1900 Wazee St., Ste. 309, Denver, CO 80202. TEL 303-292-4080. FAX 302-292-4181. *5620*

HIGHLIGHTS (EDWARDSVILLE).
Southern Illinois University at Edwardsville, Regional Research and Development Services, Campus Box 1456, Edwardsville, IL 62026-1456. TEL 618-692-3500. FAX 618-692-2886. circ. 1,000. *3584*

HILDEBRANDT REPORT.
Hildebrandt, Inc. (Somerville), 50 Division St., Somerville, NJ 08876-2900. TEL 908-725-1600. FAX 908-725-9764. circ. 5,000. *3787*

HILLSDALE MAGAZINE.
Hillsdale College, 33 E. College St., Hillsdale, MI 49242. TEL 517-437-7341. FAX 517-437-0160. circ. 24,000. *1871*

HILLTOP.
Howard University, 2251 Sherman Ave., N.W., Washington, DC 20059. TEL 202-806-6866. circ. 10,000. *1871*

HINDUSTAN CHAMBER REVIEW.
Hindustan Chamber of Commerce, 8 Kondi Chetty St., Madras 600 001, India. TEL 583134. FAX 568063. *1142*

HINE'S DIRECTORY OF INSURANCE ADJUSTERS.
Hine's, Inc., Box 143, Geneva, IL 60134-0143. TEL 708-462-9670. circ. 6,000. *3650*

HINE'S INSURANCE COUNSEL.
Hine's, Inc., Box 143, Geneva, IL 60134. TEL 708-462-9670. circ. 7,000. *3788*

HIPPOCRATES.
Heath Publishing Group 301 Howard St., 18th Fl., San Francisco, CA 94105-2252. TEL 415-512-9100. circ. 900,000. *4466*

HIROSHIMA IGAKU.
Hiroshima Igakkai, 1-1-1 Kannonhon-machi, Nishi-ku, Hiroshima 733, Japan. TEL 082-232-7211. FAX 082-293-3363. circ. 5,800. *4466*

HIROSHIMA UNIVERSITY. RESEARCH INSTITUTE FOR RADIATION BIOLOGY AND MEDICINE. PROCEEDINGS.
Hiroshima University, Research Institute for Radiation Biology and Medicine, Kasumi, Hiroshima 734, Japan. circ. 450. *4876*

HISPANIC REGISTER.
12475 Central Ave., Dept. 325, Chino, CA 91710. circ. 9,300. *2882*

HISPANIC YELLOW PAGES (MCLEAN).
Vega and Associates, 2071 Chain Bridge Rd., Ste. 50, Vienna, VA 22182-2622. TEL 703-903-9779. FAX 703-903-9788. circ. 100,000. *1614*

HISTORIC NANTUCKET.
Nantucket Historical Association, Box 1016, Nantucket, MA 02554. TEL 508-228-1894. FAX 508-558-5618. circ. 2,875. *3471*

HISTORICAL GEOGRAPHY RESEARCH PAPER SERIES.
Historical Geography Research Group, Department of Geography, University of Edinburgh, Drummond St., Edinburgh EH8 9XP, Scotland. TEL 44-131-650-2559. FAX 44-131-650-2524. circ. 450. *3260*

HISTORISCHE TATSACHEN.
Verlag fuer Volkstum und Zeitgeschichtsforschung, Hochstr. 6, 32602 Vlotho, Germany. TEL 49-5733-2157. FAX 49-5733-4419. circ. 10,000. *3416*

HISTORY OF ANTHROPOLOGY NEWSLETTER.
c/o George W. Stocking, 1126 E. 59th St., University of Chicago, Chicago, IL 60637. TEL 312-702-7702. FAX 312-702-4503. circ. 300. *311*

HITACHI ZOSEN TECHNICAL REVIEW.
Hitachi Zosen Corporation, Technical Research Institute, 3-22, Sakurajima 1-chome, Konohana-ku, Osaka-shi, Osaka 554, Japan. FAX 06-465-4040. circ. 2,800. *2601*

HITSAUSTEKNIIKKA - SVETSTEKNIK.
Suomen Hitsausteknillinen Yhdistys, Makelankatu 36A, 00510 Helsinki, Finland. TEL 358-773-21-99. FAX 358-773-26-61. circ. 5,500. *4986*

HIV FUNDING WATCH.
Department of Health, Reprographics & Library Services Division, 1100 W. 49th St., Austin, TX 78756-3199. TEL 512-458-7684. FAX 512-458-7683. *4621*

HJELPEPLEIEREN.
Norsk Hjelpepleierforbund, P.O. Box 151, Brun, N-0611 Oslo 1, Norway. FAX 645602.
circ. 48,000. *4714*

HOGAR.
Editores Nacionales, Aguirre 730 y Boyaca, Casilla 1239, Guayaquil, Ecuador. TEL 4-327-200.
circ. 35,000. *6997*

HOGARAMA.
J S A Publishing, 2601 Ocean Park Blvd., Ste. 200, Santa Monica, CA 90405. TEL 310-399-9000. FAX 310-399-1722.
circ. 1,200,000. *3523*

HOJA DEL LUNES DE ORENSE.
Region, Cardenal Quiroga 11 y 15, Orense, Spain. *3215*

HOKKAIDO UNIVERSITY. ECONOMIC JOURNAL.
Hokkaido University, Faculty of Economics, North 9, West 7, Kita-ku, Sapporo 060, Japan. TEL 011-706-4112. FAX 011-706-4947.
circ. 560. *928*

HOKKAIDO UNIVERSITY. FACULTY OF SCIENCE. JOURNAL. SERIES 4: GEOLOGY AND MINERALOGY.
Hokkaido University, Faculty of Science, Nishi-8-chome, Kita-10-jo, Kita-ku, Sapporo 060, Japan. TEL 011-706-3225. FAX 011-716-0394.
circ. 850. *2243*

HOLD PUSTEN.
Norsk Radiografforbund, Lakkegt. 19-21, N-0187 Oslo, Norway. FAX 47-22-17-52-04.
circ. 1,380. *4876*

HOLE.
Hole Magazine, 123 Irving Ave., Ottawa, ON K1Y 1Z3, Canada. TEL 403-228-6950.
circ. 300. *4217*

HOLLAND HERALD.
Media Partners International, P.O. Box 469, 1180 AL Amstelveen, Netherlands. TEL 31-20-5473550. FAX 31-20-6438581.
circ. 170,000. *6935*

HOLSTEIN FRIESIAN JOURNAL.
Holstein Friesian Society of Great Britain & Ireland, Scotsbridge House, Rickmansworth, Herts. WD3 3BB, England. TEL 44-1923-494600. FAX 44-1923-770003.
circ. 14,500. *250*

HOME & AWAY (MINNESOTA EDITION).
American Automobile Association, Minnesota State Automobile Association, Seven Travelers Trail, Burnsville, MN 55337. TEL 612-890-2500. FAX 612-894-4079.
circ. 212,000. *6891*

HOME BUILDER MAGAZINE.
Work-4 Projects Ltd., P.O. Box 400, Victoria Sta., Westmount, PQ H3Z 2V8, Canada. TEL 514-489-4941. FAX 514-489-5505.
circ. 26,042. *857*

HOME CARE PROVIDER.
Mosby - Year Book, Inc. 11830 Westline Industrial Dr., St. Louis, MO 63146-3318. TEL 314-872-8370. FAX 314-432-1380.
circ. 8,095. *4714*

HOME DIGEST (FRENCH EDITION).
Mema N.V., Wielewaalstraat 20, 2610 Wilrijk, Belgium. TEL 32-3-4480827. FAX 32-3-4480832.
circ. 11,000. *3688*

HOME ECONOMICS NEWS.
Institute of Home Economics, 21 Portland Pl., London WIN 3AF, England. TEL 44-171-436-5677.
circ. 1,700. *3523*

HOMEBRIGHT MAGAZINE.
Media Partners CPR, Northern Rock House, 20 Market Pl., Guisborough, Cleveland TS14 6HF, England. TEL 44-1287-639111. FAX 44-1287-637201.
circ. 2,000,000. *2569*

HOMEFINDERS GUIDE.
Publishing People, Inc., Alta Loma, CA 91701. FAX 800-692-3233.
circ. 45,000. *6026*

HOMEMAKERS'S MAGAZINE.
Telemedia Procom Inc., 25 Sheppard Ave. W., Ste. 100, North York, ON M2H 6S7, Canada. TEL 416-733-7600. FAX 416-218-3633.
circ. 1,600,000. *3524*

HOMES MAGAZINE.
Homes Publishing Group, 178 Main St., Unionville, ON L3R 2G9, Canada. TEL 905-479-4663. FAX 905-479-4482.
circ. 100,000. *6026*

HOMEWORLD BUSINESS.
I C D Publications, 1393 Veterans Hwy, Ste. 214 N, Hauppauge, NY 11788. TEL 516-979-7878. FAX 516-979-8182.
circ. 12,800. *3689*

HONG KONG APPAREL.
Hong Kong Trade Development Council, 36-39th Fl., Office Tower, Convention Plaza, 1 Harbour Rd., Wanchai, Hong Kong. TEL 584-4333. FAX 824-0249.
circ. 30,000. *1833*

HONG KONG EXTERNAL TRADE.
Census and Statistics Department, Wanchai Tower, 12 Harbour Rd., Central, Hong Kong. TEL 852-25988197. FAX 852-25987482.
circ. 700. *1004*

HONG KONG TOYS.
Hong Kong Trade Development Council, 36-39th Fl., Office Tower, Convention Plaza, 1 Harbour Rd., Wanchai, Hong Kong. TEL 2584-4333. FAX 2824-0249.
circ. 40,000. *3300*

HONG KONG VISITOR.
South China Morning Post Ltd., Box 47, Hong Kong, Hong Kong. TEL 5652430. FAX 5658961.
circ. 50,000. *6891*

HONOURABLE ARTILLERY COMPANY JOURNAL.
Honourable Artillery Company, Armoury House, London, EC1Y 2BQ, England. FAX 0171-628-0949.
circ. 2,800. *5033*

HOPPENSTEDT BOERSENFUEHRER.
Verlag Hoppenstedt GmbH, Havelstr. 9, 64295 Darmstadt, Germany. TEL 49-6151-380-0. FAX 49-6151-380-360.
circ. 3,000. *1099*

HORA DE CIERRE.
Inter American Press Association, 2911 N.W. 39th St., Miami, FL 33142. TEL 305-634-2465. FAX 305-635-2272.
circ. 15,000. *3704*

HORECA NEDERLAND VISIE.
Horeca Nederland, Postbus 566, 3440 AN Woerden, Netherlands. TEL 31-3480-66842. FAX 31-3480-24061.
circ. 15,750. *3562*

HORIZON AIR MAGAZINE.
Paradigm Communications Group, 2701 First Ave., Ste. 250, Seattle, WA 98121. TEL 206-441-5871. FAX 206-448-6939.
circ. 25,000. *6935*

HORIZONTES (SAN FRANCISCO).
Horizontes, 2601 Mission St., Ste. 900, San Francisco, CA 94110. TEL 415-641-6051. FAX 415-282-3320.
circ. 19,700. *2882*

HORSE BRASS.
National Horse Brass Society, 69 West Chiltern, Woodcote, Reading RG8 0SG, England. TEL 44-1491-680484.
circ. 500. *3508*

HOSHASEN EIKYO KENKYUJO HAPPYO RONBUN MOKUROKU.
Radiation Effects Research Foundation, 5-2, Hijiyama Park, Minami-ku Hiroshima-shi, Hiroshima-ken 732, Japan. FAX 81-82-263-7279. *4566*

HOSIERY STATISTICS.
National Association of Hosiery Manufacturers, 200 N. Sharon Amity Rd., Charlotte, NC 28211. TEL 704-365-0913. FAX 704-332-2056.
circ. 1,000. *1838*

HOSPICE TODAY.
Hospice of the Florida Suncoast, 300 E. Bay Dr., Largo, FL 34640. TEL 813-586-4432. FAX 813-586-5213.
circ. 55,000. *6375*

EL HOSPITAL (CINCINNATI).
Salud Publications International Inc., 2724 Erie Ave., Ste. B, Cincinnati, OH 45208-2125. TEL 513-533-5470. FAX 513-533-5474.
circ. 14,850. *4467*

HOSPITAL & HEALTHCARE NEWS.
H. Robert Jacobs Publishing Co., Inc., 2022 E. Allegheny Ave., Philadelphia, PA 19134. TEL 215-739-2033. FAX 215-426-4438.
circ. 46,700. *3547*

HOSPITAL BLUE BOOK (OFFICIAL SOUTHERN EDITION).
Billian Publishing, Inc., 2100 Powers Ferry Rd., Ste. 300, Atlanta, GA 30339. TEL 404-955-5656. FAX 404-952-0669.
circ. 10,654. *3547*

HOSPITAL DEVELOPMENT.
Wilmington Publishing, Wilmington House, Church Hill, Dartford, Kent UA2 7EF, England. TEL 44-1322-277788. FAX 44-1322-276476.
circ. 8,635. *3548*

HOSPITAL FOOD SERVICE.
American Hospital Association, One North Franklin, Chicago, IL 60606. TEL 312-422-3873. FAX 312-422-4579.
circ. 1,700. *5233*

HOSPITAL MANAGEMENT INTERNATIONAL.
Sterling Publications Ltd. P.O. Box 839, London W2 2YW, England. TEL 0171-915-9600.
circ. 10,000. *3549*

HOSPITAL MEDICINE.
Quadrant HealthCom, 105 Raider Blvd., Belle Mead, NJ 08502-1510. TEL 908-874-0707. FAX 908-874-5611.
circ. 34,000. *4467*

HOSPITALIS.
Hospitalis Verlag AG, Hermetschloostr. 75, Postfach 1632, CH-8048 Zurich, Switzerland. TEL 41-1-4330080. FAX 41-1-4330242.
circ. 12,600. *3550*

HOSPITALITY & TOURISM EDUCATOR.
Council on Hotel, Restaurant and Institutional Education, 1200 17th St., Washington, DC 20036-3047. TEL 202-331-5990. FAX 202-785-2511.
circ. 2,000. *2399*

HOSPITALITY INDUSTRY INTERNATIONAL.
B M I Publications Ltd., Suffolk House, George St., Croydon, Surrey CR9 1SR, England. TEL 44-181-649-7233. FAX 44-181-649-7234.
circ. 25,000. *3563*

HOTEL & CATERING BUSINESS.
Dewberry Boyes Ltd., 64 Woodrow, London SE18 5DH, England. TEL 44-181-317-8800. FAX 44-181-317-3636. *3563*

HOTEL BUSINESS.
I C D Publications, 1393 Veterans Hwy., Ste. 214 N., Hauppauge, NY 11788. TEL 516-979-7878.
circ. 45,000. *3563*

HOTEL INC. HOTEL PROPRIETOR.
Manor Publishing Ltd., Unit 7, Edison Rd., Highfield Industrial Estate, Hampden Park, Eastbourne, E. Sussex BN23 6PT, England. TEL 44-1323-507474. FAX 44-1323-509316.
circ. 8,000. *3564*

HOTEL UND GASTGEWERBE.
S H Z Fachverlag AG, Alte Landstr. 43, CH-8700 Kuesnacht, Switzerland. TEL 01-9108022. FAX 01-9105155.
circ. 10,000. *3564*

HOTELNEWS.
Hotelnews Edicoes e Promocoes Ltda., Rua Afonso Celso 797, 04119-060 Sao Paolo SP, Brazil. TEL 55-5745166. FAX 55-5495967. circ. 18,000. *3565*

HOUSE BUILDER.
Housebuilder Publications Ltd., 82 New Cavendish St., London W1M 8AD, England. TEL 071-580-5588. FAX 071-323-0890. circ. 19,687. *858*

HOUSE EAR INSTITUTE. REVIEW.
House Ear Institute, 2100 W. Third St., 5th Fl., Los Angeles, CA 90057. TEL 213-483-4431. FAX 213-483-8789. circ. 16,000. *4797*

HOUSE, HOME & GARDEN.
Berkeley House Enterprises, Inc., 809 Virginia Ave., Martinsburg, WV 25401. TEL 304-267-2673. circ. 15,000. *3229*

HOUSEWARES FOCUS.
Faversham House Group Ltd., Faversham House, 232a Addington Rd., South Croydon, Surrey CR2 8LE, England. TEL 44-181-651-7100. FAX 44-181-651-7117. circ. 4,825. *3689*

HOUSING IN SOUTHERN AFRICA.
Unified Communications C.C., P.O. Box 344, Westhoven 2142, South Africa. TEL 27-11-477-9760. FAX 27-11-673-6218. circ. 4,000. *3584*

HOUSING POLICY DEBATE.
Federal National Mortgage Association, 3900 Wisconsin Ave., N.W., Washington, DC 20016-2899. TEL 202-752-4422. FAX 202-752-4933. circ. 4,000. *3584*

HOUSING RESEARCH REVIEW.
Scottish Homes, Thistle House, 91 Haymarket Terrace, Edinburgh EH12 5HE, Scotland. TEL 44-131-313-0044. FAX 44-131-313-1115. circ. 7,880. *3585*

HOUSING RESEARCH SUMMARY.
Joseph Rowntree Foundation, The Homestead, 40 Water End, York YO3 6LP, England. TEL 44-1904-629241. FAX 44-1904-620072. circ. 3,000. *3585*

HOUSTON FIRE FIGHTER.
Houston Professional Firefighters Association, 1907 Freeman St., Houston, TX 77009. TEL 713-223-9166. FAX 713-237-0912. circ. 4,000. *2921*

HET HOUTBLAD.
Het Houtblad B.V., Postbus 1375, 1300 BJ Almere, Netherlands. TEL 31-36-5327331. FAX 31-36-5329708. circ. 18,500. *886*

HOW TO START YOUR OWN BUSINESS WITH 2000 TO 5000 DOLLARS.
Royal University, Ltd., 6, Lower Hatch St., Dublin 2, Ireland. circ. 20. *1576*

HOWARD UNIVERSITY MAGAZINE.
Howard University, Department of Publications, Arrupe House, 1400 Shepherd St., N.E., Washington, DC 20017. TEL 202-806-0970. FAX 202-806-4577. circ. 10,000. *2432*

HUAXIA KAOGU.
Henan Sheng Wenwu Yanjiusuo, No. 9, Longhai Bei 3 Jie, Zhengzhou, Henan 450004, People's Republic of China. TEL 6252066. circ. 5,000. *356*

HUDSON GAZETTE.
397 Main Rd., Hudson, PQ J0P 1H0, Canada. TEL 514-458-5482. FAX 514-458-3337. circ. 1,115. *3122*

HUDSON VALLEY MAGAZINE.
Suburban Publishing Co., 40 Garden St., Poughkeepsie, NY 12601-3106. TEL 914-485-7844. FAX 914-485-5975. circ. 4,000. *3230*

HULLFIRE.
Hull University, Students' Union, University House, Cottingham Rd., Hull, North Humberside HU6 7RX, England. TEL 44-1482-466269. FAX 44-1482-466280. circ. 8,000. *1871*

HUM - THE GOVERNMENT COMPUTER MAGAZINE.
557 Cambridge St., S., Ste. 202, Ottawa, ON K1S 4J4, Canada. TEL 613-237-4862. FAX 613-237-4232. circ. 13,000. *2073*

HUMAN GENOME NEWS.
Human Genome Management Information System, Oak Ridge National Laboratory, 1060 Commerce Park, Oak Ridge, TN 37830. TEL 423-576-6669. FAX 423-574-9888. circ. 12,300. *744*

HUMAN GENOME PROGRAM REPORT.
U.S. Department of Energy, Human Genome Program, Office of Health and Environmental Research, ER-72 GTN, Washington, DC 20585. TEL 301-903-6488. FAX 301-903-5051. *744*

HUMAN RESOURCE MANAGER.
Thorpe Park, Peterborough, Cambs. PE3 6JY, England. TEL 01733-316078. FAX 01733-312347. circ. 6,000. *1504*

HUMAN RESOURCE PROFESSIONAL.
Faulkner & Gray, Inc. (New York), 11 Penn Plaza, 17th Fl., New York, NY 10001. TEL 212-967-7000. FAX 212-967-7155. circ. 1,147. *1504*

HUMANES LEBEN - HUMANES STERBEN.
Gesellschaft fuer Humanes Sterben e.V., Postfach 110529, 86030 Augsburg, Germany. TEL 49-821-502350. FAX 49-821-5023555. circ. 40,000. *4468*

HUMPHREYS COLLEGE QUARTERLY NEWS BULLETIN.
Humphreys College, 6650 Inglewood Ave., Stockton, CA 95207. TEL 209-478-0800. FAX 209-478-8721. circ. 20,000. *1871*

THE HUNTED NEWS.
The Subourbon Press, Box 9101, Warwick, RI 02889. TEL 401-739-2279. circ. 250. *4218*

HUNTER EDUCATION INSTRUCTOR.
Outdoor Empire Publishing, Inc., 511 Eastlake Ave. E., Box 19000, Seattle, WA 98109. TEL 206-624-3845. circ. 10,000. *6566*

HUNTING REVIEW.
Hunting Group Management Services Ltd., 3 Cockspur St., London SW1Y 5BQ, England. TEL 0171-321-0123. FAX 0171-839-2072. circ. 12,000. *6758*

HUSTON VOICE.
811 Westheimee, Ste. 105, Houston, TX 77006. TEL 713-529-8490. FAX 713-529-9531. circ. 10,000. *3533*

HYDRA NACHTEXPRESS.
Hydra e.V., Rigaerstr. 3, 10247 Berlin, Germany. TEL 49-30-4224646. FAX 49-30-7074723. circ. 2,000. *6997*

HYDRAULICS & PNEUMATICS.
Penton Publishing Co. 1100 Superior Ave., Cleveland, OH 44114-2543. TEL 216-696-7000. FAX 216-696-8765. circ. 52,000. *2743*

HYDROCARBON TECHNOLOGY INTERNATIONAL.
Sterling Publications Ltd. 86-88 Edgware Rd., London W2 2YW, England. TEL 0171-915-9623. FAX 0171-258-0624. circ. 12,500. *5359*

HYDROPNEUMA.
F I M O P - C C I B, 500 Louisalaan, 1050 Brussels, Belgium. TEL 32-2-6407735. FAX 32-2-6408480. circ. 10,000. *2747*

HYVA ATERIA.
Fakta Oy, Hitsaajankatu 7, FIN-00081 A-Lehdet, Helsinki, Finland. TEL 358-0-75961. FAX 358-0-7596373. circ. 20,000. *3565*

I A C P - B J A POLICY ISSUES.
International Association of Chiefs of Police, Inc., 515 N. Washington St., Ste. 400, Alexandria, VA 22314-2340. TEL 703-243-6500. *2165*

I A C P TRAINING KEY.
International Association of Chiefs of Police, Inc., 515 N. Washington St., Ste. 400, Alexandria, VA 22314-2340. TEL 703-243-6500. *2165*

I A E A NEWSBRIEFS.
International Atomic Energy Agency, Division of Public Information, Wagramstr. 5, Postfach 100, A-1400 Vienna, Austria. TEL 43-1-23601286. FAX 43-1-2307610. circ. 8,500. *2577*

I A E A TECHNICAL DOCUMENTS SERIES.
International Atomic Energy Agency, Wagramerstr. 5, P.O. Box 100, A-1400 Vienna, Austria. TEL 43-1-2060-22529. FAX 43-1-2060-29302. circ. 200. *2577*

I A O STRAIGHT TALK.
International Association for Orthodontics, 1100 Lake St., Ste. 240, Oak Park, IL 60301-1035. TEL 708-445-0320. FAX 708-445-0321. circ. 2,100. *4643*

I A T A ANNUAL REPORT.
International Air Transport Association, 2000 Peel St., Montreal, PQ H3A 2R4, Canada. TEL 514-844-6311. FAX 514-844-3788. *6758*

I A T A REVIEW.
International Air Transport Association, 2000 Peel St., Montreal, PQ H3A 2R4, Canada. TEL 514-844-6311. FAX 514-844-3788. *6759*

I B E C - E S R I BUSINESS FORECAST.
Irish Business and Employers Confederation, Confederation House, 84-86 Lower Baggot St., Dublin 2, Ireland. TEL 353-1-6601011. FAX 353-1-6601717. *1521*

I B E C NEWS.
Irish Business and Employers Confederation, Confederation House, 84-86 Lower Baggot St., Dublin 2, Ireland. TEL 353-1-6601011. FAX 353-1-6601717. *1521*

I B M NIEUWS.
I B M Nederland N.V., Johan Huizingalaan 765, P.O. Box 9999, 1000 AG Amsterdam, Netherlands. TEL 31-20-5133813. FAX 31-20-6177600. circ. 15,000. *2015*

I B M - U K NEWS.
I B M United Kingdom Ltd., P.O. Box 41, North Harbour, Portsmouth PO6 3AU, England. TEL 01705-564325. FAX 01705-385081. circ. 19,000. *1991*

I B W A NEWS.
International Bottled Water Association, 113 N. Henry St., Alexandria, VA 22314. TEL 703-683-5213. FAX 703-683-4074. circ. 2,500. *506*

I B W A TECHNICAL BULLETIN.
International Bottled Water Association, 113 N. Henry St., Alexandria, VA 22314. TEL 703-683-5213. FAX 703-683-4074. circ. 2,500. *506*

I C A N COMMUNICATE.
Invalid Childrens' Aid Nationwide, Barbican City Gate, 1-3 Dufferin St., London EC1Y 8NA, England. TEL 44-171-374-4422. FAX 44-171-374-2762. circ. 1,500. *2469*

I C A NEWSLETTER.
International Communication Association, 8140 Burnet Rd., Box 9589, Austin, TX 78766. TEL 512-454-8299. FAX 512-454-4221. *1905*

I C A S A L S NEWSLETTER.
International Center for Arid and Semiarid Land Studies, Texas Tech Univ., Box 41036, Lubbock, TX 79409-1036. TEL 806-742-2218. FAX 806-742-1954. circ. 3,000. *122*

I C M R BULLETIN.
Indian Council of Medical Research, Division of
Publication & Information, P.O. Box 4911, Ansari
Nagar, New Delhi 110 029, India. TEL 91-11-
6963980. FAX 91-11-6868662.
circ. 7,200. *4468*

I C S C RESEARCH QUARTERLY.
International Council of Shopping Centers, 665 Fifth
Ave., New York, NY 10022. TEL 212-421-8181.
FAX 212-421-6464.
circ. 5,500. *6027*

I E E - AUTOMATISIERUNG UND DATENTECHNIK.
Huethig GmbH, Postfach 102869, 69018
Heidelberg, Germany. TEL 49-6221-489232.
FAX 49-6221-489482.
circ. 20,000. *2700*

I E E E SPECTRUM.
Institute of Electrical and Electronics Engineers, Inc.,
345 E. 47th St., New York, NY 10017-2394.
TEL 212-705-7569. FAX 212-705-7589.
circ. 300,000. *2703*

I E N - EUROPE.
I E N Europe N.V. Rue Verte 216, 1030 Brussels,
Belgium. TEL 32-2-2402611. FAX 32-2-2427111.
circ. 50,008. *2747*

I E S E REVISTA.
Estudios y Ediciones I E S E S.L., Juan de Alos 43,
08034 Barcelona, Spain. TEL 34-3-2044000.
FAX 34-3-2801177.
circ. 15,834. *929*

I F M A WORLD.
International Foodservice Manufacturers Association,
180 N. Stetson Ave., Ste. 4400, Chicago, IL
60601. TEL 312-540-4400. *2976*

I F S NEWSLETTER.
Institute for Fusion Studies, University of Texas,
Austin, TX 78712. TEL 512-471-4378.
circ. 400. *2577*

I G B P GLOBAL CHANGE REPORT.
Royal Swedish Academy of Sciences, International
Geosphere-Biosphere Programme, P.O. Box 50005,
S-104 05 Stockholm, Sweden. TEL 46-8-16-64-48.
FAX 46-8-16-64-05.
circ. 5,000. *2243*

I H A BULLETIN.
Independent Healthcare Association, 22 Little
Russell St., London WC1A 2HT, England. TEL 0171-
430-0537. FAX 0171-242-2681. *3550*

I L A REPORTER.
Illinois Library Association, 33 W. Grand Ave No.
301, Chicago, IL 60610. TEL 312-644-1896.
FAX 312-644-1899.
circ. 4,400. *3996*

I LAISVE.
Friends of the Lithuanian Front, 1634-49th Ave.,
Cicero, IL 60650. *2883*

**I LOVE NEW YORK: THE FINGER LAKES TRAVEL
GUIDE.**
Finger Lakes Association, Inc., 309 Lake Street,
Penn Yan, NY 14527. TEL 315-536-7488.
FAX 315-536-1237.
circ. 65,000. *6892*

I M S NEWSLETTER.
Unesco, SC-IOC-MRI, 1 rue Miollis, 75732 Paris
Cedex 15, France. FAX 40-56-93-16.
circ. 5,000. *2296*

I N D A C.
Indianapolis Athletic Club, 350 North Meridian St,
Indianapolis, IN 46204. TEL 317-634-4331.
circ. 3,500. *1850*

I N E M BULLETIN.
International Network for Environmental
Management, Bahnhofstr. 36, 22880 Wedel,
Germany. TEL 04103-84019. FAX 04103-13699.
circ. 4,000. *2801*

I N F O.
Tulsa City-County Library System, Business and
Technology Dept., 400 Civic Center, Tulsa, OK
74103. TEL 918-596-7988. FAX 918-596-7895.
circ. 1,400. *4038*

I O M NEWS.
International Organization for Migration, 17 route
des Morillons, P.O. Box 71, CH-1211 Geneva 19,
Switzerland. TEL 41-22-7179242. *5785*

I P A AKTUELL.
A. Bernecker Verlag, Unter dem Schoeneberg 1,
34212 Melsungen, Germany. TEL 49-5661-731-0.
FAX 49-5661-73189.
circ. 54,500. *2165*

I P A S E BIBLIOTECA INFORMA.
Instituto de Previdencia e Assistencia dos Servidores
do Estado, Divsao de Relacoes Publicas, Biblioteca,
Rua Pedro Lessa 36, 13 Andar, Rio de Janeiro, G
B, Brazil.
circ. 400. *4038*

I P O ANNUAL PROGRESS REPORT.
Instituut voor Ferceptie Onderzoek, P.O. Box 513,
5600 MB Eindhoven, Netherlands. TEL 31-40-
773873. FAX 31-40-773876.
circ. 1,500. *4074*

I P P F MEDICAL BULLETIN.
International Planned Parenthood Federation,
Regent's College, Inner Circle, Regent's Park,
London NW1 4NS, England. TEL 44-171-486-
0741. FAX 44-171-487-7950.
circ. 30,000. *5785*

I P P F OPEN FILE.
International Planned Parenthood Federation,
Regent's College, Inner Circle, Regent's Park,
London NW1 4NS, England. TEL 44-171-486-
0741. FAX 44-171-487-7950.
circ. 2,500. *5785*

I P P F PLANNED PARENTHOOD CHALLENGES.
International Planned Parenthood Federation,
Regent's College, Inner Circle, Regent's Park,
London SW1 4NS, England. TEL 44-171-486-0741.
FAX 44-171-487-7950. *5785*

I-PUNKT.
Echter Wuerzburg, Fraenkische
Gesellschaftsdruckerei und Verlag GmbH, Postfach
5560, 97005 Wuerzburg, Germany. TEL 49-931-
6671-171. *1377*

I.Q.S.
Institut Quimic de Sarria, 08017 Barcelona, Spain.
FAX 2056266. *1677*

I S P NEWS.
M I S Training Institute Press, Inc., 498 Concord St.,
Framingham, MA 01701. TEL 508-879-7999.
circ. 25,000. *2182*

I S S A JOURNAL.
Information Systems Security Association, 4350
DiPaolo Center, Ste. C, Glenview, IL 60025-5212.
TEL 847-699-6441. FAX 847-699-6369. *2050*

I S S A TODAY.
International Sanitary Supply Association, Inc., 7373
N. Lincoln Ave., Lincolnwood, IL 60646. TEL 847-
982-0800. FAX 847-982-1012.
circ. 4,100. *5964*

I T A A MEMBERSHIP DIRECTORY.
Information Technology Association of America,
Publications Dept., 1616 N. Ft. Myer Dr., Ste.
1300, Arlington, VA 22209-9998. TEL 410-543-
0475. FAX 410-543-2921.
circ. 10,000. *2074*

I T E M.
R & B Enterprises (West Conshohocken) 20 Clipper
Rd., West Conshohocken, PA 19428. TEL 610-
825-1960. FAX 610-825-1684.
circ. 24,325. *2707*

I T R.
Technopress Fachzeitschriften Verlagsgesellschaft
mbH, Iglaseegasse 21-23, Postfach 176, A-1191
Vienna, Austria. TEL 43-1-322551.
circ. 17,000. *6857*

I T T HARTFORD AGENT.
I T T Hartford Group, Hartford Plaza, Hartford, CT
06115. TEL 203-547-4959. FAX 203-547-3799.
circ. 9,500. *3651*

**IBARAKI DAIGAKU KYOIKU GAKUBU KIYO. SHIZEN
KAGAKU.**
Ibaraki Daigaku, Kyoikugakubu, 1-1, Bunkyo 2-
chome, Mito-shi, Ibaraki-Ken 310, Japan. TEL 81-
29-228-8282. FAX 81-29-228-8329.
circ. 300. *6246*

IBERIAN STUDIES.
University of Keele, Centre for Iberian Studies,
Keele, Staffs. ST5 5BG, England. TEL 44-1782-
621111. FAX 44-1782-613847.
circ. 300. *6327*

ICE CREAM.
Ice Cream Alliance, 5 Pelham Ct., Pelham Rd.,
Nottingham NG5 1AP, England. TEL 44-115-985-
8505. FAX 44-115-985-7985.
circ. 1,250. *3000*

**IDAHO. DEPARTMENT OF FISH AND GAME.
FEDERAL AID INVESTIGATION PROJECTS.
PROGRESS REPORTS AND PUBLICATIONS.**
Department of Fish and Game, Box 25, Boise, ID
83707. TEL 208-334-3746. FAX 208-334-2148.
2129

**IDAHO BUREAU OF LAND MANAGEMENT
TECHNICAL BULLETIN.**
U.S. Bureau of Land Management Idaho State
Office, 3380 Americana Terr., Boise, ID 83706.
TEL 208-384-3066. FAX 208-384-3075.
circ. 200. *2129*

IDAHO CITIES.
Association of Idaho Cities, 3314 Grace St., Boise,
ID 83703. TEL 208-344-8594. FAX 208-344-
8677.
circ. 2,250. *5943*

IDEAS FOR BETTER LIVING.
Boulevard Associates, Inc., 724 E. Woodrow Ave.,
Columbus, OH 43207-2057. TEL 614-449-0133.
FAX 614-449-0135.
circ. 250,000. *3524*

**ILLINOIS. HOUSING DEVELOPMENT AUTHORITY.
ANNUAL REPORT.**
Housing Development Authority, 401 N. Michigan
Ave., Chicago, IL 60611. TEL 312-336-5200.
FAX 312-836-5249.
circ. 5,000. *3585*

ILLINOIS BROKER.
Broker Publishing, Inc., 6560 N. Scottsdale Rd.,
Ste. G-203, Scottsdale, AZ 85253. TEL 602-998-
8155. FAX 602-998-8549.
circ. 61,000. *3651*

ILLINOIS DEER & TURKEY SHOW PREVIEW.
Target Communications Corp., 7626 W. Donges
Bay Rd., Mequon, WI 53097-3400. TEL 414-242-
3990. FAX 414-242-7391.
circ. 30,000. *6566*

ILLINOIS DENTAL NEWS.
Illinois State Dental Society, 1010 S. Second St.,
Springfield, IL 62705. TEL 217-525-1406.
FAX 217-525-8872.
circ. 6,300. *4643*

ILLINOIS POLICE ASSOCIATION OFFICIAL JOURNAL.
Illinois Police Association, 220 Yosemite Cir. N.,
Minneapolis, MN 55422-5032.
circ. 17,000. *2165*

ILLINOIS QUARTERLY.
University of Illinois at Urbana-Champaign, Alumni
Association, University of Illinois, 227 Illini Union,
Urbana, IL 61801. TEL 217-337-1471. FAX 217-
333-7803.
circ. 117,000. *1872*

ILLINOIS TECHNOGRAPH.
Illini Media Co., 57 E. Green St., Champaign, IL
61820. TEL 217-333-3733. FAX 217-244-6616.
circ. 4,500. *2602*

ILLINOIS WILDLIFE.
Illinois Wildlife Federation, 123 S. Chicago, Rossville,
IL 60963. TEL 217-748-6365. FAX 217-748-
6304.
circ. 12,500. *2130*

ILMAILU.
Suomen Ilmailuliitto, Malmi Airport, 00700 Helsinki
70, Finland. TEL 358-0-35093-44. FAX 358-0-
35093440.
circ. 10,600. *67*

IMAGE DE LA MAURICIE.
Publicite G.M. Inc., 564 Blvd. des Prairies, Cap-de-la-Madeleine, Que. G8T 1K9, Canada. TEL 819-378-2176.
circ. 10,000. *2152*

IMAGING BUSINESS.
Phillips Business Information, Inc., 1201 Seven Locks Rd., Potomac, MD 20854. TEL 301-424-3338. FAX 301-309-3847. *2028*

IMPACT.
Social Impact Foundation Inc., Noel St. 2948, United Paranaque III M.M., P.O. Box 2950, Metro Manila, Philippines. TEL 827-65-81. FAX 827-65-81.
circ. 300. *6327*

IMPACT (AUSTIN).
Department of Mental Health and Mental Retardation, Public Information Office, Box 12668, Austin, TX 78711. TEL 512-465-4540. FAX 512-206-4711.
circ. 30,000. *4840*

IMPACT (NORTH YORK).
Seneca College, Student Federation Council, 1750 Finch Ave. E., N. York, ON M2J 2X5, Canada.
TEL 416-491-5050.
circ. 10,000. *1872*

IMPERIAL CANCER RESEARCH FUND. SCIENTIFIC REPORT.
Imperial Cancer Research Fund, Lincoln's Inn Fields, London WC2A 3PX, England. TEL 44-171-269-3206. FAX 44-171-269-3084.
circ. 1,700. *4756*

IMPORT AUTOMOTIVE PARTS & ACCESORIES.
Meyers Publishing Corp., 6211 Van Nuys Blvd., Van Nuys, CA 91401. TEL 818-785-3900. FAX 818-785-4397.
circ. 35,000. *6788*

IN CONTACT.
British Red Cross Society, 9 Grosvenor Cresc., London SW1X 7EJ, England. TEL 44-171-235-5454. FAX 44-171-245-6315.
circ. 41,000. *6376*

IN OLTRE.
Schena Editore, Viale le Stazione 177, 72015 Fasano (BR), Italy. TEL 080-71-46-81.
FAX 80714690.
circ. 1,000. *4219*

IN ONTARIO.
Insurance Institute of Ontario, 18 King St., E., 6th Fl., Toronto, ON M5C 1C4, Canada. TEL 416-362-8586. FAX 416-362-1126.
circ. 15,000. *3651*

IN OTHER WORDS.
Wycliffe Bible Translators, Inc., Box 2727, Huntington Beach, CA 92647. TEL 714-969-4600. FAX 714-969-4661.
circ. 300,000. *6067*

IN PERSPECTIVE.
Wiltel, Box 4311, Houston, TX 77210-4311.
TEL 713-364-4139. FAX 713-367-0278.
circ. 27,000. *1906*

IN THE DRIVER'S SEAT.
Ontario Safety League, 21 Four Seasons Place, Etobicoke, Ont. M9B 6J8, Canada. TEL 416-593-2670. *6788*

INCENTIVE TAXATION.
Henry George Foundation of America, 2000 Century Plaza (238), Columbia, MD 21044.
TEL 410-740-1177. FAX 410-740-3279.
circ. 5,400. *3585*

INDEPENDENT BOOKSELLING TODAY!
Paz & Associates, 2106 20th Ave. S., Nashville, TN 37212-4312. TEL 615-298-2303. FAX 615-298-9864.
circ. 400. *5998*

INDEPENDENT BUSINESS.
Group IV Communications, Inc., 125 Auburn Ct., Ste. 100, Thousand Oaks, CA 91362-3617.
TEL 805-496-6156. FAX 805-496-5469.
circ. 600,000. *930*

INDEPENDENT GASOLINE MARKETING.
Society of Independent Gasoline Marketers of America, 11911 Freedom Dr., No. 590, Reston, VA 22090-5602. TEL 703-709-7000. FAX 703-709-7007.
circ. 5,500. *5359*

INDEPENDENT NEWSPAPER FROM RUSSIA.
Cynthia Neu, Ed. & Pub., 7338 Dartford Dr., Ste. 9, McLean, VA 22102. TEL 703-827-0414. FAX 703-827-8923.
circ. 7,000. *5753*

INDEX NEW ZEALAND.
National Library of New Zealand, P.O. Box 1467, Wellington, New Zealand. TEL 64-4-4743098.
FAX 64-4-4753124.
circ. 400. *15*

INDEX TO PHILIPPINE PERIODICALS.
University of the Philippines Diliman, University Library, Gonzalez Hall, Diliman, Quezon City 1101, Philippines. TEL 632-976061. FAX 632-992863.
circ. 93. *534*

INDIA. CENTRAL VIGILANCE COMMISSION. REPORT.
Central Vigilance Commission, No.3, Dr. Rajendra Prasad Road, New Delhi, India. *5906*

INDIA. DEPARTMENT OF SPACE. ANNUAL REPORT.
Department of Space, Antariksh Bhavan, New Bel Rd., Bangalore 560094, India. TEL 080-3334474.
FAX 080-3332253.
circ. 5,000. *67*

INDIA. MINISTRY OF EDUCATION AND SOCIAL WELFARE. DEPARTMENT OF SOCIAL WELFARE. DOCUMENTATION SERVICE BULLETIN.
Ministry of Education and Social Welfare, Department of Social Welfare, Shastri Bhavan, New Delhi 110001, India. *6357*

INDIA. MINISTRY OF EDUCATION AND SOCIAL WELFARE. PROVISIONAL STATISTICS OF EDUCATION IN THE STATES.
Ministry of Education and Social Welfare, Department of Education, Shastri Bhavan, New Delhi 110001, India. *2390*

INDIA. MINISTRY OF FINANCE. FINANCE LIBRARY. WEEKLY BULLETIN.
Ministry of Finance, Finance Library, North Block, New Delhi 110001, India. TEL 3013852. *1100*

INDIAN CHEMICALS AND PHARMACEUTICALS STATISTICS.
Ministry of Chemicals and Fertilizers, Economics and Statistics Division, New Delhi, India. *5450*

INDIAN CRUSADER.
American Indian Liberation Crusade, Inc., 4009 Halldale Ave., Los Angeles, CA 90062. TEL 213-299-1810.
circ. 4,000. *2884*

INDIAN EDUCATION ABSTRACTS.
Ministry of Education and Social Welfare, Department of Education, Shastri Bhavan, New Dehli 110001, India. *2390*

INDIAN FERTILISER STATISTICS.
Ministry of Chemicals and Fertilisers, Economics and Statistics Division, New Delhi, India. *174*

INDIAN INSTITUTE OF TROPICAL METEOROLOGY. ANNUAL REPORT.
Indian Institute of Tropical Meteorology, Dr. Homi Bhabha Rd., Pashan, Pune 411 008, India. *4998*

INDIAN JOURNAL OF MEDICAL RESEARCH. SECTION A: INFECTIOUS DISEASES.
Indian Council of Medical Research, Division of Publication & Information, P.O. Box 4911, Ansari Nagar, New Delhi 110 029, India. TEL 91-11-6963980. FAX 91-11-6868662.
circ. 700. *4470*

INDIAN PETROLEUM AND NATURAL GAS STATISTICS.
Ministry of Petroleum & Chemicals, Department of Petroleum & Natural Gas, Economics and Statistics Division, Shastri Bhawan, New Delhi 110 001, India. FAX 66235. *5383*

INDIAN VACUUM SOCIETY. BULLETIN.
Indian Vacuum Society, c/o Technical Physics & Prototype Engineering Division, Bhabha Atomic Research Centre, Bombay 400 085, India. TEL 91-22-612-2630. FAX 91-22-61205711.
circ. 800. *5551*

INDIANA CONSTRUCTOR.
I B J Corp., 431 N. Pennsylvania St., Indianapolis, IN 46204. TEL 317-634-6200. FAX 317-263-5060.
circ. 3,500. *859*

INDIANA CONTRACTOR.
Indiana Association of Plumbing - Heating - Cooling Contractors, Inc., Box 40963, Indianapolis, IN 46240. TEL 317-575-9292. FAX 317-575-9378.
circ. 5,200. *3329*

INDIANA MUSICATOR.
Indiana Music Educators Association, Ball State University, School of Music, Muncie, IN 47306.
TEL 317-285-5496. FAX 317-285-1139.
circ. 2,000. *5164*

INDIANA PUBLISHER.
Hoosier State Press Association, Inc., 300 Consolidated Building, 1 Virginia Ave., Ste. 701, Indianapolis, IN 46204-3616. TEL 317-637-3966. FAX 317-624-4428. *3705*

INDIANA UNIVERSITY. SCHOOL OF LIBRARY & INFORMATION SCIENCES. ALUMNI NEWSLETTER.
Indiana University, Alumni Association, Fountain Sq., No.219, Bloomington, IN 47402-4822. TEL 812-855-5844.
circ. 3,800. *3997*

INDO - U S BUSINESS.
Indo-American Chamber of Commerce, Vulcan Insurance Bldg., Veer Nariman Rd., Churchgate, Bombay 400 020, India.
circ. 1,800. *1143*

INDOCHINA NEWSLETTER.
Asia Resource Center, 2161 Massachusetts Ave., Cambridge, MA 02140. TEL 617-497-5273.
FAX 617-354-2832.
circ. 1,000. *5754*

INDONESIA. DIREKTORAT PERUMAHAN RAKJAT. LAPORAN KERDJA.
Direktorat Perumahan Rakjat, Jalan Wijaya I-68, Kebayoran Baru, Jakarta, Indonesia. *3585*

INDRESCO INC. MARION DIVISION. NEWS AND REVIEW.
Indresco Inc., Marion Division, 617 W. Center St., Box 505, Marion, OH 43302. TEL 614-383-5211. FAX 614-382-2052.
circ. 7,500. *4339*

INDUSTRI-NOTICIAS.
Publi-News Latinoamericana, S.A.C.V., Colima 436, psio 2, Mexico 7 D.F., Mexico. *931*

INDUSTRIA ALIMENTARIA.
Alfa Editores Tecnicos S.A., Libertad No. 107-402, 03660 Mexico DF, Mexico. TEL 525-579-3333.
FAX 525-532-9504.
circ. 5,000. *2976*

INDUSTRIA ALIMENTICIA.
Stagnito Publishing Company, 1935 Shermer Rd., Ste. 100, Northbrook, IL 60062. TEL 847-205-5660. FAX 847-205-5680.
circ. 20,000. *2977*

INDUSTRIA INTERNACIONAL.
Publicaciones Internacionales S.A., Paseo de Castellana 210, 28046 Madrid, Spain. TEL 1-457-08-06. FAX 1-457-29-38.
circ. 6,000. *1522*

INDUSTRIA PORCINA.
Watt Publishing Co., 122 S. Wesley Ave., Mt. Morris, IL 61054. TEL 815-734-4171. FAX 815-734-4201.
circ. 8,842. *273*

INDUSTRIA TURISTICA.
Charles Francis Publications, Inc., Box 52-1898, Miami, FL 33152-1898. TEL 305-592-3168.
circ. 6,000. *6893*

INDUSTRIAL AND LABOR RELATIONS REVIEW.
Cornell University, New York State School of
Industrial and Labor Relations, Ithaca, NY 14853-
3901. TEL 607-255-2732. FAX 607-255-8016.
circ. 400. *1378*

INDUSTRIAL COMPUTING.
E M A P Business & Computer Publications Ltd.,
33-39 Bowling Green Ln., London EC1R 0DA,
England. TEL 44-171-837-1212. FAX 44-171-278-
4008.
circ. 15,002. *1992*

INDUSTRIAL COMPUTING.
I S A Services, Inc., 67 Alexander Dr., Box 12277,
Research Triangle Park, NC 27709. TEL 919-549-
8411. FAX 919-832-0237.
circ. 40,000. *2015*

INDUSTRIAL ENVIRONMENTAL MANAGEMENT.
Faversham House Group Ltd., Faversham House,
232a Addington Rd., South Croydon, Surrey CR2
8LE, England. TEL 44-181-651-7100. FAX 44-181-
651-7117.
circ. 8,128. *2853*

INDUSTRIAL HEATING.
Business News Publishing Company, 755 W. Big
Beaver Rd., Ste. 1000, Troy, MI 48084. TEL 810-
362-3700. FAX 810-362-0317.
circ. 22,500. *2747*

INDUSTRIAL LOCOMOTIVE.
Industrial Locomotive Society, Byfield, Wreford's Ln.,
Exeter, Devon EX4 5BR, England. TEL 01793-
692588.
circ. 350. *6811*

INDUSTRIAL NOTTINGHAMSHIRE.
Nottinghamshire Chamber of Commerce and
Industry, 395 Mansfield Rd., Nottingham NG5 2DL,
England. TEL 0602-624624. FAX 0602-605981.
circ. 2,500. *1143*

INDUSTRIAL PROGRESS.
Donnelly Marketing 1717 Park St., Ste. 250,
Naperville, IL 60563-8479.
circ. 60,000. *6653*

INDUSTRIAL PUERTO RICO.
Antilles Publishing, 721 Hernandez St., Miramar
Towers, Apt. 12B, Santurce 00908, PR 00901.
circ. 7,500. *1522*

INDUSTRIAL SYSTEMS.
Business & Management Editions Brussels s.p.r.l.,
Rue Stephanie, 17, 1020 Brussels, Belgium.
TEL 32-2-4266115. FAX 32-2-4258226.
circ. 20,000. *2747*

INDUSTRIAL TEACHER EDUCATION DIRECTORY.
National Association of Industrial and Technical
Teacher Educators, Dept. of Industrial Technology,
University of Northern Iowa, Cedar Falls, IA 50615-
0178. TEL 319-273-2753. FAX 319-273-5818.
circ. 3,800. *2432*

INDUSTRIAL WOODWORKER.
Willowe Magazines Ltd., 47-49 Cinque Ports St.,
Rye, E. Sussex TN31 7AN, England. TEL 44-1797-
227300. FAX 44-1797-222445.
circ. 13,000. *886*

INDUSTRIE MEISTER.
Vogel Verlag und Druck GmbH & Co. KG, Max-
Planck-Str. 7-9, 97082 Wuerzburg, Germany.
TEL 0931-4182145. FAX 0931-4182640.
circ. 17,792. *1522*

INDUSTRY WEEK.
Penton Publishing Co. 1100 Superior Ave.,
Cleveland, OH 44114-2543. TEL 216-696-7000.
FAX 216-969-7670.
circ. 233,000. *1422*

INDY'S CHILD.
Indy's Child, Inc., 8900 Keystone Crossing, Ste.
538, Indianapolis, IN 46240. TEL 317-843-1494.
FAX 317-574-3233.
circ. 70,000. *1769*

INFANT NUTRITION.
Hayward Medical Communications Ltd., 44 Earlham
St., Covent Garden, London WC2H 9LA, England.
TEL 44-171-240-4493. FAX 44-171-240-4479.
4806

INFARMA.
Conselho Federal de Farmacia, SBS Quadra 01,
Bloco K, 70093-900 Brasilia D.F., Brazil. TEL 061-
224-68-49. FAX 061-224-68-25.
circ. 10,000. *5417*

INFECTIONS IN MEDICINE.
S C P Communications, Inc., 134 W. 29th St., New
York, NY 10001-5304. TEL 212-714-1740.
circ. 61,693. *4621*

INFIRMIERE DU QUEBEC.
Order of Nurses of Quebec, 4200 Dorchester Blvd.
W., Montreal, PQ H3Z 1V4, Canada. TEL 514-762-
1667. FAX 514-769-9490.
circ. 61,803. *4715*

INFO MAGAZINE
Union Pacific Railroad, Employee Communications
Department, 1416 Dodge St., Omaha, NE 68179.
circ. 78,000. *6811*

INFOPACK E & E
Ediciones Press Graph, S.L., C. Mallorca 219 5o 2o,
08008 Barcelona, Spain. TEL 34-3-3237554.
FAX 34-3-3237463.
circ. 7,000. *5300*

INFORM-ACTION.
Manitoba Teachers Society, 191 Harcourt St.,
Winnipeg, MB R3J 3H2, Canada. TEL 204-888-
7961. FAX 204-831-0877.
circ. 2,050. *4074*

INFORMAL LOGIC.
Department of Philosophy, University of Windsor,
Windsor, ON N9B 3P4, Canada. TEL 519-253-
4232. FAX 519-973-7050.
circ. 300. *5479*

INFORMATION DISPLAY.
Society for Information Display, 1526 Brookhollow
Dr., Ste. 82, Santa Ana, CA 92705-5421. TEL 714-
545-1526. FAX 714-545-1547.
circ. 10,000. *4044*

INFORMATION FUER DIE TRUPPE.
Bundesministerium der Verteidigung, Fue SI 3,
Postfach 1328, 53003 Bonn, Germany. *5033*

INFORMATION LEGISLATIVE SERVICE.
Pennsylvania School Boards Association, 774
Limekiln Rd., New Cumberland, PA 17070-2398.
TEL 717-774-2331. FAX 717-774-0718.
circ. 11,300. *2341*

**INFORMATION RESOURCES MANAGEMENT
JOURNAL.**
Idea Group Publishing, 4811 Jonestown Rd., Ste.
230, Harrisburg, PA 17109-1751. TEL 717-541-
9150. FAX 717-541-9159.
circ. 500. *1423*

**INFORMATION TECHNOLOGY FOR LOCAL
GOVERNMENT.**
Government Group Publications, Southbank House,
Black Prince Rd., London SE1 7SJ, England.
TEL 0171-582-9191. FAX 0171-587-1810.
circ. 12,403. *2069*

INFORMATION TECHNOLOGY REVIEW.
Price Waterhouse, 32 London Bridge St., London
SE1 9SY, England. TEL 44-171-939-6283. FAX 44-
171-403-5265.
circ. 25,000. *2069*

INFORMATIONEN UND BERICHTE.
Braunschweigisches Lancesmuseum, Burgplatz 1,
38100 Braunschweig, Germany. TEL 0531-
4842602. FAX 0531-4842607.
circ. 1,000. *357*

INFORMATORE AGRARIO.
Informatore Agrario s.r.l., Lungadige Galtarossa 23-
E, 37123 Verona, Italy. TEL 39-45-597855.
FAX 39-45-597510.
circ. 45,118. *124*

INFORMATORE DI VETERINARIA E ZOOTECNIA.
Organizzazione Editoriale Medico Farmaceutica, Via
Edolo 42, 20125 Milan, Italy. TEL 39-2-675051.
FAX 39-2-67505223.
circ. 45,000. *6947*

**INFORME DE OPERACION DE LAS PRINCIPALES
EMPRESAS PRODUCTORAS Y DISTRIBUIDORAS
DE ENERGIA ELECTRICA DE COSTA RICA.**
Instituto Costarricense de Electricidad (ICE), Apdo.
10032, 1000 San Jose Costa Rica. TEL 506-
207720. *2707*

INFRASTRUCTURE FINANCE.
Institutional Investor, Inc., 488 Madison Ave., New
York, NY 10022. TEL 212-224-3570. FAX 212-
224-3592.
circ. 16,000. *1309*

INGENIERIA CIVIL.
Obsidiana Editores, S.A., Czda. de Tlalpan 2365,
Col. Ciudad Jardin, 04370 Mexico DF, Mexico.
TEL 6899133.
circ. 3,900. *2662*

INGENIERIA DE COSTOS.
D'Pastrana Editores, S.A., Kepler 147-A, Mexico 5,
D.F., Mexico.
circ. 5,000. *1423*

INGENIEUR ET INDUSTRIE.
Association pour la Promotion des Publications
Scientifiques (APPS), 26 av. de l'Amarante, B-1020
Brussels, Belgium. TEL 32-2-268-29-33. FAX 32-2-
268-25-14.
circ. 20,000. *2603*

INGENJOEREN.
Ingenjoersfoerbundet, P.O. Box 3C2 25, S-104 25
Stockholm, Sweden.
circ. 8,700. *2603*

INITIATIVE.
German British Chamber of Industry and
Commerce, 16 Buckingham Gate, London SW1E
6LB, England. TEL 071-235-5656. FAX 071-233-
7835.
circ. 2,300. *1280*

INJECTION MOLDING.
55 Madison St., Ste 770, Denver, CO 80206.
TEL 303-321-2322. FAX 303-321-3552.
circ. 37,500. *5620*

INLAND.
Inland Steel Flat Product Co. 30 W. Monroe St.,
Chicago, IL 60603. TEL 312-346-0300.
circ. 12,000. *3230*

INLINE RETAILER & INDUSTRY NEWS.
Inline, Inc., 2025 Pearl St., Boulder, CO 80302.
TEL 303-440-5111. FAX 303-440-3313.
circ. 8,000. *6464*

INNER CIRCLE LETTER.
Nelson Newsletter Publishing Corp., Box 41630,
Tucson, AZ 85717-1630. TEL 520-629-0434.
FAX 520-629-0387. *3508*

INNIS HERALD.
University of Toronto, Innis College Student Society,
2 Sussex Ave., Toronto, ON L5S 1A1, Canada.
TEL 416-978-4748.
circ. 2,000. *1872*

INNISFAIL BOOSTER.
4932 4th St., Innisfail, AB T4G 1N2 Canada.
TEL 403-227-3477.
circ. 7,500. *3122*

INNOMINATE.
Sydney University Medical Society, Council of the
Sydney University Medical Society, Blackburn Bldg.
D06, University of Sydney, Sydney, N.S.W. 2006,
Australia. TEL 61-2-351263E. FAX 61-2-3516198.
circ. 1,000. *1872*

INNOVATOR (ANN ARBOR).
University of Michigan, School of Education, E. & S.
University Aves., Ann Arbor, MI 48103. TEL 313-
763-4880. FAX 313-763-4062.
circ. 49,000. *2341*

INSIDE (ALBANY).
New York State Bar Association, Corporate Counsel
Section, 1 Elk St., Albany, NY 12207-1096.
TEL 518-463-3200. FAX 518-463-8844.
circ. 1,100. *3903*

INSIDE THE VATICAN.
Urbi et Orbi Communications, 3050 Gap Knob Rd.,
New Hope, KY 40052. TEL 502-325-3061.
FAX 502-325-3091.
circ. 14,000. *6182*

INSIDE TRACKS.
93 Goulding Ave., North York, ON M2M 1L3,
Canada. TEL 416-229-9213.
circ. 5,000. *5164*

INSIDER (SKOKIE).
Innate Graphics, Inc., 4124 Oakton St., Skokie, IL
60076. TEL 708-673-3458. FAX 708-675-0591.
circ. 1,018,350. *1872*

INSIEME.
Publications Ensemble Inc., 4358 rue Charleroi,
Montreal-Nord, PQ H1H 1T3, Canada. TEL 514-
328-2062. FAX 514-328-6562.
circ. 20,000. *2884*

INSIGHT (AKRON).
Akron - Summit County Public Library, 55 S. Main
St., Akron, OH 44326. TEL 330-643-9000.
circ. 2,000. *3999*

INSIGHT (CHICAGO).
Illinois C P A Society, 222 S. Riverside Plaza, 16th
Fl., Chicago, IL 60606. TEL 312-993-0393.
FAX 312-993-7713.
circ. 26,000. *1047*

INSIGHT (SPRINGFIELD).
State Library, 300 S. Second St., Springfield, IL
62701. TEL 217-785-6925. FAX 217-785-4324.
circ. 3,900. *3999*

INSIGHTS (WASHINGTON, 1988).
Library of Congress Professional Association, Library
of Congress, Washington, DC 20540. TEL 202-
707-3635.
circ. 2,200. *3999*

INSPAIN.
InSpain Magazine, Dr. Esquerdo 35, 1F, 28028
Madrid, Spain. TEL 256-1779. FAX 256-1779.
circ. 15,000. *6893*

INSTALLATION NEWS.
Bobit Publishing Company, 2512 Artesia Blvd.,
Redondo Beach, CA 90278-3210. TEL 213-376-
8788. FAX 213-376-9043.
circ. 23,000. *1907*

INSTALLATIONS NYT.
Teknisk Forlag A - S, Skelbaekgade 4, DK-1780
Copenhagen V, Denmark. TEL 45-31-21-68-01.
FAX 45-31-21-04-01.
circ. 8,838. *2707*

INSTITUT CATHOLIQUE DE PARIS. ANNUAIRE.
Institut Catholique de Paris, 21 rue d'Assas, 75270
Paris Cedex 06, France. TEL 44-39-52-00. FAX 45-
44-27-14. *6182*

INSTITUT FUER AFRIKA-KUNDE. ARBEITEN.
Institut fuer Afrika-Kunde, Neuer Jungfernstieg 21,
20354 Hamburg, Germany. TEL 49-40-3562523.
FAX 49-40-3562511.
circ. 250. *5673*

**INSTITUT FUER ALLGEMEINE BOTANIK UND
BOTANISCHER GARTEN. MITTEILUNGEN.**
Universitaet Hamburg, Institut fuer Allgemeine
Botanik und Botanischer Garten, Ohnhorststr. 18,
22609 Hamburg, Germany. FAX 49-40-
82282254.
circ. 550. *685*

**INSTITUT FUER SCHWEIZERISCHES ARBEITSRECHT.
MITTEILUNGEN.**
Staempfli und Cie AG, Hallerstr. 7-9, CH-3001
Bern, Switzerland. TEL 41-31-3006666. FAX 41-
31-3006699.
circ. 300. *1379*

INSTITUT FUER VERKEHRSWESEN. MITTEILUNGEN.
Universitaet fuer Bodenkultur, Institut fuer
Verkehrswesen, Peter-Jordan-Str. 82, A-1190
Vienna, Austria. TEL 43-1-476545300. FAX 43-1-
476545344.
circ. 400. *6719*

**INSTITUT FUER WISSENSCHAFT UND KUNST.
MITTEILUNGEN.**
Institut fuer Wissenschaft und Kunst, Berggasse 17-
1, A-1090 Vienna, Austria.
circ. 2,000. *2433*

**INSTITUT GEOGRAPHIQUE NATIONAL. BULLETIN
D'INFORMATION.**
Institut Geographique National, Service de la
Documentation Geographique, 136 bis, rue de
Grenelle, 75700 Paris, France. TEL 43-98-80-00.
3280

INSTITUT HISTORIQUE BELGE DE ROME. BULLETIN.
N.V. Brepols, Steenweg op Tielen 68, 2300
Turnhout, Belgium. TEL 32-14-402500. FAX 32-14-
428919. *3418*

**INSTITUT INTERNATIONAL J. MARITAIN. NOTES ET
DOCUMENTS.**
Institut International Jacques Maritain, Via Quintino
Sella, 33, 00187 Rome, Italy. TEL 39-6-4874336.
FAX 39-6-4825188.
circ. 2,000. *5673*

INSTITUTA ET MONUMENTA. SERIE II: INSTITUTA.
Fondazione "Claudio Monteverdi", Via Ugolani Dati
4, 26100 Cremona, Italy. TEL 39-372-26580.
circ. 500. *5164*

**INSTITUTE FOR INTEGRATED AGRICULTURAL
DEVELOPMENT. RESEARCH REPORT.**
Institute for Integrated Agricultural Development,
Department of Agriculture Energy & Minerals, RMB
1145, Chiltern Valley Rd., Rutherglen, Vic. 3685,
Australia. TEL 61-60-304500. FAX 61-60-304600.
circ. 1,000. *125*

INSTITUTE FOR SOCIAL RESEARCH NEWSLETTER.
Institute for Social Research, York University, 4700
Keele St., North York, ON M3J 1P3, Canada.
TEL 416-736-5061. FAX 416-736-5749.
circ. 2,600. *6328*

**INSTITUTE OF ELECTROLYSIS. LIST OF QUALIFIED
OPERATORS. SYLLABUS PROSPECTUS.**
Institute of Electrolysis, 251 Seymour Grove,
Manchester M16 ODS, England. *491*

INSTITUTE OF ENERGY. JOURNAL.
Institute of Energy, 18 Devonshire St., London W1N
2AU, England. TEL 071-580-0008. FAX 071-580-
4420.
circ. 2,500. *2551*

**INSTITUTE OF ENGINEERS & TECHNICIANS
JOURNAL.**
Deeson Editorial Services Ltd., Ewell House,
Graveney Rd., Faversham, Kent ME13 8UP,
England. TEL 44-1795-535468. FAX 44-1795-
535469.
circ. 6,500. *2756*

**INSTITUTE OF MODERN RUSSIAN CULTURE
NEWSLETTER.**
Institute of Modern Russian Culture, Box 4353,
USC, Los Angeles, CA 90089-4353. TEL 213-740-
2735. FAX 213-740-8550.
circ. 1,000. *2884*

INSTITUTO BRASIL - ESTADOS UNIDOS. BOLETIM.
Instituto Brasil - Estados Unidos, Av. N.S. de
Copacabana, 690 - 11 andar, 22050-000 Rio de
Janeiro, RJ, Brazil. TEL 55-21-2558332. FAX 55-
21-2559355.
circ. 10,000. *2342*

INSTITUTO BUTANTAN. MEMORIAS.
Instituto Butantan, Av. Vital Brasil 1500, 05503-
900 Sao Paulo, Brazil. TEL 011-813-7222-2129.
FAX 011-815-1505.
circ. 800. *808*

**INSTITUTO DE ECONOMIA AGRICOLA.
INFORMACOES ECONOMICAS.**
Instituto de Economia Agricola, Av. Miguel Stefano,
3900, Caixa Postal 6802, 04301-903 Sao Paulo,
SP, Brazil. FAX 55-11-2764062. *193*

**INSTITUTO DE INVESTIGACION TEXTIL Y DE
COOPERACION INDUSTRIAL. BOLETIN INTEXTER.**
Instituto de Investigacion Textil y de Cooperacion
Industrial, Colon 15, 08222 Terrassa, Spain.
TEL 34-3-7398277. FAX 34-3-7398272.
circ. 1,000. *6679*

**INSTITUTO POLITECNICO NACIONAL. ESCUELA
NACIONAL DE CIENCIAS BIOLOGICAS. ANALES.**
Instituto Politecnico Nacional, Escuela Nacional de
Ciencias Biologicas, Carpio y Plan de Ayala, Col.
Santo Tomas, Apdo. Postal 42-186, 11340,
Mexico, D.F., Mexico. FAX 525-3963503.
circ. 1,000. *640*

**INSTYTUT TRANSPORTU SAMOCHODOWEGO.
ZESZYTY NAUKOWE.**
Instytut Transportu Samochodowego, Ul. Jagillonska
80, Warsaw, Poland. TEL 48-22-113231. FAX 48-
22-110906. *6719*

INSURANCE DIRECTORY OF NEW ZEALAND.
Mercantile Gazette Marketing, P.O. Box 20-034,
Christchurch 5, New Zealand.
circ. 3,000. *3652*

INSURANCE FIELD.
Insurance Field Company, Box 18630, Louisville, KY
40218. TEL 502-491-5857. FAX 502-491-5905.
circ. 3,000. *3652*

INSURANCE TIMES.
20 Park Plz., Ste. 1101, Boston, MA 02116-4303.
TEL 617-292-7117. FAX 617-292-0111.
circ. 6,500. *3653*

INTEGRATED SYSTEM DESIGN.
The Verecom Group, 5150 El Camino Real, Ste. D-
31, Los Altos, CA 94022-1527. TEL 415-903-
0140. FAX 415-903-0151.
circ. 55,000. *2015*

INTENSIVE CARING UNLIMITED.
Intensive Caring Unlimited (ICU), 571 Creek Rd.,
Ivyland, PA 18974. TEL 215-629-0449.
circ. 3,000. *1769*

INTER - MECANIQUE DU BATIMENT.
Corporation des Maitres Mecaniciens en Tuyauterie
du Quebec, 8175 bd. Saint-Laurent, Montreal, PQ
H2P 2M1, Canada. TEL 514-382-2668. FAX 514-
382-1566.
circ. 5,441. *3329*

**INTER-AMERICAN DEVELOPMENT BANK. INSTITUTE
FOR LATIN AMERICAN INTEGRATION. ANNUAL
REPORT.**
Banco Interamericano de Desarrollo, Instituto para la
Integracion de America Latina, Esmeralda 130,
Buenos Aires, Argentina. TEL 394-2059. FAX 394-
2293. *1309*

INTERCHANGE (PORTLAND).
Oregon Educational Media Association, 16695 S.W.
Rosa Rd., Beaverton, OR 97007. TEL 503-649-
5764. *2342*

INTERCHANGE CUSTOMER NEWSLETTER.
Nebraska Public Power District, Box 499,
Columbus, NE 68601-0499. TEL 402-563-5811.
FAX 402-563-5511.
circ. 5,000. *3230*

INTERFACE (STORRS).
University of Connecticut, Center for Instructional
Media & Technology, UCIMT, U-1, 249 Glenbrook
Rd., Storrs, CT 06269-2001. TEL 203-486-2530.
FAX 203-486-1766.
circ. 7,000. *1907*

INTERIEUR.
NOVA Kommunikation A-S, Box 146, Solvang 23,
DK-3450 Alleroed, Denmark. TEL 45-48-17-00-78.
FAX 45-48-17-13-65.
circ. 7,000. *3679*

INTERIOR DECORATORS' HANDBOOK.
Columbia Communications, Inc., 2125 Center Ave.,
Ste. 305, Fort Lee, NJ 07024-5859. TEL 212-532-
9290. FAX 212-779-8345.
circ. 20,000. *3679*

INTERIORSCAPE.
Brantwood Publications, Inc., 3023 Eastland Blvd.,
Ste. 103, Clearwater, FL 34621-4106. TEL 813-
796-3877.
circ. 7,500. *3679*

INTERMEDIAIR.
V N U Business Publications B.V., Postbus 9194,
1006 CC Amsterdam, Netherlands. TEL 31-
206175137.
circ. 195,000. *1101*

THE INTERMOUNTAIN RETAILER.
Utah Food Industry Association, 1578 W. 1700 S.,
Ste. 200, Salt Lake City, UT 84104. TEL 801-973-
9517. FAX 801-972-8712.
circ. 1,000. *3006*

INTERNAL MEDICINE WORLD REPORT.
Medical World Business Press, Inc., 241 Forsgate Dr., CN 505, Jamesburg, NJ 08831. TEL 908-656-1140. FAX 908-656-1142.
circ. 105,000. *4706*

THE INTERNATIONAL (LONDON, 1988).
Financial Times Business Information, Magazines 2 Greystoke Pl., Fetter Ln., London EC4A 1ND, England. TEL 0171-405-6969. FAX 0171-405-5276.
circ. 35,000. *1334*

INTERNATIONAL ARTHURIAN SOCIETY. NEWSLETTER.
Northeastern Illinois University, Department of English, 5500 N. St. Louis Ave., Chicago, IL 60625. TEL 202-319-5240. *4220*

INTERNATIONAL ASSOCIATION OF EDUCATORS FOR WORLD PEACE. CIRCULATION NEWSLETTER.
Peace Progress Press, Box 3282, Mastin Lake Sta., Huntsville, AL 35810-0282. TEL 205-534-5501. FAX 205-536-1018.
circ. 10,000. *2451*

INTERNATIONAL ASSOCIATION OF METEOROLOGY AND ATMOSPHERIC PHYSICS. REPORT OF PROCEEDINGS OF GENERAL ASSEMBLY.
International Association of Meteorology and Atmospheric Physics, c/o Prof. Roland List, Department of Physics, University of Toronto, Toronto, ON M5S 1A7, Canada. TEL 416-978-2982. FAX 416-978-8905. *4998*

INTERNATIONAL ASSOCIATION OF MILK CONTROL AGENCIES. PROCEEDINGS OF ANNUAL MEETINGS.
International Association of Milk Control Agencies, c/o Lyle Newcomb, New York Int'l Dept. of Agriculture and Markets, 1 Winners Circle, Albany, NY 12235. TEL 518-457-5731. FAX 518-485-5816. *251*

INTERNATIONAL ASSOCIATION OF MUSEUMS OF ARMS AND MILITARY HISTORY. CONGRESS REPORTS.
International Association of Museums of Arms and Military History, c/o Markku Melkko, P.O. Box 266, FIN-00171 Helsinki, Finland. FAX 358-0-1616390. *5123*

INTERNATIONAL ASSOCIATION OF PHYSICAL EDUCATION AND SPORTS FOR GIRLS AND WOMEN. PROCEEDINGS OF THE INTERNATIONAL CONGRESS.
Japan Association of Physical Education for Women and Girls, 6-102 O.M.Y.C., 3-1 Jinen-cho Yoyogi, Shibuya-ku, Tokyo, Japan. *6465*

INTERNATIONAL BAR NEWS.
International Bar Association, 2 Harewood Pl., Hanover Sq., London W1R 9HB, England. TEL 44-71-629-1206. FAX 44-71-409-0456.
circ. 16,000. *3933*

INTERNATIONAL BASKETBALL FEDERATION. OFFICIAL REPORT OF THE WORLD CONGRESS.
International Basketball Federation, Postfach 700607, 81306 Munich, Germany. TEL 49-89-7481580. FAX 49-89-74815833.
circ. 300. *6506*

INTERNATIONAL BIODETERIORATION & BIODEGRADATION.
Elsevier Science Ltd., P.O. Box 800, Kidlington, Oxford OX5 1DX, England. TEL 44-1865-843000. FAX 44-1865-843010. *662*

INTERNATIONAL BIOTECHNOLOGY LABORATORY.
International Scientific Communications, Inc., 30 Controls Dr., Box 870, Shelton, CT 06484-0870. TEL 203-926-9300. FAX 203-926-9310.
circ. 37,000. *662*

INTERNATIONAL BOWLING INDUSTRY.
Crown Publications, 660 Hampshire Rd., No. 200, Westlake Village, CA 91361-2504. TEL 805-371-7877. FAX 805-371-7885.
circ. 10,750. *6506*

INTERNATIONAL CABLE.
Phillips Business Information, Inc., 1201 Seven Locks Rd., Potomac, MD 20854. TEL 301-424-3338. FAX 301-309-3847. *1962*

INTERNATIONAL COMMISSION FOR THE CONSERVATION OF ATLANTIC TUNAS. COLLECTIVE VOLUME OF SCIENTIFIC PAPERS.
International Commission for the Conservation of Atlantic Tunas, Estebanez Calderon 3 8l, 28020 Madrid, Spain. TEL 34-1-5793352. FAX 34-1-5715299. *2936*

INTERNATIONAL COMMISSION FOR THE CONSERVATION OF ATLANTIC TUNAS. DATA RECORD.
International Commission for the Conservation of Atlantic Tunas, Estebanez Calderon 3 8l, 28020 Madrid, Spain. TEL 34-1-5793352. FAX 34-1-5725299. *2936*

INTERNATIONAL COMMISSION FOR THE CONSERVATION OF ATLANTIC TUNAS. STATISTICAL BULLETIN.
International Commission for the Conservation of Atlantic Tunas, Estebanez Calderon, 3 8l, 28020 Madrid, Spain. TEL 34-1-5793352. FAX 34-1-5715299. *2947*

INTERNATIONAL COMMISSION ON IRRIGATION AND DRAINAGE. REPORT.
International Commission on Irrigation and Drainage, 48 Nyaya Marg, Chanakyapuri, New Delhi 110021, India. TEL 3016837.
circ. 1,000. *6970*

INTERNATIONAL COMMUNICATOR.
Academy of Dentistry International, 5125 MacArthur Blvd., N.W., Ste. 50, Washington, DC 20016-3315. TEL 202-364-8349. FAX 202-364-8349.
circ. 2,000. *4643*

INTERNATIONAL CONFERENCE ON LASERS. PROCEEDINGS (YEAR).
STS Press, Box 245, McLean, VA 22101. TEL 703-642-5835. FAX 703-642-5838.
circ. 300. *5604*

INTERNATIONAL CONGRESS FOR STEREOLOGY. PROCEEDINGS.
International Society for Stereology, c/o Dr. Aurora Astudillo, Sec.-Treas., Tatiana, Univ. de Oviedo, Ed. Quimicas, Julian Claveria s-n, 33006 Oviedo, Spain. TEL 34-85-103658.
circ. 480. *2732*

INTERNATIONAL CONGRESS OF OPHTHALMOLOGY. ABSTRACTS.
International Federation of Ophthalmological Societies, c/o Dr. Bruce E. Spivey, Northwestern Healthcare Network, 980 N. Miichigan Ave., Ste. 1500, Chicago, IL 60511.
circ. 8,500. *4770*

INTERNATIONAL CRANES.
K H L International Ltd., Southfields, Southview Rd., Wadhurst, E. Sussex TN5 6TP, England. TEL 44-1892-784088. FAX 44-1892-784086.
circ. 14,200. *2732*

INTERNATIONAL DESALINATION AND WATER REUSE QUARTERLY.
Lineal Publishing Co., 10842 Pine Bark Ln., Boca Raton, FL 33428-2852. TEL 407-451-9429. FAX 407-451-9435.
circ. 7,259. *6970*

INTERNATIONAL DEVELOPMENT POLICIES.
Commonwealth Secretariat, Marlborough House, Pall Mall, London SW1Y 5HX, England. TEL 44-171-839-3411. FAX 44-171-747-6235.
circ. 350. *1310*

INTERNATIONAL DIABETES DIGEST.
F S G Communications Ltd., Vine House, Fair Green, Reach, Cambridge CB5 0JD, England. TEL 44-1638-743633. FAX 44-1638-743998.
circ. 5,000. *4671*

INTERNATIONAL ENVIRONMENTAL TECHNOLOGY.
International Labmate Ltd., 12 Alban Park, Hatfield Rd., St. Albans, Herts. AL4 0JJ, England. TEL 44-1727-858840. FAX 44-1727-840310.
circ. 51,072. *2837*

INTERNATIONAL FEDERATION FOR HOUSING AND PLANNING. DIRECTORY.
International Federation for Housing and Planning, Wassenaarseweg 43, 2596 CG The Hague, Netherlands.
circ. 1,500. *3585*

INTERNATIONAL FIBER JOURNAL.
McMickle Publications, Inc., 2919 Spalding Dr., Atlanta, GA 30350-4623. TEL 770-394-6098. FAX 770-393-0161.
circ. 8,900. *6679*

INTERNATIONAL FINANCIER.
International Society of Financiers, Box 18508, Asheville, NC 28814. TEL 704-252-5907. FAX 704-251-5061.
circ. 500. *1102*

INTERNATIONAL FIRE FIGHTER.
International Association of Fire Fighters, 1750 New York Ave., N.W., Washington, DC 20006-5301. TEL 202-737-8484. FAX 202-737-8418.
circ. 195,000. *2921*

INTERNATIONAL FOOD INGREDIENTS.
Miller Freeman Technical Ltd. Europe, P.O. Box 325, 3600 AH Maarssen, Netherlands. TEL 31-346-554311. FAX 31-346-550372.
circ. 9,500. *2978*

INTERNATIONAL GRAVIMETRIQUE BUREAU. BULLETIN D'INFORMATION.
Bureau Gravimetric International, 18 av. Edouard Belin, 31055 Toulouse Cedex, France. TEL 61-33-29-80. FAX 33-61-25-30-98.
circ. 350. *2275*

INTERNATIONAL GROUND WATER TECHNOLOGY.
National Trade Publications, Inc., 13 Century Hill Latham, NY 12110-2197. TEL 518-783-1281. FAX 518-783-1386.
circ. 10,000. *6970*

INTERNATIONAL HOSPITAL EQUIPMENT.
Pan European Publishing Co. Rue Verte 216, 1030 Brussels, Belgium. TEL 32 2-2402611. FAX 32-2-2427111.
circ. 30,004. *4472*

INTERNATIONAL INSTITUTE OF SEISMOLOGY AND EARTHQUAKE ENGINEERING. YEAR BOOK.
International Institute of Seismology and Earthquake Engineering, Building Research Institute-Ministry of Construction, 1 Tatehare, Tsukuba-city, Ibaraki Prefecture 305, Japan. TEL 81-298-64-2151. FAX 81-298-64-2989. *2276*

INTERNATIONAL JOURNAL OF EDUCOLOGY.
Educology Research Associates, P.O. Box 216, Terrigal, N.S.W. 2260, Australia. TEL 61-43-653120. FAX 61-43-652871.
circ. 1,500. *2399*

INTERNATIONAL JOURNAL OF FOOD SCIENCES AND NUTRITION.
Carfax Publishing Co., P.O. Box 25, Abingdon, Oxon. OX14 3UE, England. TEL 44-1235-401000. FAX 44-1235-401550.
circ. 1,000. *5234*

INTERNATIONAL JOURNAL OF INTENSIVE CARE.
Greycoat Publishing, 1 Harley St., London W1N 1DA, England. TEL 44-171-637-1828. FAX 44-171-637-3020.
circ. 25,868. *4473*

INTERNATIONAL JOURNAL OF THE SOCIOLOGY OF LANGUAGE.
Walter de Gruyter und Co., Mouton de Gruyter, Genthiner Str. 13, 10785 Berlin, Germany. TEL 49-30-26005-0. FAX 49-30-26005251.
circ. 900. *4076*

INTERNATIONAL LABORATORY.
International Scientific Communications, Inc., 30 Controls Dr., Box 870, Shelton, CT 06484-0870. TEL 203-926-9300. FAX 203-926-9310.
circ. 52,503. *1716*

INTERNATIONAL LAW PRACTICUM.
New York State Bar Association, International Law and Practice Section, 1 Elk St., Albany, NY 12207-1096. TEL 518-463-3200. FAX 518-463-8844.
circ. 2,000. *3935*

INTERNATIONAL LEADS.
American Library Association International Relations Round Table, 50 E. Huron St. Chicago, IL 60611. TEL 312-280-3200. FAX 312-944-3897.
circ. 900. *4001*

INTERNATIONAL MARKETING.
Quest Magazines Ltd., Publishing House, 652 Victoria Rd., South Ruislip, Mddx. HA4 0SX, England. TEL 44-181-842-1010. FAX 44-181-841-2557.
circ. 5,000. *1469*

THE INTERNATIONAL PRESS DIRECTORY.
The Magazine Business Ltd., 8 Tottenham Mews, London W1P 9PJ, England. TEL 44-171-436-5211. FAX 44-171-436-5290.
circ. 12,500. *5999*

INTERNATIONAL RELATIONS.
David Davies Memorial Institute of International Studies, 2 Chadwick St., London SW1P 2EP, England. TEL 44-171-222-4063. FAX 44-171-233-2863.
circ. 1,000. *5756*

INTERNATIONAL SADDLERY AND APPAREL JOURNAL.
EEMG, Inc, Box 3039, Berea, KY 40403-3039. FAX 606-986-1770.
circ. 6,863. *6548*

INTERNATIONAL SHIPPING REVIEW.
Contract Communications Ltd., Nestor House, Playhouse Yard, London EC4V 5EX, England. TEL 44-171-779-8714. FAX 44-171-779-8760.
circ. 8,000. *6837*

INTERNATIONAL SKYLINE.
I.S.P. of Canada, 3738 - 39th Ave. W., Vancouver, BC V6N 3A7, Canada.
circ. 18,750. *1908*

INTERNATIONAL SOCIETY FOR BRITISH GENEALOGY AND FAMILY HISTORY. NEWSLETTER.
International Society for British Genealogy and Family History, Box 3115, Salt Lake City, UT 84110-3115. TEL 250-477-2708. FAX 250-595-2495.
circ. 1,000. *3089*

INTERNATIONAL SOCIETY OF BLOOD TRANSFUSION. PROCEEDINGS OF THE CONGRESS.
Societe Internationale de Transfusion Sanguine, c/o C N T S, B.P. 100, 91943 Les Ulis Cedex, France. TEL 69-07-20-40. FAX 69-07-41-85. *4701*

INTERNATIONAL SOCIETY OF WEIGHING AND MEASUREMENT. MEMBERSHIP DIRECTORY & PRODUCT GUIDE.
International Society of Weighing and Measurement, 10 Kimball St., W., Winder, GA 30680. TEL 770-868-5300. FAX 770-868-5301.
circ. 1,400. *5014*

INTERNATIONAL THEATRE INSTITUTE OF THE UNITED STATES. NEWSLETTER.
International Theatre Institute of the United States, Inc., 47 Great Jones St., New York, NY 10012-1114. TEL 212-254-4141. FAX 212-254-6814.
circ. 1,500. *6697*

INTERNATIONAL TRANSPORT WORKERS' FEDERATION REPORT ON ACTIVITIES.
International Transport Workers' Federation, 49-60 Borough Rd., London SE1 1DS, England.
circ. 500. *3723*

INTERNATIONALES JAHRBUCH FUER RECHTSPHILOSOPHIE UND GESETZGEBUNG.
Manzsche Verlags- und Universitaetsbuchhandlung GmbH, Kohlmarkt 16, A-1014 Vienna, Austria. TEL 43-1-531610. FAX 43-1-53161181.
circ. 500. *3793*

INTERNETWORK.
Cardinal Business Media, Inc., 1300 Virginia Dr., Ste. 400, Fort Washington, PA 19034. TEL 215-643-8000. FAX 215-643-3901.
circ. 100,000. *2038*

INTERPLANETARY NEWS.
Interplanetary Space Travel Research Association (United Kingdom), 21 Hargwyne St., Stockwell, London SW9 9RQ, England. *69*

INTERPRETER (NASHVILLE).
United Methodist Communications, 810 12th Ave. S., Nashville, TN 37203-4744. TEL 615-742-5400. FAX 615-742-5460.
circ. 264,903. *6148*

INTERVUE.
Intergraph Corporation, LR24C2, Huntsville, AL 35894. TEL 205-730-8172. FAX 205-730-9508.
circ. 60,000. *2032*

INTO VIEW.
Youth for Christ, Cleobury Pl., Cleobury Mortimer, Kidderminster DY14 8JG, England. TEL 44-1299-270260. FAX 44-1299-271158.
circ. 6,000. *1794*

INTRODUCTION TO GRAVITATION CHEMISTRY.
Ensanian Physicochemical Institute, Box 98, Eldred, PA 16731. TEL 814-225-3296.
circ. 100. *1679*

INTRON - CANADIAN MOLECULAR BIOLOGY.
Canadian Biotechnology News Service, 340 Richmond Rd., Box 67039, Ottawa, ON K2A 0E8, Canada. TEL 613-726-0115. FAX 613-726-7344.
circ. 6,000. *662*

INUIT ART QUARTERLY.
Inuit Art Foundation, 2081 Merivale Rd., Nepean, ON K2G 1G9, Canada. TEL 613-224-8189. FAX 613-224-2907.
circ. 1,862. *435*

INVEST IN BRITAIN ANNUAL REPORT.
Invest in Britain Bureau, Kingsgate House, 66-74 Victoria St., London SW1E 6SW, England. TEL 44-71-215-2542. FAX 44-71-215-8451.
circ. 6,000. *933*

INVESTIGACION BIBLIOTECOLOGICA.
Universidad Nacional Autonoma de Mexico, Centro Universitario de Investigaciones Bibliotecologicas, Torre II de Humanidades, pisos 12 y 13, Ciudad Universitaria, 04510 Mexico, D.F., Mexico. TEL 525-6230352. FAX 525-5507461.
circ. 1,000. *4001*

INVESTIGACION Y EDUCACION EN ENFERMERIA.
Universidad de Antioquia, Facultad de Enfermeria, Apdo. Aereo 1226, Carrera 53, no. 62-65, Medellin, Colombia. TEL 5742-110058. FAX 5742-638282.
circ. 1,000. *4716*

INVESTIR.
Societe d'Information Economique et Financiere, Investir Publications, 48 rue Notre-Dame des Victoires, 75002 Paris, France. TEL 1-44-88-48-00. FAX 1-44-88-48-01.
circ. 120,000. *1103*

INVESTMENT MANAGEMENT.
Mitre House Publishing Ltd., The Clifton Centre, 110 Clifton St., London EC2A 4HD, England. TEL 071-729-6644.
circ. 8,000. *1103*

THE INVESTMENT REPORTER.
Share Holder Communication Systems, 4600 Campus Dr., Ste. 205, Newport Beach, CA 92660-1801. TEL 714-724-0444.
circ. 36,204. *1336*

IOWA. DEPARTMENT OF EMPLOYMENT SERVICES. ANNUAL REPORT.
Department of Employment Services, 1000 E. Grand Ave., Des Moines, IA 50319. TEL 515-281-3201.
circ. 2,000. *1381*

IOWA ACADEMY OF SCIENCE. JOURNAL.
Iowa Academy of Science, 175 Baker Hall, University of Northern Iowa, Cedar Falls, IA 50614. TEL 319-273-2021.
circ. 2,100. *6249*

IOWA AGRICULTURE AND HOME ECONOMICS EXPERIMENT STATION. RESEARCH BULLETIN.
Iowa State University of Science and Technology, 304 Curtiss Hall, Ames, IA 50011. TEL 515-294-5616. FAX 515-294-8662. *126*

IOWA AGRICULTURIST.
Iowa Agriculturist, Inc., Student Publications, Ames, IA 50011. TEL 515-294-9381.
circ. 2,500. *126*

IOWA CITY MAGAZINE.
Iowa City Magazine Publishing, Inc., Box 2672, Iowa City, IA 52244-2672. TEL 319-354-7738. FAX 319-354-7738.
circ. 15,000. *3230*

IOWA ENGINEER.
Iowa Engineer, Inc., c/o Advertising Director, 16G Hamilton Hall, Iowa State University, Ames, IA 50011-0001. TEL 515-294-9390.
circ. 4,000. *2606*

IOWA TRUCKING LIFELINER.
Iowa Motor Truck Association, Capital Center One, 600 E. Court, Ste. D, Des Moines, IA 50309-2020. TEL 515-244-5193. FAX 515-244-2204.
circ. 3,187. *6858*

IRAN. MINISTRY OF ECONOMY. INTERNAL WHOLESALE TRADE STATISTICS.
Ministry of Finance and Economic Affairs, Bureau of Statistics, Teheran, Iran. *1007*

IRAN. MINISTRY OF ECONOMY. INTERNATIONAL TRADE STATISTICS.
Ministry of Finance and Economic Affairs, Bureau of Statistics, Teheran, Iran. *1007*

IRELAND. DEPARTMENT OF SOCIAL WELFARE. STATISTICAL INFORMATION ON SOCIAL WELFARE.
Department of Social Welfare, Statistics Unit, Store St., 4th Fl., Dublin 1, Ireland. TEL 01-8748444. FAX 01-87043868.
circ. 1,300. *6377*

IRIS YEAR BOOK.
British Iris Society, Copper Beeches, N. End Ln., Downe, Orpington, Kent BR6 7HG, England. TEL 01689-853646.
circ. 800. *3058*

IRISH AMERICAN POST.
Irish American Post Ltd., 301 N. Water St., 3rd Floor, Milwaukee, WI 53202-5713. TEL 414-273-8132. FAX 414-273-8196.
circ. 25,000. *2885*

IRISH BANK OFFICIALS ASSOCIATION NEWSHEET.
Irish Bank Officials Association, 93 St. Stephen's Green, Dublin 2, Ireland. TEL 01-8722255. FAX 01-4780567.
circ. 11,000. *1103*

IRISH COLLEGE OF OPHTHALMOLOGISTS. YEARBOOK.
Irish College of Ophthalmologists, 10 Hagans Ct., Lad Ln., Dublin 2, Ireland. TEL 01-6785974. FAX 01-6785047.
circ. 450. *4771*

IRISH COMPANY REPORTING.
University of Ulster, School of Management, Coleraine BT52 1SA, N. Ireland. TEL 44-1232-365131. FAX 44-1232-366805.
circ. 100. *1048*

IRISH COOPERATIVE ORGANIZATION SOCIETY. ANNUAL REPORT.
Irish Cooperative Organization Society Ltd., Plunkett House, 84 Merrion Sq., Dublin 2, Ireland. TEL 0353-1-6681784. FAX 0353-1-6764783. *127*

IRISH CRIMINAL LAW JOURNAL.
The Round Hall Press, Kill Ln., Blackrock, Co. Dublin, Ireland. TEL 2892922. FAX 2893072.
circ. 350. *3910*

IRISH IN BRITAIN DIRECTORY.
Brent Irish Advisory Service, 76 Salisbury Rd., London NW6 6NY, England. TEL 44-171-328-1188. FAX 44-171-328-1198.
circ. 10,000. *2885*

IRISH JOURNAL OF EUROPEAN LAW.
The Round Hall Press, Kill Ln., Blackrock, Co. Dublin, Ireland. TEL 2892922. FAX 2893072.
circ. 300. *3794*

IRISH MEDICAL TIMES.
Medical Publications Ltd., 30 Lancaster Gate, London W2 3LP, England. *4475*

IRISH MOTOR INDUSTRY.
Jude Publications Ltd., Jude House, Tara St., Dublin 2, Ireland. TEL 01-6713500. FAX 01-6713074.
circ. 2,500. *6789*

IRON MOUNTAIN REVIEW.
Emory & Henry College, Box 64, Emory, VA 24327. TEL 540-944-4121.
circ. 450. *4221*

AL-ISLAM.
c/o Jamiat Ahl-e-Hadith, 106 Ravi Rd., Lahore, Pakistan. FAX 042-54072.
circ. 4,000. *6118*

ISLANDER.
Islander Trust, 21 Pointers Close, Isle of Dogs, London E14 3AP, England. TEL 44-171-987-8631. FAX 44-171-987-8631.
circ. 6,000. *3156*

ISRAEL. GOVERNMENT PRESS OFFICE. DAILY NEWS AND EDITORIAL SURVEY.
Government Press Office, Agron House, 37 Hillel St., Jerusalem 94581, Israel. *3182*

ISRAEL. KNESSET. HA-VA'ADA LE-INYANEI BIKORET HA-MEDINA. SIKUMEHA VE-HATSA'OTEHA SHEL HA-VA'ADA LE-INYANEI BIKORET HA-MEDINA LE-DIN VE-KHESHBON SHEL MEVAKER HA-MEDINA.
Knesset, Jerusalem, Israel. *5943*

ISRAEL. KNESSET. VA'ADAT HA-KESAFIM MISPARIM AL VA'ADAT HA-KESAFIM.
Knesset, Jerusalem, Israel. *1551*

ISRAELI MAP COLLECTORS SOCIETY. JOURNAL.
Israeli Map Collectors Society, 4 Brenner St., Jerusalem 92103, Israel. TEL 972-2-611687.
circ. 100. *3508*

ISSUES (SAN FRANCISCO).
A Messianic Jewish Perspective, Box 424885, San Francisco, CA 94142-4885. TEL 415-864-2600. FAX 415-552-8325.
circ. 40,000. *6207*

ISTITUTO RICERCHE PESCA MARITTIMA. QUADERNI.
Istituto Ricerche sulla Pesca Marittima, Molo Mandracchio, 60100 Ancona, Italy. TEL 39-71-5314. FAX 39-71-55313.
circ. 500. *2937*

ISTITUTO STORICO ARTISTICO ORVIETANO. BOLLETTINO.
Istituto Storico Artistico Orvietano, Piazza Febei N.1, 05018 Orvieto, Italy. *3420*

ITALIAN JOURNAL OF ZOOLOGY.
Mucchi Editore s.r.l., Via Emilia Est. 1527, 41100 Modena, Italy. FAX 059-223917.
circ. 500. *809*

ITALIC HANDWRITING NEWSLETTER.
Continuing Education Press, 1633 S.W. Park, Box 1491, Portland, OR 97207. TEL 503-725-4846. FAX 503-725-4840.
circ. 15,000. *2490*

ITHACA COLLEGE QUARTERLY.
Ithaca College, Alumni Hall, Ithaca, NY 14850. TEL 607-274-3830. FAX 607-274-1490.
circ. 40,000. *1873*

ITINERA GEOBOTANICA.
Universidad de Leon, Secretariado de Publicaciones, Campus de Verganza, s-n, 24007 Leon, Spain. TEL 34-87-291558. FAX 34-87-291558.
circ. 1,000. *686*

IVY LEAF.
Alpha Kappa Alpha Sorority, Inc., 5656 S. Stony Island Ave., Chicago, IL 60637. *1873*

IWATE MEDICAL UNIVERSITY SCHOOL OF LIBERAL ARTS & SCIENCES. ANNUAL REPORT.
Iwate Ika Daigaku Kyoyobu, 16-1, 3-chome, Honcho-dori, Morioka-shi, Iwate-ken 020, Japan. TEL 0196-51-5111. FAX 0196-25-5816.
circ. 330. *6250*

IX.
Verlag Heinz Heise GmbH und Co. KG, Helstorferstr. 7, 30625 Hannover, Germany. TEL 49-511-5352-0. FAX 49-511-5352-129.
circ. 31,933. *1993*

IZOTOPTECHNIKA, DIAGNOSZTIKA.
Izotop Intezet Kft., P.O. Box 77, 1525 Budapest, Hungary. TEL 361-169-9499. FAX 361-169-5087.
circ. 350. *1679*

J A M I F.
Association des Medecins Israelites de France, 11 ave. de la Republique, 94260 Fresnes, France.
circ. 8,500. *4476*

J L B SMITH INSTITUTE OF ICHTHYOLOGY. ICHTHYOLOGICAL BULLETIN.
J L B Smith Institute of Ichthyology, Private Bag 1015, Grahamstown 6140, South Africa. TEL 27-461-27124. FAX 27-461-22403.
circ. 1,000. *309*

J L B SMITH INSTITUTE OF ICHTHYOLOGY. SPECIAL PUBLICATION.
J L B Smith Institute of Ichthyology, Private Bag 1015, Grahamstown 6140, South Africa. TEL 27-461-27124. FAX 27-461-22403.
circ. 1,500. *809*

J P C NEWSLETTER.
Joint Planning Commission, Lehigh - Northampton Counties, 961 Marcon Blvd., Ste. 310, Allentown, PA 18103-9397. TEL 215-264-4544.
circ. 1,600. *3586*

J. WAYNE AND ELSIE M. GUNN CENTER FOR THE STUDY OF SCIENCE FICTION NEWSLETTER.
J. Wayne and Elsie M. Gunn Center for the Study of Science Fiction. University of Kansas, English Department, Lawrence, KS 66045. TEL 913-864-3380. FAX 913-864-4298.
circ. 1,200. *4328*

JAARBOEK NUMAGA.
Vereniging Numaga, P.O. Box 1359, 6501 BJ Nijmegen, Netherlands.
circ. 1,300. *3420*

JACKSON BUSINESS JOURNAL.
Box 12727, Jackson, MS 39236-2727. TEL 601-956-0756. FAX 601-956-4047.
circ. 4,007. *933*

JACKSONVILLE MEDICINE.
Duval County Medical Society, 515 Lomax St., Jacksonville, FL 32204. TEL 904-355-6561. FAX 904-353-5848.
circ. 1,800. *4476*

JAEGER.
Jaegerne, Danmarks Jaegerforbund, Hoejnaesvej 56, DK-2610 Reedovre, Denmark. TEL 45-38 33 29 11. FAX 45-31-19-02-41. *6567*

DER JAEGER IN BADEN-WUERTTEMBERG.
Dr. Neinhaus Verlag AG, Wollgrasweg 31, 70599 Stuttgart, Germany. TEL 49-711-4586091. FAX 49-456603.
circ. 30,000. *6567*

JAHRBUCH FUER GLOCKENKUNDE.
Deutsches Glockenmuseum, Talstr. 19, 35751 Greifenstein, Germany. TEL 06449-6460.
circ. 600. *5123*

JAMAICAN GEOGRAPHER.
Jamaican Geographical Society, c/o Geography Dept., University of the West Indies, Kingston 7, Jamaica, W.I. TEL 908-927-2129.
circ. 350. *3263*

JAMAICAN HISTORICAL REVIEW.
Jamaican Historical Society, P.O. Box 105, Kingston 977-5448, Jamaica, W.I. TEL 809-968-7280. FAX 809-926-2217.
circ. 1,000. *3473*

JAMESTOWN COLLEGE. ALUMNI & FRIENDS.
6093 College Lane, Jamestown, ND 58405. TEL 701-252-3467. FAX 701-253-4318.
circ. 12,000. *1873*

JAMI'AT AL-AZHAR. KULLIYYAT AL-LUGHAH AL-ARABIYYAH BIL-ZAGAZIG. MAJALLAH.
Jami'at al-Azhar, Kulliyyat al-Lughah al-Arabiyyah bil-Zagazig, Zagazig, Egypt. TEL 02-055-324114. FAX 02-055-330204. *4077*

JANA SANGH PATRIKA.
Bharatiya Janasangh Kerala Pradesh, M.G. Road, Cochin 11, India. *5675*

JAPAN. FORESTRY AND FOREST PRODUCTS RESEARCH INSTITUTE. ANNUAL REPORT.
Kyushu Research Center, Forestry and Forest Products Research Institute, 4-11-16 Kurokami, Kumamoto 860, Japan. TEL 096-343-3168. FAX 096-344-5054.
circ. 700. *3019*

JAPANESE BULLETIN OF ARTS THERAPY.
Societe Japonaise de Psychopathologie de l'Expression, c/o Neuropsychiatric Research Institute, 91 Bentencho, Shinjuku-ku, Tokyo 162, Japan. TEL 81-3-3260-9171.
circ. 4,500. *436*

JAPANESE GUIDE TO HAWAII.
Stone Publishing Company, 425 South, Ste. 1101, Honolulu, HI 96813.
circ. 45,000. *6895*

JAPANESE JOURNAL OF EDUCATIONAL PSYCHOLOGY.
Japanese Association of Educational Psychology c/o Faculty of Education, University of Tokyo, 7-3-1 Hongo, Bunkyo-ku, Tokyo 113, Japan. *5851*

JAPANESE JOURNAL OF ORAL AND MAXILLOFACIAL SURGERY.
Japanese Society of Oral and Maxillofacial Surgeons, 1-15-2-502 Nakasato, Kita-ku, Tokyo 114, Japan.
circ. 2,500. *4644*

JAPANESE JOURNAL OF TOXICOLOGY AND ENVIRONMENTAL HEALTH.
Pharmaceutical Society of Japan, 12-15, Shibuya 2-chome, Shibuya-ku, Tokyo 150, Japan.
circ. 1,700. *2846*

JAPANESE TELEPHONE DIRECTORY AND GUIDE OF SOUTHERN CALIFORNIA.
Japan Publicity, 19300 S Hamilton Ave., Ste. 130, Gardena, CA 90248-4403. TEL 310-515-7100. FAX 310-515-7188.
circ. 100,000. *1619*

JAZZ.
Hochuli AG, Box 4132, Murteuz, Switzerland.
circ. 10,000. *5166*

JAZZSOUTH.
Southern Arts Federation, 181 14th St., N.E., Ste. 400, Atlanta, GA 30309. TEL 404-874-7244. FAX 404-873-2148.
circ. 3,000. *5167*

JEG ARBEJDER MED.
Dansk Historisk Haandbogsorlag ApS, Buddingevej 87 A, DK-2800 Lyngby, Denmark. TEL 45-93-48-00. FAX 45-93-47-47.
circ. 2,400. *3090*

JEOPARDY.
College Hall 132, Western Washington University, Bellingham, WA 98225. TEL 360-650-3118.
circ. 1,200. *4223*

THE JERSEY.
Jersey Cattle Society of the United Kingdom, Scotsbridge House, Scots Hill, Rickmansworth, Herts WD3 3BB, England. TEL 0923-897063. FAX 0923-897691.
circ. 1,000. *274*

JERSEY AT HOME.
Royal Jersey Agricultural and Horticultural Society, Springfield, St. Helier, Jersey JE2 4JF, Channel Islands. TEL 44-1534-37227. FAX 44-1534-24692.
circ. 1,500. *251*

JERSEY EVENING POST.
P.O. Box 582, Jersey JE4 8XQ, Channel Islands, U.K. TEL 01534-73333. FAX 01534-79681.
circ. 25,000. *3224*

JERSEY JAZZ.
New Jersey Jazz Society, Box 410, Brookside, NJ 07926. TEL 201-543-2039.
circ. 1,500. *5168*

JESSE MEYERS' BEVERAGE DIGEST.
Beverage Digest Compay, LLC, Box 238, Old Greenwich, CT 06870-0238. TEL 203-358-8198. FAX 203-327-9761. *507*

JEWELLERY NEWS ASIA (CHINESE EDITION).
Miller Freeman Asia Ltd. 1025 Stanhope House, 738 King's Rd., Quarry Bay, Hong Kong. TEL 852-2805-5661. FAX 852-2960-0977.
circ. 9,000. *3697*

JEWELLERY TIME.
Ink Link Publications, Box 46-218, Herne Bay, Auckland, New Zealand. TEL 09-378 1222. FAX 09-378-1270.
circ. 1,200. *3697*

THE JEWELRY APPRAISER.
National Association of Jewelry Appraisers, Box 6558, Annapolis, MD 21401-0558. TEL 301-261-8270.
circ. 600. *3697*

JEWISH CIVIC PRESS.
924 Valmont St., New Orleans, LA 70115. TEL 504-895-8784.
circ. 5,845. *2886*

JEWISH JOURNAL (DEERFIELD BEACH).
Newspaper Network, 601 Fairway Dr., Deerfield Beach, FL 33441. TEL 305-698-6397. FAX 305-429-1207.
circ. 56,000. *2887*

JEWISH QUARTERLY.
Jewish Literary Trust Ltd., P.O. Box 1148, London NW5 2AZ, England. TEL 0171-485-4062.
circ. 3,000. *2888*

JEWISH SPORTS & FITNESS.
Jewish Sports Congress, P.O. Box 234549, Great Neck, NY 11023-4549. TEL 516-482-5550. FAX 516-482-5583.
circ. 250,000. *5531*

JEWISH STAR (SAN FRANCISCO).
Fraternal Media, 109 Minna St., Ste. 323, San Francisco, CA 94105-3701. TEL 415-421-4874. FAX 415-398-7983.
circ. 3,000. *2888*

JEWISH VEGETARIANS.
Jewish Vegetarians of North America, 6938 Reliance Rd., Federalsburg, MD 21632. TEL 410-754-5550.
circ. 520. *5235*

THE JEWISH VOICE (PROVIDENCE).
Jewish Federation of Rhode Island, 130 Sessions St., Providence, RI 02906. TEL 401-421-4111. FAX 401-331-7961.
circ. 7,500. *2888*

JEWISH WESTERN BULLETIN.
Anglo-Jewish Publishers, 3268 Heather St., Vancouver, BC V5Z 3K5, Canada. TEL 604-879-6575. FAX 604-879-6573.
circ. 2,402. *2889*

JEWS FOR JESUS NEWSLETTER.
Jews for Jesus, 60 Haight St., San Francisco, CA 94102. TEL 415-864-2600. FAX 415-552-8325.
circ. 135,000. *6207*

JIANGSU GAOJIAO.
Jiangsu Sheng Gaodeng Jiaoyu Xuehui, 207 Shanghai Rd., Nanjing, Jiangsu 210024, People's Republic of China. TEL 86-25-6638659. FAX 86-25-7714402.
circ. 5,000. *2433*

JIDOSHA HOYU SHARYOSU.
Jidosha Kensa Toroku Kyoryokukai, Toranomon Kiyoshi Bldg., 3-10, 4-chome, Toranomon, Minato-ku, Tokyo 105, Japan. TEL 03-3432-5611. FAX 03-3432-1044.
circ. 1,500. *6613*

JIEGOU GONGCHENGSHI.
Tongji Chubanshe, 1239 Siping Rd., Shanghai 200092, People's Republic of China. TEL 5455080. FAX 5458965.
circ. 2,000. *2664*

JINKO KOKYU.
Nihon Kokyurhyohou Igakkai, Fukushima Kenritsu Ika Daigaku Masuikagaku Kyoshitsu, 1, Hikarigaoka, Fukushima-shi, Fukushima-ken 960-12, Japan. TEL 81-245-48-0828. FAX 81-245-48-0828.
circ. 1,350. *4888*

JOB SHOP TECHNOLOGY.
Edwards Publishing Company, 16 Waterbury Rd., Box 7193, Prospect, CT 06712-1237. TEL 203-758-4474. FAX 203-758-4475.
circ. 100,000. *1506*

JOBMART.
American Planning Association, 122 S. Michigan Ave., Ste. 1600, Chicago, IL 60603-6107. TEL 312-431-9100. FAX 312-431-9985.
circ. 5,500. *5269*

JOHN & MABLE RINGLING MUSEUM OF ART.
John and Mable Ringling Museum of Art Foundation, 5401 Bay Shore Rd., Sarasota, FL 34243-2161. TEL 813-359-5700. FAX 813-359-5745.
circ. 5,000. *5123*

JOHNS HOPKINS A P L TECHNICAL DIGEST.
Johns Hopkins University, Applied Physics Laboratory, Johns Hopkins Rd., Laurel, MD 20723. TEL 301-953-5625. FAX 301-953-1093.
circ. 5,800. *5552*

JOINT GOVERNMENTAL SALARY AND BENEFITS SURVEY: ARIZONA.
Department of Administration, Personnel Division, 1831 W. Jefferson, Phoenix, AZ 85382. TEL 602-542-5250. *1010*

JORDANS JOURNAL.
Jordan Publishing Ltd., 21 St. Thomas St., Bristol BS1 6JS, England. TEL 0117-923-0600. FAX 0117-923-0063.
circ. 7,200. *934*

JOSLYN NEWS.
Joslyn Art Museum, 2200 Dodge St., Omaha, NE 68102. TEL 402-342-3300. FAX 402-342-2376.
circ. 7,500. *5123*

JOURNAL DE L'ILE DE LA REUNION.
Ste. France Antilles, 42 rue Alexis-de-Villeneuve, B.P. 166, 97463 Saint-Denis, Reunion. TEL 21-32-64. FAX 262-20-08-37.
circ. 26,000. *3108*

JOURNAL DES PAYS D'EN HAUT.
Les Publications Laurentiennes, P.O. Box 1890, 1012 rue Valiquette, Ste. Adele PQ J0R 1L0, Canada. TEL 514-229-6664. FAX 514-229-6063.
circ. 17,000. *3122*

JOURNAL DU BARREAU.
Barreau du Quebec, Maison du Barreau, 445 St-Laurent Blvd., Montreal, PQ H2Y 3T8, Canada. TEL 514-954-3440. FAX 514-954-3477.
circ. 21,800. *3795*

JOURNAL HOLDINGS IN THE NATIONAL CAPITAL AREA.
Interlibrary Users Association, c/o Merilee Worsey, Comsat Corp., 22300 Comsat Dr., Clarksburg, MD 20871. TEL 301-428-4512. FAX 301-428-7747.
circ. 250. *4039*

JOURNAL INDUSTRIEL DU QUEBEC.
Info-Industriel Inc., 2370 E. Boul. Henri-Bourassa, Montreal, Que. H2B 1T6, Canada. TEL 514-388-8801. FAX 514-388-7871.
circ. 25,000. *861*

JOURNAL OF AFFORDABLE HOUSING AND COMMUNITY DEVELOPMENT LAW.
American Bar Association, 750 N. Lake Shore Dr., Chicago, IL 60611. TEL 312-988-5522. FAX 312-988-5568.
circ. 1,300. *3586*

JOURNAL OF ATHLETIC TRAINING.
National Athletic Trainers Association, Inc., 2952 N. Stemmons Fwy., Dallas, TX 75247-6117. TEL 800-879-6282. FAX 214-637-2206.
circ. 21,000. *4898*

JOURNAL OF CELLULOSE SCIENCE AND TECHNOLOGY.
Guangzhou Research Institute of Chemistry, P.O. Box 1122, Wushan, Guangzhou, Guangdong Province 510650, People's Republic of China. TEL 86-20-705360. FAX 86-20-7705319.
circ. 1,000. *5322*

JOURNAL OF COLLEGE AND UNIVERSITY STUDENT HOUSING.
Association of College and University Housing Officers' International, 364 West Lane Ave., Ste. C, Columbus, OH 43201-1062. TEL 614-292-0099. FAX 614-292-3205.
circ. 3,000. *2433*

JOURNAL OF COMPUTER INFORMATION SYSTEMS.
International Association for Computer Information Systems, 217 College of Business, Oklahoma State University, Stillwater, OK 74075. TEL 405-744-5090. FAX 405-744-5180.
circ. 1,000. *2056*

JOURNAL OF COMPUTING IN TEACHER EDUCATION.
International Society for Technology in Education, 1787 Agate St., Eugene, OR 97403-1923. TEL 541-346-4414. FAX 541-346-5890.
circ. 2,500. *2406*

JOURNAL OF COOPERATIVE EDUCATION.
Cooperative Education Association, Inc., 8640 Giulford Rd., Ste. 215, Columbia, MD 21046-2615. TEL 410-290-3666. FAX 410-290-3084.
circ. 3,000. *2346*

JOURNAL OF CYTOLOGY AND GENETICS.
Society of Cytologists and Geneticists, Department of Botany, Bangalore University, Bangalore 560 056, India. TEL 3355036.
circ. 350. *745*

JOURNAL OF DATABASE MANAGEMENT.
Idea Group Publishing, 4811 Jonestown Rd., Ste. 230, Harrisburg, PA 17109-1751. TEL 717-541-9150. FAX 717-541-9159.
circ. 300. *2066*

JOURNAL OF ELECTROTOPOGRAPHY.
Electrotopograph Corporation, Box 98, Eldred, PA 16731. TEL 814-225-3296.
circ. 1,000. *5553*

JOURNAL OF EUROPEAN BUSINESS.
Faulkner & Gray, Inc. (New York), 11 Penn Plaza, 17th Fl., New York, NY 10001. TEL 212-967-7000. FAX 212-967-7155.
circ. 6,202. *937*

JOURNAL OF FAMILY LIFE.
72 Philip St., Albany, NY 12202. TEL 518-432-1578. FAX 518-462-6836.
circ. 4,000. *6419*

JOURNAL OF FINANCIAL PLANNING TODAY.
New Directions Publications, Inc., Box 6097, W. Palm Beach, FL 33405. TEL 407-434-0100. FAX 407-641-4801.
circ. 500. *1105*

JOURNAL OF GENERAL ORTHODONTICS.
International Association for Orthodontics, 1100 Lake St., Ste. 240, Oak Park, IL 60301-1035. TEL 708-445-0320. FAX 708-445-0321.
circ. 3,800. *4645*

JOURNAL OF GENETICS & BREEDING.
Istituto Sperimentale per la Cerealicoltura, Via Cassia, 176, 00191 Rome, Italy. TEL 39-6-3295705. FAX 39-6-36306022.
circ. 300. *129*

JOURNAL OF HOUSING RESEARCH.
Federal National Mortgage Association, 3900 Wisconsin Ave., N.W., Washington, DC 20016-2899. TEL 202-752-4422. FAX 202-752-4933.
circ. 3,200. *3586*

JOURNAL OF INDO-EUROPEAN STUDIES.
Institute for the Study of Man, Box 34070, N.W., Washington, DC 20043. TEL 202-371-2700. FAX 202-371-1523.
circ. 80. *6331*

JOURNAL OF INTERNATIONAL MARKETING & MARKETING RESEARCH.
European Marketing Association, 18 St. Peters Steps, Brixham, Devon, England. *1471*

JOURNAL OF KANSAS PHARMACY.
Kansas Pharmacists Association, 1308 SW. 10th Ave., Topeka, KS 66604-1299. TEL 913-232-0439. FAX 913-232-3764.
circ. 1,200. *5422*

JOURNAL OF MICROWAVE POWER AND ELECTROMAGNETIC ENERGY.
International Microwave Power Institute, 10210 Leatherleaf Ct., Manassas, VA 22111-4245. TEL 703-257-1415.
circ. 1,000. *2711*

JOURNAL OF MIND AND BEHAVIOR.
Institute of Mind & Behavior, Box 522, Village Sta., New York, NY 10014. TEL 212-595-4853.
circ. 1,208. *5858*

JOURNAL OF MYOCARDIAL ISCHEMIA.
P R R, Inc., 17 Prospect St., Huntington, NY 11743. TEL 516-424-8900. FAX 516-424-8503.
circ. 27,833. *4606*

JOURNAL OF N I H RESEARCH.
William M. Miller, 1444 I St., NW, Ste. 1000,
Washington, DC 20005. TEL 202-785-5333.
FAX 202-872-7738.
circ. 29,730. *4484*

**JOURNAL OF NUCLEAR AGRICULTURE AND
BIOLOGY.**
Indian Society for Nuclear Techniques in Agriculture
and Biology, Nuclear Research Laboratory, Indian
Agricultural Research Institute, New Delhi 110012,
India.
circ. 400. *228*

JOURNAL OF ORTHOPAEDIC SURGERY.
Hong Kong University Press, 139 Pokfulam Rd.,
Hong Kong, Hong Kong. TEL 852-2818-3761.
FAX 852-2872-8938.
circ. 2,000. *4786*

JOURNAL OF OSTEOPATHIC MEDICINE.
In Vivo Inc., Box 5262, Princeton, NJ 08543-5262.
circ. 33,000. *4786*

**JOURNAL OF PARK AND RECREATION
ADMINISTRATION.**
Sagamore Publishing Inc., 302 W. Hill St., Box 647,
Champaign, IL 61824-0647. TEL 217-359-5940.
FAX 217-359-5975.
circ. 720. *6567*

**JOURNAL OF PLANAR CHROMATOGRAPHY -
MODERN T L C.**
Research Institute for Medicinal Plants, Lupaszigeti
st. 4, P.O. Box 11, 2011 Budakalasz, Hungary.
TEL 36-1-1688042. FAX 36-26-320426.
circ. 220. *1718*

JOURNAL OF POPULATION AND HEALTH STUDIES.
Korea Institute for Population and Health, SAN 42-
14 Bulgwang-Dong, Eunpyung-Ku, Seoul 122, S.
Korea. *827*

JOURNAL OF PROTECTIVE COATINGS AND LININGS.
Technology Publishing Co., 2100 Wharton St., Ste.
31, Pittsburgh, PA 15203. TEL 412-431-8300.
FAX 412-431-5428.
circ. 15,000. *5308*

JOURNAL OF SPORTS PHILATELY.
Sports Philatelists International, c/o Margaret A.
Jones, 5310 Lindenwood Ave., St.Louis, MO 63109-
1758. TEL 314-352-0888.
circ. 500. *5458*

JOURNAL OF TOSOH RESEARCH.
Tosoh Corporation, 4560 Tonda, Shinnanyo-shi,
Yamaguchi-ken 746, Japan. FAX 81-834-62-1748.
circ. 750. *2644*

JOURNAL OF TRANSPORTATION MEDICINE.
Japanese Association of Transportation Medicine, c/
o Business Center for Academic Societies Japan, 5-
16-9 Honkomagome, Bunkyo-ku, Tokyo 113,
Japan. TEL 03-5814-5811. FAX 03-5814-5822.
circ. 600. *4787*

JOURNALIST'S HANDBOOK.
Carrick Media, 2-7 Galt House, 31 Bank St., Irvine
KA12 0LL, Scotland. TEL 44-1294-311322.
circ. 2,600. *3706*

JOURNALS OF DISSENT AND SOCIAL CHANGE.
California State University, Sacramento, Library,
2000 Jed Smith Dr., Sacramento, CA 95819.
TEL 916-278-6466. *6441*

JOURNEE VINICOLE.
Promovin, B.P. 1064, 34007 Montpellier Cedex 1,
France. TEL 67-07-91-01. FAX 67-47-93-63.
circ. 15,900. *507*

JUDARNA I F.D. SOVJET.
Svenska Kommitten foer Judarna i f.d. Sovjet, P.O.
Box 5053, S-102 42 Stockholm, Sweden. TEL 46-
8-664-53-38. FAX 46-8-664-05-91.
circ. 2,600. *5731*

JUDO.
Judo Magazine B.V., Blokhoeve 5, 3438 LC
Nieuwegein, Netherlands. TEL 31-23-325260.
FAX 31-23-342721.
circ. 60,000. *6467*

JUNIOR STATEMENT.
Junior Statesmen of America, 60 E. Third Ave., Ste.
320, San Mateo, CA 94401. TEL 415-347-1600.
FAX 415-347-7200.
circ. 20,000. *1795*

JUNTENDO MEDICAL JOURNAL.
Juntendo Medical Society, 2-1-1 Hongo, Bunkyo-ku,
Tokyo 113, Japan. FAX 3814-9100.
circ. 3,550. *4485*

JURBOOK.
Varus Verlag Birgit Laube, Koenigswintererstr. 552,
53227 Bonn, Germany. TEL 0228-440015.
FAX 0228-440017.
circ. 18,000. *3876*

JURISTISCHE SCHULUNG.
C.H. Beck'sche Verlagsbuchhandlung, Wilhelmstr. 9,
80801 Munich, Germany. TEL 089-38189-338.
FAX 089-38189-398.
circ. 24,738. *3799*

JUS-EXTRA.
Oesterreichische Staatsdruckerei, Rennweg 12a, A-
1037 Vienna, Austria. TEL 01-79789307. FAX 01-
79789419.
circ. 1,250. *3892*

K.A.C.B. AUTO REVUE.
Eclips Promotion, 53 rue d'Arlon, B-1040 Brussels,
Belgium. TEL 32-2-2870911. FAX 32-2-2307584.
circ. 40,000. *6790*

K C M S BULLETIN.
Medical Society County of Kings, Inc., 1313 Bedford
Ave., Brooklyn, NY 11216. TEL 718-467-9000.
FAX 718-778-0380.
circ. 2,800. *4485*

K F Z BETRIEB AKTUELLE WOCHENZEITUNG.
Vogel Verlag und Druck GmbH & Co. KG, Max-
Planck-Str. 7-9, 97082 Wuerzburg, Germany.
TEL 0931-4182145. FAX 0931-4182640.
circ. 34,000. *6790*

K F Z BETRIEB UNTERNEHMERMAGAZIN.
Vogel Verlag und Druck GmbH & Co. KG, Max-
Planck-Str. 7-9, 97082 Wuerzburg, Germany.
TEL 0931-4182145. FAX 0931-4182640.
circ. 33,940. *6790*

K MITTEILUNGEN.
Gesamtverband Kunststoffverarbeitende Industrie
e.V., Froschpfort 16, 56410 Montabaur, Germany.
FAX 49-2602-4308.
circ. 3,000. *5521*

K N A G NIEUWS.
Koninklijk Nederlands Aardrijkskundig Genootschap,
P.O. Box 80123, 3508 TC Utrecht, Netherlands.
TEL 31-30-532757. FAX 31-30-535523.
circ. 4,300. *3264*

**K O A DIRECTORY ROAD ATLAS AND CAMPING
GUIDE.**
Meredith Corporation, 1716 Locust St., Des Moines,
IA 50336. TEL 515-284-3412. FAX 515-284-
2700.
circ. 1,900,000. *1619*

K: REVISTA DE POESIA.
Lubio Cardozo y Juan Pinto, Eds. & Pubs., Apartado
410, Merida, Venezuela. *4309*

K W S NEWSLETTER.
Kenya Wildlife Service, Nairobi Education Centre,
P.O. Box 40241, Nairobi, Kenya. TEL 254-2-
501081. FAX 254-2-505866.
circ. 2,000. *2131*

KABAR.
Australia Indonesia Association of New South Wales,
G.P.O. Box 802, Sydney, N.S.W. 2001, Australia.
TEL 02-635-4186.
circ. 150. *5759*

KACHERE TEXTS.
University of Malawi, Chancellor College, P.O. Box
280, Zomba, Malawi. TEL 265-50-522549.
FAX 265-50-522046.
circ. 500. *6073*

KAERNTER BAUER.
Kammer fuer Land- und Forstwirtschaft Kaernten,
Museumgasse 5, A-9020 Klagenfurt, Austria.
TEL 43-463-5850. FAX 43-463-5850389.
circ. 30,000. *130*

KAGAKU GIJUTSU BUNKEN TOYAMA.
Kagaku Gijutsu Bunken Tyo Shikokai, c/o Toyama
Prefectural Library, 206-3 Chayamachi, Toyama
930-01, Japan.
circ. 500. *6672*

KAI TIAKI: NURSING NEW ZEALAND.
New Zealand Nurses' Organisation, P.O. Box 2128,
Wellington, New Zealand. TEL 64-4-385-0847.
FAX 64-4-382-9993.
circ. 24,000. *4719*

KAKU YUUGOU KAGAKU KENKYUSHO NYUSU.
Kaku Yuugou Kagaku Kenkyusho, Furocho, Chikusa-
ku, Nagoya-shi, Aichi-ken 464-01, Japan. TEL 81-
52-789-4551. FAX 81-52-789-4200.
circ. 2,650. *5596*

KALAMAZOO COLLEGE QUARTERLY.
Kalamazoo College, 1200 Academy St., Kalamazoo,
MI 49006-3295. TEL 616-377-7304. FAX 616-
337-7305.
circ. 15,300. *1873*

KALASTAJA.
Kalatalouden Keskusliitto Koydenpunojankatu 7 B
23, 00180 Helsinki 18, Finland. TEL 358-0-640-
126. FAX 358-0-608-305.
circ. 9,636. *2937*

KALEIDOSCOPE (BIRMINGHAM).
University of Alabama at Birmingham, Box 76,
University Center, Birmingham, AL 35294-1150.
TEL 205-934-3354.
circ. 8,000. *1873*

KALEVA.
Sanomalehti Kaleva, P.O. Box 70, FIN-90150 Oulu,
Finland. TEL 358-81-5377245. FAX 358-81-
5377248.
circ. 37,615. *3137*

KALOKAGATHIA.
Magyar Testnevelesi Egyetem, Alkotas u. 44, 1123
Budapest, Hungary. TEL 36-1-1554-444. FAX 36-1-
1566-337.
circ. 300. *6467*

KAN ANDERS.
Kan Anders, Werkgemeenschap voor Pacifisme,
Ekologie en Socialisme, Vamingsraat 82, 2611 LA
Delft, Netherlands. TEL 31-15-2121694.
circ. 1,000. *5759*

KANAGAWA-KEN HAKUBUTSUKAN KYOKAI KAIHO.
Kanagawa-ken Hakubutsukan Kyokai, 5-60 Minami-
Nakadori, Naka-ku, Yokohama-sh, Kanagawa-ken
231, Japan. TEL 045-201-0926. FAX 045-201-
7364. *5124*

**KANSAS. DEPARTMENT OF HEALTH AND
ENVIRONMENT. ANNUAL SUMMARY OF VITAL
STATISTICS.**
Department of Health and Environment, Center for
Health and Environmental Statistics, 900 S.W.
Jackson, Topeka, KS 66612-1290. TEL 913-296-
5640. FAX 913-296-7025.
circ. 1,000. *5787*

**KANSAS. LEGISLATIVE RESEARCH DEPARTMENT.
REPORT ON KANSAS LEGISLATIVE INTERIM
STUDIES.**
Legislative Research Department, Topeka, KS
66612. TEL 913-296-3181. *5678*

KANSAS RESTAURANT.
Kansas Restaurant Association, 359 S. Hydraulic,
Wichita, KS 67211. TEL 316-267-8383.
circ. 1,500. *3566*

KANSAS WILDFLOWER SOCIETY NEWSLETTER.
Hall Publishing Co., Mulvane Arts Center, Washburn
University, Topeka, KS 66621. TEL 913-231-1010.
FAX 913-233-2780.
circ. 550. *3059*

KANTINEN.
Kantineledernes Landsklub, Kolleruplund 63, 2665
Vallensbaek Strand, Denmark. FAX 45-43-54-34-
52.
circ. 4,347. *1850*

KAPPA ALPHA PSI JOURNAL.
McQuiddy Publishing Co., 2320 N. Broad St.,
Philadelphia, PA 19132. TEL 215-228-7184.
circ. 15,000. *1850*

KAPPA DELTA EPSILON CURRENT.
Kappa Delta Epsilon, c/o Kay Damron, Ed., Oconee County Public Schools, Box 146, School St., Watkinsville, GA 30677. TEL 706-769-6655. circ. 1,500. *1873*

KAPPA TAU ALPHA. NEWSLETTER.
Kappa Tau Alpha, U M School of Journalism, Columbia, MO 65211. TEL 573-882-7685. FAX 573-882-4823. circ. 500. *3707*

KARAYOLLARI TEKNIK BULTENI.
General Directorate of Highways, Ankara, Turkey. circ. 3,000. *2667*

DER KARTOFFELBAU.
Verlag Th. Mann, Nordring 10, 45894 Gelsenkirchen, Germany. TEL 49-209-9304184. FAX 49-209-9304185. circ. 5,232. *229*

KATES KIN.
1395 Main St., Box 8, Rarden, OH 45671. TEL 614-372-6705. circ. 800. *3090*

KATORIKKU KENKYU.
Sophia University, Theological Society, Kamishakujii 4-32-11, Nerima-ku, Tokyo 177, Japan. TEL 03-5991-0343. FAX 03-5991-6928. circ. 1,000. *6184*

KAUPPAKAMARILEHTI.
Keskuskauppakamari, P.O. Box 1000, FIN-00101 Helsinki 10, Finland. TEL 358-0-696969. FAX 358-0-650303. circ. 26,000. *1144*

KEADILAN.
Islamic University of Indonesia, Faculty of Law, Jalan Taman Siswa 158, Yogyakarta 55151, Indonesia. TEL 2978. circ. 2,500. *3800*

KEEP ON TRUCKIN' NEWS.
Mid-West Truckers Association, Inc., 2727 N. Dirksen Parkway, Springfield, IL 62702. TEL 217-525-0310. FAX 217-525-0342. circ. 3,500. *6858*

KEHITTYVAE KAUPPA.
Kauppiaitten Kustannus Oy, Kanavakatu 3.B, FIN-00160 Helsinki, Finland. TEL 358-0-228821. circ. 21,368. *1473*

KEIRYO KOKUGO GAKKAI.
Keiryo Kokugo Gakkai, c/o Tokyo Joshi Daigaku, Zenpukuji 2-6-1, Suginami-ku, Tokyo 167, Japan. TEL 03-3395-1211. circ. 600. *4081*

KEIZAIGAKU KENKYU.
Keizai Riron Gakkai, c/o Rikkyo Daigaku Keizaigakubu, 3 Ikebukuro, Toshima-ku, Tokyo 171, Japan. *938*

KEIZAIGAKU RONSHU.
University of Tokyo Press, 3-1 Hongo 7-chome, Bunkyo-ku, Tokyo 113, Japan. *938*

KELLY'S LINK.
Kelly's Directories Part of the Reed Elsevier group, Windsor Court, E. Grinstead House, E. Grinstead, W. Sussex RH19 1XB, England. TEL 01342-326972. FAX 01342-335747. circ. 50,000. *1619*

KELLY'S OIL & GAS DIRECTORY.
Kelly's Directories Part of the Reed Elsevier group, Windsor Court, E. Grinstead House, E. Grinstead, W. Sussex RH19 1XB, England. TEL 01342-326972. FAX 01342-335747. circ. 7,000. *1619*

KEMPER INSURANCE MAGAZINE.
Kemper National Insurance Cos., Publications - Community Relations, 1 Kemper Dr., Long Grove, IL 60049-0001. FAX 708-540-4279. circ. 13,600. *3655*

KENKALUSIKKA.
Suomen Kenkakauppiaiden Liitto r.y., Fredrikinkatu 67 E 42, FIN-00100 Helsinki 10, Finland. TEL 358-0-409-932. FAX 358-0-409-563. circ. 1,296. *6307*

KENTUCKY COUNCIL ON HIGHER EDUCATION. COUNCIL ACTIONS.
Kentucky Council on Higher Education, 1050 U.S. 127 S., Ste. 101, Frankfort, KY 40601-4395. TEL 502-564-3553. FAX 502-564-2063. circ. 1,200. *2435*

KENTUCKY NURSE.
Kentucky Nurses Association, Box 2616, Louisville, KY 40201. TEL 502-637-2546. FAX 502-637-8236. circ. 28,000. *4719*

KENTUCKY PRAIRIE FARMER.
Farm Progress Companies 191 S. Gary Ave., Carol Stream, IL 60188. TEL 708-690-5600. FAX 708-462-2869. circ. 10,500. *229*

KENYA SOCIETY FOR THE BLIND. ANNUAL REPORT AND ACCOUNTS.
Kenya Society for the Blind, P.O. Box 46656, Nairobi, Kenya. TEL 254-2-503757. circ. 2,000. *3320*

KERALA SABHA.
Better Life Movement, Better Life Center, Aloor, Kallettumkara, Kerala 680 683, India. circ. 2,000. *6208*

KESHEV.
Bar-Ilan University, Institute of Holocaust Research, Ramat Gan 52100, Israel. circ. 1,000. *3423*

KEY - A GUIDE TO COLLEGE AND CAREERS.
Target Marketing, Inc., 5 Victory Ln., Ste. 101, Liberty, MO 64068. TEL 816-781-7557. FAX 816-792-3892. circ. 1,400,000. *2413*

KHADYA VIGYAN.
Central Food Technological Research Institute, Mysore 570 013, India. circ. 1,500. *2981*

KINDAI EIGA.
Kindai-Eiga Corp., Owaricho Bldg., 2F, 6-8-3 Ginza, Chuo-ku, Tokyo 104, Japan. TEL 81-3-5568-2811. FAX 81-3-5568-2818. *5106*

KINGSMAN.
City University of New York, Brooklyn College, c/o Michael Golub, Box 23-0200, Brooklyn, NY 11223. TEL 718-376-1429. circ. 20,000. *1874*

KIRJASTOLEHTI.
Suomen Kirjastoseura, Kansakoulukatu 10 A 19, SF-00100 Helsinki, Finland. TEL 358-0-694-1856. FAX 358-0-694-1859. circ. 6,748. *4004*

KIRKLAND LAKE GAZETTE.
1 Duncan Ave., Kirkland Lake, ON P2N 2N8, Canada. TEL 705-568-NEWS. FAX 705-568-4444. circ. 7,479. *3122*

KITCHENS.
Maclean Hunter Ltd., Maclean Hunter House, Chalk Ln., Cockfosters Rd., Barnet, Herts EN4 0BU, England. TEL 0181-242-3000. FAX 0181-242-3185. circ. 11,499. *862*

KNOX COUNTY ILLINOIS GENEALOGICAL SOCIETY. QUARTERLY.
Knox County Illinois Genealogical Society, Box 13, Galesburg, IL 61402-0013. circ. 280. *3091*

DER KNUEPFTEPPICH.
Westdeutsche Verlagsanstalt GmbH, Ahmser Str. 190, 32052 Herford, Germany. TEL 49-5221-7750. FAX 49-5221-775215. circ. 4,000. *3679*

KOBE UNIVERSITY. SCHOOL OF BUSINESS ADMINISTRATION. ANNALS.
Kobe Daigaku, School of Business Administration, Rokkodai-cho, Nada-ku, Kobe-shi, Hyogo-ken 657, Japan. FAX 078-881-8100. *1430*

KOEBENHAVNS HAVNEBLAD.
Faellesrepraesentationen for Funktionaerer ved Koebenhavns Havnevaesen, Nordre Toldbod 7, Postboks 2083, 1013 Copenhagen K, Denmark. TEL 33 14 43 40, local 310. FAX 33-93-23-40. circ. 4,400. *6839*

KOEBENHAVNS UNIVERSITET. GEOLOGISK CENTRALINSTITUT. AARSBERETNING.
Koebenhavns Universitet, Geologisk Institut, Oester Voldgade 10, DK-1350 Copenhagen K, Denmark. TEL 33-11-22-32. circ. 525. *2247*

KOEDBRANCHEN.
Danske Slagtermestres Landsforening, P.O. Box 709, DK-5230 Odense M, Denmark. TEL 45-66-12-87-30. FAX 45-66-12-87-94. circ. 3,200. *2982*

KOKURITSU KAGAKU HAKUBUTSUKAN SENPO.
Monbusho, Kokuritsu Kagaku Hakubutsukan, 7-20 Ueno Koen, Taito-ku, Tokyo 110, Japan. circ. 1,000. *6255*

KOKURITSU KOKKAI TOSHOKAN GEPPO.
National Diet Library, 1-10-1 Nagata-cho, Chiyoda-ku, Tokyo 100, Japan. TEL 03-3581-2331. FAX 03-3597-9104. circ. 3,950. *4004*

KOKUSAIHO GAIKO ZASSHI.
Kokusaiho Gakkai, c/o Faculty of Law, University of Tokyo, 3-1, Hongo 7-chome, Bunkyo-ku, Tokyo, Japan. TEL 03-3812-2111. circ. 800. *3937*

KOLDFAX.
Air-Conditioning and Refrigeration Institute, 4301 Fairfax Dr., Ste. 425, Arlington, VA 22203-1627. TEL 703-524-8800. FAX 703-528-3816. *3330*

KOLEINU.
Habonim-Dror Organisation, 523 Finchley Rd., London NW3 7BD, England. TEL 44-171-4359033. FAX 44-171-4314503. circ. 1,500. *6127*

KOLONITRAEDGAARDEN.
Svensk Foerbund for Kolonitraedgaard och Fritidsbyar, Ringvaegen 123, 1 tr., S-116 61 Stockholm, Sweden. TEL 46-8-743-00-90. FAX 46-8-40-38-98. circ. 29,300. *3059*

KONCAR STRUCNE INFORMACIJE.
S O U R Rade Koncar, O O U R Elektrotehnicki Institut, Bastijanova ul. bb, 41001 Zagreb, Croatia. TEL 041-312222. FAX 041-334170. circ. 2,500. *2711*

KONEVIESTI.
Viestilehdet Oy, Revontulentie 8b, 02100 Espoo 10, Finland. TEL 90-131151. FAX 0-131-15209. circ. 53,500. *4340*

KONJUNKTURNI BAROMETAR.
Zavod za Trzisna Istrazivanja, Mose Pijade 8-I, 11001 Belgrade, Yugoslavia. *1525*

KONSTRUKTIONSPRAXIS.
Vogel Verlag und Druck GmbH & Co. KG, Max-Planck-Str. 7-9, 97082 Wuerzburg, Germany. TEL 0931-4182145. FAX 0931-4182640. circ. 26,827. *2736*

KONTROLLE.
Konradin Verlag Robert Kohlhammer GmbH, Ernst-Mey-Str. 8, 70771 Leinfelden-Echterdingen, Germany. TEL 49-711-7594-0. FAX 49-711-7594-390. circ. 20,525. *2608*

KOOTENAY BUSINESS JOURNAL.
Catalyst Communications Inc., 2F-601 Front St., Nelson, BC V1L 5P5, Canada. TEL 604-352-6397. FAX 604-352-2588. circ. 6,500. *940*

KOREA FORUM.
Korea-Verband im Asienhaus, Bullmannaue 11, 45327 Essen, Germany. TEL 0201-8303812. circ. 600. *5288*

KOSMETISCHE MEDIZIN.
B M V - Berliner Medizinische Verlagsanstalt GmbH,
Lietzenburgerstr. 97, 10719 Berlin, Germany.
TEL 49-30-8823569. FAX 49-30-8812225.
circ. 4,000. *4487*

KOSMOS.
International Society for Astrological Research, Inc.,
P.O. Box 38613, Los Angeles, CA 90038-0613.
TEL 805-525-0461. FAX 805-525-0461.
circ. 1,000. *472*

KOSMOS.
Deutsche Verlags-Anstalt GmbH, Postfach 106012,
70049 Stuttgart, Germany. TEL 49-711-2631-0.
FAX 49-711-2631292.
circ. 71,201. *6255*

KOTI.
Maa- ja Kotitalousnaisten Keskus, Lonnrotinkatu 13,
SF-00120 Helsinki, Finland. TEL 90-680-700.
FAX 90-680-70270.
circ. 25,365. *3524*

KRISTDEMOKRATEN.
Samhaellsgemenskaps Foerlags AB, P.O. Box
19098, S-104 32 Stockholm, Sweden. TEL 46-8-
15-05-45. FAX 46-8-612-79-53.
circ. 9,700. *5679*

KRISTELIGT DAGBLAD.
Fanoegade 15, DK-2100 Copenhagen Oe, Denmark.
TEL 45-39-27-12-35. FAX 45-39-27-15-25.
circ. 15,662. *3134*

KRITERION.
Universitaet Salzburg, Institut fuer Philosophie,
Franziskanergasse 1, A-5020 Salzburg, Austria.
FAX 43-662-8044629.
circ. 500. *5484*

KROPPSOEVING.
Landslaget Fysisk Fostring i Skolen, Moellegt. 10, N-
3111 Toensberg, N-3111 Toensberg, Norway.
TEL 47-33-31-53-00. FAX 47-33-31-52-66.
circ. 2,500. *2349*

KUENSTLER JAHRBUCH.
Verlag Disco Post GmbH, Oststr. 2, 56424 Staudt,
Germany. TEL 49-2602-70044. FAX 49-2602-
69939.
circ. 10,000. *1622*

KUKHOEBO.
National Assembly, c/o Secretary-General, 1-1
Yeoidodong, Yeongdungpo-ku, Seoul, S. Korea.
TEL 788-2058. FAX 788-3348.
circ. 5,500. *5679*

KULDE.
Skarland Press A-S, P.O. Box 5042 Maj., N-0301
Oslo, Norway. TEL 47-22-60-13-90. FAX 47-22-69-
36-50.
circ. 5,617. *3330*

KULTUR NEWS.
Kulturring in Berlin e.V., Friedrichstr. 120, 10117
Berlin, Germany. TEL 49-30-2826343. FAX 49-30-
2826343.
circ. 1,500. *438*

KULTUR UND TECHNIK.
C.H. Beck'sche Verlagsbuchhandlung, Wilhelmstr. 9,
80801 Munich, Germany. TEL 089-38189-338.
FAX 089-38189398.
circ. 12,551. *5124*

**KUNSTHISTORISCHES INSTITUT IN FLORENZ.
MITTEILUNGEN.**
Kunsthistorisches Institut in Florenz, Via G. Giusti
44, 50121 Florence, Italy. TEL 39-55-2491147.
FAX 39-55-2491155.
circ. 900. *439*

KURIER WILENSKI.
Parliament of the Republic of Lithuania, Laisves 60,
Vilnius 2056, Lithuania. TEL 42-79-01. FAX 42-72-
65.
circ. 20,000. *2891*

KURSKONTAKTE.
Flurweg 4, 83646 Bad Toelz, Germany. TEL 49-
8041-5439. FAX 49-8041-73814.
circ. 15,500. *5218*

KUSPI.
Turun Hammaslaaketieteenkandidaattiseura,
Lemminkaisenkatu 2, 20520 Turku 52, Finland.
circ. 2,600. *4547*

KUTLWANO.
Department of Information and Broadcasting,
Private Bag 0060, Gaborone, Botswana. TEL 267-
32541. FAX 267-352971.
circ. 24,000. *5679*

KUWAIT BULLETIN OF MARINE SCIENCE.
Kuwait Institute for Scientific Research, Mariculture
and Fisheries Department, P.O. Box 1638, Salmiya,
Kuwait. TEL 965-575-1984. FAX 965-571-1293.
circ. 700. *2938*

KWANSEI GAKUIN DAIGAKU RIGAKUBU TSUSHIN.
Kwansei Gakuin University, School of Science, 1-
155 Uegahara-ichiban-cho, Nishinomiya-shi, Hyogo-
ken 662, Japan. TEL 0798-53-6111. FAX 0798-
51-0914.
circ. 1,200. *1974*

KYOIKU HYORON.
Japan Teachers' Union, Nihon Kyoiku-Kaikan, 2-6-2
Hitotsubashi, Kanda, Chiyoda-ku, Tokyo, Japan.
circ. 20,000. *2349*

**KYOTO UNIVERSITY. FACULTY OF ENGINEERING.
MEMOIRS.**
Kyoto University, Faculty of Engineering, Yoshida
Hon-machi, Sakyo-ku, Kyoto 606, Japan. *2609*

**KYOTO UNIVERSITY. RESEARCH REACTOR
INSTITUTE. ANNUAL REPORTS.**
Kyoto University, Research Reactor Institute,
Kumatori-cho, Sennan-gun, Osaka 590-04, Japan.
TEL 0724-52-0901. FAX 0724-53-5810.
circ. 1,000. *2579*

KYRKOFOERFATTNINGAR.
Verbum Foerlag AB, P.O. Box 15169, S-104 65
Stockholm, Sweden. TEL 46-8-743-65-00. FAX 46-
8-641-45-85.
circ. 2,000. *6074*

KYUSHU NEURO-PSYCHIATRY.
Kyushu Association of Neuro-Psychiatry, c/o
Department of Neuro-Psychiatry, Faculty of
Medicine, Kyushu University, Maidashi, Higashi-ku,
Fukuoka 812-82, Japan. TEL 81-92-641-1151.
FAX 81-92-632-3558.
circ. 1,100. *4849*

L A N A NYT.
Lokalhistoriske Arkiver i Nordjyllands Amt, c/o
Lokalhistorisk Arkiv for Aalborg Kommune,
Arkivstraede 1, P.O. Box 1353, DK-9100 Aalborg,
Denmark. TEL 45-98-12-85-77. FAX 45-98-10-22-
48.
circ. 800. *3424*

L AE S.
Aarhus Universitet, Institut for Nordisk Sprog og
Litteratur, Niels Juelsgade 84, DK-8200 Aarhus N,
Denmark. TEL 45-89-42-11-11. FAX 45-86-10-43-
07.
circ. 700. *4227*

**L & D - LIEFERANTEN UND DIENSTLEISTER FUER
VERLAGE UND AGENTUREN.**
Presse Fachverlag, Eidelstedteweg 22, 20255
Hamburg, Germany. TEL 040-565031. FAX 040-
5602920.
circ. 3,800. *5814*

L.G. ARGOMENTI.
Comune di Genova, Civiche Biblioteche, Via
Archimede, 44, 16142 Genoa, Italy. TEL 39-10-
509181.
circ. 1,500. *4150*

L M S.
George Warman Publications (Pty.) Ltd., P.O. Box
704, Cape Town 8000, South Africa. TEL 27-21-
245320. FAX 27-21-261332.
circ. 5,800. *4681*

L T U MAGAZIN.
Westend GmbH, Westendstr. 1, 45143 Essen,
Germany. TEL 0201-1882269. FAX 0201-
1882235.
circ. 400,000. *6936*

LAB PRODUCTS INTERNATIONAL.
Pan European Publishing Co. Rue Verte 216, 1030
Brussels, Belgium. TEL 32-2-2402611. FAX 32-2-
242711.
circ. 49,750. *4682*

LAB 2000.
Ediciones Mayo, S.A., Muntaner 374, 4o, 08006
Barcelona, Spain. TEL 34-3-209C255. FAX 34-3-
2020643.
circ. 5,000. *6256*

LABMEDICA INTERNATIONAL.
Globetech Publishing, 30 Cannon Rd., Wilton, CT
06897. TEL 203-762-3432. FAX 203-762-8640.
circ. 26,000. *4682*

LABO.
Verlag Hoppenstedt GmbH, Havestr. 9, 64295
Darmstadt, Germany. TEL 49-6151-380-0. FAX 49-
6151-380-360.
circ. 25,000. *4682*

LABOR AND EMPLOYMENT UPDATE.
Reed McClure, 3600 Columbia Center, 701 Fifth
Ave., Seattle, WA 98104-7081. TEL 206-292-
4900. FAX 206-223-0152.
circ. 4,400. *1383*

**LABOR FORCE AND NONAGRICULTURAL
EMPLOYMENT ESTIMATES.**
Department of Employment Security, 500 James
Robertson Pkwy., 11th Fl., Nashville, TN 37245-
1000. TEL 615-741-1729. *1012*

LABOR LEADER.
San Diego-Imperial Counties Labor Council, 4265
Fairmount Ave., San Diego, CA 92105-1265.
circ. 33,000. *3723*

LABOR VOICE.
Australian Labor Party, Western Australia Branch,
2nd Fl., Labor Centre, 82 Beaufort St., Perth, W.A.
6000, Australia. FAX 09-2279585.
circ. 10,000. *5679*

LABORATORIET.
Institutet foer Biomedicinsk Laboratorievetenskap,
Adolf Fredriks Kyrkogata 11, S-111 37 Stockholm,
Sweden. TEL 46-8-240131. FAX 46-8-240124.
circ. 12,428. *4682*

LABORATORY PRODUCT NEWS.
Southam Magazine Group, 1450 Don Mills Rd., Don
Mills, ON M3B 2X7, Canada. TEL 416-445-6641.
FAX 416-442-2261.
circ. 20,000. *4683*

LABORPRAXIS.
Vogel Verlag und Druck GmbH & Co. KG, Max-
Planck-Str. 7-9, 97082 Wuerzburg, Germany.
TEL 0931-4182145. FAX 0931-4182640.
circ. 20,000. *4683*

LACTEOS Y CARNICOS MEXICANOS.
Alfa Editores Tecnicos S.A. Libertad No. 107-402,
03660 Mexico DF, Mexico. TEL 525-579-3333.
FAX 525-5329504.
circ. 5,000. *2982*

LADUE PUBLIC SCHOOLS BULLETIN.
Ladue Board of Education, c/o Elizabeth Schwartz,
Ed., School District of the City of Ladue, 9703
Conway Rd., St. Louis, MO 63124. TEL 314-994-
7080. FAX 314-994-0441.
circ. 12,000. *2350*

LAGOS EDUCATION REVIEW.
Joja Educational Research and Publishers Limited,
13 B Ikorodu Rd., Maryland, P.M.B. 21526, Ikeja,
Lagos State, Nigeria. TEL 234-64-933866.
circ. 3,000. *2350*

LAHN-DILL-ANZEIGER.
Anzeigenblatt Verlag Lahn-Dill, Elsa-Brandstroem-Str.
18, 35578 Wetzlar, Germany. TEL 49-6441-
75166. FAX 49-6441-75166.
circ. 370,000. *3146*

LAKE BIWA STUDY MONOGRAPHS.
Lake Biwa Research Institute, 1-10, Uchide-hama,
Otsu-shi, Shiga-ken 520, Japan. TEL 0775-26-
4800. FAX 0775-26-4803.
circ. 500. *2287*

LAMAZE PARENTS' MAGAZINE.
Lamaze Publishing Co., 372 Danbury Rd., Wilton, CT 06897-2523. TEL 203-834-2711. FAX 203-761-8696.
circ. 2,400,000. *4741*

LAMAZEBABY.
Lamaze Publishing Co., 372 Danbury Rd., Wilton, CT 06897-2523. TEL 203-834-2711. FAX 203-761-8696.
circ. 1,800,000. *4741*

LAMP (NEW YORK).
Exxon Corporation, 5959 Las Colinas Blvd., Irving, TX 75039-2298. TEL 214-444-1116. FAX 214-444-1139.
circ. 680,000. *5363*

LANCASHIRE CONSTABULARY JOURNAL.
Lancashire Constabulary, County Police Headquarters, P.O. Box 77, Hutton, Preston PR4 5SB, England. TEL 0772-618444. FAX 0772-618356.
circ. 5,000. *2168*

LANCE.
University of Windsor, Student Media Corp, Windsor, ON N9B 3P4, Canada. TEL 519-253-4232. FAX 519-971-3624.
circ. 10,000. *1874*

LAND AND LIBERTY.
Land and Liberty International Ltd., 177 Vauxhall Bridge Rd., London SW1V 1EU, England. TEL 071-834-4266. FAX 071-834-4979.
circ. 2,000. *6028*

LAND & WATER.
V N U Business Publications B.V., Postbus 9194, 1006 CC Amsterdam, Netherlands. TEL 31-20-4875515. FAX 31-20-4875735.
circ. 11,000. *2668*

LAND LINE MAGAZINE.
Owner-Operator Independent Drivers Association of America, Box L, Grain Valley, MO 64029. TEL 816-229-5791. FAX 816-229-0518.
circ. 110,000. *6858*

LANDESBIBLIOGRAPHIE VON BADEN-WUERTTEMBERG.
Kommission fuer Geschichtliche Landeskunde in Baden-Wuerttemberg, Eugenstr. 7, 70182 Stuttgart, Germany.
circ. 800. *3367*

LANDESVERSICHERUNGSANSTALT WUERTTEMBERG. MITTEILUNGEN.
W. Kohlhammer GmbH, Hessbruehlstr. 69, 70565 Stuttgart, Germany. TEL 49-711-7863-1. FAX 49-711-7863263. *6381*

LANDMAN.
American Association of Professional Landmen, 4100 Fossil Creek Blvd., Fort Worth, TX 76137-2791. TEL 817-847-7700.
circ. 10,000. *5363*

LANDSCAPE CONTRACTOR.
Maury Boyd and Associates, Inc., 2200 S. Main St., Ste. 304, Lombard, IL 60148. TEL 708-932-8443. FAX 708-932-8939.
circ. 2,200. *3060*

LANGLEY ADVANCE.
20488 Fraser Hwy., Langley, BC V3A 4G2, Canada. TEL 604-534-8641. FAX 604-534-3383.
circ. 34,500. *3122*

LANGUAGE QUARTERLY.
University of South Florida, College of Arts & Sciences, 4202 E. Fowler Ave., CPR 107, Tampa, FL 33620-5550. TEL 813-974-5618. FAX 813-974-5618.
circ. 500. *4084*

LANTERN'S CORE.
Northwestern University Library, Staff Association, 1935 Sheridan Rd., Evanston, IL 60208. TEL 312-491-7633. FAX 312-491-8306.
circ. 550. *4005*

LARGE ANIMAL VETERINARIAN.
Watt Publishing Co., 122 S. Wesley Ave., Mt. Morris, IL 61054-1497. TEL 815-734-4171.
circ. 16,438. *275*

LASER APPLICAZIONI INDUSTRIALI, TECNOLOGIE, MERCATI.
Gruppo Editoriale Jackson S.p.A., Via M. Gorki 69, 20092 Cinisello B. (MI), Italy. TEL 39-2-660341. FAX 39-2-66034238.
circ. 17,400. *5606*

LASTBILEN.
Aakerifoerlaget AB, P.O. Box 508, 182 15 Danderyd, Sweden. TEL 46-08-753-54-40. FAX 46-08-755-88-95.
circ. 16,500. *6858*

LASTEBILEN.
Norges Lastebileier-Forbund, Th. Meyersgt. 72, P.O. Box 4658 Sofienberg, N-0506 Oslo, Norway. TEL 47-22-11-01-55. FAX 47-22-20-56-15.
circ. 13,000. *6858*

LATEINAMERIKA JAHRBUCH (YEAR).
Vervuert Verlag GmbH, Wielandstr. 40, 60318 Frankfurt a.M., Germany. TEL 49-69-5974617. FAX 49-69-5978743.
circ. 200. *4150*

LATIN AMERICA - CHICAGO.
University of Chicago, Center for Latin American Studies, 5848 S. University Ave., Chicago, IL 60637. TEL 312-702-8420. FAX 312-702-1755.
circ. 1,500. *2892*

LAUREL OF PHI KAPPA TAU.
Phi Kappa Tau Fraternity, 15 N. Campus Ave., Oxford, OH 45056-0030. TEL 513-523-4193. FAX 513-523-9325.
circ. 45,000. *1874*

LAW ENFORCEMENT PRODUCT NEWS.
General Communications, Inc., 100 Garfield St., Denver, CO 80206-5550. TEL 303-322-6400. FAX 303-322-0627.
circ. 40,000. *2168*

LAW OF THE SEA INSTITUTE. OCCASIONAL PAPER.
Law of the Sea Institute, University of Hawaii - Manoa, Richardson School of Law, 2515 Dole St., Honolulu, HI 96822. TEL 808-956-3300. FAX 808-956-3307.
circ. 500. *3957*

LAW TECHNOLOGY JOURNAL.
University of Warwick, CTI Law Technology Centre, Coventry CV4 7AL, England. TEL 44-1203-523294. FAX 44-1203-524105.
circ. 600. *3890*

THE LAWYERS WEEKLY.
Butterworths Canada Ltd., Part of the Reed Elsevier group, 75 Clegg Rd., Markham, ON L6G 1A1, Canada. TEL 905-479-2665. FAX 905-479-2826.
circ. 22,500. *3807*

LEADER (STOCKPORT).
Covenanters, 11-33 Lower Hillgate, Stockport, Ches. SK1 1JQ, England. TEL 0161-474-1262. FAX 0161-474-1300.
circ. 4,300. *6075*

LEADER MAGAZINE.
Active Parenting Publishers, 810 Franklin Court, Ste. B, Marietta, GA 30067-8943. TEL 770-429-0565. FAX 770-429-0334.
circ. 55,000. *1772*

LEADERS.
Leaders Magazine, Inc., 59 E. 54th St., New York, NY 10022. TEL 212-758-0740. FAX 212-593-5194.
circ. 33,000. *1288*

LEADING EDGE.
Canadian Business Aircraft Association, 50 O'Connor St., Ste. 1317, Ottawa, ON K1P 6L2, Canada. TEL 613-236-5611. FAX 613-236-2361.
circ. 1,000. *6761*

LEADING LIGHT.
Wellington Maritime Museum, P.O. Box 893, Wellington, New Zealand. TEL 64-4-4728904. FAX 64-4-4711373.
circ. 750. *5124*

LEAN TRIMMINGS.
National Meat Association, 1970 Broadway, Ste. 825, Oakland, CA 94612. TEL 510-763-1533. FAX 510-763-6186.
circ. 1,250. *275*

LEBENSBAUM.
Markgrafenstr. 21, 91438 Bad Windsheim, Germany. TEL 09841-2974.
circ. 300. *2132*

LEBENSMITTEL PRAXIS.
Lebensmittel Praxis Verlag Neuwied GmbH, Postfach 1861, 56508 Neuwied, Germany. TEL 02631-879-0. FAX 02631-879175. *3006*

DER LEBENSMITTELKAUFMANN.
Oesterreichischer Wirtschaftsverlag, Nikolsdorfergasse 7-11, A-1051 Vienna, Austria. TEL 0222-555585.
circ. 21,200. *3006*

LEBLANC BELL.
G. Leblanc Corporation, P.O. Box 1415, Kenosha, WI 53141-1415. TEL 414-658-1644. FAX 414-658-2824.
circ. 38,000. *5171*

THE LECTURER.
N A T F H E - The University and College Lecturers' Union, 27 Britannia St., London WC1X 9JP, England. TEL 0171-837-3636. FAX 0171-837-4403.
circ. 72,000. *2400*

LEE HOWARD NEWSLETTER.
Selective Books, Inc., Box 1140, Clearwater, FL 34617. TEL 813-447-0100.
circ. 5,500. *6001*

LEEDS ON.
Mediamark Publishing International Ltd., 35 Gresse St., Rathbone Pl., London W1P 1PN, England. TEL 44-171-580-3105. FAX 44-171-580-1695.
circ. 50,000. *3965*

LEGAL EXECUTIVE.
Institute of Legal Executives, Kempston Manor, Kempston, Bedford, England. TEL 01234-840022. FAX 01234-841999.
circ. 19,997. *3808*

LEGAL MANAGEMENT.
Association of Legal Administrators, 175 E. Hawthorn Pkwy., Ste. 325, Vernon Hills, IL 60061-1428. TEL 847-247-5573. FAX 847-816-1213.
circ. 25,000. *3808*

LEGIS-MATE.
National Diet Library, 1-10-1 Nagata-cho, Chiyoda-ku, Tokyo 100, Japan. TEL 03-3581-2331. FAX 03-3597-9104.
circ. 1,800. *4006*

LEGISLACAO FEDERAL E MARGINALIA.
Lex Editora S.A., Machado de Assis, Nrs. 47-57, Caixa Postal 12888, 04106-900 Sao Paulo SP, Brazil. TEL 55-11-5490122. FAX 55-11-5759138.
circ. 20,000. *3809*

LEHEL AKTUELL.
S P D - Ortsverein Lehel, c/o Dr. Thomas Lange, Knobelstr. 30, 80538 Munich, Germany. TEL 49-89-222918.
circ. 7,200. *5679*

LEHIGH ALUMNI BULLETIN.
Lehigh University, Alumni Association, 436 Broadhead Ave., Bethlehem, PA 18015. TEL 610-758-4838. FAX 610-758-4708.
circ. 50,000. *1874*

LEHRMITTEL AKTUELL - LEHRMITTEL COMPUTER.
Westermann Schulbuchverlag GmbH, Postfach 4938, 38039 Braunschweig, Germany. TEL 49-531-708375. FAX 49-531-708127.
circ. 38,404. *2459*

LEICHHARDT HISTORICAL JOURNAL.
9 The Avenue, Balmain E., N.S.W. 2041, Australia. TEL 61-2-810-8560. FAX 61-2-555-9277.
circ. 300. *3388*

LEIPURI.
Suomen Leipuriliitto r.y., P.O. Box 115, SF-00241 Helsinki, Finland. TEL 358-0-14887304. FAX 358-0-14887301.
circ. 1,600. *3000*

LEIPZIGER WIRTSCHAFT.
Schluetersche Verlagsanstalt GmbH und Co., Hans-Boeckler-Allee 7, 30173 Hannover, Germany. TEL 0511-8550-0. FAX 0511-8550400.
circ. 38,000. *1144*

Contr Circ

LEISURE WORLD GOLDEN RAIN NEWS.
Golden Rain Foundation, Box 2338, Seal Beach, CA
90740-1338. TEL 310-430-0534. FAX 310-598-
1617.
circ. 2,392. *3292*

LEISUREWAYS.
Canada Wide Magazines Ltd. (Toronto), 2 Carlton
St., Ste. 801, Toronto, ON M5B 1J3, Canada.
TEL 416-595-5007.
circ. 634,000. *3122*

LENNOX NEWS.
Lennox International Inc., Office of Government and
Public Relations, Box 799900, Dallas, TX 75379-
9900. TEL 214-497-5258. FAX 214-497-5292.
circ. 15,000. *3330*

LESBIAN NEWS.
2953 Lincoln Blvd., Santa Monica, CA 90405.
TEL 310-392-8224. FAX 310-452-0562.
circ. 27,000. *3534*

LESBIAN REVIEW OF BOOKS.
Box 6369, Altadena, CA 91003. TEL 818-398-
4200. FAX 818-398-4200.
circ. 2,000. *4228*

**LESOTHO. MINISTRY OF NATURAL RESOURCES.
HYDROLOGICAL YEARBOOK.**
Ministry of Natural Resources, Department of Water
Affairs, P.O. Box MS 772, Maseru 100, Lesotho.
FAX 266-310437. *2287*

LETRAS DE DEUSTO.
Universidad de Deusto, Facultad de la Filosofia y
Letras, Departamento de Publicaciones, Apdo. 1,
48080 Bilbao, Spain. TEL 34-4-4453100. FAX 34-
4-445-8916.
circ. 750. *3618*

LET'S PLAY HOCKEY.
Let's Play, Inc., 2721 E. 42nd St., Minneapolis, MN
55406. TEL 612-729-0023. FAX 612-729-0259.
circ. 19,500. *6468*

LET'S TALK FAMILIES!
Family Service Canada, 600-220 Laurier Ave., W.,
Ottawa, ON K1P 5Z9, Canada. TEL 613-230-9960.
FAX 613-230-5884.
circ. 4,000. *6381*

THE LETTERBOX MARKETING HANDBOOK.
Association of Household Distributors Ltd., 36
Frogmore St., Tring, Hants. HP23 5AU, England.
TEL 44-1442-890991. FAX 44-1452-890992.
circ. 3,000. *39*

LA LETTRE D'ACTIVITES EN PAYS BASQUE.
Bayonne Chamber of Commerce, 50-51 allees
Marines, B.P. 215, 64102 Bayonne Cedex, France.
TEL 59-46-59-99. FAX 59-59-42-75. *1145*

LETTRE D'INFORMATION METAUX.
Editions Montmartre, 142 rue Montmartre, 75002
Paris, France. TEL 33-1-40-26-83-21. FAX 33-1-
40-39-97-52.
circ. 500. *4962*

LEUKEMIA SOCIETY OF AMERICA. NEWSLINE.
Leukemia Society of America, Inc., 600 Third Ave.,
4th Fl., New York, NY 10016. TEL 212-573-8484.
FAX 212-856-9686.
circ. 66,000. *4759*

LEVNEDSMIDDELBLADET - SUPERMARKEDET.
Visholm Media AS, Sydvestvej 49, P.O. Box 221,
DK-2600 Glostrup, Denmark.
circ. 3,000. *3006*

**LEXICON VEVY EUROPE SKIN CARE INSTANT
REPORTS.**
Vevy Europe S.p.A., Casella Postale 81570, 16131
Genoa, Italy. TEL 39-10-5221515. FAX 39-10-
5221530.
circ. 12,900. *4663*

LEXINGTON THEOLOGICAL QUARTERLY.
Lexington Theological Seminary, 631 S. Limestone
St., Lexington, KY 40508. FAX 606-281-6042.
circ. 2,300. *6075*

LEY.
Ediciones la Ley S.A., 1471 Tucuman, 1050
Buenos Aires, Argentina. TEL 541-495481.
FAX 541-4760953.
circ. 12,000. *3810*

LIBERAL REVIEW.
Liberal Party, 88-1 Rosmead Place, Colombo 7, Sri
Lanka. TEL 582779. FAX 588875.
circ. 1,000. *5680*

LIBRA.
Chartered Accountant Students' Society of London
(CASSL), Friendly House, 52 Tabernacle St., London
EC2A 4NB, England. TEL 44-171-490-0680.
FAX 44-171-253-4530.
circ. 6,500. *1050*

LIBRARY ASSOCIATION RECORD.
Library Association, 7 Ridgmount St., London WC1E
7AE, England. TEL 44-171-636-7543. FAX 44-
171-436-7213.
circ. 28,000. *4007*

LIBRARY DEVELOPMENTS.
Texas State Library, Library Development Division,
Box 12927, Austin, TX 78711. TEL 512-463-
5465. FAX 512-463-5436.
circ. 1,000. *4008*

LIBRARY LIAISON.
Libraries Board of South Australia, G.P.O. Box 419,
Adelaide, S.A. 5001, Australia. TEL 61-8-2077357.
FAX 61-8-2077351.
circ. 1,000. *4008*

LIBRARY MATTERS.
Queens Borough Public Library, 89-11 Merrick
Blvd., Jamaica, NY 11432. TEL 718-990-0705.
FAX 718-291-8936.
circ. 20,000. *4008*

LICENSEE AND MORNING ADVERTISER.
Licensee and Morning Advertiser, Elvian House,
Nixey Close, Slough, Berks SL1 1NQ, England.
TEL 01753-811911. FAX 01753-810503.
circ. 16,459. *508*

DAS LIEBHABERORCHESTE.
Bund Deutscher Liebhaberorchester e.V., Schlegelstr.
14, 90491 Nuernberg, Germany. TEL 49-911-
591309. FAX 49-911-594836.
circ. 4,700. *5171*

LIETUVOS RYTAS.
Lietuvos Rytas, Gedimino pr. 12A, 2001 Vilnius,
Lithuania. TEL 370-2-6226980. FAX 370-2-
227656.
circ. 40,000. *3190*

LIFE LINES.
Monumental Life Insurance Company, 2 E. Chase
St., Baltimore, MD 21202. TEL 301-685-2900.
FAX 301-347-8656.
circ. 850. *3657*

LIFT.
Association for Spina Bifida and Hydrocephalus, 42
Park Rd., Peterborough, Cambs. PE1 2UQ,
England. TEL 01733-555988. FAX 01733-
555985.
circ. 1,000. *3305*

LIGHT (WASHINGTON).
A F L - C I O, Utility Workers Union of America, 815
Sixteenth St., N.W., Washington, DC 20006.
TEL 202-347-8105. FAX 202-347-4872.
circ. 65,000. *1386*

LIGHT (WHEATON).
Christian Blind Mission International Inc., Box
19000, Greenville, SC 29602-9000. TEL 803-239-
0065. FAX 803-239-0069.
circ. 38,000. *3320*

LIJECNICKI VJESNIK.
Zbor Lijecnika Hrvatske, Subiceva 9, 41000 Zagreb,
Croatia. TEL 041-440-621.
circ. 7,400. *4490*

LIJFBLAD.
Mediselect B.V., Postbus 28091, 3828 ZH
Hoogland, Netherlands. TEL 31-33-4808020.
FAX 31-33-4805881.
circ. 10,000. *5426*

LIMITED EDITION.
Oxford County Newspapers, Newspaper House,
Osney Mead, Oxford OX2 0EJ, England. TEL 01865-
244988. FAX 01865-243382.
circ. 30,000. *3157*

**LINGUISTIC CIRCLE OF MANITOBA AND NORTH
DAKOTA. PROCEEDINGS.**
University of North Dakota, Box 7128, Grand Forks,
ND 58202-7128. TEL 701-777-2714. FAX 701-
777-3650.
circ. 500. *4230*

LINKAGE.
National Diet Library, Information Processing
Division, 1-10-1 Nagata-cho, Chiyoda-ku, Tokyo
100 Japan. TEL 03-3581-2331. FAX 03-3581-
3292.
circ. 1,000. *1995*

LINKING LIBRARIES.
Rochester Regional Library Council, Box 66160,
Fairport, NY 14450-6162. TEL 716-223-7570.
FAX 716-223-7712.
circ. 1,050. *4010*

LINKING RING.
International Brotherhood of Magicians, c/o Philip R.
Willmarth, Exec.Ed., 348 E Wilshire Ln., Arlington
Heights, IL 60004. TEL 708-577-7337. FAX 708-
577-7337.
circ. 13,000. *3509*

LITERACY ADVOCATE.
Laubach Literacy International, 1320 Jamesville
Ave., Box 131, Syracuse, NY 13210. TEL 315-422-
9121
circ. 20,000. *2400*

THE LITERARIAN.
Mercantile Library Association of the City of New
York, 17 E. 47th St., New York, NY 10017.
TEL 212-755-6711.
circ. 600. *4010*

LITERARY ONOMASTICS STUDIES.
State University of New York at Brockport, State
University College, Brockport, Brockport, NY 14420.
TEL 719-395-2269. *4230*

**LITERATURNACHRICHTEN - AFRIKA - ASIEN -
LATEINAMERIKA.**
Gesellschaft zur Foerderung der Literatur aus Afrika,
Asien und Lateinamerika e.V., Reineckstr. 3, 60313
Frankfurt a.M., Germany. TEL 49-69-2102277.
FAX 49-69-2102247.
circ. 2,900. *4232*

LITHO WEEK.
Haymarket Magazines Ltd., 38-42 Hampton Rd.,
Teddington, Middx. TW11 0JE, England. TEL 081-
943-5000.
circ. 12,832. *5814*

LIVE RAIL.
Southern Electric Group, 67 Denham Crescent,
Mitcham, Surrey CR4 4LZ, England. *6813*

LIVER UPDATE.
American Liver Foundation, 1425 Pompton Ave.,
Cedar Grove, NJ 07009-1043. TEL 201-256-
2550.
circ. 70,000. *4695*

LIVING LIGHT.
United States Catholic Conference, Office for
Publishing and Promotion Services, 3211 Fourth
St., N.E., Washington, DC 20017-1194. TEL 202-
541-3098. FAX 202-541-3089.
circ. 1,200. *6186*

LIVING MUSIC.
Living Music Foundation, Inc., Box 173, Desert Hot
Springs, CA 92240-8463. TEL 619-329-8463.
circ. 300. *5172*

LIVING TRENDS.
K.L. Publications, 2001 Killebrew Dr., Ste. 105,
Bloomington, MN 55425. TEL 512-854-0155.
FAX 612-854-9440.
circ. 1,000,000. *3231*

LIVINGFRONT.
American Cancer Society, Inc., Florida Division,
3709 W. Jetton Ave., Tampa, FL 33629. TEL 813-
253-0541. FAX 813-254-5857.
circ. 350,000. *4759*

LIVINGSTON COUNTY AGRICULTURAL NEWS.
Cooperative Extension Association of Livingston
County, Agricultural Division, 158 S. Main St.,
Mount Morris, NY 14510. TEL 716-658-4110.
FAX 716-658-4707.
circ. 250. *133*

LIVS.
Sveriges Livsmedelshandlarefoerbund (SSLF), PO Box 1311, S-111 83 Stockholm, Sweden. TEL 08-141870. FAX 08-243506.
circ. 6,307. *2982*

LIVSMEDELSTEKNIK.
Stiftelsen Svensk Livsmedelsteknik, Katarinavaegen 20, 116 45 Stockholm, Sweden. FAX 46-8-640-80-45.
circ. 2,300. *2982*

LLOYDS BANK ANNUAL REVIEW.
Lloyds Bank plc., Economics Department, P.O. Box 19, Hays Lane House, 1 Hays Ln., London SE1 2HA, England. TEL 44-171-407-1000. FAX 44-171-357-4378. *1107*

LLOYD'S SHIPPING CONNECTIONS.
L L P Limited, Sheepen Pl., Colchester, Essex CO3 3LP, England. TEL 44-1206-772277. FAX 44-1206-772118.
circ. 1,000. *1623*

LOCAL AUTHORITY WASTE & ENVIRONMENT.
Faversham House Group Ltd., Faversham House, 232a Addington Rd., South Croydon, Surrey CR2 8LE, England. TEL 44-181-651-7100. FAX 44-181-651-7117.
circ. 5,813. *2854*

LOCAL GOVERNMENT FINANCES IN MARYLAND.
Department of Fiscal Services, 90 State Circle, Annapolis, MD 21401. TEL 410-841-3710. FAX 410-841-3722. *1553*

LOCAL GOVERNMENT MANAGEMENT.
Institute of Municipal Management, P.O. Box 409, S. Melbourne, Vic. 3205, Australia. TEL 03-696-5799. FAX 03-690-4217.
circ. 5,000. *5945*

LOCAL 1010 STEELWORKER.
U S W A Local 1010, 3703 Euclid Ave., E. Chicago, IN 46312. TEL 219-398-3100. FAX 219-397-5968.
circ. 23,000. *3724*

LOCATION UPDATE.
Location Update, Inc., 7021 Hayvenhurst Ave., 205, Van Nuys, CA 91406-3802. TEL 213-461-8887. FAX 213-469-3711.
circ. 30,000. *5107*

LOCATOR OF USED MACHINERY, EQUIPMENT & PLANT SERVICES.
Machinery Information Systems, Inc., 1110 Spring St., Silver Spring, MD 20910. TEL 301-585-9498. FAX 301-585-9460. *4341*

LODGING.
American Hotel Association Directory Corp., 1201 New York Ave., N.W., Ste. 600, Washington, DC 20005-3931. TEL 202-289-3100. FAX 202-289-3199.
circ. 40,500. *3567*

LODGING HOSPITALITY.
Penton Publishing Co. 1100 Superior Ave., Cleveland, OH 44114-2543. TEL 216-696-7000. FAX 216-696-8765.
circ. 49,000. *3567*

LOGISTICA MANAGEMENT.
Edizioni Ritman s.r.l., Via Varesina 76, 20156 Milan, Italy. TEL 39-2-38008859. FAX 39-2-38008828.
circ. 5,269. *1431*

LOGISTICS FOCUS.
Institute of Logistics, Douglas House, Queen's Sq., Corby, Northants. NN17 1PL, England. TEL 44-1536-205500. FAX 44-1536-400979.
circ. 11,500. *1167*

LOGISTICS NEWS.
Bolton Publications (Pty) Ltd., P.O. Box 966, Parklands 2121, South Africa. TEL 27-11-8803520. FAX 27-11-8806574.
circ. 3,408. *6722*

LONDON COLLEGE OF MUSIC MAGAZINE.
London College of Music, Thames Valley University, St. Mary's Rd., Ealing, London W5 5RF, England. TEL 44-181-231-2364. FAX 44-181-231-2433. *5172*

LONDON PORTRAIT.
I P C Magazines, Specialist Magazine Group King's Reach Tower, Stamford St., London SE1 9LS, England. TEL 44-171-261-5000. FAX 44-1444-445599.
circ. 90,000. *3157*

LONG ISLAND PARENTING NEWS.
R D M Publishing Corporation, Box 214, Island Park, NY 11558. TEL 516-889-5510. FAX 516-889-5513.
circ. 50,000. *1772*

LONGWOOD GRADUATE PROGRAM SEMINARS.
University of Delaware, College of Agricultural Sciences, 153 Townsend Hall, Newark, DE 19717-1303. TEL 302-451-2517. FAX 302-292-3651.
circ. 800. *690*

LOOKOUT (NEW YORK).
Seamen's Church Institute of New York and New Jersey, 241 Water St., New York, NY 10038. TEL 212-349-9090. FAX 212-349-8342.
circ. 10,000. *6382*

LOS ANGELES READER.
Burnside Group, Inc., 5550 Wilshire Blvd., No. 301, Los Angeles, CA 90036. TEL 213-965-7430. FAX 213-933-0281.
circ. 83,138. *3231*

LOST TREASURE.
Lost Treasure, Inc., Box 1589, Grove, OK 74344. TEL 918-786-2182. FAX 918-786-2192.
circ. 45,832. *3509*

LOUGHTON REVIEW.
Monkswood Press, Caxton House, Old Station Rd., Loughton, Essex IG10 4PE, England. TEL 0181-502-0236. FAX 0181-508-2834.
circ. 17,700. *39*

LOUISIANA AGRICULTURE.
Louisiana State University, Agricultural Center, Box 25100, Baton Rouge, LA 70894-5100. TEL 504-388-2263. FAX 504-388-4524.
circ. 5,000. *133*

LOUISIANA STATE UNIVERSITY. LIBRARY LECTURES.
Louisiana State University, Library, Baton Rouge, LA 70803-7507. TEL 504-388-2217. FAX 504-388-6825. *4010*

LOUISIANA WATER RESOURCES RESEARCH INSTITUTE. ANNUAL REPORT.
Louisiana Water Resources Research Institute, 3418 Ceba Bldg., Louisiana State University, Baton Rouge, LA 70803. FAX 504-388-5990. *6972*

LOURDES - ROSEN.
Deutscher Lourdes-Verein, Schwalbengasse 10, 50667 Cologne, Germany. TEL 0221-2576246. FAX 0221-2576189.
circ. 25,000. *6186*

LOW BIDDER.
Associated General Contractors of America, N.Y. State Chapter, 1900 Western Ave., Albany, NY 12203. TEL 518-456-1134. FAX 518-456-1198.
circ. 1,700. *6823*

LOYOLA MAGAZINE.
Loyola University Chicago, 820 N. Michigan Ave., Chicago, IL 60611. TEL 312-915-6407. FAX 312-915-7742.
circ. 93,000. *1875*

LUBRICANTS WORLD.
Hart Publications, Inc., 4545 Post Oak Pl., Ste. 210, Houston, TX 77027. TEL 713-993-9320.
circ. 10,000. *5363*

LUCKY MEE FAMILY ASSOCIATION. YEARBOOK.
Lucky Mee Family Association, Drawer 4487, El Paso, TX 79914. TEL 915-751-7233.
circ. 180. *3092*

LUNDIAN.
M. Arthur Diakite, P.O. Box 722, S-220 07 Lund, Sweden. TEL 46-111322. FAX 46-111322.
circ. 10,000. *3218*

LUREN.
Scandinavian Philatelic Library of Southern California, Box 310, Claremont, CA 91711. TEL 909-626-1764.
circ. 250. *5458*

LUSAKA CITY LIBRARY. ANNUAL REPORT.
Lusaka City Library, P.O. Box 31304, Katondo Rd., Lusaka, Zambia. TEL 227282.
circ. 150. *4010*

LUSORAMA.
Verlag Teo Ferrer de Mesquita, Postfach 100839, 60008 Frankfurt a.M., Germany. TEL 069-282647. FAX 069-287363.
circ. 800. *4090*

LUTHERAN JOURNAL.
Outlook Publishing, Inc., 7317 Cahill Rd., Edina, MN 55439. TEL 612-941-3010. FAX 612-941-6830.
circ. 125,000. *6151*

LUXE.
Style Communications Inc., 1448 Lawrence Ave. E., Ste. 302, Toronto, ON M4A 4V6, Canada. TEL 416-755-5199. FAX 416-755-9123.
circ. 105,000. *3697*

LUXEMBOURG. MINISTERE DES FINANCES. BUDGET DE L'ETAT.
Ministere des Finances, 3 rue de la Congregation, L-1352 Luxembourg, Luxembourg. *1553*

LYCOMING COUNTY HISTORICAL SOCIETY JOURNAL.
Lycoming County Historical Society, 858 W. Fourth St., Williamsport, PA 17701. TEL 717-326-3326. FAX 717-326-3689.
circ. 1,200. *3477*

M A R G I N.
Mulini Press, P.O. Box 82, Jamison Centre, A.C.T. 2614, Australia. TEL 61-6-2512519.
circ. 200. *4234*

M.A.S.H. MAGAZINE.
Banzai Productions, Postbus 5050, 3502 JB Utrecht, Netherlands. TEL 31-30-2942988.
circ. 1,100. *6469*

M A S T.
R B Publishing Company, 2701 E. Washington Ave., Madison, WI 57304-5002. TEL 604-241-8777. FAX 608-241-8666.
circ. 36,000. *1931*

M & T - METALLHANDWERK & TECHNIK.
Charles Coleman Verlag GmbH & Co. KG, Wahmstr. 56, 23552 Luebeck, Germany. TEL 49-451-79933-0. FAX 49-451-7993399. *863*

M B.
Bitaon Publishing Co. Ltd., 15 Rambam St., P.O. Box 1480, Tel Aviv 61014, Israel. TEL 972-3-5164461. FAX 972-3-5164435.
circ. 4,000. *3182*

M C C NEWS.
Manhattan Christian College, c/o Laurin Hill, Dir. of Alumni and Public Relations, 1415 Anderson, Manhattan, KS 66502-4081. TEL 913-539-3571. FAX 913-539-0832.
circ. 15,000. *1875*

M E A T.
M E A T Communications, Inc., P.O. Box 35, Sta. O, Toronto, ON M4A 2M8, Canada. TEL 416-699-8486. FAX 416-690-6697.
circ. 35,000. *5172*

M E M C O NEWS.
Miller Electric Manufacturing Co., 1635 W. Spencer, Box 1079, Appleton, WI 54911. TEL 414-735-4249. FAX 414-735-4013.
circ. 44,000. *4987*

M E T E M - INTERNATIONAL SOCIETY OF TORONTO FOR HUNGARIAN CHURCH HISTORY. NEWSLETTER.
M E T E M - International Society of Toronto for Hungarian Church History, Regis College, 15 St. Mary St., Toronto, ON M4Y 2R5, Canada. TEL 416-922-2476. FAX 416-922-2898. *3426*

M F D REGISTER.
Milwaukee Fire Department Athletic Association, 711 W. Wells St., Milwaukee, WI 53233. TEL 414-276-5656. *5968*

M H L S NEWS.
Mid-Hudson Library System, 103 Market St., Poughkeepsie, NY 12601. TEL 914-471-6060. FAX 914-454-5940.
circ. 1,100. *4010*

M H - R V BUILDERS NEWS.
Dan Kamrow & Associates, Inc., Box 72367,
Roselle, IL 60172. TEL 708-893-8872.
circ. 10,022. *863*

M I Z - MATERIALIEN UND INFORMATIONEN ZUR ZEIT.
Alibri Verlag, Wuerzburgerstr. 18a, 63739
Aschaffenburg, Germany. TEL 49-6021-15744.
FAX 49-6021-15744.
circ. 1,200. *4153*

M K - MARKETING Y VENTAS PARA DIRECTIVOS.
Grupo Especial Directivos, C. Orense 39 2o D,
28020 Madrid, Spain. TEL 34-1-5566411. FAX 34-1-5554118.
circ. 9,637. *1475*

M L SEIDMAN MEMORIAL TOWN HALL LECTURE SERIES.
Rhodes College, 2000 N. Pkwy., Memphis, TN
38112. TEL 901-726-3818.
circ. 600. *5682*

M L T A NEWS.
Modern Language Teachers' Association of New
South Wales, c/o School of Modern Languages,
Macquarie University, N. Ryde, NSW 2113,
Australia.
circ. 650. *4090*

M O P S A NEWSLETTER.
Missouri Political Science Association, c/o George
Connor, Sect.-Treas., Dept. of Political Science,
Southwest Missouri State University, Springfield, MO
65804. TEL 417-836-6956.
circ. 80. *5682*

M P R C REPORT ON FINANCE, COMMERCE, INDUSTRY: INDONESIA.
M P R C (Asia) Sdn. Berhad, P.O. Box 10706,
50722 Kuala Lumpur, Malaysia. TEL 60-3-2217762. FAX 60-3-7564478. *1221*

M P R C REPORT ON FINANCE, COMMERCE, INDUSTRY: SINGAPORE.
M P R C (Asia) Sdn. Berhad, P.O. Box 10706,
50722 Kuala Lumpur, Malaysia. TEL 60-3-2217762. FAX 60-3-7564478. *1221*

M P R C REPORT ON FINANCE, COMMERCE, INDUSTRY: SOUTH EAST ASIA.
M P R C (Asia) Sdn. Berhad, P.O. Box 10706,
50722 Kuala Lumpur, Malaysia. TEL 60-3-2217762. FAX 60-3-7564478. *1221*

M P R C REPORT ON FINANCE, COMMERCE, INDUSTRY: THAILAND.
M P R C (Asia) Sdn. Berhad, P.O. Box 10706,
50722 Kuala Lumpur, Malaysia. TEL 60-2-2217762. FAX 60-3-7564478. *1221*

M S C KONTAKTE.
Birkenverlag der Herz-Jesu-Missionare, Postfach
1146, 83381 Freilassing, Germany. TEL 08654-9324. FAX 08654-67606.
circ. 8,000. *6186*

M S L A JOURNAL.
Manitoba School Library Association, c/o Manitoba
Teachers' Society, 191 Harcourt St., Winnipeg, Man.
R3J 3H2, Canada. TEL 204-888-7961.
circ. 250. *2494*

M S U ALUMNI MAGAZINE.
Michigan State University, Alumni Association, Rm.
108, Student Union, E. Lansing, MI 48824-1029.
TEL 517-355-8314. FAX 517-355-5265.
circ. 44,000. *1875*

M S U MATHEMATICS NEWSLETTER.
Montana State University, Mathematical Sciences
Department, Bozeman, MT 59717. TEL 406-994-3601. *4378*

M S U U NEWSLETTER: GLEANINGS.
Ministerial Sisterhood Unitarian Universalist, c/o
Universalist Unitarian Church, 740 E. Main St.,
Santa Paula, CA 93060. TEL 805-525-8859.
circ. 300. *6151*

M S W MANAGEMENT.
Forester Communications, Inc., 5638 Hollister Ave.,
Ste. 301, Goleta, CA 93117-3474. TEL 805-681-1300. FAX 805-681-1312.
circ. 24,000. *2854*

M T I REPORTER.
Madison Teachers, Inc., 821 Williamson St.,
Madison, WI 53703 TEL 608-257-0491. *2351*

M T S ECHO.
Manitoba Telephone System, 489 Empress St.,
Winnipeg, MB R3C 3V6, Canada. TEL 204-941-8256. FAX 204-775-0718.
circ. 6,000. *1947*

M T TODAY.
Valley Forge Press, 1288 Valley Forge Rd., Box
1135, Valley Forge, PA 19482. TEL 610-935-3302. FAX 215-935-3072.
circ. 60,000. *4683*

M T U FOCUS.
Motoren- und Turbinen-Union Muenchen GmbH,
Postfach 500640, 80976 Munich, Germany.
TEL 49-89-14894332. FAX 49-89-14892172.
circ. 3,000. *72*

MAANEDSBLADET PRESS.
Maanedsbladet Press, Studiestraede 24, 1, DK-1455 Copenhagen K, Denmark. TEL 45-33-11-58-11. FAX 45-33-11-68-66.
circ. 9,082. *3134*

MAANEDSMAGASINET ERHVERV - NORDJYLLAND.
Sct. Thoegersvej 8, P.O. Box 30, 7770 Vestervig,
Denmark. FAX 97-94-14-10.
circ. 16,600. *1431*

MCALLEN NEWS JOURNAL.
Advance Publishing Company, 1101 N. Cage, Twin
Palm Plaza, Ste. C1, Pharr, TX 78577. TEL 210-783-0036.
circ. 1,000. *942*

MACCABI WORLD UNION. NEWSLETTER.
Maccabi World Union, Kfar Hamaccabiah, Israel.
circ. 500. *6469*

MACHINE DESIGN.
Penton Publishing Co. 1100 Superior Ave.,
Cleveland, OH 44114-2543. TEL 216-696-7000.
FAX 216-696-8765.
circ. 180,000. *2762*

MACHINE DYNAMICS PROBLEMS.
Wydawnictwo M E T, c/o Mieczyslaw Pekalak, Ul.
Piekalkiewicza 5 m.6, 00-710 Warsaw, Poland.
TEL 48-22-490195. FAX 48-22-490306.
circ. 300. *2762*

MACHINE TOOL SELECTOR.
Nexus Media Ltd., Nexus House, Azalea Dr.,
Swanley, Kent BR8 8HY, England. TEL 01322-660070. FAX 01322-337633.
circ. 18,634. *4341*

MACHINERY & EQUIPMENT M R O.
Southam Magazine Group, 1450 Don Mills Rd., Don
Mills, ON M3B 2X7, Canada. TEL 416-445-6641.
FAX 416-442-2077.
circ. 20,200. *4341*

MACHINIST.
International Association of Machinists and
Aerospace Workers, 900 Machinists Pl., Upper
Marboro, MD 20772. TEL 301-967-4500.
circ. 700,000. *3724*

THE MCKINSEY QUARTERLY.
McKinsey & Co. Inc., 55 E. 52nd St., New York, NY
10022. TEL 212-446-7000. *1432*

MACUSER.
Ziff-Davis Publishing Co. (Foster City), 950 Tower
Ln., Foster City, CA 94404. TEL 415-378-5600.
circ. 311,253. *2097*

MADAME.
Magazinpresse Verlag GmbH, Elisenstr. 3, 80335
Munich, Germany. TEL 089-55135-0. FAX 089-55135299.
circ. 110,079. *7000*

MADENCILIK.
Turk Muhendis ve Mimar Odalari Birligi, Maden
Muhendisleri Odasi, Selanik Cad. 19-3, 06650
Ankara, Turkey. TEL 4-1251080. FAX 4-1175290.
circ. 5,000. *5069*

MAERKISCHE ZEITUNG.
Landsmannschaft Berlin-Mark Brandenburg,
Landesverband Berlin, Stresemannstr. 90, 10117
Berlin, Germany. TEL 261 046.
circ. 3,500. *5682*

DAS MAGAZIN.
Das Magazin Verlagsgesellschaft mbH, Brunnenstr.
4, 10119 Berlin, Germany. TEL 49-30-58314433.
FAX 49-30-58314444.
circ. 92,000. *3146*

MAGAZIN FESTSPIELE.
W i W Verlags GmbH, Walschgasse 14, A-1010
Vienna, Austria. TEL 01-5129230. FAX 01-5139469.
circ. 80,000. *6698*

MAGAZINE & BOOKSELLER.
North American Publishing Co. (New York), 322
Eighth Ave., 3rd Fl., New York, NY 10001.
TEL 212-620-7330. FAX 212-620-7335.
circ. 19,000. *6002*

THE MAGAZINE HANDBOOK (YEAR).
Periodical Publishers Association, Queens House, 28
Kingsway, London WC2B 6JR, England. TEL 44-171-379-6268. FAX 44-171-379-5661.
circ. 6,000. *40*

MAGAZINE NEWS.
Periodical Publishers Association, Queens House, 28
Kingsway, London WC2B 6JR, England. TEL 44-171-379-6268. FAX 44-171-379-5661.
circ. 10,194. *40*

"MAGISCHE" WELT.
Verlag W. Geissler-Werry, In den Benden 13, 52355
Dueren, Germany. TEL 02421-51567.
circ. 1,600. *3509*

THE MAGISTRATE.
Digma Publications (Pty) Ltd., 270 Main St.,
Waterkloof, Pretoria 0181 South Africa. TEL 27-12-346-3840. FAX 27-12-346-3845.
circ. 1,900. *3812*

MAGNET MARKETING.
Graham Communications, 40 Ova Rd., Quincy, MA
02170. TEL 617-328-0069. FAX 617-471-1504.
circ. 3 500. *1475*

MAGNOLIA (WINSTON-SALEM).
Southern Garden History Society, c/o Old Salem,
Inc., Drawer F, Salem Sta., Winstor-Salem, NC
27108. TEL 910-724-3125. FAX 910-721-7335.
circ. 600. *3060*

MAHARASHTRA BHUGOLSHASTRA SANSHODHAN PATRIKA.
Maharashtra Bhugolshastra Parishad, Kala Basant
Sahakari Grih. Sanstha, 80E, Shivejinagar,
Bhandarkar Rd., Prabhat Lane 15, Pune 411 004,
India. TEL 334720.
circ. 1,000. *3265*

MAHARASHTRA STATE BUDGET IN BRIEF.
Directorate of Economics and Statistics, MHADA
Bldg., Kalanagar, Bandra (E), Bombay 400051,
India. *1553*

MAILOUT.
Mailout Trust, 9 Chapel St., Holywell Green, Halifax
HX4 9AY, England. TEL 44-1422-310161. FAX 44-1422-310161.
circ. 7,500. *441*

MAINE APPRISE.
Maine Secondary School Principals' Association, Box
2468, Augusta, ME 04338-2468. FAX 207-622-1513.
circ. 480. *2459*

MAINE POTATO NEWS.
Northeast Publishing Company, Box 510, Presque
Isle, ME 04769. TEL 207-764-7033. FAX 207-764-4499.
circ. 6,000. *231*

MAINE TRAILS.
Maine Better Transportation Association, 146 State
St., Augusta, ME 04330. TEL 207-622-0526.
FAX 207-623-2928.
circ. 1,200. *2668*

MAINTENANCE TECHNOLOGY.
Applied Technology Publications, Inc., 1300 S. Grove Ave., Barrington, IL 60010. TEL 708-382-8100. FAX 708-304-8603.
circ. 72,000. *6657*

LE MAITRE IMPRIMEUR.
Association des Arts Graphiques du Quebec, Inc., 65, rue de Castelnau Ouest, Bureau 101, Montreal, PQ H2R 2W3, Canada. TEL 514-274-7446. FAX 514-274-7482.
circ. 3,959. *5814*

MAJALLAT AL-SHURTAH.
Royal Oman Police, Directorate of Public Relations, P.O. Box 2, 113 Muscat, Sultanate of Oman. TEL 968-569216. FAX 968-563352.
circ. 9,000. *2169*

MAKEDONSKI JAZIK.
Institut za Makedonski Jazik, Skopje, P.O. Box 434, 91000 Skopje, Macedonia.
circ. 1,000. *4090*

MAKERERE UNIVERSITY. ALBERT COOK LIBRARY. LIBRARY BULLETIN AND ACCESSION LIST.
Makerere University, Albert Cook Library, Makerere Medical School, Box 7072, Kampala, Uganda.
4040

MAKKAL KURAL.
Newsmen Associates Ltd., 1, First Main Rd., United India Colony, Kodambakkam, Madras 600 024, India. TEL 044-4831188. FAX 044-4832833.
circ. 1,900. *3172*

MALAWI. NATIONAL LIBRARY SERVICE BOARD. ANNUAL REPORT.
National Library Service Board, P.O. Box 30314, Lilongwe 3, Malawi. TEL 265-783700. FAX 265-783560.
circ. 300. *4011*

MALAWI. NATIONAL LIBRARY SERVICE BOARD. STAFF NEWSLETTER.
National Library Service Board, P.O. Box 30314, Lilongwe 3, Malawi. TEL 265-783700. FAX 265-783560.
circ. 400. *4011*

MALAYSIAN AGRICULTURAL JOURNAL.
Ministry of Agriculture, Publications Officer, Wisma Tani, Jalan Mahameru, 50624 Kuala Lumpur, Malaysia.
circ. 1,500. *134*

MAMAMIA.
Randersackererstr. 81, 97074 Nuernberg, Germany. TEL 49-931-15729. FAX 49-931-3552512.
circ. 10,000. *1798*

MAMMALIA.
Museum National d'Histoire Naturelle, Mammiferes et Oiseaux, 55 rue Buffon, 75005 Paris, France. TEL 40-79-30-69. FAX 40-79-30-63.
circ. 670. *813*

MANAGED CARE.
Stezzi Communications, Inc., 301 Oxford Valley Rd., Ste. 1105A, Yardley, PA 19067. TEL 215-321-6663. FAX 215-321-6670.
circ. 80,000. *4491*

MANAGEMENT.
Jemma Publications Ltd., Marino House, 53 Glasthule Rd., Sandycove, Co. Dublin, Ireland. TEL 01-800000. FAX 01-844041.
circ. 8,000. *1432*

MANAGEMENT ACCOUNTER.
Society of Management Accountants of Alberta, 1800-125 Ninth Ave., S.E., Calgary, AB T2G 0P6, Canada. TEL 403-269-5341. FAX 403-262-5477.
circ. 7,000. *1050*

MANAGEMENT BRIEFS.
Clinical Laboratory Management Association, 9 Old Lincoln Hwy., Ste. 201, Malvern, PA 19355-2135. TEL 610-647-8970. FAX 610-889-9731.
circ. 8,500. *4683*

MANAGEMENT CONSULTANTS NEWS.
Witton House, Lower Rd., Chorleywood, Herts WD3 5LD, England. TEL 01923-285323. FAX 01923-285819.
circ. 9,000. *1432*

MANAGEMENT FORUM.
International Management Council, 430 S. 20th St., No. 3, Omaha, NE 68102. TEL 402-345-1904. FAX 402-345-4480.
circ. 6,000. *1432*

MANAGEMENT OF THE CALIFORNIA STATE WATER PROJECT.
Department of Water Resources, Box 942836, Sacramento, CA 94236-0001. TEL 916-445-9248.
6972

MANAGEMENT UPDATE (DENVER).
Medical Group Management Association, 104 Inverness Terrace E., Englewood, CO 80112. TEL 303-799-1111.
circ. 22,000. *4492*

MANAGERSEMINARE.
ManagerSeminare Gerhard May Verlags GmbH, Endenicherstr. 282, 53121 Bonn, Germany. TEL 49-228-97791-0. FAX 49-228-616164.
circ. 30,000. *1435*

MANAGING AUTOMATION.
Thomas Publishing Company, Five Penn Plaza, New York, NY 10001. TEL 212-629-0500. FAX 212-629-1564.
circ. 104,000. *2016*

MANAGING OFFICE TECHNOLOGY.
Penton Publishing Co. 1100 Superior Ave., Cleveland, OH 44114-2543. TEL 216-696-7000. FAX 216-696-7648.
circ. 110,000. *1494*

MANHATTAN ARTS INTERNATIONAL.
200 E. 72nd St., Ste. 26L, New York, NY 10021. TEL 212-472-1660. FAX 212-794-0343.
circ. 40,000. *441*

MANIPULACION DE MATERIALES EN LA INDUSTRIA.
Publicaciones Internacionales S.A., P. Castellana, 210, 28046 Madrid, Spain.
circ. 2,000. *864*

MANITOBA MUSEUM OF MAN AND NATURE. ANNUAL REPORT.
Manitoba Museum of Man and Nature, 190 Rupert Ave., Winnipeg, MB R3B 0N2, Canada. TEL 204-956-2830. FAX 204-942-3679.
circ. 3,000. *5125*

MANITOBAN.
University of Manitoba, Students' Union, Rm. 105, University Centre, Winnipeg, MB R3T 2N2, Canada. TEL 204-474-6535. FAX 204-269-1299.
circ. 13,000. *1875*

MANUFACTURED HOME MERCHANDISER.
R L D Group, Inc., 203 N. Wabash, Ste. 800, Chicago, IL 60601-2476. TEL 312-236-3528.
circ. 15,000. *3588*

MANUFACTURING & PROCESS AUTOMATION.
Kerrwil Publications Ltd., 395 Matheson Blvd. E., Mississauga, ON L4Z 2H2, Canada. TEL 905-890-1846. FAX 905-890-5769.
circ. 15,600. *2016*

MANUFACTURING COMPUTER SOLUTIONS.
Findlay Publications Ltd., Hadlow House, 9 High St., Green St. Green, Orpington, Kent BR6 6BG, England. TEL 44-1689-854754. FAX 44-1689-860041.
circ. 54,000. *2680*

MANUFACTURING MANAGEMENT.
Industrial Trade Journals Ltd., 8th Fl., Tubs Hill House, London Rd., Sevenoaks, Kent TN13 1BL, England. TEL 01732-464154. FAX 01732-464454.
circ. 20,688. *2749*

MANUFACTURING SYSTEMS.
Hitchcock Publishing 191 S. Gary Ave., Carol Stream, IL 60188-2292. TEL 708-665-1000. FAX 708-462-2225.
circ. 115,000. *1526*

MAPFRE SEGURIDAD.
Editorial Mapfre, Ctra. Majadahonda a Pozuelo km. 3500, 28220 Majadahonda (Madrid), Spain. TEL 626-55-17. FAX 626-21-42.
circ. 19,510. *5253*

MAPLE LEAVES.
Canadian Philatelic Society of Great Britain, c/o David F. Sessions, Ed., 31 Eastergate Green, Rustington, Littlehampton, W. Sussex BN16 3EN, England. TEL 44-1903-830266.
circ. 500. *5458*

MAQUINAS & METAIS.
Aranda Editora Ltda., Rua D. Elisa no. 167, Perdizes, 01155-900 Sao Paulo, SP, Brazil. TEL 55-11-8264511. FAX 55-11-669585.
circ. 15,000. *4342*

MAR.
Liga Maritima de Chile, Errazurriz 471, Casilla 117-V, Valparaiso, Chile. TEL 255179.
circ. 2,000. *6840*

MARANATHA.
South African Union Conference of Seventh-Day Adventists, P.O. Box 468, Bloemfontein 9300, South Africa. TEL 27-51-4473871. FAX 27-51-4488059.
circ. 13,592. *6208*

MARCA.
Recoletos Cia. Editorial, C. Recoletos 1, 28001 Madrid, Spain. TEL 337-32-20. FAX 337-37-71.
circ. 741,000. *6469*

MARGARET SHAW LECTURES.
South African Museum, P.O. Box 61, Cape Town 8000, South Africa. TEL 27-21-243330. FAX 27-21-246716.
circ. 450. *363*

MARI - PAPEL.
Latin Press Inc., Apdo. Postal 67252, Medellin, Colombia. TEL 57-4-284-5232.
circ. 2,053. *5323*

MARINA DOCK AGE.
Preston Publications, Inc., 7800 N. Merrimac Ave., Box 48312, Niles, IL 60714-3426. TEL 847-967-1810. FAX 947-965-0056.
circ. 18,000. *6536*

MARKEE.
H J K Publications, Inc., 655 Fulton St., Ste. 9, Sanford, FL 32771. TEL 407-324-1733. FAX 407-324-1766.
circ. 18,500. *5107*

MARKET CONNECTION.
Last Mountain Times Ltd., 103 First Ave. W., Nokomis, SK S0G 3R0, Canada. TEL 306-528-2020. FAX 306-528-2090.
circ. 6,410. *3123*

MARKET VISION SUPLEMENTOS.
Aramo Editorial, S.A., Muntaner 60 2o 2a, 08011 Barcelona, Spain. TEL 34-3-4537938. FAX 34-3-3237926.
circ. 5,500. *2527*

MARKETEER.
c/o J. Cook, Ed., 1602 E. Glen Ave., Peoria, IL 61614.
circ. 2,000. *1476*

THE MARKETER.
Oklahoma Petroleum Marketers Association, 5115 N. Western, Oklahoma City, OK 73118. TEL 405-842-6625. FAX 405-842-9564.
circ. 1,300. *5363*

MARKETING HIGHER EDUCATION NEWSLETTER.
Topor & Associates, 655 Castro St., Ste. 8, Mountain View, CA 94041-2000. TEL 415-961-6121.
circ. 700. *2436*

MARKETPLACE MAGAZINE.
A D D Inc., 211 N. Lynndale Dr., Ste. 8, Appleton, WI 54913-1897. TEL 414-735-5969. FAX 414-735-5970.
circ. 16,000. *943*

MARQUETTE TRIBUNE.
Marquette University, 1131 W. Wisconsin Ave., Milwaukee, WI 53233. TEL 414-288-7057. FAX 414-288-1979.
circ. 7,500. *1876*

MARTLET.
Martlet Publishing Society, Box 3035, Victoria, BC
V8W 3P3, Canada. TEL 604-721-8358. FAX 604-
721-8361.
circ. 10,000. *1876*

**MARYLAND. STATE HIGHWAY ADMINISTRATION.
TRAFFIC TRENDS.**
State Highway Administration, Department of
Transportation, 707 Calvert St., Baltimore, MD
21203. TEL 410-787-4050. FAX 410-787-5823.
circ. 200. *6823*

MARYLAND BIRDLIFE.
Maryland Ornithological Society, Inc., Patuxent
Wildlife Research, Laurel, MD 20708. TEL 301-
497-5641. FAX 301-497-5624.
circ. 2,200. *778*

MARYLAND MEDICAL JOURNAL.
Medical and Chirurgical Faculty of Maryland, 1211
Cathedral St, Baltimore, MD 21201. TEL 410-539-
0872. FAX 410-547-0915.
circ. 7,500. *4492*

MARYLAND MUSIC EDUCATOR.
Maryland Music Educators Association, c/o Thomas
W. Fugate, Ed., 27 Meadow Ln., Thurmont, MD
21788. TEL 301-271-7269. FAX 301-271-7032.
circ. 1,400. *5172*

MARYLAND P T A BULLETIN.
Maryland Congress of Parents and Teachers, 3121
Saint Paul St., Ste. 25, Baltimore, MD 21218-
3857. TEL 301-685-0865. *2352*

MASCHINEN ANLAGEN VERFAHREN.
Konradin Verlag Robert Kohlhammer GmbH, Ernst-
Mey-Str. 8, 70771 Leinfelden-Echterdingen,
Germany. TEL 49-711-7594-0. FAX 49-711-7594-
390.
circ. 18,134. *1435*

MASCHINENMARKT.
Vogel Verlag und Druck GmbH & Co. KG, Max-
Planck-Str. 7-9, 97082 Wuerzburg, Germany.
TEL 0931-4182145. FAX 0931-4182640.
circ. 49,500. *4342*

MASKIN - AKTUELT.
Teknisk Forlag A-S, Skelbaekgade 4, DK-1717
Copenhagen V, Denmark. TEL 45-31-21-68-01.
FAX 45-31-21-04-01.
circ. 20,430. *4963*

MASKINBEFAELET.
Svenska Maskinbefaelsfoerbundet, P.O. Box 12100,
S-102 23 Stockholm, Sweden. TEL 46-8-693-56-
21. FAX 46-8-693-55-50.
circ. 4,283. *6842*

MASKINSTATIONEN OG LANDBRUGSLEDEREN.
I-S Moeller, L.P. Bechs Vej 29, DK-8240 Risskov,
Denmark. TEL 45-86-17-77-58. FAX 45-86-17-46-
80.
circ. 4,200. *205*

MASONIC WORLD.
Publishers, Inc., 500 Temple Ave., Detroit, MI
48201. TEL 313-831-6250.
circ. 12,000. *1851*

**MASSACHUSETTS COLLEGE OF PHARMACY.
BULLETIN.**
Massachusetts College of Pharmacy and Allied
Health Sciences, 179 Longwood Ave., Boston, MA
02115. TEL 617-732-2800. FAX 617-732-2801.
circ. 8,000. *5427*

**MASSACHUSETTS STATE LABOR COUNCIL A F L - C
I O NEWSLETTER.**
Massachusetts State Labor Council, A F L - C I O, 8
Beacon St., 3rd Fl., Boston, MA 02108. TEL 617-
227-8260. FAX 617-227-2010.
circ. 8,000. *3725*

MASTER LOCK NEWS TODAY.
Master Lock Co., 2600 N. 32nd St., Milwaukee, WI
53210. TEL 414-444-2800. FAX 414-449-3193.
circ. 1,900. *889*

MASTER, MATE & PILOT.
International Organization of Masters, Mates &
Pilots, 700 Maritime Blvd., Linthicum Heights, MD
21090. TEL 410-850-8700. FAX 410-850-0973.
circ. 13,000. *3725*

MASTER PLUMBER OF SOUTH AUSTRALIA.
Master Plumbers & Mechanical Services
Association, 219 Henley Rd., Torrensville, S.A.
5031, Australia.
circ. 550. *3331*

MASTERSTROKE.
Mediamark Publishing International Ltd., 35 Gresse
St., Rathbone Pl., London W1P 1PN, England.
TEL 44-171-580-3105. FAX 44-171-580-1695.
circ. 60,000. *6508*

MASTHEAD.
North Island Sound Ltd., 1606 Sedlescomb Dr., Unit
8, Mississauga, CN L4X 1M6, Canada. TEL 905-
625-7070. FAX 905-625-4856.
circ. 4,504. *6002*

MATCH NEWS.
Match International Centre, 1102-200 Elgin St.,
Ottawa, ON K2P 1L5, Canada. TEL 613-238-1312.
FAX 613-238-6867.
circ. 5,000. *7001*

MATEMATICA APLICADA E COMPUTACIONAL.
Sociedade Brasileira de Matematica Aplicada e
Computacional, Rua Lauro Muller, 455 Botafogo
CEP, 22290 Rio de Janiero RJ, Brazil. TEL 55-21-
541-2132.
circ. 700. *4410*

MATERIAL HANDLING ENGINEERING.
Penton Publishing Co. 1100 Superior Ave.,
Cleveland, OH 44114-2543. TEL 216-696-7000.
FAX 216-696-8765.
circ. 101,447. *4342*

**MATERIAL HANDLING ENGINEERING HANDBOOK
AND DIRECTORY.**
Penton Publishing Co. 1100 Superior Ave.,
Cleveland, OH 44114-2543. TEL 216-696-7000.
FAX 216-696-8765.
circ. 113,000. *4342*

MATERIALS HANDLING NEWS.
Nexus Media Ltd., Nexus House, Azalea Dr.,
Swanley, Kent BR8 8HY, England. TEL 44-1322-
660070. FAX 44-1322-667633.
circ. 20,096. *4343*

**MATERIALS ON ASIA - ACCESSION LIST AND
REVIEW.**
National Diet Library, 1-10-1 Nagata-cho, Chiyoda-
ku, Tokyo 100, Japan. TEL 03-3581-2331.
FAX 03-3597-9104.
circ. 490. *539*

MATERNAL & CHILD HEALTH.
Barker Publications Ltd., Barker House, 539 London
Rd., Isleworth, Mddx. TW7 4DA, England. TEL 44-
181-847-1774. FAX 44-181-568-2766.
circ. 25,000. *4808*

MATHEMATECH.
Parrish Platt International, Great Percy House, 26
Great Percy St., London WC1X 9QP, England.
TEL 0171-278-3650. FAX 0171-278-3659.
circ. 27,000. *4379*

MATHEMATICAL LOG.
Mu Alpha Theta, 601 Elm St., Rm. 423, Norman,
OK 73019. TEL 405-325-4489.
circ. 25,000. *4380*

MATHEMATICS TEACHING.
Association of Teachers of Mathematics, 7
Shaftesbury St., Derby DE3 8YB, England. TEL 44-
1332-346599. FAX 44-1332-204257.
circ. 3,800. *4382*

**MATHILDA AND TERENCE KENNEDY INSTITUTE OF
RHEUMATOLOGY. ANNUAL REPORT.**
Mathilda and Terence Kennedy Institute of
Rheumatology, 6 Bute Gardens, Hammersmith,
London W6 7DW, England. TEL 44-181-748-9966.
FAX 44-181-748-5090.
circ. 1,000. *4894*

MATHITIKI ESTIA.
Ministry of Education and Culture, Pancyprian
Gymnasium, P.O Box 1034, Nicosia, Cyprus.
TEL 357-2-463692. FAX 357-2-446313.
circ. 1,000. *1798*

MATTER.
G L M Publications 10 Bank St., Ste. 1200, White
Plains, NY 10606-1952. *468*

MATURE AMERICAN.
Alternative Publications, Inc., 1123 N. Water St.,
Milwaukee, WI 53202. TEL 414-276-2222.
FAX 414-276-3312.
circ. 32,000. *3292*

MAXINE'S PAGES.
Crystal Rain Research Agency, Box 866,
Manchester, GA 31816. TEL 706-846-9332.
circ. 137. *5683*

MAY TRENDS.
George S. May International Company, Management
Consultants, 303 S. Northwest Hwy., Park Ridge, IL
60068-4265. TEL 708-825-8806. FAX 708-825-
7937.
circ. 30,000. *1577*

MAYO AGRICOLA.
Distrito de Riego No. 38, Rio Mayo, Pesquiera y
Jimenez, Navojoa, Sonora, Mexico. *135*

MAYO ALUMNI.
Mayo Foundation, Mayo Clinic, Rochester, MN
55905.
circ. 14,000. *4492*

MAYO CLINIC PROCEEDINGS.
Mayo Foundation for Medical Education and
Research, Rochester, MN 55905. TEL 507-284-
2154. FAX 507-284-0252.
circ. 91,000. *4492*

ME.
Viestintaerengas Oy, c/o Eka Co-op, P.O. Box 72,
FIN-00501 Helsinki, Finland. FAX 0-733-3264.
circ 339,435. *1160*

MECHANIKA TEORETYCZNA I STOSOWANA.
Polskie Towarzystwo Mechaniki Teoretycznej i
Stosowanej, Palac Kultury, p.309, 00-901 Warsaw,
Poland.
circ. 400. *2739*

MEDBOOK.
Varus Verlag Birgit Laube Koenigswintererstr. 552,
53227 Bonn, Germany. TEL 0228-440015.
FAX 0228-440017.
circ. 16,000. *4567*

MEDECIN DU QUEBEC.
Federation des Medecins Omnipraticiens du Quebec,
1440 Rue St.Catherine Ouest, Ste. 1000, Montreal,
PQ H3G 1R8, Canada. TEL 514-878-1911.
FAX 514-878-4455.
circ. 19,600. *4492*

MEDIA MOVES.
Two-Ten Communications Ltd., Communications
House, 210 Old St., London EC1V 9UN, England.
TEL 44-171-490-8111. FAX 44-171-490-1255.
circ. 5,000. *1964*

MEDIA NEWS.
Ming Chuan College, No. 250 Chung Shan N. Rd.,
Sec. 5, Taipei, Taiwan, Republic of China. TEL 02-
882-4564. FAX 02-881-8575.
circ. 8,000. *1911*

MEDICAL CARE INTERNATIONAL.
Globetech Publishing, 30 Cannon Rd., Wilton, CT
06897. TEL 203-762-3432. FAX 203-762-8640.
circ. 30,000. *4493*

MEDICAL DEVICE & DIAGNOSTIC INDUSTRY.
Canon Communications, Inc., 3340 Ocean Park
Blvd., Ste. 1000, Santa Monica, CA 90405-3207.
TEL 310-392-5509. FAX 310-392-4920.
circ. 40,000. *3637*

MEDICAL EXPRESS REPORTS.
Cambridge Medical Publications Ltd., Wicker House,
High St., Worthing, W. Sussex BN11 1DJ, England.
TEL 01903-205884. FAX 01903-234862. *4495*

MEDICAL FOCUS.
Beta Verlag GmbH, Postfach 140121, 53056
Bonn, Germany. TEL 49-228-91937-0. FAX 49-
228-252067.
circ. 17,000. *5969*

MEDICAL FORUM REPORTER.
Cambridge Medical Publications Ltd., Wicker House,
High St., Worthing, W. Sussex BN11 1DJ, England.
TEL 01903-205884. FAX 0 903-234862. *4495*

MEDICAL IMAGING (PORTSMOUTH).
Second Source Publications, Inc., 10 Risho Ave., East Providence, RI 02914-1215. TEL 401-434-1050. FAX 401-434-1090.
circ. 17,000. *4495*

MEDICAL MARKETING & MEDIA.
C P S Communications, Inc., 7200 W. Camino Real, Ste. 215, Boca Raton, FL 33433. TEL 407-368-9301. FAX 407-368-7870.
circ. 12,800. *5427*

MEDICAL MEETINGS.
63 Great Rd., Maynard, MA 01754. TEL 508-897-5552. FAX 508-897-6824.
circ. 14,000. *4935*

MEDICAL PLASTICS AND BIOMATERIALS.
Canon Communications, Inc., 3340 Ocean Park Blvd., Ste. 1000, Santa Monica, CA 90405-3216. TEL 310-392-5509. FAX 310-392-5509.
circ. 5,000. *4496*

MEDICAL PRODUCT MANUFACTURING NEWS.
Canon Communications, Inc., 3340 Ocean Park Blvd., Ste. 1000, Santa Monica, CA 90405-3207. TEL 310-392-5509. FAX 310-392-4920.
circ. 30,000. *3637*

MEDICAL PROTECTION SOCIETY. ANNUAL REPORT.
Medical Protection Society Ltd., 50 Hallam St., London W1N 6DE, England. TEL 44-171-637-0541. FAX 44-171-636-0690.
circ. 135,000. *4496*

MEDICAL RECORD RISKS: CLAIMS & LITIGATION.
Cox Publications, Box 20316, Billings, MT 59104-0316. TEL 406-256-8822. *3658*

MEDICAL RESEARCH COUNCIL NEWSLETTER.
Medical Research Council of Canada, 1600 Scott St., Tower B, Ottawa, ON K1A 0W9, Canada. TEL 613-954-1806. FAX 613-954-6653.
circ. 4,500. *4497*

MEDICAL RESEARCH COUNCIL OF CANADA. REPORT OF THE PRESIDENT.
Medical Research Council of Canada, 1600 Scott St., Tower B, Ottawa, ON K1A 0W9, Canada. TEL 613-954-1806. FAX 613-954-6653.
circ. 2,300. *4497*

MEDICAL RESEARCH FUNDING BULLETIN.
Science Support Center, Box 7507, New York, NY 10150. TEL 212-371-3398.
circ. 3,100. *4497*

MEDICAL SCIENTIFIC UPDATE.
National Jewish Center for Immunology and Respiratory Medicine, 1400 Jackson St., Denver, CO 80206. TEL 303-388-4461. FAX 303-398-1125.
circ. 26,000. *4889*

MEDICAL SOCIETY OF LONDON. TRANSACTIONS.
Medical Society of London, 11 Chandos St., Cavendish Sq., London W1N OEB, England. TEL 44-171-580-1043. FAX 44-171-580-5793.
circ. 550. *4497*

MEDICAL TRIBUNE.
Medical Tribune, Inc., 100 Ave. of the Americas, 9th Fl., New York, NY 10013-1606. TEL 212-674-8500. FAX 212-529-8490.
circ. 130,000. *4498*

MEDICAMUNDI.
Philips Medical Systems International, P.O. Box 10000, 5680 DA Best, Netherlands. FAX 31-40-762499.
circ. 14,000. *4880*

MEDICINA DE LA EMPRESA.
Sociedad Catalana de Seguridad y Medicina del Trabajo, Tapineria, 10 pral., 08002 Barcelona, Spain. *5253*

MEDICINE INTERNATIONAL (MIDDLE EASTERN EDITION).
The Medicine Group (Journals) Ltd., Publishing House, 62 Stert St., Abingdon, Oxon OX14 3UQ, England. TEL 44-1235-555770. FAX 44-1235-554691.
circ. 20,000. *4499*

MEDICINE NORTHWEST.
University of Washington, School of Medicine, Mail Stop SC-60, Seattle, WA 98195. TEL 206-685-0381.
circ. 17,000. *4499*

MEDICINE ON THE MIDWAY.
University of Chicago Hospitals, Office of Public Affairs, 5841 S. Maryland Ave., Mail Code 6063, Chicago, IL 60637. TEL 312-702-7322. FAX 312-702-3171.
circ. 14,000. *1876*

MEDICO-LEGAL SOCIETY OF VICTORIA. PROCEEDINGS.
Medico-Legal Society of Victoria, 3 Berkeley St., Hawthorn, Vic. 3122, Australia.
circ. 600. *3885*

MEDITERRANEA. SERIE DE ESTUDIOS BIOLOGICOS.
Universidad de Alicante, Facultad de Ciencias, Apdo. 99, 03080 Alicante, Spain. TEL 96-590-3400. FAX 96-590-3464.
circ. 600. *813*

MEDIUM.
Saskatchewan Teachers' Federation, Box 1108, Saskatoon, SK S7K 3N3, Canada. TEL 306-525-0368.
circ. 400. *4012*

MEDIZINISCHE KLINIK.
Urban und Vogel, Lindwurmstr. 95, 80337 Munich, Germany. TEL 49-89-53292-0. FAX 49-89-53292-100.
circ. 10,000. *4501*

MEDLEMSTIDNINGEN INDUSTRIFACKET.
Industrifacket, P.O. Box 1120, S-111 81 Stockholm, Sweden. TEL 46-8-786-85-95. FAX 46-8-21-28-72.
circ. 125,000. *3725*

MEETING NEWS.
Miller Freeman Inc. (New York) One Penn Plaza, New York, NY 10119. TEL 212-714-1300. FAX 708-647-5972.
circ. 60,100. *4936*

MEETINGS AND CONVENTIONS ASIA PACIFIC.
Venture Asia Publishing, 10 Craig Rd., Singapore 089670, Singapore. TEL 65-223-1866. FAX 65-223-0811.
circ. 12,059. *4936*

MEETINGS MONTHLY, NEWS BULLETIN.
Publicom Inc., C.P. 365, Place d'Armes, Montreal, PQ H2Y 3H1, Canada. TEL 514-274-0004. FAX 514-274-5884.
circ. 12,703. *4936*

MEGAPHONE (CANTON).
Culver-Stockton College, Attn.: Steve Wiegenstein, Canton, MO 63435. TEL 217-231-6380. FAX 217-231-6611.
circ. 1,000. *1876*

MEHFIL MAGAZINE.
V I G Communications Inc., 301-1334 W. 6th Avenue, Vancouver, BC V6H 1A7, Canada. TEL 604-730-1352. FAX 604-731-2965.
circ. 25,000. *2894*

MELLIAND TEXTILBERICHTE.
Melliand Textilberichte GmbH, Mainzer Landstr. 251, 60326 Frankfurt a.M., Germany. TEL 49-69-75951651. FAX 49-69-75951650.
circ. 6,500. *6682*

MEMISA MEDISCH.
Memisa Medicus Mundi, Eendrachtsweg 48, 3012 LD Rotterdam, Netherlands. FAX 31-10-4047319.
circ. 4,000. *4502*

MEMO: TO THE PRESIDENT.
American Association of State Colleges and Universities, One Dupont Circle, N.W., Ste. 700, Washington, DC 20036. TEL 202-293-7070. FAX 202-296-5819. *2436*

MEMOIRES ET DOCUMENTS GEOGRAPHIE.
C N R S Editions, 20-22 rue St. Amand, 75015 Paris, France. TEL 45-33-16-00. FAX 45-33-92-13.
circ. 1,500. *3265*

MENDEL.
Mendelian Society of India, 194-B, S.K. Puri, Patna 800001, India. TEL 91-612-233741.
circ. 750. *746*

MENNINGER PERSPECTIVE.
Menninger Foundation, Box 829, Topeka, KS 66601-0829. TEL 913-350-5860. FAX 913-271-9723.
circ. 24,500. *4851*

MENORCA, DIARIO INSULAR.
Editorial Menorca, S.A., Avda. Central 5, 07714 Mahon, Baleares, Spain. TEL 971-35-16-00. FAX 971-35-38-35.
circ. 326. *3216*

MENSA BULLETIN.
American Mensa Ltd. (Brooklyn), 201 Main St., Ste. 1101, Fort Worth, TX 76102-3115. FAX 718-332-1183.
circ. 49,000. *1851*

MENTAL HEALTH MATTERS.
Northern Ireland Association for Mental Health, 80 University St., Belfast BT7 1HE, N. Ireland. FAX 0232-234940.
circ. 1,500. *5865*

MERKBLAETTER GEFAEHRLICHE ARBEITSSTOFFE.
Ecomed Verlagsgesellschaft AG & Co. KG, Rudolf-Diesel-Str. 3, 86899 Landsberg, Germany. TEL 49-8191-125-0. FAX 49-8191-125492.
circ. 10,500. *5253*

MERTON MESSENGER.
Merton Council, Civic Centre, London Rd., Morden, Surrey SM4 5DX, England. TEL 44-181-345-3366. FAX 44-181-545-4054.
circ. 80,000. *3157*

MESECHABE: THE JOURNAL OF SURREGIONALISM.
Center for Gulf South History and Culture, Inc., 1539 Crete St., New Orleans, LA 70119-3006. TEL 504-861-8832.
circ. 1,000. *5486*

MESSAGE.
Congress Centrum Mainz GmbH, Rheinstr. 66, 55116 Mainz, Germany. TEL 06131-242100. FAX 06131-242105.
circ. 25,000. *4936*

MESSAGES.
Society for Environmental Graphic Design, 401 F St., N.W., Ste. 333, Washington, DC 20001. TEL 202-638-5555. FAX 202-638-0891.
circ. 1,500. *5815*

MESSENGER.
Southeast Asia Union Mission of Seventh-Day Adventists, 251 Upper Serangoon Rd., Singapore, Singapore.
circ. 2,000. *6209*

METAL CENTER NEWS.
Hitchcock Publishing 191 S. Gary Ave., Carol Stream, IL 60188. TEL 708-665-1000. FAX 708-462-2225.
circ. 12,600. *4965*

METAL FORMING.
Precision Metal Forming Association, 27027 Chardon Rd., Richmond Hts., OH 44143. TEL 216-585-8800. FAX 216-585-2126.
circ. 60,000. *4965*

METAL HEAT TREATING.
Penton Publishing Co., 1100 Superior Ave., Cleveland, OH 44114-2543. TEL 216-696-7000.
circ. 15,873. *4965*

METALES Y METALURGIA.
Tecnipublicaciones, S.A., C. Albacete 5, 28027 Madrid, Spain. TEL 34-1-3261440. FAX 34-1-3262407.
circ. 5,000. *4966*

METALWORKING PRODUCTION & PURCHASING.
Action Communications Inc., 135 Spy Court, Markham, ON L3R 5H6, Canada. TEL 905-477-3222. FAX 905-477-4320.
circ. 18,000. *4968*

METHODIST COLLEGE TODAY.
Methodist College, 5400 Ramsey St., Fayetteville, NC 28311. TEL 919-630-7043. FAX 919-630-7119.
circ. 15,000. *1876*

METMENYS.
A M & M Publications, 306 55th Place, Downers Grove, IL 60516. TEL 630-852-3887.
circ. 1,000. *4237*

METRO (REDONDO BEACH).
Bobit Publishing Company, 2512 Artesia Blvd., Redondo Beach, CA 90278-3210. TEL 310-376-8788. FAX 310-376-9043.
circ. 17,500. *6722*

METROKIDS.
KidStuff Publication, Inc., 1080 N. Delaware Ave., Ste. 702, Philadelphia, PA 19125-4330. TEL 215-551-3200. FAX 215-551-3203.
circ. 70,000. *1772*

METROPOLITAN NASHVILLE BOARD OF EDUCATION. NEWS AND VIEWS.
Metropolitan Nashville Board of Education, 2601 Bransford Ave., Nashville, TN 37204. TEL 615-259-8400.
circ. 7,500. *2353*

METROSPORTS MAGAZINE.
Tate House Enterprises, Inc., 27 W. 24th St., New York, NY 10010. TEL 212-627-7040. FAX 212-627-7446.
circ. 170,000. *6470*

MEXICAN AMERICAN GROCERS ASSOCIATION. MAGAZINE.
Mexican American Grocers Association, 405 N. San Fernando Rd., Los Angeles, CA 90031. TEL 213-227-1565. FAX 213-227-6935.
circ. 12,500. *3007*

MEXICO BUSINESS MONTHLY.
Kal Wagenheim, Ed. & Pub., 52 Maple Ave., Maplewood, NJ 07040. TEL 201-762-1565. FAX 201-762-9585. *1290*

MEXICO CITY DAILY BULLETIN.
Edit, S.A., Gomez Farias 41, Col. San Rafael, 06470 Mexico, D.F., Mexico. TEL 905-546-5115. FAX 905-535-6060.
circ. 10,000. *6898*

MICHIGAN. DEPARTMENT OF STATE POLICE. ANNUAL REPORT.
Department of State Police, 714 S. Harrison Rd., East Lansing, MI 48823. TEL 517-332-2521. *2169*

MICHIGAN. STATE COURT ADMINISTRATOR. ANNUAL REPORT.
State Court Administrative Office, Box 30048, Lansing, MI 48909. TEL 517-373-0130. FAX 517-373-8922.
circ. 1,500. *3878*

MICHIGAN AIRPORT DIRECTORY.
Aeronautics Commission, 2700 E. Airport Service Dr., Capital City Airport, Lansing, MI 48906. TEL 517-335-8521. FAX 517-321-6422.
circ. 8,000. *6762*

MICHIGAN ASSOCIATION OF SECONDARY SCHOOL PRINCIPALS' BULLETIN.
Michigan Association of Secondary School Principals, 418 Erickson Hall, Michigan State University, E. Lansing, MI 48823. *2353*

MICHIGAN AVIATION.
Aeronautics Commission, 2700 E. Airport Service Dr., Capital City Airport, Lansing, MI 48906. TEL 517-335-9283. FAX 517-321-6422.
circ. 17,000. *72*

MICHIGAN DEER & TURKEY SHOW PREVIEW.
Target Communications Corp., 7626 W. Donges Bay Rd., Mequon, WI 53097-3400. TEL 414-242-3990. FAX 414-242-7391.
circ. 35,000. *6568*

MICHIGAN FOOD NEWS.
Michigan Grocers Association, 221 N. Walnut St., Lansing, MI 48933. TEL 517-372-6800. FAX 517-372-3002.
circ. 9,000. *2984*

MICHIGAN JOURNAL OF POLITICAL SCIENCE.
University of Michigan, Michigan Journal of Political Science, 5620 Haven Hall, Ann Arbor, MI 48109-1045. TEL 313-764-6386.
circ. 1,000. *5583*

MICHIGAN LUTHERAN.
Lutheran Church - Missouri Synod, Michigan District, 3773 Geddes Road, Ann Arbor, MI 48105. TEL 313-665-3791. FAX 313-665-0255.
circ. 76,000. *6152*

MICHIGAN STATE UNIVERSITY. AGRICULTURAL ECONOMICS REPORT.
Michigan State University, Department of Agricultural Economics, Reference Rm., East Lansing, MI 48824-1039. TEL 517-355-6650. FAX 517-432-1300.
circ. 90. *196*

MICHIGAN STATE UNIVERSITY. LIBRARY. AFRICANA: SELECT RECENT ACQUISITIONS.
Michigan State University Libraries, East Lansing, MI 48824-1048. TEL 517-355-2366. FAX 517-432-1445.
circ. 300. *539*

MICRO.
Canon Communications, Inc., 3340 Ocean Park Blvd., Ste. 1000, Santa Monica, CA 90405-3207. TEL 310-392-5509. FAX 310-392-4920.
circ. 23,000. *2527*

MICROWAVES & R F PRODUCT EXTRA.
Penton Publishing Co. (Hasbrouck Heights) 611 Rte. 46 W., Hasbrouck Heights, NJ 07604. TEL 201-393-6050.
circ. 40,000. *2713*

MID-AMERICA BANNER.
Mid-America Machine Dealers Association, 40625 N. Sunset Dr., Antioch, IL 60002. TEL 847-395-6922. FAX 847-395-6922.
circ. 1,000. *1525*

MID-AMERICA COMMERCE & INDUSTRY.
M A C I Inc., 1824 Cheyenne Rd., Topeka, KS 66604. TEL 913-272-5280.
circ. 9,483. *1222*

MID-AMERICAN REVIEW.
Bowling Green State University, Department of English, c/o George Looney, Ed., Bowling Green State University, Bowling Green, OH 43403. TEL 419-372-2725.
circ. 1,000. *4154*

MID-SOUTH FARMER.
Farm Progress Companies 191 S. Gary Ave., Carol Stream, IL 60177. TEL 708-690-5600. FAX 708-462-2869.
circ. 42,000. *196*

MIDDLE ATLANTIC PERSPECTIVE.
Middle Atlantic Region, N N - L M, New York Academy of Medicine, 1216 Fifth Ave., New York, NY 10029. TEL 212-876-8763. FAX 212-534-7042.
circ. 2,100. *4502*

MIDDLE EAST EXPATRIATE.
Al Hilal Publishing & Marketing Group, P.O. Box 224, Manama, Bahrain. TEL 973-293131. FAX 973-293400.
circ. 16,200. *3194*

MIDDLE EAST POLICY.
Middle East Policy Council, 1730 M St., N.W., Ste. 512, Washington, DC 20036. TEL 202-296-6767. FAX 202-296-5791.
circ. 7,500. *5762*

MIDDLE EAST SATELLITE TODAY.
Icom Publications Ltd., Chancery House, St. Nicholas Way, Sutton, Surrey SM1 1JB, England. TEL 44-181-642-1117. FAX 44-181-642-1941.
circ. 6,034. *1365*

MIDDLE EAST TRADE.
Middle East Trade Publications Ltd., 11 Gower St., London WC1E GHB, England. TEL 071-636-2911.
circ. 15,320. *1290*

MIDRANGE SYSTEMS.
Cardinal Business Media, Inc., 1300 Virginia Dr., Ste. 400, Fort Washington, PA 19034-3225. TEL 215-643-8000. FAX 215-643-3901.
circ. 50,000. *2092*

MIDWEST AUTOMOTIVE & AUTOBODY NEWS.
Automotive Publishing Co., 2900 W. Peterson Ave., Chicago, IL 60659. TEL 312-764-1640.
circ. 11,562. *6792*

MIDWEST EXPRESS MAGAZINE.
Paradigm Communications Group, 2701 First Ave., Ste. 250, Seattle, WA 98121. TEL 206-441-5871. FAX 206-448-6939
circ. 30,000. *6936*

MIDWEST GAS NEWS.
Gas Digest, 11246 S. Post Oak, Ste. 206, Houston, TX 77035-5741. TEL 713-723-7456.
circ. 2,000. *5363*

MIDWEST MOTORIST.
Automobile Club of Missouri, 12901 North Forty Dr., St. Louis, MO 63141. TEL 314-523-7350.
circ. 370,000. *6792*

MIDWESTERN DENTIST.
Greater Kansas City Dental Society, 5907 Raytown Trafficway, Kansas City, MO 64133. TEL 816-737-5353.
circ. 800. *4648*

MIE UNIVERSITY. FACULTY OF FISHERIES. JOURNAL.
Mie Daigaku, Suisan Gakubu, 2-80 Edobashi Tsushi, Mie-ken 514, Japan. *2938*

MIKRO P C.
Oy Talentum Ab, P.O. Box 920, FIN-00101 Helsinki Finland. TEL 358-0-148-801. FAX 358-0-6586512.
circ. 54,210. *2098*

MILITARY ADVOCATE.
Judge Advocates Association, 1815 H St. N.W., Ste. 408, Washington, DC 20006-3697. TEL 202-628-0979. FAX 202-775-0295.
circ. 700. *3958*

MILITARY & AEROSPACE ELECTRONICS.
PennWell Publishing Co. (Nashua), 10 Tara Blvd., 5th Fl., Nashua, NH 03062-2801. TEL 603-891-0123. FAX 603-891-0574.
circ. 48,000. *73*

MILITARY CLUB & HOSPITALITY.
Executive Business Media, Inc., 825 Old Country Rd. Box 1500, Westbury, NY 11590. TEL 516-334-3030.
circ. 11,000. *2984*

MILITARY EXCHANGE MAGAZINE.
Downey Communications Inc., 4800 Montgomery Lane, Bethesda, MD 20814-5341. TEL 301-718-7600. FAX 301-718-7604.
circ. 10,500. *5039*

MILITARY GROCER.
Downey Communications 4800 Montgomery Ln., Ste. 710, Bethesda, MD 20814-5341. TEL 301-718-7600. FAX 301-718-7652.
circ. 14,000. *3007*

MILITARY MARKET.
Army Times Publishing Co., 6883 Commercial Dr., Springfield, VA 22159. TEL 703-750-8676.
circ. 12,000. *5039*

MILK BULLETIN.
Scottish Milk Marketing Board, Underwood Rd., Paisley, Renfrewshire PA3 1TJ, Scotland. FAX 041-889-1225.
circ. 3,200. *252*

MILL NECK MANOR BULLETIN.
Mill Neck Foundation, Frost Mill Rd., Box 100, Mill Neck, NY 11765. TEL 516-922-4100. FAX 516-922-3759.
circ. 76,000. *3313*

MILTON KEYNES CITIZEN.
Napier House, Auckland Park, Bletchley, Milton Keynes, Bucks. MK1 1BU, England. TEL 01908-374033. FAX 01908-371115.
circ. 89,700. *3157*

MINAMI TAIHEIYO KENKYU.
Kagoshima University, Research Center for the South Pacific, 1-21-24, Korimoto, Kagoshima 890, Japan. TEL 81-99-285-7354. FAX 81-99-256-9358.
circ. 700. *6258*

MINBAR AL-TAMRID.
Ministry of Health, School of Nursing, P.O. Box 3798, Abu Dhabi, United Arab Emirates. TEL 668591. FAX 665472. circ. 1,000. *4720*

MINDANAO ART & CULTURE.
Mindanao State University, Mamitua Saber Research Center, P.O. Box 5594, Iligan City 9200, Philippines. circ. 500. *2954*

MINI DATA REPORT.
Siemens, S.A., Calle Orense No. 2, Madrid 20, Spain. *2092*

MINILAB DEVELOPMENTS.
Professional & Trade Publications Ltd., 46 Ford End, Woodford Green, Essex IG8 OEG, England. TEL 0181-506-1011. circ. 5,000. *5515*

MINING MIRROR.
Brooke Pattrick (Pty) Ltd., P.O. Box 422, Bedfordview 2008, South Africa. TEL 27-11-6224666. FAX 27-11-6167196. circ. 5,348. *5072*

MINING NEWS.
Chamber of Mines of South Africa, P.O. Box 809, Johannesburg 2000, South Africa. TEL 27-11-4987100. FAX 27-11-8368070. *5072*

MINISTERIALTIDENDE FOR KONGERIGET DANMARK.
Justisministeriet, Sekretariatet for Retsinformation, Axeltorv 6, 5. sal, DK-1609 Copenhagen V, Denmark. TEL 45-33-32-52-22. FAX 45-33-91-28-01. circ. 2,007. *5911*

MINNEAPOLIS LABOR REVIEW.
Minneapolis Central Labor Union Council, 312 Central Ave., Rm. 526, Minneapoli, MN 55414. TEL 612-379-4206. FAX 612-379-1307. circ. 50,000. *3725*

MINNEAPOLIS - ST. PAUL CITYBUSINESS.
City Media, Inc., 821 Marquette Ave., Ste. 2000, Minneapolis, MN 55402-2922. TEL 612-288-2141. FAX 612-288-2121. circ. 6,000. *944*

MINNESOTA AGRICULTURAL ECONOMIST.
University of Minnesota, Department of Applied Economics, 1994 Buford Ave., St. Paul, MN 55108. TEL 612-625-1705. FAX 612-625-6245. circ. 4,000. *196*

MINNESOTA MEDICINE.
Minnesota Medical Association, 3433 Broadway St., N.E., Ste. 300, Minneapolis, MN 55413-1761. TEL 612-378-1875. FAX 612-378-3875. circ. 10,000. *4503*

MINNESOTA P - H - C CONTRACTOR MAGAZINE.
Minnesota Master Plumber Publishing Co., Inc., c/o Paula Shelander, Ed., 8085 Wayzata Blvd., no. 109, Minneapolis, MN 55426-1456. TEL 612-546-4448. FAX 612-546-4507. circ. 2,500. *3331*

MINNESOTA SCIENCE.
University of Minnesota, Agricultural Experiment Station, 405 Coffey Hall, St. Paul, MN 55108. TEL 612-625-7290. circ. 24,000. *6259*

MINNESOTA SPORTS.
Skyway News, 33 S. Fifth St., Ste. 800, Minneapolis, MN 55402-1050. TEL 612-375-9222. FAX 612-375-9208. circ. 40,000. *6470*

MINORITY M B A.
Peterson's - C O G Publishing, 16030 Ventura Blvd., Ste. 560, Encino, CA 91436. TEL 818-789-5293. FAX 818-789-5488. circ. 13,381. *5270*

MINOTAUR.
Minotaur Press, 95 Harbormaster Rd., No. 11, S. San Francisco, CA 94080. circ. 150. *4311*

MINZU YANJIU (BEIJING, 1979).
Zhongguo Shehui Kexueyuan, Minzu Yanjiusuo, 27 Baishiqiao Lu, Beijing 100081, People's Republic of China. TEL 8022288. circ. 5,000. *5289*

MIRACULOUS MEDAL.
Central Association of the Miraculous Medal, 475 E. Chelten Ave., Philadelphia, PA 19144. TEL 215-848-1010. circ. 340,000. *6209*

MIRROR.
Graphic Corporation, Graphic Rd., P.O. Box 742, Accra, Ghana. FAX 233-21-669886. circ. 126,000. *3152*

MIRROR AND PROBE.
Dental Students' Association, University of Sri Lanka, University Park, Peradeniya, Sri Lanka. *4648*

MISNOMER.
Box 2115, Oxford, MS 38655. TEL 601-234-7635. circ. 300. *4154*

MISSET BULK.
Misset Postbus 4, 7000 BA Doetinchem, Netherlands. TEL 31-8340-49371. FAX 31-8340-43839. circ. 5,000. *6723*

MISSIONHURST.
Missionhurst, Inc., 4651 N. 25th St., Arlington, VA 22207-3500. TEL 703-528-3800. FAX 703-522-7864. circ. 80,000. *6188*

MISSISSIPPI CONGRESS OF PARENTS AND TEACHERS. PROCEEDINGS.
Mississippi Congress of Parents and Teachers, Box 1937, Jackson, MS 39215-1937. TEL 601-352-7383. *2460*

MISSISSIPPI CONGRESS OF PARENTS AND TEACHERS. YEARBOOK.
Mississippi Congress of Parents and Teachers, Box 1937, Jackson, MS 39215-1937. TEL 601-352-7383. *2460*

MISSISSIPPI UNITED METHODIST ADVOCATE.
United Methodist Church, Mississippi Conference, Box 1093, Jackson, MS 39215. TEL 601-354-0515. circ. 15,000. *6153*

MISSOURI. DIVISION OF HIGHWAY SAFETY (YEAR). HIGHWAY SAFETY PLAN.
Division of Highway Safety, Box 104808, Jefferson City, MO 65110-4808. TEL 314-751-4161. FAX 314-634-5977. circ. 50. *6823*

MISSOURI ALUMNUS.
Publications & Alumni Communication, 407 Donald. W. Renolds Alumni & Visitors Center, Columbia, MO 65211. TEL 314-882-7357. FAX 314-882-7290. circ. 119,000. *1877*

MISSOURI PIPELINE.
Missouri Petroleum Marketers Association, 238 E. High St., Jefferson City, MO 65101. TEL 314-635-7117. FAX 314-635-3575. circ. 1,400. *5364*

MISSOURI'S NEW AND EXPANDING INDUSTRY.
Department of Economic Development, Box 118, Jefferson City, MO 65102. TEL 573-751-9072. FAX 573-751-7385. circ. 800. *1526*

MITRE.
Bishop's University, Student's Representative Council, c/o Box 2133, Lennoxville, PQ J1M 1Z7, Canada. TEL 819-569-9551. *4154*

MITSUBISHI DENSEN KOGYO JIHO.
Mitsubishi Cable Industries, Ltd., Patent & Technology Administration Department, OAP Tower, 25Fl., 1-8-30, Temmabashi, Kita-ku, Osaka-shi, Osaka 530, Japan. TEL 06-881-5209. FAX 06-881-5223. circ. 6,500. *2713*

MITTEILEN.
Evangelisch-Lutherisches Missionswerk in Niedersachsen, Georg-Haccius-Str. 9, 29320 Hermannsburg, Germany. TEL 05052-69233. FAX 05052-69222. circ. 17,500. *6153*

MITTEILUNGEN DER AERZTEKAMMER FUER WIEN - WIENER ARZT.
Aerztekammer fuer Wien, Weihburggasse 10-12, A-1010 Vienna, Austria. TEL 43-1-51501223. FAX 43-1-51501289. circ. 12,000. *4503*

MITTELFRAENKISCHE WIRTSCHAFT.
Hofmann Druck Nuernberg, Postfach 120260, 90109 Nuernberg, Germany. TEL 49-911-5203-0. FAX 49-911-5203148. circ. 70,000. *1146*

HAMIZRAH HEHADASH.
Magnes Press, Hebrew University, Jerusalem, P.O. Box 7695, Jerusalem 91076, Israel. TEL 972-2-660341. FAX 972-2-633370. circ. 2,500. *5289*

MOBILE.
Verlag Herder GmbH und Co. KG, Hermann-Herder-Str. 4, 79104 Freiburg, Germany. TEL 49-761-2717-438. FAX 49-761-2717426. circ. 320,000. *1799*

MOBILE & SATELLITE SINGLE MARKET REVIEW.
Kline Publishing Ltd., 4-6 Station Parade, Balham High Rd., London SW12 9AD, England. TEL 081-673-7783. FAX 081-675-6466. circ. 22,000. *1911*

MOBILE PRODUCT ASIA.
Phillips Business Information, Inc., 1201 Seven Locks Rd., Potomac, MD 20854. TEL 301-340-1520. FAX 301-424-4297. *1947*

MOBILE PRODUCT EUROPE.
Phillips Business Information, Inc., 1201 Seven Locks Rd., Potomac, MD 20854. TEL 301-340-1520. FAX 301-424-4297. *1947*

MODEL ROCKET NEWS.
Estes Industries, 1295 H St., Penrose, CO 81240. TEL 719-372-6565. FAX 719-372-3419. *3511*

MODELL MAGAZIN.
Alba Publikationen Alf Teloeken, Roemerstr. 9, 40476 Duesseldorf, Germany. TEL 0211-469010. FAX 0211-484382. circ. 14,091. *3512*

MODERATOR.
Mt. Marty College, 1105 W. 8th St., Yankton, SD 57078. TEL 605-668-1543. circ. 1,000. *1877*

MODERN BAKING.
Donohue - Meehan Publishing Company (Des Plaines), 2700 River Rd., Des Plaines, IL 60018. TEL 708-299-4430. FAX 708-296-1968. circ. 27,000. *3001*

MODERN FARMING.
Massey Ferguson, P.O. Box 62, Floor 10, Coventry CV4 9GF, England. TEL 44-1203-851221. FAX 44-1203-851282. circ. 15,557. *136*

MODERN HEALTHCARE (YEAR).
Crain Communications, Inc. (Chicago), 740 N. Rush St., Chicago, IL 60611-2590. TEL 312-649-5341. FAX 312-280-3189. circ. 86,915. *3553*

MODERN MEDIA.
Eiken Chemical Co. Ltd., 1-33-8 Hongo, Bunkyo-ku, Tokyo 113, Japan. *763*

MODERN REPROGRAPHICS.
Avis, 1017 Wenonah Ave., Oak Park, IL 60304-1812. TEL 312-686-1238. FAX 312-868-1052. circ. 6,000. *5815*

MOEBEL-KULTUR.
Ferdinand Holzmann Verlag GmbH, Mexikoring 37, 22297 Hamburg, Germany. TEL 040-632018-0. FAX 040-6307510. *3691*

MOEBELMARKT.
Verlag Matthias Ritthammer GmbH, Andernacherstr. 5a, 90019 Nuernberg, Germany. TEL 49-911-955780. FAX 49-911-9557811. circ. 12,800. *3691*

MOISTURE MANAGER.
Munters Ltd., Blackstone Rd., Huntingdon, Cambs. PE18 6EF, England. TEL 44-1480-432243. FAX 44-1480-413147. circ. 12,500. *2810*

MONDO ECONOMICO.
Societa Editoriale Media Economici Seme S.p.A., Via P. Lomazzo, 52, 20154 Milan, Italy. TEL 39-2-331211. FAX 39-2-316905. circ. 25,744. *1223*

MONITEUR DES TRAVAUX PUBLICS ET DU BATIMENT.
Publications du Moniteur, 17 rue d'Uzes, 75002 Paris Cedex, France. TEL 1-40-13-30-30. FAX 1-40-41-94-95. circ. 76,054. *2668*

MONITORE DIOCESANO.
Curia Vescovile, 93100 Caltanissetta, Italy. circ. 450. *6188*

MONKEY.
Japan Monkey Centre, Kanrin Inuyama 26, Aichi 484, Japan. TEL 0568-61-2327. FAX 0568-62-6823. circ. 2,000. *814*

MONOCLE.
Piton Publishing House Ltd., 79-81 High St., Godalming, Surrey GU7 1AW, England. TEL 44-1483-425454. FAX 44-1483-414262. circ. 10,500. *3965*

MONTANA.
Montana Historical Society, 225 N. Roberts St., Box 201201, Helena, MT 59620-1201. TEL 406-444-4708. FAX 406-444-2696. circ. 10,000. *3479*

MONTANA FARM BUREAU SPOKESMAN.
Montana Farm Bureau Federation, 502 S. 19th, Bozeman, MT 59715. TEL 406-587-3153. circ. 7,000. *136*

MONTANA STATE LIBRARY NEWS UPDATE.
Montana State Library, 1515 E. 6th Ave., Helena, MT 59620. TEL 406-444-3115. FAX 406-444-5612. circ. 1,200. *4013*

MONTHLY BREWING INDUSTRY COMMENTARY.
Cyrus J. Lawrence, Inc., 1290 Ave. of the Americas, New York, NY 10104. TEL 212-468-5000. *1223*

MONTREAL SCOPE.
Metro Plaza Ltd., Rm. 232, 1253 McGill College, Montreal, PQ H3B 2Y5, Canada. TEL 514-933-3333. FAX 514-931-9581. circ. 40,000. *3123*

MOOREA.
Irish Garden Plant Society, c/o National Botanical Gardens, Glasnevin, Dublin 9, Ireland. FAX 337329. circ. 600. *3061*

MORE THAN MONEY.
Impact Project, 2244 Alder St., Eugene, OR 97405-8900. TEL 503-343-2420. circ. 1,000. *1343*

MORINVILLE AND DISTRICT GAZETTE.
9920 - 103 St., Morinville, AB TOG 1P0, Canada. TEL 403-939-7443. FAX 403-460-9364. circ. 6,400. *3123*

MORNING STAR.
Morning Star Ltd., 1-3 Ardleigh Rd., London N1 4HS, England. TEL 44-171-254-0033. FAX 44-171-254-5950. circ. 10,000. *3158*

MOTHERING.
Mothering Magazine, Box 1690, Santa Fe, NM 87504. FAX 505-986-8335. circ. 7,322. *6985*

MOTOR.
Forlaget Motor ApS, Firskovvej 32, P.O. Box 500, DK-2800, Lyngby. TEL 45-45-27-07-07. FAX 45-45-27-09-93. circ. 205,000. *6792*

MOTOR.
Hearst Business Publishing, 645 Stewart Ave., Garden City, NY 11530. TEL 516-227-1370. FAX 516-227-1405. circ. 140,000. *6792*

MOTOR CARAVANNER.
Motor Caravanners' Club, 71 Cricklewood Broadway, London NW2 3JR, England. *6569*

MOTOR CLUB NEWS.
Motor Club of America, c/o Marlene Timm, Ed., 484 Central Ave., Newark, NJ 07107. circ. 130,000. *6901*

MOTOR - MAGASINET.
Dansk Auto Media A-S, Hoejvangen 23, P.O. Box 159, DK-3480 Fredensborg, Denmark. TEL 45-48-485100. FAX 45-48-482015. circ. 15,200. *6793*

MOTOR TRADER.
Reed Business Publishing Group Quadrant House, The Quadrant, Sutton, Surrey SM2 5AS, England. TEL 0181-652-3276. FAX 0181-652-8982. circ. 25,070. *6794*

MOTOR TRANSPORT.
Reed Business Publishing Group Quadrant House, The Quadrant, Sutton, Surrey SM2 5AS, England. TEL 0181-652-3284. FAX 0181-652-8957. circ. 28,766. *6859*

MOTORCYCLE INDUSTRY MAGAZINE.
Industry Shopper Publishing, Inc., Box 160, Gardnerville, NV 89410-0160. TEL 702-782-0222. FAX 702-782-0266. circ. 13,200. *6526*

MOTORCYCLE PRODUCT NEWS.
M H West, Inc. 5743 Corsa Ave., Ste. 220, Westlake Village, CA 91362-4027. TEL 818-997-0664. FAX 818-997-1058. circ. 12,951. *6526*

MOTORING.
Western India Automobile Association, 76 Veer Nariman Rd., Churchgate, Bombay 20, India. circ. 30,000. *6795*

MOTORING & LEISURE.
Civil Service Motoring Association Ltd., Britannia House, 21 Station St., Brighton BN1 4DE, England. TEL 44-1273-744721. FAX 44-1273-323990. circ. 320,000. *6795*

MOTORRAD NEWS.
Syburger Verlag GmbH, Hertingerstr. 60, 59423 Unna, Germany. TEL 49-2303-98550. FAX 49-2303-98559. circ. 80,000. *5527*

MOUNTAIN CONSTRUCTOR & RECLAMATIONIST.
Phoenix Publishing Corporation, Box 6048, Denver, CO 80206-0048. TEL 303-988-2784. circ. 11,201. *866*

MOUNTAIN RIDERS.
South By Southwest Ranch, 15190 Tierra Rejada, Moor Park, CA 93021. TEL 805-523-9334. circ. 5,000. *6549*

MOUNTAIN TRAVEL - SOBEK, THE ADVENTURE COMPANY.
Mountain Travel - Sobek, 6420 Fairmount Ave., El Cerrito, CA 94530. circ. 160,000. *6901*

MOUNTAIN XPRESS.
Mountain Xpress, Inc., Box 144, Asheville, NC 28802. TEL 704-251-1333. FAX 704-251-1311. circ. 18,000. *3233*

MOVIE (YEAR).
Greater Union Organization, 49 Market St., Sydney, N.S.W. 2000, Australia. TEL 61-2-3736600. FAX 61-2-2675277. circ. 40,000. *5108*

MOVIMENTO ANAGRAFE DITTE.
Camera di Commercio Industria, Artigianato e Agricoltura di Pesaro e Urbino, Corso XI Settembre, 116, 61100 Pesaro, Italy. TEL 0721-3571. FAX 0721-31015. circ. 720. *1146*

MOVIMIENTO DE ROCK.
Zona 10, S.A., C. Bruc 65, 3o 2a, 08009 Barcelona, Spain. TEL 34-3-4883609. FAX 34-3-4876665. circ. 25,000. *5174*

MOVIN' OUT.
118 1-2 Franklin St., Box 97, Slippery Rock PA 16057. TEL 412-794-6857. FAX 412-794-1314. circ. 42,000. *6859*

MUHENDIS VE MAKINA.
Makina Muhendisleri Odasi, Sumer Sokak, 36-1-A Demirtepe, 06440 Ankara, Turkey. TEL 4-2313164. FAX 4-2313165. circ. 30,000. *2764*

MULTI-HOUSING NEWS.
Miller Freeman Inc. (New York) One Penn Plaza, New York, NY 10119. TEL 212-869-1300. FAX 212-944-7164. circ. 28,300. *866*

MULTICULTURAL PUBLISHING AND EDUCATION COUNCIL. NEWSLETTER.
Multicultural Publishing and Education Council, c/o Rennie Mau, President, 2280 Grass Valley Hwy., No.181, Auburn, CA 95603. TEL 916-889-4438. FAX 916-888-0690. circ. 1,500. *6002*

MULTIMEDIA PRODUCER.
Knowledge Industry Publications, Inc., 701 Westchester Ave., White Plains, NY 10604. TEL 914-328-9157. FAX 914-328-9093. circ. 40,000. *2039*

MUNDI MEDICINA.
Holy Cross Monastery, Box 99, West Park, NY 12493. TEL 914-384-6660. FAX 914-384-6031. circ. 6,500. *6079*

EL MUNDO.
Alameda Publishing, 630 20th St., Oakland, CA 94612. TEL 510-763-1120. FAX 510-763-9670. circ. 30,000. *2896*

MUNDO NEGRO.
Misioneros Combonianos, Congregacion Misionera, Arturo Soria, 101, 28043 Madrid, Spain. FAX 91-5192550. circ. 100,000. *6079*

MUNICIPAL ASSOCIATION OF TASMANIA. SESSION. MINUTES OF PROCEEDINGS.
Municipal Association of Tasmania, 34 Patrick St., Hobart, Tas. 7000, Australia. TEL 002-310666. FAX 002-240086. circ. 200. *5946*

MUNICIPAL ATTORNEY.
National Institute of Municipal Law Officers, 1000 Connecticut Ave., N.W., Ste. 902, Washington, DC 20036. TEL 202-466-5424. FAX 202-785-0152. circ. 2,500. *3818*

MUNICIPAL ENGINEER.
Brooke Pattrick (Pty) Ltd., P.O. Box 422, Bedfordview 2008, South Africa. TEL 27-11-6224566. FAX 27-11-6167196. circ. 4,357. *2669*

MUNRO EAGLE.
Clan Munro Association U S A, Inc , 11 Las Huertas Ridge Rd., Placitas, NM 87043. circ. 600. *3094*

MURMUR.
Cambridge University Medical Society, Department of Anatomy, Cambridge University, Cambridge CB2 9DT, England. TEL 44-1223-60160. circ. 750. *4504*

MUSEO CIVICO DI STORIA NATURALE DI TRIESTE. ATTI.
Tipografia Villaggio del Fanciullo, Via Conconello 16, Opicina 34016 Trieste, Italy. TEL 39-40-301821. FAX 39-40-302563. circ. 400. *596*

MUSEO CIVICO DI STORIA NATURALE DI VENEZIA. BOLLETTINO.
Museo Civico di Storia Naturale di Venezia, Fontego dei Turchi, S. Croce 1730, 30135 Venice, Italy. TEL 39-41-721852. FAX 39-41-5242592. circ. 1,000. *596*

MUSEUM OF THE FUR TRADE QUARTERLY.
Museum of the Fur Trade, HC-74, Box 18, Chadron, NE 69337. TEL 308-432-3843. circ. 3,000. *3479*

MUSHROOM JOURNAL.
Mushroom Growers' Association, 2 St. Pauls St., Stamford, Lincs. PE9 2BE, England. circ. 1,000. *3061*

MUSIC CRITICS ASSOCIATION. NEWSLETTER.
Music Critics Association, 7 Pine Ct., Westfield, NJ 07090. TEL 908-233-8468. FAX 908-233-8468. circ. 1,000. *5176*

MUSIC FROM CHINA. NEWS.
Music from China, 170 Park Row, Ste. 12-D, New York, NY 10038. TEL 212-962-5698. circ. 1,200. *5176*

MUSICAL HERITAGE REVIEW MAGAZINE.
Musical Heritage Society, 1710 Highway 35, Ocean, NJ 07712. TEL 201-531-7000. *5178*

MUSICAL MERCHANDISE REVIEW.
Larkin-Pluznick-Larkin, Inc., 100 Wells Ave., Box 9103, Newton, MA 02159-9103. TEL 617-964-5100. FAX 617-964-2752. circ. 12,000. *5178*

MUSIKK - FOKUS.
N M M - Nordisk Musiker- og Musikkpedagogforening, P.O. Box 210, N-4301 Sandnes, Norway. TEL 47-51-66-54-57. FAX 47-51-62-27-00. circ. 2,727. *5181*

MUTUALITE.
Association Internationale des Societes d'Assurance Mutuelle, 114 rue la Boetie, 75008 Paris, France. FAX 1-42-56-04-49. circ. 2,500. *3659*

MUZIEKHANDEL.
Nederlandse Muziek Federatie - N M F, Eikbosserweg 181, 1213 RX Hilversum, Netherlands. TEL 31-35-6248104. FAX 31-35-6214220. circ. 500. *5181*

MY CAREER.
Department of Labour, Private Bag X117, Pretoria 0001, South Africa. TEL 27-12-3106358. FAX 27-12-3222839. circ. 45,000. *5271*

MYCOPHILE.
North American Mycological Association, 3556 Oakwood, Ann Arbor, MI 48104-5213. TEL 313-971-2522. circ. 2,000. *692*

MYCOTAXON.
Mycotaxon Ltd., Box 264, Ithaca, NY 14851. TEL 607-273-4357. FAX 607-273-4357. circ. 650. *692*

N A A C NEWSLETTER.
Huts Corner, Tilford Rd., Hindhead, Surrey GU26 6SF, England. TEL 01428-605360. FAX 01428-606531. circ. 600. *136*

N A A F I NEWS.
Navy, Army & Air Force Institutes, HQ N A A F I, London Rd., Amesbury, Wilts SP4 7EN, England. TEL 0980-627043. FAX 0980-627155. circ. 11,000. *5040*

N A B P NEWSLETTER.
National Association of Boards of Pharmacy, 700 Busse Hwy., Park Ridge, IL 60068-2402. TEL 708-698-6227. circ. 1,800. *5429*

N A C R C BULLETIN.
National Association of County Recorders and Clerks, c/o National Association of Counties, 440 First St., N.W., 8th Fl., Washington, DC 20001. TEL 202-393-6226. circ. 900. *5911*

N A C W P I JOURNAL.
Simpson Publishing Co., c/o Dr. Richard Weerts, Ed., Division of Fine Arts, Northeast Missouri State University, Kirksville, MO 63501. TEL 816-785-4442. FAX 816-785-7463. circ. 6,000. *5182*

N A E B BULLETIN.
National Association of Educational Buyers, 450 Wireless Blvd., Hauppauge, NY 11788-3934. TEL 516-273-2600. FAX 516-273-2305. *2495*

N A E I R ADVANTAGE.
National Association for the Exchange of Industrial Resources, 560 McClure St., Box 8076, Galesburg, IL 61402. TEL 309-343-0704. FAX 309-343-0862. circ. 38,000. *6383*

N A F O LIST OF FISHING VESSELS.
Northwest Atlantic Fisheries Organization, P.O. Box 638, Dartmouth, NS B2Y 3Y9, Canada. TEL 902-469-9105. FAX 902-469-5729. *2939*

N A M A JOURNAL.
National Account Management Association, 150 N. Wacker Dr., Ste. 960, Chicago, IL 60606-1607. TEL 312-251-3131. FAX 312-251-3132. circ. 2,000. *1480*

N A P O PROBATION DIRECTORY.
Owen Wells Publishing Company, 23 Eaton Rd., Ilkley, W. Yorks LS29 9PU, England. TEL 44-1943-602270. FAX 44-1943-816732. circ. 10,000. *6383*

N A R D ALMANAC AND HEALTH GUIDE.
Creative Comics Syndicate, 1608 South Dakota, Sioux Falls, SD 57105. circ. 40,000. *1480*

N A R F REHABILITATION REPORT.
National Association of Rehabilitation Facilities, Box 17675, Washington, DC 20041. TEL 703-648-9300. FAX 703-648-0346. circ. 2,000. *4818*

N A R I FOCUS.
National Association of the Remodeling Industry, 4301 N. Fairfax Dr., No.310, Arlington, VA 22203. TEL 703-276-7600. FAX 703-243-3465. circ. 7,500. *866*

N B I A NEWSLETTER.
New Brunswick Institute of Agrologists, P.O. Box 20280, Fredericton, NB E3B 4Z7, Canada. TEL 506-452-3260. FAX 506-452-3316. circ. 200. *136*

N B T A NEWS.
New Brunswick Teachers' Association, Box 752, Fredericton, NB E3B 5R6, Canada. TEL 506-452-8921. FAX 506-453-9795. circ. 8,200. *2354*

N-BAHN MAGAZIN.
Alba Publikationen Alf Teloeken, Roemerstr. 9, 40476 Duesseldorf, Germany. TEL 0211-469010. FAX 0211-484382. circ. 12,412. *3512*

N C G A NEWS.
Northern California Golf Association, 3200 Lopez Rd., Box NCGA, Pebble Beach, CA 93953. TEL 408-625-4653. FAX 408-625-0150. circ. 150,000. *6471*

N D R E PUBLICATIONS.
Norwegian Defence Research Establishment, Box 25, N-2007 Kjeller, Norway. FAX 63-807159. *6260*

N E C RESEARCH AND DEVELOPMENT.
N E C Creative Ltd., 29-11, Shiba 5-chome, Minato-ku, Tokyo 108, Japan. circ. 5,000. *2714*

N E F E DIGEST.
National Endowment for Financial Education, 4695 S. Monaco St., Denver, CO 80237-3403. TEL 303-220-1200. FAX 303-220-1810. circ. 70,000. *1110*

N I C SENTINEL.
North Idaho College, 1000 W. Garden, Coeur D. Alene, ID 83814. TEL 208-769-3388. circ. 2,300. *1877*

N N F A TODAY.
National Nutritional Foods Association, 3931 MacArthur Blvd., Ste. 101, Newport Beach, CA 92660-3021. TEL 714-622-6272. FAX 714-622-6266. *5237*

N N O MAGAZINE.
Noord - Nederlands Orkest, Emmaplein 2, P.O. Box 818, 9700 AV Groningen, Netherlands. TEL 31-50-126200. FAX 31-50-138164. circ. 3,500. *5182*

N NOTICIAS.
National Association of Hispanic Journalists, 1193 National Press Bldg., 529 14th St., N.W., Washington, DC 20045. TEL 202-662-7145. FAX 202-662-7144. circ. 2,500. *3708*

N & M.
Norges Naturvernforbund, Postboks 2113 Grunerlokka, N-0505 Oslo, Norway. TEL 47-22-715520. FAX 47-22-715640. circ. 30,000. *2811*

N R E L IN REVIEW.
U.S. National Renewable Energy Laboratory, 1617 Cole Blvd., Golden, CO 80401-3393. TEL 303-275-4363. FAX 303-275-4053. circ. 7,600. *2586*

N R R I NOW.
University of Minnesota, Duluth, Natural Resources Research Institute, 5013 Miller Trunk Hwy., Duluth, MN 55811. TEL 218-720-4300. FAX 218-720-4219. circ. 4,000. *2213*

N S G A RETAIL FOCUS.
National Sporting Goods Association, 1699 Wall St., Mt. Prospect, IL 60056-5780. TEL 847-439-4000. FAX 847-439-0111. *1480*

N S R A NEWS.
Nuclear Safety Research Association, 1-2-2 Uchisaiwai-cho, Chiyoda-ku, Tokyo 107, Japan. TEL 03-3503-5785. circ. 1,500. *2579*

N S R A NEWSLETTER.
National Ski Retailers Association, 1699 Wall St., Mt. Prospect, IL 60056. TEL 847-439-4293. FAX 847-439-0111. circ. 500. *1480*

N.S.W. MASTER PLUMBER.
Master Plumbers and Mechanical Contractors Association of New South Wales, P.O. Box 65, Haberfield, N.S.W. 2045, Australia. TEL 61-2-797-7055. FAX 61-2-799-5841. circ. 1,600. *3331*

N V V K INFO.
Uitgeverij Kluwer B.V., Postbus 23, 7400 GA Deventer, Netherlands. TEL 31-570-633155. FAX 31-570-633834. circ. 1,500. *5253*

N W D A EXECUTIVE NEWSLETTER.
National Wholesale Druggists' Association, Box 2219, Reston, VA 22090. TEL 703-787-0000. FAX 703-787-6930. circ. 2,300. *5429*

N Y C - ON STAGE.
c/o Theatre Development Fund, 1501 Broadway, Rm. 2110, New York, NY 10036. TEL 212-221-0885. FAX 212-768-1563. *6699*

N.Y. REAL PROPERTY LAW JOURNAL.
New York State Bar Association, Real Property Section, 1 Elk St., Albany, NY 12207-1096. TEL 518-463-3200. FAX 518-463-8844. circ. 4,800. *6030*

N Y S S A SPHERE.
New York State Society of Anesthesiologists, Inc., 360 Lexington Ave., Ste. 1800, New York, NY 10017. TEL 212-867-7140. FAX 212-867-7153. circ. 3,200. *4592*

N Y U PHYSICIAN.
New York University School of Medicine, 550 First Ave., New York, NY 10016. FAX 212-263-8425. circ. 18,000. *1877*

NACION.
Estudios y Publicaciones Economicas y Sociales, S.A., Cerrada de Eugenia, 25, Col. del Valle, Delegacion Benito Juarez, Apartado Postal 32-470, CP 03100 Mexico DF, Mexico. TEL 536-18-31. FAX 525-687-2922.
circ. 15,000. *5685*

NADI ABU DHABI AL-SIYAHI.
Nadi Abu Dhabi al-Siyahi, P.O. Box 28, Abu Dhabi, United Arab Emirates. TEL 724954.
circ. 1,000. *1852*

NADI AL-WASL.
Nadi al-Wasl, P.O. Box 3888, Dubai, United Arab Emirates. TEL 374487.
circ. 500. *1852*

NAERINGSMIDDELINDUSTRIEN.
Skarland Press A-S, P.O. Box 5042 Maj., N-0301 Oslo, Norway. TEL 47-22-60-13-90. FAX 47-22-69-36-50.
circ. 3,766. *2985*

NAGOYA MATHEMATICAL JOURNAL.
Nagoya Daigaku, Daigakuin Tagensurikagaku Kenkyuka, Chikusa-ku, Nagoya 464-01, Japan. FAX 52-789-2829.
circ. 1,250. *4384*

NAILPRO.
Creative Age Publications, 7628 Densmore Ave., Van Nuys, CA 91406. TEL 818-782-7328. FAX 818-782-7450.
circ. 42,000. *497*

NAMO BUDDHA NEWSLETTER.
Namo Buddha Seminar, Maytrees, Aylesbury Rd., Monks Risborough, Bucks. HP27 0JT, England. TEL 08444-3642.
circ. 2,000. *6110*

NAPOLEONIC SOCIETY OF AMERICA. MEMBER'S BULLETIN.
Napoleonic Society of America, 5744 W. Irving Park Rd., Chicago, IL 60634-2623. TEL 813-586-1779. FAX 813-581-2578.
circ. 2,200. *3430*

NARA IGAKU ZASSHI.
Nara Igakkai, Nara Medical University, Kashihara 634, Nara, Japan. TEL 07442-2-3051.
circ. 1,000. *4505*

NAROD POLSKI.
Polish Roman Catholic Union of America, 984 N. Milwaukee Ave., Chicago, IL 60622. TEL 312-278-3210. FAX 312-278-4595.
circ. 30,000. *2896*

NASSAU COUNTY DENTAL SOCIETY. NEWSLETTER.
Nassau County Dental Society Headquarters, 377 Oak St., No. 205, Garden City, NY 11530-6543. TEL 516-764-9620. FAX 516-227-1114.
circ. 2,000. *4648*

NATCHEZ TRACE TRAVELER.
Natchez Trace Genealogical Society, Box 420, Florence, AL 35631-0420.
circ. 150. *3094*

NATIONAL ASSOCIATION OF BEVERAGE RETAILERS. NEWS AND VIEWS.
National Association of Beverage Retailers, 5101 River Rd., Ste. 108, Bethesda, MD 20816. TEL 301-656-1494. FAX 301-656-7539.
circ. 15,000. *509*

NATIONAL ASSOCIATION OF MEAT PURVEYORS. NEWSLETTER.
National Association of Meat Purveyors, 1920 Association Dr., Ste. 400, Reston, VA 22091-1547. TEL 703-758-1900. FAX 703-758-8001.
circ. 420. *2985*

NATIONAL ASSOCIATION OF RAILROAD PASSENGERS NEWS.
National Association of Railroad Passengers, 900 Second St., N.E., Ste. 308, Washington, DC 20002-3557. TEL 202-408-8362. FAX 202-408-8287.
circ. 2,300. *6814*

NATIONAL ASSOCIATION OF STATE PARK DIRECTORS. ANNUAL INFORMATION EXCHANGE.
National Association of State Park Directors, c/o Ney C. Landrum, Exec. Dir., 126 Mill Branch Rd, Tallahassee, FL 32312.
circ. 400. *2134*

NATIONAL ASSOCIATION OF WOMEN ARTISTS. ANNUAL EXHIBITION CATALOG.
National Association of Women Artists, 41 Union Sq., W., Rm. 906, New York, NY 10003. TEL 212-675-1616.
circ. 1,000. *444*

NATIONAL BOTANIC RESEARCH INSTITUTE, LUCKNOW. PROGRESS REPORT.
National Botanical Research Institute, Lucknow. Progress Report, Lucknow 226001, India. *692*

NATIONAL BOTANICAL INSTITUTE. REVIEW.
National Botanical Institute (Claremont), Private Bag X7, Claremont 7735, South Africa. TEL 27-21-762-1166. FAX 27-21-762-3229.
circ. 500. *692*

NATIONAL BRAILLE ASSOCIATION. GENERAL INTEREST CATALOG.
National Braille Association, Inc., 3 Townline Cir., Rochester, NY 14623. TEL 716-427-8260. *3321*

NATIONAL BRAILLE ASSOCIATION. MUSIC CATALOG.
National Braille Association, Inc., 3 Townline Cir., Rochester, NY 14623. TEL 716-427-8260. *3321*

NATIONAL BRAILLE ASSOCIATION. TEXTBOOK CATALOG.
National Braille Association, Inc., 3 Townline Cir., Rochester, NY 14623. TEL 716-427-8260. *3321*

NATIONAL BUSINESS BULLETIN.
National Business Magazines, 361 Riley St., Surry Hills, N.S.W. 2010, Australia. TEL 61-2-2125588. FAX 61-2-2122709.
circ. 41,989. *946*

NATIONAL CENTRE FOR OCCUPATIONAL HEALTH. ANNUAL REPORT.
Department of Health, National Centre for Occupational Health, P.O. Box 4788, Johannesburg 2000, South Africa. FAX 27-11-720-6608.
circ. 400. *5254*

NATIONAL CLOTHESLINE.
B P S Communications, Box 340, Willow Grove, PA 19090-0340. TEL 215-843-9795. FAX 215-843-8511.
circ. 38,000. *1829*

NATIONAL CONFERENCE OF APPELLATE COURT CLERKS. NEWSLETTER.
National Conference of Appellate Court Clerks, National Center for State Courts, 300 Newport Ave., Williamsburg, VA 23187-8798. TEL 804-253-2000.
circ. 225. *3951*

NATIONAL CONFERENCE OF STATE SOCIAL SECURITY ADMINISTRATORS. PROCEEDINGS.
National Conference of State Social Security Administrators, c/o Social Security Division, c/o Jim Larche, Deputy Dir., Employee Retirement System of Georgia, Two Northside 75, Ste. 300, Atlanta, GA 30318. TEL 404-352-6400. *6384*

NATIONAL COUNCIL OF ELECTED COUNTY EXECUTIVES.
Griffin Media Group, 505 Court St., Apt. 5M, Brooklyn, NY 11231-3952. TEL 212-481-4188. FAX 212-481-7239.
circ. 2,500. *5912*

NATIONAL COUNCIL OF TEACHERS OF MATHEMATICS. YEARBOOK.
National Council of Teachers of Mathematics, 1906 Association Dr., Reston, VA 22091. TEL 703-620-9840. FAX 703-476-2970. *4385*

NATIONAL COUNCIL OF THE PAPER INDUSTRY FOR AIR AND STREAM IMPROVEMENT. TECHNICAL BULLETIN.
National Council of the Paper Industry for Air and Stream Improvement, Inc., Box 13318, Research Triangle Park, NC 27709-3318.
circ. 1,500. *2839*

NATIONAL DAIRY COUNCIL OF CANADA. DIRECTION.
National Dairy Council of Canada, 221 Laurier Ave., E., Ottawa, ON K1N 6P1, Canada. TEL 613-238-4116. FAX 613-238-6247.
circ. 1,500. *253*

NATIONAL DEVELOPMENT.
Intercontinental Media, 25 Sylvan Rd. S., Ste. R, Box 3410, Milford, CT 06460. TEL 203-226-7463. FAX 203-222-8793.
circ. 22,000. *2669*

NATIONAL DEVELOPMENT FINANCE CORPORATION. QUARTERLY REVIEW.
National Development Finance Corporation, Finance and Trade Center, 2nd Fl., Shahrah-e Faisal, Karachi, Pakistan. FAX 525310.
circ. 1,200. *1224*

NATIONAL DIET LIBRARY. BOOKS ON JAPAN IN WESTERN LANGUAGES RECENTLY ACQUIRED.
National Diet Library, 1-10-1 Nagata-cho, Chiyoda-ku, Tokyo 100, Japan. TEL 81-3-3581-2331. FAX 81-3-3597-9104.
circ. 800. *540*

NATIONAL DIET LIBRARY. NEWSLETTER.
National Diet Library, 1-10-1 Nagata-cho, Chiyoda-ku, Tokyo 100, Japan. TEL 03-3581-2331. FAX 03-3597-9104.
circ. 1,000. *4014*

NATIONAL DIET LIBRARY. REFERENCE.
National Diet Library, 1-10-1 Nagata-cho, Chiyoda-ku, Tokyo 100, Japan. TEL 03-3581-2331. FAX 03-3597-9104.
circ. 1,700. *3819*

NATIONAL DIRECTORY OF CHIROPRACTIC.
One Directory of Chiropractic, Inc., Box 10056, Olathe, KS 66051. FAX 913-730-0658.
circ. 31,000. *1628*

NATIONAL FEDERATION OF FRUIT & POTATO TRADES. FEDERATION NEWS.
National Federation of Fruit and Potato Trades Ltd., 103-107 Market Towers, 1 Nine Elms Ln., London SW8 5NQ, England. *157*

NATIONAL FORUM (AUBURN).
Honor Society of Phi Kappa Phi (Auburn), c/o Dr. James P. Kaetz, Ed., 129 Quad Center, Mell St., Auburn, AL 36849-5306. TEL 334-844-5200. FAX 334-844-5994.
circ. 120,000. *1878*

NATIONAL FOUNDATION FOR ADVANCEMENT IN THE ARTS. ANNUAL REPORT.
National Foundation for Advancement in the Arts, 800 Brickell Ave. No. 5, Miami, FL 33131-2944. TEL 305-377-1140. FAX 305-377-1149.
circ. 1,000. *444*

NATIONAL HOG FARMER.
Intertec Publishing Corp., Webb Division, 7900 International Dr., Ste. 300, Minneapolis, MN 55425. TEL 612-851-4710. FAX 612-851-4601.
circ. 88,552. *278*

NATIONAL HOUSING REGISTER.
William D. Diemer, Ed. & Pub., 27239 Meadowbrook Dr., Davis, CA 95616-5049. TEL 916-757-6403. FAX 916-753-1768.
circ. 50. *6031*

NATIONAL INDUSTRIAL MAGAZINE.
Brymel Publications, Inc., 801 York Mills Rd., Ste. 201, Don Mills, ON M3B 1X7, Canada. TEL 416-446-1404. FAX 416-446-0502.
circ. 24,077. *1527*

NATIONAL INDUSTRIAL TRANSPORTATION LEAGUE. NOTICE.
National Industrial Transportation League, 1700 N. Moore St., Ste. 1900, Arlington, VA 22209-1904. TEL 703-524-5011. FAX 703-524-5017.
circ. 1,500. *6723*

NATIONAL INSTITUTE FOR EDUCATIONAL RESEARCH. RESEARCH BULLETIN.
National Institute for Educational Research, 6-5-22 Shimo-Meguro, Meguro-ku, Tokyo 153, Japan. *2356*

NATIONAL INSTITUTE OF WATER AND ATMOSPHERIC RESEARCH. MEMOIR.
National Institute of Water and Atmospheric Research Ltd., P.O. Box 14-901, Kilbirnie, Wellington, New Zealand. TEL 64-4-386-0300. FAX 64-4-386-2153.
circ. 500. *2301*

NATIONAL INVESTMENT BANK, GHANA. ANNUAL REPORT.
National Investment Bank, 37 Kwame Nkrumah Ave., P.O. Box 3726, Accra, Ghana. *1111*

NATIONAL MISSING PERSONS REPORT.
Search Reports, Inc., 345 Boulevard, Hasbrouck Heights, NJ 07604. TEL 201-288-4445. FAX 201-288-8055.
circ. 45,000. *2170*

NATIONAL MUSEUM OF THE PHILIPPINES. ANNUAL REPORT.
National Museum of the Philippines, Padre Burgos St., Manila, Philippines. TEL 632-527-12-15. FAX 632-530-0229.
circ. 500. *5129*

NATIONAL POLICE REVIEW.
National Police Officers Association, Box 22129, Louisville, KY 40252-0129. TEL 502-425-9215.
circ. 22,500. *2170*

THE NATIONAL PROVISIONER.
Stagnito Publishing Company, 1935 Shermer Rd., Ste. 100, Northbrook, IL 60062. TEL 847-205-5660. FAX 847-205-5680.
circ. 18,500. *2985*

NATIONAL RETIREMENT QUARTERLY.
Pierce Publications, 3 Northender Rd., Gatley, Ches. SK8 4NR, England. TEL 44-161-491-6000. FAX 44-161-491-1557.
circ. 20,000. *3158*

NATIONAL SAFETY.
Safety First Association, 7 Pitcairn Rd., Blairgowrie, Johannesburg 2194, South Africa. TEL 27-11-7827698.
circ. 3,200. *5971*

NATIONAL SECURITY REVIEW.
National Defense College of the Philippines, Fort Bonifacio, Rizal, Philippines.
circ. 2,000. *5686*

NATIONALLY COORDINATED PROGRAM OF HIGHWAY RESEARCH, DEVELOPMENT, AND TECHNOLOGY.
U.S. Federal Highway Administration, Office of Highway Information Management, Department of Transportation, 400 Seventh St., S.W., Washington, DC 20590. TEL 703-285-2101. FAX 703-285-2379.
circ. 1,500. *6824*

NATUN THIKANA.
71-4 Dr. Nilmani Sarkar St., Calcutta 50, India. *4156*

NATUR.
Natur Media GmbH, Belfortstr. 6-8, 81667 Munich, Germany.
circ. 120,696. *692*

NATURAL CHOICE MAGAZINE.
Media Partners CPR, Northern Rock House, 20 Market Pl., Guisborough, Cleveland TS14 6HF, England. TEL 44-1287-639111. FAX 44-1287-637201.
circ. 150,000. *5533*

NATURAL FOOD TRADER.
I B T M Ltd., Queensway House, 2 Queensway, Redhill, Surrey RH1 1QS, England. TEL 0737-768611. FAX 0737-760425.
circ. 4,500. *5237*

NATURAL FOODS MERCHANDISER.
New Hope Communications, Inc., 1301 Spruce St., Boulder, CO 80302-4832. TEL 303-939-8440. FAX 303-939-9559.
circ. 14,000. *1480*

NATURAL GAS FUELS.
R P Publishing, Inc., 1290 Broadway, Ste. 700, Denver, CO 80203-5607. TEL 303-863-0521. FAX 303-863-1722.
circ. 8,000. *6724*

NATURAL HISTORY MUSEUM AND INSTITUTE, CHIBA. ANNUAL REPORT.
Natural History Museum and Institute, Chiba, 955-2 Aoba-cho, Chuo-ku, Chiba 260, Japan. TEL 81-43-265-3111. FAX 81-43-266-2481.
circ. 1,000. *5129*

NATURAL HISTORY MUSEUM AND INSTITUTE, CHIBA. BULLETIN. HUMANITIES.
Natural History Museum and Institute, Chiba, 955-2 Aoba-cho, Chuo-ku, Chiba 260, Japan. TEL 81-43-265-3111. FAX 81-43-266-2481.
circ. 1,500. *3383*

NATURAL HISTORY MUSEUM AND INSTITUTE, CHIBA. JOURNAL.
Natural History Museum and Institute, Chiba, 955-2 Aoba-cho, Chuo-ku, Chiba 260, Japan. TEL 81-43-265-3111. FAX 81-43-266-2481.
circ. 1,500. *692*

NATURAL HISTORY MUSEUM AND INSTITUTE, CHIBA. JOURNAL. SPECIAL ISSUE.
Natural History Museum and Institute, Chiba, 955-2 Aoba-cho, Chuo-ku 260, Japan. TEL 81-43-265-3111. FAX 81-43-266-2481.
circ. 1,500. *693*

NATURAL HISTORY RESEARCH.
Natural History Museum and Institute, Chiba, 955-2 Aoba-cho, Chuo-ku, Chiba 260, Japan. TEL 81-43-265-3111. FAX 81-43-266-2481.
circ. 1,500. *693*

NATURAL HISTORY RESEARCH. SPECIAL ISSUE.
Natural History Museum and Institute, Chiba, 955-2 Aoba-cho, Chuo-ku, Chiba 260, Japan. TEL 81-43-265-3111. FAX 81-43-266-2481.
circ. 2,500. *693*

NATURAL WORLD.
R S N C - The Wildlife Trusts Partnership, 20 Upper Ground, London SE1 9PF, England. TEL 44-171-805-5555. FAX 44-171-805-5565.
circ. 154,200. *2135*

NATURSCHUTZ HEUTE.
Naturschutzbund Deutschland e.V., Postfach 301054, 53190 Bonn, Germany. TEL 49-228-9756141. FAX 49-228-9756194.
circ. 180,000. *2136*

NAVAL AVIATION NEWS.
U.S. Department of the Navy, Naval Historical Center, Bldg. 157-1 WNY, Washington, DC 20374-5059. TEL 202-433-4407. FAX 202-433-2343.
circ. 30,000. *73*

NAVAL WAR COLLEGE REVIEW.
U.S. Naval War College, 686 Cushing Rd., Code 32, Newport, RI 02841-1207. TEL 401-841-2236. FAX 401-841-3579.
circ. 9,500. *5041*

NAVY CHAPLAIN.
U.S. Navy, Bureau of Naval Personnel, Washington, DC 20370. TEL 804-444-7665. FAX 804-445-1006.
circ. 4,200. *5041*

NAVY SUPPLY CORPS NEWSLETTER.
U.S. Department of the Navy, Supply Systems Command, Washington, DC 20374. TEL 703-607-1301. FAX 703-607-2221.
circ. 15,000. *5042*

NAWPA PACHA.
Institute of Andean Studies, Box 9307, Berkeley, CA 94709. TEL 510-525-7816.
circ. 550. *365*

NAZARETH.
Via Filitteria 10, 06049 Spoleto, Italy.
circ. 2,000. *6079*

NEAR WEST GAZETTE.
Near West Gazette, Inc., 1335 W. Harrison St., Chicago, IL 60607-3318. TEL 312-243-4288. FAX 312-243-4270.
circ. 15,000. *3233*

NEBELSPALTER.
E. Loepfe-Benz AG, CH-9400 Rorschach, Switzerland. TEL 071-414341. FAX 071-414313.
circ. 38,864. *4156*

NEBRASKA. DEPARTMENT OF ROADS. TRAFFIC ANALYSIS UNIT. CONTINUOUS TRAFFIC COUNT DATA AND TRAFFIC CHARACTERISTICS ON NEBRASKA STREETS AND HIGHWAYS.
Department of Roads, Transportation Planning Division, 1500 Nebraska Hwy. 2, Box 94759, Lincoln, NE 68509-4759. TEL 402-471-4567. FAX 402-479-4325. *6824*

NEBRASKA. DEPARTMENT OF SOCIAL SERVICES. ANNUAL REPORT.
Department of Social Services, Research and Finance Division, Box 95026, 301 Centennial Mall So., Lincoln, NE 68509. FAX 402-471-9455.
circ. 500. *6384*

NEBRASKA HIGHWAY PROGRAM.
Nebraska Department of Roads, 1500 NE Hwy. 2, Box 94759, Lincoln, NE 68509-4759. TEL 402-479-4512. FAX 402-479-4325.
circ. 3,850. *6824*

NEBRASKA MORTAR AND PESTLE.
Nebraska Pharmacists Association, Inc., 6221 S. 58th St., Ste. A, Lincoln, NE 68516-3679. TEL 402-420-1500. FAX 402-420-1406.
circ. 1,250. *5429*

NEBRASKA MUSIC EDUCATOR.
Nebraska Music Educators Association, Box 83046, Lincoln, NE 68501-3046. TEL 402-435-6913. FAX 402-474-3250.
circ. 1,550. *5182*

NEBRASKA RETAILER.
Nebraska Retail Grocers Association, 11902 Elm St., No. 4, Omaha, NE 68144-4362. TEL 402-333-4421. FAX 402-333-4336.
circ. 500. *1480*

NEDERDUITSE GEREFORMEERDE KERK VAN NATAL GEMEENTE VRYHEID. MAANDBRIEF.
Nederduitse Gereformeerde Kerk van Natal Gemeentevryheid, Smalstraat 82, Vryheid, Natal, South Africa.
circ. 600. *6153*

NEDERDUITSE GEREFORMEERDE TEOLOGIESE TYDSKRIF.
Nederduitse Gereformeerde Kerk Uitgewers, P.O. Box 4539, Cape Town, South Africa. TEL 27-21-215540. FAX 27-21-4191865.
circ. 1,800. *6153*

NEDERLANDS ELEKTRONICA- EN RADIOGENOOTSCHAP. TIJDSCHRIFT.
Nederlands Elektronica- en Radiogenootschap, Box 39, Leidschendam, Netherlands. TEL 31-70-3325112. FAX 31-70-3326477.
circ. 900. *1912*

NEEDLE'S EYE.
Union Special Corp., 1 Union Special Plaza, Huntley, IL 60142. TEL 847-669-4334. FAX 847-669-3534.
circ. 28,600. *1836*

NEERLANDIA.
Algemeen Nederlands Verbond, J. van Nassaustraat 109, 2596 BS The Hague, Netherlands. TEL 31-70-3245514. FAX 31-70-3246186.
circ. 3,000. *4156*

NEIGHBOR.
309 W. 43rd St., Ste. 103, Sioux Falls, SD 57105-6805. TEL 605-335-7300. FAX 605-335-8141.
circ. 29,000. *137*

NEIGHBORLINE.
University of Dayton, Dayton, OH 45469. TEL 513-229-4639.
circ. 900. *6384*

NEPHROLOGY NEWS & ISSUES.
Nephrology News & Issues, Inc., 15150 N. Hayden Rd., Ste. 101, Scottsdale, AZ 85260-2514. TEL 602-443-4635. FAX 602-443-4528.
circ. 13,100. *4929*

NEPHROLOGY NEWS & ISSUES - EUROPE.
Nephrology News & Issues, Inc., 15150 N. Hayden Rd., Ste. 101, Scottsdale, AZ 85260-2514. TEL 602-443-4635. FAX 602-443-4528.
circ. 5,000. *4929*

NEPSZABADSAG.
Nepszabadsag, Ltd., Becsi ut, 1034 Budapest, Hungary. TEL 36-1-2501680. FAX 36-1-2500250.
circ. 300,000. *3164*

NEPSZAVA (BUDAPEST EDITION).
Torokvesz ut 30-A, 1022 Budapest, Hungary. TEL 361-202-7788. FAX 361-202-7798.
circ. 120,000. *3164*

NET FRIEND NEWS.
American Tennis Federation, 200 Castlewood Dr., North Palm Beach, FL 33408. TEL 407-848-1026. FAX 407-863-8984.
circ. 200. *6509*

NETNEWS MAGAZINE.
T D A Group, 289 S. San Antonio Rd., Ste. 204, Los Altos, CA 94022. TEL 415-948-3140. FAX 415-948-4280.
circ. 170,000. *2040*

NETWORK.
Canadian Controlled Media Communications, 287 MacPherson Ave., Toronto, ON M4V 1A4, Canada. TEL 416-928-2909. FAX 416-966-1181.
circ. 150,000. *3123*

NETWORK (ARLINGTON).
National School Public Relations Association, 1501 Lee Highway, Ste. 201, Arlington, VA 22209. TEL 703-528-5840. *42*

NETWORK (ATLANTA).
Presbyterian Church in America, Mission to the World, Box 29765, Atlanta, GA 30359. TEL 404-320-3373. FAX 404-325-5974.
circ. 88,000. *6080*

NETWORK (DURHAM).
Family Health International, Research Triangle Park Branch, Box 13950, Durham, NC 27709. FAX 919-544-7040.
circ. 65,000. *828*

NETWORK COMPUTING (MANHASSET).
C M P Publications, Inc., 600 Community Dr., Manhasset, NY 11030. TEL 516-562-5000. FAX 516-365-4601.
circ. 175,425. *2040*

NETWORK WORLD.
Network World Inc., 161 Worcester Rd., 5th Fl., Framingham, MA 01701. TEL 508-875-6400. FAX 508-879-3167.
circ. 150,210. *2040*

NETWORKING.
B M I Publications Ltd., Suffolk House, George St., Croydon, Surrey CR9 1SR, England. TEL 44-181-649-7233. FAX 44-181-649-7234.
circ. 27,000. *6902*

NEUE ARGUMENTE.
Arbeitsgemeinschaft Nein zur Atomenergie, Ja zur Umwelt, Postfach 27, A-2103 Langenzersdorf, Austria. TEL 43-1-4725184. FAX 43-1-278850130.
circ. 9,000. *2812*

NEUE JURISTISCHE WOCHENSCHRIFT.
C.H. Beck'sche Verlagsbuchhandlung, Wilhelmstr. 9, 80801 Munich, Germany. TEL 49-89-38189-338. FAX 49-89-38189-398.
circ. 55,858. *3821*

NEUMATICOS Y ACCESSORIOS.
General de Ediciones Especializadas, S.L., C. Juan de Olias, 11 y 13, 28020 Madrid, Spain. TEL 34-1-5719676. FAX 34-1-5210695.
circ. 3,000. *6217*

NEUROLOGICAL INSTITUTE. BULLETIN.
Kyushu Daigaku, Igakubu, 1-1, Maidashi 3-chome, Higashi-ku, Fukuoka-shi, Fukuoka-ken 812-82, Japan. TEL 81-92-641-1151. FAX 81-92-633-4306. *4854*

NEUROLOGY REVIEWS.
Partners in Medical Communication, 4 Brighton Rd., Clifton, NJ 07012. TEL 201-913-1000. FAX 201-916-0021. *4855*

NEVADA STATE MUSEUM NEWSLETTER.
Nevada State Museum, Publications Office, Capitol Complex, Carson City, NV 89710. TEL 702-687-4810.
circ. 1,000. *5130*

NEW ACCOUNTANT.
Real Estate News Corp., 3525 W. Petersen Ave., Chicago, IL 60659.
circ. 64,632. *1052*

NEW AGE RETAILER.
Continuity Publishing, Inc., 1300 N. State St., Ste. 105, Bellingham, WA 98225-4730. TEL 360-676-0789. FAX 360-676-0932.
circ. 5,800. *5219*

NEW BOOKS ON FAMILY PLANNING.
National Institute of Health and Family Welfare, New Mehrauli Rd., Munirka, New Delhi 110067, India.
circ. 1,250. *828*

NEW BRUNSWICK. DEPARTMENT OF ADVANCED EDUCATION AND LABOUR. ANNUAL REPORT.
Department of Advanced Education and Labour, P.O. Box 6000, Fredericton, NB E3B 5H1, Canada. TEL 506-453-2568. FAX 506-453-3806.
circ. 700. *1389*

NEW BRUNSWICK GOVERNMENT DOCUMENTS.
Legislative Assembly, Legislative Library, 766 King St., P.O. Box 6000, Fredericton, NB E3B 5H1, Canada. TEL 506-453-2338. FAX 506-444-5889.
circ. 200. *5933*

NEW CANTERBURY LITERARY SOCIETY NEWS.
Norman T. Gates, Ed. & Pub., 520 Woodland Ave., Haddonfield, NJ 08033.
circ. 125. *4241*

NEW CITY.
New City Press, Box 332, Manila, Philippines. FAX 02-623956.
circ. 10,000. *6080*

NEW CONVERSATIONS.
United Church Board for Homeland Ministries, 700 Prospect Ave., Cleveland, OH 44115-1100. TEL 216-736-3277. FAX 216-736-3263.
circ. 1,500. *6080*

NEW DETROIT INC. ANNUAL REPORT.
New Detroit, Inc., 2900 Penobscot Bldg., 645 Griswold St., Detroit, MI 48226-4234. TEL 313-496-2000. FAX 313-496-2071.
circ. 10,000. *6384*

NEW ELECTRONICS.
Findlay Publications Ltd., Franks Hall, Franks Ln., Horton Kirby, Kent DA4 9LL, England. TEL 44-1322-222222. FAX 44-1322-289577.
circ. 25,055. *2528*

NEW ENGLAND ECONOMIC INDICATORS.
Federal Reserve Bank of Boston, Research Department, 600 Atlantic Ave., Boston, MA 02106. TEL 617-973-3397. FAX 617-973-4292.
circ. 6,000. *1224*

NEW ENGLAND PRINTER AND PUBLISHER.
New England Printer & Publisher Inc., 12 Carleton Dr., Box 810, Newburyport, MA 01950. TEL 508-462-9461. FAX 508-462-9160.
circ. 680. *5815*

NEW ENGLAND SKIERS' GUIDE.
Ski Racing International, Box 1125, Waitsfield, VT 05673-1125. TEL 802-496-7700. FAX 802-496-7704.
circ. 90,000. *6570*

NEW EQUIPMENT DIGEST.
Penton Publishing Co. 1100 Superior Ave., Cleveland, OH 44114-2543. TEL 216-696-7000. FAX 216-696-8765.
circ. 209,041. *6659*

NEW EQUIPMENT NEWS.
Canadian Engineering Publications Ltd., 204 Richmond St. W., Ste. 415, Toronto, ON M5V 1V6, Canada. TEL 416-599-3737. FAX 416-599-3730.
circ. 23,000. *6658*

NEW ERA MAGAZINE.
New Era Magazine, 22031 Bushard, Huntington Beach, CA 92646. TEL 714-962-1351. FAX 714-962-1354.
circ. 23,606. *1829*

NEW HAMPSHIRE QUARTER NOTES.
New Hampshire Music Educators Association, Rt. 5, Box 307, Penacook, NH 03303. TEL 603-648-2692.
circ. 800. *5183*

NEW HAVEN COLONY HISTORICAL SOCIETY. JOURNAL.
New Haven Colony Historical Society, 114 Whitney Ave., New Haven, CT 06510. TEL 203-562-4183.
circ. 1,200. *3480*

NEW HOMES MAGAZINE.
New Homes, Inc., 7543 W. 85th St., Bloomington MN 55438-1308. FAX 612-933-6310.
circ. 60,000. *603*

NEW JERSEY AVIATION NEWS.
Department of Transportation, Division of Aeronautics, 1035 Parkway Ave., CN 610, Trenton, NJ 08625-0610. TEL 609-530-2914. FAX 609-530-5719.
circ. 2,000. *74*

NEW JERSEY FAMILY.
104 LaBarre Ave., Trenton, NJ 08618. TEL 609-695-5646.
circ. 30,000. *1800*

NEW JERSEY MOTOR TRUCK ASSOCIATION. BULLETIN.
New Jersey Motor Truck Association, 160 Tices Ln. E. Brunswick, NJ 08816. TEL 908-254-5000. FAX 908-613-1745.
circ. 2,100. *6860*

NEW JERSEY SAVINGS LEAGUE NEWS.
New Jersey Savings League, 411 North Ave. E., Cranford, NJ 07016. TEL 908-272-8500. FAX 908-272-6626.
circ. 1,100. *1112*

NEW JERSEY SPEECH AND HEARING ASSOCIATION. JOURNAL.
New Jersey Speech and Hearing Association, c/o Auriemma, 6 Crest Ln., Warren, NJ 07059-5110. circ. 1,100. *4507*

NEW JERSEY STATE BAR ASSOCIATION. CERTIFIED TRIAL ATTORNEYS SECTION. NEWSLETTER.
New Jersey State Bar Association, 1 Constitution Sq., New Brunswick, NJ 08901-1500. TEL 908-249-5000. FAX 908-828-0034.
circ. 400. *3951*

NEW JERSEY STATE BAR ASSOCIATION. CORPORATE AND BUSINESS LAW SECTION. NEWSLETTER.
New Jersey State Bar Association, 1 Constitution Sq., New Brunswick, NJ 08901-1500. TEL 908-249-5000. FAX 908-823-0034.
circ. 1,300. *3905*

NEW METHODS.
New Methods Co., Box 22605, San Francisco, CA 94122-0605. TEL 415-664-3469.
circ. 5,600. *6951*

NEW MOTHER.
Maclean Hunter Ltd., Maclean Hunter Bldg., 777 Bay St., Toronto, ON M5W 1A7, Canada. TEL 416-596-5230. FAX 416-593-3197.
circ. 340,000. *1773*

NEW ON THE CHARTS.
Music Business Reference, Inc., 70 Laurel Pl., New Rochelle, NY 10801. TEL 914-632-3349. FAX 914-633-7690.
circ. 2,500. *5183*

NEW PAGES.
New Pages Press, Box 438, Grand Blanc, MI 48439. TEL 313-743-8055. FAX 313-743-2730.
circ. 5,000. *6003*

NEW RESOURCES.
State Library, 1500 Senate St., Box 11469, Columbia, SC 29211. TEL 803-734-8666. FAX 803-734-8676.
circ. 575. *541*

NEW STAMPS GAZETTE.
Shield Stamp Company, Box 2977, Grand Central Sta., New York, NY 10163. TEL 212-629-7979. FAX 212-629-3350.
circ. 15,000. *5459*

NEW STEEL.
Hitchcock Publishing 191 S. Gary Ave., Carol Stream, IL 60188. TEL 708-462-4641. FAX 708-462-2205.
circ. 24,000. *4969*

NEW TECH TIMES.
New York City Technical College, 300 Jay St, Rm. A310, Brooklyn, NY 11201. TEL 718-260-5453. FAX 718-260-5455.
circ. 8,000. *1878*

NEW UNIVERSITY.
University of California, Irvine, 3100 Gateway Commons, Irvine, CA 92717. TEL 714-856-4285. FAX 714-856-4287.
circ. 13,000. *1878*

THE NEW VISION.
P.O. Box 9815, Kampala, Uganda. TEL 256-41-235846. FAX 256-41-235221.
circ. 37,000. *3223*

NEW YORK (STATE). CRIME VICTIMS BOARD. REPORT.
Crime Victims Board, 845 Central Ave., Rm. 107, Albany, NY 12206-1588. TEL 578-457-8066. FAX 578-457-8658.
circ. 2,000. *2171*

NEW YORK (STATE). DEPARTMENT OF LABOR. OPERATIONS - EMPLOYMENT SERVICE AND UNEMPLOYMENT INSURANCE.
Department of Labor, Division of Research and Statistics, 1 Main St., 9th Fl., Brooklyn, NY 11201. TEL 718-797-7703. *1389*

NEW YORK (STATE). INSURANCE DEPARTMENT. BULLETIN.
Insurance Department, Research Bureau, 160 W. Broadway, 21st Fl., New York, NY 10013. TEL 212-602-0473. FAX 212-602-0437.
circ. 5,000. *3660*

NEW YORK AGRICULTURAL STATISTICS.
Department of Agriculture and Markets, 1 Winner's Cir., Albany, NY 12235-0001. FAX 518-453-6564.
circ. 2,800. *177*

NEW YORK AUTO REPAIR NEWS.
Van Allen Publishing Co., Box 354, Hicksville, NY 11802. TEL 516-422-5521.
circ. 11,300. *6796*

NEW YORK CITY BALLET NEWS.
New York City Ballet Guild, New York City Ballet, Inc., New York State Theater, 20 Lincoln Center, New York, NY 10023. TEL 212-870-5677. FAX 212-870-4244.
circ. 6,000. *2190*

NEW YORK HOLSTEIN NEWS.
New York Holstein Association, Box 190, Ithaca, NY 14851. TEL 607-273-7591. FAX 607-273-7612.
circ. 4,300. *253*

NEW YORK INTERNATIONAL LAW REVIEW.
New York State Bar Association, International Law and Practice Section, 1 Elk St., Albany, NY 12207-1096. TEL 518-463-3200. FAX 518-463-8844.
circ. 2,000. *3939*

NEW YORK STATE BAR ASSOCIATION. ANTITRUST LAW SECTION SYMPOSIUM.
New York State Bar Association, Antitrust Law Section, 1 Elk St., Albany, NY 12207. TEL 518-463-3200. FAX 518-463-8844.
circ. 675. *3824*

NEW YORK STATE BAR ASSOCIATION. BUSINESS LAW SECTION. PROCEEDINGS OF THE ANNUAL MEETING.
New York State Bar Association, Business Law Section, One Elk St., Albany, NY 12207. TEL 518-463-3200. FAX 518-487-5699.
circ. 5,000. *3905*

NEW YORK STATE BAR ASSOCIATION. ENVIRONMENTAL LAW SECTION JOURNAL.
New York State Bar Association, Environmental Law Section, 1 Elk St., Albany, NY 12207-1096. TEL 518-463-3200. FAX 518-463-8844.
circ. 1,700. *2812*

NEW YORK STATE BAR ASSOCIATION. LABOR AND EMPLOYMENT LAW SECTION. NEWSLETTER.
New York State Bar Association, Labor and Employment Law Section, 1 Elk St., Albany, NY 12207-1096. TEL 518-463-3200. FAX 518-463-8844.
circ. 2,000. *1389*

NEW YORK STATE BAR JOURNAL.
New York State Bar Association, One Marine Midland Plaza, Binghamton, NY 13902. FAX 607-772-6093.
circ. 59,000. *3824*

THE NEW YORK STATE TROOPER.
State Police, Public Security Bldg., State Campus, Albany, NY 12226. FAX 518-485-7818.
circ. 14,000. *2171*

NEW YORK STATE URBAN DEVELOPMENT CORPORATION. ANNUAL REPORT.
Urban Development Corporation, 1515 Broadway, New York, NY 10036. TEL 212-930-0305. FAX 212-930-0444. *5913*

NEW ZEALAND. CENTRAL ADVISORY COMMITTEE ON THE APPOINTMENTS AND PROMOTION OF PRIMARY TEACHERS. REPORT TO THE MINISTER OF EDUCATION.
Government Printing Office, Private Bag, Wellington, New Zealand. *2357*

NEW ZEALAND CHILDCARE ASSOCIATION. REPORT TO ANNUAL CONFERENCE.
New Zealand Childcare Association, P.O. Box 11-863, Wellington, New Zealand.
circ. 800. *1773*

NEW ZEALAND DAIRY BOARD. ANNUAL REPORT AND STATEMENT OF ACCOUNTS.
New Zealand Dairy Board, P.O. Box 417, Wellington, New Zealand. FAX 64-4-4723691.
circ. 50,000. *253*

NEW ZEALAND HEALTH INFORMATION SERVICE. CANCER: NEW REGISTRATIONS AND DEATHS.
New Zealand Health Information Service, Ministry of Health, 133 Molesworth St., P.O. Box 5013, Wellington, New Zealand. TEL 04-496-2000. FAX 04-496-2040. *4569*

NEW ZEALAND HEALTH INFORMATION SERVICE. FETAL AND INFANT DEATHS.
New Zealand Health Information Service, Ministry of Health, 133 Molesworth St., P.O. Box 5013, Wellington, New Zealand. TEL 04-496-2188. FAX 04-496-2340. *5802*

NEW ZEALAND HEALTH INFORMATION SERVICE. MENTAL HEALTH DATA.
New Zealand Health Information Service, Ministry of Health, 133 Molesworth St., P.O. Box 5013, Wellington, New Zealand. TEL 04-496-2188. FAX 04-496-2340. *4569*

NEW ZEALAND HEALTH INFORMATION SERVICE. MORTALITY AND DEMOGRAPHIC DATA.
New Zealand Health Information Service, Ministry of Health, 133 Molesworth St., P.O. Box 5013, Wellington, New Zealand. TEL 04-469-2188. FAX 04-496-2340. *5802*

NEW ZEALAND INSTITUTE OF VALUERS. LIBRARY CATALOGUE.
New Zealand Institute of Valuers, P.O. Box 27-146, Wellington, New Zealand. TEL 64-4-3858436. FAX 64-4-3829214.
circ. 2,200. *6040*

NEW ZEALAND INSTITUTE OF VALUERS. PROPERTY DIGEST.
New Zealand Institute of Valuers, P.O. Box 27-146, Wellington, New Zealand. TEL 64-4-3858436. FAX 64-4-3829214.
circ. 2,400. *6032*

NEW ZEALAND INTERNATIONAL REVIEW.
New Zealand Institute of International Affairs, P.O. Box 600, Wellington 2, New Zealand. TEL 64-4-4715356. FAX 64-4-4731-261.
circ. 1,500. *5763*

NEW ZEALAND JOURNAL OF PHYSIOTHERAPY.
New Zealand Society of Physiotherapists (Inc.), P.O. Box 57-108, Auckland 4, New Zealand. TEL 64-9-6207566. FAX 64-9-6207566.
circ. 1,500. *4818*

NEW ZEALAND JOURNAL OF PSYCHOLOGY.
New Zealand Psychological Society, c/o Business Manager, P.O. Box 4092, Wellington, New Zealand. TEL 64-4-8015414. FAX 64-4-8015366.
circ. 900. *5867*

NEW ZEALAND JOURNAL OF SPORTS MEDICINE.
Sports Medicine New Zealand, 96 Anzac Ave., P.O. Box 6398, Dunedin, New Zealand. TEL 64-3-4886390. FAX 64-3-4792557.
circ. 1,000. *4899*

NEW ZEALAND MANUFACTURER (WELLINGTON, 1992).
New Zealand Manufacturers Federation, 3 Church St., P.O. Box 11-543, Wellington 1, New Zealand. TEL 64-4-4733-000. FAX 64-4-4733-004.
circ. 3,000. *947*

NEW ZEALAND MARINE SCIENCES SOCIETY REVIEW.
New Zealand Marine Sciences Society, P.O. Box 434, Cambridge, New Zealand. TEL 64-7-8567026. FAX 64-7-8560151.
circ. 300. *597*

NEW ZEALAND PLUMBING REVIEW.
Akron Consolidated Ltd., Box 51-182, Auckland 6, New Zealand.
circ. 1,250. *3331*

NEW ZEALAND R S A REVIEW.
New Zealand Returned Services Association, 181-183 Willis St., P.O. Box 27248, Wellington, New Zealand. TEL 64-4-3847994. FAX 64-4-3853325.
circ. 101,000. *6385*

NEWFOUNDLAND ANCESTOR.
Newfoundland and Labrador Genealogical Society Inc., Colonial Bldg., Military Rd., St. John's, NF A1C 2C9, Canada. TEL 709-754-9525.
circ. 1,100. *3095*

NEWMEDIA.
HyperMedia Communications, 901 Mariners Island, Ste. 365, San Mateo, CA 94404. TEL 415-573-5170. FAX 408-773-8309.
circ. 40,000. *1966*

NEWPORT BEACH (714).
Baker Communications, Inc., 901 Dover Dr., Ste. 231, Newport Beach, CA 92660. TEL 714-722-1286. FAX 714-722-6632.
circ. 50,000. *3234*

NEWPORT NAVALOG.
Edward A. Sherman Publishing Co., 101 Malbone Rd., Box 420, Newport, RI 02840. FAX 401-849-3300.
circ. 7,200. *5042*

NEWS ABOUT LIBRARY SERVICES FOR THE BLIND AND PHYSICALLY HANDICAPPED.
State Library, 1500 Senate St., Box 11469, Columbia, SC 29211. TEL 803-737-9970.
circ. 7,200. *3307*

NEWS & VIEWS OF LOCAL 23.
United Food and Commercial Workers, Local 23, 951 Penn Ave., Pittsburgh, PA 15222. TEL 412-261-0301. FAX 412-261-4429.
circ. 23,000. *3726*

NEWS FOR SOUTH CAROLINA LIBRARIES.
State Library, 1500 Senate St., Box 11469, Columbia, SC 29211. TEL 803-734-8666. FAX 803-734-8676.
circ. 1,800. *4016*

NEWS FROM HOPE COLLEGE.
Hope College, 141 E. 12th St., Holland, MI 49423. TEL 616-395-7860. FAX 616-395-7991.
circ. 40,000. *1878*

NEWS IN HEADACHE.
Cambridge Medical Publications Ltd., Wicker House, High St., Worthing, W. Sussex BN11 1DJ, England. TEL 01903-205884. FAX 01903-234862. *4858*

NEWS OF NORWAY.
Royal Norwegian Embassy, 2720-34th St., N.W., Washington, DC 20008. TEL 202-333-6000. FAX 202-337-0870.
circ. 19,000. *2899*

NEWSLETTER FROM DICK B. ON THE SPIRITUAL ROOTS OF ALCOHOLICS ANONYMOUS.
Good Book Publishing Co., 2747 S. Kihei Rd., D110, Kihei, HI 96753. TEL 808-874-4876.
circ. 800. *2199*

NEWSLINE (JEFFERSON CITY).
Missouri State Library, Box 387, Jefferson City, MO 65102-0387. TEL 573-751-3615. FAX 573-751-3612.
circ. 4,250. *4016*

NEWSOUTH JAPANESE MAGAZINE.
Print Graphics Services, Inc., Box 2752, Peachtree City, GA 30269. TEL 770-631-9159. FAX 770-631-8852.
circ. 40,000. *3234*

NEXUS (BOULDER).
1680 Sixth St., Ste. 6, Boulder, CO 80302. TEL 303-442-6662. FAX 303-442-7596.
circ. 50,000. *292*

NICARAGUA UPDATE.
Nicaragua Solidarity Campaign, 129 Seven Sisters Rd., London N7 7QG, England. TEL 44-171-272-9619. FAX 44-171-272-5476.
circ. 1,750. *5688*

NICHOLS NEWS.
Nichols College, Box 5000, Dudley, MA 01571. TEL 508-943-1560.
circ. 10,000. *1878*

NIEDERSAECHSISCHE GEMEINDE.
Niedersaechsischer Staedte-und Gemeindebund, Seelhorststr. 18, 30175 Hannover, Germany. TEL 0511-280720. FAX 0511-854107.
circ. 12,700. *5948*

NIET ZO BENAUWD.
Stichting Familieclub Johannes van der Linden, Salomeschouw 61, 2726 JP Zoetermeer, Netherlands. TEL 31-79-3411955.
circ. 150. *3095*

NIGERIA INDUSTRIAL DIRECTORY.
Malthouse Press Ltd., 8 Amore St. (off Toyin St.), P.O. Box 8917, Ikeja, Lagos State, Nigeria.
circ. 5,000. *1631*

NIGHTLIFE.
Data-Boy Enterprises, Inc., 6363 Santa Monica Blvd., Ste. 200, Los Angeles, CA 90038-1619. TEL 213-656-2960. FAX 213-656-7312.
circ. 44,000. *3536*

NIHON DAIGAKU RIKOGAKU KENKYUJO SHOHO.
Nihon Daigaku, Rikogaku Kenkyujo, 1-8 Kanda Surugadai, Chiyoda-ku, Tokyo 101, Japan. *6659*

NIHON DAIGAKU RIKOGAKUBU GAKUJUTSU KOENKAI KOEN RONBUNSHU.
Nihon Daigaku, Rikogakubu Rikogaku Kenkyujo, 1-8 Kanda Surugadai, Chiyoda-ku, Tokyo 101, Japan. *6659*

NIHON FUJIN KAGAKUSHA NO KAI NYUSU.
Nihon Fujin Kagakusha no Kai, Toho Daigaku Rigakubu, 2-2-1, Miyama, Funabashi-shi, Chiba-ken 274, Japan. TEL 81-474-70-1335.
circ. 1,000. *7003*

NIHON GAISHO GAKKAI ZASSHI.
Nihon Gaisho Gakkai, Teikyo Daigaku Kyumei Kyukyu Senta, 11-1, Kaga 2-chome, Itabashi-ku, Tokyo 173, Japan. TEL 81-3-3964-1211. FAX 81-3-5375-0854.
circ. 1,200. *4788*

NIHON KOTSU KEITAI KEISOKU GAKKAI ZASSHI.
Nihon Kotsu Keitai Keisoku Gakkai, Niigata Daigaku Igakubu Seikei Gekagaku Kyoshitsu, Asahimachi Dori 1 Bancho, Niigata-shi, Niigata-ken 951, Japan. TEL 81-25-223-6161. FAX 81-25-229-1675.
circ. 1,000. *4788*

NIHON SHINSEIJI GAKKAI ZASSHI.
Nihon Shinseiji Gakkai, c/o Nihon University, School of Medicine, Department of Pediatrics, 30-1 Oyaguchi-Kami-machi, Itabashi-ku, Tokyo 173, Japan.
circ. 4,000. *4809*

NIHON SUPINDORU GIHO.
Nihon Supindoru Seizo K.K., 2-30, Shioe 4-chome, Amagasaki-shi, Hyogo-ken 661, Japan. TEL 81-06-499-4304. FAX 81-06-499-5631.
circ. 1,000. *2765*

NIKKEI ELECTRONICS ASIA.
Nikkei Business Publications, Inc., Nikkei Business Publications Asia, Ltd., Unit 1404, East Point Centre (New Wing), 533 Hennessy Rd., Causeway Bay, Hong Kong. TEL 852-2575-8301. FAX 852-2574-8175.
circ. 24,245. *2528*

NIKKEI MEDICAL.
Nikkei Business Publications, Inc. 2-7-6 Hirakawa-cho, Chiyoda-ku, Tokyo 102, Japan. TEL 03-5210-8502. FAX 03-5210-8119.
circ. 104,000. *4508*

NIMBUS.
Societa Meteorologica Subalpina, V. Gioberti 88, 10128 Turin, Italy. TEL 39-11-591145. FAX 39-11-5683190.
circ. 500. *5004*

THE NINETIES MONTHLY.
Going Fine Ltd., Southward Mansion, Flats A & B, 1F, 3 Lau Li St., Causeway Bay, Hong Kong. TEL 852-2887-3997. FAX 852-2887-3897.
circ. 40,000. *3153*

NIPPON BIYO GEKA GAKKAISHI.
Nippon Biyo Geka Gakkai, 12-5, Shinbashi 1-chome, Minato-ku, Tokyo 105, Japan. TEL 03-3573-2111. FAX 03-3573-2114.
circ. 400. *4916*

NIPPON JUI CHIKUSAN DAIGAKU KENKYU HOKOKU.
Nippon Jui Chikusan Daigaku, 1-7-1 Kyonan-cho, Musashino-shi, Tokyo 180, Japan. TEL 422-31-4151. FAX 422-33-2035.
circ. 500. *6951*

NIPPON MEDICAL SCHOOL. JOURNAL.
Nippon Medical School, Medical Association, 1-1-5 Sendagi, Bunkyo-ku, Tokyo 113, Japan. TEL 81-3-3822-2131. FAX 81-3-3822-3759.
circ. 2,850. *4508*

NONESUCH.
University of Bristol, Information Office, Senate House, Tyndal Ave., Bristol BS8 1TH, England. TEL 44-117-9287777. FAX 44-117-9292396.
circ. 45,000. *1878*

NONPUBLIC SCHOOL ENROLLMENT AND STAFF, NEW YORK STATE.
Education Department, Information, Reporting & Technology Services, Education Bldg. Annex, Rm. 962, Albany, NY 12234. TEL 518-474-7082. FAX 518-474-4351. *2358*

NONSOLOBUS.
Azienda Trasporti Area Fiorentina, Viale dei Mille 115, 50131 Florence, Italy. TEL 39-55-5650241. FAX 39-55-5650243.
circ. 4,000. *6724*

NONVIOLENT SANCTIONS.
Albert Einstein Institution, 50 Church St., 3rd Fl., Cambridge, MA 02138-3726. TEL 617-876-0311. FAX 617-876-0837.
circ. 800. *5688*

NOR MARMARA.
Solakzade Sok. No. 5, Istanbul. TEL 90-212-2491989. FAX 90-212-2444736.
circ. 1,700. *3222*

NORD-EMBALLAGE.
Foerlags AB Thorsten Fahlskog, P.O. Box 25, S-162 11 Vaellingby, Sweden. TEL 46-8-870280. FAX 46-8-874815.
circ. 3,800. *5302*

NOR'EASTER (DULUTH).
Lake Superior Marine Museum Association, Box 177, Duluth, MN 55802. TEL 218-727-2497. FAX 218-720-5270.
circ. 600. *3480*

NORFOLK SOUTHERN WORLD.
Norfolk Southern Corporation, Public Relations Department, 3 Commercial Pl., Norfolk, VA 23510. TEL 804-629-2707. FAX 804-629-2822.
circ. 47,000. *6814*

NORSK IDRETT.
Norsk Idrettsforbund, N-1351 Rud, Norway.
circ. 13,000. *6472*

NORSK SKOLEBLAD.
Norsk Laererlag, Rosenkrantzgt. 15, N-0160 Oslo, Norway. TEL 47-22-00-20-00. FAX 47-22-00-21-90.
circ. 69,830. *2358*

NORSK V V S.
Skarland Press A-S, P.O. Box 5042 Maj., N-0301 Oslo, Norway. TEL 47-22-60-13-90. FAX 47-22-69-36-50.
circ. 5,007. *3331*

NORTE.
Frente de Afirmacion Hispanista A.C., Lago Como 201, 11320 Mexico DF, Mexico. TEL 525-5963328. FAX 525-5962425.
circ. 3,000. *4244*

NORTH AMERICAN ASSOCIATION OF SUMMER SESSIONS. NEWSLETTER.
North American Association of Summer Sessions, 11728 Summerhaven Dr., St. Louis, MO 63146-5444. *2461*

NORTH AMERICAN FARM EQUIPMENT JOURNAL.
G J P Enterprises Inc., 101 W. 29th St., Ste. 102, Box 1210, Marshfield, WI 54449. TEL 715-339-2234. FAX 715-389-2380.
circ. 6,050. *206*

NORTH AMERICAN MISSIONS.
Association of North American Missions, 3859 Nottingham Dr., Sarasota, FL 34235. TEL 941-955-8529. FAX 941-951-0805.
circ. 5,000. *6154*

NORTH CAROLINA. SECRETARY OF STATE. DIRECTORY OF STATE AND COUNTY OFFICIALS.
Secretary of State, 300 N. Salisbury St., Raleigh, NC 27603-5909. TEL 919-733-7355.
circ. 10,000. *5913*

NORTH CAROLINA DENTAL REVIEW.
University of North Carolina, School of Dentistry, Brauer Hall, Rm. 410, CB 7450, Chapel Hill, NC 27599-7450. TEL 919-966-2730. FAX 919-956-4049.
circ. 6,200. *4649*

NORTH CAROLINA LAWYER.
North Carolina Bar Association, Box 3688, Cary NC 27519-3688. TEL 919-677-0561. FAX 919-677-0761.
circ. 10,500. *3826*

NORTH CAROLINA MANUAL.
Secretary of State, 300 N. Salisbury St., Raleigh, NC 27603-5909. TEL 919-733-7355.
circ. 5,000. *5913*

NORTH CAROLINA PLUMBING - HEATING - COOLING FORUM.
North Carolina Association of Plumbing - Heating - Cooling Contractors, Inc., 413 Glenwood Ave., Raleigh, NC 27603. TEL 919-833-0372. FAX 919-833-0921.
circ. 4,000. *3331*

NORTH CAROLINA SEED LAW.
Department of Agriculture, Box 27647, Raleigh, NC 27611. TEL 919-733-7125. *140*

NORTH CAROLINA STATE UNIVERSITY. COLLEGE OF FOREST RESOURCES. TECHNICAL REPORT.
North Carolina State University, College of Forest Resources, Raleigh, NC 27695.
circ. 75. *3022*

NORTH CENTRAL OPTOMETRIC VIEWPOINT.
R.C. Publications, Inc. (Brookfield), Box 604, Brookfield, WI 53008-0604. TEL 414-789-2749. FAX 414-789-9458.
circ. 26,200. *4773*

NORTH COUNTRY FARM NEWS.
Clinton County Cooperative Extension, 6064 State Rte. 22, Ste. 5, Plattsburgh, NY 12901-6222.
circ. 900. *140*

NORTH DAKOTA. JUDICIAL SYSTEM. ANNUAL REPORT.
Judicial System, Office of State Court Administrator, State Capitol, Bismarck, ND 58505. TEL 701-328-4216. FAX 701-328-4480.
circ. 1,000. *3878*

NORTH DAKOTA'S HIGHWAY SAFETY PLAN.
Department of Transportation, Driver's License and Traffic Safety, Traffic Safety Programs Section, 608 E. Blvd. Ave., Bismarck, ND 58505-0700. TEL 701-224-2600. FAX 701-224-4545.
circ. 150. *6824*

NORTH GEORGIA JOURNAL.
Legacy Communications, Inc., P.O. Box 127, Roswell, GA 30077-0127. TEL 404-642-5569. FAX 404-642-6598.
circ. 2,451. *6903*

NORTH LOUISIANA HISTORICAL ASSOCIATION. JOURNAL.
North Louisiana Historical Association, Box 6701, Shreveport, LA 71136. TEL 318-797-5337.
circ. 500. *3481*

NORTH TEXAS GOLFER.
Golfer Magazines, Inc., 9182 Old Katy Rd., Ste. 212, Houston, TX 77055. TEL 713-464-0308. FAX 713-464-0129.
circ. 29,000. *6510*

NORTH THOMPSON TIMES.
Rubicon Publishing Inc., RR 1, Box 1102, Clearwater, BC VOE 1N0, Canada. TEL 604-674-3343. FAX 604-674-3777.
circ. 1,903. *3123*

NORTH WIND.
Northern Michigan University, Marquette, MI 49855. TEL 906-227-2545. *1879*

NORTHEAST DIRECTORY OF TRANSPORTATION SERVICES.
Northeast Journal of Transportation, 31 Fargo St., S. Boston, MA 02127. TEL 617-695-1660. FAX 617-695-1665. *1631*

NORTHEASTERN UNIVERSITY MAGAZINE.
Northeastern University, Office of University Relations, 360 Huntington Ave., 598 CP, Boston, MA 02115. TEL 617-373-5444. FAX 617-373-5430.
circ. 135,000. *1879*

NORTHERN AUTOMOTIVE NEWS.
13304 Stone Rd., Minnetonka, MN 55305. TEL 612-544-6805.
circ. 7,000. *6796*

NORTHERN MOSAIC.
Thunder Bay Multicultural Association, 17 N. Court St., Thunder Bay, ON P7A 4T4, Canada. TEL 807-345-0551. FAX 807-345-0173.
circ. 600. *2899*

NORTHERN NEW ENGLAND REVIEW.
Franklin Pierce College, Box 60, Rindge, NH 03461. TEL 603-899-4089. FAX 603-899-6448.
circ. 600. *4244*

NORTHERN ONTARIO BUSINESS.
Laurentian Publishing Co., 158 Elgin St., Sudbury, ON P3E 3N5, Canada. TEL 705-673-5705. FAX 705-673-9542.
circ. 10,000. *948*

NORTHWEST ASSOCIATION OF SCHOOLS AND COLLEGES. CONVENTION PROCEEDINGS.
Northwest Association of Schools and Colleges, Boise State University, Boise, ID 83725. TEL 208-334-3226. FAX 208-334-3228. *2438*

NORTHWEST ASSOCIATION OF SCHOOLS AND COLLEGES. NEWSLETTER.
Northwest Association of Schools and Colleges, Boise State University, Boise, ID 83725. TEL 208-334-3226. FAX 208-334-3228. *2358*

NORTHWEST MOTOR.
Automotive Publishing Company, Box 46937, Seattle, WA 98146-0937. TEL 206-935-3336. FAX 206-937-9732. *6796*

NORTHWEST PASSAGES.
Northwest Airlines, Inc., 5101 Northwest Dr., St. Paul, MN 55111-3034. TEL 612-726-7357. FAX 612-726-3942.
circ. 56,000. *6762*

NORTHWESTERN PERSPECTIVE.
Northwestern University, 555 Clark St., Evanston, IL 60208-1230. TEL 847-491-5000. FAX 847-491-2376.
circ. 95,624. *1879*

NORTHWESTERN UNIVERSITY. MATERIALS RESEARCH CENTER. ANNUAL TECHNICAL REPORT.
Northwestern University, Materials Research Center, 2145 Sheridan Rd., Evanston, IL 60208-3116. TEL 708-491-3606. FAX 312-491-4181. *2740*

NORWEB MAGAZINE.
Media Partners CPR, Northern Rock House, 20 Market Pl., Guisborough, Cleveland TS14 6HF, England. TEL 44-1287-639111. FAX 44-1287-637201.
circ. 1,800,000. *2570*

NORWEGIAN OFFSHORE INDEX.
Selvig Publishing A-S, P.O. Box 9070 Groenland, 0133 Oslo, Norway. TEL 22-364440. FAX 22-360550. *5383*

NOS MAISONS FAMILIALES DE VACANCES.
Federation des Maisons Familiales de Vacances, 28 place St-Georges, 75442 Paris 9, France. *6903*

NOSTALGIA MOTOR MAGAZINE.
Foerlags AB Albinsson & Sjoeberg, P.O. Box 529, S-371 23 Karlskrona, Sweden. TEL 46-455-335325. FAX 46-455-311715.
circ. 15,600. *334*

NOSTRE TOR.
Famija Albeisa - Ente Morale, Via Pierino Belli 6, 12051 Alba CN, Italy. TEL 39-173-441742.
circ. 2,250. *3620*

NOTAS.
Vervuert Verlag GmbH, Wielandstr. 40, 60318 Frankfurt a.M., Germany. TEL 49-69-5974617. FAX 49-69-5978743.
circ. 750. *4158*

NOTI S A I.
Sociedad Antioquena de Ingenieros y Arquitectos, Calle 71, No. 65-100, Apdo. Aereo 4754, Medellin, Colombia. TEL 257-3900. FAX 255-4584.
circ. 2,500. *2613*

NOTIZIARIO MOTORISTICO.
Azienda Cataloghi Italiani s.a.s., Via B. Crespi, 30-2, 20159 Milan, Italy. TEL 39-2-606052. FAX 39-2-606487.
circ. 18,072. *6796*

NOTRE DAME MAGAZINE.
University of Notre Dame, Notre Dame Magazine, Main Bldg., Rm. 415, Notre Dame, IN 46556. TEL 219-631-5335. FAX 219-631-6767.
circ. 130,000. *1879*

NOTRE DAME REPORT.
University of Notre Dame, Office of the Provost, Notre Dame, IN 46556. TEL 219-631-5337.
circ. 1,600. *1879*

NOUVEAU COMMERCE.
A C N C Nouveau Commerce, Librarie Anima, 3 rue Ravignan, 75018 Paris, France. TEL 42-64-05-25.
circ. 1,000. *4245*

NOUVEAU GLOSSAIRE NAUTIQUE D'AUGUSTIN JAL.
C N R S Editions, 20-22 rue St. Amand, 75015 Paris, France. TEL 45-33-16-00. FAX 45-33-92-13.
circ. 1,250. *2302*

NOVA SCOTIA. DEPARTMENT OF ECONOMIC DEVELOPMENT. ANNUAL REPORT.
Department of Economic Development, P.O. Box 519, Halifax, NS B3J 2R7, Canada. TEL 902-424-8922. FAX 902-424-5739.
circ. 300. *5913*

NOVAS DE ALEGRIA.
Casa Publicadora das Assembleias de Deus, Av. Alm. Gago Coutinho 158, 1700 Lisbon, Portugal.
circ. 10,400. *6210*

NOVYI ZHURNAL.
New Review Inc., 611 Broadway, Ste. 842, New York, NY 10012-2608. TEL 212-353-1478.
circ. 1,300. *2900*

NOW HEAR THIS U S S CALLAWAY NEWSLETTER.
5319 Manning Pl., N.W., Washington, DC 20013-5311. TEL 202-363-3663.
circ. 390. *5042*

NUCLEAR ENERGY.
Nuclear Energy Institute, 1776 Eye St., N.W., Ste. 400, Washington, DC 20006-3708. TEL 202-739-8000.
circ. 10,000. *2580*

NUCLEAR FORUM.
British Nuclear Industry Forum, 22 Buckingham Gate, London SW1E 6LB, England. TEL 071-828-0116. FAX 071-828-0110.
circ. 7,000. *2580*

NUCLEAR INDIA.
Department of Atomic Energy, Publications Officer, Chhatrapati Shivaji Maharaj Marg, Bombay 400039, India.
circ. 5,000. *2580*

NUEVA CARDIOLOGIA.
Obsidiana Editores, S.A., Czda. de Tlalpan 2365, Col. Ciudad Jardin, 04370 Mexico DF, Mexico. TEL 6899133.
circ. 570. *4608*

NUEVA LENTE.
Miguel J. Goni Fernandez, Ed. & Pub., Ardemans 64, Madrid, Spain.
circ. 10,000. *5515*

NUEVO SIGLO.
4809 N. Armenia Ave., Ste. 115, Tampa, FL 33603. TEL 813-872-6692. FAX 813-877-6444.
circ. 18,000. *2900*

NUMARK NEWS.
Numark Ltd., Numark House, 5-6 Fairway Ct., Amber Close, Tamworth Business Park, Tamworth, Staffs B77 4RP, England. TEL 44-1827-69269. FAX 44-1827-62369.
circ. 6,000. *5431*

NUMBER ONE.
Volunteer State Community College, Humanities Division, 1480 Nashville Pike, Gallatin, TN 37066. TEL 615-452-8600.
circ. 2,000. *4312*

THE NUMISMATIST.
American Numismatic Association, 818 N. Cascade Ave., Colorado Springs, CO 80903-3279. TEL 719-632-2646. FAX 719-634-4085.
circ. 25,000. *5226*

NUORTEN SARKA.
Suomen 4H-Liitto, Bulevardi 28, 00120 Helsinki 12, Finland. TEL 358-0-645133.
circ. 28,500. *140*

NURSCENE.
Manitoba Association of Registered Nurses, 647 Broadway, Winnipeg, MB R3C 0X2, Canada. TEL 204-774-3477. FAX 204-775-6052.
circ. 11,000. *4722*

NURSING (YEAR) CAREER DIRECTORY.
Springhouse Corporation 1111 Bethlehem Pike, Box 908, Springhouse, PA 19477-0908. TEL 215-646-8700. FAX 215-646-4399.
circ. 100,000. *1632*

NURSING B C.
Registered Nurses Association of British Columbia, 2855 Arbutus St, Vancouver, BC V6J 3Y8, Canada. TEL 604-736-7331. FAX 604-738-2272.
circ. 35,000. *4723*

NURSING IN CRITICAL CARE.
Greycoat Publishing, 1 Harley St., London W1N 1DA, England. TEL 44-171-637-1828.
circ. 1,100. *4723*

NURSING MANAGEMENT.
Springhouse Corporation 1111 Bethlehem Pike, Box 908, Springhouse, PA 19477. TEL 215-646-8700.
circ. 135,000. *4724*

NUSLECA.
Nusleca Publications, Shripney Works, Bognor Regis, W. Sussex PO22 9NQ, England. FAX 0243-868052.
circ. 5,000. *3331*

NUTRICION CLINICA.
Alpe Editores, S.A., Pedro Rico, 27, 28029 Madrid, Spain. TEL 34-1-7338811. FAX 34-1-3159652.
circ. 5,000. *5238*

NUTRITION FORUM.
Canadian Society for Nutritional Sciences, Department of Foods and Nutrition, University of Manitoba, Winnipeg, MB R3T 2N2, Canada. TEL 613-993-4484. *5238*

NUTRITION HEALTH REVIEW.
Vegetus Publications, Box 406, Haverford, PA 19041. TEL 610-896-1853. FAX 610-896-1857. circ. 280,800. *5239*

NUTRITION NEWS IN ZAMBIA.
National Food and Nutrition Commission, P.O. Box 32669, Lusaka, Zambia. circ. 5,000. *2985*

NUX.
University of Natal, Students Representative Council, P.O. Box 375, Pietermaritzburg, Natal, South Africa. circ. 2,500. *1879*

NWY NEWS.
British Gas Wales, Public Relations Dept., Helmont House, Churchill Way, Cardiff CF1 4NB, Wales. TEL 0222-239290. FAX 0222-290738. circ. 6,500. *5366*

NY TEKNIK.
Ingenjoersfoerlaget AB, S-106 12 Stockholm, Sweden. TEL 46-8-796-6650. FAX 46-8-789-6224. circ. 133,956. *2613*

NYE FAMILY NEWSLETTER.
Nye Family of America Association, Box 134, E. Sandwich, MA 02537. TEL 508-888-2368. circ. 2,400. *3096*

O A N DIRECTORY & BUYER'S GUIDE.
Oregon Association of Nurserymen, 2780 S.E. Harrison, Ste. 102, Milwaukie, OR 97222. TEL 503-653-8733. FAX 503-653-1528. circ. 5,500. *1632*

O B G MANAGEMENT.
Dowden Publishing Company, 110 Summit Ave., Montvale, NJ 07645. TEL 201-391-9100. FAX 201-391-2778. circ. 34,500. *4743*

O C D DIAMOND.
American Cyanamid Co., Organic Chemical Division, Bound Brook, NJ 08805. TEL 908-831-2000. circ. 6,500. *6659*

O D I INDEX TO DEVELOPMENT LITERATURE.
Overseas Development Institute, Regent's College, Inner Circle, Regent's Park, London NW1 4NS, England. TEL 0171-487-7413. FAX 0171-487-7590. circ. 200. *1018*

O D I NATURAL RESOURCE PERSPECTIVES.
Overseas Development Institute, Regent's College, Inner Circle, Regent's Park, London NW1 4NS, England. TEL 0171-487-7413. FAX 0171-487-7590. circ. 6,000. *1312*

O E M DESIGN.
Wilmington Publishing, Wilmington House, Church Hill, Dartford, Kent UA2 7EF, England. TEL 0322-277788. FAX 0322-276476. circ. 30,500. *2613*

O P M A OVERSEAS MEDIA GUIDE.
Overseas Press and Media Association, c/o Sinclairs, 32 Queen Anne St., London W1M 9LB, England. circ. 5,000. *1632*

O P S E U NEWS.
Ontario Public Service Employees Union, 100 Lesmill Rd., North York, ON M3B 3P8, Canada. TEL 416-443-8888. FAX 416-443-1762. circ. 20,000. *1390*

O P T I M A NEWSLETTER.
Organization for the Phyto-Taxonomic Investigation of the Mediterranean Area, Departmento Biologia Vegetal, Universidad Politecnica de Madrid, Ciudad Universitaria, 28040 Madrid, Spain. TEL 34-15445800. FAX 34-13365656. circ. 750. *694*

O R INSIGHT.
Operational Research Society, Seymour House, 12 Edward St., Birmingham B1 2RX, England. TEL 44-121-233-9300. FAX 44-121-233-0321. circ. 3,000. *2359*

O S L A NEWSLETTER.
Ontario Association of Speech - Language Pathologists and Audiologists, 410 Jarvis St., Toronto, ON M4Y 2G6, Canada. circ. 1,700. *2472*

O S M T ADVOCATE.
Ontario Society of Medical Technologists, 234 Eglinton Ave. E. Ste. 600, Toronto, Ont. M4P 1K5, Canada. circ. 4,000. *4684*

O S T C NEWS.
Ontario Shade Tree Council, 75 The Donway W., Ste. 302, Don Mills, ON M3C 2E9, Canada. TEL 416-443-1785. FAX 416-443-1418. circ. 300. *3022*

OAKLAND UNIVERSITY MAGAZINE.
Oakland University, Publications Department, 109 N. Foundation Hall, Rochester, MI 48309-4401. TEL 810-370-3184. FAX 810-370-3182. circ. 40,000. *1979*

OASIS.
WaterAid, Prince Consort House, 27-29 Albert Embankment, London SE1 7UB, England. TEL 44-171-793-4500. FAX 44-171-793-4545. circ. 90,000. *1312*

OB-GYN NEWS.
International Medical News Group, 12230 Wilkins Ave., Rockville, MD 20852. TEL 301-816-8700. circ. 31,000. *4743*

OBEROESTERREICHER-LEBENSBILDER ZUR GESCHICHTE OBEROESTERREICHS.
Oberoesterreichisches Landesarchiv, Anzengruberstr. 19, A-4020 Linz, Austria. TEL 43-732-6555230. FAX 43-732-655523-4619. circ. 500. *3432*

OBEROESTERREICHISCHES LANDESARCHIV. MITTEILUNGEN.
Oberoesterreichisches Landesarchiv, Anzengruberstr. 19, A-4020 Linz, Austria. TEL 43-732-6555230. FAX 43-732-655523-4619. circ. 500. *3432*

OBERWEIS REPORT: A MONTHLY REVIEW.
Oberweis Asset Management, Inc., 1 Constitution Dr., Aurora, IL 60506. TEL 800-323-6166. FAX 708-896-5282. circ. 4,000. *1113*

OBLATES.
Missionary Association of Mary Immaculate, 15 S. 59th St., Belleville, IL 62223-4694. TEL 618-233-2238. circ. 500,000. *6082*

OBSERVER (ANCHORAGE).
Regional Citizens' Advisory Council of Prince William Sound, 750 W. Second Ave., No. 100, Anchorage, AK 99501-2167. TEL 907-277-7222. FAX 907-277-4523. circ. 30,000. *2839*

OBSERVER (FT. LAUDERDALE).
Broward Community College Board of Trustees, 225 E. Las Olas Blvd., Ft. Lauderdale, FL 33301. TEL 305-973-2237. FAX 305-968-2448. circ. 10,000. *1879*

OCCASIONAL PAPERS IN ENTOMOLOGY.
Department of Food and Agriculture, Division of Plant Industry, 1220 N St., Sacramento, CA 95814. TEL 916-445-5421. circ. 200. *733*

OCCUPATIONAL HAZARDS.
Penton Publishing Co. 1100 Superior Ave., Cleveland, OH 44114-2543. TEL 216-696-7000. FAX 216-696-3765. circ. 60,000. *5254*

OCEAN DRILLING PROGRAM. PROCEEDINGS, PART A: INITIAL REPORTS.
Texas A&M University, Ocean Drilling Program, 1000 Discovery Dr., College Station, TX 77845-9547. TEL 409-845-2016. FAX 409-845-4857. circ. 1,550. *2302*

OCEAN DRILLING PROGRAM. SCIENTIFIC RESULTS. PROCEEDINGS. PART B: SCIENTIFIC RESULTS.
Texas A&M University, Ocean Drilling Program, 1000 Discovery Dr., College Station, TX 77845-9547. TEL 409-845-2016. FAX 409-845-4857. circ. 1,550. *2302*

OCEAN VOICE.
International Maritime Satellite Organization, 99 City Rd., London EC1Y 4AX, England. TEL 0171-728-1000. FAX 0171-728-1044. circ. 18,684. *6844*

OCEANOGRAPHIC RESEARCH INSTITUTE. INVESTIGATIONAL REPORT.
Oceanographic Research Institute, P.O. Box 10712 Marine Parade, Durban 4056, South Africa. TEL 27-31-373536. FAX 27-31-372132. circ. 400. *817*

THE OCTAGON.
American Chemical Society, Lehigh Valley Section, 744 N. Broad St., Allentown, PA 18104. TEL 610-770-7348. FAX 610-770-7348. circ. 1,000. *1687*

ODINI.
Likuni Press and Publishing House, P.O. Box 133, Lilongwe, Malawi. TEL 265-721388. FAX 265-721141. circ. 12,000. *6190*

ODONTOLOGO.
Asociacion Odontologica Panamena, Apdo. 6777, Zona 5, Panama, Panama. TEL 507-269-1603. FAX 507-269-3749. circ. 1,000. *4650*

OESTERREICHISCHE BAUERNZEITUNG.
Baeuerlicher Presseverein, Castellezgasse 20-1, A-1020 Vienna, Austria. circ. 16,000. *141*

OESTERREICHISCHE BLASMUSIK.
Tuba Musikverlag, Steinamangererstr. 187, A-7400 Oberwart, Austria. TEL 03352-33392. FAX 03352-34130. circ. 10,000. *5184*

OESTERREICHISCHE FREIBERUFS TIERARZT.
Ostag Werbung und Verlag, Wickenburggasse 17, A-1082 Vienna, Austria. TEL 43-1-4027573. FAX 43-1-4088292. circ. 2,900. *6951*

OESTERREICHISCHE INSTALLATEURZEITUNG.
Verlag Piletzky, Nikolsdorfergasse 7, A-1050 Vienna, Austria. circ. 4,600. *3331*

OESTERREICHISCHES JUGENDROTKREUZ. ARBEITSBLAETTER.
Oesterreichisches Jugendrotkreuz, Wiedner Hauptstr. 32, A-1041 Vienna 4, Austria. FAX 43-1-58900179. circ. 10,000. *6386*

OESTERREICHISCHES STAATSARCHIV. MITTEILUNGEN.
Verlag Ferdinand Berger und Soehne GmbH, Wienerstr. 21-23, A-3580 Horn, Austria. TEL 43-2982-4161232. FAX 43-2982-2317235. circ. 500. *3433*

OFF DUTY AMERICA.
Off Duty Enterprises, 3313 Harbor Blvd., Ste. C-2, Costa Mesa, CA 92626. TEL 714-549-7172. FAX 714-549-4222. circ. 400,000. *5043*

OFFICE EQUIPMENT NEWS.
Wilmington Publishing, Wilmington House, Church Hill, Dartford, Kent UA2 7EF, England. TEL 0322-277788. FAX 0322-276476. circ. 55,236. *1495*

OFFICE MAGAZINE.
Patey Doyle (Publishing) Ltd., Wilmington House, Church Hill, Wilmington, Dartford DA2 7EF, England. circ. 55,000. *1495*

OFFICE RELOCATION MAGAZINE.
O R M Group, 600 Haverford Rd., Haverford, PA 19041. TEL 610-649-6565. FAX 610-642-8020. circ. 38,000. *1495*

OFFICERS CALL.
National Officers Association, Box 4975, Reston, VA 22090-1464. TEL 703-438-3060. FAX 703-438-3072.
circ. 24,000. *5043*

OFFICEWORLD NEWS.
B U S Publications, 366 Ramtown Greenville Rd., Howell, NJ 07731-2789. TEL 908-363-0708. FAX 908-367-2426.
circ. 34,500. *1496*

OFFICIAL BRITISH THEATRE DIRECTORY SEATING PLAN GUIDE.
Richmond House Publishing Company Ltd., Douglas House, 3 Richmond Bldgs., London W1V 5AE, England. TEL 44-171-437-9556. FAX 44-171-287-3463.
circ. 3,000. *6700*

OFFICIAL GUIDE TO HOUSTON.
Desert Publications, Inc., 303 N. Indian Canyon Dr., Box 2724, Palm Springs, CA 92262. TEL 619-325-2333. FAX 619-325-7008.
circ. 600,000. *6904*

OFFICIAL MOTOR FREIGHT - SHIPPERS GUIDE.
Official Motor Freight Guide, Inc., 1700 W. Cortland St., Chicago, IL 60622-1150. TEL 312-278-2454. FAX 312-489-0482.
circ. 1,767. *6860*

OFFICIAL VISITORS GUIDE TO CENTRAL FLORIDA.
Orlando - Orange County Convention and Visitors Bureau, Inc., 6700 Forum Dr., Ste. 100, Orlando, FL 32821-8087. TEL 407-363-5800. FAX 407-363-5899.
circ. 1,000,000. *6904*

OFFSHORE (TULSA).
PennWell Publishing Co., Box 1260, Tulsa, OK 74101. TEL 918-835-3161. FAX 918-832-9295.
circ. 35,500. *5367*

OFFSHORE FINANCIAL REVIEW.
Financial Times Business Information, Magazines 2 Greystoke Pl., Fetter Ln., London EC4A 1ND, England. TEL 0171-405-6969. FAX 0171-405-5726. *1345*

OFFSHORE VISIE.
Uitgeverij Tridens, Postbus 526, 1970 AM IJmuiden, Netherlands. TEL 31-2550-30577. FAX 31-2550-30577.
circ. 3,500. *5368*

OHIO A F L - C I O NEWS AND VIEWS.
Ohio A F L - C I O, 271 E. State St., Columbus, OH 43215. TEL 614-224-8271. FAX 614-224-2671.
circ. 11,500. *3726*

OHIO BEVERAGE JOURNAL.
Midwest Beverage Publications, Inc., 3 12th St., Wheeling, WV 26003. TEL 304-232-7620. FAX 304-233-1236.
circ. 7,125. *510*

OHIO CONTRACTOR.
Triad, Inc., 6525 Busch Blvd., Columbus, OH 43229. TEL 614-846-8761. FAX 614-846-8763.
circ. 5,500. *6824*

OHIO DEER & TURKEY SHOW PREVIEW.
Target Communications Corp., 7626 W. Donges Bay Rd., Mequon, WI 53097-3400. TEL 414-242-3990. FAX 414-242-7391.
circ. 35,000. *6571*

OHIO DENTAL JOURNAL.
Ohio Dental Association, 1370 Dublin Rd., Columbus, OH 43215-1098. TEL 614-486-2700.
circ. 5,300. *4650*

OHIO ENGINEER.
Ohio Society of Professional Engineers, 445 King Ave., Columbus, OH 43201. TEL 614-424-6640. FAX 614-421-1257.
circ. 4,000. *2613*

THE OHIO FAMILY PHYSICIAN.
Ohio Academy of Family Physicians, 4075 N. High St., Columbus, OH 43214. TEL 614-267-7867.
circ. 4,000. *4510*

OHIO GENEALOGICAL SOCIETY. WOOD COUNTY CHAPTER. NEWSLETTER.
Ohio Genealogical Society, Wood County Chapter, Box 722, Bowling Green, OH 43402. TEL 419-352-4940.
circ. 150. *3096*

OHIO GRANGER.
Ohio State Grange, 1031 E. Broad St., Columbus, OH 43205. TEL 614-258-9569.
circ. 14,500. *141*

OHIO NURSES REVIEW.
Ohio Nurses Association, 4000 E. Main St., Columbus, OH 43213-2983. TEL 614-237-5414. FAX 614-237-6074.
circ. 9,000. *4725*

OHIO STATE LANTERN.
Ohio State University, School of Journalism, c/o Lee Becker, 242 W. 18th Ave., Columbus, OH 43210. TEL 614-292-2031. FAX 614-292-3722.
circ. 30,000. *1879*

OHIO STATE UNIVERSITY. COLLEGE OF MEDICINE. JOURNAL.
Ohio State University, College of Medicine, 941 Chatham Ln., Columbus, OH 43221. TEL 614-459-3909. FAX 614-293-3666.
circ. 13,700. *4510*

OHIO STATE UNIVERSITY. SCHOOL OF PUBLIC ADMINISTRATION. WORKING PAPER SERIES.
Ohio State University, Administrative Science Research, 1775 College Rd., Columbus, OH 42310. TEL 614-422-8696. *5914*

OIL CAN.
Illinois Petroleum Marketers Association, Box 12020, Springfield, IL 62791-2020. TEL 217-544-4609. FAX 217-789-0222.
circ. 1,250. *5369*

OIL, GAS & PETROCHEM EQUIPMENT.
PennWell Publishing Co., Box 1260, Tulsa, OK 74101. TEL 918-835-3161. FAX 918-832-9295.
circ. 36,000. *5369*

OILSEEDS AND INDUSTRIAL CROPS.
Processors & Growers Research Organisation, 34 Cavendish Rd., London NW6 7XP, England. TEL 0181-459-5330.
circ. 12,000. *141*

OKLAHOMA. CONSERVATION COMMISSION. BIENNIAL REPORT.
Conservation Commission, 2800 Lincoln, Ste. 160, Oklahoma City, OK 73105. TEL 405-521-2384.
circ. 175. *2137*

OKLAHOMA DAILY.
University of Oklahoma, Student Publication Board, 860 Van Vleet, Norman, OK 73019. TEL 405-325-7565. FAX 405-325-7517.
circ. 14,500. *1879*

OKLAHOMA FARM BUREAU JOURNAL.
Oklahoma Farm Bureau, 2501 N. Stiles, Oklahoma City, OK 73105. TEL 405-273-4200. FAX 405-523-2326.
circ. 111,000. *141*

OKLAHOMA SCHOOL BOARD JOURNAL.
Oklahoma State School Boards Association, 2801 N. Lincoln Blvd., Oklahoma City, OK 73105. TEL 405-528-3571. FAX 405-528-5695.
circ. 4,600. *2359*

OLD BEN NEWS.
Newsvendors' Benevolent Institution, P.O. Box 306, Dunmow, Essex CM6 1HY, England.
circ. 46,000. *1168*

OLD YORK ROAD HISTORICAL SOCIETY BULLETIN.
Old York Road Historical Society, c/o Jenkintown Library, York and Vista Rds., Jenkintown, PA 19046. TEL 215-884-0593.
circ. 265. *3482*

ON COURT.
Fourhand II, Inc., 1200 Sheppard Ave. E., Ste. 400, Willowdale, Ont. M2K 2S5, Canada. TEL 416-497-1370. FAX 416-494-5343.
circ. 50,000. *6510*

ON THE TOWN.
On the Town Publications Inc., 705 Bagley Ave., S.E., Ste. 102, Grand Rapids, MI 49506-3001. TEL 616-451-0361. FAX 616-454-4666.
circ. 35,000. *3235*

ON TRACK (WASHINGTON).
National Railroad Construction and Maintenance Association, Inc., 122 C St., NW., Ste. 850, Washington, DC 20001-2109. FAX 202-638-1045.
circ. 1,500. *6814*

ON WALL STREET.
Securities Data Publishing, 40 W. 57th St., 11th Fl., New York, NY 10019. TEL 212-765-5311. FAX 212-765-6123.
circ. 50,000. *1345*

ONCOLOGIA.
Alpe Editores, S.A., Pedro Rico, 27, 28029 Madrid, Spain. TEL 34-1-7338811. FAX 34-1-3159652.
circ. 6,000. *4761*

ONCOLOGY.
P R R, Inc., 17 Prospect St., Huntington, NY 11743. TEL 516-424-8900. FAX 516-424-8503.
circ. 26,265. *4761*

ONCOLOGY NEWS INTERNATIONAL.
Pub. Mary Schuldner, 17 Prospect St., Huntington, NY 11743. TEL 516-424-8900. FAX 516-424-8503.
circ. 26,722. *4762*

ONDERSTEPOORT JOURNAL OF VETERINARY RESEARCH.
Agricultural Research Council, Onderstepoort Veterinary Institute, Private Bag X5, Onderstepoort 0110, South Africa. TEL 27-12-5299101. FAX 27-12-5299318.
circ. 600. *6951*

ONSEI GENGO IGAKU.
Nihon Onsei Gengo Igakkai, Hakuo Bldg., 5F, 2-3-10 Kohraku, Bunkyo-ku, Tokyo 112, Japan. FAX 03-5684-5954.
circ. 1,850. *4798*

ONTARIO BEEF.
Ontario Cattlemen's Association, 130 Malcolm Rd., Guelph, ON N1K 1B1, Canada. TEL 519-824-0334. FAX 519-824-9101.
circ. 20,931. *279*

ONTARIO GOLF NEWS.
Ontario Golf News Inc., 2 Billingham Rd., Ste. 400, Toronto, ON M9B 6E1, Canada. TEL 416-232-2380. FAX 416-232-9291.
circ. 40,000. *6510*

ONTARIO GOVERNMENT LIBRARIES COUNCIL. EXCHANGE.
Ontario Government Libraries Council, 77 Wellesley St., W., 4th Fl., Ferguson Block, Toronto, ON M7A 1N3, Canada. TEL 416-327-2535. FAX 416-327-2530.
circ. 110. *4018*

ONTARIO GRAPE GROWER.
Ontario Grape Growers' Marketing Board, Box 100, Vineland, ON L0R 2E0, Canada. TEL 905-688-0990. FAX 905-688-3211.
circ. 8,000. *233*

ONTARIO MUSEUM ANNUAL.
Ontario Museum Association, George Brown House, 50 Baldwin St., Toronto, ON M5T 1L4, Canada. TEL 416-348-8672. FAX 416-348-0438.
circ. 1,500. *5130*

ONTARION.
Ontarion, Inc., University of Guelph, University Centre, Rm. 264, Guelph, ON N1G 2W1, Canada. TEL 519-824-4120. FAX 519-824-7838.
circ. 12,000. *1880*

ONZE VOGELS.
Nederlandse Bond van Vogelliefhebbers, Postbox 74, 4600 AB Bergen Op Zoom, Netherlands. TEL 31-1640-35007. FAX 31-1640-39020.
circ. 45,000. *779*

OOST-EUROPA VERKENNINGEN.
Instituut voor Publiek en Politiek, Prinsengracht 911-915, 1017 KD Amsterdam, Netherlands. TEL 31-20-5217600. FAX 31-20-6383118.
circ. 1,000. *5765*

OP CIT.
Waterstone's Publications, 26 Exeter St., Boston, MA 02116. TEL 617-859-8030. FAX 617-437-0997. circ. 25,000. *4159*

OP OOGHOOGTE.
Stichting Oogkamp Himalaya, Postbus 174, 2110 AD Aerdenhout, Netherlands. TEL 31-23-5290073. FAX 31-23-5286922. circ. 20,000. *4774*

OPEN DEUR.
Boekencentrum B.V., Postbus 29, 2700 AA Zoetermeer, Netherlands. TEL 31-79-615481. FAX 31-79-615489. *6154*

OPERNWELT.
Friedrich Kulturzeitschriftenverlag, Luetzowplatz 7, 10785 Berlin, Germany. TEL 49-30-254495-0. FAX 49-30-25449512. circ. 10,000. *5185*

LA OPINION.
Avda. 4, 16-12, Cucuta, N. de S., Colombia. TEL 75-719999. FAX 75-717869. circ. 1,500. *3131*

OPINION.
Opinion Publications, Box 681, Cape May Court House, NJ 08210-0681. circ. 3,700. *5488*

OPPORTUNITIES FOR THEATRE STAFF & OTHER SPECIALISTS.
Newton Mann Ltd., Stretton Rd., Tansley Matlock, Derbyshire DE4 5GE, England. TEL 44-1629-583941. FAX 44-1629-580479. circ. 5,000. *4725*

OPPORTUNITIES IN OPTIONS.
Box 2126, Malibu, CA 90265. FAX 310-456-3703. circ. 2,500. *1345*

OPPORTUNITY MAGAZINE.
Ashlee Publishing, 18 E. 41st St., New York, NY 10017. TEL 212-376-7722. FAX 212-376-7723. *1481*

OPTICAL PRISM.
VezCom Inc., 31 Hastings Dr., Unionville, ON L3R 4Y5, Canada. TEL 905-475-9343. FAX 905-477-2821. circ. 7,368. *4775*

OPTIMUM.
Canada Communication Group, Publishing Division, Ottawa, ON K1A 0S9, Canada. TEL 819-956-4802. circ. 1,200. *1438*

OPTIONS.
International Institute for Applied Systems Analysis, A-2361 Laxenburg, Austria. TEL 43-2236-807-0. FAX 43-2236-73149. circ. 8,000. *2083*

OPUNTIA.
Speirs Publishing, P.O. Box 6830, Calgary, AB T2P 2E7, Canada. circ. 100. *4330*

OPUS DEI AWARENESS NETWORK.
Opus Dei Awareness Network, Inc., Box 4333, Pittsfield, MA 01202. TEL 413-499-7168. FAX 413-499-7860. *6190*

ORANGE SEED TECHNICAL BULLETIN.
Department of State, Division of Library and Information Services, R.A. Gray Bldg., Tallahassee, FL 32399-0250. TEL 904-487-2651. FAX 904-488-2746. circ. 1,200. *4018*

ORBIT MAGAZINE.
Popular Amusement, Inc., 919 S. Main, No. 2001, Royal Oak, MI 48067. TEL 810-541-3900. FAX 810-541-4054. circ. 55,000. *3966*

ORD & BILD.
Stiftelsen Ord&Bild, P.O. Box 2390, S-403 16 Goeteborg, Sweden. TEL 46-31-774-17-40. FAX 46-31-701-70-60. circ. 8,000. *4159*

OREGON BUSINESS NETWORK NEWS.
Oregon Business Network, Box 5488, Portland, OR 97219. TEL 503-244-2689. FAX 503-618-8771. circ. 21,000. *949*

OREGON PSYCHOLOGY.
Oregon Psychological Association, 147 S.E. 102nd Ave., Portland, OR 97216-2703. circ. 700. *5868*

OREGON PUBLISHER.
Oregon Newspaper Publishers Association, 7150 S.W. Hampton St., Ste. 111, Portland, OR 97223. TEL 503-624-6397. FAX 503-639-9009. circ. 400. *6004*

OREGON PURCHASOR.
Purchasing Management Association of Oregon, c/o Decorators West, Box 25191, Portland, OR 97225-0191. TEL 503-245-2296. circ. 2,200. *1481*

OREGON QUARTERLY.
University of Oregon, 5228 University of Oregon, Eugene, OR 97403-5228. TEL 503-346-5047. FAX 503-346-2220. circ. 100,000. *1880*

OREGON WHEAT.
Oregon Wheat Growers League, 202 S.E. Dorion, Box 400, Pendleton, OR 97801. TEL 503-276-7330. FAX 503-276-1723. circ. 6,050. *260*

ORGAN CLUB JOURNAL.
Organ Club, c/o Philip Weston, Gen. Sec., 36 Fortismere Ave., London N10 3BL, England. *5186*

ORGANIC CONSUMER REPORT.
Eden Ranch, Box 370, Topanga, CA 90290. TEL 213-455-2065. *5240*

ORGANICA.
Organica Press, 4419 N. Manhattan Ave., Tampa, FL 33614. TEL 813-877-4186. FAX 813-876-8166. circ. 200,000. *4247*

ORIENTAL COLLEGE MAGAZINE.
Punjab University, Oriental College, Lahore, Pakistan. TEL 311496. circ. 500. *4247*

ORION (CHICO).
California State University, Chico, College of Communication, Department of Journalism, Chico, CA 95929-0600. TEL 916-898-5625. FAX 916-898-4839. circ. 10,000. *1880*

ORITA.
University of Ibadan, Department of Religious Studies, Ibadan, Oyo State, Nigeria. circ. 500. *6082*

ORIZZONTE SICILIA.
Banca Popolare Sant'Angelo, Via Ruggiero VII, no.78, 90141 Palermo, Italy. TEL 39-91-332922. FAX 39-91-584923. *1228*

ORNIS FENNICA.
Finnish Ornithological Society, University of Helsinki, Department of Ecology and Systematics, Division of Population Biology, P.O. Box 17, SF-00014 Helsinki, Finland. TEL 358-81-5531214. FAX 358-81-5531227. circ. 1,200. *779*

OSMANIA UNIVERSITY. DEPARTMENT OF PSYCHOLOGY. RESEARCH BULLETIN.
Osmania University, Department of Psychology, Hyderabad 500007, Andhra Pradesh, India. *5868*

THE OSWEGONIAN.
State University of New York, Oswego, 216 Hewitt Union, Oswego, NY 13126. TEL 315-341-3600. circ. 7,500. *1880*

OTECHESTVENNAYA GEOLOGIYA.
Varshavskoe Shosse., 129B, 113545 Moscow, Russia. TEL 7-95-3152847. FAX 7-95-3152701. circ. 1,000. *2256*

OTIS RUSH.
S A Publishing Ventures and Futures, P.O. Box 21, North Adelaide, S. Australia 5006, Australia. TEL 61-8-2117505. FAX 61-8-2117323. circ. 450. *4313*

OTTERBEIN MISCELLANY.
Otterbein College, Westerville, OH 43081. TEL 614-890-3000. circ. 300. *4159*

OUR HERITAGE.
Genealogical Society of Van Zandt County, Box 715, Canton, TX 75103-0716. TEL 903-567-5012. circ. 425. *3097*

OUR VOICE (CLEVELAND).
American Mutual Life Association, 19424 S. Waterloo Rd., Cleveland, OH 44119-3250. circ. 8,500. *3661*

OUT AND ABOUT SMITH MOUNTAIN LAKE.
Rte. 1, Box 437, Moneta, VA 24121. TEL 703-297-6444. circ. 40,000. *6905*

OUTDOOR OKLAHOMA.
Department of Wildlife Conservation, 1801 N. Lincoln, Oklahoma City, OK 73105. TEL 405-521-3855. FAX 405-521-3535. circ. 21,500. *2138*

OUTDOOR RETAILER.
Pacifica Publishing Corporation, 310 Broadway, Laguna Beach, CA 92551. TEL 714-376-8155. FAX 714-497-2093. circ. 16,191. *6572*

OUTDOOR TRADE AND INDUSTRY.
97 Front St., Whickham, Newcastle-upon-Tyne NE16 4JL, England. *6572*

OUTERWEAR.
Fur Publishing Plus, Inc., 19 W. 21st St., Ste. 403, New York, NY 10010. TEL 212-727-1210. circ. 15,000. *1836*

OUTLOOK.
General Conference of the New Church, c/o G.S. Kuphal, 20 Red Barn Rd., Brightlingsea, Colchester, Essex CO7 OSH, England. TEL 44-1206-302932. circ. 2,000. *6210*

OUTLOOK (WAKE FOREST).
Southeastern Baptist Theological Seminary, Inc., Wake Forest, NC 27587. TEL 919-556-3101. FAX 919-556-8550. circ. 13,000. *6155*

OUTLOOK MAGAZINE.
Summer and Casual Furniture Manufacturers Association, 223 S. Wrenn St., HP-7, High Point, NC 27261. TEL 910-884-5000. FAX 910-884-5303. circ. 7,000. *3691*

OUTREACH (NEW YORK).
Armenian Apostolic Church of America, 138 E. 39th St., New York, NY 10016. TEL 212-689-7810. FAX 212-689-7168. circ. 10,500. *6210*

OVERALL THERE IS A SMELL OF FRIED ONIONS.
P.O. Box 73, West PDO, Nottingham NG7 4DG, England. TEL 44-115-953-8333. FAX 44-115-953-8333. circ. 5,000. *5110*

OVERTURE.
Winnipeg Symphony Orchestra, 101-555 Main St., Winnipeg, MB R3B 1C3, Canada. TEL 204-949-3950. FAX 204-956-1271. circ. 14,000. *5186*

OVERVIEW (WOODRIDGE).
Overview Ltd., Box 211, Woodridge, NJ 07075. circ. 450. *4313*

OXFORD REVIEW.
Oxford Books, Inc., 360 Pharr Rd., N.E., Atlanta, GA 30305. TEL 404-262-3333. circ. 227,000. *4159*

OXFORDSHIRE LOCAL HISTORY.
Oxfordshire Local History Association, c/o Dr. F.B. Atkins, 8 Thornbury Rd., Eynsham, Oxon OX8 1PW, England. circ. 300. *3433*

P C DISTRIBUTOR.
Empresar Editores Ltda., Carrera 11, No. 94-02, L-123, Bogota, Colombia. TEL 2182730. FAX 610-1958. circ. 5,000. *2099*

P C I A JOURNAL.
Personal Communications Industry Association, 500 Montgomery St., Ste. 700, Alexandria, VA 22314-1560.
circ. 3,500. *1948*

P C MAGAZINE.
Gruppo Editoriale Jackson S.p.A., Via M. Gorki 69, 20092 Cinisello B. (MI), Italy. TEL 39-2-66034309. FAX 39-2-66034290.
circ. 35,105. *2099*

P C MICRO MAGAZINE.
Ecopress S.A., Rue Gabrielle 114, 1180 Brussels, Belgium. FAX 32-2-3442451.
circ. 15,000. *2100*

P C REPORT.
Boston Computer Society, IBM PC Users Group, 101 First Ave., No. 2, Waltham, MA 02154-1160. TEL 617-290-5700.
circ. 16,000. *2100*

P C SPECIAL MONTHLY.
Interface Electronic Publisher, Flat 8, 13th Fl., Yeung Yiu Chung no.8, Ind. Bldg., 20 Wang Hoi Rd., Kowloon Bay, Kowloon, Hong Kong. TEL 3-7955582. FAX 3-7952962. *2100*

P C WEEK.
Ziff-Davis Publishing Co. (Medford), One Park Ave., New York, NY 10016-5146. TEL 212-503-5100.
circ. 128,277. *2101*

P C WEEK ASIA.
Newsources Investments Ltd., 1501 Shiu Lam Bldg., 23 Luard Rd., Wanchai, Hong Kong. TEL 5284808. FAX 8656832.
circ. 21,429. *2101*

P E I T F NEWSLETTER.
Prince Edward Island Teachers Federation, P.O. Box 6000, Charlottetown, PE C1A 8B4, Canada. TEL 902-569-4157. FAX 902-569-3682.
circ. 2,400. *2360*

P F I WORLD REPORT.
Prison Fellowship International, Box 17434, Washington, DC 20041. TEL 703-481-0000. FAX 703-481-0003.
circ. 6,500. *6082*

P G A PROFILE.
In Focus Publishing, 52 Mere Green Rd., Sutton Coldfield, W. Midlands B75 5BT, England. TEL 021-323-3073. FAX 021-323-2911.
circ. 5,500. *6511*

P G W NEWSLINE.
Philadelphia Gas Works, 800 W. Montgomery Ave., Philadelphia, PA 19122. TEL 215-684-6564.
circ. 4,500. *5370*

P H - O FORUM.
P H - O Forum, c/o King - Drew Medical Center, Rm. 5101, 12021 S. Wilmington Ave., Los Angeles, CA 90059. TEL 310-668-3850. FAX 310-668-3108.
circ. 2,200. *4809*

P I M A MAGAZINE.
Paper Industry Management Association, 1699 Wall St., Ste. 212, Mt. Prospect, IL 60056-5782. TEL 847-956-0250. FAX 847-956-0520.
circ. 16,611. *5323*

P L I WARWICK JOURNAL OF PHILISOPHY.
University of Warwick, Department of Philosophy, Coventry CV4 7AL, England. TEL 44-1203-523421. FAX 44-1203-523019.
circ. 400. *5489*

P O B - POINT OF BEGINNING.
Business News Publishing Co., 755 W. Big Beaver, Ste. 1000, Troy, MI 48084. TEL 810-362-3700. FAX 610-362-0317.
circ. 54,000. *2670*

P P O UPDATE.
Lippincott - Raven Publishers 227 E. Washington Sq., Philadelphia, PA 19106. TEL 215-238-4200.
circ. 25,000. *4762*

P S.
Editorial Perpetuo Socorro, Covarrubias, 19, 28010 Madrid, Spain.
circ. 14,000. *6083*

P S A C UNION UPDATE.
Public Service Alliance of Canada, 233 Gilmour St., Ottawa, ON K2P 0P1, Canada. TEL 613-560-4241. FAX 613-236-1654.
circ. 30,000. *3726*

P S A INDUSTRIAL BULLETIN.
Public Service Association of New South Wales, G.P.O. Box 3365, Sydney, N.S.W. 2001, Australia. TEL 61-2-290-1555. FAX 61-2-262-1623.
circ. 7,000. *3726*

P S A REPORTER.
Public Service Association of New South Wales, G.P.O. Box 3365, Sydney, N.S.W. 2001, Australia. TEL 61-2-290-1555. FAX 61-2-262-1623.
circ. 7,000. *3726*

P S B A BULLETIN.
Pennsylvania School Boards Association, 774 Limekiln Rd., New Cumberland, PA 17070-2398. TEL 717-774-2331. FAX 717-774-0718.
circ. 11,300. *2461*

P S I NACHRICHTEN.
Praesent Service Institut, Neusserstr. 111, 40219 Duesseldorf, Germany. TEL 49-211-901910. FAX 49-211-9019125.
circ. 6,300. *43*

P T DISTRIBUTOR.
Penton Publishing Co. 1100 Superior Ave., Cleveland, OH 44114-2543. TEL 216-696-7000. FAX 216-696-8765.
circ. 10,000. *2766*

P T I C BULLETIN.
Patent and Trademark Institute of Canada, Box 1298, Sta. B, Ottawa, ON K1P 5R3, Canada. TEL 613-234-0516. *5342*

P T N MASTER BUYING GUIDE & DIRECTORY.
P T N Publishing Corp., 445 Broad Hollow Rd., Ste. 21, Melville, NY 11747-4722. TEL 516-845-2700. FAX 516-845-7109.
circ. 10,000. *5516*

P T S NEWS.
Philatelic Traders Society Ltd., British Philatelic Centre, 107 Charterhouse St., London EC1M 6PT, England. TEL 0171-490-1005. FAX 0171-253-0414. *5460*

P T TODAY.
Valley Forge Press, 1288 Valley Forge Rd., Ste. 50, Box 1135, Valley Forge, PA 19482. TEL 610-935-3302. FAX 610-935-3072.
circ. 50,000. *4818*

PAA KRYSS TILL RORS.
Svenska Kryssarklubben, Karlavagen 67, S-114 49 Stockholm, Sweden. TEL 46-8-663-18-60. FAX 46-8-662-95-18.
circ. 40,000. *6538*

PACIFIC COAST NURSERYMAN AND GARDEN SUPPLY DEALER.
Cox Publishing Co., 306 W. Foothill Blvd., Box 1477, Glendora, CA 91740. TEL 818-914-3916. FAX 818-914-3751.
circ. 10,200. *3064*

PACIFIC ECHO.
Neighbors of Woodcraft, Box 769, Oregon City, OR 97045-0052. TEL 503-224-3525. FAX 503-223-5140.
circ. 10,000. *1852*

PACIFIC HOSTELLER.
Canadian Hostelling Association, B.C. Region, 1515 Discovery St., Vancouver, B.C. V6R 4K5, Canada. TEL 604-224-7177. FAX 604-224-4852.
circ. 10,000. *6905*

PACK NEWS & MECHNICAL HANDLING NEWS.
Kluwer Business Press Kouterveldstraat 2, 1831 Diegem, Belgium. TEL 32-2-7231111. FAX 32-2-7231512.
circ. 9,500. *5302*

PACKAGING DIGEST EDICION LATINO AMERICANA.
Cahners Publishing Company (Des Plaines), Division of Reed Elsevier Inc., 1350 E. Touhy Ave., Box 5080, Des Plaines, IL 60018-5080. TEL 847-390-2363. FAX 847-390-2460.
circ. 30,584. *5302*

PACKAGING DIGEST MACHINERY - MATERIALS GUIDE.
Cahners Publishing Company (Des Plaines), Division of Reed Elsevier Inc., 1350 E. Touhy Ave., Box 5080, Des Plaines, IL 60611. TEL 847-635-8800. FAX 847-390-2460.
circ. 109,000. *5302*

PACKAGING DIGEST MARKETPLACE EDITION.
Cahners Publishing Comany (Des Plaines), Division of Reed Elsevier Inc., 1350 E. Touhy Ave., Box 5080, Des Plaines, IL 60018-5080. TEL 847-390-2363. FAX 847-635-6856.
circ. 150,000. *5302*

PACKPLAS INTERNATIONAL.
International Printing Communications Ltd., P.O. Box 923, Crownhill Industry, Milton Keynes, Cambs. MK8 0AY, England. TEL 44-1908-561444. FAX 44-1908-569564.
circ. 14,000. *5303*

PADOVA ECONOMICA.
Camera di Commercio, Industria, Artigianato e Agricoltura di Padova, Via E. Filiberto 34, Padua, Italy.
circ. 2,000. *1147*

PAEDAGOGISCHE HOCHSCHULE WEINGARTEN. PERSONEN- UND VORLESUNGSVERZEICHNIS.
Paedagogische Hochschule Weingarten, Kirchplatz 2, 88250 Weingarten, Germany. TEL 49-751-501240. FAX 49-751-501200.
circ. 2,500. *1880*

PAGAN DAWN.
Pagan Federation, BM Box 7097, London WC1N 3XX, England. TEL 44-181-891-1302.
circ. 4,500. *6210*

PAINOMAAILMA.
Painomaailma Oy, Loennrotinkatu 11 A, FIN-00120 Helsinki, Finland. TEL 358-0-2287-7242. FAX 358-0-603-914.
circ. 3,200. *5815*

PAINTING AND WALLCOVERING CONTRACTOR.
Finan Publishing Company, Inc., 8730 Big Bend Blvd., St. Louis, MO 63119. TEL 314-961-6644. FAX 314-961-4809.
circ. 31,000. *5309*

PAKISTAN. FINANCE DIVISION. SUPPLEMENTARY DEMANDS FOR GRANTS AND APPROPRIATIONS.
Finance Division, Islamabad, Pakistan. *1558*

PAKISTAN. OFFICE OF THE ECONOMIC ADVISER. GOVERNMENT SPONSORED CORPORATIONS AND OTHER INSTITUTIONS.
Office of the Economic Adviser, Islamabad, Pakistan. *1528*

PAKISTAN JOURNAL OF BOTANY.
Pakistan Botanical Society, Dept. of Botany, University of Karachi, Karachi 75270, Pakistan. TEL 92-21-447867. FAX 92-21-466896.
circ. 1,000. *695*

PAKISTAN JOURNAL OF HYDROCARBON RESEARCH.
Hydrocarbon Development Institute of Pakistan, 230 Nizamuddin Rd. F 7-4, P.O. Box 1308, Islamabad, Pakistan. TEL 92-51-823690. FAX 92-51-828773.
circ. 500. *5370*

PAKISTAN JOURNAL OF NEMATOLOGY.
Pakistan Nematological Society, National Nematological Research Centre, University of Karachi, Karachi 75270, Pakistan. FAX 92-21-466896.
circ. 600. *817*

PAKISTAN MANAGEMENT REVIEW.
Pakistan Institute of Management, Shahrah-Iran, Clifton, Karachi 6, Pakistan.
circ. 2,000. *1439*

PAKISTAN TEXTILE JOURNAL.
Mazhar Yusuf, Ed. & Pub., 304 Shaheen Centre, Kehkashan, Main Clifton Rd., Karachi, Pakistan. TEL 534792. FAX 572231.
circ. 2,200. *6683*

PALAEONTOLOGIA AFRICANA.
University of the Witwatersrand, Johannesburg, Bernard Price Institute for Palaeontological Research, Wits 2050, South Africa. TEL 27-11-7162870. FAX 27-11-4031423.
circ. 600. *5316*

PALAESTRA.
Via Tiglio S. Biagio, Maddaloni 81024, Italy.
circ. 1,000. *4248*

PALEORIENT.
C N R S Editions, 20-22 rue St. Amand, 75015 Paris, France. TEL 45-33-16-00. FAX 45-33-92-13.
circ. 1,500. *5317*

PALLIATIVE CARE TODAY.
C C T Healthcare Communications Ltd., 50-52 Union St., London SE1 1TD, England. TEL 0171-407-9731. FAX 0171-407-7083.
circ. 8,000. *4762*

PALMER VIDEO MAGAZINE.
Palmer Video Corp., 1767 Morris Ave., Union, NJ 07083. TEL 908-686-3030. FAX 908-686-2151.
circ. 203,915. *1977*

PALMETTO.
Florida Native Plant Society, Box 6116, Spring Hill, FL 34606-0906. TEL 407-856-2366.
circ. 2,800. *3064*

PANGOLIN PAPERS.
Turtle Press, Box 241, Nordland, WA 98358.
TEL 360-385-3626.
circ. 500. *4160*

PANNONISCHE FORSCHUNGSSTELLE OBERSCHUETZEN. ARBEITSBERICHTE - MITTEILUNGEN.
Pannonische Forschungsstelle Oberschuetzen, Postfach 12, A-7432 Oberschuetzen, Austria.
TEL 03353-669340.
circ. 500. *5187*

PAPER AGE.
Global Publications, 77 Waldron Ave., Glen Rock, NJ 07452-2830. TEL 201-666-2262. FAX 201-666-9046.
circ. 31,400. *5323*

PAPER, FILM AND FOIL CONVERTER.
Intertec Publishing Corp., 29 N. Wacker Dr., Chicago, IL 60606. TEL 312-726-2802. FAX 312-726-2574.
circ. 39,737. *5304*

PAPERWORKER.
United Paperworkers International Union, 3340 Perimeter Hill Dr., Box 1475, Nashville, TN 37202. TEL 615-834-8590. FAX 615-333-6667.
circ. 290,000. *3726*

PAPERWORLD.
American Papermaker, 57 Executive Park South, N.E., No. 30o, Atlanta, GA 30329-2213. TEL 404-841-3333. FAX 404-841-3332.
circ. 40,000. *5324*

PAPUA NEW GUINEA NATIONAL BIBLIOGRAPHY.
Papua New Guinea National Library Service, P.O. Box 5770, Boroko, N.C.D., Papua New Guinea.
FAX 675-3251331.
circ. 280. *543*

PARABAS.
21-B, Quarter-6D, Chittaranjan, West Bengal, India.
4160

PARALLELOGRAM INTERNATIONAL.
Fitzroy Publishing Ltd., 46 Old Compton St., London W1V 5BP, England. TEL 0171-437-7005.
FAX 0171-434-2225.
circ. 4,250. *2079*

PARENTS NEWS.
10 The Manor Dr., Worcester Park, Surrey KT4 7LG, England. TEL 44-181-337-6337. FAX 44-181-715-2842.
circ. 50,000. *1775*

PARISH AND COMMUNITY LIBRARIES NEWS.
Catholic Library Association, Parish Section, Box 16321, St. Paul, MN 55116. FAX 612-690-2131.
circ. 350. *4019*

PARISH MAGAZINE - ARTHUR CONAN DOYLE SOCIETY.
Arthur Conan Doyle Society, c/o Christopher Roden, Ashcroft, 2 Abbotsford Dr., Penyffordd, Ches. CH4 0JG, England. TEL 44-1244-545210.
circ. 350. *4298*

PARK-NICOLLET INSTITUTE FOR RESEARCH AND EDUCATION BULLETIN.
Park Nicollet Medical Center, 5000 W. 39th St, Minneapolis, MN 55416. TEL 612-993-3123.
circ. 9,000. *4513*

PARKING.
National Parking Association, 1112 16th St. N.W., Ste. 300, Washington, DC 20036. TEL 202-296-4336. FAX 202-331-8523.
circ. 5,000. *6798*

PARKING TECHNOLOGY.
Witter Publishing Co., Inc., 84 Park Ave., Flemington, NJ 08822. TEL 908-788-0343.
FAX 908-788-3782.
circ. 25,000. *6725*

PAROISSES ET COMMUNES DE FRANCE.
C N R S Editions, 20-22 rue St. Amand, 75015 Paris, France. TEL 45-33-16-00. FAX 45-33-92-13.
circ. 1,50C. *3434*

PARTICIPATION.
International Political Science Association, c/o University College Dublin, Department of Politics, Belfield, Dublin 4, Ireland. TEL 01-7068182. FAX 01-7061171. *5691*

PASS HERALD LTD.
Crowswest Mall, Blairmore, AB TOK OEO, Canada. TEL 403-562-2248. FAX 403-562-8379.
circ. 1,255. *3124*

THE PASSING SHOW.
Shubert Archive, 149 W. 45th St., New York, NY 10036. TEL 212-944-3895. FAX 212-944-4139.
circ. 3,000. *6700*

PASSPORT.
Briercrest Family of Schools, 510 College Dr., Caronport, SK SOH OSO, Canada. TEL 306-756-3200. FAX 306-756-3366.
circ. 27,000. *1881*

PASTE-UP.
Cedar Rapids Stamp Club, Box 2554, Cedar Rapids, IA 52406.
circ. 50. *5460*

PATENT AND TRADEMARK INSTITUTE OF CANADA. ANNUAL PROCEEDINGS.
Patent and Trademark Institute of Canada, Box 1298, Sta. B, Ottawa, ON K1P 5R3, Canada.
TEL 613-234-0516. *5343*

PATHWAYS TO HEALTH.
A.R.E. Medical Clinic, 4018 N. 40th St., Phoenix, AZ 85018. TEL 602-955-0551.
circ. 3,500. *5489*

PATIENT OUTCOMES.
Williams & Wilkins, 351 W. Camden St., Baltimore, MD 21201. TEL 410-528-4000. FAX 410-528-4312.
circ. 55,000. *4514*

PATINAGRAM.
Potomac Antique Tools and Industries Association, 13004 Clarion Rd., Ft. Washington, MD 20744. TEL 301-292-1606.
circ. 360. *334*

PATOLOGIA.
Obsidiana Editores, S.A., Czda. de Tlalpan 2365, Col. Ciudad Jardin, 04370 Mexico DF, Mexico.
TEL 6899133.
circ. 1,370. *600*

PATRIOT.
Runaway Publications, Box 1172, Ashland, OR 97520-0040. TEL 503-482-2578.
circ. 100. *4314*

PAYLOAD ASIA.
Asian Media Services Ltd., P.O. Box 3580, GPO Hong Kong, Hong Kong. TEL 852-893-3676. FAX 852-893-3676.
circ. 12,500. *6763*

PEABODY NEWS.
Johns Hopkins University, Peabody Institute, 1 E. Mt. Vernon Place, Baltimore, MD 21202-2397. TEL 301-659-8163. FAX 301-783-8576.
circ. 25,000. *188.*

PEABODY REFLECTOR.
George Peabody College for Teachers, Alumni Association, Box 161, Nashville, TN 37203.
TEL 615-322-2601.
circ. 25,000. *1881*

PEACE CORPS TIMES.
U.S. Peace Corps, 1990 K St., N.W., Washington, DC 20526. TEL 202-254-3371. FAX 202-606-3110.
circ. 19,000. *1313*

PEACE GAZETTE.
Mount Diablo Peace Center, 55 Eckley Ln., Walnut Creek, CA 94596.
circ. 2,500. *5691*

PEANUT FARMER.
Specialized Agricultural Publications, Inc., 3000 Highwoods Blvd., Ste. 300, Raleigh, NC 27604-1029. TEL 919-872-5040. FAX 919-872-6531.
circ. 20,000. *233*

THE PEANUT GROWER.
Vance Publishing Corporation, Box 83, Tifton, GA 31793. TEL 912-386-8591. FAX 912-386-9772.
circ. 25,000. *234*

PEARLS OF WISDOM.
Summit Lighthouse, Box 5000, Corwin Springs, MT 59030-5000. TEL 406-222-8300. FAX 406-222-8307. *5489*

PEAT ABSTRACTS.
Bord na Mona, Peat Research Centre, Droichead Nua, Co. Kildare, Ireland. TEL 045-31201.
FAX 045-33240.
circ. 210. *5084*

PEDIATRIA MODERNA.
Grupo Editorial Moreira Jr., Rua Henrique Martins 493, 04504 Sao Paulo SP, Brazil. TEL 884-9911. FAX 884-9993.
circ. 12,000. *4810*

PEDIATRICIAN.
E P I Inc., 8003 Old York Rd., Elkins Park, PA 19117. TEL 215-635-1700.
circ. 10,565. *4812*

PEDIATRIKA.
Alpe Editores, S.A., Pedro Rico, 27, 28029 Madrid, Spain. TEL 34-1-7338811. FAX 34-1-3159652.
circ. 6,500. *4813*

PEDOLOGIST.
Japanese Society of Pedology, c/o National Institute of Agro-Environmental Sciences, 3-1-1 Kannondai, Tsukuba, Ibaraki 305, Japan. TEL 0298-38-8275. FAX 0298-38-8199.
circ. 700. *234*

PENMEN'S NEWS LETTER.
Eileen Richardson, Ed. & Pub., 34 Broadway Ave., Ottawa, ON K1S 2V6, Canada. TEL 613-232-3014.
circ. 300. *2362*

PENN LINES.
Pennsylvania Rural Electric Association, Box 1266, 212 Locust St., Harrisburg, PA 17108. TEL 717-233-5704. FAX 717-234-1309.
circ. 176,000. *3235*

PENNSYLVANIA. CRIME COMMISSION. REPORT.
Crime Commission, 1800 Elmerton Ave., 3rd Fl., Harrisburg, PA 17110-9718. TEL 215-834-1164. FAX 215-834-0737.
circ. 40,000. *2171*

PENNSYLVANIA A F L - C I O NEWS.
c/o David H. Wilderman, Dir., 230 State St., Harrisburg, PA 17101. TEL 717-238-9351. FAX 717-238-8541.
circ. 10,000. *3726*

PENNSYLVANIA DEER & TURKEY SHOW PREVIEW.
Target Communications Corp., 7526 W. Donges Bay Rd., Mequon, WI 53097-3400. TEL 414-242-3990. FAX 414-242-7391.
circ. 35,000. *6572*

PENNSYLVANIA LAWYER.
Pennsylvania Bar Association, 100 South St., Harrisburg, PA 17108. TEL 717-238-6715. FAX 717-238-7182.
circ. 30,000. *3832*

PENNSYLVANIA MESSAGE.
Pennsylvania Association for Retarded Citizens, Inc., 2001 N. Front St., Ste. 221, Harrisburg, PA 17102-2104. FAX 717-234-7615.
circ. 8,500. *2473*

PENNSYLVANIA OSTEOPATHIC MEDICAL ASSOCIATION. JOURNAL.
Pennsylvania Osteopathic Medical Association, 1330 Eisenhower Blvd., Harrisburg, PA 17111. TEL 717-939-9318. FAX 717-939-7255.
circ. 3,400. *4514*

PENNSYLVANIA SCHOOLMASTER.
Pennsylvania Association of Secondary School Principals, 801 N. Second St., Harrisburg, PA 17102-3297. TEL 717-233-3001.
circ. 3,200. *2362*

PENNTRUX.
Pennsylvania Motor Truck Association, 910 Linda Ln, Camp Hill, PA 17011-6401. TEL 717-761-7122. FAX 717-761-8434.
circ. 2,500. *6860*

THE PENSION ACTUARY.
American Society of Pension Actuaries, 4350 N. Fairfax Dr., Ste. 820, Arlington, VA 22203-1619. TEL 703-516-9300. FAX 703-519-9308.
circ. 4,200. *3661*

PEOPLE AND THE PLANET.
Planet 21, 1 Woburn Walk, London WC1H 0JJ, England. TEL 44-171-383-4388. FAX 44-171-388-2398.
circ. 20,000. *5789*

PEPEROMIA AND EXOTIC PLANT SOCIETY. GAZETTE.
Peperomia and Exotic Plant Society, 4278 N. Hazel St., Apt. 8C, Chicago, IL 60613.
circ. 75. *3064*

PEPPER 'N SALT.
Standard Schnauzer Club of America, 1884 W. Lake Storey Rd., Galesburg, IL 61401. TEL 309-344-1140.
circ. 600. *5393*

PERCEPTIVE REPORT.
Perceptive Marketers Agency, Ltd., 1100 E. Hector St., Ste. 301, Conshohocken, PA 19428. TEL 610-825-8710. FAX 610-825-9186.
circ. 500. *1481*

PERFORMANCE.
Phillips Petroleum Co. UK Ltd., 35 Guildford Rd., Woking, Surrey GU22 7QT, England. TEL 01483-752657. FAX 01483-752607.
circ. 5,000. *5370*

PERFORMANCE FOR THE CHRYSLER CAR ENTHUSIAST.
R H O Publications, 1580 Hampton Rd., Bensalem, PA 19020-4610. TEL 215-639-4456.
circ. 60,000. *6798*

PERFORMER.
National Ballet of Canada, 157 King St., E., Toronto, ON M5C 1G9, Canada. TEL 416-362-1041. FAX 416-368-7443.
circ. 12,500. *2190*

PERFORMING ARTS.
Performing Arts Network, 10350 Santa Monica Blvd., Ste. 350, Los Angeles, CA 90025. TEL 310-839-8000. FAX 310-839-5651.
circ. 700,000. *6700*

PERFUMERY.
I C O International, 3A Barbanou, P.O. Box 190 25, 117 10 Athens, Greece. TEL 30-1-9017-806. FAX 30-1-9016-663.
circ. 10,000. *497*

LOS PERROS DEL MUNDO.
Publitecnic S.A., Calle 4, no. 188, Apdo. Postal 74-290, 09070 Mexico DF, Mexico. TEL 685-28-19. FAX 67-06318.
circ. 10,000. *5393*

PERSONAL ENGINEERING & INSTRUMENTATION NEWS.
P E C Inc., Box 430, Rye, NH 03870-0430. TEL 603-427-1377. FAX 603-427-1388.
circ. 50,000. *2102*

PERSPECTIVAS EM CIENCIA DA INFORMACAO.
Universidade Federal de Minas Gerais, Escola de Biblioteconomia, Caixa Postal 1606, 30161-970 Belo Horizonte MG, Brazil. TEL 55-31-4995227. FAX 55-31-4995200.
circ. 800. *4019*

PERSPECTIVE (INDIANAPOLIS).
Resort Condominiums International, Inc., Box 80229, Indianapolis, IN 46280-0229. TEL 317-871-9641. FAX 317-871-9507.
circ. 7,000. *6032*

PERSPECTIVES.
Chambre Francaise de Commerce et d'Industrie de Madrid, C. Ruiz de Alarcon, 7, 28014 Madrid, Spain. TEL 34-1-5226742. FAX 34-1-5233642.
circ. 2,200. *1147*

PERSPECTIVES ON MEDICAL RESEARCH.
Medical Research Modernization Committee, Box 2751, New York, NY 10163. TEL 216-832-3904. FAX 216-283-6702.
circ. 1,200. *4684*

PESARO CITTA E CONTA.
Societa Pesarese di Studi Storici, Via Abbati 30, Casella 9, 61100 Pesaro, Italy. TEL 39-721-34411.
circ. 800. *3434*

PESQUISA AGROPECUARIA BRASILEIRA.
Empresa Brasileira de Pesquisa Agropecuaria, Servico de Producao e Informacao, Caixa Postal 040315, 70770-901 Brasilia D.F., Brazil. TEL 55-62-3484236. FAX 55-61-2724168.
circ. 1,600. *144*

PESQUISA MEDICA.
Fundacao Faculdade Federal de Ciencias Medicas de Porto Alegre, Centro Academico XXII de Marco, Rua Sarmento Leite, 245, 90050-170 Porto Alegre RS, Brazil. TEL 55-512-2248822. FAX 55-512-2267913.
circ. 1,000. *4515*

PEST MANAGEMENT.
National Pest Control Association, 8100 Oak St., Dunn Loring, VA 22027. TEL 703-573-8330. FAX 703-573-4116.
circ. 5,500. *733*

PET FOCUS.
Focus Publications, Inc., Box 609, Windham, ME 04038. TEL 207-893-0058. FAX 207-893-1077.
circ. 105,000. *5393*

PET PRODUCT NEWS.
Fancy Publications, Box 6040, Mission Viejo, CA 92690. TEL 714-855-8822. FAX 714-855-3045. *5393*

PET SERVICES JOURNAL.
American Boarding Kennels Association, 4575 Galley Rd., Ste. 400A, Colorado Springs, CO 80915. TEL 719-591-1113. FAX 719-579-0006.
circ. 1,700. *5393*

PETROLEUM MARKETER.
G C I Publishing Co., Inc., 1801 Rockville Pike, Ste. 330, Rockville, MD 20852. TEL 301-984-7333.
circ. 17,000. *5372*

PETS QUARTERLY MAGAZINE.
P Q M, 151 - 8333 Jones Rd., Richmond, BC V6Y 1L5, Canada. TEL 604-244-7450. FAX 604-244-7450.
circ. 31,400. *5393*

PETSPECTIVES.
American Professional Pet Distributors, Inc., 225 E. 6th St., Ste. 230, St. Paul, MN 55101. TEL 612-293-1049.
circ. 1,000. *5393*

PFLANZENSCHUTZ KURIER.
Bayer AG, Geschaeftsbereich Pflanzenschutz, 51368 Leverkusen, Germany.
circ. 168,000. *235*

PHARE.
C.P. 369, Alouette, PQ G0V 1A0, Canada. TEL 418-677-8160. FAX 418-677-8480.
circ. 3,000. *5044*

PHARMA SELECTA.
Stichting Pharma Selecta, Postbus 122, 8430 Oosterwolde, Netherlands. TEL 31-5160-15908.
circ. 2,800. *5433*

PHARMACEUTICAL MEDICINE (WORTHING).
Cambridge Medical Publications Ltd., Wicker House, High St., Worthing, W. Sussex BN11 1DJ, England. TEL 01903-205884. FAX 01903-234862. *4515*

PHARMACEUTICAL TECHNOLOGY EUROPE - BIOPHARM.
Advanstar Communications, Advanstar House, Park West, Sealand Rd., Chester CH1 4RN, England. TEL 44-1244-378888. FAX 44-1244-370512.
circ. 19,000. *5435*

PHARMACEUTISCH WEEKBLAD.
Koninklijke Nederlandse Maatschappij ter Bevordering der Pharmacie, Alexanderstraat 11, 2514 JL The Hague, Netherlands. TEL 31-70-3624111. FAX 31-70-3106530.
circ. 4,000. *5435*

THE PHARMACIST.
Mediselect B.V., Postbus 28091, 3828 ZH Hoogland, Netherlands. TEL 31-33-4808020. FAX 31-33-4805881. *5435*

PHARMACOTHERAPY.
Pharmacotherapy Publications, Inc., New England Medical Center - Box 806, 750 Washington St., Boston, MA 02111. TEL 617-636-5390. FAX 617-636-5318.
circ. 292. *5437*

PHARMACTUEL.
Association des Pharmaciens des Etablissements de Sante du Quebec, 1470 Peel, Tour B, Bureau 900, Montreal, PQ H3A 1T1, Canada. TEL 514-286-0776. FAX 514-286-1081.
circ. 1,800. *5437*

PHARMACY NEWS.
Rajesh Publications, 1 Ansari Rd., Daryaganj, Dew Delhi 110 002, India.
circ. 12,000. *5437*

PHARMACY PRODUCTS REVIEW.
Cosmetics Communications Ltd., 335 Linen Hall, 162-168 Regent St., London W1R 5TB, England. TEL 44-171-434-1530. FAX 44-171-437-0915.
circ. 15,000. *5438*

PHARMACY TODAY.
American Pharmaceutical Association, 2215 Constitution Ave., N.W., Washington, DC 20037. TEL 202-628-4410. FAX 202-628-5425.
circ. 40,000. *5438*

PHARMACY TODAY.
Miller Freeman Publishers Ltd. Sovereign Way, Tonbridge, Kent TN9 1RW, England. TEL 01732-364422. FAX 01732-361534.
circ. 9,969. *5438*

PHARMACY WEEK.
Pharmacy Week, Box 552, Madison, WI 53701-0552. TEL 608-251-1112. FAX 608-251-1155.
circ. 11,500. *5438*

PHI ALPHA DELTA REPORTER.
Phi Alpha Delta, 10722 White Oak Ave., Granda Hills, CA 91344-4698. TEL 818-360-1941. FAX 818-363-5851.
circ. 95,000. *1852*

PHI RHO SIGMA. JOURNAL.
Phi Rho Sigma Medical Society, Box 90264, Indianapolis, IN 46290-0264. TEL 317-255-4379. FAX 317-253-5067.
circ. 16,000. *1881*

PHILADELPHIA MEDICINE.
Philadelphia County Medical Society, 2100 Spring Garden St., Philadelphia, PA 19130. TEL 215-563-5343. FAX 215-563-3627.
circ. 4,300. *4515*

PHILALETHES.
Philalethes Society, Drawer 70, 110 Quince Ave., Highland Springs, VA 23075. TEL 804-737-4498.
circ. 4,800. *1852*

PHILATELIC FOUNDATION QUARTERLY.
Philatelic Foundation, 501 Fifth Ave., No. 1901,
New York, NY 10017-6103. TEL 212-867-3699.
FAX 212-867-3984.
circ. 1,700. *5460*

**PHILIPPINE INSURANCE COMMISSION ANNUAL
REPORT.**
Insurance Commission, Insurance Commission Bldg.,
1071 United Nations Ave., P.O. Box 3589, Manila,
Philippines. TEL 632-599-221. FAX 632-522-
1434.
circ. 320. *3662*

**PHILIPPINES. FOOD AND NUTRITION RESEARCH
INSTITUTE. ANNUAL REPORT.**
Food and Nutrition Research Institute, Science
Complex, Bicutan, Tagig, Metro Manila 1604,
Philippines. TEL 837-89-34. FAX 837-89-34.
5240

**PHILIPPINES. REPUBLIC. NATIONAL MUSEUM
PAPERS.**
National Museum of the Philippines, Padre Burgos
St., Manila, Philippines. TEL 632-527-12-15.
FAX 632-530-03-06.
circ. 500. *5131*

THE PHILIPPINES: NEWS AND VIEWS.
Philippine Embassy, 1617 Massachusetts Ave.,
N.W., Washington, DC 20036. TEL 202-483-1414.
circ. 1,000. *5767*

THE PHILOSOPHER'S STONE.
Winged Feet Productions, 59 Masons Rd., Hemel
Hempstead, Herts HP2 4QU, England. TEL 44-
1442-391333.
circ. 100. *5332*

PHOENIX (MANCHESTER).
C S U (Publications) Ltd. Armstrong House, Oxford
Rd., Manchester M1 7ED, England. TEL 0161-236-
9816. FAX 0161-236-8541.
circ. 1,200. *5272*

PHOENIX TIMES.
Sam Weller Associates, 139 Kensington High St.,
London W8 6SU, England. TEL 44-171-937-0052.
FAX 44-171-937-1393.
circ. 3,650. *3041*

**PHOENIX: VOICE OF THE SCRAP RECYCLING
INDUSTRIES.**
Institute of Scrap Recycling Industries, Inc., 1325 G
St., Ste. 1000, Washington, DC 20005. TEL 202-
737-1770. FAX 202-626-0900.
circ. 45,000. *2814*

PHOTO DISTRICT NEWS.
B P I Communications, Inc. (New York), 1515
Broadway, New York, NY 10036. TEL 212-764-
7300. FAX 212-944-1719.
circ. 20,000. *5517*

PHOTO VIDEO AUDIO NEWS (FRENCH EDITION).
Mema N.V., Wielewaalstraat 20, 2610 Wilrijk,
Belgium. TEL 32-3-4480827. FAX 32-3-4480832.
circ. 6,000. *5517*

PHOTOBULLETIN DAILY.
PhotoSource International, Pine Lake Farm, Osceola,
WI 54020. TEL 715-248-3800. FAX 715-248-
7394. *5517*

PHOTOFILE.
Australian Centre for Photography, 257 Oxford St.,
Paddington, N.S.W. 2021, Australia. TEL 61-2-
3321455. FAX 61-2-3316887.
circ. 5,000. *5517*

PHOTOGRAMMETRIC COYOTE.
E. Coyote Enterprises, Inc., Rt. 3, Bldg. 228, Box
1119, Mineral Wells, TX 76067. TEL 817-325-
0757.
circ. 10,000. *3268*

PHOTOGRAPHIC JOURNAL.
Royal Photographic Society of Great Britain, Acorn
House, 74-94 Cherry Orchard Dr., Croydon CRO
6BA, England. TEL 44-181-681-8339. FAX 44-
181-681-1880.
circ. 10,000. *5518*

PHOTOGRAPHICA.
American Photographic Historical Society, 1150
Sixth Ave., 3rd Fl., New York, NY 10036-2701.
TEL 212-575-0483.
circ. 500. *5518*

PHOTOGRAPHY.
Devin - Adair Publishers, Inc., 6 N. Water St.,
Greenwich, CT 06830. TEL 203-531-7755.
FAX 203-622-6688.
circ. 4,800. *5518*

PHOTONICS SPECTRA.
Laurin Publishing Co., Inc., Box 4949, Berkshire
Common, Pittsfield, MA 01202-4949. TEL 413-
499-0514. FAX 413-442-3180.
circ. 85,000. *5611*

PHYSICIANS' DESK REFERENCE.
Medical Economics Publishing Co., Inc., 5 Paragon
Dr., Montvale, NJ 07645. TEL 201-357-7200.
FAX 201-573-1045.
circ. 485,000. *4516*

**PHYSICIANS' DESK REFERENCE FOR
NONPRESCRIPTION DRUGS.**
Medical Economics Publishing Co., Inc., 5 Paragon
Dr., Montvale, NJ 07645. TEL 201-358-7200.
FAX 201-573-1045.
circ. 315,000. *4516*

PHYSICIANS LIFESTYLE MAGAZINE.
K & K Publishing, Inc., 19 W. 34th St., Ste. 1010,
New York, NY 10001-3006. TEL 212-643-0991.
3236

PHYTON.
Fundacion Romulo Raggio, Gaspar Campos 861,
1638 Vicente Lopez, Argentina. TEL 54-1-791-
0868. FAX 54-1-796-1456.
circ. 750. *696*

PICTOU ADVOCATE.
21 George St., Box 1000, Pictou, NS B0K 1H0,
Canada. TEL 902-485-8014. FAX 902-752-4816.
circ. 188. *3124*

PIG INDUSTRY.
B C Publications, 16C Market Pl., Diss, Norfolk
IP22 3AB, England. TEL 44-1379-644200.
FAX 44-1379-650480.
circ. 7,800. *144*

PIG INTERNATIONAL.
Watt Publishing Co., 122 S. Wesley Ave., Mt.
Morris, IL 61054. TEL 815-734-4171. FAX 815-
734-4201
circ. 18,668. *280*

THE PILOT LOG.
Pilot International, 244 College Street, Macon, GA
31201. TEL 912-743-7403. FAX 912-743-2173.
circ. 17,500. *1852*

PINELLAS COUNTY REVIEW.
Warfield Media Co., Box 6130, Clearwater, FL
34618-6130. TEL 813-724-1112.
circ. 10,000. *951*

PINKER MODA.
Ediciones Tecnicas Doria, Avda. Puerta del Angel 7,
Sobreat. A - B, 08002 Barcelona, Spain. TEL 34-3-
3187489. FAX 34-3-3011105.
circ. 12,000. *6683*

THE PIONEER.
Church Army in Australia, 75 Hawkesbury Rd.,
Wetmead, N.S.W. 2145, Australia. TEL 61-2-
6355669.
circ. 4,000. *6156*

PIONIER.
C A M A - Zending, Amersfoortseweg 44, 3951 LC
Maarn, Netherlands. TEL 31-343-443392. FAX 31-
343-443392.
circ. 5,900. *6156*

PIPE DREAM.
State University of New York at Binghamton,
Student Association, Box 2002, SUNY-B,
Binghamton, NY 13902. TEL 607-777-2515.
FAX 607-777-2600.
circ. 9,000. *1882*

THE PIPE SMOKER'S EPHEMERIS.
Tom Dunn, Ed. & Pub., 20-37 120th St., College
Point, NY 11356-2128.
circ. 7,500. *6710*

PIPELINE (ROY).
Doberman Pinscher Club of America, Box 1170,
Roy, WA 98580-1170. TEL 206-843-2805.
FAX 206-843-0144.
circ. 2,150. *1852*

PIPELINES.
Plumbers - Steamfitters U A Local 38, 1621
Market St., San Francisco, CA 94103. TEL 415-
626-2000.
circ. 3,000. *3727*

PIRKKA.
Kauppiaitten Kustannus Oy, Kanavakatu 3.B, FIN-
00160 Helsinki, Finland. TEL 358-0-228821.
circ. 2,254,173. *1482*

PITT MAGAZINE.
University of Pittsburgh, Department of University
Relations, 400 Craig Hall, Pittsburgh, PA 15260.
TEL 412-624-4147 FAX 412-624-1021.
circ. 125,000. *1882*

PITTSBURGH LEGAL JOURNAL (MONTHLY EDITION).
Allegheny County Bar Association, 436 7th Ave.,
Ste. 400, Pittsburgh, PA 15219-1818. TEL 412-
261-6161. FAX 412-261-3522.
circ. 7,900. *3833*

PITTSBURGH MUSICIAN.
Pittsburgh Musicians Union, Local No.60-471,
A.F.M., 709 Forbes Ave., Pittsburgh, PA 15219.
TEL 412-281-1822.
circ. 1,200. *5188*

PIVOT.
250 Riverside Dr., Apt. No. 23, New York, NY
10025. TEL 212-222-1408.
circ. 1,500. *4314*

PLACE OF GRADUATION.
University of British Columbia, Centre for Health
Services and Policy Research No. 429 - 2194
Health Sciences Mall, Vancouver, BC V6T 1Z3,
Canada. TEL 604-822-4810 FAX 604-822-5690.
circ. 200. *4517*

PLAISANCIERS.
970 Montee de Liesse, Ville St-Laurent, PQ H4T
1W7, Canada. TEL 514-856-0788.
circ. 20,000. *6538*

PLAN AND ACTION.
Stichting Mensen in Nood - Caritas Nederland.,
Postbus 1041, 5200 BA 's-Hertogenbosch,
Netherlands. TEL 31-73-6456789. FAX 31-73-
6456700.
circ. 2,000. *6387*

PLANNING IN NORTHEASTERN ILLINOIS.
Northeastern Illinois Planning Commission, 222 S.
Riverside Plz., Ste. 1800, Chicago, IL 60606-
6001. TEL 312-454-0400. FAX 312-454-0411.
circ. 9,500. *3591*

PLANT ENGINEERING PRODUCT SUPPLIER GUIDE.
Cahners Publishing Company (Des Plaines), Division
of Reed Elsevier Inc., 1350 E. Touhy Ave., Box
5080, Des Plaines, IL 60018-5080. TEL 847-635-
8800. FAX 847-390-2536. *2614*

PLANT EQUIPMENT HIRE & RATE REVIEW.
Brooke Pattrick (Pty) Ltd., P.C. Box 422,
Bedfordview 2008, South Africa. TEL 27-11-
6224666. FAX 27-11-6167196.
circ. 4,100. *1528*

PLANT GENETIC RESOURCES NEWSLETTER.
International Plant Genetic Resources Institute, Via
delle Sette Chiese 142, 00145 Rome, Italy.
TEL 39-6-518921. FAX 39-6-5750309.
circ. 5,000. *2139*

PLANTS, SITES & PARKS.
B P I Communications, 1801 West End Ave., Ste.
400, Nashville, TN 37203. TEL 615-329-4940.
FAX 615-329-4733.
circ. 40,500. *1528*

PLAST PANORAMA SCANDINAVIA.
Teknisk Forlag A-S, Skelbaekgade 4, DK-1780
Copenhagen V, Denmark. TEL 45-31-21-68-01.
FAX 45-31-21-04-01.
circ. 4,447. *5623*

PLASTERER AND CEMENT MASON.
Plasterers & Cement Masons International, 1125
17th St., N.W., Washington, DC 20036. TEL 202-
393-6569. FAX 202-393-2514.
circ. 40,000. *3727*

PLASTI-NOTICIAS.
Publi-News Latinoamericana, S.A.C.V., Colima 436, piso 2, Mexico 7 D.F., Mexico. *5624*

PLASTICHEM.
Singapore Polytechnic Polymer Society, Dover Rd., Singapore 5, Singapore. circ. 1,000. *2646*

PLASTICS AND RUBBER WEEKLY.
E M A P Maclaren Ltd., 19 Scarbrook Rd., Croydon, Surrey CR9 1QH, England. TEL 0181-760-9690. FAX 0181-681-1672. circ. 20,584. *5624*

THE PLASTICS DISTRIBUTOR & FABRICATOR MAGAZINE.
P M D Publishing Inc., 2701 N. Pulaski Rd., Chicago, IL 60639-2119. TEL 312-235-3800. FAX 312-235-7204. circ. 25,000. *5624*

PLASTICS TECHNOLOGY.
Bill Communications, Inc., 355 Park Ave. S., 5th Fl., New York, NY 10010-1789. TEL 212-592-6200. FAX 212-592-6339. circ. 48,334. *5625*

PLASTIQUES MODERNES ET ELASTOMERES.
Editions Montmartre, 142 rue Montmartre, 75002 Paris, France. TEL 33-1-40-26-83-21. FAX 33-1-40-39-97-52. circ. 5,000. *5626*

PLASTVERARBEITER.
Huethig GmbH, Postfach 102869, 69018 Heidelberg, Germany. TEL 49-6221-489230. FAX 49-6221-489481. circ. 12,647. *5626*

PLAY GOLF (NEDERLANDSE EDITIE).
Play Golf S.A., Rue du Chatelain 49, 1050 Brussels, Belgium. TEL 32-2-6471750. FAX 32-2-6482989. *6511*

PLAY SCHOOLS NEWSLETTER.
Play Schools Association, P.O. Box 573, New York, NY 10156-0573. TEL 212-725-6540. circ. 2,500. *2363*

PLAYBACK.
Brunico Communications Inc., 366 Adelaide St. W., Ste. 500, Toronto, Ont. M5V 1R9, Canada. TEL 416-408-2300. FAX 416-408-0870. circ. 9,800. *1967*

PLAYBACK (CARLSBAD).
National Association of Music Merchants Inc., 5140 Avenida Encinas, Carlsbad, CA 92008. TEL 619-438-8001. circ. 10,500. *5188*

PLAYTIMES.
Playgroup Association of Queensland, 396 Milton Rd., Auchenflower, Qld. 4066, Australia. TEL 61-7-3718253. FAX 61-7-8700569. circ. 18,000. *1776*

PLAZA DE LA CONSTITUCION.
Ayuntamiento, Plaza de la Constitucion, 28700 San Sebastian de los Reyes, Spain. TEL 1-6526200. circ. 15,000. *5949*

PLEIN CHANT.
Editions Plein Chant, Bassac, 16120 Chateauneuf-sur-Charente, France. TEL 16-45-81-93-26. FAX 16-45-81-92-83. circ. 1,000. *4251*

PLUG.
Kunst en Cultuur Noordholland, Postbus 5348, 2000 GH Haarlem, Netherlands. TEL 31-23-5319139. FAX 31-23-5315284. circ. 35,000. *6701*

PLUMBING ENGINEER.
T M B Publishing, 1884 Techny Ct., Northbrook, IL 60062. TEL 847-564-1127. FAX 847-564-1264. circ. 23,000. *3332*

PLYMOUTH COUNTY BUSINESS REVIEW.
Plymouth County Development Council, Box 1620, Pembroke, MA 02359. TEL 617-826-3136. FAX 617-826-0444. circ. 5,000. *1168*

PNEURAMA.
Promotec s.r.l., Via A.G. Ragazzi 9, 40011 Anzola dell'Emilia (BO), Italy. TEL 39-51-733000. FAX 39-51-731886. circ. 15,000. *6217*

PODIATRIC PRODUCTS.
Novicom, Inc., 20000 Mariner Ave., Ste. 480, Torrance, CA 90503. TEL 310-793-4141. FAX 310-793-4138. circ. 13,000. *4790*

PODIATRY TODAY.
Dowden Publishing Company, 110 Summit Ave., Montvale, NJ 07625. TEL 201-391-2778. FAX 202-391-2778. circ. 16,995. *4790*

POET (MISHAWAKA).
Fine Arts Society, 2314 W. Sixth St., Mishawaka, IN 46544. circ. 1,000. *4315*

POETRY KANTO.
Kanto Poetry Center, Kanto Gakuin University, Kamariya-cho, Kanazawa-ku, Yokohama 236, Japan. TEL 045-781-2001. circ. 800. *4316*

POETS' ROUNDTABLE.
826 S. Center St., Terre Haute, IN 47807. TEL 812-234-0819. circ. 2,000. *4317*

POINT OF VIEW.
Holt Renfrew & Co., Limited, 50 Bloor St., W., Toronto, Ont. M4W 1A1, Canada. TEL 416-922-2333. FAX 416-922-3240. circ. 150,000. *1844*

POINTS NORTH.
North Country Reference & Research Resources Council, 7 Commerce Ln., Canton, NY 13617. TEL 315-386-4569. FAX 315-379-9553. circ. 200. *4019*

POLICE AND SECURITY NEWS.
Days Communications Inc., 1690 Quarry Rd., Box 330, Kulpsville, PA 19443. TEL 215-362-2233. FAX 215-368-9955. circ. 20,960. *2172*

POLICE MARTIAL ARTS ASSOCIATION NEWS.
Police Martial Arts Association, P.O. Box 7303, Sub 12, Riverview, NB E1B 4T9, Canada. TEL 506-387-5126. FAX 506-387-5126. circ. 1,000. *2172*

POLICE OFFICERS JOURNAL.
Dale Corporation, 84 Executive Dr., Troy, MI 48083-4504. TEL 313-597-9040. FAX 313-597-0082. circ. 5,000. *2172*

POLIMERY W MEDYCYNIE.
Akademia Medyczna we Wroclawiu, Zaklad Chirurgii Eksperymentalnej i Badania Biomaterialow, Ul. Poniatowskiego 2, 50-326 Wroclaw, Poland. TEL 48-71-226310. FAX 48-71-215729. circ. 200. *1743*

POLISH AMERICAN JOURNAL.
Panagraphics Corporation, 1275 Harlem Rd., Buffalo, NY 14206-1960. TEL 716-893-5771. FAX 716-893-5783. circ. 3,000. *2902*

POLISH AMERICAN WORLD.
3100 Grand Blvd., Baldwin, NY 11510. TEL 516-223-6514. FAX 516-223-6514. circ. 6,000. *2902*

POLITISCHES DENKEN JAHRBUCH (YEAR).
J.B. Metzlersche Verlagsbuchhandlung, Werastr. 21-23, 70182 Stuttgart, Germany. FAX 49-711-2194249. circ. 450. *4161*

POLLUTION ATMOSPHERIQUE.
Association pour la Prevention de la Pollution Atmospheriques, 58 rue du Rocher, 75008 Paris, France. TEL 42-93-69-30. FAX 42-93-41-99. circ. 2,000. *2839*

POLLUTION ENGINEERING.
Cahners Publishing Company (Des Plaines), Division of Reed Elsevier Inc., 1350 E. Touhy Ave., Box 5080, Des Plaines, IL 60018-5080. TEL 847-635-8800. FAX 847-390-2636. circ. 58,992. *2839*

PONDICHERRY INDUSTRIAL PROMOTION, DEVELOPMENT AND INVESTMENT CORPORATION. ANNUAL REPORTS AND ACCOUNTS.
Pondicherry Industrial Promotion, Development and Investment Corporation Ltd., 38 Romain Rolland St, Pondicherry 605001, India. *1168*

POPULAR ASTRONOMY.
Society for Popular Astronomy, 36 Fairway, Keyworth, Nottingham NG12 5DU, England. *485*

POR ESCRITO.
Editorial Unidifusion, Av. Mexico 3150, Monraz, 44670 Guadalajara, Jalisco, Mexico. TEL 3-813-1415. FAX 3-813-1465. circ. 1,500. *3193*

PORK.
Vance Publishing Corporation, 400 Knightsbridge Pkwy., Lincolnshire, IL 60069. TEL 913-438-8700. FAX 913-438-0695. circ. 76,500. *280*

PORK REPORT.
National Pork Producers Council, Box 10383, Des Moines, IA 50306. TEL 515-223-2600. FAX 513-223-2646. circ. 109,000. *280*

PORK REPORT.
S P I Marketing Group, 502 45th St. W., 2nd Fl., Saskatoon, SK S7L 6H2, Canada. TEL 306-653-3014. FAX 306-244-2918. circ. 2,100. *280*

PORT OF BALTIMORE MAGAZINE.
Maryland Port Administration, World Trade Center Baltimore, Baltimore, MD 21202. TEL 410-385-4480. FAX 410-385-4485. circ. 11,000. *6845*

PORT OF NEW ORLEANS ANNUAL DIRECTORY.
Port of New Orleans, 2 Canal St., Box 60046, New Orleans, LA 70160. TEL 504-528-3234. FAX 504-524-2196. circ. 10,300. *6725*

PORT OF ROTTERDAM MAGAZINE (NEDERLANDSE EDITIE).
FHp BV, Postbus 145, 3000 AC Rotterdam, Netherlands. TEL 31-10-4896508. circ. 16,000. *6845*

PORT PROGRESS NEWS AND EVENTS.
Port of Oakland, 530 Water St., Oakland, CA 94607. TEL 510-272-1100. FAX 510-272-1172. circ. 15,000. *6845*

PORTLAND ART MUSEUM NEWSLETTER.
Portland Art Museum, 1219 S.W. Park Ave., Portland, OR 97205. TEL 503-226-2811. FAX 503-226-2842. circ. 20,000. *5131*

PORTSIDE.
Port of Portland, Box 3529, Portland, OR 97208. TEL 503-231-5000. circ. 10,000. *6846*

PORTUGAL. INSTITUTO NACIONAL DE ESTATISTICA. SERIE ESTATISTICAS REGIONAIS.
Instituto Nacional de Estatistica, Av. Antonio Jose de Almeida, 1078 Lisbon Codex, Portugal. *6624*

POSSIBILITIES.
Publishing Directions, Inc., 5301 Wisconsin Ave., N.W., Ste. 620, Washington, DC 20015. TEL 202-364-8000. FAX 202-364-8910. circ. 300,000. *6156*

POST EAGLE.
Post Publishing Co. Inc., 800 Van Houten Ave., Clifton, NJ 07013. TEL 201-476-5414. FAX 201-473-3211. circ. 17,000. *2903*

POST OFFICE XPRESS.
S A Post Office, P.O. Box 9255, Pretoria 0001, South Africa. TEL 27-12-4217714. FAX 27-12-4217606.
circ. 33,000. *1932*

POSTAL HISTORY JOURNAL.
Postal History Society, Inc., c/o Kalman V. Illyefalvi, Sec.-Treas., 8207 Daren Ct., Pikesville, MD 21208. TEL 410-653-0665.
circ. 600. *1932*

POSTGRADUATE DOCTOR: AFRICA.
Barker Publications Ltd., Barker House, 539 London Rd., Isleworth, Mddx. TW7 4DA, England. TEL 44-181-847-1774. FAX 44-181-568-2766.
circ. 13,181. *4517*

POSTGRADUATE DOCTOR: CARIBBEAN.
Barker Publications Ltd., Barker House, 539 London Rd., Isleworth, Mddx. TW7 4DA, England. TEL 44-181-874-1774. FAX 44-181-568-2766.
circ. 3,000. *4517*

POSTGRADUATE DOCTOR: MIDDLE EAST.
Barker Publications Ltd., Barker House, 539 London Rd., Isleworth, Mddx. TW7 4DA, England. TEL 44-181-847-1774. FAX 44-181-568-2766.
circ. 21,413. *4517*

POSTHORN.
Scandinavian Collectors Club, 2316 Lakeview Dr., Fergus Falls, MN 56537-3903. TEL 218-739-3260.
circ. 1,000. *5461*

POSTMASTERS ADVOCATE.
National League of Postmasters, 1023 N. Royal St., Alexandria, VA 22314-1569. TEL 703-548-5922. FAX 703-836-8937.
circ. 23,000. *1932*

POTATO NEWSLETTER.
Department of Agriculture, Plant Industry Branch, Box 6000, Fredericton, NB E3B 5H1, Canada. TEL 506-457-7244. FAX 506-457-7267.
circ. 1,000. *236*

POTOMAC LIFE.
C E R Publications, Box 59508, Potomac, MD 20859. TEL 301-299-5183.
circ. 32,000. *3236*

POULTRY PROGRESS.
A D A S Leeds, Lawnswood, Otley Rd., Leeds LS16 5PY, England. TEL 44-113-261-1222. FAX 44-113-230-0174.
circ. 3,750. *281*

POWDER RIVER BREAKS.
Powder River Basin Resource Council, Box 1178, Douglas, WY 82633. TEL 307-358-5002.
circ. 975. *2815*

POWER DELIVERY PRODUCT NEWS.
PennWell Publishing Co., Box 1260, Tulsa, OK 74112-6619. TEL 918-835-3161. FAX 918-831-9834.
circ. 60,000. *2716*

POWER TRANSMISSION DESIGN.
Penton Publishing Co. 1100 Superior Ave., Cleveland, OH 44114-2543. TEL 216-696-7000. FAX 216-696-8765.
circ. 52,000. *2767*

POWER TRANSMISSION DESIGN HANDBOOK.
Penton Publishing Co. 1100 Superior Ave., Cleveland, OH 44114-2543. TEL 216-696-7000. FAX 216-696-8765.
circ. 52,000. *2767*

PRACTICAL DIABETOLOGY.
R.A. Rapaport Publishing, Inc., 150 W. 22nd St., New York, NY 10011. TEL 212-989-0200. FAX 212-989-4786.
circ. 52,000. *4674*

PRACTICAL GASTROENTEROLOGY.
Shugar Publishing, 32 Mill Rd., Westhampton Beach, NY 11978-0947. TEL 516-288-4404. FAX 516-288-4435.
circ. 32,000. *4695*

PRACTICAL OPTOMETRY.
Medicopea International Inc., 3333 Cote Vertu Blvd., Ste. 300, St. Laurent, PQ H4R 2N1, Canada. TEL 514-333-4561. FAX 514-336-1129.
circ. 2,300. *4776*

PRAGMA'S PRODUCT PROFILES.
Semaphore Corp., 207 Granada Dr., Aptos, CA 95003. TEL 408-688-9200.
circ. 4,000. *2079*

PRAIRIE HARVESTER.
Prairie Bible Institute, Three Hills, AB TOM 2N0, Canada. TEL 403-443-5511. FAX 403-443-5540.
circ. 13,000. *1882*

PRATTFOLIO
Pratt Institute, Office of Alumni Resources, Brooklyn, NY 11205.
circ. 27,000. *1882*

PRAXIS COMPUTER.
Deutscher Aerzte-Verlag GmbH, Postfach 400265, 50532 Cologne, Germany. TEL 49-2234-7011-0. FAX 49-2234-7011255.
circ. 40,000. *1997*

PRAXISREPORT PSYCHOLOGISCHE THERAPIEN UND PSYCHOTHERAPIEN.
Psychomedia Verlags GmbH, Postfach 465, 12214 Berlin, Germany. TEL 49-30-4927200. FAX 49-30-7749176.
circ. 500. *5870*

PRE-VUE ENTERTAINMENT MAGAZINE.
National Pre-Vue Network, 7825 Fay Ave., La Jolla, CA 92037. TEL 619-456-5577. FAX 619-542-0114.
circ. 200,000. *5110*

PREMIERE.
Bernerstr. 2 38106 Braunschweig, Germany. TEL 49-531-330218. FAX 49-531-45340.
circ. 1,000. *6701*

PRENATAL EDUCATOR.
E P I Inc., 8003 Old York Rd., Elkins Park, PA 19117. TEL 215-635-1700.
circ. 8,540. *4744*

LA PRENSA.
Editora la Prensa, S.A. de C.V., Basilio Badillo 40, 06030 Mexico, D.F., Mexico. TEL 905-228-9977. FAX 905-512-5296.
circ. 3,500. *3193*

PRESBYTERIAN COLLEGE MAGAZINE.
Presbyterian College, Office of Public Relations, Box 975, Clinton, SC 29325. TEL 864-833-2820. FAX 864-833-8481.
circ. 13,500. *1882*

PRESBYTERIAN SUN.
Synod of the Sun, 920 S. I-35 E., Denton, TX 76205-7898.
circ. 107,000. *6156*

PRESBYTERION.
Covenant Theological Seminary, 12330 Conway Rd., St. Louis, MO 63141. TEL 314-434-4044. FAX 314-434-4819.
circ. 100. *6156*

PRESENTATIONS MAGAZINE.
Lakewood Publications Inc., 50 S. Ninth St., Minneapolis, MN 55402. TEL 612-333-0471. FAX 612-333-5526.
circ. 70,000. *43*

PRESERVATION NOTES.
Society for the Preservation of Long Island Antiquities, 93 North Country Rd., Setauket, NY 11733. TEL 516-941-9444. FAX 516-941-9184.
circ. 1,800. *402*

PRESERVATION PERSPECTIVE.
Preservation New Jersey, 149 Kearny Ave., Perth Amboy, NJ 08361-4700. TEL 908-442-1100. FAX 908-442-2442.
circ. 3,000. *402*

PRESHIPMENT TESTING.
International Safe Transit Association, Box 10744, Chicago, IL 60610-0744. TEL 312-645-0083. FAX 312-645-1078.
circ. 3,200. *5304*

PRESS COUNCIL OF THE REPUBLIC OF CHINA.
National Press Council of the Republic of China, Nanchang Rd. Sec. 1, Lane 9, No. 4, 3rd Fl., Taipei, Taiwan 107, Republic of China.
circ. 4,000. *3709*

PRESS GRAPH & IMAGING.
Ediciones Press Graph, S.L., C. Mallorca, 219 5o 2o, 08008 Barcelona, Spain. TEL 34-3-2327554. FAX 34-3-3237463
circ. 12,000. *5816*

PRESSEMARKT EUROPA.
Verband Deutscher Zeitschriften Verleger, Winterstr. 50, 53117 Bonn, Germany. TEL 49-228-3820323. FAX 49-228-312219.
circ. 500. *6005*

PRETTIG WEEKEND.
Fam Press, Heerengracht 4, 1141 TR Monnickendam, Netherlands. TEL 31-299-652337 FAX 31-299-655258.
circ. 25,000. *3196*

PREVIEW (COLLINSVILLE).
Stehman Publications 300 W. Main St., Collinsville, IL 62234. TEL 618-345-7559. FAX 618-345-8915. *4652*

PREVIEW THEATER BROCHURE.
American Film Institute John F. Kennedy Center for the Performing Arts, Washington, DC 20566 TEL 202-828-4000. *5110*

PREVISOES IONOSFERICAS M U F.
Ministerio da Marinha, Diretoria de Armamento e Comunicacoes, Rua 1 de Marco, 118, Rio de Janeiro, RJ, Brazil. FAX 021-216-5048.
circ. 250. *1967*

PRIESTERJAHRHEFT.
Bonifatiuswerk der Deutschen Katholiken e.V., Postfach 1169, 3304 Paderborn, Germany. TEL 49-5251-29960. FAX 49-5251-299688.
circ. 20,000. *6192*

PRIMARY CARE & CANCER.
P P R, Inc., 17 Prospect St., Huntington, NY 11743. TEL 516-424-8900. FAX 516-424-8503.
circ. 70,440. *4762*

PRIME TIMES.
Life Newspapers, 709 Enterprise Dr., Oak Brook, IL 60521. TEL 708-368-1100. FAX 708-368-1188.
circ. 55,000. *3294*

PRIME TIMES MAGAZINE
Grote Publishing, 634 W Main St., Ste. 207, Madison, WI 53703-2634. TEL 608-257-4640. FAX 608-257-4670.
circ. 80,000. *2154*

PRIMETIME LIVING.
PrimeTime Association, 1530K Jamacho Rd., No. 278, El Cajon, CA 92019-3754. TEL 619-278-7115.
circ. 110,000. *3294*

PRINCETON ALUMNI WEEKLY.
Princeton Alumni Publications, 194 Nassau St., Princeton, NJ 08542. TEL 609-258-4885. FAX 609-258-2247.
circ. 57,000. *1882*

PRINT & GRAPHICS.
East-West Communications, 911 N. Fillmore St., Arlington, VA 22201-2127. TEL 703-525-4800. FAX 703-525-4805.
circ. 20,000. *5816*

PRINT BUYER GUIDE.
Uitgeverij Compres b.v., Postbus 55, 2300 AB Leiden, Netherlands. TEL 31-71-161515. FAX 31-71-121550.
circ. 6,500. *5304*

PRINTER'S NORTHWEST TRADER.
Eagle Newspapers, Inc., Box 450, Woodburn, OR 97071. TEL 800-426-2416. FAX 503-981-1253.
circ. 5,850. *5817*

PRINTING JOURNAL.
East-West Communications, 911 N. Fillmore St., Arlington, VA 22201-2127 TEL 703-525-4800. FAX 703-525-4805.
circ. 18,000. *5817*

PRINTING PRODUCT NEWS.
Manor Publishing Ltd., Unit 7, Edison Rd., Highfield Industrial Estate, Hampden Park, Eastbourne, E. Sussex BN23 6PT, England. TEL 44-1323-507474. FAX 44-1323-509306.
circ. 6,000. *5817*

PRISON SERVICE NEWS.
H.M. Prison Service, Rm. 302, Cleland House, Page St., London SW1P 4LN, England. TEL 44-171-217-6575. FAX 44-171-828-8692.
circ. 30,000. *2174*

PRIVATE CARRIER.
National Private Truck Council, 66 Canal Center Plaza, Ste. 600, Alexandria, VA 22314. TEL 703-683-1300. FAX 703-683-1217.
circ. 13,000. *6860*

PRIVATE LINE (ALEXANDRIA).
National Private Truck Council, 66 Canal Center Plaza, Ste. 600, Alexandria, VA 22314. TEL 703-683-1300. FAX 703-683-1217.
circ. 2,500. *6860*

PRO.
Johnson Hill Press, Inc. 1233 Janesville Ave., Ft. Atkinson, WI 53538. TEL 414-563-6388. FAX 414-563-1699.
circ. 47,500. *3065*

PRO MOTION.
Beyond the Byte, c/o Emily Laisy, Ed., 2501 Laurel Brook Rd., Box 388, Fallston, MD 21047-0388. TEL 410-877-3524. FAX 410-877-7064.
circ. 250. *1914*

PRO RE NATA.
Art Davis Associates, Box 216, Cedar Falls, IA 50613. TEL 801-322-3439.
circ. 15,000. *4726*

PRO SHOP EUROPE.
Mark Allen Publishing Ltd., Snow Hill, Dinton, Salisbury, Wiltshire SP3 5HN, England. TEL 01722-716996. FAX 01722-716926.
circ. 6,850. *6512*

PRO ZUKUNFT.
Verlag Julius Beltz GmbH, Am Hauptbahnhof 10, 69469 Weinheim, Germany. TEL 06201-60070. FAX 06201-600738.
circ. 1,800. *2815*

PROBABLE LEVELS OF R & D EXPENDITURES: FORECAST AND ANALYSIS.
Battelle Memorial Institute, Columbus Operations, 505 King Ave., Columbus, OH 43201. TEL 614-424-6424. *6661*

PROBE.
Adelaide University Dental Students Society (AUDSS), School of Dentistry, Undergraduate Mailbox, 5th Fl., Dental Hospital, Frome Rd., Adelaide, S.A. 5000, Australia. TEL 618-223-9211. FAX 61-8-232-4061.
circ. 220. *4652*

PROBLEMI DI GESTIONE.
Centro di Formazione e Studi (Formez), Via Campi Flegrei 34, Comprensorio Olivetti, 80072 Arco Felice (NA), Italy. TEL 39-81-5250111. FAX 39-81-8041348.
circ. 7,000. *1440*

PROBLEMY RODZINY.
Towarzystwo Rozwoju Rodziny, Zarzad Glowny, c/o Problemy Rodziny, Redakcja, Ul. Schillera 4-35, 00-248 Warsaw, Poland. TEL 48-2-319310.
circ. 1,200. *6425*

PROCESS INDUSTRIES CANADA.
Zanny Publications Ltd., 11966 Woodbine Ave., Gormley, ON L0H 1G0, Canada. TEL 905-887-5048. FAX 905-479-4839.
circ. 24,000. *2648*

PROCESSING.
Putman Publishing Co., 301 E. Erie St., Chicago, IL 60611. TEL 312-644-2020. FAX 312-644-1131.
circ. 110,000. *2648*

PRODUCE MERCHANDISING.
Vance Publishing Corporation (Lenexa), 10901 W. 84th Terr., Lenexa, KS 66214-1631. TEL 913-438-8700. FAX 913-438-0692.
circ. 12,200. *2988*

PRODUCT MANAGEMENT TODAY.
Product Management Today, Inc., 28 Jones Ave., Flourtown, PA 19031. TEL 215-233-9384. FAX 215-233-9320.
circ. 9,600. *1482*

PRODUCTION.
University of British Columbia, Centre for Health Services and Policy Research, No. 429 - 2194 Health Sciences Mall, Vancouver, BC V6T 1Z3, Canada. TEL 604-822-4810. FAX 604-822-5690.
circ. 300. *4519*

PRODUCTION JOURNAL.
Newspaper Society, Bloomsbury House, 74-77 Great Russell St., London WC1B 3DA, England. TEL 44-171-636-7014. FAX 44-171-631-5119.
circ. 3,000. *5818*

PRODUCTRONIC.
Huethig GmbH, Paul-Gerhardt-Allee 46, 81245 Munich, Germany. TEL 49-89-83948-0. FAX 49-89-8394848.
circ. 10,568. *2530*

PRODUITS EQUIPEMENTS INDUSTRIELS.
Editions Elsevier Thomas, 128 rue d'Aguesseau, 92100 Boulogne-Billancourt, France. TEL 41-10-40-70. FAX 48-25-14-00.
circ. 49,800. *2740*

PRODUITS POUR L'INDUSTRIE QUEBECOISE.
Action Communications Inc., 135 Spy Court, Markham, ON L3R 5H6, Canada. TEL 905-477-3222. FAX 905-477-4320.
circ. 15,050. *6661*

PRODUKTION.
Dansk Landbrugs Grovvareselskab a.m.b.a., Axelborg, DK-1503 Copenhagen V, Denmark. TEL 45-33-15-11-13. FAX 45-33-15-13-56.
circ. 126,000. *198*

PRODUKTIONS NYT.
Christtreu, Strandlodsvei 48, DK-2300 Copenhagen S, Denmark. TEL 45-32-84-48-48. FAX 45-31-58-20-55.
circ. 24,850. *4345*

PROFESSIONAL BOATBUILDER.
WoodenBoat Publications, Inc., Box 78, Brookline, ME 04616. TEL 207-359-4651. FAX 207-359-8920.
circ. 23,000. *6539*

PROFESSIONAL CAR WASHING & DETAILING.
National Trade Publications, Inc., 13 Century Hill, Latham, NY 12110-2197. TEL 518-783-1281. FAX 518-783-1386.
circ. 17,590. *6798*

PROFESSIONAL COMPUTING PLUS.
V N U Business Publications B.V., Postbus 9194, 1006 CC Amsterdam, Netherlands. TEL 31-20-5102911. FAX 31-20-6175137.
circ. 43,000. *1997*

PROFESSIONAL EDGE.
Association of Professional Engineers of Saskatchewan, 2255 13th Av., Regina, SK S4P 0V6, Canada. TEL 306-525-9547. FAX 306-525-0851.
circ. 4,000. *2616*

PROFESSIONAL FIRE FIGHTER.
Dale Corporation, 84 Executive Dr., Troy, MI 48083-4504. TEL 313-597-9040. FAX 313-597-0082.
circ. 2,500. *2922*

PROFESSIONAL FORESTER.
Ontario Professional Foresters Association, 27 West Beaver Creek Rd., Richmond Hill, ON L4B 1M8, Canada. TEL 905-764-2921. FAX 905-764-2921.
circ. 1,300. *3023*

PROFESSIONAL OFFICER.
Federated Union of Managerial and Professional Officers, Terminus House, The High, Harlow, Essex CM20 1TZ, England. TEL 44-1274-434444. FAX 44-1279-451176.
circ. 12,500. *5916*

PROFESSIONAL PADDLESPORTS ASSOCIATION NEWS.
Professional Paddlesports Association, Box 248, Butler, KY 41006-0248. TEL 606-472-2205. FAX 606-472-2030.
circ. 750. *6539*

PROFESSIONAL PILOT MAGAZINE.
Queensmith Communications Corporation, 3014 Colvin St., Alexandria, VA 22314. TEL 703-370-0606. FAX 703-370-7082.
circ. 32,000. *6764*

PROFESSIONAL SURVEYOR.
American Surveyors Publishing Co., 2300 Ninth St. S., Ste. 501, Arlington, VA 22204-2300. TEL 703-892-0733. FAX 703-920-3652.
circ. 54,725. *3270*

PROFILE (SKOKIE).
Brunswick Corporation, One N. Field Ct., Lake Forest, IL 60045-4811. TEL 708-735-4457. FAX 708-735-4455.
circ. 30,000. *1529*

PROFOTO.
Professional Photographers of Southern Africa, P.O. Box 47044, Parklands 2121, South Africa.
circ. 3,200. *5520*

PROGNOSTICO.
Instituto de Economia Agricola, Av. Miguel Stefano 3900, Caixa Postal 6802, 04301-9031 Sao Paulo SP, Brazil. FAX 55-11-2764062. *237*

PROGRAMA DE FORRAJES TROPICALES. INFORME BIANUAL.
Centro Internacional de Agricultura Tropical, Apdo. Aereo 6713, Cali, Colombia. TEL 57-2-4450000. FAX 57-2-4450273.
circ. 250. *146*

PROGRAMMA COMUNISTA.
Istituto Programma Comunista, Casella Postale 962, 20100 Milan, Italy.
circ. 2,000. *5700*

PROGRESS IN DERMATOLOGY.
Dermatology Foundation, 1560 Sherman Ave., Ste. 302, Evanston, IL 60201-4802.
circ. 3,000. *4664*

THE PROGRESS OF NATIONS.
United Nations Children's Fund (UNICEF), UNICEF House, 3 United Nations Plaza, New York, NY 10017. TEL 212-326-7000. FAX 212-888-7465.
circ. 71,500. *6387*

PROGRESSIVE GIFTS.
Max Publishing Ltd., United House, North Rd., London N7 9DP, England. TEL 44-171-700-6740. FAX 44-171-609-4222.
circ. 7,500. *3301*

PROGRESSIVE GROCER'S ANNUAL REPORT OF THE GROCERY INDUSTRY.
263 Tresser Blvd., Stamford, CT 06901. TEL 203-325-3500. FAX 203-325-4377.
circ. 70,049. *3007*

PROMAX INTERNATIONAL.
Promotion & Marketing Executives in the Electronic Media, 2029 Century Pk. E., Ste. 555, Los Angeles, CA 90067-2906. TEL 310-788-7600. FAX 310-788-7616.
circ. 2,000. *1967*

PROMPT.
Deutsche Blindenstudienanstalt e.V., Postfach 1160, 35001 Marburg, Germany. TEL 49-6421-606-0.
circ. 40. *3322*

PROP.
Oesterreichischer Aero Club, Prinz-Eugen-Str. 12, A-1040 Vienna, Austria. TEL 01-5051028.
circ. 6,000. *3514*

PROPERTY REGISTER.
Tophill Press, 49 High St., Sevenoaks, Kent TN13 1L8, England. TEL 0732-743300. FAX 0732-743006. *6033*

PROSPECT (SUTTON).
Harrington Publications, Rafferty House, 2-4 Sutton Court Rd., Sutton, Surrey SM1 4SS, England. TEL 44-181-770-9340. FAX 44-181-770-9345.
circ. 12,000. *3662*

PROSPEROUS TIMES.
Howard Publications, 417 Fayette St., Hammond, IN 46320. TEL 219-933-3253.
circ. 42,000. *3236*

PROSTHETICS AND ORTHOTICS INTERNATIONAL.
International Society for Prosthetics and Orthotics, Borgervaenget 5, DK-2100 Copenhagen OE, Denmark. TEL 45-31-20-72-60. FAX 45-31-18-16-69.
circ. 3,300. *4790*

PROTEIN INFORMATION RESOURCE NEWSLETTER.
National Biomedical Research Foundation, 3900 Reservoir Rd., N.W., Washington, DC 20007. TEL 202-687-2121. FAX 202-687-1662.
circ. 1,000. *602*

PROVEN AND POPULAR HOME PLANS.
Giroux Publishing, 102 Ellis St., Penticton, BC V2A 4L5, Canada. TEL 604-493-0942. FAX 604-493-7526.
circ. 10,000. *871*

PROVENCE GENEALOGIE.
Centre Genealogique de Midi-Provence, B.P. 30, 13243 Marseille Cedex 01, France.
circ. 1,300. *3098*

PROVINCIA NUOVA.
Amministrazione Provinciale, Corso V. Emanuele 17, 26100 Cremona, Italy. TEL 0372-406268. FAX 0372-456744.
circ. 2,000. *5916*

PROVINCIAL NEWSLETTER.
British Columbia Registered Music Teachers' Association, 197 Vancouver Ave., Penticton, BC V2A 1A1, Canada. TEL 604-492-8944. FAX 604-493-9130.
circ. 1,000. *5189*

PROYECTOS QUIMICOS.
Tecnipublicaciones, S.A., C. Albacete 5, 28027 Madrid, Spain. TEL 34-1-3261440. FAX 36-1-3262407.
circ. 3,000. *1689*

PRZEGLAD ANTROPOLOGICZNY.
Polskie Towarzystwo Antropologiczne, Ul. Marymoncka 34, 01-813 Warsaw, Poland.
circ. 500. *319*

PRZEMYSLOWY INSTYTUT ELEKTRONIKI. PRACE.
Przemyslowy Instytut Elektroniki, Ul. Dluga 44-50, 00-241 Warsaw, Poland. TEL 48-22-313839. FAX 48-22-313014.
circ. 300. *2530*

PSIONIC MEDICINE.
Psionic Medical Society, Garden Cottage, Beacon Hill Park, Hindhead, Surrey GU26 6HU, England.
circ. 100. *4520*

PSIQUIS.
Alpe Editores, S.A., Pedro Rico, 27, 28029 Madrid, Spain. TEL 34-1-7338811. FAX 34-1-3159652.
circ. 6,000. *4862*

PSYCHIATRIC FORUM.
Department of Mental Health, William S. Hall Psychiatric Institute, Box 202, Columbia, SC 29202. TEL 803-734-7154. FAX 803-734-0791.
circ. 4,000. *4862*

PSYCHIATRIC TIMES.
C M E Inc., 1924 E. Deere Ave., Santa Ana, CA 92705-5723. TEL 800-447-4474. FAX 714-250-1245.
circ. 42,445. *4863*

PSYCHOLOGY BULLETIN.
Psychology Resource Centre, Private Bag X17, Bellville 7535, South Africa. TEL 27-21-959-2283. FAX 27-21-959-3515.
circ. 1,000. *5876*

PUBLIC EDUCATION ALERT.
Public Education Association, 39 W. 32nd St., New York, NY 10001-3803. TEL 212-868-1640. FAX 212-268-7344.
circ. 5,000. *2364*

PUBLIC EMPLOYEE PRESS.
American Federation of State, County & Municipal Employees, A F L - C I O, District Council 37, 125 Barclay St., New York, NY 10007. TEL 212-815-1000. FAX 212-815-7535.
circ. 160,000. *3727*

THE PUBLIC EYE (WASHINGTON).
Public Employees Roundtable, Box 14270, Ben Franklin Sta., Washington, DC 20044-4270. TEL 202-927-5000. FAX 202-927-5001. *5916*

PUBLIC PERSPECTIVE.
Roper Center for Public Opinion Research, Box 440, Storrs, CT 06269. TEL 203-486-4440. FAX 203-486-6308.
circ. 3,000. *5701*

PUBLIC SCHOOL ENROLLMENT AND STAFF, NEW YORK STATE.
Education Department, Information, Reporting & Technology Services, Education Bldg. Annex, Rm. 962, Albany, NY 12234. TEL 518-474-7082. FAX 518-474-4351. *2365*

PUBLIC SCHOOL PROFESSIONAL PERSONNEL REPORT, NEW YORK STATE.
Education Department, Information, Reporting & Technology Services, Education Bldg. Annex, Rm. 962, Albany, NY 12234. TEL 518-474-7082. FAX 518-474-4351. *2365*

PUBLIC SECTOR.
Auburn University, Center for Governmental Services, 2232 Haley Center, Auburn University, Auburn, AL 36849. TEL 205-844-1913. FAX 205-844-1919.
circ. 3,000. *5917*

PUBLIC SECTOR PROCUREMENT AND FINANCE.
Government Group Publications, Southbank House, Black Prince Rd., London SE1 7SJ, England. TEL 0171-582-9191. FAX 0171-587-1810.
circ. 11,480. *5917*

PUBLICITY AND MEDIA RESOURCES FOR PUBLISHERS.
Association of American University Presses, Inc., 584 Broadway, Ste. 410, New York, NY 10012. TEL 212-941-6610. *44*

PUEBLO BUSINESS JOURNAL.
201 W. 8th St., Ste. 408, Box 1544, Pueblo, CO 81002. TEL 719-542-3616. FAX 719-542-4506.
circ. 6,500. *1235*

PUERTO RICO. OFICINA DE PRESUPUESTO Y GERENCIA. PRESUPUESTO (YEARS).
Oficina de Presupuesto, Box 3228, San Juan, PR 00902. TEL 809-725-9420. FAX 809-723-7308. *5918*

PUGET SOUND COMPUTERUSER.
K F H Publications Inc., 3530 Bagley Ave. N., Seattle, WA 98103. TEL 206-547-4950. FAX 206-547-5355.
circ. 85,000. *2102*

PULMONARY REVIEWS.
Partners in Medical Communication, 4 Brighton Rd., Clifton, NJ 07012. TEL 201-916-1000. FAX 201-916-0021. *4890*

PULP AND PAPER.
Miller Freeman, Inc., 600 Harrison St., San Francisco, CA 94107. TEL 415-905-2200. FAX 415-905-2232.
circ. 40,900. *5325*

PULSE (PICO RIVERA).
Southern California Veterinary Medical Association, 8338 Rosemead Blvd., Pico Rivera, CA 90660. TEL 310-948-4979.
circ. 1,100. *6952*

PULSE! (WEST SACRAMENTO).
M T S, Incorporated, Tower Records - Pulse!, 2500 Delmonte St., Bldg. C, W. Sacramento, CA 95691. TEL 916-373-2450. FAX 916-373-2480.
circ. 300,000. *5190*

PULSO.
Universidad Internacional de la Florida, Miami, Programa Centroamericano de Periodismo, Biscayne Blvd. at N.E. 151st St., North Miami, FL 33181. TEL 305-940-5672. FAX 305-956-5498.
circ. 4,500. *3710*

PUNJABI SAHITYA.
c/o H. S. Kalra, Ed., 254 Rowley Gardens, Woodberry Grove, London N4 1HW, England.
circ. 4,000. *4162*

PUPPETRY JOURNAL.
Puppeteers of America, 8005 Swallow Dr., Macedonia, OH 44056.
circ. 2,200. *6701*

PURCHASING TODAY.
National Association of Purchasing Management, 2055 E. Centennial Circle, Tempe, AZ 85285. TEL 602-752-6276. FAX 602-752-7890.
circ. 40,000. *1483*

PURDUE UNIVERSITY. OFFICE OF MANPOWER STUDIES. MANPOWER & TECHNICAL EDUCATION REQUIREMENTS REPORTS.
Purdue University, Office of Manpower Studies, Knoy Hall, W. Lafayette, IN 47907. TEL 317-494-2559. FAX 317-494-0486. *1393*

PURJEHTIJA.
Finnish Yachting Association, Raciokatu 20, SF-00240 Helsinki, Finland. TEL 358-0-1582350. FAX 358-0-1582365.
circ. 31,000. *6539*

PUROSANGUE IN ITALIE.
Associazione Nazionale Allevatori Cavalli Purosangue, Via del Caravaggio 3, 20144 Milan, Italy. TEL 39-2-48012002. FAX 39-2-48194547.
circ. 2,500. *6550*

PURPLE AND GOLD.
Chi Psi Educational Trust, 1705 Washtenaw Ave., Ann Arbor, MI 48104. TEL 313-663-4205.
circ. 17,000. *1853*

PUTTERIDGE BURY MANAGEMENT REVIEW.
University of Luton, Putteridge Bury, Hitchin Rd., Luton, Beds. LU2 8LE, England. TEL 01582-482555. FAX 01582-482689.
circ. 300. *1441*

PYRETHRUM POST.
Pyrethrum Bureau, Pyrethrum Board of Kenya, P.O. Box 420, Nakuru, Kenya. TEL 254-37-211567. FAX 254-37-45274. *548*

Q: THE PHYSICIANS GUIDE TO QUALITY.
Target Marketing, Inc., 5 Victory Ln., Ste. 101, Liberty, MO 64068. TEL 816-781-7557. FAX 816-781-3298.
circ. 60,000. *4521*

QUADERNI DI COOPERAZIONE SANITARIA.
Amici di Raoul Follereau, Via Borselli 4, 40135 Bologna, Italy. TEL 39-51-433402. FAX 39-51-434046.
circ. 2,000. *4627*

QUADERNI DI ECONOMIA E FINANZA.
Banco di Sardegna S.p.A., Servizio Studi, Viale Umberto I, 36, 07100 Sassari, Italy. TEL 39-79-226572. FAX 39-79-225579.
circ. 2,000. *1236*

QUADRANT.
Ablex, 28 E. 39th St., New York, NY 10016. TEL 212-697-6430. FAX 201-953-3989.
circ. 2,000. *5878*

QUAKER CAMPUS.
Whittier College, Quaker Campus, Box 8613, Whittier, CA 90608. TEL 310-907-4354. FAX 310-945-5301.
circ. 2,000. *1883*

QUALITY OF CARE.
Commission on Quality of Care for the Mentally Disabled, 99 Washington Ave., Ste. 1002, Albany, NY 12210. TEL 518-473-6304. FAX 518-473-6302.
circ. 11,000. *4865*

QUALITY SOURCE.
American Group Practice Association, 1422 Duke St., Alexandria, VA 22314. TEL 703-838-0033. FAX 703-548-1890. *4521*

QUANTUM (NEW YORK).
Springer-Verlag, Science Journals, 175 Fifth Ave., New York, NY 10010. TEL 212-460-1500. FAX 212-473-6272.
circ. 40,000. *6273*

QUARTERLY FORECAST OF JAPANESE ECONOMY.
Japan Center for Economic Research, Nikkei Kayabacho Bldg., 6-1 Nihonbashi Kayabacgi 2-chome, Chuo-ku, Tokyo 103, Japan. TEL 81-3-3639-2801. FAX 81-3-3639-2839. *1529*

QUARTERLY JOURNAL OF TAIWAN LAND CREDIT.
Land Bank of Taiwan, Credit Investigation & Research Department, 46 Kuan Chien Rd., Taipei, Taiwan, Republic of China. TEL 02-3613020. FAX 02-3115782.
circ. 500. *198*

QUARTERNOTE.
American Musicians Union, Inc., 8 Tobin Ct., Dumont, NJ 07628. TEL 201-384-5378.
circ. 350. *5190*

QUEBEC HOME & SCHOOL NEWS.
Quebec Federation of Home and School Associations, 3285 Cavendish Blvd., Ste. 562, Montreal, PQ H4B 2L9, Canada. TEL 514-481-5619. FAX 514-481-5619.
circ. 1,350. *2365*

QUEEN'S AWARDS MAGAZINE.
Nexus Media Ltd., Nexus House, Azalea Dr., Swanley, Kent BR8 8H4, England. TEL 44-1322-660070. FAX 44-1322-666408.
circ. 10,000. *1293*

QUEENSLAND FOREST SERVICE. RESEARCH NOTE.
Queensland Forest Service, G.P.O. Box 944, Brisbane, Qld. 4001, Australia. TEL 07-877-9727. FAX 07-371-2217.
circ. 400. *3023*

QUEENSLAND FOREST SERVICE. RESEARCH PAPER.
Queensland Forest Service, G.P.O. Box 944, Brisbane, Qld. 4001, Australia. TEL 07-877 9727. FAX 07-371-2217.
circ. 400. *3023*

QUEENSLAND FRUIT AND VEGETABLE NEWS.
Queensland Fruit and Vegetable Growers, Box 19, Brisbane Market, Brisbane, Qld. 4106, Australia. TEL 61-7-2132464. FAX 61-7-2132467.
circ. 8,000. *3065*

QUERCE.
Collegio alla Querce, Via della Piazzuola 44, 50133 Florence, Italy. TEL 39-55-573621. FAX 39-55-579655.
circ. 2,000. *2365*

QUERSCHNITTE.
Verlag fuer Kultur und Wissenschaft, Friedrichstr. 38, 53111 Bonn, Germany. TEL 49-228-638784. FAX 49-228-638784.
circ. 1,000. *6157*

QUEST (BOSTON).
Church of the Larger Fellowship, Unitarian Universalist, 25 Beacon St., Boston, MA 02108. TEL 617-742-2100. FAX 617-523-4123.
circ. 3,000. *6086*

QUEST: MANHATTAN PROPERTIES & COUNTRY ESTATES.
Quest Magazines, Inc., 1046 Madison Ave., New York, NY 10021-0137. FAX 212-288-4536.
circ. 97,000. *6033*

QUESTE.
Premier Magazines Ltd., Haymarket House, 1 Oxendon St., London SW1Y 4EE, England. TEL 44-171-925-2544. FAX 44-171-839-4491.
circ. 25,000. *6799*

QUICK TOPICS NEWSLETTER.
American Wholesale Marketers Association, 1128 16th St., N.W., Washington, DC 20036. TEL 202-463-2124. FAX 202-467-0559.
circ. 4,200. *3001*

QUIET MIRACLE.
Bible Literature International, 625 E.N. Broadway, Columbus, OH 43214-4133. TEL 614-267-3116. FAX 614-267-7110.
circ. 20,000. *6086*

QUINCY BUSINESS NEWS.
John R. Graham, Inc., 40 Oval Rd., Ste. 2, Quincy, MA 02170-3813. TEL 617-328-0069. FAX 617-471-1504.
circ. 2,850. *954*

QUIRK'S MARKETING RESEARCH REVIEW.
Quirk Enterprises, Box 23536, Minneapolis, MN 55423. TEL 612-861-1836. FAX 612-861-8051.
circ. 15,500. *1483*

QUOTARIAN.
Quota International, 1420 21st St., N.W., Washington, DC 20036. TEL 202-331-9694.
circ. 14,000. *1853*

R A C JOURNAL.
I I T Research Institute, Reliability Analysis Center, 201 Mill St., Rome, NY 13440. TEL 315-337-0900. FAX 315-337-9932.
circ. 20,000. *2616*

R A C M S A NEWS.
R A C Motor Sports Association Ltd., Motor Sports House, Riverside Park, Colnbrook, Slough SL3 0HG, England. TEL 44-1753-681736. FAX 44-1753-682938.
circ. 30,000. *6476*

R A NEWS.
Recreation Association of the Public Service of Canada, 2451 Riverside Dr., Ottawa, ON K1H 7X7, Canada. TEL 613-733-5100. FAX 613-733-3310.
circ. 40,000. *1853*

R B ELEKTRONICA.
Uitgeverij de Muiderkring B.V., Hogeweyselaan 227, 1382 JL Weesp, Netherlands. TEL 31-2940-15210. FAX 31-2940-12782.
circ. 12,000. *2531*

R E F Z.
Medialog Verlag GbR, Sabelsbergerstr. 9, 80333 Munich, Germany. TEL 49-89-282058. FAX 49-89-2802265.
circ. 19,985. *3837*

R E I D QUARTERLY.
Prudential Insurance Co. of America, Public Relations & Advertising Dept., 5 Plaza, Newark, NJ 07101. TEL 201-877-6000.
circ. 3,000. *3663*

R E R F UPDATE.
Radiation Effects Research Foundation, 5-2 Hijiyama Park, Minami-ku, Hiroshima-shi, Hiroshima-ken 732, Japan. FAX 81-82-263-7279. *4882*

R E S.
Tecnipublicaciones S.A., Fernando VI 27-1, 28004 Madrid, Spain. TEL 91-319-7889. FAX 91-410-1069.
circ. 5,000. *1117*

R I A L UPDATE.
Religion in American Life, 2 Queenston Pl., Rm. 200, Princeton, NJ 08540. TEL 609-921-3639. FAX 609-921-0551.
circ. 4,000. *6086*

R I L M ABSTRACTS OF MUSIC LITERATURE.
R I L M Abstracts, City University of New York, 33 W. 42nd St., New York, NY 10036. TEL 212-642-2709. FAX 212-642-1973.
circ. 1,500. *5209*

R I P A REPORT.
Royal Institute of Public Administration, 3 Birdcage Walk, London SW1H 9JH, England. TEL 071-222-2248. FAX 071-222-2249. *5918*

R S E NEWS.
Royal Society of Edinburgh, 22 George St., Edinburgh EH2 2PQ, Scotland. TEL 44-131-225-6057. FAX 44-131-220-6889.
circ. 1,200. *6274*

R S - MAGAZINE.
Computer Publishing Group, 320 Washington St., Brookline, MA 02146-3202. TEL 617-739-7001. FAX 617-739-7003.
circ. 40,000. *2090*

R T.
Allied Healthcare Publications, 4676 Admiralty Way, Ste. 202, Marina Del Rey, CA 90292. TEL 310-306-2206. FAX 310-301-8101.
circ. 20,000. *4890*

R T P VIEWPOINTS.
Research Triangle Park, 2 Hanes Dr., Box 12255, Research Triangle Park, NC 27709. TEL 919-549-8181. FAX 919-549-8246.
circ. 3,500. *6274*

R V BUSINESS.
T L Enterprises, Inc., 3601 Calle Tecate, Camarillo, CA 93012. TEL 805-389-0300. FAX 805-389-0484.
circ. 13,510. *6494*

R V NEWS.
D & S Media Enterprises, Inc., 6125 S. Ash Ave, Ste. 8, Tempe, AZ 85283-5608. TEL 602-839-8130. FAX 602-820-0934.
circ. 13,000. *6726*

R V TIMES.
Sheila Jones Publishing Ltd., P.O. Box 160, 129 W. Second Ave., Qualicum Beach, BC V9K 1S7, Canada. TEL 604-752-8266. FAX 604-752-8269.
circ. 45,000. *6908*

RACIAL - ETHNIC DISTRIBUTION OF PUBLIC SCHOOL STUDENTS AND STAFF, NEW YORK STATE.
Education Department, Information, Reporting & Technology Services, Education Bldg. Annex, Rm. 962, Albany, NY 12234. TEL 518-474-7082. FAX 518-474-4351. *2365*

RACQUETTE.
State University of New York, College at Potsdam, 119 Borrington Student Union, Potsdam, NY 13676. TEL 315-267-8451. FAX 315-267-2170.
circ. 3,500. *1883*

RADCLIFFE NEWS.
Radcliffe College, 10 Garden St., Cambridge, MA 02138. TEL 617-495-8608. FAX 617-496-4640.
circ. 43,000. *1883*

RADCLIFFE QUARTERLY.
Radcliffe College, 10 Garden St., Cambridge, MA 02138. TEL 617-495-8608. FAX 617-496-4640.
circ. 30,000. *1883*

RADIATION EFFECTS RESEARCH FOUNDATION. ANNUAL REPORT.
Radiation Effects Research Foundation, 5-2 Hijiyama Park, Minami-ku, Hiroshima-shi, Hiroshima-ken 732, Japan. FAX 81-82-263-7279. *4882*

RADIATION EFFECTS RESEARCH FOUNDATION. COMMENTARY AND REVIEW SERIES.
Radiation Effects Research Foundation, 5-2 Hijiyama Park, Minami-ku, Hiroshima-shi, Hiroshima-ken 732, Japan. FAX 81-82-261-7279. *4882*

RADIATION EFFECTS RESEARCH FOUNDATION NEWSLETTER.
Radiation Effects Research Foundation, 5-2, Hijiyama Park, Minami-ku, Hiroshima-shi, Hiroshima-ken 732, Japan. FAX 81-82-261-7279. *4882*

RADIO RESOURCE MAGAZINE.
Pandata Corporation, 14 Inverness Dr. E., D-136, Englewood, CO 80112. TEL 303-792-2390. FAX 303-792-2391.
circ. 35,000. *1939*

RADIO - T V INTERVIEW REPORT.
Bradley Communications Corp., Box 1206, Lansdowne, PA 19050. TEL 215-259-1070. FAX 215-284-3704.
circ. 4,000. *44*

RADIO WEEK.
National Association of Broadcasters, 1771 N St., N.W., Washington, DC 20036. TEL 202-429-5350. FAX 202-429-5406. *1940*

RADIOBOTE.
F.O. Rothy, Ed. & Pub., A-4360 Grein, Austria.
circ. 150,000. *1940*

RADIUS (ROCKFORD).
Tube and Pipe Association, International (TPA), 833 Featherstone Rd., Rockford, IL 61107. TEL 815-399-8775. FAX 815-399-7679.
circ. 1,200. *4972*

RAIL WHISPERS.
Whisper Publications, Inc., 1865 Palmer Ave., Ste. 202, Larchmont, NY 10538. TEL 914-833-3634. FAX 914-834-7651.
circ. 30,000. *3236*

RAILWAYS AFRICA.
Rail-Link C C, P.O. Box 4794, 2125 Randburg, Transvaal, South Africa. TEL 27-11-463-4330. FAX 27-11-463-4224.
circ. 2,500. *6817*

RAILWAYS INSTITUTE MAGAZINE.
Railways Institute Council, P.O. Box 8436, Perth Business Centre, Perth, W.A. 6849, Australia. TEL 61-9-3262461. FAX 61-9-3262754.
circ. 4,000. *6817*

RAINEY TIMES.
Rt. 4, Box 56, Sulphur Springs, TX 75482. TEL 903-885-3523. FAX 903-439-1081.
circ. 300. *3099*

RANDSE AFRIKAANSE UNIVERSITEIT. JAARBOEK.
Rand Afrikaans University, P.O. Box 524, Auckland Park 2006, South Africa. FAX 27-11-4892790.
2440

RANSOMER.
Guild of Our Lady of Ransom, 31 Southdown Rd., Wimbledon, London SW20 8QJ, England. TEL 44-181-947-2598. FAX 44-181-944-6208.
circ. 2,000. *6193*

RAPPORT ANNUEL SUR LA COOPERATION AU DEVELOPPEMENT - BURUNDI.
United Nations Development Program, Programme des Nations Unies pour le Developpement au Burundi, c/o Ms. Linda Schrieber, Chief, Documentation and Statistics Office, BPPE, UNDP, New York, NY 10017. *1313*

RARE COIN REVIEW.
Bowers and Merena Galleries, Inc., Box 1224, Wolfeboro, NH 03894. TEL 603-596-5095. FAX 603-569-5319. *5227*

RASSEGNA DELL'IMBALLAGGIO E CONFEZIONAMENTO.
Editrice Arti Poligrafiche Europee, Via Casella 16, 20156 Milan, Italy. TEL 39-2-392281. FAX 39-2-39214341.
circ. 11,797. *5304*

RASSEGNA ECONOMICA (NAPLES).
Banco di Napoli, Direzione Generale, Ufficio Studi, Via Roma 177-178, 80132 Naples, Italy.
circ. 5,350. *1237*

RASSEGNA GRAFICA.
Editrice Arti Poligrafiche Europee, Via Casella, 16, 20156 Milan, Italy. TEL 39-2-392281. FAX 39-2-39214341.
circ. 12,627. *5818*

RATTLE OF THETA CHI.
Theta Chi Funds for Leadership and Education, Inc., 3330 Founders Rd., Indianapolis, IN 46268. TEL 317-824-1881. FAX 317-824-1908.
circ. 85,000. *1883*

RAZZA BOVINA PIEMONTESE.
Associazione Nazionale Allevatori Bovini di Razza Piemontese, Via Valeggio 22, 10128 Turin, Italy. TEL 39-173-750791. FAX 39-173-750915.
circ. 4,000. *282*

REACH (NEW HAVEN).
Religious Education Association, 409 Prospect St., New Haven, CT 06511-2177. TEL 203-865-6142. FAX 203-865-6142.
circ. 1,000. *2366*

READER (SAN DIEGO).
Box 85803, San Diego, CA 92138. TEL 619-235-3000. FAX 619-231-0489.
circ. 131,000. *4163*

READING TIME.
Children's Book Council of Australia, P.O. Box 62, Ashmont, Wagga Wagga, N.S.W. 2650, Australia. FAX 069-25-4907.
circ. 2,200. *4256*

THE READMORE NEWSLETTER.
Readmore Publications, Inc., 22 Cortlandt St., New York, NY 10007-3194. TEL 212-349-5540. FAX 212-571-7328.
circ. 2,500. *4022*

REAL ESTATE BUSINESS.
Realtors National Marketing Institute, Real Estate Brokerage Council, Box 300, Wheaton, IL 60189-0300. TEL 708-752-0500. FAX 708-752-0525.
circ. 31,500. *6033*

REAL ESTATE FORUM.
Real Estate Forum, Inc., 111 Eighth Ave., No. 1511, New York, NY 10011-5201. TEL 212-563-6460. FAX 212-967-1498.
circ. 24,000. *5034*

REAL SOCIEDAD ARQUEOLOGICA. BOLETIN ARQUEOLOGICO.
Real Sociedad Arqueologica Tarraconense, Museo Nacional Arqueologic, Tarragona, Spain.
circ. 1,000. *369*

REALITY.
Reality Inc., 1 Canyon Dr., Alexandria, VA 22305. TEL 703-836-0565.
circ. 10,000. *6086*

RECAMBIO LIBRE.
General de Edicones Especializadas, S.L., C. Juan de Olias, 11 y 13, 28020 Madrid, Spain. TEL 34-1-5719676. FAX 34-1-5210695.
circ. 3,000. *6799*

THE RECORD OF SIGMA ALPHA EPSILON.
Sigma Alpha Epsilon National Fraternity, Box 1856, Evanston, IL 60204. TEL 708-475-1856.
circ. 81,000. *1883*

RECORDER (SEARCY).
Alpha Chi National Honor Society, Box 2249, Harding University, Searcy, AR 72149. TEL 501-268-6161.
circ. 7,500. *2440*

RECYCLAGE MAGAZINE.
Editions Montmartre, 142, rue Montmartre, 75002 Paris, France. TEL 33-1-40-26-83-21. FAX 33-1-40-39-97-52.
circ. 6,000. *2855*

RECYCLAGE RECUPERATION.
Editions Montmartre, 142 rue Montmartre, 75002 Paris, France. TEL 33-1-40-26-83-21. FAX 33-1-40-39-97-52.
circ. 6,000. *1442*

RED AND BLACK (WASHINGTON).
Washington & Jefferson College, 60 S. Lincoln St., Washington, PA 15301. TEL 412-223-6049.
circ. 1,500. *1883*

RED MEN MAGAZINE.
Improved Order of Red Men, Box 683, Waco, TX 76703. TEL 817-756-1221. FAX 817-756-4828.
circ. 27,000. *1853*

RED SHIELD NEWS.
Royal Insurance, Corporate Communications Dept., 9300 Arrowpoint Blvd., Charlotte, NC 28217. TEL 704-522-2000. FAX 704-522-2055.
circ. 10,000. *3663*

RED TAPE.
Public Service Association of New South Wales, G.P.O. Box 3365, Sydney, N.S.W. 2001, Australia. TEL 61-2-290-1555. FAX 61-2-262-1623.
circ. 45,000. *3727*

REDWOOD NEWS.
California Redwood Association, 405 Enfrente Dr., Ste. 200, Novato, CA 94949. TEL 415-382-0662. FAX 415-382-8531.
circ. 30,000. *403*

REFINISHER.
Dulux Australia, P.O. Box 60, Rosebank MDC, Clayton S., Vic. 3169, Australia. TEL 61-2-94763199. FAX 61-2-94765739.
circ. 17,000. *6793*

REFLECTIONS.
Springer-Verlag Hong Kong, Ltd., 701 Mirror Tower, 61 Mody Rd., Tsim Sha Tsui, Kowloon, Hong Kong. TEL 852-723-9698. FAX 852-724-2366.
circ. 5,000. *6007*

REFLEX MAGAZINE.
Xelfer, 105 S. Main Ste. 204, Seattle, WA 98104. TEL 206-682-7688. FAX 206-682-6912.
circ. 7,000. *449*

REFRIGERATED AND FROZEN FOODS.
Stagnito Publishing Company, 1935 Shermer Rd., Ste. 100, Northbrook, IL 60062. TEL 847-205-5660. FAX 847-205-568C.
circ. 29,500. *2985*

REGARDS SUR LE COMITE D'ETABLISSEMENT D'ORLY SUD.
Comite d'Etablissement Air France-Orly Sud, Extension Est, Batiment CRP, Aerogare d'Orly Sud France.
circ. 8,000. *75*

REGENCY INTERNATIONAL DIRECTORY.
Regency International Publications Ltd., 325 Canterbury Road, Densole, Folkestone, Kent CT18 7BB, England. TEL 0303-893488. FAX 0303-893488. *1636*

REGIONAL AIRLINE ASSOCIATION. ANNUAL REPORT.
Regional Airline Association, 1200 19th S., N.W., Ste. 300, Washington, DC 20036. TEL 202-857-1170. FAX 202-429-5113.
circ. 2,700. *6764*

REGIONAL DEVELOPMENT CORPORATION. ANNUAL REPORT.
Regional Development Corporation, P.O. Box 428, Fredericton, N.B. E3B 5R4, Canada. TEL 506-453-2277.
circ. 1,000. *1237*

THE REGIONAL REVIEW.
Yorkshire and Humberside Regional Research Observatory, University of Leeds, School of Geography, Leeds LS2 9JT, England. TEL 44-113-233-3336. FAX 44-113-233-3308.
circ. 150. *6274*

REGIONS BEYOND ADVENCE.
Regions Beyond Missionary Union International, 1431 Stuckert Rd., Warrington, PA 18976-1526. TEL 215-745-0680. FAX 215-742-3031.
circ. 11,400. *6087*

REGISTERED REPRESENTATIVE.
Plaza Communications, Inc., 18818 Teller Ave., No. 280, Irvine, CA 92715 TEL 714-851-2220. FAX 714-851-1636.
circ. 90,000. *1349*

REHAB & COMMUNITY CARE MANAGEMENT.
B C S Communications Ltd., 101 Thorncliffe Park Dr., Toronto, ON M4H 1M2, Canada. TEL 416-421-7944. FAX 416-421-0966.
circ. 25,000. *4819*

REIGN OF THE SACRED HEART.
Priests of the Sacred Heart, 6889 S. Lovers Ln., Hales Corners, WI 53130. TEL 414-425-3383. FAX 414-425-5719.
circ. 490,000. *6193*

REINSURANCE REPORTER.
Lincoln National Life Reinsurance Co., One Reinsurance Pl., P.O. Box 7808, Ft. Wayne, IN 46301. FAX 219-455-4124.
circ. 4,400. *3663*

RELAY MAGAZINE.
Florida Municipal Electric Association, Inc., Box 10114, 417 E. College Ave., Tallahassee, FL 32302-2114. TEL 904-224-3314.
circ 2,200. *2570*

REMOVALS AND STORAGE.
Quarrington-Curtis Ltd., 15-17 Canute Rd., Southampton SO14 3FJ England. TEL 44-1703-635438. FAX 44-1703-632193.
circ. 1,800. *6726*

RENDER.
Editors West, 10961 Desert Lawn Dr., No. 57, Calimesa, CA 92320. TEL 714-795-4240.
circ. 7,500. *146*

RENEWAL NEWS.
Presbyterian Renewal Publications, Box 429, Black Mountain, NC 28711-0429. TEL 704-669-7373. FAX 704-669-4880.
circ. 14,000. *6158*

RENS OG VASK.
Visholm Media AS, Sydvestvej 49, P.O. Box 221, DK-2600 Glostrup, Denmark.
circ. 3,000. *1829*

RENT I DANMARK.
Forlaget Thorsgaard ApS, Holmensvej 5, P.O. Box 5, 3600 Frederikssund, Denmark. TEL 42-31-21-05. FAX 47-38-36-33.
circ. 7,000. *1443*

RENTAL EQUIPMENT REGISTER.
Miramar Publishing Co., Box 15518, N. Hollywood, CA 91615-9773. TEL 310-337-9717.
circ. 17,500. *1483*

RENTAL PRODUCT NEWS.
Johnson Hill Press, Inc. 1233 Janesville Ave., Ft. Atkinson, WI 53538. TEL 414-563-6388. FAX 414-563-1699.
circ. 20,000. *1530*

REPORT TO BUSINESS.
Better Business Bureau of Metropolitan New York Inc., 257 Park Ave. S., New York, NY 10010. TEL 212-533-7500. *2154*

THE REPORTER (LITTLE ROCK).
Arkansas School Boards Association, 808 Dr. M.L. King Dr., Little Rock, AR 72202-3646. TEL 501-372-1415. FAX 501-375-2454.
circ. 3,500. *2462*

REPORTER ON HUMAN REPRODUCTION & THE LAW.
Legal-Medical Studies, Inc., Box 8219, Boston, MA 02114. TEL 617-742-7959. *3840*

REPORTERO INDUSTRIAL.
Keller International Publishing Corporation, 150 Great Neck Rd., Great Neck, NY 11021. TEL 516-829-9210. FAX 516-829-7265.
circ. 38,428. *4345*

REPROGRAFIA ACTUAL.
Ediciones Press Graph, S.L., C. Mallorca 219 5o 2o, 08008 Barcelona, Spain. TEL 34-3-3237554. FAX 34-3-3237463.
circ. 2,500. *5818*

RES PUBLICA NOWA.
Batory Press Sp. z o.o., P.O. Box 856, 00-950 Warsaw 1, Poland. TEL 48-22-6298934. FAX 48-22-6273668.
circ. 5,000. *4163*

RESEARCH (SAN FRANCISCO).
Research Holdings Ltd., 2201 Third St., San Francisco, CA 94107. TEL 415-621-0220. FAX 415-621-0735.
circ. 61,500. *1349*

RESEARCH & DEVELOPMENT.
Cahners Publishing Company (Des Plaines), Division of Reed Elsevier Inc., 1350 E. Touhy Ave., Box 5080, Des Plaines, IL 60018-5080. TEL 847-635-8800. FAX 847-390-2618.
circ. 100,084. *6662*

RESEARCH & DEVELOPMENT PRODUCT SOURCE TELEPHONE DIRECTORY.
Cahners Publishing Company (Des Plaines), Division of Reed Elsevier Inc., 1350 E. Touhy Ave., Box 5080, Des Plaines, IL 60018-5080. TEL 847-635-8800. FAX 847-390-2618.
circ. 100,000. *6662*

RESEARCH IN FISHERIES.
University of Washington, School of Fisheries WH-10, Seattle, WA 98195. TEL 206-543-4678. FAX 206-685-7471.
circ. 3,000. *2942*

RESEARCH - PENN STATE.
Pennsylvania State University, Senior Vice President for Research, 320 Kern Bldg., University Park, PA 16802. TEL 814-865-3477. FAX 814-863-4627.
circ. 25,000. *2441*

RESEARCHPLUS.
Market Research Society, 15 Northburgh St., London EC1V 0AH, England. TEL 44-171-490-4911. FAX 44-171-490-0608.
circ. 7,000. *1484*

RESIDENCES.
Marketing U.S.P. Inc., 554 Grosvenor, Westmount, PQ H3Y 2S4, Canada. TEL 514-935-1171. FAX 514-935-4504.
circ. 71,053. *3681*

RESIDENTIAL LIGHTING MAGAZINE.
Vance Publishing Corporation (Lincolnshire), Box 1414, Lincolnshire, IL 60069-1414. TEL 708-634-2600. FAX 708-634-4379.
circ. 11,600. *3692*

RESOURCES (NASHVILLE).
F I S I - Madison Financial Box 40726, Nashville, TN 37204. TEL 615-371-2658.
circ. 1,200,000. *2155*

RESTAURANT HOSPITALITY.
Penton Publishing Co. 1100 Superior Ave., Cleveland, OH 44114-2543. TEL 216-696-7000. FAX 216-696-8765.
circ. 124,048. *3570*

RESTORATION HERALD.
Christian Restoration Association, 5664 Cheviot Rd., Cincinnati, OH 45247. TEL 513-385-0461.
circ. 4,500. *6089*

RETAIL OBSERVER.
1442 Sierra Creek Way, San Jose, CA 95132. TEL 408-272-8974. FAX 408-272-3344.
circ. 5,100. *3692*

RETHINKING SCHOOLS.
Rethinking Schools Limited, 1001 E. Keefe Ave., Milwaukee, WI 53212. TEL 414-694-9646. FAX 414-964-7220.
circ. 33,000. *2367*

THE RETIRED OFFICER.
Retired Officers' Association, 201 N. Washington St., Alexandria, VA 22314-2539. TEL 703-838-8115. FAX 703-838-8179.
circ. 385,290. *5045*

RETIREMENT LIFE (WASHINGTON).
National Association of Retired Federal Employees, 1533 New Hampshire Ave., N.W., Washington, DC 20036. TEL 202-234-0832. FAX 202-797-9698.
circ. 1,000. *3295*

REVIEW OF AGRICULTURAL ECONOMICS.
Review of Agricultural Economics, c/o Department of Agricultural Economics, Kansas State University, Manhattan, KS 66506-4011. TEL 913-532-4488. FAX 913-532-6925.
circ. 600. *198*

REVIEW OF BUSINESS.
St. John's University, College of Business Administration, Bent Hall, 8000 Utopia Pkwy., NY 11439. TEL 718-990-6768. FAX 718-990-1868.
circ. 7,000. *955*

REVISTA A T E M C O P.
Asociacion Espanola de Tecnicos de Maquinaria para la Construccion, Obras Publicas y Mineria, c/o Cruz del Sur, No. 3 bajo, 28007 Madrid, Spain. TEL 1-574-98-18. FAX 1-573-18-00.
circ. 5,000. *2671*

REVISTA AEREA.
Strato Publishing Co., Inc., 310 E. 44th St., Ste. 1601, New York, NY 10017. TEL 212-370-1740. FAX 212-949-6756.
circ. 10,000. *76*

REVISTA ALENTEJANA.
Casa do Alentejo, Rua das Portas de Santo Antao 58, Lisbon 2, Portugal.
circ. 3,000. *4163*

REVISTA BRASILEIRA DE XADREZ POSTAL.
Clube de Xadrez Epistolar Brasileiro, Caixa Postal 317, 40001 Salvador (BA), Brazil. *6477*

REVISTA CUBANA DE INVESTIGACIONES PESQUERAS. BOLETINES BIBLIOGRAFICOS.
Direccion de Ciencia y Tecnica, Ministerio de la Industria Pesquera, 5ta Avda. y 248 Barlovento, Santa Fe, Playa, Havana, Cuba. FAX 0511345.
circ. 900. *2942*

REVISTA DE ARQUITECTURA.
Sociedad Central de Arquitectos, Montevideo 938, 1019 Buenos Aires, Argentina. TEL 54-1-812-3644. FAX 54-1-953-5508.
circ. 8,000. *403*

REVISTA DE CIENCIAS FARMACEUTICAS.
Universidade Estadual Paulista, Av. Vicente Ferreira 1278, Caixa Postal 71, 17515-901 Marilia SP, Brazil. TEL 55-144-222504. FAX 55-144-222504. *5442*

REVISTA DE ESTUDIOS SOCIALES.
Centro de Estudios Sociales de la Santa Cruz del Valle de los Caidos, Palacio Real, Bailen s-n, Apdo. de Correas 14158, Madrid 15, Spain.
circ. 2,000. *6427*

REVISTA DE HISTORIA.
Comite Provincial del Partido Comunista de Cuba, Seccion de Investigaciones Historicas, Ave. 20 Aniversario y Plaza de la Revolucion, Holguin, Cuba. TEL 462013.
circ. 3,000. *3356*

REVISTA ECONOMICA.
Universidad Nacional de la Plata, Instituto de Investigaciones Economicas, Calle 48 No. 555, Piso 5, Ofic. 523, 1900 La Plata, Argentina. TEL 54-21-43985.
circ. 1,000. *956*

REVISTA ELECTROTECNICA.
Asociacion Electrotecnia Argentina, Posadas 1659, C.P. 1112 Buenos Aires, Argentina. TEL 804-3454-1532.
circ. 1,600. *2718*

REVISTA IBEROAMERICANA DE MICOLOGIA.
Asociacion Espanola de Micologia, C. Industria 241-249, 1o 1a Escalera Izq., 08026 Barcelona, Spain. TEL 34-3-4551100. FAX 34-3-4550918.
circ. 850. *701*

REVISTA TRIMESTRAL DE JURISPRUDENCIA.
Supremo Tribunal Federal, SIG-Quadra 6-Lote 800, 70604 Brasilia, D.F., Brazil.
circ. 2,000. *3842*

REVUE ARCHEOLOGIQUE DE L'EST ET DU CENTRE-EST.
C N R S Editions, 20-22 rue St. Amand, 75015 Paris, France. TEL 45-33-16-00. FAX 45-33-92-13.
circ. 1,500. *370*

REVUE ARCHEOLOGIQUE NARBONNAISE.
C N R S Editions, 20-22 rue St. Amand, 75015 Paris, France. TEL 45-33-16-00. FAX 45-33-92-13.
circ. 1,500. *370*

REVUE D'ELEVAGE ET DE MEDECINE VETERINAIRE DES PAYS TROPICAUX.
Expansion Scientifique, 31 bd. de la Tour Maubourg, 75007 Paris, France. TEL 40-62-64-00. FAX 45-55-69-20. *6953*

REVUE D'HISTOIRE DES TEXTES.
C N R S Editions, 20-22 rue St. Amand, 75015 Paris, France. TEL 45-33-16-00. FAX 45-33-92-13.
circ. 1,250. *4259*

REVUE DE L'ALIMENTATION ANIMALE.
Gedeon Marketing Eure, B.P. 16, 29560 Telgruc sur Mer, France. TEL 33-98-27-37-66. FAX 33-98-27-37-65.
circ. 3,000. *260*

REVUE FRANCAISE DE SERVICE SOCIAL.
Association Nationale des Assistants de Service Social, 15 rue de Bruxelles, 75009 Paris, France. TEL 1-45-26-33-79. FAX 1-42-80-07-03.
circ. 2,700. *6389*

REVUE INTERNATIONALE DE CRIMINOLOGIE ET DE POLICE TECHNIQUE.
Marcel Meichtry Editions, Chemin de la Caroline 26, CH-1213 Petit-Lancy - Geneva, Switzerland. TEL 41-22-7921027. FAX 41-22-7928834.
circ. 1,500. *2175*

REVUE MEDICALE DE BRUXELLES.
Association des Medecins Anciens Etudiants de l'Universite Libre de Bruxelles (A.M.U.B.), Route de Lennik 808, Bte. 612, 1070 Brussels, Belgium. TEL 32-2-555-6062. FAX 32-2-555-6117.
circ. 2,900. *4525*

REVUE MILITAIRE SUISSE.
Association de la Revue Militaire Suisse, Case Postale 7, CH-1669 Albeuve, Switzerland.
circ. 3,105. *5046*

Contr Circ

REVUE OCCASIONS D'AFFAIRES.
Revue Occasions d'Affaires Ltee, 425 St.-Amable St., Ste. 145, Quebec, PQ G1R 5E4, Canada. TEL 418-640-1686. FAX 418-640-1687. *956*

RHODE ISLAND. DEPARTMENT OF STATE LIBRARY SERVICES. NEWSLETTER.
Department of State Library Services, 300 Richmond St., Providence, RI 02903-4222. TEL 401-277-2726. FAX 401-831-1131. circ. 800. *4023*

THE RHODE ISLAND BUILDER REPORT.
Rhode Island Builders Association, 450 Veterans Memorial Pkwy. No. 301, E. Providence, RI 02914-5380. TEL 401-438-7400. FAX 401-438-7446. circ. 3,400. *872*

RHODE ISLAND ROOTS.
Rhode Island Genealogical Society, 13 Countryside Dr., Cumberland, RI 02864. circ. 800. *3099*

RICHMOND AFRO-AMERICAN NEWSPAPER.
Afro-American Co. of Baltimore City, 2519 N. Charles St., Baltimore, MD 21218. TEL 410-554-8200. FAX 804-554-8477. circ. 30,000. *2905*

RIDER UNIVERSITY MAGAZINE.
Rider University, 2083 Lawrenceville Rd., Lawrenceville, NJ 08648-3099. TEL 609-869-5165. FAX 609-895-1678. circ. 32,500. *1884*

RINKSIDER.
Target Publishing Co., Inc. (Columbus), 2470 E. Main St., Columbus, OH 43209. TEL 614-235-1022. FAX 614-235-3584. circ. 3,000. *1444*

RIO (SAN ANTONIO).
Paseo del Rio Association of San Antonio, 213 Broadway, Ste. 5, San Antonio, TX 78205-1923. FAX 222-2673. circ. 50,000. *1148*

RIO GRANDE DO SUL, BRAZIL. PROCURADORIA GERAL DO ESTADO. REVISTA.
Procuradoria Geral do Estado, Av. Borges Medeiros 1501, 13th, Porto Alegre 90060, Brazil. FAX 0512-255496. circ. 1,500. *3844*

RIPON MAGAZINE.
Ripon College, Box 248, Ripon, WI 54971. TEL 414-748-8364. FAX 414-748-9262. circ. 14,000. *1884*

RISCONTROL.
Edition Vega Verlagsgesellschaft mbH, Postfach 11, A-3532 Rastenfeld, Austria. TEL 43-1-8185354. FAX 43-1-5132942. circ. 7,000. *3664*

RISK MANAGEMENT FOR EXECUTIVE WOMEN.
Cox Publications, Box 20316, Billings, MT 59104-0316. TEL 406-256-8822. circ. 470. *3664*

RIVISTA DELL'ARBITRATO.
Casa Editrice Dott. A. Giuffre, Via Busto Arsizio, 40, 20151 Milan, Italy. TEL 02-38089200. FAX 06-38009582. circ. 1,500. *1394*

RIVISTA TECNICA DI CINEMATOGRAFIA.
Edizione Cinemeccanica S.p.A., Viale Campania 23, Milan, Italy. TEL 39-2-718941. FAX 39-2-70100470. circ. 5,000. *5111*

ROAD AHEAD.
Road Ahead Publishing Co. Pty Ltd., G.P.O. Box 1403, Brisbane, Qld. 4001, Australia. TEL 61-7-33612340. FAX 61-7-32571863. circ. 616,033. *6800*

ROAD KING.
Hammock Publishing, Inc., 3322 W. End Ave., Ste. 700, Nashville, TN 37203-0076. TEL 615-385-9745. FAX 615-386-9349. circ. 220,000. *6860*

ROAD PATROL.
Royal Automobile Club of Western Australia, G.P.O. Box C140, Perth, W.A. 6001, Australia. TEL 61-9-4214444. FAX 61-9-2211887. circ. 360,131. *6800*

ROADSMART.
Amoco Enterprises, Inc., Amoco Motor Club, Signature Group, 200 Martingale Rd., Schaumberg, IL 60173. TEL 810-558-7275. FAX 810-558-5897. circ. 1,300,000. *6910*

ROCAS Y MINERALES.
Editorial Rocas y Minerales, C. Arturo Baldasano, 15 bajo, 28043 Madrid, Spain. TEL 34-1-4151804. FAX 34-1-4151661. circ. 6,000. *5077*

ROCKEFELLER FOUNDATION. ANNUAL REPORT.
Rockefeller Foundation, 420 Fifth Ave., New York, NY 10018. TEL 212-869-8500. FAX 212-764-3468. circ. 18,000. *6389*

ROCKET.
BAM Media, Inc., 2028 Fifth Ave., Seattle, WA 98121. TEL 206-728-7625. circ. 70,000. *5193*

ROCKETEER.
Missouri Training Center for Men, Box 7, Moberly, MO 65270. TEL 816-263-3778. circ. 2,700. *2175*

ROCKY MOUNTAIN COAL MINING INSTITUTE. PROCEEDINGS.
Rocky Mountain Coal Mining Institute, 3000 Youngfield, Ste. 324, Lakewood, CO 80215. TEL 303-238-9099. FAX 303-238-0509. circ. 1,000. *5077*

ROCKY MOUNTAIN CONSTRUCTION (SOUTH EDITION).
Rocky Mountain Construction Magazine, Inc., Associated Construction Publications, 2403 Champa, Denver, CO 80205-2694. TEL 303-295-0630. FAX 303-295-2159. circ. 7,800. *872*

ROCKY MOUNTAIN FOOD DEALER.
Rocky Mountain Food Dealers Association, 1370 Pennsylvania St., Ste. 320, Denver, CO 80203-5022. TEL 303-830-7001. circ. 1,400. *3007*

ROEH HACHESHBON.
Institute of Certified Public Accountants in Israel, P.O. Box 29281, 1 Montefiore St., Tel Aviv, Israel. TEL 972-3-5161114. FAX 972-3-5103105. circ. 2,700. *1054*

ROERFAG.
Skarland Press A-S, P.O. Box 5042 Maj., N-0301 Oslo, Norway. TEL 47-22-60-13-90. FAX 47-22-69-36-50. circ. 3,980. *3332*

THE ROLL.
Scholar Contemplationis, 3425 Forest Ln., Pfafftown, NC 27040-9545. TEL 919-924-4980. circ. 550. *5497*

ROLL CALL.
Roll Call, Inc. 900 Second St., N.E., Ste. 107, Washington, DC 20002. TEL 202-289-4900. FAX 202-289-2205. circ. 12,000. *5704*

ROMA E PROVINCIA ATTRAVERSO LA STATISTICA.
Camera di Commercio Industria Artigianato e Agricoltura di Roma, Via De'Burro 147, 00186 Rome, Italy. *6626*

ROMANIAN JOURNAL OF METEOROLOGY.
National Institute of Meteorology and Hydrology, 97 Bucuresti-Ploiesti Hwy., 71581 Bucharest, Rumania. TEL 40-1-6793240. FAX 40-1-3129843. circ. 250. *5005*

ROOFING HOLLAND.
Mandate Publishers BV, Postbus 9198, 1800 GD Alkmaar, Netherlands. TEL 31-2513-20500. circ. 14,000. *873*

ROSACRUZ.
Supreme Grand Lodge of AMORC, Inc., Rosicrucian Park, San Jose, CA 95191-0001. TEL 408-287-9171. circ. 17,000. *5497*

THE ROSE.
Royal National Rose Society, Chiswell Green, St. Albans AL2 3NR, England. TEL 44-1727-850461. FAX 44-1727-850330. circ. 19,000. *3066*

ROSKILL'S METALS DATABOOK.
Roskill Information Services Ltd., 2 Clapham Rd., London SW9 0JA, England. TEL 44-171-582-5155. FAX 44-171-793-0008. circ. 75. *5077*

ROSSING MAGAZINE.
Rossing Uranium Ltd., Corporate Affairs, P.O. Box 22391, Windhoek 9000, Namibia. TEL 061-228147. circ. 4,000. *2140*

ROTOR AND WING INTERNATIONAL.
Phillips Business Information, Inc., 1201 Seven Locks Rd., Potomac, MD 20854. TEL 301-424-3338. FAX 301-309-3847. *76*

ROUNDUP (EL PASO).
Acme Boot Co., Inc., Box 9215, El Paso, TX 79983-0216. TEL 615-552-2000. circ. 2,500. *6308*

ROYAL AIR FORCE EDUCATION BULLETIN.
Royal Air Force Training Development and Support Unit, Department of Educational and Training Technology Development, RAF Newton, Nottingham NG13 8HL, England. TEL 0949-20771. FAX 0949-21201. circ. 1,300. *5046*

ROYAL BANK LETTER.
Royal Bank of Canada, Public Affairs Department, One Place Ville Marie, 7th Fl. W., Box 6001, Montreal, PQ H3C 3A9, Canada. TEL 514-874-4883. FAX 514-874-2239. circ. 350,000. *1119*

ROYAL BOTANICAL GARDENS, HAMILTON, ONT. TECHNICAL BULLETIN.
Royal Botanical Gardens, Box 399, Hamilton, ON L8N 3H8, Canada. TEL 905-527-1158. FAX 905-577-0375. circ. 1,000. *701*

ROYAL CALEDONIAN CURLING CLUB. ANNUAL.
Royal Caledonian Curling Club, Cairnie House, Ave. K, Ingliston Showground Newbridge, Midlothian EH28 2NB, Scotland. TEL 44-131-333-3003. FAX 44-131-333-3323. circ. 3,000. *6478*

ROYAL COLLEGE OF ANAESTHETISTS. NEWSLETTER.
Royal College of Anaesthetists, 48-49 Russell Sq., London WC1B 4JY, England. TEL 44-171-813-1900. FAX 44-171-813-1876. circ. 6,000. *4593*

ROYAL COLLEGE OF PHYSICIANS OF EDINBURGH. PROCEEDINGS.
Royal College of Physicians of Edinburgh, 9 Queen St., Edinburgh EH2 1JQ, Scotland. TEL 0131-225-7324. FAX 0131-220-3939. circ. 6,100. *4527*

ROYAL COLLEGE OF SPEECH AND LANGUAGE THERAPISTS. BULLETIN.
Royal College of Speech and Language Therapists, 7 Bath Pl., London EC2 3DR, England. TEL 44-171-613-3855. FAX 44-171-613-3854. circ. 8,000. *2474*

ROYAL INSTITUTION OF GREAT BRITAIN. RECORD.
Royal Institution of Great Britain, 21 Albemarle St., London W1X 4BS, England. TEL 44-171-409-2992. circ. 3,000. *6276*

ROYAL INSTITUTION OF GREAT BRITAIN. ROYAL INSTITUTION LECTURES.
Royal Institution of Great Britain, 21 Albemarle St., London W1X 4BS, England. TEL 44-171-409-2992. circ. 4,000. *6276*

ROYAL SOCIETY NEWS.
Royal Society of London, 6 Carlton House Terrace, London SW1Y 5AG, England. TEL 44-171-839-5561. FAX 44-171-976-1837.
circ. 5,000. *6276*

RUBBER & PLASTICS NEWS.
Crain Communications Inc. (Akron), 1725 Merriman Rd., Ste. 300, Akron, OH 44313-5251. TEL 330-836-9180. FAX 330-836-1005.
circ. 16,052. *6218*

RUCH FILOZOFICZNY.
Polskie Towarzystwo Filozoficzne, c/o Uniwersytet Mikolaja Kopernika, Instytut Filozofii, Ul. Podmurna 74, 87-100 Torun, Poland. TEL 48-56-21157. FAX 48-56-21157.
circ. 530. *5497*

RUNAWAY.
Publishing People, Inc., Box 610, Alta Loma, CA 91701. FAX 800-692-3233.
circ. 287,000. *6910*

RUNDBRIEF FRAUEN IN DER LITERATURWISSENSCHAFT.
Universitaet Hamburg, Arbeitsstelle fuer Feministische Literaturwissenschaft, Von-Melle-Park 6, 20146 Hamburg, Germany. TEL 49-40-41234818. FAX 49-40-41234785.
circ. 1,000. *4261*

RUNNING & FITNEWS.
American Running and Fitness Association, 4405 East-West Hwy., Ste. 405, Bethesda, MD 20814. TEL 301-913-9517. FAX 301-913-9520.
circ. 20,000. *5535*

THE RUNNING BOARD.
Edmonton Antique Car Club, P.O. Box 102, Edmonton AB T5J 2G9, Canada.
circ. 95. *6800*

RURAL ELECTRIC NEBRASKAN.
Nebraska Rural Electric Association, 800 S. 13th St., Lincoln, NE 68501. TEL 402-475-4988.
circ. 58,000. *2570*

RURAL ROOTS.
Prince Albert Daily Herald, 30-10th St., P.O. Box 550, Prince Albert, SK S6V 5R9, Canada. TEL 306-764-4276. FAX 306-763-3331.
circ. 24,107. *149*

RUSSKOE VOZROZHDENIE.
St. Seraphim Foundation, 53 Duane Ln., Demarest, NJ 07627-1304. TEL 201-768-5424. FAX 201-768-3436.
circ. 1,500. *6113*

RUTGERS MAGAZINE.
Rutgers University, Department of University Communications, Alexander Johnston Hall, New Brunswick, NJ 08903. TEL 908-932-7315. FAX 908-932-8412.
circ. 110,000. *1884*

RX REMEDY.
Rx Remedy, Inc., 120 Post Rd. W., Westport, CT 06880. TEL 203-341-7000. FAX 203-221-4913.
circ. 2,000,000. *3295*

RX UPDATE.
Valley Forge Press, 1288 Valley Forge Rd., Box 1135, Valley Forge, PA 19482. TEL 610-935-3302. FAX 610-935-3072.
circ. 60,000. *5442*

RYERSON RAMBLER.
Ryerson Polytechnic University, Department of Development, Alumni and Community Relations, 350 Victoria St., Toronto, ON M5B 2K3, Canada. TEL 416-979-5304. FAX 416-979-5166.
circ. 50,000. *1884*

S A B S CATALOGUE.
South African Bureau of Standards, Information and Publications, Private Bag X191, Pretoria 0001, South Africa. TEL 27-12-428-7911. FAX 27-12-344-1568.
circ. 2,000. *5017*

S A CLEANING REVIEW.
George Warman Publications (Pty.) Ltd., P.O. Box 704, Cape Town 8000, South Africa. TEL 27-21-245320. FAX 27-21-261332.
circ. 1,800. *1829*

S A INSTRUMENTATION & CONTROL.
Technews (Pty) Ltd., P.O. Box 626, Kloof 3640, South Africa. TEL 27-31-7640593. FAX 27-31-7640386.
circ. 5,674. *6663*

S A L S IN BRIEF.
Southern Adirondack Library System, 22 Whitney Pl., Saratoga Springs, NY 12866. TEL 518-584-7300.
circ. 425. *4024*

S.A. MARKSMAN.
South African Pistol Association, P.O. Box 73989, Fairland 2030, South Africa.
circ. 500. *6478*

S A R A SCOPE.
Society of American Registered Architects, 1245 S. Highland Ave., Lombard, IL 60148. TEL 312-763-5767. FAX 312-763-5788.
circ. 500. *403*

S A T H NEWS.
Society for the Advancement of Travel for the Handicapped, 347 Fifth Ave., Ste. 610, New York, NY 10016. TEL 212-447-7284. FAX 212-725-8253.
circ. 1,000. *6911*

S A W E NEWSLETTER.
Society of Allied Weight Engineers, Inc., 5530 Aztec Dr., La Mesa, CA 91942-2110. TEL 619-465-1367. FAX 619-465-2561.
circ. 1,000. *76*

S C A N.
U.S. National Aeronautics and Space Administration, National Technology Transfer Center, c/o Wheeling Jesuit University, 316 Washington Ave., Wheeling, WV 26003. TEL 304-243-2440. FAX 304-243-4390. *83*

S C O U T.
U S A Volleyball, 3595 E. Fountain Blvd., Ste. I-2, Colorado Springs, CO 80910-1740. TEL 719-637-8300. FAX 719-597-6307. *6513*

S E C DOCKET.
U.S. Securities and Exchange Commission, 450 Fifth St., N.W., MISC-11, Washington, DC 20549. TEL 202-272-7460. FAX 202-272-7050.
circ. 12,500. *1350*

S E C NEWS DIGEST.
U.S. Securities and Exchange Commission, 450 Fifth St., N.W., MISC-11, Washington, DC 20549. TEL 202-272-7460. FAX 202-272-7050. *1350*

S E I U UPDATE.
Service Employees International Union, 1313 L St., N.W., Washington, DC 20005. TEL 202-898-3200. FAX 202-898-3438.
circ. 50,000. *3727*

S F E P DIRECTORY.
Society of Freelance Editors and Proofreaders, 38 Rochester Rd., London NW1 9JJ, England. TEL 44-171-813-3113.
circ. 2,500. *6007*

S H O T BUSINESS.
National Shooting Sports Foundation, 11 Mile Hill Rd., Newtown, CT 06470-2359. TEL 203-426-1320. FAX 203-426-1087.
circ. 20,000. *6575*

S I G A C T NEWS.
Association for Computing Machinery, Special Interest Group on Automata and Computability Theory, 1515 Broadway, 17th Fl., New York, NY 10036.
circ. 1,588. *2017*

S I G N U M NEWSLETTER.
Association for Computing Machinery, Special Interest Group on Numerical Mathematics, 1515 Broadway, 17th Fl., New York, NY 10036. TEL 212-869-7440.
circ. 1,800. *4412*

S K A V - FACHBLATT.
Schweizerischer Verband Christlicher Institutionen, Zaehringerstr. 19, 6000 Lucerne 7, Switzerland.
circ. 1,500. *6390*

S N E S U P BULLETIN.
Syndicat National de l'Enseignement Superieur, 78 rue du Faubourg Saint-Denis, 75010 Paris, France. *2441*

S N V BULLETIN.
Schweizerische Normen-Vereinigung, Muehlebachstr. 54, CH-8008 Zurich, Switzerland. TEL 41-1-2545454. FAX 41-1-2545474.
circ. 1,200. *5017*

S O R T BULLETIN.
American Library Association, Staff Organizations Round Table, 50 E. Huron St., Chicago, IL 60611.
circ. 550. *4024*

S P A B NEWS.
Society for the Protection of Ancient Buildings, 37 Spital Sq., London E1 6DY, England. TEL 44-171-377-1644. FAX 44-171-247-5296.
circ. 5,500. *403*

S P E E A SPOTLITE.
Seattle Professional Engineering Employees Association, 15205 52nd Ave. S., Seattle, WA 98188. TEL 206-433-0995. FAX 206-248-3990.
circ. 18,000. *3728*

S P E REVIEW.
McQuillan Young Communications, 211 Piccadilly, London W1V 9LD, England. TEL 44-171-917-2731. FAX 44-171-917-2734.
circ. 4,000. *5375*

SAAGVERKEN.
Arbor Publishing AB, P.O. Box 26212, S-100 41 Stockholm, Sweden. TEL 46-8-611-60-30. FAX 46-8-679-90-50.
circ. 3,319. *3037*

SAASTOPANKKI.
Saastopankkiliitto, Postilokero 47, SF-00101 Helsinki 10, Finland. FAX 0-1334935.
circ. 27,188. *1120*

SACERDOZIO REGALE.
Centro Sacerdozio Regale, Via Villanova, 14, Casa Betania, 33170 Pordenone, Italy. TEL 39-434-570019.
circ. 3,000. *6091*

SADO MARINE BIOLOGICAL STATION. REPORT.
Niigata Daigaku, Rigakubu Fuzoku Sado Rinkai Jikkenjo, 2-8050 Igarashi, Niigata 950-21, Japan. TEL 0259-75-2012. FAX 0259-75-2012.
circ. 600. *605*

SAFE CYCLING.
Motorcycle Safety Foundation, 2 Jenner St., Ste. 150, Irvine, CA 92718-3812. TEL 714-727-3227. FAX 714-727-4217.
circ. 6,500. *6529*

SAFE DRIVER.
Order of the Road, P.O. Box 227, Forest Row, E. Sussex RH18 5YS, England. TEL 44-1342-826536. FAX 44-1342-824847.
circ. 1,800. *6801*

SAFECO AGENT.
Safeco Corporation, Safeco Plaza, Seattle, WA 98185. TEL 206-545-6009.
circ. 11,000. *3664*

SAFETY & COMPLIANCE NEWS.
National Private Truck Council, 66 Canal Center Plaza, Ste. 600, Alexandria, VA 22314. TEL 703-683-1300. FAX 703-683-1217.
circ. 2,500. *6861*

SAFETY RESOURCES.
Gulf Atlantic Communications Corporation, Inc., Box 407000, Ft. Lauderdale, FL 33340-7000. TEL 954-489-4070. FAX 954-489-4079.
circ. 10,000. *5258*

SAFETY SIGNALS.
Industrial Safety Equipment Association, 1901 N. Moore St., Ste. 808, Arlington, VA 22209. TEL 703-525-1695. FAX 703-528-2148.
circ. 450. *5258*

SAG SERVUS IN WIEN.
Milde Verlag GmbH, Autokaderstr. 29, A-1210 Vienna, Austria. TEL 01-27703. FAX 01-2770326.
circ. 67,000. *3113*

SAGA OF SIGMA TAU GAMMA.
Sigma Tau Gamma Fraternity, Box 54, Warrensburg, MO 64093. TEL 816-747-2222. FAX 816-747-9599.
circ. 28,000. *1884*

SAGGI.
Masson S.p.A., Divisione Periodici, Via Statuto 2-4, 20121 Milan, Italy. TEL 39-2-63671. FAX 39-2-6367211.
circ. 1,000. *4867*

SAKHO & TELE.
Alssociation of Electrical Engineers in Finland, Merikasarmink. 7 J 53, SF-00160 Helsinki, Finland. TEL 358-0-171-050. FAX 358-0-657-562.
circ. 4,500. *2719*

SAIL.
Cahners Publishing Company (Newton), Consumer Division, Division of Reed Elsevier Inc., 275 Washington St., Newton, MA 02158-1630. TEL 617-964-3030. FAX 617-630-3737.
circ. 5,000. *6539*

SAILBOARD RETAILER.
Extreme Publishing, 20518 1st Ave. E., Spanaway, WA 98387-8462.
circ. 4,500. *6539*

ST. ALBERT GAZETTE.
Jamison Newspapers, Inc., 25 Chisholm Ave., Box 263, St. Albert, AB T8N 1N3, Canada. TEL 403-460-5500. FAX 403-460-8220.
circ. 14,000. *3125*

ST. AUSTELL BODMIN AND NEWQUAY PACKET.
Packet Newspapers (Cornwall) Ltd., Ponsharden, Falmouth, Cornwall TR10 8AP, England. TEL 01326-373791. FAX 01326-373887.
circ. 23,843. *3159*

ST. DUNSTAN'S ANNUAL REVIEW.
St. Dunstan's for Men and Women Blinded in the Services, P.O. Box 4XB, 12-14 Harcourt St., London W1A 4XB, England. TEL 0171-723-5021. FAX 0171-262-6199. *3323*

ST. GALLEN.
Tourist Information St. Gallen, Postfach 2242, Bahnhofplatz 1a, CH-9001 St. Gallen, Switzerland. TEL 41-71-2273737. FAX 41-71-2273767.
circ. 5,500. *6911*

ST. JOSEPH VALLEY RECORD.
Northern Indiana Historical Society, 808 W. Washington, S. Bend, IN 46601. TEL 219-235-9664. FAX 219-235-9059.
circ. 2,500. *3487*

ST. LOUIS POCKET GUIDE.
Pocket Guide Publications, Inc., 9650 Clayton Rd., St. Louis, MO 63124. TEL 314-991-5222. FAX 314-991-4118.
circ. 800,000. *6911*

SAINT LOUIS UNIVERSITY RESEARCH JOURNAL.
Saint Louis University, Graduate School of Arts and Sciences, Box 71, Baguio City 2600, Philippines.
circ. 1,000. *3624*

SALE AND ALTRINCHAM MESSENGER.
Sale and Altrincham Messenger Ltd., 46 Washway Rd., Sale, Manchester M33 1QZ, England. TEL 44-161-969-8411. FAX 44-161-976-3703.
circ. 54,575. *3159*

SALES AND MARKETING STRATEGIES & NEWS.
Hughes Communications, Inc., 211 W. State St., Box 197, Rockford, IL 61105. TEL 800-435-2937. FAX 815-963-7773.
circ. 71,000. *1485*

SALMANTICENSIS.
Universidad Pontificia, Departamento de Ediciones y Publicaciones, Apdo. de Correos 541, 37080 Salamanca, Spain. TEL 34-23-215140. FAX 34-23-215140.
circ. 2,000. *6195*

SALUS MILITIAE.
Hospital Central de las Fuerzas Armadas, San Martin, Caracas-1060, Venezuela.
circ. 1,000. *4528*

SALUTE.
Military Forces Features, Inc., 169 Lexington Ave., New York, NY 10157-0014. TEL 212-532-0660. FAX 212-779-3080.
circ. 225,000. *3237*

SALVO.
Fort Point and Presidio Historical Association, Box 29163, Presidio of San Francisco, CA 94129. TEL 415-921-8193.
circ. 900. *3487*

SAMPLE CASE.
Order of United Commercial Travelers of America, 632 N. Park St., Columbus, OH 43215. TEL 614-228-3275.
circ. 140,000. *1853*

SAMVADADHVAN.
Indian Statistical Institute, 203 Barrackpore Trunk Rd., Calcutta 700035, India.
circ. 2,500. *6627*

SAN FRANCISCO BAY VIEW.
Bay View Inc., 4401 Third St., San Francisco, CA 94124. TEL 415-695-0713. FAX 415-695-1845.
circ. 20,000. *2906*

SAN FRANCSCO CATHOLIC.
Archdiocese of San Francisco, Catholic Communications Center, 441 Church St., San Francisco, CA 94114. TEL 415-565-3630.
circ. 48,000. *6195*

SAN FRANCISCO DOWNTOWN.
Gordon Media, 215 Leidesdorff, No. 400, San Francisco, CA 94111. TEL 415-362-6641. FAX 415-362-2254.
circ. 35,000. *3237*

SAN FRANCISCO GIFTCENTER AND JEWELRYMART BUYER'S GUIDE.
Bolger Publications Inc., 3301 Como Ave., S.E., Minneapolis, MN 55414. TEL 612-645-6311. FAX 612-645-1750.
circ. 24,000. *3301*

SAN FRANCISCO PENINSULA PARENT.
Peninsula Parent Newspaper Inc., 1480 Rollins Rd., Burlingame, CA 94010-2307. TEL 415-342-9203. FAX 415-342-9276.
circ. 60,000. *1777*

SAN JOSE FILM & VIDEO PRODUCTION BINDER.
San Jose Film & Video Commission, 333 W. San Carlos St., Ste. 1000, San Jose, CA 95110. TEL 408-295-9600. FAX 408-295-3937.
circ. 1,000. *5112*

SANATORIO SAO LUCAS. BOLETIM.
Fundacao para o Progresso da Cirurgia, Rua Pirapitingui 80, Sao Paulo, Brazil.
circ. 2,000. *4919*

SANCHAR.
Sangam Paper Corporation, Sanchar Bldg., Hotgi Rd., Solapur Maharashtra 413003, India. TEL 60048 . FAX 600484.
circ. 532. *3176*

SANDLAPPER.
Sandlapper Society, Inc., Box 1108, Lexington, SC 29071. TEL 803-359-9954. FAX 803-957-8226.
circ. 7,000. *3237*

SANDUQ ABU DHABI LIL-INMA' AL-IQTISADI AL-ARABI. AL-TAQRIR AL-SANAWI.
Abu Dhabi Fund for Arab Economic Development, P.O. Box 814, Abu Dhabi, United Arab Emirates. TEL 72580C.
circ. 1,000. *1314*

SANGYO GIJUTSU JOHO YOKKAICHI.
Yokkaichi-shiritsu Toshokan, 2-42 Kubota 1-chome, Yokkaichi-shi Mie-ken 510, Japan. *6663*

SANKYO RESEARCH LABORATORIES. ANNUAL REPORT.
Sankyo Co., Ltd., Research Institute, 1-2-58 Hiro-machi, Shinagawa-ku, Tokyo 140, Japan. TEL 81-3-3492-3131. FAX 81-3-5436-8569. *5443*

SANTO CENACOLO.
Commissariato di Terra Santa, Via dell'Ospizio 15, Pistoia, Italy. TEL 39-573-236740.
circ. 2,900. *5091*

SANYO KASEI NEWS.
Sanyo Chemical Industries Ltd., 11-1 Ikkyo Nomcto-cho, Higashiyama-k., Kyoto 605, Japan.
circ. 6,000. *1692*

SAO PAULO (CITY) ARQUIVO MUNICIPAL. REVISTA.
Arquivo Municipal, Divisao de Arquivo Historico, Rua da Consolacao 1024, Sao Paulo, Brazil.
circ. 1,000. *3487*

SARAWAK ELECTRICITY SUPPLY CORPORATION. ANNUAL REPORT.
Sarawak Electricity Supply Corporation, P.O. Box 149, 93700 Kuching, Sarawak, Malaysia. TEL 082-441188. FAX 082-444082.
circ. 2,000. *2719*

SASKATCHEWAN. DEPARTMENT OF INDUSTRY AND COMMERCE. INDUSTRIAL BENEFITS FROM RESOURCE DEVELOPMENT.
Government Printing Co., 2005 8th St., Regina, Sask. S4P 3V7, Canada. TEL 306-566-9393. *958*

SASKATCHEWAN BULLETIN.
Saskatchewan Teachers' Federation, Box 1108, Saskatoon, SK S7K 3N3, Canada. TEL 306-373-1160. FAX 306-374-1122.
circ. 22,300. *2369*

SASKATCHEWAN FARM LIFE.
Farm Life Publications, 75 Lenore Dr., No. 4, Saskatoon, SK S7K 7V1, Canada. TEL 306-242-5723. FAX 306-668-5164.
circ. 160,000. *150*

SASKATCHEWAN MANUFACTURERS GUIDE.
Government Printing Co., 2005 8th St., Regina, Sask. S4P 3V7, Canada. TEL 306-566-9393. *1638*

SASKATCHEWAN RESEARCH COUNCIL. ANNUAL REPORT.
Saskatchewan Research Council, 15 Innovation Blvd., Saskatoon, SK S7N 2X8, Canada. TEL 306-933-5400. FAX 306-933-7446.
circ. 200,000. *6278*

SATVISION MAGAZINE.
Satellite Broadcasting and Communications Association, 225 Reinekers Ln., Ste. 600, Alexandria, VA 22314-2322. TEL 703-549-6990. FAX 703-549-7640.
circ. 10,000. *1968*

SCAN.
Dienst Landbouwkundig Onderzoek, Staring Centrum, Instituut voor Onderzoek van het Landelijk Gebied, P.O. Box 125, 5700 AC Wageningen, Netherlands. TEL 31-3-7-474200. FAX 31-317-424812.
circ. 2,000. *239*

SCANDINAVIAN JOURNAL OF NUTRITION.
Swedish Nutrition Foundation, Ideon, S-223 70 Lund, Sweden. TEL 46-40)-46-18-22-80. FAX 46-0-46-18-22-81.
circ. 2,500. *5241*

SCENE (CLEVELAND).
Northeast Scene, Inc., 1375 Euclid Ave., Ste. 312, Cleveland, OH 44115. TEL 216-241-7550. FAX 216-241-6275.
circ. 48,169. *3238*

SCENE (NEW YORK, 1990).
Scene, 240 E. 79th St., Ste. 10D, New York, NY 10021. TEL 212-737-5100.
circ. 1,500,000. *5112*

SCHERZO.
Scherzo Editorial, S.A., Marques de Mondejar, 11 2o D, 28028 Madrid, Spain. TEL 34-3-567622.
circ. 15,000. *5195*

SCHIFFS-INGENIEUR JOURNAL.
Verein der Schiffs-Ingenieur zu Hamburg e.V., Gurlittstr. 32, 20099 Hamburg, Germany. TEL 49-40-2803883. FAX 49-40-2803565.
circ. 1,500. *6847*

SCHOOL ADMINISTRATOR.
American Association of School Administrators, 1801 North Moore St., Arlington, VA 22209. TEL 703-528-0700. FAX 703-528-2146. *2462*

SCHOOL BUS BRIEFS.
Department of Public Instruction, Pupil Transportation Service, 125 S. Webster St., Box 7841, Madison, WI 53707-7841. *6727*

SCHOOL BUS FLEET.
Bobit Publishing Company, 2512 Artesia Blvd., Redondo Beach, CA 90278-3210. TEL 310-376-8788. FAX 310-376-9043.
circ. 20,000. *6727*

SCHOOL LIBRARIES BULLETIN.
Anambra State School Libraries Association, c/o Enugu Campus Library, University of Nigeria, Nsukka, Enugu State, Nigeria.
circ. 250. *4025*

SCHOOL PLANNING AND MANAGEMENT.
Peter Li, Inc., 330 Progress Rd., Dayton, OH 45449. TEL 573-847-5900. FAX 513-847-5910.
circ. 55,000. *2370*

SCHUETTGUT.
Trans Tech Publications, Postfach 1254, 38670 Clausthal-Zellerfeld, Germany. TEL 49-5323-9697-0. FAX 49-5323-969799.
circ. 7,500. *6663*

DER SCHWEIZER TREUHAENDER.
Treuhand-Kammer, Postfach 892, CH-8025 Zurich, Switzerland. TEL 41-1-2677575. FAX 41-1-2677555.
circ. 10,423. *1054*

SCHWEIZERISCHE FEUERWEHR-ZEITUNG.
Schweizerischer Feuerwehrverband, Ensingerstr. 37, CH-3000 Bern 16, Switzerland. TEL 41-31-3528311. FAX 41-31-3523464.
circ. 22,000. *2923*

SCHWEIZERISCHE LEHRERZEITUNG.
Zuerichsee Medien AG, Seestr. 86, CH-7612 Staefa, Switzerland. TEL 01-9285611.
circ. 16,500. *2371*

SCHWIMMBAD UND SAUNA.
Fachschriften Verlag GmbH, Hoehenstr. 17, 70736 Fellbach, Germany. TEL 0711-5206-256. FAX 0711-5281424.
circ. 20,187. *873*

SCIENCE TECHNOLOGY JOURNAL.
Institute of Science Technology, Mansell House, 22 Bore St., Lichfield, Staffs. WS13 6LP, England. TEL 01543-251346. FAX 01543-415804.
circ. 2,000. *6663*

SCOPE.
Verlag Hoppenstedt GmbH, Havelstr. 9, 64295 Darmstadt, Germany. TEL 49-6151-380-0. FAX 49-6151-380-360.
circ. 80,000. *1530*

SCOTLAND GROUP ORGANISER AND TRAVEL TRADE GUIDE.
Case Publications Ltd., Benson House, 218 St. Vincent St., Glasgow G2 5SG, Scotland. TEL 44-141-221-5521. FAX 44-141-221-5010.
circ. 10,000. *6911*

SCOTTISH LICENSED TRADE NEWS.
Peebles Publishing Group Ltd., Bergius House, Clifton St., Glasgow G3 7LA, Scotland. TEL 44-141-331-1022. FAX 44-141-331-1395.
circ. 16,000. *511*

SCOTTISH LITERARY JOURNAL.
Association for Scottish Literary Studies, Dept. of English, University of Aberdeen, Old Aberdeen AB9 2UB, Scotland. TEL 0224-272634.
circ. 820. *4263*

SCOTTISH MEDICINE.
Hermiston Publications Ltd., 9 Stonelaws, E. Linton, E. Lothian EH40 3DX, Scotland. TEL 44-1620-870313. FAX 44-1620-870313.
circ. 5,000. *4529*

SCOTTISH MUSEUM NEWS.
Scottish Museums Council, County House, 20-22 Torphichen St., Edinburgh EH3 8JB, Scotland. TEL 44-131-229-7465. FAX 44-131-229-2728.
circ. 1,500. *5132*

SCOTTISH OPTOMETRIST.
Scottish Committee of Optometrist, c/o 24 Tweed Crescent, Pean Park, Renfred, Scotland. *4777*

SCOTTISH TRAVEL AGENTS NEWS.
S & G Publishing (Scotland) Ltd., 71 Henderson St., Bridge of Allan, Stirling FK9 4HG, Scotland. TEL 44-1786-834238. FAX 44-1786-834295.
circ. 1,000. *6911*

SCREENWRITER.
L S W - Screenwriter Publications, 187 Manygate Ln., Shepperton, Middx. TW17 9ER, England. TEL 44-1932-232952.
circ. 1,250. *5112*

THE SCRIBE.
University of Bridgeport, Student Center, 244 University Ave., Bridgeport, CT 06601. TEL 203-576-4382. FAX 203-576-4941.
circ. 2,500. *1885*

SCRIBES JOURNAL OF LEGAL WRITING.
American Society of Writers on Legal Subjects, Wake Forest University, School of Law, Box 7206, Winston-Salem, NC 27109. TEL 910-759-5440. FAX 910-759-6077.
circ. 3,900. *3847*

SCRINIUM.
Verband Oesterreichischer Archivare, Postfach 164, A-1014 Vienna, Austria. *4026*

SCRIPPS RESEARCH INSTITUTE. SCIENTIFIC REPORT.
Scripps Research Institute, Office of Communications, 10666 N. Torrey Pines Rd., La Jolla, CA 92037. TEL 619-455-8263. FAX 619-554-6357.
circ. 5,000. *4529*

SCRIPTA GEOLOGICA.
Nationaal Natuurhistorisch Museum, Postbus 9517, 2300 RA Leiden, Netherlands.
circ. 575. *2260*

SCROLL OF PHI DELTA THETA.
Phi Delta Theta Fraternity, 2 So. Campus, Oxford, OH 45056. TEL 513-523-6345. FAX 513-523-9200. *1885*

SEA BREEZE.
Wachters' Organic Sea Products Corporation, 360 Shaw Rd., South San Francisco, CA 94080. FAX 415-875-1626.
circ. 50,000. *6911*

SEARCH (LONDON, 1957).
Muscular Dystrophy Group of Great Britain and Northern Ireland, 7-11 Prescott Pl., London SW4 6BS, England. TEL 0171-720-8055. FAX 0171-498-0670.
circ. 16,000. *3316*

SEARCH (YORK).
Joseph Rowntree Foundation, The Homestead, 40 Water End, York YO3 6LP, England. TEL 44-1904-629241. FAX 44-1904-620072.
circ. 8,500. *6391*

SEARCHLIGHT.
Dale Corporation, 84 Executive Dr., Troy, MI 48083-4504. TEL 313-597-9040. FAX 313-597-0082.
circ. 1,000. *2176*

SECRETARESSE.
Kluwer Editorial Kouterveld 2, B-1831 Diegem, Belgium. TEL 32-2-7231511.
circ. 5,500. *1497*

SECURITY CONCEPTS.
Terra Publishing, Inc., R.D. 1, Box 142, Center St. Ext., Salamanca, NY 14779. TEL 716-945-3488. FAX 716-945-5238.
circ. 21,000. *2184*

SECURITY INDUSTRY.
S P L, Berwick House, 8-10 Knoll Rise, Orpington, Kent BR6 0PS, England. TEL 44-1689-874025. FAX 44-1689-896847.
circ. 6,000. *2184*

SECURITY NEWS (SALAMANCA).
Terra Publishing, Inc., R.D. 1, Box 142, Center St. Ext., Salamanca, NY 14779. TEL 716-945-3488. FAX 716-945-5238.
circ. 21,000. *2184*

SECURITY PULSE.
Canadian Alarm & Security Association, 610 Alden Rd., Ste. 201, Markham, ON L3R 9Z1, Canada. TEL 905-513-0622. FAX 905-513-0624.
circ. 6,000. *2184*

SECURITY SALES.
Bobit Publishing Company, 2512 Artesia Blvd., Redondo Beach, CA 90278-3210. TEL 310-376-8788. FAX 310-376-9043.
circ. 23,500. *890*

SECURITY TECHNOLOGY & DESIGN.
Locksmith Publishing Corp., 850 Busse Hwy., Park Ridge, IL 60068. TEL 847-692-5940. FAX 847-692-4604.
circ. 28,500. *2185*

SEEDS FOR THE PARISH.
Evangelical Lutheran Church in America, 8765 W. Higgins Rd., Chicago, IL 60631-4177. TEL 312-380-2949. FAX 312-380-2406.
circ. 200,000. *6159*

THE SEEING EYE GUIDE.
The Seeing Eye, Inc., Box 375, Morristown, NJ 07963-0375. TEL 201-539-4425. FAX 201-539-0922.
circ. 25,000. *3323*

SEGAVISIONS.
Infotainment World, Inc., 951 Mariners Island Blvd., Ste. 700, San Mateo, CA 94404-1561. TEL 415-349-4300.
circ. 1,000,000. *2024*

SEIKEI KISHO KANSOKUJO HOKOKU.
Seikei Gakuen Integrated Educational Institute, 3-1, Kichijoji Kita-machi 3-chome, Musashino-shi, Tokyo 180, Japan. FAX 0422-37-3863. *5011*

SEKTOR ERZIEHUNG.
Gewerkschaft Erziehung Basel, Rebgasse 1, Postfach, CH-4005 Basel, Switzerland. TEL 061-6921400.
circ. 1,250. *1777*

DER SELBSTAENDIGE.
Bund der Selbstaendigen Deutscher Gewerbeverband e.V., Hochkreuzallee 89, 53175 Bonn, Germany. TEL 0228-311046. FAX 0228-316966.
circ. 100,000. *1579*

SELECCION.
Alpe Editores, S.A., Pedro Rico, 27, 28029 Madrid, Spain. TEL 34-1-7338811. FAX 34-1-3159652.
circ. 5,500. *4900*

SELECTA - MEDIZIN AKTUELL.
Selecta Verlagsgesellschaft mbH, Postfach 4240, 65032 Wiesbaden, Germany. TEL 0611-1705-0. FAX 0611-1705379. *4529*

SELECTED READINGS IN PLASTIC SURGERY.
411 N. Washington Ave., Ste. 6900, Dallas, TX 75246. TEL 214-824-0154. FAX 214-824-0463.
circ. 1,800. *4919*

SELF-EMPLOYED AMERICA.
National Association for the Self-employed, 2121 Precinct Line Rd., Hurst, TX 76054. FAX 800-551-4446.
circ. 320,000. *1579*

SELLING LONG-HAUL.
B M I Publications Ltd., Suffolk House, George St., Croydon, Surrey CR9 1SR, England. TEL 44-181-649-7233. FAX 44-181-649-7234.
circ. 19,000. *6912*

SEMAPHORE SIGNAL.
Semaphore Corp., 207 Granada Dr., Aptos, CA 95003. TEL 408-688-9200.
circ. 7,000. *2058*

SEMBRADOR.
Parroquia Santisima Trinidad Rufino, La Misma del Punto (8), Italia 62, Rufino, Argentina. *3110*

SENDTNERA.
Botanische Staatssammlung Muenchen, Menzingerstr. 67, 80638 Munich, Germany. *702*

Contr Circ

SENIOR BULLETIN.
Senior Publications Pty Ltd, P.O. Box 102026, Moreletapark 0044, South Africa. TEL 27-12-9971894. FAX 27-12-9971894.
circ. 15,000. *3296*

SENIOR CITIZENS POST.
Coordinating Council for Senior Citizens, 807 S. Duke St., Durham, NC 27701. TEL 919-688-8247. FAX 919-683-3406.
circ. 1,500. *3296*

SENIOR GROUP TRAVELER.
Senior Travel Publications, Inc., 750 Old Hickory Blvd., Ste. 150-Bldg. 2, Brentwood, TN 37027-4502. TEL 615-371-6181. FAX 615-221-8825.
circ. 10,700. *6912*

SENIOR NEWS.
Box 270848, Corpus Christi, TX 78427. TEL 512-852-0163. FAX 512-852-5756.
circ. 110,000. *3296*

SENIOR SUN.
New York State Electric & Gas Corp., 4500 Vestal Parkway E., Binghamton, NY 13902. TEL 607-762-4822. FAX 607-762-4189.
circ. 65,000. *2558*

SENIOR TRAVEL TIPS (SAN RAFAEL).
Senior Marketing Associates, 710 C St., Ste. 200, San Rafael, CA 94901. TEL 415-453-8481. FAX 415-453-8540.
circ. 11,000. *6912*

SENIOR TRAVEL TIPS (SCOTTS VALLEY).
5281 Scotts Valley Dr., Scotts Valley, CA 95066-3514. TEL 408-438-6085. FAX 408-438-4705.
circ. 11,500. *6912*

SENIOR WORLD OF LOS ANGELES COUNTY.
Kendell Communications Inc., Box 1565, El Cajon, CA 92022. TEL 310-820-1125.
circ. 150,000. *3296*

SENSHU SHIZEN KAGAKU KIYO.
Senshu Daigaku, Shizen Kagaku Kenkyukai, 1-1 Higashi-Mita 2-chome, Tama-ku, Kawasaki-shi, Kanagawa-ken 214, Japan. TEL 81-44-911-0588. FAX 81-44-911-1243.
circ. 350. *6284*

SENSOR REPORT.
P. Keppler Verlag GmbH und Co. KG, Industriestr. 2, 63150 Heusenstamm, Germany. TEL 49-6104-606208. FAX 49-6104-606323.
circ. 10,000. *3637*

SENSUS WATER JOURNAL.
Sensus Technologies, Inc., 450 N. Gallatin Ave., Box 487, Uniontown, PA 15401. TEL 412-439-7700. FAX 412-430-3959.
circ. 15,000. *6974*

SEOUL JOURNAL OF MEDICINE.
Seoul National University, College of Medicine, 28 Yunkun-dong, Chongro-gu, Seoul, S. Korea. TEL 82-2-745-2430. FAX 82-2-764-8340.
circ. 1,500. *4530*

SER PADRES.
Gruner & Jahr U.S.A. Publishing, 110 Fifth Ave., New York, NY 10011. TEL 212-463-1636.
circ. 325,000. *7006*

SERIALS HOLDINGS IN NEWFOUNDLAND LIBRARIES.
Memorial University of Newfoundland Library, Periodicals Division, St. John's, NF A1C 5S7, Canada. TEL 709-753-8425. FAX 709-737-4569.
546

SERICA.
Silk Association of Great Britain, c/o Rheinbergs Ltd., Morley Rd., Tonbridge TN9 1RN, England. TEL 0732-351357. FAX 0732-770217.
circ. 150. *6684*

SERPENTINE MUSE.
Adventuresses of Sherlock Holmes, c/o Evelyn Herzog, Man. Ed., 360 W. 21st St., New York, NY 10011. TEL 212-527-7789. *4298*

SERVER - PENNSYLVANIA.
Group Publications, Inc., 1816 Brownsville Rd., Pittsburgh, PA 15210-3908. TEL 412-885-7600. FAX 412-885-7617.
circ. 21,000. *3571*

SERVICE EMPLOYEES UNION.
Service Employees International Union, Local 328, 1313 L St., N.W., Washington, DC 20005. TEL 202-898-3200. FAX 202-898-3438.
circ. 1,100,000. *3728*

SEVENTY SIX.
Unocal Corporation, Box 7600, Los Angeles, CA 90051. TEL 213-977-6814.
circ. 16,000. *5375*

SEVERN TRENT PLC. ANNUAL REPORT AND ACCOUNTS (YEAR).
Severn Trent Plc., 2308 Coventry Rd., Birmingham B26 3JZ, England. TEL 0121-722-6000.
circ. 130,000. *6974*

SHALE SHAKER.
Oklahoma City Geological Society, Inc., 227-W Park Ave., Oklahoma City, OK 73102. TEL 405-236-8086. FAX 405-236-8085.
circ. 1,250. *2250*

SHALOM.
Jewish Peace Fellowship, Box 271, Nyack, NY 10960. TEL 914-358-4601. FAX 914-358-4924.
circ. 3,000. *5735*

SHARING TIMES.
Christ Truth Ministries, Box 610, Upland, CA 91785. TEL 909-981-2838. FAX 909-981-2839.
circ. 3,500. *6429*

SHELL-VENSTER.
Shell Nederland B.V., Dept. PAC/1, Hofplein 20, Rotterdam, Netherlands.
circ. 51,000. *5375*

THE SHEPHERD COLLEGE PICKET.
Shepherd College, Shepherdstown, WV 25443. TEL 304-876-2511. FAX 304-876-3262.
circ. 4,000. *1885*

SHICHOKAKU KYOIKU.
Japan Audio-Visual Education Association, 1-17-1 Toranomon, Minato-ku, Tokyo 105, Japan. FAX 81-3-3597-0564.
circ. 5,000. *2372*

SHIFT.
Shift Magazine Inc., 174 Spandina Ave., Ste. 407, Toronto, ON M5T 2C2, Canada. TEL 416-504-1887. FAX 416-504-1889.
circ. 10,000. *6663*

SHINKO PANTEC GIHO.
Shinko Pantec Co. Ltd., 1-4, 1-chome, Murotani, Nishi-ku, Kobe-shi, Hyogo-ken 651-22, Japan. TEL 81-078-992-6525. FAX 81-078-992-6504.
2769

SHIPYARD BULLETIN.
Newport News Shipbuilding, Newport News, VA 23607. TEL 804-380-2342. FAX 804-380-3867.
circ. 30,000. *6849*

SHIPYARD LOG.
Pearl Harbor Naval Shipyard, 401 Ave. E, Ste. 124, Pearl Harbor, HI 96860-5350. TEL 808-474-3214. FAX 808-471-0709.
circ. 4,500. *5047*

SHOPPING GUIDE ZURICH.
Promotion Verlag AG, Mainaustr. 35, Postfach 10, CH-8034 Zurich, Switzerland. TEL 01-3835252. FAX 01-3839233.
circ. 28,000. *6912*

SHOPTALK (ENGLEWOOD).
American Humane Association, Animal Protection Division, 63 Inverness Dr. E., Englewood, CO 80112-5117. TEL 303-792-9900. FAX 303-792-5333.
circ. 4,800. *298*

SHOWBOAT CENTENNIALS NEWSLETTER.
Showboat Centennials, 76 Glen Dr., Worthington, OH 43085. TEL 614-431-9422.
circ. 160. *6540*

SHOWCASE U S A.
Bobit Publishing Company, 2512 Artesia Blvd., Redondo Beach CA 90278-3210. TEL 310-376-8788. FAX 310-376-9043.
circ. 20,000. *1294*

SHUTTLE PLUS.
Sewing Machine Trade Association, 24 Fairlawn Grove, Chiswick, London W4 5EH, England. TEL 44-181-995-0411. FAX 44-181-742-2396.
circ. 3,200. *1836*

SIA.
Samverkande Traefacken, P.O. Box 1138, S-111 81 Stockholm, Sweden. TEL 46-8-23-04-25. FAX 46-8-411-27-42
circ. 110,000. *303?*

SICHER SCHAFFEN - LAENGER LEBEN.
Landwirtschaftliche Sozialversicherung, Postfach 310110, 86062 Augsburg, Germany. TEL 0821-4081-0. FAX 0821-4081115.
circ. 55,000. *6392*

SICHERHEITS-BESCHAFFUNGSDIENST.
Richard Boorberg Verlag (Stuttgart), Scharrstr. 2, 70563 Stuttgart, Germany. TEL 0711-73850. FAX 0711-7352244.
circ. 15,000. *2185*

SIDNEY HAUGHTON MEMORIAL LECTURES.
South African Museum, P.O. Box 61, Cape Town 8000, South Africa. TEL 27-21-243330. FAX 27-21-246716.
circ. 450. *5318*

SIETE DIAS MEDICOS.
Ediciones Mayo, S.A., Muntaner 374, 4o, 08006 Barcelona, Spain. TEL 34-3-2090255. FAX 34-3-2020643.
circ. 30,000. *4531*

SIGNATURE.
Griffin Printing and Lithograph, Co., Inc., 544 W. Colorado St., Glendale, CA 91204-1102. TEL 818-244-2128. FAX 818-242-1172.
circ. 6,500. *6008*

SIGNS OF THE TIMES (CINCINNATI).
S T Publications, 407 Gilbert Ave., Cincinnati, OH 45202. TEL 513-421-2050. FAX 513-421-5144.
circ. 4,219. *45*

SIIRTOLAISUUS.
Siirtolaisuusinstituutti, Piispankatu 3, FIN-20500 Turku, Finland. TEL 358 21-2317536. FAX 358-21-2333460.
circ. 1,400. *5792*

AL-SIJIL AL-SHAHRI LI-AHDATH AL-ALAM.
Ministry of Information and Culture, Information Department, P.O. Box 17, Abu Dhabi, United Arab Emirates. TEL 453000.
circ. 1,000. *5771*

AL-SIJIL AL-SHAHRI LI-AHDATH DAWLAT AL-IMARAT AL-ARABIYYAH AL-MUTTAHIDAH.
Ministry of Information and Culture, Information Department, P.O. Box 17, Abu Dhabi, United Arab Emirates. TEL 453000.
circ. 1,000. *5920*

SILENT ADVOCATE.
St. Rita School for the Deaf, 1720 Glendale-Milford Rd., Cincinnati, OH 45215. TEL 513-771-7600. FAX 513-771-7607.
circ. 25,000. *3314*

SILHOUETTE.
McMaster Students Union, Rm. 406, Hamilton Hall, 1280 Main St. W., Hamilton, ON L8S 4K1, Canada. TEL 905-525-9140. FAX 905-523-0107.
circ. 11,000. *4166*

SILKROAD.
Emphasis HK Ltd., 505-508 Westlands Centre, 20 Westlands Rd., Quarry Bay, Hong Kong. TEL 590-1328. FAX 590-1333.
circ. 46,425. *6937*

LE SILLON ROMAND.
Edipresse Publications SA, Av. de la Gare 33, CH-1001 Lausanne, Switzerland. TEL 021-3494545. FAX 021-3494079.
circ. 23,076. *151*

SILVER BARON'S MONEY FEVER.
S B Stocks U S A, 1 E. Camelback Rd., Ste. 680, Phoenix, AZ 85012-1051. TEL 602-265-4245. FAX 602-265-2806.
circ. 1,900. *1352*

SILVER CIRCLE.
Home Savings of America, 4900 Rivergrade Rd., Irwindale, CA 91706.
circ. 600,000. *3238*

SIMMENTALER JOURNAL.
Simmentaler Cattle Breeders' Society of S.A., P.O. Box 3868, Bloemfontein 9300, South Africa. TEL 27-51-477696. FAX 27-51-471529.
circ. 1,200. *284*

SIMMONS REVIEW.
Simmons College, 300 The Fenway, Boston, MA 02115. TEL 617-521-2363. FAX 617-521-3193.
circ. 18,500. *1886*

SINGAPORE. HOUSING AND DEVELOPMENT BOARD. ANNUAL REPORT.
Housing and Development Board, 3451 Jalan Bukit Merah, Singapore 0315, Singapore. TEL 2739090.
3594

SINGAPORE. MINISTRY OF THE ENVIRONMENT. ANNUAL REPORT.
Ministry of the Environment, Environment Bldg., 40 Scotts Rd., Singapore 0922, Singapore. TEL 065-7327733. FAX 065-7319866. *2819*

SINGAPORE CONTRACTORS' EQUIPMENT CATALOGUE.
Times Trade Directories Pte. Ltd., Times Centre, 1 New Industrial Rd., Singapore 1953, Singapore. TEL 2848844. FAX 2881186.
circ. 20,000. *1639*

SINGAPORE SOURCE BOOK FOR ARCHITECTS & DESIGNERS.
Times Trade Directories Pte. Ltd., Times Centre, 1 New Industrial Rd., Singapore 1953, Singapore. TEL 2848844. FAX 2881186.
circ. 15,000. *1639*

THE SINGER.
Rhinegold Publishing Ltd., 241 Shaftesbury Ave., London WC2H 8EH, England. TEL 44-171-333-1720. FAX 44-171-333-1769.
circ. 8,000. *5197*

SINGLE FILE MAGAZINE.
Single File Magazine, 250 Pearl St., Grand Rapids, MI 49503-2624. TEL 616-774-8100. FAX 616-774-9552.
circ. 45,000. *6311*

SINGLE PARENT.
Parents Without Partners Inc., 401 N. Michigan Ave., Chicago, IL 60611. TEL 312-644-6610. FAX 312-245-1083.
circ. 110,000. *6392*

SJOESPORT.
Sjoesport A-S, P.O. Box 576, 5001 Bergen, Norway.
circ. 21,000. *6540*

SJONVARPSVISIR.
Islenska Utvarpsfelagid hf. - Stoed 2, Lynghalsi 5, P.O. Box 10110, IS-130 Reykjavik, Iceland. TEL 354-515-6770. FAX 354-515-6870.
circ. 50,000. *1969*

SKETCH BOOK.
Kappa Pi International Honorary Art Fraternity, 9321 Paul Adrian Dr., Crestwood, MO 63126.
circ. 2,000. *452*

LE SKI (TORONTO, 1988).
Solstice Publishing Inc., 47 Soho Square, Toronto, ON M5T 2Z2, Canada. TEL 416-595-1252. FAX 416-595-7255.
circ. 21,000. *6481*

SKI COST OF DOING BUSINESS SURVEY.
National Ski Retailers Association, 1699 Wall St., Mt. Prospect, IL 60056. TEL 847-439-4293. FAX 847-439-0111.
circ. 400. *6495*

SKI - SCHWEIZER SKISPORT.
Habegger AG Druck und Verlag, Gutenbergstr. 1, CH-4552 Derendingen, Switzerland. TEL 065-411151. FAX 065-422632.
circ. 114,000. *6576*

SKI WATCH ATLAS.
C R N International, Inc., One Circular Ave., Hamden, CT 06514. TEL 203-288-2002. FAX 203-281-3291.
circ. 100,000. *6576*

SKIER'S POCKET GUIDE.
Pocket Guide Publications, Inc., 9650 Clayton Rd., St. Louis, MO 63124. TEL 314-991-5222. FAX 314-991-4118.
circ. 1,100,000. *6576*

SKOHANDLAREN.
Skohandlarens Foerlags AB, Surbrunnsgatan 12, S-114 21 Stockholm, Sweden. TEL 46-8-791-53-00. FAX 46-8-213-690.
circ. 1,900. *6309*

SKOLEFOKUS.
Laererforbundet, Wergelandsveien 15, N-0167 Oslo, Norway. TEL 47-22-03-00-00. FAX 47-22-42-65-87.
circ. 36,000. *2442*

SKOLVAERLDEN.
Laerarnas Riksfoerbund, P.O. Box 3529, 103 69 Stockholm, Sweden. TEL 46-86-13-27-00. FAX 46-84-411-01-75.
circ. 54,800. *2372*

SKOVEN.
Dansk Skovforening, Amalievej 20, 1875 Frederiksberg C, Denmark. TEL 45-31-244266. FAX 45-33-255082.
circ. 4,318. *3025*

SKUPNOST.
Slovenska Skupnost - Unione Slovena, Via G. Gallina 5, 34122 Trieste, Italy. TEL 39-40-639126.
circ. 5,000. *2908*

SKYE TERRIER CLUB OF AMERICA. BULLETIN.
Skye Terrier Club of America, 7 Fox Hill Ave., Bristol, RI 02809. TEL 401-254-0389.
circ. 200. *5395*

SKYPOWER.
Lockheed Martin, 542642 LOCKHEED MARA, 86 S. Cobb Dr., Marietta, GA 30063-0244. TEL 770-494-2406. FAX 770-494-4809.
circ. 30,000. *77*

SLOOP & RECYCLING.
Misset Postbus 4, 7000 BA Doetinchem, Netherlands. TEL 31-8340-49911. FAX 31-8340-63638.
circ. 25,000. *2857*

SMALL BUSINESS ADVOCATE (WASHINGTON).
U.S. Small Business Administration, Office of Advocacy, Mail Code 3114, 409 Third St., S.W., Washington, DC 20416. TEL 202-205-6531. FAX 202-205-6928.
circ. 9,800. *1579*

SMALL BUSINESS BULLETIN (WORCESTER).
Small Business Service Bureau, Inc., Box 1441, 554 Main St., Worcester, MA 01601. TEL 508-756-3513. FAX 508-791-4709.
circ. 35,000. *1579*

SMALL BUSINESS NEWS - AKRON.
Small Business News, Inc., 14725 Detroit Ave., Ste. 300, Cleveland, OH 44107-4103. TEL 216-228-6397. FAX 216-529-8924.
circ. 18,000. *1579*

SMALL BUSINESS NEWS - CLEVELAND.
Small Business News, Inc., 14725 Detroit Ave., Ste. 300, Cleveland, OH 44107-4103. TEL 216-228-6397. FAX 216-529-8924.
circ. 30,000. *1580*

SMART CARD NEWS.
Smart Card News Ltd., 40 Arundel Pl., Brighton BN2 1GO, England. TEL 44-1273-302503. FAX 44-1273-300991.
circ. 1,000. *2032*

SNOW.
Verlag Delius, Klasing und Co., Postfach 101671, 33516 Bielefeld, Germany. TEL 49-521-559280. FAX 49-521-559113.
circ. 70,000. *6481*

SNOW GOER.
Camar Publications Ltd., 130 Spy Court, Markham, ON L3R 5H6, Canada. TEL 416-485-8440. FAX 416-475-9246.
circ. 150,000. *6577*

SOBER TIMES.
P.O. Box 13013, Mill Creek, WA 98082-1013.
circ. 80,000. *2201*

SOBRE LOS DERIVADOS DE LA CANA DE AZUCAR.
Ediciones Cubanas, Obispo No. 527, Apdo. 605, Havana, Cuba.
circ. 1,500. *240*

SOCIAL CARE RESEARCH FINDINGS.
Joseph Rowntree Foundation, The Homestead, 40 Water End, York YO3 6LP, England. TEL 44-1904-629241. FAX 44-1904-620072.
circ. 2,500. *6392*

SOCIAL WORK IN EUROPE.
Russell House Publishing Ltd., 38 Silver St., Lyme Regis, Dorset DT7 3HS, England. TEL 44-1297-443948. FAX 44-1297-443948.
circ. 75. *6393*

SOCIALE DIENST POST.
Sociale Dienst, Vlaardingenlaan 15, 1062 HM Amsterdam, Netherlands. TEL 31-20-5160801. FAX 31-20-6141631.
circ. 75,000. *6394*

SOCIALIST PERSPECTIVE.
Council for Political Studies, 140-20E, South Sinthee Rd., 1st Fl., Calcutta 700 050, India. TEL 557-5351.
circ. 1,000. *5708*

SOCIEDAD ARGENTINA DE ESTUDIOS GEOGRAFICOS. BOLETIN.
Sociedad Argentina de Estudios Geograficos - GAEA, Rodriquez Pena 158, 4, 1020 Buenos Aires, Argentina. TEL 541-40-2076. *3273*

SOCIEDAD MATEMATICA MEXICANA. BOLETIN.
Sociedad Matematica Mexicana, Apdo. Postal 14-170, 07000 Mexico, D.F., Mexico. TEL 525-747-7103. FAX 525-747-7104.
circ. 900. *4396*

SOCIEDADE DE MEDICINA E CIRURGIA DE SAO JOSE DO RIO PRETO. REVISTA.
Sociedade de Medicina e Cirurgia de Sao Jose do Rio Preto, Rua Spinola s-n, Sao Jose da Rio Preto 15100, Brazil. *4920*

SOCIETA ECONOMICA DI CHIAVARI. ATTI.
Publipress, Via M. Vattuone 157-1, 16039 Sestri Levante (GE), Italy. *6394*

SOCIETE D'EDITION DE PERIODIQUES SPORTIFS.
Sopusi, 10 rue du Faubourg Montmartre, 75009 Paris, France.
circ. 175,000. *6481*

SOCIETE GEOGRAPHIQUE DE LIEGE. BULLETIN.
Societe Geographique de Liege, Sart Tilman B11, 4000 Liege, Belgium. TEL 32-41-665324. FAX 32-41-665700.
circ. 650. *3274*

SOCIETE HISTORIQUE NICOLAS DENYS. REVUE D'HISTOIRE.
Societe Historique Nicolas Denys, Centre Universitaire, Shippagan, NB EOB 2PO, Canada.
circ. 800. *3488*

SOCIETE J.K. HUYSMANS. BULLETIN.
Societe J.K. Huysmans, 22 rue Guynemer, 75006 Paris, France. FAX 33-1-42840587.
circ. 600. *4167*

SOCIETE NATIONALE DES CHEMINS DE FER BELGES. RAPPORT ANNUEL.
Societe Nationale des Chemins de Fer Belges, Fonsnylaan 47B, Bureau 40-231, B-1060 Brussels, Belgium. *6818*

SOCIETY FOR THE ADVANCEMENT OF SCANDINAVIAN STUDY. NEWS AND NOTES.
Ohio State University, Department of German, 314 Cunz Hall, 1841 Millikin Rd., Columbus, OH 43210. TEL 614-292-8687.
circ. 700. *6347*

SOCIETY OF ARCHER-ANTIQUARIES. JOURNAL.
Society of Archer-Antiquaries, c/o Doug Elmy, 61 Lambert Rd., Bridlington, Yorks YO16 5RD, England. TEL 44-1262-601604. *6481*

SOCIETY OF DEPRECIATION PROFESSIONALS. JOURNAL.
Society of Depreciation Professionals, 3421 M St., N.W., Ste. 218, Washington, DC 20007-3516. TEL 202-362-0680. FAX 202-966-2283.
circ. 350. *1055*

SOCIETY OF FEDERAL LINGUISTS. NEWSLETTER.
Society of Federal Linguists, Inc., Box 7765,
Washington, DC 20044.
circ. 150. *4109*

**SOCIETY OF PHOTOGRAPHER AND ARTIST
REPRESENTATIVES. NEWSLETTER.**
Society of Photographer and Artist Representatives,
60 E. 42nd St., No. 1166, New York, NY 10165-
0006. TEL 212-779-7464. *5521*

**SOCIETY OF PROFESSORS OF EDUCATION.
OCCASIONAL PAPERS.**
Society of Professors of Education, c/o Dr. Dalton B.
Curtis, Jr., Southeast Missouri State University, One
University Plz., Cape Girardeau, MO 63701.
TEL 615-974-2201. FAX 615-974-8718. *2373*

SOCIETY OF TELECOM EXECUTIVES. REVIEW.
Society of Telecom Executives, 75-79 York Rd.,
London SE1 7AQ, England. TEL 44-171-928-9951.
FAX 44-171-928-5440.
circ. 24,000. *1915*

SOCIOECONOMIC NEWSLETTER.
Institute for Socioeconomic Studies, Airport Rd.,
White Plains, NY 10604. TEL 914-428-7400.
circ. 17,500. *6432*

SOFTWARE MAGAZINE.
Sentry Publishing Company, Inc., 1 Research Dr.,
Ste. 400B, Westborough, MA 01581-3907.
TEL 508-366-2031. FAX 508-836-4732.
circ. 91,000. *2116*

SOIL SCIENCE ALERT.
Elsevier Science B.V., P.O. Box 211, 1000 AE
Amsterdam, Netherlands. TEL 31-20-4853911.
FAX 31-20-4853598. *2221*

SOKOL POLSKI.
Polish Falcons of America, 615 Iron City Dr.,
Pittsburgh, PA 15205-4397. TEL 412-922-2244.
FAX 412-922-5029.
circ. 15,300. *1854*

SOL DE PARRAL.
Sol de Parral, S.A., Colegio No. 20, 33800 Hgo. del
Parral, Chihuahua, Mexico. TEL 2-52-50. FAX 2-53-
40.
circ. 5,400. *3193*

EL SOL DE TEXAS.
Organizacion Editorial Hispana, Inc., Box 803402,
Dallas, TX 75380-3402. TEL 214-386-9120.
FAX 214-386-7125.
circ. 26,000. *2909*

SOLDIERS.
U.S. Department of the Army, Cameron Sta.,
Alexandria, VA 22304-5050. TEL 703-274-6671.
FAX 703-274-1896.
circ. 250,000. *5048*

SOLEIL DE COLOMBIE BRITANNIQUE.
1645 W. 5th Ave., Vancouver, BC V5N 1S4,
Canada. TEL 604-730-9575. FAX 604-730-9576.
circ. 2,800. *3125*

SOLID FUEL REVIEW.
Carter Spencer Publishing Ltd., Chancery Ct.,
Lincoln Rd., High Wycombe, Bucks. HP12 3RE,
England. TEL 44-1494-442424. FAX 44-1494-
472790.
circ. 7,000. *2558*

SOLID WASTE TECHNOLOGIES.
Adams - Green Industry Publishing, Inc., 2100
Powers Ferry Rd., N.W., Ste. 405, Atlanta, GA
30339-5014. TEL 770-937-0222. FAX 770-937-
0303.
circ. 33,090. *2558*

SOMMETS.
Universite de Sherbrooke, Pavillon J.S. Bourque,
2500 bd. de l'Universite, Sherbrooke, PQ J1K 2R1,
Canada. TEL 819-821-7388. FAX 819-821-7900.
circ. 50,000. *1886*

SONG OF ZION.
Jackman Music Corp., Box 1900, Orem, UT 84059-
5900. TEL 801-225-0859. FAX 801-225-0851.
circ. 17,000. *5197*

SONNTAGSANZEIGER.
Power Print Druck und Verlags KG, Holtenklinkerstr.
88-92, Postfach 800806, 21029 Hamburg
Bergedorf, Germany. TEL 49-40-724040-0.
circ. 3,200. *3149*

SONS OF ITALY NEWS.
Order of the Sons of Italy in America, Grand Lodge
of Massachusetts, 93 Concord Ave., Belmont, MA
02178-4042.
circ. 17,500. *1854*

SOPHIA.
Melkite Diocese of Newton, Sophia Editorial Office,
11245 Rye St., N. Hollywood, CA 91602-2022.
TEL 818-761-2034. FAX 818-761-2922.
circ. 13,500. *6196*

SOTAINVALIDI.
Sotainvalicien Veljesliitto, Kasarmikatu 34 A, FIN-
00130 Helsinki, Finland. TEL 358-0-478-500.
FAX 358-0-4785-0100.
circ. 51,000. *6395*

SOTILASAIKAKAUSLEHTI.
Upseeriliitto, Luotsikatu 7 A 2, FIN-00160 Helsinki,
Finland. TEL 358-0-6689-4060. FAX 358-0-6689-
4020.
circ. 6,078. *5048*

SOUND AND VIBRATION.
Acoustical Publications, Inc., Box 40416, Bay
Village, OH 44140. TEL 216-835-0101. FAX 216-
835-9303
circ. 21,000. *2769*

SOUNDINGS FROM AROUND THE WORLD.
World Neighbors, Inc., 4127 N.W. 122nd St.,
Oklahoma City, OK 73120-8869. TEL 405-752-
9700. FAX 405-752-9393.
circ. 1,700. *5771*

THE SOURCE (PRINCETON).
Construction Financial Management Association,
707 State Rd., Ste. 223, Princeton, NJ 08540-
1413. TEL 609-683-5000. FAX 609-683-4821.
circ. 5,500. *1640*

SOURCES.
Fine Arts Trade Guild, 16-18 Empress Pl., London
SW6 1TT, England. TEL 44-171-381-6616.
FAX 44-171-381-2596.
circ. 2,000. *470*

SOURCES.
Barrie Zwicker, Ec. & Pub., 4 Phipps St., Ste. 109,
Toronto, ON M4Y 1J5, Canada. TEL 416-964-
7799. FAX 416-964-8763.
circ. 13,500. *1640*

SOURCES D'HISTOIRE MEDIEVALE.
C N R S Editions, 20-22 rue St. Amand, 75015
Paris, France. TEL 45-33-16-00. FAX 45-33-92-13.
circ. 1,250. *3445*

**SOUTH AFRICA. DEPARTMENT OF AGRICULTURE
AND FISHERIES. DIVISION OF ECONOMIC
SERVICES. ABSTRACT OF AGRICULTURAL
STATISTICS.**
Department of Agriculture and Fisheries, Division of
Economic Services, Private Bag X246, Pretoria
0001, South Africa. *181*

**SOUTH AFRICA. DEPARTMENT OF AGRICULTURE
AND FISHERIES. DIVISION OF ECONOMIC
SERVICES. TRENDS IN THE AGRICULTURAL
SECTOR.**
Department of Agriculture and Fisheries, Division of
Economic Services, Private Bag X246, Pretoria
0001, South Africa. *200*

**SOUTH AFRICA. DEPARTMENT OF AGRICULTURE.
OFFICIAL LIST OF PROFESSIONAL RESEARCH
WORKERS, LECTURING STAFF AND EXTENSION
WORKERS IN THE AGRICULTURAL FIELD.**
Department of Agriculture, Private Bag X144,
Pretoria 0001, South Africa. TEL 27-12-3197141.
FAX 27-12-3232516. *152*

**SOUTH AFRICA. DEPARTMENT OF LAND AFFAIRS.
DIRECTORATE OF SURVEYS AND LAND
INFORMATION. ANNUAL REPORT OF THE CHIEF
SURVEYOR-GENERAL.**
Department of Land Affairs, Directorate of Surveys
and Land Information, Rhodes Ave., Mowbray 7705,
South Africa. TEL 27-21-6854070. FAX 27-21-
6891351.
circ. 400. *2672*

**SOUTH AFRICA. NATIONAL PARKS BOARD. ANNUAL
REPORT.**
National Parks Board, P.O. Box 787, Pretoria
0001, South Africa. TEL 27-12-343-9770. FAX 27-
12-343-9958. *2141*

**SOUTH AFRICAN ASSOCIATION FOR MARINE
BIOLOGICAL RESEARCH. BULLETIN.**
South African Association for Marine Biological
Research, P.O. Box 10712, Marine Parade 4056,
South Africa. TEL 27-31-373536. FAX 27-31-
372132.
circ. 450. *608*

SOUTH AFRICAN DRAUGHTSMAN.
South African Institute of Draughtsmen, P.O. Box
30, Bergvliet 7864, South Africa. TEL 27-21-
750156. FAX 27-21-750156.
circ. 3,000. *6664*

SOUTH AFRICAN EXPORTERS.
SAFTO, Publishing Division, P.O. Box 782706,
Sandton 2146, South Africa. TEL 27-11-883-3737.
FAX 27-11-883-6562.
circ. 14,000. *1295*

**SOUTH AFRICAN JOURNAL OF AGRICULTURAL
EXTENSION.**
South African Society for Agricultural Extension,
University of Pretoria, Pretoria 0002, South Africa.
TEL 27-12-420-3247. FAX 27-12-342-2713. *153*

**SOUTH AFRICAN JOURNAL OF OCCUPATIONAL
THERAPY.**
South African Association of Occupational
Therapists, P.O. Box 145, Rondebosch 7700, South
Africa. TEL 27-2241-42244. FAX 27-2241-42244
circ. 900. *4532*

**SOUTH AFRICAN JOURNAL OF SURVEYING AND
MAPPING.**
South African Council for Professional Land
Surveyors and Technical Surveyors, P.O. Box
62041, Marshalltown 2107, South Africa. TEL 27-
11-8346431. FAX 27-11-835-8657.
circ. 2,000. *2672*

SOUTH AFRICAN LAPIDARY MAGAZINE.
Federation of South African Gem & Mineralogical
Societies, P.O. Box 28744, Sunnyside 0132, South
Africa. TEL 27-12-44-4520.
circ. 600. *2216*

SOUTH AFRICAN MECHANICAL ENGINEER.
Promech Publishing, P.O. Box 35502, Emmarentia
2029, South Africa. TEL 27-11-7811401. FAX 27-
11-7811403.
circ. 4,310. *2769*

SOUTH AFRICAN MUSEUM. ANNALS.
South African Museum, P.O. Box 61, Cape Town
8000, South Africa. TEL 27-21-243330. FAX 27-
21-246716.
circ. 450. *609*

SOUTH AFRICAN MUSIC TEACHER.
South African Society of Music Teachers, P.O. Box
20032, Noordbrug 2522, South Africa.
circ. 2,000. *5199*

SOUTH AFRICAN TRANSPORT.
Bolton Publications (Pty) Ltd., P.O. Box 966,
Parklands 2121, South Africa. TEL 27-11-
8803520. FAX 27-11-8806574.
circ. 5,039. *6727*

SOUTH AUSTRALIAN BUILDER.
Master Builders Association of South Australia, 47
South Terrace, Adelaide, S.A. 5000, Australia.
circ. 2,000. *874*

SOUTH AUSTRALIAN TENNIS NEWS.
South Australia Hard Court Tennis League, P.O. Box
202, Goodwood, S.A. 5034, Australia. TEL 61-8-
2932347. FAX 61-8-2938024
circ. 7,000. *6514*

SOUTH BUCKS STAR.
Bucks Free Press Group, Gomm Rd., High
Wycombe, Bucks. HP13 7DW, England. TEL 44-
1494-521212. FAX 44-1494-441977.
circ. 84,000. *3159*

SOUTH CAROLINA. MARINE RESOURCES DIVISION. TECHNICAL REPORT.
Department of Natural Resources, Marine Resources Division, Box 12559, Charleston, SC 29422-2559. TEL 803-762-5026. FAX 803-762-5110.
circ. 100. *2305*

SOUTH CAROLINA LAWYER.
South Carolina Bar, Box 608, 950 Taylor St., Columbia, SC 29202. TEL 803-799-6653. FAX 803-799-4118.
circ. 8,500. *3850*

SOUTH CAROLINA MEDICAL ASSOCIATION. JOURNAL.
South Carolina Medical Association, Box 11188, Columbia, SC 29211. TEL 803-798-6207. FAX 803-772-6783.
circ. 5,300. *4533*

SOUTH CAROLINA RULES AND REGULATIONS FOR HUNTING AND FISHING LICENSES.
Atlantic Publication Group, Inc., Box 61719, Charleston, SC 29419-1719. TEL 803-747-0025. FAX 803-744-0816.
circ. 400,000. *6577*

SOUTH CAROLINA STATE LIBRARY. ANNUAL REPORT.
State Library, 1500 Senate St., Box 11469, Columbia, SC 29211. TEL 803-734-8666. FAX 803-734-8676.
circ. 500. *4028*

SOUTH CAROLINA Y F AND F F A.
South Carolina Young Farmers and Future Farmers, 914A Rutledge Bldg., 1429 Senate St., Columbia, SC 29201. TEL 803-734-8426. FAX 803-734-3525.
circ. 8,000. *153*

SOUTH COAST.
South Coast Publishing, P.O. Box 43, Bexhill-on-Sea, E. Sussex TN39 3GB, England. TEL 01424-222795. FAX 01424-211307.
circ. 11,000. *3967*

SOUTH DAKOTA ACADEMY OF SCIENCE. PROCEEDINGS.
South Dakota Academy of Science, 414 E. Clark St., Vermillion, SD 57069. TEL 605-677-6176.
circ. 350. *6288*

SOUTH DAKOTA GEOLOGICAL SURVEY. BULLETIN.
Geological Survey, Science Center University, 414 E. Clark, Vermillion, SD 57069. TEL 605-677-5227. FAX 605-677-5895. *2262*

SOUTH DAKOTA GEOLOGICAL SURVEY. CIRCULAR.
Geological Survey, Science Center University, 414 East Clark, Vermillion, SD 57069. TEL 605-677-5227. FAX 605-677-5895. *2262*

SOUTH DAKOTA GEOLOGICAL SURVEY. REPORTS OF INVESTIGATION.
Geological Survey, Science Center University, 414 East Clark, Vermillion, SD 57069. TEL 605-677-5227. FAX 605-677-5895. *2262*

SOUTH DAKOTA JOURNAL OF MEDICINE.
South Dakota State Medical Association, 1323 S. Minnesota Ave., Sioux Falls, SD 57105. TEL 605-336-1965. FAX 605-336-0270.
circ. 1,600. *4533*

SOUTH DAKOTAN.
University of South Dakota Alumni Association, University of South Dakota, 414 E. Clark St., Vermillion, SD 57069. TEL 605-677-6714. FAX 605-677-6717.
circ. 34,000. *1886*

SOUTH FLORIDA PARENTING.
Ken Roberts, Ed. & Pub., 4200 Aurora St., Ste. R, Coral Gables, FL 33146. TEL 305-448-6003. FAX 305-448-6290.
circ. 100,000. *1778*

SOUTHAMPTON CITY NEWS.
Southampton City Council, Civic Centre, Southampton SO15 7NC, England. TEL 44-1703-832000. FAX 44-1703-234537.
circ. 93,000. *5921*

SOUTH EAST EUROPEAN MONITOR.
9-12 Goldegasse, A-1040 Vienna, Austria. TEL 43-1-5055680. FAX 43-1-5055680.
circ. 1,500. *3445*

SOUTHEAST TRAVEL PROFESSIONAL.
Florida Travel Professional, 1200 N.W. 78th Ave., No. 216, Miami, FL 33126-1817. TEL 305-592-6133. FAX 305-592-9741.
circ. 10,000. *6913*

SOUTHEASTERNER.
University of Kentucky, Southeast Community College, Cumberland, KY 40823. TEL 606-589-2145.
circ. 3,500. *3711*

SOUTHERN AFRICA'S TRAVEL NEWS WEEKLY.
Travel and Trade Publishing (Pty) Ltd., P.O. Box 662, Auckland Park 2006, South Africa. TEL 27-11-7263036. FAX 27-11-7263994.
circ. 5,670. *6913*

SOUTHERN CALIFORNIA BUSINESS.
Los Angeles Area Chamber of Commerce, 350 S. Bixel St., Los Angeles, CA 90017. TEL 213-580-7571. FAX 213-580-7586.
circ. 10,000. *1149*

SOUTHERN CALIFORNIA GUIDE.
Westworld Publishing Corp., 11385 Exposition Bl., No. 102, Los Angeles, CA 90064. TEL 310-391-8255.
circ. 34,000. *6913*

SOUTHERN EXPOSURE (CARBONDALE).
Southern Illinois University at Carbondale, Library Affairs, Carbondale, IL 62901. TEL 618-453-2516.
circ. 404. *4028*

SOUTHERN ILLINOIS UNIVERSITY AT EDWARDSVILLE. REGIONAL RESEARCH AND DEVELOPMENT SERVICES. REPORT: PRIVATE SECTOR INVESTMENTS.
Southern Illinois University at Edwardsville, Regional Research and Development Services, Campus Box 1456, Edwardsville, IL 62026-1456. TEL 618-692-3500. FAX 618-692-2886.
circ. 100. *3595*

SOUTHERN LANDSCAPE & TURF.
Brantwood Publications, Inc., 3023 Eastland Blvd., Ste. 103, Clearwater, FL 34621-4106. TEL 813-796-3877.
circ. 18,000. *3067*

SOUTHERN METHODIST UNIVERSITY SCHOOL OF LAW. BRIEF.
Southern Methodist University, School of Law, Dallas, TX 75275. TEL 214-768-3341. FAX 214-768-4330.
circ. 9,000. *3851*

SOUTHERN PACIFIC BULLETIN.
Southern Pacific Lines, Southern Pacific Bldg., One Market Plaza, San Francisco, CA 94105. TEL 415-541-1656.
circ. 45,000. *6818*

SOUTHWEST BAPTIST UNIVERSITY OMNIBUS.
Southwest Baptist University, 623 Pike St., Bolivar, MO 65613. TEL 417-326-5281. FAX 417-326-1833.
circ. 1,800. *1886*

SOUTHWEST BOOSTER.
30-4th Ave. N.W., Swift Current, SK S9H 3X4, Canada. TEL 306-773-9321. FAX 306-773-9136.
circ. 19,100. *3125*

SOUTHWEST CONTRACTOR.
McGraw-Hill Companies, Southwest Contractor, 2050 E. University, Phoenix, AZ 85034. TEL 602-258-1641.
circ. 5,600. *874*

SOU'WESTER (EDWARDSVILLE).
Southern Illinois University at Edwardsville, Edwardsville, IL 62026. TEL 618-692-3190.
circ. 300. *4269*

SOVEREIGN.
Sovereign Magazine Ltd., 45 Blondvil St., Coventry CV3 5QX, England. TEL 44-1203-505339. FAX 44-1203-503135.
circ. 105,000. *6801*

THE SOWER.
Bible Society of South Africa, P.O. Box 6215, Roggebaai, Cape Town 8012, South Africa. FAX 27-21-419-4846.
circ. 68,000. *6094*

SOWITIMES.
Studenteninformationsverein Public Media, Stifterstr. 20, A-4100 Ottensheim, Austria. TEL 04234-4547.
circ. 12,000. *2442*

SOZIALES SEMINAR INFORMATIONEN.
Akademie Franz-Hitze-Haus, Kardinal-von-Galen-Ring 50, 48149 Muenster, Germany. TEL 0251-9818-0. FAX 0251-9818480.
circ. 6,000. *6197*

SPA DESTINATIONS.
Publicom Inc., C.P. 365, Place d'Armes, Montreal, PQ H2Y 3H1, Canada. TEL 514-274-0004. FAX 514-274-5884.
circ. 20,000. *6913*

SPACE BUSINESS NEWS.
Phillips Business Information, Inc., 1201 Seven Locks Rd., Potomac, MD 20854. TEL 301-424-3338. FAX 301-309-3847. *77*

SPARE TIME.
Kipen Publishing Corporation, 5810 W. Oklahoma Ave., Milwaukee, WI 53219. TEL 414-543-8110. FAX 414-543-9767.
circ. 301,000. *1352*

SPAREBANKBLADET.
Sparebankforeningens Publikasjoner AS, P.O. Box 6772, St. Olavs Plass, O-130 Oslo, Norway. FAX 22-36-25-33.
circ. 8,000. *1121*

SPEAK OUT!
Trinity College London, 16 Park Crescent, London W1N 4AP, England. TEL 44-171-323-2328. FAX 44-171-323-5201.
circ. 2,000. *2475*

SPEAK UP!
Bible Holiness Movement, Box 223, Sta. A, Vancouver, BC V6C 2M3, Canada. TEL 604-498-3895.
circ. 1,500. *5709*

SPECIAL LIBRARIES ASSOCIATION. SOCIAL SCIENCE DIVISION. BULLETIN.
Special Libraries Association, Social Science Division, 2000 15th St., N., Ste. 701, Arlington, VA 22201-2617. TEL 703-524-7802. FAX 708-524-9335.
circ. 800. *4028*

LO SPECIALISTA.
Ansid - Edit s.r.l., Viale Monte Ceneri 58, 20155 Milan, Italy. TEL 39-2-33003971. FAX 39-2-39215800.
circ. 18,000. *6801*

SPECTROSCOPY EUROPE.
I M Publications, 6 Charlton Mill, Charlton, Chichester, W. Sussex PO18 OHY, England. TEL 49-1243-811334. FAX 49-1243-811711.
circ. 21,000. *1721*

SPECTRUM.
Tzavta Publishing, P.O. Box 18287, Tel Aviv 61181, Israel. TEL 3-5622076. FAX 3-5618549.
circ. 4,000. *5612*

SPEIDEREN.
Norges Speiderforbund, Oevre Vollgate 9, N-0158 Oslo, Norway. TEL 47-22-42-26-60. FAX 47-22-42-07-04.
circ. 40,000. *1806*

SPHINCTER.
University of Liverpool, Medical School, Royal Liverpool Hospital, Box 147, Liverpool L69 3BX, England.
circ. 900. *4533*

SPICAE.
C N R S Editions, 20-22 rue St. Amand, 75015 Paris, France. TEL 45-33-16-00. FAX 45-33-92-13.
circ. 1,500. *4110*

SPIEL UND THEATER.
Deutscher Theaterverlag GmbH, Postfach 100261, 69496 Weinheim, Germany. TEL 06201-51061. FAX 06201-507082. *6703*

Contr Circ

SPIRIT.
Volunteers of America. 3939 N. Causeway, Ste. 400, Metairie, LA 70002. FAX 504-837-4200. circ. 23,000. *6395*

THE SPIRITUAL HEALER.
Harry Edwards Spiritual Healing Sanctuary Trust, Burrows Lea, Shere, Guildford, Surrey GU5 9QG, England. TEL 44-1483-202054. circ. 7,250. *5221*

SPOLETIUM.
Accademia Spoletina, Palazzo Mauri, Via Brignone 14, 06049 Spoleto (PG), Italy. TEL 0743-221203. circ. 1,500. *3626*

SPORTFISKE.
Sveriges Sportfiske- och Fiskevaardsfoerbund Sportfiskarna, P.O. Box 104, S-443 22 Lerum, Sweden. circ. 60,000. *6578*

SPORTING SCENE.
Sporting Scene, 22 Maberley Cres., West Hill, Ont. M1C 3K8, Canada. TEL 416-284-0304. FAX 416-284-1299. circ. 19,800. *6484*

SPORTING TIMES (CALGARY).
Quicksilver Communications, Box 42001, Acadia Postal Outlet, Calgary, AB T2J 7A6, Canada. TEL 403-255-8067. circ. 2,000. *6484*

SPORTS AND ENTERTAINMENT LAW NEWS.
State Bar of Wisconsin, Sports and Entertainment Law Section, 402 W. Wilson St., Madison, WI 53703. TEL 608-257-3838. FAX 608-257-5502. circ. 160. *3851*

SPORTS TREND.
Shore-Varrone, Inc., 6255 Barfield Rd. N.E., Ste. 200, Atlanta, GA 30328-4300. TEL 404-252-8831. FAX 404-252-4436. circ. 29,102. *6486*

SPORTS TURF BULLETIN.
Sports Turf Research Institute, Bingley, W. Yorks. BD16 1AU, England. TEL 44-1274-565131. FAX 44-1274-561891. circ. 4,500. *242*

SPORTSFISKEREN.
Harlang & Toksvig Bladforlag A-S, Vejle, Denmark. circ. 20,637. *2944*

SPORTSTYLE.
Fairchild Fashion & Merchandising Group 7 W. 34th St., New York, NY 10001. TEL 212-630-4870. FAX 212-630-4879. circ. 23,500. *6486*

SPRINGFIELD PUBLIC SCHOOLS. NEWS AND VIEWS.
Springfield Public Schools, Board of Education, 940 N. Jefferson, Springfield, MO 65802. circ. 50,000. *2374*

SPRINGHILLIAN.
Spring Hill College, 4000 Dauphin St., Mobile, AL 36608. TEL 334-380-3850. FAX 334-460-2185. circ. 2,100. *1886*

SPRINGS.
Spring Manufacturers Institute, Inc., 2001 Midwest Rd., Ste. 106, Oak Brook, IL 60521-1335. TEL 708-495-8588. FAX 708-495-8595. circ. 7,000. *2769*

SPRINKLER AGE.
American Fire Sprinkler Association, 12959 Jupiter Rd., Ste. 142, Dallas, TX 75238. TEL 214-349-5965. FAX 214-343-8898. circ. 3,900. *2923*

SPRINKLER BULLETIN.
Mather and Platt Ltd., Park Works, Manchester M10 6BA, England. circ. 10,000. *3666*

SQUILLA.
Francescani di Recco, Via S. Francesco 4, 16036 Recco GE, Italy. TEL 39-185-74198. circ. 6,000. *6197*

STADT DUISBURG. WAHLEN (YEAR).
Amt fuer Statistik, Stadtforschung und Europaangelegenheiten, Der Oberstadtdirektor, 47049 Duisburg, Germany. TEL 49-203-2833085. FAX 49-203-2834404. circ. 350. *5934*

STADT UND GEMEINDE.
Verlag Otto Schwartz und Co., Annastr. 7, 37075 Goettingen, Germany. TEL 49-551-31051. FAX 49-551-372812. circ. 7,000. *5921*

STADTGEMEINDE DEUTSCHLANDSBERG. MITTEILUNGEN.
Stadtgemeinde Deutschlandsberg, Hauptplatz 35, A-8530 Deutschlandsberg, Austria. TEL 03462-2011253. FAX 03462-2011262. circ. 3,600. *3113*

STAFFROOM GUIDE TO SCHOOL JOURNEYS.
E M A P - Response Publishing Ltd., Wentworth House, Wentworth St., Peterborough, Cambs. PE1 1DS, England. TEL 01733-63100. FAX 01733-62656. circ. 5,000. *2463*

STAGE.
Lusaka Theatre Club (Co-Op) Ltd., P.O. Box 30615, Lusaka, Zambia. circ. 300. *6703*

STAINLESS STEEL.
Southern Africa Stainless Steel Development Association, P.O. Box 4479, Rivonia 2128, South Africa. TEL 27-11-803-5610. FAX 27-11-803-2011. circ. 7,623. *4975*

STAINLESS STEEL BUYER'S GUIDE (YEAR).
Southern Africa Stainless Steel Development Association P.O. Box 4479, Rivonia 2128, South Africa. TEL 27-11-803-5610. FAX 27-11-803-2011. circ. 3,010. *4975*

STAMP LOVER.
National Philatelic Society, 107 Charterhouse St., London EC1M 6FT, England. TEL 44-171-251-5040. circ. 1,500. *5463*

STAND BY.
Electrical Workers Local 369, Box 36275, Louisville, KY 40233. TEL 502-368-2568. FAX 502-368-1270. circ. 2,000. *3728*

THE STANDARD.
170-176 Koroit St., Warrnambool, Vic. 3280, Australia. TEL 61-55-61-4000. FAX 61-55-62-0389. circ. 146. *3112*

STANDARD & POOR'S CORPORATION RECORDS.
Standard & Poor's 25 Broadway, New York, NY 10004. TEL 212-208-8000. FAX 212-412-0459. *1353*

STANDBEIN SPIELBEIN.
Szenario Verlag, Friesenstr. 6, 31134 Hildesheim, Germany. TEL 49-5121-33001. FAX 49-5121-34929. circ. 1,000. *5133*

STANFORD.
Stanford Alumni Association, Bowman Alumni House, Stanford, CA 94305. TEL 415-723-2021. FAX 415-725-8676. circ. 100,000. *1836*

STAR CARRIER.
National Star Route Mail Contractors Association, 324 E. Capito St., Washington, DC 20003. TEL 202-543-1661. FAX 202-543-8863. circ. 5,000. *1933*

STARK REPORT.
Stark Research, Inc., 1020 Prospect St., Ste. 3, La Jolla, CA 92037. TEL 619-459-0818. FAX 619-459-0819. circ. 250. *1354*

STARKENBURGER WIRTSCHAFT.
Industrie- und Handelskammer Darmstadt, Rheinstr. 89, 64295 Darmstadt, Germany. TEL 49-6151-871-0. FAX 49-6151-871281. circ. 15,000. *149*

STATE BAR OF NEW MEXICO. BAR BULLETIN.
State Bar of New Mexico, 121 Tijeras N.E., Albuquerque, NM 87102. TEL 505-842-6132. FAX 505-843-8765. circ. 4,700. *3852*

STATE DIRECTORY OF KENTUCKY.
Directories, Inc., Box 187, Pewee Valley, KY 40056. TEL 502-241-8256. circ. 5,000. *5923*

STATE GEOLOGISTS JOURNAL.
Association of American State Geologists, c/o Ohio Geological Survey, 4383 Fountain Sq. Dr., Columbus, OH 43224-1362. TEL 614-265-6576. FAX 614-447-1918. circ. 200. *2263*

THE STATE OF THE MARKET.
Chartered Institute of Marketing, Moor Hall, Cookham, Maidenhead, Berkshire SL6 9QH, England. TEL 44-1628-427500. FAX 44-1628-427499. circ. 25,000. *1241*

STATE OF THE UNION.
Union League Club of Chicago, 65 W. Jackson Blvd., Chicago, IL 60604. TEL 312-427-7800. circ. 4,800. *1854*

STATE PEACE OFFICERS JOURNAL.
North American Publishing Company, Box 130155 Houston, TX 77219-0155. TEL 713-526-6425. circ. 20,000. *2176*

STATE PLANNING NEWSLETTER.
Office of State Planning, 116 W. Jones St., Raleigh, NC 27603-8003. TEL 919-733-4131. FAX 919-715-3562. circ. 2,700. *6634*

STATE UNIVERSITY OF NEW YORK. RESEARCH.
State University of New York at Albany, Research Foundation, State University Plaza, Albany, NY 12246. TEL 518-434-7180. FAX 518-434-7211. circ. 13,000. *2374*

STATE UNIVERSITY OF NEW YORK AT ALBANY. ALBANY.
State University of New York at Albany, Office of University Relations, AD233, Albany, NY 12222. TEL 518-442-3070. circ. 70,000. *1887*

STATIONERY UPDATE.
Datateam Publishing, Datateam House, Tovil Hill, Maidstone, Kent ME15 6QS, England. TEL 01622-687031. FAX 01622-757646. circ. 6,000. *1497*

STATISTICAL NOTES OF JAPAN.
International Statistical Affairs Division, Statistical Standards Department, Statistics Bureau, Management and Coordination Agency, 19-1 Wakamatsu-cho, Shinjuku-ku, Tokyo, Japan. FAX 81-3-5273-1181. circ 550. *6635*

STATISTICAL REPORT ON VISITOR ARRIVALS TO INDONESIA.
Department of Tourism, Post, and Telecommunications, Jalan Kebon Sirih, No.36, Jakarta, Indonesia. TEL 021-347611. FAX 021-375409. circ. 500. *6932*

STATISTISK AARBOG FOR HOVEDSTADSREGIONEN.
Hovedstadsregionens Statistikkontor, Vester Voldgade 87, 4, DK-1552 Copenhagen, Denmark. TEL 45-33-66-24-24. FAX 45-33-91-05-02. circ. 1,000. *6637*

STAVANGER AFTENBLAD.
P.O. Box 229, N-4001 Stavanger, Norway. TEL 47-51-50-00-00. FAX 47-51-89-32-23. circ. 71,771. *3202*

STEAMBOAT VACATION GUIDE.
Mac Media L L C, Box 4328, Steamboat, CO 80477. TEL 970-879-5250. FAX 970-879-4650. circ. 110,000. *3239*

STEN.
Sveriges Stenindustrifoerbund, P.O. Box 106, S-121 22 Johanneshov, Sweden. TEL 46-08-81-86-00. FAX 46-08-81-86-02. circ. 8,600. *875*

STENOGRAFISK TIDSSKRIFT.
Dansk Stenografisk Forening, Grumstrupsalle 4, DK-8660 Skanderborg, Denmark. TEL 75-571073. *1497*

STEVENS INDICATOR.
Stevens Alumni Association, Castle Point, Hoboken, NJ 07030. TEL 201-216-5161. FAX 201-216-5374.
circ. 20. *1887*

STILL WATERS NEWSLETTER.
Still Waters Foundation, Inc., 615 Stafford Ln., Pensacola, FL 32506. TEL 904-455-9511.
circ. 2,000. *5499*

STIRPES.
Texas State Genealogical Society, 204 Glentower, San Antonio, TX 78213. TEL 210-341-8372. FAX 210-341-7529.
circ. 850. *3102*

STITCHES.
Stitches Publishing Inc., 16787 Warden Ave., R.R. 3, Newmarket, ON L3Y 4W1, Canada. TEL 905-853-1884. FAX 905-853-6565.
circ. 44,000. *4534*

STNEWS.
Chemical Abstracts Service, 240 Olentangy River Rd., Box 3012, Columbus, OH 43210-0012. TEL 614-447-3600. FAX 614-447-3713. *1711*

STOCKTON NEWS.
Stockton Borough Council, P.O. Box 11, Municipal Bldgs., Church Rd., Stockton-on-Tees TS18 1LD, England. TEL 44-1642-670067. FAX 44-1642-622005.
circ. 75,000. *5951*

STORE EQUIPMENT AND DESIGN.
S E D Publishing, Box 578249, Chicago, IL 60657-8429. TEL 312-281-4441. FAX 312-281-8275.
circ. 20,000. *3008*

STRADA MAESTRA.
Leopoldo Fusconi Editore, Piazza Roosevelt 4, 40123 Bologna, Italy. TEL 39-51-228148. FAX 39-51-220825.
circ. 500. *3360*

STRAHLENTELEX MIT ELEKTROSMOG-REPORT.
Rauxeler Weg 6, 13507 Berlin, Germany. TEL 49-30-4352840. FAX 49-30-4352840.
circ. 1,200. *2848*

STRAZ.
Polish National Union of America, 1004 Pittston Ave., Scranton, PA 18505. TEL 717-344-1513. FAX 717-961-5961.
circ. 10,000. *2909*

STRITCH M.D.
Loyola University Chicago, Stritch School of Medicine, 2160 S. First Ave., Maywood, IL 60153. TEL 708-216-6700. FAX 708-216-8199.
circ. 6,500. *1887*

STROKE NEWS.
Stroke Association, CHSA House, Whitecross St., London EC1Y 8JJ, England. TEL 44-171-490-7999. FAX 44-171-490-2686.
circ. 34,000. *4820*

STUD. MED.
Danish Medical Students Association, Blegdamsvej 3, DK-2200 Copenhagen N, Denmark.
circ. 5,000. *4534*

STUDENT B M J (SOUTH AFRICAN EDITION).
George Warman Publications (Pty.) Ltd., P.O. Box 704, Cape Town 8000, South Africa. TEL 27-21-245320. FAX 27-21-261332. *4534*

STUDENT MAGAZINE (COSTA MESA).
Box 1641, Costa Mesa, CA 92628-1641. TEL 714-548-9116.
circ. 20,000. *1887*

STUDIA PHONOLOGICA.
Kyoto University, Institution for Phonetic Sciences, c/o Mr. Shuji Doshita, Kyoto Daigaku Kogakubu Johokagakka, Yoshida Honmachi, Sakyo-ku, Kyoto 606, Japan. FAX 81-75-753-5977.
circ. 1,000. *4113*

STUDIE O RUKOPISECH.
Archiv Akademie Ved Ceske Republiky, V Zamcich 56-76, 181 00 Prague 8, Czech Republic. TEL 42-2-8541765. FAX 42-2-8541560.
circ. 300. *3448*

STUDIEN VON ZEITFRAGEN.
Peter Spengler Verlag, Postfach 101920, 60019 Frankfurt a.M., Germany. TEL 49-69-5963690. FAX 49-69-5974213.
circ. 100. *3360*

STUDIES IN AVIAN BIOLOGY.
Cooper Ornithological Society, Inc. (Riverside), Department of Biology, University of California at Riverside, Riverside, CA 92521. FAX 909-787-4286.
circ. 1,000. *781*

STUDIES IN ENGLISH LITERATURE.
English Literary Society of Japan, 501 Kenkyusha Bldg., 9 Surugadai 2-chome, Kanda, Chiyoda-ku, Tokyo 101, Japan. TEL 03-3293-7528. FAX 03-3233-3398.
circ. 3,800. *4272*

STUDIO ONE.
College of Saint Benedict, St. Joseph, MN 56374.
circ. 700. *4320*

STYLE (EDITION FRANCAISE).
N.V. Trends Magazines Bd. Louis Schmidt 97, 1040 Brussels, Belgium. TEL 32-2-7321860. FAX 32-2-7344018. *3115*

STYLE (NEDERLANDSE EDITIE).
N.V. Trends Magazines Bd. Louis Schmidt 97, 1040 Brussels, Belgium. TEL 32-2-7321860. FAX 32-2-7344018. *3115*

SUB-POSTMASTER.
National Federation of Sub-Postmasters, Evelyn House, 22 Windlesham Gardens, Shoreham-By-Sea, Sussex, England. TEL 44-1273-452324. FAX 44-1273-465403.
circ. 21,000. *1933*

SUBCONSCIOUS SOUP.
Scott Clark, Ed. & Pub., 103 Nicholas Ct., Kissimmee, FL 34758-3115. TEL 407-932-4597.
circ. 1,000. *4320*

SUBTERRANEAN SOCIOLOGY NEWSLETTER.
Subterranean Sociological Association, Department of Sociology, Eastern Michigan University, Ypsilanti, MI 48197. TEL 517-522-3551.
circ. 600. *6437*

SUD OUEST.
8 rue de Cheverus, 33000 Bordeaux, France. TEL 56-00-33-33. FAX 56-44-46-61.
circ. 14,795. *3140*

SUEDWEST PRESSE.
Neue Pressegesellschaft, Frauenstr. 77, 89073 Ulm, Germany. TEL 49-731-156500. FAX 49-731-156308.
circ. 130,000. *3149*

SUGAR MILLING RESEARCH INSTITUTE. ANNUAL REPORT.
Sugar Milling Research Institute, University of Natal, Private Bag X10, 4014 Dalbridge, South Africa. TEL 27-31-2616882. FAX 27-31-2616886.
circ. 400. *2992*

SUGAR TECHNOLOGISTS' ASSOCIATION OF TRINIDAD AND TOBAGO. PROCEEDINGS.
Sugar Manufacturers' Association of Trindad & Tobago, Suite 402, 4th Level, Mecalfab's Building, 92 Queen St., Port-of-Spain, Trinidad & Tobago, W.I. *2992*

SUGARBEET GROWER.
Sugar Publications, 503 Broadway, Fargo, ND 58102. TEL 701-237-5747. FAX 701-235-0140.
circ. 12,800. *242*

SUI YUAN WEN HSIEN.
Association of Fellow Provincials of Sui Yuan, 101 Fourth St., Chung Yang Rd., Hsin Tien, Taipei Hsien, Taiwan 23127, Republic of China. TEL 886-2-219-6633.
circ. 1,500. *2910*

SULPHUR IN AGRICULTURE.
Sulphur Institute, 1140 Connecticut Ave., N.W., Ste. 612, Washington, DC 20036. TEL 202-331-9660. FAX 202-293-2940.
circ. 3,000. *154*

SUMMARY OF STATE LAWS AND REGULATIONS RELATING TO DISTILLED SPIRITS.
Distilled Spirits Council of the United States, Inc., Legal Division, 1250 Eye St., N.W., Ste. 900, Washington, DC 20005. TEL 202-682-8825. FAX 202-682-8888. *512*

SUMMER POCKET GUIDE.
Pocket Guide Publications, Inc., 9650 Clayton Rd., St. Louis, MO 63124. TEL 314-991-5222. FAX 314-991-4118.
circ. 500,000. *6914*

SUN-DIAMOND GROWER.
Sun-Diamond Growers of California, Box 1727, Stockton, CA 95201. TEL 209-467-6219. FAX 209-467-6357.
circ. 12,000. *2992*

SUNEXPERT.
Computer Publishing Group, 320 Washington St., Brookline, MA 02146-3202. TEL 617-739-7001. FAX 617-739-7003.
circ. 69,000. *2091*

SUNNHETSBLADET.
Norsk Bokforlag A-S, Olaf Helsets vei 8, Oslo 6, Norway. TEL 22-28-52-20. FAX 22-29-85-11.
circ. 14,408. *5536*

SUO.
Suoseura, Unioninkatu 40, SF-00170 Helsinki, Finland. FAX 358-41-677405.
circ. 900. *3026*

SUOMEN KALASTUSLEHTI.
Kalatalouden Keskusliitto, Koydenpunojankatu 7 B 23, 00180 Helsinki 18, Finland. TEL 358-0-640-126. FAX 358-0-608-309.
circ. 4,392. *2944*

SUOMEN LAAKARILEHTI.
Suomen Laakariliitto, Makelankatu 2, 00500 Helsinki, Finland. TEL 358-90-393-0795.
circ. 21,500. *4534*

SUOMEN LEHDISTO.
Sanomalehtien Liitto, Lonnrothinkatu 11, FIN-00120 Helsinki, Finland. TEL 358-0-2287-7300. FAX 358-0-607-989.
circ. 3,376. *3711*

SUOMI - U S A.
Suomi-Amerikka Yhdistysten Liitto, Mechelininkatu 10A, FIN-00100 Helsinki, Finland. TEL 358-0-440711. FAX 358-0-408974.
circ. 30,275. *5773*

SUPERCONDUCTOR INDUSTRY.
Rodman Publishing Corp., 17 S. Franklin Tpk., Box 555, Ramsey, NJ 07446. TEL 201-825-2552. FAX 201-825-0553.
circ. 7,000. *2720*

SURFACE COATINGS AUSTRALIA.
Surface Coatings Association Australia Inc., 443 High St., Prahran, Vic. 3181, Australia. TEL 61-3-95106238. FAX 61-3-95296069.
circ. 1,350. *5311*

SURGICAL UPDATE.
American Association of Oral and Maxillofacial Surgeons, 9700 W. Bryn Mawr Ave., Rosemont, IL 60018. TEL 708-678-6200. FAX 708-678-6286.
circ. 150,000. *4655*

SURPLUS RECORD.
Surplus Record, Inc., 20 N. Wacker Dr., Chicago, IL 60606. TEL 312-372-9077. FAX 312-372-6537.
circ. 70,000. *4346*

SVENSK JAKT.
Svenska Jaegarefoerbundet, P.O. Box 1, S-163 21 Spaanga, Sweden. TEL 46-8-795-33-00. FAX 46-8-761-20-15.
circ. 173,400. *6579*

SVENSK PAPPERSTIDNING - NORDISK CELLULOSA.
Arbor Publishing AB, P.O. Box 26212, S-100 41 Stockholm, Sweden. TEL 46-8-611-60-30. FAX 46-8-679-90-50.
circ. 7,687. *5326*

Contr Circ

SVENSK TENNIS.
I C A Foerlaget AB, Storagatan 41, S-721 85 Vaesteraas, Sweden. TEL 46-21-19-40-00. FAX 46-21-19-42-21.
circ. 85,100. *6515*

SVENSK VAEGTIDNING.
Svenska Vaegfoereningens Foerlags AB, Wallingatan 33, S-111 24 Stockholm, Sweden. TEL 46-8-23-17-35. FAX 46-8-7918158.
circ. 3,000. *2674*

SVENSK VETERINAERTIDNING.
Sveriges Veterinaerfoerbund, P.O. Box 12 709, S-112 94 Stockholm, Sweden. TEL 08-654-2480. FAX 08-6517082.
circ. 2,600. *6954*

SVERIGES NATUR.
Svenska Naturskyddsfoereningen, P.O. Box 4625, S-116 91 Stockholm, Sweden. TEL 08-7026500. FAX 08-702-2702.
circ. 18,000. *2142*

SVETSAREN.
Esab AB, Marketing Communications, P.O. Box 8004, S-402 77 Goeteborg, Sweden. FAX 46-31-509-390.
circ. 1,600. *4988*

SVOBODNE SLOVO.
Melantrich, Inc., Vaclavske nam. 36, 112 12 Prague 1, Czech Republic.
circ. 155,000. *3133*

SWAMP GAS JOURNAL.
Ufology Research of Manitoba, Box 1918, Winnipeg General Post Office, Winnipeg, MB R3C 3R2, Canada. TEL 204-269-7553.
circ. 250. *79*

SWANSEA GEOGRAPHER.
University College of Swansea, Department of Geography, Singleton Park, Swansea, Glam. SA2 8PP, Wales. FAX 44-1792-205556.
circ. 200. *3275*

SWARTHMORE COLLEGE PHOENIX.
Swarthmore College, Swarthmore, PA 19081. TEL 215-328-8173. FAX 215-328-8674.
circ. 2,700. *1888*

SWATCHES.
National Association of Decorative Fabric Distributors, 3008 Millwood Ave., Columbia, SC 29205. TEL 803-252-5646.
circ. 17,000. *6684*

SWEET'S CANADIAN CONSTRUCTION CATALOGUE FILE.
McGraw-Hill Information Systems Company of Canada Ltd., 270 Yorkland Blvd., North York, ON M2J 1R8, Canada. TEL 416-496-3100.
circ. 7,000. *876*

SWEET'S CATALOG FILE FOR THE CIVIL ENGINEERING & RETROFIT MARKET.
Sweet's Catalog Files 1221 Ave. of the Americas, New York, NY 10020. TEL 212-512-4450. FAX 212-512-2348.
circ. 15,000. *2674*

SWEET'S CATALOG FILE FOR THE ELECTRICAL ENGINEERING AND RETROFIT MARKET.
Sweet's Catalog Files 1221 Ave. of the Americas, New York, NY 10020. TEL 212-512-4450. FAX 212-512-2348.
circ. 15,000. *2720*

SWEET'S CONTRACT INTERIORS FILE.
Sweet's Catalog Files 1221 Ave. of the Americas, New York, NY 10020. TEL 212-512-4450. FAX 212-512-2348.
circ. 10,000. *3682*

SWEET'S GENERAL BUILDING AND RENOVATION FILE.
Sweet's Catalog Files 1221 Ave. of the Americas, New York, NY 10020. TEL 212-512-4450. FAX 212-512-2348.
circ. 25,000. *876*

SWEET'S HOMEBUILDING & REMODELING FILE.
Sweet's Catalog Files 1221 Ave. of the Americas, New York, NY 10020. TEL 212-512-4450. FAX 212-512-2348.
circ. 29,000. *876*

SWEET'S INDUSTRIAL CONSTRUCTION AND RENOVATION FILE.
Sweet's Catalog Files 1221 Ave. of the Americas, New York, NY 10020. TEL 212-512-4450. FAX 212-512-2348.
circ. 25,000. *376*

SWEET'S INTERNATIONAL BUILDING PRODUCTS CATALOG FILE.
Sweet's Catalog Files 1221 Ave. of the Americas, New York, NY 10020. TEL 212-512-4450. FAX 212-512-2348.
circ. *876*

SWEET'S INTERNATIONAL PRODUCTLINE.
Sweet's Catalog Files 1221 Ave. of the Americas, New York, NY 10020. TEL 212-512-4750. FAX 212-512-4302.
circ. *876*

SWEET'S LIGHT SOURCE.
Sweet's Catalog Files, 1221 Ave. of the Americas, New York, NY 10020. TEL 212-512-4450. FAX 212-512-2348.
circ. 21,000. *876*

SWEET'S MECHANICAL ENGINEERING AND RETROFIT FILE.
Sweet's Catalog Files 1221 Ave. of the Americas, New York, NY 1C020. TEL 212-512-4450. FAX 212-512-2348.
circ. 15,000. *2770*

SWEET'S PRODUCTLINE.
Sweet's Catalog Files 1221 Ave. of the Americas, New York, NY 10020. TEL 212-512-4750. FAX 212-512-4302.
circ. 25,000. *875*

SWENSON CENTER NEWS.
Swenson Swedish Immigration Research Center, Augustana College, 639 38th St., Rock Island, IL 61201-2273. TEL 309-794-7204. FAX 309-794-7443.
circ. 4,500. *2910*

SWIFT CURRENT SUN.
55 1st Ave. N.E., Swift Current, SK S9H 2A9, Canada. TEL 306-773-3116. FAX 306-773-2653.
circ. 20,032. *3126*

SWINGER'S TODAY.
Contact Advertising, 2010 St. Lucie Blvd., Ft. Pierce, FL 34946. TEL 561-464-5447. FAX 561-466-7294.
circ. 15,000. *4946*

SWINGERS UPDATE.
Contact Advertising, 2010 St. Lucie Blvd., Ft. Pierce, FL 34946. TEL 561-464-5447. FAX 561-466-7294.
circ. 22,000. *4946*

SWINGING TIMES.
Contact Advertising, 2010 St. Lucie Blvd., Ft. Pierce, FL 34946. TEL 561-464-5447. FAX 561-466-7294.
circ. 50,000. *4946*

SWISS SURGERY.
Hans Huber AG, Laenggassstr. 76, CH-3000 Bern 9, Switzerland. TEL 41-31-3004500. FAX 41-31-3004590.
circ. 2,000. *4922*

SYKEPLEIEN. FAG.
Norsk Sykepleierforbund, P.O. Box 2633, St. Hanshaugen, N-0131 Oslo, Norway. FAX 47-22-38-35-36.
circ. 50,000. *4729*

SYKEPLEIEN. JOURNALEN.
Norsk Sykepleierforbund, P.O. Box 2633, St. Hanshaugen, N-0131 Oslo, Norway. FAX 47-22-38-35-36.
circ. 51,094. *4729*

SYMANTEC.
Symantec Corporation, 10201 Torre Ave., Cupertino, CA 95014-2132. TEL 408-253-9600. FAX 408-253-3968.
circ. 650,000. *2117*

SYNAPSE (BOSTON).
Unitarian Universalist Association, 25 Beacon St., Boston, MA 02108-2800. TEL 617-742-2100. FAX 617-367-3237.
circ. 10,500. *4168*

SYNDICAT NATIONAL DES ARCHITECTES D'INTERIEUR. BULLETIN.
Syndicat National des Architectes d'Interieur, 57, Bd. Richard Lenoir, 75011 Paris, France.
circ. 650. *405*

SYSTEMS CONTRACTOR NEWS.
Miller Freeman P S N 2 Park Ave., Ste. 1820, New York, NY 10016. TEL 212-213-3444. FAX 212-213-3484.
circ. 14,000. *2533*

SZABADSAG.
Szabadsag Ltd., Str. Napoca Nr. 16, P.O. Box 340, 3400 Cluj, Rumania. TEL 40-64-198985. FAX 40-64-197206.
circ. 500. *3208*

SZIVARVANY.
Framo Publishing, 561 W. Diversey Pkwy., Chicago, IL 60614. TEL 312-477-1485. FAX 312-477-2598.
circ. 1,500. *2910*

T A M BULLETIN.
Travelling Art Mail, c/o T A M Postbus 10388, 5000 JJ Tilburg, Netherlands. TEL 31-13-5366103. *455*

T & A M REPORT.
University of Illinois at Urbana-Champaign, Department of Theoretical and Applied Mechanics, 216 Talbot Laboratory Urbana, IL 61801. TEL 217-333-2322.
circ. 65. *2741*

T E A M HORIZONS.
Evangelical Alliance Mission, Box 969, Wheaton, IL 60189-0969. TEL 708-553-1326. FAX 708-653-1826.
circ. 45,000. *6097*

T G.
Ediciones Sohail, Velazquez 21, 28001 Madrid, Spain. TEL 1-275-38-28.
circ. 10,000. *455*

T H E JOURNAL.
Ed Warnshius Ltd., 150 El Camino Real, Ste. 112, Tustin, CA 92680-3670. TEL 714-730-4011. FAX 714-730-3739.
circ. 146,000. *2408*

T H - TRANSPORT OCH HANTERING.
T.H. Foerlag, Box 45056, S-104 30 Stockholm, Sweden. TEL 46-8-23-03-70. FAX 46-8-10-46-18.
circ. 3,400. *6727*

T I A NEWS.
Sosland Publishing Co., 4800 Main St., Ste. 100, Kansas City, MO 64112. TEL 815-756-1000. FAX 816-756-0484.
circ. 2,500. *3002*

T I F F A FREIGHT FORWARDING HANDBOOK.
Cosmic Group of Companies, 4th Fl., Phyathai Bldg., 31 Phyathai Rd., Rajthevi, Bangkok 10400, Thailand. TEL 245-3850. FAX 245-4737.
circ. 5,000. *6850*

T M A GUIDE TO TOBACCO TAXES.
Tobacco Merchants Association of the United States, Inc., 231 Clarksville Rd., Ste. 6, Box 8019, Princeton, NJ 08543-8019. TEL 609-275-4900. FAX 609-275-8379. *6710*

T M A LEAF BULLETIN.
Tobacco Merchants Association of the United States, Inc., 231 Clarksville Rd., Ste. 6, Box 8019, Princeton, NJ 08543-8019. TEL 609-275-4900. FAX 609-275-8379. *6710*

T M A TOBACCO BAROMETER.
Tobacco Merchants Association of the United States, Inc., 231 Clarksville Rd., Ste. 6, Box 8019, Princeton, NJ 08543-8019. TEL 609-275-4900. FAX 609-275-8379. *6710*

T M A TOBACCO BAROMETER. SMOKING, CHEWING, SNUFF.
Tobacco Merchants Association of the United States, Inc., 231 Clarksville Rd., Ste. 6, Box 8019, Princeton, NJ 08543-8019. TEL 609-275-4900. FAX 609-275-8379. *6710*

T M A TOBACCO TRADE BAROMETER.
Tobacco Merchants Association of the United States, Inc., 231 Clarksville Rd., Ste. 6, Box 8019, Princeton, NJ 08543-8019. TEL 609-275-4900. FAX 609-275-8379. *6710*

T N SERRURERIE - MIROITERIE.
28 rue Andre Bonnenfant, 78100 Saint-Germain en Laye, France. TEL 39-73-50-31. FAX 39-73-53-31. circ. 6,000. *890*

T N T MAGAZINE.
14-15 Child's Pl., Earls Ct., London SW5 9RX, England. TEL 44-171-373-3377. FAX 44-171-373-9457. circ. 69,504. *3160*

T.P.L. NEWS.
Toronto Public Library, 281 Front St. E., Toronto, Ont. M5A 4L2, Canada. TEL 416-393-7565. FAX 416-393-7782. circ. 900. *4029*

T S I JOURNAL OF PARTICLE INSTRUMENTATION.
T S I Incorporated, 500 Cardigan Rd., Box 64394, St. Paul, MN 55164. TEL 612-490-2833. FAX 612-490-3860. circ. 9,000. *2770*

T S S A REPORT.
Tackle & Shooting Sports Agents Association, 1033 N. Fairfax St., Ste. 200, Alexandria, VA 22314-1540. TEL 708-381-3032. FAX 708-381-9518. circ. 400. *963*

T T G ASIA HOTEL GUIDE.
Miller Freeman Pte. Ltd., 100 Beach Rd., 26-00 Shaw Towers, Singapore 0718, Singapore. TEL 65-2943366. FAX 65-2985534. circ. 60,608. *6914*

T T R A NEWS.
University of Utah, 10200 W. 44th Ave., No. 304, Wheat Ridge, CO 80033. TEL 303-422-6557. FAX 303-422-8894. circ. 900. *6914*

T T - REVUE.
Verband Oeffentlicher Verkehr, Daehlhoelzliweg 12, CH-3000 Bern 6, Switzerland. *6728*

T U C NEWS.
Trades Union Congress of Ghana, Hall of Trade Unions, P.O. Box 701, Accra, Ghana. circ. 10,000. *3729*

T V NEWS.
80 Eighth Ave., Ste. 315, New York, NY 10011. TEL 212-243-6800. FAX 212-243-7457. circ. 60,000. *1971*

T V 7 JOURS.
Trustar Ltd., 2020 rue Universite, 20th Fl., Montreal, PQ H3A 2A5, Canada. TEL 514-383-3400. FAX 514-383-1766. circ. 255. *1971*

T V TODAY.
National Association of Broadcasters, 1771 N St., N.W., Washington, DC 20036. TEL 202-429-5350. FAX 202-429-5406. *1971*

T W I C E.
Cahners Publishing Company (New York), Division of Reed Elsevier Inc., 249 W. 17th St., New York, NY 10011. TEL 212-645-0067. FAX 212-337-7066. circ. 32,988. *2533*

TABI TO TETSUDO.
Tetsudo Journal Sha, Iidabashi 4-8-6, Chiyoda-ku, Tokyo, Japan. TEL 03-3264-1891. FAX 03-3265-3597. circ. 120,000. *6914*

TACOMA - PIERCE COUNTY CHAMBER OF COMMERCE UPDATE.
Tacoma-Pierce County Chamber of Commerce, 950 Pacific Ave., Ste. 300, Box 1933, Tacoma, WA 98401. TEL 206-627-2175. FAX 206-597-7305. circ. 3,500. *1150*

TAHITI BEACH PRESS.
Tahiti Publications Touristiques, P.O. Box 887, Papeete 98713, Tahiti. TEL 689-426850. FAX 689-433356. circ. 2,700. *6914*

TAIEI TOSHI NEWS.
Invest in Britain Bureau, 1 Victoria St., London SW1H 0ET, England. TEL 44-171-215-5638. FAX 44-171-215-5651. circ. 11,300. *1355*

TAITO.
Kasi- ja Taideteollisuusliitto, P.O. Box 186, Kalevankatu 61, FIN-00181 Helsinki, Finland. TEL 358-0-694-0023. FAX 358-0-694-0067. circ. 12,000. *470*

TAIWAN HAIXIA.
Guojia Haiyang-ju, Disan Haiyang Yanjiusuo, P.O. Box 0570, Xiamen, Fujian 361005, People's Republic of China. TEL 0592-2085880. FAX 0592-2086646. circ. 1,000. *2306*

TAKE OFF.
Skandinavisk Bladforlag A-S, Frederiksberg Alle 3, DK-1621 Copenhagen V, Denmark. TEL 45-31-23-80-99. FAX 45-31-23-70-42. circ. 6,000. *6914*

TALKING PICTURES.
Valis Books, 15b Bloom Grove, West Norwood, London SE27 0HZ, England. TEL 44-181-670-6211. FAX 44-181-365-8894. circ. 500. *5114*

TALKING POINT.
Trinity College London, 16 Park Crescent, London W1N 4AP, England. TEL 44-171-323-2328. FAX 44-171-323-5201. circ. 6,000. *2503*

TALKING TO THE BOSS.
4556 Oakton St., No.200, Skokie, IL 60076-3144. TEL 708-933-9659. FAX 708-933-9667. circ. 15,000. *963*

TALLYBOARD.
Forest Products Accident Prevention Association, 690 Mc Keown Ave. P.O. Box 2050, North Bay, Ont. P1B 9P1, Canada. TEL 705-472-4120. FAX 705-472-0207. circ. 3,200. *3026*

TAMKANG JOURNAL OF MATHEMATICS.
Tamkang University Press, Tamsui, Taipei, Taiwan 25137, Republic of China. TEL 886-2-621-5656. FAX 886-2-620-2613. circ. 300. *4399*

TAMPA BAY FAMILY JOURNAL.
Family Journal Publications, Inc., Box 1100, Orlando, FL 32802-1100. TEL 813-289-4060. FAX 813-289-4585. circ. 25,000. *1778*

TANNING TRENDS.
Tanning Trends Inc., 3101 Page Ave., Jackson, MI 49203. TEL 517-784-1772. FAX 517-787-3940. circ. 20,000. *1580*

TANZANIA. BUREAU OF STANDARDS. DIRECTOR'S ANNUAL REPORT.
Bureau of Standards, P.O. Box 9524, Dar es Salaam, Tanzania. TEL 255-51-43298. FAX 255-51-43298. *5018*

TAPOVAN PRASAD.
Chinmaya Mission, No. 2, 13th Ave., Harrington Rd., Madras 600031, Tamil Nadu, India. TEL 8265641. circ. 5,000. *6115*

TAR HEEL LIBRARIES.
Department of Cultural Resources, Division of State Library, 109 E. Jones St., Raleigh, NC 27611. TEL 919-733-2570. FAX 919-733-8748. circ. 5,000. *4029*

TARHEEL BANKING TODAY.
North Carolina Bankers Association, 3709 National Dr., Box 30609, Raleigh, NC 27622-0609. TEL 919-782-6960. FAX 919-782-6701. *1123*

TASMANIA. DEPARTMENT OF PRIMARY INDUSTRY AND FISHERIES. MARINE RESOURCES DIVISION. TECHNICAL REPORT.
Department of Primary Industry and Fisheries, Marine Resources Division, P.O. Box 619F, Hobart, Tas. 7001, Australia. FAX 61-02-278035. circ. 400. *2944*

TASMANIAN BUSINESS REPORTER.
Tasmanian Chamber of Commerce and Industry, G.P.O. Box 793H, Hobart, Tas. 7001, Australia. TEL 61-02-345933. FAX 61-02-311278. circ. 16,000. *1150*

TASMANIAN EDUCATION REVIEW.
Australian Education Union, Tasmanian Branch, 32 Patrick St., Hobart, Tas., Australia. TEL 61-02-349500. FAX 61-02-343052. circ. 6,400. *3729*

TATER NEWS.
National Potato Promotion Board, 7555 E. Hampden Ave., No. 412, Denver, CO 80231-4835. TEL 303-758-7783. FAX 303-756-9256. circ. 17,000. *242*

TAX NOTES.
Tax Analysts, 6830 N. Fairfax Dr., Arlington, VA 22213. TEL 703-533-4400. FAX 703-533-4444. *1566*

TAXATION IN AUSTRALIA (BLUE EDITION).
Taxation Institute of Australia, 7th Fl., 64 Castlereagh St., Sydney, N.S.W. 2000, Australia. TEL 61-2-2323422. FAX 61-2-2216953. circ. 10,000. *1568*

TAYLOR.
Taylor University, 500 W. Reade Ave., Upland, IN 46989. TEL 317-998-2751. FAX 317-998-4910. circ. 23,500. *2443*

TEACHER IN ZIMBABWE.
Zimbabwe Publishing House, P.O. Box 350, Harare, Zimbabwe. TEL 263-4-497548. FAX 263-4-497554. circ. 55,000. *2376*

TEACHERS' MONEY MATTERS.
Teachers' Money Matters Ltd., 70 Scriven Rd., Bailieboro, Ont. K0L 1B0, Canada. TEL 705-939-1203. FAX 705-939-1179. circ. 33,000. *1123*

TEACHING EDUCATION.
University of South Carolina, College of Education, Columbia, SC 29208. TEL 803-777-6301. FAX 803-777-3090. circ. 1,200. *2376*

TEAM (LONDON).
22-24 Worple Rd., Wimbledon, London SW19 4DD, England. TEL 081-947-3131. FAX 081-944-6552. circ. 40,000. *3572*

TEAM REHAB REPORT.
Miramar Publishing Co., Box 3640, Culver City, CA 90231-3640. TEL 310-337-9717. FAX 310-337-1041. circ. 12,000. *3308*

TECAGRI NEWS.
Clark Consulting International, Inc., 14N921 Lac du Beatrice, Dundee, IL 60118-3115. TEL 847-836-5100. FAX 847-836-5140. circ. 90,000. *207*

TECH CENTER NEWS.
Springer Publishing Inc., 31201 Chicago Rd. S., Warren, MI 48093. TEL 313-939-6800. FAX 313-939-5850. circ. 17,500. *6803*

TECH DIRECTIONS.
Prakken Publications, Inc., Box 8623, Ann Arbor, MI 48107. TEL 313-769-1211. FAX 313-769-8383. circ. 44,000. *2504*

TECHNICAL EDUCATION NEWS.
Glencoe - McGraw-Hill 1221 Ave. of the Americas, New York, NY 10020. TEL 212-512-4736. FAX 212-512-6904. circ. 47,000. *2504*

TECHNION - ISRAEL INSTITUTE OF TECHNOLOGY. PRESIDENT'S REPORT.
Technion - Israel Institute of Technology, Division of Public Affairs, Haifa 3200, Israel. circ. 30,000. *6665*

TECHNISCH WEEKBLAD.
V N U Business Publications B.V., P.O. Box 90162, 1006 BD Amsterdam, Netherlands. TEL 31-20-4875459. FAX 31-20-4875731. circ. 24,241. *2620*

TECHNISCHE REVUE.
Misset Postbus 4, 7000 BA Doetinchem,
Netherlands. TEL 31-8340-49911. FAX 31-8340-
43839.
circ. 15,230. *6666*

TECHNOLOGY FOCUS.
Defence Research & Development Organization,
Metcalfe House, New Delhi 110 054, India.
TEL 011-2932252. FAX 011-2919151.
circ. 2,500. *5049*

TECHNOLOGY FOR ALASKAN TRANSPORTATION.
Alaska Transportation Technology Transfer
Program, DOT & PF T2 Program, 2301 Peger Rd.,
Fairbanks, AK 99709-5399. TEL 907-451-5320.
FAX 907-451-2313.
circ. 2,200. *6728*

TECHNOLOGY IN EDUCATION.
B & S Publications, 3 Crescent Terr., Cheltenham,
Glos. GL50 3PE, England. TEL 01242-510760.
FAX 01242-22626.
circ. 8,000. *6667*

TECNICA E INVENCION.
Princesa 14, 28008 Madrid, Spain. TEL 2414800.
circ. 3,000. *5344*

EL TECOLOTE.
Accion Latina, 766 Valencia St., San Francisco, CA
97110. TEL 415-252-5957. FAX 415-252-5701.
circ. 10,000. *2911*

TED SLANKER'S MARKET UPDATE.
Ted E. Slanker, Jr., Ed. & Pub., R.R. 2, Box 175,
Powderly, TX 75473-9740. TEL 903-732-4653.
FAX 903-732-4151.
circ. 10,650. *1355*

TEE TO GREEN.
Custom Publishing Company Ltd. 45 Station Rd.,
Redhill, Surrey RH1 1QU, England. TEL 0737-
767213. FAX 0737-771662.
circ. 11,100. *3967*

**TEESWATER SHEEP BREEDERS' ASSOCIATION.
ANNUAL FLOCK BOOK.**
Teeswater Sheep Breeders' Association, 1 The
Mount, Leyburn, N. Yorks DL8 5JA, England.
TEL 44-1969-23432.
circ. 140. *285*

TEKNISK NYT.
Teknisk Forlag A-S, Skelbaekgade 4, DK-1780
Copenhagen V, Denmark. TEL 45-31-21-68-01.
FAX 45-31-21-04-01.
circ. 18,522. *2620*

TEKSTIILIOPETTAJA.
Tekstiiliopettajaliitto, Mannerheimintie 132 B 31,
SF-00270 Helsinki, Finland.
circ. 1,500. *3527*

TELECOMMAGAZINE.
V N U Business Publications B.V., Postbus 9194,
1006 CC Amsterdam, Netherlands. TEL 31-20-
4875487.
circ. 17,000. *2070*

TELECOMMS ABSTRACTS.
Techgnosis Ltd., Blade House, Battersea Rd.,
Stockport, Cheshire SK4 3AE, England. TEL 44-
161-442-2639. FAX 44-161-443-1162. *2003*

**TELECOMMUNICATION AUTHORITY OF SINGAPORE.
SINGAPORE TELECOM ANNUAL REPORT.**
Telecommunication Authority of Singapore, 35
Robinson Rd., TAS Bldg., Singapore 0106,
Singapore. TEL 65-323-3888. FAX 65-323-0941.
1951

TELECOMMUNICATIONS AMERICAS.
Portland House, Stag Pl., London SW1E 5XT,
England. TEL 44-171-957-0030. FAX 44-171-957-
0031.
circ. 54,050. *1951*

TELEPHONY.
Telephony Publishing One I B M Plaza, Chicago, IL
60611. TEL 312-595-1080.
circ. 48,307. *1952*

TELESIS (OTTAWA).
Bell-Northern Research Ltd., 3500 Carling Ave.,
Ottawa, ON K1Y 4H7, Canada. TEL 613-765-2520.
FAX 613-763-2008.
circ. 35,000. *1952*

TELEVISION BROADCAST.
Miller Freeman P S N Inc. 2 Park Ave., 18th Fl.,
New York, NY 10016. TEL 212-213-3444.
FAX 212-213-3484.
circ. 30,800. *1973*

TELEVISION BUYER.
E M A P Media 33-39 Bowling Green Ln., London
WC1R 0DA, England. FAX 44-171-833-4519.
circ. 7,927. *1973*

TELEVISION INTERNATIONAL MAGAZINE.
Television International Publications Ltd., Box 2430,
Hollywood, CA 90028. TEL 818-795-8386.
FAX 818-795-8436.
circ. 14,000. *1973*

TELLING IT LIKE IT IS.
Transportation Communications International Union,
3 Research Pl., Rockville, MD 20850. TEL 301-
948-4910. FAX 301-948-1369.
circ. 2,200. *6819*

**TENNESSEE. DEPARTMENT OF SAFETY. ANNUAL
REPORT.**
Department of Safety, 1150 Foster Ave., Nashville,
TN 37249-100C. TEL 615-251-5313. FAX 615-
251-5242.
circ. 500. *5826*

TENNESSEE DEER & TURKEY SHOW & PREVIEW.
Target Communications Corp., 7626 W. Donges
Bay Rd., Mequon, WI 53097-3400. TEL 414-242-
3990. FAX 414-242-7391.
circ. 30,000. *6579*

TENNESSEE LAW ENFORCEMENT JOURNAL.
Tennessee Law Enforcement Officers Association, c/
o Lt. J.P. Ruff, Box 139, Ellendale, TN 38029-
0139. FAX 612-541-0435.
circ. 3,000. *2177*

TENNESSEE PARENT - TEACHER BULLETIN.
Tennessee Congress of Parents and Teachers,
1905 Acklen Ave., Nashville, TN 37212. TEL 615-
383-9740.
circ. 1,400. *2377*

TENNESSEE SCHOOL BOARD BULLETIN.
Tennessee School Boards Association, 500 13th
Ave. North, Nashville, TN 37203-2830. FAX 615-
741-2842.
circ. 1,800. *2464*

TENNESSEE TRUCKING NEWS.
Tennessee Trucking Association, 1415
Murgreesboro Rd., Ste. 672, Nashville, TN 37217.
TEL 615-360-9200. FAX 615-361-3137.
circ. 1,000. *5861*

TENNIS U S T A.
New York Times Magazine Group, Sports - Leisure
Division, 5520 Park Ave., Box 395, Trumbull, CT
06611. TEL 203-373-7155. FAX 203-371-2199.
circ. 440,000. *6516*

TENSOR.
Tensor Society, Kawaguchi Sutikenkyujo -
Kawaguchi Institute of Mathematical Sciences, 7-15,
Matsu-ga-oka 2-chome, Chigasaki-shi, Kanagawa-
ken 253, Japan.
circ. 600. *4400*

TENTH TIMES.
Texas Dental Association, Tenth District Dental
Society, 3303 Northland, No. 313, Austin, TX
78731. TEL 512-452-9296.
circ. 450. *4655*

TERMALISMO - BALNEARIOS.
Editorial J.S. Publicaciones Especiales, Santa Susana
55, 5o 1 y 2, 28033 Madrid, Spain. TEL 1-
7633401.
circ. 20,000. *3333*

TERRATECH.
Vereinigte Fachverlage GmbH, Lise-Meitner-Str. 2,
55129 Mainz, Germany. TEL 49-6131-992150.
FAX 49-6131-992100.
circ. 2,500. *2848*

TEVA VA-ARETZ.
Eretz Ha-Tzvi Inc., P.O. Box 565, Taiber 26,
Givatayim 53104, Israel. TEL 972-3-5712681.
2142

TEXAS AGRINEWS.
Big River Press, Inc., 1217 N. Conway, Box 353,
Mission, TX 78572. TEL 210-585-4893. FAX 210-
585-2304.
circ. 9,379. *156*

TEXAS BICYCLIST.
Yellow Jersey Enterprises, 12814 Azalea Creek
Trail, Houston, TX 77095-4209. TEL 713-782-
1661.
circ. 45,000. *6530*

TEXAS CIVIL ENGINEER.
American Society of Civil Engineers, Texas Section,
3501 Manor Rd., Austin, TX 78723. TEL 512-472-
8905. FAX 512-472-2934.
circ. 5,750. *2674*

TEXAS DIRECTOR.
Rector - Duncan & Associates, Box 14667, Austin,
TX 78761. TEL 512-454-5252. FAX 512-451-
9556.
circ. 1,000. *3041*

**TEXAS HIGHER EDUCATION COORDINATING BOARD.
C B POLICY PAPER.**
Texas Higher Education Coordinating Board, Box
12788, Capitol Sta., Austin, TX 78711. TEL 512-
483-6111. FAX 512-433-6127. *2444*

**TEXAS HIGHER EDUCATION COORDINATING BOARD.
C B STUDY PAPER.**
Texas Higher Education Coordinating Board, Box
12788, Capitol Sta., Austin, TX 78711. TEL 512-
483-6111. FAX 512-433-6127. *2444*

**TEXAS HIGHER EDUCATION COORDINATING BOARD.
STATUS REPORT ON HIGHER EDUCATION AND
STATISTICAL REPORT**
Texas Higher Education Coordinating Board, Box
12788, Capitol Sta., Austin, TX 78711. TEL 512-
483-6111. FAX 512-483-6127.
circ. 1,000. *2444*

TEXAS INSTRUMENTS TECHNICAL JOURNAL.
Texas Instruments, Box 350311, Mail Sta. 3940,
Dallas, TX 75265. TEL 214-917-3906. FAX 214-
917-3850.
circ. 12,300. *2620*

TEXAS LEGION TIMES.
Adcraft Agency, Box 337, Jacksboro, TX 76458-
0337. TEL 817-567-6622. FAX 817-567-6372.
circ. 100,500. *1854*

TEXAS LIBRARIES.
Texas State Library and Archives Commission, Box
12927, Austin, TX 78711. TEL 512-463-5493.
FAX 512-463-5436.
circ. 1,400. *4030*

TEXAS PETROLEUM AND C-STORE JOURNAL.
Texas Oil Marketers Association 701 W. 15th St.,
Austin, TX 78701. TEL 512-476-9547. FAX 512-
477-4239.
circ. 1,200. *5378*

TEXAS PROPANE.
Texas Propane Gas Association, Box 140735,
Austin, TX 78714-0735 TEL 512-836-8620.
FAX 512-834-0758.
circ. 1,250. *5378*

TEXAS PUBLIC LIBRARY DIRECTORY.
Texas State Library, Library Development Division,
Box 12927, Austin, TX 78711. TEL 512-463-
5465.
circ. 500. *4030*

TEXAS PUBLIC LIBRARY STATISTICS.
Texas State Library, Library Development Division,
Box 12927, Austin, TX 78711. TEL 512-463-
5465.
circ. 500. *4041*

TEXAS PUBLIC LIBRARY SUMMARY.
Texas State Library, Library Development Division,
Box 12927, Austin, TX 78711. TEL 512-463-
5465.
circ. 500. *4041*

TEXAS TOUR AND MEETING GUIDE.
Publishing Partnership Box 1569, Austin, TX
78767. TEL 512-320-6900. FAX 512-476-9007.
circ. 52,355. *6915*

TEXTIEL BEHEER.
Stichting Vakblad Textielreiniging, Rembrandtlaan 67, 3723 BH Bilthoven, Netherlands. FAX 31-30-2286885.
circ. 1,000. *1829*

TEXTIL EXPRES SUPLEMENTOS.
Aramo Editorial, S.A., Muntaner 60 2o 2a, 08011 Barcelona, Spain. TEL 34-3-4537938. FAX 34-3-3237926.
circ. 4,500. *6686*

TEXTILE WORLD.
Intertec Publishing Corp., Textile Publications, P.O. Box 12901, Overland Park, KS 66282-2901.
circ. 32,164. *6688*

THAI CHAMBER OF COMMERCE. DIRECTORY (YEAR)
.
Cosmic Group of Companies, 4th Fl., Phyathai Bldg., 31 Phyathai Rd., Rajthevi, Bangkok 10400, Thailand. TEL 662-2453850. FAX 662-2461710.
circ. 5,000. *1150*

THAI FURNITURE INDUSTRIES ASSOCIATION DIRECTORY.
Cosmic Group of Companies, 4th Fl., Phyathai Bldg., 31 Phyathai Rd., Rajthevi, Bangkok 10400, Thailand. TEL 245-3850. FAX 246-4737.
circ. 5,000. *1643*

THAI-KOREAN CHAMBER OF COMMERCE HANDBOOK & DIRECTORY.
Cosmic Group of Companies, 4th Fl., Phyathai Bldg., 31 Phyathai Rd., Rajthevi, Bangkok 10400, Thailand. TEL 662-2453850. FAX 662-2461710.
circ. 2,000. *1150*

THAILAND SHOWCASE.
Cosmic Group of Companies, 4th Fl., Phyathai Bldg., 31 Phyathai Rd., Rajthevi, Bangkok 10400, Thailand. TEL 245-3850. FAX 246-4737.
circ. 10,000. *1296*

THAQAFA WA FANN.
Cultural Foundation, Culture and Arts Department, P.O. Box 2380, Abu Dhabi, United Arab Emirates. TEL 215300. FAX 336059.
circ. 500. *455*

THAT'S MY BABY.
That's My Baby, Inc., Box 1156, Lake Oswego, OR 97035. TEL 503-620-9132. FAX 503-620-3800.
circ. 500,000. *1779*

THEATER HEUTE.
Friedrich Kulturzeitschriftenverlag, Luetzowplatz 7, 10785 Berlin, Germany. TEL 49-30-254495-0. FAX 49-30-25449512.
circ. 20,000. *6705*

THEMIS.
Zeta Tau Alpha, International Office, 3450 Founders Rd., Indianapolis, IN 46268. TEL 317-872-0540. FAX 371-876-3948.
circ. 65,000. *1888*

THEOLOGIA REFORMATA.
Drukkerij Oosterbaan en Le Cointre B.V., Postbus 25, 4460 AA Goes, Netherlands. TEL 08380-17091.
circ. 750. *6162*

THEOLOGICA XAVERIANA.
Pontificia Universidad Javeriana, Facultad de Teologia, Apdo. Aereo 54953, Carrera 10, No. 65-48, Bogota 2 D.E., Colombia. TEL 57-1-2124846. FAX 57-1-2123360. *6198*

THEOLOGY AND CULTURE NEWSLETTER.
Andover Newton Theological School, 210 Herrick Rd., Newton Centre, MA 02159. TEL 617-964-1100. FAX 508-771-7919.
circ. 3,000. *6099*

THE THIRD ALTERNATIVE.
T T A Press, 5 Martins Ln., Witcham, Ely, Cambs. CB6 2LB, England. TEL 44-1353-777931.
circ. 750. *4332*

THIRD DEGREE.
University of Regina, Communications Office, Regina, SK S4S OA2, Canada. TEL 306-585-4403. FAX 306-585-4997.
circ. 27,000. *1888*

THOMIST.
Thomist Press, 487 Michigan Ave., N.E., Washington, DC 20017. TEL 202-529-5300. FAX 202-636-4460.
circ. 1,000. *6198*

THOROUGHBRED RACING ASSOCIATIONS. DIRECTORY AND RECORD BOOK.
Thoroughbred Racing Associations, 420 Fair Hill Dr., No. 1, Elkton, MD 21921-2573. FAX 410-398-1366.
circ. 3,000. *6552*

TIDEWATER PARENT.
Windmill Publishing, Inc., 2753 Atwoodtown Rd., Virginia Beach, VA 23456. TEL 804-426-2595. FAX 804-426-5299.
circ. 40,000. *1779*

TIEFKUEHL-REPORT.
Dr. Vollmer GmbH, Siegfriedstr. 5, 63785 Obernburg a.M., Germany. TEL 06022-1604. FAX 06022-7696.
circ. 7,500. *3334*

TIEMPO LATINO.
Tiempo Latino News, 3288 21st St., Box 9, San Francisco, CA 94110. TEL 415-821-4452.
circ. 35,000. *2911*

TIERRA ADENTRO.
Instituto de Investigaciones Agropecuarias, Casilla 469, Correo 3, Santiago, Chile. TEL 56-2-5417223. FAX 56-2-5417667.
circ. 5,000. *156*

TIETOVERKKO.
Oy Talentum Ab, P.O. Box 920, SF-00101 Helsinki, Finland. TEL 358-0-148-801. FAX 358-0-6856512.
circ. 12,781. *2042*

TIETOVIIKKO.
Oy Talentum Ab, P.O. Box 920, FIN-00101 Helsinki, Finland. TEL 358-0-148-801. FAX 358-0-145109.
circ. 26,736. *1999*

TIJDSCHRIFT VOOR CRIMINOLOGIE.
Gouda Quint B.V. Postbus 1148, 6801 MK Arnhem, Netherlands.
circ. 600. *2177*

TILBURY TIMES.
McConnell Publishing Inc., P.O. Box 490, 9 Prospect St., Tilbury, ON NOP 2LO, Canada. TEL 519-682-0411. FAX 519-682-3633.
circ. 288. *3126*

TIMBER - WEST.
Timber - West Publications, Inc., Box 610, Edmonds, WA 98020. TEL 206-778-3388. FAX 206-771-3623.
circ. 10,500. *3038*

TIMBERLINES.
Canadian Forest Service, Northern Forestry Centre, 5320-122 St., Edmonton, AB T6H 3S5, Canada. TEL 403-435-7210. FAX 403-435-7359.
circ. 5,000. *3027*

TIMBROSCOPIE.
Timbropresse SA, 33 rue de Chazelles, 75850 Paris Cedex 17, France. TEL 47-66-02-13. FAX 47-66-11-34.
circ. 53,772. *5464*

TIMES BUSINESS DIRECTORY OF SINGAPORE.
Times Trade Directories Pte. Ltd., Times Centre, 1 New Industrial Rd., Singapore 1953, Singapore. TEL 2848844. FAX 2881186.
circ. 25,000. *1643*

TIMES GUIDE TO COMPUTERS.
Times Trade Directories Pte. Ltd., Times Centre, 1 New Industrial Rd., Singapore 1953, Singapore. TEL 2848844. FAX 2881186.
circ. 30,000. *1643*

TIPSICO BULLETIN.
Tipsico Coin Co., Box 1128, 2141 Broadway, N. Bend, OR 97459. TEL 503-756-7111.
circ. 1,000. *5227*

TIRE RETREADING - REPAIR JOURNAL.
Tire Industry Publication Service, Inc., Box 37203, Louisville, KY 40233-7203. TEL 502-968-8900. FAX 502-964-7859.
circ. 2,650. *6219*

TOBACCO ASSOCIATES. ANNUAL REPORT.
Tobacco Associates, Inc., 1306 Annapolis Dr., Ste. 102, Raleigh, NC 27608. TEL 919-821-7670. FAX 919-821-7674.
circ. 7,500. *6711*

TOBAKSHANDLAREN.
Tobaks- & Servicehandelns Riksfoerbund, Instrumentvaegen 10, P.O. Box 9025, S-126 00 Haegersten, Sweden. TEL 46-8-681-03-20. FAX 46-8-19-95-26.
circ. 1,800. *6711*

TODAY'S ARIZONA WOMAN (SCOTTSDALE).
Publishers West, Inc., 4425 N. Saddlebag Trail, Scottsdale, AZ 85251-3419. TEL 602-945-5000. FAX 602-941-5196.
circ. 50,000. *7008*

TODAY'S ARIZONA WOMAN (TUCSON EDITION).
Publishers West, Inc. (Tucson), 4725 E. Sunrise Dr., Ste. 406, Tucson, AZ 85718-4534. TEL 602-795-6202. FAX 602-795-6305.
circ. 20,000. *7008*

TODAY'S ASTROLOGER.
American Federation of Astrologers, Inc., 6535 S. Rural Rd., Box 22040, Tempe, AZ 85285. TEL 602-838-1751. FAX 602-838-8293.
circ. 2,700. *473*

TODAY'S CHICAGO WOMAN.
Leigh Communications, Inc., 150 E. Huron St., Ste. 1225, Chicago, IL 60611-2912. TEL 312-951-7600. FAX 312-951-9083.
circ. 100,000. *7008*

TODAY'S DISTRIBUTOR.
Johnson Hill Press, Inc. 1233 Janesville Ave., Ft. Atkinson, WI 53538. TEL 414-563-6388. FAX 414-563-1702.
circ. 42,000. *1488*

TODAY'S HEALTH CARE.
Transcontinental Publishing Inc., Box 45454, Phoenix, AZ 85064-5454. TEL 602-331-8900. FAX 602-331-8448. *4538*

TODAY'S HOSPITAL GIFT SHOP BUSINESS.
Nason & Associates, Box 8204, Asheville, NC 28814. TEL 704-298-1322. FAX 704-298-1312.
circ. 8,000. *1488*

TODAY'S REFINERY.
Percy Publishing Company, Inc., 170 King St., Box 287, Chappaqua, NY 10514. TEL 914-238-0205. FAX 914-238-0210.
circ. 10,406. *5378*

TODAY'S TIMES.
Today's Times Publications, 100 Annex, 856 Homer St., Vancouver, BC V6B 2W5, Canada. TEL 604-689-5087. FAX 604-689-5874.
circ. 30,000. *3297*

TODAY'S WOMAN IN BUSINESS.
E M C Marketing Associates, 113 Old Black River Rd., P.O. Box 1291, Saint John, NB E2L 4H8, Canada. TEL 506-658-0754. FAX 506-633-0868.
circ. 10,000. *964*

TOELEVEREN & UITBESTEDEN.
Misset Postbus 4, 7000 BA Doetinchem, Netherlands. TEL 31-8340-49911. FAX 31-8340-43839.
circ. 7,850. *4347*

TOHKAI SEIKEI GEKA GAISHO KENKYU KAISHI.
Tohkai Seikei Geka Gaisho Kenkyukai, Gifu Kenritsu Tajimi Byoin Seikei Geka, 5-161, Maebatacho, Tajimi-shi, Gifu-ken 507, Japan. TEL 0572-22-5311. FAX 0572-25-1246.
circ. 1,000. *4792*

TOHKAI SEKITSUI GEKA.
Tohkai Sekitsui Geka Konwakai, Gifu Kenritsu Tajimi Byoin, 5-161, Maebbatacho, Tajimi-shi, Gifuken 507, Japan. TEL 0572-22-5311. FAX 0572-25-1246.
circ. 600. *4792*

TOHOKU DAIGAKU SOZAI KOGAKU KENKYUJO IHO.
Tohoku Daigaku, Sozai Kogaku Kenkyujo, 1-1 Katahira 2-chome, Aoba-ku, Sendai 980, Japan. TEL 81-22-217-5166. FAX 81-22-217-5211. *4977*

TOHOKU KOGYO DAIGAKU KIYO, 1. RIKOGAKU HEN.
Tohoku Kogyo Daigaku, 35-1 Kasumi-cho,
Yagiyama, Taihaku-ku, Sendai-shi, Miyagi-ken 982,
Japan.
circ. 730. *2620*

TOHOKU NO NOGYO KISHO.
Nihon Nogyo Kisho Gakkai, Tohoku Shibu, Norin
Suisansho Tohoku Nogyo Shikenjo, 4 Akahira,
Shimokuriyagawa, Morioka-shi, Iwate-ken 020-01,
Japan. TEL 81-196-43-3461. FAX 81-196-41-
7794.
circ. 300. *5007*

TOKYO DAIGAKU TEOIN SENTA DAYORI.
Tokyo Daigaku, Teion Senta, 11-16, Yayoi 2-chome,
Bunkyo-ku, Tokyo 113, Japan. TEL 03-3812-2111.
FAX 03-3815-8389.
circ. 500. *5586*

TOKYO JOSHI IKA DAIGAKU ZASSHI.
Tokyo Joshi Ika Daigaku Gakkai, c/o Library, 8-1
Kawada-cho, Shinjuku-ku, Tokyo 162, Japan.
circ. 1,750. *4538*

TOLEDO MEDICINE.
Academy of Medicine of Toledo and Lucas County,
4428 Secor Rd., Toledo, OH 43623. TEL 419-473-
3200. FAX 419-475-6744.
circ. 1,500. *4538*

TOLSTOY FOUNDATION NEWS.
Tolstoy Foundation, Inc., 104 Lake Rd., Valley
Cottage, NY 10989-2459. TEL 212-677-7770.
FAX 914-268-6937.
circ. 10,000. *6396*

TOMAHAWK (INDIANAPOLIS).
Maury Boyd & Associates, Inc., 5783 Park Plaza
Ct., Indianapolis, IN 46220-3995.
circ. 35,000. *1889*

TOOWOOMBA AND GOLDEN WEST VISITORS' GUIDE.
Toowoomba and Golden West Regional Tourist
Association Ltd., P.O. Box 3090, Toowoomba, Qld.
4350, Australia. TEL 61-76-321988. FAX 61-76-
324404. *6916*

TOP BUSINESS.
Verlag Moderne Industrie, Justus-von-Liebig-Str. 1,
86899 Landsberg, Germany. TEL 49-8191-125-0.
FAX 49-89-8191-125312. *1448*

TOP HOTEL.
Freizeit Verlag Landsberg GmbH, Celsiusstr. 6,
86899 Landsberg, Germany. TEL 49-8191-3049.
FAX 49-8191-47685.
circ. 18,697. *3572*

TOP RAIL.
B L A Group Ltd., 5-8 Hardwick St., London EC1R
4RB, England. TEL 44-171-278-7603. FAX 44-
171-278-6246.
circ. 200,000. *6916*

TOPICS IN PEDIATRICS.
Minneapolis Children's Medical Center, 2525
Chicago Ave., S., Minneapolis, MN 55404. TEL 612-
863-6222. FAX 612-863-6674.
circ. 10,000. *4815*

TOPLINE.
McCollum-Spielman Worldwide, Inc., 235 Great
Neck Rd., Great Neck, NY 11021. TEL 516-482-
0310. FAX 516-482-3228.
circ. 5,000. *1489*

TORCH (CHICAGO).
International Association of Torch Clubs, c/o R.
Pattrick Deans, Ed., Strickland & Jones, PC, 749
Boush St., Norfolk, VA 23510-1517. TEL 804-622-
3927. FAX 804-623-9740.
circ. 2,850. *1854*

TORCH & TREFOIL.
Alpha Phi Omega, 14901 E. 42nd St.,
Independence, MO 64108. TEL 816-471-8667.
circ. 17,000. *1889*

TORONTO GARDENS.
Bayview Media Inc., 1560 Bayview Ave., Ste. 302A,
Toronto, ON M4G 3B8, Canada. TEL 416-481-
1955. FAX 416-481-2819.
circ. 50,000. *3068*

TORONTO STOCK EXCHANGE REVIEW.
Toronto Stock Exchange, 2 First Canadian Place,
Toronto, ON M5X 1J2, Canada. TEL 416-947-
4222. FAX 416-947-4585.
circ. 1,150. *1356*

TOSCANA LIONS.
Lions International, Distretto 108, Via Valdelsa 23,
53011 Castellina in Chianti, Italy. TEL 39-577-
740374.
circ. 3,500. *1854*

TOSHOKAN KYORYOKU TSUSHIN.
National Diet Library, 1-10-1 Nagata-cho, Chiyoda-
ku, Tokyo 100, Japan. TEL 03-3581-2331.
FAX 03-3597-9104.
circ. 4,600. *4030*

TOTALISATOR AGENCY BOARD. ANNUAL REPORT.
Totalisator Agency Board, 106-110 Jackson St.,
Petone, New Zealand. TEL 644-576-6999.
FAX 644-576-6942.
circ. 1,600. *5925*

TOUCHLINE.
Soccer Association for Youth U S A, 4903 Vine St.,
Cincinnati, OH 45217. TEL 513-242-4263.
FAX 513-482-7162.
circ. 100,000. *6517*

TOUCHSTONE (SPRING).
Touchstone Press, Box 8308, Spring, TX 77387-
8308.
circ. 500. *4321*

TOURS ON MOTORCOACH.
Publicom Inc., C.P. 365, Place d'Armes, Montreal,
PQ H2Y 3H1, Canada. TEL 514-274-0004.
FAX 514-274-5834.
circ. 13,302. *6919*

TOW TIMES.
T T Publications, Inc., 203 State Rd. 434, W.,
Winter Springs, FL 32708-2598. TEL 407-260-
0712. FAX 407-260-1486.
circ. 30,000. *6851*

TOWN AND COUNTRY FARMER.
Town and Country Farmer Publications Pty. Ltd.,
P.O. Box 793, Benalla, Vic. 3672, Australia. TEL 61-
57-641348. FAX 51-57-641349.
circ. 18,000. *157*

TOWN HALL.
Informed Publications Ltd., 95 Ditchling Rd.,
Brighton, Sussex BN1 4SE, England. TEL 44-1273-
571989. FAX 44-1273-623338.
circ. 1,000. *5952*

TOXICOLOGIC PATHOLOGY.
Society of Toxicologic Pathologists, c/o Dr. Carl L.
Alden, Ed., G.D. Searle & Co., 4901 Searle Pky.,
Skokie, IL 60077. TEL 708-982-7379. FAX 708-
982-7374.
circ. 845. *2848*

TOYAMA DAIGAKU KYOIKUGAKUBU KIYO, A. BUNKAKEI.
Toyama Daigaku, Kyoikugakubu, 3190 Gofuku,
Toyama-shi, Toyama-ken 930, Japan. TEL 0764-
41-1271. FAX 0764-32-4212. *4278*

TOYAMA DAIGAKU KYOIKUGAKUBU KIYO, B. RIKAKEI.
Toyama Daigaku, Kyoikugakubu, 3190 Gofuku,
Toyama-shi, Toyama-ken 930, Japan. TEL 0764-
41-1271. FAX 0764-32-4212. *6291*

TOYOTA.
Toyota Motor Corporation, International Public
Affairs Division, 4-18, Koraku 1-chome, Bunkyo-ku,
Tokyo 112, Japan. TEL 03-3817-9930. FAX 03-
3817-9017.
circ. 30,000. *6804*

TOYOTA ENGINE TECHNOLOGY.
Toyota Motor Corporation, International Public
Affairs Division, 4-18, Koraku 1-chome, Bunkyo-ku,
Tokyo 112, Japan. TEL 03-3817-9930. FAX 03-
3817-9017.
circ. 20,000. *6804*

TRACES OF INDIANA AND MIDWESTERN HISTORY.
Indiana Historical Society, 315 W. Ohio, Indianapolis,
IN 46202-3299. TEL 317-232-1878. FAX 317-
233-3109.
circ. 11,000. *3490*

TRACK AND TIRE.
29829 Greenfield Rd., Ste. 101, Southfield, MI
48076-2201. TEL 800-872-2574. FAX 313-557-
4156.
circ. 30,100. *877*

TRADE CHRONICLE.
Chronicle Publications, P.O. Box 5257, Iftikhar
Chambers, Altaf Hussain Rd. Karachi 74000,
Pakistan. TEL 92-21-218129. FAX 92-21-219190.
circ. 5,500. *1532*

TRADERS MAGAZINE.
Securities Data Publishing, 40 W. 57th St., 11th
Fl., New York, NY 10106. TEL 212-765-5311.
FAX 212-765-6123.
circ. 4,000. *1124*

TRADEWINDS NEWSLETTER.
Portuguese UK Chamber of Commerce, 22-25a
Sackville St., 4th Fl., London W1X 1DE, England.
TEL 44-171-494-1844. FAX 44-171-494-1322.
circ. 2,500. *1297*

TRAFALGAR HOUSE TODAY.
Trafalgar House Public Ltd. Co., 1 Berkeley St.,
London W1A 1BY, England. TEL 0171-499-5020.
FAX 0171-499-5359
circ. 38,000. *2621*

TRAGER INSTITUTE NEWSLETTER.
Trager Institute, 21 Locust Ave., Mill Valley, CA
94941-2805. TEL 415-388-2688.
circ. 2,000. *4820*

TRAILER.
Foerlags AB Albinsson & Sjoeberg, P.O. Box 529, S-
371 23 Karlskrona, Sweden. TEL 46-455-335325.
FAX 46-455-311715.
circ. 29,200. *6804*

TRAILER-BODY BUILDERS.
Tunnell Publications, Inc., Box 66010, Houston, TX
77266. TEL 713-523-5124. FAX 713-523-8384.
circ. 14,000. *6861*

TRAIN COLLECTORS QUARTERLY.
Train Collectors Association, Box 619, Willow Street,
PA 17584. TEL 717-687-8623.
circ. 28,200. *3517*

TRAINING AKTUELL.
ManagerSeminare Gerhard May Verlags GmbH,
Endenicherstr. 282, 53121 Bonn, Germany.
TEL 49-228-97791-0. FAX 49-228-616164.
circ. 750. *1449*

TRAINING AND CONDITIONING.
Mag, Inc., 438 W. State St., Ithaca, NY 14850.
TEL 607-272-0265. FAX 607-272-2015.
circ. 23,295. *6489*

TRANSAT.
Inmarsat, 99 City Rd., London EC1Y 1AX, England.
TEL 44-171-728-1450. FAX 44-171-728-1344.
circ. 18,000. *1919*

TRANSCEND.
Transcend Publications, 1 Daniels Farm Rd., Ste.
134, Trumbull, CT 06611.
circ. 15,000. *2911*

TRANSCULTURAL PSYCHIATRIC RESEARCH REVIEW.
McGill University, Department of Psychiatry, 1033
Pine Ave. W., Montreal, PQ H3A 1A1, Canada.
TEL 514-398-7302. FAX 514-398-4370.
circ. 600. *4870*

TRANSILVANIA.
Casa de Presa si Editura Cultura Nationala, Str. Dr.
Ion Ratiu nr.2, 2400 Sibiu, Rumania. TEL 40-24-
69413377.
circ. 3,000. *6100*

TRANSITIONS.
Center for Population Options, 1025 Vermont Ave.,
N.W., Ste. 200, Washington, DC 20005. TEL 202-
347-5700. FAX 202-347-2263.
circ. 5,000. *1779*

TRANSMISSION AND DISTRIBUTION.
Intertec Publishing Corp., 9800 Metcalf, Overland
Park, KS 66212-2215. TEL 913-341-1300.
FAX 913-967-1904.
circ. 36,400. *2721*

TRANSMISSION & DISTRIBUTION INTERNATIONAL.
Intertec Publishing Corp., 9800 Metcalf Ave.,
Overland Park, KS 66212-2215. TEL 913-341-
1300. FAX 913-967-1898.
circ. 17,000. *2721*

TRANSMISSION DIGEST.
M D Publications, Inc. (Springfield), 3057 E. Cairo,
Box 2210, Springfield, MO 65801-2210. TEL 417-
866-3917. FAX 417-866-2781.
circ. 24,000. *6804*

TRANSPONDER.
Terra Publishing, Inc., R.D. 1, Box 142, Center St.
Ext., Salamanca, NY 14779. TEL 716-945-3488.
FAX 716-945-5238.
circ. 14,500. *1974*

TRANSPORT MANAGEMENT.
Institute of Transport Administration, 32 Palmerston
Rd., Southampton SO14 1LL, England. FAX 44-
1703-634165.
circ. 3,500. *6730*

TRANSPORTARBETAREN.
Svenska Transportarbetarefoerbundet, P.O. Box
714, S-101 33 Stockholm, Sweden. TEL 46-8-723-
77-00. FAX 46-8-723-00-76.
circ. 69,000. *6731*

TRANSPORTATION & DISTRIBUTION.
Penton Publishing Co. 1100 Superior Ave.,
Cleveland, OH 44114-2543. TEL 216-696-7000.
FAX 216-696-8765.
circ. 74,138. *6731*

TRANSPORTRECHT.
Luchterhand Verlag (Kriftel), Gutenbergstr. 8,
65830 Kriftel, Germany. TEL 49-6192-408233.
FAX 49-6192-408248.
circ. 1,100. *6733*

TRAVEL AGENT.
Universal Media, Inc., 801 Second Ave., New York,
NY 10017. TEL 212-370-5050. FAX 212-370-
4491.
circ. 53,503. *6919*

TRAVEL COUNSELOR MAGAZINE.
Miller Freeman Inc. (New York) One Penn Plaza,
New York, NY 10119. TEL 212-714-1300.
FAX 212-714-1313.
circ. 28,000. *6920*

TRAVEL COURIER.
Baxter Publishing Co., 310 Dupont St., Toronto, ON
M5R 1V9, Canada. TEL 416-968-7252. FAX 416-
968-2377.
circ. 7,290. *6920*

TRAVEL DIRECTORY (YEAR).
Interasia Publications, Ltd., No. 11-01 Fortune
Centre, 190 Middle Rd., Singapore 0718,
Singapore. TEL 3397622. FAX 3398521.
circ. 3,700. *6920*

TRAVEL ON SASKATCHEWAN HIGHWAYS.
Department of Highways and Transportation,
Planning and Coordination, 1855 Victoria Ave.,
Regina, SK S4P 3V5, Canada. TEL 306-787-8334.
FAX 306-787-1007.
circ. 300. *6827*

TRAVEL RETAILER INTERNATIONAL.
Euromoney Publications plc., Nestor House,
Playhouse Yard, London EC4V 5EX, England.
TEL 44-171-799-8935. FAX 44-171-779-8541.
circ. 5,000. *1489*

TRAVEL TRADE REPORT.
Travel Press, Asia Bldg., 12th Fl., 294-1 Phya Thai
Rd., Bangkok 10400, Thailand. TEL 66-2-216-
7252. FAX 66-2-216-6599.
circ. 12,600. *6921*

TRAVELAGE EAST.
Reed Travel Group, Part of the Reed Elsevier group
500 Plaza Dr., Secaucus, NJ 07096. TEL 201-902-
2021. FAX 201-902-1967.
circ. 23,400. *6922*

TRAVELAGE MID-AMERICA.
Reed Travel Group, Part of the Reed Elsevier group
500 Plaza Dr., Secaucus, NJ 07096. TEL 201-902-
2021. FAX 201-902-1967.
circ. 17,600. *6922*

TRAVELAGE WEST.
Reed Travel Group, Part of the Reed Elsevier group
500 Plaza Dr., Secaucus, NJ 07096. TEL 201-902-
2021. FAX 201-902-1967.
circ. 31,000. *6922*

TRAX D J MUSIC GUIDE.
Trax Entertainment, 111 N. La Cienega Blvd.,
Beverly Hills, CA 90211-2206. TEL 310-659-
7852. FAX 310-659-7856.
circ. 1,000. *5202*

TRE OG MOEBLER.
John A. Antonsen A-S, Sognsveien 4, N-0451 Oslo,
Norway. TEL 47-22-69-22-99. FAX 47-22-46-50-
10.
circ. 2,535. *3693*

TREASURY & RISK MANAGEMENT.
C F O Publishing Corporation 253 Summer St.,
Boston, MA 02210. TEL 617-345-9700. FAX 617-
951-4090.
circ. 46,000. *1356*

TREE - RING BULLETIN.
Tree - Ring Society, University of Arizona, Tree -
Ring Laboratory, Tucson, AZ 85721. TEL 520-621-
1608. FAX 520-621-8229.
circ. 350. *706*

TRENDS (LIBERTY).
Target Marketing, Inc., 5 Victory Ln., Ste. 101,
Liberty, MO 64068. TEL 816-781-7557. FAX 816-
792-3892.
circ. 400,000. *5274*

TRENDS & WORDS.
Via Siepelunga 57, 40137 Bologna, Italy. TEL 39-
51-6237010. FAX 39-51-6237162.
circ. 1,000. *1919*

TRENDS MAGAZINE.
Netmar Publications Inc., 1383 Confederation St.,
Sarnia, ON N7S 5P1, Canada. TEL 519-336-1100.
FAX 519-336-1833.
circ. 5,000. *965*

TRI-CITY NEWS.
Meadowridge Publications, 1405 Broadway, Port
Coquitlam, BC V3C 5W9, Canada. TEL 604-525-
6397. FAX 604-944-0703.
circ. 45,458. *3126*

TRI-STATE REAL ESTATE JOURNAL.
Adler Group, Inc., 4002 Lincoln Drive West, Ste. G,
Marlton, NJ 08053. TEL 609-988-0092. FAX 609-
988-0093.
circ. 7,000. *6038*

TRIBULUS.
Cultural Foundation, Emirates Natural History
Group, P.O. Box 2380, Abu Dhabi, United Arab
Emirates. TEL 212900. FAX 336059.
circ. 500. *6292*

**TRIBUNAL DE JUSTICA DO ESTADO DO RIO
GRANDE DO SUL. REVISTA DE JURISPRUDENCIA.**
Tribuna de Justica, Praca Marechal Deodoro, 55, 5o
andar, 90010-908 Porto Alegre RS, Brazil. TEL 55-
51-2282444 ext. 1550.
circ. 4,650. *3859*

TRIBUNE BUSINESS WEEKLY.
South Bend Tribune, 225 W. Colfax, South Bend, IN
46626. TEL 219-235-6474. FAX 219-239-2646.
circ. 8,000. *965*

TRIBUS.
Linden-Museum Stuttgart-Staatliches Museum fuer
Voelkerkunde, Hegelplatz 1, 70174 Stuttgart,
Germany. TEL 49-711-2022400. FAX 49-711-
2022590.
circ. 800. *324*

TRIBUTE.
Tribute Publishing, Inc., 900 A Don Mills Rd., Ste.
1000, Don Mills, ON M3C 1V6, Canada. TEL 416-
445-0544. FAX 416-445-2894.
circ. 600,000. *5114*

TRINITY REVIEW.
Trinity Foundation, Box 1666, Hobbs, NM 88241-
1666. TEL 505-392-7274.
circ. 3,000. *5503*

TRITON MUSEUM OF ART. MEMBERS' BULLETIN.
Triton Museum of Art, 1505 Warburton Ave., Santa
Clara, CA 95050. TEL 408-247-3754. FAX 408-
247-3796.
circ. 1,500. *5134*

TRIVIZIER.
V B M - L K V, Mesdagstraat 118, 2596 XZ The
Hague, Netherlands. TEL 31-70-3242125. FAX 31-
70-3282000.
circ. 23,000. *5050*

TROPICAL AGRICULTURIST.
Department of Agriculture, No. 1, Sarasavi
Mawatha, P.O. Box 05, Peradeniya, Sri Lanka.
TEL 94-8-88136. FAX 94-8-88030.
circ. 850. *157*

TROPICAL FRESHWATER BIOLOGY.
Idodo Umeh Publishers Ltd., 52 Ewah Rd., P.O. Box
3441, Benin City, Edo State, Nigeria. TEL 234-52-
254404.
circ. 200. *2945*

TROPICAL MEDICINE AND HYGIENE NEWS.
American Society of Tropical Medicine and Hygiene
(Washington), 6436 31st St., N.W., Washington, DC
20015. TEL 301-496-6721. FAX 301-402-3255.
circ. 2,400. *4628*

TRUCK SALES & LEASING MAGAZINE.
Newport Communications East, Inc., 600
Reisterstown Rd., Ste. 404, Baltimore, MD 21208-
5107. TEL 410-486-7430. FAX 410-786-7478.
circ. 22,000. *6862*

TRUCKER'S CONNECTION.
5960 Crooked Creek Rd., Ste. 15, Norcross, GA
30092. TEL 404-416-0927. FAX 404-416-1734.
circ. 170,081. *6863*

TRUCKERS - U S A.
Horizon Media, Box 3168, Tuscaloosa, AL 35403-
3168. TEL 205-758-3070.
circ. 100,000. *6863*

TRUSTEE QUARTERLY.
Association of Community College Trustees, 1740
N St., N.W., Washington, DC 20036. TEL 202-775-
4667.
circ. 7,000. *2444*

TRYBUNA.
Ad Novum, Ul. Miedziana 11, 00-835 Warsaw,
Poland. TEL 48-2-625-3015. FAX 48-22-204100.
circ. 100,000. *3206*

TRZISTE STOKE I STOCIH PROIZODA.
Zavod za Trzisna Istrazivanja, Mose Pijade 8-I,
11001 Belgrade, Yugoslavia. *182*

TSUSHIN KOGYO.
Tsushin Kikai Kogyokai, Sankei Bldg. Annex, 7-2,
Ote-machi 1-chome, Chiyoda-ku, Tokyo 100, Japan.
TEL 81-3-3231-3156. FAX 81-3-3231-3110.
1952

TUCSON WEEKLY.
Tucson Weekly, Inc., Box 2429, Tucson, AZ 85702.
TEL 520-795-2143. FAX 520-792-2096.
circ. 40,000. *4170*

TUG WORLD NEWSLETTER.
Thomas Reed Publications Ltd., 38 S. John St.,
London EC1M 4AY, England.
circ. 2,500. *6851*

TULANE MEDICINE.
Tulane University, Office of University Publications,
300 Hebert Hall, New Orleans, LA 70118-5698.
TEL 504-865-5714. FAX 504-865-5621.
circ. 18,500. *4539*

TULANIAN.
Tulane University, University Relations, Hebert Hall,
Rm. 300, New Orleans, LA 70118. TEL 504-865-
5714. FAX 504-865-5621.
circ. 75,000. *1889*

TURBULENCE.
Wydawnictwo Politechniki Czestochowskiej, Ul.
Dabrowskiego 69, 42-200 Czestochowa, Poland.
TEL 48-34-250974. FAX 48-34-612385.
circ. 500. *5018*

TURF NEWS.
Turfgrass Producers International, 1855-A Hicks Rd., Rolling Meadows, IL 60008. TEL 708-705-9898. FAX 708-705-8347.
circ. 1,400. *243*

TURIST- OG RUTEBILBLADET.
Skolegade 19 A, DK-8000 Aarhus C, Denmark. TEL 45-86-118680. FAX 45-86-14-4452.
circ. 4,000. *6923*

TURNBERRY.
G S & J Publishing, Inc., 5212 N.W. 54th Ave., Pompano Beach, FL 33073-3755. TEL 305-977-5901.
circ. 5,000. *456*

TUTTI AL BAR.
Tuttopress Editrice s.r.l., Via Cagliero, 21, 20125 Milan, Italy. TEL 39-2-6682834. FAX 39-2-6072185.
circ. 170,000. *3572*

TWIN CITIES VISITOR.
Skyway Publications, 15 S. Fifth St., Ste. 800, Minneapolis, MN 55402-1050. TEL 512-375-9222. FAX 512-375-9208.
circ. 30,000. *6923*

TWINS.
Twins Magazine, Inc., 6740 Antioch, Ste.155, Merriam, KS 66204. TEL 913-722-1090. FAX 913-722-1767.
circ. 17,000. *1779*

TWO - TEN TODAY.
56 Main St., Waterdown, MA 02172. TEL 617-923-4500. FAX 617-926-6037.
circ. 12,000. *6309*

TYLER JUNIOR COLLEGE NEWS.
Tyler Junior College, Box 9020, Tyler, TX 75711. TEL 214-510-2335. FAX 903-510-2708.
circ. 3,500. *1889*

U A P D REPORT.
Union of American Physicians and Dentists, 1330 Broadway, Ste. 730, Oakland, CA 94612. TEL 510-839-0193. FAX 510-763-8756.
circ. 3,000. *3730*

U B S INTERNATIONAL FINANCE.
Union Bank of Switzerland, Bahnhofstr. 45, CH-8021 Zurich, Switzerland. TEL 01-2346544. FAX 01-2346190.
circ. 25,000. *1124*

U D I DATAGRAM.
Utility Data Institute 1200 G St., N.W., Ste. 250, Washington, DC 20005. TEL 202-942-8788. FAX 202-942-8789. *2571*

U F C W ACTION.
United Food and Commercial Workers International Union, 1775 K St., N.W., Washington, DC 20006. TEL 202-223-3111. FAX 202-466-1562.
circ. 1,300,000. *3730*

U K PRODUCT REVIEW.
Macmillan Magazines Ltd., Porters South, 4-6 Crinan St., London N1 9XW, England. TEL 44-171-833-4000. FAX 44-171-843-4640.
circ. 15,000. *650*

U N I D O LINKS.
United Nations Industrial Development Organization, Box 300, A-1400 Vienna, Austria. TEL 43-1-211-31-5538. FAX 43-1-209-2669.
circ. 12,000. *1315*

U OF L.
University of Louisville, Alumni Association, 19 Development and University Relations Bldg., University of Louisville, Louisville, KY 40292. TEL 502-852-6171. FAX 502-852-7658.
circ. 85,000. *1889*

U P E N.
University of Port Elizabeth, P.O. Box 1600, Port Elizabeth 6000, South Africa. TEL 27-41-5042173. FAX 27-41-5042574.
circ. 3,000. *1889*

U S A RICE COUNCIL REVIEW.
U S A Rice Federation, 6699 Rookin, Box 740123, Houston, TX 77274. TEL 713-270-6699. FAX 713-270-9021.
circ. 16,000. *243*

U S B E: FOR MEMBERS ONLY.
United States Book Exchange, Periodicals and Serials Division, 2969 W. 25th St., Cleveland, OH 44113.
circ. 2,100. *4031*

U S - CHINA REVIEW.
U S - China Peoples Friendship Association, 122 W. 27th St., 10th Fl., New York, NY 10001-6227. TEL 212-736-7355.
circ. 17,000. *5775*

U S TECH.
Mid-Atlantic Tech Publications, Inc., Box 957, Valley Forge, PA 19482. TEL 610-783-6100. FAX 610-783-0317.
circ. 50,000. *2534*

U: THE NATIONAL COLLEGE MAGAZINE.
American Collegiate Network, 1800 Century Park E., Ste, 820, Los Angeles, CA 90067-1511. TEL 310-551-1381. FAX 310-551-1659.
circ. 1,500,000. *2445*

UGEMAGASINET INDUSTRIEN.
Dansk Industri (DI), DK-1787 Copenhagen V, Denmark. TEL 45-33-77-33-77. FAX 45-33-77-37-70.
circ. 14,600. *1532*

UHREN KATALOG.
Hee -Verlag GmbH, Wintermuehlenhof, 53639 Koenigswinter, Germany. TEL 49-2223-9230-0. FAX 49-2223-923026.
circ. 40,000. *3699*

ULTIMO.
Akzente Salzburg, Nonntaler Hauptstr. 1, A-5020 Salzburg, Austria. TEL 0662-849291. FAX 0662-84929122.
circ. 30,000. *3113*

ULUSAL CERRAHI DERGISI.
Turkish Surgical Society, Guzelbahce Sok. 35-7, 80200 Nisantasi - Istanbul, Turkey. TEL 90-212-2475295. FAX 90-212-2470835.
circ. 1,000. *4922*

UMWELT JOURNAL.
Journal Verlag, Dietrichgasse 24b-18, A-1030 Vienna, Austria. TEL 43-1-7155827-0.
circ. 24,000 *2822*

UMWELTMAGAZIN.
Vogel Verlag und Druck GmbH & Co. KG, Max-Planck-Str. 7-9, 97082 Wuerzburg, Germany. TEL 0931-4182145. FAX 0931-4182640.
circ. 20,000. *2823*

UNDERGROUND FOREST - SELVA SUBTERRANEA.
1701 Bluebell Ave., Boulder, CO 80302. TEL 303-449-1188.
circ. 5,000. *4170*

UNDERGROUND LAMP POST.
Henry A. Pohs, Ed. & Pub., 4537 Quitman St., Denver, CO 80212. TEL 303-455-3922.
circ. 450. *335*

UNDERHOOD SERVICE.
Babcox Publications, 11 S. Forge St., Akron, OH 44304. TEL 216-536-6117. FAX 216-535-0874.
circ. 40,000. *6804*

UNDERNEATH IT ALL
Associated Utility Contractors of Maryland, 2913 Crabapple Lane, Ellicott City, MD 21042. TEL 410-750-2554. FAX 410-750-7668.
circ. 3,000. *2621*

UNDERWATER MAGAZINE.
Doyle Publishing Co., 5222 FM 1960 W., Ste. 112, Houston, TX 77069. TEL 713-440-0278. FAX 713-580-4433.
circ. 20,000. *1489*

UNDZER VEG.
Achdut Ha-Avoda-Poale Zion of Canada, 272 Codsell Ave., Downsview, Ont. M3H 3X2, Canada. circ. 4,000. *2912*

UNICUM.
Unicum Verlag GmbH, Willy-Brandt-Platz 5-7, 44787 Bochum, Germany. TEL 49-234-96151-0. FAX 49-234-60256.
circ. 333,000. *1890*

DIE UNIE.
Suid-Afrikaanse Onderwysersunie, P.O. Box 196, Cape Town 8000, South Africa. TEL 27-21-461-6340. FAX 27-21-461-9233.
circ. 7,055. *2379*

UNIFICATION.
Unification Printers & Publishers Pty. Ltd., 12 Vernon St., Strathfield N.S.W. 2135, Australia. TEL 61-2-746-8789. FAX 61-2-7642058.
circ. 4,300. *2912*

UNION ELECTRIC NEWS.
Union Electric Company, 1901 Chouteau Ave, Box 149, St. Louis, MO 63166. TEL 314-554-3120.
circ. 10,100. *2571*

UNION MATTERS.
Saskatchewan Government Employees' Union, 1440 Broadway Ave., Regina Sask. S4P 1E2, Canada. TEL 306-522-8571. FAX 306-352-1969.
circ. 17,500. *3731*

UNION MEDICALE BALKANIQUE. ARCHIVES.
Union Medicale Balkanique, Str. Gabriel Peri Nr. 1, Bucharest, Rumania.
circ. 2,000. *4540*

UNION SIGNAL.
National Woman's Christian Temperance Union, 1730 Chicago Ave., Evanston, IL 60201. TEL 847-864-1396. *2201*

UNIONE MATEMATICA ITALIANA. NOTIZIARIO.
Unione Matematica Italiana, Piazza Porta San Donato 5, 40126 Bologna, Italy. TEL 39-51-243190. FAX 39-51-2-3190
circ. 3,000. *4402*

UNITA.
Unita S.p.A., Via d'Araceli 13, 20162 Milan, Italy.
circ. 400,000. *5714*

UNITED ARAB EMIRATES. AL-MASRAF AL-MARKAZI. AL-MULHIQ AL-IHSA'I.
Central Bank, P.O. Box 854, Abu Dhabi, United Arab Emirates. TEL 652220. FAX 668483.
circ. 500. *1034*

UNITED ARAB EMIRATES. AL-MASRAF AL-MARKAZI. AL-NASHRAH AL-IQTISADIYYAH.
Central Bank, P.O. Box 854, Abu Dhabi, United Arab Emirates. TEL 652220. FAX 668483. *1125*

UNITED ARAB EMIRATES. AL-MASRAF AL-MARKAZI. AL-TAQRIR AL-SANAWI
Central Bank, P.O. Box 854, Abu Dhabi, United Arab Emirates. TEL 652220. FAX 668483. *1569*

UNITED ARAB EMIRATES. WIZARAT AL-SIHHAH. IDARAT AL-TIBB AL-WAQA'I. AL-TAQRIR AL-SANAWI.
Wizarat al-Sihhah, Idarat al-Tibb al-Waqa'i, P.O. Box 344, Abu Dhabi, United Arab Emirates. TEL 333485.
circ. 1,000. *5977*

UNITED ARAB EMIRATES. WIZARAT AL-TARBIYYAH WAL-TA'LIM. AL-TAQRIR AL-SANAWI.
Wizarat al-Tarbiyyah wal-Ta'lim, Idarat al-I'lam al-Tarbawi, P.O. Box 259, Abu Dhabi, United Arab Emirates. TEL 213800.
circ. 1,000. *2464*

UNITED NATIONS CHILDREN'S FUND. ANNUAL REPORT.
United Nations Children's Fund (UNICEF), UNICEF House, 3 United Nations, New York, NY 10017. TEL 212-326-7000. FAX 212-888-7465.
circ. 56,650. *6397*

U.S. CENTERS FOR DISEASE CONTROL. ABORTION SURVEILLANCE REPORT
U.S. Centers for Disease Control, 1600 Clifton Rd., Atlanta, GA 30333. TEL 404-639-3311. *829*

U.S. CHAMBER OF COMMERCE. ASSOCIATION AGENDA.
U.S. Chamber of Commerce, 1615 H St., N.W., Washington, DC 20062. TEL 202-463-5560. FAX 202-463-3190.
circ. 1,200. *1150*

U.S. COAST GUARD. ENVIRONMENTAL PROTECTION NEWSLETTER.
U.S. Coast Guard, 2100 Second St., S.W., Washington, DC 20593. TEL 202-267-1054.
2823

U.S. FOREST SERVICE. GENERAL TECHNICAL REPORT N C.
U.S. Forest Service, North Central Forest Experiment Sta., 1992 Folwell Ave., St. Paul, MN 55108. TEL 612-649-5259.
circ. 1,000. *3028*

U.S. FOREST SERVICE. NORTH CENTRAL FOREST EXPERIMENT STATION. LIST OF PUBLICATIONS.
U.S. Forest Service, North Central Forest Experiment Sta., 1992 Folwell Ave., St. Paul, MN 55108. TEL 612-649-5259.
circ. 1,500. *3032*

U.S. FOREST SERVICE. RESEARCH NOTE N C.
U.S. Forest Service, North Central Forest Experiment Sta., 1992 Folwell Ave., St. Paul, MN 55108. TEL 612-649-5259.
circ. 2,000. *3028*

U.S. FOREST SERVICE. RESEARCH PAPER N C.
U.S. Forest Service, North Central Forest Experiment Sta., 1992 Folwell Ave., St. Paul, MN 55108. TEL 612-649-5259.
circ. 2,000. *3028*

U.S. FOREST SERVICE. RESOURCE BULLETIN N C.
U.S. Forest Service, North Central Forest Experiment Sta., 1992 Folwell Ave., MN 55108. TEL 612-649-5259.
circ. 2,000. *3028*

U.S. NATIONAL ENDOWMENT FOR THE ARTS. ANNUAL REPORT.
U.S. National Endowment for the Arts, Public Information Office, 1100 Pennsylvania Ave., N.W., Washington, DC 20506. TEL 202-682-5400.
circ. 4,000. *456*

U.S. SMALL BUSINESS ADMINISTRATION. ANNUAL REPORT.
U.S. Small Business Administration, c/o John Ward, Ed., MC-3114, 409 Third St., S.W., Washington, DC 20416. TEL 202-205-6740.
circ. 2,000. *1581*

U.S. SURGEON GENERAL. REPORT.
U.S. Centers for Disease Control, National Center for Chronic Disease Prevention and Health Promotion, 4770 Buford Hwy., N.E., MS K-50, Atlanta, GA 30341-3724. TEL 404-488-5705. FAX 404-488-5939. *2202*

UNITED STATES AMATEUR BOXING. ANNUAL GUIDE.
United States Amateur Boxing (U S A Boxing), Inc., One Olympic Plaza, Colorado Springs, CO 80909. TEL 719-578-4506. *6491*

UNITED STATES PILOTS ASSOCIATION. NEWSLETTER.
United States Pilots Association, 483 S. Kirkwood Rd., Ste. 10, St. Louis, MO 63122. TEL 314-849-8772. *80*

UNITED WAY CANADA. DIRECTORY.
United Way of Canada, 56 Sparks St., Ste. 404, Ottawa, ON K1P 5A9, Canada. TEL 613-236-7041. *6397*

UNITS.
National Apartment Association, 201 N. Union St., No. 200, Alexandria, VA 22314. TEL 703-518-6141. FAX 703-518-6191.
circ. 37,000. *3597*

UNIVERSAL MESSAGE.
Islamic Research Academy, D-35, Block 5, Federal 'B' Area, Karachi 75950, Pakistan. TEL 92-21-6349840. FAX 92-21-422827.
circ. 1,000. *6121*

UNIVERSIDAD AUTONOMA DE SANTO DOMINGO. BIBLIOTECA CENTRAL. BOLETIN DE ADQUISICIONES.
Universidad Autonoma de Santo Domingo, Biblioteca Central, Santo Domingo, Dominican Republic. *551*

UNIVERSIDAD COMPLUTENSE DE MADRID. REVISTA MATEMATICA.
Editorial Complutense de Madrid, Donoso Cortes 65, 28015 Madrid, Spain. TEL 34-1-3946372. FAX 34-1-3946382. *4402*

UNIVERSIDAD DE ORIENTE. INSTITUTO OCEANOGRAFICO BIBLIOTECA. BOLETIN BIBLIOGRAFICO.
Universidad de Oriente, Instituto Oceanografico de Venezuela, Apdo: Postal 94, Cumana, Sucre, Venezuela.
circ. 1,000. *2221*

UNIVERSIDAD NACIONAL AUTONOMA DE MEXICO. SEMINARIO DE INVESTIGACIONES BIBLIOTECOLOGICA. PUBLICACIONES. SERIE B. BIBLIOGRAFIA.
Universidad Nacional Autonoma de Mexico, Seminario de Investigaciones Bibliotecologicas, Cuidad Universitaria, 04510 Mexico D.F., Mexico. *552*

UNIVERSIDADE DE SAO PAULO. ESCOLA DE ENFERMAGEM. REVISTA.
Universidade de Sao Paulo, Escola de Enfermagem, Av. Dr. Eneas de Carvalho Aguiar, 419, SP, Caixa Postal 5751, 05403 Sao Paolo, Brazil. FAX 011-280-8213.
circ. 1,000. *4729*

UNIVERSIDADE ESTADUAL PAULISTA. REVISTA DE ODONTOLOGIA.
Universidade Estadual Paulista, Av. Vicente Ferreira, 1278, Caixa Postal 71, 17515-901 Marilia SP, Brazil. TEL 55-144-222504. FAX 55-144-222504.
circ. 1,000. *4656*

UNIVERSIDADE FEDERAL DO CEARA. CENTRO DE CIENCIAS DA SAUDE. REVISTA DE MEDICINA.
Universidade Federal do Ceara, Centro de Ciencias da Saude, Rua Alexandre Barauna 949, Caixa Postal 3170, 60430 Fortaleza, Ceara, Brazil. TEL 085-243-9002. FAX 085-243-90-10.
circ. 2,000. *4541*

UNIVERSIDADE FEDERAL DO RIO DE JANEIRO. FACULDADE DE ODONTOLOGIA. ANAIS.
Universidade Federal do Rio de Janeiro, Faculdade de Odontologia, Ilha da Cidade Universitaria, Rio de Janeiro, Brazil. *4656*

UNIVERSIDADE FEDERAL DO RIO DE JANEIRO. INSTITUTO DE MATEMATICA. ESTUDOS E COMUNICACOES.
Universidade Federal do Rio de Janeiro, Instituto de Matematica, C.P. 68530, 21945-970 Rio de Janeiro, RJ, Brazil. TEL 55-21-5900940. FAX 55-21-2901095. *4402*

UNIVERSIDADE FEDERAL DO RIO DE JANEIRO. INSTITUTO DE MATEMATICA. MEMORIAS DE MATEMATICA.
Universidade Federal do Rio de Janeiro, Instituto de Matematica, C.P. 68530, 21945-970 Rio de Janeiro, RJ, Brazil. TEL 55-21-5900940. FAX 55-21-2901095. *4406*

UNIVERSITAET LEIPZIG.
Leipziger Universitaetsverlag GmbH, Augustusplatz 10, 04109 Leipzig, Germany. TEL 49-341-2619964. FAX 49-341-9730099.
circ. 9,000. *1890*

UNIVERSITAETSBIBLIOTHEK GIESSEN. HANDSCHRIFTENKATALOGE.
Universitaetsbibliothek Giessen, Otto-Behaghel-Str. 8, 35394 Giessen, Germany. TEL 49-641-7022330. FAX 49-641-46406.
circ. 500. *552*

UNIVERSITAS. CIENCIA.
Universidade Federal da Bahia, Centro Editorial e Didatico, Rua Augusto Viana s-n, Canela, 40000 Salvador, Bahia, Brazil. TEL 071-245-2811.
circ. 500. *6293*

UNIVERSITAS. CULTURA.
Universidade Federal da Bahia, Centro Editorial e Didatico, Rua Augusto Viana s-n, Canela, 40000 Salvador, Bahia, Brazil. TEL 071-245-2811.
circ. 500. *3629*

UNIVERSITAT DE BARCELONA. BIBLIOTECA. MEMORIA ANUAL.
Universitat de Barcelona, Biblioteca, Gran via de les Corts Catalanes, 585, 08007 Barcelona, Spain. *4032*

UNIVERSITE DE BRETAGNE OCCIDENTALE. GUIDE DE L'ETUDIANT.
Universite de Bretagne Occidentale, Rue de Archives, 29269 Brest, France. TEL 98-31-60-20. FAX 98-31-60-01. *2380*

UNIVERSITE DE MONCTON. REVUE.
Universite de Moncton, Moncton, NB E1A 3E9, Canada. TEL 506-858-4062. FAX 506-858-4103.
circ. 500. *3126*

UNIVERSITEIT UTRECHT. UNIVERSITEIT MEDIA BULLETIN.
Universiteit Utrecht, Afdeling In- en Externe Betrekkingen, Heidelberglaan 8, 3584 CS Utrecht, Netherlands. TEL 31-30-2533550. FAX 31-30-2521818.
circ. 1,700. *2446*

UNIVERSITETET I TRONDHEIM. VITENSKAPSMUSEET. RAPPORT. BOTANISK SERIE.
University of Trondheim, Museum of Natural History and Archaeology, Department of Botany, N-7004 Trondheim, Norway. TEL 47-73-59-22-60. FAX 47-73-59-22-49.
circ. 275. *707*

UNIVERSITY FINANCE TREND ANALYSIS.
Statistics Canada, Publications Sales and Services, Ottawa, Ont. K1A 0T6, Canada. FAX 613-951-1584.
circ. 200. *2394*

UNIVERSITY OF ALASKA MUSEUM. ANNUAL REPORT.
University of Alaska Museum, 907 Yukon Dr., Fairbanks, AK 99775-1200. TEL 907-474-7505. FAX 907-474-5469. *5134*

UNIVERSITY OF ALBERTA. CENTRE FOR CRIMINOLOGICAL RESEARCH. DISCUSSION PAPERS.
University of Alberta, Department of Sociology, Centre for Criminological Research, Edmonton, AB T6G 2H4, Canada. TEL 403-492-3322. FAX 403-492-7196.
circ. 150. *2178*

UNIVERSITY OF ALLAHABAD. EDUCATION DEPARTMENT. RESEARCHES AND STUDIES.
University of Allahabad, Education Department, Allahabad 211002, Uttar Pradesh, India. *2380*

UNIVERSITY OF CALIFORNIA. SEISMOGRAPHIC STATIONS. BULLETIN.
University of California at Berkeley, Seismographic Station, 475 Earth Sciences Bldg., Berkeley, CA 94720. TEL 415-642-3977. FAX 643-5811.
circ. 450. *2283*

UNIVERSITY OF CALIFORNIA AT BERKELEY. CAMPUS STATISTICS.
University of California at Berkeley, 2223 Fulton, 4th Fl., Berkeley, CA 94720. TEL 415-642-5743. FAX 415-643-6523.
circ. 500. *2394*

UNIVERSITY OF CALIFORNIA, SANTA CRUZ. INSTITUTE FOR MARINE SCIENCES. SPECIAL PUBLICATION.
University of California, Santa Cruz, Institute of Marine Sciences, Santa Cruz, CA 95064. TEL 408-429-2464. FAX 408-429-0146.
circ. 500. *2307*

UNIVERSITY OF CAPE TOWN. RESEARCH REPORT.
University of Cape Town, Research Support Services, Private Bag, Rondebosch 7700, South Africa. TEL 27-21-6502202. FAX 27-21-6502138.
circ. 600. *2447*

UNIVERSITY OF DELAWARE. STUDENT CENTER. REVIEW.
University of Delaware, Student Center, B-1 Student Ctr., Newark, DE 19716. TEL 302-451-2771. FAX 032-451-1396.
circ. 15,000. *1891*

Contr Circ

UNIVERSITY OF DENVER JOURNAL.
University of Denver, Office of Communications, Denver, CO 80208. TEL 303-871-2711. FAX 303-871-3827.
circ. 70,000. *1891*

UNIVERSITY OF GEORGIA. COLLEGE OF AGRICULTURE EXPERIMENT STATIONS. BULLETIN.
University of Georgia, College of Agriculture Experiment Stations, Connor Hall, Athens, GA 30602. TEL 404-542-3621. *160*

UNIVERSITY OF GEORGIA. COLLEGE OF AGRICULTURE EXPERIMENT STATIONS. RESEARCH REPORTS.
University of Georgia, College of Agriculture Experiment Stations, Connor Hall, Athens, GA 30602. TEL 404-542-3621.
circ. 1,500. *160*

UNIVERSITY OF HARTFORD STUDIES IN LITERATURE.
University of Hartford, English Department, 200 Bloomfield Ave., W. Hartford, CT 06117. TEL 203-243-4574.
circ. 500. *4281*

UNIVERSITY OF ILLINOIS AT URBANA-CHAMPAIGN. DEPARTMENT OF AGRICULTURAL ECONOMICS. LEASE SHARES AND FARM RETURNS.
University of Illinois at Urbana-Champaign, Department of Agricultural Economics, Urbana, IL 61801. TEL 217-333-2638. *201*

UNIVERSITY OF ILLINOIS AT URBANA-CHAMPAIGN. SCHOOL OF ART AND DESIGN. NEWSLETTER.
University of Illinois at Urbana-Champaign, Continuing Education and Public Service-Visual Arts, 123 Fine and Applied Arts Bldg., Champaign, IL 61820. TEL 217-333-2439. FAX 217-244-7388.
circ. 6,000. *457*

UNIVERSITY OF LONDON. ROYAL POSTGRADUATE MEDICAL SCHOOL. ANNUAL REPORT.
University of London, Royal Postgraduate Medical School, Hammersmith Hospital, Du Cane Rd., London W12 ONN, England. TEL 44-181-383-3201. FAX 44-181-383-3203.
circ. 6,000. *4541*

UNIVERSITY OF MANCHESTER. DEPARTMENT OF COMPUTER SCIENCE. TECHNICAL REPORT SERIES.
University of Manchester, Department of Computer Science, Oxford Rd., Manchester M13 9PL, England. TEL 44-161-275-6130. FAX 44-161-275-6236.
circ. 100. *2059*

UNIVERSITY OF MANILA LAW GAZETTE.
University of Manila, 546 Dr. M.V. de los Santos St., Sampaloc, Manila D-403, Philippines.
circ. 500. *3862*

UNIVERSITY OF NEVADA. BASQUE STUDIES PROGRAM NEWSLETTER.
University of Nevada, Basque Studies Program, Getchell Library, Reno, NV 89557-0012. TEL 702-784-4854. FAX 702-784-1355.
circ. 8,500. *2913*

UNIVERSITY OF NEWCASTLE. DEPARTMENT OF ELECTRICAL AND COMPUTER ENGINEERING. TECHNICAL REPORT EE.
University of Newcastle, Department of Electrical and Computer Engineering, Callaghan, N.S.W. 2308, Australia. TEL 61-49-216026. FAX 61-49-216993.
circ. 800. *2722*

UNIVERSITY OF OCCUPATIONAL AND ENVIRONMENTAL HEALTH. JOURNAL.
University of Occupational and Environmental Health, Japan, Iseigaoka 1-1, Yahatanishi-ku, Kita-Kyushu 807, Japan. FAX 093-692-4876.
circ. 900. *5260*

UNIVERSITY OF OXFORD. SCHOOL OF GEOGRAPHY. RESEARCH PAPERS.
University of Oxford, School of Geography, Mansfield Rd., Oxford OX1 3TB, England. TEL 01865-271919. FAX 01865-271929.
circ. 300. *3276*

UNIVERSITY OF PORT ELIZABETH. INSTITUTE FOR PLANNING RESEARCH. ANNUAL REPORT.
University of Port Elizabeth, Institute for Planning Research, P.O. Box 1600, Port Elizabeth 6000, South Africa. TEL 27-41-5042336. FAX 27-41-531769.
circ. 400. *1316*

UNIVERSITY OF RHODE ISLAND. LIBRARY. LIBRARY LETTER.
University of Rhode Island, Association of Friends of the Library, Kingston, RI 02881. *4033*

UNIVERSITY OF SINGAPORE. HISTORY SOCIETY. JOURNAL.
National University of Singapore, History Department, Kent Ridge, Singapore 0511, Singapore. TEL 772-3839.
circ. 500. *3386*

UNIVERSITY OF THE PHILIPPINES. INSTITUTE OF LIBRARY SCIENCE. NEWSLETTER.
University of the Philippines, Institute of Library Science, U.P. Diliman, Quezon City 1101, Philippines. TEL 9205303. FAX 9224714.
circ. 1,200. *4033*

UNIVERSITY OF THE PUNJAB. INSTITUTE OF GEOLOGY. GEOLOGICAL BULLETIN.
University of the Punjab, Institute of Geology, Qaid-E-Azam Campus, Lahore, Pakistan. *2266*

UNIVERSITY OF TOKYO. INSTITUTE OF APPLIED MICROBIOLOGY. REPORTS.
University of Tokyo, Institute of Applied Microbiology, 1-1-1 Yayoi, Bunkyo-ku, Tokyo 113, Japan. *625*

UNIVERSITY OF WALES AT ABERYSTWYTH. LIBRARY REPORT.
University of Wales at Aberystwyth, Library, Aberystwyth, Dyfed SY23 3DZ, Wales.
circ. 100. *4033*

UNIVERSITY OF WASHINGTON DAILY.
University of Washington, Board of Student Publications 144 Communications, Box 353720, Seattle, WA 98195. TEL 206-543-7666. FAX 206-543-2345.
circ. 18,000. *1891*

UNIVERSITY OF WATERLOO. GAZETTE.
University of Waterloo, Internal Communications Department, Waterloo, ON N2L 3G1, Canada. TEL 519-885-1211. FAX 519-746-8652.
circ. 10,000. *2390*

UNIVERSITY OF WATERLOO COURIER.
University of Waterloo, Waterloo, Ont. N2L 3G1, Canada. TEL 519-885-1211.
circ. 50,000. *1891*

UNIVERSITY OF WISCONSIN AT MADISON. COLLEGE OF ENGINEERING. ANNUAL REPORT.
University of Wisconsin at Madison, College of Engineering, 215 N. Randall Ave., Madison, WI 53706-1688. TEL 608-263-5988. FAX 608-263-9259.
circ. 6,500. *2622*

UNIX REVIEW.
Miller Freeman, Inc. 600 Harrison St., San Francisco, CA 94107. TEL 415-905-2200. FAX 415-905-2232.
circ. 77,700. *2047*

UNMUZZLED OX.
Unmuzzled Ox Foundation, Ltd., 105 Hudson St., New York, NY 10013. TEL 212-226-7170.
circ. 20,000. *4322*

UP TO DATE.
Mediamark Publishing International Ltd., 35 Gresse St., Rathbone Pl., London W1P 1PN, England. TEL 44-171-580-3105. FAX 44-171-580-1695.
circ. 370,000. *1952*

UP WITH PEOPLE REPORTS.
Up with People, Inc., 1 International Ct., Broomfield, CO 80021-9506. TEL 303-438-7391. FAX 303-438-7302.
circ. 60,000. *2453*

UPDATE (SOUTH AFRICAN EDITION).
George Warman Publications (Pty.) Ltd., P.O. Box 704, Cape Town 8000, South Africa. TEL 27-21-245320. FAX 27-21-261332.
circ. 8,400. *4541*

UPPER CASE.
National Life Insurance Company of Vermont, Montpelier, VT 05604. TEL 802-229-3333.
circ. 3,000. *3668*

UPPER TRIAD.
Upper Triad Association, Inc., Box 2050, Germantown, MD 20875. TEL 301-916-2933.
circ. 2,000. *5504*

UPSOUTH.
Upsouth, Inc., 3627 Hammett Hill Rd., Bowling Green, KY 42101. TEL 502-843-8018.
circ. 75. *4282*

UROLOGIA.
Libreria Editrice Canova, Viale della Liberazione 40, 31030 Dosson di Casier (Treviso), Italy. TEL 39-422-322393. FAX 39-422-322305.
circ. 1,300. *4931*

UROLOGY INTERNATIONAL.
Complete Medical Communications Ltd., C M C House, 19 King Edward St., Macclesfield, Ches. SK10 1AQ, England. TEL 44-1625-619855. FAX 44-1625-619812.
circ. 24,000. *4932*

USED EQUIPMENT DIRECTORY.
Penton Publishing Co. (Hasbrouck Heights) 611 Rte. 46 W., Hasbrouck Heights, NJ 07604. TEL 201-393-9558. FAX 201-393-9553.
circ. 75,000. *4347*

UTAH STATE UNIVERSITY MAGAZINE.
Utah State University, Information Services, Logan, UT 84322-0500. TEL 801-797-1353. FAX 801-797-1250.
circ. 60,000. *1892*

UTILITY CONSTRUCTION AND MAINTENANCE.
Practical Communications, Inc., Box 183, Cary, IL 60013-0183. TEL 847-639-2200. FAX 847-639-9542.
circ. 25,500. *878*

UTILITY FINANCE.
O X E R A Press, Blue Boar Ct, Alfred St., Oxford OX1 4EH, England. TEL 44-1865-251142. FAX 44-1865-201080.
circ. 1,000. *2560*

UTTAR BHARAT BHOOGOL PATRIKA.
Uttar Bharat Parishad, c/o V.K Shrivastava, Secy., Dept. of Geography, University of Gorakhpur, Gorakhpur 273 009, India. TEL 335221. *3277*

UTTAR BHARAT TIMES.
Paresh Kumar Kashyap, Ed. & Pub., Court Rd., Bijnor 246 701, U.P., India. TEL 01342-62664.
circ. 2,200. *3179*

V.C.F. NEWSLETTER.
Veterinary Christian Fellowship, 112 Lenthay Rd., Sherborne, Dorset DT9 6AG, England. TEL 01935-812872.
circ. 420. *6956*

V C OE ZEITUNG.
Verkehrsclub Oesterreich Dingelstedtgasse 15, A-1150 Vienna, Austria. TEL 43-1-8932697. FAX 43-1-8932431.
circ. 25,000. *6734*

V D E W DIE OEFFENTLICHE ELEKTRIZITAETSVERSORGUNG.
Vereinigung Deutscher Elektrizitaetswerke e.V., Stresemannallee 23, 60596 Frankfurt a.M., Germany. FAX 069-6304339. *2722*

V F A PROFIL.
Profil Verlag GmbH, Schadeweg 160B, 26127 Oldenburg, Germany. TEL 49-441-93023-0. FAX 49-441-9302320.
circ. 36,000. *406*

V F W AUXILIARY.
Veterans of Foreign Wars of the United States, Ladies Auxiliary, 406 W. 34th St., Kansas City, MO 64111. TEL 816-561-8655. FAX 816-931-4753.
circ. 775,000. *1854*

V S D A VOICE.
Video Software Dealers Association, 16530 Ventura Blvd. Encino, CA 91436-4551. TEL 609-231-7800. FAX 609-231-9791.
circ. 5,000. *1978*

V V S.
Teknisk Forlag A-S, Skelbaekgade 4, DK-1780
Copenhagen V, Denmark. TEL 45-31-21-68-01.
FAX 45-31-21-04-01.
circ. 4,876. *3334*

THE V W AUTOIST.
Volkswagen Club of America, Box 154, N. Aurora, IL
60542-0154. TEL 708-896-2803.
circ. 2,000. *6805*

VAART BLAD.
Norges Kooperative Landsforening, Kirkegt. 4, 0107
Oslo 1, Norway. TEL 22-89-95-00. FAX 22-41-11-
38.
circ. 253,355. *1161*

VAART VERN.
Krigsskoleutdannede Offiserers Landsforening, P.O.
Box 7207, Ho, N-0307 Oslo 3, Norway. TEL 02-52-
15-46. FAX 02-69-56-08.
circ. 2,000. *5051*

VACATION INDUSTRY REVIEW.
Interval International, 6262 Sunset Dr., Penthouse
1, S. Miami, FL 33143. TEL 305-666-1861.
FAX 305-663-2220.
circ. 15,000. *6924*

VAESTRA SVERIGES AFFAERER & FOERETAG.
Vaestra Sveriges Affaerer & Foeretag, P.O. Box 411,
S-401 26 Goeteborg, Sweden. TEL 46-031-
624060. FAX 46-031-624066.
circ. 7,530. *1489*

VAEXTSKYDDSKURIREN.
Bayer (Sverige) AB, Agro-Kemi, P.O. Box 50113, S-
202 11 Malmoe, Sweden.
circ. 40,000. *244*

VAKBLAD MIX.
M'Xpress vof, P.O. Box 66, 5258 ZH Berlicum,
Netherlands. TEL 31-73-5034347. FAX 31-73-
5034347.
circ. 2,000. *3604*

**VALLEYKIDS NEWSMAGAZINE FOR WEST
SUBURBAN PARENTS.**
227 N. Second St., Geneva, IL 60134-1436.
TEL 708-208-7221. FAX 708-208-7257.
circ. 32,382. *1780*

VALOER.
Foereningen Valoer, Konstvetenskapliga
Institutionen, Slottet, Soedra tornet, inngaang HO, S-
752 37 Uppsala, Sweden. TEL 46-18-182888.
FAX 46-18-182892.
circ. 50. *458*

**VANCOUVER ISLAND REGIONAL LIBRARY
NEWSLETTER.**
Vancouver Island Regional Library, Box 3333, 6250
Hammond Bay Road, Namaimo, BC V9R 5N3,
Canada. TEL 604-758-4697. FAX 604-758-2482.
circ. 389. *4034*

VANGUARD (LA HABRA).
Alpha Beta Company, 777 S. Harbor Blvd., La
Habra, CA 90631. TEL 714-738-2000.
circ. 34,000. *2993*

EL VAQUERO.
Glendale Community College, 1500 N. Verdugo Rd.,
Glendale, CA 91208-2894. TEL 818-240-1000.
FAX 818-549-9436.
circ. 3,500. *1892*

VARME OG SANITETS NYT.
Christtreu, Strandlodsvei 48, DK-2300 Copenhagen
S, Denmark. TEL 32-844848. FAX 31-582055.
circ. 12,456. *3334*

VARSITY.
S R C Press, University of Cape Town,
Rondesbosch 7700, South Africa. TEL 021
698531.
circ. 7,500. *1892*

VASAMA.
Suomen Sahkoalantyontekijain Liitto, P.O. Box 747,
33101 Tampere, Finland. TEL 358-31-2520-111.
FAX 358-31-2520-210.
circ. 31,238. *3731*

VASTGOEDMARKT.
Ten Hagen & Stam b.v. Postbus 34, 2501 AG The
Hague, Netherlands. TEL 31-70-3045700. FAX 31-
70-3045812.
circ. 7,955. *878*

VECINOS DEL VALLE.
Daily News, 21221 Oxnard St., Woodland Hills, CA
91367. TEL 818-713-3229. FAX 818-713-3024.
circ. 48,000. *2913*

THE VEGAN NEWS.
Vegan Action, Box 4353, Berkeley, CA 94704.
TEL 510-654-6297. FAX 510-595-7569.
circ. 10,000. *5242*

THE VEGAS CONNECTION.
Contact Advertising, 2010 St. Lucie Blvd., Ft. Pierce,
FL 34946. TEL 561-464-5447. FAX 561-464-
5447.
circ. 6,000. *4946*

VEILIG VLIEGEN.
Koninklijke Luchtmacht, Afdeling Bedrijfsveiligheid
Koninklijke Luchtmachtstaf, Binckhorstlaan 135,
Postbus 20703, 2500 ES The Hague, Netherlands.
TEL 70-3492358. FAX 70-3492500.
circ. 5,000. *80*

VEN'D'EST.
Editions Cooperatives du Ven'd'Est, Ltee., P.O. Box
430, Petit Rocher, NB E0B 2E0, Canada. TEL 506-
783-4097. FAX 506-783-8386.
circ. 4,500. *3126*

**VENEZUELA. OFICINA CENTRAL DE ESTADISTICA E
INFORMATICA. ENCUESTA CUALITATIVA.**
Oficina Central de Estadistica e Informatica, Apdo.
de Correos 4593, Carmelitas, Caracas 1010A,
Venezuela. TEL 58-2-782-11-33. FAX 58-2-781-
13-80. *1035*

VEREIN ZUM SCHUTZ DER BERGWELT. JAHRBUCH.
Verein zum Schutz der Bergwelt e.V., Praterinsel 5,
80538 Munich, Germany. TEL 49-89-479053.
FAX 49-89-479053. *2144*

VERKEHRSBLATT.
Verkehrsblatt Verlag Borgmann GmbH, Hohe Str.
39, 44139 Dortmund, Germany. TEL 49-231-
128047. FAX 49-231-125640.
circ. 10,000. *6827*

VERKO.
Verko Maskinkontakt AB, Datavaegen 10, S-436 32
Askim, Sweden. FAX 031-680009.
circ. 4,466. *2772*

VERMILION STANDARD.
4917 50 Ave., Box 750, Vermilion, AB T0B 4M0,
Canada. TEL 403-853-5344. FAX 403-853-5203.
circ. 82. *3126*

**VERMONT. COMMISSIONER OF BANKING
INSURANCE AND SECURITIES. ANNUAL REPORT
OF THE BANK COMMISSIONER.**
Department of Banking Insurance and Securities,
Division of Banking, 89 Main St., Drawer 20,
Montpelier, VT 05620. TEL 802-828-3301.
circ. 1,700. *1126*

VERMONT DEPARTMENT OF LIBRARIES NEWS.
Department of Libraries, Pavillion Office Bldg., 109
State St., Montpellier, VT 05609.
circ. 2,000. *4034*

**VERMONT ECONOMIC DEVELOPMENT AUTHORITY.
ANNUAL REPORT.**
Economic Development Authority, 56 E. State St.,
Montpelier, VT 05602-3012. TEL 802-223-7226.
FAX 802-223-4205.
circ. 400. *1533*

VERMONT PARENT AND CHILD MAGAZINE.
Box 4446, Burlington, VT 05406-4446. TEL 802-
425-3835.
circ. 25,000. *1780*

VERMONT PHILATELIST.
Vermont Philatelic Society, 18 Fuller St., Montpelier,
VT 05602. *5464*

VERMONT VACATION.
Travel Routes, Inc., Box 949, Chester, VT 05143-
0949. FAX 802-257-0848.
circ. 150,000. *6924*

VERSES.
Cader Publishing, Ltd., 36915 Ryan Rd., Sterling
Heights, MI 48310. TEL 810-795-3635. FAX 810-
795-9875.
circ. 5,000. *4282*

VERWARMING EN VENTILATIE.
Vereniging van Nederlandse Installatiebedrijven
(VNI), Postbus 7272, 2701 AG Zoetermeer,
Netherlands.
circ. 4,000. *3334*

**VERZEICHNIS DER KONSULARISCHEN
VERTRETUNGEN IN OESTERREICH.**
Bundesministerium fuer Auswaertige
Angelegenheiten, Ballhausplatz 2, A-1014 Vienna,
Austria. *5777*

VESAK.
Australian Buddhist Mission Inc., 16 Woodhouse
Drive, Ambarvale, N.S.W. 2560, Australia. TEL 61-
46-267420. FAX 61-2-4494657.
circ. 2,000. *6111*

VETERANPOSTEN.
Sveriges Paensionaers Foerbund - S P F, P.O. Box
26070, S-100 41 Stockholm, Sweden. TEL 46-8-
679-88-50. FAX 46-8-611-56-82.
circ. 142,500. *5052*

VETERANS' BULLETIN.
Georgia Department of Veterans Service, Floyd
Veterans Bldg., 970 East, Atlanta, GA 30334.
TEL 404-656-5933. FAX 404-656-5934.
circ. 2,400. *1855*

VETERINARY FORUM.
Forum Publications, Inc., 1610-A Frederica Rd., St.
Simons Island, GA 31522-2509. TEL 912-638-
4848. FAX 912-634-0768.
circ. 45,000. *6958*

VETS HELPING VETS.
USVMI, Golden Triangle Sales, 3738 E. First St.,
Fort Worth, TX 76111. TEL 817-834-7573.
circ. 10,000. *5052*

VIA FEDEX.
The Wells Group, 430 First Ave. N., Ste. 550,
Minneapolis, MN 55401-1735. TEL 612-338-
8300. FAX 612-338-6546.
circ. 330,000. *1919*

**VIA INTERNATIONAL PORT OF NEW YORK - NEW
JERSEY.**
Port Authority of New York and New Jersey, One
World Trade Ctr., Rm. 34E, New York, NY 10048.
TEL 212-435-6614. FAX 212-435-6032.
circ. 30,000. *6852*

VIA SATELLITE.
Phillips Business Information, Inc., 1201 Seven
Locks Rd., Potomac, MD 20854. TEL 301-424-
3338. FAX 301-340-0542. *1920*

VIBORG STIFTS FOLKEBLAD.
Viborg Stifts Folkeblad, Sct. Mathiasgade 7, DK-
8800 Viborg, Denmark. TEL 45-89-27-63-00.
FAX 45-86-62-22-20.
circ. 12,720. *3135*

VICTORIAN REAL ESTATE JOURNAL.
Real Estate Institute of Victoria Ltd., P.O. Box 443,
Camberwell, Vic. 3124, Australia. TEL 61-3-
92056666. FAX 61-3-92056699.
circ. 2,500. *6038*

VIDA RELIGIOSA.
Misioneros Hijos del Inmaculado Corazon de Maria
(Claretianos), Buen Suceso, 22, 28008 Madrid,
Spain. TEL 91-5482101.
circ. 10,000. *6200*

VIDEO RETAILER SHOWCASE.
Tel-Aire Publications, Inc., 3105 E. Carpenter Frwy.,
Irving, TX 75062. TEL 214-438-4111. FAX 214-
579-7483.
circ. 19,500. *1979*

VIE DE L'AUTO.
Elvea - La Vie de l'Auto, BP 88, 77003
Fontainbleau Cedex, France. TEL 60-71-55-55.
FAX 60-72-20-22.
circ. 68,500. *336*

VIE DE LA MOTO.
Elvea - La Vie de l'Auto, BP 19, 77302
Fontainbleau Cedex, France. TEL 60-71-55-55.
FAX 60-72-22-37.
circ. 43,000. *336*

VIE ET SANTE.
Editions Vie et Sante, 60 av. Emile Zola, 77192
Dammarie les Lys Cedex, France. FAX 64-87-00-66.
circ. 40,000. *5537*

VIE SOCIALE.
Centre d'Etudes, de Documentation, d'Information et
d'Action Sociales (CEDIAS), 5 rue Las-Cases, 75007
Paris, France. TEL 45-51-66-10.
circ. 1,750. *6439*

VIEWPOINT (LONDON, 1965).
Delane Press, 157 Vicarage Rd., London E1O 5DU,
England. TEL 44-181-539-3876. *5715*

VIHERPIHA.
A-Lehdet Oy, Hitsaajankatu 7, FIN-00081 A-Lehdet,
Finland. TEL 358-0-786858.
circ. 37,419. *3068*

**VIKING SOCIETY FOR NORTHERN RESEARCH. SAGA
BOOK.**
Viking Society for Northern Research, c/o Dept. of
Scandinavian Studies, University College, London
WC1E 6BT, England. TEL 44-171-380-7176.
circ. 650. *3454*

VIM & VIGOR.
McMurry Publishing, 1010 E. Missouri Ave.,
Phoenix, AZ 85014-2601. FAX 602-395-5853.
circ. 950,000. *5537*

VINTNERS WORLD.
Jemma Publications Ltd., Marino House, 53
Glasthule Rd., Sandycove, Co. Dublin, Ireland.
TEL 2800000. FAX 2801818.
circ. 7,500. *512*

**VIRGIN ISLANDS (U.S.). DEPARTMENT OF LABOR.
BUREAU OF LABOR STATISTICS. LABOR MARKET
REVIEW.**
Department of Labor, Bureau of Labor Statistics,
P.O. Box 3359, Charlotte Amalie, St. Thomas, VI
00803. TEL 809-776-3700. FAX 809-774-5908.
circ. 900. *1398*

VIRGINIA MARITIMER.
Port Authority, 600 World Trade Center, Norfolk, VA
23510. TEL 804-683-8000. FAX 804-683-8500.
circ. 9,500. *6852*

VIRGINIA P H C IMAGE.
Virginia Association of Plumbing - Heating - Cooling
Contractors, 1001 E. Broad St., Ste. 225,
Richmond, VA 23219-1928. TEL 804-644-5826.
FAX 804-643-5927.
circ. 4,400. *3334*

**VIRGINIA POLYTECHNIC INSTITUTE AND STATE
UNIVERSITY. DEPARTMENT OF GEOLOGICAL
SCIENCES. GEOLOGICAL GUIDEBOOKS.**
Virginia Polytechnic Institute and State University,
Department of Geological Sciences, 4044 Derring
Hall, Blacksburg, VA 24061. TEL 703-231-6521.
2267

**VIRGINIA SCHOOL BOARDS ASSOCIATION
NEWSLETTER.**
Virginia School Boards Association, 2320 Hunters
Way, Ste. B, Charlottesville, VA 22911-7931.
TEL 804-295-8722. FAX 804-295-8785.
circ. 2,300. *2464*

VIRKSOMHEDS NYT.
Christtreu, Strandlodsvei 48, DK-2300 Copenhagen
S, Denmark. TEL 32-844848. FAX 31-582055.
circ. 16,954. *6734*

VISION (STAMFORD).
Keep America Beautiful, Inc., Mill River Plaza, 9 W.
Broad St., Stamford, CT 06902-3734. TEL 203-
323-8987.
circ. 2,000. *2825*

VISION OF REALITY.
Piranesi Ltd., Bogisiceva 11, 61000 Ljubljana,
Slovenia. TEL 386-61-223-039. FAX 386-61-221-
226.
circ. 2,000. *406*

VISIONS: AM ART QUARTERLY.
L A Artcore, 420 E. Third St., Ste. 110, Los
Angeles, CA 90013-1644. TEL 213-628-6164.
FAX 213-520-1277.
circ. 12,000. *458*

EL VISITANTE DE PUERTO RICO.
Puerto Rican Catholic Conference, Box 41305,
Minillas Sta., San Juan, PR 00940-1305. TEL 809-
728-3710. FAX 809-728-3656.
circ. 59,500. *6200*

VISITOR MAGAZINE.
Fairway Group Inc., 215 Fairway Rd. S., Kitchener,
ON N2G 4E5, Canada. TEL 519-886-2831.
FAX 519-886-9383.
circ. 50,000. *6925*

VISTA MAGAZINE.
Horizon, 999 Ponce de Leon Blvd., Ste. 600, Coral
Gables, FL 33134. TEL 305-442-2462. FAX 305-
443-7650.
circ. 1,100.000. *6925*

VITA IN CAMPAGNA.
Informatore Agrario S.r.l., Lungadige Galtarossa 23-
E, 37133 Verona, Italy. TEL 39-45-597855.
FAX 39-45-597510.
circ. 80,073. *3069*

VITA TRENTINA.
Vita Trentina Editrice - Coop., s.r.l., Via S. Giovanni
Bosco, 5, 38100 Trento, Italy. TEL 39-461-
272666. FAX 39-461-272655.
circ. 15,000. *3186*

VITALITY.
Vitality, Inc., 8080 N. Central, LB 78, Dallas, TX
75206. TEL 214-591-1480.
circ. 1,500,000. *5537*

VITALITY MAGAZINE.
356 Dupont St., Toronto, ON M5R 1V9, Canada.
TEL 416-964-0528.
circ. 35,000. *293*

VIVRE ENSEMBLE.
Union Nationale des Associations de Parents et
Amis de Personnes Handicapees Mentales, 15 rue
Coysevox, 75018 Paris, France.
circ. 75,250. *2476*

VOCE SERAFICA DELLA SARDEGNA.
Frati Minori Cappuccini di Sardegna, Via S. Ignazio
da Laconi 94, 09123 Cagliari, Italy. TEL 39-70-
660303. FAX 39-70-655583.
circ. 3,000. *6200*

VOETBAL TOTAAL.
Koninklijke Nederlandsche Voetbalbond, P.O. Box
515, 3700 AM Zeist, Netherlands. TEL 31-3439-
9211. FAX 31-3439-1397.
circ. 30,500. *6518*

VOICE (ALBANY).
United University Professions, 159 Wolf Rd.,
Albany, NY 12205. TEL 518-458-7935. FAX 518-
459-3242.
circ. 20,000. *2448*

VOICE (FT. LAUDERDALE).
Cary - Joy Communications, 1405 S.E. First St., Ft.
Lauderdale, FL 33301. TEL 954-463-5556.
FAX 954-463-2674.
circ. 70,000. *4820*

VOICE OF SILENCE NEWSLETTER.
World Federation of the Deaf, 120 via Gregoria VII,
Rome 00165, Italy.
circ. 500. *3315*

VOICE OF WALDEN.
Walden Forever Wild, Inc., Box 275, Concord, MA
01742. TEL 503-429-2839. FAX 860-487-1629.
2145

VOIES DE LA CREATION THEATRALE.
C N R S Editions, 20-22 rue St. Amand, 75015
Paris, France. TEL 45-33-16-00. FAX 45-33-92-13.
circ. 1,500. *6707*

VOIX SEPHARADE.
Communaute Sepharade du Quebec, 4735 Chemin
de la Cote Ste. Catherine, Montreal, PQ H3W 1M1,
Canada. TEL 514-733-4998. FAX 514-733-3158.
circ. 6,000. *2914*

VOLKSDANS.
Landelijk Centrum Amateurdans, Postbus 452,
3500 AL Utrecht, Netherlands. TEL 31-30-334255.
FAX 31-30-332721
circ. 3,000. *2957*

THE VOLUME FRAMER.
Vic Faulkner Associates, 74a The Broadway,
Chesham, Bucks. HP5 1EG, England. TEL 01494-
791451. FAX 01494-778224.
circ. 5,000. *458*

THE VOLUNTEER LIBRARIAN.
Association of Private Libraries, c/o Sophie Mitrisin,
66 Frankfort St., Apt. 2G, New York, NY 10038-
1622. TEL 212-732-4461. *4034*

VORSCHAU.
Forschungsgesellschaft fuer Wohnen, Bauen und
Planen, Loewengasse 47, A-1030 Vienna, Austria.
TEL 0222-726251. FAX 0222-712625121. *879*

VORTEX.
American Chemical Society, California Section,
2140 Shattuck Ave., Rm. 1101, Berkeley, CA
94704. TEL 415-848-0512. *1696*

VOX ME D A L.
Dalhousie University, Dalhousie Medical Alumni
Association, Sir Charles Tupper Med. Bldg., Halifax,
NS B3H 3J5, Canada. TEL 902-494-8800.
FAX 902-494-2033.
circ. 6,000. *1893*

VOXAIR.
Canadian Forces Base Winnipeg, Westwin, MB R3J
0T0, Canada. TEL 204-889-3963. FAX 204-885-
4176.
circ. 3,600. *5052*

LA VOZ (SEATTLE).
Concilio for the Spanish Speaking, 157 Yesler Way.,
Ste 400, Seattle, WA 98104-2572. TEL 206-461-
4891. FAX 206-461-4893.
circ. 14,000. *2914*

VYZIVA A POTRAVINY.
Spolecnost pro Vyzivu, Sobeslavska 40, 130 00
Prague 3, Czech Republ c. TEL 42-2-67311280.
FAX 42-2-67310515.
circ. 5,500. *5243*

VYZOV.
Permskii Gorispolkom, Upravlenie Vnutrennikh Del,
Ul. Druzhby 34, 614600 Perm, Russia. TEL 48-39-
24. FAX 32-52-19.
circ. 50,000. *5739*

W B F IN ACTION.
Workmen's Benefit Fund of the United States of
America, 99 N. Broadway, Hicksville, NY 11801-
2905. TEL 516-938-6060.
circ. 15,000. *3669*

W C E R HIGHLIGHTS.
Wisconsin Center for Education Research, University
of Wisconsin at Madison, 1025 W. Johnston St.,
Rm. 785, Madison, WI 53706. TEL 608-263-
8814. FAX 608-263-6448.
circ. 8,900. *2464*

W D A JOURNAL.
Wisconsin Dental Association, 111 E. Wisconsin
Ave., Ste. 1300, Milwaukee, Milwaukee, WI 53202.
TEL 414-276-4520. FAX 414-276-8431.
circ. 3,100. *4656*

W E R A BROCHURE.
Western English Retailers Association, 451 E. 58th
Ave., Box 087, Denver, CO 80216. TEL 303-298-
7882. FAX 303-292-3468.
circ. 1,000. *1837*

W E R A SPECIAL NEWSLETTER.
Western English Retailers Association, 451 E. 58th
Ave., Box 087, Denver, CO 80216. TEL 303-298-
7882. FAX 303-292-3468.
circ. 300. *1837*

W E S A NEWSLETTER.
Wisconsin Electronic Sales and Service Association,
Box 09091, Milwaukee, WI 53209.
circ. 250. *1581*

W N C BUSINESS BEAT.
Nason & Associates, Box 8204, Asheville, NC
28814. TEL 704-298-1322. FAX 704-298-1312.
circ. 19,000. *969*

W P A NEWS.
Western Publications Association, 2401 Pacific
Coast Hwy., Ste. 102, Hermosa Beach, CA 90254-
2734. TEL 818-995-7338. FAX 818-995-0878.
circ. 2,200. *6011*

DIE WAAGE.
Gruenenthal GmbH, 52220 Stolberg, Germany.
TEL 02402-103345. FAX 02402-103520.
circ. 30,000. *3150*

WAGES AND BENEFITS.
Employee Futures Research, Box 15236, Colorado
Springs, CO 80935-5236.
circ. 700. *2464*

WAGONER JOURNAL.
Northwest Genealogical Society, Box 6, Alliance, NE
69301.
circ. 300. *3105*

WAKE FOREST LAW REVIEW.
Wake Forest Law Review Association, Inc., Wake
Forest University, Winston-Salem, NC 27109.
TEL 919-759-5439. FAX 919-759-4496.
circ. 1,500. *3867*

WALL STREET & TECHNOLOGY.
United News & Media, One Penn Plaza, New York,
NY 10119. TEL 212-869-1300.
circ. 25,200. *1130*

WALLACES FARMER.
Farm Progress Companies 191 S. Gary Ave., Carol
Stream, IL 60188. TEL 708-690-5600. FAX 708-
462-2869.
circ. 80,000. *162*

WANASAN.
Royal Forest Department, Vanasarn Forest Journal
Office, Bangkok, Thailand.
circ. 5,400. *3029*

**WASHINGTON (STATE). DEPARTMENT OF REVENUE.
RESEARCH DIVISION. COMPARATIVE STATE -
LOCAL TAXES.**
Department of Revenue, Research Division, Box
47459, Olympia, WA 98504-7459. TEL 360-753-
2087. FAX 360-664-0972. *1571*

**WASHINGTON (STATE). DEPARTMENT OF REVENUE.
RESEARCH DIVISION. PROPERTY TAX STATISTICS.**
Department of Revenue, Research Division, Box
47459, Olympia, WA 98504-7459. TEL 360-753-
2087. FAX 360-664-0972. *1571*

**WASHINGTON (STATE) RESEARCH COUNCIL.
NOTEBOOK.**
Washington Research Council, 1301 Fifth Ave., Ste.
350, Seattle, WA 98101-2603. TEL 206-357-
6643. FAX 206-754-2193.
circ. 2,500. *5927*

**WASHINGTON CRIME NEWS SERVICES CALENDAR
OF EVENTS.**
Washington Crime News Services, 3918 Prosperity
Ave., Ste. 318, Fairfax, VA 22031-3304. TEL 703-
573-1600. FAX 703-573-1604. *4937*

WASHINGTON OPERA MAGAZINE.
Washington Opera Guild, Kennedy Center,
Washington, DC 20566. TEL 202-416-7850.
FAX 202-416-7857.
circ. 60,000. *5205*

WASHINGTON REAL ESTATE NEWS.
Department of Licensing, Real Estate Division, Box
9015, Olympia, WA 98507. TEL 206-753-3194.
FAX 206-586-0998.
circ. 60,000. *6039*

**WASHINGTON UNIVERSITY MAGAZINE AND ALUMNI
NEWS.**
Washington University, Office of Publications,
Campus Box 1070, One Brookings Dr., St. Louis,
MO 63130-4899. TEL 314-935-5248. FAX 314-
935-4259.
circ. 108,000. *1893*

WASHINGTON'S HILL RAG.
Fagon Publishing Group, 224 Seventh St., S.E., No.
300, Washington, DC 20003. TEL 202-543-8300.
circ. 20,000. *3242*

WASTE MAGAZIN.
Bohmann Druck und Verlag GmbH & Co. KG,
Leberstr. 122, A-1110 Vienna, Austria. TEL 43-1-
74095-0. FAX 43-1-74095183.
circ. 8,000. *2858*

THE WASTE MANAGER.
Environmental Services Association, Mountbarrow
House, 6-20 Elizabeth St., London SW1W 9RB,
England. TEL 44-171-824-8882. FAX 44-171-824-
8753.
circ. 4,200. *2858*

WAT KAN ONS OPVOER'
Dramatic Artistic & Literary Rights Organisation
(Pty) Ltd., SAMRO House, Cor. de Beer & Juta
Streets, Braamfontein, South Africa.
circ. 2,000. *6707*

WATCH MAGAZINE.
Watch Magazines Inc., 245-401 Richmond St. W.,
Toronto, ON M5V 1X3, Canada. TEL 416-595-
1313. FAX 416-595-1312.
circ. 50,000. *1811*

WATER AND WASTE TREATMENT.
Faversham House Group Ltd., Faversham House,
232a Addington Rd., South Croydon, Surrey CR2
8LE, England. TEL 44-181-651-7100. FAX 44-181-
651-7117.
circ. 8,506. *6978*

WATER CONDITIONING AND PURIFICATION.
Publicom Inc., 2800 E. Ft. Lowell Rd., Tucson, AZ
85716-1518. FAX 520-323-7412.
circ. 18,537. *6978*

WATER FLYING.
Seaplane Pilots Association, 421 Aviation Way,
Frederick, MD 21701. TEL 301-695-2083.
FAX 301-695-2375.
circ. 6,500. *80*

WATER PRODUCTS.
Faversham House Group Ltd., Faversham House,
232a Addington Rd., South Croydon, Surrey CR2
8LE, England. TEL 44-181-651-7100. FAX 44-181-
651-7117. *6979*

WATER SEWAGE AND EFFLUENT.
Brooke Pattrick (Pty) Ltd., P.O. Box 422,
Bedfordview 2008, South Africa. TEL 27-11-
6224666. FAX 27-11-6167196.
circ. 3,210. *6981*

WATER SKIER.
American Water Ski Association, 799 Overlook Dr.,
Winter Haven, FL 33884. TEL 914-324-4341.
FAX 914-325-8259.
circ. 30,000. *6582*

WATER TECHNOLOGY.
National Trade Publications, Inc., 13 Century Hill,
Latham, NY 12110-2197. TEL 518-783-1281.
FAX 518-783-1386.
circ. 17,680. *6981*

WATERFRONT NORTHWEST NEWS.
Duncan McIntosh Co. Inc., 17782 Cowan, Ste. C,
Irvine, CA 92714. TEL 714-660-6150. FAX 714-
660-6172.
circ. 27,300. *6542*

AL-WATHA'IQ AL-FILASTINIYYAH.
Cultural Foundation, Centre for Documentation and
Research, P.O. Box 2380, Abu Dhabi, United Arab
Emirates. TEL 212900. FAX 541595.
circ. 1,000. *3500*

WATT.
Gruppo Editoriale Jackson S.p.A., Via M. Gorki 69,
20092 Cinisello B. (MI), Italy. TEL 39-2-6607228.
FAX 39-2-66034290.
circ. 9,804. *2722*

WAYN-E-GRAM MAGAZINE.
Continental Grain Company, Wayne Feed Division,
10 S. Riverside Plaza, Chicago, IL 60606-3708.
TEL 312-930-1050. FAX 312-466-6614.
circ. 2,500. *261*

WAYNE STATE MAGAZINE.
Wayne State University, Alumni Association, Office of
Alumni Relations, Detroit, MI 48202. TEL 313-577-
2300. FAX 313-577-2302.
circ. 13,500. *1893*

WE PROCEEDED ON.
Lewis and Clark Trail Heritage Foundation, Inc., Box
3434, Great Falls, MT 59403. TEL 406-453-2826.
circ. 1,500. *3492*

WEDDING BELLS MAGAZINE.
50 Wellington St., E., 2nd Fl., Toronto, ON M5E
1C8, Canada. TEL 416-862-8479. FAX 416-862-
2184.
circ. 107,000. *4415*

WEEKEND SPARK.
Rowland B. Martyn, Ed. & Pub., 7 Lamina Sankoh
St., Freetwon, Sierra Leone. TEL 232-22-263285.
circ. 20,000. *3210*

WEEKLY NEWS UPDATE ON THE AMERICAS.
Nicaragua Solidarity Network, 339 Lafayette St.,
New York, NY 10012. TEL 212-674-9499.
FAX 212-674-9139.
circ. 140. *3128*

WEEKLY PETROLEUM ARGUS.
Petroleum Argus Ltd., 93 Shepperton Rd., London
N1 3DF, England. TEL 0171-359-8792. FAX 0171-
226-0695. *5380*

WEHRMEDIZINISCHE MONATSSCHRIFT.
Beta Verlag GmbH, Postfach 140121, 53056
Bonn, Germany. TEL 49-228-91937-0. FAX 49-
228-252067.
circ. 5,285. *4543*

WELCOME BACK STUDENT GUIDE.
Kingston Publications, P.O. Box 1352, Kingston, ON
K7L 5C6, Canada. TEL 613-549-8442.
circ. 15,000. *1893*

WELCOME HOME MAGAZINE.
James F. & Mary Sweeney, Eds. & Pubs., 5944 S.
Kipling St., Ste. 204, Littleton, CO 80127-2590.
TEL 303-972-2584. FAX 303-972-2261.
circ. 31,000. *3242*

WELDER.
Boc-Murex, Hertford Rd., Waltham Cross, Herts.,
England.
circ. 15,500. *4988*

WELDING DESIGN AND FABRICATION.
Penton Publishing Co. 1100 Superior Ave.,
Cleveland, OH 44114-2543. TEL 216-696-7000.
FAX 216-696-8765.
circ. 40,000. *4989*

WELDING RESEARCH ABROAD.
Welding Research Council, 345 E. 47th St., New
York, NY 10017. TEL 212-705-7956.
circ. 800. *4989*

WELDING RESEARCH COUNCIL BULLETIN.
Welding Research Council, 345 E. 47th St., New
York, NY 10017. TEL 212-705-7956.
circ. 900. *4989*

WELFARE BULLETIN.
Center on Social Welfare Policy and Law, 275
Seventh Ave., Ste. 1205, New York, NY 10001-
6708. TEL 212-633-6967. FAX 212-633-6371.
circ. 600. *3879*

WELL SERVICING.
Workover-Well Servicing Publications, Inc., 6060 N.
Central Expy., Ste. 428, Dallas, TX 75206.
TEL 214-692-0771.
circ. 10,000. *5380*

**WELLINGTON REGIONAL EMPLOYERS ASSOCIATION
NEWSLETTER.**
Wellington Regional Employers Association (Inc.),
Federation House, 6th Floor, Box 1087, 95-99
Molesworth St., Wellington, New Zealand. TEL 64-4-
737224. FAX 374501. *1399*

WELSH FARMER.
Farmers' Union of Wales, Llys Amaeth, Queens Sq.,
Aberystwyth, Dyfed, Wales. TEL 44-1970-612755.
FAX 44-1970-624369.
circ. 16,000. *163*

WER - WAS - WO.
Studentenwerk Goettingen, Platz der Goettinger
Sieben 4, 37073 Goettingen, Germany. TEL 0551-
395147. FAX 0551-395186.
circ. 12,500. *1893*

WERBUNG.
Schweizerischer Reklameverband, Kappelergasse 14, CH-8022 Zurich, Switzerland. FAX 01-2118018.
circ. 2,468. *47*

WE'RE NEXT.
Box GG, Jal, NM 88252. TEL 505-395-2053.
circ. 200,000. *1812*

WERTPAPIER.
Deutsche Schutzvereinigung fuer Wertpapierbesitz e.V., Humboldtstr. 9, 40237 Dusseldorf, Germany.
circ. 34,000. *1359*

DIE WESER.
Weserbund e.V., Teerhof 34, 28199 Bremen, Germany. TEL 49-421-598290. FAX 49-421-5982940.
circ. 1,200. *2825*

WESLEYAN WORLD.
Wesleyan World Missions, 6060 Castleway West Dr., Box 50434, Box 50434, IN 46250-0434. TEL 317-595-4172. FAX 317-841-1125.
circ. 36,000. *6103*

WESPENNEST.
Rembrandtstr. 31-9, A-1020 Vienna, Austria. TEL 01-3326691. FAX 01-3332970.
circ. 5,000. *4173*

WEST CENTRAL BUSINESS JOURNAL.
Marie Howe, Ed. & Pub., 920 W. Market St., Lima, OH 45805. TEL 419-227-0511. FAX 419-224-3921.
circ. 16,000. *970*

WEST COAST LIFESTYLE MAGAZINE.
W. Bill Golding, Ed. & Pub., 14148 Burbank Blvd., Spt. 7, Van Nuys, CA 91401-4943. TEL 818-780-8400. FAX 818-780-8979.
circ. 70,000. *3242*

WEST COAST PEDDLER.
Box 5134, Whittier, CA 90607. TEL 310-698-1718. FAX 310-698-1500. *336*

WEST VIRGINIA. COMMISSION ON AGING. ANNUAL PROGRESS REPORT.
Commission on Aging, State Capitol, Charleston, WV 25305. TEL 304-348-3317.
circ. 500. *3298*

WEST VIRGINIA FOURTH ESTATESMAN.
West Virginia University, School of Journalism, 112 Martin Hall, Box 6010, Morgantown, WV 26506-6010. TEL 304-293-3505. FAX 304-293-3027.
circ. 3,800. *3712*

WESTCHESTER COMMERCE.
Suburban Publishing, Inc., 100 Clearbrook Rd., Elmsford, NY 19801. TEL 914-345-6726. FAX 914-345-3515.
circ. 10,000. *1151*

WESTCHESTER FAMILY.
New York Family Publications, Inc., 141 Halstead Ave., Ste. 3D, Mamaroneck, NY 10543-2652. TEL 914-381-7474.
circ. 35,000. *1780*

WESTENDER.
108-110 Camden High St., London NW1 0LU, England. TEL 44-171-485-6050.
circ. 40,000. *3161*

WESTERN ASSOCIATION NEWS.
Western Association News, Inc., 13274 Fiji Way, No. 416, Marina Del Rey, CA 90292-7090. TEL 310-577-3700. FAX 310-577-3715. *1450*

WESTERN ASSOCIATION OF GRADUATE SCHOOLS. PROCEEDINGS OF THE ANNUAL MEETING.
Western Association of Graduate Schools, University of Wyoming, The Graduate School, Box 3018, Laramie, WY 82071-3108. TEL 307-766-2287. FAX 307-766-4042.
circ. 500. *2448*

WESTERN AUSTRALIA. DEPARTMENT FOR COMMUNITY DEVELOPMENT. ANNUAL REPORT.
Department for Community Development, 189 Royal St., E. Perth, W.A. 6004, Australia. TEL 61-9-222-2555. FAX 61-9-222-2776.
circ. 2,000. *6399*

WESTERN AUSTRALIA. DEPARTMENT OF TRANSPORT. ANNUAL REPORT.
Department of Transport, 136-138 Stirling Highway, Nedlands, W.A. 6009, Australia. FAX 61-9-3865119.
circ. 600. *6734*

WESTERN AUSTRALIA. GEOLOGICAL SURVEY. MINERAL RESOURCES BULLETIN.
Geological Survey of Western Australia, 100 Plain St., E. Perth, W.A. 6004, Australia. TEL 61-9-222333. FAX 61-9-2223633. *5081*

WESTERN AUSTRALIAN COASTAL SHIPPING COMMISSION. ANNUAL REPORT.
Coastal Shipping Commission, P.O. Box 394, Fremantle, Australia. *6853*

WESTERN BEEF PRODUCER.
Western Farmer-Stockman Magazines Box 2160, Spokane, WA 99210-1615. TEL 509-459-5361. FAX 509-459-5102.
circ. 34,404. *287*

WESTERN CANADA HIGHWAY NEWS MAGAZINE.
Craig Kelman & Associates Ltd., 3C - 2020 Portage Ave., Winnipeg, MB R3J 0K4, Canada. TEL 204-885-7798. FAX 204-889-3576.
circ. 4,500. *6863*

WESTERN CAVER.
Western Australian Speleological Group, P.O. Box 67, Nedlands, W.A. 6909, Australia. TEL 61-9-3465550.
circ. 200. *2268*

WESTERN CLEANER AND LAUNDERER.
Wakefield Publishing Co., 100 N. Hill Ave., Ste. C, Pasadena, CA 91106-1941. TEL 818-793-2911. FAX 818-793-5540
circ. 15,000. *1830*

WESTERN GROCERY NEWS.
Sunset Publishing Corp., 3055 Wilshire Blvd., Los Angeles, CA 90010. TEL 213-380-9680. FAX 213-380-4217.
circ. 9,000. *3009*

WESTERN HOG JOURNAL.
Alberta Pork Producers Development Corp., 10319 Princess Elizabeth Ave., Edmonton, AB T5G 0Y5, Canada. TEL 403-474-8288. FAX 403-471-8065.
circ. 9,559. *287*

WESTERN POWER CORPORATION. ANNUAL REPORT.
Western Power Corporation, Perth, W.A., Australia. TEL 09-325-4597. FAX 09-326-4984.
circ. 4,000. *2560*

WESTERN ROOFING - INSULATION - SIDING.
Dodson Publications Inc., 546 Court St., Reno, NV 89501-1711. TEL 702-333-1080. FAX 702-333-1081.
circ. 20,000. *879*

WESTERN SHOW NEWS.
Bolger Publications Inc., 3301 Como Ave., S.E., Minneapolis, MN 55414. TEL 612-645-6311. FAX 612-645-1750.
circ. 30,000. *3302*

WESTERN VIKING.
Western Viking Inc., 24C5 N.W. Market St., Ste. 202, Seattle, WA 98107. TEL 206-784-4617. FAX 206-734-4856.
circ. 3,000 *2915*

WESTMINSTER MAGAZINE.
Westminster College, Office of Communication Services, New Wilmington, PA 16172. TEL 412-946-7226. FAX 412-946-7187.
circ. 20,225. *1894*

WESTMOUNT EXAMINER.
210 Victoria St., Westmount, PQ H3Z 2M4, Canada. TEL 514-484-5610. FAX 514-484-6028.
circ. 8,000. *3127*

WESTON-SUPER-MARE ADMAG.
Admag Newspapers 11 Beacons Field Rd., Weston-super-Mare, Avon BS23 1YE, England. TEL 44-1934-417921. FAX 44-1934-635031.
circ. 80,000. *3161*

WETLANDS INTERNATIONAL.
International Waterfowl and Wetlands Research, Slimbridge, Gloucester GL2 7BX, England. TEL 44-1453-890624. FAX 44-1453-890697.
circ. 1,700. *823*

WHAT'S NEW IN ELECTRONICS.
Westwick-Farrow Pty. Ltd., Cnr. Fox Valley Rd. and Kiogle St., Wahroonga, N.S.W. 2076, Australia. TEL 61-2-4872700. FAX 61-2-4891265.
circ. 9,200. *2534*

WHAT'S NEW IN PROCESS ENGINEERING.
Westwick-Farrow Pty. Ltd., Cnr. Fox Valley Rd. and Kiogle St., Wahroonga, N.S.W. 2076, Australia. TEL 61-2-4872700. FAX 61-2-4891265.
circ. 9,200. *2623*

WHAT'S NEW IN RADIO COMMUNICATIONS.
Westwick-Farrow Pty. Ltd., Cnr. Fox Valley Rd. and Kiogle St., Wahroonga, N.S.W. 2076, Australia. TEL 61-2-4872700. FAX 61-2-4891265.
circ. 5,200. *1941*

WHAT'S NEW IN SCIENTIFIC & LABORATORY TECHNOLOGY.
Westwick-Farrow Pty. Ltd., Cnr. Fox Valley Rd. and Kiogle St., Wahroonga, N.S.W. 2076, Australia. TEL 61-2-4872700. FAX 61-2-4891265.
circ. 7,200. *6670*

WHAT'S NEW IN TELECOMMUNICATIONS.
Westwick-Farrow Pty. Ltd., Crn. Fox Valley Rd. and Kogle St., Wahroonga. N.S.W. 2076, Australia. TEL 61-2-4872700. FAX 61-2-4891265.
circ. 5,335. *1953*

THE WHEEL EXTENDED.
Toyota Motor Corporation, International Public Affairs Division, 1-4-18, Koraku, Bunkyo-ku, Tokyo 112, Japan. TEL 03-3817-9930 FAX 03-3817-9017.
circ. 11,000. *6806*

WHERE ATLANTA.
Where Magazines International (Atlanta), 180 Allen Rd., 302 N. Bldg., Atlanta, GA 30328. TEL 404-843-9800. FAX 404-843-9070.
circ. 50,000. *6938*

WHERE BALTIMORE.
Where Magazines International (Baltimore), 516 N. Charles St., Ste. 300, Baltimore, MD 21201. TEL 410-539-4373. FAX 410-539-4381.
circ. 30,000. *6926*

WHERE BOSTON.
Where Magazines International (Boston), 120 Boylston St., Fl. 3, Boston, MA 02116-4611. TEL 617-482-6777. FAX 617-482 3337.
circ. 60,000. *6938*

WHERE CALGARY.
Key West Publishers Ltd. 125 Ninth Ave. S.E., Ste. 250, Calgary, AB T2G 0P6, Canada. TEL 403-299-1888. FAX 403-299-1899.
circ. 18,900. *6938*

WHERE CHICAGO.
Where Magazines International (Chicago), 1165 N. Clark St. Chicago, IL 60610-2845. TEL 312-642-1896. FAX 312-642-5467.
circ. 100,000. *6938*

WHERE EDMONTON.
Where Magazines International (Edmonton), 9343-50th St., Unit 4, Edmonton, AB T6B 2L5, Canada. TEL 403-465-3362. FAX 403-448-0424.
circ. 40,000. *6926*

WHERE HALIFAX.
Metro-Guide Publishing Box 14 5475 Spring Garden Rd., Halifax, NS B3J 3T2, Canada. TEL 902-420-9943. FAX 902-429-9058.
circ. 24,000. *6938*

WHERE LOS ANGELES.
Where Magazines International (Los Angeles), 3733 Motor Ave. Ste. 301, Los Angeles, CA 90034-6403. TEL 310-280-2880. FAX 310-836-1803.
circ. 50,000. *6938*

WHERE NEW ORLEANS.
V.I.P. 621 Decatur St., 2nd Fl., New Orleans, LA 70130. TEL 504-522-6468. FAX 504-522-0018.
circ. 70,000. *6938*

WHERE NEW YORK.
Where Magazines International (New York), 475 Park Ave. S., Fl. 2100, New York, NY 10016-6901. TEL 212-687-4646. FAX 212-687-4661. circ. 119,000. *6938*

WHERE OTTAWA - HULL.
Capital Publishers 400 Cumberland St., Ottawa, ON K1N 8X3, Canada. TEL 613-241-7888. FAX 613-241-3112. circ. 32,000. *6938*

WHERE PARIS.
6 rue de Ponthieu, 75008 Paris, France. TEL 53-83-89-40. FAX 53-83-89-50. circ. 40,000. *6938*

WHERE ROCKY MOUNTAINS.
R M V Publications Ltd., Ste. 250, One Palliser Sq., 125 Ninth Ave. S.E., Calgary, AB T2G 0P6, Canada. TEL 403-299-1888. FAX 403-299-1899. circ. 187,500. *6926*

WHERE ST. LOUIS.
Where Magazines International (St. Louis), 1750 S. Brentwood Blvd., Ste. 311, St. Louis, MO 63144. TEL 314-968-4940. FAX 314-968-0813. circ. 33,000. *6938*

WHERE SAN FRANCISCO.
Where Magazines International (San Francisco), 74 New Montgomery St., Ste. 320, San Francisco, CA 94105. TEL 415-546-6101. FAX 415-546-6108. circ. 57,000. *6938*

WHERE SEATTLE.
Where Magazines International (Seattle), 2505 Third Ave., Ste. 305, Seattle, WA 98121. TEL 206-728-2624. FAX 206-728-1423. circ. 30,000. *6927*

WHERE TORONTO.
Key Publishers Co. Ltd. 6 Church St., Toronto, ON M5E 1M1, Canada. TEL 416-364-3333. FAX 416-594-3375. circ. 79,000. *6938*

WHERE TWIN CITIES.
Minnesota Monthly Publications, 10 S. Fifth St., Ste. 1000, Minneapolis, MN 55402-1011. TEL 612-339-1619. FAX 612-371-5801. circ. 30,000. *6938*

WHERE VANCOUVER.
Where Canada, Inc. The Sixth Estate, 2208 Spruce St., Vancouver, BC V6H 2P3, Canada. TEL 604-736-5586. FAX 604-736-3465. circ. 50,000. *6938*

WHERE VICTORIA.
Key Pacific Publishers Co. Ltd. 1001 Wharf St., 3rd Fl., Victoria, BC V8W 1T6, Canada. TEL 604-388-4324. FAX 604-388-6166. circ. 22,000. *6938*

WHERE WASHINGTON, DC.
Where Magazines International (Washington, DC), 1225 19th St., N.W., Washington, DC 20036. TEL 202-463-4550. FAX 202-463-4553. circ. 90,000. *6938*

WHERE WINNIPEG.
Where Magazines International, Fanfare Communications, 128 James Ave., Ste. 300, Winnipeg, MB R3B 0N8, Canada. TEL 204-943-4439. FAX 204-947-5463. circ. 32,000. *6938*

WHICH AIRLINE? AND BUSINESS TRAVEL UPDATE.
B M I Publications Ltd., Suffolk House, George St., Croydon, Surrey CR9 1SR, England. TEL 44-181-649-7233. FAX 44-181-649-7234. circ. 45,000. *6927*

THE WHITE PAPER.
Association of Certified Fraud Examiners, 716 West Ave., Austin, TX 78701. TEL 512-478-9070. FAX 512-478-9297. circ. 14,000. *2185*

THE WHOLESALER.
T M B Publishing, 1838 Techny Ct., Northbrook, IL 60082. TEL 847-564-1127. FAX 847-564-1127. circ. 32,000. *3334*

WHO'S WHO IN CARGO HANDLING.
International Cargo Handling Coordination Association, 71 Bondway, London SW8 1SH, England. TEL 0171-793-1022. FAX 0171-820-1703. *6853*

WHO'S WHO IN ECONOMIC DEVELOPMENT.
American Economic Development Council, 9801 W. Higgins, Ste. 540, Rosemont, IL 60018-4726. TEL 847-692-9944. FAX 847-696-2990. circ. 2,700. *561*

WHO'S WHO IN RECREATION.
Society of Recreation Executives, Box 520, Gonzales, FL 32560-0520. TEL 904-477-7992. FAX 904-479-8393. circ. 4,100. *561*

WILDLANDS NEWS.
Plymouth County Wildlands Trust, Box 2282, Duxbury, MA 02331. TEL 617-934-9018. circ. 1,300. *2146*

WILDLIFE RESCUE.
Wildlife Rescue Association of British Columbia, 5216 Glencarin Dr., Burnaby, BC V5B 3C1, Canada. TEL 604-526-7275. FAX 604-524-2890. circ. 2,000. *2146*

WILTSHIRE GAZETTE AND HERALD.
Media in Wessex, 100 Victoria Rd., Swindon, Wilts. SN1 3BE, England. TEL 44-1793-528144. FAX 44-1793-542434. circ. 24,000. *3161*

WINDSPEAKER.
Aboriginal Multi-Media Society of Alberta, 15001 112th Ave., Edmonton, AB T5M 2V6, Canada. TEL 403-455-2700. FAX 403-455-7639. circ. 3,000. *2915*

WINGED HEAD.
Pittsburgh Athletic Association, 4215 Fifth Ave., Pittsburgh, PA 15213. TEL 412-621-2400. FAX 412-321-4541. circ. 3,500. *1855*

THE WINNING EDGE.
Transportation Communications International Union, 3 Research Pl., Rockville, MD 20850. TEL 301-948-4910. FAX 301-948-1369. circ. 2,200. *3732*

WIRELESS: FOR THE CORPORATE USER.
Wireless Publishing Co. 3 Wing Dr., Ste. 240, Cedar Knolls, NJ 07927. TEL 201-285-1500. FAX 201-285-1519. circ. 34,000. *1920*

WIRELESS PRODUCT NEWS.
Phillips Business Information, Inc., 1201 Seven Locks Rd., Potomac, MD 20854. TEL 301-424-3338. FAX 301-309-3847. *1953*

WIRTSCHAFT NORDHESSEN.
Industrie- und Handelskammer Kassel, Kurfuerstenstr. 9, 34117 Kassel, Germany. TEL 49-561-78910. FAX 49-561-7891290. circ. 50,000. *1151*

WISCONSIN ARCHITECT.
Wisconsin Architect, Inc., 321 S. Hamilton St., Madison, WI 53703-3606. TEL 608-257-8477. circ. 3,700. *406*

WISCONSIN CRIME AND ARRESTS (YEAR).
Office of Justice Assistance, Statistical Analysis Center, 220 State St., 2nd Fl., Madison, WI 53702. TEL 608-266-7644. FAX 608-266-6676. circ. 500. *2180*

WISCONSIN DEER & TURKEY SHOW PREVIEW.
Target Communications Corp., 7626 W. Donges Bay Rd., Mequon, WI 53092-3400. TEL 414-242-3990. FAX 414-242-7391. circ. 40,000. *6582*

WISCONSIN LAND INFORMATION NEWSLETTER.
University of Wisconsin-Madison, Land Information & Computer Graphics Facility, B102 Steenbock Library, 550 Babcock Dr., Madison, WI 53706. TEL 608-263-5534. FAX 608-262-2500. circ. 13,000. *5936*

WISCONSIN P-H-C CONTRACTOR.
Target Communications Corp., 7626 W. Donges Bay Rd., Mequon, WI 53097-3400. TEL 414-242-3990. FAX 414-242-7391. circ. 6,000. *3334*

WISCONSIN PASTORAL HANDBOOK.
Milwaukee Catholic Press Apostolate, Inc., 3501 S. Lake Dr., Box 07913, Milwaukee, WI 53207-7913. TEL 414-769-3472. circ. 2,300. *6201*

WISCONSIN SCHOOL NEWS.
Wisconsin Association of School Boards, 122 W. Washington Ave., Madison, WI 53703. TEL 608-257-2622. FAX 608-257-8386. circ. 5,700. *2464*

WITNESS (FARMINGTON HILLS).
Oakland Community College, 27055 Orchard Lake Rd., Farmington Hills, MI 48334. TEL 810-471-7740. circ. 1,500. *4173*

WOLKENRIDDER.
K L M Royal Dutch Airlines, Public Relations Bureau, Postbus 7700, 1117 ZR Schiphol Airport, Netherlands. TEL 31-20-6491126. FAX 31-20-6488200. circ. 42,000. *6927*

WOMAN ACTIVIST.
Woman Activist, Inc., 2310 Barbour Rd., Falls Church, VA 22043. circ. 600. *5739*

WOMAN'S VOICE.
Shelby J. Hoon, Ed. & Pub., Box 454, Kent, OH 44240-0454. TEL 216-673-2990. FAX 216-673-6141. circ. 20,000. *7011*

WOMEN IN THE ARTS.
National Museum of Women in the Arts, 1250 New York Ave. N.W., Washington, DC 20005-3920. TEL 202-783-5000. FAX 202-393-3235. circ. 65,000. *460*

WOMENPOLICE.
R.R. 1, Box 149, Deer Isle, ME 04627. TEL 207-348-6976. FAX 207-348-6171. circ. 3,000. *2178*

WOMEN'S CONTACT BULLETIN.
Public Service Association of New South Wales, G.P.O. Box 3365, Sydney, N.S.W. 2001, Australia. TEL 61-2-290-1555. FAX 61-2-262-1623. circ. 9,000. *3732*

WOMEN'S DIGEST.
Women's Digest, Inc., 511-6 Baymeadows Rd., Ste. 200, Jacksonville, FL 32217. TEL 904-733-2853. circ. 69,000. *7012*

WOMEN'S ENVIRONMENT AND DEVELOPMENT ORGANIZATION NEWS & VIEWS.
Women's Environment and Development Organization (WEDO), 845 Third Ave., 15th Fl., New York, NY 10022. TEL 212-759-7982. FAX 212-759-8647. circ. 20,000. *7012*

WOMEN'S HEALTH NEWSLETTER.
Women's Health, 52 Featherstone St., London EC1Y 8RT, England. TEL 44-171-251-6580. FAX 44-171-608-0928. circ. 600. *6986*

WOMEN'S HISTORY CATALOG.
National Women's History Project, 7738 Bell Rd., Windsor, CA 95492. TEL 707-838-6000. FAX 707-838-0478. circ. 300,000. *7021*

WOMEN'S STUDIES QUARTERLY.
Feminist Press at the City University of New York, 311 E. 94th St., New York, NY 10128-5603. TEL 212-360-5790. FAX 212-348-1241. circ. 3,000. *7021*

WOMEN'S VIEW.
Smith Family, 16 Larkin St., Camperdown, N.S.W. 2050, Australia. TEL 61-2-550-4422. FAX 61-2-550-4235. circ. 27,000. *7012*

WOMEN'S WORLD.
Jewish Women International, 1828 L St., N.W., Ste. 250, Washington, DC 20036. TEL 202-857-1320. FAX 202-857-1380.
circ. 60,000. *7012*

WOOD DIGEST.
Johnson Hill Press, Inc. 1233 Janesville Ave., Ft. Atkinson, WI 53538. TEL 414-563-6388. FAX 414-563-1702.
circ. 52,000. *3039*

WOOD TECHNOLOGY.
Miller Freeman, Inc. 600 Harrison St., San Francisco, CA 94107. TEL 415-905-2200. FAX 415-905-2232.
circ. 20,600. *3040*

WOODMEN.
Woodmen of the World Life Insurance Society, c/o Billie Jo Foust, Asst. Ed., 1700 Farnam St., Omaha, NE 68102. TEL 402-342-1890. FAX 402-271-7269.
circ. 508,000. *3669*

WOODWORKING.
Action Communications Inc., 135 Spy Court, Markham, ON L3R 5H6, Canada. TEL 905-477-3222. FAX 905-477-4320.
circ. 11,000. *888*

WOOL NEWS.
Wool & Woollens Export Promotion Council, 612-714 Ashoka Estate, 24 Barakhamba Rd., New Delhi 110001, India. TEL 91-11-3315512. FAX 91-11-3314626.
circ. 1,000. *6689*

WOOL SACK.
Mid-States Wool Growers Cooperative, Box 328, Brookings, SD 57006. TEL 605-692-2324. FAX 605-692-8182.
circ. 18,000. *6689*

WORCESTER BUSINESS JOURNAL.
Worcester Publishing Ltd., 172 Shrewsbury St., Worcester, MA 01604. TEL 508-755-8004. FAX 508-755-8860. *1172*

THE WORD.
Three R Publications, 13 Bevington Rd., Oxford OX2 6NB, England. TEL 44-1865-57411.
circ. 10,000. *3161*

WORD (CINCINNATI).
Word Publications, Inc., 6895 Farmbrook, Cincinnati, OH 45230. TEL 513-231-9673.
circ. 50,000. *4173*

WORD OF LIFE QUARTERLY.
Word of Life Fellowship, Rte. 9, Schroon Lake, NY 12870. TEL 518-532-7111. FAX 518-532-7421.
circ. 50,000. *6104*

WORD OF MOUTH (SAN FRANCISCO).
c/o Delta Dental Plan of CA, Box 7736, San Francisco, CA 94120. TEL 415-972-8300.
circ. 9,000. *4657*

WORDPERFECT REPORT.
WordPerfect Corporation, 1555 N. Technology Way, Orem, UT 84057. TEL 801-225-5000. FAX 801-222-5077.
circ. 2,000,000. *1157*

WORKBOAT INTERNATIONAL.
Rushton Marine Press Ltd., Woodside, Burnhams Rd., Little Bookham, Leatherhead, Surrey KT23 3BA, England. TEL 44-1372-453316. FAX 44-1372-459974.
circ. 6,500. *6853*

WORKERS EDUCATION JOURNAL.
Central Board for Workers Education, 1400 West High Court, Gokulpeth, Nagpur 440010, India.
circ. 2,000. *2403*

WORKING MOMS AND DADS.
Corporate Marketing and Publishing Inc., Box 12217, Tucson, AZ 85732-2217. TEL 520-790-4044.
circ. 25,000. *1780*

THE WORKMEN'S CIRCLE - ARBITER RING CALL.
Workmen's Circle, 45 E. 33 St., New York, NY 10016. TEL 212-898-6800. FAX 212-532-7518.
circ. 30,000. *2915*

WORLD AEROSPACE TECHNOLOGY.
Sterling Publications Ltd., 86-88 Edgware Rd., London W2 2YW, England. TEL 01-258-0066. *81*

THE WORLD & I.
News World Communications, Inc. 3600 New York Ave.. N.E., Washington, DC 20002. TEL 202-635-4000. FAX 202-269-9353.
circ. 3,523. *3242*

WORLD BROADCAST NEWS.
Intertec Publishing Corp., 9800 Metcalf, Overland Park, KS 66212-2215. TEL 913-341-1300. FAX 913-967-1898.
circ. 12,500. *1975*

WORLD FEDERATION FOR MENTAL HEALTH. ANNUAL REPORT.
World Federation for Mental Health, Sheppard & Enoch Pratt Hospital, Box 6815, Baltimore, MD 21285-6815. TEL 410-938-3180. FAX 410-938-3183.
circ. 4,000. *5887*

WORLD INDUSTRIAL REPORTER.
Keller International Publishing Corporation, 150 Great Neck Rd., Great Neck, NY 11021. TEL 516-829-9210. FAX 516-829-7265.
circ. 40,093. *4348*

WORLD M & A NETWORK.
International Executive Reports, Ltd., 717 D St., N.W., Ste. 300, Washington, DC 20004-2807. TEL 202-628-7767. FAX 202-628-6618.
circ. 15,000. *971*

WORLD OF CHABAD.
Lubavitch British Columbia, 5750 Oak St., Vancouver, BC V6M 2V9, Canada. TEL 604-266-1313. FAX 604-263-7934.
circ. 6,000. *2915*

WORLD OUTLOOK.
Baptist Men's Movement, Kingsley, Pontesbury, Shrewsbury, Shrops. SY5 0QH, England. TEL 44-1743-790377.
circ. 1,200. *6165*

WORLD PEACEMAKERS QUARTERLY.
World Peacemakers Inc., 11427 Scottsbury Terr., Germantown, MD 20876-6010. TEL 202-265-7582.
circ. 1,000. *5718*

WORLD STUDENT NEWS.
International Union of Students, 17th November St., P.O. Box 58, 11001 Prague 01, Czech Republic. *2383*

WORLD VISION.
World Vision, Box 9716, Federal Way, WA 98063-9716. TEL 206-815-1000. FAX 206-815-3445.
circ. 100,651. *6165*

WORLD WATER AND ENVIRONMENTAL ENGINEERING.
Faversham House Group Ltd., Faversham House, 232a Addington Rd., South Croydon, Surrey CR2 8LE, England. TEL 44-181-651-7100. FAX 44-181-651-7117.
circ. 9,997. *6982*

WORLD WIDE BARACA - PHILATHEA NEWS.
World Wide Baraca-Philathea Union, Tower House, Mt. Vernon, VA 22121-9999. TEL 703-780-9806.
circ. 600. *5104*

WORLD'S CHILDREN.
Save the Children Fund, Mary Datchelor House, 17 Grove Ln., London SE5 8RD, England. TEL 44-171-703-5400. FAX 44-171-703-2278.
circ. 200,000. *1780*

WORTHING GUARDIAN.
Worthing Guardian Series, 56a Chapel Rd., Worthing, W. Sussex BN11 0HJ, England. TEL 44-1903-209025. FAX 44-1903-201481.
circ. 102,000. *3161*

WPROST.
Agencja Wydawniczo-Reklamowa "Wprost", sp. z o.o. Ul. Grunwaldzka 104, 60-307 Poznan, Poland. TEL 48-61-599371. FAX 48-61-668097.
circ. 350,000. *3207*

WRITERS GUILD OF AMERICA, EAST. NEWSLETTER.
Writers Guild of America, East, Inc., 555 W. 57th St., New York, NY 10019. TEL 212-767-7800.
circ. 3,500. *4287*

WRITER'S N W.
Media Weavers 24450 N.W Hansen Rd., Hillsboro, OR 97124. TEL 503-621-3911.
circ. 75,000. *6011*

THE WRITING INSTRUCTOR.
T W I (The Writing Instructor), University of Southern California, THH 440 - MC 0354, Los Angeles, CA 90089-0354. TEL 213-740-3744. FAX 213-741-0377.
circ. 1,000. *4287*

WUQUF.
Edition Wuquf, Postfach 130652, 20106 Hamburg, Germany.
circ. 300. *3376*

WYOMING. DEPARTMENT OF ADMINISTRATION AND INFORMATION. STATE LIBRARY. ANNUAL REPORT DIGEST.
Department of Administration and Information, State Library, Supreme Court Bldg., Cheyenne, WY 82002. TEL 307-777-7281. FAX 307-777-6289. *5928*

WYOMING AGRICULTURE.
Wyoming Farm Bureau Federation, 406 S. 21st St., Box 1348, Laramie, WY 82070. TEL 307-745-4835. FAX 307-721-7790.
circ. 8,000. *164*

WYOMING MINERAL YEARBOOK.
Department of Commerce, Division of Economic and Community Development, 1601 Yellowstone Rd., Cheyenne, WY 82002. TEL 307-777-7284. FAX 307-777-5840.
circ. 1,000. *2268*

WYOMING RURAL ELECTRIC NEWS.
Wyoming Rural Electric Association, Box 380, Casper, WY 82602. TEL 307-234-6152. FAX 307-234-4115.
circ. 31,332. *2572*

X C.
B_A Group Ltd., 5-8 Hardwick St., London EC1R 4PB, England. TEL 44-171-278-7711. FAX 44-171-278-6246.
circ. 100,000. *3968*

X S.
Gold Coast Publishing, Box 14426, Ft. Lauderdale, FL 33302. TEL 305-356-4943. FAX 305-356-4949.
circ. 45,000. *3242*

XAVIER REVIEW.
Xavier University of Louisiana, Box 110C, New Orleans, LA 70125. TEL 504-483-7304. FAX 504-486-2385.
circ. 300. *4288*

XEROX DISCLOSURE JOURNAL.
Xerox Corporation, Xerox Square 05B, Rochester, NY 14644. TEL 716-423-3255.
circ. 500. *5346*

XIANDAI FAXUE.
Xiandai Faxue Zazhishe Chongqing, Sichuan 630031, People's Republic of China. TEL 0811-9861199.
circ. 50,000. *3870*

XIUCI XUEXI.
Fudan University Press, 220 Handan Rd., Shanghai 200433, People's Republic of China. TEL 86-21-5492222. FAX 86-21-5491875.
circ. 300. *4124*

XTRA!
Pink Triangle Press, 491 Church St., Ste. 200, Toronto, ON M4Y 2C6, Canada. TEL 416-925-6665. FAX 416-925-6574.
circ. 37,000. *3538*

Y A B A FRAMEWORK.
Young American Bowling Alliance, 5301 S. 76th St., Greendale, WI 53129. TEL 414-421-4700. FAX 414-421-1301.
circ. 25,000. *6519*

YALE UNIVERSITY. ECONOMIC GROWTH CENTER. THREE YEAR REPORT.
Yale University, Economic Growth Center, Box 208269, New Haven, CT 06520-8269. TEL 203-432-3610. FAX 203-432-3898. *972*

YAMAGUCHI UNIVERSITY. SCHOOL OF MEDICINE. BULLETIN.
Yamaguchi Daigaku, Igakubu, Kogushi, Ube-shi 755, Japan. *4545*

YARD AND GARDEN.
Johnson Hill Press, Inc. 1233 Janesville Ave., Ft. Atkinson, WI 53538. TEL 414-563-6388. FAX 414-563-6388.
circ. 26,000. *3069*

YEON-GU WEOLBO.
Jeon la Bug-do Gyo Yug Yeon Gu Won, Jeon Ju, S. Korea.
circ. 2,500. *2384*

YINGSHI WENXUE.
Shandong Sheng Yingshi Zhizuo Zhongxin, No. 55, Wenhua Donglu, Jinan, Shandong 250014, People's Republic of China. TEL 86-0531-657715.
circ. 8,000. *4289*

YORK JOURNAL OF CONVOCATION.
Convocation of York, c/o Synodal Secretary, Church House, West Walls, Carlishe CA3 8UE, England.
circ. 400. *6104*

YOU AND YOUR BUSINESS.
Thomas J. Martin, Ed. & Pub., 383 S. Broadway, Hicksville, NY 11801. TEL 516-681-2111. *1581*

YOUNG ARCHAEOLOGIST.
Council for British Archaeology, Bowes Morell House, 111 Walmgate, York YO1 2UA, England. TEL 44-1904-671417. FAX 44-1904-671384.
circ. 1,400. *379*

YOUNG ISRAEL VIEWPOINT.
National Council of Young Israel, 3 W. 16th St, New York, NY 10011. TEL 212-929-1525. FAX 212-727-9526.
circ. 40,000. *5718*

YOUNG MEN'S INSTITUTE. INSTITUTE JOURNAL.
Young Men's Institute, 50 Oak St., San Francisco, CA 94102. TEL 415-621-4948. FAX 415-621-0963.
circ. 4,500. *6104*

YOUNG PEOPLE NOW.
National Youth Agency, 17-23 Albion St., Leicester LE1 6GD, England. TEL 44-116-285-6789. FAX 44-116-247-1043.
circ. 5,000. *6399*

YOUNG TELEGRAPH.
Two-Can Publishing, 346 Old St., London EC1V 9NQ, England. TEL 44-171-613-3376. FAX 44-171-613-3372.
circ. 1,300,000. *1813*

YOUR CHURCH.
Christianity Today, Inc., 465 Gundersen, Carol Stream, IL 60188-2498. TEL 708-260-6200. FAX 708-260-0114.
circ. 153,000. *6105*

YOUR HEALTH.
British Columbia Lung Association, 2675 Oak St., Vancouver, BC V6H 2K2, Canada. TEL 604-731-5864. FAX 604-731-5810.
circ. 19,500. *4892*

YOUR ILLINOIS F F A.
Illinois F F A, Box 50, Roanoke, IL 61561. TEL 309-923-7413. FAX 309-923-7618.
circ. 17,000. *164*

YUCA BOLETIN INFORMATIVO.
Centro Internacional de Agricultura Tropical, Apdo. Aereo 6713, Cali, Colombia. TEL 57-2-4450000. FAX 57-2-4450273.
circ. 2,200. *164*

Z A B S REVIEW.
Bureau of Standards, P.O. Box RW 50259, Lusaka, Zambia. TEL 260-1-227171.
circ. 500. *5019*

Z M P D. KWARTALNY BIULETYN INFORMACYJNY.
Zrzeszenie Miedzynarodowych Przewoznikow Drogowych, Grojecka 17, 02-021 Warsaw, Poland. *6863*

ZAJEDNICAR.
Croatian Fraternal Union of America, 100 Delaney Dr., Pittsburgh, PA 15235. TEL 412-351-3909. FAX 412-823-1594.
circ. 40,000. *2916*

ZAKENAUTO.
Misset Postbus 4, 7000 BA Doetinchem, Netherlands. TEL 31-8340-49911. FAX 31-8340-43839.
circ. 174,000. *6807*

ZAMBIA. MINISTRY OF AGRICULTURE AND WATER DEVELOPMENT. LAND USE BRANCH. SOIL SURVEY REPORT.
Ministry of Agriculture and Water Development, Land Use Branch, c/o Soil Survey Unit, Mount Makulu Research Station, Private Bag 7, Chilanga, Zambia. TEL 260-1-278087. *246*

ZAMBIA LAW JOURNAL.
University of Zambia, School of Law, P.O. Box 32379, Lusaka, Zambia. FAX 260-1-254408.
circ. 300. *3871*

ZEITBUEHNE.
Magazin-Verlag Zachl, Lederergasse 67, A-4021 Linz, Austria. TEL 07252-67133. FAX 07252-68228.
circ. 10,000. *1247*

ZEITSCHRIFT FUER VERKEHRSERZIEHUNG.
Rot-Gelb-Gruen Lehrmittel GmbH, Theodor-Heuss-Str. 3, 38122 Braunschweig, Germany. TEL 0531-809070. FAX 0531-8090721.
circ. 5,000. *6828*

ZERO ONE.
Zero One Publications, 39 Minford Gardens, W. Kensington, London W14 0AP, England.
circ. 600. *3161*

ZGODA.
Polish National Alliance of North America, 6100 N. Cicero Ave., Chicago, IL 60646-4385. TEL 312-286-0500. FAX 312-286-0842.
circ. 72,200. *2916*

ZHIYE YU JIANKANG.
Tianjin Institute of Industrial Hygiene and Occupational Diseases, 221 Ma Chang Rd., Hexi District, Tianjin 300204, People's Republic of China. TEL 3283432.
circ. 100,000. *5980*

ZHONGGUO FANGZHI.
China National Textile Council, General Office, Rm. 302, 105 Jiangxi Zhonglu, Shanghai 200002, People's Republic of China. TEL 3233411.
circ. 20,000. *6689*

ZHONGHUA LAODONG WEISHENG ZHIYEBING ZAZHI.
Tianjin Institute of Industrial Hygiene and Occupational Diseases, 211 Ma Chang Rd., Hexi District, Tianjin 300204, People's Republic of China. TEL 86-22-3280264.
circ. 400. *5260*

ZHONGWEN XINXI.
Zhongguo Zhongwen Xinxi Xuehui, P.O. Box 263, Chendu Keji Daxue - Chengdu University of Science and Technology, Chengdu , Sichuan Province, People's Republic of China. TEL 028-581554.
circ. 5,000. *4036*

ZIMBABWE. COTTON RESEARCH INSTITUTE. ANNUAL REPORT.
Ministry of Lands, Agriculture and Rural Resettlement, Research and Specialist Services, P.O. Box 8108, Causeway, Zimbabwe.
circ. 300. *246*

ZIMBABWE RESEARCH INDEX.
Scientific Liaison Office, P.O. Box CY 294, Causeway, Harare, Zimbabwe. TEL 263-4-700573. FAX 263-4-728799.
circ. 500. *6305*

ZINBVN.
Kyoto University, Institute for Research in Humanities, Ushinomiya-cho, Yoshida, Sakyo-ku, Kyoto 606, Japan. *3631*

ZONE OUTAOUAIS.
Communications Zone Outaouais, 38 Laval, Hull PQ J8X 3G7, Canada. TEL 819-777-5538. FAX 819-777-5585.
circ. 20,000. *3127*

ZONTIAN.
Zonta International, 557 W. Randolph St., Chicago, IL 60661-2206. TEL 312-930-5848. FAX 312-930-0951.
circ. 36,000. *7013*

ZUERCHER OBERLAENDER.
Zuercher Oberlaender, Rapperswilerstr. 1, CH-8620 Wetzikon, Switzerland. TEL 01-9333333. FAX 01-9323232.
circ. 800. *3220*

ZUKUENFTE.
Klartext Verlag, Dickmannstr. 2-4, 45143 Essen, Germany. TEL 49-201-8620658. FAX 49-201-8620622.
circ. 2,000. *6670*

2 X 4.
Editions C.R. Inc., P.O. Box 1010, Victoriaville, PQ G6P 8Y1, Canada. TEL 819-752-4243. FAX 819-758-8812.
circ. 7,959. *3040*

4 WHEEL DRIVE.
Foerlags AB Albinsson & Sjoeberg, P.O. Box 529, S-371 23 Karlskrona, Sweden. TEL 46-455-335325. FAX 46-455-311715.
circ. 23,000. *6807*

20 - 20.
Canadian Table Tennis Association, 1600 James Naismith Dr., Gloucester, ON K1B 5N4, Canada. TEL 613-748-5675. FAX 613-748-5705.
circ. 3,000. *6519*

33 METAL PRODUCING.
Penton Publishing 1100 Superior Ave., Cleveland, OH 44114. TEL 216-696-7000. FAX 216-696-8765.
circ. 22,000. *4980*

40 PLUS.
Trustar Ltd., 2020 Universite, 20th Fl., Montreal, PQ H3A 2A5, Canada. TEL 514-383-3400. FAX 514-383-1766.
circ. 600. *3298*

1590 BROADCASTER.
1590 Broadcasting Corp., 502 W. Hollis St., Box 548, Nashua, NH 03061. TEL 603-889-1590. FAX 603-883-4344.
circ. 63,500. *1975*

This User's Guide refers exclusively to the U.S. Newspaper Section of Volume 5, which contains a comprehensive listing of general-interest daily and weekly newspapers published in the United States. *Subject-oriented newspapers* from the United States, and *all* newspapers from the rest of the world are subject-classified are listed in the CLASSIFIED LIST OF SERIALS, Volumes 1-3 of **Ulrich's**.

This volume is arranged in several sections: DAILY NEWSPAPERS, detailed citations of daily newspapers filed alphabetically by state, city, and newspaper name; WEEKLY NEWSPAPERS, detailed citations of weekly newspapers filed alphabetically by state, city, and name; TITLE INDEX; DAILY NEWSPAPERS INDEX, WEEKLY NEWSPAPERS INDEX, GEOGRAPHIC INDEX, and CESSATIONS INDEX.

This User's Guide is separated into three divisions for ease of use: I) Section Descriptions, II) Full Entry Content Description, and III) Alphabetizing Rules for Main Entry Title.

Section Descriptions

DAILY NEWSPAPERS

This section comprises active U.S. general-interest newspapers that are published four or more days per week. All titles are active and are arranged alphabetically by state, city, and newspaper name. A (▼) appears in front of new titles that began publication in 1994, 1995 or 1996.

WEEKLY NEWSPAPERS

This section comprises active U.S. general-interest newspapers that are published three or less days per week. All titles are active and are arranged alphabetically by state, city, and newspaper name. A (▼) appears in front of new titles that began 1994, 1995 or 1996.

TITLE INDEX

The TITLE INDEX is a major point of access to the newspapers contained in Volume 5 of **Ulrich's**. Only U.S.-based general-interest daily and weekly newspaper titles listed in Volume 5 are included in this index; the titles of other types of serials, as well as titles of subject-specific newspapers from the U.S. and all categories of newspapers from the rest of the world, can be found in the main TITLE INDEX in Volume 4 of **Ulrich's**.

The TITLE INDEX lists all current and ceased newspapers in this directory. The city and state of publication appear in parentheses next to the newspaper title. Boldface type indicates the page number where the complete entry can be found in Volume 5.

Prior to using the TITLE INDEX, a user should become familiar with title alphabetizing rules as described in the "Alphabetizing Rules for Main Entry Title" paragraphs of this User's Guide on p. liii. Newspapers with identical titles are sorted alphabetically by their two-letter state abbreviation. A (▼) appears in front of titles that began publication in 1994, 1995 or 1995. A dagger (†) appears in front of titles known to have ceased publication. No page references are listed for ceased titles, as full entries for such titles do not appear in this directory.

DAILY NEWSPAPER INDEX

The DAILY NEWSPAPER INDEX is a subset of the TITLE INDEX. Daily newspapers are segregated and listed alphabetically by title. The city and state of publication appear in parentheses next to the daily newspaper title. **Boldface** type indicates the page number where the complete entry can be found in Volume 5. Newspapers with identical titles are sorted alphabetically by their two-letter state abbreviation. A (▼) appears in front of titles that began publication in 1994, 1995 or 1996. A dagger (†) appears in front of titles known to have ceased publication. No page references are listed for ceased titles, as full entries for such titles do not appear in this directory.

WEEKLY NEWSPAPER INDEX

The WEEKLY NEWSPAPER INDEX is a subset of the TITLE INDEX. Weekly newspapers are segregated and listed alphabetically by title. The city and state of publication appear in parentheses next to the weekly newspaper title. **Boldface** type indicates the page number where the complete entry can be found in Volume 5. Newspapers with identical titles are sorted alphabetically by their two-letter state abbreviation. A (▼) appears in front of titles that began publication in 1994, 1995 or 1996. A dagger (†) appears in front of the titles known to have ceased publication. No page references are listed for ceased titles, as full entries for such titles do not appear in this directory.

GEOGRAPHIC INDEX

All daily and weekly newspaper titles are sorted alphabetically by state. The city name appears in parentheses following each title. **Boldface** type indicates the page number where the complete entry will be found in Volume 5. A (▼) appears in front of titles that began publication in 1994, 1995 or 1996. A dagger (†) appears in front of titles known to have ceased publication. No page references are listed for ceased titles, as full entries for such titles do not appear in this directory.

CESSATION INDEX

In this section, titles of newspapers known to have ceased publication are listed alphabetically by title. The city name appears in parentheses following each title. No page references are listed, as full citations for these titles do not appear in this directory.

Full Entry Content Description

Basic Information

The following items are mandatory for listing and appear in all entries: country code, main entry title, frequency of publication, address, and owner name. Other items listed are not mandatory and are also briefly described below.

Country Code

The country code is centered in the top line over each entry. The only country code appearing is "US" which is the country code for the United States.

ISSN

The ISSN for the main entry title is printed immediately following the country code. Not all publications have been assigned an ISSN, and lack of a number does not render a publication ineligible for listing.

Title Information

The main title is printed in boldfaced, uppercased lettering as the first item of an entry. Titles are listed alphabetically within their respective states and cities. Former titles, if known, are given at the end of an entry; they are preceded by a boldfaced notation "**Formerly:**."

A (▼) printed before the title indicates that the title began publishing in 1994, 1995 or 1996.

Year First Published

The year first published is given if provided by the publisher.

Frequency

The frequency of a publication is given in abbreviated form, such as "d." for daily, "w." for weekly. For newspapers published less than seven days per week, the days of the week the newspaper is published are given, if known. Abbreviations for frequency notations are listed in the "General Abbreviations" on p. liv.

Price

The price is listed in U.S. dollars. The price may be given for annual subscriptions, per copy, per month, in state, out of county, and so forth. There may be several price structures, depending on the information received from the publisher.

Address, Telephone and Fax Numbers, E-mail and Web Site Addresses

The location address, telephone and fax number, e-mail address and Uniform Resource Locator (URL), if available, are listed in each entry.

Owner Information

The name of the owner of a newspaper is listed. Usually the owner address, telephone, and fax number are also listed. Occasionally there will be more than one owner listed. The owner address may differ from the location address. This information is preceded by the boldfaced notation "**Owner(s):.**"

Editor

One name is given, preceded by the notation "Ed." This person may be the Editor-in-Chief, the Managing Editor, or another high-ranking editor. Advanced degrees and titles are omitted; the absence of a title does not mean the editor does not have one.

Publisher

One name is given preceded by the notation "Pub." Advanced degrees and titles are omitted; the absence of a title does not mean the publisher does not have one.

Advertising

If advertising is accepted or included, and no advertising contact name or advertising rate have been provided by the publisher, the abbreviation "adv." prints in the entry.

Advertising Rate and Contact Name

When provided by the publisher, an advertising contact name and/or display rate are listed. The name is preceded by the words "adv. contact:." The price is preceded by the words "adv. rate:."

Special Features

A listing of special features may include such items as book reviews or photos.

Publication Size

If known, the trim size of the newspaper is listed. The size, such as "tabloid" will be preceded by the words "pub. size:."

Circulation

All circulation figures used are approximate. Circulation is given only if provided by the publisher. Various types of circulations may be noted, such as "paid," "free," or "controlled." There may be more than one circulation figure and more than one type of circulation listed. If the type of circulation is not known, only the circulation figure will be listed. All circulation data are preceded by the notation "circ." If the circulation figures are known to pertain to either Sunday, evening, or morning circulation, or a combination thereof, such information is noted.

Wire Services

If a newspaper is known to use one or more news or photo wire services, abbreviations or names of the services are listed in the entry. Such information is preceded by the boldfaced words "**Wire Service(s):**." Abbreviations for wire services used are listed in the "General Abbreviations" on p. liv.

Alphabetizing Rules for Main Entry Title

Titles are filed in strict alphabetical order, without regard to acronyms, abbreviations, or spaces; for example:

> *Saint Louis* before *St. Louis*
>
> *Newport Daily News* before *New Rochelle Standard-Star*
>
> *St. Louis News* between *Stillwater Gazette* and *Stockton Record*.

Hyphenated titles will sort before unhyphenated titles; for example:

> *News-Tribune* before *News Advance* and *News Tribune*

Articles at the beginning of titles are omitted, or are bypassed in filing.

In an index, when two or more titles with the same name are listed, the titles will sort alphabetically on the two-letter state abbreviations.

SAMPLE ENTRY

❶ ALASKA

❷ KODIAK

❸ US   ❹ ISSN 0740-2112

❺ **KODIAK DAILY MIRROR.**   ❻ 1940.   ❼ Mon.-Fri.   ❽ $.50 newsstand; $8/mo. local.
❾ 1419 Selig St., Kodiak, AK 99615.   ❿ TEL 907-486-3227;   ⓫ FAX 907-486-3088.
⓬ E-mail: nfreeman@dailymirror.com   ⓭ **Owner(s):** Kodiak Publishing Co., Inc., 1419 Selig St., Kodiak, AK 99615, TEL 907-486-3227;   ⓮ Ed. Andy Hall;   ⓯ Pub. Nancy Freeman;
⓰ adv. contact: Amy Willis.   ⓱ adv. rate: $12.50/SAU;   ⓲ photos;
⓳ pub. size: tabloid;   ⓴ circ. evening, 3,000 (paid) Sun. 3,000 (paid).   ㉑ **Wire service(s):** AP.
㉒ **Formerly:** Kodiak Mirror

KEY

❶ State
❷ City
❸ Country Code
❹ ISSN
❺ Title
❻ First Published
❼ Frequency
❽ Price
❾ Address
❿ Telephone
⓫ Fax
⓬ E-mail
⓭ Owner(s)
⓮ Editor
⓯ Publisher
⓰ Advertising Contact
⓱ Advertising Rate
⓲ Special Features
⓳ Publication Size
⓴ Circulation
㉑ Wire Service(s)
㉒ Former Title(s)

Abbreviations
General Abbreviations and Special Symbols

3/mo.	3x/month	KNT	Knight News-Tribune News Service
3/yr.	3x/year	KR	Knight-Ridder
a.	annual	LAT-WP	Los Angeles Times-Washington Post News Service
abstr.	abstracts	LDE	London Daily News
adv.	advertising	Ln.	Lane
aft.	afternoon	LT	Times of London
am	a.m.	m.	monthly
AP	Associated Press	Mar.	March
API	Allied Press International	May	May
approx.	approximately	MG	Manchester Guardian
Apr.	April	Mgr.	Manager
assn.	association	mktg.	marketing
Asst.	Assistant	Mng.	Managing
Aug.	August	MNS	Massachusetts News Service
Ave.	Avenue	mo.	month
bi-m.	every 2 months	Mon.	Monday
bi-w.	biweekly	morn.	morning
bibl.	bibliography	mult.	multiple
Bldg.	Building	N	National News Service
Blvd.	Boulevard	N.	North
BPS	Black Press Service	NEA	Newspaper Enterprises Association
BUP	British United Press	NENS	New England News Service
BW	Business Wire	NNS	Newhouse News Service
c/o	care of	Nov.	November
CanP	Canadian Press	NWS	National Weather Service
CaNS	Catholic News Service	NYT	New York Times
CiNS	City News Service	Oct.	October
circ.	circulation	ONS	Ottawa News Service
CN	Capital News	P	Pacific News Service
CNS	Copley News Service	pg.	page
col.	column	Pkwy.	Parkway
contr.	controlled	Pl.	Place
CQ	Congressional Quarterly Service	Plz.	Plaza
CSM	Christian Science Monitor	pm	p.m.
CST	Chicago Sun Times	Pres.	President
CT-NYT	Chicago Tribune-New York Times	pub.	publication
CUP	Canadian United Press	Pub.	Publisher
cy.	county	q.	quarterly
d.	daily	Rd.	Road
Dec.	December	RN	Reuters News Agency
deliv.	delivered, delivery	Rte.	Route
Dept.	Department	s-a.	twice annually
Dir.	Director	s-m.	twice monthly
DJ	Dow Jones	s-w.	twice weekly
E.	East	S.	South
ea.	each	Sat.	Saturday
Ed.	Editor	SAU	Standard Advertising Unit
exc.	except	SC	Southern News Service
Expy.	Expressway	Sep.	September
Feb.	February	SHNA	Scripps-Howard Newspaper Alliance
Field	Field News Service (formerly Chicago Daily News Sun Times)	St.	Street
		Ste.	Suite
Fl.	Floor	Sun.	Sunday
fortn.	fortnightly	Thu.	Thursday
Fri.	Friday	Tue.	Tuesday
Gen.	General	UPI	United Press International
GNS	Gannett News Service	W.	West
HHS	Hearst Headline Service	w.	weekly
hr.	hour	wd.	word
Hwy.	Highway	Wed.	Wednesday
in.	inch	WIP	Washington International Report
IPN	International Photo News	wk.	week
irreg.	irregularly	WN	World News
ITNA	Independent Television News Association, Inc.	WNS	Women's News Service
Jan.	January	WWD	Women's Wear Daily
Jct.	Junction	yr.	year
Jul.	July	†	denotes ceased title
Jun.	June	▼	denotes newly published title
KNS	Knight News Service		

United States Abbreviations

AK	Alaska		NY	New York
AL	Alabama		OH	Ohio
AR	Arkansas		OK	Oklahoma
AZ	Arizona		OR	Oregon
CA	California		PA	Pennsylvania
CO	Colorado		RI	Rhode Island
CT	Connecticut		SC	South Carolina
DC	District of Columbia		SD	South Dakota
DE	Delaware		TN	Tennessee
FL	Florida		TX	Texas
GA	Georgia		UT	Utah
HI	Hawaii		VA	Virginia
IA	Iowa		VT	Vermont
ID	Idaho		WA	Washington
IL	Illinois		WI	Wisconsin
IN	Indiana		WV	West Virginia
KS	Kansas		WY	Wyoming
KY	Kentucky			
LA	Louisiana			
MA	Massachusetts			
MD	Maryland			
ME	Maine			
MI	Michigan			
MN	Minnesota			
MO	Missouri			
MS	Mississippi			
MT	Montana			
NC	North Carolina			
ND	North Dakota			
NE	Nebraska			
NH	New Hampshire			
NJ	New Jersey			
NM	New Mexico			
NV	Nevada			

Canadian Province Abbreviations

AB	Alberta
BC	British Columbia
MB	Manitoba
NB	New Brunswick
NF	Newfoundland
NS	Nova Scotia
NT	NW Territory
ON	Ontario
PE	Prince Edward Is and
PQ	Quebec
SK	Saskatchewan
YT	Yukon Territory

Daily Newspapers

ALABAMA

ALEXANDER CITY

US   ISSN 0738-5110

ALEXANDER CITY OUTLOOK. 1892. Tue.-Sat. $.50 newsstand; $96/yr. in cy.; $102/yr. out of cy. 548 Cherokee Rd., Alexander City, AL 35010. TEL 205-234-4281; FAX 205-234-6550. **Owner(s):** Tallapoosa Publishers, Inc., P.O. Box 999, Alexander City, AL 35010. TEL 205-234-4281; Ed. K.A. Turner; Pub. Bruce Wallace; adv. contact: Billy McGhee. photos; pub. size: broadsheet; circ morning 6,200(paid); Sun. 6,200(paid). **Wire Service(s):** AP.

ANDALUSIA

US

ANDALUSIA STAR NEWS. Tue.-Sat. $.50 newsstand; $21/3 mos. in cy.; $24/3 mos. out of cy. 207 Dunson St., Andalusia, AL 36420. TEL 334-222-2402; FAX 334-222-6597. **Owner(s):** Boone Newspapers, Inc., P.O. Box 2370, Tuscaloosa, AL 35403. TEL 407-338-3298; Ed. Greg Mc Cord; Pub. Bill Beckner; adv. contact: Ruck Ashworth. pub. size: broadsheet; circ. morning 6,500(paid).

ANNISTON

US

ANNISTON STAR. 1883. d. $.50/day newsstand; $1/Sun.; $10/mo. carrier. 216 W. Tenth St., Anniston, AL 36201. TEL 205-236-1551; FAX 205-231-0027. **Owner(s):** Consolidated Publishing Co., 216 W. Tenth St., Anniston, AL 36201. TEL 205-236-1551; FAX 205-231-0027; Ed. H. Brandt Ayers; Pub. H. Brandt Ayers; adv. contact: Ken Warren. photos; bk.rev.; pub. size: broadsheet; circ. evening 31,500(paid); Sun. 35,000(paid). **Wire Service(s):** AP, NYT, KRT.

ATHENS

US   ISSN 0739-1307

NEWS-COURIER. 1880. Tue.-Fri. & Sun. $.35/day newsstand; $1/Sun.; $50/yr.; $26.50/26 wks. Houston & Green Sts., Athens, AL 35611. TEL 205-232-2720; FAX 205-233-7753. **Owner(s):** News-Courier, Inc., P.O. Drawer 190, Cullman, AL 35056. TEL 205-232-2720; Ed. Sonny Turner; Pub. Robert Bryan; adv. contact: Belinda Williams. pub. size: broadsheet; circ. morning 8,479(paid); Sun. 8,479(paid). **Wire Service(s):** AP.

BIRMINGHAM

US   ISSN 0899-0050

BIRMINGHAM NEWS. 1888. d. $.35/day newsstand; $1.25/Sun.; $123.60/yr. local; $248.40/yr. out of state. 2200 Fourth Ave., N, Birmingham, AL 35203. TEL 205-325-2222; FAX 205-325-2283. **Owner(s):** Newhouse Newspapers, 1101 Connecticut Ave., N.W., Washington, DC 20036. TEL 202-383-7800; Ed. James E. Jacobson; Pub. Victor H. Hanson, II; adv. contact: Bil Ward. photos; bk.rev.; pub. size: broadsheet circ. morning 160,364(paid); Sun. 207,490(paid). **Wire Service(s):** AP, NNS, KNS, CSM.

US   ISSN 1040-1571

BIRMINGHAM POST-HERALD. 1870. Mon.-Fri. $.35 newsstand; $54/yr. 2200 Fourth Ave., N., Birmingham, AL 35203. TEL 205-325-2222; FAX 205-325-2410; E-mail: postherald@aol.com; URL: http://www.postherald.com. **Owner(s):** Scripps-Howard, 312 Walnut St., 26th Fl., Cincinnati, OH 45202. TEL 513-977-3000; Ed. Jim Willis. adv. contact: Bill Ward. photos; bk.rev.; pub. size: broadsheet; circ. evening 60,857(paid). **Wire Service(s):** AP, SHNS, NYT.

CULLMAN

US

CULLMAN TIMES. 1901. d. $.35/day newsstand; $1.25/Sun.; $52/yr. in cy.; $80.88/yr. out of cy. $46.80/yr. senior citizens. 300 Fourth Ave., S.E., Cullman, AL 35056. TEL 205-734-2131; FAX 205-737-1020. **Owner(s):** Robert Bryan, 300 Fourth Ave., S.E., Cullman, AL 35055. TEL 205-734-2131; FAX 205-737-1020; Ed. David Poynor; Pub. Robert Bryan; adv. contact: Robert Camp. pub. size: broadsheet; circ. morning 11,759(paid); Sun. 12,939(paid). **Wire Service(s):** AP.

DECATUR

US

DECATUR DAILY. 1912. d. $.25/day newsstand; $1.25/Sun.; $108/yr. 201 First Ave., S.E., Decatur, AL 35601. TEL 205-353-4612; FAX 205-340-2366. **Owner(s):** Tennessee Valley Printing Co., Inc.; Ed. Barrett C. Shelton, Jr.; Pub. Barrett C. Shelton, Jr.; photos; bk.rev.; pub. size: broadsheet; circ. evening 31,000(paid); Sun. 32,000(paid). **Wire Service(s):** AP, NYT, SHNA.

DOTHAN

US

DOTHAN EAGLE. d. $.50/day newsstand; $1.25/Sun. 227 N. Oates, Dothan, AL 36302. TEL 205-792-3141; FAX 205-712-7975. **Owner(s):** Thomson Newspapers, Inc., One Station Pl., Stamford, CT 06902. TEL 203-428-2500; Ed. Terry Conner; Pub. Paul P. Seveska; adv. contact: Fred Ellison. photos; pub. size: standard; circ. evening 33,000(paid); Sun. 38,000(paid). **Wire Service(s):** AP.

ENTERPRISE

US

ENTERPRISE LEDGER. 1898. Sun.-Fri. $.50/day newsstand; $1.25/Sun.; $123/yr. 106 N. Edwards St., Enterprise, AL 36330. TEL 205-347-9533; FAX 205-347-0825. **Owner(s):** Thomson Newspapers, Inc., 3150 Des Plaines Ave., Des Plaines, IL 60014. TEL 708-299-5544; Pub. Mark Cullen; adv.; pub. size: broadsheet; circ. morning 9,471(paid); Sun. 10,800(paid).

FLORENCE

US   ISSN 0743-1511

TIMES DAILY. 1869. d. $.50/day newsstand; $1.50/Sun.; $126/yr. 219 W. Tennesee St., Florence, AL 35630. TEL 205-766-3434; FAX 205-740-4717; E-mail: timesdly@timesdaily.com; URL: http://www.timesdaily.com/tdnewspa.html. **Owner(s):** New York Times Co., The, 229 W. 43rd St., New York, NY 10036. TEL 212-556-1234; Ed. Kathy Silverberg; Pub. Frank Hellderman; adv. contact: Tim Thompson. pub. size: broadsheet; circ. morning 34,000(paid); Sun. 36,000(paid). **Wire Service(s):** UPI.

FORT PAYNE

US

TIMES-JOURNAL, THE. 1879. Tue.-Sat. $.50/day newsstand; $.75/Sat. & Sun.; $55/yr. 811 Greenhill Blvd., Fort Payne, AL 35967. TEL 205-845-2550; FAX 205-845-7459. **Owner(s):** Southern Newspapers, Inc., 1050 Wilcrest Dr., Houston, TX 77042. TEL 713-266-5481; Ed. William Bynum; Pub. Ben Shurett; adv. contact: Sharon Kyle. pub. size: broadsheet; circ. evening 6,500(paid). **Wire Service(s):** AP.

GADSDEN

US

GADSDEN TIMES. 1867. d. $.50/day newsstand; $1.25/Sun.; $8.41/mo. 401 Locust, Gadsden, AL 35901. TEL 205-549-2000; FAX 205-549-2105. **Owner(s):** New York Times Co., The, 229 W. 43rd St., New York, NY 10036. TEL 212-556-1234; Ed. Ron Reeves; Pub. Roger Hawkins; pub. size: broadsheet; circ. morning 30,000(paid); evening 30,637; Sun. 33,005. **Wire Service(s):** AP, NYT.

HUNTSVILLE

US

HUNTSVILLE TIMES, THE. 1910. d. $.25/day newsstand; $1.25/Sun. newsstand; $10.50/mo. carrier; $126/yr.; $72/yr. Sun. 2317 Memorial Pkwy., S., Huntsville, AL 35801. TEL 205-532-4000; FAX 205-532-4420; E-mail: jdestel@travellers.com; URL: http://www.htimes.com. **Owner(s):** Newhouse Newspapers, 1101 Connecticut Ave., N.W., Washington, DC 20036. TEL 202-383-7800; Ed. Melinda Joiner. adv. contact: William Joyner, Jr. photos; bk.rev.; pub. size: broadsheet; circ. evening 60,000(paid); Sun. 83,000(paid). **Wire Service(s):** AP, LAT-WP, NNS, KR.

JASPER

US   ISSN 0893-0759

JASPER DAILY MOUNTAIN EAGLE. 1872. Sun.-Fri. $.35/day newsstand; $.75/Sun.; $9/mo. 1301 Viking Dr., Jasper, AL 35501. TEL 205-221-2840; FAX 205-221-2421. **Owner(s):** Cleveland Newspapers, Inc., Cleveland, TN; Ed. Steve Cox; Pub. R. Douglas Pearson, Jr.; adv.; photos; bk.rev.; pub. size: broadsheet; circ. evening 14,200(controlled & paid). **Wire Service(s):** AP.

LANETT

US

VALLEY TIMES-NEWS. 1950. Mon.-Fri. $.50 newsstand; $5.50/mo. 220 N. 12th St., Lanett, AL 36863. TEL 334-644-1101; FAX 334-644-5587. **Owner(s):** Valley Newspapers, Inc., 220 N. 12th St., Lanett, AL 36863. TEL 205-644-1101; Ed. Cy Wood; Pub. Cy Wood; adv. contact: Bridge Turner. pub. size: broadsheet; circ. evening 15,000(free & paid). **Wire Service(s):** AP.

Formerly: Lanett Valley Times-News.

MOBILE

US

MOBILE REGISTER, THE. 1932. d. $.50/day newsstand; $1/Sun.; $9.95/mo. carrier. 304 Government St., Mobile, AL 36602. TEL 334-433-1551; FAX 334-434-8662; E-mail: mobile.eds@dibbs.com; URL: http://www.mobileregister.com. **Owner(s):** Newhouse Publishing, Inc., Syracuse, NY 13321; Ed. Mike Marshall; Pub. Howard Bronson; adv. contact: Larry Wooley. photos; pub. size: broadsheet; circ. morning 110,000(paid); Sun. 128,000(paid). **Wire Service(s):** CST, NNS, AP, LAT-WP, SHNA, KNT.

MONTGOMERY

US   ISSN 0892-4457

MONTGOMERY ADVERTISER. 1827. d. $.35 newsstand; $117/yr. 200 Washington Ave., Montgomery, AL 36101-1000. TEL 334-262-1611; FAX 334-261-1505. **Owner(s):** Gannett Company, Inc., 1100 Wilson Blvd., Arlington, VA 22340. TEL 703-284-6000; Ed. Jim Tharpe; Pub. Richard Amberg, Jr.; adv. contact: Leo Pieri. photos; bk.rev.; pub. size: broadsheet; circ. morning 65,000(paid); Sun. 85,000(paid). **Wire Service(s):** AP, KR, SHNA.

Formerly: Advertiser, The.

OPELIKA

US   ISSN 1044-7539

OPELIKA-AUBURN NEWS. 1903. Sun.-Fri. $.35/day newsstand; $1/Sun.; $101.75/yr. 3505 Pepperell Pkwy., Opelika, AL 36801. TEL 334-749-6271; FAX 334-749-6271. **Owner(s):** Thomson Newspapers, Inc., 3150 Des Plaines Ave., Des Plaines, IL 60018. TEL 708-299-5544; Ed. Phil Lucas; Pub. Steven McPhaul; adv. contact: Jack Nolan. pub. size: broadsheet; circ. morning 14,000(paid); Sun. 15,800(paid). **Wire Service(s):** AP.

SCOTTSBORO

US

DAILY SENTINEL, THE. 1887. Tue.-Fri. & Sun. $69/yr. 701 Veterans Hwy., Scottsboro, AL 35768. TEL 205-259-1020; FAX 205-259-2709. **Owner(s):** Scottsboro Newspapers, Inc., 701 Veterans Hwy., Scottsboro, AL 35768. TEL 205-259-1020; Ed. Carmen Wann; Pub. Anita F. Bynum; photos; bk.rev.; pub. size: broadsheet; circ. evening 7,000(paid); Sun. 7,500(paid).

SELMA

US   ISSN 1043-9129

SELMA TIMES-JOURNAL. 1827. d. $.50/day newsstand; $1.25/Sun.; $14/yr. mailed. 1018 Water Ave., Selma, AL 36701. TEL 334-875-2110; FAX 334-872-4588. **Owner(s):** Selma Newspapers, Inc., 1018 Water Ave., Selma, AL 36701. TEL 205-875-2110; Ed. Chuck Chandler; Pub. E. Wilson Koeppel; adv. contact: George Turner. photos; bk.rev.; pub. size: broadsheet; circ. morning 9,257(paid); Sun. 9,798(paid). **Wire Service(s):** AP.

TALLADEGA

US   ISSN 1059-6461

DAILY HOME. 1867. d. $10.50/mo. in cy.; $9.50/mo. in state, $10.50/mo. out of state. 4 Sylacauga Hwy., Talladega, AL 35160. TEL 205-362-1000; FAX 205-249-4315. **Owner(s):** Consolidated Publishing Co., P.O. Box 977, Talladega, AL 35161. TEL 205-362-1000; Ed. Carol Pappas; Pub. Ed Fowler, Jr.; adv. contact: Pam Adamson. pub. size: standard; circ. evening 10,000(free & paid); Sun. 41,400(free & paid). **Wire Service(s):** AP.

TROY

US   ISSN 1044-0070

MESSENGER, THE. 1866. Tue.-Fri. & Sun. $.50/day newsstand; $1.70/Sun.; $84/yr. 918 S. Brundidge St., Troy, AL 36081. TEL 334-566-4270; FAX 334-566-4281; E-mail: troymssngr@aol.com. **Owner(s):** Troy Publications, Inc., P.O. Box 727, Troy, AL 36081. TEL 205-566-4281; Ed. Chris Day; Pub. Rick Reynolds; adv. contact: DeeDee Carter. pub. size: broadsheet; circ. morning 5,000(paid); Sun. 5,000(paid).

Formerly: Troy Messenger.

TUSCALOOSA

US

TUSCALOOSA NEWS, THE. 1818. d. $.50/day newsstand; $1.50/Sun.; $11.25/mo. 2001 Sixth St., Tuscaloosa, AL 35402. TEL 205-345-0505; FAX 205-349-0802. **Owner(s):** New York Times Co., The, 229 W. 43rd St., New York, NY 10036. TEL 212-556-1234; Ed. Ben Windham; Pub. Ron Sawyer; adv. contact: Bob Gruber. pub. size: broadsheet; circ. morning 40,316(paid); Sun. 40,929(paid). **Wire Service(s):** AP, NYT.

ALASKA

ANCHORAGE

US   ISSN 0194-6870

ANCHORAGE DAILY NEWS. 1946. d. $.50/day newsstand; $1.50/Sun.; $12.50/mo. Sun. mailed; $30/mo. mailed; $135/yr. carrier. 1001 Northway Dr., Anchorage, AK 99508. TEL 907-257-4200; FAX 907-258-2157; E-mail: 74220.2560@compuserve.com; URL: http://www.adn.com/. **Owner(s):** McClatchy Newspapers, P.O. Box 15779, Sacramento, CA 95852. TEL 916-321-1000; FAX 916-321-1869; Ed. Patrick Dougherty; Pub. Fuller A. Cowell; adv. contact: Dave Kuta. bk.rev.; pub. size: broadsheet; circ. morning 81,562(paid); Sun. 93,785(paid). **Wire Service(s):** Cox, AP, SHNA.

FAIRBANKS

US   ISSN 8750-5495

FAIRBANKS DAILY NEWS-MINER. 1903. d. $.50/day newsstand; $1.50/Sun.; $18.50/mo. mailed; $221/yr. mailed; $13.75/mo. 200 N. Cushman St., Fairbanks, AK 99701. TEL 907-456-6661; FAX 907-452-7917. **Owner(s):** Media News Group, 4888 Loop Central Dr., Ste. 525, Houston, TX 77081-2211. TEL 713-295-3800; Ed. Kelly Bostian; Pub. Paul J. Massey; adv. contact: Marilyn Romano. pub. size: broadsheet; circ. morning 20,000(paid); Sun. 25,000(paid). **Wire Service(s):** AP, NYT, McClatchey.

JUNEAU

US

JUNEAU EMPIRE. 1912. Sun.-Fri. $.50 newsstand; $52.50/3 mo. 2nd class; $49.50/mo. 1st class. 3100 Channel Dr., Juneau, AK 99801. TEL 907-586-3740; FAX 907-586-3740. **Owner(s):** Morris Communications, 3100 Channel Dr., Juneau, AK 99801. TEL 907-586-3740; Ed. Suzanne Downing; Pub. John A. Winters; adv. contact: Robin H. Paul. pub. size: broadsheet; circ. evening 7,500(paid). **Wire Service(s):** AP, KR, LAT-WP.

KENAI

US

PENINSULA CLARION. 1970. Mon.-Fri. $.50 newsstand; $78/yr. 150 Trading Bay Rd., Kenai, AK 99611. TEL 907-283-7551; FAX 907-283-3299. **Owner(s):** William Morris, III, P.O. Box 3009, Kenai, AK 99611. TEL 907-283-7551; Ed. Lori Evans; Pub. William Morris, III; adv. contact: Michelle Glaves. pub. size: tabloid; circ. morning 5,500(paid). **Wire Service(s):** AP.

KETCHIKAN

US

KETCHIKAN DAILY NEWS. 1936. Mon.-Sat. $.75 newsstand; $92/yr. local. 501 Dock St., Ketchikan, AK 99901. TEL 907-225-3157; FAX 907-225-1096. **Owner(s):** Pioneer Printing Co., 501 Dock St., Ketchikan, AK 99901. TEL 907-225-3157; Ed. Belinda Chase; Pub. Tena Williams; adv.; pub. size: broadsheet; circ. 5,823(paid). **Wire Service(s):** AP. Formerly: Ketchikan Log.

KODIAK

US   ISSN 0740-2112

KODIAK DAILY MIRROR. 1940. Mon.-Fri. $.50 newsstand; $8/mo. local. 1419 Selig St., Kodiak, AK 99615. TEL 907-486-3227; FAX 907-486-3088. **Owner(s):** Kodiak Publishing Co., Inc., 1419 Selig St., Kodiak, AK 99615. TEL 907-486-3227; Ed. Cecil Ranney; Pub. Nancy Freeman; adv. contact: Laurie Skonberg. photos; pub. size: tabloid; circ. evening 3,000(paid). **Wire Service(s):** AP.

SITKA

US

DAILY SITKA SENTINEL. 1939. Mon.-Fri. $.50 newsstand; $80/yr. local. 112 Barracks St., Sitka, AK 99835. TEL 907-747-3219; FAX 907-747-8898. **Owner(s):** Verstovia Corp., 112 Barracks St., Sitka, AK 99835. TEL 907-747-3219; Ed. Thad Poulson; Pub. Thad Poulson; adv. contact: Catherine Bagley. pub. size: broadsheet; circ. evening 2,965(paid). **Wire Service(s):** AP.

AMERICAN SAMOA

PAGO PAGO

US

SAMOA NEWS. 1969. Mon.-Fri. $200/yr. in country; $400/yr. out of country. P.O. Box 999, Pago Pago, AS 96799. TEL 684-533-5599; FAX 684-633-4854. **Owner(s):** Samoa News, P.O. Box 999, Pago Pago, AS 96799; Pub. Lewis Wolman; adv.; photos; bk.rev.; pub. size: tabloid; circ. morning 2,500(paid). **Wire Service(s):** AP, PAC News.

ARIZONA

BISBEE

US

BISBEE DAILY REVIEW. Sun.-Fri. $.50 newsstand; $105.60/yr. 12 Main St., Bisbee, AZ 85603-0127. TEL 520-432-2231; FAX 520-432-2356. **Owner(s):** Wick Communications, Inc., 333 Wilcox Dr., Ste. 302, Sierra Vista, AZ 85635. TEL 520-458-0200; Ed. John Moeur; Pub. Walter Wick; adv.; photos; bk.rev.; pub. size: broadsheet; circ. 1,300(paid).

BULLHEAD CITY

US   ISSN 1061-8589

MOHAVE VALLEY DAILY NEWS. 1926. Sun.-Fri. $.50 newsstand; $21.39/3 mos. home deliv.; $35.09/6 mos. senior citizens. P.O. Box 21209, Bullhead City, AZ 86439-8589. TEL 520-763-2505; FAX 520-763-7820. **Owner(s):** Brehm Communications, Inc., 17065 Via del Campo, Ste. 200, San Diego, CA 92127. TEL 619-451-6200; Ed. Darryle Purcell; Pub. Martin Cody; adv. contact: Steve Paterson. photos; bk.rev.; pub. size: broadsheet; circ. morning 9,200(paid); Sun. 8,500(paid). **Wire Service(s):** AP. Formerly: Bullhead City Mohave Valley News.

CASA GRANDE

US

CASA GRANDE DISPATCH. 1912. Mon.-Sat. $175/yr. in state; $195/yr. out of state. 200 W. Second St., Casa Grande, AZ 85222. TEL 602-836-7461. **Owner(s):** Casa Grande Valley Newspapers, Inc., Box 15002, Casa Grande, AZ 85230-5002. TEL 602-836-7461; Ed. Donovan Kramer, Jr.; Pub. Donovan M. Kramer, Sr.; adv. contact: Kara Bugbee. pub. size: broadsheet; circ. morning 9,027(paid); evening 9,027(paid). **Wire Service(s):** AP

CHANDLER

US   ISSN 0746-1445

CHANDLER ARIZONAN TRIBUNE. 1912. d. $.50/day newsstand; $1.75/Sun.; $10/mo. carrier. 25 S. Arizona Pl., Ste. 565, Chandler, AZ 85225. TEL 602-821-7474; FAX 602-821-7480. **Owner(s):** Cox Arizona Publications, 120 W. First Ave., Mesa, AZ 85210. TEL 602-898-6500; Ed. Susan Keaton; Pub. Sandy Schwartz; adv. contact: Tim Thomas. photos; pub. size: broadsheet; circ. morning 11,000(paid); Sun. 11,000(paid). **Wire Service(s):** AP; LAT-WP, NYT.

DOUGLAS

US

DOUGLAS DISPATCH. 1902. d. $.35/day newsstand; $.50/Sun.; $60.80/yr. 530 11th St., Douglas, AZ 85607. TEL 602-364-3424; FAX 602-364-6750. **Owner(s):** Wick Communications, Inc., 333 W. Wilcox Dr., Ste. 302, Sierra Vista, AZ 85635. TEL 602-458-0200; Ed. Sharilyn Cox; Pub. Sharilyn Cox; adv.; pub. size: broadsheet; circ. evening 16,800(free & paid); Sun. 5,900(free & paid). **Wire Service(s):** AP.

FLAGSTAFF

US   ISSN 1054-9536

ARIZONA DAILY SUN. 1883. d. $216/yr. 417 W. Santa Fe Ave., Flagstaff, AZ 86001. TEL 602-774-4545; FAX 602-773-1934. **Owner(s):** Flagstaff Publishing Co., P.O. Box 1849, Flagstaff, AZ 86002. TEL 602-774-4545; Ed. Mike Patrick; Pub. Don Rowley; adv. contact: Theresa Givens. photos; pub. size: broadsheet; circ. evening 13,222(paid); Sun. 14,792(paid). **Wire Service(s):** AP.

Dailies

GILBERT

US

GILBERT TRIBUNE. 1990. d. $.50/day newsstand; $1.75/Sun. 655 N. Gilbert Rd., Ste. 160, Gilbert, AZ 85234. TEL 602-898-5610; FAX 602-545-9241. **Owner(s):** Cox Arizona Publications, 120 W. First Ave., Mesa, AZ 85210. TEL 602-898-6500; FAX 602-898-6463; Ed. Jim Ripley; Pub. Sanford Schwartz; pub. size: broadsheet; circ. morning 5,007(paid). **Wire Service(s):** AP, LAT-WP, SHNS, NYT.

KINGMAN

US

KINGMAN DAILY MINER. 1883. Sun.-Fri. $.50/day newsstand; $1/Sun.; $6.50/mo. 3015 Stockton Hill Rd., Kingman, AZ 86401. TEL 520-753-6397; FAX 520-753-5661. **Owner(s):** Western Newspapers, Inc., P.O. Box 3909, Yuma, AZ 85365. TEL 602-753-6397; Ed. Tim Wiederaenders; Pub. Kit K. Atwell; adv.; pub. size: broadsheet; circ. morning 8,600(paid); evening 8,600(paid); Sun. 9,000(paid). **Wire Service(s):** AP.

LAKE HAVASU CITY

US   ISSN 1068-1884

LAKE HAVASU CITY HERALD. 1964. Tue.-Fri & Sun. $.50/day newsstand; $.75/Sun.; $62/yr. in cy.; $120/yr. out of cy. 2225 W. Acoma Blvd., Lake Havasu City, AZ 86403. TEL 520-855-2197; FAX 520-855-2637. **Owner(s):** Wick Communications, Inc., P.O. Box 1271, Yuma, AZ 85366. TEL 520-783-3311; Ed. Stan Usinowicz; Pub. Mike Quinn; pub. size: standard; circ. 13,500(paid).

US   ISSN 1068-1876

TODAY'S DAILY NEWS-HERALD. 1980. Tue.-Fri. & Sun. $.50/day newsstand; $.75/Sun.; $62/yr. in state; $120/yr. out of state. 2225 W. Acoma Blvd., Lake Havasu City, AZ 86403. TEL 520-855-6397; FAX 520-855-7447. **Owner(s):** Wick Communications, Inc., 333 W. Wilcox Dr., Ste. 302, Sierra Vista, AZ 85635; Western Newspapers, Inc., 290 S. First Ave., Ste. 4, Yuma, AZ 85364. TEL 520-783-3311; Ed. Stan Usinowicz; Pub. Michael Quinn; adv. contact: Kingsley Gerlach. pub. size: broadsheet; circ. morning 13,500(paid); Sun. 13,500(paid). **Wire Service(s):** AP.

Formerly: Lake Havasu City/Today's Daily News.

MESA

US

MESA TRIBUNE. d. $.50/day newsstand; $1.75/Sun.; $96/yr. 120 W. First Ave., Mesa, AZ 85210. TEL 602-898-6500; FAX 602-898-6362; E-mail: coxtrib@prodigy.com. **Owner(s):** Cox Enterprises, Inc., P.O. Box 105357, Atlanta, GA 30348. TEL 404-843-5000; Ed. Jeff Bruce; Pub. Sanford Schwartz; photos; bk.rev.; pub. size: broadsheet; circ. morning 103,516(paid); Sun. 106,757(paid). **Wire Service(s):** AP, LAT-WP, SHNS, NYT.

PHOENIX

US   ISSN 0892-8711

ARIZONA REPUBLIC. 1889. d. $.50/day newsstand; $2/Sun.; $3.50/wk. 200 E. Van Buren St., Phoenix, AZ 85004. TEL 602-271-8000; FAX 602-271-8044. **Owner(s):** Phoenix Newspapers, Inc., P.O. Box 1950, Phoenix, AZ 85001. TEL 602-271-8000; Ed. Pam Johnson; Pub. John Oppedahl; adv. contact: Jeanne Bonham. photos; bk.rev.; pub. size: standard; circ. morning 399,830(paid); Sun. 597,255(paid). **Wire Service(s):** AP, NYT, LAT-WP, KR.

US   ISSN 1064-8321

PHOENIX GAZETTE. 1880. d. $.35/day newsstand; $2/Sun. 120 E. Van Buren, Phoenix, AZ 85004. TEL 602-271-8000; FAX 602-271-8911. **Owner(s):** Phoenix Newspapers, Inc., 200 E. Van Buren St., Phoenix, AZ 85004. TEL 602-271-8000; FAX 602-271-8911; Ed. Pam Johnson. adv. contact: Cathy Davis. pub. size: broadsheet; circ. evening 87,355(paid); Sun. 587,919(paid). **Wire Service(s):** AP, LAT-WP, KR, NYT.

PRESCOTT

US

DAILY COURIER, THE. 1882. Sun.-Fri. $.50/day newsstand; $1.25/Sun.; $9.11/mo. home deliv. 147 N. Cortez, Prescott, AZ 86301. TEL 602-445-3333. **Owner(s):** Western Newspapers, Inc., 147 N. Cortez, Prescott, AZ 86301. TEL 602-445-3333; Ed. Jim Garner; Pub. Bob Gilliland; adv. contact: Pam Hood. adv.: $11.85/SAU Mon.-Fri.; $13.04/SAU Sun. photos; bk.rev.; pub. size: broadsheet; circ. evening 17,001(paid); Sun. 19,023(paid). **Wire Service(s):** AP, LAT-WP.

Formerly: Courier.

SCOTTSDALE

US   ISSN 0888-0271

SCOTTSDALE PROGRESS TRIBUNE. 1948. d. $.35/day newsstand; $1.50/Sun.; $1.85/home deliv. 7525 E. Camelback Rd., Ste. 100, Scottsdale, AZ 85251. TEL 602-941-2300; FAX 602-970-2360. **Owner(s):** Cox Arizona Publications, 120 W. First Ave., Mesa, AZ 85210. TEL 602-898-6500; Ed. Hal DeKeyser; Pub. Sanford Schwartz; adv. contact: Kristi Kollman. photos; bk.rev.; pub. size: broadsheet; circ. evening 18,979(paid). **Wire Service(s):** AP, LAT-WP, SHNS, NYT.

Formerly: Progress Tribune.

SIERRA VISTA

US   ISSN 8750-3891

SIERRA VISTA HERALD. 1956. Sun.-Fri. $.50/day newsstand; $1.25 Sun.; $8.80/mo. home deliv. 102 Fab Ave., Sierra Vista, AZ 85635. TEL 520-458-9440; FAX 520-459-0120. **Owner(s):** Wick Communications, Inc., 333 W. Wilcox Dr., Ste. 302, Sierra Vista, AZ 85635. TEL 602-458-0200; Pub. Bob Wick; adv. contact: Dennis Benth. pub. size: standard; circ. evening 10,500(paid); Sun. 18,000(paid). **Wire Service(s):** AP.

SUN CITY

US

DAILY NEWS-SUN. 1957. Mon.-Sat. $.50 newsstand; $91.20/yr. home deliv.; $125/yr. mailed. 10102 Santa Fe Dr., Sun City, AZ 85351. TEL 602-977-8351; FAX 602-876-3695. **Owner(s):** Ottaway Newspapers, Inc., P.O. Box 401, Campbell Hall, NY 10916. TEL 914-294-8181; Ed. Maryanne Leyshon; Pub. Sam L. Marocco; adv. contact: Jan McKinney. adv.: $11.50/SAU. pub. size: broadsheet; circ. evening 21,200(paid). **Wire Service(s):** AP, ONS.

TEMPE

US   ISSN 0744-2092

TEMPE DAILY NEWS TRIBUNE. 1887. d. $.50/day newsstand; $1.75/Sun.; $10/mo. carrier. 51 W. Third St., Ste. 106, Tempe, AZ 85281. TEL 602-898-5680; FAX 602-968-8030. **Owner(s):** Cox Arizona Publications, 120 W. First Ave., Mesa, AZ 85210. TEL 602-898-6500; Ed. Jim Ripley; Pub. Sanford Schwartz; pub. size: broadsheet; circ. morning 13,659(paid). **Wire Service(s):** AP, SHNA, LAT-WP, CNS.

TUCSON

US

ARIZONA DAILY STAR. 1877. d. $.50/day newsstand; $1.50/Sun.; $2.90/wk.; $150.80/yr.; $299/yr. mailed. 4850 S. Park Ave., Tucson, AZ 85714-1637. TEL 602-573-4220; FAX 602-573-4107. **Owner(s):** Star Publishing Co., 4850 S. Park Ave., Tucson, AZ 85714. TEL 602-573-4220; Ed. Bobbie Jo Buel; Pub. Michael E. Pulitzer; adv. contact: Paul Ingegneri. pub. size: broadsheet; circ. morning 98,793(paid); Sun. 174,987(paid). **Wire Service(s):** AP, NYT, KR.

US   ISSN 0888-5478

TUCSON CITIZEN. 1870. Mon.-Sat. $.35 newsstand; $3.50/wk.; $6.50/mo.; $78/yr. mailed; $182/yr. out of city. 4850 S. Park Ave., Tucson, AZ 85714. TEL 602-573-4561; FAX 602-573-4569; E-mail: tcnew@aol.com. **Owner(s):** Gannett Company, Inc., 1100 Wilson Blvd., Arlington, VA 22234. TEL 703-284-6000; Ed. Ricardo Pimentel; Pub. C. Donald Hatfield; adv. contact: Sam Adkins. photos; bk.rev.; pub. size: broadsheet; circ. evening 60,000(paid). **Wire Service(s):** AP, LAT-WP, GNS.

YUMA

US ISSN 1048-2237

YUMA DAILY SUN. 1872. d. $.50/day newsstand; $1.25/Sun.; $98/mo. 2055 S. Arizona Ave., Yuma, AZ 85364. TEL 602-783-3333; FAX 602-343-1009; E-mail: yumasun@primenet.com; URL: http://www.primenet.com/~yumasun. **Owner(s):** Cox Enterprises, Inc., P.O. Box 4689, Atlanta, GA 30302. TEL 404-526-5541; Ed. Terry L. Ross; Pub. Sam Pepper; adv. contact: Jerry Collins. photos; pub. size: broadsheet; circ. evening 27,500(paid); Sun. 34,700(paid). **Wire Service(s):** AP.

ARKANSAS

ARKADELPHIA

US

ARKADELPHIA DAILY SIFTINGS HERALD. 1886. Mon.-Fri. $.50 newsstand; $60/yr. in town; $66/yr. rural. 205 S. 26th St., Arkadelphia, AR 71923. TEL 501-246-5525; FAX 501-246-6556. **Owner(s):** Stephens Group, Inc., P.O. Box 1359, Fort Smith, AR 72910. TEL 501-785-7810; Ed. Steve Fellers; Pub. Judith Collis; adv. contact: Lois Baker. pub. size: broadsheet; circ. evening 3,980(paid). **Wire Service(s):** AP.

BATESVILLE

US ISSN 1076-4801

BATESVILLE GUARD. 1876. Mon.-Fri. $42/yr. 258 W. Main St., Batesville, AR 72501. TEL 501-793-2383; FAX 501-793-9268. **Owner(s):** Batesville Guard-Record Co., Inc., 258 W. Main St., Batesville, AR 72501; Ed. Jeff Porter; Pub. Pat Jones; adv. contact: Jim Kemp. pub. size: standard; circ. evening 9,500(paid). **Wire Service(s):** AP.

BENTON

US

BENTON COURIER. 1876. Mon.-Fri. $.35 newsstand; $5.25/mo.; $66/yr. mailed in state; $72/yr. mailed out of state. One Courier Pl., Benton, AR 72015. TEL 501-778-8228; FAX 501-776-1230. **Owner(s):** Hollinger International, Inc., 401 N. Wabash, Chicago, IL 60611. TEL 312-321-3000; Ed. Judy Smith; Pub. Rebecca H. Winburn; adv. contact: Carrol Powell. photos; bk.rev.; pub. size: broadsheet; circ. evening 9,800(paid). **Wire Service(s):** AP.

BENTONVILLE

US

BENTON COUNTY DAILY RECORD. 1886. d. $.25/day newsstand; $1/Sun.; $72/yr. mail. 104 S.W. A St., Bentonville, AR 72712. TEL 501-271-3700; FAX 501-273-7777. **Owner(s):** Community Publishers, Inc., P.O. Box 1049, Bentonville, AR 72712. TEL 501-271-3700; Ed. Kent Marts; Pub. Mike Brown; adv.; photos; bk.rev.; pub. size: broadsheet; circ. morning 9,500(paid); Sun. 10,500(paid). **Wire Service(s):** AP.

BLYTHEVILLE

US

COURIER NEWS. 1903. Sun.-Fri. $.50/day newsstand; $.50/Sun.; $7.95/mo. carrier; $75/yr.; $22.65/3 mos. mailed; $90.60/yr. N. Broadway & Moultrie, Blytheville, AR 72316. TEL 501-763-4461; FAX 501-763-6874. **Owner(s):** Tennyson Publishing, N. Broadway & Moultrie, Blytheville, AR 72316; Ed. Cynthia Jarden; Pub. David Tennyson; pub. size: broadsheet; circ. evening 5,500(paid); Sun. 5,500(paid). **Wire Service(s):** AP, NYT.

CAMDEN

US

CAMDEN NEWS. 1921. Mon.-Fri. $.35 newsstand; $75/yr. home deliv.; $90/yr. mail deliv.; $98/yr. out of cy. 113 Madison Ave., Camden, AR 71701. TEL 501-836-8192; FAX 501-837-1414. **Owner(s):** Camden News Publishing Co., 113 Madison Ave., Camden, AR 71701. TEL 501-836-8192; FAX 501-837-1414; Ed. Edward Waller; Pub. Walter E. Hussman, Jr.; adv. contact: Sue Parnell. photos; bk.rev.; pub. size: standard; circ. evening 5,000(paid). **Wire Service(s):** AP.

CONWAY

US

LOG CABIN DEMOCRAT. 1879. Sun.-Fri. $.35/day newsstand; $1/Sun.; $112/yr. out of cy. 1058 Front St., Conway AR 72032. TEL 501-327-6621; FAX 501-327-6787. **Owner(s):** Morris Communications, P.O. Box 936, Augusta, GA 30903. TEL 706-724-0851; Ed. David Keith; Pub. Mike Hengel; photos; pub. size: broadsheet; circ. evening 10,000(paid); Sun. 12,000(paid). **Wire Service(s):** AP.

DE QUEEN

US

DE QUEEN DAILY CITIZEN. 1933. Mon.-Fri. $.35 newsstand; $84/yr. 404 De Queen Ave., De Queen, AR 71832. TEL 501-642-2111; FAX 501-642-3138. **Owner(s):** De Queen Bee Co., P.O. Box 1000, De Queen, AR 71832. TEL 501-642-2111; Ed. Billy Ray McKelvy; Pub. Ray Kimball; adv. contact: Gail Mitchell. pub. size: broadsheet circ. evening 2,646(paid). **Wire Service(s):** AP, NEA.

EL DORADO

US

EL DORADO NEWS-TIMES. 1888. d. $.35/day newsstand; $1/Sun.; $23.25/3 mos. 111 N. Madison, El Dorado, AR 71730. TEL 501-862-6611; FAX 501-862-0054. **Owner(s):** Walter Husman Jr., 111 N. Madison, El Dorado, AR 71730. TEL 501-862-6611; Ed. George Arnold; Pub. Walter E. Hussman, Jr.; adv. contact: Karen Williams. pub. size: broadsheet; circ. morning 11,700(paid); Sun. 12,050(paid). **Wire Service(s):** AP.

FAYETTEVILLE

US SSN 1066-3355

FAYETTEVILLE NORTHWEST ARKANSAS TIMES. 1867. d. $72/yr. 212 N. East Ave., Fayetteville, AR 72701. TEL 501-442-1710; FAX 501-442-5477. **Owner(s):** American Publishing Co., 606 N. Van Buren, P.O. Box 520, Marion, IL 62959. TEL 618-993-1711; Pub. Rancy Cope; adv. contact: Kaye Hunton. pub. size: broadsheet; circ. morning 14,129(paid); Sun. 13,950(paid). **Wire Service(s):** AP.

FORREST CITY

US

FORREST CITY TIMES-HERALD. 1875. Mon.-Fri. $.35 newsstand; $4/mo. in cy; $4.40/mo. out of cy; $69.50/yr. local; $87.50/yr. elsewhere. 222 N. Izard St., Forrest City, AR 72335. TEL 501-633-3130; FAX 501-633-0599. **Owner(s):** Times-Herald Publishing, P.O. Box 1699, Forrest City, AR 72335. TEL 501-633-3130; Ed. Kersh Hall; Pub. Trent Bonner McCollum; adv. contact: Jim Wirski. pub. size broadsheet; circ. evening 4,750(paid). **Wire Service(s):** AP.

FORT SMITH

US

FORT SMITH SOUTHWEST TIMES RECORD. 1832. d. $8/mo. daily & Sun. 920 Rogers Ave., Fort Smith, AR 72901. TEL 501-785-7700; FAX 501-785-7741. **Owner(s)** Stephens Group, Inc., 920 Rogers Ave., Fort Smith, AR 72901. TEL 501-785-7700; Ed. Jerry Fruss; Pub. Gene Kincy; adv. contact: Ronnie Bell. pub. size: broadsheet; circ. morning 41,400(paid); Sun. 45,700(paid). **Wire Service(s):** AP.

HARRISON

US ISSN 1074-0384

HARRISON DAILY TIMES. 1876. Sun.-Fri. $80/yr. local; $89/yr. out of state. 111 W. Rush Ave., Harrison, AR 72601. TEL 501 741-2325; FAX 501-741-5632. **Owner(s):** American Publishing Co., 606 N. Van Buren, P.O. Box 520, Marion, IL 62959. TEL 618-993-1711; Ed. Dwain Lair; Pub. Jeff Christianson; adv. contact: Michelle Kennedy. pub. size: standard; circ. evening 11,500(paid); 2,000(paid). **Wire Service(s):** AP.

HELENA

US ISSN 8750-5274

HELENA DAILY WORLD. 1871. Sun.-Fri. $66/yr. 417 York St., Helena, AR 72342. TEL 501-338-9181; FAX 501-338-9184. **Owner(s):** American Publishing Co., 606 N. Van Buren, P.O. Box 520, Marion, IL 62959. TEL 618-993-1711; Ed. Larry Binz; Pub. Bill Lederman; adv. contact: Doris Freer. photos; bk.rev.; pub. size: broadsheet; circ. evening 4,010(paid); Sun. 4,216(paid). **Wire Service(s):** AP.

HOPE

US

HOPE STAR, THE. 1899. Mon.-Fri. $.50 newsstand; $63/yr. 522 W. Third St., Hope, AR 71801. TEL 501-777-8841. **Owner(s):** Newsco, Inc., 215 Mountain Dr., Ste. 101, Destin, FL 32541. TEL 904-837-4040; Ed. Pat Harris; Pub. Ronnie Cupstid; adv. contact: Richard Haycox. pub. size: broadsheet; circ. evening 5,068(paid). **Wire Service(s):** AP.

HOT SPRINGS

US

SENTINEL-RECORD, THE. 1876. d. $8.95/mo. 300 Spring, Hot Springs, AR 71901. TEL 501-623-7711; FAX 501-623-2984. **Owner(s):** Sentinel-Record, Inc., P.O. Box 580, Hot Springs, AR 71902. TEL 501-623-7711; FAX 501-623-2984; Pub. Walter E. Hussman, Jr.; adv. contact: F.E. Emerson. bk.rev.; pub. size: broadsheet; circ. morning 18,231(paid); Sun. 19,308(paid). **Wire Service(s):** AP.

JACKSONVILLE

US   ISSN 8750-7501

JACKSONVILLE PATRIOT. 1957. Mon.-Fri. $.25 newsstand; $29/yr. in cy.; $51/yr. out of cy.; $76/yr. out of state. 1108 B Main St., Jacksonville, AR 72076. TEL 501-982-6506; FAX 501-985-2054. **Owner(s):** Magie Enterprises, Inc., Cabot, AR 72023. TEL 501-843-3534; Ed. Cleo Beard; Pub. Cone Magie; adv. contact: Susie Magie. photos; pub. size: broadsheet; circ. evening 2,350(paid).
   Formerly: Jacksonville Daily News.

JONESBORO

US

JONESBORO SUN. 1903. d. $.35/day newsstand; $1/yr. Sun.; $8.50/mo. 518 Carson St., Jonesboro, AR 72401. TEL 501-935-5525; FAX 501-935-5823. **Owner(s):** Troutt Bros. Inc., 518 Carson, Jonesboro, AR 72401. TEL 501-935-5525; Ed. John Troutt, Jr.; Pub. John Troutt; adv. contact: Jerry P. Donohue. pub. size: broadsheet; circ. morning 26,900(paid); Sun. 31,000(paid). **Wire Service(s):** AP.

LITTLE ROCK

US   ISSN 1060-4332

ARKANSAS DEMOCRAT-GAZETTE. 1870. d. $.35/day newsstand; $1/Sun.; $10.75/mo.; $4.50/mo. Sun. Capitol Ave. & Scott St., Little Rock, AR 72201. TEL 501-378-3400; FAX 501-372-3908; E-mail: news@ardemgaz.com; URL: http://www.ardemgaz.com. **Owner(s):** Little Rock Newspapers, Inc., P.O. Box 2221, Little Rock, AR 72203. TEL 501-378-3400; Ed. Robert Lutgen; Pub. Walter Hussman, Jr.; adv. contact: John Mobbs. pub. size: broadsheet; circ. morning 181,126(paid); Sun. 299,172(paid). **Wire Service(s):** AP, TPNS, SHNA, NYT, KR, LAT-WP.

MAGNOLIA

US

BANNER-NEWS. 1878. d. $.35 newsstand; $71.40/yr. 134 S. Washington, Magnolia, AR 71753. TEL 501-234-5130; FAX 501-234-2551. **Owner(s):** Banner-News Publishing Co., P.O. Box 100, Magnolia, AR 71753. TEL 501-234-2551; Ed. Melissa Butler; Pub. Walter E. Hussman; adv. contact: Susan Carmichael. photos; pub. size: broadsheet; circ. evening 5,000(paid). **Wire Service(s):** AP.
   Formerly: Magnolia Banner-News.

MALVERN

US

MALVERN DAILY RECORD. 1916. Mon-Fri. $6.50/mo.; $78/yr.; $78/yr. mailed out of town. 219 Locust St., Malvern, AR 72104. TEL 501-337-7523; FAX 501-337-1226. **Owner(s):** American Publishing Co., 606 N. Van Buren, P.O. Box 520, Marion, IL 62959. TEL 618-993-1711; Ed. Steven Brawner; Pub. Ron Causey; adv.; photos; pub. size: standard; circ. evening 6,275(paid). **Wire Service(s):** AP.

MOUNTAIN HOME

US   ISSN 0745-7707

BAXTER BULLETIN. 1901. Mon.-Sat. $.50 newsstand; $68.64/yr. 16 W. Sixth St., Mountain Home, AR 72653. TEL 501-425-3133; FAX 501-425-5091. **Owner(s):** Gannett Company, Inc., P.O. Box 1688, Greenville, SC 29602; Ed. Linda Leicht; Pub. Betty Barker Smith; adv.; photos; bk.rev.; pub. size: broadsheet; circ. morning 9,900(paid). **Wire Service(s):** AP.
   Formerly: Mountain Home Baxter Bulletin.

US

DAILY NEWS. 1985. Mon.-Sat. $.35/day newsstand; $.50/Sun.; $55/yr. local. Hwy. 62, E., Mountain Home, AR 72653. TEL 501-425-6301; FAX 501-424-4488. **Owner(s):** Rupert & Sandra Phillips, 2720 Prosperity Ave., Fairfax, VA 22034-1000. TEL 703-560-4000; Ed. Joe Dobson; Pub. Chuck Pullins; adv. contact: Chuck Pullins. photos; bk.rev.; pub. size: broadsheet; circ. evening 2,000(paid); Sun. 2,000(paid). **Wire Service(s):** AP.
   Formerly: North Arkansas View-Daily News.

NEWPORT

US

NEWPORT DAILY INDEPENDENT. 1901. Mon.-Fri. $.50 newsstand; $6.75/mo. carrier; $40.50/6 mo. carrier. 2408 Hwy. 367, N., Newport, AR 72112. TEL 501-523-5855; FAX 501-523-6540. **Owner(s):** American Publishing Co., 606 N. Van Buren, P.O. Box 520, Marion, IL 62959. TEL 618-993-1711; Ed. Patricia Mays; Pub. Bill Park; adv. contact: Bill Park. photos; pub. size: broadsheet; circ. evening 3,202(paid). **Wire Service(s):** AP.

PARAGOULD

US

PARAGOULD DAILY PRESS. 1883. Tue.-Sun. $69/yr. 1401 W. Hunt St., Paragould, AR 72450. TEL 501-239-8562; FAX 501-239-8565. **Owner(s):** Paxton Media Group, Inc., P.O. Box 2300, Paducah, KY 42002. TEL 502-443-1771; Ed. Todd Nighswonger; Pub. David Mossesso; adv. contact: Dina Mason. pub. size: broadsheet; circ. evening 6,500(paid). **Wire Service(s):** AP.

PINE BLUFF

US

PINE BLUFF COMMERCIAL. 1881. d. $7.50/mo. 300 Beech St., Pine Bluff, AR 71601. TEL 501-534-3400; FAX 501-543-1455. **Owner(s):** Stephens Group, Inc., P.O. Box 1359, Fort Smith, AR 72902. TEL 501-785-7700; Ed. Byron Tate; Pub. Charles Berry; adv.; photos; bk.rev.; pub. size: broadsheet; circ. morning 22,500(paid); Sun. 22,500(paid). **Wire Service(s):** AP, KR.

RUSSELLVILLE

US   ISSN 1075-1866

COURIER, THE. 1874. Tue.-Sun. $.35/day newsstand; $1/Sun.; $7.95/mo. 201 E. Second St., Russellville, AR 72811. TEL 501-968-5252; FAX 501-968-4037. **Owner(s):** Paducah Newspapers, Inc., 408 Kentucky Ave., Paducah, KY 42002; Ed. Bill Newsom; Pub. Craig Martin; adv.; photos; bk.rev.; pub. size: broadsheet; circ. evening 11,862(paid); Sun. 14,846(paid). **Wire Service(s):** AP.

SEARCY

US   ISSN 0747-0401

DAILY CITIZEN. 1854. Sun.-Fri. $.50/day newsstand; $1/Sun.; $7.75/mo. 3000 E. Race Ave., Searcy, AR 72143. TEL 501-268-8621; FAX 501-268-6277. **Owner(s):** Paxton Media Group, Inc., P.O. Box 2300, Paducah, KY 42002. TEL 502-443-1771; FAX 502-442-8188; Ed. Tommy Jackson. adv. contact: Phil Weaver. photos; bk.rev.; pub. size: broadsheet; circ. evening 6,350(paid); Sun. 7,380(paid). **Wire Service(s):** AP.

SPRINGDALE

US   ISSN 1053-9689

MORNING NEWS OF NORTHWEST ARKANSAS. 1886. d. $.25/day newsstand; $1/Sun.; $72/yr. local. 2560 Lowell Rd., Springdale, AR 72765. TEL 501-751-6200; FAX 501-751-6209. **Owner(s):** D.R. Partners, Inc., P.O. Box 1350, Fort Smith, AR 72902. TEL 501-785-7801; Ed. Rusty Turner; Pub. Tom Stallbaumer; adv. contact: Kent Eikenberry. pub. size: broadsheet; circ. morning 33,000(paid); Sun. 36,000(paid). **Wire Service(s):** AP, LAT-WP, SHNA.
   Formerly: Morning News & Northwest Arkansas Morning News.

STUTTGART

US

STUTTGART DAILY LEADER. 1889. Mon.-Fri. $.50 newsstand; $51/yr. in cy.; $72/yr. out of cy. 111 W. Sixth St., Stuttgart, AR 72160. TEL 501-673-8533; FAX 501-673-3671. **Owner(s):** American Publishing Co., 606 N. Van Buren, P.O. Box 520, Marion, IL 62959. TEL 618-993-1711; Ed. William T. Bradow; Pub. Gene Austin; adv.; photos; pub. size: broadsheet; circ. evening 4,500(paid). **Wire Service(s):** AP.

WEST MEMPHIS

US

WEST MEMPHIS EVENING TIMES. 1931. Mon.-Fri. $.35 newsstand; $66/yr. in cy.; $72/yr. out of cy. 111 E. Bond St., West Memphis, AR 72301. TEL 501-735-1010; FAX 501-735-1020. **Owner(s):** West Memphis Evening Times, 111 E. Bond St., West Memphis, AR 72301. TEL 501-735-1010; Pub. Alexander P. Coulter; adv. contact: Bob Bruce. pub. size: broadsheet; circ. evening 9,547(paid). **Wire Service(s):** AP.

CALIFORNIA

ALAMEDA

US

ALAMEDA TIMES STAR. 1872. d. $2.90/wk. 1516 Oak St., Alameda, CA 94501. TEL 510-523-1200; FAX 510-748-0437. **Owner(s):** Alameda Publishing Corp., 116 W. Winton Ave., Hayward, CA 94544. TEL 510-521-1200; Ed. Thomas Tuttle; Pub. Thomas Tuttle; pub. size: broadsheet; circ. morning 6,908(paid). **Wire Service(s):** UPI, NYT, CNS, AP.

ANTIOCH

US

LEDGER DISPATCH. 1870. d. $.50/day newsstand; $1.25/Sun.; $9.05/mo. 1650 Cavallo Rd., Antioch, CA 94509. TEL 510-757-2525; FAX 510-706-2305. **Owner(s):** Knight-Ridder, Inc., One Herald Plz., Miami, FL 33132. TEL 305-376-3800; Ed. Bob Goll; Pub. George E. Riggs; adv.; photos; bk.rev.; pub. size: standard; circ. evening 22,950(paid); Sun. 23,533(paid). **Wire Service(s):** AP, McClatchy, NYT.
    Formerly: Daily Ledger-Post Dispatch.

AUBURN

US

AUBURN JOURNAL. 1856. Sun.-Fri. $.50/day newsstand; $.75/Sun.; $77.22/yr. carrier; $19.31/3 mos. senior citizens. 1030 High St., Auburn, CA 95603. TEL 916-885-5656; FAX 916-887-1231. **Owner(s):** Brehm Communications, Inc., 17065 Via del Campo, Ste. 200, San Diego, CA 92127. TEL 619-451-6200; Ed. Michael Ackley; Pub. Scott Little; adv. contact: Rhonda Blocker. pub. size: broadsheet; circ. morning 13,000(paid); Sun. 15,000(paid). **Wire Service(s):** AP.

BAKERSFIELD

US   ISSN 0276-5837

BAKERSFIELD CALIFORNIAN. 1866. d. $.50/day newsstand; $1.25/Sun; $12.50/mo.; $8/mo. Sat. & Sun. 1707 Eye St., Bakersfield, CA 93301. TEL 805-395-7500; FAX 805-395-7519. **Owner(s):** Bakersfield Californian Corp., 1707 Eye St., Bakersfield, CA 93301. TEL 805-395-7519; Ed. Mike Jenner; Pub. Ginger Moorhouse; photos; bk.rev.; pub. size: broadsheet; circ. morning 85,000(paid); Sun. 91,000(paid). **Wire Service(s):** AP.

BANNING

US   ISSN 0747-1521

BANNING RECORD GAZETTE. 1908. Mon.-Fri. $.35 newsstand; $5.75/mo. 218 N. Murray St., Banning, CA 92220. TEL 909-849-4586; FAX 909-849-2437. **Owner(s):** Record-Gazette, Inc., 218 N. Murray St., Banning, CA 92220. TEL 714-849-4586; Ed. Steve Tuckey; Pub. Charles Freeman; adv. contact: Steve Tuckey. pub. size: broadsheet; circ. evening 18,400(paid). **Wire Service(s):** AP.

BARSTOW

US

DESERT DISPATCH. 1910. Mon.-Sun. $.25/day newsstand; $.75/Sat.; $1.35 Sun.; $8.46/mo. 130 Coolwater Ln., Barstow, CA 92311. TEL 619-256-2257; FAX 619-256-0685. **Owner(s):** Freedom Communications, Inc., 1055 N. Main St., Ste. 901, Irvine, CA 92701. TEL 714-542-4415; Ed. Merrill McCarty; Pub. Maureen Saltzer; pub. size: broadsheet; circ. evening 8,000(paid). **Wire Service(s):** AP.
    Formerly: Barstow Desert Dispatch.

BENICIA

US

BENICIA HERALD. 1877. Tue.-Fri. & Sun. $.50 newsstand; $4.50/mo. carrier. 820 First St., Benicia, CA 94520. TEL 707-745-0733; FAX 707-557-6380. **Owner(s):** Gibson Publications, Inc., 820 First St., Benicia, CA 94510. TEL 707-745-0733; FAX 707-557-6330; Pub. David L. Payne; adv. contact: Sam Springer. photos; bk.rev.; pub. size: broadsheet; circ. morning 10,000(paid).

CHICO

US   ISSN 0746-5548

CHICO ENTERPRISE-RECORD. 1853. d. $.50/day newsstand; $1/Sun.; $8.58/mo. in town; $9.12/yr. motor carrier. 400 E. Park Ave., Chico, CA 95928. TEL 916-891-1234; FAX 916-342-3617. **Owner(s):** Stephens Group, Inc., P.O. Box 1350, Fort Smith, AR 72902. TEL 501-785-7815; Ed. Jack Winning; Pub. James Dimmitt; adv.; pub. size: broadsheet; circ. morning 31,000(paid). Sun. 33,500(paid). **Wire Service(s):** AP.

COSTA MESA

US

DAILY PILOT, THE. 1923. Mon.-Sat. $.25 newsstand; $22.50/mo. carrier. 330 W. Bay St., Costa Mesa, CA 92627-2020. TEL 714-642-4321; FAX 714-646-4170. **Owner(s):** Times-Mirror Co., Times Mirror Sq., Los Angeles, CA 90053. TEL 213-273-3700; Ed. Steve Marble; Pub. Tom Johnson; pub. size: broadsheet; circ. morning 45,000(paid).

US

ORANGE COAST DAILY PILOT. 1907. Mon.-Sat. $8.50/mo. mailed out of state. 330 W. Bay St., Costa Mesa, CA 92627. TEL 714-642-4321; FAX 714-646-4170. **Owner(s):** Orange Coast Daily Pilot, Inc., 330 W. Bay St., P.O. Box 1560, Costa Mesa, CA 92626. TEL 714-642-4321; Ed. Steve Marble; Pub. Tom Johnson; adv.; pub. size: broadsheet; circ. 48,700(paid). **Wire Service(s):** AP.

CRESCENT CITY

US   ISSN 1056-9510

DEL NORTE TRIPLICATE. 1879. Tue.-Sat. $.35/day newsstand; $.50/Sat.; $54/yr. carrier. 312 H St., Crescent City, CA 95531. TEL 707-464-2141; FAX 707-464-5102. **Owner(s):** Western Communications, Inc., 1526 N.W. Hill St., Crescent City, CA 95531. TEL 707-464-2141; Ed. John Pritchett; Pub. Geoffrey T. White; adv. contact: Patty Leonard. photos; pub. size: broadsheet; circ. morning 6,900(paid). **Wire Service(s):** AP.

DANVILLE

US

SAN RAMON VALLEY TIMES, THE. 1945. d. $.50/day newsstand; $1.25/Sun.; $9.50/mo. carrier; $5/mo. Sat. & Sun. 524 Hartz Ave., Danville, CA 94526. TEL 510-837-4257; FAX 510-837-4334. **Owner(s):** Knight-Ridder, Inc., One Herald Plz., Miami, FL 33132. TEL 305-376-3800; Ed. Karen Magnuson; Pub. David Rourds; adv. contact: Wendy Davidson. photos; pub. size: broadsheet; circ. morning 40,000(paid); Sun. 45,000(paid). **Wire Service(s):** AP.

DAVIS

US

DAVIS ENTERPRISE. 1897. Sun.-Fri. $.50 newsstand; $6.44/4 wks. 315 G St. Davis, CA 95616. TEL 916-756-0800; FAX 916-756-1668; E-mail: editor@davis.com; URL: http://www.davisenterprise.com. **Owner(s):** Davis Enterprise, The, 315 G St., Davis, CA 95616. TEL 916-756-0800; Ed. Debbie Davis; Pub. Burt McNaughton; adv. contact: Donna Okinga. pub. size: broadsheet; circ. morning 11,200(paid); Sun. 11,500(paid). **Wire Service(s):** AP, NYT.

EL CAJON

US   ISSN 0898-1817

DAILY CALIFORNIAN, THE. 1892. c. $.25/day newsstand; $.50/Sat. or Sun.; $24.94/3 mos.; $48/6 mos.; $83.46/yr. 1000 Pioneer Way, El Cajon, CA 92020. TEL 619-442-4404; FAX 619-447-6165. **Owner(s):** Kendell Communications, 1000 Pioneer Way, El Cajon, CA 92020. TEL 619-442-4404; Ed. Della Elliott; Pub. Paul Zindell; pub. size: broadsheet; circ. evening 26,500(paid); Sun. 26,500(paid). **Wire Service(s):** AP.
    Formerly: Californian, The.

EL CENTRO

US   ISSN 1072-9283

IMPERIAL VALLEY PRESS. 1901. Sun.-Fri. $1/day newsstand; $1/Sun.; $8/mo. home deliv.; $10/mo. in cy. mail; $13/mo. out of cy. mail. 205 N. Eighth St., El Centro, CA 92243. TEL 619-337-3400; FAX 619-353-3003. **Owner(s):** Associated Desert Newspapers, 205 N. Eighth St., El Centro, CA 92243. TEL 619-337-3400; FAX 619-353-3003; Ed. J.R. Fitch; Pub. J.R. Fitch; adv. contact: John Yanni. bk.rev.; pub. size: broadsheet; circ. evening 18,500(paid); Sun. 19,000(paid). **Wire Service(s):** AP.
    Formerly: Brawley News.

ESCONDIDO

US   ISSN 1059-5694
NORTH COUNTY TIMES. 1986. d. $.35/day newsstand; $1.25/Sun.; $9.80/4 wks. 207 E. Pennsylvania Ave., Escondido, CA 92025. TEL 619-433-7333; FAX 619-745-3769. **Owner(s):** South Coast Newspapers, 1722 S. Hill St., Oceanside, CA 92054. TEL 619-433-7333; Ed. W. Russel Harris; Pub. Thomas Misset; adv.; pub. size: broadsheet; circ. evening 40,000(paid); Sun. 42,000(paid). **Wire Service(s):** AP.
   Formerly: Times Advocate.

EUREKA

US
TIMES-STANDARD. 1854. d. $11/mo. 930 Sixth St., Eureka, CA 95501. TEL 707-441-0500; FAX 707-441-0565. **Owner(s):** Thomson Newspapers, Inc., 3150 Des Plaines Ave., Des Plaines, IL 60014. TEL 708-299-5544; Ed. Rex Wilson; Pub. Stephen J. Sosinski; adv. contact: Gary Siegel. pub. size: broadsheet; circ. evening 22,525(paid); Sun. 24,885(paid). **Wire Service(s):** AP.

FAIRFIELD

US   ISSN 0746-5858
DAILY REPUBLIC. 1855. d. $.35/day newsstand; $1.25/Sun.; $9.65/mo. home deliv. 1250 Texas St., Fairfield, CA 94533. TEL 707-425-4646; FAX 707-425-5924. **Owner(s):** Fairfield Publishing Co., 1250 Texas St., Fairfield, CA 94533. TEL 707-425-4646; Ed. Bill Buchanan; Pub. Foy McNaughton; pub. size: broadsheet; circ. morning 21,147(paid); Sun. 22,865(paid). **Wire Service(s):** AP.

FREMONT

US
ARGUS, THE. 1960. d. $.35/day newsstand; $1.25/Sun.; $2.70/wk. 39737 Paseo Padre Bldg., Fremont, CA 94538. TEL 510-661-2600; FAX 510-353-7029. **Owner(s):** Alameda Publishing Corp., P.O. Box 1350, Oakland, CA 94604-1350. TEL 510-763-1120; Ed. Nancy DeBolt; Pub. Peter Bernhard; adv. contact: Melinda Brown. pub. size: broadsheet; circ. morning 33,939(paid). **Wire Service(s):** AP, LAT-WP, CNS, SHNA, NYT.

FRESNO

US   ISSN 0889-6070
FRESNO BEE, THE. 1922. d. $11.45/mo; $148.19/yr. 1626 E St., Fresno, CA 93786. TEL 209-441-6111; FAX 209-441-6436. **Owner(s):** McClatchy Newspapers, P.O. Box 15779, Sacramento, CA 95852. TEL 916-446-9211; Pub. Robert Weil; photos; pub. size: standard; circ. morning 154,644(paid); Sun. 192,262(paid). **Wire Service(s):** AP, NYT, McClatchy, RN, KR, SHNA.

GILROY

US
DISPATCH, THE. 1868. Mon.-Fri. $.50 newsstand; $23.09/3 mos. carrier; $37.05/3 mos. mailed local; $39/3 mos. mailed elsewhere. 6400 Monterey St., Gilroy, CA 95020. TEL 408-842-6400; FAX 408-842-7105. **Owner(s):** McClatchy Newspapers, P.O. Box 15779, Sacramento, CA 95852. TEL 916-321-1000; Pub. Paula Mabry; adv. contact: Arleen Hudson. photos; pub. size: broadsheet; circ. morning 6,600(paid). **Wire Service(s):** AP, McClatchy News Service.

GLENDALE

US   ISSN 0746-3340
GLENDALE NEWS-PRESS. 1905. Mon.-Sat. $.25 newsstand; $7.50/mo. 425 W. Broadway, Ste. 300, Glendale, CA 91204-1269, TEL 818-241-4141; FAX 818-241-1975. **Owner(s):** Times-Mirror Co., Times-Mirror Sq., Los Angeles, CA 90053. TEL 213-237-3700; Ed. William Lobdell; Pub. Judee Kendall; adv. contact: Willa Robinson. photos; bk.rev.; pub. size: broadsheet; circ. morning 10,409(paid). **Wire Service(s):** AP, CINS.

GRASS VALLEY

US
UNION, THE. 1864. Mon.-Sat. $.50 newsstand; $8/mo.; $10.19/mo. mailed. 11464 Sutton Way, Grass Valley, CA 95945. TEL 916-273-9561; FAX 916-273-1854; E-mail: mail@theunion.com; URL: http://www.theunion.com. **Owner(s):** Nevada County Publishing Co., 131 S. Cedar, Nevada, MO 64772. TEL 417-667-8121; Ed. John Seelmyer. adv. contact: Matt Bodourian. photos; bk.rev.; pub. size: broadsheet; circ. evening 17,500(paid). **Wire Service(s):** AP.

HANFORD

US
HANFORD SENTINEL. 1886. d. $9/mo. carrier; $10/mo. motor rte. 300 W. Sixth St., Hanford, CA 93230. TEL 209-582-0471; FAX 209-582-8631. **Owner(s):** Scripps League Newspapers, Inc., P.O. Box 16B, Charlottesville, VA 22901; Ed. Leah Leach; Pub. Neil Williams; adv. contact: Bob Rankin. photos; bk.rev.; pub. size: broadsheet; circ. evening 14,375(paid); Sun. 14,640(paid). **Wire Service(s):** AP.

HAYWARD

US
DAILY REVIEW. 1892. d. $.50/day newsstand; $1.25/Sun; $10.84/mo. 116 W. Winton Ave., Hayward, CA 94544. TEL 510-783-6111; FAX 510-293-2490. **Owner(s):** Alameda Publishing Corp., 116 W. Winton Ave., Hayward, CA 94544. TEL 510-783-6111; Ed. Mario Dianda; Pub. Peter Bernhard; adv.; pub. size: broadsheet; circ. morning 41,900(paid); Sun. 50,500(paid). **Wire Service(s):** AP, LAT-WP, NYT, SHNA.

HOLLISTER

US
HOLLISTER FREE LANCE. 1873. d. $.50 newsstand; $69.28/yr. 350 Sixth St., Hollister, CA 95023. TEL 408-637-5566; FAX 408-637-4104. **Owner(s):** McClatchy Newspapers, P.O. Box 15799, Sacramento, CA 95813. TEL 916-446-9211; Ed. Mark Paxton; Pub. Paula Mabry; adv. contact: Brenda Weatherly. photos; bk.rev.; pub. size: broadsheet; circ. morning 4,231(paid). **Wire Service(s):** AP, McClatchy.

JACKSON

US
AMADOR LEDGER DISPATCH. 1853. Mon.-Wed. & Fri. $.50 newsstand; $50/yr. 10776 Argonaut Ln., Jackson, CA 95642. TEL 209-223-1767; FAX 209-223-1264. **Owner(s):** McClatchy Newspapers, P.O. Box 15779, Sacramento, CA 95852. TEL 916-321-1000; Ed. Joe Evans; Pub. K. Newton; adv. contact: Jerry Behrens. photos; pub. size: broadsheet; circ. morning 14,400(controlled & paid).
   Formerly: Amador Ledger.

LAKEPORT

US   ISSN 0746-4304
LAKE COUNTY RECORD-BEE. 1878. Tue.-Sat. $.50 newsstand; $57.80/yr. 2150 S. Main St., Lakeport, CA 95453. TEL 707-263-5636; FAX 707-263-0600. **Owner(s):** Lake County Publishing, 2150 S. Main, P.O. Box 849, Lakeport, CA 95453. TEL 707-263-5636; Ed. Thomas Monigan; Pub. Tim Timmons; adv. contact: Debbie Geissler. photos; pub. size: standard; circ. morning 9,010(paid).

LODI

US
LODI NEWS-SENTINEL. 1881. Mon.-Sat. $6.75/mo. 125 N. Church St., Lodi, CA 95240. TEL 209-369-2761. **Owner(s):** Lodi News-Sentinel, P.O. Box 1360, Lodi, CA 95241. TEL 209-369-2761; Ed. Marty Weybret. adv. contact: Dan Battilana. pub. size: broadsheet; circ. morning 18,000(free). **Wire Service(s):** AP, SJNS.

LOMPOC

US
LOMPOC RECORD. 1875. Sun.-Fri. $.50/day newsstand; $1/Sun.; $7.35/mo. 115 N. H St., Lompoc, CA 93436. TEL 805-736-2313; FAX 805-736-5654. **Owner(s):** Donrey Media Group, P.O. Box 17017, Fort Smith, AR 72902. TEL 501-785-7810; Ed. Rita Henning; Pub. Ron Hoffer; adv. contact: Dick Bausman. pub. size: broadsheet; circ. evening 8,700(paid); Sun. 10,216(paid). **Wire Service(s):** AP.

LONG BEACH

US
PRESS-TELEGRAM. 1897. d. $.35/day newsstand; $1.25/Sun.; $2.85/wk. home deliv. 604 Pine Ave., Long Beach, CA 90844-0001. TEL 310-435-1161; FAX 310-437-7892; E-mail: ptweb@ptconnect.infi.net; URL: http://www.ptconnect.com. **Owner(s):** Knight-Ridder, Inc., One Herald Plz., Miami, FL 33132. TEL 305-350-2650; Ed. Jim Crutchfield; Pub. Rick Sadowski; adv.; pub. size: broadsheet; circ. morning 132,000(paid); Sun. 153,000(paid). **Wire Service(s):** AP, NYT, KR.

LOS ANGELES

US

LOS ANGELES BULLETIN. Mon.-Fri. $.25 newsstand. 210 S. Spring St., Los Angeles, CA 90012-3710. TEL 213-628-4384; FAX 213-687-3886. **Owner(s):** Metropolitan News Co., 210 S. Spring St., Los Angeles, CA 90012-3710. TEL 213-628-4384; FAX 213-687-3886; Ed. Roger M. Grace; Pub. Roger M. Grace; adv.; photos; bk.rev.; pub. size: tabloid; circ. morning 1,500(paid). **Wire Service(s):** AP.

US   ISSN 0362-5575

LOS ANGELES DAILY JOURNAL. 1888. Mon.-Fri. $2 newsstand; $389/yr. 915 E. First St., Los Angeles, CA 90012-4042. TEL 213-229-5300; FAX 213-680-3682. **Owner(s):** Daily Journal Co., 915 E. First St., Los Angeles, CA 90012. TEL 213-229-5300; FAX 213-680-3682; Ed. Janet Shprintz; Pub. Gerald Salzman; adv. contact: Nell Fields. pub. size: broadsheet; circ. morning 17,373(paid). **Wire Service(s):** AP, RN.

US   ISSN 0458-3035

LOS ANGELES TIMES. 1881. d. $.50 newsstand; $4.04/wk. Times Mirror Sq., Los Angeles, CA 90053. TEL 213-237-5000; FAX 213-237-4712; E-mail: terry.schwadron@latimes.com; URL: http://www.latimes.com/. **Owner(s):** Times-Mirror Co., Times Mirror Sq., Los Angeles, CA 90053. TEL 213-237-3700; Ed. Michael Parks; Pub. Richard Schlosberg III; adv. contact: Lawrence M. Kline. photos; bk.rev.; pub. size: broadsheet; circ. morning 1,021,121(paid); Sun. 1,391,076(paid). Wire Service(s): AP, DJ, RN, UPI, LAT-WP, CSM, CiNS.

US

METROPOLITAN, THE. 1901. Mon.-Fri. $1 newsstand; $172/yr. mailed. 210 S. Spring St., Los Angeles, CA 90012. TEL 213-628-4384; FAX 213-687-3886. **Owner(s):** Grace Communications, 210 S. Spring St., Los Angeles, CA 90012. TEL 213-628-4384; Ed. Roger M. Grace; Pub. JoAnne W. Grace; adv. contact: Matt Lewis. pub. size: tabloid; circ. morning 2,500(paid).

MADERA

US   ISSN 8750-9571

MADERA TRIBUNE. 1885. Mon.-Sat. $.50 newsstand; $75/yr. home deliv.; $114/yr. mailed. 100 E. Seventh St., Madera, CA 93638. TEL 209-674-2424; FAX 209-673-6526. **Owner(s):** U.S. Media Group, P.O. Box 227, Crystal City, MO 63019; Ed. Paul Bittick; Pub. Danny Dean; adv. contact: Armida Roberts. pub. size: broadsheet; circ. evening 9,900(paid). **Wire Service(s):** AP.

MANTECA

US   ISSN 0745-2748

MANTECA BULLETIN. 1908. d. $.50 newsstand; $8.50/mo. carrier; $98/yr. mailed. 531 E. Yosemite Ave., Manteca, CA 95336. TEL 209-239-3531; FAX 209-239-1801. **Owner(s):** Morris Communications, P.O. Box 936, Augusta, GA 30903. TEL 706-724-0851; Ed. Drew Voros; Pub. Darrel Phillips; adv. contact: Rita Hill. pub. size: broadsheet; circ. morning 7,500(paid); Sun. 7,500(paid). **Wire Service(s):** AP.

MARYSVILLE

US

APPEAL-DEMOCRAT. 1860. d. $.35/day newsstand; $.70/Sun.; $7.50/mo. carrier. 1530 Ellis Lake Dr., Marysville, CA 95901. TEL 916-741-2345; FAX 916-741-1195; E-mail: appeal@syix.com. **Owner(s):** Freedom Communications, Inc., 17666 Fitch St., Irvine, CA 92714. TEL 716-553-9292; Ed. Julie Shirley; Pub. Robert Hardie; pub. size: broadsheet; circ. evening 24,000(paid); Sun. 24,000(paid). **Wire Service(s):** AP, NYT, KR.

Formerly: Yuba-Sutter Appeal Democrat.

MERCED

US

MERCED SUN-STAR. 1869. Mon.-Sat. $.50/day newsstand; $.75/Sat.; $85.80/yr. carrier. 3033 N. G St., Merced, CA 95340. TEL 209-722-1511; FAX 209-384-2226. **Owner(s):** U.S. Media Group, P.O. Box 227, Crystal City, MO 63019; Ed. Norman Martin, Jr.; Pub. Allan C. Portner; pub. size: broadsheet; circ. morning 20,000(paid). **Wire Service(s):** AP.

MODESTO

US

MODESTO BEE, THE. 1884. d. $.50 newsstand; $11.26/mo 1325 H St., Modesto, CA 95354. TEL 209-578-2000; FAX 209-578-2207; E-mail: eelamont@aol.com; URL: http://www.modbee.com. **Owner(s):** McClatchy Newspapers P.O. Box 15779, Sacramento, CA 95852. TEL 916-446-9211; Ed. Mark Vasche; Pub. Orage Quarles III; adv.; photos; bk.rev.; pub. size: broadsheet; circ. morning 85,000(paid); Sun. 94,000(paid). **Wire Service(s):** AP, NYT, LAT-WP, McClatchy, KR.

MONTEREY

US   ISSN 0889-3101

MONTEREY COUNTY HERALD, THE. 1922. d. $.50/day newsstand; $1.25/Sun.; $13.85/mo. carrier; $20/mo. mailed. 8 Upper Ragsdale Dr., Monterey, CA 93940. TEL 408-372-3311; FAX 408-372-8401; E-mail: herald@ix.netcom.com. **Owner(s):** Scripps-Howard, 312 Walnut St., 28th Fl., Cincinatti, OH 45202. TEL 513-977-3000; Ed. Walter Dawson. adv. contact: Jay Palmquist. pub. size: standard; circ. morning 36,905(paid); Sun. 37,685(paid). **Wire Service(s):** AP, LAT-WP, CSM.

Formerly: Monterey Peninsula Herald, The.

MOORPARK

US

MOORPARK STAR. 1983. d. $.25 newsstand; $2.50/wk. 530 Moorpark Ave., Ste. 180, Moorpark, CA 93021. TEL 805-523-7440; FAX 805-523-7316. **Owner(s):** Scripps-Howard, 312 Walnut St., 28th Fl., Cincinnati, OH 45202. TEL 513-977-3000; Ed. Debi Ryono; Pub. Debi Ryono; adv. contact: Harvey Hopkins. pub. size: broadsheet; circ. morning 2,000(free & paid).

Formerly: Moorpark News-Mirror.

NAPA

US

NAPA VALLEY REGISTER. 1863. d. $.50/day newsstand; $1.25/Sun. 1515 Second St., Napa, CA 94559. TEL 707-226-3711; FAX 707-224-3963. **Owner(s):** Napa Valley Publishing Co., 1615 Second St., Napa, CA 94559. TEL 707-224-3363; Ed. Doug Wilks; Pub. Michael Giangreco; adv. contact: Sandy Aimo. pub. size: broadsheet; circ. evening 21,600(paid). **Wire Service(s):** AP.

Formerly: Napa Register.

NOVATO

US   ISSN 0891-5164

MARIN INDEPENDENT JOURNAL. 1861. d. $.35/day newsstand; $1/Sun.; $18.02/8 wks. home deliv. 150 Alameda Del Prado, Novato, CA 94948-6150. TEL 415-883-8600; FAX 415-883-5458; E-mail: ij@well.com. **Owner(s):** Gannett Company, Inc., 1100 Wilson Blvd., Arlington, VA 22340. TEL 703-284-6000; Pub. Phyllis Pfeiffer; pub. size: broadsheet; circ. evening 37,350(paid); Sun. 41 540(paid). **Wire Service(s):** AP, GNS.

OAKLAND

US   ISSN 0745-3841

TRIBUNE, THE. 1874. d. $.50/day newsstand; $1.50/Sun. 66 Jack London Sq., Oakland, CA 94607. TEL 510-208-6300; FAX 510-208-6477. **Owner(s):** Oakland Tribune, Inc., 66 Jack London Sq., Oakland, CA 94604. TEL 510-208-6300; Ed. David Burgin; Pub. Joseph J. Haraburda; pub. size: broadsheet; circ. morning 75,480(paid); Sun. 73,000(paid). **Wire Service(s):** AP.

ONTARIO

US

INLAND VALLEY DAILY BULLETIN. 1885. d. $.35/day newsstand; $1/Sun.; $10.36/4 wks. 2041 E. Fourth St., Ontario, CA 91764. TEL 909-987-6397; FAX 909-948-9038. **Owner(s):** Stephens Group, Inc., P.O. Box 1359, Fort Smith, AR 72901 TEL 501-785-7810; Pub. Mike Ferguson; adv. contact: John Souza. bk.rev.; pub. size: broadsheet; circ. morning 82,600(free & paid); Sun. 86,000(free & paid). **Wire Service(s):** AP, KNS.

Formerly: Progress Bulletin Daily Report.

OROVILLE

US

OROVILLE MERCURY-REGISTER. 1873. Mon.-Sat. $.50 newsstand; $6.97/mo. carrier. 2081 Second St., Oroville, CA 95965. TEL 916-533-3131; FAX 916-533-3127. **Owner(s):** Donrey Media Group, P.O. Box 17017, Fort Smith, AR 72901. TEL 501-785-7810; Ed. John Fenrich; Pub. John Fenrich; adv. contact: Milt Moore. pub. size: broadsheet; circ. evening 9,894(paid). **Wire Service(s):** AP.

PALMDALE

US   ISSN 0744-5830

ANTELOPE VALLEY PRESS. 1915. Tue.-Sun. $.50/day newsstand; $1.25/Sun.; $99.95/yr. 37404 N. Sierra Hwy., Palmdale, CA 93550. TEL 805-273-2700; FAX 805-947-4870; E-mail: editor@avpress.com; URL: http://www.avpress.com. **Owner(s):** Antelope Valley Newspapers, Inc., P.O. Box 880, Palmdale, CA 93550. TEL 805-273-2700; Ed. Vern Lawson. adv.; photos; bk.rev.; pub. size: broadsheet; circ. morning 56,276(paid); Sun. 58,775(paid). **Wire Service(s):** NYT, AP.

PALM SPRINGS

US

DESERT SUN. 1927. d. $.50/day newsstand; $.75/Sat.; $1/Sun. 750 N. Gene Autry Trail, Palm Springs, CA 92262. TEL 619-322-8889; FAX 619-778-4654; E-mail: pssun@aol.com; 74111.2461@compuserve.com; URL: http://www.desert-sun.com. **Owner(s):** Gannett Company, Inc., 1100 Wilson Blvd., Arlington, VA 22234. TEL 703-284-6000; Ed. Keith Carter; Pub. Robert Dickey; adv. contact: Greg Pedersen. photos; bk.rev.; pub. size: broadsheet; circ. morning 52,733(paid); Sun. 53,669(paid). **Wire Service(s):** AP, GNS, NYT.

PALO ALTO

US

▼**PALO ALTO DAILY NEWS.** 1995. 6/wk. free. 329 Alma St., Palo Alto, CA 94301. TEL 415-327-6397; FAX 415-327-0676. **Owner(s):** Priceless LLC, 329 Alma St., Palo Alto, CA 94301. TEL 415-327-6397; FAX 415-327-0676; Ed. David Price; Pub. David Price; adv. contact: James Pavelich. photos; pub. size: tabloid; circ. evening 10,000(free).

PASADENA

US   ISSN 1069-2827

PASADENA STAR-NEWS, THE. 1886. d. $.35/day newsstand; $1/Sun.; $18/8 wks. 911 E. Colorado Blvd., Pasadena, CA 91109. TEL 818-578-6300; FAX 818-792-9413. **Owner(s):** Thomson Newspapers, Inc., 3150 Des Plaines Blvd., Des Plaines, IL 60018. TEL 708-299-5544; Ed. Lawrence Wilson; Pub. Joe Logan; pub. size: broadsheet; circ. morning 42,800(paid); Sun. 42,800(paid). **Wire Service(s):** AP, NYT.
    Formerly: Star-News.

PASO ROBLES

US

DAILY PRESS, THE. 1986. Mon.-Fri. $.50 newsstand; $81/yr. 1414 Park St., Paso Robles, CA 93446. TEL 805-238-0330; FAX 805-238-6504. **Owner(s):** U.S. Media Group, P.O. Box 227, Crystal City, MO 63019; Ed. Scott Steepleton; Pub. Pat Cavanaugh; adv. contact: John Echeubste. photos; bk.rev.; pub. size: broadsheet; circ. evening 5,300(paid). **Wire Service(s):** AP, CNS, CN.
    Formerly: Paso Robles Press.

PLACERVILLE

US

MOUNTAIN DEMOCRAT. 1851. Wed.-Fri. & Mon. $.50 newsstand; $68/yr. in cy. 1360 Broadway, Placerville, CA 95667. TEL 916-622-1255; FAX 916-622-7894; E-mail: mtdemo@calweb.com; URL: http://www.mtdemocrat.com. **Owner(s):** Mother Lode Printing & Publishing Co., 1360 Broadway, Placerville, CA 95667. TEL 916-622-1255; Ed. Michael Raffety; Pub. James Webb; adv.; photos; bk.rev.; pub. size: broadsheet; circ. morning 13,200(paid). **Wire Service(s):** NYT.
    Formerly: Mountain Democrat & Placerville Times.

PLEASANTON

US   ISSN 8750-9946

TRI-VALLEY HERALD. 1874. d. $.50/day newsstand; $1.25/Sun. 4770 Willow Rd., Pleasanton, CA 94588. TEL 510-734-8600; FAX 510-416-4850. **Owner(s):** Alameda Publishing Corp., P.O. Box 5050, Hayward, CA 94540. TEL 510-783-6111; Ed. Tim Hunt; Pub. Peter Bernhard; adv. contact: Jennine Loumena. photos; pub. size: standard; circ. morning 38,000(paid); Sun. 38,000(paid). **Wire Service(s):** AP.

US

VALLEY TIMES. d. $.50 newsstand; $53.50/yr. 127 Spring St., Pleasanton, CA 94566. TEL 510-462-4160; FAX 510-847-2189; E-mail: valleytims@aol.com. **Owner(s):** Knight-Ridder, Inc., One Herald Plz., Miami, FL 33132. TEL 305-376-3800; Ed. Karen Magnuson; Pub. George Riggs; adv. contact: Wendy Davidson. bk.rev.; pub. size: broadsheet; circ. evening 38,500(paid); Sun. 40,000(paid). **Wire Service(s):** AP, NYT, LAT-WP, McClatchy.

PORTERVILLE

US

PORTERVILLE RECORDER. 1908. Mon.-Sat. $.50/day newsstand; $.75/Sat.; $87/yr. 115 E. Oak Ave., Porterville, CA 93257. TEL 209-784-5000; FAX 209-784-1689. **Owner(s):** Freedom Communications, Inc., 1766 Fitch, Irvine, CA 92714-6022. TEL 714-253-2303; FAX 714-474-7675; Ed. Rick Elkins; Pub. James L. Lyons; adv. contact: Jonell Webb. photos; pub. size: broadsheet; circ. evening 13,000(paid). **Wire Service(s):** AP.

RED BLUFF

US

RED BLUFF DAILY NEWS. 1885. Mon.-Sat. $.50 newsstand; $89.40/yr. deliv. 545 Diamond Ave., Red Bluff, CA 96080. TEL 916-527-2151; FAX 916-527-3719. **Owner(s):** Donrey Media Group, P.O. Box 17017, Fort Smith, AR 72901. TEL 501-785-7810; Ed. Bill Goodyear; Pub. Mel Wagner; adv. contact: Jean Hanson. pub. size: standard; circ. evening 9,000(paid). **Wire Service(s):** AP.

REDDING

US

RECORD SEARCHLIGHT. 1938. d. $.50/day newsstand; $1.50/Sun. 1101 Twin View Blvd., Redding, CA 96003. TEL 916-243-2424; FAX 916-225-8212; E-mail: recsrch@snowcrest.net; URL: http://www.redding.com/. **Owner(s):** John P. Scripps Newspapers, Inc., 306 Scripps Bldg., 525 C St., San Diego, CA 92101. TEL 714-233-7231; Ed. Tom King; Pub. Tom King; adv. contact: Bill Dawson. pub. size: broadsheet; circ. morning 40,000(paid); Sun. 41,000(paid). **Wire Service(s):** AP.
    Formerly: Redding Record Searchlight.

REDLANDS

US

REDLANDS DAILY FACTS. 1890. Sun.-Fri. $.35/day newsstand; $1/Sun.; $1.61/wk. carrier. 700 Brookside Ave., Redlands, CA 92373. TEL 909-793-3221; FAX 909-793-9588. **Owner(s):** Stephens Group, Inc., P.O. Box 1359, Fort Smith, AR 72902; Ed. Carl Baker; Pub. Toebe Bush; adv. contact: Dave Berkowitz. pub. size: broadsheet; circ. evening 8,750(paid); Sun. 8,750(paid). **Wire Service(s):** AP.

RICHMOND

US   ISSN 0746-6323

WEST COUNTY TIMES. 1899. d. $.50/day newsstand; $1.50/Sun.; $10.99/mo. home deliv. 4301 Lakeside Dr., Richmond, CA 94806. TEL 510-262-2770; FAX 510-262-2776; E-mail: wctimes@aol.com. **Owner(s):** Knight Ridder, Inc., One Herald Plz., Miami, FL 33132. TEL 305-376-3800; Ed. Anthony Marquez. pub. size: broadsheet; circ. morning 34,797(paid); Sun. 35,244(paid). **Wire Service(s):** AP, NYT, LAT-WP.

RIDGECREST

US   ISSN 1076-0059

DAILY INDEPENDENT. 1928. Tue.-Fri. & Sun. $.50/day newsstand; $1/Sun.; $7/mo. carrier; $6/mo. senior citizens. 224 E. Ridgecrest Blvd., Ridgecrest, CA 93555. TEL 619-375-4481; FAX 614-375-4880. **Owner(s):** Swift Newspapers, Inc., 1802 N. Carson St., Ste. 100, Carson City, NV 89706; Ed. Scott Farwell; Pub. W. Les Hill; adv. contact: Matthew Hill. pub. size: broadsheet; circ. evening 9,000(paid); Sun. 9,200(paid). **Wire Service(s):** AP.

RIVERSIDE

US

PRESS-ENTERPRISE, THE. 1878. d. $.25/day newsstand; $1/Sun.; $2.40/wk. 3512 14th St., Riverside, CA 92501. TEL 909-684-1200; FAX 909-782-7634. **Owner(s):** Press-Enterprise Co., 3512 14th St., Riverside, CA 92501. TEL 909-684-1200; FAX 909-782-6034; Ed. Mel Opotowsky. adv. contact: David Cornwall. pub. size: broadsheet; circ. morning 163,004(paid); Sun. 171,139(paid). **Wire Service(s):** NYT, AP, KR.

SACRAMENTO

US   ISSN 0890-5738
SACRAMENTO BEE. 1857. d. $.50/day newsstand; $1.25/Sun.; $11.25/mo. carrier. 2100 Q St., Sacramento, CA 95816-6816. TEL 916-321-1000; FAX 916-321-1109; E-mail: sacbeeedit@netcom.com; URL: http://www.sacbee.com. **Owner(s):** McClatchy Newspapers, P.O. Box 15779, Sacramento, CA 95852. TEL 916-321-1850; Ed. Rick Rodriguez; Pub. James McClatchy; adv. contact: Gene Grant. photos; bk.rev.; pub. size: broadsheet; circ. morning 279,942(paid); Sun. 350,361(paid). **Wire Service(s):** AP, NYT, LAT-WP, SHNA.

SALINAS

US
CALIFORNIAN, THE. 1872. Mon.-Sat. $.35/day newsstand; $.75/Sat.; $12/mo. in cy.; $13/mo. out of cy. 123 W. Alisal St., Salinas, CA 93901. TEL 408-424-2221; FAX 408-754-4293; E-mail: valleynews@aol.com. **Owner(s):** Gannett Company, Inc., 1100 Wilson Blvd., Arlington, VA 22234. TEL 703-284-6000; Pub. Michael Chihak; adv. contact: Robert Aguilar. pub. size: broadsheet; circ. morning 23,800(paid). **Wire Service(s):** AP, GNS, NYT.

SAN BERNARDINO

US
SAN BERNARDINO COUNTY SUN. 1894. d. $.50/day newsstand; $1.50/Sun. 399 N. D St., San Bernardino, CA 92401. TEL 909-889-9666; FAX 909-885-8741. **Owner(s):** Gannett Company, Inc., 1100 Wilson Blvd., Arlington, VA 22234. TEL 703-284-6000; Ed. Catherine Hamm; Pub. Brooks Johnson; adv. contact: Robert Balzer. photos; pub. size: broadsheet; circ. morning 96,000(paid); Sun. 105,000(paid). **Wire Service(s):** AP, GNS, NYT.

SAN DIEGO

US
SAN DIEGO TRANSCRIPT. 1886. Mon.-Fri. $.75 newsstand; $45.90/3 mos.; $81.21/6 mos.; $131.82/yr.; $222.45/2 yrs. 2131 Third Ave., San Diego, CA 92101. TEL 619-232-4381; FAX 619-239-5716; E-mail: editor@sddt.com; URL: http://www.sddt.com/. **Owner(s):** Calcomco, Inc., 534 Rivard Blvd., Detroit, MI 48230. TEL 313-885-9228; Ed. Martin Kruming; Pub. Bill Revelle; adv. contact: Tom Kelleher. photos; bk.rev.; pub. size: broadsheet; circ. morning 10,100(paid). **Wire Service(s):** AP, DJ.

US
SAN DIEGO UNION-TRIBUNE. 1868. d. $.35/day newsstand; $1.50/Sun.; $10.50/mo. 350 Camino De La Reina, San Diego, CA 92108. TEL 619-299-3131; FAX 619-293-2148; E-mail: ellen.bevier@uniontrib.com; URL: http://www.uniontrib.com/. **Owner(s):** Union-Tribune Publishing Co., 350 Camino De La Reina, San Diego, CA 92108. TEL 619-299-3131; Ed. Karin Winner; Pub. Helen K. Copley; adv.; photos; bk.rev.; pub. size: broadsheet; circ. morning 376,511(paid); Sun. 453,891(paid). **Wire Service(s):** AP, UPI, CNS, DJ, RN, KR, NYT, BPI, CSM, CT-NYT.
   Formerly: San Diego Union.

SAN FRANCISCO

US
SAN FRANCISCO CHRONICLE. 1865. d. $.50 newsstand; $14.40/4 wks. 901 Mission St., San Francisco, CA 94103-2988. TEL 415-777-1111; FAX 415-896-1107; E-mail: chronletters@sfgate.com; URL: http://www.sfgate.com/. **Owner(s):** Chronicle Publishing Co., 901 Mission St., San Francisco, CA 94103. TEL 415-777-1111; Ed. Daniel Rosenheim. adv. contact: Bart Green. photos; bk.rev.; pub. size: broadsheet; circ. morning 493,942(paid); Sun. 646,171(paid). **Wire Service(s):** AP, NYT, RN, LAT-WP.

US   ISSN 1059-2636
SAN FRANCISCO DAILY JOURNAL. 1893. Mon.-Fri. $1 newsstand; $47/mo. 1390 Market St., Ste. 1210, San Francisco, CA 94102. TEL 415-252-0500; FAX 415-252-0288. **Owner(s):** Daily Journal Co., 915 E. First St., Los Angeles, CA 90012. TEL 213-229-5300; Ed. Steve Ball. adv.; pub. size: broadsheet; circ. morning 6,494(paid). **Wire Service(s):** AP, NYT.

US
SAN FRANCISCO EXAMINER. 1865. d. $.25/day newsstand; $1.50/Sun.; $12/4 wks.; $6.60/4 wks. Sun. only. 110 Fifth St., San Francisco, CA 94103. TEL 415-777-2424; FAX 415-777-2525; E-mail: letters@examiner.com; URL: http://www.sfgate.com/examiner. **Owner(s):** Hearst Corp., 959 Eighth Ave., New York, NY 10019. TEL 212-262-5700; Pub. Lee Guittar; adv. contact: Bart Green. photos; bk.rev.; pub. size: standard; circ. evening 125,000(paid); Sun. 646,171(paid). **Wire Service(s):** AP, CDN, CSM, CT, KR, RN.

SAN JACINTO

US
HEMET NEWS. 1893. d. $.25/day newsstand; $.50/Sun.; $19.47/13 wks. home deliv.; $64.65/yr. 474 W. Esplanade Ave., San Jacinto, CA 92583. TEL 909-487-2232; FAX 909-487-2250. **Owner(s):** Stephens Group, Inc., P.O. Box 1359, Fort Smith, AR 72902. TEL 501-785-7310; Ed. Craig Schultz; Pub. Jim Fredericks; adv. contact: Manny Padilla. pub. size: broadsheet; circ. morning 17,000(paid). **Wire Service(s):** AP.

SAN JOSE

US   ISSN 0747-2099
SAN JOSE MERCURY NEWS. 1851. d. $.35/day newsstand; $1.35/Sun.; $11.95/mo. home deliv. 750 Ridder Park Dr., San Jose, CA 95190. TEL 408-920-5000; FAX 408-298-1966; E-mail: jceppos@sjmercury.com; URL: http://www.sjmercury.com/. **Owner(s):** Knight-Ridder, Inc., One Herald Plz., Miami, FL 33132-1693. TEL 305-376-3800; Ed. David Yarnold; Pub. Jay Harris; adv. contact: Lou Alexander. photos; bk.rev.; pub. size: broadsheet; circ. morning 284,206(paid); Sun. 345,432(paid). **Wire Service(s):** AP, NYT, LAT-WP, KR.

SAN LUIS OBISOPO

US
SAN LUIS OBISPO COUNTY TELEGRAM-TRIBUNE. 1869. Mon.-Sat. $.35/day newsstand; $1/Sat.; $9.75/mo. 3825 S. Higuera St., San Luis Obispo, CA 93401. TEL 805-731-7800; FAX 805-781-7870; E-mail: tel-trib@slonet.org; URL: http://www.slonet.org/vv/tt. **Owner(s):** John P. Scripps Newspapers, Inc., 306 Scripps Bldg., 525 C St., San Diego, CA 92101. TEL 714-233-7231; Ed. John T. Moore. adv. contact: Butch Hughes. photos; bk.rev.; pub. size: broadsheet; circ. morning 35,000. **Wire Service(s):** AP, MMS, SHNS.

SAN MATEO

US
SAN MATEO TIMES. 1889. Mon.-Sat. $.50/day newsstand; $.75 Sat.; $7.50/mo. 1080 S. Amphlett Blvd., San Mateo, CA 94402. TEL 415-348-4321; FAX 415-348-4478; E-mail: smtimes@smtimes.com; URL: http://www.baynet.com/smtimes.html. **Owner(s):** Alameda Publishing Corp., 116 W. Winton Ave., Hayward, CA 94544. TEL 510-783-6111; Ed. Terry Greenberg; Pub. John Clinton, Jr.; adv. contact: Robert Miller. photos; bk.rev.; pub. size: broadsheet; circ. evening 40,000(paid). **Wire Service(s):** AP, NYT, SHNA, McClatchy, Cox.

SAN PEDRO

US   ISSN 0747-4180
NEWS-PILOT, THE. 1928. Mon.-Sat. $.25 newsstand; $6.50/mo. 362 W. Seventh St., San Pedro, CA 90731. TEL 310-832-0221; FAX 310-833-1540; E-mail: newspilot@aol.com. **Owner(s):** Copley Press Inc., 7776 Ivanhoe Ave., La Jolla, CA 92037; Ed. Phillip F. Sanfield; Pub. Tom Wafer; adv. contact: Charlie Mc Manis. pub. size: broadsheet; circ. morning 16,500(paid). **Wire Service(s):** AP, CNS.
   Formerly: San Pedro News-Pilot.

SANTA ANA

US   ISSN 0886-4934
ORANGE COUNTY REGISTER. 1905. d. $.30/day newsstand; $1.25/Sun.; $9.65/mo.; $5.26/Sat. & Sun. only. 625 N. Grand Ave., Santa Ana, CA 92701. TEL 714-835-1234; FAX 714-543-3904; E-mail: rworld@link.freedom.com; URL http://www.ocregister.com. **Owner(s):** Freedom Communications, Inc., 2055 N. Main St., Ste. 901, Irvine, CA 92701. TEL 714-542-4415; Ed. Tonnie Katz; Pub. R. David Threshie, Jr.; photos; bk.rev.; pub. size: broadsheet; circ. morning 358,173(paid); Sun. 407,692(paid). **Wire Service(s):** AP, NYT, KR, RN, SHNA.

SANTA BARBARA

US
SANTA BARBARA NEWS PRESS. 1855. d. $.50/day newsstand; $1/Sun.; $2.79/wk.; $133.35/yr. 715 Ana Capa, Santa Barbara, CA 93101. TEL 805-564-5200; FAX 805-564-5136. **Owner(s):** New York Times Co., 229 W. 43rd St., New York, NY 10036. TEL 212-556-1234; Ed. Tom Bolton; Pub. Steven Ainsley; adv. contact: Lynn Randolph. pub. size: broadsheet; circ. morning 53,000(paid); Sun. 58,000(paid). **Wire Service(s):** AP, NYT, KRS.

Dailies

SANTA CRUZ

US

SANTA CRUZ COUNTY SENTINEL. 1856. d. $.50/day newsstand; $1.25/Sun.; $21.39/8 wks. carrier. 207 Church St., Santa Cruz, CA 95060. TEL 408-423-4242; FAX 408-429-9620; E-mail: sented@cruzio.com; URL: http://www.cruzio.com/bus/news/sentinel.html. **Owner(s):** Ottaway Newspapers, Inc., P.O. Box 401, Campbell Hall, NY 10916. TEL 914-294-8181; Ed. Tom Honig; Pub. David B. Regan; adv. contact: Karen Carnot. pub. size: broadsheet; circ. morning 27,860(paid); Sun. 30,021(paid). **Wire Service(s):** AP, McClatchy, ONS, NYT.

   Formerly: Santa Cruz Sentinel.

SANTA MARIA

US   ISSN 0745-6166

SANTA MARIA TIMES. 1882. d. $.50/day newsstand; $1/Sun.; $8.50/mo. mailed; $10.25/mo. in state; $11.25/mo. out of state. 3200 Skyway Dr., Santa Maria, CA 93455. TEL 805-925-2691; FAX 805-928-5657; E-mail: casmt@plink.geis.com. **Owner(s):** Scripps League Newspapers, Inc., P.O. Box 1109, Herndon, VA 22070. TEL 703-713-1920; Ed. Wayne Agner; Pub. John Shields; adv. contact: Bernie Petrich. photos; bk.rev.; pub. size: broadsheet; circ. evening 22,500(paid); Sun. 24,100(paid). **Wire Service(s):** AP, CNS, SHNA, McClatchy.

SANTA MONICA

US   ISSN 0898-5375

OUTLOOK, THE. 1875. Mon.-Sat. $.25 newsstand; $6.50/mo. carrier. 1920 Colorado Ave., Santa Monica, CA 90404. TEL 310-829-6811; FAX 310-453-3085. **Owner(s):** Copley Press, Inc., 7776 Ivanhoe Ave., La Jolla, CA 92037; Ed. Lou Brancaccio; Pub. Thomas Wafer; adv. contact: Janice Sheldon. photos; pub. size: broadsheet; circ. morning 25,000(paid). **Wire Service(s):** AP, NYT, CNS, McClatchy, Cox, CiNS.

SANTA ROSA

US

SANTA ROSA PRESS DEMOCRAT. 1857. d. $2.75/wk. 427 Mendocino Ave., Santa Rosa, CA 95401. TEL 707-546-2020; FAX 707-546-7538. **Owner(s):** New York Times Co., The, 229 W. 43rd St., New York, NY 10036. TEL 212-556-1234; Ed. Peter Golis; Pub. Michael J. Parman; adv. contact: Ken Svanum. bk.rev.; pub. size: standard; circ. morning 98,000(paid); Sun. 103,000(paid). **Wire Service(s):** AP, NYT, CNS, LAT-WP.

SIMI VALLEY

US

CAMARILLO STAR. 1926. d. $2.50/wk. 888 Easy St., Simi Valley, CA 93065. TEL 805-987-5001; FAX 805-482-8631. **Owner(s):** John P. Scripps Newspapers, Inc., 525 C St., Ste. 306, San Diego, CA 92101. TEL 619-233-7231; Ed. Dave Smith; Pub. John Wilcox; pub. size: broadsheet; circ. morning 11,500(paid); Sun. 11,800(paid). **Wire Service(s):** AP.

   Formerly: Camarillo Star-Free Press.

US

SIMI VALLEY STAR. 1912. d. $.35/day newsstand; $1.50/Sun.; $98/yr. local. 888 Easy St., Simi Valley, CA 93065. TEL 805-526-6211; FAX 805-526-0479. **Owner(s):** John P. Scripps Newspapers, Inc., 888 Easy St., Simi Valley, CA 92065. TEL 805-526-6211; Ed. Tom Pfeifer; Pub. John Wilcox; adv. contact: Pepper Aarvold. pub. size: broadsheet; circ. evening 16,562(controlled & paid); Sun. 17,161(controlled & paid). **Wire Service(s):** AP.

   Formerly: Simi Valley Enterprise.

SONORA

US

UNION DEMOCRAT, THE. 1854. Mon.-Fri. $.50 newsstand; $6/mo. carrier. 84 S. Washington St., Sonora, CA 95370. TEL 209-532-7151; FAX 209-532-5139. **Owner(s):** Union Democrat Corp., 84 S. Washington St., Sonora, CA 95370. TEL 209-532-7151; Ed. Buzz Eggleston; Pub. Harvey C. McGee; adv. contact: Bud Vogel. pub. size: broadsheet; circ. evening 13,800(paid). **Wire Service(s):** AP.

SOUTH LAKE TAHOE

US   ISSN 8750-3948

TAHOE DAILY TRIBUNE. 1958. Mon.-Fri. $.50/day newsstand; $1/weekends; $90/yr. 3079 Harrison Ave., South Lake Tahoe, CA 96150. TEL 916-541-3880; FAX 916-541-0373; E-mail: tribune@tahoe.com; URL: http://www.tahoe.com. **Owner(s):** Tahoe Daily Tribune Inc., P.O. Box 1358, South Lake Tahoe, CA 96156. TEL 916-541-3880; Ed. Claire Fortier; Pub. Loren C. Abbott; adv. contact: Steve Baker. photos; pub. size: broadsheet; circ. morning 10,000(paid). **Wire Service(s):** AP.

STOCKTON

US

RECORD, THE. 1895. d. $.35/day newsstand; $1.25/Sun.; $11.31/mo. carrier. 530 E. Market St., Stockton, CA 95202. TEL 209-943-6397; FAX 209-546-8288. **Owner(s):** Omaha World-Herald Co., World-Herald Sq., 1334 Dodge St., Omaha, NE 68102. TEL 402-444-1000; Ed. Jim Gold; Pub. Terry Kroeger; adv. contact: Dave Windgarden. photos; bk.rev.; pub. size: broadsheet; circ. morning 53,748(paid); Sun. 60,503(paid). **Wire Service(s):** AP, GNS, NYT.

   Formerly: Stockton Record.

TAFT

US

DAILY MIDWAY DRILLER. 1910. Mon.-Fri. $.35 newsstand; $5.90/mo. in cy. 800 Center St., Taft, CA 93268. TEL 805-763-3171; FAX 805-763-5638. **Owner(s):** Midway Driller, Inc., 800 Center St., Taft, CA 93268. TEL 805-763-3171; FAX 805-763-5638; Ed. Dave Hook; Pub. Dorthy M. Parsons; adv.; photos; pub. size: broadsheet; circ. evening 4,700(paid). **Wire Service(s):** AP.

   Formerly: Taft Daily Midway Driller.

TEMECULA

US   ISSN 1045-5868

CALIFORNIAN, THE. 1976. d. $.25/day newsstand; $.75/Sun.; $17.51/13 wks. home deliv. 27450 Ynez Rd., Ste. 300, Temecula, CA 92591. TEL 909-676-4315; FAX 909-699-1467. **Owner(s):** South Coast Newspapers, 1722 S. Hill St., Oceanside, CA 92054. TEL 619-433-7333; Ed. James Folmer; Pub. Linda Wunerlich; adv.; photos; pub. size: broadsheet; circ. morning 14,500(paid); Sun. 14,500(paid). **Wire Service(s):** AP.

THOUSAND OAKS

US

THOUSAND OAKS STAR. 1954. d. $.35/day newsstand; $1.50/Sun. 2595 E. Thousand Oaks Blvd., Thousand Oaks, CA 91362. TEL 805-496-3211; FAX 805-379-3251. **Owner(s):** Scripps-Howard, 312 Walnut St., 28th Fl., Cincinatti, OH 45202. TEL 513-977-3000; Ed. Deann Wahl. adv. contact: Steve McConnell. pub. size: broadsheet; circ. morning 100,000(paid); Sun. 22,537(paid). **Wire Service(s):** AP, SH.

   Formerly: Thousand Oaks News-Chronicle.

TORRANCE

US

DAILY BREEZE. 1895. d. $8/mo.; $96/yr. 5215 Torrance Blvd., Torrance, CA 90503. TEL 310-540-5511; FAX 310-540-6272. **Owner(s):** Copley Press, Inc., 7776 Ivanhoe, La Jolla, CA 92037; Ed. Jean Adelsman; Pub. Thomas J. Wafer, Jr.; pub. size: broadsheet; circ. morning 80,800(paid); Sun. 119,753(paid). **Wire Service(s):** AP, CNS, NYT.

TRACY

US

TRACY PRESS. 1896. Mon.-Sat. $.25 newsstand; $50/yr. carrier. 145 W. Tenth St., Tracy, CA 95376. TEL 209-835-3030; FAX 209-835-0655. **Owner(s):** Tom, Bob, & Sam Matthews, P.O. Box 419, Tracy, CA 95378. TEL 209-835-3030; FAX 209-835-0655; Ed. Sam Matthews; Pub. Tom Matthews; adv. contact: Diane Lopez. pub. size: broadsheet; circ. morning 11,000(paid). **Wire Service(s):** AP, NYT.

TULARE

US

TULARE ADVANCE-REGISTER. 1882. Mon.-Sat. $.50 newsstand; $6.75/mo. 388 E. Cross Ave., Tulare, CA 93274. TEL 209-688-0521; FAX 209-688-7503. **Owner(s):** Gannett Company, Inc., 1100 Wilson Blvd., Arlington, VA 22234. TEL 703-284-6000; Ed. Lynda Thullen; Pub. Amy L. Pack; adv. contact: David Dakin. pub. size: broadsheet; circ. evening 9,000(paid). **Wire Service(s):** AP, SHNA.

   Formerly: Advance-Register.

TURLOCK

US

TURLOCK JOURNAL. 1904. Mon.-Sat. $.35/day newsstand; $.50/Sat.; $8.32/mo. carrier. 138 S. Center St., Turlock, CA 95380. TEL 209-634-9141; FAX 209-632-8813. **Owner(s):** Freedom Communications, Inc., 17666 Fitch, Irvine, CA 92714. TEL 714-553-9292; Pub. M. Olaf Frandsen; adv. contact: Christine Hammers. pub. size: broadsheet; circ. evening 9,700(paid). **Wire Service(s):** AP.
Formerly: Turlock Daily Journal.

UKIAH

US

UKIAH DAILY JOURNAL. 1862. Sun.-Fri. $.50/day newsstand; $1/Sun.; $7.50/mo.; $90/yr. carrier. 590 S. School St., Ukiah, CA 95482. TEL 707-468-0123; FAX 707-468-5780. **Owner(s):** Stephens Group, Inc., P.O. Box 1359, Fort Smith, AR 72901; Ed. Randy Foster; Pub. Dennis Wilson; adv. contact: John Speck. pub. size: broadsheet; circ. evening 7,609(paid); Sun. 7,727(paid). **Wire Service(s):** AP.

VACAVILLE

US   ISSN 0746-4193

REPORTER, THE. 1883. d. $.35/day newsstand; $1/Sun.; $20/2 mos. 916 Cotting Ln., Vacaville, CA 95688. TEL 707-448-6401; FAX 707-447-8411. **Owner(s):** John Rico Publishing Co., Inc., 318 Main St., Vacaville, CA 95688. TEL 707-448-6401; Ed. Diane Barney; Pub. Richard Rico; adv. contact: Jerry Billings. photos; pub. size: broadsheet; circ. morning 20,000(paid); Sun. 22,000(paid). **Wire Service(s):** AP.

VALENCIA

US

SIGNAL, THE. 1919. d. $78/yr. carrier; $150/yr. mailed. 24000 Creekside Rd., Valencia, CA 91355. TEL 805-259-1234; FAX 805-254-8068. **Owner(s):** Morris Communications, P.O. Box 8167, Savannah, GA 31412. TEL 912-233-1281; Ed. Tim Whyte; Pub. Darell Phillips; adv. contact: Ethel Nakutin. photos; bk.rev.; pub. size: broadsheet; circ. morning 44,000(paid); Sun. 44,000(paid). **Wire Service(s):** AP.
Formerly: Newhall Signal & Saugus Enterprise.

VALLEJO

US

VALLEJO TIMES-HERALD. 1875. d. $.50/day newsstand; $1/Sun.; $8.58/mo. 440 Curtola Pkwy., Vallejo, CA 94590. TEL 707-643-5217. **Owner(s):** Stephens Group, Inc., P.O. Box 1359, Fort Smith, AR 72902. TEL 501-785-7810; Ed. Joe Lowell; Pub. David Stringer; adv.; pub. size: broadsheet; circ. morning 23,000(paid); Sun. 24,000(paid). **Wire Service(s):** AP, TP.

VENTURA

US

VENTURA COUNTY STAR. 1883. d. $.35/day newsstand; $1.50/Sun.; $8/mo. carrier; $15.90/mo. mailed. 5250 Ralson St., Ventura, CA 93003. TEL 805-650-2900; FAX 805-650-2950; E-mail: vcstar@aol.com. **Owner(s):** John P. Scripps Newspapers, Inc., 525 C St., Ste. 306, San Diego, CA 92101; Ed. Joe Howry; Pub. John Wilcox; adv. contact: Harvey Hopkins. photos; bk.rev.; pub. size: broadsheet; circ. morning 54,000(paid); Sun. 59,000(paid). **Wire Service(s):** AP, NYT, MNS, SHNA.
Formerly: Ventura County Star-Free Press.

VICTORVILLE

US   ISSN 1042-8496

DAILY PRESS. 1937. d. $.35/day newsstand; $1.25/Sun.; $8/wk. carrier; $240.76/yr. 13891 Park Ave., Victorville, CA 92392-1389. TEL 619-241-7744; FAX 619-241-1860. **Owner(s):** Freedom Communications, Inc., P.O. Box 19549, Irvine, CA 92713-9549. TEL 714-553-9292; Fub. Maureen Saltzer Brotherton; adv. contact: Ray Marien. photos; bk.rev.; pub. size: broadsheet; circ. morning 27,000(paid); Sun. 30,000(paid). **Wire Service(s):** AP.
Formerly: Victor Valley Daily Press.

VISALIA

US

VISALIA TIMES-DELTA. 1859. Mon.-Sat. $.50/day newsstand, $1/Sat.; $10/mo. 330 N. West St., Visalia, CA 93291. TEL 209-734-5821; FAX 209-734-5843. **Owner(s):** Gannett Company, Inc., 1100 Wilson Blvd., Arlington, VA 22234. TEL 703-284-6000; Ed. Tom Bray; Pub. Amy L. Pack; adv. contact: David Dajin. pub. size: broadsheet; circ. morning 24,000(paid). **Wire Service(s):** AP, GNS.

WALNUT CREEK

US   ISSN 0192-0235

CONTRA COSTA TIMES. 1911. d. $.50 newsstand; $11.85/mc. 2640 Shadelands Dr., Walnut Creek, CA 94598. TEL 510-935-2525. **Owner(s):** Knight-Ridder, Inc., One Herald Plz., Miami, FL 94598. TEL 305-376-3800; Ed. Saundra Keyes; Pub. George E. Riggs; adv.; pub. size: broadsheet; circ. morning 93,334(paid); Sun. 105,503(paid). **Wire Service(s):** AP, McClatchy, NYT, LAT-WP, SHNA.

WATSONVILLE

US

REGISTER-PAJARONIAN. 1868. Mon.-Sat. $.35/day newsstand; $.50/Sat.; $7.25/mo. carrier; $10.55/mo. mailed. 1000 Main St., Watsonville, CA 95076. TEL 408-761-7300; FAX 408-722-8386; E-mail: pajaro@cruzio.com. **Owner(s):** News Media Corp., 211 Hwy. 38 E., P.O. Box 46, Rochelle, IL. TEL 815-562-2061; Pub. Douglas Leifeit; adv. contact: Nancy Moors. photos; bk.rev.; pub. size: broadsheet; circ. evening 11,000(paid). **Wire Service(s):** AP, LAT-WP, SHNA.
Formerly: Watsonville Register-Pajaronian.

WEST COVINA

US   ISSN 8755-9595

SAN GABRIEL VALLEY TRIBUNE. 1955. d. $.35/day newsstand; $1/Sun.; $2.10/wk. $130/yr. 1210 Azusa Canyon Rd., West Covina, CA 91790. TEL 818-962-8811; FAX 818-856-2758. **Owner(s):** Thomson Newspapers, Inc., Metro Ctr., One Station Pl., Stamford CT 06902; Ed. John Irby; Pub. Joe Logan; adv.; photcs; bk.rev.; pub. size: broadsheet; circ. morning 60,000(paid); Sun. 60,000(paid). **Wire Service(s):** AP, NYT, Scripps-McClatchy.

WHITTIER

US   ISSN 1069-2819

WHITTIER DAILY NEWS. 1900. d. $.25/day newsstand; $1/Sun.; $1.55/wk. 7612 Greenleaf Ave., Whittier, CA 90602. TEL 310-698-0955; FAX 310-698-0450. **Owner(s):** Thomson Newspapers, P.O. Box 1259, Covina, CA 91722. TEL 818-962-8811; Ed. Bill Bell; Pub. Bill Bell; pub. size: broadsheet; circ. evening 17,000(paid). **Wire Service(s):** AP, CINE, DJ, KR, NYT.

WOODLAND

US   ISSN 0747-1890

DAILY DEMOCRAT. 1857. d. $.50 newsstand; $6.90/mo. home deliv. 711 Main St., Woodland, CA 95695. TEL 916-662-5421; FAX 916-662-1288. **Owner(s):** Donrey Media Group, P.O. Box 17017 Fort Smith, AR 72901. TEL 501-785-7810; Ed. Jim Smith; Pub. Ron Rhea; adv. contact: Neil Rabon. pub. size: broadsheet; circ. evening 11,014(paid); Sun. 11,308(paid). **Wire Service(s):** AP.

WOODLAND HILLS

US

DAILY NEWS. 1911. d. $.25/day newsstand; $1/Sun.; $14.84/2 mos. 21221 Oxnard St., Woodland Hills, CA 91367. TEL 818-713-3000; FAX 818-713-3545. **Owner(s):** Jack Kent Cooke, Inc., 21221 Oxnard St., Woodland Hills, CA 91367. TEL 818-713-3131; Ed. Ron Kaye; Pub. Larry Beasley; adv. contact: Kevin E. Drolet. pub. size: broadsheet; circ. morning 212,252(paid); Sun. 227,054(paid).

Dailies

YREKA

US

SISKIYOU DAILY NEWS. 1941. Mon.-Fri. $.50 newsstand; $70/yr. 309 S. Broadway, Yreka, CA 96097. TEL 916-842-5777; FAX 916-842-6787. **Owner(s):** American Publishing Co., 606 N. Van Buren, P.O. Box 520, Marion, IL 62959. TEL 618-993-1711; Ed. Rebecca Weathers. adv.; photos; pub. size: broadsheet; circ. evening 6,100(paid). **Wire Service(s):** AP.

COLORADO

ALAMOSA

US   ISSN 1047-1170

VALLEY COURIER. 1925. Tue.-Sat. $.35 newsstand; $7.50/mo. 401-407 State St., Alamosa, CO 81101. TEL 719-589-2553; FAX 719-589-6573. **Owner(s):** News Media Corp., Rochelle, IL. TEL 815-562-2061; Ed. Greg Johnson; Pub. Keith R. Cerny; adv. contact: Keith R. Cerny. photos; pub. size: standard; circ. evening 5,150(paid). **Wire Service(s):** AP.

ASPEN

US

ASPEN DAILY NEWS. 1978. Mon.-Sat. free. 517 E. Hopkins, Aspen, CO 81611. TEL 970-925-2220; FAX 970-920-2118; E-mail: aspnews@infosphere.com. **Owner(s):** David Danforth, 517 E. Hopkins, Aspen, CO 81611. TEL 303-925-2220; Ed. Jim Burruf; Pub. David Danforth; adv. contact: Ross Furukowa. photos; pub. size: tabloid; circ. morning 11,700(free). **Wire Service(s):** AP.

US

ASPEN TIMES, THE. 1881. Mon.-Fri. free/Mon.-Thu. newsstand; $.25/Fri.; $32/yr. 310 E. Main St., Aspen, CO 81611. TEL 970-925-3414; FAX 970-925-6240; E-mail: aspenonline@infosphere.com; URL: http://www.aspenonline.com/clients/aspenonline/directory/times **Owner(s):** Full Court Press, Ltd., 310 E. Main St., Aspen, CO 81611. TEL 970-925-3414; FAX 970-925-6240; Ed. Andy Stone; Pub. Michael McVoy; adv. contact: Candice Welsh. photos; bk.rev.; pub. size: tabloid; circ. morning 12,500(free & paid); Sun. 11,000(free & paid). **Wire Service(s):** AP.
    Formerly: Aspen Times & Times Daily.

BOULDER

US   ISSN 0746-8733

DAILY CAMERA. 1891. d. $.25/day newsstand; $.75/Sun.; $29.25/13 wks. 1048 Pearl St., Boulder, CO 80302. TEL 303-442-1202; FAX 303-449-9358; E-mail: news@dailycamera.com. **Owner(s):** Knight-Ridder, Inc., One Herald Plz., Miami, FL 33132. TEL 305-376-3800; Ed. Gary Burns; Pub. Harold Higgins; adv. contact: Kelly Mirt. pub. size: broadsheet; circ. morning 35,000(paid); Sun. 43,000(paid). **Wire Service(s):** AP, LAT-WP, KNT, NYT.
    Formerly: Boulder Daily Camera.

CANON CITY

US   ISSN 1054-3457

DAILY RECORD. 1896. Mon.-Sat. $.35 newsstand; $6.75/mo. 523 Main St., Canon City, CO 81212. TEL 719-275-7565; FAX 719-275-1353. **Owner(s):** Royal Gorge Publishing Co., 523 Main St., Canon City, CO 81212. TEL 719-275-7565; Ed. Troy Schwindt; Pub. Ed Lehman; adv. contact: Terri Holloway. pub. size: broadsheet; circ. evening 8,794(paid). **Wire Service(s):** AP.
    Formerly: Canon City Daily Record.

COLORADO SPRINGS

US

COLORADO SPRINGS GAZETTE TELEGRAPH. 1872. d. $.50/day newsstand; $1/Sun.; $9.50/mo. home deliv. 30 S. Prospect St., Colorado Springs, CO 80903. TEL 719-632-5511; FAX 719-636-0224; E-mail: gazette@usa.net; URL: http://usa.net/gazette. **Owner(s):** Freedom Communications, Inc., 17666 Fitch St., Irvine, CA 92714. TEL 714-553-9292; Ed. Terri Fleming; Pub. N. Christian Anderson; bk.rev.; pub. size: broadsheet; circ. morning 103,945(paid); Sun. 123,051(paid). **Wire Service(s):** AP, KNT, NYT, SHNA.

CRAIG

US

NORTHWEST COLORADO DAILY PRESS. 1965. Mon.-Sat. $.25 newsstand; $5.50/mo. home deliv. 466 Yampa Ave., Craig, CO 81625. TEL 970-824-7031; FAX 970-824-6810. **Owner(s):** Yampa Valley Newspapers, Inc., P.O. Box 5, Craig, CO 81626. TEL 970-824-6810; Ed. Steve Busemeyer; Pub. Carol Beumer; adv. contact: Carol Beumer. pub. size: tabloid; circ. evening 3,500(paid). **Wire Service(s):** AP.

DENVER

US

DENVER POST. 1895. d. $.25/day newsstand; $1/Sun.; $7.25/mo. 1560 Broadway, Denver, CO80202. TEL 303-820-1010; FAX 303-820-1369; E-mail: newsroom@denverpost.com; URL: http://www.denverpost.com. **Owner(s):** Media News Group, P.O. Box 7810, Woodbury, NJ 08096; Ed. Dennis Britton; Pub. Ryan McKibben; adv. contact: Doug Barnett. photos; pub. size: broadsheet; circ. morning 284,542(paid); Sun. 456,057(paid). **Wire Service(s):** AP, LAT-WP, KR, UPI, DJ, NYT.

US

ROCKY MOUNTAIN NEWS. 1859. d. $.35/day newsstand; $.75/Sun.; $12.80/mo. 400 W. Colfax Ave., Denver, CO 80204. TEL 303-892-5000; FAX 303-892-5249; E-mail: newsdesk@denver-rmn.com; URL: http://www.denver-rmn.com. **Owner(s):** Scripps-Howard, 312 Walnut St., 28th Fl., Cincinnatti, OH 45202. TEL 513-977-3000; Ed. John Temple; Pub. Larry D. Strutton; adv. contact: Jerry Dunning. pub. size: tabloid; circ. morning 331,044(paid); Sun. 446,866(paid). **Wire Service(s):** AP, SHN, NEA.

DURANGO

US

DURANGO HERALD. 1881. Tue.-Sun. $.35/day newsstand; $.75/Sun.; $56/yr. carrier. 1275 Main Ave., Durango, CO 81301. TEL 303-247-3504; FAX 303-259-5011. **Owner(s):** Durango Herald Inc., P.O. Drawer A, Durango, CO 81302. TEL 303-247-3504; Ed. Dan Partridge; Pub. Richard G. Ballantine; adv. contact: Sharon Hermes. pub. size: broadsheet; circ. morning 8,118(paid); Sun. 10,672(paid). **Wire Service(s):** AP.

FORT COLLINS

US   ISSN 0164-9167

FORT COLLINS COLORADOAN. 1873. d. $.35/day newsstand; $1/Sun.; $32.50/13 wks. carrier. 1212 Riverside Ave., Fort Collins, CO 80524. TEL 970-224-7730; FAX 970-224-7899; E-mail: editor@fortnet.org; URL: http://www.fortnet.org/coloradoan/home.html. **Owner(s):** Gannett Company, Inc., 1100 Wilson Blvd., Arlington, VA 22234. TEL 703-284-6000; Pub. Dorothy Bland; adv. contact: Bob Williams. photos; bk.rev.; pub. size: broadsheet; circ. morning 23,500(paid); Sun. 35,000(paid). **Wire Service(s):** AP, GNS, LAT-WP.

FORT MORGAN

US

FORT MORGAN TIMES. 1884. Mon.-Sat. $.50 newsstand; $108/yr. 329 Main St., Fort Morgan, CO 80701. TEL 303-867-5651; FAX 303-867-7448. **Owner(s):** Media News Group, 309 S. Broad St., Woodbury, NJ 08096. TEL 609-845-3300; Ed. Bill Spencer; Pub. Robert W. Spencer, Jr.; adv. contact: Harold Bohm. photos; pub. size: broadsheet; circ. evening 5,429(paid). **Wire Service(s):** AP.

FRISCO

US

SUMMIT DAILY NEWS. 1989. Tue.-Sun. free newsstand; $2/wk. 40 W. Main St., Frisco, CO 80443. TEL 970-668-3998; FAX 970-668-3859. **Owner(s):** Eagle-Summit Publishing Co., P.O. Box 81, Vail, CO 81658. TEL 303-476-0555; pub. size: tabloid; circ. morning 8,000(free); Sun. 8,000(free). **Wire Service(s):** AP.

GLENWOOD SPRINGS

US

GLENWOOD POST. 1890. Mon.-Sat. $.35 newsstand; $102/yr. carrier. 2014 Grand Ave., Glenwood Springs, CO 81601. TEL 970-945-8515; FAX 970-945-4487; E-mail: glenpost@rof.net; URL: http://www.glenwoodpost.com. **Owner(s):** Morris Communications, P.O. Box 936, Augusta, GA 30903. TEL 706-724-0851; Ed. Dennis Webb; Pub. Gary Dickson; adv. contact: Bob Zanella. bk.rev.; pub. size: broadsheet; circ. evening 5,100(paid). **Wire Service(s):** AP.

GRAND JUNCTION
US

DAILY SENTINEL, THE. 1893. d. $.35/day newsstand; $1/Sun.; $2.75/wk. carrier. 734 S. Seventh St., Grand Junction, CO 81501. TEL 970-256-4256; FAX 970-241-6860. **Owner(s):** Cox Enterprises, Inc., 1400 Lake Hearn Dr., N.E., Atlanta, GA 30319. TEL 404-843-5000; Ed. Dennis Herzog; Pub. George Orbanek; adv. contact: Dennis Mitchell. pub. size: broadsheet; circ. evening 30,319(paid); Sun. 36,000(paid). **Wire Service(s):** AP, Cox, SHNA, LAT-WP.

GREELEY
US

GREELEY TRIBUNE. 1870. d. $.50/day newsstand; $.75/Sun.; $9.25/mo. local; $9.25/mo. mailed. 501 Eighth Ave., Greeley, CO 80631. TEL 303-352-0211; FAX 303-356-5780. **Owner(s):** Swift Publications, 501 Eighth Ave., Greeley, CO 80631. TEL 303-352-0211; Ed. Chris Cobler; Pub. David Trussell; adv. contact: George Snyder. photos; bk.rev.; pub. size: broadsheet; circ. evening 24,000(paid); Sun. 24,500(paid). **Wire Service(s):** AP, LAT-WP.

GUNNISON
US   ISSN 0892-1113

GUNNISON COUNTRY TIMES. 1880. Mon.-Fri. $.25 newsstand; $48/yr. in cy.; $72/yr. out of cy. 218 N. Wisconsin, Gunnison, CO 81230. TEL 970-641-1414; FAX 970-641-6515; E-mail: streed@frontier.net; URL: http://www.gunnisontimes.com/current/news.html. Owner(s): Ventana Publishing Co., Telluride, CO; Ed. Steve Reed. adv. contact: David Puddu. pub. size: tabloid; circ. 3,500(paid). **Wire Service(s):** AP.

LA JUNTA
US   ISSN 1056-4616

LA JUNTA TRIBUNE-DEMOCRAT. 1897. Mon.-Fri. $.25 newsstand; $51/yr. carrier mail in city; $57/yr. mailed 810 zip code; $79.50/yr. elsewhere. 422 Colorado Ave., La Junta, CO 81050. TEL 719-384-4475; FAX 719-384-5999. **Owner(s):** La Junta Democrat Publishing Co., Inc., P.O. Box 480, La Junta, CO 81050. TEL 719-384-4475; Ed. Wanda Lowe; Pub. John Lowe; adv. contact: Shelley Noe. photos; pub. size: tabloid; circ. evening 3,787(paid). **Wire Service(s):** AP.

LAMAR
US

LAMAR DAILY NEWS. 1907. Mon.-Fri. $.50 newsstand; $84/yr. local; $116/yr. tri-state; $126/yr. elsewhere. 310 S. Fifth St., Lamar, CO 81052. TEL 719-336-2266; FAX 719-336-2526; E-mail: ldnews@iquana.ruralnet.net. **Owner(s):** Media News Group, 309 S. Broad St., Woodbury, NJ 08096. TEL 609-845-3300; Ed. Ava Betz; Pub. Tom Betz; pub. size: broadsheet; circ. morning 4,200(paid). **Wire Service(s):** AP.

LONGMONT
US

DAILY TIMES-CALL. 1871. d. $.25/day newsstand; $.75/Sun.; $8/mo. local; $8.25/mo. elsewhere; $10/mo. mailed. 350 Terry St., Longmont, CO 80501. TEL 303-776-2244; FAX 303-678-8615. **Owner(s):** Times-Call Publishing Corp., P.O. Box 299, Longmont, CO 80502. TEL 303-776-2244; FAX 303-678-8615; Ed. Keith Briscoe; Pub. Edward Lehman; adv. contact: Linda Szaloczi. photos; pub. size: broadsheet; circ. evening 21,000(paid); Sun. 23,000(paid). **Wire Service(s):** AP, LAT-WP.
Formerly: Longmont Daily Times-Call.

LOVELAND
US

LOVELAND DAILY REPORTER-HERALD. 1880. Mon.-Sat. $.35 newsstand; $75/yr. 201 E. Fifth St., Loveland, CO 80537. TEL 970-669-5050. **Owner(s):** Loveland Publishing Co., 201 E. Fifth St., Loveland, CO 80537. TEL 970-669-5050; Ed. Ken Amundson; Pub. Edward Lehman; adv. contact: Sally Lee. photos; bk.rev.; pub. size: broadsheet; circ. evening 17,500(paid). **Wire Service(s):** AP, LAT-WP.

MONTROSE
US

MONTROSE DAILY PRESS. 1908. Mon.-Fri. $.35 newsstand; $60/yr. in state; $72/yr. out of state. 535 S. First St., Montrose, CO 81401. TEL 970-249-3444; FAX 970-249-3331. **Owner(s):** Press Publishing Co., P.O. Box 850, Montrose, CO 81402. TEL 970-249-3444; Ed. Richard E. Day; Pub. William Prescott Allen, III; pub. size: broadsheet; circ. evening 7,400(paid). **Wire Service(s):** AP.

US

▼**MONTROSE MORNING SUN.** 1996. Mon.-Fri. free. 120 N. Selig Ave., Montrose, CO 81401. TEL 970-240-4900; FAX 970-240-1842. **Owner(s):** D.P. Newspaper, LLC, 120 N. Selig Ave., Montrose, CO 81401. TEL 970-240-4900; Ed. Gary Taylor; Pub. Tony Daranyi; adv. contact: Karl Terry. pub. size: standard.

PUEBLO
US   ISSN 0747-3559

PUEBLO CHIEFTAIN. 1873. d. $.25/day newsstand; $.50/Sun.; $8/mo. 825 W. Sixth St., Pueblo, CO 81003. TEL 719-544-3520; FAX 719-546-3235. **Owner(s):** Star Journal Publishing Corp., Inc., P.O. Box 4040, Pueblo, CO 81003. TEL 719-544-3520; Ed. Robert H. Rawlings; Pub. Robert H. Rawlings; adv. contact: Jack Wyss. pub. size: broadsheet; circ. morning 51,000(paid); Sun. 56,500(paid). **Wire Service(s):** AP.

ROCKY FORD
US

ROCKY FORD DAILY GAZETTE. 1907. Mon.-Fri. $.25 newsstand $40/yr. carrier; $60/yr. mailed. 912 Elm Ave., Rocky Ford, CO 81067. TEL 719-254-3351; FAX 719-254-3354. **Owner(s):** Rocky Ford Publishing Co., 912 Elm Ave., Rocky Ford, CO 81067. TEL 303-254-3351. Ed. J.R. Thompson; Pub. Anne M. Thompson; adv. contact: Laura Thompson. pub. size: broadsheet; circ. evening 3,304(paid).

SALIDA
US

MOUNTAIN MAIL. 1880. Mon.-Fri. $.25 newsstand; $48/yr. 125-129 E. Second St. Salida, CO 81201. TEL 719-539-6591; FAX 719-539-6630; E-mail: mtnmail@rmii.com; URL: http://www.peaksnewsnet.com. **Owner(s):** Arkansas Valley Publishing Co., P.O. Box 189, Salida, CO 81201. TEL 719-539-6691; FAX 719-539-6630; Ed. Merle Baranczyk; Pub. Merle Baranczyk; adv. contact: Vickie Vigil. photos; bk.rev.; pub. size: tabloid; circ. morning 3,200(paid).

STEAMBOAT SPRINGS
US

STEAMBOAT TODAY. 1989. Mon.-Fri. free. 1041 Lincoln Ave., Steamboat Springs, CO 80477. TEL 970-879-1505; FAX 970-379-2888; E-mail: jbone@rmii.com. **Owner(s):** WorldWest Limited Liability Co., Lawrence, KS; Ed. Tom Ross; Pub. Suzanne Antinora; adv. contact: Sandy Lettunich. pub. size: tabloid; circ. morning 5,000(free). **Wire Service(s):** AP.

STERLING
US

STERLING JOURNAL-ADVOCATE. 1885. Mon.-Sat. $.50 newsstand; $71/yr. 504 N. Third St., Sterling, CO 80751. TEL 970-522-1990; FAX 970-522-2320. **Owner(s):** Media News Group, 309 S. Broad St., Woodbury, NJ 08096. TEL 609-845-3300; Pub. Bill Muldoon; adv. contact: Myron House. bk.rev.; pub. size: broadsheet; circ. evening 5,875(paid). **Wire Service(s):** AP.

TELLURIDE
US

TELLURIDE DAILY PLANET. 1993. Mon.-Fri. free. 283 S. Fir St., Telluride, CO 81435. TEL 970-728-9788; FAX 970-728-9793; E-mail: tdplanet@aol.com; URL: http://www.telluridegateway.com/current/news.html. Owner(s): D.P. Newspaper, LLC, P.O. Box 2315, Telluride, CO 81435. TEL 970-728-9788; FAX 970-728-9793; Ed. Ben Beer Pub. Tony Daranyi; adv. contact: John Douret. photos; bk.rev.; pub. size: tabloid; circ. morning 4,500(free).

TRINIDAD
US

CHRONICLE NEWS, THE. 1876. Mon.-Fri. $.25 newsstand; $42/yr. local. 200 W. Church St., Trinidad, CO 81082. TEL 719-846-3311; FAX 719-846-3612. **Owner(s):** Lake Charles American Press, 327 Board St., Lake Charles, LA 70601. TEL 318-439-2781; Ed. Cosette Henritze. pub. size: broadsheet; circ. evening 4,000(paid). **Wire Service(s):** AP.
Formerly: Trinidad Chronicle News.

VAIL

US

VAIL DAILY. 1981. d. free; $29.95/yr. mailed. 143 E. Meadow Dr., Vail, CO 81657. TEL 970-476-0555; FAX 970-476-8906; E-mail: vdail@vail.net; URL: http://www.vaildaily.com/vail. Owner(s): Swift Publications, Reno, NV; Ed. Rob Spencer; Pub. Bob Brown; adv. contact: Valerie Smith. photos; pub. size: tabloid; circ. morning 12,000(free). **Wire Service(s):** AP.

CONNECTICUT

BRIDGEPORT

US

CONNECTICUT POST. 1883. d. $.50/day newsstand; $1.50/Sun.; $180/yr. 410 State St., Bridgeport, CT 06604. TEL 203-333-0161; FAX 203-367-8158. **Owner(s):** Thomson Newspapers, Inc., 3150 Des Plaines Ave., Des Plaines, IL 60018. TEL 708-299-5544; Ed. Michael Daly; Pub. Robert Laska; adv. contact: Brenda MacDonald. pub. size: broadsheet; circ. morning 75,000(paid); Sun. 92,455(paid). **Wire Service(s):** AP, UPI, KR.
Formerly: Bridgeport Post Telegram.

BRISTOL

US   ISSN 0891-5563

BRISTOL PRESS, THE. 1871. d. $35.10/3 mos. in area; $52/3 mos. out of area. 99 Main St., Bristol, CT 06010. TEL 203-584-0501; FAX 203-585-9283. **Owner(s):** Journal Register Co., 50 W. State St., 12th Fl., Trenton, NJ 08608. TEL 609-396-2200; Ed. Robert E. Brown; Pub. James Normandin; pub. size: broadsheet; circ. evening 20,484(paid). **Wire Service(s):** AP.

DANBURY

US   ISSN 1044-4106

NEWS-TIMES. 1883. d. $.50/day newsstand; $1.50/Sun.; $3.30/wk. carrier. 333 Main St., Danbury, CT 06810-5868. TEL 203-744-5100; FAX 203-792-8730. **Owner(s):** Ottaway Newspapers, Inc., P.O. Box 401, Campbell Hall, NY 10916. TEL 914-294-8181; Ed. Paul Steinmetz, Jr.; Pub. Wayne J. Shepperd; adv. contact: Paul Evans. photos; bk.rev.; pub. size: broadsheet; circ. morning 37,939(paid); Sun. 45,563(paid). **Wire Service(s):** AP, ONS, KRTN.

GREENWICH

US   ISSN 0279-5213

GREENWICH TIME. 1861. d. $.50/day newsstand; $1.50/Sun. 20 E. Elm, Greenwich, CT 06830. TEL 203-625-4400; FAX 203-964-4419. **Owner(s):** Southern Connecticut Newspapers, Inc., 75 Tresser Blvd., P.O. Box 9307, Stamford, CT 06901. TEL 203-964-2200; Ed. Joseph Pisani; Pub. William J. Rowe; adv. contact: John Dunster. pub. size: broadsheet; circ. evening 13,407(paid); Sun. 14,300(paid). **Wire Service(s):** AP, LAT-WP, KR, CT-NYT, UPI Photo.

HARTFORD

US   ISSN 1047-4153

HARTFORD COURANT. 1764. d. $.50/day newsstand; $1.50/Sun.; $3.90/wk.; $45.50/3mos. 285 Broad St., Hartford, CT 06115-2510. TEL 203-241-6200; FAX 203-241-3865. **Owner(s):** Times Mirror Co., Times Mirror Sq., 220 W. First St., Los Angeles, CA 90012. TEL 213-237-3700; Ed. Clifford L. Teutsch; Pub. Michael E. Waller; adv. contact: Kathleen Coddington. pub. size: broadsheet; circ. morning 227,792(paid); Sun. 316,058(paid). **Wire Service(s):** AP, KR, LAT-WP, DJ, RN, Bloomberg Business News.

MANCHESTER

US

JOURNAL INQUIRER. 1968. Mon.-Sat. $.40 newsstand; $124.80/yr. carrier. 306 Progress Dr., Manchester, CT 06040. TEL 203-646-0500; FAX 203-646-9867; E-mail: journalinq@aol.com; URL: http://www.journalinquirer.com. **Owner(s):** Journal Publishing Co., 306 Progress Dr., Manchester, CT 06040. TEL 203-643-8111; Ed. Chris Powell; Pub. Elizabeth S. Ellis; adv. contact: Bill Sybert. pub. size: tabloid; circ. evening 50,000(paid). **Wire Service(s):** AP.
Formerly: Manchester Journal Inquirer.

MERIDEN

US

RECORD-JOURNAL. 1867. d. $4/wk. 11 Crown St., Meriden, CT 06450-5788. TEL 203-235-1661; FAX 203-639-0210. **Owner(s):** Record-Journal Publishing Co., 11 Crown St., Meriden, CT 06450. TEL 203-235-1661; Ed. Donald Schiller; Pub. Eliot C. White; adv. contact: Michael F. Killian. photos; bk.rev.; pub. size: broadsheet; circ. morning 30,189(paid); Sun. 30,803(paid). **Wire Service(s):** AP.

MIDDLETOWN

US

MIDDLETOWN PRESS. 1884. Mon.-Sat. $.50 newsstand; $182/yr. home deliv. Two Main St., Middletown, CT 06457. TEL 203-347-3331; FAX 203-347-3380. **Owner(s):** Journal Register Co., 50 W. State St., 12th Fl., Trenton, NJ 08608. TEL 609-396-2200; Ed. Suzanne Simoneau; Pub. James F. Normandin; adv. contact: Jamie M. Tomasic. photos; bk.rev.; pub. size: standard; circ. morning 15,200(paid). **Wire Service(s):** UPI, NYT, LAT-WP.

NAUGATUCK

US

NAUGATUCK DAILY NEWS. 1885. Mon.-Sat. $.50 newsstand; $93.60/yr. carrier; $96/yr. mailed. 71 Weid Dr., Naugatuck, CT 06770. TEL 203-729-2228; FAX 203-729-9099. **Owner(s):** American Publishing Co., 606 N. Van Buren, P.O. Box 520, Marion, IL 62959. TEL 618-993-1711; Pub. Ronald Waer; pub. size: broadsheet; circ. evening 5,250(paid). **Wire Service(s):** AP.

NEW BRITAIN

US

HERALD, THE. 1880. Mon.-Sat. $.50 newsstand; $138.60/yr. One Herald Sq., New Britain, CT 06050-2050. TEL 203-225-4601; FAX 203-225-4601. **Owner(s):** Journal Register Co., 50 W. State St., 12th Fl., Trenton, NJ 08608. TEL 609-396-2200; Pub. James Normandin; adv. contact: Mark Lane. photos; bk.rev.; pub. size: broadsheet; circ. evening 33,252(paid). **Wire Service(s):** AP.

NEW HAVEN

US

NEW HAVEN REGISTER. 1812. d. $.50/day newsstand; $1.50/Sun.; $3.50/wk. 40 Sargent Dr., New Haven, CT 06511. TEL 203-789-5440; FAX 203-865-8360. **Owner(s):** E.M. Warburg/Pincus & Co., 40 Sargent Dr., New Haven, CT 06511; Ed. David Funkhouser; Pub. William Rush; adv. contact: Charlene Chiaro. photos; pub. size: standard; circ. morning 100,089(paid); Sun. 123,922(paid). **Wire Service(s):** AP, LAT-WP, KR.

NEW LONDON

US   ISSN 0744-0499

DAY, THE. 1881. d. $.50/day newsstand; $1/Sun.; $3.10/wk. carrier; $15.38/mo. mailed; $12.40/4 wks. motor rte. 47 Eugene O'Neill Dr., New London, CT 06320. TEL 203-442-2200; FAX 203-447-1683. **Owner(s):** Day Publishing Co., The, P.O. Box 1231, New London, CT 06320. TEL 203-442-2200; FAX 203-447-1683; Ed. Lance Johnson; Pub. Reid MacCluggage; adv.; photos; bk.rev.; pub. size: broadsheet; circ. morning 42,366(paid); Sun. 48,713(paid). **Wire Service(s):** AP, NYT, KNT.
Formerly: New London Day.

NORWALK

US

HOUR, THE. 1871. Mon.-Sat. $.40 newsstand; $.75/Sat.; $117.60/yr. 346 Main Ave., Norwalk, CT 06851. TEL 203-846-3281; FAX 203-846-9897. **Owner(s):** Estate of Nellie Thomas, 346 Main Ave., Norwalk, CT 06851. TEL 203-846-3281; Ed. Mark Allison; Pub. B.J. Frazier; adv. contact: Thomas Kies. photos; pub. size: standard; circ. evening 21,500(paid). **Wire Service(s):** AP.
Formerly: Norwalk Hour.

NORWICH

US

NORWICH BULLETIN. 1791. d. $.50/day newsstand; $1/Sun.; $2.75/wk. 66 Franklin St., Norwich, CT 06360. TEL 860-887-9211; FAX 860-887-9666; E-mail: norbull@q.continuum.net; URL: http://www.ctonline.com/ctonline/nbulletin.html. **Owner(s):** Gannett Company, Inc., 1100 Wilson Blvd, Arlington, VA 22234; Pub. Richard M. Bottorf; adv.; bk.rev.; pub. size: broadsheet; circ. morning 34,000(paid); Sun. 37,000(paid). **Wire Service(s):** AP, GNS.

STAMFORD

US   ISSN 0279-5167

ADVOCATE, THE. 1829. d. $.50/day newsstand; $1.50/Sun.; $3/wk. 75 Tresser Blvd., Stamford, CT 06901. TEL 203-964-2200; FAX 203-964-2345. **Owner(s):** Times-Mirror Co., Times-Mirror Sq., 220 W. First St., Los Angeles, CA 90053. TEL 213-237-3700; Ed. Dierdre Channing; Pub. William J. Rowe; pub. size: broadsheet; circ. evening 31,000(paid); Sun. 42,000(paid). **Wire Service(s):** AP.

TORRINGTON

US   ISSN 0746-8180

REGISTER CITIZEN. 1874. d. $.50/day newsstand; $1/Sun.; $11.80/4 wks. 190 Water St., Torrington, CT 06790-0058. TEL 203-489-3121; FAX 203-489-6790. **Owner(s):** Journal Register Co., 50 W. State St., 12th Fl., Trenton, NJ 08608. TEL 609-396-2200; Pub. William Murray; adv. contact: Richard Welch. pub. size: broadsheet; circ. morning 16,585(paid). **Wire Service(s):** AP, NYT.

WATERBURY

US

WATERBURY REPUBLICAN-AMERICAN. 1990. d. $.50 newsstand; $1.50 Sun.; $2/wk. 389 Meadow St., Waterbury, CT 06722-2090. TEL 203-574-3636. **Owner(s):** Republican-American, Inc., P.O. Box 2090, Waterbury, CT 06722-2090. TEL 203-574-3636; Ed. Robert D. Veillette; Pub. William J. Pape II; adv. contact: Patrick Cox. pub. size: broadsheet; circ. morning 61,000(paid); Sun. 80,000(paid). **Wire Service(s):** AP.

WILLIMANTIC

US

CHRONICLE, THE. 1876. Mon.-Sat. $.50 newsstand; $2.10/wk. carrier. One Chronicle Rd., Willimantic, CT 06226. TEL 203-423-8466; FAX 203-423-2641. **Owner(s):** Lucy Crosby, One Chronicle Rd., Willimantic, CT 06226. TEL 203-423-8466; Ed. Barry Lewis. adv. contact: Walter Riley. pub. size: broadsheet; circ. evening 13,000(paid). **Wire Service(s):** AP. **Formerly:** Willimantic Chronicle.

DELAWARE

DOVER

US   ISSN 0745-8096

DELAWARE STATE NEWS. 1953. d. $.35 newsstand; $1.25/Sun.; $2.10/wk. Webbs Ln. & New Burton Rd., Dover, DE 19901. TEL 302-674-3600. **Owner(s):** Independent Newspapers, Inc., 8015 N. 54th St., Scottsdale, AZ 85253. TEL 602-997-5811; Ed. Michael Pelrine; Pub. Tammy Brittingham; adv. contact: Helen Downing. pub. size: standard; circ. morning 25,000(paid); Sun. 38,000(paid). **Wire Service(s):** SHNA, KNT, LAT-WP.

LEWES

US

DAILY WHALE, THE. 1975. d. $.35 newsstand; $1/Sun.; $100/yr. home deliv. Rte. 1, Midway Shopping Ctr., Lewes, DE 19958-0037. TEL 302-645-2265; FAX 302-645-2267. **Owner(s):** Independent Newspapers, Inc., P.O. Box 7001, Dover, DE 19903; Ed. Andy West; Pub. Tamra Brittingham; adv. contact: Tom Schwab. photos; pub. size: broadsheet; circ. morning 5,500(free & paid); Sun. 36,000(free & paid). **Wire Service(s):** KR, SHNA, LAT-WP.

NEW CASTLE

US   ISSN 1042-4121

NEWS JOURNAL, THE. 1880. d. $3.35/wk. home deliv. 950 W. Basin Rd., New Castle, DE 19720. TEL 302-324-2500; FAX 302-324-5509. **Owner(s):** Gannett Company, Inc., 1100 Wilson Blvd., Arlington, VA 22234. TEL 703-248-6000; Ed. Valerie Bender; Pub. W. Curtis Riddle; adv. contact: Sam Martin. photos; bk.rev.; pub. size: broadsheet; circ. morning 125,000(paid); Sun. 151,000(paid). **Wire Service(s):** AP, LAT-WP, GNS, Baltimore Sun, SHNS.

DISTRICT OF COLUMBIA

WASHINGTON

US   ISSN 0190-8286

WASHINGTON POST, THE. 1877. d. $.25/day newsstand; $1.50/Sun; $132.60/yr. 1150 15th St., N.W., Washington, DC 20071. TEL 202-334-6000; FAX 202-334-5547. **Owner(s):** Washington Post Co., 1150 15th St., N.W., Washington, DC 20071. TEL 202-334-6000; Ed. Robert Kaiser; Pub. Donald E. Graham; adv. contact: Steve Hills. pub. size: broadsheet; circ. morning 834,641(paid); Sun. 1,140,564(paid). **Wire Service(s):** AP, UPI, CT, NYNS, CDN, LAT-WP.

US   ISSN 0732-8494

WASHINGTON TIMES. 1982. d. $.25/day newsstand; $1/Sun.; $2/wk. local. 3600 New York Ave., N.E., Washington, DC 20002. TEL 202-636-3000; FAX 202-269-3419. **Owner(s):** News World Communications, Inc., 401 Fifth Ave., New York, NY 10016. TEL 212-532-8300; Ed. Josette Shiner. adv.; photos; bk.rev.; pub. size: broadsheet; circ. morning 100,000(paid); Sun. 85,000(paid). **Wire Service(s):** AP, AFP, RN, LDE.

FLORIDA

BOCA RATON

US

NEWS, THE. 1958. d. $.25/day newsstand; $.50/Sun.; $1.48/wk. 33 S.E. Third St., Boca Raton, FL 33432. TEL 407-338-4910; FAX 407-338-4944. **Owner(s):** Knight-Ridder, Inc., One Herald Plz., Miami, FL 33132. TEL 305-376-3800; Ed. John Futch; Pub. Roger Coover; adv. contact: Judy Green. photos; bk.rev.; pub. size: broadsheet; circ. morning 16,000(paid); Sun. 20,000(paid). **Wire Service(s):** AP, KNT, LAT-WP.

BRADENTON

US

BRADENTON HERALD, THE. 1922. d. $.35/day newsstand; $1/Sun.; $125.20/yr. 102 Manatee Ave., W., Bradenton, FL 34205. TEL 941-748-0411; FAX 941-745-7094. **Owner(s):** Knight-Ridder Inc., One Herald Plz., Miami, FL 33132. TEL 305-376-3800; FAX 305-376-3865; Ed. Bruce Lind. Pub. Craig Wells; adv. contact: Bruce Faulmann. photos; bk.rev.; pub. size: broadsheet; circ. morning 43,194(paid); Sun. 55,149(paid). **Wire Service(s):** AP, KR, KNT.

BROOKSVILLE

US

HERNANDO TODAY. 1987. Mon.-Sat. $.25 newsstand; $32.50/yr. 15299-A Cortez Blvd., Brooksville, FL 34613-6095. TEL 904-544-5295; FAX 904-799-3688. **Owner(s):** Media General, Inc., P.O. Box 85333, Richmond, VA 23293-0001. TEL 804-649-6000; Ed. Robert Notte. adv.; photos; bk.rev.; pub. size: broadsheet; circ. 17,000(free & paid). **Wire Service(s):** AP.

CAPE CORAL

US   ISSN 0747-4199

DAILY BREEZE, THE. 1963. Mon.-Sat. $.25 day newsstand; $45/yr. 2510 Del Prado Blvd., Cape Coral, FL 33904. TEL 941-574-1110; FAX 941-574-3403. **Owner(s):** Breeze Corp., P.O. Box 846, Cape Coral, FL 33904. TEL 941-574-1110; adv. contact: Bonnie Cook. photos; pub. size: broadsheet; circ. evening 5,000(free & paid). **Wire Service(s):** AP.

CHARLOTTE HARBOR

US   ISSN 1044-0399

CHARLOTTE SUN HERALD. 1893. d. $.50/day newsstand; $1.50/Sun. $32.37/3 mos.; $104.96/yr. 23170 Harbor View Rd., Charlotte Harbor, FL 33980. TEL 941-629-2855; FAX 941-629-2085; E-mail: cnared@aol.com; URL: http://www.charlotte-florida.com. **Owner(s):** Sun Coast Media Group, 23170 Harbor View Rd., Charlotte Harbor, FL 33980. TEL 941-629-2855; Ed. Jeff Dunr-Rankin; Pub. Derrick Dunn-Rankin; adv. contact: Jim Leatham. pub. size: broadsheet; circ. evening 26,800(paid). **Wire Service(s):** AP, Pix Stocks. **Formerly:** Charlotte Herald-News.

CRYSTAL RIVER

US

CITRUS COUNTY CHRONICLE. 1890. d. $.25/day newsstand; $.75/Sun. $89/yr. 1624 N. Meadowcrest Blvd., Crystal River, FL 34429. TEL 904-726-1441; FAX 904-563-5665; E-mail: citrus@infi.net; URL: http://www.chronicle-online.com. **Owner(s):** LCNI-Landmark Community Newspaper, P.O. Box 549, Shelbyville, KY 40066. TEL 502-633-4334; Ed. Ken Melton; Pub. Gerard Mulligan; adv. contact: Dale Bowen. photos; bk.rev.; pub. size: broadsheet; circ. morning 22,000(paid); Sun. 25,000(paid). **Wire Service(s):** AP, KR, N, LAT-WP.

DAYTONA BEACH

US

DAYTONA BEACH NEWS-JOURNAL, THE. 1904. d. $.35/day newsstand; $1/Sun.; $10.18/mo.; $132.29/yr. 901 Sixth St., Daytona Beach, FL 32117. TEL 904-252-1511; FAX 904-258-8469. **Owner(s):** News-Journal Corp., 901 Sixth St., Daytona Beach, FL 32117. TEL 904-252-1511; FAX 904-736-2714; Ed. Donald Lindley; Pub. Tippen Davidson; adv. contact: Kathy Coughlin. photos; pub. size: broadsheet; circ. morning 99,625(paid); Sun. 119,335(paid). **Wire Service(s):** AP, NYT.

ENGLEWOOD

US

ENGLEWOOD SUN HERALD. d. $.35/day newsstand; $1/Sun.; $18.50/3 mos. carrier in cy.; $26.50/3 mos. carrier Charlotte & Englewood cys. 167 W. Dearborn St., Englewood, FL 34223. TEL 941-474-5521; FAX 941-426-3576. **Owner(s):** Sun Coast Media Group, 23170 Harbor View Rd., Charlotte Harbor, FL 33980. TEL 941-629-2855; FAX 941-629-2085; Ed. Chris Portor; Pub. Derek Dun-Rankin; adv. contact: Lang Capasso. photos; bk.rev.; pub. size: broadsheet; circ. morning 35,000(paid); Sun. 40,000(paid).

Formerly: Englewood Sun-Times.

FORT LAUDERDALE

US   ISSN 0744-8139

SUN-SENTINEL. 1911. d. $.35/day newsstand; $1/Sun.; $2.45/wk. 200 E. Las Olas Blvd., Fort Lauderdale, FL 33301-2293. TEL 305-356-4000; FAX 305-356-4093. **Owner(s):** Tribune Co., 435 N. Michigan Ave., Chicago, IL 60601; Ed. Ellen Soeteber; Pub. Scott C. Smith; adv.; photos; bk.rev.; pub. size: broadsheet; circ. morning 264,300(paid); Sun. 366,200(paid). **Wire Service(s):** AP, RN, LAT-WP, KRT, DJ, NYT, CQ.

FORT MYERS

US

NEWS-PRESS, THE. 1884. d. $.50/day newsstand; $1.50/Sun.; $13.70/mo. Martin Luther King, Jr. Blvd., Fort Myers, FL 33901-2442. TEL 941-335-0200; FAX 941-334-0708. **Owner(s):** Gannett Company, Inc., 1100 Wilson Blvd., Arlington, VA 22209. TEL 703-284-6000; Ed. Vickie Kilgore; Pub. Frederick Jacobi; adv.; photos; bk.rev.; pub. size: broadsheet; circ. morning 90,000(paid); Sun. 140,000(paid). **Wire Service(s):** AP, GNS, KRT.

Formerly: Fort Myers News-Press.

FORT PIERCE

US

TRIBUNE, THE. 1903. d. $.25/day newsstand; $.75/Sun.; $1.60/wk. 600 Edwards Rd., Fort Pierce, FL 34982. TEL 407-461-2050; FAX 407-461-4447. **Owner(s):** Freedom Communications, Inc., 17666 Fitch, Irvine, CA 92714. TEL 714-553-9292; Ed. Harold Muddiman; Pub. David Rutledge; adv.; pub. size: standard; circ. morning 32,298(paid); Sun. 35,097(paid). **Wire Service(s):** UPI, AP.

Formerly: Fort Pierce & Port St. Lucie Tribune.

FORT WALTON BEACH

US

NORTHWEST FLORIDA DAILY NEWS. 1946. d. $.50/day newsstand; $1.25/Sun.; $10/mo. 200 Racetrack Rd., N.W., Fort Walton Beach, FL 32547. TEL 904-863-1111; FAX 904-862-5230. **Owner(s):** Freedom Communications, Inc., 17666 Fitch, Irvine, CA 92714. TEL 714-553-9292; Ed. Debbie Lord; Pub. Marvin DeBolt; adv. contact: Sam Childs. photos; pub. size: broadsheet; circ. morning 38,000(paid); Sun. 50,000(paid). **Wire Service(s):** AP, KRTN.

GAINESVILLE

US   ISSN 0163-4925

GAINESVILLE SUN, THE. 1876. d. $.50/day newsstand; $1.25/Sun.; $151.58/yr. 2700 S.W. 13th St., Gainesville, FL 32608. TEL 904-378-1411; FAX 904-338-3128. **Owner(s):** New York Times Co., The, 229 W. 43rd St., New York, NY 10036. TEL 212-556-1234; Ed. Curt Pierson; Pub. John W. Fitzwater; adv. contact: David Minnich. photos; bk.rev.; pub. size: broadsheet; circ. morning 55,972(paid); Sun. 61,389(paid). **Wire Service(s):** AP, NYT.

JACKSONVILLE

US   ISSN 0704-2325

FLORIDA TIMES-UNION. 1864. d. $.50/day newsstand; $1.50/Sun.; $234/yr.; $134.16/yr. Sat. & Sun. One Riverside Ave., Jacksonville, FL 32202-4904. TEL 904-359-4111; FAX 904-359-4478; E-mail: scheski@tu.infi.net; URL: http://www.times-union.com. **Owner(s):** Florida Times-Union, One Riverside Ave., Jacksonville, FL 32202-4904. TEL 904-359-4111; Ed. Mary Kress; Pub. Carl N. Cannon; adv.; photos; bk.rev.; pub. size: broadsheet; circ. morning 194,654(paid); Sun. 253,960(paid). **Wire Service(s):** AP, NYT, LAT-WP, KNS, DJ.

KEY WEST

US

KEY WEST CITIZEN. 1881. Sun.-Fri. $.25/day newsstand; $1/Sun.; $99.51/yr. carrier; $138.24/yr. elsewhere. 3420 Northside Dr., Key West, FL 33040. TEL 305-294-6641; FAX 305-294-0768. **Owner(s):** Thomson Newspapers, Inc., 3150 Des Plaines Ave., Des Plaines, IL 60018. TEL 708-299-5544; Ed. Tim Aten; Pub. Winston Burrell; adv. contact: Randy Erickson. bk.rev.; pub. size: standard; circ. morning 10,940(paid); Sun. 11,470(paid). **Wire Service(s):** AP.

LAKE CITY

US

LAKE CITY REPORTER. 1874. Mon.-Sat. $.25 newsstand; $83.46/yr. 126 E. Duval St., Lake City, FL 32055. TEL 904-752-1293; FAX 904-752-9400. **Owner(s):** New York Times Co., The, 229 W. 43rd St., New York, NY 10036. TEL 212-556-1234; Ed. Tommy Hornsby; Pub. Don L. Caldwell; adv. contact: Andy Caldwell. pub. size: broadsheet; circ. evening 10,500(paid). **Wire Service(s):** AP, NYT.

LAKELAND

US   ISSN 0163-0288

LEDGER, THE. 1924. d. $.50/day newsstand; $1/Sun.; $10.60/4 wks.; $137.80/yr. 401 S. Missouri Ave., Lakeland, FL 33801. TEL 941-687-7000; FAX 941-687-7090; E-mail: info@tsolv.com; URL: http://www.lakeland.tsolv.com. **Owner(s):** New York Times Co., The, 229 W. 43rd St., New York, NY 10036. TEL 212-556-1234; Ed. Hunter George; Pub. Don Whitworth; adv. contact: Lucy Talley. pub. size: broadsheet; circ. morning 78,200(paid); Sun. 96,000(paid). **Wire Service(s):** AP, NYT, KNT.

LEESBURG

US

DAILY COMMERCIAL. 1875. d. $.25/day newsstand; $1/Sun. 212 E. Main St., Leesburg, FL 34748. TEL 352-365-8212; FAX 352-365-1951. **Owner(s):** Better Built Media Group, Inc., P.O. Box 490007, Leesburg, FL 34749; Ed. Randy Fears; Pub. Jim Perry; adv.; photos; bk.rev.; pub. size: broadsheet; circ. morning 34,782(paid); Sun. 37,654(paid). **Wire Service(s):** AP.

MARIANNA

US

JACKSON COUNTY FLORIDAN. 1927. Tue.-Fri. & Sun. $91.20/yr. 4403 Constitution Ln., Marianna, FL 32446. TEL 904-526-3614; FAX 904-482-4478. **Owner(s):** Thomson Newspapers, Inc., Des Plaines, IL; Ed. Judy Green; Pub. Jane Benton; adv. contact: Valeria Roberts. pub. size: broadsheet; circ. evening 6,100(paid); Sun. 7,000(paid). **Wire Service(s):** AP.

MELBOURNE

US   ISSN 1051-8304

FLORIDA TODAY. 1966. d. $.50 newsstand; $13.78/mo. One Gannett Plz., Melbourne, FL 32940. TEL 407-242-3500; FAX 407-242-6620; E-mail: 71333.1616@compuserve.com; URL: http://www.flatoday.com/space. **Owner(s):** Gannett Company, Inc., 1160 Wilson Blvd., Arlington, VA 22209. TEL 703-284-6000; Ed. Melinda Meers; Pub. Michael J. Coleman; adv. contact: Mike Jung. photos; bk.rev.; pub. size: broadsheet; circ. morning 98,377(paid); Sun. 124,839(paid). **Wire Service(s):** AP, GNS.

MIAMI

US

MIAMI HERALD. 1910. d. $.35/day newsstand; $1/Sun.; $141.22/yr. in cy.; $157.10/yr. east & west coast. One Herald Plz., Miami, FL 33132-1693. TEL 305-350-2111; FAX 305-376-2072; E-mail: 74763.3324@compuserve.com; URL: http://www.herald.com/. **Owner(s):** Knight-Ridder, Inc., One Herald Plz., Miami, FL 33132. TEL 305-376-3800; Ed. Jim Hampton; Pub. David Lawrence, Jr.; adv.; photos; bk.rev.; pub. size: broadsheet; circ. morning 378,195(paid); Sun. 500,564(paid). **Wire Service(s):** AP, UPI, LAT-WP, KNT, TD.

NAPLES

US

NAPLES DAILY NEWS. 1923. d. $.35/day newsstand; $1.50/Sun.; $183.38/yr. in state; $173/yr. mailed. 1075 Central Ave., Naples, FL 33940. TEL 813-263-4770; FAX 813-263-4816. **Owner(s):** Scripps-Howard, 1100 Central Trust Tower, Cincinnati, OH 45202. TEL 513-977-3000; Ed. Phil Lewis; Pub. Corbin Wyant; pub. size: broadsheet; circ. morning 53,000(paid); Sun. 65,000(paid).

Formerly: Naples News.

NEW SMYRNA

US

NEW SMYRNA BEACH OBSERVER. 1913. Tue.-Sat. $.50 newsstand; $19.82/3 mos. 823 S. Dixie Fwy., New Smyrna, FL 32168. TEL 904-427-1000; FAX 904-428-1265. **Owner(s):** American Publishing Co., 606 N. Van Buren, P.O. Box 520, Marion, IL 62959. TEL 618-993-1711; Ed. Jim Jones; Pub. Gui Bleasley; adv.; photos; bk.rev.; pub. size: broadsheet; circ. morning 5,500(paid). **Wire Service(s):** AP.

OBSERVER, THE. 1913. Tue.-Sat. $.50 newsstand; $72.34/yr. 823 S. Dixie Fwy., New Smyrna, FL 32168. TEL 904-427-1000. **Owner(s):** American Publishing Co., 606 N. Van Buren, P.O. Box 520, Marion, IL 62959. TEL 618-993-1711; Ed. Jim Jones; Pub. David Crawley; adv. contact: Jamie Smith. photos; bk.rev.; pub. size: broadsheet; circ. 4,300(paid). **Wire Service(s):** AP.

OCALA

US   ISSN 0163-3201

OCALA STAR BANNER. 1866. d. $.25/day newsstand; $.75/Sat.; $1.25/Sun. 2121 S.W. 19th Ave. Rd., Ocala, FL 32674. TEL 904-867-4010; FAX 904-867-4018. **Owner(s):** New York Times Co., The, 229 W. 43rd St., New York, NY 10036. TEL 212-556-1234; Ed. Jay McKenzie; Pub. Charles Stout; adv. contact: Foy Maloy. photos; bk.rev.; pub. size: broadsheet; circ. morning 50,000(paid); Sun. 54,000(paid). **Wire Service(s):** AP, NYT, SHNA, KR, LAT-WP.

OKEECHOBEE

US

DAILY OKEECHOBEE NEWS, THE. 1910. d. $.35/day newsstand; $.50/Sun.; $9.01/mo. in cy.; $17.23/mo. out of cy. 107 S.W. 17th St., Ste. D, Okeechobee, FL 34974. TEL 813-763-3134; FAX 813-763-5901. **Owner(s):** Independent Newspapers, Inc., P.O. Box 7001, Dover, DE 19903. TEL 302-674-4750; Ed. Katrina Elsken; Pub. Richard Hitt; adv. contact: Judy Kasten. photos; pub. size: broadsheet; circ. morning 6,000(paid); Sun. 6,000(paid). **Wire Service(s):** AP.

Formerly: Okeechobee News.

ORANGE PARK

US

CLAY TODAY. 1974. Tue.-Sat. free newsstand; $73.83/yr. in cy. mailed. 1564 Kingsley Ave., Orange Park, FL 32073. TEL 904-264-3200; FAX 904-269-6958. **Owner(s):** Add, Inc., 600 Industrial Rd., P.O. Box 609, Waupaca, WI 54981. TEL 715-258-8450; Ed. Sandy Mulvihill; Pub. Joyce Lydon; pub. size: tabloid; circ. evening 50,000(free & paid).

ORLANDO

US   ISSN 0744-6055

ORLANDO SENTINEL. 1876. d. $.50/day newsstand; $1.50/Sun.; $3.75/wk.; $190.80/yr. 633 N. Orange Ave., Orlando, FL 32801. TEL 407-420-5000; FAX 407-420-5758. **Owner(s):** Tribune Co., 435 N. Michigan Ave., Chicago, IL 60611. TEL 312-222-3394; Ed. Jane Healy; Pub. John Puerner; adv. contact: William E. Steiger. photos; pub. size: broadsheet; circ. morning 273,761(paid); Sun. 376,003(paid). **Wire Service(s):** AP, KRTN, LAT-WP, NYT DJ, SHNA, RN.

PALATKA

US   ISSN 0163-5050

DAILY NEWS. 1885. Mon.-Fri. $.50 newsstand; $82.58/yr. 1825 St. Johns Ave., Palatka, FL 32177. TEL 904-328-2721; FAX 904-325-0663. **Owner(s):** New York Times Co., The, 229 W. 43rd St., New York, NY 10036. TEL 212-556-1234; Ed. Jim Baltzelle; Pub. Robert R. Starr; adv. contact: Garrett Wallace. pub. size: broadsheet; circ. evening 14,000(paid). Wire Service(s): AF.

PALM BEACH

US

PALM BEACH DAILY NEWS. 1897. d.: Oct.-May; Sun.-Thu.: June-Sep. $.25/day newsstand; $.50/Sun.; $1.60/wk. 265 Royal Poinciana Way, Palm Beach, FL 33480. TEL 407-820-3860; FAX 407-655-4594; E-mail: nusk64c@prodigy.com. **Owner(s):** Palm Beach Newspapers, Inc., 2751 S. Dixie, P.O. Drawer T, West Palm Beach, FL 33405. TEL 407-833-7411; Ed. Libby Wells; Pub. Joyce Harr; adv.; $32.50/SAL Sun.; $28.90/SAU daily. photos; bk.rev.; pub. size: standard; circ. morning 9,200(paid); Sun. 10,900(paid).

PANAMA CITY

US

NEWS HERALD, THE. 1970. d. $.35/day newsstand; $1.25/Sun.; $106.50/yr. 501 W. 11th St., Panama City, FL 32401. TEL 904-763-7621; FAX 904-763-4636. **Owner(s):** Freedom Communications, Inc., 1055 N. Main St., Ste. 901, Santa Ana, CA 92701. TEL 714-542-4415; Ed. Steve Bornhoft; Pub. Karen Hanes; adv.; photos; pub. size: standard; circ. morning 37 470(paid); Sun. 43,087(paid). **Wire Service(s):** AP, KR.

PENSACOLA

US

PENSACOLA NEWS JOURNAL. 1889. d. $.40/day newsstand; $1.50/Sun.; $13/mo. home deliv. 101 E. Romana St., Pensacola, FL 32501. TEL 904-435-8500; FAX 904-435-8633; E-mail: pns@gulfsurf.infi.net; URL: http://www.gulfsurf.com. **Owner(s):** Gannett Company, Inc., 1100 Wilson Blvd., Arlington, VA 22234. TEL 703-284-6000; Ed. Mike Ryan; Pub. Denise H. Bannister; adv. contact: John DiMambro. photos; pub. size: broadsheet; circ. morning 61,208(paid); Sun. 82,146(paid). **Wire Service(s):** AP, GNS, KR.

SANFORD

US   ISSN 0893-3642

SANFORD HERALD. 1908. Tue.-Fri. & Sun. $.50/day newsstand; $.75/Sun.; $3.46/yr. 300 N. French Ave., Sanford, FL 32771. TEL 407-322-2611. **Owner(s):** Martinsville Bulletin, P.O. Box 1667, Sanford, FL 32772. TEL 305-322-2611; Ed. Lacy Loar. pub. size: standard; circ. evening 7 465(paid). **Wire Service(s):** AP.

SARASOTA

US

SARASOTA HERALD TRIBUNE. 1925. d. $.50/day newsstand; $1.25/Sun. 801 S. Tamiami Trail, Sarasota, FL 34236. TEL 941-953-7755. **Owner(s):** New York Times Co., The, 229 W. 43rd St., New York, NY 10036. TEL 212-556-1234; Ed. Walco Proffitt; Pub. Lynn O. Matthews; adv.; photos; bk.rev.; pub. size: broadsheet; circ. morning 135,000(paid); Sun. 160,000(paid). **Wire Service(s):** AP, NYT, LAT-WP.

ST. AUGUSTINE

US   ISSN 1041-1577

ST. AUGUSTINE RECORD. 1894. d. $.50/day newsstand; $1/Sun.; $7/mo. 158 Cordova St., St. Augustine, FL 32084. TEL 904-829-6562; FAX 904-829-6664; E-mail: record@aug.com; URL: http://staugustine.com. **Owner(s):** Morris Communications, P.O. Box 936 Augusta, GA 30903. TEL 706-724-0851; FAX 706-722-0011; Pub. Ronnie Hughes; adv. contact: Grover Ford. photos; bk.rev.; pub. size: broadsheet; circ. evening 15,000(paid); Sun. 180,000. **Wire Service(s):** AP, KR, LAT-WP.

ST. PETERSBURG

US

ST. PETERSBURG TIMES. 1884. d. $.25/day newsstand; $1/Sun.; $29.90/3 mos. home deliv. 490 First Ave., S., St. Petersburg, FL 33701-1121. TEL 813-393-8111; FAX 813-893-8673; E-mail: sptimes@sptimes.com; URL: http://www.sptimes.com. **Owner(s):** Times Publishing Co., P.O. Box 1121, St. Petersburg, FL 33731. TEL 813-893-8111; Ed. Neil Brown. adv. contact: Richard Reeves. photos; bk.rev.; pub. size: broadsheet; circ. morning 364,810(paid); Sun. 462,103(paid). **Wire Service(s):** AP, NYT, LAT-WP, RN.

STUART

US

STUART NEWS. 1913. d. $.50/day newsstand; $1/Sun.; $9.49/mo.; $112/yr. 1939 S. Federal Hwy., Stuart, FL 34994. TEL 561-287-1550; FAX 561-221-4246. **Owner(s):** Scripps-Howard, 312 Walnut St., Cincinnati, OH 45202. TEL 513-977-3000; Ed. Nancy Smith. adv. contact: Greg Anderson. photos bk.rev. pub. size: broadsheet; circ. morning 39,104(paid); Sun. 47,214(paid). **Wire Service(s):** AP, NYT, SHNS.

TALLAHASSEE

US   ISSN 0738-5153
TALLAHASSEE DEMOCRAT. 1905. d.
$.50/newsstand; $1.25/Sun.; $154.44/yr. 277
N. Magnolia Dr., Tallahassee, FL 32301.
TEL 904-599-2100; FAX 904-599-2295; E-mail:
telltdo@tdo.infi.net; URL: http://www.tdo.com.
Owner(s): Knight-Ridder, Inc., One Herald Plz.,
Miami, FL 33132. TEL 305-376-3800; Ed. Bob
Shaw; Pub. J. Carrol Dadisman; adv.; pub. size:
broadsheet; circ. morning 58,000(paid); Sun.
78,610(paid). **Wire Service(s):** KR, AP, LAT-WP.

TAMPA

US   ISSN 1042-3761
TAMPA TRIBUNE, THE. 1895. d. $.50/day
newsstand; $1/Sun.; $91/yr. 202 S. Parker St.,
Tampa, FL 33606. TEL 813-259-7711;
FAX 813-259-7773; E-mail:
pbreckenridge@tboweb.com; URL:
http://www.tampatrib.com/. **Owner(s):** Media
General, Inc., 333 E. Grace St., Richmond, VA
23219. TEL 804-649-6671; Ed. Bruce Witwer;
Pub. Jack Butcher; adv. contact: Tony DiSalvo.
photos; bk.rev.; pub. size: broadsheet; circ.
morning 265,988(paid); Sun. 360,251(paid).
Wire Service(s): AP, AP Wire Photo.

VERO BEACH

US
PRESS-JOURNAL. 1919. d. $.35/day newsstand;
$.50/Sat. & Sun.; $84/yr. carrier. 1801 S. U.S.
Hwy. 1, Vero Beach, FL 32960.
TEL 561-562-2315; FAX 561-562-7210.
Owner(s): Scripps-Howard, 312 Walnut St., 28th
Fl., Cincinnati, OH 45202; Ed. Larry Reisman;
Pub. John J. Schumann, Jr.; adv.; photos; pub.
size: broadsheet; circ. morning 32,000(paid);
Sun. 34,500(paid). **Wire Service(s):** AP, UPI.
    Formerly: Vero Beach Press-Journal.

WEST PALM BEACH

US
PALM BEACH POST. 1923. d. $.50/day newsstand;
$1/Sun.; $2.55/wk. 2751 S. Dixie Hwy., West
Palm Beach, FL 33405. TEL 561-820-4400;
FAX 561-820-4445. **Owner(s):** Cox Enterprises,
Inc., P.O. Box 4689, Atlanta, GA 30302. TEL
404-526-5537; Ed. Tom O'Hara; Pub. Tom
Giuffrida; adv. contact: Van Esselstyn. photos;
bk.rev.; pub. size: broadsheet; circ. morning
172,000(paid); Sun. 221,000(paid). **Wire
Service(s):** AP, RN, LAT-WP, NYT, Cox.

WINTER HAVEN

US
NEWS CHIEF. 1879. d. $.25/day newsstand;
$.50/Sun.; $92.60/yr. 650 Sixth St: S.W., Winter
Haven, FL 33880. TEL 941-294-7731;
FAX 941-294-2008. **Owner(s):** Morris
Communications, P.O. Box 936, Augusta, GA
30903. TEL 706-724-0851; Pub. Joe Ben Oller;
adv. contact: Tom Duncan. bk.rev.; pub. size:
standard; circ. evening 15,000(paid); Sun.
15,000(paid). **Wire Service(s):** AP.

GEORGIA

ALBANY

US
ALBANY HERALD, THE. 1891. d. $.50/day
newsstand; $1.25/Sun.; $144/yr. 126 N.
Washington St., Albany, GA 31701.
TEL 912-888-9300; FAX 912-888-9357.
Owner(s): Gray Communications Systems, Inc.,
P.O. Box 48, Albany, GA 31703. TEL
912-888-9300; Pub. Christian R. Schilt; adv.;
photos; bk.rev.; pub. size: standard; circ. morning
34,000(paid); Sun. 40,000(paid). **Wire
Service(s):** AP.

AMERICUS

US
AMERICUS TIMES-RECORDER. 1879. Mon.-Sat. $.50
newsstand; $93/yr. 1612 Vienna Rd., Americus,
GA 31709. TEL 912-924-2751;
FAX 912-928-6344. **Owner(s):** Thomson
Newspapers, Inc., 3150 Des Plaines Ave., Des
Plaines, IL 60018. TEL 708-299-5544; Ed. Beth
Alston; Pub. Daryl Henning; adv. contact: Jeff
Masters. pub. size: broadsheet; circ. evening
8,000(paid). **Wire Service(s):** AP, AP Photo.

ATHENS

US   ISSN 0898-3712
ATHENS BANNER HERALD. 1965. d. $.25/day
newsstand; $1/Sun.; $8.67/mo. carrier;
$106/yr. One Press Pl., Athens, GA 30601.
TEL 770-549-0123; FAX 770-543-5234.
Owner(s): Morris Communications, P.O. Box 136,
Augusta, GA 30913. TEL 706-724-0851; Ed.
Les Simpson; Pub. Jeff Wilson; pub. size:
broadsheet; circ. evening 13,282(paid); Sun.
37,000(paid). **Wire Service(s):** AP, NYT, LAT-WP.

US   ISSN 0898-3712
ATHENS DAILY NEWS. 1965. d. $.25/day
newsstand; $1/Sun.; $8.67/mo. One Press Pl.,
Athens, GA 30601. TEL 770-549-0123;
FAX 770-208-2246; E-mail:
76735.26@compuserve.com; URL:
http://www.athensnewspapers.com. **Owner(s):**
Morris Communications, P.O. Box 936, Augusta,
GA. TEL 706-724-0851; Ed. Les Simpson; Pub.
Jeff Wilson; adv.; photos; bk.rev.; pub. size:
broadsheet; circ. morning 15,844(paid); Sun.
33,870(paid). **Wire Service(s):** AP, KR, LAT-WP.

ATLANTA

US   ISSN 0093-1179
ATLANTA JOURNAL-CONSTITUTION. 1883. d.
$.50/day newsstand; $2/Sun.; $149.19/yr. 72
Marietta St., Atlanta, GA 30303.
TEL 404-526-5151; FAX 404-526-5819.
Owner(s): Cox Enterprises, Inc., P.O. Box
105357, Atlanta, GA 30348. TEL
404-843-5000; Ed. John Walter; Pub. Roger
Kintzel; adv. contact: Roy Sheppard. photos;
bk.rev.; pub. size: broadsheet; circ. morning
308,984(paid); evening 161,393(paid); Sun.
715,397(paid). **Wire Service(s):** AP, UPI, LAT-WP.

AUGUSTA

US   ISSN 0747-1343
AUGUSTA CHRONICLE, THE. 1785. d. $.50/day
newsstand; $1.25/Sun.; $11/mo. home deliv.
725 Broad St., Augusta, GA 30901.
TEL 706-724-0851; FAX 706-722-7403.
Owner(s): Southeastern Newspapers Corp., P.O.
Box 1928, Augusta, GA 30903-1928. TEL
706-724-0851; Ed. John Fish; Pub. William S.
Morris, III; adv. contact: Ron Tennant. pub. size:
broadsheet; circ. morning 78,000(paid); Sun.
102,000(paid). **Wire Service(s):** AP, NYT, LAT-WP.

BRUNSWICK

US
BRUNSWICK NEWS, THE. Mon.-Sat. $.25 newsstand;
$5/mo. local; $7/mo. out of state. 3011 Altama
Ave., Brunswick, GA 31520-1557.
TEL 912-265-8320; FAX 912-264-4973.
Owner(s): Brunswick News Publishing Co., P.O.
Box 1557, Brunswick, GA 31521. TEL
912-265-8320; FAX 912-264-4973; Ed. Hank
Rowland. adv. contact: Ron Maulden. pub. size:
standard; circ. morning 16,356(paid). **Wire
Service(s):** AP.

US
GEORGIA TIMES-UNION. d. $.50/day newsstand;
$1/Sun.; $2.99/wk. deliv.; $155.48/yr. 3675
Community Rd., Brunswick, GA 31520.
TEL 912-264-0720; FAX 912-264-1407.
Owner(s): Billy Morris, Augusta, GA; Ed. Joe
Adams; Pub. Carl N. Cannon; adv.; pub. size:
broadsheet; circ. morning 20,000(paid); Sun.
7,500(paid).
    Formerly: Florida Times Union - Georgia
Edition.

CARROLLTON

US   ISSN 1049-9458
TIMES-GEORGIAN. 1872. Tue.-Sun. $.50 newsstand;
$1/Sun.; $90/yr. carrier. 901 Hays Mill Rd.,
Carrollton, GA 30117. TEL 770-834-6631;
FAX 770-834-9991. **Owner(s):** Paxton Media
Group, Inc., P.O. Box 2300, Paducah, KY 42002.
TEL 502-443-1771; Ed. Bruce Browning; Pub.
Dawn Weatherly; pub. size: broadsheet; circ.
morning 13,000(paid). **Wire Service(s):** AP.

CARTERSVILLE

US   ISSN 1049-6750
CARTERSVILLE DAILY TRIBUNE NEWS. 1946.
Sun.-Fri. $.50 newsstand; $1/Sun.; $71/yr. 251
S. Tennessee, Cartersville, GA 30120.
TEL 770-382-4545; FAX 770-382-2711.
Owner(s): Cleveland Newspapers, Inc., Cleveland,
TN; Ed. Lewis Justus; Pub. Charles E. Hurley; pub.
size: broadsheet; circ. evening 10,000(paid). **Wire
Service(s):** UPI.

US

DAILY TRIBUNE NEWS. Sun.-Fri. $.50 newsstand; $19.50/3 mos.; $35.50/6 mos.; $75/yr. 251 S. Tennessee St., Cartersville, GA 30120. TEL 770-382-4545; FAX 770-382-2711. **Owner(s):** Cleveland Newspapers, Inc., Cleveland, OH; Ed. Kevin Atwill; Pub. Charles Hurley; adv. contact: Charles Hurley. photos; bk.rev.; pub. size: broadsheet; circ. evening 10,500(paid).

COLUMBUS

US ISSN 8750-8389
COLUMBUS LEDGER-ENQUIRER. 1886. d. $.50 newsstand; $3.25/wk. 17 W. 12th St., Columbus, GA 31902. TEL 706-324-5526; FAX 706-376-6336; E-mail: leonline@leo.infi.net; URL: http://www.l-e-o.com. **Owner(s):** Knight-Ridder, Inc., One Herald Plz., Miami, FL 33132; Ed. Sam Jones; Pub. John F. Greenman; pub. size: standard; circ. evening 53,511(paid); Sun. 67,659(paid). **Wire Service(s):** AP, KNS, NYT.

CONYERS

US ISSN 1050-1401
ROCKDALE CITIZEN. 1909. Mon.-Fri. $60/yr. 969 S. Main St., Conyers, GA 30207. TEL 770-483-7108. **Owner(s):** Gray Communications Systems, Inc., P.O. Box 48, Albany, GA 31703. TEL 912-888-9300; Ed. Fred Turner; Pub. Richard T. Rae; photos; bk.rev.; pub. size: broadsheet; circ. 11,500(paid).

CORDELE

US
CORDELE DISPATCH. 1908. Mon.-Fri. $.50/newsstand; $84/yr. carrier. 306 13th Ave., W., Cordele, GA 31015. TEL 912-273-2277; FAX 912-273-7239. **Owner(s):** Thomson Newspapers, Inc., 3150 Des Plaines Ave., Des Plaines, IL 60018. TEL 708-299-5544; Ed. Bill Rungy; Pub. Randy Cox; adv. contact: Shane Belton. pub. size: broadsheet; circ. evening 6,143(free). **Wire Service(s):** AP.

DALTON

US
DAILY CITIZEN NEWS. 1800. d. $.50/day newsstand; $1/Sun.; $10.50/mo. 308 S. Thornton Ave., Dalton, GA 30720. TEL 706-278-1011; FAX 706-275-6641. **Owner(s):** Thomson Newspapers, Inc., 3150 Des Plaines Ave., Des Plaines, IL 60018. TEL 708-299-5544; Pub. Ken Fortenberry; pub. size: broadsheet; circ. morning 13,500(paid). **Wire Service(s):** AP.
   Formerly: Dalton Daily Citizen News.

DOUGLASVILLE

US
DOUGLAS COUNTY SENTINEL. 1902. Tue.-Sat. $.25 newsstand; $50/yr. carrier. 6405 Fairburn Rd., Douglasville, GA 30134. TEL 770-942-6571; FAX 770-949-7556. **Owner(s):** Paxton Media Group, Inc., P.O. Box 2300, Paducah, KY 42002. TEL 502-443-1771; Ed. Bill Fordham; Pub. Dawn Wetherby; adv. contact: Melba Daniels. pub. size: broadsheet; circ. evening 11,000(paid). **Wire Service(s):** AP.

DUBLIN

US
COURIER HERALD, THE. 1913. Mon.-Sat. $.50 newsstand; $64/yr. 115 S. Jefferson St., Dublin, GA 31021. TEL 912-272-5522; FAX 912-272-2189. **Owner(s):** DuBose Porter, 115 S. Jefferson St. Dublin, GA 31021. TEL 912-272-5522; Griffin Lovett, 115 S. Jefferson St., Dublin, GA 31201; Ed. Rodney Manley; Pub. Griffin Lovett; adv. contact: Joy Green. pub. size: broadsheet; circ. evening 13,600(paid). **Wire Service(s):** AP.
   Formerly: Dublin Courier Herald.

GAINESVILLE

US
TIMES, THE. 1947. d. $.35/day newsstand; $1.50/Sun.; $37.70/13 wks. home deliv. 345 Green St., N.W., Gainesville, GA 30501. TEL 770-532-1234 FAX 770-532-0457; E-mail: 102432.3532@compuserve.com. **Owner(s):** Gannett Company, Inc., 1100 Wilson Blvd., Arlington, VA 22234. TEL 703-284-6000; Ed. John Druckenmiller; Pub. Sandra S. Bailey; adv. contact: Brad Hagstrom. pub. size: broadsheet; circ. evening 21,005(paid); Sun. 21,005(paid). **Wire Service(s):** AP.

GRIFFIN

US ISSN 0746-3324
GRIFFIN DAILY NEWS. d. $.50/day newsstand; $1/Sun.; $9.75/mo. home deliv. 323 E. Solomon St., Griffin, GA 30223. TEL 770-227-3276; FAX 770-412-1678 E-mail: editor@griffin-news.com; URL: http://www.griffin-news.com. **Owner(s):** Thomson Newspapers, Inc., 3150 Des Plaines, IL 60018. TEL 704-299-5544; Ed. Michelle Phillips; Pub. Otis Raybon; adv. contact: Jeff Jones. pub. size: broadsheet; circ. morning 13,000(paid); Sun. 15,000(paid).

JONESBORO

US
CLAYTON NEWS DAILY. 1971. Mon.-Sat. $.50 newsstand; $7/mo. 138 Church St., Jonesboro, GA 30236. TEL 404-478-5753; FAX 404-473-9032. **Owner(s):** Southern Publishing Co., 138 Church St., Jonesboro, GA 30236. TEL 404-478-5500; Ed. Tom Kerlin; Pub. Neely Young; adv. contact: Colleen Mitchell. pub. size: broadsheet; circ. evening 25,000(paid). Wire Service(s): UPI.

LA GRANGE

US
LA GRANGE DAILY NEWS. Mon.-Sat. $.50 newsstand; $6.75/mo. home deliv. 105 Ashton St., La Grange, GA 30240. TEL 706-884-7311; FAX 706-884-8712. **Owner(s):** Mid-South Management Co., Inc., P.O. Box 929, La Grange, GA 30241. TEL 706-884-7311; Ed. C. Lee West; Pub. Louis Harvath, II; adv. contact: Jeniifer Bell. pub. size: broadsheet; circ. evening 14,765(paid). Wire Service(s): AP.

LAWRENCEVILLE

US
GWINNETT DAILY POST. 1970. Tue.-Sat. $.50 newsstand; $64.95/yr. in cy. 166 Buford Dr., Lawrenceville, GA 30245. TEL 770-963-9205; FAX 770-339-8081. **Owner(s):** Gray Communications Systems, Inc., P.O. Box 603, Lawrenceville, GA 30246. TEL 770-963-9205; FAX 770-338-7353; Ed. Howard Reed; Pub. Richard T. Rae; adv. contact: Melody Bishop. pub. size: standard; circ. morning 15,000(paid).
   Formerly: Gwinnett Post-Tribune.

MACON

US ISSN 1054-2485
MACON TELEGRAPH. 1826. d. $.50/day newsstand; $1.50/Sun. 120 Broadway, Macon, GA 31201. TEL 912-744-4200; FAX 912-744-4385; E-mail: metro@mto.infi.net; URL: http://www.macontel.com. **Owner(s):** Knight-Ridder, Inc., One Herald Plz., Miami, FL 33132. TEL 305-376-3800; Ed. Rick Thomas; Pub. Carol Hudler; adv. contact: Pete Herschberger. photos; bk.rev.; pub. size: broadsheet; circ. morning 75,000(paid); Sun. 102,000(paid). **Wire Service(s):** AP, NYT, KRN.

MARIETTA

US ISSN 8750-4618
MARIETTA DAILY JOURNAL. 1867. d. $.25 newsstand; $9.45/mo. 580 Fairground St., Marietta, GA 30060. TEL 770-428-9411; FAX 770-422-9533. **Owner(s):** Otis A. Brumby, Jr., Marietta, GA 30060; Pub. Otis Brumby; pub. size: broadsheet; circ. morning 30,000(paid); Sun. 35,000(paid). **Wire Service(s):** AP, SHNA.

MILLEDGEVILLE

US
UNION-RECORDER. 1820. Tue.-Sat. $.50 newsstand; $79.30/yr. One Union-Recorder Plz., Garrett Way, Milledgeville, GA 31061-0520. TEL 912-452-0567; FAX 912-452-9539. **Owner(s):** Knight-Ridder, Inc., One Herald Plz., Miami, FL 33132-1693. TEL 305-376-3800; Ed. Debra Evans; Pub. Susan L. Patterson; adv.; photos; bk.rev.; pub. size: broadsheet; circ. morning 9,200(paid). **Wire Service(s):** AP, KR.

MOULTRIE

US
OBSERVER, THE. Mon.-Sat. $.50 newsstand; $82/yr. 25 N. Main St., Moultrie, GA 31768. TEL 912-985-4545; FAX 912-985-3569. **Owner(s):** Gannett Company, Inc., 1100 Wilson Blvd., Arlington, VA 22340. TEL 703-284-6000; Ed. Wayne Grandy; Pub. Gary Boley; adv. contact: Kendra Walden. pub. size: broadsheet; circ. morning 8,000(paid). **Wire Service(s):** AP.
   Formerly: Moultrie Observer.

ROME

US ISSN 1060-4049
ROME NEWS-TRIBUNE. 1838. Sun.-Fr. $.50/day newsstand; $1.50/Sun.; $74/yr. in cy.; $140/yr. out of state. 305 E. Sixth Ave., Rome, GA 30161. TEL 706-291-6397; FAX 706-232-9632. **Owner(s):** News Publishing Co., P.O. Box 1633, Rome, GA 30161. TEL 706-290-5330; Ed. David Williams; Pub. B.H. Mooney, III; adv.; pub. size: broadsheet; circ. evening 24,500(paid). **Wire Service(s):** AP.

SAVANNAH

US

SAVANNAH MORNING NEWS/EVENING PRESS. 1850. d. $.25/day newsstand; $1.25/Sun.; $120/yr. 111 W. Bay St., Savannah, GA 31401. TEL 912-236-9511; FAX 912-234-6522. **Owner(s):** Southeastern Newspapers Corp., GA; Ed. J. Frank Lynch; Pub. Frank Anderson; adv. contact: Don Bailey. pub. size: broadsheet; circ. morning 56,085(paid); evening 15,360(paid); Sun. 82,463(paid). **Wire Service(s):** AP, NEA, LAT-WP.

Formerly: Savannah News-Press.

STATESBORO

US   ISSN 0746-4665

STATESBORO HERALD. 1937. d. $.50/day newsstand; $.75/Sun.; $10/mo. One Herald Sq., Statesboro, GA 30458. TEL 912-764-9031; FAX 912-489-8181. **Owner(s):** Morris Communications, Savannah, GA; Pub. Randy Morton; adv. contact: Jane Malton. pub. size: broadsheet; circ. morning 8,000(paid); Sun. 8,000(paid). **Wire Service(s):** UPI.

THOMASVILLE

US   ISSN 0746-4894

THOMASVILLE TIMES-ENTERPRISE. 1889. Tue.-Sun. $2.20/wk. only. 106 South St., Thomasville, GA 31792. TEL 912-226-2400; FAX 912-228-5863. **Owner(s):** Thomson Newspapers, Inc., 3150 Des Plains Ave., Des Plaines, IL 60018. TEL 708-299-5544; Pub. Wallace Goodman; adv. contact: Norman Bankston. pub. size: broadsheet; circ. morning 10,343(paid). **Wire Service(s):** AP.

TIFTON

US   ISSN 1065-2884

TIFTON GAZETTE. 1888. Mon.-Sat. $.50 newsstand; $8.40/mo. 211 N. Tift Ave., Tifton, GA 31794. TEL 912-382-4321; FAX 912-387-7322. **Owner(s):** Thomson Newspapers, Inc., 3150 Des Plaines Ave., Des Plaines, IL 60018. TEL 708-299-5544; Ed. Mike Jones; Pub. James S. McKee; adv. contact: Randy Blalock. bk.rev.; pub. size: broadsheet; circ. morning 9,431(paid). **Wire Service(s):** AP.

VALDOSTA

US

VALDOSTA DAILY TIMES. 1867. d. $9.50/mo. 201 N. Troup St., Valdosta, GA 31601. TEL 912-244-1880; FAX 912-244-2560. **Owner(s):** Thomson Newspapers, Inc., 3150 Des Plaines Ave., Des Plaines, IL 60018. TEL 618-937-6411; Ed. Gerald Guys; Pub. Bob Morrell; adv. contact: Daniel Sutton. pub. size: broadsheet; circ. morning 21,147(paid); Sun. 21,147(paid). **Wire Service(s):** AP.

WARNER ROBINS

US

DAILY/SUNDAY SUN, THE. 1949. Sun.-Fri. $.35/day newsstand; $.75/Sun.; $8.25/mo. carrier; $11/mo. mailed. 1553 Watson Blvd., Warner Robins, GA 31093. TEL 912-923-6432; FAX 912-328-7682. **Owner(s):** Park Communications, Inc., Vine Ctr. Office Tower, 333 W. Vine St., 17th Fl., Lexington, KY 40507. TEL 606-252-7275; Ed. Rex Sanders. adv. contact: Don Baumgart. photos; bk.rev.; pub. size: broadsheet; circ. evening 8,500(paid); Sun. 9,500(paid). **Wire Service(s):** AP.

WAYCROSS

US

WAYCROSS JOURNAL HERALD. 1914. Mon.-Sat. $.35 newsstand; $8/mo.; $96/yr. in city. 400 Isabella St., Waycross, GA 31501. TEL 912-283-2244; FAX 912-283-2815. **Owner(s):** Journal Herald Co., Inc., P.O. Box 219, Waycross, GA 31501. TEL 912-283-2244; Ed. Jack Williams, III; Pub. Roger L. Williams; adv. contact: David Tanner. pub. size: broadsheet; circ. evening 13,500(paid). **Wire Service(s):** AP.

GUAM

AGANA

US   ISSN 0196-2485

PACIFIC DAILY NEWS. 1944. d. P.O. Box DN, Agana, GU 96910. TEL 671-477-9712; FAX 671-472-1512. **Owner(s):** Pacific Daily News, Agana, GU; Ed. Joseph A. Novotny; Pub. Lee P. Webber; adv.; photos; pub. size: tabloid; circ. morning 25,232(paid); Sun. 22,981(paid). **Wire Service(s):** AP, GNS, LAT-WP.

HAWAII

HILO

US

HAWAII TRIBUNE-HERALD. 1923. Sun.-Fri. $.50/day newsstand; $1/Sun.; $9/mo. 355 Kinoole St., Hilo, HI 96720. TEL 808-935-6621; FAX 808-961-3680. **Owner(s):** Stephens Group, Inc., P.O. Box 1359, Fort Smith, AR 72902. TEL 501-785-7810; Pub. Jim D. Wilson; adv. contact: Sandy Ault. pub. size: broadsheet; circ. morning 19,688(paid); Sun. 23,888(paid). **Wire Service(s):** AP.

HONOLULU

US   ISSN 1072-7191

HONOLULU ADVERTISER. 1856. d. $.50/day newsstand; $1.50/Sun.; $26.80/4 wks. airmail. 605 Kapiolani Blvd., Honolulu, HI 96813. TEL 808-525-8000; FAX 808-525-8037. **Owner(s):** Gannett Company, Inc., 1100 Wilson Blvd., Arlington, VA 22234. TEL 703-284-6000; Ed. Gerry Keir; Pub. Larry Fuller; adv.; photos; pub. size: broadsheet; circ. morning 192,000(paid); Sun. 198,000(paid). **Wire Service(s):** AP, LAT-WP, KR.

HONOLULU STAR-BULLETIN. 1882. Sun.-Fri. $.50 newsstand; $7.50/4 wks. daily; $13.50/4 wks. daily & Sun. 605 Kapiolani Blvd., Honolulu, HI 96813. TEL 808-525-8640; FAX 808-523-8509; E-mail: davids@aloha.net; URL: http://www.starbulletin.com. **Owner(s):** Liberty Newspaper Ltd. Partnership, Honolulu, HI 96813; Ed. David Shapiro; Pub. John M. Flanagan; adv. contact: Howard Griffin. bk.rev.; pub. size: broadsheet; circ. evening 80,069(paid). **Wire Service(s):** AP, NYT, RN, SHNA, NNS.

KAILUA KONA

US   ISSN 0744-4591

WEST HAWAII TODAY. 1968. Sun.-Fri. $7.75/mo. carrier. 75-5580 Kuakini Hwy, Kailua Kona, HI 96745-0789. TEL 808-329-9311; FAX 808-329-4860; E-mail: wht@1lhawaii.net; URL: http://www.ihawaii.net/~wht. **Owner(s):** Stephens Group, Inc., P.O. Box 17017, Fort Smith, AR 72917-7017. TEL 501-785-7810; Ed. Reed Flickinger; Pub. Richard Asbach; adv. contact: Deborah Ward. pub. size: tabloid; circ. morning 13,000(paid); Sun. 13,800(paid). **Wire Service(s):** AP.

LIHUE

US

ISLAND TIMES. 1902. Sun.-Fri. $.50/day newsstand; $.75/Sun.; $7.75/mo. 3137 Kuhio Hwy., Lihue, HI 96766. TEL 808-245-3681; FAX 808-245-5286. **Owner(s):** Pulitzer Publishing Co., 900 N. Tucker Blvd., St. Louis, MO 63101. TEL 313-340-8000; Ed. Rita DeSilva; Pub. Roy Callaway; adv. contact: Christin Myreall. pub. size: standard; circ. morning 10,000(paid); Sun. 10,000(paid). **Wire Service(s):** AP.

Formerly: Garden Island Times.

WAILUKU

US

MAUI NEWS. 1900. Sun.-Fri. $.50/day newsstand; $1.50/Sun.; $72/yr. in cy. 100 Mahalani St., Wailuku, HI 96793. TEL 808-244-3981; FAX 808-242-9087; E-mail: mauinews@maui.net; URL: http://www.maui.net/~mauinews/news.html. **Owner(s):** Maui Publishing Co., Ltd., P.O. Box 550, Wailuku, HI 96793. TEL 808-244-3981; Ed. Dave Hoff; Pub. Richard Kameron; adv. contact: Dawn E. Miguel. photos; pub. size: broadsheet; circ. morning 20,300(paid); Sun. 26,900(paid). **Wire Service(s):** AP.

IDAHO

BLACKFOOT

US   ISSN 0893-3812

BLACKFOOT MORNING NEWS. 1904. Mon.-Sat. $.50 newsstand; $86.20/yr. in cy.; $97.45/yr. mailed. 34 N. Ash, Blackfoot, ID 83221. TEL 208-785-1100; FAX 208-785-4239. **Owner(s):** American Publishing Co., 606 N. Van Buren, P.O. Box 520, Marion, IL 62959. TEL 618-993-1711; Ed. Michael O'Donnell; Pub. Kaye Moses; adv. contact: Leslie Bare. photos; bk.rev.; pub. size: broadsheet; circ. morning 5,000(paid). **Wire Service(s):** AP.

BOISE

US

IDAHO STATESMAN, THE. 1864. d. $.50/day newsstand; $1.50/Sun.; $13/4 wks. 1200 N. Curtis Rd., Boise, ID 83706. TEL 208-377-6200; FAX 208-377-6309; E-mail: idastate@aol.com. **Owner(s):** Gannett Company, Inc., 1100 Wilson Blvd., Arlington, VA 22234. TEL 703-248-6000; Ed. Karen Baker; Pub. Pamela Meals; adv. contact: Deborah Pantenburg. photos; bk.rev.; pub. size: broadsheet; circ. morning 66,162(paid); Sun. 88,125(paid). **Wire Service(s):** AP, GNS, NYT.

BURLEY

US

SOUTH IDAHO PRESS. 1904. Sun.-Fri. $.50 newsstand; $7.70/mo. carrier. 230 E. Main St., Burley, ID 83318. TEL 208-678-2201; FAX 208-678-0412; E-mail: sip@cyberway.net; URL: http://www.cyberhighway.net/~sip. **Owner(s):** Retirement Systems of Alabama, 833 W. Vine St., Ste. 1700, Lexington, KY 40507. TEL 606-252-7275; Ed. Scott Logan. adv. contact: Marva Osterhout. pub. size: broadsheet; circ. evening 6,200(paid); Sun. 6,500(paid). **Wire Service(s):** AP.

Formerly: Burley South Idaho Press.

COEUR D'ALENE

US   ISSN 1041-2883

COEUR D'ALENE PRESS. 1892. d. $.50/day newsstand; $1/Sun.; $11.50/mo. carrier. 201 Second St., Coeur d'Alene, ID 83814. TEL 208-664-8176; FAX 208-664-0212. **Owner(s):** Hagadone Corp., 201 Second St., Coeur d'Alene, ID 83814. TEL 208-667-3431; Ed. Mike Feiler; Pub. Jim Thompson; adv. contact: Paul Burke. pub. size: broadsheet; circ. morning 15,000(paid); Sun. 30,000(paid). **Wire Service(s):** AP.

IDAHO FALLS

US

IDAHO FALLS POST REGISTER. 1881. Sun.-Fri. $.50/day newsstand; $1.50/Sun.; $9.50/mo. 333 Northgate Mile, Idaho Falls, ID 83401. TEL 208-522-1800; FAX 208-529-9683; E-mail: mchan@srv.net; URL: http://www.idahonews.com. **Owner(s):** Post Co., The, P.O. Box 1800, Idaho Falls, ID 83403. TEL 208-522-1800; Ed. Jerry M. Brady; Pub. Jerry M. Brady; adv. contact: David Gilchrist. photos; bk.rev.; pub. size: broadsheet; circ. evening 29,000(paid); Sun. 30,000(paid). **Wire Service(s):** AP, KR.

KELLOGG

US   ISSN 1044-9553

SHOSHONE NEWS-PRESS. 1926. Tue.-Sun. $.50 newsstand; $8.75/mo. 401 Main St., Kellogg, ID 83837. TEL 208-783-1107; FAX 208-784-6791. **Owner(s):** Hagadone Corp., 401 Main St., Kellogg, ID 83837. TEL 208-667-3431; Ed. Judy Binkley; Pub. Judy Binkley; pub. size: standard; circ. morning 5,100(paid). **Wire Service(s):** AP.

Formerly: Shoshone County News-Press.

LEWISTON

US   ISSN 0892-2586

LEWISTON MORNING TRIBUNE. 1892. d. $.50/day newsstand; $1.25/Sun.; $126/yr. local; $132/yr. motor rte.; $144/yr. mailed. 505 C St., Lewiston, ID 83501. TEL 208-743-9411; FAX 208-746-1185; E-mail: city@lmtribune.com; URL: http://www.lmtribune.com. **Owner(s):** Tribune Publishing Co., 505 C St., P.O. Box 957, Lewiston, ID 83501. TEL 208-743-9411; Ed. Paul Emerson; Pub. A.L. Alford; adv. contact: Rob Minereini. pub. size: broadsheet; circ. morning 26,500(paid); Sun. 28,500(paid). **Wire Service(s):** AP, NYT.

MOSCOW

US

MOSCOW-PULLMAN DAILY NEWS. 1981. Mon.-Sat. $.50/day newsstand; $1/Sat.; $12.25/mo. mailed. 409 S. Jackson, Moscow, ID 83843. TEL 208-882-5561; FAX 208-883-8205; E-mail: editor@moscow.com; URL: http://www.dnews.com. **Owner(s):** Kearns-Tribune Corp., 143 S. Main St., Salt Lake City, UT 84111. TEL 801-237-2031; News Review Publishing Co., 505 C. St., Lewiston, ID 83501. TEL 800-745-9411. Ed. Rick Hoover; Pub. Mark Trahant; adv. contact: Randy Pressnall. pub. size: broadsheet; circ. evening 8,900(paid). **Wire Service(s):** AP, KRTN.

Formerly: Daily News.

NAMPA

US

IDAHO PRESS-TRIBUNE. 1883. d. $.50/day newsstand; $1/Sun.; $8.50/mo. 1618 N. Midland St., Nampa, ID 83651. TEL 208-467-9252; FAX 208-467-9562. **Owner(s):** Swift-Pioneer Newspapers, 221 First Ave., W., Ste. 405, Seattle, WA 98119. TEL 206-284-4424; Ed. Vicki Holbrook; Pub. Jim Barnes; adv. contact: John Rybarczyk. pub. size: standard; circ. evening 21,000(paid); Sun. 21,000(paid). **Wire Service(s):** AP.

POCATELLO

US

IDAHO STATE JOURNAL. 1893. Sun.-Fri. $.50/day newsstand; $1.25/Sun.; $9/mo. in city; $9.75/mo. rural. 305 S. Arthur Ave., Pocatello, ID 83204. TEL 208-232-4161; FAX 208-233-8007. **Owner(s):** Idaho State Publishing, Inc., Pocatello, ID 83204; Ed. Donald H. Black; Pub. Donald J. Byrne; adv. contact: Leonard Martin. photos; pub. size: broadsheet; circ. evening 20,000(paid); Sun. 22,500(paid). **Wire Service(s):** AP.

SANDPOINT

US   ISSN 1047-6822

BONNER COUNTY DAILY BEE. 1965. Tue.-Sun. $.50/day newsstand $1.25/Sun.; $10.25/mo. in city; $10.75/mo. motor rte. 310 Church St., Sandpoint, ID 83864. TEL 208-263-9534; FAX 208-263-9091. **Owner(s):** Hagadone Corp., P.O. Box 1178, Coeur D Alene, ID 83814. TEL 208-667-3431; Ed. Bill Buley; Pub. Joe Grimes; adv. contact: Herb Offermann. pub. size: broadsheet; circ. evening 6,800(paid); Sun. 32,000(paid). **Wire Service(s):** AP.

Formerly: Sandpoint Daily Bee.

TWIN FALLS

US

TWIN FALLS TIMES-NEWS. 1905. d. $.50/day newsstand; $1.50/Sun.; $3.60/wk. home deliv. 132 Third St., W., Twin Falls, ID 83301. TEL 208-733-0931. **Owner(s):** Howard Publications, Inc., P.O. Box 570, Oceanside, CA 92049. TEL 714-433-5771; Ed. Clark Walworth; Pub. Stephen Hartgen; adv. contact: Pete York. photos; bk.rev.; pub. size: broadsheet; circ. morning 23,000(paid); Sun. 24,000(paid). **Wire Service(s):** LAT-WP, KR, AP.

ILLINOIS

ALTON

US

TELEGRAPH, THE. 1836. d. $.50/day newsstand; $1.50/Sun.; $3.25/wk; $13/4 wks. 111 E. Broadway, Alton, IL 62002. TEL 618-463-2500; FAX 618-463-9829. **Owner(s):** Journal Register Co., 50 W. State St., 12th Fl., Trenton, NJ 08603. TEL 609-396-2200; Ed. Walt Sharp; Pub. Gale Baldwin; pub. size: broadsheet; circ. morning 34,500(paid); Sun. 36,500(paid). **Wire Service(s):** AP.

ARLINGTON HEIGHTS

US

DAILY HERALD. 1872. d. $.35/day newsstand; $1.25/Sun.; $182/yr. carrier. 155 E. Algonquin Rd., Arlington Heights, IL 60005. TEL 847-427-4300; FAX 847-427-1301. **Owner(s):** Paddock Publications, P.O. Box 280, Arlington Heights, IL 60006. TEL 708-870-3600; Ed. John Lampinen. adv. contact: Jim Walsh. pub. size: broadsheet; circ. morning 125,000(paid); Sun. 119,538(paid). **Wire Service(s):** UPI, AP.

Formerly: Hanover Park Daily Herald.

AURORA

US

BEACON NEWS. 1846. d. $.35/day newsstand; $1/Sun.; $120/yr. 101 S. River St., Aurora, IL 60506. TEL 708-844-5844; FAX 708-844-5818. **Owner(s):** Copley Press, Inc., 7776 Ivanhoe St., La Jolla, CA 92037. TEL 619-454-0411; Ed. Mike Chapin. photos; pub. size: broadsheet; circ. evening 40,000(paid). **Wire Service(s):** AP.

BELLEVILLE

US   ISSN 8750-1058

BELLEVILLE NEWS-DEMOCRAT. 1858. d. $.50/day newsstand; $1.25/Sun.; $1.25/wk. home deliv.; $2.10/wk. daily; $2/wk. weekends. 120 S. Illinois St., Belleville, IL 62220. TEL 618-234-1000; FAX 618-234-5957. **Owner(s):** Walt Disney Co. 500 S. Buena Vista St., Burbank, CA 91521. TEL 818-560-5300; Ed. Greg Edwards; Pub. Gary Berkey; adv.; pub. size: broadsheet; circ. morning 50,621(paid); Sun. 61,936(paid). **Wire Service(s):** AP, NYT, CSM.

Dailies

BELVIDERE

US

BELVIDERE DAILY REPUBLICAN. 1894. Mon.-Sat. $.35 newsstand; $6.50/mo. local. 401 Whitney Blvd., Belvidere, IL 61008. TEL 815-544-9811; FAX 815-544-6334; E-mail: realibertry@aol.com; URL: http://www.members.gnn.com/lpahl/bdr.htm. **Owner(s):** Belvidere Daily Republican, 401 Whitney Blvd., Belvidere, IL 61008. TEL 815-544-9811; FAX 815-544-6334; Ed. Kathy Sterbencz. adv. contact: Sheri Aspenson. photos; bk.rev.; pub. size: broadsheet; circ. evening 5,100(paid). **Wire Service(s):** AP.

BENTON

US

EVENING NEWS. Sat.-Thu. $.50/day newsstand; $1/Sun.; $116/yr. in cy.; $136/yr. out of state. 111-115 E. Church St., Benton, IL 62812. TEL 618-438-5611; FAX 618-435-2413. **Owner(s):** American Publishing Co., 606 N. Van Buren, P.O. Box 520, Marion, IL 62959. TEL 618-993-1711; adv. contact: Nancy Winter. pub. size: broadsheet; circ. morning 4,800(paid); Sun. 4,800(paid).
  Formerly: Benton Evening News.

BLOOMINGTON

US

PANTAGRAPH, THE. 1837. d. $.50/day newsstand; $1.25/Sun.; $161.20/yr. motor rte.; $156/yr. home deliv. 301 W. Washington, Bloomington, IL 61701. TEL 309-829-9411; FAX 309-829-9104; E-mail: pantagra@pantagraph.com; URL: http://www.pantagraph.com. **Owner(s):** Chronicle Publishing Co., 901 Mission St., San Francisco, CA 94103; Ed. Jan Dennis; Pub. Donald R. Scagg; adv. contact: John Hoffman. bk.rev.; pub. size: broadsheet; circ. morning 51,626(paid); Sun. 56,284(paid). **Wire Service(s):** AP, LAT-WP, SH, Smithsonian.

CANTON

US

DAILY LEDGER. 1849. Mon.-Sat. $.50 newsstand; $99/yr. in cy.; $125.05/yr. out of cy. 53 W. Elm, Canton, IL 61520. TEL 309-647-5100; FAX 309-647-4665. **Owner(s):** American Publishing Co., 606 N. Van Buren, P.O. Box 520, Marion, IL 62959. TEL 618-993-1711; Pub. Scott Koon; adv. contact: Jackie Caulkins. photos; pub. size: broadsheet; circ. evening 6,000(paid). **Wire Service(s):** AP.

CARBONDALE

US

SOUTHERN ILLINOISAN. 1947. d. $.50/day newsstand; $1.50/Sun.; $11.80/4 wks. local. 710 N. Illinois Ave., Carbondale, IL 62901. TEL 618-529-5454; FAX 618-457-2935; E-mail: fiexpress@aol.com. **Owner(s):** Lee Enterprises, Inc., 130 E. Second St., Davenport, IA 52801. TEL 319-383-2202; Ed. Carl Rexroad; Pub. Richard Johnston; adv. contact: Jeff Barr. photos; bk.rev.; pub. size: broadsheet; circ. morning 30,000(paid); Sun. 36,000(paid). **Wire Service(s):** AP.

CARMI

US

CARMI TIMES. 1950. Mon.-Sat. $.50 newsstand; $103.40/yr. in cy. 323-325 E. Main St., Carmi, IL 62821. TEL 618-382-4176; FAX 618-384-2163. **Owner(s):** American Publishing Co., 606 N. Van Buren, P.O. Box 520, Marion, IL 62959. TEL 618-993-1711; Pub. Barry C. Cleveland; pub. size: broadsheet; circ. evening 3,800(paid). **Wire Service(s):** AP.

CENTRALIA

US

CENTRALIA SENTINEL. 1863. Sun.-Fri. $.35/day newsstand; $.75/Sun.; $78/yr. carrier; $70/yr. mailed in area; $80/yr. mailed out of area. 232 E. Broadway, Centralia, IL 62801. TEL 618-532-5604; FAX 618-532-1212. **Owner(s):** Centralia Press, Ltd., P.O. Box 627, Centralia, IL 62801. TEL 618-532-5604; FAX 618-532-1212; Ed. David L. Felts; Pub. John Perine; adv.; photos; pub. size: broadsheet; circ. morning 16,250(paid); Sun. 17,100(paid). **Wire Service(s):** AP, LAT-WP.
  Formerly: Centralia Evening & Sunday Sentinel.

CHAMPAIGN

US   ISSN 1042-3354

CHAMPAIGN NEWS GAZETTE. 1852. d. $.35/day newsstand; $1.50/Sun.; $166.40/yr. home deliv. 15 Main St., Champaign, IL 61820. TEL 217-351-5252; FAX 217-351-5291; E-mail: mcdonald@news-gazette.com; URL: http://www.news-gazette.com. **Owner(s):** Professional Impressions Media Group, 15 Main St., P.O. Box 677, Champaign, IL 61824. TEL 217-351-5252; Ed. John Foreman; Pub. Marajen Stevick Chinigo; adv. contact: Sue Trippiedi. pub. size: broadsheet; circ. evening 45,375(paid); Sun. 52,514(paid). **Wire Service(s):** AP, NYT.

CHARLESTON

US

CHARLESTON TIMES-COURIER. 1840. Mon.-Sat. $.50/day newsstand; $.75/Sat.; $2.20/wk.; $28/13 wks. mailed. 307 Sixth St., Charleston, IL 61920. TEL 217-345-7085; FAX 217-345-7090. **Owner(s):** Howard Publications, Inc., P.O. Box 570, Oceanside, CA; Ed. Bill Lair. adv. contact: Robert Yamamoto. pub. size: broadsheet; circ. morning 7,432(paid). **Wire Service(s):** AP.
  Formerly: Charleston Coles County Daily.

CHICAGO

US   ISSN 0745-7014

CHICAGO DEFENDER. 1905. Mon.-Thu. & Sat. $.50 newsstand; $55.47/6 mos.; $112.84/yr. 2400 S. Michigan Ave., Chicago, IL 60616. TEL 312-225-2400; FAX 312-225-9231. **Owner(s):** Sengstacks Enterprises, 2400 S. Michigan Ave., Chicago, IL 60616. TEL 312-225-2400; Ed. Michael Brown; Pub. Frederick D. Sengstacke; pub. size: tabloid; circ. morning 21,000(paid). **Wire Service(s):** AP.

US

CHICAGO SUN TIMES. 1948. d. $.35/day newsstand; $1.25/Sun.; $3.50/wk. carrier. 401 N. Wabash Ave., Chicago, IL 60611. TEL 312-321-3000; FAX 312-321-3084; E-mail: metro@suntimes.com; URL: http://www.suntimes.com/. **Owner(s):** American Publishing Co., 606 N. Van Buren, P.O. Box 520, Marion, IL 62959. TEL 618-993-1711; Ed. Nigel Wade; Pub. F. David Radler; photos; bk.rev.; pub. size: tabloid; circ. morning 501,115(paid); Sun. 469,161(paid). **Wire Service(s):** AP, DJ, LAT-WP, RN, GNS.

US

CHICAGO TRIBUNE. 1847. d. $.50/day newsstand; $1.75/Sun.; $3.80/wk. 435 N. Michigan Ave., Chicago, IL 60611-4041. TEL 312-222-3920; FAX 312-222-3093; E-mail: prjeff@aol.com; URL: http://www.chicago.tribune.com. **Owner(s):** Tribune Co., 435 N. Michigan Ave., Chicago, IL 60611-4041. TEL 312-222-3232; Ed. Ann Marie Lipinski; Pub. John W. Madigan; adv.; photos; bk.rev.; pub. size: broadsheet; circ. morning 667,908(paid); Sun. 1,066,393(paid). **Wire Service(s):** AP, RN, KR.

US   ISSN 1070-2040

DAILY SOUTHTOWN. 1906. d. $.35/day newsstand; $1.50/Sun.; $116/yr. carrier. 5959 S. Harlem Ave., Chicago, IL 60638-3188. TEL 312-586-8800; FAX 312-229-2900. **Owner(s):** American Publishing Co., 606 N. Van Buren, P.O. Box 520, Marion, IL 62959. TEL 618-993-1711; Ed. Michael J. Kelley; Pub. Norman A. Rosinski; adv. contact: Michael Beatty. pub. size: broadsheet; circ. evening 55,813(paid); Sun. 62,322(paid). **Wire Service(s):** AP.
  Formerly: Southtown Economist.

CLINTON

US

CLINTON DAILY JOURNAL. 1905. Mon.-Fri. $.35 newsstand; $90/yr. Rte. 54, W., Clinton, IL 61727. TEL 217-935-3171; FAX 217-935-6086. **Owner(s):** New Media Corp., 401 N. Main, Rochelle, IL 61068. TEL 815-562-4171; Ed. Cameron Maun; Pub. Terrie L. Baker; pub. size: broadsheet; circ. evening 3,760(paid). **Wire Service(s):** UPI.

CRYSTAL LAKE

US   ISSN 8750-0396

NORTHWEST HERALD. 1875. d. $.50/day newsstand; $1.25/Sun.; $2.90/wk. home deliv. 7717 S. Rte. 31, Crystal Lake, IL 60014. TEL 815-459-4040; FAX 815-459-5640. **Owner(s):** B.F. Shaw Printing Co., 113 Peoria Ave., Dixon, IL 61021; Ed. Cliff Ward; Pub. Robert A. Shaw; adv. contact: Chris Golbeck. pub. size: broadsheet; circ. morning 32,430(paid); Sun. 31,903(paid). **Wire Service(s):** AP.

DANVILLE

US   ISSN 0742-8286

COMMERCIAL-NEWS. 1866. d. $.35/day newsstand; $1.25/Sun.; $102.70/6 mos.; $207.40/yr. 17 W. North St., Danville, IL 61832. TEL 217-446-1000; FAX 217-446-6648. **Owner(s):** Gannett Company, Inc., 1100 Wilson Blvd., Arlington, VA 22340; Ed. Richard Farrant; Pub. Charles E. Morris; adv. contact: Carol Nichols. photos; pub. size: broadsheet; circ. evening 21,140(paid); Sun. 23,685(paid). **Wire Service(s):** AP, GNS.
  Formerly: Danville Commercial-News.

DECATUR

US

HERALD-REVIEW. 1878. d. $.50/day newsstand; $1.75/Sun.; $14.40/4 wks. 601 E. William, Decatur, IL 62523. TEL 217-429-5151; FAX 217-421-7965; E-mail: 74220,1412@compuserve.com. **Owner(s):** Lee Enterprises, Inc., 130 E. Second St., Davenport, IA 52801. TEL 319-383-2202; Ed. George T. Althoff; Pub. Bill Johnston; adv. contact: Kevin Haezeboreck. pub. size: broadsheet; circ. morning 44,000(paid); Sun. 55,000(paid). **Wire Service(s):** AP, KR.

DE KALB

US

DAILY CHRONICLE. 1879. Sun.-Fri. $.50/d.; $1/Sun.; $8.25/mo. 1586 Barber Green Rd., De Kalb, IL 60115. TEL 815-756-4841; FAX 815-756-2079. **Owner(s):** Northern Illinois Publishing Co., 2815 Barber Greene Rd., De Kalb, IL 60115. TEL 815-756-4841; Ed. John Secor. adv. contact: Reino Rippi. pub. size: broadsheet; circ. evening 12,599(paid); Sun. 12,825(paid). **Wire Service(s):** AP.

DES PLAINES

US

DES PLAINES JOURNAL. 1933. Wed.-Sat. & Mon. $.50 newsstand; $25/yr. in cy.; $26/yr. out of cy. 622 Graceland Ave., Des Plaines, IL 60016. TEL 708-299-5511; FAX 708-298-8549. **Owner(s):** Des Plaines Journal, Inc., 622 Graceland Ave., Des Plaines, IL 60016. TEL 708-299-5511; Ed. Todd C. Wessell; Pub. Richard C. Wessell, Sr.; adv.; pub. size: standard; circ. evening 12,000(paid).

DIXON

US   ISSN 0889-4612

TELEGRAPH, THE. 1851. Mon.-Sat. $.50/day newsstand; $1/Sat.; $98/yr. 113 Peoria Ave., Dixon, IL 61021-0409. TEL 815-284-2222; FAX 815-284-2870. **Owner(s):** B.F. Shaw Printing Co., P.O. Box 409, Dixon, IL 61021-0409. TEL 815-284-2222; FAX 815-284-2870; Ed. Mike Chapman; Pub. William E. Shaw; adv.; pub. size: broadsheet; circ. evening 10,300(paid). **Wire Service(s):** AP, CNS.
    Formerly: Dixon Telegraph.

DU QUOIN

US

DU QUOIN EVENING CALL. 1895. d. $.50/day newsstand; $1/Sun.; $86/yr. mailed in cy.; $90/yr. mailed out of cy. 9 N. Division St., Du Quoin, IL 62832. TEL 618-542-2133; FAX 618-542-2726; E-mail: dqedit@ampub.com; URL: http://www.ampub.com/~duquoin/call.html. **Owner(s):** American Publishing Co., 606 N. Van Buren, P.O. Box 520, Marion, IL 62959. TEL 618-993-1711; Ed. John Croessman; Pub. Steve Fisher; adv. contact: Doris Hottes. photos; pub. size: broadsheet; circ. evening 4,800(paid). **Wire Service(s):** AP.

EDWARDSVILLE

US   ISSN 1074-1860

EDWARDSVILLE INTELLIGENCER. 1862. Mon.-Sat. $.50/day newsstand; $.75/Sat.; $1.50/wk. carrier. 117 N. Second St., Edwardsville, IL 62025. TEL 618-656-4700; FAX 618-656-7618; E-mail: mminton@edwpub.com; URL: http://www.edwpub.com. **Owner(s):** Hearst Corp., 959 Eighth Ave., New York, NY 10019; Pub. Bruce Coury; adv. contact: Shelley Loftus. photos; pub. size: broadsheet; circ. evening 7,200(paid). **Wire Service(s):** AP.

EFFINGHAM

US

EFFINGHAM DAILY NEWS. 1899. Mon.-Sat. $.50 newsstand; $7.40/mo.; $78/yr. 201 N. Banker, Effingham, IL 62401. TEL 217-347-7151; FAX 217-342-9315. **Owner(s):** Park Communications, Inc., Vine Ctr. Office Tower, 333 W. Vine St., 17th Fl., Lexington, KY 40507. TEL 606-252-7275; Ed. Susan Duncan; Pub. Paul E. Semple; adv. contact: Carl A. Thoele. pub. size: broadsheet; circ. morning 13,000(paid); evening 13,000(paid). **Wire Service(s):** AP.

ELDORADO

US

ELDORADO DAILY JOURNAL. 1911. Mon.-Sat. $.50 newsstand; $2.10/wk.; $54/6 mos.; $104/yr. 1200 Locust St., Eldorado, IL 62930. TEL 618-273-3379 FAX 618-273-3738. **Owner(s):** American Publishing Co., 606 N. Van Buren, P.O. Box 520, Marion, IL 62959. TEL 618-993-1711; Ed. Scott Hines; Pub. George Wilson; pub. size: broadsheet; circ. evening 1,300(paid). **Wire Service(s):** AP.

ELGIN

US

COURIER-NEWS, THE. 1874. d. $.35/day newsstand; $1/Sun.; $102.90/yr. 300 Lake St., Elgin, IL 60120. TEL 708-888-7800; FAX 708-888-7836 **Owner(s):** Copley Press, Inc., 7776 Ivanhoe Ave., La Jolla, CA 92037. TEL 619-454-0411; Ed. Mike Bailey; Pub. Art Wible; adv. contact: Richard Ballschmeide. pub. size: standard; circ. evening 28,000(paid); Sun. 28,000(paid). **Wire Service(s):** AP, CNS, NYT.
    Formerly: Daily Courier-News.

FLORA

US

DAILY CLAY COUNTY ADVOCATE-PRESS. 1886. Mon.-Fri. $.50 newsstand; $7.50/yr. in cy.; $84.50/yr. out of cy. 105 W. North Ave., Flora, IL 62839. TEL 618-662-2108. **Owner(s):** American Publishing Co., 606 N. Van Buren, P.O. Box 520, Marion, IL 62959. TEL 618-993-1711; Pub. J.L. Thatcher; adv. contact: Bonnie Thatcher. pub. size: broadsheet; circ. evening 3,500(paid). **Wire Service(s):** AP.

FREEPORT

US

FREEPORT JOURNAL-STANDARD. 1847. Mon.-Sat. $.50/day newsstand; $1/Sat.; $118.92/yr. carrier. 27 S. State Ave., Freeport, IL 61032. TEL 815-232-1171; FAX 815-232-3601. **Owner(s):** Howard Publications, Inc., 1722 S. Hill, Oceanside, CA 92054. TEL 619-433-7333; Ed. John Plevka; Pub. Gary Quinn; pub. size: broadsheet; circ. evening 13,000 paid). **Wire Service(s):** AP.

GALESBURG

US

REGISTER-MAIL. 1872. Mon.-Sat. $.50 newsstand; $69/yr. carrier; $82/yr. in state; $114/yr. out of state. 140 S. Prairie St., Galesburg, IL 61401. TEL 309-343-7181; FAX 309-342-5171. **Owner(s):** Copley Press, Inc., 7776 Ivanhoe Ave., La Jolla, CA 92037. TEL 619-454-0411; Pub. John T. McConnell; adv. contact: Doris Medhurst. pub. size: broadsheet; circ. evening 19,000(paid). Wire Service(s): AP.

GENEVA

US

KANE COUNTY CHRONICLE. 1881. Tue.-Sat. $.50 newsstand; $68.85/yr. 1000 Randall Rd., Geneva, IL 60134. TEL 708-232-9222; FAX 708-232-4962. **Owner(s):** B.F. Shaw Printing Co., 444 Pine Hill Dr., P.O. Box 409, Dixon, IL 61021. TEL 815-284-2222; FAX 815-284-2870; Ed. David Heun; Pub. Roger F. Coleman; adv. contact: Jim Holm. photos; pub. size: broadsheet; circ. 15,000(paid). **Wire Service(s):** AP.

HARRISBURG

US

HARRISBURG DAILY REGISTER. 1915. Mon.-Sat. $.50/day newsstand; $1/Sun.; $69.75 in cy.; $83.45 out of cy. 35 S. Vine St., Harrisburg, IL 62946. TEL 618-253-7146; FAX 618-252-0863; E-mail: gwilson@ampub.com; URL: http://www.dailyregister.com. **Owner(s):** American Publishing Co., 606 N. Van Buren, P.O. Box 520, Marion, IL 62959. TEL 618-993-1711; Ed. Lee Smith; Pub. George Wilson; adv. contact: Sally Wofford. pub. size: broadsheet; circ. evening 6,200(paid); Sun. 6,200(paid). **Wire Service(s):** AP.

JACKSONVILLE

US

JACKSONVILLE JOURNAL-COURIER. 1830. d. $.35/day newsstand in city; $.50/day out of city; $1.25/Sun.; $2.85/wk. carrier; $136/yr. mailed. 235 W. State St., Jacksonville, IL 62650. TEL 217-245-6121; FAX 217-245-1226. **Owner(s):** Freedom Communications, Inc., 17666 Fitch, Irvine, CA 92713. TEL 714-553-9292; FAX 714-474-7675; Ed. Ted Roth; Pub. John R. Power. adv. contact: Randy Lohrenz. photos; bk.rev.; pub. size: broadsheet; circ. morning 14,500(paid); Sun. 14,500(paid). **Wire Service(s):** AP.

JOLIET

US

HERALD-NEWS, THE. 1839. d. $.35/day newsstand; $1.25/Sun.; $2.50/wk. home deliv.; $3.50/wk. mailed. 300 Caterpillar Dr., Joliet, IL 60436. TEL 815-729-6161; FAX 815-729-6031. **Owner(s):** Copley Press, Inc., 7776 Ivanhoe Ave., La Jolla, CA 92037. TEL 619-454-0411; adv. contact: Cory Bollinger. photos; bk.rev.; pub. size: broadsheet; circ. evening 49,750(paid); Sun. 50,130(paid). **Wire Service(s):** AP, CNS, SHNA.
  Formerly: Joliet Herald-News.

KANKAKEE

US

DAILY JOURNAL. 1903. Sun.-Fri. $.35/day newsstand; $1.25/Sun.; $4.70/2 wks. carrier; $117/yr. 7 cys.; $170/yr. out of state. 8 Dearborn Sq., Kankakee, IL 60901. TEL 815-937-3300; FAX 815-937-3301. **Owner(s):** Small Newspaper Group, 8 Dearborn Sq., Kankakee, IL 60901. TEL 815-937-3300; Ed. Phil Angelo; Pub. Jean Alice Small; adv. contact: Pam Dunlap. pub. size: broadsheet; circ. evening 29,162(paid); Sun. 33,400(paid). **Wire Service(s):** AP.

KEWANEE

US

KEWANEE STAR-COURIER. 1893. Mon.-Sat. $.50 newsstand; $108.70/yr. local. 105 E. Central Blvd., Kewanee, IL 61443. TEL 309-852-2181; FAX 309-852-0010. **Owner(s):** Lee Enterprises, Inc., 215 N. Main St., Davenport, IA 52801. TEL 319-383-2202; Ed. Anita Bird. pub. size: broadsheet; circ. evening 8,000(paid). **Wire Service(s):** AP.

LANSING

US

TIMES, THE. 1906. d. $.50/day newsstand; $1.75/Sun.; $3.20/wk. carrier. 2 River Pl., Ste. I, Lansing, IL 60438. TEL 708-474-2800; FAX 708-474-2897. **Owner(s):** Howard Publications, Inc., 601 W. 45th Ave., Munster, IN 46321. TEL 219-933-3200; Ed. Harry Gamble; Pub. Pat Colander; adv. contact: Joe Pepe. photos; bk.rev.; pub. size: broadsheet; circ. evening 90,658(paid); Sun. 93,476(paid). **Wire Service(s):** AP, CNS, NYT.

LA SALLE

US

NEWS-TRIBUNE. 1891. Mon.-Sat. $.50 newsstand; $84/yr. 426 Second St., La Salle, IL 61301-2366. TEL 815-223-3200; FAX 815-223-2543. **Owner(s):** Daily News-Tribune, Inc., 426 Second St., La Salle, IL 61301-2366. TEL 815-223-3200; Ed. Linda Kleezewski; Pub. Peter Miller, III; adv. contact: Bob Vickery. photos; bk.rev.; pub. size: broadsheet; circ. evening 19,550(paid). **Wire Service(s):** AP.

LAWRENCEVILLE

US

LAWRENCEVILLE DAILY RECORD. 1847. Mon.-Fri. $.25 newsstand; $59/yr. 1209 State St., Lawrenceville, IL 62439. TEL 618-943-2331; FAX 618-943-3976. **Owner(s):** Larry R. Lewis, 1209 State St., Lawrenceville, IL 62439. TEL 618-943-2331; Pub. Larry R. Lewis; adv. contact: Sandie Stafford. pub. size: broadsheet; circ. evening 4,500(paid). **Wire Service(s):** AP.

LINCOLN

US

LINCOLN COURIER. Mon.-Sat. $.35 newsstand; $2.25/wk. in cy. 601 Pulaski St., Lincoln, IL 62656. TEL 217-732-2101; FAX 217-732-7039. **Owner(s):** Copley Press, Inc., 7776 Ivanhoe, La Jolla, CA 92037. TEL 619-454-0411; Ed. Jeff Nelson; Pub. John Clarke; adv. contact: Karen Harges. pub. size: broadsheet; circ. evening 7,200(paid). **Wire Service(s):** AP.
  Formerly: Courier, The.

LITCHFIELD

US

LITCHFIELD NEWS-HERALD. 1856. Mon.-Fri. $.20 newsstand; $16/yr. in area. 112 E. Ryder St., Litchfield, IL 62056. TEL 217-324-2121; FAX 214-324-2122. **Owner(s):** Litchfield News-Herald, Inc., P.O. Box 160, Litchfield, IL 62056. TEL 217-324-2121; Ed. Micki Romanus; Pub. John C. Hanafin; adv. contact: Fred W. Jones. pub. size: broadsheet; circ. evening 5,800(paid). **Wire Service(s):** AP.

MACOMB

US

MACOMB JOURNAL. 1855. d. $.35/day newsstand; $.50/Sun.; $1.90/wk. carrier. 128 N. Lafayette, Macomb, IL 61455. TEL 309-833-2114; FAX 309-833-2346. **Owner(s):** Park Communications, Inc., Vine Ctr. Office Tower, Lexington, KY 40507. TEL 606-252-7275; Ed. Craig Kibler. adv.; bk.rev.; pub. size: broadsheet; circ. evening 7,000(paid); Sun. 7,500(paid). **Wire Service(s):** AP.

MARION

US

MARION DAILY REPUBLICAN. 1914. Mon.-Sat. $.50/day newsstand; $.75/Sat.; $8.40/mo. carrier. 502 W. Jackson St., Marion, IL 62959. TEL 618-993-2626; FAX 618-993-8326. **Owner(s):** American Publishing Co., 606 N. Van Buren, P.O. Box 520, Marion, IL 62959. TEL 618-993-1711; Ed. Richard Darby; Pub. Sam Shelton; adv. contact: Michelle Bean. photos; pub. size: broadsheet; circ. evening 4,600(paid). **Wire Service(s):** AP.

MATTOON

US

MATTOON JOURNAL GAZETTE. 1905. Mon.-Sat. $.50/day newsstand; $.75/Sat.; $106.60/yr. 100 Broadway, Mattoon, IL 61938. TEL 217-235-5656; FAX 217-235-1925. **Owner(s):** Howard Publications, Inc., 1715 S. Freeman, Oceanside, CA 92054. TEL 619-433-5771; Pub. William Hamel, Jr.; adv. contact: Robert Yamamoto. photos; bk.rev.; pub. size: broadsheet; circ. morning 12,002(paid). **Wire Service(s):** AP.

MOLINE

US

ROCK ISLAND ARGUS DISPATCH, THE. 1878. d. $.35/day; $1.25/Sun.; $135.20/yr. home deliv. 1720 Fifth Ave., Moline, IL 61265. TEL 309-764-4344; FAX 309-797-0311. **Owner(s):** Moline Dispatch Publishing, 1720 Fifth Ave., Moline, IL 61265. TEL 309-764-4344; Ed. Russell Scott; Pub. Gerald J. Taylor; photos; bk.rev.; pub. size: broadsheet; circ. evening 41,830(paid); Sun. 51,927(paid). **Wire Service(s):** UPI, KNT.
  Formerly: Rock Island Argus.

MONMOUTH

US

DAILY REVIEW ATLAS. 1924. Mon.-Sat. $.50 newsstand; $20.50/3 mos. carrier. 400 S. Main St., Monmouth, IL 61462. TEL 309-734-3176; FAX 309-734-7649. **Owner(s):** American Publishing Co., 606 N. Van Buren, P.O. Box 520, Marion, IL 62959. TEL 618-993-1700; Ed. John Stiles; Pub. Scott Champion; adv.; pub. size: broadsheet; circ. morning 3,600(paid). **Wire Service(s):** AP.

MORRIS

US

MORRIS DAILY HERALD. 1891. Mon.-Fri. $.50 newsstand; $65/yr. local. 1804 N. Division St., Morris, IL 60450. TEL 815-942-3221; FAX 815-942-0988. **Owner(s):** B.F. Shaw Printing Co., 113 Peoria Ave., Dixon, IL 61021. TEL 815-284-2222; Pub. Timothy J. West; adv.; photos; pub. size: broadsheet; circ. evening 7,900(paid). **Wire Service(s):** AP.
  Formerly: Morris Herald.

MT. CARMEL

US

MOUNT CARMEL DAILY REPUBLICAN-REGISTER. 1839. Mon.-Fri. $.50 newsstand; $57.90/yr. in cy. 115-117 E. Fourth St., Mt. Carmel, IL 62863. TEL 618-262-5144; FAX 618-263-4437. **Owner(s):** Mt. Carmel Register-Publishing Co., Inc., 115-117 E. Fourth St., Mt. Carmel, IL 62863. TEL 618-262-5144; FAX 618-263-4437; Ed. Phil Gower; Pub. Jack Rodgers; adv. contact: Sally Voigt. bk.rev.; pub. size: broadsheet; circ. evening 4,600(paid). **Wire Service(s):** AP.

MT. VERNON

US

MT. VERNON REGISTER NEWS. 1871. Mon.-Sat. $.35 newsstand; $7.50/mo. home deliv. 118 N. Ninth St., Mt. Vernon, IL 62864. TEL 618-242-0113; FAX 618-242-8286. **Owner(s):** Thomson Newspapers, Inc., One Thorn Run Center, Ste. 500, 1187 Thorn Run Rd. Extension, Corapolis, PA 15108. TEL 412-262-7870; Ed. Terry Geese; Pub. Charles E. Dietz; adv. contact: Sara Sledge. pub. size: broadsheet; circ. evening 11,900(paid). **Wire Service(s):** AP.

OLNEY

US

OLNEY DAILY MAIL. 1898. Mon.-Sat. $.50 newsstand; $90/yr. 206 Whittle Ave., Olney, IL 62450-0340. TEL 618-393-2931; FAX 618-392-2953. **Owner(s):** American Publishing Co., 606 N. Van Buren, P.O. Box 520, Marion, IL 62959. TEL 618-993-1711; Ed. Perry Dable; Pub. Steve Raymond; adv. contact: Carol Lydle. photos; pub. size: broadsheet; circ. evening 5,000(paid). **Wire Service(s):** API.

OTTAWA

US

DAILY TIMES. 1844. Mon.-Sat. $.35 newsstand; $78/yr. in city. 110 W. Jefferson St., Ottawa, IL 61350. TEL 815-433-2000; FAX 815-433-1626. **Owner(s):** Ottawa Publishing Co., 110 W. Jefferson St., Ottawa, IL 61350. TEL 815-433-2000; Ed. Lonny Cain. adv. contact: Joan Heyers. photos; pub. size: broadsheet; circ. evening 12,473(paid). **Wire Service(s):** AP.

PARIS

US

PARIS BEACON NEWS. 1848. Mon.-Sat. $.40 newsstand; $78/yr. carrier. 218 N. Main St., Paris, IL 61944. TEL 217-465-6424; FAX 217-463-1232. **Owner(s):** E.H. Jenison, 218 N. Main St., Paris, IL 61944. TEL 217-465-6424; Ed. Ned Jenison; Pub. E.H. Jenison; adv.; pub. size: broadsheet; circ. evening 7,300(paid). **Wire Service(s):** AP.

PAXTON

US

PAXTON DAILY RECORD. 1865. Mon.-Fri. $.25 newsstand; $54/yr. in cy.; $80/yr. elsewhere. 218 N. Market St., Paxton, IL 60957. TEL 217-379-2356; FAX 217-379-3104. **Owner(s):** Paxton Printing Co., 218 N. Market St., Paxton, IL 60957. TEL 217-379-4313; Ed. Bob Maney; Pub. Paul E. Anderson; adv. contact: Toni Swan. pub. size: broadsheet; circ. evening 1,550(paid).

PEKIN

US   ISSN 0745-7863

PEKIN DAILY TIMES. 1880. Mon.-Sat. $.50 newsstand; $1.75/wk. 20 S. Fourth St., Pekin, IL 61554. TEL 309-346-1111; FAX 309-346-9815. **Owner(s):** Howard Publications, Inc., P.O. Box 570, Oceanside, CA 92049; Pub. David Simpson; adv. contact: Eleanor Gibbons. pub. size: broadsheet; circ. evening 15,472(paid). **Wire Service(s):** AP.

PEORIA

US

PEORIA JOURNAL STAR. 1855. d. $.50/day newsstand; $1.50/Sun.; $200.20/yr. One News Plz., Peoria, IL 61643. TEL 309-686-3020; FAX 309-686-3265. **Owner(s):** Copley Press, Inc., 7776 Ivanhoe Ave., La Jolla, CA 92037. TEL 619-454-0411; Ed. Jack Brimeyer; Pub. John McConnell; adv. contact: Carl Arrenius. photos; bk.rev.; pub. size: broadsheet; circ. morning 79,883(paid); Sun. 107,798(paid). **Wire Service(s):** AP, KNT, NWS.

PONTIAC

US

PONTIAC DAILY LEADER. 1880. Mon.-Sat. $.50 newsstand; $2.05/wk. 318 N. Main St., Pontiac, IL 61764. TEL 815-842-1153. E-mail: pontiacdl@aol.com. **Owner(s):** American Publishing Co., 606 N. Van Buren, P.O. Box 520, Marion, IL 62959. TEL 618-933-1711; Ed. Pat Graziano; Pub. R.A. Westerfield; adv.; bk.rev.; pub. size: broadsheet; circ. morning 7,200(paid). **Wire Service(s):** AP.

QUINCY

US   ISSN 0746-6358

QUINCY HERALD-WHIG. 1835. d. $.50/day newsstand; $1.25/Sun.; $128.05/yr. 130 S. Fifth St., Quincy, IL 62301. TEL 217-223-5100; FAX 217-223-9757; E-mail: whig@bcl.net; URL: http://www.bc.net/~whig/. **Owner(s):** Quincy Newspapers, Inc., 130 S. Fifth St., Quincy, IL 62301; Ed. Michael Hilfrink; Pub. Thomas A. Oakley; adv. contact: Mel Evanoff. pub. size: broadsheet; circ. evening 25,300(paid); Sun. 30,145(paid). **Wire Service(s):** AP.

ROBINSON

US

ROBINSON DAILY NEWS. 1919. Mon.-Sat. $.35 newsstand; $71/yr. 302 S. Cross St., Robinson, IL 62454. TEL 618-544-2101; FAX 618-544-9533. **Owner(s):** Robinson Daily News, Inc., P.O. Box 639, Robinson, IL 62454; Ed. Byron Tracy; Pub. Larry H. Lewis; adv. contact: Wally Dean. photos; bk.rev.; pub. size: broadsheet; circ. evening 7,100(paid). **Wire Service(s):** AP, CNS.

ROCKFORD

US

REGISTER STAR. 1888. d. $.50/day newsstand; $1.50/Sun.; $182/yr. carrier; $195/yr. motor rte. 99 E. State St., Rockford, IL 61104-1004. TEL 815-987-1200; FAX 815-987-1365. **Owner(s):** Gannett Company, Inc., 1100 Wilson Blvd., Arlington, VA 22234. TEL 703-284-6000; Pub. Mary P. Stier; adv.; pub. size: broadsheet; circ. morning 79,000(paid); Sun. 90,000(paid). **Wire Service(s)** AP, GNS, TP.

SHELBYVILLE

US

SHELBYVILLE DAILY UNION. 1887. Mon.-Fri. $.25 newsstand; $1/wk. carrier; $50/yr. carrier. 100 W. Main St., Shelbyville, IL 62565. TEL 217-774-2161; FAX 217-774-5732. **Owner(s):** George Frazier, 100 W. Main St., Shelbyville, IL 62565; Ed. George Frazier; Pub. George Frazier adv.; pub. size: broadsheet; circ. evening 5,000(paid). **Wire Service(s):** AP.
   Formerly: Shelbyville Union.

SPRINGFIELD

US

STATE JOURNAL-REGISTER. 1831. c. $.50/day newsstand; $1.50/Sun.; $3/wk. carrier; $3.22/wk. mailed in state; $3.85/wk. mailed out of state; $139.36/yr. in state. One Copley Plz., Springfield, IL 62705-0219. TEL 217-788-1300; FAX 217-788-1551. **Owner(s):** Copley Press, Inc., 7776 Ivanhoe Ave., La Jolla, CA 92037. TEL 619-454-0411; Ed. Patrick Coburn; Pub. John P. Clarke; adv. contact: Gary Kreppert. photos; pub. size: broadsheet; circ. morning 68,048(paid); Sun. 77,270(paid). **Wire Service(s):** AP, CNS, NYT, SHNA.

STERLING

US

DAILY GAZETTE. 1854. d. $.50/day newsstand; $1/Sun.; $105/yr. home deliv. 312 Second Ave., Sterling, IL 61081. TEL 815-625-3600; FAX 815-625-9390. **Owner(s):** Shaw Newspaper Co., Peoria St., Dixon, IL 61021. TEL 815-664-4321; Ed. Jonie Larson; Pub. William E. Shaw. adv.; photos; pub. size: broadsheet; circ. evening 15,000(paid); Sun. 15,000(paid). **Wire Service(s):** AP, SHNA.
   Formerly: Sterling Daily Gazette.

STREATOR

US   ISSN 0745-5542

STREATOR TIMES-PRESS. 1927. Mon.-Sat. $.35 newsstand; $80.60/yr. 115 Oak St., Streator, IL 61364. TEL 815-673-3711; FAX 815-672-9332. **Owner(s):** Small Newspaper Group, Kankakee, IL 60901; Ed. James Russell. adv.; photos; pub. size: broadsheet; circ. evening 13,700(free & paid). **Wire Service(s):** AP.

TAYLORVILLE

US

TAYLORVILLE BREEZE-COURIER. 1894. Sun.-Fri. $.50/day newsstand; $1/Sun.; $6.85/mo. home deliv. 212 S. Main St., Taylorville, IL 62568. TEL 217-824-2233; FAX 217-824-2026. **Owner(s):** James Frank Cooper, P.O. Box 440, Taylorville, IL 62568. TEL 217-824-2233; FAX 217-824-2026; Ed. J. Robert Cooper; Pub. James F. Cooper; adv. contact: Joseph Dorr. photos; bk.rev.; pub. size: broadsheet; circ. evening 14,500(free & paid). **Wire Service(s):** AP.

WATSEKA

US

IROQUOIS COUNTY TIMES REPUBLIC. 1870. Mon.-Fri. $.50 newsstand; $72.50/yr. mailed in cy.; $91/yr. carrier. 1492 E. Walnut St., Watseka, IL 60970. TEL 815-432-5227; FAX 815-432-5159. **Owner(s):** Twin States Publishing Co., Inc., 1492 E. Walnut St., Watseka, IL 60970. TEL 815-432-5227; Ed. Carla Waters; Pub. Bette Schmid; adv. contact: Kenneth Wynn. pub. size: tabloid; circ. evening 3,660(paid). **Wire Service(s):** AP.
   Formerly: Watseka Iroquois County Daily Times Republic.

WAUKEGAN

US

NEWS-SUN, THE. 1892. Mon.-Sat. $.35/day newsstand; $1/Sat.; $2.30/wk. 100 W. Madison St., Waukegan, IL 60085. TEL 708-336-7000; FAX 708-249-7202. **Owner(s):** Copley Press, Inc., 7776 Ivanhoe Ave., La Jolla, CA 92037. TEL 619-454-0411; Ed. Chris Adams. adv.; pub. size: broadsheet; circ. evening 40,000(paid). **Wire Service(s):** AP, CNS, SHNA, NYT.

WEST FRANKFORT

US

DAILY AMERICAN. 1916. Sat.-Thu. $.50/day newsstand; $.75/Sat.; $1/Sun.; $114/yr. home deliv. 111 S. Emma St., West Frankfort, IL 62896. TEL 618-932-2146; FAX 618-937-6006. **Owner(s):** American Publishing Co., 606 N. Van Buren, P.O. Box 520, Marion, IL 62959. TEL 618-993-1711; Ed. Bob Ellis; Pub. G. David Green; adv. contact: Diann Walthes. pub. size: broadsheet; circ. evening 4,500(paid). **Wire Service(s):** AP.
Formerly: West Frankfort Daily American.

INDIANA

ANDERSON

US

HERALD BULLETIN. 1868. d. $.50/day newsstand; $1.50/Sun.; $3/wk. carrier deliv. 1133 Jackson St., Anderson, IN 46016. TEL 317-622-1212; FAX 317-640-4815; E-mail: thb@indy.net; URL: http://www.indol.com/tp.html. **Owner(s):** Thomson Newspapers, Inc., 3150 Des Plaines Ave., Des Plaines, IL 60018. TEL 708-299-5544; Ed. Elliot Tompkins; Pub. David Smith; adv.; pub. size: broadsheet; circ. morning 35,000(paid); Sun. 37,000(paid). **Wire Service(s):** AP.
Formerly: Anderson Herald Bulletin.

AUBURN

US

EVENING STAR. 1871. Mon.-Sat. $.50/day newsstand; $.75/Sat.; $62.40/6 mos. home deliv. 118 W. Ninth St., Auburn, IN 46706. TEL 219-925-2611; FAX 219-925-2625. **Owner(s):** Kendallville Publishing Co., 112 N. Main St., Kendallville, IN 46755. TEL 219-347-0400; Ed. David Kurtz; Pub. George O. Witwer; adv. contact: Martin Alexander. pub. size: broadsheet; circ. evening 9,000(paid). **Wire Service(s):** AP.
Formerly: Auburn Evening Star.

BEDFORD

US

TIMES-MAIL. 1884. Mon.-Sat. $.50 newsstand; $11.10/mo. home deliv.; $123/yr. 813 16th St., Bedford, IN 47421. TEL 812-275-3355; FAX 812-275-4191; E-mail: tmnews@tmnews.com; URL: http://www.tmnews.com. **Owner(s):** Schurz Communications, Inc., South Bend, IN 46626. TEL 219-233-6161; Ed. Carol Johnson; Pub. Scott C. Schurz; adv. contact: Ellen Ware. pub. size: broadsheet; circ. evening 15,000(paid). **Wire Service(s):** AP.

BLOOMFIELD

US

EVENING WORLD. 1930. Mon.-Fri. $.35 newsstand; $6.25/mo. carrier. 29-31 W. Main St., Bloomfield, IN 47424. TEL 812-384-3501; FAX 812-384-3741. **Owner(s):** William C. Miles, P.O. Box 311, Bloomfield, IN 47424. TEL 812-384-3501; Ed. Gayle Robbins; Pub. William C. Miles; adv.; pub. size: broadsheet; circ. evening 3,800(paid). **Wire Service(s):** AP.

BLOOMINGTON

US   ISSN 1044-4246

HERALD-TIMES. 1877. d. $.50/day newsstand; $1.50/Sun.; $11.95/mo. 1900 S. Walnut St., Bloomington, IN 47401. TEL 812-332-4401; FAX 812-331-4383. **Owner(s):** Schurz Communications, Inc., 225 W. Colfax Ave., South Bend, IN 46626. TEL 219-287-1001; Ed. Bob Zaltsberg; Pub. Scott C. Schurz; adv. contact: Lori Grass. pub. size: broadsheet; circ. morning 30,940(paid); Sun. 45,000(paid). **Wire Service(s):** AP, NYT.

BLUFFTON

US

BLUFFTON NEWS-BANNER. 1929. Mon.-Sat. $.50 newsstand; $110/yr. carrier; $135/yr. mailed. 125 N. Johnson St., Bluffton, IN 46714. TEL 219-824-0224; FAX 219-824-0700; E-mail: newsbanner@ssi.parlorcity.com. **Owner(s):** News-Banner, P. O. Box 436, Bluffton, IN 46714. TEL 219-824-0224; FAX 219-824-0700; Ed. Joel Smekens; Pub. James C. Barbieri; adv. contact: Connie Edington. photos; pub. size: broadsheet; circ. evening 5,700(paid). **Wire Service(s):** AP.

BRAZIL

US

BRAZIL TIMES. 9888. Mon.-Sat. $.50 newsstand; $84/yr. in state; $90/yr. out of state. 100 N. Meridian, Brazil, IN 47834. TEL 812-446-2216; FAX 812-446-0938. **Owner(s):** Nixon Newspapers, Inc., P.O. Box 1149, Peru, IN 46970. TEL 317-473-3091; FAX 317-473-8428; Ed. James Dressler; Pub. William Harper; adv. contact: Larry Knight. photos; bk.rev.; pub. size: broadsheet; circ. evening 5,300(paid). **Wire Service(s):** AP.

CHESTERTON

US

CHESTERTON TRIBUNE. 1884. Mon.-Fri. $.35 newsstand; $5/mo. carrier; $7/mo. mailed. 193 S. Calumet Rd., Chesterton, IN 46304. TEL 219-926-1131; FAX 219-926-6389. **Owner(s):** Warren Canright, 193 S. Calumet Rd., Chesterton, IN 46304. TEL 219-926-1131; Ed. David Canright; Pub. Warren Canright; adv. contact: Bill Mathe. pub. size: broadsheet; circ. evening 5,200(paid).

CLINTON

US

DAILY CLINTONIAN. 1912. Mon.-Fri. $.50 newsstand; $82/yr. in cy.; $86/yr. out of cy. 422 S. Main St., Clinton, IN 47842-2414. TEL 317-832-2443. **Owner(s):** Clinton Color Crafters, Inc., 422 S. Main St., Clinton, IN 47842. TEL 317-832-2443; Ed. George L. Carey; Pub. George L. Carey; adv. contact: Bob Bartlett. photos; pub. size: broadsheet; circ. evening 5,452(paid). **Wire Service(s):** AP, PhotoStream.
Formerly: Clinton Daily Clintonian.

COLUMBIA CITY

US   ISSN 0746-9950

POST & MAIL, THE. 1853. Mon.-Sat. $.50 newsstand; $115.10/yr. home deliv. 116 N. Chauncey St., Columbia City, IN 46725-2002. TEL 219-244-5153; FAX 219-244-7598. **Owner(s):** American Publishing Co., 606 N. Van Buren, P.O. Box 520, Marion, IL 62959. TEL 618-993-1711; Ed. Marilee Kreps; Pub. Doug Driscoll; adv. contact: Margarett Adams. pub. size: broadsheet; circ. evening 4,700(paid). **Wire Service(s):** AP.

COLUMBUS

US

REPUBLIC, THE. 1872. d. $.50/day newsstand; $1.50/Sun.; $10.50/mo. home deliv. 333 Second St., Columbus, IN 47201. TEL 812-372-7811; FAX 812-379-5608. **Owner(s):** Home News Enterprises, 333 Second St., Columbus, IN 47201. TEL 812-372-7811; Ed. J.K. Murphy; Pub. Don R. Bucknam; adv. contact: Pamela Wells-Lego. pub. size: broadsheet; circ. morning 22,000(paid); Sun. 26,000(paid). **Wire Service(s):** AP, KR, SHNA, NEA.
Formerly: Columbus Republic.

CONNERSVILLE

US

CONNERSVILLE NEWS-EXAMINER. 1888. Mon.-Sat. $.50 newsstand; $7.25/mo. home deliv. 406 Central Ave., Connersville, IN 47331. TEL 317-825-0585; FAX 317-825-4599. **Owner(s):** Nixon Newspapers, Inc., 33 W. Third St., Peru, IN 46970. TEL 317-473-3091; Ed. Bob Powers. adv. contact: Diane Howell. pub. size: broadsheet; circ. evening 9,200(paid). **Wire Service(s):** AP, NEA.

CRAWFORDSVILLE

US

CRAWFORDSVILLE JOURNAL REVIEW. 1841. Mon.-Sat. $.50/day newsstand; $.75/Sat.; $7.25/mo. carrier; $7.50/mo. motor rte. 119 N. Green St., Crawfordsville, IN 47933. TEL 317-362-1200; FAX 317-364-5424; E-mail: jreview@link2000.net. **Owner(s):** Freedom Communications, Inc., 17666 Fitch, Irvine, CA 92713. TEL 714-553-9292; Ed. Gaildene Hamilton; Pub. James J. McMillen; adv. contact: Randy List. photos; bk.rev.; pub. size: broadsheet; circ. morning 10,700(paid). **Wire Service(s):** AP, KTR.

DECATUR

US   ISSN 0894-2307
DECATUR DAILY DEMOCRAT. 1857. Mon.-Sat. $.50 newsstand; $104/yr. carrier. 141 S. Second St., Decatur, IN 46733. TEL 219-724-2121; FAX 219-724-7981. **Owner(s):** American Publishing Co., 606N. Van Buren, P.O. Box 520, Marion, IL 62959. TEL 618-993-1711; Ed. Bob Shraluka. adv. contact: Ron Platt. pub. size: broadsheet; circ. evening 6,100(paid). **Wire Service(s):** AP.

Formerly: Decatur Democart.

ELKHART

US   ISSN 0746-7516
ELKHART TRUTH, THE. 1889. d. $.50/day newsstand; $1.25/Sun.; $119.70/yr. home deliv.; $128.25/yr. motor rte. 421 S. Second St., Elkhart, IN 46516. TEL 219-294-1661; FAX 219-294-4014. **Owner(s):** Truth Publishing Co., 421 S. Second St., Elkhart, IN 46516. TEL 219-294-1661; Ed. Jeff Gillaspy; Pub. Anthony Biggs; adv.; pub. size: broadsheet; circ. evening 30,000(paid); Sun. 31,000(paid). **Wire Service(s):** AP, SHNA.

ELWOOD

US
CALL-LEADER. 1891. Mon.-Sat. $.35 newsstand; $105/yr. mailed out of cy. 317 S. Anderson St., Elwood, IN 46036. TEL 317-552-3355; FAX 317-552-3358. **Owner(s):** Elwood Publishing Co., Inc., 317 S. Anderson St., Elwood, IN 46036. TEL 317-552-3355; Ed. Neil Johnson; Pub. Jack L. Barnes; adv. contact: Robert Nash. pub. size: broadsheet; circ. evening 4,000(paid). **Wire Service(s):** AP.

EVANSVILLE

US
EVANSVILLE COURIER. 1845. d. $.50/day newsstand; $2/Sun.; $15.75/mo. carrier; $16.40/mo. motor rte. 300 Walnut St., Evansville, IN 47713. TEL 812-424-7711; FAX 812-422-8196. **Owner(s):** Scripps-Howard, 312 Walnut St., 28th Fl., Cincinnati, OH 45202. TEL 513-977-3000; Ed. Vince Vawter. adv. contact: Jack Pate. photos; pub. size: broadsheet; circ. morning 62,924(paid); evening 27,939(paid); Sun. 117,980(paid). **Wire Service(s):** AP, NYT, SHNA, LAT-WP.

US   ISSN 0896-6249
EVANSVILLE PRESS. 1906. Mon.-Sat. $.50 newsstand; $9.35/mo.; $112.20/yr. carrier. 300 E. Walnut St., Evansville, IN 47713. TEL 812-464-7614; FAX 812-464-7641. **Owner(s):** Hartmann Publishing Co., 300 E. Walnut St., Evansville, IN 47713. TEL 812-464-7614; Ed. Bob Gustin. adv. contact: Jack Pate. pub. size: broadsheet; circ. evening 35,000(paid). **Wire Service(s):** KNT, AP.

FISHER

US
DAILY LEDGER. 1888. Mon.-Sat. $.35 newsstand; $86/yr. motor rte; $80/yr. carrier. 13095 Publishers Dr., Fisher, IN 46030. TEL 317-773-1210; FAX 317-598-6340. **Owner(s):** Central Newspapers, Inc., 135 N. Pennsylvania St., Ste. 1200, Indianapolis, IN 46204-2400. TEL 317-231-9200; Pub. David A. Lewis; adv.; photos; pub. size: broadsheet; circ. evening 10,000(paid). **Wire Service(s):** AP.

Formerly: Noblesville Daily Ledger.

FORT WAYNE

US
FORT WAYNE NEWS-SENTINEL. 1918. Mon.-Sat. $.50 newsstand; $1.45/wk. carrier. 600 W. Main St., Fort Wayne, IN 46802. TEL 219-461-8222; FAX 219-461-8649. **Owner(s):** Knight-Ridder, Inc., One Herald Plz., Miami, FL 33132. TEL 305-376-3800; Ed. Richard Battin; Pub. Ms. Scott McGehee; adv. contact: Lisa Goodman. photos; bk.rev.; pub. size: broadsheet; circ. evening 57,000(paid). **Wire Service(s):** AP, KR.

US   ISSN 0734-3701
JOURNAL-GAZETTE, THE. d. $.50/day newsstand; $1.50/Sun. 600 W. Main St., Fort Wayne, IN 46802. TEL 219-461-8333; FAX 219-461-8648. **Owner(s):** Journal Gazette Co., The, 600 W. Main St., Fort Wayne, IN 46802. TEL 219-461-8333; Ed. Sherry Skufca; Pub. Richard G. Inskeep; adv. contact: Lisa Goodman. photos; bk.rev.; pub. size: broadsheet; circ. morning 62,000(paid); Sun. 140,000(paid). **Wire Service(s):** AP, LAT-WP, SHNA, RN.

FRANKFORT

US
FRANKFORT TIMES. 1885. Mon.-Sat. $.50 newsstand; $8/mo. carrier. 251 E. Clinton St., Frankfort, IN 46041 TEL 317-659-4622; FAX 317-654-7031 **Owner(s):** Nixon Newspapers, Inc., P.O. Box 1149, Peru, IN 46970. TEL 317-473-3091; Ed. Howard W. Hewitt; Pub. Mark Ingels; adv. contact: Greg Ludlow. pub. size: standard; circ. evening 7,600(paid). **Wire Service(s):** AP.

FRANKLIN

US
DAILY JOURNAL. 1962. Mon.-Sat. $.50/day newsstand; $.75/Sat.; $6.50/mo. carrier; $7.50/mo. motor rte. 2575 N. Morton St., Franklin, IN 46131. TEL 317-736-7101; FAX 317-736-2713. **Owner(s):** Home News Enterprises, 333 Second St., Columbus, IN 47201. TEL 812-372-7811; Ed. Jeff Owen; Pub. Howard Herron. adv. contact: J. Fred Mattingly. pub. size: broadsheet; circ. morning 17,500(paid). **Wire Service(s):** AP, SHNA.

GARY

US   ISSN 8750-3492
POST-TRIBUNE. 1907. d. $.50/day newsstand; $1.50/Sun.; $2.80/wk. carrier. 1065 Broadway, Gary, IN 46402. TEL 219-881-3000; FAX 219-881-3232. **Owner(s):** Knight-Ridder, Inc., One Herald Plz., Miami, FL 33132. TEL 305-376-3800; Pub. Scott Bosley; adv. contact: Thomas Sanders. photos; pub. size: broadsheet; circ. evening 69,000(paid); Sun. 80,000(paid). **Wire Service(s):** AP, KRI, NYT.

GOSHEN

US   ISSN 8750-3867
GOSHEN NEWS, THE. 1837. Mon.-Sat. $.50 newsstand; $93/yr. 114 S. Main St., Goshen, IN 46526. TEL 219-533-2151; FAX 219-533-0839; E-mail: goshennews@tln.net; URL: http://www.tln.ret/news/current. **Owner(s):** News Printing Co., Inc., P.O. Box 569, Goshen, IN 46526-0569. TEL 219-533-2151; Ed. Gerald Hertzler; Pub. John W. Gemmer; adv. contact: James Young. pub. size: broadsheet; circ. evening 16,423(paid). **Wire Service(s):** AP.

GREENCASTLE

US
BANNER-GRAPHIC. 1918. Mon.-Sat. $.50 newsstand; $92/yr. in state. 100 N. Jackson St., Greencastle, IN 46135. TEL 317-653-5151; FAX 317-653-2063. **Owner(s):** Truth Publishing Co., 421 S. Second St., Elkhart, IN 46516. TEL 219-294-1661; Ed. Eric Bernsee Pub. Steve Hendershot; adv. contact: Steve Hendershot. pub. size: broadsheet; circ. morning 6,500(paid). **Wire Service(s):** AP, NYT.

GREENFIELD

US
DAILY REPORTER. 1908. Mon.-Sat. $.50 newsstand; $7.50/mo. 22 W. New Rd. Greenfield, IN 46143. TEL 317-462-5528; FAX 317-467-6009. **Owner(s):** Home News Enterprises, 333 Second Street, Columbus, IN 47201. TEL 812-372-7811; Ed. Dave Scott; Pub. Larry W. Brown; adv. contact: Dave McCammon. photos; bk.rev.; pub. size: broadsheet; circ. evening 8,970(paid). **Wire Service(s):** AP.

GREENSBURG

US
GREENSBURG DAILY NEWS. 1894. Mon.-Sat. $.50 newsstand; $117/yr. carrier; $130.20/yr. mailed. 135 S. Franklin St., Greensburg, IN 47240. TEL 812-663-3111; FAX 812-663-2985. **Owner(s):** American Publishing Co., 606 N. Van Buren P.O. Box 520, Marion, IL 62959. TEL 618-993-1711; Pub. Phillip Hart; adv. contact: Pamela Able. pub. size: broadsheet; circ. evening 6,500(paid). **Wire Service(s):** AP.

HARTFORD CITY

US
HARTFORD CITY NEWS-TIMES. 1892. Mon.-Sat. $.50 newsstand; $2.20/wk. home deliv.; $125/yr. mailed. 123 S. Jefferson St., Hartford City, IN 47348. TEL 317-348-0110; FAX 317-348-0112. **Owner(s):** American Publishing Co., 606 N. Van Buren, P.O. Box 520, Marion, IL 62959. TEL 618-993-1711; Ed. Elisabeth Jones. adv. contact: Steven Crouse. pub. size: broadsheet; circ. evening 2,231(paid). **Wire Service(s):** AP.

HUNTINGTON

US
HUNTINGTON HERALD-PRESS. 1848. Sun.-Fri. $.50/day newsstand, $1.50/Sun.; $93.60/yr. carrier; $101/yr. motor rte. $127.40/yr. mailed. 7 N. Jefferson, Huntington, IN 46750-0860. TEL 219-356-6700; FAX 219-356-9026. **Owner(s):** Huntington Newspapers Inc., P.O. Box 860, Huntington, IN 46750-0860 TEL 219-356-6700; FAX 219-356-9026; Ed. Michael V. Perkins. adv. contact: Claude Good. pub. size: broadsheet; circ. morning 7,500(paid); Sun. 8,100(paid). **Wire Service(s):** AP.

INDIANAPOLIS

US
INDIANAPOLIS NEWS. 1869. Mon.-Sat. $.50 newsstand. 307 N. Pennsylvania St., Indianapolis, IN 46204. TEL 317-633-1240; FAX 317-633-1038. **Owner(s):** Central Newspapers, Inc., 135 N. Pennsylvania Ave., Ste. 1200, Indianapolis, IN 46280. TEL 317-231-9200; Ed. Nancy Comiskey; Pub. Eugene Pulliam; adv. contact: Kimberly Parker. photos; bk.rev.; pub. size: broadsheet; circ. evening 85,000(paid). **Wire Service(s):** AP, CNS, LAT-WP, SHNA, NYT.

US
INDIANAPOLIS STAR. d. $.50/day newsstand; $1.50/Sun.; $3.30/wk. carrier; $171.60/yr. carrier. 307 N. Pennsylvania St., Indianapolis, IN 46204-1899. TEL 317-633-1240; FAX 317-633-9423. **Owner(s):** Central Newspapers, Inc., 135 N. Pennsylvania Ave., Indianapolis, IN 46204. TEL 317-231-9200; Ed. Nancy Comiskey; Pub. Eugene S. Pulliam; adv. contact: Kimberly Parker. photos; pub. size: broadsheet; circ. morning 229,876(paid); Sun. 404,469(paid). **Wire Service(s):** AP, SHNA, NYT, KNT, LAT-WP.

JASPER

US
HERALD, THE. 1895. Mon.-Sat. $.50 newsstand; $8/mo. carrier; $8.25/mo. motor rte. 216 E. Fourth St., Jasper, IN 47546. TEL 812-482-2424; FAX 812-482-4104. **Owner(s):** Jasper Herald Co., 216 Fourth St., Jasper, IN 47546. TEL 812-482-2424; Ed. John A. Rumbach. adv. contact: Don Schreve. pub. size: tabloid; circ. evening 13,000(paid). **Wire Service(s):** AP.

JEFFERSONVILLE

US
JEFFERSONVILLE EVENING NEWS. 1872. Mon.-Sat. $.50 newsstand; $7.80/mo. home deliv. 221 Spring St., Jeffersonville, IN 47131. TEL 812-283-6636; FAX 812-284-7081; E-mail: jlg@iglou.com. **Owner(s):** Park Communications, Inc., Vine Ctr. Office Tower, 333 W. Vine St., 17th Fl., Lexington, KY 40507. TEL 606-252-7275; Ed. John Gilkey. adv.; bk.rev.; pub. size: broadsheet; circ. evening 18,000(paid). **Wire Service(s):** AP.

KENDALLVILLE

US   ISSN 8750-0876
KENDALLVILLE NEWS-SUN. Mon.-Sat. $.50/day newsstand; $.75/Sat.; $119.60/yr. carrier; $135.95/yr. motor rte.; $163/yr. out of state. 102 N. Main St., Kendallville, IN 46755. TEL 219-347-0400; FAX 219-347-2693. **Owner(s):** Kendallville Publishing Co., P.O. Box 39, Kendallville, IN 46755. TEL 219-347-0400; FAX 219-347-2693; Ed. James Kroemer; Pub. George O. Witwer; adv. contact: Ron Ensley. photos; bk.rev.; pub. size: broadsheet; circ. evening 8,000(paid).

KOKOMO

US   ISSN 0746-2034
KOKOMO TRIBUNE, THE. 1850. d. $.50/day newsstand; $1.50/Sun.; $3/wk.; $13/mo. 300 N. Union St., Kokomo, IN 46904. TEL 317-459-3121; FAX 317-456-3815; E-mail: ktonline@aol.com; URL: http://www.members.aol.com/ktonline/. **Owner(s):** Thomson Newspapers, Inc., 3150 Des Plaines Ave., Des Plaines, IL 60018. TEL 708-299-5544; Ed. John C. Wiles; Pub. Arden Draeger; adv. contact: Jeff Pizzano. pub. size: broadsheet; circ. evening 29,000(paid); Sun. 30,000(paid). **Wire Service(s):** AP.

LAFAYETTE

US
JOURNAL & COURIER. 1829. d. $.50/day newsstand; $1.50/Sun.; $3.25/wk. 217 N. Sixth St., Lafayette, IN 47901-1420. TEL 317-423-5511; FAX 317-423-2613; E-mail: postmaster@jandc.mdn.com; URL: http://www.jconline.com. **Owner(s):** Gannett Company, Inc., 1100 Wilson Blvd., Arlington, VA 22234. TEL 703-284-6000; Ed. Denise Richter; Pub. Richard L. Holtz; adv. contact: Ted Taylor. photos; pub. size: broadsheet; circ. morning 38,172(paid); Sun. 44,892(paid). **Wire Service(s):** AP, GNS, LAT-WP.

LA PORTE

US
LA PORTE HERALD-ARGUS. 1880. Mon.-Sat. $.50 newsstand; $93.60/yr. 701 State St., La Porte, IN 46350. TEL 219-362-2161; FAX 219-362-2166. **Owner(s):** Small Newspaper Group, 701 State St., La Porte, IN 46350-3328. TEL 219-362-2161; FAX 219-362-2166; Ed. Mark Johnson; Pub. Clem Otolski; adv. contact: Thomas P. Avery. photos; bk.rev.; pub. size: broadsheet; circ. evening 13,199(paid). **Wire Service(s):** AP, SHNS.

LEBANON

US
REPORTER, THE. 1891. Mon.-Sat. $.50 newsstand; $969/yr. mailed in cy.; $118/yr. out of cy. 117 E. Washington St., Lebanon, IN 46052. TEL 317-482-4650; FAX 317-482-4652. **Owner(s):** Lebanon Newspapers, Inc., 117 E. Washington St., Lebanon, IN 46052. TEL 317-482-4650; adv.; photos; pub. size: broadsheet; circ. evening 7,400(paid). **Wire Service(s):** AP.
Formerly: Lebanon Reporter.

LINTON

US
LINTON DAILY CITIZEN. 1900. Mon.-Fri. $.75 newsstand; $78/yr. 79 S. Main St., Linton, IN 47441. TEL 812-847-4487; FAX 812-847-9513. **Owner(s):** Hammell Newspapers Of Indiana, Inc., 79 S. Main St., Linton, IN 47441. TEL 812-847-4487; Ed. Heather Atkinson; Pub. Ron Dietz; adv. contact: Tina Cunningham. pub. size: broadsheet; circ. evening 9,500(paid). **Wire Service(s):** AP.

LOGANSPORT

US
PHAROS-TRIBUNE. 1844. Sun.-Fri. $.50/day newsstand; $1.25/Sun.; $137.80/yr. carrier; $179.40/yr. in state mailed; $192.40/yr. out of state mailed. 517 E. Broadway, Logansport, IN 46947. TEL 219-722-5000; FAX 219-722-5238. **Owner(s):** Thomson Newspapers, Inc., One Thorn Run Ctr., Ste. 500, 1187 Thorn Run Rd. Ext., Coraopolis, PA 15108. TEL 412-262-7870; Ed. Dave Long; Pub. Mark Cohen; adv. contact: David Tucker. photos; bk.rev.; pub. size: broadsheet; circ. evening 14,499(paid); Sun. 15,233(paid). **Wire Service(s):** AP,KR.

MADISON

US
MADISON COURIER. 1837. Mon.-Sat. $.50 newsstand; $67.10/yr. carrier; $82/yr. IN & KY; $88/yr. out of area. 310 Courier Sq., Madison, IN 47250. TEL 812-265-3641. **Owner(s):** Madison Courier, Inc., 310 Courier Sq., Madison, IN 47250. TEL 812-265-3641; Ed. Graham Taylor; Pub. Jane W. Jacobs; adv.; photos; bk.rev.; pub. size: broadsheet; circ. evening 9,800(paid). **Wire Service(s):** AP.

MARION

US
MARION CHRONICLE-TRIBUNE. 1886. d. $.35/day newsstand; $1.25/Sun.; $11.60/4 wks. 610 S. Adams St., Marion, IN 46953. TEL 317-664-5111; FAX 317-664-6292. **Owner(s):** Gannett Company, Inc., 1100 Wilson Blvd., Arlington, VA 22234. TEL 703-284-6000; Ed. Randolph Brandt; Pub. Victor W. Hussey; adv. contact: Mike Casuscelli. pub. size: broadsheet; circ. morning 20,812(paid); Sun. 25,050(paid).

MARTINSVILLE

US
MARTINSVILLE DAILY REPORTER. 1889. Mon.-Sat. $.50 newsstand; $1.65/wk.; $7.15/mo.; $76.50/yr. 60 S. Jefferson, Martinsville, IN 46151. TEL 317-342-3311; FAX 317-342-1446. **Owner(s):** Robert Kendall, 1290 E. Jackson, Martinsville, IN 46151; Dorothy Kendall, 1290 E. Jackson, Martinsville, IN 46151; Mark Kendall, P.O. Box 1636, Lawrenceville, NJ 08648; Harriet Tackitt, P.O. Box 1636, Lawrenceville, NJ 08648; Wendell & Kay Holt, 1290 E. Jackson, Martinsville, IN 46151. TEL 317-342-3527; Robert Adams, E. High St., Mooresville, IN 46158; Ed. Bette Nunn; Pub. Mr. Kay Selch; adv. contact: Mr. Kay Selch. pub. size: broadsheet; circ. evening 8,450(paid). **Wire Service(s):** UPI.

MICHIGAN CITY

US   ISSN 1047-6016
MICHIGAN CITY NEWS-DISPATCH. 1881. d. $.50/day newsstand; $1/Sun.; $10.25/mo. mailed; $10.55/mo. motor rte.; $129/yr. mailed in state; $171/yr. mailed out of state. 121 W. Michigan Blvd., Michigan City, IN 46360. TEL 219-874-7211; FAX 219-872-8511. **Owner(s):** Nixon Newspapers, Inc., 33 W. Third St., Peru, IN 46970. TEL 317-473-3091; Ed. Dave Hawk; Pub. Don Manaher; adv. contact: Debbie Everly. photos; pub. size: broadsheet; circ. morning 15,000(paid); Sun. 15,500(paid). **Wire Service(s):** AP.

MONTICELLO

US

HERALD-JOURNAL, THE. 1862. Mon.-Sat. $.50 newsstand; $9/mo. 114 S. Main St., Monticello, IN 47960. TEL 219-583-5121; FAX 219-583-4241. **Owner(s):** Home News Enterprises, P.O. Box 3011, Columbus, IN 47202. TEL 812-379-5658; Ed. Larry Magrath; Pub. Don Hurd; adv. contact: Kevin Lashbrook. pub. size: broadsheet; circ. evening 6,000(paid). **Wire Service(s):** UPI.

MUNCIE

US

STAR PRESS. 1904. Mon.-Sat. $.50 newsstand; $83.20/yr. carrier. 125 S. High St., Muncie, IN 47305. TEL 317-747-5730; FAX 317-747-5727. **Owner(s):** Muncie Newspapers, Inc., Muncie, IN 47307; Ed. Sally Mills; Pub. Robert G. Ellis; adv. contact: John Rice. photos; bk.rev.; pub. size: broadsheet; circ. morning 40,000(paid). **Wire Service(s):** AP, KR, SHNA.

Formerly: Muncie Star & Evening Press.

MUNSTER

US

TIMES, THE. 1906. d. $.50/day newsstand; $1.50/Sun.; $2.75/wk. 601 45th St., Munster, IN 46321. TEL 219-933-3223; FAX 219-933-3249. **Owner(s):** Howard Publications, Inc., P.O. Box 570, Oceanside, CA 92049. TEL 619-433-5771; Pub. William Howard; adv. contact: Joseph Pepe. photos; bk.rev.; pub. size: broadsheet; circ. morning 73,000(paid); Sun. 80,000(paid). **Wire Service(s):** AP, NYT, CNS.

NEW ALBANY

US

LEDGER TRIBUNE, THE. 1851. Sun.-Fri. $.50/day newsstand; $1.25/Sun.; $117/yr. 303 Scribner Dr., New Albany, IN 47150. TEL 812-944-6481; FAX 812-949-6585. **Owner(s):** American Publishing Co., 606 N. Van Buren, P.O. Box 520, Marion, IL 62959. TEL 618-993-1711; Ed. W. Curt Vincent; Pub. Russ Maroney; adv.; photos; pub. size: broadsheet; circ. evening 12,500(paid); Sun. 12,500(paid). **Wire Service(s):** AP.

Formerly: Ledger.

NEW CASTLE

US

NEW CASTLE COURIER-TIMES. 1841. Mon.-Sat. $.50 newsstand; $104/yr.; $150/yr. mailed. 201 S. 14th St., New Castle, IN 47362. TEL 317-529-1111; FAX 317-529-1731. **Owner(s):** Nixon Newspapers, Inc., 33 W. Third St., Peru, IN 46970; Ed. Darrel Radford; Pub. J. Wesley Rowe, Jr.; adv. contact: Tina West. photos; pub. size: broadsheet; circ. evening 12,000(paid). **Wire Service(s):** AP.

PERU

US

PERU TRIBUNE. 1921. Mon.-Sat. $.50 newsstand; $9.50/mo. mailed. 26 W. Third St., Peru, IN 46970. TEL 317-473-6641; FAX 317-472-4438. **Owner(s):** Nixon Newspapers, Inc., 33 W. Third St., Peru, IN 46970. TEL 317-473-3091; Ed. Jeff Ward; Pub. Raymond Moscowitz; adv.; photos; pub. size: broadsheet; circ. morning 7,800(paid). **Wire Service(s):** AP.

Formerly: Peru Daily Tribune.

PLYMOUTH

US

PILOT-NEWS. 1851. Mon.-Sat. $.35 newsstand; $78/yr. carrier; $84/yr. motor rte.; $102/yr. mail. 217-223 N. Center St., Plymouth, IN 46563. TEL 219-936-3101; FAX 219-936-3844. **Owner(s):** Park Communications, Inc., Vine Ctr. Office Tower, 333 W. Vine St., 17th Fl., Lexington, KY 40507. TEL 606-252-7275; Ed. Robert Noren. pub. size: broadsheet; circ. evening 7,600(paid). **Wire Service(s):** AP.

PORTLAND

US   ISSN 0010-3101

PORTLAND COMMERCIAL REVIEW. 1871. d. $.50 newsstand; $60/yr. 309 W. Main St., Portland, IN 47371. TEL 219-726-8141; FAX 219-726-8143. **Owner(s):** Graphic Printing Co., Inc., 309 W. Main St, P.O. Box 1049, Portland, IN 47371. TEL 219-726-8141; Ed. Jack C Ronald. Pub. Jack C. Ronald; adv. contact: Don Gillespie. pub. size: broadsheet; circ. evening 6,100(paid). **Wire Service(s):** AP.

PRINCETON

US

PRINCETON DAILY CLARION. 1846. Mon.-Fri. $.50 newsstand; $53/yr. 100 N. Gibson, Princeton, IN 47670. TEL 812-385-2525; FAX 812-386-5199. **Owner(s):** Brehm Communications, Inc., 17065 Via del Campo, Ste. 200, San Diego, CA 92197. TEL 619-451-6200; Ed. Tec Morris; Pub. Gary Blackburn; adv.; photos; pub. size: broadsheet; circ. morning 6,700(paid). **Wire Service(s):** AP.

RENSSELAER

US

RENSSELAER REPUBLICAN. 1865. Mon.-Sat. $.50 newsstand; $94/yr. home deliv. 117 N. Van Rensselaer St., Rensselaer, IN 47978. TEL 219-866-5111; FAX 219-866-3775. **Owner(s):** Kankakee Publishing Co., P.O. Box 298, Rensselaer, IN 47978; Ed. John Scheibel. adv. contact: Frank Copley. pub. size: broadsheet; circ. evening 3,500(paid). **Wire Service(s):** AP.

RICHMOND

US

RICHMOND PALLADIUM-ITEM. 1831. d. $.35/day newsstand; $1.25/Sun.; $16.25/13 wks. Sun. only; $32.50/13 wks. daily;. 1175 N. A St., Richmond, IN 47374. TEL 317-962-1575; FAX 317-966-6377. **Owner(s):** Gannett Company, Inc., 1100 Wilson Blvd., Arlington, VA 22234. TEL 703-284-6000; adv. contact: Al Bonner. pub. size: broadsheet; circ. evening 19,778(paid); Sun. 25,028(paid). **Wire Service(s):** AP, GNS.

ROCHESTER

US

ROCHESTER SENTINEL, THE. 1858. Mon.-Sat. $.50 newsstand; $93/yr. local; $117/yr. out of state. 118 E. Eighth St., Rochester, IN 46975-0260. TEL 219-223-2111; FAX 219-223-5782; E-mail: raincreek@aol.com. **Owner(s):** Sentinel Corp., 118 E. Eighth St., Rochester, IN 46975. TEL 219-223-2111; FAX 219-223-5782; Ed. W.S. Wilson; Pub. Sarah O. Wilson; adv. contact: Ryan N. Showley. photos; pub. size: broadsheet; circ. evening 4,845(paid). **Wire Service(s):** AP.

RUSHVILLE

US   ISSN 8756-6443

RUSHVILLE REPUBLICAN. 1840. Mon.-Sat. $.50 newsstand; $8.05/mo. carrier. 219 N. Perkins St., Rushville, IN 46173. TEL 317-932-2222; FAX 317-932-4358. **Owner(s):** American Publishing Co., 606 N. Van Buren, P.O. Box 520, Marion, IL 62959. TEL 6 3-993-1711; Ed. Charlie Wilson; Pub. Norman D. Voiles; adv. contact: Marilyn Land. pub. size: broadsheet; circ. evening 4,150(paid). **Wire Service(s):** AP.

SEYMOUR

US

TRIBUNE, THE. 1879. Mon.-Sat. $.50 newsstand; $112.25/yr. in state mailed; $123.65/yr. out of state. 1215 E. Tipton, Seymour, IN 47274. TEL 812-522-4871; FAX 812-522-7691. **Owner(s):** Freedom Communications, Inc., 17666 Fitch, Irvine, CA 92714. TEL 714-553-9292; Ed. W. Curt Vincent; Pub. Russell E. Maroney; adv. contact: Lisa McCory. photos; bk.rev.; pub. size: broadsheet; circ. evening 9,687(paid). **Wire Service(s):** AP.

Formerly: Seymour Tribune.

SHELBYVILLE

US

SHELBYVILLE NEWS. 1948. Mon.-Sat. $.50 newsstand; $45/6 mos. home deliv. 123 E. Washington, Shelbyville, IN 46176. TEL 317-398-6631; FAX 317-398-0194. **Owner(s):** Shelbyville Newspapers Inc., 123 E. Washington St., Shelbyville, IN 46176. TEL 317-398-6631; Ed. Scarlett Syse. Pub. John C. Deprez, Jr.; adv. contact: Dee Bonner. bk.rev.; pub. size: broadsheet; circ. evening 11,500(paid). **Wire Service(s):** AP, SHNA, NEA, RN, NYT.

SOUTH BEND

US

SOUTH BEND TRIBUNE. 1872. d. $.50/day newsstand; $1.50/Sun.; $126/yr. carrier; $135/yr. motor rte. 225 W. Colfax Ave., South Bend, IN 46626. TEL 219-235-6161; FAX 219-236-1765. **Owner(s):** Schurz Communications, Inc., 225 W. Colfax Ave., South Bend, IN 46626. TEL 219-235-6161; Ed. Tim Harmon. adv. contact: Carol A. Smith. photos; bk.rev.; pub. size: broadsheet; circ. evening 86,817(paid); Sun. 121,079(paid). **Wire Service(s):** AP, NYT, SH.

SPENCER

US   ISSN 0745-7227
SPENCER EVENING WORLD. 1927. Mon.-Fri. $.30 newsstand; $48/yr. 114 E. Franklin St., Spencer, IN 47460. TEL 812-829-2255; FAX 812-829-4666. **Owner(s):** Spencer Evening World, Inc., P.O. Box 226, Spencer, IN 47460; Ed. Tom Douglas; Pub. John T. Gillaspy; adv.; pub. size: broadsheet; circ. evening 3,600(paid).

SULLIVAN

US
SULLIVAN DAILY TIMES. 1905. Mon.-Fri. $.30 newsstand; $42/yr. in cy; $48/yr. out of cy. 115 W. Jackson, Sullivan, IN 47882. TEL 812-268-6356; FAX 812-268-3110. **Owner(s):** Pierce Oil Co., Inc., P.O. Box 130, Sullivan, IN 47882. TEL 812-268-6356; Ed. Tom P. Gettinger; Pub. Nancy Pierce Gettinger; adv. contact: B.J. White. pub. size: broadsheet; circ. evening 5,000(paid). **Wire Service(s):** AP.

TERRE HAUTE

US
TRIBUNE-STAR. 1894. d. $.50/day newsstand; $1.50/Sun.; $156/yr. home deliv. 721 Wabash Ave., Terre Haute, IN 47807. TEL 812-231-4200; FAX 812-231-4234. **Owner(s):** Thomson Newspapers, Inc., One Thorn Run Ctr., Ste. 500, 1187 Thorn Run Rd. Ext., Coraopolis, PA 15108. TEL 412-262-7870; Ed. David Cox; Pub. Jack Meany; adv. contact: Rick Schmidt. bk.rev.; pub. size: broadsheet; circ. morning 36,000(paid); Sun. 43,000(paid). **Wire Service(s):** AP.

TIPTON

US   ISSN 0746-0619
TIPTON TRIBUNE. Mon.-Sat. $.35 newsstand; $64.80/yr. in town; $75.60/yr. motor rte.; $85/yr. mailed. 110 W. Madison, Tipton, IN 46072. TEL 317-675-2115; FAX 317-675-4147. **Owner(s):** Elwood Publishing Co., Inc., 317 S. Anderson, Elwood, IN 46036; Ed. E. Neil Johnson; Pub. Jack L. Barnes; adv. contact: Jay Puterbaugh. pub. size: broadsheet; circ. evening 4,000(paid). **Wire Service(s):** AP.

VALPARAISO

US
VALPARAISO VIDETTE-TIMES. 1927. d. $.50/day newsstand; $1.75/Sun.; $9.40/mo. carrier. 1111 Glendale Blvd., Valparaiso, IN 46383. TEL 219-462-5151; FAX 219-465-7298. **Owner(s):** Thomson Newspapers, One Thorn Run Ctr., Ste. 500, 1187 Thorn Run Rd. Ext., Coraopolis, PA 15108. TEL 412-262-7870; Ed. Don Asher; Pub. Dan Blum; adv. contact: Mark Leuthart. photos; bk.rev.; pub. size: broadsheet; circ. evening 90,000(paid); Sun. 90,000(paid). **Wire Service(s):** AP, TN, SHNA.
     Formerly: Valparaiso Vidette-Messenger.

VINCENNES

US   ISSN 1072-3609
VINCENNES SUN-COMMERCIAL. 1804. Sun.-Fri. $.50/day newsstand; $1.50/Sun.; $78.80/yr. home deliv.; $98.80/yr motor rte. 702 Main St., Vincennes, IN 47591. TEL 812-886-9955; FAX 812-885-2235. **Owner(s):** Central Newspapers, Inc., 135 N. Pennsylvania, Indianapolis, IN 46204. TEL 317-231-9200; Ed. Michael E. Quayle; Pub. Michael E. Quayle; adv. contact: Robert Haven. pub. size: broadsheet; circ. evening 15,000(paid); Sun. 16,000(paid). **Wire Service(s):** AP.

WABASH

US
WABASH PLAIN DEALER. 1859. Mon.-Sat. $.50 newsstand; $6.25/mo. carrier; $6.65/mo. motor rte. 123 W. Canal St., Wabash, IN 46992. TEL 219-563-2131; FAX 219-563-0816; E-mail: wapd@holli.com; URL: http://207.2.127.1:80/newswave. **Owner(s):** Nixon Newspapers, Inc., 33 W. Third St., Peru, IN 46970. TEL 219-563-7414; Ed. Roy Church; Pub. Jim Widner; adv.; pub. size: broadsheet; circ. evening 7,500(paid). **Wire Service(s):** UPI.

WARSAW

US
TIMES-UNION. 1854. Mon.-Sat. $.50 newsstand; $8.10/mo. motor rte.; $10/mo. local mailed; $11/mo. elsewhere. Times Bldg., Warsaw, IN 46581-1448. TEL 219-267-3111. **Owner(s):** Reub Williams & Sons, Inc., P.O. Box 1448, Warsaw, IN 46581-1448. TEL 219-267-3111; Ed. Norman Hagg; Pub. M.R. Williams; adv. contact: Bill Hays. photos; pub. size: broadsheet; circ. evening 14,500(paid). **Wire Service(s):** AP, NYT.

WASHINGTON

US
WASHINGTON TIMES-HERALD. 1867. Mon.-Sat. $.50 newsstand; $81/yr. 102 E. Van Trees St., Washington, IN 47501. TEL 812-254-0480; FAX 812-254-7517. **Owner(s):** Stephens Group, Inc., P.O. Box 1359, Fort Smith, AR 72901. TEL 501-785-7810; Ed. Melody Maust; Pub. Lars Purdue; adv. contact: Don Brown. photos; bk.rev.; pub. size: standard; circ. evening 10,200(paid). **Wire Service(s):** AP.

WINCHESTER

US
NEWS-GAZETTE, THE. 1847. Mon.-Sat. $.50 newsstand; $106.20/yr. in cy.; $112/yr. mailed in cy.; $112/yr. mailed out of cy. 224 W. Franklin St., Winchester, IN 47394. TEL 317-584-4501; FAX 317-584-3066. **Owner(s):** Whitewater Publishing Co.; Ed. Michael Buckmaster; Pub. Jack J. Armstrong; adv.; photos; pub. size: broadsheet; circ. evening 5,000(paid). **Wire Service(s):** AP.

IOWA

AMES

US   ISSN 0893-7915
DAILY TRIBUNE, THE. 1867. Mon.-Sat. $.50/day newsstand; $1/Sat.; $121.70/yr. carrier in cy.; $159.10/yr. mailed in cy.; $210.15/yr. mailed out of cy. 317 Fifth St., Ames, IA 50010. TEL 515-232-2160; FAX 515-232-2364. **Owner(s):** Ames Daily Tribune, 317 Fifth. St., P.O. Box 380, Ames, IA 50010. TEL 515-232-2160; Ed. Jeff Bruner; Pub. Gary G. Gerlach; adv.; photos; pub. size: broadsheet; circ. evening 10,000(paid). **Wire Service(s):** AP, NYT.
     Formerly: Ames Daily Tribune.

ATLANTIC

US   ISSN 8756-6400
ATLANTIC NEWS-TELEGRAPH. 1871. Mon.-Sat. $.50 newsstand; $22/3 mo.; $79/yr. 410 Walnut St., Atlantic, IA 50022. TEL 712-243-2624; FAX 712-243-4988. **Owner(s):** American Publishing Co., 606 N. Van Buren, P.O. Box 520, Marion, IL 62959. TEL 618-993-1711; Ed. Christy Stinger; Pub. Ken Lingen; adv.; pub. size: broadsheet; circ. evening 5,100(paid). **Wire Service(s):** AP.

BOONE

US   ISSN 1050-4087
BOONE NEWS-REPUBLICAN. 1865. Mon.-Fri. $.50 newsstand; $72/yr. carrier in town; $80/yr. motor in cy.; $94/yr. mailed in cy.; $135/yr. mailed out of cy. 812 Keeler St., Boone, IA 50036. TEL 515-432-1234; FAX 515-432-7811. **Owner(s):** Schaub Publishing, Inc., 812 Keeler St., P.O. Box 100, Boone, IA 50036-0100. TEL 515-432-1234; FAX 515-432-7811; Ed. James A. Bachtell; Pub. R.C. Schaub; adv. contact: Susan E. Tolan. pub. size: broadsheet; circ. evening 4,000(paid). **Wire Service(s):** AP.

BURLINGTON

US   ISSN 1073-9297
HAWK EYE, THE. 1837. d. $.50/day newsstand; $1.25/Sun.; $9/mo. 800 S. Main St., Burlington, IA 52601. TEL 319-754-8461; FAX 319-754-6824. **Owner(s):** Burlington Hawk Eye Co., P.O. Box 10, Burlington, IA 52601. TEL 319-754-8461; FAX 319-754-6824; Ed. Dale Alison; Pub. Bill Mertens; adv. contact: Nelson Showalter. photos; pub. size: broadsheet; circ. evening 18,000(paid); Sun. 20,000(paid). **Wire Service(s):** AP.

CARROLL

US

CARROLL TIMES HERALD. 1928. Mon.-Fri. $.50 newsstand; $78/yr. 508 N. Court St., Carroll, IA 51401. TEL 712-792-3573; FAX 712-792-5218. **Owner(s):** James B. & Ann Wilson, 508 N. Court St., Carroll, IA 51401. TEL 712-792-3573; Ed. James B. Wilson; Pub. James B. Wilson; adv. contact: Debra Lucht. pub. size: broadsheet; circ. evening 6,500(paid). **Wire Service(s):** AP.

Formerly: Carroll Daily Times Herald.

CEDAR RAPIDS

US   ISSN 1066-0291

CEDAR RAPIDS GAZETTE. 1883. d. $.75/day newsstand; $1.75/Sun.; $197/yr. carrier. 500 Third Ave., S.E., Cedar Rapids, IA 52401. TEL 319-398-8211; FAX 319-398-5846; E-mail: gazette@infi.net; URL: http://www.fyiowa.com/gazette. **Owner(s):** Gazette Co., The, 500 Third Ave., S.E., Cedar Rapids, IA 52401. TEL 319-398-8211; Ed. Mark Bowden; Pub. Joe Hladky; adv.; photos; bk.rev.; pub. size: broadsheet; circ. morning 70,692(paid); Sun. 83,050(paid). **Wire Service(s):** AP, LAT-WP.

CENTERVILLE

US

AD EXPRESS & DAILY IOWEGIAN. 1883. Mon.-Fri. $.50 newsstand; $49/yr. local; $61/yr. out of state. 105 N. Main St., Centerville, IA 52544. TEL 515-856-6336; FAX 515-856-8118. **Owner(s):** Appanoose Publishing Co., Inc., 105 N. Main St., Centeville, IA 52544; Ed. Steve Dunn; Pub. John C. Arnold; adv. contact: Cindy Briggs. pub. size: broadsheet; circ. morning 3,100(paid).

CHARLES CITY

US   ISSN 1049-7242

CHARLES CITY PRESS. 1896. Mon.-Sat. $.50 newsstand; $88.50/yr. 801 Riverside, Charles City, IA 50616. TEL 515-228-3211; FAX 515-228-2641. **Owner(s):** American Publishing Co., 606 N. Van Buren, P.O. Box 520, Marion, IL 62959. TEL 618-993-1711; Ed. Mark Micks; Pub. Gene A. Hall; adv. contact: Rich Gifford. pub. size: broadsheet; circ. evening 3,000(paid). **Wire Service(s):** AP.

CHEROKEE

US   ISSN 0747-4776

CHEROKEE COUNTY'S DAILY TIMES. 1870. Tue.-Sat. $.50 newsstand; $60/yr. in cy.; $75/yr. out of cy. 111 S. Second St., Cherokee, IA 51012. TEL 712-225-5111; FAX 712-225-2910. **Owner(s):** Edwards Publications, P.O. Box 1193, Seneca, SC 29769; Ed. Mike Palachek; Pub. John Kern; adv. contact: Deb Reynolds. pub. size: broadsheet; circ. morning 3,000(paid). **Wire Service(s):** AP.

CLINTON

US

CLINTON HERALD. 1856. Mon.-Sat. $.50 newsstand; $80/yr. 221 Sixth Ave., S., Clinton, IA 52732. TEL 319-242-7101; FAX 319-242-3854. **Owner(s):** Stephens Group, Inc., P.O. Box 1359, Fort Smith, AR 72902. TEL 501-785-7196; Ed. Carl Gustin; Pub. Jack Dermody; adv. contact: Gary Bicker. pub. size: broadsheet; circ. evening 18,000(paid). **Wire Service(s):** AP.

COUNCIL BLUFFS

US   ISSN 1046-1833

COUNCIL BLUFFS DAILY NONPAREIL. 1857. d. $.35/day newsstand; $1.25/Sun.; $1.90/wk.; $93.60/yr. 117 Pearl St., Council Bluffs, IA 51503. TEL 712-328-1811; FAX 712-328-1597. **Owner(s):** Thomson Newspapers, Inc., One Thorn Run Ctr., Ste. 500, 1187 Thorn Run Rd. Ext., Coraopolis, PA 15108. TEL 412-262-7870; Ed. Charles Gates; Pub. Joseph Craig; adv. contact: Denny Koenders. photos; pub. size: broadsheet; circ. evening 17,855(paid); Sun. 19,815(paid). **Wire Service(s):** AP.

CRESTON

US

CRESTON NEWS ADVERTISER. 1881. Mon.-Fri. $.50 newsstand; $116.50/yr. 503 W. Adams St., Creston, IA 50801. TEL 515-782-2141; FAX 515-782-6628. **Owner(s):** Shaw Newspaper Co., 444 Pine Hill Dr., Dixon, IL 61021. TEL 815-284-4000; Ed. Jeff Young; Pub. Arvid Huisman; adv. contact: Roger Lanning. pub. size: broadsheet; circ. evening 5,632(paid). **Wire Service(s):** AP.

DAVENPORT

US   ISSN 1064-2986

QUAD-CITY TIMES. 1855. d. $.50/day newsstand; $2/Sun.; $3.95/wk. carrier; $4.90/wk. out of state. 500 E. Third St., Davenport, IA 52801. TEL 319-383-2200; FAX 319-383-2370. **Owner(s):** Lee Enterprises, Inc., 400 Putnam Bldg., Davenport, IA 52801. TEL 319-383-2100; Ed. Daniel K. Hayes; Pub. Robert A. Fusie; adv. contact: Michae Gulledge. photos; bk.rev.; pub. size: broadsheet; circ. morning 54,000(paid); Sun. 83,000(paid). **Wire Service(s):** AP.

DES MOINES

US

DES MOINES REGISTER. 1848. d. $.35/day newsstand; $1.50/Sun.; $1.75/wk. home deliv. 715 Locust, Des Moines, IA 50309. TEL 515-284-8281; FAX 515-284-8287. **Owner(s):** Gannett Company, Inc., 1100 Wilson Blvd., Arlington, VA 22209. TEL 703-284-6000; Pub. Barbara Henry; adv.; photos; bk.rev.; pub. size: broadsheet; circ. morning 185,407(paid); Sun. 319,498(paid). **Wire Service(s):** AP, CDN, DJ, LAT-WP, GNS.

DUBUQUE

US

TELEGRAPH HERALD. 1836. d. $.50/day newsstand; $1.50/Sun.; $3.25/wk. home deliv. 801 Bluff St., Dubuque, IA 52001. TEL 319-588-5611; FAX 319-588-5739; E-mail: thonline@wcinet.com; URL: http://www.thonline.com. **Owner(s):** Woodward Communications, Inc., P.O. Box 688, Dubuque, IA 52004-0688. TEL 319-588-5611; Ed. Soren Nielson; Pub. Tom Yunt; adv. contact: Jim Hart. pub. size: broadsheet; circ. evening 34,025(paid); Sun. 39,020(paid). **Wire Service(s):** KR.

ESTHERVILLE

US   ISSN 0747-0754

ESTHERVILLE DAILY NEWS. 1902. 4/wk.: Mon., Wed., Thu., Sat. $.35 newsstand; $16/3 mos.; $60/yr. 10 N. Seventh St., Estherville, IA 51334. TEL 712-362-2622; FAX 712-362-2624. **Owner(s):** Ogden Newspapers, Inc., 1500 Main St., Wheeling, WV 26003; Ed. Ron Menendez; Pub. Ron Menendez; adv.; pub. size: broadsheet; circ. morning 2,100(paid).

FAIRFIELD

US   ISSN 1061-4508

FAIRFIELD DAILY LEDGER. 1849. Mon.-Fri. $.50 newsstand; $74/yr. mailed in cy.; $99/yr. out of state. 112 E. Broadway, Fairfield, IA 52556. TEL 515-472-4129; FAX 515-472-1916. **Owner(s):** Inland Industries, Inc., P.O. Box 15999 Shawnee Mission, KS 66285; Ed. William Draper; Pub. Jeff Wilson; adv. contact: Gene Luedtke. pub. size: broadsheet; circ. evening 5,000(paid). **Wire Service(s):** AP.

FORT DODGE

US   ISSN 0740-6991

FORT DODGE MESSENGER. 1855. d. $.35/day newsstand; $.75/Sun.; $104.50/yr. 713 Central Ave., Fort Dodge, IA 50501. TEL 515-573-2141; FAX 515-573-2148. **Owner(s):** Ogden Newspapers, Inc., 1500 Main St., Wheeling, WV 26003. TEL 304-233-0100; Ed. Larry W. Johnson. adv. contact: Tim Craig. photos; bk.rev.; pub. size: standard; circ. morning 23,000(paid); Sun. 23,000(paid). **Wire Service(s)** AP.

FORT MADISON

US   ISSN 0746-4266

FORT MADISON DAILY DEMOCRAT. 1869. Mon.-Fri. $.50 newsstand; $68.25/yr. local. 1226 Ave. H, Fort Madison, IA 52627. TEL 319-372-6421; FAX 319-372-3867. **Owner(s):** Brehm Communications, Inc., P.O. Box 28429, San Diego, CA 92128. TEL 619-451-6200; Ed. Robin Delaney. adv. contact: Danna Cambel. photos; pub. size: broadsheet; circ. evening 7,500(paid). **Wire Service(s):** AP.

IOWA CITY

US

IOWA CITY PRESS-CITIZEN. 1841. Mon.-Sat. $.35/day newsstand; $.50/Sat.; $9/mo. 1725 N. Dodge St., Iowa City, IA 52245. TEL 319-337-3181; FAX 319-339-7342; E-mail: cwanninger@aol.com. **Owner(s):** Gannett Company, Inc., 1100 Wilson Blvd., Arlington, VA 22234. TEL 703-284-6000; Ed. Mike Beck; Pub. Charles T. Wanninger; adv. contact: Diana White. photos; bk.rev.; pub. size: broadsheet; circ. evening 16,500(paid). **Wire Service(s):** AP, GNS.

KEOKUK

US

KEOKUK DAILY GATE CITY. 1847. Mon.-Fri. $.50 newsstand; free Wed.; $83.20/yr. in town; $88.40/yr. elsewhere. 1016 Main St., Keokuk, IA 52632. TEL 319-524-8300; FAX 319-524-4363. **Owner(s):** Brehm Communications, Inc., P.O. Box 28429, San Diego, CA 92128. TEL 619-451-6200; Ed. Donald Ball; Pub. William D. DeLost; adv. contact: Wes Grooms. photos; bk.rev.; pub. size: broadsheet; circ. evening 6,600(paid). **Wire Service(s):** AP.

LE MARS

US
LE MARS DAILY SENTINEL. 1870. Mon.-Fri. $.50 newsstand; $96/yr. in cy.; $114/yr. in state; $182/yr. out of state. 41 First Ave., N.E., Le Mars, IA 51031. TEL 712-546-7031; FAX 712-546-7035. **Owner(s):** U.S. Media Group, P.O. Box 227, Crystal City, MO 63019. TEL 501-423-6688; Ed. John Buntsma; Pub. Tom Schmitt; adv. contact: Kevin Hook. photos; bk.rev.; pub. size: broadsheet; circ. evening 5,500(paid). **Wire Service(s):** AP.

MARSHALLTOWN

US
MARSHALLTOWN TIMES-REPUBLICAN. 1858. d. $.50/day newsstand; $.75/Sun.; $85/yr. 135 W. Main St., Marshalltown, IA 50158. TEL 515-753-6611; FAX 515-753-7221; E-mail: timesr@mrshlnet.com; URL: http://www.oweb.com/times-republican. **Owner(s):** Ogden Newspapers, Inc., 1500 Main St., Wheeling, WV 26003. TEL 304-233-0100; Ed. Dave Dawson; Pub. Mike Schlesinger; adv. contact: Reed Riskedahl. photos; bk.rev.; pub. size: broadsheet; circ. evening 12,500(paid); Sun. 12,500(paid). **Wire Service(s):** AP.

MASON CITY

US
GLOBE-GAZETTE. 1893. d. $.50/day newsstand; $1.50/Sun.; $166.40/yr. 300 N. Washington, Mason City, IA 50401-3222. TEL 515-421-0524; FAX 515-421-0516. **Owner(s):** Lee Enterprises, Inc., 215 N. Main St., Davenport, IA 52801. TEL 319-383-2202; Ed. Gary Sawyer; Pub. Howard Query; adv.; photos; pub. size: broadsheet; circ. morning 22,000(paid). **Wire Service(s):** AP, NYT.

MT. PLEASANT

US
MOUNT PLEASANT NEWS. 1978. Mon.-Fri. $.50 newsstand; $73/yr. 215 W. Monroe, Mt. Pleasant, IA 52641. TEL 319-385-3131. **Owner(s):** Mount Pleasant News, Inc., 215 W. Monroe St., Mt. Pleasant, IA 52641. TEL 319-385-3131; Pub. Emery Styron; adv.; photos; pub. size: broadsheet; circ. evening 3,700(paid). **Wire Service(s):** AP.

MUSCATINE

US
MUSCATINE JOURNAL. 1888. Mon.-Sat. $.50 newsstand; $121.75/yr. in cy. 301 E. Third St., Muscatine, IA 52761. TEL 319-263-2331; FAX 319-262-8042. **Owner(s):** Lee Enterprises, Inc., 215 N. Main St., Davenport, IA 52801. TEL 319-383-2108; Pub. David Fuselier; adv. contact: Jay Lenkersdorfer. pub. size: broadsheet; circ. evening 10,000(paid). **Wire Service(s):** AP.

NEWTON

US   ISSN 1040-1539
NEWTON DAILY NEWS. 1902. Mon.-Fri. $.50 newsstand; $70/yr. 200 First Ave., E., Newton, IA 50208. TEL 515-792-3121; FAX 515-792-5505. **Owner(s):** B.F. Shaw Printing Co., Dixon, IL 61021; Ed. Pete Hussmann; Pub. Joe McDermott; adv. contact: Dave Stanley. photos; pub. size: broadsheet; circ. evening 7,500(paid). **Wire Service(s):** UPI.

OELWEIN

US   ISSN 1074-4487
OELWEIN DAILY REGISTER. 1881. Mon.-Sat. $.50/day newsstand; $1/Sat.; $99/yr. mailed; $124.80/yr. deliv. 25 First St., S.E., Oelwein, IA 50662. TEL 319-283-2144; FAX 319-283-3268. **Owner(s):** Oelwein Publications, P.O. Box 1193, Seneca, SC 29769; Ed. James A. Morrison; Pub. Jody Perrotto; adv. contact: Martin VanEe. photos; pub. size: broadsheet; circ. evening 6,500(paid). **Wire Service(s):** AP.

OSKALOOSA

US   ISSN 0898-2066
OSKALOOSA HERALD. 1850. Mon.-Sat. $.50 newsstand; $66/yr. in cy. 1901 A Ave., W., Oskaloosa, IA 52577. TEL 515-672-2581; FAX 515-672-2294. **Owner(s):** Donrey Media Group, P.O. Box 17017, Fort Smith, AR 72902. TEL 501-785-7802; Ed. Kimberly Walker; Pub. Keith Ponder; adv.; photos; pub. size: broadsheet; circ. evening 4,800(paid).

OTTUMWA

US   ISSN 0886-4209
OTTUMWA COURIER. 1848. Mon.-Sat. $.50 newsstand; $9.75/4 wks. carrier in cy. 213 E. Second St., Ottumwa, IA 52501. TEL 515-684-4611; FAX 515-684-7834. **Owner(s):** Lee Enterprises, Inc., 215 Main St., Ste. 400, Davenport, IA 52801. TEL 319-383-2100; Ed. Russell Cunningham, Jr.; Pub. Martha Wells; adv.; photos; pub. size: broadsheet; circ. morning 19,289(paid). **Wire Service(s):** AP.

SHENANDOAH

US
VALLEY NEWS TODAY-DAILY SENTINEL. 1993. Tue.-Sat. $.50 newsstand; $2/wk. carrier. 702 W. Sheridan St., Shenandoah, IA 51601. TEL 712-246-3097; FAX 712-246-3099. **Owner(s):** Gleason-Knowles Communications, Inc., 702 W. Sheridan St., Shenandoah, IA 51601; Ed. Julia Dinvelle; Pub. Gregg Knowles; adv.; photos; pub. size: tabloid; circ. evening 3,250(paid). **Wire Service(s):** Iowa Media Link.
Formerly: Valley News Today, Shenandoah Evening Sentinel.

SIOUX CITY

US
SIOUX CITY JOURNAL. 1854. d. $.50/day newsstand; $1.50/Sun.; $12.25/mo. carrier; $49/4 mos. mailed. Sixth & Pavonia Sts., Sioux City, IA 51102. TEL 712-279-5072; FAX 712-279-5059. **Owner(s):** Sioux City Newspapers, P.O. Box 118, Sioux City, IA 51102. TEL 712-279-5072; Ed. Karen Luken; Pub. Tom Kurdy; photos; pub. size: broadsheet; circ. morning 50,000(paid); Sun. 50,000(paid). **Wire Service(s):** AP.

SPENCER

US   ISSN 0746-0872
SPENCER DAILY REPORTER. 1875. Tue.-Sat. $.75 newsstand; $65/yr. carrier. 416 First Ave., W., Spencer, IA 51301. TEL 712-262-6610; FAX 712-262-3044. **Owner(s):** Edwards Publications, Seneca, SC 51301. TEL 864-882-3718; Ed. John Payne; Pub. Joni Weerheim; adv. contact: Chris Swanson. pub. size: broadsheet; circ. morning 4,300(paid). **Wire Service(s):** AP.

STORM LAKE

US   ISSN 0893-8555
STORM LAKE PILOT TRIBUNE. 1870. Tue.-Sat. $.50 newsstand; $50/yr. 111 W. Seventh St., Storm Lake, IA 50588. TEL 712-732-3130; FAX 712-732-3152. **Owner(s):** Edwards Publications, P.O. Box 1193, Seneca, SC 29679. TEL 803-882-3272; Ed. Dana Larsen; Pub. Robert L. Madsen; adv.; photos; bk.rev.; pub. size: broadsheet; circ. morning 4,625(paid). **Wire Service(s):** AP.

VINTON

US
VINTON CEDAR VALLEY DAILY TIMES. 1889. Mon.-Fri. $.50 newsstand; $49/yr. out of town; $60/yr. in town. 108 E. Fifth St., Vinton, IA 52349. TEL 319-472-2311; FAX 319-472-4811. **Owner(s):** Mid-America Publishing Corp., 108 Third St., Ste. 350, Des Moines, IA 50309. TEL 515-282-8220; Ed. Kathy Mahr; Pub. Doug Lindner; adv. contact: Kathy Mahr. photos; bk.rev.; pub. size: broadsheet; circ. evening 3,000(paid). **Wire Service(s):** LAT-WP.

WASHINGTON

US   ISSN 0894-2552
WASHINGTON EVENING JOURNAL. 1893. Mon.-Fri. $.50 newsstand; $8.25/mo. carrier; $7.75/mo. mailed in cy.; $9.90/mo. mailed in state; $32.50/3 mos. elsewhere. 111 N. Marion Ave., Washington, IA 52353. TEL 319-653-2191. **Owner(s):** Washington Publishing Co., Inc., 111 N. Marion Ave., Washington, IA 52353. TEL 319-653-2191; Ed. Brooks Taylor; Pub. Darwin Sherman; adv. contact: Arnold Smith. photos; bk.rev.; pub. size: broadsheet; circ. evening 14,200(paid). **Wire Service(s):** AP.

WATERLOO

US
WATERLOO COURIER. 1859. Sun.-Fri. $.50/day newsstand; $1.50/Sun.; $156/yr. 501 Commercial St., Waterloo, IA 50701. TEL 319-291-1400; FAX 319-234-6405. **Owner(s):** Howard Publications, Inc., 501 Commercial St., Waterloo, IA 50701. TEL 319-291-1400; Ed. Saul Shapiro; Pub. James Lewis; adv. contact: David E. Tansey. photos; bk.rev.; pub. size: broadsheet; circ. evening 47,837(paid). **Wire Service(s):** AP, LAT-WP, SHNA, KNT, NEA.

WEBSTER CITY

US

DAILY FREEMAN JOURNAL. 1857. Mon.-Fri. $.35 newsstand; $59.80/yr. 720 Second St., Webster City, IA 50595. TEL 515-832-4350; FAX 515-832-2314. **Owner(s):** Ogden Newspapers, Inc., 1500 Main St., Wheeling, WV 26003; Ed. Lori Niles; Pub. Mike Fertig; adv.; pub. size: broadsheet; circ. evening 4,000(paid).
   Formerly: Webster City Freeman Journal.

KANSAS

ABILENE

US

ABILENE REFLECTOR-CHRONICLE. 1872. Mon.-Sat. $.50 newsstand; $6.50/mo.; $70/yr. in cy.; $79.20/yr. out of cy.; $96/yr. out of state. 303 N. Broadway, Abilene, KS 67410. TEL 913-263-1000; FAX 913-263-1645. **Owner(s):** Reflector-Chronicle Publishing Corp., 303 N. Broadway, Abilene, KS 67410. TEL 913-263-1000; FAX 913-263-1645; Ed. Dave Bergmeier; Pub. Vivien L. Sadowski; adv.; photos; bk.rev.; pub. size: broadsheet; circ. evening 4,500(paid). **Wire Service(s):** AP.

ARKANSAS CITY

US   ISSN 0888-8485

ARKANSAS CITY TRAVELER. 1873. Mon.-Sat. $.50 newsstand; $64.98/yr. 200 E. Fifth Ave., Arkansas City, KS 67005. TEL 316-442-4200; FAX 316-442-7483. **Owner(s):** Morris Communications, P.O. Box 936, Augusta, GA 30903. TEL 706-724-0851; Ed. Rick Horn; Pub. Kim Benedict; adv. contact: Lisa Fooese. pub. size: broadsheet; circ. evening 6,600(paid). **Wire Service(s):** AP.

ATCHISON

US

ATCHISON DAILY GLOBE. 1877. Mon.-Sat. $.50 newsstand; $7.45/mo. carrier; $96.00/yr. mailed. 1015 Main St., Atchison, KS 66002. TEL 913-367-0583; FAX 913-367-7531. **Owner(s):** American Publishing Co., 606 N. Van Buren, P.O. Box 520, Marion, IL 62959. TEL 618-993-1711; Ed. Jim Headley; Pub. Stan Wilson; adv.; photos; pub. size: broadsheet; circ. evening 8,651(free & paid). **Wire Service(s):** AP.

AUGUSTA

US

AUGUSTA DAILY GAZETTE. 1893. Mon.-Fri. $.50 newsstand; $70/yr. in cy.; $80.96/yr. out of cy.; $122.26/yr. elsewhere. 204 E. Fifth St., Augusta, KS 67010-0009. TEL 316-775-2218; FAX 316-775-3220. **Owner(s):** American Publishing Co., 606 N. Van Buren, P.O. Box 520, Marion, IL 62959. TEL 618-993-1711; Ed. Michael McDermott; Pub. Carter J. Zerbe; adv.; pub. size: broadsheet; circ. evening 7,815(paid). **Wire Service(s):** AP.

BELOIT

US   ISSN 8750-1791

BELOIT DAILY CALL. 1901. Mon-Fri. $.50 newsstand; $63.60/yr. 122 Court St., Beloit, KS 67420. TEL 913-738-5728; FAX 913-738-6442. **Owner(s):** Beloit Newspapers, Inc., P.O. Box 366, Beloit, KS 67420. TEL 913-738-3757; Ed. Larry Hiatt; Pub. Larry Hiatt; adv.; photos; bk.rev.; pub. size: broadsheet; circ. evening 2,174(paid). **Wire Service(s):** AP.
   Formerly: Beloit Daily Call & Posts.

CHANUTE

US

CHANUTE TRIBUNE. 1892. Mon.-Sat. $.50 newsstand; $70.20/yr. 15 N. Evergreen, Chanute, KS 66720. TEL 316-431-4100; FAX 316-431-4100. **Owner(s):** Harris Enterprises, P.O. Box 190, Hutchinson, KS 67504. TEL 316-694-5830; Pub. Thomas N. Bell; adv.; photos; bk rev.; pub. size: broadsheet; circ. evening 5,000(paid). **Wire Service(s):** AP.

CLAY CENTER

US

CLAY CENTER DISPATCH. 1873. Mon.-Fri. $.35 newsstand; $58/yr. carrier; $66/yr. in state mailed; $75/yr. out of state. 805 Fifth St., Clay Center, KS 67432. TEL 913-632-2127. **Owner(s):** Clay Center Publishing Co., P.O. Box 519, Clay Center, KS 67432. TEL 913-632-2127; Ed. Ned Valentine. adv. contact: Ken Kneper. pub. size: broadsheet; circ. evening 3,500(paid).

COFFEYVILLE

US   ISSN 0746-8202

COFFEYVILLE JOURNAL, THE. 1875. Tue.-Fri. & Sun. $.35/day newsstand $.75/Sun.; $74/yr. Eighth & Elm Sts., Coffeyville, KS 67337. TEL 316-251-3300; FAX 316-251-1905. **Owner(s):** Hometown Communications, 12 Chelsea Rd., Arlington, VA 22209. TEL 501-223-9968; Ed. Tim Flowers; Pub. Mike Thornberry; adv. contact: Chris Zimmerman. photos; pub. size: broadsheet; circ. evening 6,700(paid); Sun. 7,200(paid). **Wire Service(s):** AP.

COLBY

US

COLBY FREE PRESS. 1888. Mon.-Thu. & Sat. $.50 newsstand; $55/yr. 155 W. Fifth St., Colby, KS 67701. TEL 913-462-3963; FAX 913-462-7749. **Owner(s):** Gozia-Driver Media, P.O. Box 806, Colby, KS 67701. TEL 913-462-3963; Pub Patty Decker; adv. contact: Patty Decker. pub. size: broadsheet; circ. morning 2,500(paid). **Wire Service(s):** AP.

COLUMBUS

US   ISSN 8756-6044

COLUMBUS DAILY ADVOCATE. 1874. Mon.-Fri. $.25 newsstand; $36/yr. carrier. 215 S. Kansas, Columbus, KS 66725. TEL 316-429-2773. **Owner(s):** Columbus Publishing Co., Inc., P.O. Box 231, Columbus, KS 66725. TEL 316-429-2773; Ed. Jay M. Lacy; Pub. Jay M. Lacy; adv. contact: Jay M. Lacy. photos; pub. size: broadsheet; circ. evening 2,537(paid). **Wire Service(s):** AP.

CONCORDIA

US

CONCORDIA BLADE-EMPIRE. 1902. Mon.-Fri. $.35 newsstand; $47.66/yr. carrier; $56.02/yr. mailec. 510 Washington, Concordia, KS 66901. TEL 913-243-2424; FAX 913-243-4407. **Owner(s):** Blade-Empire Publishing Co., Inc., P.O. Box 309, Concordia, KS 66901. TEL 913-243-2424; Ed. Jim Lowell; Pub. Brad Lowell; adv. contact: Joni Regner. photos; bk.rev.; pub. size: broadsheet; circ. evening 3,100(paid). **Wire Service(s):** AP.

COUNCIL GROVE

US

COUNCIL GROVE REPUBLICAN. 1872. Mon.-Fri. $.25 newsstand; $47.40/yr. carrier in town. 208 W. Main St., Council Grove, KS 66846. TEL 316-767-5123. **Owner(s):** Council Grove Publishing Co., Inc., 208 W. Main St., Council Grove, KS 66846. TEL 316-767-5123; Ed. Craig A. McNeal; Pub. Craig A. McNeal; adv. contact: Don A. McNeal. pub. size: broadsheet; circ. evening 2,499(paid). **Wire Service(s):** AP.

DERBY

US

DAILY REPORTER, THE. 1922. Mon.-Fri. $.50 newsstand; $78/yr. carrier; $81/yr. mail. 201 S. Baltimore, Derby, KS 67037. TEL 316-788-2835; FAX 316-788-0854. **Owner(s):** American Publishing Co., 606 N. Van Buren, P.O. Box 520, Marion, IL 62959. TEL 618-993-1711; Ed. Randy Fogg; Pub. Jim Stephenson; adv.; photos; bk.rev.; pub. size: standard; circ. evening 1,830(paid). **Wire Service(s):** AP.

DODGE CITY

US   ISSN 0889-3489

DODGE CITY DAILY GLOBE. 1911. Mon.-Sat. $.50 newsstand; $104/yr. 705 Second Ave., Dodge City, KS 67801. TEL 316-225-4151; FAX 316-225-4154. **Owner(s):** Morris Communications, P.O. Box 936, Augusta, GA 30903. TEL 706-724-0851; Ed. Gary Reber; Pub. Terry Cochran; adv. contact: Linda Livingston. photos; pub. size: broadsheet; circ. morning 9,300(paid). **Wire Service(s):** AP.

EL DORADO

US   ISSN 1053-9999

EL DORADO TIMES. 1919. Mon.-Sat. $.50 newsstand; $83.40/yr. 111 N. Vine, El Dorado, KS 67042. TEL 316-321-1120; FAX 316-321-7722; E-mail eldtimes@southwind.net; URL: http://www.southwind.net/~eldtimes. **Owner(s):** American Publishing Co., 606 N. Van Buren, P.O. Box 520, Marion, IL 62959. TEL 618-993-1711; Pub. Guy P. Russell; pub. size: broadsheet; circ. evening 4,800(paid). **Wire Service(s):** AP.

EMPORIA

US

EMPORIA GAZETTE. 1890. Mon.-Sat. $.35/day newsstand; $.50/Sat.; $69/yr. 517 Merchant St., Emporia, KS 66801. TEL 316-342-4800; FAX 316-342-8108; E-mail: egazette@cadvantage.com; URL: http://www.emporiagazette.com. **Owner(s):** White Corp., Inc., 517 Merchant St., Emporia, KS 66801. TEL 316-342-4800; FAX 316-342-4800; Ed. Patrick Kelley; Pub. Paul David Walker; adv. contact: Bruce Knaak. photos; bk.rev.; pub. size: broadsheet; circ. evening 10,000(paid). **Wire Service(s):** AP, NYT.

FORT SCOTT

US   ISSN 8755-3171

FORT SCOTT TRIBUNE, THE. 1884. Mon.-Sat. $.35/newsstand; $69.85/yr. 6 E. Wall St., Fort Scott, KS 66701. TEL 316-223-1460; FAX 316-223-1469. **Owner(s):** Frank E. Emery, 6 E. Wall St., Fort Scott, KS 66701. TEL 316-223-1462; FAX 316-223-1469; Ed. Melinda Rhodes; Pub. Frank E. Emery; adv. contact: Tammie Braznell. photos; pub. size: broadsheet; circ. evening 4,452(paid). **Wire Service(s):** AP.

GARDEN CITY

US

GARDEN CITY TELEGRAM. 1929. Mon.-Sat. $.50 newsstand; $.75/Sat.; $79.58/yr. carrier. 310 N. Seventh St., Garden City, KS 67846. TEL 316-275-8500; FAX 316-275-5165. **Owner(s):** Harris Enterprises, P.O. Box 190, Hutchinson, KS 67504. TEL 316-662-3311; Affiliates Profit Sharing Trust, P.O. Box 190, Hutchinson, KS 67504. TEL 316-662-3311; Ed. Carol Crupper; Pub. James E. Bloom; adv. contact: Darla Craig. photos; pub. size: broadsheet; circ. evening 10,912(paid). **Wire Service(s):** AP, HNS.

GOODLAND

US   ISSN 0893-0562

GOODLAND DAILY NEWS. 1932. Tue.-Sat. $.50 newsstand; $59.64/yr. local; $78/yr. elsewhere. 1205 Main St., Goodland, KS 67735-0500. TEL 913-899-2338; FAX 913-899-6186. **Owner(s):** U.S. Media Group, P.O. Box 227, Crystal City, MO 63019. TEL 314-937-5200; Ed. Peter Liwoski; Pub. Randy McCants; adv. contact: Gennifer House. photos; pub. size: standard; circ. evening 2,669(free & paid). **Wire Service(s):** AP.

GREAT BEND

US   ISSN 0891-7078

GREAT BEND TRIBUNE. 1876. d. $.50/day newsstand; $1/Sun.; $23.55/3 mos. carrier in city; $94.20/yr. carrier; $24.45/3 mos. mailed; $97.50/yr. mailed. 2012 Forest Ave., Great Bend, KS 67530. TEL 316-792-1211; FAX 316-792-3441. **Owner(s):** Morris Newspaper Corp., P.O. Box 8167, Savannah, GA 31412. TEL 912-233-1281; Pub. Robert B. Werner; adv.; photos; bk.rev.; pub. size: broadsheet; circ. evening 9,500(paid). Sun. 8,500(paid). **Wire Service(s):** AP.

HAYS

US

HAYS DAILY NEWS. 1929. Sun.-Fri. $.50/day newsstand; $1/Sun.; $98/yr. carrier. 507 Main St., Hays, KS 67601. TEL 913-628-1081; FAX 913-628-8186. **Owner(s):** News Publishing Co., 507 Main St., P.O. Box 857, Hays, KS 67601. TEL 913-628-1081; FAX 913-628-8186; Ed. Greg Halling; Pub. Jim Hitch; adv. contact: Michael H. Haas. pub. size: standard; circ. evening 13,249(paid); Sun. 14,172(paid). **Wire Service(s):** AP.

HIAWATHA

US

HIAWATHA DAILY WORLD. 1908. Mon.-Fri. $.50 newsstand; $51.21/yr. carrier; $62.80/yr. out of cy. mailed. 607 Utah St., Hiawatha, KS 66434. TEL 913-742-2111; FAX 913-742-2276. **Owner(s):** Cleveland Newspapers, Inc., P.O. Box 3600, Cleveland, TN 37320; Ed. Deb Rosenberger; Pub. Barry Stokes; adv. contact: Barry Stokes. pub. size: broadsheet; circ. evening 2,800(paid).

HUTCHINSON

US

HUTCHINSON NEWS. 1872. d. $.50/day newsstand; $1.25/Sun.; $150.24/yr. 300 W. Second, Hutchinson, KS 67504-0190. TEL 316-694-5700; FAX 316-694-5767. **Owner(s):** Hutchinson Publishing Co., 300 W. Second, Hutchinson, KS 67501. TEL 316-694-5700; FAX 316-662-4186; Ed. Wayne Lee; Pub. Wayne Lee; adv. contact: Lori Beck. pub. size: broadsheet; circ. morning 37,940(paid); Sun. 41,325(paid). **Wire Service(s):** AP, NYT, LAT-WP.

INDEPENDENCE

US

INDEPENDENCE DAILY REPORTER. 1881. d. $.50/day newsstand; $1/Sun.; $81.95/yr. 320 N. Sixth St., Independence, KS 67301. TEL 316-331-3550; FAX 316-331-3550. **Owner(s):** Reporter Publishing Co., Inc., P.O. Box 869, Independence, KS 67301. TEL 316-331-3550; FAX 316-331-3550; Ed. Georgia High; Pub. Herbert A. Meyer, III; adv. contact: Steve McBride. photos; pub. size: broadsheet; circ. evening 7,541; Sun. 8,436. **Wire Service(s):** AP.

IOLA

US

IOLA REGISTER. 1867. Mon.-Sat. $.50 newsstand; $18.81/3 mos. 302 S. Washington, Iola, KS 66749. TEL 316-365-2111; FAX 316-365-6289. **Owner(s):** Mickey Lynn, 302 S. Washington, Iola, KS 66749; Jack Hastings, 302 S. Washington, Iola, KS 66749; Ed. Emerson Lynn; Pub. Emerson Lynn; adv. contact: Jack Hastings. photos; bk.rev.; pub. size: broadsheet; circ. evening 4,200(paid). **Wire Service(s):** AP.

JUNCTION CITY

US

JUNCTION CITY DAILY UNION. 1861. d. $.35/day newsstand; $1/Sun.; $6.50/mo. 222 W. Sixth St., Junction City, KS 66441. TEL 913-762-5000; FAX 913-762-4584. **Owner(s):** Montgomery Communications, Inc., 222 W. Sixth St., Junction City, KS 66441. TEL 913-762-5000; FAX 913-762-4584; Ed. Ron Hosie; Pub. John G. Montgomery; adv. contact: Steve Stevens. adv.: $8.85/SAU. photos; pub. size: broadsheet; circ. evening 7,249(paid); Sun. 8,047(paid). **Wire Service(s):** AP, CNS.

KANSAS CITY

US

KANSAS CITY KANSAN. 1921. Tue.-Fri. & Sun. $.35/day newsstand; $1/Sun.; $67.35/yr. carrier; $53.05/yr. senior citizens. 901 N. Eighth St., Kansas City, KS 66101. TEL 913-371-4300; FAX 913-342-8620. **Owner(s):** Inland Industries, Inc., 105th & Santa Fe, Shawnee, KS 66215. TEL 913-492-9050; Ed. Patrick Lowry; Pub. William E. Epperheimer; adv. contact: Joie Mellenbruch. photos; bk.rev.; pub. size: broadsheet; circ. evening 14,941(paid); Sun. 17,039(paid). **Wire Service(s):** AP.

LARNED

US   ISSN 0888-1189

TILLER & TOILER. 1879. Mon.-Fri. $.50/day newsstand; $50.02/yr. 115 W. Fifth St., Larned, KS 67550. TEL 316-285-3111; FAX 316-285-6062. **Owner(s):** Star Communications, Inc., 115 W. Fifth St., Larned, KS 67550; Ed. Dennis Martin. adv. contact: Dennis Martin. pub. size: standard; circ. evening 3,000(paid). **Wire Service(s):** AP.
Formerly: Larned Tiller & Toiler.

LAWRENCE

US

JOURNAL-WORLD, THE. 1854. d. $.50/day newsstand; $1/Sun.; $122.85/yr. 609 New Hampshire St., Lawrence, KS 66044. TEL 913-843-1000; FAX 913-843-1922; E-mail: rgage@ljworld.com; URL: http://www.ljworld.com/. **Owner(s):** World Co., 609 New Hampshire St., Lawrence, KS 66044. TEL 913-843-1000; FAX 913-832-7207; Ed. Roger Verdon; Pub. Dolph C. Simons, Jr.; adv. contact: Tom Fisher. photos; bk.rev.; pub. size: broadsheet; circ. morning 18,501(paid); Sun. 19,447(paid). **Wire Service(s):** AP, NYT, LAT-WP, KR.

LEAVENWORTH

US

LEAVENWORTH TIMES. 1857. Sun.-Fri. $.50/day newsstand; $1/Sun.; $106.36/yr. 418-22 Seneca St., Leavenworth, KS 66048. TEL 913-682-0305; FAX 913-682-1114. **Owner(s):** American Publishing Co., 606 N. Van Buren, P.O. Box 520, Marion, IL 62959. TEL 618-993-1711; Ed. Keith Robison; Pub. Barbara Trimble; adv. contact: Todd Frantz. photos; bk.rev.; pub. size: broadsheet; circ. evening 9,200(paid); Sun. 9,900(paid). **Wire Service(s):** AP.

LIBERAL

US   ISSN 0745-8916

LIBERAL SOUTHWEST DAILY TIMES. 1886. Sun.-Fri.
$.50/day newsstand; $1/Sun.; $93/yr. 16 S.
Kansas, Liberal, KS 67901. TEL 316-624-2541;
FAX 316-624-0735. **Owner(s):** Liberal
Newspapers, Inc., P.O. Box 889, Liberal, KS
67905. TEL 316-624-2541; FAX
316-624-0735; Ed. Ken Walker; Pub. Jeff
Burkhead; adv. contact: Mitch Bettis. photos; pub.
size: broadsheet; circ. evening 7,450; Sun.
6,450(paid). **Wire Service(s):** AP.

LYONS

US   ISSN 1040-1504

LYONS DAILY NEWS. 1906. Mon.-Fri. $.35
newsstand; $38/yr. 210 W. Commercial, Lyons,
KS 67554. TEL 316-257-2368;
FAX 316-257-2369. **Owner(s):** Lyons Publishing
Co., Inc., 210 W. Commercial, Lyons, KS 67554.
TEL 316-257-2368; Ed. John L. Sayler; Pub.
Paul E. Jones; adv. contact: Paul E. Jones. photos;
pub. size: broadsheet; circ. evening 2,599(paid).
Wire Service(s): AP.

MANHATTAN

US

MANHATTAN MERCURY. 1884. Sun.-Fri. $.35/day
newsstand; $.75/Sun.; $96/yr. in cy.;
$117.15/yr. out of cy. Fifth & Osage, Manhattan,
KS 66502. TEL 913-776-8805;
FAX 913-776-8807. **Owner(s):** Seaton Publishing
Co., P.O. Box 787, Manhattan, KS 66502; Pub.
Edward Seaton; adv. contact: Steve Stallwitz. pub.
size: broadsheet; circ. evening 12,850(paid); Sun.
14,000(paid). **Wire Service(s):** AP, NYT, LAT-WP.

MCPHERSON

US

MCPHERSON SENTINEL. 1887. Mon.-Sat. $.50
newsstand; $8.25/mo.; $90/yr. 301 S. Main,
McPherson, KS 67460. TEL 316-241-2422;
FAX 316-241-2425. **Owner(s):** American
Publishing Co., 606 N. Van Buren, P.O. Box 520,
Marion, IL 62959. TEL 618-993-1711; Pub.
Tom A. Throne; adv.; pub. size: broadsheet; circ.
evening 5,700(paid). **Wire Service(s):** AP.

NEWTON

US

NEWTON KANSAN. 1872. Mon.-Sat. $.50 newsstand;
$7.50/4 wks. 121 W. Sixth, Newton, KS 67114.
TEL 316-283-1500; FAX 316-283-2471; E-mail:
nkansan@southwind.net; URL:
http://www.southwind.net/nkansan. **Owner(s):**
Morris Communications, P.O. Box 936, Augusta,
GA 30903. TEL 706-724-0851; Ed. Connie
White; Pub. Douglas J. Anstaett; adv. contact:
Dennis Garrison. photos; bk.rev.; pub. size:
broadsheet; circ. evening 7,705(paid). **Wire
Service(s):** AP.

NORTON

US

NORTON DAILY TELEGRAM. 1906. Mon.-Fri.
$.25/day newsstand; $37.94/yr. local;
$43.21/yr. mailed. 215 S. Kansas, Norton, KS
67654. TEL 913-877-3361;
FAX 913-877-3732. **Owner(s):** Richard D. Boyd,
215 S. Kansas, Norton, KS 67654. TEL
913-877-3361; Ed. Richard D. Boyd; Pub.
Richard D. Boyd; adv. contact: Victor Randolph.
photos; pub. size: broadsheet; circ. evening
2,100(paid). **Wire Service(s):** AP.

OLATHE

US   ISSN 0886-9871

OLATHE DAILY NEWS. 1960. Mon.-Sat. $.50
newsstand; $7.30/mo. 514 S. Kansas, Olathe,
KS 66061. TEL 913-764-2211;
FAX 913-764-3672. **Owner(s):** Keltatim Inc.,
514 S. Kansas, Olathe, KS 66061. TEL
913-764-2211; Ed. Laird McGregor; Pub. Tim
O'Donnell; adv. contact: Rick Brown. photos; pub.
size: broadsheet; circ. morning 10,285(paid).
Wire Service(s): AP.

OTTAWA

US

OTTAWA HERALD. 1895. Mon.-Sat. $.50 newsstand;
$75.43/yr. local; $103.08/yr. out of area. 104
S. Cedar, Ottawa, KS 66067.
TEL 913-242-4700; FAX 913-242-9420.
Owner(s): Harris Enterprises, First National Bank
Bldg., Hutchinson, KS 67501. TEL
316-694-5880; Ed. Jay Bemis; Pub. John D.
Montgomery; adv. contact: Tom Love. photos;
bk.rev.; pub. size: broadsheet; circ. evening
6,100(paid). **Wire Service(s):** AP.

PARSONS

US

PARSONS SUN. 1871. Mon.-Sat. $.50 newsstand;
$78.30/yr. 220 S. 18th St., Parsons, KS
67357-0836. TEL 316-421-2000;
FAX 316-421-2217. **Owner(s):** Parsons
Publishing Co., 220 S. 18th St., Parsons, KS
67357. TEL 316-421-2000; Ed. Jim Cook; Pub.
Ann K. Charles; adv. contact: Carolyn Kennett.
photos; pub. size: broadsheet; circ. evening
7,500(paid). **Wire Service(s):** AP, Harris.

PITTSBURG

US

PITTSBURG MORNING SUN. 1887. Wed.-Sun.
$.50/day newsstand; $1/Sun.; $84/yr. 701 N.
Locust, Pittsburg, KS 66762.
TEL 316-231-2600 FAX 316-231-0645.
Owner(s): Morris Communications, P.O. Box 936,
Augusta, GA 30903. TEL 706-724-0851; Ed.
Tom Epling; Pub. Tom H. Collinson; adv. contact:
Karen L. Van Leeuwen. pub. size: broadsheet; circ.
morning 12,000(paid); Sun. 12,000(paid). **Wire
Service(s):** AP.

PRATT

US   ISSN 1048-3675

PRATT TRIBUNE. 1917. Mon.-Fri. $.50 newsstand;
$80/yr. in trade zone; $90/yr. elsewhere. 320 S.
Main St., Pratt, KS 67124. TEL 316-672-5511;
FAX 316-672-5514. **Owner(s):** Hometown
Communications, AL. Ed. Conrad Easterday; Pub.
Jim Phillips; adv. contact: Pattie Crane. pub. size:
broadsheet; circ. morning 2,700(paid). **Wire
Service(s):** AP.

RUSSELL

US

RUSSELL DAILY NEWS. 1947. Mon.-Sat. $.50/day
newsstand; $78/yr. 802 N. Maple St., Russell, KS
67665. TEL 913-483-2116;
FAX 913-483-4012 **Owner(s):** Russell
Publishing, Inc., P.O. Box 513, Russell, KS
67665. TEL 913-483-2116; Ed. Jim Joule; Pub.
Allan D. Evans; adv. contact: Cindy Reed. pub.
size: standard; circ. evening 3,900(paid).

SALINA

US

SALINA JOURNAL. 1871. d. $.50/day newsstand;
$1.50/Sun.; $15/mo. carrier; $16/mo. motor
rte.; $12/mo. in state; $22/mo. out of state.
333 S. Fourth St., Salina, KS 67401.
TEL 913-823-6363; FAX 913-827-6363.
Owner(s): Harris Publications, 300 W. Second,
Hutchinson, KS 67501. TEL 316 694-5700; FAX
316-662-4186; Ed. Scott Seirer; Pub. Harris
Rayl; adv. contact: Jeannie Sharp. photos; pub.
size: broadsheet; circ. morning 30,000(controlled
& paid); Sun. 36,000(controlled & paid). **Wire
Service(s):** AP.

TOPEKA

US   ISSN 1067-1994

CAPITAL-JOURNAL. 1879. d. $.50/day newsstand;
$1.50/Sun.; $129/yr. carrier; $53/3 mos.
mailed. 616 S.E. Jefferson St., Topeka, KS
66607. TEL 913-295-1111;
FAX 913-295-1261. **Owner(s):** Morris
Communications, P.O. Box 936, Augusta, GA
30903. TEL 706-724-0851; Pub. P. Scott
McKibben; adv. contact: Ron Burns. photos; pub.
size: broadsheet; circ. morning 70,000(paid);
Sun. 73,000(paid). **Wire Service(s):** AP, LAT-WP.

WELLINGTON

US

WELLINGTON DAILY NEWS. 1901. Mon.-Fri. $.50
newsstand; $51/yr. in city; $63/yr. out of city;
$110/yr. out of state. 113 W. Harvey,
Wellington, KS 67152-0368.
TEL 316-326-3326; FAX 316-326-3290.
Owner(s): Jack C. Mitchell, 22 Pinecrest,
Wellington, KS 67152. TEL 316-326-3326; Ed.
Janet Johnson; Pub. Jack C. Mitchell; adv. contact:
Bill Newland. photos; pub. size: broadsheet; circ.
evening 4,200(paid). **Wire Service(s):** AP.
    Formerly: Wellington Daily News Evening Paper.

WICHITA

US   ISSN 1046-3127

WICHITA EAGLE. 1872. d. $.50/day newsstand;
$1.50/Sun.; $3.15/wk. 825 E. Douglas, Wichita,
KS 67202. TEL 316-268-6000;
FAX 316-268-6627. **Owner(s):** Knight-Ridder,
Inc., One Herald Plz., Miami, FL 33132. TEL
305-376-3800; Ed. Davis Merritt. adv. contact:
Ron Davidson. photos; bk.rev.; pub. size:
broadsheet; circ. morning 120,411(paid); Sun.
197,211(paid). **Wire Service(s):** NYT, AP, KR,
LAT-WP, CNS.

WINFIELD

US   ISSN 0889-6747

WINFIELD DAILY COURIER. 1887. Mon.-Sat. $.50/day newsstand; $60.75/yr. 201 E. Ninth St., Winfield, KS 67156. TEL 316-221-1050; FAX 316-221-1101; E-mail: courier@horizon.hit.net; URL: http://www.hit.net:80/courier. **Owner(s):** Winfield Publishing Co., Inc., 201 E. Ninth St., Winfield, KS 67156; Ed. Tod Megredy; Pub. F.D. Seaton; adv. contact: Lloyd Craig. pub. size: tabloid; circ. evening 6,000(paid). **Wire Service(s):** AP.

KENTUCKY

ASHLAND

US

DAILY INDEPENDENT, THE. 1896. d. $.50/day newsstand; $1.25/Sun.; $166.40/yr. carrier; $154.40/yr. mailed. 224 17th St., Ashland, KY 41101. TEL 606-329-1717; FAX 606-324-8434. **Owner(s):** Ottaway Newspapers, Inc., P.O. Box 401, Campbell Hall, NY 10916. TEL 914-294-8181; Ed. Mike Reliford; Pub. John W. Del Santo; adv.; photos; bk.rev.; pub. size: broadsheet; circ. evening 24,889(paid); Sun. 26,933(paid). **Wire Service(s):** AP, ONS, SHNA.

BOWLING GREEN

US

DAILY NEWS. 1854. Sun.-Fri. $.50/day newsstand; $1.25/Sun.; $2.05/wk. 813 College, Bowling Green, KY 42101. TEL 502-781-1700; FAX 502-781-0726; E-mail: dnews@netam.com; URL: http://www.bowlinggreen.ky.net/dailynews. **Owner(s):** News Publishing Co., 813 College, Bowling Green, KY 42101. TEL 502-781-1700; FAX 502-781-0726; Pub. John B. Gaines; adv. contact: Roger Jones. photos; bk.rev.; pub. size: broadsheet; circ. evening 21,100(paid); Sun. 25,000(paid). **Wire Service(s):** AP.
     Formerly: Bowling Green Park City Daily News.

CORBIN

US

CORBIN TIMES-TRIBUNE. 1892. Mon.-Sat. $.50 newsstand; $102/yr. 201 N. Kentucky, Corbin, KY 40701. TEL 606-528-2464; FAX 606-528-9850. **Owner(s):** American Publishing Co., 606 N. Van Buren, P.O. Box 520, Marion, IL 62959. TEL 618-993-1711; Ed. John Whitlock; Pub. Rochelle Stidham; pub. size: broadsheet; circ. evening 7,500(paid). **Wire Service(s):** AP.

COVINGTON

US

KENTUCKY POST, THE. 1890. Mon.-Sat. $.35 newsstand; $8.95/mo. 421 Madison Ave., Covington, KY 41011. TEL 606-292-2600; FAX 606-291-2525. **Owner(s):** Scripps-Howard, 312 Walnut St., 28th Fl., Cincinnati, OH 45202. TEL 513-977-3000; Ed. Robert Kraft. adv. contact: Connie Cooper. pub. size: broadsheet; circ. evening 38,147(paid). **Wire Service(s):** AP.
     Formerly: Covington Kentucky Post.

DANVILLE

US   ISSN 0889-0056

ADVOCATE-MESSENGER. 1865. Sun.-Fri. $.50/day newsstand; $1/Sun.; $109.20/yr. local; $133.20/yr. in state; $142/yr. out of state. 330 S. Fourth St., Danville, KY 40422. TEL 606-236-2551; FAX 606-236-9566; E-mail: advocate@amnews.com; URL: http://www.amnews.com. **Owner(s):** Schurz Communications, Inc., 223 W. Colfax, South Bend, IN 46601; Ed. John T. Davis; Pub. Mary Schurz; adv. contact: Mike Elliott. photos; bk.rev.; pub. size: broadsheet; circ. evening 12,000(paid); Sun. 13,000(paid). **Wire Service(s):** AP.

ELIZABETHTOWN

US

NEWS-ENTERPRISE. 1974. Sun.-Fri. $.50/day newsstand; $1/Sun.; $92.95/yr. in cy.; $125/yr. in state. 408 W. Dixie Ave., Elizabethtown, KY 42701. TEL 502-769-2312; FAX 502-769-6965; E-mail: etown@infi.net; URL: http://www.newsenterpriseonline.com. **Owner(s):** Landmark Communications, Inc., 150 W. Brambleton Ave., Norfolk, VA 23510; Ed. David Greer; Pub. Mike Andres; adv. contact: Jamie Sizemore. pub. size: broadsheet; circ. morning 16,100(paid); Sun. 20,000(paid). **Wire Service(s):** AP.

FRANKFORT

US

FRANKFORT STATE JOURNAL. Sun.-Fri. $.50/day newsstand; $1.25/Sun.; $9.25/mo. 321 W. Main St., Frankfort, KY 40601. TEL 502-227-4556; FAX 502-227-2831. **Owner(s):** Albert Dix, 321 W. Main St., Frankfort, KY 40601; Ed. Carl West; Pub. Albert Dix; adv. contact: Wayne Dommick. pub. size: broadsheet; circ. evening 12,000(paid); Sun. 12,500(paid).

GLASGOW

US

GLASGOW DAILY TIMES. 1889. Sun.-Fri. $.50/day newsstand; $1/Sun.; $72/yr. 100 Commerce Dr., Glasgow, KY 42141. TEL 502-678-5171; FAX 502-678-5052. **Owner(s):** Stephens Group, Inc., P.O. Box 1359, Fort Smith, AR 72902. TEL 501-785-7801; Ed. Joel Wilson; Pub. William Tinsley; adv. contact: Harold Spear. pub. size: standard; circ. evening 10,000(paid); Sun. 10,000(paid).

HARLAN

US

HARLAN DAILY ENTERPRISE. 1901. Mon.-Sat. $.50 newsstand; $87/yr. carrier; $120/yr. mailed. 1548 S. US Hwy. 421, Harlan, KY 40831. TEL 606-573-4510; FAX 606-573-0042. **Owner(s):** American Publishing Co., 606 N. Van Buren, P.O. Box 520, Marion, IL 62959. TEL 618-993-1711; Ed. John Henson; Pub. James Kirby; adv. contact: Bill Combs. photos; pub. size: broadsheet; circ. evening 6,766(paid). **Wire Service(s):** AP.

HENDERSON

US

HENDERSON GLEANER. 1884. Tue.-Sun. $.50/day newsstand; $1.50/Sun.; $10.50/mo. in cy.; $11.50/mo. in state; $12.50/mo. out of state. 455 Klutey Park Plz., Henderson, KY 42420. TEL 502-827-2000; FAX 502-827-2765. **Owner(s):** Walt Dear, P.O. Box 4, Henderson, KY 42420. TEL 502-827-2000; Ed. David Dixon; Pub. Steve Austin; adv. contact: Nancy Pippin. pub. size: broadsheet; circ. morning 11,500(paid); Sun. 14,000(paid). **Wire Service(s):** AP.

HOPKINSVILLE

US

KENTUCKY NEW ERA. 1869. Mon.-Sat. $.50 newsstand; $8/mo. home deliv.; $12/mo. mailed. 1618 E. Ninth St., Hopkinsville, KY 42240. TEL 502-886-4444. **Owner(s):** Kentucky New Era, Inc., 1618 E. Ninth St., Hopkinsville, KY 42440. TEL 502-886-4444; Ed. Mike Herndon; Pub. Robert C. Carter; adv. contact: Taylor Hayes. photos; bk.rev.; pub. size: broadsheet; circ. evening 15,134(paid). **Wire Service(s):** AP.

LEXINGTON

US   ISSN 0745-4260

LEXINGTON HERALD-LEADER. 1888. d. $.50/day newsstand; $1.75/Sun.; $17.45/mo. carrier; $10.25/mo. Fri.-Sun. carrier; $17.40/4 wks. mailed in state; $7/4 wks. Sun. mailed in state;. 100 Midland Ave., Lexington, KY 40508. TEL 606-231-3100; FAX 606-231-3454. **Owner(s):** Knight-Ridder, Inc., One Herald Plz., Miami, FL 33132. TEL 305-376-3800; Ed. David Holwerk; Pub. Lewis Owens; adv.; photos; pub. size: broadsheet; circ. morning 119,078(paid); Sun. 166,237(paid). **Wire Service(s):** AP, KNS, NYT.

LOUISVILLE

US

COURIER-JOURNAL, THE. 1868. d. $.50/day newsstand; $1.50/Sun.; $15/mo. carrier; $15.50/mo. motor rte. 525 W. Broadway, Louisville, KY 40202. TEL 502-582-4011; FAX 502-582-4075; E-mail: cjletter@louisvil.gannett.com; URL: http://www.courier-journal.com. **Owner(s):** Gannett Company, Inc., 1100 Wilson Blvd., Arlington, VA 22209. TEL 703-284-6000; Ed. Stephen Ford; Pub. Edward E. Manassah; adv.; pub. size: broadsheet; circ. morning 239,907(paid); Sun. 330,022(paid). **Wire Service(s):** AP, NYT, LAT-WP, DJ.

MADISONVILLE

US

MESSENGER, THE. 1917. Mon.-Sat. $.50/day newsstand; $70/yr. 221 S. Main, Madisonville, KY 42431. TEL 502-821-6833; FAX 502-821-6855. **Owner(s):** Paxton Media Group, Inc., P.O. Box 2300, Paducah, KY 42002. TEL 502-443-1771; Ed. Tom Clinton; Pub. Bob Morris; adv. contact: Beth Baggerly. pub. size: broadsheet; circ. evening 11,322(paid). **Wire Service(s):** AP.
     Formerly: Madisonville Messenger.

MAYFIELD

US

MAYFIELD MESSENGER. 1900. Mon.-Sat. $.50/day newsstand; $5/mo. 201 N. Eighth St., Mayfield, KY 42066. TEL 502-247-5223; FAX 502-247-6336. **Owner(s):** Messenger Newspapers, Inc., P.O. Box 709, Mayfield, KY 42066. TEL 502-247-5223; Ed. Mike Turley; Pub. Bob T. Shytle; pub. size: broadsheet; circ. evening 7,600(free & paid). **Wire Service(s):** AP.

MAYSVILLE

US

LEDGER-INDEPENDENT. 1968. Mon.-Sat. $.50 newsstand; $2.25/wk. 41-43 W. Second St., Maysville, KY 41056. TEL 606-564-9091; FAX 606-564-6893; E-mail: ponto@mau-uky.campus.mcl.net; URL: http://www.trib.com/maysville. **Owner(s):** Howard Publications, Inc., 1715 S. Beeman, St., P.O. Box 570, Oceanside, CA 92079. TEL 619-433-5771; Ed. Matt Stahl; Pub. Robert Hendrickson; adv. contact: Patty Moore. pub. size: broadsheet; circ. morning 9,400(paid). **Wire Service(s):** AP.

MIDDLESBORO

US   ISSN 1041-7095

MIDDLESBORO DAILY NEWS. 1911. Mon.-Sat. $.50/day newsstand; $7.25/mo. carrier; $90.10/yr. in state; $85/yr. out of state. 120 N. 11th St., Middlesboro, KY 40965. TEL 606-248-1010; FAX 606-248-7614. **Owner(s):** American Publishing Co., 606 N. Van Buren, P.O. Box 520, Marion, IL 62959. TEL 618-993-1711; Ed. Ray Short; Pub. J.T. Hurst; adv. contact: Pat Cheek. photos; bk.rev.; pub. size: broadsheet; circ. evening 7,600(paid). **Wire Service(s):** AP.

MURRAY

US

MURRAY LEDGER & TIMES. 1879. Mon.-Sat. $.50 newsstand; $72/yr. Whitnell & Glendale, Murray, KY 42071. TEL 502-753-1916; FAX 502-753-1927. **Owner(s):** Murray Newspapers, Inc., P.O. Box 1040, Murray, KY 42071. TEL 502-753-1916; Ed. Walter Apperson; Pub. Walter Apperson; adv. contact: Mary Ann Orr. bk.rev.; pub. size: broadsheet; circ. evening 8,400(paid). **Wire Service(s):** AP.

OWENSBORO

US

OWENSBORO MESSENGER-INQUIRER. 1874. d. $.50/day newsstand; $1.50/Sun.; $131/yr. 1401 Frederica St., Owensboro, KY 42301. TEL 502-926-0123; FAX 502-686-7868. **Owner(s):** A.H. Belo Corp., 400 S. Record, Dallas, TX 75202. TEL 214-977-6606; Ed. Paul Raupp; Pub. Robert Mong; adv. contact: Frank Leto. photos; bk.rev.; pub. size: broadsheet; circ. morning 32,518(paid); Sun. 34,189(paid). **Wire Service(s):** AP, LAT-WP, KR.

PADUCAH

US   ISSN 1050-0030

PADUCAH SUN. 1929. d. $.50/day newsstand; $1.25/Sun.; $11.40/mo. carrier; $12.25/mo. mailed in region; $15/mo. mailed elsewhere. 408 Kentucky Ave., Paducah, KY 42003. TEL 502-443-1771; FAX 502-442-7859. **Owner(s):** Paxton Media Group, Inc., P.O. Box 2300, Paducah, KY 42002. TEL 502-443-1771; FAX 502-442-8188; Ed. Jim Paxton; Pub. Fred Paxton; adv.; photos; bk.rev.; pub. size: broadsheet; circ. morning 30,570(paid); Sun. 33,042(paid). **Wire Service(s):** AP, NYT.

RICHMOND

US

RICHMOND REGISTER. 1917. Mon.-Sat. $.50 newsstand; $102/yr. carrier; $108/yr. mailed in cy.; $111/yr. out of cy. 380 Big Hill Ave., Richmond, KY 40475. TEL 606-623-1669; FAX 606-623-2337. **Owner(s):** American Publishing Co., 606 N. Van Buren, P.O. Box 520, Marion, IL 62959. TEL 618-993-1711; Ed. John Butwell. adv. contact: Teresa Senters. pub. size: broadsheet; circ. evening 9,300(paid). **Wire Service(s):** AP.

SOMERSET

US   ISSN 0899-1839

COMMONWEALTH JOURNAL. 1895. Sun.-Fri. $.50/day newsstand; $1/Sun.; $83.80/yr. 110-112 E. Mount Vernon St., Somerset, KY 42501. TEL 606-678-8191; FAX 606-679-9225. **Owner(s):** Park Communications, Inc., Vine Ctr. Office Tower, 333 W. Vine St., 17th Fl., Lexington, KY 40507. TEL 606-252-7275. Ed. James T. Stratton; Pub. James T. Stratton; adv. contact: Kathy Gregory. photos; bk.rev.; pub. size: broadsheet; circ. evening 8,300(paid); Sun. 8,300(paid). **Wire Service(s):** AP.

WINCHESTER

US

WINCHESTER SUN. 1878. Mon.-Sat. $.50 newsstand; $96/yr. 20 Wall St., Winchester, KY 40392-4300. TEL 606-744-3123; FAX 606-745-0538. **Owner(s):** Winchester Sun Co., Inc., 20 Wall St., Winchester, KY 40391. TEL 606-744-3123; Ed. William S. Blakeman; Pub. Betty Berryman; adv. contact: Ann Laurence. photos; bk.rev.; pub. size: broadsheet; circ. evening 12,500(free & paid). **Wire Service(s):** AP.

LOUISIANA

ABBEVILLE

US

ABBEVILLE MERIDIONAL. 1857. Tue.-Fri. & Sun. $.50/day newsstand; $.75/Sun.; $60.96/yr. 318 N. Main St. Abbeville, LA 70510. TEL 318-893-4223; FAX 318-898-9022. **Owner(s):** Louisiana State Newspapers, 666 Jefferson, Lafayette, LA 70501. TEL 318-233-6400; Ed. Gwen Broussard; Pub. David Clevenger; adv. contact: Mike Hebert. photos; pub. size: broadsheet; circ. morning 5,200(controlled & paid); Sun. 6,000(controlled & paid). **Wire Service(s):** AP.

ALEXANDRIA

US

ALEXANDRIA DAILY TOWN TALK. 1883. d. $.50/day newsstand; $1/Sun.; $12/mo.; $144/yr. 1201 Third St., Alexandria, LA 71301. TEL 318-487-6397; FAX 318-487-6315. **Owner(s):** Central Newspapers, Inc., 135 N. Pennsylvania Ave., Indianapolis, IN 45204. TEL 317-231-9200; Ed. James R. Butler; Pub. John E. Newhouse, III; adv. contact: Bill Hertzler. photos; bk.rev.; pub. size: broadsheet; circ. morning 41,000(paid); Sun. 41,000(paid). **Wire Service(s):** AP, NYT, SHNS.

BASTROP

US

BASTROP DAILY ENTERPRISE. 1899. Mon.-Fri. $.50 newsstand; $55/yr. carrier; $69/yr. out of state mailed. 119 E. Hickory, Bastrop, LA 71220. TEL 318-281-4421; FAX 318-283-1699. **Owner(s):** Smith Newspapers, Inc., P.O. Box 27, Fort Payne, AL 35967. TEL 205-845-5510; Ed. Tim Franklin; Pub. Wally Gallian; adv. contact: Pam Glenn. pub. size: broadsheet; circ. evening 6,200(paid). **Wire Service(s):** AP.

BATON ROUGE

US   ISSN 1061-3978

ADVOCATE, THE. 1842. d. $.50 newsstand; $2.76/wk. 525 Lafayette St., Baton Rouge, LA 70802. TEL 504-383-1111; FAX 504-388-0323. **Owner(s):** Capital City Press, 525 Lafayette St., Baton Rouge, LA 70802. TEL 504-383-1111; adv. contact: Mike Nola. photos; bk.rev.; pub. size: broadsheet; circ. morning 110,000(paid); Sun. 141,000(paid). **Wire Service(s):** AP, WP-LAT, KR.
    Formerly: State Times/Morning Advocate.

BOGALUSA

US

BOGALUSA DAILY NEWS & SUNDAY NEWS. 1927. Sun.-Fri. $.50/day newsstand; $1/Sun.; $105/yr. in state mailed; $108/yr. out of state. 525 Ave. V, Bogalusa, LA 70427. TEL 504-732-2565; FAX 504-732-4006. **Owner(s):** Pontchartrain Newspapers, Inc., P.O. Box 820, Bogalusa, LA 70429. TEL 504-732-2565; Ed. Lou Major, Jr.; Pub. Lou Major, Sr.; adv. contact: Linda Clements. pub. size: broadsheet; circ. evening 8,000(paid); Sun. 9,000(paid). **Wire Service(s):** UPI.

CROWLEY

US

CROWLEY POST-SIGNAL. 1974. Tue.-Fri. & Sun. $.50/day newsstand; $.75/Sun.; $52.40/yr. carrier; $74.88/yr. mailed in state; $84/yr. out of state. 602 N. Parkerson Ave, Crowley, LA 70526. TEL 318-783-3450; FAX 318-788-0949. **Owner(s):** Moody Co., First National Bank Towers, Lafayette, LA 70501; Ed. Harold Gonzales; Pub. Milo A. Nickel; adv. contact: Glen Boudreaux. photos; pub. size: broadsheet; circ. evening 5,800(paid); Sun. 6,200(paid). **Wire Service(s):** AP.

DE RIDDER

US

BEAUREGARD DAILY NEWS. Tue.-Fri. & Sun. $.25/day newsstand; $1.25/Sun.; $52/yr. 903 W. First St., De Ridder, LA 70634. TEL 318-462-0616; FAX 318-463-5347. **Owner(s):** Erban Wise, Sulphur, LA; Ed. Bob Houston; Pub. Erban Wise; adv. contact: Beaux Victor. pub. size: broadsheet; circ. morning 13,800(paid).
Formerly: De Ridder Beauregard Daily News.

FRANKLIN

US

FRANKLIN BANNER-TRIBUNE. 1884. Mon.-Fri. $.25 newsstand; $36.40/yr. carrier; $72.80/yr. mailed elsewhere. 115 Wilson St., Franklin, LA 70538. TEL 318-828-3706; FAX 318-828-2874. **Owner(s):** Morgan City Newspapers, Inc., Morgan City, LA; Ed. Paul Godfrey; Pub. Allan R. Von Werder; adv.; photos; bk.rev.; pub. size: broadsheet; circ. evening 3,750(paid). **Wire Service(s):** AP.

HAMMOND

US   ISSN 1049-3395

HAMMOND DAILY STAR. 1959. Sun.-Fri. $.50/day newsstand; $1/Sun.; $8/mo. carrier. 725 S. Morrison Blvd., Hammond, LA 70403. TEL 504-345-2333; FAX 504-542-0242. **Owner(s):** Nixon Newspapers, Inc., 33 W. Third St., P.O. Box 1149, Peru, IN 46970; Ed. Lil Mirando; Pub. David K. Frazer; adv. contact: Liz Black. pub. size: broadsheet; circ. evening 12,163(paid); Sun. 13,636(paid). **Wire Service(s):** AP.

HOUMA

US

COURIER, THE. 1878. Sun.-Fri. $.50/day newsstand; $.75/Sun.; $90/yr. carrier; $99/yr. mailed elsewhere. 3030 Barrow St., Houma, LA 70360. TEL 504-879-1557; FAX 504-857-2244. **Owner(s):** New York Times Co., The, 229 W. 43rd St., New York, NY 10036. TEL 212-556-1234; Ed. Mike Slaughter; Pub. Miles Forrest; adv. contact: Lisa Ferrell. pub. size: broadsheet; circ. evening 22,000(paid); Sun. 22,000(paid). **Wire Service(s):** AP, NYT.
Formerly: Houma Daily Courier.

JENNINGS

US

JENNINGS DAILY NEWS. 1896. Tue.-Fri. & Sun. $.50/day newsstand; $.75/Sun.; $5.50/mo.; $16.50/3 mos.; $33/6 mos.; $66/yr. 238 Market St., Jennings, LA 70546. TEL 318-824-3011; FAX 318-824-3019. **Owner(s):** Newspaper Service Co., Inc., c/o R. H. Fackelman, P.O. Drawer 12428, Panama City, FL 32401; Ed. Jack Givo; Pub. Marc Richard; adv. contact: Paula Richard. pub. size: broadsheet; circ. evening 5,800(paid); Sun. 5,800(paid). **Wire Service(s):** AP.

LAFAYETTE

US

LAFAYETTE ADVERTISER. 1894. d. $.50/day newsstand; $1/Sun.; $14/mo. home deliv.; $168/yr. 221 Jefferson St., Lafayette, LA 70501. TEL 318-289-6300; FAX 318-233-5340. **Owner(s):** Thomson Newspapers, Inc., One Thorn Run Ctr., Ste. 500, 1187 Thorn Run Rd. Ext., Coraopolis, PA 15108. TEL 412-262-7870; Ed. Lou Zeigler; Pub. John E. Miller; adv. contact: Johnny Meche. photos; pub. size: broadsheet; circ. morning 38,000(paid); Sun. 44,000(paid).

LAKE CHARLES

US   ISSN 0739-1196

LAKE CHARLES AMERICAN PRESS. 1895. d. $.50/day newsstand; $1.50/Sun.; $12/mo. 4900 Hwy. 90, E., Lake Charles, LA 70601. TEL 318-433-3000; FAX 318-494-4008. **Owner(s):** Shearman Corp., 4900 Hwy. 90, E., Lake Charles, LA 70601. TEL 318-433-3000; FAX 318-494-4008; Ed. Bret Downer; Pub. Maynard Woodhatch; adv.; photos; bk.rev.; pub. size: broadsheet; circ. morning 37,391(paid); Sun. 42,119(paid). **Wire Service(s):** AP.

LEESVILLE

US   ISSN 1069-3548

LEESVILLE DAILY LEADER. 1870. Tue.-Fri. & Sun. $.25/day newsstand; $.75/Sun.; $52/yr. carrier; $75/yr. out of parish mailed; $85/yr. out of state mailed. 206 E. Texas St., Leesville, LA 71446. TEL 318-239-3444; FAX 318-238-1152. **Owner(s):** News Leader, Inc., P.O. Box 1999, Sulphur, LA 70664. TEL 318-238-9788; Ed. Shannon Duhon; Pub. Erbon Wise; adv. contact: George Jinks. photos; bk.rev.; pub. size: broadsheet; circ. morning 9,000(paid); Sun. 13,800(paid). **Wire Service(s):** AP.

MINDEN

US

MINDEN PRESS-HERALD. 1849. Mon.-Fri. $.50 newsstand; $84/yr. carrier; $96/yr. in parish mailed; $108/yr. out of parish mailed. 203 Gleason St., Minden, LA 71055. TEL 318-377-1866; FAX 318-377-1895. **Owner(s):** Specht Newspapers, Inc., P.O. Box 1339, Minden, LA 71058. TEL 318-377-1866; adv. contact: Billy Walker. pub. size: broadsheet; circ. evening 5,200(paid). **Wire Service(s):** AP.

MONROE

US

NEWS-STAR, THE. d. $.35/day newsstand; $1.50/Sun.; $12/mo.; $144/yr. 411 N. Fourth St., Monroe, LA 71201. TEL 318-322-5161; FAX 318-362-0273. **Owner(s):** Gannett Company, Inc., 1100 Wilson Blvd., Arlington, VA 22340. TEL 703-284-6000; Ed. Reed Eckhart; Pub. Ed Major; adv.; photos; bk.rev.; pub. size: broadsheet; circ. morning 40,000(paid); Sun. 50,000(paid). **Wire Service(s):** AP.
Formerly: The New Star.

MORGAN CITY

US

DAILY REVIEW, THE. 1872. Mon.-Fri. $.35 newsstand; $36/yr. carrier; $104/yr. mail. 1014 Front St., Morgan City, LA 70380. TEL 504-384-8370; FAX 504-384-4255. **Owner(s):** Morgan City Newspapers, Inc., 1014 Front St., Morgan City, LA 70381. TEL 504-384-8370; FAX 504-384-4255; Ed. Steve Shirley; Pub. Doyle E. Shirley; adv. contact: Steve Shirley. adv.: $6.30/SAU. photos; bk.rev.; pub. size: broadsheet; circ. evening 6,342(paid). **Wire Service(s):** AP.

NATCHITOCHES

US

NATCHITOCHES TIMES. Tue.-Fri. & Sun. $.50 newsstand; $65/yr. in cy.; $130/yr. out of cy. 904 Hwy. One, S., Natchitoches, LA 71457. TEL 318-352-3618; FAX 318-352-7842. **Owner(s):** Lovan B. & Patricia W. Thomas, P.O. Box 448, Natchitoches, LA 71458. TEL 318-352-3618; Ed. Carolyn Roy; Pub. Lovan B. Thomas; adv. contact: Charles Norman. pub. size: broadsheet; circ. 8,100(paid).

NEW IBERIA

US

DAILY IBERIAN. 1893. d. $.50/day newsstand; $1/Sun.; $96/yr. home deliv.; $134.52/yr. mailed. 926 E. Main St., New Iberia, LA 70560. TEL 318-365-6773; FAX 318-367-9640. **Owner(s):** Wick Communications, Inc., 333 W. Wilcox Dr., Ste. 302, Sierra Vista, AZ 85635; Ed. James Smith; Pub. Will Chapman; adv. contact: Jim Hornbeck. photos; bk.rev.; pub. size: broadsheet; circ. evening 29,500(free & paid); Sun. 16,100(paid). **Wire Service(s):** AP.

NEW ORLEANS

US   ISSN 1055-3053

TIMES-PICAYUNE. 1837. d. $.35/day newsstand; $1.50/Sun.; $6.20/mo. daily; $7/mo. Sun.; $11/mo. daily & Sun. deliv. 3800 Howard Ave., New Orleans, LA 70125. TEL 504-826-3279; FAX 504-826-3007; E-mail: ldennery@aol.com; URL: http://www.neworleans.net/. **Owner(s):** Times-Picayune Publishing Corp., 3800 Howard Ave., New Orleans, LA 70125. TEL 504-586-3785; Ed. Dan Shea; Pub. Ashton Phelps, Jr.; adv. contact: Robert G. O'Neill. photos; pub. size: broadsheet; circ. morning 270,228(paid); Sun. 319,119(paid). **Wire Service(s):** AP, CDN, ANS, CNS, DJ.

OPELOUSAS

US

DAILY WORLD. 1940. Sun.-Fri. $.50/day newsstand; $.75/Sun.; $90/yr. carrier; $110/yr. mailed in state; $110/yr. out of state; $36/yr. Sun. local; $69/yr. Sun. mailed elsewhere. 2781 I49 Service Rd., S., Opelousas, LA 70570-1179. TEL 318-942-4971; FAX 318-948-6572. **Owner(s):** New York Times Co., The, 229 W. 43rd St., New York, NY 10036. TEL 212-556-1234; Ed. Harlan Kirgan; Pub. Aaron Parsons; adv. contact: Bill Brownley. pub. size: broadsheet; circ. evening 14,000(paid); Sun. 15,000(paid). **Wire Service(s):** NYT.

RUSTON

US   ISSN 0891-8708

RUSTON DAILY LEADER. 1894. Sun.-Fri. $.50/day newsstand; $.75/Sun.; $6/mo. carrier; $7.25/mo. in parish mailed; $8/mo. out of parish. 208 W. Park Ave., Ruston, LA 71270. TEL 318-255-4353; FAX 318-255-4006. **Owner(s):** Ruston Newspapers, Inc., P.O. Box 520, Ruston, LA 71273. TEL 318-255-4353; Ed. Jeff Benson; Pub. Rick Hohlt; adv. contact: Jeanie McCartney. pub. size: broadsheet; circ. evening 6,800(controlled); Sun. 7,000(controlled). **Wire Service(s):** AP.

SHREVEPORT

US

TIMES, THE. 1871. d. $.50/day newsstand; $1.50/Sun.; $13.25/mo. carrier; $21/mo. mailed. 222 Lake St., Shreveport, LA 71101. TEL 318-459-3200; FAX 318-459-3462. **Owner(s):** Gannett Company, Inc., 1100 Wilson Blvd., Arlington, VA 22234. TEL 703-284-6000; Ed. Mike Whitehead; Pub. Richard Stone; adv. contact: Dan Mills. pub. size: broadsheet; circ. morning 82,637(paid); Sun. 103,747(paid). **Wire Service(s):** AP, SC, GNS.

SLIDELL

US

SLIDELL SENTRY-NEWS. 1965. Tue.-Sun. $.50/day newsstand; $1/Sun.; $101/yr.; $121.28/yr. mailed. 3648 Pontchartrain Dr., Slidell, LA 70458. TEL 504-643-4918; FAX 504-643-4966; E-mail: sentry@neosoft.com; URL: http://www.tamnet.com. **Owner(s):** Wick Communications, Inc., 333 W. Wilcox Dr., Ste. 302, Sierra Vista, AZ 85635; Ed. Kevin Chiri; Pub. Terry Maddox; adv.; photos; bk.rev.; pub. size: broadsheet; circ. morning 27,704(free & paid); Sun. 27,650(free & paid). **Wire Service(s):** AP.

SULPHUR

US

SOUTHWEST DAILY NEWS. 1930. d. $.25 newsstand; $25.75/yr. 716 E. Napoleon, Sulphur, LA 70663. TEL 318-527-7075; FAX 318-528-3044. **Owner(s):** News Leader, Inc., P.O. Box 1999, Sulphur, LA 70664-1999. TEL 318-527-7075; FAX 318-528-3044; Ed. O. Hayes; Pub. E.W. Wise; adv. contact: Susan Peveto. bk.rev.; pub. size: broadsheet; circ. morning 16,000(paid). **Wire Service(s):** AP, NEA.
   Formerly: Southwest Builder News.

THIBODAUX

US

DAILY COMET. 1889. Mon.-Fri. $.50 newsstand; $73/yr. carrier. 705 W. Fifth St., Thibodaux, LA 70301. TEL 504-447-4055; FAX 504-448 7606. **Owner(s):** New York Times Co., The, 229 W. 43rd St., New York, NY 10036; Ed. Colley Charpentier; Pub. Chris Bond; adv. contact: Alan Rini. pub. size: broadsheet; circ. evening 12,400(paid). **Wire Service(s):** AP.

MAINE

AUGUSTA

US   ISSN 0745-2039

KENNEBEC JOURNAL. 1825. d. $.50/day newsstand; $1.25/Sun.; $148/yr. carrier; $165/yr. mailed in state; $254.40 mailed out of state. 274 Western Ave., Augusta, ME 04330. TEL 207-623-3811; FAX 207-623-2167. **Owner(s):** Guy Gannett Communications, One City Ctr., Portland, ME 04101. TEL 800-442-6035; Ed. Davis Rawson. pub. size: broadsheet; circ. morning 17,700(paid); Sun. 15,037(paid). **Wire Service(s):** AP.

BANGOR

US   ISSN 0892-8738

BANGOR DAILY NEWS. 1889. Mon.-Sat. $.50/day newsstand; $1.25/Sat.; $2.60/wk. carrier. 491 Main St., Bangor, ME 04401. TEL 207-990-3000; FAX 207-941-9476; E-mail: bangornews@aol.com. **Owner(s):** Bangor Publishing Co., 491 Main St., Bangor, ME 04401; Pub. Richard J. Warren; adv. contact: Wayne Lawton. photos; pub size: standard; circ. morning 75,142(paid). **Wire Service(s):** AP, UPI, NYT.

BIDDEFORD

US

JOURNAL TRIBUNE. 1884. Mon.-Sat. $.50 newsstand; $130/yr. carrier; $135.70/yr motor rte.; $175/yr. mail. Alfred Rd., Rte. 111, Biddeford, ME 04005. TEL 207-282-1535; FAX 207-282-3138. **Owner(s):** Journal Publishing Co., P.O. Box 627, Biddeford, ME 04005. TEL 207-282-1535; Ed. Robert Saunders; Pub. Dennis J. Flaherty; adv. contact: Donald Lauzier. pub. size: broadsheet; circ. evening 14,765(paid). **Wire Service(s):** AP, SHNA, KR.

BRUNSWICK

US   ISSN 0747-1300

TIMES-RECORD. 1967. Mon.-Fri. $.50/newsstand; $105/yr. in area; $113.35 out of area. 6 Industry Rd., Brunswick, ME 04011. TEL 207-729-3311 FAX 207-729-5728. **Owner(s):** Brunswick Publishing Co., P.O. Box 10, Brunswick, ME 04011. TEL 207-729-3311; FAX 207-721-5728; Ed. Martin McKenna; Pub. Campbell B. Niven; adv. contact: John Bamford. photos; bk.rev.; pub. size: standard; circ. evening 13,500(paid). **Wire Service(s):** AP, NYT.

LEWISTON

US

SUN-JOURNAL. 1893. Mon.-Sat. $.50 newsstand; $164.42/yr. carrier. 104 Park St., Lewiston, ME 04243-4400. TEL 207-784-5411; FAX 207-777-3436. **Owner(s):** Lewiston Daily Sun, inc., 104 Park St., Lewiston, ME 04240-4400. TEL 207-784-5411; Ed. Mary Lynn Kelsch; Pub. James Costello, Sr.; adv.; photos; bk.rev.; pub. size: broadsheet; circ. morning 41,550(paid); Sun. 44,000(paid). **Wire Service(s):** AP, KR,.

PORTLAND

US

PORTLAND PRESS HERALD. 1921. d. $.60/day newsstand; $1.75/Sun.; $149.95/yr. carrier; $304/yr. mailed in state; $401/yr. mailed out of state. 390 Congress St., Portland, ME 04101. TEL 207-791-6310; FAX 207-791-6920; E-mail: joem@portland.com; URL: http://www.portland.com/. **Owner(s):** Guy Gannett Communications, One City Ctr., Portland, ME 04101; Ed. Jeannine Guttman; Pub. Made eine G. Corson; adv. contact: Gary Gagne. photos; bk.rev.; pub. size: broadsheet; circ. morning 70,000(paid); Sun. 140,000(paid). **Wire Service(s):** AP.

WATERVILLE

US

CENTRAL MAINE MORNING SENTINEL. 1904. d. $.50/day newsstand; $1.25/Sun.; $148/yr. carrier; $165/yr. mailed in state; $250.40/yr. mailed out of state. 25 Silver St., Waterville, ME 04901. TEL 207-873-3341; FAX 207-873-6145. **Owner(s):** Guy Gannett Communications, One City Ctr., Portland, ME 04101. TEL 800-442-6056; Ed. Timothy Allen. adv. contact: Molly Evans. pub. size: broadsheet; circ. morning 23,757(paid); Sun. 19,568(paid). **Wire Service(s):** AP, UPI.
   Formerly: Waterville Central Maine.

MARYLAND

ANNAPOLIS

US

CAPITAL, THE. 1727. d. $.35 day newsstand, $.79/Sun.; $2.55/wk. carrier; $45.50/13 wks. mailed. 2000 Capital Dr., Annapolis, MD 21401. TEL 410-268-5000; FAX 410-280-5953. **Owner(s):** Capital-Gazette Newspapers, 2000 Capital Dr., Annapolis, MD 21401. TEL 410-268-5000; Ed. Thomas Marquardt. adv.; pub. size: broadsheet; circ. evening 44,800(paid); Sun. 45,500(paid). **Wire Service(s):** AP, KR.
   Formerly: Annapolis Capital.

BALTIMORE

US

BALTIMORE SUN. 1837. d. $.50/day newsstand; $1.50/Sun.; $13.67/mo. carrier; $14.75/mo. mailed. 501 N. Calvert St., Baltimore, MD 21278. TEL 410-332-6000; FAX 410-752-6049. **Owner(s):** Times-Mirror Co., Times-Mirror Sq., Los Angeles, CA 90053. TEL 310-972-7000; Ed. Bill Marimow Pub. Mary E. Junck; adv.; photos; bk.rev. pub. size: broadsheet; circ. morning 337,292(paid); Sun. 488,562(paid). **Wire Service(s):** AP, RN, KNT, NYT, DJ, LAT-WP.

CAMBRIDGE

US

DAILY BANNER. 1897. Mon.-Fri. $.35 newsstand; $78/yr. carrier; $95/yr. mailed. 1000 Goodwill Rd., Cambridge, MD 21613. TEL 410-228-3131; FAX 410-228-6547; E-mail: dafb@aol.com. **Owner(s):** Independent Newspapers, Inc., P.O. Box 7001, Dover, DE 19903. TEL 302-674-3600; Ed. Debra Bierbaum. adv. contact: Debra Bierbaum. photos; bk.rev.; pub. size: broadsheet; circ. evening 7,500(paid). **Wire Service(s):** LAT-WP.

CUMBERLAND

US

CUMBERLAND TIMES-NEWS. 1869. d. $.50/day newsstand; $1.25/Sun.; $2.75/wk. home deliv. 19 Baltimore St., Cumberland, MD 21502. TEL 301-722-4600; FAX 301-722-4870; E-mail: lwhite@miworld.com; URL: http://www.times-news.com. **Owner(s):** Thomson Newspapers, Inc., One Thorn Run Ctr., Ste. 500, 1187 Thorn Run Rd. Ext., Coraopolis, PA 15108. TEL 412-262-7870; Ed. Lance White; Pub. Terry Horne; adv. contact: Stephen Stouffer. pub. size: broadsheet; circ. morning 31,800(paid); Sun. 33,923(paid). **Wire Service(s):** AP.

EASTON

US   ISSN 1065-2345

STAR-DEMOCRAT, THE. 1799. Sun.-Fri. $.50/day newsstand; $1.25/Sun.; $92.40/yr. in cy.; $96.60/yr. out of cy.; $136.50/yr. out of state. 29088 Airpark Dr., Easton, MD 21601. TEL 410-822-1500; FAX 410-820-6519. **Owner(s):** Whitney-Conn, P.O. Box 600, Easton, MD 21601. TEL 410-822-1500; Ed. Barbara Sauers; Pub. Larry Effingham; photos; bk.rev.; pub. size: broadsheet; circ. morning 17,500(paid); Sun. 18,000(paid). **Wire Service(s):** AP.

ELKTON

US   ISSN 1046-2058

CECIL WHIG. 1841. Mon.-Fri. $.40 newsstand; $68.25/yr. carrier. 601 Bridge St., Elkton, MD 21921. TEL 410-398-3311; FAX 410-398-4044. **Owner(s):** Chesapeake Publishing Corp., Airport Industrial Park, Easton, MD 21601. TEL 410-822-1500; Ed. Terry Peddicord; Pub. Tom Bradlee; adv. contact: Tina Winmill. pub. size: broadsheet; circ. morning 17,000(paid). **Wire Service(s):** AP.

FREDERICK

US

FREDERICK POST, THE. 1910. Mon.-Sat. $.50/newsstand; $88.40/yr. carrier. 200 E. Patrick St., Frederick, MD 21701-0578. TEL 301-662-1177; FAX 301-662-8299. **Owner(s):** Great Southern Printing & Mfg. Co., 200 E. Patrick St., Frederick, MD 21701. TEL 301-662-1177; Ed. Mike Powell; Pub. George B. Delaplaine; adv. contact: Jim Enright. pub. size: broadsheet; circ. morning 34,000(paid). **Wire Service(s):** AP.

US

NEWS, THE. 1883. Mon.-Sat. $.50 newsstand; $88.90/yr. home deliv. 200 E. Patrick St., Frederick, MD 21701-5632. TEL 301-662-1177; FAX 301-662-8299. **Owner(s):** Great Southern Printing & Mfg., 200 E. Patrick, Frederick, MD 21701-5632. TEL 301-662-1177; FAX 301-662-8299; Ed. Michael Powell; Pub. George Delaplaine; adv. contact: Jim Enright. pub. size: broadsheet; circ. evening 15,425(paid). **Wire Service(s):** AP.

HAGERSTOWN

US

DAILY MAIL, THE. d. $.50/day newsstand; $1.25/Sun.; $10.50/mo. carrier; $11.29/mo. motor rte. 100 Summit Ave., Hagerstown, MD 21740. **Owner(s):** Schurz Communications, Inc., 225 W. Colfax Ave., South Bend, IN 46626. TEL 219-233-6161; Ed. Gloria George; Pub. John League; adv.; photos; pub. size: broadsheet; circ. morning 38,022; evening 18,000(paid). **Wire Service(s):** AP, UPI.

US

HERALD, THE. 1828. d. $.50/day newsstand; $1.25/Sun.; $10.50/mo. carrier; $11.29/mo. motor rte. 100 Summit Ave., Hagerstown, MD 21740. TEL 301-733-5131; FAX 301-714-0245. **Owner(s):** Schurz Communications, Inc., 225 W. Colfax Ave., South Bend, IN 46626. TEL 219-233-6161; Ed. Gloria George; Pub. John League; pub. size: broadsheet; circ. morning 38,022(paid); Sun. 39,663(paid). **Wire Service(s):** AP, UPI.

   Formerly: Hagerstown Herald-Mail.

LANHAM

US

PRINCE GEORGES JOURNAL. 1975. Mon.-Fri. $.25/newsstand; $65/yr. 9410 Annapolis Rd., Lanham, MD 20706. TEL 301-459-3131; FAX 301-731-8363. **Owner(s):** Journal Newspapers, Inc., 2720 Prosperity Ave., Fairfax, VA 22034-1000. TEL 703-560-4000; Ed. Joann Gosslin; Pub. Ryan Phillips; adv. contact: Dave Hills. photos; pub. size: broadsheet; circ. morning 32,253(paid). **Wire Service(s):** AP.

ROCKVILLE

US   ISSN 0162-2080

MONTGOMERY JOURNAL, THE. 1973. Mon.-Fri. $.25/day newsstand; $21/3 mos. carrier; $39/6 mos.; $72/yr.; $62/yr senior citizens & military. 2 Research Ct., Rockville, MD 20850. TEL 301-670-1400; FAX 301-670-1421. **Owner(s):** Journal Newspapers, Inc., 2720 Prosperity Ave., Fairfax, VA 22034. TEL 703-560-4000; Ed. Julie Rasicot; Pub. Ryan E. Phillips; adv. contact: Kenneth Courter. photos; pub. size: broadsheet; circ. morning 29,378(paid). **Wire Service(s):** AP.

SALISBURY

US

DAILY TIMES. 1886. d. $.50/day newsstand; $1.25/Sun.; $3.50/wk. carrier; $132.50/yr. P.O. Box 1937, Salisbury, MD 21802-1937. TEL 410-749-7171; FAX 410-543-8736; E-mail: toadvine@shore.intercom.net; URL: http://www.intercom.net/dailytimes. **Owner(s):** Thomson Newspapers, Inc., 65 Queens St., W., Toronto, ON M5H 2M8, Canada; Ed. Mel Toadvine; Pub. Edward C. White; adv. contact: Clyde Pinson. pub. size: broadsheet; circ. morning 31,700(paid); Sun. 34,215(paid). **Wire Service(s):** AP.

WESTMINSTER

US

CARROLL COUNTY SUN. 1984. Sun.-Fri. $.50/day newsstand; $1.50/Sun.; $12.95/mo. 15 E. Main St., Winchester Exchange, Westminster, MD 21157. TEL 410-751-7900; FAX 410-751-7916. **Owner(s):** Times-Mirror Co., Times-Mirror Sq., 220 W. First St., Los Angeles, CA 90053. TEL 213-237-3700; pub. size: broadsheet; circ. morning 5,000(paid); evening 7,000(paid); Sun. 22,740(paid). **Wire Service(s):** AP, Sun, LAT-WP, RN, NYT.

US   ISSN 0746-7494

CARROLL COUNTY TIMES. 1911. d. $.50/day newsstand; $1/Sun.; $105/yr. 201 Railroad Ave., Westminster, MD 21157. TEL 410-848-4400; FAX 410-857-8749; E-mail: carolcyt@cct.infi.net; URL: http://www.infi.net/carrollcounty. **Owner(s):** Landmark Community Newspapers, Inc., P.O. Box 549, Shelbyville, KY 40065. TEL 502-633-4334; Ed. David Ammenheuser. adv. contact: Charles Baker. pub. size: broadsheet; circ. morning 23,400(paid); Sun. 23,400(paid). **Wire Service(s):** AP, SHNA, GNS.

MASSACHUSETTS

ATHOL

US

ATHOL DAILY NEWS. 1934. Mon.-Sat. $.35 day newsstand; $81/yr. carrier; $120/yr. mailed. 225 Exchange St., Athol, MA 01331. TEL 508-249-3535; FAX 508-249-9630. **Owner(s):** Athol Press, Inc., 225 Exchange St., Athol, MA 01331. TEL 508-249-3535; Ed. Cynthia Jack; Pub. Richard J. Chase, Jr.; adv. contact: Dan Mahoney. photos; bk.rev.; pub. size: broadsheet; circ. evening 6,000(paid). **Wire Service(s):** AP.

ATTLEBORO

US   ISSN 1053-7805

SUN CHRONICLE. 1973. d. $.50 newsstand; $3.50/wk. carrier; $4.25/wk. mailed. 34 S. Main, Attleboro, MA 02703. TEL 508-222-7000; FAX 508-226-5851. **Owner(s):** United Communications Corp., 715 58th St., Kenosha, WI 53410. TEL 414-657-1000; Ed. Ned Bristol; Pub. Paul Rixon; adv. contact: Paul Morrissey. pub. size: standard; circ. evening 25,000(paid); Sun. 25,000(paid). **Wire Service(s):** AP.

BEVERLY

US

SALEM EVENING NEWS. 1893. Mon.-Sat. $.50 day newsstand; $2.20/wk. carrier; $14.75/mo. mailed. 32 Dunham Rd., Beverly, MA 01915. TEL 508-922-1234; FAX 508-922-4330. **Owner(s):** Ottaway Newspapers, Inc., P.O. Box 401, Campbell Hall, NY 10916. TEL 914-294-8181; Ed. David Marcus; Pub. John Kinney; pub. size: broadsheet; circ. morning 9,101(paid). **Wire Service(s):** UPI, ONS.

   Formerly: Beverly Times.

BOSTON

US   ISSN 0743-1791

BOSTON GLOBE. 1872. d. $.50/day newsstand; $1.50/Sun.; $4.50/wk. in city; $27/mo. in state; $35.50/mo. elsewhere. 135 Morrissey Blvd., Boston, MA 02107. TEL 617-929-2000; FAX 617-929-3192. **Owner(s):** New York Times Co., The, 229 W. 43rd St., New York, NY 10036. TEL 212-556-1234; Ed. Gregory Moore; Pub. William O. Taylor; adv. contact: Robert Manning. pub. size: broadsheet; circ. morning 486,403(paid); Sun. 777,902(paid). **Wire Service(s):** AP, UPI, LAT-WP, KNT, RN.

US   ISSN 0738-5854

BOSTON HERALD. 1982. d. $.50/day newsstand; $1.50/Sun.; $3.30/wk. 300 Harrison Ave., Boston, MA 02106-2096. TEL 617-426-3000; FAX 617-542-1315. **Owner(s):** Patrick J. Purcell, One Herald Sq., Boston, MA 02106-2096. TEL 617-426-3000; Ed. Kevin Covey; Pub. Patrick J. Purcell; adv. contact: Jack Breed. photos; bk.rev.; pub. size: tabloid; circ. morning 320,000(paid); Sun. 227,040(paid). **Wire Service(s):** AP, RN, SHNA, GNS, DJ, LT, NWS, LAT-WP, CNS, CN.

BROCKTON

US   ISSN 0279-4683

BROCKTON ENTERPRISE, THE. 1880. d. $.50/day newsstand; $1.25/Sun.; $3.05/wk. carrier. 60 Main St., Brockton, MA 02401. TEL 508-586-6200; FAX 508-586-6506. **Owner(s):** Newspaper Media Corp., 60 Main St., P.O. Box 1450, Brockton, MA 02401. TEL 508-586-6200; Pub. James F. Plugh; bk.rev.; pub. size: broadsheet; circ. evening 57,000(paid); Sun. 64,900(paid). **Wire Service(s):** AP, LAT-WP, SHNA.

DEDHAM

US   ISSN 1068-1914

DAILY TRANSCRIPT. 1973. Mon.-Fri. $.50 day newsstand; $91/yr. carrier; $100/yr. mailed. 367 Washington St., Dedham, MA 02026. TEL 617-433-7800; FAX 617-326-9675. **Owner(s):** Fidelity Investments, 82 Devonshire St., Boston, MA 02019. TEL 617-728-6488; Ed. Joseph Gibbs; Pub. Asa Cole; adv. contact: Paul Farrell. pub. size: standard; circ. evening 8,000(paid). **Wire Service(s):** AP.

FALL RIVER

US

HERALD NEWS, THE. 1872. d. $.50/day newsstand, $1.75/Sun.; $3.40/wk. $176.80/yr. carrier; $286/yr. mailed. 207 Pocasset St., Fall River, MA 02721. TEL 508-676-8211; FAX 508-676-2566. **Owner(s):** Northeast Publishing, Inc., 207 Pocasset St., Fall River, MA 02721. TEL 508-676-8211; Ed. Paul Palange; Pub. Tracy R. Greene; pub. size: broadsheet; circ. evening 33,767(paid); Sun. 37,084(paid). **Wire Service(s):** AP.
Formerly: Fall River Herald News.

FITCHBURG

US   ISSN 1049-1155

SENTINEL & ENTERPRISE. 1838. d. $2.50/wk. 808 Main St., Fitchburg, MA 01420. TEL 508-343-6911; FAX 508-342-1158. **Owner(s):** Thomson Newspapers, Inc., One Thorn Run Ctr., Ste. 500, 1187 Thorn Run Rd. Ext., Coraopolis, PA 15108. TEL 412-262-7870; Ed. Michael Cleveland; Pub. William A. White; adv. contact: Janet Banville. photos; bk.rev.; pub. size: broadsheet; circ. evening 20,000(paid); Sun. 21,000(paid). **Wire Service(s):** AP.

FRAMINGHAM

US

MIDDLESEX NEWS. 1897. d. $.50/day morning; $.50/day afternoon; $1.50/Sun.; $171.60/yr. carrier; $241.80/yr. mailed. 33 New York Ave., Framingham, MA 01701. TEL 508-626-3800; FAX 508-626-4400 **Owner(s):** Fidelity Investments, 82 Devonshire St., Boston, MA 02019. TEL 617-728-6488; Ed. Andrea Haynes; Pub. Asa Cole; adv. contact: Paul Farrell. pub. size: broadsheet; circ. morning 2,000(paid); evening 34,000(paid); Sun. 44,000(paid). **Wire Service(s):** AP, RN.

US

NEWS-TRIBUNE. 1882. Mon.-Fri. $.50 day newsstand; $2./wk. home deliv.; $110/yr. mailed; $125/yr. foreign. 33 New York Ave., Framingham, MA 01701. TEL 508-433-7800; FAX 508-872-2131 **Owner(s):** Fidelity Investments, 82 Devonshire St., Boston, MA 02019. TEL 617-728-6488; Ed. Ellen Ishkanian; Pub. Asa Cole; adv. contact: Susan Robinson. pub. size: tabloid; circ. evening 8,831(paid). **Wire Service(s):** AP.

GARDNER

US   ISSN 0740-0837

GARDNER NEWS. 1869 Mon.-Sat. $.40/newsstand; $85/yr. carrier & motor rte.; $128/yr. mailed. 309 Central St., Gardner, MA 01440. TEL 508-632-8000; FAX 508-630-2231. **Owner(s):** Gardner News, Inc., The, 309 Central St., Gardner, MA 01440. TEL 508-632-8000; Ed. Rob Heenan; Pub. Alberta Bell; adv. contact: Donna Watson. photos; bk.rev.; pub. size: broadsheet; circ. evening 8,000(paid). **Wire Service(s):** AP.

GLOUCESTER

US

GLOUCESTER DAILY TIMES. 1856. Mon.-Sat. $165/yr. Whittemore St., Gloucester, MA 01930. TEL 508-283-7000; FAX 508-281-5748. **Owner(s):** Essex County Newspapers, Inc., Whittemore St., Gloucester, MA 01930. TEL 508-283-7000; Ed. Mary Wessling Herrington; Pub. John Kinney; pub. size: standard; circ. evening 14,000(paid). **Wire Service(s):** AP, ONS.

GREENFIELD

US

RECORDER, THE. 1792. Mon.-Sat. $.40/day newsstand; $2.10/wk. carrier; $10.80/mo. mailed. 14 Hope St., Greenfield, MA 01301. TEL 413-772-0261; FAX 413-774-5020. **Owner(s):** Newspapers of New England, Inc., P.O. Box 273, Greenfield, MA 01302. TEL 413-772-0261; Ed. Tim Blagg; Pub. Mike Kapusta; adv. contact: Rich Fahey. pub. size: standard; circ. morning 15,169(paid); evening 15,300(paid). **Wire Service(s):** AP, LAT-WP.

HAVERHILL

US

HAVERHILL GAZETTE. 1821. Mon.-Sat. $.50/day newsstand; $.75/Sat.; $2.40/week carrier or mailed. W. Lowell Ave., Haverhill, MA 01832. TEL 508-374-0321; FAX 508-374-9631; E-mail: hgazette@aol.com; URL: http://www.hgazette.com. **Owner(s):** Scripps League Newspapers, Inc., P.O. Box 1109, Herndon, VA 22070. TEL 703-713-1920; Ed. Robert Gates. pub. size: broadsheet; circ. evening 13,000(paid). **Wire Service(s):** UPI, AP.

HYANNIS

US   ISSN 0747-1467

CAPE COD TIMES. 1936. d. $.50/day newsstand; $1.50/Sun.; $148.50/yr. 319 Main St., Hyannis, MA 02601. TEL 508-775-1200; FAX 508-775-7337. **Owner(s):** Ottaway Newspapers, Inc., P.O. Box 401, Campbell Hall, NY 10916. TEL 914-294-8181; Ed. Timothy White; Pub. John Wilcox; adv.; photos; bk.rev.; pub. size: standard; circ. morning 48,000(paid); Sun. 55,000(paid). **Wire Service(s):** AP, NYT, ONS, WP.

LOWELL

US

LOWELL SUN. 1878. d. $.50/day newsstand, $1.50/Sun.; $3.50/wk. carrier. 15 Kearney Sq., Lowell MA 01852. TEL 508-458-7100; FAX 508-970-4600. **Owner(s):** Lowell Sun Publishing Co., 15 Kearney Sq., Lowell, MA 01852. TEL 508-458-7100; FAX 508-970-4700; Ed. Malcolm Gibson; Pub. John H. Costello, Jr.; adv. contact: Paul Schwabe. photos; bk.rev.; pub. size: broadsheet; circ. evening 52,673(paid); Sun 56,033(paid). **Wire Service(s):** AP, NYT, CHR, SHNA, LAT-WP, Cox, CNS, NEA.

LYNN

US   ISSN 8750-8249

DAILY EVENING ITEM. 1877. Mon.-Sat. $.50 day newsstand; $120/yr. home deliv. 38 Exchange St., Lynn, MA 01901. TEL 617-593-7700; FAX 617-581-3178; E-mail: lynnitem@shore.net; URL: http://www.dreamlight.com/ community/news/news.htm. Owner(s): Peter Gamage, P.O. Box 951, Lynn, MA 01903. TEL 617-593-7700; Ed. Allan T. Kort; Pub. Brian Thayer; adv. contact: Kevin J. Kelly. pub. size: broadsheet circ. evening 27,672(paid). **Wire Service(s):** AP, NEA.

MALDEN

US

DAILY NEWS-MERCURY, THE. 1908. Mon.-Fri. $.35 newsstand; $1.85/wk. carrier; $140/yr. mailed. 277 Commercial St., Malden, MA 02148. TEL 617-321-8000; FAX 617-321-8008; E-mail: newsmerc@user1.channel1.com. **Owner(s):** Eastern Middlesex Press Publishing, Inc., 277 Commercial St., Malden, MA 02148; Ed. Stephan Freker; Pub. Warren H. Jackson; pub. size: broadsheet; circ. evening 13,599(paid). **Wire Service(s):** UPI.
Formerly: Melrose News.

MILFORD

US

MILFORD DAILY NEWS. 1887. d. $.50 newsstand; $140.40/yr. home deliv.; $175/yr. mailed. 159 S. Main St., Milford, MA 01757. TEL 508-473-1111; FAX 508-478-8769. **Owner(s):** ALTA Group Newspapers, Inc., Alfred Rd., Biddeford, ME 04005. TEL 207-282-1535; Ed. Nicholas J. Tosches; Pub. Thomas C. Sawyer, Sr.; adv. contact: Richard Rae. pub. size: broadsheet; circ. evening 15,000(paid). **Wire Service(s):** AP.

NEW BEDFORD

US   ISSN 0745-3574

STANDARD-TIMES, THE. 1850. d. $.50/day newsstand; $1.65/Sun.; $202/yr. mail. 25 Elm St., New Bedford, MA 02740. TEL 508-997-7411; FAX 508-979-4541; E-mail: newsroom@s-t.com; URL: http://www.s-t.com/. **Owner(s):** Standard-Times Publishing Co., 25 Elm St., New Bedford, MA 02740; Ed. Dave Humphrey; Pub. William T. Kennedy; adv.; photos; bk.rev.; pub. size: broadsheet; circ. evening 43,448(paid); Sun. 48,992(paid). **Wire Service(s):** AP, DJ, ONS, NYT.
    Formerly: New Bedford Standard-Times.

NEWBURYPORT

US

DAILY NEWS OF NEWBURYPORT, THE. 1793. Mon.-Sat. $.50 newsstand; $9/mo. carrier; $14.75/mo. mailed. 23 Liberty St., Newburyport, MA 01950. TEL 508-462-6666; FAX 508-465-8505. **Owner(s):** Ottaway Newspapers, Inc., P.O. Box 401, Campbell Hall, NY 10916. TEL 914-294-8181; Ed. Calhoun Kleen; Pub. John Kinney; adv. contact: Mike Eramo. pub. size: broadsheet; circ. evening 14,000(paid). **Wire Service(s):** UPI, ONS.
    Formerly: Newburyport Daily News.

NORTH ADAMS

US

TRANSCRIPT, THE. 1896. Mon.-Sat. $.50 newsstand; $110/yr. American Legion Dr., North Adams, MA 01247. TEL 413-663-3741; FAX 413-662-2792. **Owner(s):** New England Newspapers, Inc., 23 Exchange St., Pawtucket, RI 02860. TEL 401-722-4000; Ed. David Nahan; Pub. David Nahan; adv. contact: Missy Tower. pub. size: broadsheet; circ. morning 10,000(paid). **Wire Service(s):** AP.

NORTHAMPTON

US   ISSN 0739-3504

DAILY HAMPSHIRE GAZETTE. 1786. d. $2.10/wk. 115 Conz St., Northampton, MA 01060. TEL 413-584-5000; FAX 413-585-5222; E-mail: gazette@crocker.com. **Owner(s):** H.S. Gere & Sons, Inc., 115 Conz St., Northampton, MA 01060. TEL 413-584-5000; Ed. Lou Groccia. adv. contact: John Ebbets. pub. size: standard; circ. evening 23,000(paid). **Wire Service(s):** AP, CSM, LAT-WP.

NORTH ANDOVER

US

EAGLE TRIBUNE, THE. 1868. d. $.35/day newsstand, $1.50/weekend; $3.05/wk. carrier; $225/yr. mailed. 100 Turnpike St., North Andover, MA 01845. TEL 508-685-1000; FAX 508-687-6045; E-mail: dwarner@eagletribune.com. **Owner(s):** Eagle Tribune Publishing Co., 100 Turnpike St., North Andover, MA 01845. TEL 508-685-1000; Ed. Gerry Molina; Pub. Irving E. Rogers, Jr.; adv. contact: V.S. Cottone. pub. size: broadsheet; circ. evening 55,754(paid). **Wire Service(s):** AP, SHNA.

PITTSFIELD

US   ISSN 0895-8793

BERKSHIRE EAGLE. 1789. d. $134.20/yr.; $207/yr. mailed. 75 S. Church St., Pittsfield, MA 01201. TEL 413-447-7311; FAX 413-449-3419; E-mail: eagle@berkshire.net. **Owner(s):** New England Newspapers, Inc., 23 Exchange St., Pawtucket, RI 02860. TEL 401-722-4000; Ed. David Scribner. adv. contact: John Gallacher. pub. size: broadsheet; circ. morning 30,500(paid); Sun. 34,000(paid). **Wire Service(s):** AP, NYT.

QUINCY

US   ISSN 0889-2253

PATRIOT LEDGER. 1837. Mon.-Sat. $.75/day newsstand; $1/Sat. $3/wk. deliv. 400 Crown Colony Dr., Quincy, MA 02169. TEL 617-786-7000; FAX 617-786-7025. **Owner(s):** George W. Prescott Publishing Co., Inc., 400 Crown Colony Dr., Quincy, MA 02169. TEL 617-786-7000; Ed. Terry Ryan; Pub. K. Prescott Low; adv.; pub. size: broadsheet; circ. morning 94,000(paid). **Wire Service(s):** AP, NYT, CSM.

READING

US

DAILY TIMES & CHRONICLE. Mon.-Fri. $.50 newsstand; $152.75/yr. in cy.; $178.75/yr. out of cy. 531 Main St., Reading, MA 01867. TEL 617-944-2200; FAX 617-942-0884. **Owner(s):** Haggerty Family, One Arrow Dr., Woburn, MA 01801. TEL 617-933-3700; Pub. Peter Haggerty; adv. contact: Judy McCoy. pub. size: broadsheet; circ. morning 41,774(paid).
    Formerly: Reading Times & Chronicle.

SOUTHBRIDGE

US

NEWS, THE. 1923. Mon.-Fri. $.45 newsstand; $80/yr. carrier; $120/yr. mailed; $156/yr. out of cy. 25 Elm St., Southbridge, MA 01550. TEL 508-764-4325; FAX 508-764-6743. **Owner(s):** Stonebridge Press Inc., 475 Washington St., Auburn, MA 01501. TEL 617-832-5876; Ed. Joe Capillo; Pub. Loren F. Ghiglione; adv.; pub. size: broadsheet; circ. evening 5,300(paid). **Wire Service(s):** AP.

SPRINGFIELD

US   ISSN 0894-2765

UNION-NEWS. d. $.50/day newsstand; $1.50/Sun.; $156/yr. daily; $78/yr. Sun. 1860 Main St., Springfield, MA 01101. TEL 413-788-1000; FAX 413-788-1301. **Owner(s):** Republican Co., 1860 Main St., Springfield, MA 01103. TEL 413-788-1000; Pub. David Starr; adv. contact: Dwight Brouillard. pub. size: standard; circ. morning 115,000(paid); Sun. 160,000(paid). **Wire Service(s):** AP, UPI.

TAUNTON

US

TAUNTON DAILY GAZETTE. 1848. Mon.-Sat. $.50 newsstand; $2.35/wk. 5 Cohannet, Taunton, MA 02780. TEL 508-880-9000; FAX 508-880-9049. **Owner(s):** Thomson Newspapers, Inc., Metro Center, One Station Pl., Stamford, CT 06902. TEL 203-425-2500; Ed. Eva T. Gaffney; Pub. Jean S. Scarborough; adv. contact: Margaret G. Vieira. bk.rev.; pub. size: broadsheet; circ. evening 15,570(paid). **Wire Service(s):** AP.

WAKEFIELD

US

WAKEFIELD ITEM. 1894. Mon.-Fri. $.35 newsstand; $11.50/mo. 26 Albion St., Wakefield, MA 01880. TEL 617-245-0080; FAX 617-246-0061. **Owner(s):** Wakefield Item Co., Inc., 26 Albion St., Wakefield, MA 01880. TEL 617-245-0080; Ed. Peter Rossi; Pub. Robert P. Dolbeare; pub. size: broadsheet; circ. evening 5,100(paid). **Wire Service(s):** AP.

WESTFIELD

US

WESTFIELD EVENING NEWS. 1932. Mon.-Sat. $.50 newsstand; $125/yr. 62-64 School St., Westfield, MA 01085. TEL 413-562-4181; FAX 413-562-4185. **Owner(s):** Westfield News Publishing Co., P.O. Box 930, Westfield, MA 01086-0930. TEL 413-562-4181; Ed. Denise King; Pub. E. Carol Mazza; adv. contact: Martha Eaillargeon. pub. size: broadsheet; circ. evening 5,500(paid). **Wire Service(s):** UPI.

WOBURN

US

DAILY TIMES CHRONICLE. 1901. Mon.-Fri. $.50 newsstand; $2.25/wk. One Arrow Dr., Woburn, MA 01801. TEL 617-933-3700; FAX 617-932-3321. **Owner(s):** Woburn Daily Times, Inc., One Arrow Dr., Woburn, MA 01801. TEL 617-933-3700; FAX 617-932-3321; Ed. James Haggerty, III; Pub. Peter Haggerty; adv. contact: Thomas R. Kirk. photos; pub. size: broadsheet; circ. evening 14,000(free & paid). **Wire Service(s):** AP.

WORCESTER

US   ISSN 1050-4184

TELEGRAM & GAZETTE. 1989. d. $.50/day newsstand; $1.50/Sun.; $3.10/wk. P.O. Box 15012, Worcester, MA 01615-0012. TEL 508-793-9100; FAX 508-793-9281; E-mail: people@telegram.infi.net; URL: http://www.telegram.com. **Owner(s):** Chronicle Publishing Co., 901 Mission St., San Francisco, CA 94103. TEL 415-777-1111; Ed. Harry T. Whitin; Pub. Bruce S. Bennett; adv.; photos; pub. size: broadsheet; circ. morning 115,129(paid); Sun. 137,655(paid). **Wire Service(s):** AP, NYT.

MICHIGAN

ADRIAN

US

DAILY TELEGRAM. 1892. d. $165/yr. mailed; $156/yr. motor rte. 133 N. Winter St., Adrian, MI 49221. TEL 517-265-5111; FAX 517-263-4152. **Owner(s):** Thomson Newspapers, Inc., 65 Queen St. W., Toronto, ON M5H 2M8, Canada; Ed. Robert Jodon; Pub. Robert Krout; adv. contact: Michelle Micklewright. pub. size: broadsheet; circ. evening 18,000(paid). Wire Service(s): AP.
Formerly: Adrian Daily Telegram.

ALBION

US   ISSN 8750-9008

ALBION RECORDER. 1908. Mon.-Sat. $.50 newsstand; $8.50/mo. in area; $9.50/mo. out of area. 111 W. Center St., Albion, MI 49224. TEL 517-629-3984; FAX 517-629-5790. **Owner(s):** Calhoun Communications, 111 W. Center St., Albion, MI 49224. TEL 517-629-3984; Ed. Stacy Henson; Pub. Richard Milliman, II; pub. size: broadsheet; circ. morning 19,400(paid). **Wire Service(s):** AP.

ALPENA

US

ALPENA NEWS. 1899. Mon.-Sat. $93.75/yr. in cy.; $148/yr. mailed out of area. 130 Park Pl., Alpena, MI 49707. TEL 517-354-3111; FAX 517-354-2096; E-mail: alpenanews@oweb.com; URL: http://www.oweb.com/upnorth/. **Owner(s):** Ogden Newspapers, Inc., 1500 Main, Wheeling, WV 26003. TEL 304-233-0100; Ed. William B. Speer; Pub. William B. Speer, Jr.; adv. contact: John Jackowiak. pub. size: broadsheet; circ. evening 13,000(paid). **Wire Service(s):** AP.

ANN ARBOR

US

ANN ARBOR NEWS. 1835. d. $.35/day newsstand; $1.25/Sun.; $132/yr.; $66/6 mos. 340 E. Huron St., Ann Arbor, MI 48104-1147. TEL 313-994-6876; FAX 313-994-6702. **Owner(s):** Newhouse Publishing, Inc., 458 Lexington Ave., New York, NY 10017; Ed. Ed Petykiewicz; Pub. Dave Wierman; adv. contact: Joe Grech. photos; bk.rev.; pub. size: broadsheet; circ. evening 57,708(paid); Sun. 74,943(paid). **Wire Service(s):** AP, LAT-WP, NYT, NNS.

BAD AXE

US

HURON DAILY TRIBUNE. 1876. Sun.-Fri. $.35 newsstand; $102/yr. in cy.; $114/yr. mailed in cy.; $126/yr. out of cy. 211 N. Heisterman, Bad Axe, MI 48413. TEL 517-269-6461; FAX 517-269-9893; E-mail: tribune@hdt.com; URL: http://www.hdtinfo.com. **Owner(s):** Hearst Corp., 959 Eighth Ave., New York, NY 10019; Ed. Sandy Sutton; Pub. H. Allen Wamsley; adv. contact: Helen Kopack. photos; bk.rev.; pub. size: broadsheet; circ. morning 10,000(paid). **Wire Service(s):** AP.

BATTLE CREEK

US

BATTLE CREEK ENQUIRER. 1900. d. $2.75/wk. local; $3/wk. out of area. 155 W. Van Buren St., Battle Creek, MI 49017. TEL 616-964-7161; FAX 616-964-0299. **Owner(s):** Gannett Company, Inc.. 1100 Wilson Blvd., Arlington, VA 22234. TEL 703-284-6000; Pub. Randy N. Miller; adv. contact: Brad Lackey. pub. size: standard; circ. evening 28,000(paid); Sun. 38,000(paid). **Wire Service(s):** AP, GNS.

BAY CITY

US

BAY CITY TIMES. d. $10.50/mo. carrier; $135/yr. motor rte. 311 Fifth St., Bay City, MI 48708. TEL 517-894-9630; FAX 517-893-0649; E-mail: newsroom@bctimes.com. **Owner(s):** Advance Publications, Inc., 485 Lexington Ave., New York, NY 10017; Ed. Paul Keep; Pub. Kevin Dykema; adv. contact: Archie Duncan. pub. size: standard; circ. morning 39,719(paid); Sun. 52,085(paid). **Wire Service(s):** AP, NYT.

BIG RAPIDS

US   ISSN 8750-5533

BIG RAPIDS PIONEER. 1862. Mon.-Sat. $.50 newsstand; $80/yr. 502 N. State, Big Rapids, MI 49307. TEL 616-796-4831; FAX 616-796-1152. **Owner(s):** Conine Publishing Co., Inc., 502 N. State, Big Rapids, MI 49307. TEL 616-796-4831; FAX 616-796-1152; Ed. Judy Hale; Pub. John A. Batdorff; adv. contact: Denise Clasen. photos; pub. size: broadsheet; circ. morning 5,900(paid). **Wire Service(s):** UPI, AP.
Formerly: Pioneer, The.

CADILLAC

US   ISSN 0745-3655

CADILLAC EVENING NEWS. 1872. Mon.-Sat. $.50 newsstand; $102.40/yr. 130 N. Mitchell, Cadillac, MI 49601-0640. TEL 616-775-6565. **Owner(s):** Thomas C. Huckle, 130 N. Mitchell, Cadillac, MI 49601-0640. TEL 616-775-6565; Ed. Mark Lagerwey; Pub. Thomas C. Huckle; adv. contact: Chris Huckle. pub. size: broadsheet; circ. morning 10,025(paid). **Wire Service(s):** AP.

CHEBOYGAN

US

CHEBOYGAN DAILY TRIBUNE. 1875. d. $.50 newsstand; $103/yr. 308 N. Main St., Cheboygan, MI 49721. TEL 616-627-7144; FAX 616-627-5331. **Owner(s):** American Publishing Co., 606 N. Van Buren, P.O. Box 520, Marion, IL 62959. TEL 618-993-1711; Ed. Carrie Stiles; Pub. Roy S. Trahan, II; adv. contact: Roy S. Trahan, II. pub. size: broadsheet; circ. morning 5,000(paid). **Wire Service(s):** UPI.

COLDWATER

US   ISSN 0745-6794

DAILY REPORTER, THE. 1896. Mon.-Sat. $.50 newsstand; $77/yr.; $82.50 mtr rte.; $144/yr. mailed. 15 W. Pearl St., Coldwater, MI 49036. TEL 517-278-2318; FAX 517-278-6041. **Owner(s):** Park Communications, Inc., Vine Ctr. Office Tower, 333 W. Vine St., 17th Fl., Lexington, KY 40507. TEL 606-252-7275; Ed. Michelle Reen. adv. contact: Mary Jo Hughes. bk.rev.; pub. size: broadsheet; circ. evening 7,915(paid). **Wire Service(s):** AP.

DETROIT

US   ISSN 1055-2758

DETROIT FREE PRESS. 1831. d. $.35/day newsstand; $1.50/Sun.; $2.50/wk. 321 Lafayette, Detroit, MI 48226. TEL 313-222-6400; FAX 313-222-5981; E-mail: 72662.1736@compuserve.com; URL: gopher://gopher.det-freepress.com:9002/. **Owner(s):** Knight-Ridder, Inc., One Herald Plz., Miami, FL 33132. TEL 305-376-3800; Ed. Chip Visci; Pub. Heath Meriwether; adv. contact: Dick McClellen. photos; bk.rev.; pub. size: broadsheet; circ. morning 531,825(paid); Sun. 1,107,645(paid). **Wire Service(s):** AP, UPI, KR, NYT.

US   ISSN 1055-2715

DETROIT NEWS. d. $.50/day newsstand; $1.50/Sun.; $117/yr. home deliv.; $494/yr. mailed in state; $530.40/yr. mailed out of state. 615 W. Lafayette, Detroit, MI 48226. TEL 313-222-6400; FAX 313-222-2335. **Owner(s):** Gannett Company, Inc., 1100 Wilson Blvd., Arlington, VA 22234. TEL 703-284-6000; Ed. Robert H. Giles; Pub. Robert H. Giles; adv.; pub. size: broadsheet; circ. evening 354,403(paid); Sun. 1,195,497(paid). **Wire Service(s):** AP, UPI, DJ, NYT.

DOWAGIAC

US

DOWAGIAC DAILY NEWS. 1897. Mon.-Fri. $.50 newsstand; $5.75/mo. carrier. 205 Spaulding St., Dowagiac, MI 49047. TEL 616-782-2101; FAX 616-782-5290. **Owner(s):** Boone/Narragansett Publishers, 205 Spaulding St., Dowagiac, MI 49047. TEL 616-782-2101; Ed. John Eby. adv. contact: Diana Kingsley. pub. size: broadsheet; circ. evening 2,737(paid). **Wire Service(s):** UPI.

ESCANABA

US

DAILY PRESS, THE. Mon.-Sat. $.50 newsstand; $139.50/yr. home deliv. 500 Ludington St., Escanaba, MI 49829. TEL 906-786-2021; FAX 906-786-3752. **Owner(s):** Thomson Newspapers, Inc., 3150 Des Plaines Ave., Des Plaines, IL 60018. TEL 708-299-5544; Ed. Peggy Bryson; Pub. Robert Gregg adv. contact: Jodi Olsen. pub. size: broadsheet; circ. evening 12,700(paid).

FLINT

US

FLINT JOURNAL. 1913. d. $.35/day newsstand; $1.25/Sun.; $10.40/mo. carrier; $11.40/mo. motor rte. 200 E. First St., Flint, MI 48502. TEL 810-766-6100; FAX 810-766-7518. **Owner(s):** Booth Newspapers, Inc., P.O. Box 2168, Grand Rapids, MI 49507. TEL 616-459-1400; Ed. Tom Lindley; Pub. Roger D. Samuel; adv. contact: Thomas Eason. bk.rev.; pub. size: broadsheet; circ. evening 106,000(paid); Sun. 124,000(paid). **Wire Service(s):** UPI, LAT-WP, NYT.

GRAND HAVEN

US

GRAND HAVEN TRIBUNE. 1885. Mon.-Sat. $1.85/wk. carrier; $1.90/wk. motor rte. 101 N. Third St., Grand Haven, MI 49417. TEL 616-842-6400; FAX 616-842-9584. **Owner(s):** Grand Haven Publishing Corp., 101 N. Third St., Grand Haven, MI 49417. TEL 616-842-6400; Ed. Fred Vandenbrand; Pub. E. Mayer Maloney; adv. contact: Paul Bedient. pub. size: broadsheet; circ. evening 11,500(paid). **Wire Service(s):** AP.

GRAND RAPIDS

US

GRAND RAPIDS PRESS, THE. 1892. d. $.50/day newsstand, $1.50/Sun.; $12/mo. carrier; $13 mo. motor rte. 155 Michigan, N.W., Grand Rapids, MI 49503. TEL 616-222-5640; FAX 616-222-5206. **Owner(s):** Advance Publications, Inc., 485 Lexington Ave., New York, NY 10017; Ed. Michael Lloyd; Pub. Danny R. Gaydou; adv. contact: Steven Westphal. pub. size: broadsheet; circ. evening 145,977(paid); Sun. 192,666(paid). **Wire Service(s):** AP, NYT, NNS.

GREENVILLE

US   ISSN 0899-6342

DAILY NEWS. 1856. Mon.-Sat. $102/yr. out of state. 109 N. Lafayette, Greenville, MI 48838. TEL 616-754-9301; FAX 616-754-8559. **Owner(s):** John Stafford, 109 N. Lafayette St., Greenville, MI 48838. TEL 616-754-9301; Ed. Alan Blanchard; Pub. John Stafford; adv. contact: Brette Mathis. pub. size: broadsheet; circ. evening 8,468(paid). **Wire Service(s):** UPI.

HILLSDALE

US

HILLSDALE DAILY NEWS. 1909. Mon.-Sat. $83.70/yr. carrier; $129.60/yr. mailed. 33 McCollum, Hillsdale, MI 49242. TEL 517-437-7351; FAX 517-437-3963. **Owner(s):** Morris Communications, P.O. Box 936, Augusta, GA 30903. TEL 706-724-0851; Ed. Marcia Loader; Pub. William K. Turner; adv. contact: Judy Gabriele. pub. size: broadsheet; circ. evening 8,500(paid). **Wire Service(s):** AP.

HOLLAND

US   ISSN 1050-4044

HOLLAND SENTINEL. 1896. d. $.50/day newsstand; $1.25/Sun.; $99.50/yr. 54 W. Eighth, Holland, MI 49423. TEL 616-392-2311; FAX 616-392-3526; E-mail: hllndstnl@aol.com; URL: http://www.macatawa.org/com/sentinel/home.html. Owner(s): Morris Communications, P.O. Box 936, Augusta, GA 30903. TEL 706-724-0851; Ed. Sue Sopel; Pub. Ron Wallace; adv. contact: Susan Temple. pub. size: broadsheet; circ. morning 19,606(paid); Sun. 20,196(paid). **Wire Service(s):** AP.

HOUGHTON

US

DAILY MINING GAZETTE. 1858. Mon.-Sat. $.50 newsstand; $2.35/wk. carrier; $10.20/mo. motor rte. 206 Shelden Ave., Houghton, MI 49931. TEL 906-482-1500; FAX 906-482-2726. **Owner(s):** Thomson Newspapers, Inc., Des Plains, IL; Ed. Cyndi Perkins; Pub. Brian McMillan; adv. contact: Karen Callaway. pub. size: broadsheet; circ. evening 13,000(paid). **Wire Service(s):** AP.

IONIA

US   ISSN 0745-2128

IONIA SENTINEL-STANDARD. 1866. Mon.-Sat. $.50 newsstand; $99/yr. 114 N. Depot, Ionia, MI 48846. TEL 616-527-2100; FAX 616-527-6860. **Owner(s):** American Publishing Co., 606 N. Van Buren, P.O. Box 520, Marion, IL 62959. TEL 618-993-1711; Ed. Brian P. Abbott; Pub. Jan Anderson; adv.; pub. size: broadsheet; circ. morning 4,082(paid). **Wire Service(s):** AP.

IRON MOUNTAIN

US

DAILY NEWS. 1921. Mon.-Sat. $.50 newsstand; $147/yr. mailed. 215 E. Ludington St., Iron Mountain, MI 49801. TEL 906-774-2772; FAX 906-774-7660. **Owner(s):** Thomson Newspapers, Inc., Des Plaines, IL; Ed. Blaine Hyska; Pub. Robert Johnson; adv.; photos; bk.rev.; pub. size: broadsheet; circ. evening 11,500(paid). **Wire Service(s):** AP.

IRONWOOD

US

IRONWOOD DAILY GLOBE. 1919. Mon.-Sat. $.50 newsstand; $9.80/mo. carrier; $11.50/mo. motor rte.; $13.50/mo. mailed. 118 E. McLeod Ave., Ironwood, MI 49938. TEL 906-932-2211; FAX 906-932-5358. **Owner(s):** Globe Publishing Co., 118 E. McLeod Ave., Ironwood, MI 49938. TEL 906-932-2211; Ed. Andrew Hill. adv. contact: Gary Mecum. pub. size: broadsheet; circ. evening 8,500(paid). **Wire Service(s):** AP.

JACKSON

US

JACKSON CITIZEN PATRIOT. 1837. d. $.35/day newsstand; $1.35/Sun.; $1.90/wk.; $8.55/mo. 214 S. Jackson St., Jackson, MI 49201-2282. TEL 517-787-2300; FAX 517-787-9711. **Owner(s):** Advance Publications, Inc., 485 Lexington Ave., New York, NY 10017. TEL 212-697-8120; Ed. Sandra D. Petykiewicz; Pub. F.T. Weaver; adv. contact: Jerry C. Gerdes. photos; bk.rev.; pub. size: broadsheet; circ. evening 38,003(paid); Sun. 42,002(paid). **Wire Service(s):** NNS, AP, SHNA.

KALAMAZOO

US

KALAMAZOO GAZETTE. 1847. d. $.50/day newsstand, $1/Sun; $11.30/mo. motor rte.; $18.25/mo. mailed. 401 S. Burdick, Kalamazoo, MI 49007. TEL 616-345-3511; FAX 616-388-8447. **Owner(s):** Newhouse Newspapers, 1101 Connecticut Ave., N.W., Washington, DC 20036. TEL 202-383-7800; Pub. George Arwady; adv. contact: Jim Coppinger. pub. size: standard; circ. evening 66,000(paid); Sun. 82,000(paid). **Wire Service(s):** AP, UPI, LAT-WP, NNS.

LANSING

US   ISSN 0274-9742

LANSING STATE JOURNAL. 1855. d. $.35/day newsstand; $1.50/Sun.; $3.25/wk. carrier or motor rte. 120 E. Lenawee, Lansing, MI 48919. TEL 517-377-1000; FAX 517-377-1298. **Owner(s):** Gannett Company, Inc., 1000 Wilson Blvd., Arlington, VA 22234. TEL 703-284-6000; Ed. Roni Rucker-Waters; Pub. Gary Suisman; adv. contact: Stan Howard. photos; bk.rev.; pub. size: standard; circ. morning 71,000(paid); Sun. 96,619(paid). **Wire Service(s):** AP, GNS.

LUDINGTON

US

LUDINGTON DAILY NEWS. 1873. d. $.50 newsstand; $89.10/yr. 202 N. Rath Ave., Ludington, MI 49431-1663. TEL 616-845-5181; FAX 616-843-4011. **Owner(s):** David R. Jackson, P.O. Box 340, Ludington, MI 49431-0340. TEL 616-845-5181; Ed. Paul S. Peterson; Pub. David R. Jackson; adv.; photos; bk.rev.; pub. size: broadsheet; circ. evening 8,115(paid). **Wire Service(s):** AP.

MANISTEE

US

MANISTEE NEWS-ADVOCATE. 1894. Mon.-Sat. $.50 newsstand; $24/3 mos. in cy.; $26/3 mos. mailed in state; $35/3 mos. mailed out of state. 75 Maple St., Manistee, MI 49660-1554. TEL 616-723-3593; FAX 616-723-4733. **Owner(s):** J.B. Publishing Co., 75 Maple St., Manistee, MI 49660-1554. TEL 616-723-3593; FAX 616-723-4733; Ed. Ken Grabowski; Pub. Jerry Fitzwater; adv. contact: Marilyn Barker. pub. size: broadsheet; circ. morning 5,200(paid). **Wire Service(s):** AP.

MARQUETTE

US   ISSN 0898-4964

MARQUETTE MINING JOURNAL. 1846. d. $.50/day newsstand, $1/Sun.; $2.50/wk. carrier; $2.65/wk. motor rte.; $2.85/wk. mailed. 249 W. Washington St., Marquette, MI 49855. TEL 906-228-2500; FAX 906-228-5556. **Owner(s):** Thomson Newspapers, Inc., 3150 Des Plaines Ave., Des Plaines, IL 60018. TEL 708-299-5544; Ed. Dave Edwards; Pub. James Reeves; adv. contact: Gail Englund. pub. size: standard; circ. evening 20,200(paid); Sun. 21,600(paid). **Wire Service(s):** AP.

MARSHALL

US

MARSHALL CHRONICLE. 1879. Mon.-Sat. $.35 newsstand; $79.50/yr. mailed in cy.; $87/yr. mailed out of cy. 115 S. Grand, Marshall, MI 49068. TEL 616-781-3943; FAX 616-781-4012. **Owner(s):** Milliman Communications, Inc., P.O. Box 160, Mason, MI 49068. TEL 517-676-9300; Pub. Dirk Milliman; pub. size: broadsheet; circ. evening 2,000(paid). **Wire Service(s):** UPI.

MIDLAND

US

MIDLAND DAILY NEWS. 1930. d. $.35/day newsstand; $.75/Sun.; $2.65/wk. carrier; $12.50/mo. mailed local; $13.50/mo. mailed out of state. 124 S. McDonald, Midland, MI 48640. TEL 517-835-7171; FAX 517-835-6991; E-mail: mdnnews2@aol.com; URL: http://www.mdn.net. **Owner(s):** Hearst Corp., 959 Eighth Ave., Pelham, NY 10803; Ed. Ralph Wirtz; Pub. Gordon Hall; pub. size: broadsheet; circ. evening 17,165(paid); Sun. 18,000(paid). **Wire Service(s):** AP.

MONROE

US

MONROE EVENING NEWS. 1825. d. $.50/day newsstand, $1.25/Sun.; $2.85/wk. carrier. 20 W. First St., Monroe, MI 48161. TEL 313-242-1100; FAX 313-242-3175. **Owner(s):** Monroe Publishing Co., Inc., 20 W. First St., Monroe, MI 48161. TEL 313-242-1100; Ed. Stephen Gray; Pub. Grattan Gray; adv. contact: Loni Peppler. photos; bk.rev.; pub. size: broadsheet; circ. evening 23,600(paid); Sun. 245,000(paid). **Wire Service(s):** AP.

MT. CLEMENS

US   ISSN 1071-1406

MACOMB DAILY. 1860. Sun.-Fri. $.50/day newsstand; $1/Sun.; $2.10/wk. carrier; $155/yr. 100 Macomb Daily Dr., Mt. Clemens, MI 48043. TEL 810-469-4510; FAX 810-469-2892; E-mail: edit@macombdaily.com; URL: http://www.macombdaily.com. **Owner(s):** Independent Newspapers, Inc., 67 Cass Ave., Mt. Clemens, MI 48043. TEL 810-469-4510; Ed. Phil VanHule; Pub. J. Gene Chambers; adv. contact: Mark Lewis. photos; bk.rev.; pub. size: broadsheet; circ. evening 50,000(paid); Sun. 60,000(paid). **Wire Service(s):** AP.

MT. PLEASANT

US

MORNING SUN. 1977. Sun.-Fri. $.50/day newsstand; $1.25/Sun.; $11.27/mo. carrier; $12.35/mo. motor rte. 215 N. Main, Mt. Pleasant, MI 48858. TEL 517-772-2971; FAX 517-773-0382. **Owner(s):** Central Michigan Newspapers, Inc., 215 N. Main, Mt. Pleasant, MI 48858. TEL 517-772-2971; Ed. Rick Mills; Pub. Ray Pike; adv. contact: Cathy Simon. photos; pub. size: broadsheet; circ. morning 8,000(paid); Sun. 12,023(paid). **Wire Service(s):** AP.
Formerly: Mt. Pleasant/Alma Morning Sun.

MUSKEGON

US

MUSKEGON CHRONICLE, THE. 1857. d. $.50/day newsstand; $1.25/Sun.; $11/mo. motor rte.; $12.50 mailed in state; $13.50 mailed out of state. 981 Third St., Muskegon, MI 49440. TEL 616-722-0320; FAX 616-722-2552. **Owner(s):** Booth Newspapers, Inc., P.O. Box 2168. Grand Rapids, MI 49500. TEL 616-459-1400; Ed. D. Gunnar Carlson; Pub. Gary Ostrom; adv. contact: Kevin Newton. pub. size: broadsheet; circ. evening 48,507(paid); Sun. 53,248(paid). **Wire Service(s):** AP, LAT-WP, NNS.

NILES

US

NILES DAILY STAR. 1886. Mon.-Sat. $.50 newsstand; $6.50/mo. carrier. 217 N. Fourth St., Niles, MI 49120. TEL 616-683-2100; FAX 616-683-2175. **Owner(s):** Boone/Narragansett Publishers, 217 N. Fourth St., Niles, MI 49120; Ed. Jan Griffey; Pub. Tom Ratterbury; adv. contact: Hal Shue. pub. size: broadsheet; circ. evening 5,000(paid). **Wire Service(s):** UP.

OWOSSO

US

ARGUS-PRESS, THE. 1854. d. $.50/day newsstand; $.75/Sun.; $8.25/mo. carrier & motor rte.; $11/mo. mailed. 201 E. Exchange St., Owosso, MI 48867. TEL 517-725-5136; FAX 517-725-6376; E-mail: argus@shianet.org; URL: http://www.shianet.org/~argus/. **Owner(s):** Argus-Press Co., 201 E. Exchange St., Owosso, MI 48867. TEL 517-725-5136; Ed. Joseph R. Peacock; Pub. Richard E. Campbell; adv. contact: Thomas Jacobs. photos; pub. size: broadsheet; circ. evening 12,500(paid); Sun. 12,500(paid). **Wire Service(s):** AP.

PETOSKEY

US

PETOSKEY NEWS-REVIEW. 1875. d. $166.15/yr. 319 State St. Petoskey, MI 49770. TEL 616-347-2544; FAX 616-347-6833. **Owner(s):** Northern Michigan Review, Inc., P.O. Box 528, Petoskey, MI 49770. TEL 616-347-2544; FAX 616-347-6833; Ed. Ken Winter; Pub. Kirk Schaller; adv.; photos; bk.rev.; pub. size: broadsheet; circ. evening 11,245(paid). **Wire Service(s):** AP.

PONTIAC

US

OAKLAND PRESS, THE. 1825. d. $.25/day newsstand; $1.25/Sun.; $2.30/wk. carrier; $13/mo. mailed in town; $21.67/mo. mailed out of town. 48 W. Huron St. Pontiac, MI 48342. TEL 810-332-8181; FAX 810-332-8885. **Owner(s):** Walt Disney Co. 500 S. Buena Vista St., Burbank, CA 91521. TEL 818-560-5300; Ed. Gary Gilbert; Pub. Dave Duncan; adv.; photos; pub. size: standard; circ. morning 78,000(paid); Sun. 100,000(paid). **Wire Service(s):** AP.

PORT HURON

US

TIMES HERALD. 1910. d. $.35/day newsstand; $1.50/Sun. 911 Military St., Port Huron, MI 48060. TEL 810-985-7171; FAX 810-989-6294. **Owner(s):** Gannett Company, Inc., 1100 Wilson Blvd., Arlington, VA 22234. TEL 703-284-6000; Pub. William Monopoli; adv. contact: Kathy Powell. photos; bk.rev.; pub. size: broadsheet; circ. evening 31,547(paid); Sun. 39,936(paid). **Wire Service(s):** AP, GNS.

ROYAL OAK

US   ISSN 1041-9977

DAILY TRIBUNE. 1902. Sun.-Fri. $.35/day newsstand; $.75/Sun.; $2.80/wk. carrier. 210 E. Third St., Royal Oak, MI 48067. TEL 810-541-3000; FAX 810-541-7903. **Owner(s):** Independent Newspapers, Inc., 100 Macomb Daily Dr., Mount Clemens, MI 48043. TEL 810-469-4510; Ed. Mike Beeson; Pub. R.D. Isham; adv. contact: Mary Vellarcita. photos; pub. size: broadsheet; circ. evening 26,300(paid); Sun. 27,000(paid). **Wire Service(s):** AP.

SAGINAW

US

SAGINAW NEWS. 1859. d. $.40/day newsstand; $1.50/Sun.; $11.50/mo. carrier; $12.50/mo. motor rte. 203 S. Washington Ave., Saginaw, MI 48607. TEL 517-752-7171; FAX 517-752-3115. **Owner(s):** Booth Newspapers, Inc., P.O. Box 2168, Grand Rapids, MI 49501. TEL 616-459-1400; Ed. Rob Hanceyside; Pub. Rex Thacher; adv. contact: Gene Bobic. photos; pub. size: broadsheet; circ. evening 55,158(paid); Sun. 65,044(paid). **Wire Service(s):** AP.

SAULT STE. MARIE

US

SAULT STE. MARIE EVENING NEWS. 1879. Sun.-Fri. $.50/day newsstand; $1/Sun.; $11/mo. carrier & motor rte.; $38/3 mo. out of area. 109 Arlington St., Sault Ste. Marie, MI 49783. TEL 906-632-2235; FAX 906-632-1222. **Owner(s):** American Publishing Co., 606 N. Van Buren, P.O. Box 520, Marion, IL 52959. TEL 618-993-1711; Ed. Ken Fazzari Pub. Howard Kaiser; adv. contact: Richard Beadle. photos; pub. size: broadsheet; circ. evening 9,784(paid); Sun. 12,067(paid). **Wire Service(s):** AP.

SOUTH HAVEN

US

SOUTH HAVEN DAILY TRIBUNE. 1899. Mon.-Fri. $.50 newsstand; $82/yr. mailed local; $88/yr. mailed out of area. 950 Bailey Ave., Ste. 4, South Haven, MI 49090. TEL 616-637-1104; FAX 616-637-8415. **Owner(s):** American Publishing Co., 606 N. Van Buren, P.O. Box 520, Marion, IL 62959. TEL 618-993-1711; Ed. Cathy Sisson; Pub. Michael Eastman; adv.; pub. size: broadsheet; circ. morning 2,500(paid). **Wire Service(s):** AP.

ST. JOSEPH

US   ISSN 0387-4400

HERALD-PALLADIUM. 1858. d. $.50/day newsstand; $1.25/Sun.; $135.20/yr. in state mailed. 3450 Hollywood Rd., St. Joseph, MI 49085. TEL 616-429-2400; FAX 616-429-7661. **Owner(s):** Herald-Palladium, The, P.O. Box 128, St. Joseph, MI 49085. TEL 616-429-2400; FAX 616-429-7661; Ed. Steve Pepple; Pub. Charles L. Casner; adv.; photos; pub. size: broadsheet; circ. evening 33,140(paid); Sun. 33,663(paid). **Wire Service(s):** AP.

STURGIS

US   ISSN 0747-3230

STURGIS JOURNAL. 1859. Mon.-Sat. $.50 newsstand; $81/yr. carrier; $90/yr. motor rte.; $10/mo. mailed. 209 John St., Sturgis, MI 49091. TEL 616-651-5407; FAX 616-651-2296; E-mail: journal@sturgisjournal.com; URL: http://www.sturgisjournal.com. **Owner(s):** Independent Media Group, Watseka, IL; Ed. Candice Phelps; Pub. Rich Piatt; adv.; pub. size: broadsheet; circ. evening 8,200(paid). **Wire Service(s):** AP, GNS.

THREE RIVERS

US

THREE RIVERS COMMERCIAL-NEWS. 1895. Mon.-Sat. $.50 newsstand $7/mo. 124 N. Main St., Three Rivers, MI 49093. TEL 616-279-7488; FAX 616-279-6007. **Owner(s):** Three Rivers Commercial, Inc., 124 N. Main St., Three Rivers, MI 49093. TEL 616-279-7488; Ed. Joseph K. Albertson; Pub. Richard L. Milliman, II; adv.; photos; pub. size: broadsheet; circ. evening 5,000(paid). **Wire Service(s):** AP.

TRAVERSE CITY

US

TRAVERSE CITY RECORD-EAGLE. 1904. d. $.50/day newsstand; $1.50/Sun.; $138.75/yr. in cy. 120 W. Front St., Traverse City, MI 49684. TEL 616-946-2000; FAX 616-946-8273. **Owner(s):** Ottaway Newspapers, Inc., P.O. Box 401, Campbell Hall, NY 10916. TEL 914-294-8181; Ed. John Tune; Pub. Frank B. Senger; adv.; photos; bk.rev.; pub. size: broadsheet; circ. morning 26,000(paid); Sun. 37,000(paid). **Wire Service(s):** AP, DJ, ONS.

UTICA

US

ADVISOR/SOURCE. 1972. Sun.-Tue. & Thu. $.50 newsstand; $26/yr. mailed locally. 48075 Van Dyke Ave., Utica, MI 48317. TEL 810-731-1000; FAX 810-781-8172. **Owner(s):** Independent Newspapers, Inc., 48075 Van Dyke Ave., Utica, MI 48317. TEL 313-731-1000; Ed. Gary Winkleman. adv. contact: Phil Marien. pub. size: broadsheet; circ. morning 113,500(paid).

MINNESOTA

ALBERT LEA

US   ISSN 1051-7421

ALBERT LEA TRIBUNE. 1897. Sun.-Fri. $.50/day newsstand; $1.25/Sun.; $9.50/mo. carrier. 808 W. Front St., Albert Lea, MN 56007. TEL 507-373-1411; FAX 507-373-0333. **Owner(s):** Boone Newspapers, Inc., P.O. Box 2370, Tuscaloosa, AL 35403. TEL 407-338-3298; Ed. Floyd Jernigan; Pub. Robert W. Brincefield; adv.; pub. size: broadsheet; circ. evening 7,300(paid); Sun. 8,500(paid). **Wire Service(s):** AP.

AUSTIN

US   ISSN 0746-9713

AUSTIN DAILY HERALD. Sun.-Fri. $.50/day newsstand, $1.25/Sun.; $9.55/mo. carrier; $9.75/mo. motor rte. or mailed. 310 Second St., N.E., Austin, MN 55912. TEL 507-433-8851; FAX 507-437-8644. **Owner(s):** Boone Newspapers, Inc., P.O. Box 2370, Tuscaloosa, AL 35403. TEL 407-338-3298; Pub. David Churchill; adv. contact: Eric Bishop. pub. size: broadsheet; circ. evening 8,000(paid); Sun. 8,000(paid). **Wire Service(s):** AP.

BEMIDJI

US   ISSN 0899-1812

PIONEER, THE. 1896. Sun.-Fri. $.50/day newsstand; $.75/Sun.; $8/mo. carrier. 1320 Neilson Ave., S.E., Bemidji, MN 56601. TEL 218-751-3740; FAX 218-751-6914. **Owner(s):** Park Communications, Inc., Vine Ctr. Office Tower, 333 W. Vine St., 17th Fl., Lexington, KY 40507. TEL 606-252-7275; Ed. Brad Swenson. adv. contact: Jeff Halvorsen. photos; pub. size: broadsheet; circ. morning 8,400(paid); Sun. 8,800(paid). **Wire Service(s):** AP.
Formerly: Bemidji Pioneer.

BRAINERD

US

BRAINERD DAILY DISPATCH. 1881. Sun.-Fri. $.50/day newsstand; $1.25/Sun; $102/yr. 506 James St., Brainerd, MN 56401. TEL 218-829-4705; FAX 218-829-7735; E-mail: dailyd@brainerd.net; URL: http://www.brainerddispatch.com. **Owner(s):** Morris Communications, P.O. Box 936, Augusta, GA 30903. TEL 706-721-0851; Ed. Roy Miller; Pub. Terry McCollough; adv. contact: Joe Smart. pub. size: broadsheet; circ. evening 14,108(paid); Sun. 16,943(paid). **Wire Service(s):** AP.

CROOKSTON

US

CROOKSTON DAILY TIMES. 1885. Mon.-Fri. $.50 newsstand; $1.75/wk. carrier; $24/3 mos. mailed in cy.; $35/3 mos. mailed MN, ND, & SD. 124 S. Broadway, Crookston, MN 56716. TEL 218-281-2730; FAX 218-281-7234. **Owner(s):** American Publishing Co., 606 N. Van Buren, P.O. Box 520, Marion, IL 62959. TEL 618-993-1711; Ed. Twylla Attepeter; Pub. Randal Hultgren; adv. contact: Michelle Rupchock. pub. size: broadsheet; circ. evening 4,600(paid). **Wire Service(s):** AP.

DULUTH

US   ISSN 0896-9418

DULUTH NEWS-TRIBUNE. 1870. d. $.50/day newsstand; $1.50/Sun.; $3.05/wk. carrier. 424 W. First St., Duluth, MN 55802. TEL 218-723-5281; FAX 218-723-4120; E-mail: mnduh@gif.com. **Owner(s):** Knight-Ridder, Inc., One Herald Plz., Miami, FL 33132. TEL 305-376-3800; Ed. Craig Gemoules; Pub. Jim Gels; adv.; pub. size: broadsheet; circ. morning 64,000(paid); Sun. 84,000(paid). **Wire Service(s):** AP.

FAIRMONT

US   ISSN 0893-3804

FAIRMONT SENTINEL. 1874. Mon.-Sat. $.50 newsstand; $67/yr. carrier; $73/yr. mail; $94.95/yr. out of area. 64 Downtown Plz., Fairmont, MN 56031-0681. TEL 507-235-3303; FAX 507-235-3718; E-mail: sentnews@rconnect.com; URL: http://www.oweb.com/sentinel. **Owner(s):** Ogden Newspapers, Inc., 1500 Main St., Wheeling, WV 26033. TEL 304-233-0100; Pub. Bryan Welch; adv. contact: Gary Andersen. pub. size: broadsheet; circ. morning 10,100(paid). **Wire Service(s):** AP.

FARIBAULT

US   ISSN 0889-8898

FARIBAULT DAILY NEWS. 1914. Tue.-Sun. $.50 newsstand; $85.25/yr. 514 Central Ave., N., Faribault, MN 55021. TEL 507-334-1853; FAX 507-334-8569. **Owner(s):** Huckle Publishing, Inc., 6291 Peninsula Dr., Traverse City, MI 49684. TEL 616-929-3571; Ed. Lisa Schwarz; Pub. David Balcom; adv. contact: Paula Patton. pub. size: broadsheet; circ. evening 7,800(paid). **Wire Service(s):** AP.

FERGUS FALLS

US

DAILY JOURNAL, THE. 1873. Mon.-Sat. $.50 newsstand; $8.25/mo. carrier & motor rte.; $7.25/mo. mailed in cy.; $8/mo. mailed out of cy.; $10/mo. mailed out of state. 914 E. Channing, Fergus Falls, MN 56537. TEL 218-736-7511; FAX 218-736-5919. **Owner(s):** Boone Newspapers, Inc., P.O. Box 2370, Tuscaloosa, AL 35403. TEL 407-338-3298; Ed. Richard Hensley; Pub. James Morgan; adv. contact: Doug Phares. bk.rev.; pub. size: broadsheet; circ. evening 10,500(paid). **Wire Service(s):** AP.
Formerly: Fergus Falls Daily Journal.

HIBBING

US   ISSN 1075-4040

HIBBING DAILY TRIBUNE. 1894. d. $.50/day newsstand; $1/Sun.; $2.52/wk. carrier & motor rte. 2142 First Ave., Hibbing, MN 55746. TEL 218-262-1011; FAX 218-262-4318. **Owner(s):** Murphy-McGinnis Media, 1226 Ogden Ave., Superior, WI 54880. TEL 715-394-4411; Ed. Pat Faherty; Pub. John Murphy; adv. contact: Terry Backstrom. photos; pub. size: broadsheet; circ. evening 10,000(paid); Sun. 18,000(paid). **Wire Service(s):** AP.

INTERNATIONAL FALLS

US

DAILY JOURNAL, THE. 1920. Mon.-Fri. $.50 newsstand; $80.40/yr. carrier. 500 Third St., International Falls, MN 56649. TEL 218-285-7411; FAX 218-285-7206. **Owner(s):** North Star Publishing Co., 500 Third St., International Falls, MN 56649. TEL 218-285-7411; Ed. Tom Klein; Pub. Arlin Albrecht; adv. contact: Harry Swendsen. photos; bk.rev.; pub. size: broadsheet; circ. evening 4,500(paid). **Wire Service(s):** AP.
   Formerly: International Falls Daily Journal.

MANKATO

US   ISSN 0893-3715

FREE PRESS. 1887. Mon.-Sat. $.50/day newsstand; $2.20/wk. carrier; $2.35/wk. motor rte.; $2.75/wk. mailed. 418 S. Second St., Mankato, MN 56001. TEL 507-625-4451; FAX 507-388-4355; E-mail: freepress@ic.mankato.mn.us; URL: http://www.mankato-freepress.com. **Owner(s):** Ottaway Newspapers, Inc., P.O. Box 401, Campbell Hall, NY. TEL 914-294-8181; Ed. Michael Larson; Pub. E. Joe Vanderhoof; adv.; pub. size: broadsheet; circ. evening 26,500(paid). Wire Service(s): AP, LAT-WP.

MARSHALL

US

MARSHALL INDEPENDENT. 1873. Mon.-Sat. $.50 newsstand; $71.50/yr. local; $96/yr. out of state. 508 W. Main St., Marshall, MN 56258. TEL 507-537-1551. **Owner(s):** Ogden Newspapers, Inc., 1500 Main St., Wheeling, WV 26033. TEL 304-233-0100; Ed. Jim Tate; Pub. Russ Labate; adv. contact: Connie Nuese. pub. size: broadsheet; circ. morning 9,300(paid). **Wire Service(s):** AP.

MINNEAPOLIS

US   ISSN 0895-2825

STAR TRIBUNE. 1867. d. $.35/day newsstand; $1.75/Sun.; $6.45/wk.; $335.40/yr. mailed. 425 Portland Ave., Minneapolis, MN 55488. TEL 612-673-4000; FAX 612-673-4359; E-mail: letters@startribune.com; URL: http://www.startribune.com. **Owner(s):** Cowles Media Co., 329 Portland Ave., Minneapolis, MN 55488. TEL 612-673-7100; FAX 612-673-7020; Ed. Pam Fine; Pub. Joel Kramer; adv.; pub. size: standard; circ. morning 388,120(paid); Sun. 682,318(paid). **Wire Service(s):** AP, NYT, LAT-WP, SHNA.

NEW ULM

US

JOURNAL, THE. 1900. d. $.50/day newsstand; $1/Sun.; $7/4 wks. carrier or motor rte. 303 N. Minnesota St., New Ulm, MN 56073-0487. TEL 507-359-2911; FAX 507-359-7362. **Owner(s):** Ogden Newspapers, Inc., 1500 Main St., Wheeling, WV 26003. TEL 304-233-0100; Ed. Kevin Sweeney; Pub. Bruce Fenske; adv. contact: Mike Stahl. pub. size: broadsheet; circ. morning 10,400(paid); Sun. 10,400(paid). **Wire Service(s):** AP.

OWATONNA

US   ISSN 0890-2860

OWATONNA PEOPLE'S PRESS. 1874. Tue.-Sun. $.50 newsstand; $96.75/yr. 135 W. Pearl St., Owatonna, MN 55060. TEL 507-451-2840; FAX 507-451-6020. **Owner(s):** Huckle Publishing, Inc., P.O. Box 346, Owatonna, MN 55060. TEL 507-451-2840; Ed. Tom Head; Pub. Ken Lyman; adv. contact: Holly Westercamp. bk.rev.; pub. size: broadsheet; circ. morning 8,000(paid); Sun. 8,000(paid). **Wire Service(s):** AP.

RED WING

US

RED WING REPUBLICAN EAGLE. 1857. Mon.-Sat. $.50 newsstand; $97/yr. 2760 N. Service Dr., Red Wing, MN 55066-0082. TEL 612-388-8235; FAX 612-388-8912. **Owner(s):** Red Wing Publishing Co., 2760 N. Service Dr., Red Wing, MN 55066. TEL 612-388-3128; FAX 612-388-8912; Ed. James Pumarlo; Pub. Arlin Albrecht; adv. contact: Vickie Winge. photos; bk.rev.; pub. size: broadsheet; circ. morning 8,450(paid). **Wire Service(s):** AP.

ROCHESTER

US

POST-BULLETIN. 1925. Mon.-Sat. $.50/day newsstand; $1.75/Sun.; $37.70/13 wks. in city; $49.95/13 wks. rural deliv. 18 First Ave., S.E., Rochester, MN 55904. TEL 507-285-7600; FAX 507-285-7772. **Owner(s):** Post-Bulletin Co., 18 First Ave. S.E., Rochester, MN 55904. TEL 507-285-7600; Ed. John Losness; Pub. William C. Boyne; adv. contact: Norm Doty. photos; bk.rev.; pub. size: broadsheet; circ. evening 41,300(paid). **Wire Service(s):** AP, NYT, KR.
   Formerly: Rochester Post-Bulletin.

ST. CLOUD

US   ISSN 0899-5028

ST. CLOUD TIMES. 1861. d. $.50/day newsstand; $1.50/Sun.; $39/3 mos. carrier; $42.90/3 mos. motor rte.; $48.75/3 mos. mail in state; $65/3 mos. mail out-of-state. 3000 Seventh St. N., St. Cloud, MN 56303. TEL 612-255-8700; FAX 612-255-8704. **Owner(s):** Gannett Company, Inc., 1100 Wilson Blvd., Arlington, VA 22234. TEL 703-284-6000; Ed. John Bodette; Pub. Sonja Sorensen Craig; adv. contact: Rhonda Barlow. pub. size: broadsheet; circ. evening 30,000(paid); Sun. 40,000(paid). **Wire Service(s):** AP, GNS.

STILLWATER

US

STILLWATER GAZETTE. 1870. Mon.-Fri. $.35 newsstand; $96/yr. mailed. 102 S. Second St., Stillwater, MN 55082. TEL 612-439-3130; FAX 612-439-4713. **Owner(s):** American Publishing Co., 606 N. Van Buren, P.O. Box 520, Marion, IL 62959. TEL 613-993-1711; Ed. Rod Aniland; Pub. Mike Mahoney; adv. contact: John Lund. photos; pub. size: broadsheet; circ. evening 4,200(free & paid). **Wire Service(s):** AP.

ST. PAUL

US   ISSN 1050-0405

ST. PAUL PIONEER PRESS. 1849. d. $.30/day newsstand; $1.50/Sun.; $3.30/wk. carrier; $4/wk. mail. 345 Cedar St., St. Paul, MN 55101. TEL 612-222-5011; FAX 612-228-5382; E-mail lundy@pioneerplanet.infi.net URL: http://www.pioneerplanet.com. **Owner(s):** Knight-Ridder, Inc., One Herald Plz., Miami, FL 33132. TEL 305-376-3800; Ed. Ken Doctor; Pub. Peter Ridder; adv.; bk.rev.; pub. size: broadsheet; circ. morning 212,000(paid); Sun. 276,055(paid).

VIRGINIA

US

MESABI DAILY NEWS. 1893. d. $.50/day newsstand; $1.50/Sun.; $16.50/6 wks. carrier; $17.10/6 wks. motor rte.; $35.75/13 wks. mailed. 704 Seventh Ave. S., Virginia, MN 55792. TEL 218-741-5544; FAX 218-741-1005. **Owner(s):** Mesabi Publishing Co., P.O. Box 956, Virginia, MN 55792. TEL 218-741-5544; Ed. Bill Hanna. adv. contact: Chris Knight. pub. size: broadsheet; circ. morning 12,245(paid); Sun. 22,165(paid). **Wire Service(s):** UPI.

WILLMAR

US

WEST CENTRAL TRIBUNE. 1895. Mon.-Sat. $.50 newsstand; $91/yr. carrier; $99/yr. mail. 2208 W. Trott Ave., Willmar, MN 56201-0839. TEL 612-235-1150; FAX 612-235-6769. **Owner(s):** Forum Communications, Inc., Fargo, ND; Ed. Paul E. London; Pub. Paul E. London; adv. contact: Marilyn Birkland. photos; bk.rev.; pub. size: broadsheet; circ. morning 17,500(paid). **Wire Service(s):** AP.

WINONA

US   ISSN 0273-9941

WINONA DAILY NEWS. 1855. c. $147.80/yr. 601 Franklin St., Winona, MN 55987. TEL 507-453-3519; FAX 507-454-1440. **Owner(s):** Lee Enterprises, Inc., 130 E. Second St., Davenport, IA 52801. TEL 313-383-2202; Ed. Jim Galewski; Pub. Howard Hoffmaster; adv.; photos; pub. size: standard; circ. morning 13,416(paid); Sun. 14,363(paid). **Wire Service(s):** AP.

WORTHINGTON

US

WORTHINGTON DAILY GLOBE. 1872. d. $.50 newsstand; $90/yr.; $99.50/yr. mailed; $112.50/yr. mailed out of area. 300 11th St., Worthington, MN 56187. TEL 507-376-9711; FAX 507-376-5202. **Owner(s):** Forum Communications, Inc., P.O. Box 2020, Fargo, ND 58207. TEL 701-223-7311; Ed. Dennis Hall; Pub. Dennis Hall; adv. contact: Denise McMillen. photos; pub. size: broadsheet; circ. morning 13,915(paid). **Wire Service(s):** AP, Thompson News Service.

MISSISSIPPI

BROOKHAVEN

US

BROOKHAVEN DAILY LEADER. 1883. Mon.-Fri. $6.25/mo.; $72/yr. 128 N. Railroad Ave., Brookhaven, MS 39601. TEL 601-833-6961; FAX 601-833-6714. **Owner(s):** Southwest Publishers, Inc., P.O. Box 551, Brookhaven, MS 39601. TEL 601-833-6961; Ed. William O. Jacobs; Pub. William O. Jacobs; adv. contact: Natalie Davis. pub. size: broadsheet; circ. evening 8,038(paid). **Wire Service(s):** AP.

CLARKSDALE

US

CLARKSDALE PRESS REGISTER. 1865. Mon.-Sat. $.50 newsstand; $6/mo.; $66/yr. 123 Second St., Clarksdale, MS 38614. TEL 601-627-2201; FAX 601-624-5125. **Owner(s):** Delta Publishing Co., Inc., 123 Second St., Clarksdale, MS 38614. TEL 601-627-2201; Ed. Clyde K. Burson; Pub. John O. Emmerich; adv. contact: Joann Stevens. pub. size: broadsheet; circ. morning 7,675(paid). **Wire Service(s):** AP.

CLEVELAND

US

CLEVELAND BOLIVAR COMMERCIAL. 1917. Mon.-Fri. $.50 newsstand; $5.50/mo. carrier & motor rte.; $6.50/mo. mailed. 821 N. Chrisman, Cleveland, MS 38732. TEL 601-843-4241; FAX 601-843-1830. **Owner(s):** Walls Newspapers, Inc., P.O. Box 530447, Birmingham, AL 35253. TEL 205-870-1684; Ed. Wayne Nicholas; Pub. Norman Van Liew; adv. contact: Ricky Nobile. pub. size: broadsheet; circ. evening 8,500(paid). **Wire Service(s):** AP.

COLUMBUS

US   ISSN 0746-7729

COMMERCIAL DISPATCH, THE. 1879. Sun.-Fri. $.25/day newsstand; $.75/Sun.; $84/yr. 516 Main St., Columbus, MS 39701-0511. TEL 601-328-2427; FAX 601-329-8937. **Owner(s):** Commercial Dispatch, Inc., 516 Main St., Columbus, OH 39701-0511. TEL 601-328-2427; FAX 601-329-8937; Ed. Birney Imes; Pub. Birney Imes; adv. contact: Gary Peeples. photos; bk.rev.; pub. size: broadsheet; circ. evening 14,836(paid); Sun. 15,980(paid). **Wire Service(s):** AP.

CORINTH

US

DAILY CORINTHIAN. 1895. Mon.-Fri. $.50 newsstand; $18/3 mos. carrier & motor rte.; $26/3 mos. mailed. 1607 S. Harper Rd., Corinth, MS 38834. TEL 601-287-6111; FAX 601-827-3525. **Owner(s):** Paxton Media Group, Inc., P.O. Box 2300, Paducah, KY 42002. TEL 502-443-1771; Ed. Mark Boehler; Pub. Tom Overton; adv. contact: Jim Burnett. pub. size: standard; circ. evening 9,400(paid). **Wire Service(s):** UPI.

Formerly: Corinth Daily Corinthian.

GREENVILLE

US

DELTA DEMOCRAT-TIMES. 1868. Sun.-Fri. $.35/day newsstand; $1/Sun.; $7.50/mo. 988 N. Broadway, Greenville, MS 38701. TEL 601-335-1155; FAX 601-335-2860. **Owner(s):** Freedom Communications, Inc., 1055 N. Main St., Ste. 901, Santa Ana, CA 92701. TEL 714-542-4415; Pub. Vernon L. DeBolt; adv. contact: Jim Kennedy. photos; bk.rev.; pub. size: standard; circ. evening 13,100(paid); Sun. 13,900(paid). **Wire Service(s):** AP.

GREENWOOD

US   ISSN 0884-4569

GREENWOOD COMMONWEALTH. 1896. Sun.-Fri. $.35/day newsstand, $1/Sun.; $7.50/mo. carrier city, $8/mo. rural carrier; $27/3 mos. mailed out of area. 329 Hwy. 82 W., Greenwood, MS 38930. TEL 601-453-5312; FAX 601-453-2908. **Owner(s):** Emmerich Newspapers, Inc., P.O. Box 8050, Greenwood, MS 38935-8050. TEL 601-453-5312; FAX 601-453-2908; Ed. Tim Kalich; Pub. Tim Kalich; adv. contact: Larry Alderman. pub. size: broadsheet; circ. evening 8,859(paid); Sun. 9,017(paid). **Wire Service(s):** AP, NYT.

GRENADA

US   ISSN 1066-7512

DAILY SENTINEL-STAR, THE. Mon.-Fri. $.50 newsstand; $5.75/mo. carrier. 158 S. Green St., Grenada, MS 38901. TEL 601-226-4321; FAX 601-226-8310. **Owner(s):** Grenada Newspapers, Inc., P.O. Box 907, Grenada, MS 38901. TEL 601-226-4321; Ed. Terri Ferguson; Pub. Joe Lee, III; pub. size: standard; circ. evening 5,200(paid). **Wire Service(s):** UPI.

Formerly: Grenada Daily Sentinel-Star.

GULFPORT

US

SUN HERALD, THE. 1884. d. $.50/day newsstand; $1.25/Sun.; $11.75/mo. 205 DeBuys Rd., Gulfport, MS 39507. TEL 601-896-2100; FAX 601-896-2104; E-mail: mtonos@sunherald.infi.net; URL: http://www.sunherald.com. **Owner(s):** Knight-Ridder, Inc., One Herald Plz., Miami, FL 33132. TEL 305-376-3800; Ed. Andrea Yaeger; Pub. Roland Weeks; adv. contact: Stone Ellis. bk.rev.; pub. size: broadsheet; circ. morning 49,059(paid); Sun. 54,980(paid). **Wire Service(s):** AP, KR.

HATTIESBURG

US

HATTIESBURG AMERICAN. 1885. d. $.35/day newsstand; $1.25/Sun.; $11/mo. 825 N. Main St., Hattiesburg, MS 39401. TEL 601-582-4321; FAX 601-583-8244. **Owner(s):** Gannett Company, Inc., 1100 Wilson Blvd., Arlington, VA 22234. TEL 703-284-6000; Ed. Ronnie Agnew; Pub. David B. Petty; adv. contact: Rick Chapman. photos; bk.rev.; pub. size: broadsheet; circ. evening 28,000(paid); Sun. 30,000(paid). **Wire Service(s):** AP, GNS.

JACKSON

US   ISSN 0744-9526

CLARION-LEDGER, THE. 1837. d. $.50/day newsstand; $1.50/Sun.; $13.50/mo. carrier; $19.50/mo. in state mailed; $21.50/mo. out of state mailed. 201 Congress St., Jackson, MS 39205. TEL 601-961-7000; FAX 601-961-7211. **Owner(s):** Gannett Company, Inc., 1100 Wilson Blvd., Arlington, VA 22234. TEL 703-284-6000; Ed. Margaret Downing; Pub. Duane McCallister; adv. contact: David Enstad. photos; bk.rev.; pub. size: broadsheet; circ. morning 109,858(paid); Sun. 128,709(paid). **Wire Service(s):** AP, KR, NYT.

LAUREL

US

LAUREL LEADER-CALL. 1911. d. $.35/day newsstand; $.75/Sun. 130 Beacon St., Laurel, MS 39440. TEL 601-428-0551; FAX 601-426-3550. **Owner(s):** American Publishing Co., 606 N. Van Buren, P.O. Box 520, Marion, IL 62959. TEL 618-993-1711; Ed. Hal Marx; Pub. Paul Barrett; adv. contact: Crystal Dupre. pub. size: broadsheet; circ. evening 10,515(paid). **Wire Service(s):** AP.

MCCOMB

US

MCCOMB ENTERPRISE-JOURNAL. 1889. Sun.-Fri. $.50/day newsstand; $1/Sun.; $8/mo. Oliver Emmerich Dr., McComb, MS 39648. TEL 601-684-2421; FAX 601-684-0836. **Owner(s):** J.O. Emmerich & Associates, Inc., Oliver Emmerich Dr., McComb, MS 39648. TEL 601-684-2421; FAX 601-684-0836; Ed. Jack Ryan; Pub. John O. Emmerich; adv. contact: Deborah W. Bean. pub. size: broadsheet; circ. evening 12,000(paid); Sun. 12,000(paid). **Wire Service(s):** AP.

MERIDIAN

US   ISSN 1064-9549

MERIDIAN STAR. 1896. d. $.50/day newsstand; $1.25/Sun.; $9.75/mo. carrier & motor rte.; $14/mo. mailed. 814 22nd Ave., Meridian, MS 39301. TEL 601-693-1551; FAX 601-485-1275. **Owner(s):** American Publishing Co., 606 N. Van Buren, P.O. Box 520, Marion, IL 62959. TEL 618-993-1711; Ed. Steve Swogetinsky; Pub. Ed Darling; adv. contact: Mike Lee. pub. size: standard; circ. evening 21,000(paid); Sun. 23,000(paid). **Wire Service(s):** AP, KR, NEA.

NATCHEZ

US   ISSN 0888-8744

NATCHEZ DEMOCRAT. 1865. d. $.50/day newsstand; $1.25/Sun.; $144/yr. carrier. 503 N. Canal St., Natchez, MS 39120. TEL 601-442-9101; FAX 601-442-9101. **Owner(s):** Boone Newspapers, Inc., P.O. Box 2370, Tuscaloosa, AL 35403. TEL 407-338-3298; Ed. Jimmy Sexton; Pub. Kenneth S. Boone; adv. contact: Brian Pierpont. pub. size: broadsheet; circ. morning 13,500(paid); Sun. 14,000(paid). **Wire Service(s):** AP.

OXFORD

US

OXFORD EAGLE. 1867. Mon.-Fri. $.35 newsstand; $5.25/mo. motor rte.; $19.50/3 mos. mailed. 916 Jackson Ave., Oxford, MS 38655. TEL 601-234-4331; FAX 601-234-4351. **Owner(s):** Oxford Eagle, Inc., 916 Jackson Ave., Oxford, MS 38655; Ed. Nina B. Goolsby; Pub. Jesse P. Phillips; adv. contact: Sandra Leake. pub. size: broadsheet; circ. evening 6,000(paid). **Wire Service(s):** AP.

PASCAGOULA

US   ISSN 1059-7166

MISSISSIPPI PRESS. 1964. Sun.-Fri. $.25/day newsstand, $1/Sun.; $5.30/mo. Mon.-Fri.; $5.35/mo. Sun.; $8/mo. daily & Sun. 405 Delmas Ave., Pascagoula, MS 39567. TEL 601-934-1408; FAX 601-934-1454. **Owner(s):** Advance Publications, Inc., 485 Lexington Ave., New York, NY 10017; Ed. Gary Holland; Pub. Wanda Henry Jacobs; adv.; photos; bk.rev.; pub. size: broadsheet; circ. evening 22,493(paid); Sun. 23,672(paid). **Wire Service(s):** AP, CST, NNS.
Formerly: Mississippi Press Register.

PICAYUNE

US

PICAYUNE ITEM. 1926. Tue.-Fri. & Sun. $.50/day newsstand; $.75/Sun. 214 N. Curran Ave., Picayune, MS 39466. TEL 601-798-4766; FAX 601-798-8602. **Owner(s):** Stephens Group, Inc., P.O. Box 17017, Fort Smith, AR 72914-7017. TEL 501-785-7810; Ed. Will Sullivan; Pub. Dave Simms; adv. contact: Tom Andrews. pub. size: standard; circ. morning 5,956(paid); Sun. 7,339(paid).

STARKVILLE

US   ISSN 1044-3657

STARKVILLE DAILY NEWS. 1901. d. $.35/day newsstand; $1/Sun.; $77/yr. home deliv. 316 University Dr., Starkville, MS 39759. TEL 601-323-1642; FAX 601-323-6586. **Owner(s):** American Publishing Co., 606 N. Van Buren, P.O. Box 520, Marion, IL 62959. TEL 618-993-1711; Ed. Pattye Archer; Pub. Rick Noffsinger; adv. contact: Suzanne Reed. pub. size: broadsheet; circ. morning 6,900(paid). **Wire Service(s):** AP.

TUPELO

US   ISSN 0744-5431

NORTHEAST MISSISSIPPI DAILY JOURNAL. 1870. d. $.50/daily; $1/Sun.; $8.90/mo. carrier; $9.55/mo. in state mailed. 1655 S. Green St., Tupelo, MS 38801-6557. TEL 601-842-2611; FAX 601-842-2233; E-mail: djuser@djournal.com; URL: http://www.djournal.com. **Owner(s):** Journal Publishing Co. P.O. Box 909, Tupelo, MS 38802. TEL 601-842-2611; Ed. Charlotte Wolfe; Pub. Billy Crews; adv. contact: Richard Crenshaw. pub. size: broadsheet; circ. morning 38,000(paid); Sun. 36,475(paid). **Wire Service(s):** AP, KR.

VICKSBURG

US   ISSN 0884-8912

VICKSBURG POST. 1883. d. $.50/day newsstand; $1.25/Sun.; $10.50/mo. home deliv. 920 South St., Vicksburg, MS 39180. TEL 601-636-4545; FAX 601-634-0897; E-mail: staff@vicksburgpost.com; URL: http://www.vicksburgpost.com. **Owner(s):** Vicksburg Printing & Publishing Co., 920 South St., Vicksburg, MS 39180. TEL 601-636-4545; FAX 601-634-0897; Ed. Charles D. Mitchell; Pub. Louis P. Cashman, II; adv. contact: David Gills. photos; bk.rev.; pub. size: broadsheet; circ. evening 15,869(paid); Sun. 16,283(paid). **Wire Service(s):** AP.
Formerly: Vicksburg Evening/Sunday Post.

WEST POINT

US

DAILY TIMES LEADER. 1929. Tue.-Fri. & Sun. $.35 newsstand; $74/yr. carrier. 227 Court West Point, West Point, MS 39773. TEL 601-494-1422; FAX 601-494-1414. **Owner(s):** American Publishing Co., 606 N. Van Buren, P.O. Box 520, Marion, IL 62959. TEL 618-993-1711; Ed. Floyd Ingram; Pub. Rick Noffsinger; adv. contact: Joyce Pierce. pub. size: broadsheet; circ. morning 4,000(paid).

MISSOURI

BLUE SPRINGS

US

BLUE SPRINGS EXAMINER. 1974. Mon.-Sat. $.50/day newsstand; $.75/Sat.; $7.90/yr. carrier. 500 W. RD Mize Rd., Blue Springs, MO 64015. TEL 816-229-9161; FAX 816-224-7245. **Owner(s):** Morris Communications, P.O. Box 936, Augusta, GA 30903. TEL 706-724-0851; Ed. Dale Brendel; Pub. Kevin Kampman; pub. size: broadsheet; circ. morning 6,500(paid). **Wire Service(s):** AP.

BOONVILLE

US

BOONVILLE DAILY NEWS. 1919. Mon.-Fri. $.50 newsstand; $10.67/mo.; $26.68/3 mos. 412 High St., Boonville, MO 65233. TEL 816-882-5335; FAX 816-882-2256. **Owner(s):** American Publishing Co., 606 N. Van Buren, P.O. Box 520, Marion, IL 62959. TEL 618-993-1711; Ed. Steve Thomas; Pub. Scott J. Jackson; adv. contact: Angela Inscore. pub. size: broadsheet; circ. evening 3,200(paid). **Wire Service(s):** AP.

BROOKFIELD

US

DAILY NEWS-BULLETIN, THE. 1879. Mon.-Fri. $.50 newsstand; $5.07/mo. carrier; $37.35/yr. carrier; $38.42/yr. mailed in cy.; $56.56/yr. mailed out of cy. 107-109 N. Main, Brookfield, MO 64628. TEL 816-258-7237 FAX 816-258-7238. **Owner(s):** American Publishing Co., 606 N. Van Buren, P.O. Box 520, Marion, IL 62959. TEL 618-993-1711; Ed. Greg Orear; Pub. Susan Abeln; adv. contact: Richard E. Abeln, Sr. photos; pub. size: broadsheet; circ. evening 3,500(free & paid). **Wire Service(s):** AP.

CAMDENTON

US   ISSN 1063-7001

LAKE SUN LEADER. 1879. Mon.-Fri. $.50 newsstand; $75.50/yr. carrier; $78/yr. mailed in state; $85/yr. mailed out of state. 450 N. Hwy. 5, Camdenton, MO 65020. TEL 314-346-2132; FAX 314-346-4508; E-mail: newsdude@is.usmo.com; URL: http://www.odd.net/lsl. **Owner(s):** American Publishing Co., 606 N. Van Buren, P.O. Box 520, Marion, IL 62959. TEL 618-993-1711; Ed. Mike Feeback; Pub. Tom Turner. adv. contact: Lisa Miller. pub. size: broadsheet; circ. evening 6,102(paid). **Wire Service(s):** AP.
Formerly: Reveille, The.

CAPE GIRARDEAU

US   ISSN 0746-4452

SOUTHEAST MISSOURIAN. 1904. d. $.50/day newsstand; $1.50/Sun. 301 Broadway, Cape Girardeau, MO 63701. TEL 314-335-6611; FAX 314-334-9258. **Owner(s):** Gary Rust, 301 Broadway, Cape Girardeau, MO 63701. TEL 314-335-9258; Ed. Joni Adams; Pub. Wally Lage; adv. contact: Pat Zellmer. pub. size: broadsheet; circ. evening 19,000(paid); Sun. 29,000(paid).

CARTHAGE

US

CARTHAGE PRESS. 1884. Mon.-Sat. $.50 newsstand; $22.33/qtr. 527 S. Main, Carthage, MO 64836. TEL 417-358-2191; FAX 417-358-7428. **Owner(s):** American Publishing Co., 606 N. Van Buren, P.O. Box 520, Marion, IL 62959. TEL 618-993-1711; Ed. Randy Turner; Pub. Jim Farley; adv. contact: Jim Farley. pub. size: standard; circ. evening 5,100(paid). **Wire Service(s):** AP.

CHILLICOTHE

US   ISSN 0746-8555

CHILLICOTHE CONSTITUTION-TRIBUNE. 1860. Mon.-Fri. $.50 newsstand; $94.99/yr. in cy.; $100.91/yr. out of cy.; $97.20/yr. out of state. 818 Washington, Chillicothe, MO 64601. TEL 816-646-2411; FAX 816-646-2028. **Owner(s):** American Publishing Co., 606 N. Van Buren, P.O. Box 520, Marion, IL 62959. TEL 618-993-1711; Ed. Charles Haney; Pub. Charles Haney; adv. contact: Rod Dixon. pub. size: broadsheet; circ. evening 4,700(paid). **Wire Service(s):** AP.

CLINTON

US

CLINTON DAILY DEMOCRAT. 1868. Mon.-Fri. $.50 newsstand; $48/yr. in cy.; $58.15/yr. out of cy.; $60/yr. out of state. 212 S. Washington St., Clinton, MO 64735. TEL 816-885-2281; FAX 816-885-2265. **Owner(s):** Democrat Publishing Co., 212 S. Washington St., Clinton, MO 64735. TEL 816-885-2281; FAX 816-885-2265; Ed. Daniel B. Miles, Jr.; Pub. K. White Miles; adv. contact: Kathleen Miles. pub. size: broadsheet; circ. evening 4,250(paid).

COLUMBIA

US

COLUMBIA DAILY TRIBUNE. 1901. d. $.50/day newsstand; $1/Sun.; $25.95/3 mo.; $49.75/6 mo.; $94/yr. 101 N. Fourth St., Columbia, MO 65201. TEL 314-449-3811; FAX 314-874-6413; E-mail: cdteditr@bigcat.missouri.edu; URL: http://www.trib.net. **Owner(s):** Tribune Publishing Co., 101 N. Fourth St., Columbia, MO 65201. TEL 314-449-3811; Ed. Jim Robertson; Pub. Henry J. Waters, III; adv. contact: Randall McMillan. pub. size: broadsheet; circ. evening 17,868(paid); Sun. 22,307(paid). **Wire Service(s):** AP, KR.

US   ISSN 0747-1874

COLUMBIA MISSOURIAN. 1908. Sun.-Fri. $.50/day newsstand; $.75/Sun.; $85/yr. 221 S. Eighth St., Columbia, MO 65201. TEL 314-882-5700; FAX 314-882-5702; E-mail: jourab@muccmail.missouri.edu; URL: http://digmo.org. **Owner(s):** Missourian Publishing Co., P.O. Box 917, Columbia, MO 65205. TEL 314-442-3161; Ed. George Kennedy; Pub. Dean Mills; adv. contact: Jack Swartz. pub. size: broadsheet; circ. morning 20,002; Sun. 26,500(paid). **Wire Service(s):** AP, NYT, SHNA.

DEXTER

US

DEXTER DAILY STATESMAN. 1898. Tue.-Fri. & Sun. $.50 newsstand; $61/yr. in cy. 33 S. Walnut, Dexter, MO 63841. TEL 314-624-4545; FAX 314-624-7449. **Owner(s):** Rust Communications, P.O. Box 699, Cape Girardeau, MO 63702-0699. TEL 314-335-6611; Ed. Debbie Renfro; Pub. Barbara Hill; adv. contact: Elaine Pursell. pub. size: broadsheet; circ. evening 5,000(paid); Sun. 5,000(paid). **Wire Service(s):** API.

US

STODDARD COUNTY NEWS. 5000. Tue., Wed., Fri. & Sun. $.50 newsstand; $65/yr. in cy. 133 S. Walnut, Dexter, MO 63841. TEL 314-624-4545. **Owner(s):** Rust Communications, P.O. Box 699, Cape Girardeau, MO 63702-0699. TEL 314-335-6611; Ed. Debbie Renfrow; Pub. Barbara Hill; pub. size: broadsheet; circ. evening 5,000(paid).

EXCELSIOR SPRINGS

US

DAILY STANDARD. 1889. Mon.-Fri. $.50 newsstand; $11.75/3 mo. carrier or mail; $14.25/3 mo. in cy.; $15.75/3 mo. out of cy. 417 Thompson, Excelsior Springs, MO 64024. TEL 816-637-3147; FAX 816-637-8411. **Owner(s):** Facklelman Publishers, LA. TEL 318-824-3011; FAX 318-824-6238; Ed. Gene Hanson; Pub. Jim Bouldin; adv. contact: Brian Rice. photos; bk.rev.; pub. size: broadsheet; circ. evening 3,000(paid). **Wire Service(s):** MissouriLink.
    Formerly: Excelsior Springs Daily Standard.

FARMINGTON

US   ISSN 1076-5832

PRESS LEADER, THE. 1950. Tue.-Sat. $.35 newsstand; $54/yr. carrier. 218 N. Washington St., Farmington, MO 63640. TEL 314-756-8927; FAX 314-756-9160; E-mail: rdennis@pressleader.com; URL: http://www.pressleader.com. **Owner(s):** American Publishing Co., 606 N. Van Buren, P.O. Box 520, Marion, IL 62959. TEL 618-993-1711; Ed. Mike Myers; Pub. Mark Griggs; pub. size: broadsheet; circ. 25,000(paid).
    Formerly: Farmington Press Greensheet.

FULTON

US   ISSN 8750-6696

FULTON SUN, THE. 1876. Tue.-Fri. & Sun. $.50 newsstand; $68.31/yr. carrier; $68.331/yr. mailed in ca; $81.82/yr. mailed in state; $86.32/yr. mailed out of cy & state; $77.68/yr. seniors. 115 E. Fifth St., Fulton, MO 65251. TEL 314-642-7272; FAX 314-642-0650. **Owner(s):** William H. Weldon, P.O. Box 420, Jefferson City, MO 65101. TEL 314-636-3131; Ed. John Egan; Pub. William H. Weldon; adv. contact: Kevin McDaniel. pub. size: broadsheet; circ. morning 5,200(paid). **Wire Service(s):** AP.

HANNIBAL

US

HANNIBAL COURIER-POST. 1838. Mon.-Sat. $.50 newsstand; $8/mo. carrier & motor rte; $12.50/mo. in state & elsewhere. 200 N. Third St., Hannibal, MO 63401. TEL 314-221-2800; FAX 314-221-1568. **Owner(s):** Morris Communications, P.O. Box 936, Augusta, GA 30903. TEL 706-724-0851; Ed. Jim Whitaker. adv. contact: Michelle Dent. pub. size: standard; circ. morning 10,000(paid). **Wire Service(s):** AP.

HOLLISTER

US

BRANSON DAILY NEWS. 1898. Tue.-Sun. $.50/day newsstand; $1/Sun.; $50/yr. in state; $55/yr. Sun. out of state; $140/yr. 6 days out of state. 200 Industrial Park Dr., Hollister, MO 65672. TEL 417-334-3161; FAX 417-334-4299. **Owner(s):** James Lancaster, P.O. Box 609, Gadsden, AL 35902; Pub. Ted Delaney; adv. contact: Sandy Wilkinson. pub. size: broadsheet; circ. morning 11,500(paid); Sun. 12,000(paid).
    Formerly: Taney County Republican.

INDEPENDENCE

US

INDEPENDENCE EXAMINER, THE. 1898. Mon.-Sat. $.50 newsstand; $.75/Sat.; $83.40/yr. carrier; $79.80/yr. out of town. 410 S. Liberty, Independence, MO 64050. TEL 816-254-8600; FAX 816-836-3805. **Owner(s):** Morris Communications, P.O. Box 936, Augusta, GA 30903. TEL 706-724-0851; Ed. Kate Lee; Pub. Ben Weir, Jr.; adv. contact: Irene Baltrusaitis. photos; bk.rev.; pub. size: broadsheet; circ. evening 21,087(paid). **Wire Service(s):** AP.

JEFFERSON CITY

US

POST-TRIBUNE. 1865. d. $.50 newsstand; $7.50/mo. 210 Monroe St., Jefferson City, MO 65101. TEL 314-636-3131; FAX 573-636-7035. **Owner(s):** News Tribune Co., P.O. Box 420, Jefferson City, MO 65101. TEL 314-636-3131; FAX 314-636-7035; Ed. Richard McGonegal; Pub. Mrs. William H. Weldon; adv. contact: Jim Ward. photos; bk.rev.; pub. size: standard; circ. evening 18,000(paid); Sun. 25,500(paid). **Wire Service(s):** AP, CNS, CQ, SHNA, NYT.

JOPLIN

US

JOPLIN GLOBE, THE. 1896. d. $.50/day newsstand; $1.50/Sun.; $141.83/yr. home deliv.; $161.76/yr. in state mailed; $175.74/yr. mailed. 117 E. Fourth St., Joplin, MO 64801. TEL 417-623-3480; FAX 417-623-8450. **Owner(s):** Ottaway Newspapers, Inc., P.O. Box 401, Campbell Hall, NY 10916. TEL 914-294-8181; Ed. Thomas P. Murray; Pub. Dan Chiodo; pub. size: broadsheet; circ. morning 36,340(paid); Sun. 45,995(paid). **Wire Service(s):** AP.

KANSAS CITY

US   ISSN 0745-1067

KANSAS CITY STAR. 1880. d. $.50/day newsstand, $1.50/Sun; $12.95/mo. carrier; $19.99/mo. mailed in state. 1729 Grand Blvd., Kansas City, MO 64108. TEL 816-234-4141; FAX 816-234-4926. **Owner(s):** Walt Disney Co., 500 S. Buena Vista St., Burbank, CA 91521. TEL 818-560-5300; Ed. Terrence Thompson; Pub. Bob Woodworth; adv.; photos; bk.rev.; pub. size: broadsheet; circ. morning 288,830(paid); Sun. 431,616(paid). **Wire Service(s):** NYT, AP, CDN, KR, LATS.

KENNETT

US   ISSN 1047-7160

DAILY DUNKLIN DEMOCRAT. 1888. Tue.-Fri. & Sun. $.50 newsstand; $5.50/mo carrier; $61/yr. carrier. 203 First St., Kennett, MO 63857. TEL 314-888-4505; FAX 314-888-5114. **Owner(s):** Delta Publishing Co., Inc., P.O. Box 669, Kennett, MO 63857. TEL 314-888-4505; Ed. Steve Gillespie; Pub. Bud Hunt; adv. contact: Terri Coleman. photos; bk.rev.; pub. size: standard; circ. evening 6,480(paid). **Wire Service(s):** AP.
    Formerly: Kennett Daily Dunklin Democrat.

KIRKSVILLE

US

KIRKSVILLE DAILY EXPRESS. 1915. Sun.-Fri. $.50/day newsstand; $.75/Sun. 110 E. McPherson St., Kirksville, MO 63501. TEL 816-665-2808; FAX 816-665-2608. **Owner(s):** Kirksville Publishing Co., 110 E. McPherson St., Kirksville, MO 63501. TEL 816-665-2808; Ed. Judy Tritz; Pub. Larry W. Freels; adv.; photos; bk.rev.; pub. size: broadsheet; circ. evening 7,400(paid); Sun. 7,900(paid). **Wire Service(s):** AP.

LEBANON

US

LEBANON DAILY RECORD. 1934. Sun.-Fri. $.50/day newsstand; $.75/Sun.; $58.29/yr. in cy.; $118.30/yr. in state; $125/yr. elsewhere. 290 S. Madison, Lebanon, MO 65536. TEL 417-532-9131; FAX 417-532-8140; E-mail: infoline@mail.llion.org; URL: http://www.llion.org/ldr/news.html. **Owner(s):** Dalton Wright, 290 S. Madison, Lebanon, MO 65536. TEL 417-532-9131; Ed. Steve Hilton; Pub. Steve Hilton; adv. contact: Rene Barker. bk.rev.; pub. size: broadsheet; circ. evening 5,281(paid); Sun. 5,642(paid). **Wire Service(s):** AP.

MACON

US

MACON CHRONICLE-HERALD. 1910. Tue.-Fri. $.50 newsstand; $10.71/mo. carrier. 217 W. Bourke, Macon, MO 63552. TEL 816-385-3121; FAX 816-385-3082. **Owner(s):** American Publishing Co., 606 N. Van Buren, P.O. Box 520, Marion, IL 62959. TEL 618-993-1711; Ed. Mark Snow; Pub. Bill Hall; adv. contact: Pat Quinly. pub. size: broadsheet; circ. evening 3,500(free). **Wire Service(s):** AP.

MARSHALL

US

MARSHALL DEMOCRAT-NEWS. 1881. Mon.-Fri. $.50 newsstand; $41.40/yr. in town. 121 N. Lafayette, Marshall, MO 65340. TEL 816-886-2233. **Owner(s):** U.S. Media Group, P.O. Box 227, Crystal City, MO 63019; Ed. Mary Jo Rieth; Pub. Shelly M. Arth; adv.; photos; bk.rev.; pub. size: broadsheet; circ. evening 4,300(paid). **Wire Service(s):** AP.

MARYVILLE

US

MARYVILLE DAILY FORUM. 1869. Tue.-Fri. & Sun. $.50/day newsstand; $.75/Sun.; $6.30/mo. 111 E. Jenkins, Maryville, MO 64468. TEL 816-562-2424; FAX 816-562-2823. **Owner(s):** Midland Media, Inc., 111 E. Jenkins, Maryville, MO 64468. TEL 816-562-2424; Ed. Steve Woolpolk; Pub. Jerry Pye; adv.; photos; bk.rev.; pub. size: broadsheet; circ. evening 4,225(paid); Sun. 4,361(paid). **Wire Service(s):** AP.

MEXICO

US

MEXICO LEDGER. 1855. d. $.50/day newsstand; $8/mo. 300 N. Washington, Ledger Plz., Mexico, MO 65265-0008. TEL 314-581-1111; FAX 314-581-2029. **Owner(s):** Hollinger, Inc.; Ed. Larry Nossaman; Pub. Joe May; adv. contact: Martin Keller. photos; bk.rev.; pub. size: broadsheet; circ. evening 10,000(paid). **Wire Service(s):** AP.

MOBERLY

US

MOBERLY MONITOR INDEX. 1869. Sun.-Fri. $.50/day newsstand; $.75/Sun.; $6/mo. carrier or mailed. 218 N. Williams St., Moberly, MO 65270. TEL 816-263-4123; FAX 816-263-3626. **Owner(s):** Stephens Group, Inc., 3600 Wheeler Ave., Fort Smith, AR 72901. TEL 501-785-7827; Ed. Ruth Carr; Pub. Bob Cunningham; adv. contact: Judy Orton. photos; bk.rev.; pub. size: standard; circ. evening 8,100(paid); Sun. 8,595(paid). **Wire Service(s):** AP.

MONETT

US

MONETT TIMES. 1888. Mon.-Fri. $.25 newsstand; $35/yr. carrier; $42/yr. mailed in cy.; $65.50/yr. out of cy.; $67.50/yr. out of state. 505 Broadway, Monett, MO 65708. TEL 417-235-3135; FAX 417-235-8852. **Owner(s):** Walls Newspapers, Inc., P.O. Box 530447, Birmingham, AL 35253. TEL 201-870-1684; Ed. Murray Bishoff; Pub. Stephen Crass; adv. contact: Mike Stubbs. pub. size: broadsheet; circ. evening 4,600(paid).

NEOSHO

US

NEOSHO DAILY NEWS. 1905. Sun.-Fri. $.50/day newsstand; $.75/Sun.; $7.50/mo. carrier. 1006 W. Harmony St., Neosho, MO 64850. TEL 417-451-1520; FAX 417-451-6408. **Owner(s):** American Publishing Co., 606 N. Van Buren, P.O. Box 520, Marion, IL 62959. TEL 618-993-1711; Ed. Christian Jackson; Pub. Valerie Praypor; adv. contact: Steve Praypor. pub. size: broadsheet; circ. evening 4,600(paid); Sun. 5,200(paid). **Wire Service(s):** AP.

NEVADA

US   ISSN 1056-3555

DAILY MAIL & SUNDAY HERALD. 1883. Tue.-Fri. & Sun. $.50 newsstand; $9/mo.; $75/yr. 131 S. Cedar St., Nevada, MO 64772. TEL 417-667-3344; FAX 417-667-8121. **Owner(s):** U.S. Media Group, P.O. Box 227, Crystal City, MO 63019. TEL 314-937-5200; FAX 314-937-7947; Ed. Jerome P. Curry. adv.; photos; bk.rev.; pub. size: broadsheet; circ. evening 4,500(paid); Sun. 4,800(paid). **Wire Service(s):** AP.

PARK HILLS

US

DAILY JOURNAL. Sun.-Fri. $.50/day newsstand, $.75/Sun. 1513 St. Joe Dr., Park Hills, MO 63601. TEL 314-431-2010; FAX 314-431-7640. **Owner(s):** Scripps League Newspapers, Inc., Eagle Hill P.O. Box 16 B, Charlottesville, VA 22901; Ed. Joseph Layden; Pub. Ron Weir; pub. size: broadsheet; circ. evening 10,300(paid) Sun. 10,300(paid). **Wire Service(s):** AP

POPLAR BLUFF

US   ISSN 1061-7116

DAILY AMERICAN REPUBLIC. 1923. Sun.-Fri. $.50/day newsstand; $1/Sun.; $82.50/yr. carrier; $144/yr. out of state. 208 Poplar St., Poplar Bluff, MO 63901. TEL 573-785-1414; FAX 573-785-2706. **Owner(s):** Butler County Publishing, 208 Poplar St., Poplar Bluff, MO 63901; Ed. Stan Berry; Pub. Don Schrieber; adv. contact: Joe Jordan. pub. size: broadsheet; circ. evening 15,000(paid); Sun. 22,000(paid). **Wire Service(s):** AP.

RICHMOND

US

DAILY NEWS. 1914. Mon.-Fri. $.50 newsstand; $51/yr. in cy.; $57/yr. in state; $57/yr. out of state. 204 W. North Main St., Richmond, MO 64085. TEL 816-776-5454; FAX 816-637-1639. **Owner(s):** Richmond News, Inc., The, 204 W. North Main St., P.O. Box 100, Richmond, MO 64085. TEL 816-776-5454; FAX 816-637-1639; Ed. Randy Roberts; Pub. Chris Sharp; adv. contact: Chris Sharp. photos; pub. size: broadsheet; circ. evening 12,888(free & paid).

ROLLA

US

ROLLA DAILY NEWS. 1942. Sun.-Fri. $.50/day newsstand; $.75/Sun.; $89/yr. carrier; $143.70/yr. out of cy.; $145/yr. out of state. 101 W. Seventh St., Rolla, MO 65401. TEL 314-364-2468; FAX 314-341-5847. **Owner(s):** American Publishing Co., 606 N. Van Buren, P.O. Box 520, Marion, IL 62959. TEL 618-993-1711; Ed. R.D. Hohenfeldt; Pub. Stephen E. Sowers; pub. size: standard; circ. evening 5,300(paid); Sun. 6,100(paid). **Wire Service(s):** UPI.

SEDALIA

US   ISSN 1061-1762

SEDALIA DEMOCRAT, THE. 1868. d. $.50/day newsstand; $1.25/Sun.; $109.20/yr. carrier. 700 S. Massachusetts, Sedalia, MO 65301. TEL 816-826-1000; FAX 816-826-2413. **Owner(s):** Freedom Communications, Inc., 1055 N. Main St., Ste. 901, Irvine, CA 92701. TEL 714-542-4415; Ed. John D. Hutchinson; Pub. Frank Lyon; adv. contact: Lisa A. Lynn. pub. size: broadsheet; circ. evening 13,723(paid); Sun. 14,455(paid). **Wire Service(s):** AF, KRT.

SIKESTON

US   ISSN 1074-4460

SIKESTON STANDARD DEMOCRAT, THE. 1913. Sun.-Fri. $.50/day newsstand; $1/Sun.; $8.40/mo. carrier; $84/r. carrier; $102.34/yr. mail out of state. 205 S. New Madrid, Sikeston, MO 63801. TEL 314-471-1137; FAX 314-471-6277. **Owner(s):** American Publishing Co., 606 N. Van Buren, P.O. Box 520, Marion, IL 62959. TEL 618-993-1711; Ed. Jill Bock; Pub. Michael Jensen; adv. contact: Deanna Nelson. pub. size: broadsheet; circ. morning 11,000(paid); Sun. 12,500(paid). **Wire Service(s):** AP.
Formerly: Standard Democrat.

SPRINGFIELD

US ISSN 0893-3448

SPRINGFIELD NEWS-LEADER, THE. 1867. d. $.50/day newsstand; $1.75/Sun.; $11.95/mo. carrier. 651 Boonville Ave., Springfield, MO 65806. TEL 417-836-1208; FAX 417-836-1147. **Owner(s):** Gannett Company, Inc., 1100 Wilson Blvd., Arlington, VA 22234. TEL 703-284-6000; Ed. Kate Marymont; Pub. Danny Martin; adv. contact: Larry Whitaker. pub. size: broadsheet; circ. morning 64,216(paid); Sun. 103,060(paid). **Wire Service(s):** AP, GNS, LAT-WP.

ST. CHARLES

US

COURIER-POST, THE. Mon.-Fri. $.50 newsstand; $55/yr. carrier. 205 N. Main St., Ste. 205, St. Charles, MO 63301. TEL 314-949-6928; FAX 314-919-6973. **Owner(s):** Legal Communications Corp., P.O. Box 88910, St. Louis, MO 63188. TEL 314-421-7880; Pub. Sue Tedesco; pub. size: tabloid; circ. morning 3,700(paid).

ST. JOSEPH

US ISSN 1063-4312

ST. JOSEPH NEWS-PRESS. 1845. d. $.50/day newsstand; $1.25/Sun.; $120.12/yr. carrier. 825 Edmond, St. Joseph, MO 64502. TEL 816-271-8500; FAX 816-271-8692. **Owner(s):** News-Press & Gazette Co., P.O. Box 29, St. Joseph, MO 64502. TEL 816-271-8500; Ed. David R. Bradley, Jr.; Pub. David R. Bradley, Jr.; adv. contact: Ron Ciani. pub. size: standard; circ. morning 44,841(paid); Sun. 50,165(paid). **Wire Service(s):** AP, NYT.
  Formerly: St. Joseph News-Press/Gazette.

ST. LOUIS

US

ST. LOUIS POST-DISPATCH. 1878. d. $.50/day newsstand; $1.25/Sun.; $3.10/wk. carrier. 900 N. Tucker Blvd., St. Louis, MO 63101. TEL 314-340-8901; FAX 314-340-3165. **Owner(s):** Pulitzer Publishing Co., 900 N. Tucker Blvd., St. Louis, MO 63101. TEL 314-340-8000; Ed. Richard Weil, Jr.; Pub. Nicholas G. Penniman, IV; adv.; pub. size: standard; circ. morning 345,700(paid); Sun. 541,991(paid). **Wire Service(s):** AP, CT-NYT, LAT-WP, KR, RN, SHNA.

US

ST. LOUIS WATCHMAN ADVOCATE. 1881. Mon.-Fri. $.50 newsstand; $50/yr. 200 S. Bemiston, Ste. 201, St. Louis, MO 63105. TEL 314-725-1515. **Owner(s):** St. Louis County Printing & Publishing Co., 200 S. Bemiston, Ste. 201, St. Louis, MO 63105. TEL 314-725-1515; Ed. Jeff Mills; Pub. Ronald W. Kuper; adv.; pub. size: tabloid; circ. morning 40,000(paid).

ST. ROBERT

US

DAILY GUIDE. 1963. Mon.-Fri. $.50 newsstand; $64/yr. 108 Holly Dr., St. Robert, MO 65583. TEL 314-336-3711; FAX 314-336-4640. **Owner(s):** American Publishing Co., 606 N. Van Buren, P.O. Box 520, Marion, IL 62959. TEL 618-993-1711; Ed. Carol Wood; Pub. Joel Goodrich; adv.; pub. size: broadsheet; circ. evening 2,800(paid); Sun. 2,800(paid). **Wire Service(s):** AP.

TRENTON

US

TRENTON REPUBLICAN TIMES. 1864. Mon.-Fri. $.50 newsstand; $53.36/yr. local. 122 E. Eighth St., Trenton, MO 64683. TEL 816-359-2212; FAX 816-359-4414. **Owner(s):** Wendell J. Lenhart, 514 Town & Country, Trenton, MO 64683. TEL 816-359-2212; Ed. Wendell J. Lenhart; Pub. Wendell J. Lenhart; adv. contact: DeLane Hein. pub. size: broadsheet; circ. evening 3,850(paid). **Wire Service(s):** AP.

WARRENSBURG

US

DAILY STAR-JOURNAL, THE. 1865. Mon.-Fri. $.50 newsstand; $48.22/yr. carrier; $58.75/yr. out of state. 135 E. Market, Warrensburg, MO 64093. TEL 816-747-8123; FAX 816-747-8741. **Owner(s):** Star-Journal Publishing Co., 135 E. Market, Warrensburg, MO 64003. TEL 816-747-8123; Ed. Avis G. Tucker; Pub. Avis G. Tucker; adv. contact: Don Kirkpatrick. photos; bk.rev.; pub. size: broadsheet; circ. evening 5,097(paid). **Wire Service(s):** AP.

WEST PLAINS

US

WEST PLAINS DAILY QUILL. 1902. Mon.-Fri. $.35 newsstand; $5.31/mo. carrier; $6/mo. out of state;. 125 N. Jefferson, West Plains, MO 65775. TEL 417-256-9191; FAX 417-256-9196. **Owner(s):** Quill Press Co., 125 Jefferson, P.O. Box 110, West Plains, MO 65775. TEL 417-256-9191; Ed. Jerry P. Womack; Pub. Frank L. Martin, III; adv. contact: Sunie K. Pace. photos; bk.rev.; pub. size: broadsheet; circ. evening 9,639(paid). **Wire Service(s):** AP.

MONTANA

BILLINGS

US

BILLINGS GAZETTE. 1885. d. $.50/day newsstand; $.75/Sat.; $1.75/Sun.; $17/4 wk. carrier; $21/4 wk. mailed MT, WY, ND. 401 N. Broadway, Billings, MT 59101. TEL 406-657-1200; FAX 406-657-1208. **Owner(s):** Lee Enterprises, Inc., 215 N. Main St., Davenport, IA 52801. TEL 319-383-2202; Ed. Richard J. Wesnick; Pub. Wayne Schile; bk.rev.; pub. size: broadsheet; circ. morning 62,370(paid); Sun. 64,064(paid). **Wire Service(s):** AP, KR.

BOZEMAN

US

BOZEMAN DAILY CHRONICLE. 1883. Sun.-Fri. $11/mo. 32 S. Rouse, Bozeman, MT 59715. TEL 406-587-4491. **Owner(s):** Big Sky Publishing Co., P.O. Box 1188, Bozeman, MT 59771. TEL 406-587-4491; Ed. Bill Wilke; Pub. Rick Coffman; adv. contact: Mike Smit. pub. size: broadsheet; circ. evening 13,100(paid); Sun. 15,800(paid). **Wire Service(s):** AP, LAT-WP.

BUTTE

US

MONTANA STANDARD. 1876. d. $.50/day newsstand; $1.50/Sun.; $3.50/wk. carrier; $4.20/wk. mail in state; $4.48/wk. mail out of state. 25 W. Granite, Butte, MT 59701-9213. TEL 406-496-5500; FAX 406-496-5551. **Owner(s):** Lee Enterprises, Inc., 400 Putnam Bldg., 215 N. Main St., Davenport, IA 52801-1924. TEL 319-383-2100; Ed. Drew Vanfossem; Pub. Norm Lewis; adv. contact: Bob Barth. pub. size: standard; circ. morning 16,000(paid); Sun. 16,600(paid). **Wire Service(s):** AP, NYT.

GREAT FALLS

US

GREAT FALLS TRIBUNE. 1884. d. $.50/day newsstand; $1.50/Sun.; $3.35/wk. carrier; $14.80/mo. mailed in state. 205 River Dr. S., Great Falls, MT 59405. TEL 406-791-1444; FAX 406-791-1431. **Owner(s):** Great Falls Tribune Co., Div. of Gannett, P.O. Box 5468, Great Falls, MT 59403. TEL 406-791-1444; Ed. Gary Moseman; Pub. Elizabeth Franz; adv. contact: Dave Gould. pub. size: broadsheet; circ. morning 35,000(paid); Sun. 41,000(paid). **Wire Service(s):** AP, NYT, SHNA, GNS.

HAMILTON

US

RAVALLI REPUBLIC. 1889. Mon.-Fri. $.50 newsstand; $75/yr. mailed in cy.; $84/yr. mailed out of cy. 232 W. Main St., Hamilton, MT 59840. TEL 406-363-3300; FAX 406-363-1767. **Owner(s):** Southwest Montana Publishing Co., P.O. Box 433, Hamilton, MT 59840. TEL 406-363-3300; Ed. Drake Kiewit; Pub. Cindy Tetrusaitis; adv. contact: Tammy Johnson. pub. size: broadsheet; circ. morning 5,200(paid). **Wire Service(s):** AP.

HAVRE

US

HAVRE DAILY NEWS. 1915. Mon.-Fri. $.50 newsstand; $96/yr. carrier; $132/yr. out of state. 119 Second St., Havre, MT 59501. TEL 406-265-6796; FAX 406-265-6798. **Owner(s):** Pioneer Press, Inc., 3701 W. Lake Ave., Glenview, IL 60025. TEL 847-486-9200; Ed. Steve Miller; Pub. Rick Weaver; adv. contact: Paula Reynolds. pub. size: standard; circ. evening 4,800(paid). **Wire Service(s):** AP.

HELENA

US

INDEPENDENT RECORD. d. $.50/day newsstand; $.75/Fri.; $1.50/Sun.; $12/mo. carrier; $156/yr. 317 Cruse St., Helena, MT 59601. TEL 406-447-4000; FAX 406-447-4052. **Owner(s):** Lee Enterprises, Inc., 120 E. Second St., Davenport, IA 52801. TEL 319-383-2202; Ed. Charles Wood; Pub. Bruce Whittenberg; adv. contact: Tom Zebrun-Gero. pub. size: broadsheet; circ. morning 14,500(paid); Sun. 15,000(paid). **Wire Service(s):** AP, NYT.
  Formerly: Helena Independent Record.

KALISPELL

US

DAILY INTER LAKE, THE. 1891. Sun.-Fri. $.50/day newsstand; $1.25/Sun.; $144/yr. carrier; $150/yr. motor rte.; $200/yr. out of state. 727 E. Idaho St., Kalispell, MT 59901. TEL 406-755-7000; FAX 406-752-6114. **Owner(s):** Hagadone Corp., P.O. Box 1178, Coeur d'Alene, ID 83814. TEL 208-667-3431; Ed. Dan Black; Pub. Ron Peterson; adv., photos; bk.rev.; pub. size: broadsheet; circ. evening 15,300(paid); Sun. 18,235(paid). **Wire Service(s):** AP.

LIVINGSTON

US

LIVINGSTON ENTERPRISE. 1883. Mon.-Fri. $.50 newsstand; $8/mo. carrier; $8.75/mo. motor rte.; $12/mo. out of state. 401 S. Main, Livingston, MT 59047. TEL 406-222-2000; FAX 406-222-8580. **Owner(s):** Yellowstone Newspapers, P.O. Box 665, Livingston, MT 59047. TEL 406-222-2000; Ed. Karin Ronnow; Pub. John Sullivan; pub. size: broadsheet; circ. evening 3,430(paid). **Wire Service(s):** AP.

MILES CITY

US   ISSN 0891-8988

MILES CITY STAR. 1910. Mon.-Fri. $.50 newsstand; $96/yr. carrier; $127/yr. mailed out of cy. 13 N. Sixth St., Miles City, MT 59301. TEL 406-232-0450; FAX 406-232-6687. **Owner(s):** Star Printing Co., MT; Ed. Mark Smidt; Pub. John Watson; adv. contact: Giff Wood. pub. size: broadsheet; circ. evening 4,150(paid). **Wire Service(s):** AP.

MISSOULA

US   ISSN 0746-4495

MISSOULIAN, THE. 1873. d. $.50/day newsstand; $1.50/Sun.; $13.80/4 wks. 500 S. Higgins Ave., Missoula, MT 59801. TEL 406-523-5200; FAX 406-523-5221. **Owner(s):** Lee Enterprises, Inc., 400 Putnam Bldg. , 215 n. Main St., Davenport, IA 52801. TEL 319-383-2100; Ed. Dave Rutter; Pub. James E. Bell; adv.; photos; pub. size: broadsheet; circ. morning 31,686(paid); Sun. 38,000(paid). **Wire Service(s):** AP, LAT-WP.

NEBRASKA

ALLIANCE

US

ALLIANCE TIMES-HERALD. 1888. Mon.-Sat. $.50 newsstand; $56/yr. carrier; $76/yr. mailed locally; $88/yr. mailed out of area. 114 E. Fourth, Alliance, NE 69301. TEL 308-762-3060. Owner(s): Alliance Publishing Co., P.O. Box G, Alliance, NE 69301. TEL 308-762-3060; Ed. Donna Price; Pub. Fred G. Kuhlman; pub. size: broadsheet; circ. evening 3,559(paid). **Wire Service(s):** AP.

BEATRICE

US

BEATRICE DAILY SUN. 1902. Mon.-Sat. $.50 newsstand; $7.75/mo. carrier NE & KS. 200 N. Seventh St., Beatrice, NE 68310. TEL 402-223-5233 FAX 402-228-3571. **Owner(s):** American Publishing Co., 606 N. Van Buren, P.O. Box 520, Marion, IL 62959. TEL 618-993-1711; Ed. Anita Meyers; Pub. Dennis M. DeRossett; adv. contact: Ronald W. Sohl. photos; pub. size: broadsheet; circ. evening 10,250(paid). **Wire Service(s):** AP.

COLUMBUS

US

COLUMBUS TELEGRAM. 1879. Sun.-Fri. $.50/day newsstand; $.75/Sun.; $87/yr. carrier; $99/yr. motor rte.; $90/yr. in state mailed; $102/yr. out of state. 1254 27th Ave., Columbus, NE 68601. TEL 402-564-2741; FAX 402-563-7500. **Owner(s):** Omaha World-Herald Co., World-Herald Sq., Columbus, NE 68601. TEL 402-444-1000; Ed. Todd Franko; Pub. Julie Speirs; adv. contact: Joe Sherbo. photos; pub. size: broadsheet; circ. evening 11,100(paid); Sun. 11,700(paid). **Wire Service(s):** AP.

FREMONT

US   ISSN 1049-8338

FREMONT TRIBUNE. 1865. Mon.-Sat. $.50 newsstand; $7/mo. carrier. 135 N. Main St., Fremont, NE 68025. TEL 402-721-5000. **Owner(s):** Independent Media Group, Watseka, IL; Ed. Brent Wasenius; Pub. Jim Holland; adv. contact: Pam Zoucha. pub. size: broadsheet; circ. evening 11,000(paid). **Wire Service(s):** AP, GNS.

GRAND ISLAND

US   ISSN 1049-3018

GRAND ISLAND INDEPENDENT. 1872. d. $.50/day newsstand; $1/Sun.; $8.50/mo. carrier. 422 W. First St., Grand Island, NE 68801. TEL 308-382-1000; FAX 308-382-8129. **Owner(s):** Morris Communications, P.O. Box 936, Augusta, GA 30903. TEL 706-724-0851; Ed. Jeff Funk; Pub. John Goossen; adv. contact: Gary Loftus. photos bk.rev.; pub. size: broadsheet; circ. morning 25,057(paid); Sun. 25,934(paid). **Wire Service(s):** AP, KNT, NEA, SHNA, CQ.

HASTINGS

US

HASTINGS DAILY TRIBUNE. 1905. Mon.-Sat. $.50 newsstand; $72/yr. carrier; $75/yr. motor rte.; $108/yr. mailed out of state. 908-912 W. Second St., Hastings, NE 68901. TEL 402-462-2131; FAX 402-461-4657; E-mail: lhavranek@neoland.cnweb.com; URL: http://www.cnweb.com.tribune. **Owner(s):** Seaton Publishing Co., P.O. Box 788, Hastings, NE 68902. TEL 402-452-2131; Ed. Gary Johansen; Pub. Donald R. Seaton; adv. contact: Ken Gettner. pub. size: broadsheet; circ. evening 15,000(paid). Wire Service(s): AP, LAT-WP, SHNA, NEA.

HOLDREGE

US

HOLDREGE DAILY CITIZEN. 1896. Mon.-Fri. $.25 newsstand; $48/yr. carrier. 418 Garfield, Holdrege, NE 68949. TEL 308-995-4441; FAX 308-995-5992. **Owner(s):** Holdrege Daily Citizen, Inc., 418 Garfield, Holdrege, NE 68949; Ed. Tunney Price; Pub. Robert King; adv. contact: Barbara J. Penrod. pub. size: broadsheet; circ. evening 4,000(paid). **Wire Service(s):** AP.

KEARNEY

US

KEARNEY HUB. 1888. Mon.-Sat. $.50/day newsstand; $1/Sat.; $91/yr. carrier; $103/yr. mailed local; $120/yr. mailed out of area. 13 E. 22nd St., Kearney, NE 68847. TEL 308-237-2152; FAX 308-234-5736. **Owner(s):** Kearney Hub Publishing Co., Inc., 13-15 E. 22nd St., Kearney, NE 68847. TEL 308-237-2152; Ed. Mike Konz. adv. contact: Gine Mortimore. bk.rev.; pub. size: broadsheet; circ. evening 26,424(paid) **Wire Service(s):** AP. **Formerly:** Kearney Saturday A.M. Hub.

LINCOLN

US   ISSN 1054-7983

LINCOLN JOURNAL STAR. 1854. d. $.50/day newsstand; $1.75/Sun.; $136/yr. carrier; $161.20/yr. mailed. 926 P St., Lincoln, NE 68508. TEL 402-475-4200; FAX 402-473-7466. **Owner(s):** Journal-Star Printing Co., P.O. Box 81859, Lincoln, NE 68501. TEL 402-475-7200; Ed. Tom White; Pub. William Roesgen; adv. contact: Jan Krueger. photos; bk.rev.; pub. size: broadsheet; circ. morning 44,144(paid); Sun. 87,148(paid). **Wire Service(s):** AP, UPI.

MCCOOK

US

MCCOOK DAILY GAZETTE. 1911. Mon.-Sat. $.50 newsstand; $59/yr. carrier. W. First & E Sts., McCook, NE 69001. TEL 308-345-4500; FAX 308-345-7881. **Owner(s):** McCook Daily Gazette, Inc., W. First & E Sts., McCook, NE 69001; Ed. Bruce Crosby; Pub. Gene O. Morris; adv. contact: Butch Mires. pub. size: broadsheet; circ. evening 8,200(paid) **Wire Service(s):** AP.

NEBRASKA CITY

US

NEBRASKA CITY NEWS-PRESS. 1854. Sun.-Fri. $.50 newsstand; $75/yr. carrier; $82/yr. mailed elsewhere. 123 S. Eighth St., Nebraska City, NE 68410. TEL 402-873-3334; FAX 402-873-5436. **Owner(s):** Midwest Newspapers, P.O. Box 380, Ames, IA 50010. TEL 515-232-2160; Ed. Dan Swanson; Pub. Doug Knight; adv. contact: Doug Knight. pub. size: broadsheet; circ. evening 2,800(paid); Sun. 2,800(paid). **Wire Service(s):** AP.

NORFOLK

US

NORFOLK DAILY NEWS. 1887. Mon.-Sat. $.50 newsstand; $90/yr. carrier or mailed; $84/yr. outside city carrier or mailed. 525 Norfolk Ave., Norfolk, NE 68701. TEL 402-371-1020; FAX 402-371-5802; E-mail: ndnews@ncfcomm.com; URL: http://www.norfolkne.com/dalynews.htm. **Owner(s):** Huse Publishing Co., Box 977, Norfolk, NE 68702. TEL 402-371-1020; Ed. Emil Reutzel; Pub. Jerry Huse; adv. contact: Larry Bartscher. pub. size: broadsheet; circ. evening 22,000(paid). **Wire Service(s):** AP.

NORTH PLATTE

US   ISSN 0747-4008

TELEGRAPH, THE. 1881. Tue.-Sun. $.50/day newsstand; $.75/Sat. & Sun.; $104.60/yr. mailed; $115/yr. mailed outside area; $150/yr. mailed out of state. 621 N. Chestnut, North Platte, NE 69101. TEL 308-532-6000; FAX 308-532-9268. **Owner(s):** Western Publishing Co., P.O. Box 1228, North Platte, NE 69103. TEL 308-532-6783; Ed. Jill Claflin; Pub. Larry Shearer; adv. contact: Dee Kline. pub. size: broadsheet; circ. morning 14,500(paid); Sun. 15,050(paid). **Wire Service(s):** AP.

OMAHA

US   ISSN 0276-4962

OMAHA WORLD-HERALD. 1885. d. $.25/day newsstand; $1.25/Sun.; $2/wk. World-Herald Sq., 1334 Dodge St., Omaha, NE 68102. TEL 402-444-1000; FAX 402-445-1299. **Owner(s):** World Newspapers Inc., Landmark Center, 15th Fl., 1299 Farnam St., Omaha, NE 68102. TEL 402-444-1000; Ed. Deanna Sands; Pub. John Gottschalk; adv. contact: Thomas Golden. photos; bk.rev.; pub. size: broadsheet; circ. morning 227,409(paid); Sun. 289,452(paid). **Wire Service(s):** AP, CDN-CST, NYT, LAT-WP.

SCOTTSBLUFF

US

STAR-HERALD. 1903. Tue.-Sun. $.50/day newsstand; $.75/Sat.-Sun.; $97.50/yr. carrier. 1405 Broadway, Scottsbluff, NE 69361. TEL 308-632-0670; FAX 308-635-1258. **Owner(s):** Western Publishing Co., P.O. Box 1228, North Platte, NE 69103. TEL 308-532-6783; Ed. Steve Miller; Pub. Steven Hungerford; adv. contact: Bernie Schutz. pub. size: broadsheet; circ. morning 16,000(paid); Sun. 16,190(paid). **Wire Service(s):** AP, SHNA.

SIDNEY

US

SIDNEY TELEGRAPH. 1873. Mon.-Fri. $61/yr.; $56/yr. senior citizens. 809 Illinois St., Sidney, NE 69162. TEL 308-254-5555; FAX 308-254-5607. **Owner(s):** Western Publishing Co.; Ed. Gordon Tustin; Pub. Don Evans; adv. contact: Sue Kilgore. photos; bk.rev.; pub. size: broadsheet; circ. evening 3,800(paid). **Wire Service(s):** AP.

YORK

US

YORK NEWS-TIMES. 1887. Mon.-Sat. $67.50/yr. mailed in cy.; $77.50/yr. mailed elsewhere. 327 Platte Ave., York, NE 68467. TEL 402-362-4478; FAX 402-362-6748. **Owner(s):** Morris Communications, P.O. Box 936, Augusta, GA 30903. TEL 706-724-0851; Ed. Mark Lile; Pub. Dan Collin; adv. contact: David H. Sjuts. pub. size: broadsheet; circ. evening 5,800(paid). **Wire Service(s):** AP.

NEVADA

CARSON CITY

US

NEVADA APPEAL. 1865. Sun.-Fri. $.35/day newsstand; $1.25/Sun.; $8/mo. carrier; $96/yr. 200 Bath St., Carson City, NV 89702-2288. TEL 702-882-2111; FAX 702-887-2426. **Owner(s):** Swift Newspapers, Inc., 437 W. Plumb Ln., Reno, NV 89509. TEL 703-333-7676; Ed. Barry Smith; Pub. Jeff Ackerman; adv. contact: Steve Reynolds. pub. size: broadsheet; circ. morning 15,000(paid); Sun. 15,000(paid). **Wire Service(s):** AP.

ELKO

US

ELKO DAILY FREE PRESS. 1883. Mon.-Sat. $.50 newsstand; $93/yr. carrier. 3720 Idaho St., Elko, NV 89801. TEL 702-738-3118; FAX 702-738-2215. **Owner(s):** Rex, Kim & Dan Steinger, 3720 Idaho St., Elko, NV 89801. TEL 702-738-3118; Ed. Dan Steninger; Pub. Rex Steninger; adv. contact: Glennis Bir. photos; pub. size: standard; circ. evening 8,000(paid). **Wire Service(s):** AP.

ELY

US

ELY DAILY TIMES. 1920. Mon-Fri. $.50 newsstand; $6.75/mo. local carrier; $108/yr. mailed out of cy. 655 Aultman St., Ely, NV 89301. TEL 702-289-4491; FAX 702-289-4566. **Owner(s):** Donrey Media Group, P.O. Box 17017, Fort Smith, AZ 72902. TEL 501-785-7801; Ed. Kent Harper; Pub. George Carnes; adv. contact: Kenneth Kliewer. pub. size: standard; circ. evening 2,600(paid). **Wire Service(s):** AP.

FALLON

US

LAHONTAN VALLEY NEWS. 1912. Mon.-Sat. $.35 newsstand; $74/yr. in cy.; $99/yr. out of cy.; $64/yr. senior citizens. 562 N. Maine St., Fallon, NV 89406. TEL 702-423-6041; FAX 702-423-0474. **Owner(s):** David & Ludie Henley, 562 N. Maine St., Fallon, NV 89406. TEL 702-423-6041; FAX 702-423-0474; Ed. Anne Pershing; Pub. Ludie Henley; adv. contact: Joyce Thompson. photos; bk.rev.; pub. size: broadsheet; circ. morning 5,000(paid). **Wire Service(s):** AP. Formerly: Fallon Lahontan Valley News.

LAS VEGAS

US

LAS VEGAS REVIEW-JOURNAL. 1905. d. $.50/day newsstand; $2.50/Sun.; $3/wk. carrier; $156/yr. 1111 W. Bonanza Rd., Las Vegas, NV 89106. TEL 702-383-0211; FAX 702-383-4665. **Owner(s):** Donrey Media Group, P.O. Box 17017, Fort Smith, AR 72902. TEL 501-785-7810; Ed. Tom Mitchell; Pub. Sherman Frederick; adv. contact: Jack Harpster. pub. size: standard; circ. morning 152,679(paid); Sun. 230,000(paid). **Wire Service(s):** AP, LAT-WP, KR.

US

LAS VEGAS SUN. 1950. d. $.50/day newsstand; $2.50/Sun.; $1.75/wk. carrier. 800 S. Valley View Blvd., Las Vegas, NV 89107. TEL 702-385-3111; FAX 702-383-7264; E-mail: bryan@lvsun.com; URL: http://www.lasvegassun.com. **Owner(s):** Las Vegas Sun, Inc., 800 S. Valley View Blvd., Las Vegas, NV 89107. TEL 702-385-3111; Ed. Sandra Thompson; Pub. Barbara Greenspun; pub. size: broadsheet; circ. evening 40,000(paid); Sun. 230,000(paid). **Wire Service(s):** AP.

RENO

US   ISSN 0745-1415

RENO GAZETTE-JOURNAL. 1870. d. $.50/day newsstand; $1.50/Sun.; $3.50/wk. carrier; $2.10/Sat. & Sun. carrier; $169/yr.; $117/yr. weekdays; $143/yr. weekends & holidays. 955 Kuenzli St., Reno, NV 89502. TEL 702-788-6200; FAX 702-788-6458. **Owner(s):** Gannett Company, Inc., 1100 Wilson Blvd., Arlington, VA 22340. TEL 703-284-6000; Ed. Tonia Cunning; Pub. Sue Clark-Johnson; adv. contact: John Zidich. pub. size: standard; circ. morning 6,630(paid); Sun. 84,335(paid). **Wire Service(s):** AP, DJ, NYT, GNS.

SPARKS

US

DAILY SPARKS TRIBUNE, THE. 1910. Sun.-Fri. $.35 newsstand; $6.50/mo. carrier. 1002 C St., Sparks, NV 89431-4929. TEL 702-358-8061; FAX 702-359-3837. **Owner(s):** Kearns-Tribune Corp., P.O. Box 887, Sparks, NV 89431. TEL 702-358-8062; FAX 702-358-3837; Ed. Bryan Jacobson. adv.; photos; pub. size: broadsheet; circ. evening 7,000(paid); Sun. 10,000(paid). **Wire Service(s):** AP.

WINNEMUCCA

US   ISSN 1082-2976

HUMBOLDT SUN. 1972. Mon.-Fri. $65/yr. in cy.; $85/yr. elsewhere. 1022 S. Grass Valley Rd., Winnemucca, NV 89445. TEL 702-623-5011; FAX 702-623-5243. **Owner(s):** Winnemucca Publishing, Inc., 1022 S. Grass Valley Rd., Winnemucca, NV 89445; Pub. Susan Brockus; adv.; pub. size: broadsheet; circ. 4,500(paid).

NEW HAMPSHIRE

BERLIN

US

BERLIN DAILY SUN. 1992. Mon.-Fri. free newsstand. 177 Main St., Berlin, NH 03570. TEL 603-752-5858; FAX 603-752-4160; E-mail: bds@moose.mcia.net. **Owner(s):** Country Club News, Inc., Seavey St., Berlin, NH 03860. TEL 603-356-2999; Ed. Rose Dodge; Pub. Mark Guerrinque; adv. contact: Rita Dube. pub. size: tabloid; circ. 7,200(free). **Wire Service(s):** AP.

US

BERLIN REPORTER, THE. 1897. Mon.-Sat. $.25/day newsstand; $.50/Wed.; $17/3 mos. carrier. 151 Main St., Berlin, NH 03570. TEL 603-752-1200; FAX 603-752-2339. **Owner(s):** Munro Enterprises, Inc., P.O. Box 38, Berlin, NH 03570. TEL 603-752-1200; Ed. Howard James; Pub. Howard James; adv. contact: Debbie Harwell. pub. size: tabloid; circ. morning 6,300(paid).
  Formerly: Daily Berlin Reporter, The.

CLAREMONT

US

EAGLE-TIMES. 1892. Sun.-Fri. $.50/day newsstand; $1/Sun.; $2.10/wk. carrier; $2.20/wk. motor rte.; $49.40/qtr. mailed; $1.60/Sun. mailed. RFD 2, Box 301, Claremont, NH 03743. TEL 603-543-3100; FAX 603-542-9705. **Owner(s):** Eagle Publications, Inc., RFD 2, Box 301, Claremont, NH 03730. TEL 603-543-3100; FAX 603-542-9705; Ed. Todd Driscoll; Pub. Harvey D. Hill; adv. contact: Robert Shomphe. photos; bk.rev.; pub. size: broadsheet; circ. evening 9,600(paid); Sun. 10,420(paid). **Wire Service(s):** AP.

CONCORD

US

CONCORD MONITOR. 1802. d. $.50/day newsstand; $1.50/Sun.; $13.65/mo. One Monitor Dr., Concord, NH 03302-1177. TEL 603-224-5301; FAX 603-228-8238; E-mail: primary@www.cmonitor.com; URL: http://www.cmonitor.com/primary. **Owner(s):** Newspapers of New England, Inc., One Monitor Dr., P.O. Box 1177, Concord, NH 03302-1177. TEL 603-224-5301; Ed. Mike Pride; Pub. Tom C. Brown; adv. contact: Roger Proulx. pub. size: broadsheet; circ. morning 22,500(paid). **Wire Service(s):** AP, LAT-WP.

DOVER

US   ISSN 0892-6026

FOSTER'S DAILY DEMOCRAT. 1873. Mon.-Sat. $.50 newsstand; $105/yr. carrier; $138/yr. mailed in state; $145/yr. mailed out of state. 333 Central Ave., Dover, NH 03820. TEL 603-742-4455; FAX 603-742-4455; E-mail: pkincade@fosters.com; URL: http://www.fosters.com. **Owner(s):** George J. Foster & Co., Inc., 333 Central Ave., Dover, NH 03820. TEL 603-742-4455; Ed. Therece D. Foster Pub. Robert H. Foster; adv. contact: Wayne Chick. pub. size: broadsheet; circ. evening 31,057(paid). **Wire Service(s):** AP, NYT.

HUDSON

US

TELEGRAPH, THE. 1832. d. $.50/day newsstand; $1.50/Sun.; $2.25/wk.; $156/yr. 17 Executive Dr., Hudson, NH 03051. TEL 603-882-2741; FAX 603-882-5138. **Owner(s):** Independent Publications, Inc., P.O. Box 1008, Nashua, NH 03061. TEL 603-882-2741; Ed. David Solomon; Pub. Terrence Williams; adv. contact: Mark Iacuessa. photos; bk.rev.; pub. size: broadsheet; circ. morning 29,000(paid); Sun. 34,000(paid). **Wire Service(s):** CSM, SHNA, AP.

KEENE

US

KEENE SENTINEL. 1799. Mon.-Sat. $.50 newsstand; $118/yr. carrier/motor rte.; $148/yr. mailed out of cy. 60 West St., Keene, NH 03431. TEL 603-352-1234; FAX 603-352-0437; E-mail: tfk@keenesentinel.com; URL: http://www.keenesentinel.com. **Owner(s):** Keene Publishing Corp., 60 West St., Keene, NH 03431. TEL 603-352-1234; Ed. James A. Rousmaniere, Jr. ; Pub. Thomas M. Ewing; adv. contact: Colin R. Lyle. bk.rev.; pub. size: broadsheet; circ. evening 15,500(paid). **Wire Service(s):** AP, LAT-WP.

LACONIA

US

CITIZEN, THE. 1925. Mon.-Sat. $.50 newsstand; $99/yr. home deliv 171 Fair St., Laconia, NH 03246. TEL 603-524-3800; FAX 603-524-6702. **Owner(s):** Robert Foster, Dover, NH. TEL 603-742-4455; adv. contact: Terry Rosseau. pub. size: standard; circ. evening 12,000(paid). **Wire Service(s):** AP.

MANCHESTER

US   ISSN 0745-5798

UNION LEADER/NEW HAMPSHIRE SUNDAY NEWS. 1863. d. $.50/day newsstand; $1.50/Sun.; $140.40/yr.; $80.08/yr. Sun. 100 William Loeb Dr., Manchester, NH 03109. TEL 603-668-4321; FAX 603-624-0727. **Owner(s):** Nackey Loeb, 100 William Loeb Dr., P.O. Box 9555, Manchester, NH 03109-9555. TEL 603-668-4321; Ed. Joseph W. McQuaid; Pub. Nackey Loeb; adv.; pub. size: standard; circ. morning 75,000(paid); Sun. 102,000(paid). **Wire Service(s):** AP.

NORTH CONWAY

US

CONWAY DAILY SUN, THE. 1989. Mon.-Sat. free newsstand; $3.50/mo.; $39/yr. 54 Seavey St., North Conway, NH 03860. TEL 603-356-2999; FAX 603-356-8774; E-mail: dailysun@mountwashingtonvalley.com; URL: http://www.mountwashingtonvalley.com. **Owner(s):** Country Club News, Inc., Seavey St., North Conway, NH 03860. TEL 603-356-2999; FAX 603-356-8774; Ed. Adam Hirshan; Pub. Mark Guerringue; adv. contact: Bob Waters. pub. size: broadsheet; circ. morning 14,000(free & paid) **Wire Service(s):** AP.

PORTSMOUTH

US   ISSN 0746-6218

PORTSMOUTH HERALD. 1889. d. $.50/day newsstand; $1.50/Sun.; $2.95/wk. home deliv.; $12.78/4 wks. mailed; $153.40/yr. 111 Maplewood Ave., Portsmouth, NH 03801. TEL 603-436-1800; FAX 603-427-0550; E-mail: pherald@nh-meseacoast.com; URL: http://www.nh-meseacoast.com. **Owner(s):** Thomson Newspapers, Inc., 3150 Des Plaines Ave., Des Plaines, IL 60018. TEL 708-299-5544; Ed. Sam Pollack. adv. contact: Gloria Bonito. pub. size: standard; circ. morning 15,000(paid); Sun. 18,600(paid). **Wire Service(s):** AP.

WEST LEBANON

US

VALLEY NEWS. 1952. d. $.50/day newsstand; $1.25/Sun. Seven Interchange Dr., West Lebanon, NH 03784. TEL 603-298-8711 FAX 603-298-0212. **Owner(s):** Newspapers of New England, Inc., Concord, NH 03302; Ed. Jim Fox; Pub. John Kuhns; adv.; pub. size: broadsheet; circ. morning 18,500(paid); Sun. 17,000(paid).

NEW JERSEY

BRIDGETON

US

BRIDGETON EVENING NEWS. 1879. Mon.-Sat. $.50 newsstand; $119.60/yr. 100 E. Commerce St., Bridgeton, NJ 08302. TEL 609-451-1000; FAX 609-451-7214. **Owner(s):** Media News Group, 309 S. Broad St., Woodbury, NJ 08096. TEL 609-845-3300; Ed. Cris Blake; Pub. John Ewing; adv.; photos; pub. size: broadsheet; circ. evening 20,000(paid). **Wire Service(s):** AP.

US

MILLVILLE NEWS. 1990. Mon.-Sat. $.50 newsstand; $1.40/wk. 100 E. Commerce St., Bridgeton, NJ 08302. TEL 609-327-1100; FAX 609-327-7214. **Owner(s):** American Publishing Co., 606 N. Van Buren, P.O. Box 520, Marion, IL 62959. TEL 618-993-1711; Ed. Jack Hummel; Pub. John M. Ewing; adv. contact: Burnie Heller. pub. size: broadsheet; circ. evening 1,500(paid). **Wire Service(s):** AP.

BRIDGEWATER

US   ISSN 0895-8785

COURIER-NEWS, THE. 1884. d. $.25/day newsstand; $.75/Sun.; $2.50/wk. home deliv.; $130/yr. 1201 Rte. 22, W., Bridgewater, NJ 08807. TEL 908-722-8800; FAX 908-707-3272. **Owner(s):** Gannett Company, Inc., 1100 Wilson Blvd., Arlington, VA 22234. TEL 703-284-6000; Ed. Laura Harrigan; Pub. Henry M. Freeman; adv. contact: Peter Ricker. photos; bk.rev.; pub. size: standard; circ. morning 50,527(paid); Sun. 53,383(paid). **Wire Service(s):** LAT-WP, GNS, AP.

CHERRY HILL

US

COURIER-POST, THE. 1875. d. $.35/day newsstand, $1.50/Sun.; $302.90/yr. mailed. 301 Cuthbert Blvd., Cherry Hill, NJ 08002. TEL 609-663-6000; FAX 609-663-3190; E-mail: cphotline@aol.com. **Owner(s):** Gannett Company, Inc., 1100 Wilson Blvd., Arlington, VA 22234. TEL 703-284-6000; Pub. Robert T. Collins; adv. contact: John E. Ziomek. bk.rev.; pub. size: broadsheet; circ. morning 89,860(paid); Sun. 100,400(paid). **Wire Service(s):** GNS, AP.

EAST BRUNSWICK

US

HOME NEWS & TRIBUNE, THE. 1879. d. $.35/day newsstand; $.50/Sun.; $1.75/wk. 35 Kennedy Blvd., East Brunswick, NJ 08816. TEL 908-246-5500; FAX 908-937-6046; E-mail: editor@injersey.com; URL: http://www.thnt.com. **Owner(s):** Asbury Park Press Corp., 3601 Hwy. 66, P.O. Box 1550, Neptune, NJ 07753. TEL 908-922-6000; Ed. Richard Hugher; Pub. E. Donald Lass; adv. contact: Robert Waitt. photos; bk.rev.; pub. size: broadsheet; circ. morning 53,084(paid); Sun. 57,000(paid). **Wire Service(s):** AP, LAT-WP, KR.
    Formerly: Home News; News Tribune.

HACKENSACK

US

RECORD, THE. 1895. d. $.50/day newsstand; $1.50/Sun. 150 River St., Hackensack, NJ 07601. TEL 201-646-4000; FAX 201-646-4135; E-mail: editor@www.bergen.com; URL: http://www.bergen.com. **Owner(s):** Macromedia Publishing, Inc., 150 River St., Hackensack, NJ 07601. TEL 201-646-4000; Ed. Vivian Waixel; Pub. Malcolm Borg; adv. contact: Cosmo DiFiore. photos; bk.rev.; pub. size: broadsheet; circ. morning 161,991(paid); Sun. 222,892(paid). **Wire Service(s):** AP, UPI, LAT-WP, RN.

JERSEY CITY

US

JERSEY JOURNAL, THE. 1879. Mon.-Sat. $.50 newsstand; $1.85/wk. home deliv.; $20/3 mos. home deliv.; $20/mo. mailed. 30 Journal Sq., Jersey City, NJ 07306. TEL 201-863-2000; FAX 201-653-1414. **Owner(s):** Advance Publications, Inc., 485 Lexington Ave., New York, NY 10017; Ed. Judith Locorriere; Pub. Scott Ring; adv.; pub. size: broadsheet; circ. morning 55,000(paid). **Wire Service(s):** AP, KR, CT-NYT.
    Formerly: Hudson Dispatch.

NEPTUNE

US

ASBURY PARK PRESS. 1879. d. $.40/day newsstand; $1.50/Sun.; $2.95/wk. 3601 Hwy. 66, Neptune, NJ 07754. TEL 908-922-6000; FAX 908-922-4818; E-mail: editor@injersey.com; URL: http://www.app.com. **Owner(s):** Asbury Park Press Corp., 3601 Highway 66, P.O. Box 1550, Neptune, NJ 07753. TEL 908-922-6000; Ed. E. Donald Lass; Pub. Donald Lass; adv.; photos; bk.rev.; pub. size: standard; circ. evening 165,000(paid); Sun. 235,000(paid). **Wire Service(s):** AP, TPS, KR, CSM, RN.

NEWARK

US

STAR-LEDGER. 1938. d. $.35/day newsstand; $1.25/Sun.; $3/wk. home deliv. One Star Ledger Plz., Newark, NJ 07102. TEL 201-877-4141; FAX 201-643-4945; E-mail: jterrito@newhouse.com; URL: http://www.nj.com/interact. **Owner(s):** Advance Publications, Inc., 485 Lexington Ave., New York, NY 10017; Ed. Charles Harrison; Pub. Martin Bartner; adv. contact: Mark Herrick. photos; pub. size: broadsheet; circ. morning 433,317(paid); Sun. 641,393(paid). **Wire Service(s):** AP, UPI, LAT-WP, RN.
    Formerly: Newark Star-Ledger.

NEWTON

US   ISSN 0893-3677

NEW JERSEY HERALD. 1829. Sun. -Fri. $.35/day newsstand; $1/Sun.; $2.15/wk. home deliv.; $98.80/yr. carrier. 2 Spring St., Newton, NJ 07860. TEL 201-383-1500; FAX 201-383-8477; E-mail: comments@njherald.com; URL: http://www.njherald.com. **Owner(s):** New Jersey Herald, P.O. Box 10, Newton, NJ 07860. TEL 201-383-1500; Pub. R. Kent Roeder; adv. contact: Dianne Ryan. photos; bk.rev.; pub. size: broadsheet; circ. evening 18,000(paid); Sun. 26,000(paid). **Wire Service(s):** AP.

PARSIPPANY

US

DAILY RECORD, THE. 1900. d. $.25/day newsstand; $1/Sun.; $2.25/wk. 629 Parsippany Rd., Parsippany, NJ 07054-0217. TEL 201-428-6200; FAX 201-428-6666; E-mail: 75141.3363@compuserve.com; URL: http://www.adone.com/dailyrecord. **Owner(s):** Goodson Newspaper Group, 1009 Lenox Dr., Lawrenceville, NJ 08648; Ed. Jack Bowie; Pub. Tom Geyer; adv.; pub. size: broadsheet; circ. morning 55,641(paid); Sun. 62,333(paid). **Wire Service(s):** AP, KNT.

PASSAIC

US   ISSN 0895-8807

NORTH JERSEY HERALD & NEWS, THE. 1872. d. $.35/day newsstand; $.50/Sun.; $2.60/wk. home deliv. 988 Main Ave., Passaic, NJ 07055. TEL 201-365-3000; FAX 201-614-0906. **Owner(s):** North Jersey Newspapers Co., 988 Main Ave., Passaic, NJ 07055. TEL 201-365-3000; Ed. Kenneth G. Pringle; Pub. Richard Vezza; adv.; photos; pub. size: broadsheet; circ. morning 54,420(paid); Sun. 52,000(paid). **Wire Service(s):** AP, LAT-WP.
    Formerly: Paterson Evening News.

PLEASANTVILLE

US

PRESS OF ATLANTIC CITY, THE. 1895. d. $.50/day newsstand; $1.50/Sun.; $3.35/wk. 11 Devins Ln., Pleasantville, NJ 08232-3806. TEL 609-645-1234; FAX 609-272-7224; E-mail: merkoski@globalent.net; URL: http://www.globalent.net/acpress. **Owner(s):** Abarta Metro Publishing Co. Inc., 1000 R.I.D.C. Plz., Pittsburgh, PA 15238. TEL 412-963-6522; Ed. Maryjane Briant; Pub. Robert McCormick; adv.; photos; pub. size: broadsheet; circ. morning 77,117(paid); Sun. 98,872(paid). **Wire Service(s):** AP, UPI, LAT-WP.

SALEM

US   ISSN 0890-9830

TODAY'S SUNBEAM. 1972. Sun.-Fri. $.35/day newsstand; $1/Sun. 93 Fifth St., Salem, NJ 08079. TEL 609-935-1500; FAX 609-845-3139. **Owner(s):** Media News Group, 309 S. Broad St., Woodbury, NJ 08096. TEL 609-845-3300; Ed. John Barna; Pub. Wayne Studer; adv. contact: Ceil Smith. photos; bk.rev.; pub. size: broadsheet; circ. morning 12,000(paid); Sun. 11,800(paid). **Wire Service(s):** AP.

TOMS RIVER

US   ISSN 0746-5416

OCEAN COUNTY'S OBSERVER. 1850. d. $.25/day newsstand; $.75/Sun.; $1.80/wk. carrier. 8 Robbins St., Toms River, NJ 08753. TEL 908-349-3000; FAX 908-349-8636. **Owner(s):** Ocean County Newspapers, Inc., 8 Robbins St., Toms River, NJ 08753. TEL 908-349-3000; Ed. Charles C. Triblehorn. adv.; pub. size: broadsheet; circ. morning 20,000(paid); Sun. 18,500(paid). **Wire Service(s):** AP.

TRENTON

US   ISSN 8750-9083

TIMES, THE. d. $.25/day newsstand; $.50/Sun.; $83.20/yr. carrier; $93.60/yr. motor rte. 500 Perry St., Trenton, NJ 08605. TEL 609-396-3232; FAX 609-394-2819; E-mail: 76666.1313@compuserve.com. **Owner(s):** Newhouse Newspapers, 140 E. 45th St., New York, NY 10018. TEL 212-697-8020; Ed. Brian Malone; Pub. Richard Bilotti; adv. contact: Sandra Lohr. pub. size: broadsheet; circ. morning 86,772(paid); Sun. 93,423(paid). **Wire Service(s):** AP, LAT-WP, NYT.
    Formerly: Trenton Times.

US

TRENTONIAN, THE. 1946. d. $.35/day newsstand; $.75/Sun.; $2.30/wk. 600 Perry St., Trenton, NJ 08618-3996. TEL 609-989-7800; FAX 609-393-6072. **Owner(s):** Journal Register Co., 50 W.State St., 12th Fl., Trenton, NJ 08608. TEL 609-396-2200; Ed. Mark H. Waligore; Pub. H.L. Schwartz, III; adv.; photos; bk.rev.; pub. size: tabloid; circ. morning 73,352(paid); Sun. 63,000(paid). **Wire Service(s):** KR, AP, SH.

VINELAND

US

DAILY JOURNAL. 1864. Mon.-Sat. $.35 newsstand; $119.60/yr. carrier. 891 E. Oak Rd., Vineland, NJ 08360. TEL 609-825-3456; FAX 609-691-2031. **Owner(s):** Times Graphics, Inc., 891 E. Oak Rd., Vineland, NJ 08360. TEL 609-691-5000; Pub. Sal Devizo; adv. contact: Al Frattura. pub. size: broadsheet; circ. evening 19,235(paid). **Wire Service(s):** AP.

WILLINGBORO

US

BURLINGTON COUNTY TIMES. 1958. d. $.35/day newsstand; $1.50/Sun.; $2.75/wk. 2284 Rte. 130, Willingboro, NJ 08046. TEL 609-871-8000; FAX 609-871-0490. **Owner(s):** Calkins Newspapers, Inc., 8400 Rte. 13, Levittown, PA 19057. TEL 215-949-4000; Ed. Jennie L. Phipps; Pub. Stanley Ellis; adv. contact: David S. Renne. pub. size: broadsheet; circ. evening 43,080(paid); Sun. 47,795(paid). **Wire Service(s):** AP.

WOODBURY

US

GLOUCESTER COUNTY TIMES. 1897. Sun.-Fri. $.35/day newsstand; $1/Sun.; $2/wk. 309 S. Broad St., Woodbury, NJ 08096. TEL 609-845-3300; FAX 609-845-2132. **Owner(s):** Media News Group, 309 S. Broad St., Woodbury, NJ 08096. TEL 609-845-3300; FAX 609-845-2132; Ed. William Long; Pub. Wayne Studer; adv.; photos; bk.rev.; pub. size: broadsheet; circ. evening 29,200(paid); Sun. 29,800(paid). **Wire Service(s):** AP.

NEW MEXICO

ALAMOGORDO

US

ALAMOGORDO DAILY NEWS. 1898. Sun.-Fri. $.50 newsstand; $7/mo. 518 24th St., Alamogordo, NM 88310. TEL 505-437-7120. **Owner(s):** DR Partners, P.O. Box 17017, Fort Smith, AR 72917. TEL 501-785-7800; Pub. Thomas W. Reeves; adv. contact: Mildred House. pub. size: broadsheet; circ. evening 8,706(paid); Sun. 9,652(paid). **Wire Service(s):** AP.

ALBUQUERQUE

US

ALBUQUERQUE JOURNAL. 1880. d. $.50/day newsstand; $1/Sun.; $10.25/mo. carrier. 7777 Jefferson, N.E., Albuquerque, NM 87109-4343. TEL 505-823-7777; FAX 505-823-3994; E-mail: journal@abqjournal.com; URL: http://www.abqjournal.com. **Owner(s):** T.H. Lang, 7777 Jefferson, N.E., Albuquerque, NM 87109. TEL 505-823-7777; Journal Publishing Co., P.O. Drawer J, Albuquerque, NM 87103. TEL 505-823-7777; Ed. Rod Deckert; Pub. T.H. Lang; adv.; photos; bk.rev.; pub. size: broadsheet; circ. morning 160,325(paid); Sun. 169,072(paid). **Wire Service(s):** AP, CSM, LAT-WP, RN.

ALBUQUERQUE TRIBUNE. 1922. Mon.-Sat. $.50 newsstand; $5.25/mo.; $31.50/6 mos. 7777 Jefferson, N.E. Albuquerque, NM 87109. TEL 505-823-7777; FAX 505-823-3689. **Owner(s):** Scripps-Howard, 312 Walnut St., 28th Fl., Cincinnati, OH 45202. TEL 513-977-3000; Ed. Scott Ware. pub. size: broadsheet; circ. evening 35,000(paid). **Wire Service(s):** AP, SHNA, NYT, LAT-WP.

ARTESIA

US

ARTESIA DAILY PRESS. 1938. Tue.-Fri. & Sun. $.35/day newsstand; $.75/Sun.; $5.75/mo. in town; $19.50/3 mos. 503 W. Main, Artesia, NM 88210. TEL 505-746-3524. **Owner(s):** Valley Newspapers, Inc., P.O. Box 179, Artesia, NM 88211. TEL 505-746-3524; Ed. Darrell Pehr; Pub. Gary Scott; pub. size: broadsheet; circ. evening 4,000(paid); Sun. 4,200(paid). **Wire Service(s):** AP.

CARLSBAD

US

CURRENT-ARGUS. 1889. Tue.-Sun. $.50/day newsstand; $1.25/Sun.; $8.75/mo. deliv. in cy. 620 S. Main, Carlsbad, NM 88220-6243. TEL 505-887-5501; FAX 505-885-1066; E-mail: argus@carlsbad.com. **Owner(s):** Omaha World-Herald Co., World-Herald Sq., 1334 Dodge St., Omaha, NE 68102. TEL 402-444-1000; Ed. Hal Miller; Pub. Sammy Lopez; pub. size: broadsheet; circ. evening 8,800(paid); Sun. 9,000(paid). **Wire Service(s):** AP.

Formerly: Carlsbad Current-Argus.

CLOVIS

US

CLOVIS NEWS JOURNAL. 1929. Sun.-Fri. $7/mo. home deliv. 501 Pile St., Clovis, NM 88101. TEL 505-763-3431; FAX 505-762-3879. **Owner(s):** Freedom Communications, Inc., 17666 Fitch, Irvine, CA 92714; Ed. Mike Wheeler; Pub. Julie Moreno; adv. contact: Wendell Jones. photos; pub. size: broadsheet; circ. evening 9,928(paid); Sun. 10,277(paid). **Wire Service(s):** AP, KR, Freedom.

DEMING

US   ISSN 0738-8349

DEMING HEADLIGHT. 1881. Mon.-Fri. $.50 newsstand; $60/yr. mailed. 219 E. Maple, Deming, NM 88030. TEL 505-546-2611; FAX 505-546-8116. **Owner(s):** WorldWest Limited Liability Co., Lawrence, KS. TEL 913-843-1000; FAX 913-832-7207; Ed. John Brennon; Pub. Tamara M. Montes; adv.; photos; pub. size: tabloid; circ. evening 11,000(free & paid). **Wire Service(s):** AP.

FARMINGTON

US

DAILY TIMES. 1894. d. $.50/day newsstand; $1/Sun.; $88/yr. carrier. 201 N. Allen, Farmington, NM 87401. TEL 505-325-4545; FAX 505-326-0234. **Owner(s):** New Mexico Newspapers, Inc., P.O. Box 450, Farmington, NM 87499. TEL 505-325-4545; Ed. Ralph Damiani; Pub. Eliot O'Brien; adv. contact: Dennis Gross. pub. size: broadsheet; circ. evening 18,706(paid); Sun. 17,401(paid). **Wire Service(s):** AP, NYT.

HOBBS

US

HOBBS DAILY NEWS-SUN. 1927. Sun.-Fri. $.50/day newsstand; $1/Sun. 201 N. Thorp, Hobbs, NM 88240. TEL 505-393-2123; FAX 505-393-5724. **Owner(s):** Sun Publishing Corp., P.O. Box 860, Hobbs, NM 88241. TEL 505-393-2123; Ed. Manny Marquez; Pub. Kathi Bearden; adv. contact: Linda Coerig. pub. size: broadsheet; circ. morning 11,908(paid); Sun. 12,716(paid). **Wire Service(s):** AP, KR.

LAS CRUCES

US

LAS CRUCES SUN-NEWS. 1937. d. $.50/day newsstand; $1.25/Sun. 256 W. Las Cruces Ave. Las Cruces, NM 88005. TEL 505-523-6414; FAX 505-527-1249. **Owner(s):** Media News Group, 4888 Loop Central Dr., Ste. 575, Houston, TX 77081. TEL 505-523-4581; Ed. Harold R. Cousland; Pub. George Smith; pub. size: broadsheet; circ. morning 21,500(paid); Sun. 23,000(paid). **Wire Service(s):** AP, NYT.

LAS VEGAS

US

LAS VEGAS DAILY OPTIC. 1879. Mor.-Fri. $59.40/yr. home deliv.; $90/yr. in cy.; $102/yr. out of cy. 614 Lincoln, Las Vegas, NM 87701. TEL 505-425-6796; FAX 505-425-1005. **Owner(s):** Las Vegas Optic Inc., 614 Lincoln, P.O. Box 2670, Las Vegas, NM 87701. TEL 505-425-6796; FAX 505-425-1005; Pub. Stuart Beck; adv. contact: Anna Huie. photos; bk.rev.; pub. size: broadsheet; circ. evening 6,248(paid). **Wire Service(s):** AP.

LOS ALAMOS

US   ISSN 0893-3456

MONITOR, THE. 1963. Tue.-Fr. & Sun. $.50 newsstand; $63.95/yr. 256 DP Rd., Los Alamos NM 87544. TEL 505-662-4185; FAX 505-662-4334; E-mail: lamonitr@rt66.com; URL: http://www.rt66.com/lamonitr. **Owner(s):** Landmark Community Newspapers, Inc., P.O. Box 549, Shelbyville, KY 40065. TEL 502-633-4334; Ed. Charmian Schaller; Pub. Evelyn Vigil; adv. contact: Sande Knight. pub. size: broadsheet; circ. evening 5,100(paid); Sun. 5,400(paid). **Wire Service(s):** AP, NYT.

Formerly: Los Alamos Monitor.

LOVINGTON

US

LOVINGTON DAILY LEADER. 1909. Tue.-Fri. & Sun. $.50 newsstand; $78/yr. in town $84/yr. in cy.; $90/yr. out of cy. 14 W. Ave. B, Lovington, NM 88260. TEL 505-396-2844; FAX 505-396-5775. **Owner(s):** Wal-Roy Publishing, Inc., P.O. Box 1717, Lovington, NM 88260. TEL 505-396-2844; Ed. John Graham; Pub. John Graham; adv. contact: Joyce Clemens. pub. size: broadsheet; circ. evening 2,100(paid); Sun. 2,400(paid). **Wire Service(s):** AP.

Dailies

PORTALES

US

PORTALES NEWS-TRIBUNE. 1957. Sun.-Fri. $.50/day newsstand; $1/Sun.; $69.75/yr. in city; $72/yr. elsewhere. 101 E. First St., Portales, NM 88130. TEL 505-356-4481; FAX 505-356-3630. **Owner(s):** Southern Newspapers, Inc., Houston, TX. TEL 713-266-5481; FAX 713-266-1847; Pub. Lone Beasley; adv. contact: Melissa Broussard. pub. size: broadsheet; circ. evening 4,200(paid); Sun. 4,500(paid). **Wire Service(s):** AP.

ROSWELL

US

ROSWELL DAILY RECORD. 1891. Sun.-Fri. $.35/day newsstand; $1/Sun.; $6.50/mo. deliv. 2301 N. Main, Roswell, NM 88201-6452. TEL 505-622-7710; FAX 505-625-0421. **Owner(s):** Roswell Daily Record, Inc., 2301 N. Main St., Roswell, NM 88201-6452. TEL 505-622-7710; FAX 505-625-0421; Ed. Greg Peretti; Pub. R. Cory Beck; adv. contact: Marion Saint. pub. size: broadsheet; circ. morning 14,500(paid); Sun. 15,000(paid). **Wire Service(s):** AP.

SANTA FE

US

SANTA FE NEW MEXICAN. 1849. d. $.50/day newsstand; $1/Sun.; $225/yr. 202 E. Marcy St., Santa Fe, NM 87501. TEL 505-983-3303; FAX 505-986-9147; E-mail: newmex@newmexico.com; URL: http://www.interart.net/zia.connection/. **Owner(s):** Robert McKinney, The New Mexican, Inc., P.O. Box 2048, Santa Fe, NM 87504. TEL 505-986-3000; Ed. Rob Dean. adv. contact: Virginia Sohn-Shahi. pub. size: broadsheet; circ. morning 25,000(paid); Sun. 26,000(paid). **Wire Service(s):** AP, NYT, LAT-WP.

SILVER CITY

US   ISSN 0891-7981

SILVER CITY DAILY PRESS & INDEPENDENT. 1896. Mon.-Sat. $.35 newsstand; $60/yr. in town; $73/yr. out of town. 300 Market St., Silver City, NM 88061. TEL 505-388-1576; FAX 505-318-1196. **Owner(s):** Silver City Daily Press & Independent Publ. Co., P.O. Box 740, Silver City, NM 88061. TEL 505-538-2794; Ed. Bill Archibald; Pub. William F. Ely; adv. contact: Francesca Wright. photos; bk.rev.; pub. size: broadsheet; circ. evening 7,450(paid). **Wire Service(s):** AP.

NEW YORK

ALBANY

US

AMSTERDAM STAR, THE. Mon.-Fri. $.50 newsstand; $6.99/mo. 9 Market St., Albany, NY 12010. TEL 518-843-3733; FAX 518-843-9104. **Owner(s):** Dave Dalfonso, 9 Market St., Albany, NY 12010. TEL 518-843-3733; FAX 518-843-9104; Brad Broyles, 9 Market St., Albany, NY 12010. TEL 518-843-3733; FAX 813-843-9104; Steve Pitcciocca, 9 Market St., Albany, NY 12010. TEL 518-843-3733; FAX 518-843-9104; Ed. Brad Broyles; Pub. Brad Broyles; pub. size: tabloid; circ. 4,000(paid). **Wire Service(s):** AP.

US

TIMES UNION. 1856. d. $.50/day newsstand; $2/Sun; $3.90/wk. home deliv. News Plz., Box 15000, Albany, NY 12212. TEL 518-454-5694; FAX 518-454-5628; E-mail: tunewsroom@aol.com. **Owner(s):** Hearst Corp., 959 Eighth Ave., New York, NY 10019. TEL 212-649-2000; Ed. Harry M. Rosenfeld; Pub. Timothy O. White; photos; bk.rev.; pub. size: broadsheet; circ. morning 106,000(paid); Sun. 168,000(paid). **Wire Service(s):** AP, LAT-WP, NYT, SHNA, KR, HHS, CNS.

AMSTERDAM

US   ISSN 0739-2540

RECORDER, THE. 1878. d. $.35/day newsstand; $.75/Sun.; $2.50/wk. One Venner Rd., Amsterdam, NY 12010. TEL 518-843-1100; FAX 518-843-1338. **Owner(s):** Wm. J. Kline & Sons, Inc., P.O. Box 640, Amsterdam, NY 12010. TEL 518-843-1100; Ed. Tony Benjamin; Pub. Frank Gappa; adv. contact: Bob Simpson. photos; bk.rev.; pub. size: broadsheet; circ. evening 11,900(paid); Sun. 11,450(paid). **Wire Service(s):** AP, Tribune.

AUBURN

US

CITIZEN, THE. 1816. Sun.-Fri. $.35/day newsstand; $1.25/Sun. 25 Dill St., Auburn, NY 13021. TEL 315-253-5311; FAX 315-253-5311. **Owner(s):** Howard Publications, Inc., P.O. Box 570, Oceanside, CA 92049; Ed. Don Rogers; Pub. Jack Palmer; adv. contact: Doris Rush. pub. size: broadsheet; circ. evening 17,800(paid); Sun. 18,400(paid). **Wire Service(s):** AP, LAT-WP. **Formerly:** Auburn Citizen.

BATAVIA

US

BATAVIA DAILY NEWS. 1878. Mon.-Sat. $.50 newsstand; $109.20/yr. carrier; $116/yr. local motor rte. 2 Apollo Dr., Batavia, NY 14020. TEL 716-343-8000; FAX 716-343-2623. **Owner(s):** Batavia Newspapers Corp., P.O. Box 360, Batavia, NY 14020. TEL 716-343-8000; Ed. Mark Graczyk; Pub. Roger Mosher; pub. size: standard; circ. evening 17,000(paid). **Wire Service(s):** AP.

BROOKLYN

US

BROOKLYN DAILY BULLETIN. 1955. Mon.-Fri. $.50 newsstand; $90/6 mos.; $150/yr. 125 Montague St., 2nd Fl., Brooklyn, NY 11201. TEL 718-625-7500; FAX 718-624-2716. **Owner(s):** Brooklyn Journal Publications, 125 Montague St., 2nd Fl., Brooklyn, NY 11201. TEL 212-608-1384; FAX 212-624-2716; Ed. Ed Goldstein; Pub. Dozier Hasty; adv. contact: Pat Higgins. pub. size: tabloid; circ. morning 5,250(paid). **Wire Service(s):** CNS.

US   ISSN 0746-8865

NEW YORK DAILY CHALLENGE. 1972. Mon.-Fri. $.35 newsstand; $65/yr. 1360 Fulton St., Brooklyn, NY 11216. TEL 718-636-9500; FAX 718-857-9115. **Owner(s):** Tom Watkins, 1360 Fulton St., Brooklyn, NY 11216; Ed. Dawad Phillip; Pub. Tom Watkins; adv. contact: Fred Hudson. pub. size: tabloid; circ. morning 79,000(paid). **Wire Service(s):** API, UPI.

BUFFALO

US   ISSN 0745-2691

BUFFALO NEWS, THE. 1880. d. $.50/day newsstand; $1.75/Sun.; $4/wk. The News Plz., Buffalo, NY 14203. TEL 716-849-4444; FAX 716-856-5150. **Owner(s):** Berkshire Hathaway, Inc., 1440 Kiewit Plz., Omaha, NE 68131. TEL 402-346-1400; adv. contact: Warren Colville. photos; bk.rev.; pub. size: broadsheet; circ. evening 284,222(paid); Sun. 365,140(paid). **Wire Service(s):** AP, KR, LAT-WP, RN.

CANANDAIGUA

US

CANANDAIGUA DAILY MESSENGER. 1796. Sun.-Fri. $.50/day newsstand; $1/Sun.; $109.20/yr. in cy. 73 Buffalo St., Canandaigua, NY 14424. TEL 716-394-0770. **Owner(s):** Canandaigua Messenger, Inc., 73 Buffalo St., Canandaigua, NY 14424. TEL 716-394-0770; Ed. Robert Matson; Pub. George M. Ewing Jr.; pub. size: broadsheet; circ. evening 14,603(paid); Sun. 14,447(paid). **Wire Service(s):** AP, Data Stream, Photo Stream, SHNA, LAT-WP.

CATSKILL

US

DAILY MAIL. 1879. Mon-Sat. $.50 newsstand; $104/yr. motor rte.; $155.16/yr. mailed. 30 Church St., Catskill, NY 12414. TEL 518-943-2100; FAX 518-943-2063. **Owner(s):** Johnson Newspaper Corp., 260 Washington St., Watertown, NY 13601; Ed. Annabar Jensis; Pub. Anthony Panetta; adv.; pub. size: broadsheet; circ. evening 5,500(paid). **Wire Service(s):** AP.

COBLESKILL

US   ISSN 1051-3841

DAILY EDITOR. Sun.-Fri. complimentary; $.75 newsstand. 59 Main St., Cobleskill, NY 12043. TEL 518-234-4368; FAX 518-234-8849. **Owner(s):** American Publishing Co., 606 N. Van Buren, P.O. Box 520, Marion, IL 62959. TEL 618-993-1711; Ed. Dana Cudmore; Pub. Ted Mike; adv. contact: Kevin O'Conner. pub. size: standard; circ. morning 18,000(paid).

CORNING

US

LEADER, THE. d. $.50/day newsstand; $1.50/Sun. 34 W. Pulteney St., Corning, NY 14830. TEL 607-936-4651; FAX 607-936-9939. **Owner(s):** Howard Publications, Inc., Oceanside, CA; Ed. Mike Gossie; Pub. William Blake; adv. contact: Mike Bartelli. pub. size: broadsheet; circ. evening 17,000(paid). **Wire Service(s):** AP.

CORTLAND

US

CORTLAND STANDARD. 1867. Mon.-Sat. $.35 newsstand; $109.20/yr. carrier; $133.10/yr. mailed. 110 Main St., Cortland, NY 13045. TEL 607-756-5665; FAX 607-756-5665. **Owner(s):** Cortland Standard Printing Co., Inc., 110 Main St., Cortland, NY 13045. TEL 607-756-5665; Pub. Kevin Howe; adv. contact: Edward J. Rounds. pub. size: broadsheet; circ. evening 12,500(paid). **Wire Service(s):** AP.

DUNKIRK
US

EVENING-OBSERVER. 1882. d. $.35/day newsstand; $.75/Sun.; $105/yr. 8-10 E. Second St., Dunkirk, NY 14048. TEL 716-366-3000; FAX 716-366-3005. **Owner(s):** Ogden Newspapers, Inc., 1500 Main St., Wheeling, WV 26033. TEL 304-233-0100; Ed. Keith Sheldon. adv. contact: Chris Bertoldson. pub. size: broadsheet; circ. evening 14,500(paid); Sun. 14,000(paid). **Wire Service(s):** AP.

ELMIRA
US

STAR-GAZETTE. d. $.50/day newsstand; $1.50/Sun.; $3.25/wk. carrier; $205.40/yr. in area; $229.32/yr. out of area mailed. 201 Baldwin St., Elmira, NY 14902. TEL 607-734-5151; FAX 607-733-4408; E-mail: sgdata@aol.com. **Owner(s):** Gannett Company, Inc., 1100 Wilson Blvd., Arlington, VA 22340; Ed. Charles W. Nutt Jr.; Pub. Margaret Buchanan; adv. contact: Mark Logsdon. pub. size: broadsheet; circ. morning 35,170(paid); Sun. 51,313(paid). **Wire Service(s):** AP, GNS.

GENEVA
US

FINGER LAKES TIMES, THE. 1872. Sun.-Fri. $.50/day newsstand; $1/Sun.; $120/yr. 218 Genesee St., Geneva, NY 14456. TEL 315-789-3333; FAX 315-789-4077. **Owner(s):** Independent Publications, Inc., Bryn Mawr, PA; Ed. Philip Beckley; Pub. George A. Park, Jr.; adv.; photos; pub. size: broadsheet; circ. evening 19,000(paid); Sun. 20,400(paid). **Wire Service(s):** AP, LAT-WP.

Formerly: Geneva Times.

GLEN FALLS
US   ISSN 0897-0505

POST-STAR. 1889. d. $.50/day newsstand; $1.50/Sun.; $3.15/wk. carrier; $3.75/wk. rural deliv.; $5/wk. mailed. Lawrence & Cooper Sts., Glen Falls, NY 12801. TEL 518-792-3131; FAX 518-743-1684; E-mail: poststar@globalone.net; URL: http://www.albany.globalone.net/poststar. **Owner(s):** Howard Publications, Inc., P.O. Box 570, Oceanside, CA 92049. TEL 619-433-5771; Ed. Steve Bennett; Pub. Jim Marshall; adv. contact: Nick Cinmano. pub. size: broadsheet; circ. morning 36,500(paid); Sun. 36,500(paid). **Wire Service(s):** AP.

GLOVERSVILLE
US

LEADER-HERALD, THE. 1887. d. $.35 newsstand; $2.20/wk. local; $2.30/wk. rural. 8-10 E. Fulton St., Gloversville, NY 12078. TEL 518-725-8616; FAX 518-725-7407. **Owner(s):** Ogden Newspapers, Inc., 1500 Main St., Wheeling, WV 26033; Ed. Tom Nevich; Pub. Joseph Bradley; bk.rev.; pub. size: broadsheet; circ. morning 15,000(paid). **Wire Service(s):** AP.

Formerly: Gloversville Leader-Herald.

HERKIMER
US

EVENING TELEGRAM. 1898. Mon.-Sat. $.50 newsstand; $2/wk. 111-113 Green St., Herkimer, NY 13350. TEL 315-866-2220; FAX 315-866-5913. **Owner(s):** American Publishing Co., 606 N. Van Buren, P.O. Box 520, Marion, IL 62959. TEL 618-993-1711; Ed. Dan Guzewich; Pub. Beth Brewer; adv. contact: Wesley Williams. pub. size: broadsheet; circ. evening 7,100(paid). **Wire Service(s):** AP.

HORNELL
US

HORNELL EVENING TRIBUNE. 1851. Sun.-Fri. $.50/day newsstand; $1.50/Sun; $10/mo. carrier; $10/mo. motor rte. 85 Canisteo St., Hornell, NY 14843. TEL 607-324-1425; FAX 607-324-1753. **Owner(s):** American Publishing Co., 606 N. Van Buren, P.O. Box 520, Marion, IL 62959. TEL 618-993-1711; Ed. Cindy Lorow; Pub. John Frungillo; adv. contact: David Broderick. pub. size: broadsheet; circ. morning 10,000(paid); Sun. 17,000(paid). **Wire Service(s):** AP.

HUDSON
US   ISSN 0747-2374

REGISTER STAR. 1785. Sun.-Fri. $.50/day newsstand; $.75/Sun.; $115/yr. home deliv. 85 Canisteo St., Hudson, NY 12534. TEL 518-828-1616; FAX 518-828-9437. **Owner(s):** Park Communications, Inc., Vine Ctr. Office Tower, 333 W. Vine St., 17th Fl., Lexington, KY 40507. TEL 606-252-7275; Ed. Jack Kehrer; Pub. William Lundquist; adv.; pub. size: broadsheet; circ. evening 15,500(paid); Sun. 15,500(paid). **Wire Service(s):** AP.

ITHACA
US

ITHACA JOURNAL, THE. 1815. Mon.-Sat. $.35/day newsstand; $.50/Sat.; $2.75/wk. home deliv.; $3/wk. motor rte. 123 W. State St., Ithaca, NY 14850. TEL 607-272-2321; FAX 607-272-4335. **Owner(s):** Gannett Company, Inc., 1100 Wilson Blvd., Arlington, VA 22234. TEL 703-284-6000; Ed. Ted Haider; Pub. Ellen Leifeld; adv. contact: Carol Becker. bk.rev.; pub. size: broadsheet; circ. morning 19,623(paid). **Wire Service(s):** AP, GNS.

JAMESTOWN
US

POST-JOURNAL, THE. 1826. d. $.35/day newsstand; $1/Sun.; $8.20/mo. motor rte. 15 W. Second St., Jamestown, NY 14701. TEL 716-487-1111; FAX 716-664-3119. **Owner(s):** Ogden Newspapers, Inc., 1500 Main St., Wheeling, WV 26033. TEL 304-233-0100; Ed. Cristie L. Herbst; Pub. Donald L. Meyer; adv. contact: Nancy Philips. pub. size: broadsheet; circ. evening 26,000(paid); Sun. 30,000(paid). **Wire Service(s):** AP.

KINGSTON
US   ISSN 0746-4932

DAILY & SUNDAY FREEMAN. 1871. Sun.-Fri. $.50/day newsstand; $1.50/Sun; $11/mo. carrier; $12/mo. motor rte. 79 Hurley Ave., Kingston, NY 12401. TEL 914-331-5000; FAX 914-331-0366. **Owner(s):** Mark Goodson Enterprises Ltd., 79 Hurley Ave., Kingston, NY 12401. TEL 914-331-5000; Ed. Sam Daleo; Pub. Ira Fusfeld; adv. contact: John Martin. photos; pub. size: broadsheet; circ. morning 23,000(paid); Sun. 32,000(paid). **Wire Service(s):** AP.

LITTLE FALLS
US

EVENING TIMES, THE. 1886. Mon.-Sat. $.40 newsstand; $2.25/wk. carrier. 347 S. Second St., Little Falls, NY 13365. TEL 315-823-3680; FAX 315-823-4086. **Owner(s):** Crowley Publishing Corp., P.O. Box 1007, Little Falls, NY 13365. TEL 315-823-3680; Ed. Larry Neely; Pub. Donald Paparella; adv. contact: Elaine McEvoy. pub. size: broadsheet; circ. evening 7,132(paid). **Wire Service(s):** AP.

Formerly: Little Falls Evening Times.

LOCKPORT
US

UNION-SUN & JOURNAL. 182_. Mon.-Sat. $.50 newsstand; $2.10/wk. home deliv. 459 S. Transit St., Lockport, NY 14094. TEL 715-439-9222; FAX 716-439-9239. **Owner(s):** Park Communications, Inc., Vine Ctr. Office Tower, 333 W. Vine St., 17th Fl., Lexington, KY 40507. TEL 606-252-7275; Ed. Daniel Kane; Pub. Thomas N. Ceravolo; adv. contact: Daniel M. Caswell. pub. size: broadsheet; circ. evening 18,000(paid). **Wire Service(s):** AP.

Formerly: Lockport Union-Sun & Journal.

MALONE
US

MALONE TELEGRAM. 1905. Mon.-Sat. $.50/day newsstand; $130/yr. in cy; $145/yr. 387 E. Main St., Malone, NY 12953. TEL 518-483-4700; FAX 518-483-8579. **Owner(s):** Johnson Newspaper Corp., 260 Washington St., Watertown, NY 13601. TEL 315-782-1000; Ed. Tom Graser; Pub. Russell F. Webster; adv.; pub. size: broadsheet; circ. evening 7,000(paid). **Wire Service(s):** AP.

MASSENA
US

DAILY COURIER OBSERVER, THE. 1891. Tue.-Sat. $.35 newsstand; $85/yr. carrier; $87/yr. motor rte. 56 1/2 Main St., Massena, NY 13662. TEL 315-769-2451; FAX 315-764-0337. **Owner(s):** Park Communications, Inc., Vine Ctr. Office Tower, 333 W. Vine St., 17th Fl., Lexington, KY 40507. TEL 606-252-7275; Ed. Ryne R. Martin. adv. contact: Mary McGee. pub. size: standard; circ. morning 7,500(paid).

Dailies

MEDINA

US

JOURNAL-REGISTER. 1903. Mon.-Fri. $.50 newsstand; $99/yr. mailed. 413 Main St., Medina, NY 14103-1416. TEL 716-798-1400; FAX 716-798-0290. **Owner(s):** Park Communications, Inc., Vine Ctr. Office Tower, 333 W. Vine St., 17th Fl., Lexington, KY 40507-1416. TEL 606-252-7275; Ed. Michael Wertman. adv. contact: Greg Kerth. pub. size: broadsheet; circ. evening 5,500(paid). **Wire Service(s):** AP.

MELVILLE

US   ISSN 0278-5587

NEWSDAY. 1940. d. $.50/day newsstand; $1.50/Sun. 235 Pinelawn Rd., Melville, NY 11747-4250. TEL 516-843-2020; FAX 516-843-2953; E-mail: esgdesk@aol.com; URL: http://www.newsday.com. **Owner(s):** Times-Mirror Co., Los Angeles, CA; Ed. Howard Schneider; Pub. Raymond A. Jansen; adv. contact: John McKeon. pub. size: tabloid; circ. morning 555,203(paid); Sun. 643,421(paid). **Wire Service(s):** AP, DJ, LAT-WP, NWS, RN, CSM.

MIDDLETOWN

US

TIMES HERALD-RECORD. 1956. d. $.50/day newsstand; $1.50/Sun.; $3.20/wk.; $12.80/mo. 40 Mulberry St., Middletown, NY 10940. TEL 914-341-1100; FAX 914-343-6414. **Owner(s):** Ottaway Newspapers, Inc., P.O. Box 401, Campbell Hall, NY 10916. TEL 914-294-8181; Ed. Jeff Storey; Pub. James A. Moss; adv. contact: Susan Krafve. photos; bk.rev.; pub. size: tabloid; circ. morning 86,141(paid); Sun. 101,954(paid). **Wire Service(s):** AP, NYT, KNT, SHNA.

NEW ROCHELLE

US   ISSN 1060-4553

DAILY ITEM, THE. 1899. d. $.50/day newsstand; $1.50/Sun.; $3.95/wk. 92 North Ave., New Rochelle, NY 10801. TEL 914-637-2200; FAX 914-637-2230. **Owner(s):** Gannett Suburban Newspapers, One Gannett Dr., White Plains, NY 10604. TEL 914-694-5000; Ed. William Carey; Pub. Ken Paulson; adv. contact: Bob Twesten. pub. size: broadsheet; circ. evening 9,200(paid); Sun. 10,300(paid). **Wire Service(s):** AP, GNS.
Formerly: Port Chester Daily Item.

US

DAILY TIMES, THE. 1925. d. $.50/day newsstand; $1.50/Sun.; $3.45/wk. 92 North Ave., New Rochelle, NY 10801. TEL 914-637-2200; FAX 914-637-2230. **Owner(s):** Gannett Suburban Newspapers, One Gannett Dr., White Plains, NY 10604. TEL 914-694-5000; Ed. William Cary; Pub. Ken Paulson; adv.; pub. size: broadsheet; circ. morning 6,500(paid); Sun. 5,700(paid). **Wire Service(s):** AP, GNS.

US   ISSN 1060-4618

STANDARD-STAR. 1926. d. $.50/day newsstand; $1.50/Sun. $3.45/wk. 92 North Ave., New Rochelle, NY 10801. TEL 914-637-2200; FAX 914-637-2230. **Owner(s):** Gannett Suburban Newspapers, One Gannett Dr., White Plains, NY 10604. TEL 914-694-5000; Ed. William Cary; Pub. Ken Paulson; adv. contact: Bob Twesten. pub. size: broadsheet; circ. morning 10,645(paid); Sun. 11,612(paid). **Wire Service(s):** AP.
Formerly: New Rochelle Standard-Star.

NEW YORK

US

NEW YORK DAILY NEWS, THE. 1919. d. $.50/day newsstand; $1.25/Sun. 450 W. 33rd St., New York, NY 10001. TEL 212-210-2100; FAX 212-661-4953. **Owner(s):** Mortimer Zuckerman, 450 W. 33rd St., New York, NY 10001; Ed. Arthur Browne; Pub. Mortimer Zuckerman; adv. contact: William D. Holiber. photos; pub. size: tabloid; circ. morning 758,509(paid); Sun. 1,010,504(paid). **Wire Service(s):** AP, RN, CT-NYT.

US

NEW YORK POST. 1801. d. $.50 newsstand; $178/yr. 1211 Ave. of the Americas, New York, NY 10036-8790. TEL 212-930-8000; FAX 212-930-8540. **Owner(s):** Rupert Murdoch/News Corp., 210 South St., New York, NY 10002; Ed. Marc Kalech; Pub. Martin Singerman; adv. contact: Patrick Judge. pub. size: tabloid; circ. evening 418,255(paid). **Wire Service(s):** AP, CDN, CST, LAT-WP, AF.

US   ISSN 0362-4331

NEW YORK TIMES, THE. 1851. d. $.60/day newsstand in area; $1/day out of area; $2.50/Sun.; $6.70/wk. deliv. 229 W. 43rd St., New York, NY 10036. TEL 212-556-1234; FAX 212-556-7389. **Owner(s):** New York Times Co., The, 229 W. 43rd St., New York, NY 10036. TEL 212-556-1234; Ed. Eugene Roberts, Jr.; Pub. Arthur Ochs Sulzberger, Jr.; adv. contact: Robert Clark. pub. size: broadsheet; circ. morning 1,157,656(paid); Sun. 1,746,707(paid). **Wire Service(s):** AP, RN, TASS, DJ, PR Newswire, NYT.

NIAGARA FALLS

US

NIAGARA GAZETTE. 1854. d. $.35/day newsstand; $1/Sun.; $3/wk. home deliv. 310 Niagara St., Niagara Falls, NY 14302-0549. TEL 716-282-2311; FAX 716-286-3895. **Owner(s):** Gannett Suburban Newspapers, One Gannett Dr., White Plains, NY 10604. TEL 914-694-5000; Pub. Mark Francis; adv. contact: Michael Kellogg. photos; bk.rev.; pub. size: broadsheet; circ. morning 27,000(paid); Sun. 30,000(paid). **Wire Service(s):** AP, GNS.

NORTH TONAWANDA

US

TONAWANDA NEWS. 1880. Mon.-Sat. $.35 newsstand; $1.70/wk. 435 River Rd., North Tonawanda, NY 14120. TEL 716-693-1000; FAX 716-693-8573. **Owner(s):** American Publishing Co., 606 N. Van Buren, P.O. Box 520, Marion, IL 62959. TEL 618-993-1711; Ed. Terry Shaw; Pub. Joseph P. Armenia; adv. contact: Frank Skally. pub. size: broadsheet; circ. evening 13,500(paid). **Wire Service(s):** AP.

NORWICH

US   ISSN 0747-0355

EVENING SUN, THE. 1891. Mon.-Fri. $.40 newsstand; $95/yr. carrier; $100/yr. motor rte. 29 Lackawanna Ave., Norwich, NY 13815. TEL 607-334-3276; FAX 607-334-8273. **Owner(s):** Snyder Communication Corp., Mechanic St., Norwich, NY 13815. TEL 607-334-3276; Ed. Jeff Genung. adv. contact: Russ Foote. photos; bk.rev.; pub. size: broadsheet; circ. evening 6,687(paid). **Wire Service(s):** AP.

OGDENSBURG

US   ISSN 0893-5149

OGDENSBURG JOURNAL. 1830. Sun.-Fri. $.35/day newsstand; $1/Sun.; $60.50/yr. home deliv. 308 Isabella, Ogdensburg, NY 13669. TEL 315-393-1000; FAX 315-393-5108. **Owner(s):** Park Communications, Inc., Vine Ctr. Office Tower, 333 W. Vine St., 17th Fl., Lexington, KY 40507. TEL 606-252-7275; Ed. James Reagen. adv.; pub. size: broadsheet; circ. morning 5,500(paid); Sun. 12,000(paid). **Wire Service(s):** AP.

OLEAN

US

OLEAN TIMES HERALD. 1860. d. $.50/day newsstand; $1.50/Sun.; $14.50/mo. 639 Norton Dr., Olean, NY 14760. TEL 716-372-3121; FAX 716-372-0740. **Owner(s):** American Publishing Co., 606 N. Van Buren, P.O. Box 520, Marion, IL 62959. TEL 618-993-1711; Ed. Charles Ward; Pub. Charles Ward; adv. contact: Larry Chiott. pub. size: broadsheet; circ. morning 25,000(paid); Sun. 25,000(paid). **Wire Service(s):** AP, UPI.

ONEIDA

US

ONEIDA DAILY DISPATCH. 1851. Mon.-Sat. $.40 newsstand; $109.40/yr. carrier; $124.80/yr. mail deliv. 130 Broad St., Oneida, NY 13421. TEL 315-363-5100; FAX 315-363-9832. **Owner(s):** Goodson Newspaper Group, P.O. Box 6490, Trenton, NJ 08648; Ed. Phyllis M. Harris; Pub. Ann Campanie; adv.; pub. size: broadsheet; circ. evening 9,400(paid). **Wire Service(s):** AP.

ONEONTA

US

DAILY STAR, THE. 1890. Mon.-Sat. $.50 newsstand; $2/wk. carrier; $99/yr. carrier. 102 Chestnut St., Oneonta, NY 13820. TEL 607-432-1000; FAX 607-432-5847. **Owner(s):** Oneonta Star Div. of Ottaway Newspapers, P.O. Box 401, Campbell Hall, NY 10916. TEL 914-294-8181; Ed. Carey Brunswick; Pub. Richard J. Anthony; adv. contact: Bill Reeves. photos; pub. size: broadsheet; circ. morning 19,800(paid). **Wire Service(s):** AP, ONS.

OSWEGO

US

PALLADIUM-TIMES, THE. 1845. Mon.-Sat. $.50 newsstand; $102/yr. home deliv. 140 W. First St., Oswego, NY 13126. TEL 315-343-3800. E-mail: frassine@knighted.com; URL: http://www.knighted.com/~palldiu. **Owner(s):** Hollinger, Inc.; Pub. Bruce P. Frassinelli; adv. contact: Jon Spauiding. photos; pub. size: broadsheet; circ. evening 11,124(paid). **Wire Service(s):** AP, SHNA.
Formerly: Oswego Palladium-Times.

PLATTSBURGH

US   ISSN 1041-4754

PRESS-REPUBLICAN. 1942. d. $.50/day newsstand; $1.50/Sun.; $204/yr. mailed. 170 Margaret St., Plattsburgh, NY 12901. TEL 518-561-2300; FAX 518-561-3362. **Owner(s):** Plattsburgh Publishing Co., 170 Margaret St., Plattsburgh, NY 12901. TEL 518-561-2300; Ed. James D. Dynko; Pub. Brenda J. Tallman; adv. contact: George Rock. bk.rev.; pub. size: broadsheet; circ. morning 24,000(paid); Sun. 25,000(paid). **Wire Service(s):** AP, DJNS, ONS, SHNS.

POUGHKEEPSIE

US

POUGHKEEPSIE JOURNAL. 1785. d. $.50/day newsstand; $1.50/Sun.; $13/mo. home deliv.; $14.50/mo. motor rte. 85 Civic Center Plz., Poughkeepsie, NY 12601. TEL 914-454-2010; FAX 914-437-4902. **Owner(s):** Gannett Company, Inc., 1100 Wilson Blvd., Arlington, VA 22234. TEL 703-284-6000; Ed. Diana Mitsu-Klos; Pub. Richard K. Wager; adv.; photos; bk.rev.; pub. size: broadsheet; circ. morning 45,000(paid); Sun. 62,500(paid). **Wire Service(s):** AP, GNS, KR.

ROCHESTER

US

ROCHESTER DEMOCRAT & CHRONICLE. 1833. d. $.35/day newsstand; $2.05/Sun.; $158.60/yr. 55 Exchange Blvd., Rochester, NY 14614. TEL 716-232-7100; FAX 716-258-9788. **Owner(s):** Gannett Company, Inc., 1100 Wilson Blvd, Arlington, VA 22234. TEL 703-284-6000; Ed. Tom Callinan; Pub. David J. Mack; adv.; photos; bk.rev.; pub. size: broadsheet; circ. morning 136,311(paid); Sun. 260,452(paid). **Wire Service(s):** AP, LAT-WP, CDN, GNS, CST, RN.

US   ISSN 0744-1851

TIMES-UNION. 1918. Mon.-Fri. $.40 newsstand; $1.50/wk. home deliv. 55 Exchange Blvd., Rochester, NY, 14614. TEL 716-232-7100; FAX 716-258-2691. **Owner(s):** Gannett Company, Inc., 1100 Wilson Blvd., Arlington, VA 22234. TEL 703-284-6000; Ed. Thomas E. Callinan; Pub. David J. Mack; adv.; pub. size: broadsheet; circ. evening 53,473(paid). **Wire Service(s):** AP, TP, GNS, NYT, Dow Jones.

ROME

US

DAILY & SUNDAY SENTINEL. 1865. d. $.50/day newsstand; free/Sun.; $124.80/yr. carrier deliv.; $130/yr. motor rte.; $143/yr. mailed. 333 W. Dominick St., Rome, NY 13440. TEL 315-337-4000; FAX 315-337-4704. **Owner(s):** Rome Sentinel Co., 333 W. Dominick St., Rome, NY 13440. TEL 315-337-4000; Ed. David G. Swanson; Pub. Stephen B. Waters; adv. contact: Ron O'Neil. photos; pub. size: broadsheet; sun. tabloid; circ. evening 17,835(paid); Sun. 27,000(free). **Wire Service(s):** AP.

SALAMANCA

US   ISSN 8755-9110

SALAMANCA PRESS. 1867. Mon.-Sat. $.50 newsstand; $9.60/mo. in cy. 36-42 River St., Salamanca, NY 14779. TEL 716-945-1644; FAX 716-945-4285. **Owner(s):** American Publishing Co., 606 N. Van Buren, P.O. Box 520, Marion, IL 62959. TEL 618-993-1711; Ed. Kevin Burleson; Pub. Pat Patterson; adv. contact: Glenda Pearson. pub. size: broadsheet; circ. evening 2,500(paid). **Wire Service(s):** AP.

SARANAC LAKE

US

ADIRONDACK DAILY ENTERPRISE. 1895. Mon.-Sat. $.35/day newsstand; $.50/Sat.; $74/yr. carrier. P.O. Box 318, Saranac Lake, NY 12983. TEL 518-891-2600; FAX 518-891-2756. **Owner(s):** Ogden Newspapers, Inc., 1500 Main St., Wheeling, WV; Ed. John Penny; Pub. Catherine Moore; adv.; photos; bk.rev.; pub. size: broadsheet; circ. evening 6,000(paid). **Wire Service(s):** AP.

SARATOGA SPRINGS

US   ISSN 1071-4448

SARATOGIAN, THE. 1865. d. $.35/day newsstand; $.75/Sun.; $29.25/3 mo. 20 Lake Ave., Saratoga Springs, NY 12866. TEL 518-584-4242; FAX 518-587-7750. **Owner(s):** Gannett Company, Inc., 1100 Wilson Blvd., Arlington, VA 22234. TEL 703-284-6901; Ed. Barbara Lombardo; Pub. Monte I. Trammer; adv. contact: Nancy Meyer. photos; pub. size: broadsheet; circ. morning 13,359(paid); Sun. 15,243(paid). **Wire Service(s):** AP, GNS.

SCHENECTADY

US   ISSN 1050-0340

DAILY GAZETTE. 1894. d. $.50/day newsstand; $1.25/Sun.; $3/wk.; $12/mo. 2345 Maxon Rd., Schenectady, NY 12301-1090. TEL 518-374-4141; FAX 518-395-3089; E-mail: gazette@dailygazette.com; URL: http://www.dailygazette.com. **Owner(s):** Daily Gazette Co., Inc., 2345 Maxon Rd., Schenectady, NY 12301-1090. TEL 518-372-4141; Ed. Thomas Woodman; Pub. John E.N. Hume, III; adv. contact: Scott Osswald. bk.rev.; pub. size: broadsheet; circ. morning 61,453(paid); Sun. 63,822(paid). **Wire Service(s):** AP, LAT-WP.

STATEN ISLAND

US

STATEN ISLAND ADVANCE. 1886. d. $.50/day newsstand; $1.50/Sun.; $2.25/wk. 950 Fingerboard Rd., Staten Island, NY 10305. TEL 718-981-1234; FAX 718-981-5679. **Owner(s):** Advance Publications, Inc., 950 Fingerboard Rd., Staten Island, NY 10305. TEL 718-981-1235; Ed. William Huus; Pub. Richard E. Diamond; adv.; photos; bk.rev.; pub. size: broadsheet; circ. evening 80,000(paid); Sun. 95,000(paid). **Wire Service(s):** AP, LAT, NNS.

SYRACUSE

US

POST-STANDARD. Mon.-Sat. $.35 newsstand; $2.10/wk. carrier; $109.20/yr. carrier. Clinton Sq., Syracuse, NY 13221. TEL 315-470-0011; FAX 315-470-3081. **Owner(s):** Syracuse Newspapers, Inc., Syracuse, NY; Ed. Rosemarry Robinson; Pub. Stephen A. Rogers; adv. contact: Klein Klaus. pub. size: broadsheet; circ. morning 89,000(paid). **Wire Service(s):** AP, LAT-WP.

US

SYRACUSE HERALD-JOURNAL/AMERICAN. 1877. d. $.35/day newsstand; $1.50/Sun.; $3.60/wk. carrier. One Clinton Sq., Syracuse, NY 13221. TEL 315-470-0011; FAX 315-470-3019. **Owner(s):** Herald Co., P.O. Box 4915, Syracuse, NY 13221. TEL 315-470-0010; Ed. Timothy Atseff; Pub. Stephen A. Rogers; adv. contact: James Kleinklaus. photos; pub. size: broadsheet; circ. evening 82,488(paid); Sun. 226,000(paid). **Wire Service(s):** NNS, KR, AP, NYT, ANS.

TROY

US

RECORD, THE. 1896. d. $.50/day newsstand; $1.50/Sun.; $2.85/wk. 501 Broadway, Troy, NY 12181. TEL 518-270-1200; FAX 518-270-1202; E-mail: troyrecord@globalone.net. URL: http://www.globalone.net/record/. **Owner(s):** Troy Publishing Co., Inc., 501 Broadway, Troy, NY 12180. TEL 518-270-1200; Ed. Charles DeLaFuente. adv. contact Michael O'Sullivan. bk.rev.; pub. size: broadsheet; circ. morning 30,000(paid); Sun. 33,000(paid). **Wire Service(s):** AP, KR.

UTICA

US

OBSERVER-DISPATCH. 1817. d. $.50/day newsstand; $1.50/Sun.; $3.30/wk. home deliv. 221 Oriskany Plz., Utica, NY 13501. TEL 315-792-5000; FAX 315-792-5033; E-mail: 76275.227@compuserve.com. **Owner(s):** Gannett Company, Inc., 1100 Wilson Blvd., Arlington, VA 22209; Pub. Donna Donovan; adv. contact: Bob Parker. pub. size: standard; circ. morning 60,000(paid); Sun. 68,321(paid). **Wire Service(s):** AP, GNS.

VESTAL

US

PRESS & SUN-BULLETIN. 1822. d. $.35/day newsstand; $1.50/Sun.; $119.60/yr. Mon.-Sat.; $171.60/yr. carrier delivery. 4421 Vestal Pkwy. E., Vestal, NY 13850. TEL 607-798-1234; FAX 607-798-1113. **Owner(s):** Gannett Company, Inc., 1100 Wilson Blvd., Arlington, VA 22234. TEL 703-284-6000; Ed. Barry Rothfeld; Pub. Bernard Griffin; adv.; bk.rev.; pub. size: broadsheet; circ. morning 70,000(paid); Sun. 90,000(paid). **Wire Service(s):** AP, GNS, LAT-WP. **Formerly:** Binghamton Press & Sun-Bulletin.

WATERTOWN

US

WATERTOWN DAILY TIMES. 1861. d. $.35/day newsstand; $1.50/Sun.; $2.85/wk. carrier; $3/wk. motor rte. 260 Washington St., Watertown, NY 13601. TEL 315-782-1000; FAX 315-782-2337. **Owner(s):** John B. Johnson, 221 Flower Ave., W., Watertown, NY 13601; Ed. John B. Johnson, Jr.; Pub. John B. Johnson; adv. contact: Robert Cornell. pub. size: broadsheet; circ. morning 40,662(paid); Sun. 44,966(paid). **Wire Service(s):** AP, NYT.

WELLSVILLE

US

WELLSVILLE DAILY REPORTER. 1880. Sun.-Fri. $.50/day newsstand; $1.50/Sun.; $7.75/mo. carrier; $8/mo. motor rte.; $9/mo. mailed in US. 159 N. Main St., Wellsville, NY 14895. TEL 716-593-5300; FAX 716-593-5303. **Owner(s):** American Publishing Co., 606 N. Van Buren, P.O. Box 520, Marion, IL 52959. TEL 618-993-1711; Ed. Nea Simon Pub. Oak Duke; pub. size: broadsheet; circ. evening 4,000(paid); Sun. 14,000(paid). **Wire Service(s):** AP.

WEST NYACK

US

ROCKLAND JOURNAL-NEWS. 1889. d. $.50/day newsstand; $1.50/Sun.; $3.45/wk. 200 N., Rte. 303, West Nyack, NY 10994. TEL 914-358-2200; FAX 914-578-2477. **Owner(s):** Gannett Company, Inc., 1100 Wilson Blvd., Arlington, VA 22234. TEL 703-284-6000; Pub. Gary Sherlock; adv. contact: Enedina Vega. photos; bk.rev.; pub. size: broadsheet; circ. evening 43,000(paid); Sun. 53,000(paid). **Wire Service(s):** AP, GNS.
   Formerly: Journal-News.

WHITE PLAINS

US

REPORTER DISPATCH, THE. 1964. d. $.50/day newsstand; $1.50/Sun.; $3.45/wk. carrier; $288/yr. mailed. One Gannett Dr., White Plains, NY 10604. TEL 914-694-9300; FAX 914-694-5018; E-mail: 73424.1275@compuserve.com. **Owner(s):** Gannett Company, Inc., 1100 Wilson Blvd., Arlington, VA 22340. TEL 703-284-6000; Ed. Kenneth A. Paulson; Pub. Gary F. Sherlock; pub. size: broadsheet; circ. morning 48,248(paid); Sun. 59,702(paid). **Wire Service(s):** AP, GNS, LAT-WP, KR.

US

TARRYTOWN DAILY NEWS. d. $.40/day newsstand; $1.50/Sun.; $3.45/wk. One Gannett Dr., White Plains, NY 10604. TEL 914-694-9300; FAX 914-694-3535. **Owner(s):** Gannett Suburban Newspapers, One Gannett Dr., White Plains, NY 10604. TEL 914-694-5000; Ed. Janet McMillan; Pub. Gary Sherlock; adv.; pub. size: broadsheet; circ. morning 6,509(paid); evening 4,200(paid); Sun. 4,800(paid). **Wire Service(s):** AP, GNS.

YONKERS

US   ISSN 1060-4723

MT. VERNON DAILY ARGUS. d. $.40/day newsstand; $1.50/Sun.; $3.45/wk. One Odell Plz., Yonkers, NY 10701. TEL 914-696-8253; FAX 914-696-8208. **Owner(s):** Gannett Suburban Newspapers, One Gannett Dr., White Plains, NY 10604. TEL 914-694-5000; Pub. Ken Paulson; adv. contact: Bob Twesten. pub. size: tabloid; circ. morning 14,000(paid); Sun. 10,300(paid). **Wire Service(s):** AP, GNS.
   Formerly: Daily Argus.

US

YONKERS HERALD STATESMAN. 1863. d. $.50/day newsstand; $1.50/Sun.; $3.45/wk. carrier. One Odell Plz., Yonkers, NY 10701. TEL 914-965-5000; FAX 914-696-8208; E-mail: 73424.1275@compuserve.com. **Owner(s):** Gannett Suburban Newspapers, One Gannett Dr., White Plains, NY 10604. TEL 914-694-5000; Pub. Gary Sherlock; adv.; pub. size: broadsheet; circ. evening 23,256(paid); Sun. 30,740(paid). **Wire Service(s):** AP, GNS, LAT-WP.

YORKTOWN HEIGHTS

US   ISSN 1060-4588

CITIZEN REGISTER. 1839. d. $.50/day newsstand; $1.50/Sun.; $3.45/wk. home deliv.; $2.20/Sun. home deliv. 1825 Commerce St., Yorktown Heights, NY 10598. TEL 914-243-3700; FAX 914-243-3703. **Owner(s):** Gannett Suburban Newspapers, One Gannett Dr., White Plains, NY 10604. TEL 914-694-5000; Pub. Gary Sherlock; adv. contact: Susan Butash. pub. size: broadsheet; circ. evening 7,900(paid); Sun. 8,800(paid). **Wire Service(s):** AP, GNS.
   Formerly: Ossining Citizen Register.

US

PEEKSKILL STAR. 1920. d. $.50/day newsstand; $1.50/Sun.; $4.50/wk. 1825 Commerce St., Yorktown Heights, NY 10598. TEL 914-243-3700; FAX 914-243-3703. **Owner(s):** Gannett Suburban Newspapers, One Gannett Dr., White Plains, NY 10604. TEL 914-694-5000; Pub. Gary Sherlock; adv. contact: Susan Butash. pub. size: broadsheet; circ. evening 12,500(paid); Sun. 13,200(paid). **Wire Service(s):** AP.

NORTH CAROLINA

ASHEBORO

US

ASHEBORO COURIER-TRIBUNE. 1876. Sun.-Fri. $.50/day newsstand; $1/Sun.; $80/yr. carrier; $140/yr. mail. 500 Sunset Ave., Asheboro, NC 27203. TEL 910-625-2102; FAX 910-626-7074; E-mail: ctnet@atomic.net; URL: http://www.atomic.net/ctnet. **Owner(s):** Donrey Media Group, P.O. Box 17017, Fort Smith, AK 72901. TEL 501-785-7810; Ed. Ray Criscoe; Pub. David Renfro; adv. contact: Chris Allen. pub. size: broadsheet; circ. evening 18,500(paid); Sun. 18,500(paid). **Wire Service(s):** AP.

ASHEVILLE

US   ISSN 1060-3255

ASHEVILLE CITIZEN-TIMES. 1870. d. $.50/day newsstand; $.75/Sat; $1.50/Sun.; $15.17/mo. 14 O'Henry Ave., Asheville, NC 28801. TEL 704-252-5611; FAX 704-251-0585. **Owner(s):** Gannett Company, Inc., 1100 Wilson Blvd., Arlington, VA 22340; Ed. Ed Dawson; Pub. Virgil L. Smith; adv.; photos; bk.rev.; pub. size: broadsheet; circ. morning 68,454(paid); Sun. 80,412(paid). **Wire Service(s):** AP, AP Leaf Desk; KNS.

BURLINGTON

US

TIMES-NEWS, THE. 1887. d. $.50/day newsstand; $1/Sun.; $7.60/mo. carrier. 707 S. Main St., Burlington, NC 27215. TEL 910-227-0131; FAX 910-229-2463. **Owner(s):** Freedom Communications, Inc., 17666 Fitch, Irvine, CA 92714. TEL 714-253-9292; FAX 714-474-7675; Ed. John Pea; Pub. Robert M. Lyons; photos; bk.rev.; pub. size: standard; circ. morning 28,789(paid); Sun. 30,848(paid). **Wire Service(s):** AP.

CHAPEL HILL

US

CHAPEL HILL HERALD. 1988. d. $.50/day newsstand; $1.50/Sun.; $13.50/mo. carrier; $18.05/mo. out of state. 106 Mallette St., Chapel Hill, NC 27516. TEL 919-967-6581; FAX 919-918-1055. **Owner(s):** Durham Herald-Sun Papers, 106 Mallette St., Chapel Hill, NC 27516. TEL 919-967-6581; Ed. William Hawkins; Pub. David Hughey; adv. contact: Beth Deacon. pub. size: standard; circ. morning 25,000(paid); Sun. 25,000(paid).

CHARLOTTE

US

CHARLOTTE OBSERVER. 1886. d. $.50/day newsstand; $1.50/Sun.; $2.50/wk. carrier in area. 600 S. Tryon St., Charlotte, NC 28202. TEL 704-358-5000; FAX 704-358-5022; E-mail: gnielson@charlotte.infi.net; URL: http://www.charlotte.com. **Owner(s):** Knight-Ridder, Inc., One Herald Plz., Miami, FL 33132. TEL 305-376-3800; Ed. Jennie Buckner; Pub. Rolfe Neill; adv. contact: Bill McNey. pub. size: broadsheet; circ. morning 232,294(paid); Sun. 298,876(paid). **Wire Service(s):** AP, AP Photo, NYT, LAT-WP.

CLINTON

US

SAMPSON INDEPENDENT, THE. 1929. Sun.-Fri. $.35/day newsstand; $.75/Sun.; $7/mo. home deliv. 303 Elizabeth St., Clinton, NC 28328. TEL 910-592-8137; FAX 910-592-8756. **Owner(s):** Park Communications, Inc., Vine Ctr. Office Tower, 333 W. Vine St., 17th Fl., Lexington, KY 40507. TEL 606-252-7275; Ed. Debbie Chiarella. adv. contact: Randy Thompson. pub. size: broadsheet; circ. evening 7,600(paid); Sun. 8,500(paid). **Wire Service(s):** AP.
   Formerly: Clinton Sampson Independent.

CONCORD

US

CONCORD TRIBUNE. 1900. Sun.-Fri. $.50/day newsstand; $1/Sun.; $7.80/mo. $93.60/yr. carrier. 125 Union St., S., Concord, NC 28025. TEL 704-782-3155; FAX 704-786-0645. **Owner(s):** Park Communications, Inc., Vine Ctr. Office Tower, 333 W. Vine St., 17th Fl., Lexington, KY 40507. TEL 606-252-7275; Ed. Dale Cline. pub. size: broadsheet; circ. evening 13,000(paid); Sun. 14,000(paid). **Wire Service(s):** AP.

DUNN

US

DUNN DAILY RECORD. 1950. Mon.-Fri. $.25 newsstand; $52/yr. carrier; $70/yr. mailed. 100 W. Broad St., Dunn, NC 28335. TEL 910-891-1234; FAX 910-891-4445. **Owner(s):** Record Publishing Co., Inc., 100 W. Broad St., Dunn, NC 28335. TEL 910-891-1234; Ed. Lisa Farmer; Pub. Bart Adams; adv. contact: Maere Kay Lashmit. photos; pub. size: broadsheet; circ. evening 10,185(paid). **Wire Service(s):** AP.

DURHAM

US ISSN 1055-4467

HERALD-SUN, THE. 1889. d. $.50/day newsstand; $1.50/Sun.; $13.50/mo. carrier; $40.50/13 wks. carrier; $60.91/13 wks. mailed in state. 2828 Pickett Rd., Durham, NC 27705. TEL 919-419-6500; FAX 919-419-6889; E-mail: jch@herald-sun.com; URL: http://www.herald-sun.com. **Owner(s):** Durham Herald Co., P.O. Box 2092, Durham, NC 27702. TEL 919-419-6500; Ed. Jon C. Ham; Pub. David Hughey; adv. contact: Gene Bobbitt. bk.rev.; pub. size: broadsheet; circ. morning 56,000(paid); Sun. 64,000(paid). **Wire Service(s):** AP, NYT, SHNA, KR, RN.

EDEN

US ISSN 1067-0874

DAILY NEWS, THE. 1924. Mon.-Fri. $.35 newsstand; $53/yr. home deliv.; $75/yr. mailed. 804 Washington St., Eden, NC 27288. TEL 910-623-2155; FAX 910-623-2228. **Owner(s):** Park Communications, Inc., Vine Ctr. Office Tower, 333 W. Vine St., 17th Fl., Lexington, KY 40507. TEL 606-252-7252; Ed. Ross Chandler. adv. contact: Maureen Craig. photos; bk.rev.; pub. size: broadsheet; circ. evening 7,878(paid). **Wire Service(s):** AP.

Formerly: Eden Daily News.

ELIZABETH CITY

US

DAILY ADVANCE. 1911. Sun.-Fri. $.50/day newsstand; $1.25/Sun.; $9.50/mo. carrier. 216 S. Poindexter, Elizabeth City, NC 27909. TEL 919-335-0841; FAX 919-335-4415. **Owner(s):** Thomson Newspapers, Inc., One Thorn Run Ctr., Ste. 500, 1187 Thorn Run Rd. Ext., Coraoipolis, PA 15108. TEL 412-262-7870; Ed. Julian Eure; Pub. Richard D. Brown; adv. contact: Greg Rapliss. pub. size: broadsheet; circ. evening 14,725(paid); Sun. 15,032(paid). **Wire Service(s):** AP.

Formerly: Elizabeth City Daily Advance.

ELIZABETHTOWN

US

BLADEN DAILY JOURNAL. 1908. Mon.-Fri. $32.50/yr. in cy.; $42/yr. out of cy.; $54/yr. out of state. 109 E. Broad St., Elizabethtown, NC 28337. TEL 919-862-4163; FAX 919-862-6602. **Owner(s):** Park Communications, Inc., Vine Ctr. Office Tower, 333 W. Vine St., 17th Fl., Lexington, KY 40507. TEL 606-252-7275; Ed. Denise D. Cross; Pub. Denise K. Cross; adv.; photos; bk.rev.; pub. size: standard; circ. evening 7,800(paid). **Wire Service(s):** AP.

FAYETTEVILLE

US ISSN 1052-9829

FAYETTEVILLE OBSERVER-TIMES. 1816. d. $.50/day newsstand; $1.50/Sun.; $10.40/mo. carrier. 458 Whitfield St., Fayetteville, NC 28306. TEL 910-323-4848; FAX 910-486-3531. **Owner(s):** Fayetteville Publishing Co., 458 Whitfield St., Fayetteville, NC 28306. TEL 919-323-4848; Pub. Ramon L. Yarborough; adv. contact: Ron Watts. pub. size: broadsheet; circ. morning 72,957(paid); Sun. 83,000(paid). **Wire Service(s):** AP, LAT-WP.

Formerly: Fayetteville Observer-Times Morning.

FOREST CITY

US

DAILY COURIER. 1978. Mon.-Fri. $.25 newsstand; $4/mo. 601 Oak St., Forest City, NC 28043. TEL 704-245-6431 FAX 704-248-2790. **Owner(s):** Ron Paris 601 Oak St., Forest City, NC 28043. TEL 704-245-6431; Bill Blair, 601 Oak St., Forest City, NC 28043. TEL 704-245-6431; FAX 704-248-2790; Ed. Amy Revis; Pub. Ron Paris; adv. contact: Jim Deviney. pub. size: broadsheet; circ. evening 11,250(paid). Wire Service(s): AP.

GASTONIA

US

GASTON GAZETTE. 1880. Mon.-Sun. $.25/day newsstand; $1/Sun.; $90/yr. home deliv. 2500 E. Franklin Blvd., Gastonia, NC 28054. TEL 704-864-3291; FAX 704-867-6988. **Owner(s):** Freedom Communications, Inc., P.O. Box 19549, Irvine, CA 92714; Ed. Jennie Lambert; Pub. Mike McMillan; adv. contact: Earl K. Brackett. photos; bk.rev.; pub. size: broadsheet; circ. morning 43,000(paid); Sun. 46,000(paid). **Wire Service(s):** AP.

GOLDSBORO

US

GOLDSBORO NEWS-ARGUS. 1885. Sun.-Fri. $.50/day newsstand; $1.25/Sun.; $7/mo. 310 N. Berkeley Blvd., Goldsboro, NC 27534. TEL 919-778-2211; FAX 919-778-9891. **Owner(s):** Wayne Printing Co., Inc., Goldsboro, NC 27532; Ed. J. Michael Rouse; Pub. Hal Tanner, Jr.; adv. contact: Nelson Mitchell. photos; bk.rev.; pub. size: broadsheet; circ. evening 22,000(paid); Sun. 25,000(paid). **Wire Service(s):** AP.

GREENSBORO

US ISSN 0747-1858

NEWS & RECORD, THE. 1972. d. $.50/day newsstand, $1.25/Sun. 200 E. Market St., Greensboro, NC 27401. TEL 910-373-7000; FAX 910-373-7067. **Owner(s):** Landmark Communications, Inc., 150 W. Brambleton Ave., Norfolk, VA 23510. TEL 804-446-2000; Ed. Patrick Yack; Pub. Van King; adv. contact: Kathy Lambeth. photos; bk.rev.; pub. size: broadsheet; circ. morning 93,348(paid); Sun. 120,300(paid). **Wire Service(s):** AP, NYT, LAT-WP.

Formerly: Greensboro Daily News.

GREENVILLE

US ISSN 1060-6130

GREENVILLE DAILY REFLECTOR. 1882. d. $.50/day newsstand; $1/Sun.; $92/yr. 209 Cotanche St., Greenville, NC 27858. TEL 919-752-6166; FAX 919-752-9583. **Owner(s):** Cox Enterprises, Inc., P.O. Box 105357, Atlanta, GA 30348. TEL 404-843-5000; Pub. D. Jordan Whichard, III; pub. size: broadsheet; circ. morning 18,846(paid); Sun. 21,117. **Wire Service(s):** AP.

HENDERSON

US

DAILY DISPATCH, THE. 1914. Tue.-Sun. $.50/day newsstand; $1/Sun.; $8.50/mo. mailed; $70/yr. 304 S. Chestnut St., Henderson, NC 27536. TEL 919-492-4001; FAX 919-430-0125. **Owner(s):** Paducah Newspapers, Inc., 408 Kentucky Ave., P.O. Box 2300, Paducah, KY 42002. TEL 302-443-1771; Ed. Laverene Jeffries; Pub. Rick Bean; adv. contact: Deborah Tuck. photos; bk.rev.; pub. size: broadsheet; circ. morning 10,500(paid); Sun. 11,000(paid). **Wire Service(s):** AP.

Formerly: Henderson Daily Dispatch.

HENDERSONVILLE

US ISSN 1042-2323

HENDERSONVILLE TIMES-NEWS. 1881. d. $.25/day newsstand; $.75/Sun.; $8.25/mo. carrier. 1717 Four Seasons Blvd., Hendersonville, NC 28792. TEL 704-692-0505; FAX 704-692-2319. **Owner(s):** New York Times Co., The, 229 W. 43rd St., New York, NY 10036. TEL 212-556-1234; Pub. Paul Bairstow; adv. contact: Mike Sternberg. pub. size: broadsheet; circ. morning 21,397(paid); Sun. 23,000(paid). **Wire Service(s):** AP, NYT.

HICKORY

US ISSN 1061-5628

HICKORY DAILY RECORD. 1915. d. $.25/day newsstand; $.75/Sun.; $91/yr. mailed. 1100 Park Pl., Hickory, NC 28602. TEL 704-322-4510; FAX 704-328-9378. **Owner(s):** Hickory Publishing Co., Inc., 1100 Park Pl., Hickory, NC 28602. TEL 704-322-4510; Ed. Elizabeth Williams; Pub. Suzanne G. Millholland; adv. contact: David Millholland. pub. size: broadsheet; circ. evening 27,258(paid); Sun. 27,258(paid). **Wire Service(s):** AP.

HIGH POINT

US ISSN 0747-1491

HIGH POINT ENTERPRISE. 1885. d. $.50/day newsstand; $1/Sun.; $7.95/mo. 210 Church Ave., High Point, NC 27262. TEL 910-888-3500; FAX 910-883-7865. **Owner(s):** High Point Enterprises, Inc., 210 Church St., High Point, NC 27262. TEL 910-888-3500; FAX 910-841-5165; Ed. Kenneth Irons; Pub. Joseph P. Rawley; adv. contact: Demi Foust. photos; bk.rev.; pub. size: broadsheet; circ. morning 31,600(paid); Sun. 32,700(paid). **Wire Service(s):** AP, KR.

JACKSONVILLE

US

JACKSONVILLE DAILY NEWS. 1953. c. $.50/day newsstand; $1.25/Sun.; $9/mo. carrier; $25.50/3 mos. carrier. 724 Bell Fork Rd., Jacksonville, NC 28540. TEL 910-353-1171; FAX 910-353-7316. **Owner(s):** Freedom Communications, Inc., 17666 Fitch, Irvine, CA 92714. TEL 714-553-9292; FAX 714-474-7675; Ed. Madison Taylor; Pub. Charles Fischer; adv. contact: W.R. Taylor. photos; bk.rev.; pub. size: broadsheet; circ. morning 23,500(paid); Sun. 25,000(paid). **Wire Service(s):** AP.

KANNAPOLIS

US

KANNAPOLIS DAILY INDEPENDENT. 1927. Sun.-Fri. $.50/day newsstand; $1/Sun.; $7.80/mo. carrier; $93.60/yr. carrier. 119-123 N. Main St., Kannapolis, NC 28081. TEL 704-932-3131; FAX 704-933-4444. Owner(s): Park Communications, Inc., Vine Ctr. Office Tower, 333 W. Vine St., 17th Fl., Lexington, KY 40507. TEL 606-252-7275; Ed. Stan Hojnacki. adv. contact: Beverly Besinger. pub. size: broadsheet; circ. evening 10,884(paid); Sun. 10,984(paid). **Wire Service(s):** AP.

KILL DEVIL HILLS

US

VIRGINIAN PILOT. d. $.50/day newsstand; $1.50/Sun.; $32.49/13 wks. 111 W. Carlton, Kill Devil Hills, NC 27948. TEL 919-441-1620; FAX 919-441-8895. Owner(s): Virginian Pilot/Ledger Star, 150 Brambleton Ave., Norfolk, VA 23510; Ed. Ronald L. Speer. adv. contact: Charles Huff. pub. size: broadsheet; circ. morning 2,694(paid); Sun. 2,923(paid).

KINSTON

US

KINSTON DAILY FREE PRESS. 1882. Sun.-Fri. $.50/day newsstand; $1/Sun.; $72/yr. 2103 N. Queen St., Kinston, NC 28501. TEL 919-527-3191; FAX 919-527-1813. Owner(s): Freedom Communications, Inc., P.O. Box 19549, Irvine, CA 92714. TEL 714-553-9292; Ed. Rick Thomason; Pub. Thomas Eugene Porter; adv. contact: Billy Moore. photos; bk.rev.; pub. size: standard; circ. evening 14,500(paid); Sun. 15,500(paid). **Wire Service(s):** AP, KR, SHNA.

LAURINBURG

US

LAURINBURG EXCHANGE. 1899. Mon.-Fri. $.50 newsstand; $63/yr. in cy.; $65/yr. out of cy. 211 Cronly St., Laurinburg, NC 28352. TEL 910-276-2311; FAX 910-276-3815. Owner(s): Mid-South Management Co., Inc., 221 Cronly St., Laurinburg, NC 28352. TEL 919-276-2311; Ed. Mark Durham; Pub. Mike Milligan; adv.; photos; pub. size: broadsheet; circ. evening 9,600(paid).

LENOIR

US

LENOIR NEWS-TOPIC. 1875. Mon.-Sat. $.50 newsstand; $90/yr. home deliv.; $108/yr. mailed. 123 Pennton Ave., Lenoir, NC 28645. TEL 704-758-7381; FAX 704-754-0110. Owner(s): Paxton Media Group, Inc., P.O. Box 2300, Paducah, KY 42002. TEL 502-443-1771; Ed. Richard Tuttell; Pub. Richard Mitchell; adv.; photos; bk.rev.; pub. size: broadsheet; circ. evening 12,300(paid). **Wire Service(s):** AP, NYT.

LEXINGTON

US   ISSN 0163-3090

LEXINGTON DISPATCH. 1882. Mon.-Sat. $.50 newsstand; $7/mo. carrier. 30 E. First Ave., Lexington, NC 27292. TEL 704-249-3981; FAX 704-249-0712. Owner(s): New York Times Co., The, 229 W. 43rd. St., New York, NY 10036. TEL 212-556-1234; Pub. Joe S. Sink, Jr.; adv. contact: Betty Barnes. pub. size: broadsheet; circ. evening 14,800(paid). **Wire Service(s):** AP, NYT.

LUMBERTON

US

ROBESONIAN, THE. 1870. Sun.-Fri. $.35/day newsstand; $.75/Sun.; $93/yr. 121 W. Fifth St., Lumberton, NC 28358. TEL 919-739-4322; FAX 919-739-6553. Owner(s): Park Communications, Inc., 1700 Vine Ctr. Office Tower, 333 W. Vine St., 17th Fl., Lexington, KY 40507. TEL 606-252-7275; Ed. John Culbreth. adv. contact: Cing King. photos; bk.rev.; pub. size: broadsheet; circ. evening 14,600(paid); Sun. 17,300(paid). **Wire Service(s):** AP.

MARION

US

MCDOWELL NEWS, THE. 1929. Mon.-Fri. $.50 newsstand; $78/yr. carrier; $91/yr. mailed in state; $85.44/yr. out of state. 26 N. Logan St., Marion, NC 28752. TEL 704-652-3313. Owner(s): Park Communications, Inc., 1700 Vine Center Office Tower, 333 W. Vine St., 17th Fl., Lexington, KY 40507. TEL 606-252-7275; Ed. Scott Hollifield. adv.; pub. size: broadsheet; circ. evening 7,200(paid). **Wire Service(s):** AP.

MONROE

US

ENQUIRER-JOURNAL, THE. 1873. Sun.-Fri. $.50/day newsstand; $.75/Sun.; $7.40/4 wks. 500 W. Jefferson St., Monroe, NC 28112. TEL 704-289-1541; FAX 704-289-2929. Owner(s): Thomson Newspapers, Inc., One Thorn Run Ctr., Ste. 500, 1187 Thorn Run Rd. Ext., Coraopolis, PA 15108. TEL 412-262-7870; Ed. Luanne Williams. adv. contact: George Hoover. pub. size: standard; circ. evening 13,273(paid); Sun. 15,163(paid). **Wire Service(s):** AP.

MORGANTON

US

NEWS HERALD, THE. 1885. Sun.-Fri. $.50/day newsstand; $.75/Sun.; $7.90/mo. carrier. 301 Collett St., Morganton, NC 28655. TEL 704-437-2161; FAX 704-437-5372. Owner(s): Park Communications, Inc., Vine Ctr. Office Tower, 333 W. Vine St., 17th Fl., Lexington, KY 40507. TEL 606-252-7275; Ed. Bill Poteat; Pub. Dorothy Park; adv. contact: Randy Hart. pub. size: broadsheet; circ. evening 12,500(paid); Sun. 13,000(paid). **Wire Service(s):** AP.

Formerly: Morganton News-Herald.

MT. AIRY

US

MOUNT AIRY NEWS. 1880. Sun.-Fri. $.50/day newsstand; $1.50/Sun.; $93.60/yr. 319 Renfro St., Mt. Airy, NC 27030. TEL 910-786-4141; FAX 910-784-2816. Owner(s): Mid-South Management Co., Inc.; Ed. Peter Williams; Pub. George W. Summerlin; adv. contact: Anthony Summerlin. pub. size: broadsheet; circ. evening 9,500(paid); Sun. 10,000(paid). **Wire Service(s):** AP.

NEW BERN

US

SUN-JOURNAL. 1871. d. $.50/day newsstand; $1/Sun.; $78/yr. 226 Pollock St., New Bern, NC 28560. TEL 919-638-8101; FAX 919-638-4664. Owner(s): Freedom Communications, Inc., P.O. Box 19549, Irvine, CA 92713. TEL 714-553-9292; Ed. Patrick Holmes; Pub. John Graham; adv. contact: Judy Zimmerman. pub. size: standard; circ. evening 18,000(paid); Sun. 18,000(paid). **Wire Service(s):** AP.

Formerly: New Bern Sun-Journal.

NEWTON

US

OBSERVER NEWS. 1879. Mon.-Fri. $.50/day newsstand; $9/3 mos.; $18/6 mos.; $33/yr. 309 N. College Ave., Newton, NC 28658. TEL 704-464-0221; FAX 704-464-1267. Owner(s): American Publishing Co., 606 N. Van Buren, P.O. Box 520, Marion, IL 62959. TEL 618-993-1711; Ed. Jennifer W. Miller; Pub. Jerry Hodge; adv. contact: Sharon Rhymer. pub. size: broadsheet; circ. evening 4,000(controlled). **Wire Service(s):** AP.

RALEIGH

US

NEWS & OBSERVER. 1865. d. $.50/day newsstand; $1.50/Sun.; $7/mo. Mon.-Sat.; $12/mo. daily & Sun.; $8/mo. Sat. & Sun.; $7/mo. Sun. 215 S. McDowell St., Raleigh, NC 27601. TEL 919-829-4500; FAX 919-829-4529; E-mail: sford@nando.com; URL: http://www.nando.net/nao/. Owner(s): McClatchy Newspapers Inc., P.O. Box 15779, Sacramento, CA 95816. TEL 916-321-1000; Ed. Frank Daniels, III; Pub. Frank Daniels, Jr.; adv.; photos; bk.rev.; pub. size: broadsheet; circ. morning 145,962(paid); Sun. 188,843(paid). **Wire Service(s):** AP, NYT, KR, LAT-WP, Tribune, Cox.

REIDSVILLE

US

REIDSVILLE REVIEW. 1888. Tue.-Fri. & Sun. $.50/day newsstand; $1/Sun.; $1.25/wk.; $65/yr. 1921 Vance St., Reidsville, NC 27320. TEL 910-349-4331; FAX 910-342-2513. Owner(s): Rockingham Newspapers, Inc., P.O. Box 2157, Reidsville, NC 27323. TEL 919-349-4331; Ed. Glenn Cook; Pub. James M. DeLapp; adv. contact: Teresa Talley. photos; bk.rev.; pub. size: broadsheet; circ. evening 7,200(paid). **Wire Service(s):** UPI.

ROANOKE RAPIDS

US

ROANOKE RAPIDS DAILY & SUNDAY HERALD. 1914. Sun.-Fri. $.50/day newsstand; $1.25/Sun. 916 Roanoke Ave., Roanoke Rapids, NC 27870. TEL 919-537-2505; FAX 919-537-2314. Owner(s): Wick Communications, Inc., 333 W, Wilcox Dr., Ste. 302, Sierra Vista, AZ 85635; Ed. Bill Moss; Pub. Steven Woody; adv. contact: Tim Frates. pub. size: broadsheet; circ. morning 13,500(paid). **Wire Service(s):** UPI.

ROCKINGHAM

US   ISSN 1050-7639

RICHMOND COUNTY DAILY JOURNAL. 1931. Sun.-Fri. $.35/day newsstand; $.50/Sun.; $84/yr. 105 E. Washington St., Rockingham, NC 28379-3639. TEL 910-997-3111; FAX 910-997-4321. **Owner(s):** Park Communications, Inc., Vine Ctr. Office Tower, 333 W. Vine St., 17th Fl., Lexington, KY 40507. TEL 606-252-7275; Ed. Bert Unger; Pub. Marvin Enderle; adv. contact: Terri Cooper. adv.: $9.20/SAU. photos; pub. size: broadsheet; circ. evening 9,800(paid); Sun. 9,800(paid). **Wire Service(s):** AP.

ROCKY MOUNT

US   ISSN 0738-5137

ROCKY MOUNT TELEGRAM. 1911. d. $.50/day newsstand; $1/Sun.; $120/yr. in town; $133.39/yr. out of town. 150 Howard St., Rocky Mount, NC 27804. TEL 919-446-5161; FAX 919-446-4057. **Owner(s):** Thomson Newspapers, Inc., 3150 Des Plaines Ave., Des Plaines, IL 60014; Ed. Jeff Herrin; Pub. Den Dickerson; adv. contact: Mark Fortune. bk.rev.; pub. size: broadsheet; circ. morning 17,000(paid); Sun. 20,000(paid). **Wire Service(s):** AP.
  Formerly: Rocky Mountain Evening Telegram.

SALISBURY

US   ISSN 0747-0738

SALISBURY POST. 1905. d. $.50/day newsstand; $1/Sun.; $8/mo. carrier. 131 W. Innes St., Salisbury, NC 28144-0105. TEL 704-633-8950; FAX 704-639-0003. **Owner(s):** Post Publishing Co., Inc., 131 W. Innes St., Salisbury, NC 28144. TEL 704-633-8950; FAX 704-633-7373; Ed. Frank Deloache; Pub. James F. Hurley III; adv. contact: Steve Johnson. photos; bk.rev.; pub. size: broadsheet; circ. evening 26,203(paid); Sun. 26,589(paid). **Wire Service(s):** AP.

SANFORD

US

SANFORD HERALD, THE. 1930. Mon.-Sat. $.50 newsstand; $60/yr. 208 St. Clair Ct., Sanford, NC 27330. TEL 919-708-9000; FAX 919-708-9001; E-mail: bhorner3@interpath.com. **Owner(s):** Sanford Herald, Inc., 208 St. Clair Ct., Sanford, NC 27330. TEL 919-708-9000; FAX 919-708-9001; Ed. Cornelia Olive; Pub. W.E. Horner, Jr.; adv. contact: James C. Banks. bk.rev.; pub. size: broadsheet; circ. evening 14,706(paid). Wire Service(s): AP.

SHELBY

US   ISSN 1043-1950

SHELBY STAR. 1894. d. $.50/day newsstand; $.75/Sun.; $10/mo. 315 E. Graham St., Shelby, NC 28150. TEL 704-484-7000; FAX 704-484-0805. **Owner(s):** Thomson Newspapers, Inc., 1 Station Pl., Stamford, CT 06902. TEL 203-428-2500; FAX 203-425-2516; Ed. Roberta Borden; Pub. R. Keith Walters; adv. contact: Charles Price. bk.rev.; pub. size: standard; circ. evening 16,800(paid); Sun. 17,400(paid). **Wire Service(s):** AP.

STATESVILLE

US   ISSN 0745-7804

STATESVILLE RECORD & LANDMARK. 1874. Sun.-Fri. $.50/day newsstand; $1/Sun.; $1.80/wk. carrier. 222 E. Broad St., Statesville, NC 28677. TEL 704-873-1451; FAX 704-872-3150. **Owner(s):** Park Communications, Inc., Vine Ctr. Office Tower, 333 W. Vine St., 17th Fl., Lexington, KY 40507. TEL 606-252-7275; Ed. Eric Millsaps. adv. contact: Dwayne Menster. pub. size: broadsheet; circ. evening 18,000(paid); Sun. 17,400(paid). Wire Service(s): AP.

TARBORO

US

DAILY SOUTHERNER, THE. 1889. Mon.-Fri. $.50 newsstand; $6.25/mo. carrier; $100/yr. mailed. 504 W. Wilson St., Tarboro, NC 27886. TEL 919-823-3106; FAX 919-823-4599. **Owner(s):** American Publishing Co., 606 N. Van Buren, P.O. Box 520, Marion, IL 62959. TEL 618-993-1711; Ed. Robert Hughes; Pub. Jerome Creech; adv. contact: Ellis W. Hooks. pub. size: broadsheet; circ. evening 6,750(paid). **Wire Service(s):** AP.

TRYON

US

TRYON DAILY BULLETIN. 1928. Mon.-Fri. $.50 newsstand; $35/yr. 106 N. Trade St., Tryon, NC 28782. TEL 704-859-9151; FAX 704-859-5575. **Owner(s):** Tryon Daily Bulletin, Inc., 106 N. Trade St., P.O. Box 790, Tryon, NC 28782. TEL 704-859-9151; Ed. Judy Lanier; Pub. Jeffrey A. Byrd; adv.; pub. size: broadsheet; circ. morning 4,400(paid).

WASHINGTON

US   ISSN 1057-7068

WASHINGTON DAILY NEWS. 1909. d. $.50/day newsstand; $.75/Sun.; $8/mo. carrier; $7.25/mo. senior citizens. 217 N. Market St., Washington, NC 27889. TEL 919-946-2144; FAX 919-946-9797. **Owner(s):** Washington News Publishing Co., P.O. Box 1788, Washington, NC 27889. TEL 919-946-2144; Ed. Mark Inabinatt; Pub. Ashley B. Futrel, Jr.; adv. contact: Eugene E. King. pub. size: broadsheet; circ. morning 10,600(paid); Sun. 10,600(paid). **Wire Service(s):** AP.

WILMINGTON

US

WILMINGTON MORNING STAR. 1867. d. $.50 newsstand; $9.95/mo.; $1.75/Sun. 1003 S. 17th St., Wilmington, NC 28401-0840. TEL 910-343-2000. E-mail: mseditor@wilmington.com; URL: http://www.wilmington.net/starnews. **Owner(s):** New York Times Co. The, 229 W. 43rd St., New York, NY 10036. TEL 212-556-1234; Ed. John Meyer; Pub. John Lynch; adv. contact: Dan Schuette. photos; bk.rev.; pub. size: broadsheet; circ. morning 53,615(paid); Sun. 65,615(paid). **Wire Service(s):** NYT, AP, KR, LAT-WP.

WILSON

US

WILSON DAILY TIMES. 1902. Mon.-Sat. $.50 newsstand; $1/Sat.; $7/mo.; $11/mo. mailed in state; $11.50/mo. out of state. 2001 Downing St. Ext., Wilson, NC 27894. TEL 919-243-5151; FAX 919-243-2999. **Owner(s):** Morgan P. & Margaret Dickerman, P.O. Box 2447, Wilson, NC 27894. TEL 919-243-5151; Ed. Hal Tarleton; Pub. Morgan Dickerman; adv. contact: Ray McKeithan. bk.rev.; pub. size: broadsheet; circ. evening 17,000(paid). **Wire Service(s):** AP.

WINSTON-SALEM

US

WINSTON-SALEM JOURNAL. 1897. d. $.50/day newsstand; $1.25/Sun. 418 N. Marshall St., Winston-Salem, NC 27101. TEL 910-727-7211; FAX 910-727-7245. **Owner(s):** Media General, Inc., 333 E. Grace St., Richmond, VA 23219. TEL 804-649-6671; Ed. Carl Crothers; Pub. Jon Witherspoon; adv. contact: Timothy Maby. photos; bk.rev.; pub. size: broadsheet; circ. morning 92,516(paid); Sun. 107,953(paid). **Wire Service(s):** AP, NYT, LAT-WP.

NORTH DAKOTA

BISMARCK

US   ISSN 0745-1091

BISMARCK TRIBUNE. 1873. d. $.50/day newsstand; $.75/Wed.; $1.75/Sun.; $162/yr. carrier. 707 E. Front Ave., Bismarck, ND 58504. TEL 701-223-2500; FAX 701-224-1412; E-mail: bismarcktribune@ndonline.com; URL: http://www.ndonline.com/ **Owner(s):** Lee Enterprises, Inc., 215 N. Main St. Davenport, IA 52801. TEL 319-383-2100; Ed. Kevin Giles; Pub. Margaret Wade; adv. contact Lani Renneau. pub. size: broadsheet; circ. evening 33,000(paid); Sun. 32,000(paid). **Wire Service(s):** AP, LAT-WP.

DEVILS LAKE

US

DEVILS LAKE JOURNAL. 1905. Mon.-Fri. $.50 newsstand; $6.50/mo. home deliv. 516 Fourth St., Devils Lake, ND 58301. TEL 701-662-2127; FAX 701-662-3115. **Owner(s):** Fark Communications, Inc., Vine Ctr. Office Tower, 333 W. Vine St., 17th Fl., Lexington, KY 40507. TEL 606-252-7275; Ed. Gordon Weixel. adv.; pub. size: broadsheet; circ. evening 5,000(paid). **Wire Service(s):** AP.

DICKINSON

US   ISSN 1049-6718

DICKINSON PRESS, THE. 1883. Tue.-Sun. $.50/day newsstand; $1/Sun.; $2.38/wk. home deliv.; $9.50/mo. home deliv. 127 W. First St., Dickinson, ND 58601. TEL 701-225-8141; FAX 701-225-4205. **Owner(s):** Forum Communications, Inc., P.O. Box 2020, Fargo, ND 58207. TEL 701-223-7311; Ed. Sharon Dietz. adv. contact: Erv Barth. pub. size: broadsheet; circ. morning 7,700(paid) Sun. 8,200(paid). **Wire Service(s):** AP.

FARGO

US   ISSN 0895-1292
FORUM, THE. 1878. d. $.50/day newsstand; $.75/Sat.; $1.75/Sun.; $171/yr. 101 N. Fifth St., Fargo, ND 58102. TEL 701-235-7311; FAX 701-241-5487; E-mail: pol@pol.org; URL: http://www.pol.org/forum. **Owner(s):** Forum Communications, Inc., P.O. Box 2020, Fargo, ND 58107. TEL 701-223-7311; Ed. Terry DeVine; Pub. William C. Marcil; adv.; bk.rev.; pub. size: standard; circ. morning 55,563(paid); Sun. 75,000(paid). **Wire Service(s):** AP, FIELD.

GRAND FORKS

US   ISSN 0745-9661
GRAND FORKS HERALD. 1876. d. $.50/day newsstand; $.75/Sat.; $1.50/Sun.; $13/4 wks. carrier. 303 Second Ave., N., Grand Forks, ND 58203. TEL 701-780-1100; FAX 701-780-1123; E-mail: gfherald@grandforks.polaristel.net. **Owner(s):** Knight-Ridder, Inc., One Herald Plz., Miami, FL 33132. TEL 305-376-3800; Ed. Jim Durkin; Pub. Michael Maidenberg; adv. contact: Tom Kuchera. photos; bk.rev.; pub. size: broadsheet; circ. morning 39,697(paid); Sun. 40,785(paid). **Wire Service(s):** AP, KR, NYT, Telephoto.

JAMESTOWN

US
JAMESTOWN SUN, THE. 1925. Mon.-Sat. $.50 newsstand; $8.85/mo carrier; $93.54/yr. in state. 122 Second St., N.W., Jamestown, ND 58401. TEL 701-252-3120; FAX 701-251-2878. **Owner(s):** American Publishing Co., 606 N. Van Buren, P.O. Box 520, Marion, IL 62959. TEL 618-993-1711; Pub. Bruce Henke; adv. contact: Gene Keller. pub. size: broadsheet; circ. morning 7,300(paid). **Wire Service(s):** AP.

MINOT

US   ISSN 0885-3053
MINOT DAILY NEWS. d. $.50/day newsstand; $1.25/Sun.; $123/yr. in cy.; $135/yr. out of cy.; $199/yr. out of state. 301 Fourth St., S.E., Minot, ND 58701. TEL 701-857-1900; FAX 701-857-1961. **Owner(s):** Ogden Newspapers, Inc., 1500 Main St., Wheeling, WV 26003. TEL 304-233-0100; Ed. Mark Hanson. adv. contact: Steve Baker. photos; bk.rev.; pub. size: standard; circ. morning 26,000(paid); Sun. 27,000(paid). **Wire Service(s):** AP.

VALLEY CITY

US
VALLEY CITY TIMES-RECORD. Mon.-Fri. $.50 newsstand; $7.50/mo. carrier; $71/yr. carrier. 146 Third St., N.E., Valley City, ND 58072. TEL 701-845-0463; FAX 701-845-0175. **Owner(s):** American Publishing Co., 606 N. Van Buren, P.O. Box 520, Marion, IL 62959. TEL 618-993-1711; Pub. Dennis L. Vernon; adv. contact: Jan Olafson. pub. size: broadsheet; circ. evening 4,000(paid). **Wire Service(s):** AP.

WAHPETON

US
DAILY NEWS. 1880. Tue.-Fri. & Sun. $.50/day newsstand; $1/Sun.; $82/yr. 601 Dakota Ave., Wahpeton, ND 58075. TEL 701-642-8585; FAX 701-642-1501. **Owner(s):** Wick Communications, Inc., 333 W. Wilcox Dr., Ste. 302, Sierra Vista, AZ 83635; Ed. Barbara Grant; Pub. Newell C. Grant; adv. contact: Roger Harty. pub. size: broadsheet; circ. morning 5,600(paid). **Wire Service(s):** AP.
    Formerly: Wahpeton-Breckenridge Daily News.

WILLISTON

US
WILLISTON HERALD. 1899. Sun.-Fri. $.50/day newsstand; $1/Sun.; $7.85/mo. carrier; $8/mo. motor rte. 14 W. Fourth St., Williston, ND 58801. TEL 701-572-2165; FAX 701-572-1965. **Owner(s):** Wick Communications, Inc., 333 W. Wilcox Dr., Ste. 302, Sierra Vista, AZ 85635. TEL 701-572-2165; FAX 701-572-1965; Ed. Ruth Newman; Pub. Don Mrachek; adv. contact: Brian Standfield. photos; pub. size: standard; circ. evening 6,600(paid); Sun. 6,750(paid). **Wire Service(s):** AP.

NORTHERN MARIANA ISLANDS

SAIPAN

US
MARIANAS VARIETY NEWS & VIEWS. 1972. Mon.-Fri. $.50 newsstand; $72/6 mo.; $144/yr. P.O. Box 231, Saipan, MP 96950. TEL 670-234-6341; FAX 670-234-9271. **Owner(s):** Younis Art Studio, Inc., P.O. Box 231, Saipan, MP 96950. TEL 670-234-6341; FAX 670-234-9271; Pub. Paz Younis; adv.; photos; bk.rev.; pub. size: standard; circ. morning 3,500(free & paid). **Wire Service(s):** Asia Wire.

US
SAIPAN TRIBUNE. 1989. Mon.-Fri. $.35 newsstand. Caller Box AAA-34, Saipan, MP 96950. TEL 670-235-6397; FAX 670-235-3733. **Owner(s):** Pacific Publications & Printing, Inc., Caller Box AAA-34, Saipan, MP 96950. TEL 011-1-670-235-2440; FAX 011-1-670-235-3733; Pub. Mark Broadhurst; adv. contact: Lizette Silva. photos; bk.rev.; pub. size: tabloid; circ. morning 3,500(paid). **Wire Service(s):** AP.

OHIO

AKRON

US
AKRON BEACON JOURNAL. 1839. d. $.35/day newsstand, $1.50/Sun.; $3.05/wk. home deliv.; $39.65/13 wks. 44 E. Exchange St., Akron, OH 44328. TEL 330-996-3000; FAX 330-376-9235. **Owner(s):** Knight-Ridder, Inc., One Herald Plz., Miami, FL 33132; Ed. Dale Allen; Pub. John L. Dotson, Jr.; pub. size: broadsheet; circ. morning 114,000(paid); Sun. 223,105(paid). **Wire Service(s):** AP, NYT, KNS, LAT-WP.

ALLIANCE

US
ALLIANCE REVIEW. 1888. Mon.-Sat. $.35 newsstand; $88/yr. carrier. 40 S. Linden Ave., Alliance, OH 44601. TEL 216-821-1300; FAX 216-821-8258. **Owner(s):** Wooster Republican Printing Co., 210 E. Liberty St., Wooster, OH 44691; Ed. Michael Patterson; Pub. Robert C. Dix Jr.; adv. contact: Don Watson. pub. size: standard; circ. evening 12,700. **Wire Service(s):** AP, NYT, Pony.

ASHLAND

US
ASHLAND TIMES-GAZETTE. 1850. Mon.-Sat. $.50 newsstand; $7.80/4 wks. in town; $8.00/4 wks. motor rte.; $9.75/4 wks. in cy. mailed; $10/4 wks. out of cy.; $10.50/4 wks. out of state. 40 E. Second St., Ashland, OH 44805. TEL 419-281-0581; FAX 419-281-5591. **Owner(s):** Ashland Publishing Co., 40 E. Second St., Ashland, OH 44805. TEL 419-281-0581; Ed. Mel McKeachie; Pub. William McKinney; adv. contact: Rhonda Geer. pub. size: broadsheet; circ. evening 12,000(paid). **Wire Service(s):** UPI, NYT.

ASHTABULA

US
ASHTABULA STAR-BEACON. 1891. d. $.35/day newsstand; $1/Sun.; $31.20/3 mos. in cy.; $32.50/3 mos. carrier; $34.45/3 mos. motor rte. 4626 Park Ave., Ashtabula, OH 44004. TEL 216-998-2323; FAX 216-992-9655. **Owner(s):** Thomson Newspapers, Inc., One Thorn Run Ctr., Ste. 500, 1187 Thorn Run Rd. Ext., Coraopolis, PA 15108. TEL 412-262-7870; Pub. Ed Looman; adv. contact: Vanessa Coper. pub. size: broadsheet; circ. morning 25,000(paid); Sun. 25,000(paid). **Wire Service(s):** UPI.

ATHENS

US   ISSN 1064-2005
ATHENS MESSENGER. 1905. Sun.-Fri. $.35 newsstand; $98/yr. carrier; $102/yr. mailed in OH. Rte. 33 N. & Johnson Rd., Athens, OH 45701. TEL 614-592-6612; FAX 614-592-4647; E-mail: messenger@seorf.ohiou.edu; URL: http://www.seorf.ohiou.edu/~xx005. **Owner(s):** Messenger Publishing Co., Inc., Rt. 33 N. & Johnson Rd., Athens, OH 45201. TEL 614-592-6612; FAX 614-592-4647; Ed. Karl Runser; Pub. G. Kenner Bush; adv. contact: Charles Douglas. bk.rev.; pub. size: broadsheet; circ. evening 14,374(paid); Sun. 17,492(paid). **Wire Service(s):** AP, SHNA.

BELLEFONTAINE

US   ISSN 0747-3273
BELLEFONTAINE EXAMINER. 1891. Mon.-Sat. free in area; $.50 newsstand; $1.85/wk. 127 E. Chillicothe Ave., Bellefontaine, OH 43311. TEL 513-592-3060. **Owner(s):** Hubbard Publishing Co., Inc., P.O. Box 40, Bellefontaine, OH 43311. TEL 513-592-3060; FAX 513-592-4463; Ed. David Wagner; Pub. T.E. Hubbard; adv. contact: Cindy Titus. photos; pub. size: broadsheet; circ. evening 11,010(paid). **Wire Service(s):** AP.

BELLEVUE

US

BELLEVUE GAZETTE. 1867. Mon.-Sat. $.50 newsstand; $1.80/wk. 107 N. Sandusky St., Bellevue, OH 44811. TEL 419-483-4190; FAX 419-483-3737. **Owner(s):** Gazette Printing Co., Inc., 107 N. Sandusky St., Bellevue, OH 44811. TEL 419-483-4190; Ed. Dennis Sabo. adv. contact: Rick Miller. pub. size: broadsheet; circ. evening 3,200(paid). **Wire Service(s):** UPI, AP.

BOWLING GREEN

US

SENTINEL-TRIBUNE. 1867. Mon.-Sat. $.35 newsstand; $1.75/wk.; $85/yr. 300 E. Poe Rd., Bowling Green, OH 43402. TEL 419-352-4611; FAX 419-354-0314. **Owner(s):** Thomas M. Haswell, P.O. Box 88, Bowling Green, OH 42402. TEL 419-352-4611; FAX 419-354-0314; Ed. David C. Miller; Pub. Thomas M. Haswell; adv. contact: Vicky Graf. photos; pub. size: broadsheet; circ. evening 13,850(paid). **Wire Service(s):** SHNA, **AP.**

BRYAN

US

BRYAN TIMES. 1949. Mon.-Sat. $.50 newsstand; $86/yr. 127 S. Walnut St., Bryan, OH 43506. TEL 419-636-1111; FAX 419-636-8937. **Owner(s):** Bryan Publishing Co., The, 127 S. Walnut St., Bryan, OH 43506. TEL 419-636-1111; FAX 419-636-8937; Ed. Linda Freed; Pub. Christopher Cullis; adv. contact: Mary Nickels. pub. size: broadsheet; circ. evening 12,000(paid). **Wire Service(s):** AP.

BUCYRUS

US

BUCYRUS TELEGRAPH-FORUM. 1923. d. $.35/day newsstand; $1.25/Sun.; $100.40/yr. mailed. 117 W. Rensselaer St., Bucyrus, OH 44820. TEL 419-562-3333; FAX 419-562-9162. **Owner(s):** Thomson Newspapers, Inc., One Station Pl., Stamford, CT 06902. TEL 203-428-2500; Ed. Lisa Miller; Pub. James F. Croneis; adv. contact: Jeanette Parker. photos; bk.rev.; pub. size: broadsheet; circ. evening 21,200(free & paid). **Wire Service(s):** AP.

CAMBRIDGE

US

DAILY JEFFERSONIAN, THE. 1824. Mon.-Sat. $.35 newsstand; $96.20/yr. 831 Wheeling Ave., Cambridge, OH 43725. TEL 614-439-3531; FAX 614-432-6219. **Owner(s):** Wooster Republican Printing Co., Wooster, OH 44691. TEL 216-264-3511; Ed. Greg Parks. adv. contact: E. Archibald. pub. size: broadsheet; circ. evening 14,150(paid). **Wire Service(s):** AP.
Formerly: Cambridge Daily Jeffersonian.

CANTON

US   ISSN 0745-7575

REPOSITORY, THE. 1815. d. $.25/day newsstand; $1.25/Sun.; $2.70/wk. home deliv. 500 Market Ave., S , Canton, OH 44702. TEL 216-454-5611. FAX 216-454-5610. **Owner(s):** Thomson Newspapers, Inc., One Thorn Run Ct., Ste. 500, 1187 Thorn Run Rd. Ext., Coraopolis, PA 15108. TEL 412-262-7870; Ed. David Kaminski; Pub. James C. Smith; adv. contact: Mark Yocum. pub. size: broadsheet; circ. morning 65,462(paid); Sun. 84,000(paid). **Wire Service(s):** AP, NYT.
Formerly: Canton Repository.

CELINA

US

CELINA DAILY STANDARD. 1848. Mon.-Sat. $.50 newsstand; $109.20/yr. in cy. 123 E. Market St., Celina, OH 45822. TEL 419-586-2371; FAX 419-586-6271 **Owner(s):** Standard Printing Co., 123 E. Market St., Celina, OH 45822. TEL 419-586-2371; FAX 419-586-6271; Ed. Mike Buettner; Pub. Frank Snyder; adv. contact: John Lake. pub. size: broadsheet; circ. evening 10,300(paid). **Wire Service(s):** AP.

CHILLICOTHE

US

CHILLICOTHE GAZETTE. 1800. Mon.-Sat. $.35/day newsstand; $.75/Sat.; $156/yr. mailed in state; $171.50/yr. mailed out of state. 50 W. Main St., Chillicothe, OH 45601. TEL 614-773-2111; FAX 614-773-2160. **Owner(s):** Gannett Company, Inc., 1100 Wilson Blvd., Arlington, VA 22340 TEL 703-284-6000; Ed. Chaz Osburn; Pub. Marvin Jones; adv.; pub. size: broadsheet; circ. evening 17,100(paid). **Wire Service(s):** AP, GNS.

CINCINNATI

US

CINCINNATI ENQUIRER. 1841. d. $.35/day newsstand; $1.50/Sun.; $15/mo. home deliv. 312 Elm St., Cincinnati, OH 45202. TEL 513-721-2700; FAX 513-768-8079; E-mail: enqedit@aol.com. **Owner(s):** Gannett Company, Inc., 1100 Wilson Blvd., Arlington, VA 22209. TEL 703-284-6000; Ed. Janet Leach; Pub. Harry M. Whipple; adv.; pub. size: broadsheet; circ. morning 198,832(paid); Sun. 348,744(paid). **Wire Service(s):** AP, NYT, LAT-WP, KNS, GNS.

US

CINCINNATI POST. 1881. Mon.-Sat. $.35 newsstand; $7.50/mo. carrier OH; $8.95/mo. carrier KY; $281.76/yr. mailed. 125 E. Court St., Cincinnati, OH 45202. TEL 513-651-4500; FAX 513-621-3962. **Owner(s):** Scripps-Howard, 312 Walnut St., 28th Fl., Cincinatti, OH 45202. TEL 513-977-3000; Ed. Robert Kraft; Pub. William Burleigh; pub. size: broadsheet; circ. evening 100,000(paid). **Wire Service(s):** AP, SHNA.

CIRCLEVILLE

US

CIRCLEVILLE HERALD. 1883. Mon.-Sat. $.50 newsstand; $96.20/yr. 210 N. Court St., Circleville, OH 43113. TEL 614-474-3131. **Owner(s):** Brown Publishing Co., P.O. Box 555, Urbana, OH 43078. TEL 513-652-2100; Ed. Willie Ehrlich; Pub. Timothy C. Kay; adv. contact: Jerry Shasteen. pub. size: broadsheet; circ. evening 8,700(paid). **Wire Service(s):** AP.

CLEVELAND

US

CLEVELAND PLAIN DEALER. 1842. d. $.35/day newsstand; $1/Sun.; $93.60/yr. 1801 Superior Ave., Cleveland, OH 44114. TEL 216-344-4500; FAX 216-999-6354. **Owner(s):** Advance Publications, Inc., 485 Lexington Ave., New York, NY 10017; Ed. Brent Larkin; Pub Alex Machaskee; adv. contact: Terry Hebert. bk.rev.; pub. size: broadsheet; circ morning 398,398(paid); Sun. 528 518(paid). **Wire Service(s):** AP, NYT, LAT-WP.

COLUMBUS

US

COLUMBUS DISPATCH. 1871. d. $.35/day newsstand; $1.75/Sun.; $5 /wk.; $156/yr. 34 S. Third St., Columbus, OH 43215. TEL 614-461-5000; FAX 614-461-8580; E-mail: letters@cd.columbus.oh.us; URL: http://www.dispatch.com. **Owner(s):** Dispatch Newspapers, Inc., 34 S. Third St., Columbus, OH 43215. TEL 614-461-5000; Ed. Robert Smith. adv. contact: Timothy Doty. photos; bk.rev.; pub. size: broadsheet; circ. morning 265,000(paid); Sun. 393,250(paid). **Wire Service(s):** AP, LAT-WP, NYT, KNT, SHNA.

US

DAILY REPORTER. 1896. Mon.-Fri. $.50 newsstand; $35/3 mos.; $55/6 mos. $80/yr.; $130/2 yrs. 329 S. Front St., Columbus OH 43215. TEL 614-224-4835; FAX 614-224-8649; E-mail: cdr@netwalk.com. **Owner(s):** Calcomco, Inc., 534 Rivard Blvd., Detroit, MI 48230. TEL 313-885-9228; Ed. Barbara G. James. pub. size: broadsheet; circ. morning 4,800(paid). **Wire Service(s):** UPI.

COSHOCTON

US

COSHOCTON TRIBUNE. 1909. d. $.35/day newsstand; $1/Sun.; $117/yr. 550 Main St., Coshocton, OH 43812. TEL 614-622-1122; FAX 614-622-7341. **Owner(s):** Thomson Newspapers, Inc., 3150 Des Plaines Ave., Des Plaines, IL 60018. TEL 708-299-5544; Ed. R. Michael Johnson; Pub. Don Miller; pub. size: standard; circ. evening 9,000(paid); Sun. 9,200(paid). **Wire Service(s):** AP.

DAYTON

US

BEAVERCREEK NEWS-CURRENT. 1959. d. $.50 newsstand; $70/yr. mailed. 1350 N. Fairfield Rd., Dayton, OH 45432. TEL 513-426-5263; FAX 513-426-4548. **Owner(s):** Amos Press, Inc., P.O. Box 4129, Sidney, OH 45365. TEL 513-435-7273; Ed. Tom Mitsoff; Pub. Mark Raymond; adv. contact: Ruth Mitsoff. photos; bk.rev.; pub. size: broadsheet; circ. evening 6,000(paid). **Wire Service(s):** AP.
Formerly: Beavercreek Daily News.

US   ISSN 0890-8931

DAYTON DAILY NEWS. 1898. d. $.50/day newsstand; $1.50/Sun.; $3/wk. 45 S. Ludlow St., Dayton, OH 45402. TEL 513-225-2424; FAX 513-225-2489. **Owner(s):** Dayton Newspapers, Inc., Fourth & Ludlow Sts., Dayton, OH 45401. TEL 513-225-2326; Ed. Steve Sidlo; Pub. Brad Tillson; adv.; photos; bk.rev.; pub. size: broadsheet; circ. morning 163,187(paid); Sun. 220,536(paid). **Wire Service(s):** AP.

DEFIANCE

US

CRESCENT-NEWS. 1878. Sun.-Fri. $.50/day newsstand; $1/Sun.; $8.50/mo. deliv. 624 W. Second St., Defiance, OH 43512. TEL 419-784-5441; FAX 419-784-1492. **Owner(s):** Defiance Publishing Co., 624 W. Second St., Defiance, OH 43512. TEL 419-784-5441; Ed. Robert M. Cummins. adv. contact: Amy Dunbar. pub. size: broadsheet; circ. evening 17,000(paid); Sun. 17,000(paid). **Wire Service(s):** AP.

DELAWARE

US   ISSN 1064-2013

DELAWARE GAZETTE. 1818. Mon.-Sat. $2.25/wk. 18 E. William St., Delaware, OH 43015. TEL 614-363-1161. **Owner(s):** W.D. Thomson, P.O. Box 100, Delaware, OH 43015. TEL 614-363-1161; FAX 614-363-6262; Ed. Tom Williams. adv. contact: Dierdre Warden. pub. size: broadsheet; circ. evening 8,760(paid). **Wire Service(s):** AP.

DELPHOS

US

DAILY HERALD. 1869. Mon.-Sat. $.50 newsstand; $1.75/wk.; $98/yr. in cy. 405 N. Main, Delphos, OH 45833. TEL 419-695-0015; FAX 419-692-7704. **Owner(s):** Delphos Newspapers, 405 N. Main St., Delphos, OH 45833. TEL 419-695-0015; FAX 419-692-7704; Ed. E. Bielawski. adv. contact: Jane Ricker. photos; bk.rev.; pub. size: broadsheet; circ. evening 4,200(controlled). **Wire Service(s):** UPI.

EAST LIVERPOOL

US

EVENING REVIEW, THE. 1879. Mon.-Sat. $.35 newsstand; $2/wk.; $104/yr. 210 E. Fourth Street, East Liverpool, OH 43920. TEL 216-385-4545; FAX 216-385-7114. **Owner(s):** Thomson Newspapers, Inc., 65 Queen St., Toronto, ON M5H 2M8, Canada. TEL 416-864-1710; Ed. Robin Webster; Pub. Charles Govey; adv. contact: Tammie McIntosh. photos; pub. size: broadsheet; circ. morning 12,170(paid). **Wire Service(s):** UPI.
    Formerly: East Liverpool Evening Review.

ELYRIA

US

ELYRIA CHRONICLE-TELEGRAM. 1829. d. $.35/day newsstand; $1/Sun.; $2.60/wk. home deliv. 225 East Ave., Elyria, OH 44035. TEL 216-329-7000; FAX 216-329-7282; E-mail: ect@ohio.net; URL: http://www.ohio.net/~ect. **Owner(s):** Lorain County Printing & Publishing Co., 225 East Ave., Elyria, OH 44035. TEL 216-329-7000; Ed. Arnold Miller; Pub. A.D. Hudnutt; adv. contact: Bill Posey. pub. size: broadsheet; circ. evening 40,000(paid); Sun. 40,000(paid). **Wire Service(s):** AP, KR, LAT-WP, SHNA.

FAIRBORN

US

FAIRBORN DAILY HERALD. Mon.-Sat. $.35 newsstand; $100/yr. mailed. One Herald Sq., Fairborn, OH 45324. TEL 513-878-3993; FAX 513-878-8314. **Owner(s):** Amos Press, Inc., 3085 Woodman Dr., Ste.170, Kettering, OH 45420. TEL 513-294-7000; Ed. Bill Flanagan; Pub. Mark Raymond; pub. size: broadsheet; circ. evening 15,300(paid). **Wire Service(s):** UPI.

FINDLAY

US

COURIER, THE. 1836. Mon.-Sat. $.50 newsstand; $104/yr. 701 W. Sandusky St., Findlay, OH 45840. TEL 419-422-5151. **Owner(s):** Findlay Publishing Co., 701 W. Sandusky St., Findlay, OH 45840. TEL 419-422-5151; Ed. Jim Harrold; Pub. Edwin L. Heminger; adv. contact: Eugene Weber. pub. size: broadsheet; circ. morning 26,000(paid). **Wire Service(s):** AP.

FOSTORIA

US

REVIEW TIMES. 1860. Mon.-Sat. $.50 newsstand; $1.85/wk. carrier; $2/wk. motor rte. 113 E. Center St., Fostoria, OH 44830. TEL 419-435-6641; FAX 419-435-9073. **Owner(s):** Spenley Newspapers, Inc., 39 S. Fourth St., Newark, OH 43055. TEL 614-345-4000; Ed. Clarence Pennington; Pub. Clarence Pennington; adv. contact: Kurt Madden. pub. size: broadsheet; circ. evening 8,000(paid). **Wire Service(s):** AP.

FREMONT

US   ISSN 0746-8148

FREMONT NEWS-MESSENGER. 1856. d. $.35 newsstand; $117/yr. 1700 Cedar St., Fremont, OH 43420. TEL 419-332-5511. **Owner(s):** Gannett Company, Inc., 1100 Wilson Blvd., Arlington, VA 22209. TEL 703-284-6000; Ed. James F. Daubel; Pub. James F. Daubel; adv. contact: Genia Lovett. photos; bk.rev.; pub. size: broadsheet; circ. evening 14,000(paid). **Wire Service(s):** AP, GNS.

GALION

US

GALION INQUIRER. 1877. Mon.-Sat. $.35 newsstand; $2.10/wk.; $109.20/yr. 378 N. Market St., Galion, OH 44833. TEL 419-468-1117; FAX 419-468-7255. **Owner(s):** Inquirer Printing Co., 378 N. Market St., Galion, OH 44833. TEL 419-468-1117; Ed. Craig Wagner; Pub. Edgar Koehl, III; pub. size: broadsheet; circ. evening 5,000(paid). **Wire Service(s):** AP.

GALLIPOLIS

US

GALLIPOLIS DAILY TRIBUNE. 1893. d. $.35/day newsstand; $1/Sun.; $97.76/yr. 825 Third Ave., Gallipolis, OH 45631. TEL 614-446-2342; FAX 614-446-3008. **Owner(s):** Multimedia, Inc., P.O. Box 1688, Greenville, SC 29602. TEL 803-298-4367; Ed. Hobart Wilson; Pub. Robert Wingett; adv. contact: Larry L. Boyer. pub. size: broadsheet; circ. evening 6,500(paid); Sun. 13,800(paid). **Wire Service(s):** AP.

GREENFIELD

US

GREENFIELD DAILY TIMES. 1932. Mon.-Fri. $.35 newsstand; $55/yr. 345 Jefferson, Greenfield, OH 45123. TEL 513-981-2141; FAX 513-981-2880. **Owner(s):** Brown Publishing Co., P.O. Box 555, Urbana, OH 43078. TEL 513-652-2100; Ed. Jeff Gilliland; Pub. Gary Schluep; adv. contact: Gary Schluep. pub. size: broadsheet; circ. evening 4,491(paid). **Wire Service(s):** AP.

GREENVILLE

US

DAILY ADVOCATE. 1883. Mon.-Sat. $.50 newsstand; $2/wk. W. Main & Sycamore, Greenville, OH 45331. TEL 513-548-3151; FAX 513-548-3913. **Owner(s):** Thomson Newspapers, Inc., One Thorn Run Ctr., Ste. 500, 1187 Thorn Run Rd. Ext., Coraopolis, PA 15108. TEL 412-262-7870; Ed. Richard Gillette; Pub. Vicki Rifenberg; adv. contact: Mary Ann Boyer. photos; bk.rev.; pub. size: broadsheet; circ. evening 22,700(free & paid). **Wire Service(s):** AP.

HAMILTON

US

JOURNAL NEWS. 1879. d. $.35/day newsstand; $1.50/Sun.; $2.50/wk. 228 Court St., Hamilton, OH 45011. TEL 513-863-8200; FAX 513-863-7988. **Owner(s):** Thomson Newspapers, Inc., One Thorn Run Ctr., Ste. 500, 1187 Thorn Run Rd. Ext., Coraopolis, PA 15108. TEL 412-262-7870; Ed. Tammy Ramsdell; Pub. Robert Murphy; adv. contact: Mike Bennett. photos; pub. size: broadsheet; circ. evening 30,000(paid); Sun. 32,000(paid). **Wire Service(s):** AP, NYT.
    Formerly: Hamilton-Fairfield Journal News.

IRONTON

US   ISSN 0279-5124

IRONTON TRIBUNE. 1850. Tue.-Fri. & Sun. $.50/day newsstand; $1/Sun.; $117/yr. mailed. 2903 S. Fifth St., Ironton, OH 45638. TEL 614-532-1441; FAX 614-532-1506. **Owner(s):** Ironton Publications, Inc., P.O. Box 647, Ironton, OH 45638. TEL 614-532-1441; Ed. Renee Carey; Pub. Jennifer J. Allen; adv. contact: Brenda Renfroe. pub. size: broadsheet; circ. evening 8,767(paid); Sun. 9,292(paid). **Wire Service(s):** AP.

KENTON

US

KENTON TIMES. 1953. Mon.-Sat. $.50 newsstand; $82.85/yr. 201 E. Columbus, Kenton, OH 43326. TEL 419-674-4066; FAX 419-673-1125. **Owner(s):** Hardin County Publishing Co., 201 E. Columbus St., Kenton, OH 43326. TEL 419-674-4066; Ed. Tim Thomas. adv. contact: Jim Grauel. bk.rev.; pub. size: standard; circ. evening 7,525(paid). **Wire Service(s):** AP.

LANCASTER

US

LANCASTER EAGLE-GAZETTE. 1807. d. $.35/day newsstand; $1.25/Sun.; $2.65/wk. carrier. 138 W. Chestnut St., Lancaster, OH 43130. TEL 614-654-1321; FAX 614-654-8271. **Owner(s):** Thomson Newspapers, Inc., One Thorn Run Ctr., Ste. 500, 1187 Thorn Run Rd. Ext., Corapolis, PA 15108. TEL 412-262-7870; Ed. Roy Youst; Pub. Russell L. McCauley; adv. contact: Janet Blair. photos; pub. size: broadsheet; circ. evening 18,000(paid); Sun. 10,000. **Wire Service(s):** AP.

LIMA

US

LIMA NEWS. 1884. d. $.35/day newsstand; $1.25/Sun.; $10/mo. home deliv. 121 E. High St., Lima, OH 45801. TEL 419-223-1010; FAX 419-229-0426; E-mail: limanews@alpha.wcoil.com; URL: http://www.limanews.com. **Owner(s):** Freedom Communications, Inc., 1055 N. High St., Ste. 9, Santa Ana, CA 92701. TEL 714-542-4415; Ed. Ray Sullivan; Pub. Thomas J. Mullen; adv. contact: Ken Carpenter. pub. size: broadsheet; circ. evening 44,484(paid); Sun. 50,221(paid). **Wire Service(s):** KNS, AP.

LISBON

US

MORNING JOURNAL. 1852. d. $.35/day newsstand; $.50/Sun. 308 Maple St., Lisbon, OH 44432. TEL 330-424-9541; FAX 330-424-0048. **Owner(s):** Buckeye Publishing Co., Inc., 308 Maple St., P.O. Box 249, Lisbon, OH 44432. TEL 216-424-9541; Ed. Dorma Tolson; Pub. John Blanchflower; adv. contact: Mace Pavelek. photos; pub. size: broadsheet; circ. morning 13,000(paid); Sun. 13,000(paid). **Wire Service(s):** AP.

LOGAN

US

LOGAN DAILY NEWS. 1842. Mon.-Sat. $.35 newsstand; $1.85/wk. city; $1.95/wk. out of city. 72 E. Main St., Logan, OH 43138. TEL 614-385-2107. **Owner(s):** Brown Publishing Co., P.O. Box 758, Logan, OH 43138. TEL 614-385-2107; Ed. Dwight Crum; Pub. Daniel P. Rodenfels; adv. contact: Keith Conner. photos; pub. size: broadsheet; circ. evening 5,900(paid). **Wire Service(s):** AP.

LONDON

US

MADISON PRESS, THE. 1845. Mon.-Fri. $.50 newsstand; $85/yr. 30 S. Oak St., London, OH 43140-0390. TEL 614-852-1616; FAX 614-852-1620. **Owner(s):** Central Ohio Printing Corp., P.O. Box 390, London, OH 43140-0390. TEL 614-852-1616; Ed. Bill McCullick; Pub. Donald L. Hartley; adv.; photos; pub. size: broadsheet; circ. evening 6,500(paid). **Wire Service(s):** AP.

Formerly: London Madison Press.

LORAIN

US

MORNING JOURNAL. 1921. d. $.50/day newsstand; $1.25/Sun.; $2.75/wk.; $117/yr. 1657 Broadway, Lorain, OH 44052. TEL 216-245-6901; FAX 216-245-5637. **Owner(s):** Journal Register Co., 50 W. State St., 12th Fl., Trenton, NJ 08608. TEL 609-396-2200; Ed. Tom Skoch; Pub. Kevin F. Walsh; adv. contact: William Cyran. photos; bk.rev.; pub. size: broadsheet; circ. morning 45,000(paid); Sun. 48,000(paid). **Wire Service(s):** AP, SHNA.

MANSFIELD

US

NEWS JOURNAL. 1933. d. $.50/day newsstand; $1.50/Sun.; $2.75/wk. 70 W. Fourth St., Mansfield, OH 44903. TEL 419-522-3311; FAX 419-522-2672. **Owner(s):** Thomson Newspapers, Inc., One Thorn Run Ctr., Ste. 500, 1187 Thorn Run Rd. Ext., Coraopolis, PA 15108. TEL 412-262-7870; Ed. Tom Brennan; Pub. Jess Allred; adv. contact: Beth Richey. photos; pub. size: broadsheet; circ. evening 40,381(paid); Sun. 54,446(paid). **Wire Service(s):** AP, KR, CSM.

Formerly: Mansfield News Journal.

MARIETTA

US

MARIETTA TIMES. 1864. Mon.-Sat. $.50/day newsstand; $.75/Sat; $2.25/wk. 700 Channel Ln., Marietta, OH 45750. TEL 614-373-2121; FAX 614-373-6251. **Owner(s):** Gannett Company, Inc., 1100 Wilson Blvd., Arlington, VA 20044. TEL 703-284-6000; Pub. David Whitehead; adv. contact: Lori Smith. pub. size: broadsheet; circ. evening 13,280(paid). **Wire Service(s):** AP, GNS.

MARION

US

MARION STAR. 1877. d. $.35/day newsstand; $1.25/Sun.; $2.40/wk. in town; $2.45/wk. in cy. 150 Court St., Marion, OH 43302. TEL 614-387-0400; FAX 614-382-2210. **Owner(s):** Thomson Newspapers, Inc., 65 Queen St., Toronto, ON M5H 2M5, Canada; Ed. Mary Lawrence; Pub. Tim Dowd; adv. contact: Donna Huffman. photos; pub. size: broadsheet; circ. evening 20,000(paid); Sun. 20,000(paid). **Wire Service(s):** AP.

Formerly: The Star.

MARTINS FERRY

US

TIMES LEADER. 1891. Sun.-Fri. $.35/day newsstand; $1/Sun.; $6.50/mo. carrier. 200 S. Fourth St., Martins Ferry, OH 43935. TEL 614-633-1131; FAX 614-633-1122. **Owner(s):** Ogden Newspapers, Inc. 1500 Main St., Wheeling, WV 26003. TEL 304-233-0100; Ed. Phyliss Sigal; Pub. Alexander F Marshall, III; adv. contact: Jeff Herr. pub. size: broadsheet; circ. evening 22,000(paid); Sun. 23,000(paid). **Wire Service(s):** AP.

MARYSVILLE

US   ISSN 1069-2207

MARYSVILLE JOURNAL-TRIBUNE. 1843. Mon.-Sat. $89/yr. in state; $90/yr. out of state. 207 N. Main St., Marysville, OH 43040. TEL 513-644-9111; FAX 513-644-9211. **Owner(s):** Mary Elizabeth Behrens, 207 N. Main St., Marysville, OH 43040. TEL 513-644-9111; Ed. Holly Zachariah; Pub. David G. Behrens; adv. contact: Marie Woodford. pub. size: broadsheet; circ. evening 6,126(paid). **Wire Service(s):** AP.

MASSILLON

US

INDEPENDENT, THE. 1863. d. $.35 newsstand; $93.60/yr. carrier. 50 North Ave., N.W., Massillon, OH 44648. TEL 216-833-2631; FAX 216-833-2635. **Owner(s):** Goodson Newspaper Group, 989 Lenox Dr., Trenton, NJ 08648. TEL 609-895-2630; Ed. Kevin D. Coffey; Pub. Jack D. Shores; pub. size: broadsheet; circ. evening 15,500(free & paid). **Wire Service(s):** SHNA, AP.

MEDINA

US

MEDINA COUNTY GAZETTE. 1832. Mon.-Sat. $.35 newsstand; $72/yr. in cy.; $78/yr. out of cy. 885 W. Liberty St., Medina, OH 44256. TEL 216-725-4166; FAX 216-725-4299. **Owner(s):** Medina County Publications, Inc., 885 W. Liberty St., P.O. Box 407, Medina, OH 44256. TEL 216-725-4166; Ed. Liz Sheaffer; Pub. George Hudnutt; adv. contact: Dennis Holsinger. pub. size: broadsheet; circ. morning 17,000(paid). **Wire Service(s):** UPI.

MIDDLETOWN

US

MIDDLETOWN JOURNAL. 1857. d. $.50/day newsstand; $1.25/Sun.; $2.50/wk.; $10.40/mo.; $135.20/yr. 52 S. Broad, Middletown, OH 45044. TEL 513-422-3611; FAX 513-423-6940. **Owner(s):** Thomson Newspapers, Inc., One Station Pl., Stamford, CT 06902. TEL 203-425-2500; Ed. Mike Williams; Pub. Carl Esposito; adv. contact: Barb Staples. photos; pub. size: broadsheet; circ. evening 23,100(paid); Sun. 24,400(paid). **Wire Service(s):** AP.

MT. VERNON

US

MOUNT VERNON NEWS. 1837. Mon.-Sat. $.50 newsstand; $124.80/yr. in state. 18 E. Vine St., Mt. Vernon, OH 43050. TEL 614-397-5333; FAX 614-397-1321. **Owner(s):** Progressive Communications Corp., 18 E. Vine St., Mt. Vernon, OH 43050. TEL 614-397-5333; Ed. Robert Nitzel; Pub. Kay Culbertson; adv. contact: John Nesbitt. pub. size: broadsheet; circ. evening 10,907(paid). **Wire Service(s):** AP.

NAPOLEON

US

NORTHWEST SIGNAL. 1966. Mon.-Fri. $.40 newsstand; $71.50/yr. in cy.; $82.50/yr. out of cy. 595 E. Riverview, Napoleon, OH 43545. TEL 419-592-5055; FAX 419-592-9778. **Owner(s):** Napoleon, Inc., P.O. Box 567, Napoleon, OH 43545. TEL 419-592-5055; Pub. James K. Kuser; adv. contact: Jim Hull. pub. size: standard; circ. morning 5,800(paid). **Wire Service(s):** UPI.

Formerly: Napoleon Northwest Signal.

NEWARK

US   ISSN 0740-2120

ADVOCATE, THE. 1821. d. $.35/day newsstand; $1/Sun.; $102/yr. in cy.; $114/yr. out of cy. 22 N. First St., Newark, OH 43055. TEL 614-345-4053; FAX 614-345-1634. **Owner(s):** Thomson Newspapers, Inc., 3150 Des Plaines Ave., Des Plaines, IL 60018. TEL 780-299-5544; Ed. Jerri Kornegay; Pub. Mark D. Richmond; adv. contact: Ronald Frailly. pub. size: broadsheet; circ. evening 23,000(paid); Sun. 23,500(paid). **Wire Service(s):** AP.

NEW PHILADELPHIA

US

TIMES-REPORTER. 1872. d. $.50/day newsstand; $1.50/Sun.; $174.20/yr. 629 Wabash Ave., N.W., New Philadelphia, OH 44663. TEL 216-364-5577. **Owner(s):** Journal Register Co., 50 W. State St., Trenton, NJ 08608. TEL 609-396-2200; Ed. Sandra Stewart; Pub. James E. Shrader; adv. contact: Mark Conrad. photos; pub. size: broadsheet; circ. morning 27,000(paid); evening 30,000(paid). **Wire Service(s):** AP, KR.

NORWALK

US   ISSN 0745-4023

NORWALK REFLECTOR. 1830. Mon.-Sat. $.35 newsstand; $91/yr. home deliv.; $110/yr. mailed. 61 E. Monroe St., Norwalk, OH 44857. TEL 419-668-3771; FAX 419-668-2424. **Owner(s):** Reflector Herald Inc., Norwalk, OH 44857; Ed. Jay Thwaite; Pub. James R. Brown; adv. contact: John Ringenberg. pub. size: broadsheet; circ. evening 9,500(paid). **Wire Service(s):** AP.

PIQUA

US

PIQUA DAILY CALL. 1883. Mon.-Sat. $.50 newsstand; $109.20/yr. in area; $135/yr. out of area. 310 Spring St., Piqua, OH 45356. TEL 513-773-2721; FAX 513-773-2782. **Owner(s):** Thomson Newspapers, Inc., One Thorn Run Ctr., Ste. 500, 1187 Thorn Run Rd. Ext., Coraopolis, PA 15108. TEL 412-262-7870; Ed. Greg Floyd; Pub. Vicky Rifenberg; adv. contact: Mary Kay Boyer. pub. size: broadsheet; circ. evening 10,000(paid). **Wire Service(s):** AP.

POMEROY

US

DAILY SENTINEL, THE. 1945. Sun.-Fri. $.35/day newsstand; $1/Sun.; $7.60/mo. 111 Court St., Pomeroy, OH 45769-1016. TEL 614-992-2156; FAX 614-992-2157. **Owner(s):** Gannett Company, Inc., 1100 Wilson Blvd., Arlington, VA 22340. TEL 703-284-6000; Ed. Charlene Hoeflich; Pub. Robert L. Wingett; adv. contact: Dave Harris. photos; bk.rev.; pub. size: broadsheet; circ. evening 6,500(paid); Sun. 14,000(paid). **Wire Service(s):** AP.

PORT CLINTON

US

NEWS-HERALD. 1865. Mon.-Sat. $.35 newsstand; $104/yr. 115 W. Second, Port Clinton, OH 43452. TEL 419-734-3141; FAX 419-734-3141. **Owner(s):** Gannett Company, Inc., 1100 Wilson Blvd., Arlington, VA 22234. TEL 703-284-6000; Ed. James Daubel; Pub. James Daubel; adv. contact: David Barth. pub. size: broadsheet; circ. evening 6,500(paid). **Wire Service(s):** AP, GNS.

PORTSMOUTH

US   ISSN 8750-6963

PORTSMOUTH DAILY TIMES. 1852. d. $.35/day newsstand; $1/Sun.; $124.80/yr. in cy.; $126/yr. out of cy. 637 Sixth St., Portsmouth, OH 45662. TEL 614-353-3101; FAX 614-353-7280. **Owner(s):** American Publishing Co., 606 N. Van Buren, P.O. Box 520, Marion, IL 62959. TEL 618-993-1711; Ed. Gary Abernathy; Pub. William J. Riley; adv. contact: Sandi Belli. pub. size: broadsheet; circ. evening 17,101(paid); Sun. 16,412(paid). **Wire Service(s):** AP.

RAVENNA

US

KENT-RAVENNA RECORD-COURIER. 1830. d. $.50/day newsstand; $1/Sun. 126 N. Chestnut St., Ravenna, OH 44266. TEL 216-296-9657; FAX 216-296-2698; E-mail: rcletters@aol.com. **Owner(s):** Record Publishing Co., Inc., 126 N. Chestnut St., P.O. Box 1201, Ravenna, OH 44266. TEL 216-296-9657; FAX 216-296-2698; Ed. Steven Harbert; Pub. David Dix; adv. contact: Ron Waite. photos; pub. size: broadsheet; circ. evening 21,500(paid); Sun. 22,500(paid). **Wire Service(s):** AP.

SALEM

US

SALEM NEWS. 1889. Mon.-Sat. $.35 newsstand; $80/yr. 161 N. Lincoln Ave., Salem, OH 44460. TEL 330-332-4601; FAX 330-332-1441. **Owner(s):** Thomson Newspapers, Inc., One Thorn Run Ctr., Ste. 500, 1187 Thorn Run Rd. Ext., Coraopolis, PA 15108. TEL 412-262-7870; Ed. J.D. Creer; Pub. Thomas Spargur; adv. contact: Jim Williams. photos; bk.rev.; pub. size: broadsheet; circ. evening 10,195(paid). **Wire Service(s):** AP.

SANDUSKY

US

SANDUSKY REGISTER. 1822. d. $.50/day newsstand; $1/Sun.; $2.10/wk. carrier. 314 W. Market St., Sandusky, OH 44870. TEL 419-625-5500; FAX 419-625-3007. **Owner(s):** Sandusky Newspapers, Inc., 314 W. Market St., Sandusky, OH 44870. TEL 419-625-5500; Ed. Rex H. Rhoades; Pub. Jim Hofmann; adv. contact: Walling Gray. pub. size: broadsheet; circ. evening 24,500(paid); Sun. 27,600(paid). **Wire Service(s):** AP.

SHELBY

US

SHELBY GLOBE. 1900. Mon.-Sat. $.30 newsstand; $71/yr. local; $95/yr. elsewhere. 37 W. Main St., Shelby, OH 44875. TEL 419-342-4276. **Owner(s):** Shelby Daily Globe, Inc., 37 W. Main St., Shelby, OH 44875. TEL 419-342-4276; Ed. Scott Gove; Pub. Scott Gove; pub. size: broadsheet; circ. evening 4,168(paid). **Wire Service(s):** AP.

SIDNEY

US

SIDNEY DAILY NEWS. 1891. Mon.-Sat. $.50 newsstand; $29.94/3 mos. home deliv.; $37.09/3 mos. students. 911 Vandemark Rd., Sidney, OH 45365. TEL 513-498-2111; FAX 513-498-0806. **Owner(s):** Amos Press, Inc., P.O. Box 150, Sidney, OH 45365. TEL 513-498-2111; Ed. Jeffrey Billiel; Pub. Linda Coffman; adv. contact: Mark Kaufman. pub. size: broadsheet; circ. evening 13,367(paid). **Wire Service(s):** AP.

SPRINGFIELD

US   ISSN 0744-6101

SPRINGFIELD NEWS-SUN. 1817. d. $.50/day newsstand; $1.25/Sun; $3.55/wk. carrier; $184.60/yr. carrier. 202 N. Limestone St., Springfield, OH 45503. TEL 513-328-0300; FAX 513-328-0328. **Owner(s):** Cox Enterprises, Inc., 1400 Lake Hearne Dr., Atlanta, GA 30319. TEL 404-843-5000; Ed. Jack Bianchi; Pub. Charles Rinehart; photos; pub. size: broadsheet; circ. morning 38,227(paid); Sun. 44,905(paid). **Wire Service(s):** AP, KR.

STEUBENVILLE

US   ISSN 0890-8656

HERALD-STAR. 1806. d. $.50/day newsstand; $1/Sun.; $2.20/wk. 401 Herald Sq., Steubenville, OH 43952. TEL 614-283-4711; FAX 614-282-4261. **Owner(s):** Thomson Newspapers, Inc., 3150 Des Plaines Ave., Des Plaines, IL 60018. TEL 708-299-5544; Ed. Judy McGovern; Pub. Robert Dunn; pub. size: broadsheet; circ. evening 21,416(paid); Sun. 21,905(paid). **Wire Service(s):** AP.

Formerly: Steubenville Herald-Star.

ST. MARYS

US   ISSN 0745-5550

EVENING LEADER, THE. 1905. Mon.-Sat. $.50 newsstand; $2.70/wk. carrier. 102 E. Spring St., St. Marys, OH 45885. TEL 419-394-7414; FAX 419-394-7202. **Owner(s):** American Publishing Co., 606 N. Van Buren, P.O. Box 520, Marion, IL 62959. TEL 618-993-1711; Ed. Jose Nogueras; Pub. David Creech; adv.; pub. size: broadsheet; circ. evening 6,600(paid). **Wire Service(s):** AP.
  Formerly: St. Marys Leader.

TIFFIN

US

ADVERTISER-TRIBUNE. 1832. d. $.50/day newsstand; $1/Sun.; $10/mo. carrier; $11.25/mo. motor rte.; $13.75/mo. mailed. 320 Nelson St., Tiffin, OH 44883. TEL 419-448-3200; FAX 419-447-3274. **Owner(s):** Ogden Newspapers, Inc., 1500 Main St., Wheeling, WV 26003. TEL 304-233-0100; Ed. John Kauffman; Pub. John Elchert; adv. contact: Pete Lynch. pub. size: broadsheet; circ. evening 11,000(paid); Sun. 11,600(paid). **Wire Service(s):** AP.
  Formerly: Tiffin Advertiser-Tribune.

TOLEDO

US

TOLEDO BLADE. 1835. d. $.50/day newsstand; $1.50/Sun.; $1.35/wk. Mon.-Sat. 541 Superior St., Toledo, OH 43660. TEL 419-245-6000; FAX 419-245-6439. **Owner(s):** Toledo Blade Co., 541 Superior St., Toledo, OH 43660. TEL 419-245-6000; Ed. John Block; Pub. John Robinson Block; adv. contact: Gerard Grabowski. photos; bk.rev.; pub. size: broadsheet; circ. evening 150,000(paid); Sun. 211,864(paid). **Wire Service(s):** AP, LAT-WP, RN, KNT, NYT, CSM, SHNA.

TROY

US

TROY DAILY NEWS. 1909. d. $.50 newsstand; $2.50/wk. 224 S. Market St., Troy, OH 45373. TEL 513-335-5634; FAX 513-335-3552. **Owner(s):** TDN Publications, Troy, OH 45373; Ed. David Lindeman; Pub. Joel H. Walker; adv. contact: Vicki Yetter. pub. size: broadsheet; circ. evening 11,087(paid); Sun. 14,000(paid). **Wire Service(s):** AP.

UPPER SANDUSKY

US

UPPER SANDUSKY DAILY CHIEF-UNION. 1936. Mon.-Sat. $.35 newsstand; $87.50/yr. 111 W. Wyandot, Upper Sandusky, OH 43351. TEL 419-294-2331; FAX 419-294-5608. **Owner(s):** Hardin County Publishing Co., 317 S. Anderson St., Elwood, IN 46036; Ed. Bette Snyder; Pub. Tom Martin; adv. contact: Tom Martin. pub. size: broadsheet; circ. evening 4,500(paid). **Wire Service(s):** AP.

URBANA

US

URBANA DAILY CITIZEN. 1837. d. $.50 newsstand; $101.40/yr. motor rte.; $124/yr. mailed in cy. 220 E. Court St., Urbana, OH 43078. TEL 513-652-1331; FAX 513-652-1336. **Owner(s):** Brown Publishing Co., 310 Patrick Ave., Urbana, OH 43078. TEL 513-652-2148; Ed. Art Kuhn; Pub. Linda Anderson; adv. contact: Debby Madison. photos; bk.rev.; pub. size: broadsheet; circ. evening 7,700(paid). **Wire Service(s):** AP.

VAN WERT

US   ISSN 8750-1503

TIMES-BULLETIN. 1845. Mon.-Sat. $.50 newsstand; $1.85/wk. in town; $1.95/wk. motor rte. 700 Fox Rd., Van Wert, OH 45891. TEL 419-238-2285; FAX 419-238-0447. **Owner(s):** Brown Publishing Co., P.O. Box 555, Urbana, OH 43078. TEL 513-652-2100; Ed. David Mosier; Pub. L.R. Joseph; adv. contact: Tracy Hoghe. photos; pub. size: broadsheet; circ. evening 7,500(paid). **Wire Service(s):** AP.

WAPAKONETA

US

WAPAKONETA DAILY NEWS. 1904. Mon.-Sat. $.50 newsstand; $126/yr. in cy.; $165/yr. mailed. 8 Willipie St., Wapakoneta, OH 45895. TEL 419-738-2128; FAX 419-738-5352; E-mail: wapakwdn@brutus.bright.net; URL: http://www.bright.net/~wapakwdn. **Owner(s):** American Publishing Co., 606 N. Van Buren, P.O. Box 520, Marion, IL 62959. TEL 618-993-1711; Ed. J. Swygart; Pub. Dianna Epperly; adv. contact: Karen Brown. photos; bk.rev.; pub. size: broadsheet; circ. evening 5,300(paid). **Wire Service(s):** AP.

WARREN

US

TRIBUNE CHRONICLE, THE. d. $.25/day newsstand; $1/Sun.; $2.25/wk. home deliv. 240 Franklin St., S.E., Warren, OH 44482-1431. TEL 216-841-1600; FAX 216-841-1721; E-mail: soravecz@cisnet.com; URL: http://www.cisnet.com/tribune. **Owner(s):** Thomson Newspapers, Inc., 3150 Des Plaines Ave., Des Plaines, IL 60018; Pub. Steven Roszczyk; adv. contact: Tim LaRose. photos; bk.rev.; pub. size: broadsheet; circ. evening 40,838(paid); Sun. 45,406(paid). **Wire Service(s):** AP, KNT.
  Formerly: Warren Tribune Chronicle.

WASHINGTON COURT HOUSE

US

RECORD HERALD. 1937. Mon.-Sat. $.50 newsstand; $8.10/mo. carrier in town. 138 S. Fayette St., Washington Court House, OH 43160. TEL 614-335-3611; FAX 614-335-5728. **Owner(s):** Brown Publishing Co., P.O. Box 555, Urbana, OH 43078. TEL 513-652-2100; Ed. Anthony Conchel; Pub. Jeff Pollard; adv.; photos; bk.rev.; pub. size: broadsheet; circ. evening 6,200(paid). **Wire Service(s):** AP.

WILLOUGHBY

US

NEWS-HERALD. 1879. d. $.50/day newsstand; $1.50/Sun.; $1.75/wk. carrier. 7085 Mentor Ave. Willoughby, OH 44094-7900. TEL 216-951-0000; FAX 216-975-2293. **Owner(s):** Journal Register Co., P.O. Box 351, Willoughby, OH 44094. TEL 216-951-0000; Ed. James Collins; Pub. Joe Cocozzo; adv.; pub. size: broadsheet; circ. evening 56,000(paid); Sun. 68,000(paid). **Wire Service(s):** AP, LAT-WP, KR.

WILMINGTON

US   SSN 8750-4847

WILMINGTON NEWS-JOURNAL. 1838. Mon.-Sat. $.50 newsstand; $85/yr. home deliv. 47 S. South St. Wilmington, OH 45177. TEL 513-382-2574; FAX 513-382-4392. **Owner(s):** Brown Publishing Co., 47 S. South St., Wilmington, OH 45177. TEL 513-382-2574; FAX 513-382-4392; Ed. Jay Carey; Pub. Clarence Graham; adv. contact: Rick Irvin. photos; bk.rev.; pub. size: broadsheet; circ. evening 7,500(paid). **Wire Service(s):** AP.

WOOSTER

US   ISSN 0892-8215

WOOSTER DAILY RECORD. 1897. d. $.50/day newsstand; $1/Sun.; $8.60/4 wks.; $160/yr. 212 E. Liberty St., Wooster, OH 44691. TEL 216-264-1125; FAX 216-264-3756. **Owner(s):** Wooster Republican Printing Co., 212 E. Liberty St., Wooster, OH 44691. TEL 216-264-1125; Ed. Melody Snure; Pub. R. Victor Dix; adv. contact: Bob Anderson. pub. size: broadsheet; circ. evening 25,695(paid). **Wire Service(s):** AP, NYT.

XENIA

US   ISSN 8750-4650

XENIA DAILY GAZETTE. 1868. Mon.-Sat. $.50 newsstand; $98.80/yr. carrier. 37 S. Detroit St., Xenia, OH 45385. TEL 513-372-4444; FAX 513-372-3385. **Owner(s):** Thomson Newspapers, Inc., One Thorn Run Ctr., Ste. 500, 1187 Thorn Run Rd. Ext., Coraopolis, PA 15108. TEL 412-262-7870; Ed. Gary Brock. adv. contact: Judy Bowermaster. pub. size: broadsheet; circ. evening 11,300(paid). **Wire Service(s):** AP.

YOUNGSTOWN

US   ISSN 0890-9857

VINDICATOR, THE. 1869. d. $.25/day newsstand; $.75/Sun.; $2/wk. carrier. 107 Vindicator Sq., Youngstown, OH 44503. TEL 216-747-1471; FAX 216-747-6712; E-mail pjvincy@aol.com. **Owner(s):** Vindicator Printing Co., P.O. Box 780, Youngstown, OH 44503. TEL 216-747-0399; Ed. Paul C. Jagnow; Pub. Betty H. Brown Jagnow; adv. contact: David Burns. photos; bk.rev.; pub. size: broadsheet; circ. evening 93,000(paid); Sun. 135,265(paid). **Wire Service(s):** AP, CT-NYT, LAT-WP, KR.

ZANESVILLE

US

TIMES RECORDER, THE. 1864. d. $.35/day newsstand; $1/Sun.; $124.80/yr. 34 S. Fourth St., Zanesville, OH 43701. TEL 614-452-4561; FAX 614-452-0750; E-mail: 75563.306@compuserve.com. **Owner(s):** Thomson Newspapers, Inc., One Thorn Run Ctr., Ste. 500, 1187 Thorn Run Rd. Ext., Coraopolis, PA 15108. TEL 412-262-7870; Ed. Richard Stubbe; Pub. John B. Raytis; adv.; photos; pub. size: broadsheet; circ. morning 24,263(paid); Sun. 23,780(paid). **Wire Service(s):** AP.

OKLAHOMA

ADA

US

ADA EVENING NEWS. 1904. Sun.-Fri. $.50/day newsstand; $1.25/Sun.; $8.20/mo. in city; $8.35/mo. in cy.; $9/mo. elsewhere. 112-120 N. Broadway, Ada, OK 74820. TEL 405-332-4433; FAX 405-332-8734. **Owner(s):** American Publishing Co., 606 N. Van Buren, P.O. Box 520, Marion, IL 62959. TEL 618-993-1711; Ed. Steve Boggs; Pub. Roy Biondi; adv. contact: Rick Cash. pub. size: broadsheet; circ. evening 10,200(paid); Sun. 9,500(paid). **Wire Service(s):** AP, Thomson.

ALTUS

US

ALTUS TIMES. 1900. d. $.50/day newsstand; $1/Sun.; $72/yr. 218 W. Commerce, Altus, OK 73521. TEL 405-482-1221; FAX 405-487-5709. **Owner(s):** Stephens Group, Inc., P.O. Box 17017, Fort Smith, AR 72917. TEL 501-785-7810; Ed. Rick Lomenick; Pub. Lyle M. Exstrom; adv. contact: Renee Carpenter. pub. size: broadsheet; circ. evening 5,500(paid); Sun. 6,000(paid). **Wire Service(s):** AP.

ALVA

US

ALVA REVIEW-COURIER. 1893. Sun.-Tue., Thu. & Fri. $.25/day newsstand; $.50/Sun.; $96/yr. in cy.; $120/yr. out of state. 620 Choctaw, Alva, OK 73717. TEL 405-327-2200; FAX 405-327-2454. **Owner(s):** Martin Broadcasting Corp., 620 Choctaw, Alva, OK 73717. TEL 405-327-2200; FAX 405-327-2454; Pub. Lynn L. Martin; adv.; photos; bk.rev.; pub. size: tabloid; circ. morning 1,700(paid); Sun. 1,700(paid). **Wire Service(s):** AP.

ANADARKO

US

ANADARKO DAILY NEWS. 1901. Mon.-Sat. $.50 newsstand; $72/yr. in cy. 117 E. Broadway, Anadarko, OK 73005-0548. TEL 405-247-3331; FAX 405-247-5571. **Owner(s):** Anadarko Publishing Co., 117 E. Broadway, Anadarko, OK 73005. TEL 405-247-3331; Ed. Paula McBride Savage; Pub. Carolyn N. McBride; adv. contact: Cindy Fletcher. bk.rev.; pub. size: broadsheet; circ. evening 5,400(paid). **Wire Service(s):** AP.

ARDMORE

US

DAILY ARDMOREITE. 1893. Sun.-Fri. $.50/day newsstand; $.75/Sun.; $60/yr. local. 117 W. Broadway, Ardmore, OK 73401. TEL 405-223-2200; FAX 405-226-2363. **Owner(s):** Morris Communications, P.O. Box 936, Augusta, GA 30903. TEL 706-724-0851; Ed. John Bridwell; Pub. Bill Stauffer; adv. contact: Barbara Winkler. photos; pub. size: broadsheet; circ. evening 11,432(paid); Sun. 13,985(paid). **Wire Service(s):** AP.

BARTLESVILLE

US   ISSN 0883-7015

BARTLESVILLE EXAMINER-ENTERPRISE. 1895. d. $.25/day newsstand; $.75/Sun.; $7/mo. carrier. 4125 S.E. Nowata Rd., Bartlesville, OK 74006. TEL 918-335-8200; FAX 918-335-3111. **Owner(s):** Stephens Group, Inc., P.O. Box 17017, Fort Smith, AR 72917-0707. TEL 501-785-7810; Ed. Susan Savage; Pub. Joseph Edwards; adv. contact: Phil Evans. pub. size: broadsheet; circ. evening 13,100(paid); Sun. 15,300(paid). **Wire Service(s):** AP.

BLACKWELL

US

BLACKWELL JOURNAL-TRIBUNE. 1893. Tue.-Fri. & Sun. $.50 newsstand; $5.50/mo. carrier; $7/mo. mailed in state. 113 E. Blackwell St., Blackwell, OK 74631. TEL 405-363-3370; FAX 405-363-4415. **Owner(s):** Stephens Group, Inc., P.O. Box 17017, Fort Smith, AR 72917. TEL 501-785-7810; Pub. Dayle McGaha; adv. contact: Tammy Zeman. pub. size: broadsheet; circ. evening 2,850(paid); Sun. 2,900(paid). **Wire Service(s):** AP.

CHICKASHA

US

CHICKASHA DAILY EXPRESS. 1889. Sun.-Fri. $.50/day newsstand; $1/Sun.; $78/yr. home deliv. 302 N. Third St., Chickasha, OK 73018. TEL 405-224-2600; FAX 405-224-7087. **Owner(s):** Stephens Group, Inc., P. O. Box 13597, Fort Smith, AR 72901; Pub. Reg Freemyer; adv. contact: Elaine Johnson. photos; bk.rev.; pub. size: broadsheet; circ. evening 5,500(paid); Sun. 6,400(paid). **Wire Service(s):** AP.

CLAREMORE

US

CLAREMORE PROGRESS. 1893. Tue.-Fri. & Sun. $.50/day newsstand; $1/Sun.; $78/yr. carrier. 315 W. Will Rogers Blvd., Claremore, OK 74017. TEL 918-341-1101; FAX 918-341-1131. **Owner(s):** Stephens Group, Inc., P.O. Box 1359, Ft. Smith, AR 72901. TEL 501-785-7810; Ed. Pat Reeder; Pub. Dave Story; adv. contact: Dave Kucifer. pub. size: broadsheet; circ. evening 6,800(paid); Sun. 7,000(paid). **Wire Service(s):** AP.

CLINTON

US

CLINTON DAILY NEWS. 1903. Sun.-Fri. $.50 newsstand; $6.25/mo. home deliv. 522 Avant Ave., Clinton, OK 73601. TEL 405-323-5151; FAX 405-323-5154. **Owner(s):** Clinton Daily News Co., 522 Avant Ave., Clinton, OK 73601. TEL 405-323-5151; FAX 405-323-5154; Ed. Steve Belcher; Pub. Charles E. Engleman; adv. contact: Carla Miller. pub. size: broadsheet; circ. evening 5,200(paid); Sun. 5,400(paid). **Wire Service(s):** AP.

CUSHING

US

CUSHING DAILY CITIZEN. 1895. Mon.-Fri. $.50 newsstand; $53/yr. 115 S. Cleveland St., Cushing, OK 74023-1031. TEL 918-225-3333; FAX 918-225-1050. **Owner(s):** Reid Newspapers, Inc., Cushing, OK; Ed. Terry Hoggett; Pub. David Reid; adv. contact: Brian Hammock. pub. size: broadsheet; circ. morning 3,200(paid). **Wire Service(s):** AP.

DUNCAN

US

DUNCAN BANNER. 1892. Sun.-Fri. $.50/day newsstand; $1/Sun.; $6.75/mo. home deliv. 1001 Elm St., Duncan, OK 73533. TEL 405-255-5354; FAX 405-255-8889. **Owner(s):** Wimberly Investments, Inc., 1001 Elm St., Duncan, OK 73533. TEL 405-255-5354; FAX 405-255-8889; Ed. Larry Gittings; Pub. Alexander J. Hruby; adv. contact: Jill Hunt. photos; bk.rev.; pub. size: broadsheet; circ. evening 10,128(paid); Sun. 10,788(paid). **Wire Service(s):** AP.

DURANT

US

DURANT DAILY DEMOCRAT. 1900. Sun.-Fri. $.50/day newsstand; $1/Sun.; $7/mo. home deliv.; $84/yr. 200 W. Beech St., Durant, OK 74701. TEL 405-924-4388; FAX 405-924-6026. **Owner(s):** DR Partners, P.O. Box 17017, Ft. Smith, AR 72917. TEL 501-785-7810; Ed. John Small; Pub. David Crouch; adv. contact: Paula M. Howell. pub. size: broadsheet; circ. evening 7,000(paid); Sun. 7,600(paid). **Wire Service(s):** AP.

EDMOND

US

EDMOND EVENING SUN. 1889. Tue.-Fri. & Sun. $.50/day newsstand; $.75/Sun.; $78/yr. home deliv.; $90/yr. mailed. 123 S. Broadway, Edmond, OK 73034. TEL 405-341-2121; FAX 405-340-7363. **Owner(s):** Edmond Publishing Co., Inc., P.O. Box 2470, Edmond, OK 13083. TEL 405-341-2121; FAX 405-340-7363; Ed. Ed Livermore; Pub. Ed Livermore; adv. contact: Tammy Claire. pub. size: broadsheet; circ. evening 10,000(paid); Sun. 11,000(paid). **Wire Service(s):** AP, NYT.

ELK CITY

US

ELK CITY DAILY NEWS. 1901. Sun.-Fri. $.50 newsstand; $6/mo. home deliv.; $65/yr. 200-206 W. Broadway, Elk City, OK 73644. TEL 405-225-3000; FAX 405-243-2414. **Owner(s):** Larry R. Wade, P.O. Box 1037, Elk City, OK 73648. TEL 405-225-3000; Mary Jane Wade, P.O. Box 1037, Elk City, OK 73648. TEL 405-225-3000; Mary Elizabeth Wade, P.O. Box 1037, Elk City, OK 73648. TEL 405-225-3000; Pub. Larry R. Wade; adv. contact: Sharon Denny. photos; bk.rev.; pub. size: broadsheet; circ. evening 6,176(paid); Sun. 10,795(paid). **Wire Service(s):** AP.

ENID

US

ENID NEWS & EAGLE. 1893. d. $.35/day newsstand; $1.50/Sun.; $10/mo. home deliv. 227 W. Broadway, Enid, OK 73701. TEL 405-233-6600; FAX 405-233-7645. **Owner(s):** Thomson Newspapers, Inc., Metro Ctr., One Station Pl., Stamford, CT 06902. TEL 203-425-2500; FAX 203-425-2516; Ed. Jerry D. Pittman; Pub. Ed J. Hauck; adv.; pub. size: broadsheet; circ. morning 25,900(paid); Sun. 26,600(paid). **Wire Service(s):** AP, Thomson News Service.
   Formerly: Enid Morning News & Enid Daily Eagle.

FREDERICK

US

FREDERICK LEADER. 1904. Tue-Fri. & Sun. $.50 newsstand; $43.20/yr. carrier; $48/yr. mailed in cy. 304 W. Grand Ave., Frederick, OK 73542. TEL 405-335-2188; FAX 405-335-2047. **Owner(s):** DonRey Media Group, P.O. Box 17017, Fort Smith, AR 72901. TEL 501-785-7810; Ed. Terri Erickson. adv. contact: Robin Coronado. pub. size: broadsheet; circ. evening 2,300(paid); Sun. 2,300(paid).
   Formerly: Frederick Daily Leader.

GROVE

US

▼**GROVE DAILY NEWS.** 1995. Tue.-Sat. $.25 newsstand; $5/mo.; $15/3 mos.; $39/yr. 22 E. Third St., Grove, OK 74344. TEL 918-786-9002; FAX 918-786-6048. **Owner(s):** David Ulrich & Francis Stipe, P.O. Box 335, Grove, OK 74344. TEL 918-786-9002; FAX 918-786-6048; Ed. Bruce Jones; Pub. David Ulrich; adv. contact: David Ulrich. photos; bk.rev.; pub. size: broadsheet; circ. morning 1,200(paid). **Wire Service(s):** AP.

GUTHRIE

US

GUTHRIE DAILY LEADER. 1889. Sun.-Fri. $.50/day newsstand; $.50/Sun.; $5.50/mo.; $66/yr. 107 W. Harrison, Guthrie, OK 73044. TEL 405-282-2222; FAX 405-282-7378. **Owner(s):** Stephens Group, Inc., P.O. Box 17017, Fort Smith, AR 72917. TEL 501-785-7810; Pub. Robert Hager; pub. size: broadsheet; circ. evening 4,208(paid); Sun. 4,373(paid).

GUYMON

US

GUYMON DAILY HERALD. 1890. Mon.-Sat. $.50 newsstand; $6/mo. home deliv.; $72/yr. 515 N. Ellison St., Guymon, OK 73942. TEL 405-338-3355; FAX 405-338-5000. **Owner(s):** Stephens Group, Inc., P.O. Box 17017, Fort Smith, AR 72917-7017. TEL 501-785-7810; Ed. Linda Holbert; Pub. William Murphy; adv. contact: Donna Stephens. photos; bk.rev.; pub. size: broadsheet; circ. evening 4,000(paid). **Wire Service(s):** AP.

HENRYETTA

US

HENRYETTA DAILY FREE-LANCE. 1901. Tue.-Fri. & Sun. $.50 newsstand; $72/yr. carrier; $72/yr. mailed in cy.; $73/yr. out of cy.; $76/yr. out of state. 812 W. Main St., Henryetta, OK 74437. TEL 918-652-3311; FAX 918-652-7347. **Owner(s):** Stephens Group, Inc., P.O. Box 1359, Fort Smith, AR 72901. TEL 501-785-7810; Ed. Mr. Chelsea Cook; Pub. Nancy Miller; adv. contact: Charlotte Klutts. photos; pub. size: broadsheet; circ. evening 2,600(paid); Sun. 2,800(paid). **Wire Service(s):** AP.

HOLDENVILLE

US

HOLDENVILLE DAILY NEWS. 1927. Tue.-Fri. & Sun. $.25 newsstand; $4/mo. carrier; $42/yr. mailed. 112 S. Creek, Holdenville, OK 74848. TEL 405-379-5411; FAX 405-379-5413. **Owner(s):** Robinson Fettis Publishing, Inc., 112 S. Creek, Holdenville, OK 74888. TEL 405-379-5411; Ed. Bill Robinson; Pub. Bill Robinson; adv. contact: Debbie Carter. pub. size: tabloid; circ. morning 2,500(paid).

HUGO

US

HUGO DAILY NEWS. 1917. Mon.-Fri. $.35 newsstand; $5/mo. carrier; $56/yr. mailed in cy. 128 E. Jackson St., Hugo, OK 74743. TEL 405-326-3311; FAX 405-326-6397. **Owner(s):** Hugo Publishing Co., 128 E. Jackson St., Hugo, OK 74743; Ed. Pam Proctor; Pub. Stan Stamper; adv. contact: Linda Packard. pub. size: broadsheet; circ. morning 35,000(paid). **Wire Service(s):** AP.

IDABEL

US

MCCURTAIN DAILY GAZETTE. 1906. Tue.-Fri. & Sun. $.25/day newsstand; $.50/Sun.; $4.10/mo. carrier. 107 S. Central St., Idabel, OK 74745. TEL 405-286-3321; FAX 405-286-2208. **Owner(s):** Gwen & Bruce Willingham, 107 S. Central, Idabel, OK 74745. TEL 405-286-3321; Ed. Bruce Willingham; Pub. Bruce Willingham; adv. contact: Margie Jones. photos; pub. size: broadsheet; circ. evening 6,200(paid); Sun. 8,400(paid). **Wire Service(s):** AP.

LAWTON

US

LAWTON CONSTITUTION. 1900. d. $.50/day newsstand; $1/Sun.; $9.50/mo. carrier. P.O. Box 2069, Lawton, OK 73502. TEL 405-353-0620; FAX 405-585-5140; E-mail: paper@sirinet.com; URL: http://www.lawton-constitution.com. **Owner(s):** Lawton Publishing Co., Inc., P.O. Box 2069, Lawton, OK 73502. TEL 405-353-0620; FAX 405-585-5140; Ed. Dennis A. Lang; Pub. Donald S. Bentley; adv. contact: Mike Owensby. photos; bk.rev.; pub. size: broadsheet; circ. morning 27,000(paid); Sun. 31,000(paid). **Wire Service(s):** AP, NYT, CNS.
   Formerly: The Lawton Constitution/Lawton Morning Press.

MCALESTER

US

MCALESTER NEWS-CAPITAL. Sun.-Fri. $.50/day newsstand; $1/Sun.; $7.50/mo. carrier. 500 S. Second St, McAlester, OK 74501. TEL 918-423-1700; FAX 918-423-3081. **Owner(s):** Park Communications, Inc., Vine Ctr. Office Tower, 333 W. Vine St., 17th Fl., Lexington, KY 40507. TEL 606-252-7275; adv. contact: Janet Grider. pub. size: broadsheet; circ. morning 13,000(paid); Sun. 13,000(paid).

MIAMI

US

MIAMI NEWS-RECORD. 1903. Sun.-Fri. $.50/day newsstand; $1.25/Sun.; $8.50/mo. home deliv.; $10.31/mo. mailed in state. 14 First Ave., N.W., Miami, OK 74354. TEL 918-542-5533; FAX 918-542-1903. **Owner(s):** Boone Newspapers, Inc., P.O. Box 2370, Tuscaloosa, AL 35403. TEL 407-338-3298; Ed. John Fox; Pub. Jerry Turner; adv. contact: Chris Rush. pub. size: broadsheet; circ. morning 7,500(paid); Sun. 8,000(paid).

MUSKOGEE

US

MUSKOGEE DAILY PHOENIX & TIMES-DEMOCRAT. 1888. d. $.35/day newsstand; $1.25/Sun.; $11.50/mo. 214 Wall St., Muskogee, OK 74401. TEL 918-684-2875 FAX 918-684-2878. **Owner(s):** Gannett Company, Inc., 1100 Wilson Blvd., Arlington, VA 22234. TEL 703-248-6000 Pub. Lawrence Corvi; adv. contact: Sheila Runnels. pub. size: broadsheet; circ. morning 19,700(paid); Sun. 21,300(paid). **Wire Service(s):** UPI, AP.

NORMAN

US

NORMAN TRANSCRIPT. 1889. d. $.50/day newsstand; $1/Sun.; $7/mo. in cy.; $14/mo. elsewhere. 215 E. Comanche Norman, OK 73069. TEL 405-321-1800; FAX 405-366-3516. **Owner(s):** Stephens Group, Inc., P.O. Box 1359, Fort Smith, AR 72902; Ed. Andy Rieger; Pub. Jim Miller; adv. contact: Walt Disney. pub. size: broadsheet; circ. evening 15,000(paid); Sun. 15,500(paid). **Wire Service(s):** AP, KNS.

OKLAHOMA CITY

US

DAILY OKLAHOMAN. 1903. d. $.50/day newsstand; $1.50/Sun.; $12.85/mo. home deliv. 9000 N. Broadway, Oklahoma City, OK 73114. TEL 405-475-3311; FAX 405-475-3183. **Owner(s):** Oklahoma Publishing Co., 9000 N. Broadway, Oklahoma City, OK 73114. TEL 405-475-3311; Ed. Ed Kelly; Pub. Edward L. Gaylord; adv. contact: David Thompson. pub. size: broadsheet; circ. morning 214,590(paid); Sun. 321,268(paid). **Wire Service(s):** AP, RN.

OKMULGEE

US

OKMULGEE TIMES. 1903. Tue.-Sun. $.50/day newsstand; $.75/Wed. & Sun.; $6/mo. home deliv.; $23.10/3 mo. mailed; $25.17/3 mos. out of state. 114 E. Seventh, Okmulgee, OK 74447. TEL 918-756-3600; FAX 918-756-8197. **Owner(s):** Stephens Group, Inc., P.O. Box 1359, Fort Smith, AR 72901-7017. TEL 501-785-7810; Pub. Jerry Quinn; adv.; photos; bk.rev.; pub. size: broadsheet; circ. morning 5,750(paid); Sun. 5,800(paid). **Wire Service(s):** AP.

PAULS VALLEY

US

PAULS VALLEY DAILY DEMOCRAT. 1904. Tue.-Fri. & Sun. $.25/day newsstand; $.50/Sun.; $5.50/mo. carrier. 108 S. Willow St., Pauls Valley, OK 73075. TEL 405-238-6464; FAX 405-238-3042. **Owner(s):** Stephens Group, Inc., P.O. Box 1359, Fort Smith, AR 72901. TEL 501-785-7810; Ed. David Vantress; Pub. Mary Anne Lynn; adv. contact: Jerry Crenshaw. bk.rev.; pub. size: broadsheet; circ. evening 4,000(paid); Sun. 4,800(paid). **Wire Service(s):** AP.
  Formerly: Pauls Valley Democrat.

PERRY

US   ISSN 0746-7559

PERRY DAILY JOURNAL. 1893. Mon.-Sat. $.35 newsstand; $5/mo. home deliv. 714 Delaware St., Perry, OK 73077. TEL 405-336-2222; FAX 405-336-3222. **Owner(s):** Perry Journal Co., 714 Delaware St., Perry, OK 73077. TEL 405-336-2222; Ed. Gene Taylor; Pub. Milo W. Watson; adv. contact: Mabel Miller. pub. size: broadsheet; circ. evening 3,250(paid). **Wire Service(s):** AP.

PONCA CITY

US

PONCA CITY NEWS. 1894. Sun.-Fri. $.35/day newsstand; $1/Sun.; $6.25/mo. carrier. 300 N. Third, Ponca City, OK 74601. TEL 405-765-3311; FAX 405-762-6397. **Owner(s):** Ponca City Publishing Co., Inc., 300 N. Third, Ponca City, OK 74601. TEL 405-765-3311; Ed. Foster Johnson; Pub. Allan W. Muchmore; adv. contact: Everett Lockwood. pub. size: standard; circ. evening 11,781(paid); Sun. 13,540(paid). **Wire Service(s):** AP.

POTEAU

US

POTEAU DAILY NEWS & SUN. 1895. Tue.-Sat. $.35/day newsstand; $1/Sat.; $53/yr. in cy. 804 N. Broadway, Poteau, OK 74953. TEL 918-647-3188; FAX 918-647-8198; E-mail: pdn&s@www.clnk.com; URL: http://www.pdns.com. **Owner(s):** LeFlore County Newspapers, P.O. Box 1237, Poteau, OK 74953. TEL 918-647-3188; Ed. Laura Young; Pub. Wallace S. Burchett; adv. contact: Janet Fox. pub. size: broadsheet; circ. morning 5,000(paid). **Wire Service(s):** AP.

PRYOR

US

PRYOR DAILY TIMES. 1940. Tue.-Fri. & Sun. $.50/day newsstand; $1/Sun.; $6.50/mo. carrier; $78/yr. 105 S. Adair St., Pryor, OK 74361. TEL 918-825-3292; FAX 918-825-1965. **Owner(s):** Pryor Publishing Co., 105 S. Adair St., Pryor, OK 74361. TEL 918-825-3292; FAX 918-852-3292; Ed. Henry Goodman. adv. contact: Diana Morgan. pub. size: broadsheet; circ. evening 5,800(paid); Sun. 7,000(paid). **Wire Service(s):** AP.

SAPULPA

US

SAPULPA DAILY HERALD. 1914. Sun.-Fri. $.50/day newsstand; $1/Sun.; $75.60/yr. home deliv. 16 S. Park, Sapulpa, OK 74066. TEL 918-224-5185; FAX 918-224-5196. **Owner(s):** Park Communications, Inc., Vine Ctr. Office Tower, 333 W. Vine St., 17th Fl., Lexington, KY 40507. TEL 606-252-7275; Ed. C.S. Lake. adv. contact: Joanita Brewer. pub. size: broadsheet; circ. evening 6,925(paid); Sun. 7,075(paid). **Wire Service(s):** AP.

SEMINOLE

US

SEMINOLE DAILY PRODUCER. 1927. Tue.-Fri. & Sun. $.35/day newsstand; $.75/Sun.; $5.50/mo. home deliv. 121 N. Main St., Seminole, OK 74868. TEL 405-382-1100; FAX 405-382-1104. **Owner(s):** Seminole Producer, Inc., P.O. Box 431, Seminole, OK 74818. TEL 405-382-1100; FAX 405-382-1104; Ed. Ken Milam; Pub. Ted Phillips; adv. contact: Jim Keisman. bk.rev.; pub. size: broadsheet; circ. evening 6,155(paid); Sun. 6,322(paid).

SHAWNEE

US

SHAWNEE NEWS-STAR. 1929. Tue.-Sun. $.50/day newsstand; $1/Sun.; $8.25/mo. carrier; $8.75/mo. city carrier; $9.00/mo. motor rte. in state; $10.25/mo. out of state. 215 N. Bell, Shawnee, OK 74801. TEL 405-273-4200; FAX 405-273-4207. **Owner(s):** Morris Communications, P.O. Box 936, Augusta, GA 30903. TEL 706-724-0851; Ed. Mike McCormick; Pub. John Tucker; adv. contact: Sherry Wilkins. photos; pub. size: broadsheet; circ. morning 14,500(paid); Sun. 15,608(paid). **Wire Service(s):** AP.

STILLWATER

US

STILLWATER NEWS-PRESS. 1940. Sun.-Fri. $.50/day newsstand; $1/Sun.; $6.25/mo. in town. 211 W. Ninth St., Stillwater, OK 74074. TEL 405-372-5000; FAX 405-372-3112. **Owner(s):** Stillwater Publishing Co., P.O. Box 2288, Stillwater, OK 74076. TEL 405-372-5000; FAX 405-372-3112; Ed. Lawrence Gibbs; Pub. L.F. Bellatti; adv. contact: Rhesa Funk. photos; pub. size: broadsheet; circ. evening 11,800(paid); Sun. 12,500(paid). **Wire Service(s):** AP, KNT.

TAHLEQUAH

US

TAHLEQUAH DAILY PRESS. 1850. Tue.-Fri. & Sun. $.35/day newsstand; $.75/Sun.; $75/yr. carrier; $69/yr. senior citizens carrier. 106 W. Second St., Tahlequah, OK 74464. TEL 918-456-8833; FAX 918-456-2019. **Owner(s):** Indian Nations Communications, Inc., 106 W. Second St., Tahlequah, OK 74464; Ed. Kim Poindexter; Pub. Brad Sugg; adv. contact: Pam Hutson. pub. size: broadsheet;
  Formerly: Tahlequah Star Citizen.

TULSA

US   ISSN 8750-5959

TULSA WORLD. 1905. d. $.50/day newsstand; $1.50/Sun.; $12.10/mo. 318 S. Main St., Tulsa, OK 74103. TEL 918-581-8300; FAX 918-581-8353; E-mail: tulsaworld@mail.webtek.com; URL: http://www.tulsaworld.com. **Owner(s):** World Publishing Co., 318 S. Main, Tulsa, OK 74103. TEL 918-581-8330; Ed. Susan Ellerbach; Pub. Robert E. Lorton; adv.; photos; bk.rev.; pub. size: broadsheet; circ. morning 170,000(paid); Sun. 240,000(paid). **Wire Service(s):** AP, LAT-WP, KR, NYT, GNS.

VINITA

US

VINITA DAILY JOURNAL. 1907. Mon.-Fri. $.50 newsstand; $5.50/mo. in town; $21.50/3 mos. in state. 130-40 S. Wilson St., Vinita, OK 74301. TEL 918-256-6422; FAX 918-256-7100. **Owner(s):** Vinita Printing Co., Inc., P.O. Box 328, Vinita, OK 74301. TEL 918-256-6422; Ed. David Burgess; Pub. Phillip Reed; adv. contact: Helen Walker. pub. size: broadsheet; circ. morning 4,250(paid). **Wire Service(s):** UPI.

WEATHERFORD

US

WEATHERFORD DAILY NEWS. 1889. Tue.-Fri. & Sun. $.50 newsstand; $58/yr. 118 S. Broadway, Weatherford, OK 73096. TEL 405-772-3301; FAX 405-772-7329; E-mail: wdn@itlnet.net; URL: http://wdn.itlnet.net. **Owner(s):** Weatherford News, Inc., P.O. Box 191, Weatherford, OK 73096. TEL 405-772-3301; Ed. Larry Adler; Pub. Philip Reid; adv. contact: Phillip Reid. photos; bk.rev.; pub. size: broadsheet; circ. evening 5,100(free & paid); Sun. 5,300(free & paid). **Wire Service(s):** AP.

WOODWARD

US   ISSN 0883-8755

WOODWARD NEWS. 1983. Tue.-Sun. $.35 newsstand; $70/yr. 904 Oklahoma Ave., Woodward, OK 73801. TEL 405-256-2200; FAX 405-245-2159. **Owner(s):** American Publishing Co., 606 N. Van Buren, P.O. Box 520, Marion, IL 62959. TEL 618-993-1711; Ed. Joel Kindel; Pub. Gloria Fletcher; adv. contact: Amy Poulson. photos; pub. size: broadsheet; circ. evening 6,500(paid); Sun. 6,500(paid). **Wire Service(s):** AP.

OREGON

ALBANY

US

ALBANY DEMOCRAT-HERALD. 1865. d. $.50/day newsstand; $.75/Sat.; $8.50/mo. 600 Lyon St., S.W., Albany, OR 97321. TEL 503-926-2211; FAX 503-926-5298. **Owner(s):** Walt Disney Co., 500 S. Buena Vista St., Burbank, CA 91521. TEL 818-560-5300; Ed. Graham Kislingbury; Pub. John E. Buchner; adv.; photos; bk.rev.; pub. size: broadsheet; circ. evening 21,657(paid). **Wire Service(s):** AP.

ASHLAND

US

ASHLAND DAILY TIDINGS. 1876. Mon.-Sat. $.50 newsstand; $6/mo. home deliv. 1661 Siskiyou Blvd., Ashland, OR 97520. TEL 503-482-3456; FAX 503-482-3688. **Owner(s):** Walt Disney Co., 500 S. Buena Vista St., Burbank, CA 91521. TEL 818-560-5300; Ed. Jeff Keating; Pub. Mike O'Brien; adv. contact: Susan Howard. photos; pub. size: broadsheet; circ. evening 6,000(paid). **Wire Service(s):** AP.

ASTORIA

US   ISSN 0739-5078

DAILY ASTORIAN. 1873. Mon.-Fri. $.50 newsstand; $6/mo. carrier; $9/mo. mailed. 949 Exchange St., Astoria, OR 97103. TEL 503-325-3211; FAX 503-325-6573. **Owner(s):** East Oregonian Publishing Co., 1089 Pendleton, Astoria, OR 97801. TEL 503-325-3211; Ed. Laura Sellers-Earl. adv. contact: Jennifer Reese. pub. size: broadsheet; circ. evening 10,000(paid). **Wire Service(s):** AP.

BAKER CITY

US

BAKER CITY HERALD. 1870. Mon.-Fri. $.35 newsstand; $87/yr. carrier; $90/yr. motor rte.; $132 yr. mailed. 1915 First St., Baker City, OR 97814-0807. TEL 541-523-3673; FAX 541-523-6426. **Owner(s):** Western Communications, Inc., 1526 N.W. Hill St., Bend, OR 97701. TEL 541-382-1811; Ed. Dean Brickey; Pub. Jack Turner; adv. contact: Lynette Perry. photos; pub. size: standard; circ. evening 12,850(paid). **Wire Service(s):** AP.

BEND

US

BULLETIN, THE. 1903. Sun.-Fri. $.35/day newsstand; $.50/Fri.; $1.25/Sun.; $9/mo. 1526 N.W. Hill St., Bend, OR 97701. TEL 541-382-1811; FAX 541-385-5802; E-mail: bulletin@bendnet.com. **Owner(s):** Western Communications, Inc., 1526 N.W. Hill St., Bend, OR 97701. TEL 541-382-1811; FAX 541-385-5802; Ed. Steve Bagwell; Pub. Gordon Black; adv. contact: Mike Thorpe. photos; bk.rev.; pub. size: standard; circ. evening 26,500(paid); Sun. 27,500(paid). **Wire Service(s):** AP, LAT-WP.

COOS BAY

US

WORLD, THE. 1878. Mon.-Sat. $.50/day newsstand; $.75/Sat.; $7/mo. 350 Commercial, Coos Bay, OR 97420. TEL 503-269-1222; FAX 503-267-0294. **Owner(s):** Scripps League Newspapers, Inc., P.O. Box 1109, Herndon, VA 22070; Ed. Veronica Combs; Pub. Don Brown; adv. contact: Juan Mejia. pub. size: broadsheet; circ. evening 17,000(paid). **Wire Service(s):** AP, SLNI, NEA.

Formerly: Coos Bay World.

CORVALLIS

US   ISSN 0746-3995

CORVALLIS GAZETTE-TIMES. 1862. d. $.35/day newsstand; $1.50/Sun.; $10.85/4 wks. home deliv. 600 S.W. Jefferson Ave., Corvallis, OR 97333. TEL 503-758-9502; FAX 503-758-9505. E-mail: gtnews@proaxis.com; URL: http://www.gtconnect.com. **Owner(s):** Lee Enterprises, Inc., 130 E. Second St., Davenport, IA 52801. TEL 319-383-2202; Pub. Beth Clark; adv. contact: Gene Fulton. photos; bk.rev.; pub. size: broadsheet; circ. morning 15,500(paid); Sun. 17,200(paid). **Wire Service(s):** AP, LAT-WP, KR.

EUGENE

US   ISSN 0739-8557

REGISTER-GUARD. 1867. d. $.35/day newsstand; $.50/Sat.; $1.25/Sun.; $9.50/mo. home deliv. 975 High St., Eugene, OR 97401. TEL 503-485-1234; FAX 503-687-6668. **Owner(s):** Guard Publishing Co., 975 High St., Eugene, OR 97401. TEL 503-343-3878; FAX 541-984-4699 Ed. Jim Godbold; Pub. Alton F. Baker, III; adv. contact: Michael Raz. bk.rev.; pub. size: broadsheet; circ. morning 75,140(paid); Sun. 78,358(paid). **Wire Service(s):** AP, NYT, LAT-WP.

GRANTS PASS

US

GRANTS PASS DAILY COURIER. 1885. Mon.-Sat. $.50 newsstand $8/mo. 409 S.E. Seventh St., Grants Pass, OR 97526. TEL 503-474-3700; FAX 503-474-3723; E-mail: courier@magik.net. **Owner(s):** Courier Publishing Co., P.O. Box 1468, Grants Pass, OR 97526. TEL 503-474-3700; FAX 503-474-3723; Ed. Dennis Roler; Pub. Dennis Mack; adv. contact: Michele Thomas. pub. size: broadsheet; circ. evening 18,520(paid). **Wire Service(s):** AP.

KLAMATH FALLS

US

HERALD & NEWS. 1906. Sun.-Fri. $.50/day newsstand; $1/Sun.; $8.75/mo. home deliv. 1301 Esplanade, Klamath Falls, OR 97601. TEL 503-885-4410; FAX 503-835-4456; E-mail: handnews@mg1.cdsnet.net; URL http://www.cdsnet.net/business/herald/news. **Owner(s):** Pioneer Press, Inc., 3701 W. Lake Ave., Glenview, IL 60025 TEL 847-486-9200; Ed. Patrick Bushey; Pub. Dwight Tracy; adv. contact: Mike Waltman. pub. size broadsheet; circ. evening 17,000(paid); Sun. 17,305(paid). **Wire Service(s):** UPI.

Formerly: Klamath Falls Herald and News.

LA GRANDE

US

OBSERVER, THE. 1896. Mon.-Sat. $.35 newsstand; $7.50/mo. carrier; $12/mo. mail. 1406 Fifth St., La Grande, OR 97850. TEL 503-963-3161; FAX 503-963-7804. **Owner(s):** Western Communications, Inc., 1525 N.W. Hill St., Bend, OR 97701. TEL 503-382-1811; FAX 503-385-1811; Ed. Ted Kramer; Pub. Robert K. Moody; adv. contact: Don Fowell. photos; bk.rev.; pub. size: broadsheet; circ. evening 7,931(paid). **Wire Service(s):** AP.

MEDFORD

US

MAIL TRIBUNE. 1906. d. $.50/day newsstand; $1/Sun.; $105/yr. 111 N. Fir St. Medford, OR 97501-0229. TEL 503-776-4411; FAX 503-776-4376. **Owner(s):** Ottaway Newspapers, Inc., P.O. Box 401, Campbell Hall, NY 10916. TEL 914-294-8181; Ed. Bob Hunter; Pub. Gregory Taylor; adv. contact: Teresa Keplinger. photos; bk.rev.; pub. size: broadsheet; circ. morning 32,000(paid); Sun. 34,000(paid). **Wire Service(s):** AP.

Formerly: Medford Mail Tribune.

ONTARIO

US

ARGUS OBSERVER. 1976. Sun.-Fri. $.50/day newsstand; $1.25/Sun.; $8/mo.; $96/yr. 1160 S.W. Fourth St., Ontario, OR 97914-0130. TEL 541-889-5387; FAX 541-889-3477. **Owner(s):** Wick Communications, Inc., 333 Wilcox, Ste. 302, Sierra Vista, AZ 85635. TEL 602-458-0200; Ed. Larry Turrle; Pub. Francis McLean; adv. contact: Linda Warren. photos; bk.rev.; pub. size: broadsheet; circ. evening 7,900(paid); Sun. 8,350(paid). **Wire Service(s):** AP.

PENDLETON

US

EAST OREGONIAN, THE. 1875. Mon.-Sat. $.50 newsstand; $12/mo. 211 S.E. Byers Ave., Pendleton, OR 97801. TEL 503-276-2211; FAX 503-276-8314. **Owner(s):** East Oregonian Publishing Co., 211 S.E. Byers Ave., Pendleton, OR 97801. TEL 503-276-2211; Ed. Dave Cash. adv. contact: Christine Moore. pub. size: standard; circ. evening 13,000(paid). **Wire Service(s):** AP.

PORTLAND

US   ISSN 8750-1317
OREGONIAN, THE. 1850. d. $.35/day newsstand; $1.50/Sun.; $11/mo. home deliv. 1320 S.W. Broadway, Portland, OR 97201. TEL 503-221-8327; FAX 503-227-5306; E-mail: letters@news.oregonian.com; URL: http://www.oregonian.com. **Owner(s):** Advance Publications, Inc., 485 Lexington Ave., New York, NY 10017. TEL 212-697-8020; Ed. Peter Bhatia; Pub. Fred A. Stickel; adv. contact: Dennis Atkins. photos; bk.rev.; pub. size: broadsheet; circ. morning 349,193(paid); Sun. 446,300(paid). **Wire Service(s):** AP, NYT, CNS, LAT-WP, NNS.

ROSEBURG

US
NEWS-REVIEW. 1867. Sun.-Fri. $.35/day newsstand; $1/Sun.; $88.75/yr. home deliv. 345 N.E. Winchester, Roseburg, OR 97470. TEL 541-672-3321; FAX 541-673-5994; E-mail: newsdesk@oregonnews.com; URL: http://www.oregonnews.com. **Owner(s):** Swift Newspapers, Inc., 345 N.E. Winchester, Roseburg, OR 97470. TEL 541-673-5994; Ed. Bart M. Smith; Pub. Ron Stewart; adv. contact: Kelly Gant. photos; pub. size: standard; circ. evening 20,638(paid); Sun. 20,767(paid). **Wire Service(s):** AP.

SALEM

US   ISSN 0739-5507
STATESMAN JOURNAL. 1851. d. $.50/day newsstand rack; $.40/day stores; $1.50/Sun.; $11.50/mo. carrier; $12.25/mo. motor rte. 280 Church St., N.E., Salem, OR 97301. TEL 503-399-6611; FAX 503-399-6706. **Owner(s):** Gannett Company, Inc., 1100 Wilson Blvd., Arlington, VA 22234. TEL 703-284-6000; Pub. Sara Bentley; adv. contact: Frank Bauer. pub. size: broadsheet; circ. morning 60,824(paid); Sun. 71,493(paid). **Wire Service(s):** AP, GNS, LAT-WP.

THE DALLES

US   ISSN 0747-3443
THE DALLES DAILY CHRONICLE. 1890. Sun.-Fri. $.35 newsstand; $6.25/mo. carrier; $6.50/mo. mailed in cy. 414 Federal St., The Dalles, OR 97058. TEL 503-296-2141; FAX 503-298-1365. **Owner(s):** Scripps League, P.O. Box 1109, Herndon, VA 22070. TEL 703-713-1920; Ed. Tom Stevenson; Pub. Harold Steininger; adv. contact: Skip Tschanz. pub. size: broadsheet; circ. evening 6,100(paid); Sun. 9,600(paid). **Wire Service(s):** AP.

PENNSYLVANIA

ALLENTOWN

US   ISSN 0884-5557
MORNING CALL, THE. 1883. d. $.50/day newsstand; $1.50/Sun.; $3.80/wk. 101 N. Sixth St., Allentown, PA 18101. TEL 610-820-6695; FAX 610-770-3766. **Owner(s):** Times-Mirror Co., Times-Mirror Sq., Los Angeles, CA 90053. TEL 213-237-3700; Ed. Raymond Holton; Pub. Gary K. Shorts; adv. contact: Howard Renner. pub. size: broadsheet; circ. morning 131,628(paid); Sun. 186,733(paid). **Wire Service(s):** AP, NYT, LAT-WP, KNT.

ALTOONA

US
ALTOONA MIRROR. 1874. d. $.50/day newsstand; $1.50/Sun.; $108/yr. home deliv. 301 Cayuga Ave., Altoona, PA 16602. TEL 814-946-7411; FAX 814-946-7539. **Owner(s):** Thomson Newspapers, Inc., 3150 Des Plaines Ave., Des Plaines, IL 60018. TEL 708-299-5544; Pub. Michael J. Miller; adv. contact: Ed Gaydos. pub. size: broadsheet; circ. evening 36,292(paid); Sun. 40,997(paid). **Wire Service(s):** AP.

BEAVER

US
BEAVER COUNTY TIMES. 1876. d. $.50/day newsstand; $1.25/Sun.; $2.70/wk. home deliv. 400 Fair Ave., Beaver, PA 15009. TEL 412-775-3200; FAX 412-775-4180; E-mail: bingle@pgh.net; URL: http://www.pgh.net/beaver/. **Owner(s):** Calkins Newspapers, Inc., Levittown, PA 19058; Ed. Dennis D. Dible; Pub. F. Wallace Gordon; adv.; bk.rev.; pub. size: broadsheet; circ. evening 48,000(paid); Sun. 57,000(paid). **Wire Service(s):** AP, KR.

BEDFORD

US   ISSN 0744-8457
BEDFORD GAZETTE/GAZETTE SUNDAY. 1805. d. $.35 newsstand; free/Sun. in cy.; $93.50/yr. 424 W. Penn St., Bedford, PA 15522. TEL 814-623-1151; FAX 814-623-5055. **Owner(s):** Edward K. Frear, 424 W. Penn St., Bedford, PA 15522. TEL 814-623-1151; Ed. Edward K. Frear; Pub. Edward K. Frear; adv. contact: Keith Landis. photos; bk.rev.; pub. size: broadsheet; circ. morning 10,145(paid). **Wire Service(s):** AP.

BLOOMSBURG

US
PRESS ENTERPRISE, THE. 1903. d. $.50/day newsstand; $.75/Sat. & Sun.; $121.55/yr. carrier deliv. 3185 Lackawanna Ave., Bloomsburg, PA 17815. TEL 717-784-2121; FAX 717-784-9226. **Owner(s):** Press-Enterprise, Inc., 3185 Lackawanna Ave., Bloomsburg, PA 17815. TEL 717-784-2121; Ed. Tim Konski; Pub. Paul R. Eyerly, III; adv. contact: Sandy Bower. photos; bk.rev.; pub. size: broadsheet; circ. morning 25,000(paid); Sun. 25,000(paid). **Wire Service(s):** AP, KNT.

BRADFORD

US
BRADFORD ERA, THE. 1877. Mon.-Sat. $.50 newsstand; $12/mo. carrier; $13/mo. motor rte. 43 Main St., Bradford, PA 16701. TEL 814-368-3173; FAX 814-362-6510. **Owner(s):** American Publishing Co., 606 N. Van Buren, P.O. Box 520, Marion, IL 62959. TEL 618-993-1711; Ed. Paul H. Reichart. adv. contact: H.L. Woodruff. pub. size: broadsheet; circ. morning 13,000(paid). **Wire Service(s):** AP.

BUTLER

US
BUTLER EAGLE. 1869. Sun.-Fri. $.35/day newsstand; $.50/Sun.; $1.50/wk. 114 W. Diamond St., Butler, PA 16001. TEL 412-282-8000; FAX 412-282-1280. **Owner(s):** Eagle Printing Co., 114 W. Diamond, Butler, PA 16001. TEL 412-282-8000; Ed. Mark Mann; Pub. Vernon L. Wise, Jr.; adv. contact: Arthur Kephart. pub. size: broadsheet; circ. evening 31,032(paid); Sun. 31,816(paid). **Wire Service(s):** AP, NYT.

CARLISLE

US
CARLISLE SENTINEL. 1861. d. $.50/day newsstand; $1/Sun.; $2.40/wk. 457 E. North St., Carlisle, PA 17013. TEL 717-243-2611; FAX 717-243-3121; E-mail: wanfried@epix.net; URL: http://www1.trib.com/cumberlink/. **Owner(s):** Howard Publications, Inc., P.O. Box 570, Oceanside, CA 92049. TEL 619-433-5771; Ed. Kurt Wanfried; Pub. Wayne Powell; adv. contact: Steve Crowley. photos; pub. size: broadsheet; circ. morning 18,500(free & paid); evening 29,000(free & paid); Sun. 21,000. **Wire Service(s):** AP.

CHAMBERSBURG

US
PUBLIC OPINION, THE. 1869. Mon.-Sat. $.35/day newsstand; $.75/Sat.; $2.25/wk. carrier; $25/2 mos. motor rte. & mailed. 77 N. Third St., Chambersburg, PA 17201. TEL 717-264-6161; FAX 717-264-0377. **Owner(s):** Gannett Company, Inc., 1100 Wilson Blvd., Arlington, VA 22234. TEL 703-284-6000; Ed. Lorrie DeFrank; Pub. Nancy Monaghan; adv.; photos; bk.rev.; pub. size: broadsheet; circ. evening 21,500(paid). **Wire Service(s):** AP, GNS, SHNA.

CLIFTON HEIGHTS

US
DELAWARE COUNTY DAILY-SUNDAY TIMES. 1876. Sun.-Fri. $.50/day newsstand; $1.25/Sun.; $3.30/wk. carrier. 500 Mildred Ave., Clifton Heights, PA 19018. TEL 610-622-8800; FAX 610-622-8829. **Owner(s):** Goodson Newspaper Group, Lawrenceville, NJ. TEL 609-895-2600; Ed. Linda DeMeglio; Pub. Frank Gothie; adv.; photos; bk.rev.; pub. size: tabloid; circ. morning 56,000(paid); Sun. 54,000(paid). **Wire Service(s):** AP.

CONNELLSVILLE

US
DAILY COURIER, THE. 1902. Mon.-Sat. $.35 newsstand; $1.80/wk. carrier; $2/wk. motor. rte.; $38.50/3 mos. mailed in cy. 127 W. Apple St., Connellsville, PA 15425. TEL 412-628-2000; FAX 412-628-5270. **Owner(s):** Thomson Newspapers, Inc., Metro Ctr., Station Pl., Stamford, CT 06902; Ed. Shawnee Culbertson. adv. contact: Nancy Henry. photos; bk.rev.; pub. size: broadsheet; circ. evening 12,000(paid). **Wire Service(s):** AP.

CORRY

US

CORRY JOURNAL. Mon.-Sat. $.35 newsstand; $9/mo. home deliv. 28 W. South St., Corry, PA 16407. TEL 814-665-8291; FAX 814-664-2288. **Owner(s):** American Publishing Co., 606 N. Van Buren, P.O. Box 520, Marion, IL 62959. TEL 618-993-1711; Ed. Kevin Downey; Pub. George R. Sample; adv. contact: Linnell Ashby. pub. size: broadsheet; circ. evening 4,353(paid). **Wire Service(s):** AP photo.

DANVILLE

US

DANVILLE NEWS. 1897. Mon.-Sat. $.50 newsstand; $83.20/yr. carrier. 14 E. Mahoning St., Danville, PA 17821. TEL 717-275-3235; FAX 717-275-7624. **Owner(s):** Stauffer Media, Inc., 14 E Mahoning St, Danville, PA 17821; Ed. Holly Brandon. adv. contact: Donna Keefer. pub. size: broadsheet; circ. evening 4,300(paid). **Wire Service(s):** AP.

DOYLESTOWN

US

INTELLIGENCER RECORD, THE. 1804. Sun.-Fri. $.35/day newsstand; $1.50/Sun.; $3.20/wk. carrier; $3.75/wk. motor rte. 333 N. Broad St., Doylestown, PA 18901. TEL 215-345-3000; FAX 215-345-3150. **Owner(s):** Calkins Newspapers, Inc., Levitown, PA. TEL 215-949-4000; Ed. Joan Bastel; Pub. Charles P. Smith; adv. contact: Rosemary Rocconi. pub. size: broadsheet; circ. morning 45,107(paid); Sun. 50,116(paid). **Wire Service(s):** AP.
Formerly: Doylestown Daily Intelligencer.

DU BOIS

US   ISSN 8750-4049

COURIER-EXPRESS. 1879. Sun.-Fri. $.50/day newsstand; $1/Sun.; $102/yr. mailed. 500 Jeffers St., Du Bois, PA 15801. TEL 814-371-4200; FAX 814-371-3241. **Owner(s):** Independent Publications, Inc., 945 Haverford Rd., Bryn Mawr, PA 19010. TEL 215-527-6330; Ed. Dennis Bonavita; Pub. W. Dock Lias; adv. contact: Linda Smith. photos; pub. size: broadsheet; circ. evening 10,750(paid); Sun. 13,400(paid). **Wire Service(s):** AP, SHNS.

EASTON

US   ISSN 1062-3620

EXPRESS-TIMES, THE. 1855. d. $.35/day newsstand; $1/Sun.; $3.10/wk. 30 N. Fourth St., Easton, PA 18042. TEL 610-258-7171; FAX 215-258-7130; E-mail: staff@express-times.com; URL: http://www.express-times.com. **Owner(s):** Media News Group, 4888 Loop Central Dr., Ste. 525, Houston, TX 77081; Ed. Joe Owens; Pub. Timothy W. Sowecke; adv. contact: Ernie Reed. pub. size: broadsheet; circ. morning 53,000(paid); Sun. 50,000(paid). **Wire Service(s):** AP, LAT-WP, KR.
Formerly: Express, The.

ELLWOOD CITY

US

ELLWOOD CITY LEDGER. 1920. Mon.-Sat. $.35 newsstand; $1.70/wk. 835 Lawrence Ave., Ellwood City, PA 16117. TEL 412-758-7529. **Owner(s):** Citizens Publishing & Printing Co., P.O. Box 471, Ellwood City, PA 16117. TEL 412-758-5573; Pub. W.R. Kegel; adv. contact: Dom A. Viccari. pub. size: broadsheet; circ. evening 7,300(paid). **Wire Service(s):** AP.

ERIE

US

ERIE DAILY TIMES/SUNDAY TIMES NEWS. 1888. d. $.35/day newsstand; $1.50/Sun. 205 W. 12th St., Erie, PA 16534. TEL 814-870-1600; FAX 814-870-1808. **Owner(s):** Times Publishing Co., 205 W. 12th St., Erie, PA 16534. TEL 814-870-1600; Ed. Jeff Pinski. adv. contact: John Andersen. pub. size: standard; circ. evening 38,585(paid); Sun. 102,298. **Wire Service(s):** AP, KNT, LAT-WP.
Formerly: Daily Times.

US

ERIE MORNING NEWS. 1957. d. $.35 newsstand; $78/yr. 205 W. 12th St., Erie, PA 16534. TEL 814-870-1600; FAX 814-870-1808. **Owner(s):** Times Publishing Co., 205 W. 12th St., Erie, PA 16534. TEL 814-870-1600; Ed. Jeff Pinski; Pub. Edward Mead; adv. contact: John Anderson. photos; pub. size: broadsheet; circ. morning 32,104(paid). **Wire Service(s):** AP, LAT.

GETTYSBURG

US

GETTYSBURG TIMES. 1902. Mon.-Sat. $.35/day newsstand; $72/yr. 1570 Fairfield Rd., Gettysburg, PA 17325. TEL 717-334-1131; FAX 717-334-4243; E-mail: times@cvn.net; URL: http://www1.infi.net/gettysburg. **Owner(s):** Times & News Publishing Co., 1570 Fairfield Rd., Gettysburg, PA 17325. TEL 717-334-1131; FAX 717-334-4243; Ed. Bill Pukmel; Pub. Philip M. Jones; adv.; pub. size: broadsheet; circ. morning 10,000(paid). **Wire Service(s):** AP.

GREENSBURG

US

STANDARD-OBSERVER. 1972. Mon.-Sat. $.35 newsstand; $62.40/yr. in state. R.D. 1, Rte. 136, Greensburg, PA 15601. TEL 412-863-3601; FAX 412-523-6805; E-mail: stdobsc@aol.com. **Owner(s):** T-R Printing & Publishing Co., P. O. Box 280, Irwin, PA 15642. TEL 412-863-3601; adv. contact: Dawn Iezzi. pub. size: broadsheet; circ. evening 16,500. **Wire Service(s):** AP.
Formerly: Irwin Standard-Observer.

US

TRIBUNE-REVIEW. 1889. d. $.35/day newsstand; $2.50/wk. Cabin Hill Dr., Greensburg, PA 15601. TEL 412-834-1151. **Owner(s):** Tribune-Review Publishing Co., P.O. Box 640, Greensburg, PA 15601. TEL 412-834-1151; Ed. George A. Beidler; Pub. Richard M. Scaife; adv.; photos; bk.rev.; pub. size: broadsheet; circ. morning 85,000(paid); Sun. 135,000(paid). **Wire Service(s):** AP, LAT-WP, RN.

GREENVILLE

US

GREENVILLE RECORD-ARGUS. 1848. Mon.-Sat. $.35 newsstand; $88.20/yr. 10 Penn Ave., Greenville, PA 15125. TEL 412-588-5000; FAX 412-588-4691. **Owner(s):** Greenville Newspapers, Inc., P.O. Box 711, Greenville, PA 16125. TEL 412-588-5000; Ed. Ron Wroughter; Pub. Robert N. Bracey; adv. contact: Steve Gargasz. photos; pub. size: standard; circ. morning 5,400(paid). **Wire Service(s):** AP News, AP laserphoto.

HANOVER

US

EVENING SUN. 1915. d. $.35/day newsstand; $1/Sun.; $2.50/wk. 135 Baltimore St., Hanover, PA 17331. TEL 717-637-3736; FAX 717-637-7730; E-mail: esun@sun-link.com; URL: http://www.sun-link.com. **Owner(s):** Thomson Newspapers, Inc., One Thorn Run Ctr., Ste. 500, 1187 Thorn Run Rd. Ext., Coraopolis, PA 15108. TEL 412-262-7870; Ed. Wayne Lowman; Pub. Edward R. Moss; pub. size: broadsheet; circ. evening 21,200(paid); Sun. 21,000(paid). **Wire Service(s):** AP.
Formerly: Hanover Sun.

HARRISBURG

US   ISSN 0887-7939

PATRIOT-NEWS. 1854. d. $.50/day newsstand; $1.75/Sun.; $.30/day deliv.; $121.68/yr. 812 Market St., Harrisburg, PA 17101. TEL 717-255-8100; FAX 717-255-8456. **Owner(s):** Advance Publications, Inc., 485 Lexington Ave., New York, NY 10017; Ed. Tom Baden; Pub. Raymond L. Gover; adv. contact: James Stephanak. bk.rev.; pub. size: broadsheet; circ. morning 105,594(paid); Sun. 177,329(paid). **Wire Service(s):** AP, NNS, NYT, LAT-WP, BS, KR.
Formerly: Patriot & Evening News.

HAZLETON

US

HAZLETON STANDARD SPEAKER. 1866. d. $.35 newsstand; $10/mo.; $25/3 mos. 21 N. Wyoming, Hazleton, PA 18201-0578. TEL 717-455-3636; FAX 717-455-4244. **Owner(s):** Hazleton Standard-Speaker, Inc., 21 N. Wyoming St., Hazleton, PA 18201. TEL 717-455-3636; Ed. Ramon Saul; Pub. Paul N. Walser; adv. contact: Gary Yacubek. pub. size: broadsheet; circ. morning 21,000(paid); Sun. 24,000(paid). **Wire Service(s):** AP, CNS.

HONESDALE

US

WAYNE INDEPENDENT, THE. 1878. Mon.-Fri. $.50 newsstand; $91/yr. carrier. 220 Eighth St., Honesdale, PA 18431. TEL 717-253-3055; FAX 717-253-5387. **Owner(s):** American Publishing Co., 606 N. Van Buren, P.O. Box 520, Marion, IL 62959. TEL 618-993-1711; Ed. Paul Quigley; Pub. Donald Doyle; adv. contact: Michelle Hessling. pub. size: broadsheet; circ. evening 6,198(paid). **Wire Service(s):** AP.

HORSHAM

US

RECORD, THE. Sun.-Fri. $.35/day newsstand; $1.40/Sun.; $175.50/yr. mailed. 145 Easton Rd., Horsham, PA 19044. TEL 215-957-8100; FAX 215-957-8165; E-mail: 75703.3217@compuserve.com. **Owner(s):** Calkins Newspapers, Inc., 8400 Rt. 13, Levittown, PA 19057. TEL 215-949-4068; Ed. Lou Sessinger. adv. contact: Kim Noble. pub. size: broadsheet; circ. morning 45,000(paid); Sun. 50,000(paid).
  Formerly: Intelligencer-Record Newspaper.

HUNTINGDON

US

DAILY NEWS. Mon.-Sat. $.50 newsstand; $110/yr. 325 Penn St., Huntingdon, PA 16652. TEL 814-643-4040; FAX 814-643-0376. **Owner(s):** Joseph F. Biddle Publishing Co., Inc., P.O. Box 384, Huntingdon, PA 16652. TEL 814-643-4040; Ed. James D. Hunt; Pub. George Sample, III; adv. contact: Carol Cutshall. pub. size: broadsheet; circ. evening 10,600(paid). **Wire Service(s):** UPI.
  Formerly: Huntingdon Daily News.

INDIANA

US

INDIANA GAZETTE. 1890. d. $.35/day newsstand; $.75/Sun.; $132/yr. 899 Water St., Indiana, PA 15701. TEL 412-465-5555; FAX 412-349-4550. **Owner(s):** Indiana Printing & Publishing Co., P.O. Box 10, Pittsburgh, PA 15201. TEL 412-465-5555; Ed. Carl Kologie. adv. contact: Carol Fletcher. photos; bk.rev.; pub. size: standard; circ. evening 20,000(paid); Sun. 10,000(paid). **Wire Service(s):** AP, NYT.

JOHNSTOWN

US

TRIBUNE DEMOCRAT, THE. 1853. d. $.50/day newsstand; $1.25/Sun. 425 Locust St., Johnstown, PA 15907. TEL 814-532-5050; FAX 814-539-1409. **Owner(s):** Johnstown Tribune Publishing Co., 425 Locust St., Johnston, PA 15907. TEL 814-532-5050; Ed. Larry Hudson; Pub. Pamela J. Mayer; adv. contact: Brian Long. photos; bk.rev.; pub. size: broadsheet; circ. morning 51,581(paid); Sun. 53,799(paid). **Wire Service(s):** AP, KR.

KANE

US

KANE REPUBLICAN. 1894. Mon.-Sat. $.50 newsstand; $11.50/mo. carrier. 200 N. Fraley St., Kane, PA 16735. TEL 814-837-6000; FAX 814-837-2227. **Owner(s):** American Publishing Co., 606 N. Van Buren, P.O. Box 520, Marion, IL 62959. TEL 618-993-1711; Pub. Kay Pearson; adv. contact: Kay Pearson. photos; bk.rev.; pub. size: broadsheet; circ. evening 2,544(paid). **Wire Service(s):** AP.

KITTANNING

US

LEADER TIMES. 1898. Mon.-Sat. $.35 newsstand; $1.75/wk. carrier; $1.90/mo. motor rte.; $127.40/yr. 115 N. Grant Ave., Kittanning, PA 16201. TEL 412-543-1303; FAX 412-545-6768. **Owner(s):** Thomson Newspapers, Inc., One Thorn Run Ctr., Ste. 500, 1187 Thorn Run Rd. Ext., Coraopolis, PA 15108. TEL 412-262-7870; Ed. Michael O'Hare; Pub. Kristy Green; adv. contact: Barbara Sheasley. pub. size: broadsheet; circ. evening 12,000(paid). **Wire Service(s):** AP.
  Formerly: Kittanning Leader Times.

LANCASTER

US

LANCASTER INTELLIGENCER JOURNAL. 1794. Mon.-Sat. $.40 newsstand; $104.20/yr. 8 W. King St., Lancaster, PA 17603-8622. TEL 717-291-8811; FAX 717-399-6507. **Owner(s):** Lancaster Newspapers, Inc., 8 W. King St., Lancaster, PA 17603. TEL 717-291-8811; Ed. William H. Cody. adv. contact: Harold E. Miller. pub. size: broadsheet; circ. morning 45,000(paid). **Wire Service(s):** AP, NYT, States News Service, Med. Tribune Service.

US

LANCASTER NEW ERA. 1877. Mon.-Sat. $.40/day newsstand; $31.20/3 mos. home deliv. 8 W. King St., Lancaster, PA 17603. TEL 717-291-8600; FAX 717-399-6506. **Owner(s):** Lancaster Newspapers, Inc., 8 W. King St., Lancaster, PA 17603. TEL 717-291-8600; Ed. Robert J. Kozak. adv. contact: Pat Hartsfield. pub. size: broadsheet; circ. evening 51,283(paid). Wire Service(s): AP, NYT, KR.
  Formerly: New Era.

LANSDALE

US   ISSN 0890-8443

REPORTER, THE. 1870. Mon.-Sat. $.35 newsstand; $2.25/wk. 307 Derstine Ave., Lansdale, PA 19446. TEL 215-855-8440; FAX 215-368-5367. **Owner(s):** Gannett Company, Inc., 1100 Wilson Blvd., Arlington, VA 22209. TEL 703-284-6000; Ed. Barbara Delp; Pub. Suzanne Bush; adv. contact: Tom Geonnotti. photos; pub. size: broadsheet; circ. morning 95,000(paid); evening 19,276(paid). **Wire Service(s):** AP, GNS.

LATROBE

US

LATROBE BULLETIN. 1902. Mon.-Sat. $.25 newsstand; $5.75/mo.; $6/mo. out of cy. 1211 Ligonier St., Latrobe, PA 15650. TEL 412-537-3351. **Owner(s):** Latrobe Printing & Publishing Co., 1211 Ligonier St., Latrobe, PA 15650. TEL 412-537-3351; Ed. Marie McCandless. adv. contact: Ken Seremet. pub. size: broadsheet; circ. evening 10,000(paid). **Wire Service(s):** AP.

LEBANON

US

LEBANON DAILY NEWS. 1872. d. $.50/day newsstand; $1.50/Sun.; $160.55/yr. carrier. 718 Poplar St., Lebanon, PA 17042. TEL 717-272-5611; FAX 717-274-1608; E-mail: lebnews@leba.net; URL: http://www.leba.net/lebnews. **Owner(s):** Thomson Newspapers, Inc., One Thorn Run Ctr., Ste. 500, 1187 Thorn Run Rd. Ext., Coraopolis, PA 15108. TEL 412-262-7870; Ed. James Burchik; Pub. Blake Sanderson; adv. contact: Karen Williams. pub. size: broadsheet; circ. evening 24,088(paid); Sun. 22,962(paid). **Wire Service(s):** UPI.

LEHIGHTON

US

TIMES NEWS. 1883. Mon.-Sat. $.50 newsstand; $8.75/mo. First & Iron Sts., Lehighton, PA 18235-0239. TEL 610-377-2051; FAX 610-377-5800; E-mail: tnonline@postoffice.ptd.net; URL: http://www.tnonline.com. **Owner(s):** Times News, Inc., 471 Delaware Ave., Palmerton, PA 18071. TEL 610-826-2115; Ed. Bob Urban. adv. contact: Don Reese. photos; pub. size: broadsheet; circ. evening 16,200(paid). **Wire Service(s):** AP.
  Formerly: Lehighton Times News.

LEVITTOWN

US

BUCKS COUNTY COURIER TIMES. 1910. Sun.-Fri. $.35/day newsstand; $1.50/Sun.; $3/wk. 8400 Rte. 13, Levittown, PA 19057. TEL 215-949-4010; FAX 215-949-4177. **Owner(s):** Courier Times, Inc., 8400 Rte. 13, Levittown, PA 19057. TEL 215-949-4010; Ed. William Steinauer; Pub. Arthur E. Mayhew; adv. contact: Tim Birch. photos; pub. size: broadsheet; circ. morning 68,500(paid); Sun. 75,100(paid). **Wire Service(s):** AP.
  Formerly: Levittown Bucks County Courier Times.

LEWISTOWN

US

SENTINEL, THE. 1903. Mon.-Sat. $.50 newsstand; $105/yr. carrier. 375 Sixth St., Lewistown, PA 17044. TEL 717-248-6741; FAX 717-248-3481. **Owner(s):** Ogden Newspapers, Inc., 1500 Main St., Wheeling, WV 26003. TEL 304-233-0100; Ed. Brad Siddons; Pub. Bart Leath; adv. contact: Diane Brown. pub. size: broadsheet; circ. 13,000(paid). **Wire Service(s):** AP.
  Formerly: Lewistown Sentinel.

LOCK HAVEN

US

LOCK HAVEN EXPRESS. 1882. Mon.-Sat. $.35 newsstand; $1.95/wk. carrier. 9-11 W. Main St., Lock Haven, PA 17745-6791. TEL 717-748-6791; FAX 717-748-1544; E-mail: express@oak.kcsd.k12.pa.us; URL: http://oak.kcsd.k12.pa.us/~express. **Owner(s):** Lock Haven Express Printing Co., P.O. Box 208, Lock Haven, PA 17745. TEL 717-748-0791; FAX 717-748-1544; Ed. Charles York; Pub. Charles R. Ryan; adv. contact: Richard Noll. pub. size: broadsheet; circ. evening 11,200(paid). **Wire Service(s):** AP.

MCKEESPORT

US

MCKEESPORT DAILY NEWS. 1884. Mon.-Sat. $.35 newsstand. 409 Walnut St., McKeesport, PA 15132-2613. TEL 412-664-9161; FAX 412-664-3972. **Owner(s):** Daily News Publishing Co., 409 Walnut St., McKeesport, PA 15132. TEL 412-664-9161; FAX 412-664-3972; Pub. Patricia M. Miles; adv. contact: Mark Caruso. photos; bk.rev.; pub. size: standard; circ. evening 33,000(paid). **Wire Service(s):** AP, LAT-WP.

MEADVILLE

US   ISSN 0747-2412

MEADVILLE TRIBUNE, THE. 1884. d. $.35 newsstand; $2.15/wk. 947 Federal Ct., Meadville, PA 16335. TEL 814-724-6370; FAX 814-724-8755. **Owner(s):** Thomson Newspapers, Inc., One Thorn Run Ctr., Ste. 500, 1187 Thorn Run Rd. Ext., Coraopolis, PA 15108. TEL 412-262-7870; Ed. Stephan Hope; Pub. Jeanne Moore-Yount; adv. contact: Marcia Martsolf. photos; pub. size: broadsheet; circ. morning 16,600(paid). **Wire Service(s):** AP, SHNA, Thomson News Service.

MILTON

US   ISSN 0895-4232

LEWISBURG DAILY JOURNAL. 1906. Mon.-Sat. $.50 newsstand; $1.95/wk.: $93.60/yr. carrier. 19 Arch St., Milton, PA 17847. TEL 717-523-1268; FAX 717-742-9876. **Owner(s):** American Publishing Co., P.O. Box 1000, West Frankfort, IL 62896. TEL 618-937-6411; Ed. Bill Kohler. adv. contact: Amy Moyer. pub. size: standard; circ. morning 11,300(paid).

US

MILTON DAILY STANDARD. 1890. Mon.-Sat. $.35 newsstand; $1.50/wk.; $78/yr. carrier. 19 Arch St., Milton, PA 17847. TEL 717-742-9671; FAX 717-742-9876. **Owner(s):** American Publishing Co., 606 N. Van Buren, P.O. Box 520, Marion, IL 62959. TEL 618-993-1711; Ed. Troy Sellers. adv. contact: Amy Moyer. photos; pub. size: broadsheet; circ. evening 2,987(paid). **Wire Service(s):** AP.

MONESSEN

US

VALLEY INDEPENDENT. 1901. Mon.-Sat. $.50 newsstand. Eastgate 19, Monessen, PA 15062. TEL 412-684-5200; FAX 412-684-8104. **Owner(s):** Thomson Newspapers, Inc., One Thorn Run Ctr., Ste. 500, 1187 Thorn Run Rd. Ext., Coraopolis, PA 15108. TEL 412-262-7870; Ed. J. Frank Jawordwski; Pub. Barbara Raitano; pub. size: standard; circ. evening 18,250(paid). **Wire Service(s):** AP.
  Formerly: Monessen Valley Independent.

MOON TOWNSHIP

US

ALLEGHENY TIMES. 1986. Sun.-Fri. $.50/day newsstand; $1.25/Sun.; $12/mo. in area. 894 Beavergrade Rd., Moon Township, PA 15108. TEL 412-269-1144; FAX 412-269-1151. **Owner(s):** Caulkins Industry, Levittown, PA; Ed. Dennis Dible; Pub. S. Wallace Gordon; pub. size: broadsheet; circ. evening 3,500(paid); Sun. 3,500(paid).

NEW CASTLE

US

NEW CASTLE NEWS. 1880. Mon.-Sat. $.35 newsstand; $2.20/wk. carrier. 27 N. Mercer St., New Castle, PA 16101. TEL 412-654-6651; FAX 412-654-9593. **Owner(s):** Thomson Newspapers, Inc., One Thorn Run Ctr., Ste. 500, 1187 Thorn Run Rc. Ext., Coraopolis, PA 15108. TEL 412-262-7870; Ed. Tim Kolodziej; Pub. Max Thomson; adv. contact: Chris D'Angelo. photos; pub. size: broadsheet; circ. evening 22,700(paid). Wire Service(s): UPI.

NORRISTOWN

US

TIMES HERALD, THE. 1799. d. $.35/day newsstand; $1/Sun. $2.85/wk. 410 Markley St., Norristown, PA 19404. TEL 610-272-2500; FAX 610-272-4003. **Owner(s):** Journal Register Co., 50 W. State St., 12th Fl., Trenton, NJ 08608. TEL 609-396-2200; Ed. Dave Gilmartin; Pub. Geoffrey L. Moser; adv.; photos; bk.rev.; pub. size: broadsheet; circ. morning 26,041; Sun. 22,512(paid). **Wire Service(s):** AP, SHNA.
  Formerly: Norristown Times Herald.

OIL CITY

US

DERRICK, THE. 1871. Mon.-Sat. $.50 newsstand; $9/mo. carrier; $11/mo. mailed. 1510 W. First St., Oil City, PA 16301. TEL 814-676-7444; FAX 814-676-7444. **Owner(s):** P.C. Boyle, P.O. Box 928, Oil City, PA 16301. TEL 814-676-7444; Ed. Glen Monkern; Pub. P.C. Boyle; adv. contact: Ned Cowart. pub. size: broadsheet; circ. morning 18,732(paid).

US

NEWS-HERALD. 1878. Mon.-Sat. $.50 newsstand; $9.95/4 wks. 1510 W. 1st St., Oil City, PA 16301. TEL 814-675-7444; FAX 814-677-8347. **Owner(s):** P.C. Boyle, P.O. Box 928, Oil City, PA 16301. TEL 814-676-7444; Ed. James Davis; Pub. P.C. Boyle; adv. contact: Ned Cowart. photos; pub. size: broadsheet; circ. morning 9,000(paid). **Wire Service(s):** AP.
  Formerly: Franklin News-Herald.

PHILADELPHIA

US

PHILADELPHIA DAILY NEWS. 1925. Mon.-Sat. $.60 newsstand; $3.60/wk. home deliv. 400 N. Broad St., Philadelphia, PA 19130. TEL 215-854-5900; FAX 215-854-5910; E-mail: dailynews.opinion@phillynews.com; URL: http://www.phillynews.com/. **Owner(s):** Philadelphia Newspapers, Inc., 400 N. Broad St., Philadelphia, PA 19130; Ed. Brian Toolan; Pub. Robert Hall; adv. contact: David Munch. pub. size: tabloid; circ. evening 200,000(paid). **Wire Service(s):** KNS, AP, RN.

US   ISSN 0885-6613

PHILADELPHIA INQUIRER. 1969. d. $.50/day newsstand; $1.50/Sun.; $4.30/wk. home deliv. 400 N. Broad St., Philadelphia, PA 19130. TEL 215-854-2000; FAX 215-854-5553; E-mail: inquirer@phillynews.com; URL: http://www.phillynews.com/. **Owner(s):** Knight-Ridder, Inc., One Herald Plz., Miami, FL 33132. TEL 305-350-2650; Ed. Max King; Pub. Robert Hall; adv. contact: Kathy McKenna. pub. size: broadsheet; circ. morning 446,842(paid); Sun. 901,891(paid). **Wire Service(s):** AP, KNS, LAT-WP.

PHOENIXVILLE

US

PHOENIX, THE. 1888. Mon.-Sat. $.35 newsstand; $1.75/wk. 225 Bridge St. Phoenixville, PA 19460. TEL 610-933-8926; FAX 610-933-1187. **Owner(s):** Journal Register Co., 50 W. State St., 12th Fl., Trenton, NJ 08608. TEL 610-396-2200; Ed. Rita Cellucci; Pub. Keith Dawn; adv. contact: Mike Joyce. pub. size: broadsheet; circ. evening 7,000(paid); Sun. 7,000(paid). **Wire Service(s):** AP.

PITTSBURGH

US

PITTSBURGH POST-GAZETTE. 1786. d. $.50/day newsstand; $1.50/Sun.; $3/wk. carrier. 34 Blvd. of the Allies, Pittsburgh, PA 15222. TEL 412-263-1100; FAX 412-391-8452. **Owner(s):** William Block, Sr., PG Publishing Co., 3450 Blvd. of the Allies, Pittsburgh, PA 15222; Ed. Madelyn Ross. adv. contact: Robert D. McCray. photos; bk.rev.; pub. size: broadsheet; circ. morning 250,000(paid); Sun. 442,471(paid). **Wire Service(s):** AP, NYT, RN.

POTTSTOWN

US

MERCURY, THE. 1931. d. $.50/day newsstand; $1/Sun. King & Hanover Sts., Pottstown, PA 19464. TEL 610-323-3000; FAX 610-970-4492. **Owner(s):** Peerless Publications, King & Hanover Sts., Pottstown, PA 19464. TEL 610-323-3000; Ed. Andy Hachadorian; Pub. Barry Hoowood; adv. contact: Dennis Pfeiffer. photos; bk.rev.; pub. size: broadsheet; circ. morning 30,000(paid); Sun. 30,000(paid). **Wire Service(s):** AP.

POTTSVILLE

US

POTTSVILLE REPUBLICAN. 1884. d. $.50/day newsstand; $.75/weekend.; $11/mo. 111-117 Mahantongo St., Pottsville, PA 17901. TEL 717-622-3456; FAX 717-628-6092; E-mail: jkane@pottsville.infi.net; URL: http://www.pottsville.com. **Owner(s):** J.H. Zerbey Newspapers, Inc., 111-117 Mahantongo St., P.O. Box 209, Pottsville, PA 17901. TEL 717-628-6092; Ed. James B. Kane; Pub. Uzal H. Martz, Jr.; adv. contact: Henry H. Nyce. photos; bk.rev.; pub. size: broadsheet; circ. evening 34,500(paid). **Wire Service(s):** AP.

PUNXSUTAWNEY

US

PUNXSUTAWNEY SPIRIT. 1873. Mon.-Sat. $.35 newsstand; $9/mo. 510 Pine St., Punxsutawney, PA 15767. TEL 814-938-8740; FAX 814-938-3794. **Owner(s):** American Publishing Co., 606 N. Van Buren, P.O. Box 520, Marion, IL 62959. TEL 618-993-1711; Ed. Wick Divelbiss; Pub. William C. Anderson; adv. contact: Mary Roberts. pub. size: broadsheet circ. morning 6,600(paid). **Wire Service(s):** AP.

READING

US

READING EAGLE & READING TIMES. 1868. d. $.50 newsstand; $124.80/yr. home deliv.; $78/yr. Sun. only. 345 Penn St., Reading, PA 19601. TEL 215-371-5000; FAX 215-371-5098. **Owner(s):** Reading Eagle Co., 345 Penn St., Reading, PA 19601. TEL 215-371-5000; Ed. Charles M. Gallagher; Pub. William S. Flippin; adv. contact: Walter Woolwine. photos; bk.rev.; pub. size: broadsheet; circ. morning 49,212(paid); evening 24,497(paid); Sun. 109,391(paid). **Wire Service(s):** AP, CNS, KNT, NEA, RN, SHNA.

RIDGWAY

US

RIDGWAY RECORD. 1892. Mon.-Sat. f cy.; $110/yr. mailed out of cy. 20 Main St., Ridgway, PA 15853-1718. TEL 814-773-3161; FAX 814-776-1086. **Owner(s):** American Publishing Co., 606 N. Van Buren, P.O. Box 520, Marion, IL 62959. TEL 618-993-1711; Ed. Bekki Guildyard; Pub. Joseph C. Piccirillo; adv. contact: Todd Stenta. pub. size: broadsheet; circ. evening 3,295(paid). **Wire Service(s):** AP.

SAYRE

US   ISSN 0746-4843

EVENING TIMES. 1891. Mon.-Sat. $.50 newsstand; $9.50/mo. carrier; $11/mo. mailed. 201 N. Lehigh Ave., Sayre, PA 18840. TEL 717-888-9643; FAX 717-888-6463. **Owner(s):** American Publishing Co., 606 N. Van Buren, P.O. Box 520, Marion, IL 62959. TEL 618-993-1711; Ed. Steve Piatt; Pub. Ted Mike, Jr.; adv. contact: Vickee Mike. pub. size: broadsheet; circ. evening 9,000(paid). **Wire Service(s):** AP.

SCRANTON

US   ISSN 1062-5844

SCRANTON TIMES/SUNDAY TIMES. 1990. d. $.35/day newsstand; $1.50/Sun.; $158.60/yr. 149 Penn Ave. & Spruce St., Scranton, PA 18503. TEL 717-348-9100; FAX 717-348-9135. **Owner(s):** Edward J. Lynett, Jr., P.O. Box 3311, Scranton, PA 18505. TEL 717-348-9100; Ed. Edward J. Lynett, Jr.; Pub. Edward J. Lynett, Jr.; adv. contact: Steve Sauder. pub. size: broadsheet; circ. evening 52,000(paid); Sun. 83,000(paid). **Wire Service(s):** AP, NYT, KNT.

US

TRIBUNE, THE. 1870. Mon.-Fri. $.40/day newsstand; $1.50/Sun.; $42.90/13 wks. in city; $44.20/13 wks. motor rte. 149 Penn Ave., Scranton, PA 18505. TEL 717-348-9100; FAX 717-348-9145. **Owner(s):** George V., William R., Edward J., Jr., Lynett, Scranton Times, Penn Ave. & Spruce St., Scranton, PA 18503. TEL 717-348-9100; Ed. Robert Burke; Pub. Edward J. Lynett, Jr.; adv. contact: Steve Sauder. pub. size: broadsheet; circ. morning 32,082(paid). **Wire Service(s):** AP, NYT, KNT.

SHAMOKIN

US

SHAMOKIN NEWS-ITEM. 1970. Mon.-Sat. $.50 newsstand; $2.20/wk. carrier. 707 N. Rock St., Shamokin, PA 17872. TEL 717-648-4641; FAX 717-644-0892. **Owner(s):** Thomson Newspapers, Inc., One Thorn Run Ctr., Ste. 500, 1187 Thorn Run Rd. Ext., Coraopolis, PA 15108. TEL 412-292-7870; Ed. M. Philip Yucha. adv. contact: John Kaminski. photos; bk.rev.; pub. size: broadsheet; circ. evening 13,134(paid). **Wire Service(s):** AP.

SHARON

US   ISSN 0744-7302

HERALD, THE. 1864. d. $.50/day newsstand; $.75/Sun.; $2.15/wk. carrier; $2.25/wk. motor rte. 52 S. Dock St., Sharon, PA 16146. TEL 412-981-6100; FAX 412-981-5116; E-mail: zavinski@pgh.net; URL: http://www.sharon-herald.com. **Owner(s):** Ottaway Newspapers, Inc., P.O. Box 401, Campbell Hall, NY 10916. TEL 914-294-8181; Ed. Peggy Dunder; Pub. John L. Lima; adv. contact: Douglas P. Homer. bk.rev.; pub. size: broadsheet; circ. evening 25,500(paid); Sun. 23,700(paid). **Wire Service(s):** AP, SHNA.
    Formerly: The Sharon Herald.

SOMERSET

US

DAILY AMERICAN. 1929. Mon.-Sat. $.35/day newsstand; $.50/Sat.; $27/3 mos.; $52/6 mos.; $100/yr. 334 W. Main St., Somerset, PA 15501. TEL 814-445-9621; FAX 814-445-2935. **Owner(s):** Somerset Newspapers, Inc., 334 W. Main St., Somerset, PA 15501. TEL 814-445-9621; Ed. James Oliver; Pub. David H. Reiley; adv. contact: Tom Koppenhofer. photos; pub. size: broadsheet; circ. morning 13,605(paid). **Wire Service(s):** AP.

STATE COLLEGE

US

CENTRE DAILY TIMES. 1898. d. $.50/day newsstand; $1.25/Sun. 3400 E. College Ave., State College, PA 16801. TEL 814-238-5000; FAX 814-237-5966. **Owner(s):** Knight-Ridder, Inc., One Herald Plz., Miami, FL 33132. TEL 305-376-3800; Pub. Lou Heldman; adv. contact: Mark Mateer. photos; bk.rev.; pub. size: broadsheet; circ. morning 26,561(paid); Sun. 34,695(paid). **Wire Service(s):** AP, KR, LAT-WP.

ST. MARYS

US

DAILY PRESS, THE. 1910. Mon.-Sat. $.50 newsstand; $128/yr. 245 Brussells St., St. Marys, PA 15857-0353. TEL 814-781-1596; FAX 814-834-7473. **Owner(s):** American Publishing Co., 606 N. Van Buren, P.O. Box 520, Marion, IL 62959. TEL 618-993-1711; Ed. Wayne Bauer; Pub. Val Mahaney; adv. contact: Robin Salbers. photos; pub. size: broadsheet; circ. evening 5,456(free & paid). **Wire Service(s):** AP.

STROUDSBURG

US

POCONO RECORD. 1894. d. $.50/day newsstand; $1.50/Sun., $156.75/yr. carrier; $166.30/yr. motor rte. 511 Lenox St., Stroudsburg, PA 18360. TEL 717-421-3000; FAX 717-424-2625. **Owner(s):** Ottaway Newspapers, Inc., P.O. Box 401, Campbell Hall, NY 10916. TEL 914-294-8181; Ed. William Kline; Pub. Carolynn Allen-Evans; adv.: $13.83/SAU (daily); $16.04/SAU (Sun.). pub. size: broadsheet; circ. morning 22,000(paid); Sun. 26,000(paid). **Wire Service(s):** AP.

SUNBURY

US

DAILY ITEM, THE. 1937. d. $.50/day newsstand; $1.40/Sun.; $117/yr. 200 Market St., Sunbury, PA 17801. TEL 717-286-5671; FAX 717-286-2570. **Owner(s):** Ottaway Newspapers, Inc., P.O. Box 401, Campbell Hall, NY 10916. TEL 914-294-8181; Ed. Leonard Ingrassia; Pub. Donald P. Micozzi; adv. contact: Martin Hughes. pub. size: broadsheet; circ. evening 25,672(paid); Sun. 28,750(paid). **Wire Service(s):** LAT-WP, AP, ONS.

TARENTUM

US

VALLEY NEWS DISPATCH. 1891. d. $.35/day newsstand; $1/Sun.; $2.75/wk. 210 Fourth Ave., Tarentum, PA 15084. TEL 412-224-4321; FAX 412-226-7787. **Owner(s):** Gannett Company, Inc., 1100 Wilson Blvd., Arlington, VA 22234. TEL 703-284-6000; Pub. Scott M. Brown; adv. contact: Randy Mooney. pub. size: broadsheet; circ. evening 35,000(paid). **Wire Service(s):** AP, GNS.

TITUSVILLE

US

TITUSVILLE HERALD. 1865. Mon.-Sat. $.50 newsstand; $9.76/mo. carrier & motor rte. 209 W. Spring St., Titusville, PA 16354. TEL 814-827-3634; FAX 814-827-2512. **Owner(s):** American Publishing Co., 606 N. Van Buren, P.O. Box 520, Marion, IL 62959. TEL 618-993-1711; Pub. Michael Sample; adv.; photos; pub. size: broadsheet; circ. morning 5,000(paid). **Wire Service(s):** AP.

TOWANDA

US

DAILY REVIEW & SUNDAY REVIEW. 1880. d. $.40/day newsstand; $1/Sun.; $117/yr. carrier; $119.60/yr. motor rte. 116 Main St., Towanda, PA 18848. TEL 717-265-2151; FAX 717-265-4200. **Owner(s):** Towanda Printing Co., 116 Main St., Towanda, PA 18848. TEL 717-265-2151; Ed. Dennis Irvine; Pub. James E. Towner; adv. contact: Laura Sylvester. pub. size: broadsheet; circ. morning 9,145(paid); Sun. 10,000(paid). **Wire Service(s):** AP.

TYRONE

US

DAILY HERALD, THE. 1857. Mon.-Sat. $.35 newsstand; $92.80/yr. 1018 Pennsylvania Ave., Tyrone, PA 16686. TEL 814-684-4000; FAX 814-684-4238. **Owner(s):** Journal Register Co., 50 W. State St., 12th Fl., Trenton, NJ 08608. TEL 609-396-2200; Pub. George Sample, III; adv. contact: Deborah Garner. photos; pub. size: broadsheet; circ. evening 4,100(paid); Sun. 6,700. **Wire Service(s):** AP.
   Formerly: The Tyrone Daily Herald.

UNIONTOWN

US

HERALD STANDARD. 1888. Sun.-Fri. $.40/day newsstand; $1.25/Sun.; $3/wk. carrier; $3.25/wk. motor rte. 8-18 E. Church St., Uniontown, PA 15401. TEL 412-439-7500; FAX 412-439-7528. **Owner(s):** Shirley Ellis, Uniontown, PA. TEL 215-752-6744; Carolyn Smith, Uniontown, PA 15401; Sandra Hardy, Uniontown, PA; Ed. Gloria Pasinski; Pub. Val J. Laub; adv. contact: Maureen Zorichak. photos; bk.rev.; pub. size: broadsheet; circ. morning 31,098(paid); Sun. 32,986(paid). **Wire Service(s):** AP.

WARREN

US

WARREN TIMES OBSERVER. 1966. Mon.-Sat. $.50 newsstand; $9.50/mo. carrier; $10/mo. motor rte. 205 Pennsylvania Ave., W., Warren, PA 16365. TEL 814-723-8200; FAX 814-723-6922. **Owner(s):** Kevin, Michael & Edward, Sr., Mead, 205 Pennsylvania Ave., W., Warren, PA 16365. TEL 814-723-8200; Ed. Jude Dippold; Pub. Kevin Mead; adv. contact: Dawn Burger. pub. size: broadsheet; circ. morning 13,500(paid). **Wire Service(s):** AP, NYT.

WARRENDALE

US   ISSN 8750-5916

NORTH HILLS NEWS RECORD. 1962. d. $.35/day newsstand; $.75/Sun.; $117/yr. carrier. 137 Commonwealth Dr., Warrendale, PA 15086. TEL 412-772-3900; FAX 412-772-3915; E-mail: metrodesk@newsrecord.com; URL: http://www.nauticom.net/www/nhnr/top.html. **Owner(s):** Gannett Company, Inc., 1100 Wilson Blvd., Arlington, VA 22340. TEL 703-284-6000; Ed. Dave Fritz; Pub. Samuel Mark Adkins; adv. contact: Jack Robb. pub. size: broadsheet; circ. morning 25,000. **Wire Service(s):** GNS.

WASHINGTON

US   ISSN 0891-0693

OBSERVER-REPORTER, WASHINGTON COUNTY EDITION. 1808. d. $.50/day newsstand; $1/Sun.; $2.70/wk. carrier; $2.85/wk. motor rte; $13/mo. motor rte. 122 S. Main St., Washington, PA 15301. TEL 412-222-2200; FAX 412-222-3982. **Owner(s):** Observer Publishing Co., 122 S. Main St., Washington, PA 15301. TEL 412-222-2200; FAX 412-222-3982; Ed. A. Parker Burroughs; Pub. John Northrop; adv. contact: Barry A. Martin. pub. size: broadsheet; circ. morning 40,500(paid); Sun. 41,500(paid). **Wire Service(s):** AP, NYT.

WAYNESBORO

US

RECORD HERALD 1847. Mon.-Sat. $.50 newsstand; $9/mo. carrier; $9.50/mo. motor rte. 30 Walnut St., Waynesboro, PA 17268. TEL 717-762-2151; FAX 717-762-3824. **Owner(s):** American Publishing Co. 606 N. Van Buren, P.O. Box 520, Marion, IL 62959. TEL 618-993-1711; Ed. Sue Ernde; Pub. Kelly Luvison; adv.; pub. size: broadsheet; circ. evening 10,200(paid). **Wire Service(s):** AP.
   Formerly: Waynesboro Record Herald.

WAYNESBURG

US

OBSERVER-REPORTER. 1808. d. $.50/day newsstand; $1/Sun. $13/mo. carrier. 32 Church St., Waynesburg, PA 15370. TEL 412-852-2602; FAX 412-852-1497. **Owner(s):** Observer Publishing Co., 122 S. Main St., Washington, PA 15301. TEL 412-222-2200; Ed. Bob Neidbalah; Pub. John Northrop; adv.; pub. size: broadsheet; circ. morning 7,500(paid); Sun. 7,500(paid). **Wire Service(s):** AP, NYT.

WEST CHESTER

US   ISSN 0163-3082

DAILY LOCAL NEWS. 1872. d. $.50/day newsstand; $1.50/Sun.; $3.95/wk. deliv. 250 N. Bradford Ave., West Chester, PA 19382-2800. TEL 610-696-1776; FAX 610-430-1180; E-mail: dlnnews@aol.com. **Owner(s):** Journal Register Co., 50 W. State St., 12th Fl., Trenton, NJ 08608. TEL 609-396-2200; Ed. Bruce Mowday; Pub. Richard Stanger; adv. contact: Regina Burkhart. photos; pub. size: broadsheet; circ. morning 35,707(paid); Sun. 34,342(paid). **Wire Service(s):** AP, CNS, NEA, SHNA.

US

DAILY RECORD, THE. 1908. d. $.50 newsstand; $3.95/wk. carrier; $2.95/wk. Mon.-Sat. 250 N. Bradford, Westchester, PA 19382. TEL 610-696-1775. **Owner(s):** Journal Register Co., 50 W. State St.,12th Fl., Trenton, NJ 08608. TEL 609-396-2200; adv. contact: Regina Burkhart. pub. size: broadsheet; circ. evening 7,800(paid). **Wire Service(s):** AP.
   Formerly: Record, The.

WILKES BARRE

US   ISSN 0896-4084

TIMES LEADER. 1810. d $.35/day newsstand; $1/Sun.; $93.60/yr. 15 N. Main St., Wilkes Barre, PA 18701. TEL 717-829-7100; FAX 717-829-2002. **Owner(s):** Walt Disney Co., 500 S. Buena Vista St., Burbank, CA 91521. TEL 818-560-5300; Ed. Allison Walzer; Pub. Mark Contreras; adv. contact: Dennis Sheely. pub. size: broadsheet; circ. morning 47,521(paid); Sun. 77,705(paid). **Wire Service(s):** AP, KRT.

US   ISSN 0163-4224

WILKES-BARRE CITIZENS' VOICE. 1978. d. $.35/day newsstand; $.75/Sun.; $2.40/wk. home deliv. 75 N. Washington St., Wilkes Barre, PA 18711. TEL 717-821-2000; FAX 717-821-2247. **Owner(s):** Citizen's Voice, Inc., 75 N. Washington St., Wilkes Barre, PA 18701. TEL 717-821-2000; Ed. Paul Golias; Pub. Ed A. Nichols, Jr.; adv. contact: Mark Altazilla. bk.rev.; pub. size: tabloid; circ. morning 45,433(paid); Sun. 45,433(paid). **Wire Service(s):** AP, SHNA.

WILLIAMSPORT

US   ISSN 1056-3083

WILLIAMSPORT SUN-GAZETTE 1801. d. $.35/day newsstand; $1/Sun.; $2/wk. carrier; $2.10/wk. motor rte; $104/yr. 252 W. Fourth St., Williamsport, PA 17701. TEL 717-326-1551; FAX 717-323-0948. **Owner(s):** Ogden Newspapers, Inc., 1500 Main St., Wheeling, WV 26003. TEL 304-233-0100; Ed. Dave Troisi; Pub. Thomas C. Briley; adv. contact: John Yahner. photos; pub. size: broadsheet; circ. evening 33,000(paid); Sun. 42,000(paid). **Wire Service(s):** AP.

YORK

US   ISSN 1043-4313

YORK DAILY RECORD. 1796. Mon-Sat. $.35 newsstand; $10/mo. carrier; $9/mo. motor rte. 1750 Industrial Hwy., York, PA 17402. TEL 717-840-4000; FAX 717-840-2009. **Owner(s):** Buckner News Alliance, 2101 Fourth Ave., Ste. 2300, Seattle, WA 98121. TEL 206-727-2727; Ed. Jim McClure; Pub. Dennis Hetzel; bk.rev.; pub. size: broadsheet; circ. morning 42,000. **Wire Service(s):** AP, KNT.

US

YORK DISPATCH/YORK SUNDAY NEWS. 1876. Sun-Fri. $.35/day newsstand; $1/Sun.; $9/mo. carrier; $10/mo. motor rte. 205 N. George St., York, PA 17401. TEL 717-854-1575. **Owner(s):** Garden State Newspapers, Inc., Woodbury, NJ; Ed. Deena Gross; Pub. Jim Sneddon; photos; bk.rev.; pub. size: broadsheet; circ. evening 40,000(paid); Sun. 90,000(paid). **Wire Service(s):** NYT, LAT-WP, AP, SHNA, Cox.

RHODE ISLAND

NEWPORT

US   ISSN 1053-2560

NEWPORT DAILY NEWS, THE. 1846. Mon.-Sat. $.50/day newsstand; $.75/Sat.; $104/yr. 101 Malbone Rd., Newport, RI 02840. TEL 401-849-3300. **Owner(s):** Edward A. Sherman Publishing Co., 101 Malbone Rd., Newport, RI 02840. TEL 401-849-3300; Ed. David Offer; Pub. Albert K. Sherman, Jr.; pub. size: broadsheet; circ. evening 15,230(paid). **Wire Service(s):** AP, Photo Wire, SHNA.

PAWTUCKET

US   ISSN 1060-2747

TIMES, THE. 1885. Mon.-Sat. $.50 newsstand; $2.50/wk. home deliv. 23 Exchange St., Pawtucket, RI 02860. TEL 401-722-4000; FAX 401-727-9252. **Owner(s):** New England Newspapers, Inc., 23 Exchange St., Pawtucket, RI 02860. TEL 401-722-4000 Ed. Karen Hupp; Pub. T. Paul Mahony; adv. contact: Steven Pitocchelli. photos; bk.rev.; pub. size: broadsheet; circ. evening 24,134(paid). **Wire Service(s):** AP.

PROVIDENCE

US

PROVIDENCE JOURNAL-BULLETIN. 1863. d. $.50/day newsstand; $1.80/Sun. 75 Fountain St., Providence, RI 02902. TEL 401-277-7136; FAX 401-277-7802. **Owner(s):** Providence Journal Co., 75 Fountain St., Providence, RI 02902. TEL 401-277-7000; adv. contact: Donald Ross. pub. size: broadsheet; circ. morning 182,000(paid); Sun. 260,000(paid). **Wire Service(s):** AP, NYT, LAT-WP, KR.

WESTERLY

US   ISSN 1065-1209

WESTERLY SUN. 1893. Sun.-Fri. $.50 newsstand; $78/26 wks.; $156/yr. 56 Main St., Westerly, RI 02891. TEL 401-596-7791; FAX 401-348-5080. **Owner(s):** Nicholas C. Utter, 56 Main St., Westerly, RI 02891. TEL 401-596-7791; Robert D. Utter, 56 Main St., Westerly, RI 02891. TEL 401-596-7791; Ed. Donald Lewis; Pub. William E. Sherman; adv. contact: Arthur B. Morin. pub. size: broadsheet; circ. morning 12,900(paid); Sun. 13,200(paid). **Wire Service(s):** AP.

WEST WARWICK

US

KENT COUNTY DAILY TIMES. 1892. Mon.-Sat. $.35 newsstand; $1.80/wk. 1353 Main St., West Warwick, RI 02893. TEL 401-821-7400; FAX 401-828-0810. **Owner(s):** Theodore Holmberg, 1353 Main St., West Warwick, RI 02893. TEL 401-821-7400; Ed. Ted Holmberg; Pub. Theodore Holmberg; adv. contact: Dan O'Neil. photos; bk.rev.; pub. size: standard; circ. evening 10,450(paid). **Wire Service(s):** AP.

WOONSOCKET

US

CALL, THE. 1892. d. $.50/day newsstand; $1.25/Sun.; $2.95/wk. home deliv.; $5/wk. mailed. 75 Main St., Woonsocket, RI 02895. TEL 401-762-3000; FAX 401-765-2834. **Owner(s):** Journal Register Co., 50 W. State St., 12th Fl., Trenton, NJ 08608. TEL 609-396-2200; Ed. Susan Hawrylur; Pub. Daniel Goodrich; adv. contact: James Sobiloff. photos; bk.rev.; pub. size: broadsheet; circ. morning 26,600(paid); Sun. 26,600(paid). **Wire Service(s):** AP.

Formerly: Woonsocket Call.

SOUTH CAROLINA

AIKEN

US   ISSN 0893-2557

AIKEN STANDARD. 1867. d. $.25/day newsstand; $.75/Sun.; $102/yr. 124 Rutland Dr., Aiken, SC 29801. TEL 803-648-2311; FAX 803-648-6052. **Owner(s):** Aiken Communications, Inc., 124 Rutland Dr., Aiken, SC 29801. TEL 803-648-2311; Evening Post Publishing Co., Charleston, SC 29801. TEL 803-577-7111; Ed. Jeffrey B. Wallace; Pub. Scott B. Hunter; adv. contact: Charles O. Grice. photos; pub. size: broadsheet; circ. evening 15,000(paid); Sun. 15,000(paid). **Wire Service(s):** AP, KR.

ANDERSON

US

ANDERSON INDEPENDENT-MAIL. 1899. d. $.50/day newsstand; $1.50/Sun.; $143.40/yr. 1000 Williamston Rd., Anderson, SC 29621. TEL 864-224-4321; FAX 864-260-1276. **Owner(s):** Harte-Hanks Communications, Inc., P.O. Box 269, San Antonio, TX 78291. TEL 864-344-8000; Ed. John Gouch; Pub. Fred L. Foster; adv. contact: Tony G. Marroni. photos; bk.rev.; pub. size: broadsheet; circ. morning 42,366(paid); Sun. 48,479(paid). **Wire Service(s):** AP, KNT, NYT.

BEAUFORT

US

BEAUFORT GAZETTE. 1897. Sun.-Fri. $.25/day newsstand; $1/Sun.; $94/yr. 1556 Salem Rd., Beaufort, SC 29902-0399. TEL 803-524-3183. **Owner(s):** McClatchy Newspapers, 2100 Q. St., P.O. Box 15774, Sacramento, CA 95816. TEL 916-321-1000; Ed. Richard Brooks; Pub. John Heath; adv. contact: Ann Robb. photos; pub. size: broadsheet; circ. morning 10,500(paid); Sun. 10,500(paid). **Wire Service(s):** AP.

CHARLESTON

US   ISSN 1061-5105

CHARLESTON POST & COURIER. 1803. d. $.50/day newsstand; $1.25/Sun.; $10.75/mo. carrier. 134 Columbus St., Charleston, SC 29403-4800. TEL 803-577-7111; FAX 803-937-5463. **Owner(s):** Evening Post Publishing Co., 134 Columbus St., Charleston, SC 29403-4800. TEL 803-577-7111; Pub. Ivan V. Anderson; adv.; photos; bk.rev.; pub. size: broadsheet; circ. morning 112,404(paid); Sun. 129,452(paid). **Wire Service(s):** AP, KNS.

Formerly: Evening Post.

COLUMBIA

US

STATE, THE. 1891. d. $.50/day newsstand; $1.50/Sun.; $3.40/wk. carrier. 1401 Shop Rd., Columbia, SC 29201. TEL 803-771-6161; FAX 803-771-8639; E-mail: cyberst@cyberstate.infi.net; URL: http://www.thestate.com. **Owner(s):** Knight-Ridder, Inc., One Herald Plz., Miami, FL 33132. TEL 305-376-3800; Ed. Paula Ellis; Pub. Frederick Mott, Jr.; adv. contact: Morton Goldstrom. pub. size: broadsheet; circ. morning 135,497(paid); evening 28,003(paid); Sun. 170,173(paid). **Wire Service(s):** AP, UPI, NYT, LAT-WP.

FLORENCE

US

FLORENCE MORNING NEWS. 1922. d. $.50/day newsstand; $1.25/Sun.; $126/yr. 310 S. Dargan St., Florence, SC 29501. TEL 803-317-6397; FAX 803-317-7292. **Owner(s):** Thomson Newspapers, Inc., One Thorn Run Ctr., Ste. 1187, 1187 Thorn Run Rd. Ext., Coraopolis, PA 15108. TEL 412-262-7870; Ed. Frank Sayles, Jr.; Pub. C. Thomas Marschel; adv. contact: David Haddad. photos; bk.rev.; pub. size: broadsheet; circ. morning 33,850(paid); Sun. 34,200(paid). **Wire Service(s):** AP, SHNA, Thomson News Service.

GREENVILLE

US

GREENVILLE NEWS. 1875. d. $.50/day newsstand; $1.50/Sun.; $3.41/wk. carrier; $13.50/mo. carrier. 305 S. Main St., Greenville, SC 29601. TEL 803-298-4100; FAX 803-298-4395. **Owner(s):** Multimedia, Inc., P.O. Box 1688, Greenville, SC 29602. TEL 803-298-4100; Ed. Ann Clark; Pub. Steve Brandt; adv. contact: David Space. photos; pub. size: broadsheet; circ. morning 112,920(paid); Sun. 142,817(paid). **Wire Service(s):** AP, LAT-WP.

GREENWOOD

US

INDEX-JOURNAL. 1919. Sun.-Fri. $.25/day newsstand; $1/Sun.; $93.60/yr.; $140/yr. mailed. 610 Phoenix St., Greenwood, SC 29646. TEL 864-223-1411. **Owner(s):** Eleanor M. Mundy & Judith M. Burns, P.O. Box 1018, Greenwood, SC 29648. TEL 803-223-1411; Pub. Eleanor M. Mundy; adv. contact: Ron Lucas. photos; bk.rev.; pub. size: standard; circ. evening 15,659(paid); Sun. 16,856(paid). **Wire Service(s):** AP.

HILTON HEAD

US

HILTON HEAD ISLAND PACKET. 1970. d. $.25/day newsstand; $1/Sun.; $84/yr. carrier. One Pope Ave., Executive Park, Hilton Head, SC 29928. TEL 803-785-4293; FAX 803-785-9424. **Owner(s):** McClatchy Newspapers, P.O. Box 15774, Sacramento, CA 95816. TEL 916-321-1000; Pub. Sara Borton; adv. contact: Phil Porter. photos; bk.rev.; pub. size: broadsheet; circ. morning 14,500(paid); Sun. 17,000(paid). **Wire Service(s):** AP, NYT.

MYRTLE BEACH

US

SUN NEWS, THE. 1935. d. $.50/day newsstand; $1.25/Sun.; $35/13 wks. 914 Frontage Rd. E., Myrtle Beach, SC 29577. TEL 803-626-8555; FAX 803-626-0328. **Owner(s):** Knight-Ridder, Inc., One Herald Plz., Miami, FL 33132. TEL 305-376-3800; Ed. Sue Deans; Pub. J. Michael Pate; adv. contact: Philip LaPorte. photos; pub. size: broadsheet; circ. morning 38,737(paid); Sun. 54,000(paid). **Wire Service(s):** AP, NYT, KRN.

ORANGEBURG

US

TIMES & DEMOCRAT, THE. 1881. d. $.35/day newsstand; $1/Sun.; $10/mo. carrier. 1010 Broughton St., S.E., Orangeburg, SC 29115. TEL 803-533-5501; FAX 803-533-5526. **Owner(s):** Howard Publications, Inc., 1715 S. Beeman St., P.O. Box 570, Oceanside, CA 92049. TEL 619-433-5771; Ed. Lee Harter; Pub. Dean B. Livingston; adv. contact: Cathy Hughes. pub. size: broadsheet; circ. morning 19,000(paid); Sun. 18,700(paid). **Wire Service(s):** AP.

Formerly: Orangeburg Times & Democrat.

ROCK HILL

US

HERALD, THE. 1878. d. $.35/day newsstand;
$.75/Sun.; $6/mo. 132 W. Main St., Rock Hill,
SC 29730. TEL 803-329-4000. **Owner(s):**
McClatchy Newspapers, P.O. Box 15774,
Sacramento, CA 95852. TEL 916-321-1000; Ed.
Betsy Lumbye; Pub. Jayne Speizer; adv. contact:
Bill Edinger. photos; pub. size: broadsheet; circ.
morning 31,000(paid); Sun. 31,500(paid). **Wire
Service(s):** AP, LAT-WP, SHNA.

SPARTANBURG

US   ISSN 0740-4743

HERALD-JOURNAL. 1844. d. $.50/day newsstand;
$1/Sun.; $9.10/mo. 189 W. Main St.,
Spartanburg, SC 29306. TEL 803-582-4511;
FAX 803-594-6349. **Owner(s):** New York Times
Co., The, 229 W. 43rd St., New York, NY 10036.
TEL 212-556-1234; Ed. Scott Kearns; Pub. Dave
Roberts; adv. contact: Bill Cranford. pub. size:
broadsheet; circ. morning 62,000(paid); Sun.
69,000(paid). **Wire Service(s):** AP.

SUMTER

US

ITEM, THE. 1894. d. $.25/day newsstand; $1/Sun.;
$86.40/yr. 20 N. Magnolia St., Sumter, SC
29150. TEL 803-775-6331;
FAX 803-775-1024. **Owner(s):** Osteen
Publishing Co., P.O. Box 1677, Sumter, SC
29151. TEL 803-775-6331; Ed. Hubert D.
Osteen, Jr.; Pub. Hubert D. Osteen, Jr.; adv.
contact: Kyle Osteen. photos; bk.rev.; pub. size:
broadsheet; circ. evening 22,180(paid); Sun.
21,500(paid). **Wire Service(s):** AP.

UNION

US

UNION DAILY TIMES. 1850. Mon.-Sat. $.50
newsstand; $6/mo.; $118.80/yr. mailed. 100
Times Blvd., Union, SC 29379.
TEL 803-427-1234; FAX 802-427-1237.
Owner(s): Mid-South Management Co., Inc., 100
Times Blvd., Union, SC 29379. TEL
803-427-1237; Ed. Graham Williams; Pub. Mike
Pippin; adv. contact: Darrell Griggs. photos;
bk.rev.; pub. size: broadsheet; circ. evening
7,000(paid). **Wire Service(s):** AP.

SOUTH DAKOTA

ABERDEEN

US

ABERDEEN AMERICAN NEWS. 1885. d. $.50/day
newsstand; $1.50/Sun. 124 S. Second St.,
Aberdeen, SD 57401. TEL 605-225-4100.
Owner(s): Knight-Ridder, Inc., One Herald Plz.,
Miami, FL 33132. TEL 305-350-2871; Ed. Anita
Meyer; Pub. Billie Smith; adv. contact: Roger
Brokke. photos; pub. size: standard; circ. morning
18,305(paid); Sun. 20,239(paid). **Wire
Service(s):** AP, KNT.

BROOKINGS

US

BROOKINGS REGISTER. 1879. Mon.-Sat. $.50
newsstand; $84/yr. local; $92/yr. out of area.
312 Fifth St., Brookings, SD 57006-0177.
TEL 605-692-6271; FAX 605-692-2979.
Owner(s): World Newspaper, Inc., 312 Fifth St.,
P.O. Box 177, Brookings, SD 57006. TEL
605-692-6271; Ed. Amy G. Dunkle. adv. contact:
Phil Dahlmeier. photos; bk.rev.; pub. size:
broadsheet; circ. evening 5,900(paid). **Wire
Service(s):** AP.

HURON

US

PLAINSMAN, THE. 1885. Tue.-Sun. $.50/day
newsstand; $1/Sun.; $8/mo. carrier. 49 E. Third
St., Huron, SD 57350. TEL 605-352-6401;
FAX 605-352-7754. **Owner(s):** World
Newspapers, Inc., World Herald Sq., Omaha, NE
68102. TEL 402-444-1000; Ed. Bette Pore; Pub.
Daryl Beall; adv. contact: Peg Mercer. pub. size:
broadsheet; circ. morning 10,500(paid); Sun.
10,700(paid). **Wire Service(s):** AP.
    Formerly: Huron Daily Plainsman.

MADISON

US

MADISON DAILY LEADER. 1890. Mon.-Fri. $.40
newsstand; $75.87/yr. in town. 214 S. Egan
Ave., Madison, SD 57042. TEL 605-256-4555;
FAX 605-256-6190. **Owner(s):** Hunter
Publishing, Inc., P.O. Box 348, Madison, SD
57042. TEL 605-256-4555; FAX
650-256-6190; Ed. Marcia Schoebert; Pub. Jon
M. Hunter; adv. contact: Glennys McCool. photos;
bk.rev.; pub. size: broadsheet; circ. evening
3,600(paid). **Wire Service(s):** AP.

MITCHELL

US

DAILY REPUBLIC. 1882 Mon.-Sat. $.50 newsstand;
$86/yr. in state mailed. 120 S. Lawler St.,
Mitchell, SD 57301. TEL 605-996-5514;
FAX 605-996-7793. **Owner(s):** Forum
Communications, Inc., P.O. Box 2020, Fargo, ND
58207. TEL 701-223-7311; Ed. Noel Hamiel;
Pub. Steve McLister; adv. contact: Linda Klein.
pub. size: broadsheet; circ. evening 12,000(paid).
Wire Service(s): AP.

PIERRE

US   ISSN 0893-5564

PIERRE CAPITAL JOURNAL. 1881. Mon.-Fri. $.50
newsstand; $70/yr. in town; $84/yr. out of town.
333 W. Dakota, Pierre, SD 57501.
TEL 605-224-7301; FAX 605-224-9210.
Owner(s): Hipple Printing Co., Inc., 333 W.
Dakota, Pierre, SD 57501. TEL 605-224-7301;
Ed. Dana Hess; Pub. Terry Hipple; adv. contact:
Terry Hipple. photos; pub. size: standard; circ.
evening 5,000(paid). **Wire Service(s):** AP.

RAPID CITY

US

RAPID CITY JOURNAL. 1878. d. $.50/day
newsstand; $1.50/Sun.; $152/yr. 507 Main,
Rapid City, SD 57701. TEL 605-394-8300;
FAX 605-342-8463. **Owner(s):** Lee Enterprises,
Inc., 130 E. Second St., Davenport, IA 52801.
TEL 319-383-2100; Ed. Steve Miller; Pub. John
Van Strydonck; adv. contact: Brenda Speth.
photos; bk.rev.; pub. size: broadsheet; circ.
morning 37,981(paid); Sun. 40,400(paid). **Wire
Service(s):** AP, NYT.

SIOUX FALLS

US

ARGUS LEADER. 1881. d. $.50/day newsstand,
$1.50/Sun.; $169/yr. carrier; $182/yr. motor
rte. 200 S. Minnesota Ave., Sioux Falls, SD
57102. TEL 605-331-2200;
FAX 605-331-2371. **Owner(s):** Gannett
Company, Inc., 1100 Wilson Blvd., Arlington, VA
22234. TEL 703-284-6000; Ed. Pete Ellis; Pub.
Mary Devish; adv. contact: Kris Kincaid. pub. size:
broadsheet; circ. morning 53,000(paid); Sun.
76,000(paid). **Wire Service(s):** AP, GNS, KR,
LAT-WP.

SPEARFISH

US   ISSN 1061-6179

BLACK HILLS PIONEER. Mon.-Sat. $.50/day
newsstand; $.50/Sat.; $7.50/mo. carrier;
$7.50/mo. motor rte. 132 E. Grant St.,
Spearfish, SD 57783. TEL 605-642-2761;
FAX 605-642-8179. **Owner(s):** Seaton Publishing
Co., P.O. Box 7, Spearfish, SD 57783. TEL
605-642-2761; Ed. Larry Weiers; Pub. Bill
Masterson, Jr.; adv. contact: Hollie Hall. pub. size:
tabloid; circ. evening 28,000(paid). **Wire
Service(s):** AP.
    Formerly: Spearfish Daily Queer County Word.

WATERTOWN

US

WATERTOWN PUBLIC OPINION. 1887. Mon.-Sat.
$.50 newsstand; $91/yr. 120 Third Ave., N.W.,
Watertown, SD 57201. TEL 605-886-6903;
FAX 605-886-4280. **Owner(s):** Watertown Public
Opinion Co., Inc., 120 Third Ave., N.W.,
Watertown, SD 57201. TEL 605-886-6901; FAX
605-836-4280; Ed. Gordon Garnos; Pub. A.W.
Johnson; adv. contact: A.W. Johnson. photos;
bk.rev. pub. size: broadsheet; circ. evening
17,500(paid). **Wire Service(s):** AP.

Dailies

YANKTON

US

YANKTON DAILY PRESS & DAKOTAN. 1861. Mon-Sat. $.50 newsstand; $87.15/yr. 319 Walnut St., Yankton, SD 57078. TEL 605-665-7811; FAX 605-665-1721. **Owner(s):** Morris Communications, P.O. Box 936, Augusta, GA 30903. TEL 706-724-0851; Ed. Don S. Smith; Pub. Don S. Smith; adv. contact: Christy Orwig. photos; bk.rev.; pub. size: standard; circ. evening 9,851(paid). **Wire Service(s):** AP.

TENNESSEE

ATHENS

US

ATHENS DAILY POST. 1848. Mon.-Fri. $.35 newsstand; $5.75/mo.; $67/yr. 320 S. Jackson, Athens, TN 37303. TEL 615-745-5664. **Owner(s):** Daily Post-Athenian Co., Inc., P.O. Box 340, Athens, TN 37371; Ed. Doug Headrick; Pub. Ralph C. Baldwin, Jr.; adv. contact: Sara Jane Locke. photos; bk.rev.; pub. size: broadsheet; circ. evening 10,982(paid). **Wire Service(s):** AP.

CHATTANOOGA

US

CHATTANOOGA FREE PRESS. 1936. d. $.50/day newsstand; $1.50/Sun.; $2.80/wk. 400 E. 11th St., Chattanooga, TN 37401-1447. TEL 615-756-6900; FAX 615-757-6383. **Owner(s):** Chattanooga Free Press, 400 E. 11th St., Chattanooga, TN 37401-1447. TEL 615-756-6900; Ed. Lee Anderson; Pub. Lee Anderson; adv. contact: Dan Nausley. photos; bk.rev.; pub. size: broadsheet; circ. evening 43,000(paid); Sun. 115,000(paid). **Wire Service(s):** AP.
  Formerly: Chattanooga News-Free Press.

US

CHATTANOOGA TIMES. 1869. Mon.-Sat. $.50/day newsstand; $1.50/Sun.; $35/13 wks. home deliv. 100 E. Tenth St., Chattanooga, TN 37402. TEL 423-756-1234; FAX 423-752-3388. **Owner(s):** Times Printing Co., 100 E. Tenth St., Chattanooga, TN 37402. TEL 423-756-1234; Ed. Ron Smith; Pub. Paul Neely; adv.; photos; bk.rev.; pub. size: broadsheet; circ. morning 42,000(paid). **Wire Service(s):** AP, NYT.

CLARKSVILLE

US

LEAF-CHRONICLE, THE. 1808. d. $.50 newsstand; $125/yr. 200 Commerce St., Clarksville, TN 37040. TEL 615-552-1808; FAX 615-648-8001; E-mail: fgeno@aol.com. **Owner(s):** Gannett Company, Inc., 1100 Wilson Blvd., Arlington, VA 22234. TEL 703-284-6000; Pub. F. Gene Washer; adv. contact: Lee Ireland. photos; bk.rev.; pub. size: broadsheet; circ. morning 22,500(paid); Sun. 24,500(paid). **Wire Service(s):** AP.

COLUMBIA

US

DAILY HERALD. 1848. Sun.-Fri. $.50/day newsstand; $1/Sun.; $18.75/3 mos.; $75/yr. prepaid. 1115 S. Main St., Columbia, TN 38401. TEL 615-388-6464; FAX 615-388-1003. **Owner(s):** Stephens Group, Inc., P.O. Box 17017, Fort Smith, AR 72902. TEL 501-785-7822; Pub. Doug Beel; adv. contact: Charles Martin. pub. size: broadsheet; circ. evening 11,567(paid); Sun. 13,344(paid). **Wire Service(s):** AP.

COOKEVILLE

US   ISSN 8750-5541

HERALD-CITIZEN. 1903. Sun.-Fri. $.50 newsstand; $70/yr. carrier; $70/yr. mailed in area. 124 S. Dixie, Cookeville, TN 38501. TEL 615-526-9715; FAX 615-526-1209. **Owner(s):** Cleveland Newspapers, Inc., P.O. Box 3600, Cleveland, TN 37320; Ed. Sam Thompson, Jr.; Pub. Sam Thompson, Jr.; adv. contact: Al Profant. photos; bk.rev.; pub. size: broadsheet; circ. evening 10,944(paid); Sun. 13,059(paid). **Wire Service(s):** AP.

DYERSBURG

US

STATE GAZETTE. 1865. Mon.-Fri. $.50 newsstand; $1/Sunday; $133.20/yr. mailed. 294 Hwy. 51 Bypass, Dyersburg, TN 38024. TEL 901-285-4091; FAX 901-285-9747. **Owner(s):** Paxton Media Group, Inc., P.O. Box 2300, Paducah, KY 42002. TEL 502-443-1771; Pub. Billy R. Smith; adv. contact: Johnny McConnell. photos; bk.rev.; pub. size: broadsheet; circ. evening 8,600(paid); Sun. 8,600(paid). **Wire Service(s):** AP, NYT.

ELIZABETHTON

US

ELIZABETHTON STAR. Sun.-Fri. $.35/day newsstand; $1/Sun.; $68/yr. home deliv.; $99/yr. mailed; $64/yr. senior citizens. 300 Sycamore St., Elizabethton, TN 37643. TEL 423-542-4151; FAX 423-542-2004. **Owner(s):** Frank Robinson, Elizabethton, TN; Ed. John Thompson; Pub. Charles Robinson; adv.; photos; bk.rev.; pub. size: broadsheet; circ. evening 9,000(paid); Sun. 10,500(paid). **Wire Service(s):** AP.

CLEVELAND

US

CLEVELAND DAILY BANNER. 1854. Sun.-Fri. $.35/day newsstand; $1/Sun.; $6.25/mo. home deliv. 1505 25th St., N.W., Cleveland, TN 37312. TEL 615-472-5041; FAX 615-476-1046. **Owner(s):** Cleveland Newspapers, Inc., 1505 25th St., N.W., Cleveland, TN 37311. TEL 615-472-5041; Ed. Pledger L. Wattenbarger; Pub. Pledger L. Wattenbarger; adv. contact: Jack Bennett. photos; bk.rev.; pub. size: broadsheet; circ. evening 16,152(paid); Sun. 18,054(paid). **Wire Service(s):** AP.

GREENEVILLE

US

GREENEVILLE SUN. 1879. Mon.-Sat. $.50 newsstand; $83/yr. carrier. 121 W. Summer St., Greeneville, TN 37743. TEL 423-638-4181; FAX 423-638-4181. **Owner(s):** Greeneville Publishing Co., P.O. Box 1630, Greeneville, TN 37744. TEL 423-638-4181; Ed. Douglas Watson; Pub. John M. Jones, Sr.; adv. contact: John E. Cash. pub. size: broadsheet; circ. evening 16,000(paid). **Wire Service(s):** AP.

JACKSON

US   ISSN 0890-9938

JACKSON SUN. 1848. d. $.35/day newsstand; $1.50/Sun.; $10.50/mo. carrier; $23.50/2 mos. in cy.; $25.50/2 mos. elsewhere. 245 W. Lafayette, Jackson, TN 38301. TEL 901-427-3333; FAX 901-425-9639. **Owner(s):** Gannett Company, Inc., 1100 Wilson Blvd., Arlington, VA 22224. TEL 703-384-6000; Ed. Patrick Rice; Pub. Michael Craft; adv. contact: Kerry Johnson. pub. size: broadsheet; circ. morning 40,000(paid); Sun. 44,000(paid). **Wire Service(s):** AP, LAT-WP.

JOHNSON CITY

US

JOHNSON CITY PRESS. 1934. d. $.35/day newsstand; $1.25/Sun.; $10/mo. carrier; $26/3 mos. 204 W. Main St., Johnson City, TN 37604. TEL 615-929-3111; FAX 615-929-7484. **Owner(s):** Press, Inc., P.O. Box 1717, Johnson City, TN 37605-1717. TEL 423-929-3111; FAX 423-461-9546; Ed. John A. Jones. adv. contact: Frank Hawkins. photos; bk.rev.; pub. size: broadsheet; circ. morning 31,600(paid); Sun. 36,000(paid). **Wire Service(s):** AP, NYT.

KINGSPORT

US

KINGSPORT DAILY NEWS. 1963. Mon.-Fri. $.25 newsstand; $36/yr. local; $48/yr. out of area. 310 E. Sullivan, Kingsport, TN 37660. TEL 423-246-4800; FAX 423-247-2502. **Owner(s):** Daily News of Kingsport, Inc., 310 E. Sullivan, Kingsport, TN 37660. TEL 615-246-4800; Ed. Pete Dykes; Pub. Steve Dykes; adv. contact: Steve Dykes. pub. size: broadsheet; circ. morning 8,000(paid). **Wire Service(s):** RP.

US

KINGSPORT TIMES-NEWS. 1918. d. $.50/day newsstand; $1.25/Sun.; $216/yr. mailed. 701 Lynn Garden Dr., Kingsport, TN 37662. TEL 423-929-2197; FAX 423-392-1392. **Owner(s):** Sandusky Newspapers, Inc., Sandusky, OH; Ed. Ted Como; Pub. Keith Wilson; adv.; photos; bk.rev.; pub. size: broadsheet; circ. evening 46,000(paid); Sun. 48,000(paid). **Wire Service(s):** AP.

KNOXVILLE

US

KNOXVILLE NEWS-SENTINEL. 1886. d. $.50/day newsstand, $2/Sun.; $17.50/mo. deliv. 208 W. Church Ave., Knoxville, TN 37902. TEL 423-523-3131; FAX 423-521-8124; E-mail: kns@knoxnews.com; URL: http://www.knoxnews.com/. **Owner(s):** Scripps-Howard, 312 Walnut St., 28th Fl., Cincinnati, OH 45202. TEL 513-977-3000; Ed. Frank Cagle. adv. contact: Debbie Smiddy. pub. size: broadsheet; circ. morning 123,000(paid); Sun. 184,000(paid). **Wire Service(s):** AP, NYT, SHNA.

LEBANON

US

LEBANON DEMOCRAT, THE. 1888. Mon.-Fri. $.35 newsstand. $11.25/3 mos. mailed; $41/yr. mailed. 402 N. Cumberland St., Lebanon, TN 37087. TEL 615-444-3952; FAX 615-444-3952. **Owner(s):** Carolton A. Jones Newspapers, Inc., Johnson City, TN 37601; Pub. Sam Hatcher; adv.; pub. size: broadsheet; circ. morning 8,933(paid). **Wire Service(s):** UPI, AP.

MARYVILLE

US

DAILY TIMES. 1883. Mon.-Fri. $.35 newsstand; $72.80/yr. motor rte.; $132/yr. mailed. 307 E. Harper Ave., Maryville, TN 37801. TEL 423-981-1100; FAX 423-981-1175. **Owner(s):** Horvitz Corp., Bellview, WA; Ed. Dean Stone; Pub. F. Max Crotser; adv. contact: Raymond Tuck. photos; pub. size: broadsheet; circ. morning 21,000(paid). **Wire Service(s):** AP. **Formerly:** Morning Daily Times.

MEMPHIS

US   ISSN 0745-4856

COMMERCIAL APPEAL, THE. 1940. d. $.50/day newsstand; $2/Sun. 495 Union Ave., Memphis, TN 38103. TEL 901-529-2345; FAX 901-529-2522. **Owner(s):** Scripps-Howard, 312 Walnut St., 28th Fl., Cincinnati, OH 45202. TEL 513-977-3000; Ed. Henry Stokes. adv. contact: David Enstad. photos; pub. size: broadsheet; circ. morning 220,000(paid); Sun. 284,949(paid). **Wire Service(s):** AP, UPI, NYT, SHNS, RN, LAT-WP.

MORRISTOWN

US

CITIZEN TRIBUNE. 1966. d. $.35/day newsstand; $1.25/Sun.; $98/yr. carrier. 1609 W. First North St., Morristown, TN 37815. TEL 615-581-5630; FAX 615-586-3061. **Owner(s):** Lakeway Publishers, Inc., P.O. Box 625, Morristown, TN 37815. TEL 615-581-5630; FAX 615-581-3061; Ed. R. Jack Fishman; Pub. R. Jack Fishman; adv. contact: Reece Sexton. bk.rev.; pub. size: broadsheet; circ. evening 20,492(paid); Sun. 24,125(paid). **Wire Service(s):** AP. **Formerly:** Morristown Citizen Tribune.

MURFREESBORO

US

MURFREESBORO DAILY NEWS JOURNAL. 1849. d. $.35/day newsstand, $1/Sun.; $114/yr. in state. 224 N. Walnut, Murfreesboro, TN 37133. TEL 615-893-5860 FAX 615-896-8702; E-mail: online@dnj.com; URL: http://www.dnj.com. **Owner(s):** Morris Communications, P.O. Box 68, Savanah, GA 31402; Ed. Mike Pirtle. adv. contact: Stacie Stamdifer. pub. size: standard; circ. evening 17,000(paid); Sun. 19,000(paid). **Wire Service(s):** AP.

NASHVILLE

US

NASHVILLE BANNER. 1876. Mon.-Fri. $.35/day newsstand, $1.50/Sun. 1100 Broadway, Nashville, TN 37203-3116. TEL 615-259-8800; FAX 615-259-8890. **Owner(s):** Nashville Banner, 1100 Broadway, Nashville, TN 37203-3116. TEL 615-259-8800; Ed. Pat Embry; Pub. Irby C. Simpkins; adv.; photos; bk.rev.; pub. size: broadsheet; circ. morning 207,658(paid); Sun. 292,859(paid). **Wire Service(s):** AP, LAT-WP, KR.

US   ISSN 1053-6590

TENNESSEAN, THE. 1812. d. $.35 newsstand; $1.50/Sun.; $3.25/wk. carrier. 1100 Broadway, Nashville, TN 37203. TEL 615-259-8000; FAX 616-259-8093. **Owner(s):** Gannett Company, Inc., 1100 Wilson Blvd., Arlington, VA 22234. TEL 703-284-6000; Ed. David Green; Pub. Craig Moon; adv. contact: Anna Bartkowski. bk.rev.; pub. size: broadsheet; circ. morning 203,805(paid); Sun. 286,956(paid). **Wire Service(s):** NYT, UPI, PS, AP.

OAK RIDGE

US   ISSN 0890-6009

OAK RIDGER, THE. 1949. Mon.-Fri. $.50/day newsstand; $.75/Fri.; $123/yr. carrier; $127/yr. mailed. 785 Oak Ridge Tpke., Oak Ridge, TN 37830. TEL 615-482-1021; FAX 615-482-7334. **Owner(s):** Morris Communications, P.O. Box 936, Augusta, GA 30903. TEL 706-724-0851; Ed. Ron Bridgeman; Pub. Pete Esser; adv. contact: Dave McCoy. pub. size: broadsheet; circ. evening 11,000(paid). **Wire Service(s):** AP.

PARIS

US   ISSN 0893-3669

PARIS POST-INTELLIGENCER, THE. 1866. Mon.-Fri. $.25 newsstand; $51/yr. carrier; $73.50/yr. mailed. 208 E. Wood St., Paris, TN 38242-0310. TEL 901-642-1162; FAX 901-642-1165. **Owner(s):** Paris Publishing Co. Inc., 208 E. Wood St., Paris, TN 38242. TEL 901-642-1162; FAX 901-642-1165; Ed. Michael Williams; Pub. Bill Williams; adv.; pub. size: broadsheet; circ. evening 8,475(paid). **Wire Service(s):** AP.

SEVIERVILLE

US   ISSN 0894-2218

MOUNTAIN PRESS, THE. 1928. d. $.50/day newsstand; $1/Sun.; $8.50/mo. carrier. 119 Riverbend Dr., Sevierville, TN 37876. TEL 423-428-0746; FAX 423-453-4913. **Owner(s):** Paxton Media Group, Inc., P.O. Box 2300, Paducah, KY 42002. TEL 502-443-1771; Ed. Anna Garber; Pub. Bob Childress; adv. contact: Linda Parham. photos; bk.rev.; pub. size: broadsheet; circ. morning 10,000(paid); Sun. 10,000(paid). **Wire Service(s):** AP.

SHELBYVILLE

US

SHELBYVILLE TIMES-GAZETTE. 1874. Mon.-Fri. $34/yr. in cy. 323 E. Depot St., Shelbyville, TN 37160-0380. TEL 615-684-1200; FAX 615-684-3228. **Owner(s):** Shelbyville Publishing Co., Inc., 323 E. Depot St., Shelbyville, TN 37160. TEL 615-684-1200; FAX 615-684-3228; Ed. Mark McGee Pub. David Segroves; adv. contact: Ruth Coop. photos; pub. size: broadsheet; circ. evening 8,699(paid). **Wire Service(s):** AP.

UNION CITY

US   ISSN 0745-5534

UNION CITY DAILY MESSENGER. 1926. Mon.-Fri. $.50 newsstand; $80/yr. 613 E. Jackson, Union City, TN 38281. TEL 901-885-0744; FAX 901-885-0782. **Owner(s):** David Critchlow, Sr., P.O. Box 430, Union City, TN 38281. TEL 901-885-0744; Scott Critchlow, P.O. Box 430, Union City, TN 38281; David Critchlow, Jr., P.O. Box 430, Union City, TN 38281; Ed. David Critchlow, Jr.; Pub. David Critchlow, Sr.; adv. contact: Gloria Chesteen. photos; bk.rev.; pub. size: broadsheet; circ. evening 8,700(paid). **Wire Service(s):** AP.

TEXAS

ABILENE

US

ABILENE REPORTER-NEWS. 1881. d. $.50/day newsstand; $1.50/Sun.; $1.50/mo. carrier. 101 Cypress St., Abilene, TX 79601. TEL 915-673-4271; FAX 915-673-1901; E-mail: reagan@texnews.com; URL: http://www.texnews.com. **Owner(s):** Harte-Hanks Communications, Inc., P.O. Box 269, San Antonio, TX 78291. TEL 512-344-8000; Ed. Danny Reagan; Pub. Frank Puckett Jr.; adv. contact: Mike Winter. pub. size: broadsheet; circ. morning 45,000(paid); Sun. 55,000(paid). **Wire Service(s):** AP, SHNA, KR.

ALICE

US

ALICE ECHO-NEWS. 1896. Sun.-Fri. $.50/day newsstand, $1.25/Sun.; $7.50/mo. local. 405 E. Main, Alice, TX 78332. TEL 512-664-6588; FAX 512-668-1030. **Owner(s):** Alice Newspapers, Inc., 405 E. Main, Alice, TX 78332. TEL 512-664-6588; Ed. Jim Terrell. Pub. Tony Morris; adv.; photos; pub. size: broadsheet; circ. evening 5,500(paid); Sun. 6,000(paid). **Wire Service(s):** AP.

AMARILLO

US

AMARILLO DAILY NEWS/SUNDAY NEWS GLOBE. 1909. d. $.50/day newsstand; $1.25/Sun.; $19.75/mo. carrier; $29.55/3 mo. carrier. 900 S. Harrison St., Amarillo, TX 79101. TEL 806-376-4488; FAX 806-373-0810. **Owner(s):** Morris Communications, P.O. Box 2091, Amarillo, TX 79166-2091. TEL 806-376-4488; Ed. Dennis Soies; Pub. Garet von Netzer; adv. contact: Steve Beasley. photos; bk.rev.; pub. size: broadsheet circ. morning 42,248(paid); Sun. 80,500(paid). **Wire Service(s):** AP, MNS, KR, LAT-WP.

AMARILLO

US

AMARILLO GLOBE TIMES. 1909. d. $.50 newsstand; $8.75/mo. carrier. 900 S. Harrison, Amarillo, TX 79101. TEL 806-376-4488; FAX 806-373-0810. **Owner(s):** Morris Communications, P.O. Box 2091, Amarillo, TX 79166-2091. TEL 806-376-4488; Ed. Dennis Spies; Pub. Garet von Netzer; adv. contact: Steve Beasley. photos; bk.rev.; pub. size: broadsheet; circ. evening 26,910(paid). **Wire Service(s):** AP, KRT, LAT-WP.

ARLINGTON

US

▼**ARLINGTON MORNING NEWS.** 1996. 5/wk.: Wed.-Sun. $4/mo. home deliv. 2201 N. Collins, Ste. 295, Arlington, TX 76011. TEL 817-461-6397. **Owner(s):** A.H. Belo Corp., 400 S. Record, Dallas, TX 75202. TEL 214-977-6606; Ed. Lawrence Young; Pub. Gary Jacobson; adv. contact: June DeRousse.

ATHENS

US   ISSN 1040-6522

ATHENS DAILY REVIEW. 1885. Sun.-Fri. $.50 newsstand; $6.50/mo. $19.25/3 mos. in cy. 201 S. Prairieville St., Athens, TX 75751. TEL 903-675-5626; FAX 903-675-9450. **Owner(s):** Stephens Group, Inc., P.O. Box 1350, Fort Smith, AR 72902. TEL 501-785-7810; Ed. Gene Lehmann; Pub. Dan Dwelle; adv. contact: Dan Youngman. photos; bk.rev.; pub. size: broadsheet; circ. evening 7,000(paid); Sun. 7,050(paid). **Wire Service(s):** AP.

AUSTIN

US   ISSN 0199-8560

AUSTIN AMERICAN-STATESMAN. 1885. d. $.50/day newsstand; $1.50/Sun.; $13.52/mo. carrier. 305 S. Congress Ave., Austin, TX 78704. TEL 512-445-3500; FAX 512-445-3557. **Owner(s):** Cox Enterprises, Inc., 72 Marietta St., N.W., Atlanta, GA 30303. TEL 404-526-5537; Ed. Kathy Warbelow. adv. contact: George Gutierrez. pub. size: broadsheet; circ. morning 182,199(paid); Sun. 271,491(paid). **Wire Service(s):** AP, LAT-WP, NYT, Cox News Line, KNT, FIELD.

BAY CITY

US

DAILY TRIBUNE, THE. 1845. Tue.-Fri. & Sun. $.50 newsstand; $69/yr. carrier in cy.; $17.25/3 mos. out of cy.; $27/3 mos. out of state. 2901 Carey Smith Blvd., Bay City, TX 77414. TEL 409-245-5555; FAX 409-244-5908. **Owner(s):** Bay City Newspapers Inc., P.O. Box 1551, Bay City, TX 77404. TEL 409-245-5555; Ed. Wendy Mohon; Pub. Eric Bauer; adv. contact: Jaime Andrews. pub. size: broadsheet; circ. evening 7,000(paid); Sun. 6,600(paid). **Wire Service(s):** AP.

BAYTOWN

US

BAYTOWN SUN. 1931. Mon.-Sat. $.50/day newsstand, $1/Sat.; $6.75/mo. home deliv.; $9/mo. mailed. 1301 Memorial Dr., Baytown, TX 77520. TEL 713-422-8302; FAX 713-427-6283. **Owner(s):** Southern Newspapers, Inc., P.O. Box 42828, Houston, TX 77242; Ed. David Eldridge; Pub. Gary Dobbs; adv. contact: Penn Neville. pub. size: broadsheet; circ. evening 16,000(paid). **Wire Service(s):** UPI, AP.

BEAUMONT

US   ISSN 0744-1207

BEAUMONT ENTERPRISE. 1880. d. $.50/day newsstand; $1.50/Sun.; $10/mo. home deliv.; $15/mo. mailed. 380 Main St., Beaumont, TX 77701. TEL 409-833-3311; FAX 409-838-2857. **Owner(s):** Hearst Corp., 959 Eighth Ave., New York, NY 10019. TEL 212-262-5700; Ed. William Mock; Pub. Aubrey L. Webb; adv. contact: Jeff Wendland. photos; pub. size: broadsheet; circ. morning 69,000(paid); Sun. 84,000(paid). **Wire Service(s):** AP, KNS.

BIG SPRING

US   ISSN 0746-6811

BIG SPRING HERALD. 1904. Sun.-Fri. $.50/day newsstand, $1.25/Sun.; $8.65/mo. carrier. 710 Scurry, Big Spring, TX 79720. TEL 915-263-7331; FAX 915-264-7205. **Owner(s):** Hollinger, Inc.; Ed. John H. Walker; Pub. Charles Williams; adv. contact: Ken Delaney. photos; bk.rev.; pub. size: broadsheet; circ. evening 8,000(paid); Sun. 9,000(paid). **Wire Service(s):** AP, SHNA.

BONHAM

US

BONHAM DAILY FAVORITE. 1894. Tue.-Fri. & Sun. $.50/day newsstand, $.75/Sun.; $90/yr. carrier; $140/yr. mailed. 314 N. Center St., Bonham, TX 75418. TEL 903-583-2124; FAX 903-583-8321. **Owner(s):** Bonham Publishers, Inc., 314 N. Center St., Bonham, TX 75418. TEL 903-583-2124; FAX 903-583-8321; Ed. John Frair; Pub. John Frair; adv. contact: Elaine Ashlock. pub. size: broadsheet; circ. evening 3,800(paid); Sun. 4,300(paid). **Wire Service(s):** AP.

BORGER

US

BORGER NEWS-HERALD. 1926. Sun.-Fri. $.50/day newsstand, $.75/Sun.; $7/mo. home deliv.; $84/yr. mailed. 207 N. Main St., Borger, TX 79007. TEL 806-273-5611; FAX 806-273-2552. **Owner(s):** Stephens Group, Inc., P.O. Box 1359, Fort Smith, AR 72902; Ed. Laura Frye; Pub. Tom Quinn; adv. contact: Helen Thomas. photos; pub. size: broadsheet; circ. evening 6,725(paid); Sun. 6,900(paid). **Wire Service(s):** AP.

BRENHAM

US   ISSN 8750-5800

BRENHAM BANNER-PRESS. 1866. Mon.-Sat. $.50 newsstand; $65/yr. 2000 Stringer, Brenham, TX 77833. TEL 409-836-7956; FAX 409-830-8577. **Owner(s):** Hartman Newspapers, Inc., P.O. Bos 1390, Rosenberg, TX 77471. TEL 713-342-4474; FAX 713-342-3219; Ed. Arthur Hahn; Pub. Charles Moser; adv.; photos; pub. size: broadsheet; circ. evening 6,500(paid). **Wire Service(s):** AP.

BROWNSVILLE

US   ISSN 0894-2064

BROWNSVILLE HERALD. 1892. d. $.35/day newsstand, $1/Sun.; $6/mo. carrier; $12/mo. elsewhere. 1135 E. Van Buren, Brownsville, TX 78520. TEL 210-542-4301; FAX 210-542-0840; E-mail: herald@hiline.net. **Owner(s):** Freedom Communications, Inc., P.O. Box 19549, Irvine, CA 92713. TEL 714-553-9292; FAX 714-474-7675; Ed. George Cox; Pub. Douglas Hardie; pub. size: standard; circ. morning 18,800(paid); Sun. 21,200(paid). **Wire Service(s):** AP.

BROWNWOOD

US

BROWNWOOD BULLETIN. 1900. Sun.-Fri. $.50/day newsstand, $1.50/Sun.; $10/mo. local; $13/mo. out of state. 700 Carnegie, Brownwood, TX 76801. TEL 915-646-2541; FAX 915-646-6835. **Owner(s):** Boone Newspapers, Inc., P.O. Box 2370, Tuscaloosa, AL 35403. TEL 407-338-3298; Ed. Gene Deason; Pub. H. Shelton Prince, Jr.; adv. contact: Jeff Littlejohn. photos; bk.rev.; pub. size: broadsheet; circ. evening 9,286(paid); Sun. 11,228(paid). **Wire Service(s):** AP.

BRYAN

US   ISSN 0739-8727

BRYAN COLLEGE STATION EAGLE. 1876. d. $.50 newsstand; $1.25/Sun.; $108/yr. 1729 Briarcrest Dr., Bryan, TX 77802. TEL 409-776-4444; FAX 409-774-0496. **Owner(s):** Eagle Printing Co., P.O. Box 3000, Bryan, TX 77805. TEL 409-776-4444; Pub. Donnis Baggett; adv. contact: Jean Wolff. pub. size: broadsheet; circ. 34,000. **Wire Service(s):** AP.

CLEBURNE

US

CLEBURNE TIMES-REVIEW. 1904. Sun.-Fri. $.50/day newsstand; $1/Sun.; $6/mo. carrier; $70/yr. in area; $73/yr. out of area. 108 S. Anglin, Cleburne, TX 76031. TEL 817-645-2441; FAX 817-645-4020. **Owner(s):** Donrey Media Group, P.O. Box 17017, Fort Smith, AK 72902. TEL 501-785-7810; Ed. Rob Fraser; Pub. Bill Rice; adv. contact: Kay Pace. pub. size: broadsheet; circ. evening 10,700(paid); Sun. 11,910(paid). **Wire Service(s):** AP.

CLUTE

US

BRAZOSPORT FACTS, THE. 1913. d. $.50/day newsstand; $1/Sun.; $8.75/mo. 720 S. Main, Clute, TX 77531. TEL 409-265-7411; FAX 409-265-9052; E-mail: thefacts@sat.net. **Owner(s):** Southern Newspapers, Inc., 720 S. Main, Clute, TX 77531. TEL 409-265-7411; FAX 409-265-9052; Ed. Wanda Garner Cash; Pub. Bill Cornwell; adv. contact: Deana Lesco. photos; bk.rev.; pub. size: broadsheet; circ. evening 19,958(paid); Sun. 21,530(paid). **Wire Service(s):** AP.

CONROE

US

CONROE COURIER, THE. 1892. d. $.50/day newsstand; $1/Sun.; $9.75/mo. carrier. 100 Ave. A, Conroe, TX 77301. TEL 409-756-6671; FAX 409-756-6676. **Owner(s):** Westward Communications, Inc., Dallas, TX; Ed. Dan Turner; Pub. Chris Eddings; adv. contact: Brenda Roy. photos; pub. size: broadsheet; circ. morning 13,701(paid); Sun. 14,760(paid). **Wire Service(s):** AP.

CORPUS CHRISTI

US   ISSN 0894-5365

CORPUS CHRISTI CALLER-TIMES. 1883. d. $.50/day newsstand; $2/Sun.; $12.95/mo. carrier. 820 Lower N. Broadway, Corpus Christi, TX 78401. TEL 512-884-2011; FAX 512-886-3732; E-mail: scottr@caller.com; URL: http://www.caller.com. **Owner(s):** Harte-Hanks Communications, Inc., P.O. Box 269, San Antonio, TX 78291. TEL 512-344-8000; Pub. Steve Sullivan; adv. contact: Leslie Wendland. photos; pub. size: broadsheet; circ. morning 67,500(paid); Sun. 96,031(paid). **Wire Service(s):** AP, CT-NYT, KR, NYT.

CORSICANA

US   ISSN 8750-2518

CORSICANA DAILY SUN. 1894. d. $.50/day newsstand; $1/Sun.; $8.25/mo. carrier; $9/mo. mailed. 405 E. Collin Ave., Corsicana, TX 75110. TEL 903-872-3931; FAX 903-872-6878. **Owner(s):** American Publishing Co., 606 N. Van Buren, P.O. Box 520-, Marion, IL 62959. TEL 618-993-1711; Ed. Rob Ludwig; Pub. Gary Connor; adv. contact: T.C. Hurst. pub. size: broadsheet; circ. evening 7,900(paid); Sun. 8,100(paid). **Wire Service(s):** AP.

DALHART

US

DALHART DAILY TEXAN. 1901. Tue.-Fri. & Sun. $.25 newsstand; $50/yr. out of state; $54.60/yr. home deliv. 410 Denrock, Dalhart, TX 79022. TEL 806-249-4511; FAX 806-249-2395. **Owner(s):** Susan J. & Robert S. Clay, 410 Denrock, Dalhart, TX 79022. TEL 806-249-4511; FAX 806-249-2395; Pub. Robert S. Clay; adv. contact: Pat Warden. bk.rev.; pub. size: broadsheet; circ. evening 2,520(paid); Sun. 2,700(paid). **Wire Service(s):** AP.

DALLAS

US

DALLAS MORNING NEWS, THE. 1885. d. $.75/day newsstand; $1.50/Sun.; $132/yr. home deliv. 400 S. Record, 4th Fl., Dallas, TX 75202. TEL 214-977-8222; FAX 214-977-8019. **Owner(s):** A.H. Belo Corp., 400 S. Record, Dallas, TX 75202. TEL 214-977-6606; Ed. Stuart Wilk; Pub. Burl Osborne; adv. contact: Jerry Coley. bk.rev.; pub. size: broadsheet; circ. morning 494,266(paid); Sun. 803,610(paid). **Wire Service(s):** AP, NYT, KNI, AFP.

DEL RIO

US

DEL RIO NEWS-HERALD. 1929. d. $.50/day newsstand; $1.25/Sun; $7.75/mo.; $46.50/6 mos.; $93/yr. 321 S. Main St., Del Rio, TX 78840. TEL 210-775-1551; FAX 210-774-2610. **Owner(s):** Hollinger, Inc.; Ed. Rosa Delgado; Pub. Joe San Miguel; adv. contact: Janie Sharp. pub. size: broadsheet; circ. evening 6,400(paid); Sun. 6,800(paid). **Wire Service(s):** AP.

DENISON

US

HERALD-DEMOCRAT. 1879. Sun.-Fri. $.25/day newsstand; $.75/Sun.; $7.50/mo. carrier; $7.75/mo. mailed. 331 W. Woodard, Denison, TX 75020. TEL 903-465-7171; FAX 903-465-7188. **Owner(s):** Stephens Group, Inc., P.O. Box 17017, Ft. Smith, AR 72917. TEL 501-785-7801; Ed. Steve Martaindale; Pub. John Wright; pub. size: standard; circ. morning 18,000(paid); Sun. 32,000(paid). **Wire Service(s):** AP.
    Formerly: Denison Herald; Sherman Democrat.

DENTON

US

DENTON RECORD-CHRONICLE. 1903. d. $.25/day newsstand; $1/Sun. $8/mo. daily carrier, $4/mo. Sun.; $16/mo. daily mailed, $11/mo. Sun. 314 E. Hickory St., Denton, TX 76201. TEL 817-387-3811; FAX 214-434-2400. **Owner(s):** Denton Publications, Inc., 314 E. Hickory St., P.O. Box 369, Denton, TX 76201. TEL 817-387-3811. Ed. Jim Flansburg; Pub. Fred Patterson; adv. contact: Sandra Kelly. pub. size: broadsheet; circ. evening 17,140(paid); Sun. 20,058(paid). **Wire Service(s):** AP.

EAGLE PASS

US

EAGLE PASS NEWS GUIDE/BRIEF. 1886. Guide: Thu. & Sun.; Brief: Mon.-Wed., Fri. & Sat. $.50/day newsstand; $19.50/yr. mailed local; $34.50/yr. mailed in state; $38.50/yr. out of state; Sun. free deliv.; Brief free distr. 1342 Main St., Eagle Pass, TX 78852. TEL 210-773-2309; FAX 217-773-3398. **Owner(s):** Guide Publishing Co., 1342 Main St., P.O. Box 764, Eagle Pass, TX 78852. TEL 512-773-2309; Ed. Maggie McBeath; Pub. Rex McBeath; adv.; pub. size: standard; circ. morning 2,500(free); Sun. 5,000(free).

EDINBURG

US

EDINBURG DAILY REVIEW. 1914. Tue.-Fri. & Sun. $.25 newsstand; $60.13/yr. 215 E. University Ave., Edinburg, TX 78539. TEL 210-383-2705. **Owner(s):** Hidalgo Publishing Co., Inc., 215 E. University, Edinburg, TX 78539. TEL 512-383-2705; Ed. Gilbert Tagle; Pub. Pearl A. Mathis; adv.; photos; bk.rev.; pub. size: standard; circ. evening 5,500(paid); Sun. 5,500(paid). **Wire Service(s):** AP.

EL PASO

US

EL PASO HERALD-POST. 1881. Mon.-Sat. $.35 newsstand; $5.50/mo. carrier. 300 N. Campbell St., El Paso, TX 79901. TEL 915-546-6100; FAX 915-546-6349. **Owner(s):** Scripps-Howard, 312 Walnut St., 28th Fl. Cincinnati, OH 45202. TEL 513-977-3000; Ed. Georgiana Vines. adv. contact: J. Michael Price. pub. size: broadsheet; circ. evening 26,168(paid). **Wire Service(s):** AP, NYT, SHNS.

US   SSN 0746-3588

EL PASO TIMES. 1881. d. $.35/day newsstand; $1.50/Sun.; $10.50/mo. carrier. 300 N. Campbell St., El Paso, TX 79901. TEL 915-546-6100; FAX 915-546-6415. **Owner(s):** Gannett Company, Inc., 1100 Wilson Blvd., Arlington, VA 22234. TEL 703-284-6000; Ed. Paula Moore; Pub. Don Flores; adv. contact: J. Michael Price. pub. size: broadsheet; circ. morning 47,000(paid); Sun. 99,000(paid). **Wire Service(s):** AP, GNS.

ENNIS

US   ISSN 8755-9056

ENNIS DAILY NEWS. 1891. Sun.-Fri. $.25 newsstand; $5/mo. carrier. 213 N. Dallas, Ennis, TX 75119. TEL 214-875-3801; FAX 214-875-9747. **Owner(s):** United Publishing Co., Inc., P.O. Drawer 100, Ennis, TX 75120. TEL 214-875-3801; FAX 214-878-8163; Ed. Charles Gentry; Pub. Charles Gentry; adv. contact: Roger Gentry. pub. size: broadsheet; circ. evening 4,500(paid); Sun. 4,500(paid). **Wire Service(s):** AP.

FORT WORTH

US

ARLINGTON STAR TELEGRAM 1883. d. $.50/day newsstand; $1.25/Sun.; $10.95/mo. carrier. 400 W. Seventh St., Fort Worth, TX 76102. TEL 817-548-5400; FAX 817-261-1193. **Owner(s):** Walt Disney Co. 500 S. Buena Vista St., Burbank, CA 91521. TEL 818-560-5300; Pub. Michael "Mac" Tully; adv. contact: Walter Owen. pub. size: broadsheet; circ. morning 47,800(paid); Sun. 70,000(paid). **Wire Service(s):** AP, RN, NYT.
    Formerly: Arlington Citizen-Journal.

US   ISSN 0889-0013

FORT WORTH STAR-TELEGRAM. 1906. d. $.50/day newsstand; $1.50/Sun.; $10.95/mo. carrier; $7.95/mo. Sat. & Sun. carrier. 400 W. Seventh St., Fort Worth, TX 76102. TEL 817-390-7400; FAX 817-390-7789. **Owner(s):** Walt Disney Co., 500 S. Buena Vista St., Burbank, CA 91521. TEL 818-560-5300; Ed. Michael Blackman; Pub. Richard Connor. bk.rev.; pub. size: broadsheet; circ. morning 256,789(paid); Sun. 350,000(paid). **Wire Service(s):** AP, LAT-WP, KNI CDN.

GAINESVILLE

US

GAINESVILLE DAILY REGISTER. 1890. Sun.-Fri. $.50/day newsstand, $.75/Sun.; $78/yr. in cy.; $90/yr. out of cy. 306 E. California, Gainesville, TX 76240. TEL 817-665-5511; FAX 817-665-0920. **Owner(s):** Stephens Group, Inc., P.O. Box 1350, Fort Smith, AR 72902. TEL 501-785-7810; Ed. Jerry Pickett; Pub. David Scott; adv. contact: Sandi Jones. pub. size: broadsheet; circ. evening 7,400(paid); Sun. 8,800(paid). **Wire Service(s):** AP.

GALVESTON

US   ISSN 0738-8047

GALVESTON COUNTY DAILY NEWS, THE. 1842. d.
$.50/day newsstand; $1/Sun.; $10.75/mo.
carrier. 8522 Teichman, Galveston, TX 77553.
TEL 409-744-3611; FAX 409-744-5233.
Owner(s): Galveston Newspapers, Inc., P.O. Box
628, Galveston, TX 77553. TEL 409-744-3611;
Ed. Dolph Tillotson; Pub. Dolph Tillotson; adv.
contact: Greg Schrader. pub. size: broadsheet;
circ. morning 28,762(paid); Sun. 29,628(paid).
Wire Service(s): AP.

HOUSTON

US

HOUSTON CHRONICLE. 1901. d. $.50/day
newsstand; $1.75/Sun.; $11/mo. home deliv.
801 Texas Ave., Houston, TX 77002.
TEL 713-220-7171; FAX 713-220-6806; E-mail:
hci@chron.com; URL: http://www.chron.com.
Owner(s): Hearst Corp., 959 Eighth Ave., New
York, NY 10019. TEL 212-262-5700; Ed. Tony
Pederson; Pub. R.J.V. Johnson; adv.; photos; pub.
size: broadsheet; circ. morning 551,553(paid);
Sun. 764,443(paid). **Wire Service(s):** AP, NYT,
LAT-WP, KNT, SHNA, Cox, NNS.

KILLEEN

US

KILLEEN DAILY HERALD. 1890. d. $.50/day
newsstand, $1/Sun.; $8.40/mo. home deliv.;
$12.10/mo. out of cy. mailed. 1809 Florence
Rd., Killeen, TX 76541. TEL 817-634-2125;
FAX 817-634-2125. **Owner(s):** F. Mayborn
Enterprises, Inc., P.O. Box 614, Temple, TX
76503. TEL 817-778-4444; Pub. Thad Byars;
adv. contact: Thad Byars. pub. size: broadsheet;
circ. morning 22,000(paid); Sun. 26,000(paid).
Wire Service(s): AP, SHNA.

GREENVILLE

US   ISSN 1042-3710

GREENVILLE HERALD BANNER. 1956. d. $.50/day
newsstand; $1/Sun.; $8/mo. 2305 King St.,
Greenville, TX 75401. TEL 214-455-4220.
Owner(s): American Publishing Co., 606 N. Van
Buren, P.O. Box 520, Marion, IL 62959. TEL
618-993-1711; Ed. Melva Geyer; Pub. Jeff
Jeffus; adv. contact: Terri McCreary. photos;
bk.rev.; pub. size: broadsheet; circ. morning
10,789(paid); Sun. 11,492(paid). **Wire
Service(s):** AP.

HUNTSVILLE

US   ISSN 0888-4145

HUNTSVILLE ITEM. 1850. d. $.50/day newsstand;
$1/Sun.; $9/mo. home deliv. 1409 Tenth St.,
Huntsville, TX 77340. TEL 409-295-4911;
FAX 409-293-3909. **Owner(s):** American
Publishing Co., 606 N. Van Buren, P.O. Box 520,
Marion, IL 62959. TEL 618-993-1711; Ed. Lisa
Trow; Pub. Arlena McLaughlin; adv. contact: Karen
Altom. pub. size: broadsheet; circ. evening
6,486(controlled & paid); Sun. 7,648(controlled
& paid). **Wire Service(s):** AP.

LAREDO

US   ISSN 0740-5227

LAREDO MORNING TIMES. 1890. d. $.35/day
newsstand; $1/Sun.; $6/mo. carrier. 111
Esperanza Dr., Laredo, TX 78041.
TEL 210-728-2500; FAX 210-723-1227; E-mail:
times@lmtonline.com; URL: http://lmtonline.com.
Owner(s): Hearst Corp., 959 Eighth Ave., New
York, NY 10019; Ed. Odie Arambula; Pub. Bill
Green; adv. contact: Frank Escoredo. pub. size:
broadsheet; circ. morning 23,500(paid); Sun.
25,000(paid). **Wire Service(s):** AP.

HARLINGEN

US

VALLEY MORNING STAR. 1911. d. $.50/day
newsstand; $1.25/Sun.; $8.50/mo. 1310 S.
Commerce, Harlingen, TX 78550.
TEL 210-423-5511; FAX 210-430-6204.
Owner(s): Freedom Communications, Inc., 17666
Fitch, Irvine, CA 92701. TEL 714-542-4415; Ed.
Patrick Canty; Pub. V. Lyle DeBolt; adv.; photos;
bk.rev.; pub. size: broadsheet; circ. morning
28,735(paid); Sun. 32,201(paid). **Wire
Service(s):** AP.
   Formerly: Harlingen Valley Morning Star.

JACKSONVILLE

US

JACKSONVILLE DAILY PROGRESS. 1910. Sun.-Fri.
$.50/day newsstand, $.75/Sun.; $8/mo. in cy.
mailed; $9/mo. out of cy. mailed. 525 E.
Commerce, Jacksonville, TX 75766.
TEL 903-586-2236; FAX 903-586-0987.
Owner(s): Stephens Group, Inc., P.O. Box 1350,
Fort Smith, AR 72901. TEL 501-785-7810; Pub.
Robb Grindstaff; adv. contact: James Hutchison.
photos; bk.rev.; pub. size: broadsheet; circ.
evening 4,953(paid); Sun. 5,137(paid). **Wire
Service(s):** AP.

LONGVIEW

US

LONGVIEW NEWS JOURNAL. 1871. d. $.50/day
newsstand, $1/Sun.; $99/yr. carrier; $14/mo.
mailed. 320 E. Methvin St., Longview, TX 75601.
TEL 903-757-3311; FAX 903-757-3742.
Owner(s): Longview Newspapers, Inc., P.O. Box
1792, Longview, TX 75606. TEL
903-757-3311; Ed. Pete Litterski. adv. contact:
Tim Hobbs. pub. size: standard; circ. morning
31,000(paid); Sun. 41,000(paid). **Wire
Service(s):** AP, NYT, CNS, SHNA.
   Formerly: Daily News.

HENDERSON

US

HENDERSON DAILY NEWS. 1931. Sun.-Fri. $.25/day
newsstand, $.75/Sun.; $6/mo. carrier. 1711
Hwy. 79, S., Henderson, TX 75653.
TEL 903-657-2501; FAX 903-657-2452.
Owner(s): Henderson Newspapers, Inc., P.O. Box
30, Henderson, TX 75653. TEL 903-657-2501;
Ed. Randy Chote; Pub. Noble Welch; adv. contact:
William Ashby. pub. size: broadsheet; circ. evening
6,500(paid); Sun. 8,000(paid). **Wire
Service(s):** AP.

KERRVILLE

US

KERRVILLE DAILY TIMES. 1908. Sun.-Fri. $.50/day
newsstand, $1/Sun.; $6.95/mo in area;
$8.10/mo. out of area; $8.85/mo. in state;
$9.60/mo. out of state. 429 Jefferson St.,
Kerrville, TX 78028. TEL 210-896-7000;
FAX 210-896-1150; E-mail: kdt@ktc.com.
Owner(s): Southern Newspapers, Inc.; Ed. Clint
Schroeder; Pub. Greg Schrader; adv. contact:
Linda Robinson. photos; bk.rev.; pub. size:
broadsheet; circ. evening 10,000(paid); Sun.
12,000(paid). **Wire Service(s):** AP.

LUBBOCK

US

LUBBOCK AVALANCHE-JOURNAL. 1904. d. $.50/day
newsstand; $1.25/Sun.; $9.75/mo. carrier;
$105/yr. carrier. 710 Ave. J, Lubbock, TX
79401. TEL 806-762-8844;
FAX 806-744-9603. **Owner(s):** Morris
Communications, P.O. Box 936, Augusta, GA
30903. TEL 706-724-0851; Ed. Burle Pettit;
Pub. David Sharp; adv. contact: Charles Evers.
photos; bk.rev.; pub. size: broadsheet; circ.
morning 72,500(paid); Sun. 82,300(paid). **Wire
Service(s):** AP, KR, LAT-WP, SHNA.

HEREFORD

US

HEREFORD BRAND. 1901. Tue.-Fri. & Sun. $.50/day
newsstand; $.75/Sun.; $52/yr. 313 Lee St.,
Hereford, TX 79045. TEL 806-364-2030;
FAX 806-364-8364. **Owner(s):** Roberts
Publishing Co., 210 E. Broadway, Andrews, TX
79714; Ed. Garry Wesner; Pub. O.G. Nieman;
adv. contact: Mauri Montgomery. photos; pub.
size: broadsheet; circ. evening 3,700(paid); Sun.
4,200(paid). **Wire Service(s):** AP.

KILGORE

US

KILGORE NEWS HERALD. 1931. Sun.-Fri. $.50/day
newsstand; $.75/Sun.; $5.50/mo. carrier. 610 E.
Main St., Kilgore, TX 75662.
TEL 903-984-2593; FAX 903-984-7462.
Owner(s): Stephens Group, Inc., P.O. Box 1359,
Fort Smith, AR 72902; Ed. Greg A. Collins; Pub.
Frank Rowe; adv. contact: Don Alexander. photos;
pub. size: broadsheet; circ. evening 5,000(paid);
Sun. 5,500(paid). **Wire Service(s):** AP.

LUFKIN

US

LUFKIN DAILY NEWS. 1906. d. $.50/day newsstand;
$1.25/Sun. 300 Ellis, Lufkin, TX 75901.
TEL 409-632-6631; FAX 409-632-6655.
Owner(s): Cox Enterprises, Inc., 72 Marietta St.,
N.W., Atlanta, GA 30303. TEL 404-843-5000;
Ed. Phil Latham; Pub. Glenn McCutchen; pub.
size: broadsheet; circ. evening 16,900(paid); Sun.
18,500(paid). **Wire Service(s):** AP, Cox.

MARSHALL

US

MARSHALL NEWS MESSENGER. Sun.-Fri. $.35/day newsstand; $1/Sun.; $8/mo. home deliv. 309 E. Austin St., Marshall, TX 75670. TEL 903-935-7914; FAX 903-935-6242. **Owner(s):** Hollinger, Inc.; Ed. Mike McNeill; Pub. Reginald Durant; adv. contact: Joe Rainwater. pub. size: standard; circ. morning 10,000(paid); Sun. 10,500(paid).

MCALLEN

US

MCALLEN MONITOR. 1911. d. $.50/day newsstand, $1.25/Sun.; $8.25/mo. carrier; $15/mo. mailed. 1101 Ash St., McAllen, TX 78501. TEL 210-686-4343; FAX 210-686-4370. **Owner(s):** Freedom Communications, Inc., 1055 N. Main, Ste. 901, Santa Anna, CA 93060; Ed. Paul Binz; Pub. Ray M. Stafford; adv. contact: Abel Fernandez. pub. size: broadsheet; circ. morning 37,823(paid); Sun. 45,034(paid). **Wire Service(s):** AP, KR.

MCKINNEY

US

MCKINNEY COURIER GAZETTE. 1847. Sun.-Fri. $.50/day newsstand; $.50/Sun.; $72/yr. in cy. mailed. 4005 W. University Dr., McKinney, TX 75070. TEL 214-542-2631; FAX 214-548-7527. **Owner(s):** McKinney Newspapers, Inc., P.O. Box 400, McKinney, TX 75069. TEL 214-542-2631; Pub. Jim Robertson; adv. contact: Pete Mulkey. pub. size: broadsheet; circ. evening 7,512(paid); Sun. 8,500(paid). **Wire Service(s):** AP.

MEXIA

US

MEXIA DAILY NEWS. 1872. Tue.-Sat. $.50 newsstand; $65/yr. in cy.; $67.60/yr. out of cy. 214 N. Railroad St., Mexia, TX 76667. TEL 817-562-2868; FAX 817-562-3121. **Owner(s):** American Publishing Co., 606 N. Van Buren, P.O. Box 520, Marion, IL 62959. TEL 618-993-1711; Ed. Bob Wright; Pub. Lynette Copley; adv.; photos; bk.rev.; pub. size: broadsheet; circ. evening 3,500(paid). **Wire Service(s):** AP.

MIDLAND

US   ISSN 0890-5932

MIDLAND REPORTER-TELEGRAM. 1929. d. $.50/day newsstand; $1.50/Sun.; $9/mo. home deliv.; $6/mo. Sat. & Sun. 201 E. Illinois, Midland, TX 79701. TEL 915-682-5311; FAX 915-682-6173; E-mail: jpatterson@basinlink.com; URL: http://www.mrt.com. **Owner(s):** Hearst Corp., 1700 Broadway, New York, NY 10019. TEL 212-649-2000; Ed. Gary Ott; Pub. Charles Spence; adv. contact: Sam Bakke. photos; bk.rev.; pub. size: broadsheet; circ. morning 24,000(paid); Sun. 29,000(paid). **Wire Service(s):** AP, LAT-WP, HHS.

MINERAL WELLS

US

MINERAL WELLS INDEX. 1900. Tue.-Fri. & Sun. $.25/day newsstand; $.75/Sun.; $55/yr. carrier; $60/yr. in cy.; $68.50/yr. out of cy.; $73.75/yr. out of state. 300 S.E. First St., Mineral Wells, TX 76067. TEL 817-325-4466; FAX 817-325-2020. **Owner(s):** Edward K. Livermore, P.O. Box 370, Mineral Wells, TX 76067. TEL 817-325-4465; Pub. Gary Adkisson; adv. contact: Bill Moore. pub. size: broadsheet; circ. evening 4,750(paid); Sun. 5,000(paid). **Wire Service(s):** AP.

MT. PLEASANT

US

MOUNT PLEASANT DAILY TRIBUNE. 1874. Sun.-Fri. $.50/day newsstand, $1/Sun.; $74/yr. in cy.; $75/yr. mailed out of cy., $80/yr. mailed out of state. 1705 Industrial Rd., Mt. Pleasant, TX 75455. TEL 903-572-1705; FAX 903-572-1705. **Owner(s):** Palmer Media, Inc., 111 E. Second St., Mt. Pleasant, TX 75455. TEL 214-572-3607; Ed. R.L. Palmer; Pub. R.B. Palmer; adv. contact: Martha McGregor. pub. size: broadsheet; circ. evening 6,500(paid); Sun. 8,000(paid). **Wire Service(s):** AP.

NACOGDOCHES

US

DAILY SENTINEL, THE. 1972. d. $.35/day newsstand; $1.25/Sun; $7.95/mo. local deliv. 4920 Colonial Dr., Nacogdoches, TX 75961. TEL 409-564-8361; FAX 409-560-4267. **Owner(s):** Cox Publishing Co., P.O. Box 68, Nacogdoches, TX 75963. TEL 409-564-8361; Ed. Erni Murray; Pub Gary Borders; adv. contact: David Lawrence. pub. size: broadsheet; circ. morning 11,000(paid); Sun. 12,500(paid). **Wire Service(s):** AP.
  Formerly: Sunday Sentinel.

NEW BRAUNFELS

US

NEW BRAUNFELS HERALD & ZEITUNG. 1852. Tue.-Fri. & Sun. $.50/day newsstand; $1/Sun.; $60/yr. carrier. 707 Landa St., New Braunfels, TX 78130. TEL 210-625-9144; FAX 210-625-1224. **Owner(s):** Southern Newspapers, Inc., 1050 Wilcrest Dr., Houston, TX 77042. TEL 713-266-5481; Ed. Doug Loveday; Pub. Doug Toney; adv. contact: Cheryl DuVall. photos; pub. size: broadsheet; circ. morning 8,600(paid); Sun. 11,000(paid). **Wire Service(s):** AP.

ODESSA

US

ODESSA AMERICAN. 1939. d. $.50/day newsstand; $1.50/Sun.; $7/mo. daily; $10/mo. carrier; $15/mo. mailed. 222 E. Fourth St., Odessa, TX 79761. TEL 915-337-4661; FAX 915-334-8671. **Owner(s):** Freedom Communications, Inc., Box 19549, Irvine, CA 92713. TEL 714-553-9292; Ed. Gary Newsom; Pub. Bill Salter; pub. size: broadsheet; circ. morning 25,692(paid); Sun. 31,858(paid). **Wire Service(s):** AP.

ORANGE

US   ISSN 0885-8047

ORANGE LEADER. 1875. d. $.35/day newsstand, $1/Sun.; $8.50/mo. home deliv. $13.00/mo. mailed. 200 Front Ave., Orange, TX 77630. TEL 409-883-3571; FAX 409-833-6342. **Owner(s):** American Publishing Co., 606 N. Van Buren, P.O. Box 520, Marion, IL 62959. TEL 618-993-1711; Pub. Jan Bromley; adv. contact: Jan Bromley. pub. size: broadsheet; circ. evening 10,013(paid); Sun. 12,500(paid). **Wire Service(s):** AP.

PALESTINE

US   ISSN 1053-5748

PALESTINE HERALD-PRESS. 1898. d. $.25/day newsstand, $.75/Sun.; $6.50/mo. carrier; $7.25/mo. in cy.; $7.75/mo. out of cy. 519 N. Elm St., Palestine, TX 75801. TEL 903-729-0281; FAX 903-729-3380. **Owner(s):** Patrick Management, P.O. Box 379, Palestine, TX 75802. TEL 903-729-0281; Ed. Bonnie Lasiter; Pub. Larry Mayo; adv. contact: Mike Whitworth. pub. size: broadsheet; circ. evening 10,076(paid); Sun. 10,471(paid). **Wire Service(s):** AP.

PAMPA

US

PAMPA NEWS. 1927. Sun.-Fri. $.50/day newsstand; $1/Sun.; $25.50/3 mos. mailed; $84/yr. carrier. 403 W. Atchison, Pampa, TX 79065. TEL 806-669-2525; FAX 806-669-2520. **Owner(s):** Freedom Communications, Inc., 17666 Fitch, Irvine, CA 92714. TEL 714-553-9292; Ed. Larry D. Hollis; Pub. Wyland Thomas; adv. contact: Rick Clark. pub. size: broadsheet; circ. evening 6,600(paid); Sun. 7,000(paid). **Wire Service(s):** AP.

PARIS

US   ISSN 8756-2081

PARIS NEWS. 1871. Sun.-Fri. $.50/day newsstand; $1.25/Sun.; $8.75/yr. carrier. 5050 S.E. Loop 286, Paris, TX 75460. TEL 903-785-8744; FAX 903-785-1263; E-mail parisnews@neto.com; URL: http://neto.com/news. Owner(s): Southern Newspapers, Inc., 1050 Wilcrest Dr., Houston, TX 77042. TEL 713-266-5481; Ed. Bill Harkins; Pub. Michael Graxiola; adv.; photos; bk.rev.; pub. size: broadsheet; circ. evening 13,800(paid); Sun. 15,631(paid). **Wire Service(s):** AP.

PASADENA

US   ISSN 0896-3320

PASADENA CITIZEN. 1947. Tue.-Sun. $.50 newsstand; $7/mo. carrier; $19/3 mos. 102 S. Shaver, Pasadena, TX 77506. TEL 713-477-0221; FAX 713-477-9090. **Owner(s):** Westward Communications, Inc., 5005 LBJ Fwy., Ste. 1040, Dallas, TX 75225. TEL 214-450-1717; Ed. Mike Simmons; Pub. Mark Singletary; adv.; photos; pub. size: broadsheet; circ. morning 8,000(paid); Sun. 15,000(paid). **Wire Service(s):** AP.

PECOS

US   ISSN 0746-4231

PECOS ENTERPRISE. 1887. Sun.-Fri. $.35/day newsstand; free Sun.; $6.50/mo. carrier; $19.50/3 mos. city deliv.; $24/3 mos. mailed. 324 S. Cedar St., Pecos, TX 79772. TEL 915-445-5475; FAX 915-445-4321. **Owner(s):** Buckner News Alliance, 2101 Fourth Ave., Ste. 2300, Seattle, WA 98121. TEL 206-727-2727; Ed. Jon Fulbright; Pub. Mac McKinnon; adv. contact: Christina Bitolas. photos; pub. size: broadsheet; circ. evening 2,550(free & paid); Sun. 4,500(free & paid). **Wire Service(s):** AP.

PLAINVIEW

US

PLAINVIEW DAILY HERALD. 1907. Sun.-Fri. $.50/day newsstand; $1.50/Sun.; $8.25/mo. carrier; $9.50/mo. mailed. 820 Broadway, Plainview, TX 79072. TEL 806-296-1300; FAX 806-296-1315; E-mail: rohyde@lonestarbbs.com; URL: http://www.texasonline.net/pageone.htm. **Owner(s):** Hearst Corp., 1700 Broadway, New York, NY 10019. TEL 212-649-2000; Ed. Danny Andrews; Pub. Rollie D. Hyde; adv. contact: Jeff Noble. photos. pub. size: standard; circ. evening 7,500(paid); Sun. 9,000(paid). **Wire Service(s):** AP, HHS.

PLANO

US   ISSN 0895-4305

PLANO STAR COURIER. 1888. Wed.-Sun. $.25/day newsstand; $1/Sun; $7/mo. 801 E. Plano Pkwy., Plano, TX 75074. TEL 214-424-6565; FAX 214-424-4388; E-mail: editorial@dal.cleaf.com; URL: http://clover.cleaf.com/~hhone/. **Owner(s):** Harte-Hanks Communications, Inc., P.O. Box 269, San Antonio, TX 78291. TEL 512-344-8000; Ed. Tim Watterson; Pub. Lynn Dickerson; adv. contact: Beth Roddy. pub. size: broadsheet; circ. evening 17,000(paid); Sun. 18,000(paid). **Wire Service(s):** AP.

PORT ARTHUR

US   ISSN 0889-6755

PORT ARTHUR NEWS. 1897. d. $.50/day newsstand, $1/Sun.; $8/mo. carrier. 549 Fourth St., Port Arthur, TX 77640. TEL 409-985-5541; FAX 409-982-4903. **Owner(s):** American Publishing Co., 606 N. Van Buren, P.O. Box 520, Marion, IL 62959. TEL 618-993-1711; Ed. Roger Cowles; Pub. Jeff Jeffus; adv. contact: Horace Fontenot. pub. size: broadsheet; circ. morning 23,000(paid); Sun. 25,000(paid). **Wire Service(s):** Laserphoto, AP, Cox.

ROSENBERG

US

HERALD COASTER. 1892. Sun.-Fri. $.50/day newsstand; $1/Sun.; $5.65/mo. motor rte.; $7/mo. deliv.; $7.25/mo. mailed; $21.75/3 mos. mailed. 1902 Fourth St., Rosenberg, TX 77471. TEL 713-342-4474; FAX 713-342-3219. **Owner(s):** Hartman Newspapers, Inc., 1904 Fourth St., Rosenberg, TX 77471. TEL 713-342-4474; FAX 713-342-3219; Ed. Bob Haenel; Pub. Clyde King; adv. contact: James Mosen. photos; bk.rev.; pub. size: broadsheet; circ. evening 8,415(paid); Sun. 9,026(paid). **Wire Service(s):** AP.

SAN ANGELO

US

SAN ANGELO STANDARD-TIMES. 1884. d. $.50/day newsstand; $1.50/Sun.; $155.40/yr. 34 W. Harris Ave., San Angelo, TX 76903. TEL 915-653-1221; FAX 915-658-7341; E-mail: comments@texaswest.com; URL: http://www.texaswest.com. **Owner(s):** San Angelo Standard, Inc., 34 W. Harris, San Angelo, TX 76903. TEL 915-653-1221; Ed. Dennis Ellsworth; Pub. Kevin J. Barry; adv. contact: Cheryl Ebright. pub. size: broadsheet; circ. morning 32,831(paid); Sun. 39,465(paid). **Wire Service(s):** AP, SHNS.

SAN ANTONIO

US   ISSN 1065-7908

SAN ANTONIO EXPRESS-NEWS. 1865. d. $.50/day newsstand; $1.50/Sun.; $9.75/mo. carrier. Ave. E & Third St., San Antonio, TX 78205. TEL 210-225-7411; FAX 210-225-8351; E-mail: jmoss@express-news.net; URL: http://www.express-news.net. **Owner(s):** Hearst Corp., 1700 Broadway, New York, NY 10019. TEL 212-649-2000; Ed. Lynnell Burkett; Pub. W. Lawrence Walker Jr.; adv.; photos; bk.rev.; pub. size: broadsheet; circ. morning 289,000(paid); Sun. 399,389(paid). **Wire Service(s):** AP, NYT, LAT-WP, SH.

SAN MARCOS

US

SAN MARCOS DAILY RECORD. 1912. Tue.-Fri. & Sun. $.50/day newsstand; $1/Sun.; $5.50/mo. carrier; $7.50/mo. mailed. 1910 I-35 S., San Marcos, TX 78666. TEL 512-392-2458; FAX 512-392-1514. **Owner(s):** American Publishing Co., 606 N. Van Buren, P.O. Box 520, Marion, IL 62959. TEL 618-993-1711; Ed. Rowe Ray; Pub. Guy Trimble; adv. contact: Janice Eaton. pub. size: broadsheet; circ. evening 7,500(paid); Sun. 8,500(paid). **Wire Service(s):** AP.

SEGUIN

US

SEGUIN GAZETTE-ENTERPRISE. 1979. Tue.-Fri. & Sun. $.50/day newsstand; $1/Sun.; $55/yr. carrier; $58.25/yr. mailed in cy. 1012 Schriewer Rd., Seguin, TX 78155. TEL 210-379-5402; FAX 210-379-8328. **Owner(s):** Southern Newspapers, Inc., P. O. Box 1200, Seguin, TX 78156-1200. TEL 512-379-5402; Ed. Kathie Ninneman; Pub. Larry Reynolds; adv. contact: Debbie Banta-Scott. pub. size: broadsheet; circ. evening 7,500(paid); Sun. 8,200(paid). **Wire Service(s):** AP.

SNYDER

US

SNYDER DAILY NEWS. 1950. Sun.-Fri. $.50 newsstand; $89.50/yr. 3600 College, Snyder, TX 79550. TEL 915-573-5486; FAX 915-573-0044. **Owner(s):** Roy McQueen, P.O. Box 949, Snyder, TX 79550. TEL 915-573-5486; FAX 915-573-0044; Ed. Bill McClellan; Pub. Roy McQueen; adv. contact: Wayne Burney. pub. size: standard; circ. evening 5,500(paid); Sun. 6,000(paid). **Wire Service(s):** AP.

STEPHENVILLE

US

STEPHENVILLE EMPIRE-TRIBUNE. 1870. Sun.-Fri. $.50/day newsstand; $1.50/Sun.; $9/mo. carrier. 590 S. Loop, Stephenville, TX 76401. TEL 817-965-3124; FAX 817-965-4269. **Owner(s):** Boone Newspapers, Inc., P.O. Box 2370, Tuscaloosa, AL 35403. TEL 407-338-3298; Ed. Jeff Osborne; Pub. Lee Leschper; adv.; photos; pub. size: broadsheet; circ. evening 6,000(paid); Sun. 6,200(paid). **Wire Service(s):** AP.

SULPHUR SPRINGS

US   ISSN 0745-6425

SULPHUR SPRINGS NEWS-TELEGRAM. 1881. Sun.-Fri. $.50/day newsstand; $.75/Fri. & Sun.; $69/yr. in city; $75/yr. out of city; $85/yr. mailed. 401 Church St., Sulphur Springs, TX 75482. TEL 903-885-8663; FAX 903-885-8768. **Owner(s):** Echo Publishing Co., 401 Church St., Sulphur Springs, TX 75482. TEL 903-885-8663; Ed. Bill Lamb; Pub. Scott Keys; adv. contact: Johnie Hardgrave. pub. size: broadsheet; circ. evening 6,900(paid); Sun. 7,400(paid). **Wire Service(s):** AP.

SWEETWATER

US

SWEETWATER REPORTER. 1881. Sun.-Fri. $.50/day newsstand; $.75/Sun.; $72/yr. home deliv. 112 W. Third St., Sweetwater, TX 79556. TEL 915-236-6677; FAX 915-235-4967. **Owner(s):** Stephens Group, Inc., Box 13507, Fort Smith, AR 72902. TEL 501-785-7810; Ed. Don Rogers; Pub. Mike Davis; adv. contact: Janice Briscoe. photos; bk.rev.; pub. size: broadsheet; circ. evening 4,000(paid); Sun. 4,500(paid). **Wire Service(s):** AP.

TAYLOR

US   ISSN 1054-3171

TAYLOR DAILY PRESS. 1912. Mon.-Fri. $.50 newsstand; $70/yr. in cy.; $96/yr. out of cy. 211 W. Third St., Taylor, TX 76574. TEL 512-352-8535; FAX 512-352-2227. **Owner(s):** Jim Chiosini, Blackland Publications, P.O. Box 1040, Taylor, TX 76574. TEL 512-352-8535; Ed. Don McAlister; Pub. Robert Swonke; adv. contact: David Ariola. pub. size: broadsheet; circ. evening 5,300(paid). **Wire Service(s):** AP.

TEMPLE

US

TEMPLE DAILY TELEGRAM. 1907. d. $.50/day newsstand; $1/Sun.; $9/mo. 10 S. Third St., Temple, TX 76501. TEL 817-778-4444; FAX 817-778-4444; E-mail: tdt@vvm.com. **Owner(s):** Frank Mayborn Enterprises, Inc., P.O. Box 6114, Temple, TX 76503-6114. TEL 817-778-4444; FAX 817-778-4444; Ed. Steve Walters; Pub. Sue Mayborn; adv. contact: Gary Garner. photos; bk.rev.; pub. size: broadsheet; circ. morning 25,500(paid); Sun. 28,500(paid). **Wire Service(s):** AP.

TERRELL

US

TERRELL TRIBUNE. 1916. Sun.-Fri. $.50 newsstand; $5.75/mo. in city; $6.25/mo. motor rte. 1125 S. Virginia St., Terrell, TX 75160. TEL 214-563-6476; FAX 214-563-6478. **Owner(s):** Hartman Newspapers, Inc., P.O. Box 1390, Rosenberg, TX 77471. TEL 713-342-4474; FAX 713-342-3219; Ed. Jim Raynes; Pub. Bill Jordan; pub. size: broadsheet; circ. evening 6,200(paid); Sun. 6,500(paid). **Wire Service(s):** AP.

TEXARKANA

US

TEXARKANA GAZETTE. 1875. d. $.35/day newsstand; $1/Sun.; $119.40/yr.; $129/yr. mailed. 315 Pine St., Texarkana, TX 75501-5655. TEL 903-794-3311; FAX 903-792-7183; E-mail: txrgaz@cei.net; URL: http://www.ardemgaz.com/txargaz. **Owner(s):** Texarkana Newspapers, Inc., P.O. Box 621, Texarkana, TX 75504. TEL 903-794-3311; Ed. Les Minor; Pub. Walter Hussman, Jr.; adv.; pub. size: broadsheet; circ. morning 32,278(paid); Sun. 36,008(paid). **Wire Service(s):** AP, SHNA, Tribune Media, KR.

TEXAS CITY

US

TEXAS CITY SUN. 1912. d. $.50/day newsstand, $.75/Sun.; $8.95/mo. carrier; $11.50/mo. mailed. 7800 Emmett Lowry Expy., Texas City, TX 77591. TEL 409-945-3441; FAX 409-935-0428. **Owner(s):** Walls Investment Co., Houston, TX. TEL 713-266-5481; Ed. Stephen Hadley; Pub. Les Daughtery, Jr.; adv. contact: Larry Cook. photos; bk.rev.; pub. size: broadsheet; circ. morning 8,800(paid); Sun. 9,100(paid). **Wire Service(s):** AP.

TYLER

US

TYLER MORNING TELEGRAPH. 1877. d. $.25/day newsstand; $.75/Sun.; $6.75/mo. carrier. 410 W. Erwin St., Tyler, TX 75702. TEL 903-597-8111; FAX 903-595-0335. **Owner(s):** T.B. Butler Publishing Co., Inc., P.O. Box 2030, Tyler, TX 75710. TEL 903-597-8111; Ed. Everett Taylor; Pub. Nelson Clyde, III; adv. contact: Nelson Clyde, IV. photos; bk.rev.; pub. size: broadsheet; circ. morning 44,000(paid); Sun. 52,000(paid). **Wire Service(s):** AP, UPI.

VERNON

US   ISSN 1046-1426

VERNON DAILY RECORD. 1923. Sun.-Fri. $.50 newsstand; $17.50/3 mos.; $32/6 mos. 3214 Wilbarger St., Vernon, TX 76384. TEL 817-552-5454; FAX 817-553-4823. **Owner(s):** Larry L. Crabtree, 3214 Wilbarger St., Vernon, TX 76384. TEL 817-552-5454; Ed. Jimmy Carr; Pub. Larry L. Crabtree; adv. contact: Jim Surber. pub. size: broadsheet; circ. evening 4,900(paid); Sun. 5,500(paid). **Wire Service(s):** AP.

VICTORIA

US

VICTORIA ADVOCATE. 1846. d. $.50/day newsstand; $1/Sun.; $9/mo. carrier. 311 E. Constitution, Victoria, TX 77901. TEL 512-575-1451; FAX 512-574-1220. **Owner(s):** Victoria Advocate Publishing Co. P.O. Box 1518, Victoria, TX 77902. TEL 512-575-1451; Ed. Jim Bishop; Pub. John Roberts; adv. contact: Fred Hornberger. photos; bk.rev.; pub. size: broadsheet; circ. morning 40,000(paid); Sun. 42,000(paid). **Wire Service(s):** AP, LAT-WP.

WACO

US

WACO TRIBUNE HERALD. 1909. d. $.50/day newsstand; $1.25/Sun.; $11.80/mo. carrier. 900 Franklin Ave., Waco, TX 76701. TEL 817-757-5757; FAX 817-757-0302. **Owner(s):** Cox Enterprises, Inc., P.O. Box 105357, Atlanta, GA 30348; Ed. Barbara Elmore; Pub. R.R. Preddy; adv. contact: Tricia Phillips. photos; bk.rev.; pub. size: broadsheet; circ. morning 50,500(paid); Sun. 65,000(paid). **Wire Service(s):** AP, NYT, Cox.

WAXAHACHIE

US   ISSN 0896-0291

WAXAHACHIE DAILY LIGHT. 1867. Sun.-Fri. $.50/day newsstand; $1.25/Sun.; $8.50/mo. 200 W. Marvin St., Waxahachie, TX 75165. TEL 214-937-3310; FAX 214-937-1139; E-mail: thelight@hachie.citylimits.net; URL: http://hachi.citylimits.net/thelight. **Owner(s):** Boone Newspapers, Inc., P.O. Box 2370, Tuscalosa, AL 35403. TEL 407-338-3298; Ed. Allan Taylor; Pub. Jeff Stumb; adv. contact: Don Wilson. pub. size: broadsheet; circ. evening 7,000(paid); Sun. 7,000(paid). **Wire Service(s):** UPI.

WEATHERFORD

US

WEATHERFORD DEMOCRAT. 1895. Sun.-Fri. $.50/day newsstand; $.75/Sun.; $5.75/mo.; $69/yr. 512 Palo Pinto St., Weatherford, TX 76086. TEL 817-594-7447; FAX 817-594-9734. **Owner(s):** Stephens Group, Inc., P.O. Box 1359, Fort Smith, AR 72902. TEL 501-785-7810. Pub. Jane Trimble; adv. contact: Carla Bandera. photos; bk.rev.; pub. size: broadsheet; circ. morning 6,000(paid); Sun. 6,700(paid). **Wire Service(s):** AP.

WICHITA FALLS

US   ISSN 0895-6138

TIMES RECORD NEWS. 1907. d. $.50 newsstand; $12.95/mo. home deliv. 1301 Lamar St., Wichita Falls, TX 76301. TEL 817-767-8341; FAX 817-767-5201; E-mail: cwilson105@aol.com; URL: http://www.wtr.com. **Owner(s):** Harte-Hanks Communications, Inc., P.O. Box 860248, Plano, TX 85086; Ed. Gary Schneeberger; Pub. Bill Guledge; adv. contact: Lori Ellington. pub. size: standard circ. morning 40,000(paid); Sun. 50,000(paid). **Wire Service(s):** AP, CTG, HHNS, KRNS.

UTAH

LOGAN

US

HERALD JOURNAL, THE. 1931. Sun.-Fri. $.50/day newsstand; $1.25/Sun.; $108/yr. in state; $114/yr. out of state. 75 W. Third, N., Logan, UT 84321. TEL 801-752-2121; FAX 801-753-6642. **Owner(s):** Pioneer Press, Inc., 221 W. First Ave., Ste 405, Seattle, WA 98119; Ed. Charles McCollum; Pub. Bruce K. Smith adv. contact: Wayne Ashcroft. pub. size: broadsheet; circ. evening 15,500(paid); Sun. 15,600(paid). **Wire Service(s):** AP, SHNA.

OGDEN

US

STANDARD-EXAMINER. 1888. d. $.50/day newsstand; $1.50/Sun.; $10.25/mo. mailed; $8.75/mo. carrier. 455 23rd St., Ogden, UT 84401. TEL 801-625-4200; FAX 801-625-4299. **Owner(s):** Sandusky Newspapers, Inc., 314 W. Market St., Sandusky, OH 44870. TEL 419-625-5500; Ed. Ronald Thornburg; Pub. Scott Trundle; adv. contact: Brad Roghaar. photos; bk.rev.; pub. size: broadsheet; circ. evening 61,000(paid); Sun. 64,000(paid). **Wire Service(s):** AP, SHNA, LAT-WP.

PROVO

US   ISSN 0891-2777

DAILY HERALD, THE. 1873. d. $9/mo. carrier; $9.25/mo. motor rte. 1555 N. 200 West, Provo, UT 84504-0717. TEL 801-373-5050; FAX 801-373-5489. **Owner(s):** Scripps League Newspapers, Inc., P.O. Box 109, Herndon, VA 22070. TEL 703-713-1920; Ed. Paul Richards; Pub. Kirk Parkinson; adv. contact: Mike Stansfield. photos; bk.rev.; pub. size: broadsheet; circ. evening 32,383(paid); Sun. 33,531(paid). **Wire Service(s):** AP.

SALT LAKE CITY

US   ISSN 0745-4724

SALT LAKE CITY DESERET NEWS. 1850. d. $.50/day newsstand; $1.50/Sun. 30 E. 100th St., Salt Lake City, UT 84110. TEL 801-237-2100; FAX 801-237-2121. **Owner(s):** Deseret News Publishing Co., P.O. Box 1257, Salt Lake City, UT 84110. TEL 801-237-2175; FAX 801-237-2121; Ed. Don C Woodward; Pub. William James Mortimer; adv. contact: Edward McCaffrey. photos; bk.rev.; pub. size: broadsheet; circ. evening 63,012(paid); Sun. 68,390(paid). **Wire Service(s):** AP, RN, NYT SHNA, UPI, LAT-WP.

US   ISSN 0746-3502

SALT LAKE TRIBUNE. 1871. d. $.50/day newsstand; $1.75/Sun.; $107/yr. carrier. 143 S. Main St., Salt Lake City, UT 84111. TEL 801-237-2045; FAX 801-521-9418; E-mail: jshelledy@sltrib.com; URL: http://www.sltrib.com/. **Owner(s):** Kearns-Tribune Corp., 143 S. Main, Salt Lake City, UT 84111. TEL 801-237-2031; Ed. James E. Shelledy; Pub. Dominic A. Welch; adv. contact: Ed McAffrey. pub. size: broadsheet; circ. morning 125,000(paid); Sun. 161,000(paid). **Wire Service(s):** NYT, LAT-WP, AP, RN, KR.

ST. GEORGE

US   ISSN 0745-6611

SPECTRUM, THE. 1963. d. $.50/day newsstand; $1.50/Sun.; $102/yr. 275 E. St. George Blvd., St. George, UT 84770. TEL 801-674-6200; FAX 801-674-6265; E-mail: rplotnow@aol.com. **Owner(s):** Thomson Newspapers, Inc., Metro Centre at One Station Pl., Stamford, CT 06902. TEL 203-425-2500; Ed. Janet Fontenot; Pub. Roger Plotnow; adv. contact: Jennie Johns. photos; bk.rev.; pub. size: broadsheet; circ. evening 22,000(paid); Sun. 22,200(paid). **Wire Service(s):** AP.

Formerly: The Daily Spectrum.

VERMONT

BARRE

US

TIMES ARGUS. 1897. d. $.50/day newsstand; $1.25/Sun.; $13.20/5 wks. carrier; $15.50/5 wks. motor rte. 540 N. Main St., Barre, VT 05641. TEL 802-479-0191; FAX 802-479-0191. **Owner(s):** Times Argus Assoc. Inc., Barre, VT 00761; Ed. Ann Gibbons; Pub. R. John Mitchell; adv. contact: Glen Dunning. pub. size: broadsheet; circ. evening 12,500(paid); Sun. 13,500(paid). **Wire Service(s):** AP, NYT, KR.

BENNINGTON

US

BENNINGTON BANNER. 1841. Mon.-Sat. $.50 newsstand; $11/mo. carrier; $13/mo. mailed. 425 Main St., Bennington, VT 05201. TEL 802-447-7567; FAX 802-442-3413. **Owner(s):** New England Newspapers, Inc., 23 Exchange St., Pawtucket, RI 02860. TEL 401-722-4000; Ed. Marlene Roderick; Pub. Mark Nesbitt; adv. contact: Brian Hewitt. pub. size: broadsheet; circ. morning 8,400(paid). **Wire Service(s):** AP.

BRATTLEBORO

US

BRATTLEBORO REFORMER. 1913. Mon.-Sat. $.50 newsstand; $105/yr. carrier; $115/yr. mailed in cy.; $140/yr. out of cy. Black Mountain Rd., Brattleboro, VT 05302-0802. TEL 802-254-2311; FAX 802-257-1305. **Owner(s):** New England Newspapers, Inc., 75 S. Church St., P.O. Box 1171, Pittsfield, MA 01201. TEL 413-447-7311; Ed. Steven Fay; Pub. Richard Macko; adv. contact: Mark Elliott. photos; bk.rev.; pub. size: broadsheet; circ. morning 11,044(paid). **Wire Service(s):** AP.

BURLINGTON

US

BURLINGTON FREE PRESS. 1827. d. $.50/day newsstand; $1.50/Sun.; $3.25/wk. carrier. 191 College St., Burlington, VT 05401. TEL 802-863-3441; FAX 802-660-1802. **Owner(s):** Gannett Company, Inc., 1100 Wilson Blvd., Arlington, VA 22234. TEL 703-284-6000; Ed. Mickey Hirten; Pub. James Carey; adv. contact: Mike Ricken. photos; bk.rev.; pub. size: broadsheet; circ. morning 53,000(paid); Sun. 69,000(paid). **Wire Service(s):** AP, GNS, LAT-WP.

NEWPORT

US

NEWPORT DAILY EXPRESS. 1936. d. $.35 newsstand; $102/yr. Hill St., Newport, VT 05855. TEL 802-334-6568; FAX 802-334-8691. **Owner(s):** Scripps League Newspapers, Inc., P.O. Box 1109, Herndon, VA 22070; Ed. Terry Albee. adv.; photos; pub. size: standard; circ. evening 4,891(paid). **Wire Service(s):** AP.

RUTLAND

US

RUTLAND HERALD. 1794. d. $.50/day newsstand; $1.50/Sun.; $3.05/wk. carrier; $3.45/wk. motor rte. 27 Wales St., Rutland, VT 05701. TEL 802-747-6121; FAX 802-775-2423. **Owner(s):** Herald Association, Inc., 27 Wales St., Rutland, VT 05701. TEL 802-747-6121; FAX 802-775-2423; Ed. John Van Hoesen; Pub. John Mitchell; adv. contact: Gracie Johnston. pub. size: broadsheet; circ. morning 22,431(paid); Sun. 23,296(paid). **Wire Service(s):** AP, NYT.

ST. ALBANS

US

ST. ALBANS MESSENGER. 1861. Mon.-Sat. $.50 newsstand; $2.10/wk. in cy.; $3/wk. out of cy.; $2.30/wk. motor route. 281 N. Main St., St. Albans, VT 05478. TEL 802-524-9771; FAX 802-527-1948. **Owner(s):** Emerson & Cynthia Lynn, French Hill Rd. 1, St. Albans, VT 05478. TEL 802-527-0800; Ed. Emerson Lynn; Pub. Emerson K. Lynn; adv. contact: Jeremy Read. bk.rev.; pub. size: broadsheet; circ. evening 5,000(paid). **Wire Service(s):** AP.

ST. JOHNSBURY

US

CALEDONIAN-RECORD, THE. 1837. Mon.-Sat. $.35 newsstand; $2.10/wk. carrier; $110/yr. mailed. 25 Federal St., St. Johnsbury, VT 05819. TEL 802-748-8121; FAX 802-748-1613. **Owner(s):** Caledonian-Record Publishing Co., Inc., P.O. Box 8, St. Johnsbury, VT 05819. TEL 802-748-8121; Ed. Ellie Dixon; Pub. Mark Smith; adv. contact: Michael Gonyaw. pub. size: broadsheet; circ. evening 11,043(paid). **Wire Service(s):** AP.

Formerly: St. Johnsbury Caledonian-Record.

VIRGIN ISLANDS

ST. CROIX

US

ST. CROIX AVIS. 1844. d. $.55/day newsstand; $.60/Sun. & Mon.; $95/yr. local; $172/yr. out of area. La Grande Princesse, Christiansted, St. Croix, VI 00820. TEL 809-773-2300; FAX 809-773-5511. **Owner(s):** St. Croix Avis, La Princesse, St. Croix, VI 00820. TEL 809-773-2300; Ed. Rena Broadhurst Knight; Pub. Rena Broadhurst Knight; adv. contact: Linda Clark. photos; bk.rev.; pub. size: tabloid; circ. morning 10,500(paid). **Wire Service(s):** AP.

ST. THOMAS

US

VIRGIN ISLANDS DAILY NEWS. 1930. d. $.60 newsstand; $254.25/yr. US mainland; $199.25/yr. Puerto Rico. 49 & 52a Estate Thomas, St. Thomas, VI 00801. TEL 809-774-8772; FAX 809-776-0740. **Owner(s):** Virgin Islands Daily News; Pub. Ariel Melchior, Jr.; adv.; photos; bk.rev.; pub. size: tabloid; circ. morning 16,623(free & paid). **Wire Service(s):** AP.

VIRGINIA

BRISTOL

US   ISSN 8750-6505

BRISTOL HERALD-COURIER, THE. 1870. d. $.50/day newsstand; $1.25/Sun.; $10.95/mo. carrier; $7/mo. weekend pkge. 320 Morrison Blvd., Bristol, VA 24201. TEL 504-669-2181; FAX 540-669-3696. **Owner(s):** Bristol Newspapers, Inc., 320 Morrison Blvd., Bristol, VA 24201. TEL 703-669-2181; Ed. Brian Reece; Pub. Arthur S. Powers; adv. contact: Joseph Adams. pub. size: broadsheet; circ. morning 47,000(paid); Sun. 47,000(paid). **Wire Service(s):** AP, SHNA, NEA.

CHARLOTTESVILLE

US   ISSN 0746-0430

DAILY PROGRESS. 1892. d. $.50/day newsstand; $1.50/Sun.; $2.80/wk. motor rte.; $145.60/yr. motor rte. 685 W. Rio Rd., Charlottesville, VA 22901. TEL 804-978-7210; FAX 804-978-7214. **Owner(s):** Media General, Inc., 333 E. Grace St., Richmond, VA 23219. TEL 804-649-6000; FAX 804-775-8090; Ed. Wayne Mogielnicki; Pub. Lawrence McConnell; adv. contact: Wanda Brickhead. photos; bk.rev.; pub. size: broadsheet; circ. evening 30,096(paid); Sun. 33,500(paid). **Wire Service(s):** AP, LAT-WP.

COVINGTON

US

VIRGINIAN REVIEW. 1914. Mon.-Sat. $.50 newsstand; $63/yr. 128 N. Maple Ave., Covington, VA 24426-0271. TEL 540-962-2121; FAX 540-962-5072. **Owner(s):** Covington Virginian Inc., 128 N. Maple Ave., Covington, VA 24426. TEL 703-962-2121; FAX 703-962-5072; Ed. Horton P. Beirne; Pub. Horton P. Beirne; adv. contact: Robert Tucker. photos; bk.rev.; pub. size: broadsheet; circ. evening 8,400(paid). **Wire Service(s):** AP.

CULPEPER

US

CULPEPER STAR EXPONENT. 1882. d. $.35/day newsstand; $1/Sun.; $98.80/yr. in cy. 122 W. Spencer St., Culpeper, VA 22701. TEL 540-825-0771; FAX 540-825-0778. **Owner(s):** Media General, Inc., 333 E. Grace St., Richmond, VA 23219. TEL 804-649-6000; FAX 804-775-8090; Pub. Peter S. Yates; adv. contact: Diane Holt. pub. size: broadsheet; circ. morning 8,010(paid). **Wire Service(s):** AP.

DANVILLE

US   ISSN 0744-3242

DANVILLE REGISTER & BEE. 1848. d. $.50/day newsstand; $1/Sun.; $8.50/mo. carrier; $11/mo. mailed. 700 Monument St., Danville, VA 24541. TEL 804-793-2311; FAX 804-797-2299; E-mail: rbnews@ns.gamewood.net; URL: http://www.gamewood.net/~rbnews. **Owner(s):** Register Publishing Co., Inc., 700 Monument St., P.O. Box 331, Danville, VA 24541. TEL 804-793-2311; Pub. Lawson Grant; adv.; photos; bk.rev.; pub. size: broadsheet; circ. morning 24,000(paid); Sun. 29,000(paid). **Wire Service(s):** AP.

FAIRFAX

US   ISSN 0162-2064

ALEXANDRIA JOURNAL. Mon.-Fri. $.25 newsstand; $72/yr. 2720 Prosperity Ave., Fairfax, VA 22034-1000. TEL 703-560-4000; FAX 703-846-8396. **Owner(s):** Journal Newspapers, Inc., 2720 Prosperity Ave., Fairfax, VA 22034-1010. TEL 703-560-4000; Ed. Jane Touzalin; Pub. Ryan Phillips; adv.; photos; bk.rev.; pub. size: broadsheet; circ. morning 5,098(paid). **Wire Service(s):** AP.

US   ISSN 0162-2072

ARLINGTON JOURNAL. 1933. Mon.-Fri. $.50 newsstand; $72/yr. 2720 Prosperity Ave., Fairfax, VA 22034. TEL 703-560-4000; FAX 703-846-8366. **Owner(s):** Journal Newspapers, Inc., 2720 Prosperity Ave., Fairfax, VA 22034. TEL 703-560-4000; Ed. Jane Touzalin; Pub. Ryan Phillips; adv.; photos; bk.rev.; pub. size: broadsheet; circ. evening 9,370(paid). **Wire Service(s):** AP.

US   ISSN 0162-2056

FAIRFAX JOURNAL. 1972. Mon.-Fri. $.25 newsstand; $21/3 mos.; $39/6 mos.; $72/yr.; $62/yr. senior citizens & military. 2720 Prosperity Ave., Fairfax, VA 22031. TEL 703-560-4000; FAX 708-846-8366. **Owner(s):** Journal Newspapers, Inc., 2720 Prosperity Ave., Fairfax, VA 22034. TEL 703-560-4000; Ed. Jane Touzalin; Pub. Ryan Phillips; adv. contact: Kenneth Courter. photos; bk.rev.; pub. size: broadsheet; circ. evening 45,088(paid). **Wire Service(s):** AP.

FREDERICKSBURG

US

FREDERICKSBURG FREE LANCE-STAR. 1885. Mon.-Sat. $.35 newsstand; $1/Sat.; $130/yr. 616 Amelia St., Fredericksburg, VA 22401. TEL 703-374-5000; FAX 703-373-8450. **Owner(s):** Free Lance-Star Publishing Co., 616 Amelia St., Fredericksburg, VA 22401. TEL 703-374-5000; Ed. Edward W. Jones; Pub.. Charles S. Rowe; adv. contact: C. Murphy Street. pub. size: broadsheet; circ. evening 45,000(paid). **Wire Service(s):** AP, KNT.

HARRISONBURG

US

DAILY NEWS-RECORD. 1897. Mon.-Sat. $.35 newsstand; $58/yr. in state; $70/yr. out of state. 231 S. Liberty St., Harrisonburg, VA 22801. TEL 540-574-6200; FAX 540-466-9112. **Owner(s):** Rockingham Publishing Co., Inc., 231 S. Liberty St., Harrisonburg, VA 22801. TEL 703-433-2702; FAX 703-433-9112; Ed. Richard R.J. Morin; Pub. Harry F. Byrd, Jr.; adv.; bk.rev.; pub. size: broadsheet; circ. morning 32,752(paid). **Wire Service(s):** AP.

HOPEWELL

US

HOPEWELL NEWS. 1926. Mon.-Fri. $.50 newsstand; $6.50/mo. carrier; $9/mo. mailed. 516 E. Randolph Rd., Hopewell, VA 23860. TEL 804-458-8511; FAX 804-458-7556. **Owner(s):** Hopewell Publishing Co., Inc., 206 S. Randolph Rd., Hopewell, VA 23860. TEL 804-458-8511; Ed. Andy Prutsok; Pub. Andy Prutsok; adv. contact: Dixie Hawkins. pub. size: broadsheet; circ. evening 7,800(paid). **Wire Service(s):** UPI.

LYNCHBURG

US

NEWS & ADVANCE. 1866. d. $.50 newsstand; $1.25/Sun.; $2.70/wk. home deliv. 101 Wyndale Dr., Lynchburg, VA 24501. TEL 804-385-5400; FAX 804-385-5538. **Owner(s):** Media General, Inc., 411 E. Franklin St., Richmond, VA 23219. TEL 804-775-8030 Ed. Joe Stinnett; Pub. Terry Hall; adv. contact: Jc Pearse. photos; bk.rev.; pub. size: broadsheet; circ. morning 40,000(paid); Sun. 46,000(paid). **Wire Service(s):** AP, NYT.

MANASSAS

US   ISSN 0745-6859

JOURNAL MESSENGER. 1869. Mon.-Sat. $.35 newsstand; $52.20/yr. 9009 Church St., Manassas, VA 22110. TEL 703-368-3101; FAX 703-368-9017. E-mail: jm@cais.com. **Owner(s):** Park Communications, Inc., Vine Ctr. Office Tower, 333 W. Vine St., 17th Fl., Lexington, KY 40507. TEL 606-252-7275; Ed. Kathryn McQuaid; Pub. Dennis Bradshaw; adv. contact: Craig Bender. pub. size: broadsheet; circ. evening 12,517(paic). **Wire Service(s):** AP.

PRINCE WILLIAM

▼**PRINCE WILLIAM JOURNA.** 1995. Mon.-Fri. $.25 newsstand; $21/3 mos.; $39/6 mos.; $72/yr. 9275 Corporate Cir., Manassas, VA 22110. TEL 703-257-4600; FAX 703-257-4960. **Owner(s):** Journal Newspapers, Inc., 2720 Prosperity Ave., Fairfax, VA 22034. TEL 703-560-4000; Ed. Mark Tapscott; Pub. Ryan Phillips; adv. contact: Cesi Myers. photos; bk.rev.; pub. size: broadsheet; circ. evening 9,500(paid). **Wire Service(s):** AP.

MARTINSVILLE

US

MARTINSVILLE BULLETIN. Sun.-Fri. $.35/day newsstand; $1/Sun.; $93 yr. carrier; $132/yr. mailed. 204 Broad St., Martinsville, VA 24112. TEL 540-638-8801; FAX 540-638-4153. **Owner(s):** Robert Haskell, 204 Broad St., Martinsville, VA 24112. TEL 703-638-8801; FAX 703-638-4153; Ed. Richard Hammerstrom; Pub. Robet Haskell; adv. contact: Robert Cox. pub. size: broadsheet; circ. evening 18,915(paid); Sun. 20,400(paid). **Wire Service(s):** AP, UPI.

NEWPORT NEWS

US

NEWPORT NEWS DAILY PRESS. 1896. d. $.35/day newsstand; $.50/Sat.; $1.50/Sun.; $2.75/wk. 7505 Warwick Blvd., Newport News, VA 23607-1517. TEL 804-247-4600; FAX 804-245-8618. **Owner(s):** Tribune Co., 435 N. Michigan Ave., Chicago, IL 60611; Ed. Will Corbin; Pub. Jack W. Davis Jr.; adv.; photos; bk.rev.; pub. size: broadsheet; circ. morning 104,000(paid); Sun. 126,000(paid). **Wire Service(s):** KNT, AP, NYT, LAT-WP.

NORFOLK

US   ISSN 0889-6127

VIRGINIAN-PILOT, THE. 1865. d. $.50/day newsstand; $1.25/Sun.; $120/yr. home deliv.; $290/yr. mail deliv. 150 W. Brambleton Ave., Norfolk, VA 23510. TEL 804-446-2000; FAX 804-446-2983. **Owner(s):** Landmark Communications, Inc., 150 W. Brambleton Ave., Norfolk, VA 23510. TEL 804-446-2000; Pub. R Bruce Bradley; adv. contact: Joe Antle. photos; bk.rev.; pub. size: broadsheet; circ. morning 199,433(paid); Sun. 238,929(paid). **Wire Service(s):** AP, LAT-WP, NYT, KR.

PETERSBURG

US

PROGRESS-INDEX. 1865. d. $9.50/mo. carrier; $12.10/mo. mailed in city; $13.50/mo. mailed out of city. 15 Franklin St. Petersburg, VA 23803. TEL 804-732-3456; FAX 804-861-9452. **Owner(s):** Thomson Newspapers, Inc., One Thorn Run Ctr., Ste. 500, 1187 Thorn Run Rd. Ext., Coraopolis, PA 15108. TEL 412-262-7870; Ed. Elizabeth Hedgepeth; Pub. George R. Fain; adv.; bk.rev.; pub. size: broadsheet; circ. evening 19,500(paid); Sun. 20,000(paid). **Wire Service(s):** AP.

Dailies

PULASKI

US

SOUTHWEST TIMES, THE. 1906. Sun.-Fri. $.35/day newsstand; $1/Sun.; $1.80/wk. carrier. 34 Fifth St., N.E., Pulaski, VA 24301. TEL 540-980-5220; FAX 540-980-3618. **Owner(s):** Southwest Publishers L.L.C., 34 Fifth St., Pulaski, VA 24301. TEL 540-980-5220; FAX 540-980-3618; Ed. Mike Williams; Pub. Syd M. Kibodeaux; adv. contact: Vickie Clayn. pub. size: broadsheet; circ. morning 6,100(paid); Sun. 6,700(paid). **Wire Service(s):** AP.

RICHMOND

US

RICHMOND TIMES-DISPATCH. 1850. d. $.50/day newsstand; $1.75/Sun.; $168/yr. carrier. 333 E. Grace St., Richmond, VA 23219. TEL 804-649-6000; FAX 804-775-8059. **Owner(s):** Media General, Inc., 411 E. Franklin St., Richmond, VA 23219-0001. TEL 804-649-6671; Ed. Louise Seals; Pub. J. Stewart Bryan III; adv.; photos; bk.rev.; pub. size: broadsheet; circ. morning 212,706(paid); Sun. 256,333(paid). **Wire Service(s):** AP, NYT, LAT-WP.

ROANOKE

US

ROANOKE TIMES, THE. 1886. d. $.35/day newsstand; $.50/Sun.; $2.40/wk. carrier. 201 W. Campbell Ave., Roanoke, VA 24011. TEL 540-981-3353; FAX 540-981-3318; E-mail: roatimes@infi.net; URL: http://www.infi.net/roatimes/index.html. **Owner(s):** Landmark Communications, Inc., 150 W. Brambleton Ave., P.O. Box 449, Norfolk, VA 23510. TEL 804-446-2000; adv. contact: Judith Perfater. photos; pub. size: broadsheet; circ. morning 115,644(paid); Sun. 126,444(paid). **Wire Service(s):** AP, LAT, WP,NYT,KRT.

    Formerly: Roanoke Times & World News.

STAUNTON

US   ISSN 0747-2501

DAILY NEWS LEADER, THE. 1904. d. $.35/day newsstand; $1/Sun.; $1.80/wk. home deliv.; $2.30/wk. mailed; $29.90/13 wks. mailed. 11 N. Central Ave., Staunton, VA 24401. TEL 540-885-7281; FAX 540-885-1094; E-mail: news@newsleader.com; URL: http://www.newleader.com/daily. **Owner(s):** Multimedia, Inc., P.O. Box 1688, Greenville, SC 29602; Ed. Rick Gunter; Pub. Wesley Wampler; adv. contact: Marty White. pub. size: broadsheet; circ. morning 18,956(paid); Sun. 23,000(paid). **Wire Service(s):** AP.

STRASBURG

US

NORTHERN VIRGINIA DAILY. 1932. Mon.-Sat. $.25 newsstand; $53/yr.; $49/yr. home deliv. 120 N. Holliday St., Strasburg, VA 22657. TEL 540-465-5137; FAX 540-465-9388. **Owner(s):** Shenandoah Publishing House, Inc., 120 N. Holliday St., Strasburg, VA 22657. TEL 703-405-5137; FAX 703-405-9388; Ed. Joe Strohmeyer. adv.; photos; pub. size: broadsheet; circ. morning 15,200(paid). **Wire Service(s):** AP.

SUFFOLK

US   ISSN 8750-9598

SUFFOLK NEWS-HERALD. 1873. Tue.-Sun. $.25/day newsstand; $.75/Sun.; $72.60/yr. in state. 130 S. Saratoga St., Suffolk, VA 23434. TEL 804-539-3437; FAX 804-539-8804. **Owner(s):** Media General, Inc., 411 E. Franklin St., Richmond, VA 23219. TEL 804-775-8030; Ed. Tim Copeland; Pub. Gaither Perry; adv. contact: Ernie Chenalt. photos; pub. size: broadsheet; circ. morning 4,200(paid); Sun. 4,300(paid).

WAYNESBORO

US   ISSN 8750-7862

WAYNESBORO NEWS-VIRGINIAN. 1892. Mon.-Sat. $.35 newsstand; $78/yr. mailed. 544 W. Main St., Waynesboro, VA 22980. TEL 703-949-8213; FAX 703-942-4542. **Owner(s):** Waynesboro Publishing Co., 544 W. Main St., Waynesboro, VA 22980. TEL 703-949-8213; Ed. Terry Smith; Pub. Wright M. Thomas; adv. contact: Harlan Phillips. pub. size: broadsheet; circ. evening 9,457(paid). **Wire Service(s):** AP.

WINCHESTER

US   ISSN 1064-0665

WINCHESTER STAR. Mon.-Sat. $.25 newsstand; $7/mo. local carrier; $58/yr. local. 2 N. Kent St., Winchester, VA 22601. TEL 540-667-3200; FAX 540-667-0012. **Owner(s):** Thomas T. Byrd, 2 N. Kent St., Winchester, VA 22601. TEL 703-667-3200; FAX 703-667-0012; Ed. Ron Morris; Pub. Thomas T. Byrd; adv. contact: Jerry Howard. pub. size: broadsheet; circ. evening 23,000(paid). **Wire Service(s):** AP, NYT.

WOODBRIDGE

US

POTOMAC NEWS. 1959. d. $.35 newsstand; $2.50/wk. 14010 Smoketown Rd., Woodbridge, VA 22193. TEL 703-878-8000; FAX 703-878-8099. **Owner(s):** Mid-State Newspapers, Inc., 14010 Smoketown Rd., Woodbridge, VA 22192. TEL 703-878-8000; Ed. Luke West; Pub. Andrew Mick; adv.; bk.rev.; pub. size: broadsheet; circ. morning 30,000(paid). **Wire Service(s):** AP, NYT, GNS.

WASHINGTON

ABERDEEN

US   ISSN 0740-3135

DAILY WORLD, THE. 0890. d. $.50/day newsstand; $.75/Sun.; $99/yr. 315 S. Michigan St., Aberdeen, WA 98520. TEL 206-532-4000; FAX 206-533-1328. **Owner(s):** Donrey Media Group, P.O. Box 17017, Fort Smith, AR 72902. TEL 501-785-7810; Ed. John C. Hughes; Pub. Ted Dixon; adv. contact: Theresa Wincewicz. photos; bk.rev.; pub. size: broadsheet; circ. evening 18,800(paid); Sun. 19,200(paid). **Wire Service(s):** AP.

BELLEVUE

US

JOURNAL AMERICAN. 1976. d. $8.50/mo. 1705 132nd St., N.E., Bellevue, WA 98005. TEL 206-455-2222; FAX 206-635-0603. **Owner(s):** Horvitz Newspapers, Inc., P.O. Box 90130, Bellevue, WA 98009; Ed. Tom Wolfe; Pub. Peter Horvitz; adv. contact: Hallie Olsen. pub. size: broadsheet; circ. morning 36,500(controlled & paid); Sun. 37,500(controlled & paid). **Wire Service(s):** AP.

BELLINGHAM

US

BELLINGHAM HERALD. 1890. d. $.35/day newsstand; $1.25/Sun.; $11.25/mo. carrier; $11.75/mo. motor rte. 1155 N. State St., Bellingham, WA 98225. TEL 360-676-2600; FAX 360-647-9260; E-mail: herald@az.com; URL: http://marie.az.com/~herald. **Owner(s):** Gannett Company, Inc., 1100 Wilson Blvd., Arlington, VA 22234. TEL 703-284-6000; Ed. Evan Miller; Pub. Robert Robbins; adv. contact: Gerry Rhea. pub. size: broadsheet; circ. evening 27,000(paid); Sun. 36,000(paid). **Wire Service(s):** AP, GNS.

BREMERTON

US   ISSN 1050-3692

SUN, THE. 1935. d. $.50/day newsstand; $1/Sun.; $102/yr. 545 Fifth St., Bremerton, WA 98337-0053. TEL 360-377-3711; FAX 360-479-7681; E-mail: mikepsun@aol.com. **Owner(s):** Scripps-Howard, 312 Walnut St., 28th Fl., Cincinnati, OH 45202. TEL 513-977-3000; Ed. Mike Phillips; Pub. Elizabeth F. Brenner; adv. contact: Earl Rush. photos; bk.rev.; pub. size: broadsheet; circ. morning 42,000(paid); Sun. 45,000(paid). **Wire Service(s):** AP, NYT, SHNA.

CENTRALIA

US

CHRONICLE, THE. 1889. Mon.-Sat. $.50 newsstand; $7/mo. 321 N. Pearl St., Centralia, WA 98531. TEL 360-736-3311; FAX 360-736-4796. **Owner(s):** Lafromboise Newspapers, Inc., 321 N. Pearl St., Centralia, WA 98531. TEL 206-736-3311; Ed. Sarah Jenkins; Pub. Dennis R. Waller; adv. contact: Tom May. photos; bk.rev.; pub. size: broadsheet; circ. evening 16,100(paid). **Wire Service(s):** AP.

    Formerly: Daily Chronicle, The.

ELLENSBURG

US

DAILY RECORD. 1909. Mon.-Sat. $.35 newsstand; $8.50/mo. in city; $15/mo. out of city. 401 N. Main St., Ellensburg, WA 98926-0248. TEL 509-925-1414; FAX 509-925-5696. **Owner(s):** McClatchy Newspapers, P.O. Box 15779, Sacramento, CA 95852. TEL 916-321-1000; Ed. Keith Love; Pub. Keith Love; adv. contact: Dave Martin. pub. size: broadsheet; circ. evening 6,000(paid). **Wire Service(s):** AP.

    Formerly: Ellensburg Daily Record.

EVERETT

US

HERALD, THE. 1891. d. $.35/day newsstand; $1.25/Sun.; $9/mo. 1213 California St., Everett, WA 98201. TEL 206-339-3000; FAX 206-339-3049. **Owner(s):** Washington Post Co., 1150 15th St., N.W., Washington, DC 20071. TEL 202-334-7100; Pub. Larry L. Hanson; photos; pub. size: broadsheet; circ. evening 53,000(paid); Sun. 64,953(paid). **Wire Service(s):** AP, NYT, LAT-WP.

KENNEWICK

US

TRI-CITY HERALD. 1947. d. $.50/day newsstand; $1.25/Sun.; $10.75/mo. 107 N. Cascade St., Kennewick, WA 99336. TEL 509-582-1500. E-mail: krobertson@tri-cityherald.com; URL: http://www.tri-cityherald.com. **Owner(s):** McClatchy Newspapers, P.O. Box 15779, Sacramento, CA 95852; Ed. Ken Robertson; Pub. Jack Briggs; adv. contact: Ellen Evans. photos; bk.rev.; pub. size: broadsheet; circ. morning 40,349(paid); Sun. 43,866(paid). **Wire Service(s):** AP, LAT-WP, McClatchy News Service, KR, NYT.

  Formerly: Pasco-Kennewick-Richland Tri-City Herald.

KENT

US   ISSN 0894-1610

VALLEY DAILY NEWS. Sun.-Fri. $.35/day newsstand; $1/Sun.; $9/4 wks.; $99/yr. 600 S. Washington, Kent, WA 98032. TEL 206-872-6600; FAX 206-854-1006; E-mail: valleyedit@aol.com. **Owner(s):** Horvitz Newspapers, Inc., 1705 132nd St., N.E., Belleview, WA 98005. TEL 206-453-4270; Ed. Dave Burch; Pub. John Perry; adv. contact: Rick Riegle. pub. size: broadsheet; circ. morning 33,000(paid); Sun. 34,000(paid).

  Formerly: Daily Globe News.

LONGVIEW

US   ISSN 0889-0005

DAILY NEWS. 1923. Mon.-Sat. $.50 newsstand; $8/mo. 770 11th Ave., Longview, WA 98632. TEL 360-577-2500; FAX 360-577-2538; E-mail: dnuz@aol.com; URL: http://www.tdn.com. **Owner(s):** Westmedia Corp., P.O. Box 189, Longview, WA 98632. TEL 360-577-2500; Ed. Robert Gaston; Pub. Ted M. Natt; pub. size: broadsheet; circ. evening 26,000(paid). **Wire Service(s):** AP.

MOSES LAKE

US   ISSN 1041-1658

COLUMBIA BASIN HERALD. Mon.-Fri. $.50 newsstand; $132/yr. in cy.; $138/yr. out of cy. 813 W. Third Ave., Moses Lake, WA 98837. TEL 509-765-4561; FAX 509-765-8659. **Owner(s):** Columbia Basin Publishing Co., Moses Lake, WA; Pub. Steve Hill; adv. contact: Steve Hill. pub. size: broadsheet; circ. evening 8,475(paid). **Wire Service(s):** AP.

MT. VERNON

US

SKAGIT VALLEY HERALD. 1884. Mon.-Sat. $.50 newsstand; $8.75/mo. 1000 E. College Way, Mt. Vernon, WA 98273-0578. TEL 206-424-3251; FAX 206-424-5300. **Owner(s):** Skagit Valley Publishing Co., P.O. Box 578, Mt. Vernon, WA 98273. TEL 360-424-3251; FAX 360-424-5300; Ed. Nancy Erickson; Pub. L. Stedem Wood; adv.; photos; bk.rev.; pub. size: broadsheet; circ. evening 20,647(paid). **Wire Service(s):** AP.

OLYMPIA

US   ISSN 0746-7575

OLYMPIAN, THE. 1889. d. $.35/day newsstand; $1.50/Sun.; $13.25/mo. carrier; $13.75/mo. motor rte. 1268 E. Fourth Ave., Olympia, WA 98506. TEL 360-754-5400; FAX 360-754-4221; E-mail: olympian@halcyon.com; URL: http://www.halcyon.com/olympian. **Owner(s):** Gannett Company, Inc., 1100 Wilson Blvd., Arlington, VA 22234. TEL 703-284-6000; Pub. Fred Hamilton; adv. contact: Dan Walker. pub. size: broadsheet; circ. morning 36,000(paid); Sun. 45,800(paid). **Wire Service(s):** AP, GNS.

PORT ANGELES

US   ISSN 1050-7000

PENINSULA DAILY NEWS. 1916. d. $.35/day newsstand; $1.25/Sun.; $8.75/mo. carrier; $9.75/mo. motor rte. 305 W. First St., Port Angeles, WA 98362. TEL 360-452-2345; FAX 360-417-3521; E-mail: pdnedit@aol.com. **Owner(s):** Horvitz Newspapers, Inc., P.O. Box 90130, Bellevue, WA 98009; Ed. Frank Ducceschi; Pub. Frank Ducceschi; adv. contact: John Huston. photos; pub. size: broadsheet; circ. evening 15,000(paid); Sun. 17,000(paid). **Wire Service(s):** AP.

SEATTLE

US

SEATTLE DAILY JOURNAL OF COMMERCE. 1893. Mon.-Sat. $1.25 newsstand; $190/yr. 83 Columbia St., Seattle, WA 98104. TEL 206-622-8272; FAX 206-622-8416. **Owner(s):** Daily Journal of Commerce, Inc., 83 Columbia St., Seattle, WA 98111. TEL 206-622-8272; Ed. Phil Brown; Pub. M.E. Brown; adv. contact: John Mihalyo. pub. size: broadsheet; circ. morning 6,544(paid). **Wire Service(s):** AP & Business Wire.

US

SEATTLE POST-INTELLIGENCER. 1863. d. $.35 newsstand; $1.50/Sun.; $10/mo. home deliv.; $2.50/wk. King, Shuhomish, Pierce & Kitsap cys.; $2.71/wk. elsewhere. 101 Elliott Ave., W., Seattle, WA 98119-4220. TEL 206-448-8000; FAX 206-448-8166. **Owner(s):** Hearst Corp., 959 Eighth Ave., New York, NY 10019. TEL 212-649-2000; Ed. Kenneth Bunting; Pub. J.D. Alexander; adv.; photos; bk.rev. pub. size: broadsheet; circ. morning 203,000(paid); Sun. 506,216(paid). **Wire Service(s):** AP, COX, NYT, HHS, RN, SHNS.

SEATTLE TIMES

US   ISSN 0745-9696

SEATTLE TIMES. 1896. d. $.35/day newsstand; $1.85/Sun.; $10/mo. carrier; $102/yr. 1120 John St., Seattle, WA 98109. TEL 206-464-2111; FAX 206-464-2261. **Owner(s):** Seattle Times Co., P.O. Box 70, Seattle, WA 98111. TEL 206-464-2111; Ed. Alex MacLeod; Pub. Michael Lemke; adv. contact: Michael Lemke. photos; pub. size: broadsheet; circ. morning 232,906(paid); Sun. 506,216(paid). **Wire Service(s):** AF, DJ, KNS, LAT-WP, CT-NYT.

SPOKANE

US

SPOKESMAN-REVIEW, THE. 1883. d. $.50/day newsstand; $1.50/Sun.; $12/mo. 999 W. Riverside Ave., Spokane, WA 99201. TEL 509-459-5000; FAX 509-459-5258; E-mail: editor@spokesman.com; URL: http://www.virtuallynw.com. **Owner(s):** Cowles Publishing Co., Review Tower, 999 W. Riverside Ave., Spokane, WA 99201. TEL 509-459-5000; FAX 509-459-5258; Ed. Chris Peck. adv.; pub. size: broadsheet; circ. morning 125,000(paid); Sun. 150,000(paid). **Wire Service(s):** AP, NYT, KR, McClatchy.

SUNNYSIDE

US   ISSN 1046-1612

DAILY SUN-NEWS. 1962. Mon.-Fri. $.35 newsstand; $4/mo. carrier; $48/yr. mailed in cy.; $50/yr. out of cy. 520 S. Seventh, Sunnyside, WA 98944. TEL 509-837-4500; FAX 509-837-6397. **Owner(s):** Eagle Newspapers, Inc., P.O. Box 12008, Salem, OR 97309. TEL 503-393-1774; FAX 503-463-9898; Ed. Olaf Elze; Pub. Tom Lanctot; adv. contact: Bob Dedolph. photos; bk.rev.; pub. size: tabloid; circ. evening 4,033(free & paid).

TACOMA

US   ISSN 1042-3621

NEWS TRIBUNE, THE. 1883. d. $.35/day newsstand; $1.50/Sun.; $10.50/mo carrier. 1950 S. State St., Tacoma, WA 98405-2830. TEL 205-597-8742; FAX 206-597-8274; E-mail: leted@p.tribnet.com; URL: http://www.tribnet.com/. **Owner(s):** McClatchy Newspapers, P.O. Box 15779, Sacramento, CA 95852. TEL 916-321-1000. Pub. Kelso Gillenwater; adv. contact: Cathy Brewis. photos; pub. size: standard; circ. morning 128,659(paid); Sun. 146,512(paid). **Wire Service(s):** AP, NYT, LAT, KNT, SHNS.

  Formerly: The Morning News Tribune.

VANCOUVER

US   ISSN 1043-4151

COLUMBIAN, THE. 1890. Sun.-Fri. $.50/day newsstand; $1.50/Sun.; $10/mo. home deliv.; $11/mo. motor rte.; $20/mo. mailed. 701 W. Eighth St., Vancouver, WA 98660-0180. TEL 360-694-3391; FAX 360-699-6033; E-mail: editors@columbian.com; URL: http://www.columbian.com. **Owner(s):** Scott Campbell, P.O. Box 180, Vancouver WA 98660. TEL 360-694-3391; FAX 360-699-6033; Ed. Tom Koenninger; Pub. Scott Campbell; adv. contact: Susan Hirtzel. photos; bk.rev.; pub. size: standard; circ. evening 56,500(paid); Sun. 66,000(paid). **Wire Service(s):** AP, LAT-WP.

WALLA WALLA

US

WALLA WALLA UNION-BULLETIN. 1968. Sun.-Fri. $.50/day newsstand; $1/Sun.; $7.50/mo. 112 S. First St., Walla Walla, WA 99362. TEL 509-525-3300; FAX 509-525-1232. **Owner(s):** Seattle Times Co., P.O. Box 1358, Walla Walla, WA 99362. TEL 509-525-3300; Ed. Rick Doyle; Pub. Debbie Frol; adv. contact: Carl Tyler. pub. size: broadsheet; circ. evening 16,000(paid); Sun. 16,300(paid). **Wire Service(s):** LAT-WP.

WENATCHEE

US

WENATCHEE WORLD. 1905. Mon.-Sat. $.50/day newsstand; $1.50/Sun.; $9.50/mo. 14 N. Mission, Wenatchee, WA 98801. TEL 509-663-5161; FAX 509-662-5413. **Owner(s):** World Publishing Co., 14 N. Mission, Wenatchee, WA 98807; Ed. Steve Lachowictz; Pub. Wilfred R. Woods; adv. contact: Jay White. pub. size: broadsheet; circ. evening 30,107(paid); Sun. 33,201(paid). **Wire Service(s):** AP.

YAKIMA

US

YAKIMA HERALD-REPUBLIC. 1903. d. $.50/day newsstand; $1.25/Sun.; $9.50/mo. carrier. 114 N. Fourth St., Yakima, WA 98901. TEL 509-248-1251; FAX 509-577-7765. **Owner(s):** Seattle Times Co., P.O. Box 70, Seattle, WA 98111; Ed. Kathleen Gilligan; Pub. Charles Cochrane, Jr.; adv. contact: Brian Vaillancourt. pub. size: standard; circ. morning 41,500(paid); Sun. 45,000(paid). **Wire Service(s):** UPI, AP, KR.

WEST VIRGINIA

BECKLEY

US   ISSN 0746-6854

REGISTER/HERALD. 1893. d. $.50/day newsstand; $1.25/Sun.; $11.95/mo. carrier. 801 N. Kanawha St., Beckley, WV 25801. TEL 304-255-4400; FAX 304-255-4427. **Owner(s):** Thomson Newspapers, Inc., 3150 Des Plaines Ave., Des Plaines, IL 60018. TEL 708-299-5544; Ed. Pat Hanna; Pub. Robert R. Hammond; adv. contact: Jack L. Scott. pub. size: broadsheet; circ. morning 33,500(paid); Sun. 34,500(paid). **Wire Service(s):** AP.

BLUEFIELD

US

BLUEFIELD DAILY TELEGRAPH. 1893. d. $.50/day newsstand; $1.25/Sun.; $11.25/mo. carrier; $13.50/mo. mailed in cy. 928 Bluefield Ave., Bluefield, WV 24701. TEL 304-327-2811; FAX 304-327-6179; E-mail: editor@bdtonline.com; URL: http://www.bdtonline.com. **Owner(s):** Thomson Newspapers, Inc., 3150 Des Plaines Ave., Des Plaines, IL 60018. TEL 708-299-5544; Ed. Tom Colley; Pub. Steve Smith; adv. contact: Terri Hale. pub. size: broadsheet; circ. morning 25,500(paid); Sun. 27,000(paid). **Wire Service(s):** AP.

CHARLESTON

US

CHARLESTON DAILY MAIL. 1920. d. $.50/day newsstand; $1.25/Sun.; $135.20/yr. 1001 E. Virginia St., Charleston, WV 25301. TEL 304-348-5140; FAX 304-348-4847. **Owner(s):** Thomson Newspapers, Inc., One Thorn Run Ctr., Ste. 500, 1187 Thorn Run Rd. Ext., Coraopolis, PA 15108. TEL 412-262-7870; Ed. Larry Aldridge; Pub. David Greenfield; adv. contact: Larry Levak. photos; pub. size: broadsheet; circ. evening 46,460(paid); Sun. 105,257(paid). **Wire Service(s):** AP, LAT-WP.

US

CHARLESTON GAZETTE, THE. 1872. d. $.50/day newsstand; $1.25/Sun.; $117/yr. carrier. 1001 Virginia St., E., Charleston, WV 25301. TEL 304-348-5100; FAX 304-348-1233. **Owner(s):** Daily Gazette Co., Inc., 1001 Virginia St., E., Charleston, WV 25301. TEL 304-348-5140; Ed. James A. Haught; Pub. Craig Selby; adv. contact: Larry Levak. photos; bk.rev.; pub. size: broadsheet; circ. morning 53,000(paid); Sun. 103,000(paid). **Wire Service(s):** NYT, AP.

CLARKSBURG

US

CLARKSBURG EXPONENT. 1927. Tue.-Sun. $.35/day newsstand; $1/Sun.; $124.80/yr. carrier. 324 Hewes Ave., Clarksburg, WV 26301. TEL 304-624-6411; FAX 304-622-3629. **Owner(s):** Clarksburg Publishing Co., 324 Hewes Ave., P.O. Box 2000, Clarksburg, WV 26301. TEL 304-624-6411; Ed. Edwin Sweeney; Pub. Cecil B. Highland, Jr.; adv. contact: Jack L. Smith. pub. size: oversize; circ. morning 6,719(paid); Sun. 24,132(paid). **Wire Service(s):** AP.

US

CLARKSBURG TELEGRAM. 1906. d. $.35/day newsstand; $1/Sun.; $140.40/yr. carrier. 324 Hewes Ave., Clarksburg, WV 26301. TEL 304-624-6411; FAX 304-622-3629. **Owner(s):** Cecil Highland, 324 Hewes Ave., Clarksburg, WV 26301. TEL 304-624-6411; Ed. Robert F. Stealey; Pub. Cecil Highland, Jr.; adv. contact: Jack L. Smith. pub. size: broadsheet; circ. evening 14,966; Sun. 24,132(paid).

ELKINS

US

INTER-MOUNTAIN, THE. 1893. Mon.-Sat. $.35 newsstand; $.50 Sat.; $81/yr. 520 Railroad Ave., Elkins, WV 26241. TEL 304-636-2121; FAX 304-636-8252. **Owner(s):** Ogden Newspapers, Inc., 1500 Main St., Wheeling, WV 26003. TEL 304-233-0100; Ed. Frank Robinson; Pub. James Hoffman; adv. contact: Michael Duplaga. pub. size: broadsheet; circ. evening 12,700(paid). **Wire Service(s):** AP.

FAIRMONT

US

TIMES WEST VIRGINIAN. 1845. d. $.50/day newsstand; $1.25/Sun.; $145.60/yr. Quincy & Ogden Sts., Fairmont, WV 26554. TEL 304-367-2500; FAX 304-367-2569; E-mail: timeswv@timeswv.com; URL: http://www.timeswv.com. **Owner(s):** Thomson Newspapers, Inc., 3150 Des Plaines Ave., Des Plaines, IL 60018. TEL 708-299-5544; Ed. Valerie Nieman; Pub. Frank Wood; adv. contact: Carolyn S. Hatting. pub. size: broadsheet; circ. morning 14,836(paid); Sun. 15,459(paid). **Wire Service(s):** AP.

HUNTINGTON

US

HUNTINGTON HERALD-DISPATCH. 1889. d. $.50/day newsstand; $1.50/Sun.; $14.08/mo. home deliv. 946 Fifth Ave., Huntington, WV 25701. TEL 304-526-4000; FAX 304-526-2857; E-mail: hdonline@access.eve.net. **Owner(s):** Gannett Company, Inc., 1100 Wilson Blvd., Arlington, VA 22234. TEL 703-284-6000; adv.; pub. size: broadsheet; circ. morning 38,516(paid); Sun. 44,087(paid). **Wire Service(s):** AP, GNS.

KEYSER

US

MINERAL DAILY TRIBUNE. Mon.-Sat. $.30 newsstand; $6.19/mo. in cy. carrier; $6.65/mo. mailed. 24 Armstong, Keyser, WV 26726. TEL 304-788-3333; FAX 304-788-3398. **Owner(s):** James Tetrick, 24 Armstrong, Keyser, WV 26726. TEL 304-788-3333; adv. contact: Robert Tetrick. pub. size: broadsheet; circ. morning 5,200(paid). **Wire Service(s):** AP.

LEWISBURG

US

WEST VIRGINIA DAILY NEWS. Mon.-Fri. $.25 newsstand; $72.08/yr. in state; $70/yr. out of state. 200 S. Court St., Lewisburg, WV 24901-0471. TEL 304-645-1206; FAX 304-645-7104. **Owner(s):** Moffitt Newspapers, Inc., P.O. Box 8565, Roanoke, VA 24014. TEL 703-344-2489; Ed. Tina Alvey; Pub. Frank Spicer; adv. contact: Judy Dowdy. photos; pub. size: broadsheet; circ. evening 4,000(paid).

LOGAN

US   ISSN 0746-0570

LOGAN BANNER. 1888. Sun.-Fri. $.50/day newsstand; $1/Sun.; $84/yr. carrier; $121/yr. mailed. 435 Stratton St., Logan, WV 25601. TEL 304-752-6950; FAX 304-752-1239. **Owner(s):** Logan Media, Inc., 435 Stratton St., Logan, WV 25601. TEL 304-752-6950; Ed. Jack McNelly; Pub. Richard Osbourne; adv. contact: Kathy Chafin. pub. size: broadsheet; circ. morning 10,000(paid); Sun. 10,000(paid). **Wire Service(s):** AP.

MARTINSBURG

US

JOURNAL, THE. 1927. d. $96/yr. local; $102/yr. mailed. 207 W. King St., Martinsburg, WV 25401. TEL 304-263-8931; FAX 304-263-8058. **Owner(s):** Ogden Newspapers, Inc., 1500 Main St., Wheeling, WV 26003. TEL 304-233-0100; Ed. William Dolittle. adv. contact: James Connors. pub. size: broadsheet; circ. morning 17,796(paid); Sun. 19,363(paid). **Wire Service(s):** UPI.
   Formerly: Evening Journal/Weekend Journal.

MORGANTOWN

US

DOMINION POST, THE. 1873. d. $.50/day newsstand; $1.25/Sun.; $156.31/yr. carrier. 1251 Earl Core Rd., Morgantown, WV 26505-6298. TEL 304-292-6301; FAX 304-291-2326. **Owner(s):** Richard G., John R., David A. Raese, 1251 Earl Core Rd., Morgantown, WV 26505. TEL 304-292-6301; FAX 304-291-2326; Ed. Ralph Brem; Pub. David Raese; adv.; pub. size: broadsheet; circ. morning 20,150(paid); Sun. 27,806(paid). **Wire Service(s):** AP.

MOUNDSVILLE

US

MOUNDSVILLE DAILY ECHO. 1891. d. $.15 newsstand; $30/yr. 713 Lafayette, Moundsville, WV 26041. TEL 304-845-2660; FAX 304-845-2661. **Owner(s):** Charles L. Walton, 713 Lafayette, Moundsville, WV 26041. TEL 304-845-2660; FAX 304-845-2661; Pub. Charles & Marian Walton; adv.; photos; pub. size: broadsheet; circ. evening 4,680(paid). **Wire Service(s):** AP.

PARKERSBURG

US   ISSN 8750-3956

PARKERSBURG SENTINEL. 1875. d. $.50/newsstand; $1/Sun.; $190.86/yr. mailed. 519 Juliana St., Parkersburg, WV 26101. TEL 304-485-1891; FAX 304-422-7134. **Owner(s):** Ogden Newspapers, Inc., 1500 Main St., Wheeling, WV 26003. TEL 304-233-0100; Ed. David Owen; Pub. Ed Kruger; adv. contact: Ed Hoffman. photos; bk.rev.; pub. size: broadsheet; circ. morning 23,400(paid); evening 10,800(paid); Sun. 43,600(paid). **Wire Service(s):** AP.
   Formerly: Parkersburg News Sentinel.

POINT PLEASANT

US

POINT PLEASANT REGISTER. Mon.-Sat. $.35 newsstand; $1.60/wk. 200 Main St., Point Pleasant, WV 25550. TEL 304-675-1333; FAX 304-675-5234. **Owner(s):** Ohio Valley Publishing Co., P.O. Box 1688, Greenville, SC 29602; Pub. Robert L. Wingett; adv. contact: Brian Billings. photos; bk.rev.; pub. size: standard; circ. evening 5,993(paid). **Wire Service(s):** AP.

WEIRTON

US

WEIRTON DAILY TIMES. 1928. d. $96.20/yr. 114 Lee Ave., Weirton, WV 26062. TEL 304-748-0606; FAX 304-748-2202. **Owner(s):** Thomson Newspapers, Inc., 3150 Des Plaines Ave., Des Plaines, IL 60018. TEL 708-299-5544; Ed. Chuck Massaro; Pub. Bob Dunn; photos; pub. size: broadsheet; circ. evening 9,000(paid). **Wire Service(s):** AP, SHNA, Thomson.

WELCH

US

WELCH DAILY NEWS. 1923. Mon.-Fri. $.30 newsstand; $75/yr. 125 Wyoming St., Welch, WV 24801. TEL 304-436-3144; FAX 304-436-3146. **Owner(s):** Jack Moffitt, 125 Wyoming St., Welch, VA 24804. TEL 304-436-3144; Ed. Mary Stillwell; Pub. W.A. Johnson; adv. contact: Vance Hayes. pub. size: broadsheet; circ. morning 6,000(paid). **Wire Service(s):** UPI.

WHEELING

US

MORNING INTELLIGENCER, THE. 1852. d. $.35/day newsstand; $1/Sun; $8/mo. carrier. 1500 Main St., Wheeling, WV 26003. TEL 304-233-0100; FAX 304-233-5718. **Owner(s):** Ogden Newspapers, Inc., 1500 Main St., Wheeling, WV 26003. TEL 304-233-0100; Ed. Bob Kelly. adv.; pub. size: broadsheet; circ. morning 23,300(paid); Sun. 54,900(paid). **Wire Service(s):** UPI.

WHEELING NEWS-REGISTER. 1890. Sun.-Fri. $.50/day newsstand; $.75/Sun.; $8/mo. carrier; $106/yr. Mon.-Sat. mailed; $57/yr. Sun. mailed. 1500 Main St., Wheeling, WV 26003. TEL 304-233-0100; FAX 304-233-0827. **Owner(s):** Ogden Newspapers, Inc., 1500 Main St., Wheeling, WV 26003. TEL 304-233-0100; Pub. G. Ogden Nutting; adv. contact: Robert H. Diehl. photos; bk.rev.; pub. size: broadsheet; circ. evening 21,300(paid); Sun. 54,900(paid). **Wire Service(s):** AP.

WILLIAMSON

US   ISSN 0883-1602

WILLIAMSON DAILY NEWS. 1904. Mon.-Sat. $.50 newsstand; $37.44/13 wks.; $68.64/26 wks. 100 Block E. Third Ave., Williamson, WV 25661. TEL 304-235-4242; FAX 304-235-0730. **Owner(s):** Williamson Daily News, Inc., Box 1660, Williamson, WV 25661. TEL 304-235-4242; Ed. Terry Richardson; Pub. Donald Wilder; adv. contact: Lisa Marcum. pub. size: broadsheet; circ. evening 11,000(paid). **Wire Service(s):** AP.

WISCONSIN

ANTIGO

US

ANTIGO DAILY JOURNAL. 1905. Mon.-Sat. $73.95/yr. in cy.; $103.40/yr. mailed. 612 Superior St., Antigo, WI 54409-2086. TEL 715-623-4191. FAX 715-623-4193. **Owner(s):** Berner Bros. Publishing Co., Inc., 612 Superior St., Antigo, WI 54409. TEL 715-623-4191; FAX 715-623-4193; Ed. Fred A. Berner; Pub. Marie F. Berner; adv.; photos; bk.rev.; pub. size: standard; circ. evening 7,000(paid). **Wire Service(s):** AP.

APPLETON

US

POST-CRESCENT. 1853. d. $.50/day newsstand; $1.50/Sun.; $.82/yr. carrier; $195/yr. mtr. rte.; $234/yr. mailed. 306 W. Washington St., Appleton, WI 54911. TEL 414-733-4411; FAX 414-733-1945. **Owner(s):** Thomson Newspapers, Inc., 3150 Des Plaines Ave., Des Plaines, IL 60018. TEL 708-299-5544; Ed. William Knutson; Pub. Donald Kampfer; adv. contact: Joel Morse. photos; pub. size: broadsheet; circ. evening 61,580(paid); Sun. 76,406(paid). **Wire Service(s):** AP, SHFS, Thomson News Service.

ASHLAND

US   ISSN 1050-4095

DAILY PRESS, THE. 1888. Mon.-Sat. $.50 newsstand; $8.50/mo. carrier. 122 W. Third St., Ashland, WI 54806. TEL 715-682-2313; FAX 715-682-4699; E-mail: ashpress@win.bright.net; URL: http://badger.win.bright.net/~wgcs/ashpress/adphome.htm. **Owner(s):** Morgan Murphy Newspapers, Inc., 1226 Ogden Ave., Superior, WI 54880. TEL 715-394-4411; Pub. John Murphy; adv. contact: Jeff Swiston. photos; bk.rev.; pub. size: broadsheet; circ. morning 7,900(paid). **Wire Service(s):** AP.

BARABOO

US

BARABOO NEWS-REPUBLIC. 1855. Sun.-Fri. $.50/day newsstand; $.75/Sun.; $8/mo. carrier; $92/yr. in state; $109.25/yr. out of state. 219 First St., Baraboo, WI 53913. TEL 608-356-4808; FAX 608-356-0344. **Owner(s):** Independent Media Group, Watseka, IL; Ed. Richard Pratt; Pub. David W. Gentry; adv. contact: Guy Beasley. photos; pub. size: standard; circ. morning 20,093(paid); evening 4,000(paid); Sun. 20,293(paid). **Wire Service(s):** AP.

BEAVER DAM

US   ISSN 0749-1379

BEAVER DAM DAILY CITIZEN. 1856. Mon.-Sat. $92.40/yr. 805 Park Ave. Beaver Dam, WI 53916. TEL 414-887-0321; FAX 414-887-8790. **Owner(s):** Citizen Publishing Co., 805 Park Ave., Beaver Dam, WI 53916. TEL 414-887-0321; FAX 414-887-8190; Ed. Jeff Hovind; Pub. James E. Comey; adv. contact: Steve Ciccantelli. pub. size: broadsheet; circ. evening 11,143(paid). **Wire Service(s):** AP, NYT.

BELOIT

US

BELOIT DAILY NEWS. 1892. Mon.-Sat. $.50 newsstand; $10.50/mo. 149 State St., Beloit, WI 53511. TEL 608-365-8811; FAX 608-365-1420. **Owner(s):** Greater Beloit Publishing Co., 149 State St., Beloit, WI 53511. TEL 608-368-8811; Ed. William Barth; Pub. Kent Eymann; adv. contact: John Wingate. pub. size: broadsheet; circ. evening 15,450(paid). **Wire Service(s):** AP.

CHIPPEWA FALLS

US   ISSN 8756-2960

CHIPPEWA HERALD-TELEGRAM. 1879. Sat.-Thu. $.50/day newsstand; $1/Sun.; $101/yr. local. 321 Frenette Dr., Chippewa Falls, WI 54729. TEL 715-723-5515; FAX 715-723-9644. **Owner(s):** Independent Media Group, 321 Frenette, Chippewa Falls, WI 54729; adv. contact: Andrew Burns. pub. size: broadsheet; circ. evening 7,500(free & paid); Sun. 20,000(free & paid). **Wire Service(s):** AP.

EAU CLAIRE

US   ISSN 0891-0227

LEADER-TELEGRAM. 1881. d. $.50 newsstand; $2.60/wk. 701 S. Farwell, Eau Claire, WI 54701. TEL 715-834-3471; FAX 715-833-9244; E-mail: leadertele@aol.com. **Owner(s):** Eau Claire Press Co., 701 S. Farwell St., Eau Claire, WI 54701. TEL 715-833-9208; Ed. Gene Ringhand; Pub. Charles Graaskamp; adv. contact: Jerry Merryfield. pub. size: standard; circ. morning 36,744(paid); evening 31,771(paid); Sun. 41,496(paid). **Wire Service(s):** AP, NYT, SH.

FOND DU LAC

US

REPORTER, THE. 1870. Sun-Fri. $.50 newsstand; $1.25 Sun.; $156/yr. 33 W. Second St., Fond Du Lac, WI 54935. TEL 414-922-4600; FAX 414-922-5388. **Owner(s):** Thomson Newspapers, Inc., 65 Queen St., Toronto, ON M5H 2M8, Canada; Ed. Richard Roesgen; Pub. Larry Antony; adv. contact: Doug Rankin. pub. size: broadsheet; circ. evening 21,000(paid); Sun. 22,000(paid). **Wire Service(s):** AP, TNS, SHNA.
    Formerly: Fond Du Lac Reporter.

FORT ATKINSON

US

DAILY JEFFERSON COUNTY UNION. 1870. Mon.-Fri. $.50 newsstand; $65/yr. 28 W. Milwaukee Ave., Fort Atkinson, WI 53538. TEL 414-563-5551; FAX 414-563-7298. **Owner(s):** W.D. Hoard & Sons Co., 28 Milwaukee Ave., W., Fort Atkinson, WI 53538. TEL 414-563-5551; Ed. Christine Spanger; Pub. B.V. Knox; adv. contact: Charles Frandson. photos; bk.rev.; pub. size: broadsheet; circ. evening 9,000(paid). **Wire Service(s):** AP.

GREEN BAY

US

GREEN BAY NEWS-CHRONICLE. 1972. Sun.-Fri. $.50 newsstand; $2/wk. 133 S. Monroe, Green Bay, WI 54301. TEL 414-432-2941; FAX 414-432-8581. **Owner(s):** Brown County Publishing Co., P.O. Box 2467, Green Bay, WI 54306. TEL 414-432-2941; Ed. Ronald Poppenhagen; Pub. Frank A. Wood; adv.; pub. size: tabloid, sun.: broadsheet; circ. morning 10,000(paid); Sun. 65,000(free). **Wire Service(s):** UPI, NYT, LAT-WP.

US

GREEN BAY PRESS-GAZETTE. 1915. d. $.35/day newsstand; $1.50/Sun.; $3.25/wk. 435 E. Walnut St., Green Bay, WI 54301. TEL 414-435-4411; FAX 414-431-8379. **Owner(s):** Gannett Company, Inc., 1100 Wilson Blvd., Arlington, VA 22234. TEL 703-284-6000; Ed. Laurie Holloway; Pub. William T. Nusbaum; adv.; photos; pub. size: broadsheet; circ. evening 61,000(paid); Sun. 86,000(paid). **Wire Service(s):** AP, GNS, KRT.

JANESVILLE

US

JANESVILLE GAZETTE. 1845. d. $.50 newsstand; $176.80/yr. One S. Parker Dr., Janesville, WI 53547. TEL 608-754-3311; FAX 608-754-8038. **Owner(s):** Bliss Communications, Inc., P.O. Box 5001, Janesville, WI 53547-5001. TEL 608-754-3311; FAX 608-754-8038; Ed. Grant Vander Velden; Pub. Sidney H. Bliss; adv.; photos; bk.rev.; pub. size: broadsheet; circ. evening 26,990(paid); Sun. 27,876(paid). **Wire Service(s):** AP.

KENOSHA

US

KENOSHA NEWS. 1894. d. $.50 newsstand; $3.50/wk. 715 58th St., Kenosha, WI 53141. TEL 414-657-1000; FAX 414-657-5101; E-mail: knews@acroment.net. **Owner(s):** United Communications Corp., 715 58th St., Kenosha, WI 53140. TEL 414-657-1000; Ed. James Meyers; Pub. Howard J. Brown; adv. contact: Frank Misureli. pub. size: broadsheet; circ. evening 31,500(paid); Sun. 31,500(paid). **Wire Service(s):** AP, LAT-WP.
    Formerly: Kenosha Evening News.

LA CROSSE

US   ISSN 0745-9793

LA CROSSE TRIBUNE. 4904. d. $.50/day newsstand; $1.75/Sun.; $208/yr. carrier; $221/yr. motor rte. 401 N. Third St., La Crosse, WI 54601. TEL 608-782-9710; FAX 608-782-8540. **Owner(s):** Lee Enterprises, Inc., 130 E. Second St., Davenport, IA 52801. TEL 319-383-2100; Ed. David Stoeffler; Pub. Jim Santori; adv. contact: Tom Kelley. pub. size: broadsheet; circ. morning 35,500(paid); Sun. 42,500(paid). **Wire Service(s):** AP, KR, SHNA.

MADISON

US   ISSN 0749-4068

CAPITAL TIMES, THE. 1917. Mon.-Sat. $.50 newsstand; $2.15/wk. carrier; $2.50/wk. mailed. 1901 Fish Hatchery Rd., Madison, WI 53713. TEL 608-252-6400; FAX 608-252-6445; E-mail: tctvoice@captimes.madison.com; URL: http://www.madison.com. **Owner(s):** Capital Times Co., 1901 Fish Hatchery Rd., Madison, WI 53713. TEL 608-252-6200; Ed. Dave Zweifel. pub. size: broadsheet; circ. evening 23,744(paid). Wire Service(s): AP, LAT-WP, SHNA.

US

WISCONSIN STATE JOURNAL. 1901. d. $.50/day newsstand; $1.75/Sun.; $95/yr.; $163/yr. motor rte. 1901 Fish Hatchery Rd., Madison, WI 53713. TEL 608-252-6100; FAX 608-252-6119. **Owner(s):** Lee Enterprises, Inc., 400 Putnam Bldg., 215 N. Main St., Davenport, IA 52801-1924. TEL 319-383-2100; Ed. Frank Denton; Pub. Phil Blake; adv.; pub. size: broadsheet; circ. morning 86,585(paid); Sun. 163,096(paid). **Wire Service(s):** AP, NYT, KR.

MANITOWOC

US

MANITOWOC HERALD-TIMES REPORTER. 1875. d. $.50/day newsstand; $1.25/Sun.; $144.40/yr. in city. 902 Franklin St., Manitowoc, WI 54220-0790. TEL 414-684-4433; FAX 414-684-4416. **Owner(s):** Thomson Newspapers, Inc., 3150 Des Plaines Ave., Des Plaines, IL 60018. TEL 708-299-5544; pub. size: broadsheet; circ. evening 19,000(paid); Sun. 18,500(paid). **Wire Service(s):** AP.

MARINETTE

US

EAGLE-HERALD. 1871. Mon.-Sat. $.50 newsstand; $9.50/mo. 1809-27 Dunlap Ave., Marinette, WI 54143. TEL 715-735-6611; FAX 715-735-7580. **Owner(s):** Eagle-Herald Publishing LLC, 1809-27 Dunlap Ave., Marinette, WI 54143; Ed. Terri Lescelius; Pub. Dennis Colling; pub. size: broadsheet; circ. evening 9,000(paid).
    Formerly: Marinette Eagle-Star & Menominee Herald Leader.

MARSHFIELD

US

MARSHFIELD NEWS HERALD. 1927. Mon.-Sat. $.35 newsstand; $.50/weekend; $79/yr. city. 111 W. Third St., Marshfield, WI 54449. TEL 715-384-3131; FAX 715-387-4175. **Owner(s):** Ogden Newspapers, Inc., 1500 Main St., Wheeling, WV; Ed. William R. Heath; Pub. James V. Eykyn; adv. contact: Karen Olson. photos; bk.rev.; pub. size: broadsheet; circ. evening 15,800(paid). **Wire Service(s):** AP.

MILWAUKEE

US   ISSN 1052-4452

MILWAUKEE JOURNAL-SENTINEL. 1882. d. $.50/day newsstand; $1.50/Sun. 333 W. State St., Milwaukee, WI 53203. TEL 414-224-2000; FAX 414-224-2047; E-mail: adrep@onwis.com; URL: http://www.onwis.com/. **Owner(s):** Journal Communications, Inc., 333 W. State St., Milwaukee, WI 53203. TEL 414-224-2000; Ed. Martin Kaiser; Pub. Keith Spore; adv.; photos; bk.rev.; pub. size: broadsheet; circ. morning 272,454(paid); Sun. 462,168(paid). **Wire Service(s):** AP, NYT, LAT-WP.
    Formerly: Milwaukee Sentinel.

MONROE

US   ISSN 1068-5820

MONROE TIMES, THE. 1898. Mon.-Sat. $.50 newsstand; $106.21/yr. 1065 Fourth Ave., W., Monroe, WI 53566. TEL 608-328-4202; FAX 608-328-4217. **Owner(s):** Monroe Publishing Co., Inc., 1065 Fourth Ave., W., Monroe, WI 53566. TEL 608-328-4202; Ed. Judie Hintzman. adv.; photos; pub. size: broadsheet; circ. evening 7,136(paid). **Wire Service(s):** AP.
    Formerly: Monroe Evening Times.

OSHKOSH

US

OSHKOSH NORTHWESTERN. 1868. d. $.50/day newsstand; $1.50/Sun. 224 State St., Oshkosh, WI 54903. TEL 414-235-7700; FAX 414-235-1316. **Owner(s):** Oshkosh Northwestern Co., 224 State St., Oshkosh, WI 54901. TEL 414-235-7700; Pub. Russell F. Sprung; adv. contact: Jim Sprung. pub. size: broadsheet; circ. morning 26,500(paid); Sun. 28,500(paid). **Wire Service(s):** AP.

PORTAGE

US   ISSN 0747-2927

DAILY REGISTER, THE. 1886. Mon.-Sat. $.50/day newsstand; $.75/Sat.; $9.25/mo. carrier. 309 DeWitt St., Portage, WI 53901. TEL 608-742-2111; FAX 608-742-8346. **Owner(s):** Independent Media Group, P.O. Box 470, Portage, WI 53901. TEL 608-742-2111; Ed. Tracy Moeller; Pub. David Gentry; adv. contact: Tom Dugan. pub. size: broadsheet; circ. morning 5,500(paid); Sun. 5,500(paid). **Wire Service(s):** AP.

RACIN E

RACINE

US   ISSN 0746-2867

JOURNAL TIMES. 1857. d. $.50/day newsstand; $1.50/Sun.; $14/mo. carrier. 212 Fourth St., Racine, WI 53403. TEL 414-634-3322; FAX 414-631-1702; E-mail: journaltimes@wi.net; URL: http://www.jtracine.com. **Owner(s):** Lee Enterprises, Inc., 130 E. Second St., Davenport, IA 52801; Ed. Alan Buncher; Pub. Peter Selkowe; pub. size: standard; circ. morning 36,385(paid); Sun. 40,000(paid). **Wire Service(s):** AP, KRTN.

RHINELANDER

US   ISSN 0746-5866

RHINELANDER DAILY NEWS. 1882. Sun.-Fri. $.50/day newsstand; $1/Sun.; $114/yr. carrier. 314 S. Courtney, Rhinelander, WI 54501. TEL 715-362-6397; FAX 715-365-6367. **Owner(s):** Scripps League Newspapers, Inc., P.O. Box 1109, Herndon, VA 22070. TEL 703-713-1920; Ed. Meredith Albright; Pub. Richard W. Timmons; adv. contact: Dennis Piotrowski. pub. size: broadsheet; circ. evening 6,400(paid); Sun. 7,000(paid). **Wire Service(s):** AP.

SHAWANO

US   ISSN 0749-7148

SHAWANO LEADER. 1881. Sun.-Fri. $.50/day newsstand; $1/Sun.; $99/yr. carrier; $135/yr. mailed. 1464 E. Green Bay St., Shawano, WI 54166. TEL 715-526-2121; FAX 715-524-3941. **Owner(s):** Independent Media Group, 321 Frenette, Chippewa Falls, WI 54729. TEL 715-723-5515; Ed. Dennis Cooley; Pub. Stephen P. Staloch; adv. contact: Guy Huffman. photos; bk.rev.; pub. size: broadsheet; circ. evening 7,500(paid); Sun. 7,500(paid). **Wire Service(s):** AP.

SHEBOYGAN

US   ISSN 0749-7121

SHEBOYGAN PRESS, THE. 1907. d. $.50/day newsstand; $1.25/Sun.; $155/yr. carrier; $208/yr. mailed. 632 Center Ave., Sheboygan, WI 53081. TEL 414-457-7711; FAX 414-457-0178. **Owner(s):** Thomson Newspapers, Inc., 3150 Des Plaines Ave., Des Plaines, IL 60018. TEL 708-299-5544; Ed. Bob Joslyn; Pub. David Gentry; adv. contact: David Leibelt. pub. size: broadsheet; circ. evening 30,500(paid); Sun. 30,500(paid). **Wire Service(s):** AP, NYT.

STEVENS POINT

US   ISSN 0748-6332

STEVENS POINT JOURNAL. 1895. Mon.-Sat. $.50 newsstand; $84.75/yr. carrier. 1200 Third Ct., Stevens Point, WI 54481. TEL 715-344-6100; FAX 715-344-7229. **Owner(s):** Journal Printing Co., 1200 3rd Ct., P.O. Box Seven, Stevens Point, WI 54481. TEL 714-344-6100; Ed. Debbie Bradley; Pub. Frank W. Leahy; adv. contact: Ken Brezinski. pub. size: broadsheet; circ. evening 15,000(paid). **Wire Service(s):** AP, NYT.

SUPERIOR

US

SUPERIOR DAILY TELEGRAM. 1890. Mon.-Sat. $.50 newsstand; $.75 Sat.; $7/mo. carrier. 1226 Ogden Ave., Superior, WI 54880. TEL 715-394-4411; FAX 715-394-9404. **Owner(s):** Daily Telegram Co., 1226 Ogden Ave., Superior, WI 54880. TEL 715-394-4411; FAX 715-394-9404; Pub. John B. Murphy; adv. contact: Randi Smith. pub. size: broadsheet; circ. evening 10,750(paid). **Wire Service(s):** AP.

Formerly: Superior Evening Telegram.

WATERTOWN

US

WATERTOWN DAILY TIMES. 1895. Mon.-Sat. $.50 newsstand; $94.80/yr. 115 Main St., Watertown, WI 53094. TEL 414-261-4949; FAX 414-261-5102. **Owner(s):** Times Publishing Co., P.O. Box 140, Watertown, WI 53094. TEL 414-261-4949; Ed. Thomas Schultz; Pub. James M. Clifford; adv. contact: Judy Christian. photos; bk.rev.; pub. size: broadsheet; circ. evening 10,100(paid). **Wire Service(s):** AP.

WAUKESHA

US   ISSN 1062-9041

FREEMAN, THE. 1858. Mon.-Sat. $.50/day newsstand; $.75/Sat.; $2.05/wk. carrier; $9.61/mo. motor rte. 801 N. Barstow St., Waukesha, WI 53187-0007. TEL 414-542-2501; FAX 414-542-2015. **Owner(s):** Thomson Newspapers, Inc., Metro Centre at One Station Pl., Stamford, CT 06902. TEL 203-425-2500; FAX 203-425-2516; Ed. Pete Kennedy; Pub. Patrick Doyle; adv.; photos; pub. size: broadsheet; circ. evening 24,000(paid). Wire Service(s): AP, KR.

Formerly: Waukesha Freeman.

WAUSAU

US   ISSN 0887-4271

WAUSAU DAILY HERALD. 1907. d. $.35/day newsstand; $1.25/Sun.; $38.35/3 mos.; $40.95/3 mos. motor rte. 800 Scott St., Wausau, WI 54401. TEL 715-842-2101; FAX 715-848-9360. **Owner(s):** Gannett Company, Inc., 1100 Wilson Blvd., Arlington, VA 22234. TEL 703-284-6000; Ed. Jim Herman; Pub. Michael Scobey; adv. contact: Victor Brabender. bk.rev.; pub. size: broadsheet; circ. evening 30,000(paid); Sun. 33,000(paid). **Wire Service(s):** AP, GNS.

WEST BEND

US   ISSN 0899-2444

DAILY NEWS. 1855. Mon.-Fri. $.50 newsstand; $9.10/mo. carrier $9.80/mo. motor rte.; $10.30/mo. mailed. 100 S. Sixth Ave., West Bend, WI 53095. TEL 414-338-0622; FAX 414-333-1984. **Owner(s):** Thomson Newspapers, Inc., 3150 Des Plaines, Des Plaines, IL 60018. TEL 618-937-6411; Ed. Steve Sandburg; Pub. Robert Gallagher; adv. contact: Barbara Swan. pub. size: broadsheet; circ. 11,300(paid).

Formerly: West Bend Daily News.

WISCONSIN RAPIDS

US

DAILY TRIBUNE, THE. 1930. Mon.-Sat. $.50 newsstand; $101.40/yr. carrier; $109.40/yr. motor rte.; $120/yr. mailed in area; $129/yr. mailed out of area; $142/yr. mailed out of state. 220 First Ave., S., Wisconsin Rapids, WI 54495-8090. TEL 715-423-7200; FAX 715-421-1545. **Owner(s):** Thomson Newspapers, Inc., One Thorn Run Ctr., Ste 500, 1187 Thorn Run Rd. Ext. Coraopolis, PA 15108. TEL 412-262-7870; Ed. Tom Enwright; Pub. Randy Graf; adv. contact: Helen Jungwirth. pub. size: broadsheet; circ. evening 14,000(paid). **Wire Service(s):** AP.

WYOMING

CASPER

US

CASPER STAR TRIBUNE. 1891. d. $.50/day newsstand; $1.25/Sun.; $12.20/mo. carrier; $3.20/wk. 170 Star Ln., Casper WY 82604. TEL 307-266-0500; FAX 307-256-0501. **Owner(s):** Howard Publications, Inc., P.O. Box 570, Oceanside, CA 92049. TEL 619-433-5771; Ed. David Hipschman; Pub. Rob Hurless; adv.; pub. size: broadsheet; circ. morning 32,658(paid); Sun. 36,847(paid). **Wire Service(s):** NYT, AP.

CHEYENNE

US   SSN 8750-0825

WYOMING TRIBUNE-EAGLE. 1867. c. $.50/day newsstand; $1.25/Sun.; $7.25/mo. carrier. 702 W. Lincoln Way, Cheyenne WY 82001. TEL 307-634-3361; FAX 307-778-7163. **Owner(s):** Cheyenne Newspapers, Inc., 702 W. Lincoln Way, Cheyenne, WY 82001. TEL 307-634-3361; Ed. Mary Woolsey; Pub. L. Michael McCraken; adv. contact: Scott Walker. photos; pub. size: broadsheet; circ. morning 16,000(paid); Sun. 18,500(paid). **Wire Service(s):** AP.

Formerly: Sunday Tribune Eagle.

GILLETTE

US   ISSN 0739-4926

NEWS-RECORD. 1904. Sun.-Fri. $.35/day newsstand; $1/Sun.; $93/yr. home deliv. 1201 W. Second St., Gillette, WY 82716. TEL 307-682-9306; FAX 307-686-9306. **Owner(s):** Betty Kennedy Gillette, WY 82716; Ron & Ann Franscell, Gillette, WY 82716; Ed. Ron Franscell; Pub. Ron Franscell; adv. contact: Roxanne Viccaro. pub. size: broadsheet; circ. evening 7,000(paid); Sun. 7,500(paid). **Wire Service(s):** AP.

LARAMIE

US

LARAMIE DAILY BOOMERANG. 1881. Tue.-Sun. $.35/day newsstand; $.75/Sun; $39/6 mos. home deliv. 314 S. Fourth St., Laramie, WY 82070-3702. TEL 307-742-2176; FAX 307-721-2973. **Owner(s):** Laramie Newspapers, Inc., 314 S. Fourth St., Laramie, WY 82070. TEL 307-742-2176; FAX 307-721-2973; Ed. Bob Wilson; Pub. Ron VanEkeren; adv. contact: Sheryl Pulse. photos; bk.rev.; pub. size: broadsheet; circ. morning 8,000(paid); Sun. 8,000(paid). **Wire Service(s):** AP.

RAWLINS

US

DAILY TIMES, THE. 1890. Tue.-Sat. $.35 newsstand; $49/yr. carrier; $59.50/yr. mailed. Sixth & Buffalo, Rawlins, WY 82301-0370. TEL 307-324-3411; FAX 307-324-2797. **Owner(s):** Rawlins Newspapers, Inc., P.O. Box 370, Rawlins, WY 82301. TEL 307-634-3361; Ed. C.H. Bowlus; Pub. David Perry; adv.; photos; bk.rev.; pub. size: tabloid; circ. morning 3,800(paid). **Wire Service(s):** AP.

RIVERTON

US

RIVERTON RANGER. 1953. Mon.-Fri. $60/yr. 421 E. Main St., Riverton, WY 82501. TEL 307-856-2244; FAX 307-856-0189. **Owner(s):** Robert & Steve Peck, 421 E. Main St., Riverton, WY 82501. TEL 307-856-2244; Ed. Dave Perry; Pub. Robert A. Peck; adv. contact: Anita Ellis. pub. size: broadsheet; circ. evening 7,280(paid). **Wire Service(s):** AP.

ROCK SPRINGS

US   ISSN 0893-3650

ROCK SPRINGS DAILY ROCKET-MINER. 1880. Tue.-Sat. $.30 newsstand; $58.20/yr. carrier; $58.60/yr. mailed in state; $62.80/yr. mailed out of state. 215 D St., Rock Springs, WY 82901. TEL 307-362-3736; FAX 307-382-2763. **Owner(s):** Rock Springs Newspapers, Inc., P.O. Box 98, Rock Springs, WY 82902. TEL 307-362-3736; Ed. Bruce Yoder; Pub. Charles Richardson; adv. contact: Garry Gouger. pub. size: broadsheet; circ. morning 7,955(paid). **Wire Service(s):** AP.

SHERIDAN

US

SHERIDAN PRESS. 1886. Mon.-Sat. $.50 newsstand; $78.50/yr. 144 Grinnell, Sheridan, WY 82801. TEL 307-672-2431; FAX 307-672-7950. **Owner(s):** Sheridan Press, The, P.O. Box 2006, Sheridan, WY 82801. TEL 307-672-2431; FAX 307-672-7950; Ed. T.D. Dreiling; Pub. Keith D. Kemper; bk.rev.; pub. size: broadsheet; circ. evening 6,348(paid). **Wire Service(s):** AP.

WORLAND

US

NORTHERN WYOMING DAILY NEWS. 1905. Tue.-Sat. $.35 newsstand; $30.25/6 mos. mail deliv. 201 N. Eighth, Worland, WY 82401. TEL 307-347-3241; FAX 307-347-4267. **Owner(s):** Big Horn Basin Newspapers, Inc., 201 N. Eighth, Worland, WY 82401. TEL 307-347-3241; Ed. Lee Lockhart; Pub. Lee Lockhart; adv.; photos; bk.rev.; pub. size: broadsheet; circ. morning 5,000(paid). **Wire Service(s):** AP.

ALABAMA

ABBEVILLE

US

ABBEVILLE HERALD. 1941. Thu. $.50 newsstand; $14.58/yr. in cy.; $18.90/yr. in state; $20/yr. out of state. 135 Kirkland St., Abbeville, AL 36310. TEL 334-585-2331; FAX 334-585-2331. **Owner(s):** J. Edward Dodd, III, P.O. Box 609, Abbeville, AL 36310. TEL 205-585-2331; Ed. J. Edward Dodd, III; Pub. J. Edward Dodd, III; adv.; pub. size: tabloid; circ. 2,200(paid).

ALBERTVILLE

US   ISSN 0889-1724

SAND MOUNTAIN REPORTER. 1955. 3/wk.: Tue., Thu., Sat. $.50 newsstand; $25/yr. 3760 U.S. Hwy. 431, Albertville, AL 35950. TEL 205-878-1311; FAX 205-878-2104. **Owner(s):** Sand Mountain Publishing Co., P.O. Box 190, Albertville, AL 35950. TEL 205-787-1311; Pub. Michael J. Hudgins; adv. contact: Debra Hedgepath. pub. size: broadsheet; circ. 13,500(paid).

ALEXANDER CITY

US

DADEVILLE RECORD. 1896. Thu. $.50 newsstand; $13/yr. in cy.; $23/yr. out of cy. 548 Cherokee Rd., Alexander City, AL 35010. TEL 205-234-4281; FAX 205-234-6550. **Owner(s):** Kenneth Boone, P.O. Box 999, Alexander City, AL 35010. TEL 205-234-4281; FAX 205-234-6550; Ed. K.A. Turner; Pub. Bruce Wallace; adv. contact: Doug Patterson. pub. size: standard; circ. 2,500(paid).

ARAB

US

ARAB TRIBUNE. 1958. Wed. $15/yr. local; $20/yr. out of area; $25/yr. out of state. 619 S. Brindlee Mountain Pkwy., Arab, AL 35016. TEL 205-586-3188; FAX 205-586-3190. **Owner(s):** Edwin H. Reed, 619 S. Brindlee Mountain Pkwy., Arab, AL 35016. TEL 205-586-3188; FAX 205-586-3190; Ed. David Moore; Pub. Edwin H. Reed; pub. size: broadsheet; circ. 7,300(paid).

ATMORE

US   ISSN 0746-1968

ATMORE ADVANCE. 1927. s-w.: Wed. & Sun. $.50 newsstand; $35/yr. carrier in area; $45/yr. out of area; $25/yr. senior citizens. 301 S. Main St., Atmore, AL 36502. TEL 205-368-2123; FAX 205-368-2124. **Owner(s):** Boone Newspapers, Inc., P.O. Box 2370, Tuscalosa, AL 35403. TEL 407-338-3298; Ed. Michele Gerlach; Pub. Michele Gerlach; adv.; photos; pub. size: broadsheet; circ. 10,000(free & paid); Sun. 3,800(free & paid)

AUBURN

US

LEE COUNTY EAGLE, THE. 1937. s-w.: Wed. & Sun. $.50 newsstand; $20/yr. 122 Tichenor Ave., Auburn, AL 36830 TEL 334-821-7150; FAX 334-887-0037. **Owner(s):** Thomson Newspapers, Inc., One Thorn Run Ctr., Ste. 500, 1187 Thorn Run Rd. Ext., Coraopolis, PA 15108. TEL 412-262-7870; Pub. Paul Seveska; adv. contact: Don Norman. pub. size: broadsheet; circ. 20,600(paid).

    Formerly: Auburn Bulletin.

BAY MINETTE

US

BALDWIN TIMES. 1890. Thu $23/yr.local; $26/yr. out of state; $17.95/yr. senior citizens. 329 Courthouse Sq., Bay Minette, AL 36507. TEL 334-937-2511; FAX 334-937-1637. **Owner(s):** Gulf Coast Newspapers, Alabama Hwy. 59, Robertsdale, AL 36567. TEL 334-947-7712; Ed. Tammy Leytham; Pub. Samantha McCaw; adv. contact: Samantha McCaw. photos; bk.rev.; pub. size: broadsheet; circ. 3,600(paid).

BESSEMER

US

WESTERN STAR. 1984. Wed. $.50 newsstand; $21/yr. local; $17/yr. senior citizens. 1709 Third Ave., Bessemer, AL 35020 TEL 205-424-7827; FAX 205-424-8118. **Owner(s):** Traibb Publications, Inc., Manchester, GA 31816; Ed. John Calure; Pub. John Calure; adv.; pub. size: broadsheet; circ. 10,000(paid).

BIRMINGHAM

US

ALABAMA MESSENGER. 1959. Sat. $10/yr. mailed. 706 Frank Nelson Bldg., Birmingham, AL 35203. TEL 205-252-3672. **Owner(s):** Eleanor Foster, 706 Frank Nelson Bldg., Birmingham, AL 35103. TEL 205-252-3672; Ed. Karen Abercrombie. adv. contact: Traci A. Smeraglia. pub. size: broadsheet; circ. 2,500(paid).

US

BIRMINGHAM WORLD. Thu. $26/yr. 407 15th St. N., Birmingham, AL 35203. TEL 205-251-6523; FAX 205-328-6729. **Owner(s):** Birmingham World, Inc., 407 15th St., N., Birmingham, AL 35203. TEL 205-251-6523; Pub. Joe Dickson; adv. contact: Clinton Mock. pub. size: broadsheet; circ. 12,600(paid). **Wire Service(s):** AP, NNS, Newsfinder.

US
COMMUNITY SHOPPER. 1977. m. free direct mail. 9229 Todd Dr., Ste. 205, Birmingham, AL 35206. TEL 205-833-8588; FAX 205-833-8589. **Owner(s):** Jarrell & Associates, Inc., 9229 Todd Dr., Ste. 205, Birmingham, AL 35206. TEL 205-833-8588; FAX 205-833-8589; Pub. Rick Jarrell; pub. size: tabloid; circ. 32,000(free).
Formerly: Shoppers Guide.

US
OVER THE MOUNTAIN JOURNAL. 1980. bi-w.: Thu. free. 3250 Independence Dr., #5, Birmingham, AL 35209. TEL 205-879-9686; FAX 205-879-4579. **Owner(s):** Maurice G. Wald, III, P.O. Box 20502, Birmingham, AL 35216. TEL 205-879-9686; FAX 205-879-4579; Ed. Cara Morrison; Pub. Maurice G. Wald, III; adv. contact: Jeff Wingo. photos; pub. size: tabloid; circ. 39,600(free & paid).

US
SAMFORD CRIMSON. Wed. $10/yr. in cy.; $12/yr. out of cy. 800 Lake Shore Dr., Birmingham, AL 35209. TEL 205-870-2998. **Owner(s):** Cook Publications, Colman, AL; Ed. Amy Walker. pub. size: tabloid; circ. 5,500(paid).

US
THRIFTY NICKEL. 1982. Thu. free. 619 Robert Jemison Rd., Ste. 200, Birmingham, AL 35209. TEL 205-942-2555; FAX 205-942-5770. **Owner(s):** Rob Puckett, 619 Robert Jemison Rd., Ste. 200, Birmingham, AL 35209; Ed. Rob Puckett. pub. size: tabloid; circ. 70,000(free).

BREWTON

US
BREWTON STANDARD, THE. 1887. s-w.: Wed. & Sun. $.50 newsstand; $30/yr. in state; $34/yr. out of state; $27/yr. senior citizens. 407 St. Nicholas Ave., Brewton, AL 36426. TEL 205-867-4876; FAX 205-867-4877. **Owner(s):** Boone Newspapers, Inc., P.O. Box 2370, Tuscaloosa, AL 35403. TEL 407-338-3298; Pub. Harris A. Pippen, III; pub. size: broadsheet; circ. 5,400(paid); Sun. 4,500(paid).

BUTLER

US
BUTLER CHOCTAW ADVOCATE. 1890. Wed. $.50 newsstand; $15/yr. in cy.; $20/yr. out of cy. 210 N. Mulberry St., Butler, AL 36904. TEL 205-459-2858; FAX 205-459-3000. **Owner(s):** Choctaw Advocate, Inc., 210 N. Mulberry St., P.O. Box 475, Butler, AL 36904. TEL 205-459-2858; Ed. Tommy J. Campbell. adv. contact: Lee Mosley. photos; bk.rev.; pub. size: standard; circ. 4,400(paid). **Wire Service(s):** AP.

CAMDEN

US
WILCOX PROGRESSIVE ERA. 1860. w. $.50 newsstand; $14/yr. in cy.; $24/yr. out of cy. P.O. Box 100; Camden, AL 36726. TEL 205-682-4422; FAX 205-682-5163. **Owner(s):** M. Hollis Curl, P.O. Box 100, Camden, AL 36726. TEL 205-682-4422; Ed. M. Hollis Curl; Pub. M. Hollis Curl; adv. contact: Melissa Dove. pub. size: standard; circ. 2,840(paid).

CARROLLTON

US
PICKENS COUNTY HERALD. 1848. Wed. $.50 newsstand; $20/yr. in cy.; $30/yr. out of state. Hwy. 17, Junkin Bldg., Carrollton, AL 35447. TEL 205-367-2217; FAX 207-367-2217. **Owner(s):** Hershel Lake, P.O. Box 390, Carrollton, AL 35447. TEL 205-367-2217; Ed. Doug Sanders; Pub. Brian Hood; pub. size: standard; circ. 4,500(paid).

CENTRE

US
CHEROKEE COUNTY HERALD. 1938. Wed. $.50 newsstand; $14/yr. in cy.; $22/yr. out of cy. 107 W. First Ave., Centre, AL 35960. TEL 205-927-5037; FAX 205-927-4853. **Owner(s):** B.H. Mooney, III, 107 W. First Ave., Centre, AL 35960. TEL 205-927-5037; FAX 205-927-4853; Ed. Paul W. Dale; Pub. B.H. Mooney; photos; pub. size: broadsheet; circ. 5,800(paid).

CENTREVILLE

US
CENTREVILLE PRESS. 1879. Wed. $.50 newsstand; $19.44/yr. mailed. 119 Court Sq. W., Centreville, AL 35042. TEL 205-926-9769; FAX 205-926-9760. **Owner(s):** Trib Publications, Inc., 119 Court Sq. W., Centreville, AL 35042. TEL 205-926-9769; Ed. Judy M. Farnetti; Pub. Robert Tribble; adv. contact: Judy M. Farnetti. pub. size: broadsheet; circ. 4,000(paid).

CHATOM

US
WASHINGTON COUNTY NEWS. 1892. Wed. $.50 newsstand; $15/yr. 305 Jordan St., Chatom, AL 36518. TEL 334-847-2599; FAX 334-847-3847. **Owner(s):** James A. Specht, P.O. Box 510, Chatom, AL 36518. TEL 334-847-2599; FAX 334-847-3847; Ed. Frank Harwell. adv. contact: Shirley Helms. photos; bk.rev.; pub. size: standard; circ. 3,700(paid).
Formerly: Call-News Dispatch.

CLANTON

US
CLANTON ADVERTISER. 1972. 3/wk.: Wed., Fri., Sun. $.75 newsstand; $56/yr. in state; $65/yr. out of state. 1109 Seventh St., N., Clanton, AL 35046. TEL 205-755-5747; FAX 205-755-5857. **Owner(s):** Boone Newspapers, Inc., P.O. Box 2370, Tuscaloosa, AL 35403. TEL 205-752-3381; Ed. Robert Basol Hughes; Pub. Michael Kelly; adv. contact: Dan Cook. pub. size: broadsheet; circ. 134,400(free & paid).

COLUMBIANA

US   ISSN 1063-9489
SHELBY COUNTY REPORTER. 1843. Wed. $.75 newsstand; $30/yr. carrier;. Main St., Columbiana, AL 35051. TEL 205-669-3131; FAX 205-669-4217. **Owner(s):** Boone Newspapers, Inc., P.O. Box 2370, Tuscaloosa, AL 35403. TEL 205-752-3381; Ed. Kim N. Price; Pub. Kim N. Price; adv. contact: Patty Bryan. pub. size: broadsheet; circ. 10,235(paid).

CULLMAN

US
CULLMAN TRIBUNE. 1874. Thu. $.50 newsstand; $18/yr. in cy.; $25/yr. out of cy. 219 Second Ave., S.E., Cullman, AL 35055. TEL 205-739-1351; FAX 205-739-4422. **Owner(s):** Delton & Barbara Blalock, P.O. Box 496, Hanceville, AL 35077; Ed. Delton Blalock; Pub. Barbara Blalock; adv. contact: Nina Hurst. photos; bk.rev.; pub. size: broadsheet; circ. 16,000(paid).

DEMOPOLIS

US
DEMOPOLIS TIMES. 1902. s-w.: Sun. & Wed. $40/yr. 315 E. Jefferson St., Demopolis, AL 36732. TEL 334-289-4017; FAX 334-289-4019. **Owner(s):** Boone Newspapers, Inc., P.O. Box 2370, Tuscaloosa, AL 35403; Ed. Danny Smith; Pub. Danny Smith; pub. size: broadsheet; circ. 2,800(paid).

DORA

US
COMMUNITY NEWS, THE. 1968. Wed. $.50 newsstand; $12.50/yr. in state; $17.50/yr. out of state; $9/yr. senior citizens. 6 Midway Plz., Dora, AL 35062. TEL 205-648-3231; FAX 205-648-3246. **Owner(s):** Lee Walls, Birmingham, AL; pub. size: broadsheet; circ. 6,000(paid).

EUFAULA

US
EUFAULA TRIBUNE. 1929. s-w.: Wed. & Sun. $26.50/yr. carrier; $34.95/yr. mailed in state; $44.95/yr. out of state. 514 E. Barbour St., Eufaula, AL 36027. TEL 334-687-3506; FAX 334-687-3229. **Owner(s):** Joel P. Smith, 325 N. Eufaula Ave., Eufaula, AL 36027; Tribune Publishing Co., P.O. Box 628, Eufaula, AL 36072-0628; Ed. Joel P. Smith; Pub. Joel P. Smith; pub. size: broadsheet; circ. 6,200(paid).

EUTAW

US
GREENE COUNTY INDEPENDENT. 1985. Wed. $.50 newsstand; $16/yr. in cy.; $22/yr. out of cy. 106 Main St., Eutaw, AL 35462. TEL 205-372-2232; FAX 205-372-2232. **Owner(s):** Greene County Independent Newspapers, Inc., 106 Main St., Eutaw, AL 35462. TEL 205-372-2232; Ed. Leewanna Parker; Pub. Betty C. Banks; adv. contact: Betty C. Banks. pub. size: broadsheet; circ. 1,500(paid).

EVERGREEN

US
EVERGREEN COURANT, THE. 1895. Thu. $15/yr. in cy.; $20/yr. out of cy. P.O. Box 440, Evergreen, AL 36401. TEL 334-578-1492; FAX 334-578-1496. **Owner(s):** Maurice G. Bozeman, P.O. Box 440, Evergreen, AL 36401. TEL 205-578-1210; Ed. Robert Bozeman, III; Pub. Maurice G. Bozeman; pub. size: standard; circ. 3,800(paid).

FAIRHOPE

US

FAIRHOPE COURIER, THE. 1894. s-w.: Wed. & Sat. $.50 newsstand; $30/yr. carrier; $32.50/yr. mailed out of state; $20.50/yr. senior citizens mailed in cy.; $25.75/yr. senior citizens mailed in state. 325 Fairhope Ave., Fairhope, AL 36532. TEL 334-928-2321; FAX 334-928-9963. **Owner(s):** Gulf Coast Newspapers, P.O. Box 509, Robertsdale, AL 36567. TEL 334-947-7712; adv.; bk.rev.; pub. size: broadsheet; circ. 33,900(paid). **Wire Service(s):** AP.

FAYETTE

US

TIMES RECORD. 1977. Wed. $.50 newsstand; $18/yr. in cy.; $20/yr. out of cy. 106 First St., S.E., Fayette, AL 35555. TEL 205-932-6271; FAX 205-932-6998. **Owner(s):** Mid-South Publishing Co., Fayette, AL 35555; Ed. Michael James; Pub. Horace Moore; adv. contact: Bobbie Cross. photos; pub. size: standard; circ. 5,000(paid).

FLOMATON

US

TRI-CITY LEDGER. 1970. Thu. $.50 newsstand; $20/yr. local; $25/yr. out of cy.; $30/yr. out of state. 20766 Hwy. 31, Flomaton, AL 36441. TEL 334-296-3491; FAX 334-296-3491. **Owner(s):** Bo Bolton, P.O. Drawer F, Flomaton, AL 36441. TEL 334-296-3491; Ed. Joe Thomas; Pub. Joe Thomas; adv. contact: Gary Murph. pub. size: broadsheet; circ. 5,500(paid).
   Formerly: Flomaton Tri-City Ledger.

FLORALA

US

FLORALA NEWS, THE. 1900. Thu. $21.60/yr. in state; $20/yr. out of state. 421 S. Fifth St., Florala, AL 36442. TEL 334-858-3342; FAX 334-858-3786. **Owner(s):** Larry Woodham, 421 S. Fifth St., Florala, AL 36442. TEL 334-858-3342; Ed. Merle Woodham; Pub. Larry Woodham; adv.; photos; pub. size: standard; circ. 2,200(paid).

FLORENCE

US

COURIER JOURNAL. 1884. Wed. free direct mail. 116 W. Mobile St., Florence, AL 35630. TEL 205-764-4268; FAX 205-760-9618. **Owner(s):** L & L Services, 301 Montgomery Ave., Sheffield, AL 35660; Ed. Tom Magazzu. adv.; photos; pub. size: tabloid; circ. 60,499(free).

FOLEY

US

ONLOOKER, THE. 1907. s-w.: Wed. & Sat. $.50 newsstand; $30/yr. in state; $32.50/yr. out of state; $25.75/yr. senior citizens in state; $28.50/yr. senior citizens out of state. 217 N. McKenzie St., Foley, AL 36535. TEL 334-943-2151; FAX 334-934-3441. **Owner(s):** Heritage Publishing, 217 N. McKenzie St., Foley, AL 36535. TEL 334-943-2151; Pub. Will Petrovich; adv.; pub. size: broadsheet; circ. 5,150(paid).

GARDENDALE

US

NORTH JEFFERSON NEWS. Thu. $.50 newsstand; $18/yr. in cy.; $25/yr. out of cy. 125 Bell St., Gardendale, AL 35071. TEL 205-631-8716; FAX 205-631-9902. **Owner(s):** Robert Bryan, 125 Bell St., Gardendale, AL 35071. TEL 205-734-2131; Ed. Tim Lassiter; Pub. Bob Bryan; adv. contact: Mona Richards. pub. size: broadsheet; circ. 4,500(paid). **Wire Service(s):** AP.

GENEVA

US

GENEVA COUNTY REAPER. 1933. Wed. $.50 newsstand; $19.44/yr. in cy.; $25./yr. out of cy. 803 E. Town Ave., Geneva, AL 36340. TEL 334-684-2280; FAX 334-684-3099. **Owner(s):** James A. Specht, P.O. Box 160, Geneva, AL 36340. TEL 205-684-2280; Pub. James A. Specht; adv. contact: Shirley Helms. photos; pub. size: broadsheet; circ. 15,000(paid).

GEORGIANA

US

BUTLER COUNTY NEWS. 1911. Thu. $13/yr. in cy.; $14/yr. out of cy. 122 Miranda Ave., Georgiana, AL 36033. TEL. 334-376-2325; FAX 334-376-9302. **Owner(s):** R.W. Pride, P.O. Box 488, Georgiana, AL 36033. TEL 205-376-2325; Ed. R.W. Pride; Pub. R.W. Pride; adv. contact: Teresa Nicholas. pub. size: standard; circ. 2,500(paid).

GREENSBORO

US

GREENSBORO WATCHMAN, THE. 1876. Thu. $18.50/yr. in cy.; $20.50/yr. in state; $26.50/yr. out of state. 1005 Market St., Greensboro, AL 36744-0550. TEL 334-624-8323; FAX 334-624-8327. **Owner(s):** E.E. Lowry, Jr., P.O. Drawer 550, Greensboro, AL 36744-0550. TEL 334-624-8323; FAX 334-624-8327; Ed. Willie L. Arrington. pub. size: broadsheet; circ. 3,100(paid).

GREENVILLE

US

GREENVILLE ADVOCATE, THE. 1865. s-w.: Wed. & Sat. $.75 newsstand; $36/yr. local; $46/yr. elsewhere. 103 Hickory St., Greenville, AL 36037. TEL 334-382-3111; FAX 335-382-7104 **Owner(s):** Greenville Newspapers, P.O. Box 507, Greenville, AL 36037. TEL 334-382-3111; Ed. Greg Fuller; Pub. Todd Carpenter adv.; photos; bk.rev.; pub. size: broadsheet; circ. 5,300(paid).

GROVE HILL

US

CLARKE COUNTY DEMOCRAT. 1856. Thu. $.50 newsstand; $16.05/yr. in cy.; $19.26/yr. out of cy.; $22/yr. out of state; $14.98/yr. senior citizens. 261 N. Jackson, Grove Hill, AL 36451. TEL 334-275-3375; FAX 334-275-3060. **Owner(s):** James A. Cox, 261 N. Jackson, Grove Hill, AL 36451. TEL 205-275-3375; Ed. James A. Cox; Pub. James A. Cox; pub. size: broadsheet; circ. 4,800(paid).

GULF SHORES

US   SSN 1041-2662

ISLANDER, THE. 1977. s-w.: Wed. & Sat. $.50 newsstand; $28.50/yr. in state; $29.95/yr. out of state; $24.50/yr. senior citizens. 128 Cove Dr., Gulf Shores, AL 36542. TEL 334-968-6414; FAX 334-968-5233. **Owner(s):** Gulf Coast Newspapers, P.O. Box 509, Robertsdale, AL 36567. TEL 334-947-7712; Pub. Denny Thomas; adv.; pub. size: broadsheet; circ. 6,000(paid).

GUNTERSVILLE

US

ADVERTISER-GLEAM. 1880. s-w.: Wed. & Sat. $.35 newsstand; $18/yr. in cy.; $32/yr. elsewhere. Taylor St., Guntersville, AL 35976. TEL 205-582-3232; FAX 205-582-3231. **Owner(s):** Sam Harvey, Taylor St., Guntersville, AL 35976. TEL 205-582-3232; FAX 205-582-3231; Don Woodward, Taylor St., Guntersville, AL 35976. TEL 205-582-3232; FAX 205-582-3231; Ed. Sam Harvey. pub. size: broadsheet; circ. 11,934(paid).

HALEYVILLE

US

NORTHWEST ALABAMIAN. 1906. s-w.: Wed. & Sat. $.50 newsstand; $25/yr. in cy.; $28/yr. out of cy. Hwy. 195, Haleyville, AL 35565. TEL 205-486-9461; FAX 205-486-4849. **Owner(s):** Hershel Lake, P.O. Box 430, Haleyville, AL 35565. TEL 205-486-9461; Pub. Horace Moore; adv. contact: Buford Thompson. photos; pub. size: broadsheet; circ. 8,600(paid).

HAMILTON

US

JOURNAL RECORD. 1970. s-w.: Wed. & Sat. $.50 newsstand; $25/yr. in cy.; $28/yr. in state; $38/yr. out of state. Hwy. 17, Hamilton, AL 35570. TEL 205-921-3114; FAX 205-921-3105. **Owner(s):** Mid-South Publishing Co., P.O. Box 430, Haleyville, AL 35565. TEL 205-486-9461; FAX 205-486-4849; Ed. Les Walters; Pub. Horace Moore; adv. contact: Sandy Ballard. photos; pub. size: broadsheet; circ. 8,500(paid).

HANCEVILLE

US

HANCEVILLE HERALD. 1977. Wed. $9.63/yr. 111 Commercial St., Hanceville, AL 35077. TEL 205-352-4775. **Owner(s):** Ginger Grantham & Violet Earing, P.O. Drawer H, Hanceville, AL 35077. TEL 205-352-4775; Ed. Ginger Grantham. adv.; pub. size: broadsheet; circ. 1,800(paid).

HARTSELLE

US

HARTSELLE ENQUIRER. 1874. Thu. $.50 newsstand; $24/yr. mailed. 407 W. Chestnut St., Hartselle, AL 35640. TEL 205-773-6566; FAX 205-773-1953; E-mail: enquirer@hiwaay.net; URL: http://www.hartselle-enquirer.com. **Owner(s):** Hartselle Enquirer, Inc., P.O. Box 929, Hartselle, AL 35640. TEL 205-773-6566; Ed. Clifton P. Knight; Pub. T. L. Beasley; adv.; photos; pub. size: broadsheet; circ. 7,800(paid).

HEADLAND
US

HEADLAND OBSERVER. 1965. Thu. $.50 newsstand; $15/yr. in cy.; $18/yr. out of cy.; $21/yr. out of state. Rte. 2, Box 707, Headland, AL 36345. TEL 334-693-3326; FAX 334-693-5224. **Owner(s):** Thomson Newspapers, Inc., One Thorn Run Ctr., Ste. 500, 1187 Thorn Run Rd. Ext., Coraopolis, PA 15108. TEL 412-262-7870; Ed. Terry Grimes; Pub. Guy Beasley; adv. contact: Betty Gamble. pub. size: broadsheet; circ. 2,000(paid).

HEFLIN
US

CLEBURNE NEWS. 1906. Thu. $.50 newsstand; $15/yr. local; $20/yr. out of cy. Hwy. 9 S., Heflin, AL 36264. TEL 205-463-2872; FAX 205-463-2872. **Owner(s):** Consolidated Publishing Co., 216 W. Tenth St., Anniston, AL 36201. TEL 205-236-1551; FAX 205-231-0027; Ed. Randy Grider; Pub. Ed Fowler; pub. size: broadsheet; circ. 7,000(paid).

JACKSON
US

SOUTH ALABAMIAN. 1887. Thu. $.50 newsstand; $16/yr. local; $24/yr. out of area. 1064 Coffeevile Rd., Jackson, AL 36545. TEL 334-246-4494; FAX 334-246-7486. **Owner(s):** Michael Breedlove, P.O. Box 68, Jackson, AL 36545. TEL 334-246-4494; Ed. Martha Ruby Motes; Pub. Michael M. Breedlove; pub. size: broadsheet; circ. 4,700(paid).

JACKSONVILLE
US

JACKSONVILLE NEWS. 1936. Wed. $.35 newsstand; $15/yr. in cy.; $22/yr. outside of cy. 203 S. Pelham Rd., Jacksonville, AL 36265. TEL 205-435-5021; FAX 205-435-1028. **Owner(s):** Consolidated Publishing Co., Tent St., Anniston, AL 36201. TEL 205-236-1551; Ed. P.A. Sanguinetti. pub. size: broadsheet; circ. 4,000(paid).

LAFAYETTE
US

LAFAYETTE SUN, THE. 1880. Wed. $.25 newsstand; $11.25/yr. in cy.; $12.50/yr. out of cy. 116 Lafayette St., Lafayette, AL 36862. TEL 334-864-8885; FAX 334-864-8310. **Owner(s):** Michael Hand, P.O. Box 378, Lafayette, AL 36862. TEL 205-864-8885; Pub. Michael Hand; adv. contact: Michael Hand. pub. size: broadsheet; circ. 2,800(paid).

LEEDS
US

LEEDS NEWS. 1939. Thu. $18/yr. 720 Parkway Dr., Leeds, AL 35094. TEL 205-699-2214; FAX 205-699-3157. **Owner(s):** Robert Bryan, 300 Fourth Ave., S.E., Cullman, AL 35055. TEL 205-734-2131; Ed. Kimberly Stark; Pub. Robert Bryan; adv. contact: Leah Hollister. pub. size: broadsheet; circ. 10,000(paid).

LINDEN
US

DEMOCRAT-REPORTER, THE. 1879. Thu. $.50 newsstand; $20/yr. in cy.; $25/yr. out of cy.; $30/yr. out of state. 108 E. Coats Ave., Linden, AL 36748. TEL 334-295-5224. **Owner(s):** Goodloe Sutton, P.O. Box 480040, Linden, AL 36748. TEL 205-295-5224; Ed. Goodloe Sutton; Pub. Goodloe Sutton; pub. size: broadsheet; circ. 5,350(paid).

LINEVILLE
US   ISSN 1053-9123

CLAY TIMES JOURNAL. 1903. w. $.50 newsstand; $18/yr. in cy.; $24/yr. out of cy. 60132 Hwy. 49, Lineville, AL 36266-0097. TEL 205-396-5760. **Owner(s):** Connie & David Proctor, P.O. Box 97, Lineville, AL 36266. TEL 205-396-5760; adv. contact: Linda McDonald. photos; bk.rev.; pub. size: standard; circ. 3,500(paid).

LIVINGSTON
US

SUMTER COUNTY RECORD-JOURNAL, THE. 1968. Thu. $15/yr. local; $18/yr. in state; $23/yr. out of state. 200 S. Washington St., Livingston, AL 35470. TEL 205-652-6100; FAX 205-652-4466. **Owner(s):** Tommy McGraw, P.O. Drawer B, Livingston, AL 35470. TEL 205-652-6100; Pub. Tommy McGraw; adv. contact: Judy Johnston. pub. size: broadsheet; circ. 3,600(paid).
  Formerly: Sumter County Record.

LUVERNE
US

LUVERNE JOURNAL & NEWS. 1888. Wed. $.50 newsstand; $15/yr. in cy.; $17/yr. out of cy. 506 Forest Ave., Luverne, AL 36049. TEL 334-335-3541; FAX 334-335-3541. **Owner(s):** Alvin Bland, P.O. Box 152, Luverne, AL 36049. TEL 334-335-3541; James Morgan, P.O. Box 152, Luverne, AL 36049. TEL 334-335-3541; Ed. Alvin Bland; Pub. James Morgan; adv. contact: James Morgan. pub. size: broadsheet; circ. 3,500(paid).

MADISON
US   ISSN 0889-4205

MADISON COUNTY RECORD. 1967. Thu. $.50 newsstand; $15/yr. in cy.; $21.50/yr. out of cy. 202 Main St., Madison, AL 35758. TEL 205-772-6677. **Owner(s):** Richard Haston, P.O. Box 175, Madison, AL 35758. TEL 205-772-8666; Ed. Jeff Dickinson; Pub. Richard A. Haston; pub. size: broadsheet; circ. 12,000(paid).

MARION
US

MARION TIMES-STANDARD. 1839. Wed. $16.20/yr. in cy.; $24.30/yr. out of cy.; $30/yr. out of state. P.O. Box 418, Marion, AL 36756. TEL 334-683-6318; FAX 334-683-4616. **Owner(s):** Robert Tribble, P.O. Box 418, Marion, AL 36756. TEL 334-683-6318; Pub. Robert Tribble; adv. contact: Lorrie Blankenship. pub. size: standard; circ. 2,400(paid).

MILLPORT
US

WEST ALABAMA GAZETTE. 1976. Thu. $.50 newsstand; $14/yr. in cy.; $17/yr. in state; $20/yr. out of state. 100 Vernon St., Millport, AL 35576. TEL 205-662-4296; FAX 205-662-4740. **Owner(s):** Peyton & Barbara Bobo, P.O. Drawer 249, Millport, AL 35576. TEL 205-662-4296; Ed. Barbara Bobo; Pub. Peyton Bobo; adv. contact: Barbara Bobo. photos; bk.rev.; pub. size: broadsheet; circ. 4,200(paid).

MOBILE
US

MOBILE BEACON. 1943. Wed. $.25 newsstand; $20/yr. 2311 Costarides, Mobile, AL 36617. TEL 205-479-0629. **Owner(s):** Mobile Beacon, P.O. Box 1407, Mobile, AL 36633. TEL 205-479-0629; Ed. Cleretta Blackmon; Pub. Lancie M. Thomas; adv. contact: Cleretta Blackmon. photos; pub. size: broadsheet; circ. 7,000(paid).

MONROEVILLE
US   ISSN 0884-8750

MONROE JOURNAL. 1866. Thu. $.50 newsstand; $26/yr. 126 Hines St., Monroeville, AL 36460. TEL 205-575-3282; FAX 205-575-3284; E-mail: monjour@monroeville.gulf.net; URL: http://www.monroeville.gulf.net/email/monjour. **Owner(s):** Southwest Alabama Publishing Co., Inc., 126 Hines St., P.O. Box 826, Monroeville, AL 36460. TEL 205-575-3282; FAX 205-575-3284; Ed. Marilyn W. Handley; Pub. Stephen E. Stewart; adv. contact: Sandra Dunn. photos; pub. size: broadsheet; circ. 6,000(paid).

MONTGOMERY
US

MONTGOMERY INDEPENDENT. 1964. Thu. $.50 newsstand; $19.90/yr. mailed. 6005-B Monticello Dr., Montgomery, AL 36117. TEL 334-213-7323; FAX 334-271-2143. **Owner(s):** Bass, Inc., 6005-B Monticello Dr., Montgomery, AL 36117. TEL 205-213-7323; Ed. Wendi Lewis. pub. size: tabloid; circ. 8,000(paid).

MOULTON
US

MOULTON ADVERTISER. 1828. Thu. $.50 newsstand; $20/yr. in cy.; $30/yr. out of cy. Main St., Moulton, AL 35650. TEL 205-974-1114. **Owner(s):** Slatcon, Inc., P.O. Box 517, Moulton, AL 35650. TEL 205-974-1114; Ed. Luke Slaton; Pub. Luke Slaton; adv. contact: Amy Thrasher. pub. size: standard; circ. 14,500(paid).

MOUNDVILLE
US

MOUNDVILLE TIMES. 1988. Thu. $.50 newsstand; $14/yr. in cy.; $16/yr. in state; $18/yr. out of state. 520 Market St., Moundville, AL 35474. TEL 205-371-2488; FAX 205-371-9010. **Owner(s):** Larry Taylor, Market St., Moundville, AL 35474. TEL 205-371-9011; FAX 205-371-9010; Ed. Austin Dare; Pub. Larry Taylor; adv.; photos; pub. size: standard; circ. 2,500(free & paid).

ONEONTA

US   ISSN 1056-4205

BLOUNT COUNTIAN, THE. 1894. Wed. $.30 newsstand; $12/yr. in cy.; $15/yr. out of cy.; $20/yr. out of state. 217 Third St., S., Oneonta, AL 35121. TEL 205-625-3231. **Owner(s):** Southern Democrat, Inc., 217 Third St., S., P.O. Box 310, Oneonta, AL 35121. TEL 205-625-3231; Ed. Lisa Ryan; Pub. Molly Howard Ryan; adv. contact: Melanie Skillman. pub. size: broadsheet; circ. 6,660(free & paid).

OPP

US

OPP NEWS. 1901. Thu. $.50 newsstand; $22/yr. in cy.; $27/yr. out of cy.; $32/yr. out of state. 200 W. Covington Ave., Opp, AL 36467. TEL 334-493-3595; FAX 334-493-4901. **Owner(s):** Covington Publishing Corp., P.O. Box 409, Opp, AL 36467. TEL 334-493-3595; Ed. Tracey Nelson; Pub. Randy Pebworth; adv. contact: Jennifer Cosby. pub. size: broadsheet; circ. 7,210(paid).

OZARK

US

SOUTHERN STAR. 1867. Wed. $.50 newsstand; $17.82/yr. in cy.; $19.98/yr. out of cy. P.O. Box 1729, Ozark, AL 36361. TEL 334-774-2715; FAX 334-774-9619. **Owner(s):** Joseph H. Adams, P.O. Box 1729, Ozark, AL 36361. TEL 205-774-2715; Ed. Joseph H. Adams; Pub. Joseph H. Adams; adv. contact: Edye Reeves. pub. size: broadsheet; circ. 5,200(paid).

PELL CITY

US

ST. CLAIR NEWS-AEGIS. 1823. Thu. $.50 newsstand; $18/yr. in cy.; $25/yr. out of cy.; $16.20/yr. senior citizens. 1820 Second Ave. N., Pell City, AL 35125. TEL 205-884-2310; FAX 205-884-2312. **Owner(s):** Bryan Publications, Cullman Times, P.O. Box 190, Cullman, AL 35055. TEL 205-734-2131; Ed. Gary Hanner. adv. contact: Stephen Adams. pub. size: standard; circ. 7,000(paid). **Wire Service(s):** UPI.

PHENIX CITY

US

PHENIX-CITIZEN. Thu. $20/yr. in state; $25/yr. out of state. 1606 Broad St., Phenix City, AL 36867. TEL 334-298-0679; FAX 334-298-7118. **Owner(s):** Mike Venable & Jill Tigner, 1606 Broad St., Phenix City, AL 36867. TEL 334-298-0679; FAX 334-298-0679; Ed. Jill Tigner; Pub. Mike Venable; pub. size: broadsheet; circ. 5,500(paid).

PIEDMONT

US   ISSN 0890-6017

PIEDMONT JOURNAL-INDEPENDENT. 1982. Wed. $.25 newsstand; $12.84/yr.; $23.54/2 yrs. 115 N. Center Ave., Piedmont, AL 36272-0203. TEL 205-447-2837; FAX 205-447-2837. **Owner(s):** Consolidated Publishing Co., P.O. Box 189, Anniston, AL 36202. TEL 205-236-1551; Lane Weatherbee, 115 N. Center Ave., Piedmont, AL 36272. TEL 205-447-2837; Ed. Lane Weatherbee; Pub. Lane Weatherbee; adv.; photos; pub. size: standard; circ. 6,600(paid).

PRATTVILLE

US

PRATTVILLE PROGRESS. 1886. s-w.: Wed. & Sat. $.50 newsstand; $24/yr. carrier. 152 W. Third St., Prattville, AL 35067. TEL 344-365-6739; FAX 344-365-1400. **Owner(s):** Multimedia, Inc., P.O. Box 1688, Greenville, SC 24602. TEL 803-298-4373; Ed. Brightman Brock; Pub. Lamar Smitherman; adv. contact: Chris Caver. pub. size: broadsheet; circ. 6,250(paid).

RAINSVILLE

US

WEEKLY POST. 1987. Thu. $15/yr. in state; $25/yr. out of state; $10/yr. senior citizens. 690 McCurdy Ave., Rainsville, AL 35986-0849. TEL 205-638-4027; FAX 205-638-2329. **Owner(s):** Carey H. Baker, 690 McCurdy Ave., Rainsville, AL 35986. TEL 205-638-4027; Pub. Carey H. Baker; adv.; photos; pub. size: standard; circ. 4,000(paid).

RED BAY

US

RED BAY NEWS. 1963. Wed. $.50 newsstand; $16/yr. local; $22/yr. elsewhere. 120 Fourth Ave. S.E., Red Bay, AL 35582. TEL 205-356-2148; FAX 205-356-2787. **Owner(s):** Harden Printers & Publishers, P.O. Box 1339, Red Bay, AL 35582. TEL 205-356-2148; FAX 205-356-2787; Ed. Tony Launius; Pub. LaVale Mills; adv. contact: LaVale Mills. photos; pub. size: broadsheet; circ. 4,020(paid). **Wire Service(s):** CNS.

ROANOKE

US

RANDOLPH LEADER. 1892. Wed. $.50 newsstand; $18/yr. local; $24/yr. elsewhere. 524 E. Main St., Roanoke, AL 36274. TEL 334-863-2819; FAX 334-863-4006. **Owner(s):** Randolph Publishers, P.O. Box 232, Roanoke, AL 36274. TEL 334-863-2819; Ed. John W. Stevenson; Pub. John W. Stevenson; pub. size: standard; circ. 6,200(paid).

ROBERTSDALE

US

INDEPENDENT, THE. 1975. Thu. $.50 newsstand; $23/yr. in state; $26/yr. out of state. P.O. Box 509, Robertsdale, AL 36567. TEL 334-947-7318; FAX 334-947-7652. **Owner(s):** Gulf Coast Newspapers, P.O. Box 509, Robertsdale, AL 36567. TEL 334-947-7712; Ed. Tammy Laytham; Pub. Stephanie Pressly; adv.; pub. size: broadsheet; circ. 3,000(paid).

ROGERSVILLE

US

EAST LAUDERDALE NEWS. 1965. Thu. $.25 newsstand; $13/yr. in state; $18/yr. out of state. E. Lee St., Rogersville, AL 35652. TEL 205-247-5565; FAX 205-247-1902. **Owner(s):** James B. & Phyllis D. Cox, P.O. Box 179, Rogersville, AL 35652. TEL 205-247-5565; FAX 205-247-1902; Ed. Phyllis D. Cox. pub. size: broadsheet; circ. 4,500(paid).

RUSSELLVILLE

US

FRANKLIN COUNTY PLUS. Wed. free. 142 Hwy. 43 By-Pass, Russellville, AL 35653. TEL 205-332-1881; FAX 205-332-1883. **Owner(s):** Franklin County Newspapers, Inc., P.O. Box 1088, Russellville, AL 35653. TEL 205-332-1881; FAX 205-332-1883; Ed. Rick Cameron; Pub. Rick Cameron; circ. 13,100(free).

US

FRANKLIN COUNTY TIMES. 1878. s-w.: Wed. & Sun. $.50 newsstand; $39.95/yr. 142 Hwy. 43 By-Pass, Russellville, AL 35653. TEL 205-332-1881; FAX 205-332-1883. **Owner(s):** Franklin County Newspapers, Inc., P.O. Box 1088, Russellville, AL 35653. TEL 205-332-1881; FAX 205-332-1883; Ed. Rick Cameron; Pub. Rick Cameron; adv.; pub. size: broadsheet; circ. 13,100(free & paid).

SAMSON

US

SAMSON LEDGER. 1899. Wed. $.50 newsstand; $17/yr. in cy.; $26/yr. out of cy. 105 W. Main St., Samson, AL 36477. TEL 334-684-2280; FAX 334-684-3099. **Owner(s):** James A. Specht, P.O. Box 66, Samson, AL 36477. TEL 334-898-2491; David Specht, P.O. Box 66, Samson, AL 36477. TEL 334-893-2491; Ed. Jay Sellsberg; Pub. James A. Specht; adv.; photos; pub. size: standard; circ. 1,500(free & paid).

SCOTTSBORO

US

VALLEY SUN, THE. Wed. free. 701 Veterans Hwy., Scottsboro, AL 35768. TEL 205-259-1020; FAX 205-259-2709. **Owner(s):** Scottsboro Newspapers, Inc., P.O. Box 220, Scottsboro, AL 35768. TEL 205-259-1020; Ed. Carmen Wann; Pub. Rick Loring; pub. size: broadsheet; circ. 7,200(free). **Wire Service(s):** AP, NEA.
    Formerly: Advertiser-Free Press.

STEVENSON

US

NORTH JACKSON PROGRESS. s-w.: Mon. & Thu. $.50 newsstand; $17/yr. 128 Oak Hill Cir., Stevenson, AL 35772. TEL 205-437-2395; FAX 205-437-2592. **Owner(s):** Larry O. Glass, P.O. Drawer 625, Stevenson, AL 35772. TEL 205-437-2395; Ed. Faye Glass; Pub. Larry O. Glass; adv. contact: Lee Glass. pub. size: standard; circ. 4,800(paid).

SULLIGENT

US

LAMAR LEADER. 1973. Wed. $.50 newsstand; $14/yr.; $16/yr. adjacent cys.; $17/yr. out of cy. 55071 Hwy. 17, Sulligent, AL 35586. TEL 205-698-8148; FAX 205-698-8146. **Owner(s):** Orman & Camille Wilson, 235 E. Main St., Sulligent, AL 35586. TEL 205-698-8148; FAX 205-698-8146; Ed. Don Dollar; Pub. Don Dollar; adv. contact: Don Dollar. pub. size: broadsheet; circ. 3,400(paid).

TALLASSEE
US
TALLASSEE TRIBUNE. 1899. Wed. $.50 newsstand; $18/yr. in cy.; $24/yr. out of state. 301 Gilmer Ave., Tallassee, AL 36078. TEL 334-283-6568; FAX 334-283-6569. **Owner(s):** Jack B. Venable, 301 Gilmer Ave., Tallassee, AL 36078; Ed. Jack B. Venable; Pub. Jack B. Venable; adv. contact: Barbara Morrow. pub. size: broadsheet; circ. 4,200(paid).

TUSCUMBIA
US
COLBERT COUNTY REPORTER. 1911. Fri. $.50 newsstand; $14/yr. mailed; $12/yr. senior citizens. 106 W. Fifth St., Tuscumbia, AL 35674. TEL 205-383-8471; FAX 205-383-8476. **Owner(s):** Jim Crawford, Jr., Lawrenceburg, TN 38464; Ed. Jim Crawford, Jr.; Pub. Jim Crawford, Jr.; adv. contact: Marcy Hill. pub. size: broadsheet; circ. 6,000(paid).

US
STANDARD & TIMES. 1829. Thu. $.50 newsstand; $14/yr. in cy. 106 W. Fifth, Tuscumbia, AL 35674. TEL 205-383-8476; FAX 205-383-8476. **Owner(s):** Jim Crawford, Jr., 106 W. Fifth, Tuscumbia, AL 35674. TEL 205-383-8476; Pub. Jim Crawford, Jr.; pub. size: broadsheet; circ. 4,500(paid).

TUSKEGEE
US
TUSKEGEE NEWS. 1865. Thu. $.50 newsstand; $22.50/yr. in cy. One Court Sq., Tuskegee, AL 36083. TEL 334-727-3020; FAX 334-727-3036. **Owner(s):** Tuskegee Newspapers, Inc., P.O. Box 60, Tuskegee, AL 36083. TEL 205-727-3020; Ed. Guy Rhodes; Pub. Paul Davis; pub. size: broadsheet; circ. 4,800(paid).

UNION SPRINGS
US
UNION SPRINGS HERALD. 1866. Wed. $.50 newsstand; $17/yr. in state; $21/yr. out of state. 104 E. Conecuh Ave., Union Springs, AL 36089. TEL 334-738-2360; FAX 334-738-2342. **Owner(s):** Terry Everett, 104 E. Conecuh Ave., Union Springs, AL 36089. TEL 334-738-2360; Pub. Thomas May; adv. contact: Neal May. pub. size: broadsheet; circ. 3,000(paid).

VERNON
US
LAMAR DEMOCRAT. 1896. Wed. $.50 newsstand; $12.50/yr in cy.; $15/yr. out of cy.; $20/yr. out of state. 125 First Ave., N.E., Vernon, AL 35592. TEL 205-695-7029; FAX 205-695-9501. **Owner(s):** Rex Rainwater, P.O. Box 587, Vernon, AL 35592. TEL 205-695-7029; Howard Reeves, P.O. Box 587, Vernon, AL 35592. TEL 205-695-7029; Ed. Howard Reeves; Pub. Rex Rainwater; pub. size: standard; circ. 4,300(paid).

WETUMPKA
US
WETUMPKA HERALD. 1898. Thu. $.50 newsstand; $16/yr. in cy.; $20/yr. in state; $24/yr. out of state. 300 Green St., Wetumpka, AL 36092-0029. TEL 334-567-7811; FAX 334-567-3284. **Owner(s):** Ellen T. Williams, 60 Tankersley Ln., Wetumpka, AL 36092. TEL 334-569-3284; Ed. Gerald Williams; Pub. Ellen T. Williams; adv. contact: Gerald M. Williams. photos; bk.rev.; pub. size: standard; circ. 4,156(free & paid).

ALASKA

ANCHORAGE
US
GREAT LANDER BUSH MAILER. 1969. m. free. 3110 Spenard Rd., Anchorage, AK 99503. TEL 907-274-0611; FAX 907-272-2105. **Owner(s):** Anchorage Printing, Inc., 3110 Spenard Rd., Anchorage, AK 99503. TEL 907-272-2213; Ed. Charles Rhodes; Pub. Charles Rhodes; adv. contact: Charles Rhodes. pub. size: tabloid; circ. 43,000(free).

US   ISSN 0049-4801
TUNDRA TIMES. 1962. bi-w. $1 newsstand; $30/yr.; $20/yr. senior citizens. 1711 E. Lore Rd., Anchorage, AK 99507. TEL 907-349-2512; FAX 907-349-0335. **Owner(s):** Eskimo, Indian, Aleut Publishing Co., P.O. Box 92247, Anchorage, AK 99507. TEL 907-349-2512; FAX 907-349-0335; Ed. Anna Pickett; Pub. Toni Kahklen-Jones; adv. contact: Anna Pickett. photos; bk.rev.; pub. size: tabloid; circ. 3,500.

BETHEL
US
TUNDRA DRUMS. 1974. Wed. $.75 newsstand; $45/yr. 660 Third Ave., Bethel, AK 99559. TEL 907-543-3500; FAX 907-543-3312; E-mail: aknewspr@alaska.net; URL: http://alaska.net/~aknewspr/drums/drums.html. **Owner(s):** Alaska Newspapers, Inc., 336 E. Fifth Ave., Anchorage, AK 99501. TEL 907-272-9830; Ed. John Plestima; Pub. Chris Casati; adv. contact: Natalie Smithson. photos; pub. size: tabloid; circ. 6,300(paid). **Wire Service(s):** AP, CSM.

CORDOVA
US
CORDOVA TIMES. 1914. Thu. $.75 newsstand; $90/yr. 1st class; $32/yr. 2nd class. P.O. Box 200, Cordova, AK 99574-0200. TEL 907-424-7181; FAX 907-424-5799; E-mail: aknewspr@alaska.net; URL: http://alaska.net/~aknewspr/cordova/cordova.html. **Owner(s):** Alaska Newspapers, Inc., 503 E. Sixth Ave., Anchorage, AK 99501. TEL 907-262-9830; Ed. Cinthia M. Stimson; Pub. Chris Casati; adv. contact: Joy Landaluce. bk.rev.; pub. size: standard; circ. 1,700(paid). **Wire Service(s):** AP.

HAINES
US
CHILKAT VALLEY NEWS. 1966. Thu. $42/yr. local; $48/yr. mailed 2nd class; $64/yr. mailed 1st class; $48/yr. Hawaii mailed. Main St., Haines, AK 99827. TEL 907-766-2688. **Owner(s):** Bonnie Hedrick, P.O. Box 630, Haines, AK 99827. TEL 907-766-2688; Ed. Bonnie Hedrick. adv.; pub. size: tabloid; circ. 1,100(paid).

HOMER
US
HOMER NEWS. 1964. Thu. $.75 newsstand; $35/yr. local; $43/yr. in state; $48/yr. out of state. 3482 Landings St., Homer, AK 99603. TEL 907-235-7767; FAX 907-235-4199; E-mail: ~haknewspr@alaska.net; URL: http://alaska.net/news/homer.html. **Owner(s):** Howard Simmons & Nancy Cohen, 3482 Landings St., Homer, AK 99603. TEL 907-235-7767; Ed. Mark Turner; Pub. Mark Turner; adv. contact: Jane Alberts. pub. size: tabloid; circ. 4,500(controlled & paid).

JUNEAU
US
CAPITAL CITY WEEKLY. 1980. w. free. 1910 Alex Holden Way, Juneau, AK 99801. TEL 907-789-4144; FAX 907-789-0987; E-mail: capweek@ptialaska.net; URL: http://www.adone.com/capcity. **Owner(s):** Summit Services, Inc., 1910 Alex Holden Way, Juneau, AK 99801; Ed. Riley Woodford; Pub. Renda Heimbigner; adv. contact: Renda Heimbigner. photos; bk.rev.; pub. size: tabloid; circ. 20,000(free & paid).

NOME
US   ISSN 0745-9106
NOME NUGGET. 1900. Thu. $.50 newsstand; $60/yr. mailed. 123 Front St., Nome, AK 99762. TEL 907-443-5235. **Owner(s):** Nancy McGuire, P.O. Box 610, Nome, AK 99762. TEL 907-443-5235; Ed. Nancy McGuire; Pub. Nancy McGuire; adv.; photos; pub. size: tabloid; circ. 4,000(paid). **Wire Service(s):** AP.

PETERSBURG
US
PETERSBURG PILOT. 1974. Thu. $1 newsstand; $36/yr. in town; $47/yr. out of town; $58/yr. out of state. 212 Harborway, Petersburg, AK 99833. TEL 907-772-9393; FAX 907-772-4871. **Owner(s):** Pilot Publishing, Inc., 212 Harborway, Petersburg, AK 99833. TEL 907-772-9393; FAX 907-772-4871; Ed. Ronald J. Loesch. pub. size: tabloid; circ. 1,800(paid).

SEWARD
US
SEWARD PHOENIX LOG. 1966. Thu. $.75 newsstand; $45/yr. 315 Fourth Ave., Seward, AK 99664. TEL 907-224-8070; FAX 907-224-3157; E-mail: aknewspr@alaska.net; URL: http://alaska.net/~aknewspr/seward/seward.html. **Owner(s):** Alaska Newspapers, Inc., 503 E. Sixth Ave., Anchorage, AK 99664. TEL 907-272-9830; FAX 907-272-9512; Ed. Chris Casati; Pub. Chris Casati; adv. contact: Bruce Swanson. photos; pub. size: tabloid; circ. 2,000(free & paid). **Wire Service(s):** AP.

VALDEZ

US

VALDEZ VANGUARD. 1976. Wed. $.75 newsstand; $45/yr. 224 Galena, Valdez, AK 99686. TEL 907-835-2211; FAX 907-835-5101; E-mail: aknewspr@alaska.net; URL: http://alaska.net/ ~a knewspr/valdez/vanguard.html. **Owner(s):** Alaska Newspapers, Inc., 336 E. Fifth Ave., Anchorage, AK 99501. TEL 907-272-9830; FAX 907-272-9512; Ed. Tony Bickert; Pub. Chris Cassati; adv.; photos; bk.rev.; pub. size: tabloid; circ. 1,650(free & paid). **Wire Service(s):** AP.

WASILLA

US

FRONTIERSMAN, THE. 1947. s-w.: Wed. & Fri. $.50 newsstand; $40/yr. in city; $65.60/yr. out of city; $70.60/yr. out of state. 1261 Seward-Meridian, Wasilla, AK 99654. TEL 907-376-5225; FAX 907-352-2277. **Owner(s):** Wick Communications, Inc., 333 W. Wilcox Dr., Ste. 302, Sierra Vista, AZ 85635. TEL 520-728-4488; FAX 520-728-6090; Ed. Vicki Naegele. adv. contact: Jerry Gamb. pub. size: broadsheet; circ. 8,000(paid). **Wire Service(s):** AP Newsfinder.

US

VALLEY SUN. Tue. free. 1261 Seward-Meridian, Wasilla, AK 99654. TEL 907-376-5225; FAX 907-352-2277. **Owner(s):** Wick Communications, Inc., 333 W. Wilcox Dr., Ste. 302, Sierra Vista, AZ 85635. TEL 520-728-4488; FAX 520-728-6090; Ed. Vicki Naegele. adv. contact: Jerry Gamb. circ. 8,200(free).

WRANGELL

US

WRANGELL SENTINEL. 1902. Thu. $.75 newsstand; $30/yr. in town; $34/yr. out of town 2nd class; $54/yr. out of town 1st class. 312 Front St., Wrangell, AK 99929. TEL 907-874-2301; FAX 907-874-2303. **Owner(s):** Wrangell Sentinel, P.O. Box 798, Wrangell, AK 99929. TEL 907-874-2301; Ed. Jodi Stephens. adv.; photos; bk.rev.; pub. size: tabloid; circ. 1,500(controlled & paid).

ARIZONA

AJO

US

AJO COPPER NEWS. 1916. Wed. $.25 newsstand; $20/yr. 10 Pajaro, Ajo, AZ 85321. TEL 520-387-7688; FAX 520-387-7688. **Owner(s):** Gabrielle, Hollister J. & Joseph D. David, P.O. Box 39, Ajo, AZ 85321. TEL 520-387-7688; Ed. Gabrielle David; Pub. Hollister J. David; adv. contact: Michelle Pacheco. photos; pub. size: tabloid; circ. 2,456(paid).

APACHE JUNCTION

US

APACHE JUNCTION INDEPENDENT. 1959. Tue. $.25 newsstand; $20/yr.; $20/3 mos. out of state. 201 W. Apache Trai , Ste. 708, Apache Junction, AZ 85220. TEL 602-982-7799; FAX 602-671-0016. **Owner(s):** Joe Smyth, 4308 E. Lakeside Ln., Scottsdale, AZ 85253. TEL 602-991-5333; Ed. James L. Files. adv.: $12.92/SAU. pub. size: broadsheet; circ. 20,000(free & paid).

US

EAST MESA INDEPENDENT. 1963. Wed. $.25 newsstand; $18/yr.; $20/3 mos. out of state. 201 W. Apache Trail, Ste. 708, Apache Junction, AZ 85220. TEL 602-982-7799; FAX 602-671-0016. **Owner(s):** Joe Smyth, 4308 E. Lakeside Ln. Scottsdale, AZ 85253. TEL 602-991-5333; Ed. Richard Dyer. adv. contact: Kurt Ploudre. adv.: $16.52/SAU. pub. size: broadsheet; circ. 37,000(paid).
    Formerly: Mesa Independent.

ARIZONA CITY

US

ARIZONA CITY INDEPENDENT. bi-w. $.50 newsstand; $8.50/yr.; $12/yr. out of state. P.O. Box 5969, Arizona City, AZ 85223. TEL 602-466-6277. **Owner(s):** Casa Grande Valley Newspapers, Inc., 200 W. Second St., Casa Grande, AZ 85222. TEL 602-836-7461; Ed. Ken Barr. circ. 2,500.

AVONDALE

US

WEST VALLEY VIEW. 1985. Wed. $.50 newsstand; $32/yr. 310 N. Dysart Rd., Avondale, AZ 85323. TEL 602-932-4361; FAX 602-932-4368. **Owner(s):** E. Freireich, 310 N. Dysart Rd., Avondale, AZ 85323. TEL 602-932-4361; FAX 602-932-4368 B. Freireich, 310 N. Dysart Rd., Avondale, AZ 85323. TEL 602-932-4361; FAX 602-932-4368 Ed. L. Painter; Pub. E. Freireich; adv.; photos; bk.rev.; pub. size: tabloid; circ. 27,000(free).

BISBEE

US

▼**BISBEE NEWS, THE.** 1995. Thu. free newsstand; $30/yr. 99 Bisbee Rd., Ste. B, Bisbee, AZ 85603. TEL 520-432-4400; FAX 520-432-4441. **Owner(s):** Bisbee Publishing Co., 99 Bisbee Rd., Ste. B, Bisbee, AZ 85603. TEL 520-432-4400; FAX 520-432-4441; adv. contact: Judy Benjamin. photos; bk.rev.; pub. size: tabloid; circ. 3,500(free & paid).

US

▼**BISBEE NOW.** 1995. q. free. 99 Bisbee Rd., Ste. B, Bisbee, AZ 85603. TEL 520-432-4400; FAX 520-432-4441. **Owner(s):** Bisbee Publishing Co., 99 Bisbee Rd., Ste. B, Bisbee, AZ 85603. TEL 520-432-4400; FAX 520-432-4441; adv. contact: Judy Benjamin. pub. size: tabloid; circ. 23,500(free).

US

BREWERY GULCH GAZETTE. 1932. Wed. $.35 newsstand; $17/yr. mailed. 99 Bisbee Rd., Ste. B, Bisbee, AZ 85603. TEL 520-432-4400; FAX 520-432-4441. **Owner(s):** Bisbee Publishing Co., 99 Bisbee Rd., Ste. B, Bisbee, AZ 85603. TEL 520-432-4400; FAX 520-432-4441; Ed. Mary Ellen Corbett. adv. contact: Judy Benjamin. bk.rev.; pub. size: tabloid; circ. 1,580(paid).

CHANDLER

US

CHANDLER INDEPENDENT. 1986. Wed. free in area; $18/yr. mailed 3rd class. 325 E Elliot Rd., Ste 21, Chandler, AZ 85225-1127. TEL 602-497-0048; FAX 602-926-1019. **Owner(s):** Joe Smyth, P.O. Box 12292, Scottsdale, AZ 85268. TEL 602-991-5333; Ed. Linda Gronemann. adv.: $13.16/SAU. pub. size: broadsheet; circ. 21,000(free & paid).

CLIFTON

US

COPPER ERA. 1889. Wed. $.35 newsstand; $17/yr. in cy.; $23/yr. in state; $28/yr. out of state. One Wards Canyon, Clifton, AZ 85533 TEL 520-865-3162; FAX 520-428-3110. **Owner(s):** Wick Communications, Inc., 333 W. Wilcox Dr., Ste. 302, Sierra Vista, AZ 85635-1357. TEL 520-453-0200; FAX 520-458-6166; Pub. Wayne Hemstreet; adv.; photos; pub. size: broadsheet; circ. 3,500(free & paid).

COOLIDGE

US

COOLIDGE EXAMINER. Wed. $.50 newsstand; $35/yr. in state; $45/yr. out of state. 353 W. Central, Coolidge, AZ 85228. TEL 602-723-5441. **Owner(s):** Casa Grande Valley Newspapers, Inc., P.O. Box 15002, Casa Grande, AZ 85230-5002. TEL 602-836-7461; Ed. Thomas Martinez. adv. contact: Bob Tuley. pub. size: broadsheet; circ. 2,288(paid).

COTTONWOOD

US

COTTONWOOD JOURNAL EXTRA 1988. Wed. controlled/home deliv. 830 S. Main, Ste. 1E, Cottonwood, AZ 86326. TEL 602-634-8551; FAX 602-282-6888. **Owner(s):** L & L Printing Co., P.O. Box 619, Sedona, AZ 86336. TEL 602-282-6809; FAX 602-282-6011; Ed. Tom Brossart; Pub. Robert Larson Jr.; adv.; pub. size: broadsheet; circ. 7,250(controlled & paid).

US

VERDE INDEPENDENT. 1947. s-w.: Wed. & Fri. $42/yr. 116 S. Main St., Cottonwood, AZ 86326. TEL 602-634-2241 FAX 602-634-2312. **Owner(s):** Western Newspapers, Inc., 2055 Arizona Ave., Yuma, AZ 85364. TEL 602-783-3333 Ed. Dan Engler; Pub. Dick Larson; adv.; pub. size: broadsheet; circ. 16,635(free & paid).

EAGAR

US

ROUND VALLEY PAPER, THE. 1988. Wed. $.25 newsstand; $18/yr. 150 N. Poverty Flat, Eagar, AZ 85925-0867. TEL 602-333-2033. **Owner(s):** Glenn & Dorothy Jacobs, P.O. Box 867, Eagar, AZ 85925-0867. TEL 602-333-2033; Pub. Dorothy Jacobs; adv.; photos; pub. size: broadsheet; circ. 1,100(free & paid).

ELOY

US

ELOY ENTERPRISE. 1947. Thu. $.50 newsstand; $35/yr. in state; $45/yr. out of state. 710 N. Main St., Eloy, AZ 85231. TEL 602-466-7333. **Owner(s):** Casa Grande Valley Newspapers, Inc., P.O. Box 15002, Casa Grande, AZ 85230-5002. TEL 602-836-7461; Ed. Joe Meahl. pub. size: broadsheet; circ. 891(paid).

GLENDALE

US

ARROW, THE. 1987. m. $15/yr. 17035 N. 67th Ave., Ste. 2, Glendale, AZ 85308. TEL 602-878-8881; FAX 602-878-8899. **Owner(s):** Phyllis C. & Elwyn W. Brown, 17035 N. 67th Ave., Ste. 2, Glendale, AZ 85308. TEL 602-878-8881; FAX 602-878-8899; Ed. Alisa Fox; Pub. Phyllis C. Brown; adv.; photos; bk.rev.; pub. size: tabloid; circ. 22,000(controlled & paid).

US   ISSN 1053-7600

GLENDALE STAR, THE. 1979. Thu. $.50 newsstand; $20/yr. 7122 N. 59th Ave., Glendale, AZ 85301. TEL 602-842-6000; FAX 602-842-6017. **Owner(s):** William V. & Darlene M. Toops, 7122 N. 59th Ave., Glendale, AZ 85301. TEL 602-842-6000; FAX 602-842-6017; Ed. Michael G. Hart; Pub. William V. Toops; adv. contact: Michael Kostelac. pub. size: tabloid; circ. 10,500(free & paid).

US

PEORIA TIMES. 1952. Fri. $.50 newsstand; $20/yr. 7122 N. 59th Ave., Glendale, AZ 85301. TEL 602-842-6000; FAX 602-842-6017. **Owner(s):** William & Darlene Toops, 7122 N. 59th Ave., Glendale, AZ 85301. TEL 602-842-6000; FAX 602-842-6017; Ed. Carolyn Dryer. adv. contact: Michael Kostelac. pub. size: tabloid; circ. 8,000(free & paid).

GLOBE

US

ARIZONA SILVER BELT. 1878. Wed. $.50 newsstand; $21/yr. in cy.; $24/yr. out of cy. 298 N. Pine, Globe, AZ 85501. TEL 520-425-7121; FAX 520-425-7001. **Owner(s):** American Publishing Co., 606 N. Van Buren, P.O. Box 520, Marion, IL 62959. TEL 618-993-1711; Ed. Ellen Kretsch; Pub. Ellen Kretsch; adv. contact: David Andrade. pub. size: broadsheet; circ. 7,000(paid). **Formerly:** Globe Arizona Silver Belt.

US

COPPER COUNTRY NEWS. 1984. Tue. free newsstand; $36/yr. 254 N. Broad, Globe, AZ 85501. TEL 602-425-0355; FAX 602-425-6535. **Owner(s):** Guy & Donna L. Anderson, 254 N. Broad, Globe, AZ 85501. TEL 602-425-0355; FAX 602-425-6535; Pub. Donna L. Anderson; adv.; photos; pub. size: tabloid; circ. 8,000(free).

GREEN VALLEY

US

GREEN VALLEY NEWS & SUN. 1964. s-w.: Wed. & Fri. $.50 newsstand; $35/yr. carrier; $50/yr. mailed. P.O. Box 567, Green Valley, AZ 85622. TEL 520-625-5511; FAX 602-625-1603. **Owner(s):** Wick Communications, Inc., 333 Wilcox Dr., Ste. 302, Sierra Vista, AZ 85635-1756. TEL 520-458-0200; Ed. Kathleen M. Engle; Pub. Frank Newel; adv.; bk.rev.; pub. size: standard; circ. 7,000(paid).

HOLBROOK

US

HOLBROOK TRIBUNE NEWS & SNOWFLAKE HERALD. 1909. s-w.: Wed. & Fri. $.35 newsstand; $25/yr. 200 E. Hopi Dr., Holbrook, AZ 86025. TEL 520-524-6203; FAX 520-524-3541. **Owner(s):** Navajo County Publishers, Inc., 200 E. Hopi Dr., Holbrook, AZ 86025. TEL 520-524-6205; Ed. Francie Payne; Pub. Paul Barger; adv. contact: Matthew Barger. photos; pub. size: broadsheet; circ. 3,476(paid).

PAGE

US

LAKE POWELL CHRONICLE. 1965. Wed. $.50 newsstand; $31/yr. in state; $40/yr. out of state. P.O. Box 1716, Page, AZ 86040. TEL 602-645-8888; FAX 602-645-2209. **Owner(s):** John & Nora McNall, Lake Powell Newspapers, Inc., P.O. Box 1716, Page, AZ 86040. TEL 602-645-8888; Ed. Scott Hoover; Pub. Susan Shenniman; pub. size: broadsheet; circ. 3,100(paid).

PARKER

US

PARKER PIONEER. 1954. Wed. $.50 newsstand; $18/yr. local; $22/yr. in state; $32/yr. out of state. 1001 12th St., Parker, AZ 85344. TEL 520-669-2275; FAX 520-669-9624. **Owner(s):** River City Newspapers, LLC, 2225 W. Acoma Blvd., Lake Havasu City, AZ 86403-1756. TEL 520-453-4237; Ed. John Moeur. adv.; pub. size: broadsheet.

PAYSON

US

PAYSON ROUNDUP. 1937. s-w.: Wed. & Fri. $.35 newsstand; $37.50/yr. in state; $44/yr. out of state. 708 N. Beeline Hwy., Payson, AZ 85547. TEL 520-474-5251; FAX 520-474-1897; E-mail: TPRoundup@aol.com; URL: http://members.aol.com/TPRoundup/index.html. **Owner(s):** WorldWest Limited Liability Co., Lawrence, KS. TEL 913-843-1000; Ed. Niki Price; Pub. David Price; adv.; photos; bk.rev.; pub. size: standard; circ. 6,200(paid). **Wire Service(s):** AP Newsfinder. **Formerly:** Payson Roundup & Rim Country News.

PHOENIX

US   ISSN 0279-3962

NEW TIMES. 1970. Wed. free newsstand; $60/yr. mailed. 1201 E. Jefferson, Phoenix, AZ 85034. TEL 602-271-0040; FAX 602-340-8806. **Owner(s):** New Times, Inc., P.O. Box 2510, Phoenix, AZ 85002. TEL 602-271-0040; FAX 602-340-8806; Ed. John Mecklin; Pub. Michele Laven; adv. contact: Mary Feldman. photos; pub. size: tabloid; circ. 140,000(free).

SAFFORD

US

EASTERN ARIZONA COURIER. 1967. Wed. $.50 newsstand; $20/yr. in state; $37/yr. out of state. 301 E. Hwy. 70, Safford, AZ 85546. TEL 520-428-2560; FAX 520-428-5396. **Owner(s):** Wick Communications, Inc., 333 W. Wilcox Dr., Ste. 302, Sierra Vista, AZ 85635. TEL 520-458-0200; FAX 520-458-6166; Ed. Wayne Hemstreet; Pub. Wayne Hemstreet; adv. contact: Ted Hecht. photos; pub. size: broadsheet; circ. 8,900(free & paid).

SCOTTSDALE

US

GILBERT INDEPENDENT. 1978. Wed. free. 11000 N. Scottsdale Rd., Ste. 210, Scottsdale, AZ 85254. TEL 602-483-0977; FAX 602-948-0496. **Owner(s):** Joe Smyth, 4308 E. Lakeside Ln., Scottsdale, AZ 85253. TEL 602-991-5333; Ed. Jeremy Handel; Pub. Ed Dulin; adv.: $11.68/SAU. pub. size: broadsheet; circ. 16,000(free).

US

PARADISE VALLEY INDEPENDENT. 1982. Wed. $20/yr. 11000 N. Scottsdale Rd., Ste. 210, Scottsdale, AZ 85254. TEL 602-483-0977; FAX 602-948-0496. **Owner(s):** Joe Smyth, Scottsdale, AZ 85253. TEL 602-991-5333; adv.: $12.72/SAU. pub. size: broadsheet; circ. 20,000(controlled & free).

US

TOWN OF PARADISE VALLEY INDEPENDENT. 1985. Wed. $.25 newsstand; $18/yr. 11000 N. Scottsdale Rd., #210, Scottsdale, AZ 85254. TEL 602-483-0977; FAX 602-948-0496. **Owner(s):** Joe Smyth, 4308 E. Lakeside Ln., Scottsdale, AZ 85253. TEL 602-991-5333; Ed. Tammy Arnold. adv.: $9.28/SAU. photos; pub. size: broadsheet; circ. 6,000(controlled & paid).

SEDONA

US

SEDONA RED ROCK NEWS. 1963. s-w.: Wed. & Fri. $.50 newsstand; $30/yr. locally; $43/yr. out of town. 298 Van Deren Rd., Sedona, AZ 86336. TEL 520-282-7795; FAX 520-282-6011. **Owner(s):** Larson Publishing, 298 Van Deven Rd., Sedona, AZ 86336. TEL 602-282-7795; Ed. Tom Brossart; Pub. Robert B. Larson; pub. size: broadsheet; circ. 7,500(paid).

SHOW LOW

US

WAMPUM SAVER. 1975. s-w.: Wed. & Sat. free. 3191 S. White Mountain Rd., Show Low, AZ 85901. TEL 602-537-5721; FAX 602-537-1780. **Owner(s):** White Mountain Publishing Co., P.O. Box 1570, Show Low, AZ 85901. TEL 602-537-5721; Pub. Greg Tock; adv. contact: Greg Tock. pub. size: tabloid; circ. 20,000(free).

US

WHITE MOUNTAIN INDEPENDENT. 1909. s-w.: Tue. & Fri. $.50 newsstand; $32/yr.; $64/2 yrs. in Navajo & Apache cys. 3191 S. White Mountain Rd., Show Low, AZ 85901. TEL 602-537-5721; FAX 602-537-1780. **Owner(s):** White Mountain Publishing Co., P.O. Box 1570, Show Low, AZ 85901; Pub. Greg Tock; adv.; photos; bk.rev.; pub. size: broadsheet; circ. morning 7,000(paid).

SUN CITY

US

▼ARROWHEAD RANCH INDEPENDENT. 1995. Wed. $.25 newsstand; free home deliv. 10327 W. Coggins Dr., Sun City, AZ 85351. TEL 602-972-6101; FAX 602-974-6004. **Owner(s):** Independent Newspapers, Inc., 11000 N. Scottsdale Rd., #210, Scottsdale, AZ 85253. TEL 602-483-0977; Pub. Bret McKeand; adv. contact: Tammi Abrahms. adv.: $10.56/SAU. photos; pub. size: broadsheet; circ. 12,000(free & paid).

US

SUN CITIES INDEPENDENT. 1960. Wed. $.25 newsstand; $80/yr.; $40/6 mos.; $20/3 mos. 10327 Coggins Dr., Sun City, AZ 85351. TEL 602-972-6101; FAX 602-974-6004. **Owner(s):** Independent Newspapers, Inc., 4308 E. Lakeside Ln., Scottsdale, AZ 85253. TEL 602-483-0977; Ed. Bret McKeand; Pub. Bret McKeand; adv. contact: Bill Siewert. photos; bk.rev.; pub. size: broadsheet; circ. 39,500(paid).

US

SUN CITY/YOUNGTOWN. Wed. free. 10327 W. Coggins Dr., Sun City, AZ 85351. TEL 602-972-6101; FAX 602-974-6004. **Owner(s):** Joe Smyth, 4308 E. Lakeside Ln., Scottsdale, AZ 85253. TEL 602-991-5333; Ed. Bret McKeand. adv.: $13.88/SAU. pub. size: broadsheet; circ. 25,000(free).

US

SUN CITY WEST. Wed. free. 10327 W. Coggins Dr., Sun City, AZ 85351. TEL 602-972-6101; FAX 602-974-6004. **Owner(s):** Joe Smyth, 4308 E. Lakeside Ln., Scottsdale, AZ 85253. TEL 602-991-5333; Ed. John Wolfe. adv.: $11/SAU. pub. size: broadsheet; circ. 14,000(free).

TOMBSTONE

US

TOMBSTONE EPITAPH, THE. 1880. m. $15/yr. 9 S. Fifth Ave., Tombstone, AZ 85638. TEL 520-457-2211. **Owner(s):** Sara E. Love, 6545 St. Andrew's Dr., Tucson, AZ 85718. TEL 602-297-7919; Wallace E. Clayton, 4610 E. Blue Mountain Dr., Tucson, AZ 85718. TEL 602-299-4657; Rudolf G. Wunderlich, 704 N. Wells St., Chicago, IL 60610; Ed. Wallace E. Clayton; Pub. Wallace E. Clayton; adv. contact: Carol Winkelmann. photos; pub. size: tabloid; circ. 12,000(paid).

WICKENBURG

US

WICKENBURG SUN. 1934. Wed. $.50 newsstand; $20/yr. in cy. 180 N. Washington St., Wickenburg, AZ 85358. TEL 520-684-5454; FAX 520-684-3185. **Owner(s):** Brehm Communications, Inc., 17065 Via del Campo, Ste. 200, P.O. Box 28429, San Diego, CA 92127. TEL 619-451-3814; Ed. Philip Swift; Pub. Kevin Cloe; adv.; photos; pub. size: broadsheet; circ. 4,000(paid).

WILLIAMS

US

WILLIAMS GRAND CANYON NEWS. 1889. Thu. $27.50/yr. 118 S. First St., Williams, AZ 86046. TEL 602-635-4426; FAX 602-635-4887. **Owner(s):** Western Newspapers, Inc., 290 S. First Ave., Ste. 4, Yuma, AZ 85364. TEL 602-783-3311; Ed. Jerry Herrmann. adv. contact: Joyce Fuller McNelly. pub. size: broadsheet; circ. 5,000(paid).

WINSLOW

US   ISSN 8750-5711

WINSLOW MAIL. 1894. s-w.: Wed & Fri. $.35 newsstand; $24/yr. in cy.; $30/yr. out of cy.; $38/yr. out of state. 208 W. First St., Winslow, AZ 86047. TEL 520-289-2467; FAX 520-524-3541. **Owner(s):** Navajo County Publishers, Inc., 200 E. Hopi Dr., Holbrook, AZ 86025. TEL 520-524-6203; Ed. Francie Paine; Pub. Paul Barger; adv. contact: Manny Maniaci. photos; pub. size: broadsheet; circ. 2,891(free & paid).

ARKANSAS

ATKINS

US

ATKINS CHRONICLE, THE. 1894. Wed. $.50 newsstand; $20/yr. in cy.; $25/yr. in state; $30/yr. out of state. 204 Ave. One, N.E., Atkins, AR 72823. TEL 501-641-7161; FAX 501-641-1604. **Owner(s):** Ginnie & Van Allen Tyson, 584 Murdoch Rd., Atkins, AR 72823. TEL 501-641-2688; FAX 501-641-1604; Ed. Van A. Tyson; Pub. Ginnie Tyson; adv. contact: Brooka Hamilton. photos; bk.rev.; pub. size: broadsheet; circ. 2,700(paid).

BEEBE

US

BEEBE NEWS. Wed. $.50 newsstand; $18/yr. in cy.; $20/yr. surrounding cys.; $25/yr. out of state. 107 E. Center, Beebe, AR 72012. TEL 501-882-5414; FAX 501-882-3576. **Owner(s):** Lee K. McLane, 107 E. Center, Beebe, AR 72012. TEL 501-882-5414; Ed. Lee K. McLane. photos; bk.rev.; pub. size: broadsheet; circ. 2,500(paid).

BERRYVILLE

US   ISSN 8750-6467

EUREKA SPRINGS TIMES-ECHO. 1879. Wed. $.50 newsstand; $20.50/yr. local; $33.75/yr. out of area. Oakview Dr., Berryville, AR 72616. TEL 501-423-6636; FAX 501-423-6640. **Owner(s):** U.S. Media Group, P.O. Box 227, Crystal City, MO 63019. TEL 314-937-5200; FAX 314-937-7947; Ed. Martha Campbell; Pub. LeRoy Gorrell; adv. contact: Pat Chaney. photos; pub. size: broadsheet; circ. 3,260(paid). **Wire Service(s):** AP.

US

GREEN FOREST TRIBUNE. 1889. Wed. $.50 newsstand; $20.50/yr. local; $33.75/yr. out of area. Oakview Dr., Berryville, AR 72616. TEL 501-423-6636; FAX 501-423-6640. **Owner(s):** U.S. Media Group, P.O. Box 227, Crystal City, MO 63019; Ed. Martha Campbell; Pub. Leroy Gorrell; adv. contact: Pat Chaney. photos; pub. size: broadsheet; circ. 1,600(paid). **Formerly:** Green Forest Carroll County Tribune.

US

STAR-PROGRESS, THE. 1873. Thu. $.50 newsstand; $20.50/yr. in cy.; $30.75/yr. in state; $33.75/yr. out of state. Oakview Dr., Berryville, AR 72616. TEL 501-423-6636; FAX 501-423-6640. **Owner(s):** U.S. Media Group, 998 E. Gannon Dr., Crystal City, MO 63019. TEL 314-937-5200; FAX 314-937-7947; Ed. Martha Cambell; Pub. LeRoy Gorrell; adv.; photos; pub. size: broadsheet; circ. 2,859(paid). **Wire Service(s):** AP.

BRINKLEY

US

BRINKLEY ARGUS. 1875. s-w.: Wed. & Fri. $.50 newsstand; $25/yr. in state; $45/yr. out of state. 308 W. Cedar, Brinkley, AR 72021. TEL 501-734-1056; FAX 501-734-2302. **Owner(s):** Franklin & Flora Jane Elledge, 308 W. Cedar, Brinkley, AR 72021. TEL 501-734-1056; Ed. Thomas Jacques. adv.; photos; pub. size: broadsheet; circ. 3,600(paid).

CALICO ROCK

US

WHITE RIVER CURRENT. 1972. Thu. $.25 newsstand; $12/yr. in cy.; $16/yr. out of cy. 105 Garden St., Calico Rock, AR 72519. TEL 501-297-8300; FAX 501-297-8799. **Owner(s):** Jeannie Day, P.O. Box 570, Calico Rock, AR 72519. TEL 501-297-8300; FAX 501-297-8799; Ed. Jeannie Day; Pub. Jeannie Day; adv. contact: Margaret Waters. photos; bk.rev.; pub. size: broadsheet; circ. 2,200(paid).

CLARKSVILLE

US

JOHNSON COUNTY GRAPHIC. 1877. Wed. $.25 newsstand; $25/yr. 203 E. Cherry, Clarksville, AR 72830. TEL 501-754-2005; FAX 501-754-2098; E-mail: rwylie@cswnet.com. **Owner(s):** Johnson County Graphic, Inc., 203 E. Cherry, Clarksville, AR 72830. TEL 501-754-2005; Ed. Margaret Wylie; Pub. Debra Grey; adv. contact: Debra Grey. photos; pub. size: standard; circ. 7,500(paid).

CLINTON

US

CLINTON VAN BUREN COUNTY DEMOCRAT. 1909. Wed. $.50 newsstand; $15/yr. in cy.; $20/yr. in state; $25/yr. out of state. 114 S. Court, Clinton, AR 72031-0119. TEL 501-745-5175; FAX 501-745-8865. **Owner(s):** Jay W. Jackson, P.O. Box 119, Clinton, AR 72031. TEL 501-745-5175; FAX 501-745-8365; Patsy Jackson, P.O. Box 119, Clinton, AR 72031. TEL 501-745-5175; FAX 501-745-8365; Pub. Jay W. Jackson; adv.; pub. size: standard; circ. 4,646(paid).

CROSSETT

US

ASHLEY COUNTY SHOPPERS GUIDE. Mon. free. 102 Pine St., Crossett, AR 71635. TEL 501-364-5186; FAX 501-364-2116. **Owner(s):** Ashley County Publishing Co., 102 Pine St., Crosssett, AR 71635. TEL 501-364-5186; FAX 501-364-2116; Ed. Steve Sanders; Pub. Larry W. Johnson; adv. contact: Charlotte Johnson. pub. size: tabloid; circ. 10,653(free).

US

ASHLEY NEWS OBSERVER. 1907. Wed. $.75 newsstand; $26/yr. in cy.; $42/yr. out of cy. 102 Pine St., Crossett, AR 71635. TEL 501-364-5186; FAX 501-364-2116. **Owner(s):** Ashley County Publishing Co., 102 Pine St., Ashley, AR 71635. TEL 501-364-5186; FAX 501-364-2116; Ed. Larry Wittnebert; Pub. Larry W. Johnson; adv. contact: Charlotte Johnson. photos; pub. size: broadsheet; circ. 5,100(paid).

DE QUEEN

US

DE QUEEN BEE. 1897. w. $.35 newsstand; $15/yr. 404 De Queen Ave., De Queen, AR 71832. TEL 501-642-2111; FAX 501-642-3138. **Owner(s):** Ray Kimball, P.O. Box 1000, De Queen, AR 71832. TEL 501-642-2111; Ed. Billy Ray McKelvy; Pub. Ray Kimball; adv. contact: Gail Mitchell. pub. size: broadsheet; circ. 5,000(paid).

DES ARC

US

WHITE RIVER JOURNAL. 1907. Thu. $.30 newsstand; $14/yr. in cy.; $22/yr. out of state. 424 Main St., Des Arc, AR 72040. TEL 501-256-4254; FAX 501-256-4254. **Owner(s):** White River Journal Corp., Fifth & Main, Des Arc, AR 72040. TEL 501-256-4254; Ed. Dean L. Walls; Pub. Dean L. Walls; adv. contact: Sandy Allred. adv.: $4.50/SAU. pub. size: broadsheet; circ. 2,650(paid).

DUMAS

US

DUMAS CLARION. 1899. Wed. $.35 newsstand; $15/yr. 136 E. Waterman, Dumas, AR 71639. TEL 501-382-4925; FAX 501-382-6421. **Owner(s):** Clarion Publishing Co., 136 E. Waterman, Dumas, AR 71639. TEL 501-382-4925; Pub. Charlotte Schexnayder; adv.; pub. size: standard; circ. 4,200(paid).

ENGLAND

US

ENGLAND DEMOCRAT. Wed. $.30 newsstand; $12/yr. in cy.; $15/yr. out of cy.; $22/yr. out of state. 121 E. Haywood, England, AR 72046. TEL 501-842-3111; FAX 501-842-3081. **Owner(s):** Jerry Jackson, P.O. Drawer 250, England, AR 72046. TEL 501-842-3111; Ed. Jerry Jackson; Pub. Jerry Jackson; pub. size: standard; circ. 1,680(paid).

GENTRY

US

DECATUR HERALD. Wed. $.50 newsstand. Main St., Gentry, AR 72734. TEL 501-736-2822; FAX 501-736-2822. **Owner(s):** Community Publishers, Inc., P.O. Box 1044, Siloam Springs, AR 72761. TEL 501-524-4131; Ed. James Garner. pub. size: broadsheet; circ. 1,050(paid).

US

GENTRY COURIER-JOURNAL. Wed. $.50 newsstand; $18/yr. Main St., Gentry, AR 72734. TEL 501-736-2822. **Owner(s):** Community Publishers, Inc., P.O. Box 1044, Siloam Springs, AR 72761. TEL 501-736-2822; Ed. James Garner. pub. size: broadsheet; circ. 1,050(paid).

GLENWOOD

US

GLENWOOD HERALD. 1926. Thu. $.50 newsstand; $15/yr. local; $30/yr. out of area; $35/yr. out of state. 204 Broadway, Glenwood, AR 71943. TEL 501-356-2111; FAX 501-356-4400. **Owner(s):** Graves Publishing Co., Inc., P.O. Box 297, Nashville, AR 71852. TEL 501-845-2010; Ed. Mike McCoy; Pub. Louie Graves; adv. contact: Theresa Parrish. pub. size: broadsheet; circ. 2,500.

GRAVETTE

US

GRAVETTE NEWS HERALD. 1894. Wed. $.50 newsstand; $16/yr. local; $22/yr. elsewhere. 123 Main St., Gravette, AR 72736. TEL 501-787-5300; FAX 501-787-5300. **Owner(s):** Community Publishers, Inc., P.O. Box 1049, Bentville, AR 72712. TEL 501-787-5300; Ed. Robert D. Evans; Pub. Mike Brown; adv. contact: Linda Milton. pub. size: broadsheet; circ. 2,100(paid).

GREENWOOD

US

GREENWOOD DEMOCRAT. 1882. Wed. $.50 newsstand; $19/yr. in cy.; $26/yr. in state; $29/yr. out of state. 38 Towne Sq., Greenwood, AR 72936. TEL 501-996-4494; FAX 501-996-4122. **Owner(s):** Westward Communications, Inc., 5005 LBJ Fwy., Dallas, TX 75244. TEL 214-450-1717; Ed. Donna R. Forst; Pub. C.A. Wells; adv.; pub. size: broadsheet; circ. 2,700(paid).

HARRISBURG

US

MODERN NEWS. 1888. Wed. $.35 newsstand; $16/yr. in cy.; $20/yr. elsewhere. 216 Main St., Harrisburg, AR 72432. TEL 501-578-2121; FAX 501-578-9415. **Owner(s):** Hazel Freeman, P.O. Box 400, Harrisburg, AR 72432. TEL 501-578-2121; Ed. Charles D. Nix. pub. size: broadsheet; circ. 2,841(paid).

HEBER SPRINGS

US   ISSN 1050-5105

SUN TIMES. 1888. s-w.: Wed. & Fri. $.50 newsstand; $29/yr. in trade zone; $36/yr. elsewhere. 107-109 N. Fourth St., Heber Springs, AR 72543. TEL 501-362-2425; FAX 501-362-5877. **Owner(s):** American Publishing Co., 606 N. Van Buren, P.O. Box 520, Marion, IL 62959. TEL 618-993-1711; Ed. Randy Kemp; Pub. Ed Trainor; adv. contact: Jerri Abbott. photos; bk.rev.; pub. size: broadsheet; circ. 4,385(paid).

HOT SPRINGS VILLAGE

US   ISSN 0747-2781

LAVILLA NEWS. 1970. Wed. $.50 newsstand; $20/yr. mailed. 121 DeSoto Ctr. Dr., Hot Springs Village, AR 71909. TEL 501-922-1900; FAX 501-922-0958. **Owner(s):** Hollinger International, Inc., 401 N. Wabash, Chicago, IL 60611. TEL 312-321-3000; Ed. Randal Hunhoff; Pub. Sam Hodges; adv. contact: Cindy Wagstaff. photos; bk.rev.; pub. size: broadsheet; circ. 4,843(free & paid).

HUNTSVILLE

US

MADISON COUNTY RECORD. 1879. Thu. $.25 newsstand; $16/yr. in cy.; $18/yr. out of cy.; $20/yr. out of state. 201 Church St., Huntsville, AR 72740. TEL 501-738-2141; FAX 501-738-1250. **Owner(s):** Alta Faubus, 201 Church St., Huntsville, AR 72740. TEL 501-738-2141; FAX 501-738-1550; Ed. Carol S. Whittemore; Pub. Alta Faubus; adv.; pub. size: broadsheet; circ. 5,500(paid).

IMBODEN

US

OZARK JOURNAL. 1915. Thu. $.25 newsstand; $10/yr. in state; $14/yr. out of state. 101 Second St., Imboden, AR 72434. TEL 501-869-2220. **Owner(s):** Ozark Journal, Inc., P.O. Box 598, Imboden, AR 72434. TEL 501-869-3159; Ed. Karen Glass; Pub. Bob Glass, Jr.; pub. size: standard; circ. 2,000(paid).

MANSFIELD

US

CITIZEN, THE. 1967. Wed. $.25 newsstand; $12/yr. local; $18/yr. in state. 112 E. Howard St., Mansfield, AR 72944-0347. TEL 501-928-5340; FAX 501-928-5340. **Owner(s):** Waldron Newspapers, Inc., P.O. Box 745, Waldron, AR 72958-0347; Ed. Marty Backus. adv. contact: Vickie Backus. pub. size: broadsheet; circ. 3,000(free & paid).

MARIANNA

US

MARIANNA COURIER INDEX. 1874. Thu. $.50 newsstand; $20/yr. in cy.; $30/yr. in state; $42/yr. out of state. 31 S. Popular St., Marianna, AR 72360. TEL 501-295-2521; FAX 501-295-9662. **Owner(s):** Times-Herald Publishing Co., P.O. Box 1699, Forrest City, AR 72335. TEL 501-633-3130; Pub. Bonner McCollum; adv. contact: Melinda Burns. pub. size: broadsheet; circ. 2,500(paid).

MARKED TREE

US

TRI-CITY TRIBUNE. 1903. Thu. $.50 newsstand; $21/yr. 18 Elm St., Marked Tree, AR 72365. TEL 501-358-2993; FAX 501-358-4538. **Owner(s):** Tri-City Tribune, Inc., P.O. Box 490, Marked Tree, AR 72365. TEL 501-358-2993; Ed. John Boxley; Pub. John Boxley; adv.; pub. size: broadsheet; circ. 2,400(paid).

MARSHALL

US

MARSHALL MOUNTAIN WAVE. 1890. Thu. $.25 newsstand; $15/yr. in cy.; $17/yr. out of cy.; $22/yr. out of state. 103 E. Main St., Marshall, AR 72650. TEL 501-448-3321; FAX 501-448-5659. **Owner(s):** Marshall Mountain Wave Publishing Co., Inc., 103 E. Main, Marshall, AR 72650. TEL 501-448-3321; FAX 501-448-5659; Ed. Debbie Horton; Pub. Jim Tilley; adv. contact: Glenda Griffith. pub. size: broadsheet; circ. 4,650(paid).

MCCRORY

US

WOODRUFF COUNTY MONITOR LEADER ADVOCATE. 1990. Wed. $.50 newsstand; $18/yr. in cy.; $25/yr. elsewhere. 301 N. Edmonds Ave., McCrory, AR 72101-0898. TEL 501-731-2263; FAX 501-731-5899. **Owner(s):** Gladys Price Press, 301 N. Edmonds Ave., McCrory, AR 72101-0898. TEL 501-731-2263; FAX 501-731-5899; Ed. Bill Riddle; Pub. Paula Davis; adv.; photos; bk.rev.; pub. size: broadsheet; circ. 2,300(paid). **Formerly:** Woodruff County Monitor.

MENA

US   ISSN 0747-1513

MENA STAR. 1898. Thu. $19/yr. local; $30/yr. elsewhere. 501-07 Mena St., Mena, AR 71953. TEL 501-394-1900; FAX 501-394-1908. **Owner(s):** Waldron Newspapers, Inc., P.O. Box 745, Gadsden, AR 72958-0347; Ed. Barney White; Pub. Barney White; adv. contact: Debbie Frost. pub. size: broadsheet; circ. evening 3,250(paid). **Wire Service(s):** AP.

MONTICELLO

US

ADVANCE-MONTICELLONIAN. 1870. Wed. $.50 newsstand; $23/yr. in state; $30/yr. out of state. 314 N. Main, Monticello, AR 71655. TEL 501-367-5325; FAX 501-367-6612. **Owner(s):** Smith Newspapers, P.O. Box 27, Fort Payne, AL 35967; Ed. Beverly Berks Rambo; Pub. Frank Jackson; adv. contact: Mary E. Jackson. pub. size: standard; circ. 5,200(paid).

MORRILTON

US

CONWAY COUNTY PETIT JEAN COUNTRY HEADLIGHT. 1874. Wed. $.50 newsstand; $27-$37/yr. 908 W. Broadway, Morrilton, AR 72110. TEL 501-354-2451; FAX 501-354-4225. **Owner(s):** Clifton T. Wells, 15 Pilot Point, Little Rock, AR 72205. TEL 501-664-4456; FAX 501-354-4225; Eddy Hodge, P.O. Box 621, Morrilton, AR 72110. TEL 501-354-5537; FAX 501-354-4225; Ed. Clifton T. Wells; Pub. Clifton T. Wells; adv. contact: Carol McKuin. pub. size: broadsheet; circ. 6,523(paid).

MOUNTAIN VIEW

US

STONE COUNTY CITIZEN. 1986. Tue. $.35 newsstand; $10/yr. in cy.; $20/yr. out of cy. P.O. Box 6, Mountain View, AR 72560. TEL 501-269-8626; FAX 501-269-4164. **Owner(s):** Dennis Brannon, P.O. Box 6, Mountain View, AR 72560. TEL 501-269-8626; Ed. Dennis Brannon; Pub. Dennis Brannon; adv. contact: Ellen Brannon. pub. size: standard; circ. 4,000(free & paid).

US

STONE COUNTY LEADER. 1951. Wed. $16/yr. in cy.; $26/yr. out of cy. 103 W. Main St., Mountain View, AR 72560. TEL 501-269-3841; FAX 501-269-2171. **Owner(s):** Stone County Publishing Co., Inc., P.O. Box 509, Mountain View, AR 72560. TEL 501-269-3841; Ed. James R. Fraser. pub. size: broadsheet; circ. 3,272(paid).

MURFREESBORO

US

MURFREESBORO DIAMOND. 1975. Wed. $.50 newsstand; $15/yr. local; $35/yr. elsewhere. On the Square, Murfreesboro, AR 71958. TEL 501-285-2723; FAX 501-285-3820. **Owner(s):** Graves Publishing Co., Inc., P.O. Box 297, Nashville, AR 71852. TEL 501-845-2010; Ed. Louie Graves. pub. size: tabloid; circ. 1,800(paid).

NASHVILLE

US

NASHVILLE NEWS. 1878. s-w.: Mon. & Thu. $.50 newsstand; $20/yr. trade area; $40/yr. elsewhere. 418 N. Main, Nashville, AR 71852. TEL 501-845-2010; FAX 501-845-5091. **Owner(s):** Graves Publishing Co., Inc., 418 N. Main, Nashville, AR 71852. TEL 501-845-2010; FAX 501-845-5091; Ed. Louie Graves. adv. contact: Tracy Bailey. pub. size: broadsheet; circ. 4,350(paid). **Wire Service(s):** AP, UPI.

NORTH LITTLE ROCK

US

TIMES, THE. 1898. Thu. $.50 newsstand; $16.50/yr. in cy.; $25/yr. in state; $30/yr. out of state. 26th & Willow Sts., North Little Rock, AR 72114. TEL 501-758-2571; FAX 501-758-2597. **Owner(s):** David & Kitty Chism, P.O. Box 428, North Little Rock, AR 72115. TEL 501-758-2571; Ed. Kitty Chism; Pub. David Chism; adv. contact: Tom Kennedy. pub. size: broadsheet; circ. 8,823(free & paid).

OSCEOLA

US

OSCEOLA TIMES. 1870. s-w.: Wed. & Sun. $15/yr. in cy.; $30/yr. elsewhere. 112 N. Poplar, Osceola, AR 72370. TEL 501-563-2615; FAX 501-563-2616. **Owner(s):** Tennyson Publishing, Blytheville, AR; Ed. Sandra Brand. adv.; pub. size: standard; circ. 12,400(free & paid). **Wire Service(s):** AP.

PARIS

US   ISSN 1071-9709

PARIS EXPRESS. 1880. Wed. $.50 newsstand; $21/yr. local. 22 S. Express St., Paris, AR 72855. TEL 501-963-2901; FAX 501-963-3062. **Owner(s):** Westward Communications, Inc., 5005 LBJ Fwy., Dallas, TX 75244. TEL 214-450-1717; FAX 214-450-1770; Ed. Roger Smith; Pub. Bill Hager; adv. contact: Vickey Wiggins. pub. size: broadsheet; circ. 3,950(paid).

PEA RIDGE

US

TIMES OF NORTHEAST BENTON COUNTY. 1966. Thu. $.50 newsstand; $14-$20/yr. 150 S. Curtis, Pea Ridge, AR 72751. TEL 501-451-1196. **Owner(s):** Mike Freeman, Pea Ridge, AR; Ed. Mike Freeman. adv.; pub. size: broadsheet; circ. 1,700(paid).

PIGGOTT

US

PIGGOTT TIMES, THE. 1967. Wed. $20/yr. in cy.; $25/yr. out of cy.; $30/yr. out of state. 209 W. Main, Piggott, AR 72454. TEL 501-598-2201; FAX 501-598-5189. **Owner(s):** K.M.B. Corp., Rector, AR. TEL 501-598-2201; FAX 501-598-5189; Ed. Ron Kemp; Pub. Ron Kemp; adv. contact: Diane Deniston. photos; bk.rev.; pub. size: standard; circ. 3,040(paid).

PINE BLUFF

US

PINE BLUFF SHOPPERS NEWS. Wed. free. 3900 Miramar Dr., Ste. B, Pine Bluff, AR 71603-3718. TEL 501-879-5450; FAX 501-879-5636. **Owner(s):** Pine Bluff News Media Group, 6130 Getty Dr., Sherwoodff, AR 72117. TEL 501-333-8300; Ed. Pat McHughes; Pub. Mike Kellar; adv. contact: Cindy Lee. pub. size: tabloid; circ. 20,000(free).

US   ISSN 0747-1572

WHITE HALL JOURNAL. 1983. Wed. $.50 newsstand; $18/yr. in cy.; $25/yr. elsewhere. 6210 Dollarway Rd., Ste. 2A, Pine Bluff, AR 71602. TEL 501-247-4700; FAX 501-247-4755. **Owner(s):** Forest Communicators, Inc., 6210 Dollarway Rd., Ste. 2A, Pine Bluff, AR 71602. TEL 501-247-4700; Ed. Frank Lightfoot; Pub. Frank Lightfoot; adv. contact: Vicki Kelly. photos; bk.rev.; pub. size: broadsheet; circ. 1,350(free & paid).

POCAHONTAS

US

POCAHONTAS STAR HERALD. 1880. Thu. $.35 newsstand; $14/yr. in cy.; $25/yr. out of cy. 109 N. Van Bibber St., Pocahontas, AR 72455. TEL 501-892-4451; FAX 501-892-4453. **Owner(s):** J.V. Rockwell, P.O. Box 128, Corning, AR 72422. TEL 501-857-3531; Ed. Kathryn T. Cheyne; Pub. J.V. Rockwell; adv. contact: Anita Murphy. pub. size: broadsheet; circ. 15,000(free & paid).

PRESCOTT

US

NEVADA COUNTY PICAYUNE. 1878. Thu. $.50 newsstand; $12.50/yr. in cy.; $20/yr. in state; $25/yr. out of state. 125 W. Main St., Prescott, AR 71857-0060. TEL 501-887-2002; FAX 501-887-2949. **Owner(s):** John & Betty Ragsdale, P.O. Box 60, Prescott, AR 71857. TEL 501-887-2002; Pub. John R. Ragsdale; adv. contact: Ricky Ragsdale. pub. size: broadsheet; circ. 2,500(paid).

SALEM

US

NEWS, THE. Thu. $.50 newsstand; $18/yr. in cy.; $23/yr. out of cy. P.O. Box 248, Salem, AR 72576. TEL 501-895-3207; FAX 501-895-4277. **Owner(s):** Paxton Media Group, Inc., P.O. Box 2300, Paducah, KY 42002. TEL 502-443-1771; Ed. Max Cates. adv. contact: Carolyn Clarke. photos; pub. size: broadsheet; circ. 3,600(paid). **Formerly:** Salem Headlight

SHERIDAN

US

SHERIDAN HEADLIGHT. 1881. Wed. $.50 newsstand; $15/yr. in cy.; $21/yr. out of cy.; $28/yr. elsewhere. 101 E. Center, Sheridan, AR 72150. TEL 501-942-2142; FAX 501-942-2143. **Owner(s):** Sheridan Headlight, P.O. Box 539, 101 E. Center, Sheridan, AR 72150. TEL 501-942-2142; Ed. Melody Moorehouse; Pub. Melody Moorehouse; adv. contact: Kathie Webb. photos; pub. size: standard; circ. 4,050(paid).

SHERWOOD

US

GREENBRIER GAZETTE. Wed. free. 6130 Getty Dr., Sherwood, AR 72117. TEL 501-833-8300; FAX 501-833-8466. **Owner(s):** Pine Bluff News Media Group, 6130 Getty Dr., Sherwood, AR 72117. TEL 501-833-8300; FAX 501-833-8466; Ed. Pat McHughes; Pub. Mike Keller; adv.; pub. size: tabloid; circ. 7,900(free).

US

JONESBORO REVIEW. Wed. free; $15/yr. mailed. 6130 Getty Dr., Sherwood, AR 72117. TEL 501-833-8300; FAX 501-833-8466. **Owner(s):** Pine Bluff News Media Group, 6130 Getty Dr., Sherwood, AR 72117. TEL 501-833-8300; FAX 501-833-8466; Ed. Ken Heard; Pub. Mike Keller; adv.; pub. size: broadsheet; circ. 8,000(controlled & free).

US

LAKE TRIBUNE. Wed. free; $15/yr. mailed. 6130 Getty Dr., Sherwood, AR 72117. TEL 501-833-8300; FAX 501-833-8466. **Owner(s):** Pine Bluff News Media Group, 6130 Getty Dr., Sherwood, AR 72117. TEL 501-833-8300; FAX 501-833-8466; Ed. Doug Dunson; Pub. Mike Kellar; adv.; pub. size: tabloid; circ. 8,400(controlled & free).

SILOAM SPRINGS

US

HERALD/LEADER. 1892. s-w.: Wed. & Sun. $.50 newsstand; $28/yr. local; $40/yr. out of area. 101 N. Mt. Olive, Siloam Springs, AR 72761. TEL 501-524-5144; FAX 501-524-3612; E-mail: Compub95@aol.com; URL: http://nwanews.com/leader.html. **Owner(s):** Community Publishers, Inc., 101 N. Mt. Olive, Siloam Springs, AR 72761. TEL 501-524-5144; Ed. Jamie West; Pub. Scott Harrell; adv.; pub. size: broadsheet; circ. 10,000(paid). **Formerly:** Siloam Springs Herald & Democrat.

STAR CITY

US

LINCOLN LEDGER. 1876. Wed. $.25 newsstand; $9/yr. in cy.; $12/yr. out of cy.; $15/yr. out of state. 2161 W. Bradley, Star City, AR 71667. TEL 501-628-4161; FAX 501-628-3802. **Owner(s):** Lincoln County Publishing Co., Inc., Town Sq., Star City, AR 71667. TEL 501-628-4161; Ed. Joe V. Mason. adv. contact: Brooke Works. pub. size: standard; circ. 2,500(paid).

TRUMANN

US

TRUMANN DEMOCRAT. 1922. Wed. $.50 newsstand; $16/yr. in cy.; $18/yr. out of cy. 200 Hwy. 463, S., Trumann, AR 72472. TEL 501-483-6317; FAX 501-483-6031. **Owner(s):** Charles Nix, Harrisburg, AR; Ed. Joyce Jaynes; Pub. Charles Nix; adv.; pub. size: broadsheet; circ. 2,200(paid).

VAN BUREN

US

ADVERTISER, THE. Wed. free. 100 N. 11th St., Van Buren, AR 72956. TEL 501-474-5215; FAX 501-471-5607. **Owner(s):** Van Buren Publishing Co., Inc., 100 N. 11th St., Van Buren, AR 72956. TEL 501-474-5215; FAX 501-471-5607; Ed. Roy Faulkenberry; Pub. Ken Richardson; adv. contact: Jim Peoples. pub. size: broadsheet; circ. 13,000(free).

US   ISSN 0885-9086

PRESS ARGUS-COURIER. 1859. s-w.: Wed. & Sat. $.50 newsstand; $34.50/yr. in area; $41.50/yr. out of area. 100 N. 11th St., Van Buren, AR 72956. TEL 501-474-5215; FAX 501-471-5607. **Owner(s):** Van Buren Publishing Co., Inc., 100 N. 11th St., Van Buren, AR 72956. TEL 501-474-5215; Ed. Roy Faulkenberry; Pub. Ken Richardson; adv. contact: Jim Peoples. photos; pub. size: broadsheet; circ. 7,000(paid).

WALDRON

US

SCOTT COUNTY ADVERTISER. 1987. Wed. free. 10 W. Second St., Waldron, AR 72958-1816. TEL 501-637-4647; FAX 501-928-5340. **Owner(s):** Waldron Newspapers, Inc., P.O. Box 745, Waldron, AR 72958-0347; Ed. Marty Backus. adv. contact: Vickie Backus. pub. size: broadsheet; circ. 4,600(free).

US

TRI-COUNTY TRADER. 1967. Wed. free. P.O. Box 745, Waldron, AR 72944. TEL 501-928-5340; FAX 501-637-4162. **Owner(s):** Waldron Newspapers, Inc., P.O. Box 745, Waldron, AR 72958-0347; Ed. Marty Backus. adv. contact: Vickie Backus. pub. size: broadsheet; circ. 5,000(free).

WALNUT RIDGE

US

TIMES DISPATCH. 1910. Wed. $.50 newsstand; $14/yr. local; $22/yr. elsewhere. 225 W. Main St., Walnut Ridge, AR 72476. TEL 501-886-2464; FAX 501-886-9369. **Owner(s):** Times Dispatch, Inc., 225 W. Main St., Walnut Ridge, AR 72476. TEL 501-886-2464; FAX 501-886-9369; Ed. John A. Bland; Pub. John A. Bland; adv. contact: Janice Hibbard. photos; bk.rev.; pub. size: broadsheet; circ. 6,200(paid). **Formerly:** Walnut Ridge Times Dispatch.

WYNNE

US

WYNNE PROGRESS. 1894. Fri. $.50 newsstand. 702 N. Falls Blvd., Wynne, AR 72396. TEL 501-238-2375; FAX 501-238-4655. **Owner(s):** Bonner McCollom, 222 N. Izzard, Forrest City, AR 72335. TEL 501-633-3130; FAX 501-633-0599; David Boger, 1328 Rowena St., Wynne, AR 72396. TEL 501-238-2375; FAX 501-238-4655; Ed. David Nichol; Pub. David M. Boger; adv. contact: Brandon Boger. photos; bk.rev.; pub. size: broadsheet; circ. 26,837(free & paid).

YELLVILLE

US

MOUNTAIN ECHO. 1886. Thu. $.50 newsstand; $21.50/yr. in cy.; $28.50/yr. out of cy.; $31.50/yr. out of state. Church St., Yellville, AR 72687. TEL 501-449-4257; FAX 501-424-4488. **Owner(s):** Journal Newspapers, Inc., 2720 Prospserity Ave., Fairfax, VA 22034-1000. TEL 703-560-4000; Ed. Ray Dean Davis; Pub. Chuck Pullins; adv.; photos; pub. size: broadsheet; circ. 2,500(paid). **Formerly:** Yellville Mountain Echo.

CALIFORNIA

ALTURAS

US

MODOC COUNTY RECORD. 1892. Thu. $.35 newsstand; $17/yr. local; $22/yr. elsewhere. 201 W. Carlos, Alturas, CA 96101. TEL 916-233-2632; FAX 916-233-5113. **Owner(s):** Rick & Jane Holloway, P.O. Box 531, Alturas, CA 96101. TEL 916-233-2632; Ed. Rick Holloway; Pub. Jane Holloway; adv.; photos; pub. size: standard; circ. 4,500(free & paid). **Formerly:** Alturas/Modoc County Record.

ANAHEIM

US

ANAHEIM BULLETIN. 1923. Thu. $6.50/mo. 1771 S. Lewis St., Anaheim, CA 92805. TEL 714-634-1567; FAX 714-704-3718. **Owner(s):** Freedom Communications, Inc., P.O. Box 19549, Irvine, CA 92713. TEL 714-553-9292; Ed. Tonnie Katz; Pub. R. David Threshie, Jr.; pub. size: tabloid; circ. 60,000(controlled & free).

US

ANAHEIM HILLS NEWS. 1969. Thu. $39/6 mos. mailed; $78/yr. mailed. 1771 S. Lewis St., Anaheim, CA 92805. TEL 714-634-1567; FAX 714-704-3714. **Owner(s):** Freedom Communications, Inc., 17666 Fitch, Irvine, CA 92714; Ed. Jannlee Watson; Pub. R. David Threshie, Jr.; adv.; pub. size: tabloid; circ. 14,000(controlled & free). **Formerly:** Anaheim Hills Highlander.

US

BREA PROGRESS. 1922. Thu. $39/6 mos. mailed; $78/yr. mailed. 1771 S. Lewis St., Anaheim, CA 92805. TEL 714-634-1567; FAX 714-704-3714. **Owner(s):** Freedom Communications, Inc., 17666 Fitch, Irvine, CA 92714. TEL 714-253-9292; Ed. Jannlee Watson; Pub. R. David Threshie, Jr.; pub. size: tabloid; circ. 10,000(controlled). **Formerly:** Brea News.

US

LA HABRA STAR. 1916. Thu. $.30 newstand. 1771 S. Lewis St., Anaheim, CA 92805. TEL 714-634-1567; FAX 714-704-3714. **Owner(s):** Freedom Communications, Inc., 17666 Fitch, Irvine, CA 92614. TEL 714-553-9292; Ed. Frank Mickadeit; Pub. R. David Threshie, Jr.; adv. contact: Lynette Harras. pub. size: broadsheet; circ. 44,000(paid). **Wire Service(s):** AP. **Formerly:** La Habra Daily Star Progress.

PLACENTIA NEWS-TIMES. 1924. Thu. free/mailed. 1771 S. Lewis, Anaheim, CA 92805. TEL 714-634-1567; FAX 714-704-3714. **Owner(s):** Freedom Communications, Inc., 17666 Fitch, Irvine, CA 92614. TEL 714-553-9292; Ed. Frank Mickadiet; Pub. R. David Threshie, Jr.; adv.; pub. size: broadsheet; circ. 12,000(controlled).
Formerly: Placentia Highlander News-Time.

ANDERSON

US

VALLEY POST. 1886. Tue. $.25 newsstand; $14/yr. in cy.; $17/yr. out of cy. 2680 Gateway, Anderson, CA 96007. TEL 916-365-2797; FAX 916-365-2829. **Owner(s):** Douglas Hirsch, 2680 Gateway, Anderson, CA 96007. TEL 916-365-2797; Ed. Loretta Carrico; Pub. Douglas Hirsch; adv.; pub. size: broadsheet; circ. 11,500(free & paid).

ARROYO GRANDE

US

FIVE CITIES TIMES-PRESS-RECORDER. 1887. s-w.: Wed. & Fri. $.50 newsstand; $42/yr. in cy.; $46/yr. in state mailed. 1052 Grand Ave., Arroyo Grande, CA 93420. TEL 805-489-4206; FAX 805-473-0571. **Owner(s):** Dick & Maxine Blankenburg, P.O. Box 460, Arroyo Grande, CA 93421. TEL 805-489-4206; Ed. Dick Blankenburg; Pub. Dick Blankenburg; adv. contact: Cindy Hodgson. photos; pub. size: broadsheet; circ. 18,500(paid).
Formerly: Arroyo Grande Five Cities Times.

ATASCADERO

US

ATASCADERO NEWS. 1916. s-w.: Wed. & Fri. $.50 newsstand; $25/yr. in cy. 5660 El Camino Real, Atascadero, CA 93422. TEL 805-466-2585; FAX 805-466-2714. **Owner(s):** James, Judson, & John Porter, P.O. Box 6068, Atascadero, CA 93424. TEL 805-466-2585; Ed. Lon Allan; Pub. James Porter; adv.; photos; pub. size: broadsheet; circ. 8,000(paid).

US

NORTH COUNTY SHOPPING NEWS. Thu. free. 5660 El Camino Real, Atascadero, CA 93422. TEL 805-466-2585; FAX 805-466-2714. **Owner(s):** James Porter, Judson Porter & John Porter, P.O. Box 6068, Atascadero, CA 93424. TEL 805-466-2585; Ed. Lon Allan; Pub. Jack Porter; adv.; pub. size: standard; circ. 2,000(free).

ATWATER

US

CHRONICLE, THE. Wed. free. 927 Atwater Blvd., Atwater, CA 20931. TEL 209-358-6431; FAX 209-357-2969. **Owner(s):** U.S. Media Group, P.O. Box 227, Crystal City, MO 63019; Ed. Ken Yancy; Pub. Al Portner; adv. contact: Cheri Mister. photos; pub. size: broadsheet; circ. 8,000(controlled & paid).

US

SIGNAL, THE. 1911. Wed. free; $.50 newsstand; $18/yr. in cy. 927 Atwater Blvd., Atwater, CA 95301. TEL 209-358-6431; FAX 209-357-2968. **Owner(s):** U.S. Media Group, P.O. Box 227, Crystal City, MO 63019; Ed. David J. Wickenhauser; Pub. Al Portner; adv. contact: Bambi Beachler. photos; pub. size: broadsheet; circ. 11,500(controlled & paid).
Formerly: Atwater Signal.

AUBURN

US

SENTINEL, THE. 1990. Thu. free newsstand; $25/yr. 1551 Lincoln Way, Auburn, CA 95603. TEL 916-823-2463; FAX 916-823-1309. **Owner(s):** Janice Forbes, 1551 Lincoln Way, Auburn, CA 95603 TEL 916-823-2463; FAX 916-823-1309; Ed. Jill Rietgens; Pub. Janice Forbes; adv. contact: Cindy Kile. photos; pub. size: broadsheet; circ. 10,000(controlled & free).

AVALON

US

AVALON BAY NEWS, THE. 1990. w. $.60 newsstand; $30/yr. 117 Whittley, Avalon, CA 90704-1809. TEL 310-510-1500; FAX 310-510-1371. **Owner(s):** Barbara L. Crow, 117 Whittley, Avalon, CA 90704. TEL 310-510-1500; FAX 310-510-1371; Ed. Barbara L. Crow; Pub. Barbara L. Crow; adv. contact: Barbara L. Crow. photos; pub. size: tabloid; circ. 2,000(free & paid).

US

CATALINA ISLANDER, THE. 1914. Fri. $.50 newsstand; $30/yr 615 Crescent Ave., Avalon, CA 90704-0428. TEL 310-510-0500; FAX 310-510-2882; E-mail: islander@lightside.com; URL: http://www.catalina.com/islander/. **Owner(s):** West Coast Community Newspapers, Inc., 2841 Loker Ave., E., Carlsbad, CA 92008. TEL 619-431-4850; FAX 619-431-4866; Pub. Sherri Walker; adv. contact: Su Marion. photos; pub. size: tabloid; circ. 6,000(free & paid).

AVENAL

US

AVENAL PROGRESS. 1986. Wed. free home deliv.; $18/yr. mailed. 141 E. King St., Avenal, CA 93204. TEL 209-386-9385; FAX 209-935-5257. **Owner(s):** Central California Publishing, P.O. Box 547, Lemoore, CA 93245-0547. TEL 800-262-3488; Ed. Laura Fairchild; Pub. Dale Anderson; adv.; photos; pub. size: broadsheet; circ. 1,200(controlled & free).

BEAUMONT

US

COMMUNITY ADVISER. 1987. Thu. $.25 newsstand; $15/yr. 795 E. Sixth St., Ste. N, Beaumont, CA 92223. TEL 909-845-9564; FAX 909-845-6713. **Owner(s):** Ken Smith, 795 E. Sixth St., Ste. N, Beaumont, CA 92223. TEL 909-845-9564; FAX 909-845-6713; Ed. Hal Lowe; Pub. Ken Smith; adv.; photos; pub. size: broadsheet; circ. 14,000(free & paid).

BEL TIBURON

US

ARK, THE. 1972. Wed. $.50 newsstand; $31/yr. in area; $41/yr. out of area. 1550 Tiburon Blvd., Bel Tiburon, CA 94920. TEL 510-435-2652; FAX 510-435-0849. **Owner(s):** Barbara Gross, 1550 Tiburon Blvd., Bel Tiburon, CA 94920. TEL 415-435-2652; FAX 415-435-0849; Marilyn Kessler, 1550 Tiburon Blvd., Bel Tiburon, CA 94920. TEL 415-435-2652; FAX 415-435-0849; Steve McNamara, 1550 Tiburon Blvd., Bel Tiburon, CA 94920. TEL 510-435-2652; Ed. Marilyn Kessler; Pub. Barbara Gross; adv. contact: Laura Wellen. pub. size: tabloid; circ. 3,000(paid).

BERKELEY

US

EAST BAY EXPRESS. 1978. Thu. free; $20/yr. mailed in cy. 931 Ashby Ave., Berkeley, CA 94709. TEL 510-540-7400; FAX 510-540-7700. **Owner(s):** Express Publishing Co., Inc., 931 Ashby Ave., Berkeley, CA 94709. TEL 510-540-7400; Ed. John Raeside; Pub. Nancy Banks; adv. contact: Robert Thomas. bk.rev.; pub. size: tabloid; circ. 64,000(free).

BEVERLY HILLS

US

BEVERLY HILLS COURIER. 1955. Fri $.50 newsstand; $75/yr. in cy. 8840 Olympic Blvd., Beverly Hills, CA 90211. TEL 310-278-1322; FAX 310-271-5118; E-mail: bhcourier@aol.com. **Owner(s):** March Schwartz, 8840 W. Olympic Blvd., Beverly Hills, CA 90211. TEL 310-278-1322; Pub. March Schwartz; adv. contact: Sande Schwartz. photos; pub. size: tabloid; circ. 48,000(paid).

BIG BEAR LAKE

US

BIG BEAR LIFE. 1941. Sat. free. 42007 Fox Farm Rd. Ste. 3, Big Bear Lake, CA 92315. TEL 909-866-3456; FAX 909-866-2302. **Owner(s):** Brehm Communications, Inc., 17065 Via del Campo, Ste. 200 San Diego, CA 92127. TEL 619-451-6200; Ed. John Emig; Pub. Jerry Wright; adv. contact: Doug Moore. pub. size: tabloid; circ. 11,051(free).

US   ISSN 1073-6867

GRIZZLY, THE. 1941. Wed. $.50 newsstand; $21/yr. in cy.; $30/yr. out of cy. $39/yr. out of state. 42007 Fox Farm Rd., Ste. 3, Big Bear Lake, CA 92315. TEL 909-866-3456; FAX 909-866-2302. **Owner(s):** Brehm Communications, Inc., 17065 Via del Campo, Ste. 200, San Diego, CA 92127. TEL 619-451-6200; Pub. Jerry Wright; adv. contact: Doug Moore. pub. size: broadsheet; circ. 10,000(paid).

BISHOP

US

REGISTER REVIEW. 1870. 3. wk.: Sun., Wed., Fri. $48/yr. local; $53/yr. out of state. 450 E. Line St., Bishop, CA 93514. TEL 619-873-3535. **Owner(s):** Bishop Chalfant Press Publications, C. Deane Funk, Bishop, CA 93514. TEL 619-873-3535; Ed. Barbara Ferry-Laughon. pub. size: standard; circ. morning 1,792(paid). **Wire Service(s):** AP.
Formerly: Inyo Register

BLYTHE

US

PALO VERDE VALLEY TIMES. 1924. s-w.: Wed. & Fri. $.50 newsstand; $38/yr. in cy.; $58/yr. out of cy. 231 N. Spring St., Blythe, CA 92225. TEL 619-922-3181; FAX 619-922-3184. **Owner(s):** Western Newspapers, Inc., P.O. Box 1271, Yuma, AZ 85366. TEL 602-783-3311; Pub. Robin Mauser; adv. contact: Dixie Allison. pub. size: broadsheet; circ. 13,000(free & paid).

BOLINAS

US

COASTAL POST. 1975. m. $20/yr. P.O. Box 31, Bolinas, CA 94924. TEL 415-868-1600; FAX 415-868-0502. **Owner(s):** Don Deane, P.O. Box 31, Bolinas, CA 94924. TEL 415-868-1600; Ed. Don Deane; Pub. Don Deane; pub. size: tabloid; circ. 12,000(free & paid).

BREA

US

HARTE-HANKS PENNYSAVER. 1962. Wed. free. 2830 Orbiter St., Brea, CA 92621. TEL 714-996-8900; FAX 714-993-4711. **Owner(s):** Harte-Hanks Communications, Inc., P.O. Box 269, San Antonio, TX 78291. TEL 210-829-9000; circ. 4,100,000(free).

BURLINGAME

US

BOUTIQUE & VILLAGER. 1965. Wed. $.25 newsstand; $18/yr. in cy. 824 Cowan Rd., Burlingame, CA 94010. TEL 415-692-9406; FAX 415-692-7587. **Owner(s):** Pan-Asian Venture Capital Corp., 1201 Evans Ave., San Francisco, CA 94124. TEL 415-826-1100; Ed. Marc Burkhardt; Pub. Ted Fang; adv. contact: Porter Deese. photos; bk.rev.; pub. size: broadsheet; circ. 13,859(paid).

US

ENQUIRER BULLETIN. 1924. Wed. $18/yr. 824 Cowan Rd., Burlingame, CA 94010. TEL 415-692-9406. **Owner(s):** Pan-Asian Venture Capital Corp., 1201 Evans Ave., San Francisco, CA 94124. TEL 415-826-1100; Ed. Alan Klapp; Pub. Leonard Sbrocco; adv.; photos; bk.rev.; pub. size: broadsheet; circ. 22,600(free).
   Formerly: San Carlos/Belmont Enquirer.

US

FOSTER CITY PROGRESS. 1966. Wed. free. 824 Cowan Rd., Burlingame, CA 94010. TEL 415-692-9406. **Owner(s):** Pan-Asian Venture Capital Corp., 1201 Evans Ave., San Francisco, CA 94124. TEL 415-826-1100; Ed. Kleyton Jones; Pub. Leonard Sbrocco; adv. contact: Alan Peterson. photos; bk.rev.; pub. size: broadsheet; circ. 10,700(controlled & free).

US

MILLBRAE & SAN BRUNO SUN. 1935. Wed. free home deliv.; $.25 newsstand. 824 Cowan Rd., Burlingame, CA 94010. TEL 415-692-9406; FAX 415-692-7587. **Owner(s):** Pan-Asian Venture Capital Corp., 1201 Evans Ave., San Francisco, CA 94124. TEL 415-826-1100; Ed. Mark Burkhardt; Pub. Ted Fang; adv. contact: Larry Boline. pub. size: broadsheet; circ. 19,000(free & paid).
   Formerly: Millbrae Sun; Millbrae-San Bruno Sun.

US

▼**PENINSULA INDEPENDENT.** 1994. Wed. free. 824 Cowan Rd., Burlingame, CA 94010. TEL 415-692-9406; FAX 415-692-7587. **Owner(s):** Pan-Asian Venture Capital Corp., 1201 Evans Ave., San Francisco, CA 94124. TEL 415-826-1100; Ed. Wendy Sykes; Pub. Leonard Sbrocco; adv. contact: Alan Peterson. photos; bk.rev.; pub. size: broadsheet; circ. 43,600(free).

US

SAN MATEO WEEKLY. Wed. free. 824 Cowan Rd., Burlingame, CA 94010. TEL 415-692-9406; FAX 415-692-7587. **Owner(s):** Pan-Asian Venture Capital Corp., 1201 Evans Ave., San Francisco, CA 94124. TEL 415-826-1100; Ed. Antonia Ehlers; Pub. Ted Fang; adv. contact: Porter Deese. photos; bk.rev.; pub. size: broadsheet; circ. 28,800(free).

BURNEY

US

INTERMOUNTAIN NEWS. 1957. Wed. $.75/newsstand; $29/yr. 36965 Main St., Burney, CA 96013. TEL 916-335-4533; FAX 916-335-5335. **Owner(s):** Craig Harrington, 36965 Main St., Burney, CA 96013. TEL 916-335-4533; Pub. Craig Harrington; adv. contact: Craig Harrington. pub. size: standard; circ. 3,335(paid).
   Formerly: Burney Intermountain News.

CALIFORNIA CITY

US   ISSN 1065-1152

MOJAVE DESERT NEWS, THE. 1938. Thu. $.50 newsstand; $20/yr. in cy.; $29/yr. out of cy.; $35/yr. out of state. 8046 California City Blvd., California City, CA 93505. TEL 619-373-4812; FAX 619-373-2941. **Owner(s):** MOCAL News Corp., 8046 California City Blvd., California City, CA 93505. TEL 619-373-4812; Ed. Connie Baker; Pub. Paul Ingram; adv. contact: Kathy Pluta. photos; bk.rev.; pub. size: standard; circ. 5,650(free & paid).
   Formerly: Enterprise, The.

CALISTOGA

US

WEEKLY CALISTOGAN. 1877. Thu. $.50 newsstand; $17.50/yr. in cy.; $23.50/yr. out of cy. 1360 Lincoln Ave., Calistoga, CA 94515. TEL 707-942-6242; FAX 707-942-4617; E-mail: WeeklyCal@aol.com; URL: http://www.sonic.net/~johnfr/Calistogan. **Owner(s):** Marjorie Brandon, 1333 Jones St., Apt. 1003B, San Fransisco, CA 94515; Ed. Pat Hampton; Pub. Bill Brenner; pub. size: broadsheet; circ. 1,000(paid).

CARLSBAD

US

CARLSBAD SUN. 1925. Thu. $.25 newsstand; $50/yr. 3rd class. 2841 Loker Ave., E, Carlsbad, CA 92008. TEL 619-431-4850; FAX 619-431-4888. **Owner(s):** West Coast Community Newspapers, Inc., 2841 Loker Ave., E., Carlsbad, CA 92008. TEL 619-431-4850; FAX 619-431-4888; Pub. Richard Fioco; adv.; pub. size: broadsheet; circ. 25,500(controlled & paid).
   Formerly: Carlsbad Journal.

CARMEL

US

CARMEL PINE CONE. 1915. Thu. free newsstand; $95/yr. Fourth St. & Mission, S.W., Carmel, CA 93921. TEL 408-624-0162; FAX 408-624-8076. **Owner(s):** Brown & Wilson, Fourth St. & Mission, S.W., Carmel, CA 93921. TEL 408-624-0162; FAX 408-624-8076; Ed. Doug Thompson; Pub. W.A. "Chip" Brown; bk.rev.; pub. size: tabloid; circ. 12,500(free & paid).

CARMICHAEL

US

CARMICHAEL TIMES. 1981. Tue. $39/yr. 4807-D El Camino Ave., Carmichael, CA 95608. TEL 916-483-0946; FAX 916-483-1902. **Owner(s):** Shirley Turner, P.O. Box 88, Carmichael, CA 95609. TEL 916-483-0946; FAX 916-483-1902; Paul O'Brien, P.O. Box 88, Carmichael, CA 95609. TEL 916-486-2908; FAX 916-483-1902; Ed. Shirley Turner. adv. contact: Shirley Turner. photos; bk.rev.; pub. size: tabloid.

CARNELIAN BAY

US

NORTH TAHOE/TRUCKEE WEEK. 1982. Thu. 5009 N. Lake Blvd., Carnelian Bay, CA 96140. TEL 916-546-5995; FAX 916-546-8113. **Owner(s):** North Tahoe Week Publishing Co., P.O. Box 49, Tahoe Vista, CA 96148. TEL 916-546-5995; FAX 916-546-8113; Ed. Patrice Parsons; Pub. David Mogilefsky; adv. contact: David Mogilefsky. pub. size: tabloid; circ. 18,000(controlled & paid).

CERES

US

CERES COURIER. 1910. s-w.: Wed. & Fri. $.25 newsstand; $30/yr. in cy.; $42/yr. mailed. 2940 Fourth St., Ceres, CA 95307. TEL 209-537-5032. **Owner(s):** Morris Communications, P.O. Box 8167, Savannah, GA 31412. TEL 912-233-1281; Ed. Jeffery Benziger; Pub. Darell Phillips; adv. contact: Bill Sanborn. pub. size: broadsheet; circ. 17,000(free & paid).

CHULA VISTA

US

CHULA VISTA STAR-NEWS. 1918. s-w.: Wed. & Sat. $.50 newsstand; $35.63/yr. in cy. 279 Third Ave., Chula Vista, CA 91911. TEL 619-427-3000; FAX 619-426-6346. **Owner(s):** West Coast Community Newspapers, Inc., 2841 Loker Ave., E., Carlsbad, CA 92008. TEL 619-431-4850; FAX 619-431-4866; Pub. Rick Fitch; adv.; photos; pub. size: broadsheet; circ. 24,000(free & paid).

US

STAR NEWS, THE. 1820. s-w.: Wed. & Sat. $.50 newsstand; $45.63/yr. in cy.; $53.10/yr. out of cy. 279 Third Ave., Chula Vista, CA 91910. TEL 619-427-3000; FAX 619-426-6346. **Owner(s):** West Coast Community Newspapers, Inc., 2841 Loker Ave., E., Carlsbad, CA. TEL 619-431-4850; Ed. Rick Fitch; Pub. Sonia Adams; adv. contact: Sonia Adams. pub. size: broadsheet; circ. 48,000(paid).
   Formerly: Imperial Beach Star News.

CITY OF COMMERCE

US

CITY TERRACE COMET. 1974. Thu. free newsstand; $75/yr. mail deliv. 2500 S. Atlantic Blvd., Bldg. B, City of Commerce, CA 90040-2004. TEL 213-263-5743. **Owner(s):** Eastern Group Publications, Inc., 2500 S. Atlantic Blvd., Bldg. B, City of Commerce, CA 90040. TEL 213-263-5743; Ed. Jonathan Sanchez; Pub. Dolores Sanchez; adv.; photos; bk.rev.; pub. size: standard; circ. 4,528(free & paid). **Wire Service(s):** CNS.

EASTSIDE SUN

US

EASTSIDE SUN. 1948. Thu. $45/6 mos.; $75/yr. 2500 S. Atlantic Blvd., Bldg. B, City of Commerce, CA 90040. TEL 213-263-5741; FAX 213-263-9161. **Owner(s):** Eastern Group Publications, Inc., 2500 S. Atlantic Blvd., Bldg. B, City of Commerce, CA 90040. TEL 213-263-5743; FAX 213-263-9169; Ed. Dolores Sanchez; Pub. Dolores Sanchez; adv.; bk.rev.; pub. size: standard; circ. 22,000(free & paid). **Wire Service(s):** CaNS.

US   ISSN 0888-7764

MEXICAN-AMERICAN SUN. 1948. Thu. $75/yr.; $42.50/6 mos. 2500 S. Atlantic Blvd., Bldg. B, City of Commerce, CA 90040. TEL 213-263-5743. **Owner(s):** Eastern Group Publications, Inc., 2500 S. Atlantic Blvd., Bldg. B, City of Commerce, CA 90040. TEL 213-263-5743; Dolores Sanchez, 2500 S. Atlantic Blvd., Bldg. B, City of Commerce, CA 90040. TEL 213-263-5743; Pub. Dolores Sanchez; adv.; photos; bk.rev.; pub. size: standard; circ. 10,978(free & paid). **Wire Service(s):** CNS.

US

NORTHEAST SUN. 1985. Thu. $75/ yr.; $42.50/6 mos. 2500 S. Atlantic Blvd., Bldg. B, City of Commerce, CA 90040. TEL 213-263-5743; FAX 213-263-9169. **Owner(s):** Eastern Group Publications, Inc., 2500 S. Atlantic Blvd., Bldg. B, City of Commerce, CA 90040. TEL 213-263-5743; Dolores Sanchez, 2500 S. Atlantic Blvd., Bldg. B, City of Commerce, CA 90040. TEL 213-263-5743; Ed. Jonathan Sanchez; Pub. Dolores Sanchez; adv.; photos; bk.rev.; pub. size: standard; circ. 17,178(controlled & free). **Wire Service(s):** CiNS.

CLAREMONT

US

CLAREMONT COURIER. 1908. Sat. $.50 newsstand; $32.50/yr. 111 S. College, Claremont, CA 91711. TEL 909-621-4761; FAX 909-621-4072. **Owner(s):** Martin & Janis Weinberger, 111 S. College, P.O. Box 820, Claremont, CA 91711. TEL 909-621-4761; FAX 909-621-4072; Ed. Martin Weinberger; Pub. Martin Weinberger; adv. contact: Phyllis Metzner. photos; pub. size: tabloid; circ. 6,025(paid).

CLEARLAKE

US

CLEAR LAKE OBSERVER-AMERICAN. 1936. s-w.: Wed. & Sat. $.25 newsstand; $19.30/yr. in cy.; $40.22/yr. out of cy. 4474 Old Hwy. 53, Clearlake, CA 95422. TEL 707-994-6444; FAX 707-994-5335. **Owner(s):** Lake County Publishing, P.O. Box 6328, Clearlake, CA 95422. TEL 707-994-6444; Ed. Debbie Geissler; Pub. Tim Timmons; adv. contact: Debbie Geissler. photos; pub. size: broadsheet; circ. 3,462(paid).

CLOVERDALE

US

CLOVERDALE REVEILLE. 1879. Wed. $.50 newsstand; $18.50/yr. 207 N. Cloverdale Blvd., Cloverdale, CA 95425. TEL 707-894-3339; FAX 707-894-3343. **Owner(s):** Hanchett Publishing, Inc., P.O. Box 157, Cloverdale, CA 95425. TEL 707-894-3339; FAX 707-894-3343; Ed. Bonny J. Hanchett; Pub. Bonny J. Hanchett; adv.; photos; pub. size: broadsheet; circ. 2,500(paid).

CLOVIS

US   ISSN 1068-5944

CLOVIS INDEPENDENT. 1906. Wed. $.50 newsstand; $21/yr. 1321 Railroad Ave., Clovis, CA 93612. TEL 209-298-8081; FAX 209-298-0459. **Owner(s):** McClatchy Newspapers, 2100 Q St., Sacramento, CA 95816. TEL 916-321-1000; Ed. Earl Wright, Jr.; Pub. Earl Wright, Jr.; adv. contact: Barbara Parnell. pub. size: broadsheet; circ. 4,000(paid).

COALINGA

US

COALINGA RECORD. 1904. Wed. $.35 newsstand; $18/yr. local; $25/yr. elsewhere; $22/yr. out of state. 152 E. Elm, Coalinga, CA 93210. TEL 209-935-2906; FAX 209-935-5257. **Owner(s):** Central California Publishing, 227 Coalinga Plz., Coalinga, CA 93210. TEL 209-935-2906; Ed. William Howell. adv. contact: Joy Redding. pub. size: standard; circ. 9,000(paid).

COLUSA

US   ISSN 0897-8743

COLUSA COUNTY SUN-HERALD. 1862. 3/wk.: Mon., Wed., Fri. $.50 newsstand; $48/yr. home deliv.; $63/yr. mailed out of cy. 825 Bridge St., Colusa, CA 95932. TEL 916-458-2121; FAX 916-458-5711. **Owner(s):** Morris Communications, P.O. Box 89, Colusa, CA 95932. TEL 916-458-2121; Pub. Darell Phillips; adv.; pub. size: broadsheet; circ. 6,500(paid).

COMPTON

US

LYNWOOD JOURNAL. 1980. Wed. $.25 newsstand; $25.60/yr. 349 W. Compton Blvd., Compton, CA 90220. TEL 310-635-6776. **Owner(s):** Rabbet Publishing Co., Inc., 349 W. Compton Blvd., Compton, CA 90220; Ed. Betty Wilson. adv.; pub. size: broadsheet; circ. 15,000(paid).

CORNING

US

CORNING OBSERVER. 1887. 3/wk.: Mon., Wed., Fri. $.50 newsstand; $38/yr. carrier. 710 Fifth St., Corning, CA 96021. TEL 916-824-5464; FAX 916-824-4804. **Owner(s):** Morris Communications, P.O. Box 1928, Augusta, GA 30903. TEL 706-724-0851; Ed. Michael Griffin; Pub. Darell Phillips; adv. contact: Patricia Begran. pub. size: broadsheet; circ. 9,800(paid).
Formerly: Corning Daily Observer.

CORONA

US   ISSN 0745-3930

CORONA-NORCO INDEPENDENT. 1887. Wed. $.25 newsstand; $9/yr. in cy.; $25/yr. out of cy. 823 S. Main St., Corona, CA 91720. TEL 909-737-1234; FAX 909-737-1572. **Owner(s):** Press-Enterprise Co., P.O. Box 792, Riverside, CA 92502; Ed. John Orr. adv. contact: Al Gould. pub. size: broadsheet; circ. 23,000(paid).

CORONADO

US

CORONADO JOURNAL. 1912. Thu. $.50 newsstand; $23.71/yr. local; $25.86/yr. in cy. 1224 Tenth St., Coronado, CA 92118. TEL 619-435-3141; FAX 619-435-3051. **Owner(s):** West Coast Community Newspapers, Inc., 2841 Loker Ave., E., Carlsbad, CA 92008. TEL 619-431-4850; FAX 619-431-4866; Ed. Maria Foster; Pub. Rick Fitch; pub. size: broadsheet; circ. 11,000(paid).

CORTE MADERA

US

TWIN CITIES TIMES. 1975. Wed. $20/yr. P.O. Box 186, Corte Madera, CA 94925. TEL 415-332-3778; FAX 415-332-8714. **Owner(s):** Marin Scope Community Newspapers, Inc., P.O. Drawer 1689, Sausalito, CA 94966. TEL 510-332-3778; Ed. Billie L. Anderson; Pub. Paul A. Anderson; adv.; pub. size: standard; circ. 6,500(controlled & paid).

CRESTLINE

US

CRESTLINE COURIER-NEWS. 1924. Thu. $.50/newsstand; $18/yr. in cy.; $30/yr. out of cy.; $45/yr. out of state. Box 3307, Crestline, CA 92325. TEL 909-338-1393; FAX 909-338-4449. **Owner(s)** Desert Community Newspapers, Yucca Valley, CA; Ed. Matthew Proietti. adv. contact: Sue Hill. pub. size: standard; circ. 3,500(paid).
Formerly: Mountain Courier-News.

CUPERTINO

US

CUPERTINO COURIER. 1947. Wed. $.50 newsstand; $20/yr. in cy.; $40/yr. out of cy.; $15/yr. senior citizens. 20465 Silverado Ave., Cupertino, CA 95014-4439. TEL 408-255-7500; FAX 408-252-3381. **Owner(s)** Select Communications, Inc., 138 Main St., Los Altos, CA; Ed. Mike Betz; Pub. Paul Nyberg; adv. contact: Susan Glaze. photos; pub. size: tabloid; circ. 18,940(free & paid).

DELANO

US

DELANO RECORD. Thu. $.35 newsstand; $19/yr. in cy. $21/yr. out of cy.; $24/yr. out of state. 1231 Jefferson, Delano, CA 93215. TEL 805-725-0600; FAX 805-725-4373. **Owner(s):** Reed Print, Inc., 5409 Aldrin Ct., Bakersfield, CA 93313; Ed. Bob Schettler; Pub. Robert Reed; adv. contact: Lonnie Lemons. pub. size: broadsheet; circ. 4,650(paid).

US

MARKET SHOPPER, THE. Wed. free. 1231 Jefferson, Delano, CA 93215. TEL 805-725-0600; FAX 805-725-4373. **Owner(s):** Reed Print, Inc., 5409 Aldrin Ct., Bakersfield, CA 93313; Ed. Bob Schettler; Pub. Robert Reed; adv. contact: Lonnie Lemons. pub. size: standard; circ. 16,150(free).

DEL MAR

US   ISSN 0191-5584
DEL MAR, SOLANA BEACH, CARMEL VALLEY, RANCHO SANTA FE SUN. 1958. Thu. $.25 newsstand; $15/yr. 1228 Camino Del Mar, Del Mar, CA 92014. TEL 619-792-3820; FAX 619-481-3312. **Owner(s):** West Coast Community Newspapers, Inc., 2841 Loker Ave., E., Carlsbad, CA 92007. TEL 619-431-4850; FAX 619-431-4888; Ed. Liam Truchard; Pub. Claire Otte; adv.; photos; pub. size: broadsheet; circ. 22,706(paid).
   Formerly: Del Mar Surfcomber.

DESERT HOT SPRINGS

US
DESERT SENTINEL, THE. 1941. Thu. $.35 newsstand; $19.40/yr. in cy. 13550 Palm Dr., Desert Hot Springs, CA 92240. TEL 619-329-1411; FAX 619-329-3860. **Owner(s):** Gannett Company, Inc., 1100 Wilson Blvd., Arlington, VA 22234. TEL 703-284-6000; Ed. John Waters, Jr.; Pub. Bob Dickey; adv.; photos; pub. size: broadsheet; circ. 2,600(free & paid).

DOWNIEVILLE

US   ISSN 0278-4394
MOUNTAIN MESSENGER. 1853. Thu. $.25 newsstand; $13/yr. in cy.; $16/yr. out of cy. 100 Main St., Downieville, CA 95936. TEL 916-289-3262; FAX 916-289-3262. **Owner(s):** Donald S. Russell, Inc., 100 Main St., Downieville, CA 95936-3262. TEL 916-289-3421; James Roos, 100 Main St., Downieville, CA 95936. TEL 510-837-0571; Don Smith, 100 Main St., Downieville, CA 95936; Pub. Donald S. Russell; adv.: $5.50/SAU. bk.rev.; pub. size: broadsheet; circ. 2,680(paid).

ELK GROVE

US
ELK GROVE CITIZEN. 1903. s-w.: Wed. & Fri. $.35 newsstand; $35/yr. in cy. 8936 Elk Grove Blvd., Elk Grove, CA 95624. TEL 916-685-5533; FAX 916-686-6675. **Owner(s):** Herburger Publications, Inc., 604 N. Lincoln, Galt, CA 95632. TEL 209-745-1551; Ed. Janell Deter; Pub. Roy E. Herburger; adv. contact: Shawn Sanderson. pub. size: broadsheet; circ. 18,000(paid).

EL MONTE

US
MID VALLEY NEWS. 1966. Wed. free; $30/yr. mailed in cy. 11001 Valley Mall, Ste. 204, El Monte, CA 91731. TEL 818-443-1753; FAX 818-443-2245. **Owner(s):** Michael DeWeese, 11001 Valley Mall, Ste. 204, El Monte, CA 91731. TEL 818-443-1753; Benson J. Hegel, 11001 Valley Mall, Ste. 204, El Monte, CA 91731. TEL 818-443-1753; Ed. Michael DeWeese; Pub. Michael DeWeese; adv. contact: Irene Ramirez. pub. size: tabloid; circ. 45,000(free & paid).

EL SEGUNDO

US
EL SEGUNDO HERALD. 1911. Thu. free; $50/yr. in cy. mailed. 312 E. Imperial Ave., El Segundo, CA 90245. TEL 310-322-1830; FAX 310-322-2787. **Owner(s):** El Segundo Herald, Inc., P.O. Box 188, El Segundo, CA 90245. TEL 310-322-1830; Ed. Heidi Maerker; Pub. Julie Spyr; adv. contact: Julie Spyr. pub. size: tabloid; circ. 15,000(controlled & free).

ENCINITAS

US
ENCINITAS SUN. 1925. Thu. free; $50/yr. 3rd class; $10/mo. 1st class out of area. 1105 Second St., Ste. 3, Encinitas, CA 92024. TEL 619-634-1534; FAX 619-634-2380. **Owner(s):** West Coast Community Newspapers, Inc., 2841 Loker Ave., E., Carlsbad, CA 92008. TEL 619-431-4850; FAX 619-431-4888; Ed. Tom Graves; Pub. Donna M. Medeiros; adv.; pub. size: broadsheet; circ. 19,479(controlled & paid).
   Formerly: Coast Dispatch.

ESCONDIDO

US
ESCONDIDO NEWS-REPORTER. 1983. s-w.: Tue. & Fri. $.50 newsstand; $30/yr. 210 S. Juniper St., Ste. 205, Escondido, CA 92025. TEL 619-747-8911; FAX 619-747-8912. **Owner(s):** Metropolitan News Co., 210 S. Spring St., Los Angeles, CA 90012-3710. TEL 213-628-4384; TEL 213-687-3886; Ed. Roger M. Grace; Pub. Roger M. Grace; adv.; pub. size: standard; circ. 9,500(paid). **Wire Service(s):** AP.

EXETER

US   ISSN 1072-1584
SUN, THE. 1903. Wed. $.50 newsstand; $17/yr. local; $23/yr. elsewhere; $25/yr. out of state. P.O. Box 7, Exeter, CA 93221-0007. TEL 209-592-3171; FAX 209-592-4308. **Owner(s):** Bill Brown, P.O. Box, Exeter, CA 93221-0007. TEL 209-592-3171; FAX 209-592-4308; Ed. Bruce Whitworth; Pub. Bill Brown; adv. contact: Marilee Stevens. pub. size: broadsheet; circ. 15,000(free & paid).

FALLBROOK

US
ENTERPRISE MOUNTAINEER, THE. 1910. Thu. $.35 newsstand; $17.95/yr. carrier; $20/yr. in cy. mailed; $22/yr. out of cy. 232 S. Main St., Fallbrook, CA 92028. TEL 619-728-5511; FAX 619-723-4967. **Owner(s):** South Coast Newspapers, 1722 S. Hill St., Oceanside, CA 92054. TEL 619-433-7333; Ed. Betty Johnston; Pub. G.L. Taylor; adv.; pub. size: standard; circ. 8,000(paid).
   Formerly: Enterprise, The.

FILLMORE

US
FILLMORE HERALD. 1907. Thu. $.35 newsstand; $22.51/yr. 606 Sespe Ave., Ste. 106, Fillmore, CA 93016. TEL 805-524-0153. **Owner(s):** Sentinel Media Publications, Inc., P.O. Box 727, Fillmore, CA 93016-0727; Ed. Doug Huff; Pub. Doug Huff; adv. contact: Doug Huff. photos; pub. size: broadsheet; circ. 3,000(controlled & paid).

FOLSOM

US
FOLSOM TELEGRAPH. 1856. Wed. $.50 newsstand; $20/yr. carrier. 555 Oakdale St., Ste. G1, Folsom, CA 95630. TEL 916-985-2581; FAX 916-985-0720. **Owner(s):** Brehm Communications, Inc., 17065 Via del Campo, Ste. 200, San Diego, CA 92127. TEL 619-451-6200; Ed. Jim Duncan; Pub. Dave Reese; adv. contact: Debbi Cornelius. pub. size: broadsheet; circ. 6,000(paid).

US
ORANGEVALE NEWS. 1956. Wed. $.50 newsstand; $20/yr. 555 Oakdale St., Ste. G1, Folsom, CA 95630-2451. TEL 916-985-2581; FAX 916-985-0720. **Owner(s):** Brehm Communications, Inc., 17065 Via del Campo, Ste. 200, San Diego, CA 92127. TEL 619-451-6200; Ed. Jim Duncan; Pub. Dave Reese; adv. contact: Debbi Cornelius. pub. size: broadsheet; circ. 6,000(paid).

FONTANA

US
FONTANA HERALD NEWS. 1923. Thu. $.50 newsstand; $18/yr. 16920 Spring St., Fontana, CA 92335. TEL 909-822-2231; FAX 909-355-9358. **Owner(s):** Herald News Publishing, Inc., 16920 Spring St., Fontana, CA 92235. TEL 909-822-2231; Ed. Russell Ingold; Pub. Jerry Bean; adv.; photos; pub. size: broadsheet; circ. evening 11,712(free & paid).

FORT BRAGG

US   ISSN 0886-8840
FORT BRAGG ADVOCATE-NEWS. 1889. Thu. $.50 newsstand; $20/yr. local. 450 N. Franklin St., Fort Bragg, CA 95437. TEL 707-964-5642; FAX 707-964-0424. **Owner(s):** Stephens Group, Inc., P.O. Box 1359, Fort Smith, AR 72902. TEL 501-785-7801; Ed. Katherine Lee; Pub. Sharon Brewer; adv.; photos; pub. size: broadsheet; circ. 5,040(paid).

FORTUNA

US
HUMBOLDT BEACON. 1902. Thu. $.50 newsstand; $10/6 mos. in cy.; $17.50/yr.; $25/yr. in state; $30/yr. out of state. 928 Main St., Fortuna, CA 95540. TEL 707-725-6166; FAX 707-725-4981. **Owner(s):** Humboldt Group, The, 928 Main St., Fortuna, CA 95540. TEL 707-725-6166; FAX 707-725-4981; Ed. Jack Hamilton; Pub. Patrick O'Dell; adv. contact: Carol Larsen. photos; bk.rev.; pub. size: standard; circ. 8,000(paid).

FRESNO

US
CALIFORNIA ADVOCATE, THE. 1967. Wed. $.50 newsstand; $20/yr. mailed. 1715 E Street, Ste. 108, Fresno, CA 93706. TEL 209-268-0941; FAX 209-268-0943. **Owner(s):** Mark Kimber, 452 Fresno St., Fresno, CA 93706. TEL 209-268-0941; Ed. Pauline Kimber; Pub. Mark Kimber; pub. size: broadsheet; circ. 25,000(paid).

GALT

US

GALT HERALD. 1903. Wed. $.35 newsstand; $18/yr. in cy. 604 N. Lincoln Way, Galt, CA 95632. TEL 209-745-1551; FAX 209-745-4492. **Owner(s):** Herburger Publications, Inc., 604 N. Lincoln Way, Galt, CA 95632. TEL 209-745-1551; Ed. John Williams; Pub. Roy Herburger; adv. contact: Dean Davy. photos; pub. size: broadsheet; circ. 9,000(free & paid).

GARDENA

US

GARDENA VALLEY NEWS. 1904. Thu. $.25 newsstand; $12/yr. home deliv.; $45/yr. mailed. 16417 S. Western Ave., Gardena, CA 90247. TEL 310-329-6351; FAX 310-329-7501. **Owner(s):** Don Algie, 16417 S. Western Ave., Gardena, CA 90247. TEL 310-329-6351; Ed. Gary Kohatsu; Pub. Don Algie; adv. contact: Dan Gagajena. photos; bk.rev.; pub. size: broadsheet; circ. 25,000(free & paid).

GARDEN GROVE

US

ORANGE COUNTY NEWS. 1909. s-w.: Wed. & Fri. $30/yr. in cy. mailed only. 9872 Chapman St., Ste. 108, Garden Grove, CA 92641. TEL 714-530-7622; FAX 714-530-7142. **Owner(s):** Orange County News Publishing Co., Inc., 9872 Chapman, Ste. 108, Garden Grove, CA 92641. TEL 714-530-7622; Ed. David Roque. adv. contact: Lois Rischel. pub. size: broadsheet; circ. 34,000(paid).

GLENDALE

US   ISSN 0008-0950

CALIFORNIA COURIER. 1958. Thu. $39/yr. P.O. Box 5390, Glendale, CA 91221. TEL 818-409-0949. Owner(s): California Courier, P.O. Box 5390, Glendale, CA 91221. TEL 818-409-0949; FAX 818-500-7372; Ed. Harut Sassounian; Pub. Harut Sassounian; adv.; bk.rev.; pub. size: tabloid; circ. 3,000(paid).

GRIDLEY

US

GRIDLEY HERALD, THE. 1880. s-w.: Wed. & Fri. $.50 newsstand; $30/yr. in cy.; $34/yr. out of cy. 630 Washington St., Gridley, CA 95948. TEL 916-846-3661; FAX 916-846-4519. **Owner(s):** Gridley Publishing Co., Inc., P.O. Box 68, Gridley, CA 95948. TEL 916-846-3661; Ed. Scotty Williams; Pub. William D. Burleson; adv. contact: Lisa Beebe. pub. size: broadsheet; circ. 4,000(paid).

HALF MOON BAY

US

HALF MOON BAY REVIEW. 1898. Wed. $.50 newsstand; $21/yr. home deliv.; $23.50/yr. mailed. 714 Kelly Ave., Half Moon Bay, CA 94019. TEL 415-726-4424; FAX 415-726-7054; E-mail: hmbreview@hmbreview.com; URL: http://www.hmbreview.com/. **Owner(s):** Wick Communications, Inc., 333 Wilcox Dr., Ste. 302, Sierra Vista, AZ 85635. TEL 602-458-0200; Ed. Marc DesJardins; Pub. Debra Godshall; adv.; pub. size: broadsheet; circ. 6,200(paid).

HEALDSBURG

US

HEALDSBURG TRIBUNE. 1856. Wed. $.50 newsstand; $21.50/yr. in cy.; $37.50/yr. out of cy.; $16/yr. senior citizens. 5 Mitchell Ln., Healdsburg, CA 95448. TEL 707-433-4451; FAX 707-431-2623. **Owner(s):** Beverly C. Reeves, 5 Mitchell Ln., Healdburg, CA 95448. TEL 707-433-4451; Ed. Dan Stebbins; Pub. Beverly Reeves; adv. contact: Lisa DeVries. photos; pub. size: broadsheet; circ. 4,650(paid).

HERMOSA BEACH

US

EASY READER. 1970. Thu. free; $40/yr. in cy. 832 Hermosa Ave., Hermosa Beach, CA 90254. TEL 310-372-4611; FAX 310-318-6292. **Owner(s):** Kevin Cody, 1233 Hermosa Ave., Hermosa Beach, CA 90254. TEL 310-372-4611; Ed. Kevin Cody; Pub. Kevin Cody; adv. contact: Maryjane Schoenheider. bk.rev.; pub. size: tabloid; circ. 70,000(free).

HESPERIA

US

APPLE VALLEY NEWS. 1965. Fri. free newsstand; $19/yr. local mailed; $21/yr. out of area. 16925 Main St., Hesperia, CA 92345. TEL 619-244-0021; FAX 619-244-6609. **Owner(s):** Raymond Pryke, 16925 Main St., Hesperia, CA 92345. TEL 619-244-0021; Ed. Joyce Bohannan; Pub. Jenny Jones; adv. contact: Patricia Ray. pub. size: broadsheet; circ. 5,000(free & paid).

US

DESERT MOUNTAIN EXPRESS. 1962. Fri. free newsstands; $19/yr. mailed local; $21/yr. mailed elsewhere. 16925 Main St., Hesperia, CA 92345. TEL 619-244-0021; FAX 619-244-6609. **Owner(s):** Raymond Pryke, 16925 Main St., Hesperia, CA 92345. TEL 619-244-0021; Ed. Joyce Bohannan; Pub. Jenny Jones; adv.; pub. size: broadsheet; circ. 18,000(free & paid).

US

HESPERIA RESORTER. 1959. Thu. free; $19/yr. mailed local; $21/yr. mailed elsewhere. 16925 Main St., Hesperia, CA 92345. TEL 619-244-0021; FAX 619-244-6609. **Owner(s):** Raymond Pryke, 16925 Main St., Hesperia, CA 92345. TEL 619-244-0021; Ed. Joyce Bohannan; Pub. Jenny Jones; adv. contact: Patricia Thomas. pub. size: broadsheet; circ. 7,000(free & paid).

HILMAR

US

HILMAR TIMES. Thu. $.25 newsstand; $17/yr. in cy. mailed; $21/yr. out of cy. mailed. 8260 Lander, Hilmar, CA 95324. TEL 209-632-4156; FAX 209-358-7108. **Owner(s):** Mid-Valley Publications, Inc., 6950 Gerard, Winton, CA 95388. TEL 209-358-5311; Ed. John Derby; Pub. John Derby; pub. size: broadsheet; circ. 6,000(paid).

HOLLISTER

US

PINNACLE, THE. 1986. Thu. free newsstand; $28/yr. 341 Tres Pinos Rd., Ste. 201, Hollister, CA 95023. TEL 408-637-6300; FAX 408-637-8174. **Owner(s):** K & S Market, Inc., P.O. Box 499, Hollister, CA 95024. TEL 408-637-6300; FAX 408-637-8174; Ed. Marvin Snow; Pub. Frank Klauer; adv.; photos; pub. size: tabloid.

HOLTVILLE

US

HOLTVILLE TRIBUNE. 1906. Thu. $.50 newsstand; $22.50/yr. in cy.; $26.50/yr. elsewhere. 523 Pine Ave., Holtville, CA 92250. TEL 619-356-2995; FAX 619-356-4915. **Owner(s):** Steve Larson, 523 Pine Ave., Holtville, CA 92250. TEL 619-356-2995; Ed. Steve Larson; Pub. Steve Larson. pub. size: tabloid; circ. 3,000(paid).

HUNTINGTON BEACH

US   ISSN 0194-6021

HUNTINGTON BEACH/FOUNTAIN VALLEY INDEPENDENT. 1966. Thu. free. 18682 Beach Blvd., Ste. 160, Huntington Beach, CA 92648. TEL 714-965-3030; FAX 714-955-7174. **Owner(s):** Los Angeles Times, Times Mirror Sq., Los Angeles, CA 90053. TEL 213-237-3700; Ed. Bill Lobdell; Pub. Tom Johnson; adv. contact: Michael Fletcher. pub. size: tabloid; circ. 65,000(free).

INDIO

US

INDIO POST. 1963. Thu. $.25 newsstand; $15/yr. in cy.; $45/yr. out of cy. 82-632 Hwy. 111, Ste. B, Indio, CA 92201. TEL 619-775-4200; FAX 619-342-7128. **Owner(s):** The Desert Sun, 750 N. Gene Autry Trail, Palm Springs, CA 92262. TEL 619-322-8839; Ed. Dick Gazi; Pub. Robert Dickey; adv. contact: Walter Hennig. photos; pub. size: standard; circ. 30,000(controlled & free).

US

PALM DESERT. 1963. Thu. $.25 newsstand; $15/yr. in cy.; $35/yr. mailed. 82-632B Hwy. 111, Indio, CA 92201. TEL 619-775-4200 **Owner(s):** The Desert Sun, 750 N. Gene Autry Trail, Palm Springs, CA 92262. TEL 619-322-8889; Pub. Robert Dickey; adv. contact: Linda Ruder. photos; pub. size: standard; circ. 30,000(controlled & free).
   Formerly: Desert Sun Community Newspaper, Desert Post.

IRVINE

US   ISSN 0195-4822

IRVINE WORLD NEWS. 1970. Thu. $60/yr. 2712 McGaw, Irvine, CA 92714. TEL 714-261-2435; FAX 714-261-2623. **Owner(s):** The Irvine Co., P.O. Box I, Newport Beach, CA 92663. TEL 714-720-2000; Ed. Don Dennis; Pub. Brien Manning; adv. contact: Tobey Anglin. pub. size: tabloid; circ. 55,000(controlled).

KERMAN

US

FIREBAUGH/MENDOTA JOURNAL. Wed. $.50 newsstand; $21.55/yr. mailed. 681 S. Madera Ave., Ste. 109, Kerman, CA 93630. TEL 209-846-6689; FAX 209-846-8045. **Owner(s):** KerWest, Inc., 681 S. Madera Ave., Ste. 109, Kerman, CA 93630. TEL 209-846-6689; Ed. Mark Kilen. adv. contact: Merlyn Wilcox. pub. size: broadsheet; circ. 7,700(free).

US

KERMAN NEWS. 1905. Wed. $.50 newsstand; $21.55/yr. 681 S. Madera Ave., Ste. 109, Kerman, CA 93630. TEL 209-846-6689; FAX 209-846-8045. **Owner(s):** KerWest, Inc., P.O. Box 336, Kerman, CA 93630. TEL 209-846-6689; Ed. Mark Kilen. adv. contact: Merlyn Wilcox. pub. size: broadsheet; circ. 2,000(paid).

US

WEST SIDE ADVANCE. 1905. Wed. free; $21.55/yr. mailed. 681 S. Madera Ave., Ste. 109, Kerman, CA 93630. TEL 209-846-6689; FAX 209-846-8045. **Owner(s):** KerWest, Inc., 681 S. Madera Ave., Ste. 109, Kerman, CA 93630. TEL 209-846-6689; Ed. Mark Kilen. adv. contact: Merlyn Wilcox. pub. size: broadsheet; circ. 2,700(free & paid).

KING CITY

US

KING CITY RUSTLER. 1901. Wed. $.50 newsstand; $23/yr. in cy.; $29/yr. out of cy. 116 S. Third St., King City, CA 93930. TEL 408-385-4880; FAX 408-385-4799. **Owner(s):** News Media Corp., 211 Hwy. 38, E., Rochelle, IL 61068; Ed. Suzi Taylor; Pub. Harry Casey; pub. size: broadsheet; circ. 4,200(paid).

KINGSBURG

US

KINGSBURG RECORDER. Wed. $.50 newsstand; $20/yr. 1467 Marion St., Kingsburg, CA 93631. TEL 209-897-2993; FAX 209-897-4868. **Owner(s):** Community Newspapers, Inc., Selma, CA. TEL 209-896-1976; FAX 209-896-9160; Ed. Tim Sheehan; Pub. Jim Brock; adv.; pub. size: standard; circ. 2,700(paid).

LA CANADA

US

LA CANADA VALLEY SUN. 1946. Thu. $.50 newsstand; $22/yr. in cy. 1061 Valley Sun Ln., La Canada, CA 91011. TEL 818-790-8774; FAX 818-790-5690. **Owner(s):** Gerald A. Bean, 1061 Valley Sun Ln., La Canada, CA 91011. TEL 818-790-8774; FAX 818-790-5690; Pub. Gerald A. Bean; adv. contact: Pat Miller. photos; pub. size: tabloid; circ. 5,900(paid).

LAFAYETTE

US

CONTRA COSTA SUN. 1938. Wed. $.75 newsstand; $30/yr. mailed. 3685 Mt. Diablo Blvd., Ste. 150, Lafayette, CA 94549. TEL 510-284-4444; FAX 510-284-1039. **Owner(s):** Knight-Ridder, Inc., One Herald Plz., Miami, FL 33132-1693. TEL 305-376-3800; Ed. Bev Britton; Pub. George Riggs; adv.; photos; pub. size: broadsheet; circ. 8,000(paid).

LAGUNA HILLS

US

LEISURE WORLD NEWS. 1965. Thu. $.50 newsstand; $12/yr. home deliv. 23522 Paseo de Valencia, Laguna Hills, CA 92653. TEL 714-837-5200; FAX 714-837-0106. **Owner(s):** Freedom Communications, Inc., 17666 Fitch, Irvine, CA 92614. TEL 714-553-9292; Ed. Cathy Lawhon. pub. size: tabloid; circ. 11,567(paid).

US

SOUTH COAST SHOPPERS/PENNY SAVERS. 1960. Wed. free. 25201 Paseo de Alicia, Ste. 120, Laguna Hills, CA 92600. TEL 714-996-8900; FAX 714-859-3469. **Owner(s):** Harte-Hanks Communications, Inc., P.O. Box 269, San Antonio, TX 78291. TEL 210-829-9000; adv.; pub. size: tabloid; circ. 4,300,000(free).
  Formerly: South Coast Shoppers.

LA JOLLA

US

LA JOLLA LIGHT. 1913. Thu. $.50 newsstand; $25/yr. 3rd class; $75/yr. 1st class. 450 Pearl St., La Jolla, CA 92037. TEL 619-459-4201; FAX 619-459-0977. **Owner(s):** West Coast Community Newspapers, Inc., 2841 Loker Ave., E., Carlsbad, CA 92008. TEL 619-431-4850; FAX 619-431-4888; Ed. Cynthia Queen; Pub. Darlene Spratt; adv.; pub. size: broadsheet; circ. 24,000(free & paid).

LAKE ARROWHEAD

US

MOUNTAIN NEWS, THE. 1920. Thu. $.50 newsstand; $22.50/yr. in cy.; $55/2 yrs.; $35/yr. out of cy.; $45/yr. out of state. 28200 Hwy. 189, Bldg. 0-1, Ste. 200, Lake Arrowhead, CA 92352. TEL 909-336-3555; FAX 909-337-5275. **Owner(s):** Brehm Communications, Inc., 17065 Via del Campo, Ste. 200, San Diego, CA 92127. TEL 619-451-3814; Ed. Matt Proietti; Pub. Phil Jaffe; adv.; pub. size: broadsheet; circ. 7,500(paid).

LAKE ELSINORE

US

LAKE ELSINORE VALLEY SUN-TRIBUNE. 1886. Thu. $.35 newsstand; $12/yr. in cy. 31900 Mission Trail, Ste. 120, Lake Elsinore, CA 92530. TEL 909-674-1535; FAX 909-674-0280. **Owner(s):** Southwest Riverside County Newspapers, Inc., P.O. Box 2108, Lake Elsinore, CA 92330. TEL 909-674-1535; Ed. Lowanna Maxwell; Pub. Tom Paradis; pub. size: broadsheet; circ. 11,069(paid).

LAKE FOREST

US

ALISO VIEJO NEWS. Thu. free. 22481 Aspan St., Lake Forest, CA 92630. TEL 714-768-3631; FAX 714-454-7354. **Owner(s):** Freedom Communications, Inc., 17666 Fitch, Irvine, CA 92614. TEL 714-553-9292; Ed. Don Chapman. pub. size: tabloid; circ. 7,247(free).

US

CAPISTRANO VALLEY NEWS. 1972. Thu. free to subscribers of Orange County Register. 22481 Aspan, Lake Forest, CA 92630. TEL 714-768-3631; FAX 714-454-7354. **Owner(s):** Orange County Register, 625 N. Grand, Santa Ana, CA 92690. TEL 714-835-1234; Ed. Steve Silverman. pub. size: tabloid; circ. 9,200(free).

US

DANA POINT NEWS. Thu. free to subscribers of Orange County Register. 22481 Aspan, Lake Forest, CA 92630. TEL 714-768-3631; FAX 714-830-9504. **Owner(s):** Orange County Register, 625 N. Grand, Santa Ana, CA 92711. TEL 714-835-1234; Ed. Steve Silverman. pub. size: tabloid; circ. 12,300(free).

US

LAGUNA NIGUEL NEWS. 1972. Thu. free. 22481 Aspan, Lake Forest, CA 92630. TEL 714-768-3631; FAX 714-454-7354. **Owner(s):** Freedom Communications, Inc., 17666 Fitch, Irvine, CA 92614. TEL 714-553-9292; Ed. Cathy Lawhon. adv. contact: Derrick Davidson. photos; pub. size: tabloid; circ. 10,400(free).

US

LAGUNA POST NEWS. 1915. Thu. free. 22481 Aspan, Lake Forest, CA 92630. TEL 714-768-3631; FAX 714-830-9504. **Owner(s):** Freedom Communications, Inc., 17666 Fitch, Irvine, CA 92714. TEL 714-553-9292; FAX 714-474-7675; Ed. Cathy Lawhon. adv. contact: Derrick Davidson. photos; pub. size: tabloid; circ. 14,213(free).
  Formerly: Laguan Beach News.

US

RANCHO SANTA MARGARITA NEWS. s-w.: Wed. & Fri. free to subscribers of Orange County Register. 22481 Aspan, Lake Forest, CA 92630. TEL 714-768-3631; FAX 714-830-9504. **Owner(s):** Orange County Register, 625 N. Grand, Santa Ana, CA 92711. TEL 714-835-1234; Ed. Cathy Lawhon. pub. size: tabloid; circ. 7,000(free).

US

SADDLEBACK VALLEY NEWS. s-w.: Wed. & Fri. free. 22481 Aspan St., Lake Forest, CA 92630. TEL 714-768-3631; FAX 714-454-7354. **Owner(s):** Orange County Register, 23811 Via Fabricante, Mission Viejo, CA 92690. TEL 714-768-3631; Ed. Cathy Lawhon. pub. size: tabloid; circ. 57,000(controlled & free).

LAKE ISABELLA

US

KERN VALLEY SUN. 1957. Wed. $.50 newsstand; $18.13/yr. home deliv.; $23.19/yr. local mailed. 6404 Lake Isabella Blvd., Lake Isabella, CA 93240. TEL 619-379-3667; FAX 619-379-4343. **Owner(s):** Wick Communications, Inc., 333 W. Wilcox Dr., Ste. 302, Sierra Vista, AZ 85635. TEL 520-458-0200; FAX 520-458-6166; Ed. Bret Bradigan; Pub. Bret Bradigan; adv.; pub. size: broadsheet; circ. 6,275(paid).

LAMONT

US

LAMONT REPORTER. Wed. free; $19/yr. in cy. mailed; $21/yr. out of cy.; $24/yr. elsewhere. 9717 Main St., Lamont, CA 93241. TEL 805-845-3704; FAX 805-832-0841. **Owner(s):** Reed Print, Inc., 5409 Aldrin Ct., Bakersfield, CA 93313; Ed. Frank W. Reed; Pub. Donald Reed; adv.; pub. size: broadsheet; circ. 8,100(free & paid).

LANCASTER

US

DESERT MAILER NEWS. 1975. Tue. free; $16/yr. mailed. 123 West Ave., Ste. J-5, Lancaster, CA 93534. TEL 805-945-8671; FAX 805-942-6418. **Owner(s):** Hamilton Diversified Services, P.O. Box 179, Pauma Valley, CA 92061. TEL 619-742-1905; FAX 619-742-1894; Pub. James Collins; adv.; photos; pub. size: tabloid; circ. 112,000(free & paid).

LEMON GROVE

US

LA MESA FORUM. Thu. free. 3434 Grove St., Lemon Grove, CA 91946. TEL 619-469-0101. **Owner(s):** Forum Publications, Inc., P.O. Box 127, Lemon Grove, CA 91946. TEL 619-469-0101; Ed. Steve Saint; Pub. Steve Saint; pub. size: tabloid; circ. 4,000(paid).

US

LEMON GROVE REVIEW. 1948. Thu. $.25 newsstand; $18/yr. P.O. Box 127, Lemon Grove, CA 91946. TEL 619-469-0101. **Owner(s):** Forum Publications, Inc., P.O. Box 127, Lemon Grove, CA 91946. TEL 619-469-0101; Pub. Steve Saint; adv.; pub. size: tabloid; circ. 2,000(paid).

US

SPRING VALLEY BULLETIN. 1949. Thu. $.25 newsstand; $18/yr. P.O. Box 127, Lemon Grove, CA 91946. TEL 619-469-0101. **Owner(s):** Forum Publications, Inc., P.O. Box 127, Lemon Grove, CA 91946. TEL 619-469-0101; Pub. Steve Saint; adv.; pub. size: tabloid; circ. 3,000(paid).

LINDEN

US

LINDEN HERALD. 1959. Thu. $.40 newsstand; $23.50/yr. 4950 N. Bonham, Linden, CA 95236. TEL 209-887-3112; FAX 209-887-3111. **Owner(s):** Brian Reilly, 4950 N. Bonham, Linden, CA 95236-0929. TEL 209-887-3112; Ed. Brian Reilly; Pub. Brian Reilly; adv.; pub. size: broadsheet; circ. 1,200(paid).

LINDSAY

US   ISSN 1072-1800

LINDSAY GAZETTE. 1901. Wed. $17/yr. in cy.; $23/yr. out of cy. 136 Honolulu, Lindsay, CA 93247. TEL 209-562-2585; FAX 209-562-2214. **Owner(s):** Mineral King Publishing Co., Lindsay, CA 93247; adv.; pub. size: broadsheet; circ. 2,300(paid).

LIVERMORE

US

INDEPENDENT, THE. 1963. Wed. free. 2250 First St., Livermore, CA 94550. TEL 510-447-8700; FAX 510-447-0212. **Owner(s):** Independent, The, 2250 First St., Livermore, CA 94550. TEL 510-447-8700; FAX 510-447-0212; Ed. Janet Armantrout; Pub. Joan Seppala; adv.; pub. size: standard; circ. 26,200(controlled).

LOCKEFORD

US

LOCKEFORD-CLEMENTS NEWS. Wed. $13.50/yr. 18540 N. Hwy. 88, Unit 22, Lockeford, CA 95237. TEL 209-727-5776. **Owner(s):** Laura J. Mays, 18540 N. Hwy. 88, Unit 22, Lockeford, CA 95237. TEL 209-727-5776; Ed. Michael L. Williams; Pub. Laura J. Mays; adv.; pub. size: tabloid; circ. 2,800(paid).

LONG BEACH

US

DOWNTOWN GAZETTE. 1978. Mon. free. 5225 E. Second St., Long Beach, CA 90803. TEL 310-433-2000; FAX 310-434-8826. **Owner(s):** Gazette Newspapers, Inc., 5225 E. Second St., Long Beach, CA 90803. TEL 310-433-2000; FAX 310-434-8826; Ed. Harry Saltzgaver; Pub. Fran Blowitz; adv.; bk.rev.; pub. size: tabloid; circ. 50,000(free).

US

GRUNION GAZETTE. 1978. Thu. free newsstand; $40/yr. 5225 E. Second St., Long Beach, CA 90803. TEL 310-433-2000; FAX 310-434-8826. **Owner(s):** Fran & John Blowitz, 5225 E. Second St., Long Beach, CA 90803. TEL 310-433-2000; FAX 310-434-8826; Pub. Fran Blowitz; adv.; bk.rev.; pub. size: tabloid; circ. 30,000(free).

US

MARINA NEWS. 1990. Thu. free. 289 Redondo Ave., Long Beach, CA 90803. TEL 714-960-2837; FAX 310-987-2251. **Owner(s):** Pat Cantalupo, 289 Redondo Ave., Long Beach, CA 90803. TEL 310-987-2246; FAX 310-987-2251; Ed. Pat Cantalupo; Pub. Pat Cantalupo; adv.; pub. size: tabloid; circ. 30,000(free).

LOS ALAMITOS

US

NEWS ENTERPRISE, THE. 1923. Thu. $.25 newsstand; $15/yr. mailed locally; $25/yr. out of state. 3622 Florista, Los Alamitos, CA 90720. TEL 714-527-8210; FAX 310-493-2310. **Owner(s):** Athena Publishing Corp., 3262 Oak Knoll Dr., Los Alamitos, CA 90720. TEL 310-431-1397; Pub. Germaine R. Erskine; adv. contact: Gerry Erskine. pub. size: standard; circ. 30,000(free & paid).
  Formerly: Seal Beach, Rossmoor, Los Alamitos, Cypress, & LaPalma News Enterprises.

LOS ALTOS

US   ISSN 8750-4588

LOS ALTOS TOWN CRIER. 1947. Wed. $.50 newsstand; $20/yr. in cy.; $40/yr. out of cy.; $15/yr. senior citizens. 138 Main St., Los Altos, CA 94022. TEL 415-948-9000; FAX 415-948-6647; E-mail: towncrier@losaltosonline.com; URL: http://www.losaltosonline.com. **Owner(s):** Select Communications, Inc., 138 Main St., Los Altos, CA 94022. TEL 415-948-4821; Ed. Bruce Barton; Pub. Paul Nyberg; adv. contact: Susan Glaze. pub. size: tabloid; circ. 16,500(controlled).

LOS ANGELES

US

ALHAMBRA POST ADVOCATE. s-w.: Wed. & Sat. $100/yr. in state. 2621 W. 54th St., Los Angeles, CA 90043. TEL 213-290-3000; FAX 213-291-0219. **Owner(s)** Wave Community Newspapers, Inc., 2621 W. 54th St., Los Angeles, CA 90043. TEL 213-727-1117; Ed. Art Aquilar; Pub. Ric Trent; circ. 25,C14(controlled).

US

ARGONAUT, THE. 1971. Thu. $85/yr. 3rd class mail; $110/yr. 1st class mail. 5355 McConnell Ave., Los Angeles, CA 90066. TEL 310-822-1629; FAX 310-821-8029. **Owner(s):** Argonaut, Inc., 5355 McConnell Ave., Los Angeles, CA 90066. TEL 310-822-1629; Ed. David Asper Johnson; Pub. David Asper Johnson; adv. contact: James Cloud. pub. size: tabloid; circ. 40,000(free & paid).

US

BELEVEDERE CITIZEN. Wed. free; $78/yr. in state. 2621 W. 54th St., Los Angeles, CA 90043. TEL 213-290-3000; FAX 213-291-0219. **Owner(s):** Wave Community Newspapers, Inc., 2621 W. 54th St., Los Angeles, CA 90043. TEL 213-727-1117; Pub. Ric Trent; circ. 15,100(free & paid).

US

BELL GARDENS REVIEW. Thu. $78/yr. in state. 2621 W. 54th St., Los Angeles, CA 90043. TEL 213-727-1117; FAX 213-292-8289. **Owner(s):** Wave Community Newspapers, Inc., 2621 W. 54th St., Los Angeles, CA 90043. TEL 213-727-1117; FAX 213-292-8289; Ed. Art Agular; Pub. Ric Trent; circ. 21,662(controlled).

US

BELL MAYWOOD CUDAHY INDUSTRIAL POST. Thu. $78/yr. in state. 2621 W. 54th St., Los Angeles, CA 90043. TEL 213-290-3000; FAX 213-727-9515. **Owner(s):** Wave Community Newspapers, Inc., 2621 W. 54th St., Los Angeles, CA 90043. TEL 213-727-1117; Ed. Art Auglar; Pub. Ric Trent; pub. size: standard; circ. 21,662(controlled).

US

CARSON WAVE. Wed. $78/yr. in state. 2621 W. 54th St., Los Angeles, CA 90043. TEL 213-290-3000; FAX 213-291-0219. **Owner(s):** Wave Community Newspapers, Inc., 2621 W. 54th St., Los Angeles, CA 90043. TEL 213-727-1117; Pub. Ric Trent; adv.; bk.rev.; pub. size: standard; circ. 14,082(paid).

US

CIVIC CENTER NEWSOURCE. Mon. $.50 newsstand; $30/yr. 210 S. Spring St., Los Angeles, CA 90012-3710. TEL 213-628-4334; FAX 213-687-3886. **Owner(s):** Metropolitan News Co., 210 S. Spring St., Los Angeles, CA 90012-3710. TEL 213-628-4334; FAX 213-687-3886; Ed. Roger M. Grace; Pub. S. John Babigian; pub. size: tabloid; circ. 7,500(paid). **Wire Service(s):** AP.

US

COMPTON WAVE. Wed. $78/yr. in state. 2621 W. 54th St., Los Angeles, CA 90043. TEL 213-290-3000; FAX 213-291-0219. **Owner(s):** Wave Community Newspapers, Inc., 2621 W. 54th St., Los Angeles, CA 90043. TEL 213-727-1117; Pub. Ric Trent; adv.; pub. size: standard; circ. 26,283(paid).

US

CULVER CITY STAR. Wed. $78/yr. in state. 2621 W. 54th St., Los Angeles, CA 90043. TEL 213-290-3000; FAX 213-292-8289. **Owner(s):** Wave Community Newspapers, Inc., 2621 W. 54th St., Los Angeles, CA 90043. TEL 213-727-1117; Pub. Ric Trent; adv. contact: Ric Trent. pub. size: standard; circ. 29,109(paid).

US

DOWNEY HERALD AMERICAN. 1953. Thu. $.25 newsstand; $78/yr. in state. 2621 W. 54th St., Los Angeles, CA 90043. TEL 213-290-3000; FAX 213-291-0219. **Owner(s):** Wave Community Newspapers, Inc., 2621 W. 54th St., Los Angeles, CA 90043; Ed. Arnold Adler; Pub. Ric Trent; adv. contact: Ric Trent. pub. size: broadsheet; circ. 25,747(paid).

US

EAGLE ROCK SENTINEL. Wed. $78/yr. in state. 2621 W. 54th St., Los Angeles, CA 90043. TEL 213-290-3000; FAX 213-292-8289. **Owner(s):** Wave Community Newspapers, Inc., 2621 W. 54th St., Los Angeles, CA 90043. TEL 213-727-1711; Ed. Roger Swanson; Pub. Rick Trent; adv. contact: Judy Kellerman. pub. size: broadsheet; circ. 8,660(paid).

US

EAST L.A./COMMERCE TRIBUNE. Wed. $78/yr. in state. 2621 W. 54th St., Los Angeles, CA 90043. TEL 213-290-3000; FAX 213-291-0219. **Owner(s):** Wave Community Newspapers, Inc., 2621 W. 54th St., Los Angeles, CA 90043. TEL 213-727-1117; Pub. Ric Trent; adv. contact: Tanner Oliver. pub. size: standard; circ. 19,059(paid).

US

EASTSIDE JOURNAL. Wed. $78/yr. in state. 2621 W. 54th St., Los Angeles, CA 90043. TEL 213-290-3000; FAX 213-291-2019. **Owner(s):** Wave Community Newspapers, Inc., 2621 W. 54th St., Los Angeles, CA 90043; Pub. C.Z. Wilson; adv. contact: Rick Billings. pub. size: standard; circ. 16,075(paid).

US

EL SERENO STAR. Wed. $78/yr. in state. 2621 W. 54th St., Los Angeles, CA 90043. TEL 213-290-3000; FAX 213-291-0219. **Owner(s):** Wave Community Newspapers, Inc., 2621 W. 54th St., Los Angeles, CA 90043; Pub. C.Z. Wilson; adv. contact: Rick Billings. pub. size: standard; circ. 7,650(paid).

US

HIGHLAND PARK NEWS/HERALD/JOURNAL. 1905. Wed. free; $78/yr. in state. 2621 W. 54th St., Los Angeles, CA 90043. TEL 213-727-1117; FAX 213-292-8289. **Owner(s):** Wave Community Newspapers, Inc., 2621 W. 54th St., Los Angeles, CA 90043; Ed. Art Aguilar; Pub. Art Aguilar; pub. size: broadsheet; circ. 15,250(free & paid).

US

HUNTINGTON PARK BULLETIN. Wed. free home deliv.; $100/yr. mailed. 2621 W. 54th St., Los Angeles, CA 90043. TEL 213-290-3000; FAX 213-219-0219. **Owner(s):** Wave Community Newspapers, Inc., 2621 W. 54th St., Los Angeles, CA 90043. TEL 213-727-1711; Ed. Eleanor Collins. pub. size: broadsheet; circ. 12,888(controlled & free). **Wire Service(s):** CNS.

US

INGLEWOOD/HAWTHORNE WAVE. Wed. $55/6 mo.; $78/yr. in state. 2621 W. 54th St., Los Angeles, CA 90043. TEL 213-290-3000; FAX 213-292-8289. **Owner(s):** Wave Community Newspapers, Inc., 2621 W. 54th St., Los Angeles, CA 90043. TEL 213-727-1117; Pub. Ric Trent; adv. contact: Ric Trent. pub. size: standard; circ. 281,000(paid).

US

L.A. WEEKLY. Thu. free; $1 newsstand Orange cy. 6715 Sunset Blvd., Los Angeles, CA 90028. TEL 213-465-9909; FAX 213-465-3220. **Owner(s):** Hartz Consumer Group, Inc., The, 667 Madison Ave., New York, NY 10021. TEL 212-308-3336; Ed. Sue Horton; Pub. Michael Sigman; adv. contact: Leslie Prentice. pub. size: broadsheet; circ. 195,000(free & paid).

US

LINCOLN HEIGHTS BULLETIN-NEWS. Wed. free; $78/yr. in state. 2621 W. 54th St., Los Angeles, CA 90043. TEL 213-290-3000; FAX 213-291-0219. **Owner(s):** Central News-Wave Publications, 621 West 54th St., Los Angeles, CA 90043; Ed. Art Aguilar; Pub. Art Aguilar; pub. size: broadsheet; circ. 9,125(free & paid).

US

LOS ANGELES INDEPENDENT. 1935. s-w.: Wed. & Sat. free; $60/yr. in cy. mailed. 4201 Wilshire Blvd., Ste. 600, Los Angeles, CA 90010. TEL 213-932-6397; FAX 213-932-8285. **Owner(s):** National Media, Inc., 4201 Wilshire Blvd., Ste. 600, Los Angeles, CA 90010. TEL 213-932-6397; Ed. Brian Lewis; Pub. Michael Laxineta; adv. contact: Mike Manning. photos; pub. size: broadsheet; circ. 200,000(controlled). **Wire Service(s):** CiNS.

US

LYNWOOD PRESS. 1922. Wed. $78/yr. in state. 2621 W. 54th St., Los Angeles, CA 90043. TEL 213-290-3000; FAX 213-291-0219. **Owner(s):** Wave Community Newspapers, Inc., 2621 W. 54th St., Los Angeles, CA 90043. TEL 213-290-3000; Pub. Ric Trent; pub. size: broadsheet; circ. 24,006(controlled).

US

MESA TRIBUNE WAVE. Wed. $78/yr. in state. 2621 W. 54th St., Los Angeles, CA 90043. TEL 213-290-3000; FAX 213-292-8289. **Owner(s):** Central News-Wave Publications, 2621 W. 54th St., Los Angeles, CA 90043. TEL 213-290-3000; Pub. Ric Trent; adv. contact: Ric Trent. pub. size: broadsheet; circ. 31,609(controlled).

US

MONTEBELLO NEWS. Wed. $78/yr. in state. 2621 W. 54th St., Los Angeles, CA 90043. TEL 213-727-1117. **Owner(s):** Wave Community Newspapers, Inc, 2621 W. 54th St., Los Angeles, CA 90043. TEL 213-290-3000; FAX 213-291-0219; Pub. Ric Trent; adv. contact: Ric Trent. pub. size: standard; circ. 17,919(paid).

US

MONTEREY PARK PROGRESS. Thu. $.25 newsstand; $78/yr. in state. 2621 W. 54th St., Los Angeles, CA 90043. TEL 213-290-3000; FAX 213-291-0219. **Owner(s):** Central News-Wave Publications, 2621 W. 54th St., Los Angeles, CA 90043. TEL 213-290-3000; Ed. Ray Babcock; Pub. Ric Trent; adv. contact: Ric Trent. pub. size: broadsheet; circ. 17,788(paid).

US

MT. WASHINGTON STAR REVIEW. Wed. $78/yr. in state. 2621 W. 54th St., Los Angeles, CA 90043. TEL 213-290-3000; FAX 213-291-0219. **Owner(s):** Wave Community Newspapers, Inc., 2621 W. 54th St., Los Angeles, CA 90043. TEL 213-727-1117; Pub. C.Z. Wilson; adv. contact: Rick Billings. pub. size: standard; circ. 5,425(paid).

US

NORWALK HERALD AMERICAN. Thu. $.25 newsstand; $78/yr. in state. 2621 W. 54th St., Los Angeles, CA 90043. TEL 213-290-3000; FAX 213-291-0219. **Owner(s):** Central News-Wave Publications, 2621 W. 54th St., Los Angeles, CA 90043. TEL 213-290-3000; Ed. Arnold Adler; Pub. Ric Trent; adv. contact: Ric Trents. pub. size: broadsheet; circ. 24,305(paid).

US

▼**OC WEEKLY.** 1995. w. 6715 Sunset Blvd., Los Angeles, CA 90028. TEL 213-465-9909; FAX 213-465-3220. **Owner(s):** The Hartz Consumer Group, Inc., 667 Madison Ave., New York, NY 10021. TEL 212-808-3336; Ed. Will Swaim; Pub. Michael Sigman; pub. size: tabloid; circ. 50,000(free).

US

PARK LABREA NEWS/BEVERLY PRESS. 1947. Thu. free; $50/yr. mailed. 142 S. Fairfax Ave., Los Angeles, CA 90036. TEL 213-933-5518; FAX 213-933-5812. **Owner(s):** Michael & Karen Villalpando, 142 S. Fairfax Ave., Los Angeles, CA 90036. TEL 213-933-5518; FAX 213-933-5812; Ed. Stan Hoskins; Pub. Michael Villalpando; adv.; pub. size: tabloid; circ. 13,100(controlled).

US

PICO RIVERA NEWS. Wed. $.25 newsstand; $100/yr. in state. 2621 W. 54th St., Los Angeles, CA 90043. TEL 213-290-3000; FAX 213-291-0219. **Owner(s):** Central News-Wave Publications, 262 W. 54th St., Los Angeles, CA 90043. TEL 213-290-3000; Ed. Art Aguilar. circ. 15,133(paid).

US

RIVERSIDE BULLETIN, THE. Thu. $.25 newsstand; $10/yr. 210 S. Spring St., Los Angeles, CA 90012-3710. TEL 213-628-4384; FAX 213-687-3886. **Owner(s):** Metropolitan News Co., 210 S. Spring St., Los Angeles, CA 90012-3710. TEL 213-628-4384; FAX 213-687-3886; Ed. Roger M. Grace; Pub. Roger M. Grace; pub. size: standard; circ. 500(paid). **Wire Service(s):** AP.

US

SAN BERNARDINO BULLETIN, THE. Tue. $.25 newsstand; $10/yr. 210 S. Spring St., Los Angeles, CA 90012-3710. TEL 213-628-4384; FAX 213-687-3886. **Owner(s):** Metropolitan News Co., 210 S. Spring St., Los Angeles, CA 90012-3710. TEL 213-628-4384; FAX 213-687-3886; Ed. Roger M. Grace; Pub. Roger M. Grace; pub. size: standard; circ. 300(paid). **Wire Service(s):** AP.

US

SAN GABRIEL PROGRESS. Wed. $78/yr. in state. 2621 W. 54th St., Los Angeles, CA 90043. TEL 213-290-3000; FAX 213-291-0219. **Owner(s):** Wave Community Newspapers, Inc., 2621 W. 54th St., Los Angeles, CA 90043. TEL 213-290-3000; Ed. Ray Babcock; Pub. Ric Trent; adv. contact: Ric Trent. bk.rev.; pub. size: standard; circ. 16,272(paid).

US
SANTA FE SPRINGS NEWS. Wed. $78/yr. in state. 2621 W. 54th St., Los Angeles, CA 90043. TEL 213-290-3000; FAX 213-291-0219. **Owner(s):** Wave Community Newspapers, Inc., 2621 W. 54th St., Los Angeles, CA 90043. TEL 213-290-3000; Ed. Ray Babcock; Pub. Ric Trent; adv. contact: Ric Trent. bk.rev.; pub. size: standard; circ. 2,530(paid).

US
SOUTH GATE PRESS. Wed. $78/yr. in state. 2621 W. 54th St., Los Angeles, CA 90043. TEL 213-290-3000; FAX 213-291-0219. **Owner(s):** Central News-Wave Publications, 2621 W. 54th St., Los Angeles, CA 90043. TEL 213-290-3000; Ed. Dennis Coffeman; Pub. Ric Trent; adv. contact: Ric Trent. circ. 23,822(controlled).

US
SOUTH SAN GABRIEL/ROSEMEAD PROGRESS. Wed. $78/yr. in state. 2621 W. 54th St., Los Angeles, CA 90043. TEL 213-290-3000; FAX 213-291-0219. **Owner(s):** Central News-Wave Publications, 2621 W. 54th St., Los Angeles, CA 90043. TEL 213-290-3000; Ed. Ray Babcock; Pub. Ric Trent; adv. contact: Ric Trent. bk.rev.; pub. size: standard; circ. 14,447(paid).

US
SOUTHSIDE JOURNAL. 1923. Wed. free. 2621 W. 54th St., Los Angeles, CA 90043. TEL 213-290-3000; FAX 213-291-0219. **Owner(s):** Wave Community Newspapers, Inc., 2621 W. 54th St., Los Angeles, CA 90043. TEL 213-290-3000; Pub. C.Z. Wilson; adv. contact: Bene Benwikere. pub. size: broadsheet; circ. 21,300(free).

US
SOUTHWEST WAVE/NEWS. 1918. Wed. free in area; $78/yr. out of area. 2621 W. 54th St., Los Angeles, CA 90043. TEL 213-290-3000; FAX 310-292-8289. **Owner(s):** Central News-Wave Publications, 2621 W. 54th St., Los Angeles, CA 90043. TEL 310-290-3000; Pub. Ric Trent; pub. size: standard; circ. 30,000(free & paid).

US
TOPICS SUN WAVE. Wed. $78/yr. in state. 2621 W. 54th St., Los Angeles, CA 90043. TEL 213-290-3000; FAX 213-292-8289. **Owner(s):** Central News-Wave Publications, 2621 W. 54th St., Los Angeles, CA 90043. TEL 213-290-3000; FAX 213-292-8289; Pub. Ric Trent; adv. contact: Ric Trent. bk.rev.; pub. size: standard; circ. 30,731(paid).

US
WESTCHESTER STAR. Wed. $78/yr. in state. 2621 W. 54th St., Los Angeles, CA 90043. TEL 213-290-3000; FAX 213-292-8289. **Owner(s):** Wave Community Newspapers, Inc., 2621 W. 54th St., Los Angeles, CA 90043; Pub. Ric Trent; adv. contact: Ric Trent. pub. size: standard; circ. 9,956(paid).

LOS BANOS

US
LOS BANOS ENTERPRISE. 1891. s-w.: Wed. & Sat. $.50 newsstand; $17.16/6 mos. in cy.; $30.03/yr. in cy.; $56.84/yr. out of cy. 1253 W. I St., Los Banos, CA 93635. TEL 209-826-3831; FAX 209-826-2005. **Owner(s):** U.S. Media Group, P.O. Box 227, Crystal City, MO 63019; Ed. Kevin Previtali. adv. contact: Rhonda Lowe. pub. size: broadsheet; circ. 7,000(paid).

LOS GATOS

US
LOS GATOS WEEKLY-TIMES. 1881. Wed. $.50 newsstand; $26/yr mailed in city; $52/yr. elsewhere. 245 Almendra Ave., Los Gatos, CA 95030. TEL 408-354-3110; FAX 408-354-3917. **Owner(s):** Metro Newspapers, Inc., 550 S. First St., San Jose, CA 95113. TEL 408-298-8000; Ed. Dale Bryant; Pub. David Cohen; pub. size: tabloid; circ. 19,000(paid).
   Formerly: Los Gatos Times Observer.

MALIBU

US   ISSN 0191-7307
MALIBU SURFSIDE NEWS. 1972. Thu. $25/yr. local; $45/yr. out of state. 28990 Pacific Coast Hwy., Malibu, CA 90265. TEL 310-457-2112; FAX 310-457-9908; E-mail: mailibunews@eworld.com. **Owner(s):** A.C. Soble/Malibu News Enterprises, 28990 Pacific Coast Hwy., Malibu, CA 90265. TEL 310-457-2112; Ed A.C. Soble; Pub. A.C. Soble; adv. contact: Christine Stoddard. pub. size: tabloid; circ. 13,500(controlled).

US   ISSN 1050-4931
MALIBU TIMES. 1946. Thu. $.25 newsstand; $35/yr. 3864 Las Flores Canyon Rd., Malibu, CA 90265. TEL 310-456-5507; FAX 310-346-8986; E-mail: agyork@malibutimes.com. **Owner(s):** Arnold G. & Karen P. York, P.O. Box 1127, Malibu, CA 90265. TEL 310-456-5507; Ed. Arnold G. York; Pub. Arnold G. York; adv.; photos; bk.rev.; pub. size: broadsheet; circ. 12,500(paid).

MAMMOTH LAKES

US
MAMMOTH TIMES. 1987. Thu. free newsstand; $40/yr. mailed. 452 Old Mammoth Rd., Mammoth Lakes, CA 93546. TEL 619-934-3929; FAX 619-934-3951; E-mail: mamtimes@ao .com. **Owner(s):** New Times Publishing, Inc., 452 Old Mammoth Rd., Mammoth Lakes, CA 93546. TEL 619-934-3929; FAX 619-934-3951; Pub. Wally Hofmann; adv. contact: Greg Myers. photos; pub. size: tabloid; circ. 12,000(free & paid).

US   ISSN 1052-5300
REVIEW HERALD, THE. 1879. s-w.: Thu. & Sun. $45/yr. local. 1566 Tavern Rd., Mammoth Lakes, CA 93546. TEL 619-934-8544; FAX 619-934-7385. **Owner(s):** Bishop Chalfant Press Publications, P.O. Box 787, Bishop, CA 93515. TEL 619-873-3535; FAX 619-873-3591; Ed. Barbara Ferry-Laughon. pub. size: broadsheet; circ. 4,500(paid). **Wire Service(s):** AP.
   Formerly: Mono Herald & Bridgeport Chronicle.

MANHATTAN BEACH

US
BEACH REPORTER, THE. 1977. Thu. free; $140/yr. in cy. mailed. 500 S. Sepulveda, Ste. 215, Manhattan Beach, CA 90266. TEL 310-374-4040; FAX 310-379-8570. **Owner(s):** National Media, Inc., P.O. Box 383, Manhattan Beach, CA 90266. TEL 310-374-4040; FAX 310-379-8570; Ed. Cara Murphy; Pub. Richard Frank; adv.; pub. size: tabloid; circ. 61,000(controlled).

MARIPOSA

US
MARIPOSA GAZETTE. 1854. Wed. $.30 newsstand; $14/yr. in cy.; $18.54/yr. out of cy. 5081 Jones St., Mariposa, CA 95338. TEL 209-966-2500; FAX 209-966-3384. **Owner(s):** C. Ruth & Dalmar J. Campbell, P.O. Box 38, Mariposa, CA 95338. TEL 209-966-2500; FAX 209-966-3384; Ed. Jerry Rankin; Pub. Dalmar J. Campbell; adv.; pub. size: broadsheet; circ. 5,100(paid).

US
MOUNTAIN LIFE. 1970. Tue. Free; $16/yr. in state; $21.45/yr. out of state. 5081 Jones St., Mariposa, CA 95338. TEL 209-966-2500; FAX 209-966-3384. **Owner(s):** Ruth & Dalmar Campbell, P.O. Box 38, Mariposa, CA 95338. TEL 209-966-2500; Ed. Jerry Rankin; Pub. Dalmar Campbell; adv.; pub. size: tabloid; circ. 12,000(free & paid).

MARTINEZ

US
MARTINEZ NEWS GAZETTE. 1858. 3/wk.: Tue., Thu., Sat. $.25 newsstand; $4/wk. carrier; $7/mo. mailed. 615 Estudillo St., Martinez, CA 94553. TEL 510-228-6400; FAX 510-228-1536. **Owner(s):** Gibson Publications, Inc., 544 Maryland St., Vallejo, CA 94589. TEL 707-643-1706; Ed. Robert V. Osmond; Pub. David Payne; adv. contact: Robert V. Osmond. photos; bk.rev.; pub. size: broadsheet; circ. 35,000(free & paid).

MENDOCINO

US
MENDOCINO BEACON, THE. 1877. Thu. $.50 newsstand; $20/yr. in cy.; $30/yr. out of cy. 45066 Ukiah St., Mendocino, CA 95460. TEL 707-937-5874; FAX 707-937-0825. **Owner(s):** Stephens Group, Inc., P.O. Box 1359, Fort Smith, AR 72902. TEL 501-785-7801; Ed. Kathryn Lee; Pub. Sharon Brewer; adv.; photos; pub. size: standard; circ. 2,400(paid).

MENLO PARK

US   ISSN 0192-0111
COUNTRY ALMANAC. 1923. Wed. $.50 newsstand; $20/yr. mailed in area; $30/yr. mailed elsewhere. 3525 Alameda De Las Pulgas, Menlo Park, CA 94025-6558. TEL 415-854-2626; FAX 415-854-0677. **Owner(s):** Embarcadero Publishing Co., 703 High St., Palo Alto, CA 94302. TEL 415-326-8210; Ed. Richard Hine; Pub. Tom Gibboney; adv. contact: Connie Colton. photos. pub. size: tabloid; circ. 21,500(free & paid).
   Formerly: Menlo Park Almanac.

MILL VALLEY

US   ISSN 0048-2641
PACIFIC SUN. 1963. Wed. free; $25/yr. in cy. mailed. 21 Corte Madera Ave., Mill Valley, CA 94941. TEL 415-383-4500; FAX 415-383-4159. **Owner(s):** Pacific Sun Publishing Co., Inc., 21 Corte Madera Ave., Mill Valley, CA 94941. TEL 415 383-4500; Ed. Linda Xiques; Pub. Stephen McNamara; adv. contact: Kathy Closs. pub. size: broadsheet; circ. 42,500(free).

MILPITAS

US

BERRYESSA SUN. 1992. bi-w.: Fri. $10/yr. 1615A S. Main St., Milpitas, CA 95035. TEL 408-262-2454; FAX 408-263-9710. **Owner(s):** Mort Levine, 1615A S. Main St., Milpitas, CA 95035. TEL 408-262-2454; Jimmy Chamoures, 1615A S. Main St., Milpitas, CA 95035. TEL 408-262-2454; Ed. Rob Devincenzi; Pub. Mort Levine; adv. contact: Linda Shmitz. pub. size: tabloid; circ. 20,000(paid).

US ISSN 0745-6212

MILPITAS POST. 1955. Thu. $.50 newsstand; $20/yr. in town; $30/yr. out of town. 1615A S. Main St., Milpitas, CA 95035. TEL 408-262-2454; FAX 408-263-9710. **Owner(s):** Mort Levine, 1615A S. Main St., Milpitas, CA 95035. TEL 408-262-2454; Jimmy Chamoures, 1615A S. Main St., Milpitas, CA 95035. TEL 408-262-2454; Ed. Rob Devincenzi; Pub. Jimmy Chamoures; adv. contact: Linda Shmitz. pub. size: tabloid; circ. 25,000(paid).

MORENO VALLEY

US

VALLEY TIMES. 1952. Thu. $.50 newsstand; $24/yr. 25873 Alessandro Blvd., Moreno Valley, CA 92553. TEL 909-242-7614; FAX 909-247-1920. **Owner(s):** Stephens Group, Inc., P.O. Box 1359, Fort Smith, AK 72902. TEL 501-785-7810; Ed. Larry Venus; Pub. Mel Harkavy; adv. contact: Bob Pay. photos; pub. size: standard; circ. 7,300(paid).
  Formerly: Butterfield Express, The.

MORGAN HILL

US

MORGAN HILL TIMES. 1894. s-w.: Tue. & Fri. $.50 newsstand; $34.40/yr. local. 30 E. Third St., Morgan Hill, CA 95037. TEL 408-779-4106; FAX 408-779-3886. **Owner(s):** McClatchy Newspapers, P.O. Box 15579, Sacramento, CA 95813. TEL 916-446-9728; Ed. Walt Glines; Pub. Paula Mabry; adv. contact: Arlene Hudson. photos; pub. size: broadsheet; circ. 3,800(controlled). **Wire Service(s):** McClatchy News Service, SHNA.

MORRO BAY

US

CENTRAL COAST SUN-BULLETIN. 1931. Wed. $.50 newsstand; $24/yr. home deliv.; $39/yr. mailed. 1149 Market St., Morro Bay, CA 93442. TEL 805-772-7346; FAX 805-772-7044. **Owner(s):** Scripps-Howard, 312 Walnut St., 28th Fl., Cincinnati, OH 45202. TEL 513-977-3000; Ed. Richard Palmer. pub. size: broadsheet; circ. 8,000(paid).

MT. SHASTA

US

MOUNT SHASTA HERALD. 1888. Wed. $.50 newsstand; $22.50/yr. in cy.; $27.50/yr. out of cy. 924 B N. Mt. Shasta Blvd., Mt. Shasta, CA 96067-0127. TEL 916-926-5214; FAX 916-926-4166. **Owner(s):** American Publishing Co., 606 N. Van Buren, P.O. Box 520, Marion, IL 62959. TEL 618-993-1711; Ed. Steve Gerace; Pub. Genny Axtman; adv. contact: Genny Axtman. pub. size: standard; circ. 4,200(paid).

NAPA

US

NAPA COUNTY RECORD. 1947. Fri. $20/yr. 1320 Second St., Napa, CA 94559. TEL 707-252-8877. **Owner(s):** David W. Barker, 520 Third St., Napa, CA 94559. TEL 707-252-8877; Ed. Melodie Ahtty; Pub. David W. Barker; adv. contact: David W. Barker. photos; bk.rev.; pub. size: broadsheet; circ. 6,000(controlled & paid).

NEEDLES

US

NEEDLES DESERT STAR. 1888. Wed. $.50 newsstand; $12.95/yr. in cy.; $26/yr. out of cy. 911 Third St., Needles, CA 92363-2935. TEL 619-326-2222; FAX 619-326-3480. **Owner(s):** News West Publishing Co., P.O. Box 28429, San Diego, CA 92198. TEL 619-326-2222; FAX 619-326-6480; Ed. Robin Richards; Pub. Lalena Stewart; adv.; photos; pub. size: broadsheet; circ. 5,000(paid).

NEWMAN

US

NEWMAN NEWS, THE. 1992. Wed. $.35 newsstand; $14/yr. 1306 O St., Newman, CA 95360. TEL 209-862-4746; FAX 209-862-4979. **Owner(s):** U.S. Media Group, P.O. Box 227, Crystal City, MO 63019; Ed. Lori Leeland. adv. contact: Karen Medeiros. photos; pub. size: standard; circ. 5,000(paid).

NOVATO

US

NOVATO ADVANCE. 1922. Wed. $3.05/mo. home deliv.; $3.75/mo. in cy. 1068 Machin Ave., Novato, CA 94945. TEL 415-898-7084; FAX 415-897-0940. **Owner(s):** Scripps League Newspapers, Inc., P.O. Box 1109, Herndon, VA 22070; Ed. John Jackson; Pub. John Burns; pub. size: standard; circ. 15,000(free & paid).

OAKDALE

US

OAKDALE LEADER. 1894. Wed. $.50 newsstand; $25/yr. in cy.; $32/yr. out of cy.; $20/yr. senior citizens. 122 S. Third Ave., Oakdale, CA 95361. TEL 209-847-3021; FAX 209-847-9750. **Owner(s):** Live Oak Publishing, 122 S. Third Ave., Oakdale, CA 95361; Ed. Steve Breen; Pub. S.L. Cook; adv. contact: John Burden. pub. size: broadsheet; circ. 10,000(free & paid).

OAKLAND

US

BAY AREA PRESS. 1970. bi-w.: Fri. free; $20/yr. mailed. Grand Lake Sta., Oakland, CA 94610. TEL 510-547-4000. **Owner(s):** Oakland Press Publications, P.O. Box 10151, Oakland, CA 94610. TEL 510-547-4000; Ed. George Epstein; Pub. George Epstein; adv.; photos; bk.rev.; pub. size: tabloid; circ. 7,000(free).

US

MONTCLARION. 1943. s-w.: Tue. & Fri. $.50 newsstand; $30/yr. in cy. 6208 La Salle Ave., Oakland, CA 94611. TEL 510-339-4060; FAX 510-339-4066. **Owner(s):** Chip & Mary Brown, 6208 La Salle Ave., Oakland, CA 94611. TEL 510-339-8777; Ed. Chris Treadway; Pub. Chip Brown; adv. contact: Jan Wasserman. photos; bk.rev.; pub. size: broadsheet; circ. 63,000(controlled). **Wire Service(s):** CNS.

US

PIEDMONTER, THE. 1916. w. $.50 newsstand; $30/yr. 5707 Redwood Rd., Oakland, CA 94619-2414. TEL 510-339-4050; FAX 510-339-4066. **Owner(s):** Hills Newspapers, Inc., 6208 LaSalle Ave., Piedmont, CA 94611. TEL 510-339-8777; Ed. Don McConnell. adv. contact: Jan Wasserman. pub. size: standard; circ. 7,000(paid).

OJAI

US

OJAI VALLEY NEWS. 1891. s-w.: Wed. & Fri. $.50 newsstand. 408 Bryant Cir., Ste. A, Ojai, CA 93023. TEL 805-646-1476; FAX 805-646-4281. **Owner(s):** Ren Adam, 408 Bryant Cir., Ste. A, Ojai, CA 93023. TEL 805-646-1476; Ed. Tim Dewar. adv. contact: Gretchen Schmidt. photos; pub. size: broadsheet; circ. 11,100(free & paid).

ORLAND

US

ORLAND PRESS-REGISTER. 1868. 3/wk.: Mon., Wed., Fri. $.50/newsstand; $48/yr. carrier; $60/yr. mailed in cy.; $63/yr. out of cy.; $40/yr. sr. citizen carrier; $50/yr. in cy.; $55/yr. out of cy. 407 Walker St., Orland, CA 95963. TEL 916-865-4433; FAX 916-865-3110. **Owner(s):** Tri-County Newspapers, Inc., 101 Airport Rd., Willows, CA 95988. TEL 916-865-4433; Ed. Virginia Webster; Pub. Darryl Phillips; adv. contact: Christine A. Stifter. pub. size: broadsheet; circ. 5,000(paid).

OROVILLE

US

DIGGER SHOPPER & NEWS, THE. 1977. Thu. free. 2057 Mitchell Ave., Oroville, CA 95966. TEL 916-533-2170; FAX 916-533-2181. **Owner(s):** David Miller, 2057 Mitchell Ave., Oroville, CA 95966. TEL 916-533-2170; Pub. David Miller; adv.; pub. size: tabloid; circ. 19,000(free).

PACIFICA

US

PACIFICA TRIBUNE. 1947. Wed. $.50 newsstand; $21/yr. carrier; $24/yr. mailed in cy.; $25/yr. in state; $27/yr. out of state; $18/yr. senior citizens. 59 Aura Vista, Pacifica, CA 94044. TEL 415-359-6666; FAX 415-359-3821; E-mail: pactrib@hax.com; URL: http://www.ci.pacifica.ca.us/TRIBUNE. **Owner(s):** Main Street Media, Houston, TX; Ed. Chris Hunter; Pub. Chris Hunter; pub. size: broadsheet; circ. 10,500(paid).

PACIFIC PALISADES

US

NORTH SHORE SHOPPER. 1928. Thu. free. 839 Via De La Paz, Pacific Palisades, CA 90272. TEL 310-454-1321; FAX 310-454-1078. **Owner(s):** Small Newspaper Group, 8 Dearborn Sq., Kankakee, IL 60901; Ed. Bill Bruns; Pub. Roberta Donohue; adv. contact: Grace Hiney. pub. size: tabloid; circ. 17,600(free).

PALM DESERT (continued)

US

PALISADIAN-POST. 1928. Thu. $.50 newsstand; $21/yr. 839 Via De La Paz, Pacific Palisades, CA 90272. TEL 310-454-1321; FAX 310-454-1078. **Owner(s):** Small Newspaper Group, Eight Dearborn Sq., Kankakee, IL 60901; Ed. Bill Bruns; Pub. Tom Small; adv. contact: Grace Hiney. pub. size: broadsheet; circ. 5,000(paid).

PALM DESERT

US

BLYTHE ADVERTISER. 1955. Tue. free. 73400 Hwy. 111, Palm Desert, CA 92260. TEL 619-346-1729. **Owner(s):** Associated Desert Shoppers, Inc., 73400 Hwy. 111, Palm Desert, CA 92260. TEL 619-345-1729; adv.; pub. size: tabloid; circ. 7,400(free).

US

BRAWLEY ADVERTISER. 1955. Wed. free. 73400 Hwy. 111, Palm Desert, CA 92260. TEL 619-346-1729; FAX 619-346-1729. **Owner(s):** Associated Desert Shoppers, Inc., 73400 Hwy. 111, Palm Desert, CA 92260. TEL 619-345-1729; FAX 619-346-1729; Pub. Hal Paradis; adv.; pub. size: tabloid; circ. 6,822(free).

US

CALEXICO ADVERTISER. 1955. w. free. 74300 Hwy. 111, Palm Desert, CA 92260. TEL 619-346-1729; FAX 619-346-7350. **Owner(s):** Associated Desert Shoppers, Inc., 73400 Hwy. 111, Palm Desert, CA 92260. TEL 619-346-1729; FAX 619-346-7350; adv.; pub. size: tabloid; circ. 7,862(free).
  Formerly: Imperial Valley Advertiser.

US

DESERT MOBILE HOME NEWS. 1955. w. free. 38-155 Story Creek, Palm Desert, CA 92261. TEL 619-568-6633; FAX 619-568-6633. **Owner(s):** Robert K. & Judith A. Brownell, 38-155 Story Creek, Palm Desert, CA 92261. TEL 619-568-6633; FAX 619-568-6633; Ed. Robert K. Brownell; Pub. Robert K. Brownell; adv. contact: Judith A. Brownell. pub. size: tabloid.

US

EAST RIVERSIDE ADVERTISER. w. free. 73400 Hwy. 111, Palm Desert, CA 92260. TEL 619-346-1729; FAX 619-346-7350. **Owner(s):** Associated Desert Shoppers, Inc., 73400 Hwy. 111, Palm Desert, CA 92260. TEL 619-346-1729; FAX 619-346-7350; adv.; pub. size: tabloid; circ. 17,000(free).

US

EL CENTRO ADVERTISER. 1955. Fri. free. 73400 Hwy. 111, Palm Desert, CA 92260. TEL 619-346-1729; FAX 619-346-7350. **Owner(s):** Associated Desert Shoppers, Inc., 73400 Hwy. 111, Palm Desert, CA 92260. TEL 619-346-1729; FAX 619-346-7350; Pub. Hal Paradis; adv.; pub. size: tabloid; circ. 18,787(free).

US

GREEN SHEET, THE. 1955. Tue. free. 73400 Hwy. 111, Palm Desert, CA 92260. TEL 619-346-1729; FAX 619-346-7350. **Owner(s):** Associated Desert Shoppers, Inc., 74300 Hwy. 111, Palm Desert, CA 92260. TEL 619-346-1729; FAX 619-346-7350; adv.; pub. size: standard; circ. 19,800(free).
  Formerly: San Bernardino Advertiser.

US

INDIO ADVERTISER. 1955. w. free. 73400 Hwy. 111, Palm Desert, CA 92260. TEL 619-346-1729; FAX 619-346-7350. **Owner(s):** Associated Desert Shoppers, Inc., 73400 Hwy. 111, Palm Desert, CA 92260. TEL 619-346-1729; FAX 619-346-7350; adv.; pub. size: tabloid; circ. 15,000(free).

US

LAKE HAVASU CITY ADVERTISER. 1955. w. free. 73400 Hwy. 111, Palm Desert, CA 92260. TEL 619-346-1729. **Owner(s):** Associated Desert Shoppers, Inc., 73400 Hwy. 111, Palm Desert, CA 92260. TEL 619-346-7350; adv.; pub. size: tabloid; circ. 13,700(free).

US

MORONGO BASIN. Wec. free. 73400 Hwy. 111, Palm Desert, CA 92260. TEL 619-346-1729; FAX 619-346-7350. **Owner(s):** Associated Desert Shoppers, Inc. 73400 Hwy. 111, Palm Desert, CA 92260. TEL 619-346-1729; FAX 619-346-7350; Ed. Hal Pardis; Pub. Hal Pardis; adv. contact: Jim McComb. pub. size: tabloid; circ. 13,900(free).

US

ONTARIO ADVERTISER. 1955. w. free. 73400 Hwy. 111, Palm Desert, CA 92260. TEL 619-346-1729; FAX 619-346-7350. **Owner(s):** Associated Desert Shoppers, Inc., 73400 Hwy. 111, Palm Desert, CA 92260. TEL 619-346-1729; FAX 619-346-7350; Pub. Hal Paradis; adv.; pub. size: tabloid; circ. 22,800(free).

US

PALM DESERT ADVERTISER. 1955. Thu. free. 74300 Hwy. 111, Palm Desert, CA 92260. TEL 619-346-1729; FAX 619-346-7350. **Owner(s):** Associated Desert Shoppers, Inc., 73400 Hwy. 111, Palm Desert, CA 92260. TEL 619-346-1729; FAX 619-346-7350; adv.; pub. size: tabloid; circ. 10,000(free).

US

PALM SPRING ADVERTISER. 1955. w. free. 73400 Hwy. 111, Palm Desert, CA 92260. TEL 619-346-1729; FAX 619-346-7350. **Owner(s):** Associated Desert Shoppers, Inc., 73400 Hwy 111, Palm Desert, CA 92260. TEL 619-346-1729; FAX 619-346-7350; adv.; pub. size: tabloid; circ. 11,250(free).

US

PARKER ADVERTISER. 1955. w. free. 73400 Hwy. 111, Palm Desert, CA 92260. TEL 619-346-1729 **Owner(s):** Associated Desert Shoppers, Inc., 73400 Hwy 111, Palm Desert, CA 92260. TEL 619-346-1729; Pub. Hal Paradis; adv.; pub. size: tabloid; circ. 7,900(free).

US

REDLANDS ADVERTISER. 1955. Thu. free. 73400 Hwy. 111, Palm Desert, CA 92260. TEL 619-346-1729 FAX 619-346-7350. **Owner(s):** Associated Desert Shoppers, Inc., 73400 Hwy. 111, Palm Desert, CA 92260. TEL 619-346-1729; FAX 619-346-7350; Pub. Hal Paradis; adv.; pub. size: tabloid; circ. 20,400(free).

US

RIVERSIDE ADVERTISER. 1955. Thu. free. 73400 Hwy. 111, Palm Desert, CA 92260. TEL 619-346-1729; FAX 619-346-7350. **Owner(s):** Associated Desert Shoppers, Inc., 73400 Hwy. 111, Palm Desert, CA 92260. TEL 619-346-1729; FAX 619-346-7350; adv.; pub. size: tabloid; circ. 13,400(free).

US

SAN BERNARDINO ADVERTISER. w. free. 73400 Hwy. 111, Palm Desert, CA 92260. TEL 619-346-1729; FAX 619-346-7350. **Owner(s):** Associated Desert Shoppers, Inc., 73400 Hwy. 111, Palm Desert, CA 92260. TEL 619-346-1729; FAX 619-346-7350; adv.; pub. size: tabloid; circ. 19,900 free).

US

TRI-STATE ADVERTISER. 1955. Tue. free. 73400 Hwy. 111, Palm Desert, CA 92250. TEL 619-346-1729. **Owner(s):** Associated Desert Shoppers, Inc., 73400 Hwy. 111, Palm Desert, CA 92260. TEL 619-346-1729; FAX 619-346-7350; Pub. Hal Paradis; adv.; pub. size: tabloid; circ. 12,900(free)

US

VICTOR VALLEY ADVERTISER. 1955. w. free. 73400 Hwy. 111, Palm Desert, CA 92250. TEL 619-346-1729. **Owner(s):** Associated Desert Shoppers, Inc., 73400 Hwy. 111, Palm Desert, CA 92260. TEL 619-346-1729; FAX 619-346-7350; Pub. Hal Paradis; adv.; pub. size: tabloid; circ. 15,500(free).

US

WEST SAN BERNARDINO ADVERTISER. 1955. Thu. free. 73400 Hwy. 111, Palm Desert, CA 92260. TEL 619-346-0601. **Owner(s):** Associated Desert Shoppers, Inc., 73400 Hwy. 111 Palm Desert, CA 92260. TEL 619-346-1729; FAX 619-346-7350; Pub. Hal Paradit; adv.; pub. size: tabloid; circ. 18,300(free).
  Formerly: White Sheet.

PALO ALTO

US   ISSN 0199-1159

PALO ALTO WEEKLY. 1979. s-w.: Wed. & Fri. $.50 newsstand; $40/yr. 703 High St., Palo Alto, CA 94301. TEL 415-326-8210; FAX 415-326-3928; E-mail: editor@paweekly.com. **Owner(s):** Embarcadero Publishing Co., P.O. Box 1610, Palo Alto, CA 94302. TEL 415-326-8210; FAX 415-326-3928; Ed. Paul Gullixson; Pub. Bill Johnson; adv. contact: Franklin Elieh. photos; bk.rev.; pub. size: tabloid; circ. 49,500(controlled & paid).

PALOS VERDES PENINSULA

US

PALOS VERDES PENINSULA NEWS. 1937. s-w.: Thu. & Sat $.25 newsstand; $41.41/yr. 655 Deep Valley Dr., Ste. 150, Palos Verdes Peninsula, CA 90274. TEL 310-377-6877; FAX 310-377-4522. **Owner(s):** National Media, Inc., P.O. Box 2609, Palos Verdes Peninsula, CA 90274. TEL 310-377-6877; Ed. Alan W. Gafford; Pub. Susan Frank; adv.; pub. size: broadsheet; circ. 19,900(free & paid). **Wire Service(s):** CiNS.

PARADISE

US

PARADISE POST. 1945. 3/wk.: Tue., Thu., Sat. $.50 newsstand; $19.30/6 mos; $36.50/yr. P.O. Box 70, Paradise, CA 95967. TEL 916-877-4413; FAX 916-877-1326. **Owner(s):** Roland Rebele, P.O. Drawer 70, Paradise, CA 95967. TEL 916-877-4413; Lowel Blankfort, P.O. Box 70, Paradise, CA 95967. TEL 916-877-4413; Ed. Linda Meilink; Pub. Randy Goldberg; adv. contact: Carol Peterson. pub. size: broadsheet; circ. 10,000(paid).

PASADENA
US
PASADENA WEEKLY. 1984. Fri. $65/yr. 50 S. De Lacey Ave., #200, Pasadena, CA 91105-1904. TEL 818-584-1500; FAX 818-795-0149. **Owner(s):** Pasadena Publications, Inc., 50 S. Delacey Ave., Rm. 200, Pasadena, CA 91105-1904. TEL 818-584-1500; FAX 818-795-0149; Ed. Bill Evans; Pub. Jim Laris; adv. contact: Fred Bankston. pub. size: tabloid; circ. 35,000(controlled & paid).

PETALUMA
US
PETALUMA ARGUS-COURIER. 1855. s-w.: Tue. & Fri. $.50 newsstand; $5/mo. carrier or motor rte.; $7/mo. mailed. 830 Petaluma Blvd., N., Petaluma, CA 94952. TEL 707-762-4541; FAX 707-765-1707. **Owner(s):** Scripps League Newspapers, Inc., P.O. Box 1104, Herndon, VA 22070. TEL 703-713-1920; Ed. Chris Samson; Pub. Dan Zimmerman; adv. contact: Michael Vail. pub. size: broadsheet; circ. 10,000(paid). **Wire Service(s):** AP.

POINT REYES STATION
US
POINT REYES LIGHT. 1948. Thu. $.50 newsstand; $22.50/yr. in cy. 11431 Hwy. 1, Point Reyes Station, CA 94956. TEL 415-663-8404; FAX 415-663-8458. **Owner(s):** David V. & Cynthia Clark Mitchell, P.O. Box 210, Point Reyes Station, CA 94956. TEL 415-663-8404; FAX 415-663-8458; Don Schinske, P.O. Box 210, Point Reyes Station, CA 94956. TEL 415-663-8404; FAX 415-663-8458; Ed. David V. Mitchell; Pub. David V. Mitchell; adv. contact: Renee Shannon. pub. size: tabloid; circ. 4,300(paid).

PRATHER
US
MOUNTAIN PRESS. 1973. Wed. $.25 newsstand; $9.50/yr. in cy.; $12.50/yr. out of cy. 29424 Auberry Rd., Ste. 118, Prather, CA 93651. TEL 209-855-8100. **Owner(s):** Homer Scott, 29424 Auberry Rd., Prather, CA 93651. TEL 209-825-8100; Ed. Alyson Nelson. adv.; photos; bk.rev.; pub. size: tabloid; circ. 2,200(paid).

RAMONA
US
RAMONA SENTINEL. 1886. Thu. $.50 newsstand; $18/yr. in cy.; $25/yr. out of cy. 611 Main St., Ramona, CA 92065. TEL 619-789-1350; FAX 619-789-4057. **Owner(s):** Calvert Communications, Inc., 13247 Poway Rd., Poway, CA 92064-4613. TEL 619-748-2311; FAX 619-748-0413; Ed. Maureen Robertson; Pub. Ann Calvert; adv. contact: Carol Kinney. photos; pub. size: broadsheet; circ. 5,344(paid).

REDWOOD CITY
US
▼**REDWOOD CITY TRIBUNE.** 1994. Wed. free deliv.; $.25 newsstand. 2317 Broadway, Ste. 110, Redwood City, CA 94010. TEL 415-367-9834; FAX 415-367-8745. **Owner(s):** Pan-Asian Venture Capital Corp., 1201 Evans Ave., San Francisco, CA 94124. TEL 415-826-1100; Ed. Marc Burkhardt; Pub. Leonard Sbrocco; adv. contact: Porter Deese. photos; bk.rev.; pub. size: broadsheet; circ. 25,600(free).

REEDLEY
US
ORANGE COVE MOUNTAIN TIMES. 1984. Wed. $.30 newsstand; $10/yr. local; $13/yr. out of cy. 1130 G St., Reedley, CA 93654. TEL 209-638-2244; FAX 209-638-5021. **Owner(s):** Reedley Exponent, P.O. Box 432, Reedley, CA 93654. TEL 209-638-2244; Ed. Doreen Rhodes; Pub. Fred Hall; adv.; pub. size: broadsheet; circ. 6,000(paid).

US
REEDLEY EXPONENT. 1891. Thu. $.50 newsstand; $17.50/ in cy. 1130 G St., Reedley, CA 93654. TEL 209-638-2244; FAX 209-638-5021. **Owner(s):** Reedley Exponent, P.O. Box 432, Reedley, CA 93654; Ed. Budd Brockett; Pub. Fred Hall; adv. contact: Janie Lucio. pub. size: tabloid; circ. 6,300(paid).

RIDGECREST
US
NEWS REVIEW. 1976. Wed. $.35 newsstand; $24/yr. in cy; $25 outside cy. 109 N. Sanders, Ridgecrest, CA 93555. TEL 619-371-4301; FAX 619-371-4304. **Owner(s):** Patricia Farris, CA; Pub. Patricia Farris; adv.; photos; bk.rev.; pub. size: tabloid; circ. 13,500(controlled).

US
SWAP SHEET. Thu. free newsstand. 619 W. Ridgecrest Blvd., Ste. D, Ridgecrest, CA 93555. TEL 619-375-5400; FAX 619-375-1901. **Owner(s):** Howard Sutton, 619 W. Ridgecrest Blvd., Ste. D, Ridgecrest, CA 93555. TEL 619-375-1901; Pub. Howard Sutton; adv.; pub. size: standard; circ. 12,000(free).

ROCKLIN
US
PLACER HERALD. 1852. Tue. $.25 newsstand; $15/yr. 5903B Sunset Blvd., Rocklin, CA 95677. TEL 916-624-9713; FAX 916-624-7469. **Owner(s):** Brehm Communications, Inc., 17065 Via del Campo, Ste. 200, San Diego, CA 92127. TEL 619-451-6200; Ed. J.T. Long; Pub. David Reese; adv.; photos; pub. size: broadsheet; circ. 5,500(paid).

ROSAMOND
US
ROSAMOND NEWS. 1988. w. $.50 newsstand; $42/yr. 2654 Diamond St., Rosamond, CA 93560-0848. TEL 805-256-0149; FAX 805-269-2139. **Owner(s):** Joyce Media, Inc., 2654 Diamond St., Rosamond, CA 93560-0848. TEL 805-256-0249; FAX 805-269-2139; Ed. Helen Dennis; Pub. John Joyce; adv. contact: Lynne Sickler. photos; bk.rev.; pub. size: tabloid; circ. 3,100(paid). **Wire Service(s):** UPI.

ROSEVILLE
US
ROSEVILLE PRESS-TRIBUNE. 1906. 3/wk.: Tue., Fri., Sun. $.50/day newsstand; $.75/Sun.; $8.75/mo. carrier. 188 Cirby Way, Roseville, CA 95678. TEL 916-786-6500; FAX 916-783-1183. **Owner(s):** Brehm Communications, Inc., 17065 Via del Campo, Ste. 200, San Diego, CA 92127. TEL 619-451-6200; Ed. Richard Walker. adv. contact: Shanda Miller. pub. size: broadsheet; circ. 14,000(paid); Sun. 14,600(paid). **Wire Service(s):** CNS.

SACRAMENTO
US
GOLD RIVER NEWS. 1989. s-w. $35/yr. 6231 Center Mall Way, Sacramento, CA 95823. TEL 916-392-5843; FAX 916-392-5843. **Owner(s):** James E. Jones, 6231 Center Mall Way, Sacramento, CA 95823. TEL 916-392-5843; FAX 916-392-5843; Ed. James Jones; Pub. James Jones; adv.; photos; pub. size: tabloid.

US
SACRAMENTO BULLETIN, THE. Tue. $.25 newsstand. 1713 J St., Ste. 202, Sacramento, CA 95814. TEL 916-445-6336; FAX 916-443-5871. **Owner(s):** Metropolitan News Co., 210 S. Spring St., Los Angeles, CA 90012-3710. TEL 213-628-4384; FAX 213-687-3886; Ed. Roger M. Grace; Pub. Roger M. Grace; pub. size: standard; **Wire Service(s):** AP.

SAN BERNARDINO
US
RIALTO RECORD. 1879. Thu. free newsstand; $29/yr. mailed in cy. 1809 S. Commer Center W., San Bernardino, CA 92408. TEL 909-381-9898; FAX 909-384-0406. **Owner(s):** Inland Empire Community Newspapers, 1809 S. Commer Center W., San Bernardino, CA 92408. TEL 909-381-9898; Ed. Lynette Jueneman; Pub. Gloria Macias-Harrison; adv.; pub. size: broadsheet; circ. 9,000(paid). **Wire Service(s):** AP.

SAN CLEMENTE
US
SUN POST NEWS. 1986. 3/wk.: Tue., Thu., Fri. $.25 newsstand; $9.75/mo. home deliv. 95 Avenida DelMar, San Clemente, CA 92672. TEL 714-492-5121; FAX 714-492-0401. **Owner(s):** Freedom Communications, Inc., 17666 Fitch, Irvine, CA 92614. TEL 714-553-9292; Ed. Morgan Sales; Pub. David Threshie, Jr.; adv. contact: Judith Kane. pub. size: broadsheet; circ. 7,500(paid).
Formerly: San Clemente News.

SAN DIEGO
US
BEACH & BAY PRESS. 1988. Thu. $38.35/yr. 4645 Cass, San Diego, CA 92109. TEL 619-270-3103; FAX 619-270-9325. **Owner(s):** Mannis Communications, Inc., P.O. Box 9550, San Diego, CA 92169. TEL 619-270-3103; FAX 619-270-3103; Ed. John Gregory; Pub. David Mannis; adv.; photos; pub. size: tabloid; circ. 22,500(free).

US
CORRIDOR NEWS. Thu. $.50 newsstand; $24/yr. in cy. 11650 Iberia Pl., Ste. 215, San Diego, CA 92128. TEL 619-487-5757; FAX 619-487-1264. **Owner(s):** Pomerado Publishing Co., Inc., 13247 Poway Rd., Poway, CA 92064; Ed. Steve Dreyer; Pub. David Calvert; pub. size: broadsheet; circ. 4,750(paid).
Formerly: Rancho Penasquitos News.

US
LOS ANGELES LOG. bi-w. $24.95/yr. 1025 Rosecrans St., San Diego, CA 92106. TEL 619-226-1608; FAX 619-226-0573. **Owner(s):** Log Newspapers, Inc., 1025 Rosecrans St., San Diego, CA 92106. TEL 619-226-1608; FAX 619-226-0573; Ed. Susan Colby. pub. size: standard; circ. 25,000(paid).

US

MIRA MESA/SCRIPPS RANCH SENTINEL. 1928. Thu. free; $35/yr. 6312 Riverdale St., San Diego, CA 92120. TEL 619-280-2985. **Owner(s):** Sarah E. Hagerty, Western States Weeklies, Inc., 6312 Riverdale St., San Diego, CA 92160. TEL 619-280-2985; Ed. Carol Burke; Pub. Sarah E. Hagerty; adv. contact: Sarah E. Hagerty. photos; bk.rev.; pub. size: tabloid; circ. 15,000(free & paid).

US

ORANGE COUNTY LOG. bi-w. $24.95. 1025 Rosecrans St., San Diego, CA 92106. TEL 619-226-1608; FAX 619-226-0573. **Owner(s):** Log Newspapers, Inc., 1025 Rosecrans St., San Diego, CA 92106. TEL 619-226-1608; FAX 619-226-0573; Ed. Susan Colby. pub. size: standard; circ. 15,000(paid).

US

PENINSULA BEACON, THE. 1981. Thu. free. 4645 Cass, San Diego, CA 92109. TEL 619-270-3103; FAX 619-270-9325. **Owner(s):** David Mannis, 4645 Cass, San Diego, CA 92109. TEL 619-270-3103; FAX 619-270-9325; Ed. John Gregory; Pub. David & Julie Mannis; adv.; photos; pub. size: tabloid; circ. 21,500(free).

US

POWAY NEWS CHIEFTAIN. Thu. $.50 newsstand; $18/yr. in cy. 11650 Iberia Pl., Ste. 215, San Diego, CA 92128. TEL 619-487-5757; FAX 619-487-1264. **Owner(s):** Pomerado Publishing Co., Inc., 13247 Poway Rd., Poway, CA 92064; Ed. Steve Dreyer; Pub. David Calvert; pub. size: broadsheet; circ. 13,700(paid).

US

RANCHO BERNARDO JOURNAL. 1970. Thu. $.50 newsstand; $24/yr. in cy. 11650 Iberia Pl., Ste. 215, San Diego, CA 92128. TEL 619-487-5757; FAX 619-487-1264. **Owner(s):** Pomerado Publishing Co., Inc., 13247 Poway Rd., Poway, CA 92064. TEL 714-748-2311; Ed. Patti Ferracone; Pub. David Calvert; adv. contact: Anne Calvert. pub. size: broadsheet; circ. 20,000(controlled & paid).

US

SAN DIEGO LOG. bi-w. $24.95/yr. 1025 Rosecrans St., San Diego, CA 92106. TEL 619-226-1608; FAX 619-226-0573. **Owner(s):** Log Newspapers, Inc., 1025 Rosecrans St., San Diego, CA 92106. TEL 619-226-1608; FAX 619-226-0573; Ed. Susan Colby. pub. size: standard; circ. 25,000(paid).

US

SAN DIEGO READER. 1972. Thu. free; $165/yr. out of cy. P.O. Box 85803, San Diego, CA 92186-0583. TEL 619-235-3000; FAX 619-231-0489. **Owner(s):** San Diego Reader, P.O. Box 85803, San Diego, CA 92186. TEL 619-235-3000; FAX 619-231-0489; Pub. James E. Holman; adv.; bk.rev.; pub. size: tabloid; circ. 134,000(free).

US

SAN DIEGO REVIEW. 1989. m. free newsstand; $15/yr. 5932 Trojan Ave., San Diego, CA 92115. TEL 619-229-8899; FAX 619-286-4026. **Owner(s):** San Diego Review, Inc., 5932 Trojan Ave., San Diego, CA 92115. TEL 619-229-8899; FAX 619-286-4026; Ed. Paul Maskut. adv.; photos; bk.rev.; pub. size: tabloid; circ. 5,000(free & paid).

US   ISSN 0898-4581

UPTOWN SAN DIEGO EXAMINER. 1937. 3/wk.: Mon., Wed., Fri. free newsstand; $25/yr. 3605 30th St., San Diego, CA 92104. TEL 619-295-5432. **Owner(s):** Examiner Group, Inc., P.O. Box 4368, San Diego, CA 92164-4368. TEL 619-295-5432; Ed. J. Specht; Pub. Arthur M. Specht; photos; pub. size: standard; circ. 250(free & paid).

SAN FERNANDO

US

RECORD LEDGER. 1921. Wed. free newsstand; $19/yr. in state; $50/yr. out of state. 1024 N. Maclay Ave., Ste. 9 San Fernando, CA 91340. TEL 818-365-3111. **Owner(s):** Valley Sun Newspapers, Inc., 1024 N. Maclay Ave., Ste. 9, San Fernando CA 91340. TEL 818-365-3111; Ed. Thelma Barrios; Pub. Thelma Barrios; adv.; pub. size: tabloid; circ. 15,000(paid).

US

SAN FERNANDO VALLEY SUN. 1904. Wed. free newsstand; $45/yr. mailed in state; $50/yr. mailed out of state. 1024 N. Maclay Ave., San Fernando, CA 91340. TEL 818-365-3111. **Owner(s):** Mission Independent Community Newspapers, 1024 N. Maclay Ave., San Fernando, CA 91340. TEL 818-365-3111; Ed. Thelma Barrios; Pub. Rick Barrios; adv.; pub. size: tabloid; circ. 10,000(paid).

SAN FRANCISCO

US

NORTH/SOUTH BEACH NOW. 1987. m. $21/yr. 470 Columbus, Ste. 206, San Francisco, CA 94133. TEL 415-391-1043; FAX 415-391-1213; E-mail: thenow@aol.com. **Owner(s):** North Beach Now, 470 Columbus, Ste. 206, San Francisco, CA 94133. TEL 415-391-1043; FAX 415-391-1213; Ed. Joan Dahlgren. adv.; photos; bk.rev.; pub. size: tabloid; circ. 3,500(free & paid).
  Formerly: North Beach Now.

US   ISSN 0036-4096

SAN FRANCISCO BAY GUARDIAN. 1966. Wed. free newsstand; $20/6 mos.; $32/yr. 520 Hampshire St., San Francisco, CA 94110-1417. TEL 415-255-3100; FAX 415-255-8955. **Owner(s):** Bruce B. Brugmann & Jean Dibble, 520 Hampshire St., San Francisco, CA 94110-1417. TEL 415-255-3100; Ed. Tim Redmond; Pub. Bruce B. Brugmann; adv.; photos; bk.rev.; pub. size: tabloid; circ. 135,000(free & paid).

US

SAN FRANCISCO INDEPENDENT. 1958. 3/wk.: Tue., Fri., Sun. free. 1201 Evans Ave., San Francisco, CA 94124. TEL 415-826-1100; FAX 415-826-5371. **Owner(s):** Pan-Asian Venture Capital Corp., 1201 Evans St., San Francisco, CA 94124. TEL 415-862-5371; Ed. Susan Herbert; Pub. Ted Fang; adv.; pub. size: broadsheet; circ. 510,000(free).

US

SAN FRANCISCO METRO REPORTER. Wed. free. 270 Francisco St., San Francisco, CA 94133. TEL 415-391-2030 FAX 415-391-2525. **Owner(s):** Garry M. Goodlett, 1366 Turk St., San Francisco, CA 94115. TEL 415-931-5778; photos; bk.rev.; pub. size: tabloid.

US

SAN FRANCISCO SENTINEL. 1974. Wed. free. 285 Shipley St., San Francisco CA 94107. TEL 415-281-3745; FAX 415-281-3714. **Owner(s):** Ray Chalker, 235 Shipley St., San Francisco, CA 94107. TEL 415-281-3745; Ed. Ray Chalker; Pub. Ray Chalker; adv. contact: Russell Rottkamp. bk.rev.; pub. size: tabloid; circ. 35,000(free). **Wire Service(s):** AP.

US

SF WEEKLY. 1981. Wed. free newsstand; $40/yr. 3rd class mailed; $80/yr. 1st class mailed. 425 Brannan St., San Francisco, CA 94107. TEL 415-541-0700; FAX 415-777-1839. **Owner(s):** New Times, Inc., 425 Brannan St., San Francisco, CA 94107. TEL 415-541-0700; Ed. John Sullivan; Pub. Jim Rizzi; adv. contact: Mary Jansen. pub. size: broadsheet; circ. 90,000(free & paid). **Wire Service(s):** Aternet, Bay City News Service.

US

SUN-REPORTER. 1944. Wed. $15/yr. 1366 Turk St., San Francisco, CA 94115. TEL 415-931-5778. **Owner(s):** Garry M. Goodlett, 1366 Turk St., San Francisco, CA 94115. TEL 415-931-5778; Ed. Amelia Ashley-Ward; Pub. Gary M. Goodlett, M.D.; adv. contact: Jessica Castle. photos; bk.rev.; pub. size: tabloid; circ. 160,000(free & paid).

US

▼**WESTERN EDITION.** 1994. m. free newsstand; $15/yr. P.O. Box 15102 San Francisco, CA 94115. TEL 415-931-6397; FAX 415-474-4160. **Owner(s):** Western Edition Publishing; Pub. Michael Martin; pub. size: tabloid; circ. 30,000(free).

SANGER

US

PARLIER POST. 1984. Wed. free; $10/yr. mailed in cy.; $13/yr. mailed out of cy. 740 N St., Sanger, CA 93657. TEL 209-875-2511. **Owner(s):** Mid-Valley Publications, Inc., P.O. Box 432, Reedley, CA 93654. TEL 209-638-2244; Ed. Dawn Pearson. adv.; bk.rev.; pub. size: standard; circ. 6,350(free & paid).

US

SANGER HERALD. 1888. Thu. $.50 newsstand; $17.50/yr. 740 N St., Sanger, CA 93657. TEL 209-875-2511; FAX 209-875-2521. **Owner(s):** Sanger Herald, Inc., 740 N St., Sanger, CA 93657; Ed. William Coleman; Pub. Fred Hall; pub. size: standard; circ. 2,600(paid).

SAN JACINTO

US

SAN JACINTO VALLEY REGISTER. 1884. Wed. free. 474 W. Esplande, San Jacinto, CA 92583-8003. TEL 909-487-2200. **Owner(s):** Stephens Group, Inc., 111 Center St., Little Rock, AR 72201. TEL 501-377-2000; Ed. Dana Straheley; Pub. Jim Fredericks; adv. contact: Manny Padilla. pub. size: tabloid; circ. 4,000(controlled).
  Formerly: San Jacinto Valley.

SAN JOSE

US   ISSN 0882-4290

METRO. 1985. Thu. free. 550 S. First St., San Jose, CA 95113. TEL 408-298-8000. **Owner(s):** Metro Publishing Co., 550 S. First St., San Jose, CA 95113. TEL 408-298-8000; Ed. Corrine Asturias; Pub. David Cohen. adv. contact: Scott Levander. bk.rev.; pub. size: tabloid; circ. 90,000(free).

SAN LUIS OBISPO

US

NEW TIMES. 1986. Thu. free newsstand; $37/yr. 197 Santa Rosa St., San Luis Obispo, CA 93405. TEL 805-546-8208; FAX 805-546-8641. **Owner(s):** Bev Johnson & Steve Moss, 197 Santa Rosa St., San Luis Obispo, CA 93405. TEL 805-546-8208; FAX 805-546-8641; Ed. Steve Moss; Pub. Steve Moss; adv.; photos; bk.rev.; pub. size: tabloid; circ. 40,000(free & paid). **Wire Service(s):** Alternet.

SAN MARCOS

US

SAN MARCOS NEWS REPORTER. 1970. Thu. free newsstand; $100/yr. mailed. 815 Grand Ave., Ste. 103, San Marcos, CA 92069. TEL 619-471-8701; FAX 619-471-2630. **Owner(s):** News Reporter, Inc., 815 W. San Marcos Blvd., San Marcos, CA 92069. TEL 619-471-8701; Ed. William Willoughby; Pub. William Willoughby; adv. contact: Jacqueline Ferris. pub. size: tabloid; circ. 10,000(free & paid).

SAN MARINO

US

SAN MARINO TRIBUNE. 1935. Thu. $.55 newsstand; $28/yr. 2260 Huntington Dr., San Marino, CA 91108. TEL 818-282-5707; FAX 818-457-6436. **Owner(s):** Clifton Smith, 2260 Huntington Dr., San Marino, CA 91108. TEL 818-792-3343; Ed. Peter Day; Pub. Clifton Smith; adv.; pub. size: broadsheet; circ. 4,000(paid).

SAN MATEO

US

COASTSIDE CHRONICLE. 1959. Sat. free. 1080 S. Amphlett Blvd., San Mateo, CA 94402. TEL 415-348-4324. **Owner(s):** Alameda Newspaper Group, 116 W. Winston Ave., Hayward, CA 94544. TEL 510-783-6111; Ed. Terry Winkler; Pub. Peter Bernhard; adv.; pub. size: standard; circ. 8,000(controlled).

US

DALY CITY RECORD. 1962. Sat. free. 1080 S. Amphlett Blvd., San Mateo, CA 94402. TEL 415-348-4324; FAX 415-348-4446. **Owner(s):** Alameda Publishing Corp., 116 W. Winton Ave., Hayward, CA 94544. TEL 510-783-6111; Ed. Terry Greenberg; Pub. John Clinton, Jr.; pub. size: standard; circ. 24,600(controlled).
   Formerly: Brisbane Bee.

US

MILLBRAE RECORDER-PROGRESS. Sat. free. 1080 S. Amplett Blvd., San Mateo, CA 94402. TEL 415-348-4321; FAX 415-348-4446. **Owner(s):** Alameda Publishing Corp., 116 W. Winton Ave., Hayward, CA 94544. TEL 510-783-6111; Ed. Will Thomas; Pub. Peter Bernard; adv.; pub. size: broadsheet; circ. 7,500(controlled).

US

SAN BRUNO HERALD. 1895. Sun. free. 1080 S. Amplett Blvd., San Mateo, CA 94402. TEL 415-348-4321; FAX 415-348-4446. **Owner(s):** Alameda Publishing Corp., 116 W. Winton Ave., Hayward, CA 94544. TEL 510-783-6111; Ed. William E. Thomas; Pub. John H. Clinton, Jr.; adv.; pub. size: broadsheet; circ. 13,000(free).

SOUTH SAN FRANCISCO ENTERPRISE-JOURNAL.
US

1895. Sat. $30/yr. 1080 Amplett Blvd., San Mateo, CA 94402. TEL 415-348-4321; FAX 415-348-4446. **Owner(s):** Alameda Publishing Corp., 116 W. Winton Ave., Hayward, CA 94544. TEL 510-783-6111; Ed. Terry Greenberg; Pub. John H. Clinton, Jr.; pub. size: broadsheet; circ. 16,150(controlled).

SAN PEDRO

US   ISSN 0891-6627

RANDOM LENGTHS NEWS. 1979. w. $20/yr. 1117 S. Pacific Ave., San Pedro, CA 90731. TEL 310-519-1016. **Owner(s):** Random Lengths News, Inc., 1117 S. Pacific Ave., San Pedro, CA 90731. TEL 310-519-1016; Ed. J. Elendorf; Pub. J.P. Allen; adv. contact: Tom Davidon. bk.rev.; pub. size: tabloid.

SAN RAFAEL

US

CLASSIFIED GAZETTE. 1968. s-w.: Wed. & Fri. free. 716 Fourth St., San Rafael, CA 94901. TEL 415-457-4151; FAX 415-454-9849. **Owner(s):** Joseph Walsh; Riley Hurd; Pub. Riley Hurd; adv.; pub. size: tabloid; circ. 54,000(free).

SANTA ANA

US   ISSN 0892-6441

TUSTIN NEWS. 1922. Thu. free in surrounding cys.; $16/yr. elsewhere. 625 N. Grand Ave., Santa Ana, CA 92701. TEL 714-953-7725; FAX 714-544-9247. **Owner(s):** Freedom Communications, Inc., 17666 Fitch, Irvine, CA 92614. TEL 714-553-9292; Ed. William A. Moses, II; Pub. Jane Lee Watson; adv. contact: Judy Duncan. pub. size: broadsheet; circ. 30,000(free).

SANTA BARBARA

US

SANTA BARBARA INDEPENDENT. 1986. Thu. free. 1221 State St., 2nd Fl., Santa Barbara, CA 93101. TEL 805-965-5205; FAX 805-965-5518. **Owner(s):** Santa Barbara Independent, The, 1221 State St., 2nd Fl., Santa Barbara, CA 93101. TEL 805-965-5205; FAX 805-965-5518; Ed. Marianne Partridge; Pub. George Thurlow; adv.; pub. size: tabloid; circ. 40,000(free & paid).

SANTA CRUZ

US   ISSN 0164-4033

GOOD TIMES. 1975. Thu. free newsstand; $85/yr. mailed. 1205 Pacific Ave., Ste. 301, Santa Cruz, CA 95060. TEL 408-458-1100; FAX 408-458-1296. **Owner(s):** West Coast Community Newspapers, Inc., P.O. Box 1885, Santa Cruz, CA 95061. TEL 408-458-1100; Ed. Matt Davidson; Pub. Carole Atkinson; adv.; bk.rev.; pub. size: tabloid; circ. 45,000(controlled).

SANTA MONICA

US

BEVERLY HILLS INDEPENDENT. 1966. Thu. free. 1920 Colorado Ave., Santa Monica, CA 90404. TEL 310-829-6811; FAX 310-453-3085. **Owner(s):** Copley Press, Inc., 5215 Torrance Blvd., Torrance, CA 90503. TEL 310-540-5511; Ed. Bea Nyburg. adv.; pub. size: broadsheet; circ. 18,400(free).

BRENTWOOD WESTWOOD PRESS.
US

1928. Thu. free. 1920 Colorado Ave., Santa Monica, CA 90404. TEL 310-829-6811; FAX 310-453-3085. **Owner(s):** Copley Press, Inc., 7776 Ivanhoe Ave., LaJolla, CA 92037. TEL 310-829-6811; Ed. Bea Nyburg. adv.; pub. size: broadsheet; circ. 20,300(free).

US

CULVER CITY-LADERA INDEPENDENT. 1961. Thu. free. 1920 Colorado Ave., Santa Monica, CA 90404. TEL 310-829-6811; FAX 310-453-3085. **Owner(s):** Copley Press, Inc., 7776 Ivanhoe Ave., LaJolla, CA 92037. TEL 619-454-0411; Ed. Bea Nyburg. adv.; pub. size: broadsheet; circ. 30,100(free).
   Formerly: Culver City-Ladera Independent & Star News.

US

OUTLOOK MAIL. 1982. Wed. free mailed. 1920 Colorado Ave., Santa Monica, CA 90404. TEL 310-829-6811; FAX 310-453-3085. **Owner(s):** Copley Press, Inc., 7776 Ivanhoe Ave., La Jolla, CA 92037. TEL 310-829-6811; Ed. Lou Branzaccio. adv. contact: Tom Pullano. pub. size: broadsheet; circ. 38,000(free). **Wire Service(s):** AP.

US

VENICE-MARINA NEWS. 1961. Thu. free. 1920 Colorado Ave., Santa Monica, CA 90404. TEL 310-829-6811; FAX 310-453-3085. **Owner(s):** Copley Press, Inc., 7776 Ivanhoe Ave., La Jolla, CA 92037. TEL 310-829-6811; Ed. Bea Nyburg. adv.; pub. size: broadsheet; circ. 15,600(free).

US

WESTCHESTER OBSERVER. 1971. Thu. free. 1920 Colorado Ave., Santa Monica, CA 90404. TEL 310-829-6811; FAX 310-829-6811. **Owner(s):** Copley Press, Inc., 7776 Ivanhoe Ave., La Jolla, CA 92037. TEL 310-829-6811; Ed. Bea Nyburg. adv.; pub. size: broadsheet; circ. 13,500(free).

US

WEST LOS ANGELES INDEPENDENT. 1928. Thu. free. 1920 Colorado Ave., Santa Monica, CA 90404. TEL 310-829-6811; FAX 310-453-3085. **Owner(s):** Copley Press, Inc., 7776 Ivanhoe Ave., La Jolla, CA 92037. TEL 310-829-6811; Ed. Bea Nyburg. adv.; pub. size: broadsheet; circ. 29,300(free).

SANTA PAULA

US

SANTA PAULA TIMES. 1993. s-w.: Wed. & Fri. $.50 newsstand; $10/mo. mailed. 944 E. Main St., Santa Paula, CA 93060. TEL 805-525-1890; FAX 805-525-7375. **Owner(s):** Donald & Debbie Johnson, 944 E. Main St., Santa Paula, CA 93060. TEL 805-525-1890; Ed. Don Johnson; Pub. Don Johnson; adv.; photos; bk.rev.; pub. size: broadsheet; circ. 9,000(free & paid).

SANTA ROSA

US

SONOMA COUNTY INDEPENDENT. 1979. Thu. free newsstand; $40/yr. in cy.; $50/yr. out of cy. 540 Mendocino Ave., Santa Rosa, CA 95401. TEL 707-527-1200; FAX 707-527-1288. **Owner(s):** Metrosa, Inc., 540 Mendocino Ave., Santa Rosa, CA 95401. TEL 707-527-1200; FAX 707-527-1288; Ed. Greg Cahill; Pub. Bob Rucker; adv.; photos; bk.rev.; pub. size: tabloid; circ. 30,000(free & paid). **Wire Service(s):** Alternet.
   Formerly: Paper, The.

SARATOGA

US   ISSN 0745-6255

SARATOGA NEWS. 1955. Wed. $.50 newsstand; $26/yr. local; $52/yr. out of area. 14375 Saratoga, Ste. E 2, Saratoga, CA 95070. TEL 408-867-6397; FAX 408-867-1010. **Owner(s):** Metro Newspapers, Inc., 550 S. First St., San Jose, CA 95113. TEL 408-298-8000; Ed. Sue Fagalde Lick. adv.; pub. size: tabloid; circ. 10,000(paid).

SAUSALITO

US

EBBTIDE. Fri. $.50 newsstand; $20/yr. 1050 Bridgeway, Sausalito, CA 94966-1689. TEL 415-332-3778; FAX 415-332-8714. **Owner(s):** Marin Scope Community Newspapers, Inc., P.O. Box 1689, Sausalito, CA 94966-1689. TEL 415-332-3778; FAX 415-332-8714; Ed. Billie Anderson; Pub. Paul A. Anderson; adv.; photos; pub. size: standard; circ. 4,500(paid).

US

MARIN SCOPE. 1971. Tue. $.50 newsstand; $20/yr. mailed. 1050 Bridgeway, Sausalito, CA 94966-1689. TEL 415-332-3778; FAX 415-332-8714. **Owner(s):** Marin Scope Community Newspapers, Inc., 1050 Bridgeway, Sausalito, CA 94966-1689. TEL 415-332-3778; FAX 415-332-8714; Ed. Billie Anderson; Pub. Paul Anderson; adv.; pub. size: standard; circ. 2,000(paid).

US

MILL VALLEY HERALD. Mon. $.50 newsstand; $20/yr. 1050 Bridgeway, Sausalito, CA 94965. **Owner(s):** Marin Scope Community Newspapers, Inc., 1050 Bridgeway, Sausalito, CA 94966. TEL 510-332-3778; Ed. Brad Foss; Pub. Paul Anderson; adv.; pub. size: standard.

US

NEWS POINTER. Wed. $.50 newsstand; $20/yr. 1050 Bridgeway, Sausalito, CA 94965. TEL 415-289-4040; FAX 415-332-8714. **Owner(s):** Marin Scope Community Newspapers, 1050 Bridgeway, Sausalito, CA 94965. TEL 415-289-4040; FAX 415-332-3778; Ed. Billie Anderson; Pub. Paul Anderson; photos; pub. size: standard; circ. 11,000(free).

US

ROSS VALLEY REPORTER. 1964. Wed. $.50 newsstand; $20/yr. 1050 Bridgeway, Sausalito, CA 94966-1689. TEL 415-289-4040; FAX 415-332-8714. **Owner(s):** Marin Scope Community Newspapers, Inc., 1050 Bridgeway, Sausalito, CA 94965. TEL 510-332-3778; Ed. Billie Anderson; Pub. Paul Anderson; adv.; pub. size: broadsheet; circ. 11,050(free & paid).

US

SAN RAFAEL NEWS POINTER. 1968. Wed. $.50 newsstand; $20/yr. 1050 Bridgeway, Sausalito, CA 94966. TEL 415-289-4040; FAX 415-332-8714. **Owner(s):** Marin Scope Community Newspapers, Inc., 1050 Bridgeway, Sausalito, CA 94966. TEL 510-332-3778; Ed. Billie Anderson; Pub. Paul Anderson; adv.; pub. size: standard; circ. 11,000(free).
   Formerly: San Rafael/Terrra Linda News.

SEAL BEACH

US

HUNTINGTON HARBOUR SUN. 1967. Thu. free home deliv.; $.25 newsstand; $45/yr. 216 Main St., Seal Beach, CA 90740. TEL 310-430-7555; FAX 310-430-3469. **Owner(s):** West Coast Community Newspapers, Inc., 2841 Loker Ave., E., Carlsbad, CA 92008. TEL 619-431-4850; Ed. Dennis Kaiser; Pub. Dar Brown; pub. size: tabloid; circ. 37,000(controlled).
   Formerly: Huntington Harbour Journal.

US

LEISURE WORLD GOLDEN RAIN NEWS. 1963. Thu. $25/yr. P.O. Box 2338, Seal Beach, CA 90740. TEL 310-430-0534 FAX 310-598-1617. **Owner(s):** Golden Rain Foundation, P.O. Box 2069, Seal Beach, CA 90740. TEL 310-431-6586; Ed. David Saunders. adv.; photos; pub. size: tabloid; circ. 8,900(free & paid).

US

SEAL BEACH SUN 1967. Thu. $.25 newsstand; $45/yr. 216 Main St., Seal Beach, CA 90740. TEL 310-430-7555 FAX 310-430-4369. **Owner(s):** West Coast Community Newspapers, Inc., 216 Main St., Seal Beach, CA 90740. TEL 310-430-7555; Pub. Dar Brown; adv.; pub. size: tabloid; circ. 37,000(controlled & paid).
   Formerly: Seal Beach Journal.

SEBASTOPAL

US

SONOMA WEST. 1889. Wed. $.50 newsstand; $25/yr. in cy.; $37.50/yr. out of cy.; $18/yr. senior citizens. 130 S. Main St., Ste. 114, Sebastopal, CA 95472. TEL 707-823-7845; FAX 707-823-7508. **Owner(s):** Sonoma West Publishers, Inc., 13C S. Main St., Ste. 114, Sebastopol, CA 95472; Ed. Barry Dugan. pub. size: standard; circ. 5,600(paid).
   Formerly: Sebastopol Times & News.

SELMA

US

SELMA ENTERPRISE. 1886. Wed. $.50 newsstand; $20/yr. in cy.; $24/yr. out of cy.; $25/yr. out of state. 2045 Grant St., Selma, CA 93662. TEL 209-896-1976; FAX 209-896-9160. **Owner(s):** Community Newspapers, Inc., P.O. Box 100, Selma, CA 93662. TEL 209-896-1976; FAX 209-896-9160; Ed. Tim Sheehan; Pub. Jim Brock; adv. contact: Gerald Latham. pub. size: broadsheet; circ. 4,000(paid).

SHAFTER

US

SHAFTER PRESS. Wed. $.35 newsstand; $19/yr. in cy.; $21/yr. out of cy.; $24/yr. out of state. 107 E. Lerdo Hwy., Shafter, CA 93263. TEL 805-746-4942; FAX 805-746-5571. **Owner(s):** Reed Print, Inc., 5409 Aldrin Ct., Bakersfield, CA 93313; Ed. Frank W. Reed; Pub. Frank W. Reed; adv. contact: Jerry Watts. pub. size: broadsheet; circ. 2,300(paid).

SHERMAN OAKS

US

VALLEY VANTAGE. 1949. Thu. free newsstand; $40/yr. mailed. 14440 Magnolia Blvd., Sherman Oaks, CA 91423-1016. TEL 818-906-2393; FAX 818-906-2129. **Owner(s):** Michael Cartel, 7443 Reseda Blvd., Reseda, CA 91335. TEL 818-881-9460; Ed. Michael Cartel; Pub. Michael Cartel; adv.; pub. size: tabloid; circ. 20,000(free & paid).

SIERRA MADRE

US

SIERRA MADRE NEWS. 1906. Thu. $.50 newsstand; $25/yr. 49 S. Baldwin Ave., Sierra Madre, CA 91024. TEL 818-355-3324; FAX 818-355-2341. **Owner(s):** Michael DeWeese, 49 S. Baldwin, Sierra Madre, CA 91024. TEL 818-355-3324; Ed. Michael DeWeese; Pub. Michael DeWeese; adv. contact: Von Raees. pub. size: broadsheet; circ. 4,000(paid).

SOLEDAD

US

GONZALES TRIBUNE. Wed. $.50 newsstand; $23/yr. in cy.; $29/yr. out of cy. 635 Front St., Soledad, CA 93960. TEL 408-678-2660; FAX 408-385-4790. **Owner(s):** News Media Corp., 211 Hwy. 38, E., Rochelle, IL 61068; Ed. Suzi Taylor; Pub. Bill Parsons; adv.; pub. size: broadsheet; circ. 710(paid).

US

SOLEDAD BEE. Wed. $.50 newsstand; $23/yr. in cy.; $29/yr. out of cy. 635 Front St., Soledad, CA 93960. TEL 408-678-2660; FAX 408-678-3676. **Owner(s):** News Media Corp., 211 Hwy. 38, E., Rochelle, IL 61068; Ed. Suzi Taylor; Pub. Bill Parsons; adv. contact: Cid Sears. pub. size: broadsheet; circ. 1,100(paid).

SOLVANG

US

SOLVANG SANTA YNEZ VALLEY NEWS. 1925. s-w.: Tue. & Thu. $.35 newsstand; $18.50/yr. 423 Second St., Solvang, CA 93463. TEL 805-688-5522; FAX 805-688-7685. **Owner(s):** Peg L. Johnson, P.O. Box 647, Solvang, CA 93464. TEL 805-688-5522; FAX 805-688-7685; Ed. Bart Ortberg. adv.; photos; pub. size: broadsheet; circ. 7,500(paid).

SONOMA

US   ISSN 8755-9498

SONOMA INDEX TRIBUNE. 1879. s-w.: Tue. & Fri. $.50 newsstand; $25/yr. in cy. 117 W. Napa St., Sonoma, CA 95476. TEL 707-938-2111; FAX 707-938-1600. **Owner(s):** Robert M. & Jean H. Lynch, P.O. Box C, Sonoma, CA 95476. TEL 707-938-2111; William E. Lynch, P.O. Box C, Sonoma, CA 95476. TEL 707-938-2111; James R. Lynch, P.O. Box C, Sonoma, CA 95476. TEL 707-938-2111; Ed. William E. Lynch; Pub. Robert M. Lynch; adv. contact: Pamela Austin. pub. size: broadsheet; circ. 11,500(paid).

Weeklies

SOUTH PASADENA
US

SOUTH PASADENA REVIEW. 1888. Wed. $.25 newsstand; $25/yr. 2nd class mail. 1024 Mission St., South Pasadena, CA 91030. TEL 818-799-1161. **Owner(s):** South Pasadena Publishing Co., 1024 Mission St., South Pasadena, CA 91030. TEL 818-799-1161; Pub. William Ericson; adv. contact: Linda McCann. pub. size: standard; circ. 5,055(paid).

ST. HELENA
US

ST. HELENA STAR. 1874. Thu. $17.50/yr. in cy.; $23.50/yr. out of cy. 1328 Main St., St. Helena, CA 94574. TEL 707-963-2731; FAX 707-963-8957. **Owner(s):** Star Publishing Co., 25 Inverness Dr., Napa, CA 94558; Ed. Jeremy Hay; Pub. Bill Brenner; pub. size: broadsheet; circ. 4,500(paid).

SUN CITY
US

MENIFEE VALLEY NEWS. 1988. Thu. $.35 newsstand; $12/yr. mailed in cy.; $32/yr. out of cy. 27070 Sun City Blvd., Sun City, CA 92586. TEL 909-679-1195; FAX 909-679-2450. **Owner(s):** Press-Enterprise Co., P.O. Box 792, Riverside, CA 92502. TEL 714-684-1200; Ed. Dennis Brosterhous; Pub. Kathleen Williams Boyer; adv.; photos; bk.rev.; pub. size: standard; circ. 7,000(free & paid).

US

SUN CITY NEWS. 1962. Thu. $.35 newsstand; $12/yr. mailed in cy.; $20/yr. out of cy. 27070 Sun City Blvd., Sun City, CA 92586. TEL 909-679-1191; FAX 909-679-2450. **Owner(s):** Press-Enterprise Co., P.O. Box 792, Riverside, CA 92502. TEL 714-684-1200; Ed. Dennis Brosterhous; Pub. Kathleen Williamson Boyer; pub. size: standard; circ. 5,400(paid).

TAHOE CITY
US

TAHOE WORLD. 1963. Thu. $.50 newsstand; $22/yr. in area; $34/yr.; outside of area. 241 N. Lake Blvd., Tahoe City, CA 96145. TEL 916-583-3488; FAX 916-583-7109; E-mail: world@tahoe.com; URL: http://www.tahoe.com. **Owner(s):** Mt. Rose Publishing, P.O. Box 138, Tahoe City, CA 96145. TEL 916-583-3488; Pub. Bill Kunerth; adv. contact: Bill Kunerth. pub. size: broadsheet; circ. 6,500(paid).

TEHACHAPI
US

TEHACHAPI NEWS. 1900. Wed. $.50 newsstand; $24/yr. in cy.; $29/yr. out of cy.; $30/yr. out of state. 411 N. Mill St., Tehachapi, CA 93561. TEL 805-822-6828; FAX 805-822-4053. **Owner(s):** William J. Mead, P.O. Box 230, Tehachapi, CA 93581. TEL 805-822-6828; Ed. Chris Rombouts; Pub. William J. Mead; adv.; photos; pub. size: broadsheet; circ. 8,000(paid).

TORRANCE
US

HARBOR EXTRA. 1992. Thu. free. 5215 Torrance Blvd., Torrance, CA 90503. TEL 310-540-5511; FAX 310-540-6272. **Owner(s):** Copley Press, Inc., 7776 Ivanhoe, La Jolla, CA 93037; Ed. Wendy Fawthrop; Pub. Thomas Wafer; adv. contact: Kevin Nolan. pub. size: tabloid; circ. 30,000(free).

US

SOUTH BAY EXTRA. 1992. Thu. free. 5215 Torrance Blvd., Torrance, CA 90503. TEL 310-540-5511; FAX 310-540-6272. **Owner(s):** Copley Press, Inc., 7776 Ivanhoe, La Jolla, CA 92037; Ed. James Box; Pub. Thomas Wafer; adv. contact: Steve Elkins. pub. size: broadsheet; circ. 133,000(free).

TRUCKEE
US

SIERRA SUN. 1869. Thu. $.50 newsstand; $22/yr. in area; $34/yr. out of area. 11429 Donner Pass Rd., Truckee, CA 96160. TEL 916-587-6061; FAX 916-587-3763; E-mail: sun@tahoe.com; URL: http://www.tahoe.com. **Owner(s):** Mt. Rose Publishing, P.O. Box 138, Tahoe City, CA 96145. TEL 916-583-3488; Ed. Peter Kostes; Pub. Bill Kunerth; pub. size: broadsheet; circ. 6,300(paid).

VALLEY CENTER
US

VALLEY ROADRUNNER. 1974. w. $.50 newsstand; $18/yr. 28904 Valley Center Rd., Valley Center, CA 92082. TEL 619-749-1112; FAX 619-749-1688. **Owner(s):** Dale & Shirley Good, 14761 Cool Valley Ranch, Valley Center, CA 92082; Ed. David Ross; Pub. Dale Good; adv. contact: Andrea Mills. photos; bk.rev.; pub. size: broadsheet; circ. 3,291(free & paid).

VENTURA
US

VENTURA COUNTY & COAST REPORTER. 1978. Thu. free; $50/yr. out of state. 1567 Spinnaker Dr., Ste. 202, Ventura, CA 93001. TEL 805-658-2244; FAX 805-658-7803. **Owner(s):** Ventura County & Coast Reporter, 1583 Spinnaker Dr., Ste. 213, Ventura, CA 93001. TEL 805-658-2244; Pub. Nancy Cloutier; pub. size: tabloid; circ. 20,000(free & paid).

VISTA
US

PENNYSAVER. 1964. Wed. free in area; $1 elsewhere. 1300 Specialty Dr., Vista, CA 92083. TEL 614-599-1484; FAX 614-598-1117. **Owner(s):** Walt Disney Co., 500 S. Buena Vista St., Burbank, CA 91521. TEL 818-560-5300; adv.; pub. size: standard; circ. 2,050,000(free).

WALNUT CREEK
US

ROSSMOOR NEWS. 1964. Wed. $25/yr. mailed. 1006 Stanley Dollar Dr., Walnut Creek, CA 94595. TEL 510-988-7800; FAX 510-935-8348. **Owner(s):** Golden Rain Foundation, P.O. Box 2190, Walnut Creek, CA 94595. TEL 510-939-1211; Ed. Maureen O'Rourke. pub. size: tabloid; circ. 8,600(paid).

WASCO
US

WASCO TRIBUNE. Wed. free. 911 Seventh St., Wasco, CA 93280. TEL 805-758-3063; FAX 805-758-3064. **Owner(s):** Reed Print, Inc., 5409 Aldrin Ct., Bakersfield, CA 93313; Ed. Frank W. Reed; Pub. Frank W. Reed; adv. contact: Jerry Watts. pub. size: broadsheet; circ. 5,600(free).

WEAVERVILLE
US

TRINITY JOURNAL. 1856. Wed. $.50 newsstand; $19/yr. in cy.; $29/yr. out of cy. 218 Main St., Weaverville, CA 96093-0340. TEL 916-623-2055; FAX 916-623-2065. **Owner(s):** Mike & Sarah Wenninger, 218 Main St., Weaverville, CA 96093. TEL 916-623-2055; FAX 916-623-2065; Ed. Mike Wenninger; Pub. Sarah Wenninger; photos; pub. size: broadsheet; circ. 4,650(paid).
   Formerly: Weaverville Weekly Trinity Journal.

WEED
US

WEED PRESS. 1925. Wed. $17/6 mos. in cy.; $25.50/yr. in cy.; $19/yr. out of cy.; $27.50/yr. out of cy. 924 N. Mt. Shasta Blvd., Weed, CA 96067. TEL 916-926-5214; FAX 916-926-4166. **Owner(s):** American Publishing Co., 606 N. Van Buren, P.O. Box 520, Marion, IL 62959. TEL 618-993-1711; Ed. Steve Derace. pub. size: standard; circ. 1,825(paid).

WEST COVINA
US

AZUSA HERALD. Thu. free; $57/yr. mailed. 1210 N. Azusa Canyon Rd., West Covina, CA 91790-1003. TEL 818-854-8700; FAX 818-338-9157. **Owner(s):** Thomson Newspapers, Inc., One Thorn Run Ctr., Ste. 500, 1187 Thorn Run Dr. Ext., Coraopolis, PA 15108. TEL 412-262-7870; Ed. John Bender; Pub. Joe Logan; pub. size: tabloid; circ. 15,000(free & paid).

US

GLENDORA PRESS. 1890. Thu. $.25 newsstand. 1210 N. Azusa Canyon Rd., West Covina, CA 91790. TEL 818-854-8700; FAX 818-854-8719. **Owner(s):** Thomson Newspapers, Inc., One Thorn Run Ctr., Ste. 500, 1187 Thorn Run Rd. Ext., Coraopolis, PA 15108. TEL 412-262-7870; Ed. John Bender. adv.; pub. size: tabloid; circ. 158,000(free).

US

HIGHLANDER. 1962. Thu. free. 1210 N. Azusa Canyon Rd., West Covina, CA 91790-1003. TEL 818-854-8700; FAX 818-854-8719. **Owner(s):** San Gabriel Valley Tribune, West Covina, CA; pub. size: tabloid; circ. 160,000(free).

WESTLAKE VILLAGE
US

ACORN, THE. 1974. Thu. $.25 newsstand; $42.50/6 mos.; $85/yr. carrier. 960 S. Westlake Blvd., Ste. 207, Westlake Village, CA 91361. TEL 805-379-0266; FAX 805-379-2164. **Owner(s):** J. Bee NP Publishing Ltd., 960 S. Westlake Blvd., Ste. 207, Westlake Village, CA 91361. TEL 805-379-0266; Ed. Joe Seldner; Pub. Jim Rule; adv. contact: Lee Tarantino. pub. size: tabloid; circ. 35,000(paid).

WEST SACRAMENTO

US

NEWS-LEDGER, THE. 1964. Wed. $15/yr. in cy.; $20/yr. out of cy. 816 W. Acres Rd., West Sacramento, CA 95691. TEL 916-371-8030. **Owner(s):** Michael P. Garten, P.O. Box 463, West Sacramento, CA 95691. TEL 916-371-8030; Ed. Steve Marschke. adv.; pub. size: broadsheet; circ. 3,800(paid).

US

WEST SACRAMENTO NEWS-LEDGER. 1964. Wed. $.50 newsstand; $15/yr. in cy.; $20/yr. elsewhere. 816 West Acres Rd., West Sacramento, CA 95691. TEL 916-371-8030; FAX 916-371-8030. **Owner(s):** Michael P. Garten, 816 West Acres Rd., West Sacramento, CA 95691. TEL 916-371-8030; Ed. Steven K. Marschke; Pub. Michael P. Garten; pub. size: broadsheet; circ. 3,600(paid).

WILLOWS

US

WILLOWS JOURNAL. 1877. 3/wk.: Mon., Wed., Fri. $.50 newsstand; $36/yr. carrier; $38/yr. mailed in cy.; $63/yr. mailed out of cy.; $40/yr. senior citizens. 1030 W. Wood St., Willows, CA 95988. TEL 916-934-6800; FAX 916-934-6815. **Owner(s):** Morris Communications, P.O. Box 936, Augusta, GA 30903; Ed. David Newton; Pub. Darell Phillips; adv. contact: Pat Begrin. pub. size: broadsheet; circ. 6,000(paid).

WINTON

US

ATWATER NEW TIMES. Thu. $.25 newsstand; $15.50/yr. in cy. mailed. 6950 Gerard, Winton, CA 95388. TEL 209-358-5311; FAX 209-358-7108. **Owner(s):** Mid-Valley Publications, Inc., 6950 Gerard, Winton, CA 95388. TEL 209-358-5311; FAX 209-358-7108; Ed. Charles Watson; Pub. John Derby; pub. size: tabloid; circ. 4,000(paid).

US

DELHI EXPRESS. Thu. $.25 newsstand; $17/yr. in cy. mailed; $21/yr. out of cy. mailed. 6950 Gerard, Winton, CA 95388. TEL 209-358-5311; FAX 209-358-7108. **Owner(s):** Mid-Valley Publications, Inc., 6950 Gerard, Winton, CA 95388. TEL 209-358-5311; Pub. John Derby; pub. size: broadsheet; circ. 3,300(paid).

US

DENAIR DISPATCH. Wed. $.25 newsstand; $17/yr. in cy. mailed. 6950 Gerard, Winton, CA 95388. TEL 209-358-5311; FAX 209-358-7108. **Owner(s):** Mid-Valley Publications, Inc., 6950 Gerard, Winton, CA 95388. TEL 209-358-5311; Ed. Mae Branagh; Pub. John Derby; pub. size: broadsheet; circ. 3,300(paid).

US

HUGHSON CHRONICLE. Tue. $.25 newsstand; $17/yr. in cy. mailed. 6950 Gerard, Winton, CA 95388. TEL 209-358-5311; FAX 209-358-7108. **Owner(s):** Mid-Valley Publications, Inc., 6950 Gerard, Winton, CA 95388. TEL 209-358-5311; Ed. Sheila Reaville; Pub. John Derby; pub. size: broadsheet; circ. 4,200(paid).

US

MERCED COUNTY TIMES, THE. Thu. $.25 newsstand; $19/yr. in cy. mailed; $23/yr. out of cy. mailed. 6950 Gerard, Winton, CA 95388. TEL 209-358-5311; FAX 209-358-7108. **Owner(s):** Mid-Valley Publications, Inc., 6950 Gerard, Winton, CA 95388. TEL 209-358-5311; Ed. Topper Smith; Pub. John Derby; pub. size: tabloid; circ. 6,000(free & paid).

US

WATERFORD NEWS. Tue. $.25 newsstand; $17/yr. in cy. mailed. 6950 Gerard, Winton, CA 95388. TEL 209-358-5311; FAX 209-358-7108. **Owner(s):** Mid-Valley Publications, Inc., 6950 Gerard, Winton, CA 95388. TEL 209-358-5311; Pub. John Derby; pub. size: broadsheet; circ. 5,200(paid).

US

WINTON TIMES. Thu. $.25 newsstand; $17/yr. in cy. mailed; $21/yr. out of cy. mailed. 6950 Gerard, Winton, CA 95388. TEL 209-358-5311; FAX 209-358-7108. **Owner(s):** Mid-Valley Publications, Inc., 6950 Gerard, Winton, CA 95388. TEL 209-358-5311; Ed. Bob Andrews; Pub. John Derby; pub. size: tabloid; circ. 3,000(paid).

WOODLAND HILLS

US   ISSN 0193-9904

LAS VIRGENES ENTERPRISE. 1980. s-m.: 1st & 15th of mo. free newsstand; $30/yr. mailed. 6324 Variel Ave., Ste. 309, Woodland Hills, CA 91367-2517. TEL 818-716-4194; FAX 818-716-6577. **Owner(s):** Center News Publishing, 6324 Variel Ave., Ste. 309, Woodland Hills, CA 91367. TEL 818-716-4194; FAX 818-716-6577; Ed. Rodger Sterling; Pub. Kathleen Sterling; adv. contact: Ruth Patin. photos; pub. size: tabloid; circ. 5,000(free).

US

▼**SOUTH OF THE BOULEVARD.** 1994. s-m.: 1st & 15th of mo. free. 6324 Variel Ave., Ste. 309, Woodland Hills, CA 91367-2517. TEL 818-716-4194; FAX 818-716-6577. **Owner(s):** Center News Publishing, 6324 Variel Ave., Ste. 309, Woodland Hills, CA 91367. TEL 818-716-4194; FAX 818-716-6577; Ed. Rodger Sterling. adv.; photos; pub. size: tabloid.

US

WARNER CENTER NEWS. 1980. s-m.: 1st & 15th. free newsstand; $30/yr. mailed. 6324 Variel Ave., Ste. 309, Woodland Hills, CA 91367-2517. TEL 818-716-4161; FAX 818-716-6577. **Owner(s):** Center News Publishing, 6324 Variel Ave., Ste. 309, Woodland Hills, CA 91367-2517. TEL 818-716-4161; FAX 818-716-6577; Ed. Rodger Sterling; Pub. Kathleen Bercsi Sterling; adv. contact: Ruth Patin. photos; pub. size: tabloid; circ. 10,000(paid).

YUCAIPA

US

YUCAIPA & CALIMESA NEWS-MIRROR. 1915. Wed. $.50 newsstand; $21/yr. 35154 Yucaipa Blvd., Yucaipa, CA 92399. TEL 909-797-9101; FAX 909-797-0502. **Owner(s):** Brehm Communications, Inc., 17065 Via del Campo, San Diego, CA 92127. TEL 619-451-6200; Ed. Bobbe Monk. pub. size: standard; circ. 15,000(paid).

YUCCA VALLEY

US

MORONGO BASIN ADVERTISER. 1955. Tue. free. 56-185 29 Palms Hwy., Yucca Valley, CA 92284. TEL 619-346-1729; FAX 619-346-7350. **Owner(s):** Associated Desert Shoppers, Inc., 73400 Hwy. 111, Palm Desert, CA 92260. TEL 619-345-1729 pub. size: tabloid; circ. 10,000(free).

US   SSN 0746-2301

YUCCA VALLEY HI-DESERT STAR. 1957. s-w.: Wed. & Sat. $.50 newsstand; $34/yr. 56445 29 Palms Hwy., Yucca Valley, CA 92284. TEL 619-365-3315; FAX 619-365-2650. **Owner(s):** Hi Desert Publishing Co., 56445 29 Palms Hwy., Yucca Valley, CA 92284. TEL 619-365-3315; FAX 619-365-2650; Ed. Alisa Hicks; Pub. Russell Cannon; adv. pub. size: standard; circ. 11,000(paid). **Wire Service(s):** AP.

COLORADO

AKRON

US

AKRON NEWS REPORTER. 1910. Thu. $.50 newsstand; $19/yr. in state, $22/yr. out of state. 69 Main, Akron, CO 80720-1439. TEL 303-345-2296; FAX 303-345-6638. **Owner(s):** Media News Group, 309 S. Broad St., Woodbury, NJ 08096. TEL 609-845-3300; Ed. Karen Ashley. adv.; photos; pub. size: broadsheet; circ. 2,174(paid).

AURORA

US

AURORA SENTINEL. 1910. Wed. $.50 newsstand; $26/yr. 1730 S. Abilene, Ste. 203, Aurora, CO 80012. TEL 303-750-7555; FAX 303-750-7699. **Owner(s):** Karen Sowell, 1730 S. Abilene, Ste. 203, Aurora, CO 80012. TEL 303-750-7555; Harrison Cochran, 1730 S. Abilene, Ste. 203, Aurora, CO 80012. TEL 303-750-7555; Ed. Jack Bacor; Pub. Karen Sowell; pub. size: tabloid; circ. 10,000(paid).

BAYFIELD

US

PINE RIVER TIMES. 1985. Thu. $.50 newsstand; $20/yr. in cy.; $26/yr. out of cy. 15 W. Mill St., Bayfield, CO 81122-0830. TEL 970-884-2331; FAX 970-884-4385. **Owner(s)** Ann McCoy, P.O. Box 830, Bayfield, CO 81122-0830. TEL 970-884-2331; FAX 970-884-4385; Pub. Ann McCoy; adv.; photos; pub. size: tabloid; circ. 1,300(paid).

BRIGHTON

US

BRIGHTON/BLADE MARKET PLACE. 1975. s-w.: Wed. & Sat. $.50 newsstand; $29/yr. 139 N. Main St., Brighton, CO 80601. TEL 303-659-1141; FAX 303-659-2901. **Owner(s):** Terry Gogerty & Anette Riesel, 139 N. Main St., Brighton, CO 80501; Ed. Morris Dinges; Pub. Terry Gogerty; adv. contact: Terry Gogerty. pub. size: broadsheet; circ. 9,300(paid).

BROOMFIELD

US

BROOMFIELD ENTERPRISE. 1975. Thu. $.50 newsstand; $52/yr. local; $52/yr. mailed. 1006 Depot Hill Rd., Ste. G, Broomfield, CO 80020. TEL 303-466-3636; FAX 303-466-8168. **Owner(s):** Boulder Publishing, Inc., Boulder, CO 80303; Ed. Noralee Taylor. adv. contact: Beth Sabo. photos; pub. size: tabloid; circ. 13,000(controlled & paid).

BRUSH

US

BRUSH NEWS-TRIBUNE. 1894. Wed. $.20 newsstand; $20/yr. 109 Clayton, Brush, CO 80723-0008. TEL 303-842-5516; FAX 303-842-5519. **Owner(s):** Media News Group, 309 S. Broad St., Woodbury, NJ 08096. TEL 609-845-3300; Ed. Darlene Doane; Pub. Darlene Doane; adv.; pub. size: tabloid; circ. 2,400(paid).

CARBONDALE

US

VALLEY JOURNAL. 1974. Thu. $.25 newsstand; $20/yr. in valley; $24/yr. out of valley; $10/yr. senior citizens. 36 N. Fourth, Carbondale, CO 81623. TEL 970-963-3211; FAX 970-963-3259. **Owner(s):** Roaring Fork Valley Journal, 36 N. Fourth, Carbondale, CO 81623. TEL 303-963-3211; FAX 303-963-3259; Ed. Patrick Noel; Pub. Robert Dundas; adv.; photos; bk.rev.; pub. size: tabloid; circ. 5,200(paid).

CASTLE ROCK

US

DAILY NEWS PRESS. 1892. s-w.: Wed. & Sat. $.50 newsstand; $38/yr. 319 Perry St., Castle Rock, CO 80104-2420. TEL 303-688-3128; FAX 303-660-0240. **Owner(s):** Westward Communications, Inc., 5005 LBJ Fwy., Ste. 1040, Dallas, TX 75244. TEL 214-450-1717; Ed. Rich Bangs; Pub. J. Tom Graham; adv. contact: Malcolm Smith. pub. size: broadsheet; circ. 4,500(paid).

US

DOUGLAS COUNTY NEWS PRESS. 1892. Wed. $.50 newsstand; $26/yr. 319 Perry St., Castle Rock, CO 80104. TEL 303-688-3128; FAX 303-660-0240. **Owner(s):** Westward Communications, Inc., 5005 L.B.J. Fwy., Ste. 1040, Dallas, TX 75244. TEL 214-450-1717; FAX 214-450-1770; Ed. Richard Bangs; Pub. J. Tom Graham; pub. size: broadsheet; circ. 17,000(paid); Sun. 4,800(paid). **Wire Service(s):** AP.

US

ELBERT COUNTY NEWS. Thu. $.50 newsstand. 319 Perry St., Castle Rock, CO 80104. TEL 303-688-3128; FAX 303-660-0240. **Owner(s):** Westward Communications, Inc., 5005 LBJ Frwy., Ste. 1040, Dallas, TX 75244; Pub. J. Tom Graham; pub. size: standard; circ. 2,900(paid).

COLORADO CITY

US

GREENHORN VALLEY NEWS. 1973. Thu. $.50 newsstand; $14/yr. in cy.; $17/yr. out of cy. P.O. Box 19041, Colorado City, CO 81019. TEL 719-676-3304; FAX 719-676-3304. **Owner(s):** Ann Enrich, P.O. Box 19041, Colorado City, CO 81019. TEL 719-676-3304; FAX 719-676-3304; Ed. Ann Enrich; Pub. Ann Enrich; adv.; photos; pub. size: tabloid; circ. 4,000(paid).

COLORADO SPRINGS

US

BLACK FOREST NEWS. 1960. Thu. $.25 newsstand; $10/yr. 2724 Airport Rd., Colorado Springs, CO 80910. TEL 719-473-4370. **Owner(s):** Electronic Publishing Services, 2545 E. Platte Pl., Colorado Springs, CO 80909. TEL 719-473-4370; Ed. Charles L.R. Mattson; Pub. Charles L.R. Mattson; adv.; photos; pub. size: tabloid; circ. 1,000(paid).

CORTEZ

US

CORTEZ MONTEZUMA VALLEY JOURNAL. 1888. 3/wk.: Tue., Thu., Sat. $.25 newsstand; $34/yr. in area; $59/yr. out of area. 37 E. Main St., Cortez, CO 81321. TEL 303-565-8527; FAX 303-565-8532. **Owner(s):** Russell D. Brown, 37 E. Main St., Cortez, CO 81321. TEL 303-565-8527; Ed. Byron McKelvie; Pub. Russell D. Brown; pub. size: standard; circ. 6,328(paid).

US

CORTEZ SENTINEL. 1936. Mon. $.25 newsstand; $34/yr. in area; $59/yr. out of area. 37 E. Main St., Cortez, CO 81321. TEL 303-565-8527; FAX 303-565-8532. **Owner(s):** Russell D. Brown, 37 E. Main St., Cortez, CO 81321. TEL 303-565-8527; Ed. Byron McKelvie; Pub. Russell D. Brown; pub. size: standard; circ. 6,328(paid).

CRAIG

US

HAYDEN VALLEY PRESS. Thu. $.25 newsstand; $14/yr. in cy.; $17/yr. out of cy. 466 Yampa Ave., Craig, CO 81625. TEL 970-824-7031; FAX 970-824-6810. **Owner(s):** Yampa Valley Newspapers, Inc., 466 Yampa Ave., P.O. Box 5, Craig, CO 81625. TEL 303-824-7031; Ed. Steve Busemeyer; Pub. Carol Beumer; pub. size: tabloid; circ. 700(paid).

DELTA

US   ISSN 0891-9704

DELTA COUNTY INDEPENDENT. 1883. Wed. $.40 newsstand; $20/yr. in state; $24/yr. out of state. 401 Meeker St., Delta, CO 81416. TEL 970-874-4421; FAX 970-874-4424; E-mail: randydci@dci-press.com; URL: http://www.dci-press.com/. **Owner(s):** Leader Publishing Co., Inc., 401 Meeker St., Delta, CO 81416. TEL 970-874-4421; FAX 970-874-4424; Ed. Pat Sunderland; Pub. Norman Sunderland; adv.; photos; pub. size: broadsheet; circ. 7,339(paid).

DENVER

US

COLORADO STATESMAN. 1898. Fri. $1 newsstand; $44/yr. 1535 Grant St., Ste. 280, Denver, CO 80203. TEL 303-837-8600; FAX 303-837-9015. **Owner(s):** Colorado Statesman, P.O. Box 18129, Denver, CO 80218. TEL 303-837-8600; FAX 303-837-9015; Pub. Jody Strogoff; adv.; pub. size: tabloid; circ. 6,000(controlled & paid).

US   ISSN 0898-1701

DENVER HERALD-DISPATCH. 1926. Thu. $.25 newsstand; $22.50/yr. 47 S. Federal Blvd., Denver, CO 80219. TEL 303-935-2453; FAX 303-936-0994. **Owner(s):** J. Ivanhoe Rosenberg, 47 S. Federal Blvd., Denver, CO 80219. TEL 303-935-2453; Ed. Charlie Leckenby; Pub. J. Ivanhoe Rosenberg; adv.; pub. size: tabloid; circ. 7,000(paid). **Wire Service(s):** AP.

US

WESTWORD. w. free. P.O. Box 5970, Denver, CO 80217. TEL 303-296-7744; FAX 303-246-2457. **Owner(s):** Westword; Ed. Patricia Calhoun. adv.; pub. size: tabloid.

DOVE CREEK

US

DOVE CREEK PRESS. 1940. Thu. $.25 newsstand; $11/yr. in cy.; $15/yr. out of cy. 321 N. Main St., Dove Creek, CO 81324. TEL 970-677-2214. **Owner(s):** Doug & Linda Funk, P.O. Box 598, Dove Creek, CO 81324; Ed. Linda Funk. adv.; pub. size: tabloid; circ. 1,100(paid).

EADS

US

KIOWA COUNTY PRESS. 1887. Fri. $.40 newsstand; $19.50/yr. in state; $22/yr. out of state. 1208 Maine St., Eads, CO 81036. TEL 719-438-5352. **Owner(s):** Christopher Sorensen, P.O. Box 248, Eads, CO 81036-0248. TEL 719-438-5352; Ed. Christopher Sorensen; Pub. Christopher Sorensen; adv.; photos; bk.rev.; pub. size: tabloid; circ. 660(paid). **Wire Service(s):** AP.

EAGLE

US

EAGLE VALLEY ENTERPRISE. 0898. Thu. $.35 newsstand; $14/yr. in cy.; $20/yr. out of cy.; $24/yr. out of state. 11 Eagle Park Dr., E., Eagle, CO 81631. TEL 303-328-6656; FAX 303-328-6393; E-mail: getnews@vail.net; URL: http://www.adone.com/enterprise. **Owner(s):** Gojan & Leslie Nikolich, P.O. Box 1000, Eagle, CO 80030. TEL 303-428-9529; Ed. Gojan Nikolich; Pub. Gojan Nikolich; adv. contact: Kim Reed. photos; bk.rev.; pub. size: tabloid; circ. 14,000(free & paid).

EAGLE-VAIL

US   ISSN 1061-1770

VAIL TRAIL. 1965. Fri. $3/mo. mailed 1st class; $25/yr. 41184 Hwy. 6 & 24, Eagle-Vail, CO 81628. TEL 970-949-4004; FAX 970-949-0199. **Owner(s):** Knox Publishing Co., P.O. Drawer 6200, Vail, CO 81658. TEL 303-949-4004; FAX 303-949-0199; Ed. Tara Flanagan; Pub. Allen Knox; adv. contact: Carolyn Knox. bk.rev.; pub. size: tabloid; circ. 14,000(controlled & paid).

ESTES PARK

US

ESTES PARK TRAIL-GAZETTE. 1915. s-w.: Wed. & Fri. $.50 newsstand; $28/yr. in cy.; $38/yr. in state; $45/yr. out of state. 251 Moraine Ave., Estes Park, CO 80517. TEL 970-586-3356; FAX 970-586-9532. **Owner(s):** Estes Park Newspapers, Inc., P.O. Box 1707, Estes Park, CO 80517. TEL 303-586-3356; Ed. Timothy Asbury; Pub. Terence K. Licence; adv. contact: Elizabeth Rogers. pub. size: broadsheet; circ. 5,800(paid).

EVERGREEN

US   ISSN 0192-0197

CANYON COURIER. 1954. Wed. $.50 newsstand; $20/yr. in cy.; $24/yr. out of cy. 4009 Hwy. 74, Evergreen, CO 80439. TEL 303-674-5534; FAX 303-674-4104. **Owner(s):** Dennis Rooker, P.O. Box 430, Evergreen, CO; Ed. Tony Messenger; Pub. Kamal Eways; adv. contact: John Ellis. pub. size: tabloid; circ. 9,300(paid).

FLORENCE

US

FLORENCE CITIZEN. Thu. $.35 newsstand; $16/yr. local; $18/yr. out of area. 200 S. Pikes Peak Ave., Florence, CO 81226. TEL 719-784-6383. **Owner(s):** Robert & Sue Wood, 200 S. Pikes Peak Ave., Florence, CO 81226. TEL 719-784-6383; Ed. Robert M. Wood; Pub. Robert M. Wood; adv.; pub. size: tabloid; circ. 1,500(paid).

FORT LUPTON

US   ISSN 1056-2419

FORT LUPTON PRESS. 1906. s-w.: Wed. & Sat. $.50 newsstand; $29/yr. 430 Denver Ave., Ste. B, Fort Lupton, CO 80621. TEL 303-857-4440; FAX 303-857-6801. **Owner(s):** Metro West Publishing Co., 139 N. Main, Brighton, CO 80601. TEL 303-659-2522; Ed. Chuck Ballou. adv.; pub. size: tabloid; circ. 5,300(paid).

FOUNTAIN

US

FOUNTAIN VALLEY NEWS & EL PASO COUNTY NEWS. 1958. w. $.75 newsstand; $20/yr.; $17/yr. senior citizens. 120 E. Ohio, Fountain, CO 80817. TEL 719-382-5613; FAX 719-382-5614. **Owner(s):** Kathryn Wiese, Shopper Press, Inc., P.O. Box 400, Fountain, CO 80817. TEL 719-382-5613; FAX 719-382-5611; Pub. Kathryn A. Wiese; adv. contact: Geof Clark. photos; pub. size: tabloid; circ. 6,500(free & paid).

FOWLER

US

FOWLER TRIBUNE, THE. 1897. Thu. $.25 newsstand; $15/yr. in cy.; $18/yr. out of cy. 112 E. Cranston St., Fowler, CO 81039. TEL 719-263-5311. **Owner(s):** Karen Turner, 112 E. Cranston St., Fowler, CO 81039. TEL 719-263-5311; Ed. Dorothy Salle. adv.; photos; pub. size: tabloid; circ. 1,520(controlled & free).

FREDERICK

US

FARMER & MINER. 1930. Wed. $19/yr. in state; $26/yr. out of state. 204 Oak St., Frederick, CO 80530. TEL 303-833-2331; FAX 303-659-2901. **Owner(s):** Terry Gogerty, 139 N. Main, Brighton, CO 80601. TEL 303-659-2522; FAX 303-659-2901; Annette Riesel, 139 N. Main Brighton, CO 80061. TEL 303-659-2522; FAX 303-659-2901; Ed. Michael Neilson; Pub. Terry Gogerty; adv.; photos; bk.rev.; pub. size: tabloid; circ. 1,100(paid).

FRISCO

US

SUMMIT COUNTY JOURNAL. 1880. Wed. $.25 newsstand; $13.50/yr. in cy.; $22/yr. out of cy. 40 W. Main St., Frisco, CO 80443. TEL 970-453-2331; FAX 970-668-0755. **Owner(s):** Eagle-Summit Publishing Co., P.O. Box 709, Frisco, CO 80443. TEL 970-668-0750; Ed. Alex Miller; Pub. Robert L. Brown; adv.; pub. size: tabloid; circ. 6,000(free & paid).

  Formerly: Breckenridge Journal.

FRUITA

US

FRUITA TIMES, THE. 1892. Fri. $.50 newsstand; $14/yr. in cy.; $20/yr. out of cy. 217 E. Aspen Ave., Fruita, CO 81521-2285. TEL 303-858-3924; FAX 303-858-7658. **Owner(s):** Eugene Thomas, 221 E. Aspen Ave., Apt. 2, Fruita, CO 81521-2285. TEL 970-858-3924; FAX 970-858-7658; Ed. Eugene Thomas; Pub. Eugene Thomas; adv.; photos; bk.rev.; pub. size: tabloid; circ. 1,300(paid).

GOLDEN

US   ISSN 0746-6382

GOLDEN TRANSCRIPT. 1866. s-w.: Tue. & Fri. $.50 newsstand; $36/yr. in cy.; $50/yr. out of cy. 1000 Tenth St., Golden, CO 80401. TEL 303-279-5541; FAX 303-279-7157. **Owner(s):** Golden Media Inc., 1000 Tenth St., Golden, CO 80401; Ed. Jacque Scott; Pub. Vince Bodiford; pub. size: broadsheet; circ. 21,800(paid).

JEFFERSON COUNTY TRANSCRIPT. 1984. Wed. $.50 newsstand; $26/yr. 1000 Tenth St., Golden, CO 80401. E-mail: trecitor@tesser.com; URL: http://www.tesser.com/transcript. **Owner(s):** Golden Media Inc., 1000 Tenth St., Golden, CO 80401; Ed. Jacque Scott; Pub. Jerry Brock; adv. contact: John Tracy photos; pub. size: standard; circ. 5,900(controlled & free).

HAXTUN

US

HAXTUN-FLEMING HERALD, THE. 1975. Wed. $18/yr. local; $19/yr. out of area. 217 S. Colorado Ave., Haxtun, CO 80731. TEL 303-774-6118. E-mail: cjc@henge.com; URL: http://www.hfherald.com. **Owner(s):** Fletcher Street, Inc., P.O. Box 128, Haxtun, CO 80731. TEL 303-774-6221; Ed. Jean Gray; Pub. Jean Gray; adv. contact: Carol Scheel. photos; pub. size: broadsheet; circ. 1,300(paid).

HIGHLANDS RANCH

US

▼**HIGHLANDER.** 1994. Thu. free. 44 Centennial Blvd., Ste. B, Highlands Ranch, CO 80126. TEL 303-688-3128; FAX 303-660-0240. **Owner(s):** Westward Communications, Inc., 5005 L.B.J. Fwy., Ste. 1040, Dallas, TX 75244. TEL 214-450-1717; Ed. Peter Lewis; Pub. J. Tom Graham; adv.; pub. size: broadsheet; circ. 11,500(paid).

HUGO

US

EASTERN COLORADO PLAINSMAN. 1912. Thu. $.30 newsstand; $13/yr. in state; $17/yr. out of state. 329 Fourth St., Hugo, CO 30821. TEL 719-743-2371; FAX 719-743-2106. **Owner(s):** Becky Osterwald, P.O. Box 98, Hugo, CO 80821. TEL 719-743-2519; Ed. Becky Osterwald; Pub. Becky Osterwald; adv. contact: Becky Osterwald. pub. size: tabloid; circ. 1,350(paid).

IDAHO SPRINGS

US

CLEAR CREEK COURANT. 1973. Wed. $.50 newsstand; $23/yr. in cy.; $28/yr. out of cy. 1634 Miner St., Idaho Springs, CO 80452-2020. TEL 303-567-4491; FAX 303-567-4492; E-mail: cccourant@aol.com. **Owner(s):** Cary Stiff & Carol Wilcox, P.O. Box 276, Idaho Springs, CO 80452. TEL 303-567-4491; FAX 303-567-4492; adv.; photos; pub. size: tabloid; circ. 3,000(paid).

JULESBURG

US

JULESBURG ADVOCATE. 1899. Thu. $.50 newsstand; $19.50/yr. in cy.; $21.75/yr. out of cy. 108 Cedar, Julesburg, CO 80737. TEL 970-474-3388; FAX 970-474-3389. **Owner(s):** Media News Group, 309 S. Broad St., Woodbury, NJ 08096. TEL 609-845-3300; adv.; photos; pub. size: broadsheet; circ. 1,833(paid).

LA JUNTA

US   ISSN 0004-1890

ARKANSAS VALLEY JOURNAL. 1949. Thu. $.50 newsstand; $28/yr. in state; $30/yr. out of state. 7 W. Fifth St., La Junta, CO 81050-0500. TEL 719-384-8121; FAX 719-384-2867. **Owner(s):** Arkansas Valley Publishing Co., P.O. Box 500, La Junta, CO 81050-0500. TEL 719-384-8121; FAX 719-384-2867; Ed. Susan Russell; Pub. Daniel R. Hyatt; adv.; pub. size: tabloid; circ. 6,597(free & paid). **Wire Service(s):** AP.

LAKEWOOD

US   ISSN 0899-2452

ARVADA JEFFERSON SENTINEL. 1967. Thu. $.75 newsstand; $39/yr. 1224 Wadsworth Blvd., Lakewood, CO 80215. TEL 303-239-9890; FAX 303-239-9808. **Owner(s):** Jefferson Sentinel Newspapers, 1224 Wadsworth Blvd., Lakewood, CO 80215. TEL 303-239-9890 FAX 303-239-9808; Ed. Jeff Whitear; Pub. Robert Cox; adv. contact: Gayla Hicks. pub. size: tabloid; circ. 24,347(paid).

  Formerly: Arvada Sentinel.

US   ISSN 1060-5215
JEFFERSON SENTINEL. Thu. $.75 newsstand;
$39/yr. 1224 Wadsworth Blvd., Lakewood, CO
80215. TEL 303-239-9890;
FAX 303-239-9808. **Owner(s):** Jefferson Sentinel
Newspapers, 1224 Wadsworth Blvd., Lakewood,
CO 80215. TEL 303-239-9890; FAX
303-239-9808; Pub. Robert Cox; pub. size:
tabloid; circ. 22,401(controlled & paid).
Formerly: Lakewood Jefferson Sentinel.

LEADVILLE

US
HERALD-DEMOCRAT. 1878. Thu. $.50 newsstand;
$19/yr. in cy.; $25/yr. out of cy. 717 Harrison
Ave., Leadville, CO 80461. TEL 719-486-0611;
FAX 719-486-0642. **Owner(s):** Arkansas Valley
Publishing Co., Salida, CO. TEL 719-539-6691;
FAX 719-539-6630; Ed. Grant Dunham. adv.
contact: Eric Guess. pub. size: tabloid; circ.
2,900(paid). **Wire Service(s):** AP.
Formerly: Leadville Herald-Democrat.

LITTLETON

US   ISSN 0745-9610
ENGLEWOOD HERALD. 1911. Thu. $.75 newsstand;
$19.95/yr. 2329 W. Main St., Littleton, CO
80120. TEL 303-794-7877;
FAX 303-794-1909. **Owner(s):** Macari-Healey
Publishing Co., 2329 W. Main St., Littleton, CO
80120. TEL 303-794-1909; Ed. Patty Burnett;
Pub. Gerard Healey; adv. contact: Gates Scott.
pub. size: tabloid; circ. 3,500(paid).
Formerly: Englewood Sentinel.

US
HIGHLANDS BRANCH HERALD. Fri. $.75 newsstand;
$24.95/yr. 2329 W. Main St., Ste. 103, Littleton,
CO 80120. TEL 303-794-7877;
FAX 303-794-1909. **Owner(s):** Macari-Healey
Publishing Co., 2329 W. Main St., Ste. 103,
Littleton, CO 80120. TEL 303-794-7877; FAX
303-794-1909; Ed. Patty Burnett; Pub. Gerard
Healey; pub. size: tabloid; circ. 11,000(paid).

US   ISSN 0899-6318
LIFE AT KEN-CARYL. 1979. bi-w.: Wed. free local;
$20/yr. outside of area. 7676 S. Continental
Divide Rd., Littleton, CO 80127.
TEL 303-979-1876. **Owner(s):** Ken-Caryl Ranch
Master Assn., 7676 S. Continental Divide Rd.,
Littleton, CO 80127. TEL 303-979-1876; FAX
303-972-1272; Ed. Eleen Laubenheim. adv.;
photos; pub. size: tabloid; circ. 3,700(free &
paid).

US
LITTLETON INDEPENDENT. 1888. Thu. $.75
newsstand; $24.95/yr. 2329 W. Main St., Ste.
103, Littleton, CO 80120. TEL 303-794-7877;
FAX 303-794-1909. **Owner(s):** Macari-Healey
Publishing Co., 2329 W. Main St., Littleton, CO
80120. TEL 303-794-1909; Ed. Patty Burnett;
Pub. Jerry Healey; adv. contact: Gates Scott. pub.
size: tabloid; circ. 9,000(paid).
Formerly: Littleton/Sentinel Independent.

LYONS

US
OLD LYONS RECORDER, THE. 1910. Thu. $.50
newsstand; $35/yr. carrier. 430 Main St., Lyons,
CO 80540-1729. TEL 303-823-6625;
FAX 303-823-6633. **Owner(s):** Old Recorder
Newspapers, P.O. Box 1729, Lyons, CO
80540-1729. TEL 303-823-6625; FAX
303-823-6633; Ed. Walter J. Kinderman; Pub.
Walter J. Kinderman; adv.; photos; bk.rev.; pub.
size: tabloid; circ. 2,400(paid).

MANCOS

US
MANCOS TIMES-TRIBUNE. 1892. Wed. $11/yr. in
cy.; $16/yr. elsewhere. 135 Grand Ave., Mancos,
CO 81328. TEL 970-533-7766;
FAX 970-565-8532. **Owner(s):** Cortez
Newspapers, Inc., P.O. Drawer O, Cortez, CO
81321. TEL 970-565-8527; FAX
970-565-8532; Ed. Julie Powell; Pub. R.D.
Brown; adv. contact: Jeanne Shrivner. photos;
bk.rev.; pub. size: tabloid; circ. 850(paid).

MANITOU SPRINGS

US
CHEYENNE MOUNTAIN JOURNAL. m.: 2nd Fri. of mo.
free mailed. 22 Ruxton Ave., Manitou Springs, CO
80829. TEL 719-685-9201;
FAX 719-685-4424. **Owner(s):** Pikes Peak
Journal, Inc., 22 Ruxton Ave., Manitou Springs,
CO 80829. TEL 719-685-9201; Ed. John G.
Graham; Pub. John G. Graham; adv. contact:
Michaela Keplinger. photos; pub. size: tabloid; circ.
6,400(free).

US
GARDEN OF THE GODS JOURNAL. m.: 4th Fri. of mo.
free mailed. 22 Ruxton Ave., Manitou Springs, CO
80829. TEL 719-685-9201;
FAX 719-685-4424. **Owner(s):** Pikes Peak
Journal, Inc., 22 Ruxton Ave., Manitou Springs,
CO 80829. TEL 719-685-9201; FAX
719-685-4424; Ed. John G. Graham; Pub. John
G. Graham; adv. contact: Michaela Keplinger.
photos; pub. size: tabloid; circ. 3,700(free).

US
MANITOU SPRINGS PIKES PEAK JOURNAL. 1882. Fri.
$.50 newsstand; $15/yr. in state; $24/yr. out of
state. 22 Ruxton Ave., Manitou Springs, CO
80829. TEL 719-685-9201;
FAX 719-685-4424. **Owner(s):** Pikes Peak
Journal, Inc., 22 Ruxton Ave., Manitou Springs,
CO 80829. TEL 719-685-9201; adv. contact:
John G. Graham. photos; pub. size: tabloid; circ.
4,800(free & paid).

US
PIKES PEAK JOURNAL. Fri. $.50 newsstand; $15/yr.
22 Ruxton Ave., Manitou Springs, CO 80829.
TEL 719-685-9201; FAX 719-685-4424.
Owner(s): Pikes Peak Journal, Inc., 22 Ruxton
Ave., Manitou Springs, CO 80829. TEL
719-685-9201; FAX 719-685-4424; Ed. John
G. Graham; Pub. John G. Graham; adv. contact:
Michaela Keplinger.

US
ROCKRIMMON JOURNAL. s-m.: 1st & 3rd Fri. free
mailed. 22 Ruxton Ave., Manitou Springs, CO
80829. TEL 719-685-9201. **Owner(s):** Pikes
Peak Journal, Inc., 22 Ruxton Ave., Manitou
Springs, CO 80829. TEL 719-685-9201; FAX
719-685-4424; Ed. John G. Graham; Pub. John
G. Graham; adv. contact: Michaela Keplinger.
photos; pub. size: tabloid; circ. 7,500(free).

MEEKER

US
MEEKER HERALD, THE. 1885. Thu. $.50 newsstand;
$25/yr. in cy.; $21/yr. senior citizens. 178 Main
St., Meeker, CO 81641-0720.
TEL 970-878-4017; FAX 970-878-4017.
Owner(s): Glenn R. & Donna L. Troester, P.O. Box
720, Meeker, CO 81641-0720. TEL
970-878-4017; FAX 970-878-4017; Ed. Glenn
R. Troester; Pub. Glenn R. Troester; adv.; photos;
pub. size: broadsheet; circ. 2,100(paid).

MONTE VISTA

US
CENTER POST DISPATCH. Wed. $.50 newsstand;
$21/yr. in cy.; $28/yr. out of cy.; $31/yr. out of
state. 229 Adams St., Monte Viste, CO 81144.
TEL 719-852-3531; FAX 719-852-3387.
Owner(s): News Media Corp., 211 Hwy. 38, E.,
P.O. Box 46, Rochelle, IL 61068; Ed. Toni
Vecchio; Pub. Keith Kerney; pub. size: tabloid; circ.
830(paid).

US
CONEJOS COUNTY CITIZEN, THE. 1892. Wed. $.50
newsstand; $18.50/yr. in cy.; $29.50/yr. out of
cy.; $32.50/yr. out of state. 229 Adams St.,
Monte Vista, CO 81144. TEL 719-852-6531;
FAX 719-852-3387. **Owner(s):** News Media
Corp., 211 Hwy. 38, E., P.O. Box 46, Rochelle, IL
61068; Pub. Keith Cerny; pub. size: tabloid; circ.
1,000(paid).

US
DEL NORTE PROSPECTOR. Wed. $.50 newsstand;
$21/yr. in cy.; $28/yr. out of cy.; $31/yr. out of
state. 229 Adams St., Monte Vista, CO 81144.
TEL 719-852-3531; FAX 719-852-3387.
Owner(s): News Media Corp., 211 Hwy. 38, E.,
P.O. Box 46, Rochelle, IL 61068; Ed. Toni
Vecchio; Pub. Keith Kerney; adv.; pub. size:
tabloid; circ. 800(paid).

US
MINERAL COUNTY MINER. Thu. $.50 newsstand;
$21/yr. in cy.; $28/yr. out of cy.; $31/yr. out of
state. 229 Adams St., Monte Vista, CO 81144.
TEL 719-852-3531; FAX 719-852-3387.
Owner(s): News Media Corp., 211 Hwy. 38, E.,
P.O. Box 46, Rochelle, IL 61068; Ed. Toni
Vecchio. pub. size: tabloid; circ. 900(paid).

US
MONTE VISTA JOURNAL. 1888. Wed. $.50
newsstand; $22.50/yr. in cy.; $29/yr. out of cy.;
$32.50/yr. out of state. 229 Adams St., Monte
Vista, CO 81144. TEL 719-852-3531;
FAX 719-852-3387. **Owner(s):** News Media
Corp., 211 Hwy. 38, E., P.O. Box 46, Rochelle, IL
61068. TEL 815-562-2061; Ed. Toni Vecchio;
Pub. Keith Cerny; adv.; pub. size: tabloid; circ.
2,500(paid).

US
SATURDAY ADVANTAGE, THE. Sat. free. 229 Adams
St., Monte Vista, CO 81144.
TEL 719-852-3531; FAX 719-852-3387.
Owner(s): News Media Corp., 211 Hwy. 38, E.,
P.O. Box 46, Rochelle, IL 61068; Ed. Toni
Vecchio; Pub. Keith Kerney; pub. size: tabloid; circ.
15,000(free).

US
SOUTH FORK TIMES. Wed. $.50 newsstand; $21/yr.
in cy.; $28/yr. out of cy.; $31/yr. out of state.
229 Adams St., Monte Vista, CO 81144.
TEL 719-852-3531; FAX 719-852-3387.
Owner(s): News Media Corp., 211 Hwy. 38, E.,
P.O. Box 46, Rochelle, IL 61068; Ed. Toni
Vecchio; Pub. Keith Kerney; adv.; pub. size:
tabloid; circ. 800(paid).

MONUMENT

US

TRIBUNE, THE. 1965. Thu. $.50 newsstand; $16.50/yr. in state; $23.50/yr. out of state. 283 Washington, Monument, CO 80132. TEL 719-481-3423. **Owner(s):** Bill Kezzizah, P.O. Box 488, Monument, CO 80132. TEL 719-481-3423; FAX 719-481-4172; Ed. Bill Kezziah; Pub. Pat Standard; adv. contact: Pat Standard. pub. size: tabloid; circ. 3,800(paid).

OURAY

US

OURAY COUNTY PLAINDEALER. 1877. Thu. $.50 newsstand; $23/yr. in cy.; $29/yr. out of cy. 333 Sixth Ave., Ouray, CO 81427. TEL 970-325-4412; FAX 970-325-4413. **Owner(s):** David Mullings, P.O. Box 607, Ouray, CO 81427. TEL 970-325-4412; Ed. David Mullings. adv.; pub. size: tabloid; circ. 1,900(paid).

US

RIDGWAY SUN. Thu. $.50 newsstand; $23/yr. in cy.; $29/yr. out of cy. 333 Sixth Ave., Ouray, CO 81427. TEL 303-325-4412; FAX 303-325-4413. **Owner(s):** David Mullings, P.O. Box 607, Ouray, CO 81427; Ed. David Mullings. adv.; pub. size: tabloid; circ. 800(paid).

PALISADE

US

PALISADE TRIBUNE. 1903. Thu. $.50 newsstand; $24/yr in cy.; $29/yr. out of cy.; $34/yr. out of state. 124 W. Third, Palisade, CO 81526. TEL 303-464-5614; FAX 303-464-5244. **Owner(s):** Bob Sweeney, P.O. Box 8, Palisade, CO 81526. TEL 303-464-5614; FAX 303-464-5244; adv.; bk.rev.; pub. size: tabloid; circ. 3,100(free & paid).

PINE

US

HIGH TIMBER TIMES. 1977. Thu. $.50 newsstand; $17/yr. local; $21/yr. elsewhere. 43 Mt. Evans Blvd., Pine, CO 80470. TEL 303-838-4884; FAX 303-838-6007. **Owner(s):** Evergreen Newspapers, Inc., 175 S. Pantops Dr., Charlottesville, VA 22901. TEL 804-977-7424; Ed. Bob Mook; Pub. Kamal P. Eways; adv. contact: John Ellis. pub. size: tabloid; circ. 3,000(paid).

RIFLE

US

CITIZEN TELEGRAM, THE. 1903. Wed. $.35 newsstand; $20/yr. in cy.; $24/yr. out of cy.; $10/yr. senior citizens. 132 E. Third St., Rifle, CO 81650. TEL 970-625-3245; FAX 970-625-3628. **Owner(s):** Community Newspapers of Colorado, Inc., 132 E. Third St., Rifle, CO 81650. TEL 970-625-3245; Ed. Suzanne Hart. adv. contact: Barb Donnely. pub. size: tabloid; circ. 3,500(controlled & paid).

SILVERTON

US

SILVERTON STANDARD & THE MINER. 1875. Thu. $.50 newsstand; $26/yr. 1257 Greene St., Silverton, CO 81433-0008. TEL 303-387-5477. **Owner(s):** Silverton Standard & The Miner, Inc., P.O. Box 8, Silverton, CO 81433. TEL 303-387-5477; Pub. Jon Denious; adv.; photos; pub. size: tabloid; circ. 1,400(paid).

STEAMBOAT SPRINGS

US

STEAMBOAT PILOT. 1885. Thu. free newsstand; $24/yr. in cy.; $32/yr. elsewhere. 1041 Lincoln Ave., Steamboat Springs, CO 80477. TEL 970-879-1502; FAX 970-879-2888. **Owner(s):** WorldWest Limited Liability Co., Lawrence, KS; Ed. Tom Ross; Pub. Suzanne Antinoro; bk.rev.; pub. size: broadsheet; circ. 7,324(free & paid). **Wire Service(s):** AP.
    Formerly: Steamboat Springs Pilot.

STRASBURG

US

EASTERN COLORADO NEWS. 1916. Thu. $18/yr. in state; $20/yr. out of state. P.O. Box 555, Strasburg, CO 80136. TEL 303-622-4417; FAX 303-622-9217. **Owner(s):** Mike Galarneau, P.O. Box 555, Strasburg, CO 80136. TEL 303-622-4417; FAX 303-622-4417; Ed. Mike Galarneau; Pub. Mike Galarneau; adv.; pub. size: broadsheet; circ. 2,000(paid).

TELLURIDE

US

TELLURIDE TIMES-JOURNAL. 1962. Thu. $.25 newsstand; $24/yr. mailed. 123 S. Spruce St., Telluride, CO 81435. TEL 303-728-4488; FAX 303-728-6090; E-mail: timesj@rmii.com; URL: http://www.adone.com/telluride/. **Owner(s):** Wick Communications, Inc., 333 W. Wilcox Dr., Ste. 302, Sierra Vista, AZ 81435. TEL 303-728-4488; FAX 303-728-6090; Ed. Margo Hecker; Pub. Tom Bonfietti; adv.; photos; bk.rev.; pub. size: tabloid; circ. 4,879(free & paid).

WALDEN

US

JACKSON COUNTY STAR. 1913. Thu. $.35 newsstand; $12/yr. in cy.; $15/yr. outside cy. 417 Fifth St., Walden, CO 80480-0397. TEL 970-723-4404; FAX 970-723-4404. **Owner(s):** Chard & Dusty Smith, 7633 State Hwy. 125, Rand, CO 80473. TEL 970-723-4404; Ed. Dusty Smith; Pub. Dusty Smith; adv. contact: Marion Trick. photos; bk.rev.; pub. size: tabloid; circ. 1,400(paid).

WESTCLIFFE

US

WET MOUNTAIN TRIBUNE. 1883. Wed. $.50 newsstand; $23/yr. 404 Main St., Westcliffe, CO 81252. TEL 719-783-2361; FAX 719-783-2879. **Owner(s):** Jim Little, 404 Main St., Westcliffe, CO 81252. TEL 719-783-2361; FAX 719-783-2879; Ed. Jim Little; Pub. Jim Little; adv. contact: Jackie Stoppe. photos; pub. size: tabloid; circ. 2,555(free & paid).

WESTMINSTER

US   ISSN 1044-4254

NORTHGLENN-THORNTON SENTINEL. 1968. Thu. $.50 newsstand; $24/yr. in cy. 7380 Lowell Blvd., Westminster, CO 80030. TEL 303-426-6000; FAX 303-430-1676. **Owner(s):** Wilbur E. Flachman, P.O. Box 215, Westminster, CO 80030. TEL 303-426-6000; FAX 303-430-1676; Ed. Karen Brown. adv. contact: Scott Bumgardner. photos; pub. size: tabloid; circ. 5,500(paid).

US   ISSN 1072-7576

WESTMINSTER WINDOW. 1947. Thu. $.50 newsstand; $24/yr. in cy. 7380 Lowell Blvd., Westminster, CO 80030. TEL 303-426-6000; FAX 303-430-1676. **Owner(s):** Wilbur E. Flachman, P.O. Box 215, Westminster, CO 80030. TEL 303-426-6000; FAX 303-430-1676; Ed. Karen Brown. adv. contact: Scott Bumgardner. photos pub. size: tabloid; circ. 5,200(paid).

WIGGINS

US

WIGGINS COURIER, THE. 1987. Thu. $.50 newsstand; $17/yr. in cy.; $18/yr. out of cy.; $20/yr. out of state. 213 Dickson, Wiggins, CO 82654. TEL 303-483-7450; FAX 303-483-7313. **Owner(s):** Verna Segelke, 213 Dickson, Wiggins, CO 80654. TEL 303-483-7460; FAX 303-483-7313; Darlene Ruyle, 213 Dickson, Wiggins, CO 80654. TEL 303-483-7460; FAX 303-483-7313; Ed. Darlene Ruyle; Pub. Verna Segelke; adv. contact: Verna Segelke. photos; pub. size: broadsheet; circ. 700(controlled & free).

WINTER PARK

US

WINTER PARK MANIFEST. 1977. Wed. $.50 newsstand; $16/yr. in cy.; $22/yr. out of cy. 78622 Winter Park Dr., Winter Park, CO 80482. TEL 970-726-5721; FAX 970-726-8789. **Owner(s):** William Potter Johnson, 445 W. Rapa Pl., Tucson, AZ 85737. TEL 520-726-5721; Ed. Harry Williamson; Pub. Patrick Brower; adv.; pub. size: tabloid; circ. 4,300(controlled).

WRAY

US

WRAY GAZETTE. 1903. Wed. $.50 newsstand; $20/yr. in area; $23/yr. out of area. 411 Main St., Wray, CO 80758. TEL 970-332-4846; FAX 970-332-4065. **Owner(s):** Wray Gazette, 411 Main St., Wray, CO 80758. TEL 303-332-4846; Ed. Ron Rieb; Pub. Ron Rieb; pub. size: oversize; circ. 3,235(paid).

YUMA

US

YUMA PIONEER. 1886. Thu. $.20/yr. 207 S. Main St., Yuma, CO 80759. TEL 970-348-2174; FAX 970-848-2895. **Owner(s):** Roger Chance, 207 S. Main St., Yuma, CO 80759. TEL 303-348-2174; Ed. Roger Chance; Pub. Roger Chance; adv.; pub. size: standard circ. 3,100(paid).

CONNECTICUT

BETHEL

US

▼**BETHEL BEACON.** 1996. Thu. $30/yr. 214 Greenwood Ave., Bethel, CT 06801. TEL 203-798-7450; FAX 203-354-2645. **Owner(s):** Housatonic Valley Publishing, 132 Darbury Rd., P.O. Box 135, New Milford, CT 06776. TEL 203-438-6544; Ed. Susan Wolf; Pub. Tripp Rothschild; adv.; bk.rev.; pub. size: broadsheet; circ. 2,200(paid).
    Formerly: Bethel Home News.

BRANFORD

US   ISSN 0888-1901
BRANFORD REVIEW. 1928. s-w.: Wed. & Sat. $.50 newsstand; $33/yr. 230 E. Main St., Branford, CT 06405. TEL 203-488-2535; FAX 203-481-4125. **Owner(s):** Journal Register Co., 50 W. State St., 12th Fl., Trenton, NJ 08608. TEL 609-396-2200; Ed. Kimberly P. Ryan. adv. contact: Greg Barden. photos; pub. size: tabloid; circ. 6,000(paid).

BRISTOL

US   ISSN 0746-9632
BLOOMFIELD JOURNAL. 1976. Fri. $.75 newsstand; $25/yr.; $20/yr. senior citizens. 99 Main St., Bristol, CT 06010. TEL 203-236-3571; FAX 203-236-0490. **Owner(s):** Journal Register Co., 50 W. State St., 12th Fl., Trenton, NJ 08608. TEL 609-396-2200; Ed. Lynn Woike. adv. contact: Frank G. Chilinski. photos; bk.rev.; pub. size: tabloid; circ. 1,750(paid).

US   ISSN 0745-0796
NEWINGTON TOWN CRIER. 1959. Fri. $.75 newsstand; $17/6 mos.; $25/yr.; $20/yr. senior citizens. 99 Main St., Bristol, CT 06010. TEL 203-236-3571; FAX 203-236-0490. **Owner(s):** Journal Register Co., 50 W. State St., 12th Fl., Trenton, NJ 08608. TEL 609-396-2200; Ed. Linda Levinson; Pub. James S. Normandin; adv. contact: Julianne Scott. photos; bk.rev.; pub. size: tabloid; circ. 2,800(paid).

US
WINDSOR LOCKS JOURNAL. 1880. Fri. $.75 newsstand; $25/yr. 99 Main St., Bristol, CT 06010. TEL 203-236-3571; FAX 203-236-0490. **Owner(s):** Imprint, Inc., 99 Main St., Bristol, CT 06010. TEL 203-236-3571; FAX 203-236-0490; Ed. Linda Tishler Levinson; Pub. Jim Normandin; adv. contact: Michael Moses. photos; bk.rev.; pub. size: tabloid; circ. 1,320(paid).

BROOKFIELD

US
BROOKFIELD JOURNAL. 1957. Fri. $.75 newsstand; $29.95/yr. in cy.; $39.95/yr. out of cy.; $36.95/yr. out of state; $22/yr. senior citizens. P.O. Box 268, Brookfield, CT 06804. TEL 203-775-2533; FAX 203-354-2645. **Owner(s):** Housatonic Valley Publishing Co., P.O. Box 1139, New Milford, CT 06776. TEL 860-354-2261; Ed. Jan Howard; Pub. Walter Rothschild, III; adv. contact: Stephanie Knowles. photos; pub. size: broadsheet; circ. 2,687(paid).

CHESHIRE

US
CHESHIRE HERALD. 1953. Thu. $.45 newsstand; $18/yr. in cy.; $26/yr. out of cy. 125 Commerce Ct., Unit 11, Cheshire, CT 06410. TEL 203-272-5316; FAX 203-250-7145. **Owner(s):** Joseph & Maureen Jakubisyn, 125 Grandview Ave., Wallingford, CT 06492; Ed. Clark Hammersley; Pub. Joseph Jakubisyn; adv. contact: Joseph Jakubisyn. pub. size: tabloid; circ. 6,800(paid).

CROMWELL

US
CROMWELL CHRONICLE. 1986. Fri. $15/yr. 615 Main St., Cromwell, CT 06416. TEL 860-635-1819; FAX 860-632-7203. **Owner(s):** Chronicle Communications, 615 Main St., Cromwell, CT 06416. TEL 860-635-1819; FAX 860-632-7203; Ed. Ron Nolan. photos; bk.rev.; pub. size: tabloid; circ. 2,000(controlled).

DARIEN

US   ISSN 0744-3862
DARIEN NEWS REVIEW. 1973. Thu. $.50 newsstand; $15/yr. in cy. Six Squab Ln., Darien, CT 06820. TEL 203-655-7476; FAX 203-655-1442. **Owner(s):** Brooks Community Newspapers, Inc., 542 Westport Ave., Norwalk, CT 06880. TEL 203-849-1600; Ed. Timothy Mahin; Pub. B.V. Brooks; pub. size: tabloid; circ. 8,000(paid).

EAST HARTFORD

US   ISSN 8750-9156
EAST HARTFORD GAZETTE, THE. 1885. Fri. free in town; $.35 newsstand; $20/yr. out of town. 1171 Main St., East Hartford, CT 06108. TEL 203-289-6468; FAX 203-289-6469. **Owner(s):** Journal Register Co., One Herald Sq., New Britain, CT 06040. TEL 203-225-4601; FAX 203-289-6469; Ed. William A. Doak; Pub. James F. Normandin; adv. contact: Mark Lane. photos; bk.rev.; pub. size: tabloid; circ. 19,678(controlled & paid).

ENFIELD

US
ENFIELD PRESS. 1880. Thu. $.50 newsstand; $20/yr. in state; $32/yr. out of state; $17/yr. senior citizens. P.O. Box 1141, Enfield, CT 06083. TEL 203-745-3348; FAX 203-745-8622. **Owner(s):** Westfield Evening News, P.O. Box 1141, Enfield, CT 06083. TEL 203-745-3348; Ed. Frank Poirot; Pub. Carol Mazza; adv. contact: Martha Baillargeon. pub. size: tabloid; circ. 2,000(paid).

FAIRFIELD

US   ISSN 0191-5134
FAIRFIELD CITIZEN NEWS. 1973. s-w.: Wed. & Fri. $.50 newsstand; $25/yr. in state; $35/yr. out of state. 220 Carter Henry Dr., Fairfield, CT 06430. TEL 203-255-4561; FAX 203-255-0456. **Owner(s):** B.V. Brooks, 542 Westport Ave., Norwalk, CT 06851. TEL 203-849-1600; Ed. Laura A. Nailen; Pub. B.V. Brooks; pub. size: tabloid; circ. 14,200(paid).

GEORGETOWN

US
REDDING PILOT, THE. 1966. Thu. $.75 newsstand; $30/yr. in cy.; $35/yr. out of cy.; $18/yr. military; $20/yr. students. 3 Main St., Georgetown, CT 06829. TEL 203-544-9519; FAX 203-544-9153. **Owner(s):** Acorn Press, Inc., 16 Bailey Ave., Ridgefield, CT 06877. TEL 203-438-6544; FAX 203-438-6014; Ed. Susan Wolf; Pub. Thomas Nash; adv.; photos; pub. size: broadsheet; circ. 2,233(free & paid). **Wire Service(s):** AP.

GLASTONBURY

US
GLASTONBURY CITIZEN. 1950. Thu. $.75 newsstand; $20/yr. in cy.; $24/yr. out of cy. 87 Nutmeg Ln., Glastonbury, CT 06033. TEL 203-633-4691; FAX 203-657-3258. **Owner(s):** Hallas Family, 1510 Main St., Glastonbury, CT 06033. TEL 203-633-4691; Ed. Kathleen Stack; Pub. James Hallas; adv. contact: Carole Saucier. pub. size: tabloid; circ. 8,900(paid).

US
RIVER EAST NEWS BULLETIN. 1984. Fri. free. 87 Nutmeg Ln., Glastonbury, CT 06033. TEL 203-633-4691; FAX 203-657-3258. **Owner(s):** Hallas Family, 1510 Main St., Glastonbury, CT 06033. TEL 203-633-4691; Ed. James Hallas; Pub. James Hallas; adv. contact: Carole Saucier. photos; pub. size: tabloid; circ. 23,000(free).

GREENWICH

US
▼**GREENWICH POST.** 1996. w. free. 22 W. Putnam Ave., Greenwich, CT 06830. TEL 203-861-9191. **Owner(s):** Hagedorn Communications, New Rochelle, NY;

HARTFORD

US   ISSN 0192-8503
HARTFORD ADVOCATE. 1973. Thu. free newsstand; $60/yr. mailed in US. 100 Constitution Plz., Hartford, CT 06103. TEL 860-548-9300; FAX 860-548-9335. **Owner(s):** New Mass Media, Inc., 87 School St., Hatfield, MA 01038. TEL 413-247-9301; Ed. Russ Hoyle; Pub. Francis Zankowski; adv. contact: Rosemary Olson. pub. size: tabloid; circ. 60,000(paid).

KENT

US
KENT GOOD TIMES DISPATCH. 1988. Fri. $.75 newsstand; $19.95/yr. in cy.; $29.95/yr. out of state. 14 Main St., Kent, CT 06757. TEL 860-927-4621; FAX 860-927-4622. **Owner(s):** Housatonic Valley Publishing Co., P.O. Box 1139, New Milford, CT 06776. TEL 860-354-2261; Ed. Lesly Ferris; Pub. Walter Rothschild; adv.; photos; pub. size: broadsheet; circ. 1,467(free & paid).

LAKEVILLE

US
LAKEVILLE JOURNAL, THE. 1897. Thu. $.75 newsstand; $27.50/yr. local. 33 Bissell St., Lakeville, CT 06039. TEL 860-435-9873; FAX 860-435-0146. **Owner(s):** Lakeville Journal Co., LLC, 33 Bissell St., Lakeville, CT 06039. TEL 203-435-9873; Ed. Kathryn Boughton; Pub. Robert A. Hatch; adv. contact: Anna Mae Kupferer. photos; pub. size: broadsheet; circ. 10,000(paid).

LITCHFIELD

US
LITCHFIELD ENQUIRER. 1825. Thu. $.75 newsstand; $29.95/yr. in cy.; $39.95/yr. in state; $41.95/yr. out of state. 43 West St., Litchfield, CT 06759. TEL 860-567-8766; FAX 860-354-2645. **Owner(s):** Housatonic Valley Publishing Co., P.O. Box 1139, New Milford, CT 06776. TEL 203-354-2261; Ed. Susan Pronovost; Pub. Walter Rothschild; adv.; photos; pub. size: broadsheet; circ. 7,730(free & paid).

MILFORD

US

CHRONICLE, THE. Thu. $16/yr. in cy.; $55/yr. out of cy. 349 New Haven Ave., Milford, CT 06516. TEL 203-876-6800; FAX 203-876-6800; E-mail: chron@neca.com; URL: http://www.thechronicle.com. **Owner(s):** Journal Register Co., 50 W. State St., 12th Fl., Trenton, NJ 08608. TEL 609-396-2200; Pub. William R. Rush; adv. contact: Ann Barnhart. circ. 8,000(free & paid).

US

EAST HAVEN ADVERTISER. Sat. $18/yr. 349 New Haven Ave., Milford, CT 06460. TEL 203-933-1000; FAX 203-876-6800. **Owner(s):** Journal Register Co., 50 W. State St., 12th Fl., Trenton, NJ 08608. TEL 609-396-2200; Ed. Cindy Boynton. circ. 3,300(free & paid).

US

NORTH HAVEN WOLLINGTON POST, THE. Thu. free; $16/yr. 349 New Haven Ave., Milford, CT 06516. TEL 203-933-1000; FAX 203-876-6800. **Owner(s):** Journal Register Co., 50 W. State St., 12th Fl., Trenton, NJ 08608. TEL 609-396-2200; Ed. Leslie Drost. circ. evening 4,000(free & paid).

US

ORANGE BULLETIN. Thu. free; $10/yr. 349 New Haven Ave., Milford, CT 06440. TEL 203-933-1000; FAX 203-876-6800. **Owner(s):** Journal Register Co., 50 W. State St., 12th Fl., Trenton, NJ 08608. TEL 609-396-2200; circ. evening 4,400(free & paid).

US   ISSN 1077-0844

STRATFORD BARD. 1970. Fri. $18/yr. in state; $50/yr. out of state. 349 New Haven Ave., Milford, CT 06460. TEL 203-876-6800; FAX 203-877-4772. **Owner(s):** Journal Register Co., 50 W. State St., 12th Fl., Trenton, NJ 08608. TEL 609-396-2200; pub. size: tabloid; circ. 17,000(free).

US

WEST HAVEN NEWS. 1931. Sat. $.35 newsstand & carrier. 349 New Haven Ave., Milford, CT 06460. TEL 203-876-6800; FAX 203-877-4772. **Owner(s):** Journal Register Co., 50 W. State St., 12th Fl., Trenton, NJ 08608. TEL 609-396-2200; pub. size: tabloid; circ. 9,000(paid).

MONROE

US

MONROE COURIER. 1965. Wed. $10/yr. P.O. Box 332, Monroe, CT 06468-0332. TEL 203-268-6234. **Owner(s):** Hometown Publications, Inc., P.O. Box 216, Monroe, CT 06468. TEL 203-268-6234; Pub. Ben Gumm; pub. size: broadsheet; circ. 4,000(paid). **Wire Service(s):** AP.

US

TRUMBULL TIMES. 1958. Thu. $.50 newsstand; $24.50/yr. in town; $30/yr. out of town. 6515 Main St., Monroe, CT 06611. TEL 203-268-6234. **Owner(s):** Hometown Publications Co., Milwaukee, WI; Ed. Tom Ebersold; Pub. Ben Gumm; adv.; pub. size: broadsheet; circ. 7,800(paid).

NEW CANAAN

US

NEW CANAAN ADVERTISER. 1908. Thu. $.70 newsstand; $28/yr. in state. 42 Vitti St., New Canaan, CT 06840. TEL 203-966-9541; FAX 203-966-8006. **Owner(s):** Hersam Publishing Co., P.O. Box 605, New Canaan, CT 06840. TEL 203-966-9541; Ed. Ed Chrostowski; Pub. V. Donald Hersam; adv.; pub. size: standard; circ. 7,430(paid).

NEW HAVEN

US   ISSN 0192-8511

NEW HAVEN ADVOCATE. 1975. Thu. $80/yr. One Long Wharf Dr., New Haven, CT 06511-5991. TEL 203-789-0010; FAX 203-787-1418; E-mail: newhadvo@pcnet.com. **Owner(s):** New Mass Media, Inc., 87 School St., Hatfield, MA 01038. TEL 413-247-9301; FAX 413-247-5439; Ed. Joshua Mamis; Pub. Gail Thompson; adv.; bk.rev.; pub. size: tabloid; circ. 55,000(free & paid).

NEW MILFORD

US

HOUSATONIC WEEKEND. 1948. Sat. free carrier. 132 Danbury Rd., New Milford, CT 06776. TEL 860-354-2261; FAX 860-354-2645. **Owner(s):** Housatonic Valley Publishing Co., P.O. Box 1139, New Milford, CT 06776. TEL 860-354-2261; Pub. Walter Rothschild; pub. size: tabloid; circ. 25,000(free).
Formerly: Advertiser, The.

US   ISSN 0028-6338

NEW MILFORD TIMES. 1914. Fri. $.75 newsstand; $29.95/yr. in cy.; $39.95/yr. in state; $41.95/yr. out of state. 132 Danbury Rd., New Milford, CT 06776. TEL 860-354-2261; FAX 860-354-2645. **Owner(s):** Housatonic Valley Publishing Co., P.O. Box 1139, New Milford, CT 06776. TEL 860-354-2261; Pub. Walter Rothchild; adv.; photos; pub. size: broadsheet; circ. 8,607(free & paid).

NEWTOWN

US

NEWTOWN BEE, THE. 1877. Fri. $.50 newsstand; $24/yr. 5 Church Hill Rd., Newtown, CT 06470. TEL 203-426-3141; FAX 203-426-1394. **Owner(s):** R. Scudder Smith, 5 Church Hill Rd., P.O. Box 5503, Newtown, CT 06470. TEL 203-426-3141; FAX 203-426-1394; Ed. R. Scudder Smith; Pub. R. Scudder Smith; pub. size: broadsheet; circ. 8,300(paid).

OLD SAYBROOK

US   ISSN 0886-6112

CLINTON RECORDER. 1900. s-w.: Tue. & Sat. $.50 newsstand; $26/yr. in cy.; $50/yr. out of cy. P.O. Drawer O, Old Saybrook, CT 06475. TEL 203-388-3441; FAX 203-388-5613. **Owner(s):** Journal Register Co., 50 W. State St., 12th Fl., Trenton, NJ 08608. TEL 609-396-2200; Ed. Karen Barretta; Pub. William Rush; pub. size: tabloid; circ. 5,000(paid).

US

PICTORIAL GAZETTE. s-w.: Tue. & Sat. $.50 newsstand; $32/yr. in cy.; $55/yr. out of cy. 162 Main St., Old Saybrook, CT 06475. TEL 203-388-3441; FAX 203-388-5613. **Owner(s):** Journal Register Co., 50 W. State St., 12th Fl., Trenton, NJ 08608. TEL 609-396-2200; Ed. Doreen Madden; Pub. William Rush; pub. size: standard; circ. 10,000(paid).

RIDGEFIELD

US

LEWISBORO LEDGER, THE. 1976. Thu. $30/yr. in cy.; $35/yr. out of cy. 16 Bailey Ave., Ridgefield, CT 06877. TEL 203-438-6545; FAX 203-438-3395. **Owner(s):** Acorn Press, Inc., 16 Bailey Ave., Ridgefield, CT 06877. TEL 203-763-8281; Pub. Thomas B. Nash; adv. contact: James DeFillipo. pub. size: broadsheet; circ. 2,077(paid). **Wire Service(s):** AP.

US

RIDGEFIELD PRESS, THE. 1875. Thu. $.75 newsstand; $30/yr. 16 Bailey Ave., Ridgefield, CT 06877. TEL 203-438-6514. E-mail: acorr@composerve.com. **Owner(s):** Acorn Press, Inc., 16 Bailey Ave., Ridgefield, CT 06877. TEL 203-438-6544; Ed. Mackin Reid; Pub. Thomas B. Nash; adv. contact: James DeFillipo. pub. size: broadsheet; circ. 7,010(paid). **Wire Service(s):** AP.

SHELTON

US

VALLEY GAZETTE. 1992. Wed. free mailed in area; $.50 newsstand. 1000 Bridgeport Ave., Shelton, CT 06484. TEL 203-926-2080; FAX 203-926-2091. **Owner(s):** Hometown Publications, Inc., 1000 Bridgeport Ave., Shelton, CT 06484. TEL 203-926-2080; FAX 203-926-2091; Ed. Nick Povinelli; Pub. Ben Gumm; adv. contact: Sally McLoran. photos; pub. size: broadsheet; circ. 15,000(free & paid).

SOUTHBURY

US   ISSN 0193-1474

VOICES. 1968. Wed. $.75 newsstand. P.O. Box 383, Southbury, CT 06488. TEL 203-263-2116; FAX 203-266-0199. **Owner(s):** Rudy Mazurosky, P. O. Box 383, Southbury, CT 06488. TEL 203-263-2116; Ed. Patty Wesley; Pub. Rudy Mazurosky; pub. size: tabloid; circ. 27,000(paid).
Formerly: Southbury Voices.

SOUTHINGTON

US

SOUTHINGTON OBSERVER. 1975. Thu. $.75 newsstand; $18/yr. local. 213 Spring St., Southington, CT 06489. TEL 860-621-6751; FAX 860-621-1841. **Owner(s):** Anthony L. Urillo, 213 Spring St., Southington, CT 06489. TEL 203-628-9645; FAX 203-621-1841; Pub. Anthony L. Urillo; adv.; photos; bk.rev.; pub. size: broadsheet; circ. 5,666(paid).

STAMFORD

US

FAIRFIELD COUNTY WEEKLY. 1979. Thu. free newsstand; $80/yr. mailed. One Dock St., Ste. 5L, Stamford, CT 06902-5838. TEL 203-406-2406; FAX 203-406-1099. **Owner(s):** New Mass Media, Inc., 50 Prospect St., Hatfield, MA 01038. TEL 413-247-9301; Ed. Lorraine Gengo; Pub. Barbara Hess; adv. contact: Kevin Heslin. photos; pub. size: tabloid; circ. 70,000(free & paid).
Formerly: Fairfield County Advocate.

VERNON

US

REMINDER, THE. 1949. Tue. free carrier. 130 Old Town Rd., Vernon, CT 06066-2156. TEL 860-875-3366; FAX 860-875-2089. **Owner(s):** Kenneth Hovland, Sr., P.O. Box 210, Vernon Rockville, CT 06066. TEL 203-872-8515; Ed. Kenneth Hovland, Jr.; Pub. Kenneth Hovland, Jr.; adv. contact: Doug Sabian. pub. size: tabloid; circ. 130,000(free).

WEST HARTFORD

US

WEST HARTFORD NEWS. 1931. Thu. $15/6 mos.; $26/yr. 20 Isham Rd., West Hartford, CT 06107. TEL 203-236-3571; FAX 203-236-0490. **Owner(s):** Journal Register Co., 50 W. State St., 12th Fl., Trenton, NJ 08608. TEL 609-396-2200; Ed. Keith Giffin; Pub. James Normandin; adv. contact: Julianne Scott. photos; pub. size: tabloid; circ. 11,000(paid).

US

WETHERSFIELD POST. 1959. Fri. $.75 newsstand; $25/yr.; $20/yr. senior citizens. 20 Isham Rd., West Hartford, CT 06127. TEL 203-236-3571; FAX 203-236-0490. **Owner(s):** Journal Register Co., 50 W. State St., 12th Fl., Trenton, NJ 08608. TEL 609-396-2200; Ed. Melanie Winters; Pub. Jim Normandin; adv. contact: Julianne Scott. photos; bk.rev.; pub. size: tabloid; circ. 3,700(paid).

US

WINDSOR JOURNAL. 1973. Fri. $.75 newsstand; $25/yr.; $20/yr. senior citizens. 20 Isham Rd., West Hartford, CT 06107. TEL 203-236-3571; FAX 203-233-2080. **Owner(s):** Journal Register Co., 50 W. State St., 12th Fl., Trenton, NJ 08608. TEL 609-396-2200; Ed. Laurie Slye; Pub. James Normandin; adv. contact: Penny Carrol. photos; bk.rev.; pub. size: tabloid; circ. 2,263(paid).

WESTON

US

WESTON FORUM, THE. 1970. Wed. $.50 newsstand; $20-$25/yr. out of town. P.O. Box 1185, Weston, CT 06883. TEL 203-544-9990; FAX 203-544-9153. **Owner(s):** Acorn Press, Inc., 16 Bailey Ave., Ridgefield, CT 06877. TEL 203-438-6544; Ed. Sybil Blau; Pub. Thomas B. Nash; adv. contact: James DeFillipo. photos; pub. size: broadsheet; circ. 3,500(controlled & paid). **Wire Service(s):** AP.

WESTPORT

US

WESTPORT NEWS. 1964. s-w.: Wed. & Fri. $.50 newsstand; $29/yr.; $20/yr. senior citizens. 136 Main St., Westport, CT 06880. TEL 203-226-6311; FAX 203-454-2765; E-mail: bcnnews3@netaxis.com; URL: http://www.townline.com/brooks/westport/news/latenews.htm. **Owner(s):** B.V. Brooks, 136 Main St., Westport, CT 06880. TEL 203-849-1600; Ed. Gary Larkin; Pub. B.V. Brooks; adv. contact: Cindy Withers. photos; bk.rev.; pub. size: tabloid; circ. 15,000(paid).

WILTON

US

WILTON BULLETIN. 1937. Wed. $.75 newsstand; $30/yr. in cy.; $35/yr. out of cy. 196 Danbury Rd., Wilton, CT 06897. TEL 203-762-5857; FAX 203-438-3395. **Owner(s):** Acorn Press, Inc., 16 Bailey Ave., Ridgefield, CT 06877. TEL 203-438-6544; Ed. Greg Bartlett; Pub. Thomas B. Nash; adv. contact: Jim DeFillipo. pub. size: broadsheet; circ. 4,500(paid). **Wire Service(s):** AP.

DELAWARE

BETHANY BEACH

US

DELAWARE WAVE. 1936. Wed. free; $35/yr. mailed 3rd class. Rte. 1, Lem Hickman Plz., Bethany Beach, DE 19930. TEL 302-537-1881; FAX 302-537-9705. **Owner(s):** Thomson Newspapers, Inc., Metro Ctr., One Station Pl., Stamford, CT 06902. TEL 203-425-2500; Ed. Steve Hoenigham; Pub. John Backe; adv. contact: Susan Lyons. photos; pub. size: tabloid; circ. 12,500(free).

GEORGETOWN

US

SUSSEX COUNTIAN. 1886. Wed. $.35 newsstand; $16/yr. in state; $20/yr. out of state. 115 N. Race St., Georgetown, DE 19947. TEL 302-856-0026; FAX 302-856-0925. **Owner(s):** Robert H. Robinson Family, P.O. Box 40, Georgetown, DE 19947. TEL 302-856-0026; Pub. Dover Post; adv.; photos; pub. size: tabloid; circ. 4,300(free & paid). **Formerly:** Georgetown Sussex Countian.

HARRINGTON

US

HARRINGTON JOURNAL, THE. 1913. Wed. $.35 newsstand; $15/yr. in state; $17/yr. out of state. 110 Center St., Harrington, DE 19952. TEL 302-398-3206; FAX 302-398-3824. **Owner(s):** Independent Newspapers, Inc., P.O. Box 7001, Dover, DE 19903. TEL 302-674-4750; Ed. Carol Ann Porter. adv. contact: Helen Downing. pub. size: broadsheet; circ. 3,000(paid).

LEWES

US

SUSSEX POST, THE. 1972. Wed. free newsstand; $13/yr. in cy.; $16/yr. elsewhere. Midway Shopping Ctr., Lewes, DE 19958. TEL 302-934-9261; FAX 302-934-8590. **Owner(s):** Independent Newspapers, Inc., P.O. Box 7001, Dover, DE 19903. TEL 800-282-8586; Ed. Andrew West; Pub. Tamra Brittingham; adv.; photos; pub. size: broadsheet; circ. 18,500(free & paid).

MILFORD

US

CHRONICLE, THE. 1878. Wed. $.50 newsstand; $18/yr. in cy.; $27/yr. elsewhere; $16/yr. senior citizens. 10 S.W. Front St., Milford, DE 19963. TEL 302-422-1200. **Owner(s):** Independent Newspapers, Inc., P.O. Box 7001, Dover, DE 19903. TEL 800-282-8586; Ed. Rosanne Pack; Pub. Rosanne Pack; adv.; pub. size: broadsheet; circ. 8,500(paid).

NEWARK

US   ISSN 1056-7658

NEWARK POST. 1910. Fri. $.50 newsstand; $15.95/yr. 153 E. Chestnut Hill Rd., Newark, DE 19713. TEL 302-737-0724; FAX 302-737-9109. **Owner(s):** Chesapeake Publishing Corp., One Airpark Dr., Easton, MD 21601. TEL 410-398-3311; FAX 410-398-4044; Ed. David G.W. Scott; Pub. James Streit; adv. contact: Tina Winmill. photos; bk.rev.; pub. size: tabloid; circ. 12,000(paid). **Formerly:** Newark Weekly Post.

REHOBOTH BEACH

US

DELAWARE BEACHCOMBER. 1968. Fri. free. P.O. Box 309, Rehoboth Beach, DE 19971. TEL 302-227-9466; FAX 302-227-9469; E-mail: dcp@dmv.com. **Owner(s):** Thomson Newspapers, Inc., Metro Ctr., One Station Pl., Stamford, CT 06902. TEL 203-425-2500; Ed. Terry Plowman. adv.; photos; bk.rev.; pub. size: tabloid; circ. 12,000(free).

US   ISSN 0740-2023

DELAWARE COAST PRESS. 1899. Wed. free newsstand; $35/yr. in cy. 3719 Highway One, Rehoboth Beach, DE 19971. TEL 302-227-9466; FAX 302-227-9469. **Owner(s):** Thomson Newspapers, Inc., Metro Ctr. 50, One Station Pl., Stamford, CT 06902. TEL 203-425-2500; Ed. Terry Plowman. adv.; photos; pub. size: tabloid; circ. 11,000(free).

SEAFORD

US

LEADER-STATE REGISTER, THE. 1890. s-w.: Wed. & Fri. $.50 newsstand; $23.50/yr. in cy.; $35/yr. elsewhere; $21/9 mos. students. 616 Water St., Seaford, DE 19973. TEL 302-629-5505; FAX 302-629-6700. **Owner(s):** Independent Newspapers, Inc., P.O. Box 7001, Dover, DE 19903. TEL 800-282-8586; Ed. Andrew West; Pub. Andrew West; adv.; pub. size: broadsheet; circ. 10,000(paid). **Formerly:** Seaford Leader-State Register.

WILMINGTON

US

WILMINGTON DEFENDER. 1962. Wed. $25/yr. 1702 Locust St., Wilmington, DE 19802. TEL 302-656-3252; FAX 302-471-1130. **Owner(s):** Wilmington Defender, 1702 Locust St., Wilmington, DE 19802; FAX 302-471-1130; Ed. A.G. Hibbert. photos; bk.rev.; pub. size: tabloid; circ. 8,000(free & paid).

DISTRICT OF COLUMBIA

WASHINGTON

US

CAPITAL SPOTLIGHT. 1936. Thu. $30/yr. 529 14th St., N.W., Ste. 2101, Washington, DC 20045. TEL 202-745-7858; FAX 202-745-7860. **Owner(s):** Bette Brooks, 529 14th St. N.W., Ste. 2101, Washington, DC 20045. TEL 202-483-4174; Ed. Bette Brook. adv.; bk.rev.; pub. size: tabloid; circ. 50,000(paid).

US

GEORGETOWN CURRENT, THE. 1967. Wed. $16/yr. 5125 McArthur Blvd., N.W., Washington, DC 20016. TEL 202-244-7223. **Owner(s):** Current Newspapers, Inc., 5125 McArthur Blvd., N.W., Washington, DC 20016. TEL 202-244-7223; Ed. Chris Kain; Pub. Davis Kennedy; adv.; photos; pub. size: tabloid; circ. 34,000(controlled & free).

US ISSN 0730-9082

GEORGETOWNER, THE. 1954. bi-w.: Fri. free. 1610 Wisconsin Ave., N.W., Washington, DC 20007. TEL 202-338-4833; FAX 202-342-0751. **Owner(s):** David Roffman, 1610 Wisconsin Ave., N.W., Washington, DC 20007. TEL 202-338-4833; FAX 202-342-0751; Ed. Gary Tishler; Pub. David Roffman; adv. contact: Karen Kemp. photos; bk.rev.; pub. size: tabloid; circ. 15,000(controlled & free).

US

NORTHWEST CURRENT, THE. 1967. Wed. $16/yr. 5125 McArthur Blvd., N.W., Washington, DC 20016. TEL 202-244-7223. **Owner(s):** Current Newspapers, Inc., 5125 McArthur Blvd., N.W., Washington, DC 20016. TEL 202-244-7223; Ed. Chris Kain; Pub. Davis Kennedy; adv.; photos; pub. size: tabloid; circ. 32,500(controlled).

US

ROCKCREEK CURRENT, THE. 1967. Wed. $16/yr. 5125 McArthur Blvd., N.W., Washington, DC 20016. TEL 202-244-7223. **Owner(s):** Current Newspapers, Inc., 5125 McArthur Blvd., N.W., Washington, DC 20016. TEL 202-244-7223; Ed. Chris Kain; Pub. Davis Kennedy; adv.; photos; pub. size: tabloid; circ. 32,500(controlled).

US

SPOTLIGHT, THE. 1955. Fri. $.85 newsstand; $38/yr. mailed. 300 Independence Ave., S.E., Washington, DC 20003. TEL 202-544-1794. **Owner(s):** Liberty Lobby, 300 Independence Ave., S.E., Washington, DC 20003. TEL 202-544-1794; Ed. Paul Croke. adv. contact: James Wolfington. pub. size: tabloid; circ. 100,000(paid).

US

WASHINGTON CITY PAPER. 1981. w. free newsstand; $35/yr. 2390 Camplain St, N.W., Washington, DC 20009. TEL 202-332-2100; FAX 202-462-8323. **Owner(s):** Tom Yoder, 11 E. Illinois St., Chicago, IL 60611. TEL 312-828-0350; Robert Roth, 11 E. Illinois St., Chicago, IL 60611. TEL 312-828-0350; Robert McCamant, 11 E. Illinois St., Chicago, IL 60611. TEL 312-828-0350; Ed. David Carr. adv. contact: Amy Austin. photos bk.rev.; pub. size: tabloid.

FEDERATED STATES OF MICRONESIA

EASTERN CAROLINE ISLANDS

US

NATIONAL UNION. 1930. m. $8/yr. newsstand local; $12/yr. elsewhere. P.O. Box PS34, Palikir, Pohnpei, Eastern Caroline Islands, FM 96941. TEL 691-320-2543; FAX 691-320-4356. **Owner(s):** FSM Information, P.O. Box PS34, Palikir, Pohnpei, Eastern Caroline Islands, FM 96941. TEL 691-320-2548; FAX 691-320-4356; pub. size: tabloid; circ. 5,000(controlled & free).

FLORIDA

ARCADIA

US

ARCADIAN, THE. 1925. Wed. free; $14.45/yr. mailed. 207 W. Oak St., Arcadia, FL 33821. TEL 941-494-2434; FAX 941-494-3533. **Owner(s):** Derrick Dunn-Rankin, 207 W. Oak St., Arcadia, FL 33821. TEL 941-492-2434; FAX 941-494-3533; Ed. Wade Hill. adv. contact: Margaret Turner. pub. size: broadsheet; circ. 9,600(controlled).

AUBURNDALE

US ISSN 0745-8363

CANADA NEWS. 1982. w.: Nov.-Apr. $1.25 newsstand; $32.50/26 wks. P.O. Box 1729, Auburndale, FL 33823. TEL 941-967-6450; FAX 941-967-1954. **Owner(s):** Canada News, P.O. Box 1729, Auburndale, FL. TEL 813-967-6450; FAX 813-967-1954; Ed. Joe Braddy; Pub. William Leeder; adv. contact: Andy Steinbergs. pub. size: tabloid; circ. 17,213(controlled & paid).

BARTOW

US

POLK COUNTY DEMOCRAT, THE. 1931. s-w.: Mon. & Thu. $.25 newsstand; $27.50/yr. out of cy.; $30/yr. out of state; $20/yr. in Polk County. 190 S. Florida Ave., Bartow, FL 33830-4701. TEL 941-533-4183; FAX 941-533-0402. **Owner(s):** Frisbie Publishing Co., Inc., P.O. Box 120, Bartow, FL 33831-0120. TEL 813-533-4183; FAX 813-533-0402; Ed. S.L. Frisbie, IV; Pub. S.L. Frisbie, IV; adv.; pub. size: broadsheet; circ. 4,336(free & paid).

BELLEVIEW

US

BELLEVIEW VOICE OF SOUTH MARION. 1969. Wed. $10/yr. in cy.; $18/yr. out of cy 11412 S.E. US 301, Belleview, FL 32620 TEL 352-245-3161. **Owner(s):** Jim Waldron, P.O. Box 700, Belleview, FL 32620. TEL 352-245-3161; Ed. Sandy Waldron; Pub. Jim Waldron; pub. size: tabloid; circ. 1,741(paid).

BOKEELIA

US

PINE ISLAND EAGLE. 1976. Wed. free home deliv.; $30/yr. mailed out of state. 10700 Stringfellow Rd., Ste. 60, Bokeelia, FL 33922. TEL 941-283-2022; FAX 941-283-0232. **Owner(s):** Breeze Corp., 10700 Stringfellow Rd., Ste. 60, Bokeelia, FL 33922. TEL 941-283-2022; Ed. Dave Holmes. pub. size: tabloid; circ. 8,500(free & paid).

BONIFAY

US

HOLMES COUNTY ADVERTISER. 1892. Wed. $.50 newsstand; $20/yr. 112 E. Virginia Ave., Bonifay, FL 32425. TEL 904-547-2270; FAX 904-547-9200. **Owner(s):** Larry Woodham, 112 W. Virginia Ave., Bonifay, FL 32425. TEL 904-547-2770; Ed. Katy Foster; Pub. Larry Woodham; pub. size: broadsheet; circ. 4,200(paid).

BONITA SPRINGS

US ISSN 0191-5479

BONITA BANNER. 1959. s-w.: Wed. & Sat. $.25 newsstand; $26/6 mos. $41.60/yr. 9102 Bonita Beach Rd., Bonita Springs, FL 33923. TEL 813-992-2110; FAX 813-992-7819. **Owner(s):** Scripps-Howard, Cincinnati, OH 45234; Ed. Cathy Cottrill. adv.; pub. size: broadsheet; circ. 30,000(paid). **Wire Service(s):** SHNA.

BRANDON

US

BRANDON NEWS, THE. 1957. Wed free. 1401 Oakfield Dr., Brandon, FL 33511-2800. TEL 813-689-7764; FAX 813-689-9545. **Owner(s):** Media General, Inc., 411 E. Franklin St., Richmond, VA 23219. TEL 804-775-8030; Ed. D'Ann White. adv. contact: Susie Howell. photos; pub. size: tabloid circ. 38,595(free).

US

▼**SOUTH TAMPA NEWS.** 1994. Wed. free. 1401 Oakfield Dr., Brandon, FL 33511-4854. TEL 813-664-0264. **Owner(s):** Media General, Inc., 333 E. Grace St., Richmond, VA 23219. TEL 804-649-6000; FAX 804-649-6898; Ed. Russell Holecek. adv. contact: Leigh Humes. pub. size: tabloid; circ. 30,000(free).

US

TEMPLE TERRACE NEWS. 1988. Wed. free. 1401 Oakfield Dr., Brandon, FL 33511-4854. TEL 813-689-7764; FAX 813-689-9545. **Owner(s):** Media General, Inc., 333 E. Grace St., Richmond, VA 23219. TEL 804-649-6000; FAX 804-649-6898; Ed. Lee Laudenberger. adv. contact: Susie Howell. pub. size: tabloid; circ. 12,900(free).

BUSHNELL

US

SUMTER COUNTY TIMES. 1881. Thu. $.35 newsstand; $15.50/yr. 204 E. McCollum Ave., Bushnell, FL 33513. TEL 904-793-2161; FAX 904-793-1486. **Owner(s):** Landmark Community Newspapers, Inc., P.O. Box 549, Shelbyville, KY 40066. TEL 502-633-4334; FAX 502-633-0852; Ed. Bob Reichman. adv.; photos; pub. size: broadsheet; circ. 4,500(paid).

CALLAHAN

US

NASSAU COUNTY RECORD. Thu. $.50 newsstand; $16.95/yr. in cy.; $23.54/yr. out of cy. 213 W. Brandies Ave., Callahan, FL 32011. TEL 904-879-2727; FAX 904-879-5155. **Owner(s):** Nassau County Record, 213 Brandies Ave., Callahan, FL 32011. TEL 904-879-2727; Ed. Winn Hardin; Pub. Jennifer Wise; adv. contact: Candy Wingo. photos; bk.rev.; pub. size: standard; circ. 4,500(paid).

CEDAR

US

CEDAR KEY BEACON. 1984. Thu. $.50 newsstand; $25/yr. in state; $25/yr. out of state. 6050 D St., Cedar, FL 32625-0998. TEL 904-543-5701; FAX 904-543-5928. **Owner(s):** Advertising Design, Inc., P.O. Box 532, Cedar Key, FL 32625. TEL 904-543-5701; FAX 904-543-5928; Ed. Connie Raftis; Pub. Michael J. Raftis; adv.; photos; bk.rev.; pub. size: tabloid; circ. 1,500(paid).

CHATTAHOOCHEE

US   ISSN 0889-2245

TWIN CITY NEWS, THE. 1964. Thu. $.30 newsstand; $15.50/yr. in cy.; $18.85/yr. elsewhere. 314 Washington St., Chattahoochee, FL 32324. TEL 904-663-2255; FAX 904-663-8102. **Owner(s):** Will I. Ramsey, Sr., 620 Morgan Ave., Chattahoochee, FL 32324. TEL 904-663-2525; FAX 904-663-2255; Ed. Stanley J. Ramsey; Pub. Stanley J. Ramsey; adv.; photos; pub. size: broadsheet; circ. 2,000(paid).

CLEWISTON

US

CLEWISTON NEWS. 1928. Wed. $16.05/yr. in cy.; $19.36/yr. out of cy. 626 W. Sugarland Hwy., Clewiston, FL 33440. TEL 941-983-9148. **Owner(s):** Joe Smyth, 4308 E. Lakeside Ln., Scottsdale, AZ 85253. TEL 602-991-5333; Ed. Tracy Whirls; Pub. Richard Hitt; adv. contact: Sandra Baker. pub. size: broadsheet; circ. 3,500(paid).

US

GLADES COUNTY DEMOCRAT. 1923. Thu. $19.08/yr. 226 W. Sugarland Hwy., Clewiston, FL 33440. TEL 813-946-0511. **Owner(s):** Independent Newspapers, Inc., P.O. Box 1236, Clewiston, FL 33440. TEL 813-983-9148; Ed. Anne Deuschle; Pub. Richard Hill; pub. size: tabloid; circ. 1,500(paid).

COCOA

US

BREVARD REPORTER, THE. 1981. Thu. $15.90/15 mos. P.O. Box 1928, Cocoa, FL 32923-1928. **Owner(s):** Will Stanley, P.O. Box 1928, Cocoa, FL 32923-1928; Ed. Stacey Schrandt. adv.; photos; pub. size: tabloid; circ. 6,000(paid).

CORAL SPRINGS

US

SUNRISE TIMES. Fri. free. 9660 W. Sample Rd., Ste. 203, Coral Springs, FL 33065. TEL 954-752-7474; FAX 954-752-7855. **Owner(s):** South Florida Newspaper Network, Inc., 601 Fairway Dr., Deerfield Beach, FL 33441. TEL 305-698-6397; FAX 305-698-6719; Ed. Van A. Gosselin; Pub. Suzanne Pemper; adv. contact: Suzanne Pemper. pub. size: tabloid; circ. 25,000(free).

US

TAMARAC FORUM. Fri. free. 9660 W. Sample Rd., Ste. 203, Coral Springs, FL 33065. TEL 305-752-7474; FAX 305-752-7855. **Owner(s):** South Florida Newspaper Network, Inc., 601 Fairway Dr., Deerfield Beach, FL 33441. TEL 305-698-6397; FAX 305-698-6719; Ed. Scott Burgess; Pub. Suzanne Pemper; circ. 25,000(free).

CRAWFORDVILLE

US

WAKULLA NEWS. 1895. Thu. $.50 newsstand; $22/yr. in cy.; $25/yr. out of cy. P.O. Box 307, Crawfordville, FL 32326. TEL 904-926-7102; FAX 904-926-3815. **Owner(s):** Wakulla Publishing Co. Board of Directors, P.O. Box 307, Crawfordville, FL 32326. TEL 904-926-7102; Ed. Shannon P. Turnbull. pub. size: broadsheet; circ. 5,000(paid).

CRESTVIEW

US

BULLETIN, THE. 1975. Wed. free local; $52/yr. mailed. 301 N. Main, Crestview, FL 32536. TEL 904-682-6524; FAX 904-682-2246. **Owner(s):** Jim Knudsen, 301 N. Main St., Crestview, FL 32536. TEL 904-682-2246; Ed. Brenda Drewery; Pub. Jim Knudsen; pub. size: tabloid; circ. 14,500(free & paid).

DADE CITY

US

PASCO NEWS. 1904. Fri. $14.84/yr. in cy.; $20.14/yr. out of cy. 13032 US 301, Dade City, FL 33525. TEL 904-567-5639; FAX 904-567-5640. **Owner(s):** Sunpress Publications, Inc., P.O. Box 187, Dade City, FL 33526. TEL 904-567-5639; FAX 904-567-5640; Ed. June Hamory; Pub. J.W. Owens; adv. contact: Donna Covert. photos; bk.rev.; pub. size: broadsheet; circ. 6,000(paid).

DEERFIELD BEACH

US

BOCA MONDAY. s-w.: Mon. & Thu. free newsstand; $22/3 mos.; $38/6 mos.; $69/yr. 601 Fairway Dr., Deerfield Beach, FL 33441. TEL 305-698-6397; FAX 305-429-1207. **Owner(s):** South Florida Newspaper Network, Inc., 601 Fairway Dr., Deerfield Beach, FL 33441. TEL 305-698-6397; FAX 305-698-6719; Ed. Richard Hayden; Pub. Bruce Warshal; adv. contact: Ron Bukley. photos; bk.rev.; pub. size: tabloid; circ. 26,000(controlled & free). **Wire Service(s):** CNS.

US

BOYNTON BEACH TIMES. 1979. Thu. free newsstand; $75/yr. 601 Fairway Dr., Deerfield Beach, FL 33441. TEL 305-698-6397; FAX 305-429-1207. **Owner(s):** Bruce Warshal & Scott Patterson, 601 Fairway Dr., Deerfield Beach, FL 33441; Ed. Richard Haydan. pub. size: tabloid; circ. 20,000(paid).

US

DEERFIELD BEACH OBSERVER. 1972. Thu. free to residents; $60/yr. out of town. 43 N.E. Second St., Deerfield Beach, FL 33441. TEL 305-428-9045; FAX 305-428-9096. **Owner(s):** Deerfield Publishing, Inc., 43 N.E. Second St., Deerfield Beach, FL 33441. TEL 305-428-9045; Ed. Judith V. Wilson; Pub. David Eller; adv.; photos; bk.rev.; pub. size: tabloid; circ. 30,000(free & paid).

US

DEERFIELD BEACH THURSDAY TIMES. Thu. free newsstand; $22/3 mos. mailed. 601 Fairway Dr., Deerfield Beach, FL 33441. TEL 305-698-6397; FAX 305-698-6719. **Owner(s):** South Florida Newspaper Network, Inc., 601 Fairway Dr., Deerfield, FL 33441. TEL 305-698-6397; Pub. Bruce Warshal; adv.; photos; bk.rev.; pub. size: tabloid; circ. 16,000(controlled & free).

US

DELRAY TIMES. 1980. s-w.: Mon. & Thu. free. 601 Fairway Dr., Deerfield Beach, FL 33441. TEL 954-698-6397; FAX 954-429-1207. **Owner(s):** South Florida Newspaper Network, Inc., 601 Fairway Dr., Deerfield Beach, FL 33487. TEL 954-698-6397; FAX 954-421-9003; Ed. Rick Haydan; Pub. Scott Patterson; adv. contact: Jim Hill. photos; bk.rev.; pub. size: tabloid; circ. 20,000(free). **Wire Service(s):** CNS.
    Formerly: Delray Monday Times.

US   ISSN 0191-7153

HI-RISER. 1967. Thu. free. 601 Fairway Dr., Deerfield Beach, FL 33441. TEL 954-563-3311; FAX 954-563-4230. **Owner(s):** Hi-Riser, 601 Fairway Dr., Deerfield Beach, FL 33441; Ed. Rick Haydan; Pub. Scott Patterson; adv. contact: Christine Beach. bk.rev.; pub. size: tabloid; circ. 35,000(free).

US

WEST BOCA TIMES. Wed. free. 601 Fairway Dr., Deerfield Beach, FL 33441. TEL 954-698-6397; FAX 954-698-6719. **Owner(s):** South Florida Newspaper Network, 601 Fairway Dr., Deerfield Beach, FL 33441. TEL 954-698-6397; FAX 954-698-6719; Ed. Richard Hayden; Pub. Scott Patterson; adv.; photos; bk.rev.; pub. size: tabloid; circ. 20,000(free). **Wire Service(s):** CNS.

DELAND

US

DELAND BEACON, THE. 1992. Wed. $.50 newsstand; $24/yr. 141 E. Indiana Ave., DeLand, FL 32724-0753. TEL 904-734-4622; FAX 904-734-4641. **Owner(s):** Barbara Shepherd, 520 N. Delaware, DeLand, FL 32720. TEL 904-736-0667; FAX 904-734-4641; Eileen Everett, 539 N. Delaware, DeLand, FL 32720. TEL 904-736-3057; FAX 904-734-4641; Joann Kramer, 141 E. Indiana, DeLand, FL 32724. TEL 904-736-5711; FAX 904-734-4641; Ed. Barbara Button. adv. contact: Eileen Everett. photos; pub. size: broadsheet; circ. 4,000(paid).

DESTIN

US

DESTIN LOG. 1974. s-w.: Wed. & Sat. $.50 newsstand; $34.98/yr. in state; $44.45/yr. out of state. 1225 Airport Rd., Destin, FL 32541. TEL 904-837-2828; FAX 904-654-5982. **Owner(s):** Scripps-Howard, Inc., 312 Walnut St., 28th Fl., Cincinnati, OH 45202. TEL 513-977-3000; Ed. Bill Runge; Pub. Michael A. Levi; adv.; pub. size: broadsheet; circ. 8,500(paid).

FERNANDINA

US

NEWS LEADER. 1858. Wed. $.50 newsstand; $19.29/yr. in cy.; $38.58/yr. out of cy. mailed; $36.40/yr. out of state. 511 Ash St., Fernandina, FL 32034. TEL 904-261-3696; FAX 904-261-3698. **Owner(s):** New York Times Co., The, 229 W. 43rd St., New York, NY 10036. TEL 212-556-1234; Ed. Mary Hurst; Pub. Steve Hopper; adv. contact: Mike Hankins. pub. size: broadsheet; circ. 11,000(paid).
   Formerly: Fernandina Beach News Leader.

FORT LAUDERDALE

US   ISSN 1065-1462

BROWARD TIMES, THE. 1990. Fri. $.50 newsstand; $35/yr. 1001 W. Cypress Creek Rd., Ste. 111, Fort Lauderdale, FL 33309. TEL 954-351-3099; FAX 954-351-3099. **Owner(s):** Broward Times, Inc., 1001 W. Cypress Creek Rd., Ste. 111, Fort Lauderdale, FL 33309. TEL 954-351-9070; FAX 954-351-3099; Pub. Keith A. Clayborne; adv.; photos; bk.rev.; pub. size: broadsheet; circ. 25,000(controlled & paid). **Wire Service(s):** AP.

FORT MEADE

US

FORT MEADE LEADER, THE. 1971. s-w.: Tue. & Fri. $.25 newsstand; $20/yr. in cy.; $27.50/yr. out of cy.; $30/yr. out of state. 25 W. Broadway, Fort Meade, FL 33841. TEL 813-285-8625; FAX 813-285-7634. **Owner(s):** Frisbie Publishing Co., Inc., P.O. Box 120, Bartow, FL 33831-0120. TEL 813-533-4183; FAX 813-533-0402; Ed. S.L. Frisbie, IV; Pub. S.L. Frisbie, IV; adv.; photos; pub. size: broadsheet; circ. 1,305(free & paid).
   Formerly: Democrat & Leader.

FORT MYERS BEACH

US

BEACH BULLETIN. 1951. Fri. free newsstand; free in cy.; $30/yr. out of cy. 19260 San Carlos Blvd., Fort Myers Beach, FL 33931. TEL 941-463-4421; FAX 941-463-1402. **Owner(s):** Breeze Corp., 2510 Del Prado Blvd., Cape Coral, FL 33904. TEL 941-574-1110; Ed. Dee McLelland. adv.; photos; bk.rev.; pub. size: tabloid, 4 color photos/art; circ. 14,000(free & paid).

US

FORT MYERS BEACH OBSERVER. 1985. Wed. free at newsstand; $25/yr. 17274 St. Carlos Blvd., Fort Myers Beach, FL 33931. TEL 941-482-7111; FAX 941-482-6365. **Owner(s):** Ogden Newspapers, Inc., 1500 Main St., Wheeling, WV 26003. TEL 304-233-0100; Ed. Dawn Grodsky. adv.; photos; pub. size: tabloid; circ. 45,000(paid).

FROSTPROOF

US

FROSTPROOF NEWS. 1914. Thu. $.50 newsstand; $13.78/yr. in cy.; $15.90/yr. out of cy. 19 S. Scenic Hwy., Frostproof, FL 33843. TEL 941-635-2171; FAX 941-635-4265. **Owner(s):** Independent Newspapers, Inc., P.O. Box 7001, Dover, DE 19903. TEL 302-674-4750; Ed. Amy Stealy; Pub. Richard Hitt; adv.; pub. size: broadsheet; circ. 2,000(paid).

FRUITLAND PARK

US

LAKE NEWS. Wed. free. 2891 Hwy. 441-27, Fruitland Park, FL 34731-2438. TEL 904-787-6277; FAX 904-357-3202. **Owner(s):** Mid-Florida Publications, P.O. Box 318, Mount Dora, FL 32757; Pub. Michael E. Tabor; pub. size: tabloid; circ. 21,500(free).

GAINESVILLE

US

RECORD, THE. 1963. Thu. $20/yr. in state; $24/yr. out of state. 620 N. Main St., Gainesville, FL 32601. TEL 904-377-2444; FAX 904-338-1986. **Owner(s):** Constance & J. Ben Rowe, P.O. Box 806, Graceville, FL 32602. TEL 352-377-2444; FAX 352-338-1986; Ed. Richard Canaday; Pub. J. Ben Rowe; adv. contact: Constance Rowe. photos; bk.rev.; pub. size: tabloid; circ. 5,000(paid).
   Formerly: Record Farm & Ranch.

GRACEVILLE

US

GRACEVILLE NEWS. 1905. Thu. $14/yr.; $12/yr. senior citizens. 1004 Tenth Ave., Graceville, FL 32440. TEL 904-263-6015. **Owner(s):** Ferrin-Cox, P.O. Box 187, Graceville, FL 32440. TEL 904-263-6015; Ed. Sharon Taylor. pub. size: standard; circ. 1,700(paid).

GULF BREEZE

US

SENTINEL, THE. 1960. Wed. $.50 newsstand; $19.26/yr. 1200 Gulf Breeze Pkwy., Gulf Breeze, FL 32562. TEL 904-932-0385; FAX 904-932-8765. **Owner(s):** Gannett Company, Inc., 1100 Wilson Blvd., Arlington, VA 22340. TEL 703-284-6000; Ed. Marlin Osborn; Pub. Marlin Osborn; adv.; pub. size: broadsheet; circ. 5,000(paid).

HALLANDALE

US

DIGEST, THE. 1963. Thu. free carrier in area; $2/wk. mailed. 224 S. Dixie Hwy., Hallandale, FL 33009. TEL 305-457-8029; FAX 305-457-1284. **Owner(s):** Dan Bluesten, 224 S. Dixie Hwy. Hollywood, FL 33020. TEL 305-457-8029; Ed. Larry Bluestein; Pub. Dan Bluesten; pub. size: broadsheet; circ. 45,000(free & paid).
   Formerly: Hallandale Digest.

HIGH SPRINGS

US   ISSN 0746-1046

HIGH SPRINGS HERALD, THE. 1951. Thu. $.25 newsstand; $15/yr. 5 N.W. First St., High Springs, FL 32655. TEL 904-454-1297; FAX 904-454-4559. **Owner(s):** Herald Publishing Co., Inc., P.C. Box 14375, Gainesville, FL 32604-3275. TEL 904-376-4446; FAX 904-376-4556; Ed. Bo Turner; Pub. Ed Barber; adv. contact: Carol Chidlow. photos; bk.rev.; pub. size: standard; circ. 3,317(free & paid). **Wire Service(s):** AP.

HOMESTEAD

US

SOUTH DADE NEWS LEADER. 1912. 3/wk.: Mon., Wed., Fri. $.50 newsstand; $19.17/13 wks.; $58.58/yr. 15 N.E. First Rd., Homestead, FL 33030. TEL 305-245-2311; FAX 305-248-0596. **Owner(s):** Homestead Newspapers, Inc., 15 N.E. First Rd., Homestead, FL 33090. TEL 305-245-2311; Ed. Yolanda Ulrich; Pub. Glen Martin; adv. contact: Charlene Russ. pub. size: broadsheet; circ. 12,514(paid). **Wire Service(s):** UPI.

JACKSONVILLE

US

JACKSONVILLE SHOPPING GUIDE. 1971. Wed. free. 3801 University Blvd., W. Jacksonville, FL 32217. TEL 904-737-7220; FAX 904-737-2274. **Owner(s):** Garry Mogach. TEL 407-249-1103; Ed. Debbie Weinelt. pub. size: tabloid; circ. 150,000(free).
   Formerly: Shopping Guide.

JACKSONVILLE BEACH

US

BEACHES LEADER. 1963. s-w.: Wed. & Fri. $.50 newsstand; $20/yr. mailed. 1114 Beach Blvd., Jacksonville Beach, FL 32250. TEL 904-249-9033. **Owner(s):** Thomas H. Wood, P.O. Box 50129, Jacksonville, FL 32250; Ed. Kathleen Feindt Bailey; Pub. Thomas H. Wood; pub. size: broadsheet; circ. 22,500(paid).

JASPER

US

JASPER NEWS. 1869. Thu. $.30 newsstand; $11/yr. in cy.; $18/yr. out of cy. P.O. Drawer D, Jasper, FL 32052. TEL 904-792-2487; FAX 904-792-3009. **Owner(s):** Ricketsons & Associates, Lake City, FL; Ed. Gail Newsome; Pub. Michael Coulter; adv. contact: Ann Hall. pub. size: standard; circ. 2,077(free & paid).

JUPITER

US   ISSN 0896-0283

JUPITER COURIER. 1958. s-w.: Wed. & Sun. $.35 newsstand; $24/yr. 800 W. Indiantown Rd., Jupiter, FL 33458. TEL 407-746-5111; FAX 407-743-0673. **Owner(s):** Scripps-Howard, 312 Walnut St., 28th Fl. Cincinnati, OH 45202. TEL 513-977-3000; Ed. Kevin Hemstock. adv.; photos; bk.rev.; pub. size: broadsheet; circ. 11,000(paid).
   Formerly: Courier Journal.

KISSIMMEE

US   ISSN 1060-1244

OSCEOLA NEWS-GAZETTE. 1895. s-w.: Thu. & Sat. $.25 newsstand; $48.15/yr. 108 Church St., Kissimmee, FL 34741. TEL 407-846-7600; FAX 407-846-8516. **Owner(s)** Florida Sun Publishing, P.O. Box 811, Bradenton, FL 34206. TEL 800-282-3953; Ed. Bill Orben. adv.; photos; pub. size: broadsheet; circ. 29,000(controlled & paid).
   Formerly: News-Gazette.

LA BELLE

US

CALOOSA BELLE. 1922. Wed. free newsstand; $16./yr. P.O. Box 518, La Belle, FL 33935. TEL 941-675-2541; FAX 941-675-1449. **Owner(s):** Independent Newspapers, Inc., P.O. Box 7001, Dover, DE 19903. TEL 813-983-9148; Ed. Patty Brant. adv. contact: Martha Briede. pub. size: broadsheet; circ. 7,500(paid).

LAKE PLACID

US

LAKE PLACID JOURNAL. 1957. Thu. $12.31/yr. 232 N. Main St., Lake Placid, FL 33852. TEL 941-465-2423; FAX 941-699-0331. **Owner(s):** Constance Delaney, P.O. Box 785, Lake Placid, FL 33852. TEL 813-465-4122; Pub. Mat Delaney; pub. size: broadsheet; circ. 4,990(paid).

LAKE WALES

US

LAKE WALES NEWS. 1926. Thu. $.25 newsstand; $14.34/yr. 140 E. Stuart Ave., Lake Wales, FL 33853. TEL 813-676-3467. **Owner(s):** Brice Printing-Sole Properties, 140 Stuart Ave., Lake Wales, FL 33853. TEL 813-676-3467; Pub. Owen B. Brice; adv.; pub. size: broadsheet; circ. 3,500(paid).

LAKE WORTH

US

LAKE WORTH HERALD COASTAL OBSERVER. 1912. Thu. $.50 newsstand; $12/6 mos.; $25/yr. 130 S. H St., Lake Worth, FL 33460. TEL 407-585-9387; FAX 407-585-5434. **Owner(s):** Karl Easton, 130 S. H St., Lake Worth, FL 33460. TEL 407-585-9387; Ed. Jay Kravetz; Pub. Karl J. Easton; adv.; photos; bk.rev.; pub. size: tabloid; circ. 40,000(free & paid). **Wire Service(s):** IPN.

LAND O' LAKES

US

LAKE AREA NEWS. Thu. free. P.O. Box 1669, Land O' Lakes, FL 34639. TEL 813-264-0170; FAX 813-265-1723. **Owner(s):** Media General, Inc., 333 E. Grace St., Richmond, VA 23219. TEL 804-649-6000; Ed. Sherri VandeSande. adv. contact: Dom Cassano. pub. size: tabloid; circ. 25,000(free).

LEHIGH ACRES

US

LEHIGH ACRES NEWS-STAR. 1962. Wed. free in cy.; $13.25/yr. out of cy.; $28/yr. out of state. 1250 Business Way, Lehigh Acres, FL 33935-0908. TEL 813-369-2191; FAX 813-369-1396. **Owner(s):** News-Star Publications, Inc., 1250 Business Way, Lehigh Acres, FL 33936. TEL 941-369-2191; FAX 941-369-1396; Ed. J. Tom Wason. adv.; photos; bk.rev.; pub. size: tabloid; circ. 12,000(controlled & free). **Formerly:** Lehigh News.

MACCLENNY

US

BAKER COUNTY PRESS, THE. 1929. Thu. $.35 newsstand; $16/yr. 104 S. Fifth St., MacClenny, FL 32063. TEL 904-259-2400. **Owner(s):** Baker County Press, Inc., 104 S. Fifth St., P.O. Box 598, MacClenny, FL 32063. TEL 904-259-2400; FAX 904-259-6502; Ed. James C. McGauley; Pub. James C. McGauley; adv. contact: Jeanie Shadd. pub. size: broadsheet; circ. 5,300(paid).

MADISON

US

MADISON COUNTY CARRIER. 1964. Wed. $.35 newsstand; $34.24/yr. in cy.; $37.45/yr. out of cy.; $35/yr. out of state. 53 South, Madison, FL 32340. TEL 904-973-4141; FAX 904-973-4121. **Owner(s):** Tommy & Mary Ellen Greene, P.O. Drawer 772, Madison, FL 32340; Ed. Robbie Burnett; Pub. Tommy Greene; adv.; pub. size: broadsheet; circ. 4,500(paid).

MADISON ENTERPRISE RECORDER. 1864. Fri. $.35 newsstand; $34.24/yr in cy. 111 S. Shelby St., Madison, FL 32341. TEL 904-973-4141; FAX 904-973-4121. **Owner(s):** Tommy & Mary Ellen Greene, P.O. Drawer 772, Madison, FL. TEL 904-973-4141; Ed. Harvey Greene; Pub. Tommy Greene; adv.; photos; bk.rev.; pub. size: broadsheet; circ. 3,500(paid).

MARATHON

US

FLORIDA KEYS KEYNOTER. 1953. s-w.: Wed. & Sat. $.25 newsstand; $30/yr. in cy.; $40/yr. elsewhere. 3015 Overseas Hwy., Marathon, FL 33050. TEL 305-743-5551; FAX 305-743-9586; E-mail: keynoter@aol.com; URL: http://florida-keys.fl.us/keynoter.htm. **Owner(s):** Knight-Ridder, Inc., One Herald Plz., Miami, FL 33132. TEL 305-376-3800; Ed. Tom Tuell; Pub. Tom Schumaker; adv.; photos; pub. size: tabloid; circ. 14,300(free & paid). **Wire Service(s):** AP Newsfinder.
    Formerly: Keynoter.

MARCO ISLAND

US

MARCO ISLAND EAGLE, THE. 1968. Wed. $.50 newsstand; $23.32/yr. in state; $42/yr. out of state. P.O. Box 579, Marco Island, FL 33969. TEL 941-394-7592; FAX 941-394-8552. **Owner(s):** New York Times Co., The, 229 W. 43rd St., New York, NY 10036. TEL 212-556-1234; Pub. Cheryl Ferrara; pub. size: tabloid; circ. 10,000(paid).

MARGATE

US

BROWARD NEWS. 1977. Thu. free newsstand; $60/yr. 767 S. State Rd. 7, Ste. 1, Margate, FL 33068-4822. TEL 305-977-7770; FAX 305-977-7779. **Owner(s):** Harvey Lustig, 767 S. State Rd. 7, Ste. 1, Margate, FL 33068. TEL 305-977-7770; FAX 305-977-7779; Ed. Mort Luxnor; Pub. Harvey Lustig; adv. contact: Shelly Lazarus. photos; pub. size: tabloid.

TRI-CITY INDEPENDENT

US

TRI-CITY INDEPENDENT. 1989. w. free; $52/yr. 340 S. State Rd. 7, Margate, FL 33068-5709. TEL 305-978-8983. **Owner(s):** Tri-City Independent, 340 S. State Rd. 7, Margate, FL 33068. TEL 305-978-8983; FAX 305-978-8983; Ed. Harry White; Pub. Pamela Donovan; adv.; photos; pub. size: tabloid; circ. 25,000(free).

MARIANNA

US

MARKETPLACE, THE. Wed. free newsstand & deliv. 4403 Constitution Ln., Marianna, FL 32448. TEL 904-526-3614; FAX 904-482-4478. **Owner(s):** Thomson Newspapers, Inc., One Thorn Run Ctr., Ste. 500, 1187 Thorn Run Rd. Ext., Coraopolis, PA 15108. TEL 412-262-7870; Ed. Judy Green; Pub. Jane Benton; pub. size: broadsheet; circ. 10,000(free).

MELBOURNE

US

BAY BULLETIN. Wed. free. One Gannett Plz., Melbourne, FL 32940. TEL 407-242-3500; FAX 407-242-0760. **Owner(s):** Gannett Company, Inc., 1100 Wilson Blvd., Arlington, VA 22340. TEL 703-284-6000; Ed. Harry McNamara; Pub. Michael Coleman; circ. 30,000(free).

LITTLE PAPER, THE. Thu. free newsstand. 835 E. New Haven Ave., Melbourne, FL 32901. TEL 407-723-5337; FAX 407-729-4210. **Owner(s):** Richard Sheffeld, 835 E. New Haven Ave., Melbourne, FL 32901. TEL 407-723-5337; Pub. Richard Sheffeld; adv.; pub. size: tabloid; circ. 50,000(free).

TIMES, THE. 1894. Wed. free. One Gannett Plz., Melbourne, FL 32940. TEL 407-242-3500; FAX 407-242-0760. **Owner(s):** Gannett Company, Inc., 1100 Wilson Blvd., Arlington, VA 22340. TEL 703-284-6000; Ed. Harry MacNamara; Pub. Michael Coleman; pub. size: broadsheet; circ. 51,493(free).

TRIBUNE, THE. 1917. Wed. free. One Gannett Plz., Melbourne, FL 32940. TEL 407-242-3500; FAX 407-242-0760. **Owner(s):** Gannett Company, Inc., 1100 Wilson Blvd., Arlington, VA 22340. TEL 703-284-6000; Ed. Harry MacNamara; Pub. Michael Coleman; pub. size: broadsheet; circ. 39,000(free).

MIAMI

US

CAROL CITY/OPA-LOCKA NEWS. 1958. Thu. $40/yr. mailed. 6796 S.W. 62nd Ave., Miami, FL 33143. TEL 305-667-7481; FAX 305-661-0954. **Owner(s):** Community Newspapers, Inc., 6796 S.W. 62nd Ave., Miami, FL 33143. TEL 305-667-7481; Ed. Michael Miller; Pub. Grant Miller; adv. contact: Grant Miller. pub. size: tabloid; circ. 3,000(controlled & paid). **Wire Service(s):** UPI.

US

CORAL GABLES NEWS. 1958. s-w.: Mon. & Thu. $.25 newsstand; $40/yr. mailed. 6796 S.W. 62nd Ave., Miami, FL 33143. TEL 305-667-7481; FAX 305-661-0954. **Owner(s):** Community Newspapers, Inc., 6796 S.W. 62nd Ave., Miami, FL 33143. TEL 305-667-7481; Ed. Michael Miller; Pub. Grant Miller; adv. contact: Grant Miller. pub. size: tabloid; circ. 8,000(controlled & paid). **Wire Service(s):** UPI.

US

HIALEAH/OPA-LACKA NEWS. 1958. s-w.: Mon. & Thu. $.25 newsstand; $40/yr. mailed. 6796 S.W. 62nd Ave., Miami, FL 33143. TEL 305-667-7481; FAX 305-661-0954. **Owner(s):** Community Newspapers, Inc., 6796 S.W. 62nd Ave., Miami, FL 33143. TEL 305-667-7481; Ed. Michael Miller; Pub. Grant Miller; adv. contact: Grant Miller. pub. size: tabloid; circ. 9,000(controlled & paid). **Wire Service(s):** UPI.
  Formerly: Hialeah-Miami Springs News.

US

HOMESTEAD/FLORIDA CITY NEWS. 1958. s-w.: Mon. & Fri. $29.92/yr. 6796 S.W. 62nd Ave., Miami, FL 33143. TEL 305-667-7481; FAX 305-661-0954. **Owner(s):** Community Newspapers, Inc., 6796 S.W. 62nd Ave., Miami, FL 33143. TEL 305-667-7481; Ed. Michael Miller; Pub. Grant Miller; adv. contact: Michael Miller. pub. size: tabloid; circ. 9,000(controlled). **Wire Service(s):** UPI.

US

KENDALL NEWS-GAZETTE. 0958. s-w.: Mon. & Thu. $.25 newsstand; $40/yr. mailed. 6796 S.W. 62nd Ave., Miami, FL 33143. TEL 305-667-7481; FAX 305-661-0954. **Owner(s):** Community Newspapers, Inc., 6796 S.W. 62nd Ave., Miami, FL 33143. TEL 305-667-7481; Ed. Michael Miller; Pub. Grant Miller; adv. contact: Grant Miller. pub. size: tabloid; circ. 25,000(controlled & paid). **Wire Service(s):** UPI.
  Formerly: Kendall-South Miami News.

US

MIAMI BEACH SUN POST. 1930. Thu. $.25 newsstand; $35/yr. 1688 Meridian Ave., Ste. 702, Miami, FL 33139. TEL 305-538-9700; FAX 305-538-6077. **Owner(s):** Prestige Publications, Inc., 1000 Lincoln Rd., Miami, FL 33139. TEL 305-538-9700; Ed. Anslie Stark; Pub. Andrew Stark; adv. contact: J.R. Stark. pub. size: tabloid; circ. 30,000(paid).

US

MIAMI SHORES NEWS. 1958. Fri. $29.92/yr. 6796 S.W. 62nd Ave., Miami, FL 33143. TEL 305-667-7481; FAX 305-661-0954. **Owner(s):** Community Newspapers, Inc., 6796 S.W. 62nd Ave., Miami, FL 33143. TEL 305-667-7481; Ed. Michael Miller; Pub. Grant Miller; adv. contact: Grant Miller. pub. size: tabloid; circ. 4,500(controlled). **Wire Service(s):** UPI.

US

MIAMI TODAY. 1983. w. $1/newsstand; $60/yr. US; $140/yr. South America, $190/yr. Europe. 710 Brickell Ave., Miami, FL 33131. TEL 305-358-1008. **Owner(s):** Today Enterprises, Inc., P.O. Box 1368, Miami, FL 33101. TEL 305-358-1008; Ed. Michael Lewis; Pub. Michael Lewis; adv.; photos; bk.rev.; pub. size: tabloid; circ. 32,665(controlled & paid). **Wire Service(s):** AP.

US

NORTH MIAMI NEWS. 1958. s-w.: Mon. & Fri. $29.92/yr. 6796 S.W. 62nd Ave., Miami, FL 33143. TEL 305-667-7481; FAX 305-661-0954. **Owner(s):** Community Newspapers, Inc., 6796 S.W. 62nd Ave., Miami, FL 33143. TEL 305-667-7481; Ed. Michael Miller; Pub. Grant Miller; adv. contact: Grant Miller. pub. size: tabloid; circ. morning 9,000(paid). **Wire Service(s):** UPI.

US

SOUTH MIAMI NEWS. 1958. s-w.: Mon. & Thu. free newsstand; $29.92/yr. local mail. 6796 S.W. 62nd Ave., Miami, FL 33143. TEL 305-667-7481; FAX 305-661-0954. **Owner(s):** Community Newspapers, Inc., 6796 S.W. 62nd Ave., Miami, FL 33143. TEL 305-661-0954; Ed. Michael Miller; Pub. Grant Miller; pub. size: broadsheet; circ. 6,500(free & paid).
  Formerly: South Miami Shore News.

MIAMI BEACH

US

SUN POST. Thu. free newsstand; $35/yr. 3rd class; $80/yr. 1st class. 1688 Meridian Ave., Ste. 702, Miami Beach, FL 33119. TEL 305-538-9700; FAX 305-538-9700. **Owner(s):** Jeanette Stark, 1688 Meridian Ave., Ste. 702, Miami Beach, FL 33119; Ed. Anslie Stark; Pub. Anslie Stark; adv. contact: Andrew Stark. photos; pub. size: tabloid; circ. 35,000(controlled).

MIAMI LAKES

US

MIAMI LAKER. 1975. m. free. 6843 Main St., Ste. 310, Miami Lakes, FL 33014. TEL 305-817-4007; FAX 305-817-4197. **Owner(s):** Graham Companies, The, 6843 Main St., Miami Lakes, FL 33014. TEL 305-821-1130; Ed. Roger Reece. adv.; pub. size: tabloid; circ. 26,500(controlled).

MILTON

US

SANTA ROSA FREE PRESS. 1975. s-w.: Mon. & Thu. $.50 newsstand. 531 W. Elva St., Milton, FL 32570. TEL 904-623-3616; FAX 904-623-2007. **Owner(s):** Jim Hill, 531 W. Elva St., Milton, FL 32570. TEL 904-623-3616; Ed. Jim Fletcher; Pub. Jim Hill; adv. contact: Jim Martin. pub. size: broadsheet; circ. 8,000(free).

US   ISSN 0273-5857

SANTA ROSA PRESS GAZETTE. 1907. s-w.: Mon. & Thu. $.50 newsstand; $24/yr. in cy.; $30/yr. out of cy. 531 W. Elva St., Milton, FL 32570. TEL 904-623-3131. **Owner(s):** Santa Rosa Press Gazette, 531 W. Elva St., Milton, FL 32572. TEL 904-623-2120; FAX 904-623-2007; Ed. Jim Fletcher. adv.; pub size: broadsheet; circ. 7,500(paid).

MONTICELLO

US   ISSN 0746-5297

MONTICELLO NEWS. 1869. s-w.: Wed. & Fri. $.25 newsstand; $29.26/yr. 100 W. Dogwood St., Monticello, FL 32344. TEL 904-997-3568; FAX 904-997-3774. **Owner(s):** Monticello Publishing Co., Inc., 100 W. Dogwood St., Monticello, FL 32344. TEL 904-997-3568; FAX 904-997-3774; Ed. Lazaro Almon; Pub. Ron Cichon; adv. contact: Shirley Rudd. photos; pub. size: broadsheet; circ. 3,000(paid).

MOUNT DORA

US

EUSTIS LAKE REGION NEWS. Thu. $.25 newsstand; $8.55/yr. in cy.; $10.17/yr. out of cy. 4645 N. Hwy. 19A, Mount Dora, FL 32757-2039. TEL 904-357-3199; FAX 904-357-3202. **Owner(s):** William Matthew, 4645 N. Hwy. 19A, Mount Dora, FL 32757-2039; Ed. Jody Harris; Pub. Michael Tabor; pub. size: broadsheet; circ. 1,500(paid).

US

TAVARES CITIZEN. 1882. Thu. $8.56/yr. in cy.; $10.17/yr. out of cy. 4645 N. Highway, 19A, Mount Dora, FL 32757-2039. TEL 904-357-3199; FAX 904-357-3202. **Owner(s):** Mid Florida Publications, Dade City, FL; Ed. C.J. Woodring; Pub. Mike Tabor; adv.; pub. size: broadsheet; circ. 400(paid).

MULBERRY

US

MULBERRY PRESS. 1909. Thu. $.50 newsstand; $24/yr. in cy. 1020 N. Church Ave., Hwy. 37-N, Mulberry, FL 33860-2040. TEL 813-425-3411. **Owner(s):** Histed Media Group, 1020 N. Church Ave., Hwy. 37-N, Mulberry, FL 33860. TEL 813-425-3411; Ed. William M. Histed. adv. contact: Barbara Wagoner. photos; bk.rev.; pub. size: broadsheet; circ. 6,500(paid).

US

POLK CITY PRESS. 1984. Thu. $.25 newsstand; $22/yr. 1020 N. Church Ave., Hwy. 37-N, Mulberry, FL 33860-2040. TEL 813-425-3411. **Owner(s):** Histed Media Group, 1020 N. Church Ave., Hwy. 37-N, Mulberry, FL 33860-2040. TEL 813-425-3411; Ed. Martha Cornell; Pub. Robert Histed; adv. contact: Barbara Wagoner. photos; bk.rev.; pub. size: broadsheet; circ. 2,500(paid).

NEW PORT RICHEY

US

SUN COAST NEWS. Sat. free in area; $5.30/mo.; $53.60/yr. 6214 U.S. Hwy. 19 New Port Richey, FL 34652. TEL 813-849-7500 FAX 813-847-2902. **Owner(s):** Sunbelt Newspapers, Inc., 6214 U.S. Hwy., New Port Richey, FL 34652; Ed. Gwen Stevenson. adv. contact: Bob Fransen. pub. size: tabloid; circ. 151,000(free & paid).
  Formerly: Tarpon Springs Leader.

NICEVILLE

US

BAY BEACON, THE. 1992. Wed. $36.50/yr. 203 W. John Sims Pkwy., Ste. 2, Niceville, FL 32578. TEL 904-678-1080; FAX 904-729-3225. **Owner(s):** Stephen W. Kent, 203 W. John Sims Pkwy., Ste. 2, Niceville, FL 32578. TEL 904-678-1080; FAX 904-729-3225; Ed. Stephen Kent; Pub. Stephen Kent; adv. contact: Sara Kent. photos; pub. size: broadsheet; circ. 12,356(free & paid).

NORTH PORT

US

SUN HERALD. s-w.: Wed. & Sun. $28.89/yr. 13644 S. Tamiami Trail, North Port, FL 34287. TEL 941-426-9544; FAX 941-423-2318. **Owner(s):** Sun Coast Media Group, 13644 S. Tamiami Trail, North Port, FL 34287. TEL 941-426-9544; Ed. Marshall Grove; Pub. Derek Dunn-Rankin; pub. size: broadsheet; circ. 7,800(paid).
  Formerly: North Port Sun Times.

ORANGE PARK

US

CLAY COUNTY CRESCENT. 1883. Thu. $.25 newsstand; $15.76/yr. mailed. 1564 Kingsley Ave., Orange Park, FL 32073. TEL 904-264-3200; FAX 904-269-6958. **Owner(s):** Add, Inc., 600 Industrial Dr., Waupaca, WI 54981. TEL 715-258-8450; Ed. Sandy Mulvhill; Pub. Joyce Lydon; adv.; photos; pub. size: tabloid; circ. 6,000(paid).

US

GAINESVILLE BUYERS GUIDE. Thu. free newsstand & home deliv. 1564 Kingsley Ave., Orange Park, FL 32073-4594. TEL 904-264-3200; FAX 904-269-6958. **Owner(s):** Add, Inc., P.O. Box 609, Waupaca, WI 54981. TEL 715-258-8450; Ed. Pierce Lehmback; Pub. Joyce Lydon; adv. contact: Tim Kult. circ. 40,000(free).

US

TODAY. 1993. s-w. Wed. & Fri. free newsstand. 1564 Kingsley Ave., Orange Park, FL 32073. TEL 904-264-3200; FAX 904-269-6958; E-mail: jlclay@jax-inter.net. **Owner(s):** Add, Inc., P.O. Box 609, Waupaca, WI 54981. TEL 715-258-8450; Ed. Sandy Muldihill; Pub. Joyce Lydon; pub. size: broadsheet; circ. 80,000(free).

ORMOND BEACH

US

DAYTONA PENNYSAVER. 1976. Wed. free. 454 S. Yonge St., Ormond Beach, FL 32174. TEL 904-677-4262; FAX 904-672-7453. **Owner(s):** News-Journal Corp., 901 Sixth St., Daytona Beach, FL 32117-8099. TEL 904-377-4262; Ed. Leonard Marsh. pub. size: tabloid; circ. 75,000(free).

OVIEDO

US

OVIEDO VOICE, THE. 1992. Thu. $.35 newsstand; $17.12/yr. 169 W. Broadway, Oviedo, FL 32765. TEL 407-366-9181; FAX 407-366-7580. **Owner(s):** Oviedo Voice, The, 169 W. Broadway, Oviedo, FL 32765; Ed. Letty Linhart; Pub. James R. Noles; adv.; photos; pub. size: tabloid; circ. 2,600(paid).

PENSACOLA

US

ESCAMBIA SUN PRESS. 1948. Thu. $.25 newsstand; $21.40/yr. in cy. 3610 Barrancas Ave., Pensacola, FL 32507. TEL 904-456-3121; FAX 904-456-0103. **Owner(s):** Michael Driver, P.O. Box 4625, Pensacola, FL 32507. TEL 904-456-3121; Ed. Michael Driver; Pub. Michael Driver; adv.; pub. size: broadsheet; circ. 3,500(paid).

US

PENSACOLA VOICE. 1865. Thu. $.50 newsstand; $20/yr. 213 E. Yonge St., Pensacola, FL 32503. TEL 904-434-6963; FAX 904-469-8745. **Owner(s):** Les Humphrey, 213 E. Yonge St., Pensacola, FL 32503. TEL 904-434-6963; Ed. Chery Johnson; Pub. Les Humphrey; adv. contact: Al Henderson. pub. size: standard; circ. 32,180(paid).

US

PERDIDO PELICAN. 1985. bi-w.: Mon. free. P.O. Box 34257, Pensacola, FL 32507. TEL 904-492-5221; FAX 904-492-7119. **Owner(s):** Gulf Breeze Publishing Co., P.O. Box 34257, Pensacola, FL 32507; Ed. Fran Thompson; Pub. Fran Thompson; adv.; photos; bk.rev.; pub. size: tabloid; circ. 10,000(free).

US

SHOPPER, THE. 1975. s-w.: Tue. & Fri. $.65 newsstand; $7/mo. 3041 E. Olive Rd., Pensacola, FL 32514. TEL 904-478-3805; FAX 904-478-2222. **Owner(s):** Susan Thibodeaux, 3041 E. Olive Rd., Pensacola, FL 32514; Ed. Susan Thibodeaux. adv.; photos; pub. size: tabloid; circ. 45,000(paid).

PENSACOLA BEACH

US

ISLANDER, THE. 1979. Wed. $.50 newsstand; $20/yr. in cy.; $25/yr. out of cy. 400 Quietwater Beach Blvd., Pensacola Beach, FL 32561. TEL 904-934-3417; FAX 904-932-7230. **Owner(s):** Island Publications of Pensacola Beach, Inc., P.O. Box 292, Gulf Breeze, FL 32562-0292. TEL 904-934-3417; Ed. Diana Nelson; Pub. Barbara Bryant; adv. contact: Karen Bryant. photos; pub. size: broadsheet; circ. 3,500(paid).

PERRY

US ISSN 0747-0967

PERRY NEWS-HERALD. 1887. Fri. $.50 newsstand; $20/yr. in cy.; $32/yr. out of cy. 123 S. Jefferson, Perry, FL 32347. TEL 904-584-5513; FAX 904-838-1566. **Owner(s):** Perry Newspapers, Inc., P.O. Box 888, Perry, FL 32347. TEL 904-584-5513; Ed. Aaron Portwood; Pub. Don Lincoln; adv. contact: Beth Mann. pub. size: broadsheet; circ. 5,100(paid).

US ISSN 0747-2358

PERRY TACO TIMES. 1962. Wed. $.50 newsstand; $20/yr. in cy.; $32/yr. out of cy. 123 S. Jefferson, Perry, FL 32347. TEL 904-584-5513; FAX 904-838-1566. **Owner(s):** Perry Newspapers, Inc., P.O. Box 888, Perry, FL 32347. TEL 904-584-5513; Ed. Aaron Portwood; Pub. Don Lincoln; adv. contact: Beth Mann. pub. size: standard; circ. 5,100(paid).

PLANT CITY

US

COURIER, THE. Thu. $.25 newsstand; $18.11/yr. 102 S. Evers St., Plant City, FL 33566. TEL 813-752-3113. **Owner(s):** Media General, Inc., 333 E. Grace St., Richmond, VA 23219. TEL 804-649-6000; Ed. Bob McClure. adv. contact: Sherry Wheeler. pub. size: tabloid; circ. 4,700(paid).

POMPANO BEACH

US

POMPANO LEDGER, THE. 1980. Thu. $.25 newsstand; $13.78/yr. 2500 S.E. Sive Ct., Pompano Beach, FL 33062. TEL 305-946-7277. E-mail: 72747.502@compuserve.com. **Owner(s):** Karen M. Foley, 660 S. Federal Hwy., Pompano Beach, FL 33062. TEL 305-946-7277; Ed. Edward J. Foley; Pub. Karen M. Foley; adv. contact: Karen M. Foley. photos; pub. size: broadsheet; circ. 20,000(free & paid). **Wire Service(s):** AP.

QUINCY

US

GADSDEN COUNTY TIMES. 1901. Thu. $.50 newsstand; $21.40/yr. in cy.; $32.10/yr. out of cy.; $30/yr. out of state. 15 S. Madison, Quincy, FL 32351. TEL 904-627-7649; FAX 904-627-7191. **Owner(s):** Timothy O. Matthew, P.O. Box 790, Quincy, FL 32353; Ed. Alice Dupont; Pub. Frederick C. Drew; adv. contact: Frederick C. Drew. pub. size: broadsheet; circ. 6,000(paid).

Formerly: Quincy Gadsden County Times.

ROYAL PALM BEACH

US

OBSERVER, THE. 1992. Wed. free. 240 Royal Palm Beach Blvd., Royal Palm Beach, FL 33411. TEL 407-791-9687; FAX 407-791-9690. **Owner(s):** Bruce H. & Mark J. Easton, 240 Royal Palm Beach Blvd., Royal Palm Beach, FL 33411. TEL 407-791-9687; FAX 407-791-9690; Ed. Mark Esterly; Pub. Bruce H. Easton; adv. contact: Bruce H. Easton. photos; bk.rev.; pub. size: tabloid; circ. 20,000(free).

RUSKIN

US

SHOPPER OBSERVER NEWS. 1958. Wed. free local carrier; $35/yr. 100 Shell Point Rd., E., Ruskin, FL 33570. TEL 813-645-3111; FAX 813-645-4118. **Owner(s):** M & M Printing Co., Inc., P.O. Box 5, Ruskin, FL 33570; Ed. Brenda Knowles; Pub. Brenda Knowles; pub. size: tabloid; circ. 22,000(free & paid).

Formerly: Ruskin Shopper & Observer News.

SANIBEL

US

ISLAND REPORTER. 1973. Fri. $.50 newsstand; $22/yr. in cy.; $28/yr. out of cy. 2340 Periwinkle Way, Sanibel, FL 33957. TEL 914-472-1587; FAX 914-472-8398. **Owner(s):** Ogden Newspapers, Inc., 1500 Main St., Wheeling, WV 26003; Ed. Ralf Kircher. adv. contact: Wendy Murray. photos; bk.rev.; pub. size: tabloid; circ. 8,500(paid).

US

SANIBEL-CAPTIVA ISLANDER. 1961. Fri. $.50 newsstand; $28/yr. 695 Tarpon Bay Rd., Sanibel, FL 33957. TEL 941-472-5185; FAX 941-472-5302. **Owner(s):** Ogden Newspapers, Inc., 1500 Main St., Wheeling, WV 26003; Ed. Scott Martell. adv. contact: Tracy Markwalter. pub. size: tabloid; circ. 7,000(paid).

SARASOTA

US

PELICAN PRESS. 1971. Thu. free newsstand; $28/yr. 230 Avenida Madera, Sarasota, FL 34242. TEL 941-349-4949; FAX 941-346-7118. **Owner(s):** John B. Davidson, 230 Avenida Madera, Sarasota, FL 34242. TEL 941-349-4949; FAX 941-346-7118; Ed. Anne Johnson; Pub. John B. Davidson; adv.; photos; bk.rev.; pub. size: tabloid.

SEBASTIAN

US

SEBASTIAN SUN. 1978. Fri. free; $18/yr. P.O. Box 1268, Sebastian, FL 32978. TEL 407-589-4566. Owner(s): Scripps-Howard, Inc., 312 Walnut St., 28th Fl., Cincinnati, OH 45202. TEL 513-977-3000; pub. size: tabloid; circ. 3,500(paid).

SEBRING

US   ISSN 0163-3988

NEWS SUN, THE. 1919. s-w.: Wed. & Sun. $.50/issue; $.75/Sun.; $36/yr. carrier; $78/yr. mailed in state; $78/yr. mailed out of state. 2227 US 27 S., Sebring, FL 33870. TEL 813-385-6155; FAX 813-385-1954. **Owner(s):** New York Times Co., The, 229 W. 43rd St., New York, NY 10036. TEL 212-556-1234; Pub. Judy Robinette; adv. contact: Jim Hyatt. photos; bk.rev.; pub. size: broadsheet; circ. 21,167(paid); Sun. 20,917(paid).

SOUTH MIAMI

US

AVENTURA NEWS. 1958. s-w.: Mon. & Wed. free; $27.50/yr. in cy. 6796 S.W. 62nd Ave., South Miami, FL 33143. TEL 305-665-8214; FAX 305-661-0954. **Owner(s):** Community Newspapers, Inc., 6796 S.W. 62nd Ave., South Miami, FL 33143. TEL 305-665-8214; Ed. David Berkowitz; Pub. Grant Miller; pub. size: tabloid; circ. 20,000(free). **Wire Service(s):** AP.

US

DOWNTOWN NEWS. 1958. s-w.: Mon. & Thu. free; $27.50/yr. in cy. mailed. 6796 S.W. 62nd Ave., South Miami, FL 33143. TEL 305-665-8214; FAX 305-661-0954. **Owner(s):** Community Newspapers, Inc., 6796 S.W. 62nd Ave., South Miami, FL 33143. TEL 305-665-8214; Ed. David Berkowitz; Pub. Grant Miller; pub. size: tabloid; circ. 4,500(free). **Wire Service(s):** AP.

US

MIAMI BEACH NEWS. 1958. s-w.: Mon. & Thu. free; $27.50/yr. in cy. mailed. 6796 S.W. 62nd Ave., South Miami, FL 33143. TEL 305-665-8214; FAX 305-661-0954. **Owner(s):** Community Newspapers, Inc., 6796 S.W. 62nd Ave., South Miami, FL 33143. TEL 305-665-8214; Ed. David Berkowitz; Pub. Grant Miller; pub. size: tabloid; circ. 4,000(controlled). **Wire Service(s):** AP.

US

NORTH BAY VILLAGE NEWS. 1958. s-w.: Mon. & Thu. free newsstand; $27.50/yr. mailed in cy. 6796 S.W. 62nd Ave., South Miami, FL 33143. TEL 305-665-8214; FAX 305-661-0954. **Owner(s):** Community Newspapers, Inc., 6796 S.W. 62nd Ave., South Miami, FL 33143; Ed. David Berkowitz; Pub. Grant Miller; adv.; pub. size: broadsheet; circ. 5,800(free). **Wire Service(s):** AP.

US

NORTH MIAMI BEACH NEWS. 1965. s-w.: Mon & Fri. $29.92/yr. 6796 S.W. 62nd Ave., South Miami, FL 33143. TEL 305-667-7481; FAX 305-661-0954. **Owner(s):** Community Newspapers, Inc., 6796 S.W. 62nd Ave., Miami, FL 33143. TEL 305-667-7481; Ed. Michael Miller; Pub. Grant Miller; pub. size: tabloid; circ. 9,000(paid). **Wire Service(s):** UPI.

US   ISSN 1048-5406

SOUTH DADE NEWS. 1958. s-w.: Mon & Fri. $29.92/yr. 6796 S.W. 62nd Ave., South Miami, FL 33143. TEL 305-667-7481; FAX 305-661-0954. **Owner(s):** Community Newspapers, Inc., 6796 S.W. 62nd Ave., Miami, FL 33143. TEL 305-667-7481; Ed. Michael Miller; Pub. Grant Miller; adv. contact: Grant Miller. pub. size: tabloid; circ. 10,500(paid). **Wire Service(s):** UPI.

US

SOUTHWEST NEWS. 1958. s-w.: Mon. & Fri. $29.92/yr. 6796 S.W. 62nd Ave., South Miami, FL 33143. TEL 305-667-7481; FAX 305-661-0954. **Owner(s):** Community Newspapers, Inc., 6796 S.W. 62nd Ave., Miami, FL 33143. TEL 305-667-7481; Ed. Michael Miller; Pub. Grant Miller; adv. contact: Grant Miller. pub. size: tabloid; circ. 10,000(controlled & paid). **Wire Service(s):** UPI.

STARKE

US

BRADFORD COUNTY TELEGRAPH. 1879. Thu. $.35 newsstand; $19.26/yr. in cy.; $21.40/yr. out of cy. 135 W. Call St., Starke, FL 32091. TEL 904-964-6305; FAX 904-964-8628; E-mail: starknet@access.net; URL: http://www.daccess.net/starknet/telegraph.htm. **Owner(s):** John M. Miller, P.O. Drawer A, Starke, FL 32091. TEL 904-964-6305; Ed. Marcia Goodge; Pub. John M. Miller; adv. contact: John M. Miller. photos; pub. size: broadsheet; circ. 6,000(paid).

ST. PETERSBURG

US

WEEKLY CHALLENGER. 1967. Thu. $.25 newsstand; $30/yr. 2500 Ninth St., S., St. Petersburg, FL 33705. TEL 813-896-2922. **Owner(s):** Cleveland Johnson, 2500 Ninth St., S., St. Petersburg, FL 33705. TEL 813-896-2922; Pub. Cleveland Johnson; pub. size: standard; circ. 37,000(paid).

SUN CITY CENTER

US

EAST BAY BREEZE. Wed. free. 1507 Sun City Ctr. Plz., Sun City Center, FL 33570. TEL 813-634-9258. **Owner(s):** Media General, Inc., 333 E. Grace St., Richmond, VA 23219. TEL 804-649-6000; FAX 804-649-6898; Ed. Penny Fletcher. adv. contact: Andrea Murray. pub. size: tabloid; circ. 15,300(free).

US

SUN, THE. Wed. free. 1507 Sun City Ctr. Plz., Sun City Center, FL 33570. TEL 813-634-9258. **Owner(s):** Media General, Inc., 333 E. Grace St., Richmond, VA 23219. TEL 804-649-6000; FAX 804-649-6898; Ed. Penny Fletcher. adv. contact: Andrea Murray. pub. size: tabloid; circ. 10,010(free).

TALLAHASSEE

US   ISSN 1062-0885

TALLAHASSEAN 1991. Fri. $.25 newsstand; $24.95/yr. 1230 N. Adams St., Tallahassee, FL 32303-6137. TEL 904-224-3805; FAX 904-561-6651. **Owner(s):** Sylvia Jordan, 1230 N. Adams St., Tallahassee, FL 32303-6137. TEL 904-224-3805; FAX 904-561-6651; Ed. Cathie Johnson; Pub. Sylvia Jordan; adv.; photos; pub. size: standard; circ. 15,000(paid).

TAMPA

US

CARROLLWOOD NEWS. 1980 Wed. free. 10029 N. Dale Mabry, Tampa, FL 33618. TEL 813-963-2660. Owner(s): Media General, Inc., 411 E. Franklin St., Richmond, VA 23219. TEL 804-775-8030; Ed. Kevin Kaley. adv. contact: David Levine. pub. size: tabloid; circ. 30,400(free).

US

FREE PRESS. 1911. Sat. $12/yr. 1010 W. Cass St., Tampa, FL 33606. TEL 813-254-5888; FAX 813-251-0511. **Owner(s):** Free Press Publishing Co., 1010 W. Cass St, Tampa, FL 33606. TEL 813-254-5838; FAX 813-251-0511; Ed. Jo Beth Harrison; Pub. John N. Harrison, III; photos; bk.rev.; pub. size: standard; circ. 700(paid).

US

LUTZ COMMUNITY NEWS. Wed. $5.95/yr. in state; $12/yr. out of state. 15431 N. Florida Ave, Tampa, FL 33613. TEL 813-963-1918. **Owner(s):** Beacon Publishing, Inc., 119 Bullard Pkwy., Tampa, FL 33617. TEL 813-988-9175; Ed. Charlie Reese; Pub. Arne McKenna; adv.; photos; pub. size: tabloid; circ. 8,000(paid). **Formerly:** Lutz Party Line.

US

TEMPLE TERRACE BEACON. Thu. $5.95/yr. in state; $12/yr. out of state. 119 Bullard Pkwy., Tampa, FL 33617. TEL 813-988-9175; FAX 813-988-9177. **Owner(s):** Beacon Publishing, Inc., 119 Bullard Pkwy., Tampa, FL 33617. TEL 813-988-9175; FAX 813-988-9177; Ed. Charlie Reese; Pub. Anne McKenna; photos; pub. size: tabloid; circ. 15,000(paid).

US

TOWN 'N COUNTRY NEWS. Wed. free. 7512 Paula Dr., Ste. 105-B, Tampa, FL 33615. TEL 813-249-0725. **Owner(s):** Media General, Inc., 411 E. Franklin St., Richmond, VA 23219. TEL 804-775-8030; Ed. Rebecca Pividal. adv. contact: Leigh Humes. pub. size: tabloid; circ. 20,520(free).

US

WEEKLY PLANET. 1988. Thu. free. 402 N. Reo St., Ste. 218, Tampa, FL 33609-1027. TEL 813-286-1600; FAX 813-289-8010. **Owner(s):** Ben Eason & Terry Garett, 750 Willoughby Way, Atlanta, GA 30312. TEL 404-588-5623; Ed. Ben Eason. adv. contact: Sharry Smith. photos; bk.rev.; pub. size: tabloid; circ. 80,000(controlled & free).

TITUSVILLE

US

STAR-ADVOCATE. 1880. Wed. free. 1100 S. Hopkins Ave., Titusville, FL 32780. TEL 407-267-4711; FAX 407-264-2228. **Owner(s):** Cape Publications, Inc., P.O. Box 419000, Melbourne, FL 32941. TEL 407-242-3500; Ed. Harry McMamara; Pub. Michael Coleman; pub. size: broadsheet; circ. 29,500(free).

VENICE

US

VENICE GONDOLIER. s-w.: Wed. & Sat. $.50 newsstand; $29.95/yr. home deliv. in state; $44.95/yr. out of state mailed. 200 E. Venice Ave., Venice, FL 34285. TEL 941-484-2611; FAX 941-485-3036. **Owner(s):** Sun Coast Media Group, 23170 Harbor View Rd., Charlotte Harbor, FL 33980. TEL 941-629-2855; FAX 941-629-2085 Pub. Bob Vedder; adv.; pub. size: broadsheet; circ. 2,500(paid).

WAUCHULA

US

HERALD-ADVOCATE. 1900. Thu. $.46 newsstand; $35.31/yr. in state; $42.80/yr. out of state. 115 S. Seventh Ave., Wauchula, FL 33873-0338. TEL 941-773-3255; FAX 941-773-0657. **Owner(s):** Mildred Kelly, Lynchburg, VA 24506; James R. Kelly, P.O. Box 338, Wauchula, FL 33873. TEL 813-773-3255; Jean C. Kelly, P.O. Box 338, Wauchula, FL 33873. TEL 813-773-3255. Ed. Cynthia Krahl; Pub. James R. Kelly; adv.; photos; pub. size: standard; circ. 5,850(paid).

WELLINGTON

US

WELLINGTON ROYAL PALM BEACH FORUM. Wed. free. 11320 Fortune Cir., Ste. G32, Wellington, FL 33414. TEL 407-791-7790; FAX 407-791-7593. **Owner(s):** South Florida Newspaper Network, Inc., 601 Fairway Dr., Deerfield Beach, FL 33441. TEL 305-698-6397; FAX 305-698-6719; Ed. Jackie Thompson; Pub. Barbara Turner; circ. 25,000(free).

WEST PALM BEACH

US

HOME TIMES FAMILY NEWSPAPER. 1980. m. $25/yr. 3676 Collin Dr., Ste. 12, West Palm Beach, FL 33406-4727. TEL 407-439-3509. **Owner(s):** Neighbor News, Inc., P.O. Box 16096, West Palm Beach, FL 33416. TEL 407-439-3509; Ed. Dennis Lombard; Pub. Dennis Lombard; adv.; photos; bk.rev.; pub. size: tabloid; circ. 5,000(free & paid).
   Formerly: Home Times Newspaper.

US

TOWN-CRIER. 1980. Thu. free. 12794 W. Forest Hill Blvd., Ste. 21, West Palm Beach, FL 33414-4757. TEL 407-793-7606; FAX 407-793-6090; E-mail: thecrier@magg.net; URL: http://www.thecrier.com. **Owner(s):** Robert C. Markey, Jr., 12794 W. Forest Hill Blvd., Ste. 21, West Palm Beach, FL 33414. TEL 407-793-3576; Ed. Robert Markey II; Pub. Robert Markey II; adv. contact: Jeff Gold. pub. size: tabloid; circ. 8,000(free).
   Formerly: Wellington Town-Crier.

WINTER GARDEN

US

WEST ORANGE TIMES. 1913. Thu. $.50 newsstand; $15/yr. in cy.; $25/yr. out of cy. 720 S. Dillard St., Winter Garden, FL 34787. TEL 407-656-2121; FAX 407-656-6075. **Owner(s):** George Bailey, 720 S. Dillard, Winter Garden, FL 34787. TEL 407-656-2121; Ed. Maryanne Swickerath; Pub. Andrew Bailey; adv.; photos; bk.rev.; pub. size: standard; circ. 8,000(paid).

WINTER PARK

US

ORLANDO WEEKLY, THE. 1990. Thu. $32.50/6 mos. 3rd class. 807 S. Orlando Ave., Ste. R, Winter Park, FL 32789. TEL 407-645-5888; FAX 407-645-2547. **Owner(s):** Alternative Media, Detroit, MI; Ed. Jeff Truesdell; Pub. Ron Williams; adv.; photos; pub. size: tabloid; circ. 50,000(controlled & free).
   Formerly: Weekly, The.

US   ISSN 1064-3605

SENIOR OBSERVER. 1989. m. $.35 newsstand; $15/yr. 609 Executive Dr., Winter Park, FL 32789. TEL 407-628-5800. **Owner(s):** Gerhard J.W. Munster, 609 Executive Dr., Winter Park, FL 32789. TEL 407-628-8500; Pub. Gerhard J.W. Munster; adv.; photos; bk.rev.; pub. size: tabloid; circ. 10,000(free & paid).

US   ISSN 1064-3613

WINTER PARK-MAITLAND OBSERVER. 1989. w. $.35 newsstand; $24/yr. 609 Executive Dr., Winter Park, FL 32789. TEL 407-628-8500. **Owner(s):** Gerhard J.W. Munster, 609 Executive Dr., Winter Park, FL 32789. TEL 407-628-8500; Ed. Gerhard J.W. Munster; Pub. Gerhard J.W. Munster; adv.; photos; bk.rev.; pub. size: tabloid; circ. 10,000(paid).
   Formerly: Winter Park Observer.

ZEPHYRHILLS

US

ZEPHYRHILLS NEWS. 1911. Thu. $.35 newsstand; $21.60/yr. local. 38333 Fifth Ave., Zephyrhills, FL 33540. TEL 813-782-1558; FAX 813-788-7987. **Owner(s):** Republic Newspapers, Inc., P.O. Box 769, Kings Mountain, NC 28086; Ed. Dave Walters; Pub. Janet Gillis; adv.; bk.rev.; pub. size: broadsheet; circ. 5,500.

GEORGIA

ADAIRSVILLE

US

NORTH BARTOW NEWS. Tue. $.25 newsstand; $20/yr. 321-B N. Main St., Adairsville, GA 30103. TEL 770-773-3754; FAX 770-773-3754. **Owner(s):** Walls Newspapers, Inc., P.O. Box 70, Cartersville, GA 30120. TEL 404-382-4545; Ed. Sheila Mullinax; Pub. Charles Hurley; adv. contact: Lisa Edwards. pub. size: broadsheet; circ. 6,000(controlled & paid).

ADEL

US

ADEL NEWS-TRIBUNE. 1888. Wed. $.50 newsstand; $19.08/yr. in cy.; $17.01/yr. senior citizens. 131 S. Hutchinson Ave., Adel, GA 31620. TEL 912-896-2233; FAX 912-896-2233. **Owner(s):** Cook Publishing Co., Inc., 131 S. Hutchinson, Adel, GA 31620. TEL 912-896-2233; pub. size: broadsheet; circ. 3,500(paid).

ALBANY

US

ALBANY JOURNAL. 1950. Fri. $.50 newsstand; $24.13/yr. local. 118 Roosevelt Ave., Albany, GA 31703. TEL 912-435-6222; FAX 912-435-0557. **Owner(s):** William O. Davis, P.O. Box 1628, 118 Roosevelt Ave., Albany, GA 31703. TEL 912-435-6222; Ed. William O. Davis; Pub. William O. Davis; pub. size: standard; circ. 7,958(paid).

ALPHARETTA

US

ALPHARETTA REVUE. 1981. Fri. $.25 newsstand; $35/yr. 319 N. Main St., Alpharetta, GA 30201. TEL 770-442-3278; FAX 770-475-1216; E-mail: tcb@mindspring.com; URL: http://www.appnews.com. **Owner(s):** Appen Newspapers, Inc., 319 N. Main St., Alpharetta, GA 30201. TEL 770-442-3278; Ed. Hatcher Hurd. pub. size: tabloid; circ. 22,500(free).

US

BUSINESS POST, THE. m. $.25 newsstand; $35/yr. 319 N. Main St., Alpharetta, GA 30201. TEL 770-442-3278. E-mail: legacybks@aol.com. **Owner(s):** Appen Newspapers, Inc., 319 N. Main St., Alpharetta, GA 30201. TEL 404-442-3278; FAX 404-475-1216; Ed. Hatcher Hurd. pub. size: standard; circ. 22,000(paid).

ATHENS

US

ATHENS OBSERVER, THE. 1974. Thu. $.50 newsstand; $6.50/13 wks.; $13/26 wks. 288 N. Lumpkin St., Athens, GA 30601. TEL 706-353-9300; FAX 706-353-1008. **Owner(s):** Athens 100 Club LLC, P.O. Box 112, Athens, GA 30603. TEL 706-353-9300; FAX 706-353-1008; Ed. Don Brown. adv. contact: Lee Owens. photos; bk.rev.; pub. size: broadsheet; circ. 2,900(free & paid).

ATLANTA

US

ATLANTA BULLETIN. 1974. Sat. free; $30/yr. mailed. 1655 Peachtree St. Ste. 1003, Atlanta, GA 30309. TEL 404-874-1968; FAX 404-874-1968. **Owner(s):** David Smith, 1655 Peachtree Rd., Ste. 102, Atlanta, GA 30309. TEL 404-874-1968; Ed. David Smith. pub. size: tabloid; circ. 50,000(free).

US

ATLANTA DAILY WORLD. 1928. 3/wk.: Sun., Tue., Thu. $.25 newsstand; $65/yr. mailed. 145 Auburn Ave., N.E., Atlanta, GA 30335-1201. TEL 404-659-1110. **Owner(s):** Atlanta Daily World, Inc., 145 Auburn Ave., N.E., Atlanta, GA 30303. TEL 404-659-1110; Ed. William Fowlkes; Pub. C.A. Scott; adv. contact: J.R. Simmons. pub. size: broadsheet; circ. 22,000(paid); Sun. 22,000(paid). **Wire Service(s):** UPI.

US

NORTHSIDE NEIGHBOR, THE. 1968. Wed. free; $112/yr. mailed. 5290 Roswell Rd., N.W., Ste. M, Atlanta, GA 30342. TEL 770-256-3100; FAX 770-256-3292. **Owner(s):** Times Journal, Inc., 580 Fairground St., P.O. Box 449, Marietta, GA 30060. TEL 770-428-9411; FAX 770-422-9533; Ed. Faye Edmundson; Pub. Otis Brumby, Jr.; adv. contact: Leo Dwyer. adv.: $27.25/SAU. photos; pub. size: broadsheet; circ. 29,000(controlled).

US
SANDY SPRINGS NEIGHBOR, THE. Wed. free. 5290 Roswell Rd., N.W., Ste. M, Atlanta, GA 30342. TEL 770-256-3100; FAX 770-256-3292. **Owner(s):** Times Journal, Inc., 580 Fairground St., Marietta, GA 30060. TEL 770-428-9411; FAX 770-422-9533; Ed. Fay Edmundson; Pub. Otis Brumby, Jr.; adv.; pub. size: broadsheet; circ. 5,000(free).

US
TUCKER-DEKALB NEIGHBOR, THE. 1969. s-w.: Wed. & Thu. free; $52/yr. mailed. 3060 Mercer University Dr., Ste. 210, Atlanta, GA 30341. TEL 770-454-9388; FAX 770-422-9533. **Owner(s):** Times Journal, Inc., 580 Fairground St., Marietta, GA 30060. TEL 770-428-9411; FAX 770-422-9533; Ed. Steven Rosenberg; Pub. Otis Brumby, Jr.; adv.; pub. size: broadsheet; circ. 200,000(controlled).

BAINBRIDGE

US
BAINBRIDGE POST-SEARCHLIGHT. 1907. s-w.: Wed. & Sat. $.50 newsstand; $27/yr. local; $40/yr. out of area. 301 N. Crawford St., Bainbridge, GA 31717. TEL 912-246-2827; FAX 912-246-7665. **Owner(s):** Sam M. Griffin, Bainbridge Post-Searchlight, 301 N. Crawford St., Bainbridge, GA 31717. TEL 912-246-2827; Ed. Jim Smith; Pub. Sam M. Griffin, Jr.; pub. size: broadsheet; circ. evening 6,100(paid).

BARNESVILLE

US
HERALD-GAZETTE, THE. Tue. $.35 newsstand; $15.90/yr. 509 Greenwood St., Barnesville, GA 30204. TEL 770-358-0754; FAX 770-358-0756. **Owner(s):** Walter Geiger, 509 Greenwood St., Barnesville, GA 30204. TEL 770-358-0754; FAX 770-358-0756; Ed. Laura Geiger; Pub. Walter Geiger; adv. contact: Laura Geiger. pub. size: broadsheet; circ. 5,000(paid).

BAXLEY

US
BAXLEY NEWS-BANNER. 1884. Wed. $.50 newsstand; $21.20/yr. 300 Parker St., Baxley, GA 31513. TEL 912-367-2468; FAX 912-367-0277. **Owner(s):** Baxley News-Banner, Inc., P.O. Box 409, Baxley, GA 31513. TEL 912-367-2468; Ed. Max Gardner; Pub. Max Gardner; pub. size: broadsheet; circ. 4,100(paid).

BLAIRSVILLE

US
NORTH GEORGIA NEWS. 1912. Wed. $.50 newsstand; $30/yr. P.O. Box 2029, Blairsville, GA 30514. TEL 706-745-6343; FAX 706-745-1830. **Owner(s):** Wanda R. West, P.O. Box 2029, Blairsville, GA 30514. TEL 706-745-6343; FAX 706-745-1830; Ed. Norman Cooper; Pub. Wanda R. West; adv. contact: Dave Wolf. pub. size: broadsheet; circ. 8,700(paid).
   Formerly: Blairsville North Georgia News.

BOSTON

US
GEORGIA SOUTH. 1993. Thu. $.35 newsstand; $24.50/yr. mailed 101 N. Main St., Boston, GA 31626. TEL 912-498-6397; FAX 912-498-1420. **Owner(s):** Georgia South Pubs. Enterprises, Inc., P.O. Box 69, Boston, GA 31626-0069. TEL 912-498-6397; FAX 912-498-1420; Ed. Dorothy Miller; Pub. Dorothy Miller; adv. contact: Savannah Miller Rogers. photos; bk.rev.; pub. size: broadsheet; circ. 6,000(free & paid).

BREMEN

US
HARALSON GATEWAY-BEACON, THE. 1895. Thu. $.50 newsstand; $15-$20/yr. in area. 222 Tallapoosa St. Bremen, GA 30110. TEL 770-537-2434; FAX 770-537-0826. **Owner(s):** Paxton Media Group, Inc., P.O. Box 2300, Paducah, KY 42002. TEL 502-443-1771; Ed. Bruce Browning; Pub. Dawn Weatherby; adv. contact: Cathy Keller. photos; pub. size: broadsheet; circ. 6,300(paid).

BRUNSWICK

US
GLYNCO OBSERVER. 1984. bi-w.: Thu. free. 5000 D Altama Ave., Brunswick, GA 31525. TEL 912-267-7878 FAX 912-264-3357. **Owner(s):** Troy Fore, 5000 D Altama Ave., Brunswick, GA 31525. TEL 912-267-7878; Ed. Troy Fore. pub. size: tabloid; circ. 3,500(free).

US
HARBOR SOUND. 1984. Wed. $3/mo. 1326 Newcastle St., Brunswick, GA 31520-0606. TEL 912-264-4521; FAX 912-264-4531. **Owner(s):** Jim Dryden, 1326 Newcastle St., Brunswick, GA 31520. TEL 912-264-4521; FAX 912-264-4531; Ed. Jim Dryden. adv.; photos; pub. size: tabloid; circ. 28,000(free).

US
JEKYLL'S GOLDEN ISLANDER. 1972. bi-m.: Thu. $15/yr. 3rd class; $25/yr. 1st class. 5000 D Altama Ave., Brunswick, GA 31525. TEL 912-267-7878; FAX 912-264-3357. **Owner(s):** Glynn Press, Inc., 5000 Altana Ave., Creola, AL 36525. TEL 912-267-7878; Ed. Troy Fore; Pub. Troy Fore; pub. size: tabloid; circ. 6,000(paid).

CAIRO

US
CAIRO MESSENGER. 1904. Wed. $.35 newsstand; $13.50/yr. loca; $16/yr. out of area; $18/yr. out of state. 31-35 First Ave., N.E., Cairo, GA 31728. TEL 912-377-2032; FAX 912-377-4640. **Owner(s):** Messenger Publishing Co., Inc., 31-35 First Ave., N.E., Cairo, GA 31728. TEL 912-377-2032; Ed. Robert H. Wind; Pub. Robert H. Wind; adv. contact: Randolph H. Wind. pub. size: broadsheet; circ. 6,200(paid).

CALHOUN

US
CALHOUN TIMES. 1870. s-w.: Wed. & Sat. $.50 newsstand; $24/yr. in cy.; $34/yr. out of cy. 215 W. Line St., Calhoun, GA 30703. TEL 706-629-2230; FAX 706-625-0899. **Owner(s):** News Publishing Co., 305 E. Sixth Ave., Rome, GA 30162. TEL 706-291-6297; Ed. Mitch Talley; Pub. Burgitt Mooney; pub. size: broadsheet; circ. 9,250(paid).

CAMILLA

US
CAMILLA ENTERPRISE. 1903. s-w.: Wed. & Fri. $.50 newsstand; $26.50/yr. in cy.; $42.50/yr. out of cy. 13 S. Scott St., Camilla, GA 31730. TEL 912-336-5265; FAX 912-336-8476. **Owner(s):** Robert Tribble P.O. Box 426, Manchester, GA; Pub. Roger Ann Jones; pub. size: broadsheet; circ. 3,400(paid).

CANTON

US
CHEROKEE TRIBUNE, THE. 1973. s-w.: Wed. & Sun. $.25/day newsstand; $.70/Sun.; $18/yr. 521 E. Main St., Canton, GA 30114. TEL 770-479-1441; FAX 770-479-3505. **Owner(s):** Times Journal, Inc., 580 Fairground St., Marietta, GA 30060. TEL 770-428-9411; FAX 770-428-7945; Ed. John Short; Pub. Otis Brumby, Jr.; adv. contact: Rebecca Hayes. bk.rev.; pub. size: broadsheet; circ. 32,000(free & paid); Sun. 32,000(free & paid).

CARTERSVILLE

US
BARTOW NEIGHBOR, THE. Wed. free. 16 Wall St., Cartersville, GA 30120. TEL 770-386-0872. **Owner(s):** Times Journal, Inc., 580 Fairground St., Marietta, GA 30060. TEL 770-428-9411; FAX 770-422-9533; Ed. Masie Underwood; Pub. Otis Brumby, Jr.; adv.; pub. size: broadsheet; circ. 7,000(free).

US
HERALD-TRIBUNE, THE. 1926 Tue. $.25 newsstand; $12/6 mos. in cy.; $20/yr. 251 S. Tennessee St., Cartersville, GA 30120. TEL 404-382-4545; FAX 404-382-2711. **Owner(s):** Cleveland Newspapers, Inc., P.O. Box 3600, Cleveland, TN 37320. TEL 423-472-504 ; Ed. Kevin Atwill; Pub. Charles Hurley; adv. contact: Charles Hurley. photos; pub. size: broadsheet; circ. 9,500(controlled & paid).

CEDARTOWN

US
CEDARTOWN STANDARD. 1869 s-w.: Tue. & Thu. $.50 newsstand; $20/yr. local; $34/yr. out of area. 213 Main St., Cedartown, GA 30125. TEL 770-748-1520. **Owner(s):** News Publishing Co., 305 E. Sixth Ave., Rome, GA 30161. TEL 404-291-6397; Ed. James M. Penney; Pub. B.H. Mooney, III; adv. contact: Tira Carter. pub. size: broadsheet; circ. 3,500(paid).

CHATSWORTH

US
CHATSWORTH TIMES, THE. 1885. Wed. $.50 newsstand; $15.75/yr. local $28/yr. out of city. 224 N. Third Ave., Chatsworth, GA 30705. TEL 706-695-4646; FAX 706-695-7181. **Owner(s):** Walls Newspapers, Inc., P.O. Box 70, Cartersville, GA 30120. TEL 404-382-4545; Ed. David L. Shelton; Pub. David L. Shelton; adv.; photos; pub. size: standard; circ. 5,800(paid).

CLAYTON
US
CLAYTON TRIBUNE. 1898. Thu. $.50 newsstand; $18/yr. in cy.; $22/yr. out of cy. Main & Oak Crescent Dr., Clayton, GA 30525. TEL 706-782-3312; FAX 706-782-4230. **Owner(s):** Community Newspapers, Inc., P.O. Box 792, Athens, GA 30603. TEL 800-226-0692; FAX 706-548-0808; Ed. Dorsey Martin; Pub. Russell Majors; adv.; pub. size: standard; circ. 6,525(controlled & paid).

COLQUITT
US
MILLER COUNTY LIBERAL. 1897. Thu. $.50 newsstand; $14.70/yr. local; $23.10/yr. elsewhere. 157 E. Main St., Colquitt, GA 31737-0037. TEL 912-758-5549; FAX 912-758-5540. **Owner(s):** Terry Toole, 157 E. Main St., P.O. Box 37, Colquitt, GA 31737. TEL 912-758-5549; FAX 912-758-5540; Ed. Debra Jones; Pub. Terry Toole; adv. contact: Betty Jo Toole. photos; bk.rev.; pub. size: broadsheet; circ. 2,800(controlled & paid). **Wire Service(s):** AP.

COLUMBUS
US
BENNING LEADER, THE. 1991. Fri. free. 17 W. 12th St., Columbus, GA 31994. TEL 706-324-5526; FAX 706-576-6234. **Owner(s):** Knight-Ridder, Inc., One Herald Plz., Miami, FL 33132. TEL 305-376-3800; Ed. Tony Adams; Pub. John Greenman; adv. contact: David Fletcher. pub. size: tabloid; circ. 25,000(controlled).
    Formerly: Benning Patriot.

COMMERCE
US
COMMERCE NEWS. 1875. Wed. $.50 newsstand; $16.50/yr. ir cy. 1672 S. Broad St., Commerce, GA 30529. TEL 706-335-2927; FAX 706-335-4531. **Owner(s):** Jackson Herald Publishing Co., P.O. Box 908, Jefferson, GA 30549. TEL 404-367-5233; Ed. Mark S. Beardsley; Pub. Herman Buffington; adv. contact: Patricia Watson. photos; pub. size: broadsheet; circ. 4,500(paid).

CONYERS
US
ROCKDALE NEIGHBOR, THE. 1969. Wed. free. 1706-D Hwy. 138, Conyers, GA 30208. TEL 770-922-8300; FAX 770-922-0879. **Owner(s):** Times Journal, Inc., 580 Fairground St., P.O. Box 449, Marietta, GA 30060. TEL 770-428-9411; FAX 770-422-9533; Ed. Anthony Rhoades; Pub. Otis Brumby; adv.; pub. size: broadsheet; circ. 17,000(free).

CORNELIA
US
NORTHEAST GEORGIAN, THE. 1892. Wed. $.50 newsstand; $17/yr. in cy.; $27/yr. out of cy. 236 Level Grove Rd., Cornelia, GA 30531. TEL 706-778-4215; FAX 706-778-4114. **Owner(s):** Community Newspapers, Inc., P.O. Box 792, Athens, GA 30603. TEL 800-226-0692; FAX 706-548-0808; Ed. Steve Avery; Pub. John D. Solesbee; adv. contact: Dalton Sirmans. pub. size: broadsheet; circ. 9,100(paid).
    Formerly: Cornelia Northeast Georgian.

COVINGTON
US
COVINGTON NEWS. 1865. 3/wk.: Tue., Thu., Sat. $.50 newsstand; $41.35/yr. in cy.; $46.64/yr. out of cy. 1166 Usher St., N.W., Covington, GA 30210. TEL 770-787-6397; FAX 770-786-6451. **Owner(s):** Morris Communications, P.O. Box 936, Augusta, GA 30903. TEL 706-724-0851; FAX 706-722-7125; Pub. Ron Stokes; adv. contact: Kim Davis. pub. size: broadsheet; circ. 7,000(controlled & paid).
    Formerly: Covington News/Multi-County Star.

US
STAR EXPRESS. Tue. free. 1166 Usher St., Covington, GA 30210. TEL 770-787-6397; FAX 770-786-6451. **Owner(s):** Morris Communications, P.O. Box 936, Augusta, GA 30903. TEL 706-724-0851; Pub. Ron Stokes; adv. contact: Kim Davis. pub. size: broadsheet; circ. 18,000(controlled).

CUMMING
US
FORSYTH COUNTY NEWS. 1908. 3/wk.: Wed., Fri., Sun. $25/yr. in cy.; $50/yr. out of cy. 121 Dahlonega St., Cumming, GA 30130. TEL 404-887-3126; FAX 404-889-6017. **Owner(s):** Swartz-Morris Media, Inc., P.O. Box 210, Cumming, GA 30128. TEL 770-887-3126; FAX 770-889-6017; Ed. Karlene Chalker; Pub. Dennis Stockton; adv. contact: Jeff Morgan. photos; bk.rev.; pub. size: broadsheet; circ. 13,000(paid); Sun. 13,200(paid). **Wire Service(s):** NYT.

DALLAS
US
DALLAS NEW ERA. 1882. Thu. $.25 newsstand; $8/yr.; $14/2 yrs. 121 W. Spring St., Dallas, GA 30132. TEL 770-445-3379. **Owner(s):** T.E. & J.T. Parker, 121 W. Spring St., Dallas, GA 30132. TEL 404-495-3379; Ed. T.E. Parker; Pub. T.E. Parker; adv. contact: Annette Manning. photos; pub. size: broadsheet; circ. 7,000(paid).

DARIEN
US
DARIEN NEWS. 1951. Wed. $.35 newsstand; $15.90/yr. in cy.; $21.20/yr. out of cy.; $25/yr. out of state. 101 Broad St., Darien, GA 31305. TEL 912-437-4251; FAX 912-437-2299. **Owner(s):** Charles M. Williamson, Jr., P.O. Box 496, Darien, GA 31305. TEL 912-437-4251; FAX 912-437-2299; Pub. Charles M. Williamson, Jr.; adv.; photos; pub. size: broadsheet; circ. 2,900(paid).

DAWSON
US
DAWSON NEWS, THE. 1866. Thu. $.35 newsstand; $18/yr. in area; $21/yr. in state; $27/yr. out of state. 139 W. Lee St., Dawson, GA 31742-0350. TEL 912-995-2175; FAX 912-995-3713. **Owner(s):** Tommy Rountree, 139 W. Lee St., Dawson, GA 31742-0350. TEL 912-995-2175; FAX 912-995-3713; Ed. Tommy Rountree. adv.; photos; pub. size: broadsheet; circ. 8,200(free & paid).

DECATUR
US
DECATUR-DEKALB NEWS/ERA. 1949. Thu. $.25 newsstand; $15.75/yr. One Town Ctr., E. Ponce De Leon, Decatur, GA 30030. TEL 404-373-4488. **Owner(s):** Decatur News Publishing Co., Inc., 739 DeKalb Industrial Way, Decatur, GA 30033. TEL 404-292-3536; Ed. John Sell; Pub. Jerry Crane; adv.; pub. size: broadsheet; circ. 9,600(paid).
    Formerly: DeKalb News/Sun.

DONALSONVILLE
US
DONALSONVILLE NEWS. 1916. Wed. $15.90/yr. local; $21.20/yr. elsewhere. 120 W. Second St., Donalsonville, GA 31745. TEL 912-524-2343; FAX 912-524-2343. **Owner(s):** Donalsonville News, Inc., Bo McLeod, Donalsonville, GA 31745. TEL 912-524-2343; Ed. Bo McLeod; Pub. Bo McLeod; pub. size: broadsheet; circ. 3,600(paid).

DOUGLAS
US
DOUGLAS ENTERPRISE. 1888. s-w.: Wed. & Sun. $.50 newsstand; $24.50/yr. in area; $55/yr. elsewhere. 1823 S. Peterson Ave., Douglas, GA 31533. TEL 912-384-2323; FAX 912-383-0218. **Owner(s):** Lovan B. & Patricia W. Thomas, 1823 S. Peterson Ave., Douglas, GA 31533. TEL 912-384-2323; Ed. Thomas Frier, Jr.; Pub. Jim Merritt; adv. contact: Jim Merritt. photos; pub. size: standard; circ. 8,100(paid); Sun. 8,100(paid).

DUNWOODY
US
CRIER NEWSPAPER. 1975. Thu. $40/yr. 17 Dunwoody Pk., Ste. 101, Dunwoody, GA 30338. TEL 770-394-4147; FAX 770-394-0019. **Owner(s):** Susan Courtemanche, 17 Dunwoody Pk., Dunwoody, GA 30338. TEL 404-394-4147; FAX 404-394-0019; Ed. Susan Courtemanche. pub. size: tabloid; circ. 22,000(controlled & free).

US
ROSWELL/ALPHARETTA CRIER NEWSPAPER. 1986. s-m.: 1st & 15th. free. 17 Dunwoody Pk., Ste. 101, Dunwoody, GA 30338. TEL 770-394-4147; FAX 770-394-0019. **Owner(s):** Susan Courtemanche, 17 Dunwood Pk., Ste. 101, Dunwoody, GA 30338; Ed. Susan Courtmanche; Pub. Susan Courtmanche; adv. contact: James Hart. pub. size: tabloid; circ. 15,000(controlled & free).

EASTMAN
US
DODGE COUNTY NEWS, THE. 1989. Wed. $.35 newsstand; $16/yr. in cy.; $21/yr. out of cy.; $26/yr. out of state. 218 Main St., S.E., Eastman, GA 31023-1650. TEL 912-374-0360; FAX 912-374-0361; E-mail: ceckles@mailpublic.lib.ga.us. **Owner(s):** Cindy Eckles, 218 Main St., S.E., Eastman, GA 31023. TEL 912-374-0360; FAX 912-374-0361; Ed. Chad Smith; Pub. Cindy Eckles; adv. contact: Cindy Eckles. photos; pub. size: broadsheet; circ. 5,515(free & paid).

US

TIMES JOURNAL-SPOTLIGHT. 1871. Wed. $.35 newsstand; $15/yr. in cy.; $20/yr. out of cy.; $24/yr. out of state. 227 College St., Eastman, GA 31023. TEL 912-374-5562; FAX 912-374-3464. **Owner(s):** Investments & Counseling Services, Inc., P.O. Drawer 4189, Eastman, GA 31023. TEL 912-374-3464; Ed. Julia J. Roberts; Pub. Julia J. Roberts; adv.; photos; pub. size: broadsheet; circ. 5,050(paid).
  Formerly: Eastman Times Journal-Spotlight.

ELBERTON

US   ISSN 8750-6734

ELBERTON STAR. 1887. Wed. $.50 newsstand; $16/yr. in cy.; $18/yr. in state; $26/yr. out of state; $14/yr. senior citizens. 14 N. Oliver St., Elberton, GA 30635-0280. TEL 706-283-3100; FAX 706-283-7841. **Owner(s):** Southern Publishing Co., Atlanta, GA; Ed. Carolyn E. Cann; Pub. Paula Pennell; adv.; photos; pub. size: broadsheet; circ. 5,600(paid).

ELLIJAY

US   ISSN 0630-0280

TIMES-COURIER. 1875. Wed. $.25 newsstand; $10/yr. in cy.; $12.50/yr. out of cy. 13 River St., Ellijay, GA 30540. TEL 706-635-4313; FAX 706-635-7006. **Owner(s):** George Bunch, P.O. Box 1076, Ellijay, GA 30540. TEL 706-635-4313; FAX 706-635-7006; Ed. George N. Bunch; Pub. George N. Bunch; adv. contact: George Bunch, Ill. photos; pub. size: broadsheet; circ. 6,550(paid).

FAYETTEVILLE

US

FAYETTE COUNTY NEWS. 1886. 3/wk: Tue., Thu., Sat. $.50 newsstand; $26.25/yr. 180 Church St., Fayetteville, GA 30214. TEL 770-461-6317; FAX 770-460-8172. **Owner(s):** Trib Publications, Inc., P.O. Box 426, Manchester, GA 31816. TEL 706-846-3188; FAX 706-846-2206; Ed. Pat Cooper; Pub. Robert Tribble; adv.; photos; pub. size: broadsheet; circ. 9,500(paid).

US

FAYETTE NEIGHBOR, THE. Wed. free. 635 N. Glynn St., Fayetteville, GA 30214. TEL 770-461-1136; FAX 770-461-1385. **Owner(s):** Times Journal, Inc., 580 Fairground St., Marietta, GA 30060. TEL 770-428-9411; FAX 770-422-9533; Ed. Joy Denton; Pub. Otis A. Brumby, Jr.; adv.; pub. size: broadsheet; circ. 16,800(free).

FITZGERALD

US

HERALD-LEADER, THE. 1895. Wed. $.50 newsstand; $30/yr. 202-204 E. Central Ave., Fitzgerald, GA 31750. TEL 912-423-9331; FAX 912-423-6533. **Owner(s):** Pryor Publications, 202-204 E. Central Ave., Fitzgerald, GA 31750. TEL 912-423-9331; FAX 912-423-6533; Ed. Barbara Ashe; Pub. Gerald W. Pryor; adv. contact: Becky Anderson. photos; pub. size: standard; circ. 5,700(paid).

FOLKSTON

US

CHARLTON COUNTY HERALD. 1898. Wed. $.30 newsstand; $14.84/yr. in cy.; $18.02/yr. out of cy. 102 W. Love St., Folkston, GA 31537. TEL 912-496-3585; FAX 912-496-4585. **Owner(s):** David Thompson, 504 S. First St., Falleston, GA 31537. TEL 912-496-7304; Ed. David Thompson. pub. size: broadsheet; circ. 2,700(paid).

FORT VALLEY

US

LEADER-TRIBUNE, THE. 1888. Wed. $.50 newsstand; $18.90/yr. in cy.; $26.50/yr. in state; $45/yr. out of state. 109 Anderson Ave., Fort Valley, GA 31030. TEL 912-825-2432; FAX 912-825-4130. **Owner(s):** Peach Publishing Co., Inc., 109 Anderson Ave., Fort Valley, GA 31030. TEL 912-825-2432; FAX 912-825-4130; Ed. Cindy Morley; Pub. Robert E. Tribble; adv.; pub. size: broadsheet; circ. 14,110(free & paid).
  Formerly: Fort Valley Leader-Tribune.

GLENNVILLE

US

GLENNVILLE SENTINEL. 1925. Thu. $.50 newsstand; $16.96 in-state; $21.20 elsewhere. P.O. Box 218, Glennville, GA 30427. TEL 912-654-2515; FAX 912-654-2527. **Owner(s):** Pam & Russell Terry Waters, P.O. Box 218, Glennville, GA 30427. TEL 912-654-2515; FAX 912-654-2527; Ed. Pam Waters; Pub. Pam Waters; adv.; pub. size: tabloid; circ. 3,450(free & paid).

GREENVILLE

US

MERIWETHER FREE PRESS. 1989. Wed. $.25 newsstand; $13/yr. in cy.; $19/yr. in state; $25/yr. out of state. 116 East Ct. Sq., Greenville, GA 30222. TEL 706-672-1753; FAX 706-672-1977. **Owner(s):** Kara Barnes Hamlott, Woodbury, GA. TEL 706-553-5601; Ed. Lee N. Howell; Pub. Lee N. Howell; adv. contact: Bryan Jeter. photos; bk.rev.; pub. size: broadsheet; circ. 2,200(free & paid).

HARTWELL

US

HARTWELL SUN, THE. 1877. Wed. $.50 newsstand; $20/yr. local; $24/yr. in state. 138 N. Forest Ave., Hartwell, GA 30643. TEL 706-376-8025; FAX 706-376-3016. **Owner(s):** Southern Crescent Newspapers, L.P., 138 Church St., Jonesboro, GA 30236; Ed. Wassie Vickery; Pub. Peggy K. Vickery; adv. contact: Rita Chapman. pub. size: broadsheet; circ. 6,300(free & paid).

HAZLEHURST

US

JEFF DAVIS LEDGER. 1940. Wed. $.50 newsstand; $15/yr. in area. 104 Lattimer St., Hazlehurst, GA 31539. TEL 912-375-4225; FAX 912-375-3704. **Owner(s):** Hazlehurst Publishing Co., P.O. Box 338, Hazlehurst, GA 31539. TEL 912-375-4225; FAX 912-375-3704; Ed. Thomas H. Purser; Pub. Kay Purser; adv. contact: Kay Purser. photos; pub. size: broadsheet; circ. 3,900(paid).

HELENA

US   ISSN 0746-4630

TELFAIR TIMES. 1952. Wed. $.25 newsstand; $10/yr. Hwy 341 N., Helena, GA 31037. TEL 912-868-5776; FAX 912-868-7255. **Owner(s):** Corbeau Publications, Inc., P.O. Box 459, Helena, GA 31037. TEL 912-868-5776; adv.; pub. size: broadsheet; circ. 2,000(paid).

US

THREE RIVERS GAZETTE. 1984. Tue. free. Hwy. 341 N., Helena, GA 31037. TEL 912-868-5776. **Owner(s):** Corbeau Publications, Inc., P.O. Box 459, Helena, GA 31037. TEL 912-868-5776; adv.; pub. size: tabloid; circ. 8,000(free).

HINESVILLE

US   ISSN 1047-6636

COASTAL COURIER. 1871. 3/wk.: Sun., Wed., Fri. $39/yr. in cy.; $41/yr. out of cy.; $46/yr. out of state. 125 S. Main St., Hinesville, GA 31313. TEL 912-876-0156; FAX 912-368-6329. **Owner(s):** Charles Morris, P.O. Box 8167, Savannah, GA 31412. TEL 912-233-1281; Ed. Pat Watkins; Pub. Mark Griffin; adv. contact: Matt Newton. photos; bk.rev.; pub. size: standard; circ. 5,600(paid).

HOMERVILLE

US

CLINCH COUNTY NEWS. 1894. Wed. $.47 newsstand; $15/yr. in cy.; $22/yr. out of cy. 210 E. Dame Ave., Homerville, GA 31634. TEL 912-487-5337; FAX 912-437-3227. **Owner(s):** Robert & Cheryl Williams, 210 E. Dame Ave., Homerville, GA 31634. TEL 912-487-5337; FAX 912-487-3227; Ed. Len Robbins; Pub. Robert Williams; adv.; photos; pub. size: broadsheet; circ. 1,900(free & paid).

JACKSON

US

JACKSON PROGRESS-ARGUS. 1873. Wed. $.50 newsstand; $18/yr. local; $34/yr. out of area. 129 Mulberry St., Jackson, GA 30233. TEL 404-775-3107; FAX 404-775-3855. **Owner(s):** Southern Publishing Co., 138 Church St., P.O. Box 368, Jonesboro, GA 30237. TEL 770-478-5753; Ed. Larry Stanford; Pub. Herman Cawthon; pub. size: standard; circ. 4,200(paid).

JEFFERSON

US

JACKSON HERALD. 1875. Wed. $.50 newsstand; $16.50/yr. in cy.; $22/yr. out of cy.; $35.35/yr. out of state. 33 Lee St., Jefferson, GA 30549. TEL 706-367-5233; FAX 706-367-8056. **Owner(s):** Herman Buffington, 162 Jett Roberts Rd., Jefferson, GA 30549. TEL 706-367-5233; Ed. Mike Buffington; Pub. Herman Buffington; adv. contact: Scott Buffington. pub. size: broadsheet; circ. 8,450(paid).

JESUP

US

PRESS-SENTINEL, THE. s-w.: Wed. & Sun. $.50 newsstand; $25/yr. mailed in cy.; $30/yr. out of state. 252 W. Walnut St., Jesup, GA 31545. TEL 912-427-3757; FAX 912-427-4092. **Owner(s):** Press-Sentinel Newspapers, Inc., P.O. Box 607, Jesup, GA 31545. TEL 912-427-3757; Ed. Drew Davis; Pub. Eric Denty; pub. size: broadsheet; circ. 7,200(paid).

LA FAYETTE

US

WALKER COUNTY MESSENGER. 1877. s-w.: Wed. & Fri. $.50 newstand; $24/yr. in cy.; $34/yr. out of area. 120 E. Patton St., La Fayette, GA 30728. TEL 706-638-1859; FAX 706-638-7045. **Owner(s):** News Publishing Co., P.O. Box 1633, Rome, GA 30162. TEL 404-291-6397; Ed. Don Stilwell; Pub. Burgett Mooney; adv. contact: Tanya Wallin. pub. size: broadsheet; circ. 3,900(paid).

LAVONIA

US

FRANKLIN COUNTY CITIZEN. 1971. Thu. $15/yr. in cy.; $20/yr. out of cy.; $24/yr. out of state. 12150 Augusta Rd., Lavonia, GA 30553. TEL 706-356-8557; FAX 706-356-2008. **Owner(s):** Community Newspapers, Inc., P.O. Box 792, Athens, GA 30603; Ed. Greg T. Pitts; Pub. Greg T. Pitts; adv.: $4.95/SAU. pub. size: broadsheet; circ. 5,418(paid).

LUDOWICI

US

LUDOWICI NEWS. 1921. Thu. $.40 newsstand; $15/yr. in cy.; $18/yr. elsewhere. 8 McDonald St., Ludowici, GA 31316. TEL 912-545-2103; FAX 912-545-2103. **Owner(s):** Ken Buchanan, 8 McDonald St., Lusowici, GA 31316. TEL 912-545-2103; Ed. Joe Parker; Pub. Ken Buchanan; adv.; pub. size: tabloid; circ. 1,000(paid).

MADISON

US

MADISONIAN, THE. 1842. Thu. $.50 newsstand; $21.20/yr. in cy.; $24.38/yr. in state; $29/yr. out of state. 131 E. Jefferson St., Madison, GA 30650. TEL 706-342-2424; FAX 706-342-1300. **Owner(s):** Robert B. Booth, P.O. Box 191, Madison, GA 30650. TEL 706-342-2424; Adelaide W. Ponder, P.O. Box 191, Madison, GA 30650. TEL 706-342-2424; Pub. Robert B. Booth; adv.; photos; bk.rev.; pub. size: broadsheet; circ. 4,800(paid).

US

OCONEE BREEZE. 1985. Sat. $.50 newsstand; $10.30/yr. mailed locally. 131 E. Jefferson St., Madison, GA 30650-0191. TEL 706-342-2424; FAX 706-342-1300. **Owner(s):** Robert B. Booth, P.O. Box 191, Madison, GA 30650. TEL 706-342-2424; Pub. Robert B. Booth; adv.; pub. size: broadsheet; circ. 6,000(free & paid).
   Formerly: Lake Oconee Free Press.

MANCHESTER

US

MANCHESTER STAR-MERCURY. 1911. Wed. $.50 newsstand; $19.08/yr. in cy.; $23.63/yr. out of cy.; $30/yr. out of state. 3051 Roosevelt Hwy., Manchester, GA 31816. TEL 706-846-3188; FAX 706-846-2206. **Owner(s):** Trib Publications, Inc., P.O. Box 426, Manchester, GA 31816. TEL 706-846-3188; Pub. Robert Tribble; adv. contact: Mike Hale. photos; pub. size: broadsheet; circ. 3,650(free & paid).

US

MERIWETHER VINDICATOR. 1876. Fri. $.35 newsstand; $15.75/yr. in cy.; $23.63/yr. in state; $30/yr. out of state. 3051 Roosevelt Hwy., Manchester, GA 31816. TEL 706-846-3188; FAX 706-846-2206. **Owner(s):** Trib Publications, Inc., P.O. Box 426, Manchester, GA 31816. TEL 706-846-3188; FAX 706-846-2206; Ed. Micky D'Avy; Pub. Robert Tribble; adv.; photos; pub. size: broadsheet; circ. 1,700(free & paid).

MARIETTA

US

ACWORTH NEIGHBOR. 1815. Thu. free local deliv.; $112/yr. mailed. 580 Fairground St., Marietta, GA 30061. TEL 770-428-9411; FAX 770-422-9533. **Owner(s):** Times Journal, Inc., 580 Fairground St., Marietta, GA 30060. TEL 770-428-9411; FAX 770-422-9533; Ed. Rodney Shumake; Pub. Otis A. Brumby, Jr.; adv.; pub. size: broadsheet; circ. 6,609(free).

US

AUSTELL NEIGHBOR. Thu. free local deliv.; $112/yr. mailed. 580 Fairground St., Marietta, GA 30060. TEL 770-428-9411; FAX 770-422-9533. **Owner(s):** Times Journal, Inc., 580 Fairground St., Marietta, GA 30060. TEL 770-428-9411; FAX 770-422-9533; Ed. Rodney Shumake; Pub. Otis A. Brumby, Jr.; adv.; pub. size: broadsheet; circ. 6,550(free).

US

CHAMBLEE-DEKALB NEIGHBOR. 1969. Wed. free; $52/yr. mailed. 580 Fairground St., Marietta, GA 30060. TEL 770-428-9411; FAX 770-422-9533. **Owner(s):** Times Journal, Inc., P.O. Box 449, Marietta, GA 30061. TEL 770-428-9411; FAX 770-422-9533; Ed. Steve Rosenberg; Pub. Otis Brumby; adv. contact: Julie Dollar. pub. size: broadsheet; circ. 5,100(controlled & free).

US

CLAYTON NEIGHBOR. 1976. Thu. free; $112/yr. mailed. 580 Fairground St., Marietta, GA 30061. TEL 770-428-9411; FAX 770-422-9533. **Owner(s):** Times Journal, Inc., 580 Fairground St., Marietta, GA 30060. TEL 770-428-9411; FAX 770-422-9533; Ed. John Marsh; Pub. Otis Brumby, Jr.; adv. contact: Judy Laney. pub. size: broadsheet; circ. 38,250(controlled).

US

DORAVILLE-DEKALB NEIGHBOR. 1969. Wed. free; $52/yr. mailed. 580 Fairgound St., Marietta, GA 30060. TEL 770-428-9411; FAX 770-422-9533. **Owner(s):** Times Journal, Inc., 580 Fairground St., Marietta, GA 30060. TEL 770-428-9411; FAX 770-422-9533; Ed. Steve Rosenberg; Pub. Otis A. Brumby, Jr.; adv.; pub. size: broadsheet; circ. 7,000(controlled).

US

DOUGLAS NEIGHBOR, THE. Thu. free. 580 Fairground St., Marietta, GA 30060. TEL 770-428-9411; FAX 770-422-9533. **Owner(s):** Times Journal, Inc., 580 Fairground St., Marietta, GA 30060. TEL 770-428-9411; FAX 770-422-9533; Ed. Joe Baggett; Pub. Otis Brumby, Jr.; adv.; pub. size: broadsheet; circ. 10,000(free).

US

DUNWOODY-DEKALB NEIGHBOR, THE. 1969. Wed. free. 580 Fairgound St., Marietta, GA 30060. TEL 770-428-9411; FAX 770-422-9533. **Owner(s):** Times Journal, Inc., P.O. Box 449, Marietta, GA 30061. TEL 770-428-9411; Pub. Otis Brumby, Jr.; adv. contact: Judy Laney. pub. size: broadsheet; circ. 10,000(controlled).

US

KENNESAW NEIGHBOR, THE. Thu. free local deliv.; $112/yr. mailed. 580 Fairground St., Marietta, GA 30060. TEL 404-428-9411; FAX 404-422-9533. **Owner(s):** Times Journal, Inc., 580 Fairground St., Marietta, GA 30060. TEL 770-428-9411; FAX 770-422-9533; Ed. Rodney Shumake; Pub. Otis A. Brumby, Jr.; adv.; pub. size: broadsheet; circ. 8,942(free).

US

MABLETON NEIGHBOR, THE. 1973. Thu. free local deliv.; $112/yr. mailed. 580 Fairground St., Marietta, GA 30060. TEL 770-428-9411; FAX 770-422-9533. **Owner(s):** Times Journal, Inc., 580 Fairground St., Marietta, GA 30060. TEL 770-428-9411; FAX 770-422-9533; Ed. Rodney Shumake; Pub. Otiis A. Brumby, Jr.; adv.; pub. size: broadsheet; circ. 6,591(free).

US

PAULDING NEIGHBOR, THE. Thu. free newsstand; $52/yr. mailed. 580 Fairground St., Marietta, GA 30060. TEL 770-428-9411; FAX 770-422-9533. **Owner(s):** Times Journal, Inc., 508 Fairgrounds, Marietta, GA 30060. TEL 770-428-9411; FAX 770-422-9533; Ed. Stan Hardegree; Pub. Otis A. Brumby, Jr.; adv. contact: Judy Laney. pub. size: broadsheet; circ. 14,750(free & paid). **Wire Service(s):** AP.

US

POWDER SPRINGS NEIGHBOR, THE. Thu. free local deliv.; $112/yr. mailed. 580 Fairground St., Marietta, GA 30060. TEL 770-428-9411; FAX 770-422-9533. **Owner(s):** Times Journal, Inc., 580 Fairground St., Marietta, GA 30060. TEL 770-428-9411; FAX 770-422-9533; Ed. Rodney Shumake; Pub. Otis A. Brumby, Jr.; adv.; pub. size: broadsheet; circ. 7,864(free).

US

SOUTH DEKALB NEIGHBOR, THE. Wed. free, $52/yr. mailed. 580 Faigound St., Marietta, GA 30060. TEL 770-428-9411; FAX 770-422-9533. **Owner(s):** Marietta Daily Journal & Neighbor Newspapers, 580 Fairground St., P.O. Box 449, Marietta, GA 30060. TEL 770-428-9411; Ed. Peggy Reeves; Pub. Otis Brumby, Jr.; adv. contact: Kathleen Gray. pub. size: broadsheet; circ. 30,500(free & paid).

US   ISSN 0192-0693

SOUTH FULTON NEIGHBOR, THE. 1968. Wed. free. 580 Fairground St., Marietta, GA 30060. TEL 770-428-9411; FAX 770-422-9533. **Owner(s):** Times Journal, Inc., 580 Fairground St., Marietta, GA 30060. TEL 770-428-9411; FAX 770-422-9533; Ed. Martha Barksdale; Pub. Otis A. Brumby, Jr.; adv. contact: Kaye Sessions. pub. size: broadsheet; circ. 22,000(free).

MARTINEZ

US

COLUMBIA NEWS TIMES. 1928. s-w.: Wed. & Fri. $.50 newsstand; $31.20/yr. in cy.; $33.25/yr. in state; $35.50/yr. out of state; $28.10/yr. senior citizens. 3919 Roberts Rd., Martinez, GA 30907. TEL 706-863-6165; FAX 706-863-9080. **Owner(s):** Karl Haywood & Phil Blanchard, 3919 Roberts Rd., Martinez, GA 30907. TEL 706-863-6165; FAX 706-863-9080; Ed. Karl Haywood; Pub. Phil Blanchard; adv.; photos; pub. size: broadsheet; circ. 14,500(paid).
   Formerly: Columbia News & Martinez-Evans Times.

MCDONOUGH

US

HENRY HERALD, THE. 1874. s-w.: Wed. & Fri. $.50 newsstand; $32/yr. in cy.; $42/yr. out of cy. 32 Macon St., McDonough, GA 30253. TEL 404-957-9161; FAX 404-954-0282. **Owner(s):** Southern Crescent Newspapers, L.P., 138 Church St., Jonesboro, GA 30236. TEL 404-478-5753; Ed. Joe Hiett; Pub. Joe Hiett; pub. size: broadsheet; circ. 7,200(paid).

MCRAE

US

TELFAIR ENTERPRISE. 1887. Wed. $.50 newsstand; $15.90/yr. in cy; $16.96/yr. in state; $20.14/yr. out of state. 237 W. Oak, McRae, GA 31055. TEL 912-868-6015; FAX 912-868-5486. **Owner(s):** Sarah J. Bowen, 237 W. Oak, P.O. Box 269, McRae, GA 31055. TEL 912-868-6015; FAX 912-868-5486; Ed. Ed Bowen, Jr. adv. contact: Ed Bowen, Jr. pub. size: standard; circ. morning 3,450.

MONROE

US

WALTON TRIBUNE. 1900. s-w.: Wed. & Sun. $.75 newsstand; $36/yr. 124 N. Broad St., Monroe, GA 30655. TEL 770-267-8371; FAX 770-267-7780. **Owner(s):** Southern Newspapers, Inc., 1050 Wilcrest Dr., Houston, TX; Ed. Wes Swietek; Pub. Robert Hale; adv.; photos; pub. size: broadsheet; circ. 5,500(paid).

NAHUNTA

US

BRANTLEY ENTERPRISE. 1920. Wed. $.35 newsstand; $15/yr. in cy.; $20/yr. out of cy. 109 Main St., Nahunta, GA 31553. TEL 912-462-6776; FAX 912-462-6776. **Owner(s):** Ken L. Buchanan, 118C N. Main St., Nahunta, GA 31553. TEL 912-462-6776; FAX 912-462-6776; Ed. Ken Buchanan; Pub. Ken Buchanan; adv.; photos; pub. size: broadsheet; circ. 2,200(paid).

NASHVILLE

US

BERRIEN PRESS. 1959. Wed. $15/yr. in cy.; $23/yr. out of cy.; $30/yr. out of state. 200 E. McPherson Ave., Nashville, GA 31639. TEL 912-686-3523; FAX 912-686-7771. **Owner(s):** Clarice Hamilton, 200 E. McPherson Ave., Nashville, GA 31639; Ed. Donald F. Boyd; Pub. Donald F. Boyd; adv.; photos; pub. size: broadsheet; circ. 4,200(paid).

NEWNAN

US

NEWNAN TIMES-HERALD. 1865. s-w.: Wed. & Sat. $.50 newsstand; $26.50/yr. local; $30.17/yr. in state; $52/yr. out of state. 16 Jefferson St., Newnan, GA 30263. TEL 770-253-1576; FAX 770-253-2538; E-mail: webmaster@newnan.com; URL: http://newnan.com. **Owner(s):** W.W. Thomasson, P.O. Box 1052, Newnan, GA 30264. TEL 770-253-1576; Ed. Marianne Thomasson; Pub. W.W. Thomasson; adv. contact: Lamar Truitt. pub. size: broadsheet; circ. 14,000(paid). **Wire Service(s):** AP.

PEACHTREE CITY

US

THIS WEEK IN PEACHTREE CITY. 1974. 3/wk.: Tue., Thu., Sat. $26.25/yr. 111 Petrol Pt., Peachtree City, GA 30269. TEL 770-487-7729; FAX 770-460-8172. **Owner(s):** Robert Tribble, Fayette Newspapers Inc., P.O. Box 2468, Peachtree City, GA 30269. TEL 770-487-7729; Ed. Janet Wells; Pub. Robert Tribble; adv.; pub. size: broadsheet; circ. 4,300(paid).

PELHAM

US

PELHAM JOURNAL. 1902. Wed. $19/yr. cy; $26.50/yr. in state; $30/yr. out of state. 310 W. Railroad St., S., Pelham, GA 31779. TEL 912-294-3661. **Owner(s):** Trib Publications, P.O. Box 426, Manchester, GA 31816. TEL 706-846-3188; Ed. Joanne Hand; Pub. Roger Anne Jones; adv.; pub. size: standard; circ. 2,500(paid).

PEMBROKE

US

BRYAN COUNTY TIMES. 1982. Wed. $.35 newsstand; $16/yr. local; $24/yr. out of state. P.O. Box 798, Pembroke, GA 31321. TEL 912-653-4570; FAX 912-653-4571. **Owner(s):** JAB, Inc., PO Box 798, Pembroke, GA 31321. TEL 912-653-4570; FAX 912-653-4571; Ed. Anne Butler; Pub. John Butler; adv. contact: Sarah Fleming. photos; pub. size: broadsheet; circ. 1,800(controlled & paid).

PERRY

US

HOUSTON TIMES-JOURNAL. 1870. Wed. $.50 newsstand; $25/yr. 807 Carroll St., Perry, GA 31069. TEL 912-987-1823; FAX 912-988-1181; E-mail: timesjrnl@aol.com. **Owner(s):** Trib Publications, Inc., P.O. Box 426, Manchester, GA 31816. TEL 706-846-3188; adv. contact: Sherri Wangler. pub. size: broadsheet; circ. 3,600(paid).

Formerly: Houston Home Journal & Perry Times.

RINCON

US

HERALD, THE. 1908. Wed. $20/yr. in state; $28/yr. out of state. P.O. Drawer 799, Rincon, GA 31326. TEL 912-826-5012; FAX 912-826-5015. **Owner(s):** Springfield Herald, Inc., P.O. Box 247, Springfield, GA 31329. TEL 912-754-6123; Ed. Steve Scholar; Pub. Ginny Anderson; adv.; pub. size: broadsheet; circ. 4,500(paid).

RINGGOLD

US

CATOOSA COUNTY NEWS. 1949. Wed. $.50 newsstand; $12/yr. in cy.; $22/yr. out of cy. 105 Maple St., Ringgold, GA 30736. TEL 706-935-2621; FAX 706-965-5349. **Owner(s):** B.H. Mooney, III, P.O. Box 1633, Rome, GA 30162. TEL 706-290-5290; Ed. Richard Ball; Pub. B.H. Mooney, III; adv. contact: Terry Morgan. pub. size: broadsheet; circ. 4,000(paid).

ROCKMART

US

ROCKMART JOURNAL. 1873. Wed. $.50 newsstand; $14/yr. in cy.; $22/yr. in cy. 240 S. Piedmont Ave., Rockmart, GA 30153. TEL 404-684-7811. **Owner(s):** B.H. Mooney, III, P.O. Box 1633, Rome, GA 30162. TEL 706-290-5290; Ed. Orbie Thaxton; Pub. B.H. Mooney, III; adv.; pub. size: broadsheet; circ. 11,000(free & paid).

ROSWELL

US   ISSN 0192-2637

ROSWELL-ALPHARETTA NEIGHBOR. 1980. Wed. $.25 newsstand; free local deliv.; $112/yr. mailed. 10479 Alpharetta St., Roswell, GA 30075. TEL 770-993-7400; FAX 770-518-6062. **Owner(s):** Times Journal, Inc., 580 Fairground St., Marietta, GA 30060. TEL 770-944-9400; FAX 770-422-9533; Ed. Rodney Shumacke; Pub. Otis Brumby, Jr.; adv. contact: Kathleen Gray. pub. size: broadsheet; circ. 37,000(controlled & paid).

Formerly: Neighborhood Newspaper Roswell-Alpharetta.

ROYSTON

US

NEWS LEADER, THE. 1978. Wed. $.25 newsstand; $13/yr. in cy. 44 Franklin Springs St., Royston, GA 30662. TEL 706-245-7351; FAX 706-245-5991. **Owner(s):** Southern Crescent Newspapers, LP, Atlanta, GA; Ed. Joe Edwards; Pub. Peggy Vickery; adv.; pub. size: broadsheet; circ. 4,000(paid).

SANDERSVILLE

US

SANDERSVILLE PROGRESS. 1887. Wed. $.50 newsstand; $21.20/yr. in cy.; $26.50/yr. out of cy.; $30/yr. out of state. 118 E. Haynes St., Sandersville, GA 31082. TEL 912-352-3161; FAX 912-552-5177. **Owner(s):** Robert Tribble, P.O. Box 431, Sandersville, GA 31082. TEL 912-552-3161; Ed. Robert Garrett. Pub. Robert Tribble; adv. contact: Melissa Brown. pub. size: broadsheet; circ. 5,300(paid).

SPARTA

US

SPARTA ISHMAELITE. 1878. Wed. $.35 newsstand; $18/yr. in cy.; $22/yr. in state; $26/yr. out of state. 109 Broad St., Sparta, GA 31087. TEL 706-444-5330; FAX 706-444-5330. **Owner(s):** R. Allen Haywood, 109 Broad St., Sparta, GA 31087. TEL 706-444-5330; FAX 706-444-5330; Ed. R. Allen Haywood; Pub. R. Allen Haywood; adv.; photos; pub. size: broadsheet; circ. 2,200(paid).

STATESBORO

US

HERALD EXTRA EXPRESS. 1971. Tue. free. 1 Herald Sq., Statesboro, GA 30458. TEL 912-764-9031; FAX 912-489-8181. **Owner(s):** Morris Newspaper Corp., Savannah, GA; Pub. Randy Morton; adv.; pub. size: broadsheet; circ. 5,300(free).

Formerly: Statesboro Southern Beacon.

ST. MARYS

US

CAMDEN COUNTY TRIBUNE. 1950. Wed. $.50 newsstand; $15/yr. in cy.; $19/yr. out of cy.; $25/yr. out of state. 707 Osborne St., St. Marys, GA 31558. TE_ 912-882-4927; FAX 912-882-6519. **Owner(s):** Community Newspapers, Inc., P.O. Box 792, Athens, GA 30603. TEL 800-226-0692; FAX 706-548-0808; Pub. Linn Hudson; adv.; photos; pub. size: broadsheet; circ. 6,300(paid).

ST. SIMONS ISLAND

US

COASTAL ILLUSTRATED. 1968. bi-w. free newsstand. 1626 Frederica Rd., St. Simons Island, GA 31522. TEL 912-638-3793; FAX 912-634-0623. **Owner(s):** Harry Kaufmann, P.O. Box 928, Sea Island, GA 31561. TEL 912-638-3793; Ed. Mary Ellen Pettigrew; Pub. Harry Kaufmann; adv.; photos; bk.rev.; pub. size: tabloid; circ. 10,000(free).

US

ISLANDER, THE. 1972. Mon. $.25 newsstand; $12.50/yr. in cy.; $14.50/yr. out of cy. 520 Wesley Oaks Cir., St. Simons Island, GA 31522. TEL 912-265-9654; FAX 912-638-2764. **Owner(s):** Islander, The, P.O. Box 20539, St. Simons Island, GA 31522. TEL 912-265-9654; Ed. M.J. Permar; Pub. M.J. Permar; adv.; photos; bk.rev.; pub. size: tabloid; circ. 1,000(paid).

SUMMERVILLE

US

CHATTOOGA PRESS. 1982. Wed. free. P.O. Box 485, Summerville, GA 30747. TEL 706-857-5433. **Owner(s):** News Publishing Co., P.O. Box 1633, Rome, GA 30162. TEL 706-290-5330; Ed. Pamella Purcell. adv.; pub. size: broadsheet; circ. 11,500(free).

US

SUMMERVILLE NEWS. 1886. Thu. $.25 newsstand; $10.60/yr. in cy. Rome Hwy., Summerville, GA 30747. TEL 706-857-2494; FAX 706-857-2393. **Owner(s):** David Espy, P.O. Box 310, Summerville, GA 30747. TEL 706-857-2494; FAX 706-857-2393; Winston Espy, P.O. Box 310, Summerville, GA 30747. TEL 706-857-2494; FAX 706-857-2393; Greg Espy, P.O. Box 310, Summerville, GA 30747. TEL 706-857-2494; FAX 706-857-2393; Ed. Gene Espy; Pub. Winston E. Espy; adv. contact: Bill Hudsputh. photos; pub. size: broadsheet; circ. 7,800(paid)

SWAINSBORO

US

BLADE, THE. 1859. s-w.: Mon. & Wed. $.35 newsstand; $20/yr. 350 W. Moring St., Swainsboro, GA 30401. TEL 912-237-9971; FAX 912-237-9451. **Owner(s):** William C. Rogers, Sr., P.O. Box 938, Swainsboro, GA 30401. TEL 912-237-9971; William C. Rogers, Jr., P.O. Box 938, Swainsboro, GA 30401. TEL 912-237-9971; Ed. Ruby Fagler; Pub. William C. Rogers, Jr.; pub. size: broadsheet; circ. 14,645(free & paid).

SYLVESTER

US

SYLVESTER LOCAL NEWS. 1884. Wed. $15/yr. in cy.; $19/yr. out of cy.; $27/yr. elsewhere. 103 E. Kelly, Sylvester, GA 31791. TEL 912-776-3991; FAX 912-776-4607. **Owner(s):** Marian A. Sumner, P.O. Box 387, Sylvester, GA 31791. TEL 912-776-7713; Ed. Marian A. Sumner; Pub. Marian A. Sumner; adv. contact: John F. Porter. pub. size: standard; circ. 3,800(paid).

THOMASTON

US

THOMASTON TIMES. 1869. 3/wk.: Mon., Wed., Fri. $.75 newsstand; $34/yr. local; $45/yr. in state; $55/yr. elsewhere. P.O. Box 430, Thomaston, GA 30286. TEL 706-647-5414; FAX 706-647-2833. **Owner(s):** Thomaston Publishing Co., Inc., P.O. Box 430, Thomaston, GA. TEL 706-647-5414; FAX 706-647-2833; Ed. Chris Smith; Pub. Chris Smith; adv.; photos; pub. size: broadsheet; circ. 6,500(free & paid).

THOMSON

US

MCDUFFIE PROGRESS, THE. 1900. s-w.: Wed. & Sun. $.50 newsstand; $25/yr. in cy.; $45/yr. out of cy. 101 Church St., S.W., Thomson, GA 30824-1090. TEL 706-595-1601; FAX 706-597-8974. **Owner(s):** McDuffie County Newspapers, Inc., P.O. Box 1090, Thomson, GA 30824. TEL 404-595-1601; Ed. Wesley King; Pub. Todd Rainwater; adv.; photos; pub. size: broadsheet; circ. 4,300(paid); Sun. 4,300(paid). **Formerly:** Thomson McDuffie Progress.

TOCCOA

US

CHIEFTAIN & TOCCOA RECORD. Thu. $.25 newsstand; $14.84/yr. in cy.; $19.08/yr. out of cy. 151 W. Doyle St., Toccoa, GA 30577. TEL 404-886-9476; FAX 706-886-2161. **Owner(s):** Century Newspapers, Inc., P.O. Drawer 1069, Toccoa, GA 30577; Ed. Tom Law. pub. size: standard; circ. 5,000(paid). **Formerly:** Chieftain, The & Toccoa Record, The.

VILLA RICA

US   ISSN 0895-7312

VILLA RICAN. 1935. Thu. $12/yr. in cy.; $15/yr. out of cy.; $10/yr. senior citizens. 215 W. Wilson St., Villa Rica, GA 30180. TEL 404-459-5166. **Owner(s):** Paxton Media Group, Inc., P.O. Box 2300, Paducah, KY 42002. TEL 502-443-1771; FAX 502-442-8188; Pub. Dawn Weatherby; adv.; photos; pub. size: broadsheet; circ. 2,170(paid).

WASHINGTON

US

WASHINGTON NEWS-REPORTER. 1919. Thu. $20.14/yr. in cy.; $26.50/yr. out of cy. 116 W. Robert Toombs Ave., Washington, GA 30673. TEL 706-678-2636; FAX 706-678-3857. **Owner(s):** Wilkes Publishing Co., 116 W. Robert Toombs Ave., Washington, GA 30673. TEL 706-678-2636; Ed. P. Smythe Newsome; Pub. P. Smythe Newsome; pub. size: standard; circ. 5,000(paid).

WAYNESBORO

US

TRUE CITIZEN, THE. 1882. Thu. $18/yr. in cy.; $23/yr. in state; $29/yr. elsewhere. 610 Academy Ave., Waynesboro, GA 30830. TEL 706-554-2111; FAX 706-554-2437. **Owner(s):** Chalker Publishing Co., 601 E. Sixth St., Waynesboro, GA 30830. TEL 706-554-7888; Ed. Jimmy Ezzell. adv.; photos; pub. size: broadsheet; circ. 4,700(paid).

WINDER

US

WINDER NEWS. 1893. Wed. $.50 newsstand; $15/yr. in cy.; $24/yr. out of cy. 189 W. Athens St., Winder, GA 30680. TEL 770-867-7557; FAX 770-867-1034. **Owner(s):** Swartz-Morris Media, Inc., Cumming, GA; Ed. Leanne T. Bell; Pub. Debbie Burgamy; adv.; photos; pub. size: broadsheet; circ. 8,000(paid). **Wire Service(s):** NYT.

WOODSTOCK

US

LAKESIDE LEDGER, THE. bi-w.: Fri. free; $15/yr. outside of area. P.O. Box 2369, Woodstock, GA 30188. TEL 770-928-0706; FAX 770-928-3152. **Owner(s):** P.C. Boyle, P.O. Box 928, Oil City, PA 16301. TEL 814-676-7444; Ed. Bob Pepalis; Pub. Dave Caughman; adv.; photos; pub. size: tabloid; circ. 31,000(free & paid).

WRIGHTSVILLE

US   ISSN 0747-3737

WRIGHTSVILLE HEADLIGHT, THE. 1880. Thu. $.35 newsstand; $15.90/yr. local; $23.85/yr. in state; $30/yr. out of state. P.O. Box 290, Wrightsville, GA 31096. TEL 912-864-3528; FAX 912-864-2166. **Owner(s):** Trib Publications, Inc., P.O. Box 426, Manchester, GA 31816. TEL 706-846-3188; Ed. Lori Brown. adv.; photos; pub. size: broadsheet; circ. 2,200(free & paid).

GUAM

AGANA

US

GUAM TRIBUNE. s-w.: Tue. & Fri. P.O. Box EG, Agana, GU 96910. TEL 671-646-5871; FAX 671-646-6702. **Owner(s):** Guam Tribune, P.O. Box EG, Agana, GU 96910; Ed. Robert Teodosio; Pub. Mark Pangilinan; adv.; pub. size: standard.

HAWAII

KANEOHE

US

MIDWEEK. Wed. free. 45-525 Luluku Rd., Kaneohe, HI 96744. TEL 808-235-5881; FAX 808-247-7246. **Owner(s):** Ken Berry, 45-525 Luluku Rd., Kaneohe, HI 96744. TEL 808-235-5881; Ed. Bill Stone; Pub. Ken Berry; adv. contact: Chris McMahon. pub. size: broadsheet; circ. 280,000(free).

US

SUN PRESS. 1961. Thu. free; $1.30/mo. voluntary.
45-525 Luluku Rd., Kaneohe, HI 96744.
TEL 808-235-5881; FAX 808-247-7246.
Owner(s): Sam Newhouse, 45-525 Luluka Rd.,
Kaneohe, HI 96744. TEL 808-235-5881; Ed. Bill
Stone; Pub. Ken Berry; adv. contact: Chris
McMahon. pub. size: broadsheet; circ.
27,000(free & paid).
   Formerly: Hawaii Sun Press.

LIHUE
US

GARDEN ISLAND EXTRA. Sat. free. 3137 Kuhio Hwy.,
Lihue, HI 96766. TEL 808-245-3681;
FAX 808-245-5286. **Owner(s):** Scripps League
Newspapers, Inc., P.O. Box 231, Lihue, HI
96766. TEL 808-245-3681; FAX
808-245-5286; Ed. Rita DeSilva; Pub. Roy
Callaway; circ. 10,000(paid).

IDAHO

ABERDEEN
US

ABERDEEN TIMES. 1911. Wed. $.50 newsstand;
$20/yr. in state; $24/yr. out of state; $19/yr.
senior citizens in state. P.O. Box X, Aberdeen, ID
83210. TEL 208-397-4440;
FAX 208-226-5295. **Owner(s):** Erma Crompton,
P.O. Box X, Aberdeen, ID 83210. TEL
208-397-4440; Ed. Julia Raben; Pub. Erma
Crompton; adv.; pub. size: standard; circ.
1,350(paid).

AMERICAN FALLS
US

POWER COUNTY PRESS. 1898. Wed. $.50
newsstand; $20/yr. P.O. Box 547, American
Falls, ID 83211. TEL 208-226-5294. **Owner(s):**
Erma & Brett Crompton, P.O. Box 547, American
Falls, ID 83211. TEL 208-226-5294; Ed. Brett
Crompton; Pub. Erma Crompton; adv.; photos;
pub. size: broadsheet; circ. 2,100(paid).

ARCO
US   ISSN 0890-1511

ARCO ADVERTISER. 1909. Thu. $.50 newsstand;
$17/yr. local; $20/yr. outside area. 146 S. Front
St., Arco, ID 83213-0803. TEL 208-527-3038;
FAX 208-527-8210. **Owner(s):** Arco Advertiser,
Inc., The, P.O. Box 803, Arco, ID 83213-0803.
TEL 208-527-3038; FAX 208-527-8210; Ed.
Charles L. Cammack; Pub. Don Cammack; adv.;
pub. size: broadsheet; circ. 1,955(paid).

BONNERS FERRY
US

BONNERS FERRY HERALD. 1891. Wed. $.50
newsstand; $28.50/yr. in state; $29.50/yr. out
of state. 213 Main St., Bonners Ferry, ID 83805.
TEL 208-267-5521; FAX 208-267-5523.
Owner(s): Penorielle Printers, Inc., San Point, ID;
Ed. David Keys; Pub. David Keys; pub. size:
broadsheet; circ. 3,000(paid).

BUHL
US

BUHL HERALD. 1909. Wed. $.30 newsstand;
$17.85/yr. in cy. 124 S. Broadway, Buhl, ID
83316. TEL 208-543-4335;
FAX 208-543-6834. **Owner(s):** Robert M. Bailey,
P.O. Box 312, Buhl, ID 83316. TEL
208-543-4335; Ed. Sandra Wisecaver; Pub.
Robert M. Bailey; pub. size: broadsheet; circ.
3,000(paid).

CAMBRIDGE
US

UPPER COUNTRY NEWS-REPORTER. 1889. Thu. $.50
newsstand; $18/yr. in cy. 155 Superior Ave.,
Cambridge, ID 83610. **Owner(s):** R. Stuart Dopf,
P.O. Box 9, Cambridge, ID 83610. TEL 208-257-3515; Ed. R. Stuart
Dopf; Pub. R. Stuart Dopf; pub. size: broadsheet;
circ. 1,100(paid).

CASCADE
US

LONG VALLEY ADVOCATE, THE. 1985. Wed. $.50
newsstand; $19/yr. in area; $24/yr. elsewhere.
112 Main St., Cascade, ID 83611.
TEL 208-382-3233; FAX 208-382-6728.
Owner(s): Michael Stewart, P.O. Box 976,
Cascade, ID 83611. TEL 208-382-4707; Fred &
Elzo O'Brien, P.O. Box 548, Cascade, ID 83611;
Michael G. Higgins, P.O. Box 957, Cascade, ID
83611; Ed. Michael Stewart; Pub. Michael
Stewart; adv. contact: Robin Simpson. photos;
pub. size: tabloid; circ. 5,000(free & paid).

CHALLIS
US

CHALLIS MESSENGER. 1881. Thu. $.50 newsstand;
$18.90/yr. in cy.; $25.20/yr. out of cy. 310 N.
Main St., Challis, ID 83226. TEL 208-879-4445.
Owner(s): Custer Publishing, Inc., P.O. Box 405,
Challis, ID 83226. TEL 208-879-4445; Ed.
Peggy Parks; Pub. Peggy Parks; pub. size: tabloid;
circ. 1,970(free & paid).

COTTONWOOD
US

COTTONWOOD CHRONICLE. 1892. Thu. $18/yr. in
state; $21/yr. out of state. 503 King St.,
Cottonwood, ID 83522-0157.
TEL 208-962-3851; FAX 208-962-7131.
Owner(s): Wherry Publishing, Inc., P.O. Box 157,
Cottonwood, ID 83522-0157. TEL
208-962-3851 FAX 208-962-7131; Ed. Greg
Wherry; Pub. Robert Wherry; adv.; pub. size:
tabloid; circ. 1,000(paid).

COUNCIL
US

RECORD, THE. 1977. Thu. $.47 newsstand; $15/yr.
in state mailed; $18/yr. out of state. 211 Illinois
Ave., Council, ID 83612. TEL 208-253-6961;
FAX 208-253-6801. **Owner(s):** Tim Blevins, P.O.
Box R, Council, ID 83612. TEL 208-253-6961;
Ed. Tim Blevins; Pub. Tim Blevins; adv.:
$3.63/SAU. photos; pub. size: broadsheet; circ.
13,000(paid).
   Formerly: Council Record.

DRIGGS
US

TETON VALLEY NEWS. 1909. Thu. $20/yr. in cy.;
$25/yr. out of cy. 60 E. Little Ave., Driggs, ID
83422. TEL 208-354-8101;
FAX 208-354-8621. **Owner(s):** Fred McCabe,
P.O. Box 49, Driggs, ID 83422. TEL
208-354-8101; FAX 208-354-8257; Ed. Jeanne
Anderson; Pub. Fred McCabe; adv.; bk.rev.; pub.
size: tabloid; circ. 2,475(paid).

EMMETT
US

MESSENGER INDEX. 1896. Wed. $21/yr. in cy.;
$34.50/yr. out of cy. 120 N. Washington,
Emmett, ID 83617. TEL 208-365-6066;
FAX 208-365-6068. **Owner(s):** Idaho
Press-Tribune, P.O. Box 577, Emmett, ID 83617.
TEL 208-467-9251; Ed. Perry Washburn. adv.;
photos; bk.rev.; pub. size: broadsheet; circ.
6,500(free & paid).

GOODING
US

GOODING COUNTY LEADER. 1908. Wed. $.50
newsstand; $21/yr. in cy.; $26/yr. out of cy.;
$16/yr. in cy. senior citizens. 200 Main St.,
Gooding, ID 83330-1186. TEL 208-934-4449;
FAX 208-934-4440. **Owner(s):** Magic Valley
Publishing, Inc., 200 Main St., Gooding, ID
83330. TEL 208-934-4449; Ed. Mary Ann
Hagen; Pub. Patty Nance; adv. photos; pub. size:
tabloid; circ. 1,200(paid).

GRANGEVILLE
US

IDAHO COUNTY FREE PRESS. 1885. Wed. $.50
newsstand; $24/yr. in cy.; $32/yr. out of cy.
318 E. Main, Grangeville, ID 83530.
TEL 208-983-1070. **Owner(s):** Eagle
Newspapers, Inc., P.O. Box 12008, Salem, OR
97309. TEL 503-393-1774; Ed. Vance Tong;
Pub. Andy McNab; adv. photos; pub. size:
broadsheet; circ. 3,850(paid).

US

SHOPPER, THE. Tue. free. 318 E. Main, Grangeville,
ID 83530. TEL 208-983-1070;
FAX 208-983-1336. **Owner(s):** Eagle
Newspapers, Inc., P.O. Box 12008, Salem, OR
97309. TEL 503-393-1774; Pub. Andy McNab;
adv.; pub. size: tabloid; circ. 9,295(free).

HAILEY
US

WOOD RIVER JOURNAL. 1881. Wed. $16/yr. in cy.;
$26/yr. out of cy. 112 S. Main, Hailey, ID
83333-0988. TEL 208-788-3444;
FAX 208-788-0083; E-mail:
wrjidaho@micron.net; URL:
http://www.sunvalleyic.com/wrj. **Owner(s):** South
Idaho Press, P.O. Box 988, Hailey, ID
83333-0988; Ed. Dan Gorham; Pub. Dan
Gorham; adv.; photos; bk.rev.; pub. size: tabloid;
circ. 12,000(free & paid). Wire Service(s): AP.

IDAHO FALLS

US

CABLE SCENE. 1971. Wed. $.50 newsstand; $15.75/yr. in cy. mailed. 587 Fourth St., Idaho Falls, ID 83401. TEL 208-523-7777; FAX 208-745-8784. **Owner(s):** Pioneer Publications, Inc., P.O. Box P, Shelley, ID 83274. TEL 208-357-7661; Pub. Terry Carr; adv. contact: Earlene Poole. pub. size: tabloid; circ. 7,000(paid).

JEROME

US

NORTH SIDE NEWS. 1907. Wed. $.50 newsstand; $21/yr. in cy.; $26/yr. out of state. 133 E. Main St., Jerome, ID 83338. TEL 208-324-3391; FAX 208-324-3391. **Owner(s):** Magic Valley Publishing, Inc., P.O. Box 468, Jerome, ID 83338; Ed. P. Marcantonio; Pub. P. Nance; adv.; bk.rev.; pub. size: tabloid; circ. 1,800(paid).

KENDRICK

US

KENDRICK-GAZETTE. 1890. Thu. $10.50/yr. P.O. Box 177, Kendrick, ID 83537. TEL 208-289-5731. **Owner(s):** William A. Roth, P.O. Box 177, Kendrick, ID 83537. TEL 208-289-5731; Ed. William A. Roth; Pub. William A. Roth; pub. size: broadsheet; circ. 930(paid).

KETCHUM

US   ISSN 0279-8964

IDAHO MOUNTAIN EXPRESS. 1974. Wed. $34/yr. 591 First Ave., N., Ketchum, ID 83340. TEL 208-726-8060; FAX 208-726-2329; E-mail: express@micron.net; URL: http://www.mtexpress.com/. **Owner(s):** Express Publishing Co., Inc., P.O. Box 1013, Ketchum, ID 83340. TEL 208-726-5060; Ed. Pam Morris; Pub. Pam Morris; adv. contact: Cheryl Beck. photos; pub. size: tabloid; circ. 13,500(paid). **Wire Service(s):** AP.

KIMBERLY

US

EAST COUNTY CHRONICLE. 1982. Fri. $.50 newsstand; $18.90/yr. in cy.; $21.53/yr. out of state. 113 N. Main, Kimberly, ID 83341. TEL 208-423-6401; FAX 208-423-4297. **Owner(s):** Barbara Homan, P.O. Box BB, Kimberly, ID 83341. TEL 208-423-6401; Ed. Mary Kopydlowski; Pub. Barbara Homan; adv.; pub. size: broadsheet; circ. 1,200(controlled & paid).

KUNA

US

KUNA-MELBA NEWS. 1983. Wed. $.30 newsstand; $18/yr. in cy.; $14/yr. senior citizens. 462 W. Third St., Kuna, ID 83634. TEL 208-466-3557; FAX 208-466-8054. **Owner(s):** Wild Horse Publishing Co., 13729 Lake Ave., Nampa, ID 83651. TEL 208-466-3557; FAX 208-466-8054; Ed. Earl L. Maggard. adv.; photos; bk.rev.; pub. size: tabloid; circ. 950(controlled & paid).

MALAD CITY

US

IDAHO ENTERPRISE. 1887. Thu. $16/yr. in cy.; $21/yr. out of cy. 100 E. 90th S., Malad City, ID 83252. TEL 208-766-4773; FAX 208-766-4774. **Owner(s):** Kris Jones, P.O. Box 205, Malad City, ID 83252; Ed. Kris Jones Smith; Pub. Kris Jones Smith; pub. size: broadsheet; circ. 1,250(paid).

MCCALL

US

STAR-NEWS, THE. 1966. Thu. $.75 newsstand; $24/yr. in area. 1000 First St., McCall, ID 83638. TEL 208-634-2123; FAX 208-634-4950. **Owner(s):** Central Idaho Publishing, Inc., P.O. Box 985, McCall, ID 83638. TEL 208-634-2123; Ed. Tom Grote; Pub. A.L. "Butch" Alford, Jr.; adv. contact: Tom Grote. pub. size: broadsheet; circ. 5,130(free & paid).

MERIDIAN

US

VALLEY NEWS. 1903. Thu. $22/yr. 815 E. First St., Meridian, ID 83642. TEL 208-888-1941; FAX 208-888-1097. **Owner(s):** AWF Publishing, 815 E. First St., Meridan, ID 83642; Pub. Tere Foley; adv.; pub. size: tabloid; circ. 1,000(paid).

MIDDLETON

US

MIDDLETON GAZETTE. m. free newsstand; $8.44/yr. 418 N. Dewey, Middleton, ID 83644-5616. TEL 208-585-3472; FAX 208-585-2582. **Owner(s):** Cheri Hess & Becky O'Meara, 8522 Hwy. 44, Middleton, ID 83644. TEL 208-585-3472; Ed. Cheri Hess; Pub. Cheri Hess; adv.; pub. size: tabloid; circ. 5,580(free & paid).

MONTPELIER

US

NEWS-EXAMINER. 1895. Wed. $.50 newsstand; $15/yr. local; $21.50/yr. out of area. 847 Washington, Montpelier, ID 83254. TEL 208-847-0552; FAX 208-847-0553. **Owner(s):** J. Walter Ross & Wayne D. Bell, 77 S. State, Preston, ID 83263. TEL 208-852-0155; FAX 208-852-0158; Ed. Rosa Moosman. adv.: $4.19/SAU. photos; pub. size: standard; circ. 2,500(paid).

MOSCOW

US

PALOUSE LIVING. 1975. Tue. free. 409 S. Jackson, Moscow, ID 83843. TEL 208-882-5561; FAX 208-883-8205. **Owner(s):** News Review Publishing Co., 408 S. Jackson, Moscow, ID 83843. TEL 208-882-5561; Ed. Randy Frisch; Pub. Randy Frisch; adv. contact: Randy Preasnell. pub. size: standard; circ. 1,800(free).
   Formerly: Palouse Shopper.

MOUNTAIN HOME

US

MOUNTAIN HOME NEWS. 1886. Wed. $23/yr. in cy.; $28/yr. out cy.; $33/yr. out of state. 195 S. Third E., Mountain Home, ID 83647. TEL 208-587-3331; FAX 208-587-9205. **Owner(s):** U.S. Media Group, Crystal City, MO; Pub. Coleen W. Swenson; adv. contact: Debra Shoemaker. pub. size: broadsheet; circ. 4,000(paid).

NEZPERCE

US

LEWIS COUNTY HERALD. 1897. Thu. $18/yr. in state. 517 Oak St., Nezperce, ID 83543-0159. TEL 208-937-2671; FAX 208-962-7131. **Owner(s):** Wherry Publishing, Inc., 517 Oak St., Nezperce, ID 83543. TEL 208-937-2671; Ed. Steve Wherry; Pub. Patricia Wherry; pub. size: tabloid; circ. 1,200(paid).

OROFINO

US

CLEARWATER TRIBUNE. 1912. Thu. $19.50/yr. in area; $23.50/yr. out of area. 161 Main St., Orofino, ID 83544. TEL 208-476-4571; FAX 208-476-0765. **Owner(s):** Clearwater Publishing Co., Inc., 161 Main St., Orofino, ID 83544. TEL 208-476-4571; Ed. Cloann Wilkins-McNall; Pub. Cloann Wilkins-McNall; adv.; pub. size: broadsheet; circ. 3,720(free & paid).
   Formerly: Orofino Clearwater.

PAYETTE

US

INDEPENDENT ENTERPRISE. 1891. Wed. $26/yr. local; $33/yr. out of area. 21 S. Main St., Payette, ID 83661-0520. TEL 208-642-3357. **Owner(s):** Wick Communications, Inc., 333 W. Wilcox Dr., Ste. 302, Sierra Vista, AZ 85635; Ed. Julie Mitchell; Pub. Eugene Rhinehart; adv.; photos; pub. size: standard; circ. 2,200(paid).

POST FALLS

US

POST FALLS TRIBUNE. 1896. Thu. $.50 newsstand; $20/yr. in cy.; $22/yr. out of cy. 318 Spokane St., Post Falls, ID 83854. TEL 208-773-7502; FAX 208-773-7002. **Owner(s):** Hagadone Corp., P.O. Box 6200, Coeur d'Alene, ID 83814. TEL 208-667-3431; Ed. Kerri Thoreson; Pub. Alissa Snider; adv. contact: Alissa Snider. pub. size: broadsheet; circ. 3,200(paid).

PRESTON

US

PRESTON CITIZEN. 1890. Wed. $.50 newsstand; $17.50/yr. in area; $24/yr. out of area. 77 S. State St., Preston, ID 83263. TEL 208-852-0155; FAX 208-852-0158. **Owner(s):** J. Walter Ross, 77 S. State St., Preston, ID 83263. TEL 208-852-0155; FAX 208-852-0158; Wayne D. Bell, 77 S. State St., Preston, ID 83263. TEL 208-852-0155; FAX 208-852-0158; Ed. Wayne D. Bell. adv. contact: J. Walter Ross. pub. size: broadsheet; circ. 5,800(free & paid).

PRIEST RIVER

US   ISSN 0740-3348

PRIEST RIVER TIMES. 1914. Wed. $18/yr. local; $25/yr. elsewhere. 221 Cottonwood Vlge., Albeny Hwy., Priest River, ID 83856. TEL 208-448-2431; FAX 208-448-2938. **Owner(s):** Hagadone Corp., P.O. Box 6200, Coeur d'Alene, ID 83814; pub. size: broadsheet; circ. 8,400(free & paid).

REXBURG

US

STANDARD JOURNAL. 1909. s-w.: Tue. & Thu. $36.75/yr. 23 S. 100 E., Rexburg, ID 83440. TEL 208-356-5441; FAX 208-356-8312. **Owner(s):** Porter Publications, Inc., P.O. Box 10, Rexburg, ID 83440. TEL 208-356-5411; Ed. Roger Porter; Pub. Roger Porter; pub. size: broadsheet; circ. 4,500(paid).
Formerly: Rexburg, The.

RIGBY

US

JEFFERSON STAR, THE. 1903. Wed. $.50 newsstand; $19.95/yr. 134 W. Main St., Rigby, ID 83442. TEL 208-745-8701; FAX 208-745-8703. **Owner(s):** Pioneer Publications, Inc., P.O. Box P, Shelley, ID 83274. TEL 208-745-8701; FAX 208-745-8703; Ed. Terry Carr; Pub. Terry Carr; adv.; photos; pub. size: broadsheet; circ. 2,300(paid).

RUPERT

US

MINIDOKA COUNTY NEWS. 1906. Wed. $.50 newsstand; $18/yr. 518 Sixth St., Rupert, ID 83350. TEL 208-436-4201; FAX 208-436-4556. **Owner(s):** Park Communications, Inc., Vine Ctr. Office Tower, 333 W. Vine St., 17th Fl., Lexington, KY 40507. TEL 606-252-7275; Ed. Judy Albertson. adv. contact: Rose Bryan. photos; bk.rev.; pub. size: broadsheet; circ. 1,414(paid).

SALMON

US

RECORDER-HERALD. 1886. Thu. $.50 newsstand; $18/yr. in state; $22/yr. out of state. 519 Van Dreff St., Salmon, ID 83467. TEL 208-756-2221; FAX 208-756-2222. **Owner(s):** Ricky G. Hodges, P.O. Box 310, Salmon, ID 83467. TEL 208-756-2221; FAX 208-756-2222; Pub. Ricky G. Hodges; adv.; pub. size: broadsheet; circ. 3,401(paid).

SHELLEY

US

SHELLEY PIONEER. 1905. Thu. $17.75/yr. in cy.; $27/yr. out of state. 154 E. Center, Shelley, ID 83274. TEL 208-357-7661. **Owner(s):** Pioneer Publications, Inc., P.O. Box P, Shelley, ID 83274. TEL 208-357-7661; Ed. Ken Carr; Pub. Ken Carr; adv.; pub. size: tabloid; circ. 1,700(paid).

SHOSHONE

US

LINCOLN COUNTY JOURNAL. 1884. Wed. $.50 newsstand; $21/yr. in cy.; $26/yr. out of cy. P.O. Box 704, Shoshone, ID 83352. TEL 208-886-2740. **Owner(s):** Lincoln County Journal, P.O. Box 704, Shoshone, ID 83352. TEL 208-886-2740; Pub. P. Nance; adv.; photos; pub. size: tabloid; circ. 1,000(paid).

SODA SPRINGS

US

CARIBOU COUNTY SUN. 1930. Thu. $.50 newsstand; $16/yr. in cy.; $20/yr. out of cy. 169 S. First W., Soda Springs, ID 83276. TEL 208-547-3260. **Owner(s):** Mark Steele, P.O. Box 815, Soda Springs, ID 83276. TEL 208-547-3260; Ed. Mark Steele; Pub. Mark Steele; adv.; pub. size: tabloid; circ. 2,900(paid).

ST. ANTHONY

US

FREMONT COUNTY HERALD-CHRONICLE. 1891. s-w.: Tue. & Thu. $.50 newsstand; $31.50/yr. local; $37/yr. out of area. 44 N. Bridge, St. Anthony, ID 83445. TEL 208-624-4455. **Owner(s):** Porter Publications, 23 S. 100 E., Rexburg, ID 83440. TEL 208-356-5441; Pub. Roger O. Porter; adv.; pub. size: broadsheet; circ. 2,300(paid).

ST. MARIES

US

ST. MARIES GAZETTE RECORD. 1906. Wed. $23.95/yr. in cy.; $35.95/yr. out of state. 127 S. Seventh, St. Maries, ID 83861. TEL 208-245-4538; FAX 208-245-4011. **Owner(s):** St. Maries Gazette Record Corp., 127 S. Seventh, St. Maries, ID 83861. TEL 208-245-4538; Ed. Robert Hammes; Pub. Dan Hammes; adv. contact: Gaye Van Winkle. pub. size: broadsheet; circ. 3,504(paid).

WEISER

US

WEISER SIGNAL AMERICAN. 1882. s-w.: Mon. & Wed. $.50 newsstand; $27/yr. in state mailed; $39/yr. out of state. 18 E. Idaho St., Weiser, ID 83672-0709. TEL 208-549-1717; FAX 208-549-1718. **Owner(s):** Signal-American Printers, Inc., P.O. Box 709, Weiser, ID 83672-0709. TEL 208-549-1717; Ed. Rob Ruth; Pub. James R. Simpson; adv. contact: Eydie Huston. photos; pub. size: broadsheet; circ. 3,000(free & paid).

ILLINOIS

ABINGDON

US

ABINGDON ARGUS. 1957. Wed. $.40 newsstand; $17/yr. in cy.; $19/yr. out of cy.; $22/yr. out of state. 405 Western Ave., Ste. 6, Abingdon, IL 61410. TEL 309-462-3189; FAX 309-462-3221. **Owner(s):** Acklin Newspaper Group, P.O. Box 32, Abingdon, IL 61410. TEL 309-462-5758; Ed. Joe Acklin; Pub. Joe Acklin; adv. contact: Marilyn Aden. pub. size: tabloid; circ. 2,500(free & paid).

US

AVON SENTINEL. 1879. Wed. $.40 newsstand; $17/yr. in cy.; $19/yr. in state; $22/yr. out of state. 405 Western Ave., Ste. 6, Abingdon, IL 61410. TEL 309-462-5758; FAX 309-462-3221. **Owner(s):** Acklin Newspaper Group, P.O. Box 32, Abingdon, IL 61410. TEL 309-462-5758; FAX 309-462-3221; Ed. Joyce Cannon; Pub. Joe Acklin; adv. contact: Marilyn Aden. photos; pub. size: tabloid; circ. 850(free & paid).

US

BLANDINSVILLE STAR GAZETTE. Thu. $.40 newsstand; $17/yr. in cy.; $18/yr. out of cy.; $22/yr. out of state. 405 Western Ave., Ste. 6, Abingdon, IL 61410. TEL 309-652-3328; FAX 309-462-3221 **Owner(s):** Acklin Newspaper Group, P.O. Box 32, Abingdon, IL 61410. TEL 309-462-5758; Ed. Pam Howard; Pub. Joe Acklin; pub. size: tabloid; circ. 650(paid).

ALEDO

US

TIMES RECORD. 1856. Wed. $.35 newsstand; $40/yr. local; $45/yr. elsewhere. 113 S. College Ave., Aledo, IL 61231. TEL 309-582-5112; FAX 309-582-5319. **Owner(s):** Trans-Continental Media, Inc., 310 N. Main St., Bicknell, IN 47512. TEL 812-735-2222; adv. contact: Teresa Larson. pub. size: broadsheet; circ. 4,000(paid).
Formerly: Aledo Times Record.

ALTAMONT

US

ALTAMONT NEWS, THE. 1881. Tue. $17.50/yr. in state; $20.50/yr. out of state. 118 N. Main, Altamont, IL 62411. TEL 618-483-6176; FAX 618-483-5177. **Owner(s):** Greg Hoskins, 118 N. Main, Altamont, IL 62411. TEL 618-483-6176; Pub. Greg Hoskins; adv. contact: Tim Gordon. pub. size: standard; circ. 2,200(paid).

AMBOY

US

AMBOY NEWS, THE. 1854. Thu. $.50 newsstand; $18/yr. local; $23/yr. elsewhere. 219 E. Main St., Amboy, IL 61310. TEL 315-857-2311; FAX 815-857-2517. **Owner(s):** John & Mary Koski, P.O. Box 162, Amboy, IL 61310. TEL 815-857-2311; FAX 815-857-2517; Pub. John Koski; adv.; photos; pub. size: tabloid; circ. 2,500(paid).

ANNA

US

GAZETTE-DEMOCRAT. 1849. Thu. $.50 newsstand; $19/yr. 112 Lafayette St., Anna, IL 62906. TEL 618-833-2158; FAX 618-833-5813. **Owner(s):** Jerry Reppert, P.O. Box 529, Anna, IL 62906; Ed. Geof Skinner; Pub. Jerry L. Reppert; adv.; pub. size: broadsheet; circ. 6,400(paid).

ARCOLA

US

ARCOLA RECORD HERALD. 1866. Thu. $.50 newsstand; $17/yr. local; $20/yr. out of state. 118 E. Main St., Arcola, IL 61910. TEL 217-268-4959. **Owner(s):** Don Rankin, 118 E. Main St., Arcola, IL 61910. TEL 217-268-4959; Ed. Don Rankin; Pub. Don Rankin; adv.; pub. size: broadsheet; circ. 2,500(paid).

ARLINGTON HEIGHTS

US

PALATINE COUNTRYSIDE. 1972. Thu. $.75 newsstand; $18.95/yr. 291 N. Dunton Ave., Arlington Heights, IL 60004. TEL 847-797-5100; FAX 847-797-5150. **Owner(s):** Pioneer Press, Inc., 3701 W. Lake Ave., Glenview, IL 60025. TEL 847-486-9200; Ed. Tom Scott; Pub. Thomas Neri; adv. contact: Anne Kelly. pub. size: tabloid; circ. 6,776(paid).

ARTHUR
US

ARTHUR GRAPHIC CLARION. 1887. Thu. $.50 newsstand; $18/yr. in cy.; $21/yr. out of cy. 113 E. Illinois St., Arthur, IL 61911. TEL 217-543-2151; FAX 217-543-2152. **Owner(s):** Arthur Graphic Clarion, Inc., 113 E. Illinois St., Arthur, IL 61911. TEL 217-543-2151; Ed. Roger Borham; Pub. Lowell Cutsinger; adv. contact: Don Newberry. photos; bk.rev.; pub. size: broadsheet; circ. 3,000(paid).

ASHTON
US

ASHTON GAZETTE. 1895. Thu. $.40 newsstand; $14/yr. in cy.; $18/yr. out of cy. 813 Main St., Ashton, IL 61006-0287. TEL 815-453-2551. **Owner(s):** David W. Townsend, 813 Main St., Ashton, IL 61006. TEL 815-453-2551; Pub. David W. Townsend; adv. contact: David W. Townsend. photos; pub. size: tabloid; circ. 1,000(paid).

ASSUMPTION
US

GOLDEN PRAIRIE NEWS. 1880. Thu. $.35 newsstand; $15/yr. 301 S. Chestnut, Assumption, IL 62510. TEL 217-226-3721; FAX 217-226-3579. **Owner(s):** Willard Raymond, 301 S. Chestnut, Assumption, IL 62510. TEL 217-226-3721; Pub. Willard Raymond; adv.; pub. size: standard circ. 2,200(paid).

ASTORIA
US

ASTORIA SOUTH FULTON ARGUS. 1959. Wed. $14.95/yr. in cy.; $19.95/yr. out of cy. 100 N. Pearl, Astoria, IL 61501-0590. TEL 309-329-2151; FAX 309-329-2344. **Owner(s):** K.K. Stevens Publishing Co., P.O. Box 590, Astoria, L 61501-0590. TEL 309-329-2151; Ed. Merrie Jean Perry; Pub. Thomas B. Stevens; adv. contact: Bonnie White. adv.: $3.80/SAU. photos; circ. 2,111(free & paid).

ATWOOD
US

ATWOOD HERALD. 1892. Wed. $.45 newsstand; $17.50/yr. 107 N. Main, Atwood, IL 61913. TEL 217-578-3213; FAX 217-578-2833. **Owner(s):** Mt. Zion Publications Inc., 107 N. Main, Atwood, IL 61913. TEL 217-578-3213; Ed. Mike Brothers; Pub. Mike Brothers; pub. size: tabloid; circ. 1,000(paid).

AUBURN
US

AUBURN CITIZEN. 1874. Thu. $.50 newsstand; $18/yr. 110 N. Fifth St., Auburn, IL 62615. TEL 217-438-6155; FAX 217-438-6156. **Owner(s):** Joe Michelich, 110 N. Fifth St., Auburn, IL 62615. TEL 217-438-6155; Ed. Joe Michelich; Pub. Joe Michelich; adv.; photos; pub. size: broadsheet; circ. 1,130(paid).

US

CHATHAM CLARION. 1962. Thu. $.50 newsstand; $18/yr. 110 N. Fifth St., Auburn, IL 62615. TEL 217-438-6155; FAX 217-438-6156. **Owner(s):** Joe Michelich, 110 N. Fifth St., Auburn, IL 62615. TEL 217-438-6155; Ed. Joe Michelich; Pub Joe Michelich; adv.; pub. size: broadsheet; circ. 1,509(paid).

US

DIVERNON NEWS. 1897. Thu. $.50 newsstand; $18/yr. 110 N. Fifth St., Auburn, IL 62615. TEL 217-438-6155; FAX 217-438-6156. **Owner(s):** Joe Michelich, 110 N. Fifth St., Auburn, IL 62615. TEL 217-438-6155; Ed. Joe Michelich; Pub. Joe Michelich; adv.; pub. size: broadsheet; circ. 312(paid).

US

PAWNEE POST. 1965. Thu. $.50 newsstand; $18/yr. 110 N. Fifth St., Auburn, IL 62615. TEL 217-438-6155; FAX 217-438-6156. **Owner(s):** Joe Michelich, 110 N. Fifth St., Auburn, IL 62615. TEL 217-438-6155; Ed. Joe Michelich; Pub. Joe Michelich; adv.; pub. size: broadsheet; circ. 475(paid).

US

ROCHESTER TIMES. Thu. $.50 newsstand; $18/yr. 110 N. Fifth St., Auburn, IL 62615. TEL 217-438-6155; FAX 217-438-6156. **Owner(s):** Joe Michelich, 110 N. Fifth St., Auburn, IL 62615; Ed. Joe Michelich; Pub. Joe Michelich; adv.; pub. size: broadsheet; circ. 774(paid).

US

SOUTH COUNTY EXPRESS. 1986. Mon. free. 110 N. Fifth St., Auburn, IL 62615. TEL 217-438-6155; FAX 217-438-6156. **Owner(s):** Joe Michelich, 110 N. Fifth St., Auburn, IL 62615. TEL 021-743-8615; Ed. Joe Michelich; Pub. Joe Michelich; adv.; pub. size: tabloid; circ. 8,000(free).

BANNOCKBURN
US

BUFFALO GROVE COUNTRYSIDE. 1977. Thu. $.75 newsstand; $18.95/yr. 2201 Waukegan Rd., Ste. E-175, Bannockburn, IL 60015. TEL 847-317-0500; FAX 847-797-5150. **Owner(s):** Pioneer Press, Inc., 3701 W. Lake Ave., Glenview, IL 60025. TEL 847-486-9200; Ed. Andis Robeznicks; Pub. Thomas Neri; adv. contact: Anne Kelly. pub. size: tabloid; circ. 5,580(paid).

US

DEERFIELD REVIEW. Thu. $1 newsstand; $36.95/yr. 2201 Waukegan Rd., Ste., E175, Bannockburn, IL 60015. TEL 847-317-0500; FAX 847-317-1022. **Owner(s):** Pioneer Press, Inc., 3701 W. Lake Ave., Glenview, IL 60025. TEL 847-486-9200; Ed. Arnold Grahl; Pub. Thomas Neri; adv.; pub. size: tabloid; circ. 6,000(paid).

US

HIGHLAND PARK NEWS. 1924. Thu. $1 newsstand; $32.95/yr. 2201 Waukegan Rd., Ste. E175, Bannockburn, IL 60015. TEL 847-317-0500; FAX 847-317-1022. **Owner(s):** Pioneer Press, Inc., 3701 W. Lake Ave., Glenview, IL 60025. TEL 847-486-9200; Ed. Kyle Leonard; Pub. Thomas Neri; adv. contact: Peggy Cunniff. pub. size: tabloid; circ. 7,635(paid).

US   ISSN 0744-7973

LAKE FORESTER. 1896. Thu. $1 newsstand; $24/yr. local. 2201 Waukegan Rd., Ste. E175, Bannockburn, IL 60025. TEL 847-486-9200; FAX 847-317-1022. **Owner(s):** American Publishing Co., 606 N. Van Buren, P.O. Box 520, Marion, IL 62959. TEL 618-993-1711; Ed. Kyle Leonard; Pub. Tom Neri; adv. contact: Lynn Schmidt. pub. size: tabloid; circ. 6,317(paid).

US

LIBERTYVILLE REVIEW. 1974. Thu. $.75 newsstand; $18.50/yr. 2201 Waukegan Rd., Ste. E175, Bannockburn, IL 60015. TEL 847-317-0500; FAX 847-317-1022. **Owner(s):** Pioneer Press, Inc., 3701 W. Lake Ave., Glenview, IL 60025. TEL 847-486-9200; Ed. Sheila Richard; Pub. Thomas Neri; pub. size: tabloid; circ. 3,800(paid).

US

MUNDELEIN REVIEW. 1974. Thu. $.75 newsstand; $18.50/yr. 2201 Waukegan Rd., Ste. E175, Bannockburn, IL 60015. TEL 847-317-0500; FAX 847-317-1022. **Owner(s):** Pioneer Press, Inc., 3701 W. Lake Ave., Glenview, IL 60025. TEL 847-486-9200; Ed. Sheila Richard; Pub. Thomas Neri; pub. size: tabloid; circ. 2,500(paid).

US

VERNON HILLS REVIEW. 1974. Thu. $1 newsstand; $36.95/yr. 2201 Waukegan Rd., Ste. E-175, Bannockburn, IL 60015. TEL 847-317-0500; FAX 847-317-1022. **Owner(s):** Pioneer Press, Inc., 3701 W. Lake Ave., Glenview, IL 60025. TEL 847-486-9200; Ed. Sheila Richard; Pub. Thomas Neri; adv.; pub. size: tabloid; circ. 2,000(paid).

BARRINGTON
US

ALGONQUIN COUNTRYSIDE. 1972. Thu. $.75 newsstand; $18.95/yr. 200 James St., Barrington, IL 60010. TEL 847-381-9200; FAX 847-381-5840. **Owner(s):** Pioneer Press, Inc., 3701 W. Lake Ave., Glenview, IL 60025. TEL 847-486-9200; Ed. Terri McHugh; Pub. Thomas Neri; adv. contact: Anne Kelly. pub. size: tabloid; circ. 2,313(paid).

US

BARRINGTON COURIER REVIEW. 1981. Thu. $.75 newsstand; $24.95/yr. 200 James St., Barrington, IL 60010. TEL 847-381-9200; FAX 847-381-5840. **Owner(s):** Pioneer Press, Inc., 3701 W. Lake Ave., Glenview, IL 60025. TEL 847-486-9200; Ed. David Kirkpatrick; Pub. Thomas Neri; adv. contact: Julie Ross. pub. size: tabloid; circ. 7,313(paid).
 Formerly: Courier, The.

US

CARY-GROVE COUNTRYSIDE. 1976. Thu. $.75 newsstand; $17.95/yr. 200 James St., Barrington, IL 60010. TEL 847-381-9200; FAX 847-381-5840. **Owner(s):** Pioneer Press, Inc., 3701 W. Lake Ave., Glenview, IL 60025. TEL 847-486-9200; Pub. Thomas Neri; adv. contact: Susan Karol. photos; pub. size: tabloid; circ. 3,049(paid).

BARRY
US

PAPER, THE. 1962. Wed. $.30 newsstand; $12/yr. in cy.; $18/yr. out of cy. 725 Bainbridge St., Barry, IL 62312. TEL 217-335-2112; FAX 217-335-2112. **Owner(s):** Debbie Harshman, 725 Bainbridge St., Barry, IL 62312. TEL 217-335-2112; Pub. Debbie Harshman; adv.; photos; pub. size: tabloid; circ. 1,600(paid).

BARTONVILLE

US

LIMESTONE INDEPENDENT NEWS. 1967. Wed. $.50 newsstand; $20/yr. 114 Roosevelt, Bartonville, IL 61607. TEL 309-697-1859; FAX 309-697-1851. **Owner(s):** Adrian Swindler, 114 Roosevelt, Bartonville, IL 61607. TEL 309-697-1859; FAX 309-697-1851; Pub. Barbara Widener; adv.; photos; pub. size: tabloid; circ. 2,500(paid).

BEARDSTOWN

US

BEARDSTOWN ILLINOIAN-STAR. 1888. Thu. $.75 newsstand; $24/yr. 1210 Wall St., Beardstown, IL 62618. TEL 217-323-1010; FAX 217-323-5402. **Owner(s):** Beardstown Newspapers, Inc., 1210 Wall St., Beardstown, IL 62618. TEL 217-323-1010; FAX 217-323-5402; Ed. Salle Lael; Pub. William Mitchell; adv.; bk.rev.; pub. size: broadsheet; circ. 2,025(paid).

US

VIRGINIA GAZETTE. 1872. Thu. $.75 newsstand; $24/yr. 1210 Wall St., Beardstown, IL 62618. TEL 217-323-1010; FAX 217-323-5402. **Owner(s):** Beardstown Newspapers, Inc., 1210 Wall St., Beardstown, IL 61618. TEL 217-323-1010; FAX 217-323-5402; Ed. Nikki Kaul; Pub. William Mitchell; adv. contact: William Mitchell. bk.rev.; pub. size: broadsheet.

BEECHER CITY

US   ISSN 1066-7970

BEECHER CITY JOURNAL. 1915. w. $.50 newsstand; 16/yr. in cy.; $18/yr. out of cy.; $20/yr. elsewhere. 104 S. Charles, Beecher City, IL 62414-0038. TEL 618-487-5634. **Owner(s):** P.J. Ryan & Cherie Ryan, 101 S. Charles, Beecher City, IL 62414. TEL 618-487-5634; Ed. P.J. Ryan; Pub. P.J. Ryan; adv.; photos; pub. size: tabloid.

BELLEVILLE

US

BELLEVILLE JOURNAL. s-w.: Wed. & Sun. free in cy.; $35/yr. out of cy. 219 N. Illinois, Belleville, IL 62220. TEL 618-277-7000; FAX 618-277-7018. **Owner(s):** Suburban Journals, 1714 Deer Tracks Trail, St. Louis, MO 63131; Ed. Scott W. Queen; Pub. Larry Johnson; adv. contact: Mark Gehrs. photos; pub. size: broadsheet; circ. 35,000(free & paid).

US

COUNTY JOURNAL. Wed. free in area; $35/yr. 219 N. Illinois, Belleville, IL 62220. TEL 618-277-7000; FAX 618-277-7018. **Owner(s):** Suburban Journals, 1714 Deer Tracks Trail, St. Louis, MO 63131; Ed. Scott W. Queen; Pub. Larry Johnson; adv. contact: Mark Gehrs. photos; pub. size: broadsheet; circ. 4,500(controlled & free).

US

FAIRVIEW HEIGHTS JOURNAL. s-w.: Wed. & Sun. free in area; $35/yr. 219 N. Illinois, Belleville, IL 62220. TEL 618-277-7000; FAX 618-277-7018. **Owner(s):** Suburban Journals, 1714 Deer Tracks Trail, St. Louis, MO 63131; Ed. Scott W. Queen; Pub. Larry Johnson; adv. contact: Dan Braun. pub. size: broadsheet; circ. 1,500(controlled & free).

BERWYN

US

BERWYN/CICERO LIFE. 1926. 3/wk.: Wed., Fri., Sun. $27/yr. 2601 S. Harlem Ave., Berwyn, IL 60402. TEL 708-484-1234. FAX 708-484-7778. **Owner(s):** Life Printing & Publishing Co., Inc., 2601 S. Harlem Ave., Berwyn, MA 60402; Ed. Robert Lifka; Pub. Jack R. Kubik; adv. contact: Dave Kuehl. pub. size: broadsheet; circ. 33,000(paid); Sun. 33,000(paid).
   Formerly: Berwyn Life.

BLOOMINGDALE

US

BLOOMINGDALE PRESS 1922. Thu. $.50 newsstand; $10.95/yr. in area; $28.95/yr. out of area. 134 S. Bloomingdale, Bloomingdale, IL 60108. TEL 708-307-1101; FAX 708-307-1190. **Owner(s):** Press Publications, Inc., 112 S. York St., Elmhurst, IL 60126. TEL 708-834-0900; FAX 708-834-0910; Ed. Bruce A. Douglas; Pub. Jack Cruger; adv.; photos bk.rev.; pub. size: tabloid; circ. 28,000(paid). **Wire Service(s):** CNS.

US

CAROL STREAM PRESS. 1900. Thu. $.50 newsstand; $10.95/yr. in area; $28.95/yr. out of area. 134 N. Bloomingdale Rd. Bloomingdale, IL 60108. TEL 708-307-1101; FAX 708-307-1190. **Owner(s):** Press Publications, Inc., 112 S. York St., Elmhurst, IL 60126. TEL 708-834-0900; Ed. Bruce A. Douglas; Pub. Jack Cruger; adv.; photos; bk.rev.; pub. size: tabloid; circ. 6,923(paid).

US

GLEN ELLYN PRESS. Thu. $.50 newsstand; $10.95/yr. in area; $28.95/yr. out of state mailed. 134 N. Bloomingdale, Bloomingdale, IL 60108. TEL 708-307-1101; FAX 708-307-1190. **Owner(s):** Press Publications, Inc., 112 S. York, Elmhurst, IL 60126. TEL 708-834-0900; Ed. Bruce A. Douglas; Pub. Jack Cruger; adv.; photos; bk.rev.; pub. size: tabloid; circ. 1,000(paid).

US

WHEATON PRESS. 1922. Thu. $.50 newsstand; $10.95/yr. in cy.; $28.95/yr. elsewhere. 134 N. Bloomingdale, Bloomingdale, IL 60108. TEL 708-307-1101; FAX 708-307-1190. **Owner(s):** Press Publications, Inc., 112 S. York St., Elmhurst, IL 60126. TEL 708-834-0900; Ed. Bruce A. Douglas; Pub. Jack Cruger; adv.; photos; bk.rev.; pub. size: tabloid; circ. 28,000(controlled & paid).

BLUE MOUND

US

BLUE MOUND LEADER. 1886. Wed. $.40 newsstand; $10/yr. in cy.; $11.50/yr. out of cy.; $13.50/yr. elsewhere. Rte. 48, Blue Mound, IL 62513-0318. TEL 217-692-2323. **Owner(s):** Cindy Stuart, P.O. Box 318, Blue Mound, IL 62513. TEL 217-692-2323; Pub. Cindy Stuart; adv. contact: Cindy Stuart. photos; pub. size: tabloid; circ. 850(free & paid).

BOLINGBROOK

US   ISSN 0885-6389

BOLINGBROOK SUN. 1963. s-w.: Wed. & Fri. $.35 newsstand; $15/yr. 339 N. Schmidt Rd., Bolingbrook, IL 60439. TEL 708-759-9169; FAX 708-759-1726. **Owner(s):** Copley Press, Inc., 7776 Ivanhoe Ave., La Jolla, CA 60540. TEL 614-454-0411; adv.; pub. size: tabloid; circ. 7,300(paid). **Wire Service(s):** CNS.

US   ISSN 0885-6397

ROMEOVILLE SUN. 1963. s-w.: Wed. & Fri. $.35 newsstand; $22.50/yr. 339 N. Schmidt Rd., Bolingbrook, IL 60439. TEL 708-759-9169; FAX 708-759-1726. **Owner(s):** Copley Press, Inc., 7776 Ivanhoe Ave., La Jolla, CA 92037; adv. contact: Rick Taden. pub. size: tabloid; circ. 7,300(paid). **Wire Service(s):** CNS

BOURBONNAIS

US

HERALD/COUNTRY MARKET, THE. 1975. Tue. $.60 newsstand; $22/yr. in state; $25/yr. out of state. 500 Brown Blvd., Bourbonnais, IL 60914-2328. TEL 815-933-1131; FAX 815-933-3785. **Owner(s):** B & B Publishing, Inc., 500 Brown Blvd., Bourbonnais, IL 60914. TEL 815-933-1131; FAX 815-933-3785; Pub. Toby Olszewski; adv. contact: Sharon Robinson. pub. size: tabloid; circ. 32,000(free & paid).
   Formerly: Country Market.

BRAIDWOOD

US

BRAIDWOOD JOURNAL, THE. 1958. Wed. $.50 newsstand; $19.50 in cy.; $22.50/yr. out of cy.; $25.50/yr. out of state. 192 E. Main, Braidwood, IL 60408. TEL 815-458-6246; FAX 815-634-2815. **Owner(s):** Sheridan Bailey, 273 S. Broadway, Coal City, IL 60416. TEL 815-634-2102; Ed. Sherican Bailey; Pub. Sheridan Bailey; adv. contact: Katie Easton. photos; pub. size: broadsheet; circ. 1,065(paid).

BREESE

US

BREESE JOURNAL. 1921. Thu. $.35 newsstand; $17.50/yr. in cy.; $21/yr. out of cy. 623-625 N. Second St., Breese, IL 62230. TEL 618-526-7211; FAX 618-526-2590. **Owner(s):** Breese Publishing Co., 623-625 N. Second St., Breese, IL 62230. TEL 618-526-7211; FAX 618-526-2590; Ed. Debbie Rehg; Pub. Dave Mahlandt; adv. contact: Vicky Albers. photos; pub. size: broadsheet; circ. 5,707(free & paid).

BRIDGEPORT

US

BRIDGEPORT LEADER. 1907. Thu. $.35 newsstand; $19.50/yr. local. 131 E. Olive, Bridgeport, IL 62417-1935. TEL 618-945-2111; FAX 618-945-2131. **Owner(s):** Louis Valbert, 424 Main, Bridgeport, IL 62417. TEL 618-945-7779; Ed. Louis Valbert; Pub. Louis Valbert; pub. size: broadsheet; circ. 3,200(paid).

BRIGHTON

US

SOUTHWESTERN JOURNAL NEWS. 1972. Thu. $.30 newsstand; $9.50/yr. in cy.; $11.50/yr. out of cy.; $13.50/yr. out of state. 117 N. Main St., Brighton, IL 62012. TEL 618-372-8451; FAX 618-372-8451. **Owner(s):** John M. Galer, 150 N. Washington, Bunker Hill, IL 62014. TEL 618-585-4411; Ed. Vera Eckhardt; Pub. John M. Galer; adv. contact: Dawn Ansell. photos; pub. size: tabloid; circ. 1,550(paid).

BUNKER HILL

US

BUNKER HILL GAZETTE NEWS. 1892. Thu. $.25 newsstand; $9 50/yr. in cy.; $11.50 out of cy.; $13.50 out of state. 150 N. Washington St., Bunker Hill, IL 52014. TEL 618-585-4411; FAX 618-585-3354. **Owner(s):** John M. Galer, 150 N. Washington, Bunker Hill, IL 62014. TEL 618-585-4411; Ed. Vera Eckhardt; Pub. John M. Galer; adv. contact: Eve Pickerill. photos; pub. size: tabloid; circ. 1,500(paid).

BUSHNELL

US

MCDONOUGH-DEMOCRAT. 1884. Mon. $17/yr. in state; $21/yr. out of state. 358 E. Main St., Bushnell, IL 61422. TEL 309-772-2129; FAX 309-772-3994. **Owner(s):** William Lorton, 358 E. Main St., Bushnell, IL 61422. TEL 309-772-2129; Pub. William Lorton; pub. size: standard; circ. 2,250(paid).

BYRON

US

NORTHERN OGLE COUNTY TEMPO. Tue. $.75 newsstand; $22/yr. 110 N. Union, Byron, IL 61010. TEL 815-234-4821; FAX 815-654-4857. **Owner(s):** Rock Valley Community Press, P.O. Box 15340, Rockford, IL 61024. TEL 815-877-4044; Ed. Michele Thomas; Pub. Craig McMullin; adv. contact: Chuck Carter. photos; pub. size: tabloid; circ. 6,000(free & paid).

CAIRO

US

CAIRO CITIZEN. 1887. Thu. $19/yr. 711 Washington, Cairo, IL 62914. TEL 618-734-4242; FAX 618-734-4244. **Owner(s):** North Scott Publishing, Inc., P.O. Box 529, Anna, IL 62906. TEL 618-833-2158; Ed. James West; Pub. Jerry L. Reppert; adv. contact: Nancy Wright. photos; pub. size: broadsheet; circ. 3,500(paid).

CAMBRIDGE

US

CAMBRIDGE CHRONICLE. 1893. Thu. $.75 newsstand; $31/yr. in state; $33/yr. out of state. 119 W. Exchange, Cambridge, IL 61238. TEL 309-937-3303; FAX 309-937-3303. **Owner(s):** Terry Newspapers, Inc., 119 W. Exchange, Cambridge, IL 61238. TEL 309-937-3303; Ed. Ty Bernier; Pub. Thomas Terry; pub. size: broadsheet; circ. 1,600(paid).

CARLINVILLE

US

CARLINVILLE DEMOCRAT. 1856. Thu. $.50 newsstand; $17/yr. in cy.; $19/yr. out of cy. 118 N. West St., Carlinville, IL 62626. TEL 217-854-2561; FAX 217-854-3366. **Owner(s):** Thomas Hatalla, P.O. Box 470, Carlinville, IL 62626. TEL 217-854-2561; FAX 217-854-3366; Edward Albracht, P.O. Box 470, Carlinville, IL 62626. TEL 217-854-2561; FAX 217-854-3366; Ed. Edward J. Albracht. adv.; photos; pub. size: standard; circ. 3,000(free & paid).

US

MACOUPIN COUNTY ENQUIRER. 1852. Thu. $.50 newsstand; $17/yr. in cy.; $19/yr. out of cy. 125 E. Main St., Carlinville, IL 62626-0200. TEL 217-854-2534; FAX 217-854-2535. **Owner(s):** Chris Schmitt, 125 E. Main St., Carlinville, IL 62626-0200. TEL 217-854-2534; FAX 217-854-2535; Ed. Chris Schmitt; Pub. Chris Schmitt; adv.; photos; pub. size: broadsheet; circ. 4,900(paid).

CARLYLE

US

CARLYLE UNION BANNER. 1863. Wed. $.35 newsstand; $17.50/yr. in cy.; $27.50/yr. out of cy. 671 Tenth St., Carlyle, IL 62231. TEL 618-594-3131; FAX 618-594-3115. **Owner(s):** Dempsey Publishing Co., 671 Tenth St., Carlyle, IL 62231. TEL 618-594-3131; Ed. Warren Dempsey; Pub. Warren Dempsey; adv. contact: Mike Langham. pub. size: broadsheet; circ. 4,800(paid).

CARROLLTON

US

CARROLLTON GAZETTE PATRIOT. 1846. Thu. $.50 newsstand; $20/yr. in cy.; $25/yr. out of cy. 428 N. Main St., Carrollton, IL 62016-0231. TEL 217-942-3626; FAX 217-942-3699. **Owner(s):** Albert W. Scott, III, 428 N. Main St., Carrollton, IL 62016. TEL 217-942-3626; FAX 217-942-3699; Pub. Albert Scott, III; adv.; photos; pub. size: broadsheet; circ. 1,701(paid).

CARTHAGE

US

HANCOCK COUNTY JOURNAL-PILOT. 1887. Wed. $.50 newsstand; $22/yr. in cy.; $35/yr. out of cy. 31 N. Washington, Carthage, IL 62321. TEL 217-357-2149; FAX 217-357-2177. **Owner(s):** Brehm Communications, Inc., 17065 Via del Campo, Ste. 200, San Diego, CA 92127. TEL 619-451-3814; Ed. Tom Martin; Pub. Bill Ferguson; photos; pub. size: broadsheet; circ. 4,200(free & paid).
  Formerly: Carthage Hancock Journal-Pilot.

CASEY

US

REPORTER, THE. 1938. s-w.: Mon. & Thu. $.50 newsstand; $35/yr. in cy.; $44/yr. out of cy.; $52/yr. out of state. 216 S. Central, Casey, IL 62420. TEL 217-932-5211; FAX 217-932-5214. **Owner(s):** Lincoln Trail Publishing Co., 216 S. Central, Casey, IL 62420. TEL 217-932-5211; Ed. Greg Bilbrey; Pub. Larry Perrotto; adv. contact: Don Cook. pub. size: broadsheet; circ. 3,500(paid).

CERRO GORDO

US

NEWS-RECORD, THE. 1889. Wed. $17/yr. 221 E. South St., Cerro Gordo, IL 61818. TEL 217-763-3541; FAX 217-578-2833. **Owner(s):** Mike Brothers, 221 E. South St., Cerro Gordo, IL 61818. TEL 217-763-3541; Pub. Mike Brothers; adv. contact: Janice Pruitt. pub. size: tabloid; circ. 1,200(paid).

CHAMPAIGN

US

THRIFTY NICKEL. 1985. Thu. free. 61 E. University Ave., Champaign, IL 61820-4109, TEL 217-356-4804; FAX 217-356-4970. **Owner(s):** Randy Cooper, 306 W. Springfield, Champaign, IL 61820; adv.; pub. size: tabloid; circ. 50,000(free).

CHESTER

US

RANDOLPH COUNTY HERALD TRIBUNE. 1926. Thu. $.50 newsstand; $19.25/yr. in cy.; $22/yr. out of cy. 624 State St., Chester, IL 62233. TEL 618-826-2385; FAX 618-826-5181. **Owner(s):** American Publishing Co., 606 N. Van Buren, P.O. Box 520, Marion, IL 62959. TEL 618-993-1711; Ed. Mary Leek. adv.; pub. size: broadsheet; circ. 4,500(paid).
  Formerly: Chester Randolph County Herald.

CHICAGO

US

BACK OF THE YARDS JOURNAL. 1932. Wed. $.20 newsstand; $40/yr. The Yards Plz., 4642 S. Damen Ave., Chicago, IL 60609. TEL 312-927-7204. **Owner(s):** Back of the Yards Journal, The Yards Plz., 4642 S. Damen Ave., Chicago, IL 60609. TEL 312-927-7940; Ed. Robert M. Lukens; Pub. Patrick J. Salmon; adv.; photos; bk.rev.; pub. size: tabloid; circ. 48,000(free & paid).

US   ISSN 0006-0410

BEVERLY REVIEW. 1905. Wed. $.50 newsstand; $18/yr. 1739 W. 99th St., Chicago, IL 60643. TEL 312-238-3366; FAX 312-238-1492. **Owner(s):** TR Communications, 1739 W. 99th St., Chicago, IL 60643. TEL 815-932-9682; Ed. Jerry Moore. adv.; pub. size: tabloid; circ. 6,000(paid).

US

BRIDGEPORT NEWS. 1943. Wed. $.20 newsstand. 3252 S. Halsted, Chicago, IL 60608. TEL 312-842-5883; FAX 312-842-5097. **Owner(s):** Chicago Bridgeport News, Inc., 3252 S. Halsted, Chicago, IL 60608. TEL 312-842-5883; FAX 312-842-5097; Ed. Janice Racinowski; Pub. Joseph L. Feldman; adv. contact: Janice Racinowski. pub. size: broadsheet; circ. 25,300(paid).
  Formerly: Chicago Bridgeport News.

US

BRIGHTON PARK-MCKINLEY PARK LIFE. 1933. Thu. $.15 newsstand; $60/yr. 1st class mail. 2949 W. 43rd St., Chicago, IL 60632. TEL 312-523-3663; FAX 312-523-3983. **Owner(s):** Albert H. Silinski, 2949 W. 43rd St., Chicago, IL 60632. TEL 312-523-3663; FAX 312-523-3983; Ed. Albert H. Silinski; Pub. Albert H. Silinski; adv.; bk.rev.; pub. size: broadsheet; circ. 30,000(controlled & paid).
  Formerly: Chicago Brighton Park-McKinley.

US

CHICAGO-LAWNDALE NEWS. 1937. s-w.: Thu. & Sun. free newsstand; $50/yr. mailed. 2300 S. Kedvale, Chicago, IL 60623. TEL 312-762-2266; FAX 312-762-5076. **Owner(s):** Chicago West Town Publications, 2300 S. Kedvale, Chicago, IL 60623. TEL 312-247-8500; Ed. Hayley Carlton; Pub. Linda Nardini; adv.; pub. size: tabloid; circ. 177,000(paid); Sun. 177,000(paid).

US

CHICAGO'S N.W. SIDE PRESS. 1940. Wed. $.35 newsstand; $85/yr. 4941 N. Milwaukee, Chicago, IL 60630. TEL 312-286-6100. **Owner(s):** Nadig Newspapers, Inc., 4941 N. Milwaukee, Chicago, IL 60640. TEL 312-286-6100; Pub. Glenn Nadig; pub. size: broadsheet; circ. 40,000(free).

US   ISSN 0028-1778

CHICAGO NEAR NORTH NEWS. 1956. Sat. $.50 newsstand; $25/yr. in cy. 222 W. Ontario St., Ste. 502, Chicago, IL 60610-3695. TEL 312-787-2677; FAX 312-787-2680. **Owner(s):** Near North News, Inc., 222 W. Ontario St., Ste. 502, Chicago, IL 60610-3695. TEL 312-787-2677; FAX 312-787-2680; Ed. Arnie Matanky; Pub. Arnie Matanky; adv.: $12.60/SAU. photos; pub. size: tabloid; circ. 7,750(free & paid).

US   ISSN 1068-8213

CHICAGO NEAR WEST GAZETTE. 1983. Wed. free newsstand; $18/yr. 1335 W. Harrison St., Chicago, IL 60607-3318. TEL 312-243-4288; FAX 312-243-4270. **Owner(s):** Mark J. Valentino, 1660 W. Ogden, Chicago, IL 60612. TEL 312-273-4288; FAX 312-243-4270; Ed. Mark J. Valentino; Pub. Mark J. Valentino; adv. contact: Laura Sorce. photos; pub. size: tabloid; circ. 15,000(controlled & free).

US

CHICAGO POST. 1984. bi-w. $12/6 mos.; $20/yr. 3647 N. Kedzie, Chicago, IL 60618. TEL 312-463-5100. **Owner(s):** Jim Boratyn, P.O. Box 18444, Chicago, IL 60618. TEL 312-463-5100; Ed. Jim Boratyn; Pub. Jim Boratyn; adv.; pub. size: tabloid; circ. 45,000(paid).

US

CHICAGO READER. 1971. Fri. free; $50/yr. 11 E. Illinois, Chicago, IL 60611. TEL 312-828-0350. **Owner(s):** Chicago Reader, Inc., 11 E. Illinois, Chicago, IL 60611. TEL 312-828-0350; Ed. Alison True; Pub. Jane Levine; adv. contact: Don Humbertson. bk.rev.; pub. size: tabloid; circ. 133,400(controlled).

US

CHICAGO WEST SIDE TIMES. 1940. s-w.: Thu. & Sun. free newsstand; $50/yr. mailed. 2300 S. Kedvale, Chicago, IL 60623. TEL 312-762-2266; FAX 312-762-5076. **Owner(s):** Chicago West Town Publications, 2300 S. Kedvale, Chicago, IL 60623. TEL 312-247-8500; Ed. Hayley Carlton; Pub. Linda Nardini; adv.; pub. size: tabloid; circ. 177,000(paid); Sun. 177,000(paid).

US

CLEAR-RIDGE REPORTER. 1961. Wed. $.50 newsstand; $75/yr. mailed. 6225 S. Kedzie Ave., Chicago, IL 60629. TEL 312-476-4800; FAX 312-476-7811. **Owner(s):** Vondrak Publishing Co., 6225 S. Kedzie Ave., Chicago, IL 60629. TEL 312-476-4800; Ed. Joseph Boyle; Pub. James C. Vondrak; adv. contact: Murphy Griffin. pub. size: tabloid; circ. 24,600(free & paid).

Formerly: Chicago-Clear-Ridge Reporter.

US

HYDE PARK HERALD. 1881. Wed. $.50 newsstand; $15/yr. 5240 S. Harper Ave., Chicago, IL 60615. TEL 312-643-8533; FAX 312-643-8542. **Owner(s):** Hyde Park Herald Newspapers, Inc., 5240 S. Harper Ave., Chicago, IL 60615. TEL 312-643-8533; Ed. Kevin Knapp; Pub. Bruce Sagan; adv.; pub. size: tabloid; circ. 26,000(paid).

US

INSIDE. 1968. Wed. free. 4710 N. Lincoln, Chicago, IL 60625. TEL 312-878-7334; FAX 312-878-0959; E-mail: insidepub@aol.com. **Owner(s):** Ronald Roenigk, 4710 N. Lincoln, Chicago, IL 60625. TEL 312-878-7334; Ed. Nancy Amdeer. adv. contact: Ron Roenigk. photos; pub. size: tabloid; circ. 65,000(free).

Formerly: Inside Gold Coast.

US

JOURNAL, THE. Sat. $.35 newsstand; $85/yr. 4941 N. Milwaukee, Chicago, IL 60630. TEL 312-286-6100. **Owner(s):** Nadig Newspapers, Inc., 4941 N. Milwaukee, Chicago, IL 60630; Ed. Randy Erickson; Pub. Glenn H. Nadig; adv.; pub. size: tabloid; circ. 1,000(controlled & free).

US

NEW CITY. 1986. Thu. free newsstand; $30/yr. mailed 3rd class; $75/yr. mailed 1st class. 770 N. Halsted, Ste. 208 Chicago, IL 60622. TEL 312-243-8786; FAX 312-243-8802. **Owner(s):** New City Communications, Inc., 770 N. Halsted, Ste. 208 Chicago, IL 60622. TEL 312-243-8786; FAX 312-243-8802; Ed. Brian Hieggelke; Pub. Jan Hieggelke; adv.; photos; bk.rev.; pub. size: tabloid; circ. 65,000(free).

US

NEWSMARKETER, THE. 1985. Wed. free. 5959 S. Harlem Ave., Chicago, IL 60638. TEL 312-229-2882; FAX 312-229-2899. **Owner(s):** American Publishing Co., 606 N. Van Buren, P.O. Box 520, Marion, IL 62959. TEL 618-993-1711; Ed. Michael Kelly; Pub. Norm Rosinski; adv. contact: Mike Beatty. pub. size: broadsheet; circ. 13,300(free).

US   ISSN 0029-2877

NORTH LOOP NEWS. 1930. Thu. free newsstand; $40.55/yr. 2nd class; $50/yr. 1st class. 1332 N. Halsted, Ste. 204, Chicago, IL 60622. TEL 312-787-5396; FAX 312-787-1616. **Owner(s):** North Loop News Corp., 800 N. Clark St., Chicago, IL 60610. TEL 312-787-5396; Ed. Deborah Madden; Pub. Michelle C. Albanese; adv. contact: Michelle C. Albanese. pub. size: tabloid; circ. 24,700(free & paid).

US

NORTHWEST LEADER. 1953. s-w.: Wed. & Sun. $.50 newsstand; $40/yr. 6010 W. Belmont Ave., Chicago, IL 60634. TEL 312-283-7900; FAX 312-283-7761. **Owner(s):** Arthur & Ramona Diaz, 6010 W. Belmont Ave., Chicago, IL 60634. TEL 312-283-7900 FAX 312-283-7761; Ed. Jackie Pledger-Skwerski. adv.; pub. size: broadsheet; circ. 25,000(paid); Sun. 6,500(paid).

US

NORTHWEST SIDE PRESS. 1940. Wed. $.35 newsstand; $85/yr. 4941 N. Milwaukee Ave., Chicago, IL 60630. TEL 312-286-6100. **Owner(s):** Nadig Newspapers, Inc., 4941 N. Milwaukee Ave., Chicago, IL 60630; Ed. Randy Erickson; Pub. Glenn H. Nadig; adv.; photos; bk.rev.; pub. size: broadsheet; circ. 40,500(controlled & free).

US

REPORTER, THE. 1964. Sat. $.35 newsstand; $85/yr. 4937 N. Milwaukee, Chicago, IL 60630. TEL 312-286-6100. **Owner(s):** Nadig Newspapers, Inc., 4941 N. Milwaukee, Chicago, IL 60630; Ed. Randy Erickson; Pub. Glenn H. Nadig; pub. size: tabloid; circ. 13,000(free).

US

RIVER NORTH NEWS. 1987. bi-w. free newsstand; $36/yr. 109 W. North Ave. 2nd Fl., Chicago, IL 60610. TEL 312-944-3300. **Owner(s):** William S. Petacque, 109 W. North Ave., 2nd Fl., Chicago IL 60610. TEL 312-944-3300; Ed. Daved Oberhelman. adv.; photos; pub. size: tabloid; circ. 12,500(free & paid).

US

SENTINEL, THE. 1911. Thu. $ newsstand; $48.95/yr. 6 N. Michigan, Ste. 905, Chicago, IL 60601. TEL 312-407-0060; FAX 312-407-0096. **Owner(s):** Sentinel Publishing Co., 6 N. Michigan, Ste 905, Chicago, IL 60601. TEL 312-407-0060; FAX 312-407-0096; Ed. Jack L. Fishbein. adv.; bk.rev.; pub. size: standard; circ. 45,500(paid). **Wire Service(s):** JTA.

US

SOUTHWEST BEACON. 1982. Tue. free home deliv. 6225 S. Kedzie Ave., Chicago, IL 60629. TEL 312-476-4800; FAX 312-476-7811. **Owner(s):** Vondrak Publishing Co. 6225 S. Kedzie, Chicago, IL 60629. TEL 312-476-4800; Ed. Joe Boyle; Pub. James C. Vondrak; adv. contact: Murphy Griffin. pub. size: tabloid; circ. 25,685(paid).

US

SOUTHWEST COURIER. 1986. Thu. free home deliv. 6225 S. Kedzie Ave., Chicago, IL 60629. TEL 312-476-4800; FAX 312-476-4800. **Owner(s):** Vondrak Publishing Co. 6225 S. Kedzie Ave., Chicago, IL 60629. TEL 312-476-4800; Ed. Timothy C. Hadac; Pub. James C. Vondrak; adv.; photos; pub. size: tabloid; circ. 13,456(paid).

US   ISSN 0038-4704

SOUTHWEST NEWS-HERALD. 1924. Thu. $18.60/6 mos. home deliv.; $21/yr. mailed. 6225 S. Kedzie Ave., Chicago, IL 60629. TEL 312-476-4800; FAX 312-476-7811. **Owner(s):** Vondrak Publishing Co. 6225 S. Kedzie Ave., Chicago, IL 60629. TEL 312-476-4800; Ed. Joe Boyle; Pub. James C. Vondrak; adv. contact: Renee Lawrence. pub. size: broadsheet; circ. 24,542(paid).

US

SOUTHWEST SHOPPER. 1960. Tue. free home deliv. 6225 S. Kedzie Ave., Chicago, IL 60629. TEL 312-476-4800. **Owner(s):** Vondrak Publishing Co., 6225 S. Kedzie Ave., Chicago, IL 60629. TEL 312-476-4800; Ed. Joe Boyle; Pub. James C. Vondrak; adv. contact: Murphy Griffin. pub. size: broadsheet; circ. 37,000(free).

US

SUBURBAN LEADER. Sun. $.50 newsstand; $40/yr. in cy. 6008 W. Belmont Ave., Chicago, IL 60634. TEL 312-283-7900; FAX 312-283-7761. **Owner(s):** Leader/Post Newspapers, Inc., 6008 W. Belmont Ave., Chicago, IL 60634. TEL 312-283-7761; Ed. Jacki Pledger. adv.; pub. size: broadsheet; circ. 11,000(paid).

US

WEST SUBURBAN POST. 1964. Fri. $.50 newsstand $40/yr. mailed. 6008 W. Belmont Ave., Chicago IL 60634. TEL 312-283-7900; FAX 312-283-7761. **Owner(s):** Leader/Post Newspapers, Inc., 6008 W. Belmont Ave., Chicago, IL 60634. TEL 312-283-7900; Ed. Jackie Pledger-Swerski; Pub. Arthur Diaz; adv. contact: Patricia Cioch. photos; pub. size: tabloid; circ. 13,000(controlled).

CHICAGO HEIGHTS

US

STAR, THE. 1901 s-w.: Thu. & Sun. $.50 newsstand; $43.20/yr. 1526 Otto Blvd., Chicago Heights, IL 60411. TEL 708-755-6161; FAX 708-755-9112. **Owner(s):** Hollinger International, 401 N. Wabash, Chicago, IL 60611. TEL 312-321-3000; Ed. Frank Shuftan; Pub. Norman Rosinski; adv. contact: Mark Lacey. photos; pub. size: broadsheet; circ. 62,758(paid); Sun. 65,995(paid).

    Formerly: Chicago Heights Star.

CHILLICOTHE

US

CHILLICOTHE BULLETIN. 1883. Wed. $.50 newsstand; $13.20/yr. in cy.; $20.80/yr. out of cy. 1008 N. Fourth St., Chillicothe, IL 61523-1504. TEL 309-274-2185; FAX 309-274-2741. **Owner(s):** Fleming Publishing Co., 100 Detroit Ave., Morton, IL 61550. TEL 309-263-2211; Ed. Beth Gehrt; Pub. Ted Fleming; adv. contact: Heidi Whitman. photos; pub. size: broadsheet; circ. 2,770(paid).

CHRISMAN

US

CHRISMAN LEADER. 1972. Thu. $.35 newsstand; $18/yr. in IL & IN; $24/yr. elsewhere. 148 W. Madison, Chrisman, IL 61924. TEL 217-269-2811. **Owner(s):** Ed Jenison, 148 W. Madison, Chrisman, IL 61924. TEL 217-269-2811; Ed. Kevin Jenison; Pub. Ed Jenison; adv.; pub. size: tabloid; circ. 2,000(paid).

CISSNA PARK

US   ISSN 0009-7543

CISSNA PARK NEWS. 1891. Thu. $.40 newsstand; $18/yr. in cy.; $20/yr. out of cy. 119 W. Garfield Ave., Cissna Park, IL 60924-0008. TEL 815-457-2245. **Owner(s):** Baier Publishing Co., 119 W. Garfield, Cissna Park, IL 60924-0008. TEL 815-457-2245; Ed. Rick A. Baier; Pub. Rick A. Baier; adv.; photos; pub. size: tabloid; circ. 1,400(paid).

US

RANKIN INDEPENDENT. 1897. Thu. $.40 newsstand; $18/yr. in cy.; $20/yr. out of cy. 119 W. Garfield St., Cissna Park, IL 60924. TEL 815-457-2245. **Owner(s):** Baier Publishing Co., 119 W. Garfield, Cissna Park, IL 60924. TEL 815-457-2245; Ed. Mary Ann Scott; Pub. Rick A. Baier; pub. size tabloid; circ. 1,750(paid).

CLIFTON

US

ADVOCATE, THE. 1883. Thu. $.40 newsstand; $14.95/yr. in state; $16.95/yr. out of state. 330 N. Fourth St., Clifton, IL 60927. TEL 815-694-2122; FAX 815-694-3770. **Owner(s):** Therese Simoneau, 330 N. Fourth St., Clifton, IL 60927. TEL 815-694-2122; Ed. Therese Simoneau; Pub. Therese Simoneau; adv.; pub. size: tabloid; circ. 2,100(controlled & paid).

COAL CITY

US

COAL CITY COURANT. 1903. Wed. $.50 newsstand; $19.50/yr. in Grundy & Will cys.; $22.50/yr. in state; $25.50/yr. out of state. 273 S. Broadway, Coal City, IL 60416. TEL 815-634-2102; FAX 815-634-2815. **Owner(s):** Bailey Printing & Publishing, 273 S. Broadway, Coal City, IL 60416. TEL 815-634-2102; Ed. Ann Gill; Pub. Sheridan Bailey; adv. contact: Katie Easton. photos; pub. size: broadsheet; circ. 2,360(paid).

US

GOOD NEWS SHOPPER. 1982. Mon. free. 273 S. Broadway, Coal City, IL 60416. TEL 815-634-2102; FAX 815-634-2815. **Owner(s):** Bailey Printing & Publishing, 273 S. Broadway, Coal City, IL 60416. TEL 815-634-2102; Ed. Sheridan Bailey; Pub. Sheridan Bailey; adv. contact: Katie Easton. pub. size: broadsheet; circ. 12,000(free).

COLCHESTER

US

COLCHESTER CHRONICLE. 1951. Thu. $.30 newsstand; $12.75/yr. in cy.; $15/yr. out of cy. 118 E. Market St., Colchester, IL 62326. TEL 309-776-3700. **Owner(s):** Stacey Nicholas & Joe Coelho, P.O. Box 356, Colchester, IL 62326. TEL 309-776-3700; Ed. Stacey Nicholas; Pub. Stacey Nicholas; adv.; photos; bk.rev.; pub. size: tabloid; circ. 600(paid).

COLLINSVILLE

US   ISSN 0883-6574

COLLINSVILLE HERALD. 1974. Thu. $.50 newsstand; $15/yr. local (includes Collinsville Journal). 113 E. Clay St., Collinsville, IL 62234. TEL 618-344-0264; FAX 618-344-3611. **Owner(s):** Suburban Journals, 1714 Deer Tracks Trail, St. Louis, MO 63131. TEL 314-821-1110; Ed. Larry Johnson; Pub. Larry Johnson; adv. contact: Bob Wilcox. pub. size: broadsheet; circ. 5,500(controlled & paid).

US

COLLINSVILLE JOURNAL. 1974. s-w.: Wed. & Sun. free distribution in cy.; $.35 newsstand; $42/yr. (with Collinsville Herald). 113 E. Clay St., Collinsville, IL 62234. TEL 618-344-0264; FAX 618-344-3611. **Owner(s):** Suburban Journals, 1714 Deer Tracks Trail, St. Louis, MO 63131. TEL 314-821-1110; Ed. Larry Johnson; Pub. Larry Johnson; adv. contact: Bob Wilcox. pub. size: broadsheet; circ. 19,000(free & paid).

COLUMBIA

US

CAHOKIA JOURNAL. 1969. s-w.: Wed. & Sun. free in area. 212 W. Locust St., Columbia, IL 62236-1732. TEL 618-281-7691; FAX 618-281-7693. **Owner(s):** Suburban Journals, 1714 Deer Tracks Trail, St. Louis, MO 63131. TEL 314-821-1110; Ed. Scott W. Queen; Pub. Larry Johnson; adv. contact: Jeff Taggert. pub. size: broadsheet; circ. 13,000(free & paid).

CLARION JOURNAL, THE

US

CLARION JOURNAL, THE. s-w.: Wed. & Sun. free in area; $50/yr. Sun.; $58/yr. Wed. 212 W. Locust St., Columbia, IL 62236. TEL 618-281-7691; FAX 618-281-7693. **Owner(s):** Suburban Journals, 1714 Deer Tracks Trail, St. Louis, MO 63131. TEL 314-821-1110; Ed. Scott W. Queen; Pub. Larry Johnson; adv. contact: Dan Braun. pub. size: broadsheet; circ. 1,500(controlled & paid); Sun. 8,500(controlled & paid).

    Formerly: Columbia Star, The.

US

EAST ST. LOUIS NEWS JOURNAL. 1954. Wed. free newsstand & home deliv. 212 W. Locust St., Columbia, IL 62236. TEL 618-281-7691; FAX 618-281-7693. **Owner(s):** Suburban Journals, 1714 Deer Tracks Trail, St. Louis, MO 63131. TEL 618-332-6000; Ed. Scott W. Queen; Pub. Larry Johnson; adv. contact: Willie Harris. pub. size: broadsheet; circ. 20,100(free).

US

MILLSTADT ENTERPRISE. Wed. free; $12/yr. in cy.; $16/yr. out of cy. 212 W. Locust St., Columbia, IL 62236. TEL 618-281-7691; FAX 618-281-7693. **Owner(s):** Suburban Journals, 1714 Deer Tracks Trail, St. Louis, MO 63131. TEL 314-821-1110; Ed. Scott W. Queen; Pub. Larry Johnson; adv. contact: Dan Braun. pub. size: broadsheet; circ. 2,000(free).

US

MONROE COUNTY CLARION. 1939. s-w.: Wed. & Sun. $.50 newsstand; $50/yr. Sun.; $58/yr. Wed. 212 W. Locust St., Columbia, IL 62236. TEL 618-281-4292; FAX 618-281-7693. **Owner(s):** Suburban Journals, 1714 Deer Tracks Trail, St. Louis, MO 63131. TEL 314-821-1110; Ed. Scott W. Queen; Pub. Larry Johnson; adv. contact: Dan Braun. pub. size: broadsheet; circ. 14,500(paid); Sun. 8,000(paid).

DALLAS CITY

US

DALLAS CITY ENTERPRISE. 1887. Wed. $.35 newsstand; $14/yr. in cy.; $15/yr. out of cy. P.O. Box 455, Dallas City, IL 62330. TEL 217-852-3511; FAX 217-852-3528. **Owner(s):** Steven & Susan Kempher, P.O. Box 455, Dallas City, IL 62330. TEL 217-852-3511; Ed. Steven A. Martin; Pub. Steven & Susan Kempher; adv. contact: Steven A. Martin. pub. size: standard; circ. 1,200(paid).

DECATUR

US

DECATUR TRIBUNE. 1969. Wed. $.50 newsstand; $25/yr. local. 240 N. Park St., Decatur, IL 62523. TEL 217-422-9702; FAX 217-422-7320. **Owner(s):** Paul V. Osbourne, 240 N. Park St., Decatur, IL 62523. TEL 217-422-9702; Pub. Paul V. Osbourne; adv. contact: Rita Gray. photos; pub. size: broadsheet; circ. 8,000(paid).

DEKALB

US

MIDWEEK, THE. 1967. Wed. free newsstand; $30/yr. out of area. P.O. Box 546, DeKalb, IL 60115. TEL 815-758-0696. **Owner(s):** Charles & Kathy Siebrasse, P.O. Box 546, DeKalb, IL 60115. TEL 815-758-0696; Ed. Sharon Emanuelson; Pub. Charles Siebrasse; adv. contact: Penny Bunnell. photos; bk.rev.; pub. size: tabloid; circ. 30,000(free & paid).

DELAVAN

US

DELAVAN TIMES, THE. 1874. Wed. $.35 newsstand; $16/yr. in state; $18/yr. out of state. 314 Locust, Delavan, IL 61734. TEL 309-244-7111. **Owner(s):** Delavan Times, Inc., 314 Locust, P.O. Box 199, Delavan, IL 61734. TEL 309-244-7111; Ed. Ruth Larimore. adv.; photos; pub. size: tabloid; circ. 1,440(paid).

DES PLAINES

US

ARLINGTON HEIGHTS JOURNAL & TOPICS. Thu. $.50 newsstand; $22/yr. in cy.; $30/yr. out of cy. 622 Graceland Ave., Des Plaines, IL 60016. TEL 847-299-5511; FAX 847-298-8549. **Owner(s):** Des Plaines Journal, Inc., 622 Graceland Ave., Des Plaines, IL 60016. TEL 847-299-5511; Ed. Todd Wessell; Pub. Richard C. Wessell, Sr.; pub. size: tabloid; circ. 12,512(paid).

US

BUFFALO GROVE JOURNAL & TOPICS. Thu. $.50 newsstand; $22/yr. in cy.; $30/yr. out of cy. 622 Graceland Ave., Des Plaines, IL 60016. TEL 847-299-5511; FAX 847-298-8549. **Owner(s):** Des Plaines Journal, Inc., 622 Graceland Ave., Des Plaines, IL 60016. TEL 847-299-5511; Ed. Todd Wessell; Pub. Richard C. Wessell, Sr.; adv.; pub. size: tabloid; circ. 3,000(paid).

US

GOLFMILL JOURNAL. s-w.: Wed. & Fri. $.50 newsstand; $25/yr. in cy.; $30/yr. out of cy. 622 Graceland Ave., Des Plaines, IL 60016. TEL 847-299-5511; FAX 847-298-8549. **Owner(s):** Des Plaines Journal, Inc., 622 Graceland Ave., Des Plaines, IL 60016. TEL 847-299-5511; Ed. Todd Wessell; Pub. Richard C. Wessell, Sr.; adv.; pub. size: tabloid; circ. 5,000(paid).

Formerly: Golfmill-Park Ridge Journal.

US

MOUNT PROSPECT JOURNAL. s-w.: Wed. & Fri. $.50 newsstand; $25/yr. in cy.; $30/yr. out of cy. 622 Graceland Ave., Des Plaines, IL 60016. TEL 847-299-5511; FAX 847-298-8549. **Owner(s):** Des Plaines Journal, Inc., 622 Graceland Ave., Des Plaines, IL 60016. TEL 847-299-5511; Ed. Todd Wessell; Pub. Richard C. Wessell, Sr.; adv.; pub. size: tabloid; circ. 6,350(paid).

US

NILES JOURNAL. Wed. $.50 newsstand; $22/yr. in cy.; $30/yr. out of cy. 622 Graceland Ave., Des Plaines, IL 60016. TEL 847-299-5511; FAX 847-298-8549. **Owner(s):** Des Plaines Journal, Inc., 622 Graceland Ave., Des Plaines, IL 60016. TEL 847-299-5511; Ed. Todd Wessell; Pub. Richard C. Wessell, Sr.; adv.; pub. size: tabloid; circ. 6,000(paid).

US

NORTHWEST JOURNAL & TOPICS. Thu. $.50 newsstand; $22/yr. in cy.; $30/yr. out of cy. 622 Graceland Ave., Des Plaines, IL 60016. TEL 847-299-5511; FAX 847-298-8549. **Owner(s):** Des Plaines Journal, Inc., 622 Graceland Ave., Des Plaines, IL 60016. TEL 847-299-5511; Ed. Todd Wessell; Pub. Richard C. Wessell, Sr.; adv.; photos; pub. size: tabloid; circ. 6,900(paid).

Formerly: Journal & Topics.

US

PALATINE JOURNAL & TOPICS. Thu. $.50 newsstand; $22/yr. in cy.; $30/yr. out of cy. 622 Graceland Ave., Des Plaines, IL 60016. TEL 847-299-5511; FAX 847-598-8549. **Owner(s):** Des Plaines Journal, Inc., 622 Graceland Ave., Des Plaines, IL 60016. TEL 847-299-5511; Ed. Todd Wessell; Pub. Richard C. Wessell, Sr.; adv.; pub. size: tabloid; circ. 3,850(paid).

US

PARK RIDGE JOURNAL. Wed. $.50 newsstand; $22/yr. in cy.; $30/yr. out of cy. mailed. 622 Graceland Ave., Des Plaines, IL 60016. TEL 847-299-5511; FAX 847-298-8549. **Owner(s):** Des Plaines Journal, Inc., 622 Graceland Ave., Des Plaines, IL 60016. TEL 847-299-5511; Ed. Todd Wessell; Pub. Richard C. Wessell, Sr.; adv.; pub. size: tabloid; circ. 5,000(paid).

US

PROSPECT HEIGHTS JOURNAL. s-w.: Wed. & Fri. $.50 newsstand; $22/yr. in cy.; $30/yr. out of cy. 622 Graceland Ave., Des Plaines, IL 60016. TEL 847-299-5511; FAX 708-298-8549. **Owner(s):** Des Plaines Journal, Inc., 622 Graceland Ave., Des Plaines, IL 60016. TEL 847-299-5511; Ed. Todd Wessell; Pub. Richard C. Wessell, Sr.; adv.; pub. size: tabloid; circ. 1,700(paid).

US

ROLLING MEADOWS JOURNAL & TOPICS. Thu. $.50 newsstand; $22/yr. in cy.; $30/yr. out of cy. 622 Graceland Ave., Des Plaines, IL 60016. TEL 847-299-5511; FAX 847-298-8549. **Owner(s):** Des Plaines Journal, Inc., 622 Graceland Ave., Des Plaines, IL 60016. TEL 847-299-5511; Ed. Todd Wessell; Pub. Richard C. Wessell, Sr.; adv.; pub. size: tabloid; circ. 5,000(paid).

US

ROSEMONT JOURNAL. s-w.: Wed. & Fri. $.50 newsstand; $22/yr. in cy.; $30/yr. out of cy. 622 Graceland Ave., Des Plaines, IL 60016. TEL 847-299-5511; FAX 847-298-8549. **Owner(s):** Des Plaines Journal, Inc., 622 Graceland Ave., Des Plaines, IL 60016. TEL 847-299-5511; Ed. Todd Wessell; Pub. Richard C. Wessell, Sr.; adv.; pub. size: tabloid; circ. 3,500(paid).

US

SUBURBAN JOURNAL. Sat. $.50 newsstand; $25/yr. in cy.; $30/yr. out of cy. 622 Graceland Ave., Des Plaines, IL 60016. TEL 847-299-5511; FAX 847-298-8549 **Owner(s):** Des Plaines Journal, Inc., 622 Graceland Ave., Des Plaines, IL 60016. TEL 847-299-5511; Ed. Todd Wessell; Pub. Richard C. Wessell, Sr.; adv.; pub. size: tabloid; circ. 6,800(paid).

Formerly: Journal & Topics.

DOWNERS GROVE

US

CLARENDON HILLS PROGRESS. 1959. s-w.: Wed. & Fri. $.50 newsstand; $19/yr. carrier. 922 Warren Ave., Downers Grove, IL 60515. TEL 630-969-0188 **Owner(s):** C.J. Winter, Jr., 922 Warren Ave., Downers Grove, IL 60515. TEL 630-969-0188; P.K. Winter, 922 Warren Ave., Downers Grove, IL 60515. TEL 630-969-0188; Craig Winter, 922 Warren Ave., Downers Grove, IL 60515; Chris Winter, 922 Warren Ave., Downer Grove, IL 60515; Ed. Robert Rockafield; Pub. P.K. Winter; adv. contact: Ed Rooney. photos; bk.rev.; pub. size: tabloid; circ. 6,087(free & paid).

US

DARIEN PROGRESS. 1959. s-w.: Wed. & Fri. $.50 newsstand; $19/yr. carrier. 922 Warren Ave., Downers Grove, IL 60515. TEL 630-969-0188. **Owner(s):** C.J. Winter, Jr., 922 Warren Ave., Downers Grove, IL 60515. TEL 630-969-0188; P.K. Winter, 922 Warren Ave., Downers Grove, IL 60515. TEL 630-969-0188; Craig Winter, 922 Warren Ave., Downers Grove, IL 60505. TEL 630-969-0188; Christopher J. Winter, 922 Warren Ave., Downers Grove, IL 60515. TEL 630-969-0188; Ed. Jennifer Parelo; Pub. C.J. Winter Jr.; photos; bk.rev.; pub. size: tabloid; circ. 10,440(free & paid).

US

DOWNERS GROVE REPORTER. 1883. s-w.: Wed. & Fri. $.50 newsstand; $19/yr. local carrier & mailed. 922 Warren Ave., Downers Grove, IL 60515. TEL 630-969-0188; FAX 630-969-0228. **Owner(s):** C.J. Winter, Jr., 922 Warren Ave., Downers Grove, IL 60515. TEL 630-969-0188; Christopher J. Winter, 922 Warren Ave., Downers Grove, IL 60515. TEL 630-969-0188; P.K. Winter, 922 Warren Ave., Downers Grove, IL 60515. TEL 630-969-0188; Craig R. Winter, 922 Warren Ave., Downers Grove, IL 60515. TEL 630-969-0188; Ed. Jennifer Parello; Pub. P.K. Winter; adv. contact: Ed Rooney. bk.rev.; pub. size: tabloid; circ. 31,464(free & paid).

US

WESTMONT PROGRESS. 1959. Thu. $.50 newsstand; $19/yr. carrier. 922 Warren Ave., Downers Grove, IL 60515. TEL 630-969-0188; FAX 630-969-0228. **Owner(s):** C.J. Winter, Jr., 922 Warren Ave., Downers Grove, IL 60515. TEL 630-969-0188; Christopher J. Winter, 922 Warren Ave., Downers Grove, IL 60515. TEL 630-969-0188; P.K. Winter, 922 Warren Ave., Downers Grove, IL 60515. TEL 630-969-0188; Craig R. Winter, 922 Warren Ave., Downers Grove, IL 60515. TEL 630-969-0188; Ed. Jennifer Parello; Pub. C.J. Winter, Jr.; adv. contact: Ed Rooney. photos; bk.rev. pub. size: tabloid; circ. 7,454(paid).

US

WOODRIDGE PROGRESS. 1965. Thu. $.50 copy; $19/yr. carrier. 922 Warren Ave., Downers Grove, IL 60515. TEL 630-969-0188; FAX 630-969-0228. **Owner(s):** C.J. Winter, Jr., 922 Warren Ave., Downers Grove, IL 60515. TEL 630-969-0188; P.K. Winter, 922 Warren Ave., Downers Grove, IL 60515. TEL 630-969-0188; Christopher J. Winter, 922 Warren Ave., Downers Grove, IL 60515. TEL 630-969-0188; Craig R. Winter, 922 Warren Ave., Downers Grove, IL 60515. TEL 630-969-0188; Ed. Robert Rockafield; Pub. C.J. Winter Jr.; adv. contact: Ed Rooney. photos; bk.rev.; pub. size: tabloid; circ. 9,133(paid).

DURAND

US

DURAND-DAKOTA VOLUNTEER. 1990. Wed. $.50 newsstand; $18/yr. in cy.; $25/yr. elsewhere. 109 E. Oak St., Durand, IL 61024. TEL 815-248-4407; FAX 815-248-9176. **Owner(s):** Volunteer, Inc., The, 109 E. Oak Street, Durand, IL 61024. TEL 815-248-4407; FAX 815-248-9176; Pub. Curt Stalheim; adv. contact: C.J. Gregg. bk.rev.; pub. size: tabloid; circ. 4,950(paid).

EARLVILLE

US

EARLVILLE LEADER. 1868. w. $.35 newsstand; $17/yr. in cy. P.O. Box 606, Earlville, IL 60518. TEL 815-246-6911; FAX 815-246-6911. **Owner(s):** Jean Albert, P.O. Box 606, Earlville, IL 60518. TEL 815-246-6911; FAX 815-246-6911; Pub. Jean Albert; adv.; pub. size: tabloid; circ. 1,158(paid).

EAST MOLINE

US

THRIFTY NICKEL WANT ADS. 1982. Thu. free. 500 42nd Ave., East Moline, IL 61244. TEL 309-792-4747; FAX 309-792-4797. **Owner(s):** Lee Enterprises, Inc., 215 N. Main St., Davenport, IA 52801-2100. TEL 319-383-2100; adv.; pub. size: tabloid; circ. 26,000(free).

EAST ST. LOUIS

US

EAST ST. LOUIS MONITOR. 1963. Thu. $.50 newsstand; $50/yr. mailed. 1501 State St., East St. Louis, IL 62205. TEL 618-271-0468. **Owner(s):** Anne E. Jordan, 1501 State St., East St. Louis, IL 62205. TEL 618-271-0468; Ed. Ernest Mercer; Pub. Anne E. Jordan; adv. contact: George Laktzian. photos; bk.rev.; pub. size: broadsheet; circ. 22,500(paid).

EDINBURG

US

HERALD-STAR, THE. 1882. Wed. $.35 newsstand; $14/yr. in state; $17/yr. out of state. 103 S. Eaton, Edinburg, IL 62531-0050. TEL 217-623-5523; FAX 217-623-4216. **Owner(s):** Glenn W. Luttrell, 103 S. Eaton, Edinburg, IL 62531. TEL 217-623-5523; Pub. Glenn W. Luttrell; adv. contact: Glenn W. Luttrell. pub. size: tabloid; circ. 750(paid).

EDWARDSVILLE

US

EDWARDSVILLE JOURNAL. 1965. Wed. free. 220 St. Louis St., Edwardsville, IL 62025. TEL 618-656-8000; FAX 618-656-5093. **Owner(s):** Madison County Publications, 1990 Troy Rd., Edwardsville, IL 62025. TEL 618-656-8000; Ed. Nicole Vaughn. adv. contact: Bob Millering. pub. size: broadsheet; circ. 12,758(free).

ELBURN

US

ELBURN HERALD. 1908. Wed. $18/yr. in cy.; $23/yr. out of cy.; $28/yr. out of state. 123 N. Main St., Elburn, IL 60119-8023. TEL 630-365-6446; FAX 630-365-2251. **Owner(s):** Kaneland Publications, Inc., P.O. Box L, Elburn, IL 60119. TEL 630-365-6446; Ed. Louise Cooper; Pub. Richard L. Cooper; adv.; pub. size: tabloid; circ. 2,500(paid).

ELIZABETH

US

GAZETTE, THE. 1834. Thu. $.75 newsstand; $23/yr. local. 240 N. Main St., Elizabeth, IL 61028. TEL 815-858-2279; FAX 815-777-3809. **Owner(s):** P. Carter & Sarah Newton, P.O. Box 319, Galena, IL 61036. TEL 815-777-0019; Pub. P. Carter Newton; adv. contact: Robin Buss. pub. size: standard; circ. 6,000(paid). **Formerly:** Northwestern Gazette.

ELIZABETHTOWN

US

HARDIN COUNTY INDEPENDENT. 1871. Thu. $.50 newsstand; $22.50/yr. 25-27 W. First St., Elizabethtown, IL 62931. TEL 618-287-2361. **Owner(s):** Noel E. Hurford, P.O. Box 328, Elizabethtown, IL 62931. TEL 618-287-2361; Ed. Noel E. Hurford; Pub. Noel E. Hurford; adv.; photos; pub. size: standard; circ. 3,000(paid). **Formerly:** Elizabeth Hardin County Independent.

ELMHURST

US

ADDISON PRESS. 1953. s-w.: Wed. & Fri. $.50 newsstand; $24.95/yr. mailed in state; $45.95/yr. mailed out of state. 112 S. York St., Elmhurst, IL 60126. TEL 630-834-0900; FAX 630-834-0910. **Owner(s):** Press Publications, Inc., 112 S. York St., Elmhurst, IL 60126. TEL 630-834-0900; Ed. Paula Widholm; Pub. John M. Cruger; adv. contact: Vince Saputo. pub. size: broadsheet; circ. 3,800(controlled).

US

BENSENVILLE PRESS. 1987. s-w.: Wed. & Fri. $.50 newsstand; $21/yr. in town; $45.95/yr. out of town. 112 S. York St., Elmhurst, IL 60126. TEL 630-834-0900; FAX 630-834-0910. **Owner(s):** Press Publications, 112 S. York St., Elmhurst, IL 60126. TEL 630-834-0900; Ed. Steve Brosinski; Pub. John M. Cruger; adv. contact: Vince Saputo. pub. size: broadsheet; circ. 865(paid).

US ISSN 1043-3236

ELMHURST PRESS. 1889. s-w.: Wed. & Fri. $.50 newsstand; $24.95/yr. in state; $45.95/yr. out of state. 112 S. York St., Elmhurst, IL 60126. TEL 630-834-0900; FAX 630-834-0910. **Owner(s):** Press Publications, Inc., 112 S. York St., Elmhurst, IL 60126. TEL 630-834-0900; Ed. Rick Nagel; Pub. John M. Cruger; adv. contact: Vince Saputo. pub. size: broadsheet; circ. 9,000(paid).

US

GLENDALE HEIGHTS PRESS. Thu. $.35 newsstand; $10.95/yr. in state; $28.95/yr. out of state mailed. 112 S. York St., Elmhurst, IL 60126. TEL 630-834-0900; FAX 630-834-0910. **Owner(s):** Press Publications, Inc., 112 S. York St., Elmhurst, IL 60126. TEL 630-834-0900; Ed. Rick Nagel; Pub. John M. Cruger; adv. contact: Vince Saputo. pub. size: tabloid; circ. 2,850(paid).

US

LOMBARD SPECTATOR. s-w.: Wed. & Fri. $.50 newsstand; $39.95/yr. mailed. 112 S. York St., Elmhurst, IL 60126. TEL 630-834-0900; FAX 630-834-0910. **Owner(s):** Press Publications, Inc., 112 S. York St., Elmhurst, IL 60126. TEL 630-834-0900; Ed. Rick Nagel; Pub. John M. Cruger; adv. contact: Vince Saputo. photos; pub. size: broadsheet; circ. 10,000(paid).

US

OAK BROOK PRESS. 1895. s-w.: Wed. & Fri. $.50 newsstand; $24.95/yr. in state; $45.95/yr. out of state. 112 S. York St., Elmhurst, IL 60126. TEL 630-834-0900; FAX 630-834-0910. **Owner(s):** Press Publications, Inc., 112 S. York St., Elmhurst, IL 60126. TEL 630-834-0900; Ed. Tammy Jensen; Pub. John M. Cruger; adv. contact: Vince Saputo. pub. size: broadsheet; circ. 500(paid).

US

VILLA PARK ARGUS. 1895. s-w.: Wed. & Fri. $.50 newsstand; $24.95/yr. in state mailed. 112 S. York St., Elmhurst, IL 60126. TEL 630-834-0900; FAX 630-834-0910. **Owner(s):** Press Publications, Inc., 112 S. York St., Elmhurst, IL 60126. TEL 630-834-0900; Ed. Rick Nagel; Pub. John M. Cruger; adv. contact: Vince Saputo. pub. size: broadsheet; circ. 3,300(controlled & paid).

US ISSN 1050-2327

WEST COOK COUNTY PRESS. 1953. Thu. $.50 newsstand; $10.95/yr. in state; $28.95/yr. out of state. 112 S. York St., Elmhurst, IL 60126. TEL 630-834-0900; FAX 630-834-0910. **Owner(s):** Press Publications, Inc., 112 S. York St., Elmhurst, IL 60126. TEL 630-834-0900; Ed. Rick Nagel; Pub. John M. Cruger; adv. contact: Vince Saputo. pub. size: broadsheet; circ. 1,200(paid).

US

WOOD DALE PRESS. 1988. s-w.: Wed. & Fri. $.50 newsstand; $21/yr. in town; $45.95/yr. out of town. 112 S. York St., Elmhurst, IL 60126. TEL 630-834-0900; FAX 630-834-0910. **Owner(s):** Press Publications, Inc., 112 S. York St., Elmhurst, IL 60126. TEL 630-834-0900; Ed. Steve Brosinski; Pub. John M. Cruger; adv. contact: Vince Saputo. pub. size: broadsheet; circ. 1,250(paid).

ELMWOOD

US

TRI-COUNTY NEWS. 1875. Thu. $16/yr. in cy.; $18/yr. out of cy. 116 S. Magnolia, Elmwood, IL 61529. TEL 309-742-2521; FAX 309-742-2511. **Owner(s):** Tri-County News, 116 S. Magnolia, Elmwood, IL 61529. TEL 309-742-2511; FAX 309-742-2511; Ed. Sue Swindler; Pub. DeEllda Swindler; adv. contact: DeEllda Swindler. pub. size: tabloid.

EL PASO

US

EL PASO JOURNAL. 1991. w. $.50 newsstand; $20/yr. in cy. 54 W. Front, El Paso, IL 61738. TEL 309-527-8595; FAX 309-527-8850. **Owner(s):** Tazewell Publishing, 100 Detroit Ave., Morton, IL 61550. TEL 309-263-2211; Pub. Ted J. Fleming; adv.; pub. size: broadsheet; circ. 1,400(paid).

ERIE

US

REVIEW, THE. 1857. Wed. $.50 newssstand; $22/yr. cy.; $28/yr. out of cy. 910 Albany St., Erie, IL 61250. TEL 309-659-2761; FAX 309-659-2761. **Owner(s):** W.N.W. Publication, 100 E. Main St., Morrison, IL 61270. TEL 815-772-7244; Ed. Judy James; Pub. Tony Komlanc; adv. contact: Gail Poss. pub. size: broadsheet; circ. 2,300(paid). **Formerly:** Erie Review.

EUREKA

US

WOODFORD COUNTY JOURNAL. 1867. Thu. $.75 newsstand; $24/yr. in cy.; $28/yr. out of cy.; $32/yr. elsewhere. 126 S. Main St., Eureka, IL 61530. TEL 309-467-3314; FAX 309-467-4563. **Owner(s):** San Francisco Chronicle, 901 Mission St., San Francisco, CA 94103; Ed. Arlene Franks; Pub. Mark Barra; adv.; photos; pub. size: broadsheet; circ. 1,857(free & paid).

EVANSTON

US   ISSN 1044-7733
EVANSTON REVIEW. 1953. Thu. $1 newsstand;
$29.95/yr. 1600 Orrington, Ste. 500, Evanston,
IL 60201. TEL 847-866-6500;
FAX 847-866-0965. **Owner(s):** Pioneer Press,
Inc., 3701 W. Lake Ave., Glenview, IL 60025. TEL
847-486-9200; Ed. Gary Taylor; Pub. Thomas
Neri; adv. contact: Lynn Schmidt. pub. size:
tabloid; circ. 13,996(paid).

US
LINCOLNWOOD REVIEW. Thu. $1 newsstand;
$17.95/yr. 1600 Orrington Ave., Evanston, IL
60201. TEL 847-866-5250;
FAX 847-866-0965. **Owner(s):** Pioneer Press,
Inc., 3701 W. Lake Ave., Glenview, IL 60025. TEL
847-486-9200; Ed. Dan Obermaier; Pub.
Thomas Neri; adv. contact: Jack Whisler. pub.
size: tabloid; circ. 1,374(paid).

US   ISSN 0193-7251
MORTON GROVE CHAMPION. 1958. Thu. $1
newsstand; $18.95/yr. 1600 Orrington Ave.,
Evanston, IL 60201. TEL 847-866-5250;
FAX 847-866-0965. **Owner(s):** Pioneer Press,
Inc., 3701 W. Lake Ave., Glenview, IL 60025. TEL
847-486-9200; Ed. Dan Obermaier; Pub.
Thomas Neri; adv.; pub. size: tabloid; circ.
3,800(paid).

US   ISSN 0192-2742
SKOKIE REVIEW. 1946. Thu. $1 newsstand;
$18.95/yr. 1600 Orrington Ave., Evanston, IL
60201. TEL 847-866-5250;
FAX 847-866-0965. **Owner(s):** Pioneer Press,
Inc., 3701 W. Lake Ave., Glenview, IL 60025. TEL
847-486-9200; Ed. Dan Obermaier; Pub.
Thomas Neri; adv. contact: Jack Whisler. pub.
size: tabloid; circ. 7,647(paid).

FAIRFIELD

US
FAIRFIELD WAYNE COUNTY PRESS. 1866. s-w.: Mon.
& Thu. $.50 newsstand; $29/yr. in cy. 213 E.
Main St., Fairfield, IL 62837.
TEL 618-842-2662; FAX 618-842-7912.
Owner(s): Wayne County Press, Inc., 213 E. Main
St., Fairfield, IL 62837. TEL 618-842-2662; FAX
618-842-7912; Ed. Tom Mathews, Jr.; Pub. Tom
Mathews, Jr.; adv. contact: Tom Mathews, Jr.
photos; pub. size: broadsheet; circ. 8,625(paid).

FARINA

US
FARINA NEWS, THE. 1882. Thu. $15/yr. in cy.;
$18/yr. out of cy.; $20/yr. out of state. 109 N.
Walnut, Farina, IL 62838. TEL 618-245-6216.
Owner(s): Shirley Ann Quick, 109 N. Walnut,
Farina, IL 62838. TEL 618-245-6216; Ed.
Shirley Ann Quick; Pub. Shirley Ann Quick; pub.
size: standard; circ. 1,300(paid).

FARMER CITY

US
FARMER CITY JOURNAL. 1872. Wed. $23.25/yr.
221 S. Main, Farmer City, IL 61842-0080.
TEL 309-928-2193; FAX 309-928-2193.
Owner(s): Illinois Valley Press, P.O. Box 80,
Farmer City, IL 61842. TEL 309-928-2193; FAX
309-928-2194; Ed. Steve Hoffman. adv.; photos;
pub. size: tabloid; circ. 3,100(paid).

FISHER

US
FISHER REPORTER. 1880. Wed. $12/yr. 118 S.
Third St., Fisher, IL 61843. TEL 217-897-1525.
Owner(s): Kenneth Sparks, P.O. Box 400, Fisher,
IL 61843. TEL 217-897-1525; Robert H. Sparks,
P.O. Box 400, Fisher, IL 61843-2170. TEL
217-897-1525; Ed. Kenneth Sparks; Pub.
Kenneth Sparks; adv. contact: Robert H. Sparks.
pub. size: broadsheet; circ. 1,100(paid).

FLANAGAN

US
FLANAGAN HOME TIMES. 1885. Wed. $22.50/yr.
home deliv.; $25/yr. in state mailed; $27.50/yr.
out of state. 112 S. Main, Flanagan, IL 61740.
TEL 815-796-2271. **Owner(s):** American
Publishing Co., 506 N. Van Buren, P.O. Box 520,
Marion, IL 62959. TEL 618-993-1711; Ed.
Debby Evans; Pub. Richard Westerfield; adv.; pub.
size: standard; circ. 1,200(paid).

FORRESTON

US
FORRESTON JOURNAL. 1865. Thu. $19.50/yr. in
state; $22.50/yr. out of state. 313 E. Main St.,
Forreston, IL 61030. TEL 815-938-3320;
FAX 815-732-4238. **Owner(s):** B.F. Shaw
Printing Co., 444 Pine Hill Dr., P.O. Box 409,
Dixon, IL 61021. TEL 815-284-2222; Ed.
Earleen Hinton; Pub. Earleen Hinton; pub. size:
broadsheet; circ. 1,000(paid).

FREEPORT

US
FREEPORT ADVERTISER SHOPPING NEWS. 1970.
Wed. free local; $20/yr. out of area. 1342 S.
Harlem Ave., Freeport, IL 61032.
TEL 815-235-4106; FAX 815-235-7077.
Owner(s): Woodward Communications, Inc.,
Eighth & Bluff, Dubuque, IA 52001. TEL
319-588-5724; pub. size: tabloid; circ.
23,000(free).

FULTON

US
FULTON JOURNAL. 1854. Wed. $.50 newsstand;
$14/yr. in cy.; $18/yr. out of cy. 408 Tenth
Ave., Fulton, IL 61252. TEL 815-589-2424.
Owner(s): Fulton Press, Inc., 408 Tenth Ave.,
Fulton, IL 61252. TEL 815-589-2424; Ed. Henry
Kramer; Pub. Henry Kramer; pub. size: standard;
circ. 2,200(paid).

US
WHITESIDE SHOPPER. 1940. Tue. free. 408 Tenth
Ave., Fulton, IL 61252. TEL 815-589-2424;
FAX 815-589-2568. **Owner(s):** Fulton Press, Inc.,
408 Tenth Ave., Fulton, IL 61252. TEL
815-589-2424; Ed. Henry Kramer; Pub. Henry
Kramer; pub. size: standard; circ. 3,300(free).

GALENA

US
GALENA GAZETTE. 1834. Wed. $1 newsstand;
$25/yr. mailed local; $40/yr. elsewhere. 716 So.
Bench St., Galena, IL 61036.
TEL 815-777-0019; FAX 815-777-3809.
Owner(s): Robert & Frances Melvold, Maquoketa
Sentinel, Maquoketa, IA 52060; P. Carter &
Sarah Newton, 301 Park Ave., Galena, IL 61036.
TEL 815-777-1765; Ed. Theresa Riniker; Pub. P.
Carter Newton; adv. contact: Robin Buss. pub.
size: tabloid; circ. 6,000(paid).

GALESBURG

US
GALESBURG POST, THE. 1928. Thu. $.25
newsstand; $9/yr. in cy.; $16/yr. out of cy.;
$18/yr. out of state. 80 S. Cherry St., Galesburg,
IL 61401-4598. TEL 309-343-5617;
FAX 309-342-1586. **Owner(s):** John P.
Creighton, 80 S. Cherry St., Galesburg, IL 61401
TEL 309-343-2552; FAX 309-342-1986; Mary
A. Creighton, 357 E. Grove St., Galesburg, IL
61401. TEL 309-343-2552; Ed. John P.
Creighton. adv.; bk.rev.; pub. size: tabloid; circ.
2,075(paid).

US
KNOXVILLE JOURNAL, THE. 1856. Thu. $.25
newsstand; $9/yr. in cy. $16/yr. out of cy.;
$18/yr. out of state. 80 S. Cherry St., Galesburg,
IL 61401-4598. TEL 309-343-5617;
FAX 309-342-1986. **Owner(s):** John P.
Creighton, 80 S. Cherry St., Galesburg, IL 61401
TEL 309-353-3527; FAX 309-342-1986; Ed.
John P. Creighton; Pub. John P. Creighton; adv.;
pub. size: tabloid; circ. 4,015(paid).

GALVA

US
GALVA NEWS. 1879. Wed. $.50 newsstand; $18/yr.
in state; $22/yr. out of state. 214 S. Exchange
St., Galva, IL 61434. TEL 309-932-2103;
FAX 309-932-3282. **Owner(s):** Copley Press
International, 7776 Ivanhoe Ave., La Jolla, CA
92037. TEL 619-454-0411; Ed. Rob Clark; Pub.
Donald Cooper; adv. contact: Stacey C. Swanson.
pub. size: broadsheet; circ. 2,400(paid).

GENESEO

US
GENESEO REPUBLIC. 1856. Fr. $.75 newsstand;
$31/yr.; $33/yr. out of state. 108 W. First St.,
Geneseo, IL 61254. TEL 309-944-2119;
FAX 309-944-6161. **Owner(s):** Terry
Newspapers, Inc., 108 W. First St., Geneseo, IL
61254. TEL 309-944-2119; Ed. Lisa Hammer.
adv. contact: Linda Venable. pub. size: broadsheet;
circ. 4,000(free & paid).

US
GENESEO SHOPPER. Wed. free. 108 W. First St.,
Geneseo, IL 61254. TEL 309-944-2119;
FAX 309-944-6161. **Owner(s):** Terry
Newspapers, Inc., 108 W. First St., Geneseo, IL
61254. TEL 309-944-2119; FAX
309-944-6161; Ed. Lisa Hammer. adv. contact:
Linda Venable. circ. 14,500(free).

GENEVA

US
GENEVA REPUBLICAN. 1847. Thu. $.75 newsstand;
$25/yr. 6 James St., Geneva, IL 60134.
TEL 630-232-2324; FAX 630-232-9974.
Owner(s): Wayne G. Woltman, 6 James St.,
Geneva, IL 60134. TEL 630-232-7400; Ed. Tim
Unzicker; Pub. Wayne G. Woltman. adv. contact:
Robert Longness. pub. size: tabloid; circ.
4,200(paid).

GEORGETOWN

US

INDEPENDENT NEWS. 1976. Wed. free local; $20/yr. out of area. 302 Mill St., Georgetown, IL 61846. TEL 217-662-2556; FAX 217-662-2484. **Owner(s):** Doyne Lenhart, 302 Mill St., Georgetown, IL 61846. TEL 217-662-2556; Ed. Vicky Delhaye; Pub. Doyne Lenhart; pub. size: tabloid; circ. 17,253(paid).

Formerly: Georgetown Independent News.

GIBSON CITY

US

GIBSON CITY COURIER. 1873. Wed. $.45 newsstand; $19.20/yr. in cy.; $20.30/yr. out of cy. 310 N. Sangamon Ave., Gibson City, IL 60936-0549. TEL 217-784-4244; FAX 217-784-4246. **Owner(s):** East Central Communications, Inc., P.O. Box 909, Rantoul, IL 61866. TEL 217-892-9615; Ed. Doris Benter; Pub. Dennis C. Kaster; pub. size: broadsheet; circ. 2,800(paid).

GILLESPIE

US

AREA NEWS, THE. Thu. $.35 newsstand; $15/yr. in cy.; $17/yr. out of cy. 112-116 W. Chestnut St., Gillespie, IL 62033. TEL 217-839-2130; FAX 217-839-2139. **Owner(s):** David & Patty Ambrose, 112 W. Chestnut St., Gillespie, IL 62033. TEL 217-839-2130; Ed. David Ambrose; Pub. David Ambrose; pub. size: broadsheet; circ. 3,175(paid).

Formerly: Gillespie Area News.

GILMAN

US

GILMAN STAR. 1869. Thu. $16/yr. in cy.; $19/yr. out of cy. 203 N. Central St., Gilman, IL 60938. TEL 815-265-7332; FAX 815-265-7880. **Owner(s):** John T. Elliot, 203 N. Central St., Gilman, IL 60938. TEL 815-265-7332; Ed. John T. Elliot; Pub. John T. Elliot; pub. size: broadsheet; circ. 2,900(paid).

GLASFORD

US

GLASFORD GAZETTE, THE. 1899. Thu. $.50 newsstand; $20.50/yr. in state; $23/yr. out of state. 401 Main St., Glasford, IL 61533-0260. TEL 309-389-2811. **Owner(s):** Gazette Printing Co., 401 Main St., Glasford, IL 61533-0260. TEL 309-389-2811; Ed. William Watkins; Pub. William Watkins; pub. size: tabloid; circ. 1,600(paid).

GLEN ELLYN

US   ISSN 1059-8146

GLEN ELLYN NEWS. 1922. s-w.: Wed. & Fri. $.50 newsstand; $34/yr. in cy.; $35/yr. out of cy.; $36/yr. out of state. 460 Pennsylvania Ave., Glen Ellyn, IL 60137. TEL 630-469-0100; FAX 630-469-4472. **Owner(s):** Glen News Printing Co., 460 Pennsylvania Ave., Glen Ellyn, IL 60137. TEL 630-469-0100; Ed. Michael Vaughn; Pub. Stuart Stone; adv. contact: Jane Rio. pub. size: tabloid; circ. 8,000(paid).

US

WHEATON LEADER. 1954. Wed. $24/yr. in cy.; $27/yr. in state; $30/yr. out of state. 460 Pennsylvania Ave., Glen Ellyn, IL 60137. TEL 630-668-7957; FAX 630-469-4472. **Owner(s):** Glen News Printing Co., 460 Pennsylvania Ave., Glen Ellyn, IL 60137. TEL 630-469-0100; Pub. Stuart Stone; adv. contact: Jane Rio. pub. size: tabloid; circ. 12,000(paid).

US

WINFIELD ESTATE. 1986. Wed. $.35 newsstand; $15/yr. 460 Pennsylvania Ave., Glen Ellyn, IL 60137. TEL 630-668-7957; FAX 630-469-4472. **Owner(s):** Glen News Printing Co., 460 Pennsylvania Ave., Glen Ellyn, IL 60137. TEL 630-469-0100; Ed. Michael Vaughn; Pub. Stuart Stone; pub. size: tabloid; circ. 3,000(free).

GLENVIEW

US

GLENVIEW ANNOUNCEMENTS. Thu. $32.95/yr. 3701 West Lake Ave., Glenview, IL 60025. TEL 847-486-9200; FAX 847-486-7451. **Owner(s):** Pioneer Press, Inc., 3701 W. Lake Ave., Glenview, IL 60025. TEL 847-486-9200; Pub. Thomas Neri; adv.; pub. size: tabloid; circ. 7,700(paid).

US   ISSN 0747-2595

MOUNT PROSPECT TIMES. 1980. Wed. $.75 newsstand; $33.15/yr. 3701 W. Lake Ave., Glenview, IL 60025. TEL 847-846-9200; FAX 847-696-3229. **Owner(s):** Pioneer Press, Inc., 3701 W. Lake Ave., Glenview, IL 60025. TEL 847-846-9200; Ed. Carroll Salman; Pub. Thomas Neri; pub. size: broadsheet; circ. 5,338(paid).

US   ISSN 0744-9550

NORTHBROOK STAR. 1935. Thu. $1 newsstand; $36.95/yr. in cy. 3701 West Lake Ave., Glenview, IL 60025. TEL 847-486-9200; FAX 847-486-7451. **Owner(s):** Pioneer Press, Inc., 3701 W. Lake Ave., Glenview, IL 60025. TEL 847-486-9200; pub. size: tabloid; circ. 7,500(paid).

US   ISSN 0745-0044

WILMETTE LIFE. Thu. $1 newsstand; $32.95/yr. 3701 W. Lake Ave., Glenview, IL 60025. TEL 847-486-9200; FAX 847-486-7451. **Owner(s):** Pioneer Press, Inc., 3701 W. Lake Ave., Glenview, IL 60025. TEL 847-486-9200; Ed. Elaine Fandell; Pub. Thomas Neri; adv.; photos; pub. size: tabloid; circ. 7,770(paid).

US

WINNETKA TALK. 1901. Thu. $1 newsstand; $32.95/yr.; $27.95/yr. senior citizens. 3701 West Lake Ave., Glenview, IL 60025. TEL 847-486-9200; FAX 847-486-7451. **Owner(s):** Pioneer Press, Inc., 3701 W. Lake Ave., Glenview, IL 60025. TEL 847-486-9200; Ed. Elaine Fandell; Pub. Thomas Neri; adv.; pub. size: tabloid; circ. 6,000(paid).

GOLCONDA

US

HERALD ENTERPRISE. 1858. Wed. $.50 newsstand; $16/yr. in cy. & adjoining area; $18/yr. out of area. Jefferson & Monroe Sts., Golconda, IL 62938-0400. TEL 618-683-3531; FAX 618-683-3531. **Owner(s):** Virginia Brenner, P.O. Box 400, Golconda, IL 62938. TEL 618-683-3531; FAX 618-683-3531; Pub. Virginia Brenner; adv. contact: Debra Carmen. adv.: $4.20/SAU. pub. size: broadsheet; circ. 2,000(paid).

GRANITE CITY

US

GRANITE CITY PRESS JOURNAL. Thu. $.50 newsstand; $18/yr. 1815 Delmar Ave., Granite City, IL 62040. TEL 618-876-2000; FAX 618-876-4240. **Owner(s):** Suburban Journals, 1714 Deer Tracks Trail, St. Louis, MO 63131. TEL 314-821-1110; Ed. Scott W. Queen; Pub. Doug Coope; adv. contact: Douglas Garbs. pub. size: broadsheet; circ. 8,000(paid).

GRANVILLE

US

PUTNAM COUNTY RECORD. Wed. $.25 newsstand; $18/yr. 318 S. McCoy St., Granville, IL 61326-0048. TEL 815-339-2321; FAX 815-339-2321. **Owner(s):** Elin Arnold, 318 S. McCoy St., Granville, IL 61326. TEL 815-339-2321; Ed. Elin Arnold; Pub. Elin Arnold; pub. size: tabloid; circ. 3,187(controlled & paid).

GRAYSLAKE

US

ANTIOCH NEWS-REPORTER. 1886. Thu. $.50 newsstand; $24.50/yr. mailed. 30 S. Whitney St., Grayslake, IL 60030. TEL 847-223-8161; FAX 847-223-8810. **Owner(s):** Lakeland Publishers, Inc., 30 S. Whitney St., Grayslake, IL 60030. TEL 847-223-8161; FAX 847-223-8810; Pub. William H. Schroder, Sr.; adv. contact: Esther Hebbard. pub. size: tabloid; circ. 4,427(paid).

US

FOX LAKE PRESS. 1934. Thu. $.50 newsstand; $24.50/yr. mailed. 30 S. Whitney St., Grayslake, IL 60030. TEL 847-223-8161; FAX 847-223-8810. **Owner(s):** Lakeland Publishers, Inc., 30 S. Whitney St., Grayslake, IL 60030. TEL 847-223-8161; FAX 847-223-8810; Ed. Rhonda Burke; Pub. William H. Schroder, Sr.; adv. contact: Esther Hebbard. pub. size: tabloid; circ. 4,982(paid).

US

GRAYSLAKE TIMES. 1900. Thu. $.50 newsstand; $24.50/yr. mailed. 30 S. Whitney St., Grayslake, IL 60030. TEL 847-223-8161; FAX 847-223-8810. **Owner(s):** Lakeland Publishers, Inc., 30 S. Whitney St., Grayslake, IL 60030. TEL 847-223-8161; FAX 847-223-8810; Ed. Rhonda Burke; Pub. William H. Schroeder, Sr.; adv. contact: Esther Hebbard. pub. size: tabloid; circ. 3,720(paid).

US

GURNEE PRESS. 1973. Thu. $.50 newsstand; $24.50/yr. mailed. 30 S. Whitney St., Grayslake, IL 60030. TEL 847-223-8161; FAX 847-223-8810. **Owner(s):** Lakeland Publishers, Inc., 30 S. Whitney St., Grayslake, IL 60030. TEL 847-223-8161; FAX 847-223-8810; Ed. Rhonda Burke; Pub. William H. Schroeder, Sr.; adv. contact: Esther Hebbard. pub. size: tabloid; circ. 3,347(paid).

US

LAKELAND PRESS. 1956. Thu. $.50 newsstand; $24.50/yr. 30 S. Whitney St., Grayslake, IL 60030. TEL 847-223-8161; FAX 847-223-8810. **Owner(s):** Lakeland Publishers, Inc., 30 S. Whitney St., Grayslake, IL 60030. TEL 847-223-8161; FAX 847-223-8810; Ed. Rhonda Burke; Pub. William H. Schroeder, Sr.; adv. contact: Esther Hebbard. pub. size: tabloid; circ. 38,724(paid).

LAKE VILLA RECORD. 1955. Thu. $.50 newsstand; $19.50/yr. mailed. 30 S. Whitney St., Grayslake, IL 60030. TEL 847-223-8161; FAX 847-223-8810. **Owner(s):** Lakeland Publishers, Inc., 30 S. Whitney St., Grayslake, IL 60030. TEL 847-223-8161; FAX 847-223-8810; Ed. Rhonda Burke; Pub. William H. Schroeder, Sr.; adv. contact: Esther Hebbard. pub. size: tabloid; circ. 2,404(paid).

US   ISSN 0895-8572
LAKE ZURICH ENTERPRISE. 1957. Thu. $.50 newsstand; $24.50/yr. mailed. 30 S. Whitney St., Grayslake, IL 60030. TEL 847-223-8161; FAX 847-223-8810. **Owner(s):** Lakeland Publishers, Inc., P.O. Box 268, Grayslake, IL 60030. TEL 847-223-8161; FAX 847-223-8810; Ed. Rhonda Burke; Pub. William H. Schroeder, Sr.; adv. contact: Esther Hebbard. pub. size: tabloid; circ. 4,043(paid).

US
LIBERTYVILLE NEWS. 1989. Thu. $.50 newsstand; $24.50/yr.; $22.50/yr. senior citizens. 30 S. Whitney St., Grayslake, IL 60030. TEL 847-223-8161; FAX 847-223-8810. **Owner(s):** Lakeland Publishers, Inc., 30 S. Whitney St., Grayslake, IL 60030. TEL 847-223-8161; FAX 847-223-8810; Ed. Rhonda Hetrick-Burke; Pub. William H. Schroeder, Sr.; adv. contact: Esther Hebbard. pub. size: tabloid; circ. 3,061(paid).

US
LINDENHURST NEWS. 1988. Thu. $.50 newsstand; $24.50/yr.; $22.50/yr. senior citizens. 30 S. Whitney St., Grayslake, IL 60030. TEL 847-223-8161; FAX 847-223-8810. **Owner(s):** Lakeland Publishers, Inc., 30 S. Whitney St., Grayslake, IL 60030. TEL 847-223-8161; FAX 847-223-8810; Pub. William H. Schroeder, Sr.; adv. contact: Esther Hebbard. pub. size: tabloid; circ. 2,800(paid).

US   ISSN 0746-8938
MUNDELEIN NEWS. 1942. Thu. $.50 newsstand; $24.50/yr. mailed. 30 S. Whitney St., Grayslake, IL 60030. TEL 847-223-8161; FAX 847-223-8810. **Owner(s):** Lakeland Publishers, Inc., 30 S. Whitney St., Grayslake, IL 60030. TEL 847-223-8161; FAX 847-223-8810; Ed. Rhonda Burke; Pub. William H. Schroeder, Sr.; adv. contact: Donna Evans. pub. size: tabloid; circ. 2,963(paid).

US
ROUND LAKE NEWS. 1938. Thu. $.50 newsstand; $24.50/yr. mailed. 30 S. Whitney St., Grayslake, IL 60030. TEL 847-223-8161; FAX 847-223-8810. **Owner(s):** Lakeland Publishers, Inc., 30 S. Whitney St., Grayslake, IL 60030. TEL 847-223-8161; FAX 847-223-8810; Ed. Rhonda Burke; Pub. William H. Schroeder, Sr.; adv. contact: Esther Hebbard. pub. size: tabloid; circ. 4,465(paid).

US
VERNON HILLS NEWS. 1958. Thu. $.50 newsstand; $24.50/yr.; $22.50/yr. senior citizens. 30 S. Whitney St., Grayslake, IL 60030. TEL 847-223-8161; FAX 847-223-8810. **Owner(s):** Lakeland Publishers, Inc., 30 S. Whitney St., Grayslake, IL 60030. TEL 847-233-8161; FAX 847-223-8110; Ed. Rhonda Hetrick-Burke; Pub. William H. Schroeder, Sr.; adv. contact: Esther Hebbard. pub. size: tabloid; circ. 2,810(paid).
   Formerly: Vernon Crier.

US   ISSN 0745-8118
WARREN-NEWPORT PRESS. 1960. Thu. $.50 newsstand; $19.50/yr. mailed. 30 S. Whitney St., Grayslake, IL 60030. TEL 847-223-8161; FAX 847-223-8810. **Owner(s):** Lakeland Publishers, Inc., 30 S. Whitney St., Grayslake, IL 60030. TEL 847-223-8161; FAX 847-223-8810; Ed. Rhonda Burke; Pub. William H. Schroeder, Sr.; adv. contact: Donna Evans. pub. size: tabloid; circ. 2,152(paid).

US
WAUCONDA LEADER. 1888. Thu. $.50 newsstand; $24.50/yr. mailed. 30 S. Whitney St., Grayslake, IL 60030. TEL 847-223-8161; FAX 847-223-8810. **Owner(s):** Lakeland Publishers, Inc., 30 S. Whitney St., Grayslake, IL 60030. TEL 847-223-8161; FAX 847-223-8810; Ed. Rhonda Burke; Pub. William H. Schroeder, Sr.; adv. contact: Esther Hebbard. pub. size: tabloid; circ. 3,961(paid).

GREENUP

US
GREENUP PRESS. 1889. Thu. $18/yr. in state; $23/yr. out of state. P.O. Box 127, Greenup, IL 62428-0127. TEL 217-923-3704; FAX 217-923-3704. **Owner(s):** William J. McMorris, P.O. Box 127, Greenup, IL 62428. TEL 217-923-3704. FAX 217-923-3704; Pub. William D. McMorris; adv. contact: Tony McMorris. photos; pub. size: standard; circ. 1,850(paid).

GREENVIEW

US
MENARD COUNTY REVIEW. 1883. Fri. $.50 newsstand; $15/yr. in state; $17/yr. out of state. 500 W. Adams, Greenview, IL 62642. TEL 217-968-5511. **Owner(s):** Petersburg Observer, P.O. Box 350, Petersburg, IL 62675. TEL 217-632-2236; Ed. Carolyn Miller; Pub. Jane Cutright; adv. contact: Carolyn Miller. pub. size: tabloid; circ. 1,650(paid).

GREENVILLE

US
GREENVILLE ADVOCATE, THE. 1858. s-w.: Tue. & Thu. $.50 newsstand; $32/yr. mailed. 305 S. Second St., Greenville IL 62246. TEL 618-664-3144. **Owner(s):** Duane L. Reeves, P. O. Box 10, Greenville, IL 62246. TEL 618-664-3144. Ed. Duane L. Reeves; Pub. Duane L. Reeves; adv.; photos; bk.rev.; pub. size: broadsheet; circ. 5,100(paid).

HARDIN

US
CALHOUN NEWS. 1915. Wed. $16/yr. in state; $24/yr. out of state. 310 S. County Rd., Hardin, IL 62047. TEL 618-576-2244; FAX 618-576-2245. **Owner(s):** Bruce Campbell, 310 S. County Rd., Hardin, IL 62047. TEL 618-576-2244. Pub. Bruce Campbell; adv. contact: Bruce Campbell. pub. size: standard; circ. 2,500(paid).
   Formerly: Hardin Calhoun News.

US
HARDIN CALHOUN HERALD. 1872. Wed. $12/yr. P.O. Box 389, Hardin IL 62047. TEL 618-576-2716. **Owner(s):** Carl Wittmond, P.O. Box 389, Hardin IL 62047. TEL 618-576-2716. FAX 618-576-2716; Pub. Carl Wittmond; adv.; photos; pub. size: standard; circ. 1,600(paid).

HAVANA

US   ISSN 1060-2437
HAVANA MASON COUNTY DEMOCRAT. 1849. Wed. $.50 newsstand; $25/yr. 2 7 W. Market St., Havana, IL 62644. TEL 309-543-3311; FAX 309-543-6844. **Owner(s):** Martin Publishing Co., Inc., 219 W. Market, Havana, IL 62644. TEL 309-543-3311; Ed. Wendy Jo Martin; Pub. Robert Martin; adv.; pub. size: broadsheet; circ. 6,300(free & paid).

HENRY

US
HENRY NEWS REPUBLICAN. 1852. Wed. $.40 newsstand; $20/yr. in Marshall & Putnam cys. 709 Third St., Henry, IL 61537. TEL 309-364-3250; FAX 309-364-3858. **Owner(s):** George Ziegler, P.O. Box 190, Henry, IL 61537. TEL 309-364-3250; FAX 309-364-3858; Ed. George Ziegler. adv.; photos; pub. size: broadsheet; circ. 2,850(paid).

US
WENONA INDEX. Wed. $.30 newsstand; $14/yr. in state; $16/yr. out of state. 709 Third St., Henry, IL 61537. TEL 309-364-3250; FAX 309-364-3858. **Owner(s):** George Ziegler, P.O. Box 190, Henry, IL 61537. TEL 309-364-3250; Pub. George Ziegler; photos; pub. size: standard; circ. 900(paid).

HERRIN

US
HERRIN SPOKESMAN. 1942. s-w.: Thu. & Sun. $21.95/yr. 106 N. 14th St., Herrin, IL 62948. TEL 618-942-5000; FAX 618-942-4630. **Owner(s):** American Publishing Co. 606 N. Van Buren, P.O. Box 520, Marion, IL 62959. TEL 618-993-1711; Ed. John Homan; Pub. G. David Green; adv. contact: Kathy Harmon. pub. size: broadsheet; circ. 2,100(paid); Sun. 2,100(paid).

HERSCHER

US
HERSCHER PILOT. 1976. Thu. $.30 newsstand; $12.50/yr. in area; $15/yr. out of area; $18/yr. out of state. P.O. Box 709, Herscher, IL 60941. TEL 815-426-2132. **Owner(s):** Robert A. Mau, P.O. Box 709, Herscher, IL 60941 TEL 815-426-2132; Ed. Robert A. Mau; Pub. Robert A. Mau adv. contact: Robert A. Mau. pub. size: tabloid; circ. 2,500(paid).

HIGHLAND

US   ISSN 8750-0007
HIGHLAND NEWS LEADER. 1861. s-w. Mon. & Thu. $.50 newsstand; $26/yr. local. 1 Woodcrest Professional Park, Highland IL 62249. TEL 618-654-2366. **Owner(s):** Walt Disney Co., 500 S. Buena Vista St., Burbank, CA 91521. TEL 818-560-5300; Pub. Kay Maue; adv.; photos; pub. size: broadsheet; circ. 15,800(free & paid).

HILLSBORO

US
HILLSBORO JOURNAL. 1853. s-w.: Mon. & Thu. $.30 newsstand; $18/yr. in cy.; $36/yr. out of cy. 431 S. Main St., Hillsboro, IL 62049. TEL 217-532-3933; FAX 217-532-3632. **Owner(s):** Phil & Nancy Galer, 431 S. Main St., Hillsboro, IL 62049. TEL 217-532-3933; John & Susie Galer, 431 S. Main St., Hillsboro, IL 62049. TEL 217-532-3933; Ed. Susie Galer; Pub. Phil Galer; pub. size: broadsheet; circ. 6,500(paid).

US

M & M JOURNAL. 1968. Mon. free. 431 S. Main St., Hillsboro, IL 62049. TEL 217-532-3933; FAX 217-532-3632. **Owner(s):** Hillsboro Journal, 431 S. Main St., Hillsboro, IL 62049. TEL 217-532-3933; Pub. Philip C. Galer; adv.; pub. size: broadsheet; circ. 14,000(free).

US

MACOUPIN & MONTGOMERY COUNTY JOURNAL. Mon. $.20 newsstand; $10/yr. 431 S. Main St., Hillsboro, IL 62049. TEL 217-532-3933; FAX 217-532-3632. **Owner(s):** Hillsboro Journal, 431 S. Main St., Hillsboro, IL 62049. TEL 217-532-3933; Ed. Philip C. Galer; Pub. Philip C. Galer; adv. contact: John Galer. pub. size: broadsheet; circ. 1,000(paid).

US

MACOUPIN COUNTY SHOPPER. 1968. Mon. free. 431 S. Main St., Hillsboro, IL 62049. TEL 217-532-3933; FAX 217-532-3632. **Owner(s):** Hillsboro Journal, 431 S. Main St., Hillsboro, IL 62049. TEL 217-532-3933; Ed. Phillip C. Galer; Pub. Phillip C. Galer; pub. size: broadsheet; circ. 13,500(free).

US

MONTGOMERY COUNTY NEWS, THE. 1869. 3/wk.: Mon., Wed., Fri. $.35 newsstand; $25/yr. 106 W. Seward, Hillsboro, IL 62049. TEL 217-532-3929; FAX 217-532-3522; E-mail: slepicka@cnmet.com. **Owner(s):** Hillsboro & Montgomery County News, Inc., P.O. Box 250, Hillsboro, IL 62049. TEL 217-532-3929; Ed. Richard L. Slepicka; Pub. Nancy B. Slepicka; adv. contact: Nancy B. Slepicka. pub. size: broadsheet; circ. 4,000(paid).

US

SORENTO NEWS. 1927. Thu. $.20 newsstand; $7/yr. in cy.; $14/yr. out of cy. 431 S. Main St., Hillsboro, IL 62049. TEL 217-532-3933; FAX 217-532-3632. **Owner(s):** Hillsboro Journal, 431 S. Main St., Hillsboro, IL 62049. TEL 217-532-3933; Ed. Philip C. Galer; Pub. Philip C. Galer; adv. contact: John Galer. pub. size: broadsheet; circ. 600(paid).

HINSDALE

US

BURR RIDGE DOINGS. s-w.: Wed. & Fri. $.75 newsstand; $41.50/yr. mailed. 118 W. First St., Hinsdale, IL 60521. TEL 708-887-0600; FAX 708-887-9646; E-mail: doingsnews@aol.com. **Owner(s):** Doings Newspapers, Inc., 118 W. First St., Hinsdale, IL 60521. TEL 708-887-0600; FAX 708-887-9645; Ed. Pat Lannom; Pub. J. Peter Teschner; adv. contact: Frieda Wolf. photos; pub. size: 4 color photos/art; circ. 11,000(paid).

US

CLARENDON HILLS DOINGS, THE. 1895. s-w.: Wed. & Fri. $.75 newsstand; $41.50/yr. mailed. 118 W. First St., Hinsdale, IL 60521. TEL 708-887-0600; FAX 708-887-9646; E-mail: doingsnews@aol.com. **Owner(s):** Doings Newspapers, Inc., 118 W. First St., Hinsdale, IL 60521. TEL 708-887-0600; FAX 708-887-9645; Ed. Pam Lannom; Pub. J. Peter Teschner; adv. contact: Frieda Wolf. photos; pub. size: tabloid; circ. 11,000(paid).

US

DARIEN DOINGS. 1895. s-w.: Wed. & Fri. $.75 newsstand; $41.50/yr. mailed. 118 W. First St., Hinsdale, IL 60521. TEL 708-887-0600; FAX 708-887-9646; E-mail: doingsnews@aol.com. **Owner(s):** Doings Newspapers, Inc., 118 W. First St., Hinsdale, IL 60521. TEL 708-887-0600; FAX 708-887-9646; Ed. Pam Lannom; Pub. J. Peter Teschner; adv. contact: Frieda Wolf. photos; pub. size: tabloid; circ. 11,000(paid).

US

HINSDALE DOINGS. 1895. s-w.: Wed. & Fri. $.75 newsstand; $41.50/yr. mailed. 118 W. First St., Hinsdale, IL 60521. TEL 708-887-0600; FAX 708-877-9646. **Owner(s):** Doings Newspapers, Inc., 118 W. First St., Hinsdale, IL 60521. TEL 708-887-0600; FAX 708-887-9646; Ed. Pam Lannom; Pub. J. Peter Teschner; adv. contact: Frieda Wolf. photos; pub. size: tabloid; circ. 11,000(paid).

US

INDIAN HEAD PARK DOINGS. s-w.: Wed. & Fri. $.75 newsstand; $41.50/yr. mailed. 118 W. First, Hinsdale, IL 60521. TEL 708-887-0600; FAX 708-887-0600; E-mail: doingsnews@aol.com. **Owner(s):** Hinsdale Doings Newspapers, Inc., 118 W. First, Hinsdale, IL 65201. TEL 708-887-0600; FAX 708-887-9646; Ed. Pam Lannom; Pub. J. Peter Treschner; adv. contact: Frieda Wolf. photos; pub. size: 4 color photos/art; circ. 11,000(paid).

US

OAK BROOK DOINGS. 1895. s-w.: Wed. & Fri. $.75 newsstand; $41.50/yr. mailed. 118 W. First St., Hinsdale, IL 60521. TEL 708-887-0600; FAX 708-887-9646. **Owner(s):** Doings Newspapers, Inc., 118 W. First St., Hinsdale, IL 60521. TEL 708-887-0600; FAX 708-887-9646; Ed. Pam Lannom; Pub. J. Peter Teschner; adv. contact: Freida Wolf. photos; pub. size: tabloid; circ. 11,000(paid).

US

OAK BROOK TERRACE DOINGS. s-w.: Wed. & Fri. $.75 newsstand; $41.50/yr. mailed. 118 W. First St., Hinsdale, IL 60521. TEL 708-887-0600; FAX 708-887-0600. **Owner(s):** Doings Newspapers, Inc., 118 W. First St., Hinsdale, IL 60521. TEL 708-887-0600; FAX 708-887-9646; Ed. Pat Lannom; Pub. J. Peter Teschner; adv. contact: Frieda Wolf. photos; pub. size: 4 color photos/art; circ. 12,000(paid).

US

WESTERN SPRINGS DOINGS. s-w.: Wed. & Fri. $.75 newsstand; $41.50/yr. mailed. 118 W. First St., Hinsdale, IL 60521. TEL 708-887-0600; FAX 708-887-9646; E-mail: doingsnews@aol.com. **Owner(s):** Doings Newspapers, Inc., 118 W. First St., Hinsdale, IL 60521. TEL 708-887-0600; FAX 708-887-9646; Ed. Pat Lannon; Pub. J. Peter Teschner; adv. contact: Frieda Wolf. photos; pub. size: 4 color photos/art; circ. 11,000(paid).

US

WILLOWBROOK DOINGS. 1895. s-w.: Wed. & Fri. $.75 newsstand; $41.50/yr. mailed. 118 W. First St., Hinsdale, IL 60521. TEL 708-887-0600; FAX 708-887-9646; E-mail: doingsnews@aol.com. **Owner(s):** Doings Newspapers, Inc., 118 W. First St., Hinsdale, IL 60521. TEL 708-887-0600; FAX 708-887-9646; Ed. Pam Lannom; Pub. J. Peter Teschner; adv. contact: Frieda Wolf. photos; pub. size: tabloid; circ. 11,000(paid).

HOOPESTON

US   ISSN 1076-4186

HOOPESTON CHRONICLE. 1872. bi-w. $28/yr. in cy.; $35/yr. elsewhere. 308 E. Main St., Hoopeston, IL 60942. TEL 217-283-5111; FAX 217-283-5846. **Owner(s):** Twin States Publishing Co., Inc., 308 E. Main St., Hoopeston, IL 60942. TEL 217-283-5111; Ed. Joann Gocking; Pub. Bette D. Schmid; adv. contact: Margie Brown. pub. size: tabloid; circ. 2,200(paid).

HUNTLEY

US

HUNTLEY FARMSIDE, THE. 1960. Thu. $.25 newsstand; $8/yr. 11801 Main, Huntley, IL 60142. TEL 847-669-5621; FAX 847-669-5623. **Owner(s):** Suzanne L. Brown, 11801 Main, Huntley, IL 60142. TEL 847-669-5621; FAX 847-669-5623; Pub. Suzanne L. Brown; adv.; photos; pub. size: tabloid; circ. 1,500(paid).

ILLIOPOLIS

US

ILLIOPOLIS SENTINEL. 1924. Thu. $15/yr.; $17.50 out of cy. P.O. Box 477, Illiopolis, IL 62539. TEL 217-486-7321. **Owner(s):** Frank Bell, P.O. Box 477, Illiopolis, IL 62539. TEL 217-486-7321; Pub. Frank Bell; adv. contact: Frank Bell. pub. size: tabloid; circ. 1,000(paid).

US

NIANTIC-HARRISTOWN COUNTY LINE OBSERVER. 1924. Fri. $9.50/yr. P.O. Box 477, Illiopolis, IL 62539. TEL 217-486-7321. **Owner(s):** Frank Bell, P.O. Box 477, Illiopolis, IL 62539. TEL 217-486-7321; Pub. Frank Bell; adv. contact: Frank Bell. pub. size: tabloid; circ. 400(paid). **Formerly:** Illinois County Line Observer.

JERSEYVILLE

US

COUNTY EDITION, THE. 1989. s-w.: Tue. & Fri. $.50 newsstand; $11.95/4 wks. 201 N. State St., Jerseyville, IL 62052. TEL 618-498-5551; FAX 618-498-3964. **Owner(s):** Journal Register Co., 50 W. State St., 12th Fl., Trenton, NJ 08608; Pub. Tom Rice; adv. contact: Doug Cooper. photos; pub. size: standard; circ. 10,000(paid). **Formerly:** Tri-County Edition, News Journal.

US

TELEGRAPH-COUNTY EDITION. 1919. s-w.: Tue. & Fri. $.50 newsstand; subscription includes The Telegraph; $13/4 wks. 201 N. State St., Jerseyville, IL 62052. TEL 618-498-5551; FAX 618-498-3964. **Owner(s):** Telegraph, 111 E. Broadway, P.O. Box 278, Alton, IL 62002. TEL 618-463-2500; FAX 618-463-9829; Ed. Tom Wrausmann; Pub. Tom Rice; adv. contact: Doug Cooper. photos; pub. size: standard; circ. 9,660(paid). **Formerly:** Tri-County Edition, News Journal.

JOLIET

US

FARMER'S WEEKLY REVIEW. 1921. Thu. $15/yr. 100 Manhattan Rd., Joliet, IL 60433. TEL 815-727-4811; FAX 815-727-5570. **Owner(s):** Patrick J. Cleary, 100 Manhattan Rd., Joliet, IL 60433. TEL 815-727-4811; Ed. Patrick J. Cleary; Pub. Patrick J. Cleary; adv. contact: Debbie Werner. bk.rev.; pub. size: tabloid; circ. 11,000(paid).

KINMUNDY

US

KINMUNDY EXPRESS. 1883. Wed. $.25; $12/yr. in state; $15/yr. elsewhere. 210 S. Madison, Kinmundy, IL 62854. TEL 618-547-3111. **Owner(s):** Rudolph Slane, 210 S. Madison, Kinmundy, IL 62854. TEL 618-547-3111; Pub. Rudolph Slane; adv. contact: Rudolph Slane. pub. size: broadsheet; circ. 990(paid).

LACON

US

LACON HOME JOURNAL. 1837. Thu. $.45 newsstand; $23/yr. 204 S. Washington St., Lacon, IL 61540. TEL 309-246-2865; FAX 309-246-3214. **Owner(s):** Marshall County Publishing Co., 204 S. Washington St., Lacon, IL 61540. TEL 309-246-2865; FAX 309-246-3214; Ed. William H. Sondag. adv.; pub. size: tabloid; circ. 2,400(paid).

LA FAYETTE

US

PRAIRIE SHOPPER, THE. 1981. Wed. $.50 newsstand; $20/yr. in state; $24/yr. out of state. 101 Jefferson St., La Fayette, IL 61449. TEL 309-995-3877; FAX 309-995-3975. **Owner(s):** Lowell McKirgan, 101 Jefferson St., La Fayette, IL 61449. TEL 309-995-3877; Pub. Lowell McKirgan; adv.; pub. size: tabloid; circ. 5,800(free & paid).

US

PRAIRIE TIMES, THE. 1984. w. $18/yr. in state; $22/yr. out of state. 101 Jefferson St., La Fayette, IL 61449. TEL 309-995-3877; FAX 309-995-3975. **Owner(s):** Lowell McKirgan, 101 Jefferson St., La Fayette, IL 61449. TEL 309-995-3877; Pub. Lowell McKirgan; pub. size: tabloid; circ. 1,000(paid).

LA HARPE

US

HANCOCK COUNTY QUILL. 1926. Wed. $.50 newsstand; $17/yr. Main St., La Harpe, IL 61450. TEL 217-659-3316; FAX 309-924-1124. **Owner(s):** Dessa Rodeffer, 702 Harmony St., Stronghurst, IL 61480. TEL 309-924-1558; FAX 309-924-1124; Belva Bell, 402 N. Broadway, Stronghurst, IL 61480. TEL 309-924-1263; FAX 309-924-1124; Ed. Belva Bell; Pub. Dessa Rodeffer; adv. contact: Shirley Linder. photos; bk.rev.; pub. size: tabloid; circ. 1,550(paid).

LAWRENCEVILLE

US

LAWRENCE COUNTY NEWS. 1842. Wed. $18/yr. P.O. Box 559, Lawrenceville, IL 62439. TEL 618-943-2331; FAX 618-943-3976. **Owner(s):** Larry L. Lewis, P.O. Box 559, Lawrenceville, IL 62439. TEL 618-943-2331; Pub. Larry L. Lewis; pub. size: standard; circ. 1,100(paid).

LEMONT

US

BOLINGBROOK METROPOLITAN. 1973. Thu. $.35 newsstand; $9.95/yr. in cy.; $15.95/yr. elsewhere. 223 Main St., Lemont, IL 60439. TEL 708-257-5300; FAX 708-257-5640. **Owner(s):** Press Publications, Inc., 112 S. York St., Elmhurst, IL 60126. TEL 708-834-0900; Ed. Michael Helenthal; Pub. Jack Crugar; adv. contact: Vince Saputo. pub. size: tabloid; circ. 17,550(paid).

US

DARIEN METROPOLITAN. 1974. Thu. $.35 newsstand; $9.95/yr. in cy.; $15.95/yr. elsewhere. 223 Main St., Lemont, IL 60439. TEL 708-257-5300; FAX 708-257-5640. **Owner(s):** Press Publications, Inc., 112 S. York St., Elmhurst, IL 60126. TEL 708-834-0900; Ed. Michael Helenthal; Pub. Jack Crugar; adv. contact: Vince Saputo. pub. size: tabloid; circ. 17,550(paid).

US

LEMONT METROPOLITAN. 1975. Thu. $.35 newsstand; $9.95/yr. in cy.; $15.95/yr. elsewhere. 223 Main St., Lemont, IL 60439. TEL 708-257-5300; FAX 708-257-5640. **Owner(s):** Press Publications, Inc., 112 S. York St., Elmhurst, IL 60126. TEL 708-834-0900; Ed. Michael Helenthal; Pub. Jack Crugar; adv. contact: Vince Saputo. pub. size: tabloid; circ. 17,550(paid).

US

LEMONT REPORTER. 1990. Wed. $.50 newsstand; $1.50/mo. carrier. 111 Illinois St., Lemont, IL 60439. TEL 708-257-1090; FAX 708-257-1093. **Owner(s):** Reporter/Progress Newspapers, 922 Warren Ave., Downers Grove, IL 60515. TEL 708-969-0188; Ed. Jennifer Parello; Pub. P.K. Winter; adv. contact: Ed Rooney. photos; bk.rev.; pub. size: tabloid; circ. 7,875(free & paid).

US

NAPERVILLE METROPOLITAN. Thu. $.35 newsstand; $9.95/yr. in cy.; $15.95/yr. elsewhere. 223 Main St., Lemont, IL 60439. TEL 708-257-5300; FAX 708-257-5640. **Owner(s):** Press Publications, Inc., 112 S. York St., Elmhurst, IL 60126. TEL 708-834-0900; Ed. Michael Helenthal; Pub. Jack Crugar; adv. contact: Vince Saputo. pub. size: tabloid; circ. 17,550(paid).

US

ORLAND METROPOLITAN. Thu. $.35 newsstand; $9.95/yr. in cy.; $15.95 elsewhere. 223 Main St., Lemont, IL 60439. TEL 708-257-5300; FAX 708-257-5640. **Owner(s):** Press Publications, Inc., 112 S. York St., Elmhurst, IL 60126. TEL 708-834-0900; Ed. Michael Helenthal; Pub. Jack Crugar; adv. contact: Vince Saputo. pub. size: tabloid; circ. 17,550(paid).

ROMEOVILLE

US

ROMEOVILLE METROPOLITAN. 1974. Thu. $.35 newsstand; $9.95/yr. in cy.; $15.95/yr. elsewhere. 223 Main St., Lemont, IL 60439. TEL 708-257-5300; FAX 708-257-5640. **Owner(s):** Press Publications, Inc., 112 S. York St., Elmhurst, IL 60126. TEL 708-334-0900; Ed. Michael Helenthal; Pub. Jack Cruger; adv. contact: Vince Saputo. pub. size: tabloid; circ. 17,550(paid).

LENA

US

NORTHWESTERN ILLINOIS FARMER. 1867. Wed. $18/yr. 119 W. Railroad, Lena, IL 61048-0536. TEL 815-369-2811; FAX 815-369-2816. **Owner(s):** Belvidere Daily Republican, Belvidere, IL; Stephenson Carroll Publishers, P.O. Box 536, Lena, IL 61048-0536. TEL 815-369-2811; Ed. Norman C. Templin; Pub. Norman C. Templin; adv.; pub. size: tabloid; circ. 11,000(paid).

LEWISTOWN

US   ISSN 1058-9619

LEWISTOWN-FULTON DEMOCRAT. 1855. Wed. $.50 newsstand; $25/yr. in cy.; $36/yr. out of cy. 165 W. Lincoln, Lewistown, IL 61542. TEL 309-547-3055; FAX 309-543-6844. **Owner(s):** Martin Publishing Co., Inc., 219 W. Market St., Havana, IL 62644. TEL 309-543-3311; Ed. Ruth Lynn; Pub. Bob Martin; adv.; pub. size: broadsheet; circ. 3,200(paid).

LINCOLNWOOD

US

ELMWOOD PARK-RIVER GROVE TIMES. 1946. Thu. $.50 newsstand; $11.95/yr. 7331 N. Lincoln Ave., Lincolnwood, IL 60645. TEL 847-329-2000; FAX 847-329-2060. **Owner(s):** Lerner Communications, Inc., 7331 N. Lincoln Ave., Lincolnwood, IL 60645. TEL 847-329-2000; FAX 847-329-2050; Ed. Brian Steele. adv.; pub. size: broadsheet; circ. 2,707(free & paid).

US

HARLEM-FOSTER-NORWOOD PARK-EDISON PARK TIMES. 1928. Thu. $.50 newsstand; $11.95/yr. 7331 N. Lincoln Ave., Lincolnwood IL 60646. TEL 847-329-2000; FAX 847-320-2060. **Owner(s):** Lerner Communications, Inc., 7331 N. Lincoln Ave, Lincolnwood, IL 60646. TEL 847-329-2000; Ed. Leigh Hanlon. adv.; pub. size: broadsheet; circ. 3,774(free & paid).

US

HARLEM-IRVING TIMES. Thu. $.50 newsstand; $11.95/yr. 7331 N. Lincoln Ave., Lincolnwood, IL 60646. TEL 847-329-2000; FAX 847-329-2060. **Owner(s):** Lerner Communications, Inc., 7331 N. Lincoln Ave., Lincolnwood, IL 60646. TEL 847-329-2000; FAX 847-329-2060; Ed. Brian Steele. adv.; pub. size: broadsheet; circ. 4,228(free & paid).

US

JEFFERSON PARK-PORTAGE PARK-BEL CRAGIN TIMES. Thu. $.50 newsstand; $11.95/yr. 7331 N. Lincoln Ave., Lincolnwood IL 60646. TEL 847-329-2000; FAX 847-329-2060. **Owner(s):** Lerner Communications, Inc., 7340 Lincoln Ave., Lincolnwood, IL 60645. TEL 847-329-2000; FAX 847-329-2050; Ed. Brian Steele. adv.; pub. size: broadsheet; circ. 6,335(free & paid). **Formerly:** Jefferson Portage Belmont Cragin.

US

LINCOLNWOOD LIFE. 1971. Thu. $.50 newsstand; $16.50/yr. 7331 N. Lincoln Ave., Lincolnwood, IL 60646. TEL 847-329-2000; FAX 847-329-2060. **Owner(s):** Lerner Communications, Inc., 7331 N. Lincoln Ave., Lincolnwood, IL 60646. TEL 847-329-2000; FAX 847-329-2060; Ed. Sarah Downey. adv.; pub. size: broadsheet; circ. 1,948(free & paid).

US   ISSN 0194-9381

MORTON GROVE-NILES LIFE. Thu. $.50 newsstand; $16.50/yr. 7331 N. Lincoln Ave., Lincolnwood, IL 60646. TEL 847-329-2000; FAX 847-329-2060. **Owner(s):** Lerner Communications, Inc., 7331 N. Lincoln Ave., Lincolnwood, IL 60646. TEL 847-329-2000; FAX 847-329-2060; Ed. Sarah Downey. adv.; pub. size: broadsheet; circ. 3,270(free & paid).
   Formerly: Morton Grove Life.

US

NEWS STAR. 1902. Wed. $.50 newsstand; $16.50/yr. 7331 N. Lincoln Ave., Lincolnwood, IL 60646. TEL 847-329-2000; FAX 847-329-2060. **Owner(s):** Lerner Communications, Inc., 7331 N. Lincoln Ave., Lincolnwood, IL 60646. TEL 847-329-2000; FAX 847-329-2060; Ed. Phil Dunn. adv.; pub. size: broadsheet; circ. 14,371(free & paid).
   Formerly: North Town News Star.

US

NILES LIFE. Thu. $.50 newsstand; $16.50/yr. 7331 N. Lincoln Ave., Lincolnwood, IL 60646. TEL 847-329-2000; FAX 847-329-2060. **Owner(s):** Lerner Communications, Inc., 7331 N. Lincoln Ave., Lincolnwood, IL 60646. TEL 847-329-2000; FAX 847-329-2061; Ed. Sara Downey; Pub. Lee Mortinson; adv. contact: Chuck Gekas. pub. size: broadsheet; circ. 907(paid).

US

NORRIDGE-HARWOOD HEIGHTS TIMES. Thu. $.50 newsstand; $11.95/yr. 7331 N. Lincoln Ave., Lincolnwood, IL 60646. TEL 847-329-2000; FAX 847-329-2060. **Owner(s):** Lerner Communications, Inc., 7331 N. Lincoln Ave., Lincolnwood, IL 60646. TEL 847-329-2000; FAX 847-329-2060; Ed. Brian Steele. adv.; pub. size: broadsheet; circ. 4,997(free & paid).
   Formerly: Norridge-Harwood Heights-Norwood Park Times.

US

NORTH CENTER-LINCOLN BELMONT-LAKE VIEW BOOSTER. Wed. $.50 newsstand; $16.50/yr. 7331 N. Lincoln Ave., Lincolnwood, IL 60646. TEL 847-329-2000; FAX 847-329-2205. **Owner(s):** Lerner Communications, Inc., 7331 N. Lincoln Ave., Lincolnwood, IL 60053. TEL 847-329-2000; FAX 847-329-2075; Ed. Phil Dunne. adv.; photos; bk.rev.; pub. size: broadsheet; circ. 7,894(free & paid).
   Formerly: Booster, The.

US

ROGERS PARK/EDGEWATER NEWS/UPTOWN NEWS STAR. 1903. s-w.: Wed. & Thu. $.50 newsstand; $16.50/yr. 7331 N. Lincoln Ave., Lincolnwood, IL 60646. TEL 847-329-2000; FAX 847-329-2060. **Owner(s):** Lerner Communications, Inc., 7331 N. Lincoln Ave., Lincolnwood, IL 60646. TEL 847-329-2000; FAX 847-329-2060; Ed. Phillip Dunn. adv. contact: Chuck Gekas. photos; bk.rev.; pub. size: broadsheet; circ. 5,888(paid); morning 16,073.

US   ISSN 1060-0217

SKOKIE LIFE. Thu. $.50 newsstand; $16.50/yr. 7331 N. Lincoln Ave., Lincolnwood, IL 60646. TEL 847-329-2000; FAX 847-329-2060. **Owner(s):** Lerner Communications, Inc., 7331 N. Lincoln Ave., Lincolnwood, IL 60646. TEL 847-329-2000; FAX 847-329-2060; Ed. Sarah Downey. adv.; pub. size: broadsheet; circ. 6,003(free & paid).

US

SKYLINE. Thu. $29.95/yr. out of area. 7331 N. Lincoln Ave., Lincolnwood, IL 60646. TEL 847-329-2000; FAX 847-329-2060. **Owner(s):** Lerner Communications, Inc., 7331 N. Lincoln Ave., Lincolnwood, IL 60646. TEL 847-329-2000; FAX 847-329-2060; Ed. Mary Marten. adv.; pub. size: broadsheet; circ. 28,503(free & paid).

LOMBARD

US

LOMBARDIAN, THE. 1957. Wed. $.45 newsstand. 613 S. Main St., Lombard, IL 60148. TEL 708-627-7010; FAX 708-627-7027; E-mail: lombardian@aol.com; URL: http://www.tccafe.com/lombardian. **Owner(s):** Scott MacKay, 613 S. Main St., Lombard, IL 60148. TEL 708-627-7010; Ed. Bonnie MacKay; Pub. Scott MacKay; adv. contact: Scott MacKay. pub. size: tabloid; circ. 14,500(paid).
   Formerly: Lombard Lombardian.

US

LOMBARDIAN VILLA PARK REVIEW. 1958. Wed. $.45 newsstand. 613 S. Main St., Lombard, IL 60148. TEL 708-627-7010; FAX 708-627-7027. **Owner(s):** Scott MacKay, 613 S. Main St., Lombard, IL 60148. TEL 708-627-7010; Ed. Bonnie MacKay; Pub. Scott MacKay; pub. size: tabloid; circ. 11,500(paid).

LOVE PARK

US

DURAND GAZETTE. 1953. Wed. $.50 newsstand; $22/yr. 2124 Harlem Rd., Ste. A, Love Park, IL 61111. TEL 815-624-6211; FAX 815-654-4857. **Owner(s):** Rock Valley Community Press, P.O. Box 15340, Rockford, IL 61132. TEL 815-248-2121; FAX 815-654-4857; Ed. Melanie Bradley; Pub. Craig McMullin; adv. contact: Randy Johnson. pub. size: tabloid; circ. 5,672(paid).

US

NEWS GAZETTE, THE. 1880. Wed. $.50 newsstand; $20/yr. carrier. 2124 Harlem Rd., Ste. A, Love Park, IL 61111. TEL 815-648-6211; FAX 815-654-4857. **Owner(s):** Rock Valley Community Press, P.O. Box 15340, Rockford, IL 61132. TEL 815-648-6211; Ed. Melanie Bradley. pub. size: tabloid; circ. 6,000(paid).

US

NORTH SUBURBAN HERALD. 1947. Wed. $22/yr. 2124 Harlem Rd., Ste. A, Loves Park, IL 61111. TEL 815-624-6211; FAX 815-654-4857. **Owner(s):** Rock Valley Community Press, P.O. Box 15340, Rockford, IL 61132. TEL 815-877-4044; FAX 815-654-4857; Ed. Denise Showers. adv. contact: Maxine Bayer. photos; bk.rev.; pub. size: tabloid; circ. 9,700(free & paid).

MARION

US

REVIEW, THE. 1990. Mon. free. P.O. Box 1111, Marion, IL 62959. TEL 618-997-2222; FAX 618-983-6227. **Owner(s):** Harry Olson, P.O. Box 1111, Marion, IL 62959. TEL 618-997-2222; Ed. Clayton Olsar; Pub. Harry Olson; adv. contact: Deborah Menley. photos; pub. size: tabloid; circ. 9,000(free).
   Formerly: Daily Review, The.

MASCOUTAH

US

CLINTON COUNTY POST. 1937. Thu. $.50 newsstand; $17.50/yr. in cy.; $20.50/yr. out of cy. 314 E. Church St., Mascoutah, IL 62258. TEL 618-588-7720; FAX 618-566-8283. **Owner(s):** Herald Publications, P.O. Drawer C, Mascoutah, IL 62258. TEL 618-566-8282; Pub. Greg Hoskins; adv.; pub. size: broadsheet.

US

COMMAND POST, THE. 1966. Fri. 314 E. Church St., Mascoutah, IL 62258. TEL 618-588-7720; FAX 618-566-8283. **Owner(s):** Herald Publications, P.O. Drawer C, Mascoutah, IL 62258. TEL 618-566-8282; Pub. Greg Hoskins; pub. size: standard; circ. 14,000(controlled & free).

US

FAIRVIEW HEIGHTS TRIBUNE. 1972. s-w.: Wed. & Thu. $.50 newsstand; $17.50/yr. in cy.; $20.50/yr. out of cy. 314 E. Church St., Mascoutah, IL 62258. TEL 618-398-8996; FAX 618-566-8283. **Owner(s):** Herald Publications, P.O. Drawer C, Mascoutah, IL 62258. TEL 618-566-8282; Ed. Les Hostetler; Pub. Greg Hoskins; adv.; pub. size: broadsheet; circ. 1,250(paid).

US

▼**LEBANON HERALD.** 1995. Thu. $.50 newsstand; $17.50 in cy.; $20.50 out of cy. 314 E. Church St., Mascoutah, IL 62258. TEL 618-588-7720; FAX 614-566-8283. **Owner(s):** Herald Publications, P.O. Drawer C, Mascoutah, IL 62258. TEL 618-566-8282; Pub. Greg Hoskins; adv.; pub. size: broadsheet; circ. 1,000(paid).

US

MASCOUTAH HERALD. 1885. Thu. $.50 newsstand; $17.50/yr. in cy.; $20.50/yr. out of cy. 314 E. Church St., Mascoutah, IL 62258. TEL 618-566-8282; FAX 618-566-8283. **Owner(s):** Herald Publications, P.O. Drawer C, Mascoutah, IL 62258. TEL 618-566-8282; Ed. Les Hostetler; Pub. Greg Hoskins; adv.; photos; bk.rev.; pub. size: broadsheet; circ. 2,400(paid).

US

SCOTT FLIER. 1987. Thu. $.50 newsstand; $17.50/yr. in cy.; $20.50/yr. out of cy. 314 E. Church St., Mascoutah, IL 62258. TEL 618-588-7720; FAX 618-566-8283. **Owner(s):** Herald Publications, P.O. Drawer C, Mascoutah, IL 62258. TEL 618-566-8282; Pub. Greg Hoskins; adv.; pub. size: broadsheet; circ. 4,000(controlled & free).

MCLEANSBORO

US

MCLEANSBORO TIMES-LEADER. 1855. Wed. & 1st Mon. of mo. $.50 newsstand; $22/yr. in cy. 123 S. Jackson, McLeansboro, IL 62859. TEL 618-643-2387. **Owner(s):** Thomson Newspapers, Inc., One Thorn Run Ctr., Ste. 500, 1187 Thorn Run Rd. Ext., Coraopolis, PA 15108. TEL 412-262-7870; Ed. Spencer Cramer; Pub. Charles Deitz; adv. contact: Kathy Metcalf. pub. size: broadsheet; circ. 3,600(paid).

MELROSE PARK

US

FRANKLIN PARK STAR-SENTINEL. 1924. Wed. $.45 newsstand; $16/yr. mailed. 1440 W. North Ave., Ste. 210, Melrose Park, IL 60160. TEL 708-345-1750; FAX 708-345-1795. **Owner(s):** Shannon Publications, Inc., P.O. Box 125, Fairbury, IL 61739. TEL 815-692-2366; Ed. David Roberts; Pub. David Roberts; adv. contact: George Bellini. pub. size: tabloid; circ. 17,000(controlled & paid).

US

MELROSE PARK STAR-SENTINEL. 1924. Wed. $.45 newsstand; $16/yr. mailed. 1440 W. North Ave., Ste. 206, Melrose Park, IL 60160. TEL 708-345-1750; FAX 708-345-1795. **Owner(s):** Shannon Publications, Inc., P.O. Box 125, Fairbury, IL 61739. TEL 815-692-2366; Ed. David Roberts; Pub. David Roberts; adv. contact: George Bellini. pub. size: tabloid; circ. 17,000(controlled & paid).

US

NORTHLAKE STAR-SENTINEL. 1924. Wed. $.45 newsstand; $16/yr. mailed. 1440 W. North Ave., Ste. 206, Melrose Park, IL 60160. TEL 708-345-1750; FAX 708-345-1795. **Owner(s):** Shannon Publications, Inc., P.O. Box 125, Fairbury, IL 61739. TEL 815-692-2366; Ed. David Roberts; Pub. David Roberts; adv. contact: George Bellini. pub. size: tabloid; circ. 17,000(controlled & paid).

US

PROVISO STAR-SENTINEL. 1924. Wed. $.45 newsstand; $16/yr. mailed. 1440 W. North Ave., Ste. 206, Melrose Park, IL 60160. TEL 708-345-1750. **Owner(s):** Shannon Publications, Inc., P.O. Box 125, Fairbury, IL 61739. TEL 815-692-2366; Ed. David Roberts; Pub. David Roberts; adv. contact: George Bellini. pub. size: tabloid; circ. 17,000(controlled & paid).

MELVIN

US

FORD COUNTY PRESS. 1918. Thu. $14/yr. local; $15 yr. out of state. 115 W. Main St., Melvin, IL 60952. TEL 217-388-7721. **Owner(s):** Fred Thackeray, 115 W. Main St., Melvin, IL 60952; adv.; photos; pub. size: standard; circ. 1,050(controlled & paid).

MENDOTA

US

MENDOTA REPORTER. 1878. Wed. $.50 newsstand; $23.95/yr. mailed; $35.95/yr. out of state. 703 Illinois Ave., Mendota, IL 61342. TEL 815-539-9396; FAX 815-539-7862. **Owner(s):** Mendota Publishing Corp., P.O. Box 300, Mendota, IL 61342. TEL 815-539-9396; Pub. Tom Cross; adv. contact: Jeff Ohlendorf. photos; pub. size: broadsheet; circ. 5,000(paid).

METAMORA

US

WASHBURN LEADER. 1892. Thu. $15/yr. 214 E. Partridge, Metamora, IL 61548. TEL 309-367-2335; FAX 309-367-2616. **Owner(s):** Metamora Woodford Publishing Co., 214 E. Partridge, Metamora, IL 61548; Ed. Larry Schultz; Pub. Melvin Nielsen; adv.; pub. size: broadsheet; circ. 925(paid).

METROPOLIS

US

METROPOLIS PLANET. 1865. Wed. $.50 newsstand; $20/yr. mailed local; $27/yr. elsewhere. 111 E. Fifth St., Metropolis, IL 62960-0820. TEL 618-524-2141; FAX 618-524-4727. **Owner(s):** Laura Harris, Richmond, KY; Ed. Clyde Wills. adv. contact: Angie Shelton. pub. size: broadsheet; circ. 5,900(paid).

MIDLOTHIAN

US

ALSIP EXPRESS. 1945. Thu. $.35 newsstand; $15/yr. in cy.; $18/yr. out of cy.; $24/yr. out of state. 3840 W. 147th St., Midlothian, IL 60445. TEL 708-388-2425; FAX 708-385-7811. **Owner(s):** Southwest Messenger Press, Inc., 3840 W. 147th St., Midlothian, IL 60445. TEL 708-388-2425; Ed. Gerald Gibbons; Pub. W.H. Lysen; adv. contact: Don Talac. pub. size: tabloid; circ. 4,970(paid).

US

BEVERLY NEWS. 1948. Thu. $.35 newsstand; $15/yr. in cy.; $18/yr. out of cy. 3840 W. 147th St., Midlothian, IL 60445. TEL 708-388-2425; FAX 708-385-7811. **Owner(s):** Southwest Messenger Press, Inc., 3840 W. 147th St., Midlothian, IL 60445. TEL 708-388-2425; Ed. Gerald Gibbons; Pub. W.H. Lysen; adv. contact: Don Talac. pub. size: tabloid; circ. 4,190(paid). **Formerly:** Chicago Beverly News.

US

BRIDGEVIEW INDEPENDENT. 1962. Wed. $.35 newsstand; $45/yr. 3840 W. 147th St., Midlothian, IL 60445 TEL 708-388-2425; FAX 708-385-7811. **Owner(s):** Southwest Messenger Press, Inc., 3840 W. 147th St., Midlothian, IL 60445 TEL 708-388-2425; Ed. Gerald Gibbons; Pub. W.H. Lysen; adv. contact: Don Talac. pub. size: tabloid; circ. 5,200(paid); evening 2,730.

US

BURBANK-STICKNEY INDEPENDENT. 1962. Thu. $.35 newsstand; $15/yr. in cy.; $18/yr. out of cy.; $24/yr. out of state. 3840 W. 147th St., Midlothian, IL 60445 TEL 708-388-2425; FAX 708-385-7811. **Owner(s):** Southwest Messenger Press, Inc., 3840 W. 147th St., Midlothian, IL 60445 TEL 708-388-2425; Ed. Gerald Gibbons; Pub. W.H. Lysen; adv. contact: Don Talac. pub. size: tabloid; circ. 6,310(paid).

US

CHICAGO RIDGE CITIZEN. 1962. Thu. $.35 newsstand; $15/yr. in cy.; $18/yr. out of cy.; $24/yr. out of state. 3840 W. 147th St., Midlothian, IL 60445 TEL 708-388-2425; FAX 708-385-7811. **Owner(s):** Southwest Messenger Press, Inc., 3840 W. 147th St., Midlothian, IL 60445 TEL 708-388-2425; Ed. Gerald Gibbons; Pub. W.H. Lysen; adv. contact: Don Talac. pub. size: tabloid; circ. 2,910(paid).

US

EVERGREEN PARK COURIER. 1930. Thu. $.35 newsstand; $15/yr. in cy.; $18/yr. out of cy.; $24/yr. out of state. 3840 W. 147th St., Midlothian, IL 60445. TEL 708-388-2425; FAX 708-385-7811. **Owner(s):** Southwest Messenger Press, Inc., 3840 W. 147th St., Midlothian, IL 60445. TEL 708-388-2425; Ed. Gerald Gibbons; Pub. W.H. Lysen; adv. contact: Don Talac. pub. size: tabloid; circ. 4,370(paid).

US

HICKORY HILLS CITIZEN. 1958. Thu. $.35 newsstand; $15/yr. in cy.; $18/yr. out of cy.; $24/yr. out of state. 3840 W. 147th St., Midlothian, IL 60445. TEL 708-388-2425; FAX 708-385-7811. **Owner(s):** Southwest Messenger Press, Inc., 3840 W. 147th St., Midlothian, IL 60445. TEL 708-388-2425; Ed. Gerald Gibbons; Pub. W.H. Lysen; adv. contact: Don Talac. pub. size: tabloid; circ. 3,430(paid).

US

MIDLOTHIAN-BREMEN MESSENGER. 1930. Thu. $.35 newsstand; $15/yr. in cy.; $18/yr. out of cy.; $24/yr. out of state. 3840 W. 147th St., Midlothian, IL 60445. TEL 708-388-2425; FAX 708-385-7811. **Owner(s):** Southwest Messenger Press, Inc., 3840 W. 147th St., Midlothian, IL 60445. TEL 708-388-2425; Ed. Gerald Gibbons; Pub. W.H. Lysen; adv. contact: Don Talac. pub. size: tabloid; circ. 10,740(paid).

US

MOUNT GREENWOOD EXPRESS. 1945. Thu. $.35 newsstand; $15/yr. in cy.; $18/yr. out of cy.; $24/yr. out of state. 3840 W. 147th St., Midlothian, IL 60445. TEL 708-388-2425; FAX 708-385-7811. **Owner(s):** Southwest Messenger Press, Inc., 3840 W. 147th St., Midlothian, IL 60445. TEL 708-388-2425; Ed. Gerald Gibbons; Pub. W.H. Lysen; adv. contact: Don Talac. pub. size: tabloid; circ. 7,320(paid).

US

OAK LAWN INDEPENDENT. 1930. Thu. $.35 newsstand; $15/yr. in cy.; $18/yr. out of cy.; $24/yr. out of state. 3840 W. 147th St., Midlothian, IL 60445. TEL 708-388-2425; FAX 708-385-7811. **Owner(s):** Southwest Messenger Press, Inc., 3840 W. 147th St., Midlothian, IL 60445. TEL 708-388-2425; Ed. Gerald Gibbons; Pub. W.H. Lysen; adv. contact: Don Talac. pub. size: tabloid; circ. 11,930(paid).

US

ORLAND TOWNSHIP MESSENGER. 1980. Thu. $.35 newsstand; $15/yr. in cy.; $18/yr. out of cy.; $24/yr. out of state. 3840 W. 147th St., Midlothian, IL 60445. TEL 708-388-2425; FAX 708-385-7811. **Owner(s):** Southwest Messenger Press, Inc., 3840 W. 147th St., Midlothian, IL 60445. TEL 708-388-2425; Ed. Gerald Gibbons; Pub. W.H. Lysen; adv. contact: Don Talac. pub. size: tabloid; circ. 3,660(paid).

US

PALOS CITIZEN. 1958. Thu. $.35 newsstand; $15/yr. in cy.; $18/yr. out of cy.; $24/yr. out of state. 3840 W. 147th St., Midlothian, IL 60445. TEL 708-388-2425; FAX 708-385-7811. **Owner(s):** Southwest Messenger Press, Inc., 3840 W. 147th St., Midlothian, IL 60445. TEL 708-388-2425; Ed. Gerald Gibbons; Pub. W.H. Lysen; adv. contact: Don Talac. pub. size: tabloid; circ. 4,720(paid).

US

SCOTTSDALE-ASHBURN INDEPENDENT. 1962. Thu. $.35 newsstand; $15/yr. in cy.; $18/yr. out of cy.; $24 out of state. 3840 W. 147th St., Midlothian, IL 60445. TEL 708-388-2425. **Owner(s):** Southwest Messenger Press, Inc., 3840 W. 147th St., Midlothian, IL 60445. TEL 708-388-2425; Ed. Gerald Gibbons; Pub. W. H. Lysen; adv.; pub. size: tabloid; circ. 5,960(paid).

US

WORTH CITIZEN. 1930. Thu. $.35 newsstand; $15/yr. in cy.; $18/yr. out of cy.; $24/yr. out of state. 3840 W. 147th St., Midlothian, IL 60445. TEL 708-388-2425; FAX 708-385-7811. **Owner(s):** Southwest Messenger Press, Inc., 3840 W. 147th St., Midlothian, IL 60445. TEL 708-385-2425; Ed. Gerald Gibbons; Pub. W.H. Lysen; adv. contact: Don Talac. pub. size: tabloid; circ. 2,810(paid).

MINIER

US

OLYMPIA REVIEW. 1967. Tue. $.35 newsstand; $22/yr. 102 S. Main, Minier, IL 61759. TEL 309-392-2414; FAX 309-392-2169. **Owner(s):** Rickard Publishing Co., P.O. Box 586, Manito, IL 61546. TEL 309-968-6705; Ed. Joe Rickard. adv.; pub. size: broadsheet; circ. 6,950(paid).

MINONK

US

MINONK NEWS DISPATCH. Thu. $.75 newsstand; $24/yr. local; $32/yr. out of state. 224 E. Fifth, Minonk, IL 61760. TEL 309-432-2505; FAX 309-432-2506. **Owner(s):** Illinois Valley Press, 301 W. Washington, Normal, IL 61761. TEL 309-829-9411; Ed. J.W. Shultz. adv.; pub. size: broadsheet; circ. 825(free & paid).

MONTICELLO

US

PIATT COUNTY JOURNAL-REPUBLICAN. 1856. Wed. $.45 newsstand; $19.20/yr. in cy.; $20.30/yr. out of cy. 118 E. Washington St., Monticello, IL 61856. TEL 217-762-2511; FAX 217-352-1722. **Owner(s):** East Central Communications, Inc., 1332 Harmon Dr., Rantoul, IL 61866. TEL 217-892-9613; Pub. Dennis Kaster; pub. size: broadsheet; circ. 3,850(paid).
  Formerly: Monticello Piatt County Journal-Republican.

MORTON

US

EAST PEORIA COURIER. 1927. Wed. free deliv.; $.50 newsstand. 100 Detroit Ave., Morton, IL 61550. TEL 309-676-2511; FAX 309-266-7385. **Owner(s):** Fleming Publishing Co., 100 Detroit Ave., P.O. Box 250, Morton, IL 61550. TEL 309-263-2211; Ed. Jill Peterson; Pub. Ted J. Fleming; pub. size: broadsheet; circ. 10,500(free & paid).

US

TAZEWELL NEWS. 1888. s-w.: Wed. & Sat. $.50 newsstand; $39.90/yr. carrier. 100 Detroit Ave., Morton, IL 61550. TEL 309-263-2211; FAX 309-266-7385. **Owner(s):** Fleming Publishing Co., 100 Detroit Ave., P.O. Box 250, Morton, IL 61550. TEL 309-263-2211; Ed. Ted W. Fleming. adv.; photos; pub. size: broadsheet; circ. 9,055(paid).
  Formerly: Morton-Tazewell News.

US

WASHINGTON REPORTER. 1840. Wed. free; $.50 newsstand. 100 Detroit Ave., Morton, IL 61550. TEL 309-676-2511; FAX 309-266-7385. **Owner(s):** Fleming Publishing Co., 100 Detroit Ave., Morton, IL 61550. TEL 309-444-2513; FAX 309-266-7385; Ed. Jeanette Kendall; Pub. Ted J. Fleming; adv.; photos; pub. size: standard; circ. evening 6,000(controlled & free). Wire Service(s): CNS.

MOUNDS

US

PULASKI ENTERPRISE. 1861. Wed. $.35 newsstand; $13/yr. in cy.; $15.60/yr. out of cy.; $18.20/yr. out of state. 315 First St., Mounds, IL 62964. TEL 618-745-6267. **Owner(s):** Edward A. Taylor, Jr., P.O. Box 459, Mounds, IL 62964. TEL 618-745-6267; Ed. Lottie M. Taylor; Pub. Edward A. Taylor, Jr.; pub. size: broadsheet; circ. 5,000(paid).

MT. OLIVE

US

MT. OLIVE HERALD, THE. 1978. Thu. $.35 newsstand; $13.30/yr. local; $14.50/yr. in cy.; $17.50/yr. out of state. 102 E. Main, Mt. Olive, IL 62069. TEL 217-999-3941; FAX 217-999-5105. **Owner(s):** John M. Galer, 150 N. Washington St., Bunker Hill, IL 62014. TEL 618-585-4411; Ed. Linda Hasquin; Pub. John M. Galer; adv.; photos; pub. size: tabloid; circ. 1,650(paid).

MT. STERLING

US

DEMOCRAT-MESSAGE. 1848. Tue. $.50 newsstand; $17/yr. in cy.; $26/yr. elsewhere. 123 W. Main St., Mt. Sterling, IL 62353. TEL 217-773-3371; FAX 217-773-3369. **Owner(s):** Coulson Publications, 123 W. Main St., Mt. Sterling, IL 62353. TEL 217-773-3371; Ed. Warren Coulson. adv. contact: Pat Webel. pub. size: tabloid; circ. 10,000(paid).

NAPERVILLE

US

FOX VALLEY SUN. 1984. 3/wk.: Wed., Fri., Sun. $36/yr. 9 W. Jackson, Naperville, IL 60566-0269. TEL 708-355-0063. **Owner(s):** Copley Press, Inc., 7776 Ivanhoe Ave., La Jolla, CA 92037. TEL 619-454-0411; adv. contact: Rick Taden. pub. size: tabloid; circ. morning 22,000(paid); Sun. 22,000(paid).

US

LISLE SUN. 1938. Thu. $36/yr. mailed. 9 W. Jackson, Naperville, IL 60540. TEL 708-968-8200; FAX 708-355-2432. **Owner(s):** Copley Press, Inc., 7776 Ivanhoe Ave., La Jolla, CA 92037. TEL 619-454-0411; adv. contact: Rick Taden. pub. size: tabloid; circ. 5,500(paid). **Wire Service(s):** IPA.

US

NAPERVILLE SUN. 1935. 3/wk.: Sun., Wed., Fri. $.50 newsstand; $36/yr. local. 9 W. Jackson, Naperville, IL 60540. TEL 708-355-0063; FAX 708-355-6703. **Owner(s):** Copley Press, Inc., 7776 Ivanhoe Ave., LaJolla, CA 92037. TEL 619-454-0411; adv. contact: Rick Taden. pub. size: tabloid; circ. 45,000(paid). **Wire Service(s):** AP, CNS.

US

WHEATON SUN. 1910. s-w.: Wed. & Fri. $.35 newsstand; $30/yr. 9 W. Jackson, Naperville, IL 60566. TEL 708-355-8012; FAX 708-355-6703. **Owner(s):** Copley Press, Inc., 7776 Ivanhoe, La Jolla, CA 92037. TEL 619-454-0411; adv. contact: Rick Taden. pub. size: tabloid; circ. 5,600(paid). Wire Service(s): AP, CNS.
  Formerly: Wheaton Journal.

NASHVILLE

US

NASHVILLE NEWS, THE. 1934. Wed. $.40 newsstand; $17.50/yr. Washington, Perry, & Jeff cys.; $21/yr. elsewhere. 211 W. St. Louis St., Nashville, IL 62263-0047. TEL 618-327-3411; FAX 618-327-3299. **Owner(s):** Richard & Constance Tomaszewski, 211 W. St. Louis St., Nashville, IL 62263-0047. TEL 618-327-3411; FAX 618-327-3299; Ed. Richard Tomaszewski. adv.; pub. size: broadsheet; circ. 5,900(paid).

NEWTON

US

NEWTON PRESS-MENTOR. 1862. s-w.: Mon. & Thu. $.30 newsstand; $25/yr. in cy. & adjoining cy.; $33.50/yr. in state; $34/yr. out of state. 101 S. Jackson St., Newton, IL 62448-9998. TEL 618-783-2324; FAX 618-783-2325. **Owner(s):** Jasper County Publishing, Co., 101 S. Jackson St., Newton, IL 62448-9998. TEL 618-783-2324; FAX 618-783-2325; Ed. Don Hecke; Pub. Don Hecke; adv. contact: Richard Bayler. pub. size: broadsheet; circ. 4,750(paid).

NILES

US

BUGLE, THE. 1957. s-w.: Thu. & Sat. $.50 newsstand; $13.50/yr. 8746 N. Shermer Rd., Niles, IL 60714. TEL 847-966-3900; FAX 847-966-0198. **Owner(s):** Besser Publications, 8746 N. Shermer Rd., Niles, IL 60714. TEL 847-966-3900; Ed. Robert Besser; Pub. Robert Besser; adv. contact; Marti Kaz. pub. size: tabloid; circ. 42,000(controlled & paid). Wire Service(s): AP.
  Formerly: Niles Bugle.

NOKOMIS

US

NOKOMIS FREE PRESS-PROGRESS. 1877. Wed. $.35 newsstand; $16.50/yr. cy. 112 W. State St., Nokomis, IL 62075. TEL 217-563-2115; FAX 217-563-7464. **Owner(s):** Free Press, Inc., 112 W. State St., Nokomis, IL 62075. TEL 217-563-2115; FAX 217-563-7464; Ed. Fred Christner; Pub. Thomas J. Phillips, Jr.; adv. contact: Cynthia Hayes. pub. size: broadsheet; circ. 2,700(paid).

O'FALLON

US

O'FALLON PROGRESS. 1895. Thu. $.50 newsstand; $20/yr. 612 E. State St., O'Fallon, IL 62269-0970. TEL 618-632-3643; FAX 618-632-6438. **Owner(s):** Walt Disney Co., 500 S. Buena Vista St., Burbank, CA 91521. TEL 818-560-5300; Ed. Jennifer Gammage; Pub. Cecil Ross; adv. contact: Pat James. adv.: $9.50/SAU. photos; pub. size: broadsheet; circ. 4,000(free & paid).

OAK BROOK

US

INDIAN HEAD PARK CITIZEN. 1947. s-w.: Wed. & Sat. $28/yr. 709 Enterprise Dr., Oak Brook, IL 60521-8814. TEL 708-368-1100; FAX 708-368-1199. **Owner(s):** Life Printing & Publishing Co., Inc., 2601 S. Harlem Ave., Berwyn, IL 60402. TEL 708-484-1234; Pub. Jack Kubik; adv. contact: Peter Manning. pub. size: broadsheet; circ. 32,500(free & paid).

US

LA GRANGE COUNTRYSIDE CITIZEN. 1949. s-w.: Wed. & Sat. $.50 newsstand; $26/yr. carrier. 709 Enterprise, Oak Brook, IL 60521. TEL 708-368-1100; FAX 708-368-1199. **Owner(s):** Life Printing & Publishing Co., Inc., 2601 S. Harlem Ave., Berwyn, IL 60402. TEL 708-484-1234; Ed. Bill Conkis; Pub. Jack R. Kubik; adv.; pub. size: broadsheet; circ. 10,624(paid).

US

LA GRANGE PARK CITIZEN. 1947. s-w.: Wed. & Sat. $28/yr. 709 Enterprise Dr., Oak Brook, IL 60521. TEL 708-368-1100; FAX 708-368-1199. **Owner(s):** Life Printing & Publishing Co., Inc., 2601 S. Harlem Ave., Berwyn, IL 60402. TEL 708-484-1234; Ed. Bill Conkis; Pub. Jack Kubik; adv. contact: Peter Manning. pub. size: broadsheet; circ. 2,810(paid).

US

LYONS CITIZEN. 1947. s-w.: Wed. & Sat. $28/yr. 709 Enterprise Dr., Oak Brook, IL 60521. TEL 708-368-1100; FAX 708-368-1199. **Owner(s):** Life Printing & Publishing Co., Inc., 2601 S. Harlem Ave., Berwyn, IL 60402. TEL 708-484-1234; Ed. Bill Conkis; Pub. Jack Kubik; adv. contact: Peter Manning. pub. size: broadsheet; circ. 3,338(paid).

US

NORTH RIVERSIDE CITIZEN. 1947. s-w.: Wed. & Sat. $.75 newsstand; $28/yr. mailed. 709 Enterprise, Oak Brook, IL 60521. TEL 708-368-1100; FAX 708-368-1199. **Owner(s):** Life Printing & Publishing Co., Inc., 2601 S. Harlem Ave., Berwyn, IL 60402. TEL 708-484-1234; Ed. Bill Conkis; Pub. Jack Kubik; adv. contact: Dave Kuehl. pub. size: broadsheet; circ. 4,964(paid).

US

SUBURBAN LIFE CITIZEN. 1926. s-w.: Wed. & Sat. $.75 newsstand; $28/yr. home deliv. 709 Enterprise Dr., Oak Brook, IL 60521-8814. TEL 708-368-8847; FAX 708-368-1188. **Owner(s):** Life Printing & Publishing Co., Inc., 2601 S. Harlem, Berwyn, IL 60402. TEL 708-484-1234; Ed. William Conkis; Pub. Jack Kubik; adv. contact: David Kuehl. pub. size: broadsheet; circ. 32,500(paid).

US

SUBURBAN LIFE GRAPHIC. 1949. s-w.: Wed. & Sat. $.75 newsstand; $29/yr. carrier; $38/yr. mailed. 709 Enterprise, Oak Brook, IL 60521. TEL 708-368-1100; FAX 708-524-1199. **Owner(s):** Lake Printing & Publishing Co., Inc., 2601 S. Harlem Ave., Berwyn, IL 60402. TEL 708-484-1234; Ed. Joseph DeRosier; Pub. Jack R. Kubik; pub. size: broadsheet; circ. 34,000(paid).

OAK PARK

US

AUSTIN WEEKLY NEWS. 1987. Thu. free newsstand; $37.50/yr. 141 S. Oak Park Ave., Oak Park, IL 60302-2972. TEL 312-626-6332; FAX 708-524-0447. **Owner(s):** Wednesday Journal, Inc., 141 S. Oak Park Ave., Oak Park, IL 60302. TEL 708-524-8300; FAX 708-524-0447; Ed. Elaine Richardson; Pub. Don Haley; adv. contact: Lorell Wallace. photos; bk.rev.; pub. size: tabloid; circ. 18,000(free).

US

ELM LEAVES. 1952. Wed. $1 newsstand; $17.95/yr. 1148 Westgate, Oak Park, IL 60301. TEL 708-383-3200; FAX 708-383-3678. **Owner(s):** Pioneer Press, Inc., 3701 W. Lake Ave., Glenview, IL 60025. TEL 847-486-9200; Ed. Rick Behren adv.; pub. size: tabloid; circ. 4,000(paid).

US

FOREST LEAVES. 1906. Wed. $1 newsstand.; $22.50/yr. 1148 Westgate, Oak Park, IL 60301. TEL 708-383-3200; FAX 708-383-3628. **Owner(s):** Pioneer Press, Inc., 3701 W. Lake Ave., Glenview, IL 60025. TEL 847-486-9200; Ed. Randy Blaser; Pub. Tom Neri; pub. size: tabloid; circ. 2,600(paid).

US

FRANKLIN PARK HERALD-JOURNAL. 1971. Wed. $1 newsstand; $17.95/yr. 1148 Westgate, Oak Park, IL 60301 TEL 708-383-3200; FAX 708-383-3678. **Owner(s):** Pioneer Press, Inc., 3701 W. Lake Ave., Glenview, IL 60025. TEL 847-486-9200; Ed. Rick Behren; Pub. Tom Neri; pub. size: tabloid; circ. 4,127(paid).

US

MAYWOOD HERALD. Wed. $1 newsstand; $18.95/yr. 1148 Westgate Oak Park, IL 60301. TEL 708-848-9710; FAX 708-383-3678. **Owner(s):** Pioneer Press, Inc., 3701 W. Lake Ave., Glenview, IL 60025. TEL 847-486-9200; Ed. Tom Ganz; Pub. Thomas Neri; adv.; pub. size: broadsheet; circ. 3,200(paid).

US

MELROSE PARK HERALD. 1902. Wed. $1 newsstand; $18.95/yr. 1148 Westgate, Oak Park, IL 60301. TEL 708-383-3200; FAX 708-383-3678. **Owner(s):** Sun Times Inc., 1232 Central Ave., Wilmette, IL 60091. TEL 708-251-4300; Ed. Greg Canfield. pub. size: standard; circ. 2,700(paid).

US

OAK LEAVES, THE. 1878. Wed. $1 newsstand; $22.50/yr. 1148 Westgate, Oak Park, IL 60301. TEL 708-383-3200; FAX 708-383-3678. **Owner(s):** Pioneer Press, Inc., 3701 W. Lake Ave., Glenview, IL 60025. TEL 847-486-9200; Ed. Randy Blaser; Pub. Tom Neri; pub. size: tabloid; circ. 11 941(paid).
   Formerly: Forest Park News.

US

WEDNESDAY JOURNAL OF OAK PARK & RIVER FOREST. 1980. Wed. $.50 newsstand; $20/yr. 141 S. Oak Park Ave., Oak Park, IL 60302. TEL 708-524-8300; FAX 708-524-0447; E-mail: wjinc@aol.com; URL: http://www.wjinc.com. **Owner(s):** Wednesday Journal, Inc., 141 S. Oak Park Ave., Oak Park, IL 60302. TEL 708-524-8300 Ed. Dan Haley. adv.; photos; pub. size: tabloid; circ. 11,500(paid).

US

WESTCHESTER HERALD. 1986. Wed. $1 newsstand; $22.50/yr. 1148 Westgate Oak Park, IL 60301. TEL 708-383-3200; FAX 708-383-3678. **Owner(s):** Sun Times, Inc., 401 N. Wabash, Chicago, IL 60611. TEL 312-321-3000; Ed. Tom Ganz. adv. contact: Tom Conradi. pub. size: standard; circ. 2,500(paid).

US

WEST PROVISO HERALD. Wed. $17.95/yr. 1148 Westgate, Oak Park, IL 60301. TEL 708-383-3200; FAX 708-383-3678. **Owner(s):** Pioneer Press, Inc., 3701 W. Lake Ave., Glenview, IL 60025. TEL 847-486-9200; Pub. Thomas Neri; adv.; pub. size: broadsheet; circ. 2,700(paid).

OREGON

US

OGLE COUNTY LIFE. 1968. Mon. free. 200 N. Third St., Ste. B, Oregon, IL 61061. TEL 815-732-2156; FAX 815-732-6154. **Owner(s):** Rochelle Newspapers, Inc., 211 Hwy. 38, E., Rochelle, IL 61068. TEL 815-562-4171; Ed. Doug Oleson; Pub. Tom Cross; adv.; pub. size: tabloid; circ. 13,000(free).

ORION

US

ORION GAZETTE. 1992. Thu. $.75 newsstand; $31/yr. 250 Tenth Ave., Orion, IL 61273. TEL 309-526-8085. **Owner(s):** Terry Newspapers, Inc., 108 W. First St., Geneseo, IL 61254. TEL 309-944-2119; Ed. Mindy Carls; Pub. Thomas Terry; adv. contact: Linda Venable. pub. size: broadsheet; circ. 1,671(paid).

OTTAWA

US

THRIF-T-NIKEL WEEKLY NEWSPAPER. 1973. Wed. free local; $50/yr. mailed elsewhere. 801 Canal St., Ottawa, IL 61350. TEL 815-433-5595; FAX 815-433-5596. **Owner(s):** F.W. Gray & Associates, Ltd., 801 Canal St., Ottawa, IL 6135C. TEL 815-433-5595; Ed. Linda K. Walter; Pub. Stephen F. Gray; adv. contact Joyce Sharp. pub. size: tabloid; circ. 19,000(controlled & paid).

US

TOWN & COUNTRY WEEKLY. 1979. Wed. $.25 newsstand; $50/yr. 801 Canal St. Ottawa, IL 6135C. TEL 815-433-5595; FAX 815-433-5596. **Owner(s):** Steve Gray & Associates Ltd., P.O. Box 279, Ottawa, IL 61350. TEL 815-433-5595; Ed. Linda Walter. pub. size: tabloid; circ. 19,000(controlled & paid).

PALOS HEIGHTS

US

OAK LAWN-EVERGREEN PARK REPORTER. 1960. Wed. $.50 newsstand; $24/yr. 12247 S. Harlem Ave., Palos Heights, IL 60463. TEL 708-448-6161. **Owner(s):** Regional Publishing Corp., 12243 S. Harlem Ave., Palos Heights, IL 60463. TEL 708-448-4000; Ed. Jack Murray; Pub. Charles Richards; adv. contact: Carol McLaughlin. photos; pub. size: broadsheet; circ. 17,424(paid).

US
PALOS HILLS-HICKORY HILLS. 1960. Thu. $.50 newsstand; $24/yr. 12247 S. Harlem Ave., Palos Heights, IL 60463. TEL 708-448-6161; FAX 708-448-4012. **Owner(s):** Regional Publishing Corp., 12243 S. Harlem Ave, Palos Heights, IL 60463. TEL 708-448-4000. Ed. Jack Murray. adv. contact: Carol McLaughlin. bk.rev.; pub. size: broadsheet; circ. 19,021(free & paid).

US
REGIONAL NEWS. 1941. Thu. $.75 newsstand; $28/yr. 12243 S. Harlem Ave., Palos Heights, IL 60463-0932. TEL 708-448-6161. **Owner(s):** Regional Publishing Corp., 12243 S. Harlem Ave., Palos Heights, IL 60463. TEL 708-448-4000; Ed. Rich Parmeter. adv. contact: Marilyn Shaw. pub. size: broadsheet; circ. 18,989(paid).

US
REPORTER, THE. 1960. Thu. $.50 newsstand; $24/yr. 12247 S. Harlem Ave., Palos Heights, IL 60463. TEL 708-448-6161. **Owner(s):** Regional Publishing Corp., 12243 S. Harlem Ave., Palos Heights, IL 60463. TEL 708-448-4000; Ed. Jack Murray; Pub. Charles Richards; adv. contact: Carol McLaughlin. pub. size: broadsheet; circ. 19,098(paid).

US
WORTH-PALOS REPORTER. 1960. Thu. $.50 newsstand; $24/yr. 12247 S. Harlem, Palos Heights, IL 60463. TEL 708-448-6161. **Owner(s):** Charles Richards, 12243 S. Harlem, Palos Heights, IL 60463. TEL 708-448-4000; Ed. Jack Murry Pub. Charles Richards; adv. contact: Carol McLaughlin. pub. size: broadsheet; circ. 17,549(paid).

US
WORTH-RIDGE REPORTER. 1960. Wed. $.50 newsstand; $24/yr. 12247 S. Harlem Ave., Palos Heights, IL 60463. TEL 708-448-6161. **Owner(s):** Regional Publishing Corp., 12243 S. Harlem Ave., Palos Heights, IL 60463. TEL 708-448-4000; Ed. Jack Murray; Pub. Charles Richards; adv. contact: Carol McLaughlin. photos; pub. size: broadsheet; circ. 17,966(paid).

PANA

US
PANA NEWS-PALLADIUM. 1869. s-w.: Mon. & Thu. $.40 newsstand; $26/yr. in cy.; $31/yr. in state; $33/yr. out of state. 205 S. Locust St., Pana, IL 62557. TEL 217-562-2113; FAX 217-562-3729. **Owner(s):** Pana News, Inc., 205 S. Locust, Pana, IL 62557. TEL 217-562-2113; FAX 217-562-3729; Ed. Tom Latonis. adv. contact: Patricia Spracklen. photos; pub. size: broadsheet; circ. 4,700(paid).

PARK RIDGE

US   ISSN 0745-8681
DES PLAINES TIMES. 1885. Thu. $20/yr. 130 S. Prospect Ave., Park Ridge, IL 60068. TEL 847-696-3133; FAX 847-696-3229. **Owner(s):** Pioneer Press, Inc., 3701 W. Lake Ave., Glenview, IL 60025. TEL 847-486-9200; Ed. Carroll Falman; Pub. Tom Neri; adv. contact: John Meyer. pub. size: broadsheet; circ. 12,000(paid).

US   ISSN 0895-0105
EDGEBROOK TIMES REVIEW. 1985. Thu. $.75 newsstand; $19.95/yr. 130 S. Prospect Ave., Park Ridge, IL 60028. TEL 847-696-3133. **Owner(s):** Pioneer Press, Inc., 3701 W. Lake Ave., Glenview, IL 60025. TEL 847-846-9200; Ed. Anne Lunde; Pub. Thomas Neri; pub. size: broadsheet; circ. 2,194(paid).

US
EDISON-NORWOOD TIMES REVIEW. 1937. Thu. $.75 newsstand; $18.95/yr. in cy. 130 S. Prospect Ave., Park Ridge, IL 60068. TEL 847-696-3133; FAX 847-696-3229. **Owner(s):** Pioneer Press, Inc., 3701 W. Lake Ave., Glen View, IL 60025. TEL 847-486-9200; Ed. Tom Ganz. adv.; photos; pub. size: broadsheet; circ. 9,300(controlled & paid).

US   ISSN 0895-0121
NILES HERALD SPECTATOR. 1986. Wed. $.75 newsstand; $18.95/yr. in cy. 130 S. Prospect Ave., Park Ridge, IL 60068. TEL 847-696-3133; FAX 847-696-3229. **Owner(s):** Pioneer Press, Inc., 3701 W. Lake Ave., Glen View, IL 60025. TEL 847-486-9200; Ed. Tom Ganz. adv.; pub. size: broadsheet; circ. 5,158(paid).

US   ISSN 0885-7814
NORRIDGE-HARWOOD HEIGHTS NEWS. 1985. Thu. $1 newsstand; $15.95/yr. 130 S. Prospect Ave., Park Ridge, IL 60068. TEL 847-696-3133; FAX 847-696-3229. **Owner(s):** Sun Times, Inc., 401 N. Wabash Ave., Chicago, IL 60611. TEL 312-321-3000; Ed. Tom Ganz. adv.; pub. size: tabloid; circ. 2,900(paid).

US   ISSN 0744-5385
PARK RIDGE HERALD ADVOCATE. 1933. Thu. $1 newsstand; $19.95/yr. 130 S. Prospect Ave., Park Ridge, IL 60068. TEL 847-696-3133; FAX 847-696-3229. **Owner(s):** American Publishing Co., 606 N. Van Buren, P.O. Box 520, Marion, IL 62959. TEL 618-993-1711; Ed. Tom Ganz. adv.; pub. size: tabloid; circ. 7,000(paid).

US   ISSN 0895-0113
ROSEMONT TIMES. 1981. Wed. $.75 newsstand; $18.95/yr. in cy. 130 S. Prospect Ave., Park Ridge, IL 60068. TEL 847-696-3133; FAX 847-696-3229. **Owner(s):** Pioneer Press, Inc., 3701 W. Lake Ave., Glen View, IL 60025. TEL 847-486-9200; Ed. Tom Ganz. adv.; pub. size: broadsheet; circ. 1,506(paid).

PAXTON

US
LODA TIMES. 1888. Wed. $.35 newsstand; $20/yr. in cy.; $25/yr. out of cy. 218 N. Market St., Paxton, IL 60957. TEL 217-379-2356; FAX 217-379-3104. **Owner(s):** Paxton Printing Co., 218 N. Market St., Paxton, IL 60957. TEL 217-379-4313; Ed. Bob Maney; Pub. Paul E. Anderson; adv. contact: Toni Swan. pub. size: broadsheet; circ. 400(paid).

US
RECORD TIMES, THE. 1865. Wed. $.35 newsstand; $20/yr. in cy.; $25/yr. out of cy. 218 N. Market St., Paxton, IL 60957. TEL 217-379-2356; FAX 217-379-3104. **Owner(s):** Paxton Printing Co., 218 N. Market St., Paxton, IL 60957. TEL 217-379-4313; Ed. Bob Maney; Pub. Paul E. Anderson; adv. contact: Toni Swan. pub. size: broadsheet; circ. 2,100(paid).

PEORIA

US
PEORIA HEIGHTS HERALD. 1940. Thu. $.35 newsstand; $15/yr. 1334 E. Samuel Ave., Peoria, IL 61614. TEL 309-688-2822. **Owner(s):** Jim Mansfield, 1334 E. Samuel Ave., Peoria, IL 61614. TEL 309-688-2822; Pub. Jim Mansfield; adv.; photos; pub. size: tabloid; circ. 1,000(paid).

US
PEORIA OBSERVER. 1962. Wed. free local; $20.80/yr. mailed. 1616 W. Pioneer Pkwy., Peoria, IL 61615. TEL 309-692-4910; FAX 309-692-6447. **Owner(s):** Fleming Publishing Co., 100 Detroit Ave., Morton, IL 61550. TEL 309-263-2211; Ed. Josh Bradshaw. adv.; photos; pub. size: tabloid; circ. 26,300(free & paid).

PERCY

US
COUNTY JOURNAL. 1980. Thu. $.50 newsstand; $17/yr. 1101 E. Pine, Percy, IL 62272. TEL 618-497-8272; FAX 618-497-2607. **Owner(s):** Gerald Willis, 1101 E. Pine, Percy, IL 62272. TEL 618-497-8272; FAX 618-497-2607; Larry Willis, 1101 E. Pine, Percy, IL 62272. TEL 618-497-8272; FAX 618-497-2607; Pub. Larry Willis; adv. contact: Judy Willis. photos; pub. size: broadsheet; circ. 6,800(controlled & free).

PETERSBURG

US
PETERSBURG OBSERVER. 1874. Thu. $.50 newsstand; $18/yr. in state. 235 E. Sangamon, Petersburg, IL 62675-0350. TEL 217-632-2236; FAX 217-632-2237. **Owner(s):** Harriett C. Shaw, P.O. Box 350, Petersburg, IL 62675. TEL 217-632-2236; Ed. Jane Shaw Cutright. adv.; pub. size: broadsheet; circ. 3,250(paid).

PLAINFIELD

US
ENTERPRISE, THE. 1887. Wed. $.40 newsstand; $15/yr. in cy.; $22/yr. out of cy.; $30/yr. out of state. 519 W. Lockport St., Plainfield, IL 60544. TEL 815-436-2431; FAX 815-436-2592. **Owner(s):** Enterprise Printing, 519 W. Lockport St., Plainfield, IL 60544. TEL 815-436-2431; FAX 815-436-2592; Ed. Deborah Danielski; Pub. Wayne Perry; adv.; photos; pub. size: tabloid; circ. 12,300(free & paid).

US
FOX VALLEY SHOPPING NEWS, THE. 1873. Thu. free local; $38/yr. elsewhere. P.O. Box 609, Plainfield, IL 60544. TEL 708-553-7431; FAX 708-553-0310. **Owner(s):** Copley Press, Inc., 7776 Ivanhoe Ave., La Jolla, CA 92037. TEL 619-454-0411; Ed. Dick Whitfield; Pub. Dick Whitfield; adv.; pub. size: tabloid; circ. 26,300(paid).
    Formerly: Sandwich Tri-County Today.

PRINCETON

US   ISSN 0894-1181

BUREAU COUNTY REPUBLICAN. 1847. 3/wk.: Tue., Thu., Sat. $.50 newsstand; $54.85/yr. local; $64.75/yr. elsewhere. P.O. Box 340, Princeton, IL 61356-0340. TEL 815-875-4461. **Owner(s):** Shaw Newspaper Co., 444 Pine Hill Dr., Dixon, IL 61021. TEL 815-284-4000; Ed. Lori Hamer; Pub. Steve Fisher; pub. size: broadsheet; circ. 8,000(paid).
   Formerly: Spring Valley's Bureau County Republican.

RANTOUL

US

RANTOUL PRESS. 1874. Wed. $.45 newsstand; $25.50/yr. 1332 E. Harmon Dr., Rantoul, IL 61866-0909. TEL 217-892-9615; FAX 217-892-9451. **Owner(s):** East Central Communications, Inc., 1332 E. Harmon Dr., Rantoul, IL 61866. TEL 217-892-9615; Ed. Chris Slack; Pub. Dennis C. Kaster; adv.; photos; pub. size: broadsheet; circ. 11,935(free & paid).

RED BUD

US

NORTH COUNTY NEWS. 1959. Thu. $.50 newsstand; $16/yr. in 3 cys.; $19/yr. out of cys. 122-124 S. Main St., Red Bud, IL 62278. TEL 618-282-3803; FAX 618-282-6134. **Owner(s):** Victor L. Mohr, P.O. Box 68, Red Bud, IL 62278; Ed. Michael Mohr; Pub. Michael Mohr; adv. contact: Toni Diewald. pub. size: broadsheet; circ. 4,000(paid).
   Formerly: Red Bud North County News.

RIVERTON

US

RIVERTON REGISTER. 1948. Wed. $.25 newsstand; $12/yr. in cy.; $14/yr. out of cy. 100 N. Sixth St., Riverton, IL 62561-0200. TEL 217-629-9247. **Owner(s):** Rhodes Publications, 100 N. Sixth St., Riverton, IL 62561-0200. TEL 217-629-9247; Ed. Barbara Rhodes; Pub. Barbara Rhodes; adv.; photos; pub. size: tabloid; circ. 2,000(paid).

US

TRI CITY REGISTER. 1948. Wed. $.25 newsstand; $12/yr. in cy.; $14/yr. out of cy. 100 N. Sixth St., Riverton, IL 62561-0200. TEL 217-629-9247. **Owner(s):** Rhodes Publications, 100 N. Sixth St., Riverton, IL 62561-0200. TEL 217-629-9247; Ed. Barbara Rhodes; Pub. Barbara Rhodes; adv.; photos; pub. size: tabloid; circ. 2,000(paid).

US

WILLIAMSVILLE SUN. 1948. Wed. $.20 newsstand; $10/yr. in cy.; $12/yr. out of cy. 100 N. Sixth St., Riverton, IL 62561-0200. TEL 217-629-9247. **Owner(s):** Rhodes Publications, 100 N. Sixth St., Riverton, IL 62561-0200. TEL 217-629-9247; Ed. Barbara Rhodes; Pub. Barbara Rhodes; adv.; photos; pub. size: tabloid; circ. 2,000(paid).

ROANOKE

US

ROANOKE REVIEW. 1913. Thu. $.75 newsstand; $24/yr. in cy.; $28/yr. in cy.; $32/yr. out of state. 105 E. Broad, Roanoke, IL 61561. TEL 309-923-5841; FAX 309-923-5841. **Owner(s):** San Francisco Chronicle, 901 Mission St., San Francisco, CA 94103; Ed. Cheryl Wolfe; Pub. Mark Barra; adv.; photos; pub. size: broadsheet; circ. 1,043(free & paid).

ROCHELLE

US

ROCHELLE NEWS LEADER. 1921. 3/wk.: Tue., Thu., Sun. $.50 newsstand; $62/yr. 211 Hwy. 38, E., Rochelle, IL 61068. TEL 815-562-4171; FAX 815-567-7048. **Owner(s):** Rochelle Newspapers, Inc. P.O. Box 46, Rochelle, IL 61068. TEL 815-562-4171; Ed. Jeff Robertson; Pub. Tom Cross; adv. contact: Pat Duffy. pub. size: broadsheet; circ. 5,500(paid).

ROSEVILLE

US

ROSEVILLE INDEPENDENT. Wed. $.40 newsstand; $17/yr. in cy.; $19/yr. out of cy.; $22/yr. out of state. Hwy. 67, Roseville, IL 61473. TEL 309-426-2255; FAX 309-462-3321. **Owner(s):** Acklin Newspaper Group, P.O. Box 32, Abington, IL 61410. TEL 309-462-5758; FAX 309-462-3221; Ed. Phil Gerding; Pub. Joe Acklin; pub. size: tabloid; circ. 850(paid).

RUSHVILLE

US

RUSHVILLE TIMES, THE. 1848. Wed. $.40 newsstand; $15/yr. in state; $24/yr. out of state. 110 E. Lafayette, Rushville, IL 62681. TEL 217-322-3321; FAX 217-322-2138. **Owner(s):** Wayne Perry, P.O. Box 226, Rushville, IL 62681. TEL 217-322-3321; Ed. Allan Icenogle; Pub. Wayne Perry; adv. contact: Pat Grate. pub. size: standard; circ. 3,375(paid).

SALEM

US

SALEM TIMES-COMMONER. 1860. 3/wk.: Mon., Wed., Fri. $.35 newsstand; $37.62/yr. carrier. 120 S. Broadway, Salem, IL 62881-0548. TEL 618-548-3330; FAX 618-548-3593. **Owner(s):** Salem Times-Commoner, 120 S. Broadway, Salem, IL 62881-0548. TEL 618-548-3330; Ed. Lela Colclasure; Pub. Francis Rees; adv.; pub. size: broadsheet; circ. 5,000(paid).

SAVANNA

US

NORTHWESTERN ILLINOIS DISPATCH. 1960. Wed. free. 121 Main St., Savanna, IL 61074. TEL 815-273-2277; **Owner(s):** Robert W. Watson, 121 Main St., Savanna, IL 61074. TEL 815-273-2277; Ed. Robert W. Watson; Pub. Robert W. Watson; adv. contact: Pat Shepherd. pub. size: tabloid; circ. 11,500(free).

SAVANNA TIMES JOURNAL

US

SAVANNA TIMES JOURNAL. 1875. Tue. $.50 newsstand; $20/yr. in cy.; $26/yr. out of cy. 121 Main St., Savanna, IL 61074. TEL 815-273-2277; FAX 815-273-2751. **Owner(s):** Robert W. Watson, 121 Main St., Savanna, IL 61074. TEL 815-273-2277; Ed. Robert W. Watson; Pub. Robert W. Watson; adv. contact: Pat Shepherd. pub. size: tabloid; circ. 2,250(paid).

SOUTH HOLLAND

US

SHOPPER, THE. 1957. Wed. free. 924 E. 162nd St., South Holland, IL 60473. TEL 708-333-5901; FAX 708-333-9630. **Owner(s):** Shopper, The, 924 E. 162nd St., South Holland, IL 60473. TEL 708-333-5901; Ed. Arlo Kalemeyn. pub. size: tabloid; circ. 48,000(free).

SPARTA

US

SPARTA NEWS PLAINDEALER. 1863. Wed. $.50 newsstand; $18/yr. in cy.; $20/yr. out of cy.; $27/yr. out of state. 116 W. Main St., Sparta, IL 62286. TEL 618-443-2145 FAX 618-443-2780. **Owner(s):** Walt Disney Co., 500 S. Buena Vista St., Burbank, CA 91521. TEL 818-560-5300; Ed. Mike Springston; Pub. J. Bart McDowell; adv. contact: Carol Mulholland. pub. size: broadsheet; circ. 5,000(paid).

SPRINGFIELD

US

ILLINOIS TIMES. 1975. Thu. free; $38/yr. 610 S. Seventh, Springfield, IL 62703. TEL 217-753-2226; FAX 217-753-2281. **Owner(s):** Illinois Times, Inc. P.O. Box 3524, Springfield, IL 62708. TEL 217-753-2226; Ed. Fletcher Farrar, Jr.; Pub. Fletcher Farrar, Jr.; pub. size: broadsheet; circ. 33,000(free & paid). **Wire Service(s):** Alternative News Service.

US

SPRINGFIELD SHOPPER. 1975. Thu. free; $20/yr. mailed. 2001 W. Monroe, Springfield, IL 62704. TEL 217-546-3295; FAX 217-546-3133. **Owner(s):** Don Hecke, P.O. Box 142, Springfield, IL 62705. TEL 217-546-3295; pub. size: tabloid; circ. evening 29,500(free & paid).

STAUNTON

US

STAUNTON STAR-TIMES. 1878. Thu. $.35 newsstand; $19/yr. 108 W. Main St., Staunton, IL 62088. TEL 618-635-2000; FAX 618-635-5281. **Owner(s):** Star-Times Publishing Co., Inc., 108 W. Main St., Staunton, IL 62088. TEL 618-635-2000; FAX 618-635-5281; Ed. Walter F. Haase. adv.; photos; bk.rev.; pub. size: broadsheet; circ. 3,900(paid).

ST. ELMO

US

SAINT ELMO BANNER. Tue. $.50 newsstand; $17.50/yr. in cy.; $20.50/yr. elsewhere. P.O. Box 10, St. Elmo, IL 62458. TEL 618-829-3246; FAX 618-829-3246. **Owner(s):** Joe Baker & Greg Hoskins, P.O. Box 10, St. Elmo, IL 62458. TEL 618-829-3246; FAX 618-829-3246; Ed. Joe Baker. adv.; photos; pub. size: tabloid; circ. 1,200(paid).

STRONGHURST

US
HENDERSON COUNTY QUILL. 1926. Wed. $.50 newsstand; $19/yr. in state; $20/yr. out of state. 102 N. Broadway, Stronghurst, IL 61480. TEL 309-924-1871; FAX 309-924-1124. **Owner(s):** Dessa Rodeffer, 702 Harmony St., Stronghurst, IL 61480. TEL 309-924-1871; FAX 309-924-1124; Belva Bell, 402 N. Broadway, Stronghurst, IL 61480. TEL 309-924-1263; FAX 309-924-1124; Ed. Belva Bell; Pub. Dessa Rodeffer; adv. contact: Shirley Linder. photos; bk.rev.; pub. size: tabloid; circ. 2,000(paid).

SULLIVAN

US
NEWS-PROGRESS. 1961. s-w.: Mon. & Wed. $.50 newsstand; $20/yr. in cy.; $25/yr. out of cy. 100 W. Monroe St., Sullivan, IL 61951. TEL 217-728-7381; FAX 217-728-2020. **Owner(s):** Marion E. Best, 1017 E. Jackson, Sullivan, IL 61951. TEL 217-728-4474; Ed. Marion E. Best; Pub. Marion E. Best; adv. contact: George Lozzi. photos; pub. size: broadsheet; **Wire Service(s):** AP.

SUMNER

US
SUMNER PRESS. 1876. Wed. $.35 newsstand; $15/yr. P.O. Box 126, Sumner, IL 62466. TEL 618-936-2212; FAX 618-936-2858. **Owner(s):** Rosco & Mary Ellen Cummingham, P.O. Box 126, Sumner, IL 62466. TEL 618-936-2212; FAX 618-936-2858; Ed. Jo Ann Dowty; Pub. Rosco Cummingham; adv.; photos; pub. size: standard; circ. 2,100(free & paid).

SYCAMORE

US   ISSN 1071-9784
GENOA-KINGSTON-KIRKLAND NEWS. 1972. Wed. $.50 newsstand; $23.50/yr. in cy. mailed; $33/yr. out of cy. mailed. 216 W. State St., Sycamore, IL 60178. TEL 815-784-5138; FAX 815-899-4329. **Owner(s):** B.F. Shaw Printing Co., 444 Pine Hill Dr., P.O. Box 409, Dixon, IL 61021. TEL 815-284-2222; FAX 815-254-9290; Ed. Gary Koehler; Pub. Roger Coleman; adv. contact: Bernice Bieber. photos; pub. size: broadsheet; circ. 2,805(paid).

US
HAMPSHIRE REGISTER NEWS. 1894. Wed. $.50 newsstand; $23.50/yr. in cy. mailed; $33/yr. out of cy. mailed. 216 W. State St., Sycamore, IL 60178. TEL 815-899-6397; FAX 815-899-4329. **Owner(s):** B.F. Shaw Printing Co., 444 Pine Hill Dr., P.O. Box 409, Dixon, IL 61021. TEL 815-284-2222; Ed. Gary Koehler; Pub. Roger Coleman; adv. contact: Bernice Bieber. photos; pub. size: broadsheet; circ. 1,700(paid).

US   ISSN 0747-3524
SYCAMORE NEWS. 1857. Wed. $.50 newsstand; $23.50/yr. in cy. mailed; $33/yr. out of cy. mailed. 216 W. State St., Sycamore, IL 60178. TEL 815-899-6397; FAX 815-899-4329. **Owner(s):** B.F. Shaw Printing Co., 444 Pine Hill Dr., P.O. Box 409, Dixon, IL 61021. TEL 815-284-2222; Ed. Gary Koehler; Pub. Roger Coleman; adv. contact: Bernice Bieber. photos; pub. size: broadsheet; circ. 10,000(free & paid). **Formerly:** Kishwaukee Independent.

THOMSON

US
CARROLL COUNTY REVIEW. 1863. Wed. $.50 newsstand; $18/yr. in cy. 809 Main St., Thomson, IL 61285. TEL 815-259-2131; FAX 815-259-3226. **Owner(s):** Jonathan K. Whitney, P.O. Box 369, Thomson, IL 61285. TEL 815-259-2131; Ed. Bill Gengenbach; Pub. Jonathan K. Whitney; adv. contact: Nancy G. Whitney. pub. size: tabloid; circ. 2,900(paid).

TINLEY PARK

US
PENNY SAVER. 1965. Tue. free. 17746 S. Oak Park Ave., Tinley Park, IL 60477. TEL 708-429-6400; FAX 708-429-7940. **Owner(s):** Shoppers Enterprise, Inc., 125 Main St., Blue Earth, MN 56013. TEL 507-526-7326; Doug Dance, 17746 S. Oak Park Ave., Tinley Park, IL 60477. TEL 708-429-6400; Ed. Anna Staten; Pub. Doug Dance; adv.; pub. size: tabloid; circ. 300,000(free).

TRENTON

US
TRENTON SUN, THE. 1880. Wed. $.35 newsstand; $15/yr. 15 W. Broadway, Trenton, IL 62293-0118. TEL 618-224-9422; FAX 618-224-9422. **Owner(s):** Sybil & Michael Conley, 15 W. Broadway, Trenton, IL 62293-0118. TEL 618-224-9422; Ed. Michael L. Conley; Pub. Michael L. Conley; adv.; pub. size: broadsheet; circ. 1,400(paid).

TUSCOLA

US
TUSCOLA REVIEW. 1875. Tue. $.50 newsstand; $20/yr. in cy.; $25/yr. out of cy. 115 W. Sale St., Tuscola, IL 61953. TEL 217-253-2358; FAX 217-253-3265. **Owner(s):** Robert Hastings, 115 W. Sale St., Tuscola, IL 61953; Beverly Hastings, 115 W. Sale St., Tuscola, IL 61953; Randy Hastings, 115 W. Sale St., Tuscola, IL 61953; Greg Hastings, 115 W. Sale St., Tuscola, IL 61953; Ed. Randy Hastings; Pub. Robert D. Hastings; adv.; pub. size: broadsheet; circ. 3,600(paid).

VANDALIA

US
VANDALIA LEADER-UNION. 1865. s-w.: Wed. & Fri. $.50 newsstand; $28/yr. 229 S. Fifth St., Vandalia, IL 62471. TEL 618-283-3374; FAX 618-283-0977. **Owner(s):** Landmark Community Newspapers, Inc., P.O. Box 549, Shelbyville, KY 40066. TEL 502-633-4334; Ed. Rich Bauer; Pub. David R. Bell; adv.; pub. size: broadsheet; circ. 5,800(paid).

VIENNA

US
VIENNA TIMES, THE. 1882. Thu. $.40 newsstand; $23/yr. 305 W. Main, Vienna, IL 62995-0457. TEL 618-658-4321. **Owner(s):** Donald L. Sanders, 305 W. Main, Vienna, IL 62995. TEL 618-658-4321; Ed. Donald L. Sanders; Pub. Donald L. Sanders; pub. size: broadsheet.

WASHINGTON

US
WASHINGTON COURIER. 1958. Wed. $22/yr. 100 Ford Ln., Washington, IL 61571. TEL 309-444-3139; FAX 309-444-8505. **Owner(s):** Hagel Publications, Inc., P.O. Box 349, Washington, IL 61571. TEL 309-444-3139; FAX 309-444-8505; Ed. Roger Hagel. adv.; pub. size: tabloid; circ. 22,000(paid).

WATERLOO

US
WATERLOO REPUBLIC-TIMES. 1890. Wed. $.30 newsstand; $18/yr. in cy.; $20/yr. out of cy.; $23/yr. out of state. 222 S. Main St., Waterloo, IL 62298. TEL 618-939-3814; FAX 618-939-3815. **Owner(s):** Walt Disney Co., 500 S. Buena Vista St., Burbank, CA 91521. TEL 818-560-5300; Ed. Marvin Cortner; Pub. Mark Schmershal; adv. contact: Karen Domyan. photos; bk.rev.; pub. size: broadsheet; circ. 4,800(paid).

WAVERLY

US
WAVERLY JOURNAL. 1872. Fri. $.50 newsstand; $20/yr. 130 S. Pearl St., Waverly, IL 62692. TEL 217-435-9221; FAX 217-435-4511. **Owner(s):** Nancy Springer, 130 S. Pearl St., Waverly, IL 62692. TEL 217-435-9221; FAX 217-435-4511; Pub. Nancy Springer; adv. contact: Nancy Springer. photos; bk.rev.; pub. size: tabloid; circ. 1,577(paid).

WEST CHICAGO

US
WARRENVILLE FREE PRESS. 1986. Thu. $.50 newsstand; $25/yr. 100 Arbor Ave., West Chicago, IL 60185. TEL 708-231-0500; FAX 708-231-6813. **Owner(s):** Wayne G. Woltman, 100 Arbor Ave., West Chicago, IL 60185. TEL 708-231-0500; Ed. Marc Alberts; Pub. Wayne G. Woltman; adv. contact: Robert Langness. pub. size: tabloid; circ. 3,000(paid).

US   ISSN 0273-6993
WINFIELD PRESS. 1980. Thu. $.50 newsstand; $25/yr. 100 Arbor Ave., West Chicago, IL 60185. TEL 708-231-0500; FAX 708-231-6813. **Owner(s):** Wayne G. Woltman, 100 Arbor Ave., West Chicago, IL 60185. TEL 708-231-0500; Ed. Marc Alberts; Pub. Wayne G. Woltman; adv. contact: Robert Langness. pub. size: tabloid; circ. 600(paid).

WHITE HALL

US
GREENE PRAIRIE PRESS. Thu. $.50 newsstand; $22/yr. in cy.; $26/yr. out of cy. 112 E. Sherman, White Hall, IL 62092. TEL 217-374-2871; FAX 217-742-3596. **Owner(s):** Elmer Fedder, 112 E. Sherman, White Hall, IL 62092. TEL 217-374-2871; Ed. Merrilyn Fedder; Pub. Elmer Fedder; adv.; pub. size: tabloid; circ. 3,000(paid).

WILMINGTON

US
BRACEVILLE EXPRESS. 1978. Wed. free. 111 S. Water St., Wilmington, IL 60481. TEL 815-476-7966; FAX 815-476-7002. **Owner(s):** George Fisher, 111 S. Water St., Wilmington, IL 60481. TEL 815-476-7966; Ed. Eric Fisher; Pub. George Fisher; adv. contact: George Fisher. pub. size: broadsheet; circ. 570(free).

US
BRAIDWOOD INDEX. 1978. Wed. free. 111 S. Water St., Wilmington, IL 60481. TEL 815-476-7966; FAX 815-476-7002. **Owner(s):** George Fisher, 111 S. Water St., Wilmington, IL 60481. TEL 815-476-7966; Ed. Eric Fisher; Pub. George Fisher; adv. contact: George Fisher. pub. size: broadsheet; circ. 2,500(free).

US
COAL CITY EXPRESS. 1978. Wed. free. 111 S. Water St., Wilmington, IL 60481. TEL 815-476-7966; FAX 815-476-7002. **Owner(s):** George Fisher, 111 S. Water Street, Wilmington, IL 60481. TEL 815-476-7966; Pub. George Fisher; adv. contact: George Fisher. pub. size: broadsheet; circ. 2,500(free).

US
ELWOOD EXPRESS. 1978. Wed. free. 111 S. Water St., Wilmington, IL 60481. TEL 815-476-7966; FAX 815-476-7002. **Owner(s):** George Fisher, 111 S. Water St., Wilmington, IL 60481. TEL 815-476-7966; Pub. George Fisher; adv. contact: George Fisher. pub. size: broadsheet; circ. 2,500(free).

US
GARDNER SOUTH WILMINGTON POST. 1978. Wed. free. 111 S. Water St., Wilmington, IL 60481. TEL 815-476-7966; FAX 815-476-7002. **Owner(s):** George Fisher, 111 S. Water Street, Wilmington, IL 60481. TEL 815-476-7966; Pub. George Fisher; adv. contact: George Fisher. pub. size: broadsheet; circ. 2,500(free).

US
WILMINGTON ADVOCATE, THE. 1853. Wed. $.50 newsstand; $18/yr. in cy.; $21/yr. out of cy.; $24/yr. out of state. 384 W. Baltimore, Wilmington, IL 60481. TEL 815-476-7511; FAX 815-476-7544. **Owner(s):** Sheridan Bailey, 273 S. Broadway, Coal City, IL 60416. TEL 815-634-2102; Ed. Sheridan Bailey; Pub. Sheridan Bailey; adv.; photos; pub. size: broadsheet; circ. 835(paid).

US
WILMINGTON EXPRESS. Wed. free. 111 S. Water St., Wilmington, IL 60481. TEL 815-476-7966; FAX 815-476-7002. **Owner(s):** George Fisher, 111 S. Water St., Wilmington, IL 60481. TEL 815-476-7966; Ed. Eric Fisher; Pub. George Fisher; adv. contact: George Fisher. pub. size: broadsheet.

US
WILMINGTON FREE PRESS. 1978. Wed. $.50 newsstand; $20/yr. out of cy.; $26/yr. out of cy.; $30/yr. out of state. 111 S. Water St., Wilmington, IL 60481. TEL 815-476-7966; FAX 815-476-7002. **Owner(s):** George Fisher, 111 S. Water St., Wilmington, IL 60481. TEL 815-476-7966; Ed. Eric Fisher; Pub. George Fisher; adv. contact: George Fisher. pub. size: broadsheet; circ. 1,775(paid).
   Formerly: Wilmington Express.

WOODSTOCK

US
WOODSTOCK INDEPENDENT, THE. 1987. Wed. $.75 newsstand; $25/yr. local. 671 E. Calhoun St., Woodstock, IL 60093-4262. TEL 815-338-8040: FAX 815-338-8177. **Owner(s):** Cheryl B. Wormley, 671 E. Calhoun, Woodstock, IL 60093. TEL 815-338-8040; FAX 815-338-8177; Denise Graff Ponstein, 671 E. Calhoun, Woodstock, IL 60098. TEL 815-338-8040; FAX 815-338-8177; Pub. Cheryl B. Wormley; adv. contact: Brent Maring. photos; pub. size: tabloid; circ. 2,500(paid).

WORDEN

US
ADVERTISER, THE. Mon. free. 125 E. Wall St., Worden, IL 62097-0490. TEL 618-459-3655; FAX 618-459-3655. **Owner(s):** Bunker Hill Publications, Inc., 150 N. Washington, Bunker Hill, IL 62014. TEL 618-585-4411; Pub. John M. Galer; adv. contact: Eve Pickerill. pub. size: broadsheet; circ. 7,187(free).

US
MADISON COUNTY CHRONICLE. 1978. Thu. $.25 newsstand; $9.50/yr. in cy.; $11.50 out of cy.; $13.50 out of state. 125 E. Wall St., Worden, IL 62097-0490. TEL 618-459-3655; FAX 618-459-3655. **Owner(s):** John M. Galer, 150 N. Washington, Bunker Hill, IL 62014. TEL 618-585-4411; Ed. Vera Eckhardt; Pub. John M. Galer; adv. contact: Eve Pickerill. photos; pub. size: tabloid; circ. 1,200(paid).

YORKVILLE

US
KENDALL COUNTY RECORD. 1864. Thu. $.50 newsstand; $21/yr. 222 S. Bridge St., Yorkville, IL 60560. TEL 708-553-7034; FAX 708-553-7085. **Owner(s):** Jeff & Kathy Farran, 222 S. Bridge St., Yorkville, IL 60560. TEL 708-553-7034; Ed. Kathy Farren; Pub. Jeff Farren; pub. size: tabloid; circ. 3,800(paid).
   Formerly: Yorkville Kendall County Record.

ZION

US
ZION-BENTON NEWS. 1929. Thu. $.50 newsstand; $16.95/yr. Lake Kenosha Cy.; $18.95/yr. out of cy. 2719 Elisha Ave. Zion, IL 60099. TEL 847-746-9000; FAX 847-746-9150. **Owner(s):** United Communications Corp., 715 58th St., Kenosha, WI 53141. TEL 414-657-1000; Ed. Mona Shannon; Pub. Frank Misureli; pub. size: tabloid; circ. 4,000(paid).

INDIANA

ALEXANDRIA

US
ALEXANDRIA TIMES-TRIBUNE. 1885. Wed. $.50 newsstand; $22/yr. in cy.; $29/yr. out of cy. One Harrison Sq., Alexandria, IN 46001. TEL 317-724-4469. **Owner(s):** Jack L. Barnes, 317 S. Anderson, Elwood, IN 46036. TEL 317-552-3355; Ed. Linda Ferris. adv. contact: Cindy Tyner. bk.rev.; pub. size: standard; circ. 3,600(paid). **Wire Service(s):** AP.

ANGOLA

US
HERALD-REPUBLICAN. 1857. s-w.: Wed. & Fri. $.50 newsstand; $39.75/yr. in cy.; $42.75/yr. out of cy. 45 S. Public Square, Angola, IN 46703. TEL 219-665-3117; FAX 219-665-2322. **Owner(s):** Home News Enterprises, 333 Second St., Columbus, IN 47201. TEL 812-372-7811; Ed. Rick Martinez. adv. contact: David Damerow. photos; pub. size: standard; circ. 6,500(free). **Wire Service(s):** CNS.

ATTICA

US   ISSN 1060-5495
FOUNTAIN COUNTY NEIGHBOR. 1851. s-w.: Tue. & Fri. $40/yr. in cy.; $51/yr. out of cy. & state. State Rd. 28 E., Attica, IN 47918. TEL 317-762-2411; FAX 317-762-2163. **Owner(s):** Twin States Publishing Co., Inc., 1322 E. Main St., Attica, IN 47918. TEL 317-762-2411; FAX 317-762-1547; Ed. Tina McGrady; Pub. Bette D. Schmid; adv. contact: Julie Lasko. pub. size: broadsheet; circ. 2,000(paid).

US
MESSENGER, THE. Tue. free. 1322 E Main St., Attica, IN 47918. TEL 317-762-2411; FAX 317-762-2163. **Owner(s):** Twin States Publishing Co., Inc., State Rd. 28, E., Attica, IN 47918. TEL 317-762-2411; Ed. Kirk Johannesen; Pub. Bette D. Schmid adv. contact: Julie Lasko. pub. size: broadsheet; circ. 11,000(free).

AUBURN

US
DEKALB COUNTY ADVERTISER. 1958. Tue. free. 118 W. Ninth St., Auburn, IN 46706. TEL 219-357-3806; FAX 219-357-3806. **Owner(s):** Kendallville Publishing Co., P.O. Box 39, Kendallville, IN 46755. TEL 219-347-0400; adv. contact: Martin Alexander. pub. size: broadsheet; circ. 18,700(free).

BATESVILLE

US
BATESVILLE HERALD-TRIBUNE. 1890. s-w.: Wed. & Sat. $.50 newsstand; $42/yr. 4 W. Pearl St., Batesville, IN 47006. TEL 812-934-4343; FAX 812-934-6406. **Owner(s):** American Publishing Co., 606 N. Van Buren, P.O. Box 520, Marion, IL 62959. TEL 615-993-1711; Ed. Don Krause; Pub. Beverly Schuld; adv. contact: Cathy Sullivan. photos; pub. size: broadsheet; circ. 7,500(paid).

BEECH GROVE

US
PERRY TOWNSHIP WEEKLY. 1928. w. free. 301 Main St., Beech Grove, IN 46107. TEL 317-787-3291; FAX 317-787-3325. **Owner(s):** Reporter-Times, Inc., 60 S. Jefferson, Martinsville, IN 46151. TEL 317-342-3311; Ed. Amy Uhls; Pub. Chris Drews; adv.; pub. size: broadsheet; circ. 25,000(free).
   Formerly: Beech Grove Perry Township Weekly.

BERNE

US

BERNE TRI-WEEKLY NEWS. 1896. 3/wk.: Mon., Wed., Fri. $.35 newsstand; $39.95/yr. 153 S. Jefferson St., Berne, IN 46711. TEL 219-589-2101; FAX 219-589-8614. **Owner(s):** EP Graphics, 153 S. Jefferson, Berne, IN 46711. TEL 219-589-2101 Pub. Carl H. Muselman; adv. contact: Jeremy Liechty. photos; bk.rev.; pub. size: broadsheet; circ 3,700(paid).

BICKNELL

US   ISSN 1060-6173

NORTH KNOX NEWS. 1864. 3/wk.: Tue., Thu., Sat. $.50 newsstand; $4/mo. in town; $90/yr. in cy.; $105/yr. out of cy. 301 W. 11th St., Bicknell, IN 47512. TEL 812-735-2230; FAX 812-735-2244. **Owner(s):** Central Newspapers, Inc., 135 N. Pennsylvania Ave., Indianapolis, IN 46204. TEL 317-231-9200; Ed. Carol Gwinnup; Pub. Michael Quayle; adv.; photos; pub. size: broadsheet; circ. morning 1,400(paid). **Wire Service(s):** AP.
   Formerly: Knox County Daily News.

BOONVILLE

US

BOONVILLE STANDARD. 1875. Wed. $.50 newsstand; $26/yr. 204 W. Locust St., P.O. Box 71, Boonville, IN 47601. TEL 812-897-2330; FAX 812-897-3703. **Owner(s):** Warrick Publishing Co., 204 W. Locust St., Boonville, IN 47601. TEL 812-897-2330; Ed. David Pearce; Pub. Myra Teal; adv.; pub. size: broadsheet; circ. 4,327(paid).

BROOKVILLE

US

BROOKVILLE AMERICAN-DEMOCRAT. 1832. Wed. $.30 newsstand; $14/yr. 533 Main St., Brookville, IN 47012. TEL 317-647-4221; FAX 317-647-4811. **Owner(s):** Whitewater Publications, P.O. Box 38, Brookville, IN 47012. TEL 317-647-4221; Ed. John L. Estridge. adv. contact: Becky Trammell. photos; pub. size: broadsheet; circ. 5,600(paid).

BROWNSTOWN

US

JACKSON COUNTY BANNER. 1869. s-w.: Tue. & Thu. $.35 newsstand; $28/yr. 116 E. Cross St., Brownstown, IN 47220. TEL 812-358-2111; FAX 812-358-5606. **Owner(s):** Jackson County Banner Inc., The, 116 E. Cross St., Brownstown, IN 47220. TEL 812-358-2111; Pub. Joseph Persinger; adv. contact: Margaret Tormoehlen. photos; pub. size: broadsheet, 4 color photos/art; circ. 4,052(paid). **Wire Service(s):** AP, Newsfinder.

CAMBRIDGE CITY

US

WESTERN WAYNE NEWS. 1991. Wed. $.35 newsstand; $14/yr. in cy.; $18/yr. out of cy.; $22/yr. out of state. 36 W. Main, Cambridge City, IN 47327. TEL 317-478-5448; FAX 317-478-5155. **Owner(s):** Ed Buhl, 36 W. Main, Cambridge City, IN 47327. TEL 317-478-5448; FAX 317-479-5155; Janis Buhl, 36 W. Main, Cambridge City, IN 47327. TEL 317-478-5448; FAX 317-478-5155; Pub. Janis Buhl; adv. contact: Janice Buhl. photos; pub. size: tabloid; circ. 2,225(free & paid).

CENTERVILLE

US

CENTERVILLE CRUSADER. 1966. Wed. $.25 newsstand; $13/yr. in cy.; $15/yr. out of cy. P.O. Box 26, Centerville, IN 47330. TEL 317-825-2728. **Owner(s):** Nancy D. Kinder, P.O. Box 26, Centerville, IN 47330. TEL 317-825-2728; Peggy Patterson, P.O. Box 26, Centerville, IN 47330. TEL 317-855-5262; Ed. Nancy D. Kinder; Pub. Peggy Patterson; adv.; photos; pub. size: tabloid; circ. 1,360(free & paid).

CHARLESTOWN

US

LEADER, THE. 1919. Wed. $15/yr. 382 Main Cross, Charlestown, IN 47111. TEL 812-256-3377; FAX 812-967-3194. **Owner(s):** Green Banner Publications, P.O. Box 38, Charleston, IN 47111. TEL 812-256-3377; Ed. Mark Grigsby; Pub. Joe Green; adv. contact: John Roberts. pub. size: tabloid; circ. 10,439(free).

CLAY CITY

US

NEWS, THE. 1912. Wed. $.35 newsstand; $16/yr. 717 Main St., Clay City, IN 47841. TEL 812-939-2163; FAX 812-939-2286. **Owner(s):** News, The, 717 Main St., Clay City, IN 47841. TEL 812-939-2163; FAX 812-939-2286; Ed. Rhonda Riggle. adv.; photos; pub. size: standard; circ. 2,000(paid).

CORYDON

US

CLARION NEWS. 1939. Wed. free local area; $.45 newsstand; $17/yr. out of area. 301 N. Capitol Ave., Corydon, IN 47112. TEL 812-738-4552; FAX 812-738-1909. **Owner(s):** O'Bannon Publishing Co., Inc., 301 N. Capitol Ave., Corydon, IN 47112. TEL 812-738-4552; Ed. Sara Combs; Pub. Dennis L. Huber; adv. contact: Mark Young. photos; pub. size: standard; circ. 15,000(free).
   Formerly: Clarion, The.

US

CORYDON DEMOCRAT. Wed. $.75 newsstand; $24/yr. in area; $23/yr. senior citizens. 301 N. Capitol Ave., Corydon, IN 47112. TEL 812-738-2211; FAX 812-738-1909. **Owner(s):** O'Bannon Publishing Co., Inc., 301 N. Capital Ave., Corydon, IN 47112. TEL 812-738-2211; Ed. Randy West; Pub. Dennis Huber; pub. size: standard; circ. 8,500(paid).

CROTHERSVILLE

US

CROTHERSVILLE TIMES. 1980. Wed. $.25 newsstand; $10/yr. 510 Moore St., Crothersville, IN 47229. TEL 812-793-2188; FAX 812-793-2188. **Owner(s):** Curt Kovener, P.O. Box 141, Crothersville, IN 47229. TEL 812-793-2188; FAX 812-793-2188; Mary A. Kovener, P.O. Box 141, Crothersville, IN 47229. TEL 812-723-2188; FAX 812-723-2188; Ed. Curt Kovener; Pub. Curt Kovener; adv.; photos; bk.rev.; pub. size: tabloid; circ. 1,200(paid).

CROWN POINT

US

LAKE COUNTY STAR. 1857. s-w.: Tue. & Thu. $.50 newsstand; $37/yr. 15 N. Court St., Crown Point, IN 46307. TEL 219-663-4212; FAX 219-663-0137. **Owner(s):** American Publishing Co., 606 N. Van Buren, P.O. Box 520, Marion, IL 62959. TEL 618-993-1711; Ed. Andrew Steele. adv.; photos; pub. size: tabloid; circ. 27,000(free & paid).
   Formerly: Crownpoint Lake County Star.

CULVER

US

CULVER CITIZEN. 1894. Wed. $.50/issue; $18/yr. in state; $21/yr. out of state. 107 S. Main St., Culver, IN 46511. TEL 219-842-3229; FAX 219-935-0083. **Owner(s):** Citizen Publications, Inc., 107 S. Main St., Culver, IN 46511. TEL 219-842-3229; FAX 219-935-0083; Ed. Judith L. Karst; Pub. Frederick A. Karst; adv.; photos; pub. size: broadsheet; circ. 1,664(controlled & paid).

DANVILLE

US

REPUBLICAN, THE. 1847. Thu. $.30 newsstand; $14/yr. 6 E. Main, Danville, IN 46122. TEL 317-745-2777; FAX 317-745-2777. **Owner(s):** Betty J. Weesner, 6 Main St., Danville, IN 46122. TEL 317-745-2777; FAX 317-745-2777; adv.; pub. size: standard; circ. 1,300(paid).

EDINBURGH

US

TRI-COUNTY NEWS. 1986. Wed. free; $35/yr. 121 E. Main Cross, Edinburgh, IN 46124. TEL 812-526-6372; FAX 812-526-6379. **Owner(s):** Gary Storie, 121 E. Main Cross, Edinburgh, IN 46124. TEL 812-526-6372; Ed. Jerry Wilson; Pub. Gary Storie; adv.; pub. size: broadsheet; circ. 8,300(paid).
   Formerly: Tri County Newspaper.

ELKHART

US

PAPER, THE. 1976. Mon. free. 229 W. Marion St., Elkhart, IN 46516. TEL 219-522-4111; FAX 219-522-7448. **Owner(s):** Della Baumgartner, P.O. Box 188, Milford, IN 46542. TEL 219-658-4815; FAX 219-658-4701; Ron & Gloria Baumgartner, P.O. Box 177, Milford, IN 46542. TEL 219-457-5000; FAX 219-658-4701; Ed. Jeri Seely; Pub. Della Baumgartner; adv. contact: Kip Schumm. photos; pub. size: tabloid; circ. 27,360(controlled & free).

ELLETTSVILLE

US

JOURNAL, THE. 1939. Wed. $.30 newsstand; $16/yr. 211 N. Sale St., Ellettsville, IN 47429. TEL 812-876-2254; FAX 812-876-2853. **Owner(s):** John T. Gillaspy, 211 N. Sale St., Ellettsville, IN 47429. TEL 812-876-2254; FAX 812-876-2853; Ed. Tom Douglas; Pub. John T. Gillaspy; adv. contact: Jane Fiscus. photos; pub. size: standard.

Weeklies

FAIRMOUNT
US

NEWS-SUN. 1872. Wed. $54/yr. 3rd class. 122 S. Main St., Fairmount, IN 46928. TEL 317-948-4165. **Owner(s):** Allen Terhune & Assoc., 122 S. Main St., Fairmount, IN 46928. TEL 317-948-4165; Ed. Allen Terhune; Pub. Jim Terhune; adv.; photos; bk.rev.; pub. size: tabloid; circ. 4,200(paid).

FERDINAND
US

DALE NEWS, THE. 1960. Fri. $.50 newsstand; $15/yr. local; $19/yr. in state; $23/yr. out of state. 113 W. Sixth St., Ferdinand, IN 47532. TEL 812-367-2041; FAX 812-367-2371. **Owner(s):** Miriam & Paul Ash, 113 W. Sixth St., Ferdinand, IN 47532; Richard & Kathy Tretter, 113 W. Sixth St., Ferdinand, IN 47532; Ed. Richard Tretter. adv.; photos; pub. size: broadsheet; circ. 1,700(paid).

FERDINAND NEWS, THE. 1906. Thu. $.50 newsstand; $17/yr. local; $19/yr. in state; $23/yr. out of state. 113 W. Sixth St., Ferdinand, IN 47532. TEL 812-367-2041; FAX 812-367-2371. **Owner(s):** Miriam & Paul Ash, 113 W. Sixth St., Ferdinand, IN 47532; Richard & Kathy Tretter, 113 W. Sixth St., Ferdinand, IN 47532; Ed. Richard Tretter. adv.; photos; pub. size: broadsheet; circ. 3,100(paid).

FISHERS
US

CARMEL NEWS TRIBUNE. 1969. Wed. free; voluntary pay subscriptions. 13095 Publishers Dr., Fishers, IN 46038. TEL 317-598-6397; FAX 317-598-6360. **Owner(s):** Central Newspapers, Inc., 135 N. Pennsylvania Ave., Ste. 1200, Indianapolis, IN 46204-2400. TEL 317-231-9200; Ed. Patricia White; Pub. David Lewis; adv. contact: Terry Coomer. photos; pub. size: broadsheet; circ. 17,750(free & paid).

US

CASTLETON BANNER. 1966. Wed. free; voluntary pay subscriptions. 13095 Publishers Dr., Fishers, IN 46038. TEL 317-598-6397; FAX 317-593-6360. **Owner(s):** Central Newspapers, Inc., 135 N. Pennsylvania Ave., Ste. 1200, Indianapolis, IN 46204-2400. TEL 317-231-9201; Ed. LeeAnn Peake; Pub. David Lewis; adv. contact: Scott Gause. photos; pub. size: broadsheet; circ. 11,700(free & paid). **Wire Service(s):** UPI.

US

FISHERS SUN-HERALD. 1980. Wed. free; voluntary pay subscriptions. 13095 Publishers Dr., Fishers, IN 46038. TEL 317-598-6397; FAX 317-598-6360. **Owner(s):** Central Newspapers, Inc., 135 N. Pennsylvania Ave., Ste. 1200, Indianapolis, IN 46204-2400. TEL 317-231-9201; Ed. Karen Peterson; Pub. Davis Lewis; adv. contact: Scott Gause. photos; pub. size: broadsheet; circ. 4,800(free & paid). **Wire Service(s):** AP.

US

GEIST GAZETTE. 1961. Wed. free; voluntary pay subscriptions. 13095 Publishers Dr., Fishers, IN 46038. TEL 317-598-6397; FAX 317-598-6360. **Owner(s):** Central Newspapers, Inc., 135 N. Pennsylvania Ave., Ste. 1200, Indianapolis, IN 46204-2400. TEL 317-231-9201; Ed. LeeAnn Peake; Pub. David Lewis; adv. contact: Scott Gause. photos; pub. size: broadsheet; circ. 2,000(free & paid).

US

GREENWOOD GAZETTE, THE. 1986. Thu. free; voluntary pay subscriptions. 13095 Publishers Dr., Fishers, IN 46038. TEL 317-598-6397; FAX 317-598-6360. **Owner(s):** Central Newspapers, Inc. 135 N. Pennsylvania St., Indianapolis, IN 46204-2400. TEL 317-231-9200; Ed. Rebecca Collier; Pub. David Lewis; adv. contact: Scott Gause. photos; bk.rev.; pub. size: broadsheet; circ. 14,000(free & paid).

US

HEIGHTS HERALD. 1981. Thu. free; voluntary pay subscriptions. 13095 Publishers Dr., Fishers, IN 46038. TEL 317-598-6397; FAX 317-598-6360. **Owner(s):** Central Newspapers, Inc. 9615 N. College Ave., Indianapolis, IN 46280. TEL 317-844-3311; Ed. Karen Peterson; Pub. David Lewis; adv. contact: Scott Gause. photos; pub. size: broadsheet; circ. 3,975(free & paid). **Wire Service(s):** UPI.

Formerly: Northern Heights Herald.

US

LAWRENCE TIMES. 1970. Wed. free; voluntary pay subscriptions. 13095 Publishers Dr, Fishers, IN 46038. TEL 317-598-6397; FAX 317-598-6360. **Owner(s):** Central Newspapers, Inc. 135 N. Pennsylvania Ave., Ste. 1200, Indianapolis, IN 46280. TEL 317-231-9200; Ed. LeeAnn Peake; Pub. David Lewis; adv. contact: Scott Gause. photos; pub. size: broadsheet; circ. 10,000(free & paid).

US

NORTH MERIDIAN OBSERVER. 1972. Wed. free; voluntary pay subscriptions. 13095 Publishers Dr., Fishers, IN 46038. TEL 317-598-6397; FAX 317-598-6360. **Owner(s):** Central Newspapers, Inc. 135 N. Pennsylvania Ave., Ste. 1200, Indianapolis, IN 46204-2400. TEL 317-231-9201; Ed. LeeAnn Peake; Pub. David Lewis; adv. contact: Scott Gause. photos; pub. size: broadsheet; circ. 3,000(free & paid).

US

NORTH SIDE TOPICS. 1961. Wed. free; voluntary pay subscriptions. 13095 Publishers Dr., Fishers, IN 46038. TEL 317-598-6397; FAX 317-598-6360. **Owner(s):** Central Newspapers, Inc. 135 N. Pennsylvania Ave., Ste. 1200, Indianapolis, IN 46204-2400. TEL 317-231-9200; Ed. LeeAnn Peake; Pub. David Lewis; adv. contact: Scott Gause. photos; pub. size: broadsheet; circ. 4,000(free & paid). **Wire Service(s):** UPI.

US

PIKE REGISTER. 1972. Wed. free; voluntary pay subscriptions. 13095 Publishers Dr., Fishers, IN 46038. TEL 317-598-6397; FAX 317-598-6360. **Owner(s):** Central Newspapers, Inc. 135 N. Pennsylvania Ave., Ste. 1200, Indianapolis, IN 46204-2400. TEL 317-231-9201; Ed. LeeAnn Peake; Pub. David Lewis; adv. contact: Scott Gause. photos; pub. size: broadsheet; circ. 3,000(free & paid). **Wire Service(s):** UPI.

US

SHERIDAN NEWS. 1982. Thu. free; voluntary pay subscriptions. 13095 Publishers Dr., Fishers, IN 46038. TEL 317-598-6397; FAX 317-598-6360. **Owner(s):** Central Newspapers, Inc. 135 N. Pennsylvania Ave., Ste. 1200, Indianapolis, IN 46204-2400. TEL 317-231-9201; Ed. Karen Peterson; Pub. David Lewis; adv. contact: Scott Gause. photos; bk.rev.; pub. size: broadsheet; circ. 1,675(free & paid). **Wire Service(s):** AP.

US

WESTFIELD ENTERPRISE. 1978. Wed. free; voluntary pay subscriptions. 13095 Publishers Dr., Fishers, IN 46038. TEL 317-773-1210; FAX 317-773-3872. **Owner(s):** Central Newspapers, Inc., 135 N. Pennsylvania Ave., Ste. 1200, Indianapolis, IN 46204-2400. TEL 317-231-9201; Ed. Patricia White; Pub. David Lewis; adv. contact: Scott Gause. photos; pub. size: broadsheet; circ. 4,300(free & paid). **Wire Service(s):** AP.

▼**WHITE RIVER GAZETTE.** 1996. Wed. free; voluntary pay subscriptions. 13095 Publishers Dr., Fishers, IN 46038. TEL 317-598-6397; FAX 317-598-6360. **Owner(s):** Central Newspapers, Inc., 135 N. Pennsylvania Ave., Ste. 1200, Indianapolis, IN 46204-2400. TEL 317-231-9201; Ed. Rebecca Collier; Pub. David Lewis; adv. contact: Scott Gause. photos; pub. size: broadsheet.

FISHERSPOLIS
US

NORA NEWS DISPATCH. 1961. Wed. free; voluntary pay subscriptions. 13095 Publishers Dr., Fisherspolis, IN 46038. TEL 317-598-6397; FAX 317-598-6360. **Owner(s):** Central Newspapers, Inc., 135 N. Pennsylvania Ave., Ste. 1200, Indianapolis, IN 46204-2400. TEL 317-231-9200; Ed. LeeAnn Peake; Pub. David Lewis; adv. contact: Scott Gause. photos; pub. size: broadsheet; circ. 8,130(free & paid).

FLORA
US

CARROLL COUNTY COMET. 1974. Wed. $.50 newsstand; $23/yr. local. 14 E. Main St., Flora, IN 46929. TEL 219-967-4135; FAX 219-967-4657. **Owner(s):** Carroll Papers, Inc., Box 26, Flora, IN 46929. TEL 219-967-4135; FAX 219-967-4657; Ed. Susan Scholl; Pub. Joseph L. Moss; adv. contact: Joseph L. Moss. pub. size: broadsheet; circ. 5,032(paid).

FOWLER
US

BENTON REVIEW, THE. 1975. Thu. $.50 newsstand; $17.50/yr. in cy.; $21/yr. out of cy. 102 E. 5th St., Fowler, IN 47944. TEL 317-884-1902; FAX 317-884-8110. **Owner(s):** Benton Review Newspaper, 102 E. 5th St., Fowler, IN 47944-0527. TEL 317-884-1902; FAX 317-884-8110; Ed. Karen Moyars; Pub. Karen Moyars; adv.; photos; bk.rev.; pub. size: broadsheet; circ. 1,890(paid).

Formerly: Fowler Benton Review.

FRENCH LICK
US

SPRINGS VALLEY HERALD. 1905. Wed. $.40 newsstand; $16.95/yr. 211 College St., French Lick, IN 47432. TEL 812-935-9630. **Owner(s):** Dorothy G. Ballard, P.O. Box 311, French Lick, IN 47432. TEL 812-936-9835. Ed. Ruth Marshall; Pub. Dorothy G. Ballard; adv.; circ. 3,000(free & paid).

GARY

US

GARY CRUSADER. Thu. $.25 newsstand; $15/yr.; $26/2 yrs. 1549 Broadway, Gary, IN 46407. TEL 219-885-4357; FAX 219-883-3317. **Owner(s):** Dorothy R. Leavell, 1549 Broadway, Gary, IN 46407. TEL 219-885-4357; Ed. David Denson; Pub. Dorothy R. Leavell; adv. contact: John Smith. pub. size: tabloid; circ. 32,000(paid).

US

GARY INFO. 1963. Thu. $.25 newsstand; $12/yr. local. 1953 Broadway, Gary, IN 46407. TEL 219-882-6711; FAX 219-886-1090. **Owner(s):** Info Printing & Publishing, Inc., 1953 Broadway, Gary, IN 46401. TEL 219-882-6711; Ed. Imogene Harris; Pub. Imogene Harris; adv. contact: Huston Pugh. pub. size: tabloid; circ. 40,000(paid).

GOSHEN

US

PAPER, THE. 1973. Tue. free. 134 S. Main St., Goshen, IN 46526. TEL 219-534-2591; FAX 219-533-4820. **Owner(s):** Della Baumgartner, P.O. Box 188, Milford, IN 46542. TEL 219-658-4815; FAX 219-658-4701; Ron & Gloria Baumgartner, P.O. Box 177, Milford, IN 46542. TEL 219-457-5000; FAX 219-658-4701; Ed. Jeri Seely; Pub. Della Baumgartner; adv. contact: Kip Schumm. photos; pub. size: tab oid; circ. 30,068(free).

GREENFIELD

US

AD-NEWS. 1979. Wed. free. P.O. Box 602, Greenfield, IN 46140-0602. TEL 317-462-7368; FAX 317-462-7779. **Owner(s):** Jim Thomas, P.O. Box 4, Greenfield, IN 46140. TEL 317-462-7368; FAX 317-462-7779; Ed. Jim Thomas; Pub. Jim Thomas; adv.; photos; bk.rev.; pub. size: tab oid; circ. 16,300(free).

US

INDY SUBURBAN NEWSPAPER. 1975. Wed. free. P.O. Box 602, Greenfield, IN 46140-0602. TEL 317-462-7368; FAX 317-462-7779. **Owner(s):** Jim Thomas, P.O. Box 4, Greenfield, IN 46140. TEL 317-462-7368; FAX 317-462-7779; Ed. Jim Thomas; Pub. Jim Thomas; adv. contact: Troy Thomas. photos; bk.rev.; pub. size: tabloid; circ. 20,000(free).

US

WESTSIDE ENTERPRISE. 1918. Wed. free. P.O. Box 602, Greenfield, IN 46140. TEL 317-462-7368; FAX 317-462-7779. **Owner(s):** Jim Thomas, P.O. Box 4, Greenfield, IN 46140. TEL 317-462-7368; FAX 317-462-7779; Ed. Jim Thomas; Pub. Jim Thomas; adv. contact: Troy Thomas. photos; bk.rev.; pub. size: tabloid; circ. 10,500(free).

GREENWOOD

US   ISSN 8750-7390

FRANKLIN CHALLENGER. 1984. Wed. $.25 newsstand; $12/yr. 152 S. Madison Ave., Greenwood, IN 46142. TEL 317-888-3376; FAX 317-888-3377. **Owner(s):** Guerrettz Industries, Inc., P.O. Box 708, Greenwood, IN 46142. TEL 317-888-3376; FAX 317-888-3377; Ed. Don Guerrettaz; Pub. Don Guerrettaz; adv.; photos; bk.rev.; pub. size: tabloid.

US

GREENWOOD & SOUTHSIDE CHALLENGER. 1972. w. $.50 newsstand; $15/yr. 152 S. Madison Ave., Greenwood, IN 46142. TEL 317-888-3376; FAX 317-888-3377. **Owner(s):** Guerrettaz Industries, Inc., 152 S. Madison Ave., Greenwood, IN 46142. TEL 317-888-3376; Ed. Don Guerrettaz; Pub. Don Guerrettaz; adv.; photos; bk.rev.; pub. size: tabloid; circ. 1,100(paid).
Formerly: Southside Challenger.

HAGERSTOWN

US

HAGERSTOWN EXPONENT, THE. 1875. Wed. $.50 newsstand; $25/yr. 99 S. Perry St., Hagerstown, IN 47346-1521. TEL 317-489-4035. **Owner(s):** Hagerstown Newspapers, Inc., 99 S. Perry St., Hagerstown, IN 47346-1521. TEL 317-489-4035; Ed. Robert A. Hansen; Pub. Patricia J. Hansen; adv.; pub. size: broadsheet; circ. 2,250(paid).

HIGHLAND

US   ISSN 1075-6981

CALUMET PRESS, THE. 1957. Wed. free; $18/yr. mailed. 8411 Kennedy Ave., Highland, IN 46322. TEL 219-838-0717; FAX 219-838-1338. **Owner(s):** Wayne & Helen Kletzing, 8220 Harrison, #301, Munster, IN 46321. TEL 219-836-8880; H.D. Van Kooten, 747 Raymond St., Griffith, IN 46319; Ed. Jeanne Larsen. adv. contact: William Palmateer. photos; pub. size: tabloid; circ. 41,193(free).

US

GRIFFITH GUIDE. Wed. free. 2747 Highway Ave., Ste. A, Highland, IN 46322-1615. TEL 219-838-5999; FAX 219-838-7999. **Owner(s):** Citizen Publishing Co., 805 Park Ave., Beaver Dam, WI 53916. TEL 414-887-0321; Ed. Rory Holscher. adv. contact: Donna Riley. pub. size: tabloid; circ. 12,000(free).
Formerly: Griffith News.

US

HIGHLAND GUIDE. Wed. free. 2747 Highway Ave., Ste. A, Highland, IN 46322. TEL 219-838-5999; FAX 219-838-7999. **Owner(s):** Citizen Publishing Co., 805 Park Ave., Beaver Dam, WI 53916. TEL 414-887-0321; FAX 414-887-2779; Ed. Rory Holscher. adv.; pub. size: tabloid; circ. 9,335(free).
Formerly: Highland News.

US

MUNSTER GUIDE. Wed. free. 2747 Highway Ave., Ste. A, Highland, IN 46322. TEL 219-838-5999; FAX 219-838-7999. **Owner(s):** Citizen Publishing Co., 805 Park Ave., Beaver Dam, WI 53916. TEL 414-887-0321; FAX 414-887-2779; Ed. Rory Holscher. adv.; pub. size: tabloid; circ. 8,450(free).
Formerly: Munster News.

US

SCHERERVILLE GUIDE. Wed. free. 2747 Highway Ave., Ste A, Highland, IN 46322-1615. TEL 219-924-5631; FAX 219-924-5671. **Owner(s):** Citizen Publishing Co., 805 Park Ave., Beaver Dam, WI 53916. TEL 414-887-0321; FAX 414-924-5671; Ed. Rory Holscher; Pub. James Hillman; pub. size: tabloid; circ. 18,889(free).
Formerly: Schererville News.

HOPE

US

STAR JOURNAL. 1912. Thu. $.50; $16/yr. in cy.; $20/yr. out of cy. 611 Harrison St., Hope, IN 47246. TEL 812-546-6113; FAX 812-546-6114. **Owner(s):** Dion Stenneski, 611 Harrison St., Hope, IN 47246. TEL 812-546-6113; Ed. Charles Biggs; Pub. Dion Stenneski; adv.; pub. size: broadsheet; circ. 1,500(paid).

INDIANAPOLIS

US

EAST SIDE HERALD. 1968. Thu. free newsstand; $45/yr. 4309 E. Michigan St., Indianapolis, IN 46201. TEL 317-356-2487; FAX 317-356-2486. **Owner(s):** East Side Communications Corp., 4309 E. Michigan St., Indianapolis, IN 46201. TEL 317-356-2487; Ed. Helen Thoele; Pub. William K. Thoele; pub. size: tabloid; circ. 38,500(controlled).

US

INDIANAPOLIS EAST SIDE HERALD. 1937. Thu. free newsstand; $20/yr. 4309 E. Michigan St., Indianapolis, IN 46201. TEL 317-356-2487. **Owner(s):** East Side Communications Corp., 4309 E. Michigan St., Indianapolis, IN 46201. TEL 317-356-2487; Ed. Ruth A. Thoele; Pub. William K. Thoele; adv. contact: Carl Thoele. pub. size: broadsheet; circ. 18,000(controlled).

US

INDIANAPOLIS RECORDER. 1895. Thu. $.75 newsstand; $39/yr.; $33/yr. senior citizens. 2901 N. Tacoma Ave., Indianapolis, IN 46218. TEL 317-924-5143; FAX 317-924-5148. **Owner(s):** William Mayes, 2901 N. Tacoma Ave., Indianapolis, IN 46218. TEL 317-924-5143; Ed. Connie Gaines-Hayes. adv.; photos; pub. size: broadsheet; circ. 15,000(paid). **Wire Service(s):** AP.

US

INDIANAPOLIS WESTSIDE ENTERPRISE. 1918. Wed. free; $13/yr. 1750 W. Morris St., Indianapolis, IN 46221. TEL 317-639-6477; FAX 317-639-6478. **Owner(s):** Jim Thomas, P.O. Box 4, Greenfield, IN 46140. TEL 317-462-7368; FAX 317-462-7779; Ed. Troy Thomas; Pub. Jim Thomas; adv.; photos; bk.rev.; pub. size: tabloid; circ. 11,000(free & paid).

US

NORTHEAST REPORTER. 1935. Thu. free newsstand; $45/yr. 4309 E. Michigan St., Indianapolis, IN 46201. TEL 317-356-2487. **Owner(s):** East Side Communications Corp., 4309 E. Michigan St., Indianapolis, IN 46201. TEL 317-356-2487; Ed. Helen Thoele; Pub. William K. Thoele; pub. size: broadsheet; circ. 16,000(controlled).

US

NUVO NEWSWEEKLY. 1990. Wed. free newsstand; $8/mo.; $95/yr. 811 E. Westfield Blvd., Indianapolis, IN 46220. TEL 317-254-2400; FAX 317-254-2405. **Owner(s):** Kevin McKinney, 811 E. Westfield Blvd., Indianapolis, IN 46220. TEL 317-254-2400; FAX 317-254-2405; Ed. Harrison J. Ullmann; Pub. Kevin K. McKinney; adv. contact: Bill Platt. photos; bk.rev.; pub. size: tabloid; circ. 40,000(free).

US

SPOTLIGHT, THE. 1939. Wed. free newsstand; $40/yr. mailed. 4217 S. Meridian, Indianapolis, IN 46217. TEL 317-788-4554. **Owner(s):** Jerry Cosby, 4217 S. Meridian St., Indianapolis, IN 46217. TEL 317-788-4554; Ed. Jerry Cosby. pub. size: broadsheet; circ. 25,000(free & paid).

Weeklies

KNIGHTSTOWN

US

WESTSIDE FLYER. 1993. Wed. $.50 newsstand; $18/yr. 7207 W. Tenth St., Indianapolis, IN 46214. TEL 317-487-1422; FAX 317-487-1158. **Owner(s):** McCarthy Media, Inc., 202 N. Mill St., Plainfield, IN 46168. TEL 317-839-5129; FAX 317-839-6546; Ed. David Beall; Pub. W. Jack McCarthy; adv. contact: Michael Schaefer. bk.rev.; pub. size: broadsheet; circ. 12,500(free & paid).

KNIGHTSTOWN

US   ISSN 0164-8640

FARMWEEK. 1955. Wed. $18.95/yr. local states. 27 N. Jefferson St., Knightstown, IN 46148. TEL 317-345-5133; FAX 800-813-1055. **Owner(s):** Mayhill Publications, Inc., 27 N. Jefferson St., Knightstown, IN 46148. TEL 317-345-5133; Ed. Nancy Searfoss; Pub. R. Thomas Mayhill; adv. contact: Freda Dudley. photos; pub. size: tabloid; circ. 28,295(paid).

TRI-COUNTY BANNER. 1962. Wed. $24/yr. local; $48/yr. outside area. 16 N. Washington St., Knightstown, IN 46148. TEL 317-345-2111; FAX 317-345-2186. **Owner(s):** Ty Swinsher Publishing Co., P.O. Box 116, Knightstown, IN 46148. TEL 317-345-2111; Ed. Eric M. Cox; Pub. Ty Swinsher; pub. size: tabloid; circ. 3,028(paid).

LA CROSSE

US

REGIONAL NEWS, THE. 1915. Thu. $.30 newsstand; $17/yr. in cy.; $20/yr. out of cy. P.O. Box 358, La Crosse, IN 46348. TEL 219-785-2442. **Owner(s):** Richard N. Slater, 9852 W. State Rd., Ste. 2, LaPorte, IN 46350. TEL 219-785-2234; Ed. Richard N. Slater; Pub. Richard N. Slater; adv.; photos; bk.rev.; pub. size: broadsheet; circ. 8,100(paid).

LAFAYETTE

US

LAFAYETTE LEADER. 1883. Thu. $1 newsstand; $40/yr. 22 N. Second St., Lafayette, IN 47902-1100. TEL 317-423-2624; FAX 317-423-4495. **Owner(s):** Dennis Dunn, 22 N. Second St., Lafayette, IN 47901. TEL 317-423-2624; Ed. Lynn Holland; Pub. Dennis Dunn; adv.; pub. size: tabloid; circ. 5,000(paid).

LA GRANGE

US

LA GRANGE STANDARD NEWS. 1856. Wed. $.50 newsstand; $25/yr. local. State Rd. 9, S., La Grange, IN 46761. TEL 219-463-2166; FAX 219-463-2734. **Owner(s):** La Grange Publishing Co., Inc., P.O. Box 148, LaGrange, IN 46761. TEL 219-463-2166; Ed. William F. Connelly; Pub. William F. Connelly; adv. contact: Norm Heign. pub. size: broadsheet; circ. 72,000(paid).

LA PORTE

US

SOUTHWEST TOWN CRIER. Mon. free. 2700 Monroe St., La Porte, IN 46350. TEL 219-362-8519; FAX 219-325-0677. **Owner(s):** Towndan Enterprises, Inc., 2700 Monroe St., La Porte, IN 46350. TEL 219-362-8519; Ed. Ralph T. Jones; Pub. Gregory L. Jones; adv.; pub. size: tabloid; circ. 5,130(paid).

US

TOWN CRIER, THE. 1933. Mon. Free; $1/wk. mailed out of area. 2700 Monroe St., La Porte, IN 46350. TEL 219-362-8519; FAX 219-325-0677. **Owner(s):** Towndan Enterprises, Inc., 2700 Monroe St., La Porte, IN 46350. TEL 219-362-8519; Ed. Ralph T. Jones. adv.; pub. size: tabloid; circ. 97,000(free).
   Formerly: Northwest Town Crier.

LAWRENCE

US

CUMBERLAND COURIER WEEKLY. 1983. Tue. free. 7962 Pendleton Pike, Lawrence, IN 46226. TEL 317-542-8149; FAX 317-542-1137. **Owner(s):** Joseph E. Zainey Enterprises, Inc., 7962 Pendleton Pike, Lawrence, IN 46226. TEL 317-542-8149; FAX 317-542-1137; Ed. Shelly Zainey; Pub. Joseph E. Zainey; adv. contact: Shelly Zainey. photos; bk.rev.; pub. size: tabloid; circ. 12,500(free).
   Formerly: Indianapolis Ad-Courier.

US

LAWRENCE TOWNSHIP JOURNAL. 1944. Wed. $.25 newsstand; $12/yr.; $18/2 yrs. 7962 Pendleton Pike, Lawrence, IN 46226. TEL 317-542-8149; FAX 317-542-1137. **Owner(s):** Joseph E. Zainey Enterprises, Inc., 7962 Pendleton Ave., Lawrence, IN 46226. TEL 317-542-1137; FAX 317-542-1137; Ed. Shelly Zainey; Pub. Joseph E. Zainey; adv. contact: Shelly Zainey. photos; pub. size: tabloid; circ. 22,500(free & paid).

LAWRENCEBURG

US

DEARBORN COUNTY REGISTER. 1825. Thu. $.75 newsstand; $23/yr. in IN, KY, OH combined w/Journal Press; $29/yr. elsewhere. 126 W. High St., Lawrenceburg, IN 47025. TEL 812-537-0063; FAX 812-537-5576. **Owner(s):** Delphos Newspapers, 405 N. Main St., Delphos, OH 45833. TEL 419-645-0015; Ed. Joe Awad; Pub. John Reiniger; adv. contact: Janet Essert. pub. size: broadsheet; circ. 8,800(paid).

US

JOURNAL PRESS. 1858. Tue. $.75 newsstand; $23/yr. in IN, OH, KY combined w/Dearborn County Register. $29/yr. elsewhere. 126 W. High St., Lawrenceburg, IN 47025. TEL 812-537-0063; FAX 812-537-5576. **Owner(s):** Register Publications, P.O. Box 328, Lawrenceburg, IN 47025. TEL 812-537-0063; Ed. Joe Awad; Pub. John Reiniger; adv. contact: Janet Essert. pub. size: broadsheet; circ. 7,685(paid).

LIGONIER

US

ADVERTISER, THE. Mon. free. 121 S. Cavin, Ligonier, IN 46767. TEL 219-894-3102; FAX 219-894-3104. **Owner(s):** Kendallville Publishing Co., 112 N. Main St., Kendallville, IN 46755. TEL 219-347-0400; Ed. Gary Kauffman; Pub. Jim Kroemer; adv. contact: Carol Arnold. pub. size: standard; circ. 14,000(free).

US

LIGONIER ADVANCE-LEADER. 1880. Thu. $.75 newsstand; $34/yr. 121 S. Cavin, Ligonier, IN 46767. TEL 219-894-3102. **Owner(s):** Kendallville Publishing Co., 112 N. Main St., Kendallville, IN 46755. TEL 219-347-0400; Ed. Gary Kauffman; Pub. Jim Kroemer; adv.; pub. size: broadsheet; circ. 2,900(paid).

LOWELL

US

CEDAR LAKE JOURNAL. Wed. free mailed. 116 Clark St., Lowell, IN 46356. TEL 219-696-7711; FAX 219-696-7713. **Owner(s):** Pilcher Publishing Co., Inc., 116 Clark St., Lowell, IN 46356; FAX 219-696-7711; Ed. L.H. Pilcher; Pub. L.H. Pilcher; adv.: $5.95/SAU. pub. size: broadsheet; circ. 5,000(free).

LOWELL

US

LOWELL TRIBUNE. 1885. Wed. $.25 newsstand; $12/yr. 116 Clark St., Lowell, IN 46356. TEL 219-696-7711; FAX 219-696-7713. **Owner(s):** Pilcher Publishing Co., Inc., 116 Clark St., P.O. Box 248, Lowell, IN 46356. TEL 219-696-7711; Ed. L.H. Pilcher; Pub. L.H. Pilcher; adv.: $5.95/SAU. pub. size: broadsheet; circ. 5,000(paid).

US

SOUTH LAKE ADVERTISER. 1885. Tue. free. 116 Clark St., Lowell, IN 46356. TEL 219-696-7711; FAX 219-696-7713. **Owner(s):** Pilcher Publishing Co., Inc., 116 Clark St., P.O. Box 248, Lowell, IN 46356. TEL 219-698-7711; Ed. L.H. Pilcher. adv.; pub. size: broadsheet; circ. 5,000(free).
   Formerly: South Lake County Advertiser.

MERRILLVILLE

US   ISSN 1044-2839

LAKE STATION HERALD. 1946. Thu. $.50 newsstand; $20/yr. in cy.; $26/yr out of cy. 3161 E. 84th Pl., Merrillville, IN 46410. TEL 219-942-8914; FAX 219-942-3925. **Owner(s):** Citizen Publishing Co., 805 Park Ave., Beaver Dam, WI 53916; Ed. R. Hoscher. adv.; pub. size: tabloid; circ. 1,500(paid).

US   ISSN 1043-9587

MERRILLVILLE HERALD. 1944. Wed. $18/yr. in cy.; $23.50/yr. out of cy. 3161 E. 84th Pl., Merrillville, IN 46410. TEL 219-942-0521; FAX 219-942-0820. **Owner(s):** Citizen Publishing Co., 805 Park Ave., Beaver Dam, WI 53916; adv. contact: Donna Riley. pub. size: tabloid; circ. 2,900(paid).

MERRIVILLE

US

HOBART GAZETTE. 1887. Wed. $20/yr. in cy.; $26/yr. out of cy. 3161 E. 84th Fl., Merriville, IN 46410. TEL 219-942-6575; FAX 219-942-0820. **Owner(s):** Citizen Publishing Co., 805 Park Ave., Beaver Dam, WI 53916. TEL 414-692-5476; Ed. Rory Holscher. adv.; pub. size: tabloid; circ. 5,700(paid).

MIDDLETOWN

US

MIDDLETOWN NEWS, THE. 1885. Wed. $.50 newsstand. 469 Locust St., Middletown, IN 47356. TEL 317-354-2221. **Owner(s):** Jack N. White, 469 Locust St., P.O Box 96 Middletown, IN 47356. TEL 317-354-2221; Ed. Cheryl Hines; Pub. Jack N. White; adv.; bk.rev.; pub. size: tabloid; circ. 1,777(paid).

MILFORD

US

MAIL-JOURNAL, THE. 1888. Wed. $.50 newsstand; $23.50/yr. 206 S. Main, Milford, IN 46542. TEL 219-658-4111; FAX 219-658-4701. **Owner(s):** Papers Inc., The, P.O. Box 188, Milford, IN 46542. TEL 219-658-4111; FAX 219-658-4701; Ed. Jeri Seely; Pub. Della Baumgartner; adv. contact: Kip Schumm. photos; pub. size: broadsheet; circ. 3,100(paid).

MISHAWAKA

US

MISHAWAKA ENTERPRISE. Thu. $.35 newsstand; $10/yr. 410 Lincoln Way, E., Ste. 6, Mishawaka, IN 46546. TEL 219-255-4789; FAX 219-255-4789. **Owner(s):** Ecom Corp., IN; Ed. William Nich. pub. size: tabloid; circ. 1,400(paid).

MOORESVILLE

US

MOORESVILLE TIMES, THE. 1871. Wed. $.50 newsstand; $18/yr. 23 E. Main St., Mooresville, IN 46158-03C8. TEL 317-831-0280; FAX 317-831-7068. **Owner(s):** Reporter-Times, Inc., 60 S. Jefferson St., Martinsville, IN 46151. TEL 317-342-3311; FAX 317-342-1446; Ed. Steve Heath; Pub. Sharon Clipp; adv. contact: Sharon Clipp. pub. size: broadsheet; circ. 6,793(paid).

MT. VERNON

US

MOUNT VERNON DEMOCRAT. 1867. Wed. $.50 newsstand; $21/yr. 425 Main St., Mt. Vernon, IN 47620. TEL 812-838-4811; FAX 812-838-3696. **Owner(s):** Landmark Community Newspapers, Inc., P.O. Box 549, Shelbyville, KY 40066; Ed. Mike Warren. adv. contact: Brenda Higgins. pub. size: broadsheet; circ. 3,500(paid).

NASHVILLE

US

BROWN COUNTY DEMOCRAT. 1870. Wed. $.50 newsstand; $24/yr. in cy.; $34/yr. out of cy. 136 N. Van Buren St., Nashville, IN 47448-0277. TEL 812-988-2221; FAX 812-988-1570. **Owner(s):** Greg Temple, P.O. Box 277, Nashville, IN 47448. TEL 812-988-2221; FAX 812-988-1570; Ed. Mike Lewis; Pub. Greg Temple; adv. contact: Keith Fleener. pub. size: broadsheet; circ. 4,495(paid).
    Formerly: Nashville Brown County Democrat.

NEWBURGH

US

NEWBURGH-CHANDLER REGISTER. 1886. Wed. $26/yr. 501 State St., Newburgh, IN 47630. TEL 812-853-3366; FAX 812-853-8685. **Owner(s):** Brehm Communications, Inc., 17065 Via del Campo, Ste. 200, San Diego, CA 92127. TEL 619-451-6200; Ed. Dave Pearce; Pub. Myra Teal; adv. contact: Joe Stoll. pub. size: standard; circ. 2,655(paid).
    Formerly: Newburgh Register.

NEW CARLISLE

US

NEW PRAIRIE TOWN CRIER. Mon. free. 115 E. Michigan St., New Carlisle, IN 46552. TEL 219-654-7468; FAX 219-325-0677. **Owner(s):** Towndan Enterprises, Inc., 2700 Monore St., La Porte, IN 46350. TEL 219-362-8519; Pub. Georgory L. Jones; circ. 4,464(free).

NEW HAVEN

US

ALLEN COUNTY TIMES. 1991. Wed. $.25 newsstand; $17.50/yr. 405 Broadway, New Haven, IN 46774-1105. TEL 219-493-2464. **Owner(s):** Ronald K. Oetting, 517 Broadway, New Haven, IN 46774. TEL 219-493-2464; Ed. Robert E. Nylund; Pub. Ronald K. Oetting; adv.; photos; pub. size: tabloid; circ. 5,000(controlled).
    Formerly: New Allen News, New Haven Mews.

NORTH MANCHESTER

US

NEWS-JOURNAL. 1873. Wed. $.50 newsstand; $39/yr. 112 W. Main St., North Manchester, IN 46962-0324. TEL 219-982-6383; FAX 219-982-8233. **Owner(s):** Susan E. Weller, 207 S. Maple St., North Manchester, IN 46962. TEL 219-982-6383; Worth H. Weller, 207 S. Maple St., North Manchester, IN 46962. TEL 219-982-6383; Ed. Rick Rogers; Pub. Worth Weller; adv. contact: Cheryl Wilson. pub. size: tabloid; circ. 2,500(paid).

NORTH VERNON

US

NORTH VERNON PLAIN DEALER. 1864. Thu. $.50 newsstand; $26/yr. local; $30.50/yr. surrounding states; $35/yr. elsewhere. 528 E. O & M Ave., North Vernon, IN 47265. TEL 812-346-3973; FAX 812-346-8368. **Owner(s):** Barbara King, P.O. Box 410, North Vernon, IN 47265. TEL 812-346-3973; Viola King, P.O. Box 410, North Vernon, IN 47265. TEL 812-346-3973; Ed. Barbara King; Pub. Barbara King; adv.; photos; pub. size: standard; circ. 6,800(paid).

US

NORTH VERNON SUN. 1876. Tue. $.50 newsstand; $26/yr. local; $30.50 in and adj. states; $35/yr. elsewhere. 528 E. O & M Ave., North Vernon, IN 47265. TEL 812-346-3973; FAX 812-346-8368. **Owner(s):** Barbara King, P.O. Box 410, North Vernon, IN 47265. TEL 812-346-3973; Viola King, P.O. Box 410, North Vernon, IN 47265. TEL 812-346-3973; Ed. Barbara King; Pub. Barbara King; adv.; photos; pub. size: standard; circ. 5,800(paid).

OSSIAN

US

OSSIAN JOURNAL. 1912. Thu. $.35 newsstand; $14.50/yr. local; $16/yr. out of area. 105 N. Jefferson St., Ossian, IN 46777. TEL 219-622-4108; FAX 219-622-4108. **Owner(s):** James Barbieri, 125 N. Johnson, P.O. Box 436, Bluffton, IN 46714. TEL 219-824-0224; FAX 219-824-0700; George Witwer, 125 N. Johnson St., P.O. Box 436, Bluffton, IN 46714. TEL 219-824-0224; FAX 219-824-0700; Ed. George B. Witwer; Pub. James C. Barbieri; adv. contact: Nila Dafforn. photos; pub. size: broadsheet; circ. 725(paid).
    Wire Service(s): AP.

US

SUNRISER NEWS. Tue. $.35 newsstand; $14.50/yr. local; $16/yr. out of area. 105 N. Jefferson St., Ossian, IN 46777. TEL 219-622-4108; FAX 219-622-4108. **Owner(s):** James Barbieri, 125 N. Johnson, P.O. Box 436, Bluffton, IN 46714. TEL 219-824-0224; George Witwer, 125 N. Johnson St., P.O. Box 436, Bluffton, IN 46714. TEL 219-824-0224; Ed. George B. Witwer; Pub. James C. Barbieri; adv. contact: Nila Dafforn. photos; pub. size: broadsheet; circ. 600(paid).

PAOLI

US

ORANGE COUNTIAN. 1984. Wed. free. 131 N.W. Court St., Paoli, IN 47454. TEL 812-723-2572; FAX 812-723-2592. **Owner(s):** Orange County Publishing Co., Inc., P.O. Box 190, Paoli, IN 47454. TEL 812-723-2572; Ed. Brenda Cornwell; Pub. Helen M. Gooch; adv.; pub. size: standard; circ. 9,150(free).

US

PAOLI NEWS. 1872. Thu. $18/yr. local; $20/yr. area cys.; $30/yr. elsewhere. 131 N.W. Court St., Paoli, IN 47454. TEL 812-723-2572; FAX 812-723-2592. **Owner(s):** Orange County Publishing Co., Inc., P.O. Box 190, Paoli, IN 47454. TEL 812-723-2572; Ed. Brenda Cornwell; Pub. F. Wendell Gooch; adv.; pub. size: broadsheet; circ. 3,100(paid).

US

PAOLI REPUBLICAN. 1872. Tue. $18/yr. local; $20/yr. surrounding cys.; $30/yr. elsewhere. 131 N.W. Court St., Paoli, IN 47454. TEL 812-723-2572; FAX 812-723-2592. **Owner(s):** Orange County Publishing Co., Inc., P.O. Box 190, Paoli, IN 47454. TEL 812-723-2572; FAX 812-723-2592; Ed. Brenda Cornwell; Pub. F. Wendell Gooch; adv.; pub. size: broadsheet; circ. 3,200(paid).

PEKIN

US   ISSN 1053-2218

AUCTIONER, THE. 1989. Wed. $.25 newsstand; $25/yr. 490 E. Hwy. 60, Pekin, IN 47165. TEL 812-967-3176; FAX 812-967-3194. **Owner(s):** Green Banner Publications, P.O. Box 38, Pekin, IN 47165. TEL 812-967-3176; Pub. Joe Green; adv. contact: John Roberts. pub. size: tabloid; circ. 500(paid).

US   ISSN 0194-3545

BANNER-GAZETTE. 1919. Wed. $.25 newsstand; $18.50/yr. 490 E. Hwy. 60, Pekin, IN 47165. TEL 812-967-3176; FAX 812-967-3194. **Owner(s):** Green Banner Publications, P.O. Box 38, Pekin, IN 47165; Ed. Mark Grigsby; Pub. Joe Green; adv. contact: John Roberts. pub. size: tabloid; circ. 14,453(free & paid).

PETERSBURG

US

PRESS-DISPATCH. 1885. Thu. $.75 newsstand; $15/yr. 820 Poplar St., Petersburg, IN 47567. TEL 812-354-8500; FAX 812-354-2014. **Owner(s):** Press Dispatch, The, P.O. Box 68, Petersburg, IN 47567. TEL 812-354-8500; FAX 812-354-2014; Ed. Andy Heuring. adv. contact: John Heuring. pub. size: broadsheet; circ. 5,800(paid).

PLAINFIELD

US   ISSN 0193-4910

HENDRICKS COUNTY FLYER. 1965. Mon. $.50 newsstand; $60/yr. in state; $70/yr. out of state. 202 N. Mill St., Plainfield, IN 46168. TEL 317-839-5129; FAX 317-839-6546. **Owner(s):** McCarthy Media, Inc., 202 N. Mill St., Plainfield, IN 46168. TEL 317-839-5129; FAX 317-839-6546; Ed. Tim Evans; Pub. W. Jack McCarthy; adv. contact: Michael Schaefer. photos; bk.rev.; pub. size: broadsheet; circ. 32,000(free & paid).

US

WEEKEND FLYER, THE. 1907. Thu. $.50 newsstand; $21/yr. 202 N. Mill, Plainfield, IN 46168. TEL 317-839-5129; FAX 317-839-6546. **Owner(s):** McCarthy Media, Inc., 202 N. Mill, P.O. Box 6, Plainfield, IN 46168. TEL 317-839-5129; FAX 317-839-6546; Ed. Tim Evans; Pub. W. Jack McCarthy; adv.; pub. size: broadsheet; circ. 9,000(paid). **Formerly:** Plainfield Messenger.

PORTAGE

US

CHESTERTON GUIDE. 1988. Wed. free. 2583 Portage Mall, Portage, IN 46368. TEL 219-762-9564; FAX 219-942-0820. **Owner(s):** Citizen Publishing Co., 805 Park Ave., Beaver Dam, WI 53916. TEL 414-887-0321; Ed. Rory Holscher; Pub. Rory Holscher; adv.; pub. size: tabloid; circ. 6,100(free). **Formerly:** Chesterton News.

US   ISSN 0746-8776

PORTAGE JOURNAL-PRESS. 1970. Thu. $20/yr. in cy.; $23/yr. out of cy. 2583 Portage Mall, Portage, IN 46368. TEL 219-762-9564; FAX 219-763-1602. **Owner(s):** Citizen Publishing Co., 805 Park Ave., Beaver Dam, WI 53916; Ed. Jim Masters. adv. contact: Donna Rileyk. pub. size: tabloid; circ. 3,500(paid).

US

VALPARAISO GUIDE. 1985. Wed. free. 2583 Portage Mall, Portage, IN 46368. TEL 219-762-9564; FAX 219-763-1602. **Owner(s):** Citizen Publishing Co., 805 Park Ave., Beaver Dam, WI 53916. TEL 414-887-0321; FAX 414-887-2779; Ed. Rory Holscher; Pub. Rory Holscher; adv.; pub. size: tabloid; circ. 17,002(free). **Formerly:** Valparaiso News.

RENSSELAER

US   ISSN 1060-5231

COURIER, THE. Wed. $.50 newsstand; $25/yr. in cy.; $27/yr. out of cy.; $32/yr. out of state. 117 N. Van Rensselaer St., Rensselaer, IN 47978. TEL 219-866-5111; FAX 219-866-3775. **Owner(s):** Kan Kakee Valley Publishing Co., 117 N. Van Rensselaer St., Rensselaer, IL 47978; Ed. William F. Kaye. adv.; photos; bk.rev.; pub. size: standard; circ. 1,000(paid).

US

REMINGTON PRESS. 1873. Wed. $.50 newsstand; $25/yr. in cy.; $27/yr. in IN.; $32/yr. out of state. 117 N. Van Rensselaer St., Rensselaer, IN 47978. TEL 219-866-5111; FAX 219-866-3775. **Owner(s):** Kankakee Valley Publishing Co., 117 N. Van Rensselaer St., Rensselaer, IN 47978; Ed. William F. Kaye. adv. contact: Frank Copley. photos; bk.rev.; pub. size: standard; circ. 1,000(paid).

RISING SUN

US

OHIO COUNTY NEWS. 1833. Thu. $.60 newsstand; $16/yr. 235 Main St., Rising Sun, IN 47040. TEL 812-438-2011; FAX 812-537-5576. **Owner(s):** Register Publications, 126 W. High St., Lawrenceburg, IN 47025. TEL 812-537-0063; Ed. Tim Hillman; Pub. John Reiniger; pub. size: broadsheet; circ. 881(free & paid).

US

RISING SUN RECORDER. 1834. Thu. $.60 newsstand; $16/yr. 235 Main St., Rising Sun, IN 47040. TEL 812-438-2011; FAX 812-537-5576. **Owner(s):** Register Publications, 126 W. High St., Lawrenceburg, IN 47025. TEL 812-537-0063; Ed. Tim Hillman; Pub. John Reiniger; pub. size: broadsheet; circ. 1,338(paid).

ROCKPORT

US

SPENCER COUNTY JOURNAL DEMOCRAT. 1850. Thu. $.50 newsstand; $21.50/yr. 541 Main St., Rockport, IN 47635. TEL 812-649-4440; FAX 812-649-9197. **Owner(s):** Landmark Community Newspapers, Inc., P.O. Box 549, Shelbyville, KY 40066. TEL 502-633-4334; Ed. Stilla Janosa McMahon. adv. contact: Kim Motteler. photos. pub. size: standard; circ. 6,100(paid). **Formerly:** Journal Democrat.

ROCKVILLE

US   ISSN 1044-7822

ROCKVILLE PARKE COUNTY SENTINEL. 1833. Wed. $.40 newsstand; $23/yr. in state; $25/yr. out of state. 125 W. High St., Rockville, IN 47872. TEL 317-569-2033. **Owner(s):** Torch Newspapers, Inc., P.O. Box 187, Rockville, IN 47872. TEL 317-569-2033; Ed. Larry Bemis; Pub. Richard E. Harney; adv.; pub. size: broadsheet; circ. 4,400(paid).

SALEM

US

SALEM DEMOCRAT, THE. 1827. Thu. $.50 newsstand; $22.50/yr. local; $31.50/yr. in state; $37.50/yr. out of state. 117 E. Walnut St., Salem, IN 47167. TEL 812-883-3282; FAX 812-883-4446. **Owner(s):** Leader Publishing Co., Inc., P.O. Box 509, Salem, IN 47167. TEL 812-883-3282; FAX 812-883-4446; Ed. Cecil J. Smith; Pub. Rodger J. Grossman; adv. contact: Patricia Robertson. photos; pub. size: broadsheet; circ. 6,100(paid).

US

SALEM LEADER. 1878. Tue. $.50 newsstand; $22.50/yr. local; $31.50/yr. in state; $37.50/yr. out of state. 117 E. Walnut St., Salem, IN 47167-0509. TEL 812-883-3281; FAX 812-883-4446. **Owner(s):** Leader Publishing Co., Inc., P.O. Box 509, Salem, IN 47167. TEL 812-883-3281; FAX 812-883-4446; Ed. Cecil J. Smith; Pub. Rodger J. Grossman; adv. contact: Patricia Robertson. pub. size: broadsheet; circ. 6,100(paid).

WASHINGTON COUNTY EDITION

WASHINGTON COUNTY EDITION. 1982. w. $15/yr. 105 E. Walnut St., Salem, IN 47167. TEL 812-883-5555; FAX 812-883-3658. **Owner(s):** Robert Green, 105 E. Walnut St., Salem, IN 47167. TEL 812-883-5555; Ed. Mark Grigsby; Pub. Joe Green; adv. contact: John Roberts. pub. size: tabloid; circ. 10,063(free & paid).

SCOTTSBURG

US

GIVEAWAY, THE. 1937. Wed. free; $15/yr. 183 E. McLain, Scottsburg, IN 47170. TEL 812-967-3176; FAX 812-752-6468. **Owner(s):** Green Banner Publications, P.O. Box 38, Pekin, IN 47165. TEL 812-967-3176; Pub. Joe Green; adv. contact: John Roberts. pub. size: tabloid; circ. 16,277(free & paid).

US

JOURNAL & AUSTIN CHRONICLE. 1882. w. $.25 newsstand; $8.75/yr. local. 183 E. McClain, Scottsburg, IN 47170. TEL 812-752-3171; FAX 812-752-6486. **Owner(s):** Green Banner Publications, P.O. Box 38, Pekin, IN 47165. TEL 812-967-3176; Ed. Mark Grigsby; Pub. Joe Green; adv. contact: John Roberts. pub. size: broadsheet; circ. 5,000(paid).

SOUTH BEND

US

SOUTH BEND TRI-COUNTY NEWS. 1923. Fri. $17.50/yr. in cy.; $25/yr. out of cy. 918 E. Jefferson Blvd., South Bend, IN 46617. TEL 219-287-0285; FAX 219-233-9991. **Owner(s):** Cherie Jolly, 918 E. Jefferson, South Bend, IN 46617. TEL 219-287-0285; Ed. Cherie Jolly; Pub. Cherie Jolly; pub. size: tabloid; circ. 1,200(paid).

SPEEDWAY

US

NORTHWEST PRESS. 1956. Wed. free. 1564 Main St., Speedway, IN 46224. TEL 317-241-4345. **Owner(s):** Speedway Northwest Press, Inc., 1564 Main St., Speedway, IN 46224. TEL 317-241-4345; Ed. Elizabeth Sullivan; Pub. Elizabeth Sullivan; adv. contact: Dale Brockin. photos; bk.rev.; pub. size: tabloid; circ. 700(free). **Formerly:** Speedway Northwest Press.

US

SPEEDWAY TOWN PRESS. 1956. w. free. 1564 Main St., Speedway, IN 46224. TEL 317-241-4345. **Owner(s):** Speedway Northwest Press, Inc., 1564 Main St., Speedway, IN 46224. TEL 317-241-4345; Ed. Elizabeth Sullivan; Pub. Elizabeth Sullivan; adv. contact: Dale Brockin. photos; bk.rev.; pub. size: tabloid; circ. 7,000(free). **Formerly:** Speedway Northwest Press.

US

WESTSIDE MESSENGER. 1915. Wed. free. 1564 Main St., Speedway, IN 46224. TEL 317-241-4345. **Owner(s):** Speedway Northwest Press, Inc., 1564 Main St., Speedway, IN 46224. TEL 317-852-5249; Ed. Elizabeth Sullivan; Pub. Elizabeth Sullivan; adv. contact: Dale Brockin. photos; bk.rev.; pub. size: tabloid; circ. 7,000(free).

TELL CITY

US

PERRY COUNTY NEWS, THE. 1891. s-w.: Mon. & Thu. $.50 newsstand; $33/yr. in cy.; $45/yr. out of cy.; $52/yr. out of state. 537 Main St., Tell City, IN 47586. TEL 812-547-3424; FAX 812-547-2847. **Owner(s):** Landmark Community Newspapers, Inc., P.O. Box 549, Shelbyville, KY 40066. TEL 502-633-4334; Ed. Mary Jeanne Schumacher; Pub. Ron Filkins; adv.; pub. size: broadsheet; circ. 7,400(paid).
Formerly: News, The.

VALPARAISO

US

CHESTERTON TOWN CRIER. 1932. Mon. free. 3 E. US Hwy. 6, Ste. 5, Valparaiso, IN 46383-8723. TEL 219-926-7685; FAX 219-926-3097. **Owner(s):** Towndan Enterprises, Inc., 2700 Monroe, La Porte, IN 46350. TEL 219-926-7685; Ed. Gregory L. Jones; Pub. Brett Alcorn; pub. size: tabloid; circ. 10,005(free).

VERSAILLES

US

OSGOOD JOURNAL. 1865. Tue. $.50 newsstand; $32/yr. in cy.; $32/yr. out of cy.; $38/yr. out of state. 115 S. Washington St., Versailles, IN 47042. TEL 812-689-6364; FAX 812-689-6508. **Owner(s):** Gene Demaree, 115 S. Washington St., Versailles, IN 47042. TEL 812-434-6946; Ed. Laura Creech; Pub. Linda Chandler; adv. contact: Linda Chandler. photos; bk.rev.; pub. size: broadsheet; circ. 5,200(paid).

US

VERSAILLES REPUBLICAN. 1856. Thu. $.50 newsstand; $32/yr. 115 Washington St., Versailles, IN 47042. TEL 812-689-6364; FAX 812-689-6508. **Owner(s):** Gene Demaree, 6709 Mad River Rd., Centerville, OH 45459. TEL 513-432-6746; Ed. Laura Creech; Pub. Linda Chandler; adv.; photos; bk.rev.; pub. size: broadsheet; circ. 5,200(paid).
Formerly: Osgood Journal & Versailles Republican.

VEVAY

US

VEVAY REVEILLE-ENTERPRISE. 1816. Thu. $.50 newsstand; $20/yr. local. 111 W. Market St., Vevay, IN 47043. TEL 812-427-2311. **Owner(s):** Vevay Newspapers, Inc., 111 W. Market St., Vevay, IN 47043. TEL 812-427-2311; Ed. Patrick Lanman; Pub. Don R. Wallis, Jr.; adv. contact: Dan Honeyman. pub. size: broadsheet; circ. 2,000(paid).
Formerly: Vevay Reveille-Enterprise & Switzerland Democrat.

WABASH

US

PAPER OF WABASH COUNTY, THE. 1977. Wed. free; $25/yr. mailed. Jct. 13 & 24, Wabash, IN 46992. TEL 219-563-8326; FAX 219-563-2863. **Owner(s):** Wayne Rees, P.O. Box 603, Wabash, IN 46992. TEL 219-563-8326; Pub. Wayne Rees; adv. contact: Julie Frieden. photos; pub. size: broadsheet; circ. 16,225(controlled & free).

WARSAW

US

PAPER, THE. 1971. Wed. free. 114 W. Market St., Warsaw, IN 46580. TEL 219-269-2932; FAX 219-269-5850. **Owner(s):** Della Baumgartner, P.O. Box 188, Milford, IN 46542. TEL 219-658-4815; FAX 219-658-4701; Ron & Gloria Baumgartner, P.O. Box 177, Milford, IN 46542. TEL 219-457-5000; FAX 219-658-4701; Ed. Jeri Seely; Pub. Della Baumgartner; adv. contact: Kip Schumm. photos; pub. size: tabloid; circ. 23,566(free).

WASHINGTON

US

HOOSIER EXPRESS. Wed. free. Memorial at N.E. 14th St., Washington, IN 47501. TEL 812-254-7322; FAX 812-254-7837. **Owner(s):** Davies County Publishing, Inc., Memorial at N.E. 14th St., Washington, IN 47501. TEL 812-254-7322; Ed. Michael Crosley; Pub. Michael Crosley; adv.; photos; bk.rev.; pub. size: broadsheet; circ. 15,500(free); Sun. 3,000(controlled & free).

WESTVILLE

US

WESTVILLE INDICATOR. 1882. Thu. $.30 newsstand; $17/yr. in cy.; $20/yr. out of cy. 9852 E. State Rd., #2, Westville, IN 46391. TEL 219-785-2234; FAX 219-785-2442. **Owner(s):** Richard N. Slater, 9852 E. State Rd., #2, Westville, IN 46391. TEL 219-785-2236; Ed. Richard N. Slater; Pub. Richard N. Slater; adv.; photos; bk.rev.; pub. size: broadsheet; circ. 5,200(controlled & paid).

WINAMAC

US

INDEPENDENT, THE. 1962. Mon. free. 114 W. Main St., Winamac, IN 46996. TEL 219-946-6629. **Owner(s):** Winamac Press, Inc., 114 W. Main St., Winamac, IN 46996. TEL 219-946-6629; Pub. Al Bundy; adv.; photos; pub. size: tabloid; circ. 7,600(free).

US

PULASKI COUNTY JOURNAL. 1872. Wed. $.75 newsstand; $20/yr. in cy. 114 W. Main St., Winamac, IN 46996. TEL 219-946-6628. **Owner(s):** Winamac Press, Inc., P.O. Box 19, Winamac, IN 46996. TEL 219-946-6628; Pub. Douglas Haley; adv. contact: Michelle Grostefon. photos; bk.rev.; pub. size: tabloid; circ. 3,800(paid).

WORTHINGTON

US

WORTHINGTON TIMES, THE. 1853. w. $.50 newsstand; $20/yr. in state; $25/yr. out of state. 12 S. Lessee, Worthington, IN 47471-0045. TEL 812-875-2141; FAX 812-875-2521. **Owner(s):** Worthington Times, P.O. Box 45, Worthington, IN 47471-0045. TEL 812-875-2141; Ed. Anna Rochelle; Pub. Anna Rochelle; adv.; photos; bk.rev.; pub. size: standard; circ. 1,000(free & paid).

ZIONSVILLE

US   ISSN 0886-4330

ZIONSVILLE TIMES SENTINEL. 1860. Wed. $.50 newsstand; $23/yr. 250 S. Elm St., Zionsville, IN 46077. TEL 317-873-6397. **Owner(s):** Jay & Paula Endress, P.O. Box 838, Zionsville, IN 46077; Ed. Paula J. Endress; Pub. Jay W. Endress; adv. contact: Jay W. Endress. pub. size: broadsheet; circ. 3,200(paid).

IOWA

AFTON

US

AFTON STAR-ENTERPRISE. 1880. Thu. $.50 newsstand; $19/yr. in state; $24/yr. out of state. 274 N. Douglas, Afton, IA 50830. TEL 515-347-8721. **Owner(s):** Afton Star-Enterprise, P.O. Box 128, Afton, IA 50830; adv.; pub. size: tabloid; circ. 1,220(paid).

ALBIA

US

ALBIA UNION-REPUBLICAN. 1862. s-w.: Tue. & Thu. $.50 newsstand; $29/yr. in state; $37/yr. out of state. 109-111 Benton Ave., E., Albia, IA 52531. TEL 515-932-7121; FAX 515-932-2822. **Owner(s):** Lancaster Management, P.O. Box 609, Gadsden, AL 35902. TEL 205-543-3417; Ed. David A. Paxton; Pub. David A. Paxton; adv. contact: Mary Ann Crall. photos; pub. size: broadsheet; circ. 3,500(paid).

US

MONROE COUNTY NEWS. 1890. s-w.: Tue. & Thu. $.50 newsstand; $29/yr. in state; $37/yr. out of state. 109-111 Benton Ave., E., Albia, IA 52531. TEL 515-932-7121; FAX 515-932-2822. **Owner(s):** Lancaster Management, P.O. Box 609, Gadsden, AL 35902. TEL 205-543-3417; Ed. David A. Paxton; Pub. David A. Paxton; adv. contact: Mary Ann Crall. photos; pub. size: broadsheet; circ. 3,400(paid).

ALGONA

US

ALGONA UPPER DES MOINES. 1866. Thu. $1 newsstand; $37/yr. 14 E. Nebraska St., Algona, IA 50511. TEL 515-295-3535; FAX 515-295-7217. **Owner(s):** Algona Publishing Co., P.O. Box 400, Algona, IA 50511. TEL 515-295-3535; Ed. Dave Thompson; Pub. Richard Plum; adv. contact: Nancy Steburg. pub. size: standard; circ. 5,300(paid).

ALTOONA

US

ALTOONA HERALD, THE. 1888. Thu. $.50 newsstand; $21/yr. in state. 809 Eighth St., S.W., Altoona, IA 50009. TEL 515-967-4224; FAX 515-967-0553. **Owner(s):** Gannett Company, Inc., 1100 Wilson Blvd., Arlington, VA 22340; Ed. Amy Duncan. adv. contact: Beth Meyer. photos; pub. size: broadsheet; circ. 10,000(controlled & paid).

ANAMOSA

US

ANAMOSA JOURNAL-EUREKA. 1854. Thu. $.50 newsstand; $21/yr. local; $27/yr. elsewhere. 208 W. Main St., Anamosa, IA 52205. TEL 319-462-3511; FAX 319-462-4540. **Owner(s):** Anamosa Publications, 208 W. Main St., Anamosa, IA 52205. TEL 319-462-3511; Ed. Nancy Gregerson; Pub. Larry K. Woellert; adv.; pub. size: tabloid; circ. 2,800(controlled & paid).

US

JONES COUNTY TOWN CRIER. Tue. free. 208 W. Main St., Anamosa, IA 52205. TEL 319-462-3511; FAX 319-462-4540. **Owner(s):** Decorah News Co., P.O. Box 350, Decorah, IA 52101. TEL 319-382-4221; Ed. Dominic Giegerich; Pub. Sid Blair; adv.; pub. size: tabloid; circ. 6,200(free).

ANKENY

US

ANKENY PRESS CITIZEN. 1955. Tue. free. 520 S.W. Third, Ankeny, IA 50021. TEL 515-964-0639; FAX 515-964-7019. **Owner(s):** Ogden Newspapers, Inc., P.O. Box 4826, Des Moines, IA 50306. TEL 515-244-4161; Ed. Dave DeValois; Pub. Roger Smed; adv.; photos; pub. size: tabloid; circ. 14,500(free). **Wire Service(s):** Iowa Link.

AUDUBON

US

NISHNA VALLEY TRIBUNE. Tue. free. 301 Broadway, Audubon, IA 50025. TEL 712-563-2661; FAX 712-563-3118. **Owner(s):** Audubon Media Corporation, 312 Broadway, Audubon, IA 50025. TEL 712-563-2661; Ed. Jeff Oakley; Pub. Keith McGlade; adv.; pub. size: broadsheet; circ. 7,000(free).

BETTENDORF

US

BETTENDORF NEWS. 1925. Thu. $.50 newsstand; $22/yr. in cy. 1704 State St., Bettendorf, IA 52722. TEL 319-355-2644; FAX 319-355-0956. **Owner(s):** Quad-City Times, 500 E. Third St., Davenport, IA 52801. TEL 319-383-2200; adv.; photos; pub. size: tabloid; circ. 3,000(paid).

BRITT

US

BRITT NEWS-TRIBUNE. 1881. Wed. $.75 newsstand; $20/yr. in cy.; $25/yr. out of cy. 42 W. Center St., Britt, IA 50423. TEL 515-843-3851; FAX 515-843-3307. **Owner(s):** Martin Bunge, 42 W. Center St., Britt, IA 50423. TEL 515-843-3851; Ed. Willy Klein; Pub. Martin Bunge; pub. size: broadsheet; circ. 2,000(paid).

BROOKLYN

US

BROOKLYN CHRONICLE. 1875. Wed. $.25 newsstand; $12/yr. 110 Jackson St., Brooklyn, IA 52211-0553. TEL 515-522-9288; FAX 515-522-7527. **Owner(s):** Brooklyn Publishing Co., 110 Jackson St., Brooklyn, IA 52211; Ed. C.V. Dunham; Pub. C.V. Dunham; adv. contact: C.V. Dunham. pub. size: broadsheet; circ. 1,450(paid).

BURLINGTON

US

SHOPPER SPREE. 1969. Wed. free. 3208 Division St., Burlington, IA 52601. TEL 319-752-4555; FAX 319-752-6410. **Owner(s):** Brehm Communications, Inc., 17065 Via Del Campo, P.O. Box 28429, San Diego, CA 92198. TEL 619-451-6200 Pub. John Lowman; adv.; pub. size: tabloid; circ. 20,300(controlled & free).

CHARITON

US

CHARITON HERALD-PATRIOT. 1857. Thu. $25/yr. 817 Braden Ave., Chariton, IA 50049. TEL 515-774-2137. **Owner(s):** Chariton Publishing Co., 817 Braden Ave., Chariton, IA 50049; Ed. Caroline Ruden; Pub. Keith Isley; adv. contact: Keith Isley. photos; pub. size: broadsheet; circ. 11,000(free).

US

CHARITON LEADER. 1867. Tue. $.50 newsstand; $29/yr. 817 Braden Ave., Chariton, IA 50049. TEL 515-774-2137; FAX 515-774-2139. **Owner(s):** Leader Publishing Co., Inc., 817 Braden Ave., Chariton IA 50049; Ed. Caroline Ruden; Pub. Keith Isley; adv. contact: Keith Isley. photos; pub. size: broadsheet; circ. 11,000(free & paid).

CLARINDA

US

CLARINDA HERALD JOURNAL. 1858. Wed. $19/yr. in state; $45/yr. out of state. 205 E. Main St., Clarinda, IA 51632. TEL 712-542-2181; FAX 712-542-5424. **Owner(s):** D.L.S., Inc., P.O. Box 278, Clarinda, IA 51632. TEL 712-542-2181; Ed. Scott Allbright; Pub. Wayne Matheny; adv. contact: Wayne Matheny. photos; pub. size: broadsheet; circ. 4,000(paid).

CLINTON

US

GATEWAY SHOPPER, THE. 1939. Sun. free. 240 Sixth Ave S., Clinton, IA 52732. TEL 319-243-1526; FAX 319-243-5035. **Owner(s):** Lee Enterprises, Inc., 130 E. Second St., Davenport, IA 52801. TEL 319-383-2202; adv.; pub. size: tabloid; circ. 22,000(free). **Formerly:** Clinton Town Talk.

CORYDON

US

CORYDON TIMES-REPUBLICAN. Tue. $.50 newsstand; $18/yr. in cy.; $21/yr. in state; $25/yr. out of state. 205 W. Jackson, Corydon, IA 50060. TEL 515-872-1234; FAX 515-872-1965. **Owner(s):** Lancaster Management, P.O. Box 609, Gadsden, AL 35902; Ed. Tammy Courter; Pub. Rhonda Bennett; pub. size: broadsheet; circ. 3,000(paid).

CRESCO

US

CRESCO TIMES-PLAIN DEALER. 1866. Wed. $.75 newsstand; $24/yr. in cy; $46/yr. out of state. 214 N. Elm St., Cresco, IA 52136. TEL 319-547-3601; FAX 319-547-4602. **Owner(s):** John Hall Publishing, Inc., P.O. Box 350, Cresco, IA 52136. TEL 319-547-3601; Ed. John Hall; Pub. John Hall; adv. contact: John Hall. pub. size: broadsheet; circ. 4,231(paid).

DAVENPORT

US

LEADER, THE. 1986. Wed. free in area; $26/yr. out of area. 423 E. 32nd St., Ste. 1, Davenport, IA 52803. TEL 319-326-5848; FAX 319-326-0356. **Owner(s):** Small Newspaper Group, 1720 Fifth Ave., Moline, IL 51265. TEL 309-764-4344; FAX 309-797-0311; Ed. Michae Romkey. adv.; photos; pub. size: broadsheet; circ. 51,000(free & paid).

DECORAH

US

DECORAH PUBLIC OPINION & JOURNAL. 1864. s-w.: Tue.: Public Opinion; Thu.: Journal. $.50 newsstand; $30-42/yr. 107 E. Water St., Decorah, IA 52101. TEL 319-382-4221; FAX 319-382-5949. **Owner(s):** Decorah News Co., P.O. Box 350, Decorah, IA 52101. TEL 319-382-4221; Ed. Richard Fromm; Pub. John Anundsen; adv.; photos; pub. size: broadsheet; circ. 6,400(free & paid). **Formerly:** Decorah Journal.

DENISON

US

DENISON BULLETIN & REVIEW. 1873. s-w.: Tue. & Fri. $.60 newsstand; $35/yr. local; $48/yr. elsewhere. 1410 Broadway Denison, IA 51442-0550. TEL 712-263-2123; FAX 712-263-2125. **Owner(s):** Denison Newspapers, Inc., 1410 Broadway, Denison, IA 51442. TEL 712-263-2122; FAX 712-263-2125; Ed. Chuck Signs; Pub. Richard R.G. Knowles; adv.; photos; pub. size: broadsheet; circ. 5,500(paid).

DES MOINES

US

DES MOINES LEE TOWN NEWS. 1958. Wed. free. 2221 E. Ovid St., Des Moines, IA 50313. TEL 515-262-1724; FAX 515-262-1825. **Owner(s):** Ogden Newspapers, Inc., 1500 Main St., Wheeling, WV 26033. TEL 304-233-0100; Ed. Dave DiValois; Pub. Roger Smed; adv. contact: Don Gimberline. pub. size: tabloid; circ. 14,207(free).

DEWITT

US   ISSN 0886-8808

DEWITT OBSERVER. 1864. s-w Wed. & Sat. $.75 newsstand; $32/yr. local. 512 Seventh St., DeWitt, IA 52742. TEL 319-659-3121; FAX 319-659-3778. **Owner(s):** Bob Parrott, 903 Seventh St., DeWitt, IA 52742. TEL 319-659-3121; Bob Melvold, 108 W. Quarry St., Maquoketa, IA 52060. TEL 319-652-2441; Frances Melvold, 108 W. Quarry St, Maquoketa, IA 52060. TEL 319-652-2441; Ed. Mary Rueter; Pub. Bob Parrott; adv. contact: Jean Bormann. photos; pub. size: tabloid; circ. 4,450(paid).

DOON

US

DOON PRESS. 1872. Thu. $.40 newsstand; $15.70/yr. in cy.; $17.70/yr. out of cy. 104 First Ave., Doon, IA 51235. TEL 712-726-3313; FAX 712-726-3313. **Owner(s):** Robert Sneller, 104 First Ave., Doon, IA 51235. TEL 712-726-3313; Ed. Harold Aardema; Pub. Robert Sneller; pub. size: tabloid; circ. 3,200(paid).

DYERSVILLE

US

DYERSVILLE COMMERCIAL. 1873. Wed. $.75 newsstand; $24/yr. local; $38/yr. out of area. 137 First Ave., E., Dyersville, IA 52040-0128. TEL 319-875-7131; FAX 319-875-2279. **Owner(s):** Northeast Iowa Publishers, Inc., 137 First Ave., E., P.O. Box 128, Dyersville, IA 52040. TEL 319-875-7131; Ed. Robert H. LeMay; Pub. Robert H. LeMay; adv. contact: Joyce Massey. pub. size: standard; circ. 4,200(paid).

EAGLE GROVE

US

EAGLE GROVE EAGLE. 1896. Wed. $.75 newsstand; $32/yr. 314 W. Broadway, Eagle Grove, IA 50533. TEL 515-448-4745; FAX 515-448-3182. **Owner(s):** Mid-America Publishing Corp., 314 W. Broadway, Eagle Grove, IA 50533. TEL 515-448-4745; FAX 515-448-3182; Pub. Gary L. Milks; adv. contact: Leigh Banwell photos; pub. size: broadsheet; circ. 2,700(paid).

EDDYVILLE

US

EDDYVILLE TRIBUNE. 1873. Thu. $18/yr. in cy.; $21/yr. out cf cy.; $24/yr. out of state. P.O. Box 228, Eddyville, IA 52553. TEL 515-969-4846; FAX 515-933-4342. **Owner(s):** Mother Wit Publishing Co., Eddyville, IA; Ed. Beverly Lehman; Pub. Jack Arnold; adv.: $374/SAU. pub. size: broadsheet; c rc. 450(paid).

EDGEWOOD

US

EDGEWOOD REMINDER. Tue. $.56 newsstand; $18/yr. in state; $21/yr. state. 105 N. Washington, Edgewood, IA 52042. TEL 319-928-6876. **Owner(s):** Roger & Donna Skattum, 105 N. Washington, Edgewood, IA 52042. TEL 319-928-6876; adv.; photos; pub. size: tabloid; circ. 1,500(free & paid).

ELDON

US

BEACON-FORUM. 1873. Thu. $15/yr. 500 Church St., Eldon, IA 52554. TEL 515-652-7612. **Owner(s):** Brian Fleck, Five Star Newspapers, P.O. Box 9, Fremont, IA 52561. TEL 515-933-4241; Ed. Donna Garber; Pub. Nancy Annis; pub. size: tabloid; circ. 1,000(paid).

ELDORA

US

ELDORA HERALD-LEADER. 1880. Tue. $.50 newsstand; $28/yr. W. Edgington Ave., Eldora, IA 50627. TEL 515-858-5051; FAX 515-858-5541. **Owner(s):** Eldora Herald-Index Publishing Co., W. Edgington Ave., Eldora, IA 50527. TEL 515-858-5051; Ed. Allyn J. Schafer; Pub. Allyn J. Schafer; pub. size: broadsheet; circ. 2,850(paid).

US

HARDIN COUNTY INDEX. 1940. Fri. $.50 newsstand; $28/yr. W. Edgington Ave., Eldora, IA 50627. TEL 515-858-5051; FAX 515-858-5541. **Owner(s):** Eldora Herald-Index Publishing Co., W. Edgington Ave., Eldora, IA 50627. TEL 515-858-5051; Ed. Allyn J. Schafer. pub. size: broadsheet; circ. 2,850(paid).

ELDRIDGE

US

NORTH SCOTT PRESS, THE. 1968. Wed. $.75 newsstand; $24/yr. in cy. 214 N. Second St., Eldridge, IA 52748. TEL 319-285-8111; FAX 319-285-8114. **Owner(s):** North Scott Press, Inc., 214 N. Second St., Eldridge, IA 52748. TEL 319-285-8111; Ed. Charles Scott Campbell; Pub. William F. "Bill" Tubbs; adv.; pub. size: tabloid; circ. 5,500(paid).

ELKADER

US

CLAYTON COUNTY REGISTER. 1878. Wed. $.75 newsstand; $23.50/yr. local. 106 Cedar, N.W., Elkader, IA 52043. TEL 319-245-1311. **Owner(s):** Griffith Press, Inc., 106 Cedar, N.W., Elkader, IA 52043. TEL 319-245-1311; FAX 319-245-1512; Ed. Robert Andersen; Pub. Robert P. Griffith; adv. contact: Robert P. Griffith. photos; pub. size: tabloid; circ. 3,000(paid).

EMMETSBURG

US

EMMETSBURG DEMOCRAT. 1877. Thu. $.40 newsstand; $22.50/yr. 1901 Main St., Emmetsburg, IA 50536. TEL 712-852-2323; FAX 712-852-3184. **Owner(s):** Ogden Newspapers, Inc., 1500 Main St., Wheeling, WV 26003; Ed. Jane Whitmore. pub. size: broadsheet; circ. evening 2,150(paid).

US

EMMETSBURG REPORTER. 1877. Tue. $.40; $22.50/yr. in cy. 1901 Main St., Emmetsburg, IA 50536. TEL 712-852-2323; FAX 712-852-3184. **Owner(s):** Ogden Newspapers, Inc., 1500 Main St., Wheeling, WV 26003; Ed. Jane Whitmore. pub. size: standard; circ. 2,286(paid).

ESSEX

US

ESSEX INDEPENDENT, THE. 1895. Thu. $.50 newsstand; $16/yr. in cy.; $21/yr. out of cy. P.O. Box 59, Essex, IA 51638-0059. TEL 712-379-3313; FAX 712-246-3099. **Owner(s):** Gleason-Knowles Communications, Inc., 702 W. Sheriden Ave., Shenandoah, IA 51601. TEL 712-246-3097; FAX 712-246-3099; Ed. Robert D. Jackson; Pub. Gregg K. Knowles; adv.; pub. size: broadsheet; circ. 600(free & paid).

FOREST CITY

US

FOREST CITY SUMMIT. 1867. Tue. $.75 newsstand; $24/yr. local; $32/yr. out of state. 105 S. Clark St., Forest City, IA 50436. TEL 515-582-2112; FAX 515-582-4442. **Owner(s):** Summit Printing Co., 105 S. Clark St., Forest City, IA 50436. TEL 515-582-2112; Ed. Cynthia Ann Carter; Pub. Martin Bunge; adv. contact: Ellen Olson. pub. size: broadsheet; circ. 10,500(paid).

FREMONT

US

FREEMONT GAZETTE. 1991. Thu. $.50 newsstand; $21/yr. P.O. Box 9, Fremont, IA 52561. TEL 515-933-4241; FAX 515-933-4341. **Owner(s):** Mother Wit Publishing Co., P.O. Box 9, Fremont, IA 52561. TEL 515-933-4241; Ed. Chris Arnold; Pub. Jack Arnold; pub. size: tabloid; circ. 1,000(paid).

GLENWOOD

US   ISSN 0746-4398

GLENWOOD OPINION-TRIBUNE. 1864. Wed. $.50 newsstand; $22.25/yr. in cy. 116 S. Walnut, Glenwood, IA 51534-0191. TEL 712-527-3191; FAX 712-587-3193. **Owner(s):** Landmark Community Newspapers, Inc., P.O. Box 549, Shelbyville, KY 40066. TEL 502-633-4334; Ed. Joe Foreman; Pub. Lois Helms; adv. contact: Lois Helms. photos; bk.rev.; pub. size: standard; circ. 3,600(paid).

GREENE

US

GREENE RECORDER, THE. 1883. Wed. $.50 newsstand; $18/yr. local; $22/yr. elsewhere. 219 N. Second St., Greene, IA 50636. TEL 515-823-4525; Sylvia J. Hawker, P.O. Box 370, Greene, IA 50636. TEL 515-823-4525; Ed. Syliva J. Hawker; Pub. Fred J. Hawker; adv.; photos; pub. size: broadsheet; circ. 1,300.

GREENFIELD

US   ISSN 1072-7523

ADAIR COUNTY FREE PRESS. 1889. Wed. $.50 newsstand; $21/yr. 108 E. Iowa St., Greenfield, IA 50849. TEL 515-743-6121; FAX 515-743-6122. **Owner(s):** Kenneth H. Sidey, 108 E. Iowa St., Greenfield, IA 50849. TEL 515-743-6121; Ed. Kenneth H. Sidey; Pub. Edwin J. Sidey; adv.; photos; pub. size: broadsheet; circ. 3,000(paid).

GRINNELL

US

GRINNELL HERALD-REGISTER. 1868. s-w.: Mon. & Thu. $.50 newsstand; $36.50/yr. local, $42/yr. out of area. 813 Fifth Ave., Grinnell, IA 50112-0360. TEL 515-236-3113; FAX 515-236-5135. **Owner(s):** Mr. & Mrs. A.J. Pinder, 813 Fifth Ave., Grinnell, IA 50112. TEL 515-236-3113; FAX 515-236-5135; Pub. A. J. Pinder; adv. contact: Jeanne Pinder. photos; bk.rev.; pub. size: broadsheet; circ. 3,550(free & paid).

GRUNDY CENTER

US

GRUNDY REGISTER. 1868. Wed. $.60 newsstand; $24/yr. 601 G Ave., Grundy Center, IA 50638. TEL 319-824-6958. **Owner(s):** Register Printing Co., 601 G Ave., Grundy Center, IA 50638. TEL 319-824-6958; Ed. Deb Workman; Pub. Ralph Kotenbeutel; adv. contact: Ralph Kotenbeutel. pub. size: broadsheet; circ. 3,000(paid).

GUTHRIE CENTER

US

TIMES GUTHRIAN. 1856. Wed. $.50 newsstand; $18/yr. in cy. 205 State, Guthrie Center, IA 50115. TEL 515-747-3511; FAX 515-747-2208. **Owner(s):** Scott P. Gonzales, 100 S. 12th St., Guthrie Center, IA 50115. TEL 515-747-3044; Ed. Scott Gonzales; Pub. Charles P. Gonzales; adv. contact: Lorence Huggins. pub. size: broadsheet; circ. 4,361(paid).

GUTTENBERG

US

GUTTENBERG PRESS. Wed. $.75 newsstand; $22/yr. local. 10 Schiller St., Guttenberg, IA 52052. TEL 319-252-2421. **Owner(s):** Howe Printing Co., P.O. Box 149, Prairie du Chien, WI 53821; adv. contact: Carl Neiers. pub. size: tabloid; circ. 2,758(free & paid).

HAMPTON

US

HAMPTON CHRONICLE & TIMES. 1876. s-w.: Tue. & Thu. $.75 newsstand; $30/yr. in cy.; $35/yr. out of cy. 9 Second St., N.W., Hampton, IA 50441. TEL 515-456-2585. **Owner(s):** Hampton Publishing Co., P.O. Box 29, Hampton, IA. TEL 515-456-2585; Ed. Joseph P. Roth; Pub. Joseph P. Roth; adv.; pub. size: broadsheet; circ. 4,000(paid).

HARLAN

US

HARLAN NEWS ADVERTISER. 1870. Fri. $.75 newsstand; $32/yr. 1114 Seventh St., Harlan, IA 51537-0721. TEL 712-755-3111; FAX 712-755-3324. **Owner(s):** Alan & Steve Mores, 1114 Seventh St., Harlan, IA 51537. TEL 712-755-3111; FAX 712-755-3324; Ed. Bob Bjoin; Pub. Alan Mores; adv. contact: Mike Kolbe. pub. size: broadsheet; circ. 5,390(paid).

US

HARLAN TRIBUNE. 1879. Tue. $.75 newsstand; $26/yr. Press Bldg., 1114 Seventh St., Harlan, IA 51537-0721. TEL 712-755-3111; FAX 712-755-3324. **Owner(s):** Alan & Steve Mores, 1114 Seventh St., Harlan, IA 51537-0721. TEL 712-755-3111; FAX 712-755-3324; Ed. Bob Bjoin; Pub. Steve Mores; adv. contact: Alan Mores. photos; pub. size: broadsheet; circ. 5,000(paid).

HUDSON

US

HUDSON HERALD, THE. 1911. Thu. $.50 newsstand; $20/yr. 411 Jefferson St., Hudson, IA 50643-0210. TEL 319-988-3855; FAX 319-988-3855. **Owner(s):** Clifford Murray, 411 Jefferson St., Hudson, IA 50643-0210. TEL 319-988-3855; Ed. Clifford Murray. adv.; photos; pub. size: broadsheet; circ. 1,500(paid).

HUMBOLDT

US

HUMBOLDT INDEPENDENT. 1889. Thu. $.60 newsstand; $27/yr. in state; $37/yr. out of state. 512 Sumner Ave., Humboldt, IA 50548. TEL 515-332-2514. E-mail: independent@trvnet.net; URL: http://www.trvnet.net/independent. **Owner(s):** Gargano Communications, Inc., 512 Sumner Ave., Humboldt, IA 50548. TEL 515-332-2514; Ed. Jeffrey Gargano; Pub. James Gargano; adv. contact: James Gargano. pub. size: broadsheet; circ. 5,825(paid).

HUMESTON

US

HUMESTON NEW ERA. 1880. w. $.40 newsstand; $14/yr. in area; $16/yr. elsewhere. RR 2, Humeston, IA 50123. TEL 515-877-3811; FAX 515-872-1234. **Owner(s):** James Lancaster, P.O. Box 609, Gadsden, AL 35901; Ed. Virginia Sponsler; Pub. Norval Lowe; adv.; pub. size: tabloid.

INDEPENDENCE

US

INDEPENDENCE BULLETIN-JOURNAL. 1860. s-w.: Wed. & Sat. $.75/Wed. newsstand; $1/Sat.; $36/yr. 116 Fifth Ave., N.E., Independence, IA 50644. TEL 319-334-2557; FAX 319-334-6752. **Owner(s):** Oelwein Publishing Co., Oelwein, IA 50304; Ed. Jim Morrison; Pub. Martin Van Ee; adv.; pub. size: broadsheet; circ. 4,500(paid).

INDIANOLA

US   ISSN 0895-3287

RECORD-HERALD & INDIANOLA TRIBUNE. 1857. Wed. $.75 newsstand; $27.50/yr. in cy.; $35/yr. elsewhere. 203 W. Salem Ave., Indianola, IA 50125. TEL 515-961-2511; FAX 515-961-4833. **Owner(s):** Des Moines Register & Tribune, P.O. Box 957, Des Moines, IA 50304. TEL 515-284-8000; Ed. Deb Belt; Pub. Tom Hawley; adv.; photos; pub. size: broadsheet; circ. 20,200(free & paid). **Wire Service(s):** Media Link, AP Newsfinder.

IOWA FALLS

US

TIMES CITIZEN. 1881. s-w.: Wed. & Sat. $.50 newsstand; $28/yr. local; $40/yr. out of state. 406 Stevens, Iowa Falls, IA 50126. TEL 515-648-2521; FAX 515-648-4765. **Owner(s):** Times Citizen, P.O. Box 640, Iowa Falls, IA 50126. TEL 515-648-2521; Ed. Elaine Loring; Pub. Mark Hamilton; pub. size: broadsheet; circ. 3,800(paid). Formerly: Iowa Falls Citizen.

JEFFERSON

US

JEFFERSON BEE. 1866. Tue. free. 214 N. Wilson Ave., Jefferson, IA 50129. TEL 515-386-4161; FAX 515-386-4162. **Owner(s):** Jefferson Bee & Herald Publishing Co., Inc., 214 N. Wilson Ave., Jefferson, IA 50129. TEL 515-386-4161; FAX 515-386-4162; Ed. Frederick G. Morain; Pub. Frederick G. Morain; adv.; pub. size: broadsheet; circ. 8,600(free).

US

JEFFERSON HERALD. 1891. Thu. $24/yr. 214 N. Wilson Ave., Jefferson, IA 50129. TEL 515-386-4161; FAX 515-386-4162. **Owner(s):** Jefferson Bee & Herald Publishing Co., Inc., 214 N. Wilson Ave., Jefferson, IA 50129. TEL 515-386-4161; FAX 515-386-4162; Ed. Frederick G. Morain. adv.; pub. size: broadsheet; circ. 3,300(paid).

KALONA

US

KALONA NEWS, THE. 1892. Wed. $.50 newsstand; $21/yr. in cy.; $23/yr. in state; $30/yr. out of state. 419 B Ave., Kalona, IA 52247-0430. TEL 319-656-2273; FAX 319-655-2299. **Owner(s):** Ronald C. Slechta, 816 Tenth St., P.O. Box 430, Kalona, IA 52247-0430. TEL 319-656-2104; FAX 319-656-2299; Helen M. Slechta, 816 Tenth St., P.O. Box 430, Kalona, IA 52247-0430. TEL 319-656-2104; FAX 319-656-2299; Ed. Ronald C. Slechta; Pub. Ronald C. Slechta; adv. contact: Ronald C. Slechta. photos; pub. size: broadsheet; circ. 3,150(paid).

KNOXVILLE

US

KNOXVILLE JOURNAL/EXPRESS. 1855. Fri. $.50 newsstand; $28/yr. 122 E. Robinson, Knoxville, IA 50138. TEL 515-842-2155; FAX 515-842-2929. **Owner(s):** Knoxville Journal-Express, Inc., 122 E. Robinson, P.O. Box 458, Knoxville, IA 50138. TEL 515-842-2155; FAX 515-842-2929; Ed. Abby St. John; Pub. Jack Crook; adv. contact: Don Abens. photos; bk.rev.; pub. size: broadsheet; circ. 3,450(paid).

LAURENS

US

LAURENS SUN, THE. Thu. $.50 newsstand; $20/yr. 119 S. Third St., Laurens, IA 50554-0125. TEL 712-845-4541. **Owner(s):** William H. & Darlene A. Chaffee, P.O. Box 125, Laurens, IA 50554-0125. TEL 712-845-4541; Ed. Dar Chaffee; Pub. William Chaffee; adv.; pub. size: broadsheet; circ. 1,550(paid).

LEON

US

LEON JOURNAL-REPORTER. 1861. Wed. $17/yr. in area; $22/yr. out of area. 110 N. Main St., Leon, IA 50144. TEL 515-446-4151. **Owner(s):** W.R. Lindsey, 110 N. Main, Leon, IA 50144. TEL 515-446-4940; Gary D. Lindsey, 802 N.W. White, Leon, IA 50144. TEL 515-446-6645; Ed. Margaret Lindsey. adv. contact: W.R. Lindsey. pub. size: standard; circ. 2,700(paid).

LIME SPRINGS

US

LIME SPRINGS HERALD. 1888. Thu. $.75 newsstand; $22.50/yr. in area; $25/yr. out of area. Main St., Lime Springs, IA 52155. TEL 319-566-2687. **Owner(s):** Barry & Sara Casebolt, P.O. Box 187, Lime Springs, IA 52155. TEL 319-566-2687; Pub. Eileen M. Evans; adv.; photos; pub. size: broadsheet; circ. 872(paid).

LOGAN

US

LOGAN HERALD OBSERVER. 1886. Wed. $.50 newsstand; $18.50/yr. in cy.; $23/yr. in state; $24.50/yr. elsewhere. 112 S. Fourth Ave., Logan, IA 51546-0148. TEL 712-644-2705; FAX 712-647-3081. **Owner(s):** Bloom Publishing Co., 112 S. Fourth Ave., Logan, IA 51546. TEL 712-644-2705; FAX 712-644-3031; Ed. Eugene A. Bloom; Pub. Eugene A. Bloom; adv.; photos; pub. size: broadsheet; circ. 2,175(paid).

LONE TREE

US

LONE TREE REPORTER, THE. 1893. Thu. $.50 newsstand; $18/yr. 117 LaVoe, Lone Tree, IA 52755. TEL 319-629-5207; FAX 319-629-5229. **Owner(s):** Slechta Communications, Inc., 117 LaVoe, Lone Tree, IA 52755. TEL 319-629-5207; FAX 319-629-5229; Ed. Cate Spears; Pub. Ronald C. Slechta; adv.; pub. size: tabloid; circ. 5,600(free & paid).

MALVERN

US

MALVERN LEADER, THE. 1874. Thu. $.50 newsstand; $16/yr. in cy.; $22/yr. out of cy. Main St., Malvern, IA 51551. TEL 712-624-8512. **Owner(s):** Mark A. Siekman, P.O. Box 129, Malvern, IA 51551. TEL 712-624-8512; Ed. Mark A. Siekman; Pub. Mark A. Siekman; adv.; photos; pub. size: broadsheet; circ. 1,300(controlled & paid).

MANCHESTER

US

MANCHESTER PRESS. 1871. Tue. $33/yr. 109 E. Delaware St., Manchester, IA 52057. TEL 319-927-2020; FAX 319-927-4945. **Owner(s):** Manchester Publishing Co., 109 E. Delaware St., Manchester, IA 52057. TEL 319-927-2020; Pub. Larry K. Woellert; adv. contact: Carol Harper. pub. size: broadsheet; circ. 4,896(paid).

MAQUOKETA

US

MAQUOKETA SENTINEL-PRESS. 1854. s-w.: Wed. & Sat. $.50 newsstand; $28/yr. in cy.; $35/yr. elsewhere. 108 W. Quarry St., Maquoketa, IA 52060. TEL 319-652-2441; FAX 319-652-6094. **Owner(s):** Maquoketa Newspapers, Inc., 108 W. Quarry, Maquoketa, IA 52060. TEL 319-652-2441; Ed. Doug Melvold; Pub. Douglas Melvold; adv.; pub. size: broadsheet; circ. 6,800(paid).

MARENGO

US

PIONEER REPUBLICAN, THE. 1853. Thu. $.75 newsstand; $24/yr. in state; $29/yr. out of state. 100 W. Main St., Marengo, IA 52301. TEL 319-642-5506; FAX 319-642-5509. **Owner(s):** Marengo Publishing Corp., 100 W. Main St., Marengo, IA 52301-0208. TEL 319-642-5506; FAX 319-642-5509; Ed. Alan Sieve; Pub. Dan DeBettignies; adv. contact: Dan De Bettignios. photos; pub. size: broadsheet; circ. 5,500(paid).

MISSOURI VALLEY

US

MISSOURI VALLEY TIMES-NEWS. 1885. s-w.: Wed. & Fri. $.50 newsstand; $38/yr. 501 E. Erie, Missouri Valley, IA 51555. TEL 712-642-2791; FAX 712-642-2595. **Owner(s):** Mark Rhoades, 138 N. 16th, Blair, NE 68008. TEL 402-426-9860; Ed. Peter Graham. adv. contact: Charles Hickman. pub. size: broadsheet; circ. 3,000(paid).

MONTEZUMA

US

MONTEZUMA REPUBLICAN, THE. 1856. Wed. $.75 newsstand; $18-$23/yr. 406 E. Main St., Montezuma, IA 50171. TEL 319-642-5506; FAX 319-642-5509. **Owner(s):** Marengo Publishing Corp., 100 W. Main St., Marengo, IA 52301-0208. TEL 319-642-5506; FAX 319-642-5509; Ed. Andrew Daughton; Pub. Dan DeBettignies; adv. contact: Roger Allen. photos; pub. size: broadsheet; circ. 5,400(free & paid).

MONTICELLO

US

MONTICELLO EXPRESS. 1865. Wed. $.75 newsstand; $24/yr. 111 E. Grand, Monticello, IA 52310. TEL 319-465-3555; FAX 319-465-4611. **Owner(s):** Monticello Express, Inc., 111 E. Grand, Monticello, IA 52310. TEL 319-465-3555; Ed. Craig Neises; Pub. Robert Goodyear; adv. contact: Mark Spensley. pub. size: tabloid; circ. 3,400(paid).

MT. AYR

US

MOUNT AYR RECORD-NEWS. 1864. Thu. $.50 newsstand; $19/yr. in cy. 122 W. Madison, Mt. Ayr, IA 50854. TEL 515-464-2440; FAX 515-464-2229. **Owner(s):** H. Alan Smith, P.O. Box 346, Mt. Ayr, IA 50854. TEL 515-464-2440; FAX 515-464-2949; Ed. H. Alan Smith; Pub. H. Alan Smith; adv. contact: Helen Terry. pub. size: broadsheet; circ. 3,875(paid).

MT. VERNON

US

SUN, THE. 1869. Wed. $.60 newsstand; $21/yr. P.O. Box 129, Mt. Vernon, IA 52314. TEL 319-895-6216. **Owner(s):** Sterling Publications, Inc., P.O. Box 129, Mt. Vernon, IA 52314. TEL 319-895-6216; FAX 319-895-6217; adv. contact: Leann Pisarik. photos; pub. size: broadsheet; circ. 2,300(paid). **Wire Service(s):** Iowa Medialink.

NASHUA

US

NASHUA REPORTER. 1878. Wed. $.50 newsstand; $19/yr. in cy.; $21/yr. in state. 216 Main St., Nashua, IA 50658. TEL 515-435-4151. **Owner(s):** Carmen Conklin, P.O. Box 67, Nashua, IA 50658. TEL 515-435-2036; Wanda Orric, P.O. Box 67, Nashua, IA 50658. TEL 515-435-2036; Ed. Conklin Orric; Pub. Carmen Conklin; adv. contact: Carmen Conklin. photos; pub. size: broadsheet; circ. 1,300(paid).

NEVADA

US

NEVADA JOURNAL. 1895. Thu. $.75 newsstand; $25/yr. 1133 Sixth St., Nevada, IA 50201. TEL 515-382-2161; FAX 515-382-4299. **Owner(s):** Partnership Press, Inc., 317 Fifth St., Ames, IA 50010. TEL 515-232-2160; adv. contact: Linette Fenimore. photos; bk.rev.; pub. size: broadsheet; circ. 3,000(paid). **Wire Service(s):** AP.

NEW HAMPTON

US

NEW HAMPTON ECONOMIST. 1930. Wed. $1 newsstand; $38/yr. 10 N. Chestnut Ave., New Hampton, IA 50659-0380. TEL 515-394-2111; FAX 515-394-2113. **Owner(s):** New Hampton Publishing Co., Inc., P.O. Box 380, New Hampton, IA 50659; Ed. Beverly Kolthoff; Pub. Dan Feuling; pub. size: broadsheet; circ. 10,000(free & paid).

NEW HAMPTON TRIBUNE. 1874. Thu. $.75 newsstand; $38/yr. 10 N. Chestnut Ave., New Hampton, IA 50659-0380. TEL 515-394-2111; FAX 515-394-2113. **Owner(s):** New Hampton Publishing Co., Inc., P.O. Box 380, New Hampton, IA 50659. TEL 515-394-2111; Ed. Beverly Kolthoff; Pub. Dan Feuling; pub. size: broadsheet; circ. 10,000(free & paid).

NEW SHARON

US

NEW SHARON STAR. 1873. Thu. $.50 newsstand; $21/yr. in cy.; $30/yr. elsewhere. 113 S. Main St., New Sharon, IA 50207. TEL 515-637-2632. **Owner(s):** Mother Wit Publishing Co., P.O. Box 90, Fremont, IA 50207. TEL 515-933-4241; Ed. Tina Reed; Pub. Jack Arnold; pub. size: tabloid; circ. 750(paid).

ONAWA

US   ISSN 0899-6520

ONAWA DEMOCRAT. 1890. Thu. $.50 newsstand; $15/yr. local; $20/yr. elsewhere. 720 Iowa Ave., Onawa, IA 51040-1628. TEL 712-423-2411; FAX 712-423-2411. **Owner(s):** Wonder & Son Publishing, 720 Iowa Ave., Onawa, IA 51040. TEL 712-423-2411; adv.; photos; pub. size: standard; circ. 3,000(paid).

US

ONAWA SENTINEL. 1885. Thu. $.35 newsstand; $14/yr. local; $17/yr. in state; $20/yr. out of state. 1014 Ninth St., Onawa, IA 51040. TEL 712-423-2021; FAX 712-423-3038. **Owner(s):** Onawa Sentinel-Verlee Sawyer, 1014 Ninth St., Onawa, IA 51040. TEL 712-423-2021; Ed. Verlee Sawyer; Pub. Verlee Sawyer; adv. contact: Larry Sawyer. pub. size: broadsheet; circ. 1,800(paid). **Wire Service(s):** Media Link.

OSAGE

US

MITCHELL COUNTY PRESS-NEWS. 1865. Wed. $26/yr. 112 N. Sixth St., Osage, IA 50461. TEL 515-732-3721; FAX 515-732-5689. **Owner(s):** Paul Bunge, 820 Main St., Osage, IA 50461. TEL 515-732-4716; Ed. Larry Kershner. adv.; pub. size: broadsheet; circ. 3,800(paid). **Formerly:** Osage Mitchell County Press-News.

OSCEOLA

US   ISSN 0745-6247

OSCEOLA SENTINEL-TRIBUNE. 1860. Thu. $.50 newsstand; $18.50/yr. local; $25/yr. elsewhere. 115 E. Washington, Osceola, IA 50213. TEL 515-342-2131; FAX 515-342-2060. **Owner(s):** Sally & Frank Morlan, 115 E. Washington, Osceola, IA 50213. TEL 515-342-2131; Ed. Frank E. Morlan. adv.; photos; bk.rev.; pub. size: broadsheet; circ. 4,200(paid). **Wire Service(s):** Iowa Media Link.

OSSIAN

US

OSSIAN BEE, THE. 1889. Wed. $.50 newsstand; $13/yr. in cy; $15/yr. out of cy. 107 W. Main St., Ossian, IA 52161-0096. TEL 319-532-9113; FAX 319-532-9081. **Owner(s):** Dirk Amundsen, 107 W. Main St., Ossian, IA 52161. TEL 319-532-9113; FAX 319-532-9081; Ed. Marlys Amundsen; Pub. Dirk Amundsen; adv.; photos; pub. size: broadsheet; circ. 1,242(paid).

PAULLINA

US

PAULLINA TIMES. 1883. Tue. $.50 newsstand; $18/yr. 144 E. Broadway, Paullina, IA 51046-0677. TEL 712-448-3622; FAX 712-448-3622. **Owner(s):** O'Shillal Enterprises, Inc., P.O. Box 637, Paullina, IA 51046-0637. TEL 712-448-3622; FAX 712-448-3622; adv.; photos; pub. size: broadsheet; circ. 1,470(free & paid). **Wire Service(s):** Iowa Media Link.

PELLA

US

PELLA CHRONICLE. 1865. Thu. $.75 newsstand; $24/yr. in area; $27/yr. out of area. 739 Franklin St., Pella, IA 50219. TEL 515-628-3882; FAX 515-628-3905. **Owner(s):** Edwards Publications, 122 E. Robinson, Knoxville, IA 50138. TEL 515-842-2155; Ed. Barry Johnson; Pub. Jack Crook; adv. contact: Don Abens. photos; bk.rev.; pub. size: broadsheet; circ. 3,600(paid).

PERRY

US ISSN 0746-7222

PERRY CHIEF. 1874. Wed. $.55 newsstand; $22-$24/yr. 1323 Second St., Perry, IA 50220. TEL 515-465-4666; FAX 515-465-3087. **Owner(s):** Stephen R. Whitehead, P.O. Box 98, Perry, IA 50220. TEL 515-465-4666; Ed. Denise Pierce. adv. contact: Ken Schumacher. pub. size: broadsheet; circ. 3,250(paid).

POCAHONTAS

US

POCAHONTAS RECORD-DEMOCRAT. 1884. Tue. $.75 newsstand; $22/yr. in cy.; $26.50/yr. out of cy.; $28.50/yr. out of state. 218 N. Main St., Pocahontas, IA 50574. TEL 712-335-3553; FAX 712-335-3856. **Owner(s):** Glenn & Wanda Schreiber, 64 Court Sq., Pocahontas, IA 50574. TEL 712-335-3553; Ed. Glenn Schreiber; Pub. Glenn Schreiber; adv. contact: Wanda Schreiber. pub. size: broadsheet; circ. 5,000(paid).

PRAIRIE CITY

US

PRAIRIE CITY NEWS. 1874. Thu. $.35 newsstand; $14/yr. in state; $17/yr. out of state. 108 E. Jefferson, Prairie City, IA 50228-0249. TEL 515-994-2349; FAX 515-994-3169. **Owner(s):** Orian Woods, 108 E. Jefferson, Prairie City, IA 50228. TEL 515-994-2349; FAX 515-994-3169; Ed. Orian Woods; Pub. Orian Woods; adv. contact: Dawn Aalbers. photos; pub. size: tabloid; circ. 1,100(paid).

RED OAK

US ISSN 0747-3281

RED OAK EXPRESS. 1867. Tue. $.75 newsstand; $22.50/yr. 2012 Commerce Dr., Red Oak, IA 51566. TEL 712-623-2566; FAX 712-623-2568. **Owner(s):** Landmark Community Newspapers, Inc., P.O. Box 549, Shelbyville, KY 40065. TEL 502-633-4334; Ed. Jan Castle Renander. adv. contact: Linda Blackburn. pub. size: broadsheet; circ. 4,800(paid).

ROCK RAPIDS

US

LYON-SIOUX PRESS. 1888. Wed. $.50 newsstand; $26/yr. in cy. & adj. cys.; $40/yr. elsewhere. 310 First Ave., Rock Rapids, IA 51246. TEL 712-472-2525; FAX 712-472-3414. **Owner(s):** New Century Press, Inc., P.O. Box 28, 310 First Ave., Rock Rapids, IA 51246. TEL 712-472-2525; Ed. Jodie Hoogendoorn; Pub. Jim Houck; pub. size: broadsheet; circ. 2,847(paid). **Formerly:** Rock Rapids County Reporter.

SCHALLER

US

SCHALLER HERALD. 1881. Wed. $.50 newsstand; $18/yr. out of state. 203 S. Main St., Schaller, IA 51053. TEL 712-275-4229. **Owner(s):** Betty Bailey, P.O. Box 129. Schaller, IA 51053. TEL 712-275-4229; Ed. Betty Bailey; Pub. Betty Bailey; adv.; pub. size: broadsheet; circ. 850(paid).

SHELDON

US

N'WEST IOWA REV EW. 1972. Sat. $.95 newsstand; $24/yr. in cy.; $36/yr. out of cy. P.O. Box 160, Sheldon, IA 51201. TEL 712-324-2514; FAX 712-324-2345. **Owner(s):** Iowa Information, Inc., P.O. Box 160, Sheldon, IA 51201. TEL 712-324-2514; Pub. Peter W. Wagner; pub. size: broadsheet.

SHELDON MAIL-SUN. 1873. Wed. $.75 newsstand; $22/yr. in cy.; $30/yr. out of cy. P.O. Box 160, Sheldon, IA 51201. TEL 712-324-2514; FAX 712-324-2345. **Owner(s):** Iowa Information, Inc., P.O. Box 160, Sheldon, IA 51201. TEL 712-324-2514; Pub. Peter W. Wagner; pub. size: broadsheet; circ. 3,400(paid). **Formerly:** Sheldon Sun.

SIBLEY

US

OSCEOLA COUNTY GAZETTE-TRIBUNE. 1872. Wed. $.50 newsstand; $19.50/yr. in cy.; $25/yr. out of cy. 201 Ninth St., Sibley, IA 51249. TEL 712-754-2551. **Owner(s):** Sibley Printing & Publishing, 201 Ninth St, Sibley, IA 51249. TEL 712-754-2551; Ed. Rosalie Block; Pub. Jerry Wiseman; adv. contact: Jay L. Mohr. pub. size: broadsheet; circ. 1,700(paid).

SIGOURNEY

US

SIGOURNEY NEWS-REVIEW. 1870. Wed. $.50 newsstand; $22/yr. in state; $25/yr. out of state. 114 E. Washington St., Sigourney, IA 52591-0285. TEL 515-622-3110; FAX 515-622-2766. **Owner(s):** Sigourney News Review, 114 E. Washington St., Sigourney, IA 52591. TEL 515-622-3110; FAX 515-622-2766; Pub. Kenneth Chaney; adv. contact: Kim Strong. pub. size: broadsheet; circ. 2,649(paid). **Wire Service(s):** Iowa Media Link.

SLATER

US ISSN 0749-7040

TRI-COUNTY TIMES, THE. 1892. Wed. $.50 newsstand; $16/yr. in state; $22/yr. out of state. 312 Main St., Slater, IA 50244. TEL 515-685-3412; FAX 515-685-3668. **Owner(s):** Edwin W. Rood, 312 Main St. Box 237, Slater, IA 50244. TEL 515-685-3412; Ed. Edwin W. Rood. photos; bk.rev.; pub. size: standard; circ. 4,800(paid). **Formerly:** Slater Tri-County Times.

SOLON

US

LEADER, THE. 1950. Wed. $.50 newsstand; $18/yr. P.O. Box 249, Solon, IA 52333. TEL 319-644-2233. **Owner(s):** Brian Fleck, Five Star Newspapers, P.O. Box 249, Solon, IA 52333. TEL 319-644-2233; Ed. Jim Wolf; Pub. Brian Fleck; pub. size: broadsheet; circ. 900(paid).

SPENCER

US

NORTHWEST IOWA SHOPPER. s-w.: Wed. & Sat. free. 416 First Ave., W., Spencer, IA 51301. TEL 712-262-6610; FAX 712-262-3044. **Owner(s):** Edward Publications, P.O. Box 1193, Seneca, SC 29679; Pub. Joni Weerheim; adv. contact: Chris Swanson. pub. size: standard; circ. 25,000(controlled & free).

SPIRIT LAKE

US

SPIRIT LAKE BEACON. 1870. Thu. $.75 newsstand; $26/yr. 1706 Ithaca St., Spirit Lake, IA 51360. TEL 712-336-1211; FAX 712-335-1219. **Owner(s):** Edwards Publications, P.O. Box 1193, Seneca, SC 29679. TEL 803-882-3272; Ed. Frank Jaquith; Pub. Lew Spence; pub. size: broadsheet; circ. 3,700(paid).

STATE CENTER

US

STATE CENTER ENTERPRISE-RECORD. 1871. w. $.75 newsstand; $22/yr. local; $26/yr. elsewhere. 130 W. Main St., State Center, IA 50247-0634. TEL 515-483-2120; FAX 515-483-2938. **Owner(s):** John & Diane Strawn, 408 Second St., S.W., State Center, IA 50247-0634. TEL 515-483-2507; Ed. John C. Strawn, II; Pub. John C. Strawn, II; adv.; photos; pub. size: broadsheet; circ. 1,250.

STORM LAKE

US

STORM LAKE TIMES. 1990. s-w.: Wed. & Sat. $.75 newsstand; $39.95/yr. in cy. 220 W. Railroad St., Storm Lake, IA 50588. TEL 712-732-4991; FAX 712-732-4331. **Owner(s):** Storm Lake Times Co., Inc., Storm Lake, IA 50588; Ed. Art Cullen; Pub. John Cullen; adv. contact: Marty Gallagher. phctos; bk.rev.; pub. size: tabloid; circ. 2,800(paid).

STORY CITY

US

STORY CITY HERALD. 1881. Wed. $.50 newsstand; $22/yr. in state; $26/yr. out of state. 423 Broad St., Story City, IA 50248. TEL 515-733-4318; FAX 515-733-4319. **Owner(s):** Eloise Thorson, 423 Broad, Story City, IA 50248. TEL 515-733-4318; FAX 515-733-4319; Ed. Todd Thorson; Pub. Todd Thorson; adv. contact: Patricia Sawyer. photos; bk.rev.; pub. size: broadsheet; circ. 2,300(free & paid).

SUMNER

US

SUMNER GAZETTE. 1800. Thu. $20/yr. carrier; $18.50/yr. in cy.; $21.50/yr elsewhere; $26.50/yr. outside. 106 E. First St., Sumner, IA 50674. TEL 319-578-3351; FAX 319-578-5784. **Owner(s):** Sumner Gazette Publishing Co., 106 E. First St., Sumner, IA 50674. TEL 319-578-3351; FAX 319-578-5784; Pub. Cal Milnes; adv.; pub. size: broadsheet; circ. 3,000(paid).

TAMA

US

TAMA NEWS-HERALD. 1925. Thu. $32/yr. in cy. 220-224 W. Third St., Tama, IA 52339. TEL 515-484-2841; FAX 515-484-5705. **Owner(s):** Ogden Newspapers, Inc., 1500 Main St., Wheeling, WV 26033. TEL 304-233-0100; Ed. Nancy Dostal; Pub. Mike Schlesinger; adv.; photos; bk.rev.; pub. size: broadsheet; circ. 3,100(paid).

THORNTON

US

SOUTHERN COUNTY NEWS. Wed. $.40 newsstand; $20/yr. in state; $25/yr. out of state. 300 Main St., Thornton, IA 50479-0096. TEL 515-998-2712; FAX 515-998-2712. **Owner(s):** Southern County News, 300 Main St., Thornton, IA 50479-0096; Ed. William Schrader. adv.; photos; pub. size: broadsheet; circ. 950(free & paid).

TIPTON

US

TIPTON CONSERVATIVE & ADVERTISER. 1846. Wed. $.75 newsstand; $24/yr. W. Fifth St., Tipton, IA 52772. TEL 319-886-2131. **Owner(s):** Ruth Clark, P.O. Box 271, Tipton, IA 52772. TEL 319-886-2131; Stuart & Sharon Clark, P.O. Box 271, Tipton, IA 52772. TEL 319-886-2131; FAX 319-886-6466; Ed. Stuart Clark; Pub. Stuart Clark; adv. contact: Mark Kuehnle. bk.rev.; pub. size: broadsheet; circ. 4,900(paid).

TRAER

US

TRAER STAR-CLIPPER. 1873. Thu. $.50 newsstand; $25/yr. in state. 625 Second St., Traer, IA 50675. TEL 319-478-2323. **Owner(s):** Marshalltown Newspaper, Inc., 135 West Main, Marshalltown, IA 50158. TEL 800-542-7893; Ed. Ellen Young. adv.; photos; pub. size: broadsheet; circ. 3,200(paid).

VICTOR

US

VICTOR ECHO. 1990. w. $.25 newsstand; $12/yr. First & Washington Sts., Victor, IA 52347. TEL 319-647-2333; FAX 319-522-7527. **Owner(s):** Brooklyn Publishing Co., First & Washington Sts., Victor, IA 52347; adv.; pub. size: broadsheet; circ. 400(paid).

WAUKON

US

WAUKON STANDARD. 1870. Wed. $.75 newsstand; $23/yr. local; $37/yr. out of area. 15 First St, N.W., Waukon, IA 52172. TEL 319-568-3431; FAX 319-568-4242. **Owner(s):** News Publishing, Inc., 1126 Mills St., Black Earth, WI 53515. TEL 319-568-3431; Ed. Dick Schilling; Pub. Tom Johnson; adv. contact: Gail Johnson. pub. size: broadsheet; circ. 4,200(paid).

WAVERLY

US

WAVERLY BREMER COUNTY INDEPENDENT. 1856. Tue. $.50 newsstand; $34/yr. 311 W. Bremer, Waverly, IA 50677. TEL 319-352-3335. **Owner(s):** Woodward Communications, Inc., Eighth & Bluff Sts., Dubuque, IA 52001. TEL 319-588-5600; Ed. Ray Locke; Pub. Jayne Hall; adv. contact: Jayne Hall. pub. size: standard; circ. 6,390(paid).

WAVERLY DEMOCRAT. 1876. Thu. $30/yr. 311 W. Bremer, Waverly, IA 50677. TEL 319-352-3335. Owner(s): Woodward Communications, Inc., Eighth & Bluff Sts., Dubuque, IA 52001. TEL 319-588-5600; Ed. Ray Locke; Pub. Jayne Hall; adv. contact: Jayne Hall. pub. size: standard; circ. 6,390(paid).

WEST BURLINGTON

US

DES MOINES COUNTY NEWS, THE. 1956. Wed. $16/yr. in cy.; $19/yr. in state; $23/yr. out of state. P.O. Box 177, West Burlington, IA 52655-0177. TEL 319-752-8328. **Owner(s):** Louisa Publishing, Box 306, Wapello, IA 52653. TEL 319-523-4631; Pub. Mike Hodges; adv. contact: Randy Bardy. photos; pub. size: tabloid; circ. 1,900(paid).

WEST LIBERTY

US

WEST LIBERTY INDEX. 1868. Thu. $.50 newsstand; $20/yr. in cy.; $22/yr. in state; $24/yr. elsewhere. 104 E. Third St., West Liberty, IA 52776. TEL 319-627-2814; FAX 319-627-2110. **Owner(s):** Wally Johnson, P.O. Box 96, West Liberty, IA 52776. TEL 319-627-2814; FAX 319-627-2110; Ed. Karen Lourens; Pub. Wally Johnson; adv.; pub. size: tabloid; circ. 3,000(paid).

WEST UNION

US

FAYETTE COUNTY UNION. 1866. Wed. $.75 newsstand; $32/yr. in cy.; $38/yr. out of state. 119 S. Vine, West Union, IA 52175-0153. TEL 319-422-3888; FAX 319-422-3488. **Owner(s):** Union, The, 119 S. Vine, West Union, IA 52175. TEL 319-422-3888; FAX 319-422-3488; Ed. Gerald H. Blue; Pub. Gerald H. Blue; adv.; photos; pub. size: broadsheet; circ. 7,200(free & paid).
  Formerly: West Union Union.

WILLIAMSBURG

US

JOURNAL TRIBUNE. Thu. $.75 newsstand; $22/yr. in cy.; $24/yr. out of cy.; $29/yr. out of state. 208 W. State St., Williamsburg, IA 52361. TEL 319-668-1240. **Owner(s):** Marengo Publishing Corp., 100 W. Main St., Marengo, IA 52301-0208. TEL 319-642-5506; FAX 319-642-5509; Ed. Ken Sweeney; Pub. Dan DeBettignies; adv. contact: Mike Simmons. photos; pub. size: broadsheet; circ. 2,000(paid).

WINTERSET

US

WINTERSET MADISONIAN. 1856. Wed. $.60 newsstand; $29.50/yr. in cy. 112 W. Court Ave., Winterset, IA 50273. TEL 515-462-2101; FAX 515-462-2102. **Owner(s):** Ted Gorman, Winterset Madisonian, 112 W. Court Ave., Winterset, IA 50273. TEL 515-462-2102; Ed. Chris Dorsey; Pub. Ted Gorman; adv.; photos; pub. size: broadsheet; circ. 4,200(paid). **Wire Service(s):** Iowa Media Link.

KANSAS

ANTHONY

US

ANTHONY REPUBLICAN, THE. 1878. Wed. $.50 newsstand; $20/yr. in surrounding cys.; $25/yr. in state. 121 E. Main St., Anthony, KS 67003. TEL 316-842-5129; FAX 316-842-5120. **Owner(s):** James W. & Vera L. Dunn, 121 E. Main St., Anthony, KS 67003. TEL 316-842-5129; Pub. James W. Dunn; adv. contact: Larry Dunn. pub. size: broadsheet; circ. 3,100(paid).

BAXTER SPRINGS

US

BAXTER SPRINGS CITIZEN. 1872. s-w.: Tue. & Fri. $.50 newsstand; $03/yr. in cy.; $37/yr. out of cy. 1010 Military Ave., Baxter Springs, KS 66713-1547. TEL 316-856-2115; FAX 316-856-3162; E-mail: kansasnews@aol.com; URL: http://www.kspress.com/baxter/baxter.html. **Owner(s):** Nichols Communications, Inc., 1010 Military Ave., Baxter Springs, KS 66713. TEL 316-856-2115; FAX 316-856-3162; Ed. Brent Fisher; Pub. Jeff Nichols; adv. contact: Mende Staggs. photos; bk.rev.; pub. size: broadsheet; circ. 2,231(paid).

BELLE PLAINE

US

BELLE PLAINE NEWS, THE. 1879. Thu. $.50 newsstand; $20/yr. 431 Merchant, Belle Plaine, KS 67013. TEL 316-488-2234; FAX 316-488-3241. **Owner(s):** William S. Clester, 431 Merchant, Belle Plaine, KS 67013. TEL 316-488-2234; FAX 316-488-3241; Ed. Marian Phipps; Pub. William S. Clester; adv. contact: Marian Phipps. photos; bk.rev.; pub. size: tabloid; circ. 1,000(paid).

US

OXFORD REGISTER, THE. 1879. Thu. $.50 newsstand; $20/yr. 431 Merchant, Belle Plaine, KS 67013. TEL 316-455-3535; FAX 316-488-3241. **Owner(s):** William Sam Clester, P.O. Box 128, Belle Plaine, KS 67013. TEL 316-488-2234; FAX 316-488-3241; Ed. Marian Phipps; Pub. William Sam Clester; adv.; photos; bk.rev.; pub. size: tabloid; circ. 500(free & paid).

BELLEVILLE

US   ISSN 0740-0985

BELLEVILLE TELESCOPE. 1870. Thu. $.50 newsstand; $23/yr. in cy. 1817 U.S. 81 Frontage Rd., Belleville, KS 66935-0349. TEL 913-527-2244; FAX 913-527-2225. **Owner(s):** Telescope, Inc., 1817 E. U.S. 81 Frontage Rd., Belleville, KS 66935. TEL 913-527-2244; Ed. Mark L. Miller; Pub. Merle M. Miller; adv. contact: Paul Hasse. pub. size: broadsheet; circ. 5,100(paid).

BIRD CITY

US

BIRD CITY TIMES. Thu. $.65 newsstand; $22/yr. P.O. Box 167, Bird City, KS 67731. TEL 913-734-2621; FAX 913-332-3001. **Owner(s):** Steve & Cynthia Haynes, 170 S. Penn, Oberlin, KS 67749. TEL 913-475-2206; FAX 913-475-2800; Ed. Steve Haynes; Pub. Cynthia Haynes; adv. contact: Nell Frohlich. pub. size: broadsheet; circ. 688(free & paid).

BONNER SPRINGS

US

BONNER SPRINGS-EDWARDSVILLE CHIEFTAIN. 1896. Thu. $.35 newsstand; $12.75/yr. in cy.; $16/yr. out of cy. P.O. Box 256, Bonner Springs, KS 66012. TEL 913-422-4048; FAX 913-422-4233. **Owner(s):** Clausie W. & Jean Smith, P.O. Box 256, Bonner Springs, KS 66012. TEL 913-422-4048; Ed. Jean Smith; Pub. Jean Smith; adv.; photos; bk.rev.; pub. size: broadsheet; circ. 13,000(controlled & free).

BURLINGAME

US   ISSN 1040-6077

OSAGE COUNTY CHRONICLE. 1863. Thu. $.50 newsstand; $21/yr. in cy.; $24/yr. out of cy. 107 E. Santa Fe, Burlingame, KS 66413-0065. TEL 913-654-3621; FAX 913-654-3438. **Owner(s):** Incunabula, Inc., 107 E. Santa Fe, Burlingame, KS 66413. TEL 913-654-3621; FAX 913-654-3438; Ed. Eric Kopp; Pub. K. Kurt Kessinger; adv. contact: Kathy Kessinger. photos; pub. size: broadsheet; circ. 5,200(paid).

BURLINGTON

US

COFFEY COUNTY TODAY. 1856. 3/wk.: Mon., Wed., Fri. $.50 newsstand; $40/yr. carrier; $46/yr. mailed in state; $50/yr. out of state. 324 Hudson St., Burlington, KS 66839. TEL 316-364-5325; FAX 316-364-2607. **Owner(s):** Glenn R. German, P.O. Drawer A, Burlington, KS 66839. TEL 316-364-8610; Ed. Mark Petterson; Pub. Glenn R. German; adv. contact: B.J. Petterson. pub. size: broadsheet; circ. 2,600(paid). **Wire Service(s):** AP.

CHENEY

US

TIMES-SENTINEL, THE. 1894. Thu. $.50 newsstand; $22/yr. 101 N. Main, Cheney, KS 67025. TEL 316-542-3111; FAX 316-542-3283. **Owner(s):** Paul Rhodes & Amy Crouch, 211 N. Garfield, Cheney, KS. TEL 316-542-0179; Ed. Paul Rhodes. adv. contact: Amy Crouch. photos; bk.rev.; pub. size: tabloid; circ. 3,550(paid).

COLUMBUS

US

TOWNE & COUNTRY SHOPPER. Thu. free. 215 S. Kansas, Columbus, KS 66725. TEL 316-429-2773; FAX 316-429-3223. **Owner(s):** Jay M. Lacy, P.O. 231, Columbus, KS 66675. TEL 316-429-2773; Ed. Al Story; Pub. Jay M. Lacey; adv. contact: Dean Lammy. pub. size: tabloid; circ. 14,000(free).

COTTONWOOD FALLS

US   ISSN 1079-8188

CHASE COUNTY LEADER-NEWS. 1871. Wed. $.75 newsstand; $23/yr. in cy.; $25/yr. out of cy. 306 Broadway Cottonwood Falls, KS 66845-0436. TEL 316-273-6391; FAX 316-273-6864. **Owner(s):** Chase County Publishing Co., Inc., 306 Broadway, Cottonwood Falls, KS 66845-0046. TEL 316-273-6391; FAX 316-273-6674; Ed. Jerry Schwilling. adv.; photos; pub. size: standard; circ. 1,700(paid).

COURTLAND

US   ISSN 0746-5750

COURTLAND JOURNAL-EMPIRE. 1891. Thu. $.35 newsstand; $12.71/yr. in cy.; $17/yr. out of state. 420 Main St., Courtland, KS 66939-0318. TEL 913-374-1428. **Owner(s):** Robert & Colleen Mainquist, 420 Main St., Courtland, KS 66939-0318. TEL 913-374-4428; pub. size: standard; circ. 650(paid).

DODGE CITY

US   ISSN 0018-1471

HIGH PLAINS JOURNAL. 1882. Mon. $56/yr. 1500 E. Wyatt Earp Blvd., Dodge City, KS 67801-0760. TEL 316-227-7171; FAX 316-227-7173. **Owner(s):** High Plains Publishers, Inc., P.O. Box 760, Dodge City, KS 67801-0760. TEL 316-227-7171; Ed. Galen Hubbs; Pub. Duane Ross; adv. contact: Tom Taylor. pub. size: negotiable; circ. 58,000(paid). **Wire Service(s)** AP, KR.

ELLSWORTH

US

ELLSWORTH REPORTER, THE. 1871. Thu. $.75 newsstand; $23.01/yr. local; $26/yr. out of state. P.O. Box 7, Ellsworth, KS 67439. TEL 913-472-3103; FAX 913-472-3268. **Owner(s):** Karl Gaston, P.O. Box 7 Ellsworth, KS 67439. TEL 913-472-3103; FAX 913-472-3268; Ed. Karl Gaston; Pub. Karl Gaston; adv.; pub. size: broadsheet; circ. 3,000(paid).

EUREKA

US

EUREKA HERALD. 1868. Thu. $.50 newsstand; $25.95/yr. in area; $36/yr. out of area. 106 W. Second, Eureka, KS 67045. TEL 316-583-5721. **Owner(s):** Greenwood County Publishing, Inc., P.O. Box 590, Eureka, KS 67045. TEL 316-583-5721; Ed. Richard W. Clasen; Pub. Richard W. Clasen; pub. size: broadsheet; circ. 3,750(paid).

FREDONIA

US

WILSON COUNTY CITIZEN. 1870. s-w.: Mon. & Thu. $.35 newsstand; $22.85/yr. 406 N. Seventh, Fredonia, KS 66736. TEL 316-378-4415. **Owner(s):** Joe & Rita Relph, 706 Madison, Fredonia, KS 66736. TEL 316-378-4415; Ed. Mina DeBarry; Pub. Joe Relph; adv.; bk.rev.; pub. size: broadsheet; circ. 3,995(paid).
    Formerly: Fredonia Wilson County Citizen.

GIRARD

US

GIRARD PRESS. 1869. Wed. $.35 newsstand; $19.25/yr. in cy.; $24.75/yr. out of cy. 102 S. Ozark, Girard, KS 66743. TEL 316-724-4426; FAX 316-724-4493. **Owner(s):** Ed & Kris McKechnie, P.O. Box 126, Girard, KS 66743. TEL 316-724-4426; Ed. Janet Beene; Pub. Ed McKechnie; adv. contact: Jim Perong. bk.rev.; pub. size: broadsheet; circ. 2,850(free & paid).

GOODLAND

US

▼**SHERMAN COUNTY STAR, THE.** 1994. Wed. $.50 newsstand; $24/yr. local; $28/yr. elsewhere. 1015 Main Ave., Goodland, KS 67735-0599. TEL 913-899-5500; FAX 913-899-6260. **Owner(s):** Top Star, Inc., P.O. Box 599, Goodland, KS 67735; Ed. Roxanne Yonkey; Pub. Eric L. Yonkey; adv. contact: Eric L. Yonkey. bk.rev.; pub. size: broadsheet; circ. 78,611(free & paid).

HILL CITY

US

HILL CITY TIMES, THE. 1886. Wed. $.35 newsstand; $16/yr. local; $17/yr. in state; $20/yr. elsewhere. 110 N. Pomeroy Ave., Hill City, KS 67642-0308. TEL 913-674-5700. **Owner(s):** Robert A. Boyd, 805 Ash, Hill City, KS 67642. TEL 913-674-2147; James E. Logback, 77 Tenth Ave., Hill City, KS 67642. TEL 913-674-2775; Ed. Jim Logback; Pub. Robert A. Boyd; adv.; photos; pub. size: broadsheet; circ. 2,600(paid).

HILLSBORO

US
HILLSBORO STAR-JOURNAL. 1933. Wed. $.75 newsstand; $33/yr. in state; $39/yr. out of state; $50/yr. foreign. 104 S. Main, Hillsboro, KS 67063. TEL 316-947-3975; FAX 316-947-3883. **Owner(s):** Hillsboro Star Journal, Inc., P.O. Box A, Hillsboro, KS 67063. TEL 316-947-3975; Ed. Stacy Stenseng; Pub. Stacy Stenseng; adv. contact: Tammy Nichol. pub. size: broadsheet; circ. 3,100(paid).

HOISINGTON

US
HOISINGTON DISPATCH. 1889. Thu. $.50 newsstand; $15.94/yr. local; $19.06/yr. in state; $22.77/yr. elsewhere. 104 N. Main, Hoisington, KS 67544. TEL 316-653-4154; FAX 316-653-4720. **Owner(s):** Brown Family Publishing, Inc. P.O. Box 330, Hoisington, KS 67544. TEL 316-653-4154; Ed. Luke Brown; Pub. Luke Brown; pub. size: oversize; circ. 2,200(paid).

HOLTON

US
HOLTON RECORDER. 1875. s-w.: Mon. & Thu. $.50 newsstand; $24/yr. in cy.; $25/yr. out of cy.; $27/yr. out of state. 109 W. Fourth St., Holton, KS 66436. TEL 913-364-3141; FAX 913-364-3422. **Owner(s):** Bryan McDaniel, 109 W. Fourth St., Holton, KS 66436. TEL 913-564-3141; Ed. Leslie McDaniel; Pub. Bryan McDaniel; adv. contact: Terri Torrey. pub. size: broadsheet; circ. 4,800(paid).

INDEPENDENCE

US   ISSN 1067-5906
INDEPENDENCE NEWS, THE. 1948. Thu. $25/yr. 210 W. Main St., Independence, KS 67301. TEL 316-331-4950; FAX 316-251-1905. **Owner(s):** John F. Vermillion, 1424 W. Eighth, Independence, KS 67301. TEL 316-331-3073; Ed. John F. Vermillion; Pub. John F. Vermillion; adv.; pub. size: broadsheet.

JETMORE

US
JETMORE REPUBLICAN. 1887. Thu. $.50 newsstand; $18.88/yr. in state; $20/yr. out of state. P.O. Box 337, Jetmore, KS 67854-0337. TEL 316-357-8316; FAX 316-357-8464. **Owner(s):** Jerry Anderson, P.O. Box 536, Cimarron, KS 67835. TEL 316-855-3902; Ed. Jerry Buxton; Pub. Jerry Anderson; pub. size: broadsheet.

JOHNSON

US
JOHNSON PIONEER. 1890. Thu. $.40 newsstand; $16.94/yr. in cy.; $19.06/yr. out of cy. 103 N. Main St., Johnson, KS 67855-0010. TEL 316-492-6244. **Owner(s):** Ronda Ford, P.O. Box 10, Johnson, KS 67855-0010. TEL 316-492-6244; Pub. Ronda Ford; adv.; bk.rev.; pub. size: broadsheet; circ. 1,100(paid).

JUNCTION CITY

US
FORT RILEY POST. 1958. Fri. $18/yr. 222 W. Sixth St., Junction City, KS 66441. TEL 913-762-5000; FAX 913-762-4584. **Owner(s):** Montgomery Communications, Inc., P.O. Box 129, Junction City, KS 66441. TEL 913-762-5000; FAX 913-762-4584; Ed. John G. Montgomery; Pub. John G. Montgomery; adv.: $12.85/SAU. pub. size: broadsheet; circ. 7,900(free).

KANSAS CITY

US
RECORD, THE. 1887. Thu. $.25 newsstand; $13.75/yr. in cy. 3414 Strong Ave., Kansas City, KS 66106. TEL 913-362-1988; FAX 913-362-1989. **Owner(s):** Jon A. Males, 3414 Strong Ave., Kansas City, KS 66106. TEL 913-362-1988; Ed. Jon A. Males; Pub. Jon A. Males; pub. size: tabloid; circ. 7,500(free & paid).

US
WYANDOTTE WEST. 1968. Thu. $.50 newsstand; $18.99/yr. 7735 Washington Ave., Kansas City, KS 66112-3312. TEL 913-788-5565; FAX 913-788-9812. **Owner(s):** Murrel W. Bland, P.O. Box 12003, Kansas City, KS 66112. TEL 913-788-5565; FAX 913-788-5565; Ed. Murrel W. Bland; Pub. Murrel W. Bland; adv. contact: Carol A. Bland. adv.: $10.36/SAU. photos; bk.rev.; pub. size: tabloid; circ. 2,839(free & paid).

KINGMAN

US
KINGMAN JOURNAL/LEADER COURIER. 1880. Tue. $30/yr. local; $33/yr. out of state. P.O. Box 353, Kingman, KS 67068. TEL 316-532-3151; FAX 316-532-3152. **Owner(s):** Robert McQuin, P.O. Box 353, Kingman, KS 67068. TEL 316-532-3151; Ed. Robert McQuin; Pub. Robert McQuin; pub. size: standard; circ. 3,400(paid).

US
LEADER-COURIER. 1885. Fri. $.50 newsstand; $30/yr. local; $33/yr. out of state. P.O. Box 353, Kingman, KS 67068. TEL 316-532-3151; FAX 316-532-3152. **Owner(s):** Robert McQuin, P.O. Box 353, Kingman, KS 67068. TEL 316-532-3151; Ed. Robert McQuin; Pub. Robert McQuin; pub. size: standard; circ. 3,400(paid).

LA CROSSE

US
RUSH COUNTY NEWS. 1940. Thu. $.50 newsstand; $21.50/yr. in state; $24.50/yr. out of state. 112 W. Eighth St., La Crosse, KS 67548. TEL 913-222-2555; FAX 913-222-2557. **Owner(s):** Rush County News, 112 W. Eighth St., La Crosse, KS 67548. TEL 913-222-2555; FAX 913-222-2557; Ed. Mary Engel; Pub. Duane Engel; adv. contact: Duane Engel. photos; pub. size: broadsheet.

LAKIN

US
LAKIN INDEPENDENT, THE. 1886. Thu. $21/yr. 118 N. Main, Lakin, KS 67860. TEL 316-355-6162. **Owner(s):** Monte E. Canfield, 118 N. Main, Lakin, KS 67860. TEL 316-355-6162; Ed. Cathy McVey. pub. size: standard; circ. 1,700(paid).

LAWRENCE

US
TELEGRAPHICS. 1883. Wed. free. 2951 Four Wheel Dr., Lawrence, KS 66046. TEL 913-749-0006; FAX 913-749-3377. **Owner(s):** TeleGraphics, Inc., P.O. Box 3127, Lawrence, KS 66046. TEL 913-749-0006; FAX 913-749-3377; Ed. Chad Lawhorn; Pub. Doris Miller; adv.; photos; bk.rev.; pub. size: broadsheet; circ. 4,500(free).

LEBANON

US
LEBANON TIMES, THE. 1887. Wed. $.35 newsstand; $11.01/yr. in cy.; $12.06/yr. in state; $12.50/yr. US. 409 Walnut, Lebanon, KS 66952. TEL 913-389-6631. **Owner(s):** Darrel & Ruth Miller, P.O. Box 157, Downs, KS 67437. TEL 913-454-3514; Ed. Phyllis Bell; Pub. Darrel E. Miller; adv.; pub. size: standard; circ. 650(free & paid).

MADISON

US
MADISON NEWS, THE. 1879. Thu. $.40 newsstand; $17.83/yr. local. 118 S. Third St., Madison, KS 66860. TEL 316-437-2433; FAX 316-437-2433. **Owner(s):** Stephen Gilman, 902 S. Fourth St., Madison, KS 66860. TEL 316-437-2029; Frances Gilman, 902 S. Fourth St., Madison, KS 66860. TEL 316-437-2029; Pub. Stephen Gilman; adv. contact: Stephen Gilman. photos; pub. size: standard; circ. 750(free & paid).

MARION

US
MARION COUNTY RECORD. 1869. Wed. $30/yr. in state; $35/yr. out of state. 117 S. Third, Marion, KS 66861-0278. TEL 316-382-2165; FAX 316-382-2262; E-mail: marcorec@southwind.net; URL: http://www2.southwind.net/~marcorec. **Owner(s):** Hoch Publishing Co., Inc., P.O. Box 278, Marion, KS 66861-0278. TEL 316-382-2165; Ed. Bill Meyer; Pub. Bill Meyer; pub. size: broadsheet; circ. 3,315(paid).

MARYSVILLE

US
MARYSVILLE ADVOCATE. 1885. Thu. $.79 newsstand; $26.23/yr. in area; $36/yr. elsewhere. 107 S. Ninth, Marysville, KS 66508-0271. TEL 913-562-2317; FAX 913-562-5589. **Owner(s):** Advocate Publishing Co., Inc., 107 S. Ninth, Marysville, KS 66508. TEL 913-562-2317; Ed. Howard D. Kessinger. adv. contact: Randy Meerian. pub. size: standard; circ. 5,982(free & paid).

MILTONVALE

US
MILTONVALE RECORD. 1899. Thu. $.30 newsstand; $15/yr. 12 Spruce St., Miltonvale, KS 67466. TEL 913-427-2680; FAX 913-427-2216. **Owner(s):** Richard Phelps, 412 Ash, Miltonvale, KS 67466. TEL 913-427-3203; Deanna Phelps, 412 Ash, Miltonvale, KS 67466. TEL 913-427-3203; Ed. Richard Phelps. adv. contact: Barbara Mikels. photos; pub. size: broadsheet; circ. 750(paid).

Weeklies

MOUNDRIDGE

US

LEDGER, THE. 1887. Thu. $18.95/yr. in state; $25/yr. out of state. 135 S. Christian, Moundridge, KS 67107. TEL 316-345-2117; FAX 316-345-2170. **Owner(s):** Davies Communications, Inc., 135 S. Christian, Moundridge, KS 67107. TEL 316-345-2117; adv.; photos; pub. size: tabloid; circ. 2,000(paid).

NEODESHA

US

NEODESHA DERRICK. 1883. Thu. $.50 newsstand; $25/yr. in state; $30/yr. out of state. 509 Main St., Neodesha, KS 66757-0356. TEL 316-325-3000; FAX 316-325-2880. **Owner(s):** JoAnne Hartley Harper, P.O. Box 356, Neodesha, KS 66757. TEL 316-325-3000; Ed. JoAnne Hartley Harper; Pub. JoAnne Hartley Harper; adv. contact: Debbie Dixon. pub. size: broadsheet; circ. 1,900(paid).

NESS CITY

US

NESS COUNTY NEWS, THE. 1884. Thu. $.40 newsstand; $17.30/yr. local; $18.36/yr. out of cy. 110 S. Kansas, Ness City, KS 67560. TEL 913-798-2213; FAX 913-798-2214. **Owner(s):** John Clarke, 110 S. Kansas, Ness City, KS 67560. TEL 913-798-2213; FAX 913-798-2214; Ed. John Clarke; Pub. John Clarke; adv. contact: John Clarke. photos; pub. size: broadsheet; circ. 2,600(paid).

OAKLEY

US

OAKLEY GRAPHIC. 1887. Wed. $20.65/yr. local; $21.71/yr. out of area. 118 Center, Oakley, KS 67748. TEL 913-672-3228; FAX 913-672-3229. **Owner(s):** J & M Enterprises, Box 528, Cimarron, KS 67835; Ed. Barbara Glover. adv. contact: Gloria Nichols. pub. size: standard; circ. 4,400(controlled & free).

OBERLIN

US

OBERLIN HERALD, THE. 1879. Wed. $.75 newsstand; $28/yr. 170 S. Penn Ave., Oberlin, KS 67749-2243. TEL 913-475-2206; FAX 913-475-2800. **Owner(s):** Steve & Cynthia Haynes, 170 S. Penn Ave., Oberlin, KS 67745-2243. TEL 913-475-2206; FAX 913-475-2800; Ed. Steve Haynes; Pub. Steve Haynes; adv. contact: Steve Highlander. photos; bk.rev.; pub. size: broadsheet; circ. 2,906(paid).

OSAWATOMIE

US

OSAWATOMIE GRAPHIC. 1887. Thu. $.50 newsstand; $22.28/yr. in cy.; $27.60/yr. out of state. 635 Main St., Osawatomie, KS 66064. TEL 913-755-4151; FAX 913-294-5535. **Owner(s):** Osawatomie Publishing Co., Inc., 635 Main St., Osawatomie, KS 66064. TEL 913-755-4151; Pub. Webster Hawkins; adv. contact: Paul L. Branson. pub. size: broadsheet; circ. 7,000(paid).

OSBORNE

US   ISSN 1040-9033

OSBORNE COUNTY FARMER. 1872. Thu. $.50 newsstand; $29.94/yr. local. 210 W. Main St., Osborne, KS 67473. TEL 913-346-5424; FAX 913-346-5400. **Owner(s):** Dale R. Worley, 203 N. Fourth, Osborne, KS 67473. TEL 913-346-5891; Ed. Kathy Worley; Pub. Dale R. Worley; adv. contact: Dale R. Worley. photos; bk.rev.; pub. size: broadsheet; circ. 2,800(paid).

OSKALOOSA

US

OSKALOOSA INDEPENDENT. 1869. Thu. $.50 newsstand; $18.17/yr. in cy.; $19.24/yr. in state; $23/yr. out of state. 607 Delaware, Oskaloosa, KS 66066. TEL 913-863-2520. **Owner(s):** Clarke Davis-Wilson Davis Publications, Inc., P.O. Box 187, Valley Falls, KS 66088. TEL 913-945-3257; Pub. Clarke Davis; adv. contact: Vickie Burke. pub. size: broadsheet; circ. 2,200(paid).

OTTAWA

US

OTTAWA TIMES. 1932. Thu. $.50 newsstand; $25.50/yr. in area. 401 S. Main St., Ste. 1, Ottawa, KS 66067-0246. TEL 913-242-9200; FAX 913-242-9595. **Owner(s):** Harris Publications, The Ottawa Herald, 104 S. Cedar, Ottawa, KS 66067. TEL 913-242-4700; Ed. Bill Gray; Pub. John Montgomery; adv. contact: Bonnie Ramsey. photos; bk.rev.; pub. size: tabloid; circ. 1,200(paid).

US

OTTAWA TIMES SHOPPER. Tue. free in area. 401 S. Main St., Ste. 1, Ottawa, KS 66067-0246. TEL 913-242-9200; FAX 913-242-9595. **Owner(s):** Harris Publications, The Ottawa Herald, 104 S. Cedar, Ottawa, KS 66067. TEL 913-242-4700; Ed. Bill Gray; Pub. John Montgomery; adv. contact: Bonnie Ramsey. pub. size: tabloid; circ. 13,500(free).

OVERLAND PARK

US

OLATHE SUN. 1950. Fri. free; voluntary pay. 7373 W. 107th St., Overland Park, KS 66212. TEL 913-381-1010; FAX 913-381-9889. **Owner(s):** Sun Publications, Inc., 7373 W. 107th St., Overland Park, KS 66212. TEL 913-381-1010; Pub. Steve Rose; adv. contact: Susan Karol. pub. size: broadsheet; circ. 101,050(paid)

PAOLA

US

MIAMI COUNTY REPUBLIC. 1871. s-w.: Mon. & Wed. $.50 newsstand; $31.50/yr. in cy.; $36.30/yr. out of cy. 121 S. Pearl St., Paola, KS 66071. TEL 913-294-2311; FAX 913-294-5318. **Owner(s):** Miami County Publishing Co., Inc., 121 S. Pearl St., Paola, KS 66071. TEL 913-294-2311; Ed. Phil McLaughlin; Pub. Phil McLaughlin; adv. contact: Lorie Zahn. pub. size: broadsheet; circ. 6,000(paid).

PARSONS

US

PARSONS NEWS. Thu. $16.95/yr. 1930 Clark St., Parsons, KS 67357-0937. TEL 316-421-2990. **Owner(s):** Toni Tippet, P.O. Box 937, Parsons, KS 67357. TEL 316-421-2990; Ed. Sherri Shire; Pub. Toni Tippet; adv. contact: Jan S. Trail. photos; pub. size: tabloid; circ. 2,500(paid).

PHILLIPSBURG

US

PHILLIPS COUNTY REVIEW. 1921. Thu. $20/yr. in area; $22.50/yr. out of area. 257 F St., Phillipsburg, KS 67661. TEL 913-543-5242. **Owner(s):** LST Publishing, Inc.; Ed. Perry Hanson; Pub. Ron Lower; adv. contact: Ron Lower. pub. size: broadsheet; circ. 3,500(paid).

PRAIRIE VILLAGE

US

▼**OTHER SIDE, THE.** 1994. m. $18/yr. 3840 W. 75th St., Prairie Village, KS 66208. TEL 913-384-2675; FAX 913-384-5068. **Owner(s):** Leathers Publishing Co. 3840 W. 75th St., Prairie Village, KS 66208. TEL 913-384-2625; FAX 913-384-5068; Ed. Barbara Thomson; Pub. Tom Leathers; adv.; bk.rev.; pub. size: standard; circ. 4,000(controlled & paid).

RUSSELL

US

RUSSELL RECORD. 1872. s-w.: Mon. & Thu. $30.75/yr. 802 N. Maple St., Russell, KS 67665. TEL 913-483-2111; FAX 913-483-4012. **Owner(s):** Russell Publishing, Inc., 802 N. Maple St., Russell, KS 67665. TEL 913-483-2111; Ed. Allen D. Evans; Pub. Allen D. Evans; adv. contact: Allen D. Evans. pub. size: standard; circ. 3,075(paid).

SHAWNEE

US

JOURNAL HERALD, THE. 1924. Thu. $.50 newsstand; $22.50/yr. in cy.; $27.50/yr. out of cy.; $32.50/yr. out of state. 11004 Johnson Dr., Shawnee, KS 66203. TEL 913-631-2550; FAX 913-631-6552. **Owner(s):** Kansan Publishing Co., 11004 Johnson Dr., Shawnee, KS 66203. TEL 913-631-2550; FAX 913-631-6552; Ed. Chuck Robinson. adv.; photos; pub. size: standard; circ. 5,000(paid).

SHAWNEE MISSION

US

JOHNSON COUNTY SUN. s-w.: Wed. & Fri. $78.28/yr. in cy. mailed; $35.38/yr. elsewhere mailed. 7373 W. 107th St. Shawnee Mission, KS 66212. TEL 913-381-1010; FAX 913-381-9889. **Owner(s):** Sun Publications, Inc., 7373 W. 107th St., Shawnee Mission, KS 66212. TEL 913-381-1010; Ed. Jack Lovelace; Pub. Steve Rose; adv. contact: Susan Karol. pub. size: broadsheet; circ. 11,000(paid).

US

LEAWOOD SUN. 1928. s-w.: Wed. & Fri. free; voluntary pay. 7373 W. 107th St. Shawnee Mission, KS 66212. TEL 913-381-1010; FAX 913-381-9889. **Owner(s):** Sun Publications, Inc., 7373 W. 107th St., Shawnee Mission, KS 66212. TEL 913-381-1010; Ed. Jack Lovelace; Pub. Steve Rose; adv. contact: Susan Karol. pub. size: broadsheet; circ. 8,000(free).

US
LENEXA SUN. 1921. s-w.: Wed. & Fri. free; voluntary pay. 7373 W. 107th St., Shawnee Mission, KS 66212. TEL 913-381-1010; FAX 913-381-9889. **Owner(s):** Sun Publications, Inc., 7373 W. 107th St., Shawnee Mission, KS 66212. TEL 913-381-1010; Ed. Jack Lovelace; Pub. Steve Rose; adv. contact: Susan Karol. pub. size: broadsheet; circ. 10,000(free).

US
NORTHEAST JOHNSON COUNTY. s-w.: Wed. & Fri. free; voluntary pay. 7373 W. 107th St., Shawnee Mission, KS 66212. TEL 913-381-1010; FAX 913-381-9889. **Owner(s):** Sun Publications, Inc., 7373 W. 107th, Overland Park, KS 66212. TEL 913-381-1010; Pub. Steve Rose; adv. contact: Susan Karol. pub. size: broadsheet; circ. 47,000(free).

US
OVERLAND PARK SUN. s-w.: Wed. & Fri. free; voluntary pay. 7373 W. 107th St., Shawnee Mission, KS 66212. TEL 913-381-1010; FAX 913-381-9889. **Owner(s):** Sun Publications, Inc., 7373 W. 107th St, Shawnee Mission, KS 66212. TEL 913-381-1010; Ed. Jack Lovelace; Pub. Steve Rose; adv. contact: Susan Karol. pub. size: broadsheet; circ. 102,100(free).

US
PRAIRIE VILLAGE SUN. s-w.: Wed. & Fri. free; voluntary pay. 7373 W. 107th St., Shawnee Mission, KS 66212. TEL 913-381-1010; FAX 913-381-9889. **Owner(s):** Sun Publications, Inc., 7373 W. 107th St., Shawnee Mission, KS 66212. TEL 913-381-1010; Pub. Steve Rose; adv. contact: Susan Karol. pub. size: broadsheet; circ. 20,000(free).

US
SHAWNEE/MERRIAM SUN. 1911. s-w.: Wed. & Fri. free; voluntary pay. 7373 W. 107th St., Shawnee Mission, KS 66212. TEL 913-381-1010; FAX 913-381-9889. **Owner(s):** Sun Publications, Inc., 7373 W. 107th, Shawnee Mission, KS 66212. TEL 913-381-1070; Ed. Jack Lovelace; Pub. Steve Rose; adv. contact: Susan Karol. pub. size: broadsheet; circ. 75,000(free).
Formerly: Merriam Sun.

SMITH CENTER

US
SMITH COUNTY PIONEER. 1871. Thu. $19/yr. in cy. 201 S. Main, Smith Center, KS 66967. TEL 913-282-3371; FAX 913-282-6383. **Owner(s):** Darrel & Ruth Miller, 201 S. Main St., Smith Center, KS 66967. TEL 913-282-3371; Ed. Darrel Miller; Pub. Darrel Miller; pub. size: standard; circ. 3,883(paid).
Formerly: Smith Center Smith County Pioneer.

ST. FRANCIS

US
ST. FRANCIS HERALD, THE. 1885. Thu. $.75 newsstand; $28/yr. P.O. Box 1050, St. Francis, KS 67756-1050. TEL 913-332-3162; FAX 913-332-3001. **Owner(s):** Steve & Cynthia Haynes, 170 S Penn, Oberlin, KS 67749. TEL 913-475-2206; FAX 913-475-2800; Ed. Karen Krien. adv. contact: Nell Frohlich. pub. size: broadsheet; circ. 3,840(free & paid).

ST. JOHN

US
ST. JOHN NEWS. 1880. Wed. $22/yr. in cy.; $32/yr. out of cy. 318 N. Main St., St. John, KS 67576. TEL 316-549-3201. **Owner(s):** Tribune Publishing Co., P.O. Box 909, Pratt, KS 67124. TEL 316-672-5511; Ed. Lisa Stevens John. pub. size: standard; circ. 1,500(paid).

ST. MARYS

US
ST. MARYS STAR. 1884. Tue. $.50 newsstand; $28.59/yr. in state; $31/yr. out of state. 517 W. Bertrand, St. Marys, KS 66536-0190. TEL 913-437-2935; FAX 913-437-2095. **Owner(s):** Anita H. Janssen, P.O. Box 190, St. Marys, KS 66536-0190. TEL 913-437-2935; FAX 913-437-2095; Ed. Anita H. Janssen; Pub. Anita H. Janssen; adv. contact: Christopher Halbkat. photos; pub. size: tabloid; circ. 2,005(paid).

ULYSSES

US
ULYSSES NEWS. 1892. Thu. $25/yr. in cy.; $28.50/yr. out of cy. 218 N. Main, Ulysses, KS 67880. TEL 316-356-1201; FAX 316-356-4610. **Owner(s):** Michael A. Pace, P.O. Box 706, Ulysses, KS 67880. TEL 316-356-1201; FAX 316-356-4610; Ed. Shirley A. Pace. adv.; photos; pub. size: broadsheet; circ. 10,400(free & paid).

VALLEY FALLS

US
VALLEY FALLS VINDICATOR. 1864. Thu. $.50 newsstand; $17/yr. 416 Broadway, Valley Falls, KS 66088. TEL 913-945-3257; FAX 913-945-3444. **Owner(s):** Wilson-Davis Publications, Inc., P.O. Box 187, Valley Falls, KS 66088-0187. TEL 913-945-3257; FAX 913-945-3444; Ed. Clarke Davis. adv.; photos; bk.rev.; pub. size: broadsheet; circ. 2,350(paid).

WASHINGTON

US
WASHINGTON COUNTY NEWS. Thu. $20/yr. in cy.; $23/yr. out of cy.; $25/yr. out of state. 211 C St., Washington, KS 66968. TEL 913-325-2219; FAX 913-325-3255; E-mail: bhays@kspress.com; URL: http://www.kspress.com/WCN/Washindex.html. **Owner(s):** Washington County News, P.O. Box 316, Washington, KS 66968. TEL 913-325-2219; Ed. William Hays. adv.; photos; pub. size: broadsheet; circ. 3,190(paid).

KENTUCKY

ALBANY

US
CLINTON COUNTY NEWS. 1949. Thu. $.30 newsstand; $12/yr. 116 Washington St., Albany, KY 42602. TEL 606-387-5144; FAX 606-387-7949. **Owner(s):** Gibson Printing Co., Inc., 116 Washington St., Albany, KY 42602. TEL 606-387-5144; FAX 606-387-7949; Ed. Alan B. Gibson. adv. contact: Janie U. Gibson. photos; pub. size: standard; circ. 3,500(paid).

BARBOURVILLE

US
BARBOURVILLE MOUNTAIN ADVOCATE. 1937. Thu. $.50 newsstand; $9/yr. in cy.; $22/yr. out of state. 214 Knox St., Barbourville, KY 40906. TEL 606-546-9225; FAX 606-546-3175. **Owner(s):** Robert K. Wilson, 214 Knox St., Barbourville, KY 40906. TEL 606-546-9225; FAX 606-546-3175; Ed. Robert K. Wilson; Pub. Cecil H. Wilson; adv. contact: Carolyn Kennedy. pub. size: broadsheet; circ. 6,800(paid).

BARDSTOWN

US   ISSN 8750-0760
KENTUCKY STANDARD. 1900. 3/wk.: Mon., Wed., Fri. $.50 newsstand; $42.50/yr. in cy.; $55.75 elsewhere; $75/yr out of state. 110 W. Stephen Foster Ave., Bardstown, KY 40004. TEL 502-348-9003; FAX 502-348-1971. **Owner(s):** Landmark Community Newspapers, Inc., P.O. Box 549, Shelbyville, KY 40065; Ed. Teresa Rice; Pub. Steve Lowery; adv. contact: Joan Hardin. pub. size: broadsheet; circ. 8,500(paid). **Wire Service(s):** AP.

US
SHOPPER'S GUIDE. Wed. free. 110 W. Stephen Foster Ave., Bardstown, KY 40004. TEL 502-348-9003; FAX 502-348-1971. **Owner(s):** Landmark Community Newspapers, Inc., P.O. Box 549, Shelbyville, KY 40065; Ed. Teresa Rice; Pub. Steve Lowery; adv. contact: Joan Hardin. pub. size: broadsheet; circ. 10,000(free).

BEAVER DAM

US
BEAVER DAM OHIO COUNTY MESSENGER. 1930. Wed. $8/yr. in cy.; $12/yr. out of cy.; $15/yr. out of state. 115 N. Main St., Beaver Dam, KY 42320. TEL 502-274-4949. **Owner(s):** Mrs. Andy Anderson, P.O. Box 187, Beaver Dam, KY 42320; Ed. Dave McBride; Pub. Mrs. Andy Anderson; adv. contact: Tressie Brown. pub. size: standard; circ. 2,100(paid).

BENTON

US
TRIBUNE COURIER. 1888. Wed. $.50 newsstand; $24/yr. in cy.; $30/yr. out of cy.; $32/yr. out of state. 308 E. 12th St., Benton, KY 42025. TEL 502-527-3162; FAX 502-527-4567. **Owner(s):** Gleaner & Journal Publishing Co., P.O. Box 4, Henderson, KY 42420. TEL 502-827-2000; Ed. Greg Travis. adv. contact: Terri Dunigan. pub. size: broadsheet; circ. 8,000(paid). **Wire Service(s):** AP.

BRANDENBURG

US
MEADE COUNTY MESSENGER. 1892. Thu. $16.90/yr. 235 Main St., Brandenburg, KY 40108. TEL 502-422-2155; FAX 502-422-2110. **Owner(s):** Mead County Messenger Corp., 235 Main St., Brandenburg, KY 40108. TEL 502-422-2155; FAX 502-422-2110; Pub. Kay McGehee; pub. size: broadsheet; circ. 7,000(paid).

BURKESVILLE

US

CUMBERLAND COUNTY NEWS. 1920. Wed. $.35 newsstand; $13/yr. 412 Courthouse Sq., Burkesville, KY 42717. TEL 502-864-3891; FAX 502-864-3497. **Owner(s):** Patsy Judd, 412 Courthouse Sq., Burkesville, KY 42717. TEL 502-286-3891; Ed. Cyndi Pritchett; Pub. Patsy Judd; adv.; photos; pub. size: broadsheet; circ. 3,000(paid).

CADIZ

US

CADIZ RECORD, THE. 1881. Wed. $.50 newsstand; $20/yr. in cy.; $23/yr. out of cy.; $30/yr. out of state. 50 Nunn Blvd., Cadiz, KY 42211. TEL 502-522-6605; FAX 502-522-3001. **Owner(s):** Kentucky Waterland Press, Inc., P.O. Box 311, Cadiz, KY 42211. TEL 502-522-6605; FAX 502-522-3001; Ed. Robin C. Stevens; Pub. Walt Dear; adv. contact: Jan C. Witty. photos; pub. size: broadsheet; circ. 4,600(paid).

CAMPBELLSVILLE

US

CENTRAL KENTUCKY NEWS-JOURNAL. 1910. s-w.: Mon. & Thu. $.50 newsstand; $32.86/yr. local; $45.05/yr. elsewhere. 428 Woodlawn Ave., Campbellsville, KY 42718. TEL 502-465-8111; FAX 502-465-2500. **Owner(s):** Landmark Community Newspapers, Inc., P.O. Box 549, Shelbyville, KY 40066. TEL 502-633-4334; Pub. Richard Robards; adv. contact: Cheryl Caulk. photos; pub. size: broadsheet; circ. 7,500(paid).

US

NEWS-JOURNAL SHOPPER. Wed. free. 428 Woodlawn Ave., Campbellsville, KY 42718. TEL 502-465-8111; FAX 502-465-2500. **Owner(s):** Landmark Community Newspapers, Inc., P.O. Box 549, Shelbyville, KY 40066; Pub. Richard Robards; adv. contact: Cheryl Caulk. pub. size: broadsheet; circ. 8,500(free).

CARLISLE

US

CARLISLE MERCURY, THE. 1867. Thu. $.50 newsstand; $16.96/yr. in cy.; $20.14/yr. out of cy.; $26/yr. out of state. 234 Locust St., Carlisle, KY 40311. TEL 606-289-2464; FAX 606-289-7900. **Owner(s):** Park Communications, Inc., Vine Ctr. Office Tower, 333 W. Vine St., 17th Fl., Lexington, KY 40507. TEL 606-252-7275; Ed. Kristie Harrod. adv. contact: Rocky Ross. pub. size: broadsheet; circ. 3,300(paid).

CARROLLTON

US

NEWS-DEMOCRAT, THE. 1867. Wed. $.50 newsstand; $21/yr. in cy.; $30/yr. out of state. 422 Main St., Carrollton, KY 41008. TEL 502-732-4261; FAX 502-732-0453. **Owner(s):** Landmark Community Newspapers, Inc., P.O. Box 549, Shelbyville, KY 40066. TEL 502-633-4334; Ed. Davette Baker Baxter. adv.; photos; pub. size: broadsheet; circ. 3,891(paid).

CAVE CITY

US   ISSN 1055-9531

PROGRESS, THE. 1935. Thu. $.25 newsstand; $6.95/yr. in cy. & adjacent cys.; $16/yr. in state; $20/yr. out of state. 604 E. Broadway, Cave City, KY 42127. TEL 502-773-3401; FAX 502-773-8950. **Owner(s):** Aubrey C. Wilson, Sr., Barren County Progress, 604 E. Broadway, Cave City, KY 42127. TEL 502-773-3401; Ed. Dorothy D. Wilson. pub. size: standard; circ. 8,200(paid).

CENTRAL CITY

US

CENTRAL CITY TIMES-ARGUS. 1906. Wed. $.25 newsstand; $9.40/yr. in cy. 202 W. Broad St., Central City, KY 42330. TEL 502-754-2331; FAX 502-754-1305. **Owner(s):** Central City Publishing Corp. 202 W. Broad St., Central City, KY 42330. TEL 502-754-2331; FAX 502-754-1805; Ed. Richard Deavers. adv.; pub. size: broadsheet; circ. 3,850(paid).

US

LEADER-NEWS. 1912. Tue. $.30 newsstand; $15.60/yr. in cy.; $17/yr. out of cy.; $20/yr. out of state. 1730 W. Everly Bros. Blvd., Central City, KY 42330. TEL 502-754-3000; FAX 502-754-9484. **Owner(s):** Vickie Anderson, P.O. Box 138, Greenville, KY 42345. TEL 502-754-3000; Ed. Carolyn Hillard; Pub. Vickie Anderson; adv. contact: Wayne Thompson. pub. size: broadsheet; circ. 9,000(paid).
   Formerly: Greenville Leader-News.

COLUMBIA

US

ADAIR PROGRESS, THE. 1988. Thu. $.35 newsstand; $11/yr. 98 Grant Ln. Columbia, KY 42728. TEL 502-384-6471; FAX 502-384-6474. **Owner(s):** Adair Progress, Inc., P.O. Box 595, Columbia, KY 42728. TEL 502-384-6471; FAX 502-384-6474; Ed. Paul Hayes; Pub. Donna Crowe; adv.; photos; bk.rev.; pub. size: broadsheet; circ. 4,900(paid).

US

ADAIR RUSSELL SHOPPER, THE. 1988. Mon. free. 98 Grant Ln., Columbia, KY 42728. TEL 502-384-6471; FAX 502-384-6474. **Owner(s):** Adair Progress, Inc., P.O. Box 595, Columbia, KY 42728. TEL 502-384-6471; FAX 502-384-6474; Ed. Paul Hayes; Pub. Donna Crowe; adv.; photos; bk.rev.; pub. size: tabloid; circ. 14,244(paid).

US

CASEY COUNTY SHOPPER, THE. 1988. Tue. free. 98 Grant Ln., Columbia, KY 42728. TEL 502-384-6471; FAX 502-384-6474. **Owner(s):** Adair Progress, Inc., P.O. Box 595, Columbia, KY 42728. TEL 502-384-6471; FAX 502-384-6474; Ed. Paul Hayes; Pub. Donna Crowe; adv.; photos; bk.rev.; pub. size: tabloid; circ. 5,626(paid).

US   ISSN 1050-4311

COLUMBIA NEWS, THE. 1988. Tue. $.35 newsstand; $11/yr. 98 Grant Ln., Columbia, KY 42728. TEL 502-384-6471; FAX 502-384-6474. **Owner(s):** Adair Progress, Inc., P.O. Box 595, Columbia, KY 42728. TEL 501-384-6471; FAX 502-384-6474; Ed. Paul Hayes; Pub. Donna Crowe; adv.; photos; bk.rev.; pub. size: broadsheet; circ. 4,200(paid).

CROMONA

US   ISSN 0899-1820

LETCHER COUNTY COMMUNITY NEWS-PRESS. 1959. Wed. $.50 newsstand; $16/yr. in cy.; $26/yr. out of cy. Rte. 805, Cromona, KY 41810. TEL 606-855-4541; FAX 606-855-9290. **Owner(s):** Superior Printing & Publishing Co., Inc., P.O. Box 156, Cromona, KY 41810. TEL 606-855-4541; Ed. Mike Whitaker. Pub. Charles Whitaker; adv.; photos; bk.rev.; pub. size: broadsheet; circ. 4,000(controlled & paid).

CUMBERLAND

US

TRI-CITY NEWS. 1929. Wed. $.35 newsstand; $15/yr. local; $20/yr. out o state. 850 E. Main St., Cumberland, KY 40823. TEL 606-589-2588; FAX 606-589-2589. **Owner(s):** Jeff Wilder, 850 E. Main St., Cumberland, KY 40823. TEL 606-589-2588; Ed. Jeff Wilder. adv. contact: Sandy Hodges. pub. size: broadsheet; circ. 3,600(paid).

CYNTHIANA

US

CYNTHIANA DEMOCRAT. 1868. Thu. $.50 newsstand; $22.26/yr. local; $21.26/yr. senior citizens. 412 Webster Ave., Cynthiana, KY 41031. TEL 606-234-1035; FAX 606-234-8096. **Owner(s):** Landmark Community Newspapers, Inc., P.O. Box 549, Shelbyville, KY 40066. TEL 502-633-4334; Ed. Becky Barnes; Pub. George Jacobs; adv. contact: Lucy Van Hook. pub. size: broadsheet; circ. 5,400(paid).

DAWSON SPRINGS

US

DAWSON SPRINGS PROGRESS. 1919. Thu. $.25 newsstand; $8/yr. in cy.; $15/yr. out of cy.; $20/yr. out of state. 131 S. Main St., Dawson Springs, KY 42408. TEL 502-797-3271; FAX 502-797-3271. **Owner(s):** Progress Publishing Co., Inc., 131 S. Main St., P.O. Box 460, Dawson Spring, KY 42408. TEL 502-797-3271; Ed. Jed Dillingham; Pub. Jed Dillingham; adv. contact: Scott Dillingham. photos; pub. size: standard; circ. 3,200(paid).

EDDYVILLE

US

HERALD LEDGER. 1905. Wed. $.50 newsstand; $17.49/yr. in cy.; $19.61/yr. out of cy.; $20.50/yr. elsewere. 214 Commerce St., Eddyville, KY 42038. TEL 502-388-2269; FAX 502-388-5540. **Owner(s):** Herald Ledger, Box 577, Eddyville, KY 42038. TEL 502-388-2269; FAX 502-388-5540; adv.; photos; pub. size: broadsheet; circ. 2,500(paid).

ELKTON

US

TODD COUNTY STANDARD. 1892. Wed. $.50 newsstand; $16/yr. P.O. Box 308, Elkton, KY 42220. TEL 502-265-2439. **Owner(s):** Mike Finch, P. O. Box 308, Elkton KY 42220. TEL 502-265-2439; FAX 502-265-2571; Ed. Mike Finch; Pub. Mike Finch; adv. contact: Jo Tribble. photos; pub. size: broadsheet; circ. 2,372(paid).

FLORENCE

US

BOONE COUNTY RECORDER. 1875. Thu. $.50 newsstand; $18.02/yr. in cy.; $23.32/yr. in state; $27.56/yr. out of state. Colonial Sq. Plz., 7736 US Hw. 42, Ste. D-4, Florence, KY 41042. TEL 606-283-0404; FAX 606-283-7285. **Owner(s):** Press Community Newspapers, 4910 Para Dr., Cincinnati, OH 45237. TEL 513-242-4300; Ed. Amy Charley; Pub. Gene A. Clabes; adv. contact: Sandra R. Cupps. photos; pub. size: broadsheet; circ. 8,000(paid).

US

DIXIE NEWS. 1962. Thu. $.25 newsstand; $13/yr. in cy. 6603 Dixie Hwy., Florence, KY 41042. TEL 606-371-6177; FAX 606-371-6306. **Owner(s):** Lee Thomas, 6603 Dixie Hwy., Florence, KY 41042. TEL 606-371-6177; Ed. Lee Thomas; Pub. Lee Thomas; pub. size: broadsheet; circ. 21,000(controlled & paid).

US

KENTON COUNTY RECORDER. 1978. Wed. $.50 newsstand; $18.02/yr. in cy.; $19/yr. out of cy.; $22/yr. in state. 7736 U.S. 42, Ste. D-4, Florence, KY 41042. TEL 606-283-0404; FAX 606-283-7285. **Owner(s):** Steppingstone Publications, Inc., 7736 U.S. 42, Florence, KY 41042. TEL 606-283-0404; Ed. Christopher Burns; Pub. Gene Clabes; pub. size: broadsheet; circ. 22,000(paid). **Wire Service(s):** AP, Newsfinder.

FORT THOMAS

US

CAMPBELL COUNTY RECORDER. 1978. Thu. $.50 newsstand; $18.02/yr. 654 Highland Ave., Ste. 27, Fort Thomas, KY 41075. TEL 606-781-4421; FAX 606-781-2703. **Owner(s):** Press Community Newspapers, 4910 Fara Dr., Cincinatti, OH 45237. TEL 513-242-4300; Ed. Steve Olding; Pub. Gene Clabes; adv. contact: Sandra Cupps. pub. size: broadsheet; circ. 3,500(paid).

FRANKLIN

US

FRANKLIN FAVORITE. 1857. Thu. $.50 newsstand; $20/yr. 103 N. High St., Franklin, KY 42135-0309. TEL 502-586-4481; FAX 502-586-6031. **Owner(s):** Gleaner & Journal Publishing Co., P.O. Box 4, Henderson, KY 42420. TEL 502-827-2000; Ed. Charles Portmann; Pub. Henry D. Stone; adv. contact: Betty Gentry. photos; pub. size: broadsheet; circ. 5,600(controlled & paid).

FULTON

US

FULTON LEADER. 1898. Thu. $.50 newsstand; $17/yr. 304 E. State Line St., Fulton, KY 42041-1200. TEL 502-472-1121; FAX 502-472-1129. **Owner(s):** Fulton Publishing Co., P.O. Box 1200, Fulton, KY 42041-1200. TEL 502-472-1121; Ed. Rita Mitchell; Pub. William Mitchell; adv. contact: Leigh Ann Moore. pub. size: broadsheet; circ. 3,100(paid).

US

FULTON SHOPPER. Wed. free. 304 E. State Line St., Fulton, KY 42041. TEL 502-472-1121; FAX 502-472-1129. **Owner(s):** Fulton Publishing Co., P.O. Box 1200, Fulton, KY 42041. TEL 502-472-1121; Ed. William Mitchell; Pub. William Mitchell; adv. contact: Leigh Ann Moore. pub. size: standard; circ. 14,500(free).

GEORGETOWN

US   ISSN 1072-9305

GEORGETOWN NEWS GRAPHIC. 1867. 3/wk.: Wed., Fri., Sun. $.50 newsstand; $45/yr. in cy.; $60/yr. out of cy.; $60/yr. out of state. 1481 Cherry Blossom Way, Georgetown, KY 40324. TEL 502-863-1111; FAX 502-863-6296. **Owner(s):** Lancaster Management, P.O. Box 609, Gadsten, AL 35902; Ed. Byron Brewer; Pub. Mike Scogin; pub. size: broadsheet; circ. 5,300(paid). Formerly: Georgetown News & Times.

GLASGOW

US

GLASGOW REPUBLICAN. Thu. $11/yr. in state; $19/yr. out of state. 100 Commerce Dr., Glasgow, KY 42141. TEL 502-678-5171; FAX 502-678-5052. **Owner(s):** Stephens Group, Inc., P.O. Box 17017, Fort Smith, AR 72917; Ed. Frances Bastien; Pub. Bill Tinsley; pub. size: standard; circ. 2,000(paid).

GRAYSON

US

GRAYSON JOURNAL-ENQUIRER. 1968. Wed. $.50 newsstand; $15.90/yr. in cy.; $30/yr. out of cy.; $35/yr. out of state. 113 Hord St., Grayson, KY 41143. TEL 606-474-5101; FAX 606-474-0013. **Owner(s):** Park Communications, Inc., Vine Ctr. Office Tower, 333 W. Vine St., 17th Fl., Lexington, KY 40507. TEL 606-252-7275; Ed. Larry Boblitt. adv. contact: Bonnie Pence. photos; pub. size: broadsheet; circ. 3,000(paid).

GREENUP

US

GREENUP COUNTY NEWS-TIMES. 1867. Thu. $.50 newsstand; $15.37/yr. in cy.; $23.32/yr. out of cy.; $24/yr. out of state. 203 Harrison St., Greenup, KY 41144. TEL 606-473-9851; FAX 606-473-7591. **Owner(s):** Park Communications, Inc., Vine Ctr. Office Tower, 333 W. Vine St., 17th Fl., Lexington, KY 40507. TEL 606-252-7252; Ed. Mason Branham. adv. contact: Betty Blevin. pub. size: broadsheet; circ. 5,700(paid).

Formerly: Greenup News.

HARDINSBURG

US

BRECKINRIDGE COUNTY HERALD-NEWS. 1874. Wed. $.50 newsstand; $15.90/yr. in cy.; $21.20/yr. in state; $25/yr. out of state. U.S. Hwy. 60, E., Hardinsburg, KY 40143. TEL 502-756-2109; FAX 502-756-1003. **Owner(s):** Brucie Beard, P.O. Box 6, Hardinsburg, KY 40143. TEL 502-756-2109; Ed. Nancy Beard; Pub. Brucie Beard; adv. contact: Barbara Masterson. pub. size: broadsheet; circ. 6,000(paid).

HARRODSBURG

US

HARRODSBURG HERALD. 1884. Thu. $.50 newsstand; $21/yr. local home deliv. 101 W. Broadway, Harrodsburg, KY 40330. TEL 606-734-2726; FAX 606-734-0737. **Owner(s):** Bill Randolph, 101 W. Broadway, Harrodsburg, KY 40330. TEL 606-734-2726; Hutton Pyles Trust, 101 W. Broadway, Harrodsburg, KY 40330. TEL 606-734-2726; Ed. Bill Randolph. adv. contact: Bill Mudd. photos; pub. size: broadsheet; circ. 6,150(paid).

HARTFORD

US

OHIO COUNTY TIMES NEWS. 1965. Thu. $.25 newsstand; $10/yr. local; $12/yr. adjoining cys.; $20/yr. out of state. 108 W. Center St., Hartford, KY 42347. TEL 502-298-7100; FAX 502-298-7592. **Owner(s):** Andy Anderson Corp., P.O. Box 226, Hartford, KY 42347. TEL 502-298-7100; Ed. Dave McBride; Pub. Gina Gibbons; adv. contact: Gina Gibbons. pub. size: broadsheet; circ. 6,800(paid).

HAWESVILLE

US

HANCOCK CLARION. 1893. Thu. $.50 newsstand; $15/yr. in cy.; $19/yr. out of cy. Main St., Hawesville, KY 42348. TEL 502-927-6945; FAX 502-927-6947. **Owner(s):** Donn K. Wimmer, P.O. Box 39, Hawesville, KY 42348. TEL 502-927-6945; FAX 502-927-6947; Ed. Donn K. Wimmer; Pub. Donn K. Wimmer; adv. contact: Kathy Sablehaus. pub. size: broadsheet; circ. 4,000(paid).

HAZARD

US

HAZARD HERALD-VOICE. 1911. Thu. $.35 newsstand; $17/yr. in state; $23/yr. elsewhere. 380 Main St., Hazard, KY 41701. TEL 606-436-5771; FAX 606-436-3140. **Owner(s):** Perry County Publishing Co., Inc., P.O. Box 869, Hazard, KY 41702. TEL 606-436-5771; FAX 606-436-3140; Pub. Jack G. Thomas; adv.; photos; pub. size: broadsheet; circ. 5,057(paid).

HODGENVILLE

US

LARUE COUNTY HERALD-NEWS. 1885. Wed. $.50 newsstand; $18.02/yr. in cy.; $23.32/yr. in state; $29.50/yr. out of state. 40 Shawnee Dr., Hodgenville, KY 42748. TEL 502-358-3118; FAX 502-358-4852. **Owner(s):** Landmark Community Newspapers, Inc., P.O. Box 549, Shelbyville, KY 40066. TEL 502-633-4335; Ed. Debby Polly; Pub. Michelle McGuffin; adv. contact: Michelle McGuffin. pub. size: broadsheet; circ. 3,975(paid).

HYDEN

US

LESLIE COUNTY NEWS. 1968. Thu. $.50 newsstand; $18.55/yr. in cy.; $26/yr. out of cy. 100 Main St., Hyden, KY 41749. TEL 606-672-2841; FAX 606-672-7409. **Owner(s):** Reba & Vernon Baker, P.O. Box 967, Hyden, KY 41749. TEL 606-672-2841; Ed. Vernon Baker; Pub. Vernon Baker; adv. contact: Bernetta York. photos; pub. size: broadsheet; circ. 5,000(paid).

US

THOUSANDSTICKS. Tue. $.50 newsstand; $18.55/yr. in cy.; $26/yr. out of cy. P.O. Box 917, Hyden, KY 41749. TEL 606-672-2841; FAX 606-672-7409. **Owner(s):** Vernon & Reba Baker, P.O. Box 967, Hyden, KY 41749. TEL 606-672-2841; Pub. Reba Baker; adv. contact: Ron Williams. pub. size: standard; circ. 4,200(paid).

INEZ

US

MOUNTAIN CITIZEN, THE. 1975. Wed. $.50 newsstand; $15/yr. in cy. Main St., Cain Bldg., Inez, KY 41224. TEL 606-298-7570; FAX 606-298-3711. **Owner(s):** New Wave Community Papers, Inc., P.O. Box 1029, Inez, KY 41224. TEL 606-298-7570; Ed. Lisa Stayton; Pub. Lisa Stayton; adv. contact: Susie Skyles. pub. size: broadsheet; circ. 5,200(paid).
   Formerly: Martin Countian & Mercury.

IRVINE

US

CITIZEN VOICE & TIMES. 1973. s-w.: Sun. & Thu. $.50 newsstand; $15.95/yr. in cy.; $23.95/yr. out of cy.; $32/yr. out of state. 108 Court St., Irvine, KY 40336-1093. TEL 606-723-5161; FAX 606-723-5509. **Owner(s):** Guy Hatfield, 108 Court St., Irvine, KY 40336-1093. TEL 606-723-5161; FAX 606-723-5509. Ed. Allen Blair; Pub. Guy Hatfield; adv. contact: Traci Cahal. pub. size: broadsheet; circ. 4,700(paid); Sun. 9,700(paid). **Wire Service(s):** AP.

US

ESTILL COUNTY TRIBUNE, THE. 1982. Wed. $.25 newsstand; $9/yr. local; $15/yr. elsewhere. 6135 Winchester Rd., Irvine, KY 40336. TEL 606-723-5012. **Owner(s):** Tracy R. Patrick, 7665 Winchester Rd., Irvine, KY 40336. TEL 606-723-7155; Ed. Delores L. Patrick; Pub. Tracy R. Patrick; pub. size: standard; circ. 2,200(paid).

LA GRANGE

US

OLDHAM ERA, THE. 1876. Thu. $.50 newsstand; $22.26/yr. in cy.; $28/yr. in state; $39.95/yr. out of state. 204 S. First St., La Grange, KY 40031-0005. TEL 502-222-7183; FAX 502-222-7194. **Owner(s):** Landmark Community Newspapers, Inc., P.O. Box 549, Shelbyville, KY 40066. TEL 502-633-4334; Ed. Kit Millay; Pub. Dorothy Abernathy; adv. contact: Doris Armstrong. photos; pub. size: broadsheet; circ. 7,000(paid).

LAWRENCEBURG

US

ANDERSON NEWS, THE. 1903. Wed. $.75 newsstand; $22.26/yr. in cy.; $29.68/yr. out of cy. 133 Main St., Lawrenceburg, KY 40342. TEL 502-839-6906; FAX 502-839-3118. **Owner(s):** Landmark Community Newspapers, Inc., P.O. Box 549, Shelbyville, KY 40065. TEL 502-633-4334; Ed. Don White; Pub. Don White; adv. contact: Bud Garrison. pub. size: broadsheet; circ. 5,300(paid).

LEBANON

US

LEBANON ENTERPRISE. 1985. Wed. $.75 newsstand; $22.26/yr. in cy.; $29.68/yr. out of cy.; $38/yr. out of state. 119 S. Proctor Knott Ave., Lebanon, KY 40033. TEL 502-692-6026; FAX 502-692-2118. **Owner(s):** Landmark Community Newspapers, Inc., P.O. Box 549, Shelbyville, KY 40066. TEL 502-633-4334; Ed. Tim Ballard; Pub. Tim Ballard; adv. contact: Mary Anne Blair. pub. size: broadsheet; circ. 6,400(paid).

LEITCHFIELD

US

GRAYSON ADVERTISER. Thu. free. 208 S. Main St., Leitchfield, KY 42754. TEL 502-259-9622; FAX 502-259-5537. **Owner(s):** Park Communications, Inc., Vine Ctr. Office Tower, 333 W. Vine St., 17th Fl., Lexington, KY 40507. TEL 606-252-7275 Ed. Carol Bond; Pub. Carol Bond; adv. contact: Nancy Farmer. pub. size: broadsheet; circ 5,000(free).

US

GRAYSON COUNTY NEWS-GAZETTE. 1881. s-w.: Mon. & Thu. $.50 newsstand; $20/yr. in cy.; $25/yr. out of cy. 208 S. Main St., Leitchfield, KY 42754. TEL 502-259-9622; FAX 502-259-5537. **Owner(s):** Park Communications, Inc., Vine Ctr. Office Tower, 333 W. Vine St., 17th Fl., Lexington, KY 40507. TEL 606-252-7252; Ed. Carol Bond. adv. contact: Nancy Farmer. pub. size: broadsheet; circ. 6,685(paid).

LIBERTY

US

CASEY COUNTY NEWS. 1904. Wed. $.50 newsstand; $22.26/yr. in cy.; $29.68. out of cy.; $36.95/yr. out of state. Campbellsville St., Liberty, KY 42539. TEL 606-787-7171; FAX 606-787-8306. **Owner(s):** Landmark Community Newspapers, Inc., P.O. Box 549, Shelbyville, KY 40065. TEL 502-633-4334; Ed. Maleena Streeval; Pub. Randall Vaught; pub. size: broadsheet; circ. 6,200(paid).
   Formerly: Liberty Casey County News.

LONDON

US

SENTINEL-ECHO. 1893. 3/wk.: Mon., Wed., Fri. $.50 newsstand; $41.34/yr. in cy. 123 W. Fifth St., London, KY 40741. TEL 606-878-7400; FAX 606-878-7404. **Owner(s):** Park Communications, Inc., Vine Ctr. Office Tower, 333 W. Vine St., 17th Fl., Lexington, KY 40507. TEL 606-252-7275; Ed. Leigh Tone. adv. contact: Rick Chandler. pub. size: broadsheet; circ. 15,100(controlled & paid).
   Formerly: London Sentinel-Echo.

LOUISA

US

ADVERTISER, THE. 1982. Thu. free. 106 Pocahantas St., Louisa, KY 41230. TEL 606-638-9957; FAX 606-638-1293 **Owner(s):** C.D. Watts, P.O. Box 129, Louisa, KY 41230. TEL 606-638-9957; FAX 606-638-9957; Ed. C.D. Watts; Pub. C.D. Watts; adv.; pub. size: tabloid; circ. 21,000(free).

US

BIG SANDY NEWS, THE. 1885. Wed. $.50 newsstand; $20/yr. in cy.; $24/yr. out of state. 101 Ricky Skaggs Blvd., Louisa, KY 41230. TEL 606-638-4581 FAX 606-638-9949. **Owner(s):** Sandy Valley Press, Inc., 101 Ricky Skaggs Blvd., Louisa, KY 41230. TEL 606-638-454 ; FAX 606-638-9949; Ed. Jerry Pennington; Pub. Allen S. Perry; adv. contact: Marjie Hale. photos; pub. size: standard; circ. 4,300(paid).

LOUISVILLE

US

LOUISVILLE DEFENDER NEWSPAPER. 1933. Thu. $.50 newsstand; $19.50/yr. in state; $21.90/yr. out of state. 1720 Dixie Hwy., Louisville, KY 40210. TEL 502-772-2591; FAX 502-772-2591. **Owner(s):** Consumer Communication Industry, 1720 Dixie Hwy., Louisville, KY 40210. TEL 502-772-2591; Ed. Yvonne Coleman. pub. size: broadsheet; circ. 8,500(paid).

US

SOUTHWEST NEWSWEEK, THE. 1954. Fri. $11/yr. 4500 Dixie Hwy., Louisville KY 40216. TEL 502-448-4581; FAX 502-447-3999. **Owner(s):** Southwest Jefferson Media, Inc., 4500 Dixie Hwy., Louisville, KY 40216. TEL 502-448-4581; Ed. Diane Vanderford; Pub. Diane Vanderford; adv.; photos; pub. size: tabloid; circ. 1,300(paid).
   Formerly: Newsweek, The

US

VOICE-TRIBUNE, THE. Wed. $.50 newsstand; $14/yr. in cy.; $16/yr. out of cy. 3518 Shelbyville Rd., Louisville, KY 40207. TEL 502-897-8900; FAX 502-897-8915. **Owner(s):** Southern Publishing Inc., 3818 Shelbyville Rd., Louisville, KY 40207. TEL 502-897-8900; Ed. Steve Rush; Pub. John Harralson; adv. contact: Don Wood. pub. size: broadsheet; circ. 5,000(paid).
   Formerly: New Voice.

MANCHESTER

US

MANCHESTER ENTERPRISE. 1890. Thu. $.75 newsstand; $22/yr. in cy.; $27/yr. elsewhere. 103 Third St., Manchester, KY 40962. TEL 606-598-2319; FAX 606-593-2330. **Owner(s):** Manchester Enterprise, P.O. Box 449, Manchester, KY 40962. TEL 606-598-2319; Ed. Mark Hoskins; Pub. Melissa Walker; adv. contact: Kay Hedricks. photos; bk.rev.; pub. size: broadsheet; circ. 8,200(paid).

MARION

US

CRITTENDEN PRESS. 1876. Thu. $.50 newsstand; $18/yr. in cy.; $21/yr. in state; $23/yr. elsewhere. 125 E. Bellville St., Marion, KY 42064. TEL 502-965-3191; FAX 502-965-2516. **Owner(s):** Nancy Mick, 125 E. Bellville St., Marion, KY 42064. TEL 502-965-3191; FAX 502-965-2516; Ed. Chris Evans; Pub. Nancy Mick; adv. contact: Marty Kares. pub. size: broadsheet; circ. 4,500(paid).

MIDDLESBORO

US

CUMBERLAND TRADING POST, THE. 1978. Thu. free; $60/yr. mailed. 110 N. 11th St., Middlesboro, KY 40965. TEL 606-248-2274; FAX 606-248-8386. **Owner(s):** American Publishing Co., 606 N. Van Buren, P.O. Box 520, Marion, IL 62959. TEL 618-993-1711; Ed. J.T. Hurst. adv. contact: Steve Bernard. pub. size: tabloid; circ. 20,000(free)

MONTICELLO

US

WAYNE COUNTY OUTLOOK. 1904. Wed. $.50
newsstand; $21/yr. local; $29/yr. elsewhere.
109 E. Columbia Ave., Monticello, KY 42633.
TEL 606-348-3338; FAX 606-348-8848.
Owner(s): Larry Traylor, Monticello, AL; Pub.
Melinda Jones; adv.; photos; pub. size:
broadsheet; circ. 6,500(paid).

MOREHEAD

US

MINIFEE COUNTY NEWS. Wed. $.50 newsstand;
$12.72/yr. in cy. 722 First St., Morehead, KY
40351. TEL 606-784-4116;
FAX 606-784-7337. **Owner(s):** Park
Communications, Inc., Vine Ctr. Office Tower, 333
W. Vine St., 17th Fl., Lexington, KY 40507. TEL
606-252-7275; Ed. Shirley Smith. adv. contact:
Brett Janke. circ. 822(paid).

US

MOREHEAD NEWS. 1883. s-w.: Tue. & Fri. $.50
newsstand; $26.50/yr. in cy. 722 W. First St.,
Morehead, KY 40351. TEL 606-784-4116;
FAX 606-784-7337. **Owner(s):** Park
Communications, Inc., Vine Ctr. Office Tower, 333
W. Vine St., 17th Fl., Lexington, KY 40507. TEL
606-252-7275; Ed. Shirley Smith. adv. contact:
Shirley Hood. pub. size: broadsheet; circ.
6,500(paid).

US

OLIVEVILLE TIMES. Wed. $.50 newsstand;
$12.72/yr. in cy. 722 W. First St., Morehead, KY
40351. TEL 606-784-4116;
FAX 606-784-7337. **Owner(s):** Park
Communications, Inc., Vine Ctr. Office Tower, 333
W. Vine St., 17th Fl., Lexington, KY 40507. TEL
606-252-7275; Ed. Mary Bobbitt. adv. contact:
Brett Janke. circ. 822(paid).

MORGANFIELD

US

UNION COUNTY ADVOCATE. 1924. Wed. $.50
newsstand; $18/yr. in cy.; $25/yr. out of cy.;
$30/yr. out of state. 214 W. Main, Morganfield,
KY 42437. TEL 502-389-1833;
FAX 502-389-3926. **Owner(s):** Union County
Advocate, P.O. Box 370, Morganfield, KY 42437.
TEL 502-389-1833; Ed. Mike Banks; Pub. Walt
Dear; adv.; photos; bk.rev.; pub. size: broadsheet;
circ. 5,500(paid).

MOUNT STERLING

US

ADVERTISER, THE. 1978. Mon. free. 40 S. Bank St.,
Mount Sterling, KY 40353. TEL 606-498-2222;
FAX 606-498-2228. **Owner(s):** Mount Sterling
Advocate, 40 S. Bank St., P.O. Box 406, Mount
Sterling, KY 40353. TEL 606-498-2222; Ed.
Glen Greene; Pub. Douglas S. Taylor; adv.; pub.
size: broadsheet; circ. 17,369(free).

MUNFORDVILLE

US   ISSN 1075-4628
HART COUNTY NEWS-HERALD. 1878. Tue. $.25
newsstand; $6.95/yr. 113 E. South St.,
Munfordville, KY 42765. TEL 502-524-2481;
FAX 502-524-2482. **Owner(s):** Aubrey C. Wilson,
Sr., 604 E. Broadway, Cave City, KY 42127. TEL
502-773-3401; Ed. Aubrey C. Wilson, Jr. adv.;
pub. size: standard; circ. 7,400(paid).

NEW CASTLE

US

HENRY COUNTY LOCAL. 1876. Wed. $.50
newsstand; $21.20/yr. Hwy. 421 & 55, New
Castle, KY 40050. TEL 502-845-2858;
FAX 502-845-2921. **Owner(s):** Landmark
Community Newspapers, Inc., P.O. Box 549,
Shelbyville, KY 40065. TEL 502-633-4334; adv.;
photos; pub. size: standard; circ. 4,500(paid).

NICHOLASVILLE

US

JESSAMINE JOURNAL. 1873. Thu. $.50 newsstand;
$18/yr. in cy.; $21.50/yr. out of cy.; $26/yr. out
of state. 507 N. Main St., Nicholasville, KY
40340. TEL 606-885-5381;
FAX 606-887-2966. **Owner(s):** Republic
Newspapers, Inc., P.O. Box 8, Nicholasville, KY
40340. TEL 606-885-5381; Ed. Randy Patrick;
Pub. Tony Cox; adv. contact: Tony Cox. photos;
pub. size: broadsheet; circ. 6,011(paid).

OLIVE HILL

US

OLIVE HILL TIMES. Wed. $.50 newsstand;
$15.90/yr. in cy.; $30/yr. out of cy.; $35/yr. out
of state. Post Office Bldg., Olive Hill, KY 41164.
TEL 606-286-4201. **Owner(s):** Park
Communications, Inc., Vine Ctr. Office Tower, 333
W. Vine St., 17th Fl., Lexington, KY 40507. TEL
606-252-7275; Ed. Mason Branham; Pub.
Ronnie Caudill; adv. contact: Elva Stamper.
photos; pub. size: broadsheet; circ. 2,350(paid).

OWINGSVILLE

US

BATH COUNTY NEWS-OUTLOOK. 1878. Thu. $.50
newsstand; $14/yr. 18 Water St., Owingsville, KY
40360. TEL 606-674-2181;
FAX 606-674-2181. **Owner(s):** Russell L. &
Margaret C. Metz, P.O. Box 577, Owingsville, KY
40360. TEL 606-674-2181; Ken E. & Gloria
Metz, P.O. Box 577, Owingsville, KY 40360. TEL
606-674-2181; Pub. Russell L. Metz; adv.
contact: Margaret C. Metz. pub. size: broadsheet;
circ. 3,600(paid).

PADUCAH

US

WEST KENTUCKY NEWS. 1967. Wed. free; $20/yr.
in cy. mailed; $25/yr. out of state mailed. 701
Jefferson St., Paducah, KY 42001-1135.
TEL 502-442-7380; FAX 502-442-5220.
Owner(s): Chris McGhee, P.O. Box 1135,
Paducah, KY 42002. TEL 502-442-7380; Pub.
Chris McGhee; adv. contact: Brian Wyatt. pub.
size: broadsheet; circ. 20,000(paid).
   Formerly: Kentucky News.

PAINTSVILLE

US

EASTERN KENTUCKY SHOPPER. Mon. free. 604 W.
Third St., Paintsville, KY 42140.
TEL 606-789-5315; FAX 606-789-9717.
Owner(s): P.T.S., Inc., P.O. Box 22, Tuscaloosa,
AL 30967; Ed. Tony Fyffe; Pub. Kate B. Dickson;
adv. contact: Chris Long. pub. size: broadsheet;
circ. 13,000(free & paid).

US

PAINTSVILLE HERALD, THE. 1901. Wed. $.50
newsstand; $25/yr. in cy. 604 W. Third St.,
Paintsville, KY 41240. TEL 606-789-5315;
FAX 606-789-9717. **Owner(s):** P.T.S., Inc., P.O.
Box 22, Tuscaloosa, AL 30967; Ed. Tony Fyffe;
Pub. Kate B. Dickson; adv. contact: Chris Long.
photos; pub. size: broadsheet; circ. 6,200(paid).

PARIS

US

ADVERTISER, THE. 1807. Mon. free; $23/yr. mailed.
123 W. Eighth St., Paris, KY 40361.
TEL 606-987-1870; FAX 606-987-3729.
Owner(s): Brannon Family, 123 W. Eighth St.,
Paris, KY 40361. TEL 606-987-1870; Ed. Jim
Brannon; Pub. Genevieve Brannon; adv.; photos;
pub. size: standard; circ. 12,800(free).
   Formerly: Citizen Advertiser.

US

BOURBON COUNTY CITIZEN. Wed. $.50 newsstand;
$16/yr.; $18/yr. out of state. 123 W. Eighth St.,
Paris, KY 40361. TEL 606-987-1870;
FAX 606-987-3729. **Owner(s):** Brannon Family,
123 Eighth St., Paris, KY 40361. TEL
606-987-1870; Ed. Jim Brannon; Pub. Genevieve
Brannon; pub. size: standard; circ. 3,400(paid).

PIKEVILLE

US

APPALACHIAN NEWS-EXPRESS. 1913. 3/wk.: Wed.,
Fri., Sun. $.50 newsstand; $52/yr. home deliv.;
$85/yr. out of area. 201 Caroline Ave., Pikeville,
KY 41501. TEL 606-437-4054;
FAX 606-437-4246. **Owner(s):** Appalachian
Newspapers, Inc., P.O. Box 802, Pikeville, KY
41502. TEL 606-437-4054; Ed. Larry Martin;
Pub. Marty Backus; adv. contact: Teresa
Fields-Branham. pub. size: broadsheet; circ.
11,300(paid).

PINEVILLE

US

PINEVILLE SUN-CUMBERLAND COURIER. 1907. Thu.
$.35 newsstand; $15/yr. in cy.; $18/yr.
elsewhere. 210 Virginia Ave., Pineville, KY
40977. TEL 606-337-2333. **Owner(s):** Pineville
Sun-Cumberland Courier, P.O. Box 250, Pineville,
KY 40977. TEL 606-337-2333; Pub. Lin
Hobbes; adv. contact: Lin Hobbes. pub. size:
broadsheet; circ. 3,250(paid).

PRESTONSBURG

US

FLOYD COUNTY TIMES. 1928. s-w.: Wed. & Fri. $.75
newsstand; $28/yr. in cy. carrier. 112 S. Central,
Prestonsburg, KY 41653. TEL 606-886-8506;
FAX 606-886-3603. **Owner(s):** Smith
Newspapers, Inc., P.O. Box 27, Fort Payne, AL
35967. TEL 205-845-5510; Ed. Janice
Sheppard; Pub. Scott Perry; adv. contact: Shawn
Hamilton. pub. size: broadsheet; circ.
12,800(paid).

PRINCETON

US

TIMES LEADER, THE. 1992. s-w.: Wed. & Sat. $.50 newsstand; $33/yr. in cy.; $39/yr. in state; $48/yr. out of state. 607 W. Washington, Princeton, KY 42445. TEL 502-365-5588; FAX 502-365-7299. **Owner(s):** Times Leader, Inc., 607 W. Washington St., Princeton, KY 42445. TEL 502-365-5588; FAX 502-365-7299; Ed. John Hutcheson, III; Pub. John Hutcheson, III; adv. contact: Ellen Franklin. photos; pub. size: broadsheet; circ. 5,800(free & paid). **Wire Service(s):** AP.
  Formerly: Caldwell County Times; Princeton Leader, The.

PROVIDENCE

US

JOURNAL-ENTERPRISE. 1899. Thu. $.25 newsstand; $12/yr. 100 Walnut St., Providence, KY 42450. TEL 502-667-2068; FAX 502-667-9160. **Owner(s):** Providence Journal-Enterprise, Inc., P.O. Box 190, Providence, KY 42450; FAX 502-667-9160; Ed. Charles Hust; Pub. Edd Hust; pub. size: standard; circ. 45,000(paid).
  Formerly: Providence Journal-Enterprise.

RADCLIFF

US

SENTINEL, THE. 1961. Thu. $.25 newsstand; $7.95/yr. 1558 Hill St., Radcliff, KY 40160. TEL 502-351-4407; FAX 502-351-4407. **Owner(s):** Sentinel, The, 1558 Hill St., Radcliff, KY 40160. TEL 502-351-4407; Ed. O.J. Royalty; Pub. O.J. Royalty; adv.; pub. size: standard; circ. 3,500(paid).

RUSSELL SPRINGS

US   ISSN 8750-1651

RUSSELL COUNTY NEWS. 1913. Sun. free newsstand; $40/yr. 120 Wilson St., Russell Springs, KY 42542-0190. TEL 502-866-3191; FAX 502-866-3198. **Owner(s):** Russell County Newspapers, Inc., 120 Wilson St., Russell Springs, KY 42642-0190. TEL 502-866-3191; FAX 502-866-3198; Ed. Dave Cazalet; Pub. Dave Cazalet; adv. contact: Kathy Ellis. pub. size: broadsheet; circ. Sun. 9,500(free & paid).

US

RUSSELL SPRINGS TIMES JOURNAL. 1949. Thu. $.50 newsstand; $17.57/yr. in cy.; $27.11/yr. out of cy.; $26/yr. out of state; $80/yr. elsewhere. 120 Wilson St., Russell Springs, KY 42642-0190. TEL 502-866-3191; FAX 502-866-3198. **Owner(s):** Russell County Newspapers, Inc., P.O. Box 190, Russell Springs, KY 42642. TEL 502-866-3191; FAX 502-866-3198; adv. contact: Kathy Ellis. photos; bk.rev.; pub. size: broadsheet; circ. 4,015(paid).

RUSSELLVILLE

US

NEWS DEMOCRAT & LEADER. 1904. s-w.: Tue. & Fri. $.50 newsstand; $25/yr. in cy.; $35/yr. out of cy. 120 Public Sq., Russellville, KY 42276. TEL 502-726-8394; FAX 502-726-8398. **Owner(s):** Park Communications, Inc., Vine Ctr. Office Tower, 333 W. Vine St., 17th Fl., Lexington, KY 40507. TEL 606-252-7275; adv.; pub. size: standard; circ. 6,800(free & paid).

SALYERSVILLE

US

SALYERSVILLE INDEPENDENT. 1921. Thu. $.50 newsstand; $18.02/yr. in cy.; $24.14/yr. out of cy; $22/yr. out of state. 7 W. Maple St., Salyersville, KY 41465. TEL 606-349-2915. **Owner(s):** Tim & Carol Bostic, P.O. Box 29, Salyersville, KY 44165. TEL 606-349-2915; Ed. Tim Bostic; Pub. Tim Bostic; pub. size: standard; circ. 4,200(paid).

SCOTTSVILLE

US

SCOTTSVILLE CITIZEN-TIMES. 1890. Thu. $.40 newsstand; $12/yr. in cy.; $15/yr. out of cy. 611 E. Main, Scottsville, KY 42164. TEL 502-237-3441; FAX 502-237-4943. **Owner(s):** Billie Hatcher & Robert B. Pitchford, III, P.O. Box 310, Scottsville, KY 42164. TEL 502-237-3441; FAX 502-237-4840; Ed. Robert B. Pitchford, III: Pub. Billie Hatcher; adv.; pub. size: standard; circ. 5,000(paid).

SHELBYVILLE

US

SHELBYVILLE SENTINEL-NEWS. 1840. s-w.: Wed. & Fri. $.50 newsstand; $31/yr. 703 Taylorsville Rd., Shelbyville, KY 40065. TEL 502-633-2526; FAX 502-633-2618. **Owner(s):** Landmark Community Newspapers, Inc., P.O. Box 549, Shelbyville, KY 40065. TEL 502-633-4334; Ed. DuAnne Puckett; Pub. James L. Edelen; adv.; photos; bk.rev.; pub size: broadsheet; circ. 7,700(paid).

US

SHOPPER/PLUS. 1983. Mon. free. 703 Taylorsville Rd., Shelbyville, KY 40065. TEL 502-633-2526; FAX 502-633-2618. **Owner(s):** Landmark Community Newspapers, Inc., P.O. Box 549, Shelbyville, KY 40055. TEL 502-633-4334; Ed. DuAnne Puckett; Pub. James L. Edelen; adv.; pub. size: broadsheet; circ. 15,600(free).

SHEPHERDSVILLE

US

PIONEER-NEWS. 1882. s-w.: Mon. & Wed. $.50 newsstand; $25.95/yr. 455 N. Buckman St., Shepherdsville, KY 40165. TEL 502-543-2288; FAX 502-955-9704. **Owner(s):** Landmark Community Newspapers, Inc., P.O. Box 549, Shelbyville, KY 40066. TEL 502-633-4334; Ed. Thomas Barr; Pub. Thomas Barr; adv. contact: Thomas Barr. pub. size: broadsheet; circ. 22,500(free & paid).

SPRINGFIELD

US

SPRINGFIELD SUN. 1904. Wed. $.75 newsstand; $22.26/yr. in cy.; $29.68/yr. out of cy.; $38/yr. out of state. 117 Cross Main, Springfield, KY 40069. TEL 606-336-3716; FAX 606-336-7718. **Owner(s):** Landmark Community Newspapers, Inc., P.O. Box 549, Shelbyville, KY 40066; Ed. Tim Ballard; Pub. Tim Ballard; pub. size: broadsheet; circ. 3,700(paid).

STANFORD

US

INTERIOR JOURNAL. 1860. Thu. $.35 newsstand; $15.50/yr. in state; $29.75/yr. out of state. 111 E. Main St., Stanford, KY 40484. TEL 606-365-2104; FAX 606-365-2105. **Owner(s):** Thomas J. Moore, 111 E. Main St., Stanford, KY 40484. TEL 606-365-2104; Sharman P. Moore, 111 E. Main St., Stanford, KY 40484. TEL 606-365-2104; Ed. Thomas J. Moore. adv.: $3.85/SAU. pub. size: broadsheet; circ. 4,339(paid).

STANTON

US

CLAY CITY TIMES, THE. 1896. Thu. $.50 newsstand; $15/yr. local; $20/yr. in state; $25/yr. out of state. 209 N. Main St., Stanton, KY 40380. TEL 606-663-5540; FAX 606-663-6397. **Owner(s):** Hatfield Newspapers, Inc., P.O. Box 766, Stanton, KY 40380-0766. TEL 606-663-5540; FAX 606-663-6397; Ed. Joe Troher; Pub. Guy Hatfield; adv.; photos; pub. size: broadsheet; circ. 4,100(paid).

STURGIS

US

STURGIS NEWS. 1885. Wed. $.35 newsstand; $9.54/yr. 617 N. Adams, Sturgis, KY 42459-0218. TEL 502-333-5545; FAX 502-333-9943. **Owner(s):** Betty P. Catlett, P.O. Box 36, Sebree, KY 42455. TEL 502-835-7521; FAX 502-825-9521; Ed. Paul J. Monsour; Pub. Betty P. Catlett; adv.; photos; pub. size: standard; circ. 3,200(paid).

TAYLORSVILLE

US

SPENCER MAGNET. Wed. $.50 newsstand. Main St., Taylorsville, KY 40071. TEL 502-477-2239; FAX 502-477-2110. **Owner(s):** Landmark Community Newspapers, Inc., P.O. Box 549, Shelbyville, KY 40065. TEL 502-633-4334; Ed. Kimberly Rich. adv.; photos; pub. size: broadsheet; circ. 2,500(paid).

TOMPKINSVILLE

US

T-VILLE NEWS TRADER. Mon. free. 105 N. Main, Tompkinsville, KY 42167. TEL 502-487-5576; FAX 502-487-8839. **Owner(s):** Monroe County Press, Inc., 105 N. Main St., Tompkinsville, KY 42167. TEL 502-487-5576; FAX 502-487-8839; Ed. Gina Kinslow; Pub. Blanche B. Trimble; adv. contact: Sharon Fister. pub. size: tabloid.

US

TOMPKINSVILLE NEWS. 1903. Thu. $.25 newsstand; $11/yr. in cy.; $15/yr. out of cy.; $20/yr. out of state. 105 N. Main, Tompkinsville, KY 42167. TEL 502-487-5576; FAX 502-487-8839. **Owner(s):** Monroe County Press Inc., 600 Magnolia Street, Tompkinsville, KY 42167. TEL 502-487-5624; FAX 502-487-8839; Ed. Gina Kinslow; Pub. Blanche B. Trimble; adv. contact: Sharon Fister. photos; pub. size: standard; circ. 4,300(paid).

VERSAILLES

US

WOODFORD SUN. 1869. Thu. $.50 newsstand; $17/yr. in cy.; $28/yr. out of state. 184 S. Main St., Versailles, KY 40383. TEL 606-873-4131; FAX 606-873-0300. **Owner(s):** Woodford Sun Co., Inc., P.O. Box 29, Versailles, KY 40383. TEL 606-873-4131; FAX 606-873-0300; Ed. H. Moss Vance; Pub. A.B. Chandler, Jr.; adv.; pub. size: broadsheet; circ. 5,900(paid).

WEST LIBERTY

US

LICKING VALLEY COURIER. 1910. Thu. $.50 newsstand; $13.50/yr. in cy.; $16/yr. out of cy.; $18/yr. out of state. 142 Prestonsburg St., West Liberty, KY 41472. TEL 606-743-3551; FAX 606-743-3565. **Owner(s):** Earl W. Kinner, P.O. Box 187, West Liberty, KY 41472. TEL 606-743-3551; Ed. Earl W. Kinner; Pub. Earl W. Kinner; adv. contact: Sue H. Kinner. pub. size: broadsheet; circ. 4,200(paid).
   Formerly: West Liberty Licking Valley Courier.

WHITESBURG

US

MOUNTAIN EAGLE, THE. 1907. Wed. $.75 newsstand; $24.50/yr. in cy.; $31.50/yr. out of cy. 367B Hazard Rd., Whitesburg, KY 41858. TEL 606-633-2252; FAX 606-633-2843. **Owner(s):** Tom Gish, P.O. Box 808, Whitesburg, KY 41858. TEL 606-633-2252; Ed. Ben Gish; Pub. Tom Gish; adv. contact: Freddy Oakes. pub. size: broadsheet; circ. 7,800(paid).
   Formerly: Whitesburg Mountain Eagle.

WHITLEY CITY

US

MCCREARY COUNTY RECORD. 1919. Tue. $.50 newsstand; $14.65/yr. in cy.; $28/yr. in state; $30/yr. out of state. Courthouse Sq., Whitley City, KY 42653-0009. TEL 606-376-5357; FAX 606-376-5357. **Owner(s):** Park Communications, Inc., Vine Ctr. Office Tower, 333 W. Vine St., 17th Fl., Lexington, KY 40507. TEL 606-252-7275; Ed. Ken Shmidheiser; Pub. James T. Stratton; adv. contact: Janie West. pub. size: broadsheet; circ. 5,400(paid).

WICKLIFFE

US

ADVANCE-YEOMAN. 1882. Wed. $.50 newsstand; $20/yr. in cy.; $25/yr. out of cy. 101 Ohio St., Wickliffe, KY 42087. TEL 502-335-3193; FAX 502-335-3560. **Owner(s):** Chris McGhee, 101 Ohio, Wickliffe, KY 42087. TEL 502-335-3193; FAX 502-335-3560; Ed. Teresa Sullivan; Pub. Chris McGhee; adv.; pub. size: standard; circ. 3,000(paid).
   Formerly: Wickliffe Advance-Yeoman.

WILLIAMSBURG

US

WHITLEY REPUBLICAN NEWS JOURNAL. 1908. Wed. $.50 newsstand; $19.10/yr. in cy.; $21.30/yr. out of cy. 105 S. Second St., Williamsburg, KY 40769. TEL 606-549-0643; FAX 606-528-9779. **Owner(s):** Terry Forcht, N. Barton & Don Estep, 105 S. Second St., Williamsburg, KY 40769. TEL 606-549-0643; Ed. Mark White; Pub. Don Estep; adv. contact: Don Estep. pub. size: broadsheet; circ. 7,600(paid).

WILLIAMSTOWN

US

GRANT COUNTY NEWS. 1906. Thu. $.50 newsstand; $15.50/yr. locally; $23/yr. in state; $30/yr. out of state. 151 N. Main St., Williamstown, KY 41097-0247. TEL 606-824-3344; FAX 606-824-5888. **Owner(s):** Landmark Community Newspapers, Inc., P.O. Box 549, Shelbyville, KY 40066. TEL 502-633-4334; Ed. Jamie Baker-Nantz; Pub. Ken Stone; adv. contact: John Hurston. photos; pub. size: broadsheet; circ. 4,470(free & paid).

LOUISIANA

ALEXANDRIA

US

ALEXANDRIA NEWS WEEKLY. 1963. Thu. $.25 newsstand; $30/yr. in state. 1746 Mason St., Alexandria, LA 71301. TEL 318-443-7664. **Owner(s):** Leon Coleman, Sr., P.O. Box 608, Alexandria, LA 71309. TEL 318-443-7664; Alice G. Coleman, 1746 Mason St., Alexandria, LA 71301. TEL 318-443-7664; Ed. Alice G. Coleman; Pub. Alice G. Coleman; adv. contact: Leon Coleman, Sr. pub. size: broadsheet; circ. 13,800(paid).

AMITE

US

AMITE TANGI DIGEST. 1928. Wed. $.50 newsstand; $20/yr. in state; $30/yr. out of state. 120 N.E. Central Ave., Amite, LA 70422. TEL 504-748-6343; FAX 504-748-7104. **Owner(s):** Louisiana State Newspapers, Lafayette, LA; Ed. Trish Adams; Pub. Carol Brookes; pub. size: standard; circ. 4,100(paid).
   Formerly: Tangi Talk/News Digest.

ARABI

US

ST. BERNARD VOICE. 1890. Fri. $.25 newsstand; $12/yr. in state; $14/yr. out of state. 234 Mehle Ave., Arabi, LA 70032. TEL 504-279-7488; FAX 504-277-2231. **Owner(s):** St. Bernard Voice, Inc., The, 234 Mehle Ave., Arabi, LA 70032. TEL 504-279-7488; FAX 504-277-2231; Ed. Edwin M. Roy, Jr.; Pub. Edwin M. Roy, Jr.; pub. size: broadsheet; circ. 3,000(paid).

ARCADIA

US

BIENVILLE DEMOCRAT & RINGGOLD RECORD. 1909. Thu. $.50 newsstand; $30/yr. in state; $25/yr. trade area. Railroad St., Arcadia, LA 71001. TEL 318-263-2922; FAX 318-263-8897. **Owner(s):** Natchitoches Times, Inc., P.O. Box 448, Natchitoches, LA 71458. TEL 318-352-3618; Ed. Wayne Dring. adv.; pub. size: broadsheet; circ. 3,500(paid).

BAKER

US

BAKER OBSERVER. 1957. Thu. $.50 newsstand; $20/yr. in cy.; $42/yr. out of state. 5240 Groom Rd., Baker, LA 70714-3126. TEL 504-775-2315; FAX 504-774-9212. **Owner(s):** Louisiana Suburban Press, P.O. Box 539, Baker, LA 70704. TEL 504-775-2315; Ed. Bill Catchings; Pub. Jack Roberts; adv. contact: Sherri Romero. photos; pub. size: broadsheet; circ. 2,100(paid).

BATON ROUGE

US

GREATER BATON ROUGE BUSINESS REPORT. 1982. bi-w: Tue. $1.50 newsstand; $39/yr. in state; $47/yr. out of state. 5757 Corporate Blvd., Ste. 402, Baton Rouge, LA 70808. TEL 504-928-1700; FAX 504-923-3448. **Owner(s):** Rolfe McCollister, 5757 Corporate Blvd., Ste. 402, Baton Rouge, LA 70808. TEL 504-928-1700; FAX 504-923-3448; Ed. Paulette Senior. adv. contact: Sara Wilensky. pub. size: tabloid; circ. 14,000(paid).

US

WEEKLY PRESS. 1981. Thu. $.25 newsstand; $25/yr. 1384 Swan Ave., Baton Rouge, LA 70807. TEL 504-775-2002. **Owner(s):** Ivory Payne, 1384 Swan Ave., Baton Rouge, LA 70807; Ed. Cassie Payne; Pub. Ivory Payne; adv.; pub. size: broadsheet; circ. 7,500(paid).

BELLE CHASSE

US

PLAQUEMINES GAZETTE. 1926. Fri. $.35 newsstand; $25/yr. 7952 Hwy. 23, Belle Chasse, LA 70037. TEL 504-392-1619; FAX 504-393-9327. **Owner(s):** Plaquemines Newspaper Publishing, Inc., 7952 Hwy. 23, Belle Chasse, LA 70037. TEL 504-392-1619; Ed. Dale Benoit. adv. contact: Norris J. Babin, Jr. pub. size: broadsheet; circ. 2,950(paid).

US

PLAQUEMINES WATCHMAN. 1981. Wed. $25/yr. in parish; $30/yr. out of parish; $35/yr. out of state. 7952 Hwy. 23, Belle Chasse, LA 70037. TEL 504-392-1619; FAX 504-393-9327. **Owner(s):** Plaquemines Newspaper Publishings, Inc., 7952 Hwy. 23, Belle Chasse, LA 70037. TEL 504-392-1619; adv.; photos; pub. size: broadsheet; circ. 2,950(paid).

BOSSIER CITY

US

BOSSIER BANNER-PROGRESS. 1859. Fri. $22/yr. in parish; $30/yr. out of parish. P.O. Box 6267, Bossier City, LA 71171. TEL 318-965-0101; FAX 318-747-5298. **Owner(s):** Robert Barton, P.O Box 6267, Bossier City, LA 71171. TEL 318-965-0101; FAX 318-747-5298; Ed. Nancy Cook; Pub. Robert Barton; adv. contact: Kathy Spivey. pub. size: broadsheet; circ. 500(paid).

US   ISSN 0747-4733

BOSSIER PRESS-TRIBUNE. 1928. Fri. $.50 newsstand; $30/yr. 409 Barksdale Blvd., Bossier City, LA 71171. TEL 318-747-7900; FAX 318-747-5298. **Owner(s):** Bossier Caddo Newspapers, Inc., 409 Barksdale Blvd., Bossier City, LA 71111. TEL 318-747-4010; Ed. Nancy Morris Cook; Pub. Bob Barton; adv. contact: Kathy Spivey. pub. size: broadsheet; circ. 7,000(controlled).

CHURCH POINT

US

CHURCH POINT NEWS. 1933. Wed. $.75 newsstand; $19.50/yr. in parish; $23.50/yr. out of parish; $30/yr. out of state. 315 N. Main, Church Point, LA 70525. TEL 318-684-5711; FAX 318-684-5793. **Owner(s):** Louisiana State Newspapers, P.O. Box 5010, Lafayette, LA 70507. TEL 318-334-3186; Ed. Diane Daigle; Pub. Willie Petre; adv. contact: Liz Harke. pub. size: broadsheet; circ. 2,146(paid).

CLINTON

US

EAST FELICIANA WATCHMAN. 1878. Wed. $.50 newsstand; $20/yr. in state. 12311 St. Helena St., Clinton Corners, Clinton, LA 70722. TEL 504-683-5195; FAX 504-683-4276. **Owner(s):** Louisiana State Newspapers, P.O. Box 5010, Lafayette, LA 70502. TEL 504-266-2100; Ed. Jack Roberts. adv. contact: Jack Roberts. photos; pub. size: standard; circ. 20,000(controlled).

    Formerly: Clinton Watchman.

COUSHATTA

US

COUSHATTA CITIZEN. 1871. Thu. $.50 newsstand; $16/yr. 1703 Ringgold Ave., Coushatta, LA 71019-1365. TEL 318-932-4201; FAX 318-932-4285. **Owner(s):** Lovan Thomas, 1703 Ringgold Ave., Coushatta, LA 71019-1365. TEL 318-932-4201; FAX 318-932-4285; Pub. Marsha Loftin; adv.; photos; pub. size: broadsheet; circ. 6,200(free & paid).

COVINGTON

US

COVINGTON ST. TAMMANY FARMER. 1874. Thu. $.35 newsstand; $15/yr. 321 N. New Hampshire St., Covington, LA 70433. TEL 504-892-2323; FAX 504-892-2325. **Owner(s):** St. Tammany Farmer, Inc., P.O. Box 269, Covington, LA 70434-0269. TEL 504-892-2323; Ed. Ron Barthet. adv.; photos; pub. size: broadsheet; circ. 4,000(paid).

US

NEWS-BANNER, THE. 1963. 3/wk.: Wed., Fri., Sun. $.75 newsstand; $72/yr. in parish mailed; $50.96/yr. home deliv.; $72/yr. elsewhere mailed. 19290 19th Ave., Covington, LA 70433. TEL 504-892-7980; FAX 504-892-8242; E-mail: banner@neosofti.com. **Owner(s):** Wick Communications, Inc., 333 W. Wilcox, Ste. 302, Sierra Vista, AZ 85632. TEL 602-458-0200; Ed. Barbara Danahy; Pub. Floyd Burckel; photos; bk.rev.; pub. size: broadsheet; circ. 26,500(paid); Sun. 21,000(paid).

DENHAM SPRINGS

US

DENHAM SPRINGS-LIVINGSTON PARISH NEWS. 1898. s-w.: Thu. & Sun. $.50 newsstand; $36.16/yr. in parish; $50.96 out of state. 688 Hatchell Ln., Denham Springs, LA 70726. TEL 504-665-5176; FAX 504-667-0167. **Owner(s):** Denham Springs Publishing Co., P.O. Box 6, Denham Springs, LA 70727. TEL 504-665-5342; Ed. Mike Dowty; Pub. Jeff M. David; adv. contact: Connie Gerstein. pub. size: broadsheet; circ. 10,544(paid).

US

LIVINGSTON LEADER. Thu. free. 688 Hatchell Ln., Denham Springs, LA 70726. TEL 504-665-5176; FAX 504-667-0167. **Owner(s):** Denham Springs Publishing Co., 688 Hatchell Ln., Denham Springs, LA 70727. TEL 504-665-5176; FAX 504-667-0167; Ed. Mike Dowty; Pub. Jeff M. David; adv. contact: Rhonda Morris. pub. size: broadsheet; circ. 5,000(free).

DE QUINCY

US

DE QUINCY NEWS. 1926. Wed. $15.45/yr. 203 E. Harrison, De Quincy, LA 70633. TEL 318-786-8004; FAX 318-786-8131. **Owner(s):** De Quincy News, 203 E. Harrison, De Quincy, LA 70633. TEL 318-786-8131; Ed. Jerry Wise; Pub. Jerry Wise; adv.; bk.rev.; pub. size: standard; circ. 3,800(paid).

DONALDSONVILLE

US

DONALDSONVILLE CHIEF. 1871. Thu. $20/yr. 402 Railroad Ave., Donaldsonville, LA 70346. TEL 504-473-3101; FAX 504-473-4060. **Owner(s):** Donaldsonville Newspapers, Inc., P.O. Box 309, Donaldsonville, LA 70346. TEL 504-473-3101; FAX 504-473-4060; Ed. Juanita Wagvespack; Pub. Ella Metrejean; adv. contact: Angela Boudreaux. pub. size: standard; circ. 3,100(paid).

EUNICE

US

EUNICE NEWS. 1904. s-w.: Thu. & Sun. $.75 newsstand; $28/yr. in parish; $38/yr. out of parish; $46/yr. elsewhere. 251 N. Second St., Eunice, LA 70535. TEL 318-457-3061; FAX 318-457-3122. **Owner(s):** Louisiana State Newspapers, P.O. Box 4033-C, Lafayette, LA 70502. TEL 313-233-7000; Ed. Jerry Hoffpauir; Pub. Willie Pitre; adv. contact: Rachel Lemoine. pub. size: broadsheet; circ. 6,000(paid); Sun. 6,500(paid).

FERRIDAY

US

CONCORDIA SENTINEL. 1876. Wed. $.50 newsstand; $20/yr. in parish; $25/yr. in state; $30/yr. out of state. 1308 N. First St., Ferriday, LA 71334. TEL 318-757-3546; FAX 318-757-3001. **Owner(s):** Hanna Publishing Co., P.O. Box 312, Ferriday, LA 71334. TEL 318-757-3646; FAX 318-757-3001 Ed. Samuel A. Hanna; Pub. Samuel A. Hanna; adv. contact: Barbara Jackson. pub. size: broadsheet; circ. 5,500(paid).

GONZALES

US

COMMUNITY MIRROR. Tue. free. 205 W. Worthey, Gonzales, LA 70737. TEL 504-647-4569; FAX 504-644-8238. **Owner(s):** Gonzales Weekly, Inc., 205 W. Worthey, Gonzales, LA 70737; Ed. Arlene E. Bishop; Pub Crawford A. Bishop; pub. size: broadsheet; circ. 20,000(free).

US

GONZALES WEEKLY. 1920. Fri. $.50 newsstand; $20/yr. in state; $25/yr. out of state. 205 W. Worthey, Gonzales, LA 70737. TEL 504-647-4569; FAX 504-644-8238. **Owner(s):** Gonzales Weekly, Inc., 205 W. Worthey, Gonzales, LA 70737. TEL 504-647-4569 Ed. Arlene E. Bishop. pub. size: broadsheet; circ. 8,000(paid).

JEANERETTE

US

JEANERETTE ENTERPRISE. 1942. Wed. $.25 newsstand; $30/yr. 808 E. Main St., Jeanerette, LA 70544. TEL 318-276-5171; FAX 318-367-9640. **Owner(s):** Wick Communications, Inc., 333 Wilcox Dr., Ste. 302, Sierra Vista, AZ 85635. TEL 520-728-4488; FAX 520-728-6090; Ed. Karma Champaigne; Pub. Will Chapman; adv. contact: Jane Collier. pub. size: standard; circ. 4,200(paid).

JENA

US

JENA TIMES OLLA-TULLOS SIGNAL. 1905. Wed. $.35 newsstand; $32/yr. P.O. Drawer 1384, Jena, LA 71342 TEL 318-992-4121; FAX 318-992-2287. **Owner(s):** Sammy J. Franklin, P.O. Box 1384, Jena, LA 71342. TEL 318-992-4121; FAX 318-992-2287; Ed. Sammy J. Franklin; Pub. Sammy J. Franklin; adv. contact: Karla Fitzgerald. pub. size: broadsheet; circ. 4,600(paid).

JONESBORO

US

JACKSON INDEPENDENT, THE. 1892. Thu. $.50 newsstand; $16.65/yr. in parish; $26.50/yr. out of parish; $32/yr. out of state. 624 Hudson Ave., Jonesboro, LA 71251. TEL 318-259-2551. **Owner(s):** T.L. Colvin, Jr., 624 Hudson Ave., Jonesboro, LA 71251; Ed. T.L. Colvin, III; Pub. T.L. Colvin, Jr.; photos; pub. size: broadsheet; circ. 3,500(free & paid).

    Formerly: Jonesboro Jackson Independent.

KENTWOOD

US

KENTWOOD NEWS-LEDGER. 1965. Wed. $.50 newsstand; $30/yr. 212 Ave. F, Kentwood, LA 70444. TEL 504-229-8607; FAX 504-748-7104. **Owner(s):** Louisiana State Newspapers, P.O. Box AD, Kentwood, LA 70444. TEL 504-229-8607; FAX 504-748-7104; Ed. Sylvia D. Jackson. adv.; photos; pub. size: broadsheet; circ. 14,646(free & paid).

LA PLACE

US

L'OBSERVATEUR. 1913. s-w.: Wed. & Sat. $.50 newsstand; $23.70/yr. 116 Newspaper Dr., La Place, LA 70068. TEL 504-652-9545; FAX 504-652-3885. **Owner(s):** Wick Communications, Inc., 333 Wilcox Dr., Ste. 302, Sierra Vista, AZ 85635. TEL 520-728-4488; FAX 520-728-6090; Ed. Michael Stout; Pub. Joy Kennon; adv. contact: Scott Madere. photos; pub. size: broadsheet; circ. 5,000(paid).

    Formerly: La Place L'Observateur.

LUTCHER

US

NEWS EXAMINER, THE. Thu. $.50 newsstand; $15.45/yr. mailed. 2290 Texas St., Lutcher, LA 70071. TEL 504-869-5784; FAX 504-869-4386. **Owner(s):** Ruhr Valley Publishing, 2290 Texas St. Lutcher, LA 70071. TEL 504-869-5784; FAX 504-869-4386; Ed. Huey Stein; Pub. Wilbur Raynaud; adv. contact: Cynthia Griffin. photos; pub. size: broadsheet; circ. 4,000(paid).

MAMOU

US

MAMOU ACADIAN PRESS. 1956. Thu. $16/yr. P.O. Drawer 260, Mamou, LA 70554. TEL 318-363-3939; FAX 318-363-2841. **Owner(s):** Louisiana State Newspapers, P.O. Drawer 260, Lafayette, LA 70501. TEL 318-363-3939; Ed. Bernice Ardoin. adv.; photos; bk.rev.; pub. size: broadsheet; circ. 2,600(free).

MANSFIELD

US

MANSFIELD ENTERPRISE. 1904. Thu. $.50 newsstand; $20/yr. in parish; $35/yr. out of parish. 202 Adams St., Mansfield, LA 71052. TEL 318-872-4120; FAX 318-872-6038. **Owner(s):** Natchitoches Times, Inc., P.O. Box 448, Natchitoches, LA 71458. TEL 318-352-5501; Ed. Keenan C. Gingles; Pub. Keenan C. Gingles; adv. contact: Bennie Hall. pub. size: broadsheet; circ. 3,800(paid).

MANY

US

SABINE BANNER. Tue. free. 850 San Antonio Ave., Many, LA 71449. TEL 318-256-3495; FAX 318-256-9151. **Owner(s):** Robert Gentry, P.O. Box 850, Many, LA 71449. TEL 318-256-3495; Ed. Shannon Clements; Pub. Robert Gentry; adv.; pub. size: tabloid; circ. 15,000(free).

US

SABINE INDEX. 1879. Wed. free; $.75 newsstand; $24/yr. in parish; $36/yr. out of parish. 850 San Antonio Ave., Many, LA 71449. TEL 318-256-3495; FAX 318-256-9151. **Owner(s):** Robert Gentry, P.O. Box 850, Many, LA 71449. TEL 318-256-3495; Ed. Shannon Clements; Pub. Robert Gentry; adv. contact: Melinda Crosier. photos; bk.rev.; pub. size: tabloid; circ. 6,200(controlled & paid).

MARKSVILLE

US

AVOYELLES JOURNAL. 1978. s-w.: Sun. & Wed. free. One N. Main St., Marksville, LA 71351. TEL 318-253-5413; FAX 318-253-7223. **Owner(s):** Avoyelles Publishing Co., P.O. Box 523, Marksville, LA 71351. TEL 318-253-5413; Ed. Randy DeCuir; Pub. Randy DeCuir; adv. contact: Kathie Lipe. pub. size: broadsheet; circ. 16,500(free).

US

WEEKLY NEWS. Thu. $13.50/yr. in parish; $24/yr. out of parish; $28/yr. out of state. 100 N. Main St., P.O. Box 523, Marksville, LA 71351. TEL 318-253-9247; FAX 318-253-9247. **Owner(s):** Avoyelles Publishing Co., P.O. Box 253, Marksville, LA 71351. TEL 318-253-9247; Ed. Randy DeCuir. pub. size: broadsheet; circ. 4,000(paid).

MORGAN CITY

US

ST. MARY JOURNAL. 1960. s-w.: Sun. & Wed. free. 1014 Front St., Morgan City, LA 70380. TEL 504-384-1350; FAX 504-384-4255. **Owner(s):** Morgan City Newspapers, Inc., P.O. Box 948, Morgan City, LA 70381. TEL 504-384-8370; Ed. Steve Shirley; Pub. Doyle E. Shirley; adv. contact: Andy Shirley. photos; pub. size: broadsheet; circ. 10,500(free).

NEW ROADS

US

POINTE COUPEE BANNER. 1880. Thu. $.50 newsstand; $20.80/yr. in state; $25/yr. out of state; $30/yr. out of cy. 123 St. Mary St., New Roads, LA 70760. TEL 504-638-7155; FAX 504-638-8442. **Owner(s):** Pointe Coupee Printing & Publishing, Inc., 123 St. Mary St., New Roads, LA 70760. TEL 504-638-7155; Pub. Mary Catherine Roy LaCour; adv. contact: Amy Braud. pub. size: standard; circ. 5,400(paid).

OAKDALE

US   ISSN 0746-5920

OAKDALE JOURNAL. 1913. Thu. $.75 newsstand; $21/yr. in area; $25/yr. in state; $31.50/yr. out of state. 122 E. Sixth Ave., Oakdale, LA 71463. TEL 318-335-0635; FAX 318-335-0431. **Owner(s):** Louisiana State Newspapers, 122 E. Sixth Ave., Oakdale, LA 71463. TEL 318-335-0635; FAX 318-335-0431; Ed. Barbara Doyle. adv.; photos; pub. size: broadsheet; circ. 14,000(paid).

OAK GROVE

US

WEST CARROLL GAZETTE. 1910. Wed. $.35 newsstand; $15/yr. in parish; $18/yr. out of parish; $27.50/yr. out of state. 512 Constitution Ave., Oak Grove, LA 71263. TEL 318-428-3207; FAX 318-428-2747. **Owner(s):** Moody Co., P.O. Box 4033C, Lafayette, LA 70502; Pub. David Clevenger; adv. contact: Bill Vaughan. photos; pub. size: standard; circ. 3,348(paid).

PLAQUEMINE

US   ISSN 1053-5691

POST SOUTH. 1957. Thu. $.50 newsstand; $20.80/yr. local. 58640 Belleview Rd., Plaquemine, LA 70764. TEL 504-687-3288; FAX 504-687-1814. **Owner(s):** Joyce S. Hebert, P.O. Box 589, Plaquemine, LA 70765-0589. TEL 504-687-3288; FAX 504-687-1814; Ed. Ellie Hebert; Pub. Joyce S. Hebert; adv.; pub. size: standard; circ. 5,800(paid).
Formerly: Plaquemine Post/Iberville South.

PONCHATOULA

US   ISSN 0889-0684

ENTERPRISE, THE. 1921. Wed. $.25 newsstand; $12/yr. 240 E. Pine St., Ponchatoula, LA 70454. TEL 504-386-6537. **Owner(s):** Don Ellzey, P.O. Box 218, Ponchatoula, LA 70454. TEL 504-386-6537; Pub. Don Ellzey; adv.; pub. size: broadsheet; circ. 2,300(paid).

US

PONCHATOULA TIMES, THE. 1981. Thu. $.50 newsstand; $11/yr. in parish; $13/yr. elsewhere. 145 W. Pine St., Ste. A, Ponchatoula, LA 70454. TEL 504-386-2877; FAX 504-386-0458. **Owner(s):** Bryan T. McMahon, 145 W. Pine St., Ste. A, Ponchatoula, LA 70454. TEL 504-386-2877; FAX 504-286-0458; adv.; photos; bk.rev.; pub. size: broadsheet; circ. 5,000(controlled & paid).

PORT ALLEN

US

WEST SIDE JOURNAL. 1938. Thu. $.35 newsstand; $10/yr. in parish; $12/yr. out of parish. 668 N. Jefferson, Port Allen, LA 70767. TEL 504-343-2540; FAX 504-344-0923. **Owner(s):** Lora Mae Young, 668 N. Jefferson, Port Allen, LA 70767. TEL 504-343-2540; Pub. Loretta Decuir; pub. size: broadsheet; circ. 4,000(paid).

RAYNE

US   ISSN 1069-2398

RAYNE ACADIAN-TRIBUNE. 1893. Thu. $.25 newsstand; $13/yr. in parish. 108 N. Adams, Rayne, LA 70578. TEL 318-334-3186; FAX 318-334-8474. **Owner(s):** Louisiana State Newspapers, 318 N. Main, P.O. Box 400, Abbeville, LA 70510. TEL 318-893-4223; Ed. Dawn Ohlenforst; Pub. Milo Nickel; adv. contact: Frances Bihm. pub. size: broadsheet; circ. 4,700(paid).

US

RAYNE INDEPENDENT. 1967. Thu. $.25 newsstand; $14/yr. 201 E. S. First St., Rayne, LA 70578. TEL 318-334-2128. **Owner(s):** Independent Publishing Corp., 201 E.S. First St., Rayne, LA 70578. TEL 318-334-2128; Ed. Jo Cart. adv. contact: Walter T. Cart. photos; pub. size: broadsheet; circ. 4,610(paid).

RAYVILLE

US

RICHLAND BEACON-NEWS. 1846. Thu. $.35 newsstand; $15/yr. local; $20/yr. in state; $25/yr. out of state. 603 N. Louisa, Rayville, LA 71269. TEL 318-728-2250; FAX 318-728-5991. **Owner(s):** Louisiana State Newspapers, P.O. Box 5010, Lafayette, LA 70507. TEL 318-334-3186; Ed. Bill Hardin; Pub. Terry Stockton; pub. size: broadsheet; circ. 5,500(paid).

SPRINGHILL

US

SPRINGHILL PRESS. Thu. $21/yr. local; $31/yr. out of parish. 127 Main St., Springhill, LA 71075. TEL 318-539-3511; FAX 318-539-3512. **Owner(s):** Lovan B. & Patricia W. Thomas, 127 Main St., Springhill, LA 71075. TEL 318-539-3511; Ed. Steve Colwell; Pub. Steve Colwell; adv. contact: Vicky Dorst. pub. size: standard; circ. 4,900(paid).
Formerly: Springhill Press & News Journal.

ST. MARTINVILLE

US

ST. MARTINVILLE TECHE NEWS. 1886. Wed. $.75 newsstand; $18.72/yr. in parish; $24.96/yr. out of parish; $30/yr. out of state. 214 N. Main St., St. Martinville, LA 70582. TEL 318-394-6232; FAX 318-394-7511. **Owner(s):** Louisiana Suburban Press, 214 N. Main St., P.O. Box 69, St. Martinville, LA 70582. TEL 318-394-6232; FAX 318-394-7511; Ed. Henri C. Bienvenu; Pub. Henri C. Bienvenu; adv. contact: Mary Johnson. photos; bk.rev.; pub. size: broadsheet; circ. 6,200(paid).

TALLULAH
US

MADISON JOURNAL. 1869. Wed. \$.35 newsstand; \$20/yr. in parish; \$23/yr. out of parish. 300 S. Chestnut St., Tallulah, LA 71282. TEL 318-574-1404; FAX 318-574-4219. **Owner(s):** L.P. Cashman, III, 300 S. Chestnut St., Tallulah, LA 71282. TEL 318-574-1404; Pub. Pete Sanders; pub. size: broadsheet; circ. 3,400(paid).

VILLE PLATTE
US

VILLE PLATTE GAZETTE. 1914. s-w.: Thu. & Sun. \$.75 newsstand; \$26/yr. local; \$30/yr. out of area. 145 Court St., Ville Platte, LA 70586. TEL 318-363-4416; FAX 318-363-2841. **Owner(s):** Louisiana State Newspapers, 122 E. Sixth Ave., Oakdale, LA 71463. TEL 318-335-0635; Ed. Danielle Wood. pub. size: broadsheet; circ. 4,000(paid).

VIVIAN
US

CADDO CITIZEN. 1912. Thu. \$23.92 in parish; \$28.08/yr. in state; \$33/yr. out of state. 105 W. Louisiana Ave., Vivian, LA 71082. TEL 318-375-3294; FAX 318-375-4578. **Owner(s):** Westward Communications, Inc., 5005 LBJ Fwy., Dallas, TX 75244. TEL 214-450-1717; FAX 214-450-1770; Ed. Linda Murray; Pub. Linda Murray; pub. size: broadsheet; circ. 2,400(paid).

WEST MONROE
US

OUACHITA CITIZEN. 1924. Thu. \$.50 newsstand; \$22/yr. in parish; \$31/yr. out of parish. 810 Natchitoches, West Monroe, LA 71291. TEL 318-322-3161; FAX 318-325-2285. **Owner(s):** Robert E. Barton, P.O. Box 758, West Monroe, LA 71294; Ed. Mark Rainwater. bk.rev.; pub. size: broadsheet; circ. 8,000(paid).

WINNFIELD
US

WINNFIELD WINN PARISH ENTERPRISE. 1925. Wed. \$.50 newsstand; \$20/yr. local. Lafayette & Long, Winnfield, LA 71483. TEL 318-628-2712; FAX 318-628-6196. **Owner(s):** Lovan B. & Patricia W. Thomas, P.O. Box 448, Natchitoches, LA 71458; Pub. Bob Holeman; adv. contact: Linda Bumbalough. pub. size: broadsheet; circ. 4,500(paid).

WINNSBORO
US

FRANKLIN SUN, THE. 1856. Wed. \$.50 newsstand; \$18.50/yr. in parish; \$27.50/yr. out of parish; \$33.50/yr. out of state. 514 Prairie, Winnsboro, LA 71295. TEL 318-435-4521; FAX 318-435-9220. **Owner(s):** Hanna Publishing Co., 514 Prairie, Winnsboro, LA 71295. TEL 318-435-4521; Ed. Leslie Young; Pub. Sam Hanna; adv. contact: Monica Huff. photos; pub. size: broadsheet; circ. 6,100(paid).

ZACHARY
US

ZACHARY PLAINSMAN-NEWS. 1953. Thu. \$.50 newsstand; \$20/yr. in parish; \$25/yr. out of parish. 5145 Main St., Ste. C, Zachary, LA 70791. TEL 504-654-6841; FAX 504-654-8271. **Owner(s):** Louisiana State Newspapers, 5240 Groom Rd., Baker, LA 70714. TEL 504-654-6841; FAX 504-654-8271; Ed. Katherine Gilbert. adv. contact: Beverly Stockwell. pub. size: broadsheet; circ. 1,600.

MAINE

AUGUSTA
US

▼**CAPITAL WEEKLY.** 1995. Thu. \$.35 newsstand; \$11.50/yr. in state \$28/yr. out of state. 173 State St., Augusta, ME 04332-2788. TEL 207-621-6000. **Owner(s):** Courier Publications, One Park Dr., Rockland, ME 04841. TEL 207-594-4401; Ed. Tom Farkas. pub. size: broadsheet; circ. 7,500(paid).

BAR HARBOR
US

BAR HARBOR TIMES. 1914. Thu. \$.75 newsstand; \$28/yr. in state; \$45/yr. out of state. 76 Cottage St., Bar Harbor, ME 04609. TEL 207-288-3311; FAX 207-288-5814. **Owner(s):** Courier Publications, One Park Dr., Rockland, ME 04841. TEL 207-594-4401; Ed. Earl Brechlin; Pub. David Morse; adv. contact: Shannon Polchies. bk.rev.; pub. size: tabloid; circ. 8,500(paid).

BELFAST
US   ISSN 0034-5075

REPUBLICAN JOURNAL 1829. Thu. \$.50 newsstand; \$18/yr. in cy. 33 High St., Belfast, ME 04915. TEL 207-338-3333; FAX 207-338-5498. **Owner(s):** Courier Publications, One Park Dr., Rockford, ME 04841. TEL 207-594-4401; Ed. Tom Groening Pub. David Morse; adv. contact: Greg Whitcomb. photos; pub. size: standard; circ. 8,000(paid).

BIDDEFORD
US

BIDDEFORD-SACO-OOB COURIER. 1989. Thu. \$.35 newsstand; \$45/yr. 5 Washington St., Biddeford, ME 04005. TEL 207-282-4337; FAX 207-282-4339. **Owner(s):** David & Carolyn Flood, 5 Washington St., Biddeford, ME 04005. TEL 207-282-4337; FAX 207-282-4339; Pub. David Flood; adv.; photos; pub. size: tabloid; circ. 22,000(controlled & free). **Wire Service(s):** AP.

BLUE HILL
US

WEEKLY PACKET. 1961. Thu. \$.60 newsstand; \$23.95/yr. in state; \$29.95/yr. out of state. Main St., Blue Hill, ME 04614. TEL 207-374-2341. **Owner(s):** Penobscot Bay Press, P.O. Box 36, Stonington, ME 04681. TEL 207-367-2200; Ed. Nathaniel W. Barrows; Pub. Nathaniel W. Barrows; adv.; photos; pub. size: tabloid; circ. 1,836(paid).

BOOTHBAY HARBOR
US

BOOTHBAY REGISTER. 1876. Thu. \$.50 newsstand; \$19/yr. in cy.; \$26/yr. out of cy 95 Townsend Ave., Boothbay Harbor, ME 04538. TEL 207-633-4620; FAX 207-633-7123. **Owner(s):** Maine-OK Enterprises, Inc., P.O. Box 357, Boothbay Harbor, ME 04538-0357. TEL 207-533-4620; Ed. Mary Brewer; Pub. Marylouise Cowan; adv.; photos; pub. size: broadsheet; circ. 5,640(paid).

BRIDGTON
US

BRIDGTON NEWS. 1870. Thu. \$.50 newsstand; \$20/yr. in state; \$24/yr. out of state. 42 Main St., Bridgton, ME 04009. TEL 207-647-2851. **Owner(s):** Bridgton News Corp., P.O. Box 244, Bridgton, ME. TEL 207-647-2851; Ed. Wayne E. Rivet; Pub. Henry A. Shorey; adv. contact: Gail Stretton. photos; pub. size: broadsheet; circ. 6,600(free & paid).

CALAIS
US

CALAIS ADVERTISER. 1836. Wed. \$27/yr. in state; \$31/yr. out of state. 14 Church St., Calais, ME 04619-0660. TEL 207-454-3561; FAX 207-454-3458. **Owner(s):** Calais Advertiser, The, P.O. Box 660, Calais, ME 04619. TEL 207-454-3561; Ed. Ferguson Calder. adv. contact: Maxine Geroux. photos; pub. size: tabloid; circ. 4,350(paid).

CAMDEN
US

CAMDEN HERALD. 1869. Thu. \$.75 newsstand; \$29/yr. in cy. 69 Elm St., Camden, ME 04843. TEL 207-236-8511; FAX 207-236-2816. **Owner(s):** Coast Papers, Inc., P.O. Box 249, Camden, ME 04843. TEL 207-236-8511; Ed. Amy Rawe; Pub. William S. Patton; adv. contact: Diane Norton. pub. size: broadsheet; circ. 4,700(paid).

CARIBOU
US

CARIBOU AROOSTOOK REPUBLICAN & NEWS. 1880. Wed. \$.75 newsstand; \$28.60/yr. in cy.; \$37/yr. out of cy.; \$39.50/yr. out of state. 159 Bennett Dr., Caribou, ME 04736. TEL 207-496-3251; FAX 207-492-4351. **Owner(s):** Northeast Publishing Co., P.O. Box 510, Presque Isle, ME 04769. TEL 207-768-4471; Ed. Reg Thompson. pub. size: broadsheet; circ. 4,800(paid).

DEXTER
US

EASTERN GAZETTE, THE. 1853. Mon. free; \$30/yr. 380 Main St., Dexter, ME 04930. TEL 207-924-7402. **Owner(s):** Robert & Janice Shank, P.O. Box 306, Dexter, ME 04930. TEL 207-924-7402; Ed. Robert Shank; Pub. Robert Shank; adv. contact: Robert Shank. photos; pub. size: tabloid; circ. 14,500(paid).

DOVER-FOXCROFT

US

COUNTY WIDE. 1977. Mon. free; $28/yr. 78 River St., Dover-Foxcroft, ME 04426. TEL 207-564-7548; FAX 207-564-7051. **Owner(s):** County Wide Communications, Inc., P.O. Box 497, Machias, ME 04654. TEL 207-564-3040; FAX 207-564-7051;.Pub. Bob Berta; adv. contact: Joyce Hartford. photos; bk.rev.; pub. size: tabloid; circ. 4,200(free & paid).

US

GUILFORD AMERICAN. 1989. Wed. $28/yr. 78 River St., Dover-Foxcroft, ME 04654. TEL 207-564-7548; FAX 207-564-7051. **Owner(s):** County Wide Communications, Inc., 78 River St., Dover-Foxcroft, ME 04426-1321. TEL 207-564-7548; Ed. Bob Berta. adv. contact: Joyce Hartford. photos; bk.rev.; pub. size: tabloid; circ. 3,200(paid).
  Formerly: Guilford Journal.

US

PISCATAQUIS OBSERVER, THE. 1838. Wed. $.60 newsstand; $23.50/yr. in cy.; $33/yr. out of state. 126 Union Sq., Dover-Foxcroft, ME 04426. TEL 207-564-8355; FAX 207-564-7056. **Owner(s):** Northeast Publishing Co., P.O. Box 510, Presque Isle, ME 04769. TEL 207-764-4471; Ed. Tom Lizotte; Pub. Richard Warren; adv.; photos; pub. size: standard; circ. 4,400(paid).

EASTPORT

US

QUODDY TIDES. 1968. bi-w.: 2nd & 4th Fri. $.75 newsstand; $22/yr. in cy.; $25/yr. elsewhere. 123 Water St., Eastport, ME 04631. TEL 207-853-4806; FAX 207-853-4095. **Owner(s):** Edward B. French, P.O. Box 213, Water St., Eastport, ME 04631. TEL 207-853-4806; Robert French, 36915 Harper Ave., Apt. 7, Mt. Clemens, MI 48035; Hugh French, 295 Brackett St., Portland, ME 04102; Ann Townsend, P.O. Box 29, Bradford, ME 04410; Ed. Edward French; Pub. Edward French; pub. size: tabloid; circ. 5,634(paid).

ELLSWORTH

US

ELLSWORTH AMERICAN, THE. 1851. Thu. $.75 newsstand; $27/yr. local; $44/yr. out of area; $40/yr. out of state. 63 Main St., Ellsworth, ME 04605-0509. TEL 207-667-2576; FAX 207-667-7656. **Owner(s):** Ellsworth American, Inc., P.O. Box 509, Ellsworth, ME 04605. TEL 207-667-2576; FAX 207-667-7656; Ed. Alan Baker; Pub. Alan Baker; adv. contact: Terry L. Young. photos; bk.rev.; pub. size: broadsheet; circ. 11,911(paid). **Wire Service(s):** API Newsfinder.

FARMINGDALE

US

COMMUNITY ADVERTISER. 1936. Mon. free newsstand; $15/yr. 324-A Maine Ave., Farmingdale, ME 04344. TEL 207-582-8486; FAX 207-582-4530. **Owner(s):** Keith Peters, 324-A Maine Ave., Farmingdale, ME 04344. TEL 207-582-8486; FAX 207-582-4530; Ed. Keith Peters. adv.; bk.rev.; pub. size: tabloid; circ. 21,000(free & paid).

FARMINGTON

US

FRANKLIN JOURNAL & FARMINGTON CHRONICLE. 1840. s-w.: Tue. & Fri. $.50 newsstand; $25/yr. in state; $35/yr. out of state. Wilton Rd., Farmington, ME 04938-0750. TEL 207-778-2075; FAX 207-778-6970. **Owner(s):** Mt. Blue Publishing Co., Inc., P.O. Box 750, Farmington, ME 04938. TEL 207-778-2075; FAX 207-778-6970; Ed. Donna Arsenault; Pub. Janet K. Warner; adv. contact: Donna-Marie Keaton. pub. size: broadsheet; circ. 9,900(paid).

FORT FAIRFIELD

US

FORT FAIRFIELD REVIEW. 1893. Wed. $.45 newsstand; $20.50/yr. in area. 128 Main St., Fort Fairfield, ME 04742. TEL 207-472-3111; FAX 207-473-7977. **Owner(s):** Eastern Publishing Ltd., P.O. Box 304, Houlton, ME 04730. TEL 207-328-8863; FAX 207-328-3208; Ed. Marcia Reed. adv.; photos; pub. size: broadsheet; circ. 2,300(paid).

HOULTON

US

HOULTON PIONEER TIMES. Wed. $28.60/yr. in cy.; $37/yr. out of cy.; $39.50/yr. out of state; $60/yr. foreign. 23 Court St., Houlton, ME 04730. TEL 207-532-2281; FAX 207-532-2403. **Owner(s):** Northeast Publishing Co., Skyway Industrial Pk., Presque Isle, ME 04769. TEL 207-764-4471; adv.; pub. size: standard; circ. 7,000(paid).

ISLESBORO

US   ISSN 1071-1473

ISLESBORO ISLAND NEWS. 1985. 11/yr. $2.25 newsstand; $24/yr. HC 60, Box 227, Islesboro, ME 04848. TEL 207-734-6745; FAX 207-734-6519. **Owner(s):** Agatha Cabaniss, HC 60, Box 227, Islesboro, ME 04848. TEL 207-754-6745; FAX 207-734-6519; Ed. Agatha Cabaniss. adv.; photos; pub. size: standard; circ. 600(free & paid).

KENNEBUNK

US

YORK COUNTY COAST STAR. 1878. Wed. $.75 newsstand; $25/yr. deliv. in cy.; $39/yr. out of cy. $80/yr. foreign. Rte. 1 S., Kennebunk, ME 04043. TEL 207-985-2961; FAX 207-985-9050. **Owner(s):** Journal Transcript Newspapers, 327 Broadway, Revere, MA 02151. TEL 617-284-2400; Ed. John Martins. pub. size: broadsheet; circ. 11,000(paid).

LINCOLN

US

LINCOLN NEWS. 1959. Thu. $.50 newsstand; $23/yr. in state; $25/yr. out of state. P.O. Box 35, Lincoln, ME 04457. TEL 207-794-6532; FAX 207-794-2004. **Owner(s):** M. Sheila Tenggren, P. O. Box 35, Lincoln, ME 04457. TEL 207-794-6532; FAX 207-794-2004; Ed. M. Sheila Tenggren; Pub. M. Sheila Tenggren; adv. contact: M. Sheila Tenggren. photos; pub. size: tabloid; circ. 5,696(paid).

LIVERMORE FALLS

US

LIVERMORE FALLS ADVERTISER. 1892. Thu. $.40 newsstand; $17/yr. in state; $24/yr. out of state. 59 Main St., Livermore Falls, ME 04254-0701. TEL 207-897-4321; FAX 207-897-4322. **Owner(s):** Mt. Blue Publishing Co., Inc., P.O. Box 750, Farmington, ME 04938. TEL 207-778-2075; Ed. Mitchell C. Thomas; Pub. Janet K. Warner; adv. contact: Carol A. Lanier. pub. size: broadsheet; circ. 3,200(paid).

MACHIAS

US

MACHIAS VALLEY NEWS OBSERVER. 1853. Wed. $.60 newsstand; $21/yr. in cy.; $22/yr. out of cy. 31 Broadway, Machias, ME 04654-0357. TEL 207-255-6561; FAX 207-255-4058. **Owner(s):** Jay B. Hinson, Robbinston, ME 04671; Eugene M. Townsend, Calais, ME 04619; Ed. Jay B. Hinson. adv.; pub. size: tabloid; circ. 3,400(paid).

MADAWASKA

US

MADAWASKA ST. JOHN VALLEY TIMES. 1957. Wed. $.60 newsstand; $30/yr. 696 W. Main St., Madawaska, ME 04756. TEL 207-728-3336; FAX 207-728-3825. **Owner(s):** Walls Newspapers, Inc., P.O. Box 7346-A, Birmingham, AL 35253. TEL 205-870-1684; Ed. Don Levesque; Pub. Emery L. Labbe; adv. contact: Don Levesque. photos; pub. size: tabloid; circ. 5,350(free & paid).

MILLINOCKET

US   ISSN 1064-0657

KATAHDIN TIMES. 1976. Tue. $.50 newsstand; $24./yr. in cy.; $31/yr. in state; $38/yr. out of state. 202 Penobscot Ave., Millinocket, ME 04462. TEL 207-723-8118; FAX 207-723-4434. **Owner(s):** David S. & Marlene Henley, P.O. Box 304, Houlton, ME 04730. TEL 207-328-8863; Ed. Barbara M. Waters; Pub. David S. Henley; adv. contact: Joe Brickham. photos; pub. size: broadsheet; circ. 4,200(free & paid).

NEWCASTLE

US

LINCOLN COUNTY NEWS. 1875. Thu. $.30 newsstand; $15/yr. in cy.; $18/yr. out of cy. Mills Rd., Newcastle, ME 04553. TEL 207-563-3171; FAX 207-563-3127. **Owner(s):** Lincoln County Publishing Co., Inc., P.O. Box 36, Damariscotta, ME 04543. TEL 207-563-3171; FAX 207-563-3127; Ed. Judi Finn; Pub. Christopher A. Roberts; adv.; pub. size: broadsheet; circ. 8,000(paid).

NORWAY

US

NORWAY ADVERTISER-DEMOCRAT. 1826. Thu. $.40 newsstand; $17.50/6 mo. in cy. Two Bridge St., Norway, ME 04268. TEL 207-743-7011; FAX 207-743-2256. **Owner(s):** Howard James, P.O. Box 269, Norway, ME 04268; Ed. Susan Reana; Pub. Howard James; pub. size: standard; circ. 7,100(paid).

OLD TOWN

US

PENOBSCOT TIMES. 1891. Thu. $.50 newsstand; $16/yr. in cy.; $24/yr. out of cy. 400 N. Main St., Old Town, ME 04468. TEL 207-827-4451; FAX 207-827-2280. **Owner(s):** David Woldstadt, Penobscot Times, Inc., 400 N. Main St., Old Town, ME 04468. TEL 207-827-4451; FAX 207-827-2280; Ed. Robert Diebold; Pub. David Wollstadt; adv. contact: Beverly King. photos; pub. size: tabloid; circ. 3,900(paid).
   Formerly: Old Town-Orono Times.

PORTLAND

US   ISSN 0025-0783

MAINE TIMES. 1968. Wed. $.95 newsstand; $1.95/seasonal guide; $25/yr. 561 Congress St., Portland, ME 04101. TEL 207-828-5432; FAX 207-828-5438. **Owner(s):** Maine Publishing, Inc.; Ed. Doug Rooks; Pub. Seth Sprague; adv.; pub. size: tabloid; circ. 20,000(paid).

PRESQUE ISLE

US

STAR-HERALD, THE. 1871. Wed. $.60 newsstand; $26/yr. in cy.; $34/yr. in state. 40 North St., Ste. B, Presque Isle, ME 04769. TEL 207-768-5431; FAX 207-764-7585. **Owner(s):** Northeast Publishing Co., P.O. Box 510, Presque Isle, ME 04769. TEL 207-764-4471; pub. size: broadsheet; circ. 8,000(paid).
   Formerly: Presque Isle Star-Herald.

ROCKLAND

US

COURIER-GAZETTE. 1846. 3/wk.: Tue., Thu., Sat. $.75 newsstand; $75/yr. in state; 95/yr. out of state. One Park Dr., Rockland, ME 04841. TEL 207-594-4401; FAX 207-596-6981. **Owner(s):** Courier Publications, One Park Dr., Rockland, ME 04841. TEL 207-594-4401; Ed. Steve Betts; Pub. David E. Morse; adv.; photos; bk.rev.; pub. size: broadsheet; circ. 9,000(paid). **Wire Service(s):** AP.

RUMFORD

US

RUMFORD FALLS TIMES. Wed. $.50 newsstand; $30/yr in cy. 71 Canal St., Rumford, ME 04276. TEL 207-364-7893; FAX 207-369-0710. **Owner(s):** James Newspapers, Bridge St., Norway, ME 04268. TEL 207-743-8996; FAX 207-743-2256; Ed. Greg Davis. adv.; photos; bk.rev.; pub. size: standard; circ. 5,000(paid).

SANFORD

US

SANFORD NEWS. 1980. Tue. $.50 newsstand; $19.99/yr. Six School St., Sanford, ME 04073. TEL 207-324-5986; FAX 207-490-1431. **Owner(s):** Buzz Dietterle, Six School St., Sanford, ME 03906. TEL 207-324-5986; FAX 207-490-1431; adv. contact: Dusty Dietterle. photos; pub. size: broadsheet; circ. evening 7,000(paid).

STONINGTON

US

ISLAND AD-VANTAGES. 1934. Thu. $.60 newsstand; $23.95/yr. in state; $29.95/yr. out of state. Main St., Stonington, ME 04681-0036. TEL 207-367-2200; FAX 207-374-2439. **Owner(s):** Penobscot Bay Press, P.O. Box 36, Stonington, ME 04681. TEL 207-367-2200; Ed. R. Nathaniel W. Barrows. adv.; photos; pub. size: tabloid; circ. 2,294(paid).

WESTBROOK

US   ISSN 0092-0119

AMERICAN JOURNAL. 1950. Wed. $.50 newsstand; $25/yr.; $44/2 yrs. 4 Dana St., Westbrook, ME 04092. TEL 207-854-2577. **Owner(s):** Durgin-Snow Publishing Co., Inc., 4 Dana St., Westbrook, ME 04092. TEL 207-854-2577; FAX 207-854-0018; Ed. Raymond M. Foote; Pub. Harry T. Foote; pub. size: tabloid; circ. 7,427(free & paid).

WINDHAM

US

SUBURBAN NEWS, THE. 1992. Tue. free newsstand; $50/yr. 690 Roosevelt Trail, Windham, ME 04062. TEL 207-892-1166; FAX 207-892-1171. **Owner(s):** Ray Roux, Gary Cooper & Bill Diamond, 690 Roosevelt Trail, Windham, ME 04062. TEL 207-892-1166; FAX 207-892-1171; Ed. Kay Soldier. adv. contact: Bill Foss. photos; pub. size: tabloid; circ. 10,000(free).

MARYLAND

BALTIMORE

US   ISSN 0748-5271

ARBUTUS TIMES. 1961. Wed. $.50 newsstand; $16/yr. 835 Frederick Rd., Baltimore, MD 21228. TEL 410-783-4500; FAX 410-788-4103. **Owner(s):** Patuxent Publishing Co., 10750 Little Patuxent Pkwy., Columbia, MD 21044. TEL 301-730-3620; Ed. Jim Joyner; Pub. Zeke Orlinsky; pub. size: tabloid; circ. 3,800(paid).

US

AVENUE NEWS. 1974. s-w.: Wed. & Thu. $.10 newsstand. 442 Eastern Blvd., Baltimore, MD 21221. TEL 410-687-7775; FAX 410-687-7881. **Owner(s):** Avenue, Inc., 442 Eastern Blvd., Baltimore, MD 21221. TEL 410-687-7775; FAX 410-687-7881; Ed. Jay Livingston; Pub. Kenneth C. Coldwell; adv.; bk.rev.; pub. size: tabloid; circ. 80,000(free & paid).

US

BALTIMORE CHRONICLE. 1973. m.: 1st Wed. $10/yr. mailed 1st class. 30 W. 25th St., Baltimore, MD 21218. TEL 410-243-4141. **Owner(s):** Schenley Press, Inc., 30 W. 25th St., Baltimore, MD 21218. TEL 410-243-4141; Ed. Alice Cherbonnier. adv.; photos; pub. size: tabloid.

US   ISSN 1041-0872

BALTIMORE MESSENGER. Wed. free; $.50 newsstand. 409 Washington Ave., Baltimore, MD 21204. TEL 410-337-2400; FAX 410-337-2490. **Owner(s):** Patuxent Publishing Co., 409 Washington Ave., Baltimore, MD 21204. TEL 410-337-2400; Ed. Len Lazarick; Pub. Zeke Orlinsky; adv. contact: Dave Tomasini. photos; bk.rev.; pub. size: tabloid; circ. 15,000(free).

US   ISSN 0748-5256

CATONSVILLE TIMES. 1881. Wed. $.50 newsstand; $19.95/yr. 405 Frederick Rd., Baltimore, MD 21228. TEL 410-788-4500; FAX 410-788-4103. **Owner(s):** Patuxent Publishing Co., 10750 Little Patuxent Pkwy., Ellicott City, MD 21043; Ed. Jim Joyner; Pub. Zeke Orlinsky; pub. size: tabloid; circ. 12,000(paid).

US

CITY PAPER. 1977. Wed. free. $50/yr. mailed. 812 Park Ave., Baltimore, MD 21201. TEL 410-523-2300; FAX 410-523-2222. **Owner(s):** Times/Shamrock Communications, 812 Park Ave., Baltimore, MD 21201. TEL 410-539-5200; Ed. Andy Markowitz; Pub. Don Farley; adv. contact: Matt Stegman. pub. size: tabloid; circ. 91,500(free & paid).

US

DUNDALK EAGLE. 1969. Thu. $.27 newsstand; $10.50/yr. local; $20/yr. out of state. 4 N. Center Pl., Baltimore, MD 21222. TEL 410-288-6060; FAX 410-283-2712. **Owner(s):** Dundalk Eagle, 4 N. Center Pl., Baltimore, MD 21222. TEL 410-288-6060; Ed. Mary G. Oelke; Pub. Kimbel E. Oelke; pub. size: tabloid. circ. 26,000(paid).

US

EAST BALTIMORE GUIDE. 1927. Thu. $15/yr. 526 S. Conkling St., Baltimore, MD 21224. TEL 410-732-6600; FAX 410-732-6336. **Owner(s):** R & B Publishing Co., 526 S. Conkling St., Baltimore, MD 21224. TEL 410-732-6600; FAX 410-732-6336; Ed. Jacqueline Watts; Pub. Richard W. Sandza; adv. contact: Cathy Hamer. photos; bk.rev.; pub. size: tabloid; circ. 40,000(controlled & free). **Wire Service(s):** AP.

US

ENTERPRISE & INNER HARBOR NEWS. 1934. Thu. free; $22/yr. mailed. 1316 Light St., Baltimore, MD 21230-4308. TEL 410-752-0711; FAX 410-752-0712. **Owner(s):** Bryan R. Moorhouse, 1316 Light St., Baltimore, MD 21230. TEL 410-752-0711; FAX 410-752-0712; R. Charles Avera, 1316 Light St., Baltimore, MD 21230. TEL 410-752-0711; FAX 410-752-0712; Ed. Bryan R. Moorhouse; Pub. Bryan R. Moorhouse; adv. contact: Darla Young. photos; pub. size: tabloid; circ. 30,000(free & paid).

US

EVERY WEDNESDAY. 1975. s-w.: Wed. & Fri. free. 2519 N. Charles St., Baltimore, MD 21218. TEL 410-554-8200; FAX 410-554-8213. **Owner(s):** John H. Murphy, II, 2519 N. Charles St., Baltimore, MD 21218; Afro-American Co., Baltimore, MS 21218; Ed. Marc Warren; Pub. John H. Murphy, III; adv.; photos; bk.rev.; pub. size: tabloid; circ. 30,000(free).

Weeklies

US
JEFFERSONIAN, THE. Thu. $.50 newsstand; $15.65/yr. in state. 409 Washington Ave., Baltimore, MD 21204. TEL 410-337-2400; FAX 410-337-2490. **Owner(s):** Patuxent Publishing Co., 409 Washington Ave., Baltimore, MD 21204. TEL 410-337-2640; Ed. Angela Bornemann; Pub. Zeke Orlinsky; adv.; pub. size: broadsheet; circ. 5,601(paid).

US
LABOR HERALD. 1936. bi-w. $.50 newsstand; $10/yr. 4005 Seven Mile Ln., Baltimore, MD 21208-6116. TEL 410-484-3832. **Owner(s):** Labor Herald Press, The, 4005 Seven Mile Ln., Baltimore, MD 21208-6116. TEL 410-484-3832; Ed. Daniel Bernstein; Pub. Daniel Bernstein; adv.; bk.rev.; pub. size: tabloid; circ. 36,000(paid).

US
NORTHWEST STAR. 1966. m.: 1st Wed. of mo. $15/yr. 7 Church Ln., Baltimore, MD 21208. TEL 410-653-3800. **Owner(s):** Northwest Star, Inc., 7 Church Ln., Baltimore, MD 21208. TEL 410-653-3800; Ed. Jonathan Berle; Pub. Jonathan Berle; pub. size: tabloid; circ. 20,000(free & paid).

US
OWINGS MILLS TIMES. 1986. Thu. free; $.50 newsstand. 409 Washington Ave., Baltimore, MD 21204. TEL 410-337-2400; FAX 410-337-2490. **Owner(s):** Patuxent Publishing Co., 10750 Little Patuxent Pkwy., Columbia, MD 21044. TEL 410-730-3620; Ed. Dan Gainor; Pub. Zeke Orlinsky; adv.; photos; pub. size: tabloid; circ. 35,000(free & paid).

BEL AIR
US
AEGIS, THE. 1856. Wed. $11.50/yr. 10 Hays St., Bel Air, MD 21014. TEL 410-838-4400; FAX 410-638-0357. **Owner(s):** Baltimore Sun, The, 501 N. Calvert St., Baltimore, MD 21278. TEL 410-332-6265; Ed. Allan Vought. adv. contact: Kay Kline. pub. size: broadsheet; circ. 34,500(paid).

BOWIE
US
BOWIE BLADE-NEWS. 1958. Thu. $.37 newsstand; $19.50/yr. 6000 Laurel-Bowie Rd., Ste. 101, Bowie, MD 20715. TEL 301-262-3700; FAX 301-464-7027. **Owner(s):** Capital-Gazette Newspapers, P.O. Drawer M, Bowie, MD 20715. TEL 301-262-3700; Ed. Susan Gross; Pub. Toni Adams; adv. contact: Toni Adams. pub. size: standard; circ. 13,000(paid). **Wire Service(s):** AP.

US
CROFTON NEWS-CRIER. 1972. Thu. $.35 newsstand; free. 6000 Laurel-Bowie Rd., Ste. 101, Bowie, MD 20715. TEL 301-262-3700; FAX 301-464-7027. **Owner(s):** Capital-Gazette Newspapers, 6800 Laurel-Bowie Rd., Bowie, MD 20715. TEL 301-262-3700; FAX 301-464-7027; Ed. Susan Gross; Pub. Philip Merrill; adv.; photos; bk.rev.; pub. size: standard; circ. 14,676(controlled & paid).

BRUNSWICK
US
BRUNSWICK CITIZEN. 1974. Wed. $.35 newsstand; $12.60/yr. in cy. 2 S. Maryland Ave., Brunswick, MD 21716. TEL 301-834-7722. **Owner(s):** Citizen Communications, 2 S. Maryland Ave., Brunswick, MD 21716. TEL 301-834-7722; Ed. Julia Maynard. pub. size: tabloid; circ. 3,500(paid).

US   ISSN 1056-7674
MIDDLETOWN VALLEY CITIZEN. 1974. w. $.25 newsstand; $12.60/yr. 2 S. Maryland Ave., Brunswick, MD 21716. TEL 301-834-7722. **Owner(s):** Citizen Newspapers, 2 S. Maryland Ave., Brunswick, MD 21716; pub. size: tabloid; circ. 1,100(paid).

BURTONSVILLE
US
SILVER SPRING GAZETTE. 1943. Wed. free. 4044 Blackburn Ln., Burtonsville, MD 20866-1171. TEL 301-421-5900; FAX 301-421-4232. **Owner(s):** Gazette Newspapers, 18705 N. Fredrich Ave., Gaithersburg, MD 20884. TEL 301-670-7100; Ed. Judy Hurz; Pub. Bill Schlossenburg; pub. size: tabloid; circ. 30,000(free).
   Formerly: Silver Spring Record.

CAMBRIDGE
US
DORCHESTER STAR. 1799. Fri. free. 300 Academy St., Cambridge, MD 21613. TEL 410-228-0222; FAX 410-228-0685. **Owner(s):** Chesapeake Publishing Corp., P.O. Box 600, Easton, MD 21601. TEL 401-822-1500; Ed. Gail Dean; Pub. Larry Effingham; adv. contact: Beverly Travers. pub. size: broadsheet; circ. 11,500(paid).

CENTREVILLE
US
QUEEN ANNE'S RECORD-OBSERVER. Wed. $16.80/yr. in cy. 114 Broadway, Centreville, MD 21617. TEL 410-758-1400; FAX 410-758-1701. **Owner(s):** Chesapeake Publishing Corp., One Airpark Dr., Easton, MD 21601. TEL 410-822-1500; Ed. William Kirby; Pub. Larry Effingham; pub. size: broadsheet; circ. 5,500(paid).

CHESTERTOWN
US
KENT COUNTY NEWS. 1793. w. $30/yr. 217 High St., Chestertown, MD 21620. TEL 410-778-2011; FAX 410-778-6522. **Owner(s):** Chesapeake Publishing Corp., One Airpark Dr., Easton, MD 21601. TEL 301-820-7070; Ed. Trish McGee; Pub. Mary Burton; pub. size: broadsheet; circ. 7,991(paid).

COLUMBIA
US
COLUMBIA FLIER. 1969. Thu. free in area; $156/yr. plus tax outside of area. 10750 Little Patuxent Pkwy., Columbia, MD 21044. TEL 410-730-3620; FAX 410-730-7053. **Owner(s):** Patuxent Publishing Co., 10750 Little Patuxent Pkwy., Columbia, MD 21044. TEL 301-730-3620; Ed. Tom Graham; Pub. S. Zeke Orlinsky; adv.; photos; bk.rev.; pub. size: tabloid; circ. 35,000(free).

US   ISSN 0748-5298
HOWARD COUNTY TIMES. 1979. Thu. $19/yr. in cy.; $21/yr. out of cy.; $25yr. out of state. 10750 Little Patuxent Pkwy., Columbia, MD 21044. TEL 410-730-3620; FAX 410-730-7053. **Owner(s):** Patuxent Publishing Co., 10750 Little Patuxent Pkwy., Columbia, MD 21044. TEL 410-730-3620; Ed. Tom Graham; Pub. Zeke Orlinsky; adv.; photos; bk.rev.; pub. size: tabloid; circ. 20,000(paid).

DENTON
US   ISSN 0746-1658
TIMES-RECORD, THE. 1922. Wed. $.50 newsstand; $16.80/yr. in cy.; $22.05 out of cy. 219 Market St., Denton, MD 21629. TEL 410-479-1800; FAX 410-479-3174. **Owner(s):** Chesapeake Publishing Corp., P.O. Box 600, Easton, MD 21601. TEL 410-822-1500; FAX 410-820-6519; Ed. Peter Howell; Pub. Larry Effingham; adv. contact: Julia Millionie. photos; pub. size: broadsheet; circ. 4,500(paid).

GAITHERSBURG
US
GAITHERSBURG GAZETTE. 1959. Wed. $12.50/mo.; $75/6 mos.; $150/yr. 18705 Frederick Rd., Gaithersburg, MD 20879. TEL 301-948-3120; FAX 301-670-7183. **Owner(s):** Washington Post Co., 1150 15th St., N.W., Washington, DC 20071. TEL 202-334-6000; Ed. Georgia MacDonald; Pub. Bill Schlossenberg; adv.; pub. size: tabloid; circ. 42,000(free & paid).

US
MONTGOMERY COUNTY SENTINEL. s-w.: Wed. & Thu. $.25 newsstand; $21/yr. 615 S. Fredrick Ave., Ste. 303, Gaithersburg, MD 20877. TEL 301-417-1200; FAX 301-417-1210. **Owner(s):** Bernard Kapiloff, P.O. Box 1272, Rockville, MD 20849. TEL 301-417-1200; Lynn G. Kapiloff, P.O. Box 1272, Rockville, MD 20849. TEL 301-417-1200; adv.; pub. size: tabloid; circ. 8,700(paid).

US
VILLAGE NEWS. 1968. s-m. $25/yr. 10120 Apple Ridge Rd., Gaithersburg, MD 20879. TEL 301-948-0110. **Owner(s):** Montgomery Village Foundation, 10120 Apple Ridge Rd., Gaithersburg, MD 20879. TEL 301-948-0110; Ed. Dagmar Kane. adv.; pub. size: tabloid; circ. 12,000(controlled & paid).
   Formerly: Montgomery Village Foundation News.

GATORSBURG
US
DAMASCUS GAZETTE. 1964. Wed. $35.50/3 mos.; $150/yr. local. 1200 Quince Orchard Blvd., Gatorsburg, MD 20878. TEL 301-253-6161; FAX 301-670-7183. **Owner(s):** Washington Post Co., 1150 15th St., N.W., Washington, DC 20071. TEL 202-334-6000; Ed. Tom Grant; Pub. Bill Schlossenberg; pub. size: tabloid; circ. 7,000(controlled).
   Formerly: Damascus Courier-Gazette.

GLEN BURNIE

US

MARYLAND GAZETTE. 1727. s-w.: Wed. & Sat. $39/yr. home deliv. 306 Crain Highway, S.W., Glen Burnie, MD 21061. TEL 410-766-3700; FAX 410-766-7031. **Owner(s):** Capital-Gazette Newspapers, 2000 Capital Dr., Annapolis, MD 21401. TEL 301-268-5000; Ed. Robert Mosier; Pub. Philip Merrill; photos; pub. size: standard; circ. 38,000(paid).

GREENBELT

US

GREENBELT NEWS REVIEW. 1937. Thu. $32/yr. 15 Crescent Rd., Greenbelt, MD 20770-0068. TEL 301-474-4131. **Owner(s):** Greenbelt Cooperative Publishing Association, Inc., P.O. Box 68, Greenbelt, MD 20768. TEL 301-474-4131; Ed. Mary Lou Williamson. adv.; photos; pub. size: tabloid; circ. 10,500(paid).

HANCOCK

US

HANCOCK NEWS. 1914. Wed. $.48 newsstand; $16.80/yr. in state; $18/yr. out of state. 263 Pennsylvania Ave., Hancock, MD 21750. TEL 301-678-6255; FAX 301-678-5520. **Owner(s):** Berkeley Springs Morgan Messenger, Mercer St., Berkeley Springs, WV 25411. TEL 304-258-1800; FAX 304-258-8441; Ed. J. Warren Buzzerd. adv.; bk.rev.; pub. size: standard; circ. 2,900(paid).

HAVRE DE GRACE

US

RECORD, THE. Fri. $.50 newsstand; $16.80/yr. in cy.; $21/yr. out of cy. 316 Saint John St., Havre De Grace, MD 21078. TEL 410-939-0400; FAX 410-939-2390. **Owner(s):** Homestead Publishing Co., Havre de Grace, MD 21078; Ed. Louis Schwalenberg. pub. size: broadsheet; circ. 5,500(paid).

LAUREL

US

LAUREL LEADER. 1897. Thu. free. 615 Main St., Laurel, MD 20707. TEL 301-725-2000; FAX 301-317-8736. **Owner(s):** Patuxent Publishing Co., 10750 Little Patuxent Pkwy., Columbia, MD 21044. TEL 301-730-3620; Ed. Joe Murchison; Pub. Zeke Orlinsky; adv. contact: David Tomasini. bk.rev.; pub. size: tabloid; circ. 28,158(controlled & free).

LEXINGTON PARK

US

ENTERPRISE, THE. 1883. s-w.: Wed. & Fri. $.75 newsstand; $37.80/yr. 235 Esperanza Shopping Ctr., Lexington Park, MD 20653. TEL 301-862-2111; FAX 301-737-2896. **Owner(s):** Chesapeake Publishing Corp., 29088 Airpark Dr., P.O. Box 600, Easton, MD 21601. TEL 410-822-1500; Ed. Donnie Morgan; Pub. Ralph Martin; adv. contact: Dave Palmer. photos; pub. size: broadsheet; circ. 16,500(free & paid).

OAKLAND

US

REPUBLICAN, THE. 1877. Thu. $.35 newsstand; $16.28/yr. local. 108 S. Second St., Oakland, MD 21550. TEL 301-334-3963; FAX 301-334-5904. **Owner(s):** Sincell Publishing Co., 108 S. Second St., Oakland, MD 21550. TEL 301-334-3963; FAX 301-334-5904; Ed. Donald W. Sincell; Pub. Robert B. Sincell; adv. contact: Lisa Rook. pub. size: broadsheet; circ. 11,500(controlled & paid).

OCEAN CITY

US

MARYLAND TIMES-PRESS. 1923. Wed. $.25 newsstand; $13.45/yr. local; $18/yr. out of area. 214 16th St., Ocean City, MD 21842. TEL 410-289-5834 FAX 410-289-6838; E-mail: atlantic@shore.intercom.net; URL: http://www.atbeach.com/mdtimes.html. **Owner(s):** Thomson Newspapers, Inc., Metro Ctr., One Station Pl., Stamford, CT 06902. TEL 203-425-2500; Ed. Stewart Dobson. adv. contact: Sue Lathbury. pub. size: tabloid; circ. 9,500(paid).

POCOMOKE CITY

US

WORCESTER COUNTY MESSENGER. 1869. Wed. $.50 newsstand; $13/yr. in cy.; $30/yr. out of cy. 129 Market St., Pocomoke City, MD 21851. TEL 410-957-1700 FAX 410-957-4314. **Owner(s):** Thomson Newspapers, Inc., Metro Ctr., One Station Pl., Stamford, CT 06902. TEL 203-425-2500; Ed. Bill Kerbin; Pub. John Backe; adv. contact: Donna Bloxom. photos; pub. size: broadsheet; circ. 3,250(paid).

POTOMAC

US

BETHESDA/CHEVY CHASE ALMANAC. Wed. free newsstand & home deliv.; $61.71/yr. mailed. 10220 River Rd., Potomac, MD 20854. TEL 301-983-3350 FAX 301-983-3923. **Owner(s):** DCI Publishing, Inc., 7670 Old Spring House Rd., McClean, VA 22101; Ed. Susan Pardys; Pub. Mary Kimm Dixon; adv. contact: Dan Laibstain. pub. size: tabloid; circ. 4,673(free & paid).

POTOMAC ALMANAC. Wed. free newsstand & home deliv.; $61.71/yr. mailed. 10220 River Rd., Potomac, MD 20854. TEL 301-983-3350; FAX 301-983-3923. **Owner(s):** DCI Publishing, Inc., 7670 Old Spring House Rd., Mc Lean, VA 22102; Ed. Susan Pardys; Pub. Mary Kimm Dixon; adv. contact: Dan Laibstain. pub. size: tabloid; circ. 20,522(free & paid).

PRINCE FREDERICK

US

RECORDER, THE. 1971. s-w.: Wed. & Fri. $.50 newsstand; $22.05/yr. in cy. 234 Merrimac Ct., Prince Frederick, MD 20678. TEL 410-535-1214 FAX 410-535-2310. **Owner(s):** Chesapeake Publishing Corp., Airpark Dr., Easton, MD 21601. TEL 410-822-1500; Ed. Kevin Conron; Pub. Ralph Martin; adv. contact: Jeannie Green. pub. size: broadsheet; circ. 8,500(paid).

PRINCE FREDRICK

US

CALVERT INDEPENDENT. 1940. Wed. $.50 newsstand; $15.75/yr. in cy.; $21/yr. out of cy. 424 Soloman's Island Rd., Prince Fredrick, MD 20678. TEL 410-535-1575; FAX 410-855-9070. **Owner(s):** News World Communications, Inc., New York, NY; adv. contact: Sandy Worsham. photos; pub. size: broadsheet; circ. 10,000(paid).

PRINCESS ANNE

US   ISSN 8756-6397

SOMERSET HERALD. 1826. Wed. $.50 newsstand; $18.90/yr.; $31.50/yr. elsewhere. 11763 Somerset Herald, Princess Anne, MD 21853. TEL 410-651-1600; FAX 410-651-3785. **Owner(s):** Thomson Newspapers, Inc., Metro Ctr. One Station Pl., Stamford, CT 06902. TEL 203-425-2500; Ed. R. Crumbacker; Pub. Darel La Prade; adv. contact: T. Sexton. photos; pub. size: broadsheet; circ. 5,800(free & paid).

SALISBURY

US

SALISBURY NEWS & ADVERTISER. 1867. Wed. free newsstand; $15/yr. 1501 Court Plz., Ste. 27, Salisbury, MD 21801. TEL 410-749-0272; FAX 410-749-5073. **Owner(s):** Independent Newspapers, Inc., 73 Dover Delaware Rd., Dover, DE 19903. TEL 302-674-4750; Ed. Robin Adamopoulos; Pub. Jim Rich; pub. size: standard; circ. morning 13,500.

SEABROOK

US

PRINCE GEORGES SENTINEL. 1932. Wed. $.25 newsstand; $15/yr. 9458 Lanham-Severn Rd., Ste. 203, Seabrook, MD 20706. TEL 301-306-9500; FAX 301-306-9596. **Owner(s):** Berlyn, Inc., P.O. Box 1247, Lanham, MD 20703. TEL 301-306-9500; FAX 301-306-9596; Ed. Lea Alexander Greve. adv.; pub. size: tabloid; circ. 104,000(fee & paid).

STEVENSVILLE

US

BAY TIMES. 1963. Wed. $.35 newsstand; $16.80/yr. in cy.; $21/yr. out of cy. 102 E. Main St., Ste. 101, Stevensville, MD 21666. TEL 410-643-7770; FAX 410-643-8374. **Owner(s):** Chesapeake Publishing Corp., P.O. Box 429, Elkton, MD 21922. TEL 410-398-3311; Ed. Angela Price; Pub. Larry Effingham; pub. size: tabloid; circ. 5,200(paid).

TIMONIUM

US

TIMES-HERALD. 1963. Thu. free; $12/yr. 2300 York Rd., Ste. 216, Timonium, MD 21093. TEL 410-453-0092; FAX 410-453-0065. **Owner(s):** JRM Incorp., 2300 York Rd., Ste. 216 Timonium, MD 21093. TEL 410-453-0092; Ed. Jim Gordon; Pub. Marina Brockman; adv.; photos; pub. size: tabloid; circ. 32,000(paid).

TOWSON

US

NORTHEAST REPORTER. 1949. Wed. free. 409 Washington Ave., Towson, MD 21204. TEL 410-337-2400; FAX 410-337-2490. **Owner(s):** Patuxent Publishing Co., 10750 Little Patuxent Pkwy., Columbia, MD 21044-3184. TEL 410-337-2400; FAX 410-337-2490; Ed. Blaise Willig. adv. contact: Karleen Pate. pub. size: tabloid; circ. 18,000.

US   ISSN 1041-0899

TOWSON TIMES. 1968. Wed. $.50 newsstand; free in cy.; $104/yr. mailed. 409 Washington Ave., Towson, MD 21204. TEL 410-337-2400; FAX 410-337-2490. **Owner(s):** Patuxent Publishing Co., 409 Washington Ave., Baltimore, MD 21204. TEL 410-337-2640; Ed. Len Lazarick; Pub. Zeke Orlinsky; adv. contact: Amy Newton. photos; pub. size: tabloid; circ. 39,000(free & paid).

UPPER MARLBORO

US

ENQUIRER-GAZETTE. Thu. $.25 newssstand; $10.50/yr. in cy.; $15.75/yr. out of cy. 14760 Main St., Upper Marlboro, MD 20773. TEL 301-627-2833; FAX 301-627-2835. **Owner(s):** Chesapeake Publishing Corp., P.O. Box 429, Elkton, MD 21922. TEL 410-398-3311; Ed. Joseph Norris; Pub. Ralph Martin; adv. contact: Joey Crossen. circ. 6,000(paid).

WALDORF

US

MARYLAND INDEPENDENT. 1872. s-w.: Wed. & Fri. $30/yr. 7 Industrial Park Dr., Waldorf, MD 20602. TEL 301-645-9480; FAX 301-645-2175. **Owner(s):** Chesapeake Publishing Corp., P.O Box 429, Elkton, MD 21922. TEL 410-398-3311; Ed. Angela Breck; Pub. Ralph Martin; adv. contact: Joey Crossen. pub. size: broadsheet; circ. 22,000(paid).

WESTMINSTER

US

COMMUNITY TIMES. 1928. Wed. $23/yr. P.O. Box 346, Westminster, MD 21158-0346. TEL 410-876-4670; FAX 410-876-7084. **Owner(s):** Landmark Community Newspapers, Inc., 201 Railroad Ave., Westminster, MD 21157. TEL 410-848-4400; FAX 410-857-1176; Ed. Brian Ditto; Pub. Robin Saul; adv. contact: Ron Thomas. photos; pub. size: broadsheet; circ. 13,580(free & paid).

MASSACHUSETTS

AMESBURY

US

AMESBURY NEWS. 1888. Fri. $.75 newsstand; $18/yr. 16 Millyard, Amesbury, MA 01913. TEL 508-388-2406; FAX 508-388-7972. **Owner(s):** Community Newspaper Co., 254 Second Ave., Meedham, MA 02194. TEL 617-433-6700; Ed. Jim Malone; Pub. Charles F. Goodrich; adv. contact: Mary Beth Gerard. pub. size: tabloid; circ. 3,557(paid).

US

MERRIMAC VALLEY SUNDAY. Sun. free. 16 Millyard, Amesbury, MA 01913. TEL 508-388-2406; FAX 508-388-7972. **Owner(s):** Community Newspaper Co., 254 Second Ave., Needham, MA 02194. TEL 508-433-6700; Ed. Jim Malone. adv. contact: Mary Beth Gerard. pub. size: standard.

ANDOVER

US

ANDOVER TOWNSMAN. 1887. Thu. $.75 newsstand; $37.50/yr. local; $42.50/yr. out of state. 33 Chestnut, Andover, MA 01810. TEL 508-475-1943; FAX 508-470-2819; E-mail: townsman2@aol.com. **Owner(s):** Irving E. Roger, Jr., 100 Turnpike St., North Andover, MA 01845. TEL 508-685-1000; Pub. Irving E. Rogers, Jr.; adv.; pub. size: tabloid; circ. 7,216(paid).

ARLINGTON

US

ARLINGTON ADVOCATE. 1872. Thu. $.75 newsstand; $25/yr.; $18.75/yr. senior citizens in cy. 5 Water St., Arlington, MA 02174. TEL 617-487-7200; FAX 617-648-4913. **Owner(s):** Community Newspaper Co., 245 Second Ave., Needham, MA 02194. TEL 617-433-6700; Ed. Tom Rose; Pub. Asa Cole; pub. size: broadsheet; circ. 10,582(free & paid).

AUBURN

US

AUBURN NEWS. 1949. Wed. $.50 newsstand; $18/yr. local; $25/yr. out of town. One St. Mark St., Auburn, MA 01501. TEL 508-832-2222; FAX 508-832-2431. **Owner(s):** Stonebridge Press Inc., 1 St. Mark St., Auburn, MA 01501. TEL 617-832-5876; Ed. Ron McGilvray; Pub. David Cutler; adv. contact: Fran Boutiliaer. pub. size: tabloid; circ. 3,000(paid).

AYER

US

GROTON LANDMARK. Thu. $.75 newsstand; $39/yr. in state; $45/yr. out of state. 69 Fitchburg Rd., Ayer, MA 01432. TEL 508-772-0777. **Owner(s):** Nashoba Publications, Inc., 69 Fitchburg Rd., Ayer, MA 01432. TEL 508-772-0777; Ed. Frank J. Hartnett, Jr.; Pub. Frank J. Hartnett, Sr.; adv. contact: Catherine Walmsley. pub. size: broadsheet.

US

HARVARD SPIRIT. Thu. $.75 newsstand; $39/yr. in state; $45/yr. out of state. 69 Fitchburg Rd., Ayer, MA 01432. TEL 508-772-0777. **Owner(s):** Nashoba Publications, Inc., 69 Fitchburg Rd., Ayer, MA 01432. TEL 508-772-0777; Ed. Frank J. Hartnett, Jr.; Pub. Frank J. Hartnett, Sr.; adv. contact: Catherine Walmsley. pub. size: broadsheet.

US

PUBLIC SPIRIT. Wed. $.75 newsstand; $39/yr. in state; $45/yr. out of state. 69 Fitchburg Rd., Ayer, MA 01432. TEL 508-772-0777. **Owner(s):** Nashoba Publications, Inc., 69 Fitchburg Rd., Ayer MA 01432. TEL 508-772-0777; Ed. Frank Hartnett, Jr.; Pub. Frank J. Hartnett, Sr.; adv. contact: Catherine Walmsley. pub. size: broadsheet.

US

TIMES FREE PRESS. 1869. Wed. $.75 newsstand; $39/yr. in state; $45/yr. out of state. 69 Fitchburg Rd., Ayer, MA 01432. TEL 508-772-0777; FAX 508-772-4012. **Owner(s):** Nashoba Publications, Inc., 69 Fitchburg Rd., Ayer, MA 01432. TEL 508-772-0777; FAX 508-772-4012; Ed. Frank Hartnett, Jr.; Pub. Frank J. Hartnett, Sr.; adv. contact: Catherine Walmsley. photos; bk.rev.; pub. size: broadsheet; circ. 34,413(free & paid).

BELCHERTOWN

US

BELCHERTOWN SENTINEL. 1915. Thu. free local; $15/yr. out of town. 10 S. Main St., Belchertown, MA 01007. TEL 413-323-7040; FAX 413-323-9424. **Owner(s):** Turley Publications, 24 Water St., Palmer, MA 01069; Ed. Chuck Wisniowski; Pub. Thomas A. Turley; adv. contact: Dave Anderson. pub. size: tabloid; circ. 8,500(paid).

BOLTON

US

BOLTON COMMON. 1988. Fri. $.75/newsstand; $28/yr. P.O. Box 8, Bolton, MA 01740. TEL 508-779-5113. **Owner(s):** Harvard Post Newspapers, Inc., 53 Bolton Rd., P.O. Box 308, Harvard, MA 01451. TEL 508-456-8122; Ed. Bill Latimer; Pub. Kathleen Cushman; adv. contact: Jodie Henderson. photos; bk.rev.; pub. size: tabloid; circ. 3,100(paid).

BOSTON

US

BAY STATE BANNER. 1965. Thu. $.40 newsstand; $15/yr.; $25/2 yrs. 68 Fargo St., Ste. 811, Boston, MA 02110-2122; FAX 617-542-7119. **Owner(s):** Banner Publications, Inc., 68 Fargo St., Ste. 1811, Boston, MA 02210. TEL 617-357-4900; FAX 617-542-7119; Ed. Yawu Miller; Pub. Melvin B. Miller; adv. contact: Sandra Casagrand. pub. size: tabloid; circ. 10,500(paid).

US   ISSN 0163-3015

BOSTON PHOENIX. 1966. Thu. $1.50 newsstand; $40/6 mos.; $75/yr. 126 Brookline Ave., Boston, MA 02215. TEL 617-536-5390; FAX 617-536-1463. **Owner(s):** Stephen M. Mindich, 126 Brookline Ave., Boston, MA 02215. TEL 617-859-3200; Ed. Marsha Pomerantz; Pub. Stephen M. Mindich; adv.; photos; bk.rev.; pub. size: tabloid; circ. 118,000(free & paid). **Wire Service(s):** AP.

US

IMPROPER BOSTONIAN, THE. 1991. bi-w. $40/yr. 45 Newbury St., Ste. 509, Boston, MA 02116-3106. TEL 617-859-1400; FAX 617-859-1446; E-mail: improperb@aol.com. **Owner(s):** Improper Publications, Inc., 45 Newbury St., Ste. 509, Boston, MA 02116. TEL 617-859-1400; FAX 617-859-1446; Ed. Danielle Dubin. adv. contact: David Dunbar. photos; bk.rev.; pub. size: tabloid; circ. 80,000(paid).

US

SOUTH BOSTON TRIBUNE. 1938. Thu. $23/yr. 395 W. Broadway, Boston, MA 02127. TEL 617-268-3440; FAX 617-268-6420. **Owner(s):** Daniel J. Horgan, P.O. Box 6, Boston, MA 02127. TEL 617-268-3440; Pub. Daniel J. Horgan; pub. size: broadsheet; circ. 8,500(paid). **Wire Service(s):** AP.

BRAINTREE

US

WEYMOUTH NEWS & GAZETTE. 1867. Wed. $.75 newsstand; $22/yr. 720 Union St., Braintree, MA 02185. TEL 617-337-1944; FAX 617-849-3319. **Owner(s):** Fidelity Investments, P.O. Box 109, Mansfield, MA 02048. TEL 508-339-8977; Ed. Patsy Murray; Pub. David S. Cutler; adv. contact: Tom Booth. pub. size: tabloid; circ. 5,400(paid).

BRIDGEWATER

US

EAST BRIDGEWATER STAR. 1812. Thu. $.50 newsstand; $17.50/yr. in cy.; $14.50/yr. senior citizens. 232 Broad St., Bridgewater, MA 02324. TEL 508-697-2881; FAX 508-947-1763. **Owner(s):** Independent Newspapers, Inc., 25 Center St., Middleboro, MA 02346. TEL 508-947-0031; Ed. Terence Egan; Pub. John Anderson; adv.; bk.rev.; pub. size: tabloid; circ. 600(paid).

CANTON

US

CANTON JOURNAL. 1876. Thu. $.75 newsstand; $22/yr. in cy.; $27/yr. out of cy. 12 Revere St., Canton, MA 02021. TEL 617-828-0006; FAX 617-828-9039. **Owner(s):** Community Newspaper Co., 254 Second Ave., Needham, MA 02194. TEL 617-433-6700; Ed. Marilyn Jackson; Pub. Margaret Smoragiewicz; adv.; pub. size: tabloid; circ. 4,500(paid).

CHELMSFORD

US

CHELMSFORD INDEPENDENT. 1952. Thu. $.50 newsstand; $18/yr. in cy.; $22/yr. out of cy. 15 Fletcher St., Chelmsford, MA 01824. TEL 508-256-7196; FAX 508-256-6111. **Owner(s):** Community Newspapers Co., 165 Enterprise Dr., Marshfield, MA 01742-6170. TEL 617-837-3500; Ed. Marlene Switzer; Pub. Mark O'Neil; adv. contact: John shimko. pub. size: tabloid; circ. 6,500(paid). **Wire Service(s):** AP.
   Formerly: Chelmsford Newsweekly.

US

WESTFORD EAGLE. 1970. Thu. $.75 newsstand; $22/yr. 15 Fletcher St., Chelmsford, MA 01824. TEL 508-256-7196; FAX 508-256-6111. **Owner(s):** Community Newspaper Co., 150 Baker Ave. Extension, Ste. 305, Concord, MA 01742; Ed. Richard Lodge; Pub. Mark O'Neil; adv. contact: Donna Nice. pub. size: broadsheet; circ. 3,700(paid).

CHICOPEE

US

CHICOPEE HERALD WEEKLY, THE. 1991. Thu. free. 143 E. Main St., Chicopee, MA 01020. TEL 413-592-1400; FAX 413-592-5286. **Owner(s):** John Maslar, P.O. Box 950, Chicopee, MA 01014. TEL 413-592-1400; FAX 413-592-5286; Ed. Joanne Despard; Pub. John Maslar; adv.; photos; pub. size: tabloid; circ. 30,000(free).
   Formerly: Herald-American.

CLINTON

US

ITEM. 1893. w. $.50 newsstand; $85.80/yr. 156 Church St., Clinton, MA 01510. TEL 508-368-0176; FAX 508-368-1151. **Owner(s):** Chronicle Publishing Co., 156 Church St., Clinton, MA 01510. TEL 508-368-0176; FAX 508-368-1157; Ed. Jan Gottesman; Pub. Frank R. Hewitt; adv. contact: Ron Chapdelaine. pub. size: broadsheet; circ. evening 4,350(paid). **Wire Service(s):** AP.
   Formerly: Daily Item.

CONCORD

US   ISSN 0744-7930

BEACON, THE. 1950. Thu. $.75 newsstand; $24/yr. in cy. 150 Baker Ave. Ext., Concord, MA 01722-9191. TEL 508-369-2800; FAX 508-371-9058. **Owner(s):** Community Newspaper Co. 82 Devonshire St., Boston, MA 02109. TEL 508-728-6553; Ed. Richard K. Lodge; Pub. Mark O'Neil; adv. contact: John Simko. pub. size: broadsheet; circ. 5,344(paid).

US

BEDFORD MINUTEMAN. 1958. Thu. $.75 newsstand; $28/yr. 150 Baker Ave. Ext., Concord, MA 01742. TEL 617-861-9110; FAX 617-863-8662. **Owner(s):** Community Newspaper Co. 254 Second Ave., Needham, MA 02194. TEL 617-837-3500; FAX 617-872-2131; Ed. Alin Gregorian; Pub. Tina Hermistone; adv.; pub. size: broadsheet; circ. 3,500(paid).

US

CONCORD JOURNAL. Thu. $.75 newsstand; $24/yr. 150 Baker Ave., Concord, MA 01720. TEL 508-369-2800; FAX 508-371-9058. **Owner(s):** Community Newspaper Co., 82 Devonshire St., Boston, MA 02109. TEL 617-728-6553; Ed. Lucile Daniels; Pub. Mark O'Neil; adv. contact: Jack Simko. pub. size: broadsheet; circ. 5,575(paid).

US

LINCOLN JOURNAL. 1985. Thu. $.75 newsstand; $28/yr. 150 Baker St., Concord, MA 01720. TEL 508-369-2800; FAX 508-371-9058. **Owner(s):** Community Newspaper Co., 82 Devonshire St., Boston, MA 02109. TEL 617-278-6553; Ed. Deb Shapiro; Pub. Mark O'Neil; adv. contact: Donna Rice. pub. size: broadsheet; circ. 1,483(paid).

US

LITTLETON INDEPENDENT. 1950. Thu. $.75 newsstand; $24/yr. in cy.; $36/yr. out of cy. 150 Baker Ave. Ext., Concord, MA 01742. TEL 508-369-2800; FAX 508-371-9058. **Owner(s):** Community Newspaper Co., 82 Devonshire St., Boston, MA 02109. TEL 617-728-6553; Ed. Marlene Switzer; Pub. Mark O'Neil; adv. contact: Donna Rice. photos; pub. size: broadsheet; circ. 1,750(paid).

US

MAYNARD BEACON. 1950. Thu. $.75 newsstand; $25/yr. in cy.; $45/2 yrs. 150 Baker Ave. Extention, Ste. 305, Concord, MA 01742. TEL 508-369-2800; FAX 508-264-9396. **Owner(s):** Community Newspapers, Inc., 100 Summer St., Boston, MA 02110. TEL 617-728-6553; Ed. June Morgon. adv. contact: Jack Simko. pub. size: broadsheet; circ. 2,743(paid).

DANVERS

US

DANVERS HERALD. 1863. Th. $.75 newsstand; $18/yr. in town; $29/yr. out of town. 152 Sylvan St., Danvers, MA 01923. TEL 508-774-0505; FAX 508-774-6365. **Owner(s):** Community Newspaper Co., 254 Second Ave., Needham, MA 02194. TEL 617-837-3500; FAX 617-872-2131; Ed. Howard Iverson; Pub. Charles F. Goodrich; adv. contact: Kristin Gongas. pub. size: tabloid; circ. 5,550(paid).

US

NORTH SHORE SUNDAY. 1977. Sat. free newsstand; $31/yr. mailed. 152 Sylvan St., Danvers, MA 01923-0293. TEL 508-774-0505; FAX 508-774-6365. **Owner(s):** Community Newspaper Co., 254 Second Ave., Needham, MA 02194-0293. TEL 617-837-3500; FAX 617-872-2131; Ed. Jim Malone; Pub. Charles F. Goodrich; adv. contact: John Vistorino. photos; pub. size: tabloid; circ. 11,000(free & paid). **Wire Service(s):** AP Newsfinder.
   Formerly: North Shore.

DEDHAM

US

PARKWAY TRANSCRIPT. 1929. Wed. $.75 newsstand; $20/yr. mailed in cy.; $25/yr. mailed out of cy. 367 Washington St., Dedham, MA 02026. TEL 617-487-7200. **Owner(s):** Community Newspaper Co. 254 Second Ave., Needham, MA 02194. TEL 617-433-6700; Ed. James Harder; Pub. Asa Cole; adv.; pub. size: broadsheet; circ. 4,500(paid).

US

WEST ROXBURY TRANSCRIPT. 1941. Wed. $.50 newsstand; $20/yr. mailed in cy.; $25/yr. mailed out of cy. 367 Washington St., Dedham, MA 02026. TEL 617-329-5008; FAX 617-326-9675. **Owner(s):** Community Newspaper Co., 254 Second Ave., Needham, MA 02194. TEL 617-433-6700; Ed. James Harder. adv. contact: Jay Pelland. pub. size: broadsheet; circ. 9,000(paid).

DRACUT

US   ISSN 8750-1341

DRACUT DISPATCH, THE. 1973. Thu. $.35 newsstand; $14/yr. 434 Textile Ave., Dracut, MA 01826. TEL 508-957-0007. **Owner(s):** William J. Themelis, 434 Textile Ave., Dracut, MA 01826; Geraldine Katin, 434 Textile Ave., Dracut, MA 01826; Ed. Geraldine Katin; Pub. William J. Themelis; adv. contact: Geraldine Katin. photos; bk.rev.; pub. size: tabloid; circ. 6,600(paid).

EDGARTOWN

US

VINEYARD GAZETTE. 1846. s w.: Tue. & Fri. summer; Fri. winter. $.50 newsstand; $37/yr. in cy. S. Summer St., Edgartown, MA 02539. TEL 508-627-4311; FAX 508-627-7444; E-mail: gazette@vineyard.net; URL: http://www.vineyard.net/biz/gazette. **Owner(s):** Richard & Mary Jo Reston, S. Summer St., Edgartown, MA 02539. TEL 508-527-4311; Ed. Richard Reston. adv.; photos; bk.rev.; pub. size: broadsheet; circ. 13,500(paid).

FALMOUTH

US   ISSN 0744-2114

ENTERPRISE, THE. 1895. s-w.: Tue. & Fri. $.50 newsstand; $42.50/yr. in cy.; $45/yr. out of cy. 50 Depot Ave., Falmouth, MA 02541. TEL 508-548-4700; FAX 508-540-8407. **Owner(s):** Falmouth Publishing, 50 Depot Ave., Falmouth, MA 01541. TEL 508-540-4700; Ed. Janice Walford; Pub. William Hough; adv. contact: Christopher Megan. pub. size: broadsheet; circ. 10,500(paid).

FOXBORO

US

FOXBORO REPORTER. 1884. Thu. $.50 newsstand; $22/yr.; $32/yr. foreign; $18/yr. senior citizens; $29/yr. senior citizens foreign. 36 Mechanic St., Foxboro, MA 02035. TEL 508-543-4851; FAX 508-543-4888. **Owner(s):** Sun Chronicle, S. Main St., Attleboro, MA 02703; Ed. Jeffrey Peterson; Pub. Paul Rixon; adv. contact: Edward Wilson. pub. size: broadsheet; circ. 5,000(paid).

GREAT BARRINGTON

US

BERKSHIRE COURIER. 1834. Thu. $.75 newsstand; $24/yr. in cy.; $31/yr. out of cy. 620 Main St., Great Barrington, MA 01230. TEL 413-528-3020; FAX 413-528-5702. **Owner(s):** Eileen & John W.P. Mooney, 620 Main St., Great Barrington, MA 01230. TEL 413-528-3020; Ed. Eileen W. Mooney; Pub. John Mooney; adv. contact: John Mooney. photos; pub. size: broadsheet; circ. 2,700(paid).

US

BERKSHIRE RECORD. 1989. Thu. $.50 newsstand; $20/yr. in cy.; $24/yr. outside cy. 21 Elm St., Great Barrington, MA 01230. TEL 413-528-5380; FAX 413-528-9449. **Owner(s):** Anthony & Donna Prisendorf, 21 Elm St., Great Barrington, MA 01230. TEL 413-528-5380; FAX 413-528-9449; Ed. Donna Prisendorf; Pub. Anthony Prisendorf; adv. contact: Jim Hurley. photos; bk.rev.; pub. size: broadsheet; circ. 4,500(paid).

HATFIELD

US

VALLEY ADVOCATE. 1973. Thu. free; $80/yr. mailed. 87 School St., Hatfield, MA 01038. TEL 413-247-9301. **Owner(s):** New Mass Media, Inc., 87 School St., Hatfield, MA 01038. TEL 413-247-9301; Ed. Dan Caccavaro; Pub. Geofrey Robinson; pub. size: standard; circ. 65,000(free & paid).

HYANNIS

US   ISSN 0744-7221

BARNSTABLE PATRIOT, THE. 1830. Thu. $.75 newsstand; $21/yr. 326 Main St., Hyannis, MA 02601. TEL 508-771-1427; FAX 508-790-3997. **Owner(s):** Robert F. & Anne G. Sennott, 326 Main St., P.O. Box 1208, Hyannis, MA 02601. TEL 508-771-1427; Ed. David Still, II; Pub. Anne G. Sennott; adv. contact: Lucinda Harrison. photos; pub. size: broadsheet; circ. 3,000(paid).

IPSWICH

US

GEORGETOWN RECORD. 1982. Wed. $.75 newsstand; $20/yr. local; $33/yr. out of area. 2 Washington St., Ipswich, MA 01938. TEL 508-352-7288; FAX 508-356-9188. **Owner(s):** Community Newspaper Co., 254 Second Ave., Needham, MA 02194. TEL 617-837-3500; FAX 617-872-2131; Ed. Ted Wadsworth; Pub. Charles Goodrich; pub. size: tabloid; circ. 1,708(paid).

US

HAMILTON-WENHAM CHRONICLE. 1949. Wed. $.75 newsstand; $26/yr. 2 Washington St., Ipswich, MA 01938. TEL 617-356-5141. **Owner(s):** Community Newspaper Co., 254 Second Ave., Needham, MA 02194. TEL 617-837-3500; FAX 617-872-2131; Ed. Sasha Paulsen; Pub. Charles Goodrich; adv. contact: John Vistorino. pub. size: tabloid; circ. 2,706(paid).

US

IPSWICH CHRONICLE. 1872. Thu. $.75 newsstand; $26/yr. 2 Washington St., Ipswich, MA 01938. TEL 508-356-5141; FAX 508-356-9188. **Owner(s):** Community Newspaper Co., 254 Second Ave., Needham, MA 02194. TEL 617-837-3500; FAX 617-872-2131; Ed. Janet McKay Smith; Pub. Charles F. Goodrich; adv.; pub. size: tabloid; circ. 4,644(paid).

US

TRI-TOWN TRANSCRIPT. 1959. Thu. $.75 newsstand; $24/yr. 2 Washington St., Ipswich, MA 01938. TEL 617-356-5141; FAX 617-807-2163. **Owner(s):** Community Newspaper Co., 254 Second Ave., Needham, MA 02194. TEL 617-837-3500; FAX 617-872-2131; Ed. Faye Raynard; Pub. Charles F. Goodrich; adv.; pub. size: tabloid; circ. 4,244(paid).

LEE

US

BERKSHIRE PENNY SAVER. 1963. Tue. free. 14 Park Pl., Lee, MA 01238-0300. TEL 413-243-2341; FAX 413-243-4662. **Owner(s):** J.W. McWhirk Publishers, Inc., 14 Park Pl., P.O. Box 300, Lee, MA 01238-0300. TEL 413-243-2341; FAX 413-243-4662; adv.; photos; pub. size: tabloid; circ. 16,000(controlled & free).

LEXINGTON

US

BURLINGTON UNION. 1956. Thu. $.50 newsstand; $22/yr. in cy.; $40/yr. out of cy. 9 Meriam St., Lexington, MA 02173. TEL 617-861-9110; FAX 617-863-8662. **Owner(s):** Community Newspaper Co., 254 Second Ave., Needham, MA 02194-5080. TEL 617-433-6700; Pub. Mark O'Neil; adv. contact: Donna Rice. pub. size: broadsheet; circ. 4,000(paid).
Formerly: Burlington News.

US

LEXINGTON MINUTEMAN. 1871. Thu. $.75 newsstand; $29/yr. 9 Meriam St., Lexington, MA 02173. TEL 617-861-9110; FAX 617-863-8662. **Owner(s):** Community Newspaper Co., 254 Second Ave., Needham, MA 02194. TEL 617-837-3500; FAX 617-872-2131; Ed. Richard K. Lodge; Pub. Mark O'Neil; adv.; pub. size: broadsheet; circ. 8,200(paid).

LYNN

US

SUNDAY POST. 1960. Sun. $.75 newsstand; $45/yr. 617-619 Chestnut St., Lynn, MA 01904. TEL 617-592-4600; FAX 617-592-1811. **Owner(s):** Community Newspaper Co., 254 Second Ave., Needham, MA 02194. TEL 617-837-3500; FAX 617-872-2131; Pub. Charles Goodrich; pub. size: broadsheet; circ. 5,000(paid); Sun. 7,500(paid).

MANSFIELD

US

MANSFIELD NEWS. 1873. Fri. $.35 newsstand; $21/yr. local; $26/yr. out of area. 154 Copeland Dr., Mansfield, MA 02048. TEL 508-339-8977; FAX 508-339-0340. **Owner(s):** Fidelity Investments, P.O. Box 109, Mansfield, MA 02048. TEL 508-339-8977; Ed. Garreth Charter; Pub. Asa Cole; adv. contact: Sean Burke. pub. size: broadsheet; circ. 3,600(paid).

MARBLEHEAD

US

MARBLEHEAD REPORTER. 1871. Thu. free home deliv.; $33/yr. mailed. 40 South St., Ste. 100, Marblehead, MA 01945. TEL 617-631-7700; FAX 617-639-2830. **Owner(s):** Community Newspaper Co., 2 Washington St., P.O. Box 192, Ipswich, MA 01938. TEL 617-356-5141; FAX 617-872-2131; Ed. Diana Montgomery; Pub. Charles F. Goodrich; adv. contact: Barbara Silva. photos; pub. size: tabloid; circ. 10,442(free & paid).

US

SWAMPSCOTT REPORTER. 1871. Thu. $.75 newsstand; $24/yr. 40 South St., Ste. 100, Marblehead, MA 01945. TEL 617-631-7700; FAX 617-639-2830. **Owner(s):** Community Newspaper Co., 254 Second Ave., Needham, MA 02194. TEL 617-837-3500; FAX 617-872-2131; Ed. Jim Malone; Pub. Charles F. Goodrich; adv. contact: Robert Tisi. pub. size: tabloid; circ. 4,000(paid).

MARION

US

ADVOCATE, THE. 1978. Thu. $.50 newsstand; $18/yr. in cy.; $28/yr. out of cy. 312 Wareham Rd., Marion, MA 02360-0959. TEL 508-748-1123; FAX 508-748-1128. **Owner(s):** G.W. Prescott Publishing Co., 400 Crown Colony Dr., Quincy, MA 02169. TEL 617-786-7000; Pub. Phyllis J. Hughes; adv.; photos; bk.rev.; pub. size: tabloid; circ. 2,202(free & paid).

US

SENTINEL, THE. 1963. Thu. $.50 newsstand; $18/yr. in cy.; $28/yr. out of cy. 312 Wareham Rd., Marion, MA 02360-0959. TEL 508-748-1123; FAX 508-748-1128. **Owner(s):** G.W. Prescott Publishing Co., 400 Crown Colony Dr., Quincy, MA 02169. TEL 617-786-7000; Ed. Mark Pothier; Pub. Phyllis J. Hughes; adv.; photos; bk.rev.; pub. size: tabloid; circ. 2,249(paid).

US

WAREHAM COURIER. 1894. Thu. $.50 newsstand; $18.50/yr. in cy.; $28/yr. out of cy. 312 Wareham Rd., Marion, MA 02360-0959. TEL 508-748-1123; FAX 508-748-1128. **Owner(s):** G.W. Prescott Publishing Co., 400 Crown Colony Dr., Quincy, MA 02169. TEL 617-786-7000; Pub. Phyllis J. Hughes; adv.; photos; bk.rev.; pub. size: tabloid; circ. 5,140(free & paid).

MARSHFIELD

US

BRAINTREE FORUM. 1877. Wed. $.75 newsstand; $20/yr. 165 Enterprise Dr., Marshfield, MA 02050. TEL 617-837-3500; FAX 617-837-9619. **Owner(s):** Community Newspaper Co., 165 Enterprise Dr., Marshfield, MA 02050. TEL 617-466-1800; Ed. Cathy Conley; Pub. Margaret Smoragiewicz; adv. contact: Judy McCaffery-Perry. pub. size: tabloid; circ. 3,500(paid).

US

COHASSET MARINER. 1978. Wed. $.50 newsstand; $25/yr. 165 Enterprise Dr., Marshfield, MA 02050. TEL 617-837-3500; FAX 617-837-9619. **Owner(s):** Community Newspaper Co., 165 Enterprise Dr., Marshfield, MA 02050. TEL 617-837-3500; Ed. Mary Fond; Pub. Margaret Smoragiewicz; adv. contact: Judy McCaffrey Perry. pub. size: tabloid; circ. 1,772(controlled & paid).

US   ISSN 0745-7960

HANOVER MARINER. 1981. Wed. $.75 newsstand; $22/yr. 165 Enterprise Dr., Marshfield, MA 02050. TEL 617-837-3500; FAX 617-837-9619. **Owner(s):** Community Newspaper Co., 165 Enterprise Dr., Marshfield, MA 02050. TEL 617-837-3500; Ed. Judy Enright; Pub. Margaret Smoragiewicz; adv. contact: Judy McCaffrey Perry. pub. size: tabloid; circ. 2,314(paid).

US

HOLBROOK SUN. 1958. Wed. $.50 newsstand; $13/yr. 165 Enterprise Dr., Marshfield, MA 02050. TEL 617-837-3500. **Owner(s):** Community Newspaper Co., 165 Enterprise Dr., Marshfield, MA 02050. TEL 617-466-1800; Ed. Cathy Conley; Pub. Margaret Smoragiewicz; adv. contact: Jim Horvath. pub. size: tabloid; circ. 1,882(paid).

US

MARINA & INDEPENDENT VOICE. 1976. Wed. free. 165 Enterprise Dr., Marshfield, MA 02050. TEL 617-837-3500; FAX 617-837-9619. **Owner(s):** Community Newspaper Co., 165 Enterprise Dr., Marshfield, MA 02050. TEL 617-466-1800; Pub. Margaret Smoragiewicz; adv.; pub. size: tabloid; circ. 3,000(controlled & paid). **Formerly:** Kingston Independent Voice.

US

MARSHFIELD MARINER. 1972. Wed. $.75 newsstand; $22/yr. 165 Enterprise Dr., Marshfield, MA 02050. TEL 617-837-3500. **Owner(s):** Community Newspaper Co., 165 Enterprise Dr., Marshfield, MA 02050. TEL 617-466-1800; Pub. Margret Smoragiewicz; adv. contact: Judy McCaffrey Perry. pub. size: tabloid; circ. 4,339(controlled & paid).

US

NORWELL MARINER. 1974. Wed. $.75 newsstand; $20/yr. in town; $25/yr. out of town; $18/yr. senior citizens. 165 Enterprise Dr., Marshfield, MA 02050. TEL 617-837-3500; FAX 617-837-9619. **Owner(s):** Community Newspaper Co., 254 Second Ave., Needham, MA 02194. TEL 617-837-3500; FAX 617-872-2131; Ed. Judy Enright; Pub. Margaret Smoragiewicz; adv. contact: Tom Booth. pub. size: tabloid; circ. 2,500(paid).

US

PEMBROKE MARINER. 1983. Wed. $.75 newsstand; $18/yr.; $16/yr. senior citizens. 165 Enterprise Dr., Marshfield, MA 02050. TEL 617-837-3500; FAX 617-837-9619. **Owner(s):** Community Newspaper Co., 165 Enterprise Dr., Marshfield, MA 02050. TEL 617-466-1800; Ed. Vicky Ogden; Pub. Margaret Fmoragiewicz; adv. contact: Jim Horvath. pub. size: tabloid; circ. 1,229(paid).

US

RANDOLPH MARINER. 1986. Thu. $.75 newsstand; $22/yr.; $20/yr. senior citizen. 165 Enterprise Dr., Marshfield, MA 02050. TEL 617-837-3500; FAX 617-837-9619. **Owner(s):** Community Newspaper Co., 165 Enterprise Dr., Marshfield, MA 02050. TEL 617-466-1800; Ed. Marilyn Jackson. adv. contact: Tom Booth. pub. size: tabloid; circ. 1,708(paid).

US

WEYMOUTH NEWS. 1867. Thu. $.50 newsstand; $20/yr. in cy; $25/yr. in state. 165 Enterprise Dr., Marshfield, MA 02050. TEL 617-837-3500; FAX 617-837-9619. **Owner(s):** Community Newspaper Co., 165 Enterprise Dr., Marshfield, MA 02050. TEL 617-466-1800; Ed. Patsy Murray; Pub. Margaret Smoragiewicz; adv. contact: Judy McCaffery-Perry. pub. size: tabloid; circ. 4,365(paid).

MELROSE

US

MELROSE FREE PRESS. 1901. Thu. $.50 newsstand; $22/yr. 40 W. Foster St., Melrose, MA 02176. TEL 617-665-4000; FAX 617-665-2195. **Owner(s):** Community Newspaper Co., 254 Second Ave., Needham, MA 02194. TEL 617-837-3500; FAX 617-872-2131; Ed. Peter Chianca. adv. contact: Chuck Goodrich. pub. size: broadsheet; circ. 7,225(paid).

US

SAUGUS ADVERTISER. 1381. Thu. $.50 newsstand; $18/yr. 40 W. Foster St., Melrose, MA 02176. TEL 617-665-4000; FAX 617-665-2195. **Owner(s):** Community Newspaper Co., 254 Second Ave., Needham, MA 02194. TEL 617-837-3500; FAX 617-872-2131; Ed. Peter Chianca; Pub. Charles Goodridge; adv. contact: Charles Goodridge. pub. size: broadsheet; circ. 8,000(paid).

MIDDLEBORO

US   ISSN 1050-0936

BRIDGEWATER INDEPENDENT. 1856. Thu. $.50 newsstand; $17.50/yr.; $14.50/yr. senior citizens. 25 Center St., Middleboro, MA 02346. TEL 508-697-2881; FAX 508-947-1763. **Owner(s):** Independent Newspapers, Inc., 25 Center St., Middleboro, MA 02346. TEL 508-947-0031 Ed. Terence Egan; Pub. John Anderson; adv.; photos; pub. size: standard; circ. 2,500(paid).

US

CAPEWAY NEWS. 1955. Tue. free delv. 25 Center St., Middleboro, MA 02346 TEL 508-947-1111; FAX 508-947-1763. **Owner(s):** Franklin Publishing Co., 65 Grove St., Middleboro, MA 02346. TEL 508-947-1763; Ed. Terrance Egan; Pub. John Anderson; adv.; photos; bk.rev.; pub. size: tabloid; circ. 22,000(free).

US

LAKEVILLE INDEPENDENT. 1985. Thu. $.50 newsstand; $17.50/yr.; $14.50/yr. senior citizens. 25 Center St., Middleboro, MA 02346. TEL 508-947-0031; FAX 508-947-1763. **Owner(s):** Independent Newspapers, Inc., 25 Center St., Middleboro, MA 02346. TEL 508-947-0031; FAX 508-947-1763; Ed. Terrence Egan; Pub. John Anderson; adv.; pub. size: tabloid; circ. 1,400(paid).

US

MIDDLEBORO GAZETTE. 1852. Thu. $.50 newsstand; $20/yr. in cy. 148 W. Grove St., Middleboro, MA 02346. TEL 508-947-1760. **Owner(s):** Hathaway Publishing Corp., 780 County St., Somerset, MA 02726. TEL 517-674-4656; Ed. Jane Lopes; Pub. Warren Hathaway; adv. contact: Jay Vogel. photos; pub. size broadsheet; circ. 6,073(paid).

US

TAUNTON INDEPENDENT. Thu. $.50 newsstand; $17.50/yr.; $14.50/yr. senior citizens. 25 Center St., Middleboro, MA 02346. TEL 508-947-0031; FAX 508-947-1763. **Owner(s):** Independent Newspapers, Inc., 25 Center St., Middleboro, MA 02346. TEL 508-947-0031; Ed. Terrence Egan; Pub. John Anderson; adv.; pub. size: tabloid; circ. 1,400(paid).

US

WEST BRIDGEWATER STAR. 1812. Thu. $.50 newsstand; $17.50/yr. in cy. 25 Center St., Middleboro, MA 02346. TEL 508-697-2881; FAX 508-947-1763. **Owner(s):** Independent Newspapers, Inc., 25 Center St., Middleboro, MA 02346. TEL 508-947-0031; Ed. Terrence Egan; Pub. John Anderson; adv.; photos; pub. size: tabloid; circ. 350(paid).

MILLBURY

US

MILLBURY/SUTTON CHRONICLE. 1986. Thu. $.35 newsstand; $9/yr. 117 Elm St., Millbury, MA 01527. TEL 508-865-1645. **Owner(s):** Andree Belisle, 117 Elm St., Millbury, MA 01527. TEL 508-865-1645; Ed. Andree Belisle; Pub. Alexander G. Belisle; adv.; photos; bk.rev.; pub. size: tabloid; circ. 2,000(paid).

MILTON VILLAGE

US

MILTON RECORD-TRANSCRIPT. 1900. Fri. $.50 newsstand; $20/yr. in cy.; $22/yr. out of cy. 26 High St., Milton Village, MA 02186. TEL 617-361-6500; FAX 617-361-8909. **Owner(s):** Tribune Publications, 1261 Hyde Park Ave., Hyde Park, MA 02136. TEL 617-361-6500; Ed. Daniel J. Horgan Jr.; Pub. Daniel J. Horgan Jr.; adv. contact: Karen Willette. photos; pub. size: broadsheet; circ. 5,900(paid).

NANTUCKET

US

INQUIRER & MIRROR, THE. 1821. Thu. $.75 newsstand; $32/yr. in area; $40/yr. out of area; $95/yr. foreign. Milestone Rd., Nantucket, MA 02554. TEL 508-228-0001; FAX 508-325-5089; E-mail: mstanton@nantucket.net; URL: http://www.nantucket.net/InkyM/. **Owner(s):** Ottaway Newspapers, Inc., P.O. Box 401, Campbell Hall, NY 10916. TEL 914-294-8181; Ed. Marianne Giffin Stanton; Pub. Marianne Giffin Stanton; adv. contact: Denese Allen. pub. size: broadsheet; circ. 8,900(paid).

US   ISSN 1046-6304

NANTUCKET BEACON. 1989. Wed. $.50 newsstand; $35/yr. 64 Old South Rd., Nantucket, MA 02554. TEL 508-228-8455; FAX 508-228-8994; E-mail: staff@NantucketBeacon.com; URL: http://www.NantucketBeacon.com. **Owner(s):** Ottaway Newspapers Inc., P.O. Box 550, Campbell Hall, NY 10916. TEL 914-294-8181; Ed. M. Vogler; Pub. Scott Himstead; adv. contact: A. Maier. photos; bk.rev.; pub. size: broadsheet; circ. 18,000(paid).

NEEDHAM

US

BELMONT CITIZEN-HERALD. 1919. Thu. $.50 newsstand; $20/yr. 254 Second Ave., Needham, MA 02194. TEL 617-433-6700. **Owner(s):** Community Newspapers Co., 254 Second Ave., Needham, MA 02194. TEL 617-433-6700; Ed. Chris Begley; Pub. Asa Cole; adv. contact: Susan Robinson. pub. size: broadsheet; circ. 5,700(paid).

US

DOVER-SHERBORN SUBURBAN PRESS. 1958. Thu. $30/yr. 992 Great Plain Ave., Needham, MA 02192. TEL 617-444-1706; FAX 617-444-1795. **Owner(s):** Suburban World, Inc., 992 Great Plain Ave., Needham, MA 02192. TEL 617-444-1706; Ed. Elizabeth Banks; Pub. William Barrett; pub. size: tabloid; circ. 6,000(paid).

US

MEDFIELD SUBURBAN PRESS. 1932. Thu. $30/yr. 992 Great Plain Ave., Needham, MA 02192. TEL 617-359-4278; FAX 617-359-4223. **Owner(s):** Suburban World, Inc., 992 Great Plain Ave., Needham, MA 02192. TEL 617-444-1706; Ed. Sandra Balzer; Pub. William Barrett; pub. size: tabloid; circ. 7,100(controlled & paid).

US

NATICK BULLETIN. 1865. Thu. $.75 newsstand; $32/yr. in town; $39/yr. out of town. 992 Great Plain Ave., Needham, MA 02192. TEL 508-653-4460; FAX 617-444-1795. **Owner(s):** Suburban World, Inc., 992 Great Plain Ave., Needham, MA 02192. TEL 617-444-1706; Ed. Joyce Bain; Pub. William Barrett; pub. size: tabloid; circ. 4,500(paid).

US

TAB, THE. 1979. Tue. free. 254 Second Ave, Needham, MA 02192. TEL 617-969-0340; FAX 617-964-2476. **Owner(s):** Tab Community Newspapers, Co., Boston, MA; Ed. George Donnolly; Pub. Kirk Davis; adv. contact: Cris Warren. pub. size: tabloid; circ. 146,000(free).

US

WATERTOWN SUN. 1921. Wed. $.50 newsstand; $20/yr. 254 Second Ave., Needham, MA 02194. TEL 617-433-6700. **Owner(s):** Community Newspapers Co., 254 Second Ave., Needham, MA 02194. TEL 617-433-6700; Ed. Ellen Ishkanian; Pub. Asa Cole; adv. contact: Susan Robinson. pub. size: tabloid; circ. 3,900(paid).

US

WAYLAND-WESTON TOWN CRIER. 1951. Thu. $27/yr.; $32.40/yr. mailed; $25/yr. senior citizens. 254 Second Ave., Needham, MA 02194. TEL 617-487-7200; FAX 617-487-7377. **Owner(s):** Fidelity Investments, P.O. Box 109, Mansfield, MA 02048. TEL 508-339-8977; Ed. Andrea Haynes; Pub. Asa Cole; pub. size: tabloid; circ. 6,500(paid).

NORTH BILLERICA

US

BILLERICA MINUTEMAN. 1971. Thu. $.50 newsstand; $24/yr. in cy. 2 Survey Cir., North Billerica, MA 01862. TEL 508-369-2800; FAX 508-262-9947. **Owner(s):** Community Newspaper Co., 254 Second Ave., Needham, MA 02194. TEL 617-837-3500; FAX 617-872-2131; Ed. Daniel Fellini; Pub. Mark O'Neil; adv. contact: Donna Rice. pub. size: broadsheet; circ. 5,403(paid).

NORTH DARTMOUTH

US

CHRONICLE, THE. 1969. Wed. $.50 newsstand; $17/yr in cy.; $26/yr. out of cy. 45 Slocum Rd., North Dartmouth, MA 02747-0268. TEL 508-992-1522; FAX 508-992-1689. **Owner(s):** Hathaway Publishing Corp., P.O. Box 80268, South Dartmouth, MA 02748-0268. TEL 617-992-1522; Ed. Susan Gonsalves; Pub. Warren Hathaway; pub. size: broadsheet; circ. 6,500(paid).

    Formerly: Dartmouth Chronicle.

ORLEANS

US

CAPE CODDER. 1946. s-w.: Tue. & Fri. $.75 newsstand; $29.50/yr. on the Cape; $44.50/yr. off the Cape. 5 Namskaket Rd., Orleans, MA 02653. TEL 508-255-2121; FAX 508-240-0333. **Owner(s):** Community Newspaper Co., 254 Second Ave., Needham, MA 02194. TEL 617-837-3500; FAX 617-872-2131; Ed. Mark Skala; Pub. Victoria Ogden; pub. size: tabloid; circ. 13,500(paid).

US

HARWICH ORACLE. 1986. Thu. $.50 newsstand; $19.95/yr. on the Cape; $26.95/yr. off the Cape. 5 Namskaket Rd., Orleans, MA 02653. TEL 508-255-1212; FAX 508-240-0333. **Owner(s):** Community Newspapers Corp., 254 Second Ave., Needham, MA 02194. TEL 617-433-6700; Ed. Craig O'Brien; Pub. Craig O'Brien; adv.; pub. size: tabloid; circ. 4,000(controlled & paid).

US

MASHPEE MESSENGER. 1985. Thu. free through request. 5 Namskaket Rd., Orleans, MA 02653. TEL 508-255-2121; FAX 508-240-0333. **Owner(s):** Community Newspapers Corp., 254 Second Ave., Needham, MA 02194. TEL 617-433-6700; adv.; pub. size: tabloid; circ. 4,600(free).

US

SANDWICH BROADSIDER. 1974. Thu. $.50 newsstand $19.95/yr. in town; $26.95/yr. out of town. 5 Namskaket Rd., Orleans, MA 02653. TEL 508-255-2121; FAX 508-240-0333. **Owner(s):** Community Newspapers Corp., 254 Second Ave., Needham, MA 02194. TEL 508-433-6700; Ed. Mark Skala. adv.; pub. size: tabloid; circ. 3,907(paid).

PALMER

US

JOURNAL REGISTER. 1850. Thu. $.50 newsstand; $28/yr. 24 Water St., Palmer, MA 01069. TEL 413-283-8393; FAX 413-289-1977. **Owner(s):** Turley Publications, Inc., 24 Water St., Palmer, MA 01069. TEL 413-283-8393; Ed. Tina Lack. pub. size: broadsheet; circ. 5,400(paid).

US

LUDLOW REGISTER. 1946. Wed. free newsstand; $25/yr. in state; $28/yr. out of state. 24 Water St., Palmer, MA 01069. TEL 413-583-3095; FAX 413-289-1977. **Owner(s):** Turley Publications, Inc., 24 Water St., Palmer, MA 01069. TEL 413-283-8393; Ed. Tina Lack. pub. size: tabloid; circ. 11,800(free).

US

STATE LINE SHOPPING GUIDE. 1962. Tue. free. 24 Water St., Palmer, MA 01069. TEL 413-283-8393; FAX 413-289-1977. **Owner(s):** Turley Publications, Inc., 24 Water St., Palmer, MA 01069. TEL 413-283-1977; Ed. Tina Lack; Pub. Patrick H. Turley; pub. size: tabloid; circ. 14,240(free).

PITTSFIELD

US

PITTSFIELD GAZETTE, THE. 1991. Thu. $25/yr. in cy.; $30/yr. out of cy.; $20 in city. 141 North St., Pittsfield, MA 01201. TEL 413-443-2010; FAX 413-443-2445. **Owner(s):** Pittsfield Gazette, Inc., 141 North St., Pittsfield, MA 01201. TEL 413-443-2010; FAX 413-443-2445; Ed. Jonathan Levine; Pub. Jonathan Levine; adv.; photos; pub. size: tabloid; circ. 8,000(free & paid).

PLYMOUTH

US

CARVER REPORTER. 1988. Wed. $.75 newsstand; $15/yr. in cy.; $30/yr. out of cy. 9 Long Pond Rd., Plymouth, MA 02360-0959. TEL 508-746-5555; FAX 508-747-2148. **Owner(s):** G.W. Prescott Publishing Co., 400 Crown Colony Dr., Quincy, MA 02169. TEL 617-786-7000; Pub. Phyllis J. Hughes; adv. contact: Gary Higgins. photos; bk.rev.; pub. size: tabloid; circ. 4,517(free & paid).

US   ISSN 0899-6229

DUXBURY REPORTER. 1987. Thu. $1 newsstand; $40/yr. 9 Long Pond Rd., Plymouth, MA 02360-0959. TEL 508-746-5555; FAX 508-747-2148. **Owner(s):** G.W. Prescott Publishing Co., 400 Crown Colony Dr., Quincy, MA 02169. TEL 617-786-7000; Ed. Nan Anastasia; Pub. Phyllis J. Hughes; adv. contact: Gary Higgins. photos; bk.rev.; pub. size: tabloid; circ. 5,500(free).

US

HALIFAX REPORTER. 1984. Thu. $.75 newsstand;
$19/yr. in cy.; $30/yr. out of cy. 9 Long Pond
Rd., Plymouth, MA 02360-0959.
TEL 508-746-5555; FAX 508-747-2148.
Owner(s): G.W. Prescott Publishing Co., 400
Crown Colony Dr., Quincy, MA 02169. TEL
617-786-7000; Pub. Phyllis J. Hughes; adv.;
photos; bk.rev.; pub. size: tabloid; circ. 1,406(free
& paid).
   Formerly: Halifax-Plympton Reporter.

US

KINGSTON REPORTER. 1984. Thu. $.75; $30/yr. 9
Long Pond Rd., Plymouth, MA 02360-0959.
TEL 508-746-5555; FAX 508-747-2148.
Owner(s): G.W. Prescott Publishing Co., 400
Crown Colony Dr., Quincy, MA 02169. TEL
617-786-7000; Pub. Phyllis J. Hughes; adv.;
photos; bk.rev.; pub. size: tabloid; circ.
3,356(free).

US

MARSHFIELD REPORTER. 1984. Thu. $.75
newsstand; $30/yr. 9 Long Pond Rd., Plymouth,
MA 02360-0959. TEL 508-746-5555;
FAX 508-747-2148. **Owner(s):** G.W. Prescott
Publishing Co., 400 Crown Colony Dr., Quincy,
MA 02169. TEL 617-786-7000; Pub. Phyllis J.
Hughes; adv.; photos; bk.rev.; pub. size: tabloid;
circ. morning 6,504(free).

US

OLD COLONY MEMORIAL. 1822. Thu. $.75
newsstand; $27/yr. in cy.; $40/yr. out of cy. 9
Long Pond Rd., Plymouth, MA 02360-0959.
TEL 508-746-5555; FAX 508-747-2148.
Owner(s): G.W. Prescott Publishing Co., 400
Crown Colony Dr., Quincy, MA 02169. TEL
617-786-7000; Pub. Phyllis J. Hughes; adv.;
photos; bk.rev.; pub. size: broadsheet; circ.
12,588(free & paid).

US

PEMBROKE REPORTER. 1983. Thu. $.75 newsstand;
$19/yr. in cy.; $30/yr. out of cy. 9 Long Pond
Rd., Plymouth, MA 02360-0959.
TEL 508-746-5555; FAX 508-747-2148.
Owner(s): G.W. Prescott Publishing Co., 400
Crown Colony Dr., Quincy, MA 02169. TEL
617-786-7000; Pub. Phyllis J. Hughes; adv.;
photos; bk.rev.; pub. size: tabloid; circ. 1,550(free
& paid).

PROVINCETOWN

US

PROVINCETOWN ADVOCATE. 1869. Thu. $1
newsstand; $28.50/yr. 100 Bradford St.,
Provincetown, MA 02657. TEL 508-487-1170;
FAX 508-487-3878. **Owner(s):** Hometown
Newspapers, 323 E. Grand River, Howell, MI
48843. TEL 517-548-2003; Ed. Peter Steele.
pub. size: tabloid; circ. 8,000(paid).

QUINCY

US   ISSN 0745-6301

HINGHAM JOURNAL & MARINER. 1867. Thu. $.75
newsstand; $22/yr. 73 South St., Quincy, MA
02043. TEL 617-749-0031;
FAX 617-740-8955. **Owner(s):** Community
Newspaper Co., 165 Enterprise Dr., Marshfield,
MA 02050. TEL 617-837-3500; Ed. Mary Ford;
Pub. David Cutler; adv. contact: Jim Horvath. pub.
size: broadsheet; circ. 4,443(controlled & paid).
   Formerly: Hingham Journal.

US

QUINCY SUN. 1968. Thu. $.35 newsstand; $13/yr.
in town; $15/yr. out of town; $18/yr. out of
state. 1372 Hancock St., Quincy, MA 02169.
TEL 617-471-3100; FAX 617-472-3963.
Owner(s): Henry W. Bosworth, 1372 Hancock St.,
Quincy, MA 02169. TEL 617-471-3100; Ed.
Robert Bosworth; Pub. Henry Bosworth; adv.
contact: Mark Crosby. pub. size: tabloid; circ.
7,000(paid).

READING

US

SUBURBAN NEWS. 1974. Sat. free in town;
$17.50/yr. out of town. 100 Main St., Reading,
MA 01867. TEL 617-944-4444;
FAX 617-944-4494. **Owner(s):** Franklin
Publishing Co., 55 Grove St., Rockland, MA
02370. TEL 617-878-5100; Ed. Rose
Thompson; Pub Richard Dalley; adv. contact:
Nancy Taylor. photos; bk.rev.; pub. size: tabloid;
circ. 35,000(free).

REVERE

US   ISSN 1054-6529

CHELSEA RECORD. 1890. s-w.: Wed. & Fri. $.35
newsstand; $29/yr. in town; $55/yr. out of town.
327 Broadway, Revere, MA 02151.
TEL 617-284-2400; FAX 617-289-5352.
Owner(s): Journal Transcript Newspapers, 327
Broadway, Revere, MA 02151. TEL
617-284-2400; Ed. Ed Coletta; Pub. Lou
McGrew; adv. contact: Charles Anderson. pub.
size: broadsheet; circ. 5,000(paid).

US

REVERE JOURNAL. 1881. Wed. $.50 newsstand;
$19/yr. local; $29/yr. elsewhere. 327 Broadway,
Revere, MA 02151. TEL 617-284-2400;
FAX 617-289-5352. **Owner(s):** Journal
Transcript Newspapers, 327 Broadway, Revere,
MA 02151. TEL 617-284-2400; Ed. Dave
Procopio; Pub. Neil P. Collins; adv. contact:
Charlie Anderson. pub. size: standard; circ.
9,000(paid).

ROCKLAND

US

SOUTH SHORE NEWS. 1965. Mon. free. 65 Grove
St., Rockland, MA 02370. TEL 617-878-5100.
Owner(s): Franklin Publishing Co., Mayflower Dr.,
Hanover, MA 02339. TEL 617-878-3444; FAX
617-878-1318 Ed. Marc Songini; Pub. Paul
Mack; adv.; photos; bk.rev.; pub. size: tabloid; circ.
70,729(controlled & paid).

SANDWICH

US

PENNYSAVER, THE. 1964. Wed. free. P.O. Box
1333, Sandwich, MA 02644-0716.
TEL 508-833-2930; FAX 508-833-0775.
Owner(s): Fidelity Investments, Boston, MA; Ed.
Margaret Smoragwiecz; Pub. Margaret
Smoragwiecz; pub. size: tabloid; circ.
151,500(free & paid).

SHARON

US

SHARON ADVOCATE. 1873. Fri. $21/yr. in town;
$26/yr. out of town. 28-A S. Main St., Sharon,
MA 02067. TEL 617-784-2131;
FAX 617-784-6724. **Owner(s):** Community
Newspapers, 28-A S. Main St., Sharon, MA
02067. TEL 617-784-2131; Ed. Gareth Charter;
Pub. Kirk Davis; adv. contact: Sean Burke. pub.
size: broadsheet; circ. 4,500(paid)

SOMERSET

US

SPECTATOR, THE. 1932. Wed. $.50 newsstand;
$22/yr. 780 County St., Somerset, MA 02726.
TEL 508-674-4656; FAX 508-677-1210.
Owner(s): Hathaway Publishing Corp., 780
County St., Somerset, MA 02726. TEL
508-674-4656; Ed. Lisa Paulo Ahesky. adv.;
bk.rev. pub. size: broadsheet; circ. 8,000(free &
paid).

SOMERVILLE

US

CAMBRIDGE CHRONICLE. 1846. Thu. $.50
newsstand; $22/yr.; $13/yr. senior citizens. 240
A. Elm St., Ste. 20, Somerville, MA 02144.
TEL 617-629-3380; FAX 617-629-3381.
Owner(s): Fidelity Investments, 82 Devonshire St.,
Boston MA 02019. TEL 617-728 6488; Ed.
John Breneman; Pub. Kirk Davis; pub. size:
broadsheet; circ. 14,119(paid).

US

WATERTOWN PRESS. 1955. Thu. $22/yr.; $13/yr.
senior citizens. 240 A. Elm St., Ste. 20,
Somerville, MA 02144. TEL 617-629-3380;
FAX 617-629-3381. **Owner(s):** Fidelity
Investments, 82 Devonshire St., Rm. 25 C,
Boston, MA 02109; Ed. Tommy Peterson; Pub.
Frank Yetter; pub. size: broadsheet circ.
5,102(paid).

SPENCER

US

NEW LEADER. 1977. Wed. $18/yr. 369 Main St.,
Spencer, MA 01562. TEL 508-885-5041;
FAX 508-885-4213. **Owner(s):** Stonebridge
Press, Inc., 475 Washington St., Auburn, MA
01501. TEL 617-832-5876; Ed. Laurie Griggs.
pub. size: tabloid; circ. 3,500(paid).

US

WICK-QUA-BOAG WEEKLY. 1955. Fri. free. 369 Main
St., Spencer, MA 01562. TEL 508-885-9402;
FAX 508-885-4213. **Owner(s):** Stonebridge
Press, Inc., One St. Mark St. Auburn, MA 01501.
TEL 617-832-5876; Ed. Laurie Griggs; Pub. John
Coots; adv.; pub. size: tabloid; circ. 15,800(free).

SPRINGFIELD

US

SPRINGFIELD ADVOCATE. 1975. Thu. free
newsstand; $60/yr. mailed. 1127 Main St.,
Springfield, MA 01103. TEL 413-781-1900;
FAX 413-781-1906. **Owner(s):** New Mass Media,
Inc., 87 School St., Hatfield, MA 01038. TEL
413-247-9301; Ed. Dan Caccavaro; Pub. Kathy
Nylic; adv. contact: Kathy Nylic. pub. size: tabloid;
circ. 38,750(free & paid).

STOUGHTON

US

ASSOCIATED NEWSPAPER. Wed. $.25 newsstand; $10/yr. 7 Cabot Pl., Stoughton, MA 02072. TEL 617-341-1111; FAX 617-341-1194. **Owner(s):** Franklin Publishing Co., 66 W. Grove St., Middleboro, MA 02346. TEL 508-697-2881; Ed. Michael Lenney; Pub. Richard Dailey; adv. contact: Chris MacDonald. photos; bk.rev.; pub. size: tabloid; circ. 40,000(paid).

US

EASTON BULLETIN. 1929. Wed. $.50 newsstand; $10/yr.; $17/2 yrs. 7 Cabot Pl., Stoughton, MA 02072. TEL 617-341-1111; FAX 617-341-1194. **Owner(s):** Richard R. Dailey, Seven Cabot Pl., Stoughton, MA 02072. TEL 617-341-1111; FAX 617-341-1194; Ed. Michael Lenney; Pub. Richard R. Dailey; adv. contact: Richard Dailey. bk.rev.; pub. size: tabloid; circ. 1,916(paid).

US

HOLBROOK TIMES. 1929. Wed. $.50 newsstand; $10/yr.; $17/2 yrs. 7 Cabot Pl., Stoughton, MA 02072. TEL 617-341-1111; FAX 617-341-1194. **Owner(s):** Associated Newspapers, 7 Cabot Pl., Stoughton, MA 02072. TEL 617-341-1111; FAX 617-341-1194; Ed. Michael Lenny; Pub. Richard Dailey; adv.; bk.rev.; pub. size: tabloid; circ. 700(paid).

US

NORTON COURIER. 1986. Wed. $.50 newsstand; $10/yr.; $17/2 yrs. 7 Cabot Pl., Stoughton, MA 02072. TEL 617-341-1111; FAX 617-341-1194. **Owner(s):** Associated Newspapers, Stoughton, MA; Ed. Michael Lenney; Pub. Richard R. Dailey; adv.; bk.rev.; pub. size: tabloid; circ. 1,270(paid).

US

RAYNHAM JOURNAL. 1982. Wed. $.50 newsstand; $10/yr.; $17/2 yrs. 7 Cabot Pl., Stoughton, MA 02072. TEL 617-341-1111; FAX 617-341-1194. **Owner(s):** Associated Newspapers, 7 Cabot Pl., Stoughton, MA 02072; bk.rev.; pub. size: tabloid; circ. 505(paid).

US

STOUGHTON CHRONICLE. 1861. Wed. $.50 newsstand; $10/yr.; $17/2 yrs. 7 Cabot Pl., Stoughton, MA 02072-0441. TEL 617-341-1111; FAX 617-341-1194. **Owner(s):** Associated Newspapers, 7 Cabot Pl., Stoughton, MA 02072. TEL 617-341-1111; FAX 617-341-1194; Ed. Michael R. Lenney. adv.; bk.rev.; pub. size: tabloid; circ. 4,469(paid).

US

WHITMAN TIMES. 1873. Wed. $10/yr.; $17/2 yrs. 7 Cabot Pl., Stoughton, MA 02072. TEL 617-341-1111; FAX 617-341-1194. **Owner(s):** Associated Newspapers, 7 Cabot Pl., Stoughton, MA 02072. TEL 617-341-1111; Ed. Michael Lenney. adv.; bk.rev.; pub. size: tabloid; circ. 2,201(paid).

TOWNSEND

US

MAIN STREET TRILOGY. 1991. Wed. $.50 newsstand; $.50/wk. deliv.; $17.50/50 wks. 8 Jefts St., Townsend, MA 01469-0571. TEL 508-597-5465; FAX 508-597-5365. **Owner(s):** Mary-Flora & Robert E. Hale, P.O. Box 571, Townsend, MA 01469. TEL 508-597-5465; FAX 508-597-5365; Ed. David Henshaw. adv.: $6.50/SAU. photos; bk.rev.; pub. size: tabloid; circ. 4,640(free & paid).

WALPOLE

US

WALPOLE TIMES, THE. 1915. Thu. $.50 newsstand; $25/yr. mailed in cy.; $30/yr. out of cy. 962 Main St., Walpole, MA 02081. TEL 508-668-0243; FAX 508-668-5174. **Owner(s):** Harris D. Lang, 257 Elm St., Walpole, MA 02081. TEL 617-668-0243; Ed. Paul Pronovost; Pub. Harris D. Lang; adv. contact: Albie Nudel. pub. size: broadsheet; circ. 6,000(paid).

WALTHAM

US   ISSN 0739-3849

NEWTON GRAPHIC. 1872. Wed. $.50 newsstand; $22/yr. in cy.; $24/yr. out of cy. 99 Moody St., Waltham, MA 02154. TEL 617-398-8000; FAX 617-398-8010. **Owner(s):** Community Newspaper Co., 254 Second Ave., Needham, MA 02194. TEL 617-433-6700; Ed. Ellen Ishkanian; Pub. Asa Cole; adv. contact: Robert Cardosa. photos; pub. size: tabloid; circ. 28,000(free & paid). **Wire Service(s):** AP.

US

SUDBURY TOWN CRIER. 1951. Thu. $.50 newsstand; $27/yr. local; $29.25 out of area; $32.40/yr. out of state. 580 Winter St., Waltham, MA 02154. TEL 617-487-7200; FAX 617-487-7377. **Owner(s):** Fidelity Investments, P.O. Box 109, Mansfield, MA 02048. TEL 508-339-8977; Ed. Andrea Haynes; Pub. Asa Cole; adv. contact: Susan Robinson. pub. size: tabloid; circ. 3,498(paid).

WARE

US

WARE RIVER NEWS. 1888. Thu. $.50 newsstand; $21/yr. 4 Church St., Ware, MA 01082. TEL 413-967-3505. **Owner(s):** Ware River News, Inc., 4 Church St., Ware, MA 01082. TEL 413-967-3505; Ed. Glenn H. Ickler; Pub. Patrick H. Turley; adv. contact: Margaret Stacy. photos; pub. size: broadsheet; circ. 4,000(paid).

WEBSTER

US

SOUTH COUNTY ADVERTISER. 1962. Sat. free. 8-10 Mechanic St., Webster, MA 01570. TEL 508-943-4800; FAX 508-943-5524. **Owner(s):** Stonebridge Press, Inc., 25 Elm St., Southbridge, MA 01550. TEL 508-764-4325; Ed. Martin Fey; Pub. Ernie Mayotte; adv.; pub. size: tabloid; circ. 17,000(free).

US

TIMES, THE. 1859. Wed. $.50 newsstand; $18/yr. in cy.; $25/yr. out of cy. 8-10 Mechanic St., Webster, MA 01570. TEL 508-943-4800; FAX 508-943-5524. **Owner(s):** Stonebridge Press, Inc., 25 Elm St., Southbridge, MA 01550. TEL 508-764-4325; Ed. Martin Fey; Pub. Ernest Mayotte; adv.; pub. size: broadsheet; circ. 5,400(paid).
  Formerly: Webster Times.

WELLESLEY

US

WELLESLEY TOWNSMAN. 1906. Thu. $.75 newsstand; $29.75 mailed local. One Crest Rd., Wellesley, MA 02181. TEL 617-235-4000; FAX 617-235-8687. **Owner(s):** Fidelity Investments, P.O. Box 109, Mansfield, MA 02048. TEL 508-339-8977; Ed. Kathy Brauner; Pub. Asa Cole; pub. size: standard; circ. 9,000.

WESTFIELD

US

LONGMEADOW NEWS. Thu. $.40 newsstand; $14/6 mos.; $20/yr.; $17/yr. senior citizens. 62-64 School St., Westfield, MA 01085. TEL 413-562-4181; FAX 413-562-4185. **Owner(s):** Westfield News Publishing Co., 62-64 School St., Westfield, MA 01085. TEL 413-562-4181; Pub. Carol Mazza; adv. contact: Martha Baillargeon. pub. size: standard; circ. 2,700(paid).

WEST SOMERVILLE

US

SOMERVILLE JOURNAL. 1870. Thu. $.50 newsstand; $22/yr.; $13/yr. senior citizens. 240 A. Elm St., Ste. 20, West Somerville, MA 02144. TEL 617-629-3380; FAX 617-629-3381. **Owner(s):** Fidelity Investments, 82 Devonshire St., R 25C, Boston, MA 02109. TEL 617-728-6488; Ed. Tom Peterson; Pub. Frank Yetter; pub. size: broadsheet; circ. 12,400(paid).

WEST SPRINGFIELD

US

WEST SPRINGFIELD RECORD. 1953. Thu. $11/yr. in cy.; $24/yr. out of cy. 516 Main St., West Springfield, MA 01089. TEL 413-736-1587. **Owner(s):** West Springfield Record, Inc., 516 Main St., W. Springfield, MA 01089. TEL 413-736-1587; Ed. Thomas Coburn. pub. size: tabloid; circ. 5,400(paid).

WHITINSVILLE

US   ISSN 0745-8673

BLACKSTONE VALLEY TRIBUNE. 1976. s-w.: Wed. & Fri. $.50 Wed. newsstand; free Fri. newsstand; $18/yr. 60 Church St., Whitinsville, MA 01588. TEL 508-234-2107; FAX 508-234-7506. **Owner(s):** Stonebridge Press Inc., 475 Washington St., Auburn, MA 01501. TEL 617-832-5876; Ed. Deborah Gauthier; Pub. David Cutler; adv.; photos; pub. size: tabloid; circ. 5,500(free & paid).

US

WEEKENDER, THE. Fri. free. 60 Church St., Whitinsville, MA 01588. TEL 508-234-2107; FAX 508-234-7506. **Owner(s):** Stonebridge Press, Inc., 25 Elm St., Southbridge, MA 01550. TEL 508-987-0754; Pub. David Cutler; pub. size: tabloid; circ. 13,000(free).

WILLIAMSTOWN

US

ADVOCATE/SOUTH ADVOCATE, THE. 1982. Wed. $35/yr. P.O. Box 95, Williamstown, MA 01267. TEL 413-458-9000; FAX 413-458-5715. **Owner(s):** Ellen J. Bernstein, P.O. Box 95, Wiliamstown, MA 01267. TEL 413-458-9000; FAX 413-458-5715; Pub. Ellen J. Bernstein; adv. contact: Gail King. photos; pub. size: tabloid; circ. 21,750(free & paid).

WILMINGTON

US

WILMINGTON-TEWKSBURY TOWN CRIER. 1955. Wed. $.50 newsstand; $20/yr. local. 104 Lowell St., Wilmington, MA 01887. TEL 508-658-2346; FAX 508-658-2266. **Owner(s):** Wilmington News Co., Inc., 104 Lowell St., Wilmington, MA 01887. TEL 508-658-2346; Ed. Jeff Nazzaro; Pub. Larz Neilson; adv. contact: John O'Neil. pub. size: broadsheet; circ. 7,081(controlled & paid).

WINCHENDON

US

JAFFREY-RINDGE CHRONICLE. 1800. Wed. $.50 newsstand; $18/yr. in cy.; $25/yr. out of cy. 20 Front St., Winchendon, MA 01475. TEL 508-297-0050; FAX 508-297-2177. **Owner(s):** Stonebridge Press, Inc., 25 Elm St., Southbridge, MA 01550. TEL 508-987-0754; Ed. Ron Muse; Pub. David Cutler; adv. contact: Cindy Janpol. pub. size: tabloid; circ. 3,000(paid).

US

WINCHENDON COURIER. 1800. Wed. $.50 newsstand; $18/yr. in cy.; $25/yr. out of cy. 20 Front St., Winchendon, MA 01475. TEL 508-297-0050; FAX 508-297-2177. **Owner(s):** Stonebridge Press, Inc., 475 Washington St., Auburn, MA 01501. TEL 617-832-5876; Ed. Kristen Spofford; Pub. David Cutler; adv. contact: Fran Boutileer. pub. size: broadsheet; circ. 2,500(paid).

WINCHESTER

US

WINCHESTER STAR. 1880. Thu. $.75 newsstand; $24/yr. mailed; $18/yr. senior citizens. 27 Waterfield Rd., Winchester, MA 01890. TEL 617-729-6100; FAX 617-729-3837. **Owner(s):** Fidelity Investments, P.O. Box 109, Mansfield, MA 02048. TEL 508-339-8977; Ed. Nancy Schwalbert; Pub. Asa Cole; adv. contact: Paul Farrell. pub. size: broadsheet; circ. 6,000(paid).

WOBURN

US   ISSN 1071-9806

WOBURN ADVOCATE. 1991. Thu. $.50 newsstand; $39/yr. 346 W. Cummings Pk., Woburn, MA 01801. TEL 617-937-8000; FAX 617-935-1990. **Owner(s):** Community Newspaper Co., 82 Devonshire St., Boston, MA 02109. TEL 617-937-8000; Ed. Larry Walsh; Pub. Mark O'Neil; adv.; photos; pub. size: tabloid; circ. 17,250(paid).

WORCESTER

US   ISSN 0191-4960

WORCESTER MAGAZINE. 1976. Wed. free newsstand; $26/yr. 3rd class. 172 Shrewsbury St., Worcester, MA 01604. TEL 508-755-8004; FAX 508-755-8860. **Owner(s):** Allen Fletcher, 172 Shrewsbury St., Worcester, MA 01604. TEL 508-755-8004; FAX 508-755-8860; Paul Giorgio, 172 Shrewsbury St., Worcester, MA 01604. TEL 508-755-8004; FAX 508-755-8860; Peter Stanton, 172 Shrewsbury St., Worcester, MA 01604. TEL 508-755-8004; FAX 508-755-8860; Ed. Walter Crockett; Pub. Peter Stanton; adv. contact: Kathy Real. photos; bk.rev.; pub. size: tabloid; circ. 40,000(free & paid).

YARMOUTHPORT

US

BOURNE COURIER. 1976. Thu. $.50 newsstand; $19.95/yr. in cy.; $26.95/yr. out of cy. 923 G, Rte. 6A, Yarmouthport, MA 02675. TEL 508-362-2111; FAX 508-240-0333. **Owner(s):** Community Newspapers Corp., 254 Second Ave., Needham, MA 02194. TEL 617-433-6700; Pub. Victoria Ogden; adv. contact: Lorrie Basler. pub. size: tabloid; circ. 7,000(paid).

US

REGISTER, THE. 1836. Thu. $.50 newsstand; $18.95/yr. mailed on Cape Cod. 923 G., Rte. 6A, Yarmouth Port, MA 02675. TEL 508-362-2111; FAX 508-362-2567. **Owner(s):** Community Newspaper Co., 923 G. Rte 6A, Yarmouth, MA 02675. TEL 508-362-2111; Ed. Mark Skala; Pub. Victoria Ogden; adv. contact: Lorrie Basler. pub. size: tabloid; circ. 12,048(paid).

Formerly: Yarmouth Register Sun.

MICHIGAN

ALLEGAN

US

ALLEGAN COUNTY NEWS. 1882. Thu. $.50 newsstand; $18/yr. in cy.; $23/yr. out of cy.; $27/yr. out of state. 235 North St., Allegan, MI 49010. TEL 616-673-5534. **Owner(s):** Kaechele Publications, Inc., P.O. Box 189, Allegan, MI 49010. TEL 616-673-5534; Ed. Dave Trinka. adv.; pub. size: broadsheet; circ. 6,500.

Formerly: Allegan County News & Gazette.

US

FENNVILLE HERALD. 1882. Thu. $.50 newsstand; $18/yr. in cy.; $23/yr. out of cy.; $27/yr. out of state. 231 Throwbridge St., Allegan, MI 49010. TEL 616-673-5534. **Owner(s):** Kaechele Publications, Inc., P.O. Box 189, Allegan, MI 49010. TEL 616-673-5534; Ed. David Trinka; Pub. Cheryl Kaechele; pub. size: broadsheet; circ. 5,000(paid).

ALPENA

US

ALPENA STAR ADVERTISER. 1972. Sun. free. 431 Ripley Blvd., Alpena, MI 49707. TEL 517-356-2121. **Owner(s):** Star Publications, P.O. Box 620, Gaylord, MI 49735. TEL 517-732-5125. Pub. James R. Glasser; adv. contact: Mike Adams. pub. size: tabloid; circ. 18,813(free).

Formerly: Alpena Ad-Vertiser.

BAY CITY

US

BAY CITY VALLEY FARMER. 1929. Thu. $.50 newsstand; $18/yr. 905 S. Henry, Bay City, MI 48706. TEL 517-893-6507. **Owner(s):** David Hebert, 905 S. Henry, Bay City, MI 48706; Ed. David B. Hebert; Pub. David B. Hebert; adv.; pub. size: tabloid; circ. 2,400(free & paid).

US

VALLEY FARMER, THE. 1929. Thu. $.50 newsstand; $18/yr. 905 S. Henry, Bay City, MI 48706. TEL 517-893-6507. **Owner(s):** David Hebert, 905 S. Henry, Bay City, MI 48706. TEL 517-893-6507; Ed. Mark Schanhals; Pub. David Hebert; adv.; photos; pub. size: tabloid.

BEULAH

US

AD-VISOR. 1966. Sun. free home deliv.; $20/yr. mailed out of area. 254 S. Benzie Blvd., Beulah, MI 49617. TEL 616-882-9613; FAX 616-882-9615. **Owner(s):** Noverr Publications Inc., P.O. Box 797, Beulah, MI 49617. TEL 616-882-9613; Ed. Joe Noverr; Pub. Frank Noverr; pub. size: tabloid; circ. 8,600(free & paid).

BIG RAPIDS

US   ISSN 0192-8678

EVART REVIEW, THE. Wed. $.50 newsstand, $18/yr. 502 N. State St., Big Rapids, MI 49307. TEL 616-796-4831; FAX 616-796-1152. **Owner(s):** Pioneer Group, 502 N. State St., Big Rapids, MI 49307. TEL 616-796-4831; FAX 616-796-1152; Ed. Jim Bruskotter. adv. contact: Denise Clasen. photos; pub. size: broadsheet; circ. 2,450(paid). **Wire Service(s):** Pioneer News Network, AP.

US

LAKE COUNTY STAR. Thu. $.50 newsstand; $16/yr. in cy. 502 N. State St., Big Rapids, MI 49307. TEL 616-796-4831; FAX 616-796-1152. **Owner(s):** Pioneer Group, 502 N. State St., Big Rapids, MI 49307. TEL 616-796-4831; FAX 616-796-1152; Ed. Jim Bruskotter. adv.; photos; pub. size: tabloid; circ. 2,850(paid). **Wire Service(s):** AP.

US

LAKEVIEW ENTERPRISE. Wed. $.50 newsstand; $16/yr. in cy. 502 N. State St., Big Rapids, MI 49307. TEL 616-796-4831; FAX 616-796-1152. **Owner(s):** Pioneer Group, 502 N. State St., Big Rapids, MI 49307. TEL 616-796-4831; FAX 616-796-1152; Ed. Judy Hale. adv. contact: Sharon Fedricks. photos; pub. size: broadsheet; circ. 5,900(paid)

BIRMINGHAM

US

BIRMINGHAM ECCENTRIC, THE. 1970. s-w.: Mon. & Thu. $.75 newsstand; $42/yr. 805 E. Maple, Birmingham, MI 48009. TEL 810-644-1100; FAX 810-644-1314. **Owner(s):** Suburban Communications Corp., 36251 Schoolcraft Rd., Livonia, MI 48150. TEL 313-591-2300; Ed. Bob Sklar. adv. contact: Kathy Hirschfield. pub. size: broadsheet; circ. 18,000(paid).

US

SOUTHFIELD ECCENTRIC. 1949. s-w.: Mon. & Thu. $.75 newsstand; $42/yr. in cy. 805 E. Maple, Birmingham, MI 48009. TEL 810-644-1100; FAX 810-591-9202. **Owner(s):** Suburban Communications Corp., 36251 Schoolcraft Rd., Livonia, MI 48150. TEL 313-591-2300; Ed. Bob Sklar. adv. contact: Kathy Hirschfield. pub. size: broadsheet; circ. 13,000(paid).

US

ST. CLAIR SHORES HERALD. 1973. Thu. $6/yr.; $10/2 yrs.; $14/3 yrs. 2648 Dorchester Rd., Birmingham, MI 48009-5989. TEL 810-649-0749. **Owner(s):** Detroit Northeast Detroiter, 2648 Dorchester Rd., Birmingham, MI 48009. TEL 810-649-0749. Ed. Lloyd Saulter; Pub. Lloyd Saulter; adv. contact: Kevin Saulter. pub. size: broadsheet; circ. 8,900(paid).

US

WEST BLOOMFIELD ECCENTRIC, THE. s-w.: Mon. & Thu. $.75 newsstand; $42/yr. in cy. 805 E. Maple, Birmingham, MI 48009. TEL 810-644-1100; FAX 810-644-1314. **Owner(s):** Suburban Communications Corp., 36251 Schoolcraft Rd., Livonia, MI 48150. TEL 313-591-2300; Ed. Bob Sklar. adv. contact: Kathy Hirschfield. pub. size: broadsheet; circ. 77,000(paid).

Formerly: Birmingham-Bloomfield Eccentric Editor.

Weeklies

BLISSFIELD

US

BLISSFIELD ADVANCE. 1874. Wed. $.50 newsstand; $18/yr. local; $28/yr. out of state. 121 Newspaper St., Blissfield, MI 49228. TEL 517-486-2400. **Owner(s):** Paul & Kelly Heidbreder, 121 Newspaper St., Blissfield, MI 49228. TEL 517-486-2400; Ed. Walt Waikowski; Pub. Paul J. Heidbreder; adv.; photos; bk.rev.; pub. size: broadsheet; circ. 2,800(paid).

BOYNE CITY

US

CITIZEN, THE. 1879. Wed. $.50 newsstand; $22/yr. in cy.; $32/yr. out of cy. 112 S. Park, Boyne City, MI 49712. TEL 616-582-6761; FAX 616-582-6762. **Owner(s):** Husan Publishing Co., P.O. Box A, Boyne City, MI 49712. TEL 616-582-6761; FAX 616-582-6762; Pub. Hugh Conklin; adv.; photos; bk.rev.; pub. size: broadsheet; circ. 3,275(free & paid).
  Formerly: Charlevoix County Press.

BRIGHTON

US

BRIGHTON ARGUS. Wed. $.50 newsstand; $26/yr. mailed in cy. 113 E. Grand River, Brighton, MI 48116. TEL 810-227-0171; FAX 810-227-0175. **Owner(s):** Hometown Newspapers, 323 E. Grand River, Howell, MI 48843. TEL 517-548-2000. adv. contact: John Utter. pub. size: broadsheet; circ. 13,000(paid).

BROOKLYN

US

EXPONENT, THE. 1881. Tue. $.50 newsstand; $25/yr. 160 S. Main St., Brooklyn, MI 49230. TEL 517-592-2122; FAX 517-592-3241. **Owner(s):** Schepeler Corp., 160 S. Main, Brooklyn, MI 49230. TEL 517-592-2122; Ed. Joyce Brown; Pub. Matt Schepeler; adv. contact: Sharon Coffman. pub. size: tabloid; circ. 5,000(paid).

BUCHANAN

US

BERRIEN COUNTY RECORD. 1867. Wed. $.75 newsstand; $25/yr. in cy.; $32/yr. out of cy. 109 Days Ave,, Buchanan, MI 49107-1612. TEL 616-695-3878; FAX 616-695-3880. **Owner(s):** Donald W. Holmes, 408 W. Roe St., Buchanan, MI 49107. TEL 616-695-1133; Pub. Donald W. Holmes; adv.; photos; pub. size: broadsheet; circ. 2,600(free & paid).

CADILLAC

US ISSN 0194-3014

NORTHERN MICHIGAN NEWS. 1972. Mon. free. 130 N. Mitchell, Cadillac, MI 49601-0640. TEL 616-775-6565. **Owner(s):** Thomas C. Huckle, 130 N. Mitchell, Cadillac, MI 49601-0640. TEL 616-775-6565; Ed. Mark Lagerwey; Pub. Thomas C. Huckle; pub. size: broadsheet; circ. 17,690(controlled).

CAMDEN

US

FARMERS' ADVANCE. 1898. Wed. $1 newsstand; $28/yr. mailed. 331 E. Bell, Camden, MI 49232. TEL 517-368-0365; FAX 517-368-5131. **Owner(s):** Suburban Communications Corp., 36251 Schoolcraft Rd., Livonia, MI 48150. TEL 313-591-2300; pub. size: tabloid; circ. 25,000(paid).

CARO

US

TUSCOLA COUNTY ADVERTISER. 1868. Wed. $.75 newsstand; $24/yr. 344 N. State St., Caro, MI 48723. TEL 517-673-3181; FAX 517-673-5662. **Owner(s):** Edwards Publications, P.O. Box 1193, Seneca, SC 29679. TEL 803-882-3272; Ed. Dean Bohn; Pub. Brett McLaughlin; adv. contact: Jamie McCoy. photos; pub. size: broadsheet; circ. 9,950(paid).

CASS CITY

US

CASS CITY CHRONICLE. 1917. Wed. $.50 newsstand; $15/yr. local; $18/yr. in state; $20/yr. elsewhere. 6550 Main St., Cass City, MI 48726. TEL 517-872-2010; FAX 517-872-2010. **Owner(s):** John Haire, 6550 Main St., Cass City, MI 48726. TEL 517-872-2010; FAX 517-872-2010; Ed. Tom Montgomery; Pub. John Haire; adv.; photos; pub. size: broadsheet; circ. 3,875(paid).

CHARLEVOIX

US

CHARLEVOIX COURIER. 1883. Wed. $47/yr. 112 Mason St., Charlevoix, MI 49720-0117. TEL 616-547-6558; FAX 616-547-4992. **Owner(s):** Charlevoix Courier, 319 State St., Petoskey, MI 49770. TEL 616-347-2544; FAX 616-347-6833; Ed. Scott Swanson. adv. contact: Kim Taylor. pub. size: tabloid; circ. 2,026(paid).

US

NORTH WOODS CALL. 1953. bi-w.: Wed. $1 newsstand; $25/yr. mailed. Rte. 1, 00509 Turkey Run, Charlevoix, MI 49720. TEL 616-547-9797; FAX 616-547-0367. **Owner(s):** North Woods Call, Inc., Rte. 1, 00509 Turkey Run, Charlevoix, MI 49720. TEL 616-547-9797; FAX 616-547-0367; Ed. Glen Sheppard. adv.; bk.rev.; pub. size: tabloid; circ. 16,500(paid).

CHARLOTTE

US

CHARLOTTE SHOPPING GUIDE. 1948. Sun. free newsstand; $104/yr. 1st class mailed. 239 Cochran Ave., Charlotte, MI 48813. TEL 517-543-9913; FAX 517-543-0665. **Owner(s):** Suburban Communications Corp., 36251 Schoolcraft Rd., Livonia, MI 48150. TEL 313-591-2300; Ed. Joe Warner; Pub. Pete Cantine; adv.; pub. size: tabloid; circ. 18,000(controlled).

US

EATON COUNTY NEWS. 1854. Sat. free newsstand; $32.50/yr. 239 S. Cochran, Charlotte, MI 48813. TEL 517-543-9913; FAX 517-543-3677. **Owner(s):** Suburban Communications Corp., 36251 Schoolcraft Rd., Livonia, MI 48150. TEL 313-591-2300; Ed. Joe Warner; Pub. Tricia Johnson; adv.; pub. size: tabloid; circ. 17,000(free & paid).

CHATHAM

US

PORCUPINE PRESS. 1989. Wed. $.75 newsstand; $24/yr. E. 3724 Autrain St., Chatham, MI 49816. TEL 906-439-5111; FAX 906-439-5337; E-mail: porkypress@aol.com. **Owner(s):** Porcupine Press, Inc., P.O. Box 200, Chatham, MI 49816. TEL 906-439-5111; FAX 906-439-5337; Ed. Michael J. VanDenBranden; Pub. Michael J. VanDenBranden; adv.; photos; pub. size: tabloid; circ. 4,665(paid). **Wire Service(s):** AP.

CHEBOYGAN

US

STRAITS AREA STAR. 1986. Sun. free. 111 N. Main, Cheboygan, MI 49721. TEL 616-627-3151. **Owner(s):** Star Publications, P.O. Box 620, Gaylord, MI 49735. TEL 517-732-5125; Pub. James R. Glasser; adv. contact: Chris Hebel. pub. size: tabloid; circ. 14,571(free).
  Formerly: Community Shopper.

CHELSEA

US

CHELSEA STANDARD, THE. 1871. Wed. $.50 newsstand; $15/yr. in cy.; $18/yr. in state; $20/yr. out of state. 101 N. Main, Chelsea, MI 48118. TEL 313-475-1371; FAX 313-475-1371. **Owner(s):** Heritage Newspapers, Inc., 101 N. Main St., Chelsea, MI 48118. TEL 313-475-1371; FAX 313-475-1413; Ed. Walter P. Leonard; Pub. Walter P. Leonard; adv.; photos; pub. size: broadsheet; circ. 5,800(paid).

CHESANING

US

TRI-COUNTY CITIZEN. 1983. Sun. free; $3/mo. out of area. 9996 E. M-57, Chesaning, MI 48616. TEL 517-845-7403; FAX 517-845-4397. **Owner(s):** Daniel Lea, 9996-E. M-27, Chesaning, MI 48616. TEL 517-845-7403; FAX 517-845-4397; Ed. Carol Coty; Pub. Daniel Lea; adv.; photos; pub. size: tabloid; circ. 18,200(free).

CLARE

US

CLARE SENTINEL. 1897. Tue. $.50 newsstand; $19.50/yr. 112 W. Fourth St., Clare, MI 48617. TEL 517-386-9937. **Owner(s):** Clare Sentinel, 112 W. Fourth St., Clare, MI 48617. TEL 517-386-9937; Ed. Alfred R. Bransdorfer; Pub. Alfred R. Bransdorfer; pub. size: broadsheet; circ. 3,500(paid).

CLARKSTON

US

CLARKSTON NEWS. 1930. Wed. $.50 newsstand; $16/yr. mailed. 5 S. Main St., Clarkston, MI 48346. TEL 810-625-3370; FAX 810-625-0706. **Owner(s):** Sherman Publications, Inc., 666 S. Lapeer, Oxford, MI 48371. TEL 810-628-4801; FAX 810-628-9750; Ed. Annette Kingsbury; Pub. James A. Sherman, Jr.; adv. contact: Eric Lewis. photos; pub. size: tabloid; circ. 4,465(free & paid).

CROSWELL

US

JEFFERSONIAN, THE. 1858. Mon. $16.95/yr. mailed in cy. 14 Wells St., Croswell, MI 48422. TEL 810-679-4500; FAX 810-679-4504. **Owner(s):** John D. Johnson, 465 N. Sandusky Rd., Sandusky, MI 48471. TEL 810-648-4000; Ed. John D. Johnson. adv. contact: Carlene Soroka. pub. size: tabloid; circ. 7,700(paid).
  Formerly: Croswell Sanilac Jeffersonian.

CRYSTAL FALLS

US

DIAMOND DRILL, THE. 1887. Wed. $.50 newsstand; $20/yr. in cy.; $25/yr. out of cy. 229 Superior Ave., Crystal Falls, MI 49920. TEL 906-875-6633; FAX 906-575-3021. **Owner(s):** Vacationland Enterprises, Rudolph J. Dalpra, 1801 Fargo Dr., Safford, AZ 85546. TEL 602-428-1525; FAX 602-428-3501; Ed. Robert Dalpra. adv.: $3.75/SAU. photos; pub. size: broadsheet; circ. 3,153(controlled & paid).

DAVISON

US

DAVISON INDEX, THE. 1889. Wed. $.50 newsstand; $15/yr. in area. 220 N. Main St., Davison, MI 48423. TEL 810-653-3511. **Owner(s):** Jim Sherman, P.O. Box 100, Davison, MI 48423-0100. TEL 810-653-3511; Ed. Don Schelske. adv.; photos; pub. size: tabloid; circ. 9,500(free & paid).

DEARBORN

US

DEARBORN PRESS & GUIDE. 1918. Thu. $.75 newsstand; $36/yr. 15340 Michigan Ave., Dearborn, MI 48126. TEL 313-943-4250; FAX 313-846-5531. **Owner(s):** Heritage Newspapers, Inc., 15340 Michigan Ave., Dearborn, MI 48126. TEL 313-943-4250; Pub. Robert Riddell; adv. contact: Judy Rogers. photos; bk.rev.; circ. 48,000(controlled & paid).

US   ISSN 0193-0230

DEARBORN TIMES-HERALD. 1963. s-w.: Wed. & Sun. $.50 newsstand; $24.95/yr. 13730 Michigan Ave., Dearborn, MI 48126-3520. TEL 313-584-4000; FAX 313-584-1357. **Owner(s):** Dearborn Management Co., 13730 Michigan Ave., Dearborn, MI 48126-3520. TEL 313-584-4000; Ed. Tom Edwards; Pub. Frank N. Bewick; adv. contact: Louise Parker. photos; bk.rev.; pub. size: broadsheet; circ. 28,000(paid); Sun. 34,000(paid). **Wire Service(s):** Newsfinder.

US

HEIGHTS TIMES-HERALD. 1963. s-w.: Wed. & Sun. $.50 newsstand; $24.95/yr. 13730 Michigan, Dearborn, MI 48126-3520. TEL 313-584-4000; FAX 313-584-1357. **Owner(s):** Laurie Bewick, 13730 Michigan, Dearborn, MI 48126-3520. TEL 313-584-4000; FAX 313-584-1357; Scott Bewick, 13730 Michigan, Dearborn, MI 48126-3520. TEL 313-584-4000; FAX 313-584-1357; Ed. Tom Edward; Pub. Frank H. Bewick; adv. contact: Louise Parker. photos; bk.rev.; pub. size: broadsheet; circ. 27,000(free & paid); Sun. 37,000(free & paid). **Wire Service(s):** ARI, United Media.

DETROIT

US

DETROIT METRO TIMES. Wed. free; $30/6 mo. third class mail; $65/6 mo. first class mail. 733 Saint Antoine St., Detroit, MI 48226. TEL 313-961-4060; FAX 313-961-6598. **Owner(s):** Ron Williams, Detroit Metro Times, 743 Beaubien, Detroit, MI 48226. TEL 313-961-4060; FAX 313-961-6598; Pub. Ron Williams; adv. contact: Jim Cohen. pub. size: tabloid; circ. 101,000(paid). **Wire Service(s):** Alternet.

US

MICHIGAN CHRONICLE. 1936. Wed. $.50 newsstand; $25/yr. 479 Ledyard St., Detroit, MI 48201. TEL 313-963-5522; FAX 313-963-8788. **Owner(s):** John S. Sengstacke, 2400 S. Michigan Ave., Chicago, IL 60616. TEL 312-225-2400; Ed. Carol Archer; Pub. Sam Logan; adv.; photos; bk.rev.; pub. size: broadsheet; circ. 30,000(paid). **Wire Service(s):** AP, API, GNS, N, UPI.

US

NEW CENTER NEWS. 1933. Mon. free. 1-218 General Motors Bldg. Detroit, MI 48202. TEL 313-872-7100; FAX 313-872-2093. **Owner(s):** Monday Morning Newspapers, Inc., Warren, MI; Ed. Peter Salinas; Pub. Bill Springer; adv. contact: Doug Miller. pub. size: tabloid; circ. 7,000(controlled & free).

DURAND

US

DURAND EXPRESS. 1887. Thu. $.35 newsstand; $20/yr. 219 N. Saginaw St., Durand, MI 48429. TEL 517-288-3164; FAX 517-288-4666. **Owner(s):** Ower Rood, 5271 Bancroft Rd., Durand, MI 48429. TEL 517-288-3164; Ed. Bryan Myrkle; Pub. Owen Rood; pub. size: broadsheet; circ. 3,000(paid).

EAST LANSING

US

TOWNE COURIER. 1972. Sat. $.50 newsstand; $26/yr. mailed in cy.; $30/yr. out of cy.; $40/yr. out of state. 210 Abbott, Ste. 28, East Lansing, MI 48823. TEL 517-333-7272; FAX 517-333-7275. **Owner(s):** Ingham Newspapers, P.O. Box 160, Mason, MI 48854; Ed. Dirk Milliman; Pub. Dirk Milliman; pub. size: tabloid; circ. 20,000(paid).

EAST TAWAS

US

IOSCO COUNTY NEWS HERALD. Wed. $.50 newsstand; $20/yr. mailed local; $24/yr. in state; $30/yr. out of state. 110 W. State St., East Tawas, MI 48730. TEL 517-362-3456; FAX 517-362-6601. **Owner(s):** J. Berkeley Smith, News Press Publishing Co., P.O. Box 72, East Tawas, MI 48730. TEL 517-362-3456; Neal Miller, New Press Publishing Co., P.O Box 72, East Tawas, MI 48730. TEL 517-362-3456; Ed. Neal Miller; Pub. Neal Miller; pub. size: tabloid; circ. 7,500(paid).
  Formerly: Tawas City Tawas Herald.

FARMINGTON

US

FARMINGTON OBSERVER. s-w.: Mon. & Thu. $.75 newsstand; $42/yr. in cy. 33411 Grand River Ave., Farmington, MI 48335-3521. TEL 313-591-2300; FAX 313-591-7279. **Owner(s):** Suburban Communications Corp., 36251 Schoolcraft Rd., Livonia, MI 48150. TEL 313-591-2300; Ed. Bob Sklar; Pub. Tom Bird; adv. contact: Rich Ficorelli. pub. size: broadsheet; circ. 150,000(paid).

FLINT

US

INDEPENDENT, THE. 1868. s-w.: Thu. & Sun. free locally. $12/mo. mailed. 5085 Miller Rd., Flint, MI 48507. TEL 810-733-2239; FAX 810-733-2688. **Owner(s):** Advance Newspapers, Inc., 5085 Miller Rd. Flint, MI 48507. TEL 810-733-2239; Ed. Dennis Setter; Pub. Joel Holland; adv. contact: Tom Reynolds. pub. size: broadsheet; circ. 15,000(paid).

US

WEST VALLEY NEWS/SUNDAY ADVANCE. s-w.: Thu. & Sun. free newsstand; $12/mo. mailed. 5085 Miller Rd., Flint, MI 48507. TEL 810-733-2239; FAX 810-733-2688. **Owner(s):** Advance Newspapers, Inc., 5085 Miller Rd., Flint, MI 48507. TEL 810-733-2239; Ed. Dennis Setter; Pub. Gary Neal; adv. contact: Tom Reynolds. pub. size: broadsheet; circ. 13,000(free & paid).

FRANKENMUTH

US

FRANKENMUTH NEWS. 1906. Wed. $.50 newsstand; $21/yr. in cy.; $21.50/yr. in state; $22/yr. out of state. 231 Hubinger St., Frankenmuth, MI 48734. TEL 517-652-3246; FAX 517-652-3247. **Owner(s):** Frankenmuth News, 410 E. Tuscola, Frankenmuth, MI 48734. TEL 517-652-6773; FAX 517-652-3247; Ed. Scott A. Wenzel; Pub. Steve Grainger; adv. contact: Douglas Knoll. photos; pub. size: broadsheet; circ. 5,000(paid).

FREMONT

US

TIMES-INDICATOR. 1878. Wed. $.50 newsstand; $22/yr. in cy.; $30/yr. out of cy. 44 W. Main St., Fremont, MI 49412. TEL 616-924-4400; FAX 616-924-4066. **Owner(s):** T.I. Publication, P.O. Box 387, Morrison, IL 61270. TEL 815-772-4123; Ed. Richard Wheater; Pub. Richard Wheater; adv. contact: Debbie Reinhold. photos; bk.rev.; pub. size: broadsheet; circ. 7,500(paid).

GAYLORD

US

GAYLORD HERALD TIMES. 1875. Thu. $.75 newsstand; $31/yr. local; $43.50/yr. out of area. 2066 Old 27, S., Gaylord, MI 49735-0598. TEL 517-732-1111; FAX 517-732-3490. **Owner(s):** Otsego County Herald Times, Inc., P.O. Box 598, Gaylord, MI 49735. TEL 517-732-1111; Ed. Mary Barker; Pub. James L. Grisso; adv. contact: Nancy Foster. photos; pub. size: broadsheet; circ. 24,500(free & paid). **Wire Service(s):** AP, Newsfinder.

US

NORTHERN STAR. 1960. Sun. free. 1966 Old 27, S., Gaylord, MI 49735. TEL 517-732-5125; FAX 517-732-9323. **Owner(s):** Star Publications, P.O. Box 620, Gaylord, MI 49735. TEL 517-732-5125; FAX 517-732-9323; Pub. James R. Glasser; adv. contact: David G. Baragrey. pub. size: tabloid; circ. 16,682(free).
Formerly: Gaylord Northern Star.

US

PRESQUE ISLE STAR. 1975. Sun. free. 1966 Old 27, S., Gaylord, MI 49735. TEL 517-732-5125; FAX 517-732-9323. **Owner(s):** Star Publications, P.O. Box 620, Gaylord, MI 49735. TEL 517-732-5125; Ed. Mike Adams; Pub. James R. Glasser; adv. contact: Mike Adams. pub. size: tabloid; circ. 7,575(free).
Formerly: Huron Shores Buyers Guide.

GLADWIN

GLADWIN COUNTY RECORD & BEAVERTON CLARION. 1877. Wed. $.50 newsstand; $16/yr. 700 E. Cedar Ave., Gladwin, MI 48624-0425. TEL 517-426-9411; FAX 517-426-2027. **Owner(s):** Gladwin County Newspapers, LLC, Fort Payne, AL; Ed. Ronald Przystas; Pub. Ronald Przystas; pub. size: broadsheet; circ. 9,000(free & paid).

GOBLES

US

VAN BUREN COUNTY ADVERTISER. 1946. Wed. free. 205 S. State St., Gobles, MI 49055. TEL 616-628-5122; FAX 616-628-5198. **Owner(s):** Michigan Printing Co., P.O. Box 278, Bloomingdale, MI 49026. TEL 616-521-4464; Ed. Pam Harris. pub. size: tabloid; circ. 6,100(controlled & free).

GRAND LEDGE

US

DELTA WAVERLY NEWS HERALD, THE. 1984. Wed. free newsstand; $104/yr. 1st class mail. 219 S. Bridge St., Grand Ledge, MI 48837. TEL 517-627-6085; FAX 517-627-3497. **Owner(s):** Community Newspapers, 239 S. Cochran, Charlotte, MI 48113. TEL 517-543-9913; Ed. Nancy Zeimen; Pub. JoAnne Jacobs; adv.; photos; pub. size: broadsheet; circ. 9,000(free & paid).

US

GRAND LEDGE INDEPENDENT, THE. 1869. Tue. free newsstand & home deliv.; $104/yr. 1st class mail. 219 S. Bridge St., Grand Ledge, MI 48837. TEL 517-627-6085; FAX 517-627-3497. **Owner(s):** Community Newspapers, 239 S. Cochran, Charlotte, MI 48813. TEL 517-543-9913; Ed. Michelle Munson. adv.; photos; bk.rev.; pub. size: standard; circ. 17,000(free & paid).

US

PORTLAND REVIEW & OBSERVER. 1867. Mon. free newsstand; $104/yr. 1st class mail. 219 S. Bridge St., Grand Ledge, MI 48837. TEL 517-627-6085; FAX 517-627-3497. **Owner(s):** Lansing Suburban Newspaper Network, Inc., 239 S. Cochran, Charlotte, MI 48813. TEL 517-627-6085; Ed. Nan Simons; Pub. JoAnne Jacobs; adv.; pub. size: tabloid; circ. 7,631(free & paid).

GRAND MARAIS

US

GRAND MARAIS PILOT & PICTURED ROCKS REVIEW. 1971. m. free statewide; $20/yr. mailed. Lake Ave., Grand Marais, MI 49839. TEL 906-494-2391; FAX 906-494-2527. **Owner(s):** Rick & Marge Capogrossa, P.O. Box 339, Grand Marais, MI 49839. TEL 906-494-2391; FAX 906-494-2527; Ed. Rick Capogrossa; Pub. Marge Capogrossa; adv. contact: Marge Capogrossa. pub. size: tabloid; circ. 40,000(free).

US

GREAT LAKES PILOT. m. free. Lake Ave., Grand Marais, MI 49839. TEL 906-494-2391; FAX 906-494-2527. **Owner(s):** Rick & Marge Capogrossa, P.O. Box 339, Grand Marais, MI 49839. TEL 906-494-2391; Ed. Rick Capogrossa; Pub. Marge Capogrossa; adv. contact: Marge Capogrossa. pub. size: tabloid.

GROSSE ILE

US

ILE CAMERA, THE. 1945. Fri. $.50 newsstand; $24/yr. 8801 Macomb, Grosse Ile, MI 48138. TEL 313-676-0515; FAX 313-676-0638. **Owner(s):** Heritage Newspapers, Inc., One Heritage Pl., Southgate, MI 48195. TEL 313-246-7800; FAX 313-284-2028; Ed. Michael Raveane; Pub. Fred Manuel; adv. contact: Lee Atkinson. photos; pub. size: tabloid.

GROSSE POINT

US

CONNECTION, THE. 1991. Thu. free. 96 Kercheval Rd., Grosse Point, MI 48236. TEL 313-882-3500; FAX 313-882-1585. **Owner(s):** Robert G. Edgar, 96 Kercheval Rd., Grosse Point, MI 48236. TEL 313-882-3500; Pub. Robert G. Edgar; adv. contact: Roger Hages. pub. size: broadsheet; circ. 35,000(controlled & free).

GROSSE POINTE FARM

US

GROSSE POINTE NEWS. 1940. Thu. $.75 newsstand; $29/yr. 1n state; $35/yr. out of state. 96 Kercheval Ave., Grosse Pointe Farm, MI 48236. TEL 313-882-6900; FAX 313-882-1585. **Owner(s):** Anteebo Publishers, 96 Kercheval, Grosse Pointe, MI 48236. TEL 313-882-6900; Ed. John Minnis; Pub. Robert G. Edgar; adv. contact: Roger Hages. photos; bk.rev.; pub. size: broadsheet; circ. 18,556(paid).

HAMTRAMCK

US   ISSN 1042-6906
HAMTRAMCK CITIZEN. 1934. Thu. $.50 newsstand; $18/yr. in cy.; $21/yr. out of cy. 11901 Joseph Campau, Hamtramck, MI 48212-3099. TEL 313-365-9500. **Owner(s):** Hamtramck Citizen, Inc., 11901 Joseph Campau, Hamtramck, MI 48212-3099. TEL 313-365-9500; Ed. Karen Kargol Spang; Pub. Karen Kargol Spang; adv.; photos; pub. size: broadsheet; circ. 9,765(controlled & paid).

HARBOR BEACH

US

HARBOR BEACH TIMES. 1834. Thu. $.50 newsstand; $18/yr. 123 N. First St., Harbor Beach, MI 48441. TEL 517-479-3605; FAX 517-479-9697. **Owner(s):** Harbor Beach Times, 123 N. First St., Harbor Beach, MI 48441; Ed. Michael & Kathy Murphy; Pub. Michael & Kathy Murphy; adv.; pub. size: broadsheet; circ. 3,200(paid).

HART

OCEANA'S HERALD-JOURNAL. 1981. Thu. $.50 newsstand; $18/yr. in cy.; $21/yr. out of cy.; $26/yr. out of state. 123 State St., Hart, MI 49420. TEL 616-873-5602; FAX 616-873-4775. **Owner(s):** Maxine Huggard, 86 Fourth St., Shelby, MI 49455. TEL 616-861-2946; Richard Lound, 3335 W. Johnson, Shelby, MI 49455. TEL 616-861-4235; Ed. Mary Sanford. adv. contact: James O. Young. photos; pub. size: broadsheet; circ. 7,400(paid).

HASTINGS

US

BATTLE CREEK SHOPPER. 1947. Thu. free in area. 1952 N. Broadway, Hastings, MI 49015. TEL 616-965-3955; FAX 616-945-5192. **Owner(s):** J-Ad Graphics, Inc., 1952 N. Broadway, Hastings, MI 49058. TEL 616-965-3955; FAX 616-945-5192; Ed. Joyce Ryan; Pub. Fred Jacobs; adv.; photos; bk.rev.; pub. size: tabloid; circ. 50,855(controlled & paid).

US

HASTINGS BANNER. 1856. Thu. $.50 newsstand; $25/yr. mailed in cy.; $27/yr. mailed in area. 1952 N. Broadway, Hastings, MI 49058. TEL 616-948-8051; FAX 616-945-5192. **Owner(s):** J-Ad Graphics, Inc., 1952 N. Broadway, Hastings, MI 49058. TEL 616-945-9554; Ed. David T. Young; Pub. Melvin F. Jacobs; adv. contact: Scott Ommen. pub. size: broadsheet; circ. 7,000(paid). **Wire Service(s):** AP.

US

HASTINGS REMINDER. Tue. free; $28/yr. 1952 N. Broadway, Hastings, MI 49058. TEL 616-945-9554; FAX 616-945-5192. **Owner(s):** Melvin Jacobs, 1952 N. Broadway, Hastings, MI 49058. TEL 616-945-9554; FAX 616-945-5192; Fredric Jacobs, 1952 N. Broadway, Hastings, MI 49058. TEL 616-945-9554; FAX 616-945-5192; Joyce Ryan, 1952 N. Broadway, Hastings, MI 49508. TEL 616-945-9554; FAX 616-945-5192; Stephan Jacobs, 1952 N. Broadway, Hastings, MI 49058. TEL 616-945-9554; FAX 616-645-5192; Ed. David Youngs. adv.; photos; bk.rev.; pub. size: tabloid; circ. 28,000(free & paid).

US

MAPLE VALLEY NEWS. 1975. Tue. free newsstand; $20/yr. mailed. 1952 N. Broadway, Hastings, MI 49058. TEL 616-945-9554; FAX 616-945-5192. **Owner(s):** J-Ad Graphics, Inc., 1952 N. Broadway, Hastings, MI 49058. TEL 616-945-9554; Ed. Jack Worner. adv. contact: Jerry Johnson. pub. size: tabloid; circ. 3,200(free).

US
SUN & NEWS, THE. Tue. free newsstand; $20/yr. 1952 N. Broadway, Hastings, MI 49058. TEL 616-795-3345; FAX 616-945-5192. **Owner(s):** John Jacobs, 1952 N. Broadway, Hastings, MI 49058. TEL 616-945-9554; FAX 616-945-5192; Ed. David Young; Pub. John Jacobs; adv.; photos; bk.rev.; pub. size: tabloid; circ. 8,000(free).

HOLT

US
HOLT COMMUNITY NEWS. Sun. $.35 newsstand; free home deliv. 2068 Cedar St., Holt, MI 48842. TEL 517-694-8484; FAX 517-694-3497. **Owner(s):** Lansing Suburban Newspaper Network, Inc., 239 S. Cochran, Charlotte, MI 48113. TEL 517-627-6085; Ed. Eric Bean; Pub. Peter Cantine; pub. size: broadsheet; circ. 10,600(free & paid).

HOUGHTON LAKE

US
HOUGHTON LAKE RESORTER. 1939. Thu. $18/yr. in cy.; $22/yr. out of cy. 4049 W. Houghton Lake Dr., Houghton Lake, MI 48629. TEL 517-366-5341; FAX 517-366-4472. **Owner(s):** Houghton Lake Resorter, Inc., 4049 W. Houghton Lake Dr., Houghton Lake, MI 48629; Ed. Robert J. Hamp. adv.; photos; pub. size: broadsheet; circ. 7,500(paid). **Wire Service(s):** AP.

HOWELL

US
FOWLERVILLE REVIEW SHOPPING GUIDE. 1874. Wed. free newsstand. 323 E. Grand River, Howell, MI 48843. TEL 517-548-2000; FAX 517-548-3005. **Owner(s):** Hometown Newspapers, 323 E. Grand River, Howell, MI 48843. TEL 517-548-2000; adv. contact: Michael Preville. pub. size: tabloid; circ. 9,000(free).

US
HARTLAND HERALD SHOPPING GUIDE. 1980. Wed. free. 323 E. Grand River, Howell, MI 48843. TEL 517-548-2000; FAX 517-548-3005. **Owner(s):** Hometown Newspapers, 323 E. Grand River, Howell, MI 48843. TEL 517-548-2000; adv. contact: Michael Preville. pub. size: tabloid; circ. 7,500(free).

IMLAY CITY

US
TRI-CITY TIMES. 1977. Wed. $.50 newsstand; $13/yr. mailed in cy.; $15/yr. out of cy.; $24/yr. out of state. 594 N. Almont Ave., Imlay City, MI 48444. TEL 810-724-6191; FAX 810-724-8552. **Owner(s):** Delores Heim, P.O. Box 278, Imlay City, MI 48444; Ed. Cathy Barringer-Rourke; Pub. Delores Heim; adv. contact: Kim Jorgensen. pub. size: broadsheet; circ. 8,760(paid).

IRON MOUNTAIN

US
ADVERTISER, THE. 1975. Tue. free. 333 S. Stephenson Ave., Iron Mountain, MI 49801. TEL 906-774-3708; FAX 906-774-1088. **Owner(s):** Advertiser, The, 1026 Prospect, Iron Mountain, MI 49801. TEL 906-774-9641; Pub. John Lutz; adv.; photos; pub. size: tabloid; circ. 20,600(free).

IRON RIVER

US
IRON RIVER REPORTER. 1885. Wed. $.75 newsstand; $36/yr. out of cy. 801 W. Adams St., Iron River, MI 49935. TEL 906-265-9927; FAX 906-265-5755. **Owner(s):** Northland Publishers, Inc., P.O. Box 311, Iron River, MI 49935. TEL 906-265-9927; FAX 906-265-5755; Ed. Edward J. Erickson, III. adv.; photos; pub. size: broadsheet; circ. 5,000(paid).

IRONWOOD

US
NORTH COUNTRY SUN. 1977. Mon. free in area; $25/yr. mailed. 216 E. Aurora St., Ironwood, MI 49938. TEL 906-932-3530; FAX 906-932-3074. **Owner(s):** La Pean Publications, 417 Ninth Ave., W., Ashland, WI 54806. TEL 715-682-8131; FAX 715-682-6400; Ed. Gary La Pean; Pub. Gary La Pean; pub. size: tabloid; circ. 16,739(free & paid).

ITHACA

US
GRATIOT COUNTY HERALD. 1887. Thu. $.50 newsstand; $21/yr. in cy.; $23/yr. out of cy.; $26/yr. out of state. 123 N. Main St., Ithaca, MI 48847. TEL 517-875-4151; FAX 517-875-3159. **Owner(s):** Patricia R. MacDonald, 123 N. Main St., Ithaca, MI 48847. TEL 517-875-4151; Thomas P. MacDonald, 123 N. Main St., Ithaca, NY 48847. TEL 517-875-4151; Ed. Randy Williams; Pub. Thomas P. MacDonald; adv.; photos; pub. size: tabloid; circ. 6,000(paid).

JACKSON

US
BLAZER NEWS. 1963. Wed. $15/yr. 3419 S. Meridian Rd., Jackson, MI 49203. TEL 517-787-0450; FAX 517-787-2907. **Owner(s):** Ben & Ruth Wade, 3419 S. Meridian Rd., Jackson, MI 49203. TEL 517-787-0450; FAX 517-787-2907; Ed. Ruth Wade; Pub. Ben Wade; adv. contact: Ron Davis. photos; bk.rev.; pub. size: tabloid; circ. 5,000(free).

JENISON

US
ADA/CASCADE/FOREST HILLS ADVANCE. Tue. $.35 newsstand. 2141 Port Sheldon Rd., Jenison, MI 49428. TEL 616-669-2700; FAX 616-669-1162. **Owner(s):** Valley Media, Inc., 2141 Port Sheldon Rd., Jenison, MI 49428. TEL 616-669-2700; FAX 616-669-1162; Ed. Tim Gortsema; Pub. Joel Holland; pub. size: tabloid; circ. 12,450(free & paid).

US
CALEDONIA/GAINES ADVANCE. Tue. free. 2141 Port Sheldon Rd., Jenison, MI 49428. TEL 616-669-2700; FAX 616-669-1162. **Owner(s):** John Badoud, 2141 Port Sheldon Rd., Jenison, MI 49428. TEL 616-669-2700; FAX 616-669-1162 Ed. Mike Wyngarden; Pub. Joel Holland; adv.; pub. size: broadsheet; circ. 6,300(free).

US
EAST GRAND RAPIDS CADENCE. Tue. free. 2141 Port Sheldon Rd., Jenison, MI 49428. TEL 616-669-2700; FAX 616-669-1162. **Owner(s):** Valley Media, Inc., 2141 Port Sheldon Rd., Jenison, MI 49428. TEL 616-669-2700; FAX 616-669-1162; Ed. Mike Wyngarden; Pub. Joel Holland; pub. size: tabloid; circ. 5,250(free).

US
GRAND RAPIDS ADVANCE. s-w.: Tue. & Wed. $.35 newsstand; 30/yr. mailed; $20/6 mos. mailed. 2141 Port Sheldon Rd., Jenison, MI 49428. TEL 616-669-2700; FAX 616-669-1162. **Owner(s):** Valley Media, Inc., 2141 Port Sheldon Rd., Jenison, MI 49428. TEL 616-669-2700; FAX 616-669-1162; Ed. Mike Windgarden; Pub. Joel Holland; pub. size: tabloid; circ. 52,846(paid).

US
GRAND VALLEY ADVANCE. 1966. Tue. free. 2141 Port Sheldon Rd., Jenison, MI 49428. TEL 616-669-2700; FAX 616-669-1162. **Owner(s):** Valley Media, Inc., 2141 Port Sheldon Rd., Jenison, MI 49428. TEL 616-669-2700; FAX 616-669-1162; Ed. Mike Wyngarden; Pub. Joel Holland; pub. size: tabloid; circ. 23,636(free).

US
KENTWOOD ADVANCE. 1982. Tue. free. 2141 Port Sheldon Rd., Jenison, MI 49428. TEL 616-669-2700; FAX 616-669-1162. **Owner(s):** Valley Media, Inc., 2141 Port Sheldon Rd., Jenison, MI 49428. TEL 616-669-2700; FAX 616-669-1162; Ed. Mike Wyngarden; Pub. Joel Holland; pub. size: tabloid; circ. 141,500(free).

US
NORTHFIELD ADVANCE. 1982. s-w.: Tue & Wed. free. 2141 Port Sheldon Rd., Jenison, MI 49428. TEL 616-669-2700; FAX 616-669-1162. **Owner(s):** Valley Media, Inc., 2141 Port Sheldon Rd., Jenison, MI 49428. TEL 616-669-2700; FAX 616-669-1162; Ed. Mike Wyngarden; Pub. Joel Holland; pub. size: tabloid; circ. 19,650(free).

US
OTTAWA ADVANCE. 1968. Tue. free. 2141 Port Sheldon Rd., Jenison, MI 49428. TEL 616-669-2700; FAX 616-669-1162. **Owner(s):** Valley Media, Inc., 2141 Port Sheldon Rd., Jenison, MI 49428. TEL 616-669-2700; FAX 616-669-1162; Ed. Mike Wyngarden; Pub. Joel Holland; pub. size: tabloid; circ. 8,200(free).

US
ROCKFORD/CEDAR SPRINGS ADVANCE. 1989. Tue. free. 2141 Port Sheldon Rd., Jenison, MI 49428. TEL 616-669-2700; FAX 616-669-1162. **Owner(s):** Valley Media, Inc. 2141 Port Sheldon Rd., Jenison, MI 49428. TEL 616-669-2700; FAX 616-669-1162; Ed. Mike Wyngarden; Pub. Joel Holland; pub. size: tabloid; circ. 13,475(free).

US
WALKER-WESTSIDE ADVANCE. 1968. Tue. free. 2141 Port Sheldon Rd., Jenison, MI 49428. TEL 616-669-2700; FAX 616-669-1162. **Owner(s):** Valley Media, Inc. 2141 Port Sheldon Rd., Jenison, MI 49428. TEL 616-669-2700; FAX 616-669-1162; Ed. Mike Wyngarden; Pub. Joel Holland; pub. size: tabloid; circ. 23,865(free).

US

WYOMING ADVANCE. 1982. Tue. free. 2141 Port
Sheldon Rd., Jenison, MI 49428.
TEL 616-669-2700; FAX 616-669-3930.
Owner(s): Valley Media, Inc., 2141 Port Sheldon
Rd., Jenison, MI 49428. TEL 616-669-2700;
FAX 616-669-1162; Ed. Mike Wyngarden; Pub.
Joel Holland; pub. size: tabloid; circ. 22,600(free).

KALKASKA

US

STAR ADVERTISER. 1970. Sun. free. 134 S. Cedar,
Kalkaska, MI 49646. TEL 616-258-3226;
FAX 616-732-9323. **Owner(s):** Star Publications,
P.O. Box 620, Gaylord, MI 49735. TEL
517-732-5125; Advertiser, Inc., 600 Charlevoix
Ave., Petoskey, MI 49770. TEL 616-347-8186;
Pub. James R. Glasser; adv. contact: David G.
Baragrey. pub. size: tabloid; circ. 20,617(free).

L'ANSE

US

L'ANSE SENTINEL. 1880. Wed. $28/yr. local;
$31/yr. in state; $34/yr. out of state. 202 N.
Main, L'Anse, MI 49946. TEL 906-524-6194.
Owner(s): LDJ Publishers, Inc., 636 Broad St.,
L'Anse, MI 49946. TEL 906-524-7132; Ed. Barry
Drue; Pub. Ed Danner; adv. contact: Gale Eilola.
photos; pub. size: broadsheet; circ. 3,800(paid).

LAKE CITY

US

WATERFRONT OF MISSAUKEE COUNTY. 1972. Tue.
$16/yr. in cy. 101 N. Main St., Lake City, MI
49651. TEL 616-839-4315;
FAX 616-839-4994. **Owner(s):** Waterfront, Inc.,
P.O. Box L, Lake City, MI 49651. TEL
616-839-4315; Robert C. Redman, Lake City, MI
49651. TEL 616-839-7272; Ed. Robert C.
Redman; Pub. Robert C. Redman; adv.; pub. size:
tabloid; circ. 3,500(paid).
　　Formerly: Lake City Waterfront.

LANSING

US

AD-VISOR. 1963. m. free. 1521 S. Pennsylvania,
Lansing, MI 48910. TEL 517-372-8433.
Owner(s): Jeanne & Manuel Castro, 1521 S.
Pennsylvania, Lansing, MI; Ed. Manuel Castro;
Pub. Manuel Castro; adv. contact: Jeanne Castro.
bk.rev.; pub. size: tabloid; circ. 15,000(free).

LAPEER

US　　ISSN 8750-4561

COUNTY PRESS, THE. 1839. s-w.: Sun & Wed.
$29.50/yr. in cy.; $32/yr. out of cy. 1521 Imlay
City Rd., Lapeer, MI 48446. TEL 810-664-0811;
FAX 810-664-5852. **Owner(s):** Walt Disney Co.,
500 S. Buena Vista St., Burbank, CA 91521. TEL
818-560-5300; Ed. Mark Haney; Pub. Ernest
Slade; pub. size: broadsheet; circ. 11,000(paid).
　　Formerly: Lapeer County Press.

LELAND

US

LEELANAU ENTERPRISE. 1877. Thu. $.50
newsstand; $17/yr. in cy.; $33/yr. out of cy.
112 Chandler St., Leland, MI 49654-0527.
TEL 616-256-9827. **Owner(s):** Leelanau
Publishing Co., Inc., P.O. Box 527, Leland, MI
49654. TEL 616-256-9827; Ed. Dick Kerr; Pub.
R.C. Kerr; adv.; pub. size: tabloid; circ.
7,637(paid).

LESLIE

US

LESLIE LOCAL INDEPENDENT. 1869. Tue. $.25
newsstand; $12/yr. in state; $14/yr. out of state.
109 Carney, Leslie, MI 49251.
TEL 517-589-8228; FAX 517-589-8526.
Owner(s): S.G. Publications, 140 E. Ash St.,
Mason, MI 48854. TEL 517-676-5100; FAX
517-676-6753; Ed. Larry Hook; Pub. George
Raymond; adv. contact: Linda Gregory. bk.rev.;
pub. size: tabloid; circ. 9,051(free & paid).

LIVONIA

US

GARDEN CITY OBSERVER. s-w.: Mon. & Thu. $.75
newsstand; $42/yr. in cy. 36251 Schoolcraft Rd.,
Livonia, MI 48150. TEL 313-591-2300;
FAX 313-591-7279. **Owner(s):** Suburban
Communications Corp., 36251 Schoolcraft Rd.,
Livonia, MI 48150. TEL 313-591-2300; Ed. Sue
Rosiek; Pub. Banks Dishman; adv. contact: Peg
Knoespel. pub. size: broadsheet; circ. 8,500(paid).

US

LIVONIA OBSERVER. s-w.: Mon. & Thu. $.75
newsstand; $42/yr. in cy. 36251 Schoolcraft Rd.,
Livonia, MI 48150. TEL 313-591-2300;
FAX 313-951-7279. **Owner(s):** Suburban
Communications Corp., 36251 Schoolcraft Rd.,
Livonia, MI 48150. TEL 313-591-2300; Ed. Sue
Rosiek; Pub. Banks Dishman; adv. contact: Peg
Knoespel. pub. size: broadsheet; circ.
29,500(paid).

US

REDFORD OBSERVER. s-w.: Mon. & Thu. $.75
newsstand; $42/yr. in cy. 36251 Schoolcraft Rd.,
Livonia, MI 48150. TEL 313-591-2300;
FAX 313-591-7279. **Owner(s):** Suburban
Communications Corp., 36251 Schoolcraft Rd.,
Livonia, MI 48150. TEL 313-591-2300; Ed. Tedd Schneider; Pub.
Philip Power; adv.; pub. size: broadsheet; circ.
12,600(paid).

US

WESTLAND OBSERVER. 1965. s-w.: Mon. & Thu.
$.75 newsstand; $43.20/yr. in cy. 36251
Schoolcraft Rd., Livonia, MI 48150.
TEL 313-591-2300; FAX 313-591-7279.
Owner(s): Suburban Communications Corp.,
36251 Schoolcraft Rd., Livonia, MI 48150. TEL
313-591-2300; Ed. Bob Sklar. adv. contact:
Kathy Hirshfield. pub. size: broadsheet; circ.
12,000(paid).

LOWELL

US

LOWELL LEDGER. 1956. Wed. $.35 newsstand;
$12.50/yr. mailed. 105 N. Broadway, Lowell, MI
49331. TEL 616-897-9261;
FAX 616-897-4809. **Owner(s):** Roger K. Brown,
105 N. Broadway, Lowell, MI 49331. TEL
616-897-9261; Ed. Roger K. Brown; Pub. Roger
K. Brown; adv.; pub. size: broadsheet; circ.
2,700(paid).

MANISTEE

US

MANISTEE OBSERVER. Sun. free local; $18/yr.
voluntary pay. 75 Maple St., Manistee, MI
49660. TEL 616-723-3593;
FAX 616-723-4733. **Owner(s):** J.B. Publishing
Co., 75 Maple St., Manistee, MI 49660. TEL
616-723-3593; FAX 616-723-4733; Ed. Ken
Grabowski; Pub. Terry Fitzwater; adv. contact:
Marilyn Barker. photos; pub. size: tabloid; circ.
Sun. 18,000(paid).

MANISTIQUE

US

MANISTIQUE PIONEER-TRIBUNE. 1876. Wed.
$17.50/yr. in cy.; $22.50/yr. out of cy. 212
Walnut St., Manistique, MI 49854.
TEL 906-341-5200. **Owner(s):** Leanne
Trebilcock, 212 Walnut, Manistique, MI 49854.
TEL 906-341-5200; Pub. Leanne Trebilcock; adv.
contact: Leanne Trebilcock. pub. size: broadsheet;
circ. 3,800(paid).

MARSHALL

US

COMMUNITY ADVISOR. 1969. Wed. free newsstand;
$26/yr. mailed. 215 W. Michigan Ave., Marshall,
MI 49068. TEL 616-781-5444;
FAX 616-781-7766. **Owner(s):** J-Ad Graphics,
Inc., 1952 N. Broadway, Hastings, MI 49058; Ed.
Tom Isham; Pub. John Jacobs; adv.; pub. size:
tabloid; circ. 19,500(free & paid).

MASON

US

ENTERPRISE, THE. Wed. $.50 newsstand; $20/yr.
624 S. Cedar, Mason, MI 48854.
TEL 517-676-9393; FAX 517-676-9402.
Owner(s): Milliman Communications, Inc., P.O.
Box 160, Mason, MI; Ed. George Pinkerton; Pub.
Dirk Milliman; adv.; pub. size: tabloid; circ.
1,800(paid).

US

INGHAM COUNTY NEWS. 1858. Wed. $.50
newsstand; $20/yr. 624 S. Cedar St., Mason, MI
48854. TEL 517-676-9393;
FAX 517-676-9402. **Owner(s):** Milliman
Communications, Inc., P.O. Box 160, Mason, MI
48854. TEL 517-676-9393; Ed. George
Pinkerton; Pub. Dirk Milliman; adv.; pub. size:
tabloid; circ. 3,000(paid).

MAYVILLE

US

MAYVILLE MONITOR. 1884. Thu. $.35 newsstand;
$13/yr. in cy.; $15/yr. elsewhere in state;
$18/yr. out of state. 6071 Fulton St., Mayville,
MI 48744-0299. TEL 517-843-6441;
FAX 517-843-0054. **Owner(s):** Gale & Debra
Langford, 6071 Fulton St., Mayville, MI
08744-0299. TEL 517-843-6441; FAX
517-843-0054; Ed. Gale Langford; Pub. Gale
Langford; adv.; photos; bk.rev.; pub. size: tabloid;
circ. 1,300(paid).

MILAN

US

MILAN AREA LEADER. 1881. Wed. $.30 newsstand;
$14/yr. Washtenaw & Monroe cys; $16/yr. out of
cys. 37 E. Main St., Milan, MI 48160-0017.
TEL 313-439-8150; FAX 313-439-2278.
Owner(s): Milan Area Leader, 37 E. Main, Milan,
MI 48160. TEL 313-439-8150; FAX
313-439-2278; Pub. G.R. Jones; adv. contact:
Timothy Troin. photos; bk.rev.; pub. size: tabloid;
circ. 3,725(paid).

MILFORD

US

MILFORD TIMES. 1871. Thu. $.50 newsstand; $26/yr. mailed locally. 405 N. Main St., Milford, MI 48381. TEL 810-685-1509; FAX 810-437-9460. **Owner(s):** Hometown Newspapers, 323 E. Grand River Ave., Howell, MI 48843. TEL 517-548-2000; Ed. Frank Eichenlaub. adv. contact: Michael Preville. pub. size: broadsheet; circ. 5,577(paid).

MORENCI

US

MORENCI OBSERVER. 1872. Wed. $.50 newsstand; $17/yr. in area; $20/yr. out of area. 120 North St., Morenci, MI 49256. TEL 517-458-6811; FAX 517-458-6811. **Owner(s):** David Green, 120 North St., Morenci, MI 49256. TEL 517-458-6811; Ed. David Green; Pub. David Green; adv.; pub. size: tabloid; circ. 2,550(paid).

MUNISING

US   ISSN 1074-0201

MUNISING NEWS. 1896. Wed. $20/yr. in cy.; $25/yr. out of cy. P.O. Box 38, Munising, MI 49862-0038. TEL 906-387-3282. **Owner(s):** Esley M. Mattson, Munising, MI; John Williams, Munising, MI; Ed. Dan Wilson. pub. size: broadsheet; circ. 3,450(paid).

MUSKEGON

US

LAKE MICHIGAN EXAMINER, THE. 1968. Wed. $.50 newsstand; $24/yr. 3494 Peninsula Dr., Muskegon, MI 49444. TEL 616-739-6397; FAX 616-737-1520; E-mail: examiner95@aol.com. **Owner(s):** SCS Publishing, Inc., 3494 Peninsula Dr., Muskegon, MI 49444. TEL 616-739-6397; FAX 616-737-1520; Ed. Susan Carrington. adv.; photos; bk.rev.; pub. size: tabloid; circ. 13,750(free & paid). **Wire Service(s):** AP.

    Formerly: Examiner, The.

NEW BALTIMORE

US   ISSN 8750-7188

BAY VOICE. 1983. Wed. $21/yr. 31950 23 Mile Rd., New Baltimore, MI 48047. TEL 810-949-7900; FAX 810-949-2217. **Owner(s):** Tom & Beth Stanton, P.O. Box 760, New Baltimore, MI 48047. TEL 810-949-7900; FAX 810-949-2217; Dorothy & Joe Stabile, P.O. Box 760, New Baltimore, MI 48047; Ed. Tom Stanton. adv.; photos; pub. size: tabloid; circ. 22,000(paid).

US

BLUE WATER VOICE. 1985. Wed. $21/yr. 31950 23 Mile Rd., New Baltimore, MI 48047. TEL 810-765-4059; FAX 810-949-2217. **Owner(s):** Tom & Beth Stanton, 31950 23 Mile Rd., New Baltimore, MI 48047. TEL 810-765-4059; Joe & Dorothy Stabile, 31950 23 Mile Rd., New Baltimore, MI 48047; Ed. Tom Stanton. photos; pub. size: tabloid; circ. 11,000(paid).

US

DOWNRIVER VOICE. 1985. Wed. $21/yr. 31950 23 Mile Rd., Box 760, New Baltimore, MI 48047. TEL 810-765-4059. **Owner(s):** Tom & Beth Stanton, 31950 23 Mile Rd., Box 760, New Baltimore, MI 48047; Joe & Dorothy Stabile, 31950 23 Mile Rd., New Baltimore, MI 48047; Ed. Donna Remer. adv. contact: Debbie Loggins. photos; pub. size: tabloid; circ. 11,000(paid).

US

MACOMB VOICE, THE. 1985. Wed. free in area; $21/yr. out of area. P.O. Box 760, New Baltimore, MI 48047. TEL 810-949-7900; FAX 810-949-2217. **Owner(s):** Tom & Beth Stanton, 31950 23 Mile Rd., New Baltimore, MI 48047. TEL 810-949-7900; Joe & Dorothy Stabile, 31950 23 Mile Rd., New Baltimore, MI 48047; Ed. Donna Remer. adv. contact: Debbie Loggins. photos; pub. size: tabloid; circ. 56,909(controlled & paid).

US

NORTH MACOMB VOICE. 1985. Wed. $25/yr. 31950 23 Mile Rd., New Baltimore, MI 48047. TEL 313-765-4059. **Owner(s):** Tom & Beth Stanton, 31950 23 Mile Rd., New Baltimore, MI 48047; Joe & Dorothy Stabile, 31950 23 Mile Rd., New Baltimore, MI 48047; Ed. Donna Remer. adv.; photos; pub. size: tabloid; circ. 9,000(paid).

NEW BUFFALO

US

NEW BUFFALO TIMES. 1943. Wed. $.50 newsstand; $26/yr. 102 S. Whittaker St., New Buffalo, MI 49117. TEL 616-469-1100; FAX 616-469-4812. **Owner(s):** M.B. Moriarty, P.O. Box 369, New Buffalo, MI 49117. TEL 616-469-1100; Ed. M.B. Moriarty; Pub. M.B. Moriarty; pub. size: tabloid; circ. 3,500(paid).

NORTHVILLE

US   ISSN 1050-2467

NORTHVILLE RECORD. 1869. Thu. $.50 newsstand; $26/yr. mailed. 104 W. Main St., Northville, MI 48167. TEL 810-349-1700; FAX 810-349-1050. **Owner(s):** Hometown Newspapers, 323 E. Grand River, Howell, MI 48843. TEL 517-548-2003; Pub. Rich Perlberg; adv. contact: Michael Preville. pub. size: broadsheet; circ. 5,781(paid).

US

NOVI NEWS. 1977. Thu. $22/yr. 104 W. Main St., Northville, MI 48167. TEL 313-349-1700; FAX 313-349-1050; E-mail: mikem@oeonline.com. **Owner(s):** Suburban Communications Corp., 36251 Schoolcraft, Livonia, MI 48150. TEL 313-591-2300; Ed. Mike Malott. adv. contact: Michael Preville. pub. size: broadsheet; circ. 6,500(paid).

NORWAY

US   ISSN 1071-2607

NORWAY CURRENT. 1885. Wed. $.40 newsstand; $21/yr. 723 Main St. Norway, MI 49870. TEL 906-563-5212; FAX 906-563-5904. **Owner(s):** Larry & Vicki Underhill, 723 Main St., Norway, MI 49870. TEL 906-563-5212; FAX 906-563-5904; Ed. Vicki Underhill; Pub. L.A. Underhill; adv. contact L.A. Underhill. photos; bk.rev.; pub. size: tabloid; circ. 1,500(controlled & paid).

ONAWAY

US

ONAWAY OUTLOOK. 1974. Wed. $.35 newsstand; $21/yr. local mailed. 319 Washington Ave., Onaway, MI 49765. TEL 517-733-6543. **Owner(s):** Milliman Communications, Inc., P.O. Box 160, Mason, MI 48854. TEL 517-676-1260; Ed. Bill Breed; Pub. Richard Lamb; pub. size: tabloid; circ. 2,400(paid).

ONTONAGON

US

ONTONAGON HERALD. 1881. Wed. $.60 newsstand; $24/yr. in cy.; $28/yr. out of cy. 326 River St., Ontonagon, MI 49953-0058. TEL 906-884-2826; FAX 906-884-2939. **Owner(s):** Maureen Guzek, Ontonagon, MI. TEL 906-884-2826; FAX 906-884-2939; Ed. Maureen Guzek; Pub. Maureen Guzek; adv.; photos; bk.rev.; pub. size: broadsheet; circ. 3,700(paid).

ORTONVILLE

US

COUNTY LINE REMINDER. 1953. Sun. free. 48 South St., Ortonville, MI 48462. TEL 810-627-2843; FAX 810-627-3473. **Owner(s):** Walt Disney Co., 500 S. Buena Vista St., Burbank, CA 91521. TEL 818-560-5300; Ed. Kathleen Steffen. adv.; photos; pub. size: broadsheet; circ. 10,000(free).

OSCODA

US

OSCODA PRESS. 1800. Wed. $.50 newsstand; $20/yr. in cy.; $24/yr. out of cy.; $30/yr. out of state. 311 S. State, Oscoda MI 48750. TEL 517-739-2055; FAX 517-739-3201. **Owner(s):** News Press Publishers, P.O. Box 663, Oscoda, MI 48750. TEL 517-739-3201; Neal Miller, P.O. Box 663, Oscoda, MI 48750. TEL 517-739-3201; Pub. J. Berkeley Smith; pub. size: tabloid; circ. 5,900(paid).

OWOSSO

US

SUNDAY INDEPENDENT, THE. 1968. Sun. $20/6 mos.; $30/yr. 1907 W M-21, Owosso, MI 48867-9317. TEL 517-723-1118; FAX 517-725-1834. **Owner(s):** Michael Flores, 1907 W M-21, Owosso, MI 48867. TEL 517-723-1118; FAX 517-725-7925; Leonard Krawczyk, 1106 S. Washington, Owosso, MI 48867. TEL 517-725-5322; FAX 517-725-2971; Ed. Bill Constine; Pub. Michael Flores; adv.; pub. size: tabloid; circ. 40,577(free).

PARMA

US

COUNTY PRESS. 1868. Wed. $.50 newsstand; $20/yr. 123 W. Main St., Parma, MI 49269. TEL 517-531-4542; FAX 517-531-3576. **Owner(s):** Schepeler Corp., 123 W. Main St., Parma, MI 49269. TEL 517-531-4542; FAX 517-531-3576; Ed. Ed Freundl; Pub. Matthew Schepeler; adv. contact: Lori Immanen. photos; pub. size: tabloid; circ. 1,800(free & paid).

    Formerly: Parma News, West County Press.

PAW PAW

US

PAW PAW COURIER-LEADER. 1844. Fri. $.50 newsstand; $14/yr. local; $15/yr. elsewhere. 32280 Red Arrow, Paw Paw, MI 49079-0129. TEL 616-657-3072; FAX 616-657-5723. **Owner(s):** Vineyard Press, Inc., Box 129, Paw Paw, MI 49079. TEL 616-657-3072; FAX 616-657-5723; Ed. Felix A. Racette. adv.; photos; pub. size: broadsheet; circ. 4,100(paid).

PERRY

US

SHIAWASSEE COUNTY JOURNAL. 1893. Wed. $.35 newsstand; $20/yr. mailed; $18/yr. senior citizens. 130 N. Main St., Perry, MI 48872. TEL 517-625-3181; FAX 517-288-4666. **Owner(s):** Owen & Arlene Rood, 219 N. Saginaw, Durand, MI 48429. TEL 517-288-3164; Ed. Bryan Myrkle; Pub. Owen Rood; adv. contact: Dan Dolihanti. pub. size: tabloid; circ. 6,035(paid).

PINCKNEY

US

PINCKNEY POST SHOPPING GUIDE. 1980. Wed. free. 107 E. Main St., Pinckney, MI 48169. TEL 313-878-3107; FAX 313-878-9247. **Owner(s):** Hometown Newspapers, 323 E. Grand River, Howell, MI 48843. TEL 517-548-2000; FAX 517-548-3005; Pub. Richard Perlberg; adv. contact: Michael Preville. pub. size: tabloid; circ. 10,400(free).

PLAINWELL

US

UNION ENTERPRISE. 1869. Thu. $.35 newsstand; $15/yr. in cy.; $18/yr. out of cy.; $22/yr. out of state. 352 12th St., Plainwell, MI 49080. TEL 616-685-9571. **Owner(s):** Union Enterprise, P.O. Box 417, Plainwell, MI 49080. TEL 616-685-9571; Ed. Dave Trinka; Pub. Cheryl Kaechele; adv.; pub. size: tabloid; circ. 5,625(free & paid).

PLYMOUTH

US

CANTON OBSERVER. s-w.: Mon & Thu. $.75 newsstand; $42/yr. in cy. 744 Wing St., Plymouth, MI 48170. TEL 313-459-2700; FAX 313-459-4224. **Owner(s):** Suburban Communications Corp., 36251 Schoolcraft Rd., Livonia, MI 48150. TEL 313-591-2300; Ed. Sue Rosiek; Pub. Banks Dishman; adv. contact: Pat Knoepsel. pub. size: broadsheet; circ. 6,000(paid).

US

PLYMOUTH OBSERVER. 1967. s-w.: Mon. & Thu. $.75 newsstand; $42/yr. in cy. 744 Wing St., Plymouth, MI 48170. TEL 313-459-2700; FAX 313-459-4224. **Owner(s):** Suburban Communications Corp., 36251 Schoolcraft Rd., Livonia, MI 48150. TEL 313-591-2300; Ed. Sue Rosiek; Pub. Banks Dishman; adv. contact: Peg Knoepsel. pub. size: broadsheet; circ. 10,000(paid).

PONTIAC

US

REMINDER, THE. Thu. free newsstand; $79/yr. mailed. 48 W. Huron St., Pontiac, MI 48342. TEL 810-745-4626; FAX 810-332-8885. **Owner(s):** Walt Disney Co., 500 S. Buena Vista St., Burbank, CA 91521. TEL 818-560-5300; Ed. Al Adler. adv. contact: Kerry Davis. pub. size: broadsheet; circ. 142,000(free).

REED CITY

US

HERALD NEWS, THE. Thu. $.50 newsstand; $18/yr. in cy.; $28/yr. out of cy.; $38/yr. out of state. 101 W. Slosson St., Reed City, MI 49677. TEL 616-832-5566; FAX 616-832-5558. **Owner(s):** Pioneer Group, 502 N. State St., Big Rapids, MI 49307. TEL 616-796-4831; Ed. Ned Adamson; Pub. Jack Batdorff; adv.; photos; pub. size: broadsheet; circ. 3,000(paid).
    Formerly: Reed City Osceola County Herald.

RICHMOND

US

REVIEW, THE. 1876. Mon. $.50 newsstand; $19.95/yr. mailed locally. 68834 S. Main St., Richmond, MI 48062. TEL 810-727-3745; FAX 810-727-3929. **Owner(s):** Sanilac Publishing, Inc., 4325 S. Sandusky Rd., Sandusky, MI 48471. TEL 810-648-4000; Ed. Jeff Payne; Pub. John D. Johnson; adv. contact: Mary Stevens. pub. size: tabloid; circ. 8,500(free & paid).

ROCHESTER

US

ROCHESTER CLARION. 1898. Thu. $.50 newsstand; $19/yr. in cy.; $24/yr. out of cy. 313 Main St., Rochester, MI 48308. TEL 810-651-4321; FAX 810-651-8243. **Owner(s):** Justin W. Wilcox, P.O. Box 9, Rochester, MI 48307. TEL 313-651-4321; Ed. Tony Manolatos. pub. size: broadsheet; circ. 10,000(paid).

ROCHESTER HILLS

US

ROCHESTER ECCENTRIC. 1972. s-w.: Mon. & Thu. $.75 newsstand; $42/yr. in cy. 1814 S. Rochester Rd., Rochester Hills, MI 48307. TEL 810-651-7575; FAX 810-651-9080. **Owner(s):** Suburban Communications Corp., 36251 Schoolcraft Rd., Livonia, MI 48150. TEL 313-591-2300; Ed. Bob Sklar. adv. contact: Bob Kampf. pub. size: broadsheet; circ. 10,000(paid).

US

TROY ECCENTRIC. 1972. s-w.: Mon. & Thu. $.50 newsstand; $36.40/yr. in cy. 1814 S. Rochester Rd., Rochester Hills, MI 48307. TEL 810-651-7575; FAX 810-651-9080. **Owner(s):** Suburban Communications Corp., 36251 Schoolcraft Rd., Livonia, MI 48150. TEL 313-591-2300; Ed. Bob Sklar. adv. contact: Tom Byrd. photos; bk.rev.; pub. size: broadsheet; circ. 10,500(paid).

ROCKFORD

US

ROCKFORD SQUIRE. 1983. Thu. free local; $20/yr. mailed. 51 E. Bridge St., Rockford, MI 49341. TEL 616-866-4465; FAX 616-866-3810. **Owner(s):** Rockford Publishing Co., 51 E. Bridge St., Rockford, MI 48341. TEL 616-866-3810; Pub. Roger Allen; adv. contact: Joanne Klukowski. bk.rev.; pub. size: tabloid; circ. 8,700(free & paid).

ROGERS CITY

US

PRESQUE ISLE ADVANCE. 1878. Thu. $.50 newsstand; $23/yr. in cy.; $24/yr. in state; $25/yr. out of state. 104 S. Third St., Rogers City, MI 49779. TEL 517-734-2105. **Owner(s):** Presque Isle Newspapers, Inc., 104 S. Third, Rogers City, MI 49779. TEL 517-734-2105; Ed. Richard Lamb; Pub. Richard Lamb; pub. size: broadsheet; circ. 4,300(paid).

ROMEO

US

ROMEO OBSERVER. 1866. Wed. $.50 newsstand; $10/yr. 124 W. St. Clair, Romeo, MI 48065-0096. TEL 810-752-3524. **Owner(s):** Romeo Observer Inc., 124 W. St. Clair, Romeo, MI 48065. TEL 313-752-3524; Ed. Jim Wallington; Pub. Melvin E. Bleich; pub. size: standard; circ. 16,900(paid).

ROSCOMMON

US

ROSCOMMON COUNTY HERALD-NEWS. 1875. Sun. $.50 newsstand; $25/yr. mailed in state; $30/yr. out of state. 905 Lake St., Roscommon, MI 48653. TEL 517-275-5100. **Owner(s):** Robert Perlberg, P.O. Box 247, West Branch, MI 48661; Ed. Cindy Gibbs; Pub. Robert Perlberg; pub. size: broadsheet; circ. 15,000(paid).

ROYAL OAK

US

TRIBUNE PLUS. Sun. free; voluntary contribution. 210 E. Third St., Royal Oak, MI 48067. TEL 810-541-3000; FAX 810-541-7903. **Owner(s):** Independent Newspapers, Inc., 100 Macomb Daily Dr., Mount Clemens, MI 48043. TEL 810-469-4510; Pub. R.D. Isham; adv. contact: Mary Vellardita. pub. size: standard; circ. 101,000(free).

SAGINAW

US

SAGINAW PRESS, THE. 1912. Fri. $.25 newsstand; $10/yr. 410 Hancock St., Saginaw, MI 48602. TEL 517-793-8070; FAX 517-793-7225. **Owner(s):** Saginaw Publishing Co., 410 Hancock St., Saginaw, MI 48602. TEL 517-793-8070; Ed. George W. Baxter, III. adv.; pub. size: standard; circ. 700(controlled & paid).

US

TOWNSHIP TIMES. 1964. Wed. $.50 newsstand; $24/yr. 2089 Wieneke Rd., Saginaw, MI 48603-3338. TEL 517-799-3200; FAX 517-799-7085. **Owner(s):** Saginaw Community News, 2089 Wienke Rd., Saginaw, MI 48603. TEL 517-799-3200; Pub. Edward Belles; adv. contact: Bob Grnak. photos; pub. size: tabloid; circ. 10,000(free & paid).

SALINE

US

SALINE REPORTER. 1948. Wed. $.35 newsstand; $14/yr. in city; $17/yr. out of city. 106 W. Michigan Ave., Saline, MI 48176. TEL 313-429-7380; FAX 313-429-3621. **Owner(s):** Heritage News, Inc., Southgate, MI 48195. TEL 313-246-0800; pub. size: broadsheet; circ. 4,800(paid).

SANDUSKY

US

SANILAC COUNTY NEWS. 1971. Wed. $.75 newsstand; $17.75/yr. mailed in cy.; $32.50/yr. out of cy.; $16.50/yr. senior citizens. 432 S. Sandusky Rd., Sandusky, MI 48471. TEL 810-648-4000; FAX 810-648-4002. **Owner(s):** Sanilac Publishing, Inc., 432 S. Sandusky Rd., Sandusky, MI 48471. TEL 810-648-4000; Ed. Eric Levine; Pub. John D. Johnson; adv. contact: Carlene Soroka. pub. size: tabloid; circ. 32,500(free & paid).
    Formerly: Sandusky Sanilac County News.

SAUGATUCK

US

COMMERCIAL RECORD. 1882. Thu. $.50 newsstand; $15/yr. in cy. P.O. Box 246, Saugatuck, MI 49453. TEL 616-857-2570. **Owner(s):** Kaechele Publications, Inc., P.O. Box 189, Allegan, MI 49010. TEL 616-673-5534; Ed. Donita Hunt; Pub. Cheryl Kaechele; adv.; photos; pub. size: broadsheet; circ. 5,000(paid).

SEBEWAING

US

NEWSWEEKLY. 1890. Tue. $.50 newsstand; $21/yr. mailed locally; $31/yr. elsewhere. 236 N. Center St., Sebewaing, MI 48759. TEL 517-883-3100; FAX 517-883-9211. **Owner(s):** Walt Disney Co., 500 S. Buena Vista St., Burbank, CA 91521. TEL 818-560-5300; Ed. Mark Rummel. adv. contact: Lorrine Kuhl. pub. size: tabloid; circ. 7,200(paid).
    Formerly: Blade & Progress Newsweekly.

SOUTHGATE

US

NEWS-HERALD, THE. s-w.: Wed. & Sun. $.75 newsstand; $48/yr. home deliv.; $78/yr. mailed. One Heritage Pl., Ste. 100, Southgate, MI 48195. TEL 313-246-0800; FAX 313-284-2028. **Owner(s):** Heritage Newspapers, Inc., One Heritage Pl., Ste. 100, Southgate, MI 48195. TEL 313-246-0800; Ed. Karl Ziomek; Pub. Fredrick Manuel; adv. contact: Darrell Futo. photos; pub. size: broadsheet; circ. 84,902(controlled & paid); Sun. 89,540(controlled & paid).
    Formerly: Lincoln Park News-Herald, The.

SOUTH LYON

US

SOUTH LYON HERALD. 1880. Thu. $.50 newsstand; $26/yr. in cy.; $32/yr. out of cy. 101 N. Lafayette, South Lyon, MI 48178. TEL 810-437-2011; FAX 810-437-9460. **Owner(s):** Hometown Newspapers, 323 E. Grand River, Howell, MI 48843. TEL 517-548-2000; Ed. Rick Byrne; Pub. Rich Perlberg; adv. contact: Lisa M. Dranginis. pub. size: broadsheet; circ. 6,000(paid).

SPARTA

US

SPARTA/KENT CITY ADVANCE. 1989. Tue. free in area; $20/6 mos. out of area; $30/yr. out of area. 151 E. Division, Sparta, MI 49345. TEL 616-887-8400; FAX 616-887-7230. **Owner(s):** Valley Media, Inc., 2141 Port Sheldon Rd., Jenison, MI 49428. TEL 616-669-2700; FAX 616-669-1162; Ed. Mike Wyngarden; Pub. Joel Holland; pub. size: tabloid; circ. 12,075(free & paid).

STANDISH

US

ARENAC COUNTY INDEPENDENT. 1883. Wed. $.50 newsstand; $18/yr. mailed in cy. $25/yr. out of cy.; $30/yr. out of state. 203 E. Cedar, Standish, MI 48658. TEL 517-846-4531; FAX 517-846-9868. **Owner(s):** R.E. Perlberg, P.O. Box 699, Standish, MI 48658. TEL 517-846-4531; Ed. Ben Welmers; Pub. Robert Perlberg; adv. contact: Kip Pamransky. pub. size: broadsheet; circ. 6,000(paid).
    Formerly: Standish Arenac County Independent.

ST. IGNACE

US

ST. IGNACE NEWS, THE. 1878. Thu. $.50 newsstand; $24/yr. 359 Reagon St., St. Ignace, MI 49781-0277. TEL 906-643-9150; FAX 906-643-9122. **Owner(s):** St. Ignace News, 359 Reagon St., St. Ignace, MI 49781-0277. TEL 906-643-9150; Ed. Wesley H. Maurer, Jr.; Pub. Wesley H. Maurer; adv. contact: Richard Hayden. photos; bk.rev.; pub. size: broadsheet; circ. 6,700(paid).

ST. JOHNS

US

CLINTON COUNTY NEWS. 1930. Sun. free newsstand & local deliv.; $1.04/yr. mailed first class. 215 N. Clinton Ave., St. Johns, MI 48879. TEL 517-224-2361; FAX 517-224-4452. **Owner(s):** Community Newspapers, Inc., 239 S. Cochran St., Charlotte, MI 48813; Ed. Al Wilson; Pub. Preston Odette; pub. size: tabloid; circ. 13,767(free & paid).

US

DEWITT BATH REVIEW. 1979. Sun. $.35 newsstand; free home deliv. 215 N. Clinton, St. Johns, MI 48879. TEL 517-224-2361; FAX 517-224-4452. **Owner(s):** Lansing Suburban Newspaper Network, Inc., 239 S. Cochran, Charlotte, MI 48113. TEL 517-627-6085; Ed. Jennifer Vincent; Pub. Preston O'Dette; adv.; pub. size: broadsheet; circ. 8,050(free).

US

ST. JOHNS REMINDER. 1949. Sat. free newsstand; $32/yr. 109 W. Higham, St. Johns, MI 48879. TEL 517-224-8356; FAX 517-224-9458. **Owner(s):** Clinton Distribution, Inc., P.O. Box 473, St. Johns, MI 48879. TEL 517-224-8357; Pub. Rebecca Wood; adv.; pub. size: tabloid; circ. 14,500(paid).

STOCKBRIDGE

US

TOWN CRIER. 1967. Tue. $15/yr. in state; $20/yr. out of state. 510 Water St., Stockbridge, MI 49285-0548. TEL 517-851-7833; FAX 517-851-4641. **Owner(s):** Charlotte Camp, Stockbridge, MI 49285; Ed. Ruth Camp Wellman; Pub. Ruth Camp Wellman; adv.; pub. size: tabloid; circ. 9,000(paid).

SWARTZ CREEK

US

DAVISON FLAGSTAFF. s-w.: Thu. & Sun. free deliv.; $.25 newsstand. P.O. Box 497, Swartz Creek, MI 48473. TEL 810-733-2239; FAX 810-733-2688. **Owner(s):** Flint Advance Newspapers, G 5085 Miller Rd., Flint, MI 48507. TEL 810-238-5070; Ed. Dennis Setter; Pub. Joel Holland; adv. contact: Tom Reynolds. pub. size: broadsheet; circ. 9,300(free).

TECUMSEH

US

TECUMSEH HERALD. 1850. Thu. $.50 newsstand; $22/yr. in cy.; $24/yr. out of cy. 110 E. Logan St., Tecumseh, MI 49286. TEL 517-423-2174; FAX 517-423-6258. **Owner(s):** James C., Dorothy L., & James L. Lincoln, 459 Seminole Dr., Tecumseh, MI 49286. TEL 517-423-7096; Ed. James L. Lincoln; Pub. James C. Lincoln; pub. size: broadsheet; circ. 5,500(paid).

THREE RIVERS

US

PENNY SAVER. 1985. Sun. free. 124 N. Main St., Three Rivers, MI 49093. TEL 616-279-7488; FAX 616-279-6007. **Owner(s):** Richard L. Milliman, 124 N. Main St., Three Rivers, MI 49093. TEL 616-279-7488; Ed. Joe Albertson; Pub. Lori Bogda; adv. contact: Lori Bogda. pub. size: tabloid; circ. 16,400(free). **Wire Service(s):** AP, NEA, CNS.

TROY

US

TROY-SOMERSET GAZETTE. 1980. Mon. free newsstand; $.75/wk. mailed. 1903 E. Wattles, Troy, MI 48098. TEL 810-524-4858; FAX 810-524-9140. **Owner(s):** Claire M. Springer, 6506 Tanglewood, Troy, MI 48098. TEL 810-828-8523; Ed. Cynthia Knett; Pub. Claire M. Springer; adv. contact: Kathy Troshyski. photos; pub. size: tabloid, 4 color photos/art; circ. 25,000(free). **Wire Service(s):** PR.

VANDERBILT

US

OUR HOME TOWN. 1956. Thu. $.25 newsstand; $14/yr. local. 540 E. Main St., Vanderbilt, MI 49795. TEL 517-732-7167. **Owner(s):** Tom Serino, P.O. Box 101, Vanderbilt, MI 49795-0101. TEL 517-983-4132. Ed. Tom Serino; Pub. Tom Serino; adv.; photos; bk.rev.; pub. size: tabloid; circ. 1,100(paid).

VASSAR

US

VASSAR PIONEER TIMES. 1857. Wed. $12/yr. 113 S. Main St., Vassar, MI 48768. TEL 517-823-8579; FAX 517-823-8778. **Owner(s):** Hearst Corp., 959 Eighth Ave., New York, NY 10019. TEL 216-642-5516; Ed. Sandy Walker. pub. size: tabloid; circ. 1,813(paid).

VICKSBURG

US

COMMERCIAL-EXPRESS. 1879. Wed. $.50 newsstand; $18/yr. 109 S. Main, Vicksburg, MI 49097. TEL 616-649-2333; FAX 616-649-2335. **Owner(s):** McGraw Publishing Inc., 109 S. Main, Vicksburg, MI 49097. TEL 616-649-2333; Ed. Jodie DeGrave; Pub. Scott McGraw; pub. size: tabloid; circ. 2,000(paid).

WARREN

US

TECH CENTER NEWS. 1976. Mon. free. 31201 Chicago Rd., B-300, Warren, MI 48093. TEL 810-939-6800; FAX 810-939-5850. **Owner(s):** Monday Morning Newspapers, Inc., 31201 Chicago Rd., S., Ste. B-300, Warren, MI 48093. TEL 810-939-6800; FAX 810-939-5850; Ed. Peter Salinas; Pub. Bill Springer; adv.; pub. size: broadsheet; circ. 16,200(controlled & free).

WATERFORD

US

SPINAL COLUMN NEWSWEEKLY. 1960. Wed. $.50 newsstand; $26/yr. in area. 7196 Cooley Lake Rd., Waterford, MI 48327. TEL 810-360-6397. **Owner(s):** Union Lake Spinal Column, 7196 Cooley Lake Rd., Union Lake, MI 48327. TEL 313-360-6397; Ed. Tim Dmoch; Pub. James W. Fancy; pub. size: tabloid; circ. 50,000(controlled).

WATERVLIET

US

TRI-CITY RECORD, THE. 1882. Thu. $.50 newsstand; $21/yr. in cy.; $23/yr. out of cy.; $26/yr. out of state. 138 N. Main St., Watervliet, MI 49098. TEL 616-463-6397; FAX 616-463-8329. **Owner(s):** Anne & Karl Bayer, 138 N. Main St., Watervliet, MI 49098; Ed. Karl Bayer; Pub. Anne Bayer; adv.; pub. size: broadsheet; circ. 2,700(paid).

WAYNE

US

BELLEVILLE ENTERPRISE. 1886. s-w.: Thu. & Sun. $.50 newsstand; $24/yr. 35540 Michigan Ave. W., Wayne, MI 48184. TEL 313-729-4000; FAX 313-729-6088. **Owner(s):** Mike Wilcox, P.O. Box 578, Wayne, MI 48184. TEL 313-729-4000; Ed. Joan Byer-Zinner; Pub. Mike Wilcox; pub. size: broadsheet; circ. 5,241(paid).

US

CANTON EAGLE. 1945. s-w.: Thu. & Sun. $.50 newsstand; $26/yr. 35540 Michigan Ave., Wayne, MI 48184. TEL 313-729-4000; FAX 313-729-6088. **Owner(s):** Michigan Community Newspaper, 35540 Michigan Ave., Wayne, MI 48184; Ed. Joan Dyer-Zinner; Pub. Mike Wilcox; adv. contact: Ron Spielman. pub. size: broadsheet; circ. 10,148(controlled).

US

INKSTER LEDGER-STAR. 1945. s-w.: Thu. & Sun. $24/yr. local; $48/yr. elsewhere. 35540 Michigan Ave., Wayne, MI 48184. TEL 313-729-4000; FAX 313-729-6088. **Owner(s):** Michigan Community Newspaper, 35540 Michigan Ave., Wayne, MI 48184. TEL 313-729-4000; FAX 313-729-6088; Ed. Mike Wilcox; Pub. Mike Wilcox; pub. size: broadsheet; circ. 4,500(paid).

US

ROMULUS ROMAN. 1885. s-w.: Thu. & Sun. $.50 newsstand; $24/yr. 5540 Michigan Ave. W., Wayne, MI 48184. TEL 313-729-4000; FAX 313-729-6088. **Owner(s):** Mike Wilcox, P.O. Box 578, Wayne, MI 48184. TEL 313-729-4000; Ed. Joan Byer-Zinner; Pub. Mike Wilcox; pub. size: broadsheet; circ. 5,039(paid).

US

WAYNE EAGLE. 1945. s-w.: Thu. & Sun. $.50 newsstand; $26/yr. 35540 Michigan Ave. W., Wayne, MI 48184. TEL 313-729-4000; FAX 313-729-6088. **Owner(s):** Mike Wilcox, P.O. Box 578, Wayne, MI 48184. TEL 313-729-4000; Ed. Joan Dyer-Zinner; Pub. Mike Wilcox; pub. size: broadsheet; circ. 6,069(paid).

US

WESTLAND EAGLE. 1945. s-w.: Thu. & Sun. $.50 newsstand; $26/yr. 35540 Michigan Ave., Wayne, MI 48184. TEL 313-729-4000; FAX 313-729-6088. **Owner(s):** Michigan Community Newspapers, 35540 Michigan Ave., Wayne, MI 48184. TEL 313-729-4000; Ed. Mike Wilcox; Pub. Mike Wilcox; pub. size: broadsheet; circ. 17,459(paid).

WEST BRANCH

US

OGEMAW COUNTY HERALD. 1880. Thu. $18/yr. in cy.; $25/yr. out of cy.; $30/yr. out of state. 215 W. Houghton Ave., West Branch, MI 48661. TEL 517-345-0044. **Owner(s):** Robert Perlberg, 215 W. Houghton Ave., West Branch, MI 48661. TEL 517-345-0044; Ed. Cindy Gibbs; Pub. Robert Pearlberg; adv. contact: Kipp Pomranky. pub. size: broadsheet; circ. 10,000(paid).

US

STAR BUYERS GUIDE. 1972. Sun. free. 420 W. Houghton Ave., West Branch, MI 48661. TEL 517-345-0510; FAX 517-732-5125. **Owner(s):** Star Publications, P.O. Box 620, Gaylord, MI 49735. TEL 517-732-5105; FAX 517-732-9322; Pub. James R. Glasser; adv. contact: David Baragrey. pub. size: tabloid; circ. 25,858(free).

WHITEHALL

US

WHITE LAKE BEACON. 1983. Mon. $.35 newsstand; free. 432 Spring St., Whitehall, MI 49461. TEL 616-894-5356; FAX 616-894-2174. **Owner(s):** White Lake Beacon, Inc., 432 Spring St., Whitehall, MI 49461. TEL 616-894-5356; FAX 616-894-2174; Ed. Gregory N. Means. adv. contact: James Young. photos; pub. size: tabloid; circ. 11,700(free).

MINNESOTA

ADA

US

ADA NORMAN COUNTY INDEX. 1880. Tue. $.75 newsstand; $21/yr. in cy.; $26/yr. in state; $30/yr. out of state. 307 W. Main St., Ada, MN 56510-0148. TEL 218-784-2541; FAX 218-784-2551. **Owner(s):** Index Printing, Inc., 307 W. Main St., Ada, MN 56510. TEL 218-784-2541; Ed. Ross D. Pfund; Pub. John R. Pfund; adv.; photos; pub. size: standard; circ. 2,450(free & paid).

AITKIN

US

AITKIN INDEPENDENT AGE. 1883. Wed. $25/yr. local; $30/yr. out of cy.; $35/yr. out of state. 213 Minnesota Ave., N., Aitkin, MN 56431. TEL 218-927-3761; FAX 218-927-3763. **Owner(s):** Mead Trust, 526 N. First St., Seward, NE 68434. TEL 402-643-4411; Evelyn Mead, 526 N. First St., Seward, NE 68434. TEL 402-643-4411; Evonne Agnello, 1214 N. Frace, Tacoma, WA 98406. TEL 206-752-8083; Ed. Ann Schwartz. adv. contact: Eric Heglund. pub. size: broadsheet; circ. 5,860(paid).

ALEXANDRIA

US

ECHO PRESS, THE. 1875. s-w.: Wed. & Fri. $.75 newsstand; $39/yr. mailed in state; $52/yr. out of state. 225 Seventh Ave. E., Alexandria, MN 56308. TEL 612-763-3133; FAX 612-763-3258. **Owner(s):** Forum Communications, Inc., 101 Fifth St. N., Fargo, ND 58102; Ed. Al Edenloff; Pub. Jon O. Haaven; adv. contact: Jody Hansen. pub. size: broadsheet; circ. 10,000(paid).
Formerly: Echo, The.

BAGLEY

US   ISSN 0889-3470

FARMERS INDEPENDENT. 1918. Wed. $.50 newsstand; $16/yr. in cy.; $20/yr. out of cy. 102 N. Main, Bagley, MN 56621. TEL 218-694-6265. **Owner(s):** Farmers Independent, 102 N. Main, Bagley, MN 56621. TEL 218-694-6265; Ed. Tom Burford; Pub. Tom Burford; adv.; photos; pub. size: broadsheet; circ. 2,650(free & paid).

BAUDETTE

US

BAUDETTE REGION, THE. 1902. w. $.50 newsstand; $20/yr. local; $26/yr. out of area. P.O. Drawer C, Baudette, MN 56623-0240. TEL 218-634-1722; FAX 218-634-1224. **Owner(s):** North Star Publishing Co., International Falls, MN 56649. TEL 218-285-7411; Ed. John C. Oren; Pub. John C. Oren; adv.: $4.10/SAU. photos; pub. size: broadsheet; circ. 2,201(free & paid).

BELGRADE

US

OBSERVER, THE. 1969. w. $.35 newsstand; $12/yr. in cy.; $14/yr. elsewhere. 303 Washburn Ave., Belgrade, MN 56312. TEL 612-254-8250; FAX 612-254-3215. **Owner(s):** Jim Lemmer, 303 Washburn, Belgrade, MN 56326-0720; Ed. Jim Lemmer; Pub. Jim Lemmer; adv. contact: Grace Scheel. photos; pub. size: tabloid; circ. 1,200(controlled & paid).

BEMIDJI

US

ADVERTISER, THE. s-w.: Wed. & Sun. free. 1320 Neilson Ave., S.E., Bemidji, MN 56601. TEL 218-751-3740; FAX 218-751-6914. **Owner(s):** Park Communications, Inc., Vine Ctr. Office Tower, 333 W. Vine St., 17th Fl., Lexington, KY 40507. TEL 606-252-7275; adv. contact: Jeff Halversen. pub. size: standard; circ. 20,000(free).

BENSON

US

BENSON SWIFT COUNTY MONITOR-NEWS. 1887. Wed. $25/yr. local; $29/yr. in state; $33/yr. out of state. 101 12th St., S., Benson, MN 56215. TEL 320-843-4111; FAX 320-843-3246. **Owner(s):** Reed Anfinson, 101 12th St., S., Benson, MN 56215. TEL 320-843-4111; Rob Anfinson, 101 12th St., S., Benson, MN 56215. TEL 320-843-4111; Ed. Reed Anfinson. pub. size: broadsheet; circ. 3,104(paid).

BIRD ISLAND

US

BIRD ISLAND UNION. 1881. Wed. $.65 newsstand; $24/yr. in cy.; $27/yr. out of cy.; $32/yr. out of state. 750 Ash Ave., Bird Island, MN 55310. TEL 612-365-3266; FAX 612-365-3266. **Owner(s):** Hubin Publishing, 201 Main St., Hector, MN. TEL 612-848-2248; FAX 612-848-2249; Ed. Bren McDowell; Pub. John Hubin; adv.; photos; pub. size: broadsheet; circ. 1,000(paid).

BLAINE

US

BLAINE BANNER. 1985. m.: 1st Wed. free newsstand; $22/yr. 12570 Radisson Rd. N.E., Blaine, MN 55449. **Owner(s):** Blaine Banner, 12570 Raddison Rd. NE, Blaine, MN 55449; adv.; photos; pub. size: tabloid; circ. 10,000(free & paid).

BLOOMINGTON

US

BLOOMINGTON SUN-CURRENT. 1954. Wed. $.75 newsstand; voluntary subscription; $40/yr. mailed. 7831 E. Bush Lake Rd., Bloomington, MN 55439. TEL 612-896-4700; FAX 612-896-4728. **Owner(s):** Minnesota Sun Publications LLC, 7831 E. Bush Lake Rd., Minneapolis, MN 55439. TEL 612-896-4700; Ed. Yvonne Klinnert; Pub. Denis Mindak; adv.; pub. size: tabloid; circ. 29,510(free & paid).

US

EDEN PRAIRIE SUN-CURRENT. 1932. Wed. $.75 newsstand; voluntary subscription; $40/yr. mailed. 7831 E. Bushlake Rd., Bloomington, MN 55439. TEL 612-896-4700; FAX 612-896-4728. **Owner(s):** Minnesota Sun Publications LLC, 7831 E. Bush Lake Rd., Bloomington, MN 55439. TEL 612-896-4700; Ed. Yvonne Klinnert; Pub. Denis Mindak; adv.; pub. size: tabloid; circ. 12,840(free & paid).

US

RICHFIELD SUN-CURRENT. Wed. free newsstand; $25/yr. mailed. 7831 E. Bush Lake Rd., Bloomington, MN 55439. TEL 612-896-4700; FAX 612-896-4728. **Owner(s):** Minnesota Sun Publications LLC, 7831 E. Bush Lake Rd., Minneapolis, MN 55439. TEL 612-896-4700; Ed. Yvonne Klinnert; Pub. Denis Mindak; pub. size: tabloid; circ. 13,514(free & paid).

BLUE EARTH

US

FARIBAULT COUNTY REGISTER. 1869. Mon. $.75 newsstand; $24.50/yr. in cy.; $29.50/yr. out of cy. 125 N. Main St. Blue Earth, MN 56013. TEL 507-526-7324; FAX 507-526-4080. **Owner(s):** Darwin & Bonnie Oordt, P.O. Box 100, Blue Earth, MN 56013. TEL 507-526-7324; FAX 507-526-4080; Ed. Kyle MacArthur; Pub. Bonnie Oordt; adv.; photos; bk.rev.; pub. size: tabloid; circ. 3,500(paid).

BUFFALO

US

WRIGHT COUNTY JOURNAL-PRESS. 1887. Thu. $25/yr. in state; $32/yr. out of state. 108 Central Ave., Buffalo MN 55313. TEL 612-682-1221; FAX 612-682-5458. **Owner(s):** James P. McDonnell, Jr., 108 Central Ave., Buffalo, MN 55313. TEL 612-545-8000; Ed. James P. McDonnell; Pub. James P. McDonnell; pub. size: broadsheet; circ. 6,500(paid).

BURNSVILLE

US

APPLE VALLEY/ROSEMONT SUN-CURRENT. 1975. Wed. free locally; $.75 newsstand; voluntary subscription; $40/yr. mailed. 1209 E. Cliff Rd., Burnsville, MN 55337. TEL 612-890-4456; FAX 612-890-4970. **Owner(s):** Minnesota Sun Publications LLC, 7831 E. Bush Lake Rd., Bloomington, MN 55439. TEL 612-896-4700; Ed. Yvonne Klinnert; Pub. Denis Mindak; adv.; pub. size: tabloid; circ. 15,043(free & paid).

US

BURNSVILLE SUN-CURRENT. 1976. Wed. free deliv.; $.75 newsstand; voluntary subscription; $40/yr. mailed. 1209 E. Cliff Rd., Burnsville, MN 55337. TEL 612-890-4456; FAX 612-890-4970. **Owner(s):** Minnesota Sun Publications LLC, 7831 E. Bush Lake Rd., Minneapolis, MN 55439. TEL 612-896-4700; Ed. Yvonne Klinnert; Pub. Denis Mindak; adv. contact: Mike Maslow. pub. size: tabloid; circ. 19,920(free & paid).

US   ISSN 8750-2895

DAKOTA COUNTY TRIBUNE. 1884. Thu. $.50 newsstand; $24/yr. 1525 E. Hwy. 13, Burnsville, MN 55337. TEL 612-894-1111; FAX 612-894-1859. **Owner(s):** Joseph R. Clay, 1525 E. Hwy. 13, Burnsville, MN 55337. TEL 612-894-1111; Daniel H. Clay, 1525 E. Hwy. 13, Burnsville, MN 55337. TEL 612-894-1111; Ed. B. Haugen. adv. contact: Cindy Warweg. pub. size: tabloid; circ. 2,000(paid).

US

EAGAN SUN-CURRENT. Wed. free; $.75 newsstand; voluntary subscription; $40/yr. mailed. 1209 E. Cliff Rd., Burnsville, MN 55337. TEL 612-890-4456; FAX 612-890-4970. **Owner(s):** Minnesota Sun Publications LLC, 7831 E. Bush Lake Rd., Minneapolis, MN 55439. TEL 612-896-4700 Ed. Yvonne Klinnert; Pub. Denis Mindak; adv. contact: Mike Maslow. pub. size: tabloid; circ. 17,855(free & paid).

Formerly: Eagan Chronicle.

LAKEVILLE

US

LAKEVILLE SUN-CURRENT. 1975. Wed. free; $.75 newsstand; voluntary subscription; $40/yr. in state. 1209 E. Cliff Rd., Burnsville, MN 55337. TEL 612-888-2240; FAX 612-890-4970. **Owner(s):** Minnesota Sun Publications LLC, 7831 E. Bush Lake Rd., Bloomington, MN 55439. TEL 612-896-4700; Ed. Yvonne Klinnert; Pub. Denis Mindak; adv. contact: Mike Maslow. pub. size: tabloid; circ. 20,000(free & paid).

SOUTH ST. PAUL/INVER GROVE HEIGHTS

US

SOUTH ST. PAUL/INVER GROVE HEIGHTS SUN-CURRENT. 1950. Wed. $.75 newsstand; voluntary subscription; $40/yr. mailed. 1209 E. Cliff Rd., Burnsville, MN 55337. TEL 612-890-4465; FAX 612-890-4970. **Owner(s):** Minnesota Sun Publications LLC, 7831 E. Bush Lake Rd., Edina, MN 55439. TEL 612-896-4700; Ed. Yvonne Klinnert; Pub. Denis Mindak; adv.; photos; pub. size: tabloid; circ. 14,500(free & paid).

WEST ST. PAUL/MENDOTA HEIGHTS

US

WEST ST. PAUL/MENDOTA HEIGHTS SUN-CURRENT. Wed. $.75 newsstand; voluntary subscription; $40/yr. mailed. 1209 E. Cliff Rd. Burnsville, MN 55337. TEL 612-890-4456; FAX 612-890-4970. **Owner(s):** Minnesota Sun Publications LLC, 7831 E. Bush Lake Rd., Minneapolis, MN 55439. TEL 612-896-4700; Ed. Yvonne Klinnert; Pub. Denis Mindak; adv.; pub. size: tabloid; circ. 10,200(free & paid).

CANBY

US

CANBY NEWS. 1878. Wed. $20/yr. in cy.; $23/yr. out of cy. 123 First St., E., Canby, MN 56220. TEL 507-223-5303; FAX 507-223-5404. **Owner(s):** Don & Ellie Berman, P.O. Box 129, Canby MN 56220. TEL 507-223-5303; Ed. Bridget Buesing. pub. size: broadsheet; circ. 3,947(paid).

CHANHASSEN

US

CHANHASSEN VILLAGER. 1985. Thu. free to residents; $22/yr. in cy. mailed; $33/yr. out of cy. 80 W. 78th St., Chanhassen, MN 55317. TEL 612-445-3333; FAX 612-934-7960. **Owner(s):** Southwest Suburban Publishing Co., P.O. Box 8, 327 Marschall Rd., Shakopee, MN 55379; Ed. Dean Trippler; Pub. Mark Weber; adv. contact: Gary Klatt. photos. pub. size: broadsheet; circ. 5,000(free & paid).

CHASKA

US

CHASKA HERALD. 1862. Thu. $22/yr. in cy. P.O. Box 113, Chaska, MN 55318. TEL 612-448-2650. **Owner(s):** Southwest Suburban Publishing, MN; Ed. LaVonne Barac; Pub. Stan Rolfsrud; pub. size: broadsheet; circ. 4,700(paid).

CHISHOLM

US

CHISHOLM FREE PRESS & TRIBUNE PRESS. 1947. s-w.: Tue. & Thu. $.30 newsstand; $20/yr. in cy.; $24/yr. out of cy. 216 W. Lake St., Chisholm, MN 55719. TEL 218-254-4432; FAX 218-254-4432. **Owner(s):** County Journal, Inc., 216 W. Lake St., Chisholm, MN 55719; Ed. Brian Anderson; Pub. Brian Anderson; adv.; photos; pub. size: tabloid; circ. 5,600(paid).

CLARISSA

US   ISSN 1065-0628

INDEPENDENT NEWS HERALD. 1891. Wed. $.50 newsstand; $20/yr. 310 W. Main St., Clarissa, MN 56440. TEL 218-756-2131; FAX 218-756-2126. **Owner(s):** Ernest & Diane Silbernagel, 310 W. Main St., Clarissa, MN 56440. TEL 218-756-2131; FAX 218-756-2126; Pub. Ernest J. Silbernagel; adv.; photos; bk.rev.; pub. size: broadsheet; circ. 2,557(paid).
    Formerly: News Herald.

CLINTON

US

NORTHERN STAR, THE. 1965. Thu. $.50 newsstand; $20/yr. in cy.; $23/yr. elsewhere. Main St., Clinton, MN 56225-0368. TEL 612-325-5152; FAX 612-325-5280. **Owner(s):** Kaercher Publications, Inc., Ortonville, MN 56278. TEL 612-839-6163; Ed. Lois Torgerson; Pub. James D. Kaercher; adv. contact: Denese Gustafson. pub. size: broadsheet; circ. 2,200(paid).

CLOQUET

US

CLOQUET BILLBOARD SHOPPER. 1962. Fri. free. 1418 S. Hwy. 33, Cloquet, MN 55720. TEL 218-879-6761; FAX 218-879-6696. **Owner(s):** Cloquet Newspapers, Inc., 1418 S. Hwy. 33, Cloquet, MN 55720. TEL 218-879-6761; Ed. Scott L. Elwood; Pub. Scott L. Elwood; adv. contact: Karen Bakke. pub. size: broadsheet; circ. 20,100(free).

US

CLOQUET PINE KNOT. 1884. s-w.: Thu. & Sat. $.50 newsstand; $23/yr. mailed in cy.; $29/yr. out of cy. 1418 S. Hwy. 33, Cloquet, MN 55720. TEL 218-879-6761. **Owner(s):** Cloquet Newspapers, Inc., 1418 S. Hwy 33, Cloquet, MN 55720. TEL 218-879-6761; Ed. Scott L. Elwood; Pub. Scott L. Elwood; adv. contact: Karen Bakke. pub. size: broadsheet; circ. 6,500(paid).

COON RAPIDS

US   ISSN 1059-9525

ANOKA COUNTY UNION. 1865. Fri. $.60 newsstand; $21/yr. 4101 Coon Rapids Blvd., Coon Rapids, MN 55433. TEL 612-421-4444; FAX 612-421-4315. **Owner(s):** ECM Publishers, Inc., 4101 Coon Rapids Blvd., Coon Rapids, MN 55433. TEL 612-421-4444; FAX 612-421-4315; Ed. Peter Bodley; Pub. Elmer L. Andersen; adv. contact: Hugh Campbell. photos; pub. size: broadsheet; circ. 5,800(paid).

US   ISSN 1059-9533

BLAINE-SPRING LAKE PARK LIFE. 1961. Fri. $.60 newsstand; $21/yr. 4101 Coon Rapids Blvd., Coon Rapids, MN 55433. TEL 612-421-4444; FAX 612-421-4315. **Owner(s):** ECM Publishers, Inc., 4101 Coon Rapids Blvd., Coon Rapids, MN 55433. TEL 612-421-4444; FAX 612-421-4315; Ed. Peter Bodley; Pub. Elmer L. Andersen; adv. contact: Hugh Campbell. photos; pub. size: broadsheet; circ. 2,100(paid).

US   ISSN 1059-9541

COON RAPIDS HERALD. 1875. Fri. $.60 newsstand; $21/yr. 4101 Coon Rapids Blvd., Coon Rapids, MN 55433. TEL 612-421-4444; FAX 612-421-4315. **Owner(s):** ECM Publishers, Inc., 4101 Coon Rapids Blvd., Coon Rapids, MN 55433. TEL 612-421-4444; FAX 612-421-4315; Ed. Peter G. Bailey; Pub. Elmer L. Andersen; adv. contact: Hugh Campbell. photos; pub. size: broadsheet; circ. 4,000(paid).

DETROIT LAKES

US

BECKER COUNTY RECORD. 1871. Sun. $.75 newsstand; free local carrier. 511 Washington Ave., Detroit Lakes, MN 56501. TEL 218-847-3151; FAX 218-847-9409. **Owner(s):** Detroit Lakes Printing Co., P.O. Box 826, Detroit Lakes, MN 56502. TEL 218-847-3151; Ed. Jamie Marks; Pub. Dennis Winskowski; adv. contact: Dave Aune. pub. size: broadsheet; circ. 20,000(free & paid).

US

DETROIT LAKES TRIBUNE. 1907. Thu. $.75 newsstand; $25.50/yr. mailed & motor rte. in cy.; $31/yr. out of cy.; $38/yr. in state. 511 Washington St., Detroit Lakes, MN 56501. TEL 218-847-3151; FAX 218-847-9409. **Owner(s):** Detroit Lakes Printing Co., P.O. Box 826, Detroit Lakes, MN 56502. TEL 218-847-3151; Ed. Jamie Marks; Pub. Dennis Winskowski; adv. contact: Dave Aune. pub. size: broadsheet; circ. 7,000(paid).

DULUTH

US

BUDGETEER PRESS/SKYWORLD DULUTH NEWS. 1931. Sun. $15/yr. 5807 Grand Ave., Duluth, MN 55807-2459. TEL 218-624-3665; FAX 218-624-7927. **Owner(s):** Murphy Newspapers, Inc., 1226 Ogden Avenue, Superior, MN 54880. TEL 715-394-4411; Ed. Richard Palmer. adv. contact: Jeff Swor. pub. size: broadsheet; circ. 60,000(controlled & paid).
    Formerly: Duluth Budgeteer/Skyworld Duluth News/Uptowner.

EDGERTON

US

EDGERTON ENTERPRISE, THE. 1883. Wed. $.50 newsstand; $20/yr. in cy.; $25/yr. elsewhere. P.O. Box 397, 831 Main St., Edgerton, MN 56128-0397. TEL 507-442-6161; FAX 507-442-6161. **Owner(s):** Melvin DeBoer, 831 Main St., Edgerton, MN 56128-0397. TEL 507-442-6161; FAX 507-442-6161; Ed. Melvin DeBoer; Pub. Melvin DeBoer; adv. contact: Melvin DeBoer. photos; pub. size: broadsheet; circ. 2,000(paid).

ELY

US   ISSN 0746-7087

ELY ECHO. 1972. Mon. $.75 newsstand; $20/yr. in cy.; $30/yr. out of cy.; $40/yr. out of state. 2 E. Sheridan St., Ely, MN 55731-1257. TEL 218-365-3141; FAX 218-365-3142. **Owner(s):** Milestones, Inc., 2 East Sheridan, Ely, MN 55731. TEL 218-365-3141; FAX 218-365-3142; Ed. Tom Coombe; Pub. Anne Wognum; adv. contact: Anne Wognum. pub. size: broadsheet; circ. 4,403(paid).

ERSKINE

US

ERSKINE ECHO, THE. 1902. w. $.50 newsstand; $16/yr. 309 First St., Erskine, MN 56535-0016. TEL 218-687-3775. **Owner(s):** Robert M. Hole, 309 First St., Erskine, MN 56535. TEL 218-687-3775; photos; pub. size: standard.

FAIRMONT

US

FAIRMONT PHOTO PRESS. 1963. Wed. free carrier & motor rte.; $33.35/yr. mailed. 112 E. First St., Fairmont, MN 56031. TEL 507-238-9456; FAX 507-238-9457. **Owner(s):** Wayne L. Schroeder, 112 E. First St., Fairmont, MN 56031. TEL 507-235-3855; Sherman L. Kumba, 238 Amber Lake Dr., Fairmont, MN 56031. TEL 507-238-1192; Ed. Sherman L. Kumba; Pub. Wayne L. Schroeder; pub. size: tabloid; circ. 11,750(free & paid).

FOREST LAKE

US   ISSN 0892-1784

ST. CROIX VALLEY PEACH. 1954. Mon. free in area; $.65/issue out of area; $81/yr. out of area. 880 SW. 15th St., Forest Lake, MN 55025-1381. TEL 612-464-4601; FAX 612-464-4605. **Owner(s):** ECM Publishers, Inc., Princeton, MN; adv. contact: Roxie Muehlberg. pub. size: tabloid; circ. 33,684(paid).

US

TIMES, THE. 1904. Thu. $.65 newsstand; $29/yr. in state; $36/yr. out of state. 880 S.W. 15th St., Forest Lake, MN 55025. TEL 612-464-4601; FAX 612-464-4605. **Owner(s):** ECM Publishers, Inc., 1201 15th Ave., S., Princeton, MN 55371. TEL 612-464-4601; Pub. Carol Deitner; adv. contact: Carol Deitner. pub. size: tabloid; circ. 3,903(paid).

FOSSTON

US

FOSSTON THIRTEEN TOWNS. 1884. Mon. $.50 newsstand; $16-$20/yr. 116 2nd St., N.W., Fosston, MN 56542. TEL 218-435-1313; FAX 218-435-1309. **Owner(s):** C & K Publishing, Inc., 606 2nd St. N.W., Fosston, MN 56542. TEL 218-435-1313; FAX 218-435-1309; Ed. David S. Carr. pub. size: broadsheet; circ. 3,100(paid).

GLENCOE

US

GLENCOE ENTERPRISE. 1873. Thu. $22/yr. in cy.; $25/yr. out of cy. 831 11th St., Glencoe, MN 55336. TEL 612-864-4715; FAX 612-864-6472. **Owner(s):** Annamarie Tudhope, P.O. Box 97, Glencoe, MN 55336. TEL 612-864-4715; Ed. Annamarie Tudhope; Pub. Annamarie Tudhope; adv.; photos; bk.rev.; pub. size: standard; circ. 4,200(paid).

GLENWOOD

US

POPE COUNTY TRIBUNE. 1920. Mon. $.75 newsstand; $21/yr. 108 S. Franklin, Glenwood, MN 56334. TEL 612-634-4571; FAX 612-634-5522. **Owner(s):** John R. Stone, P.O. Box 157, Glenwood, MN 56334. TEL 612-634-4571; Pub. John R. Stone; adv. contact: Stacy Gerdes. photos; pub. size: broadsheet; circ. 4,000(paid).
    Formerly: Glenwood Pope County Tribune.

GONVICK

US

LEADER-RECORD. w. $.75 newsstand; $18/yr. in cy.; $23/yr. out of cy. P.O. Box 159, Gonvick, MN 56644. TEL 218-776-3665; FAX 218-487-5251. **Owner(s):** Richard Richards, Box 159, Gonvick, MN 56644. TEL 218-487-5225; Ed. C. J. Richards; Pub. Dick Richards; adv.; photos; bk.rev.; pub. size: tabloid; circ. 2,252(paid).

GRAND RAPIDS

US

GRAND RAPIDS HERALD-REVIEW. 1894. s-w.: Sun. & Wed. $.75 newsstand; $38/yr. carrier; $40/yr. motor rte.; $45/yr. mailed. 301 First Ave., N.W., Grand Rapids, MN 55744. TEL 218-326-6623; FAX 218-326-6627. **Owner(s):** Murphy-McGinnis Media, 625 First Bank Pl., 130 W. Superior St., Duluth, MN 55802. TEL 218-723-8000; Ed. Wanda Moeller. adv. contact: Steve Lynch. photos; pub. size: tabloid; circ. 21,000(paid).

GRANITE FALLS

US

GRANITE FALLS/CLERKFIELD ADVOCATE TRIBUNE. 1883. w. $30/yr. 138 Eighth Ave., Granite Falls, MN 56241. TEL 320-564-2126; FAX 320-564-4293. **Owner(s):** Mainstream Publications, Northfield, MN; Ed. Tim Johnson; Pub. Tim Douglass; pub. size: broadsheet; circ. 4,100(paid).
    Formerly: Granite Falls Tribune.

GRYGLA

US

GRYGLA EAGLE. 1973. Thu. $18/yr. in trade area; $23/yr. outside of area. Main St., Grygla, MN 56727. TEL 218-294-6220; FAX 218-294-6220. **Owner(s):** Richards Publishing Co., Inc., Box 159, Gonvick, MN 56644. TEL 218-487-5225; Ed. Joy Nordby; Pub. Dick Richards; adv.; pub. size: tabloid; circ. 1,000(paid).

HASTINGS

US

HASTINGS STAR GAZETTE. 1857. Thu. $1 newsstand; $31.50/yr. local. 741 Spiral Blvd., Hastings, MN 55033. TEL 612-437-6153; FAX 612-437-5911. **Owner(s):** Arlin Albright, Red Wing, MN 55066; Ed. Doug Schult; Pub. Steve Messick; adv. contact: Ross Ulrich. pub. size: broadsheet; circ. 6,500(paid).

HAWLEY

US

HAWLEY HERALD. 1890. Mon. $.65 newsstand; $20/yr. in cy.; $22.50/yr. out of cy. 608 Main St., Hawley, MN 56549. TEL 218-483-3306; FAX 218-483-4457. **Owner(s):** Eugene Prim, P.O. Box 709, Hawley, MN 56549. TEL 218-483-3306; Ed. Linda Walter; Pub. Tom Jensen; pub. size: broadsheet; circ. 1,700(paid).

HUTCHINSON

US

HUTCHINSON LEADER. 1882. s-w.: Tue. & Thu. $39/yr. local. 36 Washington Ave., W., Hutchinson, MN 55350-2240. TEL 612-587-5000; FAX 612-587-6104. **Owner(s):** Red Wing Publishing Co., P.O. Box 82, Red Wing, MN 55066 TEL 612-388-8235; FAX 612-388-8912; Ten Part, 36 Washington Ave., W., Hutchinson, MN 55350. TEL 612-587-5000; Ed. Richard Crawford. adv.; photos; bk.rev.; pub. size: broadsheet; circ. 5,011(paid).

JACKSON

US

JACKSON COUNTY LIVEWIRE. 1929. Mon. free in area; $14/yr. out of area. 310 Second St., Jackson, MN 56143-0208. TEL 507-847-3771; FAX 507-847-5822. **Owner(s):** Jim Keul, P.O. Box 208, Jackson, MN 56143-0208. TEL 507-847-3771; FAX 507-847-5822; Ed. Jarrod Igou; Pub. Jim Keul; adv. contact: Dallas Luhmann. pub. size: tabloid; circ. 9,200(free & paid).

JASPER

US   ISSN 0744-3110

JASPER JOURNAL. 1888. Mon. $.50 newsstand; $16.50/yr. local $21/yr. elsewhere. P.O. Box 188, Jasper, MN 56144. TEL 507-348-4176; FAX 507-825-2168. **Owner(s):** Pipestone Publishing Co., P.O. Box 277, Pipestone, MN 56164. TEL 507-825-3333; Ed. Charles Draper; Pub. Charles Draper; adv. contact: Deloris Quissell. pub. size: tabloid; circ. 933(paid).

KENYON

US

KENYON LEADER. 1885. Wed. $.50 newsstand; $18/yr. in cy.; $20/yr. in state; $24/yr. out of state. 638 Second St., Kenyon, MN 55946. TEL 507-789-6161; FAX 507-789-6161. **Owner(s):** Noah Publishing, Inc., 638 Second St., Kenyon, MN 55946. TEL 507-789-6161; FAX 507-789-6161; Ed. Douglas A. Noah; Pub. Robert Noah; adv.; photos; pub. size: broadsheet; circ. 1,949(free & paid).

LAKEFIELD

US

LAKEFIELD STANDARD. 1884. Wed. $.75 newsstand; $21/yr. in cy.; $24.50/yr. out of cy. 403 Main St., Lakefield, MN 56150. TEL 507-662-5555; FAX 507-662-6770. **Owner(s):** Lakefield Publishing Co., P.O. Box 249, Lakefield, MN 56150. TEL 507-662-5555; FAX 507-662-6375; Ed. Mark O. Erickson; Pub. Jim Keul; pub. size: broadsheet; circ. 1,750(paid).

LAKEVILLE

US

LAKEVILLE LIFE & TIMES. 1979. Sat. $.50 newsstand; $1.50/wk. 20777 Holyoke Ave. W., Lakeville, MN 55044. TEL 612-469-2181; FAX 612-469-2184; E-mail: lkvlpub@aol.com. **Owner(s):** Richard M. Sherman, 14135 Guthrie Ave., Apple Valley, MN 55124-6720; Barbara W. Sherman, 14135 Guthrie Ave., Apple Valley, MN 55124-6720; Ed. Richard M. Sherman; Pub. Richard M. Sherman; adv.; photos; pub. size: tabloid; circ. 17,970(free & paid).

LAMBERTON

US

LAMBERTON NEWS. 1923. Wed. $.50 newsstand; $17.50/yr. local; $20/yr. in state; $22.50/yr. out of state. 218 Main St., Lamberton, MN 56152. TEL 507-752-7181. FAX 507-752-7181. **Owner(s):** Joseph G. Dietl, 218 Main St., Lamberton, MN 56152. TEL 507-752-7181; FAX 507-752-7181; Pub. Joseph G. Dietl; adv.; photos; pub. size: standard.

LE CENTER

US

LE CENTER LEADER. 1895. Wed. $1 newsstand; $27.50/yr. in state; $37.50/yr. out of state. 62 E. Minnesota St., Le Center, MN 56057. TEL 612-357-2233; FAX 612-357-6656. **Owner(s):** Bob Bradford, 62 E. Minnesota St., Le Center, MN 56057. TEL 612-357-2233; Ed. Steve Jessop; Pub. Steve Jessop; adv. contact: Steve Jessop. pub. size: broadsheet; circ. 2,000(paid).

LEWISTON

US

LEWISTON JOURNAL. 1929. Tue. $20/yr. in cy.; $27/yr. out of cy. 220 E. Main, Lewiston, MN 55952. TEL 507-523-2119 FAX 507-523-2891. **Owner(s):** Mack Publishing, 924 Whitewater Ave., St. Charles, MN 55972. TEL 507-932-3663; Ed. Susan Schossel-Halter; Pub. Tim Mack; adv. contact: Tim Mack. pub. size: broadsheet; circ. 1,700(paid).

LINDSTROM

US

CHICAGO COUNTY PRESS. 1898. Thu. $.65 newsstand; $30,59/yr. in cy. $35/yr. out of cy. 12615 Lake Blvd., Lindstrom, MN 55045-0748. TEL 612-257-5115; FAX 612-257-5500. **Owner(s):** John A. Silver, 12615 Lake Blvd., P.O. Box 748, Lindstrom, MN 55045. TEL 612-257-5115; FAX 612-257-5500; Ed. Ellen Glenna; Pub. John A. Silver; adv. contact: Ellen Glenna. photos; bk.rev.; pub. size: broadsheet; circ. 4,333(free & paid).

LITCHFIELD

US

LITCHFIELD INDEPENDENT REVIEW. 1876. Thu. $.60 newsstand; $20/yr. in cy. $25/yr. out of cy. $28/yr. out of state. P.O. Box 921, Litchfield, MN 55355. TEL 612-693-3266; FAX 613-693-9177. **Owner(s):** Vernon Madson, P.O. Box 921, Litchfield, MN 55355. TEL 612-693-9177; Stanley Roeser, P.O. Box 921, Litchfield, MN 55355; pub. size: broadsheet; circ. 4,200(paid).

LONG PRAIRIE

US

LONG PRAIRIE LEADER. 1887. Wed. $.75 newsstand; $20/yr. in cy. 2 Third St., S., Long Prairie, MN 56347. TEL 612-732-2151; FAX 612-732-2152. **Owner(s):** Gary & Sharon Brown, P.O. Box 479, Long Prairie, MN 56387. TEL 612-732-2151; Ed. Sue Farmer; Pub. Gary Brown; adv.; pub. size: broadsheet; circ. 3,500(paid).

LUVERNE

US

ROCK COUNTY STAR HERALD. 1873. Thu. $.75 newsstand; $27/yr. in cy.; $35/yr. out of cy. 117 W. Main, Luverne, MN 56156. TEL 507-283-2333; FAX 507-283-2335. **Owner(s):** Tollefson Publishing, P.O. Box 327, Luverne, MN 56156. TEL 507-283-2333; Pub. Roger S. Tollefson; adv.; photos; pub. size: broadsheet; circ. 4,200(paid).

MADISON

US

MADISON WESTERN GUARD, THE. 1892. Wed. $.75 newsstand; $25/yr. 216 Sixth Ave., Madison, MN 56256. TEL 612-598-7521; FAX 612-598-7523. **Owner(s):** RBM Publications, Main St., Wheaton, MN 56296; Ed. Richard Gail; Pub. Richard Gail; adv. contact: Missy Schmidt. photos; pub. size: broadsheet; circ. 3,200(paid).

MAHNOMEN

US

MAHNOMEN PIONEER, THE. 1905. w. $.40 newsstand; $20/yr. P.O. Box 219, Mahnomen, MN 56557. TEL 218-935-5296. **Owner(s):** Patrick D. Kelly, P.O. Box 219, Mahnomen, MN 56557. TEL 218-935-5296; Ed. Sue Gruman. adv. contact: Patrick Kelly. photos; pub. size: broadsheet.

MCINTOSH

US

MCINTOSH TIMES. 1888. Wed. $18/yr. local; $23/yr. out of cy. 115 Broadway, N.W., McIntosh, MN 56556. TEL 218-563-3585; FAX 218-487-5251. **Owner(s):** Richard Richards, P.O. Box 159, Gonvick, MN 56644. TEL 218-487-5225; Ed. Mary Horacek. adv.; photos; pub. size: tabloid; circ. 1,350(paid).

MELROSE

US

MELROSE BEACON. 1890. Mon. $.50 newsstand; $19/yr. in area; $25/yr. in state; $30/yr. out of state. 408 E. Main St., Melrose, MN 56352. TEL 612-256-3240; FAX 612-256-3363. **Owner(s):** Stearns County Publishing, Inc., P.O. Box 186, Melrose, MN 56352. TEL 612-256-3240; Ed. Mike Kosik; Pub. Don Larson; adv. contact: Richard Raeker. photos; pub. size: broadsheet; circ. 4,500(paid).

MIDDLE RIVER

US ISSN 0747-4407

NEW RIVER RECORD. 1902. Thu. $15/yr.; $20/yr. out of area. Hill Ave., Middle River, MN 56737. TEL 218-222-3514. **Owner(s):** Richard Richards, P.O. Box 159, Gonvick, MN 56644. TEL 218-487-5225; Ed. Becky Rantanen. adv.; pub. size: tabloid; circ. 1,275(paid).

MILACA

US

MILLE LACS COUNTY TIMES. 1892. Wed. $.60 newsstand; $21/yr. local & surrounding cys.; $25/yr. in state; $30/yr. out of state. 225 S.W. Second St., Milaca, MN 56353. TEL 612-983-6111; FAX 612-983-6112. **Owner(s):** Elmer L. Andersen, 800 Rosedale Towers, St. Paul, MN 55113; Ed. Gary Larson. adv.; pub. size: broadsheet; circ. 3,500(paid).

MINNEAPOLIS

US

BROOKLYN CENTER SUN POST. 1956. Wed. $.75 newsstand; voluntary subscription; $40/yr. mailed. 4080 W. Broadway, Ste. 113, Minneapolis, MN 55428. TEL 612-896-4700; FAX 612-536-7519. **Owner(s):** Minnesota Sun Publications LLC, 7831 E. Bush Lake Rd., Bloomington, MN 55439. TEL 612-896-4700; Ed. Yvonne Klinnert; Pub. Denis Mindak; adv.; pub. size: tabloid; circ. 9,551(controlled & free).

US

BROOKLYN PARK SUN POST. 1965. Wed. $.75 newsstand; voluntary subscription; $40/yr. mailed. 4080 W. Broadway, Ste. 113, Minneapolis, MN 55422. TEL 612-896-4700; FAX 612-536-7519. **Owner(s):** Minnesota Sun Publications LLC, 7831 E. Bush Lake Rd., Bloomington, MN 55439. TEL 612-896-4700; Ed. Yvonne Klinnert; Pub. Denis Mindak; adv.; pub. size: tabloid; circ. 16,357(controlled & free).
Formerly: Brooklyn Park Post.

US

EDINA SUN-CURRENT. 1932. Wed. $.75 newsstand; voluntary subscription; $40/yr. mailed. 4080 W. Broadway, Ste. 113, Minneapolis, MN 55422. TEL 612-896-4700; FAX 612-536-7519. **Owner(s):** Minnesota Suburban Publishing, 7831 E. Bush Lake Rd., Bloomington, MN 55439. TEL 617-896-4700; Ed. Yvonne Klinnert; Pub. Denis Mindak; adv.; pub. size: tabloid; circ. 12,375(free & paid).

US

NEW HOPE-GOLDEN VALLEY SUN POST. 1974. Wed. $.75 newsstand; voluntary subscription; $40/yr. mailed. 4080 W. Broadway, Ste. 113, Minneapolis, MN 55422. TEL 612-536-7500; FAX 612-536-7519. **Owner(s):** Minnesota Sun Publications LLC, 7831 E. Bush Lake Rd., Bloomington, MN 55439. TEL 612-896-4700; Ed. Yvonne Klinnert; Pub. Denis Mindak; adv.; pub. size: tabloid; circ. 13,400(free & paid).

US

NORTH MINNEAPOLIS SUN POST. Wed. $.75 newsstand; voluntary subscription; $40/yr. mailed. 4080 W. Broadway Ave., Ste. 113, Minneapolis, MN 55422-5605. TEL 612-896-4700; FAX 612-536-7519. **Owner(s):** Minnesota Sun Publications LLC, 7831 E. Bush Lake Rd., Bloomington, MN 55439. TEL 612-896-4700; Ed. Yvonne Klinnert; Pub. Denis Mindak; adv.; pub. size: tabloid; circ. 9,334(controlled & paid).

US ISSN 0193-2802

TWIN CITIES READER. 1977. Wed. $30/yr. 10 S. 5th St., Ste. 200, Minneapolis, MN 55402-1012. TEL 612-321-7300; FAX 612-321-7333. **Owner(s):** City Media, Inc., 821 Marquette Ave. South, Ste. 2000, Minneapolis, MN 55402. TEL 612-359-2100; Ed. Claude Peck; Pub. R.T. Rybak; adv. contact: Matt Farley. photos; bk.rev.; pub. size: tabloid; circ. 95,000(free).

MINNETONKA

US

EXCELSIOR/SHOREWOOD SUN-SAILOR. Wed. free; $.75 newsstand; voluntary subscription; $40/yr. mailed. W. Wind Plz., 4785 Hwy. 101, S., Minnetonka, MN 55345. TEL 612-896-4700; FAX 612-935-1452. **Owner(s):** Minnesota Suburban Publications, 7831 E. Bush Lake Rd., Bloomington, MN 55439. TEL 612-896-4700; Ed. Yvonne Klinnert; Pub. Denis Mindak; adv.; pub. size: tabloid; circ. 6,132(free & paid).

US

HOPKINS SUN-SAILOR. Wed. free; $.75 newsstand; voluntary subscription; $40/yr. mailed. W. Wind Plz., 4785 Hwy. 101, S., Minnetonka, MN 55435. TEL 612-932-6660; FAX 612-935-1452. **Owner(s):** Minnesoa Sun Publications LLC, 7831 E. Bush Lake Rd., Bloomington, MN 55439. TEL 612-896-4700; FAX 612-536-7519; Ed. Yvonne Klinnert; Pub. Denis Mindak; adv.; pub. size: tabloid; circ. 4,158(free).
Formerly: Westonka Sailor.

US

MINNETONKA SUN-SAILOR. Wed. free; $.75 newsstand; voluntary subscription; $40/yr. W. Wind Plz., 4785 Hwy. 101, S., Minnetonka, MN 55435. TEL 612-896-4700; FAX 612-896-4728. **Owner(s):** Minnesota Sun Publications LLC, 7831 E. Bush Lake Rd., Bloomington, MN 55439. TEL 612-896-4700; Ed. Yvonne Klinnert; Pub. Denis Mindak; adv.; pub. size: tabloid; circ. 16,650(free).

US

PLYMOUTH SUN-SAILOR. Wed. free; $.75 newsstand; voluntary subscription; $40/yr. mailed. W. Wind Plz., 4785 Hwy. 101, S., Minnetonka, MN 55345. TEL 612-932-6660; FAX 612-935-1452. **Owner(s):** Minnesota Sun Publications LLC, 7831 E. Bush Lake Rd., Bloomington, MN 55439. TEL 612-895-4700; FAX 612-896-4728; Ed. Yvonne Klinnert; Pub. Denis Mindak; adv.; pub. size: tabloid; circ. 17,500(free).

US

ST. LOUIS PARK SUN-SAILOR. 1984. Wed. free; $.75 newsstand; voluntary subscription; $40/yr. mailed. W. Wind Plz., 4785 Hwy. 10l, S., Minnetonka, MN 55345. TEL 612-932-6660; FAX 612-935-1452. **Owner(s):** Minnesota Sun Publications LLC, 7831 E. Bush Lake Rd., Minneapolis, MN 55439. TEL 612-896-4700; Ed. Yvonne Klinnert; Pub. Denis Mindak; adv. contact: Mike Maslow. pub. size: tabloid; circ. 11,728(free).

US

WAYZATA/ORONO/LONG LAKE SUN-SAILOR. Wed. free; $.75 newsstand; voluntary subscription; $40/yr. mailed. W. Wind Plz., 4785 Hwy. 101, S., Minnetonka, MN 55345. TEL 612-932-6660; FAX 612-935-1452. **Owner(s):** Minnesota Sun Publications LLC, 7831 E. Bush Lake Rd., Bloomington, MN 55439. TEL 612-896-4700; Ed. Yvonne Klinnert; Pub. Denis Mindak; adv. contact: Mike Maslow. pub. size: tabloid; circ. 5,000(free).

MONTEVIDEO

US

MONTEVIDEO AMERICAN-NEWS. 1911. Thu. $1 newsstand; $32/yr. local. 223 S. First St., Montevideo, MN 56265. TEL 612-269-2156; FAX 612-269-2159. **Owner(s):** Montevideo Publishing Co., Inc., P.O. Box 736, Montevideo, MN 56265. TEL 612-269-2156; Pub. Patrick Schmidt; adv. contact: Kurt Dahl. photos; pub. size: broadsheet; circ. 5,025(paid).

MOOSE LAKE

US   ISSN 0746-2980

MOOSE LAKE STAR-GAZETTE. 1095. w. $.50 newsstand; $20/yr. local. 308 Elm Ave., Moose Lake, MN 55767. TEL 218-485-4406; FAX 218-485-0237. **Owner(s):** Jerry DeRungs, 212 4th St., Moose Lake, MN 55767; Ed. Jerry DeRungs; Pub. Jerry DeRungs; adv.; photos; pub. size: broadsheet; circ. 2,800(controlled & paid).

MORA

US

KANABEC COUNTY TIMES. 1884. Thu. $.65 newsstand; $22/yr. in cy; $28.50/yr. out of cy. 106 N.W. Railroad Ave., Mora, MN 55051. TEL 612-679-2661; FAX 612-679-2663. **Owner(s):** Eugene Johnson, P.O. Box 5, Mora, MN 55051; Ed. Lee Ostrom; Pub. Wade Weber; adv. contact: Annette Krist. pub. size: broadsheet; circ. 3,000(paid).

MORRIS

US

MORRIS SUN. Tue. $.50 newsstand; $27/yr. in area with Morris Tribune; $36/yr. out of area. 108 E. Sixth St., Morris, MN 56267-0470. TEL 612-589-2525; FAX 612-589-4357. **Owner(s):** Morris Tribune, Inc., P.O. Box 470, Morris, MN 56267; Ed. Jim Morrison. adv. contact: Anne Erickson. pub. size: broadsheet; circ. 3,900(paid).

US

MORRIS TRIBUNE. Thu. $.50 newsstand; $27/yr. in area with Morris Sun; $36/yr. out of area. 108 E. Sixth St., Morris, MN 56267-0470. TEL 612-589-2525; FAX 612-589-4357. **Owner(s):** Morris Tribune, Inc., P.O. Box 470, Morris, MN 56267. TEL 612-589-2525; Ed. Jim Morrison. adv. contact: Anne Erickson. pub. size: broadsheet; circ. 3,900(paid).

NEW PRAGUE

US

NEW PRAGUE TIMES. 1889. Thu. $.75 newsstand; $20/yr. in cy.; $25/yr. in state; $30/yr. out of state. 200 E. Main St., New Prague, MN 56071. TEL 612-758-4435; FAX 612-758-4135. **Owner(s):** Suel Printing Co., P.O. Box 25, New Prague, MN 56071. TEL 612-758-4435; Ed. Lois Suel Wann; Pub. E. Charles Wann; adv. contact: Mark Slavik. pub. size: broadsheet; circ. 4,500(paid).

NORTH BRANCH

US   ISSN 0891-0731

ECM POST-REVIEW. 1875. Thu. $.65 newsstand; $24/yr. 612 Main St., North Branch, MN 55056-0366. TEL 612-674-7025; FAX 612-674-7026. **Owner(s):** ECM Publishers, Inc., 1201 15th Ave. S., Princeton, MN 55373-2306. TEL 612-333-2980; Ed. Twyla Ring; Pub. Elmer L. Andersen; adv. contact: Mary Eslinger. pub. size: tabloid; circ. 2,500(paid).

NORTHFIELD

US

NORTHFIELD NEWS. 1876. s-w.: Wed. & Fri. $32/yr. in state; $38/yr. out of state. 115 W. Fifth St., Northfield, MN 55057. TEL 507-645-5615. **Owner(s):** Bradford Family, 1118 Lia Court, Northfield, MN 55057. TEL 507-645-5615; Ed. James Lynch; Pub. Robert Bradford; adv. contact: Doug Fitzgerald. photos; bk.rev.; pub. size: broadsheet; circ. 6,000(paid).

NORTHOME

US

NORTHOME RECORD & MIZPAH MESSAGE. 1901. Tue. $.35 newsstand; $16.50/yr. in cy.; $20/yr. in state; $22.50/yr. out of state. Main St., Northome, MN 56661-0025. TEL 218-897-5278. **Owner(s):** Bernard & Kathryn E. Elhard, Northome, MN 56601; Pub. Kathryn E. Elhard; adv.; pub. size: tabloid; circ. 1,000(paid).

NORTH ST. PAUL

US

EAST SIDE REVIEW. 1938. Mon. free in area. 2515 E. Seventh Ave., North St. Paul, MN 55109-3098. TEL 612-777-8800; FAX 612-777-8288. **Owner(s):** Lillie Suburban Newspapers, Inc., 2515 E. Seventh Ave., St. Paul, MN 55109. TEL 612-777-8800; FAX 612-777-8200; Ed. Mary Lee Hagert; Pub. N. Ted Lillie; adv. contact: Mark Beckstrom. pub. size: broadsheet; circ. 19,822(free).

US

NEW BRIGHTON-MOUNDS VIEW BULLETIN. 1938. Wed. $.50 newsstand; free home deliv.; $21.95/yr. out of area. 2515 E. Seventh Ave., North St. Paul, MN 55109. TEL 612-777-8800; FAX 612-777-8200. **Owner(s):** Lillie Suburban Newspapers, Inc., 2515 E. Seventh Ave., St. Paul, MN 55109-3093. TEL 612-777-8800; FAX 612-777-8288; Ed. Mary Lee Hagert; Pub. N. Ted Lillie; adv. contact: Mark Beckstrom. pub. size: broadsheet; circ. 10,000(paid).

US

ST. ANTHONY BULLETIN. 1938. Wed. $.50 newsstand; free home deliv.; $21.95/yr. out of area. 2515 E. Seventh Ave., North St. Paul, MN 55109. TEL 612-777-8800; FAX 612-777-8200. **Owner(s):** Lillie Suburban Newspapers, Inc. 2515 E. Seventh Ave., St. Paul, MN 55109-3093. TEL 612-777-8800; FAX 612-777-8288; Ed. Mary Lee Hagert; Pub. N. Ted Lillie; adv. contact: Mark Beckstrom. pub. size: broadsheet; circ. 3,000(free & paid).

OAKDALE

US

OAKDALE CLARION. 1992. Fri. $19/yr. mailed in state; $21/yr. out of state. 1979 Geneva Ave. N., Oakdale, MN 55128. TEL 612-730-9116; FAX 612-730-0340. **Owner(s):** Oakdale Clarion; Pub. Lisa Heikkila; adv.: $6.50/SAU. circ. 2,000(paid).

OKLEE

US

OKLEE HERALD. 1917. Wed. $.75 newsstand; $18/yr. in cy.; $23/yr. out of cy. Main St., Oklee, MN 56742. TEL 218-796-5181; FAX 218-487-5251. **Owner(s):** Richards Publishing Co., Inc., Box 159, Gonvick, MN 56644. TEL 218-487-5225; Ed. Marilyn Whyte; Pub. Dick Richards; adv.; photos; pub. size: tabloid; circ. 1,200(paid).

OLIVIA

US

OLIVIA TIMES JOURNAL. Mon. $.75 newsstand; $24/yr. in cy. 816 E. Lincoln Ave., Olivia, MN 56277. TEL 612-523-2032. **Owner(s):** Olivia Publishing, Inc., 816 E. Lincoln, Olivia, MN. TEL 612-523-2032; Ed. Pat Kelly. adv.; photos; pub. size: broadsheet; circ. 1,810(controlled & paid).

US

RENVILLE COUNTY SHOPPER. 1967. Mon. free. 816 E. Lincoln, Olivia, MN 56277. TEL 612-523-2032; FAX 612-523-2033. **Owner(s):** Olivia Publishing, Inc., 816 E. Lincoln, Olivia, MN 56277; Pub. Rose Hettig; adv.; pub. size: broadsheet; circ. 5,100(free).

ORTONVILLE

US

ORTONVILLE INDEPENDENT. 1920. Tue. $.50 newsstand; $22/yr. in cy.; $26.50/yr. out of cy.; $28.50/yr. out of state. 29 N.W. Second St., Ortonville, MN 56278. TEL 612-839-6163; FAX 612-839-6173. **Owner(s):** James D., Jeannette & Sue Kaercher, P.O. Box 336, Ortonville, MN 56278. TEL 612-839-6163; Ed. James D. Kaercher; Pub. Jeannette Kaercher; adv.; pub. size: broadsheet; circ. 3,700(controlled & paid).

OSAKIS

US   ISSN 1040-6069

OSAKIS REVIEW, THE. 1890. Tue. $.50 newsstand; $20/yr. in cy.; $23/yr. in state; $26/yr. out of state. 28 E. Main St., Osakis, MN 56360-0220. TEL 612-859-2143; FAX 612-859-2054. **Owner(s):** John & Roberta Olson, 23 E. Main St., Osakis, MN 56360. TEL 612-859-2143; Pub. John Olson; adv. contact: John Olson. pub. size: tabloid; circ. 1,350(controlled & free).

OWATONNA

US

OWATONNA WEEKLY SHOPPER. Sat. free. 135 W. Pearl St., Owatonna, MN 55060. TEL 507-451-2840; FAX 507-451-6020. **Owner(s):** Huckle Publishing, Inc., P.O. Box 346, Owatonna, MN 55060; Pub. Ken Lynam; adv. contact: Holly Westercamp. pub. size: standard; circ. Sun. 18,000(free).

PARK RAPIDS

US

PARK RAPIDS ENTERPRISE. 1882. s-w. Wed. & Sat. $30/yr. in cy.; $40/yr. out of cy.; $42/yr. out of state. 402 Pleasant Ave., Park Rapids, MN 56470. TEL 218-732-3364; FAX 218-732-8757. **Owner(s):** Forum Communications, Inc., P.O. Box 2020, Fargo, ND 58107. TEL 701-241-5400; Ed. LuAnn Hurd-Lof. adv.; photos; pub. size: broadsheet; circ. 6,000(paid).

PAYNESVILLE

US

PAYNESVILLE PRESS, THE. 1887. Wed. $.60 newsstand; $19/yr. local. 211 Washburne, Paynesville, MN 56362. TEL 612-243-3772. E-mail: paypress@lkdllink.net; URL: http://www.edtechweb.com/paynesvillearea. **Owner(s):** Paynesville Press, The, P.O. Box 54, Paynesville, MN 56362. TEL 612-243-3772; Pub. Peter J. Jacobsa; adv.; pub. size: broadsheet; circ. 2,970(paid).

PELICAN RAPIDS

US

PELICAN RAPIDS PRESS. 1897. Wed. $.50 newsstand; $22/yr. 29 West Mill, Pelican Rapids, MN 56572-0632. TEL 218-863-1421; FAX 218-863-1423. **Owner(s):** Gary E. & Richard E. Peterson, P.O. Box L, Pelican Rapids, MN 56572. TEL 218-863-1421; FAX 218-863-1423; Ed. Gary E. Peterson; Pub. Richard E. Peterson; adv.; pub. size: standard; circ. 3,468(paid).

PERHAM

US

PERHAM ENTERPRISE-BULLETIN. 1882. Thu. $.75 newsstand; $22/yr. in cy.; $24/yr. out of cy.; $26/yr. out of state. 135 E. Main St., Perham, MN 56573. TEL 218-346-5900; FAX 218-346-5901. **Owner(s):** Mike Parta, Parta Printers, 135 E. Main St., New York Mills, MN 56567. TEL 218-385-2275; Ed. Charles Johnson; Pub. Mike Parta; adv. contact: Cleone Stewart. photos; pub. size: broadsheet; circ. 3,200(paid).

PIPESTONE

US

PIPESTONE COUNTY STAR. 1879. Wed. $.75 newsstand; $26/yr. in cy.; $32/yr. out of cy. 101 Second St., N.E., Pipestone, MN 56164. TEL 507-825-3333; FAX 507-825-2168. **Owner(s):** Pipestone Publishing Co., P.O. Box 277, Pipestone, MN 56164-0277. TEL 507-825-3333; Ed. Mark Fode; Pub. Chuck Draper; adv. contact: Ray Fuder. pub. size: broadsheet; circ. 4,040(paid).

PLAINVIEW

US

PLAINVIEW NEWS. Tue. $.50 newsstand; $20/yr. in surrounding cys.; $27/yr. elsewhere. 409 W. Broadway, Plainview, MN 55964. TEL 507-534-3121. **Owner(s):** Timothy Mack, P.O. Box 457, Plainview, MN 55964; Ed. Janet Mack; Pub. Timothy Mack; adv. contact: Julie Stoning. pub. size: broadsheet; circ. 2,500(paid).

PRINCETON

US

PRINCETON UNION-EAGLE. 1876. Thu. $.60 newsstand; $21/yr. in cy.; $16/yr. senior citizens. 208 N. LaGrande, Princeton, MN 55371. TEL 612-389-1222; FAX 612-389-1728. **Owner(s):** ECM Publishers, Inc., 208 N. LaGrande, Princeton, MN 55371. TEL 612-389-1222; Ed. Luther Dorr; Pub. Elmer L. Andersen; adv.; photos; pub. size: broadsheet; circ. 3,600(paid).

PROCTOR

US

PROCTOR JOURNAL. 1906. Thu. $.75 newsstand; $20.50/yr. 215 Fifth St., Proctor, MN 55810-1686. TEL 218-624-3344; FAX 218-624-7037. **Owner(s):** Jake Benson, 215 Fifth St., Proctor, MN 55810-1686. TEL 218-624-3344; FAX 218-624-7037; Pub. Jake Benson; adv. contact: Diane Giuliani. photos; pub. size: tabloid; circ. 2,000(paid).

RED WING

US

HIAWATHA VALLEY SHOPPER. 1955. Sun. free. P.O. Box 324, Red Wing, MN 55066. TEL 715-792-2880; FAX 715-273-4769; E-mail: helmprint@aol.com. **Owner(s):** Helmer Printing Co., Inc., P.O. Box 40, Beldoneville, WI 54003; Ed. Milton Helmer; Pub. W.M.A. Helmer; adv.; photos; pub. size: tabloid; circ. 41,000(free).

REDWOOD FALLS

US

REDWOOD GAZETTE, THE. 1869. s-w.: Mon. & Thu. $1 newsstand; $42/yr. in surrounding cys.; $52/yr. out of area. 140 E. Second St., Redwood Falls, MN 56283. TEL 507-637-2929; FAX 507-637-3175. **Owner(s):** Bob Bradford, P.O. Box 299, Redwood Falls, MN 36283. TEL 507-637-2929; Ed. Rick Peterson; Pub. Rick Peterson; adv. contact: Shelly Doering. pub. size: broadsheet; circ. 5,500(paid).

ROSEAU

US

ROSEAU TIMES-REGION. 1889. Tue. $21/yr. in cy.; $28/yr. out of cy. 106 W. Center St., Roseau, MN 56751. TEL 218-463-1521; FAX 218-463-1530. **Owner(s):** Warren Sheaf Publishing Co., P.O. Box 45, Warren, MN 56762. TEL 218-745-5174; Ed. Dick Melvin. adv. contact: Jodi Wiskow. pub. size: broadsheet; circ. 4,450(paid).

ROSEVILLE

US

COLUMBIA HEIGHTS-FINDLEY FOCUS. Thu. free newsstand; $75/yr. mailed. 2819 N. Hamline Ave., Ste. 101, Roseville, MN 55113-7118. TEL 612-633-3434; FAX 612-633-9550. **Owner(s):** Focus Newspapers, 7401 Bush Lake Rd., Minneapolis, MN 55439. TEL 612-831-1200; Ed. Mac Meade; Pub. Richard Roberts; adv. contact: Collette Roberts. pub. size: broadsheet; circ. 11,425(free).

US

FRIDLEY FOCUS. Thu. free newsstand; $75/yr. 2819 Hamline Ave., N., Ste. 101, Roseville, MN 55113-7118. TEL 612-633-3434; FAX 612-571-1026. **Owner(s):** Focus Newspapers, 7401 Bush Lake Rd., Minneapolis, MN 55439. TEL 612-831-1200; Ed. Mac Meade; Pub. Richard Roberts; adv. contact: Collette Roberts. pub. size: tabloid; circ. 10,168(free).
Formerly: Fridley/Columbia Heights Focus.

US

MOUNDS VIEW-NEW BRIGHTON-ST. ANTHONY FOCUS. 1985. Thu. free newsstand; $75/yr. mailed. 2819 N. Hamline Ave., Ste. 101, Roseville, MN 55113-7118. TEL 612-633-3434; FAX 612-633-9550. **Owner(s):** Focus Newspapers, Minneapolis, MN; Ed. Collette Roberts; Pub. Richard Roberts; adv. contact: Collette Roberts. pub. size: tabloid; circ. 52,000(free).
Formerly: Shoreview/Moundsview/Arden Hills Focus.

US

ROSEVILLE-FALCON HEIGHTS-ARDEN HILLS FOCUS. 1985. Thu. free newsstand; $75/yr. mailed. 2819 N. Hamline Ave., n., Ste. 101, Roseville, MN 55113-7118. TEL 612-633-3434; FAX 612-633-9550. **Owner(s):** Focus Newspapers, Minneapolis, MN 55428. TEL 612-536-7500; Ed. Pam Hentges; Pub. Richard Roberts; adv. contact: Collette Roberts. pub. size: tabloid; circ. 13,579(free).

RUSHFORD

US

TRI-COUNTY RECORD. 1915. Thu. $.60 newsstand; $21/yr.; $25/yr. out of cy. 300 S. Mill St., Rushford, MN 55971. TEL 507-864-7700. **Owner(s):** Tri-County Publishing, Inc., 300 S. Mill St., Rushford, MN 55971; Ed. Myron J. Schober; Pub. Darlene J. Schober; adv.; photos; pub. size: broadsheet; circ. 1,750(paid).

RUTHTON

US

BUFFALO RIDGE GAZETTE, THE. 1974. Wed. $.50 newsstand; $17/yr. 320 Aetna, Ruthton, MN 56170. TEL 507-658-3919; FAX 507-247-5502. **Owner(s):** Hunt & Hunt Newspapers, 151 N. Tyler St., Tyler, MN 56178. TEL 507-247-5502; FAX 507-247-5502; Ed. Lorry Sanderson; Pub. Charles Hunt; adv.; photos; pub. size: broadsheet; circ. 500(paid).

SAUK CENTRE

US

SAUK CENTRE HERALD. 1867. Tue. $.50 newsstand; $20/yr. in area; $24/yr. out of area; $25/yr. out of state. 522 Sinclair Lewis Ave., Sauk Centre, MN 56378. TEL 612-352-6577; FAX 612-352-5647. **Owner(s):** Dave Simpkins, 522 Sinclair Lewis Ave., Sauk Centre, MN 56378. TEL 612-352-2345; Pub. Dave Simpkins; adv. contact: Glenn Domine. pub. size: broadsheet; circ. 3,550(paid).

SEBEKA

US

SEBEKA/MENAHGA REVIEW MESSENGER. 1898. Wed. $.60 newsstand; $19.06/yr. in trade area; $22.50/yr. in state; $27/yr. out of state. 112 Minnesota Ave., W., Sebeka, MN 56477-0309. TEL 218-837-5558; FAX 218-837-5560. **Owner(s):** Marjon Printers, Inc., Box 309, Sebeka, MN 56477. TEL 218-837-5558; FAX 218-837-5560; Ed. T.M. Bloomquist. adv.: $5.25/SAU. photos; pub. size: broadsheet; circ. 3,545(free & paid).

SHAKOPEE

US

SHAKOPEE VALLEY NEWS. 1900. Thu. $.75 newsstand; $22/yr. in cy.; $33/yr. out of cy. 327 Marschall Rd., Shakopee, MN 55379. TEL 612-445-3333. **Owner(s):** Southwest Suburban Publishing, P.O. Box 8, Shakopee, MN 55379. TEL 612-445-3333; Ed. Pat Minelli; Pub. Stan Rolffrug; pub. size: broadsheet; circ. 4,009(paid).

SHERBURN

US   ISSN 1056-8999

WEST MARTIN WEEKLY NEWS. 1888. Wed. $.75 newsstand; $21/yr. in cy. 10 N. Main St., Sherburn, MN 56171. TEL 507-764-6681; FAX 507-764-2756. **Owner(s):** Harwood & Polly Schaffer, P.O. Box 820, Sherburn, MN 56171. TEL 507-764-6681; FAX 507-764-2756; adv.; photos; pub. size: broadsheet; circ. 2,000(paid).

SLAYTON

US

MURRAY COUNTY WHEEL HERALD. Mon. $.50 newsstand; $22/yr. in cy. 2734 Broadway Ave., Slayton, MN 56172. TEL 507-836-8726; FAX 507-836-8726. **Owner(s):** Will Beers, P.O. Box 263, Slayton, MN 36172. TEL 507-386-8726; Ed. Randy Beers; Pub. Will Beers; adv. contact: Randy Beers. pub. size: broadsheet; circ. 7,100(paid).

SPOONER

US

EVERGREEN SHOPPING GUIDE. w. 509 Front St., Spooner, MN 54801. TEL 715-635-2181; FAX 715-635-2186. **Owner(s):** Northwest Wisconsin Media, Inc., P.O. Box 338, Spooner, MN 54801. TEL 715-635-2181; FAX 715-635-2186; circ. 16,800(free & paid).

SPRINGFIELD

US

SPRINGFIELD ADVANCE-PRESS. 1896. Wed. $.75 newsstand; $23.50/yr. 13 S. Marshall Ave., Springfield, MN 56087. TEL 507-723-4225; FAX 507-723-4400. **Owner(s):** Don R. Peterson, 135 Interlaken Rd., Fairmont, MN 56031; D.J. Hepstrom, 518 N. Marshall Ave., Springfield, MN 56087. TEL 507-723-5078; FAX 507-723-6534; Ed. Peter Hedstrom; Pub. Peter C. Hedstrom; adv. contact: Peter Hedstrom. photos; pub. size: broadsheet; circ. 232,906(paid).

SPRING VALLEY

US

RIVER VALLEY SHOPPER. Mon. free. 141 S. Broadway, Spring Valley, MN 55975-0112. TEL 507-346-7365; FAX 507-346-7366. **Owner(s):** Phillips Publishing, Inc., P.O. Box 112, Spring Valley, MN 55975. TEL 507-346-7365; Pub. David Phillips; adv.; pub. size: standard; circ. 13,785(free).

US

SPRING VALLEY TRIBUNE. 1880. Wed. $.60 newsstand; $18/yr. locally. 141 S. Broadway, Spring Valley, MN 55975-0112. TEL 507-346-7365; FAX 507-346-7366. **Owner(s):** Phillips Publishing, Inc., P.O. Box 112, Spring Valley, MN 55975. TEL 507-346-7365; FAX 507-346-7366; Pub. David Phillips; photos; pub. size: broadsheet; circ. 2,000(paid).

STAPLES

US

STAPLES WORLD. 1890. Thu. $.75 newsstand; $22/yr. in surrounding cys.; $26/yr. in state; $30/yr. out of state. 224 Fourth St., N., Staples, MN 56479. TEL 218-894-1112; FAX 218-894-3570. **Owner(s):** Devlin Newspapers, Inc., 224 Fourth St., Staples, MN 56479-0100. TEL 218-894-1112; FAX 218-894-3570; Ed. Tom Crawford; Pub. Russ Devlin; adv. contact: Gary Mueller. photos; pub. size: broadsheet; circ. 2,728(free & paid).

ST. CHARLES

US

ST. CHARLES PRESS. 1877. Tue. $.50 newsstand; $20/yr. in cy.; $27/yr. out of cy. 924 Whitewater Ave. St. Charles, MN 55972. TEL 507-932-3663; FAX 507-932-5537. **Owner(s):** Mack Publishing, 924 Whitewater Ave., St. Charles, MN 55972. TEL 507-932-3663; Ed. Julie Smith; Pub. Tim Mack; adv.; pub. size: broadsheet; circ. 2,700(paid).

ST. JAMES

US

ST. JAMES PLAINDEALER. 1891. Thu. $1 newsstand; $27/yr. in cy. 604 First Ave., S., St. James, MN 56081. TEL 507-375-3161; FAX 507-375-3221. **Owner(s):** Robert Bradford, Northfield, MN 55057; FAX 507-375-3221; Ed. Pat Beck; Pub. R. Joseph Flanagan; adv. contact: R. Joseph Flanagan. pub. size: broadsheet; circ. 3,000(paid).

ST. PAUL

US

FOREST LAKE PRESS. Fri. $.50 newsstand; $25/yr. in cy. 4779 Bloom Ave., St. Paul, MN 55110. TEL 612-429-7781; FAX 612-429-1242. **Owner(s):** Press Publications, Inc., 4779 Bloom Ave., St. Paul, MN 55110. TEL 612-429-7781; Ed. Paul Wahl; Pub. Eugene D. Johnson; adv. contact: Michelle Larson. pub. size: broadsheet; circ. 14,020(paid).

US

GRAND GAZETTE. 1972. m. free newsstand; $15/yr. out of area mailed. 757 S. Snelling Ave., St. Paul, MN 55116-2250. TEL 612-699-1462; FAX 612-699-6501. **Owner(s):** Michael Mischke, 757 S. Snelling Ave., St. Paul, MN 55116-2250. TEL 612-699-1462; FAX 612-699-6501; Ed. Dale Mischke; Pub. Michael Mischke; adv.; photos; bk.rev.; pub. size: tabloid; circ. 22,500(free & paid).

US

LILLIE SUBURBAN SHOPPING REVIEW. 1938. Mon. free. 2515 E. Seventh Ave., St. Paul, MN 55109-3098. TEL 612-777-8800; FAX 612-777-8288. **Owner(s):** Lillie Suburban Newspapers, Inc., 2515 E. Seventh Ave., St. Paul, MN 55109-3098. TEL 612-777-8800; FAX 612-777-8288; Ed. Mary Lee Hagert; Pub. Jeff Enright; adv. contact: Mark Beckstrom. pub. size: broadsheet; circ. 20,000(free).

US

MAPLEWOOD REVIEW. 1938. Wed. $.50 newsstand; $19.95/yr. in area; $23.95/yr. out of area. 2515 E. Seventh Ave., St. Paul, MN 55109-3098. TEL 612-777-8800; FAX 612-777-8288. **Owner(s):** Lillie Suburban Newspapers, Inc., 2515 E. Seventh Ave., St. Paul, MN 55109. TEL 612-777-8800; FAX 612-777-8288; Ed. Mary Lee Hagert; Pub. N. Ted Lillie; adv. contact: Mark Beckstrom. pub. size: broadsheet; circ. 1,100(free & paid).

US

OAKDALE-LAKE ELMO REVIEW. 1938. Wed. $.50 newsstand; $19.95/yr. in area; $23.95/yr. out of area. 2515 E. Seventh Ave., St. Paul, MN 55109. TEL 612-777-8800; FAX 612-777-8288. **Owner(s):** Lillie Suburban Newspapers, Inc., 2515 E. Seventh Ave., St. Paul, MN 55109. TEL 612-777-8800; Ed. Mary Lee Hagert; Pub. N. Ted Lillie; adv. contact: Mark Beckstrom. pub. size: broadsheet; circ. 780(free & paid).

US

RAMSEY COUNTY REVIEW. 1938. Wed. $.50 newsstand; $16/yr. in area. $20/yr. out of area. 2515 E. Seventh Ave., St. Paul, MN 55109-3098. TEL 612-777-8800; FAX 612-777-8288. **Owner(s):** Lillie Suburban Newspapers, Inc., 2515 E. Seventh Ave., St. Paul, MN 55109. TEL 612-777-8800; FAX 612-777-8288; Ed. Mary Lee Hagert; Pub. N. Ted Lillie; adv. contact: Mark Beckstrom. pub. size: broadsheet; circ. 1,500(free & paid).

US

ROOSEVELT REVIEW. 1938. Tue. $.40 newsstand; $19.95/yr. in cy.; $23.95/yr. out of cy. 2515 E. Seventh Ave., St. Paul, MN 55109. TEL 612-777-8800; FAX 612-777-8288. **Owner(s):** Lillie Suburban Newspapers, Inc., 2515 E. Seventh Ave., St. Paul, MN 55109. TEL 612-777-8800; FAX 612-777-8200; Ed. Mary Lee Hagert; Pub. Ted Lillie; adv. contact: Paula Green. pub. size: broadsheet. circ. 16,000(paid).

US

ROSEVILLE REVIEW. 1938. Tue. free in area; $1/wk. out of area mailed. 2515 E. Seventh Ave., St. Paul, MN 55109-3098. TEL 612-777-8800; FAX 612-777-8288. **Owner(s):** Lillie Suburban Newspapers, Inc., 2515 E. Seventh Ave., St. Paul, MN 55109-3098. TEL 612-777-8300; FAX 612-777-8288; Ed. Mary Lee Hagert; Pub. N. Ted Lillie; adv. contact: Mark Beckstrom. photos; pub. size: broadsheet; circ. 15,684(free).

US

SHOREVIEW-ARDEN HILLS BULLETIN. 1938. Wed. $.50 newsstand; free in area; $21.95/yr. out of area. 2515 E. Seventh Ave., St. Paul, MN 55109-3098. TEL 612-777-8800; FAX 612-777-8288. **Owner(s):** Lillie Suburban Newspapers, Inc., 2515 E. Seventh Ave., St. Paul, MN 55109-3098. TEL 612-777-8300; FAX 612-777-8288; Ed. Mary Lee Hagert; Pub. N. Ted Lillie; adv. contact: Mark Beckstrom. pub. size: broadsheet; circ. 16,214(free & paid).

US

SHOREVIEW PRESS. Tue. $.50 newsstand; $25/yr. in cy. 4779 Bloom Ave., St. Paul, MN 55110. TEL 612-429-7781; FAX 612-429-1242. **Owner(s):** Press Publications Inc., 4779 Bloom Ave., St. Paul, MN 55110. TEL 612-429-7781; Ed. Paul Wahl; Pub. Eugene D. Johnson; adv. contact: Michelle Larson. pub. size: broadsheet.

US

SOUTH-WEST REVIEW. 1938. Sun. free. 2515 E.
Seventh Ave., St. Paul, MN 55109-3098.
TEL 612-777-8800; FAX 612-777-8288.
Owner(s): Lillie Suburban Newspapers, Inc., 2515
E. Seventh Ave., St. Paul, MN 55109-3098. TEL
612-777-8800; FAX 612-777-8288; Ed. Mary
Lee Hagert; Pub. N. Ted Lillie; adv. contact: Mark
Beckstrom. pub. size: broadsheet; circ.
22,509(free).

US

ST. CROIX VALLEY PRESS. 1978. Wed. $.50
newsstand; $25/yr. in area. 4779 Bloom Ave.,
St. Paul, MN 55100. TEL 612-429-7781;
FAX 612-429-1242. **Owner(s):** Press
Publications, Inc., 4779 Bloom Ave., St. Paul, MN
55110. TEL 612-429-7781; Ed. Paul Wahl; Pub.
Eugene D. Johnson; adv. contact: Michelle Larson.
pub. size: broadsheet; circ. 12,899(paid).

US

VADNAIS HEIGHTS PRESS. Wed. $.50 newsstand;
$25/yr. in cy. 4779 Bloom Ave., St. Paul, MN
55110. TEL 612-429-7781;
FAX 612-429-1242. **Owner(s):** Press
Publications, Inc., 4779 Bloom Ave., St. Paul, MN
55110. TEL 612-429-7781; Ed. Paul Wahl; Pub.
Eugene D. Johnson; adv. contact: Michelle Larson.
pub. size: broadsheet.

US

VILLAGER. s-m.: Wed. free; $25/yr out of area
mailed. 757 S. Snelling Ave., St. Paul, MN
55116. TEL 612-699-1462;
FAX 612-699-6501. **Owner(s):** Michael Mischke,
757 S. Snelling Ave., St. Paul, MN 55116. TEL
612-699-1462; Ed. Dale Mischke; Pub. Michael
Mischke; adv.; photos; bk.rev.; circ.
44,500(controlled & free).

US

WOODBURY-SOUTH MAPLEWOOD REVIEW. 1938.
Mon. free in area. 2515 E. Seventh Ave., St. Paul,
MN 55109-3098. TEL 612-777-8800;
FAX 612-777-8288. **Owner(s):** Lillie Suburban
Newspapers, Inc., 2515 E. Seventh Ave., St. Paul,
MN 55109-3098. TEL 612-777-8800; FAX
612-777-8288; Ed. Mary Lee Hagert; Pub. N.
Ted Lillie; adv. contact: Mark Bechstrom. photos;
pub. size: broadsheet; circ. 9,510(free).

ST. PETER

US

ST. PETER HERALD. 1884. Thu. $1 newsstand;
$30/yr in cy.; $35/yr. out of cy.; $45/yr. out of
state. 311 S. Minnesota Ave., St. Peter, MN
56082. TEL 507-931-4520;
FAX 507-931-4522. **Owner(s):** St. Peter
Publishing Co., 311 S. Minnesota Ave., St. Peter,
MN 56082. TEL 507-931-4520; Pub. Peggy
Palmer; adv.; photos; pub. size: broadsheet; circ.
2,900(paid).

THIEF RIVER FALLS

US

NORTHERN WATCH. 1991. Sat. free in trade area;
$.75/copy outside of trade area. 324 N. Main
Ave., Thief River Falls, MN 56701.
TEL 218-681-4450; FAX 218-681-4455.
Owner(s): Thief River Falls Times, Inc., 324 N.
Main Ave., Thief River Falls, MN 56701. TEL
218-681-4450; FAX 218-681-4455; Ed. Marvin
Lundin; Pub. John Mattson; adv. contact: Denise
Laymon. adv.: $8/SAU. pub. size: broadsheet;
circ. 22,500(free).

US   ISSN 8750-3883

THIEF RIVER FALLS TIMES, THE. 1910. Wed. $.75
newsstand; $24/yr. in area; $29/yr. out of area.
324 N. Main Ave., Thief River Falls, MN 56701.
TEL 218-681-4450; FAX 218-681-4455.
Owner(s): Thief River Falls Times, Inc., 324 N.
Main Ave., Thief River Falls, MN 56701-0100.
TEL 218-681-4450; FAX 218-681-4455; Ed.
Marvin Lundin; Pub. John P. Mattson; adv.
contact: Denise Laymon. adv.: $5.50/SAU. pub.
size: broadsheet; circ. 5,800(paid).
    Formerly: Times, The.

TRACY

US

TRACY HEADLIGHT-HERALD. 1879. Wed. $.75
newsstand; $25/yr. in cy.; $32/yr. out of cy.
207 Fourth St., Tracy, MN 56175.
TEL 507-629-4300; FAX 507-629-4301.
Owner(s): James Keul, 207 Fourth St., Tracy, MN
56175. TEL 507-629-4300; Seth Schmidt, 207
Fourth St., Tracy, MN 56175. TEL
507-629-4300; Ed. Seth Schmidt; Pub. Seth
Schmidt; adv. contact: Lisa Sell. pub. size:
broadsheet; circ. 2,300(paid).

TWO HARBORS

US

LAKE COUNTY NEWS-CHRONICLE. 1895. Thu. $.75
newsstand; $24/yr. in cy.; $29/yr. out of cy.;
$32/yr. out of state. 109 Waterfront Dr., Two
Harbors, MN 55616. TEL 218-834-2141.
Owner(s): Mary E. Williams, 109 Waterfront Dr.,
Two Harbors, MN 55616. TEL 218-834-2141;
George Williams, Jr., 109 Waterfront Dr., Two
Harbors, MN 55616. TEL 218-834-2141; Ed.
Forrest Johnson; Pub. Forrest Johnson; adv.
contact: Donna Carlson. pub. size: broadsheet;
circ. 3,350(paid).

TYLER

US

TYLER TRIBUTE. 1972. Thu. $.50 newsstand;
$19/yr. in cy.; $23/yr. in state. 151 N. Tyler St.,
Tyler, MN 56178-0466. TEL 507-247-5502;
FAX 507-247-5502; E-mail:
103216.3660@compuserve.com. **Owner(s):**
Hunt & Hunt Newspapers, 151 N. Tyler St., Tyler,
MN 56178. TEL 507-247-5502; FAX
507-247-5502; Ed. Charles R. Hunt; Pub.
Charles R. Hunt; adv.; photos; pub. size:
broadsheet; circ. 1,680(paid).
    Formerly: Tyler Tribune.

WACONIA

US

WACONIA PATRIOT. 1895. Thu. $.75 nesstand;
$25.60/yr. carrier in state; $32.90/yr. out of
state. 8 Elm St., S., Waconia, MN 55387.
TEL 612-442-4414; FAX 612-442-4428.
Owner(s): Carver County News, Inc., Watertown,
MN 55388. TEL 612-955-1111; Ed. Keith
Anderson; Pub. James Berreth; adv. contact:
Karen Miller. pub. size: broadsheet; circ.
4,200(paid).

WADENA

US

WADENA PIONEER JOURNAL. 1878. Thu. $.75
newsstand; $22/yr. in area; $26/yr. in state;
$31/yr. out state. 314 S. Jefferson, Wadena, MN
56482. TEL 218-631-2561;
FAX 218-631-1621. **Owner(s):** Fargo Forum
Communications, 101 Fifth St., N., P.O. Box
2020, Fargo, ND 58102. TEL 701-241-5404;
Ed. Miranda Bryant; Pub. Randy Mohs; adv.
contact: Krista Lien. pub. size: broadsheet; circ.
4,000(paid).

WARREN

US

WARREN SHEAF. 6880. Wed. $.50 newsstand;
$21/yr. local; $25/yr. out of cy. 127 W. Johnson
Ave., Warren, MN 56762. TEL 218-745-5174;
FAX 218-745-5175. **Owner(s):** Warren Sheaf
Publishing Co., P.O. Box 45, Warren, MN 56762.
TEL 218-745-5174; FAX 218-745-5174; Ed.
Eric Mattson; Pub. Eric Mattson; pub. size:
broadsheet; circ. 3,500(paid).

WASECA

US   ISSN 0745-8177

WASECA COUNTY NEWS. 1981. s-w.: Tue. & Thu. $1
newsstand; $35/yr. in area; $46/yr. out of area.
213 Second St. N.W., Waseca, MN 56093-0465.
TEL 507-835-3380; FAX 507-835-3435.
Owner(s): Waseca Publishing Co., Inc., 108
Second Ave. NW, Waseca, MN 56093. TEL
507-835-3380; FAX 507-835-3435; Ed. Tom
West; Pub. Tom West; adv. contact: Cheryl Neid.
photos; bk.rev.; pub. size: broadsheet; circ.
7,236(paid). **Wire Service(s):** AP, Datafinder.

WAYZATA

US

LAKESHORE WEEKLY NEWS. 1982. Thu. free
newsstand; $16/6 mos.; $28/yr. 18178
Minnetonka Blvd., Wayzata, MN 55391.
TEL 612-473-0890; FAX 612-473-0895.
Owner(s): Peter H. May, 240 Minnesota Ave.,
Wayzata, MN 55391. TEL 612-473-0890; FAX
612-473-0895; Pub. Peter H. May; adv. contact:
Mark Gardner. pub. size: tabloid; circ.
25,000(controlled & free); morning
32,000(controlled). **Wire Service(s):** AP,
Newsfinder.
    Formerly: Weekly News.

WELLS

US

WELLS MIRROR, THE. 1913. Thu. $.60 newsstand;
$24/yr. in cy. 40 W. Franklin, Wells, MN 56097.
TEL 507-553-3131; FAX 507-553-3132.
Owner(s): Wells Mirror Co., 40 W. Franklin, Wells,
MN 56097. TEL 507-553-3131; FAX
507-553-3132; Ed. Tracy Madden; Pub. Mike
Johnson; adv. contact: Tammy Madsen. photos;
pub. size: standard; circ. 2,000(paid).

WHITE BEAR LAKE

US

QUAD COMMUNITY PRESS. 1983. Tue. $.50
newsstand; $25/yr. 4779 Bloom Ave., White Bear
Lake, MN 55110. TEL 612-429-7781;
FAX 612-429-1242. **Owner(s):** Press
Publications, Inc., 4779 Bloom Ave., St. Paul, MN
55110. TEL 612-429-7781; Pub. Eugene D.
Johnson; adv. contact: Michelle Larson. pub. size:
broadsheet; circ. 7,000(paid).

WINDOM

US

WINDOM COTTONWOOD COUNTY CITIZEN. Wed. $.75 newsstand; $29.95/yr. in area; $41.95/yr. out of area. 260 Tenth St., Windom, MN 56101. TEL 507-831-3455; FAX 507-831-3740. **Owner(s):** Kim Anderson, 260 Tenth St., Windom, MN 56101; Ed. Rahn Larson. adv.; pub. size: broadsheet; circ. 4,000(paid).

MISSISSIPPI

ABERDEEN

US

ABERDEEN EXAMINER. 1866. Wed. $.50 newsstand; $18/yr. in cy.; $25/yr. out of cy.; $32/yr. out of state. 209 E. Commerce St., Aberdeen, MS 39730. TEL 601-369-4507; FAX 601-369-4508. **Owner(s):** Northeast Mississippi Community Newspapers, Inc., P.O. Box 909, Tupelo, MS 38802. TEL 601-842-2611; Ed. Barry Burleson; Pub. Barry Burleson; adv. contact: Jimmy Willis. pub. size: broadsheet; circ. 5,000(paid).

AMORY

US   ISSN 0899-0085

AMORY ADVERTISER, THE. 1917. Wed. $.50 newsstand; $18/yr. in cy. 113 S. Main St., Amory, MS 38821. TEL 601-256-5647; FAX 601-256-5701. **Owner(s):** Northeast Mississippi Community Newspapers, Inc., P.O. Box 519, Amory, MS 38821. TEL 601-256-5647; Ed. Chris Wilson. adv. contact: Bonnie Parham. photos; bk.rev.; pub. size: broadsheet; circ. 5,800(paid).

BATESVILLE

US

▼**PANOLIAN ADVANTAGE, THE.** 1996. Wed. free. 174 Hwy. 51, N., Batesville, MS 38606. TEL 601-563-4591; FAX 601-563-5610. **Owner(s):** John H. Howell, 174 Hwy. 51, N., P.O. Box 393, Batesville, MS 38606. TEL 601-563-4591; Rupert K. Howell, 174 Hwy. 51, N., P.O. Box 393, Batesville, MS 38606. TEL 601-563-4591; Ed. Tawanda Tinkersley; Pub. Tawanda Tinkersley; adv. contact: Sandy Richardson. circ. 10,700(free).

US

PANOLIAN, THE. 1882. Wed. $.75 newsstand; $20/yr. in state; $30.50/yr. out of state. 174 Hwy. 51, N., Batesville, MS 38606. TEL 601-563-4591; FAX 601-563-5610. **Owner(s):** John H. Howell, 174 Hwy. 51, N., P.O. Box 393, Batesville, MS 38606. TEL 601-563-4591; Rupert K. Howell, 174 Hwy. 51, N., P.O. Box 393, Batesville, MS 38606. TEL 601-563-4591; Ed. Tawanda Tinkersley; Pub. Tawanda Tinkersley; adv. contact: Sandy Richardson. pub. size: standard; circ. 10,000(paid).

BAY SPRINGS

US

JASPER COUNTY NEWS, THE. 1920. Wed. $13/yr. in cy.; $17/yr. out of cy.; $20/yr. out of state. Hwy. 15 N., Industrial Park, Bay Springs, MS 39422. TEL 601-764-3104; FAX 601-764-3106. **Owner(s):** Ronnie L. Buckley, P.O. Box 449, Bay Springs, MS 39422. TEL 601-764-2388; Ed. Kevin Williams; Pub. Ronnie L. Buckley; pub. size: standard; circ. 4,200(paid).
    Formerly: Bay Springs Jasper County News.

BAY ST. LOUIS

US

BAY ST. LOUIS SEA COAST ECHO. 1892. Thu. & Sun. $.50 newsstand; $34/yr. in cy.; $49/yr. out of cy.; $59/yr. out of state. 124 Court St., Bay St. Louis, MS 39520. TEL 601-467-5474; FAX 601-467-0333. **Owner(s):** Bay St. Louis Newspapers, Inc., P.O. Box 2009, Bay St. Louis, MS 39521. TEL 601-467-5474; Ed. Richard Meek; Pub. Ellis C. Cuevas; pub. size: standard; circ. 7,800(paid).

BOONEVILLE

US

BOONEVILLE BANNER-INDEPENDENT. 1898. Thu. $.50 newsstand; $20/yr. local; $30/yr. elsewhere. 208 Main St., Booneville, MS 38829. TEL 601-728-6214; FAX 601-728-1636. **Owner(s):** Paxton Media Group, Inc., P.O. Box 2300, Paducah, KY 42002. TEL 502-443-1771; Ed. Kenny Gooda; Pub. Tom Overton; adv. contact: Jim Burnett. pub. size: broadsheet; circ. 5,600(paid).

BRANDON

US

RANKIN COUNTY NEWS, THE. 1848. Wed. $.50 newsstand; $15/yr. in cy.; $20/yr. out of cy. Town Sq., 207 Government St., Brandon, MS 39042. TEL 601-825-8333; FAX 601-825-8334. **Owner(s):** RCN Corporation, P.O. Box 107, Brandon, MS 39043. TEL 601-825-8333; Ed. Marcus Bowers, Jr.; Pub. Marcus Bowers, Jr.; adv. contact: Marcus Bowers, Jr. pub. size: broadsheet; circ. 6,000(paid).

BRUCE

US

BRUCE CALHOUN COUNTY JOURNAL. 1953. Thu. $.50 newsstand $16/yr. 207 N. Newberger St., Bruce, MS 38915. TEL 601-983-2570; FAX 601-983-7567. **Owner(s):** S. Gale Denley, P.O. Box 278, Bruce, MS 38915; Ed. Celia Denley-Hillhouse Pub. S. Gale Denley; pub. size: broadsheet; circ. 3,500(paid).

CANTON

US

MADISON COUNTY HERALD. 1906. Thu. $.25 newsstand; $12/yr. in cy.; $15/yr. out of cy. 159 E. Center St., Canton, MS 39046. TEL 601-859-1221; FAX 601-859-9409. **Owner(s):** Mississippi Publishers Corp., P.O. Box 40, Jackson, MS 39205. TEL 601-961-7022; pub. size: broadsheet; circ. 5,000(paid).

CARROLLTON

US

CONSERVATIVE, THE. 1864. Thu. $.25 newsstand; $14/yr. Lexington Ave., Carrollton, MS 38917. TEL 601-283-1131. **Owner(s):** Montgomery Publishing Co., P.O. Box 345, Carrollton, MS 38917. TEL 601-283-113.; Ed. Tim Beeland; Pub. Tim Beeland; circ. 1,000(paid).

CARTHAGE

US

CARTHAGINIAN, THE. 1872. Thu. $.50 newsstand; $20/yr. 122 W. Franklin St., Carthage, MS 39051. TEL 601-267-45C.; FAX 601-267-5290. **Owner(s):** John H. Keith, The Carthaginian, 122 Franklin St. Carthage, MS 39051. TEL 601-267-45C.; Ed. Wade Prather; Pub. John H. Keith; adv.; pub. size: broadsheet; circ. 5,400(paid).

COLUMBIA

US

COLUMBIAN-PROGRESS. 1882. Thu. & Sat. $.50 newsstand; $30/yr. in cy.; $35/yr. in state; $40/yr. out of state. 318 Second St., Columbia, MS 39429. TEL 601-736-2611; FAX 601-736-4507. **Owner(s):** John Emmerich, 318 Second St., Columbia, MS 39429. TEL 601-736-2611; Ed. Ken Prillhart; Pub. Ken Prillhart; adv. contact: Bonnie Hudson. pub. size: standard; circ. 12,900(paid).

COLUMBUS

US

GOLDEN TRIANGLE SHOPPER. Tue. free. 516 Main St., Columbus, MS 39701. TEL 601-328-2424; FAX 601-329-8937. **Owner(s):** Commercial Dispatch, Inc., 516 Main St., Columbus, MS 39701. TEL 601-328-2424; adv. contact: Gary Peeples. bk.rev.; pub. size: standard; circ. 15,000(free). **Wire Service(s:** AP.

D'IBERVILLE

US

BILOXI-D'IBERVILLE PRESS. 1973. Wed. $.25 newsstand; $14/yr. mailed in Harrison & Jackson cys.; $12/yr. senior citizens; $25/yr. elsewhere. 9450 Central Ave., D'Iberville, MS 39532. TEL 601-392-3307; FAX 601-392-7043. **Owner(s):** S & F Publishing Co., Inc., P.O. Box 194, Biloxi, MS 39533. TEL 601-392-3307; Ed. Walter Fountain; Pub. Charles R. Stein, Sr.; pub. size: broadsheet; circ. 6,000(paid).

DEKALB

US

KEMPER COUNTY MESSENGER. 1940. Thu. $.50 newsstand; $12/yr. in cy.; $15/yr. out of cy.; $18/yr. out of state. Main St., DeKalb, MS 39328 TEL 601-743-576.; FAX 601-743-2760. **Owner(s):** Jeff & Jayne Jowers, P.O. Box 546, DeKalb, MS 39328. TEL 601-743-5760; James & Eettye Sedge, 107 Lavern, Crystal Springs, MS 39059. TEL 601-892-5510; Ed. Jeff Jowers; Pub. James L. Sledge, Jr.; adv. contact: Patty Jowers. bk.rev.; pub. size: broadsheet; circ. 2,200(free & paid).

EUPORA

US

WEBSTER PROGRESS-TIMES. 1879. Wed. $.50 newsstand; $22/yr. in state; $30/yr. out of state. 122 Dunn St., Eupora, MS 39744. TEL 601-258-7532; FAX 601-258-6474. **Owner(s):** American Publishing Co., 606 N. Van Buren, P.O. Box 520, Marion, IL 62959. TEL 618-993-1711; Ed. Betsy Mordecai; Pub. Timothy R. James; adv. contact: Timothy R. James. photos; pub. size: broadsheet; circ. 2,638(paid).

FOREST

US

SCOTT COUNTY TIMES. 1939. Wed. $.50 newsstand; $21/yr. in cy.; $24/yr. in state; $27/yr. out of state. 311 Smith St., Forest, MS 39074. TEL 601-469-2561; FAX 601-469-2004. **Owner(s):** Scott Publishing, Inc., P.O. Box 89, Forest, MS 39074. TEL 601-469-2561; Ed. S.L. Salter; Pub. S.L. Salter; adv. contact: Nicole Nichols. pub. size: broadsheet; circ. 5,200(paid).

FULTON

US

ITAWAMBA COUNTY TIMES, THE. 1945. Wed. $.50 newsstand; $18/yr. 106 W. Main St., Fulton, MS 38843-5149. TEL 601-862-3141; FAX 601-862-7804. **Owner(s):** Journal Publishing Co., P.O. Box 909, Tupelo, MS 38801. TEL 601-862-2611; FAX 601-862-7804; Pub. Rubye Del Harden; adv.; pub. size: broadsheet; circ. 6,600(paid).

HAZLEHURST

US

COPIAH COUNTY COURIER. 1884. Wed. $.50 newsstand; $14/yr. 103 S. Ragsdale Ave., Hazlehurst, MS 39083-0135. TEL 601-894-3141; FAX 601-894-3144. **Owner(s):** James & Wilma S. Lambert, 103 S. Ragsdale Ave., Hazlehurst, MS 39083; Ed. James Lambert; Pub. James Lambert; adv.; photos; pub. size: standard; circ. 6,036(free & paid).

HOLLY SPRINGS

US

SOUTH REPORTER, THE. 1865. Thu. $.50 newsstand; $17/yr. in cy.; $22/yr. out of cy. 157 S. Center St., Holly Springs, MS 38635. TEL 601-252-4261; FAX 601-252-3388. **Owner(s):** Walter W. Webb, 157 S. Center St., Holly Springs, MS 38635. TEL 601-252-4261; Ed. Walter W. Webb; Pub. Walter W. Webb; pub. size: broadsheet; circ. 6,300(paid).

HOUSTON

US

TIMES POST, THE. 1906. Wed. $.50 newsstand; $24/yr. in cy.; $30/yr. in state; $40/yr. out of state. 225 E. Madison, Houston, MS 38851. TEL 601-456-3771; FAX 601-456-5202. **Owner(s):** Houston Newspapers, Inc., 225 E. Madison, Houston, MS 38851. TEL 601-456-3771; Ed. Kenny Hoblitzell; Pub. Kenny Hoblitzell; adv. contact: Laura Bray. pub. size: broadsheet; circ. 9,300(paid).

IUKA

US

IUKA TISHOMINGO COUNTY NEWS. 1885. Thu. $.35 newsstand; $15/yr. in state; $25/yr. out of state. 120 W. Front St., Iuka, MS 38852. TEL 601-423-2211; FAX 601-423-3667. **Owner(s):** John H. Biggs, 120 W. Front St., Iuka, MS 38852. TEL 601-423-3666; Caroline Morris, Sheffield, AL; Ed. John H. Biggs; Pub. John H. Biggs; pub. size: standard; circ. 6,000(paid).

JACKSON

US

NORTHSIDE SUN, THE. 1967. Thu. $.50 newsstand; $16/yr. in cy. 269 Briarwood, Jackson, MS 39206. TEL 601-957-1122; FAX 601-957-1533. **Owner(s):** Sunland Publishing Co., Inc., P.O. Box 16709, Jackson, MS 39236. TEL 601-957-1122; FAX 601-957-1533; Ed. Jimmye Sweat. adv. contact: Jonni Webb. photos; bk.rev.; pub. size: broadsheet; circ. 9,500(paid).
Formerly: Sunland.

KOSCIUSKO

US

STAR-HERALD, THE. 1866. Thu. $.50 newsstand; $28/yr. local. 317 N. Madison, Kosciusko, MS 39090. TEL 601-289-2251; FAX 601-289-2254. **Owner(s):** American Publishing Co., 606 N. Van Buren, P.O. Box 520, Marion, IL 62959. TEL 618-993-1711; Ed. Jack Weatherly; Pub. Neal H. Turnage; adv. contact: Donna Peeples. pub. size: broadsheet; circ. 9,100(paid).
Formerly: Kosciusko Star-Herald.

LAUREL

US

IMPACT OF LAUREL. 1976. Wed. & Sun. free. 1010 N. 16th Ave., Laurel, MS 39440. TEL 601-649-1129. **Owner(s):** Buckley Newspapers, Inc., Box 449, Bay Springs, MS 39422. TEL 601-764-3104; Ed. Ronnie L. Buckley. adv. contact: James H. Luper. pub. size: tabloid; circ. 51,279(free).

LIBERTY

US   ISSN 0893-3790

SOUTHERN HERALD, THE. 1825. Thu. $.50 newsstand; $15/yr. in cy.; $20/yr. out of cy. & state. 258 Main St., Liberty, MS 39645. TEL 601-657-4818; FAX 601-657-4818. **Owner(s):** Richard H. Stratton, P.O. Box 674, Liberty, MS 39645. TEL 601-657-4818; Ed. Richard H. Stratton; Pub. Richard H. Stratton; adv.; photos; pub. size: standard; circ. 1,100(free & paid).
Formerly: Liberty Southern Herald.

LOUISVILLE

US

LOUISVILLE WINSTON COUNTY JOURNAL. 1892. Wed. $.75 newsstand; $20.50/yr. in cy.; $31/yr. out of cy. 119 N. Court Ave., Louisville, MS 39339. TEL 601-773-6241; FAX 601-773-6242. **Owner(s):** Louisville Newspapers, Inc., P.O. Box 469, Louisville, MS 39339. TEL 601-773-6241; Ed. Lori Clendenning; Pub. Jerry Shiverdecker; pub. size: broadsheet; circ. 5,300(paid).

US

SHOPPER'S GUIDE, THE. 1892. Wed. free. 119 N. Court Ave., Louisville, MS 39339. TEL 601-773-6241; FAX 601-773-6242. **Owner(s):** Louisville Newspapers, Inc., P.O. Box 469, Louisville, MS 39339; Ed. Lori Clendening; Pub. Jerry Shiverdecker; circ. 9,600(free & paid).

LUCEDALE

US

GEORGE COUNTY TIMES. Thu. $.25 newsstand; $11/yr. in cy.; $15/yr. in state; $18/yr. out of state. P.O. Box 238, Lucedale, MS 39452. TEL 601-947-2967; FAX 601-947-6828. **Owner(s):** O.G. Sellers, P.O. Box 238, Lucedale, MS 39452. TEL 601-947-7967; Ed. O.G. Sellers; Pub. O.G. Sellers; pub. size: standard; circ. 5,000(paid).
Formerly: Lucedale George County Times.

MACON

US

MACON BEACON, THE. 1849. Thu. $.50 newsstand; $17/yr. in state; $20/yr. out of state. 403 S. Jefferson, Macon, MS 39341. TEL 601-726-4747; FAX 601-726-4742. **Owner(s):** R. Scott Boyd, P.O. Box 32, Macon, MS 39341. TEL 601-726-4747; FAX 601-726-4742; Ed. R. Scott Boyd; Pub. R. Scott Boyd; pub. size: broadsheet; circ. 2,900(paid).

MAGEE

US

MAGEE COURIER. 1899. Thu. $.50 newsstand; $18/yr. in cy. 206 N. Main St., Magee, MS 39111. TEL 601-849-3434; FAX 601-849-6828. **Owner(s):** Simpson Publishing Co., Inc., P.O. Box 338, Magee, MS 39111. TEL 601-849-3434; FAX 601-849-6828; Ed. Pat Brown; Pub. Pat Brown; adv. contact: Jeau Butler. photos; pub. size: broadsheet; circ. 3,500(paid).

MAGNOLIA

US

MAGNOLIA GAZETTE, THE. 1874. Thu. $.50 newsstand; $10/yr. in cy.; $20/yr. out of state. 279 E. Bay, Magnolia, MS 39652. TEL 601-783-2441; FAX 504-748-7104. **Owner(s):** Louisiana State Newspapers, Abbeyville, LA; Ed. Chellette Simmons. adv. contact: Sally Nagle. photos; pub. size: broadsheet; circ. 1,200(paid).

NEW ALBANY

US

NEW ALBANY GAZETTE. 1887. Wed. & Fri. $.50 newsstand; $31.50/yr. local. 713 Carter Ave., New Albany, MS 38652. TEL 601-534-6321; FAX 601-534-6355. **Owner(s):** Landmark Community Newspapers, Inc., Hwy. 55, S., Shelbyville, KY 40065; Ed. Betty Jo Stewart. pub. size: broadsheet; circ. 16,000(paid).

NEWTON

US

NEWTON RECORD. 1901. Wed. $.50 newsstand; $22/yr. in cy.; $27/yr. out of cy.; $32/yr. out of state. 120 S. Main St., Newton, MS 39345. TEL 601-683-2001; FAX 601-683-2360. **Owner(s):** American Publishing Co., 606 N. Van Buren, P.O. Box 520, Marion, IL 62959. TEL 618-993-1711; Ed. J.E. Strange; Pub. J.E. Strange; adv.; photos; pub. size: broadsheet; circ. 2,674(paid).

US

SHOPPING NEWS, THE. 1980. Wed. free. 120 S. Main St., Newton, MS 39345. TEL 601-683-2001; FAX 601-683-2360. **Owner(s):** American Publishing Co., 606 N. Van Buren, P.O. Box 520, Marion, IL 62959. TEL 618-993-1711; Ed. J.E. Strange; Pub. J.E. Strange; adv.; pub. size: broadsheet; circ. 8,600(free).

OCEAN SPRINGS

US

OCEAN SPRINGS RECORD. 1965. Thu. $.50 newsstand; $19.75/yr. in cy. 715 Cox Ave., Ocean Springs, MS 39564. TEL 601-875-2791; FAX 601-875-9569. **Owner(s):** Gannett Company, Inc., 1100 Wilson Blvd., Arlington, VA 22234. TEL 703-284-6000; Pub. James Ricketts; adv. contact: Peter D. Logan. photos; pub. size: standard; circ. 3,600(paid).

PHILADELPHIA

US

NESHOBA DEMOCRAT, THE. 1881. Wed. $.50 newsstand; $21/yr. in cy.; $27/yr. out of cy. 439 Beacon St., Philadelphia, MS 39350. TEL 601-656-4000; FAX 601-656-6379. **Owner(s):** Neshoba Democrat Publishing Co., P.O. Box 30, Philadelphia, MS 39350. TEL 601-656-4000; Ed. Stanley Dearman; Pub. Stanley Dearman; adv.; photos; bk.rev.; pub. size: standard; circ. 7,500(paid).

PONTOTOC

US

PONTOTOC PROGRESS. 1929. Thu. $.50 newsstand; $23/yr. in cy.; $28/yr. elsewhere. 19 S. Liberty, Pontotoc, MS 38863. TEL 601-489-3511; FAX 601-489-6714. **Owner(s):** Daily Journal Newspapers, Tupelo, MS 38801. TEL 601-937-6411; Ed. David Helms; Pub. Gary Andrews; pub. size: broadsheet; circ. 6,800(paid).

PORT GIBSON

US

PORT GIBSON REVEILLE. 1851. Thu. $.35 newsstand; $14/yr. in state; $19.50/yr. out of state. 708 Main St., Port Gibson, MS 39150. TEL 601-437-5103; FAX 601-437-4410. **Owner(s):** Edgar T. Crisler, Jr., P.O. Box 1002, Port Gibson, MS 39150. TEL 601-437-5103; FAX 601-437-4410; Ed. Edgar T. Crisler, Jr.; Pub. Edgar T. Crisler, Jr.; adv. contact: Janice Bufkin. photos; bk.rev.; pub. size: standard; circ. 2,247(free & paid).

QUITMAN

US

CLARKE COUNTY TRIBUNE. 1908. Wed. $18/yr. in cy.; $20/yr. out of cy.; $22/yr. out of state. 101 Main St., Quitman, MS 39355. TEL 601-776-3726; FAX 601-776-5793. **Owner(s):** James T. Speed, 101 Main St., Quitman, MS 39355. TEL 601-776-3726; Ed. Carol Owens; Pub. James T. Speed; adv.; pub. size: standard; circ. 4,000(paid).

RALEIGH

US

SMITH COUNTY REFORMER. 1889. Wed. $.50 newsstand; $15/yr. in cy.; $20/yr. out of cy.; $23/yr. out of state. Main St., Raleigh, MS 39153. TEL 601-782-4358; FAX 601-764-3106. **Owner(s):** Ronnie L. Buckley, Buckley Newspapers, P.O. Box 449, Bay Springs, MS 39422. TEL 601-764-3104; Ed. Blenda Singleton. adv contact: Brenda Ingram. bk.rev.; pub. size: standard; circ. 3,800(paid).

RICHTON

US

RICHTON DISPATCH, THE. 1905. Thu. $.25 newsstand; $12/yr. in cy.; $15/yr. out of cy. 110 Walnut St., Richton, MS 39476-0019. TEL 601-788-6031; FAX 601-788-6031. **Owner(s):** Richton Dispatch, P.O. Drawer X, Richton, KS 39476-1521. TEL 601-788-6031; FAX 601-788-6031; Ed. Larry A. Wilson. adv.; photos; pub. size: standard; circ. 1,600(paid).

RIPLEY

US

RIPLEY SOUTHERN SENTINEL. 1879. s-w.: Wed. & Sat. $.50 newsstand; $38.50/yr. in cy.; $45.50/yr. out of cy.; $56/yr. out of state. 701 City Ave. N., Ripley, MS 38663. TEL 601-837-8111; FAX 601-837-4504. **Owner(s):** Sentinel, Inc., P.O. Box 558, Ripley, MS 38663. TEL 601-837-8111; adv. contact: Jane Matthews. pub. size: broadsheet; circ. 7,200(paid).

SENATOBIA

US

DEMOCRAT, THE. 1881. Tues. $.50 newsstand; $18/yr. local; $23/yr. in state; $28/yr. out of state. 219 E. Main St., Senatobia, MS 38668-0369. TEL 601-562-4414; FAX 601-562-8366. **Owner(s):** North Mississippi Newspapers, Inc.; Ed. Sarah Bondurant; Pub. Joe Lee, III; adv. contact: Sarah Bondurant. photos; bk.rev.; pub. size: broadsheet; circ. 5,000(free & paid).
Formerly: Tate County Democrat.

SOUTHAVEN

US

DE SOTO TIMES. 1939. w. $22/yr. in cy.; $35/yr. out of cy. 1283 Stateline, Southaven, MS 38671. TEL 601-393-6397; FAX 601-393-6463. **Owner(s):** Bailey Publications, Inc., P.O. Box 100, Hernando, MS 38671 Ed. William Bailey. adv.; photos; pub. size: standard; circ. 6,559(paid).

TYLERTOWN

US

TYLERTOWN TIMES. 1907. Thu. $15/yr. 727 Beulah Ave., Tylertown, MS 39667 TEL 601-876-5111; FAX 601-876-5280. **Owner(s):** Tylertown Times, 727 Beulah Ave., Tylertown MS 39667; Ed. Carolyn Dillon. pub. size: broadsheet; circ. 3,950(paid).

WAYNESBORO

US

WAYNE COUNTY NEWS. 1891 Thu. $.50 newsstand; $14/yr. local. 608 Station St., Waynesboro, MS 39367. TEL 601-735-434 ; FAX 601-735-1111. **Owner(s):** News Publishing Co. of Mississippi, P.O. Box 509, Waynesboro, MS 39367. TEL 601-735-434 ; Ed. Tom White. adv.; pub. size: broadsheet; circ. 5,000(paid).

WIGGINS

US

STONE COUNTY ENTERPRISE. 1906. Wed. $.35 newsstand; $15/yr. in cy.; $20/yr. out of cy.; $23/yr. out of state. 143 First St., Wiggins, MS 39577. TEL 601-928-4802; FAX 601-928-2191. **Owner(s):** Stone County Enterprise, P.O. Box 157, Wiggins, MS 39577. TEL 601-928-4802; Ed. Don Groves; Pub. Don Groves. adv. contact: Christy Groves. pub. size: broadsheet; circ. 2,700(paid).

WINONA

US

WINONA TIMES. Thu. $.50 newsstand $20/yr. in cy.; $25/yr. out of cy. 401 Summit St., Winona, MS 38967. TEL 601-283-1131. **Owner(s):** Montgomery Publishing Co. P.O. Box 151, Winona, MS 38967. TEL 601-283-1131; Ed. Tim Beeland; Pub. Tim Beeland; pub. size: broadsheet; circ. 3,600(paid).

YAZOO CITY

US

YAZOO HERALD. 1872. s-w.: Wed. & Sat. $.50 newsstand; $26/yr. in state; $38/yr. out of state. 1035 Grand Ave., Yazoo City, MS 39194. TEL 601-746-4911; FAX 601-746-4915. **Owner(s):** Yazoo Newspaper Co., Inc., P.O. Box 720, Yazoo City, MS 39194. TEL 601-746-4911; Ed. Roy Thomas; Pub. Roy Thomas; adv. contact: Phyllis Thomas. pub. size: broadsheet; circ. 4,200(paid).

MISSOURI

ALBANY

US

ALBANY LEDGER, THE. 1868. Wed. $.50 newsstand; $20/yr. in cy.; $24/yr. in state; $28/yr. out of state. P.O. Box 247, Albany MO 64402. TEL 816-726-3997; FAX 816-726-3997. **Owner(s):** Terry and Nancy Holub, Smith & Clay Sts., P.O. Box 247, Albany, MO 64402. TEL 816-726-3997; Ed. James Avey; Pub. Jack Pitzer; adv.; pub. size: broadsheet; circ. 1,600(paid).
Formerly: Ledger-Highlight The.

ARNOLD

US

JEFFERSON COUNTY JOURNAL. s-w.: Sun. & Wed. free. 27 Fox Valley Ctr., Arnold, MO 63010. TEL 314-296-2800; FAX 314-296-2800. **Owner(s):** Suburban Journals, P.O. Box 309, Festus, MO 63028. TEL 314-296-1800; Ed. Jennifer Florian. pub. size: broadsheet; circ. 19,000(free).

ASHLAND

US

BOONE COUNTY JOURNAL. 1969. Wed. $16/yr. in state; $20/yr. out of state. 104 W. Broadway, Ashland, MO 65010. TEL 314-657-2334; FAX 314-657-2002. **Owner(s):** Richard Flink, 104 W. Broadway, Ashland, MO 65010. TEL 314-657-2334; Ed. Jane Flink; Pub. Richard Flink; adv.; pub. size: broadsheet; circ. 1,700(paid).

AURORA

US   ISSN 1041-1275

AURORA ADVERTISER. 1886. 3/wk.: Mon., Wed., Fri. $.35 newsstand; $16/yr. in cy. 226 W. Church St., Aurora, MO 65605. TEL 417-678-2115. **Owner(s):** Lawrence County Newspapers, Inc., 32 W. Olive, Aurora, MO 65605. TEL 417-678-2115; Ed. Paul E. Donley; Pub. Paul E. Donley; adv. contact: Jowell Bagby. photos; bk.rev.; pub. size: standard; circ. 3,500(paid).

AVA

US

DOUGLAS COUNTY HERALD. 1887. Thu. $.35 newsstand; $14/yr. in cy.; $19/yr. out of cy. 304 E. Washington Ave., Ava, MO 65608-0577. TEL 417-683-4181. **Owner(s):** James E. Curry, 304 E. Washington Ave., Ava, MO 65608; D. Keith Moore, 304 E. Washington Ave., Ava, MO 65608. TEL 417-683-4181; Ed. D. Keith Moore; Pub. James Curry; adv. contact: Burrely Loftin. pub. size: broadsheet; circ. 5,000(paid).

BELLE

US

BELLE BANNER. 1907. Wed. $.40 newsstand; $17.61/yr. local; $20.28/yr. in state; $20/yr. out of state. 307 S. Alvarado Ave., Belle, MO 65013-0711. TEL 314-859-3328; FAX 314-859-6274. **Owner(s):** Tri-County Newspapers, 307 Alvarado, P.O. Box 711, Belle, MO 65013-0711. TEL 314-859-3328; FAX 314-859-6274; Ed. Ron Lewis; Pub. Ron Lewis; adv.; photos; pub. size: broadsheet; circ. 2,750(paid).

US

BLAND COURIER. 1901. Wed. $.40 newsstand; $17.61/yr. local; $20.28/yr. in state; $20/yr. out of state. 307 Alvarado, Belle, MO 65014. TEL 314-646-3312; FAX 314-859-6274. **Owner(s):** Tri-County Newspapers, 307 Alvarado, P.O. Box 711, Belle, MO 65013-0711. TEL 314-859-3328; FAX 314-859-6274; Ed. Ron Lewis; Pub. Ron Lewis; adv.; photos; pub. size: broadsheet; circ. 900(paid).

BELTON

US

STAR-HERALD. 1892. Thu. $.50 newsstand; $19/yr. in cy.; $26/yr. out of cy. & KS; $31/yr. out of state. 419 Main St., Belton, MO 64012. TEL 816-331-5353. **Owner(s):** Belton Publishing Co., Inc., 419 Main St., Belton, MO 64012. TEL 816-331-5353; Ed. Mark E. Cox; Pub. Mark E. Cox; adv. contact: Vicki Daniel. pub. size: broadsheet; circ. 5,348(paid).

BETHANY

US

BETHANY REPUBLICAN-CLIPPER. 1873. Wed. $.50 newsstand; $25/yr. 214 N. 16th St., Bethany, MO 64424. TEL 816-425-6325; FAX 816-425-3441. **Owner(s):** Bethany Printing Co., P.O. Box 351, Bethany, MO 64424. TEL 816-425-6325; FAX 816-425-3441; Ed. Philip Conger; Pub. Philip Conger; adv. contact: Kathy Conger. photos; pub. size: broadsheet; circ. 20,900(free & paid).

US

HARRISON COUNTY ADVISOR. 1967. Tue. free in cy.; $35/yr. out of cy.; $13/yr. mailed 3rd class. 303 N. 25th, Bethany, MO 64424. TEL 816-425-3433; FAX 816-425-6984. **Owner(s):** Harrison County Advisor, Inc., P.O. Box 106, Bethany, MO 64424. TEL 816-425-3433; adv.; pub. size: tabloid; circ. 7,000(free).

BOLIVAR

US

BOLIVAR HERALD-FREE PRESS. 1868. Wed. $.50 newsstand; $25/yr. in cy. 335 S. Springfield, Bolivar, MO 65613-0330. TEL 417-326-7636; FAX 417-326-8701. **Owner(s):** Sterling Media, Ltd., Rt. 3, Box 559, Bolivar, MO 65613. TEL 417-326-7636; Ed. Judy Kallenbach. adv. contact: Sue Roweton. pub. size: broadsheet; circ. 7,400(paid).

BOONVILLE

US

RECORD, THE. Tue. $.50 newsstand; $32.09/yr. 412 High St., Boonville, MO 65233. TEL 816-882-5335; FAX 816-882-2256. **Owner(s):** American Publishing Co., 606 N. Van Buren, P.O. Box 520, Marion, IL 62959. TEL 816-993-1711; Ed. Steve Thomas; Pub. Scott Jackson; adv. contact: Angela Inscore. photos; pub. size: broadsheet; circ. 10,000(paid).

BOWLING GREEN

US

BOWLING GREEN TIMES. 1874. Wed. $21/yr. in cy.; $31/yr. out of cy. 106 W. Main, Bowling Green, MO 63334. TEL 573-324-2222; FAX 573-324-3991. **Owner(s):** Smith Newspapers, Inc., P.O. Box 27, Fort Payne, AL 35967. TEL 205-845-5510; Pub. Candace Velvin; pub. size: broadsheet; circ. 3,125(paid).

BUFFALO

US

BUFFALO REFLEX. 1869. Wed. $.50 newsstand; $20.88/yr. local; $38/yr. out of state. 114 E. Lincoln, Buffalo, MO 65622. TEL 417-345-2224; FAX 417-345-2235. **Owner(s):** James Sterling, P.O. Box 330, Bolivar, MO 65622. TEL 417-325-7636; FAX 417-326-8701; Ed. Dave Abner; Pub. James Hamilton; adv. contact: Linda Lopez. bk.rev.; pub. size: broadsheet; circ. 4,700(paid).

BUTLER

US

NEWS-X PRESS. 1984. Fri. $.42 newsstand; $20.09/yr. in cy.; $23.36/yr. out of cy.; $21.15/yr. out of state. 5 N. Main, Butler, MO 64730-0210. TEL 816-679-6126; FAX 816-679-4905. **Owner(s):** Jim & Carol Peters, 5 N. Main St., Butler, MO 64730; Ed. C.A. Moore. adv. contact: Paula Shenengerdt. pub. size: standard; circ. 3,800(paid).

CALIFORNIA

US

CALIFORNIA DEMOCRAT. 1858. Wed. $21.75/yr. in cy.; $24/yr. in state; $26.50/yr. out of state. 319 S. High St., California, MO 65018. TEL 573-796-2135; FAX 573-796-4220. **Owner(s):** Freedom Communications, Inc., 17666 Fitch, Irvine, CA 92714. TEL 714-553-9292; FAX 714-474-7675; Ed. Connie Bestgen; Pub. Ray Grimes; pub. size: broadsheet; circ. 4,000(paid).

CAMERON

US

CAMERON CITIZEN OBSERVER. Thu. $.50 newsstand; $20/yr. in cy.; $22/yr. out of cy.; $28/yr. out of state. P.O. Box 70, Cameron, MO 64429. TEL 816-632-7281; FAX 816-632-4508. **Owner(s):** Smith Publishing Co., P.O. Box 70, Cameron, MO 64429. TEL 816-632-7281; Ed. Craig Watkins; Pub. Craig Watkins; pub. size: broadsheet; circ. 2,500(paid).

CANTON

US

PRESS-NEWS JOURNAL. 1863. Thu. $.50 newsstand; $20-$23/yr. 130 N. Fourth St., Canton, MO 63435. TEL 573-288-5668. **Owner(s):** Americanton Enterprises Inc., 130 N. Fourth St., Canton, MO 63435. TEL 573-288-5668; FAX 573-288-0000; Ed. David Steinbeck; Pub. David Steinbeck; pub. size: broadsheet; circ. 3,500(paid). **Formerly:** Canton Press-News Journal.

CARROLLTON

US

CARROLLTON DEMOCRAT. 1881. s-w.: Tue. & Fri. $.50 newsstand; $49.39/yr. carrier; $55.77/yr. mailed in cy.; $70.64/yr. mailed out of cy.; $66.50/yr. mailed out of state. Hwy. 65 & 24 S., Carrollton, MO 64633. TEL 816-542-0881; FAX 816-542-2580. **Owner(s):** Standard Herald, Inc.; Ed. Ray Scherer. Pub. Jack Krier; adv. contact: Judy Stroud. pub. size: broadsheet; circ. evening 2,800(paid). **Formerly:** Carrollton Daily Democrat.

CARUTHERSVILLE

US

DEMOCRAT-ARGUS, THE. 1868. s-w.: Wed. & Fri. $30/yr. 111 E. Fifth St., Caruthersville, MO 63830. TEL 314-333-4336; FAX 314-333-2307. **Owner(s):** Rust Communications, P.O. Box 699, Cape Girardeau, MO 63702-0699. TEL 800-879-1210; Ed. Jennifer Dodson. adv. contact: Sheila Roufe. pub. size: broadsheet; circ. 16,000(free & paid).

CASSVILLE

US   ISSN 0194-1542

BARRY COUNTY ADVERTISER. 1966. w. $.25 newsstand; $30/yr. 904 West St., Cassville, MO 65625. TEL 417-847-3155; FAX 417-847-4523. **Owner(s):** Barry County Advertiser, 904 West St., P.O. Box 488, Cassville, MO 65625. TEL 417-847-4475; FAX 417-847-4523; Ed. Jennie Herrin. adv.; photos; pub. size: tabloid; circ. 10,500(paid).

US

CASSVILLE DEMOCRAT. 1872. Wed. $.30 newsstand; $25/yr. 600 Main St., Cassville, MO 65625. TEL 417-847-2610; FAX 417-847-3092. **Owner(s):** Mike & Lisa Schlichtman, P.O. Box 486, Cassville, MO 65625. TEL 417-847-2610; Ed. Mike Schlichtman. adv.; pub. size: broadsheet; circ. 3,500(paid).

CENTRALIA

US

CENTRALIA FIRESIDE GUARD. 1868. Wed. $20/yr. local; $22.50/yr. in state; $27/yr. out of state. 118 W. Sneed, Centralia, MO 65240. TEL 314-682-2133; FAX 314-682-3361. **Owner(s):** Charles & Janann Hedberg, 118 W. Sneed, Centralia, MO 65240; Ed. Janann Hedberg; Pub. Charles Hedberg; pub. size: broadsheet; circ. 4,300(paid).

CHARLESTON

US

CHARLESTON ENTERPRISE-COURIER. 1874. Thu. $.30 newsstand; $18.70/yr. out of state; $20/yr. in state. 206 S. Main St., Charleston, MO 63834. TEL 314-683-3351; FAX 314-683-2217. **Owner(s):** Enterprise-Courier, Inc., P.O. Box 69, Charleston, MO 63834; Ed. Jim Anderson; Pub. Mildred Wallhausen; adv. contact: Vanessa Shankle. pub. size: broadsheet; circ. 3,500(paid).

CLINTON

US

CLINTON EYE, THE. Thu. $.30 newsstand. 212 S. Washington St., Clinton, MO 64735-0586. TEL 816-885-2281; FAX 816-885-2265. **Owner(s):** Democrat Publishing Co., 212 S. Washington St., Clinton, MO 64735-0586. TEL 816-885-2281; FAX 816-885-2265; Ed. Kathleen Miles; Pub. Kathleen K. White; adv. contact: Kathy Jo Johnson. pub. size: broadsheet; circ. 665(paid).

US

KAYO, THE. Tue. free. 212 S. Washington St., Clinton, MO 64735-0586. TEL 816-885-2281; FAX 816-885-2265. **Owner(s):** Democrat Publishing Co., 212 S. Washington St., Clinton, MO 64735-0586. TEL 816-885-2281; FAX 816-885-2265; Ed. Kathleen Miles; Pub. Kathleen K. White; adv. contact: Kathy Jo Johnson. pub. size: broadsheet; circ. 14,000(free).

COLUMBIA

US   ISSN 0026-6671

MISSOURI PRESS NEWS. 1938. m. $7.50/yr. 802 Locust, Columbia, MO 65201. TEL 573-449-4167; FAX 573-874-5894. **Owner(s):** Missouri Press Association, 802 Locust, Columbia, MO 65201. TEL 573-449-4167; Ed. Kent M. Ford; Pub. Doug Crews; adv.; photos; pub. size: standard; circ. 900.

US

WHEELS 'N DEALS. bi-m. free. 1203 Wilks Blvd., Columbia, MO 65201. TEL 314-443-6014; FAX 314-874-9594. **Owner(s):** Tom Ridge, P.O. Box 256, Columbia, MO 65201. TEL 314-443-6014; Ed. Tom Ridge; Pub. Tom Ridge; pub. size: broadsheet circ. 17,000(free).

CUBA

US

CUBA FREE PRESS. 1960. Thu. $.50 newsstand; $18.16/yr. 110 S. Buchanan, Cuba, MO 65453. TEL 314-885-7460; FAX 314-885-3803. **Owner(s):** Cuba Free Press, Inc., 110 S. Buchanan, Cuba, MO 65453. TEL 314-885-7460; Ed. Percy Pascoe; Pub. Percy Pascoe; adv. contact: Sherry Wycoff. pub. size: broadsheet; circ. 3,657(free & paid).

DIXON

US

DIXON PILOT. 1910. Thu. $.35 newsstand; $18/yr. in cy. 302 Locust St., Dixon, MO 65459. TEL 314-759-2127. **Owner(s):** Rick Blackburn, 302 Locust St., P.O. Drawer V, Dixon, MA 65459. TEL 314-759-2127; Ed. Ralph Nelson; Pub. Rick Blackburn; adv. contact: Connie Blackburn. pub. size: broadsheet; circ. 2,500(paid).

DONIPHAN

US

PROSPECT-NEWS, THE. 1874. Wed. $.50 newsstand; $15/yr. local; $25/yr. elsewhere. 110 Washington, Doniphar, MO 63935. TEL 573-996-2103; FAX 573-996-2217. **Owner(s):** Rust Communications, P.O. Box 600, Cape Girardeau, MO 63702. TEL 314-335-6611; Ed. Barbara Horton; Pub. Butler County; adv.; pub. size: broadsheet; circ. 5,300(paid).

US

PROSPECTOR, THE. Wed. free home deliv. in cy.; $25/yr. outside area. 110 Washington St., Doniphan, MO 63935. TEL 314-996-2103; FAX 314-996-2217. **Owner(s):** Butler County Publishing, 208 Poplar St., Poplar Bluff, MO 63901. TEL 573-785-1414; Ed. Barbara Horton; Pub. Don Schrieber; adv.; pub. size: broadsheet; circ. 6,800(free).

ELDON

US

ELDON ADVERTISER. 1894. Wed. $.50 newsstand; $22/yr. in cy.; $27/yr. out of cy.; $33/yr. out of state. 409-15 S. Maple St., Eldon, MO 65026-0315. TEL 314-392-5658; FAX 314-392-7755. **Owner(s):** Vernon Publishing, Inc., 409-15 S. Maple St., Eldon, MO 65026. TEL 573-392-5659; Ed. Ginny Duffield; Pub. Jeffrey D. Vernor; adv.; photos; pub. size: broadsheet; circ. 5,600(paid).

ELLINGTON

US

REYNOLDS COUNTY COURIER. 1876. Thu. $.35 newsstand; $16.50/yr. in surrounding cys.; $26/yr. elsewhere. 130 Main St., Ellington, MO 63638. TEL 314-663-2243; FAX 314-663-2763. **Owner(s):** Ellinghouse Publishing Co., Inc., 101 W. Elm, Piedmont, MO 63957. TEL 314-223-7122; FAX 314-223-7871; Pub. Mary Beth Stivers; adv. contact: Debbie Shrum. photos; pub. size: broadsheet; circ. 2,850(paid). **Wire Service(s):** AP.

FAYETTE

US   ISSN 0746-9934

DEMOCRAT-LEADER. 1874. Sa. $.30 newsstand; $12/yr. in cy.; $29/yr. in state; $34/yr. out of state. 202 E. Morrison St., Fayette, MO 65248-0032. TEL 816-248-2235; FAX 816-298-1200. **Owner(s):** Wood Creek Corp., 202 E. Morrison St., Fayette, MO 65248. TEL 816-248-5223; FAX 816-298-1200; Ed. H. Denny Davis; Pub. H. Denny Davis; adv.; pub. size: standard; circ. 2,512(free & paid).

US   ISSN 0746-9942

FAYETTE ADVERTISER, THE. 1840. Wed. $.30 newsstand; $12/yr. in cy.; $18/yr. 202 E. Morrison St., Fayette, MO 65248. TEL 816-248-2235; FAX 816-248-1200. **Owner(s):** Wood Creek Corp., 202 E. Morrison St., Fayette, MO 65248. TEL 816-248-5223; FAX 816-248-1200; Ed. H. Denny Davis; Pub. H. Denny Davis; adv.; pub. size: standard; circ. 4,912(paid).

FESTUS

US

NEWS DEMOCRAT JOURNAL. 1865. s-w.: Sun. & Wed. $.50 newsstand; free home deliv. 988 E. Gannon Dr., Festus, MO 63028. TEL 314-937-9811; FAX 314-931-2638. **Owner(s):** Suburban Journals, 1714 Deer Tracks Trail, St. Louis, MO 63131. TEL 314-821-1110; Ed. Lois Kendal; Pub. Thomas Rice; adv. contact: Carla Leara. pub. size: broadsheet; circ. 23,800(paid).

FLORISSANT

US

FLORISSANT VALLEY REPORTER. 1950. Tue. $.50 newsstand; $12.95/yr. in cy.; $17.95/yr. out of cy. 525 Rue St. Francois, Florissant, MO 63031. TEL 314-839-1111. **Owner(s):** Reynolds Publishing Co., Inc, P.O. Box 69, Florissant, MO 63032. TEL 314-839-1111; Ed. David L. Reynolds; Pub. David L. Reynolds; adv.; photos; bk.rev.; pub. size: tabloid; circ. 9,000(paid).

FORSYTH

US

▼**TANEY COUNTY TIMES.** 1995. w. $.35 newsstand; $15/yr. in cy.; $25/yr. out of cy. 253 Main St., Forsyth, MO 65653. TEL 417-546-3305; FAX 417-546-2326. **Owner(s):** Pat & Wendy Fitzgerald, P.O. Box 220, Forsyth, MO 65653. TEL 417-546-3305; FAX 417-546-2326; Ed. Patrick D. Fitzgerald; Pub. Patrick D. Fitzgerald; adv.; photos; pub. size: broadsheet; circ. 2,400(free & paid).

FREDERICKTOWN

US

FREDERICKTOWN DEMOCRAT-NEWS. 1870. Wed. $25/yr. in state; $31/yr. out of state. 131 S. Main, Fredericktown, MO 63645. TEL 573-783-3366; FAX 573-783-6890. **Owner(s):** American Publishing Co., 606 N. Van Buren, P.O. Box 520, Marion, IL 62959. TEL 618-993-1711; Ed. Alan Kopitsky; Pub. Mary Cissell; adv.; photos; bk.rev.; pub. size: broadsheet; circ. 3,400(paid).

GAINESVILLE

US

OZARK COUNTY TIMES. 1883. Wed. $.50 newsstand. P.O. Box 188, Gainesville, MO 65655. TEL 417-679-4641; FAX 417-679-3423. **Owner(s):** Danton Wright, P.O. Box 188, Gainesville, MO. TEL 417-679-4641; FAX 417-679-3423; Ed. Rhonda Sprague; Pub. Walt Sanders; adv. contact: Walt Sanders. photos; bk.rev.; pub. size: broadsheet; circ. 11,400(free & paid).

GALLATIN

US

NORTH MISSOURIAN. 1864. Wed. $.50 newsstand; $18-$24/yr. 203 N. Main, Gallatin, MO 64640. TEL 816-663-2154; FAX 816-663-2054. **Owner(s):** Gallatin Publishing Co., 203 N. Main, P.O. Box 37, Gallatin, MO 64640. TEL 816-663-2154; FAX 816-663-2498; Ed. Darryl Wilkinson. adv.; photos; bk.rev.; pub. size: tabloid; circ. 2,600(paid).

HARRISONVILLE

US

HARRISONVILLE CASS COUNTY DEMOCRAT MISSOURIAN. 1881. Fri. $.50 newsstand; $24.50. plus tax. 310 S. Lexington, Harrisonville, MO 64701. TEL 816-380-3228; FAX 816-380-2095. **Owner(s):** Clark O. Murray, P.O. Box 15999, Shawnee Mission, KS 66285. TEL 913-492-9050; Ed. William E. James. adv. contact: Gavin Fenwick. photos; pub. size: broadsheet; circ. 6,181(paid).

HERMANN

US

HERMANN ADVERTISER-COURIER. 1854. Wed. $.50 newsstand; $23/yr. in cy.; $28/yr. out of cy.; $35/yr. out of state. 136 E. Fourth St., Hermann, MO 65041-0350. TEL 314-486-5418; FAX 314-486-5524. **Owner(s):** Spirit Newspapers of Missouri, Inc., 136 E. Fourth St., Hermann, MO 65041. TEL 314-486-5418; Ed. Don Kruse. adv. contact: Helen Davis. pub. size: broadsheet; circ. 4,400(paid).

HERMITAGE

US

HERMITAGE INDEX. 1885. Thu. $.50 newsstand; $18.50/yr. in cy.; $24/yr. out of cy.; $30/yr. out of state. P.O. Box 127, Hermitage, MO 65668. TEL 417-745-6404; FAX 417-745-2222. **Owner(s):** Earl & Willa Mae Jenkins, P.O. Box 127, Hermitage, MO 65668. TEL 417-745-6404; FAX 417-745-2222; Ed. Don Ginnings; Pub. Earl Jenkins; adv. contact: Don Ginnings. pub. size: broadsheet; circ. 4,400(paid).

HOLDEN

US

HOLDEN IMAGE-PROGRESS, THE. 1904. Wed. $.50 newsstand; $18/yr. local; $29/yr. out of state. 117 E. 2nd St., Holden, MO 64040. TEL 816-732-5552; FAX 816-732-4696. **Owner(s):** Rusty Hartwell, 117 E. 2nd St., Holden, MO 64040. TEL 816-732-5552; FAX 816-732-4696; Pub. Rusty Hartwell; adv. contact: Cindy Reynolds. pub. size: standard; circ. 7,700(free & paid).

Formerly: Holden Progress, The.

HOLTS SUMMIT

US

▼**CALLAWAY COURIER.** 1994. Wed. $.35 newsstand; $15/yr. in cy.; $20/yr. out of cy. P.O. Box 635, Holts Summit, MO 65043. TEL 573-896-9311; FAX 573-896-8725. **Owner(s):** Callaway Courier, Inc., P.O. Box 635, Holts Summit, MO 65043. TEL 573-896-9311; Ed. Dwight Warren. adv.; photos; pub. size: broadsheet; circ. 3,000(paid).

HOPKINS

US

HOPKINS JOURNAL, THE. 1874. Wed. $.35 newsstand; $12.57/yr. 117 N. Third St., Hopkins, MO 64461. TEL 816-778-3464; FAX 816-778-3345. **Owner(s):** Paul E. Thompson, P.O. Box 167, Hopkins, MO 64461. TEL 816-778-3464; FAX 816-778-3345; Ed. Darla Thompson; Pub. Paul E. Thompson; adv. contact: Paul Thompson. photos; pub. size: standard.

HOUSTON

US

HOUSTON HERALD & REPUBLICAN. 1878. Thu. $.50 newsstand; $18.65/yr. in cy.; $29/yr. out of cy.; $27.55/yr. elsewhere in MO. 113 N. Grand, Houston, MO 65483. TEL 417-967-2000; FAX 417-967-2096. **Owner(s):** Houston Newspapers, Inc., P.O. Box 70, Houston, MO 65483. TEL 412-967-2000; Ed. Bradley G. Gentry. adv.; pub. size: broadsheet; circ. 9,800(free & paid).

IRONTON

US

MOUNTAIN ECHO. 1937. w. $.50 newsstand; $21/yr. local; $33/yr. out of area; $33/yr. out of state. 110 N. Main St., Ironton, MO 63650-0025. TEL 314-546-3917; FAX 314-546-3919. **Owner(s):** Iron County Newspaper, 110 N. Main St., Ironton, MO 63650-0025. TEL 314-546-3917; FAX 314-546-3919; Ed. Mark Cheaney; Pub. Judy Schaaf; adv.; photos; pub. size: broadsheet; circ. 6,650(free & paid).

JACKSON

US

JACKSON CASH-BOOK JOURNAL. 1870. Wed. $.35 newsstand; $12/yr. in cy.; $14/yr. in surrounding cys.; $18/yr. in state; $27/yr. out of state. 210 W. Main St., Jackson, MO 63755. TEL 573-243-3515; FAX 573-243-3517. **Owner(s):** Gerald Jones, P.O. Box 369, Jackson, MO 63755. TEL 573-243-3515; Ed. David Bloom; Pub. Gerald Jones, II; adv. contact: Pam Jones. photos; pub. size: broadsheet; circ. 8,000(free & paid).

KANSAS CITY

US

CLAY DISPATCH-TRIBUNE. 1964. Wed. $.50 newsstand; $18/yr. 7007 N.E. Parvin Rd., Kansas City, MO 64117. TEL 816-454-9660; FAX 816-454-7523. **Owner(s):** Townsend Communications, Inc., 7007 N.E. Parvin Road, Kansas City, MO 64117. TEL 816-454-9660; Ed. Linn Brown; Pub. Harold G. Townsend, Jr.; adv. contact: Dorothy Baum. pub. size: broadsheet; circ. 61,000(paid).

US

LIBERTY TRIBUNE. Wed. $.50 newsstand; $18/yr. 7007 N.E. Parvin Rd., Kansas City, MO 64117. TEL 816-454-9660; FAX 816-454-7523. **Owner(s):** Townsend Communications, Inc., 7007 N.E. Parvin Rd., Kansas City, MO 64117. TEL 816-454-9660; Ed. Linn Brown; Pub. Harold G. Townsend, Jr.; adv.; pub. size: broadsheet; circ. 10,200(paid).

US

NEW TIMES, THE. 1991. Wed. free newsstand; $40/yr. mailed. 207 Westport Rd., Ste. 201, Kansas City, MO 64111. TEL 816-753-7880; FAX 816-561-6252. **Owner(s):** J. Patrick O'Connor & Steven A. Glorioso, 207 Westport Rd., Ste. 201, Kansas City, MO 64111. TEL 816-753-7880; FAX 816-561-6252; Ed. C.J. Janovy; Pub. Steven A. Glorioso; adv.; photos; bk.rev.; pub. size: tabloid.

US

PITCH WEEKLY. 1980. Thu. free newsstand; $35/yr. 3535 Broadway, Ste. 400, Kansas City, MO 64111. TEL 816-561-6061; FAX 816-756-0502; E-mail: pitchwee@qni.com; URL: http://www.qni.com/pitch/. **Owner(s):** Hal Brody, 3535 Broadway, Ste. 400, Kansas City, MO 64111. TEL 816-561-6061; FAX 816-756-0502; Ed. Jeffrey Drake; Pub. Hal Brody; adv. contact: Julie Brecht. photos; bk.rev.; pub. size: tabloid; circ. 85,000(controlled & free).

US

PLATTE DISPATCH TRIBUNE. 1914. Wed. $.50 newsstand; $15/yr. in cy. 7007 N.E. Parvin Rd., Kansas City, MO 64117. TEL 816-454-9660; FAX 816-452-5889. **Owner(s):** Townsend Communications, Inc., 7007 N.E. Parvin Road, Kansas City, MO 64117. TEL 816-454-9660; FAX 816-452-5889; Ed. Linn Brown; Pub. Harold G. Townsend, Jr.; adv. contact: Dorothy Baum. pub. size: broadsheet; circ. 13,400(paid).

US

PRESS DISPATCH. 1914. Wed. $.50 newsstand; $17/yr. in cy.; $20/yr. out of cy. 7007 N.E. Parvin Rd., Kansas City, MO 64117. TEL 816-454-9660; FAX 816-452-5889. **Owner(s):** Townsend Communications, Inc., 7007 N.E. Parvin Road, Kansas City, MO 64117. TEL 816-454-9660; FAX 816-452-9660; Ed. Linn Brown; Pub. Harold G. Townsend, Jr.; adv. contact: Dorothy Baum. pub. size: broadsheet; circ. 1,770(paid).

US

WEDNESDAY MAGAZINE. 1937. Wed. free newsstand; $20/yr. in cy.; $35/2 yrs. 20 E. Gregory Blvd., Kansas City, MO 64114. TEL 816-361-0616; FAX 816-822-1856. **Owner(s):** Townsend Communications, Inc., 7007 N.E. Parvin Rd., Kansas City, MO 64116. TEL 816-454-9660; Ed. David Knopf; Pub. Harold G. Townsend, Jr.; adv. contact: Lori Richmond. pub. size: tabloid; circ. 34,000(paid).

KIMBERLING CITY

US

ISSN 0894-0568

TABLE ROCK GAZETTE. 1961. Thu. $.50 newsstand; $20.77/yr. in cy.; $28.62/yr. out of cy.; $31.62/yr. out of state. Kimberling City Shopping Center, Hwy. 13, Kimberling City, MO 65686. TEL 417-739-4694; FAX 417-739-4695. **Owner(s):** Jack & Kathy Krier, P.O. Box 432, Kimberling City, MO; Ed. Pam Soetaert; Pub. Jack Krier; adv.; pub. size: broadsheet; circ. 3,791(paid).

Formerly: Kimberling City Table Rock Gazette.

LAMAR

US

LAMAR DEMOCRAT. 1870. s-w.: Wed. & Sat. $.50 newsstand; $34.50/yr. 900 N. Gulf St., Lamar, MO 64759. TEL 417-682-5529; FAX 417-682-5595. **Owner(s):** Lamar Democrat, Inc., 900 N. Gulf, Lamar, MO 64759. TEL 417-682-5529; Pub. Douglas D. Davis; adv. contact: Douglas D. Davis. photos; bk.rev.; pub. size: broadsheet; circ. evening 3,800(paid).

LEE'S SUMMIT

US

LEE'S SUMMIT JOURNAL. 1881. 3/wk.: Mon., Wed., Fri. $.50 newsstand; $36/yr. in cy.; $47/yr. out of cy. 415 S. Douglas St., Lee's Summit, MO 64063. TEL 816-524-2345; FAX 816-524-5136. **Owner(s):** Inland Industries, Inc., 105th & Santa Fe, Shawnee, KS 66215. TEL 913-492-9050; Ed. Ken Hatfield; Pub. W. Ferrell Shuck; adv. contact: Jane Drummond. pub. size: broadsheet; circ. 7,650(paid). **Wire Service(s):** AP.

LEXINGTON

US

LEXINGTON NEWS. 1800. s-w.: Wed. & Fri. $.50 newsstand; $25.61/yr. local; $40/yr. out of state. 925 Main St., Lexington, MO 64067. TEL 816-259-2266; FAX 816-259-4870. **Owner(s):** Jack Krier, P.O. Box 69, Carrollton, MO 64633. TEL 816-542-0881; Ed. Eric Crane; Pub. Frank Mercer; adv. contact: Jamie Krier. photos; bk.rev.; pub. size: standard; circ. 3,500(paid).

LINN

US

LINN UNTERRIFIED DEMOCRAT. 1866. Wed. $.50 newsstand; $21/yr. in cy.; $27/yr. out of cy.; $30/yr. out of state. 300 E. Main St., Linn, MO 65051. TEL 314-897-3150; FAX 314-897-0076. **Owner(s):** Jerrilynn Voss, 300 E. Main St., Linn, MO 65051; Ed. Paul Slater; Pub. Jerrilynn Voss; adv.; pub. size: broadsheet; circ. 4,750(paid).

LOUISIANA

US

LOUISIANA PRESS-JOURNAL. 1855. Wed. $.50 newsstand; $21/yr. local. 3406 Georgia St., Louisiana, MO 63353. TEL 573-754-5566; FAX 573-754-4749. **Owner(s):** Press-Journal Publishing Co., Inc., 3406 Georgia St., Louisiana, MO 63353. TEL 573-754-5566; Ed. Walt Gilbert; Pub. Walt Gilbert; adv. contact: Walt Gilbert. photos; pub. size: broadsheet; circ. 3,500(paid).

MARBLE HILL

US

BOLLINGER COUNTY BANNER-PRESS. 1881. Thu. $.50 newsstand; $15/yr. local. 103 Walnut St., Marble Hill, MC 63764. TEL 314-238-2821; FAX 314-238-0020 **Owner(s):** Concord Publishing, 301 Broadway, Cape Girardeau, MO 63701. TEL 314-334-7100; Ed. Jim McIntosh; Pub. Wally Lage; adv.; photos; bk.rev.; pub. size: broadsheet; circ. 4,500(paid).

Formerly: Marble Hill Bollinger County Banner-Press.

MARCELINE

US

MARCELINE PRESS. 1966. Thu. $.50 newsstand; $33/yr. 123 S. Kansas, Marceline, MO 64658. TEL 816-376-3508; FAX 816-376-2757; E-mail: bllevans@aol.com. **Owner(s):** American Publishing Co., 606 N. Van Buren, P.O. Box 520, Marion, IL 62959. TEL 618-993-1711; Ed. Cathy Lenny. adv.; pub. size: broadsheet; circ. 16,650(free & paid).

MARSHFIELD

US

MARSHFIELD MAIL. 1892. Wed. $.50 newsstand; $21/yr. local; $30/yr. elsewhere. 225 N. Clay St., Marshfield, MO 65706-1652. TEL 417-468-2013; FAX 417-859-7930. **Owner(s):** Gordon E. Nordquist, 9164 Riverview Dr., Rogersville, MO 65742. TEL 417-753-7083; Beverly Hickey, 853 Queen St., Maize, KS 67101; Robert Bolitho Design Benefit Trust No. 1, P.O. Box 3008, Palm Beach, FL 33480; Ed. Gordon Nordquist. adv.; photos; pub. size: standard; circ. 5,500(free & paid).

MARTHASVILLE

US

MARTHASVILLE RECORD, THE. 1896. Thu. $.35 newsstand; $18.50 local; $20.65 in state; $20.50 out of state. 203 W. South St., Marthasville, MO 63357-0077. TEL 314-433-2223. **Owner(s):** Rueben Eichmeyer, P.O. Box 77, Marthasville, MO 63357-0077. TEL 314-433-2223; Mabel Eichmeyer, P.O. Box 77, Marthasville, MO 63357-0077. TEL 314-433-2223; adv.; pub. size: broadsheet; circ. 784(paid).

MILAN

US

MILAN STANDARD, THE. 1872. Thu. $.40 newsstand; $15.06/yr. in cy.; $17.88/yr. out of cy.; $21/yr. out of state. 105 S. Market St., Milan, MO 63556. TEL 816-265-4244; FAX 816-265-3180. **Owner(s):** Bertha B. Wilson, 431 E. Second St., Milan, MO 63556. TEL 816-265-3122; R.W Wilson, 431 E. Second St., Milan, MO 63556. TEL 816-265-4323; Mary Ann Cowgill, 402 S. Water, Milan, MO 63556. TEL 816-265-4524; Ed. Robert W. Wilson; Pub. Robert W. Wilson; adv. contact: David T. Wilson. photos; pub. size: broadsheet; circ. 3,993(paid).

MONTGOMERY CITY

US

MONTGOMERY STANDARD. 1858. Wed. $.25 newsstand; $12/yr. in cy.; $16/yr. out of cy. 115 W. Second St., Montgomery City, MO 63361. TEL 573-564-2339. **Owner(s):** Montgomery Standard, Inc., 115 W. Second St., Montgomery City, MO 63361. TEL 573-564-2339; Ed. John Fisher. adv. pub. size: broadsheet; circ. 3,500(paid).

MOUND CITY

US

MOUND CITY NEWS. 1879. Thu. $.50 newsstand; $18/yr. in cy.; $20/yr. in state; $22/yr. elsewhere. 511 State St., Mound City, MO 64470-0175. TEL 816-442-5423; FAX 816-442-5423. **Owner(s):** Mound City News, Inc., 511 State St., Mound City, MO 64470-0175. TEL 816-442-5423; Pub. Linda Boultinghouse; adv.; photos pub. size: broadsheet; circ. 2,409(paid).

Formerly: Mound City News Independent.

MOUNTAIN GROVE

US

MOUNTAIN GROVE NEWS-JOURNAL. 1890. Wed. $.45 newsstand; $15.50/yr. local $18.50/yr. out of area; $22/yr. out of state. 150 E. First St. Mountain Grove, MO 65711. TEL 417-926-5148; FAX 417-925-6648. **Owner(s):** Dean DeVries, 150 E. First St., Mountain Grove, MO 65711. TEL 417-926-5148; Ed. Doug Berger; Pub. Dean DeVries; adv. contact: Sandy Anderson. photos; bk.rev.; pub. size: broadsheet; circ. 12,200(free & paid).

MT. VERNON

US

LAWRENCE COUNTY RECORD. 1875. Wed. $.50 newsstand; $16.50/yr. local; $24/yr. out of state. 312 S. Hickory, Mt. Vernon, MO 65712. TEL 417-466-2185; FAX 417-465-2187. **Owner(s):** Stephen & Kathy Fairchild, P.O. Box 348, Mt. Vernon, MO 65712. TEL 417-466-2185; Ed. Kathy S. Fairchild; Pub. Stephen C. Fairchild; adv. contact: Rosemary Hailey. pub. size: broadsheet; circ. 3,400(paid).

O'FALLON

US

O'FALLON JOURNAL. 1963. 3/wk.: Wed., Fri., Sun. free local; $56.25/yr. elsewhere. 216 E. Elm St., O'Fallon, MO 63366. TEL 314-240-4949; FAX 314-272-7913. **Owner(s):** Suburban Journals, 1714 Deer Tracks Trail, St. Louis, MO 63131. TEL 314-821-1110; Ed. Scott Queen; Pub. Tom Rice; adv. contact Shelley Jefts. photos; bk.rev.; pub. size: broadsheet; circ. 13,000(free).

Formerly: O'Fallon Tribune Journal.

Weeklies

OWENSVILLE

US

GASCONADE COUNTY REPUBLICAN. 1904. Wed. $.50 newsstand; $25.25/yr. 106 E. Washington Ave., Owensville, MO 65066. TEL 573-437-2323; FAX 573-437-3033. **Owner(s):** Warden Publishing Co., Inc., P.O. Box 540, Owensville, MO 65066. TEL 573-437-2323; Ed. Thomas C. Warden; Pub. Thomas C. Warden; adv. contact: Don Warden. pub. size: standard; circ. 7,700(free & paid).
Formerly: Owensville Gasconade County Republican.

OZARK

US

CHRISTIAN COUNTY HEADLINER NEWS. 1967. s-w.: Wed. & Sat. $.50 newsstand; $29/yr. carrier. 427 E. South St., Ozark, MO 65721. TEL 417-581-3541; FAX 417-581-3577. **Owner(s):** Lancaster Management, P.O. Box 609, Gadsen, AL 35209. TEL 205-543-3417; Ed. Robert Kornfeld; Pub. Roger Frieze; pub. size: broadsheet; circ. 4,500(paid).
Formerly: Ozark Headliner.

PACIFIC

US   ISSN 0746-1712

TRI-COUNTY JOURNAL. 1962. Wed. $.50 newsstand; $39/6 mos.; $78/yr. 111 W. St. Louis St., Pacific, MO 63069. TEL 314-227-1286; FAX 314-227-1272. **Owner(s):** Suburban Journals, 1714 Deer Tracks Trail, St. Louis, MO 63131. TEL 314-821-1110; Ed. Danette Thompson; Pub. Laurie Samo; adv.; photos; pub. size: broadsheet; circ. 13,000(free).

PALMYRA

US

PALMYRA SPECTATOR. 1839. Wed. $22.50/yr. 304 S. Main, Palmyra, MO 63461. TEL 573-769-3111; FAX 573-769-3554. **Owner(s):** Keck Enterprises Inc., P.O. Box 431, Palmyra, MO 63461. TEL 573-769-3111; Ed. Lee Keck. pub. size: broadsheet; circ. 3,300(paid).

PARIS

US

MONROE COUNTY APPEAL. 1865. Thu. $.50 newsstand; $20.50/yr. in area; $22.50/yr. in state; $23.50/yr. out of state. 230 N. Main St., Paris, MO 65275. TEL 816-327-4192; FAX 816-327-4847. **Owner(s):** Richard Fredrick, P.O. Box 207, Paris, MO 65275. TEL 816-327-4192; Pub. Richard Fredrick; adv.; photos; pub. size: broadsheet; circ. 2,300(paid).

PARKVILLE

US   ISSN 0899-5737

PLATTE COUNTY GAZETTE. 1885. Wed. $.35 newsstand; $15/yr. 6201 N.W. Hwy. 9, Parkville, MO 64512. TEL 816-741-9530; FAX 816-741-9593. **Owner(s):** Dan O'Dell, 6201 N.W. Hwy. 9, Parkville, MO 64512. TEL 816-781-1044; FAX 816-781-1755; Ed. Jason Offutt; Pub. Randall Battagler; adv. contact: Carol Allen. photos; bk.rev.; pub. size: standard; circ. 15,588(free & paid).

PERRYVILLE

US

PERRY COUNTY REPUBLIC-MONITOR, THE. 1889. s-w.: Tue. & Thu. $.75 newsstand; $35.05/yr. in cy.; $45.68/yr. out of cy.; $55/yr. out of state. 10 W. St. Maries, Perryville, MO 63775. TEL 314-547-4567; FAX 314-547-1643. **Owner(s):** P.T.S., Inc., P.O. Box 32040, Tuscaloosa, AL 30967. TEL 205-752-7500; FAX 205-752-5600; Ed. Randall J. Pribble; Pub. Randall J. Pribble; adv. contact: Randall J. Pribble. photos; pub. size: broadsheet; circ. 11,457(free & paid).

US

SUN TIMES. 1989. Wed. $.50 newsstand; $19.12/yr. 10 Perry Plz., Perryville, MO 63775. TEL 314-883-2980; FAX 314-547-8085. **Owner(s):** Elmo Donze, 10 Perry Plz., Perryville, MO 63775; Ed. John Meacham; Pub. Elmo Donze; adv. contact: Bob Scott. photos; pub. size: broadsheet; circ. 3,000(controlled & paid).

PIEDMONT

US

WAYNE COUNTY JOURNAL-BANNER. 1876. Thu. $.50 newsstand; $21/yr. local; $31/yr. elsewhere. 101 W. Elm St., Piedmont, MO 63957. TEL 573-223-7122; FAX 573-223-7871. **Owner(s):** Harold Ellinghouse, 101 W. Elm St., Piedmont, MO 63957. TEL 573-223-7122; FAX 573-223-7871; Mary B. Stivers, 101 W. Elm St., Piedmont, MO 63957. TEL 573-223-7122; FAX 573-223-7871; Ed. Harold T. Ellinghouse; Pub. Harold T. Ellinghouse; adv.; photos; pub. size: broadsheet; circ. 5,500(paid). **Wire Service(s):** AP.

PIERCE CITY

US

PIERCE CITY LEADER-JOURNAL. 1905. Thu. $.35 newsstand; $14.92/yr. local. 105 W. Commercial St., Pierce City, MO 64862. TEL 417-476-2232. **Owner(s):** Linda Eck Elderton, R.R. 2, Box 345A, Sarcoxie, MO 64862. TEL 417-548-3311; adv. contact: Marlene Gisn. bk.rev.; pub. size: tabloid; circ. 1,000(paid).

POTOSI

US

INDEPENDENT-JOURNAL, THE. 1872. Thu. $.50 newsstand; $24/yr. 119 E. High St., Potosi, MO 63664-0340. TEL 314-438-5141; FAX 314-438-4472. **Owner(s):** Independent-Journal, Inc., P.O. Box 340, 119 E. High St., Potosi, MO 63664. TEL 314-438-5141; FAX 314-438-4472; Ed. Neil Richards. adv.; photos; bk.rev.; pub. size: broadsheet; circ. 5,479(free & paid).

RAYTOWN

US

RAYTOWN DISPATCH TRIBUNE. 1926. Wed. $.50 newsstand; $17/yr. in state; $20/yr. out of state. 10227 E. 61st St., Raytown, MO 64133. TEL 816-358-6398; FAX 816-358-5141. **Owner(s):** Townsend Communications, Inc., 7007 N.E. Parvin Rd., Kansas City, MO 64117. TEL 816-454-9660; Ed. Gene Gentrup; Pub. Harold G. Townsend, Jr.; adv. contact: Lori Richmond. pub. size: broadsheet; circ. 25,300(paid).

ROCK PORT

US

ATCHISON COUNTY MAIL, THE. 1848. Thu. $.50 newsstand; $21/yr. in cy.; $26.50/yr. elsewhere. 300 S. Main St., Rock Port, MO 64482. TEL 816-744-6245; FAX 816-744-2645. **Owner(s):** William W. & Marilyn S. Farmer, 300 S. Main St., Rock Port, MO 64482. TEL 816-744-6245; FAX 816-744-2645; Ed. William C. Farmer; Pub. William W. Farmer; adv. contact: Michael P. Farmer. adv.: $3.75/SAU. photos; bk.rev.; pub. size: broadsheet; circ. 2,550(paid). **Wire Service(s):** MO Line.

SALEM

US

SALEM NEWS. 1923. s-w.: Tue. & Thu. $.53 newsstand; $32.77/yr. 500 N. Washington St., Salem, MO 65560-0798. TEL 573-729-4126; FAX 573-729-4920. **Owner(s):** Salem Publishing Co., P.O. Box 798, Salem, MO 65560. TEL 573-729-4126; Ed. Donald Dodd; Pub. W. Ray Vickery; adv. contact: Karen Barred. pub. size: broadsheet; circ. 3,800(paid).

SARCOXIE

US

SARCOXIE RECORD, THE. 1901. Thu. $.35 newsstand; $17.99/yr. 101 N. Sixth St., Sarcoxie, MO 64862. TEL 417-548-3311. **Owner(s):** Linda Eck Elderton, R.R. 2, Box 345A, Sarcoxie, MO 64862. TEL 417-548-3311; adv. contact: Marlene Gish. photos; pub. size: tabloid; circ. 1,400(paid).

SAVANNAH

US

SAVANNAH REPORTER & ANDREW COUNTY DEMOCRAT. 1876. Thu. $.35 newsstand; $18/yr. local; $21/yr. in state; $23/yr. out of state. 115 S. Fourth St., Savannah, MO 64485. TEL 816-324-3149; FAX 816-324-3632. **Owner(s):** L & T Development, Inc., Savannah Reporter, Inc., 115 S. Fourth, Savannah, MO 64485. TEL 816-324-3149; Ed. Twila Miller; Pub. Larry Miller; adv.; photos; pub. size: standard; circ. 4,050(paid).

SEDALIA

US

CENTRAL MISSOURI NEWS. 1985. Wed. $22/yr. in cy.; $26/yr. out of cy.; $30/yr. out of state. 406 S. Ohio, Sedalia, MO 65301. TEL 816-827-2425; FAX 816-827-2427. **Owner(s):** Melton Publishing Co., 406 S. Ohio St., Sedalia, MO 65301. TEL 816-827-2425; FAX 816-827-2427; Ed. Pete Daniels; Pub. Greg Melton; adv.; photos; bk.rev.; pub. size: broadsheet; circ. 4,000(paid).

US

PLAINSMAN WEEKLY NEWS. 1980. Wed. free. 700 S. Massachusetts, Sedalia, MO 65301-2305. TEL 816-826-1000; FAX 816-826-3913. **Owner(s):** Sedalia Democrat Co., 700 S. Massachusetts, Sedalia, MO 65301. TEL 816-826-1000; Pub. Howard A. Cochran; adv.; pub. size: tabloid; circ. 61,784(free).

SEYMOUR

US

WEBSTER COUNTY CITIZEN. 1907. Wed. $.50 newsstand; $12-$25/yr. 221 S. Commercial, Seymour, MO 65746-0190. TEL 417-935-2257. Owner(s): Gary & Helen Sosniecki, 221 S. Commercial, Seymour, MO 65746-0190. TEL 417-935-2257; Pub. Helen Sosniecki; adv.: $3.00/SAU. pub. size: broadsheet; circ. 4,783(free & paid). Wire Service(s): AP.

SHELBYVILLE

US

SHELBY COUNTY HERALD. 1870. Wed. $.50 newsstand; $20/yr. local; $25/yr. elsewhere. 106 E. Main St., Shelbyville, MO 63469-0225. TEL 314-633-2261; FAX 314-633-2133. **Owner(s):** W. Rogers Hewitt, 207 S. Cleveland, Shelbyville, MO 63469. TEL 314-633-2261; FAX 314-633-2133; Ed. W. Rogers Hewitt; Pub. W. Rogers Hewitt; adv. contact: Betty Thrasher. photos; pub. size: broadsheet; circ. 2,500(paid).

SHERIDAN

US   ISSN 0747-0444

QUAD RIVER NEWS. 1983. Wed. $.35 newsstand; $12/yr. R.R. 1, Box 16, Sheridan, MO 64486. TEL 816-799-3735; FAX 816-564-3707. **Owner(s):** Joe & Elise Stark, R.R. 1, Box 16, Sheridan, MO 64486. TEL 816-799-3735; FAX 816-564-3707; Ed. Joe Stark; Pub. Joe Stark; adv.: $2/SAU. pub. size: broadsheet; circ. 750(paid).

SMITHVILLE

US

SMITHVILLE LAKE DEMOCRAT-HERALD, THE. 1888. Wed. $.50 newsstand; $15/yr. in cy.; $18/yr. out of cy.; $25/yr. out of state. 110 N. Bridge St., Smithville, MO 64089-0209. TEL 816-532-4444; FAX 816-532-4918. **Owner(s):** David T. Peery, P.O. Box 269, Smithville, MO 64089-0269. TEL 816-532-4444; FAX 816-532-4918; Ed. David T. Peery; Pub. David T. Peery; adv.: $4/SAU. photos; pub. size: broadsheet; circ. 2,380(paid).

ST. CHARLES

US

ST. CHARLES JOURNAL. 1957. 3/wk.: Sun., Wed., Fri. free. 1529 Old Hwy. 94, S., Ste. 108, St. Charles, MO 63303-3707. TEL 314-724-1111; FAX 314-946-5955. **Owner(s):** Suburban Journals, 1417 Deer Tracks Trail, St. Louis, MO 63113. TEL 314-821-1110; Ed. Scott Queen. adv. contact: Tom McCullen. pub. size: broadsheet; circ. 78,000(controlled).

ST. CLAIR

US

ST. CLAIR MISSOURIAN. 1924. s-w.: Wed. & Sat. $.50 newsstand Sat.; $.75 newsstand Wed.; $29.61/yr. in cy.; $32.46/yr. adjacent cy.; $50/yr. out of state. 465 St. Claire St., St. Clair, MO 63077. TEL 314-629-1027; FAX 314-629-2810. **Owner(s):** Missourian Publishing Co., 14 W. Main St., Washington, MO 63090. TEL 314-239-7701; Ed. William Miller. adv. contact: Laurie Pinnell. pub. size: broadsheet; circ. 26,945(paid). **Wire Service(s):** AP.

STEEL

US

STEELE ENTERPRISE. 1921. Thu. $.35 newsstand; $12.50/yr. in cy; $30/yr. out of cy. 227 W. Main, Steel, MO 63877. TEL 573-695-3415; FAX 573-695-2114. **Owner(s):** David Tennyson, 677 N. Hwy. 131, Blytheville, AR 72315. TEL 314-695-3415; FAX 314-695-2114; Ed. Karen Tennyson. adv.; photos; bk.rev.; pub. size: standard; circ. 2,450(paid).

STEELVILLE

US

STEELVILLE STAR/CRAWFORD MIRROR. 1872. Wed. $.50 newsstand; $12.76/yr. in cy. 106 S. First St., Steelville, MO 65565. TEL 573-775-5454; FAX 573-885-3803. **Owner(s):** Percy Pascoe, P.O. Box BG, Steelville, MO 65565; Ed. Ava Viehman; Pub. Percy Pascoe; pub. size: tabloid; circ. 3,100(paid).

STE. GENEVIEVE

US

STE. GENEVIEVE HERALD. 1881. Wed. $.50 newsstand; $19/yr. in cy.; $27/yr. out of area. 330 Market St., Ste. Genevieve, MO 63670. TEL 573-883-2222; FAX 573-883-2833. **Owner(s):** Ste. Genevieve Newspapers, Inc., 330 Market St., Ste. Genevieve, MO 63670. TEL 573-883-2222; Ed. Jean Rissover; Pub. Bob Burr; pub. size: standard; circ. 5,000(paid). **Wire Service(s):** Mo. Medialink.

ST. JAMES

US

ST. JAMES LEADER JOURNAL. 1896. Wed. $.50 newsstand; $18.25/yr. in cy.; $21.50/yr. out of cy.; $22/yr. out of state. 125 W. Springfield Ave., St. James, MO 65559. TEL 573-265-3321; FAX 573-265-3197. **Owner(s):** American Publishing Co., 606 N. Van Buren, P.O. Box 520, Marion, IL 62959. TEL 618-993-1711; Ed. Joe Arnold; Pub. Joe Arnold; adv.; photos; bk.rev.; pub. size: broadsheet; circ. 2,000(paid). **Wire Service(s):** AP.

ST. JOSEPH

US

ST. JOSEPH TELEGRAPH, THE. 1989. Thu. $1 newsstand; $28/yr. 620 Frances St., Rm. 318, St. Joseph, MO 64501. TEL 816-364-1323; FAX 816-364-3083. **Owner(s):** Leo S. Johnson, P.O. Box 1087 St. Joseph, MO 64052-1087. TEL 816-364-1323; FAX 816-364-3083; Pub. Scott Johnson; adv.; photos; bk.rev.; pub. size: broadsheet; circ. 2,100(free & paid).

ST. LOUIS

US

CENTRAL WEST END JOURNAL. 1984. s-w.: Wed. & Sun. free. 1714 Deer Tracks Trail, St. Louis, MO 63131. TEL 314-821-2462; FAX 314-821-0843. **Owner(s):** Suburban Journals, 1714 Deer Tracks Trail, St. Louis, MO 63131. TEL 314-821-1110; Ed. Dan Barger. adv. contact: Dave Wittman. pub. size: broadsheet; circ. 7,500(free).

US

CHESTERFIELD JOURNAL. 1990. s-w. Wed. & Sun. free. 1714 Deer Tracks Trail, St. Louis, MO 63131-1825. TEL 314-821-2462; FAX 314-821-0843. **Owner(s):** Suburban Journals, 1714 Deer Tracks Trail, St. Louis, MO 63131-1825. TEL 314-821-1110; Ed. Mary Shapiro. adv. contact: Dave Wittman. pub. size: broadsheet; circ. 15,220(free).

US

CITIZEN JOURNAL. 1968. s-w. Sun. & Wed. free. 1714 Deer Tracks Trail, St. Louis, MO 63131. TEL 314-821-2462; FAX 314-821-0843. **Owner(s):** Suburban Journals, 1714 Deer Tracks Trail, Saint Louis, MO 63131. TEL 314-821-1110; Ed. Dan Barger. adv. contact: Dave Wittman. pub. size: broadsheet; circ. 23,000(free).

US

COMMUNITY NEWS. 1921. Wed. $5.6/yr. 5748 Helen Ave., St. Louis, MO 63136. TEL 314-261-5555; FAX 314-261-2776. **Owner(s):** Huneke Publications, Inc., 5748 Helen Ave., St. Louis, MO 63136. TEL 314-261-5555; FAX 314-261-2776; Ed. C.R. Boeckskopf; Pub. Robert Huneke, Jr.; adv.: $20/SAU. photos; pub. size: tabloid; circ. 30,000(free).

US

COUNTY STAR JOURNAL EAST. 1993. s-w.: Sun. & Wed. free; $26/3 mos. mailed. 4305 Woodson Rd., St. Louis, MO 63134. TEL 314-426-2222; FAX 314-426-4911. **Owner(s):** Suburban Journals, 1714 Deer Tracks Trail, St. Louis, MO 63131. TEL 314-821-1110; Ed. Dan Barger. adv. contact: Mark Gehrs. photos; pub. size: broadsheet; circ. 31,005(free & paid).

US

COUNTY STAR JOURNAL WEST. 1993. s-w.: Sun. & Wed. free; $26/3 mos. mailed. 4305 Woodson Rd., St. Louis, MO 63134. TEL 314-426-2222; FAX 314-426-3911. **Owner(s):** Suburban Journals, 1714 Deer Tracks Trail, St. Louis, MO 63131. TEL 314-821-1110; Ed. Dan Barger. adv. contact: Denny Shea. photos; pub. size: broadsheet; circ. 16,290(free & paid). Formerly: Maryland Heights Bridgeton Journal.

US

MID-COUNTY JOURNAL. s-w.: Sun. & Wed. free. 1714 Deer Tracks Trail, St. Louis, MO 63131. TEL 314-821-2462; FAX 314-821-0843. **Owner(s):** Suburban Journals, 1714 Deer Tracks Trail, St. Louis, MO 63131. TEL 314-821-1110; Ed. Dan Barger. adv. contact: Dave Wittman. pub. size: broadsheet.

US

NORTH COUNTY JOURNAL EAST. 1960. s-w.: Sun. & Wed. free; $26/3 mos. mailed. 4305 Woodson Rd., St. Louis, MO 63134. TEL 314-426-2222; FAX 314-426-4911. **Owner(s):** Suburban Journals, 1714 Deer Tracks Trail, St. Louis, MO 63131. TEL 314-821-1100; Ed. Dan Barger. adv. contact: Mark Gehrs. photos; pub. size: broadsheet; circ. 47,982(free & paid). Formerly: North County Journal

US

NORTH COUNTY JOURNAL WEST. 1993. s-w.: Sun. & Wed. free; $26/3 mos. mailed. 4305 Woodson Rd., St. Louis, MO 63134. TEL 314-426-2222; FAX 314-426-4911. **Owner(s):** Suburban Journals, 1714 Deer Tracks Trail, St. Louis, MO 63131. TEL 314-821-1110; Ed. Dan Barger. adv. contact: Mark Gehrs. photos; pub. size: broadsheet; circ. 59,000(free & paid).

US

NORTHSIDE JOURNAL. 1993. s-w.: Sun. & Wed. free; $26/3 mos. mailed. 4305 Woodson Rd., St. Louis, MO 63134. TEL 314-426-2222; FAX 314-426-4911. **Owner(s):** Suburban Journals, 1714 Deer Tracks Trail, St. Louis, MO 63131. TEL 314-821-1110; Ed. Dan Barger. adv. contact: Mark Gehrs. photos; pub. size: broadsheet; circ. 36,000(free & paid).

US

OAKVILLE-MEHVILLE JOURNAL. s-w.: Sun. & Wed. free. 4210 Chippewa, St. Louis, MO 63116. TEL 314-664-2700; FAX 314-664-8533. **Owner(s):** Suburban Journals, 1714 Deer Tracks Trail, St. Louis, MO 63131. TEL 314-821-1110; Ed. Lois Kendall. pub. size: broadsheet.

US

PRESS JOURNAL. s-w.: Sun. & Wed. free. 1714 Deer Tracks Trail, St. Louis, MO 63131. TEL 314-821-2462; FAX 314-821-0843. **Owner(s):** Suburban Journals, 1714 Deer Tracks Trail, St. Louis, MO 63131. TEL 314-821-2462; Ed. Dan Barger. adv. contact: Dave Wittman. pub. size: broadsheet.

US

SOUTH CITY JOURNAL. Wed. free. 4210 Chippewa, St. Louis, MO 63131. TEL 314-664-2700; FAX 314-664-8533. **Owner(s):** Suburban Journals, 1714 Deer Tracks Trail, St. Louis, MO 63131. TEL 314-821-1110; Ed. Lois Kendall. pub. size: broadsheet.

US

SOUTH COUNTY JOURNAL. 1965. s-w.: Sun. & Wed. free. 4210 Chippewa, St. Louis, MO 63116. TEL 314-664-2700; FAX 314-664-8533. **Owner(s):** Suburban Journals, 1714 Deer Tracks Trail, St. Louis, MO 63131. TEL 314-821-1110; Ed. Lois Kendall. pub. size: broadsheet; circ. 63,705(free).

US

SOUTHSIDE JOURNAL. s-w.: Sun. & Wed. free. 4210 Chippewa, St. Louis, MO 63131. TEL 314-664-2700; FAX 314-664-8533. **Owner(s):** Suburban Journals, 1714 Deer Tracks Trail, St. Louis, MO 63131. TEL 314-821-1110; Ed. Lois Kendall. pub. size: broadsheet.

US

SOUTHWEST CITY JOURNAL. 1921. s-w.: Sun. & Wed. free. 4210 Chippewa, St. Louis, MO 63119. TEL 314-664-2700; FAX 314-664-9777. **Owner(s):** Suburban Journals, 1714 Deer Tracks Trail, St. Louis, MO 63131. TEL 314-821-1110; Ed. Lois Kendall. pub. size: broadsheet; circ. 27,450(free).

US

SOUTHWEST COUNTY JOURNAL. 1990. s-w.: Sun. & Wed. free. 4210 Chippewa, St. Louis, MO 63116. TEL 314-644-2700; FAX 314-644-4777. **Owner(s):** Suburban Journals, 1714 Deer Tracks Trail, St. Louis, MO 63131. TEL 314-821-1110; Ed. Lois Kendall. pub. size: broadsheet; circ. 29,907(free).

US

ST. LOUIS AMERICAN NEWSPAPER. 1928. Thu. $30/yr. in cy. 4144 Lindell Ave., Ste. B-5, St. Louis, MO 63108. TEL 314-533-8000; FAX 314-533-0038. **Owner(s):** Donald M. Suggs, 4144 Lindell Ave., St. Louis, MO 63108. TEL 314-533-8000; Ed. Eric Clark; Pub. Dr. Donald M. Suggs; pub. size: broadsheet; circ. 65,500(paid). **Wire Service(s):** AP.

US

ST. LOUIS SENTINEL NEWSPAPER. 1968. Thu. $25/yr. 2900 N. Market, St. Louis, MO 63106. TEL 314-531-2691; FAX 314-531-4442. **Owner(s):** Woods Publications, 2900 N. Market, St. Louis, MO 63106. TEL 314-531-2101; Ed. Michael Williams. photos; bk.rev.; pub. size: broadsheet; circ. 38,000(controlled & paid).

US

WEST COUNTY JOURNAL. s-w.: Sun. & Wed. free. 1714 Deer Tracks Trail, St. Louis, MO 63131. TEL 314-821-2462; FAX 314-821-0843. **Owner(s):** Suburban Journals, 1714 Deer Tracks Trail, St. Louis, MO 63131. TEL 314-821-1110; Ed. Dan Barger; Pub. Dan Barger; pub. size: broadsheet; circ. 30,000(free).

STOCKTON

US

CEDAR COUNTY REPUBLICAN. 1888. Wed. $.50 newsstand; $17/yr. in cy.; $32/yr. out of cy.; $39/yr. out of state. 108 S.E. Arcad St., Stockton, MO 65785. TEL 417-276-4211; FAX 417-276-5760. **Owner(s):** Sterling Media, Ltd., Rt. 3, Box 559, Bolivar, MO 65613. TEL 417-326-7636; Ed. Anita Todd; Pub. Jeff Jasper; adv. contact: Jeff Jasper. pub. size: broadsheet; circ. 2,800(paid).

SULLIVAN

US

SULLIVAN INDEPENDENT NEWS. 1962. Wed. $.50 newsstand; $20.50/yr. in cy.; $26/yr. out of cy.; $30/yr. out of state. Scottsdale & Springfield Rd., Sullivan, MO 63080. TEL 314-468-6511; FAX 314-468-4046. **Owner(s):** Kathleen Manion, Scottsdale & Springfield Rd., Sullivan, MO 63080. TEL 314-468-6511; Ed. Jim Bartle; Pub. Kathleen Manion; adv. contact: Jim Bartle. photos; bk.rev.; pub. size: tabloid; circ. 7,000(paid).

TARKIO

US

TARKIO AVALANCHE. 1884. Thu. $.50 newsstand; $21/yr. surrounding cys; $26.50/yr. elsewhere. 107 N. Third, Tarkio, MO 64491-0278. TEL 816-736-4111; FAX 816-736-5700. **Owner(s):** Will Johnson, 107 N. Third, Tarkio, MO 64491. TEL 816-736-4111; FAX 816-736-5700; Ed. Will Johnson. adv. contact: Will Johnson. photos; pub. size: broadsheet; circ. evening 1,760(controlled & paid). **Wire Service(s):** AP.

THAYER

US

SOUTH MISSOURIAN NEWS. 1991. Thu. $.50 newsstand; $18-$23/yr. 101 Chestnut St., Thayer, MO 65791. TEL 417-264-3085; FAX 417-264-3814. **Owner(s):** Paducah Newspapers, Inc., 408 Kentucky Ave., Paducah, KY 42002. TEL 502-443-1771; FAX 502-442-1771; Ed. Max Cates; Pub. Janie Flynn; adv. contact: Carolyn Clarke. photos; pub. size: broadsheet; circ. 1,532(paid).

TRENTON

US

GREEN HILLS WEEKLY. 1972. Wed. free. 122 E. Eighth St., Trenton, MO 64683. TEL 816-359-2212; FAX 816-359-4414. **Owner(s):** Wendell J. Lenhart, P.O. Box 548, Trenton, MO 64683. TEL 816-359-2212; Ed. Diane Raines; Pub. Wendell Lenhart; adv. contact: DeLane Hein. pub. size: broadsheet; circ. 13,000(free).

TROY

US

TROY FREE PRESS & SILEX INDEX. Wed. $.50 newsstand; $23/yr. in cy.; $35/yr. out of cy.; $18/yr. in cy. senior citizens; $30/yr. out of cy. senior citizens. 615 E. Cherry St., Troy, MO 63379. TEL 314-462-4720; FAX 314-528-6694. **Owner(s):** Smith Publishing Co., 615 E. Cherry St., Troy, MO 63379; Ed. Bob Simons; Pub. Pat Whiteside; pub. size: broadsheet; circ. 3,000(paid).

UNIONVILLE

US

UNIONVILLE REPUBLICAN, THE. 1865. Wed. $15/yr. in cy; $18/yr. out of cy. 111 S. 16th St., Unionville, MO 63565-0365. TEL 816-947-2222; FAX 816-947-2223. **Owner(s):** Ron & Theresa Kinzler, 111 S. 16th St., Unionville, MO 63565. TEL 816-947-2222; Ed. Theresa Kinzler; Pub. Ron Kinzler; pub. size: standard; circ. 3,800(paid).

VERSAILLES

US

VERSAILLES LEADER-STATESMAN. 1887. Thu. $.50 newsstand; $38/yr. 104 W. Jasper, Versailles, MO 65084. TEL 314-378-5441. **Owner(s):** Dane Vernon, P.O. Box 348, Versailles, MO 65084-0348. TEL 314-378-5441; Ed. Duane Johnson; Pub. Dane Vernon; adv.; photos; pub. size: broadsheet; circ. 3,900(paid).

VIENNA

US

MARIES COUNTY GAZETTE. 1876. Wed. $.40 newsstand; $17.61/yr. local; $20.28/yr. in state; $20/yr. out of state. Courthouse Sq., Vienna, MO 65582. TEL 314-422-3441; FAX 314-859-6274. **Owner(s):** Tri-County Newspapers, 307 Alvarado, Belle, MO 65013. TEL 314-859-3328; Pub. Ron Lewis; adv.; photos; pub. size: broadsheet; circ. 2,300(paid).

WARRENTON

US

WARRENTON NEWS-JOURNAL. 1973. Wed. free. 111 W. Main, Warrenton, MO 63383. TEL 314-456-3481; FAX 314-456-3020. **Owner(s):** Suburban Journals, 1714 Deer Tracks Trail, St. Louis, MO 63131. TEL 314-821-1110; Ed. Marie Hollenbuck; Pub. Don Miller; adv. contact: Shelly Jefts. pub. size: broadsheet; circ. 12,272(free).

WARSAW

US

WARSAW BENTON COUNTY ENTERPRISE. 1879. Thu. $19.95/yr. in cy.; $25/yr. out of cy.; $25/yr. out of state. 107 Main St., Warsaw, MO 65355. TEL 816-438-6312; FAX 816-438-3464. **Owner(s):** M.K. White, 107 Main St., Warsaw, MO 65355. TEL 816-438-5933; Ed. M.K. White; Pub. M.K. White; adv. contact: M.K. White. pub. size: standard; circ. 5,200(paid).

WASHINGTON

US

WASHINGTON MISSOURIAN. 1860. s-w.: Wed. & Sat. $.50/Sat. newsstand; $.75/Wed. newsstand; $29.61/yr. in cy.; $32.46/yr. out of cy.; $50/yr. out of state. 14 W. Main, Washington, MO 63090. TEL 314-239-7701; FAX 314-239-0915. **Owner(s):** Missourian Publishing Co., 14 W. Main, Washington, MO 63090. TEL 314-239-7701; Ed. William L. Miller; Pub. Tom L. Miller; adv. contact: Tom L. Miller. pub. size: broadsheet; circ. morning 26,024(paid). **Wire Service(s):** AP.

WENTZVILLE

US   ISSN 0192-6896

WENTZVILLE JOURNAL. 1966. 3/wk.: Wed., Fri., Sun. free local; $56.25/yr. elsewhere. 501 E. Pearce Blvd., Wentzville, MO 63385. TEL 314-327-6463; FAX 314-327-6411. **Owner(s):** Suburban Journals, 1714 Deer Tracks Trail, St. Louis, MO 63131. TEL 314-821-1110; Ed. Tammy Tucker; Pub. Tom Rice; adv. contact: Shelley Jefts. pub. size: broadsheet; circ. 30,200(free & paid). **Formerly:** Wentzville Messenger.

WINDSOR

US

WINDSOR REVIEW. 1870. Thu. $15.95/yr. in cy.; $18.50/yr. out of cy. 205 S. Main, Windsor, MO 65360. TEL 816-647-2121; FAX 816-647-2122. **Owner(s):** Jack Krier, 205 S. Main, Windsor, MO 65360. TEL 816-647-2121; Pub. Jack Krier; adv.; photos; bk.rev.; pub. size: broadsheet; circ. 1,500(paid).

MONTANA

ANACONDA

US

ANACONDA LEADER. 1969. s-w.: Wed. & Fri. $25.50/yr. 121 Main St., Anaconda, MT 59711. TEL 406-563-5283; FAX 406-563-5284. **Owner(s):** Leader Printing & Supply, Inc., 121 Main St., Anaconda, MT 59711. TEL 406-563-5283; Ed. Dick Crockford; Pub. Dean A. Neitz; adv. contact: Micky Gee. photos; pub. size: broadsheet; circ. 4,000(free & paid).

BIGFORK

US

BIG FORK EAGLE. 1979. Wed. $.50 newsstand; $17/yr. in cy.; $22/yr. out of cy.; $30/yr. out of state. P.O. Box 406, Bigfork, MT 59911. TEL 406-837-5131; FAX 406-837-1132; E-mail: marcus@netrix.net; URL: http://www.townnews.com/mt/mteagle. **Owner(s):** Marc Wilson, P.O. Box 406, Bigfork, MT 59911. TEL 406-837-5131; Ed. Marc Wilson; Pub. Marc Wilson; pub. size: broadsheet; circ. 3,500(paid).

BIG SANDY

US

MOUNTAINEER, THE. 1911. Wed. $.50 newsstand; $22/yr. in cy.; $24/yr. in state; $26/yr. out of state. 123 Main St., Big Sandy, MT 59520. TEL 406-378-2176; FAX 406-378-2176. **Owner(s):** Rettig Publishing, Inc., P.O. Box 529, Big Sandy, MT 59520. TEL 406-378-2176; FAX 406-378-2176. Ed. James L. Rettig; Pub. James L. Rettig; pub. size: broadsheet; circ. 1,200(paid). **Formerly:** Big Sandy Mountaineer.

COLUMBIA FALLS

US

HUNGRY HORSE NEWS. 1946. Thu. $.75 newsstand; $23/yr. local; $30/yr. out of area; $39/yr. out of state. 926 Nucleus Ave., Columbia Falls, MT 59912. TEL 406-892-2151; FAX 406-892-5600. **Owner(s):** Brian & Carol Kennedy, 926 Nucleus Ave., Coumbia Falls, MT 59912. TEL 406-892-2151; Ed. Brian M. Kennedy. adv. contact: Noreen Hanson. pub. size: broadsheet; circ. 7,200(paid).

CUT BANK

US

WESTERN BREEZE. 1942. s-w.: Tue. & Fri. $.50 newsstand; $25/yr. in cy.; $27.50/yr. out of cy.; $30/yr. out of state. 32 S. Central Ave., Cut Bank, MT 59427-1253. TEL 406-873-4128; FAX 406-873-4129. **Owner(s):** James O'Day, P.O. Box 1253, Cut Bank, MT 59427-1253. TEL 406-873-4128; FAX 406-873-4129; Ed. James M. O'Day; Pub. James M. O'Day; adv. contact: Penne Swenson. photos; pub. size: tabloid; circ. 1,950(paid).

FORT BENTON

US

RIVER PRESS, THE. 1880. Wed. $.50 newsstand; $18/yr. in cy.; $22/yr. out of cy. 1114 Front St., Fort Benton, MT 59442-0069. TEL 406-622-3311; FAX 406-622-5446. **Owner(s):** Stanley E. & Esther C. Tichenor, P.O. Box 69, Fort Benton, MT 59442. TEL 406-622-3311; FAX 406-622-5446; Ed. Tim Burmister; Pub. Esther Tichenor; adv.; photos; bk.rev.; pub. size: standard; circ. 2,100(paid).

GLASGOW

US

GLASGOW COURIER, THE. 1913. Thu. $.75 newsstand; $33/yr. in cy.; $37/yr. out of cy.; $47/yr. out of state. 341 Third Ave., S., Glasgow, MT 59230. TEL 406-228-9301; FAX 406-228-2665. **Owner(s):** Bruce Wright, MT; John Stanislaw, MT; Ed. Scott Ross; Pub. John Stanislaw; pub. size: standard; circ. 4,200(paid).

GLENDIVE

US

GLENDIVE RANGER-REVIEW. 1881. s-w.: Sun. & Thu. $.75 newsstand; $36/yr. carrier; $46/yr. mailed; $49.30/yr. out of state. 119 W. Bell St., Glendive, MT 59330. TEL 406-365-3303. **Owner(s):** Yellowstone Newspapers, P.O. Box 665, Livingston, MT 59047. TEL 406-222-2000; Ed. Mervir Mecklenberg; Pub. G.R. Zander; pub. size: broadsheet; circ. 4,100(paid).

HARLOWTON

US   ISSN 0889-5627

TIMES-CLARION, THE. 1917. Thu. $.50 newsstand; $20/yr. in cy.; $23/yr. in state. 1 1 S. Central St., Harlowton, MT 59036-0307. TEL 406-632-5633; FAX 406-632-5644. **Owner(s):** Gerald H. & Audrey J. Miller, 14 W. Division, Harlowton, MT 59036. TEL 406-632-5566; FAX 406-632-5644; Ed. Gerald H. Miller; Pub. Gerald H. Miller; adv.; photos; pub. size: standard; circ. 1,675(paid). **Wire Service(s):** AP.

HAVRE

US

SENTINEL, THE. Wed. free deliv. 119 Second St., Havre, MT 59501. TEL 406-265-6796; FAX 406-265-6798. **Owner(s):** Pioneer Press, Inc., 3701 W. Lake Ave., Glenview, IL 60025. TEL 847-486-9200; Ed. Steve Miller; Pub. Rick Weaver; adv. contact: Paula Reynolds. pub. size: tabloid. circ. 7,500(free).

LEWISTOWN

US

LEWISTOWN NEWS-ARGUS. 1883. s-w.: Wed. & Sun. $.35 newsstand; $32.12/yr. local. 521 W. Main St., Lewistown, MT 59457-0900. TEL 406-538-3401; FAX 406-538-3405. **Owner(s):** Central Montana Publishing, P.O. Box 900, Lewistown, MT 59457; Ed. Lori Jacobs; Pub. Ken Byerly; adv. contact: Mitch Kottas. pub. size: standard; circ. 5,000(paid).

LIBBY

US

WESTERN NEWS. 1900. s-w.: Wed. & Fri. $.50 newsstand; $19.50/yr. in cy.; $26/yr. out of cy. 311 California Ave., Libby, MT 59923. TEL 406-293-4124; FAX 406-293-7187. **Owner(s):** Cabinet Publishing Co., P.O. Box 1377, Libby, MT 59923; Ed. Roger Morris; Pub. Mark McMahon; adv. contact: Lee Bothman. pub. size: broadsheet; circ. 4,600(paid).

PHILIPSBURG

US

PHILIPSBURG MAIL, THE. 1886. Wed. $.50 newsstand; $20/yr. 123 Broadway, Philipsburg, MT 59858-0160. TEL 406-859-3223; FAX 406-859-3113. **Owner(s):** James J. & Lee Tracy, 123 Broadway, Philipsburg. MT 59858-0160. TEL 406-859-3223; Pub. Lee Tracy; adv.; photos; pub. size: broadsheet; circ. 1,500(paid).

RONAN

US

LAKE COUNTY LEADER. 1910. Thu. $.50 newsstand; $20.95/yr. in cy.; $24.95/yr. out of cy.; $26.95/yr. out of state. 229 Main St., S.W., Ronan, MT 59864. TEL 406-676-3800; FAX 406-676-3801. **Owner(s):** Todd Mowbray, Courier/Pioneer/Advertiser, P.O. Box 1091, Polson, MT 59860. TEL 406-883-4343; Pub. John Schnase; pub. size: broadsheet; circ. 5,900(paid).

SIDNEY

US

SIDNEY HERALD-LEADER. 1908. s-w.: Sun. & Wed. $34/yr. in cy. 310 Second Ave., N.E., Sidney, MT 59270. TEL 406-482-2706; FAX 406-482-7802. **Owner(s):** Wick Communications, Inc., 333 Wilcox Dr., Ste. 302, Sierra Vista, AZ 85635. TEL 520-458-0200; FAX 520-458-6166; Ed. Sharon Dunham; Pub. Rick Schneider; adv. contact: Dianne Swanson. pub. size: broadsheet; circ. 4,500(paid).

WHITEFISH

US

WHITEFISH PILOT. 1902. Thu. $.75 newsstand; $23/yr. in cy.; $35/yr. out of cy. P.O. Box 488, Whitefish, MT 59937. TEL 406-862-3505; FAX 406-862-3636. **Owner(s):** Betty Kennedy, P.O. Box 189, Columbia Falls, MT; Ed. Brian Kennedy; Pub. Brian Kennedy; adv. contact: Jolene Shima. pub. size: broadsheet; circ. 4,400(paid).

WOLF POINT

US

HERALD-NEWS. 1913. Thu. $.75 newsstand; $2517/yr. local; $31/yr. in state; $325/yr. out of state; $46.80/yr. foreign. 408 Main St., Wolf Point, MT 59201. TEL 406-653-2222; FAX 406-653-2222. **Owner(s):** Herald-News, Inc., Box 639, Wolf Point, MT 59201. TEL 406-653-2222; Ed. Greg Little. adv.; photos; pub. size: broadsheet; circ. 3,500(paid).

NEBRASKA

ALBION

US

ALBION NEWS. 1879. Wed. $.50 newsstand; $17/yr. local; $20/yr. out of state. 328 W. Church St., Albion, NE 68620. TEL 402-395-2115; FAX 402-395-2772. **Owner(s):** Albion News, P.O. Box 431, Albion, NE 68620. TEL 402-395-2115; FAX 402-395-2772; Ed. Jean Kaup. adv.; photos; bk.rev.; pub. size: broadsheet; circ. 3,200(paid).

ALMA

US

HARLAN COUNTY JOURNAL. 1896. Thu. $.50 newsstand; $20/yr. local; $22/yr. elsewhere. 713 W. Main St., Alma, NE 68920. TEL 308-928-2143. **Owner(s):** Wayne & Marilyn Lingg, 900 Brown, Alma, NE 68920. TEL 308-928-2710; Ed. Wayne Lingg; Pub. Wayne Lingg; adv.; photos; pub. size: broadsheet; circ. 2,230(paid).

ARAPAHOE

US

ARAPAHOE PUBLIC MIRROR. 1880. Wed. $.50 newsstand; $16-$20/yr. 420 Nebraska Ave., Arapahoe, NE 68922-0660. TEL 308-962-7261; FAX 308-962-7262. **Owner(s):** Arapahoe Public Mirror, 420 Nebraska Ave., Arapahoe, NE 68922-0660. TEL 308-962-7261; FAX 308-962-7262; Ed. Gayle Gill Schutz; Pub. T.M. Gill; adv.; pub. size: broadsheet.

ARTHUR

US

ARTHUR ENTERPRISE, THE. 1911. w. $.25 newsstand; $10/yr. in cy.; $11.50/yr. in state; $13/yr. out of state. P.O. Box 165, Arthur, NE 69121-0165. TEL 308-764-2402. **Owner(s):** Robert J. Crouse, Arthur, NE 69121. TEL 308-764-2402; Ed. Robert J. Crouse; Pub. Robert J. Crouse; adv. contact: Karen A. Sizer. photos; pub. size: tabloid; circ. 480(free & paid).

ATKINSON

US

ATKINSON GRAPHIC, THE. 1882. Wed. $.50 newsstand; $14.50/yr. in state; $20/yr. out of state. 207 E. State St., Atkinson, NE 68713. TEL 402-925-5411. **Owner(s):** G.Z. & Roxanne Hollingsworth, 306 W. First St., Atkinson, NE 68713. TEL 402-925-5411; Pub. G.Z. Hollingsworth; pub. size: broadsheet; circ. 2,300(paid).

AUBURN

US

AUBURN PRESS TRIBUNE. 1882. Tue. $21/yr. in cy.; $27/yr. out of cy. 830 Central Ave., Auburn, NE 68305. TEL 402-274-3185. **Owner(s):** Auburn Newspapers, 830 Central Ave., Auburn, NE 68305. TEL 402-274-3185; FAX 402-274-3185; Ed. Darrell Wellman; Pub. Mark A. Cramer; pub. size: broadsheet; circ. 3,650(paid).

US

NEMAHA COUNTY HERALD. 1888. Tue. $.35 newsstand; $22/yr. local; $27/yr. out of area. 830 Central Ave., Auburn, NE 68305. TEL 402-274-3185; FAX 402-274-3273. **Owner(s):** Mark A. Cramer, P.O. Box 250, Auburn, NE 68305. TEL 402-274-3185; Ed. Darrell Wellman; Pub. Mark Cramer; adv. contact: Don Chapin. pub. size: broadsheet; circ. 3,700(paid).

AURORA

US

AURORA NEWS-REGISTER. 1870. Wed. $20/yr. in cy.; $24/yr. out of cy.; $27/yr. out of state. 1312 K. St., Aurora, NE 68818. TEL 402-694-2131; FAX 402-694-2133; E-mail: NewsRegister@hamilton.net; URL: http://www.hamilton.net/aurora/newsreg/anewsreg.htm. Owner(s): Aurora Publishing Co., 1312 K St., Aurora, NE 68818. TEL 402-694-2131; Ed. Hap Fruits; Pub. Ron Furse; pub. size: standard; circ. 4,000(paid).

BELLEVUE

US   ISSN 0193-0389

BELLEVUE LEADER. 1973. Wed. $.50 newsstand; $28/yr. in cy. 604 Fort Crook Rd., N., Bellevue, NE 68005. TEL 402-733-7300; FAX 402-733-9116. **Owner(s):** Bellevue Leader Co., 604 Fort Crook Rd., N., Bellevue, NE 68005. TEL 402-733-7300; FAX 402-733-9116; Ed. Ron Petak; Pub. Dixie Cavner; adv.; photos; pub. size: broadsheet; circ. 24,500(free & paid).

BLAIR

US

ARLINGTON CITIZEN. 1954. Wed. $.50 newsstand; $9/yr. 138 N. 16th St., Blair, NE 68008. TEL 402-426-2121; FAX 402-426-2227. **Owner(s):** Blair Enterprise Co., Inc., 138 N. 16th, Blair, NE 68008. TEL 402-426-2121; Ed. Carrie Larkins; Pub. Kenneth H. Rhoades; adv. contact: Lynette Hansen. photos; pub. size: broadsheet; circ. 746(paid).

US

BLAIR ENTERPRISE. 1892. Thu. $.50 newsstand; $19.95/yr. in cy.; $29.95/yr. out of cy.; $32/yr. out of state. 138 N. 16th, Blair, NE 68008. TEL 402-426-2121; FAX 402-426-2227. **Owner(s):** Blair Enterprise Co., Inc., 138 N. 16th, Blair, NE 68008. TEL 402-426-2121; Ed. Kathy Schwartz; Pub. Kenneth H. Rhoades; adv. contact: Lynette Hanson. photos; pub. size: broadsheet; circ. 4,200(controlled & paid).

US

BLAIR PILOT-TRIBUNE. 1905. s-w.: Tue. & Thu. $.50 newsstand; $19.95/yr. in cy.; $29.95/yr. out of cy.; $32/yr. out of state. 16th & Front St., Blair, NE 68008. TEL 402-426-2121; FAX 402-426-2227. **Owner(s):** Blair Enterprise Co., Inc., 138 N. 16th, Blair, NE 68008. TEL 402-426-3144; Ed. Mark Rhoades; Pub. Kenneth H. Rhoades; adv. contact: Lynette Hansen. photos; pub. size: broadsheet; circ. 14,000(controlled & paid).

BROKEN BOW

US

CUSTER COUNTY CHIEF. 1892. s-w.: Mon. & Thu. $28/yr. in area; $38/yr. out of area. 305 S. 10th, Broken Bow, NE 68822. TEL 308-872-2471; FAX 308-872-2415. **Owner(s):** Smith Newspapers, Inc., P.O. Box 27, Fort Payne, AL 35967. TEL 205-845-5510; Ed. Jeff Billser; Pub. Charley Najacht; adv. contact: Mary Coffman. pub. size: broadsheet; circ. morning 3,300(paid).

BURWELL

US

BURWELL TRIBUNE. 1892. Wed. $20/yr. in state; $24/yr. out of state. 757 H St., Burwell, NE 68823. TEL 308-346-4504; FAX 308-346-4018. **Owner(s):** Kendall Neiman, P.O. Box 547, Burwell, NE 68823. TEL 308-346-4504; Ed. Kendall Neiman; Pub. Kendall Neiman; pub. size: broadsheet; circ. 2,400(paid).

US

SARGENT LEADER. Wed. $.50 newsstand; $20/yr. local; $24/yr. elsewhere. 757 H. St., Burwell, NE 68823. TEL 308-346-4504; FAX 307-346-4018. **Owner(s):** Kendall Neiman, P.O. Box 547, Burwell, NE 68823. TEL 308-346-4504; FAX 308-346-4018; Steve DeLashmutt, P.O. Box 547, Burwell, NE 68823. TEL 308-346-4504; FAX 308-346-4018; Ed. Kendall Neiman; Pub. Steve DeLashmutt; pub. size: broadsheet; circ. 1,500(paid).

US

TAYLOR CLARION. 1884. Wed. $.50 newsstand; $20/yr. local; $22/yr. in region; $24/yr. out of state. 757 H St., Burwell, NE 68823. TEL 308-346-4504; FAX 308-346-4018. **Owner(s):** Kendall Neiman, P.O. Box 547, Burwell, NE 68823. TEL 308-346-4504; FAX 308-346-4018; Steve DeLashmutt, P.O. Box 547, Burwell, NE 68823. TEL 308-346-4504; FAX 308-346-4018; Ed. Kendall Neiman; Pub. Steve DeLashmutt; pub. size: broadsheet; circ. 1,500(paid).

US

WHEELER COUNTY INDEPENDENT. 1890. Wed. $.50 newsstand; $20/yr. local; $22/yr. elsewhere. 757 H St., Burwell, NE 68823. TEL 308-346-4504. **Owner(s):** Kendall Neiman, P.O. Box 547, Burwell, NE 68823. TEL 308-346-4504; FAX 308-346-4018; Steve DeLashmutt, P.O. Box 547, Burwell, NE 68823. TEL 308-346-4504; FAX 308-346-4018; Ed. Kendall Neiman; Pub. Kendall Neiman; pub. size: broadsheet; circ. 510(paid).

CENTRAL CITY

US

CENTRAL CITY REPUBLICAN NONPAREIL. 1893. Thu. $17.50/yr. local; 19.50/yr. in state; $23/yr. out of state. 802 C. Ave., Central City, NE 68826. TEL 308-946-3081; FAX 308-946-3082. **Owner(s):** Robert M. Jensen, 802 C Ave., Central City, NE 68826. TEL 308-946-3081; Ed. Robert M. Jensen; Pub. Robert M. Jensen; adv. contact: Ronna Cutles. pub. size: broadsheet; circ. 2,000(paid).

COZAD

US

TRI-CITY TRIB. 1965. Thu. $19.50/yr. 320 W. Eighth St., Cozad, NE 69130. TEL 308-784-3644; FAX 308-784-3647. **Owner(s):** Tri-City Trib, 320 W. Eighth St., Cozad, NE 69130; Ed. Dean Dorsey. adv.; photos; pub. size: tabloid; circ. 4,950(paid).

CRETE

US

CRETE NEWS, THE. 1871. Wed. $24.75/yr. in cy.; $35/yr. out of cy. 1201 Linden, Crete, NE 68333. TEL 402-826-2147; FAX 402-826-5072. **Owner(s):** Crete News, Inc., P.O. Box 40, Crete, NE 68333. TEL 402-826-2147; Pub. Lloyd Reeves; pub. size: broadsheet; circ. 4,400(paid).

DAVID CITY

US

DAVID CITY BANNER-PRESS, THE. 1873. Thu. $20/yr. local; $24/yr. in state; $28/yr. out of state. 331 E St., David City, NE 68632. TEL 402-367-3054; FAX 402-367-3055. **Owner(s):** Banner Press Publishing Co., Inc., Box 407, David City NE 68632. TEL 402-367-3054; Ed. Zean Carney; Pub. Zean Carney; pub. size: broadsheet; circ. 4,300(paid).

DESHLER

US

DESHLER RUSTLER, THE. 1986. Wed. $.45 newsstand; $17.50/yr. in state; $20/yr. out of state. 706 Fourth St. Deshler, NE 68340. TEL 402-365-7221; FAX 402-365-7228. **Owner(s):** Harod W. Struve, 307 Alice St., Deshler, NE 68340. TEL 402-365-7575; FAX 402-365-7228; Ed. Harold W. Struve; Pub. Harold W. Struve; adv.; photos; pub. size: standard; circ. 1,600(paid).

ELKHORN

US   ISSN 0746-1437

DOUGLAS COUNTY POST GAZETTE. 1895. Tue. $.50 newsstand; $18.75/yr. in cy.; $24/yr. out of cy.; $28.50/yr. out of state. 113 Hillrise, Elkhorn, NE 68022. TEL 402-289-2329; FAX 402-289-0861. **Owner(s):** Penny Overmann, 113 Hillrise, Elkhorn, NE 68022. TEL 402-289-2329; FAX 402-289-0861; Ed. Mark Thiessen. adv. contact: Penny Overmann. photos; bk.rev.; pub. size: broadsheet; circ. 7,800(free & paid).

FAIRBURY

US

FAIRBURY JOURNAL-NEWS, THE. 1892. s-w.: Tue. & Fri. $28/yr. 516 Fifth St., Fairbury, NE 68352. TEL 402-729-6141; FAX 402-729-3892. **Owner(s):** McBattas Co., 516 Fifth St., Fairbury, NE 68352. TEL 402-729-6141; Pub. Fred A. Arnold, Jr.; adv. contact: Darrel Junker. photos; pub. size: standard; circ. 4,808(paid).

FALLS CITY

US

FALLS CITY JOURNAL. 1857. s-w.: Tue. & Fri. $.50 newsstand; $30/yr. carrier & mailed. 1810 Harlan St., Falls City NE 68355. TEL 402-245-2431 FAX 402-245-4404. **Owner(s):** Journal Publishing Co., 1810 Harlan St., P.O. Box 128, Falls City, NE 68355. TEL 402-245-2431; Ed. Bill Schock. adv. contact: Lori Harring. pub. size: broadsheet; circ. 4,100(paid).

GENEVA

US

NEBRASKA SIGNAL. 1874. Wed. $22/yr. local; $26/yr. out of area. 131 N. Ninth, Geneva, NE 68361. TEL 402-759-3117; FAX 402-759-4214. **Owner(s):** John Edgecombe, Jr., 131 N. Ninth, Geneva, NE 68361. TEL 402-759-3117; FAX 402-759-4214; Ed. John F. Edgecombe, Jr.; Pub. John F. Edgecombe, Jr.; adv.; photos; pub. size: broadsheet; circ. 3,707(paid).

GERING

US

GERING COURIER. 1887. Thu. $.50 newsstand; $21.75/yr. in cy.; $29.75/yr. out of cy. 1428 Tenth St., Gering, NE 69341. TEL 308-436-2222. **Owner(s):** Jack & Carol Ann Lewis, 1428 Tenth St., Gering, NE 69341; Ed. Jack Lewis; Pub. Carol Ann Lewis; pub. size: broadsheet; circ. 2,361(paid).

LEXINGTON

US

CLIPPER-HERALD. 1891. s-w.: Wed. & Sat. $.50 newsstand; $29/yr. in cy.; $39/yr. out of cy. 114 W. Fifth St., Lexington NE 68850-0599. TEL 308-324-5511; FAX 308-324-5240. **Owner(s):** Western Publishing Co., P.O. Box 1228, North Platte, NE 69103-1228; Pub. Peter J. Cook; adv.; bk.rev.; pub. size: broadsheet; circ. 4,100(paid).

LYONS

US

LYONS MIRROR-SUN. 1883. Thu. $.50 newsstand; $21-26/yr. P.O. Box 59, Lyons, NE 68038. TEL 402-687-2616. **Owner(s):** Bobbie & Dewaine Gahan, 215 N. Engdahl Ave., Oakland, NE 68045. TEL 402-685-6229; Ed. Anne O'Mara; Pub. Dewaine Gahan; adv.; pub. size: broadsheet; circ. 1,500(paid).

MINDEN

US

MINDEN COURIER. 1890. w. $.50 newsstand; $20/yr. 317 N. Minden Ave., Minden, NE 68959-0379. TEL 308-832-2222; FAX 308-832-2221. **Owner(s):** John & JoAnn Edgecombe, 317 N. Minden Ave., Minden, NE 68959. TEL 308-832-2222; FAX 308-832-2221; Ed. Julinne Gasseling; Pub. John Edgecombe, Jr.; adv. contact: JoAnn Edgecombe. photos; pub. size: broadsheet; circ. 2,800(paid).

O'NEILL

US

FRONTIER & HOLT COUNTY INDEPENDENT. Thu. $22.50/yr. in cy.; $27.50/yr. out of cy.; $35/yr. out of state. 114 N. Fourth St., O'Neill, NE 68763. TEL 402-336-1220; FAX 402-336-1222. **Owner(s):** G.A. Miles, P.O. Box 360, O'Neill, NE 68763. TEL 402-336-1220; Ed. Burnell McCulloch; Pub. G.A. Miles; adv. contact: George T. Miles. pub. size: broadsheet; circ. 4,870(paid).

OAKLAND

US

OAKLAND INDPENDENT. 1880. Thu. $.50 newsstand; $25-$32/yr. 217 N. Oakland Ave., Oakland, NE 68045-0085. TEL 402-685-5624; FAX 402-685-5625. **Owner(s):** Bobbie & Dewaine Gahan, 215 N. Engdahl Ave., Oakland, NE 68045. TEL 402-685-5229; Pub. Dewaine Gahan; adv.; pub. size: standard; circ. 1,913(paid).

OGALLALA
US
KEITH COUNTY NEWS. 1885. s-w.: Mon. & Wed. $28/yr. 116 W. A St., Ogallala, NE 69153. TEL 308-284-4046; FAX 308-284-4048. **Owner(s):** Jack Pollock, 116 W. A St., Ogallala, NE 69153. TEL 308-284-4046; FAX 308-284-4048; Ed. Tom Huddleson; Pub. Jack Pollock; adv. contact: Marilee Perlinger. pub. size: broadsheet; circ. 4,500(paid).
Formerly: Ogallala Keith County News.

OMAHA
US
OMAHA STAR. 1938. Thu. $.35 newsstand; $24/yr. local; $26/yr. out of area. 2216 N. 24th St., Omaha, NE 68110. TEL 402-346-4041. **Owner(s):** Marquerita Washington, 2216 N. 24th St., Omaha, NE 68110. TEL 402-346-4041; adv.; bk.rev.; pub. size: standard; circ. 30,000(paid).

ORD
US
ORD QUIZ. 1882. Thu. $.75 newsstand; $27.50/yr. in state; $30/yr. out of state. 305 S. 16th St., Ord, NE 68862-0197. TEL 308-728-3262; FAX 308-728-5715. **Owner(s):** Quiz Graphic Arts, Inc., 305 S. 16th St., Ord, NE 68862. TEL 308-728-3262; FAX 308-728-5715; Ed. Doug Barber; Pub. Kerry E. Leggett; adv. contact: Lynn Griffith. photos; pub. size: broadsheet; circ. 2,904(paid).

OVERTON
US
BEACON OBSERVER, THE. 1898. Wed. $.35 newsstand; $29/yr. P.O. Box 330, Overton, NE 68863. TEL 308-987-2451; FAX 308-987-2452. **Owner(s):** Norman G. & Polly A. Taylor, P.O. Box 330, Overton, NE 68863. TEL 308-907-2451; FAX 308-987-2452; Pub. Polly Taylor; adv.; photos; pub. size: broadsheet; circ. 1,518(controlled & paid).

PAPILLION
US
PAPILLION TIMES. 1874. Thu. $23.40/yr. in cy.; $31.20/yr. elsewhere. 138 N. Washington, Papillion, NE 68046. TEL 402-339-3331; FAX 402-339-8562. **Owner(s):** Papillion Times Printing Co., 138 N. Washington St., Papillion, NE 68046. TEL 402-339-3331; Ed. Chris Poore; Pub. James Negen; adv. contact: Joni Bartak. pub. size: broadsheet; circ. 4,200(paid).

PLAINVIEW
US
PLAINVIEW NEWS. 1892. Wed. $.50 newsstand; $21/yr. 508 W. Locust, Plainview, NE 68769. TEL 402-582-4921; FAX 402-582-4922. **Owner(s):** Lee Warneke, P.O. Box 9, Plainview, NE 68769-0009. TEL 402-582-4921; FAX 402-582-4922; Pub. Lee Warneke; adv.; photos; pub. size: broadsheet; circ. 1,814(paid).

PLATTSMOUTH
US
PLATTSMOUTH JOURNAL. 1882. s-w.: Mon. & Thu. $.40 newsstand; $27/yr. in cy.; $34/yr. elsewhere. 410 Main St., Plattsmouth, NE 68048. TEL 402-296-2141; FAX 402-296-3401. **Owner(s):** Plattsmouth Journal Company, 410 Main St., Plattsmouth, NE 68048. TEL 402-296-2141; Pub. Lou Prohaska; adv. contact: Kathy Herndon. pub. size: standard; circ. evening 5,400.

SCHUYLER
US
SCHUYLER SUN. 1871. Thu. $.50 newsstand; $25/yr. in cy.; $27/yr. out of state. 1112 C St., Schuyler, NE 68661. TEL 402-352-2424; FAX 402-352-3332. **Owner(s):** Francis Svoboda, P.O. Box 506, Schuyler, NE 68661. TEL 402-352-2424; FAX 402-352-3332; Ed. Michael Rea; Pub. Francis Svoboda; adv. contact: Curt Mentzer. pub. size: broadsheet; circ. 3,800(paid).

SEWARD
US
SEWARD COUNTY INDEPENDENT. 1897. Wed. $.75 newsstand; $23/yr. in cy.; $25/yr. out of cy.; $36/yr. out of state. 129 S. Sixth St., Seward, NE 68434. TEL 402-643-3676; FAX 402-643-6774. **Owner(s):** Rhoades Publishing, Blair, NE 68008. TEL 402-426-2121; Ed. Lori Shriner; Pub. Mark Rhoades; adv. contact: Lynn Dance. photos; pub. size: broadsheet; circ. 3,683(paid).

SOUTH SIOUX CITY
US
SOUTH SIOUX CITY STAR. 1909. Thu. $.50 newsstand; $22.50/yr. in state; $26/yr. out of state. 2520 Dakota Ave., South Sioux City, NE 68776-0157. TEL 402-494-4264; FAX 402-494-2414. **Owner(s):** Star Printing & Publishing, 2520 Dakota Ave., South Sioux City, NE 68776. TEL 402-494-4264; FAX 402-494-2414; Ed. Peggy Williams. adv.; photos; pub. size: broadsheet; circ. 6,513(paid).

SPRINGVIEW
US
SPRINGVIEW HERALD. 1886. Thu. $.35 newsstand; $16/yr. local; $18/yr. in state; $20/yr. out of state. W. L St., Springview, NE 68778-0369. TEL 402-497-3651; FAX 402-497-2651. **Owner(s):** Springview Herald, P.O. Box 369, Springview, NE 68778-0369. TEL 402-497-3651; FAX 402-497-2651; Ed. Karen Kurzenberger; Pub. Karen Kurzenberger; adv. contact: Karen Kurzenberger. photos; pub. size: tabloid; circ. 900(free & paid).

SUPERIOR
US   ISSN 0740-0969
SUPERIOR EXPRESS, THE. 1900. Thu. $.35 newsstand; $14/yr. local.   48 E. Third St., Superior, NE 68978. TEL 402-879-3291; FAX 402-879-3293. **Owner(s):** Superior Publishing Co., P.O. Box 408, Superior, NE 68978. TEL 402-879-3291; Pub. Bill Blauvelt; adv. contact: Sherri Nun. photos; pub. size: broadsheet; circ. 4,150(paid).

SUTHERLAND
US
COURIER-TIMES. 1895. Thu. $.25 newsstand; 12/yr. 824 First, Sutherland, NE 69165. TEL 308-386-4617; FAX 308-386-2426. **Owner(s):** Courier-Times, 824 First, Sutherland, NE 69165. TEL 308-386-4617; FAX 308-386-2426; Pub. Russell Masters; adv.; pub. size: tabloid.

SYRACUSE
US
SYRACUSE JOURNAL-DEMOCRAT. 1878. Thu. $18/yr. 123 W. 17th St., Syracuse, NE 68446. TEL 402-269-2135; FAX 402-269-2392. **Owner(s):** Midwest Newspapers, Inc., P.O. Box 380, Ames, IA 50010. TEL 515-232-2160; Ed. David Swanson; Pub. W.R. Welsh; adv. contact: Vanessa Rudolph. pub. size: tabloid; circ. 3,415(paid).

VALENTINE
US
VALENTINE NEWSPAPER. 1887. Wed. $18-$22/yr. 610 N. Main St., Valentine, NE 69201-1530. TEL 402-376-3742. **Owner(s):** Valentine Newspaper, P.O. Box 450, Valentine, NE 69201. TEL 402-376-3742; Ed. Ray K. Dover; Pub. Ray K. Dover; pub. size: broadsheet; circ. 2,600(paid).

WAHOO
US
WAHOO NEWSPAPER. 1885. Thu. $28/yr. 564 N. Broadway, Wahoo, NE 68066. TEL 402-443-4162; FAX 402-443-4459. **Owner(s):** Saunders County Publishing, Inc., 564 N. Broadway, P.O. Box 147, Wahoo, NE 68066. TEL 402-443-4162; Ed. Zean Carney; Pub. Zean Carney; pub. size: broadsheet; circ. 4,500(paid).

WAYNE
US
WAYNE HERALD. 1876. Thu. $.50 newsstand; $20/yr. in area; $30/yr. in state; $40/yr. out of state. 114 Main St., Wayne, NE 68787-0070. TEL 402-375-2600; FAX 402-375-1888. **Owner(s):** Northeast Nebraska Media, Inc., 114 Main St., Wayne, NE 68787. TEL 402-375-2600; FAX 402-375-1888; Pub. Lester J. Mann; pub. size: standard; circ. morning 2,600(paid). **Wire Service(s):** AP, Newsfinder.

WEST POINT

US

WEST POINT NEWS. 1870. Wed. $29.50/yr. 134 E. Grove St., West Point, NE 68788. TEL 402-372-2461; FAX 402-372-3530. **Owner(s):** Tom Kelly, P.O. Box 40, West Point, NE 68788. TEL 402-372-2461; Ed. Willis Mahannah; Pub. Tom Kelly; pub. size: broadsheet; circ. 4,205(paid).

NEVADA

BOULDER CITY

US

BOULDER CITY NEWS. 1937. Thu. $.25 newsstand; $20/yr. home deliv.; $25/yr. mailed. 1227 Arizona St., Boulder City, NV 89005. TEL 702-293-2302; FAX 702-294-0977. **Owner(s):** HBC Publications, Two Commerce Center, Henderson, NV 89014. TEL 702-564-1881; Ed. Paul Szydelko; Pub. Mike O'Callaghan; adv. contact: Anne Picking. pub. size: broadsheet; circ. 5,500(paid).

CARSON CITY

US

CHRONICLE, THE. 1927. Wed. free. 200 Bath St., Carson City, NV 89702. TEL 702-882-2111; FAX 702-887-2420. **Owner(s):** Scores, Inc., P.O. Box 3209, Carson City, NV 89702-3209. TEL 702-883-8282; Ed. Barry Smith; Pub. Jeff Ackerman; adv. contact: Steve Reynolds. pub. size: broadsheet; circ. 34,000(free). **Wire Service(s):** AP.

HAWTHORNE

US

MINERAL COUNTY INDEPENDENT-NEWS. 1928. Wed. $.35 newsstand; $25/yr. 501 D St., Hawthorne, NV 89415. TEL 702-945-2414; FAX 702-945-1270. **Owner(s):** Mineral County Independent, 501 D St., Hawthorne, NV 89415. TEL 702-945-2414; Mineral County Independent, MCIN, Inc., 501 D St., Hawthorn, NY 89415. TEL 702-945-2414; FAX 702-945-1270; Ed. Ted Hughes. adv.; photos; pub. size: broadsheet; circ. 2,900(free).

INCLINE VILLAGE

US

NORTH LAKE TAHOE BONANZA. 1959. s-w.: Wed. & Fri. $.50 newsstand; $36/yr. 917 Tahoe Blvd., Ste. 100, Incline Village, NV 89452. TEL 702-831-4666; FAX 916-546-2507; E-mail: bonanza@tahoe.com; URL: http://www.tahoe.com. **Owner(s):** North Lake Tahoe Bonanza, P.O. Box 7820, Incline Village, NV 89452. TEL 702-831-4666; Ed. Patrick McCartney. adv.; photos; pub. size: standard; circ. 7,900(free & paid).

LAS VEGAS

US

LAS VEGAS TODAY. 1975. Thu. free newsstand; $75/yr. 4440 S. Arville, Ste. 12, Las Vegas, NV 89103. TEL 702-221-5000; FAX 702-221-5099. **Owner(s):** Desert Media Group, 4440 S. Arville, Ste. 12, Las Vegas, NV 89103. TEL 702-221-5000; Ed. Tom W. Westmoreland. pub. size: oversize; circ. 50,000(controlled).

LOVELOCK

US

LOVELOCK REVIEW-MINER. 1903. Thu. $.35 newsstand; $18/yr. in state; $25/yr. out of state. 230 Main St., Lovelock, NV 89419. TEL 702-273-7245. **Owner(s):** Lovelock Review-Miner, 230 Main St., Lovelock, NV 89419. TEL 702-273-7245; FAX 702-273-0500; Ed. Gwendolyn Bogh Carter; Pub. Gwendolyn Bogh Carter; adv.; pub. size: broadsheet; circ. 1,500(paid).

TONOPAH

US

EUREKA SENTINEL. 1870. Thu. $.25 newsstand; $20/yr. 150 Main St., Tonopah, NV 89049. TEL 702-482-3365; FAX 702-482-5042. **Owner(s):** Central Nevada Newspapers, Inc., P.O. Box 193, Tonopah, NV 89049. TEL 702-482-3365; Ed. William G. Roberts; Pub. William G. Roberts; pub. size: tabloid; circ. 550(paid).

US

TONOPAH TIMES-BONANZA & GOLDFIELD NEWS. 1900. Thu. $.25 newsstand; $20/yr. 150 Main St., Tonopah, NV 89049. TEL 702-482-3365; FAX 702-482-5042. **Owner(s):** Central Nevada Newspapers, Inc., P.O. Box 193, Tonopah, NV 89049. TEL 702-482-3365; Ed. William G. Roberts; Pub. William G. Roberts; pub. size: tabloid; circ. 2,300(paid).

YERINGTON

US

FERNLEY LEADER-DAYTON COURIER. 1983. Wed. $.35 newsstand; $16.95/yr. 41 N. Main St., Yerington, NV 89447. TEL 702-463-4242; FAX 702-463-5547. **Owner(s):** Mason Valley News, Inc., 41 N. Main, Yerington, NV 89447. TEL 702-463-4242; Ed. Laura Tennant; Pub. Bob Sanford; adv.; photos; pub. size: broadsheet; circ. 2,600(controlled & paid).

US

MASON VALLEY NEWS. 1917. Fri. $.50 newsstand; $22.50/yr. 41 N. Main St., Yerington, NV 89447. TEL 702-463-4242; FAX 702-463-5547. **Owner(s):** Mason Valley News, Inc., 41 N. Main, Yerington, NV 89447. TEL 702-463-4242; FAX 702-463-5547; Ed. David Sanford; Pub. Bob Sanford; adv.: $5.60/SAU. photos. pub. size: broadsheet; circ. 4,000(controlled & paid). **Formerly:** Yerington Mason Valley News.

NEW HAMPSHIRE

CENTER OSSIPEE

US

CARROLL COUNTY INDEPENDENT. 1881. Wed. $20/yr. in cy.; $28/yr. out of cy. Moultonville Rd., Center Ossipee, NH 03814. TEL 603-539-4111; FAX 603-539-5564. **Owner(s):** Jacob J. & Ann Burghardt, 324 Wentworth Hill Rd., Sandwich, NH 03270. TEL 603-284-7001; Pub. Jacob J. Burghardt; adv. contact: Robin DeMello. photos; pub. size: broadsheet; circ. 5,500(paid).

COLEBROOK

US

NEWS & SENTINEL, THE. 1870 Wed. $.60 newsstand; $28/yr. One Bridge St., Colebrook, NH 03576. TEL 603-237-5501. E-mail: sentinel@colbsent.com; URL http://www.colbsent.com. **Owner(s):** John D. Harrigan, P.O. Box 39, Colebrook, NH 03576. TEL 603-237-5001; FAX 603-237-5060; Ed. Dennis Joos; Pub. John D. Harrigan; adv.; photos; pub. size: tabloid; circ. 4,454(free & paid).

CONWAY

US

MT. WASHINGTON VALLEY MOUNTAIN EAR. 1976. Wed. free newsstand; $30./yr. out of area. Mt. River Village, Rte. 16, Conway, NH 03818. TEL 603-447-6336; FAX 603-447-5474. **Owner(s):** R. Stephen Eastman, Mt. River Village, Rte. 16, Conway, NH 038 3. TEL 603-447-6336; FAX 603-447-5474; Sarah W. Eastman, Mt. River Village, Rte. 16, Conway, NH 03818. TEL 603-447-6335; FAX 603-447-5474; Ed. R. Stephen Eastman. adv. contact: Paula Tetreault. photos; pub. size: tabloid; circ. 12,000(free).

DERRY

US

DERRY NEWS. 1880. s-w.: Wed. & Fr. $.50 newsstand; $32/yr. 46 W Broadway, Derry, NH 03033. TEL 603-437-7000; FAX 603-432-4510. **Owner(s):** Derry Publishing Co., Inc., 46 W. Broadway, Derry, NH 03038. TEL 603-432-3363; Ed. Steve Stevens; Pub. Tom Kirk; adv. contact: Tom Kirk. pub. size: broadsheet; circ. 10,700(paid).

DOVER

US

TRANSCRIPT, THE. 1975. Thu. $.35 newsstand; $18.50/yr. 563 Central Ave., Dover, NH 03820. TEL 603-742-3735; FAX 603-742-6442. **Owner(s):** Tri-Town Publisher, Inc., 563 Central Ave., Dover, NH 03820. TEL 603-742-3735; FAX 603-742-6442; adv. $10.75/SAU. photos; pub. size: broadsheet; circ. 6,700(paid).

HILLSBOROUGH

US

NEW HAMPSHIRE WEEK IN REVIEW. 1868. Mon. free. 202 W. Main St., Hillsborough, NH 03244-1190. TEL 603-464-5588. **Owner(s):** Granite Quill Publishers, P.O. Box 917, Hillsborough, NH 03244. TEL 603-464-5588; Ed. Joyce Bosse; Pub. Leigh Bosse; adv.; pub. size: tabloid; circ. 22,500(free & paid).

HUDSON

US

HUDSON-LITCHFIELD NEWS. 1990. Fri. free. 222 Central St., Ste. 5, Hudson, NH 03051. TEL 603-883-1432. **Owner(s):** PBR Enterprises, Inc., 222 Central St., Hudson, NH 03051. TEL 603-880-1516; Ed. Diane Thorns. adv. contact: Ed Koenig. photos; pub. size: tabloid; circ. 9,800(free).

LANCASTER

US

COOS COUNTY DEMOCRAT. 1838. Wed. $.60 newsstand; $25/yr. in NH & VT; $28/yr. 79 Main St., Lancaster, NH 03584. TEL 603-788-4939; FAX 603-788-3022. **Owner(s):** North Country Publishing Inc., P.O. Box 28, Lancaster, NH 03584. TEL 603-788-4939; Ed. Eugene Ehlert; Pub. John D. Harrigan; adv.; photos; pub. size: broadsheet; circ. 6,500(paid).

LITTLETON

US

COURIER, THE. 1889. Wed. $.50 newsstand; $21/yr. in cy.; $28/yr. out of cy. 365 Union St., Littleton, NH 03561. TEL 603-444-3927; FAX 603-444-3920. **Owner(s):** White Mountain Publishing Partnership, P.O. Box 230, Littleton, NH; Ed. Tim McCarthy; Pub. Thomas C. Hepner; adv. contact: Georgia Golden. photos; bk.rev.; pub. size: broadsheet; circ. 7,000(paid).

MILFORD

US   ISSN 1071-9206

MILFORD CABINET & WILTON JOURNAL. 1802. Wed. $.50 newsstand; $21/yr. in state; $28/yr. out of state. 54 School St., Milford, NH 03055-0180. TEL 603-673-3100; FAX 603-673-8250; E-mail: Cabinet@jlc.net; URL: http://www.cabinet.com. **Owner(s):** Frank & Martha Manley, P.O. Box 180, Milford, NH 03055. TEL 603-673-3100; FAX 603-673-8250; Ed. Robert Mackintosh; Pub. Frank Manley; adv.; pub. size: broadsheet; circ. 9,000(paid).

NASHUA

US   ISSN 0192-8597

1590 BROADCASTER. 1964. Wed. free. 502 W. Hollis St., Nashua, NH 03062-0548. TEL 603-889-1590; FAX 603-883-4344. **Owner(s):** 1590 Broadcasting Corp., 502 W. Hollis St., Nashua, NH 03062. TEL 603-889-1590; Ed. Maurice R. Parent; Pub. Maurice R. Parent; adv. contact: Maurice R. Parent. photos; pub. size: tabloid; circ. 64,000(free).

NEWPORT

US

ARGUS-CHAMPION, THE. 1825. Thu. $.50 newsstand; $19.95/yr. in state; $24.95/yr. out of state. 86 Sunapee St., Newport, NH 03773. TEL 603-863-1776; FAX 603-863-0066. **Owner(s):** Dirk Ippen, 86 Sunapee St., Newport, NH 03773; Ed. Allan Stein. adv. contact: Robert Shomphe. pub. size: broadsheet; circ. 5,100(paid).

NORTH HAMPTON

US

HAMPTON UNION. 1901. s-w.: Tue. & Fri. $.75 newsstand; $36.40/yr. Fern Crossing Mall, North Hampton, NH 03862. TEL 603-926-4511; FAX 603-964-5661. **Owner(s):** Ottaway Newspapers, Inc., P.O. Box 401, Campbell Hall, NY 10916. TEL 914-294-8181; Ed. Thomas Lynch; Pub. John Tabor; pub. size: broadsheet; circ. 7,200(paid).

PETERBOROUGH

US

MONADNOCK LEDGER. 1953. Thu. $.50 newsstand; $24/yr. in state; $30/yr. out of state. 20 Grove St., Peterborough, NH 03458. TEL 603-924-7172; FAX 603-924-3681. **Owner(s):** Newspapers of New England, Inc., 3 North State St., Concord, NH 03301. TEL 603-224-5301; Pub. Heather McKernan; pub. size: broadsheet; circ. 7,000(paid).

US

PETERBOROUGH TRANSCRIPT. 1849. Thu. $.50 newsstand; $20/yr. in state; $24/yr. out of state. 43 Grove St., Peterborough, NH 03458. TEL 603-924-3333; FAX 603-924-7946. **Owner(s):** Joseph D. Cummings, 220 Sand Hill Rd., Peterborough, NH 03458. TEL 603-924-6486; Paul C. Cummings, Jr., 220 Sand Hill Rd., Peterborough, NH 03458. TEL 603-924-6486; Ed. John Franklin; Pub. Jospeh D. Cummings; adv. contact: Heidi Bourgeois. pub. size: broadsheet; circ. 5,900(paid).

PLYMOUTH

US

RECORD ENTERPRISE. Wed. $.50 newsstand; $21/yr. in cy.; $26/yr. out of cy. 111 Main St., Plymouth, NH 03264. TEL 603-536-1311; FAX 603-536-1311. **Owner(s):** White Mountain Publishing Partnership, P.O. Box 230, Littleton, NH 03561. TEL 603-444-3927; Ed. William York; Pub. Thomas Hepner; adv. contact: Georgia Golden. photos; bk.rev.; pub. size: tabloid; circ. 6,500(paid).

ROCHESTER

US

ROCHESTER TIMES, THE. 1993. Thu. $28/yr. 77 N. Main St., Rochester, NH 03867. TEL 603-332-2300; FAX 603-330-0718. **Owner(s):** Lou McGrew, 77 N. Main St., Rochester, NH 03870. TEL 603-332-2300; FAX 603-330-0718; Ed. John Nolan; Pub. Lou McGrew; adv. contact: Lou McGrew. photos; pub. size: tabloid.

SALEM

US

SALEM OBSERVER. 1966. Wed. $.50 newsstand; $18/yr. in state; $21/yr. out of state. 380 Main St., Salem, NH 03079. TEL 603-893-4356; FAX 603-898-0249; E-mail: soart@aol.com. **Owner(s):** Observer, Inc., The, P.O. Box 720, Salem, NH 03079. TEL 603-893-4356; FAX 603-898-0249; Ed. Monique J. Duhamel; Pub. Arthur Mueller, Jr.; adv. contact: Armand Beliveau. photos; bk.rev.; pub. size: broadsheet; circ. 6,000(paid).

STRATHAM

US

EXETER NEWS-LETTER. 1831. s-w.: Tue. & Fri. $.75 newsstand; $36.40/yr. in cy. 7 Portsmouth Ave., Stratham, NH 03885. TEL 603-772-6000; FAX 603-772-3830. **Owner(s):** Ottaway Newspapers, Inc., P.O. Box 401, Campbell, NY 10916; Ed. Thomas Lynch; Pub. John Tabor; adv. contact: Michael Rabideau. pub. size: broadsheet; circ. morning 7,125(paid). **Wire Service(s):** AP, Newsfinder.

WOLFEBORO

US   ISSN 1060-0590

GRANITE STATE NEWS. 1859. Wed. $.50 newsstand; $20/yr. in cy.; $28/yr. out of cy. 10 Endicott Street, Wolfeboro, NH 03894. TEL 603-569-3126; FAX 603-569-4743. **Owner(s):** Jacob J. & Ann Burghardt, 324 Wentworth Hill Rd., Sandwich, NH 03270. TEL 603-284-7001; Ed. Jeanne Tempest; Pub. Jacob J. Burghardt; adv. contact: Jeffry Morris. photos; pub. size: broadsheet; circ. 5,500(paid).

NEW JERSEY

BAYONNE

US

BAYONNE COMMUNITY NEWS. 1978. Wed. $60/yr. 13 E. 21st St., Bayonne, NJ 07002. TEL 201-437-2460; FAX 201-437-7127. **Owner(s):** Edward M. Kukowski, Bayonne, NJ; Victor J. Ruggiero, Bayonne, NJ; Pub. Edward M. Kukowski; adv. contact: Renee Pavlick. photos; pub. size: tabloid; circ. 28,525(controlled & free).

BELVIDERE

US

NEWS, THE. 1962. Wed. $.35 newsstand; $21/yr. P.O. Box 265, Belvidere, NJ 07823. TEL 908-475-1848; FAX 908-362-9223. **Owner(s):** North Jersey Newspapers Co., 988 Main St., Passaic, NJ 07005. TEL 201-365-3000; FAX 201-365-5887; Ed. Ivan Boccolini; Pub. Rosemarie Maio; adv. contact: Rosemarie Maio. photos; pub. size: broadsheet; circ. 1,300(paid).

BERLIN

US

JOURNAL, THE. 1973. Fri. $.30 newsstand; $15/yr.; $12/yr. senior citizens. 131 S. White Horse Pike, Berlin, NJ 08009-0399. TEL 609-767-1640; FAX 609-768-4320. **Owner(s):** Community Newspaper, Inc., 131 S. White Horse Pike, Berlin, NJ 08009. TEL 609-767-1640; FAX 609-768-4320; Ed. Lewis A. Chimenti; Pub. Ed McCartney; adv.; photos; pub. size: tabloid; circ. evening 15,000(free & paid).

BERNARDSVILLE

US

BERNARDSVILLE NEWS. 1896. Wed. $.60 newsstand; $25/yr. in cy. 17-19 Morristown Rd., Bernardsville, NJ 07924. TEL 908-766-3900; FAX 908-766-6365. **Owner(s):** Recorder Publishing Co., 17-19 Morristown Rd., Bernardsville, NJ 07924. TEL 908-766-3900; Ed. Charles Zavalick; Pub. Cortland Parker; adv. contact: Allison Spinella. photos; bk.rev.; pub. size: broadsheet; circ. 11,800(paid).

US

RANDOLPH REPORTER. Thu. $.50 newsstand; $15/yr. in cy.; $25/yr. out of cy. 17-19 Morristown Rd., Bernardsville, NJ 07924. TEL 908-766-3900; FAX 201-691-2396. **Owner(s):** Recorder Publishing Co., 17-19 Morristown Rd., Bernardsville, NJ 07924. TEL 201-766-3900; Ed. Claire Seedburg; Pub. Cortland Parker; pub. size: standard; circ. 4,043(paid).

Weeklies

BLACKWOOD

US

NEWS REPORT. 1960. Thu. $.50 newsstand; $16/yr. Black Horse Pike & Turnersville Fwy., Blackwood, NJ 08012. TEL 609-228-7300; FAX 609-227-1205. **Owner(s):** Intercounty Newspaper Group, P.O. Box 67, Blackwood, NJ 08012. TEL 609-228-7300; Ed. John Worthington; Pub. Art Thompson; adv.; photos; bk.rev.; pub. size: tabloid; circ. 3,500(paid).

US

RECORD-BREEZE. 1919. Thu. $17/yr. in cy.; $20/yr. out of cy. Black Horse Pike. & Turnersville Fwy, Blackwood, NJ 08012. TEL 609-228-7300; FAX 609-227-1207. **Owner(s):** Associated Utilities Service, 155 Gathor Blvd., Medford, NJ 08055; Ed. John Worthington; Pub. Art Thompson; adv. contact: Mark Mulle. photos; bk.rev.; pub. size: tabloid; circ. 3,500(paid).

BLAIRSTOWN

US

BLAIRSTOWN PRESS. 1877. Wed. $.50 newsstand; $21/yr. in cy. 122 Rte. 94, Blairstown, NJ 07825. TEL 908-362-6161; FAX 908-362-9223. **Owner(s):** North Jersey Newspapers Co., 988 Main Ave., Passaic, NJ 07005. TEL 201-365-3000; FAX 201-365-5887; Ed. Paul Avery; Pub. Rosemarie Maio; pub. size: broadsheet; circ. 4,000(paid).

BLOOMFIELD

US

BELLEVILLE POST. 1982. Thu. $22/yr. in cy. 266 Liberty St., Bloomfield, NJ 07003. TEL 201-743-4040; FAX 201-680-8848. **Owner(s):** Worrall Community Newspapers, Inc., P.O. Box 3109, Union, NJ 07083. TEL 908-686-7700; Pub. David Worrall; adv. contact: Peter Worrall. pub. size: broadsheet; circ. 12,000(paid).

US

GLEN RIDGE PAPER, THE. 1935. Thu. $22/yr. in cy. 266 Liberty St., Bloomfield, NJ 07003. TEL 201-743-4040; FAX 201-674-2038. **Owner(s):** Worrall Community Newspapers, Inc., P.O. Box 3109, Union, NJ 07083. TEL 908-686-7700; Ed. Russell Roemmele; Pub. David Worrall; adv. contact: Peter Worrall. pub. size: broadsheet; circ. 1,512(paid).

US

INDEPENDENT PRESS OF BLOOMFIELD, THE. 1883. Thu. $22/yr. in cy. 266 Liberty St., Bloomfield, NJ 07003. TEL 201-743-4040; FAX 201-674-2038. **Owner(s):** Worrall Community Newspapers, Inc., P.O. Box 3109, Union, NJ 07083. TEL 908-686-7700; Ed. Russell Roemmele; Pub. David Worrall; adv. contact: Peter Worrall. pub. size: broadsheet; circ. 3,976(paid).

US

NUTLEY JOURNAL. 1982. Thu. $22/yr. in cy. 266 Liberty St., Bloomfield, NJ 07003. TEL 201-743-4040; FAX 201-680-8848. **Owner(s):** Worrall Community Newspapers, Inc., P.O. Box 3109, Union, NJ 07083. TEL 908-686-7700; Pub. David Worrall; adv. contact: Peter Worrall. pub. size: broadsheet; circ. 10,400(paid).

BORDENTOWN

US

REGISTER-NEWS. 1845. Thu. $.25 newsstand; $13/yr. in state $16.50/yr. out of state; $11/yr. senior citizens. 137 Farnsworth Ave., Bordentown, NJ 08505. TEL 609-298-7111; FAX 609-298-7107. **Owner(s):** Lorraine Publishing, Inc., 137 Farnsworth Ave., P.O. Box 189, Bordentown, NJ 08505. TEL 609-298-7111; FAX 609-298-7107; Ed. Jennifer L. Collins; Pub. Hershel M. Brown; adv. contact: Michael Atkins. photos; pub. size: tabloid; circ. 7,800(paid).

BRICK

US

BRICK TOWNSHIP TOWN NEWS. 1980. Thu. $.35 newsstand; $9/yr. in town; $14/yr. out of town. 526 Jackson Ave., Brick, NJ 08723. TEL 908-477-9110; FAX 908-477-8305. **Owner(s):** Brick Township Town News, 526 Jackson N.E., Brick, NJ 08723. TEL 908-477-9110; FAX 908-477-8305; Pub. Edward C. Mueller; adv.; photos; bk.rev.; pub. size: tabloid; circ. 5,000(free & paid).

BUDD LAKE

US

MT. OLIVE CHRONICLE. Thu. $.50 newsstand; $15/yr. mailed in cy. 336 Rte. 46, Budd Lake, NJ 07828. TEL 201-691-8181; FAX 201-691-2396. **Owner(s):** Recorder Publishing Co., 17-19 Morristown Rd., Bernardsville, NJ 07924. TEL 908-766-3900; Ed. Phillip J. Nardone; Pub. Cortland Parker; adv.; pub. size: standard; circ. 5,000(paid).

BUTLER

US

LAKELAND TODAY. 1961. s-w.: Wed. & Sun. free. 10 Park Pl., Butler, NJ 07405. TEL 201-283-5507; FAX 201-838-1495. **Owner(s):** North Jersey Newspapers Co., 988 Main Ave., Passaic, NJ 07055; Pub. Richard Vezza; adv.; pub. size: standard; circ. 23,000(free & paid).

US

PASSAIC VALLEY TODAY. s-w.: Wed. & Sun. $.25 newsstand; free home deliv. 10 Park Pl., Butler, NJ 07405. TEL 201-283-5507; FAX 201-838-1495. **Owner(s):** North Jersey Newspapers Co., 988 Main Ave., Passaic, NJ 07055. TEL 201-365-3000; Ed. Nancy Rubenstein; Pub. Richard J. Vezza; adv. contact: Tony Roselli. pub. size: broadsheet; circ. 10,926(paid).

US

SUBURBAN LIFE. 1961. Wed. $31/yr. 10 Park Pl., Butler, NJ 07405. TEL 201-283-5511; FAX 201-838-1495. **Owner(s):** North Jersey Newspapers Co., 988 Main Ave., Passaic, NJ 07055. TEL 201-365-3000; Ed. Robert Errera; Pub. Richard Vezza; adv. contact: Tony Viggiano. pub. size: broadsheet; circ. 32,579(paid). **Wire Service(s):** AP.

Formerly: Suburban Life Today.

US

SUBURBAN TRENDS. 1955. s-w.: Sun. & Wed. $54.60/yr. 10 Park Pl., Butler, NJ 07405-1377. TEL 201-838-9000; FAX 201-838-1495. **Owner(s):** North Jersey Newspapers Co., 998 Main Ave., Passaic, NJ 07055. TEL 201-492-3500; Ed. John Carle. adv. contact: Joseph Onegri. photos; bk.rev.; pub. size: broadsheet; circ. 12,160(paid); Sur. 14,287(paid).

US

WAYNE TODAY. 1962. s-w.: Sun. & Wed. $31.20/yr. 10 Park Pl., Butler, NJ 07415. TEL 201-283-5507; FAX 201-492-3548. **Owner(s):** North Jersey Newspapers Co., 988 Main Ave., Passaic, NJ 07055. TEL 201-365-3000; Ed. Nancy Rubenstein; Pub. Richard Vezza; adv.; photos; pub. size: broadsheet; circ. 48,000(controlled & paid).

BYRAM

US

SUSSEX COUNTY CHRONICLE. 1993. Wed. $.35 newsstand; $21/yr. 23 Rte 206, Byram, NJ 07874. TEL 201-691-9532; FAX 201-852-9320. **Owner(s):** North Jersey Newspapers Co., 988 Main Ave., Passaic, NJ 07055. TEL 201-492-3000; Pub. Rosemarie Maio; adv.; photos; pub. size: broadsheet; circ. 2,400(paid).

CALDWELL

US

PROGRESS, THE. 1911. Thu. $15/yr. in cy. 6 Brookside Ave., Caldwell, NJ 07006-0072. TEL 201-226-8900; FAX 201-226-0553. **Owner(s):** John A. Sullivan, II & Jean E. Conlon, 6 Brookside Ave., Caldwell, NJ 07006. TEL 201-226-8900; Ed. Jean E. Conlon. adv. contact: Roger White. pub. size: broadsheet; circ. 9,300(paid).

CAMDEN

US

CAMDEN COUNTY RECORD. 1959. Thu. $.15 newsstand; $18/yr. 519 Federal St., Ste. 207, Camden, NJ 08103. TEL 609-757-9200; FAX 609-541-4036. **Owner(s):** Tymes Publishing, P.O. Box 389, Camden, NJ 08011. TEL 609-757-9200; FAX 609-541-4036; Ed. Nina France; Pub. Jeffrey Gunning; pub. size: tabloid; circ. 12,000(paid).

CAPE MAY

US

CAPE MAY STAR & WAVE. 1854. Thu. $.50 newsstand; $22/yr. in cy.; $25/yr. out of cy. 513 Washington Mall, Cape May, NJ 08204. TEL 609-884-3466; FAX 609-884-2893; E-mail: rcooper@acy.digex.net; URL: http://www.acy.digex.net/~crmwave. **Owner(s):** American Publishing Co., 605 N. Van Buren, P.O. Box 520, Marion, IL 62959. TEL 618-993-1711; Ed. Mary Keely; Pub. Ralph Cooper; adv. contact: Roseanne Merrick-Borgo. pub. size: standard; circ. 7,800(paid).

CHERRY HILL
US

THIS WEEK. 1991. Thu. free. 301 Cuthbert Blvd., Cherry Hill, NJ 08002. TEL 609-663-4200; FAX 609-663-7664. **Owner(s):** Gannett Company, Inc., 1100 Wilson Blvd., Arlington, VA 22234. TEL 703-284-6000; Ed. Tom Engleman; Pub. Robert Collins; adv. contact: Dennis Watson. pub. size: broadsheet; circ. 4,800(free).
  Formerly: Suburban, The.

CHESTER
US

OBSERVER-TRIBUNE. 1936. Thu. $.75 newsstand; $28/yr. in cy.; $30/yr. out of cy.; $38/yr. out of state. 530 E. Main St., Chester, NJ 07930. TEL 908-879-4100; FAX 908-879-6141. **Owner(s):** Recorder Publishing Co., 17-19 Morristown Rd., Bernardsville, NJ 07924. TEL 201-766-3900; Ed. Philip Nardone; Pub. Cortlandt Parker; adv. contact: Alison Spinella. pub. size: broadsheet; circ. 6,877(paid).

CLIFTON
US   ISSN 0745-8908

NORTH JERSEY PROSPECTOR. 1933. Thu. $.35 newsstand; $30/yr. 85 Crooks Ave., Clifton, NJ 07011. TEL 201-773-8300. **Owner(s):** North Jersey Prospector, Inc., 85 Crooks Ave., Clifton, NJ 07011. TEL 201-773-8300; Ed. Alex Bidnik, Jr.; Pub. Blanche Kubat; adv. contact: Rich Grudzinski. photos; bk.rev.; pub. size: tabloid; circ. 109,023(controlled & paid).

CLOSTER
US

SUBURBANITE, THE. 1958. Wed. free home deliv. 231 Herbert Ave., Closter, NJ 07624. TEL 201-784-0903; FAX 201-784-2592. **Owner(s):** North Jersey Newspapers Co., 998 Main Ave., Passaic, NJ 07055. TEL 201-492-3000; Ed. David Savastino; Pub. Sherwood Spitz; pub. size: tabloid; circ. 49,000(free).
  Formerly: Northern N.J. Suburbanite.

COLLINGSWOOD
US

RETROSPECT, THE. 1902. Fri. $.35 newsstand; $13/yr. 732 Haddon Ave., Collingswood, NJ 08108-0296. TEL 609-854-1400. **Owner(s):** Retrospect, Inc., 732 Haddon Ave., Camden, NJ 08108. TEL 609-854-1400; Ed. Kenneth W. Roberts. adv.; pub. size: tabloid; circ. 4,300(paid).

COLOGNE
US

SOUTH JERSEY ADVISOR. 1970. Thu. free; $35/yr. 644 W. White Horse Pike, Cologne, NJ 08213. TEL 609-646-5843; FAX 609-965-2814. **Owner(s):** Ronald G. Moissinac, 509 S. Fourth Ave., Absecon, NJ 08201. TEL 609-646-5843; FAX 609-965-2814; Ed. Kenneth Platt; Pub. Ronald G. Moissinac; adv. contact: Terry Wheland. photos; pub. size: tabloid; circ. 22,481(free & paid).

CRANFORD
US

CRANFORD CHRONICLE. 1893. Wed. $.50 newsstand; $25/yr. in cy. 102 Walnut Ave., Cranford, NJ 07016. TEL 908-276-6000; FAX 908-276-6220. **Owner(s):** Forbes Newspapers, Inc., 44 Veterans Memorial Dr., E., Somerville, NJ 08876. TEL 908-722-3000; Ed. Ed Carroll; Pub. Louis Barsony; adv. contact: Margaret Ames. pub. size: broadsheet; circ. 7,331(paid).

DAYTON
US

CENTRAL POST. 1958. Thu. $.60 newsstand; $29/yr. 397 Ridge Rd., Ste. 4, Dayton, NJ 08810. TEL 908-329-9214; FAX 908-329-9286. **Owner(s):** Princeton Packet, Inc., 300 Witherspoon St., Princeton, NJ 08540. TEL 609-924-3244; Ed. Helene Ragovin; Pub. James Kilgore; adv. contact: Martin Hillson. pub. size: broadsheet; circ. 5,000(paid).

US

CRANBURY PRESS. Wed. $.60 newsstand; $29/yr. 397 Ridge Rd., Ste. 4, Dayton, NJ 08810. TEL 908-329-9216; FAX 908-329-9286. **Owner(s):** Princeton Packet, Inc., 300 Witherspoon St., Princeton, NJ 08540. TEL 609-924-3244; Ed. Helene Ragovin; Pub. James Kilgore; adv. contact: Martin Hillson. pub. size: broadsheet; circ. 5,000(paid).

US

NORTH BRUNSWICK POST. Fri. Free; $29/yr. 397 Ridge Rd., Ste. 4, Dayton, NJ 08810. TEL 908-329-9216; FAX 908-329-9286. **Owner(s):** Princeton Packet, Inc., 300 Witherspoon St., Princeton, NJ 08540. TEL 609-924-3244; Ed. Helen Ragovin; Pub. James Kilgore; circ. 2,700(paid).

DENVILLE
US

CITIZEN OF MORRIS COUNTY. Wed. $15/yr. in cy.; $25/yr. out of cy. 124 E. Main St., Denville, NJ 07834. TEL 201-627-0400. **Owner(s):** Andis, Inc., 125 E. Main St., Denville, NJ 07834. TEL 201-627-0400; Ed. Audrey Davie. adv. contact: Diane Goldthwait. pub. size: broadsheet; circ. 7,000(paid).

FAIR LAWN
US

NEWS BEACON. 1959. Thu. $.25 newsstand; $9/yr. 12-38 River Rd., Fair Lawn, NJ 07410. TEL 201-791-8400; FAX 201-794-3259. **Owner(s):** North Jersey Newspapers Co., 988 Main Ave., Passaic, NJ 07055. TEL 201-492-3500; Pub. Joseph Gioioso; adv. contact: Sharon Puser. pub. size: tabloid; circ. 36,400(controlled).

FLEMINGTON
US

HUNTERDON COUNTY DEMOCRAT. Thu. $.75/newsstand; $29/yr. P.O. Box 32, Flemington, NJ 08822-0032. TEL 908-782-4747; FAX 908-782-6572. **Owner(s):** Hunterdon County Democrat, P.O. Box 32, Flemington, NJ 08822-0032; Ed. Sally Graziano; Pub. Catherine Langley; circ. 25,000(paid).

FRANKLINVILLE
US   ISSN 0016-0040

FRANKLIN TOWNSHIP SENTINEL. 1942. Thu. $.35 newsstand; $15/yr. P.O. Box 367, Franklinville, NJ 08322. TEL 609-694-1600; FAX 609-694-0469. **Owner(s):** James R. Kinkade, RD 2, P. O. Box 670, Elmer, NJ 08318; Ed. James R. Kinkade; Pub. James R. Kinkade; adv. contact: Monica Billings. pub. size: broadsheet; circ. 4,700(paid).
  Formerly: Franklinville Sentinel.

FRENCHTOWN
US

DELAWARE VALLEY NEWS. 1879. Thu. $.40 newsstand; $18/yr. 207 Harrison St., Frenchtown, NJ 08825. TEL 908-996-4047; FAX 908-996-2238. **Owner(s):** Hunterdon County Democrat, P.O. Box 32, Flemington, NJ 08822. TEL 908-782-4747; Ed. Nick DiGiovanni; Pub. Catherine Langley; adv. contact: Jane Leuthauser. pub. size: broadsheet; circ. 4,800(paid).

GARFIELD
US

MESSENGER, THE. 1940. Thu. $10/yr. mailed only. 48 Harrison Ave., Garfield, NJ 07026. TEL 201-473-1927; FAX 201-546-4233. **Owner(s):** James & Nancy Huffman, 629 Victoria Ave., Paramus, NJ 07652. TEL 201-652-6155; FAX 201-652-7126; Ed. James A. Huffman. adv.; pub. size: tabloid; circ. 1,500(paid).

GLOUCESTER CITY
US

GLOUCESTER CITY NEWS. 1927. Thu. $.50 newsstand; $14/yr. 34 S. Broadway, Gloucester City, NJ 08030. TEL 609-456-1199; FAX 609-456-1330. **Owner(s):** William E. Cleary, P.O. Box 151, Gloucester City, NJ 08030. TEL 609-456-1199; FAX 609-456-1330; Ed. William E. Cleary; Pub. William E. Cleary; photos; bk.rev.; pub. size: tabloid; circ. 5,000(free & paid).

HACKETTSTOWN
US

COMMUNITY FORUM. 1972. Fri. free. 106 E. Moore St., Hackettstown, NJ 07840. TEL 908-852-1212; FAX 908-852-9320. **Owner(s):** North Jersey Newspapers Co., 988 Main Ave., Passaic, NJ 07055. TEL 201-492-3000; Ed. Dan Hirshberg. pub. size: broadsheet; circ. 53,511(free & paid).
  Formerly: Forum, The.

US

STAR GAZETTE. Thu. $.50 newsstand; $21/yr. in cy.; $23/yr. out of cy. 106 E. Moore St., Hackettstown, NJ 07840. TEL 908-852-1212; FAX 908-852-9320. **Owner(s):** North Jersey Newspapers Co., 988 Main Ave., Passaic, NJ 07005. TEL 201-365-3000; Ed. Dan Hirshberg. adv.; photos; pub. size: broadsheet; circ. 4,300(paid).

HAMMONTON
US

ATLANTIC COUNTY RECORD. Thu. $21/yr. 12th St. & West End Ave., Hammonton, NJ 08037. TEL 609-641-3100; FAX 609-646-0516. **Owner(s):** Gannett Company, Inc., 1100 Wilson Blvd., Arlington, VA 22340. TEL 703-284-6000; adv.; pub. size: broadsheet; circ. 3,500(paid).

Weeklies

US   ISSN 0746-7036
EGG HARBOR NEWS. 1911. Thu. $21/yr. 12th St. & West End Ave., Hammonton, NJ 08037. TEL 609-561-2300; FAX 609-567-2269. **Owner(s):** Gannett Company, Inc., 1100 Wilson Blvd., Arlington, VA 22340. TEL 703-284-6000; adv.; pub. size: broadsheet; circ. 2,000(paid).

US
HAMMONTON NEWS. 1858. Thu. $.50 newsstand; $21/yr. 12th St. & West End Ave., Hammonton, NJ 08037. TEL 609-561-2300; FAX 609-646-0561. **Owner(s):** Gannett Company, Inc., 1100 Wilson Blvd., Arlington, VA 22340. TEL 703-284-6000; Pub. Ron Jacovini; adv.; photos; pub. size: broadsheet; circ. 6,500(paid).

US
MAINLAND JOURNAL. 1894. Thu. $21/yr. 12th St. & West End Ave., Hammonton, NJ 08037. TEL 609-641-3100; FAX 609-646-0516. **Owner(s):** Gannett Company, Inc., 1100 Wilson Blvd., Arlington, VA 22340. TEL 703-284-6000; adv.; pub. size: broadsheet; circ. 5,000(paid).
  Formerly: Pleasantville Mainland Journal.

HAWTHORNE

US
HAWTHORNE PRESS. 1924. Thu. $.25 newsstand; $15/yr. local; $18/yr. in state; $22/yr. out of state. 463 Lafayette Ave., Hawthorne, NJ 07506. TEL 201-427-3330. **Owner(s):** William R. Missonellie, P.O. Box 1, Hawthorne, NJ 07506; Ed. Linda Missonellie; Pub. William R. Missonellie; adv.; pub. size: tabloid; circ. 5,600(paid).

HIGHTSTOWN

US
MESSENGER-PRESS. 1903. Thu. $.60 newsstand; $16/6 mos. in cy.; $20/yr. in cy. 510 Rte. 130, S., Hightstown, NJ 08520. TEL 609-448-2100; FAX 609-448-8044. **Owner(s):** Princeton Packet, Inc., 300 Witherspoon, Princeton, NJ 08540; Ed. Frank Herrick; Pub. James Kilgore; adv. contact: Debra Richford. pub. size: broadsheet; circ. 5,000(paid).

HOBOKEN

US
HOBOKEN REPORTER. 1983. Sun. $50/yr. 1321 Washington St., Hoboken, NJ 07030. TEL 201-798-7800; FAX 201-798-0018. **Owner(s):** Joseph Barry, 1321 Washington St., Hoboken, NJ 07030. TEL 201-798-7800; adv. contact: David Unger. bk.rev.; pub. size: tabloid; circ. 17,800(controlled).

US
HUDSON REPORTER. 1983. s-w.: Thu. & Sun. free newsstand; $25/yr. 1400 Washington St., Hoboken, NJ 07030. TEL 201-798-7800; FAX 201-798-0018. **Owner(s):** Joseph Barry, 1400 Washington St., Hoboken, NJ 07030; Ed. Michael Richardson; Pub. Lucha M. Malato; adv. contact: David S. Unger. pub. size: tabloid; circ. 25,000(free & paid); Sun. 65,000(free & paid).

US
JERSEY CITY REPORTER. 1982. Sun. free; $50/yr. out of area. 1321 Washington St., Hoboken, NJ 07030. TEL 201-798-7800; FAX 201-798-0018. **Owner(s):** Joseph Barry, 1321 Washington St., Hoboken, NJ 07030. TEL 201-798-7800; Ed. Michael Richardson. bk.rev.; pub. size: tabloid; circ. 19,200(controlled).

US
NORTH BERGEN/NORTH HUDSON REPORTER. 1985. Sun. $20/3 mos.; $35/6 mos; $50/yr. 1321 Washington St., Hoboken, NJ 07030. TEL 201-798-7800 FAX 201-798-0018. **Owner(s):** Joseph Barry, 1321 Washington St., Hoboken, NJ 07030. TEL 201-798-7800; Pub. David Unger; adv. contact: David Unger. pub. size: tabloid; circ. 31,585(controlled).
  Formerly: North Hudson Reporter.

US
WEEHAWKEN REPORTER. 1986. Sun. free newsstand; $50/yr. 1400 Washington St., Hoboken, NJ 07030. TEL 201-798-7800; FAX 201-798-0018. **Owner(s):** Joseph Barry, 1321 Washington St., Hoboken, NJ 07030. TEL 201-798-7800; Ed. Michael Richardson; Pub. Joseph Barry; adv. contact: David Unger. pub. size: tabloid; circ. 18,000(free & paid).

HOPEWELL

US
BEACON-RECORD. 1845. Wed. $26/yr. in state; $49/yr. out of state; $21/yr. senior citizens. P.O. Box 8, Hopewell, NJ 08525. TEL 609-466-1190; FAX 609-466-2123 **Owner(s):** Princeton Packet, Inc., 300 Witherspoon St., Princeton, NJ 08540; Ed. Mae Rhine. pub. size: broadsheet; circ. 3,500(paid).

KEARNY

US
OBSERVER, THE. 1887. Wed. free; $30/yr. 531 Kearny Ave., Kearny, NJ 07032. TEL 201-991-1600; FAX 201-991-8941. **Owner(s):** Observer, The, 531 Kearny Ave., Kearny, NJ 07032. TEL 201-991-1600; FAX 201-991-8941; Pub. Mary Tortoreti; adv. contact: Antoinette Zuest. photos; pub. size: broadsheet; circ. 25,000(free & paid).
  Formerly: Kearny Observer.

LAKEHURST

US
ADVANCE NEWS. 1968. Wed. $.15 newsstand; $7.50/yr.; $15/2 yrs.; $22.50/3 yrs. 2048 Rte. 37, Lakehurst, NJ 08733. TEL 908-657-8936; FAX 908-657-2970. **Owner(s):** Advance Nickel Dime News, 2048 Rte. 37, Lakehurst, NJ 08733. TEL 908-657-8936; Pub. Jerri T. Varelli; adv. contact: Rose Mauder. photos; bk.rev.; pub. size: tabloid; circ. 25,000(paid).

LEBANON

US
HUNTERDON REVIEW. 1868. Wed. $.50 newsstand; $20/yr. local. 1128 Rte. 31 N., Lebanon, NJ 08833. TEL 908-735-4081; FAX 908-735-2945. **Owner(s):** Recorder Publishing Co., 17-19 Morristown Rd., Bernardsville, NJ 07924. TEL 201-766-3900; Ed. Richard Hartten; Pub. Cortlandt Parker; adv. contact: Joyce Flyan. pub. size: broadsheet; circ. 4,900(paid).

LEDGEWOOD

US
WEST MORRIS STAR-JOURNAL. 1962. Wed. $.35 newsstand; $21/yr. in cy.; $24/yr. out of cy.; $28/yr. out of state. 50 Main St. Ledgewood, NJ 07852. TEL 201-584-7176; FAX 201-584-7403. **Owner(s):** North Jersey Newspapers Inc., 988 Main Ave., Passaic, NJ 07005. TEL 201-362-3000; FAX 201-365-5887; Ed. Dan Hirschberg; Pub. Rosemarie Maio; pub. size: broadsheet; circ. 6,000(paid).

LIVINGSTON

US
WEST ESSEX TRIBUNE. 1929. Thu. $.40 newsstand; $17/yr. in cy.; $20/yr. out of cy.; $23/yr. out of state. 495 S. Livingston Ave., Livingston, NJ 07039-0065. TEL 201-992-1771; FAX 201-992-7015. **Owner(s):** E. Christopher Cone, 18 Midway Dr., Livingston, NJ 07039. TEL 201-992-1771; FAX 201-992-7015; Ed. Nancy B. Dinar; Pub. E. Christopher Cone; adv. contact: Judith Dressel. pub. size: broadsheet; circ. 8,000(paid).

MADISON

US
CHATHAM COURIER. 1930. Thu. $.50 newsstand; $21/yr. in cy.; $25/yr. out of cy.; $30/yr. out of state. 155 Main St., Madison, NJ 07940. TEL 201-377-2000; FAX 201-377-7721. **Owner(s):** Parker Publishing Co., 17-19 Morristown Rd., Bernardsville, NJ 07924. TEL 908-766-3900; Ed. Gene Robbins; Pub. Cortlandt Parker; adv. contact: Carmel Clancy. pub. size: standard; circ. 4,200(paid).

US
FLORHAM PARK EAGLE. 1882. Thu. $21/yr. in cy.; $30/yr. out of cy.; $20/college yr. students. 155 Main St., Madison, NJ 07940. TEL 201-377-2000; FAX 201-377-7721. **Owner(s):** Recorder Publishing Co, 17-19 Morristown Rd., Bernardsville, NJ 07924. TEL 908-766-3900; Ed. Gene Robbins; Pub. Cortlandt Parker; adv. contact: Carmel Clancy. photos; pub. size: broadsheet; circ. 1,892(paid).
  Formerly: Florham Park Eagle & Community News.

US
HANOVER EAGLE & REGIONAL NEWS. 1956. Thu. $.50 newsstand; $18/yr. in cy.; $25/yr. out of cy.; $30/yr. out of state. 155 Main St., Madison, NJ 07940. TEL 201-377-2000; FAX 201-377-7721. **Owner(s):** Recorder Publishing Co., 17-19 Morristown Rd., Bernardsville, NJ 07924. TEL 908-766-3900; Ed. Gene Robbins; Pub. Cortlandt Parker; adv. contact: Carmel Clancy. pub. size: tabloid; circ. 4,500(paid).

US
MADISON EAGLE. 1880. Thu. $21/yr. in cy.; $25/yr. out of cy.; $30/yr. out of state; $20/college year. 155 Main St., Madison, NJ 07940. TEL 201-377-2000; FAX 201-377-7721. **Owner(s):** Recorder Publishing Co., 17-19 Morristown Rd., Bernardsville, NJ 07924. TEL 908-766-3900; Ed. Gene Robbins; Pub. Cortlandt Parker; adv. contact: Carmel Clancy. pub. size: broadsheet; circ. 3,315(paid).

US

MORRIS NEWS BEE. 1946. Thu. $.50 newsstand; $18/yr. in cy.; $25/yr. out of cy.; $30/yr. out of state. 155 Main St., Madison, NJ 07940. TEL 201-377-2000; FAX 201-377-7721. **Owner(s):** Recorder Publishing Co., 17-19 Morristown Rd., Bernardsville, NJ 07924. TEL 908-766-3900; Ed. Gene Robbins; Pub. Cortlandt Parker; adv. contact: Carmel Clancy. pub. size: broadsheet; circ. 4,500(paid).

MANAHAWKIN

US

BEACH HAVEN TIMES. 1923. Wed. $24/yr. in cy.; $28/yr. out of cy. 345 E. Bay Ave., Manahawkin, NJ 08050. TEL 609-597-3211; FAX 609-597-8169. **Owner(s):** Manahawkin Times-Beacon Co., 395 E. Bay Ave., Manahawkin, NJ 08050. TEL 609-597-3211; Ed. Jan Zollinger; Pub. J. Peter Lindquist; adv. contact: Tim Wallace. pub. size: broadsheet; circ. 7,819(paid).

US

BEACON, THE. 1889. Thu. $24/yr. in cy.; $28/yr. out of cy. 345 E. Bay Ave., Manahawkin, NJ 08050. TEL 609-597-3211; FAX 609-597-8169. **Owner(s):** Manahawkin Times-Beacon Co., 345 E. Bay Ave., Manahawkin, NJ 08050. TEL 609-597-3211; Ed. Jan Zollinger; Pub. J. Peter Lindquist; adv. contact: Tim Wallace. photos; pub. size: broadsheet; circ. 13,000(controlled).

MAPLE SHADE

US

MAPLE SHADE PROGRESS. 1918. Thu. $.35 newsstand; $15/yr. 306 E. Main St., Maple Shade, NJ 08052. TEL 609-779-7788. **Owner(s):** Frank E. Gerkens, 306 E. Main St., Maple Shade, NJ 08502. TEL 609-779-7788; Ed. Frank E. Gerkens; Pub. Frank E. Gerkens; pub. size: broadsheet; circ. 10,000(free & paid).

US

MT. LAUREL PROGRESS PRESS. Thu. $.35 newsstand; $12/yr. 306 E. Main St., Maple Shade, NJ 08052. TEL 609-779-7788. **Owner(s):** Frank E. Gerkens, 306 E. Main St., Maple Shade, NJ 08502. TEL 609-779-7788; Ed. Frank E. Gerkens; Pub. Frank E. Gerkens; pub. size: broadsheet; circ. 5,000(free & paid).

MAPLEWOOD

US

NEWS-RECORD OF MAPLEWOOD & SOUTH ORANGE. 1986. Thu. $22/yr. in cy. 463 Valley St., Maplewood, NJ 07040. TEL 201-763-0700; FAX 201-674-2038. **Owner(s):** Worrall Community Newspapers, Inc., 1291 Stuyvesant Ave., Union, NJ 07083. TEL 908-686-7700; Ed. Anthony Puglisi; Pub. David Worrall; adv. contact: Peter Worrall. pub. size: broadsheet; circ. 6,745(paid).

US

VAILSBURG LEADER. 1950. Thu. $.50 newsstand; $22/yr. 463 Valley St., Maplewood, NJ 07040. TEL 908-686-7700; FAX 908-763-2557. **Owner(s):** Worrall Community Newspapers, Inc., 1291 Stuyvesant Ave., Union, NJ 07083. TEL 908-686-7700; Ed. Yolanda McBride; Pub. David Worrall; adv. contact: Peter Worrall. pub. size: standard; circ. 1,500(paid).

MAYWOOD

US   ISSN 0048-2404

OUR TOWN. 1948. Thu. $.35 newsstand; $12/yr.; $22/2 yrs. 58 W. Pleasant Ave., Maywood, NJ 07607. TEL 201-843-5700. **Owner(s):** Jim & Kathy Panos, 680 Jersey Ave., Maywood, NJ 07607; Ed. Katherine J. Panos. adv.; pub. size: tabloid; circ. 3,500(free & paid).

MEDFORD

US   ISSN 0745-7030

CENTRAL RECORD. 1896. Thu. $.35 newsstand; $16/yr. Old Marlton Pike, Medford, NJ 08055. TEL 609-654-5000. **Owner(s):** Central Record, Inc., The, P.O. Box 1027, Medford, NJ 08055. TEL 908-654-5000; FAX 908-654-8237; Ed. Patricia E. Haughey. adv.; pub. size: broadsheet; circ. 12,000(paid).

MIDDLETOWN

US

MIDDLETOWN COURIER. 1955. Thu. $.40 newsstand; $13/yr. in state; $16/yr. out of state. 320 Kings Hwy., E., Middletown, NJ 07748. TEL 908-957-0070; FAX 908-957-0143. **Owner(s):** Bayshore Press, Inc., 320 Kings Hwy., E., Middletown, NJ 07748. TEL 201-957-0070; Ed. Bonnie Walling; Pub. John Famulary; adv.; photos; pub. size: tabloid; circ. 11,000(paid).

MILLBURN

US

MILLBURN & SHORT HILLS ITEM. 1888. Thu. $.50 newsstand; $18/yr. 100 Millburn Ave., Millburn, NJ 07041. TEL 201-376-1200; FAX 201-376-8556. **Owner(s):** BAL Communications, Inc., 100 Millburn Ave., Millburn, NJ 07041. TEL 201-376-1200; FAX 201-376-8550; Ed. Carter J. Bennett; Pub. Barbara A. Lewis; adv. contact: Tracy DuPuis. pub. size: broadsheet; circ. 5,000(paid).

MONTCLAIR

US

MONTCLAIR TIMES, THE. 1877. Thu. $.50 newsstand; $18/yr. 114 Valley Rd., Montclair, NJ 07042. TEL 201-746-1100; FAX 201-746-0995. **Owner(s):** Montclair Newspapers, Inc., 114 Valley Rd., Montclair, NJ 07042. TEL 201-746-1100; FAX 201-746-8131; Ed. Lucinda Smith; Pub. Barbara A. Lewis; adv. contact: Sara Singleton. photos; pub. size: broadsheet; circ. 12,003(paid).

MORGANVILLE

US

INDEPENDENT, THE. 1970. Wed. free deliv. 25 Kilmer Dr., Ste. 109, Morganville, NJ 07751-1561. TEL 908-254-7000; FAX 908-254-0456. **Owner(s):** Greater Media, Inc., 2 Kennedy Blvd., East Brunswick, NJ 08816. TEL 908-247-6161; Ed. Marilyn Duff; Pub. Kevin Wittman; adv.; pub. size: tabloid; circ. 34,000(free). **Wire Service(s):** AP, Newsfinder.

US

NEWS TRANSCRIPT. 1888. Wed. $.40 newsstand; $32/yr. 25 Kilmer Dr., Ste. 109, Morganville, NJ 07751. TEL 908-972-6740; FAX 908-972-6746. **Owner(s):** Greater Media, Inc., 2 Kennedy Blvd., East Brunswick, NJ 07728. TEL 908-247-6161; Ed. Mark Rosman; Pub. Kevin Wittman; adv. contact: Gerry Haggerty. photos; pub. size: tabloid; circ. 40,000.

MORRIS PLAINS

US

PARSIPPANY FOCUS. 1989. Thu. $.30 newsstand; $12/yr. in cy. 25109 Rte. 10, Morris Plains, NJ 07950. TEL 201-984-5100; FAX 201-984-3003. **Owner(s):** Parsippany Focus, Inc., 25109 Rte. 10, Morris Plains, NJ 07950. TEL 201-984-5100; FAX 201-984-3003; Ed. Cathy Haddon; Pub. Frank L. Cahill; adv. contact: John Caroperso. photos; bk.rev.; pub. size: broadsheet; circ. 30,500(free & paid).

MT. HOLLY

US

GAZETTE, THE. 1986. Thu. $.35 newsstand; $15/yr. 69 High St., Mt. Holly, NJ 08060. TEL 609-261-7341; FAX 609-261-7392. **Owner(s):** Robert Reichenbach, 69 High St., Mt. Holly, NJ 08060. TEL 609-261-7341; FAX 609-261-7392; Ed. Paul Fowler; Pub. Robert Reichenbach; adv. contact: Elda Goss. photos; pub. size: tabloid; circ. 3,000(paid).

MT. LAUREL

US

NEWS WEEKLY. 1966. Thu. $.50 newsstand; $14/yr. in cy.; $20/yr. out of cy. 155 Gaither Dr., Mt. Laurel, NJ 08054. TEL 609-231-7600; FAX 609-231-4333. **Owner(s):** Intercounty Newspaper Group, 6220 Ridge Ave., Philadelphia, PA 19128. TEL 215-483-7300; Ed. Sandra McGuire; Pub. Fred W. Donaldson; adv. contact: John Brookover. photos; bk.rev.; pub. size: tabloid; circ. 8,600(paid).

NETCONG

US

NETCONG NEWS-LEADER. Wed. $.35 newsstand; $18/yr. P.O. Box 637, Netcong, NJ 07857. TEL 201-347-0300; FAX 201-362-9223. **Owner(s):** North Jersey Newspapers Co., 988 Main Ave., Passiac, NJ 07005. TEL 201-365-3000; FAX 201-365-5887; Ed. Shawn Cupolo; Pub. Rosemarie Maio; pub. size: broadsheet; circ. 3,000(paid).

NEW PROVIDENCE

US

CHATHAM INDEPENDENT PRESS. 1969. Wed. free; $75/yr. mailed. 80 South St., New Providence, NJ 07974. TEL 908-464-1025; FAX 908-464-9085. **Owner(s):** North Jersey Newspapers Co., 988 Main Ave., Passaic, NJ 07055. TEL 201-365-3000; FAX 201-365-5887; Ed. Christopher Moore; Pub. Michael J. Kelly; adv. contact: Brad Tomlinson. pub. size: broadsheet; circ. 43,200(free & paid).

US

DISPATCH, THE. 1950. Sat. $16.50/yr. 80 South St., New Providence, NJ 07974. TEL 908-464-1025; FAX 908-464-9085. **Owner(s):** North Jersey Newspapers Co., 988 Main Ave., Passaic, NJ 07055. TEL 201-365-3000; FAX 201-365-5887; Ed. Christopher Moore; Pub. Michael Kelly; pub. size: broadsheet; circ. 3,000(paid).

US

INDEPENDENT PRESS. 1964. Wed. free home deliv.; $.50 newsstand; $75/yr. mailed. 80 South St., New Providence, NJ 07974. TEL 908-464-1025; FAX 908-464-9085. **Owner(s):** North Jersey Newspapers Co., 988 Main Ave., Passaic, NJ 07005. TEL 201-365-3000; FAX 201-365-5887; Ed. Christopher Moore; Pub. Michael J. Kelly; adv. contact: Brad Tomilson. photos; bk.rev.; pub. size: broadsheet; circ. 38,455(free & paid).

US

MADISON INDEPENDENT PRESS. 1964. Wed. free; $30//yr. in state; $35/yr. out of state. 80 South St., New Providence, NJ 07974. TEL 908-464-1025; FAX 908-464-9085. **Owner(s):** North Jersey Newspapers Co., 988 Main Ave., Passaic, NJ 07055. TEL 201-365-3000; FAX 201-365-5887; Ed. Christopher Moore; Pub. Michael J. Kelly; adv. contact: Brad Tomlinson. photos; bk.rev.; pub. size: broadsheet; circ. 3,900(free & paid).

US

MILLBURN-SHORT HILLS INDEPENDENT PRESS. 1978. Wed. free; $75/yr. mailed. 80 South St., New Providence, NJ 07974. TEL 908-464-1025; FAX 908-464-9085. **Owner(s):** North Jersey Newspapers Co., 988 Main St., Passaic, NJ 07005. TEL 201-365-3000; FAX 201-365-5887; Pub. Michael Kelly; adv. contact: Brad Tomilson. pub. size: broadsheet; circ. 6,500(free & paid).
  Formerly: Short Hills-Millburn Independent.

US

SUMMIT INDEPENDENT PRESS. 1967. Thu. free; $20/yr. mailed. 80 South St., New Providence, NJ 07974. TEL 908-464-1025; FAX 908-464-9085. **Owner(s):** North Jersey Newspapers Co., 988 Main Ave., Passaic, NJ 07055. TEL 201-365-3000; FAX 201-365-5887; Ed. Christopher Moore; Pub. Michael J. Kelly; adv. contact: Brad Tomlinson. photos; pub. size: broadsheet; circ. 9,300(free & paid).

NUTLEY

US

BELLEVILLE TIMES NEWS. 1909. Thu. $.50 newsstand; $16/yr. in state; $18/yr. out of state. 800 Bloomfield Ave., Nutley, NJ 07110. TEL 201-759-3200; FAX 201-667-3904. **Owner(s):** Orechio Publications, 155A Washington Ave., Belleville, NJ 07109. TEL 201-759-3200; Ed. Richard Dickon; Pub. Frank Orechio; pub. size: standard; circ. 7,000(paid).

US

BLOOMFIELD LIFE. 1980. Thu. $.50 newsstand; $16/yr.; $8/yr. senior citizens. 800 Bloomfield Ave., Nutley, NJ 07110. TEL 201-759-3200; FAX 201-667-3904. **Owner(s):** Orechio Publications, 800 Bloomfield Ave., Nutley, NJ 07110. TEL 201-759-3200; Ed. Steve Galvacky; Pub. Frank A. Orechio; adv. contact: Maria Paladino. pub. size: broadsheet; circ. 5,000(paid).

US

NUTLEY SUN. 1895. Thu. $.50 newsstand; $16/yr. mailed in state; $18/yr. out of state. 800 Bloomfield Ave., Nutley, NJ 07110. TEL 201-759-3200; FAX 201-667-3904. **Owner(s):** Orechio Publications, 800 Bloomfield Ave., Nutley, NJ 07110. TEL 201-759-3200; Ed. James Zocolli; Pub. Frank Orechio; adv. contact: Celeste Federico. pub. size: broadsheet; circ. 8,000(paid).

OCEAN CITY

US

SENTINEL-LEDGER THE. 1881. Thu. (Sep.-May); s-w.: Tue. & Fri. (Jun.-Aug.). $.50 newsstand; $25/yr. in cy.; $29/yr. out of cy.; $29/yr. out of state; $33/yr. west of MS; $21/yr. military. 112 E. Eighth St., Ocean City, NJ 08226-0238. TEL 609-399-5411; FAX 609-399-0416; E-mail: rcooper@acy.digex.net; URL: http://www.acy.digex.net. **Owner(s):** American Publishing Co., 606 N. Van Buren, P.O. Box 520, Marion, IL 62959. TEL 618-993-1711; Ed. John H. Andrus, II; Pub. Ralph J. Cooper; adv. contact: Barbara Bradley. photos; bk.rev.; pub. size: broadsheet; circ. 10,764(paid).

ORANGE

US

EAST ORANGE RECORD. 1899. Thu. $22/yr. in cy. 170 Scotland Rd., Orange, NJ 07050. TEL 201-674-8000; FAX 201-674-2038. **Owner(s):** Worrall Community Newspapers, Inc., 1291 Stuyvesant Ave., Union, NJ 07083. TEL 908-686-7700; Ed. Anthony Puglisi; Pub. David Worrall; adv. contact: Peter Worrall. pub. size: broadsheet; circ. 2,531(paid).

US

ORANGE TRANSCRIPT. 1898. Thu. $22/yr. in cy. 170 Scotland Rd., Orange, NJ 07050. TEL 201-674-8000; FAX 201-674-2038. **Owner(s):** Worrall Community Newspapers, Inc., P.O. Box 3109, Union, NJ 07083. TEL 908-686-7700; Ed. Anthony Puglisi; Pub. David Worrall; adv. contact: Peter Worrall. pub. size: broadsheet; circ. 2,500(paid).

US

WEST ORANGE CHRONICLE. 1931. Thu. $22/yr. in cy. 170 Scotland Rd., Orange, NJ 07050. TEL 201-674-8000; FAX 201-674-2038. **Owner(s):** Worrall Community Newspapers, Inc., P.O. Box 3109, Union, NJ 07083. TEL 908-686-7700; Ed. Rose Manzo; Pub. David Worrall; adv. contact: Peter Worrall. pub. size: broadsheet; circ. 6,000(paid).

PALISADES PARK

US

BERGEN NEWS, THE. 1950. Wed. $.50 newsstand; $32/yr. in state; $42/yr. out of state. 111 Grand Ave., Palisades Park, NJ 07650. TEL 201-947-5000; FAX 201-947-6968. **Owner(s):** News Publishing Group, 111 Grand Ave., Palisades Park, NJ 07650. TEL 201-947-5000; FAX 201-947-6968; Ed. Eleanor Marra; Pub. William Cohen; adv.; photos; pub. size: tabloid; circ. 38,962(controlled).
  Formerly: Bergen News-Palisades, South & Valley Editions.

US

PRESS JOURNAL, THE. 1874. Thu. $.50 newsstand; $32/yr. in cy.; $42/yr. out of cy. 111 Grand Ave., Palisades Park, NJ 07650. TEL 201-871-6900. **Owner(s):** News Publishing Co., 111 Grand Ave., Palisades Park, NJ 07650. TEL 201-947-5000; FAX 201-947-0968; Ed. Eleanor Marra; Pub. William Cohen; adv.; photos; pub. size: broadsheet; circ. 10,987(controlled & paid).
  Formerly: Press Journal-North & South Editions.

US

RAMSEY-MAHWAH REPORTER. 1976. Fri. $.50 newsstand; $30/yr. in town; $42/yr. out of town. 111 Grand Ave., Palisades Park, NJ 07650. TEL 201-825-3737; FAX 201-947-6968. **Owner(s):** News Publishing Group, 111 Grand Ave., Palisades Park, NJ 07650. TEL 201-947-5000; Ed. Eleanor Marra; Pub. William Cohen; adv. contact: Jill Cohen. photos; pub. size: tabloid; circ. 4,468(paid).

US

REPORTER, THE. Fri. $.35 newsstand; $25/yr. 111 Grand Ave., Palisades Park, NJ 07650. TEL 201-947-5000; FAX 201-947-6968. **Owner(s):** News Publishing Group, 111 Grand Ave., Palisades Park, NJ 07650. TEL 201-947-5000; FAX 201-947-6968; Ed. Eleanor Marra; Pub. William Cohen; adv.; photos; pub. size: tabloid; circ. 10,000(paid).

US

SUN-BULLETIN, THE. 1893. Fri. $.50 newsstand; $32/yr. in state; $42/yr. out of state. 111 Grand Ave., Palisades Park, NJ 07650. TEL 201-947-5000; FAX 201-947-6968. **Owner(s):** News Publishing Group, 111 Grand Ave., Palisades Park, NJ 07650. TEL 201-947-5000; FAX 201-947-6968; Ed. Eleanor Marra; Pub. William Cohen; adv. contact: Lesley Ann Cohen. photos; pub. size: tabloid; circ. 18,454(paid).
  Formerly: Sun-Bulletin-East & Central Editions.

PARAMUS

US

POST REVIEW, THE. s-w.: Sun. & Thu. $.50 newsstand; $39/yr. in cy. Includes The Review. 50 Eisenhower Dr., Paramus, NJ 07652. TEL 201-843-0500; FAX 201-291-5905. **Owner(s):** North Jersey Newspapers Co., 988 Main Ave., Passaic, NJ 07055. TEL 201-365-3000; FAX 201-365-5887; Ed. Ellen Walsh. adv. contact: Brian Winterberg. pub. size: broadsheet; circ. Sun. 10,000(paid).
  Formerly: Sunday Post.

US

REVIEW, THE. 1920. Thu. $.35 newsstand; $39/yr. includes Sunday Post. 50 Eisenhower Dr., Paramus, NJ 07652. TEL 201-843-0500; FAX 201-843-2388. **Owner(s):** North Jersey Newspapers Co., 988 Main Ave., Passaic, NJ 07055. TEL 201-365-3000; Ed. Christina Rossi; Pub. Joe Giosio; adv. contact: Briar Winterberg. pub. size: tabloid; circ. 10,000(paid).

US

RIDGEWOOD NEWS. 1889. s-w.: Sun. & Thu. $.35/Thu.; $.50/Sun.; $15.50/yr. Thu. only; $23.40/yr. Sun. only; $39/yr. both editions. 50 Eisenhower Dr., Paramus, NJ 07652. TEL 201-843-0500; FAX 201-368-0706. **Owner(s):** North Jersey Newspapers Co., 988 Main Ave., Passaic, NJ 07055. TEL 201-365-3000; Ed. Ellen Walsh. adv.; pub. size: broadsheet; circ. 8,900(paid); Sun. 12,000(paid).
  Formerly: Sunday News.

US

SUBURBAN TOWN NEWS. 1952. Wed. free. 50 Eisenhower Dr., Paramus, NJ 07652. TEL 201-368-0100; FAX 201-368-0706. **Owner(s):** North Jersey Newspapers Co., 988 Main Ave., Passaic, NJ 07055. TEL 201-365-3000; FAX 201-365-5887; Ed. Paul Rabin; Pub. S. Spitz; adv.; pub. size: tabloid; circ. 114,000(free). **Wire Service(s):** SNS.

PASSAIC

US

PASSAIC CITIZEN. 1921. Thu. $.25 newsstand;
$16/yr. in state; $18/yr. out of state. 298
Passaic St., Passaic, NJ 07055.
TEL 201-779-7500. **Owner(s):** D & H
Communications, Inc., P.O. Box 453, East
Rutherford, NJ 07073. TEL 201-779-7500; Ed.
Helen Gately; Pub. Renata Helstoski; adv.; photos;
pub. size: tabloid; circ. 10,000(paid).

PENNINGTON

US   ISSN 0746-1771

LAWRENCE LEDGER. 1969. Thu. $.60 newsstand;
$32/yr. 53 Pennington-Hopewell Rd., Pennington,
NJ 08534. TEL 609-466-8650;
FAX 609-466-2123. **Owner(s):** Princeton Packet,
Inc., 300 Witherspoon, P.O. Box 350, Princeton,
NJ 08540. TEL 609-924-3244; Ed. Tom
Lederer. pub. size: standard; circ. 3,100(paid).

PHILLIPSBURG

US

PHILLIPSBURG FREE PRESS. 1961. Thu. $.40
newsstand; $18/yr. in NJ & PA; $23/yr.
elsewhere. 198 Chamber St., Phillipsburg, NJ
08865. TEL 908-859-4444;
FAX 908-859-3084. **Owner(s):** Montclair
Newspapers, Inc., Montclair, NJ; Ed. Michael C.
O'Connor; Pub. Rosemary Maio; adv.; pub. size:
tabloid; circ. 3,100(paid).

POINT PLEASANT BEACH

US

LEADER, THE. 1916. Thu. $.50 newsstand;
$17.50/yr. 707 Arnold Ave., Point Pleasant
Beach, NJ 08742. TEL 908-899-1000;
FAX 908-899-2135. **Owner(s):** Rockfleet Media,
Inc., Point Pleasant Beach, NJ; Ed. Andrew Mills.
pub. size: broadsheet; circ. 8,500(paid).

US

REVIEW, THE. Thu. $.50 newsstand; $17.50/yr.
707 Arnold Ave., Point Pleasant Beach, NJ
08742. TEL 908-899-1000;
FAX 908-899-2135. **Owner(s):** Rockfleet Media,
Inc., Point Pleasant Beach, NJ 08742; Ed. Andrew
Mills. pub. size: broadsheet; circ. 8,000(paid).

US   ISSN 1053-4555

SEASIDE HEIGHTS OCEAN COUNTY REVIEW. 1913.
Thu. $.50 newsstand; $17.50/yr. 707 Arnold
Ave., Point Pleasant Beach, NJ 08742.
TEL 908-899-1000; FAX 908-899-2135.
Owner(s): Rockfleet Media, Inc., Point Pleasant
Beach, NJ; Ed. Andrew Mills; Pub. Sheila O'Malley;
adv.; photos; bk.rev.; pub. size: broadsheet; circ.
8,500(paid).

PRINCETON

US

FRANKLIN NEWS-RECORD. Fri. free; $27/yr. out of
area. 300 Witherspoon St., Princeton, NJ 08542.
TEL 609-924-3244; FAX 609-924-3842.
Owner(s): Princeton Packet, Inc., 300
Witherspoon St., Princeton, NJ 08540. TEL
609-924-3244; Ed. Cindy Maylor. adv. contact:
Allison Spinella. pub. size: standard; circ.
4,900(free & paid).

US

PRINCETON PACKET, THE. 1786. s-w.: Tue. & Fri.
$.60 newsstand; $37/yr. 300 Witherspoon St.,
Princeton, NJ 08542. TEL 609-924-3244;
FAX 609-921-2714. **Owner(s):** Princeton Packet,
Inc., 300 Witherspoon St., P.O. Box 350,
Princeton, NJ 08542. TEL 609-924-3244; Ed.
Fred Egeznof. adv.; photos; bk.rev.; pub. size:
broadsheet; circ. 14,420(paid).

US   ISSN 0191-7056

TOWN TOPICS. 1946. Wed. $.50 newsstand;
$20/yr. local; $25/yr. elsewhere. 4 Mercer St.,
Princeton, NJ 08540. TEL 609-924-2200.
Owner(s): Donald C. Stuart, III, 4 Mercer St.,
Princeton, NJ 08540; Ed. Donald C. Stuart, III.
adv. contact: Linda Sproehnle. pub. size: tabloid;
circ. 14,435(free & paid).

RAHWAY

US

CLARK PATRIOT. 1965. Thu. $.25 newsstand;
$15/yr. 219 Central Ave., Rahway, NJ 07065.
TEL 908-574-1200; FAX 908-388-4143.
Owner(s): Tabloid Lithographers, Inc., P.O. Box
1061, Rahway, NJ 07065. TEL 908-574-1200;
Ed. Ellen Vigilante; Pub. Ellen Vigilante; adv.;
photos; pub. size: broadsheet; circ. 1,300(free &
paid).

US

RAHWAY NEWS-RECORD. 1822. Thu. $.25
newsstand; $15/yr. 219 Central Ave., Rahway,
NJ 07065. TEL 908-574-1200;
FAX 908-388-4143. **Owner(s):** Tabloid
Lithographers, Inc., P.O. Box 1061, Rahway, NJ
07065. TEL 908-574-1200; Ed. Ellen Vigilante;
Pub. Ellen Vigilante; adv.; photos; pub. size:
broadsheet; circ. 1,877(paid).

RAMSEY

US

RAMSEY HOME & STORE NEWS. 1960. Wed. free. 6A
E. Main St., Ramsey, NJ 07446-0329.
TEL 201-327-1212; FAX 201-327-3684.
Owner(s): Arthur Aldrich, P.O. Box 329, Ramsey,
NJ 07446-0329. TEL 201-327-1212; FAX
201-327-3684; Ed. Arthur Aldrich; Pub. Arthur
Aldrich; adv. contact: Jo Bosakowski. photos; pub.
size: tabloid; circ. 25,947(free).

RIO GRANDE

US

CAPE MAY HERALD DISPATCH. 1984. Wed. $15/yr.
1508 Rte. 47, S., Rio Grande, NJ 08242.
TEL 609-886-8600; FAX 609-886-1879.
Owner(s): Seawave Corp., P.O. Box 400, Rio
Grande, NJ 08242. TEL 609-886-8600; FAX
609-886-1879; Ed. Joseph R. Zelnik; Pub. Arthur
R. Hall; adv. contact: Beth Huber. photos; bk.rev.;
pub. size: tabloid; circ. 29,206(free & paid).

US

LOWER TOWNSHIP LANTERN. 1979. Wed. free
newsstand; $15/yr. 1508 Rte. 47, S., Rio
Grande, NJ 08242. TEL 609-886-8600;
FAX 609-886-1879. **Owner(s):** Seawave Corp.,
P.O. Box 400, Rio Grande, NJ 08242. TEL
609-886-8600; Ed. Joseph R. Zelnik; Pub. Arthur
R. Hall; adv. contact: Beth Huber. photos; bk.rev.;
pub. size: tabloid; circ. 29,000(free & paid).

RUTHERFORD

US

SOUTH BERGENITE. 1970. Wed. free. 71 Union Ave.,
Rutherford, NJ 07070. TEL 201-933-1166;
FAX 201-933-5496. **Owner(s):** North Jersey
Newspapers Co., 988 Main Ave., Passaic, NJ
07005. TEL 201-365-3000; FAX
201-365-5887; Ed. Edward Kensik; Pub. Joseph
Gioioso; adv. contact: Sharon Puser. pub. size:
tabloid; circ. 36,178(free).

SALEM

US

SALEM COUNTY RECORD. 1819. Fri. free. 93 Fifth
St., Salem, NJ 08079. TEL 609-935-1500;
FAX 609-845-3139. **Owner(s):** Media News
Group, 309 S. Broad St., Woodbury, NJ 08096.
TEL 609-845-3300; Ed. John Barna; Pub. Wayne
Studer; adv. contact: Ceil Smith. pub. size:
broadsheet; circ. 7,000(free).

SECAUCUS

US

SECAUCUS HOME NEWS. 1910. Thu. $.35
newsstand; $12/yr. in cy.; $13/yr. in state;
$14/yr. out of state. 766 Irving Pl., Secaucus, NJ
07094. TEL 201-867-2071;
FAX 201-865-3806. **Owner(s):** Gretchen Henkel,
766 Irving Pl., Secaucus, NJ 07094. TEL
201-867-2071; Ed. Gretchen Henkel; Pub.
Gretchen Henkel; adv. contact: Debbie Zapoluch.
pub. size: tabloid; circ. 5,500(paid).

SOMERSET

US

SOMERSET SPECTATOR. 1969. Thu. $.25
newsstand; $14.95/yr. 102 Walnut Ave.,
Somerset, NJ 08873-5717. TEL 908-247-8700;
FAX 908-247-3707. **Owner(s):** Somerset
Spectator, Inc., P.O. Box 5717, Somerset, NJ
08875. TEL 908-247-8700; FAX
908-247-3707; adv.; pub. size: standard; circ.
4,900(paid).

SOMERVILLE

US

BOUND BROOK CHRONICLE. 1866. Thu. $.50
newsstand; $25/yr. in cy.; $28/yr. out of cy. 44
Veterans Memorial Dr., E., Somerville, NJ 08876.
TEL 908-722-3000; FAX 908-231-1385.
Owner(s): Forbes Newspapers, Inc., P.O. Box 95,
Bedminster, NJ 07921; Ed. Michael Deak; Pub.
Louis Barsony; adv. contact: Rick Kestenbaum.
pub. size: broadsheet; circ. 2,700(paid).

US

CHRONICLE, THE. 1956. Thu. $.50 newsstand;
$25/yr. 44 Veterans Memorial Dr., E., Somerville,
NJ 08876. TEL 908-722-3000;
FAX 908-526-2509. **Owner(s):** Forbes
Newspapers, Inc., P.O. Box 95, Bedminster, NJ
07921; Pub. Louis Barsony; adv. contact: Lena
Moore. pub. size: broadsheet; circ. 3,268(paid).
Formerly: Middlesex Chronicle.

US

HILLSBOROUGH BEACON. 1956. Thu. $32/yr. 307
Omni Dr., Somerville, NJ 08876.
TEL 908-359-0850; FAX 908-359-3930.
Owner(s): Princeton Packet, Inc., 300
Witherspoon, Princeton, NJ 08540. TEL
609-924-3244; Ed. Jon Steele. adv.; bk.rev.; pub.
size: broadsheet; circ. 4,000(paid).

US   ISSN 1058-6857
MANVILLE NEWS. 1945. Thu. $22/yr. 307 Omni Dr., Somerville, NJ 08876. TEL 908-359-3930; FAX 908-359-3936. **Owner(s):** Princeton Packet, Inc., 300 Witherspoon St., Princeton, NJ 08540. TEL 609-924-3244; Ed. Jon Steele. adv.; pub. size: broadsheet; circ. 1,400(paid).

US
SOMERSET MESSENGER GAZETTE. 1823. Thu. $.60 newsstand; $16/yr. 44 Veterans Memorial Dr. E., Somerville, NJ 08876. TEL 908-722-3000; FAX 908-526-2509. **Owner(s):** Forbes Newspapers, Inc., P.O. Box 95, Bedminster, NJ 07921. TEL 908-722-3000; Ed. Andrew Simpson; Pub. Louis Barsony; adv. contact: Rich McComb. pub. size: broadsheet; circ. 20,000(paid).

SPARTA

US
SPARTA INDEPENDENT. 1985. Thu. free. 270 Sparta Ave., Ste. 101, Sparta, NJ 07871. TEL 201-729-7620; FAX 201-729-0513. **Owner(s):** Straus Media of New Jersey, Inc., 328-C Sparta Ave., Sparta, NJ 07871. TEL 201-729-7620; Ed. David Slavin; Pub. David Slavin; adv.; photos; pub. size: tabloid; circ. 8,600(free).

STIRLING

US
ECHOES-SENTINEL. 1954. Wed. $.50 newsstand; $22/yr. in cy.; $40/yr. out of cy. 254 Mercer St., Stirling, NJ 07980. TEL 908-647-1134; FAX 908-647-7679. **Owner(s):** Recorder Publishing Co., 17-19 Morristown Road, Bernardsville, NJ 07924. TEL 908-766-3900; Ed. Jeff French; Pub. Cortlandt Parker; adv. contact: Allison Spinello. pub. size: broadsheet; circ. 6,500(paid).

SURF CITY

US   ISSN 0194-6307
BEACHCOMBER, THE. 1950. Fri. (May-Sep.). free. 1816 Long Beach Blvd., Surf City, NJ 08008. TEL 609-494-5900; FAX 609-494-1437. **Owner(s):** Jersey Shore News Magazines, Inc., 1816 Long Beach Blvd., Ship Bottom, NJ 08008. TEL 609-494-5900; FAX 609-494-1437; Ed. Marion Figley; Pub. Margaret Buchholz; adv. contact: Norman Scull. bk.rev.; pub. size: tabloid; circ. 12,000(free).

TOMS RIVER

US
OCEAN COUNTY REPORTER. 1956. s-w.: Thu. & Sat. free. 8 Robbins St., Toms River, NJ 08753. TEL 908-349-1501; FAX 908-240-0545. **Owner(s):** Goodson Newspaper Group, 1009 Lenox Dr., Lawrenceville, NJ 08648. TEL 609-895-2600; Pub. Robert Juzwiak; adv. contact: Paul Haney. photos; pub. size: tabloid; circ. 100,107(free). **Wire Service(s):** CNS.

TURNERSVILLE

US
PLAIN DEALER. 1926. Thu. $17/yr. Black Horse Pike & North South Fwy., Turnersville, NJ 08012. TEL 609-228-7300; FAX 609-227-1207. **Owner(s):** Intercounty Newspaper Group, P.O. Box 67, Blackwood, NJ 08012. TEL 609-228-7300; Ed. John Worthington; Pub. Art Thompson; adv. contact: James Pearce. photos; bk.rev.; pub. size: tabloid; circ. 6,200(paid).

UNION

US
CLARK EAGLE. 1930. Thu. $.25 newsstand; $13/yr. 1291 Stuyvesant Ave., Union, NJ 07083. TEL 908-686-7700. **Owner(s):** Worrall Community Newspapers, Inc., 1291 Stuyvesant Ave., Union, NJ 07083. TEL 908-686-7700; Ed. Tom Canavan; Pub. David Worrall; adv. contact: Peter Worrall. photos bk.rev.; pub. size: broadsheet; circ. 1,500(free & paid).

US
HILLSIDE LEADER. 1990. Thu. $.50 newsstand; $22/yr. 1291 Stuyvesant Ave., Union, NJ 07083. TEL 908-686-7700. **Owner(s):** Worrall Community Newspapers, Inc., 1291 Stuyvesant Ave., Union, NJ 07083. TEL 908-686-7700; Ed. Tom Canavan; Pub. David Worrall; adv. contact: Peter Worrall. photos bk.rev.; pub. size: broadsheet; circ. 1,500(paid).

US   ISSN 8750-8664
KENILWORTH LEADER. 1945. Thu. $.50 newsstand; $22/yr. 1291 Stuyvesant Ave., Union, NJ 07083. TEL 908-686-7700. **Owner(s):** Worrall Community Newspapers, Inc., 1291 Stuyvesant Ave., Union, NJ 07083. TEL 908-686-7700; Ed. Thomas Canavan. adv. contact: Peter Worrall. photos; bk.rev.; pub. size: broadsheet; circ. 1,200(paid).

US
LINDEN LEADER. Thu. $.50 newsstand; $22/yr. 1291 Stuyvesant Ave., Union, NJ 07083. TEL 908-686-7700. **Owner(s):** Worrall Community Newspapers, Inc., 1291 Stuyvesant Ave., Union, NJ 07083. TEL 908-686-7700; Ed. Thomas Canavan. adv. contact: Nancy Antheil. photos; bk.rev.; pub. size: broadsheet; circ. 2,650(paid).

US
MOUNTAINSIDE ECHO. Thu. $.50 newsstand; $20/yr. 1291 Stuyvesant Ave., Union, NJ 07083. TEL 908-686-7700; FAX 908-686-4169. **Owner(s):** Worrall Community Newspapers, Inc., 1291 Stuyvesant Ave., Union, NJ 07083. TEL 908-686-7700; Ed. Thomas Canavan; Pub. Raymond Worrall; pub. size: broadsheet; circ. 850(paid).

US
RAHWAY PROGRESS. 1990. Thu. $.25 newsstand; 13/yr. 1291 Stuyvesant Ave., Union, NJ 07083. TEL 908-686-7700. **Owner(s):** Worrall Community Newspapers, Inc., 1291 Stuyvesant Ave., Union, NJ 07083. TEL 908-686-7700; Ed. Thomas Canavan; Pub. David Worrall; adv. contact: Peter Worrall. photos; bk.rev.; pub. size: broadsheet; circ. 1,500(paid).

US
ROSELLE PARK LEADER. 1990. Thu. $.50 newsstand; $22/yr. 1291 Stuyvesant Ave., Union, NJ 07083. TEL 908-686-7700. **Owner(s):** Worrall Community Newspapers, Inc., 1291 Stuyvesant Ave., Union, NJ 07083. TEL 908-686-7700; Ed. Thomas Canavan; Pub. David Worrall; adv. contact: Peter Worrall. photos; bk.rev.; pub. size: broadsheet; circ. 1,000(paid).

US
ROSELLE SPECTATOR. 1917. Thu. $.50 newsstand; $22/yr. 1291 Stuyvesant Ave., Union, NJ 07083. TEL 908-686-7700; FAX 908-686-4169. **Owner(s):** Worrall Community Newspapers, Inc., 1291 Stuyvesant Ave., Union, NJ 07083. TEL 908-686-7700; Ed. Thomas Canavan; Pub. David Worrall; adv. contact: Peter Worrall. photos; pub. size: broadsheet; circ. 1,000(paid).

US
SPRINGFIELD LEADER. 1945. Thu. $.50 newsstand; $22/yr. 1291 Stuyvesant Ave., Union, NJ 07083. TEL 908-686-7700. **Owner(s):** Worrall Community Newspapers, Inc., 1291 Stuyvesant Ave., Union, NJ 07083. TEL 908-686-7700; Ed. Thomas Canavan. adv. contact: Peter Worrall. photos; bk.rev.; pub. size: broadsheet; circ. 2,250(paid).

US
SUMMIT OBSERVER. Thu. $.50 newsstand; $20/yr. mailed in cy.; $35/2 yrs. mailed in cy. 1291 Stuyvesant Ave., Union, NJ 07083. TEL 908-686-7700; FAX 908-686-4169; E-mail wcn22@aol.com. **Owner(s):** Worrall Community Newspapers, 1291 Stuyvesant Ave., Union, NJ 07083. TEL 908-686-7700; Ed. Tom Canavan; Pub. David Worrall; adv. contact: Peter Worrall bk.rev.; pub. size: broadsheet; circ. 1,000(paid).

US
UNION LEADER. 1928. Wed. $.50 newsstand; $22/yr. 1291 Stuyvesant Ave., Union, NJ 07083. TEL 908-686-7700. **Owner(s):** Worrall Community Newspapers, Inc., 1291 Stuyvesant Ave., Union, NJ 07083. TEL 908-686-7700; Ed. Tom Canavan; Pub. David Worrall; adv. contact: Peter Worrall. photos; bk.rev.; pub. size: broadsheet; circ. 8,125(paid).

VERONA

US
VERONA-CEDAR GROVE TIMES. 1948. Thu. $.50 newsstand; $18/yr.; $10/yr. senior citizens. 685 Bloomfield Ave., Verona, NJ 07044. TEL 201-239-0900; FAX 201-239-7739. **Owner(s):** Montclair Newspapers, Inc., 114 Valley Rd., Montclair, NJ 07042. TEL 201-746-1100; Ed. Ward Miele. adv.; photos; pub. size: broadsheet; circ. 6,000(paid).

WEST CALDWELL

US
FAIRFIELD CHRONICLE, THE. Wed. $.20 newsstand; $6/yr. in cy.; $12/yr. in state; $24/yr. out of state. P.O. Box 6123, West Caldwell, NJ 07007-6123. TEL 201-227-4433; FAX 201-882-8553. **Owner(s):** Reboli Publishing Co., P.O. Box 6123, West Caldwell, NJ 07007. TEL 201-227-4433; FAX 201-882-8553; Ed. Kelly J. Kilborn; Pub. John A. Reboli; adv. contact: Joan C. Beechey. photos; bk.rev.; pub. size: tabloid

US
MORRISTOWN NEWS, THE. Wed. $.20 newsstand; $6/yr. in area; $12/yr. in state; $24/yr. out of state. P.O. Box 6123, West Caldwell, NJ 07007-6123. TEL 201-227-4433; FAX 201-882-8553. **Owner(s):** Reboli Publishing Co., P.O. Box 6123, West Caldwell, NJ 07007-6123. TEL 201-227-4433; FAX 201-832-8553; Ed. Kelly J. Kilborn; Pub. John A. Reboli; adv. contact: Joan C. Beechey. photos; bk.rev. pub. size: tabloid; **Wire Service(s):** Parsippany News Service, NJ Wire Service.

US
PARSIPPANY NEWS, THE. Thu. $.20 newsstand. P.O. Box 6123, West Caldwell, NJ 07007-6123. TEL 201-227-4433; FAX 201-882-8553. **Owner(s):** Reboli Publishing Co., P.O. Box 6123, West Caldwell, NJ 07007. TEL 201-227-4433; FAX 201-882-8553; Ed. Kelly J. Kilborn; Pub. John A. Reboli; adv. contact: Joan C. Beechey. photos; bk.rev.; pub. size: tabloid; **Wire Service(s):** Parsippany News Service, NJ Wire Service.

WESTFIELD

US
TIMES, THE. Thu. $.50 newsstand; $20/yr. in cy.; $24/yr. out of cy. 50 Elm St., Westfield, NJ 07090. TEL 908-232-4407. **Owner(s):** Carmelo Montalbano, 50 Elm St., Westfield, NJ 07090. TEL 908-232-4407; Ed. Paul J. Peyton; Pub. Carmelo Montalbano; pub. size: tabloid; circ. 5,500(paid).
    Formerly: Scotch Plains Times.

US
WESTFIELD LEADER. 1890. Thu. $20/yr. in cy.; $24/yr. out of cy. 50 Elm St., Westfield, NJ 07090. TEL 908-232-4407. **Owner(s):** Kurt C. Bauer, 50 Elm St., Westfield, NJ 07090. TEL 908-232-4407; Ed. Paul J. Peyton; Pub. Jeffrey L. Bauer; adv. contact: Kathleen L. Norman. pub. size: standard; circ. 7,300(paid).

WESTWOOD

US
PASCACK VALLEY COMMUNITY LIFE. 1928. Wed. $6/yr. 345 Kinderkamack Rd., Westwood, NJ 07675. TEL 201-664-2501; FAX 201-664-1332. **Owner(s):** North Jersey Newspapers Co., 988 Main Ave., Passaic, NJ 07005. TEL 201-365-3000; FAX 201-365-5887; Ed. Barbara J. Stewart. adv.; photos; pub. size: tabloid; circ. 26,000(paid).
    Formerly: Pascack Valley News.

WILDWOOD

US
CAPE MAY COUNTY GAZETTE LEADER. 1976. Wed. $.50 newsstand; $18/yr. in cy.; $21.50/yr. out of cy. 1212 Atlantic Ave., Wildwood, NJ 08260. TEL 609-522-3423; FAX 609-522-7451. **Owner(s):** Jersey Shore News Magazines, Inc., 1816 Long Beach Blvd., Ship Bottom, NJ 08008. TEL 609-494-5900; FAX 609-494-1437; Ed. Rob Seitzinger; Pub. Rick Travers; adv. contact: Marylou Trottnow. photos; pub. size: broadsheet; circ. 7,000(paid).
    Formerly: Gazette Leader.

US
FREE TIME. Wed. free. 1212 Atlantic Ave., Wildwood, NJ 08260. TEL 609-522-3423; FAX 609-522-3423. **Owner(s):** Jersey Shore News Magazines, Inc., 1816 Long Beach Blvd., Ship Bottom, NJ 08008. TEL 609-494-5900; FAX 609-494-1437; Ed. Jean Barracalough; Pub. Will Petrovicz; pub. size: standard; circ. 25,000(free).

US
WILDWOOD LEADER. Wed. $.50 newsstand; $22/yr. 1212 Atlantic Ave., Wildwood, NJ 08260. TEL 609-522-3423; FAX 609-522-7451. **Owner(s):** Travers Brothers, Jersey Shore News Magazines/Gazette Leader Publ. TEL 804-977-7520; Ed. Rob Seitzinger; Pub. Rick Travers; pub. size: standard; circ. 8,000(paid).

NEW MEXICO

ALBUQUERQUE

US
ALBUQUERQUE STREET NEWS. 1990. s-m.: 1st & 16th. $.75/copy; $.10 wholesale to vendors. 1019 Second St., S.W., Albuquerque, NM 87125. TEL 505-842-8314. **Owner(s):** Albuquerque Help for the Homeless, P.O. Box 26896, Albuquerque, NM 87125. TEL 505-842-8314; Pub. Karen Krueger; adv.; photos; bk.rev.; pub. size: tabloid; circ. 6,000(free).

BELEN

US
VALENCIA COUNTY NEWS-BULLETIN. 1911. 3/wk.: Tue., Wed., Sat. $.50 newsstand; $36/yr. in cy.; $42/yr. elsewhere. 1837 Sosimo Padilla Blvd., Belen, NM 87002. TEL 505-864-4472; FAX 505-864-3549; E-mail: cristop555@aol.com. **Owner(s):** WorldWest Limited Liability Co., 609 New Hampshire, P.O. Box 688, Lawrence, KS 66044. TEL 913-843-1000; FAX 913-832-7207; Ed. Sandy Battin; Pub. Chris Baker; adv.; photos; bk.rev.; pub. size: broadsheet; circ. 5,200(free & paid). **Wire Service(s):** AP.

ESPANOLA

US
RIO GRANDE SUN. 1956. Thu. $.40 newsstand; $15/yr. 238 N. Railroad, Espanola, NM 87532. TEL 505-753-2126. **Owner(s):** Sun Co., Inc., P.O. Box 790, Espanola, NM 87532. TEL 505-753-2126; Ed. Robert E. Trapp; Pub. Robert E. Trapp; adv. contact: Robert B. Trapp. pub. size: broadsheet; circ. 10,800(paid).

ESTANCIA

US
ESTANCIA VALLEY CITIZEN. 1958. Thu. $.50 newsstand; $16/yr. in state; $22/yr. elsewhere. 400 S. Fifth St., Estancia, NM 87016-0288. TEL 505-384-2744. **Owner(s):** Carolyn Appelman, P.O. Box 288, Estancia, NM 87016-0288. TEL 505-384-2744; Ed. Morrow Hall; Pub. Carolyn Appelman; adv.; photos; bk.rev.; pub. size: broadsheet; circ. 2,400(free & paid).
    Formerly: Torrance County Citizen.

GRANTS

US
CIBOLA COUNTY BEACON. 1941. s-w.: Wed. & Fri. $.50 newsstand; $48/yr. 300 N. Second St., Grants, NM 87020. TEL 505-287-4411; FAX 505-287-7822. **Owner(s):** Grants Publishing Co., Inc., 300 N. Second St., Grants, NM 87020. TEL 505-287-4411; Ed. J.D. Meisner; Pub. Jamie Honeycutt; adv.; photos; pub. size: broadsheet; circ. 3,500(paid).

HOBBS

US
HOBBS FLARE. 1948. Wed. $.50 newsstand; $18/yr. in cy.; $24/yr. out of cy.; $30/yr. out of state. 114 E. Dunnam, Hobbs, NM 88240. TEL 505-393-5141; FAX 505-393-1831. **Owner(s):** Clyde & Judy McLaughlin, 114 E. Dunnam, Hobbs, NM 88240. TEL 505-393-5141; Ed. Rick McLaughlin; Pub. Rick McLaughlin; pub. size: standard; circ. 3,700(paid).

US
QUIK QUARTER WANT ADS. Thu. free. 3932 S.Dalmont St., Hobbs, NM 88240. TEL 505-397-4591; FAX 505-397-4592. **Owner(s):** Quik Quarter Want Ads, 107 W. Alston, Hobbs, NM 88240. TEL 505-397-4591; FAX 505-397-4592; Pub. Cindy Yearout; adv. contact: Cindy Yearout. pub. size: tabloid; circ. 15,000(free).

RATON

US   ISSN 0896-1093
RATON RANGE, THE. 1881. s-w.: Tue. & Fri. $.75 newsstand; $40/yr. in cy.; $45/yr. out of cy. 208 S. Third St., Raton, NM 87740. TEL 505-445-2721; FAX 505-445-2723. **Owner(s):** Raton Newspaper Inc., 208 S. Third St., Raton, NM 87740. TEL 505-445-2721; FAX 505-445-2723; Ed. Todd Wildermuth; Pub. Curtis Williams; adv. contact: Paula Pachorek. photos; pub. size: broadsheet; circ. 3,000(paid).

RIO RANCHO

US   ISSN 1049-7374
OBSERVER, THE. 1973. s-w.: Wed. & Fri. $.50 newsstand; $22/yr. 1594 Sara Rd., Rio Rancho, NM 87124. TEL 505-892-8080; FAX 505-892-5719. **Owner(s):** Wick Communications, Inc., 333 Wilcox Dr., Ste. 302, Sierra Vista, AZ 85635-1756. TEL 520-458-0200; FAX 520-458-6166; Pub. Michael J. Ryan; adv. contact: Marisa Gilles. photos; bk.rev.; pub. size: broadsheet; circ. 8,000(controlled & paid).

RUIDOSO

US
RUIDOSO NEWS, THE. 1946. s-w.: Wed. & Fri. $.50 newsstand; $34/yr. mailed; $68/yr. home deliv. 104 Park Ave., Ruidoso, NM 88345. TEL 505-257-4001; FAX 505-257-7053; E-mail: ruidosonws@aol.com. **Owner(s):** WorldWest Limited Liability Co., 609 New Hampshire, Lawrence, KS 66044; Ed. Joanna Dodder; Pub. Keith Green; adv.; photos; pub. size: broadsheet; circ. evening 5,800(paid).

SANTA FE

US
SANTA FE REPORTER, THE. 1974. Wed. free newsstand; $50/yr. mailed in US. 132 E. Marcy St., Santa Fe, NM 87501. TEL 505-988-5541; FAX 505-988-5348. **Owner(s):** Santa Fe Reporter, Inc., The, P.O. Box 2306, Santa Fe, NM 87504; Ed. Hope Aldrich; Pub. Hope Aldrich; adv.; pub. size: tabloid; circ. 25,000. **Wire Service(s):** Alternet.

SOCORRO

US   ISSN 0011-7633

DEFENSOR CHIEFTAIN. 1865. s-w.: Wed. & Sun. $.35 newsstand; $28/yr. in cy.; $38/yr. elsewhere. 200 Winkler, S.W., Socorro, NM 87801. TEL 505-835-0520; FAX 505-835-1837; E-mail: defensorcor@aol.com. **Owner(s):** WorldWest Limited Liability Co., Lawrence, KS; Ed. Gwen Roath; Pub. Gwen Roath; adv. contact: Daniel Gaines. pub. size: broadsheet; circ. 2,800(paid).

TAOS

US

TAOS NEWS. 1893. Thu. $.50 newsstand; $35/yr. 120 Camino de la Placita, Taos, NM 87571. TEL 505-758-2241; FAX 505-758-9647. **Owner(s):** Robin McKinney Martin, P.O. Box U, Taos, NM 87571. TEL 505-758-2241; Ed. Deborah Ensor; Pub. George Fellows; adv. contact: Joanne Crass. pub. size: broadsheet; circ. 10,500(paid).

TRUTH OR CONSEQUENCES

US

HERALD, THE. 1916. Wed. $.50 newsstand; $20/yr. in cy.; $30/yr. out of cy. 1204 N. Date St., Truth or Consequences, NM 87901-0752. TEL 505-894-2143; FAX 505-894-7824. **Owner(s):** Herald Publishing Co., Inc., 1204 N. Date, Truth or Consequences, NM 87901-0752. TEL 505-894-2143; FAX 505-894-7824; Pub. Bob Tooley; adv. contact: Maureen Tooley. photos; pub. size: broadsheet; circ. 4,500(paid).

US

SIERRA COUNTY SENTINEL. 1967. Wed. $.50 newsstand; $30/yr. local; $25/yr. in cy. 1747 E. Third, Truth or Consequences, NM 87901. TEL 505-894-3088; FAX 505-894-3998. **Owner(s):** Myrna Baird, P.O. Box 351, Truth or Consequences, NM 87901. TEL 505-894-3088; Ed. Bill Johnson; Pub. Myrna Baird; adv. contact: Myrna Baird. pub. size: standard; circ. 4,300(paid).

TUCUMCARI

US

QUAY COUNTY SUN. 1975. s-w.: Wed. & Sat. $.50 newsstand; $36/yr. 902 S. First St., Tucumcari, NM 88401-1408. TEL 505-461-1952; FAX 505-461-1965. **Owner(s):** Southern Newspapers, Inc., 1050 Wilcrest, Houston, TX 77042. TEL 713-266-5481; Ed. Ron V. Wilmet; Pub. Ron V. Wilmet; adv.; photos; pub. size: broadsheet; circ. 3,600(paid).

NEW YORK

ADAMS

US

JEFFERSON COUNTY JOURNAL. 1844. Wed. $.35 newsstand; $18/yr. in cy.; $22/yr. out of cy.; $24/yr. out of state. 7 Main St., Adams, NY 13605-0068. TEL 315-232-2141; FAX 315-232-4586. **Owner(s):** Journal Publishing Co., 7 Main St., Adams, NY 13605. TEL 315-232-2141; FAX 315-232-4586; Ed. Karl Fowler; Pub. Karl Fowler; adv. contact: Rick Sidman. photos; pub. size: broadsheet; circ. 3,000(controlled).

ALBION

US

ALBION ADVERTISER. 1824. Wed. $.50 newsstand; $27/yr. 116 N. Mair St., Albion, NY 14411. TEL 716-589-4455; FAX 716-589-4488. **Owner(s):** Park Communications, Inc., Vine Ctr. Office Tower, 333 W. Vine St., 17th Fl., Lexington, KY 40507. TEL 606-252-7275; Ed. Owen P. Toale. adv. contact: Gregory Kerth. pub. size: broadsheet; circ. 2,000(paid).

ALDEN

US

WEISBECK, THE. 1914. Thu. $.50 newsstand; $18/yr. 13200 Broadway, Alden, NY 14004. TEL 716-937-9226. **Owner(s):** Weisbeck Publishing & Printing Inc., 13200 Broadway, Alden, NY 14004. TEL 716-937-9226; Ed. Leonard A. Weisbeck, Sr.; Pub. Leonard A. Weisbeck, Jr.; adv.; pub. size: tabloid; circ. 3,588(paid).

ALEXANDRIA BAY

US

THOUSAND ISLANDS SUN. 1901. Wed. $.50 newsstand; $22/yr. in cy.; $26/yr. out of cy; $32/yr. Canada. P.O Box 277, Alexandria Bay, NY 13607-0277. TEL 315-482-2581; FAX 315-482-6315. **Owner(s):** Thousand Islands Printing Co., Inc., P.O. Box 277, Alexandria Bay, NY 13607. TEL 315-482-2581; FAX 315-482-6315; Ed. Jeanne Snow; Pub. Jeanne Snow; adv. contact: Craig Snow. photos; pub. size: standard; circ. 6,422(paid).

ALTAMONT

US   ISSN 0890-6025

ALTAMONT ENTERPRISE, THE. 1884. Thu. $.50 newsstand; $24/yr. in cy.; $26/yr. out of cy. 123 Maple Ave., Altamont, NY 12009. TEL 518-861-6641; FAX 518-861-5105. **Owner(s):** James E. Gardner, 123 Maple Ave., Altamont, NY 12009. TEL 518-861-6641; FAX 518-861-5105; Ed. Chris Sanford; Pub. James E. Gardner; adv.; bk.rev.; pub. size: tabloid; circ. 7,200(paid).

AMENIA

US

HARLEM VALLEY TIMES. 1852. Thu. $.60 newsstand; $29.50/yr. E. Main St., Amenia, NY 12501. TEL 914-373-8084; FAX 914-373-8908. **Owner(s):** Taconic Media, Inc., P.O. Box 316, Millbrook, NY 12545. TEL 914-677-8241; Ed. Bob Lomicky; Pub. Hamilton Meserve; adv.; pub. size: broadsheet; circ. 3,800(paid).

AMITYVILLE

US

AMITYVILLE RECORD. 1904. Wed. $.35 newsstand; $14/yr. 85 Broadway, Amityville, NY 11701. TEL 516-264-0077; FAX 516-264-5310. **Owner(s):** ACJ Communications, Inc., 85 Broadway, Amityville, NY 11701. TEL 516-264-0077; Ed. Jim Custer; Pub. Alfred James; adv.; photos; pub. size: tabloid; circ. 8,000(paid).

BABYLON

US

BEACON NEWSPAPER. 1966. Thu. $.50 newsstand; $17/yr.; $29/2 yrs.; $42/3 yrs. 65 Deerpark Ave., Babylon, NY 11702. TEL 516-587-5612; FAX 516-587-0198. **Owner(s):** Beacon Newspapers, Inc., 65 Deerpark Ave., Babylon, NY 11702. TEL 516-587-5612; Ed. Terry Bouquet; Pub. John Mangano; adv.; photos; pub. size: tabloid circ. 52,000(free & paid). **Formerly:** Babylon Beacon.

BALDWINSVILLE

US

BALDWINSVILLE MESSENGER. 1846. Wed. $.75 newsstand; $21/yr.; $13/yr. students; $21/yr. senior citizens. 7-11 E. Genesee St., Baldwinsville, NY 13027. TEL 315-635-3921; FAX 315-635-3914. **Owner(s):** Eagle Newspapers, Inc., P.O. Box 65, Fayetteville, NY 13066. TEL 315-637-3127; Ed. Rebecca Sernett; Pub. Stewart F. Hancock, II; adv.; photos; pub. size: broadsheet; circ. 7,500(paid).

US

CAMILLUS ADVOCATE. 1926. Wed. $.75 newsstand; $24/yr.; $13/yr. students; $21/yr. senior citizens. 7-11 E. Genesee St., Baldwinsville, NY 13027. TEL 315-635-3921; FAX 315-635-3914. **Owner(s):** Eagle Newspapers, Inc., P.O. Box 65, Fayetteville, NY 13066. TEL 315-637-3127; Ed. Richard Palmer; Pub. Stewart Hancock; adv. contact: Tammy Grashof. photos; pub. size: broadsheet; circ. 3,475(paid).

US

LIVERPOOL REVIEW. 1926. Wed. $.75 newsstand; $25/yr.; $13/yr. student; $13/yr. students; $21/yr. senior citizens. 7-11 E. Genesee St., Baldwinsville, NY 13027. TEL 315-635-3921; FAX 315-635-3914. **Owner(s):** Eagle Newspapers, Inc., 7-11 E. Genesee St., P.O. Box 270, Baldwinsville, NY 13027. TEL 315-635-3921; Ed. Ali Holzapple; Pub. Stewart Hancock; adv. contact: Jack Mott. photos; pub. size: broadsheet; circ. 14,916(paid). **Formerly:** Review, The.

BALLSTON SPA

US

BALLSTON JOURNAL. 1798. Wed. $.50 newsstand; $15/yr. in cy.; $18/yr. out of cy.; $20/yr. out of state. 72 W. High St., Ballston Spa, NY 12020. TEL 518-885-4341. **Owner(s):** Journal Newspapers, Inc., 72 W. High St., Ballston Spa, NY 12020. TEL 518-885-4341; Ed. Charles Hogan; Pub. Charles Hogan. adv. contact: Nancy Rochford. pub. size: broadsheet; circ. 2,200(paid).

US

MALTA MESSENGER. Mon. free. 72 W. High St., Ballston Spa, NY 12020. TEL 518-885-4341. **Owner(s):** Journal Newspapers, Inc., 72 W. High St., Ballston Spa, NY 12020. TEL 518-885-4341; Ed. Charles Hogan; Pub. Charles Hogan. adv.; pub. size: standard; circ. 6,000(free).

US

MONEYSAVER, THE. 1969. Tue. free. 72 W. High St., Ballston Spa, NY 12020-1927. TEL 518-885-4341. **Owner(s):** Journal Newspapers, Inc., 72 W. High St., Ballston Spa, NY 12020-1927. TEL 518-885-4341; Ed. Charles Hogan; Pub. Charles Hogan; adv. contact: Charles Hogan. pub. size: tabloid; circ. 15,000(free).

BATH

US
STEUBEN COURIER-ADVOCATE. 1843. Sun. free in cy. 10 W. Steuben St., Bath, NY 14810. TEL 607-776-2121; FAX 607-776-3967. **Owner(s):** Greenhow Newspapers, Inc., 85 Canisteo St., Hornell, NY 14843. TEL 607-324-1425; Ed. Mark Raven; Pub. Colleen Neeley; adv. contact: Colleen Neeley. pub. size: broadsheet; circ. Sun. 11,313(free).

BAYSIDE

US
BAYSIDE TIMES, THE. 1934. Thu. $.50 newsstand; $15/yr. local; $29/2 yrs. in cy.; $19/yr. elsewhere. 41-02 Bell Blvd., 2nd Fl., Bayside, NY 11361. TEL 718-229-0300; FAX 718-225-7117. **Owner(s):** Queens Publishing Corp., 41-02 Bell Blvd., 2nd Fl., Bayside, NY 11361. TEL 718-229-0300; FAX 718-225-7117; Ed. Roz Liston; Pub. Steve Blank; adv.; photos; pub. size: tabloid; circ. 11,044(paid).

US
FLUSHING TIMES, THE. 1992. Thu. $.50 newsstand; $19/yr.; $35/2 yrs. in cy. 41-02 Bell Blvd., 2nd Fl., Bayside, NY 11361. TEL 718-229-0300; FAX 718-225-7117. **Owner(s):** Queens Publishing Corp., 41-02 Bell Blvd., 2nd Fl., Bayside, NY 11361. TEL 718-229-0300; FAX 718-225-7117; Ed. Roz Liston; Pub. Steve Blank; adv. contact: Howard Swensler. photos; pub. size: tabloid; circ. 4,845(paid).

US
WHITESTONE TIMES, THE. 1991. Thu. $.50 newsstand; $19/yr. in cy.; $35/2 yrs. in cy. 41-02 Bell Blvd., 2nd Fl., Bayside, NY 11361. TEL 718-229-0300; FAX 718-225-7117. **Owner(s):** Queens Publishing Corp., 41-02 Bell Blvd., 2nd Fl., Bayside, NY 11361. TEL 718-229-0300; FAX 718-225-7117; Ed. Roz Liston; Pub. Steven Blank; adv.; photos; pub. size: tabloid; circ. 3,603(paid).

BELLMORE

US
BELLMORE-MERRICK OBSERVER. 1949. Thu. $7/yr. 2262 Centre Ave., Bellmore, NY 11710. TEL 516-679-9888. **Owner(s):** Observer Newspapers, Inc., 2262 Centre Ave., Bellmore, NY; Ed. Jackson B. Pokress; Pub. Wilma J. Pokress; adv.; photos; bk.rev.; pub. size: tabloid; circ. 5,000(paid).

US
BELLMORE LIFE. 1964. Wed. $.35 newsstand; $14.50/yr. 2818 Merrick Rd., Bellmore, NY 11710. TEL 516-826-0333. **Owner(s):** L & M Publications, Inc., 1840 Merrick Avenue, Merrick, NY 11566. TEL 516-378-5320; Ed. Paul Laursen; Pub. Linda Toscano; adv. contact: Mike Diller. pub. size: tabloid; circ. 5,127(free & paid).

US
SEAFORD-WANTAGH OBSERVER. 1949. Thu. $7/yr. in cy.; $9/yr. out of cy. 2262 Centre Ave., Bellmore, NY 11710. TEL 516-679-9888. **Owner(s):** Bellmore-Merrick Observer, 2262 Centre Ave., Bellmore, NY 11710. TEL 516-679-9888; Ed. Jackson B. Pokress; Pub. Wilma J. Pokress; adv.; photos; bk.rev.; pub. size: tabloid; circ. 5,000(paid).

US
WANTAGH-SEAFORD CITIZEN. 1953. Thu. $.25 newsstand; $11.50/yr. 2818 Merrick Rd., Bellmore, NY 11710. TEL 516-826-0812; FAX 516-826-0814. **Owner(s):** L & M Publications, Inc., 1840 Merrick Ave., Merrick, NY 11566. TEL 516-378-5320; Ed. Paul Laursen; Pub. Linda Laursen Toscano; adv. contact: Carole Friedman. photos; pub. size: tabloid; circ. 4,137(free & paid).

BERLIN

US
ECHO, THE. 1940. Thu. $.50 newsstand; $19.50/yr. local; $21.50/yr. out of state. Rte. 22, Berlin, NY 12022. TEL 518-658-2777; FAX 518-658-2266. **Owner(s):** Ralph G. deLeon, P.O. Box 270, Berlin, NY 12022. TEL 518-658-2777; Pub. Ralph G. deLeon; adv.; photos; bk.rev.; pub. size: tabloid; circ. 2,000(paid).

BOONVILLE

US
BOONVILLE HERALD. 1852. Wed. $.40 newsstand; $16/yr. surrounding cys. $18/yr. elsewhere. E. Schuyler St., Boonville, NY 13309. TEL 315-942-4449. **Owner(s):** Irene Lansing, Jackson Hill Rd., Boonville, NY 13309. TEL 315-942-4844; Ed. Irene Lansing. adv.; photos; pub. size: broadsheet; circ. 3,400(free & paid).

BRIDGEHAMPTON

US
DAN'S PAPERS. 1960. Thu. free; $26/yr. 2221 Montauk Hwy., Bridgehampton, NY 11932. TEL 516-537-0500; FAX 516-537-3330. **Owner(s):** News Communications, Inc., 174-15 Harding Expy., Queens, NY 11365. TEL 718-357-7400; Ed. Dan Rattiner; Pub. Dan Rattiner; adv. contact: Leslie Halligan. photos; bk.rev.; pub. size: tabloid; circ. 120,000(free).

BROCKPORT

US
BROCKPORT POST, THE. 1968. Thu. $21/yr. 2 S. Main St., Brockport, NY 14420. TEL 716-381-3300; FAX 716-637-5637. **Owner(s):** Wolfe Publications, Inc., P.O. Box C, Fishers, NY 14453; Ed. Andrew D. Wolfe; Pub. Andrew D. Wolfe; pub. size: broadsheet; circ. 1,600(paid).

US
TRI-COUNTY ADVERTISER. 1957. Mon. free. 15 Main St., Brockport, NY 14420. TEL 716-637-5100; FAX 716-637-0111. **Owner(s):** Sally A. Becht, 15 Main St., Brockport, NY 14420. TEL 716-637-5100; Ed. Sally A. Becht. adv. contact: David G. Abrams. pub. size: tabloid; circ. 16,000(free).

BRONX

US
BRONX NEWS. 1982. Thu. $10/yr. 135 Dreiser Loop, Bronx, NY 10475. TEL 718-671-1234. **Owner(s):** C.G. Hagedorn, 135 Dreiser Loop, Bronx, NY 10475. TEL 718-671-1234; Pub. C.G. Hagedorn; adv.; pub. size: tabloid; circ. 8,000(paid).

US
BRONX PRESS-REVIEW. 1940. Thu. $.35 newsstand; $9/yr. 170 W. 233rd St., Bronx, NY 10463. TEL 718-543-5200; FAX 718-543-4206. **Owner(s):** Parkchester Publishing, Inc., 170 W. 233rd St., Bronx, NY 10463. TEL 718-543-5200; Pub. Andrew Wolf; adv.; bk.rev.; pub. size: tabloid; circ. 12,000(paid).

US
CITY NEWS. 1969. Sat. free. 135 Dreiser Loop, Bronx, NY 10475. TEL 718-671-1234. **Owner(s):** C.G. Hagedorn, 135 Dreiser Loop, Bronx, NY 10475. TEL 718-671-1234; Ed. C.G. Hagedorn; Pub. C.G. Hagedorn; adv.; pub. size: tabloid; circ. 15,500(free).

US
PARKCHESTER NEWS. 1974. Fri. free. 135 Dreiser Loop, Bronx, NY 10475. TEL 718-671-1234. **Owner(s):** C.G. Hagedorn, 135 Dreiser Loop, Bronx, NY 10475. TEL 718-671-1234; Ed. C.G. Hagedorn; Pub. C.G. Hagedorn; adv.; pub. size: tabloid; circ. 12,500(free).

US
RIVERDALE PRESS. 1950. Thu. $.75 newsstand; $19/yr.; $33/2 yrs. 6155 Broadway, Bronx, NY 10471. TEL 718-543-6065. **Owner(s):** Dale Press, Inc., 6155 Broadway, Bronx, NY 10471. TEL 212-543-6065; Ed. Bernard L. Stein; Pub. Bernard L. Stein; adv. contact: Phyllis Steele. photos; pub. size: broadsheet; circ. 14,500(paid).

BROOKLYN

US
BAY NEWS. 1945. Mon. $.50 newsstand; $20/yr. 1733 Sheepshead Bay Rd., Brooklyn, NY 11235. TEL 718-769-4400; FAX 718-769-5048. **Owner(s):** Courier-Life, Inc., 1733 Sheepshead Bay Rd., Brooklyn, NY 11235; Ed. Ken Brown; Pub. Edward E. Luster; adv. contact: Clifford Luster. photos; bk.rev.; pub. size: tabloid; circ. 76,000(controlled & paid).

US
BAY RIDGE COURIER. 1978. Thu. $.50 newsstand; $20/yr. mailed. 1733 Sheepshead Bay Rd., Brooklyn, NY 11235. TEL 718-769-4400; FAX 718-769-5048. **Owner(s):** Courier-Life, Inc., 1733 Sheepshead Bay Rd., Brooklyn, NY 11235. TEL 718-769-4400; Ed. Kenneth Brown; Pub. Edward Luster; adv. contact: Clifford Luster. photos; bk.rev.; pub. size: tabloid; circ. 79,000(controlled & paid).

US
BROOKLYN GRAPHIC. 1953. Wed. $6/yr. 1733 Sheepshead Bay Rd., Brooklyn, NY 11235. TEL 718-769-4400; FAX 718-769-5048. **Owner(s):** Courier-Life, Inc., 1733 Sheepshead Bay Rd., Brooklyn, NY 11235. TEL 718-769-4400; Ed. Kenneth Brown; Pub. Edward Luster; adv. contact: Clifford Luster. pub. size: tabloid; circ. 13,500(paid).

US
BROOKLYN HEIGHTS COURIER. 1990. bi-w.: Mon. free. 1733 Sheepshead Bay Rd., Brooklyn, NY 11235. TEL 718-769-4400; FAX 718-769-5048. **Owner(s):** Courier-Life, Inc., 1733 Sheepshead Bay Rd., Brooklyn, NY 11235. TEL 718-769-4400; Ed. Kenneth Brown; Pub. Edward Luster; adv. contact: Clifford Luster. photos; bk.rev.; pub. size: tabloid; circ. 72,000(free).

US

BROOKLYN HEIGHTS PRESS. 1937. Thu. \$.50 newsstand; \$25/yr. 125 Montague St., Lower Level, Brooklyn, NY 11201. TEL 718-624-0536; FAX 718-624-2716. **Owner(s):** Brooklyn Journal Publications, 125 Montague St., Lower Level, Brooklyn, NY 11201. TEL 718-624-0536; Ed. Henrik Krogius; Pub. Dozier Hasty; adv. contact: Patricia Higgins. pub. size: tabloid; circ. 19,500(paid).

US

BROOKLYN HOME REPORTER & SUNSET NEWS. 1953. Fri. \$.50 newsstand; \$35/yr. 8723 Third Ave., Brooklyn, NY 11209. TEL 718-238-6600; FAX 718-238-6630. **Owner(s):** Modern Media, Inc., 8723 Third Ave., Brooklyn, NY 11209; Ed. Sara Otey; Pub. J. Frank Griffin; adv.; pub. size: tabloid; circ. 18,452(paid).

US   ISSN 0740-2643

BROOKLYN RECORD. 1938. Fri. \$25/yr. 125 Montague St., Brooklyn, NY 11201. TEL 718-624-6033; FAX 718-624-2716. **Owner(s):** Fredrick Halla, 125 Montague St., Brooklyn, NY 11201; Ed. Fredrick Halla; Pub. Fredrick Halla; adv.; bk.rev.; pub. size: tabloid; circ. 4,500(paid).

US

BROOKLYN SPECTATOR. 1933. Wed. \$.30 newsstand; \$15/yr. 8723 Third Ave., Brooklyn, NY 11209. TEL 718-238-6603; FAX 718-238-6630. **Owner(s):** Modern Media, Inc., 8723 Third Ave., Brooklyn, NY 11209; Ed. Sara Otey; Pub. J. Frank Griffin; pub. size: tabloid; circ. 18,000(paid).

US

CANARSIE COURIER. 1921. Thu. \$.25 newsstand; \$11.50/yr. local; \$17/yr. out of town. 1142 E. 92nd St., Brooklyn, NY 11236. TEL 718-257-0600; FAX 718-272-0870. **Owner(s):** Mary Samitz, 1142 E. 92 St., Brooklyn, NY 11236. TEL 212-257-0600; Ed. Charles Rogers; Pub. Mary Samitz; adv.; photos; pub. size: tabloid; circ. 15,000(paid).

US

CANARSIE DIGEST. 1959. Thu. \$.50 newsstand; \$20/yr. 1733 Sheepshead Bay Rd., Brooklyn, NY 11235. TEL 718-769-4400; FAX 718-769-5408. **Owner(s):** Courier-Life, Inc., 1733 Sheepshead Bay Rd., Brooklyn, NY 11235. TEL 718-769-4400; Ed. Ken Brown; Pub. Edward Luster; adv. contact: Clifford Luster. photos; bk.rev.; pub. size: tabloid; circ. 10,900(paid).

US

CARROLL GARDENS/COBBLE HILL COURIER. 1990. bi-w.: Mon. free. 1733 Sheepshead Bay Rd., Brooklyn, NY 11235. TEL 718-769-4400; FAX 718-769-5408. **Owner(s):** Courier-Life, Inc., 1733 Sheepshead Bay Rd., Brooklyn, NY 11235. TEL 718-769-4400; Ed. Ken Brown; Pub. Edward Luster; adv. contact: Clifford Luster. photos; bk.rev.; pub. size: tabloid; circ. 81,000(free).

US

FLATBUSH LIFE. 1956. Thu. \$.50 newsstand; \$20/yr. 1733 Sheepshead Bay Rd., Brooklyn, NY 11235. TEL 718-769-4400. **Owner(s):** Courier-Life, Inc., 1733 Sheepshead Bay Rd., Brooklyn, NY 11235. TEL 718-769-4400; Ed. Kenneth Brown; Pub. Edward Luster; adv. contact: Clifford Luster. photos; bk.rev.; pub. size: tabloid; circ. 13,600(paid).

US

GREENPOINT GAZETTE/ADVERTISER. 1973. Wed. \$.25 newsstand; \$20/yr. in Brooklyn; \$25/yr. out of Brooklyn. 597 Manhattan Ave., Brooklyn, NY 11222-3919. TEL 718-389-6067; FAX 718-349-3471. **Owner(s):** Community Gazette, Inc., 597 Manhattan Ave., Brooklyn, NY 11222-3919. TEL 718-389-6067; FAX 718-349-3471; Ed. Rick Haines. adv.; photos; bk.rev.; pub. size: tabloid; circ. 5,010(free & paid). **Wire Service(s):** CNS.

US

HARBORWATCH. 1989. Thu. free to military; \$15/yr. mailed. 1733 Sheepshead Bay Rd., Brooklyn, NY 11235. TEL 718-769-4400; FAX 718-769-5048. **Owner(s):** Courier-Life, Inc., 1733 Sheepshead Bay Road, Brooklyn, NY 11235. TEL 718-769-4400; Ed. Kenneth Brown; Pub. Edward Luster; adv. contact: Clifford Luster. photos; bk.rev.; pub. size: tabloid; circ. 12,000(controlled & paid).

US

KINGS COUNTY NEWS. 1976. Mon. \$.50 newsstand; \$26/yr. 2446 E. 65th St., Brooklyn, NY 11234. TEL 718-763-7034; FAX 718-763-7035. **Owner(s):** EWA Publications, 275 Bay 37th St., Brooklyn, NY 11214. TEL 718-996-5406; FAX 718-373-1352; Ed. Kevin Browne. adv.; photos; bk.rev.; pub. size: tabloid; circ. 71,000(controlled & paid).

US

KINGS COURIER. 1951. Mon. \$.50 newsstand; \$20/yr. 1733 Sheepshead Bay Rd., Brooklyn, NY 11235. TEL 718-769-4400; FAX 718-769-5408. **Owner(s):** Courier-Life, Inc., 1733 Sheepshead Bay Rd., Brooklyn, NY 11235; Ed. Ken Brown; Pub. Edward Luster; adv. contact: Clifford Luster. photos; bk.rev.; pub. size: tabloid; circ. 10,700(controlled & paid).

US

METROPOLITAN NEWS. 1970. Fri. \$.50 newsstand; \$26/yr. 2446 E. 65th St., Brooklyn, NY 11234. TEL 718-763-7034; FAX 718-763-7035. **Owner(s):** EWA Publications, 2446 E. 65th St., Brooklyn, NY 11234. TEL 718-763-7034; FAX 718-763-7035; photos; bk.rev.; pub. size: tabloid; circ. 132,000(controlled & paid).

US

NEW YORK METROPOLITAN NEWS. 1962. Mon. \$.50 newsstand; \$26/yr. 2446 E. 65th St., Brooklyn, NY 11234. TEL 718-763-7034; FAX 718-763-7035. **Owner(s):** EWA Publications, 2446 E. 65th St., Brooklyn, NY 11234. TEL 718-763-7034; FAX 718-763-7035; Ed. Kevin Browne. photos; bk.rev.; pub. size: tabloid; circ. 216,000(controlled & paid).

US

PARK SLOPE COURIER. 1990. bi-w.: Mon. free. 1733 Sheepshead Bay Rd., Brooklyn, NY 11235. TEL 718-769-4400; FAX 718-769-5048. **Owner(s):** Courier-Life, Inc., 1733 Sheepshead Bay Rd., Brooklyn, NY 11235. TEL 718-769-4400; Ed. Kevin Brown; Pub. Edward Luster; adv. contact: Clifford Luster. photos; bk.rev.; pub. size: tabloid; circ. 101,000(free).

US

PHOENIX NEWSPAPER, THE. 1972. Mon. \$.50 newsstand; \$18/yr. 33 Flatbush Ave., Brooklyn, NY 11217. TEL 718-643-1400; FAX 718-643-1033. **Owner(s):** Dnynia Armstrong, 453 State St., Brooklyn, NY 11217. TEL 718-643-1400; FAX 718-643-1033; Ed. Dennis Holt. adv. contact: Conni Hannon. photos; pub. size: tabloid; circ. 13,000(paid).

BUFFALO

US

AMHERST BEE. 1879. Wed. \$.75 newsstand; \$32/yr. in cy. 5564 Main St., Buffalo, NY 14231-0150. TEL 716-632-4700; FAX 716-633-8601. **Owner(s):** Bee Publications, Inc., P.O. Box 150, Williamsville, NY 14221. TEL 716-632-4700; FAX 716-633-8601; Ed. David Sherman; Pub. Trey Measer; pub. size: tabloid; circ. 10,000(paid).

US

BUFFALO ROCKET. 1969. Wed. \$30/yr. 2503 Delaware, Buffalo, NY 14216. TEL 716-873-2594; FAX 716-873-0809. **Owner(s):** David Gallagher, 2503 Delaware, Buffalo, NY 14216. TEL 716-873-2594; Ed. Craig W. Turner; Pub. David H. Gallagher; adv.; pub. size: tabloid; circ. 15,000(paid).

US

KEN-TON BEE. 1892. Wed. \$.75 newsstand; \$29/yr. in cy. 564 Main St., Buffalo, NY 14221. TEL 716-632-4700; FAX 716-633-8601. **Owner(s):** Bee Publications, nc., 5564 Main St., Buffalo, NY 14221. TEL 716-632-4700; Ed. David Sherman; Pub. Trey Measer; adv.; pub. size: tabloid; circ. 1,800(paid).

US

RIVERSIDE REVIEW. 1923. Wed. free newsstand; \$39.50/yr. mailed. 215 Military Rd., Buffalo, NY 14207. TEL 716-877-8400; FAX 716-877-8742. **Owner(s):** Worrall Community Newspapers, Inc., 1291 Stuyvesant Ave., Union, NJ 07083. TEL 908-686-7700; Ed. Richard Mack; Pub. Kevin Worral; adv. contact: James Smith. pub. size: tabloid; circ. 14,300(free & paid).

US

WEST SIDE TIMES. 1893. Tue. \$30/yr. 2503 Delaware, Buffalo, NY 14215. TEL 716-873-2594; FAX 716-873-0809. **Owner(s):** David H. Gallagher, 2503 Delaware Ave., Buffalo, NY 14216. TEL 716-873-2594 FAX 716-873-0809; Ed. Dennis Gallagher; Pub. David H. Gallagher; adv.; photos; pub. size: tabloid; circ. 13,000(free).

CAMBRIDGE

US   ISSN 0745-9531

EAGLE, THE. 1981. Wed. \$24/yr. in state; \$25/yr. out of state. P.O. Box 36, Cambridge, NY 12816. TEL 518-677-5158; FAX 518-677-8323. **Owner(s):** Eagle, The, P.O. Box 36 Cambridge, NY 12816. TEL 518-677-5158; FAX 518-677-8323; Ed. Richard F. Farrell; Pub. Richard F. Farrell; adv.; photos; bk.rev.; pub. size: tabloid; circ. 3,725(free & paid).

CANASTOTA

US

CANASTOTA BEE-JOURNAL. Wed. \$.75 newsstand; \$25/yr.; \$13/yr. student; \$21/yr. senior citizen. 114 Canal St., Canastota, NY 13032. **Owner(s):** Eagle Newspapers, Inc., P.O. Box 65, Fayetteville, NY 13066, free & paid. TEL 315-637-3121; Ed. Rich Petrillo; Pub. Stewart Hancock; pub. size: broadsheet.

Weeklies

US
CHITTENANGO-BRIDGEPORT TIMES. 1910. Wed.
$.75 newsstand; $25/yr.; $13/yr. student;
$21/yr. senior citizen. 114 Canal St., Canastota,
NY 13032. TEL 315-687-3887;
FAX 315-637-3124. **Owner(s):** Eagle
Newspapers, Inc., P.O. Box 65, Fayetteville, NY
13066. TEL 315-637-3121; Ed. Pete Anderson;
Pub. Stewart Hancock; adv. contact: Becky
Cooper. pub. size: broadsheet; circ. 2,206(paid).

CANTON

US
ST. LAWRENCE PLAINDEALER. Tue. $18.90/yr. in
cy.; $19.95/yr. out of cy. 75 Main St., Canton,
NY 13617. TEL 315-386-8521;
FAX 315-386-8887. **Owner(s):** Park
Communications, Inc., Vine Ctr. Office Tower, 333
W. Vine St., 17th Fl., Lexington, KY 40507. TEL
606-252-7252; Ed. Paul Mitchell. pub. size:
broadsheet; circ. 3,500(paid).

CARMEL

US   ISSN 0890-1147
PUTNAM COURIER-TRADER, THE. 1841. Thu. $.50
newsstand; $24.95/yr. in cy.; $34.95/yr. out of
cy.; $16/yr. senior citizens. 73 Gleneida, Carmel,
NY 10512. TEL 914-225-3633;
FAX 914-225-1914. **Owner(s):** Housatonic Valley
Publishing Co., P.O. Box 1139, New Milford, CT
06776. TEL 860-354-2261; Ed. Barbara Gallo
Farrell; Pub. John Norton; adv. contact: Joan
Byrnes. photos; pub. size: broadsheet; circ.
6,200(paid).

CARTHAGE

US
CARTHAGE REPUBLICAN TRIBUNE. 1860. Wed. $.75
newsstand; $29/yr.local; $35/yr. elsewhere. 3
Front St., Carthage, NY 13619.
TEL 315-493-1270. **Owner(s):** Johnson
Newspaper Corp., 260 Washington St.,
Watertown, NY 13601. TEL 315-782-1000; adv.
contact: Charles Howlett. photos; bk.rev.; pub.
size: broadsheet; circ. 3,000(paid).

CAZENOVIA

US
CAZENOVIA REPUBLICAN. 1794. Wed. $.75
newsstand; $25/yr. in cy.; $21/yr. senior
citizens; $13/yr. students. 72 Albany St.,
Cazenovia, NY 13035. TEL 315-655-3415;
FAX 315-637-3124. **Owner(s):** Eagle
Newspapers, Inc., P.O. Box 65, Fayetteville, NY
13066. TEL 315-637-3121; Ed. Jennifer
Kovalich; Pub. Stewart Hancock; adv. contact:
Pam Kennedy. pub. size: broadsheet; circ.
3,871(paid).

CHATHAM

US   ISSN 1064-4644
CHATHAM COURIER-ROUGHNOTES. 1825. Thu. $.50
newsstand; $32/yr. in cy. 24 Park Row,
Chatham, NY 12037. TEL 518-392-4141;
FAX 518-392-7322. **Owner(s):** Park
Communications, Inc., Vine Ctr. Office Tower, 333
W. Vine St., 17th Fl., Lexington, KY 40507. TEL
606-252-7252; Ed. Anne M. Sheehan. adv.;
photos; pub. size: tabloid; circ. 6,000(paid). **Wire
Service(s):** AP.

CHEEKTOWAGA

US
CHEEKTOWAGA TIMES. 1946. Thu. $.75 newsstand;
$25/yr. 343 Maryvale Dr., Cheektowaga, NY
14225. TEL 716-892-5323;
FAX 716-892-4925. **Owner(s):** Eve J. Allis, 403
Walton Drive, Cheektowaga, NY 14225. TEL
716-892-5323; adv.; photos; pub. size: tabloid;
circ. 5,600(paid).

CLIFTON PARK

US
COMMUNITY NEWS. 1969. Fri. free. Clifton
Corporate Park, Bldg. 400, Ste. 479, Clifton
Park, NY 12065. TEL 518-371-7108;
FAX 518-371-0933. **Owner(s):** Gannett
Company, Inc., 1100 Wilson Blvd., Arlington, VA
22234. TEL 703-284-6000; Ed. Jim Rogalski;
Pub. Monte Trammer; adv. contact: Winifred
Getty. photos; pub. size: broadsheet; circ.
26,000(controlled & free). **Wire Service(s):** AP,
GNS.

CLINTON

US
CLINTON COURIER. 1846. Wed. $.75 newsstand;
$25/yr. in cy.; $30/yr. out of cy.; $19.75/yr.
student. 32 College St., Clinton, NY 13323.
TEL 315-853-3490; FAX 315-853-3522.
Owner(s): Charles & Cynthia Kershner, 32
College St., Clinton, NY 13323-0294. TEL
315-853-3490; FAX 315-853-3522; Ed. Charles
J. Kershner; Pub. Cynthia Kershner; adv.; bk.rev.;
pub. size: tabloid; circ. 2,170(paid).

COBLESKILL

US
COBLESKILL TIMES JOURNAL. 1876. Wed. $.50
newsstand; $20/yr. in cy.; $35/yr. out of cy. 19
Division St., Cobleskill, NY 12043.
TEL 518-234-2515; FAX 518-234-7898.
Owner(s): Jim Poole, P.O. Box 339, Cobleskill,
NY 12043. TEL 518-234-2515; Ed. Patsy
Nicosia; Pub. Jim Poole; adv. contact: Marilyn
Swartout. photos; pub. size: broadsheet; circ.
6,000(paid).

CONKLIN

US   ISSN 1065-5891
COUNTRY COURIER, THE. 1976. Wed. $.45
newsstand; $19/yr. mailed in cy. 1035 Conklin
Rd., Conklin, NY 13748. TEL 607-775-0472;
FAX 607-775-5863. **Owner(s):** Masthead
Publications, Inc., 1035 Conklin Rd., Conklin, NY
13748. TEL 607-775-0472; FAX
607-775-5863; Ed. Elizabeth Einstein; Pub. Don
Einstein; adv.; photos; pub. size: tabloid; circ.
1,600(paid).

US   ISSN 1051-3574
VESTAL TOWN CRIER. 1989. Wed. $.45 newsstand;
$19/yr. mailed in cy.; $20/yr. out of cy. 1035
Conklin Rd., Conklin, NY 13748.
TEL 607-775-0472; FAX 607-775-5863.
Owner(s): Masthead Publications, Inc., P.O. Box
208, Conklin, NY 13748. TEL 607-775-0472;
FAX 607-775-5863; Ed. Elizabeth Einstein; Pub.
Don Einstein; adv.; photos; pub. size: tabloid; circ.
1,400(paid).

WINDSOR

US   ISSN 1059-5449
WINDSOR STANDARD. 1879. Wed. $.45 newsstand;
$19/yr. in cy.; $20/yr. out of cy. 1035 Conklin
Rd., Conklin, NY 13748. TEL 607-775-0472;
FAX 607-775-5863. **Owner(s):** Masthead
Publications, Inc., P.O. Box 208, Conklin, NY
13748. TEL 607-775-0472; FAX
607-775-5863; Ed. Elizabeth Einstein; Pub. Don
Einstein; adv.; photos; pub. size: tabloid; circ.
15,600(paid).

COOPERSTOWN

US
FREEMAN'S JOURNAL. 1808. Sun. $.50 newsstand;
$22/yr. 89 Main St., Cooperstown, NY 13326.
TEL 607-547-2545; FAX 607-547-5587; E-mail:
fj808@magnum.wpe.com; URL:
http://www.wpe.com/~fj808. **Owner(s):** Robert &
Judy Miller, P.O. Box 790, Cooperstown, NY
13326. TEL 607-547-2545; Ed. Dan Sheridan;
Pub. Robert Miller; adv. contact: Robert Miller.
pub. size: broadsheet; circ. 14,500(paid).

CORAM

US
YANKEE TRADER. 1966. Wed. free. One Glenmere
Ln., Coram, NY 11727. TEL 516-331-3300;
FAX 516-331-3481. **Owner(s):** John W. Sutter,
One Glenmere Ln., Coram, NY 11727. TEL
516-331-3300; Pub. John W. Sutter; adv.; pub.
size: tabloid; circ. 252,399(free).

CROSS RIVER

US   ISSN 0746-1836
PATENT TRADER. 1956. Thu. $.75 newsstand;
$45/yr. Cross River Shopping Plz., Corner Rts.
121 & 35, Cross River, NY 10518.
TEL 914-763-3200; FAX 914-763-3911.
Owner(s): Tucker Communications, Inc., Cross
River Shopping Plz., P.O. Box 1000, Cross River,
NY 10518. TEL 914-763-3200; Ed. Susan
Pronovost; Pub. Carll Tucker; adv.; pub. size:
broadsheet; circ. 16,000(paid). **Wire
Service(s):** AP.

CUBA

US
PATRIOT & FREE PRESS. 1862. Wed. $.50
newsstand; $21/yr. in cy.; $23/yr. out of cy. 34
Water St., Cuba, NY 14727-1490.
TEL 716-968-2580; FAX 716-968-2622.
Owner(s): Empire Phoenix Corp., 97 Pennsylvania
Ave., Friendship, NY 14739. TEL 716-973-2025;
Ed. John Arden-Hopkins; Pub. Christina
Arden-Hopkins; adv.; photos; pub. size:
broadsheet; circ. 3,050(paid).
    Formerly: Cuba Patriot & Free Press; New
Patriot; Free Press.

DANSVILLE

US
DANSVILLE GENESEE COUNTRY EXPRESS. 1851.
Thu. $.75 newsstand; $27/yr. in cy. 113 Main
St., Dansville, NY 14437. TEL 716-335-2272;
FAX 716-335-6957. **Owner(s):** American
Publishing Co., 606 N. Van Buren, P.O. Box 520,
Marion, IL 61959. TEL 618-993-1711; Ed. Tami
Bacon; Pub. Frederick W. Kurtz; adv. contact:
Barbara Nagle. pub. size: broadsheet; circ.
14,842(free & paid).

DELHI

US   ISSN 0745-0206

DELAWARE COUNTY TIMES. 1978. Fri. $.35 newsstand; $17.50/yr. in cy. 56 Main St., Delhi, NY 13752. TEL 607-746-2176; FAX 607-746-3135. **Owner(s):** Donald F. Bishop, Hobart, NY 13788. TEL 607-746-2176; FAX 607-746-3235; Pub. Donald F. Bishop; adv. contact: Kathy Rogers. photos; bk.rev.; pub. size: broadsheet; circ. 1,500(paid).

DELMAR

US

COLONIE SPOTLIGHT. Wed. $.50 newsstand; $24/yr in cy. 125 Adams St., Delmar, NY 12054. TEL 518-439-4949; FAX 518-439-0609. **Owner(s):** Spotlight Newspapers, Inc., 125 Adams St., Delmar, NY 12054. TEL 518-439-4949; Ed. Martin Kelly; Pub. Richard A. Ahlstrom; pub. size: tabloid; circ. 4,000(paid).

US

LOUDENVILLE WEEKLY. Wed. $.50 newsstand; free in area; $24/yr. in cy. 125 Adams St., Delmar, NY 12054. TEL 518-439-4949; FAX 518-439-0609. **Owner(s):** Spotlight Newspapers, Inc., 125 Adams St., Delmar, NY 12054. TEL 518-439-4949; Ed. Martin Kelly; Pub. Richard A. Ahlstrom; pub. size: tabloid; circ. 5,000(free & paid).

US

SPOTLIGHT, THE. 1955. Wed. $.50 newsstand; $24/yr. in cy.; $32/yr. out of cy. 125 Adams St., Delmar, NY 12054. TEL 518-439-4949; FAX 518-439-0609. **Owner(s):** Spotlight Newspapers, Inc., 125 Adams St., Delmar, NY 12054. TEL 518-439-4949; Ed. Susan Graves; Pub. Richard A. Ahlstrom; adv.; pub. size: tabloid; circ. 7,000(paid).

DEPOSIT

US

DEPOSIT COURIER. 1848. w. $.50 newsstand; $16/yr. in cy.; $19/yr. out of cy. 138 Front St., Deposit, NY 13754. TEL 607-467-3600; FAX 607-467-5330. **Owner(s):** Hilton A. Evans, 138 Front St., Deposit, NY 13754. TEL 607-467-3600; Ed. Hilton A. Evans. pub. size: broadsheet; circ. 2,200(paid).

DUNDEE

US

DUNDEE OBSERVER. 1878. Wed. $.60 newsstand; $23/yr. in state; $27/yr. out of state. 45 Water St., Dundee, NY 14837. TEL 607-243-8351; FAX 607-243-5833. **Owner(s):** Mary Geo Tomion, 45 Water St., Dundee, NY 14837. TEL 607-243-8351; FAX 607-243-5833; Ed. Mary Geo Tomion; Pub. Mary Geo Tomion; adv. contact: Lori Knapp. photos; pub. size: tabloid; circ. 3,200(free & paid).

EAST AURORA

US

EAST AURORA ADVERTISER. 1872. Tue. $.50 newsstand; $18/yr. in cy.; $25/yr. out of cy. 710 Main St., East Aurora, NY 14052. TEL 716-652-0320. **Owner(s):** Grant M. Hamilton, 710 Main St., East Aurora, NY 14052. TEL 716-652-0320; Ed. Grant M. Hamilton; Pub. Grant M. Hamilton; adv.; pub. size: broadsheet; circ. 4,400(paid).

US

ELMA REVIEW. 1972. Wed. $.25 newsstand; $13/yr. in cy.; $15/yr. out of cy. 710 Main St., East Aurora, NY 14052. TEL 716-652-0327. **Owner(s):** Grant M. Hamilton, P.O. Box 118, Elma, NY 14052. TEL 716-652-0327; Ed. Grant M. Hamilton; Pub. Grant M. Hamilton; adv. contact: Sharon Nieman. pub. size: tabloid; circ. 1,200(paid).

EAST HAMPTON

US

EAST HAMPTON STAR. 1885. Thu. $1 newsstand; $30/yr. in cy.; $40/yr. out of cy.; $45/yr. Manhattan deliv. 153 Main St., East Hampton, NY 11937. TEL 516-324-0002; FAX 516-324-7943. **Owner(s):** Helen S. Rattray, P.O. Box 5002, East Hampton, NY 11937. TEL 516-324-0002; FAX 516-324-7943; Arthur L. Carter, 54 E. 64th St., New York, NY 10021. TEL 212-755-2400; Ed. Helen S. Rattray; Pub. Arthur L. Carter; adv. contact: Gregg Robinson. photos; bk.rev.; pub. size: broadsheet; circ. 14,223(paid).

EAST SETAUKET

US

THREE VILLAGE HERALD. 1954. Wed. $.50 newsstand; $18/yr. in cy.; $24/yr. out of cy. 60 Rt. 25A, East Setauket, NY 11733. TEL 516-751-1550; FAX 516-751-8592. **Owner(s):** North Suffolk Publishing Co., P.O. Box BH, Stony Brook, NY 11790; Ed. Sue Bridson; Pub. Gardner Cowles, III; adv. contact: Aileen Heugen. pub. size: tabloid; circ. 9,000(paid).

ELIZABETHTOWN

US

NORTH COUNTRYMAN, THE. 1928. Sat. $25/yr. in cy.; $30/yr. out of cy. P.O. Box 338, Elizabethtown, NY 12932. TEL 518-873-6368; FAX 518-873-6360. **Owner(s):** Elizabethtown Denton Publications, Inc., P.O. Box 338, Elizabethtown, NY 12932. TEL 518-873-6368; Ed. John Gereau; Pub. Dan Alexander; pub. size: tabloid; circ. 3,000(paid).
Formerly: Rouses Point North Countryman.

US

TIMES OF TI. 1974. s-w.: Wed. & Sat. $25/yr. in cy.; $30/yr. out of cy. P.O. Box 338, Elizabethtown, NY 12932. TEL 518-585-6204; FAX 518-873-6360. **Owner(s):** Denton Publications, Inc., P.O. Box 338, Elizabethtown, NY 12932. TEL 518-873-6368; Ed. John Gereau; Pub. Dan Alexander; adv. contact: Scarlet Keller. pub. size: tabloid; circ. 9,392(paid).
Formerly: Ticonderoga Times of Ti.

US

VALLEY NEWS. 1939. Wed. $25/yr. in cy.; $30/yr. out of cy. P.O. Box 338, Elizabethtown, NY 12932. TEL 518-873-6368; FAX 518-873-6360. **Owner(s):** Denton Publications, Inc., P.O. Box 338, Elizabethtown, NY 12932. TEL 518-873-6368; Ed. John Gereau; Pub. Dan Alexander; pub. size: tabloid; circ. 4,800(paid).

US

WARRENSBURG-LAKE GEORGE NEWS. 1868. Wed. $25/yr. in cy.; $30/yr. out of cy. P.O. Box 338, Elizabethtown, NY 12932. TEL 518-623-3411; FAX 518-623-9264. **Owner(s):** Denton Publications, Inc., P.O. Box 338, Elizabethtown, NY 12932. TEL 518-873-6368; Ed. John Gereau; Pub. Dan Alexander; adv. contact: John McGlire. pub. size: tabloid; circ. 3,000(paid).

ELLENVILLE

US   ISSN 1077-6133

ELLENVILLE PRESS. 1873. Wed. $.35 newsstand $16.50/yr. 7 Cape Ave., Ellenville, NY 12428 TEL 914-647-7222. **Owner(s):** Rondout Valley Publishing Co., Inc., P.O. Box 31, Ellenville, NY 12428. TEL 914-647-7222; Ed. Minnie L. Wainer. Pub. Minnie L. Wainer; adv.; photos; bk.rev.; pub. size: tabloid; circ. 1,970(paid).

ELMONT

US

ELMONT HERALD. 1978. Fri. $.35 newsstand; $14/yr. in cy.; $16/yr. out of cy. 591 Bauer Ct., Elmont, NY 11003-4312. TEL 516-354-3373; FAX 516-328-8586. **Owner(s):** Rita Mezzapelle, 591 Bauer Ct., Elmont, NY 11003. TEL 516-354-3379; FAX 516-328-8586; Ed. Roy J. Mezzapelle; Pub. Roy J. Mezzapelle; adv. contact: Roy J. Mezzapelle. photos; pub. size: tabloid; circ. 5,000(paid).

ELMSFORD

US

PENNYSAVER. 1985. Sat. free. 101 Executive Blvd., Elmsford, NY 10523. TEL 914-592-5222; FAX 914-592-4816. **Owner(s):** Pennysaver Group, Inc., 101 Executive Blvd., P.O. Box 481, Elmsford, NY 10523. TEL 914-592-5222; Ed. Steve Traub; Pub. Steve Traub; adv.; pub. size: standard; circ. 353,500(controlled & free).
Formerly: Pennysaver/Westchester Life.

ENDWELL

US

VALLEY NEWS, THE. 1989. Fri. $.75 newsstand; $32/yr. 3128 Watson Blvd., Endwell, NY 13760-3532. TEL 607-757-0753; FAX 607-757-0784. **Owner(s):** Brad Manchester, 3128 Watson Blvd., Endwell, NY 13760. TEL 607-757-0753; FAX 607-757-0784; Keith Manchester, 3128 Watson Blvd., Endwell, NY 13760. TEL 607-757-0753; FAX 607-757-0784; Ed. Tom Melville. Pub. Brad Manchester; adv. contact: Brad Manchester. photos; bk.rev.; pub. size: broadsheet; circ. 1,500(paid).

FAIRPORT

US

SHOPPING NEWS. 1948. Tue. free in area; $15/yr. out of area. 149 Main St., N., Fairport, NY 14450. TEL 716-388-1050; FAX 716-388-0114. **Owner(s):** American Publishing Corp., 111 S. Emma St., West Frankfort, IL 62896. TEL 618-937-6411; pub. size: tabloid; circ. 16,000(free & paid).

FAYETTEVILLE

US

DEWITT TIMES. 1970. Wed. $.75 newsstand; $21/yr. 117 Highbridge Rd., Fayetteville, NY 13066. TEL 315-637-3121; FAX 315-637-3124. **Owner(s):** Eagle Newspapers, Inc., P.O. Box 270, Baldwinsville, NY 13027. TEL 315-635-9321; Ed. Chris Donton; Pub. Stewart Hancock; adv. contact: Michele Hunt. pub. size: tabloid; circ. 1,703(paid).
Formerly: De Witt Suburban Times.

US
EAGLE BULLETIN. 1850. Wed. $.75 newsstand; $21/yr. in cy.; $13/yr. students. 117 Highbridge St., Fayetteville, NY 13066. TEL 315-637-3121; FAX 315-637-3124. **Owner(s):** Eagle Newspapers, Inc., 7 E. Genesee St., P.O. Box 270, Baldwinsville, NY 13027. TEL 315-635-9321; Ed. Chris Donlon; Pub. Stewart Hancock; adv. contact: John Mott. pub. size: tabloid; circ. 7,032(paid).

FISHERS

US
BRIGHTON-PITTSFORD POST, THE. 1932. Wed. $.75 newsstand; $28/yr. P.O. Box C, Fishers, NY 14453. TEL 716-381-3300; FAX 716-924-7734. **Owner(s):** Wolfe Publications, Inc., P.O. Box C, Fishers, NY 14453. TEL 716-924-4040; Ed. Andrew D. Wolfe; Pub. Andrew D. Wolfe; pub. size: broadsheet; circ. 12,500(paid).

US
EAST ROCHESTER POST-HERALD. 1989. Thu. $.45 newsstand; $18/yr. mailed. P.O. Box C, Fishers, NY 14453. TEL 716-924-4040; FAX 716-924-7734. **Owner(s):** Wolfe Publications, Inc., P.O. Box C, Fishers, NY 14453. TEL 716-924-4040; Ed. John S. Wolfe; Pub. Andrew D. Wolfe; pub. size: broadsheet; circ. 1,100(paid).

US
GREECE POST, THE. 1960. Thu. $.50 newsstand; $21/yr. P.O. Box C, Fishers, NY 14453. TEL 716-381-3300; FAX 716-924-7734. **Owner(s):** Wolfe Publications, Inc., P.O. Box C, Fishers, NY 14453. TEL 716-924-4040; Ed. Andrew D. Wolfe; Pub. Andrew D. Wolfe; pub. size: broadsheet; circ. 8,500(paid).

US
HENRIETTA POST. 1964. Wed. $.50 newsstand; $21/yr. mailed. P.O. Box C, Fishers, NY 14453. TEL 716-381-3300; FAX 716-924-7734. **Owner(s):** Wolfe Publications, Inc., P.O. Box C, Fishers, NY 14453. TEL 716-924-4040; Ed. Andrew D. Wolfe; Pub. Andrew D. Wolfe; pub. size: broadsheet; circ. 2,500(paid).

US
PENFIELD POST REPUBLICAN, THE. 1950. Thu. $.50 newsstand; $21/yr. P.O. Box C, Fishers, NY 14453. TEL 716-381-3300; FAX 716-924-7734. **Owner(s):** Wolfe Publications, Inc., P.O. Box C, Fishers, NY 14453. TEL 716-924-4040; Ed. Andrew D. Wolfe; Pub. Andrew D. Wolfe; adv.; pub. size: broadsheet; circ. 3,800(paid).

FLORAL PARK

US
FLORAL PARK BULLETIN. 1941. w. $.35 newsstand; $15/yr. P.O. Box 227, Floral Park, NY 11001. **Owner(s):** Carla Cohen, P.O. Box 227, Floral Park, NY 11001; Ed. Carla Cohen; Pub. Carla Cohen; adv. contact: Janis Murphy. pub. size: tabloid.

US
FRANKLIN SQUARE BULLETIN. 1938. Thu. $.35 newsstand; $15/yr. 139 Tulip Ave., Floral Park, NY 11001. TEL 516-775-7700. **Owner(s):** Nassau Border Papers, Inc., P.O. Box 155, Franklin Square, NY 11010. TEL 516-775-7700; Ed. Carla Cohen; Pub. Carla Cohen; adv. contact: Janis Murphy. photos; pub. size: tabloid; circ. 8,700(paid).

US
GATEWAY, THE. 1926. Wed. $15/yr. P.O. Box 227, Floral Park, NY 11002. TEL 516-775-2700. **Owner(s):** Carla Cohen, P.O. Box 227, Floral Park, NY 11002. TEL 516-775-2700; Ed. Carla Cohen. adv.; photos; pub. size: tabloid; circ. 12,000(paid).

FLUSHING

US
FRESH MEADOWS TIMES, THE. 1993. Thu. $.50 newsstand; $19/yr.; $35/2 yrs. in cy. 41-02 Bell Blvd., 2nd Fl., Flushing, NY 11361. TEL 718-229-0300; FAX 718-225-7117. **Owner(s):** Queens Publishing Corp., 41-02 Bell Blvd., Second Fl., Flushing, NY 11361. TEL 718-229-0300; Ed. Roz Liston; Pub. Steve Blank; adv.; photos; pub. size: tabloid; circ. 1,552(paid).

US
GLEN OAKS LEDGER, THE. 1993. Thu. $.50 newsstand; $15/yr.; $29/2 yr. in cy. 41-02 Bell Blvd., 2nd Fl., Flushing, NY 11361. TEL 718-229-0300; FAX 718-225-7117. **Owner(s):** Queens Publishing Corp., 214-11 41st Ave., Flushing, NY 11361. TEL 718-229-0300; FAX 718-225-7171; Ed. Roz Liston; Pub. Steven Blank; adv.; photos; pub. size: tabloid; circ. 2,424(paid).

US
▼**JAMAICA TIMES, THE.** 1995. Thu. $.50 newsstand; $19/yr.; $25/2 yrs. in cy. 41-02 Bell Blvd., 2nd Fl., Flushing, NY 11361. TEL 718-229-0300; FAX 718-225-7117. **Owner(s):** Queens Publishing Corp., 214-11 41st Ave., Flushing, NY 11361. TEL 718-229-0300; Ed. Roz Liston; Pub. Steve Blank; adv.; photos; pub. size: tabloid; circ. 1,019.

US
LITTLE NECK LEDGER, THE. 1919. Thu. $.50 newsstand; $19/yr.; $35/2 yrs. 41-02 Bell Blvd., 2nd Fl., Flushing, NY 11361. TEL 718-229-0300; FAX 718-225-7117. **Owner(s):** Queens Publishing Corp., 214-11 41st Ave., Flushing, NY 11361. TEL 718-229-0300; Ed. Roz Liston; Pub. Steven Blank; adv.; photos; pub. size: tabloid; circ. 3,723(paid).

US
▼**QUEEN VILLAGE TIMES, THE.** 1994. Thu. $.50 newsstand; $19/yr.; $35/2 yrs. in cy. 41-02 Bell Blvd., 2nd Fl., Flushing, NY 11361. TEL 718-229-0300; FAX 718-225-7117. **Owner(s):** Queens Publishing Corp., 41-02 Bell Blvd., 2nd Fl., Flushing, NY 11361. TEL 718-229-0300; Ed. Roz Liston; Pub. Steve Blank; adv.; photos; pub. size: tabloid; circ. 2,039(paid).

FORT PLAIN

US
COURIER-STANDARD-ENTERPRISE. 1876. Wed. $.50 newsstand; $18/yr. in cy. 41 Main St., Fort Plain, NY 13339. TEL 518-993-2321; FAX 518-993-4919. **Owner(s):** Tri-Village Publishers, Inc., 1 Venner Rd., Amsterdam, NY 12010. TEL 518-843-1100; Ed. Robert P. Lindsay; Pub. Richard A. Barker; adv. contact: Carrie Hazzard. photos; pub. size: broadsheet; circ. 4,700(paid).

FREEPORT

US
FREEPORT BALDWIN LEADER, THE. 1935. Thu. $.30 newsstand; $11.50/yr. 30 S. Ocean Ave., Ste. 204, Freeport, NY 11520. TEL 516-378-3133; FAX 516-378-3139. **Owner(s):** L & M Publications, Inc., 1840 Merrick Ave., Merrick, NY 11566. TEL 516-378-5320; FAX 516-378-0287; Ed. Laura Shofer; Pub. Linda L. Toscano; adv. contact: Mark Treske. pub. size: tabloid; circ. 2,700(paid).

US
LEADER, THE. 1935. Thu. $11.50/yr. 30 S. Ocean Ave., Ste. 204, Freeport, NY 11520. TEL 516-378-3133. **Owner(s):** L & M Publications, Inc., 1840 Merrick Ave., Merrick, NY 11566. TEL 516-378-5320; Ed. Paul Laursen; Pub. Linda Toscano; pub. size: tabloid; circ. 3,000(paid).

US
VALLEY STREAM COURIER. 1966. Thu. $16/yr. 244 Whaley St., Freeport, NY 11520. TEL 516-378-5002. **Owner(s):** Rosemary McCarthy, Freeport, NY. TEL 516-378-5002; Ed. Rosemary A. McCarthy; Pub. Rosemary A. McCarthy; pub. size: tabloid; circ. 9,000(paid).

FRESH MEADOWS

US
QUEENS TRIBUNE. 1970. Thu. $12/yr.; $21/2 yrs.; $29/3 yrs. 174-15 Horace Harding Expwy., Fresh Meadows, NY 11365. TEL 718-357-7400; FAX 718-357-9417. **Owner(s):** News Communications, Inc., Fresh Meadows, NY; Ed. David Oats; Pub. Steven Goldstein; adv. contact: Steven Goldstein. pub. size: tabloid; circ. 146,000(free & paid).

FULTON

US
FULTON PATRIOT. 1823. Mon. free newsstand; $7/yr. in cy.; $14/yr. out of cy. P.O. Box 299, Fulton, NY 13069. TEL 315-592-2459. **Owner(s):** Fulton Newspapers, Inc., P.O. Box 805, Fulton, NY 13069. TEL 315-598-6397; Pub. Roy N. Hodge; pub. size: standard; circ. 6,235(paid).

US   ISSN 1067-7755
VALLEY NEWS. 1947. s-w.: Mon. & Thu. $.35 newsstand; $17/yr. in cy. 117 Oneida St., Fulton, NY 13069. TEL 315-598-6397. **Owner(s):** Fulton Newspapers, Inc., P.O. Box 805, Fulton, NY 13069. TEL 315-598-6397; Ed. Ronald L. Caravan; Pub. Isabelle Caravan; adv. contact: Allison McManus. pub. size: tabloid; circ. 10,000(paid).

GLENS FALLS

US
CHRONICLE, THE. 1980. Thu. free; $35/yr. P.O. Box 153, Glens Falls, NY 12801. TEL 518-792-1126. **Owner(s):** Chronicle, The, P.O. Box 153, Glens Falls, NY 12801. TEL 518-792-1126; Ed. Mark Frost; Pub. Patricia Maddock; adv.; photos; bk.rev.; pub. size: tabloid; circ. 25,000(free & paid).

GOSHEN

US

INDEPENDENT REPUBLICAN. 1812. Wed. $.50 newsstand; $20/yr. in cy.; $22/yr. out of cy. 132 W. Main, Goshen, NY 10924-0628. TEL 914-294-6111; FAX 914-294-0532. **Owner(s):** Betty J. Wright, 132 W. Main, Goshen, NY 10924-0628. TEL 914-294-6111; FAX 914-294-0532; Ed. Betty Jane Wright. adv.; photos; pub. size: tabloid; circ. 3,800(paid).

GOUVERNEUR

US

GOUVERNEUR TRIBUNE PRESS. 1886. Wed. $.50 newsstand; $18/yr. in state; $25/yr. out of state. 74 Trinity Ave., Gouverneur, NY 13642. TEL 315-287-2100; FAX 315-287-2101. **Owner(s):** Gouverneur Tribune Press, Inc., 74 Trinity Ave., Gouverneur, NY 13642. TEL 315-287-2100; Pub. M. Dan McClellan; adv. contact: Colin Graves. bk.rev.; pub. size: standard; circ. 5,000(paid).

GOWANDA

US

GOWANDA PENNYSAVER NEWS. 1939. Mon. free. 62 W. Main St., Gowanda, NY 14070. TEL 716-532-2288; FAX 716-532-3056. **Owner(s):** H & K Publications, Inc., 50 Buffalo St., Hamburg, NY 14075. TEL 716-649-4413; Ed. Maureen Spockdale; Pub. H & K Publication; pub. size: tabloid; circ. 11,800(free).

GRAND ISLAND

US

GRAND ISLAND PENNYSAVER. 1949. Tue. free. 1854C Whitehaven Rd., Grand Island, NY 14072-0130. TEL 716-773-7676; FAX 716-773-7190. **Owner(s):** Niagara Frontier Publications, Inc., 1854C Whitehaven Rd., Grand Island, NY 14072. TEL 716-773-7676; FAX 716-773-7190; Ed. Michele Ramstetter; Pub. Arthur J. Mazenauer; adv.; photos; pub. size: tabloid; circ. 7,000(free).

US

ISLAND DISPATCH. 1944. Fri. $.65 newsstand; $20.95/yr. in cy.; $25.95/yr, out of cy. 1854C Whitehaven Rd., Grand Island, NY 14072-0130. TEL 716-773-7676; FAX 716-773-7190. **Owner(s):** Niagara Frontier Publications, Inc., 1845C Whitehaven Rd., Grand Island, NY 14072. TEL 716-773-7676; FAX 716-773-7190; Ed. Michele Ramstetter; Pub. Arthur J. Mazenauer; adv.; photos; pub. size: tabloid; circ. 3,700(paid). **Wire Service(s):** NY Press Assn.

US

LEWISTON-PORTER SENTINEL. 1987. Sat. free. 1854C Whitehaven Rd., Grand Island, NY 14072. TEL 716-773-7676; FAX 716-773-7190. **Owner(s):** Niagara Frontier Publications, Inc., 1854C Whitehaven Rd., Grand Island, NY 14072. TEL 716-773-7676; FAX 716-773-7190; Ed. Michele Ramstetter; Pub. Arthur J. Mazenauer; adv.; photos; pub. size: tabloid; circ. 15,000(free). Wire Service(s): NY Press Assn.

US

NIAGARA/WHEATFIELD TRIBUNE. Thu. free. 1854C Whitehaven Rd., Grand Island, NY 14072-0130. TEL 716-773-7676; FAX 716-773-7190. **Owner(s):** Niagara Frontier Publications, Inc., 1854C Whitehaven Rd., Grand Island, NY 14072. TEL 716-773-7676; FAX 716-773-7190; Ed. Michele Ramstetter; Pub. Arthur J. Mazenauer; adv.; photos; pub. size: tabloid; circ. 15,000(free). Wire Service(s): NY Press Assn.

GRANVILLE

US

GRANVILLE SENTINEL. 1875. Wed. $20/yr. in NY-New England; $30/yr. elsewhere. 14 E. Main St., Granville, NY 12832. TEL 518-642-1234; FAX 518-642-1344. **Owner(s):** Manchester Newspapers, Inc., 6 North St., Granville, NY 12832; Ed. John Manchester; Pub. John Manchester; adv. contact: John Manchester. pub. size: broadsheet; circ. 3,300(paid).

US

NORTH COUNTRY FREE PRESS. 1985. Sat. free. 14 E. Main St., Granville, NY 12832. TEL 518-642-1234; FAX 518-642-1344. **Owner(s):** Manchester Newspapers, Inc., 6 North St., Granville, NY 12832; Ed. Stella Wood; Pub. John Manchester; adv. contact: John Manchester. pub. size: tabloid; circ. 22,000(paid). **Formerly:** Free Press.

GREAT NECK

US

GREAT NECK NEWS. 1925. Fri. $.35 newsstand; $9.50/yr. 643 Middle Neck Rd., Great Neck, NY 11023. TEL 516-487-1100; FAX 516-487-1100. **Owner(s):** Litmore Publications, Inc., P.O. Box 398, Great Neck, NY 11022. TEL 516-931-0012; Ed. Karen Rubin; Pub. Margaret Morgan; pub. size: tabloid; circ. 6,700(paid).

GREENE

US

CHENANGO AMERICAN. 1855. Tue. $14/yr. in city; $16/yr. in cy.; $20/yr. out of cy. 12 S. Chenango St., Greene, NY 13778. TEL 607-656-4511; FAX 607-563-7118. **Owner(s):** Kenneth S. Paden & Paul Hamilton, Sr., 5 Winkler Rd., Sidney, NY 13838. TEL 607-563-3526; Ed. Pete Mansheffer; Pub. Kenneth S. Paden; adv.; pub. size: broadsheet; circ. 3,500(paid).

US

OXFORD REVIEW-TIMES. 1960. Tue. $16/yr. in area; $20/yr. out of area. 12 S. Chenango St., Greene, NY 13778. TEL 607-656-4511; FAX 607-563-7118. **Owner(s):** Kenneth S. Paden & Paul Hamilton, Sr., 12 S. Chenango St., Greene, NY 13778. TEL 607-563-3526; Ed. Pete Mansheffer; Pub. Ken Paden; adv.; photos; pub. size: broadsheet; circ. 3,500(paid).

US

WHITNEY POINT REPORTER. 1850. Tue. $16/yr. local; $20/yr. out of area. 12 S. Chenango St., Greene, NY 13778. TEL 607-656-4511; FAX 607-563-7118. **Owner(s):** Kenneth S. Paden & Paul Hamilton, Sr., 12 S. Chenango St., Greene, NY 13778; Ed. Peter Mansheffer; Pub. Kenneth Paden adv.; pub. size: broadsheet; circ. 3,500(paid).

GREENWICH

US

GREENWICH JOURNAL & SALEM PRESS. 1842. Thu. $.60 newsstand; $23/yr. in cy.; $26/yr. elsewhere. 35 Salem St., Greenwich, NY 12834. TEL 518-692-2266. **Owner(s):** Sally B. Tefft, 35 Salem St., P.O. Box 185, Greenwich, NY 12834. TEL 518-692-2266; Pub. Sally B. Tefft; adv. contact: Culver S. Tefft. pub. size: broadsheet; circ. 3,816(paid).

GREENWOOD LAKE

US

GREENWOOD LAKE & WEST MILFORD NEWS. 1964. Wed. $26/yr. in cy.; $29.50/yr. out of cy. Windermere Ave., Greenwood Lake, NY 10925. TEL 914-477-2575; FAX 914-477-2577. **Owner(s):** Greenwood Lake News, Inc., P.O. Box 1117, Greenwood Lake, NY 10925. TEL 914-477-2575; Pub. Ann Chaimowitz; adv. contact: Ann Chaimowitz. pub. size: tabloid; circ. 4,000(paid).

HAMBURG

US

SUN & ERIE COUNTY INDEPENDENT, THE. 1875. Thu. $.75 newsstand; $17.50/yr. 46 Buffalo St., Hamburg, NY 14075. TEL 716-649-4040; FAX 716-649-6374. **Owner(s):** H & K Publications, Inc., P.O. Box 590, Hamburg, NY 14075. TEL 716-649-4040; Ed. Eileen Hotho. adv.; photos; bk.rev.; pub. size: tabloid; circ. 10,000(paid). **Wire Service(s):** Empire News Service.

HAMILTON

US

HAMILTON MID-YORK WEEKLY. 1828. Thu. free newsstand; $19/yr. outside area. 55 Utica St., Hamilton, NY 13346. TEL 315-824-2150; FAX 315-824-4220. **Owner(s):** Oneida Madison Pennysaver, The, P.O. Box 203, Clinton, NY 13323. TEL 315-853-6103; Ed. Carolyn Godfrey; Pub. Wayne Cleary; adv. contact: Bonny Bean. pub. size: broadsheet; circ. 9,000(free & paid).

US

HAMILTON TRIBUNE. Wed. $.75 newsstand; $25/yr. $21/yr. senior citizens; $13/yr. students. 45 Lebanon, Hamilton, NY 13346. TEL 315-824-3147. **Owner(s):** Eagle Newspapers, Inc., P.O. Box 55, Fayetteville, NY 13066. TEL 315-637-3121; Ed. Andrew Larison Pub. Stewart Hancock; adv. pub. size: broadsheet.

HASTINGS-ON-HUDSON

US   ISSN 0745-3477

ENTERPRISE, THE. Fri. $24/yr. in cy.; $30/yr. out of cy. 5 Boulanger Plz., Hastings-on-Hudson, NY 10706. TEL 914-478-2787; FAX 914-478-2863. **Owner(s):** Deborah White, P.O. Box 278, Hastings-on-Hudson, NY 10706. TEL 914-478-2787; Ed. Terri Salvatore; Pub. Deborah White; pub. size: standard; circ. 4,900(paid). **Formerly:** Hastings Enterprise.

HAVERSTRAW

US

ROCKLAND COUNTY TIMES. 1889. Thu. $.50 newsstand; $21/yr. in cy.; $27/yr. out of cy. 11 New Main St., Haverstraw, NY 10927. TEL 914-429-2000; FAX 914-429-8990. **Owner(s):** RCT Publishing Co., Inc., 11 New Main St., Haverstraw, NY 10927. TEL 914-429-2000; FAX 914-429-8990; Ed. Evelyn Davis; Pub. Evelyn Davis; adv. contact: Evelyn Davis. photos; bk.rev.; pub. size: broadsheet; circ. 8,000(paid).

HICKSVILLE

US

EAST MEADOW BEACON. 1950. Thu. $9.50/yr. One Jonathan Ave., Hicksville, NY 11801-5201. TEL 516-931-1400. **Owner(s):** Nassau County Publications, Inc., One Jonathan Ave., Hicksville, NY 11801; Ed. Peter Hoegl; Pub. Peter Hoegl; adv.; photos; bk.rev.; pub. size: tabloid; circ. 5,800(paid).

US

HEMPSTEAD BEACON. 1951. Fri. $9.50/yr. One Jonathan Ave., Hicksville, NY 11801-5201. TEL 516-931-1400. **Owner(s):** Nassau County Publications, Inc., One Jonathan Ave., Hicksville, NY 11801. TEL 516-931-1400; Pub. Pete Hoegl; adv.; photos; bk.rev.; pub. size: tabloid; circ. 5,100(paid).

US

MERRICK BEACON. 1950. Fri. $9.50/yr. One Jonathan Ave., Hicksville, NY 11801-5201. TEL 516-931-1400. **Owner(s):** Nassau County Publications, Inc., One Jonathan Ave., Hicksville, NY 11801; Ed. Peter Hoegl; Pub. Peter Hoegl; adv.; photos; bk.rev.; pub. size: tabloid; circ. 4,000(paid).

US   ISSN 0747-4741

MID-ISLAND TIMES. Fri. $.35/newsstand; $9.50/yr. mailed. 81 E. Barclay St., Hicksville, NY 11801. TEL 516-931-0012. **Owner(s):** Litmore Publications, Inc., 81 E. Barclay St., Hicksville, NY 11801. TEL 516-931-0012; Ed. Meg Norris; Pub. Meg Norris; adv.; pub. size: tabloid; circ. 5,685(paid).

US

UNIONDALE BEACON. 1951. Fri. $9.50/yr. One Jonathan Ave., Hicksville, NY 11801-5201. TEL 516-931-1400. **Owner(s):** Nassau County Publications, Inc., One Jonathan Ave., Hicksville, NY 11801-5201. TEL 516-931-1400; Pub. Peter Hoegl; adv.; photos; bk.rev.; pub. size: tabloid; circ. 5,300(paid).

US

WEST HEMPSTEAD BEACON. 1951. Fri. $.35 newsstand; $9.50/yr. local; $12/yr. elsewhere. One Jonathan Ave., Hicksville, NY 11801-5201. TEL 516-931-1400. **Owner(s):** Nassau County Publications, Inc., One Jonathan Ave., Hicksville, NY 11801. TEL 516-931-1400; Ed. Peter Hoegl; Pub. Peter Hoegl; adv.; photos; bk.rev.; pub. size: tabloid; circ. 5,200(paid).

HIGHLAND FALLS

US

NEWS OF THE HIGHLANDS. 1891. Wed. $.50 newsstand; $21/yr. Webb Ln., Highland Falls, NY 10928. TEL 914-446-4519. **Owner(s):** News of the Highlands, Inc., P.O. Box 278, Highland Falls, NY 10928. TEL 914-446-4519; FAX 914-446-0532; Ed. Frederick Brennan. pub. size: broadsheet; circ. 3,000(paid).
  Formerly: Highland Falls News of the Highlands.

HORSEHEADS

US   ISSN 1064-4091

CHEMUNG VALLEY REPORTER. 1856. Thu. $.50 newsstand; $20/yr. in cy.; $22/yr. out of cy. 126 S. Main St., Horseheads, NY 14845. TEL 607-739-3001; FAX 607-739-2935. **Owner(s):** Roots & Wings, Inc., P.O. Box 474, Horseheads, NY 14845. TEL 607-739-3001; FAX 607-739-2935; Ed. Thomas Bohlert; Pub. Patricia Powers; adv. contact: Karen Ketter. photos; bk.rev.; pub. size: tabloid; circ. 1,500(free & paid).

HUNTINGTON

US

HUNTINGTON RECORD. 1932. Thu. $15/yr. 322 Main St., Huntington, NY 11743. TEL 516-427-7000; FAX 516-427-5820. **Owner(s):** James Kous, 135 Liberty Ave., Mineola, NY 11501. TEL 516-747-8282; Ed. Peter Sloggatt; Pub. James Koutsis; pub. size: tabloid; circ. 60,000(paid).
  Formerly: Record, The.

HYDE PARK

US

HYDE PARK TOWNSMAN. 1959. Thu. $.60 newsstand; $29/yr. 639 Albany Post Rd., Hyde Park, NY 12538. TEL 914-229-7126; FAX 914-229-6283. **Owner(s):** Taconic Media, Inc., P.O. Box 316, Millbrook, NY 12545. TEL 914-677-8241; Ed. Dan Barton; Pub. Hamilton W. Meserve; pub. size: broadsheet; circ. 2,000(paid).

IRVINGTON

US

IRVINGTON VIEWPOINT, THE. 1990. m. free; $15/yr. out of town. 37 Barney Park, Irvington, NY 10533. TEL 914-591-3700; FAX 914-591-9226. **Owner(s):** Berger Communications, Inc., 37 Barney Park, Irvington, NY 10533. TEL 914-591-3700; FAX 914-591-9226; Ed. George Berger; Pub. George Berger; adv.; pub. size: tabloid; circ. 6,500(controlled & free).

ITHACA

US

ITHACA TIMES. 1972. Thu. $22.95/yr. P.O. Box 27, Ithaca, NY 14851-0027. TEL 607-277-7000; FAX 607-277-1012. **Owner(s):** Ithaca Times; Pub. James Bilinski; adv.; pub. size: tabloid; circ. 20,012.

LACKAWANNA

US

FRONT PAGE. 1959. Wed. $14/yr. in cy.; $22/yr. out of cy. 2703 S. Park Ave., Lackawanna, NY 14218. TEL 716-823-8222; FAX 716-821-0550. **Owner(s):** Front Page Group, Inc., 2703 S. Park Ave., Lackawanna, NY 14218. TEL 716-823-8222; Pub. William Delmont; photos; pub. size: tabloid; circ. 15,800(paid).

US

SOUTH BUFFALO NEWS. 1919. Wed. $14/yr. in cy; $22/yr. out of cy. 2703 S. Park Ave., Lackawanna, NY 14218. TEL 716-823-8222; FAX 716-821-0550. **Owner(s):** Front Page Group, Inc., 2703 S. Park Ave., Lackawanna, NY 14218. TEL 716-823-8222; Pub. William Delmont; adv.; photos; pub. size: tabloid; circ. 5,500(paid).

LAKE PLACID

US

LAKE PLACID NEWS. 1905. Fri. $.50 newsstand; $30-$33/yr. 412 S. Main St., Lake Placid, NY 12946. TEL 518-523-4401; FAX 518-523-1531. **Owner(s):** Ogden Newspapers, Inc., 1500 Main St., Wheeling, WV 26033. TEL 304-233-0100; Ed. Julie Stowell. adv. contact: Susan Harrington. photos; pub. size: broadsheet; circ. 3,200(paid).

LAWRENCE

US

BALDWIN HERALD. 1943. Wed. $.75 newsstand; $22/yr. in cy.; $30/yr. out of cy. 379 Central Ave., Lawrence, NY 11559. TEL 516-569-4000; FAX 516-569-4942. **Owner(s):** Richner Communications, Inc., 379 Central Ave., Lawrence, NY 11559. TEL 516-569-4000; FAX 516-569-4942; Ed. Alison Zesko. adv.; photos; bk.rev.; pub. size: broadsheet; circ. 1,328(free & paid).
  Formerly: South Shore Reporter-Baldwin.

US

LONG ISLAND GRAPHIC-ROOSEVELT PRESS. Thu. $.75 newsstand; $22/yr. 379 Central Ave., Lawrence, NY 11559. TEL 516-569-4000; FAX 516-569-4942. **Owner(s):** Richner Communications, Inc., 379 Central Ave., Lawrence, NY 11559. TEL 516-569-4000; FAX 516-569-4942; Ed. Jean Graham. adv.; photos; bk.rev.; pub. size: tabloid; circ. 1,170(paid).

US

LYNBROOK HERALD. 1964. Thu. $.50 newsstand; $12/yr. in cy.; $18/yr. out of cy. 379 Central Ave., Lawrence, NY 11559. TEL 516-569-4000; FAX 516-569-4942. **Owner(s):** Richner Communications, Inc., 379 Central Ave., Lawrence, NY 11559. TEL 516-569-4000; FAX 516-569-4942; Ed. Bob Clark. adv. contact: Barbara Klein. pub. size: tabloid; circ. 6,100(paid).

US

MEADOWBROOK TIMES. 1964. Wed. $22/yr. in cy.; $30/yr. out of cy. 379 Central Ave., Lawrence, NY 11559. TEL 516-569-4000; FAX 516-569-4942. **Owner(s):** Richner Communications, Inc., 379 Central Ave., Lawrence, NY 11559. TEL 516-569-4000; FAX 516-569-4942; Ed. Hanna Bennett; Pub. Clifford Richner; adv. contact: Barbara Klein. pub. size: tabloid; circ. 3,000(paid).

US

NASSAU HERALD. 1924. Thu. $18/yr. in cy.; $26/yr. out of cy. 379 Central Ave., Lawrence, NY 11559. TEL 516-569-4000; FAX 516-569-4942. **Owner(s):** Richner Communications, Inc., 379 Central Ave., Lawrence, NY 11559. TEL 516-569-4000; FAX 516-569-4942; Ed. Randy Kress; Pub. Clifford Richner; pub. size: tabloid; circ. 12,500(paid).
 Formerly: Nassau Herald-Lawrence.

US

PRIMETIME. 1987. Fri. free. 379 Central Ave., Lawrence, NY 11559. TEL 516-569-4444; FAX 516-569-4942. **Owner(s):** Richner Communications, Inc., 379 Central Ave., Lawrence, NY 11559. TEL 516-569-4444; FAX 516-569-4942; Pub. Clifford Richner; pub. size: tabloid; circ. 110,000(free).

US

ROCKAWAY JOURNAL. 1883. Wed. $12/yr. in cy.; $18/yr. out of cy. 379 Central Ave., Lawrence, NY 11559. TEL 516-569-4000; FAX 516-569-4942. **Owner(s):** Richner Communications, Inc., 379 Central Ave., Lawrence, NY 11559. TEL 516-569-4000; FAX 516-569-4942; Ed. Ceena Weisman; Pub. Cliff Richner; pub. size: tabloid; circ. 1,917(paid).

US

ROCKVILLE CENTRE HERALD. 1991. Thu. $.75 newsstand; $18/yr. in town; $26/yr. elsewhere. 379 Central Ave., Lawrence, NY 11559. TEL 516-569-4000; FAX 516-569-4942. **Owner(s):** Richner Communications, Inc., 379 Central Ave., Lawrence, NY 11559. TEL 516-569-4000; FAX 516-569-4942; Ed. Jeff Kleuwer; Pub. Clifford Richner; adv. contact: Barbara Klein. pub. size: tabloid; circ. 5,400(paid).

US

VALLEY STREAM HERALD. 1990. Thu. $.75 newsstand; $22/yr.; $36/2 yrs.; $44/3 yrs.; $30/yr. out of cy. 379 Central Ave., Lawrence, NY 11559. TEL 516-569-4000; FAX 516-569-4942. **Owner(s):** Richner Communications, Inc., 379 Central Ave., Lawrence, NY 11559. TEL 516-569-4000; FAX 516-569-4942; Ed. Fran Evans; Pub. Clifford Richner; adv. contact: Barbara Klien. pub. size: tabloid; circ. 9,121(paid).

LINDENHURST

US

SOUTH BAY'S NEWSPAPER. 1953. Wed. $.25 newsstand; $12.50/yr. 150 W. Hoffman Ave., Lindenhurst, NY 11757-4043. TEL 516-226-2636. **Owner(s):** Excel Promotions Corp., 150 W. Hoffman Ave., Lindenhurst, NY 11757-4043. TEL 516-226-2636; FAX 516-226-2680; Ed. J.M. Freedman. adv.; photos; bk.rev.; pub. size: tabloid; circ. 93,410(free).

US

SOUTH BAY'S SHOPPER. 1953. Wed. $.25 newsstand; $12.50/yr. deliv. 150 W. Hoffman Ave., Lindenhurst, NY 11757. TEL 516-226-2636; FAX 516-226-2680. **Owner(s):** Excel Promotions Corp., 150 W. Hoffman Ave., Lindenhurst, NY 11757. TEL 516-226-2636; FAX 516-226-2680; Ed. J.M. Freedman. adv.; photos; pub. size: tabloid; circ. 93,410(free).

LOCKPORT

US

TRI-COUNTY NEWS. Sat. free. 459-491 S. Transit St., Lockport, NY 14094. TEL 716-439-9222; FAX 716-439-9249. **Owner(s):** Park Communications, Inc., Vine Ctr. Office Tower, 333 W. Vine St., 17th Fl., Lexington, KY 40507. TEL 606-252-7252 Ed. Dan Kane. pub. size: broadsheet; circ. 8,000(free).
 Formerly: Lockport Tri-County News.

LOCUST VALLEY

US

LOCUST VALLEY LEADER. 1946. Thu. $.40 newsstand; $18/yr. 160 Birch Hill Rd., Locust Valley, NY 11560. TEL 516-676-1434; FAX 516-671-7442. **Owner(s):** Edith Hay Wyckoff, 160 Birch Hill Rd., Locust Valley, NY 11560. TEL 516-671-7442; Ed. Edith Hay Wyckoff; Pub. Edith Hay Wyckoff; adv. contact: Claudia De Vecchi. pub. size: tabloid; circ. 3,800(paid).

LONG BEACH

US

LONG BEACH HERALD. 1990. Thu. $.75 newsstand; $22/yr. in town; $30/yr. elsewhere. 143 E. Park Ave., Long Beach, NY 11561. TEL 516-431-3400; FAX 516-889-4419. **Owner(s):** Richner Publications, Inc., 379 Central Ave., Lawrence, NY 11559. TEL 516-569-4000; FAX 516-569-4942; Ed. Mike Harrison; Pub. Clifford Richner. adv. contact: Barbara Klein. photos; bk.rev.; pub. size: tabloid; circ. 6,228(paid).

US

LONG BEACH INDEPENDENT VOICE. 1932. Thu. $.35 newsstand; $11/yr.; $19/2 yrs. 78 W. Park Ave., Long Beach, NY 11561. TEL 516-897-8800; FAX 516-739-5404. **Owner(s):** Barry Manning, 216 E. Second St., Mineola, NY 11501. TEL 516-739-6400; FAX 516-739-5404; Pub. Barry Manning; pub. size: tabloid; circ. 5,000(paid).

US

OCEANSIDE/ISLAND PARK HERALD. 1966. Wed. $.50 newsstand; $18/yr. 143 E. Park Ave., Long Beach, NY 11561. TEL 516-431-3400; FAX 516-889-4419. **Owner(s):** Richner Publications, Inc., 379 Central Ave., Lawrence, NY 11559. TEL 516-569-4000; FAX 516-569-4942; Ed. Greg Slater; Pub. Clifford Richner; adv.; photos bk.rev.; pub. size: broadsheet; circ. 5,500(paid).

LOWVILLE

US

JOURNAL & REPUBLICAN. 1830. Wed. $.75 newsstand; $29/yr. in state; $35/yr. out of state. 7556 State St., Lowville, NY 13367. TEL 315-376-3525; FAX 315-376-4136. **Owner(s):** Lowville Newspapers Corp./Johnson Newspaper Corp., 7556 State St., Lowville, NY 13367. TEL 315-376-3525; FAX 315-376-4136; Ed. Gordon H. Allen; Pub. Pamala J. Spry adv. contact: Bonnie Franklin. pub. size: broadsheet; circ. 6,273(paid).

LYONS

US ISSN 1064-7619

WAYNE COUNTY STAR. 1821. s-w. Wed. & Sat. $.50 newsstand; $27/yr. in cy.; $38/yr. out of cy. 36 B Canal St., Lyons, NY 14489-0430. TEL 315-946-9701; FAX 315-946-4382. **Owner(s):** Wayuga Community Newspapers, Inc., Main St., Red Creek, NY 13143-0031. TEL 315-754-6229; FAX 315-754-6431; Ed. Mary K. Henderberg; Pub. Christopher M. Palermo; adv.; photos; pub. size: tabloid; circ. 4,700(free & paid). **Wire Service(s):** Newsfinder.
 Formerly: Lyons Wayne County Star.

MAHOPAC

US

BEACON LIGHT. Wed. $.20 newsstand; $10/yr. in cy.; $20/yr. out of cy. 83 E. Lake Blvd., Mahopac, NY 10541. TEL 914-628-8400. **Owner(s):** Gateway Papers, Inc., P.O. Drawer H, Mahopac, NY 10541. TEL 914-628-8400; Ed. Karen Placek; Pub. Don Hall; adv. contact: Don Hall. pub. size: tabloid; circ. 2,700(paid).

US

BREWSTER TIMES. Wed. $.20 newsstand; $10/yr. in cy.; $20/yr. out of cy. 83 E. Lake Blvd., Mahopac, NY 10541. TEL 914-628-8400. **Owner(s):** Gateway Papers, Inc., P.O. Drawer H, Mahopac, NY 10541. TEL 914-628-8400; Ed. Karen Placek Pub. Don Hall; adv. contact: Don Hall. pub. size: tabloid; circ. 8,200(paid).

US

CARMEL TIMES. Wed. $.20 newsstand; $10/yr. in cy.; $20/yr. out of cy. 83 E. Lake Blvd., Mahopac, NY 10541. TEL 914-628-8400; FAX 914-628-8400. **Owner(s):** Gateway Papers, Inc., P.O. Drawer H, Mahopac, NY 10541. TEL 914-628-8400; Ed. Karen Placek. Pub. Don Hall; adv. contact: Don Hall. pub. size: tabloid; circ. 11,800(paid).

US

EAST FISHKILL RECORD. 1858. Wed. $.20 newsstand; $10/yr. in cy.; $20/yr. out of cy. 83 E. Lake Blvd., Mahopac, NY 10541. TEL 914-628-8400. **Owner(s):** Gateway Papers, Inc., P.O. Drawer H, Mahopac, NY 10541. TEL 914-628-8400; Ed. Karen Placek Pub. Don Hall; adv. contact: Don Hall. pub. size: tabloid; circ. 3,100(paid).

US

FISHKILL STANDARD. Wed. $.20 newsstand; $10/yr. in cy.; $20/yr. out of cy. 83 E. Lake Blvd., Mahopac, NY 10541. TEL 914-628-8400. **Owner(s):** Gateway Papers, Inc., P.O. Drawer H, Mahopac, NY 10541. TEL 914-628-8400; Ed. Karen Placek; Pub. Don Hall; adv. contact: Don Hall. pub. size: tabloid; circ. 6,200(paid).

US

LA GRANGE INDEPENDENT. Wed. $.10 newsstand; $5/yr. in cy.; $20/yr. out of cy. 83 E. Lake Blvd., Mahopac, NY 10541. TEL 914-628-8400. **Owner(s):** Gateway Papers, Inc., P.O. Drawer H, Mahopac, NY 10541. TEL 914-628-8400; Ed. Karen Placek; Pub. Don Hall; adv. contact: Don Hall. pub. size: tabloid; circ. 2,600(paid).

US

MAHOPAC PRESS. Wed. $.20 newsstand; $10/yr. in cy.; $20/yr. out of cy. 83 E. Lake Blvd., Mahopac, NY 10541. TEL 914-628-8400; FAX 914-628-8400. **Owner(s):** Gateway Papers, Inc., P.O. Drawer H, Mahopac, NY 10541. TEL 914-628-8400; Ed. Karen Placek; Pub. Don Hall; adv. contact: Don Hall. pub. size: tabloid; circ. 3,200(paid).

MARATHON

US
CORTLAND DEMOCRAT. 1864. Sun. $.50 newsstand; $20/yr. in state; $21/yr. out of state. P.O. Box 878, Marathon, NY 13803-0878. TEL 607-849-4555; FAX 607-849-4654. **Owner(s):** Lakeside Printing, Inc., P.O. Box 150, 819 W. Genesee St., Skaneateles, NY 13152. TEL 315-685-8904; Ed. Sharon Fox. adv. contact: David Chubb. pub. size: tabloid; circ. 1,250(paid).

MASPETH

US
▼**FOREST HILLS/REGO PARK TIMES.** 1995. Thu. $.35 newsstand; $12/yr. 5551 69th St., Maspeth, NY 11378. TEL 718-639-7000; FAX 718-429-1234. **Owner(s):** Walter H. Sanchez, II, 5551 69th St., Maspeth, NY 11378. TEL 718-639-7000; FAX 718-429-1234; Ed. Alice Wenz; Pub. Walter H. Sanchez, II; adv.; pub. size: tabloid; circ. 8,000(paid).

US
GLENDALE REGISTER. 1847. Thu. $12/yr. in area; $16/yr. out of area. 5551 69th St., Maspeth, NY 11378. TEL 718-639-7000; FAX 718-429-1234. **Owner(s):** Walter H. Sanchez, II, 5551 69th St., Maspeth, NY 11378. TEL 718-639-7000; FAX 718-429-1234; Ed. Alice Wenz; Pub. Walter H. Sanchez, II; pub. size: tabloid; circ. 10,000(paid).

US
▼**HOWARD BEACH RESIDENT.** 1996. Thu. $.35 newsstand; $12/yr. 5551 69th St., Maspeth, NY 11378. TEL 718-639-7000; FAX 718-429-1234. **Owner(s):** Walter H. Sanchez, II, 5551 69th St., Maspeth, NY 11378. TEL 718-639-7000; FAX 718-429-1234; Ed. Alice Wenz; Pub. Walter H. Sanchez, II; adv.; pub. size: tabloid.

US
JACKSON HEIGHTS NEWS. Thu. $.35 newsstand; $12/yr. 5551 69th St., Maspeth, NY 11378. TEL 718-639-7000; FAX 718-429-1234. **Owner(s):** Walter H. Sanchez, II, 5551 69th St., Maspeth, NY 11378. TEL 718-639-7000; FAX 718-429-1234; Ed. Alice Wenz; Pub. Walter H. Sanchez, II; adv.; pub. size: tabloid; circ. 25,000(paid).

US
LEADER OBSERVER. 1909. Thu. $.35 newsstand; $12/1 yr. in cy. 5551 69th St., Maspeth, NY 11378. TEL 718-639-7000; FAX 718-429-1234. **Owner(s):** Walter H. Sanchez, II, 5551 69th St., Maspeth, NY 11378. TEL 718-639-7000; FAX 718-429-1234; Ed. Alice Wenz; Pub. Walter H. Sanchez, II; adv.; pub. size: tabloid; circ. 7,000(paid).

US
LONG ISLAND CITY/ASTORIA JOURNAL. 1838. Thu. $.35 newsstand; $12/yr. in cy.; $16/yr. out of cy. 5551 69th St., Maspeth, NY 11378. TEL 718-639-7000; FAX 718-429-1234. **Owner(s):** Walter H. Sanchez, II, 5551 69th St., Maspeth, NY 11378. TEL 718-639-7000; FAX 718-429-1234; Ed. Alice Wenz; Pub. Walter H. Sanchez, II; adv.; pub. size: tabloid; circ. 32,000(paid).
Formerly: Long Island City Journal.

US
QUEENS LEDGER. 1873. Thu. $.35 newsstand; $12/yr. in cy.; $16/yr. out of cy. 5551 69th St., Maspeth, NY 11378. TEL 718-639-7000; FAX 718-429-1234. **Owner(s):** Walter H. Sanchez, II, 5551 69th St., Maspeth, NY 11378. TEL 718-639-7000; FAX 718-429-1234; Ed. Alice Wenz; Pub. Walter H. Sanchez, II; adv.; pub. size: tabloid; circ. 10,000(paid).

MASSAPEQUA PARK

US
MASSAPEQUA POST. 1954. Wed. $.35 newsstand; $15/yr. 1045B Park Blvd., Massapequa Park, NY 11762. TEL 516-798-5100; FAX 516-798-5296; E-mail: recpost@aol.com. **Owner(s):** ACJ Communications, 197 Broadway, Amityville, NY 11701. TEL 516-264-0077; FAX 516-264-5310; Ed. Mary Capone; Pub. Carolyn James; adv.; photos; pub. size: tabloid; circ. 8,000(paid).

MASSENA

US
FREE TRADER. 1981. Thu. free. W. Hatfield St., Massena, NY 13662. TEL 315-769-7149; FAX 315-764-7440. **Owner(s):** Bob Noreault, W. Hatfield St., Massena, NY 13662. TEL 315-769-7149; Ed. Bob Noreault; Pub. Bob Noreault; adv.; pub. size: tabloid; circ. 14,000(controlled).

MATTITUCK

US
NEWS-REVIEW, THE. 1950. Thu. $1 newsstand; $35/yr. in cy.; $44/yr. out of cy. 7785 Main Rd., Mattituck, NY 11952. TEL 516-298-3200; FAX 516-298-3287. **Owner(s):** Times/Review Newspapers, P.O. Box 1500, Mattituck, NY 11952. TEL 516-298-3200; Ed. Ruth Jernick; Pub. Troy Gustavson; pub. size: tabloid; circ. 5,000(paid).

US
SUFFOLK TIMES. 1857. Thu. $1 newsstand; $35/yr. in cy.; $44/yr. out of cy. 7785 Main Rd., Mattituck, NY 11952. TEL 516-298-3200; FAX 516-298-3287; E-mail: stnrnews@aol.com. **Owner(s):** Times/Review Newspapers, P.O. Box 1500, Mattituck, NY 11952. TEL 516-298-3200; Pub. Troy Gustavson; adv.; photos; bk.rev.; pub. size: tabloid; circ. 10,450(free & paid).

MERRICK

US
MERRICK LIFE. 1938. Thu. $.40 newsstand; $17/yr. 1840 Merrick Ave., Merrick, NY 11566. TEL 516-378-5320; FAX 516-378-0287. **Owner(s):** L & M Publications, Inc., 1840 Merrick Ave., Merrick, NY 11566. TEL 516-378-5320; Ed. Paul Laursen; Pub. Linda Toscano; adv. contact: Lois Roos. pub. size: tabloid; circ. 6,268(free & paid).

MEXICO

US
CITIZEN OUTLET. Wed. $.50 newsstand; $10/yr. N. Jefferson St., Mexico, NY 13114. TEL 315-963-7813; FAX 315-963-4087. **Owner(s):** Mark Backus, P.O. Box 129, Mexico, NY 13114. TEL 315-963-7813; Pub. Mark Backus; pub. size: tabloid; circ. 16,000(paid).

US
INDEPENDENT MIRROR. 1861. Wed. $10/yr. P.O. Box 129, Mexico, NY 13114. TEL 315-963-7813. **Owner(s):** Mark Backus, P.O. Box 129, Mexico, NY 13114. TEL 315-963-7813; FAX 315-963-4087; Ed. Rose Ann Parsons. pub. size: tabloid; circ. 3,100(paid).

MILLBROOK

US
MILLBROOK ROUND TABLE. 1888. Thu. $.60 newsstand; $29/yr. Front St. & Merritt Ave., Millbrook, NY 12545. TEL 914-677-8241; FAX 914-677-6337. **Owner(s):** Taconic Media, Inc., P.O. Box 316, Millbrook, NY 12545. TEL 914-677-8241; Ed. Diane Zucker; Pub. Helen Meserve; adv. contact: Marty Sweeney. pub. size: broadsheet; circ. 2,500(paid).

US
VOICE LEDGER, THE. 1969. Thu. $.60 newsstand; $29/yr. Front St., Millbrook, NY 12545. TEL 914-677-8241; FAX 914-677-6337. **Owner(s):** Taconic Media, Inc., P.O. Box 316, Millbrook, NY 12545. TEL 914-677-8241; Ed. Dan Barton; Pub. Hamilton Meserve; adv. contact: Marty Sweeney. photos; bk.rev.; pub. size: broadsheet; circ. 2,500(paid).
Formerly: Pleasant Valley Voice.

MILLERTON

US
MILLERTON NEWS, THE. 1934. Thu. $27.50/yr. in cy.; $35/yr. in NY, CT, MA; $43.50/yr. elsewhere. Main St., Millerton, NY 12546. TEL 518-789-4401; FAX 518-789-9247; E-mail: mnews@aol.com. **Owner(s):** Lakeville Journal Co., LLC, 33 Bissell St., P.O. Box 353, Lakeville, CT 06039. TEL 860-435-9873; Ed. Kathryn Boughton; Pub. A. Whitney Ellsworth; adv. contact: Anna Mae Kupferer. photos; bk.rev.; pub. size: broadsheet; circ. 6,400(paid).

MINEOLA

US
BALDWIN CITIZEN. 1925. Thu. $.35 newsstand; $15/yr.; $19/2 yrs. 216 E. Second St., Mineola, NY 11501. TEL 516-739-6400; FAX 516-739-5404. **Owner(s):** Nassau Community Newspaper Group, Inc., 216 E. Second St., Mineola, NY 11501. TEL 516-739-6400; FAX 516-739-5404; Ed. Michelle Gothels; Pub. Barry Manning; pub. size: tabloid; circ. 5,500(paid).

US ISSN 0746-2093
EAST ROCKAWAY OBSERVER. 1967. Thu. $.40 newsstand; $15/yr. 216 E. Second St., Mineola, NY 11501. TEL 516-739-6400; FAX 516-739-5404. **Owner(s):** Nassau Community Newspaper Group, Inc., 216 E. Second St., Mineola, NY 11501. TEL 516-739-6400; Ed. Patricia Horwell; Pub. Barry Manning; adv. contact: Rhonda Glickman. pub. size: tabloid; circ. 4,500(paid).
Formerly: East Rockaway/Lynbrook Observer.

US
FARMINGDALE OBSERVER. 1962. Thu. $.75 newsstand; $18/yr. in state; $28/yr. out of state. 132 E. Second St., Mineola, NY 11501. TEL 516-747-8282; FAX 516-742-5867. **Owner(s):** Anton Publications, 132 E. Second St., Mineola, NY 11501. TEL 516-747-8287; Ed. Christine Leonard; Pub. Karl V. Anton; adv. contact: Harriett Heffernan. photos; bk.rev.; pub. size: tabloid; circ. 3,471(paid).

GLEN COVE RECORD PILOT

GLEN COVE RECORD PILOT. 1875. Thu. $.75 newsstand; $21/yr.; $31/yr. out of state. 132 E. Second St., Mineola, NY 11501. TEL 516-747-8282; FAX 516-742-5867. **Owner(s):** Anton Publications, 135 Liberty St., Mineola, NY 11501. TEL 516-747-8282; Ed. Dan McCue; Pub. Karl V. Anton, Jr.; pub. size: tabloid; circ. 7,735(paid).

GREAT NECK RECORD. Thu. $.75 newsstand; $21/yr.; $31 out of state. 132 E. Second St., Mineola, NY 11501. TEL 516-747-8282; FAX 516-742-5867. **Owner(s):** Anton Publications, 132 E. Second St., Mineola, NY 11501. TEL 516-747-8282; Ed. Dan McCue; Pub. Karl V. Anton, Jr.; adv. contact: Maggie Polk. pub. size: tabloid; circ. 6,734(paid).

HICKSVILLE ILLUSTRATED NEWS. Thu. $.75 newsstand; $28/yr. out of state. 132 E. Second St., Mineola, NY 11501. TEL 516-747-8282. **Owner(s):** Anton Publications, 132 E. Second St., Mineola, NY 11501; Ed. Tricia Clark; Pub. Karl V. Anton, Jr.; pub. size: tabloid; circ. 5,500(paid).
Formerly: Hicksville Mid-Island Herald.

LEVITTOWN TRIBUNE. 1947. Fri. $.75 newsstand; $18/yr. in state; $28/yr. out of state. 132 E. Second St., Mineola, NY 11501. TEL 516-747-8282. **Owner(s):** Anton Publications, 132 E. Second St., Mineola, NY 11501. TEL 516-747-8282; FAX 516-742-5867; Ed. Peter Modia; Pub. Karl V. Anton, Jr.; adv. contact: Harriet Heffernan. bk.rev.; pub. size: tabloid; circ. 4,900(paid).

LYNBROOK USA. Wed. $.35 newsstand; $15/yr.; $23/2 yrs. 216 E. Second St., Mineola, NY 11501. TEL 516-739-6400; FAX 516-739-5404. **Owner(s):** News Communications, Inc., 174-15 Hoarce Harding Expy., Fresh Meadows, NY 11365. TEL 718-357-3380; Pub. Barry Manning; pub. size: tabloid; circ. 10,000(paid).

MALVERNE TIMES. Wed. $.35 newsstand; $15/yr.; $23/2 yrs. 216 E. Second St., Mineola, NY 11501. TEL 516-739-6400; FAX 516-739-5404. **Owner(s):** News Communications, Inc., 174-15 Hoarce Harding Expy., Fresh Meadows, NY 11365. TEL 718-357-3380; Ed. Jo-An Denoy; Pub. Barry Manning; pub. size: tabloid; circ. 10,000(paid).

MANHASSET PRESS. 1958. Thu. $.75 newsstand; $21/yr.; $31/yr. out of state. 132 E. Second St., Mineola, NY 11501. TEL 516-747-8282; FAX 516-742-5867. **Owner(s):** Anton Publications, 132 E. Second St., Mineola, NY 11501. TEL 516-747-8282; Ed. Dan McCue. pub. size: tabloid; circ. 4,700(paid).

MASSAPEQUAN OBSERVER. 1957. Thu. $.75 newsstand; $18/yr.; $28 out of state. 132 E. 2nd. St., Mineola, NY 11501. TEL 516-747-8282; FAX 516-742-5867. **Owner(s):** Anton Publications, 132 E. 2nd. St., Mineola, NY 11501. TEL 516-747-8282; Ed. Caroline Smith; Pub. Karl Anton, Jr.; adv. contact: Christopher Westman. pub. size: tabloid; circ. 3,023(paid).

MINEOLA AMERICAN. 1952. Wed. $12/yr. local; $22/yr. out of area. 135 Liberty Ave., Mineola, NY 11501. TEL 516-747-8282. **Owner(s):** Anton Publications, 135 Liberty Ave, Mineola, NY 11501. TEL 516-747-8282; Ed. Maggie Whitely; Pub. Louis C. Sanders; pub. size: tabloid; circ. 3,975(paid).

OCEANSIDE CENTRE BEACON. 1935. Thu. $.35 newsstand; $15/yr. 216 E. Second St., Mineola, NY 11501. TEL 516-739-6400; FAX 516-739-5404. **Owner(s):** Nassau Community Newspaper Group., Inc., 100 E. Second St., Mineola, NY 11501. TEL 516-739-6400; Ed. Pat Horwell; Pub. Barry Manning; pub. size: tabloid; circ. 6,500(paid).
Formerly: Oceanside-Rockville Centre Beacon.

OYSTER BAY ENTERPRISE PILOT. 1885. Thu. $.75 newsstand; $21/yr. 132 E. Second Ave., Mineola, NY 11501. TEL 516-747-8282; FAX 516-742-5867. **Owner(s):** Anton Publications, 132 E. Second St., Mineola, NY 11501. TEL 516-747-8282; Ed. Dagmar Fors Karppi; Pub. Karl V. Anton; pub. size: tabloid; circ. 2,200(paid).

ROCKVILLE CENTRE LONG ISLAND NEWS & OWL. 1908. Wed. $15/yr. 216 E. Second St., Mineola, NY 11501. TEL 516-739-6400; FAX 516-739-5404. **Owner(s):** Long Island News Group, 216 E. Second Ave., Mineola, NY 11501. TEL 516-739-6400; Ed. Helen Shrimpton. pub. size: tabloid; circ. 3,900(paid).

SYOSSET JERICHO TRIBUNE. Fri. $.75/newsstand; $18/yr. in area; $18/yr. sr. citizen; $31/2 yrs. 132 E. Second St., Mineola, NY 11501. TEL 516-747-8282; FAX 516-742-5867. **Owner(s):** Anton Publications, 135 Liberty Ave., Mineola, NY 11501. TEL 516-747-8282; Ed. Kathy Gerber; Pub. Carl V. Anton, Jr.; adv. contact: Harriet Heffernan. pub. size: tabloid; circ. 5,800(paid).
Formerly: Syosset Tribune.

THREE VILLAGE TIMES. 1948. Fri. $12/yr.; $21.25/2 yrs.; $30/3 yrs. 132 E. Second St., Mineola, NY 11501. TEL 516-747-8282; FAX 516-742-5367. **Owner(s):** Anton Publications, 132 E. Second St., Mineola, NY 11501. TEL 516-747-8282; Ed. Danny McCue; Pub. Karl V. Anton, Jr.; adv. contact: Harriet Heffernan. pub. size: tabloid; circ. 1,563(paid).

VALLEY STREAM MAILEADER. 1923. Wed. $.35 newsstand; $15/yr. 216 E. Second St., Mineola, NY 11501. TEL 516-739-6400; FAX 516-739-5404. **Owner(s):** Nassau Community Newspapers, P.O. Box 159, Valley Stream, NY 11582. TEL 516-825-0155; Ed. Patricia Horwell; Pub. Barry Manning; adv.; photos; pub. size: tabloid; circ. 8,800(paid).

WESTBURY TIMES. 1964. Thu. $18/yr. in state; $23/yr. out of state. 132 E. Second St., Mineola, NY 11501. TEL 516-747-8282; FAX 516-742-5287. **Owner(s):** Anton Publications, 132 E. Second St., Mineola, NY 11501. TEL 516-747-8282; Ed. Danny McCue. adv. contact: Harriet Heffernan. pub. size: tabloid; circ. 3,575(paid).

MONROE

PHOTO NEWS. 1967. Wed. $.50 newsstand; $21/yr in cy.; $25/yr. out of cy. 45 Gilbert St., Monroe, NY 10950. TEL 914-782-4000; FAX 914-782-1711. **Owner(s):** Straus Communications, P.O. Box 190, Warwick, NY 10990. TEL 914-986-2061; Ed. Stan Martin; Pub. Stan Martin; pub. size: tabloid; circ. 4,900(paid).
Formerly: Monroe-Woodbury Photo News.

MORAVIA

JOURNAL COURIER. Wed. $.45 newsstand; $12/yr. in cy.; $16/yr. out of cy. 6 Central St., Moravia, NY 13118. TEL 315-497-1551; FAX 315-497-1551. **Owner(s):** Community Newspapers, 6 Central St., Moravia, NY 13118. TEL 315-497-1551; Ed. Bernard McGuerty, III; Pub. Bernard McGuerty, III; adv.; photos; pub. size tabloid; circ. 2,500(paid).

MORAVIA REPUBLICAN REGISTER. 1863. Wed. $16/yr. in cy.; $20/yr. out of cy. 6 Central St., Moravia, NY 13118. TEL 315-497-1551. **Owner(s):** Community Newspapers, 6 Central St., Moravia, NY 13118. TEL 315-497-1551; Ed. Bernard McGuerty, III. adv.; photos; pub. size: tabloid; circ. 2,500(paid).

SOUTHERN CAYUGA TRIBUNE. Wed. $.45 newsstand; $16/yr. in cy.; $20/yr. out of cy. 6 Central St., Moravia, NY 13118. TEL 315-497-1551; FAX 315-497-1551. **Owner(s):** Community Newspapers, 6 Central St., P.O. Box 591, Moravia, NY 13118. TEL 315-497-1551; Ed. Bernard McGuerty, III; Pub. Bernard McGuerty, II; photos; pub. size: tabloid; circ. 2,500(paid).

NAPLES

NAPLES RECORD, THE. 1870. Wed. $.50 newsstand; $24/yr. in state; $30/yr. out of state. 23 Mill St., Naples, NY 14512. TEL 716-374-5260. **Owner(s):** Naples Record, P.O. Box 370, Naples, NY 14512. TEL 716-374-5260; Ed. Mike Fowler; Pub. Mike Fowler; adv.; photos; bk.rev.; pub. size: tabloid; circ. 1,350(paid).

NARROWSBURG

RIVER REPORTER, THE. 1975. Thu. $.60 newsstand; $22/yr. 8 Main St., Narrowsburg, NY 12764. TEL 914-252-7414; FAX 914-252-3298; E-mail: riverrep@zelacom.com. **Owner(s):** Suart Communications, Inc., P.O. Box 20, Narrowsburg, NY 12764. TEL 914-252-7414; FAX 914-252-3298; Ed. Pam Chergotis. adv.; photos; bk.rev.; pub. size: tabloid; circ. 3,700(paid).

NEWARK

COURIER GAZETTE. 1846. Fri. $.50 newsstand; $19/yr. in cy.; $26/yr. out of cy. 613 S. Main St., Newark, NY 14513. TEL 315-331-1000; FAX 315-331-1053. **Owner(s):** Ad Group, Inc., 613 S. Main St., Newark, NY 14513. TEL 315-331-6956; Ed. Sandra Marcaro; Pub. John H. VanDusen; pub. size: broadsheet; circ. 4,000(paid).

NEW ROCHELLE

US
TOMORROW. 1983. m. $10/yr. 459 Main St., Ste. 204, New Rochelle, NY 10801. TEL 914-636-4646. **Owner(s):** Marketing Tomorrow, Inc., 459 Main St., New Rochelle, NY 10801. TEL 914-636-4646; Ed. Glenda Palmer; Pub. Philip Wanderman; pub. size: oversize; circ. 47,000(paid).

NEW YORK

US
CHELSEA CLINTON NEWS. 1939. Thu. $.50 newsstand; $24/yr. 242 W. 30th St., 5th Fl., New York, NY 10001. TEL 212-268-3087; FAX 212-268-2935. **Owner(s):** News Communications, Inc., 242 W. 30th St., 5th Fl., New York, NY 10001. TEL 212-268-3087; FAX 212-268-2935; Ed. Larry O'Connor. pub. size: tabloid; circ. 12,000(paid).

US
DOWNTOWN EXPRESS. 1986. bi-w.: Tue. free. 80 Eighth Ave., Ste. 312, New York, NY 10011. TEL 212-242-6162. **Owner(s):** Clean Slate Corp., 80 Eighth Ave., Ste. 312, New York, NY 10011. TEL 212-242-6162; Ed. Thomas Butson. adv. contact: Loren Granville. photos; pub. size: tabloid; circ. 15,000(free).

US
NEW YORK BEACON. 1976. Thu. $.60 newsstand; $32/yr. 15 E. 40th St., Ste. 402, New York, NY 10016. TEL 212-213-8585; FAX 212-213-6291. **Owner(s):** Walter Smith, 15 E. 40th St., Ste. 402, New York, NY 10016. TEL 212-213-8585; Ed. Walter Smith; Pub. Walter Smith; adv. contact: Miatta Haj. photos; bk.rev.; pub. size: tabloid; circ. 63,750(paid). **Wire Service(s):** AP.

US
NEW YORK OBSERVER. 1987. Wed. $1 newsstand; $22/yr. mailed. 54 E. 64th St., New York, NY 10021. TEL 212-755-2400; FAX 212-688-4889; E-mail: editorial@observer.con. **Owner(s):** Arthur Carter, 54 E. 64th St., New York, NY 10021. TEL 212-755-2400; FAX 212-688-4889; Ed. Peter Kaplan; Pub. Arthur Carter; pub. size: broadsheet; circ. 51,000(paid).

US
NEW YORK PRESS. 1988. Tue. free; $25/yr. mailed. 295 Lafayette St., 9th Fl., New York, NY 10012-3920. TEL 212-941-1130; FAX 212-941-7824. **Owner(s):** New York Press, Inc., 295 Lafayette St., 9th Fl., New York, NY 10012-3920. TEL 212-941-1130; FAX 212-941-7824; Ed. Russ Smith; Pub. Ron Mann; adv. contact: J.P. Weiner. pub. size: tabloid; circ. 100,000(controlled & free).

US   ISSN 0473-5900
OUR TOWN. 1970. Wed. free newsstand; $60/yr. mailed. 242 W. 30th St., 5th Fl., New York, NY 10001. TEL 212-268-8600; FAX 212-268-0614. **Owner(s):** News Communications, Inc., 363 Seventh Ave., New York, NY 10001. TEL 212-268-8600; FAX 212-268-0614; Ed. Doug Simpson; Pub. Tom Allon; pub. size: tabloid; circ. 118,000(free).

US   ISSN 1076-0091
PEOPLE'S WEEKLY WORLD. 1967. Thu. $.50 newsstand; $20/yr. 235 W. 23rd St., New York, NY 10011. TEL 212-924-2523; FAX 212-645-5436. **Owner(s):** Long View Publishing Co. Inc., 239 W. 23rd St., New York, NY 10011. TEL 212-924-2523; Ed. Carolyn Rummel. adv.; pub. size: tabloid; circ. 60,000(paid). **Wire Service(s):** UPI, TASS.
   Formerly: People's Daily World.

US
▼**RESIDENT COMMUNITY NEWS.** 1996. m. 215 Lexington Ave., 13th Fl., New York, NY 10016. TEL 212-679-4970. **Owner(s):** Resident Publications; Pub. Pat Stevenson;

US   ISSN 0042-6202
VILLAGER, THE. 1933. Wed. $.50 newsstand; $21/yr. 80 Eighth Ave., Ste. 312, New York, NY 10011. TEL 212-229-1890; FAX 212-229-2790. **Owner(s):** Clean Slate Corp., 80 Eighth Ave., New York, NY 10011. TEL 212-229-1890; Ed. Thomas Butson; Pub. Elizabeth Butson; adv.; photos; pub. size: tabloid; circ. 20,000(paid).

US   ISSN 0042-6180
VILLAGE VOICE, THE. 1955. Wed. free in Manhattan; $1.25 newsstand; $47.95/yr. 36 Cooper Sq., New York, NY 10003. TEL 212-475-3300; FAX 212-475-8944. **Owner(s):** Leonard Stern, 36 Cooper Sq., New York, NY 10003. TEL 212-475-3300; Ed. Karen Durbin. adv.; photos; bk.rev.; pub. size: tabloid; circ. 156,272(paid). **Wire Service(s):** AP.

US
WESTSIDER, THE. 1973. Thu. $22/yr. 242 W. 30th St., 5th Fl., New York, NY 10001. TEL 212-268-3087; FAX 212-268-2935. **Owner(s):** News Communications, Inc., 242 W. 30th St., 5th Fl., New York, NY 10001. TEL 212-268-3087; Ed. Larry O'Connor. pub. size: tabloid; circ. 15,000(paid).

NORTHPORT

US
OBSERVER, THE. 1922. Thu. $.75 newsstand; $20/yr. 160 Main St., Northport, NY 11768. TEL 516-261-6124; FAX 516-265-6237. **Owner(s):** North Shore News Group, P.O. Box 805, Smithtown, NY 11787. TEL 516-265-2100; Ed. David Ambro; Pub. Bernard Paley; adv. contact: Jennifer Paley. pub. size: tabloid; circ. 10,000(paid).

NORTH SYRACUSE

US
STAR-NEWS, THE. 1924. Wed. $.75 newsstand; $25/yr. 428 S. Main St., North Syracuse, NY 13212. TEL 315-458-4406; FAX 315-458-4407. **Owner(s):** Eagle Newspapers, Inc., P.O. Box 270, Baldwinsville, NY 13027. TEL 315-635-3921; FAX 315-635-3914; Ed. Maria Forastiero. adv. contact: John Mott. photos; pub. size: broadsheet; circ. 7,200(paid).

NORTH TONAWANDA

US
RECORD-ADVERTISER. 1914. Wed. free. 435 River Rd., North Tonawanda, NY 14120. TEL 716-693-1000; FAX 716-693-8573. **Owner(s):** Tonawanda News, 435 River Rd., North Tonawanda, NY. TEL 716-693-1000; Ed. Terry Shaw; Pub. Joseph P. Armenia; pub. size: broadsheet; circ. 33,000(free). **Wire Service(s):** AP.

ORCHARD PARK

US
SOUTHTOWNS CITIZEN. 1932. Sat. $.60 newsstand; $25/yr. 6519 E. Quaker St., Orchard Park, NY 14127. TEL 716-662-0001; FAX 716-667-3002. **Owner(s):** Coleman Communications Corp., 6519 E. Quaker St., Orchard Park, NY 14127. TEL 716-662-0001; Ed. Christopher Coleman; Pub. Christopher Coleman; adv. contact: Steve Frick. pub. size: tabloid; circ. 5,000(paid).

OWEGO

US
TIOGA COUNTY GAZETTE & TIMES. 1800. Thu. $.50 newsstand; $18/yr. in cy.; $22 out of cy. 181-183 Front St., Owego, NY 13827. TEL 607-687-2434; FAX 607-687-2931. **Owner(s):** Owego Pennysaver Press, P.O. Box 149, Owego, NY 13827. TEL 607-687-2434; Ed. Kim Depew. pub. size: standard; circ. 1,500(paid).

OYSTER BAY

US
OYSTER BAY-SYOSSET GUARDIAN. 1899. Fri. $.50 newsstand; $20/yr. 102 Audrey Ave., Oyster Bay, NY 11771. TEL 516-922-4215; FAX 516-922-4227. **Owner(s):** Oyster Bay Publishing Co., Inc., P.O. Box 28, Oyster Bay, NY 11771. TEL 516-922-4215; Ed. Gloria O'Rourke. adv. contact: Lucy Minicozzi. pub. size: broadsheet; circ. 30,000(paid).

OZONE PARK

US
FORUM OF QUEENS. 1977. w. free; $65/yr. 137-05 Cross Bay Blvd., Ozone Park, NY 11417. TEL 718-845-3221; FAX 718-738-7645. **Owner(s):** Queens Herald Corp., 137-05 Cross Bay Blvd., Ozone Park, NY 11417. TEL 718-845-3221; FAX 718-738-7645; Ed. Denis J. Waszak, Jr.; Pub. Thomas J. LaVecchia; adv.; photos; bk.rev.; pub. size: tabloid; circ. 25,000(free & paid).
   Formerly: Forum of South Queens.

PALMYRA

US
COURIER-JOURNAL. 1838. Wed. $.35 newsstand; $14.50/yr. 612 E. Main St., Palmyra, NY 14522. TEL 315-597-6655; FAX 315-597-6947. **Owner(s):** Suburban Circle Publications, Inc., 2808 Dewey Ave., Rochester, NY 14616. TEL 716-663-0068; Ed. Stephen Buchiere; Pub. Lawrence Lucieer; pub. size: tabloid; circ. 2,700(paid).

PATCHOGUE

US

LONG ISLAND ADVANCE. 1871. Thu. $24/yr. 20 Medford Ave., Patchogue, NY 11772. TEL 516-475-1000; FAX 516-475-1565. **Owner(s):** John T. Tuthill, III, P.O. Box 780, Patchogue, NY 11772. TEL 516-475-1000; Ed. Kevin Molloy; Pub. John T. Tuthill, III; pub. size: tabloid; circ. 10,500(paid).

PAWLING

US   ISSN 0747-2188

PAWLING NEWS CHRONICLE. 1870. Thu. $.60 newsstand; $18.65/yr. in cy. 3 Memorial Ave., Pawling, NY 12564. TEL 914-855-1100; FAX 914-855-1106. **Owner(s):** Taconic Media, Inc., P.O. Box 316, Millbrook, NY 12545. TEL 203-354-2261; Pub. Hamilton & John Meserve; adv.; photos; pub. size: tabloid; circ. 2,357(paid).

PEARL RIVER

US

CLARKSTOWN COURIER, THE. 1992. Wed. $.50 newsstand; $100/yr. 25 West Central Ave., Pearl River, NY 10965. TEL 914-732-8200; FAX 914-732-9214. **Owner(s):** Aldrich Family Trust, 25 W. Central Ave., Pearl River, NY 10965. TEL 914-732-8200; FAX 914-732-9214; Sluys Family Trust, 25 W. Central Ave., Pearl River, NY 10965. TEL 914-732-8200; FAX 914-732-9214; Ed. Arthur R. Aldrich; Pub. Arthur R. Aldrich; adv. contact: Judith C. Haber. bk.rev.; pub. size: tabloid; circ. 45,000(free).

US

OUR TOWN. 1973. Wed. free. 25 W. Central Ave., Pearl River, NY 10965. TEL 914-732-8200; FAX 914-732-9214. **Owner(s):** Community Media, Inc., 25 W. Central Ave., Pearl River, NY 10965. TEL 914-732-8200; FAX 914-732-9214; Ed. Arthur R. Aldrich; Pub. Arthur R. Aldrich; adv. contact: Judith C. Haber. bk.rev.; pub. size: tabloid; circ. 22,000(free).

US

ROCKLAND INDEPENDENT, THE. 1992. Wed. $.50 newsstand; $100/yr. 25 West Central Avenue, Pearl River, NY 10965. TEL 914-732-8200; FAX 914-732-9214. **Owner(s):** Aldrich Family Trust, 25 W. Central Ave., Pearl River, NY 10965. TEL 914-732-8200; FAX 914-732-9214; Sluys Family Trust, 25 W. Central Ave., Pearl River, NY 10965. TEL 914-732-8200; FAX 914-732-9214; Ed. Arthur R. Aldrich; Pub. Arthur R. Aldrich; adv. contact: Judith C. Haber. bk.rev.; pub. size: tabloid; circ. 45,000(free).

PEEKSKILL

US

PEEKSKILL HERALD. 1986. w. $30/yr. local; $40/yr. out of area. 927 South St., Peekskill, NY 10566. TEL 914-737-7747. **Owner(s):** Highland Publications, Inc., P.O. Box 2250, Peekskill, NY 10566; Ed. Kathy Daley. pub. size: tabloid; circ. 5,000(paid).

PENN YAN

US

CHRONICLE-EXPRESS. 1824. Wed. $.75 newsstand; $28/yr. 138 Main St., Penn Yan, NY 14527. TEL 315-536-4422. **Owner(s):** Greenhow Newspapers, Inc., 85 Canisteo St., Hornell, NY 14843. TEL 607-324-1425; Ed. Gwen Chamberlin; Pub. Gregg Morris; adv. contact: Gregg Morris. pub. size: broadsheet; circ. 4,550(paid).

PHOENIX

US

PHOENIX REGISTER. 1912. Wed. $.50 newsstand; $10/yr. 71 State St., Phoenix, NY 13135. TEL 315-695-4771; FAX 315-695-4771. **Owner(s):** Oswego County Weeklies, P.O. Box 129, Mexico, NY 13114. TEL 315-963-7813; FAX 315-963-4087; Ed. Kim McGrath. adv. contact: Charles Seaman. pub. size: tabloid; circ. 3,400(paid).

PINE PLAINS

US

PINE PLAINS REGISTER-HERALD. 1859. Thu. $29/yr. Main St., Pine Plains, NY 12567. TEL 518-398-1313; FAX 518-677-6337. **Owner(s):** Taconic Media, Inc., P.O. Box 316, Millbrook, NY 12545. TEL 914-677-8241; Ed. Diane Zucker; Pub. Hamilton W. Meserve; pub. size: broadsheet; circ. 1,850(paid).

PITTSFORD

US

PERINTON-FAIRPORT POST, THE. 1932. Wed. $.75 newsstand; $25/yr. mailed. 4 S. Main St., Pittsford, NY 14534. TEL 716-924-4040; FAX 716-924-7734. **Owner(s):** Wolfe Community News, P.O. Drawer C, Pittsford, NY 14453. TEL 716-924-4040; FAX 716-924-7734; Pub. Andrew D. Wolfe; pub. size: broadsheet; circ. 4,500(paid).

PORT CHESTER

US   ISSN 0680-0660

WESTMORE NEWS. 1964. Thu. $.50 newsstand; $18/yr. 38 Broad St., Port Chester, NY 10573-4197. TEL 914-939-6864. **Owner(s):** Westmore News, Inc., 38 Broad St., Port Chester, NY 10573. TEL 914-939-6864; Ed. Jananne Abel; Pub. Richard Abe; adv.; photos; pub. size: tabloid; circ. 3,000(paid).

PORT JERVIS

US

GAZETTE, THE. 1850. Fri. $.50 newsstand; $18.50/yr. deliv. & mailed. 84-88 Fowler St., Port Jervis, NY 12771. TEL 914-856-5383; FAX 914-858-8484. **Owner(s):** Ottaway Newspapers, Inc., P.O. Box 401, Campbell Hall, NY 10916. TEL 914-294-8181; Ed. Janis Osborne. adv.; photos; pub. size: tabloid; circ. 9,500(paid).
Formerly: Tri-State Gazette.

PORT WASHINGTON

US

PORT WASHINGTON NEWS. 1903. Thu. $.75 newsstand; $21/yr. 270 Main St., Port Washington, NY 11050. TEL 516-767-0035; FAX 516-944-7743. **Owner(s):** Long Island Community Newpapers, P.O. Box 1578, Mineola, NY 11501; Ed. Christina Cronin Southard; Pub. Karl V. Anton; adv. contact: Richard Gaudet. pub. size: tabloid; circ. 6,969(paid).

POTSDAM

US

CLARKSON INTEGRATOR. 1920. Mon. $10/yr. Clarkson Ave., Potsdam, NY 13699. TEL 315-265-9050; FAX 315-268-7661. **Owner(s):** Clarkson Integrator, P.O. Box 8710, Potsdam, NY 13699-8710. TEL 315-265-9050; FAX 315-268-7661; Ed. Wayne Devoid. adv.; photos; bk.rev.; pub. size: tabloid; circ. 6,000(controlled & paid). Wire Service(s): AP.

POUND RIDGE

US

COUNTRY SHOPPER. m. free. P.O. Box 190, Pound Ridge, NY 10576. TEL 914-764-4678; FAX 914-764-4662. **Owner(s):** Country Shopper, P.O. Box 190, Pound Ridge, NY 10576. TEL 914-764-4678; Ed. Lillian Petruccione. pub. size: tabloid; circ. 31,000(free).

PULASKI

US

SALMON RIVER NEWS. 1973. Tue. $.50 newsstand; $10/yr. 7549 Broad St., Pulaski, NY 13142. TEL 315-963-7813; FAX 315-963-7813. **Owner(s):** Oswego County Weeklies, P.O. Box 129, Mexico, NY 13114. TEL 315-963-7813; FAX 315-963-4087; Ed. Roseanne Parsons; Pub. Mark Backus; adv. contact: Charles Seaman. pub. size: tabloid; circ. 8,000(paid).

RAVENA

US

GREENVILLE LOCAL. 1932. Thu. $19/yr. local; $21/yr. out of cy. 164 Main St., Ravena, NY 12143. TEL 518-756-2030; FAX 518-756-8555. **Owner(s):** Bleezarde Publishing, Inc., 314 S. Jefferson, Ravena, NY 12143. TEL 518-756-2030; Pub. Richard G. Bleezarde; pub. size: tabloid; circ. 1,800(paid).

US

RAVENA NEWS HERALD. Thu. $19/yr. 164 Main St., Ravena, NY 12143. TEL 518-756-2030; FAX 518-756-8555. **Owner(s):** Bleezarde Publishing, Inc., 164 Main St., Ravena, NY 12143-0307. TEL 518-756-2030; FAX 518-756-8555; Ed. Stacy Meizels; Pub. Richard G. Bleezarde; adv.; photos; pub. size: tabloid; circ. 5,025(paid); morning 1,800(paid).

RED CREEK

US

POST-HERALD. 1894. Thu. $.45 newsstand; $20/yr. local; $30/yr. out of state. Main St., Red Creek, NY 13143-0199. TEL 315-754-6229; FAX 315-754-6431. **Owner(s):** Angelo G. Palermo, Main St., Red Creek, NY 13143. TEL 315-754-6229; Pub. Christopher Palermo; adv. contact: Charles Palermo. pub. size: tabloid; circ. 3,700(paid). **Wire Service(s):** Empire Information System.

   Formerly: Red Creek Herald, Fair Haven Register, Cato Citizen.

REGO PARK

US

QUEENS CHRONICLE. 1979. Thu. $75/yr. 62-33 Woodhaven Blvd., Rego Park, NY 11374. TEL 718-205-8000; FAX 718-205-0150. **Owner(s):** Susan Merzon, 151-15 84th St., Howard Beach, NY 11414. TEL 718-738-1704; Ed. Stanley Merzon; Pub. Susan Merzon; adv. contact: Mark Weidler. photos; bk.rev.; pub. size: tabloid; circ. 5,500(controlled & free). **Wire Service(s):** CNS.

RHINEBECK

US

GAZETTE-ADVERTISER. 1846. Thu. $.60 newsstand; $29/yr. in state; $35/yr. out of state. 7 Livingston St., Rhinebeck, NY 12572. TEL 914-876-3033; FAX 914-876-3033. **Owner(s):** Taconic Media, Inc., Front St. & Merrit Ave., Millbrook, NY 12545; Ed. John Zych; Pub. Hamilton W. Meserve; adv. contact: Marty Sweeney. pub. size: broadsheet; circ. 4,500(paid).

RIDGEWOOD

US

TIMES NEWSWEEKLY. 1908. Thu. $.30 newsstand; $10/yr. local; $12/yr. out of area. 6658 Fresh Pond Rd., Ridgewood, NY 11385. TEL 718-821-7500; FAX 718-456-0120. **Owner(s):** Ridgewood Times Printing & Publishing Co., P.O. Box C-299, Flushing, NY 11385; Ed. James P. Devlin; Pub. Maureen E. Walthers; adv.; pub. size: tabloid; circ. 23,000(paid).

   Formerly: Ridgewood Times.

ROCHESTER

US

GATES-CHILI NEWS. 1958. Wed. $.35 newsstand; $15/yr.; $29/2 yrs. 2361 Chili Ave., Rochester, NY 14624-3319. TEL 716-247-9200; FAX 716-247-9210. **Owner(s):** Patricia Smith, 2361 Chili Ave., Rochester, NY 14624. TEL 716-247-9200; Ed. Michael Murphy; Pub. Patricia M. Smith; adv.; photos; pub. size: tabloid; circ. 9,800(controlled & paid).

US

GOLDEN TIMES. 1976. s-m.: 1st & 3rd Wed. $15/yr.; $25/2 yrs. 80 Rockwood Pl., Rochester, NY 14610. TEL 716-242-9930; FAX 716-256-2765. **Owner(s):** Carmen J. Viglucci, 80 Rockwood Pl., Rochester, NY 14610; Ed. Carmen J. Viglucci. adv. contact: Ralph Hyman. photos; bk.rev.; pub. size: tabloid; circ. 20,000(free & paid); morning 500.

US

IRONDEQUOIT PRESS. 1932. Thu. $.50 newsstand; $21/yr.; $18/yr. senior citizens. 657 Titus Ave., Rochester, NY 14617. TEL 716-342-9450; FAX 716-342-6146. **Owner(s):** Wolfe Publications, Inc., 666 Phillips Rd., Fishers, NY 14453. TEL 716-924-4040; Ed. Linda Quinlan; Pub. Andrew D. Wolfe, Sr.; pub. size: broadsheet; circ. 7,700(paid).

SAUGERTIES

US

SATURDAY POST-STAR. 1877. Sat. $.75 newsstand; $30/yr.; $35/yr. out of cy. 141 Ulster Ave., Saugerties, NY 12477. TEL 914-246-4985; FAX 914-246-5108. **Owner(s):** American Publishing Co., 606 N. Van Buren, P.O. Box 520, Marion, IL 62959. TEL 618-993-1711; Pub. Paul Scott; circ. 3,000(paid).

US

SAUGERTIES POST STAR. 1877. Sun. $30/yr. in cy.; $35/yr. out of cy. 141 Ulster Ave., Saugerties, NY 12477. TEL 914-246-4985; FAX 914-246-5108. **Owner(s):** American Publishing Co., 606 N. Van Buren, P.O. Box 520, Marion, IL 62959. TEL 618-993-1711; Ed. Donna Gomez. pub. size: tabloid; circ. 2,500(paid).

   Formerly: Sunday Old Dutch Post-Star.

SAYVILLE

US

FIRE ISLAND TIDE. 1976. bi-w. (May-Sep.). $1 newsstand; $10/yr. 49 Main St., Sayville, NY 11782. TEL 516-567-7470. **Owner(s):** Fire Island Tide, Inc., P.O. Box 8, Patchogue, NY 11772. TEL 516-567-7470; Pub. Warren C. McDowell; adv.; photos; bk.rev.; pub. size: tabloid; circ. 15,000(paid).

US

ISLIP BULLETIN. 1946. Thu. $.50 newsstand; $20/yr. P.O. Box 367, Sayville, NY 11782. TEL 516-589-6200; FAX 516-475-1565. **Owner(s):** John-Lor Publications, P.O. Box 780, Patchogue, NY 11772. TEL 516-475-1000; Ed. Hank Shaw; Pub. John T. Tuthill, III; pub. size: tabloid; circ. 10,000(paid).

US

SUFFOLK COUNTY NEWS. 1884. Thu. $.75 newsstand; $24/yr. 23 Candee Ave., Sayville, NY 11782. TEL 516-589-6200; FAX 516-589-3246. **Owner(s):** John-Lor Publications, P.O. Box 780, Patchogue, NY 11772. TEL 516-475-1000; Ed. Hank Shaw; Pub. John Tuthill; adv. contact: John Tuthill. pub. size: tabloid; circ. 10,000(paid).

SCARSDALE

US

SCARSDALE INQUIRER, THE. 1901. Fri. $.75 newsstand; $33/yr. The Harwood Bldg., Ste. 510, Scarsdale, NY 10583. TEL 914-725-2500; FAX 914-725-1552. **Owner(s):** S.I. Communications, Inc., P.O. Box 418, Scarsdale, NY 10583. TEL 914-725-2500; FAX 914-725-1552; Ed. Linda Leavitt; Pub. Deborah White; adv.; photos; pub. size: broadsheet; circ. 7,500(free & paid).

SENECA FALLS

US

REVEILLE/BETWEEN THE LAKES. 1855. Thu. $.50 newsstand; $24.95/yr. 2024 Rte. 5 & 20, Seneca Falls, NY 13148-0557. TEL 315-568-6400; FAX 315-568-4200; E-mail: lakes@vivanet.com. **Owner(s):** Reveille Publishing Co., Inc., 2024 Rte. 5 & 20, Seneca Falls, NY 13148. TEL 315-568-6400; FAX 315-568-4200; Pub. Joe Siccardi; adv.; photos; bk.rev.; pub. size: tabloid; circ. 1,845(paid).

   Formerly: Seneca Falls-Waterloo Reveille.

SETAUKET

US

PORT TIMES-RECORD, THE. 1989. Thu. $.75 newsstand; $23/yr. in cy. 185 Rte. 25A, Setauket, NY 11733. TEL 516-751-7744. **Owner(s):** Leah S. Dunaief, P.O. Box 707, Setauket, NY 11733. TEL 516-751-7744; FAX 516-751-4165; Ed. Denise Alfieri; Pub. Leah S. Dunaief; adv.; photos; bk.rev.; pub. size: tabloid; circ. 7,680(paid).

   Formerly: Port Times.

US

TIMES OF NESCONSET, THE. Thu. $.75 newsstand; $27/yr. 185 Rte. 25A, Setauket, NY 11733. TEL 516-751-7744; FAX 516-751-4165. **Owner(s):** Leah S. Dunaief, P.O. Box 707, Setauket, NY 11733. TEL 516-751-7744; FAX 516-751-4165; Ed. Joan Cipriano; Pub. Leah S. Dunaief; adv.; photos; bk.rev.; pub. size: tabloid; circ. 4,000(paid).

US

TIMES OF SMITHTOWN. 1993. Thu. $.75 newsstand; $23/yr. in cy.; $31/yr. out of cy. 185 Rte. 25A, Setauket, NY 11733. TEL 516-751-7744; FAX 516-751-4165. **Owner(s):** Leah S. Dunaief, P.O. Box 707, Setauket, NY 11733. TEL 516-751-7744; FAX 516-751-4165; Ed. Marie Murtagh; Pub. Leah S. Dunaief; adv.; photos; bk.rev.; pub. size: tabloid; circ. 23,000(paid).

US

TIMES OF ST. JAMES. 1989. Thu. $.75 newsstand; $23/yr. in cy.; $31/yr. out of cy. 185 Rte. 25A, Setauket, NY 11733. TEL 516-751-7744; FAX 516-751-4165. **Owner(s):** Leah S. Dunaief, P.O. Box 707, Setauket, NY 11733. TEL 516-751-7744; FAX 516-751-4165; Ed. Marie Murtagh; Pub. Leah S. Dunaief; adv.; photos; bk.rev.; pub. size: tabloid; circ. 32,000(paid).

US

VILLAGE BEACON-RECORD, THE. 1986. Thu. $.75 newsstand; $22/yr. 185 Rte. 25A, Setauket, NY 11733. TEL 516-331-1154; FAX 516-751-4165. **Owner(s):** Leah S. Dunaief, P.O. Box 707, Setauket, NY 11733. TEL 516-751-7744; FAX 516-751-4165; Ed. Leah S. Dunaief; Pub. Leah S. Dunaief; adv.; photos; bk.rev.; pub. size: tabloid; circ. 35,000(paid).

US   ISSN 0889-8677

VILLAGE TIMES, THE. 1976. Thu. $.75 newsstand; $27/yr. 185 Rte. 25A, Setauket, NY 11733. TEL 516-751-7744; FAX 516-751-4165. **Owner(s):** Leah S. Dunaief, P.O. Box 707, Setauket, NY 11733. TEL 516-751-7744; FAX 516-751-4165; Ed. Leah S. Dunaief; Pub. Leah S. Dunaief; adv.; photos; bk.rev.; pub. size: tabloid; circ. 10,000(paid).

SHELTER ISLAND HEIGHTS

US   ISSN 0746-0668
SHELTER ISLAND REPORTER. 1959. Thu. $.75 newsstand; $20/yr. in cy.; $25/yr. out of cy. 9 Grand Ave., Shelter Island Heights, NY 11965. TEL 516-749-1000; FAX 516-749-0144. **Owner(s):** Gardner Cowles, III, P.O. Box 3020, Shelter Island Heights, NY 11965. TEL 516-749-1000; Ed. Elizabeth A. Bonora; Pub. Gardner Cowles, III; adv. contact: Maria Loconsolo. pub. size: tabloid; circ. 2,800(paid).

SIDNEY

US
TRI-TOWN NEWS. Wed. $.50 newsstand; $19/yr. local; $22/yr. out of area. 5 Winkler Rd., Sidney, NY 13838. TEL 607-563-3526; FAX 607-563-7118. **Owner(s):** Paul Hamilton, Sr. & Ken Paden, P.O. Box 388, Sidney, NY 13838. TEL 607-563-3526; Ed. Nancy Burns. adv. contact: Anna Ritchey. photos; pub. size: standard; circ. 6,000(paid).

SKANEATELES

US   ISSN 1066-1352
MARCELLUS OBSERVER. 1879. Wed. $.75 newsstand; $25/yr. 2 Fennel St., Skaneateles, NY 13152. TEL 315-685-8338; FAX 315-685-8338. **Owner(s):** Eagle Newspapers, Inc., P.O. Box 65, Fayetteville, NY 13066. TEL 315-637-3121; Ed. Helen MacDonald; Pub. Stewart Hancock; adv. contact: Laurie Smart. pub. size: broadsheet; circ. 1,418(paid).

US
SKANEATELES PRESS. 1939. Wed. $.75 newsstand; $21/yr. 2 Fennel St., Skaneateles, NY 13152. TEL 315-685-8338; FAX 315-685-8338. **Owner(s):** Eagle Newspapers, Inc., P.O. Box 65, Fayetteville, NY 13066. TEL 315-637-3121; Ed. Helen MacDonald; Pub. Stewart Hancock; adv. contact: Laurie Smart. pub. size: broadsheet; circ. 4,000(paid).

SMITHTOWN

US
BROOKHAVEN REVIEW. 1888. Thu. $.50 newsstand; $15.50/yr. 127 E. Main St., Smithtown, NY 11787. TEL 516-265-3500; FAX 516-265-3504. **Owner(s):** ESP Publications, P.O. Box 925, Smithtown, NY 11787; Pub. Diane Capuano; adv. contact: Diane Capuano. pub. size: tabloid; circ. 3,000(paid).

US
COMMACK NEWS. 1964. Thu. $.75 newsstand; $20/yr. One Brookside Dr., Smithtown, NY 11787. TEL 516-265-2100; FAX 516-265-6237. **Owner(s):** North Shore News Group, P.O. Box 805, Smithtown, NY 11787. TEL 516-265-2100; Pub. Bernard Paley; adv.; photos; pub. size: tabloid; circ. 4,500(paid).

US
ISLIP NEWS. 1950. Thu. $.75 newsstand; $20/yr. One Brookside Dr., Smithtown, NY 11787. TEL 516-265-2100; FAX 516-265-6237. **Owner(s):** Northshore News Group, P.O. Box 805, Smithtown, NY 11787. TEL 516-265-2100; Ed. Jennifer Paley. adv.; pub. size: tabloid; circ. 3,100(paid).

US
SMITHTOWN MESSENGER. 1887. Thu. $.50 newsstand; $15.50/yr. in cy. 127 E. Main St., Smithtown, NY 11787. TEL 516-265-3500; FAX 516-265-3504. **Owner(s):** Sal Diperi, 127 E. Main St., Smithtown, NY 11787. TEL 516-265-3500; Ed. Terry Gilberti. adv. contact: Phil Sciarillo. photos; pub. size: tabloid; circ. 9,820(paid).

US
SMITHTOWN NEWS THE. 1945. Thu. $.75 newsstand; $20/yr. One Brookside Dr., Smithtown, NY 11787. TEL 516-265-2100; FAX 516-265-6237. **Owner(s):** North Shore News Group, One Brookside Dr., Smithtown, NY 11787. TEL 516-265-2100; Ed. David Ambro. adv.; photos; bk rev.; pub. size: tabloid; circ. 9,650(paid).

SOUTHAMPTON

US   ISSN 0745-6484
SOUTHAMPTON PRESS. 1898. Thu. $.75 newsstand; $28/yr. in cy.; $36/yr. out of cy. 135 Windmill Ln., Southampton, NY 11968. TEL 516-283-4100. **Owner(s):** Southampton Press Publishing Co., Inc., 135 Windmill Ln., Southampton, NY 11968. TEL 516-283-4100; FAX 516-283-4927; Ed. Peter B. Boody; Pub. Donald H. Louchheim adv.; photos; bk.rev.; pub. size: broadsheet; circ. 12,000(controlled & paid).

SOUTHOLD

US
TRAVELER/WATCHMAN. 1824. Thu. $30/yr. in cy.; $38/yr. out of cy. Traveler St., Southold, NY 11971. TEL 516-765-3425; FAX 516-765-1756. **Owner(s):** Emanuel Konto Kosta, Traveler St., Southold, NY 11971. TEL 516-765-3425; FAX 516-756-1756; Ed. Joey MacLellan; Pub. Emanuel Konto Kosta; adv. contact: Pat Lollot. pub. size: broadsheet; circ. 10,000(paid).

SPECULATOR

US
HAMILTON COUNTY NEWS. 1947. Tue. $.50 newsstand; $20/yr. in cy.; $22/yr. out of cy.; $25/yr. out of state. Rte. 8 & 30, Speculator, NY 12164. TEL 518-548-6898; FAX 518-548-5305 **Owner(s):** Wm. J. Kline & Sons, Inc., Rte. 8 & 30, Speculator, NY 12164. TEL 518-548-6898; FAX 518-548-5305; Ed. Cristine Meixner; Pub. Richard Barker; adv. contact: Arthur Simmons. photos; pub. size: tabloid; circ. 3,960(paid).

SPENCERPORT

US
BROCKPORT/HOLLEY SUBURBAN NEWS. 1989. Mon. free; $35/yr. 1835 N. Union St., Spencerport, NY 14559. TEL 716-352-3411; FAX 716-352-4811. **Owner(s):** Keith A. Ryan, 1835 N. Union St., Spencerport, NY 14559. TEL 716-352-3411; FAX 716-352-4811; Pub. Keith A. Ryan; adv.; photos; pub. size: tabloid; circ. 7,355(free & paid).

US
SUBURBAN NEWS. 1953. Mon free; $35/yr. 1835 N. Union St., Spencerport, NY 14559. TEL 716-352-3411; FAX 716-352-4811. **Owner(s):** Keith A. Ryan, P.O. Box 106, Spencerport, NY 14559-0106. TEL 716-352-3411; Ed. Evelyn Dow; Pub. Keith A. Ryan; adv.; photos; pub. size tabloid; circ. 32,000(free & paid).
Formerly: Spencerport Suburban News.

SPRINGVILLE

US
SPRINGVILLE JOURNAL. 1867. Thu. $.75/newsstand; $17.50/yr. in state; $14/yr. senior citizens & military. 35 E. Main St., Springville, NY 14141-0095. TEL 716-592-4550; FAX 716-592-4663. **Owner(s):** H & K Publications, Inc., 50 Buffalo St., Hamburg, NY 14075. TEL 716-649-4413; Ed. David Pierce; Pub. Steve Kluckhohn; adv.; photos; bk.rev.; pub. size: tabloid; circ. 4,368(free & paid).

STATEN ISLAND

US
STATEN ISLAND REGISTER. 1966. Tue. $.50 newsstand; $20/yr. locally. 2100 Clove Rd., Staten Island, NY 10305. TEL 718-447-4700; FAX 718-816-7719. **Owner(s):** Joseph Sclafani & Diane Sclafani, 2100 Clove Rd., Staten Island, NY 10305. TEL 718-447-4700; FAX 718-816-7719; Ed. Diane Sclafani; Pub. Joanne Lent; adv.; photos; pub. size: tabloid; circ. 75,000(paid). **Wire Service(s):** SHNA.

SUNNYSIDE

US
WOODSIDE HERALD. 1935. Fri. $.25 newsstand; $15/yr. 43-11 Greenpoint Ave., Sunnyside, NY 11104. TEL 718-729-3444; FAX 718-718-7294. **Owner(s):** Joseph Sabba, 43-11 Greenpoint Ave., Sunnyside, NY 11104. TEL 718-729-3444; Ed. Douglas Kennedy; Pub. Joseph Sabba; adv. contact: Joseph Sabba. pub. size: tabloid; circ. 14,212(paid).

SYRACUSE

US
NORTH SYRACUSE STAR-NEWS. 1924. Wed. $.75 newsstand; $21/yr. in cy.; $13/yr. students. 428 S. Main St., Syracuse, NY 13212. TEL 315-458-4406; FAX 315-458-4407. **Owner(s):** Eagle Newspapers, Inc. P.O. Box 65, Fayetteville, NY 13066. TEL 315-637-3121; Ed. Todd Fielding; Pub. Stewart Hancock; adv.; photos; pub. size: broadsheet; circ. 5,275(paid).
Formerly: Star News.

US
ONONDAGA VALLEY NEWS. 1956. Mon. free; $.25 newsstand; $15/yr. mailed. 250 Bear St., W., Syracuse, NY 13204. TEL 315-472-7825; FAX 315-478-1434. **Owner(s):** John Badoud, 250 Bear St., W., Syracuse, NY 13221. TEL 315-472-7825; Ed. Ann C. Allen; Pub. A. Loren Colburn; adv.; $6.18/SAU photos; bk.rev.; pub. size: tabloid; circ. 8,785(controlled & free).

US

SCOTSMAN PRESS, THE. 1954. Mon. free; $.30 newsstand; $15/yr. mailed. 450 Bear St., W., Syracuse, NY 13204. TEL 315-472-7825; FAX 315-478-1434. **Owner(s):** John Badoud, 250 Bear St., W., Syracuse, NY 13204. TEL 315-472-7825; FAX 315-478-1434; Ed. A. Allen; Pub. A. Loren Colburn; adv.: $5.09/SAU. photos; bk.rev.; pub. size: tabloid; circ. 19,700(controlled & free).

US

SYRACUSE NEW TIMES. 1969. Wed. free; $24.95/yr. 1415 W. Genesee St., Syracuse, NY 13204-2156. TEL 315-422-7011; FAX 315-422-1721; E-mail: newtimes@ras.com. **Owner(s):** Art Zimmer, Ltd., 1415 W. Genesee St., Syracuse, NY 13204-2156. TEL 315-422-7011; FAX 315-422-1721; Ed. Mike Greenstein; Pub. Art Zimmer; adv. contact: Karen Belgrader. photos; bk.rev.; pub. size: tabloid; circ. 45,000(controlled & free). **Wire Service(s):** Alternet.

US

VILLAGER, THE. Mon. free; $.30 newsstand; $15/yr. local mailed. 250 Bear St., W., Syracuse, NY 13221. TEL 315-472-7825; FAX 315-478-1434. **Owner(s):** John Badoud, 250 Bear St., W., Syracuse, NY 13221. TEL 315-472-7825; FAX 315-478-1434; Ed. Ann Allen; Pub. A. Loren Colburn; adv.: $5.09/SAU. photos; bk.rev.; pub. size: broadsheet; circ. 11,841(controlled & free).

TANNERSVILLE

US

MOUNTAIN EAGLE. 1982. Thu. $.75 newsstand; $35/yr. in state; $45/yr. out of state. Railroad Ave., Tannersville, NY 12485. TEL 518-589-7007; FAX 518-589-7028. **Owner(s):** Eagle Newspapers, Inc., P.O. Box 65, Fayetteville, NY 13066. TEL 315-637-3121; Ed. Paul Smart. adv.; pub. size: broadsheet; circ. 6,500(paid).

TRUMANSBURG

US

CANDOR CHRONICLE. Wed. $.50 newsstamd; $20/yr. in cy.; $24/yr. out of cy.; $19/yr. senior citizens. 51 N. Main St., Trumansburg, NY 14886. TEL 607-387-3181; FAX 607-387-9421. **Owner(s):** Finger Lakes Community Newspapers, Inc., P.O. Box 6475, Ithaca, NY 14851. TEL 607-277-7000; Ed. Cliff Creech; Pub. James Bilinski; adv. contact: Jim Graney. photos; pub. size: tabloid; circ. 10,000(paid).

US

INTERLAKEN REVIEW. Wed. $.50 newsstand; $20/yr. in cy.; $24/yr. out of cy.; $19/yr. senior citizens. 51 N. Main St., Trumansburg, NY 14886. TEL 607-387-3181; FAX 607-387-9421. **Owner(s):** Finger Lakes Community Newspapers, Inc., P.O. Box 6475, Ithaca, NY 14851. TEL 607-277-7000; Ed. Cliff Creech; Pub. James Bilinski; adv. contact: Jim Graney. photos; pub. size: tabloid; circ. 10,000(paid).

US

NEWFIELD NEWS. Wed. $.50 newsstand; $20/yr. in cy.; $24/yr. out of cy.; $19/yr. senior citizens. 51 N. Main St., Trumansburg, NY 14886. TEL 607-387-3181; FAX 607-387-9421. **Owner(s):** Finger Lakes Community Newspapers, Inc., P.O. Box 6475, Ithaca, NY 14851. TEL 607-277-7000; Ed. Cliff Creech; Pub. James Bilinski; adv. contact: Jim Graney. pub. size: tabloid; circ. 5,000(paid).

US

OVID GAZETTE. Wed. $.50 newsstand; $20/yr. in cy.; $24/yr. out of cy.; $19/yr. senior citizens. 51 N. Main St., Trumansburg, NY 14886. TEL 607-387-3181; FAX 607-387-9421. **Owner(s):** Finger Lakes Community Newspapers, Inc., P.O. Box 6475, Ithaca, NY 14851. TEL 607-277-7000; Ed. Cliff Creech; Pub. James Bilinski; adv. contact: Jim Graney. photos; pub. size: tabloid; circ. 7,000(paid).

US

SPENCER RANDOM HARVEST WEEKLY. Wed. $.50 newsstand; $20/yr. in cy.; $24/yr. out of cy.; $19/yr. senior citizens. 51 N. Main St., Trumansburg, NY 14886. TEL 607-387-3181; FAX 607-387-9421. **Owner(s):** Finger Lakes Community Newspapers, Inc., P.O. Box 6475, Ithaca, NY 14851. TEL 607-277-7000; Ed. Cliff Creech; Pub. James Bilinski; adv. contact: Jim Graney. photos; pub. size: tabloid; circ. 7,000(paid).

US

TRUMANSBURG FREE PRESS. Wed. $.50 newsstand; $20/yr. in cy.; $24/yr. out of cy.; $19/yr. senior citizens. 51 N. Main St., Trumansburg, NY 14886. TEL 607-387-3181; FAX 607-387-9421. **Owner(s):** Finger Lakes Community Newspapers, Inc., P.O. Box 6475, Ithaca, NY 14851. TEL 607-277-7000; Ed. Cliff Creech; Pub. James Bilinski; adv. contact: Jim Graney. pub. size: tabloid; circ. 6,000(paid).

TUPPER LAKE

US

TUPPER LAKE FREE PRESS & HERALD. 1895. Wed. $.50/newsstand; $25/yr. in cy.; $26/yr. out of cy. 136 Park St., Tupper Lake, NY 12986. TEL 518-359-2166. **Owner(s):** M. Dan McClelland & Elizabeth J. Bell, P.O. Box 1210, Tupper Lake, NY 12989. TEL 518-359-2166; Ed. Sue Mitchell. adv. contact: Betty Bell. pub. size: broadsheet; circ. 3,700(free & paid).

WADING RIVER

US

COMMUNITY JOURNAL. 1978. Wed. $.10 newsstand. Rte. 25A & Dogwood Dr., Wading River, NY 11792. TEL 516-929-8882. **Owner(s):** Bernadette Smith Budd, Rte. 25A & Dogwood Dr., Wading River, NY 11792. TEL 516-929-8882; Ed. Bernadette Smith Budd; Pub. Bernadette Smith Budd; photos; pub. size: tabloid.

WALDEN

US

MID HUDSON TIMES. Wed. $.75 newsstand; $24/yr. 23 E. Main St., Walden, NY 12586. TEL 914-778-2181; FAX 914-778-1196. **Owner(s):** Wallkill Valley Publications, Inc., P.O. Box 446, Walden, NY 12586; Ed. Carl J. Aiello; Pub. Carl J. Aiello; adv. contact: Nick Licata. circ. 3,500(paid).

US

WALLKILL VALLEY TIMES, THE. 1983. Wed. $.50 newsstand; $21/yr. 23 E. Main St., Walden, NY 12586. TEL 914-778-2181; FAX 914-778-1196. **Owner(s):** Wallkill Valley Publications, Inc., P.O. Box 446, Walden, NY 12586. TEL 914-778-2181; Ed. Carl J. Aiello; Pub. Carl J. Aiello; adv. contact: Nicholas Licata. photos; bk.rev.; pub. size: tabloid; circ. 5,000(paid).

WALTON

US

REPORTER, THE. 1881. Wed. $.75 newsstand; $26/yr. in cy.; $30/yr. out of cy. 181 Delaware St., Walton, NY 13856. TEL 607-865-4131; FAX 607-865-8983. **Owner(s):** Reporter Co., Inc., The, 181 Delaware St., Walton, NY 13856. TEL 607-865-4131; Ed. Patricia Breakey. adv. contact: David MacDonald. photos; pub. size: tabloid; circ. 7,491(paid).

WAPPINGERS FALLS

US

BEACON FREE PRESS. 1962. Wed. $25/yr. 84 E. Main St., Wappingers Falls, NY 12590-2599. TEL 914-297-3723; FAX 914-297-6810; E-mail: newsplace@aol.com. **Owner(s):** Wappingers Falls Shopper, Inc., 84 E. Main St., Wappingers Falls, NY 12590. TEL 914-297-3723; FAX 914-297-6810; Ed. Albert Osten; Pub. Albert Osten; adv.; pub. size: broadsheet; circ. 8,300(paid).

US   ISSN 0192-9631

SOUTHERN DUTCHESS NEWS. 1958. Wed. $23/yr. 84 E. Main St., Wappingers Falls, NY 12590-2599. TEL 914-297-3723; FAX 914-297-6810; E-mail: newsplace@aol.com. Owner(s): Wappingers Falls Shopper, Inc., 84 E. Main St., Wappingers Falls, NY 12590. TEL 914-297-3723; FAX 914-297-6810; Pub. Albert Osten; adv.; pub. size: broadsheet; circ. 20,000(controlled & paid).

US

SPACKENKILL SENTINEL. 1972. Wed. $25/yr. 84 E. Main St., Wappingers Falls, NY 12590. TEL 914-297-3723; FAX 914-297-6810; E-mail: newsplace@aol.com. **Owner(s):** Wappingers Falls Shopper, Inc., 84 E. Main St., Wappingers Falls, NY 12590. TEL 914-297-3723; FAX 914-297-6810; Ed. Albert Osten; Pub. Albert Osten; adv.; pub. size: broadsheet; circ. 4,000(paid).

WARWICK

US

WARWICK ADVERTISER, THE. 1866. Wed. $.50 newsstand; $21/yr. 10 Oakland Ave., Warwick, NY 10990. TEL 914-986-2061; FAX 914-986-2063. **Owner(s):** Straus Communications, P.O. Box 190, Warwick, NY 10990. TEL 914-986-2061; Ed. Stan Martin; Pub. Stan Martin; pub. size: tabloid; circ. 4,800(paid).

US

WARWICK VALLEY DISPATCH. 1885. Wed. $.50 newsstand; $20/yr. in cy.; $22/yr. out of cy. 2 Oakland Ave., Warwick, NY 10990. TEL 914-986-2216. **Owner(s):** Betty Jane Wright, 2 Oakland Ave., Warwick, NY 10990; Ed. Betty Jane Wright; Pub. Betty Jane Wright; pub. size: tabloid; circ. 3,000(paid).

WATKINS GLEN

US   ISSN 1041-6250

WATKINS REVIEW & EXPRESS. 1854. Wed. $.50 newsstand; $18/yr. in cy.; $20/yr. in state; $22/yr. out of state. 210 N. Franklin, Watkins Glen, NY 14891. TEL 607-535-2711; FAX 607-535-2500. **Owner(s):** Gary R. Herzig, 210 N. Franklin St., Watkins Glen, NY 14891. TEL 607-535-2711; Lynn B. Hevzig, 210 N. Franklin St., Watkins Glen, NY 14891. TEL 607-535-2711; Ed. Glenda Gephart. adv.; photos; bk.rev.; pub. size: tabloid; circ. 3,000(paid).

WEBSTER

US   ISSN 0745-7685

WAYNE COUNTY MAIL. 1887. Thu. $.25 newsstand; $12.50/yr. 2010 Empire Blvd., Webster, NY 14580. TEL 716-671-1533; FAX 716-671-7067. **Owner(s):** Richard Calus & W. David Young, 2010 Empire Blvd., Webster, NY 14580. TEL 716-671-1533; Ed. James J. Gertner. adv. contact: Jenifer Calus. photos; pub. size: tabloid; circ. 2,500(paid).

US   ISSN 0745-1377

WEBSTER HERALD. 1899. Wed. $.40 newsstand; $18/yr. 2010 Empire Blvd., Webster, NY 14580. TEL 716-671-1533; FAX 716-000-0007. **Owner(s):** Empire State Weeklies, 2010 Empire Blvd., Webster, NY 14580. TEL 716-671-1533; FAX 716-671-7061; Ed. James J. Gertner; Pub. James J. Gertner; adv. contact: Jan Glende. photos; pub. size: tabloid; circ. 4,897(paid).

US

WEBSTER POST, THE. 1992. Wed. $.50 newsstand; $21/yr. mailed. 40 North Ave., Webster, NY 14580. TEL 716-872-2221; FAX 716-872-0494. **Owner(s):** Wolfe Publications, Inc., P.O. Box C, Fishers, NY 14453. TEL 716-924-4040; Ed. Andrew D. Wolfe; Pub. Andrew D. Wolfe; adv.; pub. size: broadsheet; circ. 2,700(paid).

WESTFIELD

US

MAYVILLE SENTINEL/CHAUTAUQUA NEWS. 1834. Thu. $.35 newsstand; $19/yr. in cy.; $20/yr. out of cy. 41 E. Main St., Westfield, NY 14787. TEL 716-326-3163; FAX 716-326-3165. **Owner(s):** Ogden Newspapers, Inc., 1500 Main St., Wheeling, WV 26033. TEL 304-233-0100; Ed. Bob Houston; Pub. Donald L. Meyer; adv. contact: Cindy Reese. photos; bk.rev.; pub. size: broadsheet; circ. 1,100(paid).

US   ISSN 1071-1074

WESTFIELD REPUBLICAN. 1855. Thu. $.40 newsstand; $21.50/yr. in cy.; $24/yr. out of cy. 41 E. Main St., Westfield, NY 14787. TEL 716-326-3163; FAX 716-326-3165. **Owner(s):** Ogden Newspapers, Inc., 1500 Main St., Wheeling, WV 26033. TEL 304-233-0100; Ed. Bob Houston; Pub. Donald L. Meyer; adv. contact: Cindy Reese. photos; pub. size: broadsheet; circ. 2,000(paid).

WESTHAMPTON BEACH

US

HAMPTON CHRONICLE-NEWS. 1907. Thu. $.75 newsstand; $24/yr. in cy.; $30/yr. out of cy. 12 Mitchell Rd., Westhampton Beach, NY 11978. TEL 516-288-1100; FAX 516-288-4965. **Owner(s):** Donald H. Louchheim, P. O. Box 1071, Westhampton Beach, NY 11978; Ed. W. Michael Pitcher; Pub. Donald H. Louchheim; adv. contact: Carol Mantell. photos; pub. size: broadsheet; circ. 8,000(paid).

WHITEHALL

US

WHITEHALL TIMES. 1815. Thu. $.60 newsstand; $20/yr. 126 Main St., Whitehall, NY 12887. TEL 518-499-1500; FAX 518-499-1500. **Owner(s):** Manchester Newspapers, Inc., P.O. Box 330, Grandville, NY 12832. TEL 518-642-1234; FAX 518-642-1344; Ed. Stella Wood; Pub. John Manchester; adv.; photos; pub. size: tabloid; circ. 2,300(paid).

WHITE PLAINS

US

SUBURBAN STREET NEWS. 1976. m. $25/yr. 199 Main St., White Plains, NY 10601. TEL 914-428-0930; FAX 914-428-9077. **Owner(s):** Suburban Street News, Inc., 199 Main St., White Plains, NY 10601. TEL 914-428-0930; Ed. James Benerofe; Pub. James Benerofe; pub. size: tabloid; circ. 25,000(paid).

WILLIAMSVILLE

US

CHEEKTOWAGA BEE. 1977. Thu. $.75 newsstand; $29/yr. 5564 Main St., Williamsville, NY 14221. TEL 716-632-4700; FAX 716-633-8601. **Owner(s):** Bee Publications, Inc., P.O. Box 150, Williamsville, NY 14231-0150. TEL 716-632-4700; FAX 716-633-8601; Ed. David Sherman; Pub. Trey Measer; pub. size: tabloid; circ. 1,900(paid).

US

CLARENCE BEE. 1937. Wed. $.75 newsstand; $29/yr. in cy.; $32/yr. out of state. 5564 Main St., Williamsville, NY 14221. TEL 716-632-4700. Owner(s): Bee Publications, Inc., 5564 Main St., Williamsville, NY 14221. TEL 716-632-4700; Ed. David Sherman; Pub. Trey Measer; adv.; pub. size: tabloid; circ. 4,700(paid).

US

DEPEW BEE. 1893. Thu. $.75 newsstand; $29/yr. in cy.; $32/yr. out of state. 5564 Main St., Williamsville, NY 14231-0150. TEL 716-632-4700; FAX 716-633-8601. **Owner(s):** Bee Publications, Inc., P.O. Box 150, Williamsville, NY 14221. TEL 716-632-4700; Ed. David Sherman; Pub. Trey Measer; adv.; pub. size: tabloid; circ. 2,000(paid).

US

EAST AURORA BEE. 1987. Thu. free. 5564 Main St., Williamsville, NY 14221. TEL 716-632-4700; FAX 716-633-8601 **Owner(s):** Bee Publications, Inc., P.O. Box 150, Williamsville, NY 14221. TEL 716-632-4700; Ed. David Sherman; Pub. Trey Measer; pub. size: tabloid; circ. 11,000(free).

US

LANCASTER BEE. 1877. Thu. $.75 newsstand; $29/yr. in cy. 5564 Main St., Williamsville, NY 14221. TEL 716-632-4700; FAX 716-633-8601. **Owner(s):** Bee Publications, Inc., P.O. Box 150, Williamsville, NY 14221; Ed. David Sherman; Pub. Trey Measer; adv.; pub. size: tabloid; circ. 3,712(paid).

US

ORCHARD PARK BEE. 1986. s-w.: Wed. & Thu. $.75 newsstand; $29/yr.; $26/yr. senior citizens. 5564 Main St., Williamsville, NY 14221. TEL 716-632-4700; FAX 716-633-8601. **Owner(s):** Bee Publications, Inc., P.O. Box 150, Williamsville, NY 14221. TEL 716-632-4700; Ed Joe Iannarelli; Pub. Trey Measer; adv. contact: Dean Hutter. pub. size: tabloid; circ. 11,000(free)

US

WEST SENECA BEE. 1980. Thu. $.75 newsstand; $29/yr. 5564 Main St., Williamsville, NY 14221. TEL 716-632-4700; FAX 716-633-8601. **Owner(s):** Bee Publications, Inc., P.O. Box 150, Williamsville, NY 14221. TEL 716-632-4700; Ed. David Sherman; Pub. Trey Measer; pub. size: tabloid; circ. 4,100(paid).

WINDHAM

US

WINDHAM JOURNAL. 1857. Thu. $.75 newsstand; $29.20/yr. in cy.; $35/yr. out of cy. Main St., Windham, NY 12496. TEL 518-734-4400; FAX 518-734-5179. **Owner(s):** Catskill Daily Mail, 30 Church St., Catskill, NY 12414; Ed. Laurie Anander; Pub. A. Paretta; adv.; pub. size: broadsheet; circ. 1,950(paid).

WOODMERE

US

SOUTH SHORE RECORD. 1953. Thu. $.50 newsstand; $20/yr. 990 Railroad Ave., Woodmere, NY 11598. TEL 516-374-9200; FAX 516-374-9209. **Owner(s):** Florence B. Schwartzberg, 990 Railroad Ave., Woodmere, NY 11598. TEL 516-374-9200; Ed. Florence B. Schwartzberg. adv.; pub. size: tabloid; circ. 22,000(free & paid).

WOODSTOCK

US

ULSTER COUNTY TOWNSMAN. 1953. Thu. $.40 newsstand; $24/yr. in cy.; $28/yr. out of cy. 18 Rock City Rd., Woodstock, NY 12498-0308. TEL 914-679-2145; FAX 914-589-7028. **Owner(s):** J. Blake Killin, P.O. Box 308, Woodstock, NY 12498. TEL 914-679-2145; Ed. J. Blake Killin; Pub. J. Blake Killin; adv.; pub. size: broadsheet; circ. 2,500(paid).

YONKERS

US

EASTCHESTER RECORD. Thu. $.75 newsstand; $25/yr. 40 Larkin Plz., Yonkers, NY 10701. TEL 914-965-4000; FAX 914-965-4026. **Owner(s):** Martinelli Publications, 40 Larkin Plz., Yonkers, NY 10701. TEL 914-965-4000; Ed. Louise Montclare; Pub. Ralph R. Martinelli; adv. contact: John Alfieri. pub. size: broadsheet; circ. 4,058(paid).

US
HARRISON INDEPENDENT. 1962. Thu. $.75 newsstand; $25/yr. 40 Larkin Plz., Yonkers, NY 10701. TEL 914-965-4000; FAX 914-965-4026. **Owner(s):** Martinelli Publications, 40 Larkin Plz., Yonkers, NY 10701. TEL 914-965-4000; Ed. Louise Montclare; Pub. Ralph Martinelli; adv. contact: John Alfieri. pub. size: broadsheet; circ. 4,300(paid).

US
MOUNT VERNON INDEPENDENT. Thu. $.75 newsstand; $25/yr. 40 Larkin Plz., Yonkers, NY 10701. TEL 914-965-4000; FAX 914-965-4026. **Owner(s):** Martinelli Publications, 40 Larkin Plz., Yonkers, NY 10701. TEL 914-965-4000; Ed. Louise Montclare; Pub. Ralph R. Martinelli; adv. contact: John Alfieri. pub. size: broadsheet; circ. 6,000(paid).

US
NORTH CASTLE NEWS. 1963. Thu. $.75 newsstand; $25/yr. 40 Larkin Plz., Yonkers, NY 10701. TEL 914-965-4000; FAX 914-965-4026. **Owner(s):** Martinelli Publications, 40 Larkin Plz., Yonkers, NY 10701. TEL 914-965-4000; Ed. Louise Montclare; Pub. Ralph R. Martinelli; adv. contact: John Alfieri. pub. size: broadsheet; circ. 3,300(paid).

US
PELHAM SUN. 1910. Thu. $.75 newsstand; $25/yr. 40 Larkin Plz., Yonkers, NY 10701. TEL 914-965-4000; FAX 914-965-2892. **Owner(s):** Martinelli Publications, 40 Larkin Plz., Yonkers, NY 10701. TEL 914-965-4000; Ed. Louise Montclaire; Pub. Ralph R. Martinelli; adv. contact: Pete Roth. pub. size: broadsheet; circ. 3,606(paid).

US
REVIEW PRESS REPORTER. 1902. Thu. $.35 newsstand; $26/yr. One Odell Plz., Yonkers, NY 10701. TEL 914-696-8245; FAX 914-696-8208. **Owner(s):** Gannett Company, Inc., 1100 Wilson Blvd., Arlington, VA 22340; Ed. Meryl Harris. adv.; photos; pub. size: broadsheet; circ. 2,200(paid).

US
RYE CHRONICLE. 1905. Thu. $.75 newsstand; $25/yr. 40 Larkin Plz., Yonkers, NY 10701. TEL 914-965-4000; FAX 914-965-2892. **Owner(s):** Martinelli Publications, 40 Larkin Plz., Yonkers, NY 10701. TEL 914-965-4000; Ed. Louise Montclare; Pub. Ralph R. Martinelli; adv. contact: John Alfieri. pub. size: broadsheet; circ. 3,966(paid).

US
SOUND VIEW NEWS. Thu. $.75 newsstand; $25/yr. 40 Larkin Plz., Yonkers, NY 10701. TEL 914-965-4000; FAX 914-965-4026. **Owner(s):** Martinelli Publications, 40 Larkin Plz., Yonkers, NY 10701. TEL 914-965-4000; Ed. Louise Montclare; Pub. Ralph R. Martinelli; adv. contact: John Alfieri. pub. size: broadsheet; circ. 6,000(paid).

US
YONKERS HOME NEWS & TIMES. Fri. $.75 newsstand; $25/yr. carrier. 40 Larkin Plz., Yonkers, NY 10701. TEL 914-965-4000; FAX 914-965-4026. **Owner(s):** Martinelli Publications, 40 Larkin Plz., Yonkers, NY 10701. TEL 914-965-4000; Ed. Louise Montclare; Pub. Ralph Martinelli; adv. contact: John Alfieri. photos; pub. size: broadsheet; circ. 20,100(paid).
Formerly: Home News & Times.

YORKTOWN HEIGHTS

US
NORTH COUNTY NEWS. 1966. Wed. $.75 newsstand; $35/yr. local; $40/yr. elsewhere. 1520 Front St., Yorktown Heights, NY 10598. TEL 914-962-4748; FAX 914-962-6763. **Owner(s):** Northern Tier Publishing Corp., 1520 Front St., Yorktown Heights, NY 10598. TEL 914-962-4748; Ed. Nancy Haggerty; Pub. Cynthia Smith; adv. contact: Jeannie Goldman. pub. size: tabloid; circ. 10,000(paid).

US
PENNYSAVER. 1958. Wed. free. 1520 Front St., Yorktown Heights, NY 10598. TEL 914-962-3871; FAX 914-962-5123. **Owner(s):** Yorktown Printing & Pennysaver Corp., 1520 Front St., Yorktown Heights, NY 10598. TEL 914-962-3871; Pub. John W. Chase; adv. contact: Chuck Young. pub. size: tabloid; circ. 320,550(free).

NORTH CAROLINA

AHOSKIE

US
NEWS-HERALD, THE. 1909. 3/wk.: Tue., Thu., Sat. $.50 newsstand; $53.42/yr. in state; $62.40/yr. out of state. 801 Parker Ave., Ahoskie, NC 27910. TEL 919-332-2123; FAX 919-332-3940. **Owner(s):** Park Communications, Inc., Vine Ctr. Office Tower, 333 W. Vine St., 17th Fl., Lexington, KY 40507. TEL 606-252-7275; Ed. Jay Jenkins. adv. contact: Phyllis Frynier. pub. size: broadsheet; circ. 6,780(paid).

ALBEMARLE

US
STANLY NEWS & PRESS. 1880. 3/wk.: Tue., Thu., Sun. $.50/day newsstand; $.75/Sun.; $44.40/yr. local; $67/yr. out of state. 237 W. North St., Albemarle, NC 28001. TEL 704-982-2121; FAX 704-983-7999. **Owner(s):** Stanly County Newspapers, Inc., 237 W. North St., Albemarle, NC 28001. TEL 704-982-2121; Ed. David Deese; Pub. J.L. Waggoner; pub. size: broadsheet; circ. 14,400(paid).

ANGIER

US
ANGIER INDEPENDENT. 1972. Tue. $15/yr. P.O. Box 878, Angier, NC 27501. TEL 919-639-4913; FAX 919-639-9919. **Owner(s):** Angier Independent, Inc., P.O. Box 878, Angier, NC 27501. TEL 919-639-4913; Ed. Terri Brooks; Pub. Bart Adams; adv.; photos; pub. size: broadsheet; circ. 5,000(paid).

APEX

US
APEX HERALD, THE. 1956. Wed. $17/yr. in cy.; $25/yr. out of cy. 616 W. Chatham St., Apex, NC 27502. TEL 919-362-8356; FAX 919-362-8356. **Owner(s):** Kirkland Newspapers, Inc., 1577 Haermitage Ct., Durham, NC 27707; Ed. Sandy Barnes; Pub. Jim Small; adv.; pub. size: broadsheet; circ. 4,000(paid).
Formerly: Western Wake Herald.

ASHEBORO

US
RANDOLPH GUIDE, THE. 1954. Wed. $.50 newsstand; $17.50/yr. in cy.; $25/yr. elsewhere. 431 S. Fayetteville St., Asheboro, NC 27203. TEL 919-625-5576; FAX 919-675-5577. **Owner(s):** Robert M. Derr, Jr., P.O. Box 1044, Asheboro, NC 27204. TEL 919-625-5577; Ed. Kathie Keyes. adv.; photos; bk.rev.; pub. size: broadsheet; circ. 2,789(free & paid).

ASHEVILLE

US
MOUNTAIN XPRESS. Wed. free newsstand. P.O. Box 144, Asheville, NC 28802. TEL 704-251-1333; FAX 704-251-1311. **Owner(s):** Green Lined Media, Inc., P.O. Box 144, Asheville, NC 28802. TEL 704-251-1333; FAX 704-251-1311; Ed. Jeff Fobes. adv.; photos; bk.rev.; pub. size: tabloid; circ. 18,100(controlled & paid).
Formerly: Green Line.

BELMONT

US
BELMONT BANNER. 1929. Wed. $.50 newsstand; $18.02/yr. in cy.; $20.14/yr. out of cy.; $23.32/yr. out of state. 812 Woodlawn St., Belmont, NC 28012. TEL 704-827-7526; FAX 704-739-0611. **Owner(s):** Republic Newspapers, Inc., P.O. Box 769, Kings Mountain, NC 28086; Ed. Jim Hefner; Pub. Dean Ridings; adv.; photos; pub. size: broadsheet; circ. 5,000(controlled).

US
MOUNT HOLLY NEWS. 1929. Wed. $.50 newsstand; $18.02/yr. in cy.; $20.14/yr out of cy.; $22.32/yr. out of state. 812 Woodlawn St., Belmont, NC 28012. TEL 704-827-7526; FAX 704-827-1037. **Owner(s):** Republic Newspapers, Inc., P.O. Box 769, Kings Mountain, NC 28086; Ed. Jim Heffner; Pub. Dean Ridings; adv.; photos; pub. size: broadsheet; circ. 2,300(paid).

BENSON

US
FOUR OAKS-BENSON NEWS IN REVIEW. 1910. Wed. $.50 newsstand; $11.50/yr. in cy.; $9.50/yr. out of cy. 113 S. Market St., Benson, NC 27504. TEL 919-894-3331; FAX 919-894-1069. **Owner(s):** Ralph E. Delano, P.O. Box 9, Benson, NC 27504. TEL 919-894-3331; Ed. Mike Dart; Pub. Norman Delano; adv. contact: Phil Burgess. pub. size: broadsheet; circ. 4,500(paid).
Formerly: Benson Review, The.

BLACK MOUNTAIN

US
BLACK MOUNTAIN NEWS. 1945. Thu. $.35 newsstand; $15/yr. in cy.; $22/yr. out of cy.; $25/yr. out of state. Cherry St., Black Mountain, NC 28711. TEL 704-669-8727; FAX 704-669-8619. **Owner(s):** Gannett Company, Inc., 1100 Wilson Blvd., Arlington, VA 22340. TEL 703-284-6000; Ed. James Aycock. adv.; photos; pub. size: broadsheet; circ. 4,500(free & paid).

BLOWING ROCK

US   ISSN 1071-0574
BLOWING ROCKET, THE. 1932. Thu. $.50 newsstand; $19/yr. in state; $23/yr. out of state. 452 Sunset Dr., Blowing Rock, NC 28605. TEL 704-295-7522; FAX 704-295-7507. **Owner(s):** Watauga Newspaper, Inc., 300 W. King St., Boone, NC 28607. TEL 704-264-3612; Ed. Jerry W. Burns. adv.; photos; bk.rev.; pub. size: broadsheet; circ. 4,500(paid).

BOONE

US
BOONE WATAUGA DEMOCRAT. 1888. 3/wk.: Mon., Wed., Fri. $.50 newsstand; $41/yr. home deliv.; $76/yr. out of state mailed. 474 Industrial Park Dr., Boone, NC 28607. TEL 704-264-3612; FAX 704-262-0282. **Owner(s):** Watauga Newspapers, Inc., P.O. Box 3050, Boone, NC 28607; Ed. Sandra Shook; Pub. William S. Cummings, III; adv. contact: Lana Brantz. photos; pub. size: broadsheet; circ. 13,500(paid). **Wire Service(s):** AP.

BREVARD

US
TRANSYLVANIA TIMES, THE. 1900. s-w.: Mon. & Thu. $.35 newsstand; $23/yr. in cy.; $26/yr. out of cy. 100 N. Broad St., Brevard, NC 28712. TEL 704-883-8156; FAX 704-883-8158. **Owner(s):** Stella A. Trapp, 100 N. Broad St., Brevard, LA 28712. TEL 704-833-8156; FAX 704-883-8158; Ed. Stella Trapp; Pub. Stella Trapp; adv.; photos; pub. size: broadsheet; circ. 8,300(paid).

BURGAW

US
PENDER CHRONICLE. 1896. Wed. $.25/newsstand; $15/yr. in cy.; $22/yr. out of cy; $26/yr. out of state. 110 Courthouse Ave., Burgaw, NC 28425. TEL 910-259-2351; FAX 910-285-3179. **Owner(s):** H.L. Oswald Enterprises, Inc., P.O. Box 699, Wallace, NC 28466. TEL 919-285-2178; Pub. H. L. Oswald; adv.; photos; pub. size: standard; circ. 6,300(paid).

US
PENDER POST. 1971. Wed. $.25 newsstand; $15/yr. in cy.; $20/yr. out of cy. 210 Fremont St., Burgaw, NC 28425. TEL 910-259-9111; FAX 910-259-9112. **Owner(s):** Post Newspapers, Inc., P.O. Box 955, Burgaw, NC 28425; Ed. Patrick Thomas; Pub. Patrick Thomas; pub. size: broadsheet; circ. 5,000(paid).

BURNSVILLE

US
YANCEY COMMON TIMES JOURNAL. 1920. Wed. $.50 newsstand; $15.90/yr. in cy.; $23.85/yr. in state; $30/yr. out of state. 5 Town Sq., Burnsville, NC 28714. TEL 704-682-2120; FAX 704-682-3701. **Owner(s):** Trib Publications, Inc., P.O. Box 426, Manchester, GA 31816. TEL 404-846-3188; Ed. Jody Higgins; Pub. Jody Higgins; adv. contact: Pat Randolph. pub. size: broadsheet; circ. 7,000(paid).
   Formerly: Yancey Journal, The.

CANTON

US
ENTERPRISE MOUNTAINEER, THE. 1903. Wed. $.25 newsstand; $10/yr. in cy.; $16/yr. in state. 119 Main St., Cantor, NC 28716. TEL 704-253-7416. **Owner(s):** Mountaineer Publishing Co., Inc., 413 N. Main St., P.O. Box 129, Waynesville, NC 28786. TEL 704-452-0661; FAX 704-452-0665; Ed. Peggy Gosselin. adv.; photos bk.rev.; pub. size: broadsheet; circ. 1,912(paid).
   Formerly: Enterprise, The.

CARY

US
CARY NEWS. 1963 s-w.: Sat. & Wed. $.50 newsstand; $24/yr. 212 E. Chatham St., Cary, NC 27511. TEL 919-460-2600; FAX 919-460-6034. **Owner(s):** McClatchy Newspapers, P.O. Box 15774, Sacramento, CA 95816. TEL 915-321-1000; Ed. Jane Paige; Pub. Jack Andrews; pub. size: standard; circ. 10,200(paid).

CHAPEL HILL

US   ISSN 1070-2741
CHAPEL HILL NEWS. 1923. 3/wk: Sun., Wed., Fri. free. 505 W. Franklin St., Chapel Hill, NC 27516. TEL 919-967-7045; FAX 919-968-4935. **Owner(s):** McClatchy Newspapers, P.O. Box 15774, Sacramento, CA 95816. TEL 916-321-1000; Ed. Richard Hart; Pub. Ted Vaden; adv. contact: Peter Tompkins. photos; pub. size: broadsheet circ. 25,000(paid); Sun. 25,000(paid). **Wire Service(s):** NYT, AP.
   Formerly: Chapel Hill Newspaper.

US
VILLAGE ADVOCATE. 1969. s-w.: Sun. & Wed. free newsstand; $20/mo. 38 McClamroch Cir., Chapel Hill, NC 27514. TEL 919-968-4801; FAX 919-942-2326. **Owner(s):** Village Companies, 88 McClamroch Cir., Chapel Hill, NC 27514. TEL 919-968-4801; Pub. Doug Rogers; adv.; photos; pub. size: tabloid; circ. 35,000(free & paid).

CHERRYVILLE

US
CHERRYVILLE EAGLE. 1906. Wed. $.50 newsstand; $16/yr. in cy.; $18/yr. out of cy.; $21/yr. out of state. P.O. Box 699, Cherryville, NC 28021. TEL 704-435-6752; FAX 704-739-0611. **Owner(s):** Republic Newspapers, Inc., P.O. Box 769, Kings Mountain, NC 28086. TEL 704-739-7496; Ed. Marsha Martin. adv.; photos; pub. size: broadsheet; circ. 3,000(paid).

CLAYTON

US
CLAYTON NEWS-STAR. 1911. Tue. $.50 newsstand; $11.50/yr. in cy.; $13.50/yr. out of cy.; $16.25 yr. out of state. 222 W. Main St., Clayton, NC 27520. TEL 919-553-7234; FAX 919-553-5358. **Owner(s):** Ralph E. Delano, P.O. Box 9, Benson, NC 27504. TEL 919-894-3331; Ed. Michele Moore; Pub. Ralph E. Delano; adv. contact: Shirley Johnson. photos; pub. size: broadsheet; circ. 3,500(paid).
   Formerly: Clayton News.

CLEMMONS

US
CLEMMONS COURIER. 1960. Thu. $.50 newsstand; $15/yr. in state; $20/yr. out of state. 3600 Clemmons Rd., Clemmons, NC 27012. TEL 910-766-4126; FAX 910-766-7350. **Owner(s):** Dwight Spark, 3600 Clemmons Rd., Clemmons, NC 27012. TEL 919-766-4126; Ed. Dwight Sparks; Pub. Dwight Sparks pub. size: standard; circ. 3,200(paid).

CREEDMOOR

US
BUTNER-CREEDMOOR NEWS, THE. 1965. Thu. $.50 newsstand; $22.26/yr. in state; $25/yr. out of state. 418 N. Main, Creedmoor, NC 27522. TEL 919-528-2393; FAX 919-528-0288. **Owner(s):** Harry R. Coleman P.O. Box 726, Creedmoor, NC 27522; Ed. Harry R. Coleman; Pub. Harry R. Coleman; adv. contact: Tracy Byrd. photos; pub. size: standard; circ. 4,400(paid).

DAVIDSON

US
MECKLENBURG GAZETTE. 1945. Wed. $.50 newsstand; $18.50/yr. 108 S. Main St., Davidson, NC 28036. TEL 704-892-8809; FAX 704-664-3614. **Owner(s):** Park Communications, Inc., Vine Ctr. Office Tower, 333 W. Vine St., 17th Fl., Lexington, KY 40507. TEL 606-252-7252; Ed. Sam Knowlton; adv. contact: Lou Sullivan. photos; bk.rev.; pub. size: broadsheet; circ. 3,000(paid).

DURHAM

US
CAROLINA TIMES. 1926. Thu. $.30 newsstand; $19.08/yr. in cy.; $22.32/yr. out of cy.; $22/yr. out of state. 923 Old Fayetteville St., Durham, NC 27701 TEL 919-682-2913. FAX 919-682-2913. **Owner(s):** United Publishers, Inc., P.O. Box 3825, Durham, NC 27702 TEL 919-682-2913; Ed. V.A. Edmonds; Pub. V.A. Edmonds; adv. contact: Kenneth Edmonds. pub. size: broadsheet; circ. 5,800(paid).

US
INDEPENDENT, THE. 1983. Wed. free newsstand; $29/yr. mailed. 2810 Hillsborough Rd., Durham, NC 27715. TEL 919-286-1972; FAX 919-286-4274. **Owner(s):** Carolina Independent Publications, P.O. Box 2690, Durham, NC 27715. TEL 919-286-1972; Ed. Bob Moser; Pub. Steve Schewel; adv. contact: Susan Watson. pub. size: tabloid; circ. 50,000(free & paid).

ELKIN

US
TRIBUNE, THE. 1911. 3/wk.: Mon., Wed., Fri. $.50 newsstand; $35/yr. home deliv.; $33.92/yr. out of state. 214 E. Main St., Elkin, NC 28621. TEL 910-835-1513; FAX 910-835-8742. **Owner(s):** Mid-South Management Co., Inc., P.O. Box 1634, Spartanburg, SC 29304. TEL 803-583-2907; Ed. Bill Watson; Pub. R. Fletcher Good IV; adv. contact: Sarah Byrd. pub. size: broadsheet; circ. 11,000(paid).

FRANKLIN

US

FRANKLIN PRESS. 1886. s-w.: Wed. & Fri. $.50 newsstand; $22.50/yr. in cy.; $36/yr. out of cy. 40 Depot St., Franklin, NC 28734. TEL 704-524-2010; FAX 704-524-8821. **Owner(s):** Community Newspapers, Inc., P.O. Box 792, Athens, GA 30603. TEL 706-548-0010; FAX 706-548-0808; Ed. Scott McRae; Pub. Kenneth Hudgins; adv. contact: Tom Brown. photos; pub. size: broadsheet; circ. 8,000(paid).

FREMONT

US

WAYNE WILSON NEWS LEADER. Wed. $.50 newsstand; $12/yr. local; $16.50/yr. out of area. 113 N. Wilson St., Fremont, NC 27830. TEL 919-965-2033; FAX 919-965-5903. **Owner(s):** Barry Merrill, P.O. Box 278, Selma, NC 25756. TEL 919-965-2033; Ed. Barry Merrill; Pub. Barry Merrill; adv.; pub. size: standard; circ. 1,500(paid).

GARNER

US

GARNER NEWS. 1962. Wed. $.50 newsstand; $17/yr. in cy. 503-L U.S. Hwy. 70, Garner, NC 27529. TEL 919-772-1166; FAX 919-779-7824. **Owner(s):** William Kirkland, 503-L U.S. Hwy 70, Garner, NC 27529; Ed. Sandy Barnes; Pub. Jim Small; pub. size: broadsheet; circ. 6,000(paid).

GATESVILLE

US

GATES COUNTY INDEX. 1932. Wed. $.50 newsstand; $19.08/yr. in cy.; $25.18/yr. out of cy. West Maple St., Gatesville, NC 27938. TEL 919-357-0960; FAX 919-332-3940. **Owner(s):** Park Communications, Inc., Vine Ctr. Office Tower, 333 W. Vine St., 17th Fl., Lexington, KY 40507. TEL 606-252-7252; Ed. Helene Knight. adv. contact: Tammy Perry. pub. size: broadsheet; circ. 2,750(paid).

GOLDSBORO

US

EASTERN CAROLINA TIMES-INQUIRER. 1975. Wed. free newsstand. P.O. Box 1659, Goldsboro, NC 27533. TEL 919-734-5444; FAX 919-734-0290. **Owner(s):** Joe C. Dougherty, P.O. Box 1659, Goldsboro, NC 27533. TEL 919-734-5444; FAX 919-734-0290; Ed. Ken Plummer. adv.; photos; bk.rev.; pub. size: tabloid; circ. 35,000(free).
Formerly: Goldsboro Times Newspaper.

GRAHAM

US

ALAMANCE NEWS. 1875. Thu. $.50 newsstand; $20/yr. in cy.; $29/yr. out of cy. 114 W. Elm St., Graham, NC 27253-0431. TEL 910-228-7851; FAX 910-229-9602. **Owner(s):** Boney Publishers, Inc., P.O. Box 431, Graham, NC 27253. TEL 919-228-7851; Ed. Tom Boney, Jr.; Pub. Tom Boney, Jr.; adv.; pub. size: standard; circ. 7,429(paid).

HERTFORD

US

PERQUIMANS WEEKLY. 1932. Thu. $.35 newsstand; $24.20/yr. in state; $26.40/yr. out of state. 119 W. Grubb St., Hertford, NC 27944. TEL 919-426-5728. **Owner(s):** Thomson Newspapers, Inc., One Thorn Run Ctr., Ste. 500, 1187 Thorn Run Rd. Ext., Coraopolis, PA 15108. TEL 412-262-7870; Ed. Susan Harris; Pub. Richard Brown; adv. contact: Anzie Ziemba. pub. size: standard; circ. 2,000(paid).

HICKORY

US

HICKORY NEWS/EXTRA, THE. 1970. Thu. $.50 newsstand; $20/yr. in area; $25/yr. out of state. 270 Union Sq. Common, Hickory, NC 28601. TEL 704-328-6164; FAX 704-322-6398. **Owner(s):** Charles H. Deal, P.O. Box 2650, Hickory, NC 28603. TEL 704-328-6164; Valerie M. Deal, P.O. Box 2650, Hickory, NC 28603. TEL 704-328-6164; Ed. Charles H. Deal; Pub. Charles H. Deal; adv. contact: Mickey L. Price. photos; bk.rev.; pub. size: broadsheet; circ. 16,000(free & paid).

HILLSBOROUGH

US   ISSN 1071-1716

NEWS OF ORANGE COUNTY, THE. 1893. Wed. $.50 newsstand; $18.93/yr. Churton St., Hillsborough, NC 27278. TEL 919-732-2171; FAX 919-732-4852. **Owner(s):** Womack Publishing Co., Inc., P.O. Box 111, Chatham, VA 24531. TEL 804-432-1654; Ed. Jonathan Butler; Pub. Charles A. Womack, Jr.; adv.; pub. size: broadsheet; circ. 4,600(free & paid).

JACKSON

US

ROANOKE-CHOWAN NEWS-HERALD. 1892. 3/wk.: Tue., Thu., Sat. $.50 newsstand; $53.42/yr. in cy. 202 W. Jefferson, Jackson, NC 27845. TEL 919-534-6911. **Owner(s):** Park Communications, Inc., Vine Ctr. Office Tower, 333 W. Vine St., 17th Fl., Lexington, KY 40507. TEL 606-252-7275; adv. contact: Judy Farmer. pub. size: standard; circ. 8,894(paid).
Formerly: Northampton News.

KENLY

US

KENLY NEWS. Wed. $.50 newsstand; $15/yr. 201 W. Second St., Kenly, NC 27542. TEL 919-284-2295. **Owner(s):** Richard D. Stewart, P.O. Box 39, Kenly, NC 27542. TEL 919-284-2295; Pub. Richard D. Stewart; adv. contact: Karen B. Stewart. photos; bk.rev.; pub. size: broadsheet; circ. 3,200(paid).

KERNERSVILLE

US

KERNERSVILLE NEWS. 1938. 3/wk.: Tue., Thu., Sat. Tue. free; $.50 newsstand; $27.95/yr. local. 300 E. Mountain St., Kernersville, NC 27284. TEL 910-993-2161; FAX 910-993-0931. **Owner(s):** Carter Publishing Co., 300 E. Mountain St., Kernersville, NC 27284. TEL 919-993-2161; Ed. John Staples; Pub. John Owensby; adv. contact: J.C. Grose. pub. size: standard; circ. 19,900(free & paid).

KING

US

KING TIMES NEWS. 1961. Thu. $.50 newsstand; $17.50/yr. in cy.; $21.50/yr. out of cy.; $25.50/yr. out of state; $15.50/yr. senior citizens. 141 Pineview Dr., King, NC 27021. TEL 910-983-3109; FAX 910-983-8203. **Owner(s):** CM Publishing Co., 141 Pineview Dr., King, NC 27021. TEL 919-983-3109; Ed. Karen McConkey; Pub. T.J. "Turk" Tergliafera; adv.; pub. size: broadsheet; circ. 6,800(paid).

KINGS MOUNTAIN

US

BESSEMER CITY RECORD. 1956. Wed. $.50 newsstand; $16/yr. in cy.; $18/yr. out of cy.; $21/yr. out of state. E. King St. & Canterbury Rd., Kings Mountain, NC 28086. TEL 704-629-2376; FAX 704-739-0611. **Owner(s):** Republic Newspapers, Inc., P.O. Box 769, Kings Mountain, NC 28086; Ed. Jim Hefner; Pub. Bob Rop; adv. contact: Darrell Austin. photos; pub. size: broadsheet; circ. 1,200(paid).

US

KINGS MOUNTAIN HERALD. 1888. Thu. $.50 newsstand; $17/yr. in cy.; $19/yr. out of cy.; $22/yr. out of state. E. King St. & Canterbury Rd., Kings Mountain, NC 28086. TEL 704-739-7496; FAX 704-739-0611. **Owner(s):** Republic Newspapers, Inc., P.O. Box 769, Kings Mountain, NC 28086; Ed. Gary and Lib Stewart; Pub. Bob Rop; adv.; photos; pub. size: broadsheet; circ. 6,500(paid).

LINCOLNTON

US

LINCOLN TIMES-NEWS. 1903. 3/wk.: Mon., Wed., Fri. $.35 newsstand; $31.20/yr. 119 W. Water St., Lincolnton, NC 28092. TEL 704-735-3031; FAX 704-735-3037. **Owner(s):** Western Carolina Publishing Co., P.O. Box 40, Lincolnton, NC 28093. TEL 704-735-3031; FAX 704-735-3037; Ed. Kathryn Yarboro; Pub. Jerry G. Leedy; adv. contact: Robert Parker. photos; bk.rev.; pub. size: standard; circ. 10,600(paid). **Wire Service(s):** AP.

LITTLETON

US

LITTLETON OBSERVER. 1955. Thu. $.50 newsstand; $14.84/yr. in cy.; $16.96/yr. out of cy.;. 101 E.S. Main St., Littleton, NC 27850-0417. TEL 919-586-6397. **Owner(s):** Jack Sharpe, P.O. Box 417, Littleton, NC 27850. TEL 919-586-6397; Pub. Hal Sharpe; adv. contact: Jane Boney. photos; pub. size: broadsheet; circ. 2,500(paid).

LOUISBURG

US

FRANKLIN TIMES. 1870. s-w.: Wed. & Sat. $.50 newsstand; $25/yr. 109 S. Bickett Blvd., Louisburg, NC 27549. TEL 919-496-6503; FAX 919-496-1689. **Owner(s):** Gary Cunard, P.O. Box 119, Louisburg, NC 27549. TEL 919-496-6503; Ed. Anna Meadows; Pub. Gary Cunard; adv.; pub. size: broadsheet; circ. 8,700(paid).

MADISON

US   ISSN 0892-1814

MESSENGER, THE. 1915. s-w.: Wed. & Fri. $.50 newsstand; $40/yr. in state; $52/yr. out of state. 208 W. Murphy St., Madison, NC 27025. TEL 910-548-6047; FAX 910-548-2853. **Owner(s):** Rockingham Newspapers, Inc., P.O. Box 508, Madison, NC 27025. TEL 910-548-6047; FAX 910-548-2853; Ed. Bruce A. Webb; Pub. Bruce A. Webb; adv. contact: Wendy Hayden. photos; bk.rev.; pub. size: broadsheet; circ. 7,600(paid).

MANTEO

US

COASTLAND TIMES. 1935. 3/wk.: Tue., Thu., Sun. $.50 newsstand; $25.66/yr. in cy. 501 Budleigh St., Manteo, NC 27954. TEL 919-473-2105; FAX 919-473-1515. **Owner(s):** Times Printing Co., 501 Budleigh St., Manteo, NC 27454. TEL 919-473-2105; Ed. F.W. Meekins; Pub. F.W. Meekins; adv. contact: V.H. Meekins. pub. size: broadsheet; circ. 12,000(paid). **Wire Service(s):** AP.

MARSHVILLE

US

HOME NEWS, THE. 1892. Thu. $.50 newsstand; $14/yr. in Union & Anson cys.; $22/yr. elsewhere. 123 E. Union St., Marshville, NC 28103. TEL 704-624-5068. **Owner(s):** Beaver Dam Press, Inc., P.O. Box 100, Marshville, NC 28103. TEL 704-624-5068; Ed. Rosemary Osborn. adv. contact: William Osborn. photos; pub. size: broadsheet; circ. 2,950(paid).

MEBANE

US

MEBANE ENTERPRISE. 1908. Wed. $.50 newsstand; $18.43/yr. 106 N. Fourth St., Mebane, NC 27302. TEL 919-563-3555; FAX 919-563-9242. **Owner(s):** Womack Publishing Co., Inc., P.O. Box 111, Chatham, VA 24531. TEL 804-432-1654; Ed. Kitty Brandon. adv.; photos; pub. size: standard; circ. 2,100(paid).

MOCKSVILLE

US

DAVIE COUNTY ENTERPRISE-RECORD. 1916. Thu. $.50 newsstand; $20/yr. in state; $25/yr. out of state. S. Main St., Mocksville, NC 27028. TEL 704-634-2129; FAX 704-634-9760. **Owner(s):** Davie County Publishing Co., Inc., P.O. Box 525, Mocksville, NC 27028. TEL 704-634-2129; Ed. Mike Barnhardt; Pub. Dwight Sparks; adv. contact: Becky Snyder. photos; pub. size: broadsheet; circ. 8,000(paid).

  Formerly: Mocksville Davie County Enterprise.

MOORESVILLE

US

MOORESVILLE TRIBUNE. Wed. $.50 newsstand; $18.37/yr. locally; $21/yr. out of state. 147 E. Center Ave., Mooresville, NC 28115. TEL 704-664-5554; FAX 704-664-3614. **Owner(s):** Park Communications, Inc., Vine Ctr. Office Tower, 333 W. Vine St., 17th Fl., Lexington, KY 40507. TEL 606-242-7252; Ed. Annette Privette. adv. contact: Lou Sullivan. photos; bk.rev.; pub. size: broadsheet; circ. 25,304(paid).

MOREHEAD CITY

US

CARTERET COUNTY NEWS-TIMES. 1912. 3/wk.: Sun., Wed., Fri. $.50 newsstand; $52/yr. in cy. 4034 Arendell St., Morehead City, NC 28557. TEL 919-726-7081; FAX 919-726-6016. **Owner(s):** Carteret Publishing, Inc., 4034 Arendell St., Morehead City, NC 28557. TEL 919-726-7081 Ed. Walter D. Phillips. adv.; photos; bk.rev.; pub. size: broadsheet; circ. 12,800(paid); Sun. 13,700(paid). **Wire Service(s):** AP.

  Formerly: Morehead City Carteret County News-Times.

MORGANTON

US

BURKE COUNTY OBSERVER. Wed. free. 301 Collett St., Morganton, NC 28655. TEL 704-437-2161; FAX 704-437-5372. **Owner(s):** Park Communications, Inc., Vine Ctr. Office Tower, 333 W. Vine St., 17th Fl., Lexington, KY 40507. TEL 606-252-7275; Ed. Bill Poteat. adv. contact: Randy Hart. pub. size: broadsheet; circ. 8,000(free).

VALDESE NEWS. 1935. Wed. $.25 newsstand. 301 Collett St., Morganton, NC 28655. TEL 704-437-2161; FAX 704-437-5372; E-mail: ann@tsl.dana.edu. **Owner(s):** Park Communications Inc., Vine Ctr. Office Tower, 333 W. Vine St., 17th Fl., Lexington, KY 40507. TEL 606-252-7275; Ed. Eugene Willard. adv. contact: Randy Hart. pub. size: broadsheet; circ. 4,000(paid).

MOUNT AIRY

US

SURRY SCENE, THE. 1981. Tue. free. 319 Renfro St., Mount Airy, NC 27030. TEL 910-786-4141; FAX 910-789-2816. **Owner(s):** Mount Airy Newspapers, Inc. P.O. Box 808, Mount Airy, NC 27030. TEL 919-786-4141; Pub. George W. Summerlin; adv. contact: Bernard Flippin. pub. size: tabloid; circ. 20,000(free).

MT. OLIVE

US

MOUNT OLIVE TRIBUNE. 1904. s-w.: Tue. & Fri. $.50 newsstand; $21.20/yr in cy.; $31.09/yr. out of cy. 301 Hwy. 55 W., Mt. Olive, NC 28365. TEL 919-658-9456; FAX 919-658-9559. **Owner(s):** McClatchy Newspapers, P.O. Box 15779, Sacramento, CA 95816. TEL 916-321-1000; Ed. Steve Herring; Pub. S.B. Pierce, Jr.; adv. contact: Gary Scott. pub. size: broadsheet; circ. 5,000(paid).

MURPHY

US   ISSN 0746-3987

CHEROKEE SCOUT. 1891. Tue. $14/yr in cy.; $22/yr. out of cy. One Church St., Murphy, NC 28906. TEL 704-837-5122; FAX 704-837-5832. **Owner(s):** Community Newspapers, Inc., Miami, FL 33152; Ed. Patty Little. photos; bk.rev.; pub. size: broadsheet; circ. 8,000(paid).

  Formerly: Cherokee Scout.

NASHVILLE

US

NASHVILLE GRAPHIC. 1895. Thu. $.50 newsstand; $18.70/yr. in cy. 106 N. Boddie St., Nashville, NC 27356. TEL 919-459-7101; FAX 919-459-3052. **Owner(s):** Nash County Newspapers, Inc.; Pub. Hal Sharp; adv. contact: Sam Taylor. photos; bk.rev. pub. size: broadsheet; circ. 4,500(controlled & paid).

NORTH WILKESBORO

US

JOURNAL-PATRIOT. 1906. s-w.: Mon. & Thu. $.35 newsstand; $29.68/yr. in cy; $31.80/yr. out of cy. 711 Main St., North Wilkesboro NC 28659. TEL 910-838-4117; FAX 910-838-9864. **Owner(s):** Carter-Hubbard Publishing Co., Inc., 711 Main St., North Wilkesboro, NC 28659. TEL 919-838-4117; Ed. Charles Williams; Pub. John Hubbard; adv. contact: Carolyn Barker. photos; pub. size: broadsheet; circ. 7,600(paid).

OLD FORT

US

NEWS BULLETIN, THE. 1973. Wed. $.25 newsstand; $15/yr. in cy.; $20/yr. out of cy. P.O. Box 638, Old Fort, NC 28762-0638. TEL 704-668-4783; FAX 704-668-4722. **Owner(s):** McDowell Publishing Associates, Inc., P.O. Box 305, Marion, NC 28752-0305. TEL 704-668-4783; adv.; photos; pub. size: standard; circ. 2,000(controlled & paid).

  Formerly: Old Fort Bulletin.

OXFORD

US

OXFORD PUBLIC LEDGER. 1881. s-w.: Mon. & Thu. $.50 newsstand; $21.20/yr in cy.; $24.38/yr. in state; $26.50/yr. out of state. 200 W. Spring St., Oxford, NC 27565. TEL 919-693-2646; FAX 919-693-3704. **Owner(s):** Royster Critcher, 200 W. Spring St., Oxford, NC 27565. TEL 919-693-2646; FAX 919-693-3704; Ed. Johnny Whitfield. adv. contact: Ronald N. Critcher. pub. size: broadsheet; circ. 8,200(paid).

PLYMOUTH

US

ROANOKE BEACON. 1889. Wed $.50 newsstand; $21.73/yr. 210-212 W. Water St., Plymouth, NC 27962. TEL 919-793-2123. **Owner(s):** Hote Jones, P.O. Box 726, Plymouth, NC 27962. TEL 919-793-2123; Ed. Doward H. Jones, Jr. adv.; pub. size: broadsheet; circ. 4,700(paid).

PRINCETON

US

PRINCETON NEWS LEADER. Wed. $.50 newsstand; $12/yr. local; $16.50/yr. out of area. 109 S. Center St., Princeton, NC 27569. TEL 919-965-2033; FAX 919-965-5903. **Owner(s):** Barry Merrill, P.O. Box 273, Selma, NC 27576. TEL 919-965-2033 Ed. Barry Merrill; Pub. Barry Merrill; circ. 1,500(paid).

RAEFORD

US

RAEFORD NEWS-JOURNAL, THE. 1905. Wed. $.50 newsstand; $14/yr. in cy.; $17/yr. in state; $20/yr. out of state. 119 W. Elwood Ave., Raeford, NC 28376. TEL 910-875-2121; FAX 910-875-7256; E-mail: njournal@coastalnet.com; URL: http://www3.coastalnet.com/cnmedia/fbpost/NJ.html. **Owner(s):** Dickson Press, Inc., P.O. Box 550, Raeford, NC 28376. TEL 910-875-2121; FAX 910-875-7256; Ed. Amy Clarkson; Pub. Louis H. Fogleman; adv. contact: Susan Stauffer. photos; pub. size: broadsheet; circ. 4,200(paid).

RALEIGH

US   ISSN 0045-5873

CAROLINIAN, THE. 1940. s-w.: Mon. & Thu. $.50 newsstand; $30/yr. locally. 649 Maywood Ave., Raleigh, NC 27603. TEL 919-834-5558; FAX 919-832-3243. **Owner(s):** Prentice Monroe, 649 Maywood Ave., Raleigh, NC 27603. TEL 919-834-5558; FAX 919-832-3243; Ed. Prentice Monroe; Pub. Prentice Monroe; pub. size: standard; circ. 17,500(paid).

US   ISSN 0896-3363

SPECTATOR. 1978. Thu. free newsstand; $30/yr. mailed. 1318 Dale St., Raleigh, NC 27605. TEL 919-828-7393; FAX 919-831-9217. **Owner(s):** Spectator Publications, Inc., 1315 Dale St., Raleigh, NC 27605. TEL 919-828-7393; photos; bk.rev.; pub. size: tabloid; circ. 60,000.

RANDLEMAN

US   ISSN 1074-5157

RANDLEMAN REPORTER. 1982. Wed. $.35 newsstand; $16.50/yr. 125 W. Academy St., Randleman, NC 27317. TEL 910-498-4151; FAX 910-498-4152. **Owner(s):** Randolph Publishing Co., P.O. Box 1044, Asheboro, NC 27204-1044; Ed. Sandra Cooper; Pub. Robert M. Deer, Jr.; adv.; photos; pub. size: broadsheet; circ. 2,150(controlled & paid).

RICHLANDS

US

RICHLANDS-BEULAVILLE ADVERTISER-NEWS. 1975. Wed. $.25 newsstand; $15/yr. in cy.; $22/yr. out of cy.; $26/yr. out of state. 105 W. Frank St., Richlands, NC 28574. TEL 910-324-5062; FAX 910-285-3179. **Owner(s):** H.L. Oswald Enterprises, Inc., 107 N. College St., Wallace, NC 28466. TEL 910-285-2178; FAX 910-285-3179; Ed. Sammie Carter; Pub. H.L. Oswald, III; adv. contact: Mary Hart Oswald. photos; pub. size: broadsheet; circ. 4,200(paid).

ROXBORO

US

COURIER-TIMES, THE. 1881. s-w.: Wed. & Sat. $.50 newsstand; $34.95/yr. in state; $38.22/yr. out of state. 109 Clayton Ave., Roxboro, NC 27573. TEL 910-599-0162; FAX 910-597-2773. **Owner(s):** Jerry M. Clayton, P.O. Box 311, Roxboro, NC 27573. TEL 910-599-0162; FAX 910-597-2773; Ed. Neal F. Rattican; Pub. Jerry M. Clayton; adv.; photos; bk.rev.; pub. size: broadsheet; circ. 7,900(paid). **Wire Service(s):** AP. Formerly: Roxboro Courier-Times.

RUTHERFORDTON

US

COUNTY NEWS ENTERPRISE. 1926. Wed. free. 218 W. First St., Rutherfordton, NC 28139. TEL 704-287-3327; FAX 704-287-9371. **Owner(s):** Forest City Publishing, 1111 Oak St., Forest City, NC 28043; Ed. Jean Gordon; Pub. Jim Deviney; adv. contact: Jim Deviney. photos; pub. size: broadsheet; circ. 12,000(free). Formerly: Enterprise; Rutherford County News Enterprise.

SCOTLAND NECK

US

COMMONWEALTH PROGRESS. Wed. $.50 newsstand; $19.08/yr. 1107 Main St., Scotland Neck, NC 27874. TEL 919-826-2111; FAX 919-826-2111. **Owner(s):** Park Communications, Inc., 1700 Vine Ctr. Office Tower, 333 W. Vine St., 17th Fl., Lexington, KY 40507. TEL 606-252-7275; Ed. Sylvia Hughes; Pub. Marie Jernigan; adv. contact: Marie Jernigan. pub. size: broadsheet; circ. 1,050(paid). Formerly: Enfield Progress.

SELMA

US

JOHNSTONIAN SUN. 1887. Thu. $.50 newsstand; $12/yr. local; $16.50/yr. out of area. 101 N. Webb St., Selma, NC 27576. TEL 919-965-2033; FAX 919-965-5903. **Owner(s):** Barry Merrill, P.O. Box 278, Selma, NC 27576. TEL 919-965-2033; Ed. Barry Merrill; Pub. Barry Merrill; pub. size: broadsheet; circ. 4,000(paid).

SHALLOTTE

US

BRUNSWICK BEACON, THE. 1962. Thu. $.50 newsstand; $12.25/yr. in cy.; $18.30/yr. out of cy.; $20.90/yr. out of state. 4709 Main St., Shallotte, NC 28459. TEL 910-754-6890; FAX 910-754-5407. **Owner(s):** Brunswick Beacon, Inc., The, 4709 Main St., P.O. Box 2558, Shallotte, NC 28459. TEL 910-754-6890; FAX 910-754-5407; Ed. Lynn S. Carlson. adv.; pub. size: broadsheet; circ. 15,000(paid).

SHELBY

US

CLEVELAND TIMES. 1941. Thu. $.25 newsstand; $12.72/yr. 824-1 E. King at Canterbury Rd., Shelby, NC 28151. TEL 704-481-8202; FAX 704-481-1031. **Owner(s):** Republic Newspapers, Inc., 824-1 E. King at Canterbury Rd., Shelby, NC 28151; Ed. Michelle Hill; Pub. Dean Ridings; adv. contact: Aron Goss. photos; pub. size: broadsheet; circ. 2,500(free & paid).

SILER CITY

US

CHATHAM NEWS, THE. Thu. $.50 newsstand; $17/yr. in cy.; $20/yr. out of cy. 303 W. Raleigh, Siler City, NC 27344. TEL 919-663-3232; FAX 919-663-4042. **Owner(s):** Chatham News Publishing Co., 303 W. Raleigh, Siler City, NC 27344. TEL 919-663-3232; Ed. Alan D. Resch; Pub. Alan D. Resch; adv. contact: Georgia Trogdon. photos; pub. size: broadsheet; circ. 9,100(paid). Formerly: Siler City Chatham News.

SMITHFIELD

US

SMITHFIELD HERALD. 1882. s-w.: Tue. & Fri. $.50 newsstand; $48/yr. out of state mailed. 125 S. Fourth St., Smithfield, NC 27577. TEL 919-934-2176; FAX 919-989-7093. **Owner(s):** McClatchy Newspapers, P.O. Box 15774, Sacramento, CA 95816. TEL 916-321-1000; Ed. Scott Bolejack; Pub. S.E. Thorndyke, Sr.; adv. contact: Robert Dixon. pub. size: broadsheet; circ. 14,420(paid).

SOUTHERN PINES

US

▼**SANDHILLS LIVING.** 1996. s-w.: Wed. & Sat. $.50 newsstand. 140 W. Vermont Ave., Southern Pines, NC 28388. TEL 910-693-7707; FAX 910-693-1103. **Owner(s):** Park Communications, Inc., Vine Ctr. Office Tower, 333 W. Vine St., 17th Fl., Lexington, KY 40507. TEL 606-252-7275; Ed. Kevin Scotti. adv. contact: Ellen Pfan. pub. size: standard; circ. 2,000(paid).

US

SOUTHERN PINES PILOT. 1920. s-w.: Mon. & Thu. $.50 newsstand; $30/yr. in cy.; $35/yr. out of cy. 145 W. Pennsylvania Ave., Southern Pines, NC 28387. TEL 910-692-7271; FAX 910-692-9382. **Owner(s):** Sam & Marjorie Ragan, P.O. Box 58, Southern Pines, NC 28387. TEL 910-692-7271; Ed. Sam Ragan; Pub. Sam Ragan; adv. contact: John Hubbard. photos; bk.rev.; pub. size: broadsheet; circ. 15,000(paid).

SOUTHPORT

US

STATE PORT PILOT, THE. 1928. Wed. $.50 newsstand; $10.87/yr. in cy.; $16.47/yr. out of cy.; $19/yr. out of state. 105 S. Howe St., Southport, NC 28461-0548. TEL 910-457-4568; FAX 910-457-9427; E-mail: stateport@aol.com; URL: http://www.southport.net. **Owner(s):** Margaret Harper, P.O. Box 10548, Southport, NC 28461. TEL 910-457-4568; FAX 910-457-9427; Ed. Ed Harper. adv. contact: Kim Adams. pub. size: broadsheet; circ. 7,400(free & paid).

SPRING HOPE

US

SPRING HOPE ENTERPRISE. 1947. Thu. $18/yr. in cy.; $30/yr. out of cy. 113 Ash St., Spring Hope, NC 27882. TEL 919-478-3651; FAX 919-478-3075. **Owner(s):** Spring Hope Enterprise, P.O. Box 399, Spring Hope, NC 27882. TEL 919-478-3651; FAX 919-478-3075; Ed. Ken Ripley; Pub. Ken Ripley; adv. contact: Greg White. photos; pub. size: standard; circ. 6,500(free & paid).

SPRUCE PINE

US

MITCHELL NEWS JOURNAL. 1927. Wed. $.50 newsstand; $17/yr. in cy.; $25/yr. out of cy.; $30/yr. out of state. 401 Locust St., Spruce Pine, NC 28777. TEL 704-765-2071; FAX 704-765-1616. **Owner(s):** CNI Newspapers, Inc., P.O. Box 1492, Spartanburg, SC 29304; Ed. Rachel Hoskins; Pub. Rick Bacon; adv.; pub. size: broadsheet; circ. 6,500(paid).

SYLVA

US ISSN 0531-0300

SYLVA HERALD & RURALITE. 1926. Thu. $.50 newsstand; $18/yr. 539 W. Main St., Sylva, NC 28779. TEL 704-586-2611; FAX 704-586-2637. **Owner(s):** Sylva Herald Publishing Co., Inc., P.O. Box 307, Sylva, NC 28779-0307. TEL 704-586-2611; FAX 704-586-2637; Ed. J.A. Gray. adv.; photos; pub. size: broadsheet; circ. 7,000(paid).

TABOR CITY

US

TRIBUNE, THE. 1946. Wed. $.25 newsstand; $9.98/yr. in town; $13/yr. out of town. Hwy. 701, N., Tabor City, NC 28463. TEL 910-653-3153; FAX 910-653-9440. **Owner(s):** W. Horace Carter, P.O. Box 67, Tabor City, NC 28463. TEL 919-653-3153; Ed. Deuce Niven; Pub. Deuce Niven; adv. contact: Penny Holmes. pub. size: broadsheet; circ. 3,800(paid).
Formerly: Tabor City Tribune.

TAYLORSVILLE

US

TAYLORSVILLE TIMES, THE. 1886. s-w.: Wed. & Sat. $.50 newsstand; $18.50/yr. in cy.; $27.50/yr. out of cy. 106 E. Main St., Taylorsville, NC 28681. TEL 704-632-2532; FAX 704-632-8233. **Owner(s):** Walter L. Sharpe, 106 E. Main St., Taylorsville, NC 28681. TEL 704-632-2532; FAX 704-632-8233; Ed. David Icenhour; Pub. Walter L. Sharpe; adv. contact: Linda Jones. pub. size: broadsheet; circ. 7,000(paid).

THOMASVILLE

US

THOMASVILLE TIMES. 1890. 3/wk.: Tue., Thu., Sat. $.50 newsstand; $3.50/mo. carrier. 512 Turner St., Thomasville, NC 27360. TEL 910-472-9500; FAX 910-476-7272. **Owner(s):** High Point Enterprises, Inc., 210 Church St., High Point, NC 27262. TEL 910-888-3500; Ed. Sarah Sue Ingram; Pub. Robert Schoolfield; adv.; pub. size: broadsheet; circ. 7,000(paid). **Wire Service(s):** AP.

TROY

US

MONTGOMERY HERALD. 1884. Wed. $.50 newsstand; $19.08/yr. in cy.; $27.56/yr. out of cy. 139 Bruton St., Troy, NC 27371. TEL 910-576-6051; FAX 910-576-1050. **Owner(s):** TMS Publishing, Inc., P.O. Box 426, Troy, NC 27371. TEL 919-576-6051; Ed. Gary Evans; Pub. Tim Bula; adv. contact: Tim Bula. pub. size: broadsheet; circ. 7,075(paid).

WADESBORO

US

ANSON RECORD, THE. 1881. Wed. $.50 newsstand; $18/yr. in cy.; $22/yr. in zones 1 & 2; $25/yr. in zones 3-10. 210 E. Morgan, Wadesboro, NC 28170. TEL 704-694-2161; FAX 704-694-7060. **Owner(s):** Community Newspapers, Inc., P.O. Box 792, Athens, GA 30603. TEL 800-226-0692; FAX 706-548-0808; Ed. Sandy Bruney; Pub. Michael Leonard; adv.; pub. size: broadsheet; circ. 7,500(paid).

WAKE FOREST

US

WAKE WEEKLY, THE. 1947. Thu. $.50 newsstand; $21.20/yr. in Wake, Franklin & Durham cys.; $29.04/yr. out of area.; $30/yr. out of state. 229 E. Owen, Wake Forest, NC 27587. TEL 919-556-3182; FAX 919-556-2233. **Owner(s):** Robert W. Allen, 229 E. Owen, Wake Forest, NC 27537. TEL 919-556-3182; Ed. Margret Allen; Pub. Robert W. Allen; adv.; pub. size: broadsheet; circ. 7,500(paid).

WALLACE

US

WALLACE ENTERPRISE. 1923. s-w.: Mon. & Thu. $.25 newsstand; $25/yr. local; $40/yr. out of cy.; $50/yr. out of state. 107 N. College St., Wallace, NC 28466. TEL 910-285-2178; FAX 910-285-3179. **Owner(s):** H.L. Oswald Enterprises, Inc., 107 N. College St., Wallace, NC 28466. TEL 910-285-2178; Ed. Sammie Carter; Pub. H.L. Oswald, III; adv. contact: Mary Hart Oswald. photos; pub. size: broadsheet; circ. 7,500(paid).

US

WARSAW-FAISON NEWS. 1955. Thu. $.25 newsstand; $15/yr. in cy.; $22/yr. out of cy.; $26/yr. out of state. 107 N. College St., Wallace, NC 28466. TEL 910-285-2178; FAX 910-285-3179. **Owner(s):** H.L. Oswald Enterprises, Inc., 107 N. College St., Wallace, NC 28466. TEL 910-285-2178; FAX 910-285-3179; Ed. Sammie Carter; Pub. H.L. Oswald, III; adv. contact: Mary Hart Oswald. photos; pub. size: broadsheet; circ. 4,000(paid).

WALNUT COVE

US

DANBURY REPORTER. 1872. Thu. $.50 newsstand; $17.50/yr. in cy.; $21.50/yr. out of cy.; $15.50/yr. senior citizens. Main St., Walnut Cove, NC 27052. TEL 910-591-8191. **Owner(s):** C.M. Publishing, P.O. Box 545, King, NC 27021. TEL 910-983-3109; FAX 910-983-8203; Ed. Denise Petree; Pub. T.J. Terglaser; adv.; pub. size: broadsheet; circ. 6,500(paid).

WARRENTON

US

WARREN RECORD, THE. 1896. Wed. $.50 newsstand; $20/yr. in cy.; $26/yr. out of cy. 123 S. Main St., Warrenton, NC 27589. TEL 919-257-3341; FAX 919-257-1413. **Owner(s):** Record Publishing Co., Inc., P.O. Box 70, Warrenton, NC 27589. TEL 919-257-3341; Ed. Howard Jones; Pub. Howard Jones; adv. contact: Jean Reid. photos; pub. size: broadsheet; circ. 5,700(paid).

WENDELL

US

GOLD LEAF FARMER, THE. 1924. Thu. $.50 newsstand; $14.34/yr. in cy. 10 S. Main St., Wendell, NC 27591. TEL 919-365-6262; FAX 919-269-8383. **Owner(s):** McClatchy Newspapers, P.O. Box 15779, Sacramento, CA 95816. TEL 916-321-1000; Ed. Matt Shaw; Pub. D. Mark Wilson; adv.; photos; pub. size: broadsheet; circ. 4,700(paid).

WEST JEFFERSON

US

JEFFERSON POST. 1929. s-w.: Tue. & Thu. $.50 newsstand; $20.80/yr. in cy.; $36.95/yr. out of cy. 203 S. Second Ave., West Jefferson, NC 28694. TEL 910-246-4121; FAX 910-246-7165. **Owner(s):** Mid-South Management Co., Inc., P.O. Box 334, Spartanburg, NC 29304. TEL 919-583-2907; Ed. Sandy Hurley; Pub. Sandy Hurley; adv. contact: Rex Goss. photos; pub. size: broadsheet; circ. 11,700(free & paid).
Formerly: Skyland Post.

WHITEVILLE

US

WHITEVILLE NEWS REPORTER. 1896. s-w.: Mon. & Thu. $.50 newsstand; $22.50/yr. in cy.; $35/yr. out of cy.; $42/yr. out of state. 127 W. Columbus St., Whiteville, NC 28472. TEL 910-642-4104; FAX 910-642-1856. **Owner(s):** News Reporter, Inc., P.O. Box 707, Whiteville, NC 28472. TEL 910-642-4104; FAX 910-642-1856; Ed. Jim High. adv. contact: Max N. Greer, Jr. photos; pub. size: broadsheet; circ. 10,100(free & paid). **Wire Service(s):** AP.

WILLIAMSTON

US

ENTERPRISE, THE. s-w.: Tue. & Thu. $.50 newsstand; $29.95/yr. 108 W. Main St., Williamston, NC 27892. TEL 919-792-1181; FAX 919-792-1921. **Owner(s):** Cox Communications, Inc., P.O. Box 105357, Atlanta, GA 30348. TEL 404-843-5000; Ed. Bobby Burns; Pub. Dallas F. Coltrain; adv. contact: Dallas F. Coltrain. pub. size: broadsheet; circ. 4,500(paid).

US

ROBERSONVILLE WEEKLY HERALD. 1914. Wed. $.35 newsstand; $11-$15/yr. 108 W. Main St., Williamston, NC 27892. TEL 919-792-1181; FAX 919-792-1921. **Owner(s):** Cox Communications, Inc., P.O. Box 105357, Atlanta, GA 30348. TEL 404-843-5000; Ed. Bobby Burns; Pub. Dallas F. Coltrain; adv. contact: Dallas F. Coltrain. photos; pub. size: standard; circ. 600(paid).

US

WILLIAMSTON ENTERPRISE. 1899. s-w.: Tue. & Thu. $.50 newsstand; $29.95/yr. in cy.; $39.95/yr. out of cy. 106-108 W. Main St., Williamston, NC 27892. TEL 919-792-1181; FAX 919-792-1921. **Owner(s):** Cox North Carolina Publications, Inc., 106-108 Main St., Williamston, NC 27892; Ed. Bobby Burns. adv. contact: Dallas F. Coltrain. photos; pub. size: standard; circ. 5,600(paid).

WILMINGTON

US

WILMINGTON JOURNAL. 1927. Thu. $.50 newsstand; $22/yr. mailed in U.S. 412 S. Seventh St., Wilmington, NC 28401. TEL 910-762-5502; FAX 910-343-1334. **Owner(s):** Katherine J. Tate, P.O. Box 1618, Wilmington, NC 28402; Ed. Katherine J. Tate; Pub. Katherine J. Tate; adv.; photos; pub. size: standard; circ. 6,000(paid).

WINDSOR

US

BERTIE LEDGER-ADVANCE. 1928. Thu. $.50 newsstand; $15.90/yr. in cy.; $23.32/yr. in state; $25/yr. out of state. 124 S. King, Windsor, NC 27983-0069. TEL 919-794-3185; FAX 919-794-2835. **Owner(s):** Cox Enterprises, Inc., P.O. Box 105357, Atlanta, GA 30348. TEL 404-843-5000; Ed. Laura Harrell; Pub. Laura Harrell; adv. contact: Sue Brett. pub. size: standard; circ. 4,450(paid).

YADKINVILLE

US

YADKIN RIPPLE, THE. 1892. Thu. $.25 newsstand; $12/yr. in cy.; $12/yr. out of cy.; $18/yr. out of state. P.O. Box 7, Yadkinville, NC 27055. TEL 910-679-2341; FAX 910-679-2340. **Owner(s):** Craig Rutledge, Jr., P.O. Box 7, Yadkinville, NC 27055. TEL 910-679-2341; FAX 910-679-2340; Ed. Charles Mathis; Pub. Craig Rutledge; adv. contact: Carol Rutledge. pub. size: standard; circ. 5,850(paid).

YANCEYVILLE

US

CASWELL MESSENGER. 1926. Wed. $.50 newsstand; $19.79/yr. in cy. 137 Main St., Yanceyville, NC 27379. TEL 910-694-4145; FAX 910-694-5637. **Owner(s):** Womack Publishing Co., Inc., P.O. Box 111, Chatham, VA 24531. TEL 804-432-1654; Ed. Gordon Bendall; Pub. Charles A. Womack, Jr.; adv. contact: Pam Durham. pub. size: broadsheet; circ. 4,800(paid).
   Formerly: Yancyville Caswell Messenger.

ZEBULON

US

ZEBULON RECORD, THE. 1925. Thu. $.50 newsstand; $14.84/yr. local; $18.55/yr. in state; $21/yr. out of state. 110 N. Ardendell Ave., Zebulon, NC 27597. TEL 919-269-6101; FAX 919-269-8383; E-mail: zrecord@merlin.nando.com. **Owner(s):** McClatchy Newspapers, P.O. Box 15774, Sacramento, CA 95816. TEL 916-321-1000; Ed. Marty Coward; Pub. D. Mark Wilson; adv.; photos; pub. size: broadsheet; circ. 3,450(paid).

NORTH DAKOTA

BEULAH

US

BEULAH BEACON. 1970. Thu. $.50 newsstand; $23/yr. in state; $30/yr. out of state. 324 Second Ave., N.E., Beulah, ND 58523-0609. TEL 701-873-4381. **Owner(s):** BHG, Inc., P.O. Box 309, Garrison, ND 58540; Pub. Mike Gackle; adv. contact: Ken Beauchamp. photos; bk.rev.; pub. size: broadsheet; circ. 2,500(paid).

BOTTINEAU

US

COURANT, THE. 1885. Tue. $22/yr. in state; $30/yr. out of state. 419 Main St., Bottineau, ND 58318. TEL 701-228-2605; FAX 701-228-5864. **Owner(s):** Hills & Plains Free Press, Inc., P.O. Box 29, Bottineau, ND 58318. TEL 701-228-2605; Ed. Terry Aman; Pub. Mike Getzloff; adv. contact: Jackie Bullinger. pub. size: standard; circ. 3,500(paid).

BOWMAN

US

BOWMAN FINDER. 1962. Wed. free in surrounding cys.; $25/yr. out of area. 18 S. Main St., Bowman, ND 58623. TEL 701-523-5623; FAX 701-523-3441. **Owner(s):** Dickson Media, Inc., P.O. Drawer F, Bowman, ND 58623. TEL 701-523-5623; Ed. Jeff Schumacher; Pub. Jeff Schumacher; adv.; pub. size: standard; circ. 11,500(free & paid).

CASSELTON

US   ISSN 1074-1801

CASS COUNTY REPORTER. 1881. Wed. $.50 newsstand; $22/yr. local; $29.50/yr. elsewhere. 122 Sixth Ave., N., Casselton, ND 58012-0190. TEL 701-347-4493; FAX 701-347-4495. **Owner(s):** Sean & Cheryl Kelly, 122 Sixth Ave., N., Casselton, ND 58012. TEL 701-347-4493; FAX 701-347-4495; Ed. Michael Utt; Pub. Sean Kelly; adv. contact: Peggy Hanson. pub. size: broadsheet; circ. 3,400(controlled & paid).

CROSBY

US

JOURNAL, THE. 1902. Wed. $.50 newsstand; $23/yr. in area; $32/yr. out of area. 217 N. Main, Crosby, ND 58730. TEL 701-965-6088; FAX 701-965-6089. **Owner(s):** Journal, The, P.O. Box E, Crosby, ND 58730. TEL 701-965-6088; Ed. Steve Andrist; Pub. Steve Andrist; pub. size: broadsheet; circ. 3,000(paid).

ELGIN

US

CARSON PRESS. 1905. Wed. $20/yr. in cy.; $23/yr. in state; $26/yr. out of state. 119 Main St., Elgin, ND 58533. TEL 701-584-2900. **Owner(s):** Duane & Gail Schatz, P.O. Box 100, Elgin, ND 58533. TEL 701-584-2900; Ed. Duane Schatz; Pub. Gail Schatz; pub. size: broadsheet; circ. 1,200(paid).

US

GRANT COUNTY NEWS. 1910. Wed. $.75 newsstand; $17/yr. in cy.; $20/yr. in state; $23/yr. out of state. 119 Main St., Elgin, ND 58533. TEL 701-584-2900; FAX 701-584-2900. **Owner(s):** Duane & Gail Schatz, 119 Main St., Elgin, ND 58533. TEL 701-584-2900; FAX 701-584-2900; Ed. Duane Schatz; Pub. Duane Schatz; adv.; pub. size: broadsheet; circ. 2,312(free & paid).

ENDERLIN

US

ENDERLIN INDEPENDENT. 1882. Wed. $.50 newsstand; $22/yr. in state; $26/yr. out of state. 209 Fourth Ave., Enderlin, ND 58027. TEL 701-437-3131; FAX 701-437-3131. **Owner(s):** Ruth E. McCleerey, 209 Fourth Ave., Enderlin, ND 58027. TEL 701-437-3131; FAX 701-437-3131; Gerald P. Harris, P.O. Box 196, La Moure, ND 58458. TEL 701-884-5393; Ed. Ruth McCleerey; Pub. Ruth McCleerey; adv. contact: Ruth McCleerey. photos; bk.rev.; pub. size: broadsheet; circ. 1,000(paid).

GARRISON

US

MCLEAN COUNTY INDEPENDENT. 1905. Thu. $23/yr. in area; $30/yr. out of state. 59 N. Main St., Garrison, ND 58540. TEL 701-463-2201. **Owner(s):** BHG, Inc., P.O. Box 309, Garrison, ND 58540. TEL 701-463-2201; Ed. Alan Reed; Pub. Don Gackle; adv. contact: Jude Iverson. pub. size: tabloid; circ. 3,875(paid).

GRAFTON

US   ISSN 1067-5922

WALSH COUNTY RECORD, THE. 1889. Tue. $.75 newsstand; $29/yr. in area. 402 Hill Ave., Grafton, ND 58237. TEL 701-352-0640. **Owner(s):** Morgan Publishing Co., 420 Hill Ave., Grafton, ND 58237. TEL 701-352-0640; Ed. John A. Strand; Pub. Jackie Thompson; adv.; pub. size: broadsheet; circ. 3,600(paid).
   Formerly: Grafton Record.

HARVEY

US

HERALD PRESS. 1897. Mon. $.75 newsstand; $24/yr. in cy.; $25/yr. in state; $34/yr. out of state. 1015 Lincoln Ave., Harvey, ND 58341. TEL 701-324-4646; FAX 701-324-4647. **Owner(s):** Charles & Marion Eldredge, 1015 Lincoln, Harvey, ND 58341. TEL 701-324-4646; Pub. Charles Eldredge; adv.; pub. size: broadsheet; circ. 3,728(paid).

HAZEN

US

HAZEN STAR. 1914. Thu. $.50 newsstand; $23/yr. in state; $30/yr. out of state. 26 E. Main St., Hazen, ND 58545. TEL 701-748-2255. **Owner(s):** BHG, Inc., P.O. Box 309, Garrison, ND 58540; Ed. Lauren Donovan. adv. contact: Doreen Ost. photos; bk.rev.; pub. size: broadsheet; circ. 2,300(paid).

JAMESTOWN

US

PRAIRIE POST. 1972. Tue. free. 217 First Ave., N., Jamestown, ND 58401. TEL 701-252-2796; FAX 701-251-2873. **Owner(s):** American Publishing Co., 606 N. Van Buren, P.O. Box 520, Marion, IL 62959. TEL 618-993-1711; Ed. Diane Adams; Pub. Bruce Henke; adv. contact: Zenithe Mayer. pub. size: tabloid; circ. 19,000(free).

LANGDON

US

CAVALIER COUNTY REPUBLICAN. 1888. Mon. $.75 newsstand; $23/yr. in city. 710 Third St., Langdon, ND 58249. TEL 701-256-5311; FAX 701-256-5841. **Owner(s):** Dickson Media, 710 Third St., Langdon, ND 58249. TEL 701-256-5311; FAX 701-256-5841; Ed. Marvin Baker; Pub. Marvin Baker; adv.; bk.rev.; pub. size: broadsheet; circ. 2,700(paid).

LINTON

US

LINTON EMMONS COUNTY RECORD. 1884. Tue. $.75 newsstand; $21/yr. in area; $30/yr. out of state. 201 N. Broadway, Linton, ND 58552-0038. TEL 701-254-4537; FAX 701-254-4909. **Owner(s):** Allan Burke, P.O. Box 38, Linton, ND 58552; Leah Burke, P.O. Box 38, Linton, ND 58552; Ed. Allan C. Burke; Pub. Allan C. Burke; adv.: $4.10/SAU. photos; pub. size: broadsheet; circ. 2,930(paid).

LISBON

US

LISBON RANSOM COUNTY GAZETTE & ENTERPRISE. 1882. Mon. $.50 newsstand; $26/yr. in state; $30/yr. out of state. 310 Main St., Lisbon, ND 58054. TEL 701-683-4128; FAX 701-683-4129. **Owner(s):** Sean W. Kelly, 310 Main St., Lisbon, ND 58054. TEL 701-683-4128; Ed. Sean W. Kelly; Pub. Sean W. Kelly; adv. contact: Cheryl A. Kelly. pub. size: broadsheet; circ. 3,600(paid).

MANDAN

US

FINDER, THE. Wed. free in town; $.25/copy. 303 First St., N.E., Mandan, ND 58554. TEL 701-663-6823; FAX 701-663-6823. **Owner(s):** Lee Enterprises, Inc., 130 E. Second St., Davenport, IA 52801; pub. size: tabloid; circ. 39,000(controlled & free).

US

MANDAN NEWS. 1975. Thu. $.50 newsstand; $25/yr. 303 First St., N.E., Mandan, ND 58554. TEL 701-663-6823; FAX 701-663-2442. **Owner(s):** Lee Enterprises, Inc., 130 E. Second St., Davenport, IA 52801; pub. size: tabloid; circ. 1,800(paid).

MINNEWAUKAN

US

BENSON COUNTY FARMERS PRESS. 1884. Wed. $.60 newsstand; $30/yr. in state; $36/yr. out of state; $42/yr. foreign. 120 B Ave., N., Minnewaukan, ND 58351-0098. TEL 701-473-5436; FAX 701-473-5736. **Owner(s):** Benson County Farmers Press, Inc., 120 B Ave., N., Minnewaukan, ND 58351. TEL 701-473-5436; FAX 701-473-5736; Consolidated Newspapers, Inc., 120 B Ave., N., Minnewaukan, ND 58351. TEL 701-473-5436; Ed. Richard M. Peterson; Pub. Richard M. Peterson; adv.; photos; bk.rev.; pub. size: broadsheet; circ. 3,005(free & paid).

NORTHWOOD

US

LARIMORE PIONEER. Wed. $.50 newsstand; $21.75/yr. in state; $29.50/yr. out of state. 22 N. Main St., Northwood, ND 58267. TEL 701-587-6126; FAX 701-587-5219. **Owner(s):** David & Leslie Pfeifle, 22 N. Main St., Northwood, ND 58267. TEL 701-587-6126; FAX 701-587-5219; Pub. David Pfeifle; pub. size: broadsheet; circ. 1,000(paid).

US

LEADER, THE. Wed. $.50 newsstand; $21.75/yr. 22 N. Main St., Northwood, ND 58367. TEL 701-587-6126; FAX 701-587-5219. **Owner(s):** David & Leslie Pfeifle, 22 N. Main St., Northwood, ND 58267. TEL 701-587-6126; FAX 701-587-5219; Pub. David Pfeifle; pub. size: broadsheet; circ. 5,000(paid).

NORTHWOOD GLEANER

US (NORTHWOOD GLEANER)

NORTHWOOD GLEANER. 1890. Wed. $.50 newsstand; $21.75/yr. in state; $29.50/yr. out of state. 22 N. Main St., Northwood, ND 58267. TEL 701-587-6126; FAX 701-587-5219. **Owner(s):** David & Leslie Pfeifle, 22 N. Main St., Northwood, ND 58267. TEL 701-587-5697; FAX 701-587-5134; Pub. David Pfeifle; pub. size: broadsheet; circ. 1,650(paid).

PARK RIVER

US

WALSH COUNTY PRESS. 1881. Sat. $.90 newsstand; $36/yr. in cy.; $56/yr. in state; $56/yr. out of state. 404 Briggs Ave., S., Park River, ND 58270. TEL 701-284-6333; FAX 701-284-6091. **Owner(s):** Walsh County Press, Inc., 404 Briggs Ave., S., Park River, SD 58270. TEL 701-284-6333; FAX 701-284-6091; Ed. Holly Anderson; Pub. H.W. Kelly; adv. contact: Joan Schumacher. pub. size: broadsheet; circ. 3,800(paid).

ROLLA

US

TURTLE MOUNTAIN STAR, THE. 1888. Mon. $.50 newsstand; $24/yr. in cy.; $26/yr. out of cy.; $34/yr. out of state. 11 First Ave., N.E., Rolla, ND 58367. TEL 701-477-6495; FAX 701-477-3182. **Owner(s):** Roger Bailey, P.O. Box 849, Rolla, ND 58367; Ed. Roger Bailey; Pub. Roger Bailey; pub. size: broadsheet; circ. 4,000(paid).

    Formerly: Rolla Turtle Mountain Star.

RUGBY

US

PIERCE COUNTY TRIBUNE. 1887. Mon. $.50 newsstand; $22/yr. in state; $28/yr. out of state. 219 S. Main Ave., Rugby, ND 58368. TEL 701-776-5252; FAX 701-776-2159. **Owner(s):** Prairie Publishing, Inc., 219 S. Main Ave., Rugby, ND 58368. TEL 701-776-5252; Ed. Matt Mullalley. adv. contact: Kim Brown. pub. size: broadsheet; circ 3,200(paid).

TURTLE LAKE

US

MCLEAN COUNTY JOURNAL. 1902. w. $.50 newsstand; $19.50/yr. in state; $27.50/yr. out of state. 210 Main St., Turtle Lake, ND 58575-0220. TEL 701-448-2649; FAX 701-448-2649. **Owner(s):** Gerald W. Anderson, 210 Main St., Turtle Lake, ND 58575-0220. TEL 701-448-2649; Pub. Gerald W. Anderson; adv.; photos; pub. size: tabloid; circ. 925(controlled & free).

UNDERWOOD

US

UNDERWOOD NEWS. Thu. $.50 newsstand; $20/yr. in state; $25/yr. out of state. P.O. Box 179, Underwood, ND 58576. TEL 701-442-5535. **Owner(s):** BHG, Inc., Garrison, ND 58540. TEL 701-463-2201. Ed. Linda Hermanson; Pub. Mike Gackle; pub. size: broadsheet; circ. 1,000(paid).

WASHBURN

US

CENTER REPUBLICAN. 1906. Thu. $.50 newsstand; $20/yr. in cy.; $24/yr. out of cy. P.O. Box 340, Washburn, ND 58577. TEL 701-452-8126. **Owner(s):** BHG, Inc., Garrison, ND 58540. TEL 701-463-2201; Ed. Lucille Gullickson; Pub. Mike Gackle adv.; photos; bk.rev. pub. size: standard; circ. 800(paid).

US   ISSN 0888-0220

LEADER-NEWS. Thu. $20/yr. in town; $23/yr. out of town; $30/yr. out of state. Box 340, Washburn, ND 58577. TEL 701-462-8126. **Owner(s):** BHG, Inc., Garrison, ND 58540. TEL 701-463-2201; Ed. Joe Froleich; Pub. Mike Gackle; adv.; photos; bk.rev.; pub. size: tabloid; circ. 2,500(paid).

WEST FARGO

US

MIDWEEK EAGLE. 1970. Mon. free in cy.; $75/yr. outside cy. 322 Sheyenne St., West Fargo, ND 58078. TEL 701-282-2443; FAX 701-282-9248. **Owner(s):** Donovan C. Witham, 322 Sheyenne St., West Fargo, ND 58078. TEL 701-282-2443; Ed. Donovan C. Witham; Pub. Donovan C. Witham; adv. contact: Dave Braton. pub. size: tabloid; circ. 63,000(free & paid).

US

MIDWEEK PLUS. 1970. Thu. free in cy. $50/yr. elsewhere. 322 Sheyenne St., West Fargo, ND 58078. TEL 701-282-2443; FAX 701-282-9248. **Owner(s):** Donovan C. Witham, 322 Sheyenne St., West Fargo, ND 58078. TEL 701-282-2443; Ed. Donovan C. Witham; Pub. Donovan C. Witham; adv. contact: Dave Braton. pub. size: tabloid; circ. 45,900(free & paid).

US

WEST FARGO PIONEER. 1967. Wed. $.35 newsstand; $15/yr. in cy.; $18/yr. out of cy. 322 Sheyenne St., West Fargo, ND 58078. TEL 701-282-2443; FAX 701-282-9248. **Owner(s):** Pioneer Press, Inc., P.O. Box 457, West Fargo, ND 58078; Ed. Thomas Jensen; Pub. Donovan C. Witham; adv.; photos; pub. size: tabloid; circ. 3,300(paid).

WILLISTON

US

WILLISTON PLAINS REPORTER. Wed. free. 14 W. Fourth St., Williston, ND 58801. TEL 701-572-6311; FAX 701-572-1965. **Owner(s):** Wick Communications, Inc., 333 W. Wilcox Dr., Ste. 302, Sierra Vista, AZ 85635; Ed. Donald J. Mrachek; Pub. Donald J. Mrachek; adv.; photos; pub. size: broadsheet; circ. 3,900(free).

NORTHERN MARIANA ISLANDS

SAIPAN

US

MARIANAS REVIEW. 1979. w. P.O. Box 1074, Saipan, MP 96950. TEL 01-234-7160. **Owner(s):** Marianas Review Saipan, MP; Ed. Ruth L. Tighe; Pub. Luis Benavente; circ. 1,700.

    Formerly: Commonwealth Examiner.

US
PALAU TRIBUNE. w. Tribune, Saipan, MP 96950.
Owner(s): United Micronesian Development
Association, Saipan, MP 96950;

OHIO

AKRON

US
SUBURBANITE, THE. 1968. Mon. $.25 newsstand;
$20/yr. local; $25/yr. out of state. 3830 S. Main
St., Akron, OH 44319. TEL 216-644-2249;
FAX 216-644-6037. **Owner(s):** Thomson
Newspapers, Inc., One Thorn Run Ctr., Ste. 500,
1187 Thorn Run Rd. Ext., Coraopolis, PA 15108.
TEL 412-262-7870; Ed. Paul R. Harbaugh; Pub.
Ron Thrash; pub. size: tabloid; circ. 26,000(paid).

AMHERST

US
NEWS TIMES. 1874. Wed. $.50 newsstand; $20/yr.
155 N. Leavitt, Amherst, OH 44001.
TEL 216-988-2801; FAX 216-988-2802.
Owner(s): Gazette Publishing Co., 607 N.
Sandusky St., Bellvue, OH 44811. TEL
419-483-4190; Ed. Kathleen Koshar; Pub. Tom
Smith; adv. contact: Dorri Sturges. pub. size:
standard; circ. 2,500(paid).

ANDOVER

US
PYMATUNING AREA NEWS. 1970. Wed. $.50
newsstand; $20/yr. in cy.; $30/yr. out of cy. 37
Public Sq., Andover, OH 44003.
TEL 216-293-6097; FAX 216-293-7374.
Owner(s): Gazette Newspapers, Inc., P.O. Box
166, Jefferson, OH 44047. TEL 216-576-9115;
Ed. Mark Owens; Pub. John Lampson; adv.
contact: Robert Halstead. pub. size: tabloid; circ.
2,100(paid).

ARCANUM

US
DARKE COUNTY EARLY BIRD, THE. 1968. Sun. free;
$.50 newsstand. 114 W. George St., Arcanum,
OH 45304. TEL 513-692-5102;
FAX 513-692-8291. **Owner(s):** John F. & Carol
L. Ball, 5312 Sebring Warner Rd., Greenville, OH
45331. TEL 513-548-3330; FAX
513-548-3376; Ed. Norma Jenkins; Pub. Carol L.
Ball; adv.; photos; pub. size: broadsheet; circ.
26,625(free).

ARCHBOLD

US
ARCHBOLD BUCKEYE. 1905. Wed. $.75 newsstand;
$29/yr. in state; $34/yr. out of state. 207 N.
Defiance St., Archbold, OH 43502.
TEL 419-445-4466; FAX 419-445-4177.
Owner(s): Archbold Buckeye, Inc., 207 N.
Defiance St., Archbold, OH 43502. TEL
419-445-4466; FAX 419-445-4177; Pub. Ross
Wm. Taylor; adv. contact: Mary Huber. pub. size:
broadsheet; circ. 3,250(paid).

US   ISSN 0093-5832
FARMLAND NEWS. 1959. Tue. $.60 newsstand;
$21/yr. local. 104 Depot St., Archbold, OH
43502-0240. TEL 419-445-9456;
FAX 419-445-4444. **Owner(s):** O. Roger Taylor,
309 Murbach St., Archbold, OH 43502. TEL
419-445-5411; Ed. Jeremy J. Rohrs; Pub. O.
Roger Taylor; adv. contact: Doug Nutter. photos;
pub. size: tabloid; circ. 7,322(paid).

ATHENS

US
ATHENS NEWS. 1977. s-w.: Mon. & Thu. free. 14 N.
Court St., Athens, OH 45701.
TEL 614-594-8219; FAX 614-592-5695.
Owner(s): Athens News Inc., The, 14 N. Court St.,
Athens, OH 45701. TEL 614-594-8219; Ed.
Terry Smith; Pub. Bruce Mitchell; pub. size:
tabloid; circ. 17,500(free).

ATTICA

US
ATTICA HUB. 1896. Thu. $.50 newsstand;
$18.50/yr. 26 N. Main St., Attica, OH 44807.
TEL 419-426-3491; FAX 419-426-3491.
Owner(s): Jeffrey Cook, 309 Moore St., Bellevue,
OH 44811. TEL 419-483-3530; Ed. Dawn
Martin; Pub. Jeffery Cook; adv.; pub. size:
broadsheet; circ. 2,800(paid).

US
BLOOMVILLE GAZETTE. 1901. Thu. $.50 newsstand;
$18.50/yr. 26 N. Main St., Attica, OH 44807.
TEL 419-426-3491; FAX 419-426-3491.
Owner(s): Seneca Publishing, 309 Moore St.,
Bellevue, OH 44811. TEL 419-483-3530; Ed.
Dawn Martin; Pub. Jeffery Cook; adv.; pub. size:
broadsheet; circ. 500(paid).

AVON LAKE

US
AVON LAKE PRESS. Wed. $.60 newsstand; $2/mo.
carrier; $25/yr. mailed in area; $30/yr. mailed
out of area. 158 Lear Rd., Avon Lake, OH
44012. TEL 216-933-5100;
FAX 216-933-7904. **Owner(s):** Richard Hemmer,
Jr., 158 Lear Rd., Avon Lake, OH 44012. TEL
216-935-5100; Ed. Richard Hemmer, Jr.; Pub.
Richard Hemmer, Jr.; adv. contact: Linda
Hemmer. pub. size: tabloid; circ. 13,000(paid).

BARBERTON

US
BARBERTON HERALD. 1927. Thu. $.50 newsstand;
$15/yr. mailed in 4 cys. area; $24/yr. mailed
out of area. 70 Fourth St., N.W., Barberton, OH
44203. TEL 330-753-1068;
FAX 330-753-1021. **Owner(s):** Richardson
Publishing Co., 70 Fourth St., N.W., Barberton, OH
44203. TEL 216-753-1068; Ed. D.A. Richardson;
Pub. D.A. Richardson; adv. contact: Rosalie
Marquette. pub. size: broadsheet; circ.
7,500(paid).

BARNESVILLE

US
BARNESVILLE ENTERPRISE. 1866. Wed. $.60
newsstand; $19.50/yr. in state; $23/yr. out of
state. 166 E. Main St., Barnesville, OH 43713.
TEL 614-425-1912; FAX 614-425-2545.
Owner(s): Dix News Media, P.O. Box 30,
Barnesville, OH 43713. TEL 614-425-1912; Ed.
Bruce Yarnall; Pub. Robert C. Dix; adv. contact:
Connie Burkhart. pub. size: standard; circ.
5,000(paid).

BATAVIA

US
CLERMONT SUN. 1828. Thu. $.35 newsstand;
$15/yr. 465 E. Main St., Batavia, OH 45103.
TEL 513-732-2511; FAX 513-732-6344.
Owner(s): Clermont Sun Publishing Co., P.O. Box
366, Batavia, OH 45103. TEL 513-732-2511;
Ed. Jean Kowalski; Pub. William Latham; adv.
contact: Carla Marasek. bk.rev.; pub. size:
broadsheet; circ. 5,000(paid).

BEACHWOOD

US
SOLON HERALD SUN. 1946. Thu. $.60 newsstand;
$32.50/yr. 3355 Richmond Rd., Ste. 171,
Beachwood, OH 44122. TEL 216-464-6397;
FAX 216-464-8816. **Owner(s):** Sun Media, Inc.,
510 Cloverleaf Pkwy., Cleveland, OH 44125. TEL
216-524-0830; FAX 216-642-5547; Ed. Mary
Jane Skala. adv. contact: John Zeigler. pub. size:
broadsheet; circ. 4,000(paid).

BEDFORD

US
BEDFORD TIME REGISTER. Thu. $14/yr. mailed. 711
Broadway, Bedford, OH 44146.
TEL 216-232-4055; FAX 216-232-8861.
Owner(s): Record Publishing Co., Inc., 1619
Commerce Dr., Cuyahoga Falls, OH 44224; Ed.
Mindy Gabarik. pub. size: tabloid; circ.
3,400(paid).

US
BULLETIN, THE. Thu. $.50 newsstand; $16/yr. 711
Broadway, Bedford, OH 44146.
TEL 216-232-4055; FAX 216-232-8861.
Owner(s): Record Publishing Co., Inc., 1619
Commerce Dr., Cuyahoga Falls, OH 44224; adv.
contact: Pam Holtz. pub. size: tabloid; circ.
7,000(paid).

US
MAPLE HEIGHTS PRESS. 1948. Thu. $.50
newsstand; $14/yr. 711 Broadway, Bedford, OH
44146. TEL 216-232-4055;
FAX 216-232-8861. **Owner(s):** Record Publishing
Co., Inc., 1619 Commerce Dr., Stow, OH 44224.
TEL 216-688-0088; Ed. Mindi Gabarik; Pub.
David Dix; pub. size: tabloid; circ. 5,500(paid).

BELLEVUE

US
RFD NEWS, THE. 1958. s-m.: 2nd & 4th Mon.
$12/yr. 131 E. Main St., Bellevue, OH 44811.
TEL 419-483-7410; FAX 419-483-3617.
Owner(s): Gazette Publishing Co., 127 N.
Sandusky Ave., Bellevue, OH 44811. TEL
419-483-3737; Ed. Thomas L. Ackerman. adv.;
bk.rev.; pub. size: tabloid; circ. 75,331(controlled
& paid).

BLUFFTON

US
BLUFFTON NEWS, THE. 1875. Thu. $30/yr. in state;
$35/yr. out of state. 101 N. Main St., Bluffton,
OH 45817. TEL 419-358-8010;
FAX 419-358-5027. **Owner(s):** Bluffton News
Printing & Publishing Co., 103 N. Main St.,
Bluffton, OH 45817. TEL 419-358-8010; Ed.
Fred Steiner; Pub. Tom Edwards; adv.; bk.rev.;
pub. size: standard; circ. 2,800(paid).

BOARDMAN
US

BOARDMAN NEWS. 1947. Thu. $.25 newsstand; $15/yr. renewal; $20/yr. 6221 Market St., Boardman, OH 44512. TEL 216-758-2658; FAX 216-758-2658. **Owner(s):** John A. Darnell, Sr. & John A. Darnell, Jr., 6221 Market St., Youngstown, OH 44512. TEL 216-758-2658; Ed. John Darnell; Pub. Jack Darnell; adv. contact: Richard Bingham. photos; bk.rev.; pub. size: broadsheet; circ. 9,000(paid).

BRYAN
US

COUNTYLINE, THE. 1967. Sun. free; $7.90/yr. mailed. 127 S. Walnut St., Bryan, OH 43506. TEL 419-636-1111. **Owner(s):** Bryan Publishing Co., The, 127 S. Walnut St., Bryan, OH 43506. TEL 419-636-1111; adv.; pub. size: tabloid; circ. Sun. 23,871(free & paid).

CADIZ
US

HARRISON NEWS-HERALD, THE. 1968. Mon. $.50 newsstand; $16.50/yr. local; $36.50/yr. out of cy.; $47/yr. out of state. P.O. Box 127, Cadiz, OH 43907. TEL 614-942-2118; FAX 614-942-4667. **Owner(s):** Patricia O'Grady, P.O. Box 127, Cadiz, OH 43907. TEL 614-942-2796; Pub. Patricia O'Grady; adv.; pub. size: broadsheet; circ. 8,000(paid).
   Formerly: Cadiz Harrison News-Herald.

CALDWELL
US

JOURNAL-LEADER. 1859. Mon. $.50 newsstand; $22/yr. in cy.; $24/yr. out of cy. 309 Main St., Caldwell, OH 43724. TEL 614-732-2341; FAX 614-732-7288. **Owner(s):** Southeast Publications, Inc., 309 Main St., Caldwell, OH 43724. TEL 614-732-2341; FAX 614-732-7288; Pub. David Evans; adv.; photos; pub. size: broadsheet; circ. 5,000(controlled & paid).

CANAL FULTON
US

SIGNAL, THE. 1879. Sun. free; $45/yr. 117A Canal St., Canal Fulton, OH 44614. TEL 216-854-4549; FAX 216-854-1928. **Owner(s):** Buckeye Publishing Co., Inc., 308 W. Maple St., Lisbon, OH 44432. TEL 216-424-9541; Ed. Marsha Kolega; Pub. John Blanchflower; adv. contact: Mace Pavelek. pub. size: broadsheet; circ. 12,600(free).

CANTON
US

FREE PRESS, THE. Sun. free in cy. 808 Monument Rd., N.W., Canton, OH 44703. TEL 216-456-0040; FAX 216-456-1153. **Owner(s):** Youngstown Vindicator, Youngstown, OH; pub. size: broadsheet; circ. 11,000(free).

CARDINGTON
US

MORROW COUNTY INDEPENDENT. 1848. Wed. $.35 newsstand; $23/yr. in cy.; $25/yr. out of cy.; $27/yr. out or state. 123 E. Main St., Cardington, OH 43315. TEL 419-864-6046; FAX 419-947-7241. **Owner(s):** Hirt Publishing, P.O. Box 303, Bellvue, OH 44811. TEL 419-483-7000; Ed. Susie Dye. adv.; photos; pub. size: broadsheet; circ. 1,100(free & paid).

CAREY
US

CAREY PROGRESSOR-TIMES, THE. 1873. Wed. $.50 newsstand; $25/yr. in state; $30/yr. out of state. 1198 E. Findlay St., Carey, OH 43316-0037. TEL 419-396-7567; FAX 419-396-7527. **Owner(s):** Stephen C. Zender, 1198 E. Findlay St., P.O. Box 37, Carey, OH 43316-0037. TEL 419-396-7567; FAX 419-396-7527; Ed. Stephen C. Zender; Pub. Stephen C. Zender; adv. contact: Susana Frey. pub. size: standard; circ. 4,200(paid).

CARROLL
US

LANCASTER FAIRFIELD ADVERTISER. 1974. Wed. free. 3675 Dolson Ct., Carroll, OH 43112. TEL 614-654-6856; FAX 614-654-5617. **Owner(s):** Add, Inc., 500 Industrial Dr., Waupaca, WI 54981. TEL 715-258-8450; pub. size: tabloid; circ. 38,450(free).

CARROLLTON
US

FREE PRESS STANDARD. 1831. Thu. $.50 newsstand; $17.50/yr. local; $35/yr. out of area; $45/yr. out of state. 43 E. Main St., Carrollton, OH 44615. TEL 216-627-5591; FAX 216-627-3195 **Owner(s):** Maynard A. Buck, Jr., 135 Poplar Ln., Cadiz, OH 43907. TEL 614-942-2796; Ed. Carol McIntire; Pub. Maynard A. Buck, Jr.; adv. contact: Judith Ray. photos; pub. size: broadsheet; circ. 8,100(free & paid).
   Formerly: Carrollton Free Press Standard.

CHAGRIN FALLS
US   ISSN 0194-3685

CHAGRIN VALLEY TIMES. 1971. Thu. $.50 newsstand; $24.75/yr. 525 E. Washington St., Chagrin Falls, OH 44022. TEL 216-247-5335; FAX 216-247-5615. **Owner(s):** Chagrin Valley Publishing Co., 525 E. Washington St., Chagrin Falls, OH 44022. TEL 216-247-5335; FAX 216-247-5615; Ed. David C. Lange. adv.; photos; pub. size: tabloid; circ. 18,000(paid).

US   ISSN 0194-3677

SOLON TIMES, THE. 1977. Thu. $.50 newsstand; $24.75/yr. 525 E. Washington St., Chagrin Falls, OH 44022. TEL 216-247-5335. **Owner(s):** Chagrin Valley Publishing Co., 525 W. Washington St., Chagrin Falls, OH 44022. TEL 216-247-5335; Ed. David C. Lange. adv.; photos; pub. size: tabloid; circ. 3,544(paid).

CHESTERLAND
US

CHESTERLAND NEWS. 1967. Wed. free in area; $15/yr. out of area. 8525 Herrick Dr., Chesterland, OH 44026. TEL 216-729-7667. **Owner(s):** Pamela Gable, 8525 Herrick Dr., Chesterland, OH 44026. TEL 216-729-7667; Pub. Pamela Gable; adv.; photos; pub. size: tabloid circ. 6,000(free).

CHILLICOTHE

ADVERTISER, THE. 1913. Sun. free. 147 W. Water St., Chillicothe, OH 45601. TEL 614-773-5010; FAX 614-773-5021. **Owner(s):** Add, Inc., 600 Industrial Dr., Waupaca, WI 54981. TEL 715-258-8450; Pub. Gordon Lowry; adv. contact: David Moore. pub. size: tabloid; circ. 30,000(free).

CINCINNATI
US

DELHI PRESS. 1924. Wed. $.50 newsstand; $2/4 wks.; $105/yr. mailed. 5552 Cheviot Rd., Cincinnati, OH 45247. TEL 513-923-3111; FAX 513-923-1806. **Owner(s):** Press Community Newspapers, 4910 Para Dr., Cincinnati, OH 45237. TEL 513-242-4300; Pub Tony Schad; adv. contact: Gary Hughes. photos; pub. size: broadsheet; circ. 11,000(free & paid).

US

HILLTOP NEWS-PRESS. 1918. Wed. $.50 newsstand; $2/4 wks.; $105/yr. mailed. 5552 Cheviot Rd., Cincinnati, OH 45247. TEL 513-923-3111. **Owner(s):** Press Community Newspapers, 4910 Para Dr., Cincinnati, OH 45237; Pub. Tony Schad. adv. contact: Gary Hughes. pub. size: broadsheet; circ. 20,000(controlled & paid).

US

NORTHEAST SUBURBAN LIFE PRESS. 1963. Wed. $.50 newsstand; $2/4 wks.; $105/yr. mailed. 9121 Union Cemetery Rd., Cincinnati, OH 45249. TEL 513-248-8600; FAX 513-677-4690. **Owner(s):** Suburban Communications Corp., 36251 Schoolcraft Rd., Livonia, MI 48150. TEL 313-591-2300; Ed. Mark Emarl; Pub. Christopher Bukvic; adv. contact: Greg Benker. photos; pub. size: broadsheet; circ. 8,900(paid).

US

NORTHWEST PRESS. 1918. Wed. $.50 newsstand; $2/4 wks.; $105./yr. mailed. 5552 Cheviot Rd., Cincinnati, OH 45247. TEL 513-923-3111. **Owner(s):** Press Community Newspapers, 4910 Para Dr., Cincinnati, OH 45237. TEL 513-242-4300; Pub. Tony Schad; adv. contact: Gary Hughes. pub. size: broadsheet; circ. 18,000(paid).

US

PRICE HILL PRESS. 1924. Wed. $.50 newsstand; $2/4 wks.; $105/yr. mailed. 5552 Cheviot Rd., Cincinnati, OH 45247. TEL 513-923-3111. **Owner(s):** Press Community Newspapers, 4910 Para Dr., Cincinnati, OH 45237. TEL 513-242-4300; Pub. Tony Schad; adv. contact: Gary Hughes. pub. size: broadsheet; circ. 9,000(paid).

US
TRI-COUNTY PRESS. Wed. $.50 newsstand; $2/4 wks. voluntary pay; $105/yr. mailed. 5552 Cheviot Rd., Cincinnati, OH 45247. TEL 513-923-3111; FAX 513-923-1806. **Owner(s):** Press Community Newspapers, 4910 Para Dr., Cincinnati, OH 45237. TEL 513-242-4300; Pub. Tony Schad; adv. contact: Gary Hughes. pub. size: broadsheet; circ. 9,200(paid).

US
WESTERN HILLS PRESS. 1924. Wed. $.50 newsstand; $2/4 wks. voluntary pay; $105/yr. mailed. 5552 Cheviot Rd., Cincinnati, OH 45247. TEL 513-923-3111. **Owner(s):** Press Community Newspapers, 4910 Para Dr., Cincinnati, OH 45237. TEL 513-242-4300; Pub. Tony Schad; adv. contact: Gary Hughes. pub. size: broadsheet; circ. 18,000(paid).

CLEVELAND

US
BEDFORD SUN BANNER. 1970. Thu. $.60 newsstand; $32.50/yr. 5510 Cloverleaf Pkwy., Cleveland, OH 44125-4887. TEL 216-524-0830; FAX 216-524-7792. **Owner(s):** Sun Media, Inc., 5510 Cloverleaf Pkwy., Cleveland, OH 44125-4887. TEL 216-524-0830; FAX 216-642-5547; adv.; photos; pub. size: broadsheet; circ. 5,589(paid).

US
BRECKSVILLE GAZETTE. 1975. s-m.: 2nd & 4th wks. $.30 newsstand; $7/yr.; $12/2 yrs. 7014 Mill Rd., Cleveland, OH 44141. TEL 216-526-7977; FAX 216-526-7114. **Owner(s):** Gazette Newspapers, 7014 Mill Rd., Cleveland, OH 44141. TEL 216-526-7977; pub. size: tabloid; circ. 8,000(paid).

US
BROOKLYN SUN JOURNAL. 1918. Thu. $.60 newsstand; $32.50/yr. 5510 Cloverleaf Pkwy., Cleveland, OH 44125-4887. TEL 216-524-0830; FAX 216-524-7792. **Owner(s):** Sun Media, Inc., 5510 Cloverleaf Pkwy., Cleveland, OH 44125-4887. TEL 216-524-0830; FAX 216-642-5547; adv.; photos; bk.rev.; pub. size: broadsheet; circ. 9,768(paid).

US   ISSN 0894-1645
BRUNSWICK SUN TIMES. Thu. $.60 newsstand; $32.50/yr. 5510 Cloverleaf Pkwy., Cleveland, OH 44125-4887. TEL 216-524-0830; FAX 216-524-7792. **Owner(s):** Sun Media, Inc., 5510 Cloverleaf Pkwy., Cleveland, OH 44125-4887. TEL 216-524-0830; FAX 216-642-5547; adv.; photos; bk.rev.; pub. size: broadsheet; circ. 6,682(paid).

US
CHAGRIN HERALD SUN. 1946. Thu. $.60 newsstand; $32.50/yr. 5510 Cloverleaf Pkwy., Cleveland, OH 44125-4887. TEL 216-524-0830; FAX 216-524-7792. **Owner(s):** Sun Media, Inc., 5510 Cloverleaf Pkwy., Cleveland, OH 44125-4887. TEL 216-524-0830; FAX 216-642-5547; adv.; photos; bk.rev.; pub. size: broadsheet; circ. 18,127(paid).
  Formerly: Chagrin Valley Herald Sun.

US
EUCLID SUN JOURNAL. 1945. Thu. $.60 newsstand; $32.50/yr. 5510 Cloverleaf Pkwy., Cleveland, OH 44125-4887. TEL 216-524-0830; FAX 216-524-7792. **Owner(s):** Sun Media, Inc., 5510 Clovereleaf Pkwy., Cleveland, OH 44125-4887. TEL 216-524-0830; FAX 216-642-5547; adv.; photos; bk.rev.; pub. size: broadsheet; circ. 12,548(paid).

US
GARFIELD MAPLE-SUN. 1918. Thu. $.60 newsstand; $32.50/yr. 5510 Cloverleaf Pkwy., Cleveland, OH 44125-4887. TEL 216-524-0830; FAX 216-524-7792. **Owner(s):** Sun Media, Inc., 5510 Cloverleaf Pkwy., Cleveland, OH 44125-4887. TEL 216-524-0830; FAX 216-642-5547; adv.; photos; pub. size: broadsheet; circ. 11,079(paid).
  Formerly: Garfield Sun-Banner.

US
GAZETTE SHOPPER. 1975. m.: 1st. Wed. free. 7014 Mill Rd., Cleveland, OH 44141. TEL 216-526-7977; FAX 216-526-7114. **Owner(s):** Brecksville-Broadview Hts. & Independence Gazette, 7014 Mill Rd., Cleveland, OH 44141. TEL 216-526-7977; Ed. Joyce McFadden. circ. evening 18,900(free & paid).

US
LAKEWOOD SUN POST. 1918. Thu. $.60 newsstand; $32.50/yr. 5510 Cloverleaf Pkwy., Cleveland, OH 44125-4887. TEL 216-524-0830; FAX 216-524-7792. **Owner(s):** Sun Media, Inc., 5510 Cloverleaf Pkwy., Cleveland, OH 44125-4887. TEL 216-524-0830; FAX 216-642-5547; adv.; photos; bk.rev.; pub. size: broadsheet; circ. 12,135(paid).

US
LEADER, THE. 1946. Thu. $15/yr. 4818 Turney Rd., Cleveland, OH 44125. TEL 216-883-0300; FAX 216-271-7447. **Owner(s):** William Kleinschmidt, 4818 Turney Rd., Cleveland, OH 44125. TEL 216-883-0300; FAX 216-271-7447; Ed. William Kleinschmidt. adv. contact: Heather Kleinschmidt. pub. size: broadsheet; circ. 6,000(paid).

US
▼**MEDINA SUN, THE.** 1995. Thu. $.60 newsstand; $32.50/yr. 5510 Cloverleaf Pkwy., Cleveland, OH 44125-4887. TEL 216-524-0830; FAX 216-524-7792. **Owner(s):** Sun Media, Inc., 5510 Cloverlef Pkwy., Cleveland, OH 44125. TEL 216-524-0830; adv.; photos; bk.rev.; pub. size: broadsheet; circ. 11,851(free).

US
NEWS SUN, THE. 1918. Thu. $.60 newsstand; $32.50/yr. 5510 Cloverleaf Pkwy., Cleveland, OH 44125-4887. TEL 216-524-0830; FAX 216-524-7792. **Owner(s):** Sun Media, Inc., 5510 Cloverleaf Pkwy., Cleveland, OH 44125-4887. TEL 216-524-0830; FAX 216-642-5547; Ed. Linda Kinsey. adv.; photos; bk.rev.; pub. size: broadsheet; circ. 17,274(paid).

US
▼**NORDONIA HILLS SUN.** 1994. Thu. $.60 newsstand. 5510 Cloverleaf Pkwy., Cleveland, OH 44125-4887. TEL 216-524-0830; FAX 216-524-7792. **Owner(s):** Sun Media, Inc., 5510 Cloverleaf Pkwy., Cleveland, OH 44125-4887. TEL 216-524-0830; FAX 216-642-5547; adv.; photos; pub. size: broadsheet; circ. 5,516(paid).

US
PARMA SUN POST. 1918. Thu. $.60 newsstand; $32.50/yr. 5510 Cloverleaf Pkwy., Cleveland, OH 44125-4887. TEL 216-524-0830; FAX 216-524-7792. **Owner(s):** Sun Media, Inc., 5510 Cloverleaf Pkwy., Cleveland, OH 44125-4887. TEL 216-524-0830; FAX 216-642-5547; adv.; photos; pub. size: broadsheet; circ. 27,947(paid).

US
SUN BANNER PRIDE. 1865. Thu. $.60 newsstand; $32.50/yr. 5510 Cloverleaf Pkwy., Cleveland, OH 44125-4887. TEL 216-524-0830; FAX 216-524-7792. **Owner(s):** Sun Media, Inc., 5510 Cloverleaf Pkwy., Cleveland, OH 44125-4887. TEL 216-524-0830; FAX 216-642-5547; adv.; photos; bk.rev.; pub. size: broadsheet; circ. 4,491(paid).

US
SUN COURIER, THE. 1966. Thu. $.60 newsstand; $32.50/yr. 5510 Cloverleaf Pkwy., Cleveland, OH 44125-4887. TEL 216-524-0830; FAX 216-524-7792. **Owner(s):** Sun Media, Inc., 5510 Cloverleaf Pkwy., Cleveland, OH 44125-4887. TEL 216-524-0830; FAX 216-642-5547; adv.; photos; bk.rev.; pub. size: broadsheet; circ. 6,693(paid).

US
SUN HERALD, THE. 1918. Thu. $.60 newsstand; $32.50/yr. 5510 Cloverleaf Pkwy, Cleveland, OH 44125-4887. TEL 216-524-0830; FAX 216-524-7792. **Owner(s):** Sun Media, Inc., 5510 Cloverleaf Pkwy., Cleveland, OH 44125-4887. TEL 216-524-0830; FAX 216-642-5547; adv.; photos; pub. size: broadsheet; circ. 17,864(paid).

US
SUN MESSENGER, THE. 1947. Thu. $.60 newsstand; $32.50/yr. 5510 Cloverleaf Pkwy., Cleveland, OH 44125-4887. TEL 216-524-0830. **Owner(s):** Sun Media, Inc., 5510 Cloverleaf Pkwy., Cleveland, OH 44125-4887. TEL 216-524-0830; FAX 216-642-5547; adv.; pub. size: broadsheet; circ. 15,033(paid).

US
SUN PRESS. 1947. Thu. $.60 newsstand; $32.50/yr. 5510 Cloverleaf Pkwy., Cleveland, OH 44125-4887. TEL 216-524-0830; FAX 216-524-7792. **Owner(s):** Sun Media, Inc., 5510 Cloverleaf Pkwy., Cleveland, OH 44125-4887. TEL 216-524-0830; FAX 216-642-5547; adv.; photos; bk.rev.; pub. size: broadsheet; circ. 20,754(paid).

US
SUN SCOOP JOURNAL. 1919. Thu. $.60 newsstand; $32.50/yr. 5510 Cloverleaf Pkwy., Cleveland, OH 44125-4887. TEL 216-524-0830; FAX 216-524-7792. **Owner(s):** Sun Media, Inc., 5510 Cloverleaf Pkwy., Cleveland, OH 44125-4887. TEL 216-524-0830; FAX 216-642-5547; adv.; photos; bk.rev.; pub. size: broadsheet; circ. 5,018(paid).

US
SUN STAR, THE. 1918. Thu. $.60 newsstand; $32.50/yr. 5510 Cloverleaf Pkwy., Cleveland, OH 44125-4887. TEL 216-524-0830; FAX 216-524-7792. **Owner(s):** Sun Media, Inc., 5510 Cloverleaf Pkwy., Cleveland, OH 44125-4887. TEL 216-524-0830; FAX 216-642-5547; adv.; photos; bk.rev.; pub. size: broadsheet; circ. 12,088(paid).

Weeklies

US

SUN, THE. 1990. Thu. $.60 newsstand; $32.50/yr. 5510 Cloverleaf Pkwy., Cleveland, OH 44125-4887. TEL 216-524-0830; FAX 216-524-7792. **Owner(s):** Sun Media, Inc., 5510 Cloverleaf Pkwy., Cleveland, OH 44125-4887. TEL 216-524-0830; FAX 216-642-5547; adv.; photos; bk.rev.; pub. size: broadsheet; circ. 7,511(paid).

US

▼**TWINSBURG SUN, THE.** 1994. Thu. $.60 newsstand; $32.50/yr. 5510 Cloverleaf Pkwy., Cleveland, OH 44125-4887. TEL 216-524-0830; FAX 216-524-7792. **Owner(s):** Sun Media, Inc., 5510 Cloverleaf Pkwy., Cleveland, OH 44125-4887. TEL 216-524-0830; FAX 216-642-5547; adv.; photos; bk.rev.; pub. size: broadsheet; circ. 5,516(free & paid).

US

▼**WEST GEAUGA SUN.** 1994. Thu. $.60 newsstand; $32.50/yr. 5510 Cloverleaf Pkwy., Cleveland, OH 44125-4887. TEL 216-524-0830; FAX 216-524-7792. **Owner(s):** Sun Media, Inc., 5510 Cloverleaf Pkwy., Cleveland, OH 44125-4887. TEL 216-524-0830; FAX 216-642-5547; adv.; photos; pub. size: broadsheet; circ. 18,127(paid).

US

WEST LIFE. 1958. Wed. $.60 newsstand; $27.50/yr. in cy.; $29.50/yr. out of cy. 27006 Center Ridge, Cleveland, OH 44145. TEL 216-871-5797; FAX 216-871-3824. **Owner(s):** Photojournal, Inc., 520 Warren St., Sandusky, OH 44870. TEL 419-625-5825; Ed. Mary Slama; Pub. Kenneth Douthit III; adv. contact: Kathleen Webb. pub. size: tabloid; circ. 15,000(paid).

US

WEST SIDE SUN NEWS. 1918. Thu. $.60 newsstand; $32.50/yr. 5510 Cloverleaf Pkwy., Cleveland, OH 44125-4887. TEL 216-524-0830; FAX 216-524-7792. **Owner(s):** Sun Media, Inc., 5510 Cloverleaf Pkwy., Cleveland, OH 44125-4887. TEL 216-524-0830; FAX 216-642-5547; adv.; photos; pub. size: broadsheet; circ. 17,926(paid).

CLYDE

US

CLYDE ENTERPRISE. 1878. Wed. $.65 newsstand; $25/yr. 107 S. Main St., Clyde, OH 43410. TEL 419-547-9194. **Owner(s):** Gazette Publishing Co., Bellevue, OH. TEL 419-483-4190; Ed. John W. Brewer; Pub. Thomas Smith; adv.; photos; pub. size: broadsheet; circ. 2,950(paid).

COLDWATER

US

MERCER COUNTY CHRONICLE. 1902. Wed. $.60 newsstand; $24/yr. in cy.; $27/yr. out of cy; $32/yr. out of state. 16 W. Main St., Coldwater, OH 45828-0105. TEL 419-678-2324; FAX 419-678-4659. **Owner(s):** Delphos Newspapers, 405 N. Main St., Delphos, OH 45833. TEL 419-695-0015; Ed. Bonnie J. VanDeMark; Pub. Bonnie J. VanDeMark; adv.; photos; pub. size: broadsheet; circ. 2,900(paid).

COLUMBIANA

US

EAST PALESTINE HERITAGE, THE. 1987. Wed. $.50 newsstand; $25/yr. F.O. Box 448, Columbiana, OH 44408. TEL 216-482-0600; FAX 216-482-1400. **Owner(s):** Heritage Associates, Inc., P.O. Box 448, Columbiana, OH 44408. TEL 216-482-0600; FAX 216-482-1400; Ed. Michael Hill; Pub. Geoffrey S. Goll; adv.; photos; pub. size: tabloid; circ. 2,800(paid).

COLUMBIA STATION

US

RURAL-URBAN RECORD. 1955. Mon. free locally; $20/yr. out of area. 24487 Squires Rd., Columbia Station, OH 44028. TEL 216-236-8982. **Owner(s):** Rural-Urban-Record, Inc., P.O. Box 966, Columbia Sta., OH 44028. TEL 216-238-8982; Ed. Leonard Boise; Pub. Leonard Boise; adv.; pub. size: tabloid; circ. 15 744(free & paid).

COLUMBUS

US

BEXLEY NEWS. 1964. Wed. $.25 newsstand; $20/yr. in cy.; $25/yr. out of cy. 5257 Sinclair Rd., Columbus, OH 43229. TEL 614-785-1212; FAX 614-842-4760. **Owner(s):** Suburban News Publications, 5257 Sinclair Rd., Columbus, OH 43229. TEL 614-785-1212; Ed. Joe Meyer; Pub. James Toms; adv. contact: Carol Zimmer. pub. size: broadsheet; circ. 6,000(paid).

US

BOOSTER, THE. 1933. Wed. $.40 newsstand; $20/yr. in cy.; $25/yr. elsewhere. 5257 Sinclair Rd., Columbus, OH 43229. TEL 614-785-1212; FAX 614-842-4760. **Owner(s):** Suburban News Publications, 5257 Sinclair Rd., Columbus, OH 43229. TEL 614-785-1212; Ed. Joe Meyer; Pub. James Toms; adv.; pub. size: tabloid; circ. 18,500(paid).

US

COLUMBUS ALIVE! 1984. Wed. free newsstand; $35/yr. mailed. 17 Brickel St., Columbus, OH 43215-0309. TEL 614-221-2449; FAX 614-221-2456. **Owner(s):** Columbus Alive, Inc., P.O. Box 15309, Columbus, OH 43215-0309. TEL 614-221-2449; FAX 614-221-2456; Ed. Sally Crane MacPhail; Pub. Angus MacPhail; adv.; photos; bk.rev.; pub. size: tabloid; circ. 33,000(free & paid).

US

COLUMBUS MESSENGER. 1974. Mon. $52/yr. mailed. 3378 Sullivant Ave., Columbus, OH 43204. TEL 614-272-5422; FAX 614-272-0684. **Owner(s):** Columbus Messenger, 3378 Sullivant Ave., Columbus, OH 43204. TEL 614-272-5422; Pub. Earle F. Moore; adv.; pub. size: tabloid; circ. 151,000(controlled & free).

US

DUBLIN SUBURBIA NEWS. 1978. Wed. $.40 newsstand; $20/yr. in cy.; $25/yr. out of cy. 5257 Sinclair Rd., Columbus, OH 43229. TEL 614-785-1212; FAX 614-842-4760. **Owner(s):** Suburban News Publications, 5257 Sinclair Rd., Columbus, OH 43229. TEL 614-785-1212; FAX 614-842-4760; Ed. Joe Meyer; Pub. James Toms; adv.; pub. size: tabloid; circ. 16,500(free & paid).

US

GROVE CITY RECORD. 1927. w: Wed. $.50 newsstand; $21/yr. mailed. P.O. Box 341890, Columbus, OH 43234-1890. TEL 614-438-8100; FAX 614-438-8110. **Owner(s):** John Wolf, P.O. Box 341890, Columbus, OH 43234-1890. TEL 614-438-8100; FAX 614-438-8110; Ed. Craig McDonald. adv. contact: Jerry O'Connell. photos; pub. size: broadsheet; circ. 5,630(free).

US

JOHNSTOWN INDEPENDENT. 1984. w: Wed. $.50 newsstand; $21/yr. mailed. P.O. Box 341890, Columbus, OH 43234-1890. TEL 614-438-8100; FAX 614-438-8110. **Owner(s):** John Wolf, P.O. Box 341890, Columbus, OH 43234-1890. TEL 614-438-8100; FAX 614-438-8110; Ed. Craig McDonald. adv. contact: Jerry O'Connell. photos; pub. size: broadsheet; circ. 2,185(free).

US

NORTHLAND NEWS. Wed. $.40 newsstand; $25/yr. in cy.; $30/yr. out of cy. 5257 Sinclair Rd., Columbus, OH 43229. TEL 614-785-1212. **Owner(s):** Suburban News Publications, 5257 Sinclair Rd., Columbus, OH 43229. TEL 614-785-1212; Ed. Joe Meyer; Pub. James Toms; adv. contact: Carol Zimmer. pub. size: broadsheet; circ. 21,400(paid).

US

NORTHWEST COLUMBUS NEWS. 1980. Wed. $.40 newsstand; $20/yr. in cy.; $25/yr. out of cy. 5257 Sinclair Rd., Columbus, OH 43229. TEL 614-785-1212; FAX 614-842-4760. **Owner(s):** Suburban News Publications, 5257 Sinclair Rd., Columbus, OH 43229. TEL 614-785-1214; FAX 614-842-4760; Ed. Joe Meyer; Pub. James Toms; adv.; pub. size: tabloid; circ. 9,000(paid).

US

PICKERINGTON TIMES-SUN. Wed. $.40 newsstand; $15/yr. mailed. 5257 Sinclair Rd., Columbus, OH 43229. TEL 614-237-2500; FAX 614-837-3441. **Owner(s):** Suburban News Publications, 5257 Sinclair Rd., Columbus, OH 43229. TEL 614-785-1212; Ed. Joe Meyer; Pub. James Toms; adv. contact: Carol Zimmer. pub. size: tabloid; circ. 8,700(paid).

US

▼**ROCKY FORK ENTERPRISE.** 1994. w.: Thu. free. P.O. Box 341890, Columbus, OH 43234-1890. TEL 614-438-8100; FAX 614-438-8110. **Owner(s):** John Wolf, P.O. Box 341890, Columbus, OH 43234-1890. TEL 614-438-8100; FAX 614-438-8110; Ed. Craig McDonald. adv. contact: Jerry O'Connell. photos; pub. size: broadsheet; circ. 12,208(free).

US

THIS WEEK IN BEXLEY. 1990. Mon. free newsstand; $75/yr. mailed. P.O. Box 341890, Columbus, OH 43234-1890. TEL 614-438-8100; FAX 614-438-8110. **Owner(s):** John Wolf, P.O. Box 341890, Columbus, OH 43234-1890. TEL 614-438-8100; FAX 614-438-8110; Ed. Craig McDonald. adv. contact: Jerry O'Connell. photos; pub. size: tabloid; circ. 9,226(free).

US
THIS WEEK IN CLINTONVILLE. 1990. Mon. free newsstand; $75/yr. mailed. P.O. Box 341890, Columbus, OH 43234-1890. TEL 614-438-8100; FAX 614-438-8110. **Owner(s):** John Wolf, P.O. Box 341890, Columbus, OH 43234-1890. TEL 614-438-8100; FAX 614-438-8110; Ed. Craig McDonald. adv. contact: Jerry O'Connell. photos; pub. size: tabloid; circ. 14,959(free).

US
THIS WEEK IN DELAWARE. 1990. Mon. free newsstand; $75/yr. mailed. P.O. Box 341890, Columbus, OH 43234-1890. TEL 614-438-8100; FAX 614-438-8110. **Owner(s):** John Wolf, P.O. Box 341890, Columbus, OH 43234-1890. TEL 614-438-8100; FAX 614-438-8110; Ed. Craig McDonald. adv. contact: Jerry O'Connell. photos; pub. size: tabloid; circ. 17,755(free).

US
THIS WEEK IN EASTSIDE. 1990. Mon. free newsstand; $75/yr. mailed. P.O. Box 341890, Columbus, OH 43234-1890. TEL 614-438-8100; FAX 614-438-8110. **Owner(s):** John Wolf, P.O. Box 341890, Columbus, OH 43234-1890. TEL 614-438-8100; FAX 614-438-8110; Ed. Craig McDonald. adv. contact: Jerry O'Connell. photos; pub. size: tabloid; circ. 13,998(free).

US
THIS WEEK IN GRANDVIEW. 1990. Mon. free newsstand; $75/yr. mailed. P.O. Box 341890, Columbus, OH 43230-1890. TEL 614-438-8100; FAX 614-438-8110. **Owner(s):** John Wolf, P.O. Box 341890, Columbus, OH 43234-1890. TEL 614-438-8100; FAX 614-438-8110; Ed. Craig McDonald. adv. contact: Jerry O'Connell. photos; pub. size: tabloid; circ. 6,008(free).

US
THIS WEEK IN HILLIARD. 1990. Mon. free newsstand; $75/yr. mailed. P.O. Box 341890, Columbus, OH 43234-1890. TEL 614-438-8100; FAX 614-438-8110. **Owner(s):** John Wolf, P.O. Box 341890, Columbus, OH 43234-1890. TEL 614-438-8100; FAX 614-438-8110; Ed. Craig McDonald. adv. contact: Jerry O'Connell. photos; pub. size: tabloid; circ. 20,542(free).

US
THIS WEEK IN NEW ALBANY. 1993. Mon. free newsstand; $75/yr. mailed. P.O. Box 341890, Columbus, OH 43234-1890. TEL 614-438-8100; FAX 614-438-8110. **Owner(s):** John Wolf, P.O. Box 341890, Columbus, OH 43234-1890. TEL 614-438-8100; FAX 614-438-8110; Ed. Craig McDonald. adv. contact: Jerry O'Connell. photos; pub. size: tabloid; circ. 3,263(free).

US
THIS WEEK IN NORTHLAND. 1990. Mon. free newsstands; $75/yr. mailed. P.O. Box 341890, Columbus, OH 43234-1890. TEL 614-438-8100; FAX 614-438-8110. **Owner(s):** John Wolf, P.O. Box 341890, Columbus, OH 43234-1890. TEL 614-438-8100; FAX 614-438-8110; Ed. Craig McDonald. adv. contact: Jerry O'Connell. photos; pub. size: tabloid; circ. 25,861(free).

US
THIS WEEK IN PICKERINGTON. 1990. Mon. free newsstand; $75/yr. mailed. P.O. Box 341890, Columbus, OH 43234-1890. TEL 614-438-8100; FAX 614-438-8110. **Owner(s):** John Wolf, P.O. Box 341890, Columbus, OH 43234-1890. TEL 614-438-8100; FAX 614-438-8110; Ed. Craig McDonald. adv. contact: Jerry O'Connell. photos; pub. size: tabloid; circ. 15,243(free).

US
THIS WEEK IN POWELL. 1990. Mon. free newsstand; $75/yr mailed. P.O. Box 341890, Columbus, OH 43234-1890. TEL 614-438-8100; FAX 614-438-8110. **Owner(s):** John Wolf, P.O. Box 341890, Columbus, OH 43234-1890. TEL 614-438-8100; FAX 614-438-8110; Ed. Jerry O'Connell. adv. contact: Jerry O'Connell. photos; pub. size: tabloid; circ. 8,158(free).

US
THIS WEEK IN REYNOLDSBURG. 1990. Mon. free newsstand; $75/yr. mailed. P.O. Box 341890, Columbus, OH 43234-1890. TEL 614-438-8100; FAX 614-438-8110. **Owner(s):** John Wolf, P.O. Box 341890, Columbus, OH 43234-1890. TEL 614-438-8100; FAX 614-438-8110; Ed. Craig McDonald. adv. contact: Jerry O'Connell. photos; pub. size: tabloid; circ. 13,919(free).

US
THIS WEEK IN SOUTHSIDE. 1990. Mon. free newsstand; $75/yr. mailed. P.O. Box 341890, Columbus, OH 43234-1890. TEL 614-438-8100; FAX 614-438-8110. **Owner(s):** John Wolf, P.O. Box 341890, Columbus, OH 43234-1890. TEL 614-438-8100; FAX 614-438-8110; Ed. Craig McDonald. adv. contact: Jerry O'Connell. photos; pub. size: tabloid; circ. 25,530(free).

US
THIS WEEK IN UNION COUNTY. 1990. Sun. free newsstand. P.O. Box 341890, Columbus, OH 43234-1890. TEL 614-438-8100; FAX 614-438-8110. **Owner(s):** John Wolf, P.O. Box 3471890, Columbus, OH 43234-1890. TEL 614-438-8100; FAX 614-438-8110; Ed. Craig McDonald. adv. contact: Jerry O'Connell. photos; pub. size: tabloid; circ. 6,749(free).

US
THIS WEEK IN WESTERVILLE. 1990. Mon. free newsstand; $75/yr. mailed. P.O. Box 341890, Columbus, OH 43234-1890. TEL 614-438-8100; FAX 614-438-8110. **Owner(s):** John Wolf, P.O. Box 34189, Columbus, OH 43234-1890. TEL 614-438-8100; FAX 614-438-8110; Ed. Craig McDonald. adv. contact: Jerry O'Connell. photos; pub. size: tabloid; circ. 25,571(free).

US
THIS WEEK IN WESTSIDE. 1990. Mon. free newsstand; $75/yr. mailed. P.O. Box 341890, Columbus, OH 43234-1890. TEL 614-438-8100; FAX 614-438-8110. **Owner(s):** John Wolf, P.O. Box 341890, Columbus, OH 43234-1890. TEL 614-438-8100; FAX 614-438-8110; Ed. Craig McDonald. adv. contact: Jerry O'Connel. photos; pub. size: tabloid; circ. 13,306.

US
THIS WEEK IN WORTHINGTON. 1990. Mon. free newsstand; $75/yr. mailed. P.O. Box 341890, Columbus, OH 43234-1890. TEL 614-438-8100; FAX 614-438-8110. **Owner(s):** John Wolf, P.O. Box 341890, Columbus, OH 43234-1890. TEL 614-438-8100; FAX 614-438-8110; Ed. Craig McDonald. adv. contact: Jerry O'Connell. photos; pub. size: tabloid; circ. 24,697(free).

US
TIMES, THE. 1871. Wed. $.40 newsstand; $12/yr. in cy.; $15/yr. out of cy. 1415-D South Hamilton Rd., Columbus, OH 43227. TEL 614-237-2500; FAX 614-237-1888. **Owner(s):** Suburban News Publications, 5257 Sinclair Rd., Columbus, OH 43229. TEL 614-785-1212; Ed. Joe Meyer; Pub. James Toms; adv.; pub. size: broadsheet; circ. 2,500(paid).
Formerly: Canal Winchester Times.

US
TRI-VILLAGE NEWS. 1931. Wed. $.25 newsstand; $20/yr. in cy.; $25/yr. out of cy. 5257 Sinclair Rd., Columbus, OH 43229. TEL 614-785-1212; FAX 614-842-4760. **Owner(s):** Suburban News Publications, 5257 Sinclair Rd., Columbus, OH 43229. TEL 614-785-1212; FAX 614-842-4760; Ed. Joe Meyer; Pub. James Toms; adv.; pub. size: tabloid; circ. 4,100(paid).

US
UA THIS WEEK. 1990. Mon. free newsstand; $75/yr. mailed. P.O. Box 341890, Columbus, OH 43234-1890. TEL 614-438-8100; FAX 614-438-8110. **Owner(s):** John Wolf, P.O. Box 341890, Columbus, OH 43234-1890. TEL 614-438-8100; FAX 614-438-8110; Ed. Craig McDonald. adv. contact: Jerry O'Connell. photos; pub. size: tabloid; circ. 22,956(free).

US
UPPER ARLINGTON NEWS. 1933. Wed. $.25 newsstand; $20/yr. in cy.; $25/yr. out of cy. 5257 Sinclair Rd., Columbus, OH 43229. TEL 614-785-1212; FAX 614-842-4760. **Owner(s):** Suburban News Publications, 5257 Sinclair Rd., Columbus, OH 43229. TEL 614-785-1212; Ed. Joe Meyer; Pub. James Toms; adv. contact: Carol Zimmer. pub. size: tabloid; circ. 17,000(paid).

US
WHITEHALL NEWS. 1986. Wed. $.25 newsstand; $20/yr. in cy.; $25/yr. out of cy. 5257 Sinclair Rd., Columbus, OH 43229. TEL 614-785-1212; FAX 614-842-4760. **Owner(s):** Suburban News Publications, 5257 Sinclair Rd., Columbus, OH 43229. TEL 614-785-1212; FAX 614-842-4760; Ed. Joe Meyer; Pub. James Toms; adv. contact: Carol Zimmer. photos; pub. size: tabloid; circ. 10,237(free).

US
WORTHINGTON SUBURBIA NEWS. 1926. Wed. $.40 newsstand; $20/yr. in cy.; $25/yr. out of cy. 5257 Sinclair Rd., Columbus, OH 43229. TEL 614-785-1212; FAX 614-842-4760. **Owner(s):** Suburban News Publications, 5257 Sinclair Rd., Columbus, OH 43229. TEL 614-785-1212; FAX 614-842-4760; Ed. Joe Meyer; Pub. James Toms; adv.; pub. size: tabloid; circ. 18,200(paid).

COLUMBUS GROVE

US

PUTNAM COUNTY VIDETTE. 1873. Wed. $.50/issue; $23/yr. in cy.; $25/ yr. in state; $27/yr. elsewhere. 111 E. Sycamore St., Columbus Grove, OH 45830. TEL 419-659-2173; FAX 419-659-2760. **Owner(s):** Hirt Publishing, P.O. Box 352, Bellevue, OH 44811. TEL 419-483-7000; Ed. Paul K. Muckley. adv.; photos; pub. size: broadsheet; circ. 2,000(paid).

CONNEAUT

US

COURIER, THE. 1992. Wed. $.50 newsstand; $20/yr.; $30/yr. out of town. 218 Washington St., Conneaut, OH 44030. TEL 216-593-6030; FAX 216-593-6061. **Owner(s):** Gazette Printing Co., Inc., P.O. Box 166, Jefferson, OH 44047. TEL 216-576-9115; FAX 216-576-2735; Ed. Patrick Williams; Pub. John Lampson; adv. contact: Bill Creed. pub. size: tabloid; circ. 1,650(paid).

COVINGTON

US

PENNY SAVER. Mon. $.25 newsstand; $13/yr. mailed. 395 S. High St., Covington, OH 45318. TEL 513-473-2028; FAX 513-473-3299. **Owner(s):** Covington Arens Corp., P.O. Box 69, Covington, OH 45318; Ed. Carol Wood; Pub. Gary Godfrey; pub. size: tabloid; circ. 10,200(paid).

US

STILLWATER VALLEY ADVERTISER. 1954. Wed. $.25 newsstand; $13/yr. mailed. 395 S. High St., Covington, OH 45318. TEL 513-473-2028; FAX 513-473-3299. **Owner(s):** Covington Arens Corp., P.O. Box 69, Covington, OH 45318. TEL 513-473-2028; Ed. Carol Wood; Pub. Gary L. Godfrey; adv.; pub. size: tabloid; circ. 10,500(paid).

CRESTLINE

US

CRESTLINE ADVOCATE. 1869. Wed. $.50 newsstand; $25/yr. 312 N. Seltzer St., Crestline, OH 44827-0226. TEL 419-683-3355. **Owner(s):** Brouwer-Marken, Inc., 312 N. Seltzer St., Crestline, OH 44827. TEL 419-683-3355; Ed. Joseph J. Petti. adv.; photos; pub. size: standard; circ. 2,300(paid).

DALTON

US

DALTON GAZETTE & KIDRON NEWS. 1875. w. $.35 newsstand; $14.50/yr. in cy.; $15/yr. in state; $15.50/yr. out of state. P.O. Box 495, Dalton, OH 44618-0495. TEL 216-828-8401. **Owner(s):** Francis Woodruff, P.O. Box 495, Dalton, OH 44618. TEL 216-828-8401; Pub. Francis Woodruff; adv.; photos; pub. size: tabloid; circ. 1,300(paid).

DAYTON

US

HUBER HEIGHTS COURIER. 1960. Wed. $.50/newsstand; $24/yr. local; $26/yr. in cy. mailed; $31/yr. out of cy. mailed. 7089 Taylorsville Rd., Dayton, OH 45424. TEL 513-236-4990; FAX 513-236-4176. **Owner(s):** Bowling-Mooreman Publications, Inc., 1455 W. Main St., Tipp City, OH 45371. TEL 513-667-2214; Ed. Chuck Vosskuehler; Pub. Vernon T. Bowling; acv.; photos; pub. size: broadsheet; circ. 12,000(controlled & free).

DELTA

US

DELTA ATLAS. 1882. Tue. $.40 newsstand; $14/yr.; $13/yr. senior citizens. 212 Main St., Delta, OH 43515. TEL 419-822-3231. **Owner(s):** Bernice T. Mack, 212 Main St., Delta, OH 43515. TEL 419-822-3231; Ed. Thomas W. Mack. adv. contact: Larry Favorite. pub. size: broadsheet; circ. 2,100(paid).

EATON

US

REGISTER-HERALD. 1820. Wed. $.50 newsstand; $26/yr. in cy.; $33/yr. out of cy.; $37/yr. out of state. 542 N. Barron, Eaton, OH 45320. TEL 513-456-5553; FAX 513-456-3558. **Owner(s):** Brown Publishing Co., P.O. Box 555, Urbana, OH 43078. TEL 513-652-2100; Ed. Deron Newman; Pub. James R. Hardin; adv. contact: Nona J. Wigger. pub. size: broadsheet; circ. 18,100(paid).

FAIRFIELD

US

FAIRFIELD ECHO. 1956. Wed. free. 5120 Dixie Hwy., Fairfield, OH 45014. TEL 513-829-7900; FAX 513-829-7950. **Owner(s):** Thomson Newspapers, Inc., One Thorn Run Ctr., Ste. 500, 1187 Thorn Run Rd. Ext., Coraopolis, PA 15108. TEL 412-262-7870; Ed. Emily York; Pub. Bob Murphy; photos; bk.rev.; pub. size: broadsheet; circ. 19,000(free).

Formerly: Fairfield Echo/Journal-News.

FAYETTE

US   ISSN 1065-0083

FAYETTE REVIEW, THE. 1901. w. $17.50-$19.50/yr. 118 W. Main, Fayette, OH 43521-0219. TEL 419-237-2591. **Owner(s):** Fayette Review, The, P.O. Box 219, Fayette, OH 43521. TEL 419-237-2591; Ed. Don Potter. adv.; circ. 1,300(paid).

FRANKLIN

US

FRANKLIN CHRONICLE. 1875. Tue. $.35 newsstand; $15.60/yr. in cy.; $17.60/yr. out of cy. 42 E. Fourth St., Franklin, OH 45005. TEL 513-746-3691; FAX 513-746-6013. **Owner(s):** Thomson Newspapers, Inc., One Thorn Run Ctr., Ste 500, 1187 Thorn Run Rd. Ext., Coraopolis, PA 15108. TEL 412-262-7870; Ed. Dan Darragh. adv. contact: Barb Stapies. pub. size: standard; circ. 3,000(paid).

GAHANNA

US

GAHANNA VILLAGE POST. 193_. Thu. $.35 newsstand; $15/yr. local. 110 N. High St., Gahanna, OH 43230. TEL 614-471-1600; FAX 614-471-1764. **Owner(s):** This Week Newspapers, 670 Lakeview Plz. Blvd., Ste. F, Worthington, OH 43085; Ed. Gaylon Vickers. pub. size: broadsheet; circ. 12,908(paid).

GRANVILLE

US

COMMUNITY BOOSTER, THE. 1949. Mon. free newsstand; $20/yr. in cy.; $25/yr. out of cy. 110 E. Elm St., Granville, OH 43023. TEL 614-587-3397; FAX 614-587-3398. **Owner(s):** Thomson Newspapers, 55 Queen St. Toronto, ON, M5H 2M2 Canada; Ed. Millie Entrekin. adv.; photos; bk.rev.; pub. size: tabloid; circ. 10,000(controlled & free).

Formerly: Granville Booster, The.

US

GRANVILLE SENTINEL, THE. 1970. Thu. $.50 newsstand; $20/yr. in cy.; $25 out of cy. 110 E Elm St., Granville, OH 43023. TEL 614-587-3397; FAX 614-587-3398. **Owner(s):** Thomson Newspapers, One Thorn Run Ctr., Ste. 500, 1187 Thorn Run Rd. Ext., Coraopolis, PA 15108. TEL 412-262-7870; Ed. Chuck Peterson; Pub. Barbara Griesse. adv.; photos; bk.rev.; pub. size: tabloid; circ. 2,000(paid).

HARTVILLE

US

HARTVILLE NEWS. 1930. Wed. $.50 newsstand; $22/yr. in area; $24/yr. elsewhere. 316 E. Maple St., Hartville, OH 44632. TEL 216-877-9345; FAX 216-877-1364. **Owner(s):** The Knowles Press, Inc., 316 E. Maple St., Hartville, OH 44632. TEL 216-877-9345; Ed. Rosalee Haines. adv.; pub. size: tabloid; circ. 3,000(paid).

HEATH

US

ACE NEWS, THE. 1963. Thu. $.30 newsstand; $14/yr. in cy.; $20/yr. out of cy. 619 Industrial Pkwy., Heath, OH 43056. TEL 614-522-8566. **Owner(s):** Boeckman Communications, 409 S. 22nd St., Heath, OH 43056. TEL 614-522-8566; Ed. Elaine Landis; Pub. Ron Boeckman; pub. size: tabloid; circ. 5,000(paid).

HILLIARD

US

HILLIARD NORTHWEST NEWS. Wed. $.40 newsstand; $1/mo. out of area. 5314 Center St., Hilliard, OH 43026. TEL 614-876-5607; FAX 614-847-0085. **Owner(s):** Suburban News Publications, 5257 Sinclair Rd., Columbus, OH 43229. TEL 614-451-1212; Ed. Martin Rozenman; Pub. Jim Torrs; adv. contact: Carol Zimmer. pub. size: tabloid; circ. 15,800(free & paid).

HILLSBORO

US   ISSN 8750-8168
PRESS GAZETTE, THE. 1818. s-w.: Tue. & Thu. $.40 newsstand; $38.50/yr. in cy. 209 S. High St., Hillsboro, OH 45133. TEL 513-393-3456; FAX 513-393-2059. **Owner(s):** Brown Publishing Co., P.O. Box 9239, Cincinnati, OH 45209. TEL 513-871-1202; Ed. Rory Ryan; Pub. Phillip A. Roberts; adv.; photos; pub. size: broadsheet; circ. 7,000(paid).

JACKSON

US
JACKSON-VINTON JOURNAL-HERALD. 1925. 3/wk.: Wed., Fri., Sat. $.50 newsstand; $51.75/yr. home deliv.; $67.38/yr. mailed; $49.16/yr. senior citizens. 295 Broadway St., Jackson, OH 45640. TEL 614-286-2187; FAX 614-286-5854. **Owner(s):** Mid-South Management Co., Inc., 314 Pine St., P.O. Box 1634, Spartanburg, SC 29304. TEL 614-286-2187; Ed. Bob Farley; Pub. P. Dale Gardener, Jr.; adv. contact: Jeanne Gillum. pub. size: broadsheet; circ. 7,100(paid).
   Formerly: Jackson Journal Herald & Vinton County Courier.

US
PIKE COUNTY NEWS WATCHMAN. s-w.: Wed. & Sun. $40.25/yr.; $49/yr. mailed; $38.24/yr. senior citizens. 295 E. Broadway, Jackson, OH 45640. TEL 614-286-2187; FAX 614-286-5854. **Owner(s):** Jackson Publishing Co., Inc., 295 E. Broadway, Jackson, OH 45640. TEL 614-286-2187; Ed. Bob Farley; Pub. P. Dale Gardener; pub. size: standard.

JEFFERSON

US
GAZETTE, THE. 1876. Wed. $.50 newsstand; $20/yr. local; $30/yr. out of state. 46 W. Jefferson St., Jefferson, OH 44047. TEL 216-576-9115; FAX 216-576-2735. **Owner(s):** Gazette Printing Co., Inc., P.O. Box 166, Jefferson, OH 44047-0166. TEL 216-576-9115; FAX 216-576-2735; Ed. Lucille Donley; Pub. John Lampson; pub. size: broadsheet; circ. 3,058(paid).

US
SENTINEL, THE. 1968. Fri. $.25 newsstand; $15/yr. mailed. 46 W. Jefferson St., Jefferson, OH 44047. TEL 216-576-9115; FAX 216-576-2735. **Owner(s):** Gazette Printing Co., Inc., 46 W. Jefferson St., P.O. Box 166, Jefferson, OH 44047. TEL 216-576-9115; FAX 216-576-2735; Ed. Chuck Altonen; Pub. John Lampson; adv.; pub. size: broadsheet; circ. 2,500(free & paid).

US
VALLEY NEWS, THE. 1895. Wed. $.50 newsstand; $20/yr. P.O. Box 166, Jefferson, OH 44047. TEL 800-860-2775; FAX 216-437-6532. **Owner(s):** Gazette Printing Co., Inc., P.O. Box 166, Jefferson, OH 44047-0166. TEL 216-576-9115; FAX 216-576-2734; Ed. Lucille Donelly; Pub. John Lampson; pub. size: tabloid; circ. 1,227(free & paid).

KETTERING

US   ISSN 1049-8117
CENTERVILLE-BELLBROOK TIMES. 1984. s-w.: Wed. & Sat. free Wed.; $.50/newsstand Sat.; $32/yr. 3085 Woodman Dr., Ste. 170, Kettering, OH 45420. TEL 513-294-7000; FAX 513-294-2981. **Owner(s):** Amos Press, Inc., 3085 Woodman Dr., Kettering, OH 45420. TEL 513-294-7000; FAX 513-294-6981; Ed. Mark Kellam; Pub. Mark Raymond; adv. contact: John Carnahan. pub. size: broadsheet; circ. 20,000(free & paid).

US   ISSN 8750-8141
KETTERING-OAKWOOD TIMES. 1956. s-w.: Wed. & Sat. $.50 newsstand; $32/yr. 3085 Woodman Dr., Ste. 170, Kettering, OH 45420. TEL 513-294-7000; FAX 513-294-2981. **Owner(s):** Amos Press, Inc., 3085 Woodman Dr., Ste. 170, Kettering, OH 45420. TEL 513-294-7000; Ed. Mark Kellam; Pub. Mark Raymond; adv. contact: John Carnahan. pub. size: broadsheet; circ. 6,000(paid).

LEBANON

US
WESTERN STAR. 1807. Wed. $.50 newsstand. 200 Harmon Ave., Lebanon, OH 45036. TEL 513-932-3010; FAX 513-932-6056. **Owner(s):** Brown Publishing Co., P.O. Box 555, Urbana, OH 43078. TEL 513-652-2100; Pub. Fred Gibson; adv.; photos; bk.rev.; pub. size: broadsheet; circ. 8,926(paid).

LIBERTY CENTER

US
LIBERTY PRESS, THE. 1882. w.: Wed. $.40 newsstand; $17/yr. 107-1 East St., Liberty Center, OH 43532. TEL 419-533-2401. **Owner(s):** Donald & Susan Mickens, 107-1 East St., Liberty Corner, OH 43532-0006. TEL 419-533-2401; Pub. Donald Mickens; adv.; pub. size: broadsheet; circ. 1,300(paid).

LIMA

US
SENIOR'S BEACON, THE. 1962. m. free; $5/yr. mailed. 800 E. Bible Rd., Lima, OH 45801. TEL 419-227-0430. **Owner(s):** Robert McDowell, 800 E. Bible Rd., P.O. Box 1102, Lima, OH 45802. TEL 419-227-0430; Ed. Pam White; Pub. Robert McDowell; adv.; photos; pub. size: tabloid; circ. 5,500(paid).
   Formerly: Enterprise & Senior.

LOGAN

US
HOCKING VALLEY ADVERTISER. 1984. Sun. free. 62 N. Mulberry St., Logan, OH 43138. TEL 614-385-1969; FAX 614-385-8758. **Owner(s):** Add, Inc., 600 Industrial Dr., P.O. Box 609, Waupaca, WI 54981. TEL 715-258-8450; pub. size: tabloid; circ. 9,441(free).

LOUDONVILLE

US
LOUDONVILLE TIMES, THE. 1873. Tue. $.50 newsstand; $20/yr. in cy.; $21/yr. in state; $25/yr. out of state. 425 E. Haskell St., Loudonville, OH 44842. TEL 419-994-4166; FAX 419-994-4617. **Owner(s):** Truax Printing, Inc., 425 E. Haskell St., Loudonville, OH 44842. TEL 419-994-4166; FAX 419-994-4617; Ed. Jim Brewer; Pub. John Truax; adv.; photos; bk.rev.; pub. size: broadsheet; circ. 2,300(paid).

LOUISVILLE

US
LOUISVILLE HERALD, THE. 1887. Thu. $.50 newsstand; $19/yr. in cy. 308 S. Mill St., Louisville, OH 44641-0170. TEL 216-875-5610; FAX 216-875-4475. **Owner(s):** Paul M. & Shirley J. Clapper, P.O. Box 170, Louisville, OH 44641-0170. TEL 216-875-5610; FAX 216-875-4475; Ed. Frank H. Clapper; Pub. Paul M. Clapper; adv. contact: Shirley J. Clapper. photos; pub. size: broadsheet; circ. 3,427(paid).

LOVELAND

US   ISSN 1066-7458
BETHEL JOURNAL, THE. 1899. Thu. $15/yr. mailed. 394 Wards Corner Rd., Ste. 170, Loveland, OH 45140-6300. TEL 513-753-1111; FAX 513-753-1117. **Owner(s):** Press Community Newspapers, 4910 Para Dr., Cincinnati, OH 45237. TEL 513-242-4300; Pub. Thomas E. Niehaus; adv.; photos; pub. size: broadsheet; circ. 1,750(free & paid).
   Formerly: Bethel Journal-Press, The.

US
COMMUNITY JOURNAL, SOUTH. 1970. Wed. $2/4 wks.; $105/yr. mailed. 394 Wards Corner Rd, Ste. 170, Loveland, OH 45140-8300. TEL 513-753-1111; FAX 513-753-1117. **Owner(s):** Press Community Newspapers, 4910 Para Dr., Cincinnati, OH 45237. TEL 513-242-4300; Ed. Gary L. Presley; Pub. Thomas F. Niehaus; adv.; photos; pub. size: broadsheet; circ. 26,141(free & paid).
   Formerly: Community Journal-Press.

US
COMMUNITY PRESS, MASON. 1988. Wed. $.50 newsstand; $2/4 wks.; $105/yr. mailed. 394 Wards Corner Rd., Loveland, OH 45140. TEL 513-683-5115; FAX 513-677-4690. **Owner(s):** Suburban Communications Corp., 36251 Schoolcraft Rd., Livonia, MI 48150. TEL 313-591-2300; Ed. Gary L. Presley; Pub. Thomas E. Niehaus; adv.; photos; pub. size: broadsheet; circ. 8,000(free).
   Formerly: Community Press.

US
EASTERN HILLS JOURNAL. 1935. Wed. $.50 newsstand; voluntary pay; $105/yr. mailed. 394 Wards Corner Rd., Loveland, OH 45140. TEL 513-683-5115; FAX 513-677-4690. **Owner(s):** Suburban Communications Corp., 36251 Schoolcraft Rd., Livonia, MI 48150. TEL 313-591-2300; Ed. Gary L. Presley; Pub. Thomas E. Niehaus; adv.; photos; pub. size: broadsheet; circ. 14,400(paid).

US

FOREST HILLS JOURNAL. 1961. Wed. $2/4 wks.; $104/yr. mailed. 394 Wards Corner Rd., Ste. 170, Loveland, OH 45140-8300. TEL 513-248-8600; FAX 513-248-1938; E-mail: localmail@aol.com. **Owner(s):** Press Community Newspapers, 4910 Para Dr., Cincinnati, OH 45237. TEL 513-242-4300; Ed. Gary Presley; Pub. Thomas E. Niehaus; adv. contact: Ruth A. Cody. pub. size: broadsheet; circ. 16,600(paid).
   Formerly: Forest Hills Journal-Press.

US   ISSN 0745-2756

LOVELAND HERALD PRESS. 1916. Wed. $.50 newsstand; $2/4 wks. vol. rate; $105/yr. by mail. 394 Wards Corner Rd., Loveland, OH 45140. TEL 513-248-8600; FAX 513-248-1938. **Owner(s):** Suburban Communications Corp., 36251 Schoolcraft Rd., Livonia, MI 48150. TEL 313-591-2300; Ed. Gary Presley; Pub. Tom Niehaus; pub. size: broadsheet; circ. 4,942.
   Formerly: Loveland Herald.

US   ISSN 0745-2764

MILFORD ADVERTISER. 1951. Wed. $.50 newsstand; $2/4 wks.; $105/yr. mailed. 394 Wards Corner Rd., Ste. 170, Loveland, OH 45140-6300. TEL 513-753-1111; FAX 513-753-1117. **Owner(s):** Suburban Communications Corp., 36251 Schoolcraft Rd., Livonia, MI 48150. TEL 313-591-2300; Pub. Thomas E. Niehaus; adv.; pub. size: broadsheet; circ. 8,900(paid).
   Formerly: Milford Advertiser-Press.

US

NORTH CLERMONT COMMUNITY JOURNAL. 1970. Wed. $2/4 wks.; $104/yr. mailed. 394 Wards Corner Rd., Ste. 170, Loveland, OH 45140-8300. TEL 513-753-1111; FAX 513-753-1117. **Owner(s):** Press Community Newspapers, 4910 Para Dr., Cincinnati, OH 45237. TEL 513-242-4300; Ed. Gary Presley; Pub. Thomas E. Niehaus; adv. contact: Ruth A. Cody. pub. size: broadsheet; circ. 6,800(paid).
   Formerly: Community Journal Press, North.

US

SUBURBAN LIFE. 1961. Wed. $.50 newsstand; $2/4 wks. voluntary rate; $105/yr. by mail. 394 Wards Corner Rd., Loveland, OH 45140-8300. TEL 513-683-5115; FAX 513-677-4690. **Owner(s):** Suburban Communications Corp., 36251 Schoolcraft Rd., Livonia, MI 48150. TEL 313-591-2300; Ed. Gary L. Presley; Pub. Thomas E. Niehaus; adv.; photos; pub. size: broadsheet; circ. 11,200(free & paid).

MANCHESTER

US

MANCHESTER SIGNAL. 1883. Thu. $.35 newsstand; $11/yr. in cy.; $14/yr. out of cy. 414 E. Seventh St., Manchester, OH 45144-1402. TEL 513-549-2800; FAX 513-549-3611. **Owner(s):** Wm. G. Woolard, Jr., 414 E. Seventh St., Manchester, OH 45144. TEL 513-549-2800; Ed. William G. Woolard, Jr.; Pub. William G. Woolard, Jr.; adv. contact: Nicolle Politt. photos; bk.rev.; pub. size: broadsheet; circ. 5,100(paid).

MASON

US

PULSE-JOURNAL. 1976. Wed. free; $.50 newsstand; voluntary pay. 1074 Reading Rd., Mason, OH 45040. TEL 513-398-8856; FAX 513-459-7965. **Owner(s):** Thomson Newspapers, Inc., One Thorn Run Ctr., Ste. 500, 1187 Thorn Run Rd. Ext., Coraopolis, PA 15108. TEL 412-262-7870; Ed. Mary Hitt; Pub. Rhonda L. Ford; pub. size: broadsheet; circ. 25,000(free & paid).

MCCONNELSVILLE

US

MORGAN COUNTY HERALD. 1844. Wed. $.60 newsstand; $26/yr. 89 W. Main St., McConnelsville, OH 43756-0268. TEL 614-962-3377. **Owner(s):** Morgan County Publishing Co., 89 W. Main St., P.O. Box 268, McConnelsville, OH 43756. TEL 614-962-3377; Ed. Don Keller. pub. size: broadsheet; circ. 5,100(free & paid).

MIAMISBURG

US

MIAMISBURG NEWS. 1880. Wed. $.50 newsstand; $26/yr. in cy. 230 S. Second St., Miamisburg, OH 45342. TEL 513-866-3331; FAX 513-652-2448 **Owner(s):** Brown Publishing Co., P.O. Box 555, Urbana, OH 43078. TEL 513-652-2100; Ed. Jim Pickering; Pub. Kimm Mote; adv. contact: Fuemel Lambke. photos; pub. size: broadsheet; circ. 7,000(paid). **Wire Service(s):** CNS.

MILLBURY

US

METRO PRESS. 1971. Mon. $.35 newsstand; $15/yr. 1550 Woodville Rd., Millbury, OH 43447. TEL 419-836-2221; FAX 419-836-1319. **Owner(s):** Photojournal, Inc., 620 Warren, Sandusky, OH 44870. TEL 419-625-5825; Ed. John Szozda. pub. size: tabloid; circ. 19,676(paid).

US

SUBURBAN PRESS. 1971. Mon. free in area; $.50 newsstand; $24/yr. out of state. 1550 Woodville Rd., Millbury, OH 43447. TEL 419-836-2221; FAX 419-836-1319. **Owner(s):** Photojournal, Inc., 620 Warren, Sandusky, OH 44870. TEL 419-625-5825; Ed. John Szozda. pub. size: tabloid; circ. 15,224(free).

MILLERSBURG

US

HOLMES COUNTY HUB. 1825. Thu. $.75 newsstand; $28/yr. in area; $33/yr. out of area. 25 N. Clay St., Millersburg, OH 44654. TEL 216-674-5676; FAX 216-674-3780. **Owner(s):** Wooster Republican Printing Co., 212 E. Liberty St., Wooster, OH 44691. TEL 216-264-1811; Ed. Jeanine Kendle; Pub. R. Victor Dix; adv. contact: Jeff Massaro. pub. size: broadsheet; circ. 4,800(paid).

MINERVA

US

MALVERN COMMUNITY NEWS. 1920. Thu. $.50 newsstand; $21/yr. in state; $33/yr. out of state. 177 Curry St., Minerva, OH 44657. TEL 216-868-3408; FAX 216-868-3273. **Owner(s):** Alliance Publishing Co., P.O. Box 2180, Alliance, OH 44601. TEL 216-821-1200; FAX 216-821-8258; Ed. Sarah Reed. adv. contact: Don Watson. pub. size: broadsheet; circ. 1,100(paid).

US   ISSN 1078-0858

MINERVA LEADER. 1937. Thu. $.50 newsstand; $21/yr. in state; $33/yr. out of state. 177 Curry St., Minerva, OH 44657-0030. TEL 216-868-5164; FAX 216-863-5164. **Owner(s):** Alliance Publishing Co., P.O. Box 2180, Alliance, OH 44601. TEL 216-821-1200; FAX 216-821-8258; Ed. Sarah Reed. adv. contact: Karen Cappelli. pub. size: broadsheet; circ. 4,000(paid).

US

PRESS-NEWS, THE. 1897. Thu. $.50 newsstand; $21/yr. in state; $33/yr. out of state. 177 Curry St., Minerva, OH 44657. TEL 216-868-5164; FAX 216-868-3273. **Owner(s):** Alliance Publishing Co., P.O. Box 2180, Alliance, OH 44601. TEL 216-821-1200; FAX 216-821-8258; Ed. Karen Mundy. Pub. Chuck Dix; adv. contact: Linda Stark. pub. size: standard; circ. 3,000(paid).

MONTPELIER

US

LEADER ENTERPRISE. 1880. Wed. $.50 newsstand; $17.50/yr. in cy.; $20.50/yr. out of cy. 319 W. Main, Montpelier, OH 43543. TEL 419-485-3113; FAX 419-636-8937. **Owner(s):** Bryan Publishing Co., The, Walnut St., Bryan, OH 43506. TEL 419-636-1111; Ed. David Belden. adv.; photos. pub. size: standard; circ. 2,000(paid).

MT. GILEAD

US

MORROW COUNTY ADVERTISER. Sun. free newsstand & home deliv. 255 Neal Ave., Mt. Gilead, OH 43338. TEL 419-946-3010; FAX 419-947-7241. **Owner(s):** Hirt Publishing, P.O. Box 352, Bellevue, OH 44811. TEL 419-483-7000; Pub. William Kreeger; adv. contact: Nancy Daehnke. pub. size: tabloid; circ. 13,380(free).

US

MORROW COUNTY SENTINEL. 1848. Wed. $27/yr. in cy.; $29/yr. out of cy.; $31/yr. out of state. 255 Neal Ave., Mt. Gilead, OH 43338. TEL 419-946-3010; FAX 419-947-7241. **Owner(s):** Hirt Publishing, P.O. Box 352, Bellevue, OH 44811. TEL 419-483-7000; Pub. William Kreeger; adv. contact: Amy Springer. photos; pub. size: broadsheet; circ. 4,100(paid).

MT. ORAB

US

BROWN COUNTY PRESS. 1973. Mon. $.25 newsstand; free. 106 N. High St., Mt. Orab, OH 45154. TEL 513-444-3411; FAX 513-444-2652. **Owner(s):** Batavia Buying Guide, The, 470 W. Main St., Mt. Orab, OH 45154. TEL 513-444-3411; FAX 513-444-2652; Ed. Eunice Ott. adv.; photos; pub. size: broadsheet; circ. 14,350(free & paid).

NEWARK

US
NEWARK/LICKING ADVERTISER. 1978. Sat. free.
195 Union St., Newark, OH 43055.
TEL 614-522-2502; FAX 614-522-2498.
Owner(s): Add, Inc., 300 Industrial Dr., Waupaca,
WI 54981. TEL 715-258-8450; Ed. Roman
Dymerski; Pub. Add, Inc.; adv.; pub. size: tabloid;
circ. 42,260(free).

NEW CARLISLE

US
NEW CARLISLE SUN. 1882. Wed. $.50 newsstand;
$26/yr. in cy.; $31/yr. out of cy. 225 S. Main
St., New Carlisle, OH 45344.
TEL 513-845-3861; FAX 513-845-3577.
Owner(s): Bowling-Mooreman Publications, Inc.,
1455 W. Main St., Tipp City, OH 45371. TEL
513-667-8512; Ed. Gary Gregory; Pub. David
Copen; pub. size: broadsheet; circ. 4,800(free &
paid).

NEWCOMERSTOWN

US
NEWCOMERSTOWN NEWS. 1898. Wed. $.50
newsstand; $20/yr. in state; $30/yr. out of state.
140 Main St., Newcomerstown, OH
43832-0030. TEL 614-498-7117;
FAX 614-498-5624. **Owner(s):** Wooster
Republican Printing Co., Wooster, OH 44691; Ed.
R.H. Booth. adv.; photos; bk.rev.; pub. size:
broadsheet; circ. 3,700(paid).

NEW LEXINGTON

US
PERRY COUNTY TRIBUNE. 1940. Wed. $1
newsstand; $31/yr. in area; $35/yr. out of area.
117 S. Main St., New Lexington, OH 43764.
TEL 614-342-4121; FAX 614-342-4131.
Owner(s): Hirt Publishing, P.O. Box 352, Bellevue,
OH 44811. TEL 419-483-7000; Ed. Carl
Burnett. adv. contact: David Schubert. pub. size:
broadsheet; circ. 4,150(paid).

US
TRIBUNE SHOPPING NEWS. Sun. free. 117 S. Main
St., New Lexington, OH 43764.
TEL 614-342-4121; FAX 614-342-4131.
Owner(s): Hirt Publishing, P.O. Box 352, Bellevue,
OH 44811. TEL 419-483-7000; Ed. Carl
Burnett; Pub. Gary Hirt; adv. contact: David
Schubert. circ. 15,150(free).

NORTH CANTON

US
SUN JOURNAL, THE. 1922. Wed. $.25 newsstand;
$13/yr. 7215 Whipple Ave., N.W., North Canton,
OH 44720. TEL 216-966-1121;
FAX 216-966-1202. **Owner(s):** Suarez Corp.,
7215 Whipple Ave., N.W., North Canton, OH
44720. TEL 216-966-1121; FAX
216-966-1202; Ed. Ginny Adams. adv.; pub.
size: broadsheet; circ. 6,000(paid).
Formerly: The Sun.

NORTH RIDGEVILLE

US
PRESS & LIGHT. 1983. Wed. $.50 newsstand;
$23.50/yr. local; $25.50/yr. elsewhere. 34100
Center Ridge Rd., North Ridgeville, OH 44039.
TEL 216-327-7543; FAX 216-327-2499.
Owner(s): Douthit Communications, Inc., P.O. Box
760, Sandusky, OH 44871. TEL 419-625-5825;
Ed. Carol Klear. adv. contact: Toni Musgrove. pub.
size: tabloid; circ. 7,200(paid).

OAK HARBOR

US
OTTAWA COUNTY EXPONENT, THE. 1871. Wed.
$15/yr. in town; $22/yr. in state; $25/yr. out of
state. 264 W. Water St., Oak Harbor, OH 43449.
TEL 419-898-5361; FAX 419-898-0501.
Owner(s): Catherine M. Freed, P.O. Box 70, Oak
Harbor, OH 43449. TEL 419-898-5361; FAX
419-848-0501; Ed. Kimra Traynor Herb; Pub.
Catherine M. Freed; adv. contact: Julie Lynn
Biggert. photos; pub. size: tabloid; circ.
2,700(paid).
Formerly: Exponent, The.

ONTARIO

US
TRIBUNE-COURIER. 1961. Thu. $.35 newsstand;
$12/yr. local; $18/yr. elsewhere. 347 Allen Dr.,
Ontario, OH 44862. TEL 419-529-2847.
Owner(s): Frank & Betty Stumbo, 347 Allen Dr.,
Ontario, OH 44862. TEL 419-529-2847; Ed.
John J. Kirschenheiter; Pub. Frank A. Stumbo;
adv. contact: Betty Stumbo. photos; bk.rev.; pub.
size: broadsheet; circ. 2,600(paid).

OTTAWA

US
PUTNAM COUNTY SENTINEL. 1855. Wed. $1
newsstand; $35/yr. mailed. 232 E. Main St.,
Ottawa, OH 45875. TEL 419-523-5709.
Owner(s): Hirt Publishing, P.O. Box 352, Bellevue,
OH 44811. TEL 419-483-7000; Ed. Nancy
Kline. pub. size: broadsheet; circ. 8,700(paid).

OXFORD

US
OXFORD PRESS. 1932. Thu. $.50 newsstand;
$20/yr. local. 15 S. Beech St., Oxford, OH
45056. TEL 513-523-4139;
FAX 513-523-1935; E-mail: oxforpress@aol.com.
Owner(s): Thomson Newspapers, Inc., 3150 Des
Plaines Ave., Des Plaines, IL 60018. TEL
708-299-5544; Ed. Robert A. Ratterman; Pub.
William Cusack; adv.; photos; pub. size:
broadsheet; circ. 4,000(paid).

PATASKALA

US
PATASKALA STANDARD. 1886. Wed. $.35
newsstand; $18/yr. in cy.; $20/yr. out of state.
350 S. Main St., Pataskala, OH 43062-0007.
TEL 614-927-2991; FAX 614-927-2930.
Owner(s): T.W. Caw, 285 Poplar St., Pataskala,
OH 43062-0007. TEL 614-927-2991; Margaret
J. Caw, 285 Poplar St., Pataskala, OH
43062-0007. TEL 614-927-2991; Ed. T.W.
Caw; Pub. T.W. Caw; adv.; photos; pub. size:
standard; circ. 4,500(paid).

PAULDING

US
PAULDING PROGRESS. 1945. Wed. $.70 newsstand;
$21/yr. in cy.; $26/yr. out of cy. 113 S. Williams
St., Paulding, OH 45879. TEL 419-399-4015;
FAX 419-399-4030. **Owner(s):** Delphos
Newspapers, 405 N. Main St., Delphos, OH
45833. TEL 419-695-0015; Ed. Anna Brewster;
Pub. Anna Brewster; pub. size: broadsheet; circ.
4,200(paid).

US
WEEKLY REMINDER. Tue. free. 113 S. Williams St.,
Paulding, OH 45879. TEL 419-399-4015;
FAX 419-399-4030. **Owner(s):** Delphos
Newspapers, 405 N. Main St., Delphos, OH
45833. TEL 419-695-0015; Ed. Anna Brewster;
Pub. Anna Brewster; pub. size: broadsheet; circ.
8,800(free).

PERRYSBURG

US   ISSN 1064-2021
PERRYSBURG MESSENGER-JOURNAL. 1853. Wed.
$.50 newsstand; $18/yr. in cy. 117 E. Second
St., Perrysburg, OH 43551. TEL 419-874-2528.
Owner(s): Welch Publishing Co., P.O. Box 267,
Perrysburg, OH 42552. TEL 419-874-2528; Ed.
Robert C. Welch; Pub. Robert C. Welch; adv.
contact: Matt Welch. photos; bk.rev.; pub. size:
broadsheet; circ. 13,000(free & paid).

US
ROSSFORD RECORD-JOURNAL. 1939. Thu. $.50
newsstand; $12/yr. in cy.; $15/yr. out of cy.
117 E. 2nd. St., Perrysburg, OH 43551.
TEL 419-874-4491. **Owner(s):** Welch Publishing
Co., P.O. Box 267, Perrysburg, OH 43552. TEL
419-874-2528; Ed. Robert C. Welch; Pub. Robert
C. Welch; adv.; pub. size: broadsheet; circ.
1,600(paid).

PORT CLINTON

US
BEACON, THE. 1983. Thu. free in cy.; $24/yr.
mailed out of cy. 106 W. Perry St., Port Clinton,
OH 43452. TEL 419-732-2154;
FAX 419-734-5382. **Owner(s):** John R.
Schaffner, P.O. Box 87, Clinton, OH 43452; Pub.
John R. Schaffner; pub. size: tabloid; circ.
17,000(free & paid).

ROCKY RIVER

US
LORAIN COUNTY TIMES, THE. 1968. Thu. $.35
newsstand; $29.50/yr. 21010 Center Ridge Rd.,
Ste. G8, Rocky River, OH 44116.
TEL 216-356-0920; FAX 216-356-0515.
Owner(s): Gottschalk Publishing Co., Inc., 21010
Center Ridge Rd., Ste. G8, Rocky River, OH
44116. TEL 216-356-0920; FAX
216-356-0515; Ed. Aharon Bucholtz; Pub.
Eleanor Gottschalk; adv.; photos; bk.rev.; pub.
size: broadsheet; circ. 3,000(free & paid).

US
WESTLAKER TIMES, THE. 1983. Thu. $.35
newsstand; $29.50/yr. 21010 Center Ridge Rd.,
Ste. G8, Rocky River, OH 44116.
TEL 216-356-0920; FAX 216-356-0515.
Owner(s): Gottschalk Publishing Co., Inc., 21010
Center Ridge Rd., Suite G8, Rocky River, OH
44116. TEL 216-356-0920; FAX
216-356-0515; Ed. Aharon Bucholtz; Pub.
Eleanor Gottschalk; adv.: $15.44/col. in. photos;
bk.rev.; pub. size: broadsheet; circ. 3,000(free &
paid).
Formerly: Bay Times.

SABINA

US

SABINA ADVERTISER. 1948. Fri. free. 58 N. Howard, Sabina, OH 45169. TEL 513-584-2122. **Owner(s):** Gaskins Printing, 58 N. Howard, Sabina, OH 45169. TEL 513-584-2122; FAX 513-584-2122; Ed. Brenda Gaskins May. adv.; photos; pub. size: tabloid; circ. 4,900(free).

SPENCERVILLE

US

JOURNAL NEWS. Thu. $.35 newsstand; $15/yr. in cy.; $18/yr. out of cy.; $21/yr. out of state. 126 N. Broadway, Spencerville, OH 45887. TEL 419-647-4981. **Owner(s):** The Journal News, 126 N. Broadway, Spencerville, OH 45887. TEL 419-647-4981; Pub. Doris Beebe; adv.; pub. size: standard.

SPRINGBORO

US

STAR PRESS. 1976. s-w.: Tue. & Sun. $.50 newsstand; $20/yr. local; $26/yr. in state. 25 E. Central, Springboro, OH 45066. TEL 513-748-2550; FAX 513-748-1165. **Owner(s):** Brown Publishing Co., P.O. Box 555, Urbanna, OH 43078. TEL 513-652-2100; Ed. Terry Baver; Pub. Fred Gibson; adv. contact: Barbara Parks. pub. size: broadsheet; circ. 14,000(paid).

ST. MARYS

US

EXTRA MERCHANDISER. 1982. Wed. free. 102 Spring St., St. Marys, OH 45885. TEL 419-394-7414; FAX 419-394-7202. **Owner(s):** American Publishing Co., 606 N. Van Buren, P.O. Box 520, Marion, IL 62959. TEL 618-993-1711; Ed. Jose Nogueran; Pub. David Creech; adv. contact: David Creech. pub. size: broadsheet; circ. 10,500(free).
  Formerly: West Auglaize Merchandiser.

STOW

US

AURORA ADVOCATE. 1972. Wed. $.50 newsstand; $18/yr. in cy. carrier; $40/yr. mailed. 1619 Commerce Dr., Stow, OH 44224. TEL 216-688-0088; FAX 216-688-1588. **Owner(s):** Record Publishing Co., Inc., 126 N. Chestnut St., Ravenna, OH 44266. TEL 216-296-9657; Ed. Ken Lahmers; Pub. David Dix; adv. contact: Larry Kinney. pub. size: tabloid; circ. 5,700(free & paid).

US

FALLS NEWS-PRESS. 1929. Sun. $.35 newsstand; $14/yr. carrier; $20/yr. mailed. 1619 Commerce Dr., Stow, OH 44224. TEL 216-688-0088; FAX 216-688-1588. **Owner(s):** Record Publishing Co., Inc., 126 N. Chestnut St., Ravenna, OH 44266. TEL 216-296-9657; Ed. Ellin Walsh; Pub. David Dix; adv.; pub. size: tabloid; circ. 24,400(paid).

US

HUDSON HUB-TIMES. s-w.: Wed. & Sun. $.35 newsstand; $18/yr. carrier; $40/yr. mailed. 1619 Commerce Dr., Stow, OH 44224. TEL 216-688-0088; FAX 216-688-1588. **Owner(s):** Record Publishing Co., Inc., 126 N. Chestnut St., Ravenna, OH 44266. TEL 216-296-9657; Ed. Debbie DiMafcio; Pub. David Dix; adv. contact: Larry Kinney. pub. size: tabloid; circ. 6,600(free & paid).

US

NEWS LEADER. Wed. $.35 newsstand; $14/yr. carrier; $20/yr. mail. 1619 Commerce Dr., Stow, OH 44224. TEL 216-688-0088; FAX 216-688-1588. **Owner(s):** Record Publishing Co., Inc., 126 N. Chestnut St., Ravenna, OH 44266. TEL 216-296-9657; Ed. Linda Hoy; Pub. David Dix; adv.; pub. size: tabloid; circ. 11,106(free & paid).

US   ISSN 0192-9410

STOW SENTRY. 1969. Sun. $.50 newsstand; $20/yr. 1619 Commerce Dr., Stow, OH 44224. TEL 216-688-0088; FAX 216-688-1588. **Owner(s):** Record Publishing Co., Inc., 125 N. Chestnut St., Ravenna, OH 44266. TEL 216-296-9657; Ed. Beverly Ocasek; Pub. David Dix; adv. contact: Pam Holtz. photos; pub. size: tabloid; circ. Sun. 13,416(paid).

US

TALLMADGE EXPRESS. Sun. $.35 newsstand; $18/yr. carrier; $40/yr. mailed. 1619 Commerce Dr., Stow, OH 44224. TEL 216-688-0088; FAX 216-688-1588. **Owner(s):** Record Publishing Co., Inc., 126 N. Chestnut St., Ravenna, OH 44266. TEL 216-296-9657; Pub. David Dix; adv. contact: Larry Kinney. pub. size: tabloid; circ. 6,416(free & paid).

STREETSBORO

US

GATEWAY NEWS, THE. 1918. Wed. $.50 newsstand; $12/yr. carrier. 9276 State Rte. 14, Streetsboro, OH 44241. TEL 330-626-5558; FAX 330-626-5550. **Owner(s):** Record Publishing Co., Inc., 126 N. Chestnut St., Ravenna, OH 44266. TEL 216-296-9657; Ed. Laura White; Pub. David Dix; pub. size: tabloid; circ. 11,000(free & paid).
  Formerly: Record-News.

STRUTHERS

US

JOURNAL, THE. Thu. $16.50/yr. 23 Lowellville Road, Struthers, OH 44471. TEL 216-755-2155. **Owner(s):** Journal Publishing Co., 23 Lowellville Rd., Struthers, OH 44471. TEL 216-755-2155; Ed. Karen Spaite; Pub. Lawrence McCarthy; adv. contact: Karen Spaite. pub. size: standard.

SUNBURY

US

SUNBURY NEWS. 1873. Thu. $.50 newsstand; $18/yr. 40 S. Vernor St., Sunbury, OH 43074. TEL 614-965-3391; FAX 614-965-3992. **Owner(s):** Delaware Gazette, 18 E. William St., Delaware, OH; Ed. Susan Wright; Pub. W.D. Thompson; adv. contact: Don Cardwell. pub. size: broadsheet; circ 3,200(paid).

SWANTON

US

SWANTON ENTERPRISE. 1886. Tue. $28/yr. 97 N. Main St., Swanton, OH 43558. TEL 419-826-3580; FAX 419-826-3590. **Owner(s):** Gazette Publishing Co., 107 N. Sandusky St., Bellevue, OH 44811. TEL 419-483-4190 Ed. Debbie Katterheinrich. pub. size: broadsheet; circ. 2,000(paid).

TIPP CITY

US

TIPP CITY HERALD. 1859. Tue. $.50 newsstand; $26/yr. in cy.; $31/yr. out of cy. 1455 W. Main St., Tipp City, OH 45371. TEL 513-667-2214; FAX 513-667-8987. **Owner(s):** Vernon T. Bowling, P.O. Box 430, Tipp City, OH 45371; Ed. Tom Barnett; Pub. Vernon T. Bowling; adv. contact Logan Rogers. pub. size: broadsheet; circ. 7,100(paid).

TOLEDO

US

POINT & SHORELAND JOURNAL. 1978. Tue. free in area; $.50 newsstand; $15/yr. mailed. 5198 N. Summit St., Toledo, OH 43611. TEL 419-729-2855. **Owner(s):** Welch Publishing Co., P.O. Box 267, Perrysburg, OH 43552. TEL 419-874-2528; Ed. James Welch; Pub. Robert C. Welch; adv.; photos; bk.rev.; pub. size: broadsheet; circ. 12,000(free & paid).

US

SYLVANIA HERALD. 1910. Wed. $.25 newsstand; $12/yr. 4444 W. Alexis St., Toledo, OH 43623. TEL 419-475-6000; FAX 419-472-7774. **Owner(s):** Herald Newspapers, 4444 W. Alexis Rd., Toledo, OH 43623. TEL 419-475-1501; Ed. Christine McKean; Pub. Allen C. Foster; adv.; photos; bk.rev.; pub. size: standard; circ. 2,500(paid).

US

WEST TOLEDO HERALD. 1970. Wed. $.25 newsstand; $15/yr. mailed. 4444 N. Alexis Rd., Toledo, OH 43623. TEL 419-475-6000; FAX 419-472-7774. **Owner(s):** Herald Newspapers, 4444 Alexis Rd., Toledo, OH 43623; Ed. Mike Bright; Pub. Allen C. Foster; adv.; photos; pub. size: broadsheet; circ. 37,000(paid).
  Formerly: Toledo Edition.

UTICA

US

UTICA HERALD. 1878. w. $.25 newsstand; $10/yr. in cy.; $12/yr. out of cy.; $14/yr. out of state. 120 S. Main St., Utica, OH 43080 TEL 614-892-2771. **Owner(s):** Nelson A. Smith, 120 S. Main, Utica, OH 43080. TEL 614-892-2771; adv.; photos; pub. size: broadsheet; circ. 2,100(paid).

VERMILION

US

VERMILION PHOTOJOURNAL. 1959. Tue. $.50 newsstand; $24/yr. 630 N. Main St., Vermilion, OH 44089. TEL 216-967-5268; FAX 216-967-2535. **Owner(s):** Photojournal, Inc., 520 Warren St., Sandusky, OH 44870. TEL 419-625-5825; Ed. Karen Cornelius. adv.; photos; pub. size: tabloid; circ. 3,500(free & paid).

VERSAILLES

US

VERSAILLES POLICY, THE. 1875. Tue. $.50 newsstand; $18/yr. in state $21/yr. out of state. P.O. Box 74, Versailles, OH 45380. TEL 513-526-9131; FAX 513-526-9131. **Owner(s):** Scott Langston, 1080 Aubert Dr., Versailles, OH 45380; Ed. Scott Langston; Pub. Scott Langston; adv.; photos bk.rev.; pub. size: standard; circ. 2,450(paid)

WAPAKONETA

US

SHELBY REVIEW. 1978. Tue. $15/yr. 8 Willipie St., Wapakoneta, OH 45895. TEL 419-738-2128; FAX 419-738-5352. **Owner(s):** American Publishing Co., 606 N. Van Buren, P.O. Box 520, Marion, IL 62959. TEL 618-993-1711; Ed. Dianna Epperly. adv. contact: Karen Brown. pub. size: broadsheet; circ. 4,550.

WAUSEON

US

FULTON COUNTY EXPOSITOR. 1854. s-w.: Tue. & Thu. $.50 newsstand; $32/yr. mailed in cy.; $40.50/yr. out of cy.; $44.50/yr. out of state. 201 N. Fulton, Wauseon, OH 43567. TEL 419-335-2010; FAX 419-335-2030. **Owner(s):** Gazette Publishing Co., 107 N. Sandsky St., Bellview, OH 44811; Ed. Brian Liskai; Pub. Robert Krumm; adv. contact: Sherry Garrison. pub. size: broadsheet; circ. 7,500(paid).

WAVERLY

US

NEWS WATCHMAN, THE. 1975. s-w.: Wed. & Sun. $.50 newsstand; $40.25/yr. in cy.; $49/yr. out of cy. 101 W. Second St., Waverly, OH 45690. TEL 614-947-2149; FAX 614-947-1344. **Owner(s):** Mid-South Management Co., Inc., 314 Pine St., Spartanburg, SC 29302. TEL 803-573-7640; FAX 803-573-7640; Ed. Betty McAdow; Pub. David H. Corcoran; adv. contact: Jane Gillum. photos; bk.rev.; pub. size: broadsheet; circ. 3,800(paid).

WELLSTON

US

WELLSTON TELEGRAM, THE. 1896. Thu. free newsstand; $25/yr. 12 S. Ohio Ave., Wellston, OH 45692. TEL 614-384-6102; FAX 614-384-3063. **Owner(s):** Steven P. Keller, 12. S. Ohio Ave., Wellston, OH 45692. TEL 614-384-6102; FAX 614-384-3063; Ed. Steven P. Keller; Pub. Steven P. Keller; adv. contact: Steven P. Keller. pub. size: broadsheet; circ. 5,200(free & paid).

WESTERVILLE

US

WESTERVILLE NEWS & PUBLIC OPINION. 1867. Wed. $.40 newsstand; $25/yr. in cy.; $30/yr. out of state. 130 Graphic Way, Westerville, OH 43081. TEL 614-882-2244. **Owner(s):** Suburban News Publications, 5257 Sinclair Rd., Columbus, OH 43229. TEL 614-464-4567; Ed. Martin Rozeman; Pub. James A. Toms; pub. size: broadsheet; circ. 20,515(free & paid).
Formerly: Westerville Public Opinion & News.

WEST MILTON

US

WEST MILTON RECORD. Wed. $.50/copy; $18.20/yr. local; $26/yr. in cy.; $31/yr. out of cy. 2 S. Miami St., West Milton, OH 45383. TEL 513-698-4451; FAX 513-667-8987. **Owner(s):** Vernon Bowling, 1455 W. Main, Tipp City, OH 45371. TEL 513-698-8512; Ed. Erik Shrewsberry; Pub. David Copen; adv. contact: Ivan Funk. pub. size: broadsheet; circ. 3,000(paid).

WEST UNION

US

PEOPLE'S DEFENDER, THE. 1866. Wed. $.40 newsstand; $13/yr. in cy.; $14/yr. out of cy. 229 N. Cross St., West Union, OH 45693. TEL 513-544-2391; FAX 513-544-2298. **Owner(s):** Defender Publishing Co., 229 N. Cross St., P.O. Box 308, West Union, OH 45693. TEL 513-544-2391; FAX 513-544-2298; Ed. Herbert H. Lax; Pub. Herbert H. Lax; adv. contact: Darlene Pettit. pub. size: broadsheet; circ. 8,900(paid).

WHEELERSBURG

US

SCIOTO VOICE. 1973. Thu. $.50 newsstand; $15/yr. in cy.; $22/yr. out of cy. 8019 Hayport Rd., Wheelersburg, OH 45694-0400. TEL 614-574-8494; FAX 614-574-2329. **Owner(s):** Voice Newspapers, Inc., P.O. Box 400, Wheerlersburg, OH 45694; Ed. James G. Kegley; Pub. James G. Kegley; adv.; pub. size: broadsheet; circ. 5,400(paid).

WILLARD

US

WILLARD TIMES-JUNCTION. 1883. s-w.: Mon. & Thu. $.35 newsstand; $30/yr. in cy.; $37.50/yr. out of cy. 211 Myrtle Ave., Willard, OH 44890. TEL 419-935-0184; FAX 419-933-2031. **Owner(s):** Shelby Daily Globe, Inc., 37 W. Main, Shelby, OH 44875. TEL 419-342-4276; Pub. Ken Gove; pub. size: broadsheet; circ. 4,200(paid).

WILLSHIRE

US

PHOTO STAR. 1895. Wed. free; $25/yr. mailed. 307 State St., Willshire, OH 45898. TEL 419-495-2696; FAX 419-495-2143. **Owner(s):** Judith Bunner, 307 State St., Willshire, OH 45898. TEL 419-495-2696; Ed. Judith Bunner; Pub. Judith Bunner; pub. size: tabloid; circ. 11,600(paid).

WILMINGTON

US

CLINTON COUNTY SHOPPERS GUIDE. 1986. Wed. free. 47 S. South St., Wilmington, OH 45177-2213. TEL 513-382-6761; FAX 513-382-4392. **Owner(s):** Brown Publishing Co., P.O. Box 555, Urbana, OH 43078. TEL 513-652-2100; Ed. Jay Carey; Pub. Clarence Graham; adv.; bk.rev.; pub. size: tabloid; circ. 16,500(free).

US

STAR REPUBLICAN. 1870. Mon. $18.75/yr. 47 S. South St., Wilmington, OH 45177. TEL 513-382-7796; FAX 513-382-4392. **Owner(s):** Brown Publishing Co., P.O. Box 555, Urbanna, OH 43078. TEL 513-652-2100; Ed. Rose Cooper; Pub. Clarence Graham; adv. contact: Rick Irvin. photos; pub. size: broadsheet; circ. 22,000(free & paid).

WOODSFIELD

US

MONROE COUNTY BEACON. 1937. Thu. $.75 newsstand; $22/yr. in school district; $39/yr. elsewhere; $19/yr. senior citizens. P.O. Box 70, Woodsfield, OH 43793-0070. TEL 614-472-0734; FAX 614-472-0735. **Owner(s):** Delphos Newspapers, 405 N. Main St., Delphos, OH 45833. TEL 419-695-0015; Ed. Arlene Selvey; Pub. Robert F. Gates; adv.; photos; pub. size: broadsheet; circ. 5,650(paid).

WORTHINGTON

US

DUBLIN VILLAGER. Mon. free newsstand; $75/yr. mailed. 670 Lakeview Plz. Blvd., Ste. F, Worthington, OH 43085. TEL 614-841-1781; FAX 614-841-0436. **Owner(s):** Dispatch Newspapers, Inc., 34 S. Third St., Columbus, OH 43229. TEL 614-461-5000; Ed. Craig McDonald; Pub. Ben Carson; adv. contact: Jerry O'Connell. photos; pub. size: tabloid; circ. 22,441(free).

YOUNGSTOWN

US

BUCKEYE REVIEW, THE. 1937. Fri. $.35 newsstand; $20/yr. 1555 Belmont Ave., Youngstown, OH 44501-0287. TEL 216-743-2250; FAX 216-746-2340. **Owner(s):** The Buckeye Publishing Co., 1555 Belmont Ave., Youngstown, OH 44501-0287. TEL 216-743-2250; FAX 216-746-2360; Ed. M. Mike McNair; Pub. M. Mike McNair; adv. contact: John Harper. photos; bk.rev.; pub. size: tabloid; circ. 20,100(free & paid).
Formerly: Youngstown Buckeye Review.

ZANESVILLE

US

ZANESVILLE MUSKINGUM ADVERTISER. 1976. Sat. free. 760 Linden Ave., Zanesville, OH 43701. TEL 614-453-0615; FAX 614-453-9504. **Owner(s):** Add, Inc., 600 Industrial Dr., Waupaca, WI 54981. TEL 715-258-8450; Ed. Ernie Bruns. pub. size: tabloid; circ. 36,055(free).

OKLAHOMA

ATOKA

US

ATOKA COUNTY TIMES. Wed. $.50 newsstand; $20/yr. in cy. mailed; $27.50/yr. out of cy.; $35/yr. out of state. 100 E. Second St., Atoka, OK 74525. TEL 405-889-3319; FAX 405-889-2300. **Owner(s):** Foster & Louise Cain, 100 E. Second St., Atoka, OK 74525. TEL 405-889-3319; Ed. Kenneth Hamilton; Pub. Louise Cain; adv. contact: Ron Linscott. pub. size: broadsheet; circ. 4,190(paid).

BETHANY

US

TRIBUNE, THE. 1923. Thu. $.35 newsstand;
$16.50/yr. in cy.; $19.50/yr. out of cy.;
$24.50/yr. out of state; $14/yr. senior citizens.
3813 N. College St., Bethany, OK 73008.
TEL 405-789-1962; FAX 405-789-4253.
Owner(s): K. Brett Wesner, P.O. Box 40, Bethany,
OK 73008. TEL 405-789-1962; FAX
405-789-4253; Ed. Lyne Gardner; Pub. K. Brett
Wesner; adv. contact: Terry Barnett. bk.rev.; pub.
size: broadsheet; circ. 3,000(paid).

BOISE CITY

US

BOISE CITY NEWS, THE. 1898. Wed. $.50
newsstand; $21.50/yr. 105 W. Main St., Boise
City, OK 73933. TEL 405-544-2222;
FAX 405-544-3281. **Owner(s):** Jim Rosebery,
105 W. Main, Boise City, OK 73933. TEL
405-544-2222; FAX 405-544-3281; Ed. Jim
Rosebery; Pub. Jim Rosebery; adv. contact: Deb
Crabtree. photos; circ. 1,800(paid).

BRISTOW

US

BRISTOW NEWS. 1948. Wed. $.35 newsstand;
$18/yr. in cy.; $24/yr. out of cy.; $31/yr. out of
state. 112 W. Sixth Ave., Bristow, OK 74010.
TEL 918-367-2282; FAX 918-367-2724.
Owner(s): Bristow Publishers, Inc., McAllister, OK
74501; adv.; pub. size: broadstreet; circ.
3,300(free & paid).

US

RECORD-CITIZEN, THE. 1898. Fri. $18/yr. in cy.;
$24/yr. out of cy.; $31/yr. out of state. 112 W.
Sixth Ave., Bristow, OK 74010.
TEL 918-367-2282. **Owner(s):** Bristow
Publishers, Inc., McAllister, OK; pub. size:
broadsheet; circ. morning 3,175(paid).

BROKEN ARROW

US

BROKEN ARROW LEDGER & SCOUT. 1903. 3/wk.:
Tue., Thu., Sun. $.50 newsstand; $45/yr. home
deliv. 110 W. Kenosh, Broken Arrow, OK 74012.
TEL 918-258-7171; FAX 918-258-9908.
Owner(s): Retherford Publications, Inc., 8584 E.
41st St., Tulsa, OK 74145. TEL 918-663-1414;
FAX 918-664-8161; Ed. Wayne Bishop; Pub. Bill
Rutherford; adv. contact: Sandy Cagle. pub. size:
broadsheet; circ. 12,000(paid); Sun. 17,000.
   Formerly: Broken Arrow Daily Ledger.

CATOOSA

US

CATOOSA TIMES HERALD. 1965. Wed. $15./yr.
local. 650 S. Cherokee, Catoosa, OK 74015.
TEL 918-266-3664; FAX 918-266-3666.
Owner(s): NEOK Publishing, Catoosa, OK 74015;
Ed. John Kester; Pub. Eula Kester; pub. size:
standard; circ. 1,400(paid).

CHANDLER

US

LINCOLN COUNTY NEWS. 1891. Thu. $.50
newsstand; $17/yr. in cy.; $19/yr. out of cy.;
$23/yr. out of state. 718 Manvel Ave., Chandler,
OK 74834. TEL 405-258-1818;
FAX 405-258-1824. **Owner(s):** Stephen E.
Mathis, P.O. Box 248, Chandler, OK 74834. TEL
405-258-1818; FAX 405-258-1824; Ed.
Stephen E. Mathis; Pub. Stephen E. Mathis; adv.
contact: P. Dawn Mathis. photos; bk.rev.; pub.
size: standard; circ. 4 100(paid).
   Formerly: Chandler Lincoln County News.

CHEROKEE

US

CHEROKEE MESSENGER & REPUBLICAN. 1900. Thu.
$.50 newsstand; $16/yr. in cy.; $25/yr. out of
cy. 216 S. Grand, Cherokee, OK 73728.
TEL 405-596-3344. **Owner(s):** Larry Hammer,
P.O. Box 245, Cherokee, OK 73728. TEL
405-596-3344. Ed. Carol Angle; Pub. Larry
Hammer; adv.; bk.rev.; pub. size: broadsheet; circ.
2,500(paid).
   Formerly: Cherokee Messenger.

CORDELL

US

CORDELL BEACON, THE. Wed. $.35 newsstand;
$16.20/yr. in cy.; $21.60/yr. out of cy.; $25/yr.
out of state. 115 E. Main St., Cordell, OK 73632.
TEL 405-832-3333. **Owner(s):** Wesner
Publications, 115 E. Main St., Cordell, OK 73632.
TEL 405-832-3333; Ed. Jason McCarty; Pub.
Brett Wesner; adv. contact: Kay Igo. pub. size:
standard; circ. 3,700(paid).

COVINGTON

US   ISSN 0746-6633

COVINGTON RECORD. 1905. Thu. $.35 newsstand;
$15.50/yr. 310 Main St., Covington, OK
73730-0535. TEL 405-864-7612;
FAX 405-864-7612. **Owner(s):** Covington
Publishing Corp., 310 Main St., Covington, OK
73730. TEL 405-864-7612; Ed. Janet Smith;
Pub. Roger L. Miller; adv. contact: Nancy Miller.
photos; bk.rev.; pub. size: tabloid; circ. 900(paid).

COWETA

US

COWETA AMERICAN. 1903. Wed. $.50 newsstand;
$16.50/yr. 107 S. Broadway, Coweta, OK
74429. TEL 918-486-4444;
FAX 918-486-3827. **Owner(s):** Retherford
Publishing, 8545 E. 41st St., Tulsa, OK 74145;
Ed. Christy Wheeland. adv. contact: Linda Miller.
pub. size: broadsheet; circ. 2,500(paid).

DURANT

US

BRYAN COUNTY STAR. Thu. $.25 newsstand;
$12/yr. P.O. Box 1427, Durant, OK 74702.
TEL 405-924-6499; FAX 405-924-6664.
Owner(s): Cecil Plyler, P.O. Box 1427, Durant,
OK 74702. TEL 405-924-6499; FAX
405-924-6664 Ed. Matt Swearengin. adv.; pub.
size: standard; circ. 5 000(paid).

US

SHOPPER ZONE I. 1976. Wed. free. 120 N. 12th St.,
Durant, OK 74701. TEL 405-924-1770;
FAX 405-924-1792. **Owner(s):** Cox Publishing
Co., 4905 Hwy. 75, S., Denison, TX 75020. TEL
903-465-1400; Pub. H. Wayne Cox; pub. size:
tabloid; circ. 15,000(free).

US   ISSN 0747-2633

SOUTHERN OKLAHOMA LEADER. 1905. Tue. free.
P.O. Box 1427, Durant, OK 74702.
TEL 405-924-6499; FAX 405-924-6664.
Owner(s): Cecil Plyler, P.O. Box 1427, Durant,
OK 74702. TEL 405-924-6499; FAX
405-924-6664; Ed. Matt Swearengin. adv.; pub.
size: standard; circ. 11,400(controlled & paid).

EAKLY

US   ISSN 0746-4789

COUNTRY CONNECTION NEWS. 1982. Wed. $.50
newsstand; $21-$24/yr. 315 Main St., Eakly, OK
73033. TEL 405-797-3648;
FAX 405-797-3663; E-mail
bblock@prodigy.com. **Owner(s):** Joyce Carney,
315 Main St., Eakly, OK 73033. TEL
405-797-3648; FAX 405-797-3653; Ed. Joyce
Carney Pub. Joyce Carney; adv. contact: Brenda
Howerton. photos; pub. size: broadsheet; circ.
2,000(paid).

EL RENO

US

EL RENO TRIBUNE. 1934. s-w.: Sun. & Wed. $.50
newsstand; $3/mo. home deliv.; $8.75/4 mos.
home deliv. 201 N. Rock Island, El Reno, OK
73036. TEL 405-262-5180;
FAX 405-262-3541. **Owner(s):** Tribune Corp.,
P.O. Box 9, El Reno, OK 73036. TEL
405-262-5180; FAX 405-262-3541; Ed. Pat
Dyer; Pub. Sean Dyer; adv. contact: Erin Dyer.
pub. size: broadsheet; circ. 4,500(paid); Sun.
5,200(paid).

FAIRVIEW

US

FAIRVIEW REPUBLICAN. 1900. Thu. $.50 newsstand;
$19/yr. in cy.; $27/yr. out of cy.; $32/yr. out of
state. 112 N. Main St., Fairview, OK 73737.
TEL 405-227-4439; FAX 405-227-4430.
Owner(s): Larry Hammer, P.O. Box 245,
Cherokee, OK 73728. TEL 405-596-3344; Pub.
Larry Hammer; adv.; pub. size: broadsheet; circ.
3,500(controlled & paid).

GROVE

US

GROVE SUN. 1898. 3/wk.: Tue., Thu., Fri. $.50
newsstand; $35/yr. in cy.; $45/yr. out of cy.;
$55/yr. out of state. 14 W. Third St., Grove, OK
74344. TEL 918-786-2228;
FAX 918-786-2156. **Owner(s):** Grove Sun
Newspaper Co., 14 W. Third St., Grove, OK
74344. TEL 918-786-2228; Ed. Randy Webb;
Pub. M. Gerald Stone; adv.; pub. size: broadsheet;
circ. 6,000(paid).

HARRAH

US

HARRAH NEWS, THE. 1959. Thu. $.25 newsstand; $18/yr. out of state. 1069 N. Harrah Rd., Harrah, OK 73045. TEL 405-454-2451; FAX 405-454-3567. **Owner(s):** Harrah News, Inc., P.O. Box 448, Harrah, OK 73045. TEL 405-454-2451; FAX 405-454-3567; Pub. Shirley Quaid; adv.; photos; bk.rev.; pub. size: tabloid; circ. 1,969(paid).

HOBART

US

HOBART DEMOCRAT-CHIEF. 1901. Thu. $.50 newsstand; $18/yr. in cy.; $28/yr. in state. 407 S. Main St., Hobart, OK 73651. TEL 405-726-3333. **Owner(s):** Democrat-Chief Publishing Co., 407 S. Main St., Hobart, OK 73651. TEL 405-726-3333; Pub. Joe Hancock; adv.; photos; pub. size: broadsheet; circ. 3,400(paid).

HOMINY

US

HOMINY NEWS-PROGRESS. 1973. Wed. $.35 newsstand; $13.50/yr. 115 W. Main St., Hominy, OK 74035. TEL 918-885-2101. **Owner(s):** Ferguson & Ferguson, S. Broadway, Cleveland, OK 74020; Ed. Ramona Brown; Pub. Romona Brown; pub. size: standard; circ. 1,550(paid).

KINGFISHER

US

KINGFISHER TIMES & FREE PRESS. 1889. s-w.: Sun. & Wed. $.50 newsstand; $26/yr. 323 N. Main St., Kingfisher, OK 73750. TEL 405-375-3220; FAX 405-375-3222. **Owner(s):** Kingfisher Newspapers Inc., 323 N. Main St., Kingfisher, OK 73750. TEL 405-375-3220; FAX 405-375-3222; Ed. Gary Reid; Pub. Gary Reid; adv.; photos; pub. size: broadsheet; circ. 4,200(paid).
Formerly: Kingfisher Times.

KONAWA

US

KONAWA LEADER. 1893. Thu. $.35 newsstand; $15/yr. 102 N. Broadway, Konawa, OK 74849. TEL 405-925-3187; FAX 405-925-3729. **Owner(s):** Ed Gallagher, P.O. Box 157, Konawa, OK 74849. TEL 405-925-3187; FAX 405-925-3729; Ed. Ed Gallagher; Pub. Ed Gallagher; pub. size: broadsheet; circ. 2,000(paid).

US

STRATFORD STAR. Thu. $.35 newsstand; $15/yr. 102 N. Broadway, Konawa, OK 74849. TEL 405-925-3187; FAX 405-925-3729. **Owner(s):** Ed Gallagher, P.O. Box 157, Konowa, OK. TEL 405-925-3187; FAX 405-925-3729; Ed. Ed Gallagher; Pub. Ed Gallagher; adv.; pub. size: standard; circ. 2,000(paid).

MADILL

US

MADILL RECORD. 1895. Thu. $20/yr. in cy.; $27/yr. in OK & TX; $32/yr. elsewhere. 211 Plaza, Madill, OK 73446. TEL 405-795-3355; FAX 405-795-3530. **Owner(s):** John D. Montgomery, P.O. Box 529, Madill, OK 73446. TEL 405-795-3355; FAX 405-795-3530; G. Montgomery, S. Codner, M. Codner, P.O. Box 529, Madill, OK 73446; Ed. Mark Codner; Pub. Mark Codner; adv.; photos; pub. size: broadsheet; circ. 4,450(paid).

MOORE

US   ISSN 0747-1947

MOORE AMERICAN. 1935. s-w.: Wed & Fri. free Wed.; $.25/Fri.; $15.50/yr. 623 N. Broadway, Moore, OK 73160. TEL 405-794-5555; FAX 405-799-8046. **Owner(s):** Redden Inc., 325 W. I-35 Service Rd., S., Moore, OK 73160. TEL 405-794-5555; FAX 405-799-8046; Ed. Oran C. Redden; Pub. Oran C. Redden; adv.; photos; pub. size: broadsheet; circ. 20,500(free & paid). **Wire Service(s):** AP.

NEWCASTLE

US

NEWCASTLE PACER, THE. 1978. Thu. $.35 newsstand; $12/yr. local; $13.50/yr. elsewhere. 120 N.E. Second St., Ste. 102, Newcastle, OK 73065. TEL 405-387-5277. **Owner(s):** Newcastle Pacer, Inc., P.O. Box 429, Newcastle, OK 73065. TEL 405-387-5277; Ed. Marvin Leyerle; Pub. Marvine Leyerle; adv. contact: Jocile Leyerle. pub. size: broadsheet; circ. 1,500(controlled & paid).

NOWATA

US

NOWATA STAR. 1904. Wed. $.50 newsstand; $18/yr. 213 N. Maple St., Nowata, OK 74048. TEL 918-273-2446. **Owner(s):** Nowata Newspapers, Inc., P.O. Box 429, Nowata, OK 74048. TEL 918-273-2446; Ed. Dave Altman; Pub. David Reid; adv. contact: Pat Morrison. pub. size: broadsheet; circ. 2,700(free & paid).

OKLAHOMA CITY

US

CAPITOL HILL BEACON. 1905. Thu. $.25 newsstand; $25/yr. mailed. 124 W. Commerce, Oklahoma City, OK 73109. TEL 405-232-4151; FAX 405-235-0818. **Owner(s):** Beacon Publishing Co., 124 W. Commerce, Oklahoma City, OK 73109; Ed. David Sellers; Pub. David Sellers; adv. contact: Mitch Sellers. pub. size: standard; circ. 23,000(paid).

US

OKLAHOMA CITY FRIDAY. 1974. Fri. $20/yr. in cy. 10801 N. Quail Plaza Dr., Oklahoma City, OK 73120. TEL 405-755-3311. **Owner(s):** Nichols Hills Publishing Co., 1605 W. Wilshire, Oklahoma City, OK 73116; Ed. Gordon Walker; Pub. J. Leland Gourley; adv. contact: Cindy Shea. bk.rev.; pub. size: broadsheet; circ. 8,119(paid).

OOLOGAH

US   ISSN 0688-0470

OOLOGAH LAKE LEADER. 1982. Thu. $.50 newsstand; $17/yr. in cy.; $20/yr. in state; $30/yr. out of state. 109 S. Maple, Oologah, OK 74053. TEL 918-443-2428. **Owner(s):** John M. Wylie, II, 109 S. Maple, Oologah, OK 74053. TEL 918-443-2428; FAX 918-443-2429; Ed. John M. Wylie, II; Pub. John M. Wylie, II; adv. contact: Harriet Estep. photos; bk.rev.; pub. size: broadsheet; circ. 3,560(free & paid).

OWASSO

US

OWASSO REPORTER. 1970. Thu. $.50 newsstand; $17.50/yr. 202 E. Second Ave., Owasso, OK 74055. TEL 918-272-1155. **Owner(s):** Retherford Publications, Inc., 8545 E. 41st St., Tulsa, OK 74145. TEL 918-663-1414; Ed. Ralph Schaefer; Pub. Bill R. Retherford; adv. contact: Charles Cagle. pub. size: broadsheet; circ. 5,000(paid).

PAWHUSKA

US

PAWHUSKA JOURNAL-CAPITAL. 1904. s-w.: Wed. & Sat. $.50 newsstand; $40/yr. in cy.; $60/yr. out of cy. 700 Kihekaa, Pawhuska, OK 74056. TEL 918-287-1590; FAX 918-287-1804. **Owner(s):** Stephens Group, Inc., P.O. Box 17017, Fort Smith, AR 72917. TEL 501-785-7810; Ed. Libby Meyer. adv. contact: Terry Collins. pub. size: broadsheet; circ. 2,400(paid).

PRYOR

US

PRYOR JEFFERSONIAN. 1907. Thu. free. 105 S. Adair St., Pryor, OK 74362. TEL 918-825-3292; FAX 918-825-1965. **Owner(s):** Daily Times, 105 S. Adair St., P.O. Box 308, Pryor, OK 74361. TEL 918-825-3292; Ed. Henry Goodman; Pub. Henry Goodman; pub. size: broadsheet; circ. 6,000(free).

PURCELL

US

PURCELL REGISTER. 1887. Thu. $.50 newsstand; $18/yr. 225 W. Main St., Purcell, OK 73080. TEL 405-527-2126; FAX 405-527-3299. **Owner(s):** McClain County Publishing Co., Inc., P.O. Box 191, Purcell, OK 73080. TEL 405-527-2126; FAX 405-527-3299; Ed. Bill Moakley. adv. contact: Vickie Foraker. photos; pub. size: broadsheet; circ. 6,200(paid).

SALLISAW

US

SEQUOYAH COUNTY TIMES. 1932. s-w.: Thu. & Sun. $.35 newsstand; $17/yr. in OK. & adjoining states; $44/yr. elsewhere. 111 N. Oak St., Sallisaw, OK 74955. TEL 918-775-4433; FAX 918-775-3023. **Owner(s):** Cookson Hills Publishers, Inc., 11 N. Oak St., Sallisaw, OK 74955. TEL 918-775-4433; Ed. Jim Mayo; Pub. Jim Mayo; adv. contact: Delanna Nutter. pub. size: broadsheet; circ. 6,948(free & paid).

SAND SPRINGS

US

SAND SPRINGS LEADER. 1912. s-w.: Sun. & Wed. $.50 newsstand; $25/yr. local. 303 N. McKinley Ave., Sand Springs, OK 74063. TEL 918-245-6634; FAX 918-241-3610. **Owner(s):** Retherford Publications, Inc., 8545 E. 41st St., Tulsa, OK 74145. TEL 918-663-1414; Ed. Don Cease. adv. contact: Dan Rodgers. pub. size: broadsheet; circ. 5,228(paid).

SAYRE

US

SAYRE JOURNAL. 1891. Thu. $.35 newsstand; $19.26/yr. in area; $24.50/yr. elsewhere. 110 N. Fourth St., Sayre, OK 73662. TEL 405-928-3372. **Owner(s):** To-Mo-Ca Comm., Inc., P.O. Box 340, Sayre, OK 73662-0340. TEL 405-928-3372; Ed. Sonya Blackshear; Pub. Tom Higley; adv.; photos; pub. size: broadsheet; circ. 2,125(paid).

SKIATOOK

US

SKIATOOK JOURNAL. 1985. Wed. $.50 newsstand; $13.75/yr. local. 501 W. Rogers, Skiatook, OK 74070. TEL 918-396-1616. **Owner(s):** Retherford Publications, Inc., 8545 E. 41st St., Tulsa, OK 74145. TEL 918-663-1414; Ed. Ralph Schaefer; Pub. Bill R. Retherford; adv.: $6.85/SAU. pub. size: broadsheet; circ. 2,321(paid).

STIGLER

US

COUNTY STAR. Thu. free. 204 S. Broadway, Stigler, OK 74462. TEL 918-967-4655; FAX 918-967-4289. **Owner(s):** Linus G. Williams, 204 S. Broadway, Stigler, OK 74462. TEL 918-967-4655; Ed. Sharon Johnson; Pub. Linus G. Williams; adv. contact: Mike Higley. pub. size: broadsheet; circ. 4,000(free).

US

STIGLER NEWS-SENTINEL. 1930. Thu. $.50 newsstand; $20/yr. 204 S. Broadway, Stigler, OK 74462. TEL 918-967-4655; FAX 918-967-4289. **Owner(s):** Linus G. Williams, 204 S. Broadway, Stigler, OK 74462. TEL 918-967-4655; Ed. Sharon Johnson; Pub. Linus G. Williams; adv. contact: Mike Higley. pub. size: broadsheet; circ. 3,900(paid).

STILWELL

US

STILWELL DEMOCRAT-JOURNAL. 1897. Thu. $.50 newsstand; $23/yr. out of state. 118 N. Second St., Stilwell, OK 74960. TEL 918-696-2228; FAX 918-696-7066. **Owner(s):** Indian Nations Communications, Inc., P.O. Box 508, Stilwell, OK 74960. TEL 918-696-2228; adv. contact: Pam Muskrat. pub. size: standard; circ. 5,700(paid).

TISHOMINGO

US

JOHNSTON COUNTY CAPITAL-DEMOCRAT. 1900. Thu. $.35 newsstand; $15/yr. in cy.; $25/yr. out of cy.; $30/yr. out of state. 103 N. Neshoba, Tishomingo, OK 73460. TEL 405-371-2356. **Owner(s):** Ray Lokey, P.O. Box 400, Tishomingo, OK 73460. TEL 405-371-2356; Ed. Ray Lokey; Pub. Ray Lokey; adv.; pub. size: broadsheet; circ. 3,150(paid).

TONKAWA

US

TONKAWA NEWS, THE. 1894. Thu. $.50 newsstand; 19.50/yr. 108 N. Seventh St., Tonkawa, OK 74653-0250. TEL 405-628-2532; FAX 405-628-4044. **Owner(s):** H. Lyle Becker, 108 N. Seventh St., Tonkawa, OK 74653-0250. TEL 405-628-2532; FAX 405-628-4044; Ed. H. Lyle Becker; Pub. H. Lyle Becker; adv.; photos; bk.rev.; pub. size: broadsheet; circ. 1,800(paid).

TULSA

US

BIXBY BULLETIN. 1905. Thu. $15.50/yr. in cy.; $29/yr. out of cy.; $36/yr. out of state. 8545 41st St., Tulsa, OK 74145. TEL 918-663-1414; FAX 918-664-8161. **Owner(s):** Retherford Publications, 8545 E. 41st St., Tulsa, OK 74145. TEL 918-663-1414; Ed. Ralph Schaefer; Pub. Bill R. Rutherford; adv.: $6.25/SAU. pub. size: standard; circ. 1,463(paid).

US   ISSN 0890-9040

COLLINSVILLE NEWS. 1899. Wed. $.50 newsstand; $16.50/yr. in cy.; $24/yr. out of cy. 9545 E. 41st St., Tulsa, OK 74145. TEL 918-663-1414. **Owner(s):** Retherford Publications, Inc., 8545 E. 41st St., Tulsa, OK 74145. TEL 918-663-1414; Ed. Ralph Schaefer; Pub. Bill R. Retherford; adv.: $6.85/SAU. pub. size: broadsheet; circ. 2,000(paid).

US

JENKS JOURNAL. 1957. w. $.50 newsstand; $15.50/yr. 8545 E. 41st., Tulsa, OK 74145. TEL 918-663-1414; FAX 918-664-8161. **Owner(s):** Retherford Publications, Inc., 8545 E. 41st St., Tulsa, OK 74145. TEL 918-663-1414; FAX 918-664-8161; Pub. Bill R. Retherford; adv. contact: John Line. photos; pub. size: broadsheet; circ. 1,300(paid).

US

OKLAHOMA EAGLE. 1921. Thu. $.50 newsstand; $23/yr. 624 E. Archer St., Tulsa, OK 74120. TEL 918-582-7124; FAX 918-582-8905. **Owner(s):** James O. Goodwin, 624 E. Archer, Tulsa, OK 74120. TEL 918-582-7124; Edward L. Goodwin, Jr., 624 E. Archer St., Tulsa, OK 74120. TEL 918-582-7124; Ed. Daryl Wilson; Pub. James G. Goodwin; pub. size: standard; circ. 12,800(paid).

US

SOUTHWEST TULSA NEWS. Thu. $.50 newsstand; $13.75/yr. 8545 E. 41st St., Tulsa, OK 74145. TEL 918-663-1414. **Owner(s):** Retherford Publications, Inc., 8545 E. 41st St., Tulsa, OK 74145. TEL 918-663-1414; Ed. Ralph Schaefer. adv.: $6.25/SAU. pub. size: tabloid; circ. 3,800(paid). **Formerly:** Tulsa County News.

WAGONER

US

WAGONER TRIBUNE, THE. 1894. Thu. $17.50/yr. 221 E. Cherokee, Wagoner, OK 74467. TEL 918-485-5505; FAX 918-485-8442. **Owner(s):** Retherford Publications, Inc., 8545 E. 41st St., Tulsa, OK 74145; Ed. Ralph Schaefer. pub. size: broadsheet circ. 3,700(paid).

WATONGA

US

WATONGA REPUBLICAN, THE. 1892. Wed. $.50 newsstand; $26/yr. in state; $30/yr. out of state. 104 E. Main, Watonga, OK 73772. TEL 405-623-4922. **Owner(s):** Mr. & Mrs. Tim Curtin, 802 N. Prouty, Watonga, OK 73772. TEL 405-623-4922; Ed. Tim Curtin; Pub. Tim Curtin; adv. contact: Tim Curtin. pub. size: broadsheet; circ. 3,552(paid).

WETUMKA

US

HUGHES COUNTY TIMES. 1930. Thu. $.25 newsstand; $17.50/yr. in cy.; $22.50/yr. out of cy.; $27.50 out of state. 120 S. Main, Wetumka, OK 74883. TEL 405-452-3294; FAX 405-452-3329. **Owner(s):** William C. Morgan, 120 S. Main, Wetumka, OK 74883. TEL 405-452-3294; Ed. William C. Morgan; Pub. William C. Morgan; adv. contact: Donna Ramsey. pub. size: broadsheet; circ. 2,300(paid).

WEWOKA

US

WEWOKA TIMES. 1926. Wed. $.50 newsstand; $48/yr. mailed; $42/yr. in cy.; $43/yr. out of cy. 210 S. Wewoka St., Wewoka, OK 74884. TEL 405-257-3341; FAX 405-257-3313. **Owner(s):** Robinson Pettis Publishing, Inc., 210 S. Wewoka, Wewoka, AR 74884; Ed. Bill Robinson; Pub. Bill Robinson; adv. contact: Kelly Robinson. photos; pub. size: tabloid; circ. evering 1,200(paid).

YALE

US

YALE NEWS, THE. 1902. Wed. $.35 newsstand; $15.50/yr. 103 N. Main St., Yale, OK 74085. TEL 918-387-2125. E-mail: yale-news@okpress.tfnet.org **Owner(s):** Beth & Homer Ray, 103 N. Main St., P.O. Box 307, Yale, OK 74085. TEL 918-387-2125; adv.; photos; bk.rev.; pub. size: standard; circ. 1,500(paid).

YUKON

US

YUKON REVIEW. 1963. s-w.: Wed. & Sat. $.50 newsstand; $26/yr. 110 S. Fifth, Yukon, OK 73099. TEL 405-354-5264; FAX 405-350-3044. **Owner(s):** Randel & Karen Grigsby, 110 S. Fifth, Yukon, OK 73099. TEL 405-354-5264; Ed. Conrad Dudderar; Pub. Randel Grigsby; adv.; photos. pub. size: broadsheet; circ. 7,100(paid).

OREGON

BAKER CITY

US

BAKER RECORD-COURIER. 1901. Thu. $15/yr. local; $18/yr. out of area. 1718 720 Main, Baker City, OR 97814-0070. TEL 541-523-5353. **Owner(s):** Byron Brinton, 2517 Valley, Baker City, OR 97314. TEL 503-523-4395; Ed. Byron Brinton; Pub. Byron Brinton; adv. contact: Jay Sublett. pub. size: broadsheet; circ. 5,040(paid).

BANDON

US

WESTERN WORLD. 1905. Wed. $.50 newsstand; $18/yr. local; $22/yr. out of cy. $30/yr. out of state. 1185 Baltimore St., Bandon, OR 97411. TEL 541-347-2423; FAX 541-347-2424. **Owner(s):** Western World Publishing Co., Inc., P.O. Box 248, Bandon, OR 97411. TEL 541-347-2423; FAX 541-347-2424; Ed. Bill Ketsdever. adv. contact: Susan Price. photos; pub. size: broadsheet; circ. 2,796(paid).

BROOKINGS

US

CURRY COASTAL PILOT. 1946. s-w.: Wed. & Sat. $.50 newsstand; $34/yr. local; $44/yr. elsewhere. 507 Chetco Ave., Brookings, OR 97415. TEL 541-469-3123; FAX 541-469-4679. **Owner(s):** Western Communications, Inc., 1526 N.W. Hill St., Bend, OR 97701. TEL 541-382-1811; Ed. Jerry Teague; Pub. Judy Zelmer Smith; adv. contact: Judy Zelmer Smith. pub. size: broadsheet; circ. 7,055(free & paid).

BURNS

US

BURNS TIMES-HERALD. 1887. Wed. $.50 newsstand; $25/yr. in cy.; $30/yr. out of cy. 355 N. Broadway, Burns, OR 97720. TEL 503-573-2022; FAX 503-573-3915. **Owner(s):** Western Communications, Inc., 1526 N.W. Hill St., Bend, OR 97701. TEL 541-382-1811; Ed. Pauline Braymen; Pub. Donna Clark; adv.; photos; pub. size: broadsheet; circ. 3,200(paid).

CANBY

US

CANBY HERALD. 1906. Wed. $.50 newsstand; $22/yr. in cy.; $30/yr. out of cy. 241 N. Grant St., Canby, OR 97013. TEL 503-266-6831. **Owner(s):** Eagle Newspapers, Inc., 4901 Indian School Rd., N.E., Salem, OR 97305. TEL 503-393-1774; Ed. Cam Silvesind; Pub. William D. Cassel; adv. contact: William D. Cassel. pub. size: standard; circ. 10,200(paid).

CONDON

US

TIMES-JOURNAL, THE. 1886. Thu. $.35 newsstand; $19/yr. 319 S. Main St., Condon, OR 97823-0746. TEL 541-384-2421. **Owner(s):** McLaren & Janet Stinchfield, 319 S. Main St., Condon, OR 97823. TEL 541-384-2421; Ed. McLaren Stinchfield; Pub. McLaren Stinchfield; adv.; photos; bk.rev.; pub. size: standard; circ. 1,650(paid).

COQUILLE

US

COQUILLE VALLEY SENTINEL. 1882. Wed. $.50 newsstand; $16/yr. in cy. One Barton's Alley, Coquille, OR 97423. TEL 503-396-3191; FAX 503-396-3624. **Owner(s):** Coquille Valley Publishing, P.O. Box 400, Coquille, OR 97423; Ed. Frederick Taylor; Pub. Frederick Taylor; adv.; pub. size: standard; circ. 1,900(paid).

COTTAGE GROVE

US

COTTAGE GROVE SENTINEL. 1889. Wed. $20.50/yr. in area; $26/yr. out of area. 116 N. 6th St., Cottage Grove, OR 97424. TEL 503-942-3325; FAX 503-942-3328. **Owner(s):** Walt Disney Co., 500 S. Buena Vista St., Burbank, CA 91521. TEL 818-560-5300; Ed. Mark Bowder; Pub. Jody Rolnick; adv. contact: Brad Chambers. pub. size: standard; circ. 5,000(paid).

CRESWELL

US   ISSN 0739-9758

CHRONICLE, THE. 1966. Wed. $.75 newsstand; $18/yr. in cy.; $21/yr. out of cy. 244 W. Oregon Ave., Creswell, OR 97426. TEL 503-895-2197. **Owner(s):** Gerri O'Rourke, P.O. Box 428, Creswell, OR 97426. TEL 503-895-2197; Ed. Gerri O'Rourke; Pub. Gerri O'Rourke; adv. contact: Gerri O'Rourke. pub. size: tabloid; circ. 3,400(free & paid).

   Formerly: Creswell Chronicle.

DALLAS

US

DALLAS POLK COUNTY ITEMIZER-OBSERVER. 1875. Wed. $.50 newsstand; $18/yr. in cy.; $24/yr. out of cy.; $30/yr. out of state. 147 S.E. Court St., Dallas, OR 97338. TEL 503-623-2373; FAX 503-623-2395. **Owner(s):** Eagle Newspapers, Inc., 4901 Indian School Rd., N.E., Salem, OR 97305. TEL 503-393-1774; Ed. Virginia Henderson; Pub. Nancy J. Adams; adv. contact: Korri Miller. photos; pub. size: tabloid; circ. 13,700(free & paid).

DAYTON

US

DAYTON TRIBUNE. 1912. Thu. $.10 newsstand; $6/yr. 408 Fourth St., Dayton, OR 97114-0069. TEL 503-864-2310; FAX 503-864-2310. **Owner(s):** George & Edwina Meitzen, P.O. Box 69, Dayton, OR 97114-0069. TEL 503-864-2310; FAX 503-864-2310; Ed. George Meitzen. adv.; pub. size: tabloid; circ. 600(paid).

DRAIN

US

DRAIN ENTERPRISE. 1950. Wed. $.30 newsstand; $11/yr. in cy. 309 First St., Drain, OR 97435-8361. TEL 503-836-2241. **Owner(s):** Betty Anderson, P.O. Box 26, Drain, OR 97435; Ed. Sue Anderson. adv.; pub. size: tabloid; circ. 1,200(paid).

EAGLE POINT

US

UPPER ROGUE INDEPENDENT. 1976. Tue. $.25 newsstand; $11.50/yr. in area; $8.65/yr. senior citizens; $23/yr. out of area. 11136 Hwy. 62, Eagle Point, OR 97524. TEL 503-826-7700; FAX 503-826-1340. **Owner(s):** Nancy Leonard, 11136 Hwy. 62, Eagle Point, OR 97524. TEL 503-826-7700; FAX 503-826-1340; Ed. Nancy Leonard; Pub. Nancy Leonard; adv.; photos; pub. size: tabloid; circ. 10,000(free & paid).

FLORENCE

US

SIUSLAW NEWS, THE. 1890. Wed. $.50 newsstand; $20/yr. in cy.; $30/yr. out of cy.; $55/yr. out of state. 148 Maple St., Florence, OR 97439. TEL 541-997-3441; FAX 541-997-7979. **Owner(s):** Mr. & Mrs. Paul R. Holman, 1490 Myrtle Loop, Florence, OR 97439. TEL 541-997-6615; Ed. Bob Serra; Pub. Paul R. Holman; adv. contact: Pam Girard. pub. size: broadsheet; circ. 6,085(paid).

FOREST GROVE

US   ISSN 1042-8518

NEWS TIMES. 1887. Wed. $24/yr. in cy.; $37/yr. out of cy. 2038 Pacific Ave., Forest Grove, OR 97116-0408. TEL 503-357-3181; FAX 503-359-8456. **Owner(s):** Community Newspapers, Inc., 2038 Pacific Ave., Forest Grove, OR 97116. TEL 503-357-3181; Ed. Jim Hart. pub. size: standard; circ. 9,100(free & paid).

GOLD BEACH

US

GOLD BEACH CURRY COUNTY REPORTER. 1914. Wed. $.50 newsstand; $17/yr. 29835 Ellensburg, Gold Beach, OR 97444-0028. TEL 541-247-6643; FAX 541-247-6644. **Owner(s):** Curry County Reporter, Inc., P.O. Box 766, Gold Beach, OR 97444. TEL 541-247-6643; Ed. Robert Van Leer. adv.; pub. size: broadsheet; circ. 3,241(paid).

GRANTS PASS

US

CENTRAL VALLEY TIMES. Wed. $15/yr. home deliv. P.O. Box 1468, Grants Pass, OR 97526. TEL 503-474-3700; FAX 503-664-7000. **Owner(s):** Courier Publishing Co., P.O. Box 1468, Grants Pass, OR 97526. TEL 503-474-3700; FAX 503-474-3723; Ed. Steve Baily; Pub. Dennis Mack; adv. contact: Michele Thomas. pub. size: broadsheet; circ. 15,000(paid).

US

COUNTRY WEEKLY. Wed. free. 409 S.E. Seventh St., Grants Pass, OR 97526. TEL 503-474-3700; FAX 503-474-3824. **Owner(s):** Courier Publishing Co., P.O. Box 1468, Grants Pass, OR 97526. TEL 503-474-3700; FAX 503-474-3723; Ed. Barbara Hahn; Pub. Dennis Mack; adv. contact: Michele Thomas. pub. size: broadsheet; circ. 21,750(free).

GRESHAM

US

GRESHAM OUTLOOK. 1911. s-w.: Wed. & Sat. $.50 newsstand; $30/yr. carrier; $34/yr. in cy. mailed; $38/yr. out of cy. 1190 N.E. Division St., Gresham, OR 97030. TEL 503-665-2181; FAX 503-665-2187. **Owner(s):** Walt Disney Co., 500 S. Buena Vista St., Burbank, CA 91521. TEL 818-560-5300; Ed. Dave Magnuson; Pub. William R. Hunter; adv. contact: Bruce Tarbet. pub. size: standard; circ. 12,500(paid).

HERMISTON

US
HERMISTON HERALD. 1906. Tue. $.75 newsstand;
$18.50/yr. local; $16.50/yr. senior citizens. 193
E. Main St., Hermiston, OR 97838.
TEL 503-567-6457; FAX 503-567-4125.
Owner(s): Western Communications, Inc., 1526
N.W. Hill St., Bend, OR 97701. TEL
541-382-1811; Ed. Michael Kane. adv.; photos;
pub. size: broadsheet; circ. 13,500(free & paid).
Wire Service(s): AP.

HILLSBORO

US
ALOHA BREEZE. 1974. Wed. free. 150 S.E. Third
Ave., Hillsboro, OR 97123. TEL 503-648-1131;
FAX 503-648-9191. **Owner(s):** Hillsboro Argus,
150 S.E. Third Ave., P.O. Box 588, Hillsboro, OR
97123. TEL 503-648-1131; Ed. Val Hess; Pub.
Walter V. McKinney; adv. contact: Kent Johnson.
pub. size: standard; circ. 5,450(free).

US   ISSN 8750-5479
HILLSBORO ARGUS. 1873. s-w.: Tue. & Thu. $.50
newsstand; $30/yr. 150 S.E. Third Ave.,
Hillsboro, OR 97123. TEL 503-648-1131;
FAX 503-648-9191. **Owner(s):** McKinney
Publishing Co., 150 S.E. Third Ave., Hillsboro, OR
97123-0588. TEL 503-648-1131; FAX
503-648-9191; Ed. Val Hess. adv. contact: Kent
Johnson. photos; pub. size: broadsheet; circ.
15,271(free & paid).

US
WEST VALLEY COURIER. 1965. Wed. free. 150 S.E.
Third Ave., Hillsboro, OR 97123.
TEL 503-648-1131. **Owner(s):** McKinney
Publishing Co., 150 S.E. Third Ave., Hillsboro, OR
97123. TEL 503-648-1131; FAX
503-648-9191; Ed. Val Hess. adv. contact: Kent
Johnson. pub. size: broadsheet; circ.
28,310(free).

HOOD RIVER

US
HOOD RIVER NEWS. 1905. s-w.: Wed. & Sat. $.50
newsstand; $34/yr. local; $28/yr. senior citizens
local; $57/yr. elsewhere. 419 Oak St., Hood
River, OR 97031. TEL 503-386-1234;
FAX 503-386-6796. **Owner(s):** Eagle
Newspapers, Inc., P.O. Box 12008, Salem, OR
97309; Pub. James Kelly; pub. size: broadsheet;
circ. 5,973(paid).

LAKE OSWEGO

US   ISSN 0889-2369
LAKE OSWEGO REVIEW. Thu. $.75 newsstand;
$24/yr. tri-cy. area; $37/yr. out of state. 111 A
Ave., Lake Oswego, OR 97034.
TEL 503-635-8811; FAX 503-635-8817.
Owner(s): Community Newspapers, Inc., P.O. Box
792, Athens, GA 30603. TEL 706-548-0010;
FAX 706-548-0808; Ed. Dana Haynes; Pub. Bob
Bigelow; pub. size: standard; circ. 9,400(paid).

US
WEST LINN TIDINGS. 1981. Thu. $.50 newsstand;
$22/yr. 111 A Ave., Lake Oswego, OR 97034.
TEL 503-635-8811; FAX 503-635-8817.
Owner(s): Community News, Inc., 6975 S.W.
Sandburg Rd., Beaverton, OR 97075. TEL
503-684-0360; FAX 503-620-3433; Ed. Dana
Haynes; Pub. Bob Bigelow. pub. size: standard;
circ. 6,925(paid).

LAKEVIEW

US   ISSN 1062-5313
LAKE COUNTY EXAMINER. Thu. $.45 newsstand;
$20/yr. in cy.; $24/yr. out of cy. 305 N. F St.,
Lakeview, OR 97630. TEL 503-947-3378;
FAX 503-947-4359. **Owner(s):** Clamath
Publishing Co., P.O. Box 271, Lakeview, OR
97630. TEL 503-947-3378; FAX
503-947-4359; Ed. Eric Hogstrom; Pub. Tillie
Flynn; adv.; pub. size: broadsheet; circ.
3,100(paid).

LEBANON

US
LEBANON EXPRESS. 1887. Wed. $.35 newsstand;
$18.50/yr. local 90 E. Grant St., Lebanon, OR
97355. TEL 541-258-3151;
FAX 541-259-3569. **Owner(s):** Walt Disney Co.,
500 S. Buena Vista St., Burbank, CA 91521. TEL
818-560-5300; Ed. Robert Oster; Pub. Mary Jo
Parker; pub. size: broadsheet; circ. 4,500(paid).

LINCOLN CITY

US
NEWS GUARD, THE. 1965. Wed. $.50 newsstand;
$24/yr. in cy.; $36/yr. out of cy. 930 S.E. Hwy.
101, Lincoln City, OR 97367.
TEL 503-994-2178; FAX 503-994-7613.
Owner(s): Pacific Coast Newspapers, Inc., P.O.
Box 848, Lincoln City, OR 97367. TEL
503-842-7535; Ed. Steve Mims; Pub. Jim Moore;
adv. contact: Heather Hatton. pub. size:
broadsheet; circ. 6,500(paid).

MADRAS

US
MADRAS PIONEER, THE. 1904. Wed. $.50
newsstand; $18/yr. in cy.; $24/yr. out of cy.
241 S.E. Sixth St., Madras, OR 97741-1635.
TEL 503-475-2275; FAX 503-475-3710.
Owner(s): Eagle Newspapers, Inc., P.O. Box
12008, Salem, OR 97309. TEL 503-393-1774;
Ed. Susan Matheny; Pub. Tony Ahern; adv.
contact: Teena Hubbard. pub. size: standard; circ.
3,400(paid).

MCMINNVILLE

US
NEWS-REGISTER. 1866. 3/wk.: Tue., Thu., Sat. $.50
newsstand; $5/mo. 611 E. Third St., McMinnville,
OR 97128. TEL 503-472-5114;
FAX 503-472-9151. **Owner(s):** Bladine Family,
611 Third Ave., McMinnville, OR 97128. TEL
503-472-5114; Ed. Jeb Bladine; Pub. Jeb
Bladine; adv. contact: Rick McDonald. pub. size:
broadsheet; circ. 10,400(paid).

MERRILL

US
BUTTE VALLEY STAR. 1927. Tue. $.30 newsstand;
$13.50/yr. 365 Front St., Merrill, OR 97633.
TEL 503-798-5668; FAX 503-798-5668.
Owner(s): Beth Carleton & Carol McKay, P.O. Box
768, Merrill, OR 97633. TEL 916-397-2601; Ed.
Beth Carleton; Pub. Beth Carleton; adv.; pub. size:
broadsheet; circ. 3,000(free & paid).

US
LOST RIVER STAR. 1927. Wed. $.30 newsstand;
$13.50/yr. 365 Front St., Merrill, OR 97633.
TEL 541-798-5668; FAX 541-798-5668.
Owner(s): Beth Carleton & Carol McKay, P.O. Box
768, Merrill, OR 97633; Ed. Beth Carleton. adv.;
pub. size: broadsheet; circ. 3,500(free & paid).

MILWAUKEE

US
CLACKAMAS COUNTY REVIEW. 1922. Fri. $.25
newsstand; $15/yr. in cy.; $12/yr. out of cy.;
$14/yr. senior citizens. 7007 Lake Rd.,
Milwaukee, OR 97267-7501.
TEL 503-786-1996; FAX 503-656-8979.
Owner(s): Columbia River Newspapers, Inc., P.O.
Box 1520, Clackamas, OR 97015. TEL
503-656-4101; Ed. Chuck Beister; Pub. Rick
Skayhan; pub. size: tabloid; circ. 9,000(paid).

MYRTLE CREEK

US   ISSN 0745-7588
UMPQUA FREE PRESS. 1902. Thu. $.35 newsstand;
$16/yr. in cy.; $20/yr. out of cy. 119 S. Main
St., Myrtle Creek, OR 97457.
TEL 503-863-5233. **Owner(s):** Umpqua Free
Press, Inc., P.O. Box 729, Myrtle Creek, OR
97457. TEL 503-863-5233; Pub. Robert F.
Scherer. pub. size: tabloid; circ. 2,900(paid).

NEWBERG

US
NEWBERG GRAPHIC. 1888. s-w.: Wed. & Sat. $.50
newsstand; $30/yr. in cy. 109 N. School St.,
Newberg, OR 97132. TEL 503-538-2181;
FAX 503-538-1632. **Owner(s):** Eagle
Newspapers, Inc., 4091 Indian School Rd., N.E.,
Salem, OR 97305. TEL 503-393-1774; FAX
503-463-9898; Ed. David Thouvenel; Pub. David
Thouvenel; adv.; photos; bk.rev.; pub. size:
broadsheet; circ. 10,400(free & paid).

NEWPORT

US
NEWS-TIMES. 1892. s-w.: Wed. & Fri. $.50
newsstand; $52/yr. in cy.; $104/yr. out of cy.
831 N.E. Avery, Newport, OR 97365.
TEL 503-265-8571; FAX 503-265-3103.
Owner(s): Walt Disney Co., 500 S. Buena Vista
St., Burbank, CA 91521. TEL 818-560-5300;
Ed. Leslie O'Donnell; Pub. Mary Jo Parker; adv.
contact: Mary Jo Parker. photos; pub. size:
broadsheet; circ. 10,500(controlled & paid).
Formerly: Newport News Times.

PENDLETON

US
PENDLETON RECORD, THE. 1911. Thu. $20/yr. 809
S.E. Court, Pendleton, OR 97801-9998.
TEL 503-276-2853. **Owner(s):** Pendleton
Record, The, 809 S.E. Court, Pendleton, OR
97801. TEL 503-276-2853; Ed. R.E. Maznaritz;
Pub. Margaret Maznaritz; adv. contact: Margaret
Maznaritz. pub. size: standard; circ. 1,000(paid).

PHILOMATH

US
BENTON BULLETIN. 1976. Thu. $.50 newsstand;
$21/yr.; $35/yr. out of state. P.O. Box 340,
Philomath, OR 97370-0340
TEL 541-929-3043; FAX 541-929-3043.
Owner(s): Edward Hawley, 20527 Dunham, P.O.
Box 183, Veneta, OR 97377. TEL
541-929-3043; FAX 541-929-3043; Ed. Troy
Hunt; Pub. Edward Hawley; adv. contact: Patricia
Hunt; photos; bk.rev.; pub. size: tabloid; circ.
1,100(paid).

PORTLAND

US

BEAVERTON VALLEY TIMES. 1920. Thu. $.50 newsstand; $22/yr. 6975 Tigard Dr., S.W., Portland, OR 97223. TEL 503-684-0360; FAX 503-620-3433. **Owner(s):** Community Newspapers, Inc., 6975 Tigard Dr., S.W., Portland, OR 97223. TEL 503-684-0360; Ed. Mikel Kelly; Pub. Steve Clark; adv. contact: Steve Clark. pub. size: broadsheet; circ. 5,972(paid).

US

BEE, THE. 1906. m.: 3rd Thu. free newsstand; $12/yr. mailed. P.O. Box 82127, Portland, OR 97282-0127. TEL 503-692-8527; FAX 503-692-8527. **Owner(s):** Three Rivers Communicatiions, Inc., 17605 S.W. 108th Pl., Tualatin, OR 97062. TEL 503-692-8527; FAX 503-692-8527; Ed. John F. Dillin, Jr.; Pub. John F. Dillin, Jr.; adv. contact: John F. Dillin, Jr. photos; bk.rev.; pub. size: tabloid; circ. 12,000(free & paid).

US

ISLAND CONNECTION. m. free. 700 N. Haden Island Dr., Ste. 210, Portland, OR 97217. TEL 503-283-5086; FAX 503-735-1446. **Owner(s):** Gayla Whitman, 700 N. Haden Island Dr., Portland, OR 97217. TEL 503-283-5086; FAX 503-735-1446; Ed. Gayla Whitman; Pub. Gayla Whitman; adv.; pub. size: tabloid.

US

ST. JOHNS REVIEW. 1904. bi-w.: Fri. $12/yr. 700 N. Haden Island Dr., Ste. 210, Portland, OR 97217. TEL 503-283-5086; FAX 503-735-1446. **Owner(s):** Gayla Whitman, 700 N. Haden Island Dr., Portland, OR 97217. TEL 503-283-5865; FAX 503-735-1446; Ed. Ty Walker; Pub. Gayla Whitman; pub. size: tabloid; circ. 3,500(paid).

US

WILLAMETTE WEEK. 1974. Wed. free newsstand; $90/yr. mailed in OR & WA. 822 S.W. 10th Ave., Portland, OR 97205-2519. TEL 503-243-2122; FAX 503-243-1115; E-mail: rmeeker@wweek.com. **Owner(s):** City of Roses Newspaper Co., 822 S.W. 10th Ave., Portland, OR 97205. TEL 503-243-2122; Ed. Mark L. Zusman; Pub. Richard H. Meeker; adv. contact: Russ Martineau. photos; bk.rev.; pub. size: tabloid; circ. 75,000(free & paid). **Wire Service(s):** AlterNet.

PRINEVILLE

US

CENTRAL OREGONIAN, THE. 1881. s-w.: Tue. & Thu. $.50 newsstand; $24/yr. 558 N. Main St., Prineville, OR 97754. TEL 503-447-6205; FAX 503-447-1754. **Owner(s):** Eagle Newspapers, Inc., P.O. Box 12008, Salem, OR 97309. TEL 503-393-7980; Ed. James O. Smith; Pub. James O. Smith; adv.; pub. size: broadsheet; circ. 6,300(free & paid).
Formerly: Prineville Central Oregonian.

REDMOND

US

REDMOND SPOKESMAN. 1910. w. $.35 newsstand; $18/yr. in state; $25/yr. out of state. 226 N. Sixth St., Redmond, OR 97756. TEL 541-548-2184; FAX 541-548-3203. **Owner(s):** Western Communications, Inc., 1526 N.W. Hill St., Bend, OR 97701. TEL 541-382-1811; Ed. Scott Maben; Pub. Carl Vertrees; adv. contact: Lane Jorgenson. photos; bk.rev.; pub. size: broadsheet; circ. 4,200(paid).

REEDSPORT

US

COURIER, THE. Thu. $.50 newsstand; $19/yr. in cy.; $21/yr. out of cy. 174 N. 16th St., Reedsport, OR 97467. TEL 503-271-3633. **Owner(s):** Carl Olson, 174 N. 16th St., Reedsport, OR 97467; Ed. Carl Olson; Pub. Carl Olson; adv.; photos; pub. size: broadsheet; circ. 2,900(paid).

ROGUE RIVER

US

RIVER PRESS. 1962. Wed. $.50 newsstand; $18/yr. in cy.; $28/yr. out of cy. 105 Gardiner St., Rogue River, OR 97537. TEL 541-582-1707; FAX 541-582-0201. **Owner(s):** River Press Publishers, Inc., 105 Gardiner St., Rogue River, OR 97537. TEL 541-582-1707; Ed. Dave Ehrhardt; Pub. Heidi Ehrhardt; adv.; photos; bk.rev.; pub. size: broadsheet; circ. 2,000(free & paid).

SANDY

US

SANDY POST. Wed. $.35 newsstand; $15/yr. mailed in cy.; $18/yr. out of cy.; $23/yr. out of state. 17270 S.E. Bluff Rd., Sandy, OR 97055. TEL 503-668-5548; FAX 503-665-2187. **Owner(s):** Walt Disney Co., 500 S. Buena Vista St., Burbank, CA 91521. TEL 818-560-5300; Ed. Dave Magnuson; Pub. William R. Hunter; adv. contact: Bruce Tarbet. pub. size: standard; circ. 3,000(paid).

SEASIDE

US

SEASIDE SIGNAL. 1905. Thu. $.50 newsstand; $20/yr. in cy.; $30/yr. outside of cy. 113 N. Holladay, Seaside, OR 97138. TEL 503-738-5561; FAX 503-738-5672. **Owner(s):** Pacific Coast Newspapers, Inc., 1902 Second, Tillamook, OR 97141. TEL 503-842-7535; Ed. Linda Lanham; Pub. Kevin Widdison; adv. contact: Gayle Vernon. photos; bk.rev.; pub. size: broadsheet; circ. 3,408(paid).

SILVERTON

US

SILVERTON APPEAL-TRIBUNE/MT. ANGEL NEWS. 1881. Wed. $.50 newsstand; $24/yr. mailed. 399 S. Water St., Silverton, OR 97381. TEL 503-873-8385; FAX 503-873-8064. **Owner(s):** East Valley Newspapers, P.O. Box 35, Silverton, OR 97381. TEL 503-873-8385; Ed. Joe Petshow; Pub. Brad Fenison; adv. contact: Linda Bye. photos; pub. size: standard; circ. 7,800(free & paid).

SPRINGFIELD

US

SPRINGFIELD NEWS, THE. 1903. s-w.: Wed. & Sat. $.35 newsstand; $29/yr. carrier; $48/yr. out of cy. 1887 Laura St., Springfield, OR 97477. TEL 503-746-1671; FAX 503-746-0633; E-mail: thenews@axessnw.com; URL: http://www.axessnw.com/~henews. **Owner(s):** Walt Disney Co., 500 S. Buena Vista, Burbank, CA 91521. TEL 818-560-5300; Pub. Mark Garber; adv. contact: Tom Chastain. pub. size: broadsheet; circ. 10,000(paid). **Wire Service(s):** UPI.

STAYTON

US

STAYTON MAIL. 1892. Tue. $.50 newsstand; $15/yr. P.O. Box 400, Stayton, OR 97383. TEL 503-769-6338; FAX 503-769-6207. **Owner(s):** Gannett Company, Inc., 1100 Wilson Blvd., Arlington, VA 22234. TEL 703-284-6000; Pub. Brad Fenison; adv.; pub. size: broadsheet; circ. 2,700(paid).

ST. HELENS

US

ST. HELENS CHRONICLE. 1881. s-w.: Wed. & Sat. $.35 newsstand; $22/yr. in cy. 195 S. 15th St., St. Helens, OR 97051. TEL 503-397-0116; FAX 503-397-4093. **Owner(s):** Parsons Associates, Inc., P.O. Box 1153, St. Helens, OR 97051. TEL 503-397-0116; FAX 503-397-4093; Pub. Pamela Petersen; adv.; pub. size: standard; circ. 17,300(free & paid).

SWEET HOME

US

NEW ERA, THE. 1929. Wed. $.50 newsstand; $23/yr. in cy.; $29/yr. out of cy. 313 Main, Sweet Home, OR 97386. TEL 514-367-2135; FAX 514-367-2137. **Owner(s):** Alex & Debra Paul, P.O. Box 39, Sweet Home, OR 97386. TEL 503-367-8426; Ed. Alex Paul; Pub. Alex Paul; adv. contact: Debra Paul. pub. size: broadsheet; circ. 3,400(paid).
Formerly: Sweet Home New Era.

TIGARD

US

TIGARD TIMES. 1956. Thu. $.50 newsstand; $22/yr. 6975 S.W. Sandburg Rd., Tigard, OR 97223. TEL 503-684-0360; FAX 503-620-3433. **Owner(s):** Community Newspapers, Inc., 6975 S.W. Sandburg Rd., Portland, OR 97223. TEL 503-684-0360; Ed. Mikel Kelly; Pub. Steve Clark; adv. contact: Fred Board. pub. size: broadsheet; circ. 9,603(paid).

TILLAMOOK

US

HEADLIGHT-HERALD. 1888. Wed. $.50 newsstand; $24/yr. in cy.; $36/yr. out of cy. 1908 Second St., Tillamook, OR 97141. TEL 503-842-7535; FAX 503-842-8842. **Owner(s):** Pacific Coast Newspapers, Inc., P.O. Box 444, Tillamook, OR 97141. TEL 503-842-7535; FAX 503-842-8842; Ed. Scott Frank; Pub. Linda Shaffer; adv. contact: Mary K. Hanthorn. photos; pub. size: broadsheet; circ. 8,052(paid).

VALE

US

MALHEUR ENTERPRISE. 1909. Wed. $.50 newsstand; $20/yr. in cy.; $30/yr. out of cy.; $15/yr. senior citizens; $15/yr. student. P.O. Box 310, Vale, OR 97918. TEL 541-473-3377; FAX 541-473-3268. **Owner(s):** Z.D. Auyer, P.O. Box 310, Vale, OR 97918. TEL 503-473-3377; FAX 503-473-3268; pub. size: broadsheet; circ. 2,350(paid).

PALAU

KOROR

US

PALAU GAZETTE. 1980. m. free. Palau Government, Koror, PW 96940. TEL 680-488-3257; FAX 680-488-1662. **Owner(s):** Palau Government/Office of the President, P.O. Box 100, Koror, PW 96940, paid. TEL 680-488-3257; FAX 680-488-1662; Ed. Roman Yano; Pub. Kunkod Nakamura; photos; pub. size: standard; circ. 1,500(free).

PENNSYLVANIA

ALBION

US

ALBION NEWS, THE. 1921. Wed. $.45 newsstand; $16/yr. 16 Market St., Albion, PA 16401. TEL 814-756-4133; FAX 814-756-5643. **Owner(s):** Penn-Ohio Graphics, Inc., P.O. Box 245, Jefferson, OH 44047. TEL 216-576-9115; FAX 216-576-2735; Ed. Vickie Canfield Peters; Pub. John Lampson; adv. contact: Daniel Sasko. photos; bk.rev.; pub. size: tabloid; circ. 3,550(paid).

ALIQUIPPA

US

NEWS, THE. 1961. Thu. free. 1181 Airport Rd., Aliquippa, PA 15001-0629. TEL 412-375-6611. **Owner(s):** R.A. Palket Co., Inc., P.O. Box 629, Aliquippa, PA 15001-0629; Pub. R.A. Palket; adv.; pub. size: tabloid; circ. 67,180(free).

ALLENTOWN

US

EAST PENN PRESS. 1959. Wed. $.50 newsstand; $20.80/yr. 1633 N. 26th St., Allentown, PA 18104. TEL 610-740-0944; FAX 610-740-0947. **Owner(s):** Pencor Services, Inc., P.O. Box 215, Palmerton, PA 18071. TEL 215-826-2551; Ed. Julia Paxson; Pub. Fred Masenheimer; adv. contact: Peg Stocking. pub. size: broadsheet; circ. 7,100(paid).

ARDMORE

US

MAINLINE LIFE. 1988. Thu. $.50 newsstand; $19.95/yr. local. 110 Ardmore Ave., Ardmore, PA 19003. TEL 610-896-9555; FAX 610-896-9560. **Owner(s):** Montgomery Publishing Co., Fort Washington, PA; Ed. Warren Patton; Pub. Art Howe; adv. contact: Harriet Gratz. pub. size: broadsheet; circ. 26,100(paid).
Formerly: Mainliner, The.

US

MAIN LINE TIMES. 1930. Thu. $.50 newsstand; $31.20/yr. carrier; mail rate by zone. 311 E. Lancaster Ave., Ardmore, PA 19003. TEL 610-642-4300; FAX 610-649-9318. **Owner(s):** Acme Newspapers, Inc., 311 E. Lancaster Ave., Ardmore, PA 19003. TEL 215-642-4300; Ed. Daniel A. Eisenhuth; Pub. Deborah Shaw; adv. contact: Joyce Sullivan. photos; pub. size: broadsheet; circ. 14,800(controlled & paid).
Formerly: Main Line Times/Main Line Sunday.

BANGOR

US

SLATEBELT HOMETOWN NEWS, THE. 1893. Thu. $.25 newsstand; $15/yr. in Slatebelt area; $17/yr. out of area. 13-15 S. Main St., Bangor, PA 18013. TEL 610-588-2196. **Owner(s):** Janson Publishing Cc., Inc., 13-15 S. Main St., Bangor, PA 18013. TEL 610-588-2196; Ed. Kathleen J. McFall; Pub. Kathleen J. McFall; adv. contact: Candi Martir. pub. size: tabloid; circ. 1,700(paid).

BARNESBORO

US

BARNESBORO STAR, THE. 1902. Wed. $.45 newsstand; $19.75/yr. in cy.; $23/yr. out of cy.; $26/yr. out of state. 520 Philadelphia Ave., Barnesboro, PA 15714. TEL 814-948-6210; FAX 814-948-7563. **Owner(s):** Sedloff Publications, Inc., P.O. Box 395, Portage, PA 15946. TEL 814-736-9666; Ed. Connie Miller. adv.; pub. size: broadsheet; circ. 5,404(paid).

BOYERTOWN

US

BOYERTOWN AREA TIMES. 1857. Thu. $.50 newsstand; $24/yr. 124 N. Chestnut St., Boyertown, PA 19512. TEL 610-367-6041; FAX 610-369-0233. **Owner(s):** Berks-Mont Newspapers, Inc., 124 N. Chestnut St., Boyertown, PA 19512. TEL 610-367-6041; Ed. Jeff Bell; Pub. James C. Webb; adv. contact: James Davidheiser. photos; pub. size: broadsheet; circ. 6,500(free & paid).

US

NEWS OF SOUTHERN BERKS, THE. 1885. Wed. $.50 newsstand; $20/yr. 124 N. Chestnut St., Boyertown, PA 19512. TEL 610-367-6041; FAX 610-369-0233. **Owner(s):** Berks-Mont Newspapers, Inc., 124 N. Chestnut St., Boyertown, PA 19512. TEL 610-367-6041; FAX 610-369-0233; Ed. Kathy Ritz. adv. contact: James Davidheiser. photos; pub. size: broadsheet; circ. 2,000(paid).

BRADDOCK

US

FREE PRESS, THE. 1913. Thu. free newsstand; $27/yr. 522 Braddock Ave., Braddock, PA 15104-1807. TEL 412-271-0622; FAX 412-351-1593. **Owner(s):** Woodland Publishing Co., 522 Braddock Ave., Braddock, PA 15104-1807. TEL 412-271-0622; Ed. Anthony Munson. adv.; pub. size: tabloid; circ. 20,410(free & paid).

BRADFORD

US

BRADFORD JOURNAL/MINER. 1832. Thu. $.45 newsstand; $23/yr. local; $33/yr. out of cy. 265 South Ave., Bradford, PA 16701. TEL 814-362-6563; FAX 814-363-8202. **Owner(s):** Grant & Debra Nichols, P.O. Box 17, Bradford, PA 16701. TEL 814-362-6563; Michelle Sherrick, P.O. Box 17, Bradford, PA 16701. TEL 814-362-6563; Adam & Steve Nichols, P.O. Box 17, Bradford, PA 16701. TEL 814-352-6563; Ed. Grant Nichols. adv. contact: Grant Nichols. photos; bk.rev.; pub. size: tabloid; circ. 5,500(paid).
Formerly: McKean County Miner.

BRISTOL

US

BRISTOL PILOT. 1986. Thu. $.35 newsstand; $18/yr. 2100 Frost Rd., Bristol, PA 19007. TEL 215-788-1682. **Owner(s):** Intercounty Newspaper Group, 6220 Ridge Ave., Philadelphia, PA 19128. TEL 215-483-7300; Ed. Kathleen Fratti; Pub. R. Arthur Thompson; adv. contact: Linda Tecce. pub. size: tabloid; circ. 4,200(paid).

BROOKVILLE

US

JEFFERSONIAN DEMOCRAT. 1839. Thu. $.50 newsstand; $26/yr. mailed. 301 Main St., Brookville, PA 15825. TEL 814-849-5339; FAX 814-849-4333. **Owner(s):** Independent Publications, Inc., 175 Main St., Brookville, PA 15825. TEL 814-949-5333; Ed. Randy Bartley; Pub. Dock Lias; adv. contact: Linda Smith. pub. size: broadsheet; circ. 4,500(paid).

CANTON

US

CANTON INDEPENDENT-SENTINEL. 1842. Thu. $.40 newsstand; $22-$25/yr. 4 Lycoming St., Canton, PA 17724-0127. TEL 717-673-5151; FAX 717-673-4315. **Owner(s):** John Shaffer, 70 Union St., Canton, PA 17724. TEL 717-673-4296; Ed. John Shaffer; Pub. John Shaffer; adv. contact: Janie Riggs. photos; pub. size: broadsheet; circ. 1,600(free & paid).

CARBONDALE

US   ISSN 0746-3510

CARBONDALE NEWS. 1872. Wed. $.16/yr. local; $24/yr. out of state. 41 N. Church St., Carbondale, PA 18407. TEL 717-282-3300. **Owner(s):** Hometown Publications, Inc., 41 N. Church St., Carbondale, PA 18407. TEL 717-282-3300; Ed. Rosemary Heth; Pub. Philip T. Heth; adv.: $4.80/SAU. pub. size: broadsheet; circ. 6,500(paid).

CLARION

US

CLARION NEWS. 1840. s-w.: Tue. & Thu. $.50 newsstand; $32.50/yr. 645 Main St., Clarion, PA 16214. TEL 814-226-7000; FAX 814-226-7518. **Owner(s):** Western Penn Newspapers, 645 Main St., Clarion, PA 16214. TEL 814-226-7000; Ed. Paul Hambke; Pub. Patrick C. Boyle; adv. contact: Mary Logue. pub. size: broadsheet; circ. 7,000(paid).

CLARKS SUMMIT

US   ISSN 1058-6865

ABINGTON JOURNAL. 1929. Wed. $.50 newsstand;
$18/yr. 211 S. State St., Clarks Summit, PA
18411. TEL 717-587-1148;
FAX 717-586-3980. **Owner(s):** Bartsen Media,
Inc., P.O. Box 366, Dallas, PA 18612. TEL
717-675-5211; Ed. Kenneth Books; Pub. Ronald
Bartizek; adv. contact: Kevin Brislin. photos;
bk.rev.; pub. size: broadsheet; circ. 3,800(paid).

CLAYSVILLE

US

WEEKLY RECORDER, THE. 1888. Fri. $.50
newsstand; $22/yr. in state; $24/yr. elsewhere.
256 Main St., Claysville, PA 15323-0506.
TEL 412-663-7742. **Owner(s):** Weekly Recorder,
P.O. Box F, Claysville, PA 15323. TEL
412-663-7742; Ed. Douglas R. Teagarden; Pub.
Douglas R. Teagarden; adv. contact: Susan Burd.
pub. size: tabloid; circ. 3,500(paid).

COLLEGEVILLE

US

INDEPENDENT, THE. 1875. Tue. $.35 newsstand;
$18/yr. in cy.; $20/yr. out of cy.; $24/yr. out of
state. 350 Walnut St., Collegeville, PA 19426.
TEL 610-489-3001; FAX 610-489-8633.
Owner(s): Montgomery Transcript Publishing Co.,
P.O. Box 39, Collegeville, PA 19426. TEL
610-489-3001; Ed. James T. Stewart; Pub. John
Stewart; pub. size: broadsheet; circ. 6,300(paid).
Formerly: Independent News, The.

CONSHOHOCKEN

US

RECORDER, THE. 1869. Thu. $.50 newsstand;
$13/yr. in cy.; $18/yr. out of cy. Seventh &
Fayette, Conshohocken, PA 19428.
TEL 610-828-4600. **Owner(s):** Intercounty
Newspaper Group, 6220 Ridge Ave., Philadelphia,
PA 19128. TEL 215-483-7300; Ed. Nancy
O'Brien; Pub. Fred W. Donaldson; adv. contact:
Mike Cooper. photos; pub. size: tabloid; circ.
3,500(paid).

CORAOPOLIS

US   ISSN 1047-0689

RECORD, THE. 1903. Wed. $.50 newsstand;
$.40/wk. home deliv.; $25.00/yr. 705 Fifth Ave.,
Coraopolis, PA 15108. TEL 412-264-4140;
FAX 412-264-8269. **Owner(s):** Trinity Holdings,
Inc., 610 Beatty Rd., Monroeville, PA 15146. TEL
412-856-7400; FAX 412-856-7954; Ed. Harry
Funk; Pub. Kevin Aylmer. adv.; pub. size: tabloid;
circ. 4,800(paid).

COUDERSPORT

US

POTTER LEADER-ENTERPRISE. 1874. Wed. $.75
newsstand; $23/yr. in cy.; $26/yr. in state;
$28/yr. out of state. 6 W. Second St.,
Coudersport, PA 16915. TEL 814-274-8044;
FAX 814-274-8120. **Owner(s):** Leader Publishing
Co., Inc., P.O. Box 29, Coudersport, PA 16915.
TEL 814-274-8141; Ed. Teri L. McDowell; Pub.
Joseph Majot; adv.; photos; pub. size: broadsheet;
circ. 12,000(paid).

CRESSON

US   ISSN 0745-7499

CRESSON-GALLITZIN MAINLINER, THE. Wed. $.45
newsstand; $19.75/yr. in cy.; $23/yr. in state;
$26/yr. out of state. 719 Front St., Cresson, PA
16630. TEL 814-886-2117. **Owner(s):** Sedloff
Publications, Inc., P.O. Box 395, Portage, PA
15946. TEL 814-736-9666; Ed. Connie Miller;
Pub. Jim Kissell; adv. contact: Jim Kissell. bk.rev.;
pub. size: broadsheet; circ. 3,642(paid).

DALLAS

US

DALLAS POST. 1889. Wed. $.50 newsstand;
$20/yr. in state. 45 Main Rd., Dallas, PA 18612.
TEL 717-675-5211. **Owner(s):** Bartsen Media,
Inc., P.O. Box 366, Dallas, PA 18612. TEL
717-675-5211; Ed. Ronald Bartizek. adv.; pub.
size: broadsheet; circ. 3,000(paid).

DREXEL HILL

US

MARCUS HOOK PRESS. 1916. Thu. $7/yr. 3245
Garrett Rd., Drexel Hill, PA 19026.
TEL 610-259-4141. **Owner(s):** Press Publishing
Co., 3245 Garrett Rd., Drexel Hill, PA 19026.
TEL 610-259-4141; Ed. M.M. Girard. adv.;
photos; pub. size: tabloid; circ. 3,500(paid).

US

RIDLEY PRESS. 1963. Thu. $7/yr. 3245 Garrett Rd.,
Drexel Hill, PA 19026. TEL 610-259-4141.
Owner(s): Press Publishing Co., 3245 Garrett
Rd., Drexel Hill, PA 19026. TEL 610-259-4141;
Ed. P.A. Girard; Pub. P.A. Girard; adv.; photos;
pub. size: tabloid; circ. 7,000(paid).

US

UPPER DARBY PRESS. 1926. Thu. $7/yr. 3245
Garrett Rd., Drexel Hill, PA 19026.
TEL 610-259-4141. **Owner(s):** Press Publishing
Co., 3245 Garrett Rd., Drexel Hill, PA 19026.
TEL 610-259-4141; Ed. P.A. Girard. adv.; photos;
pub. size: tabloid; circ. 4,000(paid).

DUSHORE

US

SULLIVAN REVIEW. 1878. Thu. $.50 newsstand;
$20/yr. in cy.; $25/yr. out of cy. Main & Water
Sts., Dushore, PA 18614. TEL 717-928-8403;
FAX 717-928-8006. **Owner(s):** John A.
Shoemaker, P.O. Box 305, Dushore, PA 18614.
TEL 717-928-8403; Christine S. Shoemaker, P.O.
Box 305, Dushore, PA 18614; Ed. T.W.
Shoemaker; Pub. T.W. Shoemaker; adv. contact:
Carmela Walosin. pub. size: broadsheet; circ.
7,000(paid).

EAST STROUDSBURG

US

POCONO SHOPPER. 1975. Wed. free. 96 S.
Courtland St., East Stroudsburg, PA 18301.
TEL 717-421-4800; FAX 717-421-4255.
Owner(s): Scranton Times, Penn Ave., Scranton,
PA; adv. contact: David Barry. bk.rev.; pub. size:
tabloid; circ. 38,000(controlled & free).

EBENSBURG

US

EBENSBURG NEWS LEADER, THE. Wed. $.45
newsstand; $19.75/yr. in cy.; $23/yr. out og cy.;
$26/yr. out of state. 975 Rowena Dr.,
Ebensburg, PA 15931. TEL 814-472-4110.
Owner(s): Sedloff Publications, Inc., Mainline
Newspapers, P.O. Box 395, Portage, PA 15946.
TEL 814-472-4110; Ed. Connie Miller. adv.
contact: Barbara Cordoro. photos; pub. size:
broadsheet; circ. 2,225(paid).

US

MOUNTAINEER-HERALD, THE. 1853. Wed. $.45
newsstand; $23.40/yr. in cy.; $26/yr. out of cy.
113 S. Center St., Ebensburg, PA 15931.
TEL 814-472-8240. **Owner(s):** David Thompson,
P.O. Box 359, Ebensburg, PA 15931. TEL
814-472-8240; Ed. Kathleen P. Nikolishen; Pub.
David E. Thompson; adv.; photos; bk.rev.; pub.
size: standard; circ. 3,200(paid).

ELIZABETHTOWN

US   ISSN 0745-9122

ELIZABETHTOWN CHRONICLE. 1869. Thu. $.50
newsstand; $18/yr. in state; $25/yr. out of state.
25 Center Sq., Elizabethtown, PA 17022-2014.
TEL 717-367-7152; FAX 717-367-3655.
Owner(s): Reid Newspapers, Inc., 513 Chocolate
Ave., Hershey, PA 17033. TEL 717-533-2900;
FAX 717-531-2561; Ed. Jeff Clouser; Pub. Barb
Smith; adv. contact: Barb Smith. pub. size:
broadsheet; circ. 3,520(free & paid).
Formerly: Chronicle, The.

EMPORIUM

US

CAMERON COUNTY ECHO. 1963. Tue. $.75
newsstand; $28/yr. 300 S. Broad St., Emporium,
PA 15834. TEL 814-486-3711;
FAX 814-486-0990. **Owner(s):** Cameron County
Echo, P.O. Box 308, Emporium, PA 15834. TEL
814-486-3711; Ed. David A. Brown. adv. contact:
Nancy A. Brown. photos; bk.rev.; pub. size:
broadsheet; circ. 4,000(paid).

EPHRATA

US

EPHRATA REVIEW. Wed. $.30 newsstand;
$15.50/yr. in cy.; $18/yr. out of cy.; $21/yr. out
of state. One E. Main St., Ephrata, PA 17522.
TEL 717-733-6397; FAX 717-733-6058.
Owner(s): Lancaster Newspapers, Inc., Eight W.
King St., Lancaster, PA 17603. TEL
717-733-6397; Ed. Andy Fasnacht. adv. contact:
Doug Dussinger. pub. size: standard; circ.
13,000(paid).

ERIE

US

MILK CREEK SUN. Sun. $.60 newsstand; $20/yr.;
$18/yr. senior citizen. 2126 Filmore Ave., Erie,
PA 16506-2941. TEL 814-838-7666;
FAX 814-838-9802. **Owner(s):** Brown-Thompson
Newspapers, W. High St. Extension, Union City,
PA 16438; Ed. Claudia Mosso. adv.; photos; pub.
size: standard; circ. 52,000(paid).

FOLSOM

US

DELAWARE COUNTY JOURNAL. Wed. free newsstand. 1300 MacDade Blvd., Folsom, PA 19033. TEL 610-583-4432; FAX 610-583-0503. **Owner(s):** Wing Publications, 1300 MacDade Blvd., Folsom, PA 19033. TEL 610-583-4432; Ed. Phil Anderson; Pub. Lewis Lax; adv. contact: Marian Asel. pub. size: tabloid; circ. 15,000(free).

US

TOWN TALK. 1963. Wed. free newsstand & carrier. 1300 MacDade Blvd., Folsom, PA 19033. TEL 610-583-4432; FAX 610-583-0503. **Owner(s):** Wing Publications, 1300 MacDade Blvd., Folsom, PA 19033. TEL 610-583-4432; Ed. Phil Anderson; Pub. Lewis Lax; adv. contact: Marian Asel. pub. size: tabloid; circ. 50,000(free).

FORT WASHINGTON

US

AMBLER GAZETTE. 1882. Wed. $.75 newsstand; $31.20/yr. mailed. 290 Commerce Dr., Fort Washington, PA 19034. TEL 215-542-0200; FAX 215-643-9475. **Owner(s):** Montgomery Publishing Co., 290 Commerce Dr., Fort Washington, PA 19034. TEL 215-542-0200; Ed. Gillian H. Gordon; Pub. Arthur W. Howe, IV; adv. contact: Michael Fisher. pub. size: standard; circ. 11,600(paid).

US

COLONIAL, THE. 1961. Thu. $.50 newsstand; $14/yr. home deliv. 290 Commerce Dr., Fort Washington, PA 19034. TEL 215-542-0200; FAX 215-643-9475. **Owner(s):** Montgomery Publishing Co., 290 Commerce Dr., Fort Washington, PA 19034. TEL 215-542-0200; Ed. Gillian Gordon; Pub. Arthur W. Howe, IV; adv. contact: Mike Fisher. pub. size: tabloid; circ. 6,000(paid).

US

MONTGOMERYVILLE SPIRIT. 1974. Wed. $.50 newsstand; $26/yr. carrier; $31.20/yr. mailed. 290 Commerce Dr., Fort Washington, PA 19034. TEL 215-542-0200; FAX 215-643-9457. **Owner(s):** Montgomery Publishing Co., 290 Commerce Dr., Fort Washington, PA 19034. TEL 215-542-0200; Ed. Elaine Abse; Pub. Arthur W. Howe, IV; adv. contact: Michael Fisher. pub. size: broadsheet; circ. 20,164(paid).

US

SPRINGFIELD SUN. 1946. Thu. $.75 newsstand; $26/yr. carrier; $31.50/yr. mailed. 290 Commerce Dr., Fort Washington, PA 19034. TEL 215-646-5100; FAX 215-643-9475. **Owner(s):** Montgomery Publishing Co., 290 Commerce Dr., Fort Washington, PA 19034. TEL 215-646-5100; Ed. Gillian H. Gordon; Pub. Arthur W. Howe, IV; adv. contact: Michael Fisher. pub. size: broadsheet; circ. 2,900(paid).

GIRARD

US

COSMOPOLITE-HERALD. 1866. Sun. $.60 newsstand; $20/yr.; $18/yr. senior citizens. P.O. Box 403, Girard, PA 16437. TEL 814-774-9648; FAX 814-774-9648. **Owner(s):** Brown-Thompson Newspapers, W. High St. Extension, Union City, PA 16438. TEL 814-438-7666; Ed. Peggy J. Machinski. adv.; pub. size: broadsheet; circ. 3,770(paid).
   Formerly: Girard Cosmopolite-Herald.

GROVE CITY

US

ALLIED NEWS. 1879. Wed. $.50 newsstand; $15/yr. carrier & motor rte.; $16/yr. mailed in area; $19/yr. mailed out of area; $14/yr. senior citizens. 201A Erie St., Grove City, PA 16127. TEL 412-458-5010; FAX 412-458-1609. **Owner(s):** Ottaway Newspapers, Inc., P.O. Box 401, Campbell Hall, NY 10916. TEL 914-294-8181; Ed. Brian David; Pub. John Lima; adv.; pub. size: broadsheet; circ. 15,000(paid).

HAMBURG

US

HAMBURG ITEM. 1875. Wed. $16/yr. local; $20/yr. out of cy. P.O. Box 31, Hamburg, PA 19526. TEL 610-562-7515; FAX 610-562-7516. **Owner(s):** Avery D. Piersons, P.O. Box 31, Hamburg, PA 19526. TEL 610-562-7515; Ed. Avery D. Piersons; Pub. Avery D. Piersons; adv. contact: William Colunio. pub. size: standard; circ. 4,200(paid).

HATBORO

US

PUBLIC SPIRIT. 1873. Wed. $.75 newsstand; $31.20/yr. 101 N. York Rd., Hatboro, PA 19040. TEL 215-675-3430; FAX 215-675-9024. **Owner(s):** Montgomery Publishing Co., 290 Commerce Dr., Fort Washington, PA 19034. TEL 215-646-5100; Ed. Christina Hecker; Pub. Arthur W. Howe, IV; adv.; pub. size: broadsheet; circ. 12,086(paid).
   Formerly: Hatboro-Warminster Today's Spirit.

US

WILLOW GROVE GUIDE. 1925. Wed. $.75 newsstand; $28.60/yr. carrier; $34/yr. mailed. 101 N. York Rd., Hatboro, PA 19040. TEL 215-542-0200; FAX 215-659-6567. **Owner(s):** Montgomery Publishing Co., 290 Commerce Drive, Fort Washington, PA 19034. TEL 215-646-5100; Ed. Dan Nephin; Pub. Arthur W. Howe, IV; adv. contact: Leslie Hamada. pub. size: broadsheet; circ. 1,553(paid).

HAVERTOWN

US

NEWS OF DELAWARE COUNTY. 1930. Wed. $26/yr. Manoa Shopping Ctr., W. Chester Pike, Havertown, PA 19083. TEL 610-446-8700; FAX 610-449-0419. **Owner(s):** Acme Newspapers, Inc., 311 E. Lancaster Ave., Ardmore, PA 19003. TEL 610-642-4300; Ed. Joan C. Toenniessen; Pub. Deb Shaw; adv. contact: Kelly Colea. photos; bk.rev.; pub. size: broadsheet; circ. 46,000(free & paid).

HAWLEY

US

NEWS EAGLE. 1957. 3/wk.: Tue., Thu., Sat. $38/yr. Wayne & Pike cys.; $60/yr. out of cy. 522 Spring St., Hawley, PA 18428. TEL 717-226-4547; FAX 717-226-4548. **Owner(s):** News Eagle, Inc., P.O. Box E, Hawley, PA 18428. TEL 717-226-4547; Pub. John C. Dyson, Jr.; adv. contact: Glenn Khoury. photos; pub. size: broadsheet; circ. 7,300(paid). **Wire Service(s):** AP.

HERSHEY

US   ISSN 8750-8753

HERSHEY CHRONICLE, THE. 1934. Thu. $.50 newsstand; $18/yr. in state $30/yr. out of state. 513 W. Chocolate Ave., Hershey, PA 17033. TEL 717-533-2900; FAX 717-531-2561. **Owner(s):** Reid Newspapers Inc., 513 W. Chocolate Ave., Hershey, PA 17033. TEL 717-533-2900; Ed. Susan Erbamer; Pub. Wanda S. Reid; adv.; photos; pub. size: broadsheet; circ. 4,000(paid).

HONESDALE

US   ISSN 1063-2794

WEEKLY ALMANAC, THE. 1990. Wed. $.45 newsstand; $24/yr. mailed. 709 Church St., Honesdale, PA 18431-1831. TEL 717-253-9270; FAX 717-253-8937. **Owner(s):** James A. Kalbaugh, 709 Church St., Honesdale, PA 18431-1831. TEL 717-253-9270; FAX 717-253-8937; Judie G. Kalbaugh, 709 Church St., Honesdale, PA 18431-1831. TEL 717-253-9270; FAX 717-253-8937; Ed. James A. Kalbaugh; Pub. James A. Kalbaugh; adv. contact: Bill Megivern. photos; bk.rev.; pub. size: tabloid; circ. 4,500(paid).

HORSHAM

US

BUCKS COUNTY TRIBUNE. 1961. Wed. free newsstand & carrier; $59/yr. mailed out of area. 390 Easton Rd., Horsham, PA 19044-2592. TEL 215-675-6600; FAX 215-675-8251. **Owner(s):** Progress Newspapers, Inc., 390 Easton Rd., Horsham, PA 19044. TEL 215-368-8600; Ed. Sandra L. Petersohn; Pub. Matthew Petersohn. adv. contact: Matthew Petersohn. adv.: $21.83/SAU. pub. size: tabloid; circ. 17,000(controlled & paid).

US

MONTGOMERY COUNTY PROGRESS. 1953. Wed. free newsstand & carrier; $59/yr. mailed. 390 Easton Rd., Horsham, PA 19044. TEL 215-675-8250; FAX 215-675-8251. **Owner(s):** Progress Newspapers, Inc., 390 Easton Rd., Horsham, PA 19044. TEL 215-368-8600; Ed. Sandra L. Petersohn; Pub. Matthew Petersohn; adv. contact: Matthew Petersohn. adv.: $21.88/SAU. pub. size: tabloid; circ. 17,200(free & paid).

US

SUNDAY BUCKS COUNTY TELEGRAPH. 1982. Sun. free newsstand & carrier; $59/yr. mailed. 390 Easton Rd., Horsham, PA 19044. TEL 215-675-8250; FAX 215-675-8251. **Owner(s):** Progress Newspapers, Inc., 390 Easton Rd., Horsham, PA 19044. TEL 215-368-8600; Ed. Sandra L. Petersohn; Pub. Matthew Petersohn; adv. contact: Matthew Petersohn. adv.: $34/SAU. pub. size: tabloid; circ. Sun 8,100(free & paid).
   Formerly: Bucks County Telegraph.

HUMMELSTOWN

US

SUN, THE. 1871. Wed. $.45 newsstand; $15/yr. in state; $18/yr. out of state 115-117 S. Water St., Hummelstown, PA 17036. TEL 717-566-3251; FAX 717-566-6196. **Owner(s):** William S. & Rosemary K. Jackson, 1406 Bradley Ave., Hummelstown, PA 17036. TEL 717-566-8958; Ed. William S. Jackson; Pub. Rosemary Jackson; adv. contact: Rosemary Jackson. photos; bk.rev.; pub. size: broadsheet; circ. 5,800(free & paid).

JEANNETTE

US   ISSN 0746-5971
JEANNETTE SPIRIT. 1983. Wed. $.40 newsstand; $20.60/yr. in cy.; $28.50/yr. out of cy.; $30.60/yr. out of state. 107 S. Second St., Jeannette, PA 15644. TEL 412-527-2868; FAX 412-887-5115. **Owner(s):** Laurel Group Press, 229 Pittsburgh St., Scottdale, PA 15683. TEL 412-887-7400; Ed. Gregory L. Stock; Pub. Ralph Heanrley; adv. contact: B.R. Cunningham. photos; pub. size: standard; circ. 2,300(paid).

JENKINTOWN

US
GLENSIDE NEWS. 1923. Wed. $.75 newsstand; $31.20/yr. 101 Greenwood Ave., Ste. 130, Jenkintown, PA 19046. TEL 215-885-1345; FAX 215-884-9112. **Owner(s):** Montgomery Publishing Co., 290 Commerce Dr., Fort Washington, PA 19034. TEL 215-542-0200; Ed. Regis D'Angiolini; Pub. Arthur W. Howe, IV; adv. contact: Leslie Hamada. pub. size: broadsheet; circ. 3,200(paid).

US
GLOBE, THE. 1927. Thu. $.75 newsstand; $31.20/yr. mailed. 101 Greenwood Ave., Ste. 130, Jenkintown, PA 19046. TEL 215-885-1345; FAX 215-884-9112. **Owner(s):** Montgomery Publishing Co., 290 Commerce Dr., Fort Washington, PA 19034. TEL 215-646-5100; Ed. Regis D'Angiolini; Pub. Arthur W. Howe, IV; adv. contact: Leslie Hamada. pub. size: broadsheet; circ. 4,000(paid).

US
TIMES CHRONICLE. 1894. Wed. $.75 newsstand; $26/yr. carrier; $31.20/yr. mailed. 101 Greenwood Ave., Ste. 130, Jenkintown, PA 19046. TEL 215-885-1345; FAX 215-884-9112. **Owner(s):** Montgomery Publishing Co., 290 Commerce Dr., Fort Washington, PA 19034. TEL 215-646-8170; Ed. Regis D'Angiolini; Pub. Arthur W. Howe, IV; adv. contact: Leslie Hamada. pub. size: broadsheet; circ. 10,000(paid).

JOHNSONBURG

US
JOHNSONBURG PRESS. 1900. Wed. $.60 newsstand; $22-$25.50/yr. 517 Market St., Johnsonburg, PA 15845. TEL 814-965-2503; FAX 814-965-2504. **Owner(s):** Johnsonburg Press Inc., 517 Market St., Johnsonburg, PA 15845. TEL 814-965-2503; FAX 814-965-2504; Ed. Frances Fowler. adv.; photos; pub. size: standard; circ. 2,500(paid).

KING OF PRUSSIA

US
KING OF PRUSSIA COURIER. 1960. Wed. $.50 newsstand; free delivery. 707 W. Dekalb Pike, King of Prussia, PA 19406. TEL 610-265-0775; FAX 610-265-0776; E-mail: kpcourier@aol.com. **Owner(s):** Suburban Publications, 134 N. Wayne Ave., Wayne, PA 19087. TEL 610-688-3000; FAX 610-254-8522; Ed. James Lewis; Pub. Bill Burgess; adv.; photos; pub. size: broadsheet; circ. 9,000(free & paid).

KUTZTOWN

US   ISSN 1041-4029
PATRIOT, THE. 1874. Thu. $.50 newsstand; $18/yr. 15076 Kutztown Rd., Kutztown, PA 19530. TEL 610-683-7343; FAX 610-683-5136. **Owner(s):** Kutztown Publishing Co., P.O. Box 346, Kutztown, PA 19530. TEL 610-683-7343; FAX 610-683-5136; Ed. Tony Phyrillas; Pub. Jacob R. Esser; adv. contact: Lois Esser. photos; pub. size: standard; circ. 4,700(paid).

LANSFORD

US   ISSN 1056-4853
VALLEY GAZETTE. 1972. m. $.75 newsstand; $16/yr. mailed. 102 W. Water St., Lansford, PA 18232-1920. TEL 717-645-4692. **Owner(s):** Gazette Publications, 102 W. Water St., Lansford, PA 18232. TEL 717-645-4692; Ed. Edward Gildea. adv.; photos; bk.rev.; pub. size: tabloid; circ. 1,500(paid).

LEWISBURG

US   ISSN 0888-0999
VALLEY TRADER. 1980. w. $25/yr. 637 Market St., Lewisburg, PA 17837-1451. TEL 800-800-4047; FAX 717-529-4048; E-mail: oberpub@theway2sell.com. **Owner(s):** Oberdorf Publishing Co., 637 Market St., Lewisburg, PA 17837-1451. TEL 717-524-9850; Ed. Max Oberdorf. adv.; photos; bk.rev.; circ. 16,000(controlled & free).

LIBRARY

US
PARK NEWS. 1981. m. $5/yr. 2550 Brownsville, Library, PA 15129. TEL 412-831-2588; FAX 412-831-2588. **Owner(s):** Wayne Perry, 3104 Trapper Dr., Library, PA 15129. TEL 412-348-6773; FAX 412-831-2588; Constance Perry, 3104 Trapper Dr., Library, PA 15129. TEL 412-348-6773; FAX 412-831-2588; Ed. Wayne Perry. adv.; photos; pub. size: tabloid; circ. 7,500(controlled & free).

LIGONIER

US
LIGONIER ECHO. 1888. Wed. $.45 newsstand; $23.60/yr. 112 W. Main St., Ligonier, PA 15658. TEL 412-238-2111; FAX 412-887-5115. **Owner(s):** Laurel Group Press, 229 Pittsburgh St., Scottdale, PA 15683-0222. TEL 412-887-7400; Ed. Richard P. Schwab. pub. size: broadsheet; circ. 4,734(paid).

US
LIGONIER FREE GAZETTE, THE. 1990. q. free distributed & mailed. P.O. Box G, Ligonier, PA 15658-1607. TEL 412-238-5749; FAX 412-238-5190; E-mail: ekmyers@third-wave.com. **Owner(s):** E. Kay Myers Advertising/PR, P.O. Box G, Ligonier, PA 15658-1607. TEL 412-238-5749; FAX 412-238-5190; Pub. E. Kay Myers; adv.; photos; pub. size: tabloid; circ. 15,000(controlled & free).

LITITZ

US
LITITZ RECORD EXPRESS, THE. 1877. Thu. $.30 newsstand; $9.50/yr. 22 E. Main St., Lititz, PA 17543. TEL 717-626-2191; FAX 717-733-6058. **Owner(s):** Lancaster Newspapers, Inc., Eight W. King St., Lancaster, PA 17603. TEL 717-291-8811; FAX 717-399-6518; adv. contact: Donald Campbell. photos; pub. size: broadsheet; circ. 7,200(free & paid).

MARTINSBURG

US
MORRISONS COVE HERALD. 1885. Thu. $.50 newsstand; $20/yr. in state; $23/yr. out of state. 113 N. Market St., Martinsburg, PA 16662. TEL 814-793-2144; FAX 814-793-4882. **Owner(s):** Morrisons Cove Herald, Inc., P.O. Box 277, Martinsburg, PA 16662. TEL 814-793-2144; FAX 814-793-4882; Pub. David Snyder; adv. contact: Richard L. Weicht. photos; pub. size: standard; circ. 6,000(paid).

MCCONNELLSBURG

US
MCCONNELLSBURG FULTON COUNTY NEWS. 1899. Thu. $15/yr. in cy.; $16/yr. out of cy.; $17.50/yr. out of state. E. Market & Fifth, McConnellsburg, PA 17233. TEL 717-485-3811; FAX 717-485-5187. **Owner(s):** Jamie S. Greathead, 321 S. Second, McConnellsburg, PA 17233. TEL 717-485-4513; FAX 717-485-5187; Ed. Bob Saul. adv. contact: Tina Gress. pub. size: standard; circ. 6,300(paid). **Wire Service(s):** AP.

MCDONALD

US
RECORD-ENTERPRISE. 1886. Wed. $30/yr. mailed; $26/yr. by carrier. 116 E. Lincoln Ave., McDonald, PA 15057. TEL 412-926-2111; FAX 412-926-2123. **Owner(s):** Observer Publishing Co., S. Main St., Washington, PA 15301. TEL 412-222-2200; Ed. Eliza A. Northrop. adv.; photos; pub. size: broadsheet; circ. 4,500(paid).
  Formerly: Record-Outlook & Enterprise.

MCKEES ROCKS

US
SUBURBAN GAZETTE. 1892. Wed. $20/yr. in cy.; $32/yr. out of cy. 421 Locust St., McKees Rocks, PA 15136-3599. TEL 412-331-2645. **Owner(s):** Virginia A. Schramm, 421 Locust St., McKees Rocks, PA 15136. TEL 412-331-2645; Ed. James C. DiNardo. pub. size: tabloid; circ. 8,700(paid).

MCMURRAY

US
ADVERTISER, THE. 1965. Thu. free; $22.50/yr. out of area. 3801 Washington Rd., McMurray, PA 15317. TEL 412-941-7725; FAX 412-941-8685. **Owner(s):** Observer-Reporter, 122 S. Main St., Washington, PA 15301. TEL 412-222-2200; Ed. Debbie Popp. adv. contact: Alice Bonnim. pub. size: broadsheet; circ. 34,641(free & paid).

US

ALMANAC, THE. 1968. Wed. free local; $22.50/yr. elsewhere. 3801 Washington Rd., McMurray, PA 15317. TEL 412-561-0700; FAX 412-941-8685. **Owner(s):** Observer-Reporter, 122 S. Main St., Washington, PA 15301. TEL 412-222-2200; Ed. Debbie Popp. adv. contact: Alice Bonnim. pub. size: broadsheet; circ. 33,279(free & paid).

MEDIA

US

TOWN TALK. 1965. Wed. free newsstand & carrier. 39 Old State Rd., Media, PA 19063. TEL 215-566-6755; FAX 215-566-1261. **Owner(s):** Town Talk Newspapers, P.O. Box 110, Media, PA 19063. TEL 215-566-6755; FAX 215-566-1261; Ed. Chris Parker; Pub. Edward Berman; adv.; photos; bk.rev.; pub. size: tabloid; circ. 85,000(free).

MIDDLEBURG

US

POST, THE. 1856. Wed. $17/yr. in cy.; $22.75/yr. out of cy.; $31.85/yr. out of state. 14 W. Market St., Middleburg, PA 17842. TEL 717-837-6065; FAX 717-374-6080. **Owner(s):** Swank-Fowler Publications, Inc., P.O. Box A, Duncannon, PA 17020. TEL 717-834-4616; Ed. Wade Fowler; Pub. Rick White; pub. size: broadsheet; circ. 2,500(paid).

MIDDLETOWN

US

PRESS & JOURNAL, THE. 1854. Wed. $.50 newsstand; $22/yr. in state; $34/yr. out of state. 20 S. Union St., Middletown, PA 17057. TEL 717-944-4628; FAX 717-944-2083. **Owner(s):** Joseph G. Sukle, P.O. Box 310, Middletown, PA 17057. TEL 717-944-4628; David Graybill, P.O. Box 310, Middletown, PA 17057. TEL 717-944-4628; Mike Graybill, P.O. Box 310, Middletown, PA 17057. TEL 717-944-4628; Louise Sukle, P.O. Box 310, Middletown, PA 17057. TEL 717-944-4628; Ed. Joseph G. Sukle; Pub. Joseph G. Sukle; adv. contact: Maxine J. Etter. photos; pub. size: broadsheet; circ. 11,400(controlled & paid). **Formerly:** Middletown Press & Journal.

MIFFLINBURG

US

MIFFLINBURG TELEGRAPH, THE. 1862. Thu. $.25 newsstand; $8/yr. in cy; $9/yr. out of cy. 358 Walnut St., Mifflinburg, PA 17844. TEL 717-966-2255; FAX 717-966-9706. **Owner(s):** John Stamm, 358 Walnut St., Mifflinburg, PA 17844. TEL 717-966-2255; FAX 717-966-9706; Pub. John Stamm; adv.; photos; pub. size: tabloid; circ. 756(paid).

MIFFLINTOWN

US

JUNIATA SENTINEL. 1846. Wed. $.50 newsstand; $15/yr. in cy.; $20/yr. out of cy. Old Rte. 22, R.D. 1, Mifflintown, PA 17059. TEL 717-436-8206; FAX 717-436-5174. **Owner(s):** Swank-Fowler Publications, Inc., P.O. Box 127, Mifflintown, PA 17059. TEL 717-436-8206; FAX 717-436-5174; Ed. Polly Digen; Pub. William A. Gilliland; adv.; pub. size: standard.

MILFORD

US   ISSN 1059-2377

PIKE COUNTY DISPATCH. 1856. Thu. $24/yr. in state; $27/yr. out of state. 105 W. Catharine St., Milford, PA 18337. TEL 717-296-6641; FAX 717-296-2610. **Owner(s):** Sue Doty-Lloyd, P.O. Box 186, Milford, PA 18337. TEL 717-296-6641; Ed. Rick Freeman; Pub. Sue Doty-Lloyd; adv. photos; pub. size: broadsheet; circ. 5,200(paid).

MILLERSBURG

US

UPPER DAUPHIN SENTINEL. 1972. Tue. $.50 newsstand; $21/yr. in state. 510 Union St., Millersburg, PA 17061. TEL 717-692-4737; FAX 717-692-2420. **Owner(s):** Kocher Enterprises, Inc., P.O. Box 169, Millersburg, PA 17061. TEL 717-692-4737; FAX 717-692-2420; Ed. Duane Good; Pub. Ben L. Kocher; adv. contact: Ben L. Kocher. photos; pub. size: broadsheet; circ. 9,500(paid).

MONROEVILLE

US

ADVANCE LEADER. 1901. Wed. $.50 newsstand; $25/yr. 610 Beatty Rd., Monroeville, PA 15146. TEL 412-856-7400; FAX 412-856-7954. **Owner(s):** Trinity Holdings, Inc., 610 Beatty Rd., Monroeville, PA 15146. TEL 412-856-7400; FAX 412-856-7954; Pub. Kevin Aylmer; adv.; photos; pub. size: broadsheet; circ. 5,790(paid).

US   ISSN 1047-0670

BRIDGEVILLE AREA NEWS. 1926. Wed. $.50 newsstand; $25/yr. 610 Beatty Rd., Monroeville, PA 15146. TEL 412-221-6397. E-mail: newsitem@ghplus.infi.net; URL: http://www.ghplus.com/hometown/bridgeville. **Owner(s):** Trinity Holdings, Inc., 600 Beatty Rd., Monroeville, PA 15146. TEL 412-856-7400; FAX 412-856-7954; Ed. Donna Selling; Pub. Kevin Aylmer; adv.; pub. size: tabloid; circ. 4,585(paid).

US

MURRYSVILLE AREA STAR. 1972. Wed. $.50 newsstand; $25/yr. 610 Beatty Rd., Monroeville, PA 15146. TEL 412-856-7400; FAX 412-856-7954. **Owner(s):** Trinity Holdings, Inc., 610 Beatty Rd., Monroeville, PA 15146. TEL 412-856-7400; FAX 412-856-7954; Pub. Kevin Aylmer; adv.; pub. size: broadsheet; circ. 5,925(free & paid).

US

PROGRESS, THE. 1948. Wed. $.50 newsstand; $25/yr. 610 Beatty Rd., Monroeville, PA 15146. TEL 412-856-7400; FAX 412-856-7954. **Owner(s):** Trinity Holdings, Inc., 610 Beatty Rd., Monroeville, PA 15146. TEL 412-856-7400; FAX 412-856-7954; Pub. Kevin Aylmer; adv.; photos; pub. size: broadsheet; circ. 7,355(paid).

US   ISSN 1047-0697

SEWICKLEY HERALD. 1903. Wed. $.50 newsstand; $25/yr. 610 Beatty Rd., Monroeville, PA 15146. TEL 412-856-7400; FAX 412-856-7954. **Owner(s):** Trinity Holdings, Inc., 610 Beatty Rd., Monroeville, PA 15146. TEL 412-856-7400; FAX 412-856-7954; Ed. Frank Tiboni; Pub. Kevin Aylmer; adv.; pub. size: tabloid; circ. 3,965(paid).

US   ISSN 1047-0662

SIGNAL-ITEM. 1873. Wed. $.50 newsstand; $25/yr. 610 Beatty Rd., Monroeville, PA 15146. TEL 412-856-7400; FAX 412-856-7954; E-mail: newsitem@ghplus.com; URL: http://www.ghplus.com/hometown/signal. **Owner(s):** Trinity Holdings, Inc., 610 Beatty Rd., Monroeville, PA 15146. TEL 412-856-7400; FAX 412-856-7954; Ed. Donna Selling. Pub. Kevin Aylmer; adv.; pub. size: tabloid; circ. 4,322(paid).

US

TIMES-EXPRESS. 1893. Wed. $.50 newsstand; $25/yr. home deliv. 610 Beatty Rd., Monroeville, PA 15146. TEL 412-856-7400; FAX 412-856-7954. **Owner(s):** Trinity Holdings, Inc., 610 Beatty Rd., Monroeville, PA 15146. TEL 412-856-7400; FAX 412-856-7954; Pub. Kevin Aylmer; adv.; photos; pub. size: broadsheet; circ. 6,000(paid).

MONTROSE

US

INDEPENDENT, THE. Wed. $.55 newsstand; $21/yr.; $25 out of cy. 24 S. Main St., Montrose, PA 18801. TEL 717-278-6397; FAX 717-278-6397. **Owner(s):** County Publishers Corp., 24 S. Main St., Montrose, PA 18801. TEL 717-278-6397; Ed. Teri Olcott; Pub. Elizabeth Taylor; adv. contact: Debbie Oaks. photos; pub. size: tabloid; circ. 1,500(paid).

US

SUSQUEHANNA COUNTY INDEPENDENT. 1816. Wed. $.55 newsstand; $21/yr. in cy.; $25/yr. out of cy. 24 S. Main St., Montrose, PA 18801. TEL 717-278-6397; FAX 717-278-4305. **Owner(s):** Earl Wootton, County Publishers Corp. 24 S. Main St., Montrose, PA 18801. TEL 717-278-6397; Robert Wootton, County Publishers Corp., 24 S. Main St., Montrose, PA 18801. TEL 717-278-6397; Ed. Elizabeth Taylor; Pub. Elizabeth Taylor; adv. pub. size: tabloid; circ. 5,000(paid).

US

WEEKEND NEWS. 1990. Sat. free. 24 S. Main St., Montrose, PA 18801. TEL 717-278-6397; FAX 717-278-6397. **Owner(s):** County Publishers Corp., 24 S. Main St., Montrose, PA 18801. TEL 717-278-6397; Ed. Teri Olcott; Pub. Elizabeth Taylor; adv. contact: Debbie Oaks. pub. size: tabloid; circ. 19,500(free).

MOSCOW

US

VILLAGER, THE. 1961. Wed. $16/yr. in state; $20/yr. out of state. R.D. 2, Box 2186B, Moscow, PA 18444. TEL 717-842-8789. **Owner(s):** Hometown Publications, Inc., 41 N. Church St., Carbondale, PA 18407. TEL 717-282-3300; Ed. Nicole Boni; Pub. Philip Hetn; adv.: $4.60/SAU. pub. size: broadsheet; circ. 4,300(paid). **Formerly:** Moscow Hamlin Villager.

MOUNTAIN TOP

US

MOUNTAINTOP EAGLE. 1969. Wed. $.50 newsstand; $18/yr. 85 S. Main Rd., Mountain Top, PA 18707. TEL 717-474-6397; FAX 717-474-9272. **Owner(s):** Stephanie Grubert, 13 Wilderness Dr., Mountain Top, PA 18707. TEL 717-868-3617; Ed. Kathy Flower; Pub. Stephanie Grubert; adv. contact: Stephanie Grubert. pub. size: broadsheet; circ. 2,850(paid).

MT. JOY

US

MOUNT JOY MERCHANDISER. 1975. Wed. $36/yr. 3rd class mailed; $70/yr. 1st class. 1425 W. Main St., Mt. Joy, PA 17552. TEL 717-653-1835; FAX 717-653-6165. **Owner(s):** Charles & Pauline Engle, P.O. Box 500, Mt. Joy, PA 17552. TEL 717-653-1833; Ed. Joanna Smith; Pub. Charles Engle; adv.; pub. size: tabloid; circ. 17,287(free).

MT. PLEASANT

US

ADVISOR, THE. 1978. Wed. $.35 newsstand; $18.60/yr. 23-33 S. Church St., Mt. Pleasant, PA 15666. TEL 412-547-5722; FAX 412-887-5115. **Owner(s):** Laurel Group Press, 229 Pittsburgh St., Scottdale, PA 15683-0222. TEL 412-887-7400; Ed. Jonna L. Stairs. pub. size: broadsheet; circ. 3,018(paid).

US

MOUNT PLEASANT JOURNAL. 1873. Wed. $.45 newsstand; $23.60/yr. 23 S. Church St., Mt. Pleasant, PA 15666. TEL 412-547-5722; FAX 412-887-5115. **Owner(s):** Laurel Group Press, 229 Pittsburgh St., Scottdale, PA 15683. TEL 412-887-7400; Ed. Marsha L. Forys. adv. contact: Charles D. Hixson. pub. size: broadsheet; circ. 5,935(paid).

NANTY GLO

US   ISSN 0746-4037

NANTY GLO JOURNAL, THE. Wed. $.45 newsstand; $19.75/yr. in cy.; $23/yr. in state; $26/yr. out of state. 975 Roberts St., Nanty Glo, PA 15943. TEL 814-749-8631. **Owner(s):** Sedloff Publications, Inc., P.O. Box 395, Portage, PA 15946; Ed. Connie Miller; Pub. Barbara Cordoro; adv. contact: Barbara Cordoro. photos; bk.rev.; pub. size: broadsheet; circ. 3,088(paid).

NEW BETHLEHEM

US

LEADER-VINDICATOR, THE. 1885. Wed. $.35 newsstand; $16/yr. in state; $40/yr. out of state. 435 Broad St., New Bethlehem, PA 16242. TEL 814-275-3131; FAX 814-275-3531. **Owner(s):** Southern Clarion County Newspapers, Inc., 435 Broad St., New Bethlehem, PA 16242. TEL 814-275-3131; Pub. James R. Shaffer; adv. contact: James R. Shaffer. pub. size: standard; circ. 5,200(paid).

NEW BLOOMFIELD

US

DUNCANNON RECORD. 1886. Thu. $17/yr. 51 N. Church St., New Bloomfield, PA 17068. TEL 717-582-4305. **Owner(s):** Swank-Fowler Publications, Inc., P.O. Box 130, New Bloomfield, PA 17068; Ed. Gary Thomas; Pub. Rick White; circ. evening 3,609(paid).

US   ISSN 0889-3810

NEWS-SUN, THE. 1868. Wed. $17/yr. in state. P.O. Box 130, New Bloomfield, PA 17068. TEL 717-582-4305; FAX 717-582-7933. **Owner(s):** Swank-Fowler Publications, Inc., 51 N. Church St., New Bloomfield, PA 17068. TEL 717-582-4305; Ed. Gary Thomas; Pub. Rick White; adv.; bk.rev.; pub. size: standard; circ. 3,239(paid).

US

PERRY COUNTY TIMES. 1886. Thu. $17/yr. in cy. 51 N. Church St., New Bloomfield, PA 17068. TEL 717-582-4305. **Owner(s):** Swank-Fowler Publications, Inc., P.O. Box 130, New Bloomfield, PA 17068. TEL 717-582-4305; Ed. Gary Thomas; Pub. Rick White; adv.; bk.rev.; pub. size: broadsheet; circ. 5,770(paid).

NEW HOPE

US

NEW HOPE GAZETTE. 1948. Thu. $18.50/yr.; $23/yr. out of cy.; $32/2 yrs. 170 Old York Rd., New Hope, PA 18938. TEL 215-862-9435; FAX 215-862-2160. **Owner(s):** Intercounty Newspaper Group, 6220 Ridge Ave., Philadelphia, PA 19128. TEL 215-483-7300; Ed. Bridget Wingert; Pub. R.A. Thompson; adv. contact: Patty Mangiaracina. pub. size: tabloid; circ. 4,000(paid).

NEWTOWN

US

ADVANCE OF BUCKS COUNTY. 1877. Thu. $.50 newsstand; $22/yr. 9 W. Centre Ave., Newtown, PA 18940. TEL 215-968-2244; FAX 215-968-2244. **Owner(s):** Intercounty Newspaper Group, 6220 Ridge Ave., Philadelphia, PA 19128. TEL 215-483-7300; Ed. Diana Bowen; Pub. Art Thompson; adv. contact: Kay Williams. photos; pub. size: tabloid; circ. 6,000(paid).

NEWTOWN SQUARE

US

COUNTY PRESS. 1931. Wed. $18/yr.; $30/2 yrs.; $42/3 yrs. 3732 West Chester Pike, Newtown Square, PA 19073-0249. TEL 610-356-6664; FAX 610-353-5321. **Owner(s):** Richard Crowe, 3732 West Chester Pike, Newtown Square, PA 19073. TEL 610-356-6664; William Lawrence, 3732 West Chester Pike, Newtown Square, PA 19073. TEL 610-356-6664; Ed. William W. Lawrence; Pub. Richard L. Crowe; adv.; pub. size: tabloid; circ. 8,250(free & paid).

US

DREXEL HILL PRESS. 1990. Wed. free deliv.; $.35 newsstand; $15/yr. 3732 West Chester Pike, Newtown Square, PA 19073. TEL 610-356-6664; FAX 610-353-5321. **Owner(s):** Richard Crowe, 3732 West Chester Pike, Newton Square, PA 19073; William Lawrence, 3732 West Chester Pike, Newtown Square, PA 19073; Ed. William Lawrence; Pub. Richard Crowe; adv.; pub. size: tabloid; circ. 2,800(free & paid).

US

HAVERFORD PRESS. 1985. Wed. $.50 newsstand; $18/yr. 3732 West Chester Pike, Newtown Square, PA 19073-0249. TEL 610-356-3820; FAX 610-353-5321. **Owner(s):** Richard Crowe, 3732 West Chester Pike, Newton Square, PA 19073. TEL 610-356-6664; William Lawrence, 3732 West Chester Pike, Newton Square, PA 19073. TEL 610-356-6664; Reese Crowe, 3732 West Chester Pike, Newton Square, PA 19073; Ed. William Lawrence; Pub. Richard Crowe; adv.; pub. size: tabloid; circ. 2,800(free & paid).

NEWVILLE

US

VALLEY TIMES-STAR. 1858. Wed. $.40 newsstand; $18.20/yr. 23 W. Big Spring Ave., Newville, PA 17241. TEL 717-776-3197; FAX 717-776-9290. **Owner(s):** Shippensburg News-Chronicle Co., Inc., P.O. Box 100, Shippensburg, PA 17257. TEL 717-532-4101; FAX 717-532-3020; Ed. Barbara Thompson; Pub. Kenneth W. Wolfrom; adv. contact: Steve Helm. photos; pub. size: broadsheet; circ. 3,500(paid).

NORRISTOWN

US

MONTGOMERY POST, THE. 1961. Thu. $.50 newsstand; $12.00/yr. 416 Egypt Rd., Norristown, PA 19403. TEL 610-630-6200; FAX 610-630-9765. **Owner(s):** Montgomery Publishing Co., 290 Commerce Dr., Fort Washington, PA 19034. TEL 215-542-0200; Ed. Lisa Lombardo; Pub. Arthur Howe, IV; adv.; pub. size: broadsheet; circ. 15,000(paid).
   Formerly: Post, The.

NORTH EAST

US

NORTH EAST BREEZE. 1868. Fri. $.60 newsstand; $20/yr. 35-39 S. Lake St., North East, PA 16428. TEL 814-725-4557. **Owner(s):** Brown-Thompson Newspapers, W. High St. Extension, Union City, PA 16438. TEL 814-438-7666; Ed. Peggy Hopkins. adv.; pub. size: broadsheet; circ. 3,368(paid).

ORBISONIA

US

VALLEY LOG, THE. 1980. Wed. $.50 newsstand; $18/yr. Water St., Orbisonia, PA 17243-0219. TEL 814-447-5506; FAX 814-447-3050. **Owner(s):** C. Arnold McClure, RDI, Shirleysburg, PA 17260. TEL 814-542-2588; FAX 814-447-3050; Ed. Lloyd M. Dell; Pub. C. Arnold McClure; adv.; photos; pub. size: broadsheet; circ. 3,061(paid).

OXFORD

US

BRANDYWINE CHRONICLE. 1982. Thu. free. 5000 Limestone Rd., Oxford, PA 19363-0520. TEL 610-932-2444; FAX 610-932-2246. **Owner(s):** Andrew & Randall Lieberman, P.O. Box 520, Oxford, PA 19363-0520. TEL 215-932-2444; pub. size: tabloid; circ. 20,000(free). **Wire Service(s):** AP.
   Formerly: Chronicle News Magazine.

US

CHESTER COUNTY PRESS. 1866. Fri. $.50 newsstand; $20/yr. in cy.; $35/yr. out of cy. 5000 Limestone Rd., Oxford, PA 19363-0520. TEL 610-932-2444; FAX 610-932-2246; E-mail: mfmm182@prodigy.com. **Owner(s):** AdPro, Inc., P.O. Box 520, Oxford, PA 19363. TEL 610-932-2444; Ed. Monika Saladino; Pub. Andrew H. Lieberman; adv. contact: Alan E. Tuens. photos; bk.rev.; pub. size: broadsheet; circ. 15,200(paid). **Wire Service(s):** AP.
   Formerly: The Chronicle.

US

UNIDA LATINA. bi-w.: Mon. free. 5000 Limestone Rd., Oxford, PA 19363. TEL 610-932-2444; FAX 610-932-2246. **Owner(s):** AdPro, Inc., P.O. Box 520, Oxford, PA 19363. TEL 610-932-2444; Ed. Nanette Lindner; Pub. Nancy Bististis; adv.; pub. size: tabloid; circ. 7,000(free).
   Formerly: La Voz.

PATTON

US

UNION PRESS-COURIER. 1906. Thu. $.40 newsstand; $19/yr. in cy.; $22/yr. in state; $23/yr. out of state. 452 Magee Ave., Patton, PA 16668. TEL 814-674-3666; FAX 814-674-3628. **Owner(s):** Frank J. Cammarata, P.O. Box 116, Patton, PA 16668. TEL 814-674-3666; FAX 814-674-3628; Ed. Mary Domalik; Pub. Cheryl Vescovi; adv.; photos; pub. size: standard; circ. 2,585(free).

PENNSBURG

US

TOWN & COUNTRY. 1899. Thu. $.50 newsstand; $26/yr. in state; $31.20/yr. out of state. Rte. 663 & Dotts St., Pennsburg, PA 18073. TEL 215-679-9561; FAX 215-679-9563. **Owner(s):** Gannett Satellite Information Network, Inc., 1100 Wilson Blvd., Arlington, VA 22234. TEL 703-284-6000; Pub. Suzanne Bush; adv.; photos; pub. size: broadsheet; circ. 5,000(paid). **Wire Service(s):** GNS.

PERKASIE

US

PERKASIE NEWS-HERALD. 1881. Wed. $.50 newsstand; $24/yr. in state; $30/yr. out of state. 320 S. Seventh St., Perkasie, PA 18944. TEL 215-257-6839; FAX 215-257-8701. **Owner(s):** Baum Publishing Co., 320 S. Seventh St., Perkasie, PA 18944. TEL 215-257-6839; FAX 215-257-8701; Ed. John A. Gerner. adv. contact: Eric L. Brunner. pub. size: broadsheet; circ. 7,000(free & paid).

PHILADELPHIA

US   ISSN 0009-3394

CHESTNUT HILL LOCAL. 1958. Thu. $.50 newsstand; $20/yr. mailed. 8434 Germantown Ave., Philadelphia, PA 19118. TEL 215-248-8800; FAX 215-248-8814; E-mail: chestnuthill@membrane.com; URL: http://membrane.com/chestnuthill/local/index.html. **Owner(s):** Chestnut Hill Community Association, 8434 Germantown Ave., Philadelphia, PA 19118. TEL 215-248-8800; Ed. Marie Reinhart Jones. adv. contact: Jason Scarpello. photos; pub. size: tabloid; circ. 10,000(paid).

US

FISHTOWN STAR. Wed. free; $85/yr. mailed. 250 W. Girard Ave., Philadelphia, PA 19123. TEL 215-925-7827; FAX 215-925-2339. **Owner(s):** News Star, Inc., 250 W. Girard Ave., Philadelphia, PA 19123. TEL 215-925-7827; Ed. Debbie Szumowski; Pub. Jonathan Stern; adv. contact: Pat Buzine. photos; bk.rev.; pub. size: tabloid; circ. 12,000(controlled & paid).

US

GERMANTOWN COURIER. 1936. Wed. $.35 newsstand; $20/yr. 6622 Germantown Ave., Philadelphia, PA 19119-0971. TEL 215-848-4300; FAX 215-848-9160. **Owner(s):** Acme Newspapers, Inc., 311 E. Lancaster Ave., Ardmore, PA 19003. TEL 215-642-4300; Ed. Sharon Bender; Pub. V. Clark McNeight; adv. contact: Allan Ash. photos; bk.rev.; pub. size: tabloid; circ. 21,000(controlled & paid).

US

GERMANTOWN PAPER. 1980. Wed. $48/yr. 2923 W. Cheltenham, Philadelphia, PA 19150. TEL 215-885-4111. **Owner(s):** Intercounty Newspaper Group, 6220 Ridge Ave., Philadelphia, PA 19128. TEL 215-483-7300; Ed. Marshall Rothman; Pub. Fred W. Donaldson; adv. contact: Leslie Sharpless. photos; pub. size: tabloid; circ. 8,000(controlled).

US

GIRARD HOME NEWS. 1937. Thu. free; $85/yr. mailed. 250 W. Girard Ave., Philadelphia, PA 19123. TEL 215-925-7827; FAX 215-925-2339. **Owner(s):** News Star, Inc., 250 W. Girard Ave., Philadelphia, PA 19123. TEL 215-923-8087; Ed. Mark Brakeman; Pub. Jonathan Stern; adv. contact: Pat Buzine. photos; pub. size: tabloid; circ. 13,500(free).
   Formerly: Philadelphia Girard Home News.

US

JUNIATA NEWS. 1934. Tue. $.25 newsstand; $49/yr. 2241 N. Fifth St., Philadelphia, PA 19133-2599. TEL 215-739-8197; FAX 215-739-9290. **Owner(s):** Juniata News, 2241 N. Fifth St., Philadelphia, PA 19133. TEL 215-739-8197; FAX 215-739-9290; Ed. Gerard R. Lineman; Pub. Gerard Lineman; adv.; photos; pub. size: tabloid; circ. 10,000(free & paid).

US

LEADER, THE. 1963. Wed. $.50 newsstand; $48/yr. 2385 W. Cheltenham Ave., Ste. 182, Philadelphia, PA 19150-1506. TEL 215-885-4111; FAX 215-885-0226. **Owner(s):** Intercounty Newspaper Group, 6220 Ridge Ave., Philadelphia, PA 19128. TEL 215-483-7300; Ed. Marshall Rothman; Pub. Fred W. Donaldson; adv. contact: Leslie Sharpless. photos; pub. size: tabloid; circ. 29,000(controlled & paid).
   Formerly: West Oak Lane Leader.

US

MT. AIRY TIMES. 1991. Wed. free in area; $.35 newsstand; $20/yr. 6622 Germantown Ave., Philadelphia, PA 19119. TEL 215-848-4300; FAX 215-848-9160. **Owner(s):** Acme Newspapers, Inc., 311 E. Lancaster Ave., Ardmore, PA 19003. TEL 215-642-4300; Ed. Sharon Bender. Pub. Deborah Shaw; adv. contact: Allan Ash. photos; bk.rev.; pub. size: tabloid; circ. 14,000(free & paid).
   Formerly: Mt. Airy Times Express.

US

NEWS GLEANER PUBLICATIONS. 1882. Wed. free; $.25 newsstand; $90/yr. mailed. 1612 Margaret St., Philadelphia, PA 19124. TEL 215-535-4275; FAX 215-533-0566. **Owner(s):** Coulston S. Henry, 1612 Margaret St., Philadelphia, PA 19124. TEL 215-535-4275; Pub. Coulston S. Henry; adv. contact: John Steinruck. pub. size: broadsheet; circ. 109,262(free & paid). **Wire Service(s):** AP.

US

NORTHEAST TIMES. 1934. s-w.: Wed. & Thu. $25/yr. 8001 Roosevelt Blvd., Ste. 401, Philadelphia, PA 19152. TEL 215-332-3300. **Owner(s):** Times Newspapers, Inc., 8001 Roosevelt Blvd., Ste. 401, Philadelphia, PA 19152. TEL 215-332-3300; Ed. John J. Scanlon; Pub. Robert T. Smylie; adv. contact Timothy Smylie. pub. size: tabloid; circ. 116,000(free & paid).

US

NORTH STAR. Wed. free; $85/yr. mailed. 250 W. Girard Ave., Philadelphia, PA 19123. TEL 215-925-7827; FAX 215-925-2339. **Owner(s):** News Star, Inc., 250 W. Girard Ave., Philadelphia, PA 19123. TEL 215-925-7827; FAX 215-925-2339; Ed. Debbie Szumowski; Pub. Jonathan Stern; adv. contact: Pat Buzine. photos; bk.rev. pub. size: tabloid; circ. 6,000(controlled & free).

US

OLNEY TIMES. 1909. Thu. free deliv.; $60/yr. mailed. 5703 N. Fifth St., Philadelphia, PA 19120. TEL 215-424-0700; FAX 215-424-4082. **Owner(s):** Olney Times, 5703 N. Fifth St., Philadelphia, PA 19120. TEL 215-424-0700; adv.; pub. size: broadsheet; circ. 25,000(free).

US   ISSN 0733-6349

PHILADELPHIA CITY PAPER. 1981. w. $52/yr. 206 S. 13th St., Philadelphia, PA 19146. TEL 215-735-8444; FAX 215-732-9033. **Owner(s):** City Communications, Inc., 206 S. 13th St., Philadelphia, PA 19146; Ed. David Warner; Pub. Paul Curci; adv. contact: Paul Curci. bk.rev.; pub. size: tabloid; circ. 75,000.

US

PHILADELPHIA GUIDE NEWSPAPER. 1939. s-w.: Thu. & Fri. $50/yr. 2022 E. Allegheny Ave., Philadelphia, PA 19134. TEL 215-423-1000; FAX 215-426-4438. **Owner(s):** H. Robert Jacobs, Jr., 47 Bank St., Medford, NJ 08055. TEL 609-654-0726; H. Robert Jacobs, Sr., 5550 Gulfstream Way Indian River, Stuart, FL 34996. TEL 609-654-9644; Graphic News, Inc., AKA Guide Newspapers, 2022 E. Allegheny Ave., Philadelphia, PA 19134. TEL 215-423-1000; Ed. H.R. Jacobs, Jr.; Pub. Michelle O'Connell; adv. contact: Michelle O'Connell. pub. size: tabloid; circ. morning 51,000(free & paid).

US

PHILADELPHIA WEEKLY. 197_. Wed. $30/6 mos.; $55/yr. 1701 Walnut St., Philadelphia, PA 19103-5220. TEL 215-563-7400; FAX 215-563-6799. **Owner(s):** Review Publishing, Ltd., 1701 Walnut St., 3rd Fl., Philadelphia, PA 19103-5220. TEL 215-563-7400; FAX 215-563-6799; Ed. Sara Kelly; Pub. Michael Cohen; adv. contact: Nicholas Riggio. photos; bk.rev.; pub. size: tabloid; circ. 112,000(controlled).
   Formerly: Philadelphia Welcomat.

US

PORT RICHMOND STAR. Wed. free; $35/yr. mailed. 250 W. Girard Ave., Philadelphia, PA 19123. TEL 215-925-7827; FAX 215-925-2339. **Owner(s):** News Star, Inc., 250 W. Girard Ave., Philadelphia, PA 19123. TEL 215-925-7827; FAX 215-925-2339; Ed. Debbie Szumowski; Pub. Jonathan Stern; adv. contact: Pat Buzine. photos; bk.rev.; pub. size: tabloid; circ. 12,000(controlled & free).

US

ROXBOROUGH REVIEW. 1902. Wed. $.50 newsstand; $85/yr. 6220 Ridge Ave., Philadelphia, PA 19128. TEL 215-483-7300. **Owner(s):** Intercounty Newspaper Group, 6220 Ridge Ave., Philadelphia, PA 19128. TEL 215-483-7300; Ed. George Beetham. adv. contact: Peter Damato. photos; pub. size: broadsheet; circ. 23,500(paid).

US

SOUTH PHILADELPHIA CHRONICLE. 1947. Thu. free newsstand; $60/yr. 12th & Porter Sts., N.W. Corner, Philadelphia, PA 19148. TEL 215-336-2500; FAX 215-336-1112. **Owner(s):** Review Publishing, Ltd., 12th & Porter, P.O. Box 2427, Philadelphia, PA 19148. TEL 215-336-2500; Ed. Dave Kramer; Pub. Michael Cohen; adv. contact: John Gallo. pub. size: tabloid; circ. 74,050(free & paid).

US

SOUTH PHILADELPHIA REVIEW. 1947. Thu. free newsstand; $60/yr. 12th & Porter Sts., Philadelphia, PA 19148. TEL 215-336-2500; FAX 215-336-1112. **Owner(s):** Review Publishing, Ltd., 12th & Porter Sts., P.O. Box 2027, Philadelphia, PA 19148. TEL 215-336-2500; Ed. Sandra Philips; Pub. Michael Cohen; adv. contact: John Gallo. pub. size: tabloid; circ. 72,000(paid).

US

SOUTHWEST GLOBE TIMES. 1945. Wed. free newsstand; $50/yr. deliv. 6330 Paschall Ave., Philadelphia, PA 19142. TEL 215-727-7777; FAX 215-727-5116. **Owner(s):** Southwest Globe Times, 6330 Paschall Ave., Philadelphia, PA 19142. TEL 215-727-7777; Ed. Lenora Iannuzzelli; Pub. Joseph Bartash; adv. contact: Theresa Nichols. photos; pub. size: tabloid; circ. 18,500(free & paid).

US

THREE STAR EDITION. Wed. free; $85/yr. mailed. 250 W. Girard Ave., Philadelphia, PA 19123. TEL 215-925-7827; FAX 215-925-2339. **Owner(s):** News Star, Inc., 250 W. Girard Ave., Philadelphia, PA 19123. TEL 215-925-7827; FAX 215-925-2339; Ed. Debbie Szumowski; Pub. Jonathan Stern; adv.; photos; bk.rev.; pub. size: tabloid; circ. 6,000(controlled & paid).

PHOENIXVILLE

US

VOICE, THE. Thu. free. 225 Bridge St., Phoenixville, PA 19460. TEL 610-933-8926; FAX 610-933-1187. **Owner(s):** Journal Register Co., 50 W. State St., 12th Fl., Trenton, NJ. TEL 609-396-2200; Ed. Rita Cellucci. pub. size: broadsheet; circ. 30,000(free).

PINE GROVE

US

PRESS HERALD. 1877. Thu. $.50 newsstand; $24/yr. in cy.; $30/yr. out of cy.; $35/yr. out of state. 181 S. Tulpehocken, Pine Grove, PA 17963. TEL 717-345-4455; FAX 717-345-8467. **Owner(s):** Call Newspapers, Inc., Pine Grove, PA; Ed. Paula Schaeffer. pub. size: standard; circ. 3,157(paid).

PITTSBURGH

US

HERALD, THE. Wed. $.50 newsstand; $30/yr. in cy.; $35/yr. out of cy. 101 Emerson Ave., Pittsburgh, PA 15215. TEL 412-782-2121; FAX 412-782-1195. **Owner(s):** Gannett Company, Inc., One Gannett Dr., White Plains, NY 10604. TEL 914-694-9300; Ed. Matthew Clark; Pub. Scott Brown; adv.; pub. size: broadsheet; circ. 5,000(paid).

US

ISDA UNIONE. bi-w.: Mon. $7/yr. 1719 Liberty Ave., Pittsburgh, PA 15222. TEL 412-281-8533; FAX 412-281-2898. **Owner(s):** L & R Frediani, 1719 Liberty Ave., Pittsburgh, PA 15222. TEL 412-281-8533; Ed. James V. Tortola; Pub. Lawrence Frediani; pub. size: standard; circ. 12,000(paid).

US   ISSN 1066-0062

PITTSBURGH CITY PAPER. 1991. Wed. free newsstand; $50/yr. 911 Penn Ave., 6th Fl., Pittsburgh, PA 15222. TEL 412-560-2489; FAX 412-281-1962. **Owner(s):** Brad Witherell, 1582 S. Parker Rd., Ste. 212, Denver, CO 80231. TEL 303-750-3865; FAX 303-696-4271; Andy March, 1582 S. Parker Rd., Ste. 212, Denver, CO 80231. TEL 303-750-3865; FAX 303-696-2471; Ed. John Hayes; Pub. Brad Witherell; adv. contact: Greg Brozovich. photos; bk.rev.; pub. size: tabloid; circ. 82,000(free & paid).

US

PITTSBURGH RENAISSANCE NEWS. 1965. Wed. $15/6 mos. 1516 Fifth Ave., Pittsburgh, PA 15219. TEL 412-391-8208; FAX 412-391-8006. **Owner(s):** Connie Portis, 1516 Fifth Ave., Pittsburgh, PA 15219. TEL 412-391-8208; FAX 412-391-8006; Ed. Connie Portis; Pub. Connie Portis; adv.; photos; bk.rev.; pub. size: tabloid; circ. 30,000(free & paid).

US

SOUTH HILLS RECORD. 1903. Thu. $.50 newsstand; $20.80/yr. carrier; $25/yr. mailed in cy.; $40/yr. out of cy. 3623 Brownsville, Pittsburgh, PA 15227. TEL 412-884-3111; FAX 412-884-3106. **Owner(s):** Trinity Holdings, Inc., 610 Beatty Rd., Monroeville, PA 15146. TEL 412-856-7400; FAX 412-856-7954; Ed. Jeff Jones; Pub. Kevin Aylmer; adv.; pub. size: tabloid; circ. 6,309(paid).

US

SOUTH PITTSBURGH REPORTER. 1939. Tue. $36/yr. 1301 E. Carson St., Pittsburgh, PA 15203-0285. TEL 412-481-0266; FAX 412-488-8011. **Owner(s):** South Pittsburgh Reporter, P.O. Box 4285, Pittsburgh, PA 15203-0285. TEL 412-481-0266; Ed. Roberta F. Smith; Pub. Roberta F. Smith; adv.; photos; pub. size: tabloid; circ. 12,000(controlled & free).

PITTSTON

US

SUNDAY DISPATCH. 1948. Sun. $1 newsstand; $52/yr. 109 New St., Pittston, PA 18640. TEL 717-655-1418; FAX 717-883-1266. **Owner(s):** Walt Disney Co., 500 S. Buena Vista St., Burbank, CA 91521. TEL 818-560-5300; Ed. Dave Jankosky; Pub. John Watson; adv. contact: Laurie Nocito. pub. size: tabloid; circ. Sun. 13,000(paid).
Formerly: Pittston Sunday Dispatch.

PORTAGE

US

PORTAGE DISPATCH, THE. 1904. Wed. $.45 newsstand; $19.75/yr. in cy.; $23/yr. in state; $26/yr. out of state. 722 Dulancey Dr., Portage, PA 15946. TEL 814-736-9666. **Owner(s):** Sedloff Publications, Inc., P.O. Box 395, Portage, PA 15946. TEL 814-472-4110; Ed. Connie Miller. adv.; photos; bk.rev.; pub. size: broadsheet; circ. 5,303(paid).

PORT ROYAL

US

TIMES, THE. 1876. Wed. $.35 newsstand; $12/yr. in cy.; $18/yr. out of cy. 111 W. Fourth St., Port Royal, PA 17082. TEL 717-527-2213; FAX 717-527-2787. **Owner(s):** David E. Wade, 111 W. Fourth St., Port Royal, PA 17082. TEL 717-527-2213; Ed. David E. Wade; Pub. David E. Wade; adv. contact: Elizabeth Wade. pub. size: standard; circ. 3,900(paid).
Formerly: Port Royal Times.

PUNXSUTAWNEY

US

COUNTY NEIGHBORS. 1991. Wed. $19/yr. in cy.; $29/yr. out of cy. 510 Pine St., Punxsutawney, PA 15767. TEL 814-938-8740; FAX 814-938-3794. **Owner(s):** American Publishing Co., 606 N. Van Buren, P.O. Box 520, Marion, IL 62959. TEL 618-993-1711; Ed. Wick Divelbiss; Pub. William Anderson; adv. contact: Valerie Pasternak. photos; pub. size: standard; circ. 5,500(free & paid). **Wire Service(s):** AP.

QUAKERTOWN

US

QUAKERTOWN FREE PRESS. 1881. Thu. $.40 newsstand; $18/yr. 312 W. Broad St., Quakertown, PA 18951. TEL 215-536-6820; FAX 215-536-6820. **Owner(s):** Franklin & Meredith, Inc., 312 W. Broad St., Quakertown, PA 18951. TEL 215-536-6820; Pub. Charles (Ty) Meredith, IV; pub. size: tabloid; circ. 5,000(paid).
Formerly: Free Press.

ROCKLEDGE

US

BREEZE, THE. 1927. Thu. $.50 newsstand; $42/yr. 54 Park Ave., Rockledge, PA 19046. TEL 215-379-5500. **Owner(s):** Intercounty Newspaper Group, 6220 Ridge Ave., Philadelphia, PA 19128. TEL 215-483-7300; Ed. Nancy Mortimer; Pub. Fred W. Donaldson; adv.; pub. size: tabloid; circ. 2,200(paid).

ROYERSFORD

US

REPORTER OF THE SPRING-FORD AREA. 1872. Thu. $.50 newsstand; $16/yr. carrier local; $20/yr. mail local; $21/yr. mail elsewhere. Park Towne Plz., Royersford, PA 19468. TEL 610-948-4850; FAX 610-948-5914. **Owner(s):** Montgomery Publishing Co., 290 Commerce Dr., Fort Washington, PA 19034. TEL 610-542-0200; Ed. Alethea Lynch; Pub. Arthur Howe; adv. contact: Gurry Gould. photos; pub. size: broadsheet; circ. 5,008(free & paid).

SAXTON

US

BROAD TOP BULLETIN. 1947. Wed. $.40 newsstand; $19/yr. 900 Sixth St., P.O. Box 188, Saxton, PA 16678-0188. TEL 814-635-2851. **Owner(s):** Jon Baughman, P.O. Box 215, Dudley, PA 16634. TEL 814-635-2851; Judy Baughman, P.O. Box 215, Dudley, PA 16634. TEL 814-635-2851; Ed. Jon Baughman; Pub. Jon Baughman; adv. contact: Peggy Whited. adv.: $3.50/SAU. photos; pub. size: broadsheet; circ. 3,250(paid).

SCHUYLKILL HAVEN

US

CALL, THE. 1891. Thu. $.50 newsstand; $24/yr. in cy.; $30/yr. out of cy.; $35/yr. out of state. 960 E. Main St., Schuylkill Haven, PA 17972. TEL 717-385-3120; FAX 717-385-0725. **Owner(s):** Call Newspapers, Inc., P.O. Box 178, Schuylkill Haven, PA 17972; Ed. LaJeune Steidle. pub. size: standard; circ. 5,100(paid).
Formerly: Schuylkill Haven Call.

SCOTTDALE

US

INDEPENDENT OBSERVER, THE. 1879. Wed. $.45 newsstand; $23.60/yr. in cy. 229 Pittsburgh St., Scottdale, PA 15683-0222. TEL 412-887-6101; FAX 412-887-5115. **Owner(s):** Laurel Group Press, 229 Pittsburgh St., Scottdale, PA 15683. TEL 412-887-7400; Ed. Dirk W. Kaufman. pub. size: broadsheet; circ. 3,473(paid).

US

SOUTHWESTERN PENNSYLVANIA SCENE. 1971. bi-m. $1.50 newsstand; $9/yr. 229 Pittsburgh St., Scottdale, PA 15683. TEL 412-887-7400. **Owner(s):** Laurel Group Press, 229 Pittsburgh St., Scottdale, PA 15683. TEL 412-887-7400; Ed. Dirk W. Kaufman; Pub. Ralph Hernley; adv.; pub. size: standard; circ. 8,000(free & paid).
Formerly: Laurel Highlands Scene.

SHIPPENSBURG

US

SHIPPENSBURG NEWS-CHRONICLE. 1875. s-w.: Mon. & Thu. $.40 newsstand; $36.40/yr. in cy.; $47.80/yr. zones 1-5; $52/yr. zones 6-8. 1011 Ritner Hwy., Shippensburg, PA 17257. TEL 717-532-4101; FAX 717-532-3020. **Owner(s):** News Chronicle Co., Inc., P.O. Box 100, Shippensburg, PA 17257. TEL 717-532-4101; Ed. James Curtis. adv. contact: Steve Helm. photos; bk.rev.; pub. size: broadsheet; circ. 6,100(free & paid). **Wire Service(s):** CNS.

SOUDERTON

US

SOUDERTON INDEPENDENT. 1878. Wed. $.50 newsstand; $17/yr. 673 E. Broad St., Souderton, PA 18964. TEL 215-723-4801; FAX 215-723-8779. **Owner(s):** Montgomery Publishing Co., 290 Commerce Dr., Fort Washington, PA 19034. TEL 215-542-0200; Ed. Barbara McClennen; Pub. Art Howe; adv. contact: John Derr. photos; pub. size: broadsheet; circ. 5,400(paid).

SPRINGBORO

US

AREA SHOPPER. 1953. Mon. $18/yr. home deliv. Lake St., Springboro, PA 16435. TEL 814-587-2032; FAX 814-587-3720. **Owner(s):** H. Jesse Haas, 102 Main St., Conneautville, PA 16406; Ed. H. Jesse Haas; Pub. H. Jesse Haas; pub. size: standard; circ. 221,000(paid).

US

CONNEAUTVILLE COURIER. Thu. $18/yr. Lake St., Springboro, PA 16435. TEL 814-587-2032; FAX 814-587-3720. **Owner(s):** H. Jesse Haas, Springboro, PA 16435; Ed. Peggy McMillan. pub. size: tabloid; circ. 1,000(free & paid).

SPRINGFIELD

US

SPRINGFIELD PRESS. 1931. Wed. $.50 newsstand; $18/yr. 204 Ballymore Rd., Springfield, PA 19064. TEL 610-544-6660; FAX 610-544-4530. **Owner(s):** Crowe Printers & Publishers, P.O. Box 291, Springfield, PA 19064. TEL 610-544-6660; Ed. Dorothy B. Koetzle; Pub. Reese Crowe, Jr.; adv. contact: Reese Crowe, Jr. pub. size: tabloid; circ. 7,000(paid).

SUSQUEHANNA

US

COUNTY TRANSCRIPT. 1886. Thu. $.50 newsstand; $20/yr. Exchange St., Susquehanna, PA 18847. TEL 717-853-3134; FAX 717-853-4707. **Owner(s):** Charles W. Ficarro, R.D. 2, Box 152 A1, Susquehanna, PA 18847. TEL 717-853-3284; FAX 717-853-4707; Pub. Charles W. Ficarro; adv.; photos; pub. size: tabloid; circ. 3,500(paid).
Formerly: Susquehanna Transcript.

TIONESTA

US

FOREST PRESS. 1867. Wed. $.50 newsstand; $19/yr. in cy. $22/yr. out of cy. 165 Elm St., Tionesta, PA 16353-0366. TEL 814-755-4900; FAX 814-755-4429. **Owner(s):** Edwin R. Patrick, P.O. Box 366, Tionesta, PA 16353. TEL 814-755-4900; Ed. Virginia Patrick; Pub. Edwin R. Patrick; adv. contact: Leslie Holt. photos; pub. size: tabloid; circ. 4,500(paid).

TOWER CITY

US

WEST SCHUYLKILL HERALD. 1898. Thu. $.50 newsstand; $28/yr. in cy.; $31/yr. in state; $35/yr. out of state. E13 E. Grand Ave., Tower City, PA 17980. TEL 717-647-2191; FAX 717-647-2420. **Owner(s):** Call Newspapers, Inc., P.O. Box 17980, Schuylkill, PA 17972. TEL 717-385-3120; Ed. June Reibsane. pub. size: standard; circ. 2,250(paid).

TUNKHANNOCK

US

TUNKHANNOCK NEW AGE-EXAMINER. 1870. s-w.: Tue. & Fri. $.50 newsstand; $35/yr. 16 E. Tioga St., Tunkhannock, PA 18657. TEL 717-836-2123; FAX 717-836-3378. **Owner(s):** Scranton Times, 149 Penn Ave., Scranton, PA 18503. TEL 717-348-9101; Ed. Mary Baldwin; Pub. James E. Towner; adv. contact: Nancy Kaufmann. pub. size: standard; circ. 5,400(paid).

UNION CITY

US

TIMES-LEADER. 1872. Sun. $.50 newsstand; $20/yr. 8230 W. High St. Extension, Union City, PA 16438. TEL 814-438-7566; FAX 814-438-2898. **Owner(s):** Erie Times, Erie, PA; Ed. John Sinnerty; Pub. Mark Laskowski; pub. size: standard; circ. 3,400(paid).

VALLEY VIEW

US

CITIZEN-STANDARD, THE. 1932. s-m. $.35 newsstand; $24/yr. in cy.; $25/yr. out of cy. 100 W. Main St., Valley View, PA 17983. TEL 717-682-9081; FAX 717-682-8734. **Owner(s):** Thomson Newspapers, Inc., 3150 Des Plaines Ave., Des Plaines, IL 60018. TEL 717-682-9081; Pub. Gregory J. Zyla; adv. contact: Wendy Knorr. bk.rev.; pub. size: broadsheet; circ. 4,640(free & paid). **Wire Service(s):** AP.

VANDERGRIFT

US

VANDERGRIFT NEWS. 1905. s-w.: Wed. & Sat. $.50 newsstand; $31.20/yr. mail ed. 143 Washington Ave., Vandergrift, PA 15690. TEL 412-567-5656; FAX 412-568-3818. **Owner(s):** Buttermilk Falls, 143 Washington Ave., Vandergrift, PA 15690. TEL 412-567-5656; FAX 412-568-3818; Ed. JoJo Bodnar; Pub. Donald Cole; adv. contact: Kurt Amendola. pub. size: broadsheet; circ. 3,000(paid).

WAYNE

US

SUBURBAN & WAYNE TIMES. 1385. Thu. $.50 newsstand; $35.95/yr. carrier in state; $41.95 mail in state. 134 N. Wayne Ave., Wayne, PA 19087. TEL 610-688-3000; FAX 610-254-8522. **Owner(s):** Journal Register Co., 50 W. State St., 12th Fl. Trenton, NJ 08608. TEL 609-396-2200; Ed. Jim Lewis; Pub. Bill Burgess; adv. contact: Dan Lionetti. pub. size: broadsheet; circ. 16,000(paid).

US

SUBURBAN ADVERTISER. 1961. Thu. $.50 newsstand; $41.95/yr. in state; $51.50/yr. out of state. 134 N. Wayne Ave., Wayne, PA 19087. TEL 610-688-3000. **Owner(s):** Journal Register Co., 134 N. Wayne Ave., Wayne, PA 19087. TEL 610-683-3000; Ed. Jim Lewis; Pub. Bill Burgess; adv. contact: Shelly Meenan. pub. size: broadsheet; circ. 18,000(controlled & free).

WEEDVILLE

US

BENNETTS VALLEY NEWS. 1953. Thu. $17/yr. in state; $20/yr. out of state. P.O. Box 158, Weedville, PA 15868. TEL 814-787-4454. **Owner(s):** Jim Leonard, P.O. Box 158, Weedville, PA 15868. TEL 814-787-4454; adv.; pub. size: standard; circ. 1,000(paid).

WELLSBORO

US

WELLSBORO GAZETTE. 1874. Wed. $.75 newsstand; $36/yr. in cy.; $40/yr. out of cy. 25 East Ave., Wellsboro, PA 16901. TEL 717-724-2287; FAX 717-724-2278. **Owner(s):** Tioga Printing Corp., 25 East Ave., Wellsboro, PA 16901. TEL 717-724-2287; Ed. Jeffrey A. Fetzer. adv. contact: Robert Miller. pub. size: broadsheet; circ. 6,850(paid).

WESTFIELD

US

FREE PRESS-COURIER. 1878. Wed. $.60 newsstand; $22/yr. in of state; $24/yr. out of state. 119 Main St., Westfield, PA 16950-0515. TEL 814-367-2230; FAX 814-367-5092. **Owner(s):** Tioga Printing Corp., Wellsboro, PA 16901. TEL 717-724-2287; FAX 717-724-2278; Ed. Marie Pepero. adv.; photos; pub. size: standard; circ. 4,000(paid).
    Formerly: Westfield Free Press-Courier.

WEST NEWTON

US

TIMES-SUN, THE. 1878. Wed. $.45 newsstand; $23.60/yr. in cy.; $35.60/yr. out of cy.; $37.60/yr. out of state. 205 E. Main St., West Newton, PA 15089-1153. TEL 412-872-6800; FAX 412-887-5115. **Owner(s):** Laurel Group Press, 229 Pittsburgh St., Scottsdale, PA 15683-0222. TEL 412-887-7400; FAX 412-887-5115; Ed. Colleen A. Pollock; Pub. H. Ralph Hernley; adv. contact: Bob Cunningham. photos; pub. size: broadsheet; circ. 3,200(paid).

WHITE HAVEN

US

JOURNAL-HERALD, THE. 1879. Thu. $.40 newsstand; $20/yr. 211 Main St., White Haven, PA 18661. TEL 717-443-9131. **Owner(s):** Jay & Clara Holder, 211 Main St., White Haven, PA 18661. TEL 717-443-9131; Seth & Ruth Isenberg, 403 Second St., Weatherly, PA 18255. TEL 717-427-4433; Pub. Clara Holder; adv. contact: Seth Isenberg. adv.: $3/SAU. photos; pub. size: broadsheet; circ. 1,780(paid).

US

▼**JOURNAL/VALLEY VIEWS.** 1994. m. $6/yr. 211 Main St., White Haven, PA 18861. TEL 717-443-9131. **Owner(s):** Jay & Clara Holder, 211 Main St., White Haven, PA 18661. TEL 717-443-9131; Seth & Ruth Isenberg, 403 Second St., Weatherly, PA 18255. TEL 717-427-4433; Ed. Ruth Isenberg. adv.: $7/SAU. photos; pub. size: standard; circ. 5,500(controlled & free).

YARDLEY

US

YARDLEY NEWS. 1946. Thu. $.50 newsstand; $18.50/yr. 10 Penn Valley Dr., Unit B, Yardley, PA 19067. TEL 215-493-2794. **Owner(s):** Intercounty Newspaper Group, 6220 Ridge Ave., Philadelphia, PA 19128. TEL 215-483-7300; Ed. Jeffrey Werner; Pub. Art Thompson; adv. contact: Resa Hall. photos; pub. size: tabloid; circ. 6,000(controlled & paid).

YEAGERTOWN

US

COUNTY OBSERVER. 1975. Wed. $.50 newsstand; $18/yr. in cy.; $25/yr. out of cy. 310 S. Main St., Yeagertown Plz., Ste. A-1, Yeagertown, PA 17099. TEL 717-248-9366; FAX 717-248-9377. **Owner(s):** Ogden Newspapers, Inc., 1500 Main St., Wheeling, WV 26003. TEL 304-233-0100; Ed. Susan Rupe. adv.; pub. size: broadsheet; circ. 6,200(paid).

RHODE ISLAND

BRISTOL

US

BRISTOL PHOENIX. 1837. Thu. $.60 newsstand; $24/yr. in cy.; $35/yr. out of cy.; $40/yr. elsewhere. One Bradford St., Bristol, RI 02809. TEL 401-253-6000; FAX 401-253-2838. **Owner(s):** Roswell Bosworth, Jr., P.O. Box 90, Bristol, RI 02809-0090. TEL 401-253-6000; Ed. Matthew Hayes; Pub. Roswell Bosworth, Jr.; adv. contact: Jane McHenry. photos; pub. size: tabloid; circ. 6,100(paid).

CRANSTON

US

CRANSTON HERALD. 1921. Thu. $.50 newsstand; $23/yr. 798 Park Ave., Cranston, RI 02910. TEL 401-781-4240; FAX 401-781-4241. **Owner(s):** Beacon Communications Corp., 1944 Warwick Ave., Warwick, RI 02889. TEL 401-732-3100; Ed. Sue Leibowitz; Pub. John Howell; pub. size: standard; circ. 5,200(paid).

EAST GREENWICH

US

EAST GREENWICH PENDULUM. 1854. Thu. $.75 newsstand; $30/yr. 580 Main St., East Greenwich, RI 02818. TEL 401-884-4662; FAX 401-884-9819. **Owner(s):** Southern Rhode Island Newspaper, 187 Main St., Wakefield, RI 02880. TEL 401-789-9744; Ed. Anne S. Davidson; Pub. Marc Romanow; adv.; photos; pub. size: broadsheet; circ. 4,000(paid).

EAST PROVIDENCE

US

EAST PROVIDENCE POST. 1906. Thu. $.35 newsstand; $12/yr. 1000A Waterman Ave., East Providence, RI 02914. TEL 401-434-7210; FAX 401-434-9469. **Owner(s):** Herald Press, 99 Webster St., Pautucket, RI 72644; Ed. David Howard. adv. contact: Mary Whelan. bk.rev.; pub. size: tabloid; circ. 12,000(paid).

US

SEEKONK STAR. Thu. $.35 newsstand; $12/yr. 1000 A. Waterman Ave., East Providence, RI 02914. TEL 401-434-7210; FAX 401-726-5820. **Owner(s):** Herald Press, 99 Webster St., Pawtucket, RI 02914. TEL 401-434-7110; Ed. David Howard; Pub. Mary Whelon; adv. contact: Mary Whelon. photos; bk.rev.; pub. size: tabloid; circ. 4,000(paid).

GREENVILLE

US

OBSERVER, THE. 1956. Thu. $.50 newsstand; $22.50/yr. One Whipple Ln., Greenville, RI 02828. TEL 401-949-2700; FAX 401-949-2420. **Owner(s):** Observer Publishing Co., One Whipple Ln., Greenville, RI 02828. TEL 401-949-2700; FAX 401-949-2420; Ed. Laurence Sasso, Jr. photos; bk.rev.; pub. size: tabloid; circ. 10,500(paid).

JAMESTOWN

US

JAMESTOWN PRESS, THE. 1989. Thu. free; $30/yr. voluntary. 42 Narragansett Ave., Jamestown, RI 02835. TEL 401-423-3200; FAX 401-423-1661; E-mail: jtownpress@aol.com. **Owner(s):** Jeff McDonough, 42 Narragansett Ave., Jamestown, RI 02835. TEL 401-423-3200; FAX 401-423-1661; Ed. Jeff McDonough; Pub. Jeff McDonough; adv. contact: Jeff McDonough. photos; bk.rev.; pub. size: tabloid; circ. 5,600(controlled & free).

NEWPORT

US ISSN 1052-6935

NEWPORT MERCURY. 1758. Fri. $.50 newsstand; $45/yr. 101 Malbone Rd., Newport, RI 02840. TEL 401-849-3300. **Owner(s):** E.A. Sherman Publishing Co., 101 Malbone Rd., Newport, RI 02840. TEL 401-849-3300; Ed. David B. Offer; Pub. Albert K. Sherman, Jr.; pub. size: broadsheet; circ. 1,273(paid).

US

NEWPORT THIS WEEK. 1973. Thu. free newsstand; $20/yr. 3rd class; $50/yr. 1st class. 38 Bellevue Ave., Newport, RI 02840. TEL 401-847-7766; FAX 401-846-4974. **Owner(s):** Lisette Prince, P.O. Box 159, Newport, RI 02840. TEL 401-847-7766; Pub. Lisette Prince; adv. contact: Jenny Fontes. photos; pub. size: tabloid; circ. 12,000(free & paid).

NORTH KINGSTOWN

US

STANDARD-TIMES. 1888. Thu. $.75 newsstand; $34/yr. in cy.; $55/yr. out of cy. 13 W. Main St., North Kingstown, RI 02852. TEL 401-294-4576; FAX 401-294-9736. **Owner(s):** Journal Register Co., 50 W. State St.,12th Fl., Trenton, NJ 08608. TEL 609-396-2200; Ed. Rudi Hempe; Pub. Marc Romanow; adv. contact: Laurie Ramaker. bk.rev.; pub. size: broadsheet; circ. 6,500(paid).

PORTSMOUTH

US

SAKONNET TIMES. 1966. Thu. $.60 newsstand; $24/yr. in cy.; $35/yr. out of cy.; $40/yr. elsewhere. 2829 East Main Rd., Portsmouth, RI 02871. TEL 401-683-1000; FAX 401-683-6688. **Owner(s):** Phoenix-Times Publishing Co., One Bradford St., Bristol, RI 02809. TEL 401-253-6000; Ed. Matthew Hayes; Pub. Roswell Bosworth, Jr.; adv. contact: Jane McHenry. pub. size: tabloid; circ. 6,378(paid).

PROVIDENCE

US

EASTSIDE MONTHLY. 1976. m. free; $12/yr. mailed. One Park Row, Providence, RI 02903. TEL 401-521-0023; FAX 401-453-3926. **Owner(s):** Barry Fain, 48 Congdon St., Providence, RI 02906. TEL 401-751-7078; John Howell, 3288 Post Rd., Warwick, RI 02886. TEL 401-732-3100; Ed. Barry Fain. adv. contact: Alice Stanelun. photos; bk.rev.; pub. size: tabloid; circ. 20,000(controlled & free).

WAKEFIELD

US   ISSN 1040-1938

NARRAGANSETT TIMES. 1855. s-w.: Wed. & Fri. $.70 newsstand; $40/yr. in state; $70/yr. out of state. 187 Main St., Wakefield, RI 02879. TEL 401-789-1081; FAX 401-783-5610. **Owner(s):** Journal Register Co., 50 W. State St., 12th Fl., Trenton, NJ 08608. TEL 609-396-2200; Ed. Betty J. Cotter; Pub. F.J. Wilson, III; adv. contact: Laurie Ramaker. photos; pub. size: broadsheet; circ. 10,000(paid).

WARREN

US

BARRINGTON TIMES. 1958. Wed. $.60 newsstand; $24/yr. in cy.; $35/yr. in New England; $40/yr. elsewhere. 139 Main St., Warren, RI 02885. TEL 401-245-6000. **Owner(s):** Phoenix-Times Publishing Co., One Bradford St., Bristol, RI 02809. TEL 401-253-6000; Ed. Patti Hart; Pub. Roswell Bosworth, Jr.; adv. contact: Marcia Bosworth. pub. size: tabloid; circ. 5,300(paid).

US

WARREN TIMES GAZETTE. 1866. Wed. $.60 newsstand; $24/yr. in cy.; $35/yr. out of state; $40/yr. elsewhere. 139 Main St., Warren, RI 02885. TEL 401-245-6002. **Owner(s):** East Bay Newspapers, P.O. Box 90, Bristol, RI 02809. TEL 401-253-6000; Ed. Patti Hart. pub. size: tabloid; circ. 3,094(paid).

WARWICK

US

WARWICK BEACON. 1952. s-w.: Tue. & Thu. $.50 newsstand; $36/yr. 1944 Warwick Ave., Warwick, RI 02889. TEL 401-732-3100; FAX 401-732-3110. **Owner(s):** Beacon Communications Corp., 1944 Warwick Ave., Warwick, RI 02889. TEL 401-732-3100; Ed. John I. Howell; Pub. John I. Howell; adv. contact: Alice Stanelun. pub. size: broadsheet; circ. 12,500(paid).

SOUTH CAROLINA

BAMBERG

US

ADVERTIZER-HERALD, THE. 1967. Thu. $.50 newsstand; $20/yr. in cy.; $22/yr. out of cy. 102 McGee St., Bamberg, SC 29003. TEL 803-245-5204; FAX 803-245-3900. **Owner(s):** UpState Newspapers Inc., Manchester, GA; Ed. Carol B. Barker; Pub. Betty S. Kilgus; adv. contact: Cindy Wise. pub. size: broadsheet; circ. 4,350(paid).

BARNWELL

US

PEOPLE-SENTINEL. 1877. Wed. $.50 newsstand; $20/yr. in cy.; $26/yr. out of cy. 1411 Dunbarton Blvd., Barnwell, SC 29812. TEL 803-259-3501; FAX 803-259-2703. **Owner(s):** Community Newspapers, Inc., P.O. Box 1777, Spartanburg, SC 29304. TEL 803-585-3678; Ed. Sharon Taylor; Pub. Rick Bacon; pub. size: broadsheet; circ. 6,000(paid). **Formerly:** Barnwell People-Sentinel.

BATESBURG-LEESVILLE

US

TWIN-CITY NEWS, THE. 1925. Wed. $.50 newsstand; $15/yr. local; $25/yr. out of state. 114 E. Columbia Ave., Batesburg-Leesville, SC 29006. TEL 803-532-6203; FAX 803-532-6204. **Owner(s):** Bruner Press, P.O. Box 311, Batesburg, SC 29006. TEL 803-532-6203; Pub. Sara F. Bruner; adv.; photos; pub. size: standard; circ. 5,500(paid).

BEAUFORT

US

BEAUFORT SHOPPER. 1972. Wed. free. 3052-C Boundary St., Beaufort, SC 29903. TEL 803-524-3494. **Owner(s):** Beaufort Gazette, P.O. Box 4549, Beaufort, SC 29903. TEL 803-524-3183; adv.; pub. size: tabloid; circ. 17,300(free).

BENNETTSVILLE

US

MARLBORO HERALD-ADVOCATE. 1874. s-w.: Mon. & Thu. $.50 newsstand; $30/yr. local; $35/yr. out of cy. 100 Fayetteville Ave., Bennettsville, SC 29512. TEL 803-479-3815; FAX 803-479-7571. **Owner(s):** Marlboro Publishing Co., Inc., 100 Fayetteville Ave., Bennettsville, SC 29512. TEL 803-479-3815; Ed. William L. Kinney, Jr.; Pub. William L. Kinney, Jr.; adv. contact: Linda Wilson. photos; bk.rev.; pub. size: broadsheet; circ. 6,800(paid).

US

MARLBORO SHOPPER. 1984. Wed. free. 100 Fayetteville Ave., Bennettsville, SC 29512. TEL 803-479-3815; FAX 803-479-7671. **Owner(s):** Marlboro Publishing Co., Inc., P.O. Box 656, Bennettsville, SC 29512. TEL 803-479-3815; Ed. Bill Kinney, Jr. adv.; pub. size: standard; circ. 13,000(free).

BISHOPVILLE

US

LEE COUNTY OBSERVER. 1977. Wed. $.50 newsstand; $14/yr. in cy.; $16/yr. out of cy.; $20/yr. out of state. 218 N. Main St., Bishopville, SC 29010. TEL 803-484-9431; FAX 803-484-5055. **Owner(s):** J.W. Scott, P.O. Box 567, Bishopville, SC 29010. TEL 803-484-9431; Ed. Carpenter King; Pub. Millie Watson; adv. contact: Millie Watson. pub. size: broadsheet; circ. 4,000(paid).

CAMDEN

US

CHRONICLE-INDEPENDENT. 1888. 3/wk.: Mon., Wed., Fri. $.35 newsstand; $46/yr. mailed. 909 W. Dekalb St., Camden, SC 29020 TEL 803-432-6157; FAX 803-432-7609. **Owner(s):** Camden Media Co., P.O. Box 1137, Camden, SC 29020. TEL 803-432-6157; Ed. Martha Bruce; Pub. Glenn Tucker; pub. size: broadsheet; circ. 8,000(paid).

CHARLESTON

US

CHARLESTON CHRONICLE, THE. 1971. Wed. $.50 newsstand; $25/yr. 1109 King St. Charleston, SC 29403. TEL 803-723-2785; FAX 803-577-6099. **Owner(s):** Jim French, P.O. Box 20548, Charleston, SC 29413. TEL 803-723-2785; Ed. Jim French; Pub. Jim French; pub. size: broadsheet; circ. 5,000(paid).

US

COASTAL TIMES. 1983. Wed. $.35 newsstand; $18/yr. local; $20/yr. out of region. 2106 Mt. Pleasant St., Ste. 3, Charleston, SC 29403. TEL 803-723-5318; FAX 803-723-5326. **Owner(s):** Mignon Clyburn, 2106 Mt. Pleasant St., Ste. 1, Charleston, SC 29403. TEL 803-723-5318; Pub. Mignon Clyburn; bk.rev.; pub. size: broadsheet; circ. 5,000(controlled & free).

CHERAW

US   ISSN 0889-0617

CHERAW CHRONICLE, THE. 1885. Thu. $.50 newsstand; $18/yr. 114 Front St., Cheraw, SC 29520 TEL 803-537-5261; FAX 803-537-4518. **Owner(s):** Community Newspapers, Inc., 1233 Boiling Springs Rd., Spartanburg, SC 29304. TEL 803-585-3678; Ed. Margaret E. Jackson; Pub. Margaret E. Jackson; adv.; photos; bk.rev.; pub. size: standard; circ. 5,150(free & paid).

CHESTER

US

CHESTER NEWS & REPORTER. 1869. s-w.: Wed. & Fri. $.50 newsstand; $26/yr. in cy.; $47/yr. in state. 104 York St., Chester, SC 29706. TEL 803-385-3177; FAX 803-581-2518. **Owner(s):** Landmark Community Newspapers, Inc., P.O. Box 549, Shelbyville, KY 40066. TEL 502-633-4334; Ed. L.D. McKeown adv. contact: Fran T. Dodds. photos; pub. size: broadsheet; circ. 7,500(paid).

CLEMSON

US

MESSENGER, THE. 1954. s-w.: Wed. & Sat. $35/yr.; $50/yr. out of state. By Pass 123 Tiger Blvd., Clemson, SC 29631. TEL 803-654-2451; FAX 803-882-2381. **Owner(s):** Edwards Publications, P.O. Box 547, Seneca, SC 29679. TEL 803-882-2375; Pub. Steve Edwards; adv. contact: Jerry Turner. pub. size: standard; circ. 4,000(free & paid).

CLINTON

US

CLINTON CHRONICLE, THE. 1900. Wed. $.50 newsstand; $24/yr. 513 N. Broad St., Clinton, SC 29325. TEL 803-833-1900; FAX 803-833-1902. **Owner(s):** Laurens County Newspapers, Inc., P.O. Box 180, Clinton, SC 29325. TEL 803-833-1900; Ed. Rick Hendricks; Pub. Larry B. Franklin; adv.; pub. size: broadsheet; circ. 5,000(controlled & paid).

CLOVER

US

CLOVER HERALD. 1928. Thu. $.25 newsstand; $14/yr. in cy.; $18/yr. out of cy. P.O. Box 38, Clover, SC 29710. TEL 803-684-9903; FAX 803-628-0300. **Owner(s):** McClatchy Newspapers, P.O. Box 15774, Sacramento, CA 95852. TEL 916-321-1006; adv.; bk.rev.; pub. size: broadsheet; circ. 2,800(paid).

CONWAY

US

HORRY INDEPENDENT. 1980. Thu. $22/yr. 2510 Main St., Conway, SC 29526. TEL 803-248-6882. **Owner(s):** Waccamaw Publishers, P.O. Box 740, Conway, SC 29526. TEL 803-248-6671; Ed. Kathy Ropp; Pub. Steve Robertson; adv.; photos; pub. size: broadsheet; circ. 6,000(free & paid).

DARLINGTON

US

NEWS & PRESS, THE. 1874. Thu. $14/yr. in cy.; $16/yr. in state; $20/yr. out of state. 141 S. Main St., Darlington, SC 29532. TEL 803-393-3811; FAX 803-393-6811. **Owner(s):** Morrell L. Thomas, Jr., P. O. Box 513, Darlington, SC 29532. TEL 803-393-3811; FAX 803-393-6811; Ed. Jim Faile; Pub. Morrell L. Thomas, Jr.; adv. contact: Crystal Eisson. pub. size: standard; circ. 6,000(paid).
   Formerly: Darlington News & Press.

DILLON

US

DILLON HERALD, THE. 1894. s-w.: Tue. & Thu. $.50 newsstand; $24/yr. local; $32.75/yr. elsewhere. 505 Hwy. 301, N., Dillon, SC 29536. TEL 803-774-3311; FAX 803-841-1930. **Owner(s):** Herald Publishing Co., Inc., P.O. Box 1288, Dillon, SC 29536-1288. TEL 803-774-3311; FAX 803-841-1930; Ed. Paul Jones. adv. contact: Johnnie Daniels. photos; pub. size: broadsheet; circ. 6,034(free & paid). **Wire Service(s):** AP.

EASLEY

US

EASLEY PROGRESS. 1902. Wed. $.50 newsstand; $12.50/yr.in cy. 205 Russell St., Easley, SC 29640. TEL 864-855-0355; FAX 864-855-6825. **Owner(s):** Crescent Communications, Inc., P.O. Box 709, Easley, SC 29641. TEL 864-855-0355; Ed. Warren Wise; Pub. Jerry D. Vickery; adv. contact: Jane Jones. photos; bk.rev.; pub. size: broadsheet; circ. 9,000(controlled & paid).

FORT MILL

US

FORT MILL TIMES. 1892. Wed. $18/yr. 116 Main St., Fort Mill, SC 29715. TEL 803-547-2353; FAX 803-547-2321. **Owner(s):** Mantle Publications, Inc., P.O. Box 250, Fort Mill, SC 29716. TEL 803-547-2353; Ed. Jerry McGuire; Pub. John E. Mantle; adv. contact: Carol Mantle. pub. size: broadsheet; circ. 7,000(paid).

FOUNTAIN INN

US   ISSN 0747-1165

TRIBUNE-TIMES. 1909. Wed. $.25 newsstand; $15/yr. in cy. 1314 N. Main St., Fountain Inn, SC 29644. TEL 864-967-9580; FAX 864-967-9585. **Owner(s):** Multimedia, Inc., 305 S. Main St., Greenville, SC 29601: TEL 864-298-4000; Ed. Ernie Castner; Pub. Sudie Buchanan; adv. contact: Laura G. Campbell. photos; bk.rev.; pub. size: broadsheet; circ. 7,300(paid).

GAFFNEY

US

GAFFNEY LEDGER, THE. 1894. 3/wk.: Mon., Wed., Fri. $.50 newsstand; $33/yr. in cy.; $55/yr. out of cy. 1604 Baker Blvd., Gaffney, SC 29342. TEL 864-489-1131; FAX 864-487-7667. **Owner(s):** Louis Sossamon, The Gaffney Ledger, Inc., P.O. Box 670, Gaffney, SC 29342. TEL 864-489-1131; FAX 864-487-7667; Cody Sossamon, The Gaffney Ledger, Inc., P.O. Box 670, Gaffney, SC 29342. TEL 864-489-1131; FAX 864-487-7667; Ed. Klonie Jordan; Pub. Louis Sossamon; adv. contact: Robert Martin. photos; bk.rev.; pub. size: standard; circ. 20,242(paid). **Wire Service(s):** AP.

GEORGETOWN

US

GEORGETOWN TIMES, THE. 1797. 3/wk.: Tue., Thu., Sat. $.25 newsstand; $24/yr. in cy. 615 Front St., Georgetown, SC 29440. TEL 803-546-4148; FAX 803-546-2395. **Owner(s):** Georgetown Communications, Inc., 615 Front St., Georgetown, SC 29440. TEL 803-546-4148; Ed. Jesse Tullos; Pub. Cathy Wilkerson; adv.; photos; pub. size: broadsheet; circ. 6,700(paid). **Wire Service(s):** AP.

GREER

US

GREER CITIZEN, THE. 1918. Wed. $.50 newsstand; $12-$24/yr. 105 Victoria, Greer, SC 29651. TEL 864-877-2076; FAX 864-877-3563. **Owner(s):** W.M. Burch, 105 Victoria, Greer, SC 29651. TEL 864-877-2076; Leland E. Burch, 105 Victoria, Greer, SC 29651. TEL 864-877-2076; Ed. Leland E. Burch; Pub. Walter M. Burch; adv.; photos; pub. size: standard; circ. 11,350(paid).

HARTSVILLE

US

DARCO NEWS & BUYERS GUIDE. Wed. free. 416 W. California Ave., Hartsville, SC 29550-4524. TEL 803-667-9656. **Owner(s):** News-Journal, Inc., 146 W. Evans St., Florence, SC 29501. TEL 803-667-9656; Pub. Jim Harris; adv. contact: Carl Campbell. pub. size: broadsheet; circ. 17,333(controlled & free).

US

HARTSVILLE MESSENGER, THE. 1893. s-w.: Mon. & Wed. $.25 newsstand; $20/yr. in cy.; $30/yr. out of cy. 207 E. Carolina Ave., Hartsville, SC 29550. TEL 803-332-6545; FAX 803-332-1341. **Owner(s):** H.D. Osteen, Jr., 207 E. Carolina St., Hartsville, SC 29550; Ed. Dennie Truesdale; Pub. H.D. Osteen, Jr.; adv. contact: Myrtleen Tyner. pub. size: broadsheet; circ. 5,000(paid).

HEMINGWAY

US

WEEKLY OBSERVER, THE. 1973. Thu. $12/yr.; $10/yr. senior citizens. 108 N. Main St., Hemingway, SC 29554. TEL 803-558-3323; FAX 803-558-9601. **Owner(s):** Community Newspapers, Inc., P.O. Box 792, Athens, GA 30601. TEL 706-548-0010; FAX 706-548-0808; Ed. Russ Pace; Pub. Robert Ryder; adv.; photos; pub. size: broadsheet; circ. 2,450(paid).

HOLLY HILL

US

OBSERVER, THE. 1972. Wed. $.25 newsstand; $15/yr. in Orangeburg cy.; $17 out of cy.; $20 out of state. 605 Gardner Blvd., Holly Hill, SC 29059-0715. TEL 803-496-3242; FAX 803-496-3242. **Owner(s):** William Magill Owens, St. George, SC 29477. TEL 803-563-3121; Pub. William M. Owens; adv.; photos; pub. size: broadsheet; circ. 3,000(paid).
   Formerly: Holly Hill Observer, The.

KINGSTREE

US

NEWS, THE. 0972. Wed. $.50 newsstand; $15/yr. in cy.; $18/yr. out of cy.; $24/yr. out of state. 107 E. Mill St., Kingstree, SC 29556-0574. TEL 803-354-7454; FAX 803-354-6530. **Owner(s):** Evening Post Publishing Co., 134 Columbus St., Charleston, SC 29403. TEL 803-577-7111; Pub. Vickey Boyd; adv.; pub. size: standard; circ. 5,200(paid).
   Formerly: Kingstree News.

LADSON

US

GOOSE CREEK GAZETTE. 1978. Wed. $.25 newsstand; $12/yr. mailed in US. 549B College Park Rd., Ladson, SC 29456. TEL 803-572-0511; FAX 803-572-0312. **Owner(s):** William C. Collins, P.O. Box 715, Summerville, SC 29484. TEL 803-572-0511; John Veronelson, P.O. Box 304, Goose Creek, SC 29445. TEL 803-572-0511; Ed. John Vernelson; Pub. John Vernelson; adv. contact: William C. Collins. photos; pub. size: broadsheet; circ. 7,350(controlled & paid).

LANCASTER

US   ISSN 0745-7421

LANCASTER NEWS. 1852. 3/wk.: Wed., Fri., Sun. $.50 newsstand; $42/yr. 701 N. White St., Lancaster, SC 29720. TEL 803-283-1133. **Owner(s):** Landmark Communications, Inc., 701 N. White St., Lancaster, SC 29720. TEL 803-283-1133; Ed. Mike Foley; Pub. David L. Ernest; adv. contact: Susan Rowell. pub. size: standard; circ. 13,000(paid). **Wire Service(s):** AP.

LANDRUM

US

NEWS LEADER, THE. 1955. Wed. $.35 newsstand; $15/yr. local. 146 Trade Ave., Landrum, SC 29356. TEL 864-457-3337; FAX 864-472-6900. **Owner(s):** Trib Publications, Inc., P.O. Box 426, Manchester, GA 31816; Ed. John F. Lawrence; Pub. John F. Lawrence; adv. contact: Larry Hamrick. pub. size: broadsheet; circ. 4,600(paid).

LAURENS

US

LAURENS COUNTY ADVERTISER. 1885. 3/wk.: Wed., Fri., Sun. $.50 newsstand; $29/yr. in cy.; $45/yr. in state; $55/yr. out of state. 226 W. Laurens, Laurens, SC 29360. TEL 864-984-2586; FAX 864-984-4039. **Owner(s):** W.J. Brown, P.O. Box 490, Laurens, SC 29360. TEL 864-984-2586; FAX 864-984-4039; Ed. Rich Browne; Pub. W.J. Brown; adv. contact: James D. Brown. pub. size: broadsheet; circ. 8,100(paid).

LEXINGTON

US

DISPATCH-NEWS, THE. 1870. Wed. $.50 newsstand; $20/yr. in state; $26/yr. out of state. 115 E. Main St., Lexington, SC 29072. TEL 803-359-3195; FAX 803-359-1378. **Owner(s):** Community Newspapers, Inc., P.O. Box 792, Athens, GA 30603. TEL 800-226-0692; FAX 706-548-0808; Ed. Tim Chamberlin; Pub. Rick Bacon; adv. contact: Linda Melton. photos; pub. size: broadsheet; circ. 9,300(paid).

US

LAKE EDITION, THE. 1993. Fri. $.50 newsstand; $14/yr. P.O. Box 502, Lexington, SC 29071. TEL 803-730-8383; FAX 803-892-5757. **Owner(s):** Jackie Black, P.O. Box 1015, Irmo, SC 29063. TEL 803-781-1210; FAX 803-892-5757; Sam Bruce, P.O. Box 502, Lexington, SC 29071. TEL 803-551-1551; FAX 803-892-5757; Ed. Jackie Black; Pub. Jackie Black; adv. contact: R.K. King. photos; bk.rev.; pub. size: standard; circ. 7,350(free & paid). **Formerly:** Irmo Independent News.

LORIS

US

LORIS TIMES. 1991. Tue. $.25 newsstand; $11/yr. in cy.; $15/yr. out of cy.; $23/yr. out of state. 4111 Walnut St., Loris, SC 29569. TEL 803-756-7224; FAX 803-756-7812. **Owner(s):** Pauline L. Lowman, P.O. Box 725, North Myrtle Beach, SC 29597. TEL 803-249-3525; FAX 803-249-7012; Ed. Polly Lowman; Pub. Pauline L. Lowman; adv.; photos; bk.rev.; pub. size: standard; circ. 4,500(paid).

MARION

US

MARION STAR & MULLINS ENTERPRISE. Wed. $18/yr. in cy.; $28/yr. out of cy. 211 Railroad Ave., Marion, SC 29571. TEL 803-423-2050; FAX 803-423-2542. **Owner(s):** Community Newspapers, Inc., P.O. Box 792, Athens, SC 30603. TEL 800-226-0692; FAX 706-548-0808; Ed. Tim Chamberlin; Pub. Robert Rider; pub. size: broadsheet; circ. 12,000(paid). **Formerly:** Marion Star.

MONCKS CORNER

US

BERKELEY INDEPENDENT. 1987. Wed. $.50 newsstand; $18/yr. 320 E. Main St., Moncks Corner, SC 29461. TEL 803-761-6397; FAX 803-899-6996. **Owner(s):** Berkeley Independent, P.O. Box 427, Moncks Corner, SC 29461. TEL 803-761-6397; FAX 803-899-6996; Manuel Cohen, P.O. Box 427, Moncks Corner, SC 29461. TEL 803-761-6397; FAX 803-899-6996; Estate of Ted Robison, P.O. Box 427, Moncks Corner, SC 29461. TEL 803-761-6397 FAX 803-899-6996; Allen & Tony Morris, P.O. Box 427, Moncks Corner, SC 29461. TEL 803-761-6397; FAX 803-899-6996 Pub. H. Allen Morris; adv. contact: Deidre Lynch photos; bk.rev.; pub. size: broadsheet; circ 11,200(paid).

MT. PLEASANT

US

JOURNAL, THE. 1968. bi-w.: Thu. $.25 newsstand; $7/yr. 1558 Ben Sawyer Blvd., Ste. B, Mt. Pleasant, SC 29464-4538. TEL 803-849-1778; FAX 803-849-0214. **Owner(s):** Community Press, Inc., 1558 Ben Sawyer Blvd., Ste. B, Mt. Pleasant, SC 29464-4538. TEL 803-849-1778; FAX 803-849-0214; Ed. Charles P. Diggle; Pub. Charles P. Diggle; adv.; bk.rev.; pub. size: broadsheet; circ. 3,200(free & paid).

US

MOULTRIE NEWS, THE. 1968. bi-w.: Wed. $.25 newsstand; $7/yr. 1558 Ben Sawyer Blvd., Ste. B, Mt. Pleasant, SC 29464-4538. TEL 803-849-1779; FAX 803-849-0214. **Owner(s):** Community Press, Inc., 1558 Ben Sawyer Blvd., Ste. B, Mt. Pleasant, SC 29464-4538. TEL 803-849-1778; FAX 803-849-0214; Ed. Charles P. Diggle; Pub. Charles P. Diggle; adv.; bk.rev.; pub. size: broadsheet; circ. 16,000(free & paid).

MYRTLE BEACH

US

ALTERNATIVES. 1987. fortn. $21.95/yr. Drawer 2485, Myrtle Beach, SC 29578. TEL 803-444-5556; FAX 803-444-5558. **Owner(s):** Alternative Publications, Ltd., Drawer 2485, Myrtle Beach, SC 29578. TEL 803-444-5556; FAX 803-444-5558; Ed. Ray Bartlett; Pub. William E. Darry; pub. size: standard; circ. 20,000(paid).

NEWBERRY

US

NEWBERRY OBSERVER, THE. 1865. 3/wk.: Mon., Wed., Fri. $.35 newsstand; $22/yr. mailed. 1716 Main St., Newberry, SC 29108. TEL 803-276-0625; FAX 803-276-1517. **Owner(s):** Knight-Ridder, Inc., One Herald Plz., Miami, FL 33132. TEL 305-376-3800; Ed. Vic MacDonald; Pub. Frank Mott; adv. contact: Debbie Waldrop. photos; pub. size: standard; circ. 6,543(paid).

NORTH CHARLESTON

US

HANAHAN NEWS. 1959. Wed. $.25 newsstand; $12/yr. mailed in US. 1924 E. Montaque Ave., North Charleston, SC 29405. TEL 803-747-5773; FAX 803-744-5505. **Owner(s):** Carl Meynardie, P.O. Box 60580, Charleston, SC 29419. TEL 803-747-5773; Ed. Carl Meynardie; Pub. Carl Meynardie; adv. contact: Paul Meynardie. pub. size: tabloid; circ. 20,500(paid).

NORTH MYRTLE BEACH

US

NORTH MYRTLE BEACH TIMES. 1971. Thu. $.50 newsstand; $25/yr. local; $30/yr. out of cy.; $40/yr. out of state. 203 N. Kings Hwy., North Myrtle Beach, SC 29582. TEL 803-249-3525; FAX 803-249-7012. **Owner(s):** Pauline L. Lowman, P.O. Box 725, N. Myrtle Beach, SC 29597. TEL 803-249-3525; FAX 803-249-7012; Ed. Pauline L. Lowman; Pub. Pauline L. Lowman; adv. contact: Diane Valas. bk.rev.; pub. size: standard; circ. 20,000(paid).

PAGELAND

US   ISSN 1063-8415

PAGELAND PROGRESSIVE-JOURNAL, THE. 1910. Tue. $.30 newsstand; $10/yr. in cy.; $15/yr. out of cy. Hwy. 9 E., Pageland, SC 29728. TEL 803-672-2358; FAX 803-672-5593. **Owner(s):** Brian & Jane Hough, 937 E. Maynard St., Pageland, SC 29728. TEL 803-672-2367; Ed. Brian Hough; Pub. Brian Hough; adv. contact: Jane Hough. photos; pub. size: broadsheet; circ. 4,000(paid).

PICKENS

US

PICKENS SENTINEL. 1872. Wed. $.50 newsstand; $12/yr. in cy.; $20/yr. out of cy. 102 Garvin St., Pickens, SC 29671. TEL 803-878-2453; FAX 803-878-2454. **Owner(s):** Pickens County Publishing, Inc., P.O. Box 95, Pickens, SC 29671. TEL 803-878-2453; FAX 803-878-2454; Pub. Jerry Alexander; adv.; photos pub. size: broadsheet; circ. 7,000(paid).

RIDGELAND

US   ISSN 1072-3986

JASPER COUNTY SUN. 1993. Wed. $.35 newsstand; $16.50/yr. in cy.; $25/yr. out of cy. 200 W. Main St., Ridgeland, SC 29936. TEL 803-726-6161; FAX 803-726-8661. **Owner(s):** Larry & Renee Miller, P.O. Box 788, Ridgeland, SC 29936. TEL 803-726-6161; FAX 803-726-8661; Ed. Larry Miller. adv. contact: Renee Miller. photos; bk.rev.; pub. size: broadsheet; circ. 3,000(paid).

SALUDA

US

SALUDA STANDARD SENTINEL. 1946. Thu. $.25 newsstand; $10/yr. in cy.; $13/yr. out of cy. P.O. Box 676, Saluda, SC 29138. TEL 803-445-2527; FAX 803-445-8679. **Owner(s):** Ralph B. Shealy, P.O. Box 676, Saluda, SC 29138. TEL 803-445-2527; FAX 803-445-8679; Ed. Ralph Shealy; Pub. Ralph Shealy; adv.; photos; bk.rev.; pub. size: standard; circ. 4,300(paid).

SENECA

US

JOURNAL TRIBUNE. s-w.: Wed. & Sat. $.50 newsstand; $34.95/yr. in cy.; $42/yr. out of cy. 210 W. North First St., Seneca, SC 29678. TEL 864-882-2375; FAX 864-882-0903. **Owner(s):** Edwards Publications, 210 W. North First St., Seneca, SC 29678. TEL 864-882-3272; FAX 864-882-0903; Ed. Dan Brannan; Pub. Steve Edwards; pub. size: broadsheet; circ. 2,000(paid).
   Formerly: Seneca Journal & Tribune.

SPARTANBURG

US

▼**YOUR PAPER.** 1994. Tue. free at newsstand only. 1855 E. Main St., Ste. 100, Spartanburg, SC 29307. TEL 803-573-8505; FAX 803-573-6605. **Owner(s):** Your Paper, Inc., P.O. Box 2524, Spartanburg, SC 29302. TEL 803-573-8505; Ed. Jeff Hayes. adv.; photos; pub. size: tabloid; circ. 12,000(free).

ST. GEORGE

US

DORCHESTER EAGLE RECORD. 1899. Thu. $.35 newsstand; $14/yr. in cy.; $16/yr. out of cy. 5549 Memorial Blvd., St. George, SC 29477. TEL 803-563-3121. **Owner(s):** William Magill Owens, 5549 Memorial Blvd., St. George, SC 29477. TEL 803-563-3121; Ed. William M. Owens; Pub. William M. Owens; adv.; photos; pub. size: broadsheet; circ. 3,100(paid).

SUMMERVILLE

US

SUMMERVILLE JOURNAL SCENE. 1972. s-w.: Wed. & Fri. $.50 newsstand; $25/yr. in state; $40/yr. out of state. 104 E. Doty Ave., Summerville, SC 29483. TEL 803-873-9424. **Owner(s):** Journal Co., P.O. Box 715, Summerville, SC 29484. TEL 803-873-9424; Ed. William C. Collins; Pub. William C. Collins; adv. contact: Shirley Hunnicutt. photos; pub. size: broadsheet; circ. 9,000(paid).

WALTERBORO

US

PRESS & STANDARD, THE. 1877. s-w.: Tue. & Fri. $.50 newsstand; $32/yr. in cy.; $44/yr. out of cy. 113 E. Washington St., Walterboro, SC 29488-3915. TEL 803-549-2586; FAX 803-549-2446. **Owner(s):** Smith Newspapers, Inc., P.O. Box 27, Fort Payne, AL 35967. TEL 205-845-5510; Ed. Taylor M. Smith; Pub. Taylor M. Smith; adv. contact: Anne Padget. adv.: $6/SAU. pub. size: broadsheet; circ. 5,750(paid).

WILLIAMSTON

US

JOURNAL, THE. 1955. Wed. $.50 newsstand; $15/yr. in cy.; $17.50/yr. out of cy.; $22/yr. out of state. 106 W. Main St., Williamston, SC 29697. TEL 864-847-7361; FAX 864-847-9879. **Owner(s):** William C. Meade, P.O. Box 369, Williamston, SC 29697. TEL 864-847-7361; Ed. Sharon Crout; Pub. David Meade; adv. contact: David Meade. photos; pub. size: broadsheet; circ. 5,600(paid).

WINNSBORO

US

HERALD-INDEPENDENT, THE. 1844. Thu. $.50 newsstand; $15/yr. in cy.; $25/yr. out of state. 127 N. Congress St., Winnsboro, SC 29180. TEL 803-635-4016; FAX 803-635-2948. **Owner(s):** Community Newspapers, Inc., P.O. Box 792, Athens, GA 30603. TEL 800-226-0692; FAX 706-548-0808; Pub. Lamon Warrock; adv. contact: Mary Douglas. photos; bk.rev.; pub. size: broadsheet; circ. 4,800(free & paid). **Wire Service(s):** AP.

YORK

US

YORKVILLE ENQUIRER. 1855. Thu. $.25 newsstand; $14/yr. in cy.; $18/yr. out of cy. 20 W. Liberty St., York, SC 29745. TEL 803-684-9903; FAX 803-628-0300. **Owner(s):** McClatchy Newspapers, 2100 Q St., Sacramento, CA 95816. TEL 916-321-1000; Ed. Gene Graham; Pub. Ray Jimison; adv.; bk.rev.; pub. size: standard; circ. 3,200(paid).

SOUTH DAKOTA

BELLE FOURCHE

US

BELLE FOURCHE POST. 1902. s-w.: Wed. & Sat. $.75 newsstand; $33.92/yr. local; $38. 48/yr. mailed. 1004 Fifth Ave., Belle Fourche, SD 57717. TEL 605-892-2528; FAX 605-892-2529. **Owner(s):** Dickson Media, Inc., Charlottesville, VA; Ed. Tim Velder; Pub. Tim Velder; adv. contact: Chrisann Mateer. pub. size: broadsheet; circ. 3,000(paid).

BUFFALO

US

NATION'S CENTER NEWS. 1979. Wed. $.55 newsstand; $26/yr. in state; $25/yr. out of state. 507 W. Fifth St., Buffalo, SD 57720. TEL 605-375-3228; FAX 605-375-3318. **Owner(s):** Linda & Walter Stephens, 507 W. Fifth St., Buffalo, SD 57720. TEL 605-375-3228; Ed. Walter Stephens; Pub. Linda Stephens; adv.; pub. size: broadsheet; circ. 3,200(controlled & paid).

CANISTOTA

US

CANISTOTA CLIPPER. 1902. Thu. $.50 newsstand; $21.20/yr. in state; $25/yr. out of state. P.O. Box 128, Canistota, SD 57012. TEL 605-296-3181; FAX 605-296-3289. **Owner(s):** Wendell Anderson, P.O. Box 128, Canistota, SD 57012. TEL 605-296-3181; Ed. Matt Anderson; Pub. Matt Anderson; pub. size: broadsheet; circ. 775(paid).

US

HARTFORD AREA NEWS. 1902. Thu. $.50 newsstand; $16.96/yr. in cy.; $22/yr. out of state. P.O. Box 128, Canistota, SD 57012. TEL 605-296-3181; FAX 605-296-3289. **Owner(s):** Wendell Anderson, P.O. Box 128, Canistota, SD 57012. TEL 605-296-3181; Ed. Matt Anderson; Pub. Matt Anderson; adv.; pub. size: broadsheet; circ. 640(paid).

US

HUMBOLT JOURNAL. 1902. Thu. $16/yr. in cy. Main St., Canistota, SD 57012. TEL 605-296-3181; FAX 605-296-3289. **Owner(s):** Wendell Anderson, P.O. Box 128, Canistota, SD 57012. TEL 605-396-3181; Ed. Wendell Anderson; Pub. Matt Anderson; adv.; photos; pub. size: broadsheet; circ. 600(paid).

US

MONTROSE HERALD. Thu. $.50 newsstand; $16/yr. in state; $22/yr. out of state. P.O. Box 128, Canistota, SD 57012. TEL 605-296-3181; FAX 605-296-3289. **Owner(s):** Wendell Anderson, P.O. Box 128, Canistota, SD 57012. TEL 605-296-3181; Ed. Wendell Anderson; Pub. Wendell Anderson; adv.; pub. size: broadsheet; circ. 560(paid).

DEADWOOD

US

LAWRENCE COUNTY CENTENNIAL. 1973. s-w.: Wed. & Sat. $.75 newsstand; $32/yr. 68 Sherman St., Deadwood, SD 57732. TEL 605-578-3305; FAX 605-578-2023. **Owner(s):** Dickson Media, Inc., 2568 Ivy Rd., Ste. D, Charlottesville, VA 22903. TEL 804-971-8350; Ed. Julie Bender; Pub. Bill Derby; adv. contact: Barb Shepardson. pub. size: broadsheet; circ. 2,675(paid). **Wire Service(s):** UPI.

DELL RAPIDS

US

BALTIC BEACON. 1889. Wed. $.50 newsstand; $24/yr. local; $29/yr. elsewhere. 414 Fourth St., Dell Rapids, SD 57022. TEL 605-428-5441; FAX 605-428-5992. **Owner(s):** Prairie Publishing, Inc., P.O. Box 99, Dell Rapids, SD 57022. TEL 605-428-5441; Ed. Shaun Marko. adv. contact: James Wilber. pub. size: tabloid; circ. 500(paid).

US

BRANDON VALLEY CHALLENGER. 1985. Wed. $.50 newsstand; $24/yr. in cy.; $29/yr. out of cy. 414 Fourth St., Dell Rapids, SD 57022. TEL 605-428-5441; FAX 605-428-5992. **Owner(s):** James Wilber, 414 Fourth St., Dell Rapids, SD 57022. TEL 605-428-5441; Ed. Alica Thiele; Pub. Jim Wilber; adv.; photos; pub. size: tabloid; circ. 1,000(paid).

US

DELL RAPIDS TRIBUNE. 1985. Wed. $.50 newsstand; $24/yr. in cy.; $29/yr. out of cy. mailed. 414 Fourth St., Dell Rapids, SD 57022. TEL 605-428-5441; FAX 605-428-5992. **Owner(s):** Jaimes Wilber, 414 Fourth St., Dell Rapids, SD 57022. TEL 605-428-5441; Ed. Shaun Marko; Pub. James Wilber; adv.; photos; pub. size: tabloid; circ. 3,119(free & paid).

EUREKA

US

NORTHWEST BLADE, THE. 1884. Wed. $.50 newsstand; $21/yr. local; $25/yr. elsewhere. P.O. Box 797, Eureka, SD 57437-0797. TEL 605-284-2631; FAX 605-284-2501. **Owner(s):** Arlo & Bonnie Mehlhaff, P.O. Box 797, Eureka, SD 57437. TEL 605-284-2631; Ed. Bonnie Mehlhaff; Pub. Arlo Mehlhaff; adv. contact: Arlo Mehlhaff. pub. size: broadsheet; circ. 1,750(paid).

FLANDREAU

US

MOODY COUNTY ENTERPRISE. 1885. Wed. $.50 newsstand; $21/yr. in area; $27/yr. elsewhere. 107 Second St., Flandreau, SD 57028. TEL 605-997-3725; FAX 605-997-3194. **Owner(s):** Chuck Cecil, 1209 Second St., Brookings, SD 57006. TEL 605-692-2329; Ed. C.F. Cecil; Pub. C.F. Cecil; adv. contact: Roger Janssen. photos; bk.rev.; pub. size: broadsheet; circ. 3,600(paid).

HILL CITY

US

PENNINGTON COUNTY PREVAILER-NEWS. 1972. Wed. $.40 newsstand; $18/yr. in state; $24/yr. out of state. 114 Main St., Ste. 1, Hill City, SD 57745-0266. TEL 605-574-2538. **Owner(s):** Custer Chronicle, Custer, SD; Ed. Don Gerken. adv.; photos; pub. size: standard; circ. 1,600(free & paid).

IPSWICH

US

IPSWICH TRIBUNE. Wed. $20/yr. in cy.; $23/yr. in state; $25/yr. out of state. 103 Main St., Ipswich, SD 57451-0007. **Owner(s):** Dwain Gibson, 103 Main St., Ipswirch, SD 57451-0007. TEL 605-426-6471; Ed. Tena Gibson; Pub. Dwain Gibson; adv.; pub. size: broadsheet; circ. 1,105(paid).

US

ROSCOE HOSMER INDEPENDENT. Wed. $20/yr. in cy.; $23/yr. in state; $25/yr. out of state. 103 Main St., Ipswich, SD 57451-0007. TEL 605-426-6471; FAX 605-426-6471. **Owner(s):** Gibson Publishing, 103 Main St., Ipswich, SD 57451-0007. TEL 605-426-6471; Ed. Tena Gibson; Pub. Dwain Gibson; adv.; pub. size: broadsheet; circ. 700(paid).

MENNO

US

HUTCHINSON HERALD. 1882. Wed. $.40 newsstand; $20/yr. in state; $22/yr. out of state. 154 E. Poplar St., Menno, SD 57045-0537. TEL 605-387-5158; FAX 605-387-5148. **Owner(s):** William J. Headley, P.O. Box 537, Menno, SD 57045. TEL 605-387-5270; Ed. William J. Headley; Pub. William J. Headley; adv.; photos; bk.rev.; pub. size: standard; circ. 1,145(free & paid).

MILBANK

US

GRANT COUNTY REVIEW. 1880. Wed. $.50 newsstand; $23/yr. in cy.; $28/out of cy. 225 S. Main St., Milbank, SD 57252-0390. TEL 605-432-4516. **Owner(s):** Phyllis Justice, P.O. Box 390, Milbank, SD 57252. TEL 605-432-4516; Ed. Phyllis Justice; Pub. Phyllis Justice; adv. contact: Phyllis Justice. pub. size: broadsheet; circ. 4,450(paid).
Formerly: Milbank Grant County Review.

NEWELL

US

BUTTE COUNTY VALLEY IRRIGATOR. 1900. Wed. $22/yr. in cy.; $26/yr. out of cy.; $30/yr. out of state. 119 Third St., Newell, SD 57760. TEL 605-456-2585; FAX 605-456-2585. **Owner(s):** Dickson Media, Inc., 2568 Ivy Rd., Ste. D, Charlottesville, VA 22903. TEL 804-971-8350; Ed. Tim Veldor; Pub. Tim Veldor; adv. contact: Austin Fost. pub. size: broadsheet; circ. 1,400(free). **Wire Service(s):** UP.

PIERRE

US

PIERRE TIMES, THE. 1875. Thu. $22/yr. 333 W. Dakota, P.O. Box 878, Pierre, SD 57501. TEL 605-224-7301; FAX 605-224-9210. **Owner(s):** Hipple Printing Co., Inc., P.O. Box 878, Pierre, SD 57501. TEL 605-224-7301; FAX 605-225-9210 Ed. Dana Hess; Pub. Terry Hipple; adv.; photos; pub. size: broadsheet; circ. 1,600(paid). **Wire Service(s):** AP.

REDFIELD

US

REDFIELD PRESS. 1898. Wed. $25/yr. in trade area; $32/yr. out of area. 16 E. Seventh Ave., Redfield, SD 57469. TEL 605-472-0822; FAX 605-472-3534. **Owner(s):** Walter Mundstock, Redfield Press, P.O. Box 440, Redfield, SD 57469. TEL 605-692-6826; Ed. Ling Leeds; Pub. Walter Mundstock; adv. contact: Walter Mundstock. bk.rev.; pub. size: broadsheet; circ. 3,662(paid).

SELBY

US

SELBY RECORD. 1888. Wed. $.50 newsstand; $20/yr. local; $26.50/yr. elsewhere. P.O. Box 421, Selby, SD 57472-0421. TEL 605-649-7866; FAX 605-649-7054. **Owner(s):** Leah & Allan Burke, P.O. Box 38, Linton, ND 58552; Ed. LeAnda Staebner; Pub. Allan & Leah Burke; adv.; pub. size: tabloid; circ. 1,400(free & paid).

SISSETON

US

SISSETON COURIER. 1892. Wed. $27-$32/yr. 117 E. Oak, Sisseton, SD 57262. TEL 605-698-7642; FAX 605-698-3641. **Owner(s):** Harley Deutsch, Eeutsch Courier, Inc., 117 E. Oak, Sisseton, SD 57262. TEL 605-698-7642; Ed. Harley Deutsch; Pub. Harley Deutsch; pub. size: broadsheet; circ. 3,941(paid).

STURGIS

US

BLACK HILLS PRESS. 1900. Sat. $.75 newsstand; $32/yr. 1238 Main, Sturgis, SD 57785. TEL 605-347-2503. **Owner(s):** Dickson Media, Inc., Charlottesville, VA; Ed. Doreen Creed. pub. size: broadsheet; circ. 4,500(paid).

US

MEADE COUNTY TIMES-TRIBUNE. 1930. Wed. $.75 newsstand; $32/yr. in cy.; $37/yr. out of cy.; $44/yr. out of state. 1238 Main St., Sturgis, SD 57785. TEL 605-347-2503; FAX 605-347-2321. **Owner(s):** Dickson Media, Inc., 2568 Ivy Rd., Ste. D, Charlottesville, VA 22903. TEL 804-971-8350; Ed. Jerry Steinley; Pub. Bill Derby; adv.; pub. size: broadsheet; circ. 3,800(free & paid).

WEBSTER

US

WEBSTER REPORTER & FARMER. 1881. Mon. $.75 newsstand; $22/yr. in area; $28/yr. out of area. 624 Main St., Webster, SD 57274-0030. TEL 605-345-3356; FAX 605-345-3739. **Owner(s):** Larry & Janet Ingalls, 450 W. Eighth Ave., P.O. Box 30, Webster, SD. TEL 605-345-3356; FAX 605-345-3739; Ed. Larry Ingalls. adv. contact: John Sahr. photos; pub. size: broadsheet; circ. 3,837(paid).

WESSINGTON SPRINGS

US

DAKATAN, THE. 1975. Tue. $25/yr. in state; $35/yr. out of state. 113 E. Main, Wessington Springs, SD 57382. TEL 605-539-1281; FAX 605-539-9315. **Owner(s):** J. Craig Wenzel, P.O. Box 305, Wessington Springs, SD 57382. TEL 605-539-1281; FAX 605-539-9315; Dennis P. Wenzel, P.O. Box T, Wessington Springs, SD 57382. TEL 605-539-1281; FAX 605-539-9315; Ed. J. Craig Wenzel. adv.; photos; pub. size: broadsheet; circ. 1,800(paid).

WINNER

US

ADVOCATE. 1910. Wed. $31.75/yr. local; $40.23/yr. elsewhere. 125 W. Third St., Winner, SD 57580. TEL 605-842-1481; FAX 605-842-1979. **Owner(s):** Bill Sniffin, 28 Boulder Loop, Lander, WY 82520; Ed. Dan Bechtold; Pub. Mylan Schroeder; adv. contact: Mylan Schroeder. pub. size: broadsheet; circ. 4,000(paid).
Formerly: Winner Advocate.

TENNESSEE

ALAMO

US

CROCKETT TIMES, THE. 1873. Wed. $15/yr. in cy.; $20/yr. out of cy. 128 W. Main, Alamo, TN 38001. TEL 901-696-4558 FAX 901-696-4550. **Owner(s):** Robert B. Sims, 128 W. Main, Alamo, TX 38001; pub. size: broadsheet; circ. 4,200(paid).

BLOUNTVILLE

US

SULLIVAN COUNTY NEWS. 1944. Thu. $.50 newsstand; $17/yr. 3200 Hwy. 126, Blountville, TN 37617. TEL 423-323-5700; FAX 423-323-1681. **Owner(s):** T.E. Worrell, Sr., c/o Bristol Newspapers, Bristol, VA 24201. TEL 703-669-2181; Ed. David McGee. adv. contact: Wayne Richardson. photos; bk.rev.; pub. size: broadsheet; circ. 4,800(paid).

BOLIVAR

US

BOLIVAR BULLETIN-TIMES. 1865. Wed. $.75 newsstand; $23/yr. in cy.; $28/yr. in state; $41/yr. out of state. 410 W. Market, Bolivar, TN 38008. TEL 901-658-3691; FAX 901-658-7222. **Owner(s):** Delphos Newspapers, 405 N. Main, Delphos, OH 45833. TEL 419-692-5050; Ed. Anne Ingle. Pub. Richard Fry; adv. contact: Rita Blackard. pub. size: broadsheet; circ. 6,200(paid).

BRENTWOOD

US

BRENTWOOD JOURNAL. 1813. Thu. $.50 newsstand; $18/yr. carrier; $25/yr. mailed. 750 Old Hickory Blvd., Bldg. 2, Ste. 150, Brentwood, TN 37027. TEL 615-373-0445; FAX 615-377-3130. **Owner(s):** Morris Communications, P.O. Box 8167, Savannah, GA 31412; Ed. Lauren Lexa; Pub. Betty Brooks. adv. contact: Betty Brooks. photos; pub. size: broadsheet; circ. 11,000(free & paid). **Wire Service(s):** AP.
Formerly: Review Appeal.

BROWNSVILLE

US   ISSN 0893-3839

BROWNSVILLE STATES-GRAPHIC. 1867. Thu. $.50 newsstand; $16.50/yr. in cy.; $20.50/yr. in state; $28.50/yr. out of state. 42 S. Washington, Brownsville, TN 38012. TEL 901-772-1172. **Owner(s):** Wireless Group, Inc., 42 S. Washington, P.O. Box 198, Brownsville, TN 38012. TEL 901-772-1172; Ed. Christy Smith. adv.; photos; bk.rev.; pub. size: standard; circ. 5,000(paid).

BYRDSTOWN

US

PICKETT COUNTY PRESS. 1974. Thu. $.50 newsstand; $15/yr. Main St., P.O. Box 268, Byrdstown, TN 38549. TEL 615-864-3675. **Owner(s):** James E. Hill, Main St., P.O. Box 268, Byrdstown, TN 38549. TEL 615-864-3675; Pub. James E. Hill; pub. size: broadsheet.

CAMDEN

US

CAMDEN CHRONICLE, THE. 1889. Wed. $.50 newsstand; $17/yr. in cy.; $16.50/yr. in state; $20/yr. out of state; $12/yr. senior citizens. 144 W. Main St., Camden, TN 38320. TEL 901-584-7200; FAX 901-584-4943. **Owner(s):** Dennis & Lisa Richardson, 144 W. Main St., Camden, TN 38320. TEL 901-584-7200; Elton C. & Joan T. Hatley, 144 W. Main St., Camden, TN 38320. TEL 901-584-7200; Ed. Joan Hatley; Pub. Lisa Richardson; adv. contact: Vanessa Bell. pub. size: broadsheet; circ. 5,000(paid).

US

MAJIC VALLEY SHOPPER'S NEWS. 1979. Tue. $.35 newsstand; free mailed. P.O. Box 307, Camden, TN 38320. TEL 901-584-8700; FAX 901-584-4943. **Owner(s):** John Churchwell, P.O. Box 307, Camden, TN 38320. TEL 901-584-8700; Ed. Fredia Garrin; Pub. John Churchwell; adv. contact: Christy Brasher. pub. size: broadsheet; circ. 8,700.

CARTHAGE

US

CARTHAGE COURIER. 1807. Thu. $.35 newsstand; $12/yr. in cy.; $14/yr. out of cy.; $17/yr. out of state. 509 Main, Carthage, TN 37030-0239. TEL 615-735-1110; FAX 615-735-0635. **Owner(s):** Hershel Lake, P.O. Box 239, Carthage, TN 37030. TEL 615-735-1110; Ed. Eddie West; Pub. Scott Winfree; adv. contact: Scott Winfree. pub. size: broadsheet; circ. 5,152(paid).

CLINTON

US

COURIER-NEWS. 1887. s-w.: Wed. & Sun. $.50 newsstand; $30/yr. in cy.; $32/yr. in surrounding cys.; $42/yr. out of area. 233 N. Hicks St., Clinton, TN 37716. TEL 423-457-2515; FAX 423-457-1586. **Owner(s):** Courier Publications, P.O. Box 1630, Greeneville, TN 37744. TEL 615-638-4181; Ed. Doug Morris; Pub. Doug Morris; adv.; photos; pub. size: standard; circ. 17,112(controlled & paid).

COLLIERVILLE

US   ISSN 0746-5939

COLLIERVILLE HERALD, THE. 1870. Thu. $.50 newsstand; $15/yr. in cy.; $18/yr. out of cy. 139 N. Main St., Collierville, TN 38017. TEL 901-853-2241; FAX 901-853-8507. **Owner(s):** Van Pritchartt, P.O. Box 427, Collierville, TN 38027. TEL 901-853-2241; Thomas Hart, P.O. Box 427, Collierville, TN 38027; Frayser Humphreys, P.O. Box 427, Collierville, TN 38027; Ed. Van Pritchartt; Pub. Van Pritchartt; adv.; photos; bk.rev.; pub. size: broadsheet; circ. 5,500(paid).

US

INDEPENDENT. 1982. Wed. $.50 newsstand; $15/yr. 151 N. Main St., Collierville, TN 38017-2617. TEL 901-853-7060. **Owner(s):** Shoppers Press of Memphis, 622 S. Highland St., Memphis, TN 38111. TEL 901-458-8030; Ed. J. Barry Heifner. adv.; pub. size: broadsheet; circ. 12,400(free & paid).

COVINGTON

US

COVINGTON LEADER. 1886. Wed. $.50 newsstand; $14/yr. in cy.; $20/yr. out of cy.; $26/yr. out of state. 2001 Hwy. 51 S., Covington, TN 38019. TEL 901-476-7116; FAX 901-476-0373. **Owner(s):** Press Holding Corp., P.O. Box 529, Covington, TN 38019-0529. TEL 901-476-7116; FAX 901-476-0373; Ed. George T. Whitley; Pub. George T. Whitley; adv. contact: Larry Whitley. photos; bk.rev.; pub. size: broadsheet; circ. 8,100(paid).

CROSSVILLE

US

CROSSVILLE CHRONICLE. 1886. 3/wk.: Tue., Wed., Fri. $.50 newsstand; $43/yr. in state; $50/yr. out of state; $35/yr. senior citizens. 312 S. Main St., Crossville, TN 38557. TEL 615-484-5145; FAX 615-456-7683. **Owner(s):** American Publishing Co., 606 N. Van Buren, P.O. Box 520, Marion, IL 62959. TEL 618-993-1711; Ed. Mike Moser; Pub. Pauline Sherrer; photos; bk.rev.; pub. size: broadsheet; circ. 89,000(paid).

DAYTON

US

HERALD-NEWS. 1898. s-w.: Sun. & Wed. $.50 newsstand; $30/yr. in cy.; $42/yr. in state; $40/yr. out of state. 3687 Rhea County Hwy., Dayton, TN 37321. TEL 423-775-6111; FAX 423-775-8218. **Owner(s):** Media Services Group, Inc., P.O. Box 1630, Greeneville, TN 37744. TEL 615-638-4181; Ed. John Carpenter; Pub. Ed Emens; adv. contact: Jim Kinser. pub. size: broadsheet; circ. Sun. 13,000(paid).

DICKSON

US

DICKSON HERALD, THE. 1907. s-w.: Wed. & Fri. $.50 newsstand; $20/yr. in cy. 104 Church St., Dickson, TN 37055. TEL 615-446-2811; FAX 615-446-5560. **Owner(s):** Leaf Chronicle Co., 200 Commerce St., Clarksville, TN 37040. TEL 615-552-1808; FAX 615-648-8001; Ed. Chris Norman. adv.; photos; pub. size: broadsheet; circ. 19,500(free & paid).

DRESDEN

US   ISSN 0016-1040

DRESDEN ENTERPRISE. 1883. Wed. $14/yr. in cy.; $16/yr. out of cy.; $24/yr. out of state. 113 Wilson, Dresden, TN 38225-0139. TEL 901-364-2234; FAX 901-364-5774. **Owner(s):** Ramona Washburn, P.O. Box 100, McKenzie, TN 38201. TEL 901-352-3323; Jeff Washburn, P.O. Box 139, Dresden, TN 38225. TEL 901-364-2234; Joel Washburn, P.O. Box 100, McKenzie, TN 38201. TEL 901-352-3323; Ed. Jeff Washburn; Pub. Ramona Washburn; adv.; photos; pub. size: broadsheet; circ. 6,200(paid).

DYER

US

TRI-CITY REPORTER. 1892. Thu. $.50 newsstand; $16.50/yr. in cy.; $20/yr. in state; $26/yr. elsewhere. 101 N. Main St., Dyer, TN 38330. TEL 901-692-3506; FAX 901-692-4844. **Owner(s):** Warmath Communications, P.O. Box 408, Humboldt, TN 38343. TEL 901-784-1563; Ed. April Jackson; Pub. Frank Warmath; adv.; photos; pub. size: broadsheet; circ. 3,500(paid).

ERWIN

US

ERWIN RECORD. 1927. Wed. $.35 newsstand; $14/yr. in cy.; $22/yr. out of cy. 218 Gay St., Erwin, TN 37650. TEL 423-743-4112; FAX 423-743-6125. **Owner(s):** Press Holding Corp., 218 Gay St., Erwin, TN 37650. TEL 423-743-4112; FAX 423-743-6125; Ed. Tom Harris; Pub. Tom Harris; adv.; photos; pub. size: standard; circ. 4,500(paid).

FAYETTEVILLE

US

ELK VALLEY TIMES. 1965. Wed. $.50 newsstand; $17/yr. local; $23/yr. elswhere. 418 N. Elk Ave., Fayetteville, TN 37334. TEL 615-433-6151; FAX 615-433-6151. **Owner(s):** Lakeway Publishers, Inc., P.O. Box 625, Morristown, TN 37815. TEL 615-581-5630; Ed. Lucy A. Carter; Pub. Lucy A. Carter; adv. contact: Lucy A. Carter. pub. size: broadsheet; circ. 8,100(paid).

FRANKLIN

US

WILLIAMSON LEADER, THE. 1973. Thu. $.25 newsstand; $15/yr. in state; $25/yr. out of state. 128 Holiday Court, Ste. 121, Franklin, TN 37067. TEL 615-794-4564; FAX 615-794-9581. **Owner(s):** Williamson Leader, Inc., P.O. Box 729, Franklin, TN 37065-0729. TEL 615-794-4564; FAX 615-794-9581; Ed. Bailey Leopard; Pub. Bailey Leopard; adv.; photos; pub. size: broadsheet; circ. 6,100(paid).

GALLATIN

US

NEWS-EXAMINER. 1840. 3/wk.: Mon., Wed., Fri. $.50 newsstand; $36/yr. One Examiner Ct., Gallatin, TN 37066. TEL 615-452-2561; FAX 615-452-9110. **Owner(s):** Gannett Company, Inc., 1100 Wilson Blvd., Arlington, VA 22234. TEL 703-284-6000; Ed. Steve Rogers; Pub. Bob Atkins; adv.; photos; bk.rev.; pub. size: broadsheet; circ. 10,800(paid). **Wire Service(s):** AP.

GERMANTOWN

US

GERMANTOWN NEWS, THE. 1974. Thu. $.50 newsstand; $25/yr. 7545 North St., Germantown, TN 38138. TEL 901-754-0337; FAX 901-754-2961. **Owner(s):** Ricketson Publishing, 7545 North St., Memphis, TN 38138. TEL 901-754-0337; FAX 901-754-2961; adv.; photos; pub. size: broadsheet; circ. 8,000(paid).

US

SHELBY SUN TIMES. 1987. Thu. $.25 newsstand; $20/yr. mailed. 7508 Capital Dr, Ste. 2, Germantown, TN 38138. TEL 901-755-7386; FAX 901-755-0827. **Owner(s):** Garry Summerford, 7508 Capital Dr., Germantown, TN 38138. TEL 901-755-7386; FAX 901-755-0827; Lynn H. Sanders, 7508 Capital Dr., Germantown, TN 38138. TEL 901-755-7386; FAX 901-755-0827; Ed. Patricia Pair; Pub. Garry Summerford; adv. contact: Rick Smith. photos; pub. size: tabloid; circ. 22,400(paid).

HARTSVILLE

US

HARTSVILLE VIDETTE, THE. 1862. Thu. $.25 newsstand; $7/yr. in cy.; $15/yr. out of cy. One Marlene St., Hartsville, TN 37074. TEL 615-374-3556. **Owner(s):** Lebanon Democrat, Lebanon, TN 37087. TEL 615-444-3952; Pub. Angelene Anderson; adv. contact: Rosemary Denham. photos; pub. size: standard; circ. 2,300(paid).

HENDERSONVILLE

US   ISSN 0193-5143

HENDERSONVILLE STAR NEWS. 1951. s-w.: Wed. & Fri. $.25 newsstand; $10/yr. mailed; $15/yr. out of state. 110 Sanders Ferry, Hendersonville, TN 37077. TEL 615-824-8480; FAX 615-824-3126. **Owner(s):** Gannett Company, Inc., 1100 Wilson Blvd., Arlington, VA 22340. TEL 615-824-8480; Ed. Mike McClanahan. adv.; photos; pub. size: broadsheet; circ. 13,300(paid). **Wire Service(s):** AP.

HUMBOLDT

US

CHRONICLE, THE. 1887. Wed. $16.50/yr. in cy.; $22/yr. in state; $27.50/yr. out of state. 2606 E. End Dr., Humboldt, TN 38343. TEL 901-784-2531; FAX 901-784-2533. **Owner(s):** Chronicle, Inc., 2606 E. End Dr., Humboldt, TN 38343. TEL 901-784-2531; FAX 901-784-2533; Ed. Martha Dodson; Pub. Frank Warmath; adv.; photos; pub. size: broadsheet; circ. 4,000(paid).

Formerly: Courier Chronicle, The.

HUNTINGDON

US

CARROLL COUNTY NEWS-LEADER. 1887. Wed. $.50 newsstand; $17/yr. in cy.; $22/yr. out of cy.; $27/yr. out of state. 163 Court Sq., Huntingdon, TN 38344. TEL 901-986-2253; FAX 901-986-3585. **Owner(s):** Dennis & Lisa Richardson, P.C. Box 389, Huntington, TN 38344. TEL 901-986-2253; Elton C. & Joan T. Hatley, P.O. Box 389, Huntington, TN 38344. TEL 901-986-2253; Ed. Shirley Nanney. pub. size: broadsheet; circ. 6,700(paid).

Formerly: Huntington Carroll News.

JASPER

US

JASPER JOURNAL. 1938. Tue. $.75 newsstand; $21/yr. in cy.; $26/yr. out of cy. 6615 Hwy. 41, Jasper, TN 37347. TEL 423-942-2433; FAX 423-942-8835. **Owner(s):** Marin County Newspapers, 6615 Hwy. 41, Jasper, TN 37347. TEL 615-942-2348; Ed. Linda Rector; Pub. Allen Kirk; adv. contact: Allen Kirk. pub. size: standard; circ. 3,600(paid).

JEFFERSON

US

STANDARD BANNER. 1927. s-w.: Tue. & Thu. $.50 newsstand; $25/yr. in cy.; $40/yr. out of cy. 122 W. Andrew Johnson Hwy., Jefferson, TN 37760-0310. TEL 615-475-2081; FAX 615-475-8539. **Owner(s):** Jefferson County Standard Publishing Co., Inc., P.O. Box 310, Jefferson, TN 37760-0310. TEL 615-475-2081; FAX 615-475-8539; Ed. Dale Gentry; Pub. Tom Gentry; adv. contact: Kathryn Hodges. pub. size: broadsheet; circ. 6,400(paid).

JONESBOROUGH

US

HERALD & TRIBUNE. 1869. Wed. $.25 newsstand; $10/yr. mailed. 702 W. Jackson Blvd., Jonesborough, TN 37559. TEL 615-753-3136; FAX 615-753-6528. **Owner(s):** Johnson City Press, P.O. Box 277, Johnson City, TN; Ed. Kelly Arnold. adv. contact: Lois Hicks. pub. size: broadsheet; circ. 4,500(paid).

KINGSTON

US

HARRIMAN RECORD. 1865. Tue. $.35 newsstand; $7.95/yr. 204 Franklin St., Kingston, TN 37763. TEL 423-376-3481; FAX 423-376-1945. **Owner(s):** Landmark Community Newspapers, Inc., P.O. Box 549, Shelbyville, KY 40066. TEL 502-633-4334; Ed. Darrell Richardson. adv. contact: Amy Hicks. pub. size: broadsheet; circ. 850(paid).

US

ROANE COUNTY NEWS, THE. 1957. 3/wk.: Mon., Wed., Fri. $.50 newsstand; $32.95/yr. in cy.; $50/yr. out of cy.; $70/yr. out of state. 204 Franklin St., Kingston, TN 37763. TEL 423-376-3481; FAX 423-376-1945. **Owner(s):** Landmark Community Newspapers, Inc., P.O. Box 549, Shelbyville, KY 40066. TEL 502-633-4334; Ed. Darrell Richardson. adv. contact: Amy Hicks. pub. size: broadsheet; circ. 8,937(paid).

US

ROCKWOOD TIMES. Tue. $.35 newsstand; $9.95/yr. P.O. Box 610, Kingston, TN 37763. TEL 423-376-3481; FAX 423-375-1945. **Owner(s):** Landmark Community Newspapers, Inc., P.O. Box 549, Shelbyville, KY 40066. TEL 502-633-4334; Ed. Darrell Richardson. adv. contact: Amy Hicks. photos; bk.rev.; pub. size: broadsheet; circ. morning 631(controlled & paid).

KNOXVILLE

US

TRI-COUNTY NEWS. 1956. Wed. $.30 newsstand; $15/yr. 9010 Chapman Hwy., Knoxville, TN 37920. TEL 423-577-5935; FAX 423-577-9896. **Owner(s):** Gladys E. Hamilton, P.O. Box 130, Seymour, TN 37865. TEL 615-577-5935; FAX 615-577-9896; Ed. Gladys E. Hamilton; Pub. Gladys E. Hamilton; pub. size: tabloid; circ. 6,500(free & paid).

LAFAYETTE

US   ISSN 0745-5976

MACON COUNTY TIMES. 1919. Thu. $.50 newsstand; $15/yr. 200 Times Ave., Lafayette, TN 37083. TEL 615-666-2440; FAX 615-666-4909. **Owner(s):** Macon County Newspapers, Inc., P.O. Box 69, Lafayette, TN 37083. TEL 615-666-2440; Ed. Truett Langston; Pub. Truett Langston; adv.; pub. size: broadsheet; circ. 6,400(paid).

LA FOLLETTE

US

JELLICO ADVANCE SENTINEL. 1880. Wed. $.25 newsstand; $8.50/yr. in cy; $10.50/yr. elsewhere. P.O. Box 1261, La Follette, TN 37766. TEL 423-562-8468; FAX 423-566-7060. **Owner(s):** La Follette Press, Inc., P.O. Box 1261, La Follette, TN 37766. TEL 615-562-8468; Ed. Rex Hickey; Pub. Larry K. Smith; circ. 850(paid).

US

LA FOLLETTE PRESS. 1910. Thu. $.50 newsstand; $15.25/yr. local; $27.50/yr. out of state. 220 N. First St., La Follette, TN 37766. TEL 615-562-8468; FAX 615-566-7060. **Owner(s):** La Follette Press, Inc., P.O. Box 1261, La Follette, TN 37766. TEL 615-562-8468; Ed. Charles Winfrey; Pub. Larry Smith; adv. contact: Larry Dilbeck. pub. size: standard; circ. 8,300(paid).

US

LAKE CITY TOWN CRIER. 1910. Tue. $.15 newsstand; $7/yr. in cy.; $9/yr. out of cy. 220 N. First St., La Follette, TN 37766. TEL 423-562-8468; FAX 423-566-7060. **Owner(s):** La Follette Press, Inc., P.O. Box 1261, La Follette, TN 37766. TEL 423-562-8468; Ed. Rex Hickey; Pub. Larry Smith; pub. size: tabloid; circ. 1,500(paid).

LAWRENCEBURG

US

DEMOCRAT-UNION. 1884. s-w. Tue. & Fri. $.25 newsstand; $18/yr. 238 Hughes St., Lawrenceburg, TN 38464. TEL 615-762-2222; FAX 615-762-4191. **Owner(s):** Jim Crawford, Jr., P.O. Box 685, Goodspring, TN 38450. TEL 615-762-2222; Ed. Charlie Crawford; Pub. Jim Crawford, Jr.; adv. contact: Charlie Crawford. pub. size: broadsheet; circ. 10,000(paid).

LEBANON

US

WILSON WORLD, THE. 1978. Thu. $.25 newsstand; $5/yr. local. 115-A East Main St., Lebanon, TN 37087. TEL 615-444-6008; FAX 615-444-6018. **Owner(s):** Tommy A. Bryan, 115-A East Main St., Lebanon, TN 37087. TEL 615-444-6008; FAX 615-444-6018; John B. Bryan, 115-A East Main St., Lebanon, TN 37087. TEL 615-444-6008; FAX 615-444-6018; W. Troy Putman, 115-A East Main St., Lebanon, TN 37087. TEL 615-444-6008; FAX 615-444-6018; Ed. Tommy A. Bryan; Pub. Tommy A. Bryan; adv. contact: John B. Bryan. photos; pub. size: tabloid; circ. 5,400(paid).

LENOIR CITY

US

NEWS HERALD. 1885. s-w.: Mon. & Thu. $.50 newsstand; $40/yr. 508 E. Broadway, Lenoir City, TN 37771. TEL 615-986-6581; FAX 615-988-3261. **Owner(s):** Loudon Publishing Co., 508 E. Broadway, Lenoir City, TN 37771. TEL 615-988-3261; Ed. Linda Brewer. adv. contact: Phylis Burnette. photos; bk.rev.; pub. size: broadsheet; circ. 14,892(free & paid).

LEWISBURG

US

LEWISBURG TRIBUNE. s-w.: Tue. & Thu. $.35 newsstand; $22/yr. in cy.; $28/yr. out of cy. 121 First Ave., S., Lewisburg, TN 37091. TEL 615-359-1188; FAX 615-359-1847. **Owner(s):** Lewisburg Tribune, Inc., 121 First Ave., S., Lewisburg, TN 37091. TEL 615-359-1188; Ed. Betty Orr; Pub. Tommy Hawkins, III; adv. contact: Bonnie Phillips. pub. size: standard; circ. 7,800(paid).

US

MARSHALL GAZETTE. Tue. $.35 newsstand; $22/yr. in cy.; $29/yr. out of cy. 121 First Ave. S., Lewisburg, TN 37091. TEL 615-359-1188. **Owner(s):** Lewisburg Tribune, Inc., 121 First Ave. S., Lewisburg, TN 37091. TEL 615-359-1188; Ed. Betty Orr; Pub. Tommy Hawkins, III; adv. contact: Bonnie Phillips. pub. size: broadsheet; circ. 7,800(paid).

LEXINGTON

US

LEXINGTON PROGRESS. Wed. $.50 newsstand; $13/yr. in cy.; $18/yr. in state; $22/yr. out of state. 60 S. Broad St., Lexington, TN 38351. TEL 901-968-6397; FAX 901-968-9560. **Owner(s):** Lexington Progress Inc., 60 S. Broad St., Lexington, TN 38351; Ed. Mike Reed; Pub. Tom Franklin; pub. size: broadsheet; circ. 8,300(paid).

LINDEN

US

BUFFALO RIVER REVIEW. 1976. Wed. $.35 newsstand; $13/yr. 115 S. Mill St., Linden, TN 37096. TEL 615-589-2169; FAX 615-589-3858. **Owner(s):** Buffalo Review, P.O. Box 914, Linden, TN 37096. TEL 615-589-2169; FAX 615-589-3858; Ed. Randy Mackin. adv. contact: Mary Perry. pub. size: broadsheet; circ. 3,000(paid).

LIVINGSTON

US

LIVINGSTON ENTERPRISE. 1892. Wed. $.50 newsstand; $15/yr. in area; $30/yr. out of area. 203 S. Church St., Livingston, TN 38570. TEL 615-823-1274; FAX 615-268-9125. **Owner(s):** Richard F. Knight, 203 S. Church St., P.O. Box 129, Livingston, TN 38570; Ed. Richard F. Knight; Pub. Richard F. Knight; adv. contact: Mickey Ledbetter. photos; pub. size: standard; circ. 5,300(paid).

MADISON

US

MESSENGER, THE. 1982. Wed. free. 322 E. Old Hickory Blvd., Madison, TN 37115. TEL 615-868-0475; FAX 615-868-6888. **Owner(s):** Bill C. Robinson, P.O. Box 626, Madison, TN 37116. TEL 615-868-0475; Ed. Susan Rotkiewcz; Pub. Bill Robinson; adv.; photos; pub. size: broadsheet; circ. 13,600(free).

MADISONVILLE

US

ADVOCATE DEMOCRAT. 1870. 3/wk.: Wed., Fri., Sun. $.50 newsstand; $36/yr. in cy.; $60/yr. out of area. 509 Cook St., Madisonville, TN 37354. TEL 423-442-4575; FAX 423-442-1416. **Owner(s):** Advocate Democrat, 509 Cook St., Madisonville, TN 37354. TEL 423-337-7101; Ed. Ann Wallace; Pub. Thomas G. Wilson, III; adv. contact: Ann Roberts. pub. size: broadsheet; circ. 5,000(paid); Sun. 15,000(paid).
Formerly: Democrat/Laker.

MANCHESTER

US

MANCHESTER TIMES. 1881. Wed. $.50 newsstand; $18/yr. local; $32/yr. out of area. 300 N. Spring St., Manchester, TN 37355. TEL 615-728-7577; FAX 615-728-7614. **Owner(s):** Lakeway Publishers, Inc., Morristown, TN; Ed. Robert Long; Pub. Chuck Cunningham; adv. contact: Susie Gilliam. pub. size: broadsheet; circ. 6,500(paid).

MARTIN

US

WEAKLEY COUNTY PRESS. 1885. s-w.: Tue. & Thu. $.50 newsstand; $18/yr. 235 Lindell, Martin, TN 38237. TEL 901-587-3144; FAX 901-587-3147. **Owner(s):** David Critchlow, P.O. Box 410, Martin, TN 38237; Ed. Joe Lofaro; Pub. David Critchlow; adv. contact: Donna Wright. pub. size: standard; circ. 5,700(paid).
Formerly: Martin Weakley County Press.

MCKENZIE

US

MCKENZIE BANNER. 1870. Wed. $.50 newsstand; $15/yr. surrounding cys.; $19/yr. in state; $25/yr. elsewhere. 3 Banner Row, McKenzie, TN 38201-0100. TEL 901-352-3323. **Owner(s):** Jeff Washburn, P.O. Box 139, Dresden, TN 38225. TEL 901-364-2234; Joel Washburn, P.O. Box 125, McKenzie, TN 38201. TEL 901-352-3323; Ramona Washburn, P.O. Box 28, McKenzie, TN 38201. TEL 901-352-3323; FAX 901-352-3322; Ed. Joel Washburn; Pub. Ramona Washburn; adv.; photos; pub. size: broadsheet; circ. 5,500(paid). **Wire Service(s):** AP.

MCMINNVILLE

US

SOUTHERN STANDARD. 1879. 3/wk.: Sun., Wed., Fri. $.50 newsstand; $48/yr. deliv. 105 College St., McMinnville, TN 37110. TEL 615-473-2191; FAX 615-473-6823. **Owner(s):** Morris Communications, P.O. Box 8167, Savannah, GA 31412. TEL 912-233-1281; Ed. Steve Weldsmith; Pub. William R. Fryar; adv. contact: Sharon Patrick. photos; bk.rev.; pub. size: broadsheet; circ. 8,400(paid).

MILAN

US

MIRROR-EXCHANGE. 1964. Tue. $.50 newsstand; $15/yr. in cy.; $20/yr. out of cy.; $25/yr. out of state. 1104 S. Main, Milan, TN 38358. TEL 901-686-8114; FAX 901-686-9005. **Owner(s):** Mirror-Exchange, Inc., P.O. Box 549, Milan, TN 38358. TEL 901-686-1632; Ed. Bob Parkins; Pub. Bob Parkins; adv. contact: Melanie Day. photos; pub. size: broadsheet; circ. 5,500(paid).
Formerly: Milan Mirror-Exchange.

MILLINGTON

US

MILLINGTON STAR, THE. 1952. Wed. $.50 newsstand; $15/yr. 5107 Easley, Millington, TN 38053-0305. TEL 901-872-2286; FAX 901-872-2965. **Owner(s):** J.T.S. Inc., P.O. Box 305, Millington, TN 38083-0305. TEL 901-872-2965; FAX 901-872-2965; Ed. Harry L. Hix, Jr.; Pub. Harry L. Hix, Jr.; adv. contact: Doyle Fagan. photos; pub. size: broadsheet; circ. 2,178(paid).

MOUNTAIN CITY

US

TOMAHAWK, THE. 1874. Wed. $.35 newsstand; $22/yr. in cy.; $30/yr. out of cy.; $18/yr. senior citizens. 118 S. Church St., Mountain City, TN 37683. TEL 423-727-6121; FAX 423-727-4833. **Owner(s):** Press, Inc., P.O. Box 1717, Johnson City, TN 37605. TEL 615-929-3111; Ed. Deidra Smith. adv. contact: Rita Corrett. bk.rev.; pub. size: standard; circ. 5,900(paid).
Formerly: Mountain City Tomahawk.

MURFREESBORO

US

COVER STORY, THE. 1975. Wed. free. 224 N. Walnut St., Murfreesboro, TN 37130. TEL 615-893-5860; FAX 615-896-8702. **Owner(s):** Morris Communications, P.O. Box 8167, Savannah, GA 31412. TEL 912-233-1281; Ed. Mike Pirtle. pub. size: tabloid; circ. 24,000(free).
Formerly: Merchant's Advocate.

NEWBERN

US

DYER COUNTY TENNESSEAN. 1888. Thu. $14/yr. in cy.; $16.50/yr. in state; $19/yr. out of state. 113 Jefferson, Newbern, TN 38059. TEL 901-627-3247. **Owner(s):** Concord Publishing House, Inc.; Ed. Chris Rimal; Pub. John Rust; adv.; pub. size: broadsheet; circ. 2,800(paid).

NEWPORT

US

PLAIN TALK. 1900. 3/wk.: Mon., Wed., Fri. $.50 newsstand; $40/yr. in cy.; $60/yr. out of cy. 145 E. Broadway, Newport, TN 37821. TEL 423-623-6171; FAX 423-625-1995. **Owner(s):** Newport Publishing Co., 145 E. Broadway, Newport, RI 37821. TEL 615-623-6171; FAX 615-625-1995; Pub. John M. Jones; adv.; bk.rev.; pub. size: broadsheet; circ. 95,000(paid).

ONEIDA

US   ISSN 8750-5940

SCOTT COUNTY NEWS. 1916. Thu. $13/yr. in cy.; $15/yr. in state; $18/yr. out of cy. 224 Alberta Ave., Oneida, TN 37841. TEL 423-569-8351; FAX 423-569-4500. **Owner(s):** Bell Press, Inc., P.O. Box 4399, Oneida, TN 37841. TEL 615-569-8351; FAX 615-569-4500; Ed. Richard Magyar, Jr.; Pub. Shelia K. Erwin; adv. contact: Gary Hollis. pub. size: standard; circ. 7,000(controlled & paid).
   Formerly: Oneida Scott County News.

PARSONS

US

NEWS LEADER, THE. 1926. Wed. $10/yr. in cy.; $16/yr. out of cy.; $20/yr. out of state. 113 S. Tennessee Ave., Parsons, TN 38363-0340. TEL 901-847-6354; FAX 901-847-9120. **Owner(s):** Sam Kennedy, P.O. Box 340, Parsons, TN 38363. TEL 901-847-6354; FAX 901-847-9120; Ed. Mary Alexander. adv.; pub. size: broadsheet; circ. 4,833(paid).
   Formerly: Parson News Leader.

PULASKI

US

CITIZEN/PRESS PLUS. 1982. Tue. free. 308 W. College, Pulaski, TN 38478. TEL 615-363-3544; FAX 615-363-4319. **Owner(s):** S. Hershel Lake, 308 W. College St., Pulaski, TN 38478. TEL 615-363-3544; Ed. Joe Collins; Pub. S. Hershel Lake; adv.; photos; pub. size: broadsheet; circ. 5,400(free).

US

PULASKI CITIZEN. 1854. Tue. $.50 newsstand; $24/yr. 308 W. College, Pulaski, TN 38478. TEL 615-363-4548; FAX 615-363-4319. **Owner(s):** S. Hershel Lake, P.O. Box E, Pulaski, TN 38478. TEL 615-363-3544; adv.; pub. size: broadsheet; circ. 8,200(paid).

US

PULASKI GILES FREE PRESS. 1961. Thu. $.50 newsstand; $24/yr. in cy. 308 W. College, Pulaski, TN 38478. TEL 615-363-4548; FAX 615-363-4319. **Owner(s):** S. Hershel Lake, P.O. Box E, Pulaski, TN 38478. TEL 615-363-4548; FAX 615-363-4319; Ed. Dana Keeton; Pub. S. Hershel Lake; adv. contact: Juanita Hoover. pub. size: broadsheet; circ. 8,400(paid).

RIPLEY

US

HALLS GRAPHIC. 1894. Thu. $10/yr. in cy.; $12/yr. elsewhere. 145 E. Jackson, Ripley, TN 38063. TEL 901-635-1771; FAX 901-635-2111. **Owner(s):** William A. Klutts, 145 E. Jackson, Ripley, TN 38063. TEL 901-635-1771; Ed. William A. Klutts; Pub. William A. Klutts; pub. size: broadsheet; circ. 1,231(paid).

US

LAUDERDALE COUNTY ENTERPRISE. 1885. Thu. $.35 newsstand; $15/yr. in cy.; $18/yr. out of cy.; $24/yr. out of state. 145 E. Jackson Ave., Ripley, TN 38063. TEL 901-635-1771; FAX 901-635-2111. **Owner(s):** William A. Klutts, P.O. Box 289, Ripley, TN 38063. TEL 901-635-1771 Ed. William A. Klutts; Pub. William A. Klutts; pub. size: standard; circ. 4,800(paid).

ROGERSVILLE

US

ROGERSVILLE REVIEW. 1885. s-w.: Wed. & Sat. $.50 newsstand; $24/yr. in cy.; $26/yr. out of cy.; $31/yr. elsewhere. 207 Washington St., Rogersville, TN 37857. TEL 423-272-7422; FAX 423-272-7889. **Owner(s):** Hawkins County Publishers, Inc., P.O. Box 100, Rogersville, TN 37857. TEL 615-272-7422; Pub. Ellen Addison; adv. contact: Ben Addison. pub. size: standard; circ. 7,012(paid).

RUTLEDGE

US

GRAINGER COUNTY NEWS. 1928. Wed. $.35 newsstand; $10/yr. in cy. Cherry St., Rutledge, TN 37861. TEL 423-828-5254. **Owner(s):** Linda Witt, P.O. Box 218, Rutledge, TN 37861. TEL 615-828-5254; Ed. Linda Witt; Pub. Linda Witt; adv. contact: Kim Carpenter. pub. size: broadsheet; circ. 3,500(paid).

SAVANNAH

US

COURIER, THE. 1884. Thu. $.50 newsstand; $13/yr. local; $21/yr. out of area; $27/yr. out of state. 801 Main St., Savannah, TN 38372. TEL 901-925-6397; FAX 901-925-6310. **Owner(s):** Savannah Publishing Co., Inc., P.O. Box 340, Savannah, TN 38372. TEL 901-925-6397; Ed. Jim Thompson; Pub. Kathryn Craddock; adv. contact: Beth Jernolds. pub. size: broadsheet; circ. 9,000(paid).
   Formerly: Savannah Courier.

SELMER

US

INDEPENDENT APPEAL. 1902. Thu. $.55 newsstand; $12/yr. in cy.; $18/yr. out of cy.; $25/yr. out of state. 111 N. Second St., Selmer, TN 38375. TEL 901-645-5346; FAX 901-645-3591. **Owner(s):** William Rail, 111 N. Second St., Selmer, TN 38375. TEL 901-645-5346; Pub. Bill Rail; adv. contact: Tena Turner. pub. size: broadsheet; circ. 7,500(paid).
   Formerly: Selmer Independent Appeal.

SMITHVILLE

US

SMITHVILLE REVIEW. 1892. Wed. $.50 newsstand; $18/yr. in cy.; $24/yr. elsewhere. 106 S. First St., Smithville, TN 37166. TEL 615-597-5485. **Owner(s):** Morris Communications, P.O. Box 8167, Savannah, GA 31412. TEL 912-233-1281; Ed. Dennis Stanley; Pub. William R. Fryar; pub. size broadsheet; circ. 4,400(paid).

SMYRNA

US

RUTHERFORD COURIER, THE. 1931. Thu. $.35 newsstand; $18/yr. 103 Front St., Smyrna, TN 37167. TEL 615-459-386E; FAX 615-459-3878. **Owner(s):** Charles H. Morris, P.O. Box 8167, Savannah, GA 31412. TEL 912-233-1281; Ed. Ric Gross pub. size: broadsheet; circ. 3,400(paid).

SOMERVILLE

US

EAST SHELBY REVIEW. 1989. Wed. $.35 newsstand; mailed free in area. 16814 Hwy. 64, Somerville, TN 38068. TEL 901-867-2306; FAX 901-465-5493. **Owner(s):** Don Dowdle, P.O. Box 423, Somerville, TN 38068. TEL 901-465-4042; FAX 901-465-5493; Ed. Stuart Chapman; Pub. Don Dowdle adv.; photos; bk.rev.; pub. size: broadsheet; circ. 5,400(free).

US

FAYETTE COUNTY REVIEW. Wed. $.35 newsstand; free/mailed in area. 16814 Hwy. 64, Somerville, TN 38068. TEL 901-465-4042; FAX 901-465-5493. **Owner(s):** Don Dowdle, 16814 Hwy. 64, P.O. Box 230, Somerville, TN 38068. TEL 901-465-4042 FAX 901-465-5493; Ed. Don Dowdle. pub. size: broadsheet; circ. 8,214.

US

FAYETTE FALCON, THE. 1837. Wed. $.25 newsstand; $10/yr. in cy.; $17/yr. out of state. 101 W. Court Sq., Somerville, TN 38068. TEL 901-465-3567; FAX 901-465-3568. **Owner(s):** Carl A. Jones, P.C. Box 1717, Johnson City, TN 37605; Ed. Butch Plea. adv. contact: Debby Smith. photos; pub. size: standard; circ. 4,000(free & paid). **Wire Service(s):** AP.

US

MID-SOUTH HORSE REVIEW. m. free; $36/yr. 1st class; $18/yr. 2nd class. 16814 Hwy. 64, Somerville, TN 38068. TEL 901-465-4042; FAX 901-465-5493. **Owner(s):** Don Dowdle, 16814 Hwy. 64, P.O. Box 519, Somerville, TN 38068. TEL 901-465-4042 FAX 901-465-5493; Ed. Sharon Keith; Pub. Don Dowdle; pub. size: tabloid; circ. 13,500(free).

SOUTH PITTSBURG

US

HUSTLER, THE. 1899. Thu. $.75 newsstand; $21/yr. in cy.; $28/yr. out of cy. 307 1/2 Elm Ave., South Pittsburg, TN 37380. TEL 615-837-6312; FAX 615-837-3715. **Owner(s):** Marion County Newspapers, Inc., 307 1/2 Elm St., South Pittsburg, TN 37380. TEL 615-837-6312; Ed. Chris Smith; Pub. Jim Shanks; adv. contact: Chris Long. circ. 3,800(paid).
   Formerly: South Pittsburg Hustler.

SPARTA

US   ISSN 0745-6026

SPARTA EXPOSITOR. 1876. s-w. Mon. & Thu. $.50 newsstand; $29/yr. local; $35/yr. out of area; $40/yr. out of state; $26/yr. senior citizens. 34 W. Bockman Way, Sparta, TN 38583. TEL 615-836-3284. **Owner(s):** Smith Newspapers, Inc., P.O. Box 27, Fort Payne, AL 35967. TEL 205-845-5510; Ed. Suzanne Dickerson; Pub. Suzann Dickerson; adv.; photos; bk.rev.; pub. size: broadsheet; circ. 11,900(free & paid).

SPRINGFIELD

US

ROBERTSON COUNTY TIMES. 1922. Wed. $.50 newsstand; $16/yr. in cy.; $30/yr. out of cy.; $30/yr. out of state. West Court Sq., Springfield, TN 37172. TEL 615-384-3567; FAX 615-384-1221. **Owner(s):** Gannett Company, Inc., P.O. Box 637, Springfield, TN 37172. TEL 615-384-3567; Ed. Tom Beesley; Pub. Hugh Braddock; adv. contact: Hugh Braddock. pub. size: broadsheet; circ. 10,000(paid).

SWEETWATER

US

ADVOCATE PENNY SAVER. 1927. Sun. free in cy. P.O. Box 389, Sweetwater, TN 37874. TEL 423-337-7101; FAX 423-442-1416. **Owner(s):** County Publishers, Inc., P.O. Box 389, Sweetwater, TN 37874. TEL 423-337-7101; Ed. Ann Wallace; Pub. Thomas G. Wilson, III; adv. contact: Ann Roberts. pub. size: broadsheet; circ. Sun. 20,000(free).

TAZEWELL

US

CLAIBORNE PROGRESS. 1887. Wed. $.50 newsstand; $17/yr. in cy.; $19.25/yr. out of cy.; $21/yr. out of state. 1001 Main St., Tazewell, TN 37879. TEL 423-626-3222; FAX 423-626-6868. **Owner(s):** American Publishing Co., 606 N. Van Buren, P.O. Box 520, Marion, IL 62959. TEL 618-993-1711; Ed. Ron Morgan. adv. contact: Judy Buchanan. photos; pub. size: broadsheet; circ. 7,000(paid).

TRACY CITY

US

GRUNDY COUNTY HERALD. 1932. Thu. $.50 newsstand; $17/yr. in cy. Oak St., Tracy City, TN 37387. TEL 615-592-2781. **Owner(s):** Grundy County Herald, Oak St., P.O. Box 189, Tracy City, TN 37387. TEL 615-592-2781; FAX 615-598-5812; Ed. Dawn J. Brothers; Pub. Dawn J. Brothers; adv. contact: Misty Reid. pub. size: broadsheet; circ. 4,800(paid).

TRENTON

US

HERALD GAZETTE, THE. 1968. Wed. $.50 newsstand; $15/yr. in cy.; $20/yr. in state; $25/yr. out of state. 111 E. First St., Trenton, TN 38382. TEL 901-855-1711; FAX 901-855-9587. **Owner(s):** Herald Gazette, Inc., The, P.O. Box 7, Trenton, TN 38382. TEL 901-855-1711; Ed. Danny Jones; Pub. Danny Jones; adv. contact: Danny Jones. pub. size: broadsheet; circ. 5,000(paid).

TULLAHOMA

US

TULLAHOMA NEWS. 1946. 3/wk.: Sun., Wed., Fri. $.50/day newsstand; $.75/Sun.; $38/yr. local; $48/yr. elsewhere. 505 Lakeway Pl., Tullahoma, TN 37388. TEL 615-455-4545; FAX 615-455-9229. **Owner(s):** Lakeway Publishers, Inc., Morristown, TN; Ed. Bob Kyer; Pub. Terry Craig; adv. contact: Harry Hill. pub. size: standard; circ. 8,500(paid); Sun. 9,500(paid).

WARTBURG

US

MORGAN COUNTY NEWS. Thu. $.50 newsstand; $15.95/yr. Maiden & Aliza St., Wartburg, TN 37887. TEL 423-346-6225; FAX 423-346-5788. **Owner(s):** Landmark Community Newspapers, Inc., P.O. Box 549, Shelbyville, KY 40066. TEL 502-633-4334; Ed. Judy Underwood; Pub. Doug Morris; pub. size: standard; circ. 4,300(paid).

WAYNESBORO

US

WAYNE COUNTY NEWS. 1857. Wed. $.25 newsstand; $9/yr.; $11/yr. out of cy. 119 E. Hollis St., Waynesboro, TN 38485. TEL 615-722-5429; FAX 615-722-5429. **Owner(s):** Nelle B. Cole, P.O. Box 156, Waynesboro, TN 38485. TEL 615-722-5429; Ed. Kathy Brison; Pub. Nelle B. Cole; adv. contact: Kathy Brison. pub. size: broadsheet; circ. 7,000(paid).

WINCHESTER

US

HERALD-CHRONICLE, THE. 1845. s-w.: Mon. & Thu. $.50 newsstand; $24/yr. in cy.; $32/yr. out of cy. 906 Dinah Shore Blvd., Winchester, TN 37398. TEL 615-967-2272; FAX 615-967-2299. **Owner(s):** Franklin County Publishing Co., Inc., 906 Dinah Shore Ave., Winchester, TN 37398. TEL 615-967-2272; Ed. Dick Wolff; Pub. Charles Sons; adv. contact: Jerry Ogle. pub. size: broadsheet; circ. 10,000(paid).
   Formerly: Winchester Herald-Chronicle.

TEXAS

ABERNATHY

US   ISSN 0895-4291

ABERNATHY WEEKLY REVIEW. 1921. Fri. $.50 newsstand; $17/yr. in cy.; $24/yr. out of cy. 916 Ave. D, Abernathy, TX 79311. TEL 806-298-2033. **Owner(s):** Scott & Judy Luce, 411 13th St., Abernathy, TX 79311. TEL 806-298-2909; Ed. Scott Luce; Pub. Scott Luce; adv. contact: Judy Luce. photos; pub. size: broadsheet; circ. 1,032(paid).

ALPINE

US

ALPINE AVALANCHE. 1890. Thu. $20/yr. in cy.; $24/yr. out of cy. 112 N. Fifth, Alpine, TX 79830. TEL 915-837-3334; FAX 915-837-7181. **Owner(s):** Earl & Sheila Plagens, Colorado City, TX; Ed. Burnis Lawrence; Pub. Burnis Lawrence; pub. size: broadsheet; circ. 4,050(paid).

ALVARADO

US

ALVARADO POST. Thu. $.50 newsstand; $16.50/yr. mailed. 206 N. Parkway, Alvarado, TX 76009. TEL 817-790-8717; FAX 817-783-7606. **Owner(s):** Alvarado Newspapers, Inc., 206 N. Parkway, Alvarado, TX 76009. TEL 817-790-8717; Pub. Roland Welch; adv.; pub. size: broadsheet; circ. 2,600(paid).

ALVIN

US

ALVIN ADVERTISER. 1891. 3/wk.: Sun., Mon., Wed. free. 201 E. House St., Alvin, TX 77511. TEL 713-331-4421; FAX 713-585-3504. **Owner(s):** Henderson Newspapers, Inc., 201 E. House St., Alvin, TX. TEL 713-331-4421; Ed. Wendy Mohon; Pub. Jim Schwind; adv. contact: Priscilla Hawkins. pub. size: broadsheet; circ. 17,300(free).

US

ALVIN SUN. 1891. 3/wk.: Sun., Mon., Wed. $.50 newsstand; $18/yr. 201 E. House St., Alvin, TX 77511. TEL 713-331-4421; FAX 713-331-4424. **Owner(s):** Henderson Newspapers, Inc., 201 E. House, Alvin, TX 77511. TEL 713-331-4421; Ed. Brandi Chionsini; Pub. Jim Schwind; adv. contact: Priscilla Hawkins. photos; pub. size: broadsheet; circ. morning 2,500(paid); evening 17,500(free); Sun. 10,500(free).

ANAHUAC

US

PROGRESS, THE. 1908. Wed. $.50 newsstand; $17.50/yr. in cy. 209 Willcox St., Anahuac, TX 77514. TEL 409-267-6131; FAX 409-336-3345. **Owner(s):** Hartman Newspapers, Inc., P.O. Box 1390, Rosenberg, TX 77471. TEL 713-342-4474; FAX 713-342-3219; Pub. E.E. Zieschang; adv. contact: Sue Hawthorne. pub. size: broadsheet; circ. 2,200(paid).

ANDREWS

US

ANDREWS COUNTY NEWS. 1934. s-w.: Wed.& Sun. $.50 newsstand; $16.90/yr. in cy.; $34.90/yr. surrounding cys.; $34.90/yr. out of area. 210 E. Broadway, Andrews, TX 79714. TEL 915-523-2085; FAX 915-523-9492. **Owner(s):** James Roberts, 210 E. Broadway, Andrews, TX 79714; Ed. James Roberts; Pub. James Roberts; adv. contact: James Egan. bk.rev.; pub. size: standard; circ. 6,500(controlled & free).

ANGLETON

US

ANGLETON TIMES. 1893. s-w.: Wed. & Sat. $.50 newsstand; $42/yr. carrier. 700 Western Ave., Angleton, TX 77515. TEL 409-849-8581; FAX 409-849-0230. **Owner(s):** Southern Newspapers, Inc., 1050 Wilcrest, Houston, TX 77042; Ed. Tommy D. Crow. adv.; photos; pub. size: broadsheet; circ. 4,000(paid). **Wire Service(s):** UPI.

ARLINGTON

US   ISSN 1044-0097

GRAND PRAIRIE NEWS. 1906. s-w.: Thu. & Sun. $.50 newsstand; $28/yr. 1000 Ave. H, E., Arlington, TX 76011. TEL 817-695-0500; FAX 817-695-0555. **Owner(s):** DFW Suburban Newspapers, Inc., 1000 Ave. H, E., Arlington, TX 76011. TEL 817-695-0500; Ed. Herb Booth; Pub. Dan Crowe; adv. contact: Greg Cashman. photos; pub. size: broadsheet; circ. 7,000(paid); Sun. 7,500(paid). **Wire Service(s):** Southwest Business Wire.

US   ISSN 8750-7870
IRVING NEWS. 1956. s-w.: Thu. & Sun. $.50 newsstand; $7/mo. mailed; $13.50/3 mos. carrier. 1000 Ave. H. E., Arlington, TX 76011. TEL 817-695-0483; FAX 817-695-0555. **Owner(s):** DFW Suburban Newspapers, Inc., 1000 Ave. H, E., Arlington, TX 76011. TEL 817-633-0500; Ed. Donnie Jackson. adv. contact: Richard Conley. pub. size: broadsheet; circ. 10,425(paid); Sun. 9,472(paid).

US
LA VIDA NEWS. 1957. Thu. free. 1401 W. Pioneer Pkwy., Ste. 100, Arlington, TX 76013. TEL 817-543-2095; FAX 817-274-8023. **Owner(s):** Ted Pruitt, 1401 W. Pioneer Pkwy., Ste. 100, Arlington, TX 76013. TEL 817-543-2095; FAX 817-860-0027; Ed. Ted Pruitt. adv.; photos; bk.rev.; pub. size: broadsheet; circ. 35,000(free). **Wire Service(s):** UPI.
Formerly: La Vida News Starships.

US   ISSN 8750-6440
MID-CITIES NEWS. 1909. s-w.: Thu. & Sun. $.50 newsstand; $4.50/mo. carrier; $7/mo. mailed. 1000 Ave. H, E., Arlington, TX 76011. TEL 817-695-0500; FAX 817-695-0555. **Owner(s):** DFW Suburban Newspapers, Inc., 1000 Ave. H, E., Arlington, TX 76011. TEL 817-695-0500; Ed. James Kunke. adv. contact: Louis Blackmon. pub. size: broadsheet; circ. 8,500(paid). **Wire Service(s):** AP.
Formerly: Mid-Cities Daily.

ATLANTA

US
ATLANTA CITIZENS JOURNAL. 1879. s-w.: Sun. & Wed. $.50 newsstand; $42/yr. local; $47/yr. elsewhere. 306 W. Main St., Atlanta, TX 75551. TEL 903-796-7133; FAX 903-796-3294. **Owner(s):** Westward Communications, Inc., 5005 LBJ Freeway, Ste. 1040, Dallas, TX 75244. TEL 214-450-1717; Ed. Jane Beckerdite; Pub. Debbie Milton. adv. contact: Debbie Milton. pub. size: broadsheet; circ. 4,300(paid).

AUSTIN

US   ISSN 1074-0740
AUSTIN CHRONICLE. 1981. Fri. free local; $60/yr. bulk mail; $135/yr. 1st class mail. 4000 N. IH-35 N., Austin, TX 78751. TEL 512-454-5766; FAX 512-458-6910. **Owner(s):** Austin Chronicle Corp., 4000 N. IH-35, Austin, TX 78751. TEL 512-454-5766; Ed. Louis Black; Pub. Nick Barbaro; adv.; photos; bk.rev.; pub. size: tabloid; circ. 80,000(controlled & free).

US   ISSN 0040-4519
TEXAS OBSERVER. 1954. bi-w.: Fri. $1.75 newsstand; $32/yr. 307 W. Seventh St., Austin, TX 78701. TEL 512-477-0746. **Owner(s):** Texas Democracy Foundation, 307 W. Seventh St., Austin, TX 78701. TEL 512-477-0746; Ed. Louis Dubose; Pub. Geoffrey Rips; adv. contact: Cliff Olofson. photos; bk.rev.; pub. size: broadsheet; circ. 8,300(paid).

US
VILLAGER NEWSPAPER. 1973. Fri. free; $20/yr. 1223-A Rosewood Ave., Austin, TX 78702. TEL 512-476-0082; FAX 512-476-0179. **Owner(s):** T.L. Wyatt, 1223-A Rosewood Ave., Austin, TX 78702. TEL 512-476-0082; Ed. T.L. Wyatt; Pub. T.L. Wyatt; pub. size: broadsheet; circ. 6,000(free & paid).

US
WESTLAKE PICAYUNE. 1977. Wed. $.50 newsstand; $31/yr. in cy.; $36/yr. outside of cy. 3103 Bee Cave Rd., Ste. 102, Austin, TX 78746. TEL 512-327-2990; FAX 512-328-6470. **Owner(s):** Westward Communications, Inc., 5005 LBJ Fwy., #1040, Dallas, TX 75244. TEL 214-450-1717; Pub. Jason Jared; adv. contact: Betty Wilson. pub. size: tabloid; circ. 3,500(paid).

AZLE

US   ISSN 0546-0920
AZLE NEWS. 1953. Thu. $.50 newsstand; $19.76/yr. in cy. 1121 S.E. Parkway, Azle, TX 76020. TEL 817-237-1184; FAX 817-238-9617. **Owner(s):** Azle Tri-County Advertiser, Inc., 1121 S.E. Parkway, Azle, TX 76020. TEL 817-237-1184; FAX 817-238-9617 Ed. Bob Buckel; Pub. Bob Buckel; adv.; pub. size: broadsheet; circ. 4,866(free & paid).

BALCH SPRINGS

US
SUBURBAN TRIBUNE. 1951. Fri. $.50 newsstand; $16/yr. in cy.; $18/yr. out of cy. 11401 Elam Rd., Ste. 106, Balch Springs, TX 75180. TEL 214-286-8350; FAX 214-286-8862. **Owner(s):** Mary Freeman, 11401 Elam Rd., Ste. 106, Balch Springs, TX 75180. TEL 214-286-8550; Ed. Mary Freeman; Pub. Mary Freeman; adv.; pub. size: tabloid; circ. 4,500(paid).

BEEVILLE

US   ISSN 0889-8618
BEEVILLE BEE-PICAYUNE. 1886. s-w.: Wed. & Sat. $.50 newsstand $44.25/yr. in cy.; $57.20/yr. out of cy.; $59.28/yr. elsewhere. 111 N. Washington St., Beeville, TX 78102. TEL 512-358-2550; FAX 512-358-5323. **Owner(s):** F.C. Latcham III, P.O. Box 10, Beeville, TX 78102. TEL 512-358-9478; FAX 512-358-5323; Fred C. Latcham, Jr., P.O. Box 10, Beeville, TX 78102. TEL 512-358-2232; FAX 512-358-5323; G.G. (Jeff) Latcham, P.O. Box 10, Beeville, TX 78102. TEL 512-358-2232; FAX 512-358-5323; Joyce Latcham, P.O. Box 10, Beeville, TX 78102. TEL 512-358-2232; FAX 512-358-5323; Ed. F.C. (Chip) Latcham, III; Pub. Fred C. Latcham, Jr.; adv. contact: Richard Carter. photos; pub. size: broadsheet; circ. 5,403(free & paid).

BELLVILLE

US
BELLVILLE TIMES. 1879. Thu. $.50 newsstand; $18.50/yr. in cy.; $23.50/yr. out of cy.; $26/yr. out of state. 106 E. Palm St., Bellville, TX 77418. TEL 409-865-3131. **Owner(s):** Austin County Publishing Co., Inc., 106 E. Palm, Bellville, TX 77418. TEL 409-865-3131; Ed. James R. Maler; Pub. Bruce White; adv.; pub. size: broadsheet; circ. 4,200(paid).

BLANCO

US   ISSN 1049-2216
BLANCO COUNTY NEWS. 1932 Wed. $.50 newsstand; $19/yr. P.O. Box 429, Blanco, TX 78606. TEL 210-833-4812; FAX 210-833-4246. **Owner(s):** Rcy McNett, P.O. Box 429, Blanco, TX 78606. TEL 210-833-4812; FAX 210-833-4246; Pub. Roy McNett; adv. contact: Tammy Mumme. photos; bk.rev.; pub. size: broadsheet; circ. 27,500(controlled & paid). **Wire Service(s):** AP.

BOOKER

US
BOOKER NEWS, THE. 1921. Wed. $.30 newsstand; $13/yr. in cy.; $15/yr. elsewhere. 204 S. Main, Booker, TX 79005. TEL 806-658-4732. **Owner(s):** Ben & Clara Boren, 204 S. Main, Booker, TX 79005. TEL 806-658-4732; Ed. Ben Bowen; Pub. Clara Boren; adv.; photos; pub. size: standard; circ. 1,150(free & paid).

BOWIE

US
BOWIE NEWS. 1920. s-w.: Sun. & Thu. $.50 newsstand; $20/yr. in cy.; $25/yr. out of cy.; $30/yr. out of state. 218 W. Tarrant, Bowie, TX 76230. TEL 817-872-2247; FAX 817-872-4812. **Owner(s):** James H. Winter, P.O. Box 831, Bowie, TX 76230. TEL 817-872-2247; Ed. Jim Winter. adv.; pub. size: broadsheet; circ. morning 4,500(paid).

US
MONTAGUE COUNTY SHOPPER, THE. 1980. w. free in cy.; $10/yr. mailed outside of cy. 114 Mason St., Bowie, TX 76230. TEL 817-872-6186; FAX 817-872-3559. **Owner(s):** Montague County Shopper, 114 N. Mason, Bowie, TX 76230. TEL 817-872-6186; Pub. Lynn Morgan. adv. contact: Kelly Pae. pub. size: tabloid; circ. 11,900(free & paid).

BRACKETTVILLE

US
BRACKETT NEWS THE. 1989. Thu. $.50 newsstand; $20/yr. in state; $27.50yr. out of state. P.O. Box 1039, Brackettville, TX 78832-1039. TEL 210-563-2852; FAX 210-563-9538. **Owner(s):** Jewel F. Robinson, P.O. Box 1039, Brackettville, TX 78832. TEL 210-563-2852; FAX 210-563-9538; Ed. Lynda Comrey; Pub. Jewel F. Robinson; adv.; photos; pub. size: standard; circ. 1,100(free & paid).

BRADY

US
BRADY STANDARD. 1909. s-w.: Tue. & Fri. $.50 newsstand; $22/yr. in cy.; $26/yr. in state; $32/yr. out of state. 201 S. Bridge Brady, TX 76825. TEL 915-597-2959 FAX 915-597-1434. **Owner(s):** Brady Standard-Herald Publishing Inc., 201 S. Bridge St., Brady, TX 76825. TEL 915-597-2959; Ed. Larry Smith; Pub. Larry Smith; adv.; pub. size: broadsheet; circ. 3,500(paid).

BRIDGEPORT

US

BRIDGEPORT INDEX. 1898. Thu. $15/yr. in cy.; $18/yr. out of cy. 916 Halsell, Bridgeport, TX 76426. TEL 817-683-4021; FAX 817-683-3841. **Owner(s):** Bridwell Publishing Co., 916 Halsell, Bridgeport, TX 76426. TEL 817-683-4021; Ed. Harlan Bridwell; Pub. Harlan Bridwell; adv.; pub. size: broadsheet; circ. 3,400(paid).

BROWNFIELD

US

BROWNFIELD NEWS. 1904. s-w.: Wed. & Sun. $.50 newsstand; $23.80/yr. in cy.; $28.75/yr. in state; $34.10/yr. out of state. 409 W. Hill St., Brownfield, TX 79316. TEL 806-637-4535; FAX 806-637-3795. **Owner(s):** Lynn Brisendine, 409 W. Hill St., Brownfield, TX 79316. TEL 806-637-4535; FAX 806-637-3795; Ed. Lynn Brisendine. adv.; photos; bk.rev.; pub. size: broadsheet; circ. 3,100(paid).

BRYAN

US

BRYAN COLLEGE STATION PRESS. 1966. Thu. free. 2606 Texas Ave., Bryan, TX 77802. TEL 409-823-0088; FAX 409-822-3649. **Owner(s):** A.H. Belo Corp., Dallas, TX; Ed. Mark Beal; Pub. Greg Huchingson; adv. contact: W.F. Moore, Jr. photos; pub. size: broadsheet; circ. 34,000(free).

BURLESON

US

BURLESON STAR. 1965. s-w.: Mon. & Thu. $.50 newsstand; $29.95/yr. 319 N. Burleson Blvd., Burleson, TX 76028. TEL 817-295-0486; FAX 817-295-5278; E-mail: burlstar@onramp.net. **Owner(s):** Susan Hutson, P.O. Drawer 909, Burleson, TX 76028. TEL 817-295-0486; James Moody, P.O. Drawer 909, Burleson, TX 76028. TEL 817-295-0486; Ed. Sally Ellertson; Pub. James Moody; adv. contact: Cathy Smith. pub. size: broadsheet; circ. 7,400(paid).

US   ISSN 1041-3081

CROWLEY REVIEW. 1970. Thu. $.25 newsstand; $13.50/yr. 319 N. Burleson Blvd., Burleson, TX 76028. TEL 817-295-0486; FAX 817-295-5278; E-mail: burlstar@onramp.net. **Owner(s):** James Moody, 952 Dorsey, Burleson, TX 76028. TEL 817-295-1623; Susan Hutson, 125 Cliffside Dr., N., Burleson, TX 76028. TEL 817-295-1654; Ed. Nancy Huckaby; Pub. James Moody; adv. contact: Cathy Smith. pub. size: broadsheet; circ. 3,000(paid).

BURNET

US

BURNET BULLETIN. 1873. Wed. $.50 newsstand; $21/yr. in cy.; $30/yr. out of cy. 101 E. Jackson, Burnet, TX 78611. TEL 512-756-6136; FAX 512-756-8911. **Owner(s):** Dixie Newspapers, 1022 B. North Blvd. Ste. 204, Horseshoe Bay, TX 75901. TEL 210-598-2163; Ed. Sara Wartes; Pub. R. Darin Brock; adv. contact: Tim Prince. pub. size: broadsheet; circ. 4,400(paid).

CALDWELL

US

BURLESON COUNTY CITIZEN TRIBUNE. 1898. Thu. $.60 newsstand; $25/yr. in cy.; $30/yr. out of cy.; $25/yr. out of state. 205 W. Buck, Caldwell, TX 77836. TEL 409-567-3286; FAX 409-567-7898. **Owner(s):** Burleson County Publishing Co., 205 W. Buck, Caldwell, TX 77836. TEL 409-567-3286; Ed. Sam Preuss. circ. 3,995(paid).

US

CALDWELL BURLESON COUNTY CITIZEN-TRIBUNE. 1898. Thu. $.60 newsstand; $19.50/yr. in cy.; $25/yr. in state; $30/yr. out-of-state. 205 W. Buck, Caldwell, TX 77836. TEL 409-567-3286; FAX 409-567-7898. **Owner(s):** Caldwell Burleson County Citizen-Tribune, 205 W. Buck, Caldwell, TX 77836. TEL 409-567-3286; Ed. Sam Preuss. adv.; pub. size: broadsheet; circ. 4,100(paid).

CAMERON

US

CAMERON HERALD. 1860. Thu. $.50 newsstand; $18/yr in cy.; $21/yr. out of cy. 108 E. First St., Cameron, TX 76520. TEL 817-697-6671; FAX 817-697-4902. **Owner(s):** Dixie Newspapers Group, 1022 B North Blvd., Ste. 204, Horseshoe Bay, TX 78657. TEL 210-598-2163; Pub. Wayne E. Green; adv. contact: Jacquie Green. pub. size: broadsheet; circ. 4,077(paid).

CANYON

US

CANYON NEWS. 1896. s-w.: Thu. & Sun. $.50 newsstand; $24/yr. local; $34/yr. elsewhere. 1500 Fifth Ave., Canyon, TX 79015. TEL 806-655-7121; FAX 806-655-0823; E-mail: canyonnews@hal.amaonline.com; URL: http://www.canyonnews.com. **Owner(s):** Randall County Publishing Co., 1500 Fifth Ave., Canyon, TX 79015. TEL 806-655-7121; FAX 806-655-0823; Ed. Brad Tooley. adv. contact: Brad Tooley. photos; bk.rev.; pub. size: broadsheet; circ. 4,300(free & paid); Sun. 4,300(free & paid).

CARROLLTON

US

METROCREST NEWS. 1960. Thu. $.50 newsstand; $48/yr. mailed. 1720 N. Josey Ln., Ste. 100, Carrollton, TX 75006. TEL 214-418-9999; FAX 214-418-1620. **Owner(s):** Dallas-Fort Worth Suburban Newspapers, Inc., 1000 Avenue H, Arlington, TX 76011. TEL 817-695-0500; Ed. Rodger Cramer. adv. contact: Judith Terry. pub. size: broadsheet; circ. 48,000(paid).

CARTHAGE

US

PANOLA WATCHMAN. 1873. s-w.: Wed. & Sun. $.50 newsstand; $32/yr. in cy. 109 W. Panola St., Carthage, TX 75633. TEL 903-693-7888; FAX 903-693-5857. **Owner(s):** Westward Communications, Inc., P.O. Box 518, Dallas, TX 75633; Ed. Ted Leach; Pub. Bill Holder; adv. contact: Bill Holder. photos; bk.rev.; pub. size: standard; circ. 5,000(paid); Sun. 5,000(paid). **Formerly:** Carthage Panola Watchman.

CENTER

US

LIGHT & CHAMPION. 1877. s-w.: Tue & Fri. $.75 newsstand; $30/yr. in cy.; $55/yr. elsewhere. 137 San Augustine St., Center, TX 75935. TEL 409-598-3377; FAX 409-598-6394. **Owner(s):** Smith Newspapers, Inc., P.O. Box 27, Fort Payne, AL 35967. TEL 205-845-5510; Ed. Candace Velvin; Pub. Bobby Windham; adv.; photos; pub. size: broadsheet; circ. 5,300(paid).

CHILDRESS

US

CHILDRESS INDEX. 1888. 3/wk.: Sun., Tue., Thu. $.50 newsstand; $36/yr. carrier; $38/yr. mailed. 226 Main St., Childress, TX 79201. TEL 817-937-2525; FAX 817-937-2239. **Owner(s):** Childress Index, Inc., 226 Main St., Childress, TX 79201. TEL 817-937-2525; Ed. Christopher Blackburn. pub. size: standard; circ. evening 3,300(paid); Sun. 3,275(paid). **Wire Service(s):** AP.

CISCO

US

CISCO PRESS. 1870. s-w.: Sun. & Thu. $.50 newsstand; $22/yr. in cy.; $28/yr. in state; $40/yr. out state. 700 Conrad Hilton Ave., Cisco, TX 76437. TEL 817-442-2244; FAX 817-629-2092. **Owner(s):** H.V. O'Brien, 215 S. Seman, Eastland, TX 76448. TEL 817-629-1707; Ed. Richard Kurklin; Pub. H.V. O'Brien; pub. size: broadsheet; circ. 1,800(paid).

CLARKSVILLE

US   ISSN 1040-2489

CLARKSVILLE TIMES, THE. 1875. Thu. $.25 newsstand; $15/yr. in cy.; $24/yr. out of cy. 106 E. Main St., Clarksville, TX 75426. TEL 903-427-5616; FAX 903-427-5617. **Owner(s):** Red River Media, Mt. Pleasant, TX; Ed. Ben Black. adv. contact: Barbara Mitchell. photos; bk.rev.; pub. size: broadsheet; circ. 3,500(paid).

CLEVELAND

US

CLEVELAND ADVOCATE. 1917. Wed. $.50 newsstand; $22/yr. 106 W. Hanson St., Cleveland, TX 77327. TEL 713-592-2626; FAX 713-592-2629. **Owner(s):** Westward Communications, Inc., P.O. Box 609, Conroe, TX 77305. TEL 713-477-0221; Ed. Jerry Vincent; Pub. Diana Lobner; adv. contact: Diana Lobner. photos; pub. size: broadsheet; circ. 2,700(free & paid).

COLEMAN

US

COLEMAN CHRONICLE & DEMOCRAT VOICE. 1933. s-w.: Tue. & Thu. $.35 newsstand; $25.95/yr. in cy.; $36.95/yr. out of cy. 208-212 W. Pecan, Coleman, TX 76834. TEL 915-625-4128; FAX 915-625-4129. **Owner(s):** Brett Autry, P.O. Box 840, Coleman, TX 76834. TEL 915-625-4128; FAX 915-625-4129; Stan Brudney, P.O. Box 840, Coleman, TX 76834. TEL 915-625-4128; FAX 915-625-4129; Ed. Brett Autry; Pub. Brett Autry; adv. contact: Stan Autry. pub. size: broadsheet; circ. 3,600(paid). **Formerly:** Coleman County Chronicle.

COLUMBUS

US   ISSN 0891-1118
BANNER PRESS NEWSPAPER, THE. 1985. Thu. $.50 newsstand; $21/yr. in cy.; $25/yr. in state; $30/yr. out of state. 1038 Milam, Columbus, TX 78934. TEL 409-732-6243; FAX 409-732-6245. **Owner(s):** Regional Newspapers, Inc., 1038 Milam, P.O. Box 490, Columbus, OH 78934. TEL 409-732-6243; Ed. Chad Ferguson. adv.; photos; bk.rev.; pub. size: broadsheet; circ. 4,700.
   Formerly: Banner Newspaper, The.

COMANCHE

US
COMANCHE CHIEF. 1873. Thu. $.50 newsstand; $17/yr. in cy.; $18.50/yr. out of cy.; $20/yr. out of state. 203 W. Grand St., Comanche, TX 76442. TEL 915-356-2636; FAX 915-356-5380. **Owner(s):** James C. & Mary Wilkerson, 205 W. Grand St., Comanche, TX 76442; Ed. James C. Wilkerson; Pub. James C. Wilkerson; adv.; pub. size: broadsheet; circ. 4,300(paid).

COMMERCE

US
COMMERCE JOURNAL. 1889. s-w.: Sun. & Wed. $.50 newsstand; $24/yr. 1219 Washington St., Commerce, TX 75428. TEL 903-886-3196; FAX 903-886-3198. **Owner(s):** American Publishing Co., 606 N. Van Buren, P.O. Box 520, Marion, IL 62959. TEL 618-993-1711; Ed. Warren Morrison; Pub. Paul Harris; adv. contact: Paul Harris. bk.rev.; pub. size: broadsheet; circ. Sun. 2,817(paid).

COPPELL

US
CITIZENS' ADVOCATE NEWSPAPER. 1984. Fri. $.35 newsstand; $15/yr. 936 S. Belt Line, Coppell, TX 75019. TEL 214-462-8192. **Owner(s):** Dan Mara Corp., 936 S. Belt Line, Coppell, TX 75019. TEL 214-420-8808; Ed. Jean Murph; Pub. Jean Murph; pub. size: standard; circ. 4,500(paid).

COPPERAS COVE

US
COPPERAS COVE LEADER PRESS. 1895. Thu. $.35 newsstand; $15/yr. local. 115 W. Ave D, Copperas Cove, TX 76522. TEL 817-547-4207; FAX 817-542-3299. **Owner(s):** Roberts Publishing Co., Andrews, TX; Ed. Connie Landmann; Pub. David Landmann; adv. contact: Bob McInerney. adv.: $5.20/SAU. pub. size: broadsheet; circ. 3,100(free & paid).

CORRIGAN

US
CORRIGAN TIMES, THE. 1954. Thu. $.50 newsstand; $13/yr. in cy.; $16/yr in state; $19/yr. out of state. 202 E. Front St., Corrigan, TX 75939. TEL 409-398-2535; FAX 409-327-7156. **Owner(s):** Polk County Publishing Co., P.O. Box 1276, Livingston, TX 77351. TEL 409-327-4357; FAX 409-327-7156; Ed. Gregory L. Peak; Pub. Alvin Holley; adv.; pub. size: broadsheet; circ. 1,450(paid).

CRANE

US
CRANE NEWS. 1947. Thu. $.50 newsstand; $18/yr. in cy.; $21/yr. in TX; $24/yr. outside of TX. 401 S. Gaston, Crane, TX 79731. TEL 915-558-3541; FAX 915-558-2676. **Owner(s):** Skip & Paula Nichols, 607 E. 24th, Crane, TX 79731. TEL 915-558-3541; FAX 915-558-2676; Ed. Skip Nichols; Pub. Skip Nichols; adv. contact: Paula Nichols. photos; bk.rev.; pub. size: broadsheet; circ. 1,758(paid).

CROCKETT

US
HOUSTON COUNTY COURIER. 1890. s-w.: Sun. & Thu. $.50 newsstand; $16.95/yr. local; $18.95/yr. in state; $20.95/yr. out state. 102 S. Seventh St., Crockett, TX 75835. TEL 409-544-2238; FAX 409-544-4088. **Owner(s):** Polk County Publishing Co., P.O. Box 1276, Livingston, TX 77351; Ed. LaDeanne Smith; Pub. Bassett Keller; adv. contact: Billy Clark. pub. size: broadsheet; circ. 56,000(paid).

CUERO

US
CUERO RECORD. 1894. Wed. $.50 newsstand; $24/yr. out of cy.; $19/yr. in cy. 119 E. Main St., Cuero, TX 77954. TEL 512-275-3464; FAX 512-275-3131. **Owner(s):** Hartman Newspapers, Inc., 1904 Fourth St., Roseberg, TX 77471. TEL 713-342-4474; Ed. Glenn Rea; Pub. Glenn Rea; adv. contact: Connie Young. pub. size: broadsheet; circ. 3,450(paid).

DALLAS

US
DALLAS PARK CITIES NEWS. 1943. Thu. $.25 newsstand; $25/yr. in state; $40/yr. out of state. 8115 Preston Rd., Ste. 120, LB10, Dallas, TX 75225. TEL 214-369-7570; FAX 214-369-7736. **Owner(s):** Marjorie B. Waters, 8115 Preston Rd., Dallas, TX 75225; Thomas R. Waters, 8115 Preston Rd., Dallas, TX 75225. TEL 214-369-7570; Ed. Pete Waters. pub. size: broadsheet; circ. 8,000(paid).

US   ISSN 1049-3387
DALLAS WHITE ROCKER NEWS. 1945. Thu. $.35 newsstand; $17/yr.; $30/2 yrs.; $45/3 yrs. P.O. Box 180698, 10809 Garland Rd., Dallas, TX 75218-0698. TEL 214-327-9335. **Owner(s):** Retta Hanie, 10809 Garland Rd., Dallas, TX 75218. TEL 214-327-9335; Ed. Retta Hanie. adv. contact: Frances Gunter. bk.rev.; pub. size: broadsheet; circ. 4,008(paid).

US
OAK CLIFF TRIBUNE. 1903. bi-w.: Thu. $.50 newsstand; $20/yr. 400 S. Zang, Ste. C101, Dallas, TX 75208. TEL 214-943-7755; FAX 214-943-7775. **Owner(s):** Oak Cliff Tribune, Inc., 400 S. Zang, Ste. C101, Dallas, TX 75200; Ed. Kathy Magers; Pub. Joseph D. Whitney; pub. size: tabloid; circ. 9,700(paid).

DECATUR

US   ISSN 0746-8679
WISE COUNTY MESSENGER. 1880. s-w.: Thu. & Sun. $.50 newsstand; $30/yr. 115 S. Trinity, Decatur, TX 76234-0149. TEL 817-627-5987; FAX 817-627-1004. **Owner(s):** Wise County Messenger, Inc., P.O. Box 149, Decatur, TX 76234. TEL 817-627-5987; FAX 817-627-1004; Ed. Julie Porter; Pub. Roy Eaton; adv. contact: Denny Deady. photos. pub. size: broadsheet; circ. 23,500(free & paid); Sun. 5,500(paid).

DEER PARK

US
DEER PARK BROADCASTER, THE. 1957. Wed. free. 102 W. Pasadena Blvd., Deer Park, TX 77536. TEL 713-479-2760; FAX 713-479-3415. **Owner(s):** Larry & B.J. Power, Broadcaster Publications, Inc., P.O. Box 369, Deer Park, TX 77536. TEL 713-479-2760; FAX 713-479-3415; Ed. Mary Ellen Wilson; Pub. Larry Power; adv. contact: Randy Wilson. pub. size: broadsheet; circ. 11,000(free & paid).

US
DEER PARK PROGRESS, THE. Sat. $.50 newsstand; $18/yr. in cy. 102 W. Pasadena Blvd., Deer Park, TX 77536. TEL 713-479-2760; FAX 713-479-3415. **Owner(s):** Larry & B.J. Power, Broadcaster Publications, Inc., P.O. Box 369, Deer Park, TX 77536. TEL 713-479-2760; FAX 713-479-3415; Ed. Mary Ellen Wilson; Pub. Larry Power; adv. contact: Randy Wilson. circ. 11,000(paid).

DENISON

US
GRAYSON COUNTY SHOPPER. 1970. Wed. free. 4101 Texoma Pkwy., Denison, TX 75020. TEL 903-465-1400; FAX 903-465-1453. **Owner(s):** Cox Publishing Co., P.O. Box 1249, Denison, TX 75021. TEL 903-465-1403; Ed. H. Wayne Cox; Pub. H. Wayne Cox; pub. size: tabloid; circ. 47,000(free).

US
SHOPPER ZONE II. 1986. Wed. free. 4101 Texoma Pky., Denison, TX 75020. TEL 903-465-1400. **Owner(s):** H. Wayne Cox, P.O. Box 1249, Denison, TX 75021. TEL 903-465-1400; Pub. H. Wayne Cox; pub. size: tabloid; circ. 9,191(free).

DESOTO

US
CEDAR HILL TODAY. 1965. Thu. $.50 newsstand; $22/yr. in city; $31/yr. out of city. 1701 N. Hampton, Ste. A, DeSoto, TX 75115. TEL 214-298-4211; FAX 214-298-5369. **Owner(s):** Richard Collins, P.O. Box 381029, Duncanville, TX 75138. TEL 214-298-4211; Ed. Mark Victry; Pub. Richard Collins; adv. contact: Linda Nasche. photos; pub. size: standard; circ. 5,400(free & paid).
   Formerly: Cedar Hill Chronicle.

US   ISSN 0704-0428
DESOTO TODAY. 1977. Thu. $.50 newsstand; $22/yr. in city; $31/yr. out of city. 1701 N. Hampton, Ste. A, DeSoto, TX 75115. TEL 214-298-4211. **Owner(s):** Richard Collins, 1701 N. Hampton, Ste. A, Duncanville, TX 75115. TEL 214-298-4211 Ed. Mark Victory; Pub. Richard Collins; adv. contact: Linda Nasche. pub. size: standard; circ. 8,900(free & paid).
   Formerly: DeSoto News Advertiser

US   ISSN 0888-1960
DUNCANVILLE TODAY. 1960. Thu. $.50 newsstand; $22/yr. in city; $31/yr. out of city. 1701 N. Hampton, Ste. A, DeSoto, TX 75115. TEL 214-298-4211; FAX 214-298-6369. **Owner(s):** Richard Collins, 1701 N. Hampton, Ste. A, Dallas, TX 75115. TEL 214-298-4211; Ed. Mark Victry; Pub. Richard Collins; adv. contact: Leslie Nasche. pub. size: broadsheet; circ. 10,500(paid).
　　Formerly: Duncanville Suburban.

US   ISSN 1065-0644
LANCASTER TODAY. 1975. Thu. $.50 newsstand; $22/yr. in city; $31/yr. out of city. 1701 N. Hampton, Ste. A, DeSoto, TX 75115. TEL 214-298-4211; FAX 214-298-6369. **Owner(s):** Richard Collins, 1701 N. Hampton, Ste. A, Duncanville, TX 75115. TEL 214-298-4211; Ed. Mark Victry; Pub. Richard Collins; adv. contact: Leslie Nasche. pub. size: standard; circ. 4,500(free & paid).
　　Formerly: Lancaster News.

US
MIDLOTHIAN TODAY. 1968. Thu. $.50 newsstand; $17/yr. in city; $21/yr. out of city. 1701 N. Hampton, Ste. A., DeSoto, TX 75115. TEL 214-775-2371; FAX 214-298-6369. **Owner(s):** Today Newspapers, Inc., P.O. Box 381029, Duncanville, TX 75138. TEL 214-298-4211; FAX 214-298-6369; Ed. Mark Victry; Pub. Richard Collins; adv. contact: Leslie Nashe. photos; bk.rev.; pub. size: standard; circ. 1,725(paid).
　　Formerly: Midlothian Reporter.

DIBOLL

US
ANGELINA FREE PRESS. 1953. Thu. $.50 newsstand; $16/yr. in cy.; $20/yr. out of cy. 201 N. Temple Dr., Diboll, TX 75941. TEL 409-829-1801; FAX 409-829-1811. **Owner(s):** Temple-Inland, Inc., 30 S. Temple Dr., Diboll, TX 75941. TEL 800-262-5512; Ed. Gary Willmon; Pub. Gary Willmon; adv. contact: Betty Jo Jared. pub. size: broadsheet; circ. 3,561(free).

DRIPPING SPRINGS

US
DRIPPING SPRINGS DISPATCH. 1982. Thu. $.50 newsstand; $18/yr. Promenade Ctr., Ste. 4, Dripping Springs, TX 78620. TEL 512-858-7893; FAX 512-858-4828. **Owner(s):** Dale Roberson, P.O. Box 550, Dripping Springs, TX 78620. TEL 512-858-7893; FAX 512-858-4828; Ed. Dale Roberson; Pub. Dale Roberson; adv. contact: Joyce Kovacs. photos; pub. size: tabloid; circ. 2,000(paid).

DUMAS

US
MOORE COUNTY NEWS-PRESS. 1927. s-w.: Thu. & Sun. $.50 newsstand; $24/yr. in cy.; $44/yr. out of cy. Seventh & Meredith Sts., Dumas, TX 79029. TEL 806-935-4111. **Owner(s):** Southern Newspapers, Inc., Houston, TX; Ed. Todd Helpler; Pub. Mike Coggins; adv. contact: Mike Coggins. photos; pub. size: broadsheet; circ. 4,881(free & paid).

EAGLE LAKE

US
EAGLE LAKE HEADLIGHT. 1903. Thu. $.35 newsstand; $12/yr. in cy.; $15/yr. out of cy. 220 E. Main St., Eagle Lake, TX 77434. TEL 409-234-5521. **Owner(s):** Jeannine Fearing, P.O. Box 67, Eagle Lake, TX 77434. TEL 713-234-5521; Ed. Jeannine Fearing; Pub. Jeannine Fearing; adv.; photos; pub. size: broadsheet; circ. 2,200(paid).

EASTLAND

US
EASTLAND TELEGRAM. 1968. s-w.: Thu. & Sun. $.50 newsstand; $19/yr. in cy. 215 S. Seaman St., Eastland, TX 76448-0029. TEL 817-629-1707. **Owner(s):** Eastland County Newspapers, Inc., P.O. Box 29, Eastland, TX 76448. TEL 817-629-1707; Ed. H.V. O'Brien; Pub. H.V. O'Brien; adv.; bk.rev.; pub. size: broadsheet; circ. 3,300(paid); Sun. 3,500(paid).

EDGEWOOD

US
EDGEWOOD ENTERPRISE. Thu. $.25 newsstand; $16.50/yr. in cy.; $22/yr. out of cy. 109 Front St., Edgewood, TX 75117. TEL 903-896-4401; FAX 903-962-3660. **Owner(s):** Westward Communications, Inc., 5005 L.B.J. Fwy., Ste. 1040, Dallas, TX 25244. TEL 214-450-1717; Ed. Glenda Lee. adv.; pub. size: broadsheet; circ. 1,500(paid).

EDNA

US
JACKSON COUNTY HERALD/TRIBUNE. 1906. Thu. $.50 newsstand; $21.50/yr. in cy.; $31.50/yr. out of cy; $35.50/yr. out of state. 306 N. Wells St., Edna, TX 77957. TEL 512-782-3547; FAX 512-782-6002. **Owner(s):** Dennis Simons, 201 1/2 N. Wells, Edna, TX 77957. TEL 512-782-3504; Joe Hermes, 606 N. Wells, Edna, TX 77957; Harrison Stafford, II, 508 Gilbert, Edna, TX 77957; Mark Rose, 105 E. Main, Edna, TX 77957. TEL 512-782-5274; David Rose, 105 E. Main, Edna, TX 77957. TEL 512-782-5274; Willard Ulbricht, 114 W. Main, Edna, TX 77957. TEL 512-782-5655; Ed. Bert West; Pub. Bert West; adv. contact: Pam Harvey. pub. size: standard; circ. 4,300(paid).

EL CAMPO

US
EL CAMPO LEADER-NEWS. 1885. s-w.: Wed. & Sat. $.50 newsstand; $25/yr. in cy. 203 E. Jackson, El Campo, TX 77437-1180. TEL 409-543-3363; FAX 409-543-0097. **Owner(s):** El Campo Newspapers, Inc., P.O. Box 1180, El Campo, TX 77437. TEL 409-543-3363; FAX 409-543-0097; Ed. Chris F. Barbee; Pub. Fred V. Barbee, Jr.; adv. contact: Donna Anderson. photos; pub. size: broadsheet; circ. 6,350(paid).

EULESS

US
D/FW PEOPLE. 1983. Thu. free to airport employees; $75/yr. mailed. 400 Fuller-Wiser, Ste. 125, Euless, TX 76039. TEL 817-540-4666; FAX 817-685-7562. **Owner(s):** Wood Publications, Atlanta, GA 30301; Ed. Bill Leader; Pub. Jim Wood; adv. contact: Janie Ross. pub. size: tabloid; circ. 13,000(free & paid).

EVERMAN

US
EVERMAN TIMES. 1962. Thu. $.35 newsstand; $12/yr. in cy.; $17/yr. out of cy. 833 E. Enon, Everman, TX 76140. TEL 817-478-4661. **Owner(s):** B & B Publishing, Inc., P.O. Box 40230, Ft. Worth, TX 76140. TEL 817-478-4661; Ed. Gene S. Blessing; Pub. Gene S. Blessing; adv.; photos; bk.rev.; pub. size: broadsheet; circ. 494(paid).

US
FOREST HILL NEWS. 1945. Thu. free newsstand; $45/yr. mailed. 833 E. Enon, Everman, TX 76140. TEL 817-478-4661. **Owner(s):** B & B Publishing, Inc., P.O. Box 40230, Everman, TX 76140. TEL 817-478-4661; Ed. Shirley Fowkes; Pub. Gene S. Blessing; adv.; photos; bk.rev.; pub. size: broadsheet; circ. 7,000(free & paid).

US
KENNEDALE NEWS. 1965. Thu. $.35 newsstand; $12/yr. in cy.; $17/yr. out of cy. 833 E. Enon, Everman, TX 76140-3523. TEL 817-478-4661. **Owner(s):** B & B Publishing, Inc., P.O. Box 40230, Fort Worth, TX 76140. TEL 817-478-4661; Ed. Gene S. Blessing; Pub. Gene S. Blessing; adv.; photos; bk.rev.; pub. size: broadsheet; circ. 350(paid).

FALFURRIAS

US
FALFURRIAS FACTS. 1906. Thu. $.50 newsstand; $20/yr. local; $22/yr. out of area. 219 E. Rice St., Falfurrias, TX 78355. TEL 512-325-2200. **Owner(s):** Facts Publishing Co., Inc., 219 E. Rice, P.O. Box 619, Falfurrias, TX 78355. TEL 512-325-2200; FAX 512-325-2200; Ed. Marcelo Silva; Pub. Marcelo Silva; adv. contact: SanJuanita Olivarez. pub. size: broadsheet; circ. 2,247(paid).

FLORESVILLE

US
FLORESVILLE CHRONICLE-JOURNAL. 1877. Wed. $.40 newsstand; $20/yr. 1433 Third, Floresville, TX 78114-0820. TEL 210-393-2111; FAX 210-393-9012. **Owner(s):** Joe H. & Marjorie Fietsam, 1401 Hospital Blvd., Floresville, TX 78114. TEL 210-393-6521; FAX 210-393-9012; Ed. Marjorie Fietsam. adv. contact: James Fietsam. pub. size: broadsheet; circ. 4,000(controlled & paid).

FLOYDADA

US
FLOYD COUNTY HESPERIAN-BEACON. 1896. Thu. $.50 newsstand; $16/yr. in cy.; $18/yr. out of cy.; $19/yr. out of state. 111 E. Missouri, Floydada, TX 79235. TEL 806-983-3737. **Owner(s):** Caprock-Sentinel Corp., 706 Barton Blvd., Austin, TX 78704. TEL 512-443-7918; Ed. Alice Towery Gilroy; Pub. Alice Towery Gilroy; pub. size: broadsheet; circ. 2,430(controlled & paid).

FORT STOCKTON

US
FORT STOCKTON PIONEER. 1908. Thu. $.50 newsstand; $21/yr. in cy.; $25/yr. out of cy.; $33/yr. out of state. 210 N. Nelson St., Fort Stockton, TX 79735. TEL 915-336-2281; FAX 915-336-6432. **Owner(s):** Big Bend Communications, Inc., P.O. Box 1528, Ft. Stockton, TX 79735. TEL 915-336-2281; Ed. David McCuffity; Pub. John Cordsen; pub. size: broadsheet; circ. 4,200(paid).

FORT WORTH

US

BENBROOK NEWS. 1939. Thu. free in cy.; $40/yr. out of cy. mailed. 7820 Wyatt Dr., Fort Worth, TX 76108-2533. TEL 817-246-2473; FAX 817-246-2474. **Owner(s):** Suburban Newspapers, Inc., 7820 Wyatt Dr., Fort Worth, TX 76108. TEL 817-246-2473; Ed. Janice Underwood; Pub. Janice Underwood; photos; pub. size: tabloid; circ. 6,000(free & paid).

US

RIVER OAKS NEWS. 1940. Thu. free in cy.; $40/yr. out of cy. mailed. 7820 Wyatt Dr., Fort Worth, TX 76108-2533. TEL 817-246-2473; FAX 817-246-2474. **Owner(s):** Suburban Newspapers, Inc., 7820 Wyatt Dr., Fort Worth, TX 76108. TEL 817-247-2474; Ed. Janice Underwood; Pub. Janice Underwood; adv.; photos; pub. size: tabloid; circ. 7,000(free).

US

SOUTH COUNTY NEWS & ADVERTISER. 1975. Thu. free; $45/yr. mailed. 833 E. Enon, Fort Worth, TX 76140. TEL 817-478-4661. **Owner(s):** B & B Publishing, Inc., P.O. Box 40230, Fort Worth, TX 76140. TEL 817-478-4661; Ed. Gene S. Blessing; Pub. Gene S. Blessing; adv.; pub. size: broadsheet; circ. 7,000(free).

US

WHITE SETTLEMENT NEWS. 1941. Thu. free in cy.; $40/yr. out of cy. mailed. 7820 Wyatt Dr., Fort Worth, TX 76108-2533. TEL 817-246-2473; FAX 817-246-2474. **Owner(s):** Suburban Newspapers, Inc., 7820 Wyatt Dr., Fort Worth, TX 76108. TEL 817-246-2473; Ed. Janice Underwood; Pub. Janice Underwood; photos; pub. size: tabloid; circ. 6,000(free & paid).

FREDERICKSBURG

US   ISSN 0747-0061

FREDERICKSBURG STANDARD/RADIO POST. 1888. Wed. $.50 newsstand; $18/yr.; $22/yr. elsewhere. 108 E. Main, Fredericksburg, TX 78624-0473. TEL 210-997-2155; FAX 210-997-9955. **Owner(s):** Fredericksburg Publishing Co, Inc., P.O. Box 473, Fredericksbrg, TX 78624. TEL 210-997-2155; Ed. Terrill D. Collier; Pub. Arthur H. Kowert; adv. contact: Elaine Kanz. photos; bk.rev.; pub. size: broadsheet; circ. 9,587(paid).

GARLAND

US   ISSN 1045-3997

GARLAND NEWS. 1887. s-w.: Thu. & Sun. $.50 newsstand; $4.50/mo.; $40.50/yr. 613 State St., Garland, TX 75040. TEL 214-272-6591; FAX 214-487-0655. **Owner(s):** DFW Suburban Newspapers, Inc., 1000 Ave. H, E., Arlington, TX 76011. TEL 817-633-0500; Ed. Ray Leszcynski. adv. contact: Neil Tait. pub. size: standard; circ. 10,750(paid). **Wire Service(s):** Southwest News. **Formerly:** Garland Daily News.

GATESVILLE

US   ISSN 0894-4954

GATESVILLE MESSENGER. 1881. Thu. $.50 newsstand; $15.44/yr. in cy. 116 S. Sixth St., Gatesville, TX 76528. TEL 817-865-5212; FAX 817-865-2361. **Owner(s):** Danny Hukel, P.O. Box 799, Gatesville, TX 76528. TEL 817-865-2352; Ed. Larry Kennedy; Pub. Marshall Day; adv. contact: Debbie Day. photos; bk.rev.; pub. size: broadsheet; circ. 5,000(paid).

GEORGETOWN

US

SUNDAY SUN. 1975. Sat. $.50 newsstand; $14/yr. in cy.; $21.50/yr. out of cy. 707 Main St., Georgetown, TX 78626. TEL 512-930-4824; FAX 512-863-2474. **Owner(s):** Linda Scarbrough, P.O. Box 39, Georgetown, TX 78627-0039. TEL 512-930-4824; Donna Josey, P.O. Box 39, Georgetown, TX 78627-0039. TEL 512-930-4824; Ed. Linda Scarbrough; Pub. Clark Thurmond; adv. contact: Clark Thurmond. photos; pub. size: broadsheet; circ. 7,500(paid).

US

WILLIAMSON COUNTY SUN. 1877. w. $.50 newsstand; $28/yr. in cy. 709 Main St., Georgetown, TX 78626-0039. TEL 512-930-4824. **Owner(s):** Williamson County Sun, Inc., P.O. Box 39, Georgetown, TX 78627. TEL 512-930-4824; Ed. Brian Pearson. adv.; photos; pub. size: broadsheet; circ. 7,400(paid).

GIDDINGS

US

GIDDINGS TIMES & NEWS. 1888. Thu. $22.50/yr. in cy.; $25.00/yr. out of cy.; $35.00/yr. out of state. 170 N. Knox Ave., Giddings, TX 78942. TEL 409-542-2222. **Owner(s):** Preuss Printing Co., 170 N. Knox Ave. Giddings, TX 78942; Ed. David True; Pub. L. M. Preuss; pub. size: broadsheet; circ. 6,200(paid).

GILMER

US   ISSN 8750-0884

GILMER MIRROR. 1877. s-w.: Wed. & Sat. $.50 newsstand; $27/yr. in cy.; $31/yr. out of cy; $35/yr. out of state. 214 E. Marshall St., Gilmer, TX 75644. TEL 903-843-2503; FAX 903-843-5123. **Owner(s):** Greeneway Enterprises, P.O. Box 250, Gilmer, TX 75644. TEL 903-843-2503; Ed. Sarah Greene; Pub. Sarah Greene; adv. contact: Patti Harris. photos; bk.rev.; pub. size: broadsheet; circ. 5,400(paid).

GLADEWATER

US

GLADEWATER MIRROR. 1949. Wed. $.50 newsstand; $26/yr. in cy.; $28/yr. out of cy.; $36.50/yr. out of state. 201 S. Dean St., Gladewater, TX 75647. TEL 903-845-2235; FAX 903-845-2237. **Owner(s):** Westward Communications, Inc., 5005 LBJ Freeway #1040, Dallas, TX 75244. TEL 214-450-1717; FAX 214-450-1770; Ed. John Gore; Pub. Floydell Borchardt; adv.; pub. size: broadsheet; circ. 1,850(paid).

GLEN ROSE

US

GLEN ROSE REPORTER. 1887. Thu. $13.50/yr in cy; $18/yr. out of cy.: $28/yr. out of state. 100 S.W. Vernon St., Glen Rose, TX 76043. TEL 817-897-2282; FAX 817-897-9423. **Owner(s):** Glen Rose Publishing Co., P.O. Box 2009, Glen Rose TX 76043. TEL 817-897-2282; FAX 817-897-9423; Ed. Dan McCarty. adv.; photos; pub. size: broadsheet; circ. 2,900(paid).

GONZALES

US

GONZALES INQUIRER. 1853. s-w.: Tue. & Fri. $.50 newsstand; $28/yr. in cy.; $33/yr. out of cy. 622 St. Paul St., Gonzales, TX 78629. TEL 210-672-2861; FAX 210-672 7029. **Owner(s):** Dixie Newspapers, 1022-B North Blvd., Ste. 204, Horseshoe Bay, TX 78654; Ed. Charles Wood; Pub. Jim Cunningham. adv. contact: Kathy Gillett. pub. size: broadsheet; circ. 4,000(paid).

GORMAN

US

GORMAN PROGRESS, THE. 1900. Wed. $.30 newsstand; $10/yr. in cy.; $14.50/yr. in state; $16.50/yr. out of state. 105 S. Kent, Gorman, TX 76454-0068. TEL 817-734-2410; FAX 817-734-2799. **Owner(s):** Joe Bennett, 106 S. Kent St., P.O. Box 68, Gorman, TX 76454-0068. TEL 817-734-2410; FAX 817-734-2799; Ed. Herman Bennett; Pub. Joe Bennett; adv.; pub. size: broadsheet; circ. 1,000(paid).

GRANBURY

US

HOOD COUNTY NEWS. 1886. s-w.: Wed. & Sat. $.50 newsstand; $26/yr. in cy.; $39/yr. out of cy.; $52/yr. out of state. 1501 E. Morgan St., Granbury, TX 76048. TEL 817-573-7066; FAX 817-573-6579. **Owner(s):** Jerry Tidwell, 1419 S. Morgan, Granbury, TX 76048; Ed. Jerry Tidwell; Pub. Jerry Tidwell; adv. contact: Cherri Medcalf. pub. size: broadsheet; circ. 10,034(paid).

GRAND SALINE

US

GRAND SALINE SUN. 1894. Wed. $.50 newsstand; $19.50/yr. in cy.; $28.50/yr. out of cy.; $32.50/yr. out of state. 116 N. Main St., Grand Saline, TX 75140. TEL 903-962-4275; FAX 903-962-3660. **Owner(s):** Westward Communications, Inc., 5005 LBJ Freeway, Ste. 1040, Dallas, TX 75244. TEL 214-450-1717; Ed. Jan Adamson. adv.; pub. size: broadsheet; circ. 2,500(paid).

GREENVILLE

US

HUNT COUNTY SHOPPER. 1965. w. free newsstand; $8.50/yr. out of area. 3617 Wesley, Greenville, TX 75401. TEL 903-455-5254; FAX 903-455-3297. **Owner(s):** Hunt County Shopper, 3617 Wesley, Greenville, TX 75401. TEL 903-455-5254; FAX 903-455-3297; Ed. Warren Hope; Pub. Warren Hope; adv.; pub. size: tabloid; circ. 24,047(free & paid).

GROESBECK

US

GROESBECK JOURNAL. 1892. Thu. $.40 newsstand; $12/yr. in cy.; $15/yr. in state; $17/yr. out of state; $19/yr. foreign. 115-117 N. Ellis, Groesbeck, TX 76642. TEL 817-729-5103; FAX 817-729-5555. **Owner(s):** Groesbeck Journal, Inc., P.O. Box 440, Groesbeck, TX 76642. TEL 817-729-5103; Ed. Thomas E. Hawkins. Pub. Thomas E. Hawkins; pub. size: broadsheet; circ. 4,600(paid).

GUN BARREL CITY

US ISSN 1046-8633
CEDAR CREEK PILOT. 1970. s-w.: Thu. & Sun. $.50 newsstand; $22/yr. 828 W. Main St., Gun Barrel City, TX 75147. TEL 903-432-3132. **Owner(s):** Stephens Group, Inc., P.O. Box 1359, Fort Smith, AR 72901-7017. TEL 501-785-7810; Ed. Chip Souza; Pub. Dan Dwelle; adv. contact: Kathi Nailling. photos; pub. size: broadsheet; circ. 5,300(paid); Sun. 6,150(paid).

HALLETTSVILLE

US
HALLETTSVILLE TRIBUNE-HERALD. 1931. Wed.21. $.60 newsstand; $19.50/yr. in cy.; $28.50/yr. out of cy.; $30/yr. out of state. 108 S. Texana, Hallettsville, TX 77964. TEL 512-798-2481; FAX 512-798-9902. **Owner(s):** L.M. Preuss, 170 N. Knox, Giddings, TX 78942. TEL 409-542-2222; Pub. Larry Rothbauer; adv. contact: Anne Kubicek. pub. size: standard; circ. 4,000(paid).

HAMILTON

US
HAMILTON HERALD-NEWS. 1875. Thu. $.40 newsstand; $20/yr. in cy.; $25/yr. out of cy. 112 E. Main, Hamilton, TX 76531. TEL 817-386-3145; FAX 817-386-3001. **Owner(s):** Hamilton Publishing Co., Inc., 112 E. Main, Hamilton, TX 76531. TEL 817-386-3145; Ed. Roger P. Miller; Pub. Kenneth Miller; pub. size: broadsheet; circ. 3,700(paid).

HASKELL

US
HASKELL FREE PRESS. 1886. Thu. $.50 newsstand; $20/yr. in cy.; $28/yr. elsewhere. 401 S. First St., Haskell, TX 79521. TEL 817-864-2686. **Owner(s):** John McDougal, 401 S. First St., Haskell, TX 79521. TEL 817-864-2686; Ed. Joyce Jones; Pub. John McDougal; adv. contact: John McDougal. pub. size: broadsheet; circ. 2,800(paid).

HEMPHILL

US
SABINE COUNTY REPORTER-RAMBLER. 1883. Wed. $.75 newsstand; $20/yr. in cy.; $30/yr. out of cy. 211 Worth St., Hemphill, TX 75948. TEL 409-787-2643; FAX 409-787-4300. **Owner(s):** Smith Newspapers, Inc., P.O. Box 27, Fort Payne, AL 35967. TEL 205-845-5510; Ed. Stephanie Corley; Pub. Stephanie Corley; pub. size: standard; circ. 4,000(paid).
   Formerly: San Augustine Rambler.

HEMPSTEAD

US ISSN 0164-4203
WALLER COUNTY NEWS-CITIZEN. 1890. Wed. $.50 newsstand; $22/yr. in cy.; $26/yr. out of cy. 705 12th St., Hempstead, TX 77445. TEL 409-826-3361; FAX 409-826-3361. **Owner(s):** Gulf Coast Newspapers, 705 12th St., Hempstead, TX 77445. TEL 409-826-3361; FAX 409-826-3361; Ed. Jim Belew; Pub. Jim Belew; adv.; photos; pub. size: broadsheet; circ. 3,500(paid).

HONDO

US
HONDO ANVIL HERALD. 1886. Thu. $.50 newsstand; $15/yr. local; $25/yr. out of area. 1601 Ave. K, Hondo, TX 78861. TEL 210-426-3346; FAX 210-426-3348. **Owner(s):** Associated Texas Newspapers, Inc., 1801 Exposition, Austin, TX 78703. TEL 512-476-3950; FAX 512-476-6356; Pub. William E. Berger; adv.; bk.rev.; pub. size: broadsheet; circ. 3,917(paid); morning 8,300.

US
SABINAL SAMPLER. 1950. Wed. free in area. 1601 Ave. K, Hondo, TX 78861. TEL 210-426-3346; FAX 210-426-3348. **Owner(s):** W.E. Berger, P.O. Box 400, Hondo, TX 78861. TEL 210-426-3346; FAX 210-426-3348; Ed. Frances Guinn. adv.: $2.00/SAU. pub. size: broadsheet; circ. 1,483(free).

HOUSTON

US
CITIZEN, THE. 1960. Wed. $.50 newsstand; $18/6 mos. mailed in area. 17511 El Camino Real, Houston, TX 77058. TEL 713-488-1108; FAX 713-286-0750. **Owner(s):** Gulf Coast Newspapers, 17511 El Camino Real, Houston, TX 77058. TEL 713-488-1108; FAX 713-286-0750; Ed. Lori Williams; Pub. Lonnie Clement; adv.; pub. size: broadsheet.

US
HOUSTON FORWARD TIMES. 1960. Wed. $.50 newsstand; $13.50/6 mos. in cy.; $25/yr. in cy. 4411 Almeda, Houston, TX 77004. TEL 713-526-4727; FAX 713-526-3170. **Owner(s):** Lenora Carter, 411 Almeda, Houston, TX 77004; Ed. Bud Johnson; Pub. Lenora Carter; adv. contact: Henrietta Smith. pub. size: broadsheet; circ. 60,000(paid).

US
HOUSTON INFORMER. 1893. Tue. $1/wk. newsstand; $32/yr. in cy. 4209 Dowling, Houston, TX 77004. TEL 713-527-8261; FAX 713-524-7028. **Owner(s):** Lorenza P. Butler, Jr., 3906 Daphne St., Houston, TX 77021. TEL 713-527-8261; Ed. George McElroy; Pub. Lorenza P. Butler, Jr.; pub. size: broadsheet; circ. 23,000(paid).

HOWE

US
HOWE ENTERPRISE. 1963. Thu. $.50 newsstand; $15/yr. in cy.; $20/yr. out of cy. 106 E. Haning St., Howe, TX 75459-0488. TEL 903-532-6012. E-mail: howeenterprise@texoma.com; URL: http://www.texoma.com/newspapers/howe-enterprise. Owner(s): Dale Rideout, 106 E. Haning St., Howe, TX 75459-0488. TEL 903-532-6012; Ed. Lana Rideout; Pub. Dale Rideout; adv. contact: Dale Rideout. photos; bk.rev.; pub. size: standard; circ. 650(free & paid).

HUMBLE

US
HUMBLE SUN. Wed. free. 20202 Hwy. 59, N., Ste. 195, Humble, TX 77338. TEL 713-446-3733; FAX 713-446-0201. **Owner(s):** Houston Community Newspapers, Inc., P.O. Box 280, Channelview, TX 77530. TEL 713-452-0530; Ed. Norm Rowland; Pub. Tony Burt, Jr.; adv.; photos; pub. size: broadsheet; circ. 17,998(controlled & free).
   Formerly: Humble Echo.

US
KINGWOOD SUN. 1942. Wed. free. 20202 Hwy. 59, N., Humble, TX 77338. TEL 713-446-3733; FAX 713-446-0201. **Owner(s):** Houston Community Newspapers, Inc., P.O. Box 280, Channelview, TX 77530. TEL 713-452-0530; Ed. Norm Rowland; Pub. Tony Burt, Jr.; adv.; photos; pub. size: broadsheet; circ. 15,975(controlled & free).
   Formerly: Kingwood Echo/New Caney Echo.

US
PORTER/NEW CANEY SUN. 1942. Wed. free. 20202 Hwy. 59, N., Humble, TX 77347. TEL 713-446-3733; FAX 713-446-0201. **Owner(s):** Houston Community Newspapers, Inc., P.O. Box 280, Channelview, TX 77530. TEL 713-452-0530; Ed. Norm Rowland; Pub. Kelli Roberts; adv.; photos; pub. size: broadsheet; circ. 12,000(controlled & free).
   Formerly: Porter/New Caney Echo.

IDALOU

US
IDALOU BEACON. 1957. w. $.50 newsstand; $15/yr. local; $17/yr. out of cy. & state. 818 Frontage Rd., Idalou, TX 79329. TEL 806-892-2233. **Owner(s):** Scott & July Luce, 411 13th St., Abernathy, TX 79311. TEL 806-298-2909; Ed. Scott Luce; Pub. Scott Luce; adv.; photos; pub. size: broadsheet; circ. 675(free & paid).

IOWA PARK

US
IOWA PARK LEADER. 1969. Thu. $.50 newsstand; $15/yr. in cy.; $17/yr. out of cy.; $20/yr out of state. P.O. Box 430, Iowa Park, TX 76367. TEL 817-592-4431. **Owner(s):** Bob & Dolores Hamilton, P.O. Box 430, Iowa Park, TX 76367. TEL 817-592-4431; adv.; photos; pub. size: standard; circ. 2,560(paid).

JASPER

US
JASPER NEWS-BOY. 1865. s-w.: Wed. & Sun. $.25 newsstand; $10/yr. in cy.; $12/yr. out of cy.; $15/yr. elsewhere. 302 N. Wheeler, Jasper, TX 75951. TEL 409-384-3441; FAX 409-384-8803. **Owner(s):** Hearst Corp., 959 Eighth Ave., New York, NY 10019; Ed. Donna Price; Pub. Willis Webb; pub. size: broadsheet; circ. 6,122(paid).

US
JASPER NEWS-BOY SHOPPER. Wed. $.25/newsstand. 302 N. Wheeler, Jasper, TX 75951. TEL 409-384-3441; FAX 409-384-8803. **Owner(s):** Enterprise Co., P.O. Box 3071, Beaumont, TX 77704. TEL 409-833-3311; Pub. Willis Webb; pub. size: broadsheet; circ. 17,700(free).

JEFFERSON

US ISSN 1060-3476
JEFFERSON JIMPLECUTE. 1848. Thu. $.50 newsstand; $18/yr. in cy.; $22.50/yr. in state; $26/yr. out of state. 205 W. Austin, Jefferson, TX 75657. TEL 903-665-2462; FAX 903-665-3802. **Owner(s):** American Publishing Co., 606 N. Van Buren, P.O. Box 520, Marion, IL 62959. TEL 618-993-1711; Ed. Lou Anne Suber; Pub. Joe Wayne Dennis; pub. size: broadsheet; circ. 2,500(paid).

JUNCTION

US

JUNCTION EAGLE, THE. 1882. Wed. $.50 newsstand; $17/yr. in cy.; $19/yr. out of cy.; $20/yr. out of state. 215 N. Sixth St., Junction, TX 76849. TEL 915-446-2610; FAX 915-446-4025. **Owner(s):** Whittemore Cooper, 215 N. Sixth St., Junction, TX 76849. TEL 915-446-2610; FAX 915-446-4025; Ed. Whittemore Cooper; Pub. Whittemore Cooper; adv. contact: Roy Cooper. bk.rev.; pub. size: standard.

KARNES CITY

US

KARNES CITATION. 1895. Wed. $.50 newsstand; $20/yr. in cy.; $26/yr. out of cy. 110 S. Market St., Karnes City, TX 78118. TEL 210-780-3924. **Owner(s):** Karnes Multimedia, Inc., 110 S. Market St., Karnes City, TX 78118. TEL 210-780-3924; Ed. Bill DeFries; Pub. Bill DeFries; adv. contact: Sharon Menn. pub. size: standard; circ. 2,550(paid).

US

KENNEDY ADVANCED TIMES. Wed. $.50 newsstand; $20/yr. in cy.; $26/yr. out of cy. 110 S. Market, Karnes City, TX 78118. TEL 210-780-3924. **Owner(s):** Karnes Multimedia, Inc., 110 S. Market St., Karnes City, TX 78118. TEL 210-780-3924; Ed. Bill DeFries; Pub. Bill DeFries; adv. contact: Sharon Menn. pub. size: standard; circ. 1,900(paid).

KAUFMAN

US

KAUFMAN HERALD, THE. 1886. Thu. $.50 newsstand; $18/yr. in cy.; $21/yr. out of cy. 300 N. Washington, Kaufman, TX 75142. TEL 214-932-2171; FAX 214-932-2172. **Owner(s):** Hartman Newspapers, Inc., P.O. Box 1390, Rosenberg, TX 77471. TEL 713-342-8691; Ed. Pam High. adv.; pub. size: broadsheet; circ. 4,200(paid).

KELLER

US

KELLER CITIZEN, THE. 1980. Tue. $.25 newsstand; $25/yr. 538 E. Price St., Keller, TX 76248. TEL 817-431-2231; FAX 817-431-2231; E-mail: billlewis@eworld.com. **Owner(s):** William C. Lewis, P.O. Box 615, Keller, TX 76244. TEL 817-431-2231; FAX 817-431-2231; Pub. William C. Lewis; adv. contact: Sandra S. Lewis. adv.: $7/SAU. photos; pub. size: broadsheet; circ. 14,700(free & paid).

KERMIT

US

WINKLER COUNTY NEWS. 1936. Thu. $16/yr. deliv. in cy.; $27/yr. mailed out of cy. 109 S. Poplar, Kermit, TX 79745. TEL 915-586-2561; FAX 915-586-2562. **Owner(s):** Golden West Publishing, Inc., 109 S. Poplar, Kermit, TX 79745. TEL 915-586-2561; Ed. Bert Brewer; Pub. Richard E. McLaughlin; adv. contact: Lura Gower. pub. size: standard; circ. 3,700(paid).

KERRVILLE

US

MOUNTAIN SUN, THE. 1881. Wed. $.50 newsstand; $20/yr. in cy.; $22.50/yr. out of cy.; $25/yr. out of state. 516 Quinlan, Kerrville, TX 78028. TEL 210-257-3300; FAX 210-257-3329. **Owner(s):** Sun Co., Inc., P.O. Box 790, Espanola, NM 87532. TEL 505-753-2126; Pub. Robert Trapp Jr.; adv.; photos; pub. size: broadsheet; circ. 6,050(paid).

KINGSVILLE

US

KINGSVILLE RECORD, THE. 1906. s-w.: Sun. & Wed. $26/yr. home deliv.; $33.50/yr. mailed. 105 S. Fifth St., Kingsville, TX 78363. TEL 512-592-4304; FAX 512-592-1015. **Owner(s):** Kingsville Publishing Co., P.O. Box 951, Kingsville, TX 78364. TEL 512-592-4304; Ed. Bob Odom; Pub. Bob Odom; pub. size: broadsheet; circ. 6,500(paid).

LA FERIA

US   ISSN 1084-2578

LA FERIA NEWS. 1923. Wed. $.50 newsstand; $22/yr. in cy.; $27/yr. in state. 116 W. Oleander St., La Feria, TX 78559-0308. TEL 210-797-1813; FAX 210-797-9217. **Owner(s):** Golden Media, Inc., P.O. Box 308, La Feria, TX 78559 TEL 210-797-1813; FAX 210-797-9217; Ed. Vincent W. Bodiford; Pub. Vincent W. Bodiford; adv.; photos; bk.rev.; pub. size: broadsheet; circ. 3,450(free & paid).

LA GRANGE

US

FAYETTE COUNTY RECORD, THE. 1922. s-w.: Tue. & Fri. $.50 newsstand; $17.50/yr. 127 S. Washington, La Grange, TX 78945. TEL 409-968-3155; FAX 409-968-6767. **Owner(s):** Richard L. Barton, P.O. Box 400, La Grange, TX 78945. TEL 409-968-3155; FAX 409-968-6767; Ed. Richard L. Barton, Jr.; Pub. Richard L. Barton Jr.; adv.; photos; pub. size: broadsheet; circ. 5,966(paid).

LAKE DALLAS

US

ARGYLE SUN, THE. 1986. Thu. free. 275 Market St., Lake Dallas, TX 75065. TEL 817-497-4141. **Owner(s):** Sun Newspapers, 275 Market St., P.O. Box 879, Lake Dallas, TX 75065. TEL 817-497-4141; Pub. Terry Lantrip; adv. contact: Willie Kelling. photos; pub. size: broadsheet; circ. 1,600(free).

US

DENTON COUNTY EXPRESS. 1992. Wed. included with The Lake Cities Sun & The Argyle Sun. 275 Market St., Lake Dallas, TX 75065. TEL 817-497-4141. **Owner(s):** Sun Newspapers, 275 Market St., Lake Dallas, TX 75065; Pub. Terry Lantrip; adv. contact: Willie Kelling. photos; pub. size: broadsheet; circ. 3,000(free).

US

LAKE CITIES SUN, THE. 1974. Wed. $.50 newsstand; $18/yr. in cy.; $26/yr. in state. 275 Market St., Lake Dallas, TX 75065. TEL 817-497-4141. **Owner(s):** Sun Newspapers, 275 Market St., P.O. Box 879, Lake Dallas, TX 75065; Pub. Terry Lantrip; adv. contact: Willie Kelling. photos; pub. size: broadsheet; circ. 1,500(paid).

LA MARQUE

US

LA MARQUE TIMES. 1946. Wed. $.25 newsstand; $16/yr. in cy. 1118 Bayou Rd., La Marque, TX 77568. TEL 409-935-243. FAX 409-925-1399. **Owner(s):** Santa Fe Newspapers, Inc., P.O. Box 158, La Marque, TX 77568. TEL 409-935-251. Ed. Harry Monych; Pub. Harry Monych; adv. contact: Harry Monych. pub. size: broadsheet; circ. 6,042(paid).

LAMESA

US

LAMESA PRESS-REPORTER. 1905. s-w. Wed. & Sun. $.50 newsstand; $25.25/yr. 523 N. First St., Lamesa, TX 79331. TEL 806-872-2177; FAX 806-872-2623. **Owner(s):** Roberts Publishing Co., 210 E. Broadway, Andrews, TX 79714. TEL 915-523-3232 Walter Buckel, 523 N. First St., Lamesa, TX 79331. TEL 806-872-2177; Russell Skiles, 523 N. First St., Lamesa, TX 79331. TEL 806-872-2177; B. McCorrick, 523 N. First St. Lamesa, TX 79331. TEL 806-872-2177; B. Buckel, 523 N. First St., Lamesa, TX 79331. TEL 806-872-2177; Barbara Buckel, 523 N. First St., Lamesa, TX 79331. TEL 806-872-2177 Venita Wade, 523 N. First St., Lamesa, TX 79331. TEL 806-872-2177; Ed. Russel Skiles; Pub. Russel Skiles; pub. size: broadsheet circ. 4,224(free & paid).

LA PORTE

US

BAYSHORE SUN. 1947. s-w.: Wed. & Sun. $.25 newsstand; $25/yr. in cy. 1200 Hwy. 146, S., Ste. 150, La Porte, TX 77571. TEL 713-471-1234; FAX 713-471-5763. **Owner(s):** Hartman Newspapers, Inc., P.O. Box 1390, Rosenberg, TX 77471. Ed. John Black; Pub. John Black; pub. size: broadsheet; circ. 13,000(paid); Sun. 5,300(paid).

LEAKEY

US

REAL AMERICAN. 1951. w. $.50 newsstand; $15/yr. in cy.; $20/yr. out of cy. Main St., Leakey, TX 78873. TEL 210-232-5204; FAX 210-232-5630. **Owner(s):** Vice Stadter, Main St. P.O. Box 1140, Leakey, TX 78873. TEL 210-232-5204; FAX 210-232-5630; Ed. Pat Thurmond; Pub. Vic Stadter; adv. contact: Pat Thurmond. photos; pub. size: standard; circ. 1,250(controlled & paid).

LEVELLAND

US

LEVELLAND HOCKLEY COUNTY NEWS-PRESS. 1925. s-w.: Wed. & Sun. $.50 newsstand; $24/yr. 711 Austin St., Levelland, TX 79336. TEL 806-894-3121; FAX 806-894-7957. **Owner(s):** Stephen & Pat Enterprises, Drawer 1628, Levelland, TX 79336 TEL 806-894-3121; FAX 806-894-7957; Ed. Stephen A. Henry; Pub. Stephen & Pat Henry; adv.; photos; pub. size: standard; circ. 4,761(free & paid); Sun. 5,045(free & paid).

LEWISVILLE

US

COPPELL GAZETTE. Thu. $.50 newsstand; $36/yr. mailed. 1165 S. Stemmons, Ste. 100, Lewisville, TX 75067. TEL 214-436-3566; FAX 214-219-0719. **Owner(s):** Harte-Hanks Communications, Inc., P.O. Box 269, San Antonio, TX 78291. TEL 512-344-8000; Ed. Tim Waterson; Pub. Lynn Dickerson; adv. contact: Debbie Rauen. pub. size: broadsheet; circ. 4,200(paid).

US   ISSN 0745-6174

LEWISVILLE LEADER. 1895. s-w.: Wed. & Sat. free. 1165 S. Stemmons, Ste. 100, Lewisville, TX 75057. TEL 214-436-3566; FAX 214-436-7432. **Owner(s):** Harte-Hanks Communications, Inc., P.O. Box 269, San Antonio, TX 78291; Ed. Kristine Hughes; Pub. Lynn Dickerson; adv. contact: Debbie Raven. pub. size: broadsheet; circ. 26,500(controlled & free); Sun. 23,500(controlled & free). **Wire Service(s):** UPI.
   Formerly: Lewisville Daily Leader.

LIBERTY

US

LIBERTY GAZETTE. 1960. Wed. free. 314 Main St., Liberty, TX 77575. TEL 409-336-6416; FAX 409-336-9400. **Owner(s):** Lawrence & Cynthia Kuslich, 314 Main St., Liberty, TX 77575. TEL 409-336-6416; FAX 409-336-9400; Ed. Edith Smith; Pub. Lawrence Kuslich; adv.; pub. size: broadsheet; circ. 8,800(free).

US

PONY EXPRESS MAIL. 1981. Tue. free. 314 Main St., Liberty, TX 77575. TEL 409-336-6416; FAX 409-336-9400. **Owner(s):** Lawrence & Cynthia Kuslich, 314 Main St., Liberty, TX 77575. TEL 409-336-6416; FAX 409-336-9400; Ed. Edith Smith; Pub. Lawrence Kuslich; adv.; pub. size: broadsheet; circ. 8,012(free).

US   ISSN 0746-6838

VINDICATOR, THE. 1887. s-w.: Wed. & Sun. $.50 newsstand; $30/yr. in cy. 301 Vera Ln., Liberty, TX 77575. TEL 409-336-3611; FAX 409-336-3345. **Owner(s):** Hartman Newspapers, Inc., P.O. Box 1390, Rosenberg, TX 77471. TEL 713-342-8691; Ed. Ernie E. Zieschang; Pub. Ernie E. Zieschang; adv. contact: Jeff Meadows. photos; circ. 4,745(free & paid).
   Formerly: Vindicator Advertiser, The.

LITTLEFIELD

US

LAMB COUNTY LEADER-NEWS. 1923. s-w.: Wed. & Sun. $.50 newsstand; $22/yr. in cy.; $28/yr. out of cy.; $32/ out of state. 313 W. Fourth St., Littlefield, TX 79339. TEL 806-385-4481; FAX 806-385-4640. **Owner(s):** Stephen & Pat Enterprises, P.O. Drawer 1628, Levelland, TX 79336. TEL 806-385-4481; Ed. Joella Lovvorn; Pub. Stephen A. Henry; adv.; photos; pub. size: standard; circ. 2,465(free & paid); Sun. 2,755(free & paid).

LIVINGSTON

US

POLK COUNTY ENTERPRISE. 1882. s-w.: Thu. & Sun. $.50 newsstand; $20/yr. in cy.; $22/yr. out of cy.; $24/yr. out of state. 100 Calhoun, Livingston, TX 77351. TEL 409-327-4357; FAX 409-327-7156. **Owner(s):** Polk County Publishing Co., P.O. Box 1276, Livingston, TX 77351. TEL 409-327-4357; Ed. Barbara White; Pub. Alvin Holly; pub. size: broadsheet; circ. 8,100(paid).
   Formerly: Livingston Polk County Enterprise.

LLANO

US

LLANO NEWS. 1889. Thu. $.50 newsstand; $19/yr. in cy.; $26/yr. rest of state; $40/yr. out of state. 813 Berry St., Llano, TX 78643. TEL 915-247-4433; FAX 915-247-4433. **Owner(s):** Walter L. Buckner, P.O. Box 187, Llano, TX 78643. TEL 915-247-4433; FAX 915-247-4433; Ed. Jimmy Stephenson; Pub. Walter L. Buckner; adv. contact: Walter L. Buckner. pub. size: standard; circ. 3,300(paid).

LOCKHART

US

LOCKHART POST REGISTER. 1872. Thu. $.50 newsstand; $35/yr. 111 S. Church St., Lockhart, TX 78644. TEL 512-398-4886; FAX 512-398-4888. **Owner(s):** Dana Garrett, 111 S. Church St., Lockhart, TX 78644. TEL 512-398-4886; Pub. Dana Garrett; adv. contact: Wayne Bock. pub. size: broadsheet; circ. 3,800(paid).

LORENZO

US

LORENZO EXAMINER. 1986. Fri. $.35 newsstand; $12/yr. in cy.; $13.50/yr. in state; $16/yr. out of state. 513 Harrison, Lorenzo, TX 79343. TEL 806-634-5390; FAX 806-634-5390. **Owner(s):** Bill & Charlotte Gibbs, 1106 Fifth, P.O. Box 331, Lorenzo, TX 79343. TEL 806-634-5390; FAX 806-634-5390; Ed. Bill Gibbs; Pub. Bill Gibbs; adv. contact: Charlotte Gibbs. pub. size: standard; circ. 650(paid).

LULING

US

LULING NEWSBOY & SIGNAL. 1940. Thu. $20.50/yr. local. 415 E. Davis, Luling, TX 78648. TEL 210-875-2116; FAX 210-875-2124. **Owner(s):** Luling Publishing Co., Inc., 415 E. Davis, Luling, TX 78648. TEL 210-875-2116; FAX 210-875-2124; Ed. Karen G. McCrary. adv.; photos; bk.rev.; pub. size: broadsheet; circ. 2,500(paid).

MABANK

US   ISSN 1049-3409

MONITOR, THE. Wed. $.25 newsstand; $15/yr. 1316 S. Third St., Mabank, TX 75147-7680. TEL 903-887-4511; FAX 903-887-4510. **Owner(s):** Charlotte Whitaker, P.O. Box 1144, Mabank, TX 75147. TEL 903-887-4511; FAX 903-887-4510; Ed. Jim McKee; Pub. Charlotte Whitaker; adv. contact: Jim McKee. photos; pub. size: broadsheet; circ. 20,750(free & paid).

MANSFIELD

US   ISSN 0746-3847

MANSFIELD NEWS-MIRROR. 1883. s-w.: Mon. & Thu. $.50 newsstand; $32.95/yr. in cy. 119 N. Main, Mansfield, TX 76063. TEL 817-473-4451; FAX 810-473-0730. **Owner(s):** Jerry T. Ebensbertger, P.O. Box 337, Mansfield, TX 76063. TEL 817-473-4451; Ed. Jerry T. Ebensberger; Pub. Jerry T. Ebensberger; adv.; pub. size: broadsheet; circ. 4,000(paid).

MARBLE FALLS

US

MARBLE FALLS HIGHLANDER. 1956. s-w.: Tue. & Fri. $.50 newsstand; $35/yr. 208 Main, Marble Falls, TX 78654. TEL 210-693-4367; FAX 210-693-3650. **Owner(s):** Dixie Newspapers, 1022-B North Blvd., Ste. 204, Horshoe Bay, TX 78657. TEL 210-598-2163; Ed. Billy Berkenbile; Pub. Jim Chionsini; adv.; photos; bk.rev.; pub. size: broadsheet; circ. 6,500(paid).

MASON

US

MASON COUNTY NEWS. 1877. Wed. $.50 newsstand; $16/yr. in cy.; $18/yr. out of cy.; $20 elsewhere. 110 Live Oak, Mason, TX 76856. TEL 915-347-5757; FAX 915-347-5668. **Owner(s):** G.W. Lyon, 110 Live Oak, Mason, TX 76856. TEL 915-347-5157; FAX 915-347-5668; Ed. G.W. Lyon; Pub. G.W. Lyon; adv.; pub. size: broadsheet; circ. 2,750(paid).

MATADOR

US   ISSN 0897-4322

MOTLEY COUNTY TRIBUNE. 1892. w. $.50 newsstand. Hwy. 70, E., Matador, TX 79244-0490. TEL 806-347-2400. **Owner(s):** Barbara B. Armstrong, Hwy. 70 East, Matador, TX 79244. TEL 806-347-2400; Ed. Barbara D. Armstrong. adv.; photos; pub. size: standard; circ. 1,200(paid).

MATHIS

US

MATHIS NEWS. 1914. Thu. $23.50/yr. 620 E. San Patricio Ave., Mathis, TX 78368. TEL 512-547-3274; FAX 512-547-3275. **Owner(s):** San Patricio Publishing Co., Inc., P.O. Drawer B, Sinton, TX 78387. TEL 512-364-1270; Ed. Charles Sullivan; Pub. John Tracy; adv. contact: Charles Sullivan. photos; pub. size: broadsheet; circ. 2,550(paid).

MCALLEN

US

VALLEY TOWN CRIER. 1964. Wed. free. 1811 N. 23rd St., McAllen, TX 78501. TEL 210-682-2423; FAX 210-630-6371. **Owner(s):** Valley Media, Inc., 1811 N. 23rd St., McAllen, TX 78501. TEL 512-682-2423; Pub. Mike McKinney; adv. contact: Jack Wilson. pub. size: broadsheet; circ. 90,000(free).

MENARD

US

MENARD NEWS & MESSENGER, THE. 1893. Thu. $.50 newsstand; $18/yr. in cy.; $22/yr. in state; $25/yr. out of state. 220 Gay St., Menard, TX 76859. TEL 915-396-2243. **Owner(s):** Dan Feather, Jr., 220 Gay St., Menard, TX 76859; Ed. Dorothy Kerns; Pub. Dan Feather, Jr.; adv.; photos; pub. size: standard; circ. 1,272(paid).

MERIDIAN

US

BOSQUE COUNTY NEWS. 1990. Wed. $.50 newsstand; $20/yr. in cy.; $24/yr. out of cy. 114 N. Main St., Meridian, TX 76665. TEL 817-435-6333; FAX 817-435-6335. **Owner(s):** Robby James, 114 N. Main St., Meridian, TX 76665. TEL 817-435-6333; FAX 817-435-6335; Ed. Robby James; Pub. Robby James; adv. contact: Alana Metker. bk.rev.; pub. size: standard; circ. 1,300(controlled & paid). **Wire Service(s):** TPA.
   Formerly: Meridian Tribune.

MESQUITE

US   ISSN 0746-4126

MESQUITE NEWS. 1882. Thu. $.50 newsstand. 303 N. Galloway, Mesquite, TX 75149. TEL 214-285-6301; FAX 214-288-9383. **Owner(s):** Harte-Hanks Communications, Inc., P.O. Box 269, San Antonio, TX 78291; Ed. Tim Watterson; Pub. Lynn Dickerson; adv. contact: Bob Tilford. photos; bk.rev.; pub. size: broadsheet; circ. 30,000(free & paid).

MEXIA

US   ISSN 1067-7305

HUBBARD CITY NEWS. 1881. Thu. $.50 newsstand; $14/yr. in cy.; $16/yr. out of cy.; $18yr. out of state. 214 N. Railroad, Mexia, TX 76667. TEL 817-562-2868; FAX 817-562-3121. **Owner(s):** American Publishing Co., 606 N. Van Buren, P.O. Box 520, Marion, IL 62959. TEL 618-993-1711; Ed. Barbara Minze; Pub. Dick Canaday; adv.; bk.rev.; pub. size: broadsheet; circ. 2,000(paid).

MIAMI

US   ISSN 0746-0082

MIAMI CHIEF, THE. 1899. Thu. $.50 newsstand; $16/yr. local; $24/yr. elsewhere. 401 E. Commercial St., Miami, TX 79059-0396. TEL 806-868-2521; FAX 806-868-5381. **Owner(s):** Valda G. Traughber, P.O. Box 396, Miami, TX 79059-0396. TEL 806-868-2521; FAX 806-868-5381; Clarence L. Traughber, P.O. Box 396, Miami, TX 79059-0396. TEL 806-868-2521; FAX 806-868-5381; Ed. Valda G. Traughber; Pub. Clarence L. Traughber; adv.; bk.rev.; pub. size: tabloid; circ. 602(paid).

MIDLOTHIAN

US

MIDLOTHIAN MIRROR. 1882. Thu. $.25 newsstand; $12/yr. in cy.; $14/yr. in state; $17/yr. out of state. 214 W. Ave. F, Midlothian, TX 76065. TEL 214-775-3322. **Owner(s):** Midlothian Mirror, 214 W. Ave. F, Midlothian, TX 76065. TEL 214-775-3322; Pub. Barham Alderdice; adv.; pub. size: standard.

MONAHANS

US

MONAHANS NEWS. 1931. Thu. $22/yr. in cy. 107 W. Second, Monahans, TX 79756. TEL 915-943-4313; FAX 915-943-4314. **Owner(s):** Ward Newspapers, Inc., 107 W. Second, Monahans, TX 79756; Pub. Pearson Cooper; adv.; photos; pub. size: broadsheet; circ. 4,000(paid).

MOODY

US

MOODY COURIER, THE. 1890. Thu. $.25 newsstand; $12/yr. in cy.; $14/yr. out of cy.; $16/yr. out of state. 502 Ave. E., Moody, TX 76557. TEL 817-853-2801; FAX 817-754-3541. **Owner(s):** Bill Foster, P.O. Box 3280, Waco, TX. TEL 817-754-3511; FAX 817-754-3541; Ed. Jennifer Latham; Pub. Bill Foster; adv. contact: Jennifer Latham. photos; bk.rev.; pub. size: broadsheet; circ. 800(controlled & paid).

MUNDAY

US   ISSN 8750-6750

MUNDAY COURIER, THE. 1971. Thu. $.50 newsstand; $15/yr. in cy.; $20/yr. out of cy. 111 E. B St., Munday, TX 76371-0130. TEL 817-422-4314; FAX 817-422-4314. **Owner(s):** Munday Courier, The, 111 E. B St., Munday, TX 76371. TEL 817-422-4314; FAX 817-422-4314; Ed. Mattie Waggoner; Pub. Michael L. Waggoner; adv.; photos; pub. size: broadsheet; circ. 1,340(free & paid).

NAVASOTA

US

NAVASOTA EXAMINER REVIEW. 1894. Thu. $.50 newsstand; $20/yr. in cy.; $23/yr. in state; $27/yr. out of state. 115 Railroad St., Navasota, TX 77868. TEL 409-825-6484; FAX 409-825-2230. **Owner(s):** Whitten & Son, Inc., P.O. Box 751, Navasota, TX 77868. TEL 409-825-6484; FAX 409-825-2230; Ed. Clark Whitten; Pub. Daphne Kopycinski; adv. contact: Daphne Kopycinski. photos; pub. size: broadsheet; circ. 5,602(free & paid).

NEDERLAND

US

MIDCOUNTY CHRONICLE. 1931. Wed. free; $26/yr. mailed. 2112 Nederland Ave., Nederland, TX 77627. TEL 409-722-0479; FAX 409-729-7626. **Owner(s):** Hearst Corp., 959 Eighth Ave., New York, NY 10019. TEL 212-262-5700; Ed. Regina Throop; Pub. John Butten; pub. size: broadsheet; circ. 25,000(controlled & free).

NEW ULM

US

NEW ULM ENTERPRISE. 1910. Thu. $.50 newsstand; $14/yr. 200 Hwy. 109, S., New Ulm, TX 78950-0128. TEL 409-992-3351. **Owner(s):** Raymond L. Dungen, Jr., P.O. Box 128, New Ulm, TX 78950-0128. TEL 409-992-3351; Ed. Raymond L. Dungen, Jr. adv.; pub. size: standard; circ. 1,203(paid).

OLNEY

US

OLNEY ENTERPRISE, THE. 1910. Thu. $.25 newsstand; $11/yr. 213 E. Main St., Olney, TX 76374. **Owner(s):** David H. Penn, 213 E. Main St., Olney, TX 76374. TEL 817-564-5558; Pub. David H. Penn; adv.; photos; pub. size: broadsheet; circ. 2,518(paid).

PALACIOS

US

PALACIOS BEACON. 1906. Wed. $.50 newsstand; $18.00/yr. in cy.; $24.00 out of cy. 453 Commerce St., Palacios, TX 77465-3009. TEL 512-972-2610; FAX 512-972-2610. **Owner(s):** Toney Publishing, 113 E. Bernard, West Columbia, TX 77486. TEL 409-345-3128; Ed. Nick West; Pub. Nick West; adv. contact: Lucy White. photos; bk.rev.; pub. size: standard; circ. 1,700(paid).

PEARLAND

US

FRIENDSWOOD & PEARLAND REPORTER NEWS. 1970. Wed. $.50 newsstand; $25/yr. 2404 S. Park, Pearland, TX 77581. TEL 713-485-7501; FAX 713-485-6397. **Owner(s):** Randy & Laura Emmons, 2404 S. Park, Pearland, TX 77581. TEL 713-485-7501; FAX 713-485-6397; Ed. Laura Emmons; Pub. Laura Emmons; adv. contact: Marguerite Atkinson. photos; pub. size: broadsheet; circ. 12,500(free & paid).
   Formerly: Friendswood Reporter News.

PITTSBURG

US

PITTSBURG GAZETTE. 1884. Thu. $.50 newsstand; $26/yr. in cy.; $32/yr. out of cy.; $40/yr. out of state. 112 Quitman St., Pittsburg, TX 75686. TEL 903-856-6629; FAX 903-856-0510. **Owner(s):** Westward Communications, Inc., 5005 LBJ Fwy., Ste. 1048, Dallas, TX 75244; Ed. Susan Taft; Pub. Debbie Knox; adv. contact: Debbie Knox. photos; bk.rev.; pub. size: standard; circ. 3,400(paid).

PLEASANTON

US

PLEASANTON EXPRESS. 1909. Wed. $20/yr. senior citizens; $.50 newsstand; $23/yr. in cy.; $28/yr. out of cy; $33/yr. out of state. 114 Goodwin, Pleasanton, TX 78064. TEL 210-281-2341; FAX 210-569-6100. **Owner(s):** Wilkerson Publishing Co., 89 Pulliam, Pleasanton, TX 78064; Ed. David B. Wilkerson; Pub. Wm. B. Wilkerson; adv. contact: Mary Gallegos. pub. size: broadsheet; circ. 7,500(paid).

PORT ISABEL

US

PORT ISABEL-SOUTH PADRE PRESS. 1950. s-w.: Mon. & Thu. $.35 newsstand; $22/yr. in cy.; $36/yr. out of cy. 101 Mazan, Port Isabel, TX 78578. TEL 210-943-5545; FAX 210-943-4782. **Owner(s):** New Horizon Publishers, Inc., P.O. Box 1791, San Benito, TX 78586. TEL 210-399-2435; FAX 210-233-9604; Ed. Dave Hamerly; Pub. Ben Brooks; adv.; pub. size: broadsheet; circ. 4,500(free & paid).

PORTLAND

US

PORTLAND NEWS. Thu. $.50 newsstand; $23.50/yr. in cy.; $29.60/yr. out of cy.; $30.60/yr. out of state. 101 Cedar Pl., Ste. G, Portland, TX 78374. TEL 512-643-1566; FAX 512-643-1567. **Owner(s):** San Patricio Publishing Co., Inc., P.O. Drawer B, Sinton, TX 78387. TEL 512-364-1270; Ed. Lisa Donaghue; Pub. John Tracy; adv.; pub. size: broadsheet; circ. 2,500(paid).

PORT LAVACA

US

PORT LAVACA WAVE. 1890. s-w.: Wed. & Sat. $.50 newsstand; $27/yr. in cy.; $40/yr. out of cy. 107 E. Austin, Port Lavaca, TX 77979-0088. TEL 512-552-9788; FAX 512-552-3108. **Owner(s):** Port Lavaca Wave, Inc., P.O. Box 88, Port Lavaca, TX 77979-0088. TEL 512-552-9788; FAX 512-552-3108; Ed. Steve Bales; Pub. Steve Bales; adv. contact: Cathy Buehring. photos; bk.rev.; pub. size: broadsheet; circ. 4,500(free & paid).

POTTSBORO

US

POTTSBORO PRESS. 1984. Thu. $15/yr. in cy.; $20/yr. in state; $25/yr. out of state. P.O. Box 837, Pottsboro, TX 75076-0837. TEL 903-786-4051. **Owner(s):** Pottsboro Press, P.O. Box 837, Pottsboro, TX 75076-0837. TEL 903-786-4051; Ed. Melissa Hill; Pub. Lori Conary; bk.rev.; pub. size: standard; circ. 1,355(paid).

QUITMAN

US

WOOD COUNTY DEMOCRAT. 1893. Wed. $.50 newsstand; $24/yr. in cy.; $32/yr. in state; $37/yr. out of state. 111 W. Lipscomb, Quitman, TX 75783. TEL 903-763-4522; FAX 903-763-4522. **Owner(s):** Westward Communications, Inc., 5005 L.B.J. Fwy., Ste. 1040, Dallas, TX 25244. TEL 214-450-1717; Ed. Larry Tucker; Pub. Nell French; adv. contact: Monte Coleman. pub. size: broadsheet; circ. 3,500(paid).

RICHARDSON

US   ISSN 1045-4004

RICHARDSON NEWS. 1958. s-w.: Thu. & Sun. $.50 newsstand; $36/yr. carrier. 409 Belle Grove, Richardson, TX 75080. TEL 214-234-3198; FAX 214-234-6906. **Owner(s):** Dallas-Fort Worth Suburban Newspapers, Inc., 1000 Ave. H, E., Arlington, TX 76011. TEL 817-695-0500; Ed. Lois Wetzel Brown. adv. contact: Lisa Redford. pub. size: broadsheet; circ. 10,000(paid); Sun. 10,000(paid).
    Formerly: Richardson Daily News.

RISING STAR

US

RISING STAR, THE. 1892. Thu. $.50 newsstand; $1.25/mo.; $7.50/6.mos.; $15/yr. local; $18/yr. Texas Cy.; $21/yr. out of state. 105 N. Main St., Rising Star, TX 76471. TEL 817-643-4141; FAX 817-629-2029. **Owner(s):** Eastland County Newspapers, Inc., P.O. Box 29, Eastland, TX 76448. TEL 817-629-1707; Ed. Elaine Coleman; Pub. H.V. O'Brien; adv.; photos; bk.rev.; pub. size: standard; circ. 747(free & paid).

ROBSTOWN

US

NUECES COUNTY RECORD STAR. 1919. Thu. $25.50/yr. 104 N. Fifth St., Robstown, TX 78380. TEL 512-387-4511. **Owner(s):** Keach & Co., Inc., P.O. Box 1192, Robstown, TX 78380. TEL 512-387-4511; FAX 512-387-2276; Ed. Sam Keach; Pub. Sam Keach; adv. contact: Darrell Keach. photos; bk.rev.; pub. size: broadsheet; circ. 15,000(paid).

ROCKDALE

US

ROCKDALE REPORTER. 1873. Thu. $.50 newsstand; $20/yr. local; $24/yr. in state; $28/yr. out of state. 221-225 E. Cameron, Rockdale, TX 76567. TEL 512-446-5838; FAX 512-446-5317. **Owner(s):** J.W. Cooke, P.O. Box 552, Rockdale, TX 76567-0552. TEL 512-446-5838; FAX 512-446-5317; Ed. J.W. Cooke; Pub. J.W. Cooke; adv. contact: Judy Lehmkuhl. adv.: $5/SAU. pub. size: broadsheet; circ. 4,564(paid).

ROSENBERG

US

FORT BEND MIRROR. 1956. Thu. $.25 newsstand; $15/yr. 1902 Fourth St., Rosenberg, TX 77471. TEL 713-242-9104; FAX 713-342-3219. **Owner(s):** Hartman Newspapers, Inc., P.O. Box 1088, Rosenberg, TX 77471. TEL 409-342-8691; Ed. Cheryl Skinner; Pub. Clyde King; pub. size: broadsheet; circ. 3,000(paid).

ROUND ROCK

US   ISSN 0164-9124

ROUND ROCK LEADER. 1876. s-w.: Mon. & Thu. $.50 newsstand; $10/3 mos.; $25/yr. 105 S. Blair, Round Rock, TX 78664. TEL 512-255-5827; FAX 512-255-3733. **Owner(s):** Todd Publications, Inc., 2304 Hancock Dr., Austin, TX 78756. TEL 512-451-3900; Ed. Will Hampton; Pub. Ken Long; adv. contact: Bobby Seiferman. photos; pub. size: broadsheet; circ. 5,719(paid).

SAN ANTONIO

US

RECORDER TIMES, THE. 1971. Thu. free; $.50 newsstand; $175.95/yr. 8603 Botts Ln., San Antonio, TX 78217. TEL 210-828-3321; FAX 210-828-3787. **Owner(s):** Prime Time, Inc., 8603 Botts Ln., San Antonio, TX 78217. TEL 512-828-3321; Ed. Steve Henry; Pub. Robert Jones; adv. contact: Jim Williams. photos; bk.rev.; pub. size: broadsheet; circ. 90,000(paid).

SAN AUGUSTINE

US

SAN AUGUSTINE TRIBUNE. 1909. Thu. $.25 newsstand; $6/yr. in cy.; $9/yr. out of cy. 315 W. Columbia St., San Augustine, TX 75972. TEL 409-275-2181. **Owner(s):** Arlan Hays, P.O. Box M, San Augustine, TX 75972. TEL 409-275-2181; Ed. Arlan Hays; Pub. Arlan Hays; adv.; photos; bk.rev.; pub. size: standard; circ. 5,600(paid).

SAN BENITO

US

SAN BENITO NEWS. 1946. s-w.: Wed. & Sun. $.50 newsstand; $20/yr. in cy. mailed; $32/yr. out of cy. mailed; $24/yr. carrier. 356 N. Sam Houston, San Benito, TX 78586. TEL 210-399-2436; FAX 210-233-9604. **Owner(s):** New Horizon Publishers, Inc., P.O. Box 1791, San Benito, TX 78586. TEL 512-399-2436; Ed. Martha McClain; Pub. Jim Elam; pub. size: broadsheet; circ. 5,100(paid).

SANTA FE

US

BULLETIN, THE. 1969. Wed. free in area; $80/yr. mailed elsewhere. 13201 Hwy. 6, Santa Fe, TX 77510. TEL 409-925-2517; FAX 409-925-1399. **Owner(s):** Santa Fe Newspapers, Inc., Drawer 730, Santa Fe, TX 77510. TEL 409-925-2517; FAX 409-925-1399; Ed. Harry Monych; Pub. Harry Monych; adv.; photos; pub. size: broadsheet; circ. 9,100(free & paid).

SEALY

US

SEALY NEWS. 1887. Thu. $.50 newsstand; $20/yr. local; $25/yr. in state; $50/yr. out of state. 111 Main St., Sealy, TX 77474-2390. TEL 409-885-3562; FAX 409-885-3564. **Owner(s):** Sealy News, Inc., 111 Main St., Sealy, TX 77474. TEL 409-885-3562; Ed. Wilma Petrusek; Pub. Richard Pennel; adv. contact: Joanie Griffin. pub. size: broadsheet; circ. 5,500(paid).

SEYMOUR

US

BAYLOR COUNTY BANNER. 1895. Thu. $.50 newsstand; $15/yr. in cy.; $18/yr. out of cy.; $20/yr. out of state. 109 E. Morris St., Seymour, TX 76380-0912. TEL 817-888-2616; FAX 817-888-3610. **Owner(s):** Earl Gwinn, 109 E. Morris, P.O. Box 912, Seymour, TX 76380-0912. TEL 817-888-2616; FAX 817-888-3610; Ed. Earl Gwinn; Pub. Earl Gwinn; adv. contact: Lita Slaggle. photos; bk.rev.; pub. size: standard; circ. 2,800(paid).

SILSBEE

US

SILSBEE BEE. 1919. Thu. $.35 newsstand; $12/yr. locally; $17.50/yr. elsewhere. 410 Hwy. 96, S., Silsbee, TX 77656. TEL 409-385-5278; FAX 409-385-5270. **Owner(s):** Danny Reneau, P.O. Box 547, Silsbee, TX 77656. TEL 409-385-2151; Ed. Danny Reneau; Pub. Danny Reneau; adv. contact: Jan Reneau. pub. size: broadsheet; circ. 7,200(paid).

SINTON

US

ODEM-EDROY TIMES. 1948. Thu. $.40 newsstand; $23.50/yr. 117 S. Rachal St., Sinton, TX 78387. TEL 512-364-1270; FAX 512-364-3833. **Owner(s):** San Patricio Publishing Co., Inc., P.O. Drawer B, Sinton, TX 78387. TEL 512-364-1270; Ed. Jim McElhaney; Pub. Helen S. Tracy; adv.; pub. size: broadsheet; circ. 650(paid).

US

SAN PATRICIO COUNTY NEWS. 1908. Wed. $.50 newsstand; $23.50/yr. 117 S. Rachal St., Sinton, TX 78387. TEL 512-364-1270; FAX 512-364-3833. **Owner(s):** San Patricio Publishing Co., Inc., P.O. Drawer B, Sinton, TX 78387. TEL 512-364-1270; Ed. James F. Tracy, Jr. adv.; pub. size: broadsheet; circ. 2,800(paid).

SOUTH PADRE ISLAND

US

COASTAL CURRENT, THE. 1990. Fri. free. 1004 Padre Blvd., South Padre Island, TX 78597. TEL 210-761-9341; FAX 210-761-1436. **Owner(s):** Jim Goller, 116 W. Esperanza, South Padre Island, TX 78597. TEL 210-761-2421; FAX 210-761-9436; Jonathan Deeley, 203 Huisache, South Padre Island, TX. TEL 210-761-9417; FAX 210-761-1436; Ed. Lori Todd; Pub. Jonathan Deeley; adv. contact: Stan Hulse. photos; bk.rev.; pub. size: tabloid; circ. 10,000(controlled & free).

SPEARMAN

US

HANSFORD COUNTY REPORTER-STATESMAN. 1907. Thu. $.50 newsstand; $19.95/yr. in cy.; $24.95/yr. out of cy. 213 Main St., Spearman, TX 79081. TEL 806-659-3434; FAX 806-659-3368. **Owner(s):** Gary Smith, 16607 Blanco Rd., Ste. 100, San Antonio, TX 78232. TEL 210-490-3715; Ed. Angela Jones; Pub. Molly Zimmerman; adv. contact: Debra McNeely. pub. size: standard; circ. 3,500(paid).

SPRINGTOWN

US

SPRINGTOWN EPIGRAPH, THE. w. $.50 newsstand. 109 N. First St., Springtown, TX 76086. TEL 817-220-7217. **Owner(s):** Azle Tri-County Advertiser, Inc., 1121 S.E. Parkway, Azle, TX 76020. TEL 817-237-1184; Ed. Bob Buckel; Pub. Bob Buckel; adv.; photos; pub. size: broadsheet; circ. 1,884(free & paid).

STAMFORD

US

STAMFORD AMERICAN. 1922. Thu. $.50 newsstand; $15/yr. in cy.; $17/yr. out of cy.; $20/yr. out of state. 112 E. Hamilton, Stamford, TX 79553. TEL 915-773-3621; FAX 915-773-3622. **Owner(s):** Lewis & Becky Alambar, P.O. Box 1207, Stamford, TX 79553. TEL 915-773-3621; FAX 915-773-3622; Ed. Michelle Sanchez. adv. contact: Timmy Sanchez. pub. size: standard; circ. 2,500(paid).

SUGAR LAND

US

FORT BEND SUN. 1967. Thu. free home deliv.; $.35 newsstand; $10/mo. local mailed. 13735 Southwest Fwy., Sugar Land, TX 77478. TEL 713-242-1812; FAX 713-242-1891. **Owner(s):** Houston Community Newspapers, Inc., 1136 Sheldon Rd., Channelview, TX 77530; Ed. Stacy Hyde; Pub. Chris Colihan; adv.; pub. size: tabloid; circ. 4,200(free & paid).
Formerly: Fort Bend Advocate.

US

SOUTHWEST SUN. 1967. Thu. free newsstand; $10/mo. carrier. 13735 Southwest Frwy., Sugar Land, TX 77478. TEL 713-242-1812; FAX 713-242-1891. **Owner(s):** Houston Community Newspapers, Inc., 1136 Sheldon Rd., Channelview, TX 72530. TEL 713-452-0530; Ed. Stacey Hyde. adv.; pub. size: broadsheet; circ. 29,000(free & paid).
Formerly: Southwest Advocate.

TAFT

US

TAFT TRIBUNE. 1922. Thu. $.50 newsstand; $23.50/yr. in cy.; $29.60/out of cy.; $30.60/yr. out of state. 325 Green Ave., Taft, TX 78390. TEL 512-528-2515; FAX 512-364-3833. **Owner(s):** San Patricio Publishing Co., Inc., P.O. Drawer B, Sinton, TX 78387. TEL 512-364-1270; Ed. Belinda Tracy; Pub. John Henry Tracy; adv. contact: Belinda Tracy. pub. size: broadsheet; circ. 1,200(paid).

TRENTON

US

TRENTON TRIBUNE. 1909. Thu. $.25 newsstand; $18-$23/yr. 115 Hamilton, Trenton, TX 75490-0043. TEL 903-989-2325. **Owner(s):** Tom M. Holmes, 115 Hamilton, Trenton, TX 75490-0043. TEL 903-989-2325; Pub. Tom M. Holmes; adv.; pub. size: standard; circ. 1,100(paid).

UVALDE

US

UVALDE LEADER-NEWS. 1879. s-w.: Thu. & Sun. $.50 newsstand; $28.50/yr. in cy.; $48/yr. out of state. 110 N. East St., Uvalde, TX 78801. TEL 210-278-3335; FAX 210-278-9191. **Owner(s):** Craig K. Garnett, P.O. Box 740, Uvalde, TX 78802. TEL 210-278-3335; Ed. Bill Cockerill; Pub. Craig K Garnett; adv. contact: Steve Balke. pub. size: broadsheet; circ. 6,000(paid); Sun. 6,500(paid).

VAN HORN

US

VAN HORN ADVOCATE. 1910. Thu. $.40 newsstand; $20/yr. 701 W. Broadway, Van Horn, TX 79855-0008. TEL 915-283-2003; FAX 915-283-2920. **Owner(s):** Larry Simpson, P.O. Box 8, Van Horn, TX 79855. TEL 915-283-2003; FAX 915-283-2920; Pub. Larry Simpson; adv.; pub. size: standard.

VEGA

US

VEGA ENTERPRISE, THE. Thu. $.25 newsstand; $15/yr. 116 S. Main St., Vega, TX 79092. TEL 806-267-2230. **Owner(s):** Imogene Galbraith, 116 S. Main St., Vega, TX 79092; Pub. Imogene Galbraith; adv.; photos; pub. size: standard.

VIDOR

US

VIDORIAN, THE. 1959. s-w.: Wed. & Fri. $.25 newsstand; $12.50/yr. 450 W. Bolivar, Vidor, TX 77662. TEL 409-769-5428; FAX 409-769-2600. **Owner(s):** A. Randall Luker, 450 W. Bolivar, Vidor, TX 77662; Ed. A. Randall Luker; Pub. A. Merle Luker; adv. contact: Adair Luker. bk.rev.; pub. size: standard; circ. 12,700(free & paid).

WACO

US

WACO CITIZEN, THE. 1946. s-w.: Wed. & Sun. $.25 newsstand; $26/yr. in cy.; $31/yr. out of cy. 1020 N. 25th St., Waco, TX 76707. TEL 817-754-3511; FAX 817-754-3541. **Owner(s):** Citizen Newspaper, Inc., 1020 N. 25th St., Waco, TX 76700. TEL 817-754-3511; FAX 817-754-3541; Pub. Bill C. Foster; adv. contact: Bill C. Foster. photos; bk.rev.; pub. size: broadsheet; circ. 3,700(paid).

WALLIS

US

WALLIS NEWS-REVIEW. Thu. $.50 newsstand; $14/yr. $16 out of state. 609 Commerce, Wallis, TX 77485. TEL 409-478-6412. **Owner(s):** Raymond L. Dungen, Jr., P.O. Box 128, New Ulm, TX 78950-0128. TEL 409-992-3351; Ed. Lucille Jemela. pub. size: broadsheet.

WEIMAR

US   **ISSN 1071-0329**

WEIMAR MERCURY. 1888. Thu. $.50 newsstand; $17/yr. in cy.; $18/yr. out of cy.; $19/yr. out of state. 200 W. Main, Weimar TX 78962. TEL 409-725-9595; FAX 409-725-9051. **Owner(s):** Weimar Mercury, 200 W. Main, Weimer, TX 78962. TEL 409-725-9595; Ed. Bruce Beal; Pub. Bruce Beal; pub. size: standard; circ. 3,500(paid).

WESLACO

US

MID VALLEY TOWN CRIER. 1967. s-w.: Wed. & Sat. free newsstand & home deliv. 401 S. Iowa, Weslaco, TX 78596. TEL 210-969-2543; FAX 210-968-0855. **Owner(s):** P.T.S., Inc., Tuscaloosa, AL 35401; Ed. James Beaver; Pub. James Beaver; adv.; pub. size: broadsheet; circ. 23,500(free).

WEST

US

WEST NEWS. 1890. Thu. $.35 newsstand; $21/yr. 214 W. Oak, West, TX 76691. TEL 817-826-3718. **Owner(s):** Cechoslovak Publishing Co., P.O. Box 38, West, TX 76691. TEL 817-826-3718; Ed. Larry Knapek; Pub. Linn Pescaia; adv. contact: Sue Pescaia. bk.rev.; pub. size: broadsheet; circ. 3,100(paid).

WEST COLUMBIA

US

GULF COAST TRIBUNE, THE. 1962. w. $.35 newsstand; $25/yr. 113 E. Bernard St., West Columbia, TX 77486. TEL 409-345-3127. **Owner(s):** David Toney, P.O. Box 488, West Columbia, TX 77486. TEL 409-345-3127; Ed. Richard Kotrla; Pub. David Toney; adv. contact: Jeri Mager. pub. size: broadsheet; circ. 1,400(paid).

US

WEST COLUMBIA BRAZORIA COUNTY NEWS. 1962. Thu. $.35 newsstand; $40/yr. 113 E. Bernard St., West Columbia, TX 77436. TEL 713-345-3127. **Owner(s):** David Toney, P.O. Box 488, West Columbia, TX 77485; Ed. David Toney. adv.; photos; pub. size: broadsheet; circ. 10,300(free & paid).

WHARTON

US   ISSN 1076-7266
WHARTON JOURNAL-SPECTATOR. 1888. s-w.: Wed. & Sat. $.50 newsstand; $30/yr. in cy.; $40/yr. in state; $45/yr. out of state. 115 W. Burleson St., Wharton, TX 77488. TEL 409-532-8840; FAX 409-532-8845. **Owner(s):** River Publishers, Inc., P.O. Box 111, Wharton, TX 77488. TEL 713-532-8840; FAX 713-532-8845; Ed. Ron Sanders. adv. contact: Missy Justice. pub. size: broadsheet; circ. 5,000(paid).

WHITE OAK

US   ISSN 1053-1513
WHITE OAK INDEPENDENT. 1990. Thu. $.50 newsstand; $20/yr. 201-B Hwy. 80, E., White Oak, TX 75693. TEL 903-759-4410; FAX 903-759-8100; E-mail: newman@rapidramp.com. **Owner(s):** Jeff & Winnie Newman, 201-B Hwy. 80, E., White Oak, TX 75693. TEL 903-759-4410; FAX 903-759-8100; Ed. Jeff Newman; Pub. Jeff Newman; adv.; photos; pub. size: broadsheet; circ. 1,200(paid).

WHITEWRIGHT

US   ISSN 0886-4322
WHITEWRIGHT SUN, THE. 1884. Thu. $.50 newsstand; $15/yr. in cy.; $18/yr. out of cy.; $22/yr. out of state. 121 Grand Ave., Whitewright, TX 75491. TEL 903-364-2276; FAX 903-364-2276. **Owner(s):** Dennis & Clara Combs, 121 Grand Ave., Whitewright, TX 75491. TEL 903-364-2276; Ed. Clara Combs; Pub. Clara Combs; adv.; photos; pub. size: standard; circ. 1,000(paid).

WIMBERLEY

US
WIMBERLEY VALLEY-NEWS. 1985. Thu. free; $20/yr. out of area. P.O. Box 989, Wimberley, TX 78676. TEL 512-858-7893; FAX 512-858-4828. **Owner(s):** Dale Roberson, P.O. Box 989, Wimberley, TX 78676. TEL 512-858-7893; FAX 512-858-4828; Ed. Dale Roberson; Pub. Dale Roberson; adv. contact: Joyce Kovacs. photos; pub. size: tabloid; circ. 1,900(controlled & paid).

WINNSBORO

US
WINNSBORO NEWS. 1908. Thu. $18/yr. in cy.; $25/yr. elsewhere. 105 E. Locust, Winnsboro, TX 75494. TEL 903-342-5247. **Owner(s):** Pen-Wheel Press, P.O. Box 87, Winnsboro, TX 75494. TEL 903-342-5247; Ed. Karen W. Pendergast; Pub. Thomas F. Pendergast; adv. contact: Linda Henry. photos; pub. size: standard; circ. 4,150(paid).

WOODVILLE

US   ISSN 1043-0350
TYLER COUNTY BOOSTER. 1930. Wed. $.50 newsstand; $13.75/yr. local. 205 W. Bluff St., Woodville, TX 75979. TEL 409-283-2516; FAX 409-283-2560. **Owner(s):** Polk County Publishing Co., P.O. Box 1276, Livingston, TX 77351. TEL 409-327-4357; FAX 409-327-7156; Ed. Gregory Peak; Pub. Alvin Holley; adv. contact: John Morrison. photos; pub. size: broadsheet; circ. 18,400(free & paid).
Formerly: Woodville Tyler County Booster.

WYLIE

US
WYLIE NEWS, THE. 1947. Wed. $.25 newsstand; $15/yr. local; $17/yr. out of cy. 113 W. Oak, Wylie, TX 75098. TEL 214-442-5515; FAX 214-442-4318. **Owner(s):** C & S Media, Inc., P.O. Box 369, Wylie, TX 75098. TEL 214-442-5515; Ed. Margaret Cook; Pub. Chad B. Engbrock; adv. contact: Chad B. Engbrock. photos; bk.rev.; pub. size: broadsheet; circ. 3,950(paid).

YOAKUM

US
YOAKUM HERALD-TIMES & FOUR STAR REPORTER. 1892. Wed. $.50 newsstand; 18.50/yr. in cy.; $25/yr. out of cy.; $30/yr. elsewhere. 312 Lott St., Yoakum, TX 77995. TEL 512-293-2335; FAX 512-293-5267. **Owner(s):** L.M. Preuss, III, P.O. Box 798, Yoakum, TX 77995. TEL 512-293-2335; Pub. Bob Anderson; adv. contact: Anne Kubicek. photos; pub. size: broadsheet; circ. 2,900(paid).
Formerly: Yoakum Herald-Times.

UTAH

AMERICAN FORK

US
CITIZEN. 1903. Wed. $.50 newsstand; $24/yr. 59 W. Main St., American Fork, UT 84003-0007. TEL 801-756-7669; FAX 801-756-5274. **Owner(s):** Newtah News Group, P.O. Box 7, American Fork, UT 84003. TEL 801-756-7669; FAX 801-756-5274; Ed. Marc Haddock; Pub. Brett Bezzant; adv. contact: Tom Hollingsworth. pub. size: broadsheet; circ. 4,200(paid).
Formerly: American Fork Citizen.

US
LEHI FREE PRESS. 1903. Wed. $.50 newsstand; $24/yr. in cy. 59 W. Main St., American Fork, UT 84003. TEL 801-756-7669; FAX 801-756-5274. **Owner(s):** Newtah News Group, P.O. Box 7, American Fork, UT 84003. TEL 801-756-7669; FAX 801-756-5274; Ed. Mark Haddock; Pub. Brett Bezzant; adv. contact: Tom Hollingsworth. adv.: $11/SAU. pub. size: broadsheet; circ. 3,200(paid).

US
NORTH UTAH COUNTY SHOPPER. Wed. free. 59 W. Main St., American Fork, UT 84003. TEL 801-756-7669; FAX 801-756-5274. **Owner(s):** Newtah News Group, P.O. Box 7, American Fork, UT 84003. TEL 801-756-7669; FAX 801-756-5274; Ed. Mark Haddock; Pub. Brett Bezzant; adv. contact: Tom Hollingsworth. adv.: $11/SAU. pub. size: broadsheet; circ. 21,000(free).

US
PLEASANT GROVE REVIEW. 1905. Wed. $.50 newsstand; $24/yr. in cy. 59 W. Main St., American Fork, UT 84003. TEL 801-756-7669; FAX 801-756-5274. **Owner(s):** Newtah News Group, P.O. Box 7, American Fork, UT 84003. TEL 801-756-7669; FAX 801-756-5274; Ed. Mark Haddock; Pub. Brett Bezzant; adv. contact: Tom Hollingsworth. adv.: $11/SAU. pub. size: broadsheet; circ. 3,000(paid).

BOUNTIFUL

US   ISSN 1061-1223
DAVIS COUNTY CLIPPER. 1891. s-w.: Tue. & Fri. $.50 newsstand; $25/yr. in cy.; $35/yr. out of cy. 1370 S. 500 W., Bountiful, UT 84010. TEL 801-295-2251; FAX 801-295-3044. **Owner(s):** Gail Stahle, 125 W. First S., Bountiful, UT 84010. TEL 801-295-2001; Ed. Judy Jensen; Pub. Gail Stahle; adv.; photos; bk.rev.; pub. size: standard; circ. 30,000(free & paid).

US
WEST VALLEY EAGLE. 1927. Thu. free newsstand; $1/mo. voluntary; $15/yr. mailed. 1370 S. Fifth W., Bountiful, UT 84010. TEL 801-292-1088; FAX 801-295-3044. **Owner(s):** Spectrum Press, Inc., 1370 S. Fifth W., Bountiful, UT 84010; Ed. Darren Tucker; Pub. Gail Stahle; pub. size: broadsheet; circ. 60,000(free & paid).
Formerly: West Valley View.

BRIGHAM CITY

US
BOX ELDER NEWS JOURNAL. 1896. Wed. $.50 newsstand; $25/yr. in cy.; $35/yr. out of cy. 55 S. 100 W., Brigham City, UT 84302. TEL 801-723-3471; FAX 801-723-5247. **Owner(s):** Box Elder News & Journal, Inc., P.O. Box 370, Brigham City, UT 84302. TEL 801-723-3471; FAX 801-723-5247; Ed. Sarah Yates; Pub. Charles C. Claybaugh; adv.; photos; pub. size: broadsheet; circ. 10,000(free & paid).

CASTLE DALE

US
EMERY COUNTY PROGRESS. Tue. $.50 newsstand; $21/yr. in cy.; $25/yr. out of cy. 190 Main St., Castle Dale, UT 84513. TEL 801-381-2431; FAX 801-381-5431. **Owner(s):** Brehm Communications, Inc., P.O. Box 28429, San Diego, CA 92128. TEL 619-451-6200; Ed. Scott Niendorf; Pub. Kevin Ashby; adv.; photos; bk.rev.; pub. size: broadsheet; circ. 2,500(controlled).

FILLMORE

US
MILLARD COUNTY GAZETTE. 1978. Tue. free in cy.; $.25 newsstand; $1 out of cy. 58 E. Center, Fillmore, UT 84631. TEL 801-743-6983; FAX 801-864-4050. **Owner(s):** Dale Whipple, 250 W. 2855 S., Salt Lake City, UT 84115. TEL 801-486-8999; FAX 801-466-8806; pub. size: tabloid; circ. 5,000(free & paid).

MAGNA

US
MAGNA TIMES. Thu. $.50 newsstand; $15/yr. 8980 W. 2700 S., Magna, UT 84044. TEL 801-250-5656; FAX 801-250-5685. **Owner(s):** Howard Stahle, 8980 W. 2700 S., Magna, UT 84044. TEL 801-250-5656; Ed. Gary R. Blodgett; Pub. J. Howard Stahle; adv. contact: Bonnie Stahle. pub. size: tabloid; circ. 2,500(paid).

US
WEST VALLEY NEWS. Thu. $.50 newsstand; $18/yr. 8980 W. 2700 S., Magna, UT 84044. TEL 801-250-5656. **Owner(s):** Howard H. Stahle, 8980 W. 2700 S., Magna, UT 84044. TEL 801-250-5656; Ed. Gary R. Blodgett; Pub. J. Howard Stahle; adv. contact: Bonnie Stahle. pub. size: tabloid; circ. 2,500(paid).

MT. PLEASANT

US

PYRAMID, THE. 1892. Wed. $.50 newsstand; $20/yr. in cy.; $23/yr. out of cy. 49 W. Main St., Mt. Pleasant, UT 84647. TEL 801-462-2134; FAX 801-462-2459. **Owner(s):** Pyramid Publishing, Inc., 49 W. Main St., Mt. Pleasant, UT 84647. TEL 801-462-2134; FAX 801-462-2459; Ed. Penny Hamilton; Pub. Martin Conover; adv. contact: Paul Hamilton. pub. size: broadsheet; circ. 2,500(paid).

OREM

US

OREM-GENEVA TIMES. 1937. Wed. $.50 newsstand; $13/yr.; $21/2 yrs. 546 S. State St., Orem, UT 84058. TEL 801-225-1340; FAX 801-225-1341. **Owner(s):** Brent Sumner, P.O. Box 65, Orem, UT 84059. TEL 801-225-1340; Ed. Brent Sumner; Pub. Brent Sumner; adv.; pub. size: standard; circ. 3,700(free).

PARK CITY

US   ISSN 0745-9483

PARK RECORD, THE. 1880. s-w. Wed. & Sat. $.50 newsstand; $32/yr. local; $60/yr. elsewhere. 1670 Bonanza Dr., Park City, UT 84060-3688. TEL 801-649-9014; FAX 801-649-4942. **Owner(s):** Peter Bernharad, 1670 Bonanza Drive, Park City, UT 84060-3688. TEL 801-649-9014; FAX 801-649-4942; Ed. Nan Chalat-Noaker; Pub. Andy Bernhard; adv. contact: Tracy Harden. pub. size: broadsheet; circ. 8,500(controlled & paid).

PRICE

US

SUN ADVOCATE. 1891. s-w.: Tue. & Thu. $.50 newsstand; $35/yr. in state. 76 W. Main St., Price, UT 84501. TEL 801-637-0732; FAX 801-637-2716; E-mail: kashbysisna.com. **Owner(s):** Brehm Communications, Inc., P.O. Box 28429, San Diego, CA 92128. TEL 619-451-6200; Ed. Lynnda Johnson; Pub. Kevin Ashby; adv.; photos; pub. size: broadsheet; circ. 5,400(free & paid).

RICHFIELD

US

REAPER EXTRA. 1964. Wed. free. 65 W. Center, Richfield, UT 84701. TEL 801-896-5476; FAX 801-896-8123. **Owner(s):** Gull Communications, Inc., 65 W. Center, Richfield, UT 84701. TEL 801-896-5476; Ed. Hal Edwards; Pub. Mark Fuellenbach; adv. contact: Charles Hawley. pub. size: broadsheet; circ. 6,600(free).
   Formerly: Rooster Valley Shopper.

US

RICHFIELD REAPER. 1888. Wed. $.25 newsstand; $24/yr. in area; $34/yr. out of area. 65 W. Center St., Richfield, UT 84701. TEL 801-896-5476; FAX 801-896-8123. **Owner(s):** Gull Communications, Inc., 65 W. Center St., Richfield, UT 84701. TEL 801-896-5476; Ed. Hal Edwards; Pub. Mark Fuellenbach; pub. size: broadsheet; circ. 5,400(paid).

ROOSEVELT

US

UINTAH BASIN STANDARD. 1913. Tue. $.50 newsstand; $20/yr. in area; $32/yr. out of area. 268 S. 200 E., Roosevelt, UT 84066. TEL 801-722-5131; FAX 801-722-4140. **Owner(s):** Craig Ashby, 268 S. 200 E., Roosevelt, UT 84066. TEL 801-722-5131; Ed. Mike Ross; Pub. Craig Ashby; pub. size: broadsheet; circ. 3,850(paid).

SALT LAKE CITY

US

PRIVATE EYE WEEKLY. 1984. Wed. free newsstand; $30/yr. mailed. 60 W. 400 S., Salt Lake City, UT 84101. TEL 801-575-7003; FAX 801-575-6106. **Owner(s):** John Saltas, 68 W. 400 S., Salt Lake City, UT 84101. TEL 801-575-7003; FAX 801-575-6106; adv.; photos; bk.rev.; pub. size: tabloid; circ. 50,000(controlled & free).

TOOELE

US

TOOELE TRANSCRIPT-BULLETIN. 1894. s-w.: Tue. & Thu. $.50 newsstand; $30/yr. carrier; $35/yr. in cy. mailed; $38/yr. out of cy. mailed. 58 N. Main, Tooele, UT 84074. TEL 801-882-0050; FAX 801-882-6123. **Owner(s):** Joel Dunn, P.O. Box 390, Tooele UT 84074. TEL 801-882-0050; Ed. David Bern; Pub. Scott C. Dunn; adv. contact: Clayton Dunn. bk.rev.; pub. size: broadsheet; circ. 6,850(paid).

TREMONTON

US   ISSN 0747-1416

LEADER, THE. 1914. Wed. $.50 newsstand; $18.50/yr. in cy.; $24.50/yr. out of cy. 119 E. Main St., Tremonton, UT 84337. TEL 801-257-5182. **Owner(s):** J. Walter Ross & Wayne D. Bell, 77 S. State, Preston, ID 83263. TEL 208-852-0155; Ed. Diana Myers; Pub. Greg Madson; adv. contact: Laura Hinsley. pub. size: standard; circ. 5,500(free & paid).

VERNAL

US   ISSN 0892-1091

VERNAL EXPRESS. 1891. Wed. $.50 newsstand; $19/yr. local; $30/yr. out of area; $33/yr. out of state. 54 N. Vernal Ave., Vernal, UT 84078. TEL 801-789-3511; FAX 801-789-8690. **Owner(s):** Vernal Express Publishing Co., P.O. Box 1000, Vernal, UT 84078. TEL 801-789-3511; FAX 801-789-8690; Ed. Steven R. Wallis. adv. contact: Janet D. Wallis. pub. size: broadsheet; circ. 4,466(paid)

VERMONT

BELLOWS FALLS

US

BELLOWS FALLS TOWN CRIER. 1984. Fri. free newsstand; $12.50/3 mos. mailed; $20/6 mos. mailed. 63 Square, Bellows Falls, VT 05101-0459. TEL 802-463-9591; FAX 802-463-9818. **Owner(s):** Roger Miller, Putney Rd., Brattleboro VT 05301. TEL 802-257-7771; FAX 802-257-2211; Ed. Steve Crimmin; Pub. Bil Bedard; adv.; photos; pub. size: tabloid.

BENNINGTON

US

PENNYSAVER PRESS. 1958. F.. free. 109 South St., Bennington, VT 05201. TEL 802-447-3381; FAX 802-447-3270. **Owner(s):** Acd, Inc., 600 Industrial Dr., Waupaca, WI 54981 TEL 715-258-8450; Ed. Kelly Nesbitt; Pub. Dan McKay; pub. size: tabloid; circ. 37,000(free).

BRADFORD

US   ISSN 0746-1674

JOURNAL OPINION. 1866. Wed. $.50 newsstand; $15/yr. Main St., Bradford, VT 05033. TEL 802-222-5281; FAX 802-222-5438. **Owner(s):** Robert F. Huminski, P.O. Box 378, Bradford, VT 05033. TEL 802-222-5281; FAX 802-222-5281; Ed. Charles Glazer; Pub. Robert F. Huminski; adv. contact: Jim Jung. photos; bk.rev.; pub. size: broadsheet; circ. 4,500(paid).

CHESTER

US

MESSAGE FOR THE WEEK. 1972. Tue. free. Elm St., Chester, VT 05143. TEL 802-875-4790; FAX 802-875-4792. **Owner(s):** Wes & Teresa Johnson, P.O. Box 759, Chester, VT 05147. TEL 802-875-4790; FAX 802-875-4792; Ed. Wes Johnson; Pub. Wes Johnson. adv. contact: Teresa Johnson. pub. size: tabloid; circ. 17,500(controlled & free).

ENOSBURG FALLS

US

COUNTY COURIER. 4895. Wed. $.75 newsstand; $20/yr. in cy.; $25/yr. out of cy. 209 Main St., Enosburg Falls, VT 05450-0398. TEL 802-933-4375; FAX 802-933-4907. **Owner(s):** Franklin Press, 209 Main St., Enosburg Falls, VT 05450-0398. TEL 802-933-4375; FAX 802-933-4907; Ed. Mathias Dubilier. adv.: $4.95/SAU. bk.rev.; pub. size: tabloid; circ. 3,462(free & paid).
   Formerly: Franklin County Courier.

HARDWICK

US   ISSN 0744-5512

HARDWICK GAZETTE. 1889. Wed. $.50 newsstand; $21/2yr. in state; $26/yr. out of state. Main St., Hardwick, VT 05843. TEL 802-472-6521. **Owner(s):** Hardwick Publishing Co., Inc., P.O. Box 367, Hardwick, VT 05843. TEL 802-472-6521; Ed. Ross Connelly; Pub. Ross Connelly; adv. contact: Kenneth Williams. photos; bk.rev.; pub. size: broadsheet; circ. 3,100(paid).

KILLINGTON

US

MOUNTAIN TIMES. 1971. Wed. $65/yr P.O. Box 183, Killington, VT 05751. TEL 802-422-2399; FAX 802-422-2395. **Owner(s):** BRC Corp., P.O. Box 183, Killington, VT 05751. TEL 802-422-2399; FAX 802-422-2395; Ed. Royal Barnard; Pub. Royal Barnard; adv. contact: Zip Barnard. photos; pub. size: tabloid; circ. 13,000(free & paid).

MANCHESTER CENTER

US ISSN 1062-5070

MANCHESTER JOURNAL. 1861. Wed. $.50 newsstand; $36/yr. P.O. Box 569, Manchester Center, VT 05255-0569. TEL 802-362-2222; FAX 802-362-5327. **Owner(s):** New England Newspapers, Inc., 23 Exchange St., Pittsfield, MA 02860; Ed. Adam Teschorn. adv.; photos; bk.rev.; pub. size: broadsheet; circ. 5,000(paid).

US

VERMONT NEWS GUIDE. 1960. Tue. free in state; $35/yr. out of state mailed. Rte. 7, Manchester Center, VT 05255. TEL 802-362-3535; FAX 802-362-5368. **Owner(s):** Add, Inc., 600 Industrial Dr., Waupaca, WI 54981. TEL 715-258-8450; Ed. David Lewis. adv.; pub. size: tabloid; circ. 16,000(free & paid).

MIDDLEBURY

US

ADDISON COUNTY INDEPENDENT. 1946. s-w.: Mon. & Thu. $.50 newsstand; $27.50/yr. in state; $38/yr. out of state. 4 Maple St., Middlebury, VT 05753. TEL 802-388-4944. **Owner(s):** Addison Press, Inc., P.O. Box 31, Middlebury, VT 05753. TEL 802-388-4944; Pub. Angelo S. Lynn; adv. contact: Jane Spencer. pub. size: tabloid; circ. 9,000(controlled & paid). **Wire Service(s):** AP.

MORRISVILLE

US

TRANSCRIPT, THE. 1973. Mon. free. Brooklyn St., Morrisville, VT 05661. TEL 802-888-2212; FAX 802-888-2173. **Owner(s):** Bradley Limoge Publishers, Inc., Brooklyn St., Morrisville, VT 05661. TEL 802-888-2212; Ed. Paulette Wallace; Pub. Bradley A. Limoge; adv. contact: Ramona Audet. pub. size: tabloid; circ. 12,045(free).
Formerly: Morrisville Transcript.

RANDOLPH

US

HERALD OF RANDOLPH. 1874. Thu. $.65 newsstand; $20/yr. local; $23/yr. out of VT & NH. 30 Pleasant St., Randolph, VT 05060. TEL 802-728-3232; FAX 802-728-9275. **Owner(s):** M.D. Drysdale, RFD 2, Randolph, VT 05060; Ed. M.D. Drysdale; Pub. M.D. Drysdale; pub. size: broadsheet; circ. 6,600(paid).

RUTLAND

US

▼**POULTNEY NEWS, THE.** 1995. Fri. free; $15/yr. 98 Allen St., Rutland, VT 05701. TEL 802-287-2043. **Owner(s):** Robert Maguire, 98 Allen St., Rutland, VT 05701. TEL 802-775-4221; FAX 802-775-9535; Pub. Lorraine Marcille; adv. contact: Lorraine Marcille. photos; pub. size: tabloid; circ. 5,700(free).

US

RUTLAND TRIBUNE, THE. 1966. Fri. free; $15/yr. 98 Allen St., Rutland, VT 05701. TEL 802-775-4221; FAX 802-775-9535; E-mail: ruttrib@sover.net; URL: http://www.rutlandvt.com. Owner(s): Robert Maguire, 98 Allen St., Rutland, VT 05701. TEL 802-775-4221; FAX 802-775-9535; Pub. Lorraine Marcille; adv. contact: Lorraine Marcille. photos; pub. size: tabloid; circ. 16,000(free).

SHELBURNE

US

VERMONT TIMES. 1990. Wed. free newsstand; $25/yr. 3rd class; $75/yr. 1st class. One Pine Haven Shore Rd., Shelburne, VT 05482. TEL 802-985-2400; FAX 802-985-2490; E-mail: vt times@ad.com. **Owner(s):** New Market Press, P.O. Box 940, Shelburne, VT 05482-0940. TEL 802-985-2400; FAX 802-985-2490; Ed. Dan Hickey; Pub. Jim Duncan; adv. contact: Jim Duncan. photos; bk.rev.; pub. size: tabloid; circ. 23,000(free).

SOUTH HERO

US

ISLANDER, THE. 1975. Tue. free; $1.25/wk. out of area. Sunset View Rd., South Hero, VT 05486. TEL 802-372-5600; FAX 802-372-3025. **Owner(s):** Northern Champlain Islander, Inc., P.O. Box 212, South Hero, VT 05486. TEL 802-372-5600; FAX 802-372-5600; Ed. George D. Fowler. adv.; photos; bk.rev.; pub. size: tabloid; circ. 7,000(free & paid).

SPRINGFIELD

US

SPRINGFIELD REPORTER, THE. 1976. Wed. $.50 newsstand; $28/yr. 151 Summer St., Springfield, VT 05156-3507. TEL 802-885-2246; FAX 802-885-9821; E-mail: reporter@vermontel.com. **Owner(s):** Rodney W. Arnold, 151 Sumner St., Springfield, VT 05156-3507. TEL 802-885-2246; FAX 802-885-2246; Ed. Rodney W. Arnold; Pub. Rodney W. Arnold; adv.; photos; bk.rev.; pub. size: tabloid; circ. 2,000(paid).

STOWE

US

STOWE REPORTER. 1958. Thu. $.50 newsstand; $17/yr. in state; $25/yr. out of state; $32/yr. Canada. School St., Stowe, VT 05672. TEL 802-253-2101; FAX 802-253-8332. **Owner(s):** Reporter Press, Inc., P.O. Box 489, Stowe, VT 05672-0489. TEL 802-253-2101; FAX 802-253-8332; Ed. Gregory Popa; Pub. D. Trowbridge Elliman; adv. contact: Janka Heath. adv.: $6.16/SAU. photos; bk.rev.; pub. size: tabloid; circ. 5,600(paid). **Wire Service(s):** AP.

WAITSFIELD

US

VALLEY REPORTER, THE. 1971. Thu. $.50 newsstand; $14.50/yr. in state; $24/yr. out of state. P.O. Box 119, Waitsfield, VT 05673-0119. TEL 802-496-3928. **Owner(s):** Valley Reporter, Inc., P.O. Box 119, Mad River Valley, Waitsfield, VT 05673-0119. TEL 802-456-3607; Ed. Al Benjamin. adv.; photos; pub. size: tabloid; circ. 2,950(free & paid).

VIRGIN ISLANDS

ST. JOHN

US ISSN 0895-0970

TRADEWINDS. 1977. bi-w. $.50 newsstand; $30/yr. P.O. Box 1500, Cruz Bay, St. John, VI 00831. TEL 809-776-6496; FAX 809-693-8885. **Owner(s):** Drum Communications, P.O. Box 500, Cruz Bay, St. John, VI 00830; Ed. Tom Oat. circ. 3,000(paid).

VIRGINIA

ABINGDON

US

ABINGDON VIRGINIAN. 1841. Wed. $20/yr. in cy.; $25/yr. out of cy. 170 E. Main St., Abingdon, VA 24210. TEL 703-628-2962. **Owner(s):** Martha M. Weisfeld, 170 E. Main St., Abingdon, VA 24210. TEL 703-628-2962; Ed. Martha M. Weisfeld; Pub. Martha M. Weisfeld; adv.; pub. size: standard; circ. 4,500(paid).

US

WASHINGTON COUNTY NEWS. 1948. Wed. $.50 newsstand; $21/yr. 143 W. Main St., Abingdon, VA 24210. TEL 540-628-7101; FAX 540-628-9396. **Owner(s):** Abingdon Newspapers, Inc., 143 W. Main St., Abingdon, VA 24210. TEL 703-628-7101; Ed. Dan Kegley; Pub. Donna Moore; adv. contact: Bill Thomas. photos; bk.rev.; pub. size: standard; circ. 5,138(paid).

ALEXANDRIA

US

ALEXANDRIA GAZETTE PACKET. 1784. Thu. $.25 newsstand; $25/yr. carrier. 1700 Diagonal Rd., Ste. 410, Alexandria, VA 22314. TEL 703-549-7185; FAX 703-548-2228. **Owner(s):** Peter Labovitz, 1700 Diagonal Rd., Ste. 410, Alexandria, VA 22314. TEL 703-549-0004; Ed. Christa Watters; Pub. Jerry Vernon; pub. size: tabloid; circ. 20,000(controlled & paid).

ALTAVISTA

US

ALTAVISTA JOURNAL. 1909. Wed. $.50 newsstand; $20/yr. in cy.; $24/yr. out of cy. 600 Main St., Altavista, VA 24517. TEL 804-369-6688; FAX 804-369-6689. **Owner(s):** Womack Publishing Co., Inc., P.O. Box 111, Chatham, VA 24531. TEL 804-432-1654; Ed. Betty Gilliam. adv. contact: Terri Osborne. pub. size: broadsheet; circ. 6,600(paid).

AMELIA COURT HOUSE

US   ISSN 0746-1798

AMELIA BULLETIN MONITOR, THE. 1973. Thu. $.25 newsstand; $16/yr. in state; $22/yr. out of state. 16301 Goodesbridge Rd., Amelia Court House, VA 23002. TEL 804-561-3655; FAX 804-561-2065. **Owner(s):** Ann B. Salster, P.O. Box 123, Amelia Court House, VA 23002. TEL 804-561-3655; Ed. Michael D. Salster; Pub. Ann B. Salster; adv.; photos; bk.rev.; pub. size: tabloid; circ. 8,300(free & paid).

AMHERST

US

AMHERST NEW ERA-PROGRESS. 1881. Thu. $.50 newsstand; $14/yr. in cy.; $20/yr. out of cy. 113 Second St., Amherst, VA 24521. TEL 804-946-7195; FAX 804-946-2684. **Owner(s):** Thomas T. Byrd, 2 N. Kent St., Winchester, VA 22601. TEL 703-667-3200; Ed. Nancy Cruthfield; Pub. Thomas T. Byrd; pub. size: broadsheet; circ. 5,000(paid).

APPOMATTOX

US

APPOMATTOX TIMES-VIRGINIAN. 1892. Wed. $.50 newsstand; $20/yr. local; $24/yr. out of state. 507 Court St., Appomattox, VA 24522. TEL 804-352-8215; FAX 804-355-2216. **Owner(s):** Womack Publishing Co., Inc., P.O. Box 111, Chatham, VA 24531. TEL 804-432-1654; Ed. Louis Wood; Pub. Charles Wolmack; adv. contact: Peggy Kidd. photos; pub. size: broadsheet; circ. 3,800(paid).

ARLINGTON

US

ARLINGTON COURIER, THE. 1988. Wed. $.25 newsstand; $10/yr. local; $20/yr. elsewhere. 3440 N. Fairfax Dr., Arlington, VA 22201. TEL 703-522-9898; FAX 703-522-8788. **Owner(s):** Emily Schlesinger, P.O. Box 10089, Arlington, VA 22210. TEL 703-522-9898; FAX 703-522-8788; Ed. Joe Farruggia. adv.; photos; bk.rev.; pub. size: tabloid; circ. 27,661(controlled & paid).

ASHLAND

US

HANOVER HERALD-PROGRESS. 1881. s-w.: Mon. & Thu. $.50 newsstand; $20/yr. in cy.; $26/yr. out of cy. 11293 Air Park Rd., Ashland, VA 23005-3203. TEL 804-798-9031; FAX 804-798-9036. **Owner(s):** Herald-Progress, Inc., 11293 Air Park Rd., Ashland, VA 23005. TEL 804-798-9031; FAX 804-798-9036; Pub. J.M. Pace, III; adv. contact: Janice Henicheck. pub. size: broadsheet; circ. 8,400(free & paid). **Wire Service(s):** AP.

BEDFORD

US

BEDFORD BULLETIN. 1857. Wed. $.50 newsstand; $22/yr. in cy.; $27/yr. out of cy.; $32/yr. out of state. 402 E. Main St., Bedford, VA 24523. TEL 540-586-8612; FAX 540-586-0834. **Owner(s):** Landmark Community Newspapers, Inc., P.O. Box 549, Shelbyville, KY 40065; Ed. Rebecca Jackson-Clause; Pub. Jay Bondurant; adv. contact: Lynn Hurst. photos; pub. size: broadsheet; circ. 8,500(paid).

BIG STONE GAP

US

POST, THE. 1890. Wed. $.40 newsstand; $20/yr. in cy.; $40/yr. elsewhere 215 Wood Ave., Big Stone Gap, VA 24219. TEL 703-523-1141; FAX 703-523-1175; E-mail: thepost@compunet.com. **Owner(s):** Wise Printing Co., P.O. Box 250, Big Stone Gap, VA 24219. TEL 703-523-1141; Ed. Jeff Moore; Pub. Robbie G. Tate; adv.; pub. size: broadsheet; circ. 4,942(free & paid). **Wire Service(s):** AP.

BLACKSTONE

US

BLACKSTONE COURIER-RECORD. 1898. Wed. $.50 newsstand; $15/yr. 207 S. Main St., Blackstone, VA 23824. TEL 804-292-3019; FAX 804-292-5966. **Owner(s):** Nottoway Publishing Co., Inc., 207 S. Main, P.O. Box 450, Blackstone, VA 23824. TEL 804-292-3019; FAX 804-292-5966; Ed. James D. Coleburn. adv.; photos; pub. size: standard; circ. 7,100(free & paid).

BOWLING GREEN

US

CAROLINE PROGRESS, THE. 1919. Wed. $.40 newsstand; $19/yr. in cy.; $34/yr. out of cy. 121 Court House Ln., Bowling Green, VA 22427. TEL 804-633-5005; FAX 804-633-6740. **Owner(s):** Chesapeake Publishing Corp., Williamsburg, VA 23188. TEL 804-220-1736; Ed. Jay Plotkin. adv. contact: Karen Oyler. pub. size: broadsheet; circ. 9,000(paid).

CHARLOTTESVILLE

US

CHARLOTTESVILLE-ALBEMARLE TRIBUNE. 1954. Thu. $.50 newsstand; $25/yr. 407 E. Seventh St., Charlottesville, VA 22902. TEL 804-979-0373; FAX 804-971-5821. **Owner(s):** Agnes White, 407 E. Seventh St., Charlottesville, VA 22902. TEL 804-979-0373; Ed. Agnes White; Pub. David White; adv.; pub. size: broadsheet; circ. 4,000(paid).

US

RURAL VIRGINIAN. Wed. free. 685 W. Rio Rd., Charlottesville, VA 22906. TEL 804-978-7200; FAX 804-978-7223. **Owner(s):** Media General, Inc., 411 E. Franklin St., Richmond, VA 23219; Ed. Robert Knapp; Pub. Lawrence McConnell; adv. contact: Wanda Birckhead. pub. size: tabloid; circ. 10,700(paid).

CHASE CITY

US

NEWS-PROGRESS, THE. 1888. s-w.: Mon. & Wed. $.25 newsstand; $16/yr. in cy.; $30/yr. out of cy. 850 E. Second St., Chase City, VA 23924. TEL 804-372-5156; FAX 804-372-3911. **Owner(s):** Mecklenburg News, Inc., P.O. Box 337, Chase City, VA 23924. TEL 804-374-0103; Ed. Douglas E. Loftis; Pub. Keith A. Shelton; adv.; photos; pub. size: broadsheet; circ. 7,675(paid).
Formerly: Clarksville Mecklenberg News.

CHATHAM

US   ISSN 1074-5114

STAR-TRIBUNE. 1869. Wed. $.50 newsstand; $20/yr. in cy.; $24/yr. out of cy. 30 N. Main St., Chatham, VA 24531. TEL 804-432-2791; FAX 804-432-4033. **Owner(s):** Womack Publishing Co., Inc., P.O. Box 111, Chatham, VA 24531. TEL 804-432-1654; Ed. Tim Davis; Pub. Charles Womack, Jr.; adv. contact: Margie Dawson. photos; pub. size: broadsheet; circ. 8,900(paid).

CHESAPEAKE

US

CHESAPEAKE POST. 1962. Fri. $.35 newsstand; $14.95/yr. in cy. 1024 N. Battlefield Blvd., Chesapeake, VA 23320. TEL 804-547-4571; FAX 804-548-0390. **Owner(s):** Byerly Publications, Inc., 1000 Armory Dr., Franklin, VA 23851. TEL 804-562-3187; Ed. Victoria Hecht; Pub. Hanes Byerly; adv. contact: Sandra Snelley. photos; pub. size: broadsheet; circ. 8,425(paid).

US

PORTSMOUTH TIMES. Fri. $.35 newsstand; $14.95/yr. in cy. 1024 N. Battlefield Blvd., Chesapeake, VA 23320. TEL 804-397-7606; FAX 804-548-0390. **Owner(s):** Byerly Publications, Inc., 1000 Armory Dr., Franklin, VA 23851. TEL 804-562-3187; Ed. Victoria Hecht; Pub. Hanes Byerly; adv. contact: Sandra Snelley. photos; pub. size: broadsheet; circ. 7,000(paid).

CHRISTIANSBURG

US

NEWS MESSENGER, THE. 1884. s-w.: Wed., Sat. $.50 newsstand. 3325 N. Franklin St., Christiansburg, VA 24073. TEL 540-382-6171; FAX 540-382-3009. **Owner(s):** New River Newspaper, LLC, One S. Ocean Blvd. Ste. 203, Boca Raton, FL 33432; Ed. Gene Morrell; Pub. John Reynolds; adv. contact: Shellby Roope. photos; pub. size: broadsheet; circ. 13,200(paid); Sun. 13,200(paid). **Wire Service(s):** AP.
Formerly: News Journal.

CLARKSVILLE

US

MECKLENBURG SUN. 1976. Wed. $.25 newsstand; $7/yr. in cy. 602 Virginia Ave., Clarksville, VA 23927. TEL 804-374-8152; FAX 804-374-8153. **Owner(s):** Tucker W. Mclaughlin, Sr., P.O. Drawer 100, South Boston, VA 24592. TEL 804-572-2928; Hugh M. Moore, P.O. Drawer 100, South Boston, VA 24592. TEL 804-572-2928; Ed. Tom McLaughlin, Jr.; Pub. Hugh M. Moore; adv.; photos. pub. size: broadsheet; circ. 5,200(paid).

CLINTWOOD

US

DICKENSON STAR/CUMBERLAND TIMES, THE. 1966. Wed. $.35 newsstand; $10/yr. in cy ; $28/yr. out of cy. Main St., Clintwood, VA 24228-0707. TEL 540-926-8816; FAX 540-926-8827; E-mail: npimedici@compunet.net. **Owner(s):** Robbie G. Tate, 564 Oak Ave., Norton, VA 24273. TEL 703-679-1056; Michael N. & Jenay Tate, P.O. Box 380 Norton, VA 24273 TEL 703-679-1101; Ed. Jenay Tate; Pub. Robbie G. Tate; adv. contact: Bill Endean photos; bk.rev.; pub. size: standard; circ. 6,800(paid). **Wire Service(s):** AP.

CREWE

US　　　ISSN 8755-9463

CREWE-BURKEVILLE JOURNAL. 1959. Thu. $.50 newsstand; $15/yr. in state; $19/yr. out of state. 107 W. Carolina Ave., Crewe, VA 23930. TEL 804-645-7534; FAX 804-645-1848. **Owner(s):** Jim R. Eanes, Eanes & Hudgins Publishing Co., Inc., 107 W. Carolina Ave., Crewe, VA 23930; Ed. Jim R. Eanes. adv.; photos; pub. size: standard; circ. 7,000(paid).

CULPEPER

US

CULPEPER NEWS. 1975. Thu. $.50 newsstand; $24/yr. in cy.; $28/yr. out of cy. 605 S. Main St., Culpeper, VA 22701. TEL 540-825-3232; FAX 540-825-5670. **Owner(s):** Virginia Newspapers, Inc., 333 E. Grace St., Richmond, VA 23219. TEL 804-649-6000; FAX 804-775-8090; Ed. Theresa Knight. adv. contact: Sherri Lutz. photos; pub. size: broadsheet; circ. 5,000(controlled & paid).

US

NORTHERN PIEDMONT EXPRESS. Wed. free. 122 W. Spencer St., Culpeper, VA 22701. TEL 540-825-0771; FAX 540-825-0771. **Owner(s):** Media General, Inc., 411 E. Franklin St., Richmond, VA 23219. TEL 804-775-8030; Pub. Peter S. Yates; adv. contact: Diane Holt. pub. size: standard; circ. 20,000(controlled & free).

DRAKES BRANCH

US

CHARLOTTE GAZETTE. 1873. Thu. $.50 newsstand; $12/yr. in cy. Main St., Drakes Branch, VA 23937. TEL 804-568-3341; FAX 804-568-3731. **Owner(s):** Dorothy C. Tucker, P.O. Box 214, Drakes Branch, VA 23937. TEL 804-568-3341; Ed. O.O. Tucker, III; Pub. Dorothy C. Tucker; pub. size: broadsheet; circ. 3,300(paid).

ELKTON

US

VALLEY BANNER, THE. 1966. Thu. $.25 newsstand; $12/yr. local; $18/yr. elsewhere. 157 W. Spotswood Ave., Elkton, VA 22827-0126. TEL 540-298-9444; FAX 540-298-2560; E-mail: frontpg@aol.com. **Owner(s):** Rockingham Publishing Co., Inc., P.O. Box 193, Harrisonburg, VA 22801. TEL 540-298-9444; FAX 540-298-2560; Ed. R.C. Murphey, IV. adv. contact: Carol Campbell. adv.: $6/SAU. photos; pub. size: standard; circ. 4,500(free & paid).

EMPORIA

US

INDEPENDENT-MESSENGER. 1896. s-w.: Sun. & Thu. $.35 newsstand; $21.85/yr. in cy.; $29.75/yr. in VA & NC; $38/yr. elsewhere. 441 S. Main St., Emporia, VA 23847. TEL 804-634-4153; FAX 804-634-0783. **Owner(s):** Byerly Publications, Inc., 1000 Armory Dr., Franklin, VA 23851. TEL 804-562-3187; Ed. Jamie Brown; Pub. Hanes Bylerly; adv. contact: Bill Edwards. photos; pub. size: broadsheet; circ. 6,800(paid).

FAIRFAX

US　　　ISSN 1065-1632

NORTHERN VIRGINIA SUN, THE. 1937. s-w.: Tue. & Fri. $.25 newsstand; $24/yr. 2710 C Prosperity Ave., Fairfax, VA 22031. TEL 703-204-2800; FAX 703-204-3455. **Owner(s):** Sun Newspapers, Inc., 2710C Prosperity Ave., Fairfax, VA 22031. TEL 703-204-2800; Ed. Henry Dunbar; Pub. David Blakeslee; adv.; pub. size: tabloid; circ. 81,000(paid). **Wire Service(s):** AP. Formerly: Arlington Northern Virginia Sun.

FALLS CHURCH

US

FALLS CHURCH NEWS-PRESS. 1991. Wed. free newsstand; $39/yr. 929 W. Broad St., Ste. 200, Falls Church, VA 22046. TEL 703-532-3267; FAX 703-532-3396. **Owner(s):** Century News Service, Inc., 929 W. Broad St., Ste. 200, Falls Church, VA 22046. TEL 703-532-3267; FAX 703-532-3396; Ed. Nicholas Benton. adv.; bk.rev.; pub. size: tabloid; circ. 8,000(free).

FARMVILLE

US

FARMVILLE HERALD, THE. 1890. 3/wk.: Wed., Fri., Sun. $.35 newsstand; $24/yr. in cy.; $35/yr. out of cy. 114 North St., Farmville, VA 23901. TEL 804-392-4151; FAX 804-392-6298. **Owner(s):** William B. Wall, 114 North St., Farmville, VA 23901. TEL 804-392-4151; Ed. Ken Woodley; Pub. Steven E. Wall; pub. size: broadsheet; circ. 8,200(paid).

US

FREE NEWS, THE. Mon. free. 114 North St., Farmville, VA 23901. TEL 804-392-4151; FAX 804-392-6298. **Owner(s):** William B. Wall, 114 North St., Farmville, VA 23901; Ed. Kim Woodley; Pub. Steven E. Wall; pub. size: broadsheet; circ. 15,000(free).

FINCASTLE

US

FINCASTLE HERALD, THE. 1866. Wed. $.50 newsstand; $20/yr. 211 Catawba St., Fincastle, VA 24090. TEL 703-473-2741; FAX 703-473-2741. **Owner(s):** Salem Publishing Co., 1633 W. Main St., Salem, VA 24153. TEL 703-389-9355; FAX 703-389-2930; Ed. Edwin Taylor; Pub. Ray Robinson; adv. contact: Joan Bowles. photos; bk.rev.; pub. size: standard; circ. 5,900(paid). Formerly: Botetourt County News.

FLOYD

US

FLOYD PRESS. 1891. Thu. $.50 newsstand; $20/yr. in cy.; $25/yr. out of cy. 710 E. Main St., Floyd, VA 24091. TEL 540-745-2127; FAX 540-745-2126. **Owner(s):** William B. & Dorothy V. Sumner, 710 E. Main St., Floyd, VA 24091. TEL 703-745-2127; Ed. Wanda Combs; Pub. Dorothy V. Sumner; adv. contact: Carman Harman. photos; pub. size: standard; circ. 5,000(paid).

GALAX

US

GALAX GAZETTE, THE. 1876. 3/wk.: Mon., Wed., Fri. $.50 newsstand; $38/yr. local. 108 W. Stuart Dr., Galax, VA 24333. TEL 540-236-5178; FAX 540-236-0756. **Owner(s):** Landmark Community Newspapers, Inc., P.O. Box 549, Shelbyville, KY 40066. TEL 502-633-4334; Ed. Amy Hauslohner; Pub. Chuck Burress; adv. contact: Robin Porter. photos; pub. size: broadsheet; circ. 8,600(paid).

GLOUCESTER

US

GLOUCESTER-MATHEWS GAZETTE JOURNAL. 1904. Thu. $.50 newsstand; $20/yr. in cy.; $24/yr. out of cy. Main St. & Lewis Ave., Gloucester, VA 23061. TEL 804-693-3101; FAX 804-693-7844. **Owner(s):** Tidewater Newspapers, Inc., P.O. Box J, Gloucester, VA 23061. TEL 804-693-3101; Ed. Elsa V. Cooke-Verbyla; Pub. John W. Cooke; adv. contact: June Byrd. photos; pub. size: broadsheet; circ. 10,500(paid). **Wire Service(s):** AP, Newsfinder.

GOOCHLAND

US

GOOCHLAND GAZETTE. 1955. Sat. $.50 newsstand; $20/yr. in cy.; $30/yr. out of cy. 3052 River Rd., W., Goochland, VA 23063. TEL 804-556-3135; FAX 804-556-4237. **Owner(s):** JGF Media, Inc., Charlottesville, VA; Ed. McGregor McCance; Pub. J. Grey Ferguson; adv. contact: Tom Haynie. photos; bk.rev.; pub. size: broadsheet; circ. 3,400(paid).

GRUNDY

US

VIRGINIA MOUNTAINEER. 1922. Thu. $.50 newsstand; $18/yr. in cy.; $25/yr. out of cy. 105 Main St., Grundy, VA 24614-2040. TEL 540-935-2123; FAX 540-935-2125. **Owner(s):** Mountaineer Publishing Co., Inc., P.O. Box 2040, Grundy, VA 24614. TEL 540-935-2123; FAX 540-935-2125; Ed. Lodge Compton; Pub. Lodge Compton; adv. contact: John Whited. pub. size: broadsheet; circ. 8,600(paid).

HEATHSVILLE

US

NORTHUMBERLAND ECHO. 1902. Wed. $.35 newsstand; $17/yr. in cy.; $32/yr. out of cy. Rt. 360, Echo Bldg., Heathsville, VA 22473. TEL 804-580-3444; FAX 804-580-6826. **Owner(s):** Chesapeake Publishing Corp., Airport Industrial Park, Easton, MD 21601. TEL 301-822-1500; Ed. Priscilla Dawson; Pub. William C. O'Donovan; pub. size: broadsheet; circ. 5,000(paid).

HILLSVILLE

US

CARROLL NEWS, THE. 1920. Wed. $.35 newsstand; $20.50/yr. 1026 W. Stuart Dr., Hillsville, VA 24343. TEL 540-728-7311; FAX 540-728-4119. **Owner(s):** Wayne Brockenbrough, P. O. Box 57, Christiansberg, VA 24073; Ed. Wendy Turner; Pub. Ina Horton; adv. contact: Joyce Cromer. pub. size: broadsheet; circ. 5,700(paid).

INDEPENDENCE

US

DECLARATION, THE. 1980. Wed. $.50 newsstand; $19/yr. local; $30/yr. out of area. 304 Davis St., Independence, VA 24348-0070. TEL 703-773-2222; FAX 703-773-2287. **Owner(s):** John E. North, 304 Davis St., Independence, VA 24348. TEL 703-773-2222; FAX 703-773-2287; Ed. John E. North; Pub. John E. North; adv. contact: Sherrie LaRue. photos; bk.rev.; pub. size: broadsheet; circ. 3,500(free & paid).

KILMARNOCK

US

RAPPAHANNOCK RECORD. 1916. Thu. $.50 newsstand; $18/yr. in cty.; $26/yr. out of cty. 27 Main St., Kilmarnock, VA 22482. TEL 804-435-1701; FAX 804-435-2632. **Owner(s):** Rappahannock Record, 27 Main St., Kilmarnock, VA 22482. TEL 804-435-1701; FAX 804-435-2632; Ed. John C. Wilson; Pub. Fred A. Gaskins; adv. contact: Linda Troise. pub. size: broadsheet; circ. 8,027(free & paid).

LAWRENCEVILLE

US

BRUNSWICK TIMES-GAZETTE. 1887. Wed. $.35 newsstand; $12/yr. in cy. 213 Main St., Lawrenceville, VA 23868. TEL 804-848-2114; FAX 804-848-2115. **Owner(s):** Byerly Publications, Inc., 1000 Armory Dr., Franklin, VA 23851. TEL 804-562-3187; Ed. Jennifer Sullivan; Pub. Hanes Byerly; adv. contact: Tom Childrey. photos; pub. size: broadsheet; circ. 5,800(paid).

LEBANON

US

LEBANON NEWS. 1880. Wed. $.50 newsstand; $20/yr. in cy.; $26/yr. out of cy. 308 Main St., Lebanon, VA 24266. TEL 540-889-2112; FAX 540-889-5017. **Owner(s):** Jerry E. Lark, P.O. Box 1268, Lebanon, VA 24266. TEL 703-889-2112; A.G. Griffith, P.O. Box 1268, Lebanon, PA 24266; Bob Hillman, P.O. Box 1268, Lebanon, PA 24266; Bill McFarlane, P.O. Box 1268, Lebanon, PA 24266; Ed. Jerry E. Lark; Pub. Jerry E. Lark; adv.; photos; pub. size: broadsheet; circ. 5,600(paid).

LEESBURG

US

LEESBURG TODAY. 1988. Wed. free newsstand; $80/yr. 1st class. 112-Q South St., S.E., Leesburg, VA 22075. TEL 703-771-8800; FAX 703-771-8833. **Owner(s):** Amendment I, Inc., 112-Q South St., S.E., Leesburg, VA 22075. TEL 703-771-8800; FAX 703-771-8833; Pub. Brett Phillips; adv. contact: Ruth Fifield. pub. size: tabloid; circ. 28,059(controlled & free).

US

LOUDOUN TIMES-MIRROR. 1798. Thu. $.50 newsstand; $23.95/yr. in cy. carrier; $29.95/yr. in cy. mailed; $39.95/yr. out of cy. 9 E. Market St., Leesburg, VA 22075. TEL 703-777-1111; FAX 703-771-0036. **Owner(s):** Arcom Publications Co., Inc., 1760 Reston Pkwy., Ste. 411, Reston, VA 22091. TEL 703-437-5400; FAX 703-437-6019; Ed. Martin Casey; Pub. Arthur W. Arundel; adv. contact: Martie Curran. photos; pub. size: broadsheet; circ. 18,000(paid).

LEXINGTON

US

NEWS-GAZETTE. 1801. Wed. $.50 newsstand; $18/yr. in cy.; $30/yr. out of cy. 20 W. Nelson St., Lexington, VA 24450. TEL 540-463-3113; FAX 540-464-6397. **Owner(s):** News-Gazette Corp., 20 W. Nelson St., Lexington, VA 24450. TEL 540-463-3113; Ed. Darryl Woodson; Pub. M.W. Paxton, IV; adv. contact: Marsha Rexrode. pub. size: broadsheet; circ. 9,364(paid).

US   ISSN 1064-7759

ROCKBRIDGE WEEKLY. 1981. Wed. $.50 newsstand; $15/yr. in area; $26/yr. out of area. College Square Shopping Ctr., Lexington, VA 24450. TEL 540-464-6600; FAX 540-464-6603. **Owner(s):** Jerry Clark, P.O. Box 791, Buena Vista, VA 24416; Ed. Jerry Clark; Pub. Jerry Clark; adv.; photos; pub. size: broadsheet; circ. 13,300(paid).

US

WEEKENDER, THE. 1989. Sat. free. 20 W. Nelson St., Lexington, VA 24450. TEL 540-463-3113; FAX 540-464-6397. **Owner(s):** News-Gazette Corp., 20 W. Nelson St., Lexington, VA 00623. TEL 540-463-3113; Ed. Darryl Woodson; Pub. M.W. Paxton, IV; adv. contact: Marshal Rexrode. pub. size: broadsheet circ. 13,800(controlled).

LOUISA

US

CENTRAL VIRGINIAN, THE. 1912. Thu. $.50 newsstand; $17/yr. in cy.; $22/yr. in state; $25/yr. out of state. 101 Elm Ave., Louisa, VA 23093. TEL 703-967-0368; FAX 703-967-0457. **Owner(s):** C.V. Corp. of Virginia, P.O. Box 464, Louisa, VA 23093. TEL 703-967-0368; FAX 703-967-0457; Ed. Hilda D. Miller; Pub. Hilda D. Miller; adv. contact: Doug Miller. photos; pub. size: broadsheet; circ. 7,000(paid).

LOVINGSTON

US

NELSON COUNTY TIMES. Thu. $.50 newsstand; $14/yr. in cy.; $20/yr. out of cy. 113 Second St., Lovingston, VA 22521. TEL 804-946-7195; FAX 804-946-2684. **Owner(s):** Thomas Byrd, Amherst Nelson Publishing Co., 90 Amherst, Lovingston, VA 22521. TEL 703-946-7195; Ed. Jim Manner; Pub. Thomas Byrd; pub. size: standard; circ. 4,700(paid).

LURAY

US

LURAY PAGE NEWS & COURIER. 1867. Thu. $.50 newsstand; $12/yr. in cy.; $15/yr. out of cy. 17 S. Broad St., Luray, VA 22835. TEL 703-743-5123. **Owner(s):** Page-Shenandoah Newspaper Corp., Inc. 17 S. Broad St., Luray, VA 22835. TEL 703-743-5123; Ed. R. Cort Kirkwood. adv.; photos; bk.rev.; pub. size: standard; circ. 7,200(paid).

MADISON

US

MADISON COUNTY EAGLE. 1911. Thu. $.50 newsstand; $24/yr. in cy. 200 Main St., Madison, VA 22727. TEL 540-948-5121; FAX 540-948-3045. **Owner(s):** Media General, Inc., 333 E. Grace St., Richmond, VA 23219. TEL 804-649-6000; FAX 804-775-8090; Ed. Greg K. Glassner. adv. contact: Sherri Lutz. photos; bk.rev.; pub. size: broadsheet; circ. 4,500(paid).

MARION

US

NEWS BUYERS CATALOG. 1980. Sat. free. 119 Sheffey St., Marion, VA 24354. TEL 540-783-5121; FAX 540-783-9713. **Owner(s):** D. Gregory Rooker, 460 W. Main St., Wytheville, VA 24382. TEL 703-228-6611; FAX 703-228-7260; Pub. Debbie Maxwell; adv.; pub. size: tabloid; circ. 9,800(free).
Formerly: Appalachian Shopper.

US   ISSN 0744-0766

SMYTH COUNTY NEWS & MESSENGER. 1884. s-w.: Wed. & Sat. $.50 newsstand; $30/yr. in cy.; $43/yr. in state; $51.20/yr. out of state. Corner of Cherry & Sheffey Sts., Marion, VA 24354. TEL 540-783-5121; FAX 540-783-9713. **Owner(s):** Family Community Newspapers, 460 W. Main St., Wytheville, VA 24382. TEL 540-228-6611; FAX 540-228-7260; Pub. D. Gregory Rooker; adv. contact: D. Gregory Rooker. photos pub. size: broadsheet; circ. 8,100(paid).

MCLEAN

US

FAIRFAX CONNECTION. 1987. w. free. 7670 Old Springhouse Rd., McLean, VA 22102. TEL 703-917-6444; FAX 703-917-0991. **Owner(s):** DCI Publishing, Inc., 7670 Old Springhouse Rd., McLean, VA 22102; Ed. Mary Caimm Dickson. adv.; circ. 22,050(controlled).

MONETA

US

SMITH MOUNTAIN EAGLE. Wed. $.50 newsstand; $20/yr. in area; $24/yr. out of area. Rte. 122, Moneta, VA 24121. TEL 540-297-1222. **Owner(s):** Womack Publishing Co., Inc., P.O. Box 111, Chatham, VA 24531; Ed. Rob Lyon; Pub. Charles Womack; adv.; pub. size: broadsheet; circ. 3,800(paid).

MONTEREY

US   ISSN 0888-9473

RECORDER, THE. 1877. Fri. $.50 newsstand; $19/yr. in cy.; $24/yr. in state; $26/yr. out of state. 3 Water St., Monterey, VA 24465. TEL 540-468-2147; FAX 540-468-2048. **Owner(s):** Recorder Publishing of Virginia, Inc., P.O. Box 10, Monterey, VA 24465. TEL 540-468-2147; Ed. Chris Pugh; Pub. Chris Pugh; adv.; pub. size: tabloid; circ. 5,600(paid).

MONTROSS

US

WESTMORELAND NEWS. 1947. Thu. $.40 newsstand; $19/yr. in cy.; $34/yr. out of cy. Courthouse Ln., Montross, VA 22520. TEL 804-493-8096; FAX 804-493-8009. **Owner(s):** Chesapeake Publishing Corp., Airport Industrial Park, Easton, MD 21601. TEL 301-822-1500; Ed. Lynn Norris; Pub. William C. O'Donovan; adv. contact: Crystal Preston. pub. size: broadsheet; circ. 5,000(paid).

NEW CASTLE

US

NEW CASTLE RECORD. 1885. Wed. $.50 newsstand; $20/yr. local; $24/yr. out of cy.; $28/yr. out of state. P.O. Box 116, New Castle, VA 24127. TEL 540-864-5944; FAX 540-864-5944. **Owner(s):** Salem Publishing Co., 1633 W. Main St., Salem, VA 24153. TEL 703-389-9355; FAX 703-389-2930; Ed. Chris Moody; Pub. Ray Robinson; pub. size: broadsheet; circ. 1,750(paid).

NORFOLK

US

METRO WEEKENDERS, THE. Fri. free. 362 Campastella Rd., Norfolk, VA 23523. TEL 804-543-6531; FAX 804-543-7620. **Owner(s):** Brenda H. Andrews, 362 Campastella Rd., Norfolk, VA 23523. TEL 804-543-6531; Ed. Leonard Colvin; Pub. Brenda H. Andrews; pub. size: broadsheet; circ. 25,000(free).

NORTON

US　　　ISSN 0889-3330

COALFIELD PROGRESS. 1911. s-w.: Tue. & Thu. $.50 newsstand; $40/yr. in cy. 725 Park Ave., Norton, VA 24273-0380. TEL 540-679-1101; FAX 540-679-5922; E-mail: npimedia@compunet.net. **Owner(s):** Norton Press, Inc., P.O. Box 380, Norton, VA 24273. TEL 703-679-1101; Ed. Jenay Tate; Pub. Robbie G. Tate; adv. contact: Bill Endean. photos; bk.rev.; pub. size: broadsheet; circ. 8,885(free & paid). **Wire Service(s):** AP.

ORANGE

US

ORANGE COUNTY REVIEW. 1931. Thu. $.50 newsstand; $24/yr. in cy.; $26/yr. out of cy. 110 Berry Hill Rd., Orange, VA 22960. TEL 540-672-1266; FAX 540-672-5831. **Owner(s):** Media General, Inc., 333 E. Grace St., Richmond, VA 23219. TEL 804-649-6000; FAX 804-775-8090; Ed. Jeff Poole; Pub. Peter S. Yates; adv. contact: Stacey Weakley. pub. size: broadsheet; circ. 7,450(paid).

PEARISBURG

US

VIRGINIAN-LEADER. 1857. Wed. $.50 newsstand; $21/yr. 511 Mountain Lake Ave., Pearisburg, VA 24134. TEL 703-921-3434; FAX 703-921-2563. **Owner(s):** Virginian Leader Corp., P.O. Drawer C, Pearisburg, VA 24134. TEL 703-921-3434; Ed. Mike Wade; Pub. Kenneth Rakes; adv.; photos; pub. size: standard; circ. 6,240(paid).

PENNINGTON GAP

US

POWELL VALLEY NEWS. 1920. Wed. $.50 newsstand; $25/yr. in surrounding cys.; $30/yr. out of area. 125 E. Morgan Ave., Pennington Gap, VA 24277. TEL 540-546-1210; FAX 540-546-5468. **Owner(s):** Donald R. & Shirley A. Watson, P.O. Box 459, Pennington Gap, VA 24277. TEL 540-546-1210; Ed. Donald R. Watson; Pub. Donald R. Watson; adv. contact: Rick L. Watson. photos; pub. size: broadsheet; circ. 7,537(paid).
　　Formerly: Pennington Gap Powell Valley.

PURCELLVILLE

US

BLUE RIDGE LEADER, THE. 1984. Fri. $.25 newsstand; $20/yr. subscription only. 769 E. Main St., Purcellville, VA 22132-3129. TEL 703-338-6200; FAX 703-338-2647. **Owner(s):** Philip Y. Hahn, 769 E. Main St., Purcellville, VA 22132. TEL 703-338-6200; FAX 703-338-2647; Ed. Philip Y. Hahn; Pub. Philip Y. Hahn; adv. contact: Lorie Keating. photos; bk.rev.; pub. size: tabloid; circ. 20,000(controlled & paid).

RESTON

US

BURKE TIMES, THE. Thu. $.25 newsstand; $29.95/yr. in cy.; $39.95/yr. out of cy. 1760 Reston Pkwy., Ste. 411, Reston, VA 22090. TEL 703-437-5400; FAX 703-437-6019. **Owner(s):** Arcom Publications Co., Inc., 1760 Reston Pkwy., Ste. 411, Reston, VA 22091. TEL 703-437-5400; FAX 703-437-6019; Ed. Marcia McAllister. adv. contact: Dianne Shelton. pub. size: broadsheet; circ. 13,006(controlled & paid).

US

CENTREVILLE TIMES. Thu. $.25 newsstand; $29.95/yr. in cy.; $39.95/yr. out of cy. 1760 Reston Pkwy., Ste. 411, Reston, VA 22091. TEL 703-437-5400; FAX 703-437-6019. **Owner(s):** Arcom Publications Co., Inc., 1760 Reston Pkwy., Ste. 411, Reston, VA 22091. TEL 703-437-5400; FAX 703-437-6019; Ed. Janet Rems; Pub. Arthur W. Arundel; adv. contact: Donna Hirsch. pub. size: broadsheet; circ. 13,948(free & paid).
　　Formerly: Centreville Times Mirror.

US

CHANTILLY TIMES. Thu. $.25 newsstand; $29.95/yr. in cy.; $39.95/yr. out of cy. 1760 Reston Pkwy., Ste. 411, Reston, VA 22090. TEL 703-437-5400; FAX 703-437-6019. **Owner(s):** Arcom Publications Co., Inc., 1760 Reston Pkwy., Ste. 411, Reston, VA 22091. TEL 703-437-5400; FAX 703-437-6019; Ed. Janet Rems; Pub. Arthur W. Arundel; adv. contact: Donna Hirsch. pub. size: broadsheet; circ. 6,980(free & paid).
　　Formerly: Chantilly Times Mirror.

US

CLARK COURIER. Thu. $.50 newsstand; $16/yr. in cy.; $20/yr. out of cy. 1760 Reston Blvd., Ste. 411, Reston, VA 22090. TEL 703-437-5400; FAX 703-437-6019. **Owner(s):** Arcom Publications Co., Onc., 1760 Reston Blvd., Ste. 411, Reston, VA 22090. TEL 703-437-5400; FAX 703-437-6019; Ed. Janet Rems, Mng. Ed.; Pub. Arthur W. Arundel; pub. size: broadsheet.

US

FAIRFAX STATION TIMES. Thu. $.25 newsstand; $29.95/yr. in cy.; $39.95/yr. out of cy. 1760 Reston Pkwy., Reston, VA 22090. TEL 703-437-5400; FAX 703-437-6019. **Owner(s):** Arcom Publications Co., Inc., 1760 Reston Pkwy., Ste. 411, Reston, VA 22091. TEL 703-437-5400; FAX 703-437-6019; Ed. Matt Brown; Pub. Arthur W. Arundel; adv. contact: Oscar Ycaza. pub. size: broadsheet; circ. 5,250(controlled & paid).

US

FAIRFAX TIMES. Thu. $.25 newsstand; $29.95/yr. in cy.; $39.95/yr. out of cy. 1760 Reston Pkwy., Ste. 411, Reston, VA 22090. TEL 703-437-5400; FAX 703-437-6019. **Owner(s):** Arcom Publications Co., Inc., 1760 Reston Pkwy., Ste. 411, Reston, VA 22091. TEL 703-437-5400; FAX 703-437-6019; Ed. Janet Rems; Pub. Arthur W. Arundel; adv. contact: Oscar Ycaza. pub. size: broadsheet; circ. 19,150(controlled & paid).

US

GREAT FALLS TIMES. 1986. Wed. $13.50/yr. in cy.; $20/yr. out of cy. 1760 Reston Pkwy., Ste. 411, Reston, VA 22090-3303. TEL 703-437-5400; FAX 703-437-6019; E-mail: nvtimes@aol.com. **Owner(s):** Arcom Publications Co., Inc., 1760 Reston Pkwy., Ste. 411, Reston, VA 22090. TEL 703-437-5400; FAX 703-435-6019; Ed. Janet Rems; Pub. Arthur W. Arundel; adv. contact: Donna Hirsch. photos; pub. size: tabloid; circ. 4,000(free).
　　Formerly: Great Falls Current.

US

HERNDON TIMES. Wed. $.25 newsstand; $29.95/yr. in cy.; $39.95/yr. out of cy. 1760 Reston Pkwy., Ste. 411, Reston, VA 22090. TEL 703-437-5400; FAX 703-437-6019. **Owner(s):** Arcom Publications Co., Inc., 1760 Reston Pkwy., Ste. 411, Reston, VA 22090-3285. TEL 703-437-5400; FAX 703-437-6019; Ed. Janet Rems; Pub. Arthur W. Arundel; adv. contact: Donna Hirsch. pub. size: broadsheet; circ. 12,041(free & paid).
　　Formerly: Herndon Times Mirror.

US

MCLEAN PROVIDENCE JOURNAL. Wed. $13.50/yr. in cy.; $20/yr. out of cy. 1760 Reston Pkwy, Ste. 411, Reston, VA 22090-3303. TEL 703-437-5400; FAX 703-437-6019; E-mail: nvtimes.aol.com. **Owner(s):** Arcom Publications Co., Inc., 1760 Reston Pkwy., Ste. 411, Reston, VA 22091-3285. TEL 703-437-5400; FAX 703-437-6019; Ed. Janet Rems; Pub. Arthur W. Arundel; adv. contact: Donna Hirsch. photos; pub. size: tabloid; circ. 14,000(free).

US

RAPPAHANNOCK NEWS. Thu. $.50 newsstand; $19/yr. in cy.; $24/yr. out of cy. 1760 Reston Pkway., Ste. 411, Reston, VA 22090. TEL 703-437-5400; FAX 703-437-6019. **Owner(s):** Arcom Publications Co., Inc., 1760 Reston Pkwy., Ste. 411, Reston, VA 22090. TEL 703-437-5400; FAX 703-437-6019; Ed. Janet Rems; Pub. Arthur W. Arundel; pub. size: broadsheet.

US

RESTON TIMES. 1965. Wed. $.25 newsstand; $29.95/yr. in cy.; $39.95/yr. out of cy. 1760 Reston Pkwy., Ste. 411, Reston, VA 22090. TEL 703-437-5400; FAX 703-437-6019. **Owner(s):** Arcom Publications Co., Inc., 1760 Reston Pkwy., Ste. 411, Reston, VA 22091. TEL 703-437-5400; FAX 703-437-6019; Ed. Janet Rems; Pub. Arthur W. Arundel; adv. contact: Donna Hirsch. photos; pub. size: broadsheet; circ. 16,527(free & paid).
　　Formerly: Reston Times Mirror.

US

SPRINGFIELD TIMES COURIER. Thu. $.25 newsstand; $29.95/yr. in cy.; $39.95/yr. out of cy. 1760 Reston Pkwy., Ste. 411, Reston, VA 22090. TEL 703-437-5400; FAX 703-437-6019. **Owner(s):** Arcom Publications Co., Inc., 1760 Reston Pkwy., Ste. 411, Reston, VA 22090. TEL 703-437-5400; FAX 703-437-6019; Ed. Marcia McAllister; Pub. Arthur W. Arundel; adv. contact: Oscar Ycaza. pub. size: broadsheet; circ. 23,500(controlled & paid).

VIENNA TIMES. 1985. Thu. $.25 newsstand; $29.95/yr. in cy.; $39.95/yr. out of cy. 1760 Reston Pkwy., Ste. 411, Reston, VA 22090. TEL 703-437-5400; FAX 703-437-6019. **Owner(s):** Arcom Publications Co., Inc., 1760 Reston Pkwy., Ste. 411, Reston, VA 22091-3285. TEL 703-437-5400; FAX 703-437-6019; Ed. Janet Rems; Pub. Arthur W. Arundel; adv. contact: Donna Hirsch. pub. size: broadsheet; circ. 11,339(free & paid).
Formerly: Vienna Times Mirror.

RICHLANDS

US

MOUNTAIN ADVISOR. Sat. free. 1206 Second St., Richlands, VA 24641. TEL 540-963-1081; FAX 540-963-0123. **Owner(s):** Media General, Inc., 333 E. Grace St., Richmond, VA 23126. TEL 804-649-6000; Pub. William H. Hall; adv. contact: Audira Leffel. pub. size: broadsheet; circ. 14,000(free).

US

RICHLANDS NEWS PRESS. 1933. Wed. $.50 newsstand; $26/yr. in cy. 1206 Second St., Richlands, VA 24641. TEL 540-963-1081; FAX 540-963-0123. **Owner(s):** Media General, Inc., 333 E. Grace St., Richmond, VA 23126. TEL 804-649-6000; FAX 804-775-8090; Pub. William H. Hall; adv. contact: Audria Leffel. photos; pub. size: broadsheet; circ. 7,900(paid).

US

TAZEWELL COUNTY FREE PRESS. 1976. Wed. free newsstand; $20/6 mos. 1249 Front St., Richlands, VA 24641. TEL 703-963-0127; FAX 703-963-0127. **Owner(s):** Loren & Lynna Mitchell, 406 Buchanan St., Richlands, VA 24641. TEL 703-963-2308; Ed. Loren Mitchell; Pub. Loren Mitchell; adv. contact: Lynna Mitchell. photos; bk.rev.; pub. size: standard; circ. 13,000(controlled & free). **Wire Service(s):** AP.

ROCKY MOUNT

US

FRANKLIN NEWS-POST. 1905. 3/wk.: Mon., Wed., Fri. $.50 newsstand; $40/yr. in cy.; $45/yr. out of cy. 121 Main St., Rocky Mount, VA 24151. TEL 540-483-5113; FAX 540-483-8013. **Owner(s):** Franklin County Newspapers, Inc., P.O. Box 250, Rocky Mount, VA 24151. TEL 540-483-5113; Ed. R.B. Hundley; Pub. R.B. Hundley; adv. contact: Ken Bradley. photos; pub. size: broadsheet; circ. 8,600(paid).

SALEM

US

SALEM TIMES-REGISTER. 1854. Thu. $.50 newsstand; $18/yr. in town; $22/yr. out of town; $26/yr. out of state. 1633 W. Main St., Salem, VA 24153. TEL 703-389-9355; FAX 703-389-2930. **Owner(s):** Ray Robinson, 1633 W. Main St., Salem, VA 24153. TEL 703-389-9355; FAX 703-389-2930; Ed. Christian Moody; Pub. Ray Robinson; adv. contact: Judy Bradshaw. photos; pub. size: broadsheet; circ. 5,000(paid).

SOUTH BOSTON

US

SOUTH BOSTON GAZETTE-VIRGINIAN. 1903. 3/wk.: Mon., Wed., Fri. $.25 newsstand; $20/yr. in cy.; $36/yr. out of cy. 3201 Halifax Rd., South Boston, VA 24592. TEL 804-572-3945; FAX 804-572-1173. **Owner(s):** Keith A. Shelton, 3201 Halifax Rd., South Boston, VA 24592. TEL 804-572-3492; Ed. Hugh M. Moore; Pub. Keith A. Shelton; adv. contact: Dell Satterfield. photos; bk.rev.; pub. size: broadsheet; circ. 11,500(paid).

US

SOUTH BOSTON NEWS & RECORD. 1892. s-w.: Mon. & Thu. $.25 newsstand; $12/yr. in cy.; $24/yr. out of cy. Halifax Sq. Shopping Ctr., Rte. 501, N., South Boston, VA 24592. TEL 804-572-2928; FAX 804-572-2920. **Owner(s):** Tucker W. McLaughlin, Sr., P.O. Drawer 100, South Boston, VA 24592. TEL 804-572-2928; Hugh M. Moore, P.O. Drawer 100, South Boston, VA 24592. TEL 804-572-2928; Ed. Sylvia McLaughlin; Pub. Tucker McLaughlin, Sr.; adv. contact: Carl Samford. pub. size: broadsheet; circ. 7,600(paid).

SOUTH HILL

US

SOUTH HILL ENTERPRISE. Wed. $.50 newsstand; $18/yr. in cy.; $25/yr. out of cy. 914 W. Danville St., South Hill, VA 23970. TEL 804-447-3178; FAX 804-447-5931. **Owner(s):** South Hill Enterprise, P.O. Box 60, South Hill, VA 23970. TEL 804-447-3178; Ed. Frank L. Nanney, Jr.; Pub. Harry J. Nanney; pub. size: broadsheet; circ. 8,575(paid).

STANARDSVILLE

US

GREENE COUNTY RECORD. 1914. Thu. $.50 newsstand; $22/yr. Main St., Stanardsville, VA 22973. TEL 804-985-2315; FAX 804-985-8356. **Owner(s):** Central Virginia Weekly Group, 333 E. Grace St., Richmond, VA 23219. TEL 804-649-6000; FAX 804-775-8090; Ed. Chris R. Brasted; Pub. Peter S. Yates; adv.; bk.rev.; pub. size: broadsheet; circ. 3,100(paid).

STUART

US

ENTERPRISE, THE. 1876. Wed. $.35 newsstand; $15/yr. local; $20/yr. elsewhere. 22 E. Main St., Stuart, VA 24171-0348. TEL 540-694-3101; FAX 540-694-3102. **Owner(s):** Gail M. Harding, 22 E. Main St., Stuart, VA 24171-0348. TEL 540-694-3101; Ed. Nancy M. Lindsey; Pub. Gail M. Harding; adv.; pub. size: broadsheet; circ. 5,900(paid).

TAZEWELL

US

CLINCH VALLEY NEWS. 1845. Wed. $.50 newsstand; $26/yr. in cy. 119 Fincastle Tpke. Tazewell, VA 24651. TEL 540-988-4770; FAX 540-963-0123. **Owner(s):** Media General, Inc., 333 E. Grace St., Richmond, VA 23219. TEL 804-649-6000; FAX 804-775-8090; Pub. William H. Hall; adv. contact: Audria Leffel. photos; pub. size: broadsheet; circ. 3,900(paid).

URBANNA

US

SOUTHSIDE SENTINEL. 1896. Thu. $.50 newsstand; $17/yr. in cy.; $23/yr. out of cy. 276 Virginia St., Urbanna, VA 23175. TEL 804-758-2328; FAX 804-758-5896. **Owner(s):** Frederick & Elizabeth Lee Gaskins, P.O. Box 549, Urbanna, VA 23175. TEL 804-758-2328; Ed. John T. Hardin; Pub. Frederick A. Gaskins; adv. contact: Anita Minuth. photos; bk.rev.; pub. size: broadsheet; circ. 5,416(free & paid).
Formerly: Urbanna Southside Sentinel.

VICTORIA

US

KENBRIDGE-VICTORIA DISPATCH. 1970. Thu. $.50 newsstand; $18/yr. in cy.; $20/yr out of cy.; $18/yr. out of state. 1404 Nottoway Blvd., Victoria, VA 23974. TEL 804-696-5550; FAX 804-696-2958. **Owner(s):** Dorothy C. Tucker, P.O. Box 40, Victoria, VA 23974. TEL 804-696-5550; Ed. Dorothy C. Tucker. adv.; pub. size: broadsheet; circ. 3,500(paid).

VINTON

### US									ISSN 8750-7919

VINTON MESSENGER. 1962. Thu. $.50 newsstand; $18/yr. in city; $22/yr. out of city; $26/yr. out of state. 118 Lee Ave., Vinton, VA 24179. TEL 703-343-0720; FAX 703-343-2648. **Owner(s):** Salem Publishing Co., 1533 W. Main St., Salem, VA 24153. TEL 703-339-9355; FAX 703-389-2930; Ed. Anne Paelti; Pub. Ray Robinson; adv.; photos; pub. size: standard; circ. 2,500(paid).

VIRGINIA BEACH

US

VIRGINIA BEACH SUN. 1925. Fri. $.35 newsstand; $14.95/yr. in cy. 209 Rosemont Rd., Virginia Beach, VA 23452. TEL 804-486-3430; FAX 804-548-0390. **Owner(s):** Byerly Publications, Inc., 1000 Armory Dr., Franklin, VA 23851. TEL 804-562-3187; Ed. Victoria Hecht; Pub. Hanes Byerly; adv. contact: Sandra Snelley. photos; pub. size: broadsheet; circ. 7,500(paid).

WAKEFIELD

### US									ISSN 0745-9467

SUSSEX-SURRY DISPATCH. 1888. Wed. $.35 newsstand; $19/yr. in cy.; $34/yr out of cy. 228 Fleetwood St., Wakefield, VA 23888. TEL 804-899-6397; FAX 804-899-7312. **Owner(s):** Chesapeake Publishing Corp., Airport Industrial Park, Easton, MD 21601. TEL 301-822-1500; Ed. Brian Rafferty; adv. contact: Lorrie Smith. photos; pub. size: broadsheet; circ. 3,200(paid).

WARRENTON

US

FAUQUIER TIMES-DEMOCRAT. 1817. Wed. $.50 newsstand; $29.95/yr. local; $39.95/yr. out of state. 39 Culpepper St., Warrenton, VA 22186. TEL 540-347-4222; FAX 540-349-8676. **Owner(s):** Arcom Publications Co., Inc., 1760 Reston Pkwy., Ste. 411, Reston, VA 22091. TEL 703-437-5400; FAX 703-437-6019; Pub. Arthur W. Arundel; adv. contact: John Toler. pub. size: broadsheet; circ. 16,000(paid).

WEST POINT

US

TIDEWATER REVIEW. 1889. Wed. $.35 newsstand; $15/yr. in cy.; $30/yr. out of cy. 702 Main St., West Point, VA 23181. TEL 804-843-2282; FAX 814-843-4404. **Owner(s):** Chesapeake Publishing Corp., Airport Industrial Park, Easton, MD 21601. TEL 301-822-1500; Ed. Roy Spears, III; Pub. William C. O'Donovan; adv. contact: Rosemary Sims. pub. size: broadsheet; circ. 4,950(paid).

WILLIAMSBURG

US   ISSN 0049-6480

VIRGINIA GAZETTE. 1736. s-w.: Wed. & Sat. $.50 newsstand; $27/yr. home deliv.; $41/yr. in state mailed; $50/yr. out of state. 216 Ironbound Rd., Williamsburg, VA 23188. TEL 804-220-1736; FAX 804-220-1665. **Owner(s):** Chesapeake Publishing Corp., Airport Industrial Park, Easton, MD 21601. TEL 410-822-1500; Ed. Susan Bruno; Pub. William C. O'Donovan; adv. contact: Michael Curry. pub. size: broadsheet; circ. 14,500(paid).

WOODSTOCK

US   ISSN 0746-6846

SHENANDOAH VALLEY-HERALD, THE. 1806. Wed. $12/yr. 207 N. Main St., Woodstock, VA 22664. TEL 540-459-4078; FAX 540-459-4077. **Owner(s):** Page-Shenandoah Newspaper Corp., P.O. Box 507, Woodstock, VA 22664. TEL 540-459-4078; FAX 540-459-4077; Ed. C.L. Earehart. adv. contact: Delores Kagey. pub. size: broadsheet; circ. 6,400(paid).

WYTHEVILLE

US

BLAND MESSENGER. 1922. Thu. $.50 newsstand; $19/yr. in cy. 460 W. Main St., Wytheville, VA 24382. TEL 540-688-3338; FAX 540-228-7260. **Owner(s):** Family Community Newspapers, 460 W. Main St., Wytheville, VA 24382. TEL 540-228-6611; FAX 540-228-7260; Ed. Stephanie Porter-Nichols; Pub. D. Gregory Rooker; adv.; photos; pub. size: broadsheet; circ. 2,500(paid).

ENTERPRISE BUYER'S CATALOGUE. 1986. Fri. free. 460 W. Main St., Wytheville, VA 24382. TEL 540-228-6611; FAX 540-228-7260. **Owner(s):** Family Community Newspapers, 460 W. Main St., Wytheville, VA 14382. TEL 540-228-6611; FAX 540-228-7260; Ed. Stephanie Porter-Nichols; Pub. D. Gregory Rooker; adv. contact: Linda Crigger. pub. size: tabloid; circ. 7,350(free). **Formerly:** Penny Saver.

US

NEWS BUYER'S CATALOGUE. Fri. free. 460 W. Main St., Wytheville, VA 24382. TEL 540-228-6611; FAX 540-228-7260. **Owner(s):** Family Community Newspapers, 460 W. Main St., Wytheville, VA 24382. TEL 540-228-6611; FAX 540-228-7260; Pub. D. Gregory Rooker; adv. contact: Debbie Overbay. pub. size: tabloid; circ. 9,800(free).

US

SOUTHWEST VIRGINIA ENTERPRISE. 1870. s-w.: Wed. & Sat. $.50 newsstand; $43.24/yr. in cy.; $51.20/yr. out of cy.; $51.20/yr. out of state. 460 W. Main St., Wytheville, VA 24382. TEL 540-228-6611; FAX 540-228-7260. **Owner(s):** Family Community Newspapers, 460 W. Main St., Wytheville, VA 24382. TEL 540-228-6611; FAX 540-228-7260; Ed. Stephanie Porter-Nichols; Pub. D. Gregory Rooker; adv.; pub. size: broadsheet; circ. 7,900(paid).

YORKTOWN

US

DENBIGH GAZETTE. 1987. Thu. $.35 newsstand; $15/yr. mailed in state; $20/yr. out of state. 4824 George Washington Hwy., Yorktown, VA 23692. TEL 804-898-7225; FAX 804-890-0119. **Owner(s):** Media General, Inc., Richmond, VA. TEL 804-649-6000; Ed. Beth Meisner; Pub. Gaither Perry; adv. contact: Peggy Brown. photos; pub. size: broadsheet; circ. 5,000(controlled & paid).

US

POQUOSON POST. Wed. $.25 newsstand; $40/yr. in state; $16/yr. out of state. 4824 George Washington Hwy., Yorktown, VA 23692. TEL 804-898-9240; FAX 804-890-0119. **Owner(s):** Poquoson Post, P.O. Box 978, Yorktown, VA 23692; Ed. Beth Meisner; Pub. Gaither Perry; adv. contact: Peggy Brown. pub. size: tabloid.

US

YORK TOWN CRIER. 1978. Wed. $.25/newsstand; $10/yr. in state; $16/yr. out of state. 4824 George Washington Hwy., Yorktown, VA 23692. TEL 804-898-7225; FAX 804-890-0119. **Owner(s):** Worrell Enterprises, Inc., 1450 S. Dixie Hwy., Boca Raton, FL 33432. TEL 407-338-3298; FAX 407-338-7732; Ed. Beth Meisner; Pub. D. Gaither Perry; adv. contact: Peggy Brown. photos; bk.rev.; pub. size: broadsheet; circ. 16,300(free & paid).

WASHINGTON

ANACORTES

US

ANACORTES AMERICAN. 1890. Wed. $.50 newsstand; $30/yr. in cy.; $40/yr. out of cy. Sixth & Q Sts., Anacortes, WA 98221. TEL 360-293-3122; FAX 360-293-5000. **Owner(s):** Skagit Valley Publishing Co., P.O. Box 578, Mt. Vernon, WA 92873; Ed. Duncan Frazier; Pub. Duncan Frazier; adv. contact: Ginny Tomasko. pub. size: broadsheet; circ. 4,500(paid).

ARLINGTON

US

NORTH SNOHOMISH WEEKLY. 1981. Thu. $.50 newsstand; $55/yr. 3611 168th St., N.E., Arlington, WA 98223-3187. TEL 360-653-8000; FAX 360-653-9848. **Owner(s):** Skagit Valley Publishing Co., 1000 E. College Way, Mount Vernon, WA 98273. TEL 206-424-3251; FAX 206-424-5300; Ed. Kristin Kinnamon; Pub. Leighton P. Wood; adv. contact: Jerry Starcevic. pub. size: broadsheet; circ. 23,000(controlled & free).

BAINBRIDGE ISLAND

US   ISSN 0745-7391

BAINBRIDGE REVIEW. 1926. s-w.: Wed. & Sat. $32.50/yr. in cy.; $42/yr. out of cy.; $72/yr. out of state. 221 Winslow Way W., Bainbridge Island, WA 98110. TEL 206-842-6613; FAX 206-842-5867. **Owner(s):** Sound Publishing, Inc., 7689 N.E. Day Rd., Bainbridge Island, WA 98110; Ed. Becky Fox-Marshall; Pub. Christiana C. Allen; adv.; pub. size: tabloid; circ. 6,100(paid).

BATTLE GROUND

US

REFLECTOR, THE. 1909. Wed. $.35 newsstand; $20/yr. in cy. mailed. 21914 N.E. 112th Ave., Battle Ground, WA 98604-2020. TEL 360-687-5151; FAX 360-687-5162. **Owner(s):** Case Publishing Co., Inc., 21914 N.E. 12th Ave., Battle Ground, WA 98604. TEL 206-687-5151; Pub. Marvin F. Case; adv. contact: Darlene Carr. photos; pub. size: broadsheet; circ. 29,000(free & paid).

BOTHELL

US   ISSN 0739-9286

NORTHSHORE CITIZEN. 1903. Wed. $.50 newsstand; $24/yr. in area. 18120 Bothell Way, N.E., Bothell, WA 98011. TEL 206-486-1231; FAX 206-483-3286. **Owner(s):** Horvitz Newspapers, Inc., P.O. Box 90130, Bellevue, WA 98009-0130. TEL 206-624-2233; Ed. John Merrill; Pub. Howard Mullenary; adv. contact: Melina Wozniak. photos; pub. size: broadsheet; circ. 5,000(paid).

BURIEN

US

HIGHLINE NEWS. 1946. s-w.: Wed. & Sat. $.50 newsstand; $36/yr. home deliv. 207 S.W. 150th St., Burien, WA 98166. TEL 206-242-0100; FAX 206-241-2788. **Owner(s):** Seattle Times Co., P.O. Box 70, Seattle, WA 98111; Ed. Rob Smith; Pub. Craig Dennis; adv. contact: Craig McMurray. photos; pub. size: broadsheet; circ. 26,000(paid). **Formerly:** Highline Times.

CAMAS

US

CAMAS/WASHOUGAL POST RECORD. 1905. Tue. $.50 newsstand; $18/yr. in cy.; $30/yr. out of cy. 425 N.E. Fourth Ave., Camas, WA 98607. TEL 206-834-2141; FAX 206-834-3423. **Owner(s):** Eagle Newspapers, Inc., P.O. Box 12008, Salem, OR 97309; Ed. Craig Clohessy; Pub. Michael Gallagher; adv. contact: Don Dire. pub. size: broadsheet; circ. 8,200(paid).

CASHMERE

US

CASHMERE VALLEY RECORD. Wed. $.50 newsstand; $19/yr. in cy. mailed. P.O. Box N, Cashmere, WA 98815. TEL 509-782-3781; FAX 509-548-4789. **Owner(s):** Prairie Media, Inc., 215 14th St., Leavenworth, WA 98826. TEL 509-548-5286; Ed. Vern Ahrendes. adv. contact: Lisa Staudinger. pub. size: broadsheet; circ. 1,800(paid).

CATHLAMET

US

WAHKIAKUM COUNTY EAGLE, THE. 1891. Thu. $.50 newsstand. 77 Main St., Cathlamet, WA 98612-0368. TEL 360-795-3391; FAX 360-795-3983. **Owner(s):** Eric R. Nelson, 77 Main St., Cathlamet, WA 98612. TEL 360-795-3391; FAX 360-795-3983; Ed. Eric R. Nelson. adv. contact: Eric R. Nelson. bk.rev.; pub. size: broadsheet; circ. 1,510(paid).

CHENEY

US

CHENEY FREE PRESS. 1896. Thu. $.50 newsstand; $20/yr. in cy. 1616 W. First St., Cheney, WA 99004. TEL 509-235-6184; FAX 509-235-2887. **Owner(s):** Journal News Publishing Co., 1855 First St., Cheney, WA 99004. TEL 509-747-7395; Ed. Kevin Hanson; Pub. William Ifft; adv. contact: Mary Mossman. pub. size: broadsheet; circ. 2,500(paid).

COLFAX

US

WHITMAN COUNTY GAZETTE. 1877. Thu. $.50 newsstand; $21/yr. in cy.; $30/yr. out of cy. 211 N. Main St., Colfax, WA 99111. TEL 509-397-4333; FAX 509-397-4527. **Owner(s):** Tribune Publishing Co., P.O. Box 957, Lewiston, ID 83501. TEL 208-743-9411; Ed. Jerry Jones; Pub. Gordon Forgey; adv. contact: Dick Bruce. pub. size: broadsheet; circ. 4,450(paid).

   Formerly: Colfax Gazette.

COLVILLE

US

STATESMAN-EXAMINER. 1948. Wed. $.60 newsstand; $23/yr. in cy.; $30/yr. out of cy. 220 S. Main St., Colville, WA 99114. TEL 509-684-4567; FAX 509-684-3849. **Owner(s):** American Publishing Co., 606 N. Van Buren, P.O. Box 520, Marion, IL 62959. TEL 618-993-1711; Ed. Chris Cowbrough; Pub. Don Birch; adv. contact: Marty Deubel. pub. size: broadsheet; circ. 6,535(free & paid).

   Formerly: Colville Statesman-Examiner.

CONNELL

US

FRANKLIN COUNTY GRAPHIC. Thu. $.40 newsstand; $20/yr. in cy.; $25/yr. out of cy. 346 S. Columbia, Connell, WA 99326-0160. TEL 509-234-3181; FAX 509-234-3182. **Owner(s):** Duane & Dee Russer, 346 S. Columbia, Connell, WA 99326. TEL 509-234-3181; FAX 509-234-3182; Ed. Kathy Valdez; Pub. Duane Russer; pub. size: broadsheet; circ. 2,676(free & paid).

DAYTON

US

DAYTON CHRONICLE. 1877. w. $.50 newsstand; $20/yr. local; $25/yr. OR, WA, ID; $29/yr. elsewhere. 358 E. Main St., Dayton, WA 99328. TEL 509-382-2221. **Owner(s):** Jack Williams, 358 E. Main St., Dayton, WA 99328. TEL 509-382-2221; Pub. Jackie Williams; adv.; bk.rev.; pub. size: standard; circ. 1,500(controlled & paid).

DEER PARK

US

TRIBUNE. 1906. Wed. $.50 newsstand; $20/yr. local; $28/yr. out of state. 104 N. Main St., Deer Park, WA 99006. TEL 509-276-5043; FAX 509-276-2041. **Owner(s):** American Publishing Co., 606 N. Van Buren, P.O. Box 520, Marion, IL 62959. TEL 618-993-1711; Ed. Tom Costigan Pub. Barbara Hanna; adv.: $6.45/SAU. pub. size: broadsheet; circ. 8,728(paid).

ENUMCLAW

US

ENUMCLAW COURIER-HERALD. 1901. Wed. $.50 newsstand; $21/yr. in King & Pierce cys.; $25/yr. in state; $28/yr. out of state. 1627 Cole St., Enumclaw, WA 98022. TEL 360-825-2555; FAX 360-825-1092. **Owner(s):** Ted Natt, P.O. Box 157, Enumclaw, WA 98022. TEL 360-825-2555; Pub. Jack Darnton; adv. contact: Bill Hinrichsen. pub. size: broadsheet; circ. 6,500(paid).

EPHRATA

US

GRANT COUNTY JOURNAL. 1907. s-w.: Mon. & Thu. $.50 newsstand; $28/yr. in cy. carrier or mailed; $38/yr. out of cy. mailed. 29 Alder, S.W., Ephrata, WA 98823. TEL 509-754-4636; FAX 509-754-5112. **Owner(s):** Jeffrey G. Fletcher, P.O. Box 993, Ephrata, WA 98823. TEL 509-754-4636; Ed. Randy Bracht; Pub. Jeffrey G. Fletcher; adv. contact: Steve Wallace. photos; pub. size: broadsheet; circ. 3,500(controlled & paid).

   Formerly: Ephrata Grant County Journal.

FEDERAL WAY

US

FEDERAL WAY NEWS. 1954. s-w.: Sat. & Wed. $.50 newsstand; $36/yr. 1634 S. 312th St., Federal Way, WA 98003. TEL 206-529-2300; FAX 206-529-2324. **Owner(s):** Times Community News, 207 S.W. 150th, Seattle, WA 98166. TEL 206-241-2700; Ed. Rob Smith; Pub. Craig Dennis; adv. contact: Carla Royter. pub. size: broadsheet; circ 45,962(free & paid).

FERNDALE

US

WESTSIDE RECORD-JOURNAL. 1885. Wed. $.50 newsstand; $20/yr. 2008 Main St., Ferndale, WA 98248-0038. TEL 360-384-1411; FAX 360-384-1417. **Owner(s):** Ferndale Record, Inc., P.O. Box 38, Ferndale, WA 98248. TEL 360-384-1411; Pub. Michael D. Lewis; adv. contact: Kim Winjum. photos; pub. size: broadsheet; circ. 8,350(free & paid).

FRIDAY HARBOR

US   ISSN 0734-3809

JOURNAL OF THE SAN JUAN ISLANDS. 1906. Wed. $.75 newsstand; $29/yr. in cy.; $43/yr. out of cy. 580 Guard St., Friday Harbor, WA 98250-0519. TEL 206-378-4191; FAX 206-378-4103; E-mail: journal@pacificrim.net; URL: http://www.pacificrim.net/~journal. **Owner(s):** John McKenna, P.O. Box 519, Friday Harbor, WA 98250. TEL 206-378-4191 FAX 206-378-4103; Lower Main and Publishing Ltd., 1970 Alberta St., Vancouver BC, Canada. TEL 604-872-8155; FAX 604-879-1483; Ed. Mike Hagan. adv. contact: Julie Greene. photos; pub. size: tabloid; circ. 6,000(free & paid).

GIG HARBOR

US

BUSINESS EXAMINER. 1985. bi-w. $20/yr. 3123 56th St., N.W., Ste. 6, Gig Harbor, WA 98335-1311. TEL 206-851-3705. **Owner(s):** Pierce County Business Examiner, 3123 56th St., N.W., Ste. 6, Gig Harbor, WA 98335-1311. TEL 206-851-3705; Pub. Jeff Rounce; pub. size: tabloid; circ. 16,500(controlled & paid). **Wire Service(s):** AP.

US

PENINSULA GATEWAY. 1917. Wed. $.50 newsstand; $20/yr. in cy. mailed; $40/yr. in state mailed; $50/yr. out of state mailed. 7521 Pioneer Way, Gig Harbor, WA 98335. TEL 206-851-9921; FAX 206-851-3939. **Owner(s):** McClately Newspapers, Inc., P.O. Box 407, Gig Harbor, WA 98335. TEL 206-851-9921; Ed. Tony Hazarian; Pub. Tom Taylor; adv. contact: Teri Kester. adv.: $17.00/SAU. photos; pub. size: broadsheet; circ. 24,000(free & paid).

GOLDENDALE

US

GOLDENDALE SENTINEL. Thu. $25/yr. in cy.; $34/yr. out of cy. 117 W. Main, Goldendale, WA 98620. TEL 509-773-3777; FAX 509-773-4737. **Owner(s):** Andrew J. McNab. 117 W. Main St., Goldendale, WA 98620. TEL 509-773-3777; Ed. Kevin McCallum; Pub. Andrew J. McNab; pub. size: standard; circ. 3,500(paid).

GRANDVIEW

US

GRANDVIEW HERALD. 1922. Wed. $.50 newsstand; $24/yr. local. 107 Division, Grandview, WA 98930. TEL 509-882-3712; FAX 509-786-1779. **Owner(s):** Fournier Media Services, P.O. Box 750, Prosser, WA 99350. TEL 509-832-3712; Ed. Scott Blanchard; Pub. John Fournier Jr.; adv. contact: Diane Buxton. pub. size: standard; circ. 2,750(paid).

ISSAQUAH

US

ISSAQUAH PRESS. 1900. Wed. $.50 newsstand; $20/yr. mailed in cy.; $35/yr. out of cy. 45 Front St., S., Issaquah, WA 98027-1328. TEL 206-392-6434; FAX 206-391-1541; E-mail: ispress@accessone.com; URL: http://www.blueworld.com/bl/isspress. **Owner(s):** Seattle Times Co., P.O. Box 70, Seattle, WA 98111. TEL 206-464-2111; Ed. Karl Kunkel; Pub. Deborah L. Berto; adv. contact: Brian Bretland. pub. size: broadsheet; circ. 8,600(paid).

LEAVENWORTH

US

LEAVENWORTH ECHO. 1906. Wed. $.50 newsstand; $19/yr. in cy. mailed. 215 14th St., Leavenworth, WA 98826. TEL 509-548-5286; FAX 509-548-4789. **Owner(s):** Prairie Media, Inc., 215 14th St., Leavenworth, WA 98826; Ed. Vern Ahrendes. adv. contact: Lisa Staudinger. pub. size: broadsheet; circ. 2,400.

LONG BEACH

US ISSN 0739-9200

LONG BEACH CHINOOK OBSERVER. 1900. Tue. $.50 newsstand; $20/yr. in cy.; $30/yr. out of cy. 212 S. Oregon St., Long Beach, WA 98631. TEL 360-642-8181; FAX 360-642-8105. **Owner(s):** East Oregonian Publishing Co., 211 S.E. Byers Ave., P.O. Box 1089, Pendleton, OR 97801. TEL 503-276-2211; Ed. Matt Winters. pub. size: broadsheet; circ. 7,200(paid). **Wire Service(s):** AP.

LYNDEN

US

LYNDEN TRIBUNE. 1888. Wed. $.75 newsstand; $23/yr. in cy.; $32/yr. out of cy.; $35/yr. out of state. 113 N. Sixth St., Lynden, WA 98264. TEL 360-354-4444; FAX 360-734-0575; E-mail: lyndentrib@nas.com; URL: http://lyndentrib.com. **Owner(s):** Lewis Publishing Co., Inc., P.O. Box 153, Lynden, WA 98264. TEL 360-354-4444; FAX 360-734-0575; Ed. Dave Brumbaugh; Pub. Michael D. Lewis; adv. contact: Pam Richardson. bk.rev.; pub. size: broadsheet; circ. 14,265(free & paid).

LYNNWOOD

US

ENTERPRISE, THE. 1958. Wed. free; $20/yr. mailed. 7300E 196th St., S.W., Lynnwood, WA 98036. TEL 206-775-7521; FAX 206-774-8622. **Owner(s):** Lafromboise Newspapers, Inc., Pearl & Maple, Centralia, WA 98531. TEL 206-622-3847; Ed. Tom Pearce; Pub. Dennis Waller; adv.; photos; pub. size: broadsheet; circ. 57,000(paid).

MAPLE VALLEY

US

VOICE OF THE VALLEY. 1968. Wed. free; $20/yr. P.O. Box 307, Maple Valley, WA 98038. TEL 206-432-9696; FAX 206-432-0701. **Owner(s):** S. Hipple, P.O. Box 307, Maple Valley, WA 98038. TEL 206-432-9696; FAX 206-432-0701; Pub. S. Hipple; adv. contact: R.B. Hipple. photos; pub. size: tabloid; circ. 17,000(free & paid).

MERCER ISLAND

US

MERCER ISLAND REPORTER. 1954. Wed. $.75 newsstand; $36/yr. 7845 S.E. 30th St., Mercer Island, WA 98040. TEL 206-232-1215; FAX 206-232-1284. **Owner(s):** Horvitz Newspapers, Inc., P.O. Box 3110, Bellevue, WA 98004. TEL 206-455-2222; Ed. Jane Meyer; Pub. Peter A. Horvitz; adv. contact: Diana Reul. pub. size: standard; circ. 5,000(paid).

NEWPORT

US

GEM STATE MINER. 1901. Wed. $.50 newsstand; $17/yr. in cy.; $26/yr. out of cy. 317 S. Union St., Newport, WA 99156. TEL 509-447-2433; FAX 509-447-9222. **Owner(s):** Northeast Washington Associates, P.O. Box 349, Newport, WV 99156. TEL 509-447-2433; Pub. Fred J. Willenbrock, II; pub. size: broadsheet; circ. 6,000(paid).

US

NEWPORT MINER. 1901. Wed. $.50 newsstand; $17.50/yr. mailed in cy.; $26.50/yr. out of cy. 317 S. Union St., Newport, WA 99156. TEL 509-447-2433; FAX 509-447-9222. **Owner(s):** Northeast Washington Associates, P.O. Box 349, Newport, WA 99156. TEL 509-447-2433; Ed. Mike Denuty; Pub. Fred J. Willenbrock, II; pub. size: broadsheet; circ. 6,500(paid).

OAK HARBOR

US

WHIDBEY NEWS-TIMES. 1891. s-w.: Wed. & Sat. $.50 newsstand; $36/yr. carrier; $46/yr. mailed in cy.; $64/yr. mailed out of cy. 3098 300th Ave., W., Oak Harbor, WA 98277. TEL 360-675-6611; FAX 360-679-2695. **Owner(s):** Sound Publishing, Inc., Bainbridge Island, WA 98110; Ed. Dave Fisher; Pub. Gregg McConnell; adv. contact: Malissa Saylors. pub. size: broadsheet; circ. 9,400(paid).

OMAK

US

OMAK-OKANOGAN COUNTY CHRONICLE. 1910. Wed. $.50 newsstand; $19/yr. home deliv.; $35/yr. mailed out of state. 618 Okoma Dr., Omak, WA 98841. TEL 509-826-1110; FAX 509-826-5819. **Owner(s):** Omak Chronicle, Inc., P.O. Box 553, Omak, WA 98841. TEL 509-826-1110; Pub. John E. Andrist; pub. size: broadsheet; circ. 16,000(paid).

OTHELLO

US ISSN 1056-8328

OTHELLO OUTLOOK, THE. 1951. Wed. $.75 newsstand; $25/yr. 180 E. Main St., Othello, WA 99344. TEL 509-488-3342; FAX 509-488-3345. **Owner(s):** Zaser-Longston, 1802-136th Pl. N.E., Seattle, WA 98005. TEL 206-562-7997; FAX 206-562-4785; Ed. Mark Grim; Pub. Bill Edlin; adv. contact: Richard Rex. pub. size: standard; circ. 2,700(paid).

PORT ORCHARD

US

PORT ORCHARD INDEPENDENT. 1886. s-w.: Wed. & Sat. $.50 newsstand; $26/yr. carrier. 1035 Bethel Ave., Port Orchard, WA 98366. TEL 360-876-4414; FAX 360-292-9521. **Owner(s):** Whidbey Press, Inc., P.O. Box 27, Port Orchard, WA 98366. TEL 360-876-4414; FAX 360-876-4458; Ed. Pat Jenkins; Pub. Mike Shepard; adv.; pub. size: tabloid; circ. 18,150(free & paid).

PORT TOWNSEND

US ISSN 1050-1460

PORT TOWNSEND/JEFFERSON COUNTY LEADER. 1889. Wed. $.75 newsstand; $19/yr. in cy.; $30/yr. out of cy. 226 Adams St., Port Townsend, WA 98368. TEL 360-385-2900. E-mail: leader@olympus.net; URL: http://www.olympus.net/biz/leader. **Owner(s):** Port Townsend Publishing Co., Inc., 226 Adams St., Port Townsend, WA 98368. TEL 360-385-2900; Ed. Frank W. Garred. adv. contact: Kathy Busic-Potocki. pub. size: broadsheet; circ. 9,247(paid).

POULSBO

US

NORTH KITSAP HERALD. 1901. b-w. $.50 newsstand; $26/yr. 19062 Hwy. 305, Ste. 203, Poulsbo, WA 98370. TEL 360-779-4464; FAX 360-682-1107. **Owner(s):** David Black, Kitsap Newspaper Group, 7689 NE. Day Rd., Bainbridge Island, WA 98110. TEL 360-842-8305; FAX 360-682-1107; Ed. Ray Miller; Pub. Doug Weese; photos; pub. size: tabloid; circ. 10,500(free & paid).

RAYMOND

US ISSN 1065-3805

WILLAPA HARBOR HERALD. 1906. Wed. $17/yr. in cy.; $22/yr. out of cy. 335 Third St., Raymond, WA 98577. TEL 206-942-3466; FAX 206-942-3487. **Owner(s):** Flannery Publications; Ed. Meredith Nicholson. adv. contact: Lora Nicholson. pub. size: broadsheet; circ. 4,302(free & paid).

REDMOND

US

REDMOND SAMMAMISH VALLEY NEWS. 1946. Wed. free; $25/yr. in cy.; $35/yr. out of cy.; $35/yr. out of cy.; $20/yr. senior citizen. 14796 N.E. 95th St., Redmond, WA 98052. TEL 206-883-7187; FAX 206-881-9567. **Owner(s):** Pacific Publishing Co., 2314 Third Ave., Seattle, WA. TEL 206-461-1300; FAX 206-461-1347; Ed. Daven Rosener; Pub. Kim Nolan; adv. contact: Laurie Dugan. photos; bk.rev.; pub. size: tabloid; circ. 11,700(free & paid).

ROYAL CITY

US

ROYAL REVIEW. 1985. Wed. $.50 newsstand; $14.50/yr. 321 Camelia St., Royal City, WA 99357-0219. TEL 509-346-9723; FAX 509-346-9453. **Owner(s):** Andrew & Rachel Perkins, 321 Camilia St., Royal City, WA 99357. TEL 509-346-9723; FAX 509-346-9453; Ed. Rachel Perkins; Pub. Rachel Perkins; adv.; photos.

SEATTLE

US

BEACON HILL NEWS, THE/SOUTH DISTRICT JOURNAL. 1924. Wed. $.35 newsstand; $24/yr. 2314 Third Ave., Seattle, WA 98121. TEL 206-461-1300; FAX 206-461-1340. **Owner(s):** Pacific Publishing Co., 2314 Third Ave., Seattle, WA 98121. TEL 206-461-1300; Ed. Jenny Yim; Pub. Brenda French; adv.; photos; pub. size: tabloid; circ. 20,000(paid).

US

CAPITOL HILL TIMES. 1926. Wed. $.35 newsstand; $15/yr. home deliv.; $24/yr. mailed. 2314 Third Ave., Seattle, WA 98121. TEL 206-461-1300; FAX 206-461-1340. **Owner(s):** Pacific Publishing Co., 2314 Third Ave., Seattle, WA 98121. TEL 206-461-1300; Ed. Dennis Fitzgerald; Pub. Brenda French; adv.; photos; pub. size: tabloid; circ. 17,000(controlled & paid).

US

DES MOINES NEWS. 1959. s-w.: Wed. & Sat. $.50 newsstand; $36/yr. home deliv. 207 S.W. 150th St., Seattle, WA 98166. TEL 206-242-0100; FAX 206-241-2788. **Owner(s):** Seattle Times Co., P.O. Box 70, Seattle, WA 98166; Ed. Rob Smith; Pub. Craig Dennis; adv. contact: Craig McMurray. pub. size: broadsheet; circ. 11,883(paid).

US

MADISON PARK TIMES. 1925. m. $.35 newsstand. 2314 Third Ave., Seattle, WA 98121. TEL 206-461-1300. **Owner(s):** Pacific Media Group, 2314 Third Ave., Seattle, WA 98121; Ed. Linnea Lundgren; Pub. Brenda L. French; circ. 6,000(paid).

US

NORTH CENTRAL OUTLOOK. 1917. Wed. $.35 newsstand; $24/yr. 2314 Third Ave., Seattle, WA 98121. TEL 206-461-1300. **Owner(s):** Pacific Publishing Co., 2314 Third Ave., Seattle, WA 98121. TEL 206-461-1300; Ed. Linnea Lundgren; Pub. Brenda L. French; adv.; photos; bk.rev.; pub. size: tabloid; circ. 9,500(controlled & paid).

US

QUEEN ANNE-MAGNOLIA NEWS. 1919. Wed. $.50 newsstand; $12/yr. 529 Warren Ave., N., Seattle, WA 98109-4527. TEL 206-282-0900; FAX 206-285-1085. **Owner(s):** Pacific Publishing Co., 2314 Third Ave., Seattle, WA 98121. TEL 206-461-1300; Ed. Jack Arends; Pub. Mike Dillon; adv.; photos; pub. size: tabloid; circ. 21,800(controlled & paid).

US

SEATTLE FACTS. 1961. Wed. $60/yr. mailed. 2765 E. Cherry, Seattle, WA 98122. TEL 206-324-0552; FAX 206-324-1007. **Owner(s):** Elizabeth Beaver Fitzgerald, P.O. Box 22015, Seattle, WA 98122. TEL 206-324-0552; Ed. Elizabeth Beaver; Pub. Elizabeth Beaver; pub. size: oversize; circ. 50,000(paid).

US

SEATTLE SKANNER, THE. 1990. Wed. $35/yr. 1326 5th Ave Ste. 825, Seattle, WA 98101. TEL 206-233-9888; FAX 206-233-9795. **Owner(s):** Bernard V. Foster, 2337 N. Williams, Portland, OR 97227-1989. TEL 503-287-3562; FAX 503-284-8200; Bobbie Dore Foster, 2337 N. Williams, Portland, OR 97227-1989. TEL 503-287-3562; FAX 503-284-8200; Ed. Bobbie Dore Foster; Pub. Bernard V. Foster; adv. contact: Ted Banks. photos; bk.rev.; pub. size: tabloid; circ. 25,000(free & paid).

US

SEATTLE WEEKLY. 1976. Wed. free. 1008 Western Ave., Ste. 300, Seattle, WA 98104. TEL 206-623-0500; FAX 206-467-4377. **Owner(s):** Quickfish Media, Inc., 1008 Western Ave., Ste. 300, Seattle, WA 98104; Ed. David Brewster; Pub. David Brewster; adv. contact: Ellen Cole. photos; bk.rev.; pub. size: tabloid; circ. 62,000(free & paid).

US

SOUTH DISTRICT JOURNAL. 1924. Wed. $.35 newsstand; $24/yr. 2314 Third Ave., Seattle, WA 98121. TEL 206-461-1300; FAX 206-461-1340. **Owner(s):** Pacific Publishing Co., 2314 Third Ave., Seattle, WA 98121. TEL 206-461-1311; Ed. Jenny Yim; Pub. Brenda French; adv.; photos; pub. size: tabloid; circ. 20,000(controlled & paid).

US

UNIVERSITY HERALD. 1925. Wed. $.35 newsstand; $24/yr. 2314 Third Ave., Seattle, WA 98121. TEL 206-461-1346. **Owner(s):** Pacific Publishing Co., 2314 Third Ave., Seattle, WA 98121. TEL 206-461-1346; Ed. Linnea Lundgren; Pub. Brenda L. French; adv.; photos; pub. size: tabloid; circ. 11,500(controlled & paid).

US

WEST SEATTLE HERALD. 1923. Wed. $.50 newsstand; $24/yr. home deliv.; $40/yr. mailed. 3500 S.W. Alaska St., Seattle, WA 98126. TEL 206-932-0300; FAX 206-937-1223. **Owner(s):** West Seattle Herald, Inc., 3500 SW Alaska St., Seattle, WA 98126. TEL 206-932-0300; Ed. Adam Worcester; Pub. Jerry Robinson; pub. size: standard; circ. 16,000(paid).
  Formerly: West Seattle Herald/White Center News.

SEQUIM

US

SEQUIM GAZETTE. 1974. Wed. $.50 newsstand; $18/yr. local; $25/yr. elsewhere. 147 W. Washington, Sequim, WA 98382. TEL 360-683-3311; FAX 360-683-6670. **Owner(s):** Olympic View Publishing Co., P.O. Box 1750, Sequim, WA 98382. TEL 206-683-3311; Ed. James Manders; Pub. Brown M. Maloney; pub. size: tabloid; circ. 11,000(paid).

SHELTON

US

SHELTON-MASON COUNTY JOURNAL. 1886. Thu. $.50 newsstand; $22/yr. in cy.; $30/yr. out of cy.; $38/yr. out of state. Third & Cota, Shelton, WA 98584. TEL 206-426-4412. **Owner(s):** Henry G. Gay, P.O. Box 430, Shelton, WA 98584. TEL 206-426-4412; Ed. Charles Gay; Pub. Henry G. Gay; pub. size: broadsheet; circ. 9,977(paid).

SNOHOMISH

US

SNOHOMISH COUNTY TRIBUNE. 1891. Wed. $.50 newsstand; $20/yr. mailed in cy.; $28/yr. out of cy. 127 Ave. C, Snohomish, WA 98290. TEL 206-568-4121; FAX 206-568-1484. **Owner(s):** Mach Publishing, P.O. Box 499, Snohomish, WA 98291. TEL 206-568-4121; Ed. Leslie Hynes; Pub. Dave Mach; adv. contact: Becky Reed. pub. size: tabloid; circ. 30,000(paid).

SPOKANE

US

SENIOR TIMES. 1976. m. $18/yr. 7802 E. Mission, Spokane, WA 99212-2598. TEL 509-928-1677; FAX 509-924-3720. **Owner(s):** Senior Times, Inc., 7802 E. Mission, Spokane, WA 99212. TEL 509-928-1677; FAX 509-924-3720; Pub. James C. Osman; adv. contact: Cathy Weyand. photos; bk.rev.; pub. size: tabloid; circ. 2,500(controlled & paid).

US

VALLEY HERALD, THE. 1920. Thu. $26/yr. in cy.; $30/yr. out of cy. 8940 E. Sprague Ave., Spokane, WA 99212. TEL 509-924-2440; FAX 509-928-3168. **Owner(s):** Clark E. Hager, Sr., 8940 E. Sprague Ave., Spokane, WA 99212. TEL 509-924-2440; Ed. Charlie Plumb; Pub. Clark E. Hager; pub. size: broadsheet; circ. 5,000(paid).
  Formerly: Spokane Valley Herald.

SPRAGUE

US

SPRAGUE ADVOCATE, THE. 1883. Thu. $.50 newsstand; $26/yr. in state; $25/yr. senior citizens; $29/yr. out of state. 113 N. C St., Sprague, WA 99032-0327. TEL 509-257-2928. **Owner(s):** Tess Canaday, Box 68, Sprague, WA 99032. TEL 509-257-2928. Pub. Tess Canaday; adv.; photos; pub. size: broadsheet; circ. 232,906(paid).

TENINO

US

ROCHESTER SUN NEWS, THE. 1922. Wed. free. P.O. Box 4004, Tenino, WA 98589-4004. TEL 360-264-2500; FAX 360-264-2955. **Owner(s):** DeVaul Publishing, Inc., 107 N. Tower, Ste. 5, Tenino, WA 98531. TEL 360-736-3580; FAX 360-736-3581; Ed. Glen Dickason; Pub. Frank DeVaul; adv.; pub. size: tabloid; circ. 1,800(free).
  Formerly: Sun, The.

US

TENINO INDEPENDENT. 1922. Fri. $.50 newsstand; $18/yr. in cy.; $21/yr. in state; $26/yr. out of state. P.O. Box 4004, Tenino, WA 98589-4004. TEL 360-264-2500; FAX 360-264-2955. **Owner(s):** DeVaul Publishing, Inc., 107 N. Tower, Ste. 5, Centralia, WA 98531. TEL 360-736-3580; FAX 360-736-3581; Ed. Glen E. Dickason; Pub. Frank DeVaul; adv. photos; pub. size: tabloid; circ. 3,000(paid).

TOPPENISH

US

TOPPENISH REVIEW. 1905. Wed. $20/yr. in cy.; $25/yr. out of cy. 11 E. Toppenish Ave., Toppenish, WA 98948. TEL 509-365-4055; FAX 509-865-2655. **Owner(s):** James A. Flint, 11 E. Toppenish Ave., Toppenish, WA 98948; Ed. Pat Jones; Pub. James Flint; pub. size: broadsheet; circ. 6,000(paid).

VASHON

US

VASHON-MAURY ISLAND BEACHCOMBER. 1957. Wed. $.50 newsstand; $20/yr. on island; $34/yr. off island; $18/yr. senior citizens. 17502 Vashon Hwy., S.W., Vashon, WA 98070. TEL 206-463-9195; FAX 206-463-6122. **Owner(s):** Sound Publishing, Inc., 7689 N.E. Day Rd., Bainbridge Island, WA 98110; Ed. Allison Arthur; Pub. Jim Long; adv. contact: Todd Brown. photos; pub. size: tabloid; circ. 4,500(paid).

WAITSBURG

US
TIMES, THE. 1878. Thu. $.50 newsstand; $20/yr. in Walla Walla & Columbia cys.; $22/yr. in state; $25/yr. out of state. 139 Main St., Waitsburg, WA 99361-0097. TEL 509-337-6631; FAX 509-337-6045. **Owner(s):** Jane A. & Ron Smith, 139 Main St., Waitsburg, WA 99361-0097. TEL 509-337-6631; FAX 509-337-6045; Ed. Ron Smith; Pub. Ron Smith; adv. contact: Jane A. Smith. pub. size: standard; circ. 1,850(paid).

WAPATO

US
WAPATO INDEPENDENT. 1906. Wed. $.50 newsstand; $20/yr. in cy.; $25/yr. out of cy.; $18/yr. senior citizens. 113 S. Wapato Ave., Wapato, WA 98951-0067. TEL 509-877-3322; FAX 509-877-2577. **Owner(s):** James A. Flint, P.O. Box 511, Toppenish, WA 98948. TEL 509-865-4055; FAX 509-862-2655; Ed. Stephen McFadden; Pub. James A. Flint; adv. contact: Larry Watkins. pub. size: broadsheet; circ. 2,100(paid).

WOODLAND

US
WOODLAND LEWIS RIVER NEWS. 1919. Wed. $35/yr. 435 Davidson St., Woodland, WA 98674. TEL 360-225-8287; FAX 360-225-8289. **Owner(s):** Stern Wheeler Publishing Co., P. O. Box 368, Castle Rock, WA 98611. TEL 360-225-8287; FAX 360-225-8289; Pub. John Hayden; pub. size: broadsheet; circ. 7,371(paid).

YELM

US
NISQUALLY VALLEY NEWS. 1921. Thu. $.50 newsstand; $23/yr. in state; $30/yr. out of state. 207 Yelm Ave., W., Yelm, WA 98597. TEL 360-458-2681; FAX 360-458-5741. **Owner(s):** Lafromboise Newspapers, Inc., 321 N. Pearl St., Centralia, WA 98531. TEL 360-736-3311; Ed. Lorraine Stensager; Pub. Dennis R. Waller; adv.; photos; bk.rev.; pub. size: standard; circ. 3,600(paid).

WEST VIRGINIA

BERKELEY SPRINGS

US   ISSN 0895-1594
MORGAN MESSENGER, THE. 1893. Wed. $.50 newsstand; $18.02/yr. in town. P.O. Box 567, Berkeley Springs, WV 25411. TEL 304-258-1800; FAX 304-258-8441. **Owner(s):** Morgan Messenger, Inc., P.O. Box 567, Berkeley Springs, WV 25411. TEL 304-258-1800; FAX 304-258-8441; Ed. J. Warren Buzzerd; Pub. J. Warren Buzzerd; adv. contact: Sandy Buzzerd. photos; pub. size: standard; circ. 5,450(paid).

BUCKHANNON

US
RECORD-DELTA, THE. 1976. 3/wk.: Mon., Wed., Fri. $59/yr. in state; $65/yr. out of state. 2-B Clarksburg Rd., Buckhannon, WV 26201. TEL 304-472-2800; FAX 304-472-0537. **Owner(s):** Mountaineer Newspapers, 2-B Clarksburg Rd., Buckhannon, WV 26201. TEL 304-472-2800; Pub. Doug Leifheit; adv. contact: Mark Davis. pub. size: broadsheet; circ. 5,000(paid).
Formerly: Buckhannon Record-Delta.

CHARLES TOWN

US
SPIRIT OF JEFFERSON-ADVOCATE. 1844. Thu. $.45 newsstand; $22/yr. in state; $23/yr. out of state. 210 N. George St., Charles Town, WV 25414-0966. TEL 304-725-2046. **Owner(s):** Jefferson Publishing Co., Inc., P.O. Box 966, Charles Town, WV 25414-0966. TEL 304-725-2046; Ed. Edward W. Dockeney, Jr. adv. contact: R. Meade Dorsey. adv.: $6.60/SAU. photos; pub. size: broadsheet; circ. 4,893(free & paid).

CLAY

US
CLAY COUNTY FREE PRESS. 1888. Wed. $.50 newsstand; $12/yr. in cy.; $15/yr. out of cy.; $18/yr. out of state. P.O. Box 180, Clay, WV 25043-0180. TEL 304-587-4250; FAX 304-587-7329. **Owner(s):** Clinton Nichols, P.O. Box 180, Clay, WV 02503-0180. TEL 304-587-4250; FAX 304-587-7329; Ed. Aaron Nichols; Pub. Clinton Nichols; pub. size: tabloid; circ. 4,000(paid).

CULLODEN

US
CABELL RECORD. 1898. Thu. $12/yr. in state; $20/yr. out of state. 2085 Rte. 60, Culloden, WV 25510. TEL 304-743-1222; FAX 304-267-1556. **Owner(s):** Cabell Record Publishing Co., Inc., 2406 Locust Lane-Millpoint, Martinsburg, WV 25401. TEL 304-267-1556; Ed. W.O. Robinson. adv. contact: Jim Drown. pub. size: broadsheet; circ. 2,525(paid).

US
PUTNAM POST-CABELL BULLETIN. 1955. Sun. free in area; $20/yr. out of area. 2085 Rte. 60, Culloden, WV 25510. TEL 304-562-6214; FAX 304-562-6214. **Owner(s):** W.O. Robinson, P.C. Publishing Company, P.O. Box 186, Culloden, WV 25510. TEL 304-562-6214; Phyllis C. Robinson, P.C. Publishing Company, P.O. Box 186, Culloden, WV 25510. TEL 304-562-6214; Ed. W.O. Robinson. adv. contact: Jim Drown. pub. size: tabloid; circ. 27,022(controlled & paid).

DANVILLE

US
COAL VALLEY NEWS. 1925. Wed. $.50 newsstand; $24/yr. mailed in state; $33/yr. out of state; $21/yr. senior citizens. One Smoot Ave., Danville, WV 25053. TEL 304-369-1165; FAX 304-369-1166. **Owner(s):** Smith Newspapers, Inc., P.O. Box 27, Fort Payne, AL 35967. TEL 205-845-5510; Ed. Marc Glenn; Pub. Marc Glenn; adv. contact: Pam Glenn. pub. size: broadsheet; circ. 6,000(paid).
Formerly: Madison Coal Valley News.

FRANKLIN

US
FRANKLIN PENDLETON TIMES. 1913. Thu. $.30 newsstand; $14/yr. mailed anywhere. Main St., Franklin, WV 26807. TEL 304-358-2304; FAX 304-358-2304. **Owner(s):** William McCoy, Jr., P.O. Box 906, Franklin, WV 26807. TEL 304-358-2261; Ed. William McCoy, Jr.; Pub. William McCoy, Jr.; adv.; pub. size: standard; circ. 5,500(paid).

GLENVILLE

US
GLENVILLE DEMOCRAT, THE. 1906. Thu. $16.96/yr. in cy.; $20/yr. out of cy.; $22/yr. out of state. 206 E. Main St., Glenville, WV 26351. TEL 304-462-7309. **Owner(s):** David Corcoran, P.O. Box 458, Glenville, WV 26351; Pub. David Corcoran; adv. contact: Angela McHenry. pub. size: broadsheet; circ. 3,300(paid).

US
GLENVILLE PATHFINDER. Thu. $16.96/yr. in cy.; $20/yr. in state; $22/yr. out of state. 109 E. Main St., Glenville, WV 26351. TEL 304-462-7309. **Owner(s):** Gilmer County Publishing, Inc., P.O. Box 458, Glenville, WV 26351. TEL 304-462-7309; Pub. Robert D. Arnold; adv. contact: Avon L. Arnold. pub. size: broadsheet; circ. 100(paid).

GRAFTON

US   ISSN 0745-1334
MOUNTAIN STATESMAN. 3/wk.: Mon., Wed., Fri. $.35 newsstand; $54/yr. home deliv. in cy. 914 W. Main St., Grafton, WV 26354. TEL 304-265-3333; FAX 304-265-3342. **Owner(s):** News Media Corp., Rochelle, IL 61068. TEL 815-562-2061; Ed. Marvin Gelhausen; Pub. Mark Davis; pub. size: broadsheet; circ. 3,300(paid).

GRANTSVILLE

US
CALHOUN CHRONICLE. 1883. Thu. $15.90/yr. in cy.; $20.67/yr. out of cy.; $23/yr. out of state. 353 Main St., Grantsville, WV 26147. TEL 304-354-6917; FAX 304-354-7142. **Owner(s):** Carl Morris, 353 Main St., Grantsville, WV 26147. TEL 304-354-6672; FAX 304-354-7142; Ed. Newton Nichols. adv. contact: Michelle Patrick. photos; pub. size: standard; circ. 3,300(paid).

HAMLIN

US
LINCOLN JOURNAL. Wed. $.50 newsstand; $21/yr. in cy.; $28.50/yr. out of cy.; $37.30/yr. out of state. 328 Walnut St., Hamlin, WV 25523. TEL 304-824-5101; FAX 304-824-5210. **Owner(s):** Lincoln Journal, Inc., 328 Walnut St., Hamlin, WV 25523. TEL 304-824-5101; FAX 304-824-5210; Ed. M. Sisco; Pub. Thomas A. Robinson; adv. contact: Patty Pritchard. pub. size: broadsheet; circ. 5,200(paid). **Wire Service(s):** WV Press Assn.

HARRISVILLE

US

RITCHIE GAZETTE. 1873. Thu. $15.37/yr. in cy.; $19.61/yr. in state; $22/yr. out of state. 112-116 E. Main St., Harrisville, WV 26362. TEL 304-643-2221. **Owner(s):** Delores J. Smith, P.O. Box 215, Harrisville, WV 26362. TEL 304-643-2221; Ed. Delores J. Smith. adv. contact: Judith Newbrough. photos; pub. size: standard; circ. 3,820(paid).

HINTON

US

HINTON NEWS. 1901. Tue. $16.43/yr. in cy.; $18/yr. out of state. 210 Second Ave., Hinton, WV 25951. TEL 304-466-0005. **Owner(s):** Hinton Publishing Co., Inc., 210 Second Ave., Hinton, WV 25951. TEL 304-466-0005; Ed. Fred Long; Pub. Fred Long; adv. contact: Fred Long. pub. size: broadsheet; circ. 4,200(paid).

HURRICANE

US

HURRICANE BREEZE. 1900. Thu. $.35 newsstand; $12.72/yr. in cy.; $16.96/yr. in state; $19.08/yr. out of state. 488 Hurricane Creek Rd., Hurricane, WV 25526. TEL 304-562-9881. **Owner(s):** Cookie Allen, 488 Hurricane Creek Rd., Hurricane, WV 25526. TEL 304-562-9881; Ed. Ron Allen; Pub. Cookie Allen; adv. contact: Ron Allen. pub. size: broadsheet; circ. 1,500(paid).

KINGWOOD

US   ISSN 1072-0057

PRESTON COUNTY NEWS. 1866. Sat. $.35 newsstand; $18/yr. in cy.; $23/yr. out of cy. 110 W. Main St., Kingwood, WV 26537. TEL 304-329-0090; FAX 304-329-2450. **Owner(s):** Preston Publications, Inc., 110 W. Main St., Kingwood, WV 26537. TEL 304-329-0090; Ed. Tina Bolyard; Pub. Gary Bolyard; adv. contact: Carol Peters. pub. size: broadsheet; circ. 5,400(paid).

LEWISBURG

US

GREENBRIER VALLEY RANGER. 1981. s-w.: Wed. & Sun. free. 200 S. Court St., Lewisburg, WV 24901-0471. TEL 304-645-1206; FAX 304-645-7104. **Owner(s):** Moffitt Newspapers, Inc., P.O. Box 8565, Roanoke, VA 24014. TEL 540-344-2489; Ed. Joyce Arbaugh; Pub. Frank Spicer; adv. contact: Judy Dowdy. photos; pub. size: broadsheet; circ. 26,762(free).

US

MOUNTAIN MESSENGER. 1985. Sun. $15/yr. carrier; $19.08/yr. mailed; $24/yr. out of state. 122 N. Court St., Lewisburg, WV 24901. TEL 304-647-5724; FAX 304-647-5767. **Owner(s):** Michael Showell, 122 N. Court St., Lewisburg, WV 24901. TEL 304-647-5724; Ed. Carol Hall; Pub. Michael Showell; adv. contact: Michael Showell. photos; bk.rev.; pub. size: broadsheet; circ. Sun. 5,000(paid). **Wire Service(s):** AP.

US

POST REPORT, THE. 1965. Thu. $.50 newsstand; $13/yr. in state. 204C W. Washington St., Lewisburg, WV 24901. TEL 304-645-1915; FAX 304-645-4853. **Owner(s):** Thomson Newspapers, Inc., 3150 Des Plaines Ave., Des Plaines, IL 60018. TEL 847-299-5544; Ed. Van Page; Pub. Rob Hammon; adv. contact: Barb Cordial. pub. size: standard; circ. 13,200(paid).

MADISON

US

HOMETOWN NEWS. 1986. w. $.50 newsstand; $21/yr. 475 Main St., Lower Level, Madison, WV 25130. TEL 304-369-5175; FAX 304-369-5176. **Owner(s):** Hometown News, Box 597, Madison, WV 25130. TEL 304-369-5175; FAX 304-369-5176; Ed. Janet Yeager; Pub. Janet Yeager; adv. contact: Arthur Bias. photos; pub. size: broadsheet; circ. 4,500(paid).

MARLINTON

US   ISSN 0738-8373

POCAHONTAS TIMES. 1883. w. $.30 newsstand; $16/yr. 810 Second Ave., Marlinton, WV 24954. TEL 304-799-4973. **Owner(s):** Jane P. Sharp, 1118 Second Ave., Marlinton, WV 24954. TEL 304-799-4913; William P. McNeel, 1118 Second Ave., Marlinton, WV 24954; Russell D. Jessee, 810 Second Ave., Marlinton, WV 24954; Ed. Pamela E. Pritt. adv.; bk.rev.; pub. size: standard; circ. 6,500(free & paid).

MONTGOMERY

US

MONTGOMERY HERALD. 1940. Wed. $18/yr. in state; $19.50/yr. out of state. 406 Lee St., Montgomery, WV 25136. TEL 304-442-4156; FAX 304-442-8753 **Owner(s):** Thomson Newspapers, Inc., 3150 Des Plaines Ave., Des Plaines, IL 60018. TEL 708-299-5544; Ed. Cheryl Keenan; Pub. Tom James; adv. contact: Nancy Shelton. pub. size: broadsheet; circ. 4,700(paid).

MOOREFIELD

US

MOOREFIELD EXAMINER. 1845. Wed. $.35 newsstand; $15.90/yr. in cy.; $19.50/yr. out of state. 132 S. Main St., Moorefield, WV 26836-0380. TEL 304-538-2342; FAX 304-538-7294. **Owner(s):** R.E. Fisher Co., Inc., 132 S. Main St., P.O. Box 380, Moorefield, WV 26836-0380. TEL 304-538-2342; FAX 304-538-7294; Ed. Phoebe F. Heishman; Pub. Phoebe F. Heishman; adv. contact: Melvin Shook. photos; bk.rev.; pub. size: standard; circ. 4,400(paid).

MOUNDSVILLE

US

GREEN TAB. 1926. Sun. free. 518 Seventh St., Moundsville, WV 26041. TEL 304-845-4050; FAX 304-845-4312. **Owner(s):** Robert W. Munn, Jr., 518 7th St., Moundsville, WV 26041. TEL 304-845-4050; Ed. Robert W. Munn, Jr. adv. contact: Ralph DeRemigio. pub. size: tabloid; circ. 60,000(free).

MULLEN

US

MULLENS ADVOCATE. 1913. Tue. $.25 newsstand; $11/yr. in cy.; $15/yr. out of cy. 217 Moran Ave., Mullen, WV 25882. TEL 304-294-4144. **Owner(s):** Jack Moffitt, 217 Moran Ave., Mullen, WV 25882. TEL 304-294-4144; Pub. W.A. Tony Johnson; adv.; pub. size: broadsheet; circ. 3,500(paid).

NEW MARTINSVILLE

US

WETZEL CHRONICLE. 1888. Wed. $.47 newsstand; $25/yr. mailed in state; $25/yr. out of state. 1100 Third St., New Martinsville, WV 26155. TEL 304-455-3300; FAX 304-455-1275. **Owner(s):** Wetzel Chronicle Co., 1100 Third St., New Martinsville, WV 26155. TEL 304-455-3300; Ed. Donald Smith; Pub. Kenneth M. Sicke; adv. contact: Michael Galluzzo. pub. size: standard; circ. 7,000(paid).

OAK HILL

US

FAYETTE TRIBUNE. 1897. Mon. & Thu. $.35 newsstand; $30/yr. 417 Main St., Oak Hill, WV 25901. TEL 304-469-3373; FAX 304-469-4105. **Owner(s):** Thomson Newspapers, Inc., 1 Thorn Run Ctr, Ste. 500, 1187 Thorn Run Rd. Ext., Coraopolis, PA 15108. TEL 412-262-7870; Ed. Cheryl Keenan; Pub. Tom James; adv.; pub. size: broadsheet; circ. 6,000(paid).

PARSONS

US   ISSN 0747-3303

PARSONS ADVOCATE. 1896. Wed. $.50 newsstand; $20/yr. in state; $25/yr. out of state. 212 Main St., Parsons, WV 26287. TEL 304-478-3533; FAX 304-478-4658. **Owner(s):** George & Mariwyn Smith, 134 Penn. Ave., Parsons, WV 26287; Ed. Mariwyn M. Smith. adv.; pub. size: standard; circ. 3,900(paid).

PENNSBORO

US

PENNSBORO NEWS. 1892. Wed. $.50 newsstand; $7.47/yr. in cy.; $12.72/yr. out of cy. P.O. Box 386, Pennsboro, WV 26415. TEL 304-659-2441; FAX 304-659-2441. **Owner(s):** James McGoldrick, 409 Main St., Pennsboro, WV 26415. TEL 304-659-2441; Ed. James McGoldrick; Pub. James McGoldrick; pub. size: broadsheet; circ. 5,100(paid).

PETERSBURG

US

GRANT COUNTY PRESS. 1896. Tue. $15.90/yr. in cy.; $16.96/yr. in state; $19.50/yr. out of state. 47 S. Main, Petersburg, WV 26847. TEL 304-257-1844; FAX 304-257-1691. **Owner(s):** Potomac Valley Press Inc., 47 S. Main, Petersburg, WV 26847; Ed. William E. Fouch. adv. contact: Jodi Fouch. pub. size: broadsheet; circ. 4,875(paid).

PHILIPPI

US

BARBOUR DEMOCRAT, THE. 1893. Wed. $19.08/yr. in state; $21.50/yr. out of state. 113 Church St., Philippi, WV 26416. TEL 304-457-2222; FAX 304-457-2703. **Owner(s):** Barbour Pub ishing Co., Inc., 113 Church St., Philippi, WV 24616; Ed. Robert A. Byrne. pub. size: standard; circ. 5,300(paid). **Formerly:** Philippi Barbour Democrat.

PIEDMONT

US

PIEDMONT HERALD. Tue. $20/yr. in cy.; $21/yr. out of cy. 34 Railroad St., Piedmont, WV 26750. TEL 304-355-2381; FAX 304-355-2383. **Owner(s):** Herald Printing House, Piedmont, WV. TEL 304-355-2381; FAX 304-355-2383; Ed. Margaret J. Hood; Pub. William T. Hood; pub. size: standard; circ. 2,000(paid).

PINEVILLE

US

INDEPENDENT HERALD, THE. 1914. Wed. $8.48/yr. in cy.; $12.72/yr. out of cy. Rte. 10, Pineville, WV 24874. TEL 304-732-6060; FAX 304-732-8228. **Owner(s):** Charles R. Cline, Rte. 10, Pineville, WV 24874. TEL 304-732-6060; Ed. Ron Mullens; Pub. Charles R. Cline; pub. size: standard; circ. 5,000(paid).

PRINCETON

US

PRINCETON TIMES. 1961. Thu. $15/yr. in state; $20/yr. out of state. 109 Thorn St., Princeton, WV 24740. TEL 304-425-8191; FAX 304-487-1632. **Owner(s):** Thomson Newspapers, Inc., 3150 Des Plaines Ave., Des Plaines, IL 60018. TEL 847-299-5544; Ed. Anita Rosen. adv. contact: Jerry L. Morgan. pub. size: broadsheet; circ. 3,000(paid).

RAVENSWOOD

US

JACKSON STAR NEWS. 1955. s-w.: Wed. & Sat. $.75 newsstand; $29.15/yr. in cy. 237 Washington St., Ravenswood, WV 26164. TEL 304-273-9333; FAX 304-273-3401. **Owner(s):** Smith Newspapers, Inc., P.O. Box 27, Fort Payne, AL 35967. TEL 205-845-5510; Ed. Greg Matics; Pub. Greg Matics; pub. size: broadsheet; circ. 14,500(paid).

RICHWOOD

US

NEWS LEADER. 1946. Wed. $.35 newsstand; $21/yr. in state; $25/yr. out of state. 4 Railroad Ave., Richwood, WV 26261. TEL 304-846-2666; FAX 304-846-4972. **Owner(s):** Jim Comstock, P.O. Box 430, Richwood, WV 26261. TEL 304-846-2667; Jay Comstock, P.O. Box 430, Richmond, VA 26261. TEL 304-846-2667; Ed. Russell McCauley; Pub. Jay Comstock; adv.; pub. size: broadsheet; circ. 4,200(paid).

US

WEST VIRGINIA HILLBILLY. 1958. Wed. $30/yr. 4 Railroad Ave., Richwood, WV 26261. TEL 304-846-2667; FAX 304-846-4972. **Owner(s):** Russell McCulley, P.O. Box 430, Richwood, WV 26261. TEL 304-846-2667; Pub. Russell McCulley; adv. contact: Russell McCulley. pub. size: tabloid; circ. 5,000(paid).

RIPLEY

US

RIPLEY JACKSON HERALD. 1877. s-w.: Wed. & Sat. $.75 newsstand; $29.15/yr. in cy.; $34.98/yr. out of cy.; $47.70/yr. out of state. 117 Court St., Ripley, WV 25271. TEL 304-372-2421; FAX 304-372-8240. **Owner(s):** Ripley Newspapers, Inc., P.O. Box 27, Fort Payne, AL 35967; Ed. Mike Ruben; Pub. Carol Haun; adv.; photos; pub. size: broadsheet; circ. 7,000(free & paid).

ROMNEY

US

HAMPSHIRE REVIEW. 1829. Wed. $.50 newsstand; $25.44/yr. mailed in cy.; $26.50/yr. in state; $27.56/yr. out of state. 25 S. Grafton St., Romney, WV 26757. TEL 304-822-3871; FAX 304-822-4487. **Owner(s):** Cornwell & Ailes, Inc., 25 S. Grafton St., Romney, WV 26757. TEL 304-822-3871; Ed. Charles See. adv. contact: Lana Bean. pub. size: broadsheet; circ. 6,100(paid).

SHEPHERDSTOWN

US

SHEPHERDSTOWN CHRONICLE. 1991. Fri. $.35 newsstand; $13.50/yr. in cy.; $22.50/yr. out of cy. Duke & Washington Sts., Shepherdstown, WV 25443. TEL 304-876-3380; FAX 304-876-1957. **Owner(s):** Corcoran Publications, Ltd., P.O. Box 2088, Shepherdstown, WV 25443. TEL 304-876-3380; FAX 304-876-3380; Ed. Mary Lehman; Pub. John Lehman; adv. contact: John Lehman. photos; pub. size: tabloid; circ. 1,500(paid).

SISTERSVILLE

US

TYLER STAR NEWS. 1878. Wed. $25/yr. in state; $28/yr. out of state. 727 Wells St., Sistersville, WV 26175. TEL 304-652-4141; FAX 304-652-1454. **Owner(s):** Ogden Newspapers, Inc., 1500 Main St., Wheeling, WV 26003. TEL 304-233-0100; Ed. Charles A. Mason; Pub. Kenneth Sickle; adv. contact: Michael Galluzzo. bk.rev.; pub. size: standard; circ. 4,200(paid).

SPENCER

US

ROANE COUNTY REPORTER. 1915. Thu. $.50 newsstand; $21/yr. in state; $25/yr. out of state. 210 E. Main St., Spencer, WV 25276-0647. TEL 304-927-2360. **Owner(s):** Spencer Newspapers, Inc., P.O. Box 647, Spencer, WV 25276. TEL 304-927-2360; Ed. Jim Cooper; Pub. David J. Hedges; adv. contact: Danny Jarvis. pub. size: broadsheet; circ. 2,456(free & paid).

US

TIMES RECORD. 1914. Thu. $.50 newsstand; $21/yr. in state; $25/yr. out of state. 210 E. Main St., Spencer, WV 25276. TEL 304-927-2360; FAX 304-927-2361. **Owner(s):** Spencer Newspapers, Inc., P.O. Box 647, Spencer, WV 25276. TEL 304-927-2360; Ed. Jim Cooper; Pub. David J. Hedges; adv. contact: Danny Jarvis. pub. size: broadsheet; circ. 3,562(free & paid).

SUMMERSVILLE

US

NICHOLAS CHRONICLE. 1880. Thu. $.50 newsstand; $25/yr. in state; $30/yr. out of state. 603 Church St., Summersville, WV 26651. TEL 304-872-2251; FAX 304-872-2254. **Owner(s):** Nicholas County Publishing Co., Inc., P.O. Box 503, Summersville, WV 26651. TEL 304-872-2251; FAX 304-872-2254; Ed. Matthew R. Yeager; Pub. Charles Yeager; adv.; photos; bk.rev.; pub. size: standard; circ. 5,000(paid). **Wire Service(s):** AP.

SUTTON

US

BRAXTON CITIZEN'S NEWS. 1976. Mon. $.16 newsstand; $10/yr. in cy.; $9/yr. senior citizens. 501 Main St., Sutton, WV 26601. TEL 304-765-5193; FAX 304-765-2754. **Owner(s):** Ed Given, 501 Main St., Sutton, WV 26601. TEL 304-765-5193; FAX 304-765-2754; Ed. Del Thayer; Pub. Ed Given; adv. contact: Jeanine Given. photos; pub. size: tabloid; circ. 6,500(paid).

US

BRAXTON DEMOCRAT-CENTRAL. 1883. Thu. $9.50/yr. in cy.; $14/yr. out of cy.; $15.50/yr. out of state. 205 Main St., Sutton, WV 26601-1399. TEL 304-765-5555; FAX 304-765-5555. **Owner(s):** Craig A. Smith, 205 Main St., Sutton, WV 26601. TEL 304-765-5555; Ed. Craig A. Smith; Pub. Craig A. Smith; adv. contact: Joan Bias. pub. size: broadsheet; circ. 4,200(paid).

UNION

US

MONROE WATCHMAN. 1872. Thu. $.50 newsstand; $18.55/yr. in state; $20/yr. out of state. Main St., Union, WV 24983. TEL 304-772-3016. **Owner(s):** Harry Mohler, Main St., Union, WV 24983. TEL 304-772-3016; pub. size: broadsheet; circ. 4,000(paid).

WAYNE

US

WAYNE COUNTY NEWS. 1874. Wed. $.50 newsstand; $22.95/yr. in cy.; $25.44/yr. out of cy.; $28.80/yr. out of state. 310 Central Ave., Wayne, WV 25570. TEL 304-272-3433; FAX 304-522-3910. **Owner(s):** Thomas J. George, 310 Central Ave., Wayne, WV 25570. TEL 304-272-3433; Pub. Thomas J. George; adv.; pub. size: broadsheet; circ. 4,600(paid).

WEBSTER SPRINGS

US

WEBSTER REPUBLICAN. 1882. Wed. $.48 newsstand; $22.81/yr. mailed in cy.; $28.69/yr. out of state. Back Fork St., Webster Springs, WV 26288. TEL 304-847-5828; FAX 304-847-5991. **Owner(s):** D. Boyd Dotson, Jr., Back Fork St., Webster Springs, WV 26288. TEL 304-847-5828; Ed. Elizabeth Tracy; Pub. D. Boyd Dotson, Jr.; pub. size: broadsheet; circ. 1,800(paid).

WELLSBURG

US

BROOKE COUNTY REVIEW. 1937. Thu. $.25 newsstand; $14/yr. mailed. 319 Charles St., Wellsburg, WV 26070. TEL 304-737-0946; FAX 304-737-1852. **Owner(s):** Brooke Publishing Inc., 319 Charles St., Wellsburg, WV 26070. TEL 304-737-0946; Pub. J.W. George Wallace; adv.; photos; pub. size: broadsheet; circ. 2,000(paid). **Wire Service(s):** WV Pressnet. **Formerly:** Brooke News & Follansbee Review.

WESTON

US

WESTON DEMOCRAT, THE. 1867. Wed. $.33 newsstand; $14.83/yr. in state; $18/yr. out of state. 238 Main Ave., Weston, WV 26452. TEL 304-269-1600; FAX 304-269-4035. **Owner(s):** Robert Billeter, P.O. Box 968, Weston, WV 26452. TEL 304-269-1600; FAX 304-269-4035; Ed. George Whelan; Pub. Robert Billeter; adv. contact: Julia Spelsberg. photos; bk.rev.; pub. size: standard; circ. 8,000(paid).

WEST UNION

US

HERALD RECORD. Tue. $.35 newsstand; $10.60/yr. local; $11.66/yr. out of cy.; $12/yr. out of state. 202 E. Main St., West Union, WV 26456. TEL 304-873-1600. **Owner(s):** Virginia Nicholson, 202 E. Main St., West Union, WV 26456. TEL 304-873-1600; Ed. Virginia Nicholson. adv.; pub. size: standard; circ. 3,150(paid).

WISCONSIN

ABBOTSFORD

US

ABBOTSFORD TRIBUNE-PHONOGRAPH. w. $.75 newsstand; $23/yr. in state; $26/yr. in IA, IL, MI, & MN; $32/yr. elsewhere. P.O. Box 677, Abbotsford, WI 54405. TEL 715-223-2342; FAX 715-223-3505. **Owner(s):** J.A. O'Leary, P.O. Box 677, Abbotsford, WI 54405. TEL 715-223-2342; Ed. Charles Runnoe; Pub. J.A. O'Leary; pub. size: tabloid; circ. 2,300(paid).

US

RECORD-REVIEW. 1964. Wed. $.50 newsstand; $20/yr. in state; $23/yr. out of state. 103 W. Spruce St., Abbotsford, WI 54405. TEL 715-223-2342; FAX 715-223-3505. **Owner(s):** J.A. & Carol O'Leary, 103 W. Spruce, Abbotsford, WI 54405. TEL 715-223-2342; FAX 715-223-3505; Ed. Peter Weinschenk; Pub. J.A. O'Leary; adv. contact: Carol O'Leary. photos; pub. size: tabloid; circ. 1,900(paid).

ADAMS

US

ADAMS COUNTY TIMES. 1940. Wed. $24/yr. in cy.; $28/yr. out of cy.; $35/yr. out of state. 116 S. Main St., Adams, WI 53910. TEL 608-339-7844; FAX 608-339-3903. **Owner(s):** Richard A. Hannagan, P.O. Box 99, Adams, WI 53910. TEL 608-339-7844; Pub. Richard A. Hannagan; pub. size: standard; circ. 4,200(paid).

ALGOMA

US

ALGOMA RECORD HERALD. s-w.: Wed. & Sun. $.50 newsstand; $20/yr. local; $25/yr. out of state. 602 Third St., Algoma, WI 54201. TEL 414-487-2222; FAX 414-487-3194. **Owner(s):** Frank Wood, P.O. Box 68, Algoma, WI 54201; Ed. Lee Lawrenz; Pub. Frank Wood; adv.; pub. size: broadsheet; circ. 4,200(paid).

    Formerly: Record Herald.

AMERY

US

AMERY FREE PRESS. 1889. Tue. $.75 newsstand; $25/yr. in cy.; $30/yr. out of cy.; $35/yr. out of state. 215 S. Keller, Amery, WI 54001. TEL 715-268-8101; FAX 715-268-8125. **Owner(s):** Sondreal Enterprises, Inc., 215 S. Keller, Amery, WI 54001. TEL 715-268-8101; Ed. Palmer Sondreal; Pub. Palmer Sondreal; adv. contact: Pamela Humpal. pub. size: broadsheet; circ. 5,000(paid). **Wire Service(s):** UPI.

ANTIGO

US

ANTIGO AREA SHOPPERS GUIDE. 1954. Tue. free local. 813 Fifth Ave., Antigo, WI 54409. TEL 715-623-5024; FAX 715-623-5389. **Owner(s):** Antigo Area Shoppers Guide, Inc., 813 Fifth Ave., Antigo, WI 54409. TEL 715-623-5024; FAX 715-623-5389; adv.; pub. size: tabloid; circ. 12,969(free).

ARCADIA

US

ARCADIA NEWS-LEADER. 1875. Thu. $.75 newsstand; $20/yr. in cy.; $22/yr. in state; $26/yr. out of state. 625 Dettloff Dr., Arcadia, WI 54612-0220. TEL 608-323-3366; FAX 608-323-2185. **Owner(s):** Blaschko Enterprises, P.O. Box 220, Arcadia, WI 54612. TEL 608-323-3366; Pub. Chuck Blaschko; adv. contact: Lisa Wolfe. photos; pub. size: standard; circ. 2,500(paid).

ARGYLE

US

ARGYLE AGENDA. 1961. Wed., local; Thu., rural. $.50 newsstand; $18/yr. mailed in state; $25/yr. mailed out of state. 101 N. State St., Argyle, WI 53504-0426. TEL 608-543-3773. **Owner(s):** Dan Witte & Mark Witte, Mt. Horeb, WI 53572. TEL 608-437-5553; Pub. Dan Witte; adv.; photos; bk.rev.; pub. size: tabloid; circ. 1,000(paid).

AUGUSTA

US   ISSN 0749-7083

AUGUSTA AREA TIMES. 1900. Wed. $.50 newsstand; $16/yr. in area; $19/yr. out of area; $23/yr. out of state. 156 E. Lincoln, Augusta, WI 54722. TEL 715-286-2655; FAX 715-286-2655. **Owner(s):** Michael D. Jensen, P.O. Box 465, Augusta, WI 54722. TEL 715-286-2655; FAX 715-597-8705; Ed. Beth Ellie; Pub. Michael D. Jensen; adv. contact: Tamy Cuddy. pub. size: standard; circ. 1,500(paid).

BALDWIN

US

BALDWIN BULLETIN. 1872. Tue. $15/yr. in cy.; $20/yr. out of cy.; $22/yr. out of state. 805 Main St., Baldwin, WI 54002. TEL 715-684-2484; FAX 715-684-4937. **Owner(s):** Thomas A. Hawley, P.O. Box 66, Baldwin, WI 54002. TEL 715-684-2484; Peter C. Hawley, P.O. Box 66, Baldwin, WI 54002; Muriel Hawley, P.O. Box 66, Baldwin, WI 54002; Ed. Thomas A. Hawley; Pub. Thomas A. Hawley; pub. size: broadsheet; circ. 3,000(paid).

BARRON

US

BARRON COUNTY NEWS SHIELD. 1876. Wed. $.75 newsstand; $20/yr. local; $21.50/yr. out of cy.; $25/yr. out of state. 219 E. La Salle, Barron, WI 54812. TEL 715-537-3117; FAX 715-537-5640. **Owner(s):** Bell Press, Inc., P.O. Box 189, Barron, WI 54812. TEL 715-532-5591; Ed. Robert Groshong; Pub. James Bell; pub. size: broadsheet; circ. 4,200(paid).

BELLEVILLE

US

BELLEVILLE RECORDER. 1885. w. $18.50/yr. in state; $22.50/yr. out of state; $.50 newsstand. 38 River St., Belleville, WI 53508. TEL 608-424-3232. **Owner(s):** Stuart M. Shapiro, P.O. Box 50, Belleville, WI 53508. TEL 608-424-3232; Pub. Stuart Shapiro; adv. contact: Stuart Shapiro. pub. size: tabloid; circ. 1,450(paid).

BERLIN

US

BERLIN BUYERS' GUIDE. 1945. Tue. free local; $52/yr. elsewhere. 124 W. Huron St., Berlin, WI 54923. TEL 414-361-2444; FAX 414-361-4959. **Owner(s):** Journal Communications, Inc., P.O. Box 661, Milwaukee, WI 53201; Ed. David Schrader. adv.; pub. size: tabloid; circ. 22,400(free).

US   ISSN 8755-4003

BERLIN JOURNAL. 1870. Thu. $.75 newsstand; $24/yr. in cy.; $42/yr. out of cy. 301 June St., Berlin, WI 54923. TEL 414-361-1515; FAX 414-361-1518. **Owner(s):** Berlin Journal Co., 301 June St., Berlin, WI 54923; Ed. Jim Wolff; Pub. G.M. Gonyo; pub. size: tabloid; circ. 4,100(paid).

US

BILLBOARD, THE. Tue. free. 301 June St., Berlin, WI 54923. TEL 414-928-2626. **Owner(s):** R.M. Gonyo, 135 E. Moore, Berlin, WI 54923. TEL 414-361-0377; Ed. Jim Wolff; Pub. R.M. Gonyo; pub. size: tabloid.

US

FOX LAKE REPRESENTATIVE. 1868. Thu. $.75 newsstand; $24/yr. local; $42/yr. in state; $55/yr. out of state. 301 June St., Berlin, WI 54923. TEL 414-928-2626. **Owner(s):** R.M. Gonyo, 135 E. Moore, Berlin, WI 54923. TEL 414-361-0377; Ed. Jim Wolff; Pub. R.M. Gonyo; pub. size: tabloid; circ. 850(paid).

BLACK RIVER FALLS

US

BANNER JOURNAL. 1856. Wed. $28/yr. local. 409 E. Main St., Black River Falls, WI 54615. TEL 715-284-4304; FAX 715-284-4634. **Owner(s):** News Publishing Co., 1126 Mills St., Black Earth, WI 53515. TEL 603-767-3655; Ed. Jeanette Ruxton; Pub. Dan Witte; adv.; photos; pub. size: tabloid; circ. 4,400(paid).

BLAIR

US

BLAIR PRESS. 1893. Thu. $.50 newsstand; $18/yr. in cy.; $20/yr. out of cy.; $24/yr. out of state. 109 N. Gilbert St., Blair, WI 54616. TEL 608-989-2531; FAX 608-989-2531. **Owner(s):** Gerald Hjornevik, P.O. Box 187, Blair, WI 54616. TEL 608-989-2531; FAX 608-989-2531; Pub. Gerald Hjornevik; adv. contact: Liz Hjornevik. photos; pub. size: broadsheet; circ. 2,150(paid).

BLANCHARDVILLE

US

BLADE ATLAS. 1888. Thu. $.40 newsstand; $15/yr. mailed in state; $18/yr. mailed out of state. 205 S. Main St., Blanchardville, WI 53516. TEL 608-523-4284; FAX 608-523-1019. **Owner(s):** John P. Riley & Thomas M. Riley, Dodgeville, WI 53533. TEL 608-935-2331; Ed. Gary McKenzie. adv.; pub. size: tabloid; circ. 1,300(paid).

BLOOMER

US

BLOOMER ADVANCE. 1888. Wed. $.50 newsstand; $17/yr. in cy.; $19/yr. out of cy. 1202 15th Ave., Bloomer, WI 54724. TEL 715-568-3100; FAX 715-568-3111. **Owner(s):** Don Bell, 1202 15th St., Bloomer, WI 54724. TEL 715-568-3100; FAX 715-568-3111; Pub. Al Bauer; pub. size: standard; circ. 3,900.

BOSCOBEL

US

BOSCOBEL DIAL. 1872. Thu. $.50 newsstand; $23/yr. mailed in state; $28/yr. out of state. 805 Wisconsin Ave., Boscobel, WI 53805. TEL 608-375-4458; FAX 608-375-2369. **Owner(s):** Kirkland Newspapers, Inc., Durham, NC 27701; Ed. David Krier. adv. contact: Jean Roth. photos; pub. size: broadsheet; circ. 6,300(paid).

BRILLION

US   ISSN 0749-7210

BRILLION NEWS. 1894. Wed. $.40 newsstand; $20/yr. 425 W. Ryan St., Brillion, WI 54110. TEL 414-756-2222; FAX 414-756-2701. **Owner(s):** Zander Press, Inc., 425 W. Ryan St., Brillion, WI 54110. TEL 414-756-2222; FAX 414-756-2701; Pub. Zane Zander; adv. contact: Zane Zander. photos; pub. size: tabloid; circ. 2,100(paid).

BRODHEAD

US

INDEPENDENT-REGISTER, THE. 1861. w. $.70 newsstand; $19/yr. in cy.; $21/yr. in state; $28/yr. out of state. 922 Exchange St., Brodhead, WI 53520. TEL 608-897-2193; FAX 608-897-4137. **Owner(s):** M.D. Markham, 922 Exchange St., Brodhead, WI 53520. TEL 608-897-2193; FAX 608-897-4137; Pub. Kim Markham; adv. contact: M.D. Markham. bk.rev.; pub. size: tabloid; circ. 7,900(free & paid).

BURLINGTON

US

BURLINGTON STANDARD PRESS. 1863. s-w.: Sun. & Wed. $.75 newsstand; $28/yr. mailed locally; $29.50/yr. in cy.; $47.50/yr. out of state. 140 Commerce St., Burlington, WI 53105. TEL 414-763-3511; FAX 414-763-2238. **Owner(s):** Robert Branen, 140 Commerce St., Burlington, WI 35105. TEL 414-763-3511; Pub. Robert Branen; adv. contact: Dave Wright. pub. size: broadsheet; circ. 9,846(paid).

CADOTT

US   ISSN 0885-0798

CADOTT SENTINEL. 1917. Thu. $.75 newsstand; $20/yr. local; $22/yr. in state; $28/yr. elsewhere. 327 Main St., Cadott, WI 54727. TEL 715-289-4978; FAX 715-239-6200. **Owner(s):** Trygg J. Hansen, P.O. Box 70, Cadott, WI 54727. TEL 715-289-4978; FAX 715-239-6200; Ed. Heather Hill; Pub. Trygg Hansen; adv.; pub. size: broadsheet; circ. 3,000(paid).

CAMBRIDGE

US   ISSN 0749-7202

CAMBRIDGE NEWS. 1892. Wed. $.50 newsstand; $20/yr. in cy.; $24/yr. elsewhere. 201 W. North St., Cambridge, WI 53523. TEL 608-423-3213; FAX 414-648-8187. **Owner(s):** Leader Printing Co., P.O. Box 60, Lake Mills, WI 53551. TEL 414-648-2334; FAX 414-648-8187; Pub. Dennis Hawkes; adv. contact: Karen DeWall. pub. size: tabloid; circ. 2,000(paid).

CAMPBELLSPORT

US

CAMPBELLSPORT NEWS. 1899. Thu. $.40 newsstand; $20/yr. in state; $22/yr. out of state. 101 N. Fond du Lac Ave., Campbellsport, WI 53010. TEL 414-533-8338; FAX 414-533-5579. **Owner(s):** Gerald F. Ninneman, P.O. Box 138, Campbellsport, WI 53010. TEL 414-533-8338; Pub. Gerald F. Ninneman; adv. contact: James Ninneman. pub. size: tabloid; circ. 2,300(paid).

CASHTON

US

CASHTON RECORD. 1896. Wed. $.50 newsstand; $16/yr. local; $24/yr. out of state. 713 Broadway, Cashton, WI 54619-0100. TEL 608-654-7330. **Owner(s):** Gerald Eddy, P.O. Box 100, Cashton, WI 54619. TEL 608-654-7330; Pub. Gerald Eddy; adv. contact: Rose Eddy. pub. size: tabloid; circ. 1,500(free & paid).

CEDARBURG

US   ISSN 1056-9006

OZAUKEE COUNTY NEWS GRAPHIC. 1883. s-w.: Mon. & Thu. $.75 newsstand; $28.97/yr. mailed. N19-W6733 Commerce Ct., Cedarburg, WI 53012. TEL 414-375-5100; FAX 414-375-5107. **Owner(s):** Lakeshore Newspapers, Inc., Beaver Dam, WI 53916; Pub. Phil Paige; adv. contact: Jim Baumgart. pub. size: tabloid; circ. 10,000(paid).
  Formerly: News Graphic Pilot.

US

OZAUKEE GUIDE. Wed. free. N19 W6733 Commerce Ct., Cedarburg, WI 53012. TEL 414-375-5100; FAX 414-375-5107. **Owner(s):** Lake Shore Newspapers, Inc., Beaver Dam, WI; Ed. Mark Jaegar; Pub. Phil Paige; adv. contact: Jim Barengart. pub. size: tabloid; circ. 35,000(free).

CHETEK

US

CHETEK ALERT, THE. 1882. Thu. $.50 newsstand; $16/yr. in cy.; $20/yr. out of cy.; $26/yr. out of state. 312 Knapp St., Chetek, WI 54728. TEL 715-924-4118; FAX 715-924-4122. **Owner(s):** Paul H. Lange, P.O. Box 5, Chetek, WI 54728. TEL 715-924-3032; Melodee A. Eckerman, P.O. Box 5, Chetek, WI 54728. TEL 715-924-2922; Ed. Melodee A. Eckerman; Pub. Paul H. Lange; pub. size: broadsheet; circ. 3,600(paid).

CHILTON

US

CHILTON TIMES-JOURNAL. 1857. Thu. $.50 newsstand; $15.50/yr. in cy. 19 E. Main St., Chilton, WI 53014. TEL 414-849-7036; FAX 414-849-4651. **Owner(s):** Vercauteren Publishing, 19 E. Main, Chilton, WI 53014. TEL 414-849-7036; FAX 414-849-4651; Ed. Debbie Dins; Pub. Gary Vercauteren; adv.; photos; pub. size: broadsheet; circ. 3,800(paid).

CLINTON

US

CLINTON TOPPER. 1938. Thu. $.50 newsstand; $17/yr. in cy.; $22/yr. out of cy. 400-B Front St., Clinton, WI 53525. TEL 608-676-4664; FAX 608-676-4664. **Owner(s):** Independent Newspapers Corp., 400-B Front St., Clinton, WI 53525. TEL 608-676-4664; FAX 608-676-4664; Ed. Robert Gard; Pub. Henry W. Schroeder; adv. contact: Sharon Bobolz. photos; pub. size: tabloid; circ. 1,500(paid).

CLINTONVILLE

US

CLINTONVILLE TRIBUNE-GAZETTE. 1881. Thu. $.50 newsstand; $22.50/yr. in cy.; $27.50/yr. in state; $32.50/yr. out of state. 13 11th St., Clintonville, WI 54929. TEL 715-823-3151. E-mail: teegee@mail.atw.fullfeed.com; URL: http://www.clintonville-online.com. **Owner(s):** Clintonville Publishing Co., 13 11th St., Clintonville, WI 54929. TEL 718-823-3151; Ed. Scott McGraw; Pub. Scott McGraw; adv. contact: Jeff Vollendorf. pub. size: broadsheet; circ. 3,450(paid).

COCHRANE

US

BUFFALO COUNTY JOURNAL. 1861. Thu. $.50 newsstand; $19/yr. surrounding area; $22/yr. out of cy.; $28/yr. out of state. 104 Fifth St., Cochrane, WI 54622-0046. TEL 608-248-2451; FAX 608-248-2422. **Owner(s):** Valley Publications, P.O. Box 109, Wabasha, MN 55981. TEL 612-565-3368; Ed. Ed McFarlaine; Pub. Gary Stumpf; adv.; pub. size: tabloid; circ. 875(paid).

COLFAX

US

COLFAX MESSENGER. 1897. Wed. $.50 newsstand; $20/yr. mailed in cy.; $24/yr. mailed out of cy. P.O. Box 517, Colfax, WI 54730-0517. TEL 715-962-3535; FAX 715-962-3535. **Owner(s):** Ellis Bloomfield, P.O. Box 517, Colfax, WI 54730-0517. TEL 715-962-3535; Ed. Ellis Bloomfield; Pub. Ellis Bloomfield; adv.; photos; pub. size: broadsheet; circ. 1,250(paid).

COLUMBUS

US

COLUMBUS JOURNAL. 1861. Mon. $.75 newsstand; $25/yr. in state; $35/yr. out of state. 101 S. Ludington St., Columbus, WI 53925. TEL 414-623-3160; FAX 414-623-9383. **Owner(s):** Citizen Publishing Co., 805 Park Ave., Beaver Dam, WI 53916; Ed. Patti Hoselton; Pub. Marshall Bernhagen; adv. contact: Bridget Gifford. pub. size: tabloid; circ. 2,000(paid).
   Formerly: Columbus Journal-Republican.

CORNELL

US

CORNELL & LAKE HOLCOMBE COURIER. 1915. Thu. $.50 newsstand; $20/yr. local; $22/yr. in state; $28/yr. out of state. P.O. Box 546, Cornell, WI 54732. TEL 715-239-6688; FAX 715-239-6200. **Owner(s):** Trygg J. Hansen, P.O. Box 546, Cornell, WI 54732-0546. TEL 715-239-6688; FAX 715-239-6200; Ed. Heather Hill; Pub. Trygg J. Hansen; adv.; pub. size: broadsheet; circ. 3,100(paid).

CRANDON

US

FOREST REPUBLICAN, THE. 1885. Wed. $.50 newsstand; $14.50/yr. in cy.; $17.50/yr. out of cy. 108-110 W. Madison St., Crandon, WI 54520. TEL 715-478-3315; FAX 715-478-5385. **Owner(s):** Russell H. Steel, P.O. Box 367, Crandon, WI 54520. TEL 715-478-3315; Ed. Russell H. Steel; Pub. Russell H. Steel; pub. size: broadsheet; circ. 3,900(paid).

CUBA CITY

US

TRI-COUNTY PRESS. 1894. Wed. $.75 newsstand; $22/yr. in state; $24/yr. in IA & IL; $35/yr. other states. 301 S. Main, Cuba City, WI 53807. TEL 608-744-2107; FAX 608-744-2108. **Owner(s):** Tri-County Publications, Inc., 301 S. Main St., Cuba City, WI 53807. TEL 608-744-2107; Ed. Craig Kowalski; Pub. William S. Hale; adv. contact: Rick Goldthorpe. pub. size: tabloid; circ. 3,000(paid).
   Formerly: Cuba City Tri-County Press.

CUMBERLAND

US

CUMBERLAND ADVOCATE. 1881. w. $.60 newsstand; $19/yr. 1375 Second Ave., Cumberland, WI 54829. TEL 715-822-4469. **Owner(s):** Jackson County Publications, Inc., P.O. Box 637, Cumberland, WI 54829. TEL 715-234-2121; Ed. Sharon Bucher; Pub. Craig Bucher; adv.; photos; pub. size: broadsheet; circ. 3,000(paid).

DARLINGTON

US

REPUBLICAN-JOURNAL. 1862. Thu. $.75 newsstand; $25/yr. in area; $32/yr. out of area. 316 S. Main St., Darlington, WI 53530. TEL 608-776-4425; FAX 608-776-4301. **Owner(s):** Darlington Publishing Co., Inc., 316 Main St., Darlington, WI 53530. TEL 608-776-4425; Ed. Cindy Lund; Pub. Brian A. Lund; adv. contact: Nancy Fink. pub. size: broadsheet; circ. 4,000(paid).

DEERFIELD

US

INDEPENDENT. 1885. Thu. $.60 newsstand; $20/yr. 7 S. Main St., Deerfield, WI 53531. TEL 608-764-5515; FAX 608-764-8214. **Owner(s):** Hometown News, L.P., 112 Market St., Sun Prairie, WI 53590. TEL 608-837-2521; Ed. Mary Pohlman; Pub. Brian Knox; pub. size: broadsheet; circ. 1,500(paid).
   Formerly: Deerfield Independent.

DE FOREST

US

FOREST TIMES-TRIBUNE. 1895. Thu. $.60 newsstand; $21/yr. in cy.; $24.50/yr. out of state; $17.50/yr. students. 108 Market St., De Forest, WI 53532. TEL 608-846-5576; FAX 608-846-5757. **Owner(s):** Richard H. & Molly Emerson, 108 Market Street, De Forest, WI 53532. TEL 608-846-5576; FAX 608-846-5757; Ed. Richard H. Emerson; Pub. Richard H. Emerson; pub. size: broadsheet; circ. 2,300(paid).

DELAVAN

US

DELAVAN ENTERPRISE. 1878. Wed. $.75 newsstand; $23.50/yr. mailed in cy.; $26.50/yr. out of cy.; $32/yr. out of state. 1436 Mound Rd., Delavan, WI 53115. TEL 414-728-3411; FAX 414-728-5706. **Owner(s):** Bliss Communications, Inc., One S. Parker Dr., Janesville, WI 53545. TEL 414-754-3311; Ed. Tom Sheeham; Pub. Tom Sheehan; adv. contact: Dave Erickson. pub. size: tabloid; circ. 5,000(paid).

DENMARK

US

DENMARK PRESS. 1883. Tue. $.50 newsstand; $20/yr. in state; $25/yr. out of state. 138 Main St., Denmark, WI 54208. TEL 414-863-2154; FAX 414-863-6102. **Owner(s):** Frank Wood, P.O. Box 610, Denmark, WI 54208. TEL 414-863-2154; FAX 414-863-6102; Pub. Frank Wood; adv.; photos; pub. size: tabloid; circ. 2,700(paid).

DE PERE

US   ISSN 0748-6219

DE PERE JOURNAL. 1871. Thu. $.50 newsstand; $14/yr. local carrier. 126 S. Broadway, De Pere, WI 54115-0188. TEL 414-336-4221. **Owner(s):** Journal Publishing Co., 126 S. Broadway, De Pere, WI 54115. TEL 414-336-4221; Ed. Marie S. Creviere; Pub. Paul J. Creviere, Sr.; adv.; photos; pub. size: broadsheet; circ. 3,895(paid).

DODGEVILLE

US

DODGEVILLE CHRONICLE, INC. 1862. Thu. $.50 newsstand; $21/yr. mailed. 106 W. Merrimac St., Dodgeville, WI 53533-0095. TEL 608-935-2331; FAX 608-935-9531. **Owner(s):** Reilly & Reilly, Inc., P.O. Box 96, Dodgeville, WI 53533. TEL 608-935-2331; FAX 608-935-9531; Ed. J. Patrick Reilly; Pub. Pat Reilly; adv. contact: Todd Novak. photos; bk.rev.; pub. size: broadsheet; circ. 5,600(paid).

DURAND

US

COURIER-WEDGE. 1861. Thu. $.50 newsstand; $21/yr. in cy. 103 W. Main St., Durand, WI 54736. TEL 715-672-4252; FAX 715-672-4254. **Owner(s):** Gary Stumpf, 200 Main St., Wabasha, MN 55981; Ed. Mary Trettin; Pub. Gary Stumpf; pub. size: broadsheet; circ. 4,300(paid).
   Formerly: Durand Courier-Wedge.

EAGLE RIVER

US

VILAS COUNTY NEWS-REVIEW. 1886. Wed. $1 newsstand; $32/yr. local; $36/yr. in state; $44/yr. out of state. 346 W. Division St., Eagle River, WI 54521-1929. TEL 715-479-4421; FAX 715-479-6242. **Owner(s):** Delphos Newspapers, 405 N. Main St., Delphos, OH 45833. TEL 419-692-5050; Ed. Kurt Krueger; Pub. Byron McNutt; adv.; photos; pub. size: broadsheet; circ. 10,250(paid).

EAST TROY

US   ISSN 0749-5943

EAST TROY NEWS. 1893. w. $.75 newsstand; $14.35/yr. 2100 Church St., East Troy, WI 53120. TEL 414-642-7451; FAX 414-763-2238. **Owner(s):** Zimmermann & Sons, Inc., P.O. Box 47, East Troy, WI 53120. TEL 414-642-7451; Pub. Robert Branen; adv. contact: David Wright. pub. size: tabloid; circ. 2,344(paid).

EDGERTON

US

EDGERTON REPORTER. 1923. Wed. $.75 newsstand; $22/yr. in cy.; $23/yr. out of cy.; $25/yr. out of state. 21 N. Henry St., Edgerton WI 53534. TEL 608-884-3367. **Owner(s):** The Reporter Co., Inc., 21 N. Henry St., Edgerton, WI 53534. TEL 608-884-3367; Ed. Helen Everson; Pub. Helen Everson; pub. size: broadsheet; circ. 3,812(paid).

ELKHORN

US   ISSN 1076-4569

ELKHORN INDEPENDENT. 1853. Wed. $.75 newsstand; $25.50/yr. in area; $27/yr. in surrounding cys.; $30/yr. in state; $19.50 senior rate. 11 W. Walworth St., Elkhorn, WI 53121. TEL 414-723-2250; FAX 414-723-7424. **Owner(s):** Southern Lakes Media, Inc., WI; Ed. Nancy Jacobson; Pub. Robert Brannen; adv. contact: Scott Johnson. pub. size: broadsheet; circ. 5,500(controlled & paid).

ELLSWORTH

US

PIERCE COUNTY HERALD. 1867. Wed. $.75 newsstand; $25/yr. in cy.; $40/yr. out of cy. 126 S. Chestnut St., Ellsworth, WI 54011. TEL 715-273-4334; FAX 715-273-4335. **Owner(s):** Western Wisconsin Publishing Co., 226 Locust, Hudson, WI 54016. TEL 715-386-9333; Ed. Bill Kirk; Pub. Steve Dzubay; adv. contact: Robin Kruse. photos; pub. size: standard; circ. 4,500(paid).

ELROY

US

KEYSTONE TRIBUNE. Thu. $.50 newsstand; $20/yr. in cy.; $22/yr. out of cy. 249 Main St., Elroy, WI 53929. TEL 608-462-8224; FAX 608-462-5678. **Owner(s):** South Central Wisconsin Newspapers, Inc., P.O. Box 470, Portage, WI 53901. TEL 608-742-2111; Ed. Bill Smith; Pub. John Burgess; adv. contact: Sharon Tyler. pub. size: tabloid; circ. 2,242(paid).

US

WONEWOC REPORTER. Wed. & Sat. $.75 newsstand; $35/yr. 249 Main St., Elroy, WI 53929. TEL 608-462-8224; FAX 608-462-5678. **Owner(s):** South Central Wisconsin Newspapers Inc., 309 DeWitt St., Portage, WI 53901. TEL 608-742-2111; Ed. Bill Smith. adv. contact: Sharon Tyler. pub. size: tabloid; circ. 2,000(paid).

FENNIMORE

US

FENNIMORE TIMES. 1881. Thu. $18/yr. 1150 Lincoln Ave., Fennimore, WI 53809. TEL 608-822-3912. **Owner(s):** William S. Hale, 1196 Lincoln Ave., Fennimore, WI 53809. TEL 608-723-2151; Ed. Matthew Johnson; Pub. William S. Hale; pub. size: broadsheet; circ. 2,000(paid).

FITCHBURG

US

FITCHBURG STAR. 1974. Thu. $.50 newsstand; $28/yr. 2934 Fish Hatchery Rd., Ste. 226, Fitchburg, WI 53713. TEL 608-273-3576. **Owner(s):** Henry W. Schroeder, 2752 Cross Country Cir., Verona, WI 53593. TEL 608-845-9559; Pub. Henry W. Schroeder; adv. contact: Chuck Nowles. pub. size: tabloid; circ. 100,000(paid).

FLORENCE

US

FLORENCE MINING NEWS. 1880. Wed. $.60 newsstand; $23/yr. in area; $26/yr. surrounding cys.; $29/yr. out cy. 140 Florence Ave., Florence, WI 54121. TEL 715-696-3400; FAX 715-528-4986. **Owner(s):** Nancy Gomez & Margie Yadro, 140 Florence Ave., Florence, WI 54121. TEL 715-528-3276; Ed. Nancy Gomez; Pub. Nancy Gomez; adv.; photos; pub. size: tabloid; circ. 2,200(paid).

FOND DU LAC

US

ACTION ADVERTISER. 1970. s-w.: Sun. & Wed. free newsstand; $59/yr. mailed. 6637 N. Rolling Meadows Dr., Fond Du Lac, WI 54935-9452. TEL 414-922-8640; FAX 414-922-0125. **Owner(s):** James Carew, 6637 N. Rolling Meadows Dr., Fond Du Lac, WI 54937. TEL 414-922-8640; Ed. Scott Witchow; Pub. Robert Carew; adv. contact: Paul Krasin. pub. size: tabloid; circ. 34,000(free & paid).

FREDERIC

US

INDIANHEAD ADVERTISER. Mon. free. 303 N. Wisconsin Ave., Frederic, WI 54837. TEL 715-327-4236; FAX 715-327-4870. **Owner(s):** Inter-County Cooperative Publishing Association, P.O. Box 490, Frederic, WI 54837. TEL 715-327-4236; adv.; pub. size: tabloid; circ. 18,200(free).

US

INTER-COUNTY LEADER. 1933. Wed. $.75 newsstand; $18/yr. mailed in cy.; $19/yr. out of cy.; $21/yr. elsewhere. 303 N. Wisconsin Ave., Frederic, WI 54837. TEL 715-327-4236; FAX 715-327-4870. **Owner(s):** Inter-County Cooperative Publishing Association, P.O. Box 490, Frederic, WI 54837. TEL 715-327-4236; Ed. Gary King; Pub. Doug Panek; adv. contact: Wayne Boniface. pub. size: tabloid; circ. 5,000(paid). **Formerly:** Frederic Inter-County Leader.

GALESVILLE

US

GALESVILLE REPUBLICAN. 1874. Wed. $20/yr. in cy.; $25/yr. out of cy.; $35/yr. out of state. 19852 Court Ave., Galesville, WI 54630-0695. TEL 608-582-2330. **Owner(s):** John P. Graf, 139 S. Davis, Galesville, WI 54630. TEL 608-582-2330; Pub. John P. Graf; pub. size: tabloid; circ. 1,875(paid).

GAY MILLS

US

CRAWFORD COUNTY INDEPENDENT-KICKAPOO SCOUT. Thu. $.50 newsstand; $17/yr. in state; $24/yr. out of state. Rebecca St., Gay Mills, WI 54631. TEL 608-375-4458. **Owner(s):** Kirkland Newspapers, Inc., Durham, NC 22701; Ed. David Kirer. adv. contact: Bonnie Olson. pub. size: broadsheet; circ. 2,600(paid).

GLENWOOD CITY

US

TRIBUNE PRESS REPORTER. 1889. Wed. $.50 newsstand; $18/yr. 217 Oak St., Glenwood City, WI 54013-0038. TEL 715-265-4646; FAX 715-265-7496. **Owner(s):** Carlton DeWitt, 215 Oak St., Glenwood City, WI 54013. TEL 715-265-4646; FAX 715-265-7496; Pub. Carlton DeWitt; adv. contact: Shawn DeWitt. photos; pub. size: broadsheet; circ. 2,800(paid).

GLIDDEN

US

GLIDDEN ENTERPRISE. 1906. Wed. $.50 newsstand; $18/yr. in cy.; $21/yr. out of cy. P.O. Box 128, Glidden, WI 54527. TEL 715-264-3481. **Owner(s):** Glidden Enterprises, Inc., P.O. Box 128, Glidden, WI 54527. TEL 715-264-3481; Ed. Matthew Hart; Pub. Matthew Hart; adv.; pub. size: broadsheet; circ. 1,450(paid).

GRANTSBURG

US

BURNETT COUNTY SENTINEL. 1962. Wed. $1 newsstand; $25/yr. in state; $32/yr. out of state. 114 Madison Ave., Grantsburg, WI 54840-0397. TEL 715-463-2341. **Owner(s):** Mainstream Publications, 114 Madison Ave., Grantsburg, WI 54840. TEL 715-463-2341; Pub. Byron Higgin; adv. contact: Sandy Eng. pub. size: broadsheet; circ. 4,500(paid). **Wire Service(s):** AP.

GREEN LAKE

US

GREEN LAKE COUNTY REPORTER. 1900. Thu. $.75 newsstand; $24/yr. local; $42/yr. in state; $55/yr. out of state. 535 Mill, Green Lake, WI 54941. TEL 414-361-1515; FAX 414-361-1518. **Owner(s):** R.M. Gonyo, 135 E. Moore, Berlin, WI 54923. TEL 414-316-0377; Ed. Jim Wolff; Pub. R.M. Gonyo; circ. 1,350(paid).

HAMMOND

US

CENTRAL SAINT CROIX NEWS. 1873. Wed. $.50 newsstand; $15/yr. in cy.; $18/yr. out of cy. 815 Davis St., Hammond, WI 54015. TEL 715-796-2355. **Owner(s):** Barbara & Robert Gardner, P.O. Box 206, Hammond, WI 54015. TEL 715-796-2355; Ed. Barbara Gardner; Pub. Barbara Gardner; adv.; photos; bk.rev.; pub. size: broadsheet; circ. 1,215(paid).

HARTFORD

US

TIMES-PRESS. 1876. Thu. $.50 newsstand; $18/yr. home deliv. & mailed. 225 N. Main St., Hartford, WI 53027. TEL 414-673-3500; FAX 414-673-5260. **Owner(s):** John McLoone, 225 N. Main St., Hartford, WI 53027. TEL 414-673-3500; Ed. John McLoone; Pub. John McLoone; adv. contact: Ken Ubert. pub. size: tabloid; circ. 7,100(paid). **Formerly:** Hartford Times-Press.

HARTLAND

US

KETTLE MORAINE INDEX. 1942. Thu. $19.20/yr. in cy.; $22.10/yr. out of cy.; $25.75/yr. out of state. 440 Cardinal Ln., Hartland, WI 53029. TEL 414-367-3272; FAX 414-367-7414; E-mail: lake@mke.follfeed.com. **Owner(s):** Add, Inc., 600 Industrial Dr., Waupaca, WI 54981. TEL 715-258-8450; Ed. Scott Peterson. adv.; photos; pub. size: tabloid; circ. 1,725(paid).

US

LAKE COUNTRY REPORTER. 1960. s-w.: Tue. & Thu. $.50 newsstand; $27.75/yr. in cy.; $33.60/yr. in state; $38.85/yr. out of state. 440 Cardinal Ln., Hartland, WI 53029. TEL 414-367-3272; FAX 414-367-7414. **Owner(s):** Add, Inc., 600 Industrial Dr., P.O. Box 609, Waupaca, WI 54981. TEL 715-258-8450; Ed. Scott Peterson; Pub. Gary Jasiek; adv. contact: Jody Medinger. pub. size: tabloid; circ. 8,011(paid).

US   ISSN 1064-2102

SUSSEX SUN. 1963. Tue. $.50 newsstand; $19.20/yr. in cy.; $22.10/yr. out of cy.; $25.75/yr. out of state. 440 Cardinal Ln., Hartland, WI 53029. TEL 414-367-3272; FAX 414-367-7414. **Owner(s):** Add, Inc., 600 Industrial Dr., Waupaca, WI 54981. TEL 715-258-8450; Ed. Scott Peterson. pub. size: tabloid; circ. 2,800(paid).

HAYWARD

US

SAWYER COUNTY RECORD. 1893. Wed. $.75
newsstand; $29/yr. mailed locally; $45/yr. out of
area. 220 W. First St., Hayward, WI 54843.
TEL 715-634-4881; FAX 715-634-8191.
Owner(s): Northwest Wisconsin Media, Inc., 220
First St., Hayward, WI 54843. TEL
715-634-4881; Ed. Kris Sorensen; Pub. Gary
Pennington; adv. contact: Gary Pennington. pub.
size: broadsheet; circ. 7,000(paid).

HILLSBORO

US   ISSN 0749-7016

HILLSBORO SENTRY-ENTERPRISE. 1885. Thu. $.60
newsstand; $20/yr. in area; $24/yr. in state;
$30/yr. out of state. 839 Water Ave., Hillsboro,
WI 54634. TEL 608-489-2264;
FAX 608-489-2348. **Owner(s):** Jack Knowles,
P.O. Box 469, Hillsboro, WI 54634. TEL
608-489-2264; Ed. Jack Knowles; Pub. Jack
Knowles; adv. contact: Kelli Mitchell. photos;
bk.rev.; pub. size: tabloid; circ. 2,200(controlled &
paid).

HORICON

US   ISSN 1053-9972

HORICON REPORTER. 1883. Thu. $.50 newsstand;
$18/yr. in cy.; $19/yr. out of cy.; $19/yr. out of
state. 319 E. Lake St., Horicon, WI 53032.
TEL 414-485-2016; FAX 414-485-4820.
Owner(s): Wisconsin Free Press, Inc., 126 Bridge
St., Mayville, WI 53050; Ed. Edward J. Zagorski
III; Pub. Andrew Johnson; adv. contact: Tina
Stambough. photos; bk.rev.; pub. size: broadsheet;
circ. 2,100(paid).

HUDSON

US   ISSN 0749-7008

HUDSON STAR-OBSERVER. 1854. Wed. $1
newsstand; $32/yr. carrier. 226 Locust St.,
Hudson, WI 54016-0147. TEL 715-386-9333;
FAX 715-386-9891. **Owner(s):** Star-Observer
Publishing Co., 226 Locust St., Hudson, WI
54016-0147. TEL 715-386-9333; FAX
715-386-9891; Ed. Robert Zientara; Pub. Steve
Dzubay; adv. contact: Robin Kavitz. photos; pub.
size: broadsheet; circ. 5,600(paid). **Wire
Service(s):** AP.

HURLEY

US

IRON COUNTY MINER. 1885. Thu. $.50 newsstand;
$24/yr. 216 Copper, Hurley, WI 54534.
TEL 715-561-3405; FAX 715-561-3799.
Owner(s): Iron County Miner, 216 Copper,
Hurley, WI 54534; Ed. H.M. Moore. adv.; photos;
pub. size: broadsheet; circ. 3,000(paid).

INDEPENDENCE

US

INDEPENDENCE NEWS-WAVE. 1878. Wed. $18/yr. in
cy.; $20/yr. out of cy.; $22/yr. elsewhere.
23703 Washington St., Independence, WI 54747.
TEL 715-985-3815; FAX 715-985-9330.
Owner(s): O.J. Evenson, P.O. Box 47,
Independence, WI 54747. TEL 715-985-3815;
Pub. O.J. Evenson; adv. contact: O.J. Evenson.
pub. size: broadsheet; circ. 1,150(paid).

IOLA

US   ISSN 0886-8360

IOLA HERALD. 1891. Thu. $.75 newsstand; $20/yr.
local; $24/yr. out of area. 165 N. Main St., Iola,
WI 54945-0235. TEL 715-445-3415;
FAX 715-445-3988. **Owner(s):** Trey & Mary
Foerster, P.O. Box 235, Iola, WI 54945. TEL
715-445-3415; FAX 715-445-3988; Pub. Trey
Foerster; adv. contact: Trey Foerster. photos; pub.
size: tabloid; circ. 1,300(paid).

JUNEAU

US

DODGE COUNTY INDEPENDENT-NEWS. 1893. Thu.
$.50 newsstand; $17/yr. local. 122 S. Main St.,
Juneau, WI 53039. TEL 414-386-2421;
FAX 414-386-2421. **Owner(s):** Independent
Publishing Corp., 122 S. Main St., Juneau, WI
53039. TEL 414-386-2421; Ed. Bonnie
Fitzgerald; Pub. Scott Fitzgerald; adv. contact: Joe
Hartzeim. photos; pub. size: broadsheet; circ.
2,100(paid).

KAUKAUNA

US

KAUKAUNA TIMES. 1880. s-w.: Tue. & Thu. $.30
newsstand; $18/yr. home deliv.; $24/yr. mailed
in WI. 1900 Crooks Ave., Kaukauna, WI
54130-0109. TEL 414-766-4651;
FAX 414-766-4736. **Owner(s):** James W. Lang,
1900 Crooks Ave., Kaukauna, WI 54130. TEL
414-766-4651; FAX 414-766-4736; Glenn P. &
Lyle J. Hansen, 1900 Crooks Ave., Kaukauna, WI
54130-0109. TEL 414-766-4651; FAX
414-766-4736; Ed. Joyce Schubring. adv.
contact: George Kailhofer. pub. size: broadsheet;
circ. 6,800(free & paid).

KENOSHA

US

BULLETIN, THE. 1981. Mon. free. 715 58th St.,
Lower Level, Kenosha, WI 53140.
TEL 414-656-1101; FAX 414-656-1255.
Owner(s): United Communications, Inc., 715
58th St., Kenosha, WI 53140. TEL
414-657-1000; Ed. Darren Hillock. adv.; photos;
pub. size: tabloid; circ. 108,500(free).

KEWASKUM

US

KEWASKUM STATESMAN. 1895. Thu. $.40
newsstand; $19/yr. in state; $22/yr. out of state.
250 Main St., Kewaskum, WI 53040.
TEL 414-626-2626; FAX 414-626-2626.
Owner(s): Lana Kuehl, 250 Main St., Kewaskum,
WI 53040. TEL 414-626-3312; FAX
414-626-2626; Ed. Lana Kuehl. adv.; photos;
bk.rev.; pub. size: standard; circ. 3,500(paid).

KEWAUNEE

US

KEWAUNEE ENTERPRISE. 1859. Wed. $.50
newsstand; $20/yr. in cy.; $25/yr. out of cy.
206 Ellis St., Kewaunee, WI 54216.
TEL 414-388-3175; FAX 414-388-0609.
Owner(s): Brown County Publishing Co.,
Denmark, WI 52503; Pub. Frank Wood; adv.
contact: Gayle Barrett. photos; pub. size:
broadsheet; circ. 2,650(paid).

KIEL

US

KIEL TRI-COUNTY RECORD. 1893. Thu. $17/yr. in
tri-county; $25/yr. out of cy.; $35/yr. out of
state. 705 Seventh St., Kiel, WI 53042.
TEL 414-894-2828; FAX 414-894-2161.
Owner(s): Delta Publications Co., Inc., P.O. Box 7,
Kiel, WI 53042. TEL 414-894-2828; Pub. Mike
Mathes; adv. contact: Joe Mathes. pub. size:
tabloid circ. 2,063(paid).

LADYSMITH

US

LADYSMITH NEWS. 1895. Thu. $.75 newsstand;
$23/yr. in surrounding cys. $29/yr. elsewhere.
120 W. Third St., S., Ladysmith, WI 54848.
TEL 715-532-5591. **Owner(s):** Donald L. Bell,
P.O. Box 189, Ladysmith, WI 54848. TEL
715-532-5591; Thomas D. & James L. Bell, P.O.
Box 189, Ladysmith, WI 54848. TEL
715-532-5591; Michael D. & Audrey M. Bell,
P.O. Box 189, Ladysmith, WI 54848. TEL
715-532-5591; Ed. John N. Terrill; Pub. Thomas
D. Bell. adv. contact: Christine Bell. pub. size:
broadsheet; circ. 5,700(paid).

LAKE GENEVA

US

LAKE GENEVA REGIONAL NEWS. 1873. Thu. $.50
newsstand; $20/yr. mailed in cy.; $25/yr. in
state; $35/yr. elsewhere. 315 Broad St., Lake
Geneva, WI 53147. TEL 414-248-4444;
FAX 414-248-4476. **Owner(s):** D.W. Bearder,
315 Broad St., Lake Geneva, WI 53147. TEL
414-248-4444; Pub. Donald W. Bearder; adv.
contact: Donald W. Bearder. pub. size: standard;
circ. 7,000(paid).

LAKE MILLS

US

LAKE MILLS LEADER. 1878. w. $.50 newsstand;
$20/yr. 322 N. Main St., Lake Mills, WI 53551.
TEL 414-648-2334; FAX 414-648-8187.
Owner(s): Dennis Hawkes, 322 N. Main, Lake
Mills, WI 53551. TEL 414-648-2334; Pub.
Dennis Hawkes; adv. contact: Arlys Hawkes.
photos; pub. size: broadsheet; circ. 3,200(paid).

LANCASTER

US

GRANT COUNTY HERALD INDEPENDENT. 1843. Thu.
$.75 newsstand; $26/yr. in cy.; $23/yr. out of
cy.; $35/yr. out of state. 208 W. Cherry,
Lancaster, WI 53813-0310. TEL 608-723-2151.
Owner(s): Lancaster Newspapers P.O. Box 310,
Lancaster, WI 53813. TEL 608-723-2151; Ed.
John D. Ingebritsen; Pub. W.S. Hale; adv. contact:
Kevin Kelly. pub. size: broadsheet. circ.
4,450(paid).

LODI

US

LODI ENTERPRISE. 1894. Thu. $27/yr. in cy.;
$33/yr. out of area. 146 S. Main St., Lodi, WI
53555. TEL 608-592-3261;
FAX 608-592-3866. **Owner(s):** Bill Haupt, P.O.
Box 16, Lodi, WI 53555. TEL 608-592-3261;
Pub. Bill Haupt; adv. contact: Mary Olson. pub.
size: broadsheet; circ. 2,400(paid).

LOYAL

US

LOYAL TRIBUNE-RECORD-GLEANER. 1894. Wed. $.75 newsstand; $24/yr. in state. 318 N. Main St., Loyal, WI 54446-0187. TEL 715-255-8531; FAX 715-255-8357. **Owner(s):** TRG, Inc., 318 N. Main, Loyal, WI 54446-0187. TEL 715-255-8357; Ed. Dean Lesar. adv.; pub. size: broadsheet; circ. 3,612(paid).

LUXEMBURG

US

LUXEMBURG NEWS. 1909. Wed. $.50 newsstand; $20/yr. in state; $25/yr. out of state. 406 Elm St., P.O. Box 130, Luxemburg, WI 54217-0130. TEL 414-845-2525; FAX 414-845-2525. **Owner(s):** Brown County Publishing Co., 138 Main St., Denmark, WI 54208; Ed. Lee Lawrenz. pub. size: broadsheet; circ. 1,100(paid).

MADISON

US   ISSN 1081-4043

ISTHMUS. 1976. w. $25/yr. 101 King St., Madison, WI 53703. TEL 608-251-5627; FAX 608-251-2165. **Owner(s):** Vincent O'Hern, 101 King St., Madison, WI 53703. TEL 608-251-5627; Ed. Marc Eisen; Pub. Vincent O'Hern; adv. contact: Linda Baldwin O'Hern. photos; bk.rev.; pub. size: tabloid; circ. 62,000(free & paid).

MANITOWOC

US

LAKESHORE CHRONICLE. 1972. Wed. & Sun. free home deliv.; $10 voluntary subscription. 909 S. 29th St., Manitowoc, WI 54220. TEL 414-682-5231; FAX 414-682-1804. **Owner(s):** Thomson Newspapers, Inc., 138 Main St., Chicago, IL 60652. TEL 414-863-2154; Ed. Debra Horn; Pub. John Clark; adv.; photos; pub. size: broadsheet; circ. 32,500(free). **Wire Service(s):** AP.

MARION

US

MARION ADVERTISER. 1895. Thu. $.50 newsstand; $17/yr. in surrounding cys.; $20/yr. in state; $22/yr. elsewhere. 109 N. Main, Marion, WI 54950. TEL 715-754-5444. **Owner(s):** Daniel S. Brandenburg, 109 N. Main, Marion, WI 54950. TEL 715-754-5444; Ed. Patsy Brandenburg; Pub. Daniel Brandenburg; pub. size: broadsheet; circ. 2,850(paid).

MARKESAN

US

HERALD, THE. 1881. w. $.75 newsstand; $21/yr. in state; $35/yr. out of state. 51 E. John St., Markesan, WI 53946. TEL 414-398-2334; FAX 414-398-3835. **Owner(s):** Citizen Publishing Co., 51 E. John St., Markesan, WI 53946. TEL 414-398-2334; FAX 414-398-2334; Pub. Marshall Bernhagen; adv. contact: Matt Gorsuch. pub. size: tabloid; circ. 1,831(free & paid).

MAUSTON

US

BUYER'S GUIDE CENT SAVER. Sat. free. 500 La Crosse St., Mauston, WI 53948. TEL 608-847-6224; FAX 608-847-5457. **Owner(s):** South Central Wisconsin Newspapers, Inc., P.O. Box 470, Portage, WI 53901. TEL 608-742-2111; Pub. David Gentry; adv. contact: Ed Miller. pub. size: tabloid; circ. 15,263(free).

US

JUNEAU COUNTY STAR-TIMES. s-w. Wed. & Sat. $.75 newsstand; $37/yr. in cy.; $39/yr. out of cy.; $50/yr. out of state. 500 La Crosse St., Mauston, WI 53948. TEL 608-847-6224; FAX 608-847-5457. **Owner(s):** South Central Wisconsin Newspapers, Inc., P.O. Box 470, Portage, WI 53901. TEL 608-742-2111; Ed. Pat Peckham; Pub. David Gentry; adv. contact: Timothy Benson. pub. size: tabloid; circ. 5,000(paid).

MAYVILLE

US

MAYVILLE NEWS. 1892. Thu. $.50 newsstand; $18/yr. 126 Bridge St., Mayville, WI 53050. TEL 414-387-2211; FAX 414-337-5515. **Owner(s):** Andrew Johnson, P.O. Box 271, Mayville, WI 53050. TEL 414-387-5515; Ed. Ken Thomas; Pub. Andrew Johnson; pub. size: broadsheet; circ. 4,333(paid).

MEDFORD

US

STAR NEWS, THE. 1875. Wed. $1 newsstand; $27.50/yr. in cy.; $31/yr. in state; $40/yr. out of state. 116 S. Wisconsin Ave., Medford, WI 54451. TEL 715-748-2626; FAX 715-748-2299. **Owner(s):** Jay O'Leary, P.O. Box 180, Medford, WI 54451. TEL 713-748-2626; Ed. Don Woerpel; Pub. Jay O'Leary; pub. size: tabloid; circ. 6,900(paid). Formerly: Medford Star News.

MELROSE

US

MELROSE CHRONICLE. 1895. Wed. $.75 newsstand; $26/yr. in state; $35/yr. out of state. P.O. Box 8, Melrose, WI 54642. TEL 608-488-3201; FAX 608-488-7851. **Owner(s):** Tom Besl, P.O. Box 8, Melrose, WI 54642. TEL 608-488-3201; Pub. Tom Besl; adv.; pub. size: tabloid; circ. 4,200(paid).

MENOMONIE

US

DUNN COUNTY NEWS. 1860. s-w.: Wed. & Sun. $.75 newsstand; $42/yr. in cy.; $56/yr. in state; $63/yr. out of state. 710 Main St., Menomonie, WI 54751. TEL 715-235-3411; FAX 715-235-0936. **Owner(s):** Independent Media Group, 321 Frenette, Chippewa Falls, WI 54729; Ed. Peg Zaemisch; Pub. Jules Molenda; adv. contact: Denny Boduh. photos; bk.rev.; pub. size: broadsheet; circ. Sun. 5,000(paid).

MERRILL

US   ISSN 0191-8958

FOTO NEWS. 1953. Wed. free newsstand; $.25 at office; $30/yr. mailed in US. 805 E. Main St., Merrill, WI 54452. TEL 715-536-7121. **Owner(s):** James O'Day, 805 E. Main St., Merrill, WI 54452. TEL 715-536-7121; Ed. Lauree O'Day; Pub. L. James O'Day; adv.; photos; pub. size: tabloid; circ. 17,100(paid).

MERRIMAC

US

SHOPPER STOPPER. 1970. Tue. free. 327 Palisade St., Merrimac, WI 53561. TEL 608-493-2291; FAX 608-493-2074. **Owner(s):** Shopper Stopper, Inc., 327 Palisade St., Merrimac, WI 53561. TEL 608-493-2291; FAX 608-493-2074; adv.; pub. size: tabloid; circ. 127,000(free).

MIDDLETON

US

MIDDLETON TIMES-TRIBUNE. 1893. Thu. $.75 newsstand; $29/yr. mailed in state; $44/yr. mailed out of state. 7507 Hubbard Ave., Ste. 102, Middleton, WI 53562. TEL 608-836-1601; FAX 608-836-3759. **Owner(s):** News Publishing Co., 1126 Mill St., Black Earth, WI 53515. TEL 608-767-3655; Ed. Mike Keeney. adv. contact: Candy Tracy. pub. size: broadsheet; circ. 2,575(paid).

MILTON

US

MILTON COURIER. 1879. Wed. $.50 newsstand; $17/yr. in state; $20/yr. out of state. 513 Vernal, Milton, WI 53563. TEL 608-868-2442; FAX 608-869-4664. **Owner(s):** Hometown News, L.P., 28 W. Milwaukee Ave., Fort Atkinson, WI 53538. TEL 414-563-5551; Pub. Brian Knox; adv. contact: Doug Welch. pub. size: tabloid; circ. 3,000(paid).

MILWAUKEE

US

BARGAIN EXPRESS NEWSPAPER. 1980. Tue. free home deliv. 10001 W. Lisbon Ave., Milwaukee, WI 53222. TEL 414-466-3933. **Owner(s):** Ads Express Publications, 10001 W. Lisbon Ave., Milwaukee, WI 53222. TEL 414-466-3933; pub. size: tabloid; circ. 162,000(free).

US

MILWAUKEE STAR. 1960. Thu. free; $12.50/yr. 3815 N. Teutonia Ave., Milwaukee, WI 53206. TEL 414-449-4870; FAX 414-449-4872. **Owner(s):** Jerrel Jones, P.O. Box 06279 St., Milwaukee, WI 53206. TEL 414-449-4870; Ed. Walter Jones; Pub. Carole Geary; adv. contact: Faithe Colas. pub. size: tabloid; circ. 5,000(free).

MINERAL POINT

US

DEMOCRAT TRIBUNE, THE. 1892. Thu. $15/yr. in state; $18/yr. out of state. 334 High St., Mineral Point, WI 53565. TEL 608-987-2141. **Owner(s):** T. Michael Reilly & J. Patrick Reilly. 334 High St., Mineral Point, WI 53565. TEL 608-987-2141; Ed. Jeanie Lewis; Pub. T. Michael Reilly; adv. contact: Mike Reilly. pub. size: tabloid; circ. 1,196(paid).

MINOCQUA

US   ISSN 0746-4274

LAKELAND TIMES. 1891. s-w.: Tue. & Fri. $.75 newsstand; $31/yr. in cy.; $40/yr. out of cy. Chippewa & Milwaukee Sts., Minocqua, WI 54548. TEL 715-356-5236; FAX 715-358-2121. **Owner(s):** Lakeland Printing Co., P.O. Box 790, Minocqua, WI 54548. TEL 715-356-5236; Pub. Don Walker; adv.; photos; pub. size: tabloid; circ. 10,500(paid).

MONDOVI

US

MONDOVI HERALD NEWS. 1900. Thu. $18/yr. in cy.; $21/yr. out of cy.; $25/yr. out of state. 123 W. Main St., Mondovi, WI 54755. TEL 715-926-4970; FAX 715-926-4928. **Owner(s):** Perry Nyseth, P.O. Box 67, Mondovi, WI 54755. TEL 715-926-4970; Pub. Perry Nyseth; adv. contact: Perry Nyseth. pub. size: standard; circ. 3,500(paid).

MONONA

US   ISSN 0745-6646

COMMUNITY HERALD. 1968. Wed. $24/yr. 6041 Monona Dr., Monona, WI 53716. TEL 608-221-1544. **Owner(s):** Community Herald Newspapers Corp., 6041 Monona Dr., Monona, WI 53716. TEL 608-221-1544; Ed. Lisa Avellaya; Pub. Henry W. Schroeder; pub. size: tabloid; circ. 1,710(paid).

US   ISSN 0883-6566

MCFARLAND COMMUNITY LIFE. 1966. Thu. $.75 newsstand; $24/yr. 6041 Monona Dr., Monona, WI 53716. TEL 608-221-1544; FAX 608-221-0463. **Owner(s):** Community Herald Newspapers Corp., 6041 Monona Dr., Monona, WI 53716. TEL 608-221-1544; Pub. Henry W. Schroeder; pub. size: tabloid; circ. 1,629(paid).

US

MCFARLAND LEADER. 1993. Mon. free. 6041 Monona Dr., Monona, WI 53716. TEL 608-221-1544; FAX 608-221-0468. **Owner(s):** Community Herald Newspapers Corp., 6041 Monona Dr., Monona, WI 53716. TEL 608-221-1544; Pub. Henry W. Schroeder; pub. size: tabloid; circ. 5,500(free).

MONTELLO

US

MARQUETTE COUNTY TRIBUNE. 1859. Thu. $.50 newsstand; $17/yr. in state; $21/yr. out of state. 120 Underwood Ave., Montello, WI 53949. TEL 608-297-2424; FAX 608-297-9293. **Owner(s):** News Publishing Co., 1126 Mills St., Black Earth, WI 53515. TEL 608-767-3655; FAX 608-767-2222; Ed. Mary Faltz; Pub. Mark Witte; adv.; photos; pub. size: tabloid; circ. 4,500(free & paid).

MOSINEE

US   ISSN 0748-8297

MOSINEE TIMES, THE. 1895. Thu. $.35 newsstand; $14/yr. in cy.; $19/yr. in state; $21/yr. out of state. 407 Third St., Mosinee, WI 54455-1495. TEL 715-693-2300; FAX 715-693-1574. **Owner(s):** Mosinee Publishing Inc., 407 Third St., Mosinee, WI 54455-1495. TEL 715-693-2300; FAX 715-693-1574; Pub. John Durst; adv. contact: Jim Kress. pub. size: broadsheet; circ. 2,300(paid).

MUKWONAGO

US

MUKWONAGO CHIEF. 1889. Wed. $.50 newsstand; $22/yr. in cy. 555 Bay View Rd., Mukwonago, WI 53149-0204. TEL 414-363-4045; FAX 414-363-8573. **Owner(s):** Add, Inc., 600 Industrial Dr., Waupaca, WI 54891. TEL 715-258-8450; Ed. Jim Flaherty; Pub. Terri Blazek; adv. contact: Terri Blazek. pub. size: tabloid; circ. 4,500(controlled & paid).

NEILLSVILLE

US

CLARK COUNTY PRESS. 1989. Thu. $.75 newsstand; $26/yr. in cy.; 30/yr. out of cy.; $39/yr. elsewhere. 614 Hewitt, Neillsville, WI 54456. TEL 715-743-2600; FAX 715-743-5460. **Owner(s):** News Publishing Co., 1126 Mills St., Black Earth, WI 53515. TEL 715-743-2600; Pub. Dan Witte; adv. contact: Kathy Potter. photos; pub. size: tabloid; circ. 3,200(paid).

NEW HOLSTEIN

US

NEW HOLSTEIN REPORTER. 1905. Thu. $.75 newsstand; $20/yr. local cys.; $28/yr. in state; $38/yr. out of state. 2118 Wisconsin Ave., New Holstein, WI 53061. TEL 414-898-4276; FAX 414-894-2161. **Owner(s):** Mark Sherry, Mike Mathes & Joe Mathes, 1803 Park Ave., New Holstein, WI 53061. TEL 414-898-4276; Pub. Mark Sherry; adv. contact: Greg Fictum. pub. size: tabloid; circ. 2,200(paid).

NEW LONDON

US

PRESS-STAR. 1891. Fri. $.75 newsstand; $20/yr. in cy.; $26/yr. in state; $32/yr. out of state. 416 N. Water St., New London, WI 54961-0283. TEL 414-982-4321; FAX 414-982-7672. **Owner(s):** Add, Inc., 600 Industrial Dr., Waupaca, WI 54981. TEL 715-258-8450; Ed. Nancy Wieneke; Pub. William Melendes; adv. contact: William Melendes. pub. size: tabloid; circ. 2,630(free & paid).
  Formerly: New London Press-Star.

NEW RICHMOND

US

NEW RICHMOND NEWS. 1869. Thu. $1 newsstand; $30/yr. mailed in state; $37/yr. out of state. 127 S. Knowles Ave., New Richmond, WI 54017. TEL 715-246-6881; FAX 715-246-7117. **Owner(s):** Robert Bradford, 127 S. Knowles Ave., New Richmond, WI 54017. TEL 715-246-6881; Ed. Linda Peterson; Pub. Michael Burke; adv. contact: Rene Findlay. pub. size: broadsheet; circ. 5,000(paid).

OCONOMOWOC

US

OCONOMOWOC ENTERPRISE. 1888. Wed. $.50 newsstand; $20/yr. in city; $35/yr. out of city. 212 E. Wisconsin Ave., Oconomowoc, WI 53066. TEL 414-567-5511; FAX 414-567-4422. **Owner(s):** Thomson Newspapers, Inc., 3150 Des Plaines Ave., Des Plaines, IL 60018. TEL 847-299-5544; Ed. Pat Walker; Pub. Steve Jahn; adv. contact: Jan Gust. photos; pub. size: broadsheet; circ. 8,000(paid).

OCONTO FALLS

US

OCONTO COUNTY TIMES-HERALD. 1890. Wed. $.50 newsstand; $20/yr. 107 S. Main St., Oconto Falls, WI 54154-0128. TEL 414-846-3427; FAX 414-846-3430. **Owner(s):** Roger F. Shellman, 107 S. Main St., Oconto Falls, WI 54154-0128. TEL 414-846-3427; FAX 414-846-3430; Ed. Roger F. Shellman; Pub. Roger F. Shellman; adv. contact: Gayle Smoot. photos; pub. size: broadsheet; circ. 5,500(controlled & paid).

OMRO

US

OMRO HERALD. 1895. Thu. $.75 newsstand; $24/yr. local; $42/yr. in state; $55/yr. out of state. 127 W. Main St., Omro, WI 54963. TEL 414-685-2707. **Owner(s):** R.M. Gonyo, 135 E. Moore, Berlin, WI 54923. TEL 414-316-0377; Berlin Journal Co., P.O. Box 502, Omro, WI 54963; Ed. Jim Wolff. pub. size: tabloid; circ. 1,125(paid).

OREGON

US

OREGON OBSERVER. 1844. Wed. $.75 newsstand; $28/yr. 845 Market St., Oregon, WI 53575. TEL 608-251-3252; FAX 608-251-0582. **Owner(s):** Henry W. Schroeder, 120 W. Vernona Ave., P.O. Box 6, Verona, WI 53575. TEL 608-251-3252; FAX 608-251-0582; Pub. Henry Schroeder; adv.; pub. size: tabloid; circ. 2,950(paid).

OSCEOLA

US

OSCEOLA SUN. 1897. w. $.50 newsstand; $15/yr. 108 Cascade St., Osceola, WI 54020-0248. TEL 715-294-2314; FAX 715-755-3314. **Owner(s):** Jeff & Julie Holmquist, 508 Cascade St., Osceola, WI 54020-0248. TEL 715-294-4580; Ed. Julie Holmquist; Pub. Jeff Holmquist; adv.; pub. size: broadsheet; circ. 2,000(paid).

OSHKOSH

US

OSHKOSH BUYERS GUIDE. 1937. s-w. Wed. & Sun. free newsstand & home deliv.; $1.25/copy mailed in US. 314 N. Koeller St., Oshkosh, WI 54901. TEL 414-235-1790; FAX 414-235-1833. **Owner(s):** Add, Inc., 600 Industrial Dr., Waupaca, WI 54981. TEL 715-258-8450; adv.; photos; pub. size: tabloid; circ. 32,000(free); Sun. 32,000(free).

OSSEO

US

TRI-COUNTY NEWS. 1900. Wed. 172 Omaha St., Osseo, WI 54758. TEL 715-597-3313; FAX 715-597-2705. **Owner(s):** Michael D. Jensen, P.O. Box 460, Osseo, WI 54758. TEL 715-597-3313; Pub. Michael D. Jensen; pub. size: standard; circ. 3,500(paid).
  Formerly: Osseo Tri-County News.

PARK FALLS

US

PARK FALLS HERALD. 1900. Thu. $.75 newsstand; $25/yr. in cy.; $30/yr. out of cy.; $35/yr. out of state. 259 Second Ave., N., Park Falls, WI 54552. TEL 715-762-4940. **Owner(s):** Bee Hive Press, Inc., P.O. Box 170, Phillips, WI 54555. TEL 715-339-3036; Ed. Kenneth Dischler; Pub. Kenneth Dischler; adv. contact: Wilma Thier. pub. size: tabloid; circ. 3,437(paid).

PESHTIGO

US

PESHTIGO TIMES. Wed. $.35 newsstand; $15/yr. in cy.; $25/yr. in state; $27/yr. out of state. 481 Maple Ave., Peshtigo, WI 54157. TEL 715-582-4541; FAX 715-582-4662. **Owner(s):** Pesch Publishing Co., Inc., P.O. Box 410, Peshtigo, WI 54157. TEL 715-582-4541; Ed. Leo Pesch; Pub. Mary Ann Gardon; adv. contact: Chuck Gardon. photos; pub. size: broadsheet; circ. 12,000(paid).

PHILLIPS

US

BEE, THE. 1884. Thu. $.75 newsstand; $25-$35/yr. 115 N. Lake, Phillips, WI 54555. TEL 715-339-3036; FAX 715-339-4300. **Owner(s):** Bee Hive Press, Inc., P.O. Box 170, Phillips, WI 54555. TEL 715-339-3036; Pub. T.L. Kempkes; adv. contact: J.P. Kempkes. photos; pub. size: tabloid; circ. 4,700(paid).

PLATTEVILLE

US

PLATTEVILLE JOURNAL. 1899. s-w.: Tue. & Thu. $.75 newsstand; $22/yr. in cy.; $29/yr. out of cy. 1190 U.S. Hwy. 151, Platteville, WI 53818. TEL 608-348-3006; FAX 608-348-3066. **Owner(s):** Richard Brockman, 855 N. Elm, Platteville, WI 53818. TEL 608-348-3006; Ed. Richard Brockman; Pub. Richard Brokman; adv.; pub. size: broadsheet; circ. 7,000(paid).

US

SHOPPING NEWS. 1950. Tue. free; $35/yr. out of area. 11 Means Dr., Platteville, WI 53818. TEL 608-348-2374; FAX 608-348-3388. **Owner(s):** Woodward Communications, Inc., P.O. Box 688, Dubuque, IA 52004. TEL 319-588-5611; Ed. George Louthain; Pub. George Louthain; adv. contact: Kathy Neumeister. pub. size: tabloid; circ. 37,877(free).

PLYMOUTH

US

REVIEW, THE. s-w.: Tue & Thu. $.75 newsstand; $28/yr. in cy.; $45/yr. out of cy. & state. 113 E. Mill St., Plymouth, WI 53073-1776. TEL 414-893-6411; FAX 414-893-5505. **Owner(s):** Wisconsin News Press Inc., 113 E. Mill St., Plymouth, WI 53073-1776. TEL 414-893-6411; FAX 414-893-5505; Ed. Emmett Feldner; Pub. Barry S. Johanson; adv. contact: Nancy Juskey. pub. size: broadsheet.

PORT WASHINGTON

US   ISSN 0749-7164

OZAUKEE PRESS. 1939. Thu. $1 newsstand; $26/yr. 125 E. Main St., Port Washington, WI 53074. TEL 414-284-3494; FAX 414-284-0067. **Owner(s):** Port Publications, 125 E. Main St., Port Washington, WI 53074. TEL 414-284-3494; FAX 414-284-0067; Ed. William Schanen Jr.; Pub. William Schanen Jr.; adv. contact: Ray Haverkamps. pub. size: tabloid; circ. 15,000(paid).

PRAIRIE DU CHIEN

US

COURIER PRESS. 1845. s-w.: Mon. & Wed. $37.50/yr. in area; $47.50/yr out of area. 132 S. Beaumont Rd., Prairie du Chien, WI 53821. TEL 608-326-2441; FAX 608-326-2443. **Owner(s):** Howe Printing Co., P.O. Box 149, Prairie du Chien, WI; Ed. William Howe; Pub. E.B. Howe; adv. contact: Gary J. Howe. photos; bk.rev.; pub. size: tabloid; circ. 13,500(controlled).

PRESCOTT

US

PRESCOTT JOURNAL. 1855. Thu. $22/yr. in cy.; $35/yr. elsewhere. 311 Dakota St., Prescott, WI 54021. TEL 715-262-5454; FAX 715-262-5474. **Owner(s):** Gary B. Rawn, 255 Lawrence St., Prescott, WI 54021. TEL 715-262-5454; Ed. Robert Herman; Pub. Gary B. Rawn; adv. contact: Rita Kemp. photos; bk.rev.; pub. size: standard; circ. 3,200(paid).

PRESQUE ISLE

US

NORTH STAR JOURNAL. 1976. Thu. $.65 newsstand; $27.50/yr. in state. 8378 Lake St., Presque Isle, WI 54557. TEL 715-686-2525; FAX 715-686-2080. **Owner(s):** Thomas Forster, 8378 Lake St., Presque Isle, WI 54557. TEL 715-686-2938; Ed. Thomas Forster; Pub. Thomas Forster; adv.; pub. size: tabloid; circ. 2,800(paid).

PRINCETON

US

PRINCETON TIMES-REPUBLIC. Thu. $.75 newsstand; $24/yr. local; $42/yr. in state; $55/yr. out of state. 439 W. Water, Princeton, WI 54968. TEL 414-295-6261; FAX 414-295-0110. **Owner(s):** R.M. Gonyo, 135 E. Moore, Berlin, WI 54923. TEL 414-361-0377; Ed. Jim Wolff; Pub. R.M. Gonyo; pub. size: broadsheet; circ. 1,475(paid).

RANDOLPH

US

ADVANCE, THE. 1883. w. $.75 newsstand; $17/yr. in state; $25/yr. out of state. 115 Williams St., Randolph, WI 53956. TEL 414-326-5151. **Owner(s):** Citizen Publishing Co., 805 Park Ave., Beaver Dam, WI 53956. TEL 414-887-0321; Ed. John Wiersma; Pub. Marshall Bernhagen; adv. contact: Francine Weatherwax. pub. size: tabloid; circ. 1,700(paid). **Wire Service(s):** AP.

RANDOM LAKE

US

SOUNDER, THE. 1918. Thu. $.50 newsstand; $13/yr. in state; $18/yr. out of state. 405 Second St., Random Lake, WI 53075-0346. TEL 414-994-9244; FAX 414-994-4817. **Owner(s):** Times Printing Co., Inc., 100 Industrial Dr., Random Lake, WI 53075-1636. TEL 414-994-4396; FAX 414-994-2088; Ed. Gary J. Feider. adv. contact: Gary J. Feider. photos; pub. size: tabloid; circ. 2,768(paid).

REEDSBURG

US

REEDSBURG TIMES-PRESS. 1860. s-w.: Wed. & Sat. $.60 newsstand; $22/yr. in cy.; $24/yr. out of cy. 117 S. Walnut St., Reedsburg, WI 53959. TEL 608-524-4336; FAX 608-524-4337. **Owner(s):** South Central Wisconsin Newspapers, Inc., P.O. Box 470, Portage, WI 53901. TEL 608-742-2111; Ed. Pete Margolis; Pub. David Gentry; adv. contact: Larry Crawford. pub. size: tabloid; circ. 4,400(paid).

RICE LAKE

US

RICE LAKE CHRONOTYPE. 1874. Wed. $20/yr. 28 S. Main St., Rice Lake, WI 54868. TEL 715-234-2121; FAX 715-234-5232. **Owner(s):** Chronotype Publishing, Inc., 28 S. Main St., Rice Lake, WI 54868. TEL 715-234-2121; Ed. Sam Finazzo; Pub. Warren Dorrance; pub. size: broadsheet; circ. 9,013(paid). **Wire Service(s):** AP Newsfinder.

RICHLAND CENTER

US

RICHLAND CENTER OBSERVER. 1854. Thu. $.60 newsstand; $16/yr. in state; $26/yr. out of state. 172 E. Court St., Richland Center, WI 53581. TEL 608-647-6141. **Owner(s):** Erik R. Olson, 172 E. Court St., P.O. Box 31, Richland Center, WI 53581. TEL 608-647-6141; Ed. Erik R. Olson; Pub. Erik R. Olson; adv. contact: Michael Lee. pub. size: tabloid; circ. 5,100(paid).

RIPON

US

FIVE COUNTY/BUYER'S GUIDE. Tue. free newsstand & home deliv.; $1/copy mailed out of area. 321 Watson St., Ripon, WI 54971. TEL 414-748-2848; FAX 414-748-2750. **Owner(s):** Add, Inc., P.O. Box 609, Waupaca, WI 54981. TEL 715-258-8450; Ed. David R. Schroeder; Pub. David R. Schroeder; pub. size: standard; circ. 21,500(free). **Formerly:** Five County Shopping News.

US   ISSN 0748-6863

RIPON COMMONWEALTH PRESS. 1864. Thu. $26/yr. in cy.; $32/yr. out of cy.; $39/yr. out of state. 656 Douglas St., Ripon, WI 54971. TEL 414-748-3017; FAX 414-748-3028. **Owner(s):** Ripon Community Publications, 646 Douglas St., P.O. Box 344, Ripon, WI 54971. TEL 414-748-3017; Pub. Tim Lyke; adv.; pub. size: broadsheet; circ. 3,700(paid).

RIVER FALLS

US

RIVER FALLS JOURNAL. 1854. Thu. $1 newsstand; $29/yr. in cy.; $51/yr. out of cy. 112 E. Walnut St., River Falls, WI 54022-0025. TEL 715-425-1561; FAX 715-425-5666. **Owner(s):** Arlin Albrecht, 112 E. Walnut St., River Falls, WI 54022. TEL 715-425-1561; Ed. Phil Pfuehler; Pub. Steve Dzubay; adv. contact: Paul Charbonneau. pub. size: standard; circ. 4,362(paid). **Wire Service(s):** AP Newsfinder, WNA.

SAUK CITY

US

SAUK-PRAIRIE STAR. 1844. Thu. $.75 newsstand; $24/yr. in state; $39/yr. out of state. 801 Water St., Sauk City, WI 53583. TEL 608-643-3444; FAX 608-643-4988. **Owner(s):** News Publishing Co., Black Earth, WI 53515; Ed. Dan Satran, Jr.; Pub. Dan Witte; adv. contact: Diane Baumgartner. pub. size: tabloid; circ. 3,000(paid).

SEYMOUR

US

TIMES-PRESS. 1886. Thu. $.50 newsstand; $20/yr. 205 N. Main St., Seymour, WI 54165-0128. TEL 414-833-2517. **Owner(s):** Journal-Sentinel, P.O. Box 661, Milwaukee, WI 53201. TEL 414-224-2115; Ed. Bettyann Kowalski. adv.; photos; bk.rev.; pub. size: tabloid; circ. 2,400(paid).

SHARON

US

SHARON REPORTER, THE. 1878. Wed. $.50 newsstand; $20/yr. in cy.; $24/yr. in state; $28/yr. in IL; $32/yr. other states. 213 Baldwin, Sharon, WI 53585-0508. TEL 414-736-4380; FAX 414-275-5259. **Owner(s):** Walworth Papers, 630 Kenosha St., Walworth, WI 53184. TEL 414-275-2166; FAX 414-275-5259; Ed. Mabel Jackson. adv.; pub. size: broadsheet; circ. 850(paid).

SHEBOYGAN

US

SHORELINE CHRONICLE. 1976. Tue. free. 614 N. Sixth St., Sheboygan, WI 53081. TEL 414-459-8820; FAX 414-459-7449. **Owner(s):** Thomson Newspapers, Inc., One Thorn Run Ctr., Ste. 500, 1187 Thorn Run Rd. Ext., Coraopolis, PA 15108. TEL 412-262-7870; Pub. Dennis Brooks; adv. contact: Larry Tuzinekewich. pub. size: tabloid; circ. 40,200(free).

SHEBOYGAN FALLS

US   ISSN 0897-4543

SHEBOYGAN FALLS NEWS. 1980. Wed. $.50 newsstand; $22/yr. in cy.; $35/yr. out cy. P.O. Box 183, Sheboygan Falls, WI 53085. TEL 414-467-6591; FAX 414-893-5505. **Owner(s):** Wisconsin News Press Inc., 113 E. Mill St., Plymouth, WI 53073; Ed. Sandra Kimball; Pub. Barry Johnson; adv. contact: Nancy Jusky. pub. size: broadsheet; circ. 2,200(paid).

SHELL LAKE

US   ISSN 8755-0520

WASHBURN COUNTY REGISTER. 1889. Thu. $.60 newsstand; $18.75/yr. in cy.; $29.50/yr. out of cy. 133 W. Fifth Ave., Shell Lake, WI 54871. TEL 715-468-2314; FAX 715-468-2314. **Owner(s):** Marc & Connie Parentau, P.O. Box 455, Shell Lake, WI 54871. TEL 715-468-2314; FAX 715-468-2314 Ed. Marc Parentau; Pub. Marc Parentau; adv. contact: Connie Parentau. photos; pub. size: tabloid; circ. 1,950(paid).

SPARTA

US

FOXXY SHOPPER. 1975. Tue. free newsstand; $55/yr. P.O. Box 526, Sparta, WI 54656. TEL 608-269-5054; FAX 608-269-1488. **Owner(s):** Lee Enterprises, Inc., 400 Putnam Bldg., 215 N. Main St., Davenport, IA 52801. TEL 312-383-2100; Ed. Lynn Schultz. pub. size: tabloid; circ. 74,000(paid).

US

MONROE COUNTY DEMOCRAT. 1859. Thu. $27/yr. in cy.; $30/yr. out o' cy.; $31 out of state. 114 W. Oak St., Sparta, WI 54656. TEL 608-269-3186; FAX 608-269-6876. **Owner(s):** Sparta Monroe County Publishers, Inc., P.O. Box 252, Sparta, WI 54656. TEL 608-269-3186; Ed. William Gleiss; Pub. William Gleiss; adv. contact: Jill Bisinger. photos; bk.rev.; pub. size: broadsheet; circ. 5,600(paid).

US

SPARTA HERALD. 1858. Mon. $.75 newsstand; $27/yr. locally mailed; $30/yr. in state; $37/yr. out of state. 114 W. Oak St., Sparta, WI 54656-0252. TEL 608-269-3186; FAX 608-269-6876. **Owner(s):** Sparta Monroe County Publishers, Inc., P.O. Box 252, Sparta, WI 54656. TEL 608-269-3186; Ed. Theodore C. Radde; Pub. Theodore C. Radde; adv.; pub. size: broadsheet; circ. 5,050(paid).

SPOONER

US   ISSN 8755-6995

SPOONER ADVOCATE. 1901. Thu. $.75 newsstand; $29/yr. in area; $44/yr. out of area. 509 Front St., Spooner, WI 54801. TEL 715-635-2181; FAX 715-635-2186. **Owner(s):** Northwest Wisconsin Media, Inc., P.O. Box 338, Spooner, WI 54801. TEL 715-635-2181; FAX 715-635-2186; Ed. William Thornley; Pub. Janet Krokson; adv. contact: Janet Krokson. photos; pub. size: broadsheet; circ. 5,039(paid).

SPRING VALLEY

US

ELMWOOD ARGUS. 1921. Wed. $.25 newsstand; $11/yr in cy.; $15/yr. out of cy. 216 S. McKay Ave., Spring Valley, WI 54767. TEL 715-778-4395. **Owner(s):** Duane Kelley, 216 S. McKay Ave., Spring Valley, WI 54767. TEL 715-778-4395; Ed. Duane Kelley; Pub. Duane Kelley; adv.; photos; pub. size: broadsheet; circ. 500(paid).

US

SPRING VALLEY SUN. 1921. Wed. $.25 newsstand; $11/yr in cy.; $15/yr. out of cy. 216 S. McKay Ave., Spring Valley, WI 54767. TEL 715-778-4395. **Owner(s):** Duane Kelley, 216 S. McKay Ave., Spring Valley, WI 54767. TEL 715-778-4395; Ed. Duane Kelley; Pub. Duane Kelley; adv.; photos; pub. size: tabloid; circ. 700(paid).

US

VALLEY VALUE SHOPPER. Tue. free. 216 S. McKay Ave., Spring Valley, WI 54767. TEL 715-778-4395. **Owner(s):** Duane Kelley, 216 S. McKay Ave., Spring Valley, WI 54767. TEL 715-778-4395; Ed. Duane Kelley; Pub. Duane Kelley; adv.: $4.50/SAU. pub. size: tabloid; circ. 2,000(controlled).

STANLEY

US

STANLEY REPUBLICAN. 1895. Thu. $18/yr. in area; $20/yr. in state; $27/yr. out of state. 131 E. First Ave., Stanley, WI 54768-0114. TEL 715-644-3319; FAX 715-644-5452. **Owner(s):** B.J. Fazendin, 131 E. First Ave., Stanley, WI 54768. TEL 715-644-3319; Ed. B.J. Fazendin. adv.; photos; pub. size: standard; circ. 2,500(paid).

STOUGHTON

US   ISSN 1049-0655

COURIER HUB. 1867. Thu. $.75 newsstand; $26.50/yr. in cy.; $35/yr. out of cy. 301 W. Main St., Stoughton, WI 53589-0577. TEL 608-873-6671; FAX 608-873-3473. **Owner(s):** Woodward Communications, Inc., P.O. Box 688, Dubuque, IA 52004-0688. TEL 319-588-5687; FAX 319-588-5739; Ed. Eric Neuwirth; Pub. Walt Handy; adv. contact: Mary Hanson. bk.rev.; pub. size: tabloid; circ. 4,374(paid).

STRATFORD

US

STRATFORD JOURNAL. 1914. Wed. $15/yr. local; $22.50/yr. in state; $30/yr. out of state. P.O. Box 5, Stratford, WI 54484. TEL 715-687-4112. **Owner(s):** Paul Hale, P.O. Box 5, Stratford, WI 54484. TEL 715-687-4112; Pub. Paul Hale; adv. contact: Paul Hale. adv.: $7.16/SAU. photos; pub. size: tabloid; circ. 750(paid).

STURGEON BAY

US   ISSN 0749-7180

DOOR COUNTY ADVOCATE. 1862. s-w.: Tue. & Fri. $.50 newsstand; $32/yr. home deliv.; $36/yr. mailed in state; $42/yr. out of state. 233 N. Third Ave., Sturgeon Bay, WI 54235-0130. TEL 414-743-3321; FAX 414-743-5817. **Owner(s):** Brown County Publishing Co., P.O. Box 278, Denmark, WI 54208. TEL 414-863-2154; Ed. Richard McCord; Pub. Frank A. Wood; adv.; photos; pub. size: broadsheet; circ. 15,384(free & paid).

Formerly: Sturgeon Bay Door County Advocate.

SUN PRAIRIE

US

COURIER, THE. 1870. Thu. $.50 newsstand; $20/yr. in cy.; $28/yr. out of cy. 114 Columbus St., Sun Prairie WI 53590-2243. TEL 608-478-2188; FAX 608-478-3618. **Owner(s):** Hometown News, L.P., 114 Columbus St., Sun Prairie, WI 53590. TEL 608-837-2521; Ed. Pam Chickoring. adv.; photos; pub. size: broadsheet; circ. 2,300(paid).

US

STAR, THE. 1877. Thu. $.60 newsstand; $22.50/yr. in cy.; $30.50/yr. out of cy. 114 Columbus St., Sun Prairie, WI 53590-2243. TEL 608-837-2521; FAX 608-825-4460. **Owner(s):** Hometown News, L.P., 114 Columbus St., Sun Prairie, WI 53590. TEL 608-837-2521; Ed. Chris Mertes. adv.; photos; pub. size: broadsheet; circ. 5,050(paid).

THORP

US   ISSN 0885-2375

THORP COURIER. 1883. Thu. $.50 newsstand; $16/yr. in cy.; $21/yr. out of cy.; $24/yr. out of state. 403 N. Washington, Thorp, WI 54771-0487. TEL 715-669-5525; FAX 715-669-5596. **Owner(s):** Thorp Courier Printing Publications, Inc., P.O. Box 487, Thorp, WI 54771. TEL 715-669-5525; Ed. Mark J. LaGasse; Pub. Mark J. LaGasse; adv.; pub. size: broadsheet; circ. 3,100(free & paid).

TOMAH

US

JOURNAL & MONITOR HERALD. 1867. s-w.: Mon. & Thu. $.75 newsstand; $27/yr. in cy.; $32/yr. in state; $40/yr. out of state. 1108 Superior Ave., Tomah, WI 54660-0190. TEL 608-372-4123; FAX 608-372-2791. **Owner(s):** John Kenny, 1108 Superior Ave., Tomah, WI 54660. TEL 608-372-4123; FAX 608-372-2791; Ed. John Froelich; Pub. John Kenny; adv.; pub. size: broadsheet; circ. 5,600(paid).

US

TOMAH JOURNAL. 1867. Thu. $.75 newsstand; $27/yr. in cy. mailed subscription incl. Tomah Monitor-Herald. 1108 Superior Ave., Tomah, WI 54660. TEL 608-372-4123; FAX 608-372-2791. **Owner(s):** Tomah Journal Printing Co., Inc., 1108 Superior Ave., Tomah, WI 54660. TEL 608-372-4729; Ed. John Froelich; Pub. John R. Kenny; adv. contact: P.J. Adler. pub. size: broadsheet; circ. 5,500(paid). **Wire Service(s):** AP.

US

TOMAH MONITOR-HERALD. 1881. Mon. $.75 newsstand; $27/yr. in cy. mailed subscription incl. Tomah Journal. 1108 Superior Ave., Tomah, WI 54660. TEL 608-372-4123; FAX 608-372-2791. **Owner(s):** Tomah Journal Printing Co., Inc., 1108 Superior Ave., Tomah, WI 54660. TEL 608-372-4729; Ed. John R. Kenny; Pub. John R. Kenny; adv. contact: P.J. Adler. pub. size: broadsheet; circ. 5,500(paid). **Wire Service(s):** AP.

TOMAHAWK

US

TOMAHAWK LEADER. 1886. Tue. $.75 newsstand; $22/yr. in area; $31/yr. in state; $41/yr. out of state. 315 W. Wisconsin Ave., Tomahawk, WI 54487. TEL 715-453-2151. **Owner(s):** Larry & Kathy Tobin, P.O. Box 345, Tomahawk, WI 54487. TEL 715-453-2151; Ed. Kathy Tobin; Pub. Kathy Tobin; adv. contact: Larry Tobin. pub. size: broadsheet; circ. 8,050(free & paid).

TURTLE LAKE

US

TURTLE LAKE TIMES, THE. 1900. Thu. $.40 newsstand; $12/yr. in surrounding cys.; $15/yr. elsewhere. 419 S. Maple, Turtle Lake, WI 54889. TEL 715-986-4675. **Owner(s):** James P. Slack, P.O. Box 88, Turtle Lake, WI 54889. TEL 715-986-4675; Ed. Anne Slack; Pub. James P. Slack; adv. contact: Denise Slack. pub. size: standard; circ. 1,250(paid).

TWIN LAKES

US

WESTOSHA REPORT. 1956. Mon. $.75 newsstand; $16.50/yr. mailed in state; $38/yr. mailed out of state. 316 N. Lake Ave., Twin Lakes, WI 53181. TEL 414-877-2813; FAX 414-877-3619. **Owner(s):** Southern Lakes Media, Inc., P.O. Box 437, Burlington, WI 53105. TEL 414-763-3511; FAX 414-763-2238; Ed. Diane Jahnke; Pub. Robert Branen; adv. contact: Dave Wright. photos; pub. size: broadsheet; circ. 12,000(paid).

UNION GROVE

US   ISSN 0749-6990

WESTINE REPORT. 1869. Wed. $.75 newsstand; $14.85/yr. in cy.; $28.05/yr. in state; $42.35/yr. out of state. 1113 Main St., Union Grove, WI 53182. TEL 414-878-1300; FAX 414-763-2238. **Owner(s):** Zimmermann & Sons, Inc., 140 Commerce St., Burlington, WI 53105. TEL 414-763-3511; Ed. Rosalyn Calek; Pub. Robert Branen; adv. contact: David Wright. pub. size: tabloid; circ. 2,200(paid).

VALDERS

US

VALDERS JOURNAL. 1940. Thu. $15/yr. in cy.; $22/yr. out of cy. 204 N. Liberty St., Valders, WI 54245. TEL 414-775-4431. **Owner(s):** Marion F. Brockman, 332 N. Jackson St., Valders, WI 54245. TEL 414-775-4316; Brian Thomsen, 204B N. Liberty St., Valders, WI 54245. TEL 414-775-9268; Ed. Brian Thomsen; Pub. Marion F. Brockman; adv. contact: Brian Thomsen. pub. size: tabloid; circ. 2,175(paid). **Wire Service(s):** AP.

VERONA

US

VERONA PRESS. 1965. Thu. $.75 newsstand; $28/yr. in cy.; $30/yr. out of cy.; $38/yr. out of state. 120 W. Verona Ave., Verona, WI 53593-0006. TEL 608-845-9559; FAX 608-845-9550. **Owner(s):** Henry W. Schroeder, 120 W. Verona Ave., Verona, WI 53593. TEL 608-845-9559; FAX 608-845-9550; Pub. Henry W. Schroeder; adv. contact: Terry Leonard. pub. size: tabloid; circ. 6,274(free & paid).

VIROQUA

US

VERNON COUNTY BROADCASTER. 1856. Thu. $.75 newsstand; $24/yr. local; $28/yr. out of cy.; $33/yr. out of state. 122 W. Jefferson St., Viroqua, WI 54665. TEL 608-637-3137; FAX 608-637-8557. **Owner(s):** Peter L. Hollister, P.O. Box 472, Viroqua, WI 54665. TEL 608-637-3137; Mary M. Hollister, P.O. Box 472, Viroqua, WI 54665. TEL 608-637-3137; Ed. Mary Hollister; Pub. Peter Hollister; adv. contact: Peter Hollister. pub. size: broadsheet; circ. 6,180(paid).

WALWORTH

US

WALWORTH TIMES, THE. 1904. Wed. $.75 newsstand; $20/yr. in cy. 325 Kenosha St., Walworth, WI 53184-0129. TEL 414-275-2166; FAX 414-275-5259. **Owner(s):** Robert Branen, P.O. Box 129, Walworth, WI 53184. TEL 414-275-2166; Ed. Kent Johnson. adv.; photos; pub. size: broadsheet; circ. 4,000(paid).

WASHBURN

US   ISSN 1041-9942

COUNTY JOURNAL, THE. 1984. Wed. $.50 newsstand; $23/yr. in 548 zip code; $28/yr. out of area. P.O. Box 637, Washburn, WI 54891-0637. TEL 715-373-5500; FAX 715-373-5546. **Owner(s):** Country Journal, Inc., P.O. Box 637, Washburn, WI 54891. TEL 715-373-5500; FAX 715-373-5546; Ed. Darrell Pendergrass. adv.; photos; pub. size: broadsheet; circ. 4,547(free & paid).
   Formerly: Bayfield County Journal.

WATERFORD

US

WATERFORD POST. 1877. Sun. $.75 newsstand; $21.50/yr. 224A N. Milwaukee St., Waterford, WI 53185. TEL 414-534-4668. **Owner(s):** Zimmermann & Sons, Inc., 140 Commerce St., Burlington, WI 53105; Ed. Pete Wicklund; Pub. Robert Branen; adv. contact: David Wright. pub. size: tabloid; circ. 1,500(paid).

WAUNAKEE

US

WAUNAKEE TRIBUNE. 1920. Thu. $.60 newsstand; $25/yr. 105 South St., Waunakee, WI 53597. TEL 608-849-5227; FAX 608-849-4225. **Owner(s):** Arthur M. Drake, 105 South St., Waunakee, WI 53597. TEL 608-849-5227; Ed. Arthur M. Drake; Pub. Arthur M. Drake; adv. contact: Arthur M. Drake. pub. size: broadsheet; circ. 3,500(paid).

WAUPACA

US

PICTURE POST. Fri. free. 717 Tenth St., Waupaca, WI 54981. TEL 715-258-5546; FAX 715-258-8162. **Owner(s):** Waupaca Publishing Co., P.O. Box 152, Waupaca, WI 54981. TEL 715-258-5546; Ed. Scott Turner. adv.; pub. size: broadsheet.

US

WISCONSIN STATE FARMER. 1956. Fri. $.50 newsstand; $18/yr. mailed. 717 Tenth St., Waupaca, WI 54981. TEL 715-258-5546; FAX 715-258-8162. **Owner(s):** Waupaca Publishing Co., P.O. Box 152, Waupaca, WI 54981. TEL 715-258-8162; Ed. Carla Gunst; Pub. Scott B. Turner; adv. contact: Tom Barton. pub. size: broadsheet; circ. 30,160(paid). **Wire Service(s):** AP.

WAUPUN

US

WAUPUN LEADER NEWS. 1881. Wed. $.75 newsstand; $21/yr. in state; $25/yr. out of state. 520 E. Main St., Waupun, WI 53963. TEL 414-324-5555; FAX 414-324-8582. **Owner(s):** Citizen Publishing Co., 805 Park Ave., Beaver Dam, WI 53956. TEL 414-887-0321; Ed. Kevin Passon. adv.; pub. size: tabloid; circ. 10,483(free & paid).

WAUTOMA

US

WAUSHARA ARGUS. 1859. Wed. $.70 newsstand; $23/yr. mailed locally. Hwy. 21 & 73 E., Wautoma, WI 54982. TEL 414-787-3334; FAX 414-787-2883. **Owner(s):** Delphos Newspapers, Delphos, OH 45833. TEL 419-695-0015; Ed. Mary Kunasch; Pub. Mary Kunasch. photos; adv. contact: Mary Kunasch. photos; pub. size: broadsheet; circ. 6,800(paid).
Formerly: Wautoma Waushara Argus.

WAUWATOSA

US   ISSN 0895-2817

BAY VIEWER, THE. 1976. Thu. $.50 newsstand; $19.50/yr. local; $43.50/yr. out of area; $64.50/yr. elsewhere. 11063 W. Blue Mound Rd., Wauwatosa, WI 53226. TEL 414-778-5000; FAX 414-778-5012. **Owner(s):** Sun Media, Inc., 5510 Cloverleaf Pkwy., Cleveland, OH 44125. TEL 216-642-5516; Ed. Jeanne Wieland; Pub. Wayne Toske; adv.; photos; pub. size: tabloid; circ. 1,527(paid).

US

BROOKFIELD NEWS. Thu. $.50 newsstand; $20.50/yr. local; $43.50/yr. out of area; $64.50/yr. elsewhere. 11063 W. Blue Mound Rd., Wauwatosa, WI 53226. TEL 414-788-5000; FAX 414-788-5012. **Owner(s):** Sun Media, Inc., 5510 Cloverleaf Pkwy., Cleveland, OH 44125. TEL 216-642-5516; Ed. Mary Lou Stover; Pub. Wayne Toske; adv.; photos; bk.rev.; pub. size: tabloid; circ. 6,807(paid).

US

BROWN DEER HERALD. Thu. $.50 newsstand; $20.50/yr. local; $43.50/yr. out of area; $64.50/yr. elsewhere. 11063 W. Blue Mound Rd., Wauwatosa, WI 53226. TEL 414-778-5000; FAX 414-778-5012. **Owner(s):** Sun Media, Inc., 5510 Cloverleaf Pkwy., Cleveland, OH 44125. TEL 216-642-5516; Ed. Mary Lou Stover; Pub. Mark Toske; pub. size: tabloid; circ. 1,500(paid).

US

CUDAHY REMINDER-ENTERPRISE. Thu. $.50 newsstand; $19.50/yr. local; $43.50/yr. out of area; $64.50/yr. elsewhere. 11063 W. Blue Mound Rd., Wauwatosa, WI 53226. TEL 414-778-5000; FAX 414-778-5012. **Owner(s):** Sun Media, Inc., 5510 Cloverleaf Pkwy., Cleveland, OH 44125. TEL 216-642-5516; Ed. Mary Lou Stover; Pub. Wayne Toske; adv.; photos; pub. size: tabloid; circ. 5,175(paid).

US

ELM LEAVES. Thu. $.50 newsstand; $20.50/yr. local; $43.50/yr. out of area; $64.50/yr. elsewhere. 11063 W. Blue Mound Rd., Wauwatosa, WI 53226. TEL 414-778-5000; FAX 414-778-5012. **Owner(s):** Sun Media, Inc., 5510 Cloverleaf Pkwy., Cleveland, OH 44125. TEL 216-642-5516; Ed. Mary Lou Stover; Pub. Wayne Toske; adv.; photos; bk.rev.; pub. size: tabloid; circ. 1,581(paid).

US

FOX POINT, BAYSIDE, RIVER HILLS HERALD. Thu. $.50 newsstand; $20.50/yr. local; $43.50/yr. out of area; $64.50/yr. elsewhere. 11063 W. Blue Mound Rd., Wauwatosa, WI 53226. TEL 414-778-5000; FAX 414-778-5012. **Owner(s):** Sun Media, Inc., 5510 Cloverleaf Pkwy., Cleveland, OH 44125. TEL 216-642-5516; Ed. Jeanne Wieland; Pub. Wayne Toske; adv.; photos; bk.rev.; pub. size: tabloid; circ. 2,053(paid).

US

FRANKLIN-HALES CORNER HUB. Thu. $.50 newsstand; $20.50/yr. local; $43.50/yr. out of area; $64.50/yr. elsewhere. 11063 W. Blue Mound Rd., Wauwatosa, WI 53226. TEL 414-778-5000; FAX 414-778-5012. **Owner(s):** Sun Media, Inc., 5510 Cloverleaf Pkwy., Cleveland, OH 44125. TEL 216-642-5516; Ed. Mary Lou Stover; Pub. Wayne Toske; adv.; photos; bk.rev.; pub. size: tabloid; circ. 4,491(paid).

US

GERMANTOWN BANNER-PRESS. 1975. Thu. $.50 newsstand; $20.50/yr. local; $43.50/yr. out of area; $64.50/yr. elsewhere. 11063 W. Blue Mound Rd., Wauwatosa, WI 53226. TEL 414-778-5000; FAX 414-778-5012. **Owner(s):** Sun Media, Inc., 5510 Cloverleaf Pkwy., Cleveland, OH 44125. TEL 216-642-5516; Ed. Mary Lou Stover; Pub. Wayne Toske; adv. contact: Howard Hoerl. photos; bk.rev.; pub. size: tabloid; circ. 2,238(paid).

US

GLENDALE HERALD. Thu. $.50 newsstand; $20.50/yr. local; $43.50/yr. out of area; $64.50/yr. elsewhere. 11063 W. Blue Mound Rd., Wauwatosa, WI 53229. TEL 414-778-5000; FAX 414-778-5012. **Owner(s):** Sun Media, Inc., 5510 Cloverleaf Pkwy., Cleveland, OH 44125. TEL 216-642-5516; Ed. Jeanne Wieland; Pub. Mark Toske; adv.; photos; pub. size: tabloid; circ. 1,714(paid).

US

GREENDALE VILLAGE LIFE. Thu. $.50 newsstand; $20.50/yr. local; $43.50/yr. out of area; $64.50/yr. elsewhere. 11063 W. Blue Mound Rd., Wauwatosa, WI 53226. TEL 414-778-5000; FAX 414-778-5012. **Owner(s):** Sun Media, Inc., 5510 Cloverleaf Pkwy., Cleveland, OH 44125. TEL 216-642-5516; Ed. Jeanne Wieland; Pub. Wayne Toske; adv.; photos; pub. size: tabloid; circ. 2,768(paid).

US

GREENFIELD OBSERVER. Thu. $.50 newsstand; $20.50/yr. local; $43.50/yr. out of area; $64.50/yr. elsewhere. 11063 W. Blue Mound Rd., Wauwatosa, WI 53226. TEL 414-778-5000; FAX 414-778-5012. **Owner(s):** Sun Media, Inc., 5510 Cloverleaf Pkwy., Cleveland, OH 44125. TEL 216-642-5516; Ed. Mary Lou Stover; Pub. Wayne Toske; adv.; photos; pub. size: tabloid; circ. 3,326(paid).

US

MENOMONEE FALLS NEWS. 1894. Thu. $.50 newsstand; $20.50/yr. local; $43.50/yr. out of area; $64.50/yr. elsewhere. 11063 W. Blue Mound Rd., Wauwatosa, WI 53226. TEL 414-778-5000; FAX 414-778-5012. **Owner(s):** Sun Media, Inc., 5510 Cloverleaf Pkwy., Cleveland, OH 44125; Ed. Jeffrey Potter; Pub. Thomas Kreckel; adv. contact: Howard Hoerl. pub. size: tabloid; circ. 5,024(paid).

US

MEQUON-THIENSVILLE COURANT. Thu. $.50 newsstand; $20.50/yr. local; $43.50/yr. out of area; $64.50/yr. elsewhere. 11063 W. Blue Mound Rd., Wauwatosa, WI 53226. TEL 414-778-5000; FAX 414-778-5012. **Owner(s):** Sun Media, Inc., 5510 Cloverleaf Pkwy., Cleveland, OH 44125. TEL 216-642-5516; Ed. Mary Lou Stover; Pub. Wayne Toske; adv.; photos; bk.rev.; pub. size: tabloid; circ. 3,000(paid).

US

MUSKEGO SUN. Thu. $.50 newsstand; $20.50/yr. local; $43.50/yr. out of area; $64.50/yr. elsewhere. 11063 W. Blue Mound Rd., Wauwatosa, WI 53213. TEL 414-778-5000; FAX 414-778-5012. **Owner(s):** Sun Media, Inc., 5510 Cloverleaf Pkwy., Cleveland, OH 44125. TEL 216-624-5516; Ed. Patrick Fitzmaurice; Pub. Wayne Toske; adv.; photos; bk.rev.; pub. size: tabloid; circ. 3,309(paid).

US

NEW BERLIN CITIZEN. Thu. $.50 newsstand; $20.50/yr. local; $43.50/yr. out of area; $64.50/yr. elsewhere. 11063 W. Blue Mound Rd., Wauwatosa, WI 53226. TEL 414-778-5000; FAX 414-778-5012. **Owner(s):** Sun Media, Inc., 5510 Cloverleaf Pkwy., Cleveland, OH 44125. TEL 216-642-5516; Ed. Mary Lou Stover; Pub. Wayne Toske; adv.; photos; bk.rev.; pub. size: tabloid; circ. 4,491(paid).

US

NORTH SHORE HERALDS. Thu. $.50 newsstand; $20.50/yr. local. P.O. Box 13155, Wauwatosa, WI 53213. TEL 414-778-5000; FAX 414-778-5012. **Owner(s):** Sun Media, Inc., 5510 Cloverleaf Pkwy., Cleveland, OH 44125. TEL 216-642-5516; Ed. Mary Schuchmann. pub. size: standard; circ. 9,636(paid).

US

OAK CREEK PICTORIAL. Thu. $.50 newsstand; $20.50/yr. local; $43.50/yr. out of area; $64.50/yr. elsewhere. 11063 W. Blue Mound Rd., Wauwatosa, WI 53226. TEL 414-778-5000; FAX 414-778-5012. **Owner(s):** Sun Media, Inc., 5510 Cloverleaf Pkwy., Cleveland, OH 44125. TEL 216-642-5516; Ed. Jeanne Wieland; Pub. Wayne Toske; adv.; photos; bk.rev.; pub. size: tabloid; circ. 4,536(paid).

US

SHOREWOOD HERALD. Thu. $.50 newsstand; $20.50/yr. local; $43.50/yr. out of area; $64.50/yr. elsewhere. 11063 W. Blue Mound Rd., Wauwatosa, WI 53226. TEL 414-778-5000; FAX 414-778-5012. **Owner(s):** Sun Media, Inc., 5510 Cloverleaf Pkwy., Cleveland, OH 44125. TEL 216-642-5516; Ed. Mary Lou Stover; Pub. Wayne Toske; adv.; photos; pub. size: tabloid; circ. 1,700(paid).

US

SOUTH MILWAUKEE VOICE GRAPHIC. Thu. $.50 newsstand; $19.50/yr. local; $43.50/yr. out of area; $64.50/yr. elsewhere. 11063 W. Blue Mound Rd., Wauwatosa, WI 53226. TEL 414-778-5000; FAX 414-778-5012. **Owner(s):** Sun Media, Inc., 5510 Cloverleaf Pkwy., Cleveland, OH 44125. TEL 216-642-5516; Ed. Mary Lou Stover; Pub. Wayne Toske; adv.; photos; bk.rev.; pub. size: tabloid; circ. 4,140(paid).

US

ST. FRANCIS REMINDER-ENTERPRISE. Thu. $.50 newsstand; $20.50/yr. local; $43.50/yr. out of area; $64.50/yr. elsewhere. 11063 W. Blue Mound Rd., Wauwatosa, WI 53226. TEL 414-778-5000; FAX 414-778-5012. **Owner(s):** Sun Media, Inc., 5510 Cloverleaf Pkwy., Cleveland, OH 44125. TEL 216-642-5516; Ed. Mary Lou Stover; Pub. Wayne Toske; photos; pub. size: tabloid; circ. 5,120(paid).
Formerly: St. Francis Free Press Reminder.

Weeklies

US
SUSSEX-LANNON-LISBON NEWS. Thu. $.50 newsstand; $20.50/yr. local; $43.50/yr. out of area; $64.50/yr. elsewhere. 11063 W. Blue Mound Rd., Wauwatosa, WI 53226. TEL 414-778-5000; FAX 414-778-5012. **Owner(s):** Sun Media, Inc., 5510 Cloverleaf Pkwy., Cleveland, OH 44125. TEL 216-642-5516; Ed. Mary Lou Stover; Pub. Wayne Toske; pub. size: tabloid; circ. 500(paid).

US
WAUWATOSA NEWS-TIMES. Thu. $.50 newsstand; $20.50/yr. local; $43.50/yr. out of area; $64.50/yr. elsewhere. 11063 W. Blue Mound Rd., Wauwatosa, WI 53226. TEL 414-768-5800; FAX 414-778-5012. **Owner(s):** Sun Media, Inc., 5510 Cloverleaf Pkwy., Cleveland, OH 44125. TEL 216-642-5516; Ed. Mary Lou Stover; Pub. Wayne Toske; pub. size: tabloid; circ. 6,760(paid).

US
WEST ALLIS STAR. Thu. $.50 newsstand; $20.50/yr. local; $43.50/yr. out of area; $64.50/yr. elsewhere. 11063 W. Blue Mound Rd., Wauwatosa, WI 53226. TEL 414-778-5000; FAX 414-778-5012. **Owner(s):** Sun Media, Inc., 5510 Cloverleaf Pkwy., Cleveland, OH 44125. TEL 216-642-5516; Ed. Mary Lou Stover; Pub. Wayne Toske; pub. size: tabloid; circ. 4,143(paid).

US
WHITEFISH BAY HERALD. Thu. $.50 newsstand; $20.50/yr. local; $43.50/yr. out of area; $64.50/yr. elsewhere. 11063 W. Blue Mound Rd., Wauwatosa, WI 53226. TEL 414-778-5000; FAX 414-778-5012. **Owner(s):** Sun Media, Inc., 5510 Cloverleaf Pkwy., Cleveland, OH 44125. TEL 216-642-5516; Ed. Mary Lou Stover; Pub. Wayne Toske; adv.; photos; bk.rev.; pub. size: tabloid; circ. 2,900(paid).

WESTBY

US
TIMES, THE. 1895. Wed. $21/yr. local; $24/yr. in state; $30/yr. out of state. 005 E. First St., Westby, WI 54667. TEL 608-634-4317; FAX 608-637-8557. **Owner(s):** Peter L. Hollister, 105 E. First St., Westby, WI 54667. TEL 608-634-4317; Mary Bormann Hollister, 105 E. First St., Westby, WI 54667. TEL 608-634-4317; Pub. Peter Hollister; adv. contact: Peter Hollister. pub. size: broadsheet; circ. 2,500(paid).

WEST SALEM

US
LA CROSSE COUNTY COUNTRYMAN. 1879. Thu. $.75 newsstand; $25/yr. in cy.; $27/yr. out of cy.; $40/yr. out of state. 153 S. Leonard St., West Salem, WI 54669. TEL 608-786-1950; FAX 608-786-1670. **Owner(s):** South Central Wisconsin Newspapers, Inc., P.O. Box 470, Portage, WI 53901. TEL 608-742-2111; Ed. Ron Marose; Pub. Dave Gentry; adv. contact: Ben Baker. photos; pub. size: tabloid; circ. 4,000(paid).

WHITEHALL

US
WHITEHALL TIMES. 1861. Thu. $.75 newsstand; $20/yr. in cy.; $26/yr. out of state. 36435 Main St., Whitehall, WI 54773. TEL 715-538-4765; FAX 715-538-4540. **Owner(s):** Charles Gauger, P.O. Box 95, Whitehall, WI 54773. TEL 715-538-4765; Ed. Scott Thomson; Pub. Robert Gauger; adv. contact: Charles Gauger. pub. size: standard; circ. 2,450(paid).

WINNECONNE

US
WINNECONNE NEWS. 1930. Wed. $15/yr. in cy.; $20/yr. out of state. 908 E. Main St., Winneconne, WI 54986. TEL 414-582-4541; FAX 414-582-4417. **Owner(s):** John Rogers, 140 Main St., Winneconne, WI 54986. TEL 414-582-4541; Ed. Margaret Rogers; Pub. John Rogers; pub. size: tabloid; circ. 1,750(paid).

WINTER

US
SAWYER COUNTY GAZETTE. 1908. Wed. $.35 newsstand; $15/yr. in cy.; $17.50/yr. out of cy. P.O. Box 99, Winter, WI 54896-0099. TEL 715-266-2511; FAX 715-266-2511. **Owner(s):** Meredith Rickert, P.O. Box 99, Winter, WI 54896-0099. TEL 715-266-2511; Pub. Meredith Rickert; adv. contact: Meredith Rickert. photos; pub. size: standard; circ. 2,250(free & paid).

WISCONSIN DELLS

US
WISCONSIN DELLS EVENTS. 1896. s-w. Wed. & Sat. $.75 newsstand; $37/yr. in cy.; $39/yr. out of cy.; $50/yr. out of state. 716 Elm St., Wisconsin Dells, WI 53965. TEL 608-254-8327; FAX 608-254-8328. **Owner(s):** South Central Wisconsin Newspapers, Inc., P.O. Box 470, Portage, WI 53901. TEL 608-742-2111; Ed. Kay J. James; Pub. David Gentry; adv. contact: Al Miller. photos; pub. size: tabloid; circ. 3,000(paid).

WITHEE

US ISSN 1047-8361
O-W ENTERPRISE. 1910. Wed. $.75 newsstand; $25/yr. in cy.; $30/yr. in state; $35/yr. elsewhere. 1006 Division St., Withee, WI 54498. TEL 715-229-2103; FAX 715-229-2104. **Owner(s):** Larry Shimono, 1006 Division St., Withee, WI 54498; Ed. Larry Shimono; Pub. Larry Shimono; adv.; pub. size: tabloid; circ. 1,100(paid).

Formerly: Owen Enterprise.

WITTENBERG

US
WITTENBERG ENTERPRISE NEWS. 1893. w. $.35 newsstand; $16.25/yr. in state; $17.75/yr. out of state. 110 W. Vinal St., Wittenberg, WI 54499-0190. TEL 715-253-2737; FAX 715-253-2700. **Owner(s):** Gordon C. & Sally Boldig, P.O. Box 190, Wittenberg, WI 54499. TEL 715-253-2737; Steve & Darlene Block, P.O. Box 190, Wittenberg, WI 54499. TEL 715-253-2737; Pub. Gordon C. Boldig; adv. contact: Darlene Block. photos; pub. size: standard; circ. 2,000(paid).

WYOMING

BUFFALO

US
BUFFALO BULLETIN. 1891. Thu. $.50 newsstand; $18/yr. in state; $26/yr. out of state. 58 N. Lobban, Buffalo, WY 82834. TEL 307-684-2223. Owner(s): Buffalo Bulletin, P.O. Box 730, Buffalo, WY 82834. TEL 307-684-2223; Ed. James F. Hicks; Pub. James F. Hicks; adv. contact: Marilyn Connolly. photos; bk.rev.; pub. size: standard; circ. 4,150(paid).

CHEYENNE

US
SENTINEL. Fri. free newsstand; $42/yr. 1810 Westland Rd., Cheyenne, WY 82001. TEL 307-632-5666; FAX 307-632-1554. **Owner(s):** News Media Corp., P.O. Box 46, Peoria, IL 61650. TEL 307-532-7097; Pub. Jim Wood; adv.; pub. size: tabloid; circ. 5,200(free & paid).

CODY

US ISSN 0747-2498
CODY ENTERPRISE. 1899. s-w.: Mon. & Wed. $.50 newsstand; $26/yr. 1549 Sheridan, Cody, WY 82414. TEL 307-587-2231; FAX 307-587-5208. **Owner(s):** Sage Publishing Co., Inc., P.O. Box 1090, Cody, WY 82414. TEL 307-587-2231; Ed. Bruce McCormack; Pub. Bruce McCormack; adv. contact: John Malmberg. pub. size: broadsheet; circ. 5,999(controlled & paid).

EVANSTON

US
UINTA COUNTY HERALD. 1938. s-w.: Tue. & Fri. $.50 newsstand; $42.50/yr. mailed in state; $45.50/yr. out of state. 1565 S. Hwy. 150, Ste. D, Evanston, WY 82930-0210. TEL 307-789-6560; FAX 307-789-2700. **Owner(s):** Wyoming Newspapers, Inc., 1565 S. Hwy. 150, Ste. D, Evanston, WY 82930. TEL 307-789-6560; FAX 307-789-6560; Ed. Shawn Hubbell; Pub. Mike Jensen; adv.: $7.78/SAU. photos; pub. size: standard; circ. 7,700(free & paid). **Wire Service(s):** AP.

Formerly: Evanston Uinta County Herald.

GUERNSEY

US　　　　ISSN 1061-1789
GUERNSEY GAZETTE/LINGLE GUIDE. 1902. Tue. $.50 newsstand; $18.95/yr. in cy.; $22.95/yr. out of cy. 40 S. Wyoming, Guernsey, WY 82214. TEL 307-836-2021; FAX 307-837-2255. **Owner(s):** Wyoming Newspapers, Inc., 2025 Main St., Torrington, WY 82240. TEL 307-532-2184; Ed. Sandra Hansen; Pub. Bill Hanson; adv.; photos; pub. size: tabloid; circ. 800(paid).

JACKSON

US
JACKSON HOLE GUIDE. 1952. Wed. $.75 newsstand; $20/yr. in cy.; $26/yr. out of cy. 185 N. Glenwood, Jackson, WY 83001. TEL 307-733-2430; FAX 307-733-7841. **Owner(s):** Grand Teton Printing & Publishing Co., 185 N. Glenwood, Jackson, WY 83001. TEL 307-733-2430; Ed. Tom Hacker; Pub. Curtis Hubbard; adv. contact: Monty Nethercott. photos; bk.rev.; pub. size: tabloid; circ. 8,000(paid). **Wire Service(s):** AP.

US
JACKSON HOLE NEWS. 1970. Wed. $.50 newsstand; $26/yr. in cy. mailed; $33/yr. out of cy. 1225 Maple Way, Jackson, WY 83001. TEL 307-733-2047; FAX 307-733-2138. **Owner(s):** Jackson Hole News, Inc., P.O. Box 7445, Jackson, WY 83001. TEL 307-733-2047; FAX 307-733-2138; Ed. Angus M. Thuemer Jr.; Pub. Michael Sellett; adv. contact: Wayne Marsee. pub. size: tabloid; circ. 9,000(paid). **Wire Service(s):** AP.

KEMMERER

US
KEMMERER GAZETTE. 1901. Thu. $.35 newsstand; $22.50/yr. 708 J.C. Penny Dr., Kemmerer, WY 83101-0030. TEL 307-877-3347; FAX 307-877-3736. **Owner(s):** Mark Steele, P.O. Box 815, Soda Springs, ID 83276. TEL 208-547-3260; Ed. Don Kominsky; Pub. Mark Steele; adv. contact: Stacy Batista. photos; pub. size: standard; circ. morning 2,000(free & paid).

LANDER

US
LANDER WYOMING STATE JOURNAL. 1886. s-w.: Mon. & Wed. $.50 newsstand; $32.95/yr. mailed in cy.; $40.95/yr. out of cy. 453 Main St., Lander, WY 82520. TEL 307-332-2323; FAX 307-332-9332. **Owner(s):** WCS Corp., P.O. Box 900, Lander, WY 82520. TEL 307-332-2323; FAX 307-332-9332; Ed. William Sniffin; Pub. William Sniffin; adv. contact: Bob Scholl. photos. pub. size: broadsheet; circ. 4,750(paid).

US
WIND RIVER NEWS. 1978. Thu. $.50 newsstand; $18.75/yr. in cy.; $21.75/yr. out of cy. 453 Main St., Lander, WY 82520. TEL 307-332-2323; FAX 307-332-9332. **Owner(s):** William Sniffin, P.O. Box 900, Lander, WY 82520. TEL 307-332-2323; Ed. Cynthia Beckwith; Pub. William Sniffin; pub. size: broadsheet; circ. 3,000(paid). **Formerly:** Lander-Wind River News.

US
WYOMING STATE JOURNAL. 1978. s-w.: Mon. & Wed. $32.95/yr. 453 Main St., Lander, WY 82520. TEL 307-332-2323; FAX 307-332-9332. **Owner(s):** Swift Newspapers, Inc., P.O. Box 900, Lander, WY 82520. TEL 307-332-2323; Ed. Cynthia Beckwith. circ. morning 3,000; evening 4,200(paid).

LOVELL

US
LOVELL CHRONICLE, THE. 1906. Thu. $.50 newsstand; $14/yr. n cy.; $22/yr. in state; $25/yr. out of state. 234 E. Main St., Lovell, WY 82431. TEL 307-548-2217. **Owner(s):** David & Susan Peck, P.O. Box 787, Lovell, WY 82431. TEL 307-548-2217 Margaret Peck, 1002 W. Park Ave., Riverton, WY 82501; Pub. David H. Peck; adv. contact: David H. Peck. pub. size: broadsheet; circ. 2,167(free & paid).

LUSK

US
LUSK HERALD. 1886. Wed. $32.95/yr. in cy.; $37.75/yr. out of cy. 227 S. Main St., Lusk, WY 82225. TEL 307-334-2867; FAX 307-334-2514. **Owner(s):** Wyoming Newspapers, Inc., P.O. Box 1058, Torrington, WY 82240. TEL 307-532-7097; Pub. Bill Hanson; pub. size: tabloid; circ. 1,650(paid).

LYMAN

US
BRIDGER VALLEY PIONEER. 1976. Fri. $.50 newsstand; $17.95/yr. P.O. Box 538, Lyman, WY 82937. TEL 307-787-3229; FAX 307-787-6795. **Owner(s):** Wyoming Newspapers, Inc., P.O. Box 46, Rochelle, IL 61068. TEL 815-562-2061; Ed. Wade Williams; Pub. Debbie Smith; adv. contact: Debbie Smith. pub. size: broadsheet; circ. 1,800(paid). **Formerly:** Uinta County Pioneer.

MOORCROFT

US
MOORCROFT LEADER. 1912. Thu. $.50 newsstand; $14/yr. in cy.; $15.50/yr. out of cy. 304 Riley, Moorcroft, WY 82721-0067. TEL 307-756-3371; FAX 307-756-9827. **Owner(s):** Edith Shepherd, 145 Prairie Rd., Moorcroft, WY 82721. TEL 307-756-9812; Clayton O. Jarred, 610 Rockpile Blvd., Gillette, WY 82721. TEL 307-682-2073; Ed. Edith Shepherd; Pub. Edith Shepherd; adv. contact: Margaret Larson photos; bk.rev.; pub. size: tabloid; circ. 1,100.

NEWCASTLE

US
NEWS LETTER JOURNAL. 1889. Wed. $.50 newsstand; $19/yr. local; $24/yr. elsewhere. 14 W. Main St., Newcastle, WY 82701. TEL 307-746-2777; FAX 307-745-2660. **Owner(s):** Robb Hicks, P.O. Box 40, Newcastle, WY 82701. TEL 307-746-2777; FAX 307-746-2660; Pub. Robb Hicks; adv.: $6/SAU. photos; pub. size: standard; circ. 2,700(paid).

SARATOGA

US
SARATOGA SUN. 1888. Wed. $.50 newsstand; $20/yr. in cy.; $28/yr. out of state. 116 E. Bridge St., Saratoga, WY 82331. TEL 307-326-8311. **Owner(s):** Saratoga Sun Ltd. Liability Co., Inc., 116 E. Bridge St., Saratoga, WY 82331. TEL 307-326-8311; Ed. Gary Stevenson; Pub. Gary Stevenson; adv.; pub. size: tabloid; circ. 1,825(paid).

TORRINGTON

US
TORRINGTON TELEGRAM. 1907. s-w: Wed. & Fri. $49.50/yr. in cy.; $55.95/yr. out of cy. 2025 Main St., Torrington, WY 82240. TEL 307-532-2184; FAX 307-532-2283. **Owner(s):** Wyoming Newspapers, Inc., P.O. Box 1058, Torrington, WY 82240. TEL 307-532-7097; Ed. Sandra Hanson; Pub. Bill Hanson; adv. contact: Bill Hanson. pub. size: broadsheet; circ. 3,400(paid). **Wire Service(s):** AP.

WHEATLAND

US
PLATTE COUNTY RECORD-TIMES. 1900. Wed. $.50 newsstand; $29.95/yr. in cy.; $36/yr. out of cy. 1007 Eighth St., Wheatland, WY 82201. TEL 307-322-2627; FAX 307-322-9612. **Owner(s):** Wyoming Newspapers Inc., P.O. Box 1054, Torrington, WY 82240. TEL 307-532-7097; Ed. Dana Biber; Pub. Jim Woods; adv. contact: Ken Barnes photos; bk.rev.; pub. size: broadsheet; circ. 2,800(paid).

Title Index

A

Abbeville Herald (Abbeville, AL) **10057**
Abbeville Meridional (Abbeville, LA) **9993**
Abbotsford Tribune-Phonograph
  (Abbotsford, WI) **10297**
Aberdeen American News
  (Aberdeen, SD) **10039**
Aberdeen Examiner (Aberdeen, MS) **10185**
Aberdeen Times (Aberdeen, ID) **10107**
Abernathy Weekly Review
  (Abernathy, TX) **10270**
Abilene Reflector-Chronicle (Abilene, KS) **9989**
Abilene Reporter-News (Abilene, TX) **10041**
Abingdon Argus (Abingdon, IL) **10109**
Abingdon Virginian (Abingdon, VA) **10284**
Abington Journal (Clarks Summit, PA) **10252**
Ace News, The (Heath, OH) **10239**
Acorn, The (Westlake Village, CA) **10084**
Action Advertiser (Fond Du Lac, WI) **10300**
Acworth Neighbor (Marietta, GA) **10104**
Ad-News (Greenfield, IN) **10132**
Ad-Visor (Beulah, MI) **10167**
Ad-Visor (Lansing, MI) **10172**
Ada/Cascade/Forest Hills Advance
  (Jenison, MI) **10171**
Ada Evening News (Ada, OK) **10028**
Adair County Free Press
  (Greenfield, IA) **10138**
Adair Progress, The (Columbia, KY) **10147**

Adair Russell Shopper, The
  (Columbia, KY) **10147**
† Adams County Leader (Council, ID)
Adams County Times (Adams, WI) **10297**
Ada Norman County Index (Ada, MN) **10176**
Addison County Independent
  (Middlebury, VT) **10284**
Addison Press (Elmhurst, IL) **10116**
† Adelanto Bulletin, The (Adelanto, CA)
Adel News-Tribune (Adel, GA) **10100**
Ad Express & Daily Iowegian
  (Centerville, IA) **9987**
Adirondack Daily Enterprise (Saranac
  Lake, NY) **10017**
Advance-Monticellonian
  (Monticello, AR) **10067**
Advance-Yeoman (Wickliffe, KY) **10152**
Advance Leader (Monroeville, PA) **10255**
Advance News (Lakehurst, NJ) **10203**
Advance of Bucks County
  (Newtown, PA) **10256**
Advance, The (Randolph, WI) **10304**
Advertiser-Gleam (Guntersville, AL) **10059**
Advertiser-Tribune (Tiffin, OH) **10027**
Advertiser, The (Van Buren, AR) **10068**
Advertiser, The (Worden, IL) **10129**
Advertiser, The (Ligonier, IN) **10133**
Advertiser, The (Louisa, KY) **10149**
Advertiser, The (Mount Sterling, KY) **10150**
Advertiser, The (Paris, KY) **10150**

Advertiser, The (Iron Mountain, MI) **10171**
Advertiser, The (Bemidji, MN) **10176**
Advertiser, The (Chillicothe, OH) **10235**
Advertiser, The (McMurray, PA) **10254**
Advertizer-Herald, The (Bamberg, SC) **10261**
Advisor/Source (Utica, MI) **10002**
Advisor, The (Mt. Pleasant, PA) **10256**
Advocate (Winner, SD) **10265**
Advocate-Messenger (Danville, KY) **9992**
Advocate/South Advocate, The
   (Williamstown, MA) **10166**
Advocate Democrat (Madisonville, TN) **10268**
Advocate Penny Saver
   (Sweetwater, TN) **10270**
Advocate, The (Stamford, CT) **9971**
Advocate, The (Clifton, IL) **10114**
Advocate, The (Baton Rouge, LA) **9993**
Advocate, The (Marion, MA) **10162**
Advocate, The (Newark, OH) **10026**
Aegis, The (Bel Air, MD) **10158**
Afton Star-Enterprise (Afton, IA) **10136**
Aiken Standard (Aiken, SC) **10038**
Aitkin Independent Age (Aitkin, MN) **10176**
Ajo Copper News (Ajo, AZ) **10063**
Akron Beacon Journal (Akron, OH) **10022**
Akron News Reporter (Akron, CO) **10085**
† Alabama Journal (Montgomery, AL)
Alabama Messenger (Birmingham, AL) **10057**
Alamance News (Graham, NC) **10228**
Alameda Times Star (Alameda, CA) **9961**
Alamogordo Daily News
   (Alamogordo, NM) **10013**
Albany Democrat-Herald (Albany, OR) **10031**
Albany Herald, The (Albany, GA) **9974**
Albany Journal (Albany, GA) **10100**
Albany Ledger, The (Albany, MO) **10187**
Albert Lea Tribune (Albert Lea, MN) **10002**
Albia Union-Republican (Albia, IA) **10136**
Albion Advertiser (Albion, NY) **10209**
Albion News (Albion, NE) **10196**
Albion News, The (Albion, PA) **10251**
Albion Recorder (Albion, MI) **9999**
Albuquerque Journal
   (Albuquerque, NM) **10013**
Albuquerque Street News
   (Albuquerque, NM) **10208**
Albuquerque Tribune
   (Albuquerque, NM) **10013**
Alexander City Outlook (Alexander
   City, AL) **9955**
Alexandria Daily Town Talk
   (Alexandria, LA) **9993**
Alexandria Gazette Packet
   (Alexandria, VA) **10284**
Alexandria Journal (Fairfax, VA) **10049**

Alexandria News Weekly
   (Alexandria, LA) **10152**
Alexandria Times-Tribune
   (Alexandria, IN) **10129**
Algoma Record Herald (Algoma, WI) **10297**
† Algonac Courier Journal (Marine City, MI)
Algona Upper Des Moines (Algona, IA) **10136**
Algonquin Countryside (Barrington, IL) **10110**
Alhambra Post Advocate (Los
   Angeles, CA) **10075**
Alice Echo-News (Alice, TX) **10041**
Aliso Viejo News (Lake Forest, CA) **10074**
Allegan County News (Allegan, MI) **10167**
Allegheny Times (Moon Township, PA) **10035**
Allen County Times (New Haven, IN) **10134**
Alliance Review (Alliance, OH) **10022**
Alliance Times-Herald (Alliance, NE) **10009**
Allied News (Grove City, PA) **10253**
Almanac, The (McMurray, PA) **10255**
Aloha Breeze (Hillsboro, OR) **10249**
† Alpena Journal (Wessington Springs, SD)
Alpena News (Alpena, MI) **9999**
Alpena Star Advertiser (Alpena, MI) **10167**
Alpharetta Revue (Alpharetta, GA) **10100**
Alpine Avalanche (Alpine, TX) **10270**
Alsip Express (Midlothian, IL) **10123**
Altamont Enterprise, The
   (Altamont, NY) **10209**
Altamont News, The (Altamont, IL) **10109**
Altavista Journal (Altavista, VA) **10284**
Alternatives (Myrtle Beach, SC) **10263**
Altoona Herald, The (Altoona, IA) **10136**
Altoona Mirror (Altoona, PA) **10032**
Altus Times (Altus, OK) **10028**
Alvarado Post (Alvarado, TX) **10270**
Alva Review-Courier (Alva, OK) **10028**
Alvin Advertiser (Alvin, TX) **10270**
Alvin Sun (Alvin, TX) **10270**
† Alvin Tiller (Lamont, CA)
Amador Ledger Dispatch (Jackson, CA) **9962**
Amarillo Daily News/Sunday News Globe
   (Amarillo, TX) **10041**
Amarillo Globe Times (Amarillo, TX) **10042**
Ambler Gazette (Fort Washington, PA) **10253**
Amboy News, The (Amboy, IL) **10109**
Amelia Bulletin Monitor, The (Amelia Court
   House, VA) **10285**
American Journal (Westbrook, ME) **10157**
Americus Times-Recorder
   (Americus, GA) **9974**
Amery Free Press (Amery, WI) **10297**
Amesbury News (Amesbury, MA) **10160**
Amherst Bee (Buffalo, NY) **10211**
Amherst New Era-Progress
   (Amherst, VA) **10285**
Amite Tangi Digest (Amite, LA) **10152**

Amityville Record (Amityville, NY) **10209**
Amory Advertiser, The (Amory, MS) **10185**
Amsterdam Star, The (Albany, NY) **10014**
Anaconda Leader (Anaconda, MT) **10195**
Anacortes American (Anacortes, WA) **10290**
Anadarko Daily News (Anadarko, OK) **10028**
Anaheim Bulletin (Anaheim, CA) **10068**
Anaheim Hills News (Anaheim, CA) **10068**
Anamosa Journal-Eureka (Anamosa, IA) **10137**
Anchorage Daily News (Anchorage, AK) **9957**
† Anchor Bay Beacon (New Baltimore, MI)
Andalusia Star News (Andalusia, AL) **9955**
† Anderson Countian (Garnett, KS)
Anderson Independent-Mail
   (Anderson, SC) **10038**
Anderson News, The
   (Lawrenceburg, KY) **10149**
Andover Townsman (Andover, MA) **10160**
Andrews County News (Andrews, TX) **10270**
Angelina Free Press (Diboll, TX) **10274**
Angier Independent (Angier, NC) **10226**
Angleton Times (Angleton, TX) **10270**
Ankeny Press Citizen (Ankeny, IA) **10137**
Ann Arbor News (Ann Arbor, MI) **9999**
Anniston Star (Anniston, AL) **9955**
Anoka County Union (Coon
   Rapids, MN) **10178**
Anson Record, The (Wadesboro, NC) **10231**
Antelope Valley Press (Palmdale, CA) **9964**
Anthony Republican, The (Anthony, KS) **10142**
Antigo Area Shoppers Guide
   (Antigo, WI) **10297**
Antigo Daily Journal (Antigo, WI) **10053**
Antioch News-Reporter (Grayslake, IL) **10118**
Apache Junction Independent (Apache
   Junction, AZ) **10063**
Apex Herald, The (Apex, NC) **10226**
Appalachian News-Express
   (Pikeville, KY) **10150**
Appeal-Democrat (Marysville, CA) **9963**
Apple Valley/Rosemont Sun-Current
   (Burnsville, MN) **10177**
Apple Valley News (Hesperia, CA) **10073**
† Applewood/Wheat Ridge Transcript
   (Golden, CO)
Appomattox Times-Virginian
   (Appomattox, VA) **10285**
Arab Tribune (Arab, AL) **10057**
Arapahoe Public Mirror (Arapahoe, NE) **10196**
Arbutus Times (Baltimore, MD) **10157**
Arcadia News-Leader (Arcadia, WI) **10297**
Arcadian, The (Arcadia, FL) **10093**
† Arcadia Tribune (Arcadia, CA)
Archbold Buckeye (Archbold, OH) **10234**
Arco Advertiser (Arco, ID) **10107**
Arcola Record Herald (Arcola, IL) **10109**

Area News, The (Gillespie, IL) **10118**
Area Shopper (Springboro, PA) **10259**
Arenac County Independent
   (Standish, MI) **10175**
Argonaut, The (Los Angeles, CA) **10075**
Argus-Champion, The (Newport, NH) **10200**
Argus-Press, The (Owosso, MI) **10001**
Argus Leader (Sioux Falls, SD) **10039**
Argus Observer (Ontario, OR) **10031**
Argus, The (Fremont, CA) **9962**
Argyle Agenda (Argyle, WI) **10297**
Argyle Sun, The (Lake Dallas, TX) **10277**
Arizona City Independent (Arizona
   City, AZ) **10063**
Arizona Daily Star (Tucson, AZ) **9958**
Arizona Daily Sun (Flagstaff, AZ) **9957**
Arizona Republic (Phoenix, AZ) **9958**
Arizona Silver Belt (Globe, AZ) **10064**
Arkadelphia Daily Siftings Herald
   (Arkadelphia, AR) **9959**
Arkansas City Traveler (Arkansas
   City, KS) **9989**
Arkansas Democrat-Gazette (Little
   Rock, AR) **9960**
Arkansas Valley Journal (La Junta, CO) **10087**
Ark, The (Bel Tiburon, CA) **10069**
Arlington Advocate (Arlington, MA) **10160**
Arlington Citizen (Blair, NE) **10196**
Arlington Courier, The (Arlington, VA) **10285**
Arlington Heights Journal & Topics (Des
   Plaines, IL) **10115**
Arlington Journal (Fairfax, VA) **10049**
▼Arlington Morning News
   (Arlington, TX) **10042**
Arlington Star Telegram (Fort
   Worth, TX) **10043**
▼Arrowhead Ranch Independent (Sun
   City, AZ) **10064**
Arrow, The (Glendale, AZ) **10064**
Artesia Daily Press (Artesia, NM) **10013**
Arthur Enterprise, The (Arthur, NE) **10196**
Arthur Graphic Clarion (Arthur, IL) **10110**
Arvada Jefferson Sentinel
   (Lakewood, CO) **10087**
Asbury Park Press (Neptune, NJ) **10012**
Asheboro Courier-Tribune
   (Asheboro, NC) **10018**
Asheville Citizen-Times (Asheville, NC) **10018**
Ashland Daily Tidings (Ashland, OR) **10031**
Ashland Times-Gazette (Ashland, OH) **10022**
Ashley County Shoppers Guide
   (Crossett, AR) **10065**
Ashley News Observer (Crossett, AR) **10065**
Ashtabula Star-Beacon (Ashtabula, OH) **10022**
Ashton Gazette (Ashton, IL) **10110**
Aspen Daily News (Aspen, CO) **9968**

Aspen Times, The (Aspen, CO) **9968**
Associated Newspaper (Stoughton, MA) **10166**
Astoria South Fulton Argus (Astoria, IL) **10110**
Atascadero News (Atascadero, CA) **10069**
Atchison County Mail, The (Rock
  Port, MO) **10192**
Atchison Daily Globe (Atchison, KS) **9989**
Athens Banner Herald (Athens, GA) **9974**
Athens Daily News (Athens, GA) **9974**
Athens Daily Post (Athens, TN) **10040**
Athens Daily Review (Athens, TX) **10042**
Athens Messenger (Athens, OH) **10022**
Athens News (Athens, OH) **10234**
Athens Observer, The (Athens, GA) **10100**
Athol Daily News (Athol, MA) **9996**
Atkins Chronicle, The (Atkins, AR) **10065**
Atkinson Graphic, The (Atkinson, NE) **10196**
Atlanta Bulletin (Atlanta, GA) **10100**
Atlanta Citizens Journal (Atlanta, TX) **10271**
Atlanta Daily World (Atlanta, GA) **10100**
Atlanta Journal-Constitution
  (Atlanta, GA) **9974**
Atlantic County Record
  (Hammonton, NJ) **10202**
Atlantic News-Telegraph (Atlantic, IA) **9986**
Atmore Advance (Atmore, AL) **10057**
Atoka County Times (Atoka, OK) **10244**
Attica Hub (Attica, OH) **10234**
Atwater New Times (Winton, CA) **10085**
Atwood Herald (Atwood, IL) **10110**
Auburn Citizen (Auburn, IL) **10110**
Auburn Journal (Auburn, CA) **9961**
Auburn News (Auburn, MA) **10160**
Auburn Press Tribune (Auburn, NE) **10196**
Auctioner, The (Pekin, IN) **10134**
Augusta Area Times (Augusta, WI) **10297**
Augusta Chronicle, The (Augusta, GA) **9974**
Augusta Daily Gazette (Augusta, KS) **9989**
† Augusta Herald (Augusta, GA)
Aurora Advertiser (Aurora, MO) **10188**
Aurora Advocate (Stow, OH) **10243**
Aurora News-Register (Aurora, NE) **10196**
Aurora Sentinel (Aurora, CO) **10085**
† Ausable Forks Adirondack Record Post
  (Elizabethtown, NY)
Austell Neighbor (Marietta, GA) **10104**
Austin American-Statesman
  (Austin, TX) **10042**
Austin Chronicle (Austin, TX) **10271**
Austin Daily Herald (Austin, MN) **10002**
† Austintown Leader (Niles, OH)
Austin Weekly News (Oak Park, IL) **10125**
Avalon Bay News, The (Avalon, CA) **10069**
Avenal Progress (Avenal, CA) **10069**
Aventura News (South Miami, FL) **10099**
Avenue News (Baltimore, MD) **10157**

Avon Lake Press (Avon Lake, OH) **10234**
Avon Sentinel (Abingdon, IL) **10109**
Avoyelles Journal (Marksville, LA) **10154**
† Azalea City News & Review (Bayou
  Labatre, AL)
Azle News (Azle, TX) **10271**
Azusa Herald (West Covina, CA) **10084**

B

Back of the Yards Journal (Chicago, IL) **10112**
Bainbridge Post-Searchlight
  (Bainbridge, GA) **10101**
Bainbridge Review (Bainbridge
  Island, WA) **10290**
Baker City Herald (Baker City, OR) **10031**
Baker County Press, The
  (MacClenny, FL) **10096**
Baker Observer (Baker, LA) **10152**
Baker Record-Courier (Baker City, OR) **10247**
Bakersfield Californian (Bakersfield, CA) **9961**
Baldwin Bulletin (Baldwin, WI) **10297**
Baldwin Citizen (Mineola, NY) **10218**
Baldwin Herald (Lawrence, NY) **10216**
Baldwinsville Messenger
  (Baldwinsville, NY) **10209**
Baldwin Times (Bay Minette, AL) **10057**
† Bal Harbor/Bay Harbour News (South
  Miami, FL)
Ballston Journal (Ballston Spa, NY) **10209**
Baltic Beacon (Dell Rapids, SD) **10264**
Baltimore Chronicle (Baltimore, MD) **10157**
Baltimore Messenger (Baltimore, MD) **10157**
Baltimore Sun (Baltimore, MD) **9995**
Bangor Daily News (Bangor, ME) **9995**
Banner-Gazette (Pekin, IN) **10134**
Banner-Graphic (Greencastle, IN) **9983**
Banner-News (Magnolia, AR) **9960**
Banner Journal (Black River Falls, WI) **10297**
Banner Press Newspaper, The
  (Columbus, TX) **10273**
Banning Record Gazette (Banning, CA) **9961**
Baraboo News-Republic (Baraboo, WI) **10053**
Barberton Herald (Barberton, OH) **10234**
Barbour Democrat, The (Philippi, WV) **10295**
Barbourville Mountain Advocate
  (Barbourville, KY) **10146**
Bargain Express Newspaper
  (Milwaukee, WI) **10302**
Bar Harbor Times (Bar Harbor, ME) **10155**
Barnesboro Star, The (Barnesboro, PA) **10251**
Barnesville Enterprise (Barnesville, OH) **10234**
Barnstable Patriot, The (Hyannis, MA) **10162**
Barrington Courier Review
  (Barrington, IL) **10110**
Barrington Times (Warren, RI) **10261**

Barron County News Shield
(Barron, WI) **10297**
Barry County Advertiser (Cassville, MO) **10189**
Bartlesville Examiner-Enterprise
(Bartlesville, OK) **10028**
Bartow Neighbor, The (Cartersville, GA) **10101**
Bastrop Daily Enterprise (Bastrop, LA) **9993**
Batavia Daily News (Batavia, NY) **10014**
Batesville Guard (Batesville, AR) **9959**
Batesville Herald-Tribune
(Batesville, IN) **10129**
Bath County News-Outlook
(Owingsville, KY) **10150**
Battle Creek Enquirer (Battle Creek, MI) **9999**
Battle Creek Shopper (Hastings, MI) **10170**
Baudette Region, The (Baudette, MN) **10176**
Baxley News-Banner (Baxley, GA) **10101**
Baxter Bulletin (Mountain Home, AR) **9960**
Baxter Springs Citizen (Baxter
Springs, KS) **10142**
Bay Area Press (Oakland, CA) **10078**
Bay Beacon, The (Niceville, FL) **10097**
Bay Bulletin (Melbourne, FL) **10096**
Bay City Times (Bay City, MI) **9999**
Bay City Valley Farmer (Bay City, MI) **10167**
Baylor County Banner (Seymour, TX) **10280**
Bay News (Brooklyn, NY) **10210**
Bayonne Community News
(Bayonne, NJ) **10200**
Bay Ridge Courier (Brooklyn, NY) **10210**
Bayshore Sun (La Porte, TX) **10277**
Bayside Times, The (Bayside, NY) **10210**
Bay State Banner (Boston, MA) **10160**
Bay St. Louis Sea Coast Echo (Bay St.
Louis, MS) **10185**
Bay Times (Stevensville, MD) **10159**
Baytown Sun (Baytown, TX) **10042**
Bay Viewer, The (Wauwatosa, WI) **10307**
Bay Voice (New Baltimore, MI) **10173**
Beach & Bay Press (San Diego, CA) **10080**
Beach Bulletin (Fort Myers Beach, FL) **10095**
Beachcomber, The (Surf City, NJ) **10207**
Beaches Leader (Jacksonville
Beach, FL) **10095**
Beach Haven Times (Manahawkin, NJ) **10204**
Beach Reporter, The (Manhattan
Beach, CA) **10077**
Beacon-Forum (Eldon, IA) **10138**
Beacon-Record (Hopewell, NJ) **10203**
Beacon Free Press (Wappingers
Falls, NY) **10224**
Beacon Hill News, The/South District Journal
(Seattle, WA) **10292**
Beacon Light (Mahopac, NY) **10217**
Beacon News (Aurora, IL) **9977**
Beacon Newspaper (Babylon, NY) **10209**

Beacon Observer, The (Overton, NE) **10198**
Beacon, The (Concord, MA) **10161**
Beacon, The (Manahawkin, NJ) **10204**
Beacon, The (Port Clinton, OH) **10242**
Beardstown Illinoian-Star
(Beardstown, IL) **10111**
Beatrice Daily Sun (Beatrice, NE) **10009**
Beaufort Gazette (Beaufort, SC) **10038**
Beaufort Shopper (Beaufort, SC) **10261**
Beaumont Enterprise (Beaumont, TX) **10042**
Beauregard Daily News (De Ridder, LA) **9994**
Beaver County Times (Beaver, PA) **10032**
Beavercreek News-Current
(Dayton, OH) **10023**
Beaver Dam Daily Citizen (Beaver
Dam, WI) **10053**
Beaver Dam Ohio County Messenger (Beaver
Dam, KY) **10146**
Beaverton Valley Times (Portland, OR) **10249**
Becker County Record (Detroit
Lakes, MN) **10178**
Bedford Bulletin (Bedford, VA) **10285**
Bedford Gazette/Gazette Sunday
(Bedford, PA) **10032**
Bedford Minuteman (Concord, MA) **10161**
Bedford Sun Banner (Cleveland, OH) **10236**
Bedford Time Register (Bedford, OH) **10234**
Beebe News (Beebe, AR) **10065**
Beecher City Journal (Beecher City, IL) **10111**
Bee, The (Portland, OR) **10250**
Bee, The (Phillips, WI) **10304**
Beeville Bee-Picayune (Beeville, TX) **10271**
Belchertown Sentinel
(Belchertown, MA) **10160**
Belevedere Citizen (Los Angeles, CA) **10075**
Belle Banner (Belle, MO) **10183**
Bellefontaine Examiner
(Bellefontaine, OH) **10022**
Belle Fourche Post (Belle Fourche, SD) **10264**
Belle Plaine News, The (Belle
Plaine, KS) **10143**
Belleview Voice of South Marion
(Belleview, FL) **10093**
Belleville Enterprise (Wayne, MI) **10176**
Belleville Journal (Belleville, IL) **10111**
Belleville News-Democrat (Belleville, IL) **9977**
Belleville Post (Bloomfield, NJ) **10201**
Belleville Recorder (Belleville, WI) **10297**
Belleville Telescope (Belleville, KS) **10143**
Belleville Times News (Nutley, NJ) **10205**
Bellevue Gazette (Bellevue, OH) **10023**
Bellevue Leader (Bellevue, NE) **10196**
Bell Gardens Review (Los Angeles, CA) **10075**
Bellingham Herald (Bellingham, WA) **10050**
Bell Maywood Cudahy Industrial Post (Los
Angeles, CA) **10075**

Bellmore-Merrick Observer
  (Bellmore, NY) **10210**
Bellmore Life (Bellmore, NY) **10210**
Bellows Falls Town Crier (Bellows
  Falls, VT) **10283**
Bellville Times (Bellville, TX) **10271**
Belmont Banner (Belmont, NC) **10226**
Belmont Citizen-Herald (Needham, MA) **10164**
Beloit Daily Call (Beloit, KS) **9989**
Beloit Daily News (Beloit, WI) **10053**
Belvidere Daily Republican (Belvidere, IL) **9978**
Benbrook News (Fort Worth, TX) **10275**
Benicia Herald (Benicia, CA) **9961**
Bennetts Valley News (Weedville, PA) **10259**
Benning Leader, The (Columbus, GA) **10102**
Bennington Banner (Bennington, VT) **10048**
Bensenville Press (Elmhurst, IL) **10116**
Benson County Farmers Press
  (Minnewaukan, ND) **10233**
Benson Swift County Monitor-News
  (Benson, MN) **10177**
Benton Bulletin (Philomath, OR) **10249**
Benton County Daily Record
  (Bentonville, AR) **9959**
Benton Courier (Benton, AR) **9959**
Benton Review, The (Fowler, IN) **10131**
Bergen News, The (Palisades Park, NJ) **10205**
Berkeley Independent (Moncks
  Corner, SC) **10263**
Berkshire Courier (Great
  Barrington, MA) **10162**
Berkshire Eagle (Pittsfield, MA) **9998**
Berkshire Penny Saver (Lee, MA) **10162**
Berkshire Record (Great
  Barrington, MA) **10162**
Berlin Buyers' Guide (Berlin, WI) **10297**
Berlin Daily Sun (Berlin, NH) **10011**
Berlin Journal (Berlin, WI) **10297**
Berlin Reporter, The (Berlin, NH) **10011**
Bernardsville News (Bernardsville, NJ) **10200**
Berne Tri-Weekly News (Berne, IN) **10130**
Berrien County Record (Buchanan, MI) **10168**
Berrien Press (Nashville, GA) **10105**
Berryessa Sun (Milpitas, CA) **10078**
Bertie Ledger-Advance (Windsor, NC) **10232**
Berwyn/Cicero Life (Berwyn, IL) **10111**
Bessemer City Record (Kings
  Mountain, NC) **10228**
Bethany Republican-Clipper
  (Bethany, MO) **10188**
▼Bethel Beacon (Bethel, CT) **10089**
Bethel Journal, The (Loveland, OH) **10240**
Bethesda/Chevy Chase Almanac
  (Potomac, MD) **10159**
Bettendorf News (Bettendorf, IA) **10137**
Beulah Beacon (Beulah, ND) **10232**

Beverly Hills Courier (Beverly Hills, CA) **10069**
Beverly Hills Independent (Santa
  Monica, CA) **10082**
Beverly News (Midlothian, IL) **10123**
Beverly Review (Chicago, IL) **10112**
Bexley News (Columbus, OH) **10237**
Biddeford-Saco-OOB Courier
  (Biddeford, ME) **10155**
Bienville Democrat & Ringgold Record
  (Arcadia, LA) **10152**
Big Bear Life (Big Bear Lake, CA) **10069**
Big Fork Eagle (Bigfork, MT) **10195**
Big Rapids Pioneer (Big Rapids, MI) **9999**
Big Sandy News, The (Louisa, KY) **10149**
Big Spring Herald (Big Spring, TX) **10042**
Billboard, The (Berlin, WI) **10297**
Billerica Minuteman (North
  Billerica, MA) **10164**
Billings Gazette (Billings, MT) **10008**
Biloxi-D'Iberville Press (D'Iberville, MS) **10185**
Bird City Times (Bird City, KS) **10143**
Bird Island Union (Bird Island, MN) **10177**
Birmingham Eccentric, The
  (Birmingham, MI) **10167**
† Birmingham Free Press (Birmingham, AL)
Birmingham News (Birmingham, AL) **9955**
Birmingham Post-Herald
  (Birmingham, AL) **9955**
Birmingham World (Birmingham, AL) **10057**
Bisbee Daily Review (Bisbee, AZ) **9957**
▼Bisbee News, The (Bisbee, AZ) **10063**
▼Bisbee Now (Bisbee, AZ) **10063**
Bismarck Tribune (Bismarck, ND) **10021**
Bixby Bulletin (Tulsa, OK) **10247**
† Biz (Oxford, PA)
Blackfoot Morning News (Blackfoot, ID) **9976**
Black Forest News (Colorado
  Springs, CO) **10086**
Black Hills Pioneer (Spearfish, SD) **10039**
Black Hills Press (Sturgis, SD) **10265**
Black Mountain News (Black
  Mountain, NC) **10226**
Blackstone Courier-Record
  (Blackstone, VA) **10285**
Blackstone Valley Tribune
  (Whitinsville, MA) **10166**
Blackwell Journal-Tribune
  (Blackwell, OK) **10028**
Blade Atlas (Blanchardville, WI) **10298**
Bladen Daily Journal
  (Elizabethtown, NC) **10019**
Blade, The (Swainsboro, GA) **10106**
Blaine-Spring Lake Park Life (Coon
  Rapids, MN) **10178**
Blaine Banner (Blaine, MN) **10177**
Blair Enterprise (Blair, NE) **10196**

Blair Pilot-Tribune (Blair, NE) **10196**
Blair Press (Blair, WI) **10298**
Blairstown Press (Blairstown, NJ) **10201**
Blanco County News (Blanco, TX) **10271**
Bland Courier (Belle, MO) **10188**
Blandinsville Star Gazette
  (Abingdon, IL) **10109**
Bland Messenger (Wytheville, VA) **10290**
Blazer News (Jackson, MI) **10171**
Blissfield Advance (Blissfield, MI) **10167**
Bloomer Advance (Bloomer, WI) **10298**
Bloomfield Journal (Bristol, CT) **10090**
Bloomfield Life (Nutley, NJ) **10205**
Bloomingdale Press (Bloomingdale, IL) **10111**
Bloomington Sun-Current
  (Bloomington, MN) **10177**
Bloomville Gazette (Attica, OH) **10234**
Blount Countian, The (Oneonta, AL) **10061**
Blowing Rocket, The (Blowing
  Rock, NC) **10227**
Bluefield Daily Telegraph
  (Bluefield, WV) **10052**
Blue Mound Leader (Blue Mound, IL) **10111**
Blue Ridge Leader, The
  (Purcellville, VA) **10288**
Blue Springs Examiner (Blue
  Springs, MO) **10005**
Blue Water Voice (New Baltimore, MI) **10173**
Bluffton News-Banner (Bluffton, IN) **9982**
Bluffton News, The (Bluffton, OH) **10234**
Blythe Advertiser (Palm Desert, CA) **10079**
Boardman News (Boardman, OH) **10235**
Boca Monday (Deerfield Beach, FL) **10094**
Bogalusa Daily News & Sunday News
  (Bogalusa, LA) **9993**
Boise City News, The (Boise City, OK) **10245**
Bolingbrook Metropolitan (Lemont, IL) **10121**
Bolingbrook Sun (Bolingbrook, IL) **10111**
Bolivar Bulletin-Times (Bolivar, TN) **10265**
Bolivar Herald-Free Press (Bolivar, MO) **10188**
Bollinger County Banner-Press (Marble
  Hill, MO) **10191**
Bolton Common (Bolton, MA) **10160**
Bonham Daily Favorite (Bonham, TX) **10042**
Bonita Banner (Bonita Springs, FL) **10093**
Bonner County Daily Bee (Sandpoint, ID) **9977**
Bonners Ferry Herald (Bonners
  Ferry, ID) **10107**
Bonner Springs-Edwardsville Chieftain (Bonner
  Springs, KS) **10143**
Booker News, The (Booker, TX) **10271**
Boone County Journal (Ashland, MO) **10188**
Boone County Recorder (Florence, KY) **10148**
Boone News-Republican (Boone, IA) **9986**
Booneville Banner-Independent
  (Booneville, MS) **10185**

Boone Watauga Democrat (Boone, NC) **10227**
Boonville Daily News (Boonville, MO) **10005**
Boonville Herald (Boonville, NY) **10210**
Boonville Standard (Boonville, IN) **10130**
Booster, The (Columbus, OH) **10237**
Boothbay Register (Boothbay
  Harbor, ME) **10155**
Borger News-Herald (Borger, TX) **10042**
Boscobel Dial (Boscobel, WI) **10298**
Bosque County News (Meridian, TX) **10279**
Bossier Banner-Progress (Bossier
  City, LA) **10152**
Bossier Press-Tribune (Bossier
  City, LA) **10152**
Boston Globe (Boston, MA) **9997**
Boston Herald (Boston, MA) **9997**
Boston Phoenix (Boston, MA) **10160**
Boulder City News (Boulder City, NV) **10199**
Bound Brook Chronicle (Somerville, NJ) **10206**
Bourbon County Citizen (Paris, KY) **10150**
Bourne Courier (Yarmouthport, MA) **10167**
Boutique & Villager (Burlingame, CA) **10070**
Bowie Blade-News (Bowie, MD) **10158**
Bowie News (Bowie, TX) **10271**
Bowling Green Times (Bowling
  Green, MO) **10188**
Bowman Finder (Bowman, ND) **10232**
Box Elder News Journal (Brigham
  City, UT) **10282**
Boyertown Area Times (Boyertown, PA) **10251**
Boynton Beach Times (Deerfield
  Beach, FL) **10094**
Bozeman Daily Chronicle
  (Bozeman, MT) **10008**
Braceville Express (Wilmington, IL) **10129**
Brackett News The (Brackettville, TX) **10271**
Bradenton Herald, The (Bradenton, FL) **9971**
Bradford County Telegraph (Starke, FL) **10099**
Bradford Era, The (Bradford, PA) **10032**
Bradford Journal/Miner (Bradford, PA) **10251**
Brady Standard (Brady, TX) **10271**
Braidwood Index (Wilmington, IL) **10129**
Braidwood Journal, The (Braidwood, IL) **10111**
Brainerd Daily Dispatch (Brainerd, MN) **10002**
Braintree Forum (Marshfield, MA) **10163**
Brandon News, The (Brandon, FL) **10093**
Brandon Valley Challenger (Dell
  Rapids, SD) **10264**
Brandywine Chronicle (Oxford, PA) **10256**
Branford Review (Branford, CT) **10090**
Branson Daily News (Hollister, MO) **10006**
Brantley Enterprise (Nahunta, GA) **10105**
Brattleboro Reformer (Brattleboro, VT) **10048**
Brawley Advertiser (Palm Desert, CA) **10079**
Braxton Citizen's News (Sutton, WV) **10296**
Braxton Democrat-Central (Sutton, WV) **10296**

Brazil Times (Brazil, IN) **9982**
Brazosport Facts, The (Clute, TX) **10042**
Brea Progress (Anaheim, CA) **10068**
Breckinridge County Herald-News
   (Hardinsburg, KY) **10148**
Brecksville Gazette (Cleveland, OH) **10236**
Breese Journal (Breese, IL) **10111**
† Breeze Herald (Conneut Lake Park, PA)
Breeze, The (Rockledge, PA) **10258**
Brenham Banner-Press (Brenham, TX) **10042**
Brentwood Journal (Brentwood, TN) **10266**
Brentwood Westwood Press (Santa
   Monica, CA) **10082**
Brevard Reporter, The (Cocoa, FL) **10094**
Brewery Gulch Gazette (Bisbee, AZ) **10063**
Brewster Times (Mahopac, NY) **10217**
Brewton Standard, The (Brewton, AL) **10058**
Brick Township Town News (Brick, NJ) **10201**
Bridgeport Index (Bridgeport, TX) **10272**
Bridgeport Leader (Bridgeport, IL) **10111**
Bridgeport News (Chicago, IL) **10112**
Bridger Valley Pioneer (Lyman, WY) **10309**
Bridgeton Evening News
   (Bridgeton, NJ) **10011**
Bridgeview Independent (Midlothian, IL) **10123**
Bridgeville Area News (Monroeville, PA) **10255**
Bridgewater Independent
   (Middleboro, MA) **10163**
† Bridgewater Townsman (Bridgewater, MA)
Bridgton News (Bridgton, ME) **10155**
Brighton-Pittsford Post, The
   (Fishers, NY) **10214**
Brighton/Blade Market Place
   (Brighton, CO) **10085**
Brighton Argus (Brighton, MI) **10168**
Brighton Park-McKinley Park Life
   (Chicago, IL) **10112**
Brillion News (Brillion, WI) **10298**
Brinkley Argus (Brinkley, AR) **10065**
Bristol Herald-Courier, The (Bristol, VA) **10048**
Bristol Phoenix (Bristol, RI) **10260**
Bristol Pilot (Bristol, PA) **10251**
Bristol Press, The (Bristol, CT) **9970**
Bristow News (Bristow, OK) **10245**
Britt News-Tribune (Britt, IA) **10137**
Broad Top Bulletin (Saxton, PA) **10259**
Brockport/Holley Suburban News
   (Spencerport, NY) **10223**
Brockport Post, The (Brockport, NY) **10210**
Brockton Enterprise, The (Brockton, MA) **9997**
Broken Arrow Ledger & Scout (Broken
   Arrow, OK) **10245**
† Broken Arrow Scout (Broken Arrow, OK)
Bronx News (Bronx, NY) **10210**
Bronx Press-Review (Bronx, NY) **10210**
Brooke County Review (Wellsburg, WV) **10296**

Brookfield Journal (Brookfield, CT) **10090**
Brookfield News (Wauwatosa, WI) **10307**
Brookhaven Daily Leader
   (Brookhaven, MS) **10004**
Brookhaven Review (Smithtown, NY) **10223**
Brookings Register (Brookings, SD) **10039**
Brooklyn Center Sun Post
   (Minneapolis, MN) **10180**
Brooklyn Chronicle (Brooklyn, IA) **10137**
Brooklyn Daily Bulletin (Brooklyn, NY) **10014**
Brooklyn Graphic (Brooklyn, NY) **10210**
Brooklyn Heights Courier
   (Brooklyn, NY) **10210**
Brooklyn Heights Press (Brooklyn, NY) **10211**
Brooklyn Home Reporter & Sunset News
   (Brooklyn, NY) **10211**
Brooklyn Park Sun Post
   (Minneapolis, MN) **10180**
Brooklyn Record (Brooklyn, NY) **10211**
Brooklyn Spectator (Brooklyn, NY) **10211**
Brooklyn Sun Journal (Cleveland, OH) **10236**
† Brooklyn Times (Brooklyn, NY)
† Brooksville Sun Journal (Brooksville, FL)
† Brookville American (Brookville, PA)
Brookville American-Democrat
   (Brookville, IN) **10130**
Broomfield Enterprise (Broomfield, CO) **10086**
Broward News (Margate, FL) **10096**
Broward Times, The (Fort
   Lauderdale, FL) **10095**
Brown County Democrat (Nashville, IN) **10134**
Brown County Press (Mt. Orab, OH) **10241**
Brown Deer Herald (Wauwatosa, WI) **10307**
Brownfield News (Brownfield, TX) **10272**
Brownsville Herald (Brownsville, TX) **10042**
Brownsville States-Graphic
   (Brownsville, TN) **10266**
Brownwood Bulletin (Brownwood, TX) **10042**
Bruce Calhoun County Journal
   (Bruce, MS) **10185**
Brunswick Beacon, The (Shallotte, NC) **10230**
Brunswick Citizen (Brunswick, MD) **10158**
Brunswick News, The (Brunswick, GA) **9974**
Brunswick Sun Times (Cleveland, OH) **10236**
Brunswick Times-Gazette
   (Lawrenceville, VA) **10287**
Brush News-Tribune (Brush, CO) **10086**
Bryan College Station Eagle (Bryan, TX) **10042**
Bryan College Station Press (Bryan, TX) **10272**
Bryan County Star (Durant, OK) **10245**
Bryan County Times (Pembroke, GA) **10105**
Bryan Times (Bryan, OH) **10023**
Buckeye Review, The (Youngstown, OH) **10244**
Bucks County Courier Times
   (Levittown, PA) **10034**
Bucks County Tribune (Horsham, PA) **10253**

Bucyrus Telegraph-Forum
(Bucyrus, OH)   **10023**
Budgeteer Press/Skyworld Duluth News
(Duluth, MN)   **10178**
Buffalo Bulletin (Buffalo, WY)   **10308**
Buffalo County Journal (Cochrane, WI)   **10298**
Buffalo Grove Countryside
(Bannockburn, IL)   **10110**
Buffalo Grove Journal & Topics (Des
Plaines, IL)   **10115**
Buffalo News, The (Buffalo, NY)   **10014**
Buffalo Reflex (Buffalo, MO)   **10188**
Buffalo Ridge Gazette, The
(Ruthton, MN)   **10182**
Buffalo River Review (Linden, TN)   **10268**
Buffalo Rocket (Buffalo, NY)   **10211**
Bugle, The (Niles, IL)   **10124**
Buhl Herald (Buhl, ID)   **10107**
Bulletin, The (Crestview, FL)   **10094**
Bulletin, The (Bedford, OH)   **10234**
Bulletin, The (Bend, OR)   **10031**
Bulletin, The (Santa Fe, TX)   **10280**
Bulletin, The (Kenosha, WI)   **10301**
Bunker Hill Gazette News (Bunker
Hill, IL)   **10112**
Burbank-Stickney Independent
(Midlothian, IL)   **10123**
Bureau County Republican
(Princeton, IL)   **10127**
Burke County Observer
(Morganton, NC)   **10229**
Burke Times, The (Reston, VA)   **10288**
Burleson County Citizen Tribune
(Caldwell, TX)   **10272**
Burleson Star (Burleson, TX)   **10272**
Burlington County Times
(Willingboro, NJ)   **10013**
Burlington Free Press (Burlington, VT)   **10048**
Burlington Standard Press
(Burlington, WI)   **10298**
Burlington Union (Lexington, MA)   **10162**
Burnet Bulletin (Burnet, TX)   **10272**
Burnett County Sentinel
(Grantsburg, WI)   **10300**
Burns Times-Herald (Burns, OR)   **10248**
Burnsville Sun-Current (Burnsville, MN)   **10177**
Burr Ridge Doings (Hinsdale, IL)   **10120**
Burwell Tribune (Burwell, NE)   **10196**
Business Examiner (Gig Harbor, WA)   **10291**
Business Post, The (Alpharetta, GA)   **10100**
Butler Choctaw Advocate (Butler, AL)   **10058**
Butler County News (Georgiana, AL)   **10059**
Butler Eagle (Butler, PA)   **10032**
Butner-Creedmoor News, The
(Creedmoor, NC)   **10227**

Butte County Valley Irrigator
(Newell, SD)   **10265**
Butte Valley Star (Merrill, OR)   **10249**
† Buyer's Guide (Napa, CA)
Buyer's Guide Cent Saver
(Mauston, WI)   **10302**
† Byron Center/Dorr Advance (Jenison, MI)

C

Cabell Record (Culloden, WV)   **10294**
Cable Scene (Idaho Falls, ID)   **10108**
Caddo Citizen (Vivian, LA)   **10155**
Cadillac Evening News (Cadillac, MI)   **9999**
Cadiz Record, The (Cadiz, KY)   **10147**
Cadott Sentinel (Cadott, WI)   **10298**
Cahokia Journal (Columbia, IL)   **10114**
Cairo Citizen (Cairo, IL)   **10112**
Cairo Messenger (Cairo, GA)   **10101**
Calais Advertiser (Calais, ME)   **10155**
Caldwell Burleson County Citizen-Tribune
(Caldwell, TX)   **10272**
Caledonia/Gaines Advance
(Jenison, MI)   **10171**
Caledonian-Record, The (St.
Johnsbury, VT)   **10048**
Calexico Advertiser (Palm Desert, CA)   **10079**
Calhoun Chronicle (Grantsville, WV)   **10294**
Calhoun News (Hardin, IL)   **10119**
Calhoun Times (Calhoun, GA)   **10101**
California Advocate, The (Fresno, CA)   **10072**
California Courier (Glendale, CA)   **10073**
California Democrat (California, MO)   **10188**
Californian, The (Salinas, CA)   **9965**
Californian, The (Temecula, CA)   **9966**
Call-Leader (Elwood, IN)   **9983**
▼Callaway Courier (Holts Summit, MO)   **10190**
Call, The (Schuylkill Haven, PA)   **10259**
Call, The (Woonsocket, RI)   **10038**
Caloosa Belle (La Belle, FL)   **10096**
Calumet Press, The (Highland, IN)   **10132**
Calvert Independent (Prince
Fredrick, MD)   **10159**
Camarillo Star (Simi Valley, CA)   **9966**
Camas/Washougal Post Record
(Camas, WA)   **10290**
Cambridge Chronicle (Cambridge, IL)   **10112**
Cambridge Chronicle (Somerville, MA)   **10165**
Cambridge News (Cambridge, WI)   **10298**
Camden Chronicle, The (Camden, TN)   **10266**
Camden County Record (Camden, NJ)   **10201**
Camden County Tribune (St.
Marys, GA)   **10106**
Camden Herald (Camden, ME)   **10155**
Camden News (Camden, AR)   **9959**

Cameron Citizen Observer
(Cameron, MO) **10188**
Cameron County Echo (Emporium, PA) **10252**
Cameron Herald (Cameron, TX) **10272**
Camilla Enterprise (Camilla, GA) **10101**
Camillus Advocate (Baldwinsville, NY) **10209**
Campbell County Recorder (Fort
Thomas, KY) **10148**
Campbellsport News
(Campbellsport, WI) **10298**
Canada News (Auburndale, FL) **10093**
Canandaigua Daily Messenger
(Canandaigua, NY) **10014**
Canarsie Courier (Brooklyn, NY) **10211**
Canarsie Digest (Brooklyn, NY) **10211**
Canastota Bee-Journal (Canastota, NY) **10211**
Canby Herald (Canby, OR) **10248**
Canby News (Canby, MN) **10177**
Candor Chronicle (Trumansburg, NY) **10224**
Canistota Clipper (Canistota, SD) **10264**
Canton Eagle (Wayne, MI) **10176**
Canton Independent-Sentinel
(Canton, PA) **10251**
Canton Journal (Canton, MA) **10161**
Canton Observer (Plymouth, MI) **10174**
Canyon Courier (Evergreen, CO) **10087**
Canyon News (Canyon, TX) **10272**
Cape Codder (Orleans, MA) **10164**
† Cape Cod News (Yarmouth Port, MA)
Cape Cod Times (Hyannis, MA) **9997**
Cape May County Gazette Leader
(Wildwood, NJ) **10208**
Cape May Herald Dispatch (Rio
Grande, NJ) **10206**
Cape May Star & Wave (Cape May, NJ) **10201**
Capeway News (Middleboro, MA) **10163**
Capistrano Valley News (Lake
Forest, CA) **10074**
Capital-Journal (Topeka, KS) **9991**
Capital City Weekly (Juneau, AK) **10062**
Capital Spotlight (Washington, DC) **10092**
Capital, The (Annapolis, MD) **9995**
Capital Times, The (Madison, WI) **10054**
▼Capital Weekly (Augusta, ME) **10155**
Capitol Hill Beacon (Oklahoma
City, OK) **10246**
Capitol Hill Times (Seattle, WA) **10293**
Carbondale News (Carbondale, PA) **10251**
Carey Progressor-Times, The
(Carey, OH) **10235**
Caribou Aroostook Republican & News
(Caribou, ME) **10155**
Caribou County Sun (Soda Springs, ID) **10109**
Carlinville Democrat (Carlinville, IL) **10112**
Carlisle Mercury, The (Carlisle, KY) **10147**
Carlisle Sentinel (Carlisle, PA) **10032**

Carlsbad Sun (Carlsbad, CA) **10070**
Carlyle Union Banner (Carlyle, IL) **10112**
Carmel News Tribune (Fishers, IN) **10131**
Carmel Pine Cone (Carmel, CA) **10070**
Carmel Times (Mahopac, NY) **10217**
Carmichael Times (Carmichael, CA) **10070**
Carmi Times (Carmi, IL) **9978**
Carol City/Opa-Locka News (Miami, FL) **10096**
Carolina Times (Durham, NC) **10227**
Caroline Progress, The (Bowling
Green, VA) **10285**
Carolinian, The (Raleigh, NC) **10230**
Carol Stream Press (Bloomingdale, IL) **10111**
† Carpinteria Herald (Goleta, CA)
Carroll County Comet (Flora, IN) **10131**
Carroll County Independent (Center
Ossipee, NH) **10199**
Carroll County News-Leader
(Huntingdon, TN) **10267**
Carroll County Review (Thomson, IL) **10128**
Carroll County Sun (Westminster, MD) **9996**
Carroll County Times (Westminster, MD) **9996**
Carroll Gardens/Cobble Hill Courier
(Brooklyn, NY) **10211**
Carroll News, The (Hillsville, VA) **10286**
Carroll Times Herald (Carroll, IA) **9987**
† Carrollton Chronicle (Carrollton, TX)
Carrollton Democrat (Carrollton, MO) **10188**
Carrollton Gazette Patriot
(Carrollton, IL) **10112**
Carrollwood News (Tampa, FL) **10099**
Carson Press (Elgin, ND) **10232**
Carson Wave (Los Angeles, CA) **10075**
Carteret County News-Times (Morehead
City, NC) **10229**
Cartersville Daily Tribune News
(Cartersville, GA) **9974**
Carthage Courier (Carthage, TN) **10266**
Carthage Press (Carthage, MO) **10005**
Carthage Republican Tribune
(Carthage, NY) **10212**
Carthaginian, The (Carthage, MS) **10185**
Carver Reporter (Plymouth, MA) **10164**
Cary-Grove Countryside (Barrington, IL) **10110**
Cary News (Cary, NC) **10227**
Casa Grande Dispatch (Casa
Grande, AZ) **9957**
Casey County News (Liberty, KY) **10149**
Casey County Shopper, The
(Columbia, KY) **10147**
Cashmere Valley Record
(Cashmere, WA) **10291**
Cashton Record (Cashton, WI) **10298**
Casper Star Tribune (Casper, WY) **10055**
Cass City Chronicle (Cass City, MI) **10168**
Cass County Reporter (Casselton, ND) **10232**

Cassville Democrat (Cassville, MO) **10189**
Castleton Banner (Fishers, IN) **10131**
Caswell Messenger (Yanceyville, NC) **10232**
Catalina Islander, The (Avalon, CA) **10069**
† Cato Citizen (Red Creek, NY)
Catonsville Times (Baltimore, MD) **10157**
Catoosa County News (Ringgold, GA) **10105**
Catoosa Times Herald (Catoosa, OK) **10245**
Cavalier County Republican
   (Langdon, ND) **10232**
Cazenovia Republican (Cazenovia, NY) **10212**
Cecil Whig (Elkton, MD) **9996**
Cedar County Republican
   (Stockton, MO) **10194**
Cedar Creek Pilot (Gun Barrel City, TX) **10276**
Cedar Hill Today (DeSoto, TX) **10273**
Cedar Key Beacon (Cedar, FL) **10094**
Cedar Lake Journal (Lowell, IN) **10133**
Cedar Rapids Gazette (Cedar Rapids, IA) **9987**
Cedartown Standard (Cedartown, GA) **10101**
Celina Daily Standard (Celina, OH) **10023**
Center Post Dispatch (Monte Vista, CO) **10088**
Center Republican (Washburn, ND) **10233**
Centerville-Bellbrook Times
   (Kettering, OH) **10240**
Centerville Crusader (Centerville, IN) **10130**
Central City Republican Nonpareil (Central
   City, NE) **10197**
Central City Times-Argus (Central
   City, KY) **10147**
Central Coast Sun-Bulletin (Morro
   Bay, CA) **10078**
† Central Coast Times (Paso Robles, CA)
Centralia Fireside Guard
   (Centralia, MO) **10189**
Centralia Sentinel (Centralia, IL) **9978**
Central Kentucky News-Journal
   (Campbellsville, KY) **10147**
Central Maine Morning Sentinel
   (Waterville, ME) **9995**
Central Missouri News (Sedalia, MO) **10192**
Central Oregonian, The (Prineville, OR) **10250**
Central Post (Dayton, NJ) **10202**
Central Record (Medford, NJ) **10204**
Central Saint Croix News
   (Hammond, WI) **10300**
Central Valley Times (Grants Pass, OR) **10248**
Central Virginian, The (Louisa, VA) **10287**
Central West End Journal (St.
   Louis, MO) **10193**
Centre Daily Times (State College, PA) **10036**
Centreville Press (Centreville, AL) **10058**
Centreville Times (Reston, VA) **10288**
Ceres Courier (Ceres, CA) **10070**
Chagrin Herald Sun (Cleveland, OH) **10236**

Chagrin Valley Times (Chagrin
   Falls, OH) **10235**
Challis Messenger (Challis, ID) **10107**
Chamblee-DeKalb Neighbor
   (Marietta, GA) **10104**
Champaign News Gazette
   (Champaign, IL) **9978**
Chandler Arizonan Tribune
   (Chandler, AZ) **9957**
Chandler Independent (Chandler, AZ) **10063**
† Chandler Post (Boonville, IN)
Chanhassen Villager (Chanhassen, MN) **10177**
Chantilly Times (Reston, VA) **10288**
Chanute Tribune (Chanute, KS) **9989**
Chapel Hill Herald (Chapel Hill, NC) **10018**
Chapel Hill News (Chapel Hill, NC) **10227**
Chariton Herald-Patriot (Chariton, IA) **10137**
Chariton Leader (Chariton, IA) **10137**
Charles City Press (Charles City, IA) **9987**
Charleston Chronicle, The
   (Charleston, SC) **10261**
Charleston Daily Mail (Charleston, WV) **10052**
Charleston Enterprise-Courier
   (Charleston, MO) **10189**
Charleston Gazette, The
   (Charleston, WV) **10052**
Charleston Post & Courier
   (Charleston, SC) **10038**
Charleston Times-Courier
   (Charleston, IL) **9978**
† Charlestown Citizen (Brookline, MA)
Charlevoix Courier (Charlevoix, MI) **10168**
Charlotte Gazette (Drakes Branch, VA) **10286**
Charlotte Observer (Charlotte, NC) **10018**
Charlotte Shopping Guide
   (Charlotte, MI) **10168**
Charlotte Sun Herald (Charlotte
   Harbor, FL) **9971**
Charlottesville-Albemarle Tribune
   (Charlottesville, VA) **10285**
Charlton County Herald (Folkston, GA) **10103**
Chase County Leader-News (Cottonwood
   Falls, KS) **10143**
Chaska Herald (Chaska, MN) **10177**
† Chateaugay Record (Chateaugay, NY)
Chatham Clarion (Auburn, IL) **10110**
Chatham Courier (Madison, NJ) **10203**
Chatham Courier-Roughnotes
   (Chatham, NY) **10212**
Chatham Independent Press (New
   Providence, NJ) **10204**
Chatham News, The (Siler City, NC) **10230**
Chatsworth Times, The
   (Chatsworth, GA) **10101**
Chattanooga Free Press
   (Chattanooga, TN) **10040**

Chattanooga Times (Chattanooga, TN) **10040**
Chattooga Press (Summerville, GA) **10106**
Cheboygan Daily Tribune
 (Cheboygan, MI) **9999**
Cheektowaga Bee (Williamsville, NY) **10225**
Cheektowaga Times (Cheektowaga, NY) **10212**
Chelmsford Independent
 (Chelmsford, MA) **10161**
Chelsea Clinton News (New York, NY) **10220**
Chelsea Record (Revere, MA) **10165**
Chelsea Standard, The (Chelsea, MI) **10168**
Chemung Valley Reporter
 (Horseheads, NY) **10216**
Chenango American (Greene, NY) **10215**
Cheney Free Press (Cheney, WA) **10291**
Cheraw Chronicle, The (Cheraw, SC) **10261**
Cherokee County's Daily Times
 (Cherokee, IA) **9987**
Cherokee County Herald (Centre, AL) **10058**
Cherokee Messenger & Republican
 (Cherokee, OK) **10245**
Cherokee Scout (Murphy, NC) **10229**
Cherokee Tribune, The (Canton, GA) **10101**
† Cherry Hill News (Cherry Hill, NJ)
Cherryville Eagle (Cherryville, NC) **10227**
Chesapeake Post (Chesapeake, VA) **10285**
Cheshire Herald (Cheshire, CT) **10090**
Chester County Press (Oxford, PA) **10256**
Chesterfield Journal (St. Louis, MO) **10193**
Chesterland News (Chesterland, OH) **10235**
Chester News & Reporter (Chester, SC) **10261**
Chesterton Guide (Portage, IN) **10135**
Chesterton Town Crier (Valparaiso, IN) **10136**
Chesterton Tribune (Chesterton, IN) **9982**
Chestnut Hill Local (Philadelphia, PA) **10257**
Chetek Alert, The (Chetek, WI) **10298**
Cheyenne Mountain Journal (Manitou
 Springs, CO) **10088**
Chicago-Lawndale News (Chicago, IL) **10112**
Chicago's N.W. Side Press (Chicago, IL) **10113**
Chicago County Press (Lindstrom, MN) **10179**
Chicago Defender (Chicago, IL) **9978**
Chicago Near North News (Chicago, IL) **10113**
Chicago Near West Gazette
 (Chicago, IL) **10113**
Chicago Post (Chicago, IL) **10113**
Chicago Reader (Chicago, IL) **10113**
Chicago Ridge Citizen (Midlothian, IL) **10123**
Chicago Sun Times (Chicago, IL) **9978**
Chicago Tribune (Chicago, IL) **9978**
Chicago West Side Times (Chicago, IL) **10113**
Chickasha Daily Express
 (Chickasha, OK) **10028**
Chico Enterprise-Record (Chico, CA) **9961**
Chicopee Herald Weekly, The
 (Chicopee, MA) **10161**

Chieftain & Toccoa Record
 (Toccoa, GA) **10106**
Childress Index (Childress, TX) **10272**
Chilkat Valley News (Haines, AK) **10062**
Chillicothe Bulletin (Chillicothe, IL) **10114**
Chillicothe Constitution-Tribune
 (Chillicothe, MO) **10005**
Chillicothe Gazette (Chillicothe, OH) **10023**
Chilton Times-Journal (Chilton, WI) **10298**
Chippewa Herald-Telegram (Chippewa
 Falls, WI) **10053**
Chisholm Free Press & Tribune Press
 (Chisholm, MN) **10177**
Chittenango-Bridgeport Times
 (Canastota, NY) **10212**
Chrisman Leader (Chrisman, IL) **10114**
Christian County Headliner News
 (Ozark, MO) **10192**
Chronicle-Express (Penn Yan, NY) **10221**
Chronicle-Independent (Camden, SC) **10261**
Chronicle News, The (Trinidad, CO) **9969**
Chronicle, The (Atwater, CA) **10069**
Chronicle, The (Milford, CT) **10091**
Chronicle, The (Willimantic, CT) **9971**
Chronicle, The (Milford, DE) **10092**
Chronicle, The (North Dartmouth, MA) **10164**
Chronicle, The (Somerville, NJ) **10206**
Chronicle, The (Carson City, NV) **10199**
Chronicle, The (Glens Falls, NY) **10214**
Chronicle, The (Creswell, OR) **10248**
Chronicle, The (Humboldt, TN) **10267**
Chronicle, The (Centralia, WA) **10050**
Chula Vista Star-News (Chula
 Vista, CA) **10070**
Church Point News (Church Point, LA) **10153**
Cibola County Beacon (Grants, NM) **10208**
Cincinnati Enquirer (Cincinnati, OH) **10023**
Cincinnati Post (Cincinnati, OH) **10023**
Circleville Herald (Circleville, OH) **10023**
Cisco Press (Cisco, TX) **10272**
Cissna Park News (Cissna Park, IL) **10114**
Citizen (American Fork, UT) **10282**
Citizen-Standard, The (Valley View, PA) **10259**
Citizen/Press Plus (Pulaski, TN) **10269**
Citizen Journal (St. Louis, MO) **10193**
Citizen of Morris County (Denville, NJ) **10202**
Citizen Outlet (Mexico, NY) **10218**
Citizen Register (Yorktown Heights, NY) **10018**
Citizens' Advocate Newspaper
 (Coppell, TX) **10273**
Citizen Telegram, The (Rifle, CO) **10089**
Citizen, The (Mansfield, AR) **10066**
Citizen, The (Boyne City, MI) **10168**
Citizen, The (Laconia, NH) **10011**
Citizen, The (Auburn, NY) **10014**
Citizen, The (Houston, TX) **10276**

Citizen Tribune (Morristown, TN) **10041**
Citizen Voice & Times (Irvine, KY) **10149**
Citrus County Chronicle (Crystal
  River, FL) **9971**
City News (Bronx, NY) **10210**
City Paper (Baltimore, MD) **10157**
City Terrace Comet (City of
  Commerce, CA) **10070**
Civic Center NEWSource (Los
  Angeles, CA) **10075**
Clackamas County Review
  (Milwaukee, OR) **10249**
Claiborne Progress (Tazewell, TN) **10270**
Clanton Advertiser (Clanton, AL) **10058**
Claremont Courier (Claremont, CA) **10071**
Claremore Progress (Claremore, OK) **10028**
Clarence Bee (Williamsville, NY) **10225**
Clarendon Hills Doings, The
  (Hinsdale, IL) **10120**
Clarendon Hills Progress (Downers
  Grove, IL) **10115**
Clare Sentinel (Clare, MI) **10168**
Clarinda Herald Journal (Clarinda, IA) **10137**
Clarion-Ledger, The (Jackson, MS) **10004**
Clarion Journal, The (Columbia, IL) **10114**
Clarion News (Corydon, IN) **10130**
Clarion News (Clarion, PA) **10251**
Clark County Press (Neillsville, WI) **10303**
Clark Courier (Reston, VA) **10288**
Clark Eagle (Union, NJ) **10207**
Clarke County Democrat (Grove
  Hill, AL) **10059**
Clarke County Tribune (Quitman, MS) **10187**
Clark Patriot (Rahway, NJ) **10206**
Clarksburg Exponent (Clarksburg, WV) **10052**
Clarksburg Telegram (Clarksburg, WV) **10052**
Clarksdale Press Register
  (Clarksdale, MS) **10004**
Clarkson Integrator (Potsdam, NY) **10221**
Clarkston News (Clarkston, MI) **10168**
Clarkstown Courier, The (Pearl
  River, NY) **10221**
Clarksville Times, The (Clarksville, TX) **10272**
Classified Gazette (San Rafael, CA) **10082**
Clay Center Dispatch (Clay Center, KS) **9989**
Clay City Times, The (Stanton, KY) **10151**
† Clay Countian (Orange Park, FL)
Clay County Crescent (Orange
  Park, FL) **10098**
Clay County Free Press (Clay, WV) **10294**
Clay Dispatch-Tribune (Kansas
  City, MO) **10190**
Clay Times Journal (Lineville, AL) **10060**
Clay Today (Orange Park, FL) **9973**
Clayton County Register (Elkader, IA) **10138**
Clayton Neighbor (Marietta, GA) **10104**

Clayton News-Star (Clayton, NC) **10227**
Clayton News Daily (Jonesboro, GA) **9975**
† Clayton Sun (Atlanta, GA)
Clayton Tribune (Clayton, GA) **10102**
Clear-Ridge Reporter (Chicago, IL) **10113**
Clear Creek Courant (Idaho
  Springs, CO) **10087**
Clear Lake Observer-American
  (Clearlake, CA) **10071**
Clearwater Tribune (Orofino, ID) **10108**
Cleburne News (Heflin, AL) **10050**
Cleburne Times-Review (Cleburne, TX) **10042**
Clemmons Courier (Clemmons, NC) **10227**
† Clermont County Review (Cincinnati OH)
† Clermont Courier (Cincinnati, OH)
Clermont Sun (Batavia, OH) **10234**
Cleveland Advocate (Cleveland, TX) **10272**
Cleveland Bolivar Commercial
  (Cleveland, MS) **10004**
Cleveland Daily Banner (Cleveland, TN) **10040**
Cleveland Plain Dealer (Cleveland, OH) **10023**
Cleveland Times (Shelby, NC) **10230**
Clewiston News (Clewiston, FL) **10094**
Clinch County News (Homerville, GA) **10103**
Clinch Valley News (Tazewell, VA) **10289**
Clinton Chronicle, The (Clinton, SC) **10262**
Clinton County News (Albany, KY) **10146**
Clinton County News (St. Johns, MI) **10175**
Clinton County Post (Mascoutah, IL) **10122**
Clinton County Shoppers Guide
  (Wilmington, OH) **10244**
Clinton Courier (Clinton, NY) **10212**
Clinton Daily Democrat (Clinton, MO) **10006**
Clinton Daily Journal (Clinton, IL) **9978**
Clinton Daily News (Clinton, OK) **10028**
Clinton Eye, The (Clinton, MO) **10189**
Clinton Herald (Clinton, IA) **9987**
Clinton Recorder (Old Saybrook, CT) **10091**
Clinton Topper (Clinton, WI) **10298**
Clinton Van Buren County Democrat
  (Clinton, AR) **10065**
Clintonville Tribune-Gazette
  (Clintonville, WI) **10298**
Clipper-Herald (Lexington, NE) **10197**
Cloquet Billboard Shopper
  (Cloquet, MN) **10178**
Cloquet Pine Knot (Cloquet, MN) **10178**
Cloverdale Reveille (Cloverdale, CA) **10071**
Clover Herald (Clover, SC) **10262**
Clovis Independent (Clovis, CA) **10071**
Clovis News Journal (Clovis, NM) **10013**
Clyde Enterprise (Clyde, OH) **10237**
Coal City Courant (Coal City, IL) **10114**
Coal City Express (Wilmington, IL) **10129**
Coalfield Progress (Norton, VA) **10288**
Coalinga Record (Coalinga, CA) **10071**

Coal Valley News (Danville, WV) **10294**
Coastal Courier (Hinesville, GA) **10103**
Coastal Current, The (South Padre
  Island, TX) **10281**
Coastal Illustrated (St. Simons
  Island, GA) **10106**
Coastal Post (Bolinas, CA) **10070**
Coastal Times (Charleston, SC) **10261**
Coastland Times (Manteo, NC) **10229**
Coastside Chronicle (San Mateo, CA) **10082**
Cobleskill Times Journal
  (Cobleskill, NY) **10212**
Cody Enterprise (Cody, WY) **10308**
Coeur d'Alene Press (Coeur d'Alene, ID) **9977**
Coffey County Today (Burlington, KS) **10143**
Coffeyville Journal, The (Coffeyville, KS) **9989**
Cohasset Mariner (Marshfield, MA) **10163**
Colbert County Reporter
  (Tuscumbia, AL) **10062**
Colby Free Press (Colby, KS) **9989**
Colchester Chronicle (Colchester, IL) **10114**
Coleman Chronicle & Democrat Voice
  (Coleman, TX) **10272**
Colfax Messenger (Colfax, WI) **10299**
Collierville Herald, The (Collierville, TN) **10266**
Collinsville Herald (Collinsville, IL) **10114**
Collinsville Journal (Collinsville, IL) **10114**
Collinsville News (Tulsa, OK) **10247**
Colonial, The (Fort Washington, PA) **10253**
Colonie Spotlight (Delmar, NY) **10213**
Colorado Springs Gazette Telegraph (Colorado
  Springs, CO) **9968**
Colorado Statesman (Denver, CO) **10086**
Columbia Basin Herald (Moses
  Lake, WA) **10051**
Columbia Daily Tribune (Columbia, MO) **10006**
Columbia Flier (Columbia, MD) **10158**
Columbia Heights-Findley Focus
  (Roseville, MN) **10182**
Columbia Missourian (Columbia, MO) **10006**
Columbian-Progress (Columbia, MS) **10185**
Columbia News, The (Columbia, KY) **10147**
Columbia News Times (Martinez, GA) **10104**
Columbian, The (Vancouver, WA) **10051**
Columbus Alive! (Columbus, OH) **10237**
Columbus Daily Advocate
  (Columbus, KS) **9989**
Columbus Dispatch (Columbus, OH) **10023**
Columbus Journal (Columbus, WI) **10299**
Columbus Ledger-Enquirer
  (Columbus, GA) **9975**
Columbus Messenger (Columbus, OH) **10237**
Columbus Telegram (Columbus, NE) **10009**
Colusa County Sun-Herald (Colusa, CA) **10071**
Comanche Chief (Comanche, TX) **10273**
Commack News (Smithtown, NY) **10223**

Command Post, The (Mascoutah, IL) **10122**
Commerce Journal (Commerce, TX) **10273**
Commerce News (Commerce, GA) **10102**
Commercial-Express (Vicksburg, MI) **10175**
Commercial-News (Danville, IL) **9978**
Commercial Appeal, The
  (Memphis, TN) **10041**
Commercial Dispatch, The
  (Columbus, MS) **10004**
Commercial Record (Saugatuck, MI) **10175**
Commonwealth Journal (Somerset, KY) **9993**
Commonwealth Progress (Scotland
  Neck, NC) **10230**
† Communicator Community News (Reno, NV)
Community Advertiser
  (Farmingdale, ME) **10156**
Community Adviser (Beaumont, CA) **10069**
Community Advisor (Marshall, MI) **10172**
Community Booster, The
  (Granville, OH) **10239**
Community Forum (Hackettstown, NJ) **10202**
Community Herald (Monona, WI) **10303**
Community Journal (Wading River, NY) **10224**
Community Journal, South
  (Loveland, OH) **10240**
Community Mirror (Gonzales, LA) **10153**
Community News (St. Louis, MO) **10193**
Community News (Clifton Park, NY) **10212**
Community News, The (Dora, AL) **10058**
Community Press, Mason
  (Loveland, OH) **10240**
† Community Press, West Chester
  (Loveland, OH)
Community Shopper (Birmingham, AL) **10058**
Community Times (Westminster, MD) **10160**
Compton Wave (Los Angeles, CA) **10075**
Concordia Blade-Empire (Concordia, KS) **9989**
Concordia Sentinel (Ferriday, LA) **10153**
Concord Journal (Concord, MA) **10161**
Concord Monitor (Concord, NH) **10011**
Concord Tribune (Concord, NC) **10018**
Conejos County Citizen, The (Monte
  Vista, CO) **10088**
† Conneaut News-Herald (Conneaut, OH)
Conneautville Courier (Springboro, PA) **10259**
Connecticut Post (Bridgeport, CT) **9970**
Connection, The (Grosse Point, MI) **10170**
Connersville News-Examiner
  (Connersville, IN) **9982**
Conroe Courier, The (Conroe, TX) **10043**
Conservative, The (Carrollton, MS) **10185**
Contra Costa Sun (Lafayette, CA) **10074**
Contra Costa Times (Walnut Creek, CA) **9967**
Conway County Petit Jean Country Headlight
  (Morrilton, AR) **10067**

Conway Daily Sun, The (North
   Conway, NH) 10011
† Conway Field & Herald (Conway, SC)
Coolidge Examiner (Coolidge, AZ) 10063
Coon Rapids Herald (Coon Rapids, MN) 10178
Coos County Democrat (Lancaster, NH) 10200
Copiah County Courier
   (Hazlehurst, MS) 10186
Coppell Gazette (Lewisville, TX) 10278
Copperas Cove Leader Press (Copperas
   Cove, TX) 10273
Copper Country News (Globe, AZ) 10064
Copper Era (Clifton, AZ) 10063
Coquille Valley Sentinel (Coquille, OR) 10248
Coral Gables News (Miami, FL) 10097
Corbin Times-Tribune (Corbin, KY) 9992
Cordele Dispatch (Cordele, GA) 9975
Cordell Beacon, The (Cordell, OK) 10245
Cordova Times (Cordova, AK) 10062
Cornell & Lake Holcombe Courier
   (Cornell, WI) 10299
Corning Observer (Corning, CA) 10071
Corona-Norco Independent
   (Corona, CA) 10071
Coronado Journal (Coronado, CA) 10071
Corpus Christi Caller-Times (Corpus
   Christi, TX) 10043
Corridor News (San Diego, CA) 10080
Corrigan Times, The (Corrigan, TX) 10273
Corry Journal (Corry, PA) 10033
Corsicana Daily Sun (Corsicana, TX) 10043
Cortez Montezuma Valley Journal
   (Cortez, CO) 10086
Cortez Sentinel (Cortez, CO) 10086
Cortland Democrat (Marathon, NY) 10218
Cortland Standard (Cortland, NY) 10014
Corvallis Gazette-Times (Corvallis, OR) 10031
Corydon Democrat (Corydon, IN) 10130
Corydon Times-Republican
   (Corydon, IA) 10137
Coshocton Tribune (Coshocton, OH) 10023
Cosmopolite-Herald (Girard, PA) 10253
Cottage Grove Sentinel (Cottage
   Grove, OR) 10248
Cottonwood Chronicle (Cottonwood, ID) 10107
Cottonwood Journal Extra
   (Cottonwood, AZ) 10063
Council Bluffs Daily Nonpareil (Council
   Bluffs, IA) 9987
Council Grove Republican (Council
   Grove, KS) 9989
Country Almanac (Menlo Park, CA) 10077
Country Connection News (Eakly, OK) 10245
Country Courier, The (Conklin, NY) 10212
Country Shopper (Pound Ridge, NY) 10221
Country Weekly (Grants Pass, OR) 10248

County Courier (Enosburg Falls, VT) 10283
County Edition, The (Jerseyville, IL) 10120
County Journal (Belleville, IL) 10111
County Journal (Percy, IL) 10125
County Journal, The (Washburn, WI) 10306
County Line Reminder (Ortonville, MI) 10173
Countyline, The (Bryan, OH) 10235
County Neighbors (Punxsutawney, PA) 10258
County News Enterprise
   (Rutherfordton, NC) 10230
County Observer (Yeagertown, PA) 10260
County Press (Parma, MI) 10173
County Press (Newtown Square, PA) 10256
County Press, The (Lapeer, MI) 10172
County Star (Stigler, OK) 10247
County Star Journal East (St.
   Louis, MO) 10193
County Star Journal West (St.
   Louis, MO) 10193
County Transcript (Susquehanna, PA) 10259
County Wide (Dover-Foxcroft, ME) 10156
† Countywide News (Westminster, MD)
Courant, The (Bottineau, ND) 10232
Courier-Express (Du Bois, PA) 10033
Courier-Gazette (Rockland, ME) 10157
Courier-Journal (Palmyra, NY) 10220
Courier-Journal, The (Louisville, KY) 9992
Courier-News (Clinton, TN) 10266
Courier-News, The (Elgin, IL) 9979
Courier-News, The (Bridgewater, NJ) 10012
Courier-Post, The (St. Charles, MO) 10008
Courier-Post, The (Cherry Hill, NJ) 10012
Courier-Standard-Enterprise (Fort
   Plain, NY) 10214
Courier-Times (Sutherland, NE) 10198
Courier-Times, The (Roxboro, NC) 10230
Courier-Wedge (Durand, WI) 10299
Courier Gazette (Newark, NY) 10219
Courier Herald, The (Dublin, GA) 9975
Courier Hub (Stoughton, WI) 10305
Courier Journal (Florence, AL) 10059
Courier News (Blytheville, AR) 9959
Courier Press (Prairie du Chien, WI) 10304
Courier, The (Russellville, AR) 9960
Courier, The (Plant City, FL) 10098
† Courier, The (Thomasville, GA)
Courier, The (Rensselaer, IN) 10135
Courier, The (Houma, LA) 9994
Courier, The (Littleton, NH) 10200
Courier, The (Conneaut, OH) 10239
Courier, The (Findlay, OH) 10024
Courier, The (Reedsport, OR) 10250
Courier, The (Savannah, TN) 10269
Courier, The (Sun Prairie, WI) 10305
Courtland Journal-Empire
   (Courtland, KS) 10143

Coushatta Citizen (Coushatta, LA) **10153**
Cover Story, The (Murfreesboro, TN) **10268**
Covington Leader (Covington, TN) **10266**
Covington News (Covington, GA) **10102**
Covington Record (Covington, OK) **10245**
Covington St. Tammany Farmer
  (Covington, LA) **10153**
Coweta American (Coweta, OK) **10245**
Cranbury Press (Dayton, NJ) **10202**
Crane News (Crane, TX) **10273**
Cranford Chronicle (Cranford, NJ) **10202**
Cranston Herald (Cranston, RI) **10260**
Crawford County Independent-Kickapoo Scout
  (Gay Mills, WI) **10300**
Crawfordsville Journal Review
  (Crawfordsville, IN) **9982**
Crescent-News (Defiance, OH) **10024**
Cresco Times-Plain Dealer (Cresco, IA) **10137**
Cresson-Gallitzin Mainliner, The
  (Cresson, PA) **10252**
Crestline Advocate (Crestline, OH) **10239**
Crestline Courier-News (Crestline, CA) **10071**
Creston News Advertiser (Creston, IA) **9987**
† Crestview Okaloosa-News Journal
  (Crestview, FL)
Crete News, The (Crete, NE) **10197**
Crewe-Burkeville Journal (Crewe, VA) **10286**
Crier Newspaper (Dunwoody, GA) **10102**
Crittenden Press (Marion, KY) **10149**
Crockett Times, The (Alamo, TN) **10265**
Crofton News-Crier (Bowie, MD) **10158**
Cromwell Chronicle (Cromwell, CT) **10090**
Crookston Daily Times (Crookston, MN) **10002**
Crossville Chronicle (Crossville, TN) **10266**
Crothersville Times (Crothersville, IN) **10130**
Crowley Post-Signal (Crowley, LA) **9993**
Crowley Review (Burleson, TX) **10272**
Cuba Free Press (Cuba, MO) **10189**
† Cuba Journal (Cuba, IL)
Cudahy Reminder-Enterprise
  (Wauwatosa, WI) **10307**
Cuero Record (Cuero, TX) **10273**
Cullman Times (Cullman, AL) **9955**
Cullman Tribune (Cullman, AL) **10058**
Culpeper News (Culpeper, VA) **10286**
Culpeper Star Exponent (Culpeper, VA) **10049**
Culver Citizen (Culver, IN) **10130**
Culver City-Ladera Independent (Santa
  Monica, CA) **10082**
Culver City Star (Los Angeles, CA) **10076**
Cumberland Advocate
  (Cumberland, WI) **10299**
Cumberland County News
  (Burkesville, KY) **10147**
Cumberland Courier Weekly
  (Lawrence, IN) **10133**

† Cumberland Times (Crossville, TN)
Cumberland Times-News
  (Cumberland, MD) **9996**
Cumberland Trading Post, The
  (Middlesboro, KY) **10149**
Cupertino Courier (Cupertino, CA) **10071**
† Current (Potsdam, NY)
Current-Argus (Carlsbad, NM) **10013**
Curry Coastal Pilot (Brookings, OR) **10248**
Cushing Daily Citizen (Cushing, OK) **10028**
Custer County Chief (Broken Bow, NE) **10196**
Cynthiana Democrat (Cynthiana, KY) **10147**

D

D/FW People (Euless, TX) **10274**
Dadeville Record (Alexander City, AL) **10057**
Daily & Sunday Freeman (Kingston, NY) **10015**
Daily & Sunday Sentinel (Rome, NY) **10017**
Daily/Sunday Sun, The (Warner
  Robins, GA) **9976**
Daily Advance (Elizabeth City, NC) **10019**
Daily Advocate (Greenville, OH) **10024**
Daily American (West Frankfort, IL) **9982**
Daily American (Somerset, PA) **10036**
Daily American Republic (Poplar
  Bluff, MO) **10007**
Daily Ardmoreite (Ardmore, OK) **10028**
Daily Astorian (Astoria, OR) **10031**
Daily Banner (Cambridge, MD) **9996**
Daily Breeze (Torrance, CA) **9966**
Daily Breeze, The (Cape Coral, FL) **9971**
Daily Californian, The (El Cajon, CA) **9961**
Daily Camera (Boulder, CO) **9968**
Daily Chronicle (De Kalb, IL) **9979**
Daily Citizen (Searcy, AR) **9960**
Daily Citizen News (Dalton, GA) **9975**
Daily Clay County Advocate-Press
  (Flora, IL) **9979**
Daily Clintonian (Clinton, IN) **9982**
Daily Comet (Thibodaux, LA) **9995**
Daily Commercial (Leesburg, FL) **9972**
Daily Corinthian (Corinth, MS) **10004**
Daily Courier (Forest City, NC) **10019**
Daily Courier Observer, The
  (Massena, NY) **10015**
Daily Courier, The (Prescott, AZ) **9958**
Daily Courier, The (Connellsville, PA) **10032**
Daily Democrat (Woodland, CA) **9967**
Daily Dispatch, The (Henderson, NC) **10019**
Daily Dunklin Democrat (Kennett, MO) **10006**
Daily Editor (Cobleskill, NY) **10014**
Daily Evening Item (Lynn, MA) **9997**
Daily Freeman Journal (Webster City, IA) **9989**
Daily Gazette (Sterling, IL) **9981**
Daily Gazette (Schenectady, NY) **10017**

Daily Guide (St. Robert, MO) **10008**
Daily Hampshire Gazette
  (Northampton, MA) **9998**
Daily Herald (Arlington Heights, IL) **9977**
Daily Herald (Delphos, OH) **10024**
Daily Herald (Columbia, TN) **10040**
Daily Herald, The (Tyrone, PA) **10037**
Daily Herald, The (Provo, UT) **10047**
Daily Home (Talladega, AL) **9956**
Daily Iberian (New Iberia, LA) **9994**
Daily Independent (Ridgecrest, CA) **9964**
Daily Independent, The (Ashland, KY) **9992**
Daily Inter Lake, The (Kalispell, MT) **10009**
Daily Item, The (New Rochelle, NY) **10016**
Daily Item, The (Sunbury, PA) **10036**
Daily Jefferson County Union (Fort
  Atkinson, WI) **10054**
Daily Jeffersonian, The
  (Cambridge, OH) **10023**
Daily Journal (Kankakee, IL) **9980**
Daily Journal (Franklin, IN) **9983**
Daily Journal (Park Hills, MO) **10007**
† Daily Journal (Elizabeth, NJ)
Daily Journal (Vineland, NJ) **10013**
Daily Journal, The (Fergus Falls, MN) **10002**
Daily Journal, The (International
  Falls, MN) **10003**
Daily Ledger (Canton, IL) **9978**
Daily Ledger (Fisher, IN) **9983**
Daily Local News (West Chester, PA) **10037**
Daily Mail (Catskill, NY) **10014**
Daily Mail & Sunday Herald
  (Nevada, MO) **10007**
Daily Mail, The (Hagerstown, MD) **9996**
Daily Midway Driller (Taft, CA) **9966**
† Daily Milford Citizen (Milford, CT)
Daily Mining Gazette (Houghton, MI) **10000**
Daily News (Mountain Home, AR) **9960**
Daily News (Woodland Hills, CA) **9967**
Daily News (Palatka, FL) **9973**
Daily News (Bowling Green, KY) **9992**
Daily News (Greenville, MI) **10000**
Daily News (Iron Mountain, MI) **10000**
Daily News (Richmond, MO) **10007**
Daily News (Wahpeton, ND) **10022**
Daily News (Huntingdon, PA) **10034**
Daily News (Longview, WA) **10051**
Daily News (West Bend, WI) **10055**
Daily News-Bulletin, The
  (Brookfield, MO) **10005**
Daily News-Mercury, The (Malden, MA) **9997**
Daily News-Record (Harrisonburg, VA) **10049**
Daily News-Sun (Sun City, AZ) **9958**
Daily News Leader, The (Staunton, VA) **10050**
Daily News of Newburyport, The
  (Newburyport, MA) **9998**

Daily News Press (Castle Rock, CO) **10086**
Daily News, The (Eden, NC) **10019**
Daily Okeechobee News, The
  (Okeechobee, FL) **9973**
Daily Oklahoman (Oklahoma City, OK) **10030**
Daily Pilot, The (Costa Mesa, CA) **9951**
Daily Press (Victorville, CA) **9967**
Daily Press, The (Paso Robles, CA) **9964**
Daily Press, The (Escanaba, MI) **9999**
Daily Press, The (St. Marys, PA) **10036**
Daily Press, The (Ashland, WI) **10053**
Daily Progress (Charlottesville, VA) **10049**
Daily Record (Canon City, CO) **9968**
Daily Record (Ellensburg, WA) **10050**
Daily Record, The (Parsippany, NJ) **10012**
Daily Record, The (Westchester, PA) **10037**
Daily Register, The (Portage, WI) **10054**
Daily Reporter (Greenfield, IN) **9983**
Daily Reporter (Columbus, OH) **10023**
Daily Reporter, The (Derby, KS) **9989**
Daily Reporter, The (Coldwater, MI) **9999**
Daily Republic (Fairfield, CA) **9962**
Daily Republic (Mitchell, SD) **10039**
Daily Review (Hayward, CA) **9962**
Daily Review & Sunday Review
  (Towanda, PA) **10036**
Daily Review Atlas (Monmouth, IL) **9980**
Daily Review, The (Morgan City, LA) **9994**
Daily Sentinel-Star, The (Grenada, MS) **10004**
Daily Sentinel, The (Scottsboro, AL) **9956**
Daily Sentinel, The (Grand Junction, CO) **9969**
Daily Sentinel, The (Pomeroy, OH) **10026**
Daily Sentinel, The (Nacogdoches, TX) **10045**
Daily Sitka Sentinel (Sitka, AK) **9957**
Daily Southerner, The (Tarboro, NC) **10021**
Daily Southtown (Chicago, IL) **9978**
Daily Sparks Tribune, The (Sparks, NV) **10010**
Daily Standard (Excelsior Springs, MO) **10006**
Daily Star-Journal, The
  (Warrensburg, MO) **10008**
Daily Star, The (Oneonta, NY) **10016**
Daily Sun-News (Sunnyside, WA) **10051**
Daily Telegram (Adrian, MI) **9999**
Daily Times (Ottawa, IL) **9981**
Daily Times (Salisbury, MD) **9996**
Daily Times (Farmington, NM) **10013**
Daily Times (Maryville, TN) **10041**
Daily Times & Chronicle (Reading, MA) **9998**
Daily Times-Call (Longmont, CO) **9969**
Daily Times Chronicle (Woburn, MA) **9998**
Daily Times Leader (West Point, MS) **10005**
Daily Times, The (New Rochelle, NY) **10016**
Daily Times, The (Rawlins, WY) **10056**
Daily Transcript (Dedham, MA) **9997**
Daily Tribune (Royal Oak, MI) **10001**
Daily Tribune News (Cartersville, GA) **9975**

Daily Tribune, The (Ames, IA) **9986**
Daily Tribune, The (Bay City, TX) **10042**
Daily Tribune, The (Wisconsin
  Rapids, WI) **10055**
Daily Whale, The (Lewes, DE) **9971**
Daily World (Opelousas, LA) **9994**
Daily World, The (Aberdeen, WA) **10050**
Dakatan, The (Wessington Springs, SD) **10265**
Dakota County Tribune (Burnsville, MN) **10177**
Dale News, The (Ferdinand, IN) **10131**
Dalhart Daily Texan (Dalhart, TX) **10043**
Dallas City Enterprise (Dallas City, IL) **10114**
Dallas Morning News, The (Dallas, TX) **10043**
Dallas New Era (Dallas, GA) **10102**
Dallas Park Cities News (Dallas, TX) **10273**
Dallas Polk County Itemizer-Observer
  (Dallas, OR) **10248**
Dallas Post (Dallas, PA) **10252**
Dallas White Rocker News (Dallas, TX) **10273**
Dalton Gazette & Kidron News
  (Dalton, OH) **10239**
Daly City Record (San Mateo, CA) **10082**
Damascus Gazette (Gatorsburg, MD) **10158**
Dan's Papers (Bridgehampton, NY) **10210**
Dana Point News (Lake Forest, CA) **10074**
Danbury Reporter (Walnut Cove, NC) **10231**
Dansville Genesee Country Express
  (Dansville, NY) **10212**
Danvers Herald (Danvers, MA) **10161**
Danville News (Danville, PA) **10033**
Danville Register & Bee (Danville, VA) **10049**
Darco News & Buyers Guide
  (Hartsville, SC) **10262**
Darien Doings (Hinsdale, IL) **10120**
Darien Metropolitan (Lemont, IL) **10121**
Darien News (Darien, GA) **10102**
Darien News Review (Darien, CT) **10090**
Darien Progress (Downers Grove, IL) **10115**
Darke County Early Bird, The
  (Arcanum, OH) **10234**
David City Banner-Press, The (David
  City, NE) **10197**
Davie County Enterprise-Record
  (Mocksville, NC) **10229**
Davis County Clipper (Bountiful, UT) **10282**
Davis Enterprise (Davis, CA) **9961**
Davison Flagstaff (Swartz Creek, MI) **10175**
Davison Index, The (Davison, MI) **10169**
Dawson News, The (Dawson, GA) **10102**
Dawson Springs Progress (Dawson
  Springs, KY) **10147**
Day, The (New London, CT) **9970**
Daytona Beach News-Journal, The (Daytona
  Beach, FL) **9972**
Daytona Pennysaver (Ormond
  Beach, FL) **10098**

Dayton Chronicle (Dayton, WA) **10291**
Dayton Daily News (Dayton, OH) **10023**
Dayton Tribune (Dayton, OR) **10248**
Dearborn County Register
  (Lawrenceburg, IN) **10133**
Dearborn Press & Guide
  (Dearborn, MI) **10169**
Dearborn Times-Herald (Dearborn, MI) **10169**
Decatur-DeKalb News/Era
  (Decatur, GA) **10102**
Decatur Daily (Decatur, AL) **9955**
Decatur Daily Democrat (Decatur, IN) **9983**
Decatur Herald (Gentry, AR) **10066**
Decatur Tribune (Decatur, IL) **10114**
Declaration, The (Independence, VA) **10287**
Decorah Public Opinion & Journal
  (Decorah, IA) **10137**
Deerfield Beach Observer (Deerfield
  Beach, FL) **10094**
Deerfield Beach Thursday Times (Deerfield
  Beach, FL) **10094**
Deerfield Review (Bannockburn, IL) **10110**
Deer Park Broadcaster, The (Deer
  Park, TX) **10273**
Deer Park Progress, The (Deer
  Park, TX) **10273**
Defensor Chieftain (Socorro, NM) **10209**
DeKalb County Advertiser (Auburn, IN) **10129**
† DeKalb News/Sun (Decatur, GA)
DeLand Beacon, The (DeLand, FL) **10094**
Delano Record (Delano, CA) **10071**
Delavan Enterprise (Delavan, WI) **10299**
Delavan Times, The (Delavan, IL) **10115**
Delaware Beachcomber (Rehoboth
  Beach, DE) **10092**
Delaware Coast Press (Rehoboth
  Beach, DE) **10092**
Delaware County Daily-Sunday Times (Clifton
  Heights, PA) **10032**
Delaware County Journal (Folsom, PA) **10253**
Delaware County Times (Delhi, NY) **10213**
Delaware Gazette (Delaware, OH) **10024**
Delaware State News (Dover, DE) **9971**
Delaware Valley News (Frenchtown, NJ) **10202**
Delaware Wave (Bethany Beach, DE) **10092**
Delhi Express (Winton, CA) **10085**
Delhi Press (Cincinnati, OH) **10235**
Dell Rapids Tribune (Dell Rapids, SD) **10264**
Del Mar, Solana Beach, Carmel Valley, Rancho
  Santa Fe Sun (Del Mar, CA) **10072**
Del Norte Prospector (Monte Vista, CO) **10088**
Del Norte Triplicate (Crescent City, CA) **9961**
Delray Times (Deerfield Beach, FL) **10094**
Del Rio News-Herald (Del Rio, TX) **10043**
Delta Atlas (Delta, OH) **10239**
Delta County Independent (Delta, CO) **10086**

Delta Democrat-Times (Greenville, MS) **10004**
Delta Waverly News Herald, The (Grand Ledge, MI) **10170**
Deming Headlight (Deming, NM) **10013**
Democrat-Argus, The (Caruthersville, MO) **10189**
Democrat-Leader (Fayette, MO) **10189**
Democrat-Message (Mt. Sterling, IL) **10124**
Democrat-Reporter, The (Linden, AL) **10060**
Democrat-Union (Lawrenceburg, TN) **10267**
Democrat, The (Senatobia, MS) **10187**
Democrat Tribune, The (Mineral Point, WI) **10302**
Demopolis Times (Demopolis, AL) **10058**
Denair Dispatch (Winton, CA) **10085**
Denbigh Gazette (Yorktown, VA) **10290**
Denham Springs-Livingston Parish News (Denham Springs, LA) **10153**
Denison Bulletin & Review (Denison, IA) **10137**
Denmark Press (Denmark, WI) **10299**
† Dennis Bulletin (South Yarmouth, MA)
Denton County Express (Lake Dallas, TX) **10277**
Denton Record-Chronicle (Denton, TX) **10043**
Denver Herald-Dispatch (Denver, CO) **10086**
Denver Post (Denver, CO) **9968**
De Pere Journal (De Pere, WI) **10299**
Depew Bee (Williamsville, NY) **10225**
Deposit Courier (Deposit, NY) **10213**
De Queen Bee (De Queen, AR) **10066**
De Queen Daily Citizen (De Queen, AR) **9959**
De Quincy News (De Quincy, LA) **10153**
Derrick, The (Oil City, PA) **10035**
Derry News (Derry, NH) **10199**
Desert Dispatch (Barstow, CA) **9961**
Desert Mailer News (Lancaster, CA) **10075**
Desert Mobile Home News (Palm Desert, CA) **10079**
Desert Mountain Express (Hesperia, CA) **10073**
Desert Sentinel, The (Desert Hot Springs, CA) **10072**
Desert Sun (Palm Springs, CA) **9964**
Deshler Rustler, The (Deshler, NE) **10197**
Des Moines County News, The (West Burlington, IA) **10142**
Des Moines Lee Town News (Des Moines, IA) **10137**
Des Moines News (Seattle, WA) **10293**
Des Moines Register (Des Moines, IA) **9987**
De Soto Times (Southaven, MS) **10187**
DeSoto Today (DeSoto, TX) **10273**
Des Plaines Journal (Des Plaines, IL) **9979**
Des Plaines Times (Park Ridge, IL) **10126**
Destin Log (Destin, FL) **10094**
Detroit Free Press (Detroit, MI) **9999**

Detroit Lakes Tribune (Detroit Lakes, MN) **10178**
Detroit Metro Times (Detroit, MI) **10169**
Detroit News (Detroit, MI) **9999**
Devils Lake Journal (Devils Lake, ND) **10021**
DeWitt Bath Review (St. Johns, MI) **10175**
DeWitt Observer (DeWitt, IA) **10137**
DeWitt Times (Fayetteville, NY) **10213**
Dexter Daily Statesman (Dexter, MO) **10006**
Diamond Drill, The (Crystal Falls, MI) **10169**
Dickenson Star/Cumberland Times, The (Clintwood, VA) **10285**
Dickinson Press, The (Dickinson, ND) **10021**
Dickson Herald, The (Dickson, TN) **10266**
Digest, The (Hallandale, FL) **10095**
Digger Shopper & News, The (Oroville, CA) **10078**
Dillon Herald, The (Dillon, SC) **10262**
Dispatch-News, The (Lexington, SC) **10263**
Dispatch, The (Gilroy, CA) **9962**
Dispatch, The (New Providence, NJ) **10204**
† Dispatch, The (Cookeville, TN)
Divernon News (Auburn, IL) **10110**
Dixie News (Florence, KY) **10143**
Dixon Pilot (Dixon, MO) **10189**
Dodge City Daily Globe (Dodge City, KS) **9989**
Dodge County Independent-News (Juneau, WI) **10301**
Dodge County News, The (Eastman, GA) **10102**
Dodgeville Chronicle, Inc. (Dodgeville, WI) **10299**

Dominion Post, The (Morgantown, WV) **10053**
Donaldsonville Chief (Donaldsonville, LA) **10153**
Donalsonville News (Donalsonville, GA) **10102**
Doon Press (Doon, IA) **10137**
Door County Advocate (Sturgeon Bay, WI) **10305**
Doraville-DeKalb Neighbor (Marietta, GA) **10104**
Dorchester Eagle Record (St. George, SC) **10264**
Dorchester Star (Cambridge, MD) **10158**
Dothan Eagle (Dothan, AL) **9955**
Douglas County Herald (Ava, MO) **10188**
Douglas County News Press (Castle Rock, CO) **10086**
Douglas County Post Gazette (Elkhorn, NE) **10197**
Douglas County Sentinel (Douglasville, GA) **9975**
Douglas Dispatch (Douglas, AZ) **9957**
Douglas Enterprise (Douglas, GA) **10102**
Douglas Neighbor, The (Marietta, GA) **10104**

Dove Creek Press (Dove Creek, CO) **10086**
Dover-Sherborn Suburban Press
   (Needham, MA) **10164**
Dowagiac Daily News (Dowagiac, MI) **9999**
Downers Grove Reporter (Downers
   Grove, IL) **10115**
Downey Herald American (Los
   Angeles, CA) **10076**
Downriver Voice (New Baltimore, MI) **10173**
Downtown Express (New York, NY) **10220**
Downtown Gazette (Long Beach, CA) **10075**
Downtown News (South Miami, FL) **10099**
Dracut Dispatch, The (Dracut, MA) **10161**
Drain Enterprise (Drain, OR) **10248**
Dresden Enterprise (Dresden, TN) **10266**
Drexel Hill Press (Newtown Square, PA) **10256**
Dripping Springs Dispatch (Dripping
   Springs, TX) **10274**
Dublin Suburbia News (Columbus, OH) **10237**
Dublin Villager (Worthington, OH) **10244**
Duluth News-Tribune (Duluth, MN) **10002**
Dumas Clarion (Dumas, AR) **10066**
Duncan Banner (Duncan, OK) **10028**
Duncannon Record (New
   Bloomfield, PA) **10256**
Duncanville Today (DeSoto, TX) **10274**
Dundalk Eagle (Baltimore, MD) **10157**
Dundee Observer (Dundee, NY) **10213**
Dunn County News (Menomonie, WI) **10302**
Dunn Daily Record (Dunn, NC) **10018**
Dunwoody-DeKalb Neighbor, The
   (Marietta, GA) **10104**
† DuPage Press Service (Wheaton, IL)
Du Quoin Evening Call (Du Quoin, IL) **9979**
Durand-Dakota Volunteer (Durand, IL) **10115**
Durand Express (Durand, MI) **10169**
Durand Gazette (Love Park, IL) **10122**
Durango Herald (Durango, CO) **9968**
Durant Daily Democrat (Durant, OK) **10028**
Duxbury Reporter (Plymouth, MA) **10164**
Dyer County Tennessean
   (Newbern, TN) **10268**
Dyersville Commercial (Dyersville, IA) **10138**

E

Eagan Sun-Current (Burnsville, MN) **10177**
Eagle-Herald (Marinette, WI) **10054**
Eagle-Times (Claremont, NH) **10011**
Eagle Bulletin (Fayetteville, NY) **10214**
Eagle Grove Eagle (Eagle Grove, IA) **10138**
Eagle Lake Headlight (Eagle Lake, TX) **10274**
Eagle Pass News Guide/Brief (Eagle
   Pass, TX) **10043**
Eagle Rock Sentinel (Los Angeles, CA) **10076**
Eagle, The (Cambridge, NY) **10211**

Eagle Tribune, The (North Andover, MA) **9998**
Eagle Valley Enterprise (Eagle, CO) **10086**
Earlville Leader (Earlville, IL) **10116**
Easley Progress (Easley, SC) **10262**
East Aurora Advertiser (East
   Aurora, NY) **10213**
East Aurora Bee (Williamsville, NY) **10225**
East Baltimore Guide (Baltimore, MD) **10157**
East Bay Breeze (Sun City Center, FL) **10099**
East Bay Express (Berkeley, CA) **10069**
East Bridgewater Star
   (Bridgewater, MA) **10161**
Eastchester Record (Yonkers, NY) **10225**
East County Chronicle (Kimberly, ID) **10108**
Eastern Arizona Courier (Safford, AZ) **10064**
Eastern Carolina Times-Inquirer
   (Goldsboro, NC) **10228**
Eastern Colorado News (Strasburg, CO) **10089**
Eastern Colorado Plainsman
   (Hugo, CO) **10087**
Eastern Gazette, The (Dexter, ME) **10155**
Eastern Hills Journal (Loveland, OH) **10240**
Eastern Kentucky Shopper
   (Paintsville, KY) **10150**
East Feliciana Watchman (Clinton, LA) **10153**
East Fishkill Record (Mahopac, NY) **10217**
East Grand Rapids Cadence
   (Jenison, MI) **10171**
East Greenwich Pendulum (East
   Greenwich, RI) **10260**
East Hampton Star (East Hampton, NY) **10213**
East Hartford Gazette, The (East
   Hartford, CT) **10090**
East Haven Advertiser (Milford, CT) **10091**
East L.A./Commerce Tribune (Los
   Angeles, CA) **10076**
Eastland Telegram (Eastland, TX) **10274**
East Lauderdale News (Rogersville, AL) **10061**
† East Los Angeles Gazette (South Gate, CA)
† East Los Angeles Tribune (South Gate, CA)
East Meadow Beacon (Hicksville, NY) **10216**
East Mesa Independent (Apache
   Junction, AZ) **10063**
Easton Bulletin (Stoughton, MA) **10166**
East Orange Record (Orange, NJ) **10205**
East Oregonian, The (Pendleton, OR) **10031**
East Palestine Heritage, The
   (Columbiana, OH) **10237**
East Penn Press (Allentown, PA) **10251**
East Peoria Courier (Morton, IL) **10124**
East Providence Post (East
   Providence, RI) **10260**
East Riverside Advertiser (Palm
   Desert, CA) **10079**
East Rochester Post-Herald
   (Fishers, NY) **10214**

East Rockaway Observer (Mineola, NY) **10218**
East Shelby Review (Somerville, TN) **10269**
East Side Herald (Indianapolis, IN) **10132**
Eastside Journal (Los Angeles, CA) **10076**
Eastside Monthly (Providence, RI) **10261**
East Side Review (North St. Paul, MN) **10181**
Eastside Sun (City of Commerce, CA) **10071**
† Eastside Times (Tulsa, OK)
East St. Louis Monitor (East St.
  Louis, IL) **10116**
East St. Louis News Journal
  (Columbia, IL) **10114**
East Troy News (East Troy, WI) **10299**
Easy Reader (Hermosa Beach, CA) **10073**
Eaton County News (Charlotte, MI) **10168**
Ebbtide (Sausalito, CA) **10083**
Ebensburg News Leader, The
  (Ebensburg, PA) **10252**
Echoes-Sentinel (Stirling, NJ) **10207**
Echo Press, The (Alexandria, MN) **10176**
Echo, The (Berlin, NY) **10210**
ECM Post-Review (North Branch, MN) **10181**
Eddyville Tribune (Eddyville, IA) **10138**
Eden Prairie Sun-Current
  (Bloomington, MN) **10177**
Edgebrook Times Review (Park
  Ridge, IL) **10126**
Edgerton Enterprise, The
  (Edgerton, MN) **10178**
Edgerton Reporter (Edgerton, WI) **10299**
Edgewood Enterprise (Edgewood, TX) **10274**
Edgewood Reminder (Edgewood, IA) **10138**
Edina Sun-Current (Minneapolis, MN) **10180**
Edinburg Daily Review (Edinburg, TX) **10043**
Edison-Norwood Times Review (Park
  Ridge, IL) **10126**
Edmond Evening Sun (Edmond, OK) **10028**
Edwardsville Intelligencer
  (Edwardsville, IL) **9979**
Edwardsville Journal (Edwardsville, IL) **10116**
Effingham Daily News (Effingham, IL) **9979**
Egg Harbor News (Hammonton, NJ) **10203**
Elbert County News (Castle Rock, CO) **10086**
Elberton Star (Elberton, GA) **10103**
Elburn Herald (Elburn, IL) **10116**
El Campo Leader-News (El Campo, TX) **10274**
El Centro Advertiser (Palm Desert, CA) **10079**
Eldon Advertiser (Eldon, MO) **10189**
Eldorado Daily Journal (Eldorado, IL) **9979**
El Dorado News-Times (El Dorado, AR) **9959**
El Dorado Times (El Dorado, KS) **9989**
Eldora Herald-Leader (Eldora, IA) **10138**
Elizabethton Star (Elizabethton, TN) **10040**
Elizabethtown Chronicle
  (Elizabethtown, PA) **10252**
Elk City Daily News (Elk City, OK) **10029**

Elk Grove Citizen (Elk Grove, CA) **10072**
Elkhart Truth, The (Elkhart, IN) **9983**
Elkhorn Independent (Elkhorn, WI) **10299**
Elko Daily Free Press (Elko, NV) **10010**
Elk Valley Times (Fayetteville, TN) **10266**
Ellenville Press (Ellenville, NY) **10213**
Ellsworth American, The
  (Ellsworth, ME) **10156**
Ellsworth Reporter, The (Ellsworth, KS) **10143**
Ellwood City Ledger (Ellwood City, PA) **10033**
Elma Review (East Aurora, NY) **10213**
Elmhurst Press (Elmhurst, IL) **10116**
Elm Leaves (Oak Park, IL) **10125**
Elm Leaves (Wauwatosa, WI) **10307**
Elmont Herald (Elmont, NY) **10213**
Elmwood Argus (Spring Valley, WI) **10305**
Elmwood Park-River Grove Times
  (Lincolnwood, IL) **10121**
Eloy Enterprise (Eloy, AZ) **10064**
El Paso Herald-Post (El Paso, TX) **10043**
El Paso Journal (El Paso, IL) **10116**
El Paso Times (El Paso, TX) **10043**
El Reno Tribune (El Reno, OK) **10245**
El Segundo Herald (El Segundo, CA) **10072**
El Sereno Star (Los Angeles, CA) **10076**
Elwood Express (Wilmington, IL) **10129**
Ely Daily Times (Ely, NV) **10010**
Ely Echo (Ely, MN) **10178**
Elyria Chronicle-Telegram (Elyria, OH) **10024**
Emery County Progress (Castle
  Dale, UT) **10282**
Emmetsburg Democrat
  (Emmetsburg, IA) **10138**
Emmetsburg Reporter
  (Emmetsburg, IA) **10138**
Emporia Gazette (Emporia, KS) **9990**
Encinitas Sun (Encinitas, CA) **10072**
Enderlin Independent (Enderlin, ND) **10232**
Enfield Press (Enfield, CT) **10090**
England Democrat (England, AR) **10066**
Englewood Herald (Littleton, CO) **10088**
Englewood Sun Herald (Englewood, FL) **9972**
Enid News & Eagle (Enid, OK) **10029**
Ennis Daily News (Ennis, TX) **10043**
Enquirer-Gazette (Upper Marlboro, MD) **10160**
Enquirer-Journal, The (Monroe, NC) **10020**
Enquirer Bulletin (Burlingame, CA) **10070**
Enterprise & Inner Harbor News
  (Baltimore, MD) **10157**
Enterprise Buyer's Catalogue
  (Wytheville, VA) **10290**
Enterprise Ledger (Enterprise, AL) **9956**
Enterprise Mountaineer, The
  (Fallbrook, CA) **10072**
Enterprise Mountaineer, The
  (Canton, NC) **10227**

† Enterprise News (Pixley, CA)
† Enterprise Sun (Marlborough, MA)
Enterprise, The (Plainfield, IL) **10126**
Enterprise, The (Ponchatoula, LA) **10154**
Enterprise, The (Falmouth, MA) **10162**
Enterprise, The (Lexington Park, MD) **10159**
Enterprise, The (Mason, MI) **10172**
Enterprise, The (Williamston, NC) **10231**
Enterprise, The
   (Hastings-on-Hudson, NY) **10215**
Enterprise, The (Stuart, VA) **10289**
Enterprise, The (Lynnwood, WA) **10292**
Enumclaw Courier-Herald
   (Enumclaw, WA) **10291**
Ephrata Review (Ephrata, PA) **10252**
† Erie County Reporter (Huron, OH)
Erie Daily Times/Sunday Times News
   (Erie, PA) **10033**
Erie Morning News (Erie, PA) **10033**
Erskine Echo, The (Erskine, MN) **10178**
Erwin Record (Erwin, TN) **10266**
Escambia Sun Press (Pensacola, FL) **10098**
Escondido News-Reporter
   (Escondido, CA) **10072**
Essex Independent, The (Essex, IA) **10138**
Estancia Valley Citizen (Estancia, NM) **10208**
Estes Park Trail-Gazette (Estes
   Park, CO) **10087**
Estherville Daily News (Estherville, IA) **9987**
Estill County Tribune, The (Irvine, KY) **10149**
Euclid Sun Journal (Cleveland, OH) **10236**
Eufaula Tribune (Eufaula, AL) **10058**
Eunice News (Eunice, LA) **10153**
Eureka Herald (Eureka, KS) **10143**
Eureka Sentinel (Tonopah, NV) **10199**
Eureka Springs Times-Echo
   (Berryville, AR) **10065**
Eustis Lake Region News (Mount
   Dora, FL) **10097**
Evanston Review (Evanston, IL) **10117**
Evansville Courier (Evansville, IN) **9983**
Evansville Press (Evansville, IN) **9983**
Evart Review, The (Big Rapids, MI) **10167**
Evening-Observer (Dunkirk, NY) **10015**
† Evening Express (Portland, ME)
Evening Leader, The (St. Marys, OH) **10027**
Evening News (Benton, IL) **9978**
Evening Review, The (East
   Liverpool, OH) **10024**
† Evening Sentinel (Ansonia, CT)
Evening Star (Auburn, IN) **9982**
Evening Sun (Hanover, PA) **10033**
Evening Sun, The (Norwich, NY) **10016**
Evening Telegram (Herkimer, NY) **10015**
Evening Times (Sayre, PA) **10036**
Evening Times, The (Little Falls, NY) **10015**

Evening World (Bloomfield, IN) **9982**
Evergreen Courant, The
   (Evergreen, AL) **10058**
Evergreen Park Courier (Midlothian, IL) **10123**
Evergreen Shopping Guide
   (Spooner, MN) **10183**
Everman Times (Everman, TX) **10274**
Every Wednesday (Baltimore, MD) **10157**
Excelsior/Shorewood Sun-Sailor
   (Minnetonka, MN) **10180**
Exeter News-Letter (Stratham, NH) **10200**
Exponent, The (Brooklyn, MI) **10168**
Express-Times, The (Easton, PA) **10033**
Extra Merchandiser (St. Marys, OH) **10243**

F

Fairbanks Daily News-Miner
   (Fairbanks, AK) **9957**
Fairborn Daily Herald (Fairborn, OH) **10024**
Fairbury Journal-News, The
   (Fairbury, NE) **10197**
† Fairchild Strikehawk (Spokane, WA)
Fairfax Connection (McLean, VA) **10287**
Fairfax Journal (Fairfax, VA) **10049**
Fairfax Station Times (Reston, VA) **10288**
Fairfax Times (Reston, VA) **10288**
Fairfield Chronicle, The (West
   Caldwell, NJ) **10207**
Fairfield Citizen News (Fairfield, CT) **10090**
Fairfield County Weekly (Stamford, CT) **10091**
Fairfield Daily Ledger (Fairfield, IA) **9987**
Fairfield Echo (Fairfield, OH) **10239**
Fairfield Wayne County Press
   (Fairfield, IL) **10117**
† Fair Haven Register (Red Creek, NY)
Fairhope Courier, The (Fairhope, AL) **10059**
Fairmont Photo Press (Fairmont, MN) **10178**
Fairmont Sentinel (Fairmont, MN) **10002**
† Fairport-Perinton Herald-Mail (Webster, NY)
Fairview Heights Journal (Belleville, IL) **10111**
Fairview Heights Tribune
   (Mascoutah, IL) **10122**
Fairview Republican (Fairview, OK) **10245**
Falfurrias Facts (Falfurrias, TX) **10274**
† Fallon Eagle Standard (Fallon, NV)
Falls Church News-Press (Falls
   Church, VA) **10286**
Falls City Journal (Falls City, NE) **10197**
Falls News-Press (Stow, OH) **10243**
Faribault County Register (Blue
   Earth, MN) **10177**
Faribault Daily News (Faribault, MN) **10002**
Farina News, The (Farina, IL) **10117**
Farmer & Miner (Frederick, CO) **10087**
Farmer's Weekly Review (Joliet, IL) **10121**

Farmer City Journal (Farmer City, IL) **10117**
Farmers' Advance (Camden, MI) **10168**
† Farmers Branch Times (Carrollton, TX)
Farmers Independent (Bagley, MN) **10176**
Farmingdale Observer (Mineola, NY) **10218**
Farmington Observer (Farmington, MI) **10169**
† Farmington Valley Herald (Simsbury, CT)
Farmland News (Archbold, OH) **10234**
Farmville Herald, The (Farmville, VA) **10286**
Farmweek (Knightstown, IN) **10133**
Fauquier Times-Democrat
   (Warrenton, VA) **10290**
Fayette Advertiser, The (Fayette, MO) **10189**
Fayette County News (Fayetteville, GA) **10103**
Fayette County Record, The (La
   Grange, TX) **10277**
Fayette County Review (Somerville, TN) **10269**
Fayette County Union (West Union, IA) **10142**
Fayette Falcon, The (Somerville, TN) **10269**
Fayette Neighbor, The (Fayetteville, GA) **10103**
Fayette Review, The (Fayette, OH) **10239**
† Fayette Sun (Fayetteville, GA)
Fayette Tribune (Oak Hill, WV) **10295**
Fayetteville Northwest Arkansas Times
   (Fayetteville, AR) **9959**
Fayetteville Observer-Times
   (Fayetteville, NC) **10019**
Federal Way News (Federal Way, WA) **10291**
Fennimore Times (Fennimore, WI) **10300**
Fennville Herald (Allegan, MI) **10167**
Ferdinand News, The (Ferdinand, IN) **10131**
Fernley Leader-Dayton Courier
   (Yerington, NV) **10199**
Fillmore Herald (Fillmore, CA) **10072**
Fincastle Herald, The (Fincastle, VA) **10286**
Finder, The (Mandan, ND) **10233**
Finger Lakes Times, The (Geneva, NY) **10015**
Firebaugh/Mendota Journal
   (Kerman, CA) **10074**
Fire Island Tide (Sayville, NY) **10222**
Fisher Reporter (Fisher, IL) **10117**
Fishers Sun-Herald (Fishers, IN) **10131**
Fishkill Standard (Mahopac, NY) **10217**
Fishtown Star (Philadelphia, PA) **10257**
Fitchburg Star (Fitchburg, WI) **10300**
Five Cities Times-Press-Recorder (Arroyo
   Grande, CA) **10069**
Five County/Buyer's Guide (Ripon, WI) **10304**
Flanagan Home Times (Flanagan, IL) **10117**
Flatbush Life (Brooklyn, NY) **10211**
† Flat River Lead Belt News (Flat River, MO)
Flint Journal (Flint, MI) **10000**
Florala News, The (Florala, AL) **10059**
Floral Park Bulletin (Floral Park, NY) **10214**
Florence Citizen (Florence, CO) **10087**
Florence Mining News (Florence, WI) **10300**

Florence Morning News (Florence, SC) **10038**
Floresville Chronicle-Journal
   (Floresville, TX) **10274**
Florham Park Eagle (Madison, NJ) **10203**
Florida Keys Keynoter (Marathon, FL) **10096**
Florida Times-Union (Jacksonville, FL) **9972**
Florida Today (Melbourne, FL) **9972**
Florissant Valley Reporter
   (Florissant, MO) **10189**
Floyd County Hesperian-Beacon
   (Floydada, TX) **10274**
Floyd County Times (Prestonsburg, KY) **10150**
Floyd Press (Floyd, VA) **10286**
Flushing Times, The (Bayside, NY) **10210**
Folsom Telegraph (Folsom, CA) **10072**
Fontana Herald News (Fontana, CA) **10072**
Ford County Press (Melvin, IL) **10123**
Forest City Summit (Forest City, IA) **10138**
Forest Hill News (Everman, TX) **10274**
▼Forest Hills/Rego Park Times
   (Maspeth, NY) **10218**
Forest Hills Journal (Loveland, OH) **10241**
Forest Lake Press (St. Paul, MN) **10183**
Forest Leaves (Oak Park, IL) **10125**
Forest Press (Tionesta, PA) **10259**
Forest Republican, The (Crandon, WI) **10299**
Forest Times-Tribune (De Forest, WI) **10299**
Forrest City Times-Herald (Forrest
   City, AR) **9959**
Forreston Journal (Forreston, IL) **10117**
Forsyth County News (Cumming, GA) **10102**
Fort Bend Mirror (Rosenberg, TX) **10280**
Fort Bend Sun (Sugar Land, TX) **10281**
Fort Bragg Advocate-News (Fort
   Bragg, CA) **10072**
Fort Collins Coloradoan (Fort
   Collins, CO) **9968**
Fort Dodge Messenger (Fort Dodge, IA) **9987**
Fort Fairfield Review (Fort
   Fairfield, ME) **10156**
Fort Lupton Press (Fort Lupton, CO) **10087**
Fort Madison Daily Democrat (Fort
   Madison, IA) **9987**
Fort Meade Leader, The (Fort
   Meade, FL) **10095**
Fort Mill Times (Fort Mill, SC) **10262**
Fort Morgan Times (Fort Morgan, CO) **9968**
Fort Myers Beach Observer (Fort Myers
   Beach, FL) **10095**
Fort Riley Post (Junction City, KS) **10144**
Fort Scott Tribune, The (Fort Scott, KS) **9990**
Fort Smith Southwest Times Record (Fort
   Smith, AR) **9959**
Fort Stockton Pioneer (Fort
   Stockton, TX) **10274**

Title

Fort Wayne News-Sentinel (Fort
Wayne, IN) **9983**
Fort Worth Star-Telegram (Fort
Worth, TX) **10043**
Forum of Queens (Ozone Park, NY) **10220**
Forum, The (Fargo, ND) **10022**
Fosston Thirteen Towns (Fosston, MN) **10178**
Foster's Daily Democrat (Dover, NH) **10011**
Foster City Progress (Burlingame, CA) **10070**
Foto News (Merrill, WI) **10302**
Fountain County Neighbor (Attica, IN) **10129**
Fountain Valley News & El Paso County News
(Fountain, CO) **10087**
Four Oaks-Benson News in Review
(Benson, NC) **10226**
Fowler Tribune, The (Fowler, CO) **10087**
Fowlerville Review Shopping Guide
(Howell, MI) **10171**
Foxboro Reporter (Foxboro, MA) **10162**
Fox Lake Press (Grayslake, IL) **10118**
Fox Lake Representative (Berlin, WI) **10297**
Fox Point, Bayside, River Hills Herald
(Wauwatosa, WI) **10307**
Fox Valley Shopping News, The
(Plainfield, IL) **10126**
Fox Valley Sun (Naperville, IL) **10124**
Foxxy Shopper (Sparta, WI) **10305**
Frankenmuth News (Frankenmuth, MI) **10169**
Frankfort State Journal (Frankfort, KY) **9992**
Frankfort Times (Frankfort, IN) **9983**
Franklin-Hales Corner Hub
(Wauwatosa, WI) **10307**
Franklin Banner-Tribune (Franklin, LA) **9994**
Franklin Challenger (Greenwood, IN) **10132**
Franklin Chronicle (Franklin, OH) **10239**
Franklin County Citizen (Lavonia, GA) **10104**
Franklin County Graphic (Connell, WA) **10291**
Franklin County Plus (Russellville, AL) **10061**
Franklin County Times (Russellville, AL) **10061**
Franklin Favorite (Franklin, KY) **10148**
Franklin Journal & Farmington Chronicle
(Farmington, ME) **10156**
Franklin News-Post (Rocky Mount, VA) **10289**
Franklin News-Record (Princeton, NJ) **10206**
Franklin Park Herald-Journal (Oak
Park, IL) **10125**
Franklin Park Star-Sentinel (Melrose
Park, IL) **10123**
Franklin Pendleton Times
(Franklin, WV) **10294**
Franklin Press (Franklin, NC) **10228**
Franklin Square Bulletin (Floral
Park, NY) **10214**
Franklin Sun, The (Winnsboro, LA) **10155**
Franklin Times (Louisburg, NC) **10228**

Franklin Township Sentinel
(Franklinville, NJ) **10202**
Frederick Leader (Frederick, OK) **10029**
Frederick Post, The (Frederick, MD) **9996**
Fredericksburg Free Lance-Star
(Fredericksburg, VA) **10049**
Fredericksburg Standard/Radio Post
(Fredericksburg, TX) **10275**
Fredericktown Democrat-News
(Fredericktown, MO) **10189**
† Freeborn County Register (Albert Lea, MN)
Freeman's Journal (Cooperstown, NY) **10212**
Freeman, The (Waukesha, WI) **10055**
Freemont Gazette (Fremont, IA) **10138**
Free News, The (Farmville, VA) **10286**
Freeport Advertiser Shopping News
(Freeport, IL) **10117**
Freeport Baldwin Leader, The
(Freeport, NY) **10214**
Freeport Journal-Standard (Freeport, IL) **9979**
Free Press (Tampa, FL) **10099**
Free Press (Mankato, MN) **10003**
Free Press-Courier (Westfield, PA) **10260**
Free Press Standard (Carrollton, OH) **10235**
Free Press, The (Canton, OH) **10235**
Free Press, The (Braddock, PA) **10251**
Free Time (Wildwood, NJ) **10208**
Free Trader (Massena, NY) **10218**
Fremont County Herald-Chronicle (St.
Anthony, ID) **10109**
Fremont News-Messenger
(Fremont, OH) **10024**
Fremont Tribune (Fremont, NE) **10009**
Fresh Meadows Times, The
(Flushing, NY) **10214**
Fresno Bee, The (Fresno, CA) **9962**
Fridley Focus (Roseville, MN) **10182**
Friendswood & Pearland Reporter News
(Pearland, TX) **10279**
Frontier & Holt County Independent
(O'Neill, NE) **10197**
Frontiersman, The (Wasilla, AK) **10063**
Front Page (Lackawanna, NY) **10216**
Frostproof News (Frostproof, FL) **10095**
Fruita Times, The (Fruita, CO) **10087**
Fulton County Expositor (Wauseon, OH) **10244**
Fulton Journal (Fulton, IL) **10117**
Fulton Leader (Fulton, KY) **10148**
Fulton Patriot (Fulton, NY) **10214**
Fulton Shopper (Fulton, KY) **10148**
Fulton Sun, The (Fulton, MO) **10006**

G

Gadsden County Times (Quincy, FL) **10098**
Gadsden Times (Gadsden, AL) **9956**

Gaffney Ledger, The (Gaffney, SC) **10262**
Gahanna Village Post (Gahanna, OH) **10239**
Gainesville Buyers Guide (Orange
   Park, FL) **10098**
Gainesville Daily Register
   (Gainesville, TX) **10043**
Gainesville Sun, The (Gainesville, FL) **9972**
Gaithersburg Gazette
   (Gaithersburg, MD) **10158**
Galax Gazette, The (Galax, VA) **10286**
Galena Gazette (Galena, IL) **10117**
Galesburg Post, The (Galesburg, IL) **10117**
Galesville Republican (Galesville, WI) **10300**
Galion Inquirer (Galion, OH) **10024**
Gallipolis Daily Tribune (Gallipolis, OH) **10024**
Galt Herald (Galt, CA) **10073**
Galva News (Galva, IL) **10117**
Galveston County Daily News, The
   (Galveston, TX) **10044**
Gardena Valley News (Gardena, CA) **10073**
Garden City Observer (Livonia, MI) **10172**
Garden City Telegram (Garden City, KS) **9990**
Garden Island Extra (Lihue, HI) **10107**
Garden of the Gods Journal (Manitou
   Springs, CO) **10088**
Gardner News (Gardner, MA) **9997**
Gardner South Wilmington Post
   (Wilmington, IL) **10129**
Garfield Maple-Sun (Cleveland, OH) **10236**
Garland News (Garland, TX) **10275**
Garner News (Garner, NC) **10228**
† Garnett Review (Garnett, KS)
Gary Crusader (Gary, IN) **10132**
Gary Info (Gary, IN) **10132**
Gasconade County Republican
   (Owensville, MO) **10192**
Gaston Gazette (Gastonia, NC) **10019**
Gates-Chili News (Rochester, NY) **10222**
Gates County Index (Gatesville, NC) **10228**
Gatesville Messenger (Gatesville, TX) **10275**
Gateway News, The (Streetsboro, OH) **10243**
Gateway Shopper, The (Clinton, IA) **10137**
Gateway, The (Floral Park, NY) **10214**
Gaylord Herald Times (Gaylord, MI) **10169**
Gazette-Advertiser (Rhinebeck, NY) **10222**
Gazette-Democrat (Anna, IL) **10109**
Gazette Shopper (Cleveland, OH) **10236**
Gazette, The (Elizabeth, IL) **10116**
Gazette, The (Mt. Holly, NJ) **10204**
Gazette, The (Port Jervis, NY) **10221**
Gazette, The (Jefferson, OH) **10240**
† Geauga Times-Leader (Chardon, OH)
Geist Gazette (Fishers, IN) **10131**
Gem State Miner (Newport, WA) **10292**
Geneseo Republic (Geneseo, IL) **10117**
Geneseo Shopper (Geneseo, IL) **10117**

Geneva County Reaper (Geneva, AL) **10059**
Geneva Republican (Geneva, IL) **10117**
Genoa-Kingston-Kirkland News
   (Sycamore, IL) **10128**
Gentry Courier-Journal (Gentry, AR) **10066**
George County Times (Lucedale, MS) **10186**
Georgetown Current, The
   (Washington, DC) **10093**
Georgetowner, The (Washington, DC) **10093**
Georgetown News Graphic
   (Georgetown, KY) **10148**
Georgetown Record (Ipswich, MA) **10162**
Georgetown Times, The
   (Georgetown, SC) **10262**
Georgia South (Boston, GA) **10101**
Georgia Times-Union (Brunswick, GA) **9974**
Gering Courier (Gering, NE) **10197**
Germantown Banner-Press
   (Wauwatosa, WI) **10307**
Germantown Courier (Philadelphia, PA) **10257**
Germantown News, The
   (Germantown, TN) **10267**
Germantown Paper (Philadelphia, PA) **10257**
Gettysburg Times (Gettysburg, PA) **10033**
Gibson City Courier (Gibson City, IL) **10118**
Giddings Times & News (Giddings, TX) **10275**
Gilbert Independent (Scottsdale, AZ) **10064**
Gilbert Tribune (Gilbert, AZ) **9958**
Gilman Star (Gilman, IL) **10118**
Gilmer Mirror (Gilmer, TX) **10275**
Girard Home News (Philadelphia, PA) **10257**
† Girard News (Niles, OH)
Girard Press (Girard, KS) **10143**
Giveaway, The (Scottsburg, IN) **10135**
Glades County Democrat
   (Clewiston, FL) **10094**
Gladewater Mirror (Gladewater, TX) **10275**
† Gladstone Delta Reporter (Escanaba, MI)
Gladwin County Record & Beaverton Clarion
   (Gladwin, MI) **10170**
Glasford Gazette, The (Glasford, IL) **10118**
Glasgow Courier, The (Glasgow, MT) **10195**
Glasgow Daily Times (Glasgow, KY) **9992**
Glasgow Republican (Glasgow, KY) **10148**
Glastonbury Citizen (Glastonbury, CT) **10090**
Glencoe Enterprise (Glencoe, MN) **10178**
Glen Cove Record Pilot (Mineola, NY) **10219**
Glendale Heights Press (Elmhurst, IL) **10116**
Glendale Herald (Wauwatosa, WI) **10307**
Glendale News-Press (Glendale, CA) **9962**
Glendale Register (Maspeth, NY) **10218**
Glendale Star, The (Glendale, AZ) **10064**
Glendive Ranger-Review (Glendive, MT) **10195**
Glendora Press (West Covina, CA) **10084**
Glen Ellyn News (Glen Ellyn, IL) **10118**
Glen Ellyn Press (Bloomingdale, IL) **10111**

Glennville Sentinel (Glennville, GA) **10103**
Glen Oaks Ledger, The (Flushing, NY) **10214**
Glen Ridge Paper, The (Bloomfield, NJ) **10201**
Glen Rose Reporter (Glen Rose, TX) **10275**
Glenside News (Jenkintown, PA) **10254**
Glenview Announcements (Glenview, IL) **10118**
Glenville Democrat, The (Glenville, WV) **10294**
Glenville Pathfinder (Glenville, WV) **10294**
Glenwood Herald (Glenwood, AR) **10066**
Glenwood Opinion-Tribune
  (Glenwood, IA) **10138**
Glenwood Post (Glenwood Springs, CO) **9968**
Glidden Enterprise (Glidden, WI) **10300**
Globe-Gazette (Mason City, IA) **9988**
Globe, The (Jenkintown, PA) **10254**
Gloucester-Mathews Gazette Journal
  (Gloucester, VA) **10286**
Gloucester City News (Gloucester
  City, NJ) **10202**
Gloucester County Times
  (Woodbury, NJ) **10013**
Gloucester Daily Times (Gloucester, MA) **9997**
Glynco Observer (Brunswick, GA) **10101**
Gold Beach Curry County Reporter (Gold
  Beach, OR) **10248**
Goldendale Sentinel (Goldendale, WA) **10291**
Golden Prairie News (Assumption, IL) **10110**
Golden Times (Rochester, NY) **10222**
Golden Transcript (Golden, CO) **10087**
Golden Triangle Shopper
  (Columbus, MS) **10185**
Gold Leaf Farmer, The (Wendell, NC) **10231**
Gold River News (Sacramento, CA) **10080**
Goldsboro News-Argus (Goldsboro, NC) **10019**
† Goleta Review (Goleta, CA)
† Goleta Sun (Santa Barbara, CA)
Golfmill Journal (Des Plaines, IL) **10115**
Gonzales Inquirer (Gonzales, TX) **10275**
Gonzales Tribune (Soledad, CA) **10083**
Gonzales Weekly (Gonzales, LA) **10153**
Goochland Gazette (Goochland, VA) **10286**
Gooding County Leader (Gooding, ID) **10107**
Goodland Daily News (Goodland, KS) **9990**
Good News Shopper (Coal City, IL) **10114**
Good Times (Santa Cruz, CA) **10082**
† Good Times News (Fayette, MO)
Goose Creek Gazette (Ladson, SC) **10262**
Gorman Progress, The (Gorman, TX) **10275**
Goshen News, The (Goshen, IN) **9983**
Gouverneur Tribune Press
  (Gouverneur, NY) **10215**
Gowanda Pennysaver News
  (Gowanda, NY) **10215**
† Grace Citizen (Preston, ID)
Graceville News (Graceville, FL) **10095**
Grainger County News (Rutledge, TN) **10269**

Grand Forks Herald (Grand Forks, ND) **10022**
Grand Gazette (St. Paul, MN) **10183**
Grand Haven Tribune (Grand
  Haven, MI) **10000**
Grand Island Independent (Grand
  Island, NE) **10009**
Grand Island Pennysaver (Grand
  Island, NY) **10215**
Grand Ledge Independent, The (Grand
  Ledge, MI) **10170**
Grand Marais Pilot & Pictured Rocks Review
  (Grand Marais, MI) **10170**
Grand Prairie News (Arlington, TX) **10270**
Grand Rapids Advance (Jenison, MI) **10171**
Grand Rapids Herald-Review (Grand
  Rapids, MN) **10179**
Grand Rapids Press, The (Grand
  Rapids, MI) **10000**
Grand Saline Sun (Grand Saline, TX) **10275**
Grand Valley Advance (Jenison, MI) **10171**
Grandview Herald (Grandview, WA) **10291**
Granite City Press Journal (Granite
  City, IL) **10118**
Granite Falls/Clerkfield Advocate Tribune
  (Granite Falls, MN) **10179**
Granite State News (Wolfeboro, NH) **10200**
Grant County Herald Independent
  (Lancaster, WI) **10301**
Grant County Journal (Ephrata, WA) **10291**
Grant County News (Williamstown, KY) **10152**
Grant County News (Elgin, ND) **10232**
Grant County Press (Petersburg, WV) **10295**
Grant County Review (Milbank, SD) **10265**
Grants Pass Daily Courier (Grants
  Pass, OR) **10031**
Granville Sentinel (Granville, NY) **10215**
Granville Sentinel, The (Granville, OH) **10239**
Gratiot County Herald (Ithaca, MI) **10171**
Gravette News Herald (Gravette, AR) **10066**
Grayslake Times (Grayslake, IL) **10118**
Grayson Advertiser (Leitchfield, KY) **10149**
Grayson County News-Gazette
  (Leitchfield, KY) **10149**
Grayson County Shopper (Denison, TX) **10273**
Grayson Journal-Enquirer
  (Grayson, KY) **10148**
Great Bend Tribune (Great Bend, KS) **9990**
Greater Baton Rouge Business Report (Baton
  Rouge, LA) **10152**
Great Falls Times (Reston, VA) **10288**
Great Falls Tribune (Great Falls, MT) **10008**
Great Lakes Pilot (Grand Marais, MI) **10170**
Great Lander Bush Mailer
  (Anchorage, AK) **10062**
Great Neck News (Great Neck, NY) **10215**
Great Neck Record (Mineola, NY) **10219**

Greece Post, The (Fishers, NY) **10214**
Greeley Tribune (Greeley, CO) **9969**
Green Bay News-Chronicle (Green
   Bay, WI) **10054**
Green Bay Press-Gazette (Green
   Bay, WI) **10054**
Greenbelt News Review
   (Greenbelt, MD) **10159**
Greenbrier Gazette (Sherwood, AR) **10068**
Greenbrier Valley Ranger
   (Lewisburg, WV) **10295**
Greendale Village Life (Wauwatosa, WI) **10307**
Greene County Independent
   (Eutaw, AL) **10058**
Greene County Record
   (Stanardsville, VA) **10289**
Greene Prairie Press (White Hall, IL) **10128**
Greene Recorder, The (Greene, IA) **10138**
Greeneville Sun (Greeneville, TN) **10040**
Greenfield Daily Times (Greenfield, OH) **10024**
Greenfield Observer (Wauwatosa, WI) **10307**
Green Forest Tribune (Berryville, AR) **10065**
Green Hills Weekly (Trenton, MO) **10194**
Greenhorn Valley News (Colorado
   City, CO) **10086**
Green Lake County Reporter (Green
   Lake, WI) **10300**
Greenpoint Gazette/Advertiser
   (Brooklyn, NY) **10211**
† Green River Republican (Morgantown, KY)
Greensboro Watchman, The
   (Greensboro, AL) **10059**
Greensburg Daily News (Greensburg, IN) **9983**
Green Sheet, The (Palm Desert, CA) **10079**
Green Tab (Moundsville, WV) **10295**
Greenup County News-Times
   (Greenup, KY) **10148**
Greenup Press (Greenup, IL) **10119**
Green Valley News & Sun (Green
   Valley, AZ) **10064**
Greenville Advocate, The
   (Greenville, AL) **10059**
Greenville Advocate, The
   (Greenville, IL) **10119**
Greenville Daily Reflector
   (Greenville, NC) **10019**
Greenville Herald Banner
   (Greenville, TX) **10044**
Greenville Local (Ravena, NY) **10221**
Greenville News (Greenville, SC) **10038**
† Greenville Piedmont (Greenville, SC)
Greenville Record-Argus
   (Greenville, PA) **10033**
Greenwich Journal & Salem Press
   (Greenwich, NY) **10215**
† Greenwich News (Greenwich, CT)

▼Greenwich Post (Greenwich, CT) **10090**
Greenwich Time (Greenwich, CT) **9970**
Greenwood & Southside Challenger
   (Greenwood, IN) **10132**
Greenwood Commonwealth
   (Greenwood, MS) **10004**
Greenwood Democrat (Greenwood, AR) **10066**
Greenwood Gazette, The (Fishers, IN) **10131**
Greenwood Lake & West Milford News
   (Greenwood Lake, NY) **10215**
Greer Citizen, The (Greer, SC) **10262**
Gresham Outlook (Gresham, OR) **10248**
Gridley Herald, The (Gridley, CA) **10073**
Griffin Daily News (Griffin, GA) **9975**
Griffith Guide (Highland, IN) **10132**
Grinnell Herald-Register (Grinnell, IA) **10138**
Grizzly, The (Big Bear Lake, CA) **10069**
Groesbeck Journal (Groesbeck, TX) **10275**
Grosse Pointe News (Grosse Pointe
   Farm, MI) **10170**
Groton Landmark (Ayer, MA) **10160**
Grove City Record (Columbus, OH) **10237**
▼Grove Daily News (Grove, OK) **10029**
Grove Sun (Grove, OK) **10245**
Grundy County Herald (Tracy City, TN) **10270**
Grundy Register (Grundy Center, IA) **10138**
Grunion Gazette (Long Beach, CA) **10075**
Grygla Eagle (Grygla, MN) **10179**
Guam Tribune (Agana, GU) **10106**
Guernsey Gazette/Lingle Guide
   (Guernsey, WY) **10309**
Guilford American (Dover-Foxcroft, ME) **10156**
Gulf Coast Tribune, The (West
   Columbia, TX) **10281**
Gunnison Country Times (Gunnison, CO) **9969**
Gurnee Press (Grayslake, IL) **10118**
Guthrie Daily Leader (Guthrie, OK) **10029**
Guttenberg Press (Guttenberg, IA) **10139**
Guymon Daily Herald (Guymon, OK) **10029**
† Gwinnett Daily News (Lawrenceville, GA)
Gwinnett Daily Post (Lawrenceville, GA) **9975**

H

† Haddon Gazette (Cherry Hill, NJ)
Hagerstown Exponent, The
   (Hagerstown, IN) **10132**
† Haines City Herald (Haines City, FL)
Half Moon Bay Review (Half Moon
   Bay, CA) **10073**
Halifax Reporter (Plymouth, MA) **10165**
Hallettsville Tribune-Herald
   (Hallettsville, TX) **10276**
Halls Graphic (Ripley, TN) **10269**
Hamburg Item (Hamburg, PA) **10253**

Hamilton-Wenham Chronicle
(Ipswich, MA) **10162**
† Hamilton County News (Elizabethtown, NY)
Hamilton County News (Speculator, NY) **10223**
Hamilton Herald-News (Hamilton, TX) **10276**
Hamilton Mid-York Weekly
(Hamilton, NY) **10215**
Hamilton Tribune (Hamilton, NY) **10215**
Hammond Daily Star (Hammond, LA) **9994**
Hammonton News (Hammonton, NJ) **10203**
Hampshire Register News
(Sycamore, IL) **10128**
Hampshire Review (Romney, WV) **10296**
Hampton Chronicle & Times
(Hampton, IA) **10139**
Hampton Chronicle-News (Westhampton
Beach, NY) **10225**
Hampton Union (North Hampton, NH) **10200**
Hamtramck Citizen (Hamtramck, MI) **10170**
Hanahan News (North Charleston, SC) **10263**
Hanceville Herald (Hanceville, AL) **10059**
Hancock Clarion (Hawesville, KY) **10148**
Hancock County Journal-Pilot
(Carthage, IL) **10112**
Hancock County Quill (La Harpe, IL) **10121**
Hancock News (Hancock, MD) **10159**
Hanford Sentinel (Hanford, CA) **9962**
Hannibal Courier-Post (Hannibal, MO) **10006**
Hanover Eagle & Regional News
(Madison, NJ) **10203**
Hanover Herald-Progress (Ashland, VA) **10285**
Hanover Mariner (Marshfield, MA) **10163**
† Hanover Park Township Times (Carol
Stream, IL)
Hansford County Reporter-Statesman
(Spearman, TX) **10281**
Haralson Gateway-Beacon, The
(Bremen, GA) **10101**
Harbor Beach Times (Harbor
Beach, MI) **10170**
Harbor Extra (Torrance, CA) **10084**
Harbor Sound (Brunswick, GA) **10101**
Harborwatch (Brooklyn, NY) **10211**
Hardin Calhoun Herald (Hardin, IL) **10119**
Hardin County Independent
(Elizabethtown, IL) **10116**
Hardin County Index (Eldora, IA) **10138**
Hardwick Gazette (Hardwick, VT) **10283**
Harlan County Journal (Alma, NE) **10196**
Harlan Daily Enterprise (Harlan, KY) **9992**
Harlan News Advertiser (Harlan, IA) **10139**
Harlan Tribune (Harlan, IA) **10139**
Harlem-Foster-Norwood Park-Edison Park Times
(Lincolnwood, IL) **10121**
Harlem-Irving Times (Lincolnwood, IL) **10121**
Harlem Valley Times (Amenia, NY) **10209**

† Harper Woods Herald (Birmingham, MI)
Harrah News, The (Harrah, OK) **10246**
Harriman Record (Kingston, TN) **10267**
Harrington Journal, The
(Harrington, DE) **10092**
Harrisburg Daily Register
(Harrisburg, IL) **9979**
Harrison County Advisor (Bethany, MO) **10188**
Harrison Daily Times (Harrison, AR) **9959**
Harrison Independent (Yonkers, NY) **10226**
Harrison News-Herald, The (Cadiz, OH) **10235**
Harrisonville Cass County Democrat Missourian
(Harrisonville, MO) **10190**
Harrodsburg Herald (Harrodsburg, KY) **10148**
Hart County News-Herald
(Munfordville, KY) **10150**
Harte-Hanks Pennysaver (Brea, CA) **10070**
Hartford Advocate (Hartford, CT) **10090**
Hartford Area News (Canistota, SD) **10264**
Hartford City News-Times (Hartford
City, IN) **9983**
Hartford Courant (Hartford, CT) **9970**
Hartland Herald Shopping Guide
(Howell, MI) **10171**
Hartselle Enquirer (Hartselle, AL) **10059**
Hartsville Messenger, The
(Hartsville, SC) **10262**
Hartsville Vidette, The (Hartsville, TN) **10267**
Hartville News (Hartville, OH) **10239**
Hartwell Sun, The (Hartwell, GA) **10103**
Harvard Spirit (Ayer, MA) **10160**
Harwich Oracle (Orleans, MA) **10164**
† Harwood Heights News (Park Ridge, IL)
Haskell Free Press (Haskell, TX) **10276**
Hastings Banner (Hastings, MI) **10170**
Hastings Daily Tribune (Hastings, NE) **10009**
Hastings Reminder (Hastings, MI) **10170**
Hastings Star Gazette (Hastings, MN) **10179**
Hattiesburg American
(Hattiesburg, MS) **10004**
Havana Mason County Democrat
(Havana, IL) **10119**
Haverford Press (Newtown Square, PA) **10256**
Haverhill Gazette (Haverhill, MA) **9997**
Havre Daily News (Havre, MT) **10008**
Hawaii Tribune-Herald (Hilo, HI) **9976**
Hawk Eye, The (Burlington, IA) **9986**
Hawley Herald (Hawley, MN) **10179**
Hawthorne Press (Hawthorne, NJ) **10203**
Haxtun-Fleming Herald, The
(Haxtun, CO) **10087**
Hayden Valley Press (Craig, CO) **10086**
Hays Daily News (Hays, KS) **9990**
Hazard Herald-Voice (Hazard, KY) **10148**
Hazen Star (Hazen, ND) **10232**

Hazleton Standard Speaker
(Hazleton, PA)   **10033**
Headland Observer (Headland, AL)   **10060**
Headlight-Herald (Tillamook, OR)   **10250**
Healdsburg Tribune (Healdsburg, CA)   **10073**
Heights Herald (Fishers, IN)   **10131**
Heights Times-Herald (Dearborn, MI)   **10169**
Helena Daily World (Helena, AR)   **9959**
Hemet News (San Jacinto, CA)   **9965**
Hempstead Beacon (Hicksville, NY)   **10216**
Henderson County Quill
(Stronghurst, IL)   **10128**
Henderson Daily News (Henderson, TX)   **10044**
Henderson Gleaner (Henderson, KY)   **9992**
† Hendersonville Free Press
(Hendersonville, TN)
Hendersonville Star News
(Hendersonville, TN)   **10267**
Hendersonville Times-News
(Hendersonville, NC)   **10019**
Hendricks County Flyer (Plainfield, IN)   **10135**
† Hendricks County Guide Gazette
(Plainfield, IN)
† Henrico Gazette (Richmond, VA)
Henrietta Post (Fishers, NY)   **10214**
Henry County Local (New Castle, KY)   **10150**
Henryetta Daily Free-Lance
(Henryetta, OK)   **10029**
Henry Herald, The (McDonough, GA)   **10105**
Henry News Republican (Henry, IL)   **10119**
Herald & News (Klamath Falls, OR)   **10031**
Herald & Tribune (Jonesborough, TN)   **10267**
Herald-Advocate (Wauchula, FL)   **10100**
Herald-Chronicle, The (Winchester, TN)   **10270**
Herald-Citizen (Cookeville, TN)   **10040**
Herald-Democrat (Leadville, CO)   **10088**
Herald-Democrat (Denison, TX)   **10043**
Herald-Gazette, The (Barnesville, GA)   **10101**
Herald-Independent, The
(Winnsboro, SC)   **10264**
Herald-Journal (Spartanburg, SC)   **10039**
Herald-Journal, The (Monticello, IN)   **9985**
Herald-Leader, The (Fitzgerald, GA)   **10103**
Herald-News (Wolf Point, MT)   **10196**
Herald-News (Dayton, TN)   **10266**
Herald-News, The (Joliet, IL)   **9980**
Herald-Palladium (St. Joseph, MI)   **10002**
Herald-Republican (Angola, IN)   **10129**
Herald-Review (Decatur, IL)   **9979**
Herald-Star (Steubenville, OH)   **10026**
Herald-Star, The (Edinburg, IL)   **10116**
Herald-Sun, The (Durham, NC)   **10019**
Herald-Times (Bloomington, IN)   **9982**
Herald-Tribune, The (Cartersville, GA)   **10101**
Herald/Country Market, The
(Bourbonnais, IL)   **10111**

Herald/Leader (Siloam Springs, AR)   **10068**
Herald Bulletin (Anderson, IN)   **9982**
Herald Coaster (Rosenberg, TX)   **10046**
Herald Enterprise (Golconda, IL)   **10118**
Herald Extra Express (Statesboro, GA)   **10105**
Herald Gazette, The (Trenton, TN)   **10270**
Herald Journal, The (Logan, UT)   **10047**
Herald Ledger (Eddyville, KY)   **10147**
Herald News, The (Fall River, MA)   **9997**
Herald News, The (Reed City, MI)   **10174**
Herald of Randolph (Randolph, VT)   **10284**
Herald Press (Harvey, ND)   **10232**
Herald Record (West Union, WV)   **10297**
Herald Standard (Uniontown, PA)   **10037**
Herald, The (New Britain, CT)   **9970**
† Herald, The (Tarpon Springs, FL)
Herald, The (Rincon, GA)   **10105**
Herald, The (Jasper, IN)   **9984**
Herald, The (Hagerstown, MD)   **9996**
Herald, The (Truth or
Consequences, NM)   **10209**
Herald, The (Pittsburgh, PA)   **10258**
Herald, The (Sharon, PA)   **10036**
Herald, The (Rock Hill, SC)   **10039**
Herald, The (Everett, WA)   **10051**
Herald, The (Markesan, WI)   **10302**
Hereford Brand (Hereford, TX)   **10044**
Hermann Advertiser-Courier
(Hermann, MO)   **10190**
Hermiston Herald (Hermiston, OR)   **10249**
Hermitage Index (Hermitage, MO)   **10190**
Hernando Today (Brooksville, FL)   **9971**
Herndon Times (Reston, VA)   **10288**
Herrin Spokesman (Herrin, IL)   **10119**
Herscher Pilot (Herscher, IL)   **10119**
Hershey Chronicle, The (Hershey, PA)   **10253**
Hesperia Resorter (Hesperia, CA)   **10073**
Hi-Riser (Deerfield Beach, FL)   **10094**
Hialeah/Opa-Lacka News (Miami, FL)   **10097**
Hiawatha Daily World (Hiawatha, KS)   **9990**
Hiawatha Valley Shopper (Red
Wing, MN)   **10182**
Hibbing Daily Tribune (Hibbing, MN)   **10003**
Hickory Daily Record (Hickory, NC)   **10019**
Hickory Hills Citizen (Midlothian, IL)   **10123**
Hickory News/Extra, The (Hickory, NC)   **10228**
Hicksville Illustrated News
(Mineola, NY)   **10219**
Highlander (West Covina, CA)   **10084**
▼Highlander (Highlands Ranch, CO)   **10087**
Highland Guide (Highland, IN)   **10132**
Highland News Leader (Highland, IL)   **10119**
Highland Park News (Bannockburn, IL)   **10110**
Highland Park News/Herald/Journal (Los
Angeles, CA)   **10076**
Highlands Branch Herald (Littleton, CO)   **10088**

† Highlands Press (Mulberry, FL)
Highline News (Burien, WA) **10290**
High Plains Journal (Dodge City, KS) **10143**
High Point Enterprise (High Point, NC) **10019**
High Springs Herald, The (High
  Springs, FL) **10095**
High Timber Times (Pine, CO) **10089**
Hill City Times, The (Hill City, KS) **10143**
Hilliard Northwest News (Hilliard, OH) **10239**
Hillsboro Argus (Hillsboro, OR) **10249**
Hillsboro Journal (Hillsboro, IL) **10119**
Hillsboro Sentry-Enterprise
  (Hillsboro, WI) **10301**
Hillsboro Star-Journal (Hillsboro, KS) **10144**
Hillsborough Beacon (Somerville, NJ) **10206**
Hillsdale Daily News (Hillsdale, MI) **10000**
Hillside Leader (Union, NJ) **10207**
Hilltop News-Press (Cincinnati, OH) **10235**
Hilmar Times (Hilmar, CA) **10073**
Hilton Head Island Packet (Hilton
  Head, SC) **10038**
Hingham Journal & Mariner
  (Quincy, MA) **10165**
Hinsdale Doings (Hinsdale, IL) **10120**
Hinton News (Hinton, WV) **10295**
Hobart Democrat-Chief (Hobart, OK) **10246**
Hobart Gazette (Merriville, IN) **10133**
Hobbs Daily News-Sun (Hobbs, NM) **10013**
Hobbs Flare (Hobbs, NM) **10208**
Hoboken Reporter (Hoboken, NJ) **10203**
Hocking Valley Advertiser (Logan, OH) **10240**
† Hodgkins Citizen (La Grange, IL)
Hoisington Dispatch (Hoisington, KS) **10144**
Holbrook Sun (Marshfield, MA) **10163**
Holbrook Times (Stoughton, MA) **10166**
Holbrook Tribune News & Snowflake Herald
  (Holbrook, AZ) **10064**
Holden Image-Progress, The
  (Holden, MO) **10190**
Holdenville Daily News
  (Holdenville, OK) **10029**
Holdrege Daily Citizen (Holdrege, NE) **10009**
Holland Sentinel (Holland, MI) **10000**
Hollister Free Lance (Hollister, CA) **9962**
† Hollywood Citizen News (Los Angeles, CA)
† Hollywood Sun (Hollywood, FL)
Holmes County Advertiser (Bonifay, FL) **10093**
Holmes County Hub (Millersburg, OH) **10241**
Holt Community News (Holt, MI) **10171**
Holton Recorder (Holton, KS) **10144**
Holtville Tribune (Holtville, CA) **10073**
Home News & Tribune, The (East
  Brunswick, NJ) **10012**
Home News, The (Marshville, NC) **10229**
Homer News (Homer, AK) **10062**

Homestead/Florida City News
  (Miami, FL) **10097**
Home Times Family Newspaper (West Palm
  Beach, FL) **10100**
Hometown News (Madison, WV) **10295**
Hominy News-Progress (Hominy, OK) **10246**
Hondo Anvil Herald (Hondo, TX) **10276**
Honolulu Advertiser (Honolulu, HI) **9976**
Honolulu Star-Bulletin (Honolulu, HI) **9976**
Hood County News (Granbury, TX) **10275**
Hood River News (Hood River, OR) **10249**
Hoopeston Chronicle (Hoopeston, IL) **10120**
Hoosier Express (Washington, IN) **10136**
Hope Star, The (Hope, AR) **9959**
Hopewell News (Hopewell, VA) **10049**
Hopkins Journal, The (Hopkins, MO) **10190**
Hopkins Sun-Sailor (Minnetonka, MN) **10180**
Horicon Reporter (Horicon, WI) **10301**
Hornell Evening Tribune (Hornell, NY) **10015**
Horry Independent (Conway, SC) **10262**
Houghton Lake Resorter (Houghton
  Lake, MI) **10171**
Houlton Pioneer Times (Houlton, ME) **10156**
Hour, The (Norwalk, CT) **9970**
Housatonic Weekend (New Milford, CT) **10091**
Houston Chronicle (Houston, TX) **10044**
Houston County Courier (Crockett, TX) **10273**
Houston Forward Times (Houston, TX) **10276**
Houston Herald & Republican
  (Houston, MO) **10190**
Houston Informer (Houston, TX) **10276**
† Houston Post (Houston, TX)
Houston Times-Journal (Perry, GA) **10105**
▼Howard Beach Resident
  (Maspeth, NY) **10218**
Howard County Times (Columbia, MD) **10158**
Howe Enterprise (Howe, TX) **10276**
Hubbard City News (Mexia, TX) **10279**
† Hubbard News (Niles, OH)
Huber Heights Courier (Dayton, OH) **10239**
Hudson-Litchfield News (Hudson, NH) **10199**
Hudson Herald, The (Hudson, IA) **10139**
Hudson Hub-Times (Stow, OH) **10243**
Hudson Reporter (Hoboken, NJ) **10203**
Hudson Star-Observer (Hudson, WI) **10301**
Hughes County Times (Wetumka, OK) **10247**
Hughson Chronicle (Winton, CA) **10085**
Hugo Daily News (Hugo, OK) **10029**
Humble Sun (Humble, TX) **10276**
Humboldt Beacon (Fortuna, CA) **10072**
Humboldt Independent (Humboldt, IA) **10139**
† Humboldt Republican (Humboldt, IA)
Humboldt Sun (Winnemucca, NV) **10011**
Humbolt Journal (Canistota, SD) **10264**
Humeston New Era (Humeston, IA) **10139**

Hungry Horse News (Columbia
    Falls, MT) **10195**
Hunt County Shopper (Greenville, TX) **10275**
Hunterdon County Democrat
    (Flemington, NJ) **10202**
Hunterdon Review (Lebanon, NJ) **10203**
† Huntingdon Carroll Leader (Huntingdon, TN)
Huntington Beach/Fountain Valley Independent
    (Huntington Beach, CA) **10073**
Huntington Harbour Sun (Seal
    Beach, CA) **10083**
Huntington Herald-Dispatch
    (Huntington, WV) **10052**
Huntington Herald-Press
    (Huntington, IN) **9983**
Huntington Park Bulletin (Los
    Angeles, CA) **10076**
Huntington Record (Huntington, NY) **10216**
Huntley Farmside, The (Huntley, IL) **10120**
Huntsville Item (Huntsville, TX) **10044**
† Huntsville News (Huntsville, AL)
Huntsville Times, The (Huntsville, AL) **9956**
Huron Daily Tribune (Bad Axe, MI) **9999**
Hurricane Breeze (Hurricane, WV) **10295**
Hustler, The (South Pittsburg, TN) **10269**
Hutchinson Herald (Menno, SD) **10265**
Hutchinson Leader (Hutchinson, MN) **10179**
Hutchinson News (Hutchinson, KS) **9990**
Hyde Park Herald (Chicago, IL) **10113**
Hyde Park Townsman (Hyde Park, NY) **10216**

I

Idaho County Free Press
    (Grangeville, ID) **10107**
Idaho Enterprise (Malad City, ID) **10108**
Idaho Falls Post Register (Idaho
    Falls, ID) **9977**
Idaho Mountain Express (Ketchum, ID) **10108**
Idaho Press-Tribune (Nampa, ID) **9977**
Idaho State Journal (Pocatello, ID) **9977**
Idaho Statesman, The (Boise, ID) **9976**
Idalou Beacon (Idalou, TX) **10276**
Ile Camera, The (Grosse Ile, MI) **10170**
Illinois Times (Springfield, IL) **10127**
Illiopolis Sentinel (Illiopolis, IL) **10120**
Impact of Laurel (Laurel, MS) **10186**
Imperial Valley Press (El Centro, CA) **9961**
Improper Bostonian, The (Boston, MA) **10160**
Independence Bulletin-Journal
    (Independence, IA) **10139**
Independence Daily Reporter
    (Independence, KS) **9990**
Independence Examiner, The
    (Independence, MO) **10006**

Independence News-Wave
    (Independence, WI) **10301**
Independence News, The
    (Independence, KS) **10144**
Independent (Collierville, TN) **10266**
Independent (Deerfield, WI) **10299**
Independent-Journal, The (Potosi, MO) **10192**
Independent-Messenger (Emporia VA) **10286**
Independent-Register, The
    (Brodhead, WI) **10298**
Independent Appeal (Selmer, TN) **10269**
Independent Enterprise (Payette, ID) **10108**
Independent Herald, The (Pineville, WV) **10296**
Independent Mirror (Mexico, NY) **10218**
Independent News (Georgetown, IL) **10118**
Independent News Herald
    (Clarissa, MN) **10178**
Independent Observer, The
    (Scottdale, PA) **10259**
† Independent Press (Marine City, MI)
Independent Press (New
    Providence, NJ) **10205**
Independent Press of Bloomfield, The
    (Bloomfield, NJ) **10201**
Independent Record (Helena, MT) **10008**
Independent Republican (Goshen, NY) **10215**
Independent, The (Robertsdale, AL) **10061**
Independent, The (Livermore, CA) **10075**
Independent, The (Winamac, IN) **10136**
Independent, The (Flint, MI) **10159**
Independent, The (Durham, NC) **10227**
Independent, The (Morganville, NJ) **10204**
Independent, The (Massillon, OH) **10025**
Independent, The (Collegeville, PA) **10252**
Independent, The (Montrose, PA) **10255**
Index-Journal (Greenwood, SC) **10038**
Indiana Gazette (Indiana, PA) **10034**
Indianapolis East Side Herald
    (Indianapolis, IN) **10132**
Indianapolis News (Indianapolis, IN) **9984**
Indianapolis Recorder (Indianapolis, IN) **10132**
Indianapolis Star (Indianapolis, IN) **9984**
Indianapolis Westside Enterprise
    (Indianapolis, IN) **10132**
Indianhead Advertiser (Frederic, WI) **10300**
Indian Head Park Citizen (Oak
    Brook, IL) **10125**
Indian Head Park Doings (Hinsdale, IL) **10120**
Indio Advertiser (Palm Desert, CA) **10079**
Indio Post (Indio, CA) **10073**
Indy Suburban Newspaper
    (Greenfield, IN) **10132**
Ingham County News (Mason, MI) **10172**
Inglewood/Hawthorne Wave (Los
    Angeles, CA) **10076**
Inkster Ledger-Star (Wayne, MI) **10176**

Inland Valley Daily Bulletin (Ontario, CA) **9963**

Inquirer & Mirror, The (Nantucket, MA) **10164**

Inside (Chicago, IL) **10113**

† Inside Ravenswood (Chicago, IL)

Intelligencer Record, The
   (Doylestown, PA) **10033**

Inter-County Leader (Frederic, WI) **10300**

Inter-Mountain, The (Elkins, WV) **10052**

† Interboro News (Prospect Park, PA)

Interior Journal (Stanford, KY) **10151**

Interlaken Review (Trumansburg, NY) **10224**

Intermountain News (Burney, CA) **10070**

Iola Herald (Iola, WI) **10301**

Iola Register (Iola, KS) **9990**

Ionia Sentinel-Standard (Ionia, MI) **10000**

Iosco County News Herald (East
   Tawas, MI) **10169**

Iowa City Press-Citizen (Iowa City, IA) **9987**

Iowa Park Leader (Iowa Park, TX) **10276**

Ipswich Chronicle (Ipswich, MA) **10162**

Ipswich Tribune (Ipswich, SD) **10265**

Iron County Miner (Hurley, WI) **10301**

Irondequoit Press (Rochester, NY) **10222**

Iron River Reporter (Iron River, MI) **10171**

Ironton Tribune (Ironton, OH) **10024**

Ironwood Daily Globe (Ironwood, MI) **10000**

Iroquois County Times Republic
   (Watseka, IL) **9981**

Irvine World News (Irvine, CA) **10073**

Irving News (Arlington, TX) **10271**

Irvington Viewpoint, The (Irvington, NY) **10216**

ISDA Unione (Pittsburgh, PA) **10258**

Island Ad-Vantages (Stonington, ME) **10157**

Island Connection (Portland, OR) **10250**

Island Dispatch (Grand Island, NY) **10215**

Islander, The (Gulf Shores, AL) **10059**

Islander, The (Pensacola Beach, FL) **10098**

Islander, The (St. Simons Island, GA) **10106**

Islander, The (South Hero, VT) **10284**

Island Reporter (Sanibel, FL) **10098**

Island Times (Lihue, HI) **9976**

Islesboro Island News (Islesboro, ME) **10156**

Islip Bulletin (Sayville, NY) **10222**

Islip News (Smithtown, NY) **10223**

Issaquah Press (Issaquah, WA) **10291**

Isthmus (Madison, WI) **10302**

Itawamba County Times, The
   (Fulton, MS) **10186**

Item (Clinton, MA) **10161**

Item, The (Sumter, SC) **10039**

Ithaca Journal, The (Ithaca, NY) **10015**

Ithaca Times (Ithaca, NY) **10216**

Iuka Tishomingo County News
   (Iuka, MS) **10186**

J

Jackson-Vinton Journal-Herald
   (Jackson, OH) **10240**

Jackson Cash-Book Journal
   (Jackson, MO) **10190**

Jackson Citizen Patriot (Jackson, MI) **10000**

Jackson County Banner
   (Brownstown, IN) **10130**

Jackson County Floridan (Marianna, FL) **9972**

Jackson County Herald/Tribune
   (Edna, TX) **10274**

Jackson County Livewire (Jackson, MN) **10179**

Jackson County Star (Walden, CO) **10089**

Jackson Heights News (Maspeth, NY) **10218**

Jackson Herald (Jefferson, GA) **10103**

Jackson Hole Guide (Jackson, WY) **10309**

Jackson Hole News (Jackson, WY) **10309**

Jackson Independent, The
   (Jonesboro, LA) **10153**

Jackson Progress-Argus (Jackson, GA) **10103**

Jackson Star News (Ravenswood, WV) **10296**

Jackson Sun (Jackson, TN) **10040**

Jacksonville Daily News
   (Jacksonville, NC) **10019**

Jacksonville Daily Progress
   (Jacksonville, TX) **10044**

Jacksonville Journal-Courier
   (Jacksonville, IL) **9979**

Jacksonville News (Jacksonville, AL) **10060**

Jacksonville Patriot (Jacksonville, AR) **9960**

Jacksonville Shopping Guide
   (Jacksonville, FL) **10095**

Jaffrey-Rindge Chronicle
   (Winchendon, MA) **10167**

▼Jamaica Times, The (Flushing, NY) **10214**

Jamestown Press, The (Jamestown, RI) **10260**

Jamestown Sun, The (Jamestown, ND) **10022**

Janesville Gazette (Janesville, WI) **10054**

Jasper County News, The (Bay
   Springs, MS) **10185**

Jasper County Sun (Ridgeland, SC) **10263**

Jasper Daily Mountain Eagle (Jasper, AL) **9956**

Jasper Journal (Jasper, MN) **10179**

Jasper Journal (Jasper, TN) **10267**

Jasper News (Jasper, FL) **10095**

Jasper News-Boy (Jasper, TX) **10276**

Jasper News-Boy Shopper (Jasper, TX) **10276**

Jeanerette Enterprise (Jeanerette, LA) **10153**

Jeannette Spirit (Jeannette, PA) **10254**

Jeff Davis Ledger (Hazlehurst, GA) **10103**

Jefferson Bee (Jefferson, IA) **10139**

Jefferson County Journal (Arnold, MO) **10188**

Jefferson County Journal (Adams, NY) **10209**

Jefferson County Transcript
   (Golden, CO) **10087**

Jefferson Herald (Jefferson, IA) **10139**

Jeffersonian Democrat (Brookville, PA) **10251**
Jeffersonian, The (Baltimore, MD) **10158**
Jeffersonian, The (Croswell, MI) **10169**
Jefferson Jimplecute (Jefferson, TX) **10276**
Jefferson Park-Portage Park-Bel Cragin Times
   (Lincolnwood, IL) **10121**
Jefferson Post (West Jefferson, NC) **10231**
† Jefferson Republic, The (De Soto, MO)
Jefferson Sentinel (Lakewood, CO) **10088**
Jefferson Star, The (Rigby, ID) **10109**
Jeffersonville Evening News
   (Jeffersonville, IN) **9984**
Jekyll's Golden Islander
   (Brunswick, GA) **10101**
Jellico Advance Sentinel (La
   Follette, TN) **10267**
Jena Times Olla-Tullos Signal
   (Jena, LA) **10153**
Jenks Journal (Tulsa, OK) **10247**
Jennings Daily News (Jennings, LA) **9994**
Jersey City Reporter (Hoboken, NJ) **10203**
Jersey Journal, The (Jersey City, NJ) **10012**
Jessamine Journal (Nicholasville, KY) **10150**
† Jet Gazette (Austin, TX)
Jetmore Republican (Jetmore, KS) **10144**
† Jet Visitor (Cherokee, OK)
Johnsonburg Press (Johnsonburg, PA) **10254**
Johnson City Press (Johnson City, TN) **10040**
Johnson County Graphic
   (Clarksville, AR) **10065**
Johnson County Sun (Shawnee
   Mission, KS) **10145**
Johnson Pioneer (Johnson, KS) **10144**
Johnston County Capital-Democrat
   (Tishomingo, OK) **10247**
Johnstonian Sun (Selma, NC) **10230**
Johnstown Independent
   (Columbus, OH) **10237**
Jonesboro Review (Sherwood, AR) **10068**
Jonesboro Sun (Jonesboro, AR) **9960**
Jones County Town Crier
   (Anamosa, IA) **10137**
Joplin Globe, The (Joplin, MO) **10006**
Journal & Austin Chronicle
   (Scottsburg, IN) **10135**
Journal & Courier (Lafayette, IN) **9984**
Journal & Monitor Herald (Tomah, WI) **10306**
Journal & Republican (Lowville, NY) **10217**
Journal-Enterprise (Providence, KY) **10151**
Journal-Gazette, The (Fort Wayne, IN) **9983**
Journal-Herald, The (White Haven, PA) **10260**
Journal-Leader (Caldwell, OH) **10235**
Journal-Patriot (North Wilkesboro, NC) **10229**
Journal-Register (Medina, NY) **10016**
Journal-World, The (Lawrence, KS) **9990**

▼ Journal/Valley Views (White
   Haven, PA) **10260**
Journal American (Bellevue, WA) **10050**
Journal Courier (Moravia, NY) **10219**
Journal Herald, The (Shawnee, KS) **10145**
Journal Inquirer (Manchester, CT) **9970**
Journal Messenger (Manassas, VA) **10049**
Journal News (Hamilton, OH) **10024**
Journal News (Spencerville, OH) **10243**
Journal of the San Juan Islands (Friday
   Harbor, WA) **10291**
Journal Opinion (Bradford, VT) **10283**
Journal Press (Lawrenceburg, IN) **10133**
Journal Record (Hamilton, AL) **10059**
Journal Register (Palmer, MA) **10164**
Journal, The (Chicago, IL) **10113**
Journal, The (Ellettsville, IN) **10130**
Journal, The (New Ulm, MN) **10003**
Journal, The (Crosby, ND) **10232**
Journal, The (Berlin, NJ) **10200**
Journal, The (Struthers, OH) **10243**
Journal, The (Mt. Pleasant, SC) **10253**
Journal, The (Williamston, SC) **10264**
Journal, The (Martinsburg, WV) **10052**
Journal Times (Racine, WI) **10055**
† Journal Transcript (Franklin, NH)
Journal Tribune (Williamsburg, IA) **10142**
Journal Tribune (Biddeford, ME) **9995**
Journal Tribune (Seneca, SC) **10264**
Julesburg Advocate (Julesburg, CO) **10087**
Junction City Daily Union (Junction
   City, KS) **9990**
Junction Eagle, The (Junction, TX) **10277**
Juneau County Star-Times
   (Mauston, WI) **10302**
Juneau Empire (Juneau, AK) **9957**
Juniata News (Philadelphia, PA) **10257**
Juniata Sentinel (Mifflintown, PA) **10255**
Jupiter Courier (Jupiter, FL) **10095**

K

Kalamazoo Gazette (Kalamazoo, MI) **10000**
Kalona News, The (Kalona, IA) **10139**
Kanabec County Times (Mora, MN) **10181**
Kane County Chronicle (Geneva, IL) **9979**
Kane Republican (Kane, PA) **10034**
Kannapolis Daily Independent
   (Kannapolis, NC) **10020**
† Kansas Business News (Augusta, KS)
† Kansas City Evening News (Shawnee
   Mission, KS)
Kansas City Kansan (Kansas City, KS) **9990**
Kansas City Star (Kansas City, MO) **10006**
Karnes Citation (Karnes City, TX) **10277**
Katahdin Times (Millinocket, ME) **10156**

Kaufman Herald, The (Kaufman, TX) **10277**
Kaukauna Times (Kaukauna, WI) **10301**
Kayo, The (Clinton, MO) **10189**
Kearney Hub (Kearney, NE) **10009**
Keene Sentinel (Keene, NH) **10011**
Keith County News (Ogallala, NE) **10198**
Keller Citizen, The (Keller, TX) **10277**
Kemmerer Gazette (Kemmerer, WY) **10309**
Kemper County Messenger
   (DeKalb, MS) **10185**
Ken-Ton Bee (Buffalo, NY) **10211**
Kenbridge-Victoria Dispatch
   (Victoria, VA) **10289**
Kendall County Record (Yorkville, IL) **10129**
Kendall News-Gazette (Miami, FL) **10097**
Kendallville News-Sun (Kendallville, IN) **9984**
Kendrick-Gazette (Kendrick, ID) **10108**
Kenilworth Leader (Union, NJ) **10207**
Kenly News (Kenly, NC) **10228**
Kennebec Journal (Augusta, ME) **9995**
Kennedale News (Everman, TX) **10274**
Kennedy Advanced Times (Karnes
   City, TX) **10277**
Kennesaw Neighbor, The (Marietta, GA) **10104**
Kenosha News (Kenosha, WI) **10054**
Kent-Ravenna Record-Courier
   (Ravenna, OH) **10026**
Kent County Daily Times (West
   Warwick, RI) **10038**
Kent County News (Chestertown, MD) **10158**
Kent Good Times Dispatch (Kent, CT) **10090**
Kenton County Recorder (Florence, KY) **10148**
Kenton Times (Kenton, OH) **10024**
Kentucky New Era (Hopkinsville, KY) **9992**
Kentucky Post, The (Covington, KY) **9992**
Kentucky Standard (Bardstown, KY) **10146**
Kentwood Advance (Jenison, MI) **10171**
Kentwood News-Ledger (Kentwood, LA) **10153**
Kenyon Leader (Kenyon, MN) **10179**
Keokuk Daily Gate City (Keokuk, IA) **9987**
Kerman News (Kerman, CA) **10074**
Kernersville News (Kernersville, NC) **10228**
Kern Valley Sun (Lake Isabella, CA) **10074**
Kerrville Daily Times (Kerrville, TX) **10044**
Ketchikan Daily News (Ketchikan, AK) **9957**
Kettering-Oakwood Times
   (Kettering, OH) **10240**
Kettle Moraine Index (Hartland, WI) **10300**
Kewanee Star-Courier (Kewanee, IL) **9980**
Kewaskum Statesman (Kewaskum, WI) **10301**
Kewaunee Enterprise (Kewaunee, WI) **10301**
Keystone Tribune (Elroy, WI) **10300**
Key West Citizen (Key West, FL) **9972**
Kiel Tri-County Record (Kiel, WI) **10301**
Kilgore News Herald (Kilgore, TX) **10044**
Killeen Daily Herald (Killeen, TX) **10044**

King City Rustler (King City, CA) **10074**
Kingfisher Times & Free Press
   (Kingfisher, OK) **10246**
Kingman Daily Miner (Kingman, AZ) **9958**
Kingman Journal/Leader Courier
   (Kingman, KS) **10144**
King of Prussia Courier (King of
   Prussia, PA) **10254**
Kingsburg Recorder (Kingsburg, CA) **10074**
Kings County News (Brooklyn, NY) **10211**
Kings Courier (Brooklyn, NY) **10211**
Kings Mountain Herald (Kings
   Mountain, NC) **10228**
Kingsport Daily News (Kingsport, TN) **10040**
Kingsport Times-News (Kingsport, TN) **10040**
Kingston Reporter (Plymouth, MA) **10165**
Kingsville Record, The (Kingsville, TX) **10277**
King Times News (King, NC) **10228**
Kingwood Sun (Humble, TX) **10276**
Kinmundy Express (Kinmundy, IL) **10121**
Kinston Daily Free Press (Kinston, NC) **10020**
Kiowa County Press (Eads, CO) **10086**
Kirksville Daily Express (Kirksville, MO) **10007**
† Kirtland Enterprise (Willoughby, OH)
Knoxville Journal/Express
   (Knoxville, IA) **10139**
Knoxville Journal, The (Galesburg, IL) **10117**
Knoxville News-Sentinel (Knoxville, TN) **10041**
Kodiak Daily Mirror (Kodiak, AK) **9957**
Kokomo Tribune, The (Kokomo, IN) **9984**
Konawa Leader (Konawa, OK) **10246**
† Kossuth County Advance (Algona, IA)
Kuna-Melba News (Kuna, ID) **10108**

L

L'Anse Sentinel (L'Anse, MI) **10172**
L'Observateur (La Place, LA) **10153**
Labor Herald (Baltimore, MD) **10158**
La Canada Valley Sun (La Canada, CA) **10074**
Lacon Home Journal (Lacon, IL) **10121**
La Crosse County Countryman (West
   Salem, WI) **10308**
La Crosse Tribune (La Crosse, WI) **10054**
Ladysmith News (Ladysmith, WI) **10301**
Lafayette Advertiser (Lafayette, LA) **9994**
Lafayette Leader (Lafayette, IN) **10133**
Lafayette Sun, The (Lafayette, AL) **10060**
La Feria News (La Feria, TX) **10277**
La Follette Press (La Follette, TN) **10267**
La Grange Countryside Citizen (Oak
   Brook, IL) **10125**
La Grange Daily News (La Grange, GA) **9975**
La Grange Independent (Mahopac, NY) **10217**
La Grange Park Citizen (Oak Brook, IL) **10125**

La Grange Standard News (La
   Grange, IN) **10133**
Laguna Niguel News (Lake Forest, CA) **10074**
Laguna Post News (Lake Forest, CA) **10074**
La Habra Star (Anaheim, CA) **10068**
Lahontan Valley News (Fallon, NV) **10010**
La Jolla Light (La Jolla, CA) **10074**
La Junta Tribune-Democrat (La
   Junta, CO) **9969**
† Lake Alfred Press (Mulberry, FL)
Lake Area News (Land O' Lakes, FL) **10096**
Lake Charles American Press (Lake
   Charles, LA) **9994**
Lake Cities Sun, The (Lake Dallas, TX) **10277**
Lake City Reporter (Lake City, FL) **9972**
Lake City Town Crier (La Follette, TN) **10267**
† Lake Country Chronicle (Buchanan, MI)
Lake Country Reporter (Hartland, WI) **10300**
Lake County Examiner (Lakeview, OR) **10249**
Lake County Leader (Ronan, MT) **10196**
Lake County News-Chronicle (Two
   Harbors, MN) **10184**
Lake County Record-Bee (Lakeport, CA) **9962**
Lake County Star (Crown Point, IN) **10130**
Lake County Star (Big Rapids, MI) **10167**
Lake Edition, The (Lexington, SC) **10263**
Lake Elsinore Valley Sun-Tribune (Lake
   Elsinore, CA) **10074**
Lakefield Standard (Lakefield, MN) **10179**
Lake Forester (Bannockburn, IL) **10110**
Lake Geneva Regional News (Lake
   Geneva, WI) **10301**
Lake Havasu City Advertiser (Palm
   Desert, CA) **10079**
Lake Havasu City Herald (Lake Havasu
   City, AZ) **9958**
Lakeland Press (Grayslake, IL) **10118**
Lakeland Times (Minocqua, WI) **10303**
Lakeland Today (Butler, NJ) **10201**
Lake Michigan Examiner, The
   (Muskegon, MI) **10173**
Lake Mills Leader (Lake Mills, WI) **10301**
Lake News (Fruitland Park, FL) **10095**
Lake Oswego Review (Lake
   Oswego, OR) **10249**
Lake Placid Journal (Lake Placid, FL) **10096**
Lake Placid News (Lake Placid, NY) **10216**
Lake Powell Chronicle (Page, AZ) **10064**
Lakeshore Chronicle (Manitowoc, WI) **10302**
Lakeshore Weekly News (Wayzata, MN) **10184**
Lakeside Ledger, The (Woodstock, GA) **10106**
Lake Station Herald (Merrillville, IN) **10133**
Lake Sun Leader (Camdenton, MO) **10005**
Lake Tribune (Sherwood, AR) **10068**
Lakeview Enterprise (Big Rapids, MI) **10167**
Lake Villa Record (Grayslake, IL) **10119**

Lakeville Independent (Middleboro, MA) **10163**
Lakeville Journal, The (Lakeville, CT) **10090**
Lakeville Life & Times (Lakeville, MN) **10179**
Lakeville Sun-Current (Burnsville, MN) **10177**
† Lake Wales Highlander (Winter Haven, FL)
Lake Wales News (Lake Wales, FL) **10096**
Lakewood Sun Post (Cleveland, OH) **10236**
Lake Worth Herald Coastal Observer (Lake
   Worth, FL) **10096**
Lake Zurich Enterprise (Grayslake, IL) **10119**
Lakin Independent, The (Lakin, KS) **10144**
Lamar Daily News (Lamar, CO) **9969**
Lamar Democrat (Vernon, AL) **10062**
Lamar Democrat (Lamar, MO) **10191**
Lamar Leader (Sulligent, AL) **10061**
La Marque Times (La Marque, TX) **10277**
Lamb County Leader-News
   (Littlefield, TX) **10278**
Lamberton News (Lamberton, MN) **10179**
La Mesa Forum (Lemon Grove, CA) **10075**
Lamesa Press-Reporter (Lamesa, TX) **10277**
Lamont Reporter (Lamont, CA) **10074**
Lancaster Bee (Williamsville, NY) **10225**
Lancaster Eagle-Gazette
   (Lancaster, OH) **10025**
Lancaster Fairfield Advertiser
   (Carroll, OH) **10235**
Lancaster Intelligencer Journal
   (Lancaster, PA) **10034**
Lancaster New Era (Lancaster, PA) **10034**
Lancaster News (Lancaster, SC) **10262**
Lancaster Today (DeSoto, TX) **10274**
Lander Wyoming State Journal
   (Lander, WY) **10309**
Lansing State Journal (Lansing, MI) **10000**
La Porte Herald-Argus (La Porte, IN) **9984**
Laramie Daily Boomerang
   (Laramie, WY) **10055**
Laredo Morning Times (Laredo, TX) **10044**
Larimore Pioneer (Northwood, ND) **10233**
LaRue County Herald-News
   (Hodgenville, KY) **10148**
Las Cruces Sun-News (Las Cruces, NM) **10013**
Las Vegas Daily Optic (Las Vegas, NM) **10013**
Las Vegas Review-Journal (Las
   Vegas, NV) **10010**
Las Vegas Sun (Las Vegas, NV) **10010**
Las Vegas Today (Las Vegas, NV) **10199**
Las Virgenes Enterprise (Woodland
   Hills, CA) **10085**
Latrobe Bulletin (Latrobe, PA) **10034**
Lauderdale County Enterprise
   (Ripley, TN) **10269**
Laurel Leader (Laurel, MD) **10159**
Laurel Leader-Call (Laurel, MS) **10004**

Laurens County Advertiser
   (Laurens, SC) 10263
Laurens Sun, The (Laurens, IA) 10139
Laurinburg Exchange (Laurinburg, NC) 10020
La Vida News (Arlington, TX) 10271
LaVilla News (Hot Springs Village, AR) 10066
L.A. Weekly (Los Angeles, CA) 10076
Lawrence County Centennial
   (Deadwood, SD) 10264
Lawrence County News
   (Lawrenceville, IL) 10121
Lawrence County Record (Mt.
   Vernon, MO) 10191
Lawrence Ledger (Pennington, NJ) 10206
Lawrence Times (Fishers, IN) 10131
Lawrence Township Journal
   (Lawrence, IN) 10133
Lawrenceville Daily Record
   (Lawrenceville, IL) 9980
Lawton Constitution (Lawton, OK) 10029
† Lead Call (Lead, SD)
Leader-Courier (Kingman, KS) 10144
Leader-Herald, The (Gloversville, NY) 10015
Leader-News (Central City, KY) 10147
Leader-News (Washburn, ND) 10233
Leader-Record (Gonvick, MN) 10179
Leader-State Register, The
   (Seaford, DE) 10092
Leader-Telegram (Eau Claire, WI) 10054
Leader-Tribune, The (Fort Valley, GA) 10103
Leader-Vindicator, The (New
   Bethlehem, PA) 10256
Leader Enterprise (Montpelier, OH) 10241
Leader Observer (Maspeth, NY) 10218
Leader, The (Davenport, IA) 10137
Leader, The (Solon, IA) 10141
Leader, The (Charlestown, IN) 10130
† Leader, The (Lansing, KS)
Leader, The (Northwood, ND) 10233
Leader, The (Point Pleasant Beach, NJ) 10206
Leader, The (Corning, NY) 10014
Leader, The (Freeport, NY) 10214
Leader, The (Cleveland, OH) 10236
† Leader, The (East Palestine, OH)
Leader, The (Philadelphia, PA) 10257
Leader, The (Tremonton, UT) 10283
Leader Times (Kittanning, PA) 10034
Leaf-Chronicle, The (Clarksville, TN) 10040
Leavenworth Echo (Leavenworth, WA) 10292
Leavenworth Times (Leavenworth, KS) 9990
Leawood Sun (Shawnee Mission, KS) 10145
† Lebanon Connecticut Valley Reporter
   (Lebanon, NH)
Lebanon Daily News (Lebanon, PA) 10034
Lebanon Daily Record (Lebanon, MO) 10007
Lebanon Democrat, The (Lebanon, TN) 10041

Lebanon Enterprise (Lebanon, KY) 10149
Lebanon Express (Lebanon, OR) 10249
▼Lebanon Herald (Mascoutah, IL) 10122
Lebanon News (Lebanon, VA) 10287
Lebanon Times, The (Lebanon, KS) 10144
Le Center Leader (Le Center, MN) 10179
Ledger-Independent (Maysville, KY) 9993
† Ledger-Star (Norfolk, VA)
Ledger Dispatch (Antioch, CA) 9961
Ledger, The (Lakeland, FL) 9972
Ledger, The (Moundridge, KS) 10145
Ledger Tribune, The (New Albany, IN) 9985
Lee's Summit Journal (Lee's
   Summit, MO) 10191
Lee County Eagle, The (Auburn, AL) 10057
Lee County Observer (Bishopville, SC) 10261
Leeds News (Leeds, AL) 10060
Leelanau Enterprise (Leland, MI) 10172
Leesburg Today (Leesburg, VA) 10287
Leesville Daily Leader (Leesville, LA) 9994
Lehi Free Press (American Fork, UT) 10282
Lehigh Acres News-Star (Lehigh
   Acres, FL) 10096
Leisure World Golden Rain News (Seal
   Beach, CA) 10083
Leisure World News (Laguna Hills, CA) 10074
Le Mars Daily Sentinel (Le Mars, IA) 9988
Lemon Grove Review (Lemon
   Grove, CA) 10075
Lemont Metropolitan (Lemont, IL) 10121
Lemont Reporter (Lemont, IL) 10121
Lenexa Sun (Shawnee Mission, KS) 10146
Lenoir News-Topic (Lenoir, NC) 10020
Leon Journal-Reporter (Leon, IA) 10139
Leslie County News (Hyden, KY) 10148
Leslie Local Independent (Leslie, MI) 10172
Letcher County Community News-Press
   (Cromona, KY) 10147
Levelland Hockley County News-Press
   (Levelland, TX) 10277
Levittown Tribune (Mineola, NY) 10219
Lewisboro Ledger, The (Ridgefield, CT) 10091
Lewisburg Daily Journal (Milton, PA) 10035
Lewisburg Tribune (Lewisburg, TN) 10268
Lewis County Herald (Nezperce, ID) 10108
Lewiston-Porter Sentinel (Grand
   Island, NY) 10215
Lewiston Journal (Lewiston, MN) 10179
Lewiston Morning Tribune (Lewiston, ID) 9977
Lewistown-Fulton Democrat
   (Lewistown, IL) 10121
Lewistown News-Argus (Lewistown, MT) 10195
Lewisville Leader (Lewisville, TX) 10278
Lexington Dispatch (Lexington, NC) 10020
Lexington Herald-Leader (Lexington, KY) 9992
Lexington Minuteman (Lexington, MA) 10162

Lexington News (Lexington, MO) **10191**
Lexington Progress (Lexington, TN) **10268**
Liberal Southwest Daily Times
   (Liberal, KS) **9991**
Liberty Gazette (Liberty, TX) **10278**
† Liberty News (Niles, OH)
Liberty Press, The (Liberty Center, OH) **10240**
Liberty Tribune (Kansas City, MO) **10190**
Libertyville News (Grayslake, IL) **10119**
Libertyville Review (Bannockburn, IL) **10110**
† Licking Countian (Newark, OH)
Licking Valley Courier (West
   Liberty, KY) **10152**
Life at Ken-Caryl (Littleton, CO) **10088**
Light & Champion (Center, TX) **10272**
Ligonier Advance-Leader (Ligonier, IN) **10133**
Ligonier Echo (Ligonier, PA) **10254**
Ligonier Free Gazette, The
   (Ligonier, PA) **10254**
Lillie Suburban Shopping Review (St.
   Paul, MN) **10183**
Lima News (Lima, OH) **10025**
Lime Springs Herald (Lime Springs, IA) **10139**
Limestone Independent News
   (Bartonville, IL) **10111**
† Lincoln-Belmont Booster (Chicago, IL)
Lincoln County Journal (Shoshone, ID) **10109**
Lincoln County News (Newcastle, ME) **10156**
Lincoln County News (Chandler, OK) **10245**
Lincoln Courier (Lincoln, IL) **9980**
Lincoln Heights Bulletin-News (Los
   Angeles, CA) **10076**
Lincoln Journal (Concord, MA) **10161**
Lincoln Journal (Hamlin, WV) **10294**
Lincoln Journal Star (Lincoln, NE) **10009**
Lincoln Ledger (Star City, AR) **10068**
Lincoln News (Lincoln, ME) **10156**
Lincoln Times-News (Lincolnton, NC) **10228**
Lincolnwood Life (Lincolnwood, IL) **10122**
Lincolnwood Review (Evanston, IL) **10117**
Linden Herald (Linden, CA) **10075**
Lindenhurst News (Grayslake, IL) **10119**
Linden Leader (Union, NJ) **10207**
Lindsay Gazette (Lindsay, CA) **10075**
† Linesville Herald (Conneaut Lake, PA)
Linn Unterrified Democrat (Linn, MO) **10191**
Linton Daily Citizen (Linton, IN) **9984**
Linton Emmons County Record
   (Linton, ND) **10233**
Lisbon Ransom County Gazette & Enterprise
   (Lisbon, ND) **10233**
Lisle Sun (Naperville, IL) **10124**
Litchfield Enquirer (Litchfield, CT) **10090**
Litchfield Independent Review
   (Litchfield, MN) **10179**
Litchfield News-Herald (Litchfield, IL) **9980**

Lititz Record Express, The (Lititz, PA) **10254**
† Little Falls Transcript (Little Falls, MN)
Little Neck Ledger, The (Flushing, NY) **10214**
Little Paper, The (Melbourne, FL) **10096**
Littleton Independent (Littleton, CO) **10088**
Littleton Independent (Concord, MA) **10161**
Littleton Observer (Littleton, NC) **10228**
† Littleton Times (Littleton, CO)
Livermore Falls Advertiser (Livermore
   Falls, ME) **10156**
Liverpool Review (Baldwinsville, NY) **10209**
† Livingston East Texas Eye (Livingston, TX)
Livingston Enterprise (Livingston, MT) **10009**
Livingston Enterprise (Livingston, TN) **10268**
Livingston Leader (Denham
   Springs, LA) **10153**
Livonia Observer (Livonia, MI) **10172**
Llano News (Llano, TX) **10278**
Lockeford-Clements News
   (Lockeford, CA) **10075**
Lockhart Post Register (Lockhart, TX) **10278**
Lock Haven Express (Lock Haven, PA) **10034**
Locust Valley Leader (Locust
   Valley, NY) **10217**
Loda Times (Paxton, IL) **10126**
Lodi Enterprise (Lodi, WI) **10301**
Lodi News-Sentinel (Lodi, CA) **9962**
Logan Banner (Logan, WV) **10052**
Logan Daily News (Logan, OH) **10025**
Logan Herald Observer (Logan, IA) **10139**
Log Cabin Democrat (Conway, AR) **9959**
Lombardian, The (Lombard, IL) **10122**
Lombardian Villa Park Review
   (Lombard, IL) **10122**
Lombard Spectator (Elmhurst, IL) **10116**
Lompoc Record (Lompoc, CA) **9962**
† London Mills Times (Roseville, IL)
Lone Tree Reporter, The (Lone
   Tree, IA) **10140**
Long Beach Chinook Observer (Long
   Beach, WA) **10292**
† Long Beach Community News (Long
   Beach, CA)
Long Beach Herald (Long Beach, NY) **10217**
Long Beach Independent Voice (Long
   Beach, NY) **10217**
Long Island Advance (Patchogue, NY) **10221**
Long Island City/Astoria Journal
   (Maspeth, NY) **10218**
Long Island Graphic-Roosevelt Press
   (Lawrence, NY) **10216**
† Long Island Journal Newspaper Group (Long
   Beach, NY)
Longmeadow News (Westfield, MA) **10166**
Long Prairie Leader (Long Prairie, MN) **10179**

Long Valley Advocate, The
   (Cascade, ID) **10107**
Longview News Journal (Longview, TX) **10044**
Lorain County Times, The (Rocky
   River, OH) **10242**
Lorenzo Examiner (Lorenzo, TX) **10278**
Loris Times (Loris, SC) **10263**
Los Altos Town Crier (Los Altos, CA) **10075**
Los Angeles Bulletin (Los Angeles, CA) **9963**
Los Angeles Daily Journal (Los
   Angeles, CA) **9963**
Los Angeles Independent (Los
   Angeles, CA) **10076**
Los Angeles Log (San Diego, CA) **10080**
Los Angeles Times (Los Angeles, CA) **9963**
Los Banos Enterprise (Los Banos, CA) **10077**
Los Gatos Weekly-Times (Los
   Gatos, CA) **10077**
Lost River Star (Merrill, OR) **10249**
Loudenville Weekly (Delmar, NY) **10213**
Loudonville Times, The
   (Loudonville, OH) **10240**
Loudoun Times-Mirror (Leesburg, VA) **10287**
Louisiana Press-Journal
   (Louisiana, MO) **10191**
Louisville Defender Newspaper
   (Louisville, KY) **10149**
Louisville Herald, The (Louisville, OH) **10240**
Louisville Winston County Journal
   (Louisville, MS) **10186**
Loveland Daily Reporter-Herald
   (Loveland, CO) **9969**
Loveland Herald Press (Loveland, OH) **10241**
Lovell Chronicle, The (Lovell, WY) **10309**
Lovelock Review-Miner (Lovelock, NV) **10199**
Lovington Daily Leader (Lovington, NM) **10013**
Lowell Ledger (Lowell, MI) **10172**
Lowell Sun (Lowell, MA) **9997**
Lowell Tribune (Lowell, IN) **10133**
Lower Township Lantern (Rio
   Grande, NJ) **10206**
Loyal Tribune-Record-Gleaner
   (Loyal, WI) **10302**
Lubbock Avalanche-Journal
   (Lubbock, TX) **10044**
Ludington Daily News (Ludington, MI) **10000**
Ludlow Register (Palmer, MA) **10164**
Ludowici News (Ludowici, GA) **10104**
Lufkin Daily News (Lufkin, TX) **10044**
Luling Newsboy & Signal (Luling, TX) **10278**
Luray Page News & Courier (Luray, VA) **10287**
Lusk Herald (Lusk, WY) **10309**
Lutz Community News (Tampa, FL) **10099**
Luverne Journal & News (Luverne, AL) **10060**
Luxemburg News (Luxemburg, WI) **10302**
Lynbrook Herald (Lawrence, NY) **10216**

Lynbrook USA (Mineola, NY) **10219**
Lynden Tribune (Lynden, WA) **10292**
Lynwood Journal (Compton, CA) **10071**
Lynwood Press (Los Angeles, CA) **10076**
Lyon-Sioux Press (Rock Rapids, IA) **10141**
Lyons Citizen (Oak Brook, IL) **10125**
Lyons Daily News (Lyons, KS) **9991**
Lyons Mirror-Sun (Lyons, NE) **10197**

M

M & M Journal (Hillsboro, IL) **10120**
Mableton Neighbor, The (Marietta, GA) **10104**
Machias Valley News Observer
   (Machias, ME) **10156**
Macomb Daily (Mt. Clemens, MI) **10001**
Macomb Journal (Macomb, IL) **9980**
Macomb Voice, The (New
   Baltimore, MI) **10173**
Macon Beacon, The (Macon, MS) **10186**
Macon Chronicle-Herald (Macon, MO) **10007**
Macon County Times (Lafayette, TN) **10267**
Macon Telegraph (Macon, GA) **9975**
Macoupin & Montgomery County Journal
   (Hillsboro, IL) **10120**
Macoupin County Enquirer
   (Carlinville, IL) **10112**
Macoupin County Shopper
   (Hillsboro, IL) **10120**
Madawaska St. John Valley Times
   (Madawaska, ME) **10156**
Madera Tribune (Madera, CA) **9963**
Madill Record (Madill, OK) **10246**
Madison County Carrier (Madison, FL) **10096**
Madison County Chronicle (Worden, IL) **10129**
Madison County Eagle (Madison, VA) **10287**
Madison County Herald (Canton, MS) **10185**
Madison County Record (Madison, AL) **10060**
Madison County Record
   (Huntsville, AR) **10066**
Madison Courier (Madison, IN) **9984**
Madison Daily Leader (Madison, SD) **10039**
Madison Eagle (Madison, NJ) **10203**
Madison Enterprise Recorder
   (Madison, FL) **10096**
Madisonian, The (Madison, GA) **10104**
Madison Independent Press (New
   Providence, NJ) **10205**
Madison Journal (Tallulah, LA) **10155**
Madison News, The (Madison, KS) **10144**
Madison Park Times (Seattle, WA) **10293**
Madison Press, The (London, OH) **10025**
† Madison Tribune (Ontario, OH)
Madison Western Guard, The
   (Madison, MN) **10180**
Madras Pioneer, The (Madras, OR) **10249**

Magee Courier (Magee, MS)   **10186**
Magna Times (Magna, UT)   **10282**
Magnolia Gazette, The (Magnolia, MS)   **10186**
Mahnomen Pioneer, The
   (Mahnomen, MN)   **10180**
Mahopac Press (Mahopac, NY)   **10217**
Mail-Journal, The (Milford, IN)   **10134**
Mail Tribune (Medford, OR)   **10031**
Maine Times (Portland, ME)   **10157**
Mainland Journal (Hammonton, NJ)   **10203**
† Main Line Chronicle (West Chester, PA)
Mainline Life (Ardmore, PA)   **10251**
Main Line Times (Ardmore, PA)   **10251**
Main Street Trilogy (Townsend, MA)   **10166**
Majic Valley Shopper's News
   (Camden, TN)   **10266**
† Malden Press-Merit (Malden, MO)
Malheur Enterprise (Vale, OR)   **10251**
Malibu Surfside News (Malibu, CA)   **10077**
Malibu Times (Malibu, CA)   **10077**
Malone Telegram (Malone, NY)   **10015**
Malta Messenger (Ballston Spa, NY)   **10209**
Malvern Community News
   (Minerva, OH)   **10241**
Malvern Daily Record (Malvern, AR)   **9960**
Malverne Times (Mineola, NY)   **10219**
Malvern Leader, The (Malvern, IA)   **10140**
† Mammoth Lakes Review/Mono Herald
   (Mammoth Lakes, CA)
Mammoth Times (Mammoth Lakes, CA)   **10077**
Mamou Acadian Press (Mamou, LA)   **10154**
Manchester Enterprise
   (Manchester, KY)   **10149**
Manchester Journal (Manchester
   Center, VT)   **10284**
Manchester Press (Manchester, IA)   **10140**
Manchester Signal (Manchester, OH)   **10241**
Manchester Star-Mercury
   (Manchester, GA)   **10104**
Manchester Times (Manchester, TN)   **10268**
Mancos Times-Tribune (Mancos, CO)   **10088**
Mandan News (Mandan, ND)   **10233**
Manhasset Press (Mineola, NY)   **10219**
Manhattan Mercury (Manhattan, KS)   **9991**
Manistee News-Advocate (Manistee, MI)   **10000**
Manistee Observer (Manistee, MI)   **10172**
Manistique Pioneer-Tribune
   (Manistique, MI)   **10172**
Manitou Springs Pikes Peak Journal (Manitou
   Springs, CO)   **10088**
Manitowoc Herald-Times Reporter
   (Manitowoc, WI)   **10054**
Mansfield Enterprise (Mansfield, LA)   **10154**
Mansfield News (Mansfield, MA)   **10162**
Mansfield News-Mirror (Mansfield, TX)   **10278**
Manteca Bulletin (Manteca, CA)   **9963**

Manville News (Somerville, NJ)   **10207**
Maple Heights Press (Bedford, OH)   **10234**
Maple Shade Progress (Maple
   Shade, NJ)   **10204**
Maple Valley News (Hastings, MI)   **10170**
Maplewood Review (St. Paul, MN)   **10183**
Maquoketa Sentinel-Press
   (Maquoketa, IA)   **10140**
† Marathon Independent Newspaper
   (Marathon, NY)
Marble Falls Highlander (Marble
   Falls, TX)   **10278**
Marblehead Reporter (Marblehead, MA)   **10162**
Marceline Press (Marceline, MO)   **10191**
Marcellus Observer (Skaneateles, NY)   **10223**
Marco Island Eagle, The (Marco
   Island, FL)   **10096**
Marcus Hook Press (Drexel Hill, PA)   **10252**
Marianas Review (Saipan, MP)   **10233**
Marianas Variety News & Views
   (Saipan, MP)   **10022**
Marianna Courier Index (Marianna, AR)   **10066**
Maries County Gazette (Vienna, MO)   **10194**
Marietta Daily Journal (Marietta, GA)   **9975**
Marietta Times (Marietta, OH)   **10025**
Marina & Independent Voice
   (Marshfield, MA)   **10163**
Marina News (Long Beach, CA)   **10075**
† Marin County Daily Recording (San
   Rafael, CA)
Marin Independent Journal (Novato, CA)   **9963**
Marin Scope (Sausalito, CA)   **10083**
Marion Advertiser (Marion, WI)   **10302**
Marion Chronicle-Tribune (Marion, IN)   **9984**
Marion County Record (Marion, KS)   **10144**
Marion Daily Republican (Marion, IL)   **9980**
Marion Star (Marion, OH)   **10025**
Marion Star & Mullins Enterprise
   (Marion, SC)   **10263**
Marion Times-Standard (Marion, AL)   **10060**
Mariposa Gazette (Mariposa, CA)   **10077**
† Market Place (Vandergrift, PA)
Marketplace, The (Marianna, FL)   **10096**
Market Shopper, The (Delano, CA)   **10071**
Marlboro Herald-Advocate
   (Bennettsville, SC)   **10261**
Marlboro Shopper (Bennettsville, SC)   **10261**
Marquette County Tribune
   (Montello, WI)   **10303**
Marquette Mining Journal
   (Marquette, MI)   **10001**
Marshall Chronicle (Marshall, MI)   **10001**
† Marshall County Life (Culver, IN)
Marshall Democrat-News
   (Marshall, MO)   **10007**
Marshall Gazette (Lewisburg, TN)   **10268**

Marshall Independent (Marshall, MN) **10003**
Marshall Mountain Wave (Marshall, AR) **10066**
Marshall News Messenger
  (Marshall, TX) **10045**
Marshalltown Times-Republican
  (Marshalltown, IA) **9988**
Marshfield Mail (Marshfield, MO) **10191**
Marshfield Mariner (Marshfield, MA) **10163**
Marshfield News Herald
  (Marshfield, WI) **10054**
Marshfield Reporter (Plymouth, MA) **10165**
Marthasville Record, The
  (Marthasville, MO) **10191**
† Mart Herald (Mart, TX)
† Martin County News (Stuart, FL)
Martinez News Gazette (Martinez, CA) **10077**
Martinsville Bulletin (Martinsville, VA) **10049**
Martinsville Daily Reporter
  (Martinsville, IN) **9984**
Maryland Gazette (Glen Burnie, MD) **10159**
Maryland Independent (Waldorf, MD) **10160**
Maryland Times-Press (Ocean
  City, MD) **10159**
Marysville Advocate (Marysville, KS) **10144**
Marysville Journal-Tribune
  (Marysville, OH) **10025**
Maryville Daily Forum (Maryville, MO) **10007**
Mascoutah Herald (Mascoutah, IL) **10122**
Mashpee Messenger (Orleans, MA) **10164**
Mason County News (Mason, TX) **10278**
Mason Valley News (Yerington, NV) **10199**
Massapequan Observer (Mineola, NY) **10219**
Massapequa Post (Massapequa
  Park, NY) **10218**
Mathis News (Mathis, TX) **10278**
† Matthews News (Matthews, NC)
Mattoon Journal Gazette (Mattoon, IL) **9980**
Maui News (Wailuku, HI) **9976**
† Maumee Valley Herald (Toledo, OH)
Mayfield Messenger (Mayfield, KY) **9993**
Maynard Beacon (Concord, MA) **10161**
Mayville Monitor (Mayville, MI) **10172**
Mayville News (Mayville, WI) **10302**
Mayville Sentinel/Chautauqua News
  (Westfield, NY) **10225**
Maywood Herald (Oak Park, IL) **10125**
McAlester News-Capital
  (McAlester, OK) **10029**
McAllen Monitor (McAllen, TX) **10045**
McComb Enterprise-Journal
  (McComb, MS) **10004**
McConnellsburg Fulton County News
  (McConnellsburg, PA) **10254**
McCook Daily Gazette (McCook, NE) **10009**
McCreary County Record (Whitley
  City, KY) **10152**

McCurtain Daily Gazette (Idabel, OK) **10029**
McDonough-Democrat (Bushnell, IL) **10112**
McDowell News, The (Marion, NC) **10020**
McDuffie Progress, The (Thomson, GA) **10106**
McFarland Community Life
  (Monona, WI) **10303**
McFarland Leader (Monona, WI) **10303**
McIntosh Times (McIntosh, MN) **10180**
McKeesport Daily News
  (McKeesport, PA) **10035**
McKenzie Banner (McKenzie, TN) **10268**
McKinney Courier Gazette
  (McKinney, TX) **10045**
McLean County Independent
  (Garrison, ND) **10232**
McLean County Journal (Turtle
  Lake, ND) **10233**
McLean Providence Journal
  (Reston, VA) **10288**
McLeansboro Times-Leader
  (McLeansboro, IL) **10123**
McPherson Sentinel (McPherson, KS) **9991**
Meade County Messenger
  (Brandenburg, KY) **10146**
Meade County Times-Tribune
  (Sturgis, SD) **10265**
Meadowbrook Times (Lawrence, NY) **10216**
Meadville Tribune, The (Meadville, PA) **10035**
Mebane Enterprise (Mebane, NC) **10229**
Mecklenburg Gazette (Davidson, NC) **10227**
Mecklenburg Sun (Clarksville, VA) **10285**
Medfield Suburban Press
  (Needham, MA) **10164**
Medina County Gazette (Medina, OH) **10025**
▼Medina Sun, The (Cleveland, OH) **10236**
Meeker Herald, The (Meeker, CO) **10088**
Melrose Beacon (Melrose, MN) **10180**
Melrose Chronicle (Melrose, WI) **10302**
Melrose Free Press (Melrose, MA) **10163**
Melrose Park Herald (Oak Park, IL) **10125**
Melrose Park Star-Sentinel (Melrose
  Park, IL) **10123**
† Melrose Shoppers News (Stoneham, MA)
Menard County Review (Greenview, IL) **10119**
Menard News & Messenger, The
  (Menard, TX) **10279**
Mena Star (Mena, AR) **10067**
Mendocino Beacon, The
  (Mendocino, CA) **10077**
Mendota Reporter (Mendota, IL) **10123**
Menifee Valley News (Sun City, CA) **10084**
Menomonee Falls News
  (Wauwatosa, WI) **10307**
Mequon-Thiensville Courant
  (Wauwatosa, WI) **10307**

Merced County Times, The
  (Winton, CA) **10085**
Merced Sun-Star (Merced, CA) **9963**
Mercer County Chronicle
  (Coldwater, OH) **10237**
Mercer Island Reporter (Mercer
  Island, WA) **10292**
Mercury, The (Pottstown, PA) **10035**
Meridian Star (Meridian, MS) **10004**
Meriwether Free Press (Greenville, GA) **10103**
Meriwether Vindicator
  (Manchester, GA) **10104**
Merrick Beacon (Hicksville, NY) **10216**
Merrick Life (Merrick, NY) **10218**
Merrillville Herald (Merrillville, IN) **10133**
Merrimac Valley Sunday
  (Amesbury, MA) **10160**
Mesabi Daily News (Virginia, MN) **10003**
Mesa Tribune (Mesa, AZ) **9958**
Mesa Tribune Wave (Los Angeles, CA) **10076**
Mesquite News (Mesquite, TX) **10279**
Message for the Week (Chester, VT) **10283**
Messenger-Press (Hightstown, NJ) **10203**
Messenger Index (Emmett, ID) **10107**
Messenger, The (Troy, AL) **9956**
Messenger, The (Attica, IN) **10129**
Messenger, The (Madisonville, KY) **9992**
Messenger, The (Madison, NC) **10229**
Messenger, The (Garfield, NJ) **10202**
Messenger, The (Clemson, SC) **10261**
Messenger, The (Madison, TN) **10268**
Metro (San Jose, CA) **10081**
Metrocrest News (Carrollton, TX) **10272**
Metropolis Planet (Metropolis, IL) **10123**
Metropolitan News (Brooklyn, NY) **10211**
Metropolitan, The (Los Angeles, CA) **9963**
Metro Press (Millbury, OH) **10241**
Metro Weekenders, The (Norfolk, VA) **10288**
Mexia Daily News (Mexia, TX) **10045**
Mexican-American Sun (City of
  Commerce, CA) **10071**
Mexico Ledger (Mexico, MO) **10007**
Miami Beach News (South Miami, FL) **10099**
Miami Beach Sun Post (Miami, FL) **10097**
Miami Chief, The (Miami, TX) **10279**
Miami County Republic (Paola, KS) **10145**
Miami Herald (Miami, FL) **9972**
Miami Laker (Miami Lakes, FL) **10097**
Miami News-Record (Miami, OK) **10029**
Miamisburg News (Miamisburg, OH) **10241**
Miami Shores News (Miami, FL) **10097**
Miami Today (Miami, FL) **10097**
Michigan Chronicle (Detroit, MI) **10169**
Michigan City News-Dispatch (Michigan
  City, IN) **9984**
Mid-Cities News (Arlington, TX) **10271**

Mid-County Journal (St. Louis, MO) **10193**
† Mid-County Times (Pardeeville, WI)
Mid-Island Times (Hicksville, NY) **10216**
Mid-South Horse Review
  (Somerville, TN) **10269**
Midcounty Chronicle (Nederland, TX) **10279**
Middleboro Gazette (Middleboro, MA) **10163**
Middlesboro Daily News
  (Middlesboro, KY) **9993**
Middlesex News (Framingham, MA) **9997**
Middleton Gazette (Middleton, ID) **10108**
Middleton Times-Tribune
  (Middleton, WI) **10302**
Middletown Courier (Middletown, NJ) **10204**
Middletown Journal (Middletown, OH) **10025**
Middletown News, The (Middletown, IN) **10133**
Middletown Press (Middletown, CT) **9970**
Middletown Valley Citizen
  (Brunswick, MD) **10158**
Mid Hudson Times (Walden, NY) **10224**
Midland Daily News (Midland, MI) **10001**
Midland Reporter-Telegram
  (Midland, TX) **10045**
Midlothian-Bremen Messenger
  (Midlothian, IL) **10123**
Midlothian Mirror (Midlothian, TX) **10279**
Midlothian Today (DeSoto, TX) **10274**
† MidMon Observer (Washington, PA)
Mid Valley News (El Monte, CA) **10072**
Mid Valley Town Crier (Weslaco, TX) **10281**
MidWeek (Kaneohe, HI) **10106**
Midweek Eagle (West Fargo, ND) **10233**
Midweek Plus (West Fargo, ND) **10233**
MidWeek, The (DeKalb, IL) **10114**
Mifflinburg Telegraph, The
  (Mifflinburg, PA) **10255**
Milan Area Leader (Milan, MI) **10172**
Milan Standard, The (Milan, MO) **10191**
Miles City Star (Miles City, MT) **10009**
Milford Advertiser (Loveland, OH) **10241**
Milford Cabinet & Wilton Journal
  (Milford, NH) **10200**
† Milford Citizen (Milford, CT)
Milford Daily News (Milford, MA) **9998**
Milford Times (Milford, MI) **10173**
Milk Creek Sun (Erie, PA) **10252**
Millard County Gazette (Fillmore, UT) **10282**
Millbrae & San Bruno Sun
  (Burlingame, CA) **10070**
Millbrae Recorder-Progress (San
  Mateo, CA) **10082**
Millbrook Round Table (Millbrook, NY) **10218**
Millburn & Short Hills Item
  (Millburn, NJ) **10204**
Millburn-Short Hills Independent Press (New
  Providence, NJ) **10205**

Millbury/Sutton Chronicle
   (Millbury, MA) **10163**
Mille Lacs County Times (Milaca, MN) **10180**
Miller County Liberal (Colquitt, GA) **10102**
Millerton News, The (Millerton, NY) **10218**
Millington Star, The (Millington, TN) **10268**
Millstadt Enterprise (Columbia, IL) **10114**
Mill Valley Herald (Sausalito, CA) **10083**
Milpitas Post (Milpitas, CA) **10078**
Milton Courier (Milton, WI) **10302**
Milton Daily Standard (Milton, PA) **10035**
Milton Record-Transcript (Milton
   Village, MA) **10163**
Miltonvale Record (Miltonvale, KS) **10144**
Milville News (Bridgeton, NJ) **10011**
Milwaukee Journal-Sentinel
   (Milwaukee, WI) **10054**
Milwaukee Star (Milwaukee, WI) **10302**
Minden Courier (Minden, NE) **10197**
Minden Press-Herald (Minden, LA) **9994**
Mineola American (Mineola, NY) **10219**
Mineral County Independent-News
   (Hawthorne, NV) **10199**
Mineral County Miner (Monte
   Vista, CO) **10088**
Mineral Daily Tribune (Keyser, WV) **10052**
Mineral Wells Index (Mineral Wells, TX) **10045**
Minerva Leader (Minerva, OH) **10241**
Minidoka County News (Rupert, ID) **10109**
Minifee County News (Morehead, KY) **10150**
Minnetonka Sun-Sailor
   (Minnetonka, MN) **10180**
Minonk News Dispatch (Minonk, IL) **10124**
Minot Daily News (Minot, ND) **10022**
Mira Mesa/Scripps Ranch Sentinel (San
   Diego, CA) **10081**
Mirror-Exchange (Milan, TN) **10268**
† Mirror-Recorder (Stamford, NY)
Mishawaka Enterprise (Mishawaka, IN) **10134**
Mississippi Press (Pascagoula, MS) **10005**
Missoulian, The (Missoula, MT) **10009**
Missouri Press News (Columbia, MO) **10189**
Missouri Valley Times-News (Missouri
   Valley, IA) **10140**
Mitchell County Press-News (Osage, IA) **10140**
Mitchell News Journal (Spruce
   Pine, NC) **10230**
Moberly Monitor Index (Moberly, MO) **10007**
Mobile Beacon (Mobile, AL) **10060**
Mobile Register, The (Mobile, AL) **9956**
Modern News (Harrisburg, AR) **10066**
Modesto Bee, The (Modesto, CA) **9963**
Modoc County Record (Alturas, CA) **10068**
Mohave Valley Daily News (Bullhead
   City, AZ) **9957**

Mojave Desert News, The (California
   City, CA) **10070**
Monadnock Ledger (Peterborough, NH) **10200**
Monahans News (Monahans, TX) **10279**
Mondovi Herald News (Mondovi, WI) **10303**
Monett Times (Monett, MO) **10007**
Moneysaver, The (Ballston Spa, NY) **10209**
Monitor, The (Los Alamos, NM) **10013**
Monitor, The (Mabank, TX) **10278**
Monroe County Appeal (Paris, MO) **10192**
Monroe County Beacon
   (Woodsfield, OH) **10244**
Monroe County Clarion (Columbia, IL) **10114**
Monroe County Democrat (Sparta, WI) **10305**
Monroe County News (Albia, IA) **10136**
† Monroe County Sentinel (Woodsfield, OH)
Monroe Courier (Monroe, CT) **10091**
Monroe Evening News (Monroe, MI) **10001**
Monroe Journal (Monroeville, AL) **10060**
Monroe Times, The (Monroe, WI) **10054**
Monroe Watchman (Union, WV) **10296**
Montague County Shopper, The
   (Bowie, TX) **10271**
Montana Standard (Butte, MT) **10008**
Montclair Times, The (Montclair, NJ) **10204**
Montclarion (Oakland, CA) **10078**
Montebello News (Los Angeles, CA) **10076**
† Montecito Life (Goleta, CA)
Monterey County Herald, The
   (Monterey, CA) **9963**
Monterey Park Progress (Los
   Angeles, CA) **10076**
Montevideo American-News
   (Montevideo, MN) **10180**
Monte Vista Journal (Monte Vista, CO) **10088**
Montezuma Republican, The
   (Montezuma, IA) **10140**
Montgomery Advertiser
   (Montgomery, AL) **9956**
Montgomery County News, The
   (Hillsboro, IL) **10120**
Montgomery County Progress
   (Horsham, PA) **10253**
Montgomery County Sentinel
   (Gaithersburg, MD) **10158**
Montgomery Herald (Troy, NC) **10231**
Montgomery Herald (Montgomery, WV) **10295**
Montgomery Independent
   (Montgomery, AL) **10060**
Montgomery Journal, The (Rockville, MD) **9996**
Montgomery Post, The
   (Norristown, PA) **10256**
Montgomery Standard (Montgomery
   City, MO) **10191**
Montgomeryville Spirit (Fort
   Washington, PA) **10253**

Monticello Express (Monticello, IA) **10140**
Monticello News (Monticello, FL) **10097**
Montrose Daily Press (Montrose, CO) **9969**
Montrose Herald (Canistota, SD) **10264**
▼Montrose Morning Sun (Montrose, CO) **9969**
Moody County Enterprise
  (Flandreau, SD) **10265**
Moody Courier, The (Moody, TX) **10279**
Moorcroft Leader (Moorcroft, WY) **10309**
Moore American (Moore, OK) **10246**
Moore County News-Press (Dumas, TX) **10274**
Moorefield Examiner (Moorefield, WV) **10295**
Mooresville Times, The
  (Mooresville, IN) **10134**
Mooresville Tribune (Mooresville, NC) **10229**
Moorpark Star (Moorpark, CA) **9963**
Moose Lake Star-Gazette (Moose
  Lake, MN) **10181**
Moravia Republican Register
  (Moravia, NY) **10219**
Morehead News (Morehead, KY) **10150**
Morenci Observer (Morenci, MI) **10173**
Morgan County Herald
  (McConnelsville, OH) **10241**
Morgan County News (Wartburg, TN) **10270**
Morgan Hill Times (Morgan Hill, CA) **10078**
Morgan Messenger, The (Berkeley
  Springs, WV) **10294**
Morning Call, The (Allentown, PA) **10032**
Morning Intelligencer, The
  (Wheeling, WV) **10053**
Morning Journal (Lisbon, OH) **10025**
Morning Journal (Lorain, OH) **10025**
Morning News of Northwest Arkansas
  (Springdale, AR) **9960**
Morning Sun (Mt. Pleasant, MI) **10001**
Morongo Basin (Palm Desert, CA) **10079**
Morongo Basin Advertiser (Yucca
  Valley, CA) **10085**
Morris Daily Herald (Morris, IL) **9980**
Morris News Bee (Madison, NJ) **10204**
Morrisons Cove Herald
  (Martinsburg, PA) **10254**
Morris Sun (Morris, MN) **10181**
Morristown News, The (West
  Caldwell, NJ) **10207**
Morris Tribune (Morris, MN) **10181**
Morrow County Advertiser (Mt.
  Gilead, OH) **10241**
Morrow County Independent
  (Cardington, OH) **10235**
Morrow County Sentinel (Mt.
  Gilead, OH) **10241**
Morton Grove-Niles Life
  (Lincolnwood, IL) **10122**
Morton Grove Champion (Evanston, IL) **10117**

Moscow-Pullman Daily News
  (Moscow, ID) **9977**
Mosinee Times, The (Mosinee, WI) **10303**
Motley County Tribune (Matador, TX) **10278**
Moulton Advertiser (Moulton, AL) **10060**
Moultrie News, The (Mt. Pleasant SC) **10263**
Mound City News (Mound City, MO) **10191**
Mounds View-New Brighton-St. Anthony Focus
  (Roseville, MN) **10182**
Moundsville Daily Echo
  (Moundsville, WV) **10053**
Moundville Times (Moundville, AL) **10060**
Mountain Advisor (Richlands, VA) **10289**
Mountain Citizen, The (Inez, KY) **10148**
Mountain Democrat (Placerville, CA) **9964**
Mountain Eagle (Tannersville, NY) **10224**
Mountain Eagle, The (Whitesburg KY) **10152**
Mountain Echo (Yellville, AR) **10068**
Mountain Echo (Ironton, MO) **10190**
Mountaineer-Herald, The
  (Ebensburg, PA) **10252**
Mountaineer, The (Big Sandy, MT) **10195**
† Mountaineer, The (Waynesville, NC)
Mountain Grove News-Journal (Mountain
  Grove, MO) **10191**
Mountain Home News (Mountain
  Home, ID) **10108**
Mountain Life (Mariposa, CA) **10077**
Mountain Mail (Salida, CO) **9969**
Mountain Messenger (Downieville CA) **10072**
Mountain Messenger (Lewisburg, WV) **10295**
Mountain News, The (Lake
  Arrowhead, CA) **10074**
Mountain Press (Prather, CA) **10080**
Mountain Press, The (Sevierville, TN) **10041**
Mountainside Echo (Union, NJ) **10207**
Mountain Statesman (Grafton, WV) **10294**
Mountain Sun, The (Kerrville, TX) **10277**
Mountain Times (Killington, VT) **10283**
Mountaintop Eagle (Mountain Top, PA) **10255**
† Mountain Visitor (Sevierville, TN)
Mountain Xpress (Asheville, NC) **10226**
Mount Airy News (Mt. Airy, NC) **10020**
Mount Ayr Record-News (Mt. Ayr IA) **10140**
Mount Carmel Daily Republican-Register (Mt.
  Carmel, IL) **9980**
Mount Greenwood Express
  (Midlothian, IL) **10123**
Mount Holly News (Belmont, NC) **10226**
Mount Joy Merchandiser (Mt. Joy, PA) **10256**
Mount Olive Tribune (Mt. Olive, NC) **10229**
Mount Pleasant Daily Tribune (Mt.
  Pleasant, TX) **10045**
Mount Pleasant Journal (Mt.
  Pleasant, PA) **10256**
Mount Pleasant News (Mt. Pleasant, IA) **9988**

Mount Prospect Journal (Des Plaines, IL) **10115**
Mount Prospect Times (Glenview, IL) **10118**
Mount Shasta Herald (Mt. Shasta, CA) **10078**
Mount Vernon Democrat (Mt. Vernon, IN) **10134**
Mount Vernon Independent (Yonkers, NY) **10226**
Mount Vernon News (Mt. Vernon, OH) **10025**
Mt. Airy Times (Philadelphia, PA) **10257**
Mt. Laurel Progress Press (Maple Shade, NJ) **10204**
Mt. Olive Chronicle (Budd Lake, NJ) **10201**
Mt. Olive Herald, The (Mt. Olive, IL) **10124**
Mt. Vernon Daily Argus (Yonkers, NY) **10018**
Mt. Vernon Register News (Mt. Vernon, IL) **9980**
† Mt. Washington Press (Cincinnati, OH)
Mt. Washington Star Review (Los Angeles, CA) **10076**
Mt. Washington Valley Mountain Ear (Conway, NH) **10199**
Mukwonago Chief (Mukwonago, WI) **10303**
Mulberry Press (Mulberry, FL) **10097**
Mullens Advocate (Mullen, WV) **10295**
Munday Courier, The (Munday, TX) **10279**
Mundelein News (Grayslake, IL) **10119**
Mundelein Review (Bannockburn, IL) **10110**
Munising News (Munising, MI) **10173**
Munster Guide (Highland, IN) **10132**
Murfreesboro Daily News Journal (Murfreesboro, TN) **10041**
Murfreesboro Diamond (Murfreesboro, AR) **10067**
Murray County Wheel Herald (Slayton, MN) **10183**
† Murray Eagle (Salt Lake City, UT)
Murray Ledger & Times (Murray, KY) **9993**
Murrysville Area Star (Monroeville, PA) **10255**
Muscatine Journal (Muscatine, IA) **9988**
Muskegon Chronicle, The (Muskegon, MI) **10001**
Muskego Sun (Wauwatosa, WI) **10307**
Muskogee Daily Phoenix & Times-Democrat (Muskogee, OK) **10029**

N

N'West Iowa Review (Sheldon, IA) **10141**
Nantucket Beacon (Nantucket, MA) **10164**
Nanty Glo Journal, The (Nanty Glo, PA) **10256**
Napa County Record (Napa, CA) **10078**
Napa Valley Register (Napa, CA) **9963**
Naperville Metropolitan (Lemont, IL) **10121**
Naperville Sun (Naperville, IL) **10124**
Naples Daily News (Naples, FL) **9973**
Naples Record, The (Naples, NY) **10219**
Narragansett Times (Wakefield, RI) **10261**
Nashua Reporter (Nashua, IA) **10140**
Nashville Banner (Nashville, TN) **10041**
Nashville Graphic (Nashville, NC) **10229**
Nashville News (Nashville, AR) **10067**
Nashville News, The (Nashville, IL) **10124**
Nassau County Record (Callahan, FL) **10094**
Nassau Herald (Lawrence, NY) **10217**
Natchez Democrat (Natchez, MS) **10005**
Natchitoches Times (Natchitoches, LA) **9994**
Natick Bulletin (Needham, MA) **10164**
Nation's Center News (Buffalo, SD) **10264**
National Union (Eastern Caroline Islands, FM) **10093**
Naugatuck Daily News (Naugatuck, CT) **9970**
Navasota Examiner Review (Navasota, TX) **10279**
† Near South Herald (Chicago, IL)
Nebraska City News-Press (Nebraska City, NE) **10009**
Nebraska Signal (Geneva, NE) **10197**
Needles Desert Star (Needles, CA) **10078**
Nelson County Times (Lovingston, VA) **10287**
Nemaha County Herald (Auburn, NE) **10196**
Neodesha Derrick (Neodesha, KS) **10145**
Neosho Daily News (Neosho, MO) **10007**
Neshoba Democrat, The (Philadelphia, MS) **10187**
Ness County News, The (Ness City, KS) **10145**
Netcong News-Leader (Netcong, NJ) **10204**
Nevada Appeal (Carson City, NV) **10010**
Nevada County Picayune (Prescott, AR) **10067**
Nevada Journal (Nevada, IA) **10140**
† New Alaskan (Ketchikan, AK)
New Albany Gazette (New Albany, MS) **10186**
Newark/Licking Advertiser (Newark, OH) **10242**
Newark Post (Newark, DE) **10092**
Newberg Graphic (Newberg, OR) **10249**
New Berlin Citizen (Wauwatosa, WI) **10307**
Newberry Observer, The (Newberry, SC) **10263**
New Braunfels Herald & Zeitung (New Braunfels, TX) **10045**
New Brighton-Mounds View Bulletin (North St. Paul, MN) **10181**
New Buffalo Times (New Buffalo, MI) **10173**
Newburgh-Chandler Register (Newburgh, IN) **10134**
† Newburgh Evening News (Newburgh, NY)
New Canaan Advertiser (New Canaan, CT) **10091**
New Carlisle Sun (New Carlisle, OH) **10242**
New Castle Courier-Times (New Castle, IN) **9985**

New Castle News (New Castle, PA) **10035**
Newcastle Pacer, The (Newcastle, OK) **10246**
New Castle Record (New Castle, VA) **10288**
New Center News (Detroit, MI) **10169**
New City (Chicago, IL) **10113**
Newcomerstown News
  (Newcomerstown, OH) **10242**
New Era, The (Sweet Home, OR) **10250**
Newfield News (Trumansburg, NY) **10224**
New Hampshire Week in Review
  (Hillsborough, NH) **10199**
New Hampton Economist (New
  Hampton, IA) **10140**
New Hampton Tribune (New
  Hampton, IA) **10140**
New Haven Advocate (New Haven, CT) **10091**
New Haven Register (New Haven, CT) **9970**
New Holstein Reporter (New
  Holstein, WI) **10303**
New Hope-Golden Valley Sun Post
  (Minneapolis, MN) **10180**
New Hope Gazette (New Hope, PA) **10256**
Newington Town Crier (Bristol, CT) **10090**
New Jersey Herald (Newton, NJ) **10012**
New Leader (Spencer, MA) **10165**
Newman News, The (Newman, CA) **10078**
New Milford Times (New Milford, CT) **10091**
Newnan Times-Herald (Newnan, GA) **10105**
Newport Daily Express (Newport, VT) **10048**
Newport Daily Independent
  (Newport, AR) **9960**
Newport Daily News, The (Newport, RI) **10037**
Newport Mercury (Newport, RI) **10260**
Newport Miner (Newport, WA) **10292**
Newport News Daily Press (Newport
  News, VA) **10049**
Newport This Week (Newport, RI) **10260**
New Prague Times (New Prague, MN) **10181**
New Prairie Town Crier (New
  Carlisle, IN) **10134**
New Richmond News (New
  Richmond, WI) **10303**
New River Record (Middle River, MN) **10180**
News & Advance (Lynchburg, VA) **10049**
News & Observer (Raleigh, NC) **10020**
News & Press, The (Darlington, SC) **10262**
News & Record, The (Greensboro, NC) **10019**
News & Sentinel, The (Colebrook, NH) **10199**
News-Banner, The (Covington, LA) **10153**
News-Courier (Athens, AL) **9955**
News-Democrat, The (Carrollton, KY) **10147**
News-Enterprise (Elizabethtown, KY) **9992**
News-Examiner (Montpelier, ID) **10108**
News-Examiner (Gallatin, TN) **10267**
News-Gazette (Lexington, VA) **10287**
News-Gazette, The (Winchester, IN) **9986**

News-Herald (Port Clinton, OH) **10026**
News-Herald (Willoughby, OH) **10027**
News-Herald (Oil City, PA) **10035**
News-Herald, The (Southgate, MI) **10175**
News-Herald, The (Ahoskie, NC) **10226**
News-Journal (North Manchester, IN) **10134**
News-Journal Shopper
  (Campbellsville, KY) **10147**
News-Ledger, The (West
  Sacramento, CA) **10085**
† News-Messenger, The (Rockingham, NC)
News-Pilot, The (San Pedro, CA) **9965**
News-Press, The (Fort Myers, FL) **9972**
News-Progress (Sullivan, IL) **10128**
News-Progress, The (Chase City, VA) **10285**
News-Record (Gillette, WY) **10055**
News-Record of Maplewood & South Orange
  (Maplewood, NJ) **10204**
News-Record, The (Cerro Gordo, IL) **10112**
News-Register (McMinnville, OR) **10249**
News-Review (Roseburg, OR) **10032**
News-Review, The (Mattituck, NY) **10218**
News-Star, The (Monroe, LA) **9994**
News-Sun (Fairmount, IN) **10131**
News-Sun, The (Waukegan, IL) **9982**
News-Sun, The (New Bloomfield, PA) **10256**
News-Times (Danbury, CT) **9970**
News-Times (Newport, OR) **10249**
News-Tribune (La Salle, IL) **9980**
News-Tribune (Framingham, MA) **9997**
News-X Press (Butler, MO) **10188**
News Beacon (Fair Lawn, NJ) **10202**
News Bulletin, The (Old Fort, NC) **10229**
News Buyer's Catalogue
  (Wytheville, VA) **10290**
News Buyers Catalog (Marion, VA) **10287**
News Chief (Winter Haven, FL) **9974**
Newsday (Melville, NY) **10016**
News Democrat & Leader
  (Russellville, KY) **10151**
News Democrat Journal (Festus, MO) **10189**
News Eagle (Hawley, PA) **10253**
† NewsEAST (Columbus, OH)
News Enterprise, The (Los
  Alamitos, CA) **10075**
News Examiner, The (Lutcher, LA) **10153**
News Gazette, The (Love Park, IL) **10122**
News Gleaner Publications
  (Philadelphia, PA) **10257**
News Guard, The (Lincoln City, OR) **10249**
New Sharon Star (New Sharon, IA) **10140**
News Herald (Lenoir City, TN) **10268**
† News Herald, The (Mobile, AL)
News Herald, The (Panama City, FL) **9973**
News Herald, The (Morganton, NC) **10020**
News Journal (Mansfield, OH) **10025**

News Journal, The (New Castle, DE) **9971**
News Leader (Fernandina, FL) **10095**
News Leader (Stow, OH) **10243**
News Leader (Richwood, WV) **10296**
News Leader, The (Royston, GA) **10105**
News Leader, The (Landrum, SC) **10263**
News Leader, The (Parsons, TN) **10269**
News Letter Journal (Newcastle, WY) **10309**
NewsMarketer, The (Chicago, IL) **10113**
News Messenger, The
  (Christiansburg, VA) **10285**
New Smyrna Beach Observer (New
  Smyrna, FL) **9973**
News of Delaware County
  (Havertown, PA) **10253**
News of Orange County, The
  (Hillsborough, NC) **10228**
† News of Paterson (Passaic, NJ)
News of Southern Berks, The
  (Boyertown, PA) **10251**
News of the Highlands (Highland
  Falls, NY) **10216**
† News Outlook (Aberdeen, NC)
News Pointer (Sausalito, CA) **10083**
News Report (Blackwood, NJ) **10201**
News Review (Ridgecrest, CA) **10080**
News Star (Lincolnwood, IL) **10122**
News Sun, The (Sebring, FL) **10099**
News Sun, The (Cleveland, OH) **10236**
News, The (Salem, AR) **10067**
News, The (Boca Raton, FL) **9971**
News, The (Clay City, IN) **10130**
News, The (Southbridge, MA) **9998**
News, The (Frederick, MD) **9996**
News, The (Belvidere, NJ) **10200**
News, The (Aliquippa, PA) **10251**
News, The (Kingstree, SC) **10262**
News Times (Amherst, OH) **10234**
News Times (Forest Grove, OR) **10248**
News Transcript (Morganville, NJ) **10204**
News Tribune, The (Tacoma, WA) **10051**
News Watchman, The (Waverly, OH) **10244**
Newsweekly (Sebewaing, MI) **10175**
News Weekly (Mt. Laurel, NJ) **10204**
New Times (Phoenix, AZ) **10064**
New Times (San Luis Obispo, CA) **10082**
New Times, The (Kansas City, MO) **10190**
Newton Daily News (Newton, IA) **9988**
Newton Graphic (Waltham, MA) **10166**
Newton Kansan (Newton, KS) **9991**
Newton Press-Mentor (Newton, IL) **10124**
Newton Record (Newton, MS) **10187**
Newtown Bee, The (Newtown, CT) **10091**
New Ulm Enterprise (New Ulm, TX) **10279**
New York Beacon (New York, NY) **10220**
† New York City Tribune (New York, NY)

New York Daily Challenge
  (Brooklyn, NY) **10014**
New York Daily News, The (New
  York, NY) **10016**
New York Metropolitan News
  (Brooklyn, NY) **10211**
† New York Newsday (New York, NY)
New York Observer (New York, NY) **10220**
New York Post (New York, NY) **10016**
New York Press (New York, NY) **10220**
New York Times, The (New York, NY) **10016**
Niagara/Wheatfield Tribune (Grand
  Island, NY) **10215**
Niagara Gazette (Niagara Falls, NY) **10016**
Niantic-Harristown County Line Observer
  (Illiopolis, IL) **10120**
† Niantic News (East Lyme, CT)
Nicholas Chronicle (Summersville, WV) **10296**
Niles Daily Star (Niles, MI) **10001**
Niles Herald Spectator (Park Ridge, IL) **10126**
Niles Journal (Des Plaines, IL) **10115**
Niles Life (Lincolnwood, IL) **10122**
Nishna Valley Tribune (Audubon, IA) **10137**
Nisqually Valley News (Yelm, WA) **10294**
Nokomis Free Press-Progress
  (Nokomis, IL) **10124**
Nome Nugget (Nome, AK) **10062**
Nora News Dispatch (Fisherspolis, IN) **10131**
▼Nordonia Hills Sun (Cleveland, OH) **10236**
Norfolk Daily News (Norfolk, NE) **10010**
Norman Transcript (Norman, OK) **10029**
Norridge-Harwood Heights News (Park
  Ridge, IL) **10126**
Norridge-Harwood Heights Times
  (Lincolnwood, IL) **10122**
North/South Beach Now (San
  Francisco, CA) **10081**
North Bartow News (Adairsville, GA) **10100**
North Bay Village News (South
  Miami, FL) **10099**
North Bergen/North Hudson Reporter
  (Hoboken, NJ) **10203**
Northbrook Star (Glenview, IL) **10118**
North Brunswick Post (Dayton, NJ) **10202**
North Castle News (Yonkers, NY) **10226**
North Center-Lincoln Belmont-Lake View Booster
  (Lincolnwood, IL) **10122**
North Central Outlook (Seattle, WA) **10293**
North Clermont Community Journal
  (Loveland, OH) **10241**
North Country Free Press
  (Granville, NY) **10215**
North Countryman, The
  (Elizabethtown, NY) **10213**
North Country Sun (Ironwood, MI) **10171**

North County Journal East (St. Louis, MO) **10193**

North County Journal West (St. Louis, MO) **10193**

North County News (Red Bud, IL) **10127**

North County News (Yorktown Heights, NY) **10226**

North County Shopping News (Atascadero, CA) **10069**

North County Times (Escondido, CA) **9962**

North East Breeze (North East, PA) **10256**

† Northeast Detroiter (Detroit, MI)

Northeast Georgian, The (Cornelia, GA) **10102**

Northeast Johnson County (Shawnee Mission, KS) **10146**

Northeast Mississippi Daily Journal (Tupelo, MS) **10005**

Northeast Reporter (Indianapolis, IN) **10132**

Northeast Reporter (Towson, MD) **10160**

Northeast Suburban Life Press (Cincinnati, OH) **10235**

Northeast Sun (City of Commerce, CA) **10071**

Northeast Times (Philadelphia, PA) **10257**

Northern Michigan News (Cadillac, MI) **10168**

Northern Ogle County Tempo (Byron, IL) **10112**

Northern Piedmont Express (Culpeper, VA) **10286**

Northern Star (Gaylord, MI) **10170**

Northern Star, The (Clinton, MN) **10178**

Northern Virginia Daily (Strasburg, VA) **10050**

Northern Virginia Sun, The (Fairfax, VA) **10286**

Northern Watch (Thief River Falls, MN) **10184**

Northern Wyoming Daily News (Worland, WY) **10056**

Northfield Advance (Jenison, MI) **10171**

Northfield News (Northfield, MN) **10181**

North Georgia News (Blairsville, GA) **10101**

Northglenn-Thornton Sentinel (Westminster, CO) **10089**

North Haven Wollington Post, The (Milford, CT) **10091**

North Hills News Record (Warrendale, PA) **10037**

North Jackson Progress (Stevenson, AL) **10061**

North Jefferson News (Gardendale, AL) **10059**

North Jersey Herald & News, The (Passaic, NJ) **10012**

North Jersey Prospector (Clifton, NJ) **10202**

North Kitsap Herald (Poulsbo, WA) **10292**

North Knox News (Bicknell, IN) **10130**

Northlake Star-Sentinel (Melrose Park, IL) **10123**

North Lake Tahoe Bonanza (Incline Village, NV) **10199**

Northland News (Columbus, OH) **10237**

North Loop News (Chicago, IL) **10113**

North Macomb Voice (New Baltimore, MI) **10173**

North Meridian Observer (Fishers, IN) **10131**

North Miami Beach News (South Miami, FL) **10099**

North Miami News (Miami, FL) **10097**

North Minneapolis Sun Post (Minneapolis, MN) **10180**

North Missourian (Gallatin, MO) **10190**

North Myrtle Beach Times (North Myrtle Beach, SC) **10263**

Northome Record & Mizpah Message (Northome, MN) **10181**

North Riverside Citizen (Oak Brook, IL) **10125**

North Scott Press, The (Eldridge, IA) **10138**

† North Scottsdale Independent (Scottsdale, AZ)

Northshore Citizen (Bothell, WA) **10290**

North Shore Heralds (Wauwatosa, WI) **10307**

North Shore Shopper (Pacific Palisades, CA) **10078**

North Shore Sunday (Danvers, MA) **10161**

Northside Journal (St. Louis, MO) **10194**

Northside Neighbor, The (Atlanta, GA) **10100**

North Side News (Jerome, ID) **10108**

Northside Sun, The (Jackson, MS) **10186**

North Side Topics (Fishers, IN) **10131**

North Snohomish Weekly (Arlington, WA) **10290**

North Star (Philadelphia, PA) **10257**

North Star Journal (Presque Isle, WI) **10304**

North Suburban Herald (Love Park, IL) **10122**

North Syracuse Star-News (Syracuse, NY) **10223**

North Tahoe/Truckee Week (Carnelian Bay, CA) **10070**

Northumberland Echo (Heathsville, VA) **10286**

North Utah County Shopper (American Fork, UT) **10282**

North Vernon Plain Dealer (North Vernon, IN) **10134**

North Vernon Sun (North Vernon, IN) **10134**

Northville Record (Northville, MI) **10173**

Northwest Alabamian (Haleyville, AL) **10059**

Northwest Blade, The (Eureka, SD) **10264**

Northwest Colorado Daily Press (Craig, CO) **9968**

Northwest Columbus News (Columbus, OH) **10237**

Northwest Current, The (Washington, DC) **10093**

Northwestern Illinois Dispatch
(Savanna, IL) **10127**
Northwestern Illinois Farmer (Lena, IL) **10121**
Northwest Florida Daily News (Fort Walton
Beach, FL) **9972**
Northwest Herald (Crystal Lake, IL) **9978**
Northwest Iowa Shopper (Spencer, IA) **10141**
Northwest Journal & Topics (Des
Plaines, IL) **10115**
Northwest Leader (Chicago, IL) **10113**
Northwest Press (Speedway, IN) **10135**
Northwest Press (Cincinnati, OH) **10235**
Northwest Side Press (Chicago, IL) **10113**
Northwest Signal (Napoleon, OH) **10026**
Northwest Star (Baltimore, MD) **10158**
Northwood Gleaner (Northwood, ND) **10233**
North Woods Call (Charlevoix, MI) **10168**
Norton Courier (Stoughton, MA) **10166**
Norton Daily Telegram (Norton, KS) **9991**
Norwalk Herald American (Los
Angeles, CA) **10076**
† Norwalk News (Westport, CT)
Norwalk Reflector (Norwalk, OH) **10026**
Norway Advertiser-Democrat
(Norway, ME) **10156**
Norway Current (Norway, MI) **10173**
Norwell Mariner (Marshfield, MA) **10163**
Norwich Bulletin (Norwich, CT) **9970**
Novato Advance (Novato, CA) **10078**
Novi News (Northville, MI) **10173**
Nowata Star (Nowata, OK) **10246**
Nueces County Record Star
(Robstown, TX) **10280**
Nutley Journal (Bloomfield, NJ) **10201**
Nutley Sun (Nutley, NJ) **10205**
NUVO Newsweekly (Indianapolis, IN) **10132**

O

O-W Enterprise (Withee, WI) **10308**
O'Fallon Journal (O'Fallon, MO) **10191**
O'Fallon Progress (O'Fallon, IL) **10124**
Oak Brook Doings (Hinsdale, IL) **10120**
Oak Brook Press (Elmhurst, IL) **10116**
Oak Brook Terrace Doings
(Hinsdale, IL) **10120**
Oak Cliff Tribune (Dallas, TX) **10273**
Oak Creek Pictorial (Wauwatosa, WI) **10307**
Oakdale-Lake Elmo Review (St.
Paul, MN) **10183**
Oakdale Clarion (Oakdale, MN) **10181**
Oakdale Journal (Oakdale, LA) **10154**
Oakdale Leader (Oakdale, CA) **10078**
Oakland Indpendent (Oakland, NE) **10197**
Oakland Press, The (Pontiac, MI) **10001**

Oak Lawn-Evergreen Park Reporter (Palos
Heights, IL) **10125**
Oak Lawn Independent (Midlothian, IL) **10123**
Oak Leaves, The (Oak Park, IL) **10125**
Oakley Graphic (Oakley, KS) **10145**
Oak Ridger, The (Oak Ridge, TN) **10041**
Oakville-Mehville Journal (St.
Louis, MO) **10194**
Oberlin Herald, The (Oberlin, KS) **10145**
Observer-Dispatch (Utica, NY) **10017**
† Observer-Patriot (Putnam, CT)
Observer-Reporter (Waynesburg, PA) **10037**
Observer-Reporter, Washington County Edition
(Washington, PA) **10037**
Observer-Tribune (Chester, NJ) **10202**
Observer News (Newton, NC) **10020**
Observer, The (New Smyrna, FL) **9973**
Observer, The (Royal Palm Beach, FL) **10098**
Observer, The (Moultrie, GA) **9975**
Observer, The (Belgrade, MN) **10176**
† Observer, The (Blackwood, NJ)
Observer, The (Kearny, NJ) **10203**
Observer, The (Rio Rancho, NM) **10208**
Observer, The (Northport, NY) **10220**
Observer, The (La Grande, OR) **10031**
Observer, The (Greenville, RI) **10260**
Observer, The (Holly Hill, SC) **10262**
Ocala Star Banner (Ocala, FL) **9973**
Oceana's Herald-Journal (Hart, MI) **10170**
Ocean County's Observer (Toms
River, NJ) **10012**
Ocean County Reporter (Toms
River, NJ) **10207**
Oceanside/Island Park Herald (Long
Beach, NY) **10217**
Oceanside Centre Beacon (Mineola, NY) **10219**
Ocean Springs Record (Ocean
Springs, MS) **10187**
Oconee Breeze (Madison, GA) **10104**
Oconomowoc Enterprise
(Oconomowoc, WI) **10303**
Oconto County Times-Herald (Oconto
Falls, WI) **10303**
▼OC Weekly (Los Angeles, CA) **10076**
Odem-Edroy Times (Sinton, TX) **10280**
Odessa American (Odessa, TX) **10045**
Oelwein Daily Register (Oelwein, IA) **9988**
Ogdensburg Journal (Ogdensburg, NY) **10016**
Ogemaw County Herald (West
Branch, MI) **10176**
Ogle County Life (Oregon, IL) **10125**
Ohio County News (Rising Sun, IN) **10135**
Ohio County Times News
(Hartford, KY) **10148**
Ojai Valley News (Ojai, CA) **10078**

Oklahoma City Friday (Oklahoma City, OK) **10246**
Oklahoma Eagle (Tulsa, OK) **10247**
Oklee Herald (Oklee, MN) **10181**
Okmulgee Times (Okmulgee, OK) **10030**
Olathe Daily News (Olathe, KS) **9991**
Olathe Sun (Overland Park, KS) **10145**
Old Colony Memorial (Plymouth, MA) **10165**
Oldham Era, The (La Grange, KY) **10149**
Old Lyons Recorder, The (Lyons, CO) **10088**
Olean Times Herald (Olean, NY) **10016**
Olive Hill Times (Olive Hill, KY) **10150**
Oliveville Times (Morehead, KY) **10150**
Olivia Times Journal (Olivia, MN) **10181**
Olney Daily Mail (Olney, IL) **9981**
Olney Enterprise, The (Olney, TX) **10279**
Olney Times (Philadelphia, PA) **10257**
Olympian, The (Olympia, WA) **10051**
Olympia Review (Minier, IL) **10124**
Omaha Star (Omaha, NE) **10198**
Omaha World-Herald (Omaha, NE) **10010**
Omak-Okanogan County Chronicle (Omak, WA) **10292**
Omro Herald (Omro, WI) **10303**
Onawa Democrat (Onawa, IA) **10140**
Onawa Sentinel (Onawa, IA) **10140**
Onaway Outlook (Onaway, MI) **10173**
Oneida Daily Dispatch (Oneida, NY) **10016**
Onlooker, The (Foley, AL) **10059**
Onondaga Valley News (Syracuse, NY) **10223**
Ontario Advertiser (Palm Desert, CA) **10079**
Ontonagon Herald (Ontonagon, MI) **10173**
Oologah Lake Leader (Oologah, OK) **10246**
Opelika-Auburn News (Opelika, AL) **9956**
Opp News (Opp, AL) **10061**
Orange Bulletin (Milford, CT) **10091**
Orange Coast Daily Pilot (Costa Mesa, CA) **9961**
Orange Countian (Paoli, IN) **10134**
Orange County Log (San Diego, CA) **10081**
Orange County News (Garden Grove, CA) **10073**
Orange County Register (Santa Ana, CA) **9965**
Orange County Review (Orange, VA) **10288**
Orange Cove Mountain Times (Reedley, CA) **10080**
Orange Leader (Orange, TX) **10045**
Orange Transcript (Orange, NJ) **10205**
Orangevale News (Folsom, CA) **10072**
Orchard Park Bee (Williamsville, NY) **10225**
Ord Quiz (Ord, NE) **10198**
Oregonian, The (Portland, OR) **10032**
Oregon Observer (Oregon, WI) **10303**
Orem-Geneva Times (Orem, UT) **10283**
Orion Gazette (Orion, IL) **10125**
† Orion Times (Orion, IL)

Orland Metropolitan (Lemont, IL) **10121**
Orlando Sentinel (Orlando, FL) **9973**
Orlando Weekly, The (Winter Park, FL) **10100**
Orland Press-Register (Orland, CA) **10078**
Orland Township Messenger (Midlothian, IL) **10123**
Oroville Mercury-Register (Oroville, CA) **9963**
† Orrville Courier-Crescent (Orrville, OH)
Ortonville Independent (Ortonville, MN) **10181**
Osage County Chronicle (Burlingame, KS) **10143**
Osakis Review, The (Osakis, MN) **10181**
Osawatomie Graphic (Osawatomie, KS) **10145**
Osborne County Farmer (Osborne, KS) **10145**
Osceola County Gazette-Tribune (Sibley, IA) **10141**
Osceola News-Gazette (Kissimmee, FL) **10095**
Osceola Sentinel-Tribune (Osceola, IA) **10140**
Osceola Sun (Osceola, WI) **10303**
Osceola Times (Osceola, AR) **10067**
Oscoda Press (Oscoda, MI) **10173**
Osgood Journal (Versailles, IN) **10136**
Oshkosh Buyers Guide (Oshkosh, WI) **10303**
Oshkosh Northwestern (Oshkosh, WI) **10054**
Oskaloosa Herald (Oskaloosa, IA) **9988**
Oskaloosa Independent (Oskaloosa, KS) **10145**
Ossian Bee, The (Ossian, IA) **10141**
Ossian Journal (Ossian, IN) **10134**
Othello Outlook, The (Othello, WA) **10292**
▼Other Side, The (Prairie Village, KS) **10145**
Ottawa Advance (Jenison, MI) **10171**
Ottawa County Exponent, The (Oak Harbor, OH) **10242**
Ottawa Herald (Ottawa, KS) **9991**
Ottawa Times (Ottawa, KS) **10145**
Ottawa Times Shopper (Ottawa, KS) **10145**
Ottumwa Courier (Ottumwa, IA) **9988**
Ouachita Citizen (West Monroe, LA) **10155**
Ouray County Plaindealer (Ouray, CO) **10089**
Our Home Town (Vanderbilt, MI) **10175**
Our Town (Maywood, NJ) **10204**
Our Town (New York, NY) **10220**
Our Town (Pearl River, NY) **10221**
Outlook Mail (Santa Monica, CA) **10082**
Outlook, The (Santa Monica, CA) **9966**
Overland Park Sun (Shawnee Mission, KS) **10146**
Over the Mountain Journal (Birmingham, AL) **10058**
Ovid Gazette (Trumansburg, NY) **10224**
Oviedo Voice, The (Oviedo, FL) **10098**
Owasso Reporter (Owasso, OK) **10246**
Owatonna People's Press (Owatonna, MN) **10003**
Owatonna Weekly Shopper (Owatonna, MN) **10181**

Owensboro Messenger-Inquirer
 (Owensboro, KY) **9993**
Owings Mills Times (Baltimore, MD) **10158**
Oxford Eagle (Oxford, MS) **10005**
Oxford Press (Oxford, OH) **10242**
Oxford Public Ledger (Oxford, NC) **10229**
Oxford Register, The (Belle Plaine, KS) **10143**
Oxford Review-Times (Greene, NY) **10215**
† Oxnard Press-Courier (Oxnard, CA)
Oyster Bay-Syosset Guardian (Oyster
 Bay, NY) **10220**
Oyster Bay Enterprise Pilot
 (Mineola, NY) **10219**
Ozark County Times (Gainesville, MO) **10190**
Ozark Journal (Imboden, AR) **10066**
Ozaukee County News Graphic
 (Cedarburg, WI) **10298**
Ozaukee Guide (Cedarburg, WI) **10298**
Ozaukee Press (Port Washington, WI) **10304**

P

Pacifica Tribune (Pacifica, CA) **10078**
Pacific Daily News (Agana, GU) **9976**
Pacific Sun (Mill Valley, CA) **10077**
Paducah Sun (Paducah, KY) **9993**
Pageland Progressive-Journal, The
 (Pageland, SC) **10263**
Paintsville Herald, The (Paintsville, KY) **10150**
Palacios Beacon (Palacios, TX) **10279**
Palatine Countryside (Arlington
 Heights, IL) **10109**
Palatine Journal & Topics (Des
 Plaines, IL) **10115**
Palau Gazette (Koror, PW) **10251**
Palau Tribune (Saipan, MP) **10234**
Palestine Herald-Press (Palestine, TX) **10045**
Palisade Tribune (Palisade, CO) **10089**
Palisadian-Post (Pacific Palisades, CA) **10079**
Palladium-Times, The (Oswego, NY) **10016**
Palm Beach Daily News (Palm Beach, FL) **9973**
Palm Beach Post (West Palm Beach, FL) **9974**
Palm Desert (Indio, CA) **10073**
Palm Desert Advertiser (Palm
 Desert, CA) **10079**
Palm Spring Advertiser (Palm
 Desert, CA) **10079**
Palmyra Spectator (Palmyra, MO) **10192**
▼Palo Alto Daily News (Palo Alto, CA) **9964**
Palo Alto Weekly (Palo Alto, CA) **10079**
Palos Citizen (Midlothian, IL) **10123**
Palos Hills-Hickory Hills (Palos
 Heights, IL) **10126**
Palos Verdes Peninsula News (Palos Verdes
 Peninsula, CA) **10079**
Palouse Living (Moscow, ID) **10108**

Palo Verde Valley Times (Blythe, CA) **10069**
Pampa News (Pampa, TX) **10045**
Pana News-Palladium (Pana, IL) **10126**
† Panhandle Press (Chester, WV)
Panola Watchman (Carthage, TX) **10272**
▼Panolian ADvantage, The
 (Batesville, MS) **10185**
Panolian, The (Batesville, MS) **10185**
Pantagraph, The (Bloomington, IL) **9978**
Paoli News (Paoli, IN) **10134**
Paoli Republican (Paoli, IN) **10134**
Paper of Wabash County, The
 (Wabash, IN) **10136**
Paper, The (Barry, IL) **10110**
Paper, The (Elkhart, IN) **10130**
Paper, The (Goshen, IN) **10132**
Paper, The (Warsaw, IN) **10136**
† Paper, The (Spartanburg, SC)
Papillion Times (Papillion, NE) **10198**
Paradise Post (Paradise, CA) **10079**
Paradise Valley Independent
 (Scottsdale, AZ) **10064**
Paragould Daily Press (Paragould, AR) **9960**
Paris Beacon News (Paris, IL) **9981**
Paris Express (Paris, AR) **10067**
Paris News (Paris, TX) **10045**
Paris Post-Intelligencer, The (Paris, TN) **10041**
Parkchester News (Bronx, NY) **10210**
Parker Advertiser (Palm Desert, CA) **10079**
Parker Pioneer (Parker, AZ) **10064**
Parkersburg Sentinel
 (Parkersburg, WV) **10053**
Park Falls Herald (Park Falls, WI) **10304**
Park LaBrea News/Beverly Press (Los
 Angeles, CA) **10076**
Park News (Library, PA) **10254**
Park Rapids Enterprise (Park
 Rapids, MN) **10181**
Park Record, The (Park City, UT) **10283**
Park Ridge Herald Advocate (Park
 Ridge, IL) **10126**
Park Ridge Journal (Des Plaines, IL) **10115**
Park Slope Courier (Brooklyn, NY) **10211**
Parkway Transcript (Dedham, MA) **10161**
Parlier Post (Sanger, CA) **10081**
Parma Sun Post (Cleveland, OH) **10236**
Parsippany Focus (Morris Plains, NJ) **10204**
Parsippany News, The (West
 Caldwell, NJ) **10208**
Parsons Advocate (Parsons, WV) **10295**
Parsons News (Parsons, KS) **10145**
Parsons Sun (Parsons, KS) **9991**
Pasadena Citizen (Pasadena, TX) **10045**
Pasadena Star-News, The
 (Pasadena, CA) **9964**
Pasadena Weekly (Pasadena, CA) **10080**

Pascack Valley Community Life
  (Westwood, NJ) **10208**
Pasco News (Dade City, FL) **10094**
Passaic Citizen (Passaic, NJ) **10206**
Passaic Valley Today (Butler, NJ) **10201**
Pataskala Standard (Pataskala, OH) **10242**
Patent Trader (Cross River, NY) **10212**
Patriot & Free Press (Cuba, NY) **10212**
Patriot-News (Harrisburg, PA) **10033**
Patriot Ledger (Quincy, MA) **9998**
Patriot, The (Kutztown, PA) **10254**
Paulding Neighbor, The (Marietta, GA) **10104**
Paulding Progress (Paulding, OH) **10242**
Paullina Times (Paullina, IA) **10141**
Pauls Valley Daily Democrat (Pauls
  Valley, OK) **10030**
Pawhuska Journal-Capital
  (Pawhuska, OK) **10246**
Pawling News Chronicle (Pawling, NY) **10221**
Pawnee Post (Auburn, IL) **10110**
Paw Paw Courier-Leader (Paw Paw, MI) **10173**
Paxton Daily Record (Paxton, IL) **9981**
Paynesville Press, The
  (Paynesville, MN) **10182**
Payson Roundup (Payson, AZ) **10064**
† Peabody Times (Peabody, MA)
Pecos Enterprise (Pecos, TX) **10046**
Peekskill Herald (Peekskill, NY) **10221**
Peekskill Star (Yorktown Heights, NY) **10018**
Pekin Daily Times (Pekin, IL) **9981**
Pelham Journal (Pelham, GA) **10105**
Pelham Sun (Yonkers, NY) **10226**
Pelican Press (Sarasota, FL) **10098**
Pelican Rapids Press (Pelican
  Rapids, MN) **10182**
Pella Chronicle (Pella, IA) **10141**
Pembroke Mariner (Marshfield, MA) **10163**
Pembroke Reporter (Plymouth, MA) **10165**
Pender Chronicle (Burgaw, NC) **10227**
Pender Post (Burgaw, NC) **10227**
Pendleton Record, The (Pendleton, OR) **10249**
Penfield Post Republican, The
  (Fishers, NY) **10214**
Peninsula Beacon, The (San Diego, CA) **10081**
Peninsula Clarion (Kenai, AK) **9957**
Peninsula Daily News (Port
  Angeles, WA) **10051**
Peninsula Gateway (Gig Harbor, WA) **10291**
▼Peninsula Independent
  (Burlingame, CA) **10070**
† Peninsula Review, The (Carmel, CA)
Pennington County Prevailer-News (Hill
  City, SD) **10265**
Pennsboro News (Pennsboro, WV) **10295**
Pennysaver (Vista, CA) **10084**
Penny Saver (Tinley Park, IL) **10128**

Penny Saver (Three Rivers, MI) **10175**
Pennysaver (Elmsford, NY) **10213**
Pennysaver (Yorktown Heights, NY) **10226**
Penny Saver (Covington, OH) **10239**
Pennysaver Press (Bennington, VT) **10283**
Pennysaver, The (Sandwich, MA) **10165**
Penobscot Times (Old Town, ME) **10157**
Pensacola News Journal (Pensacola, FL) **9973**
Pensacola Voice (Pensacola, FL) **10098**
People-Sentinel (Barnwell, SC) **10261**
People's Defender, The (West
  Union, OH) **10244**
People's Weekly World (New York, NY) **10220**
Peoria Heights Herald (Peoria, IL) **10126**
Peoria Journal Star (Peoria, IL) **9981**
Peoria Observer (Peoria, IL) **10126**
Peoria Times (Glendale, AZ) **10064**
Perdido Pelican (Pensacola, FL) **10098**
Perham Enterprise-Bulletin
  (Perham, MN) **10182**
Perinton-Fairport Post, The
  (Pittsford, NY) **10221**
Perkasie News-Herald (Perkasie, PA) **10257**
Perquimans Weekly (Hertford, NC) **10228**
Perry Chief (Perry, IA) **10141**
Perry County News, The (Tell City, IN) **10136**
Perry County Republic-Monitor, The
  (Perryville, MO) **10192**
Perry County Times (New
  Bloomfield, PA) **10256**
Perry County Tribune (New
  Lexington, OH) **10242**
Perry Daily Journal (Perry, OK) **10030**
Perry News-Herald (Perry, FL) **10098**
Perrysburg Messenger-Journal
  (Perrysburg, OH) **10242**
Perry Taco Times (Perry, FL) **10098**
Perry Township Weekly (Beech
  Grove, IN) **10129**
Peru Tribune (Peru, IN) **9985**
Peshtigo Times (Peshtigo, WI) **10304**
Petaluma Argus-Courier (Petaluma, CA) **10080**
Peterborough Transcript
  (Peterborough, NH) **10200**
Petersburg Observer (Petersburg, IL) **10126**
Petersburg Pilot (Petersburg, AK) **10062**
Petoskey News-Review (Petoskey, MI) **10001**
Pharos-Tribune (Logansport, IN) **9984**
Phenix-Citizen (Phenix City, AL) **10061**
Philadelphia City Paper
  (Philadelphia, PA) **10257**
Philadelphia Daily News
  (Philadelphia, PA) **10035**
Philadelphia Guide Newspaper
  (Philadelphia, PA) **10257**
Philadelphia Inquirer (Philadelphia, PA) **10035**

Philadelphia Weekly (Philadelphia, PA) **10257**
Philipsburg Mail, The (Philipsburg, MT) **10195**
Phillipsburg Free Press
  (Phillipsburg, NJ) **10206**
Phillips County Review
  (Phillipsburg, KS) **10145**
Phoenix Gazette (Phoenix, AZ) **9958**
Phoenix Newspaper, The (Brooklyn, NY) **10211**
Phoenix Register (Phoenix, NY) **10221**
Phoenix, The (Phoenixville, PA) **10035**
Photo News (Monroe, NY) **10219**
Photo Star (Willshire, OH) **10244**
Piatt County Journal-Republican
  (Monticello, IL) **10124**
Picayune Item (Picayune, MS) **10005**
Pickens County Herald (Carrollton, AL) **10058**
Pickens Sentinel (Pickens, SC) **10263**
Pickerington Times-Sun
  (Columbus, OH) **10237**
Pickett County Press (Byrdstown, TN) **10266**
Pico Rivera News (Los Angeles, CA) **10076**
Pictorial Gazette (Old Saybrook, CT) **10091**
† Pictorial Press (Tahlequah, OK)
Picture Post (Waupaca, WI) **10306**
Piedmonter, The (Oakland, CA) **10078**
Piedmont Herald (Piedmont, WV) **10296**
Piedmont Journal-Independent
  (Piedmont, AL) **10061**
Pierce City Leader-Journal (Pierce
  City, MO) **10192**
Pierce County Herald (Ellsworth, WI) **10300**
Pierce County Tribune (Rugby, ND) **10233**
Pierre Capital Journal (Pierre, SD) **10039**
Pierre Times, The (Pierre, SD) **10265**
Piggott Times, The (Piggott, AR) **10067**
Pike County Dispatch (Milford, PA) **10255**
Pike County News Watchman
  (Jackson, OH) **10240**
Pike Register (Fishers, IN) **10131**
Pikes Peak Journal (Manitou
  Springs, CO) **10088**
Pilot-News (Plymouth, IN) **9985**
Pinckney Post Shopping Guide
  (Pinckney, MI) **10174**
Pine Bluff Commercial (Pine Bluff, AR) **9960**
† Pine Bluff News (Pine Bluff, AR)
Pine Bluff Shoppers News (Pine
  Bluff, AR) **10067**
Pine Island Eagle (Bokeelia, FL) **10093**
Pine Plains Register-Herald (Pine
  Plains, NY) **10221**
Pine River Times (Bayfield, CO) **10085**
Pineville Sun-Cumberland Courier
  (Pineville, KY) **10150**
Pinnacle, The (Hollister, CA) **10073**
Pioneer-News (Shepherdsville, KY) **10151**

Pioneer Republican, The (Marengo, IA) **10140**
Pioneer, The (Bemidji, MN) **10002**
Pipestone County Star (Pipestone, MN) **10182**
Piqua Daily Call (Piqua, OH) **10026**
Piscataquis Observer, The
  (Dover-Foxcroft, ME) **10156**
Pitch Weekly (Kansas City, MO) **10190**
Pittsburg Gazette (Pittsburg, TX) **10279**
Pittsburgh City Paper (Pittsburgh, PA) **10258**
Pittsburgh Post-Gazette
  (Pittsburgh, PA) **10035**
† Pittsburgh Press (Pittsburgh, PA)
Pittsburgh Renaissance News
  (Pittsburgh, PA) **10258**
Pittsburg Morning Sun (Pittsburg, KS) **9991**
Pittsfield Gazette, The (Pittsfield, MA) **10164**
Placentia News-Times (Anaheim, CA) **10069**
Placer Herald (Rocklin, CA) **10080**
Plain Dealer (Turnersville, NJ) **10207**
Plainsman, The (Huron, SD) **10039**
Plainsman Weekly News (Sedalia, MO) **10192**
Plain Talk (Newport, TN) **10269**
Plainview Daily Herald (Plainview, TX) **10046**
Plainview News (Plainview, MN) **10182**
Plainview News (Plainview, NE) **10198**
Plano Star Courier (Plano, TX) **10046**
Plaquemines Gazette (Belle Chasse, LA) **10152**
Plaquemines Watchman (Belle
  Chasse, LA) **10152**
Platte County Gazette (Parkville, MO) **10192**
Platte County Record-Times
  (Wheatland, WY) **10309**
Platte Dispatch Tribune (Kansas
  City, MO) **10190**
Platteville Journal (Platteville, WI) **10304**
Plattsmouth Journal (Plattsmouth, NE) **10198**
Pleasant Grove Review (American
  Fork, UT) **10282**
Pleasanton Express (Pleasanton, TX) **10279**
Plymouth Observer (Plymouth, MI) **10174**
Plymouth Sun-Sailor (Minnetonka, MN) **10180**
Pocahontas Record-Democrat
  (Pocahontas, IA) **10141**
Pocahontas Star Herald
  (Pocahontas, AR) **10067**
Pocahontas Times (Marlinton, WV) **10295**
Pocono Record (Stroudsburg, PA) **10036**
Pocono Shopper (East
  Stroudsburg, PA) **10252**
Point & Shoreland Journal (Toledo, OH) **10243**
Pointe Coupee Banner (New Roads, LA) **10154**
Point Pleasant Register (Point
  Pleasant, WV) **10053**
Point Reyes Light (Point Reyes
  Station, CA) **10080**
† Poland Leader (Niles, OH)

Polk City Press (Mulberry, FL) **10097**
Polk County Democrat, The
  (Bartow, FL) **10093**
Polk County Enterprise (Livingston, TX) **10278**
Pompano Ledger, The (Pompano
  Beach, FL) **10098**
Ponca City News (Ponca City, OK) **10030**
Ponchatoula Times, The
  (Ponchatoula, LA) **10154**
Pontiac Daily Leader (Pontiac, IL) **9981**
Pontotoc Progress (Pontotoc, MS) **10187**
Pony Express Mail (Liberty, TX) **10278**
Pope County Tribune (Glenwood, MN) **10178**
Poquoson Post (Yorktown, VA) **10290**
Porcupine Press (Chatham, MI) **10168**
Portage Dispatch, The (Portage, PA) **10258**
Portage Journal-Press (Portage, IN) **10135**
Portales News-Tribune (Portales, NM) **10014**
Port Arthur News (Port Arthur, TX) **10046**
Porter/New Caney Sun (Humble, TX) **10276**
Porterville Recorder (Porterville, CA) **9964**
Port Gibson Reveille (Port Gibson, MS) **10187**
Port Isabel-South Padre Press (Port
  Isabel, TX) **10279**
Portland Commercial Review
  (Portland, IN) **9985**
Portland News (Portland, TX) **10280**
Portland Press Herald (Portland, ME) **9995**
Portland Review & Observer (Grand
  Ledge, MI) **10170**
Port Lavaca Wave (Port Lavaca, TX) **10280**
Port Orchard Independent (Port
  Orchard, WA) **10292**
Port Richmond Star (Philadelphia, PA) **10257**
Portsmouth Daily Times
  (Portsmouth, OH) **10026**
Portsmouth Herald (Portsmouth, NH) **10011**
Portsmouth Times (Chesapeake, VA) **10285**
Port Times-Record, The (Setauket, NY) **10222**
Port Townsend/Jefferson County Leader (Port
  Townsend, WA) **10292**
Port Washington News (Port
  Washington, NY) **10221**
Post & Mail, The (Columbia City, IN) **9982**
Post-Bulletin (Rochester, MN) **10003**
Post-Crescent (Appleton, WI) **10053**
Post-Herald (Red Creek, NY) **10222**
Post-Journal, The (Jamestown, NY) **10015**
Post-Standard (Syracuse, NY) **10017**
Post-Star (Glen Falls, NY) **10015**
Post-Tribune (Gary, IN) **9983**
Post-Tribune (Jefferson City, MO) **10006**
Post Falls Tribune (Post Falls, ID) **10108**
Post Report, The (Lewisburg, WV) **10295**
Post Review, The (Paramus, NJ) **10205**
Post South (Plaquemine, LA) **10154**

Post, The (Middleburg, PA) **10255**
Post, The (Big Stone Gap, VA) **10285**
Poteau Daily News & Sun (Poteau, OK) **10030**
Potomac Almanac (Potomac, MD) **10159**
Potomac News (Woodbridge, VA) **10050**
Potter Leader-Enterprise
  (Coudersport, PA) **10252**
Pottsboro Press (Pottsboro, TX) **10280**
Pottsville Republican (Pottsville, PA) **10035**
Poughkeepsie Journal
  (Poughkeepsie, NY) **10017**
▼Poultney News, The (Rutland, VT) **10284**
Poway News Chieftain (San Diego, CA) **10081**
Powder Springs Neighbor, The
  (Marietta, GA) **10104**
Powell Valley News (Pennington
  Gap, VA) **10288**
Power County Press (American
  Falls, ID) **10107**
Prairie City News (Prairie City, IA) **10141**
Prairie Post (Jamestown, ND) **10232**
Prairie Shopper, The (La Fayette, IL) **10121**
Prairie Times, The (La Fayette, IL) **10121**
Prairie Village Sun (Shawnee
  Mission, KS) **10146**
Pratt Tribune (Pratt, KS) **9991**
Prattville Progress (Prattville, AL) **10061**
Prescott Journal (Prescott, WI) **10304**
Presque Isle Advance (Rogers City, MI) **10174**
Presque Isle Star (Gaylord, MI) **10170**
Press & Journal, The (Middletown, PA) **10255**
Press & Light (North Ridgeville, OH) **10242**
Press & Standard, The
  (Walterboro, SC) **10264**
Press & Sun-Bulletin (Vestal, NY) **10017**
Press-Dispatch (Petersburg, IN) **10134**
Press-Enterprise, The (Riverside, CA) **9964**
Press-Journal (Vero Beach, FL) **9974**
Press-News Journal (Canton, MO) **10188**
Press-News, The (Minerva, OH) **10241**
Press-Republican (Plattsburgh, NY) **10016**
Press-Sentinel, The (Jesup, GA) **10103**
Press-Star (New London, WI) **10303**
Press-Telegram (Long Beach, CA) **9962**
Press Argus-Courier (Van Buren, AR) **10068**
Press Dispatch (Kansas City, MO) **10190**
Press Enterprise, The (Bloomsburg, PA) **10032**
Press Gazette, The (Hillsboro, OH) **10240**
Press Herald (Pine Grove, PA) **10258**
Press Journal (St. Louis, MO) **10194**
Press Journal, The (Palisades Park, NJ) **10205**
Press Leader, The (Farmington, MO) **10006**
Press of Atlantic City, The
  (Pleasantville, NJ) **10012**
† Press, The (Alexandria, MN)
Preston Citizen (Preston, ID) **10108**

Preston County News (Kingwood, WV) **10295**
Price Hill Press (Cincinnati, OH) **10235**
Priest River Times (Priest River, ID) **10108**
PrimeTime (Lawrence, NY) **10217**
Prince Georges Journal (Lanham, MD) **9996**
Prince Georges Sentinel
  (Seabrook, MD) **10159**
Princeton Daily Clarion (Princeton, IN) **9985**
Princeton News Leader (Princeton, NC) **10229**
Princeton Packet, The (Princeton, NJ) **10206**
Princeton Times (Princeton, WV) **10296**
Princeton Times-Republic
  (Princeton, WI) **10304**
Princeton Union-Eagle (Princeton, MN) **10182**
▼Prince William Journal
  (Manassas, VA) **10049**
Private Eye Weekly (Salt Lake City, UT) **10283**
Proctor Journal (Proctor, MN) **10182**
Progress-Index (Petersburg, VA) **10049**
Progress, The (Cave City, KY) **10147**
Progress, The (Caldwell, NJ) **10201**
† Progress, The (Clearfield, PA)
Progress, The (Monroeville, PA) **10255**
Progress, The (Anahuac, TX) **10270**
Prospect-News, The (Doniphan, MO) **10189**
Prospect Heights Journal (Des
  Plaines, IL) **10115**
Prospector, The (Doniphan, MO) **10189**
Providence Journal-Bulletin
  (Providence, RI) **10038**
Provincetown Advocate
  (Provincetown, MA) **10165**
Proviso Star-Sentinel (Melrose Park, IL) **10123**
Pryor Daily Times (Pryor, OK) **10030**
Pryor Jeffersonian (Pryor, OK) **10246**
Public Opinion, The
  (Chambersburg, PA) **10032**
Public Spirit (Ayer, MA) **10160**
Public Spirit (Hatboro, PA) **10253**
Pueblo Chieftain (Pueblo, CO) **9969**
Pulaski Citizen (Pulaski, TN) **10269**
Pulaski County Journal (Winamac, IN) **10136**
Pulaski Enterprise (Mounds, IL) **10124**
Pulaski Giles Free Press (Pulaski, TN) **10269**
Pulse-Journal (Mason, OH) **10241**
Punxsutawney Spirit
  (Punxsutawney, PA) **10035**
Purcell Register (Purcell, OK) **10246**
Putnam County Record (Granville, IL) **10118**
Putnam County Sentinel (Ottawa, OH) **10242**
Putnam County Vidette (Columbus
  Grove, OH) **10239**
Putnam Courier-Trader, The
  (Carmel, NY) **10212**
Putnam Post-Cabell Bulletin
  (Culloden, WV) **10294**

Pymatuning Area News (Andover, OH) **10234**
Pyramid, The (Mt. Pleasant, UT) **10283**

Q

Quad-City Times (Davenport, IA) **9987**
Quad Community Press (White Bear
  Lake, MN) **10184**
Quad River News (Sheridan, MO) **10193**
Quakertown Free Press
  (Quakertown, PA) **10258**
Quay County Sun (Tucumcari, NM) **10209**
Queen Anne-Magnolia News
  (Seattle, WA) **10293**
Queen Anne's Record-Observer
  (Centreville, MD) **10158**
Queens Chronicle (Rego Park, NY) **10222**
Queens Ledger (Maspeth, NY) **10218**
Queens Tribune (Fresh Meadows, NY) **10214**
▼Queen Village Times, The
  (Flushing, NY) **10214**
Quik Quarter Want Ads (Hobbs, NM) **10208**
Quincy Herald-Whig (Quincy, IL) **9981**
Quincy Sun (Quincy, MA) **10165**
Quoddy Tides (Eastport, ME) **10156**

R

Raeford News-Journal, The
  (Raeford, NC) **10230**
Rahway News-Record (Rahway, NJ) **10206**
Rahway Progress (Union, NJ) **10207**
Ramona Sentinel (Ramona, CA) **10080**
Ramsey-Mahwah Reporter (Palisades
  Park, NJ) **10205**
Ramsey County Review (St. Paul, MN) **10183**
Ramsey Home & Store News
  (Ramsey, NJ) **10206**
Rancho Bernardo Journal (San
  Diego, CA) **10081**
Rancho Santa Margarita News (Lake
  Forest, CA) **10074**
Randleman Reporter (Randleman, NC) **10230**
Randolph County Herald Tribune
  (Chester, IL) **10112**
† Randolph County Times-Herald (Moberly, MO)
Randolph Guide, The (Asheboro, NC) **10226**
Randolph Leader (Roanoke, AL) **10061**
Randolph Mariner (Marshfield, MA) **10163**
Randolph Reporter (Bernardsville, NJ) **10200**
Random Lengths News (San Pedro, CA) **10082**
Rankin County News, The
  (Brandon, MS) **10185**
Rankin Independent (Cissna Park, IL) **10114**
† Rantoul Pacesetter (Rantoul, IL)
Rantoul Press (Rantoul, IL) **10127**
Rapid City Journal (Rapid City, SD) **10039**

Rappahannock News (Reston, VA) **10288**
Rappahannock Record
  (Kilmarnock, VA) **10287**
Raton Range, The (Raton, NM) **10208**
Ravalli Republic (Hamilton, MT) **10008**
Ravena News Herald (Ravena, NY) **10221**
Rayne Acadian-Tribune (Rayne, LA) **10154**
Rayne Independent (Rayne, LA) **10154**
Raynham Journal (Stoughton, MA) **10166**
Raytown Dispatch Tribune
  (Raytown, MO) **10192**
Reading Eagle & Reading Times
  (Reading, PA) **10036**
Real American (Leakey, TX) **10277**
Reaper Extra (Richfield, UT) **10283**
Record-Advertiser (North
  Tonawanda, NY) **10220**
Record-Breeze (Blackwood, NJ) **10201**
Record-Citizen, The (Bristow, OK) **10245**
Record-Delta, The (Buckhannon, WV) **10294**
Record-Enterprise (McDonald, PA) **10254**
Record-Herald & Indianola Tribune
  (Indianola, IA) **10139**
Record-Journal (Meriden, CT) **9970**
Record-Review (Abbotsford, WI) **10297**
Record Enterprise (Plymouth, NH) **10200**
Recorder-Herald (Salmon, ID) **10109**
Recorder, The (Greenfield, MA) **9997**
Recorder, The (Prince Frederick, MD) **10159**
Recorder, The (Amsterdam, NY) **10014**
Recorder, The (Conshohocken, PA) **10252**
Recorder, The (Monterey, VA) **10287**
Recorder Times, The (San Antonio, TX) **10280**
Record Herald (Washington Court
  House, OH) **10027**
Record Herald (Waynesboro, PA) **10037**
Record Ledger (San Fernando, CA) **10081**
Record Searchlight (Redding, CA) **9964**
Record, The (Stockton, CA) **9966**
Record, The (Gainesville, FL) **10095**
Record, The (Council, ID) **10107**
Record, The (Kansas City, KS) **10144**
Record, The (Havre De Grace, MD) **10159**
Record, The (Boonville, MO) **10188**
Record, The (Hackensack, NJ) **10012**
Record, The (Troy, NY) **10017**
Record, The (Coraopolis, PA) **10252**
Record, The (Horsham, PA) **10034**
Record Times, The (Paxton, IL) **10126**
Red Bay News (Red Bay, AL) **10061**
Red Bluff Daily News (Red Bluff, CA) **9964**
Redding Pilot, The (Georgetown, CT) **10090**
Redfield Press (Redfield, SD) **10265**
Redford Observer (Livonia, MI) **10172**
Redlands Advertiser (Palm Desert, CA) **10079**
Redlands Daily Facts (Redlands, CA) **9964**

Redmond Sammamish Valley News
  (Redmond, WA) **10292**
Redmond Spokesman (Redmond OR) **10250**
Red Oak Express (Red Oak, IA) **10141**
Red Wing Republican Eagle (Red
  Wing, MN) **10003**
▼Redwood City Tribune (Redwood
  City, CA) **10080**
Redwood Gazette, The (Redwood
  Falls, MN) **10182**
Reedley Exponent (Reedley, CA) **10080**
Reedsburg Times-Press
  (Reedsburg, WI) **10304**
Reflector, The (Battle Ground, WA) **10290**
Regional News (Palos Heights, IL) **10126**
Regional News, The (La Crosse, WI) **10133**
Register-Guard (Eugene, OR) **10031**
Register-Herald (Eaton, OH) **10239**
Register-Mail (Galesburg, IL) **9979**
Register-News (Bordentown, NJ) **10201**
Register-Pajaronian (Watsonville, CA) **9967**
Register/Herald (Beckley, WV) **10052**
Register Citizen (Torrington, CT) **9971**
Register Review (Bishop, CA) **10069**
Register Star (Rockford, IL) **9981**
Register Star (Hudson, NY) **10015**
Register, The (Yarmouth Port, MA) **10167**
† Register, The (Shrewsbury, NJ)
Reidsville Review (Reidsville, NC) **10020**
Reminder, The (Vernon, CT) **10092**
Reminder, The (Pontiac, MI) **10174**
Remington Press (Rensselaer, IN) **10135**
Reno Gazette-Journal (Reno, NV) **10010**
Rensselaer Republican (Rensselaer, IN) **9985**
Renville County Shopper (Olivia, MN) **10181**
Reporter Dispatch, The (White
  Plains, NY) **10018**
Reporter of the Spring-Ford Area
  (Royersford, PA) **10258**
Reporter, The (Vacaville, CA) **9967**
† Reporter, The (Tampa, FL)
Reporter, The (Casey, IL) **10112**
Reporter, The (Chicago, IL) **10113**
Reporter, The (Palos Heights, IL) **10126**
Reporter, The (Lebanon, IN) **9984**
Reporter, The (Palisades Park, NJ) **10205**
Reporter, The (Walton, NY) **10224**
Reporter, The (Lansdale, PA) **10034**
Reporter, The (Fond Du Lac, WI) **10054**
Repository, The (Canton, OH) **10023**
Republican-Journal (Darlington, WI) **10299**
Republican Journal (Belfast, ME) **10155**
Republican, The (Danville, IN) **10130**
Republican, The (Oakland, MD) **10159**
Republic, The (Columbus, IN) **9982**

▼Resident Community News (New York, NY) **10220**
Reston Times (Reston, VA) **10288**
Retrospect, The (Collingswood, NJ) **10202**
Reveille/Between the Lakes (Seneca Falls, NY) **10222**
Revere Journal (Revere, MA) **10165**
† Review-Enterprise (Blackwood, NJ)
Review Herald, The (Mammoth Lakes, CA) **10077**
Review Press Reporter (Yonkers, NY) **10226**
Review, The (Erie, IL) **10116**
Review, The (Marion, IL) **10122**
Review, The (Richmond, MI) **10174**
Review, The (Paramus, NJ) **10205**
Review, The (Point Pleasant Beach, NJ) **10206**
Review, The (Plymouth, WI) **10304**
Review Times (Fostoria, OH) **10024**
Reynolds County Courier (Ellington, MO) **10189**
RFD News, The (Bellevue, OH) **10234**
Rhinelander Daily News (Rhinelander, WI) **10055**
Rialto Record (San Bernardino, CA) **10080**
Rice Lake Chronotype (Rice Lake, WI) **10304**
Richardson News (Richardson, TX) **10280**
Richfield Reaper (Richfield, UT) **10283**
Richfield Sun-Current (Bloomington, MN) **10177**
Richland Beacon-News (Rayville, LA) **10154**
Richland Center Observer (Richland Center, WI) **10304**
Richlands-Beulaville Advertiser-News (Richlands, NC) **10230**
Richlands News Press (Richlands, VA) **10289**
Richmond County Daily Journal (Rockingham, NC) **10021**
Richmond Palladium-Item (Richmond, IN) **9985**
Richmond Register (Richmond, KY) **9993**
Richmond Times-Dispatch (Richmond, VA) **10050**
Richton Dispatch, The (Richton, MS) **10187**
Ridgefield Press, The (Ridgefield, CT) **10091**
Ridgewood News (Paramus, NJ) **10205**
Ridgway Record (Ridgway, PA) **10036**
Ridgway Sun (Ouray, CO) **10089**
Ridley Press (Drexel Hill, PA) **10252**
Rio Grande Sun (Espanola, NM) **10208**
Ripley Jackson Herald (Ripley, WV) **10296**
Ripley Southern Sentinel (Ripley, MS) **10187**
Ripon Commonwealth Press (Ripon, WI) **10304**
Rising Star, The (Rising Star, TX) **10280**
Rising Sun Recorder (Rising Sun, IN) **10135**
Ritchie Gazette (Harrisville, WV) **10295**

Riverdale Press (Bronx, NY) **10210**
River East News Bulletin (Glastonbury, CT) **10090**
River Falls Journal (River Falls, WI) **10305**
River North News (Chicago, IL) **10113**
River Oaks News (Fort Worth, TX) **10275**
River Press (Rogue River, OR) **10250**
River Press, The (Fort Benton, MT) **10195**
River Reporter, The (Narrowsburg, NY) **10219**
Riverside Advertiser (Palm Desert, CA) **10079**
Riverside Bulletin, The (Los Angeles, CA) **10076**
Riverside Review (Buffalo, NY) **10211**
Riverton Ranger (Riverton, WY) **10056**
Riverton Register (Riverton, IL) **10127**
River Valley Shopper (Spring Valley, MN) **10183**
Roane County News, The (Kingston, TN) **10267**
Roane County Reporter (Spencer, WV) **10296**
Roanoke-Chowan News-Herald (Jackson, NC) **10228**
Roanoke Beacon (Plymouth, NC) **10229**
Roanoke Rapids Daily & Sunday Herald (Roanoke Rapids, NC) **10020**
Roanoke Review (Roanoke, IL) **10127**
Roanoke Times, The (Roanoke, VA) **10050**
Robersonville Weekly Herald (Williamston, NC) **10231**
Robertson County Times (Springfield, TN) **10270**
Robesonian, The (Lumberton, NC) **10020**
Robinson Daily News (Robinson, IL) **9981**
Rochelle News Leader (Rochelle, IL) **10127**
Rochester Clarion (Rochester, MI) **10174**
† Rochester Courier (Rochester, NH)
Rochester Democrat & Chronicle (Rochester, NY) **10017**
Rochester Eccentric (Rochester Hills, MI) **10174**
Rochester Sentinel, The (Rochester, IN) **9985**
Rochester Sun News, The (Tenino, WA) **10293**
Rochester Times (Auburn, IL) **10110**
Rochester Times, The (Rochester, NH) **10200**
Rockaway Journal (Lawrence, NY) **10217**
Rockbridge Weekly (Lexington, VA) **10287**
Rock County Star Herald (Luverne, MN) **10180**
Rockcreek Current, The (Washington, DC) **10093**
Rockdale Citizen (Conyers, GA) **9975**
Rockdale Neighbor, The (Conyers, GA) **10102**
Rockdale Reporter (Rockdale, TX) **10280**
Rockford/Cedar Springs Advance (Jenison, MI) **10171**
Rockford Squire (Rockford, MI) **10174**

Rock Island Argus Dispatch, The
(Moline, IL) **9980**
Rockland County Times
(Haverstraw, NY) **10216**
Rockland Independent, The (Pearl
River, NY) **10221**
Rockland Journal-News (West
Nyack, NY) **10018**
Rockmart Journal (Rockmart, GA) **10105**
Rockrimmon Journal (Manitou
Springs, CO) **10088**
Rock Springs Daily Rocket-Miner (Rock
Springs, WY) **10056**
Rockville Centre Herald (Lawrence, NY) **10217**
Rockville Centre Long Island News & Owl
(Mineola, NY) **10219**
Rockville Parke County Sentinel
(Rockville, IN) **10135**
Rockwood Times (Kingston, TN) **10267**
Rocky Ford Daily Gazette (Rocky
Ford, CO) **9969**
▼Rocky Fork Enterprise
(Columbus, OH) **10237**
Rocky Mountain News (Denver, CO) **9968**
Rocky Mount Telegram (Rocky
Mount, NC) **10021**
Rogers Park/Edgewater News/Uptown News
Star (Lincolnwood, IL) **10122**
Rogersville Review (Rogersville, TN) **10269**
† Rohnert Park Cotati Clarion (Cotati, CA)
Rolla Daily News (Rolla, MO) **10007**
Rolling Meadows Journal & Topics (Des
Plaines, IL) **10115**
Rome News-Tribune (Rome, GA) **9975**
Romeo Observer (Romeo, MI) **10174**
Romeoville Metropolitan (Lemont, IL) **10121**
Romeoville Sun (Bolingbrook, IL) **10111**
Romulus Roman (Wayne, MI) **10176**
Roosevelt Review (St. Paul, MN) **10183**
Rosamond News (Rosamond, CA) **10080**
Roscoe Hosmer Independent
(Ipswich, SD) **10265**
Roscommon County Herald-News
(Roscommon, MI) **10174**
Roseau Times-Region (Roseau, MN) **10182**
Roselle Park Leader (Union, NJ) **10207**
† Roselle Record (Carol Stream, IL)
Roselle Spectator (Union, NJ) **10207**
Rosemont Journal (Des Plaines, IL) **10115**
Rosemont Times (Park Ridge, IL) **10126**
Roseville-Falcon Heights-Arden Hills Focus
(Roseville, MN) **10182**
Roseville Independent (Roseville, IL) **10127**
Roseville Press-Tribune (Roseville, CA) **10080**
Roseville Review (St. Paul, MN) **10183**

Rossford Record-Journal
(Perrysburg, OH) **10242**
Rossmoor News (Walnut Creek, CA) **10084**
Ross Valley Reporter (Sausalito, CA) **10083**
Roswell-Alpharetta Neighbor
(Roswell, GA) **10105**
Roswell/Alpharetta Crier Newspaper
(Dunwoody, GA) **10102**
Roswell Daily Record (Roswell, NM) **10014**
Round Lake News (Grayslake, IL) **10119**
Round Rock Leader (Round Rock, TX) **10280**
Round Valley Paper, The (Eagar, AZ) **10063**
Roxborough Review (Philadelphia, PA) **10258**
Royal Review (Royal City, WA) **10292**
Ruidoso News, The (Ruidoso, NM) **10208**
Rumford Falls Times (Rumford, ME) **10157**
Rural-Urban Record (Columbia
Station, OH) **10237**
Rural Virginian (Charlottesville, VA) **10285**
Rush County News (La Crosse, KS) **10144**
Rushville Republican (Rushville, IN) **9985**
Rushville Times, The (Rushville, IL) **10127**
Russell County News (Russell
Springs, KY) **10151**
Russell Daily News (Russell, KS) **9991**
Russell Record (Russell, KS) **10145**
Russell Springs Times Journal (Russell
Springs, KY) **10151**
Ruston Daily Leader (Ruston, LA) **9995**
Rutherford Courier, The (Smyrna, TN) **10269**
Rutland Herald (Rutland, VT) **10048**
Rutland Tribune, The (Rutland, VT) **10284**
Rye Chronicle (Yonkers, NY) **10226**

S

Sabina Advertiser (Sabina, OH) **10243**
Sabinal Sampler (Hondo, TX) **10276**
Sabine Banner (Many, LA) **10154**
Sabine County Reporter-Rambler
(Hemphill, TX) **10276**
Sabine Index (Many, LA) **10154**
Sacramento Bee (Sacramento, CA) **9965**
Sacramento Bulletin, The
(Sacramento, CA) **10080**
† Sacramento Union (Sacramento, CA)
Saddleback Valley News (Lake
Forest, CA) **10074**
Saginaw News (Saginaw, MI) **10001**
Saginaw Press, The (Saginaw, MI) **10174**
Saint Elmo Banner (St. Elmo, IL) **10127**
Saipan Tribune (Saipan, MP) **10022**
Sakonnet Times (Portsmouth, RI) **10260**
Salamanca Press (Salamanca, NY) **10017**
Salem County Record (Salem, NJ) **10206**
Salem Democrat, The (Salem, IN) **10135**

Salem Evening News (Beverly, MA) **9996**
Salem Leader (Salem, IN) **10135**
Salem News (Salem, MO) **10192**
Salem News (Salem, OH) **10026**
Salem Observer (Salem, NH) **10200**
Salem Times-Commoner (Salem, IL) **10127**
Salem Times-Register (Salem, VA) **10289**
Salina Journal (Salina, KS) **9991**
Saline Reporter (Saline, MI) **10174**
Salisbury News & Advertiser
   (Salisbury, MD) **10159**
Salisbury Post (Salisbury, NC) **10021**
Salmon River News (Pulaski, NY) **10221**
Salt Lake City Deseret News (Salt Lake
   City, UT) **10047**
Salt Lake Tribune (Salt Lake City, UT) **10048**
Saluda Standard Sentinel (Saluda, SC) **10263**
Salyersville Independent
   (Salyersville, KY) **10151**
Samford Crimson (Birmingham, AL) **10058**
Samoa News (Pago Pago, AS) **9957**
Sampson Independent, The
   (Clinton, NC) **10018**
Samson Ledger (Samson, AL) **10061**
San Angelo Standard-Times (San
   Angelo, TX) **10046**
San Antonio Express-News (San
   Antonio, TX) **10046**
† San Antonio Light (San Antonio, TX)
San Augustine Tribune (San
   Augustine, TX) **10280**
San Benito News (San Benito, TX) **10280**
San Bernardino Advertiser (Palm
   Desert, CA) **10079**
San Bernardino Bulletin, The (Los
   Angeles, CA) **10076**
San Bernardino County Sun (San
   Bernardino, CA) **9965**
San Bruno Herald (San Mateo, CA) **10082**
† San Clemente News (San Clemente, CA)
Sandersville Progress
   (Sandersville, GA) **10105**
▼Sandhills Living (Southern Pines, NC) **10230**
† San Diego Bulletin (Los Angeles, CA)
San Diego Log (San Diego, CA) **10081**
San Diego Reader (San Diego, CA) **10081**
San Diego Review (San Diego, CA) **10081**
San Diego Transcript (San Diego, CA) **9965**
San Diego Union-Tribune (San
   Diego, CA) **9965**
Sand Mountain Reporter
   (Albertville, AL) **10057**
† Sandpoint News-Bulletin (Sandpoint, ID)
Sand Springs Leader (Sand
   Springs, OK) **10247**
Sandusky Register (Sandusky, OH) **10026**

Sandwich Broadsider (Orleans, MA) **10164**
Sandy Post (Sandy, OR) **10250**
Sandy Springs Neighbor, The
   (Atlanta, GA) **10101**
San Fernando Valley Sun (San
   Fernando, CA) **10081**
Sanford Herald (Sanford, FL) **9973**
Sanford Herald, The (Sanford, NC) **10021**
Sanford News (Sanford, ME) **10157**
San Francisco Bay Guardian (San
   Francisco, CA) **10081**
San Francisco Chronicle (San
   Francisco, CA) **9965**
San Francisco Daily Journal (San
   Francisco, CA) **9965**
San Francisco Examiner (San
   Francisco, CA) **9965**
San Francisco Independent (San
   Francisco, CA) **10081**
San Francisco Metro Reporter (San
   Francisco, CA) **10081**
San Francisco Sentinel (San
   Francisco, CA) **10081**
San Gabriel Progress (Los Angeles, CA) **10076**
San Gabriel Valley Tribune (West
   Covina, CA) **9967**
Sanger Herald (Sanger, CA) **10081**
Sanibel-Captiva Islander (Sanibel, FL) **10098**
Sanilac County News (Sandusky, MI) **10175**
San Jacinto Valley Register (San
   Jacinto, CA) **10081**
San Jose Mercury News (San Jose, CA) **9965**
San Luis Obispo County Telegram-Tribune (San
   Luis Obisopo, CA) **9965**
San Marcos Daily Record (San
   Marcos, TX) **10046**
San Marcos News Reporter (San
   Marcos, CA) **10082**
San Marino Tribune (San Marino, CA) **10082**
San Mateo Times (San Mateo, CA) **9965**
San Mateo Weekly (Burlingame, CA) **10070**
San Patricio County News (Sinton, TX) **10281**
San Rafael News Pointer
   (Sausalito, CA) **10083**
San Ramon Valley Times, The
   (Danville, CA) **9961**
Santa Barbara Independent (Santa
   Barbara, CA) **10082**
Santa Barbara News Press (Santa
   Barbara, CA) **9965**
Santa Cruz County Sentinel (Santa
   Cruz, CA) **9966**
Santa Fe New Mexican (Santa Fe, NM) **10014**
Santa Fe Reporter, The (Santa Fe, NM) **10208**
Santa Fe Springs News (Los
   Angeles, CA) **10077**

Santa Maria Times (Santa Maria, CA) **9966**
† Santa Monica Life (Santa Monica, CA)
Santa Paula Times (Santa Paula, CA) **10082**
Santa Rosa Free Press (Milton, FL) **10097**
Santa Rosa Press Democrat (Santa
  Rosa, CA) **9966**
Santa Rosa Press Gazette (Milton, FL) **10097**
Sapulpa Daily Herald (Sapulpa, OK) **10030**
Sarasota Herald Tribune (Sarasota, FL) **9973**
Saratoga News (Saratoga, CA) **10083**
Saratoga Sun (Saratoga, WY) **10309**
Saratogian, The (Saratoga Springs, NY) **10017**
Sarcoxie Record, The (Sarcoxie, MO) **10192**
Sargent Leader (Burwell, NE) **10197**
Saturday Advantage, The (Monte
  Vista, CO) **10088**
Saturday Post-Star (Saugerties, NY) **10222**
Saugerties Post Star (Saugerties, NY) **10222**
Saugus Advertiser (Melrose, MA) **10163**
Sauk-Prairie Star (Sauk City, WI) **10305**
Sauk Centre Herald (Sauk Centre, MN) **10182**
Sault Ste. Marie Evening News (Sault Ste.
  Marie, MI) **10001**
Savannah Morning News/Evening Press
  (Savannah, GA) **9976**
Savannah Reporter & Andrew County Democrat
  (Savannah, MO) **10192**
Savanna Times Journal (Savanna, IL) **10127**
Sawyer County Gazette (Winter, WI) **10308**
Sawyer County Record (Hayward, WI) **10301**
Sayre Journal (Sayre, OK) **10247**
Scarsdale Inquirer, The (Scarsdale, NY) **10222**
Schaller Herald (Schaller, IA) **10141**
Schererville Guide (Highland, IN) **10132**
Schuyler Sun (Schuyler, NE) **10198**
Scioto Voice (Wheelersburg, OH) **10244**
Scotsman Press, The (Syracuse, NY) **10224**
Scott County Advertiser (Waldron, AR) **10068**
Scott County News (Oneida, TN) **10269**
Scott County Times (Forest, MS) **10186**
Scott Flier (Mascoutah, IL) **10122**
Scottsdale-Ashburn Independent
  (Midlothian, IL) **10124**
Scottsdale Progress Tribune
  (Scottsdale, AZ) **9958**
Scottsville Citizen-Times
  (Scottsville, KY) **10151**
Scranton Times/Sunday Times
  (Scranton, PA) **10036**
Seaford-Wantagh Observer
  (Bellmore, NY) **10210**
Seal Beach Sun (Seal Beach, CA) **10083**
Sealy News (Sealy, TX) **10280**
Seaside Heights Ocean County Review (Point
  Pleasant Beach, NJ) **10206**
Seaside Signal (Seaside, OR) **10250**

Seattle Daily Journal of Commerce
  (Seattle, WA) **10051**
Seattle Facts (Seattle, WA) **10293**
Seattle Post-Intelligencer (Seattle, WA) **10051**
Seattle Skanner, The (Seattle, WA) **10293**
Seattle Times (Seattle, WA) **10051**
Seattle Weekly (Seattle, WA) **10293**
Sebastian Sun (Sebastian, FL) **10099**
Sebeka/Menahga Review Messenger
  (Sebeka, MN) **10182**
Secaucus Home News (Secaucus, NJ) **10206**
Sedalia Democrat, The (Sedalia, MO) **10007**
Sedona Red Rock News (Sedona, AZ) **10064**
Seekonk Star (East Providence, RI) **10260**
Seguin Gazette-Enterprise (Seguin, TX) **10046**
Selby Record (Selby, SD) **10265**
Selma Enterprise (Selma, CA) **10083**
Selma Times-Journal (Selma, AL) **9956**
Seminole Daily Producer
  (Seminole, OK) **10030**
† Seminole Outlook (Oviedo, FL)
Senior's Beacon, The (Lima, OH) **10240**
Senior Observer (Winter Park, FL) **10100**
Senior Times (Spokane, WA) **10293**
Sentinel (Cheyenne, WY) **10308**
Sentinel & Enterprise (Fitchburg, MA) **9997**
Sentinel-Echo (London, KY) **10149**
Sentinel-Ledger, The (Ocean City, NJ) **10205**
Sentinel-Record, The (Hot Springs, AR) **9960**
Sentinel-Tribune (Bowling Green, OH) **10023**
† Sentinel/Altitudes (Frisco, CO)
Sentinel, The (Auburn, CA) **10069**
Sentinel, The (Gulf Breeze, FL) **10095**
Sentinel, The (Chicago, IL) **10113**
Sentinel, The (Radcliff, KY) **10151**
Sentinel, The (Marion, MA) **10162**
Sentinel, The (Havre, MT) **10195**
Sentinel, The (Jefferson, OH) **10240**
Sentinel, The (Lewistown, PA) **10034**
Sequim Gazette (Sequim, WA) **10293**
Sequoyah County Times (Sallisaw, OK) **10246**
Seward County Independent
  (Seward, NE) **10198**
Seward Phoenix Log (Seward, AK) **10062**
Sewickley Herald (Monroeville, PA) **10255**
SF Weekly (San Francisco, CA) **10081**
Shafter Press (Shafter, CA) **10083**
Shakopee Valley News (Shakopee, MN) **10183**
Shamokin News-Item (Shamokin, PA) **10036**
Sharon Advocate (Sharon, MA) **10165**
Sharon Reporter, The (Sharon, WI) **10305**
Shawano Leader (Shawano, WI) **10055**
† Shawnee-Cridersville Press (Wapakoneta, OH)
Shawnee/Merriam Sun (Shawnee
  Mission, KS) **10146**
Shawnee News-Star (Shawnee, OK) **10030**

Title

Sheboygan Falls News (Sheboygan Falls, WI) **10305**
Sheboygan Press, The (Sheboygan, WI) **10055**
Shelby County Herald (Shelbyville, MO) **10193**
Shelby County Reporter (Columbiana, AL) **10058**
Shelby Globe (Shelby, OH) **10026**
Shelby Review (Wapakoneta, OH) **10244**
Shelby Star (Shelby, NC) **10021**
Shelby Sun Times (Germantown, TN) **10267**
Shelbyville Daily Union (Shelbyville, IL) **9981**
Shelbyville News (Shelbyville, IN) **9985**
Shelbyville Sentinel-News (Shelbyville, KY) **10151**
Shelbyville Times-Gazette (Shelbyville, TN) **10041**
Sheldon Mail-Sun (Sheldon, IA) **10141**
Shelley Pioneer (Shelley, ID) **10109**
Shelter Island Reporter (Shelter Island Heights, NY) **10223**
Shelton-Mason County Journal (Shelton, WA) **10293**
Shenandoah Valley-Herald, The (Woodstock, VA) **10290**
Shepherdstown Chronicle (Shepherdstown, WV) **10296**
Sheridan Headlight (Sheridan, AR) **10067**
Sheridan News (Fishers, IN) **10131**
Sheridan Press (Sheridan, WY) **10056**
▼ Sherman County Star, The (Goodland, KS) **10143**
Shiawassee County Journal (Perry, MI) **10174**
Shippensburg News-Chronicle (Shippensburg, PA) **10259**
Shopper/PLUS (Shelbyville, KY) **10151**
Shopper's Guide (Bardstown, KY) **10146**
Shopper's Guide, The (Louisville, MS) **10186**
Shopper Observer News (Ruskin, FL) **10098**
Shopper Spree (Burlington, IA) **10137**
Shopper Stopper (Merrimac, WI) **10302**
Shopper, The (Pensacola, FL) **10098**
Shopper, The (Grangeville, ID) **10107**
Shopper, The (South Holland, IL) **10127**
Shopper Zone I (Durant, OK) **10245**
Shopper Zone II (Denison, TX) **10273**
Shopping News (Fairport, NY) **10213**
Shopping News (Platteville, WI) **10304**
Shopping News, The (Newton, MS) **10187**
Shoreline Chronicle (Sheboygan, WI) **10305**
Shoreview-Arden Hills Bulletin (St. Paul, MN) **10183**
Shoreview Press (St. Paul, MN) **10183**
Shorewood Herald (Wauwatosa, WI) **10307**
Shoshone News-Press (Kellogg, ID) **9977**
† Shreveport Journal (Shreveport, LA)
Sidney Daily News (Sidney, OH) **10026**

Sidney Herald-Leader (Sidney, MT) **10196**
Sidney Telegraph (Sidney, NE) **10010**
Sierra County Sentinel (Truth or Consequences, NM) **10209**
Sierra Madre News (Sierra Madre, CA) **10083**
Sierra Sun (Truckee, CA) **10084**
Sierra Vista Herald (Sierra Vista, AZ) **9958**
Signal-Item (Monroeville, PA) **10255**
Signal, The (Atwater, CA) **10069**
Signal, The (Valencia, CA) **9967**
Signal, The (Canal Fulton, OH) **10235**
Sigourney News-Review (Sigourney, IA) **10141**
Sikeston Standard Democrat, The (Sikeston, MO) **10007**
Silsbee Bee (Silsbee, TX) **10280**
Silver City Daily Press & Independent (Silver City, NM) **10014**
Silver Spring Gazette (Burtonsville, MD) **10158**
Silverton Appeal-Tribune/Mt. Angel News (Silverton, OR) **10250**
Silverton Standard & The Miner (Silverton, CO) **10089**
Simi Valley Star (Simi Valley, CA) **9966**
Sioux City Journal (Sioux City, IA) **9988**
Siskiyou Daily News (Yreka, CA) **9968**
Sisseton Courier (Sisseton, SD) **10265**
Siuslaw News, The (Florence, OR) **10248**
Skagit Valley Herald (Mt. Vernon, WA) **10051**
Skaneateles Press (Skaneateles, NY) **10223**
Skiatook Journal (Skiatook, OK) **10247**
Skokie Life (Lincolnwood, IL) **10122**
Skokie Review (Evanston, IL) **10117**
Skyline (Lincolnwood, IL) **10122**
Slatebelt Hometown News, The (Bangor, PA) **10251**
Slidell Sentry-News (Slidell, LA) **9995**
Smith County Pioneer (Smith Center, KS) **10146**
Smith County Reformer (Raleigh, MS) **10187**
Smithfield Herald (Smithfield, NC) **10230**
Smith Mountain Eagle (Moneta, VA) **10287**
Smithtown Messenger (Smithtown, NY) **10223**
Smithtown News, The (Smithtown, NY) **10223**
Smithville Lake Democrat-Herald, The (Smithville, MO) **10193**
Smithville Review (Smithville, TN) **10269**
Smyth County News & Messenger (Marion, VA) **10287**
† Snake River Press (Craig, CO)
Snohomish County Tribune (Snohomish, WA) **10293**
Snyder Daily News (Snyder, TX) **10046**
Soledad Bee (Soledad, CA) **10083**
Solon Herald Sun (Beachwood, OH) **10234**
Solon Times, The (Chagrin Falls, OH) **10235**

Solvang Santa Ynez Valley News (Solvang, CA) **10083**
Somerset Herald (Princess Anne, MD) **10159**
Somerset Messenger Gazette (Somerville, NJ) **10207**
Somerset Spectator (Somerset, NJ) **10206**
Somerville Journal (West Somerville, MA) **10166**
Sonoma County Independent (Santa Rosa, CA) **10083**
Sonoma Index Tribune (Sonoma, CA) **10083**
Sonoma West (Sebastopal, CA) **10083**
Sorento News (Hillsboro, IL) **10120**
Souderton Independent (Souderton, PA) **10259**
Sounder, The (Random Lake, WI) **10304**
Sound View News (Yonkers, NY) **10226**
South-West Review (St. Paul, MN) **10184**
South Alabamian (Jackson, AL) **10060**
Southampton Press (Southampton, NY) **10223**
South Bay's Newspaper (Lindenhurst, NY) **10217**
South Bay's Shopper (Lindenhurst, NY) **10217**
South Bay Extra (Torrance, CA) **10084**
South Bend Tri-County News (South Bend, IN) **10135**
South Bend Tribune (South Bend, IN) **9985**
South Bergenite (Rutherford, NJ) **10206**
South Boston Gazette-Virginian (South Boston, VA) **10289**
South Boston News & Record (South Boston, VA) **10289**
South Boston Tribune (Boston, MA) **10160**
South Buffalo News (Lackawanna, NY) **10216**
South City Journal (St. Louis, MO) **10194**
South Coast Shoppers/Penny Savers (Laguna Hills, CA) **10074**
South County Advertiser (Webster, MA) **10166**
South County Express (Auburn, IL) **10110**
South County Journal (St. Louis, MO) **10194**
South County News & Advertiser (Fort Worth, TX) **10275**
South Dade News (South Miami, FL) **10099**
South Dade News Leader (Homestead, FL) **10095**
South Dekalb Neighbor, The (Marietta, GA) **10104**
South District Journal (Seattle, WA) **10293**
† South East Metro Shopper (Cottage Grove, MN)
Southeast Missourian (Cape Girardeau, MO) **10005**
Southern Cayuga Tribune (Moravia, NY) **10219**
Southern County News (Thornton, IA) **10142**
Southern Dutchess News (Wappingers Falls, NY) **10224**

Southern Herald, The (Liberty, MS) **10186**
Southern Illinoisan (Carbondale, IL) **9978**
Southern Oklahoma Leader (Durant, OK) **10245**
Southern Pines Pilot (Southern Pines, NC) **10230**
Southern Standard (McMinnville, TN) **10268**
Southern Star (Ozark, AL) **10061**
Southfield Eccentric (Birmingham, MI) **10167**
South Fork Times (Monte Vista, CO) **10088**
South Fulton Neighbor, The (Marietta, GA) **10104**
South Gate Press (Los Angeles, CA) **10077**
South Haven Daily Tribune (South Haven, MI) **10002**
South Hill Enterprise (South Hill, VA) **10289**
South Hills Record (Pittsburgh, PA) **10258**
South Idaho Press (Burley, ID) **9977**
Southington Observer (Southington, CT) **10091**
South Jersey Advisor (Cologne, NJ) **10202**
South Lake Advertiser (Lowell, IN) **10133**
South Lyon Herald (South Lyon, MI) **10175**
South Miami News (Miami, FL) **10097**
South Milwaukee Voice Graphic (Wauwatosa, WI) **10307**
South Missourian News (Thayer, MO) **10194**
▼South Of The Boulevard (Woodland Hills, CA) **10085**
† South Pasadena Journal (Los Angeles, CA)
South Pasadena Review (South Pasadena, CA) **10084**
South Philadelphia Chronicle (Philadelphia, PA) **10258**
South Philadelphia Review (Philadelphia, PA) **10258**
South Pittsburgh Reporter (Pittsburgh, PA) **10258**
South Reporter, The (Holly Springs, MS) **10186**
South San Francisco Enterprise-Journal (San Mateo, CA) **10082**
South San Gabriel/Rosemead Progress (Los Angeles, CA) **10077**
South Shore News (Rockland, MA) **10165**
South Shore Record (Woodmere, NY) **10225**
Southside Journal (Los Angeles, CA) **10077**
Southside Journal (St. Louis, MO) **10194**
Southside Sentinel (Urbanna, VA) **10289**
† Southside Sun (East Point, GA)
South Sioux City Star (South Sioux City, NE) **10198**
South St. Paul/Inver Grove Heights Sun-Current (Burnsville, MN) **10177**
▼South Tampa News (Brandon, FL) **10093**
Southtowns Citizen (Orchard Park, NY) **10220**

Title

† South Valley Eagle (Salt Lake City, UT)
Southwest Beacon (Chicago, IL) **10113**
Southwest City Journal (St. Louis, MO) **10194**
Southwest County Journal (St. Louis, MO) **10194**
Southwest Courier (Chicago, IL) **10113**
Southwest Daily News (Sulphur, LA) **9995**
Southwestern Journal News (Brighton, IL) **10111**
Southwestern Pennsylvania Scene (Scottdale, PA) **10259**
Southwest Globe Times (Philadelphia, PA) **10258**
Southwest News (South Miami, FL) **10099**
Southwest News-Herald (Chicago, IL) **10113**
Southwest Newsweek, The (Louisville, KY) **10149**
Southwest Shopper (Chicago, IL) **10113**
Southwest Sun (Sugar Land, TX) **10281**
Southwest Times, The (Pulaski, VA) **10050**
Southwest Town Crier (La Porte, IN) **10133**
Southwest Tulsa News (Tulsa, OK) **10247**
Southwest Virginia Enterprise (Wytheville, VA) **10290**
Southwest Wave/News (Los Angeles, CA) **10077**
Spackenkill Sentinel (Wappingers Falls, NY) **10224**
Sparta/Kent City Advance (Sparta, MI) **10175**
Sparta Expositor (Sparta, TN) **10269**
Sparta Herald (Sparta, WI) **10305**
Sparta Independent (Sparta, NJ) **10207**
Sparta Ishmaelite (Sparta, GA) **10105**
Sparta News Plaindealer (Sparta, IL) **10127**
Spectator (Raleigh, NC) **10230**
Spectator, The (Somerset, MA) **10165**
Spectrum, The (St. George, UT) **10048**
Speedway Town Press (Speedway, IN) **10135**
Spencer County Journal Democrat (Rockport, IN) **10135**
Spencer Daily Reporter (Spencer, IA) **9988**
Spencer Evening World (Spencer, IN) **9986**
Spencer Magnet (Taylorsville, KY) **10151**
Spencer Random Harvest Weekly (Trumansburg, NY) **10224**
Spinal Column Newsweekly (Waterford, MI) **10176**
Spirit Lake Beacon (Spirit Lake, IA) **10141**
† Spirit of Bucks County (Hatboro, PA)
Spirit of Jefferson-Advocate (Charles Town, WV) **10294**
Spokesman-Review, The (Spokane, WA) **10051**
Spooner Advocate (Spooner, WI) **10305**
Spotlight, The (Washington, DC) **10093**
Spotlight, The (Indianapolis, IN) **10132**
Spotlight, The (Delmar, NY) **10213**

Sprague Advocate, The (Sprague, WA) **10293**
Springfield Advance-Press (Springfield, MN) **10183**
Springfield Advocate (Springfield, MA) **10165**
Springfield Leader (Union, NJ) **10207**
Springfield News-Leader, The (Springfield, MO) **10008**
Springfield News-Sun (Springfield, OH) **10026**
Springfield News, The (Springfield, OR) **10250**
Springfield Press (Springfield, PA) **10259**
Springfield Reporter, The (Springfield, VT) **10284**
Springfield Shopper (Springfield, IL) **10127**
Springfield Sun (Springfield, KY) **10151**
Springfield Sun (Fort Washington, PA) **10253**
Springfield Times Courier (Reston, VA) **10289**
Springhill Press (Springhill, LA) **10154**
Spring Hope Enterprise (Spring Hope, NC) **10230**
Springs Valley Herald (French Lick, IN) **10131**
Springtown Epigraph, The (Springtown, TX) **10281**
Spring Valley Bulletin (Lemon Grove, CA) **10075**
Spring Valley Sun (Spring Valley, WI) **10305**
Spring Valley Tribune (Spring Valley, MN) **10183**
Springview Herald (Springview, NE) **10198**
Springville Journal (Springville, NY) **10223**
† Squire, The (Prairie Village, KS)
St. Albans Messenger (St. Albans, VT) **10048**
Stamford American (Stamford, TX) **10281**
Standard & Times (Tuscumbia, AL) **10062**
Standard-Examiner (Ogden, UT) **10047**
Standard-Observer (Greensburg, PA) **10033**
Standard-Star (New Rochelle, NY) **10016**
Standard-Times (North Kingstown, RI) **10260**
Standard-Times, The (New Bedford, MA) **9998**
Standard Banner (Jefferson, TN) **10267**
Standard Journal (Rexburg, ID) **10109**
Stanley Republican (Stanley, WI) **10305**
Stanly News & Press (Albemarle, NC) **10226**
St. Anthony Bulletin (North St. Paul, MN) **10181**
Staples World (Staples, MN) **10183**
Star-Advocate (Titusville, FL) **10099**
Star-Democrat, The (Easton, MD) **9996**
Star-Gazette (Elmira, NY) **10015**
Star-Herald (Belton, MO) **10188**
Star-Herald (Scottsbluff, NE) **10010**
Star-Herald, The (Presque Isle, ME) **10157**
Star-Herald, The (Kosciusko, MS) **10186**
Star-Ledger (Newark, NJ) **10012**
Star-News, The (McCall, ID) **10108**
Star-News, The (North Syracuse, NY) **10220**
Star-Progress, The (Berryville, AR) **10065**

Star-Tribune (Chatham, VA) **10285**
Star Advertiser (Kalkaska, MI) **10172**
Star Buyers Guide (West Branch, MI) **10176**
Star Express (Covington, GA) **10102**
Star Gazette (Hackettstown, NJ) **10202**
Star Journal (Hope, IN) **10132**
Starkville Daily News (Starkville, MS) **10005**
Star News, The (Chula Vista, CA) **10070**
Star News, The (Medford, WI) **10302**
Star Press (Muncie, IN) **9985**
Star Press (Springboro, OH) **10243**
Star Republican (Wilmington, OH) **10244**
Star, The (Chicago Heights, IL) **10114**
Star, The (Sun Prairie, WI) **10306**
Star Tribune (Minneapolis, MN) **10003**
State Center Enterprise-Record (State
  Center, IA) **10141**
State Gazette (Dyersburg, TN) **10040**
State Journal-Register (Springfield, IL) **9981**
State Line Shopping Guide
  (Palmer, MA) **10164**
Staten Island Advance (Staten
  Island, NY) **10017**
Staten Island Register (Staten
  Island, NY) **10223**
State Port Pilot, The (Southport, NC) **10230**
Statesboro Herald (Statesboro, GA) **9976**
Statesman-Examiner (Colville, WA) **10291**
Statesman Journal (Salem, OR) **10032**
Statesville Record & Landmark
  (Statesville, NC) **10021**
State, The (Columbia, SC) **10038**
St. Augustine Record (St. Augustine, FL) **9973**
Staunton Star-Times (Staunton, IL) **10127**
Stayton Mail (Stayton, OR) **10250**
St. Bernard Voice (Arabi, LA) **10152**
St. Charles Journal (St. Charles, MO) **10193**
St. Charles Press (St. Charles, MN) **10183**
St. Clair Missourian (St. Clair, MO) **10193**
St. Clair News-Aegis (Pell City, AL) **10061**
St. Clair Shores Herald
  (Birmingham, MI) **10167**
St. Cloud Times (St. Cloud, MN) **10003**
St. Croix Avis (St. Croix, VI) **10048**
St. Croix Valley Peach (Forest
  Lake, MN) **10178**
St. Croix Valley Press (St. Paul, MN) **10184**
Steamboat Pilot (Steamboat
  Springs, CO) **10089**
Steamboat Today (Steamboat
  Springs, CO) **9969**
Steele Enterprise (Steel, MO) **10193**
Steelville Star/Crawford Mirror
  (Steelville, MO) **10193**
Ste. Genevieve Herald (Ste.
  Genevieve, MO) **10193**

Stephenville Empire-Tribune
  (Stephenville, TX) **10046**
Sterling Journal-Advocate (Sterling, CO) **9969**
Steuben Courier-Advocate (Bath, NY) **10210**
Stevens Point Journal (Stevens
  Point, WI) **10055**
St. Francis Herald, The (St.
  Francis, KS) **10146**
St. Francis Reminder-Enterprise
  (Wauwatosa, WI) **10307**
St. Helena Star (St. Helena, CA) **10084**
St. Helens Chronicle (St. Helens, OR) **10250**
Stigler News-Sentinel (Stigler, OK) **10247**
St. Ignace News, The (St. Ignace, MI) **10175**
Stillwater Gazette (Stillwater, MN) **10003**
Stillwater News-Press (Stillwater, OK) **10030**
Stillwater Valley Advertiser
  (Covington, OH) **10239**
Stilwell Democrat-Journal (Stilwell, OK) **10247**
St. James Leader Journal (St.
  James, MO) **10193**
St. James Plaindealer (St. James, MN) **10183**
St. John News (St. John, KS) **10146**
St. Johns Reminder (St. Johns, MI) **10175**
St. Johns Review (Portland, OR) **10250**
St. Joseph News-Press (St.
  Joseph, MO) **10008**
St. Joseph Telegraph, The (St.
  Joseph, MO) **10193**
St. Lawrence Plaindealer (Canton, NY) **10212**
St. Louis American Newspaper (St.
  Louis, MO) **10194**
† St. Louis Naborhood Link News (St.
  Louis, MO)
St. Louis Park Sun-Sailor
  (Minnetonka, MN) **10180**
St. Louis Post-Dispatch (St. Louis, MO) **10008**
St. Louis Sentinel Newspaper (St.
  Louis, MO) **10194**
† St. Louis South St. Louis County News (St.
  Louis, MO)
St. Louis Watchman Advocate (St.
  Louis, MO) **10008**
St. Maries Gazette Record (St.
  Maries, ID) **10109**
St. Martinville Teche News (St.
  Martinville, LA) **10154**
St. Mary Journal (Morgan City, LA) **10154**
St. Marys Star (St. Marys, KS) **10146**
Stoddard County News (Dexter, MO) **10006**
Stone County Citizen (Mountain
  View, AR) **10067**
Stone County Enterprise (Wiggins, MS) **10187**
Stone County Leader (Mountain
  View, AR) **10067**
† Stoneham Weekender News (Stoneham, MA)

Storm Lake Pilot Tribune (Storm Lake, IA) **9988**
Storm Lake Times (Storm Lake, IA) **10142**
Story City Herald (Story City, IA) **10142**
Stoughton Chronicle (Stoughton, MA) **10166**
Stowe Reporter (Stowe, VT) **10284**
Stow Sentry (Stow, OH) **10243**
St. Paul Pioneer Press (St. Paul, MN) **10003**
St. Peter Herald (St. Peter, MN) **10184**
St. Petersburg Times (St. Petersburg, FL) **9973**
Straits Area Star (Cheboygan, MI) **10168**
Stratford Bard (Milford, CT) **10091**
Stratford Journal (Stratford, WI) **10305**
Stratford Star (Konawa, OK) **10246**
Streator Times-Press (Streator, IL) **9981**
Stuart News (Stuart, FL) **9973**
Sturgis Journal (Sturgis, MI) **10002**
Sturgis News (Sturgis, KY) **10151**
Stuttgart Daily Leader (Stuttgart, AR) **9960**
Suburban & Wayne Times (Wayne, PA) **10259**
Suburban Advertiser (Wayne, PA) **10259**
Suburban Gazette (McKees Rocks, PA) **10254**
Suburbanite, The (Closter, NJ) **10202**
Suburbanite, The (Akron, OH) **10234**
Suburban Journal (Des Plaines, IL) **10115**
Suburban Leader (Chicago, IL) **10113**
Suburban Life (Butler, NJ) **10201**
Suburban Life (Loveland, OH) **10241**
Suburban Life Citizen (Oak Brook, IL) **10125**
Suburban Life Graphic (Oak Brook, IL) **10125**
Suburban News (Reading, MA) **10165**
Suburban News (Spencerport, NY) **10223**
Suburban News, The (Windham, ME) **10157**
Suburban Press (Millbury, OH) **10241**
Suburban Street News (White Plains, NY) **10225**
Suburban Town News (Paramus, NJ) **10205**
Suburban Trends (Butler, NJ) **10201**
Suburban Tribune (Balch Springs, TX) **10271**
Sudbury Town Crier (Waltham, MA) **10166**
Suffolk County News (Sayville, NY) **10222**
Suffolk News-Herald (Suffolk, VA) **10050**
Suffolk Times (Mattituck, NY) **10218**
Sullivan County News (Blountville, TN) **10265**
Sullivan Daily Times (Sullivan, IN) **9986**
Sullivan Independent News (Sullivan, MO) **10194**
Sullivan Review (Dushore, PA) **10252**
Sulphur Springs News-Telegram (Sulphur Springs, TX) **10046**
Summerville Journal Scene (Summerville, SC) **10264**
Summerville News (Summerville, GA) **10106**
Summit County Journal (Frisco, CO) **10087**
Summit Daily News (Frisco, CO) **9968**

Summit Independent Press (New Providence, NJ) **10205**
Summit Observer (Union, NJ) **10207**
Sumner Gazette (Sumner, IA) **10142**
Sumner Press (Sumner, IL) **10128**
Sumter County Record-Journal, The (Livingston, AL) **10060**
Sumter County Times (Bushnell, FL) **10094**
Sun & Erie County Independent, The (Hamburg, NY) **10215**
Sun & News, The (Hastings, MI) **10171**
Sun-Bulletin, The (Palisades Park, NJ) **10205**
Sun-Journal (Lewiston, ME) **9995**
Sun-Journal (New Bern, NC) **10020**
Sun-Reporter (San Francisco, CA) **10081**
Sun-Sentinel (Fort Lauderdale, FL) **9972**
Sun Advocate (Price, UT) **10283**
Sun Banner Pride (Cleveland, OH) **10236**
Sunbury News (Sunbury, OH) **10243**
Sun Chronicle (Attleboro, MA) **9996**
Sun Cities Independent (Sun City, AZ) **10065**
Sun City/Youngtown (Sun City, AZ) **10065**
Sun City News (Sun City, CA) **10084**
Sun City West (Sun City, AZ) **10065**
Sun Coast News (New Port Richey, FL) **10097**
Sun Courier, The (Cleveland, OH) **10236**
Sunday Bucks County Telegraph (Horsham, PA) **10253**
Sunday Dispatch (Pittston, PA) **10258**
† Sunday Glades Trend (Clewiston, FL)
Sunday Independent, The (Owosso, MI) **10173**
Sunday Post (Lynn, MA) **10162**
† Sunday Sun (Scranton, PA)
Sunday Sun (Georgetown, TX) **10275**
Sun Herald (North Port, FL) **10097**
Sun Herald, The (Gulfport, MS) **10004**
Sun Herald, The (Cleveland, OH) **10236**
Sun Journal, The (North Canton, OH) **10242**
Sun Messenger, The (Cleveland, OH) **10236**
Sun News, The (Myrtle Beach, SC) **10038**
Sun Post (Miami Beach, FL) **10097**
Sun Post News (San Clemente, CA) **10080**
Sun Press (Kaneohe, HI) **10107**
Sun Press (Cleveland, OH) **10236**
Sunriser News (Ossian, IN) **10134**
Sunrise Times (Coral Springs, FL) **10094**
Sun Scoop Journal (Cleveland, OH) **10236**
Sun Star, The (Cleveland, OH) **10236**
Sun, The (Exeter, CA) **10072**
Sun, The (Sun City Center, FL) **10099**
Sun, The (Mt. Vernon, IA) **10140**
Sun, The (Cleveland, OH) **10237**
Sun, The (Hummelstown, PA) **10253**
Sun, The (Bremerton, WA) **10050**
Sun Times (Heber Springs, AR) **10066**
Sun Times (Perryville, MO) **10192**

Superior Daily Telegram (Superior, WI) **10055**
Superior Express, The (Superior, NE) **10198**
† Surfside News (South Miami, FL)
Surry Scene, The (Mount Airy, NC) **10229**
Susquehanna County Independent
   (Montrose, PA) **10255**
Sussex-Lannon-Lisbon News
   (Wauwatosa, WI) **10308**
Sussex-Surry Dispatch (Wakefield, VA) **10289**
Sussex Countian (Georgetown, DE) **10092**
Sussex County Chronicle (Byram, NJ) **10201**
Sussex Post, The (Lewes, DE) **10092**
Sussex Sun (Hartland, WI) **10300**
Swampscott Reporter
   (Marblehead, MA) **10162**
Swanton Enterprise (Swanton, OH) **10243**
Swap Sheet (Ridgecrest, CA) **10080**
Sweetwater Reporter (Sweetwater, TX) **10046**
† Sycamore Messenger (Cincinnati, OH)
Sycamore News (Sycamore, IL) **10128**
Sylva Herald & Ruralite (Sylva, NC) **10231**
Sylvania Herald (Toledo, OH) **10243**
Sylvester Local News (Sylvester, GA) **10106**
Syosset Jericho Tribune (Mineola, NY) **10219**
Syracuse Herald-Journal/American
   (Syracuse, NY) **10017**
Syracuse Journal-Democrat
   (Syracuse, NE) **10198**
Syracuse New Times (Syracuse, NY) **10224**

T

T-Ville News Trader (Tompkinsville, KY) **10151**
Table Rock Gazette (Kimberling
   City, MO) **10191**
Tab, The (Needham, MA) **10164**
Taft Tribune (Taft, TX) **10281**
Tahlequah Daily Press (Tahlequah, OK) **10030**
Tahoe Daily Tribune (South Lake
   Tahoe, CA) **9966**
Tahoe World (Tahoe City, CA) **10084**
Tallahassean (Tallahassee, FL) **10099**
Tallahassee Democrat (Tallahassee, FL) **9974**
Tallassee Tribune (Tallassee, AL) **10062**
Tallmadge Express (Stow, OH) **10243**
Tama News-Herald (Tama, IA) **10142**
Tamarac Forum (Coral Springs, FL) **10094**
Tampa Tribune, The (Tampa, FL) **9974**
▼Taney County Times (Forsyth, MO) **10189**
Taos News (Taos, NM) **10209**
Tarkio Avalanche (Tarkio, MO) **10194**
Tarrytown Daily News (White
   Plains, NY) **10018**
Taunton Daily Gazette (Taunton, MA) **9998**
Taunton Independent (Middleboro, MA) **10163**
Tavares Citizen (Mount Dora, FL) **10097**

Taylor Clarion (Burwell, NE) **10197**
Taylor Daily Press (Taylor, TX) **10046**
Taylorsville Times, The
   (Taylorsville, NC) **10231**
Taylorville Breeze-Courier (Taylorville, IL) **9981**
Tazewell County Free Press
   (Richlands, VA) **10289**
Tazewell News (Morton, IL) **10124**
Tech Center News (Warren, MI) **10176**
Tecumseh Herald (Tecumseh, MI) **10175**
Tehachapi News (Tehachapi, CA) **10084**
Telegram & Gazette (Worcester, MA) **9999**
Telegraph-County Edition
   (Jerseyville, IL) **10120**
Telegraph Herald (Dubuque, IA) **9987**
TeleGraphics (Lawrence, KS) **10144**
Telegraph, The (Alton, IL) **9977**
Telegraph, The (Dixon, IL) **9979**
Telegraph, The (North Platte, NE) **10010**
Telegraph, The (Hudson, NH) **10011**
Telfair Enterprise (McRae, GA) **10105**
Telfair Times (Helena, GA) **10103**
Telluride Daily Planet (Telluride, CO) **9969**
Telluride Times-Journal (Telluride, CO) **10089**
Tempe Daily News Tribune (Tempe, AZ) **9958**
Temple Daily Telegram (Temple, TX) **10046**
Temple Terrace Beacon (Tampa, FL) **10099**
Temple Terrace News (Brandon, FL) **10093**
Tenino Independent (Tenino, WA) **10293**
Tennessean, The (Nashville, TN) **10041**
Terrell Tribune (Terrell, TX) **10047**
Teton Valley News (Driggs, ID) **10107**
Texarkana Gazette (Texarkana, TX) **10047**
Texas City Sun (Texas City, TX) **10047**
Texas Observer (Austin, TX) **10271**
The Dalles Daily Chronicle (The
   Dalles, OR) **10032**
Thief River Falls Times, The (Thief River
   Falls, MN) **10184**
† This Week (Aledo, IL)
This Week (Cherry Hill, NJ) **10202**
This Week In Bexley (Columbus, OH) **10237**
This Week In Clintonville
   (Columbus, OH) **10238**
This Week In Delaware (Columbus, OH) **10238**
This Week In Eastside (Columbus, OH) **10238**
This Week In Grandview
   (Columbus, OH) **10238**
This Week In Hilliard (Columbus, OH) **10238**
This Week In New Albany
   (Columbus, OH) **10238**
This Week In Northland
   (Columbus, OH) **10238**
This Week In Peachtree City (Peachtree
   City, GA) **10105**

This Week In Pickerington
(Columbus, OH) **10238**
This Week In Powell (Columbus, OH) **10238**
This Week In Reynoldsburg
(Columbus, OH) **10238**
This Week In Southside
(Columbus, OH) **10238**
This Week In Union County
(Columbus, OH) **10238**
This Week In Westerville
(Columbus, OH) **10238**
This Week In Westside (Columbus, OH) **10238**
This Week In Worthington
(Columbus, OH) **10238**
Thomaston Times (Thomaston, GA) **10106**
Thomasville Times (Thomasville, NC) **10231**
Thomasville Times-Enterprise
(Thomasville, GA) **9976**
Thorp Courier (Thorp, WI) **10306**
Thousand Islands Sun (Alexandria
Bay, NY) **10209**
Thousand Oaks Star (Thousand
Oaks, CA) **9966**
Thousandsticks (Hyden, KY) **10148**
Three Rivers Commercial-News (Three
Rivers, MI) **10002**
Three Rivers Gazette (Helena, GA) **10103**
Three Star Edition (Philadelphia, PA) **10258**
Three Village Herald (East
Setauket, NY) **10213**
Three Village Times (Mineola, NY) **10219**
Thrif-T-Nikel Weekly Newspaper
(Ottawa, IL) **10125**
Thrifty Nickel (Birmingham, AL) **10058**
Thrifty Nickel (Champaign, IL) **10112**
Thrifty Nickel Want Ads (East
Moline, IL) **10116**
Tidewater Review (West Point, VA) **10290**
Tifton Gazette (Tifton, GA) **9976**
Tigard Times (Tigard, OR) **10250**
Tiller & Toiler (Larned, KS) **9990**
Times & Democrat, The
(Orangeburg, SC) **10038**
Times-Bulletin (Van Wert, OH) **10027**
Times-Clarion, The (Harlowton, MT) **10195**
Times-Courier (Ellijay, GA) **10103**
Times-Express (Monroeville, PA) **10255**
Times-Georgian (Carrollton, GA) **9974**
Times-Herald (Timonium, MD) **10159**
Times-Indicator (Fremont, MI) **10169**
Times-Journal, The (Fort Payne, AL) **9956**
Times-Journal, The (Condon, OR) **10248**
Times-Leader (Union City, PA) **10259**
Times-Mail (Bedford, IN) **9982**
Times-News, The (Burlington, NC) **10018**
Times-Picayune (New Orleans, LA) **9994**

Times-Press (Hartford, WI) **10300**
Times-Press (Seymour, WI) **10305**
Times-Record (Brunswick, ME) **9995**
Times-Record, The (Denton, MD) **10158**
Times-Reporter (New Philadelphia, OH) **10026**
Times-Sentinel, The (Cheney, KS) **10143**
Times-Standard (Eureka, CA) **9962**
Times-Sun, The (West Newton, PA) **10260**
Times-Union (Warsaw, IN) **9986**
Times-Union (Rochester, NY) **10017**
Times Argus (Barre, VT) **10048**
Times Chronicle (Jenkintown, PA) **10254**
Times Citizen (Iowa Falls, IA) **10139**
Times Daily (Florence, AL) **9956**
Times Dispatch (Walnut Ridge, AR) **10068**
Times Free Press (Ayer, MA) **10160**
Times Guthrian (Guthrie Center, IA) **10138**
Times Herald (Port Huron, MI) **10001**
Times Herald-Record (Middletown, NY) **10016**
Times Herald, The (Norristown, PA) **10035**
Times Journal-Spotlight (Eastman, GA) **10103**
Times Leader (Martins Ferry, OH) **10025**
Times Leader (Wilkes Barre, PA) **10037**
Times Leader, The (Princeton, KY) **10151**
Times News (Lehighton, PA) **10034**
Times Newsweekly (Ridgewood, NY) **10222**
Times of Nesconset, The
(Setauket, NY) **10222**
Times of Northeast Benton County (Pea
Ridge, AR) **10067**
Times of Smithtown (Setauket, NY) **10222**
Times of St. James (Setauket, NY) **10222**
Times of Ti (Elizabethtown, NY) **10213**
Times Post, The (Houston, MS) **10186**
Times Record (Fayette, AL) **10059**
Times Record (Aledo, IL) **10109**
Times Record (Spencer, WV) **10296**
Times Recorder, The (Zanesville, OH) **10028**
Times Record News (Wichita Falls, TX) **10047**
Times, The (North Little Rock, AR) **10067**
Times, The (Melbourne, FL) **10096**
Times, The (Gainesville, GA) **9975**
Times, The (Lansing, IL) **9980**
Times, The (Munster, IN) **9985**
† Times, The (Augusta, KY)
Times, The (Shreveport, LA) **9995**
Times, The (Webster, MA) **10166**
Times, The (Forest Lake, MN) **10178**
Times, The (Trenton, NJ) **10012**
Times, The (Westfield, NJ) **10208**
Times, The (Columbus, OH) **10238**
Times, The (Port Royal, PA) **10258**
Times, The (Pawtucket, RI) **10037**
Times, The (Waitsburg, WA) **10294**
Times, The (Westby, WI) **10308**
† Times Tribune (Palo Alto, CA)

Times Union (Albany, NY) **10014**
Times West Virginian (Fairmont, WV) **10052**
Tioga County Gazette & Times
(Owego, NY) **10220**
Tipp City Herald (Tipp City, OH) **10243**
Tipton Conservative & Advertiser
(Tipton, IA) **10142**
† Tipton News Leader (Altus, OK)
Tipton Tribune (Tipton, IN) **9986**
Titusville Herald (Titusville, PA) **10036**
Today (Orange Park, FL) **10098**
Today's Daily News-Herald (Lake Havasu
City, AZ) **9958**
Today's Sunbeam (Salem, NJ) **10012**
Todd County Standard (Elkton, KY) **10147**
Toledo Blade (Toledo, OH) **10027**
Tomahawk Leader (Tomahawk, WI) **10306**
Tomahawk, The (Mountain City, TN) **10268**
Tomah Journal (Tomah, WI) **10306**
Tomah Monitor-Herald (Tomah, WI) **10306**
Tombstone Epitaph, The
(Tombstone, AZ) **10065**
Tomorrow (New Rochelle, NY) **10220**
Tompkinsville News (Tompkinsville, KY) **10151**
Tonawanda News (North
Tonawanda, NY) **10016**
Tonkawa News, The (Tonkawa, OK) **10247**
Tonopah Times-Bonanza & Goldfield News
(Tonopah, NV) **10199**
Tooele Transcript-Bulletin (Tooele, UT) **10283**
Topics Sun Wave (Los Angeles, CA) **10077**
Toppenish Review (Toppenish, WA) **10293**
Torrington Telegram (Torrington, WY) **10309**
† Total, The (Heflin, AL)
† Town & Country (Bradford, PA)
Town & Country (Pennsburg, PA) **10257**
Town & Country Weekly (Ottawa, IL) **10125**
Town-Crier (West Palm Beach, FL) **10100**
Town 'n Country News (Tampa, FL) **10099**
Town Crier (Stockbridge, MI) **10175**
Town Crier, The (La Porte, IN) **10133**
Towne & Country Shopper
(Columbus, KS) **10143**
Towne Courier (East Lansing, MI) **10169**
Town of Paradise Valley Independent
(Scottsdale, AZ) **10064**
Township Times (Saginaw, MI) **10174**
Town Talk (Folsom, PA) **10253**
Town Talk (Media, PA) **10255**
Town Topics (Princeton, NJ) **10206**
Towson Times (Towson, MD) **10160**
Tracy Headlight-Herald (Tracy, MN) **10184**
Tracy Press (Tracy, CA) **9966**
Tradewinds (St. John, VI) **10284**
Traer Star-Clipper (Traer, IA) **10142**
† Transcript-Telegram (Holyoke, MA)

Transcript, The (North Adams, MA) **9998**
Transcript, The (Dover, NH) **10199**
Transcript, The (Morrisville, VT) **10284**
Transylvania Times, The (Brevard, NC) **10227**
Traveler/Watchman (Southold, NY) **10223**
Traverse City Record-Eagle (Traverse
City, MI) **10002**
Trentonian, The (Trenton, NJ) **10012**
Trenton Republican Times
(Trenton, MO) **10008**
Trenton Sun, The (Trenton, IL) **10128**
Trenton Tribune (Trenton, TX) **10281**
Tri-City Herald (Kennewick, WA) **10051**
Tri-City Independent (Margate, FL) **10096**
Tri-City Ledger (Flomaton, AL) **10059**
Tri-City News (Cumberland, KY) **10147**
Tri-City Record, The (Watervliet, MI) **10176**
Tri-City Reporter (Dyer, TN) **10266**
† Tri-City Times (Geraldine, AL)
Tri-City Times (Imlay City, MI) **10171**
Tri-City Trib (Cozad, NE) **10197**
Tri-City Tribune (Marked Tree, AR) **10066**
Tri-County Advertiser (Brockport, NY) **10210**
Tri-County Banner (Knightstown, IN) **10133**
Tri-County Citizen (Chesaning, MI) **10168**
Tri-County Journal (Pacific, MO) **10192**
Tri-County News (Elmwood, IL) **10116**
Tri-County News (Edinburgh, IN) **10130**
Tri-County News (Lockport, NY) **10217**
Tri-County News (Knoxville, TN) **10267**
Tri-County News (Osseo, WI) **10303**
Tri-County Press (Cincinnati, OH) **10236**
Tri-County Press (Cuba City, WI) **10299**
Tri-County Record (Rushford, MN) **10182**
Tri-County Times, The (Slater, IA) **10141**
Tri-County Trader (Waldron, AR) **10068**
Tri-State Advertiser (Palm Desert, CA) **10079**
Tri-Town News (Sidney, NY) **10223**
Tri-Town Transcript (Ipswich, MA) **10162**
Tri-Valley Herald (Pleasanton, CA) **9964**
Tri-Village News (Columbus, OH) **10238**
Tribune (Deer Park, WA) **10291**
Tribune-Courier (Ontario, OH) **10242**
Tribune-Review (Greensburg, PA) **10033**
Tribune-Star (Terre Haute, IN) **9986**
Tribune-Times (Fountain Inn, SC) **10262**
Tribune Chronicle, The (Warren, OH) **10027**
Tribune Courier (Benton, KY) **10146**
Tribune Democrat, The
(Johnstown, PA) **10034**
Tribune Plus (Royal Oak, MI) **10174**
Tribune Press Reporter (Glenwood
City, WI) **10300**
Tribune Shopping News (New
Lexington, OH) **10242**
Tribune, The (Oakland, CA) **9963**

Tribune, The (Monument, CO) **10089**
Tribune, The (Fort Pierce, FL) **9972**
Tribune, The (Melbourne, FL) **10096**
Tribune, The (Seymour, IN) **9985**
Tribune, The (Elkin, NC) **10227**
Tribune, The (Tabor City, NC) **10231**
Tribune, The (Bethany, OK) **10245**
Tribune, The (Scranton, PA) **10036**
Tri City Register (Riverton, IL) **10127**
Trinity Journal (Weaverville, CA) **10084**
Troy-Somerset Gazette (Troy, MI) **10175**
Troy Daily News (Troy, OH) **10027**
Troy Eccentric (Rochester Hills, MI) **10174**
Troy Free Press & Silex Index
   (Troy, MO) **10194**
True Citizen, The (Waynesboro, GA) **10106**
Trumann Democrat (Trumann, AR) **10068**
Trumansburg Free Press
   (Trumansburg, NY) **10224**
Trumbull Times (Monroe, CT) **10091**
Tryon Daily Bulletin (Tryon, NC) **10021**
Tucker-DeKalb Neighbor, The
   (Atlanta, GA) **10101**
Tucson Citizen (Tucson, AZ) **9958**
Tulare Advance-Register (Tulare, CA) **9966**
Tullahoma News (Tullahoma, TN) **10270**
Tulsa World (Tulsa, OK) **10030**
Tundra Drums (Bethel, AK) **10062**
Tundra Times (Anchorage, AK) **10062**
Tunkhannock New Age-Examiner
   (Tunkhannock, PA) **10259**
Tupper Lake Free Press & Herald (Tupper
   Lake, NY) **10224**
Turlock Journal (Turlock, CA) **9967**
Turtle Lake Times, The (Turtle
   Lake, WI) **10306**
Turtle Mountain Star, The (Rolla, ND) **10233**
Tuscaloosa News, The (Tuscaloosa, AL) **9957**
Tuscola County Advertiser (Caro, MI) **10168**
Tuscola Review (Tuscola, IL) **10128**
Tuskegee News (Tuskegee, AL) **10062**
Tustin News (Santa Ana, CA) **10082**
Twin-City News, The
   (Batesburg-Leesville, SC) **10261**
Twin Cities Reader (Minneapolis, MN) **10180**
Twin Cities Times (Corte Madera, CA) **10071**
Twin City News, The
   (Chattahoochee, FL) **10094**
Twin Falls Times-News (Twin Falls, ID) **9977**
▼Twinsburg Sun, The (Cleveland, OH) **10237**
Tyler County Booster (Woodville, TX) **10282**
Tyler Morning Telegraph (Tyler, TX) **10047**
Tyler Star News (Sistersville, WV) **10296**
Tylertown Times (Tylertown, MS) **10187**
Tyler Tribune (Tyler, MN) **10184**

U

UA This Week (Columbus, OH) **10238**
Uinta County Herald (Evanston, WY) **10308**
Uintah Basin Standard (Roosevelt, UT) **10283**
Ukiah Daily Journal (Ukiah, CA) **9967**
Ulster County Townsman
   (Woodstock, NY) **10225**
Ulysses News (Ulysses, KS) **10146**
Umpqua Free Press (Myrtle Creek, OR) **10249**
Underwood News (Underwood, ND) **10233**
Unida Latina (Oxford, PA) **10257**
Union-News (Springfield, MA) **9998**
Union-Recorder (Milledgeville, GA) **9975**
Union-Sun & Journal (Lockport, NY) **10015**
Union City Daily Messenger (Union
   City, TN) **10041**
Union County Advocate
   (Morganfield, KY) **10150**
Union Daily Times (Union, SC) **10039**
Uniondale Beacon (Hicksville, NY) **10216**
Union Democrat, The (Sonora, CA) **9966**
Union Enterprise (Plainwell, MI) **10174**
Union Leader (Union, NJ) **10207**
Union Leader/New Hampshire Sunday News
   (Manchester, NH) **10011**
Union Press-Courier (Patton, PA) **10257**
† Union Shopper, The (Arcata, CA)
Union Springs Herald (Union
   Springs, AL) **10062**
† Union, The (Arcata, CA)
Union, The (Grass Valley, CA) **9962**
Unionville Republican, The
   (Unionville, MO) **10194**
University Herald (Seattle, WA) **10293**
Upper Arlington News (Columbus, OH) **10238**
Upper Country News-Reporter
   (Cambridge, ID) **10107**
Upper Darby Press (Drexel Hill, PA) **10252**
Upper Dauphin Sentinel
   (Millersburg, PA) **10255**
Upper Rogue Independent (Eagle
   Point, OR) **10248**
Upper Sandusky Daily Chief-Union (Upper
   Sandusky, OH) **10027**
Uptown San Diego Examiner (San
   Diego, CA) **10081**
Urbana Daily Citizen (Urbana, OH) **10027**
Utica Herald (Utica, OH) **10243**
Uvalde Leader-News (Uvalde, TX) **10281**

V

Vadnais Heights Press (St. Paul, MN) **10184**
Vail Daily (Vail, CO) **9970**
Vailsburg Leader (Maplewood, NJ) **10204**
Vail Trail (Eagle-Vail, CO) **10086**

Valders Journal (Valders, WI) **10306**
Valdese News (Morganton, NC) **10229**
Valdez Vanguard (Valdez, AK) **10063**
Valdosta Daily Times (Valdosta, GA) **9976**
Valencia County News-Bulletin
  (Belen, NM) **10208**
Valentine Newspaper (Valentine, NE) **10198**
Vallejo Times-Herald (Vallejo, CA) **9967**
Valley Advocate (Hatfield, MA) **10162**
Valley Banner, The (Elkton, VA) **10286**
Valley City Times-Record (Valley
  City, ND) **10022**
Valley Courier (Alamosa, CO) **9968**
Valley Daily News (Kent, WA) **10051**
Valley Falls Vindicator (Valley Falls, KS) **10146**
Valley Farmer, The (Bay City, MI) **10167**
Valley Gazette (Shelton, CT) **10091**
Valley Gazette (Lansford, PA) **10254**
Valley Herald, The (Spokane, WA) **10293**
Valley Independent (Monessen, PA) **10035**
Valley Journal (Carbondale, CO) **10086**
Valley Log, The (Orbisonia, PA) **10256**
Valley Morning Star (Harlingen, TX) **10044**
Valley News (Meridian, ID) **10108**
Valley News (West Lebanon, NH) **10011**
Valley News (Elizabethtown, NY) **10213**
Valley News (Fulton, NY) **10214**
Valley News Dispatch (Tarentum, PA) **10036**
Valley News, The (Endwell, NY) **10213**
Valley News, The (Jefferson, OH) **10240**
Valley News Today-Daily Sentinel
  (Shenandoah, IA) **9988**
Valley Post (Anderson, CA) **10069**
Valley Reporter, The (Waitsfield, VT) **10284**
Valley Roadrunner (Valley Center, CA) **10084**
Valley Stream Courier (Freeport, NY) **10214**
Valley Stream Herald (Lawrence, NY) **10217**
Valley Stream Maileader (Mineola, NY) **10219**
Valley Sun (Wasilla, AK) **10063**
Valley Sun, The (Scottsboro, AL) **10061**
Valley Times (Moreno Valley, CA) **10078**
Valley Times (Pleasanton, CA) **9964**
Valley Times-News (Lanett, AL) **9956**
Valley Times-Star (Newville, PA) **10256**
Valley Town Crier (McAllen, TX) **10278**
Valley Trader (Lewisburg, PA) **10254**
Valley Value Shopper (Spring
  Valley, WI) **10305**
Valley Vantage (Sherman Oaks, CA) **10083**
Valparaiso Guide (Portage, IN) **10135**
Valparaiso Vidette-Times (Valparaiso, IN) **9986**
Van Buren County Advertiser
  (Gobles, MI) **10170**
Vandalia Leader-Union (Vandalia, IL) **10128**
Vandergrift News (Vandergrift, PA) **10259**
Van Horn Advocate (Van Horn, TX) **10281**

Vashon-Maury Island Beachcomber
  (Vashon, WA) **10293**
Vassar Pioneer Times (Vassar, MI) **10175**
Vega Enterprise, The (Vega, TX) **10281**
Venice-Marina News (Santa
  Monica, CA) **10082**
Venice Gondolier (Venice, FL) **10100**
† Ventura Bulletin, The (Los Angeles, CA)
Ventura County & Coast Reporter
  (Ventura, CA) **10084**
Ventura County Star (Ventura, CA) **9967**
Verde Independent (Cottonwood, AZ) **10063**
Vermilion Photojournal (Vermilion, OH) **10243**
Vermont News Guide (Manchester
  Center, VT) **10284**
Vermont Times (Shelburne, VT) **10284**
Vernal Express (Vernal, UT) **10283**
Vernon County Broadcaster
  (Viroqua, WI) **10306**
Vernon Daily Record (Vernon, TX) **10047**
Vernon Hills News (Grayslake, IL) **10119**
Vernon Hills Review (Bannockburn, IL) **10110**
Verona-Cedar Grove Times
  (Verona, NJ) **10207**
Verona Press (Verona, WI) **10306**
Versailles Leader-Statesman
  (Versailles, MO) **10194**
Versailles Policy, The (Versailles OH) **10243**
Versailles Republican (Versailles, IN) **10136**
Vestal Town Crier (Conklin, NY) **10212**
Vevay Reveille-Enterprise (Vevay, IN) **10136**
Vicksburg Post (Vicksburg, MS) **10005**
† Victor-Farmington Herald (Webster, NY)
Victor Echo (Victor, IA) **10142**
Victoria Advocate (Victoria, TX) **10047**
Victor Valley Advertiser (Palm
  Desert, CA) **10079**
† Victor Valley Living (Hesperia, CA)
Vidorian, The (Vidor, TX) **10281**
Vienna Times (Reston, VA) **10289**
Vienna Times, The (Vienna, IL) **10128**
Vilas County News-Review (Eagle
  River, WI) **10299**
Village Advocate (Chapel Hill, NC) **10227**
Village Beacon-Record, The
  (Setauket, NY) **10222**
† Village Journal (Osterville, MA)
Village News (Gaithersburg, MD) **10158**
Villager (St. Paul, MN) **10184**
Villager Newspaper (Austin, TX) **10271**
Villager, The (New York, NY) **10220**
Villager, The (Syracuse, NY) **10224**
Villager, The (Moscow, PA) **10255**
Village Times, The (Setauket, NY) **10222**
Village Voice, The (New York, NY) **10220**
Villa Park Argus (Elmhurst, IL) **10116**

Villa Rican (Villa Rica, GA) **10106**
Ville Platte Gazette (Ville Platte, LA) **10155**
Vincennes Sun-Commercial
  (Vincennes, IN) **9986**
† Vincennes Valley Advance (Vincennes, IN)
Vindicator, The (Youngstown, OH) **10027**
Vindicator, The (Liberty, TX) **10278**
Vineyard Gazette (Edgartown, MA) **10161**
Vinita Daily Journal (Vinita, OK) **10030**
Vinton Cedar Valley Daily Times
  (Vinton, IA) **9988**
† Vinton County Courier (McArthur, OH)
Vinton Messenger (Vinton, VA) **10289**
Virginia Beach Sun (Virginia Beach, VA) **10289**
Virginia Gazette (Beardstown, IL) **10111**
Virginia Gazette (Williamsburg, VA) **10290**
Virginia Mountaineer (Grundy, VA) **10286**
Virginian-Leader (Pearisburg, VA) **10288**
Virginian-Pilot, The (Norfolk, VA) **10049**
Virginian Pilot (Kill Devil Hills, NC) **10020**
Virginian Review (Covington, VA) **10049**
Virgin Islands Daily News (St.
  Thomas, VI) **10048**
Visalia Times-Delta (Visalia, CA) **9967**
† Vista Press (Kansas City, MO)
Voice-Tribune, The (Louisville, KY) **10149**
Voice Ledger, The (Millbrook, NY) **10218**
Voice of the Valley (Maple Valley, WA) **10292**
Voices (Southbury, CT) **10091**
Voice, The (Phoenixville, PA) **10258**

W

Wabash Plain Dealer (Wabash, IN) **9986**
Waco Citizen, The (Waco, TX) **10281**
Waconia Patriot (Waconia, MN) **10184**
Waco Tribune Herald (Waco, TX) **10047**
Wadena Pioneer Journal (Wadena, MN) **10184**
Wagoner Tribune, The (Wagoner, OK) **10247**
Wahkiakum County Eagle, The
  (Cathlamet, WA) **10291**
Wahoo Newspaper (Wahoo, NE) **10198**
Wakefield Item (Wakefield, MA) **9998**
Wake Weekly, The (Wake Forest, NC) **10231**
Wakulla News (Crawfordville, FL) **10094**
Walker-Westside Advance (Jenison, MI) **10171**
Walker County Messenger (La
  Fayette, GA) **10104**
Wallace Enterprise (Wallace, NC) **10231**
† Wallace Miner (Kellogg, ID)
Walla Walla Union-Bulletin (Walla
  Walla, WA) **10052**
Waller County News-Citizen
  (Hempstead, TX) **10276**
Wallis News-Review (Wallis, TX) **10281**
Wallkill Valley Times, The (Walden, NY) **10224**

Walpole Times, The (Walpole, MA) **10166**
Walsh County Press (Park River, ND) **10233**
Walsh County Record, The
  (Grafton, ND) **10232**
Walton Tribune (Monroe, GA) **10105**
Walworth Times, The (Walworth, WI) **10306**
Wampum Saver (Show Low, AZ) **10064**
Wantagh-Seaford Citizen (Bellmore, NY) **10210**
Wapakoneta Daily News
  (Wapakoneta, OH) **10027**
Wapato Independent (Wapato, WA) **10294**
Wareham Courier (Marion, MA) **10163**
Ware River News (Ware, MA) **10166**
Warner Center News (Woodland
  Hills, CA) **10085**
Warren-Newport Press (Grayslake, IL) **10119**
Warren Record, The (Warrenton, NC) **10231**
Warrensburg-Lake George News
  (Elizabethtown, NY) **10213**
Warren Sheaf (Warren, MN) **10184**
Warren Times Gazette (Warren, RI) **10261**
Warren Times Observer (Warren, PA) **10037**
† Warrenton Banner (Warrenton, MO)
Warrenton News-Journal
  (Warrenton, MO) **10194**
Warrenville Free Press (West
  Chicago, IL) **10128**
Warsaw-Faison News (Wallace, NC) **10231**
Warsaw Benton County Enterprise
  (Warsaw, MO) **10195**
Warwick Advertiser, The (Warwick, NY) **10224**
Warwick Beacon (Warwick, RI) **10261**
Warwick Valley Dispatch (Warwick, NY) **10224**
Wasco Tribune (Wasco, CA) **10084**
Waseca County News (Waseca, MN) **10184**
Washburn County Register (Shell
  Lake, WI) **10305**
Washburn Leader (Metamora, IL) **10123**
Washington City Paper
  (Washington, DC) **10093**
Washington County Edition (Salem, IN) **10135**
Washington County News (Chatom, AL) **10058**
Washington County News
  (Washington, KS) **10146**
Washington County News
  (Abingdon, VA) **10284**
Washington Courier (Washington, IL) **10128**
Washington Daily News
  (Washington, NC) **10021**
Washington Evening Journal
  (Washington, IA) **9988**
Washington Missourian
  (Washington, MO) **10195**
Washington News-Reporter
  (Washington, GA) **10106**
Washington Post, The (Washington, DC) **9971**

Washington Reporter (Morton, IL) **10124**
Washington Times (Washington, DC) **9971**
Washington Times-Herald
  (Washington, IN) **9986**
Waterbury Republican-American
  (Waterbury, CT) **9971**
Waterford News (Winton, CA) **10085**
Waterford Post (Waterford, WI) **10306**
Waterfront of Missaukee County (Lake
  City, MI) **10172**
Waterloo Courier (Waterloo, IA) **9988**
Waterloo Republic-Times (Waterloo, IL) **10128**
Watertown Daily Times
  (Watertown, NY) **10017**
Watertown Daily Times (Watertown, WI) **10055**
Watertown Press (Somerville, MA) **10165**
Watertown Public Opinion
  (Watertown, SD) **10039**
Watertown Sun (Needham, MA) **10164**
Watkins Review & Express (Watkins
  Glen, NY) **10225**
Watonga Republican, The
  (Watonga, OK) **10247**
Wauconda Leader (Grayslake, IL) **10119**
Waukon Standard (Waukon, IA) **10142**
Waunakee Tribune (Waunakee, WI) **10306**
Waupun Leader News (Waupun, WI) **10306**
Wausau Daily Herald (Wausau, WI) **10055**
Waushara Argus (Wautoma, WI) **10307**
Wauwatosa News-Times
  (Wauwatosa, WI) **10308**
Waverly Bremer County Independent
  (Waverly, IA) **10142**
Waverly Democrat (Waverly, IA) **10142**
Waverly Journal (Waverly, IL) **10128**
Waxahachie Daily Light
  (Waxahachie, TX) **10047**
Waycross Journal Herald (Waycross, GA) **9976**
Wayland-Weston Town Crier
  (Needham, MA) **10164**
Wayne County Journal-Banner
  (Piedmont, MO) **10192**
Wayne County Mail (Webster, NY) **10225**
Wayne County News (Waynesboro, MS) **10187**
Wayne County News (Waynesboro, TN) **10270**
Wayne County News (Wayne, WV) **10296**
Wayne County Outlook (Monticello, KY) **10150**
Wayne County Star (Lyons, NY) **10217**
Wayne Eagle (Wayne, MI) **10176**
Wayne Herald (Wayne, NE) **10198**
Wayne Independent, The
  (Honesdale, PA) **10033**
Waynesboro News-Virginian
  (Waynesboro, VA) **10050**
Wayne Today (Butler, NJ) **10201**

Wayne Wilson News Leader
  (Fremont, NC) **10228**
Wayzata/Orono/Long Lake Sun-Sailor
  (Minnetonka, MN) **10180**
Weakley County Press (Martin, TN) **10268**
Weatherford Daily News
  (Weatherford, OK) **10030**
Weatherford Democrat
  (Weatherford, TX) **10047**
Webster County Citizen (Seymour, MO) **10193**
Webster Herald (Webster, NY) **10225**
Webster Post, The (Webster, NY) **10225**
Webster Progress-Times (Eupora, MS) **10186**
Webster Reporter & Farmer
  (Webster, SD) **10265**
Webster Republican (Webster
  Springs, WV) **10296**
Wednesday Journal of Oak Park & River Forest
  (Oak Park, IL) **10125**
Wednesday Magazine (Kansas
  City, MO) **10190**
Weed Press (Weed, CA) **10084**
Weehawken Reporter (Hoboken, NJ) **10203**
† Weekender Enquirer (Boonville, IN)
Weekender, The (Whitinsville, MA) **10166**
† Weekender, The (Bronx, NY)
Weekender, The (Lexington, VA) **10287**
Weekend Flyer, The (Plainfield, IN) **10135**
Weekend News (Montrose, PA) **10255**
Weekly Almanac, The (Honesdale, PA) **10253**
Weekly Calistogan (Calistoga, CA) **10070**
Weekly Challenger (St. Petersburg, FL) **10099**
Weekly News (Marksville, LA) **10154**
Weekly Observer, The (Hemingway, SC) **10262**
Weekly Packet (Blue Hill, ME) **10155**
Weekly Planet (Tampa, FL) **10099**
Weekly Post (Rainsville, AL) **10061**
Weekly Press (Baton Rouge, LA) **10152**
Weekly Recorder, The (Claysville, PA) **10252**
Weekly Reminder (Paulding, OH) **10242**
† Weekly Territorial (Tucson, AZ)
Weimar Mercury (Weimar, TX) **10281**
Weirton Daily Times (Weirton, WV) **10053**
Weisbeck, The (Alden, NY) **10209**
Weiser Signal American (Weiser, ID) **10109**
Welch Daily News (Welch, WV) **10053**
Wellesley Townsman (Wellesley, MA) **10166**
Wellington Daily News (Wellington, KS) **9991**
Wellington Royal Palm Beach Forum
  (Wellington, FL) **10100**
Wellsboro Gazette (Wellsboro, PA) **10260**
Wells Mirror, The (Wells, MN) **10184**
† Wellston Sentry (Wellston, OH)
Wellston Telegram, The (Wellston, OH) **10244**
Wellsville Daily Reporter (Wellsville, NY) **10017**
Wenatchee World (Wenatchee, WA) **10052**

Wenona Index (Henry, IL) **10119**
Wentzville Journal (Wentzville, MO) **10195**
West Alabama Gazette (Millport, AL) **10060**
West Allis Star (Wauwatosa, WI) **10308**
West Bloomfield Eccentric, The
  (Birmingham, MI) **10167**
West Boca Times (Deerfield Beach, FL) **10094**
West Bridgewater Star
  (Middleboro, MA) **10163**
Westbury Times (Mineola, NY) **10219**
West Carroll Gazette (Oak Grove, LA) **10154**
West Central Tribune (Willmar, MN) **10003**
Westchester Herald (Oak Park, IL) **10125**
Westchester Observer (Santa
  Monica, CA) **10082**
Westchester Star (Los Angeles, CA) **10077**
West Columbia Brazoria County News (West
  Columbia, TX) **10281**
West Cook County Press (Elmhurst, IL) **10116**
West County Journal (St. Louis, MO) **10194**
West County Times (Richmond, CA) **9964**
Westerly Sun (Westerly, RI) **10038**
Western Breeze (Cut Bank, MT) **10195**
▼Western Edition (San Francisco, CA) **10081**
Western Hills Press (Cincinnati, OH) **10236**
Western News (Libby, MT) **10195**
Western Springs Doings (Hinsdale, IL) **10120**
Western Star (Bessemer, AL) **10057**
Western Star (Lebanon, OH) **10240**
Western Wayne News (Cambridge
  City, IN) **10130**
Western World (Bandon, OR) **10248**
Westerville News & Public Opinion
  (Westerville, OH) **10244**
West Essex Tribune (Livingston, NJ) **10203**
West Fargo Pioneer (West Fargo, ND) **10233**
Westfield Enterprise (Fishers, IN) **10131**
Westfield Evening News (Westfield, MA) **9998**
Westfield Leader (Westfield, NJ) **10208**
Westfield Republican (Westfield, NY) **10225**
Westford Eagle (Chelmsford, MA) **10161**
▼West Geauga Sun (Cleveland, OH) **10237**
West Hartford News (West
  Hartford, CT) **10092**
West Haven News (Milford, CT) **10091**
West Hawaii Today (Kailua Kona, HI) **9976**
West Hempstead Beacon
  (Hicksville, NY) **10216**
Westine Report (Union Grove, WI) **10306**
West Kentucky News (Paducah, KY) **10150**
Westlake Picayune (Austin, TX) **10271**
Westlaker Times, The (Rocky
  River, OH) **10242**
Westland Eagle (Wayne, MI) **10176**
Westland Observer (Livonia, MI) **10172**
West Liberty Index (West Liberty, IA) **10142**

West Life (Cleveland, OH) **10237**
West Linn Tidings (Lake Oswego, OR) **10249**
West Los Angeles Independent (Santa
  Monica, CA) **10082**
West Martin Weekly News
  (Sherburn, MN) **10183**
West Memphis Evening Times (West
  Memphis, AR) **9961**
West Milton Record (West Milton, OH) **10244**
Westminster Window
  (Westminster, CO) **10089**
Westmont Progress (Downers
  Grove, IL) **10115**
Westmoreland News (Montross, VA) **10287**
Westmore News (Port Chester, NY) **10221**
West Morris Star-Journal
  (Ledgewood, NJ) **10203**
West News (West, TX) **10281**
Weston Democrat, The (Weston, WV) **10297**
Weston Forum, The (Weston, CT) **10092**
West Orange Chronicle (Orange, NJ) **10205**
West Orange Times (Winter
  Garden, FL) **10100**
Westosha Report (Twin Lakes, WI) **10306**
West Plains Daily Quill (West
  Plains, MO) **10008**
† West Plains Tribune (Spokane, WA)
West Point News (West Point, NE) **10199**
Westport News (Westport, CT) **10092**
West Proviso Herald (Oak Park, IL) **10125**
West Roxbury Transcript
  (Dedham, MA) **10161**
West Sacramento News-Ledger (West
  Sacramento, CA) **10085**
West San Bernardino Advertiser (Palm
  Desert, CA) **10079**
West Schuylkill Herald (Tower City, PA) **10259**
West Seattle Herald (Seattle, WA) **10293**
West Seneca Bee (Williamsville, NY) **10225**
West Side Advance (Kerman, CA) **10074**
Westside Enterprise (Greenfield, IN) **10132**
Westside Flyer (Indianapolis, IN) **10133**
West Side Journal (Port Allen, LA) **10154**
Westside Messenger (Speedway, IN) **10135**
Westside Record-Journal
  (Ferndale, WA) **10291**
Westsider, The (New York, NY) **10220**
West Side Sun News (Cleveland, OH) **10237**
West Side Times (Buffalo, NY) **10211**
West Springfield Record (West
  Springfield, MA) **10166**
West St. Paul/Mendota Heights Sun-Current
  (Burnsville, MN) **10177**
West Suburban Post (Chicago, IL) **10113**
West Toledo Herald (Toledo, OH) **10243**
West Valley Courier (Hillsboro, OR) **10249**

West Valley Eagle (Bountiful, UT) **10282**
West Valley News (Magna, UT) **10282**
West Valley News/Sunday Advance
   (Flint, MI) **10169**
West Valley View (Avondale, AZ) **10063**
Westville Indicator (Westville, IN) **10136**
West Virginia Daily News
   (Lewisburg, WV) **10052**
West Virginia Hillbilly (Richwood, WV) **10296**
Westword (Denver, CO) **10086**
Wethersfield Post (West Hartford, CT) **10092**
Wet Mountain Tribune (Westcliffe, CO) **10089**
Wetumpka Herald (Wetumpka, AL) **10062**
Wetzel Chronicle (New
   Martinsville, WV) **10295**
Wewoka Times (Wewoka, OK) **10247**
Weymouth News (Marshfield, MA) **10163**
Weymouth News & Gazette
   (Braintree, MA) **10161**
Wharton Journal-Spectator
   (Wharton, TX) **10282**
Wheaton Leader (Glen Ellyn, IL) **10118**
Wheaton Press (Bloomingdale, IL) **10111**
Wheaton Sun (Naperville, IL) **10124**
† Wheat Ridge Sentinel (Lakewood, CO)
Wheeler County Independent
   (Burwell, NE) **10197**
Wheeling News-Register (Wheeling, WV) **10053**
Wheels 'N Deals (Columbia, MO) **10189**
Whidbey News-Times (Oak Harbor, WA) **10292**
Whitefish Bay Herald (Wauwatosa, WI) **10308**
Whitefish Pilot (Whitefish, MT) **10196**
White Hall Journal (Pine Bluff, AR) **10067**
Whitehall News (Columbus, OH) **10238**
Whitehall Times (Whitehall, NY) **10225**
Whitehall Times (Whitehall, WI) **10308**
White Lake Beacon (Whitehall, MI) **10176**
White Mountain Independent (Show
   Low, AZ) **10064**
White Oak Independent (White
   Oak, TX) **10282**
White River Current (Calico Rock, AR) **10065**
▼White River Gazette (Fishers, IN) **10131**
White River Journal (Des Arc, AR) **10066**
White Settlement News (Fort
   Worth, TX) **10275**
Whiteside Shopper (Fulton, IL) **10117**
Whitestone Times, The (Bayside, NY) **10210**
Whiteville News Reporter
   (Whiteville, NC) **10231**
Whitewright Sun, The (Whitewright, TX) **10282**
Whitley Republican News Journal
   (Williamsburg, KY) **10152**
Whitman County Gazette (Colfax, WA) **10291**
Whitman Times (Stoughton, MA) **10166**
Whitney Point Reporter (Greene, NY) **10215**

Whittier Daily News (Whittier, CA) **9967**
Wichita Eagle (Wichita, KS) **9991**
Wick-Qua-Boag Weekly (Spencer, MA) **10165**
Wickenburg Sun (Wickenburg, AZ) **10065**
Wiggins Courier, The (Wiggins, CO) **10089**
Wilcox Progressive Era (Camden, AL) **10058**
Wildwood Leader (Wildwood, NJ) **10208**
Wilkes-Barre Citizens' Voice (Wilkes
   Barre, PA) **10037**
† Wilkes-Barre Sunday Independent (Wilkes
   Barre, PA)
Willamette Week (Portland, OR) **10250**
Willapa Harbor Herald (Raymond, WA) **10292**
Willard Times-Junction (Willard, OH) **10244**
Williams Grand Canyon News
   (Williams, AZ) **10065**
Williamson County Sun
   (Georgetown, TX) **10275**
Williamson Daily News (Williamson, WV) **10053**
Williamson Leader, The (Franklin, TN) **10266**
Williamsport Sun-Gazette
   (Williamsport, PA) **10037**
Williamston Enterprise
   (Williamston, NC) **10231**
Williamsville Sun (Riverton, IL) **10127**
Williston Herald (Williston, ND) **10022**
Williston Plains Reporter (Williston, ND) **10233**
Willowbrook Doings (Hinsdale, IL) **10120**
Willow Grove Guide (Hatboro, PA) **10253**
Willows Journal (Willows, CA) **10085**
Wilmette Life (Glenview, IL) **10118**
Wilmington-Tewksbury Town Crier
   (Wilmington, MA) **10166**
Wilmington Advocate, The
   (Wilmington, IL) **10129**
Wilmington Defender (Wilmington, DE) **10092**
Wilmington Express (Wilmington, IL) **10129**
Wilmington Free Press (Wilmington, IL) **10129**
Wilmington Journal (Wilmington, NC) **10231**
Wilmington Morning Star
   (Wilmington, NC) **10021**
Wilmington News-Journal
   (Wilmington, OH) **10027**
Wilson County Citizen (Fredonia, KS) **10143**
Wilson Daily Times (Wilson, NC) **10021**
Wilson World, The (Lebanon, TN) **10268**
Wilton Bulletin (Wilton, CT) **10092**
Wimberley Valley-News (Wimberley, TX) **10282**
Winchendon Courier (Winchendon, MA) **10167**
Winchester Star (Winchester, MA) **10167**
Winchester Star (Winchester, VA) **10050**
Winchester Sun (Winchester, KY) **9993**
Winder News (Winder, GA) **10106**
Windham Journal (Windham, NY) **10225**
Windom Cottonwood County Citizen
   (Windom, MN) **10185**

Wind River News (Lander, WY) **10309**
Windsor Journal (West Hartford, CT) **10092**
Windsor Locks Journal (Bristol, CT) **10090**
Windsor Review (Windsor, MO) **10195**
Windsor Standard (Conklin, NY) **10212**
Winfield Daily Courier (Winfield, KS) **9992**
Winfield Estate (Glen Ellyn, IL) **10118**
Winfield Press (West Chicago, IL) **10128**
Winkler County News (Kermit, TX) **10277**
Winneconne News (Winneconne, WI) **10308**
Winnetka Talk (Glenview, IL) **10118**
Winnfield Winn Parish Enterprise
   (Winnfield, LA) **10155**
Winnsboro News (Winnsboro, TX) **10282**
Winona Daily News (Winona, MN) **10003**
Winona Times (Winona, MS) **10187**
Winslow Mail (Winslow, AZ) **10065**
Winston-Salem Journal
   (Winston-Salem, NC) **10021**
Winter Park-Maitland Observer (Winter
   Park, FL) **10100**
Winter Park Manifest (Winter Park, CO) **10089**
Winterset Madisonian (Winterset, IA) **10142**
† Winter Visitor Independent (Mesa, AZ)
Winton Times (Winton, CA) **10085**
Wisconsin Dells Events (Wisconsin
   Dells, WI) **10308**
Wisconsin State Farmer (Waupaca, WI) **10306**
Wisconsin State Journal (Madison, WI) **10054**
Wise County Messenger (Decatur, TX) **10273**
Wittenberg Enterprise News
   (Wittenberg, WI) **10308**
Woburn Advocate (Woburn, MA) **10167**
Wonewoc Reporter (Elroy, WI) **10300**
Woodbury-South Maplewood Review (St.
   Paul, MN) **10184**
Wood County Democrat (Quitman, TX) **10280**
Wood Dale Press (Elmhurst, IL) **10116**
Woodford County Journal (Eureka, IL) **10116**
Woodford Sun (Versailles, KY) **10152**
Woodland Lewis River News
   (Woodland, WA) **10294**
Woodridge Progress (Downers
   Grove, IL) **10115**
Wood River Journal (Hailey, ID) **10107**
Woodruff County Monitor Leader Advocate
   (McCrory, AR) **10066**
Woodside Herald (Sunnyside, NY) **10223**
Woodstock Independent, The
   (Woodstock, IL) **10129**
Woodward News (Woodward, OK) **10031**
Wooster Daily Record (Wooster, OH) **10027**
Worcester County Messenger (Pocomoke
   City, MD) **10159**
Worcester Magazine (Worcester, MA) **10167**
World, The (Coos Bay, OR) **10031**

Worth-Palos Reporter (Palos
   Heights, IL) **10126**
Worth-Ridge Reporter (Palos
   Heights, IL) **10126**
Worth Citizen (Midlothian, IL) **10124**
Worthington Daily Globe
   (Worthington, MN) **10004**
Worthington Suburbia News
   (Columbus, OH) **10238**
Worthington Times, The
   (Worthington, IN) **10136**
Wrangell Sentinel (Wrangell, AK) **10063**
Wray Gazette (Wray, CO) **10089**
Wright County Journal-Press
   (Buffalo, MN) **10177**
Wrightsville Headlight, The
   (Wrightsville, GA) **10106**
† Wrova Reporter (Galva, IL)
Wyandotte West (Kansas City, KS) **10144**
Wylie News, The (Wylie, TX) **10282**
Wynne Progress (Wynne, AR) **10068**
Wyoming Advance (Jenison, MI) **10172**
Wyoming State Journal (Lander, WY) **10309**
Wyoming Tribune-Eagle
   (Cheyenne, WY) **10055**

X

Xenia Daily Gazette (Xenia, OH) **10027**

Y

Yadkin Ripple, The (Yadkinville, NC) **10232**
Yakima Herald-Republic (Yakima, WA) **10052**
Yale News, The (Yale, OK) **10247**
Yancey Common Times Journal
   (Burnsville, NC) **10227**
Yankee Trader (Coram, NY) **10212**
Yankton Daily Press & Dakotan
   (Yankton, SD) **10040**
Yardley News (Yardley, PA) **10260**
† Yarmouth Sun (Yarmouth Port, MA)
Yazoo Herald (Yazoo City, MS) **10187**
Yoakum Herald-Times & Four Star Reporter
   (Yoakum, TX) **10282**
Yonkers Herald Statesman
   (Yonkers, NY) **10018**
Yonkers Home News & Times
   (Yonkers, NY) **10226**
York County Coast Star
   (Kennebunk, ME) **10156**
York Daily Record (York, PA) **10037**
York Dispatch/York Sunday News
   (York, PA) **10037**
York News-Times (York, NE) **10010**
York Town Crier (Yorktown, VA) **10290**
Yorkville Enquirer (York, SC) **10264**

▼Your Paper (Spartanburg, SC) **10264**
Yucaipa & Calimesa News-Mirror
  (Yucaipa, CA) **10085**
Yucca Valley Hi-Desert Star (Yucca
  Valley, CA) **10085**
Yukon Review (Yukon, OK) **10247**
Yuma Daily Sun (Yuma, AZ) **9959**
Yuma Pioneer (Yuma, CO) **10089**

Z

Zachary Plainsman-News (Zachary, LA) **10155**
Zanesville Muskingum Advertiser
  (Zanesville, OH) **10244**
Zebulon Record, The (Zebulon, NC) **10232**
Zephyrhills News (Zephyrhills, FL) **10100**
Zion-Benton News (Zion, IL) **10129**
† Zionsville Eagle (Indianapolis, IN)
Zionsville Times Sentinel (Zionsville, IN) **10136**
1590 Broadcaster (Nashua, NH) **10200**

Daily Newspapers Index

Abbeville Meridional (Abbeville, LA) **9993**
Aberdeen American News
  (Aberdeen, SD) **10039**
Abilene Reflector-Chronicle (Abilene, KS) **9989**
Abilene Reporter-News (Abilene, TX) **10041**
Ada Evening News (Ada, OK) **10028**
Ad Express & Daily Iowegian
  (Centerville, IA) **9987**
Adirondack Daily Enterprise (Saranac
  Lake, NY) **10017**
Advertiser-Tribune (Tiffin, OH) **10027**
Advisor/Source (Utica, MI) **10002**
Advocate-Messenger (Danville, KY) **9992**
Advocate, The (Stamford, CT) **9971**
Advocate, The (Baton Rouge, LA) **9993**
Advocate, The (Newark, OH) **10026**
Aiken Standard (Aiken, SC) **10038**
Akron Beacon Journal (Akron, OH) **10022**
† Alabama Journal (Montgomery, AL)
Alameda Times Star (Alameda, CA) **9961**
Alamogordo Daily News
  (Alamogordo, NM) **10013**
Albany Democrat-Herald (Albany, OR) **10031**
Albany Herald, The (Albany, GA) **9974**
Albert Lea Tribune (Albert Lea, MN) **10002**
Albion Recorder (Albion, MI) **9999**
Albuquerque Journal
  (Albuquerque, NM) **10013**
Albuquerque Tribune
  (Albuquerque, NM) **10013**

Alexander City Outlook (Alexander
  City, AL) **9955**
Alexandria Daily Town Talk
  (Alexandria, LA) **9993**
Alexandria Journal (Fairfax, VA) **10049**
Alice Echo-News (Alice, TX) **10041**
Allegheny Times (Moon Township, PA) **10035**
Alliance Review (Alliance, OH) **10022**
Alliance Times-Herald (Alliance, NE) **10009**
Alpena News (Alpena, MI) **9999**
Altoona Mirror (Altoona, PA) **10032**
Altus Times (Altus, OK) **10028**
Alva Review-Courier (Alva, OK) **10028**
Amador Ledger Dispatch (Jackson, CA) **9962**
Amarillo Daily News/Sunday News Globe
  (Amarillo, TX) **10041**
Amarillo Globe Times (Amarillo, TX) **10042**
Americus Times-Recorder
  (Americus, GA) **9974**
Amsterdam Star, The (Albany, NY) **10014**
Anadarko Daily News (Anadarko, OK) **10028**
Anchorage Daily News (Anchorage, AK) **9957**
Andalusia Star News (Andalusia AL) **9955**
Anderson Independent-Mail
  (Anderson, SC) **10038**
Ann Arbor News (Ann Arbor, MI) **9999**
Anniston Star (Anniston, AL) **9955**
Antelope Valley Press (Palmdale CA) **9964**
Antigo Daily Journal (Antigo, WI) **10053**
Appeal-Democrat (Marysville, CA) **9963**

Argus-Press, The (Owosso, MI) **10001**
Argus Leader (Sioux Falls, SD) **10039**
Argus Observer (Ontario, OR) **10031**
Argus, The (Fremont, CA) **9962**
Arizona Daily Star (Tucson, AZ) **9958**
Arizona Daily Sun (Flagstaff, AZ) **9957**
Arizona Republic (Phoenix, AZ) **9958**
Arkadelphia Daily Siftings Herald
  (Arkadelphia, AR) **9959**
Arkansas City Traveler (Arkansas
  City, KS) **9989**
Arkansas Democrat-Gazette (Little
  Rock, AR) **9960**
Arlington Journal (Fairfax, VA) **10049**
▼Arlington Morning News
  (Arlington, TX) **10042**
Arlington Star Telegram (Fort
  Worth, TX) **10043**
Artesia Daily Press (Artesia, NM) **10013**
Asbury Park Press (Neptune, NJ) **10012**
Asheboro Courier-Tribune
  (Asheboro, NC) **10018**
Asheville Citizen-Times (Asheville, NC) **10018**
Ashland Daily Tidings (Ashland, OR) **10031**
Ashland Times-Gazette (Ashland, OH) **10022**
Ashtabula Star-Beacon (Ashtabula, OH) **10022**
Aspen Daily News (Aspen, CO) **9968**
Aspen Times, The (Aspen, CO) **9968**
Atchison Daily Globe (Atchison, KS) **9989**
Athens Banner Herald (Athens, GA) **9974**
Athens Daily News (Athens, GA) **9974**
Athens Daily Post (Athens, TN) **10040**
Athens Daily Review (Athens, TX) **10042**
Athens Messenger (Athens, OH) **10022**
Athol Daily News (Athol, MA) **9996**
Atlanta Journal-Constitution
  (Atlanta, GA) **9974**
Atlantic News-Telegraph (Atlantic, IA) **9986**
Auburn Journal (Auburn, CA) **9961**
Augusta Chronicle, The (Augusta, GA) **9974**
Augusta Daily Gazette (Augusta, KS) **9989**
† Augusta Herald (Augusta, GA)
Austin American-Statesman
  (Austin, TX) **10042**
Austin Daily Herald (Austin, MN) **10002**
Baker City Herald (Baker City, OR) **10031**
Bakersfield Californian (Bakersfield, CA) **9961**
Baltimore Sun (Baltimore, MD) **9995**
Bangor Daily News (Bangor, ME) **9995**
Banner-Graphic (Greencastle, IN) **9983**
Banner-News (Magnolia, AR) **9960**
Banning Record Gazette (Banning, CA) **9961**
Baraboo News-Republic (Baraboo, WI) **10053**
Bartlesville Examiner-Enterprise
  (Bartlesville, OK) **10028**
Bastrop Daily Enterprise (Bastrop, LA) **9993**

Batavia Daily News (Batavia, NY) **10014**
Batesville Guard (Batesville, AR) **9959**
Battle Creek Enquirer (Battle Creek, MI) **9999**
Baxter Bulletin (Mountain Home, AR) **9960**
Bay City Times (Bay City, MI) **9999**
Baytown Sun (Baytown, TX) **10042**
Beacon News (Aurora, IL) **9977**
Beatrice Daily Sun (Beatrice, NE) **10009**
Beaufort Gazette (Beaufort, SC) **10038**
Beaumont Enterprise (Beaumont, TX) **10042**
Beauregard Daily News (De Ridder, LA) **9994**
Beaver County Times (Beaver, PA) **10032**
Beavercreek News-Current
  (Dayton, OH) **10023**
Beaver Dam Daily Citizen (Beaver
  Dam, WI) **10053**
Bedford Gazette/Gazette Sunday
  (Bedford, PA) **10032**
Bellefontaine Examiner
  (Bellefontaine, OH) **10022**
Belleville News-Democrat (Belleville, IL) **9977**
Bellevue Gazette (Bellevue, OH) **10023**
Bellingham Herald (Bellingham, WA) **10050**
Beloit Daily Call (Beloit, KS) **9989**
Beloit Daily News (Beloit, WI) **10053**
Belvidere Daily Republican (Belvidere, IL) **9978**
Benicia Herald (Benicia, CA) **9961**
Bennington Banner (Bennington, VT) **10048**
Benton County Daily Record
  (Bentonville, AR) **9959**
Benton Courier (Benton, AR) **9959**
Berkshire Eagle (Pittsfield, MA) **9998**
Berlin Daily Sun (Berlin, NH) **10011**
Berlin Reporter, The (Berlin, NH) **10011**
Big Rapids Pioneer (Big Rapids, MI) **9999**
Big Spring Herald (Big Spring, TX) **10042**
Billings Gazette (Billings, MT) **10008**
Birmingham News (Birmingham, AL) **9955**
Birmingham Post-Herald
  (Birmingham, AL) **9955**
Bisbee Daily Review (Bisbee, AZ) **9957**
Bismarck Tribune (Bismarck, ND) **10021**
Blackfoot Morning News (Blackfoot, ID) **9976**
Black Hills Pioneer (Spearfish, SD) **10039**
Blackwell Journal-Tribune
  (Blackwell, OK) **10028**
Bladen Daily Journal
  (Elizabethtown, NC) **10019**
Bluefield Daily Telegraph
  (Bluefield, WV) **10052**
Blue Springs Examiner (Blue
  Springs, MO) **10005**
Bluffton News-Banner (Bluffton, IN) **9982**
Bogalusa Daily News & Sunday News
  (Bogalusa, LA) **9993**
Bonham Daily Favorite (Bonham, TX) **10042**

Bonner County Daily Bee (Sandpoint, ID) **9977**
Boone News-Republican (Boone, IA) **9986**
Boonville Daily News (Boonville, MO) **10005**
Borger News-Herald (Borger, TX) **10042**
Boston Globe (Boston, MA) **9997**
Boston Herald (Boston, MA) **9997**
Bozeman Daily Chronicle
   (Bozeman, MT) **10008**
Bradenton Herald, The (Bradenton, FL) **9971**
Bradford Era, The (Bradford, PA) **10032**
Brainerd Daily Dispatch (Brainerd, MN) **10002**
Branson Daily News (Hollister, MO) **10006**
Brattleboro Reformer (Brattleboro, VT) **10048**
Brazil Times (Brazil, IN) **9982**
Brazosport Facts, The (Clute, TX) **10042**
Brenham Banner-Press (Brenham, TX) **10042**
Bridgeton Evening News
   (Bridgeton, NJ) **10011**
Bristol Herald-Courier, The (Bristol, VA) **10048**
Bristol Press, The (Bristol, CT) **9970**
Brockton Enterprise, The (Brockton, MA) **9997**
Brookhaven Daily Leader
   (Brookhaven, MS) **10004**
Brookings Register (Brookings, SD) **10039**
Brooklyn Daily Bulletin (Brooklyn, NY) **10014**
Brownsville Herald (Brownsville, TX) **10042**
Brownwood Bulletin (Brownwood, TX) **10042**
Brunswick News, The (Brunswick, GA) **9974**
Bryan College Station Eagle (Bryan, TX) **10042**
Bryan Times (Bryan, OH) **10023**
Bucks County Courier Times
   (Levittown, PA) **10034**
Bucyrus Telegraph-Forum
   (Bucyrus, OH) **10023**
Buffalo News, The (Buffalo, NY) **10014**
Bulletin, The (Bend, OR) **10031**
Burlington County Times
   (Willingboro, NJ) **10013**
Burlington Free Press (Burlington, VT) **10048**
Butler Eagle (Butler, PA) **10032**
Cadillac Evening News (Cadillac, MI) **9999**
Caledonian-Record, The (St.
   Johnsbury, VT) **10048**
Californian, The (Salinas, CA) **9965**
Californian, The (Temecula, CA) **9966**
Call-Leader (Elwood, IN) **9983**
Call, The (Woonsocket, RI) **10038**
Camarillo Star (Simi Valley, CA) **9966**
Camden News (Camden, AR) **9959**
Canandaigua Daily Messenger
   (Canandaigua, NY) **10014**
Cape Cod Times (Hyannis, MA) **9997**
Capital-Journal (Topeka, KS) **9991**
Capital, The (Annapolis, MD) **9995**
Capital Times, The (Madison, WI) **10054**
Carlisle Sentinel (Carlisle, PA) **10032**

Carmi Times (Carmi, IL) **9978**
Carroll County Sun (Westminster, MD) **9996**
Carroll County Times (Westminster, MD) **9996**
Carroll Times Herald (Carroll, IA) **9987**
Cartersville Daily Tribune News
   (Cartersville, GA) **9974**
Carthage Press (Carthage, MO) **10005**
Casa Grande Dispatch (Casa
   Grande, AZ) **9957**
Casper Star Tribune (Casper, WY) **10055**
Cecil Whig (Elkton, MD) **9996**
Cedar Rapids Gazette (Cedar Rapids, IA) **9987**
Celina Daily Standard (Celina, OH) **10023**
Centralia Sentinel (Centralia, IL) **9978**
Central Maine Morning Sentinel
   (Waterville, ME) **9995**
Centre Daily Times (State College, PA) **10036**
Champaign News Gazette
   (Champaign, IL) **9978**
Chandler Arizonan Tribune
   (Chandler, AZ) **9957**
Chanute Tribune (Chanute, KS) **9989**
Chapel Hill Herald (Chapel Hill, NC) **10018**
Charles City Press (Charles City, IA) **9987**
Charleston Daily Mail (Charleston, WV) **10052**
Charleston Gazette, The
   (Charleston, WV) **10052**
Charleston Post & Courier
   (Charleston, SC) **10038**
Charleston Times-Courier
   (Charleston, IL) **9978**
Charlotte Observer (Charlotte, NC) **10018**
Charlotte Sun Herald (Charlotte
   Harbor, FL) **9971**
Chattanooga Free Press
   (Chattanooga, TN) **10040**
Chattanooga Times (Chattanooga, TN) **10040**
Cheboygan Daily Tribune
   (Cheboygan, MI) **9999**
Cherokee County's Daily Times
   (Cherokee, IA) **9987**
Chesterton Tribune (Chesterton, IN) **9982**
Chicago Defender (Chicago, IL) **9978**
Chicago Sun Times (Chicago, IL) **9978**
Chicago Tribune (Chicago, IL) **9978**
Chickasha Daily Express
   (Chickasha, OK) **10028**
Chico Enterprise-Record (Chico, CA) **9961**
Chillicothe Constitution-Tribune
   (Chillicothe, MO) **10005**
Chillicothe Gazette (Chillicothe, OH) **10023**
Chippewa Herald-Telegram (Chippewa
   Falls, WI) **10053**
Chronicle News, The (Trinidad, CO) **9969**
Chronicle, The (Willimantic, CT) **9971**
Chronicle, The (Centralia, WA) **10050**

Cincinnati Enquirer (Cincinnati, OH) **10023**
Cincinnati Post (Cincinnati, OH) **10023**
Circleville Herald (Circleville, OH) **10023**
Citizen Register (Yorktown Heights, NY) **10018**
Citizen, The (Laconia, NH) **10011**
Citizen, The (Auburn, NY) **10014**
Citizen Tribune (Morristown, TN) **10041**
Citrus County Chronicle (Crystal River, FL) **9971**
Claremore Progress (Claremore, OK) **10028**
Clarion-Ledger, The (Jackson, MS) **10004**
Clarksburg Exponent (Clarksburg, WV) **10052**
Clarksburg Telegram (Clarksburg, WV) **10052**
Clarksdale Press Register (Clarksdale, MS) **10004**
Clay Center Dispatch (Clay Center, KS) **9989**
Clay Today (Orange Park, FL) **9973**
Clayton News Daily (Jonesboro, GA) **9975**
Cleburne Times-Review (Cleburne, TX) **10042**
Cleveland Bolivar Commercial (Cleveland, MS) **10004**
Cleveland Daily Banner (Cleveland, TN) **10040**
Cleveland Plain Dealer (Cleveland, OH) **10023**
Clinton Daily Democrat (Clinton, MO) **10006**
Clinton Daily Journal (Clinton, IL) **9978**
Clinton Daily News (Clinton, OK) **10028**
Clinton Herald (Clinton, IA) **9987**
Clovis News Journal (Clovis, NM) **10013**
Coeur d'Alene Press (Coeur d'Alene, ID) **9977**
Coffeyville Journal, The (Coffeyville, KS) **9989**
Colby Free Press (Colby, KS) **9989**
Colorado Springs Gazette Telegraph (Colorado Springs, CO) **9968**
Columbia Basin Herald (Moses Lake, WA) **10051**
Columbia Daily Tribune (Columbia, MO) **10006**
Columbia Missourian (Columbia, MO) **10006**
Columbian, The (Vancouver, WA) **10051**
Columbus Daily Advocate (Columbus, KS) **9989**
Columbus Dispatch (Columbus, OH) **10023**
Columbus Ledger-Enquirer (Columbus, GA) **9975**
Columbus Telegram (Columbus, NE) **10009**
Commercial-News (Danville, IL) **9978**
Commercial Appeal, The (Memphis, TN) **10041**
Commercial Dispatch, The (Columbus, MS) **10004**
Commonwealth Journal (Somerset, KY) **9993**
Concordia Blade-Empire (Concordia, KS) **9989**
Concord Monitor (Concord, NH) **10011**
Concord Tribune (Concord, NC) **10018**
† Conneaut News-Herald (Conneaut, OH)
Connecticut Post (Bridgeport, CT) **9970**
Connersville News-Examiner (Connersville, IN) **9982**
Conroe Courier, The (Conroe, TX) **10043**
Contra Costa Times (Walnut Creek, CA) **9967**
Conway Daily Sun, The (North Conway, NH) **10011**
Corbin Times-Tribune (Corbin, KY) **9992**
Cordele Dispatch (Cordele, GA) **9975**
Corpus Christi Caller-Times (Corpus Christi, TX) **10043**
Corry Journal (Corry, PA) **10033**
Corsicana Daily Sun (Corsicana, TX) **10043**
Cortland Standard (Cortland, NY) **10014**
Corvallis Gazette-Times (Corvallis, OR) **10031**
Coshocton Tribune (Coshocton, OH) **10023**
Council Bluffs Daily Nonpareil (Council Bluffs, IA) **9987**
Council Grove Republican (Council Grove, KS) **9989**
† Countywide News (Westminster, MD)
Courier-Express (Du Bois, PA) **10033**
Courier-Journal, The (Louisville, KY) **9992**
Courier-News, The (Elgin, IL) **9979**
Courier-News, The (Bridgewater, NJ) **10012**
Courier-Post, The (St. Charles, MO) **10008**
Courier-Post, The (Cherry Hill, NJ) **10012**
Courier Herald, The (Dublin, GA) **9975**
Courier News (Blytheville, AR) **9959**
Courier, The (Russellville, AR) **9960**
Courier, The (Houma, LA) **9994**
Courier, The (Findlay, OH) **10024**
Crawfordsville Journal Review (Crawfordsville, IN) **9982**
Crescent-News (Defiance, OH) **10024**
Creston News Advertiser (Creston, IA) **9987**
Crookston Daily Times (Crookston, MN) **10002**
Crowley Post-Signal (Crowley, LA) **9993**
Cullman Times (Cullman, AL) **9955**
Culpeper Star Exponent (Culpeper, VA) **10049**
Cumberland Times-News (Cumberland, MD) **9996**
Current-Argus (Carlsbad, NM) **10013**
Cushing Daily Citizen (Cushing, OK) **10028**
Daily & Sunday Freeman (Kingston, NY) **10015**
Daily & Sunday Sentinel (Rome, NY) **10017**
Daily/Sunday Sun, The (Warner Robins, GA) **9976**
Daily Advance (Elizabeth City, NC) **10019**
Daily Advocate (Greenville, OH) **10024**
Daily American (West Frankfort, IL) **9982**
Daily American (Somerset, PA) **10036**
Daily American Republic (Poplar Bluff, MO) **10007**
Daily Ardmoreite (Ardmore, OK) **10028**
Daily Astorian (Astoria, OR) **10031**
Daily Banner (Cambridge, MD) **9996**

Daily Breeze (Torrance, CA) **9966**
Daily Breeze, The (Cape Coral, FL) **9971**
Daily Californian, The (El Cajon, CA) **9961**
Daily Camera (Boulder, CO) **9968**
Daily Chronicle (De Kalb, IL) **9979**
Daily Citizen (Searcy, AR) **9960**
Daily Citizen News (Dalton, GA) **9975**
Daily Clay County Advocate-Press
  (Flora, IL) **9979**
Daily Clintonian (Clinton, IN) **9982**
Daily Comet (Thibodaux, LA) **9995**
Daily Commercial (Leesburg, FL) **9972**
Daily Corinthian (Corinth, MS) **10004**
Daily Courier (Forest City, NC) **10019**
Daily Courier Observer, The
  (Massena, NY) **10015**
Daily Courier, The (Prescott, AZ) **9958**
Daily Courier, The (Connellsville, PA) **10032**
Daily Democrat (Woodland, CA) **9967**
Daily Dispatch, The (Henderson, NC) **10019**
Daily Dunklin Democrat (Kennett, MO) **10006**
Daily Editor (Cobleskill, NY) **10014**
Daily Evening Item (Lynn, MA) **9997**
Daily Freeman Journal (Webster City, IA) **9989**
Daily Gazette (Sterling, IL) **9981**
Daily Gazette (Schenectady, NY) **10017**
Daily Guide (St. Robert, MO) **10008**
Daily Hampshire Gazette
  (Northampton, MA) **9998**
Daily Herald (Arlington Heights, IL) **9977**
Daily Herald (Delphos, OH) **10024**
Daily Herald (Columbia, TN) **10040**
Daily Herald, The (Tyrone, PA) **10037**
Daily Herald, The (Provo, UT) **10047**
Daily Home (Talladega, AL) **9956**
Daily Iberian (New Iberia, LA) **9994**
Daily Independent (Ridgecrest, CA) **9964**
Daily Independent, The (Ashland, KY) **9992**
Daily Inter Lake, The (Kalispell, MT) **10009**
Daily Item, The (New Rochelle, NY) **10016**
Daily Item, The (Sunbury, PA) **10036**
Daily Jefferson County Union (Fort
  Atkinson, WI) **10054**
Daily Jeffersonian, The
  (Cambridge, OH) **10023**
Daily Journal (Kankakee, IL) **9980**
Daily Journal (Franklin, IN) **9983**
Daily Journal (Park Hills, MO) **10007**
† Daily Journal (Elizabeth, NJ)
Daily Journal (Vineland, NJ) **10013**
Daily Journal, The (Fergus Falls, MN) **10002**
Daily Journal, The (International
  Falls, MN) **10003**
Daily Ledger (Canton, IL) **9978**
Daily Ledger (Fisher, IN) **9983**
Daily Local News (West Chester, PA) **10037**

Daily Mail (Catskill, NY) **10014**
Daily Mail & Sunday Herald
  (Nevada, MO) **10007**
Daily Mail, The (Hagerstown, MD) **9996**
Daily Midway Driller (Taft, CA) **9966**
Daily Mining Gazette (Houghton, MI) **10000**
Daily News (Mountain Home, AR) **9960**
Daily News (Woodland Hills, CA) **9967**
Daily News (Palatka, FL) **9973**
Daily News (Bowling Green, KY) **9992**
Daily News (Greenville, MI) **10000**
Daily News (Iron Mountain, MI) **10000**
Daily News (Richmond, MO) **10007**
Daily News (Wahpeton, ND) **10022**
Daily News (Huntingdon, PA) **10034**
Daily News (Longview, WA) **10051**
Daily News (West Bend, WI) **10055**
Daily News-Bulletin, The
  (Brookfield, MO) **10005**
Daily News-Mercury, The (Malden, MA) **9997**
Daily News-Record (Harrisonburg, VA) **10049**
Daily News-Sun (Sun City, AZ) **9958**
Daily News Leader, The (Staunton, VA) **10050**
Daily News of Newburyport, The
  (Newburyport, MA) **9998**
Daily News, The (Eden, NC) **10019**
Daily Okeechobee News, The
  (Okeechobee, FL) **9973**
Daily Oklahoman (Oklahoma City, OK) **10030**
Daily Pilot, The (Costa Mesa, CA) **9961**
Daily Press (Victorville, CA) **9967**
Daily Press, The (Paso Robles, CA) **9964**
Daily Press, The (Escanaba, MI) **9999**
Daily Press, The (St. Marys, PA) **10036**
Daily Press, The (Ashland, WI) **10053**
Daily Progress (Charlottesville, VA) **10049**
Daily Record (Canon City, CO) **9968**
Daily Record (Ellensburg, WA) **10050**
Daily Record, The (Parsippany, NJ) **10012**
Daily Record, The (Westchester, PA) **10037**
Daily Register, The (Portage, WI) **10054**
Daily Reporter (Greenfield, IN) **9983**
Daily Reporter (Columbus, OH) **10023**
Daily Reporter, The (Derby, KS) **9989**
Daily Reporter, The (Coldwater, MI) **9999**
Daily Republic (Fairfield, CA) **9962**
Daily Republic (Mitchell, SD) **10039**
Daily Review (Hayward, CA) **9962**
Daily Review & Sunday Review
  (Towanda, PA) **10036**
Daily Review Atlas (Monmouth, IL) **9980**
Daily Review, The (Morgan City, LA) **9994**
Daily Sentinel-Star, The (Grenada, MS) **10004**
Daily Sentinel, The (Scottsboro, AL) **9956**
Daily Sentinel, The (Grand Junction, CO) **9969**
Daily Sentinel, The (Pomeroy, OH) **10026**

Daily Sentinel, The (Nacogdoches, TX) **10045**
Daily Sitka Sentinel (Sitka, AK) **9957**
Daily Southerner, The (Tarboro, NC) **10021**
Daily Southtown (Chicago, IL) **9978**
Daily Sparks Tribune, The (Sparks, NV) **10010**
Daily Standard (Excelsior Springs, MO) **10006**
Daily Star-Journal, The
  (Warrensburg, MO) **10008**
Daily Star, The (Oneonta, NY) **10016**
Daily Sun-News (Sunnyside, WA) **10051**
Daily Telegram (Adrian, MI) **9999**
Daily Times (Ottawa, IL) **9981**
Daily Times (Salisbury, MD) **9996**
Daily Times (Farmington, NM) **10013**
Daily Times (Maryville, TN) **10041**
Daily Times & Chronicle (Reading, MA) **9998**
Daily Times-Call (Longmont, CO) **9969**
Daily Times Chronicle (Woburn, MA) **9998**
Daily Times Leader (West Point, MS) **10005**
Daily Times, The (New Rochelle, NY) **10016**
Daily Times, The (Rawlins, WY) **10056**
Daily Transcript (Dedham, MA) **9997**
Daily Tribune (Royal Oak, MI) **10001**
Daily Tribune News (Cartersville, GA) **9975**
Daily Tribune, The (Ames, IA) **9986**
Daily Tribune, The (Bay City, TX) **10042**
Daily Tribune, The (Wisconsin
  Rapids, WI) **10055**
Daily Whale, The (Lewes, DE) **9971**
Daily World (Opelousas, LA) **9994**
Daily World, The (Aberdeen, WA) **10050**
Dalhart Daily Texan (Dalhart, TX) **10043**
Dallas Morning News, The (Dallas, TX) **10043**
Danville News (Danville, PA) **10033**
Danville Register & Bee (Danville, VA) **10049**
Davis Enterprise (Davis, CA) **9961**
Day, The (New London, CT) **9970**
Daytona Beach News-Journal, The (Daytona
  Beach, FL) **9972**
Dayton Daily News (Dayton, OH) **10023**
Decatur Daily (Decatur, AL) **9955**
Decatur Daily Democrat (Decatur, IN) **9983**
Delaware County Daily-Sunday Times (Clifton
  Heights, PA) **10032**
Delaware Gazette (Delaware, OH) **10024**
Delaware State News (Dover, DE) **9971**
Del Norte Triplicate (Crescent City, CA) **9961**
Del Rio News-Herald (Del Rio, TX) **10043**
Delta Democrat-Times (Greenville, MS) **10004**
Deming Headlight (Deming, NM) **10013**
Denton Record-Chronicle (Denton, TX) **10043**
Denver Post (Denver, CO) **9968**
De Queen Daily Citizen (De Queen, AR) **9959**
Derrick, The (Oil City, PA) **10035**
Desert Dispatch (Barstow, CA) **9961**
Desert Sun (Palm Springs, CA) **9964**

Des Moines Register (Des Moines, IA) **9987**
Des Plaines Journal (Des Plaines, IL) **9979**
Detroit Free Press (Detroit, MI) **9999**
Detroit News (Detroit, MI) **9999**
Devils Lake Journal (Devils Lake, ND) **10021**
Dexter Daily Statesman (Dexter, MO) **10006**
Dickinson Press, The (Dickinson, ND) **10021**
Dispatch, The (Gilroy, CA) **9962**
Dodge City Daily Globe (Dodge City, KS) **9989**
Dominion Post, The (Morgantown, WV) **10053**
Dothan Eagle (Dothan, AL) **9955**
Douglas County Sentinel
  (Douglasville, GA) **9975**
Douglas Dispatch (Douglas, AZ) **9957**
Dowagiac Daily News (Dowagiac, MI) **9999**
Duluth News-Tribune (Duluth, MN) **10002**
Duncan Banner (Duncan, OK) **10028**
Dunn Daily Record (Dunn, NC) **10018**
Du Quoin Evening Call (Du Quoin, IL) **9979**
Durango Herald (Durango, CO) **9968**
Durant Daily Democrat (Durant, OK) **10028**
Eagle-Herald (Marinette, WI) **10054**
Eagle-Times (Claremont, NH) **10011**
Eagle Pass News Guide/Brief (Eagle
  Pass, TX) **10043**
Eagle Tribune, The (North Andover, MA) **9998**
East Oregonian, The (Pendleton, OR) **10031**
Edinburg Daily Review (Edinburg, TX) **10043**
Edmond Evening Sun (Edmond, OK) **10028**
Edwardsville Intelligencer
  (Edwardsville, IL) **9979**
Effingham Daily News (Effingham, IL) **9979**
Eldorado Daily Journal (Eldorado, IL) **9979**
El Dorado News-Times (El Dorado, AR) **9959**
El Dorado Times (El Dorado, KS) **9989**
Elizabethton Star (Elizabethton, TN) **10040**
Elk City Daily News (Elk City, OK) **10029**
Elkhart Truth, The (Elkhart, IN) **9983**
Elko Daily Free Press (Elko, NV) **10010**
Ellwood City Ledger (Ellwood City, PA) **10033**
El Paso Herald-Post (El Paso, TX) **10043**
El Paso Times (El Paso, TX) **10043**
Ely Daily Times (Ely, NV) **10010**
Elyria Chronicle-Telegram (Elyria, OH) **10024**
Emporia Gazette (Emporia, KS) **9990**
Englewood Sun Herald (Englewood, FL) **9972**
Enid News & Eagle (Enid, OK) **10029**
Ennis Daily News (Ennis, TX) **10043**
Enquirer-Journal, The (Monroe, NC) **10020**
Enterprise Ledger (Enterprise, AL) **9956**
† Enterprise Sun (Marlborough, MA)
Erie Daily Times/Sunday Times News
  (Erie, PA) **10033**
Erie Morning News (Erie, PA) **10033**
Estherville Daily News (Estherville, IA) **9987**
Evansville Courier (Evansville, IN) **9983**

Evansville Press (Evansville, IN) **9983**
Evening-Observer (Dunkirk, NY) **10015**
† Evening Express (Portland, ME)
Evening Leader, The (St. Marys, OH) **10027**
Evening News (Benton, IL) **9978**
Evening Review, The (East
  Liverpool, OH) **10024**
† Evening Sentinel (Ansonia, CT)
Evening Star (Auburn, IN) **9982**
Evening Sun (Hanover, PA) **10033**
Evening Sun, The (Norwich, NY) **10016**
Evening Telegram (Herkimer, NY) **10015**
Evening Times (Sayre, PA) **10036**
Evening Times, The (Little Falls, NY) **10015**
Evening World (Bloomfield, IN) **9982**
Express-Times, The (Easton, PA) **10033**
Fairbanks Daily News-Miner
  (Fairbanks, AK) **9957**
Fairborn Daily Herald (Fairborn, OH) **10024**
Fairfax Journal (Fairfax, VA) **10049**
Fairfield Daily Ledger (Fairfield, IA) **9987**
Fairmont Sentinel (Fairmont, MN) **10002**
† Fallon Eagle Standard (Fallon, NV)
Faribault Daily News (Faribault, MN) **10002**
Fayetteville Northwest Arkansas Times
  (Fayetteville, AR) **9959**
Fayetteville Observer-Times
  (Fayetteville, NC) **10019**
Finger Lakes Times, The (Geneva, NY) **10015**
Flint Journal (Flint, MI) **10000**
Florence Morning News (Florence, SC) **10038**
Florida Times-Union (Jacksonville, FL) **9972**
Florida Today (Melbourne, FL) **9972**
Forrest City Times-Herald (Forrest
  City, AR) **9959**
Fort Collins Coloradoan (Fort
  Collins, CO) **9968**
Fort Dodge Messenger (Fort Dodge, IA) **9987**
Fort Madison Daily Democrat (Fort
  Madison, IA) **9987**
Fort Morgan Times (Fort Morgan, CO) **9968**
Fort Scott Tribune, The (Fort Scott, KS) **9990**
Fort Smith Southwest Times Record (Fort
  Smith, AR) **9959**
Fort Wayne News-Sentinel (Fort
  Wayne, IN) **9983**
Fort Worth Star-Telegram (Fort
  Worth, TX) **10043**
Forum, The (Fargo, ND) **10022**
Foster's Daily Democrat (Dover, NH) **10011**
Frankfort State Journal (Frankfort, KY) **9992**
Frankfort Times (Frankfort, IN) **9983**
Franklin Banner-Tribune (Franklin, LA) **9994**
Frederick Leader (Frederick, OK) **10029**
Frederick Post, The (Frederick, MD) **9996**

Fredericksburg Free Lance-Star
  (Fredericksburg, VA) **10049**
Freeman, The (Waukesha, WI) **10055**
Freeport Journal-Standard (Freeport, IL) **9979**
Free Press (Mankato, MN) **10003**
Fremont News-Messenger
  (Fremont, OH) **10024**
Fremont Tribune (Fremont, NE) **10009**
Fresno Bee, The (Fresno, CA) **9962**
Fulton Sun, The (Fulton, MO) **10006**
Gadsden Times (Gadsden, AL) **9956**
Gainesville Daily Register
  (Gainesville, TX) **10043**
Gainesville Sun, The (Gainesville, FL) **9972**
Galion Inquirer (Galion, OH) **10024**
Gallipolis Daily Tribune (Gallipolis, OH) **10024**
Galveston County Daily News, The
  (Galveston, TX) **10044**
Garden City Telegram (Garden City, KS) **9990**
Gardner News (Gardner, MA) **9997**
Gaston Gazette (Gastonia, NC) **10019**
† Geauga Times-Leader (Chardon, OH)
Georgia Times-Union (Brunswick, GA) **9974**
Gettysburg Times (Gettysburg, PA) **10033**
Gilbert Tribune (Gilbert, AZ) **9958**
Glasgow Daily Times (Glasgow, KY) **9992**
Glendale News-Press (Glendale, CA) **9962**
Glenwood Post (Glenwood Springs, CO) **9968**
Globe-Gazette (Mason City, IA) **9988**
Gloucester County Times
  (Woodbury, NJ) **10013**
Gloucester Daily Times (Gloucester, MA) **9997**
Goldsboro News-Argus (Goldsboro, NC) **10019**
Goodland Daily News (Goodland, KS) **9990**
Goshen News, The (Goshen, IN) **9983**
Grand Forks Herald (Grand Forks, ND) **10022**
Grand Haven Tribune (Grand
  Haven, MI) **10000**
Grand Island Independent (Grand
  Island, NE) **10009**
Grand Rapids Press, The (Grand
  Rapids, MI) **10000**
Grants Pass Daily Courier (Grants
  Pass, OR) **10031**
Great Bend Tribune (Great Bend, KS) **9990**
Great Falls Tribune (Great Falls, MT) **10008**
Greeley Tribune (Greeley, CO) **9969**
Green Bay News-Chronicle (Green
  Bay, WI) **10054**
Green Bay Press-Gazette (Green
  Bay, WI) **10054**
Greeneville Sun (Greeneville, TN) **10040**
Greenfield Daily Times (Greenfield, OH) **10024**
Greensburg Daily News (Greensburg, IN) **9983**
Greenville Daily Reflector
  (Greenville, NC) **10019**

Greenville Herald Banner
   (Greenville, TX) **10044**
Greenville News (Greenville, SC) **10038**
† Greenville Piedmont (Greenville, SC)
Greenville Record-Argus
   (Greenville, PA) **10033**
Greenwich Time (Greenwich, CT) **9970**
Greenwood Commonwealth
   (Greenwood, MS) **10004**
Griffin Daily News (Griffin, GA) **9975**
▼ Grove Daily News (Grove, OK) **10029**
Gunnison Country Times (Gunnison, CO) **9969**
Guthrie Daily Leader (Guthrie, OK) **10029**
Guymon Daily Herald (Guymon, OK) **10029**
† Gwinnett Daily News (Lawrenceville, GA)
Gwinnett Daily Post (Lawrenceville, GA) **9975**
Hammond Daily Star (Hammond, LA) **9994**
Hanford Sentinel (Hanford, CA) **9962**
Hannibal Courier-Post (Hannibal, MO) **10006**
Harlan Daily Enterprise (Harlan, KY) **9992**
Harrisburg Daily Register
   (Harrisburg, IL) **9979**
Harrison Daily Times (Harrison, AR) **9959**
Hartford City News-Times (Hartford
   City, IN) **9983**
Hartford Courant (Hartford, CT) **9970**
Hastings Daily Tribune (Hastings, NE) **10009**
Hattiesburg American
   (Hattiesburg, MS) **10004**
Haverhill Gazette (Haverhill, MA) **9997**
Havre Daily News (Havre, MT) **10008**
Hawaii Tribune-Herald (Hilo, HI) **9976**
Hawk Eye, The (Burlington, IA) **9986**
Hays Daily News (Hays, KS) **9990**
Hazleton Standard Speaker
   (Hazleton, PA) **10033**
Helena Daily World (Helena, AR) **9959**
Hemet News (San Jacinto, CA) **9965**
Henderson Daily News (Henderson, TX) **10044**
Henderson Gleaner (Henderson, KY) **9992**
Hendersonville Times-News
   (Hendersonville, NC) **10019**
Henryetta Daily Free-Lance
   (Henryetta, OK) **10029**
Herald & News (Klamath Falls, OR) **10031**
Herald-Citizen (Cookeville, TN) **10040**
Herald-Democrat (Denison, TX) **10043**
Herald-Journal (Spartanburg, SC) **10039**
Herald-Journal, The (Monticello, IN) **9985**
Herald-News, The (Joliet, IL) **9980**
Herald-Palladium (St. Joseph, MI) **10002**
Herald-Review (Decatur, IL) **9979**
Herald-Star (Steubenville, OH) **10026**
Herald-Sun, The (Durham, NC) **10019**
Herald-Times (Bloomington, IN) **9982**
Herald Bulletin (Anderson, IN) **9982**

Herald Coaster (Rosenberg, TX) **10046**
Herald Journal, The (Logan, UT) **10047**
Herald News, The (Fall River, MA) **9997**
Herald Standard (Uniontown, PA) **10037**
Herald, The (New Britain, CT) **9970**
Herald, The (Jasper, IN) **9984**
Herald, The (Hagerstown, MD) **9996**
Herald, The (Sharon, PA) **10036**
Herald, The (Rock Hill, SC) **10039**
Herald, The (Everett, WA) **10051**
Hereford Brand (Hereford, TX) **10044**
Hernando Today (Brooksville, FL) **9971**
Hiawatha Daily World (Hiawatha, KS) **9990**
Hibbing Daily Tribune (Hibbing, MN) **10003**
Hickory Daily Record (Hickory, NC) **10019**
High Point Enterprise (High Point, NC) **10019**
Hillsdale Daily News (Hillsdale, MI) **10000**
Hilton Head Island Packet (Hilton
   Head, SC) **10038**
Hobbs Daily News-Sun (Hobbs, NM) **10013**
Holdenville Daily News
   (Holdenville, OK) **10029**
Holdrege Daily Citizen (Holdrege, NE) **10009**
Holland Sentinel (Holland, MI) **10000**
Hollister Free Lance (Hollister, CA) **9962**
† Hollywood Sun (Hollywood, FL)
Home News & Tribune, The (East
   Brunswick, NJ) **10012**
Honolulu Advertiser (Honolulu, HI) **9976**
Honolulu Star-Bulletin (Honolulu, HI) **9976**
Hope Star, The (Hope, AR) **9959**
Hopewell News (Hopewell, VA) **10049**
Hornell Evening Tribune (Hornell, NY) **10015**
Hour, The (Norwalk, CT) **9970**
Houston Chronicle (Houston, TX) **10044**
† Houston Post (Houston, TX)
Hugo Daily News (Hugo, OK) **10029**
Humboldt Sun (Winnemucca, NV) **10011**
Huntington Herald-Dispatch
   (Huntington, WV) **10052**
Huntington Herald-Press
   (Huntington, IN) **9983**
Huntsville Item (Huntsville, TX) **10044**
† Huntsville News (Huntsville, AL)
Huntsville Times, The (Huntsville, AL) **9956**
Huron Daily Tribune (Bad Axe, MI) **9999**
Hutchinson News (Hutchinson, KS) **9990**
Idaho Falls Post Register (Idaho
   Falls, ID) **9977**
Idaho Press-Tribune (Nampa, ID) **9977**
Idaho State Journal (Pocatello, ID) **9977**
Idaho Statesman, The (Boise, ID) **9976**
Imperial Valley Press (El Centro, CA) **9961**
Independence Daily Reporter
   (Independence, KS) **9990**

Independence Examiner, The
  (Independence, MO) **10006**
Independent Record (Helena, MT) **10008**
Independent, The (Massillon, OH) **10025**
Index-Journal (Greenwood, SC) **10038**
Indiana Gazette (Indiana, PA) **10034**
Indianapolis News (Indianapolis, IN) **9984**
Indianapolis Star (Indianapolis, IN) **9984**
Inland Valley Daily Bulletin (Ontario, CA) **9963**
Intelligencer Record, The
  (Doylestown, PA) **10033**
Inter-Mountain, The (Elkins, WV) **10052**
Iola Register (Iola, KS) **9990**
Ionia Sentinel-Standard (Ionia, MI) **10000**
Iowa City Press-Citizen (Iowa City, IA) **9987**
Ironton Tribune (Ironton, OH) **10024**
Ironwood Daily Globe (Ironwood, MI) **10000**
Iroquois County Times Republic
  (Watseka, IL) **9981**
Island Times (Lihue, HI) **9976**
Item, The (Sumter, SC) **10039**
Ithaca Journal, The (Ithaca, NY) **10015**
Jackson Citizen Patriot (Jackson, MI) **10000**
Jackson County Floridan (Marianna, FL) **9972**
Jackson Sun (Jackson, TN) **10040**
Jacksonville Daily News
  (Jacksonville, NC) **10019**
Jacksonville Daily Progress
  (Jacksonville, TX) **10044**
Jacksonville Journal-Courier
  (Jacksonville, IL) **9979**
Jacksonville Patriot (Jacksonville, AR) **9960**
Jamestown Sun, The (Jamestown, ND) **10022**
Janesville Gazette (Janesville, WI) **10054**
Jasper Daily Mountain Eagle (Jasper, AL) **9956**
Jeffersonville Evening News
  (Jeffersonville, IN) **9984**
Jennings Daily News (Jennings, LA) **9994**
Jersey Journal, The (Jersey City, NJ) **10012**
Johnson City Press (Johnson City, TN) **10040**
Jonesboro Sun (Jonesboro, AR) **9960**
Joplin Globe, The (Joplin, MO) **10006**
Journal & Courier (Lafayette, IN) **9984**
Journal-Gazette, The (Fort Wayne, IN) **9983**
Journal-Register (Medina, NY) **10016**
Journal-World, The (Lawrence, KS) **9990**
Journal American (Bellevue, WA) **10050**
Journal Inquirer (Manchester, CT) **9970**
Journal Messenger (Manassas, VA) **10049**
Journal News (Hamilton, OH) **10024**
Journal, The (New Ulm, MN) **10003**
Journal, The (Martinsburg, WV) **10052**
Journal Times (Racine, WI) **10055**
Journal Tribune (Biddeford, ME) **9995**
Junction City Daily Union (Junction
  City, KS) **9990**

Juneau Empire (Juneau, AK) **9957**
Kalamazoo Gazette (Kalamazoo, MI) **10000**
Kane County Chronicle (Geneva, IL) **9979**
Kane Republican (Kane, PA) **10034**
Kannapolis Daily Independent
  (Kannapolis, NC) **10020**
† Kansas City Evening News (Shawnee
  Mission, KS)
Kansas City Kansan (Kansas City, KS) **9990**
Kansas City Star (Kansas City, MO) **10006**
Kearney Hub (Kearney, NE) **10009**
Keene Sentinel (Keene, NH) **10011**
Kendallville News-Sun (Kendallville, IN) **9984**
Kennebec Journal (Augusta, ME) **9995**
Kenosha News (Kenosha, WI) **10054**
Kent-Ravenna Record-Courier
  (Ravenna, OH) **10026**
Kent County Daily Times (West
  Warwick, RI) **10038**
Kenton Times (Kenton, OH) **10024**
Kentucky New Era (Hopkinsville, KY) **9992**
Kentucky Post, The (Covington, KY) **9992**
Keokuk Daily Gate City (Keokuk, IA) **9987**
Kerrville Daily Times (Kerrville, TX) **10044**
Ketchikan Daily News (Ketchikan, AK) **9957**
Kewanee Star-Courier (Kewanee, IL) **9980**
Key West Citizen (Key West, FL) **9972**
Kilgore News Herald (Kilgore, TX) **10044**
Killeen Daily Herald (Killeen, TX) **10044**
Kingman Daily Miner (Kingman, AZ) **9958**
Kingsport Daily News (Kingsport, TN) **10040**
Kingsport Times-News (Kingsport, TN) **10040**
Kinston Daily Free Press (Kinston, NC) **10020**
Kirksville Daily Express (Kirksville, MO) **10007**
Knoxville News-Sentinel (Knoxville, TN) **10041**
Kodiak Daily Mirror (Kodiak, AK) **9957**
Kokomo Tribune, The (Kokomo, IN) **9984**
La Crosse Tribune (La Crosse, WI) **10054**
Lafayette Advertiser (Lafayette, LA) **9994**
La Grange Daily News (La Grange, GA) **9975**
Lahontan Valley News (Fallon, NV) **10010**
La Junta Tribune-Democrat (La
  Junta, CO) **9969**
Lake Charles American Press (Lake
  Charles, LA) **9994**
Lake City Reporter (Lake City, FL) **9972**
Lake County Record-Bee (Lakeport, CA) **9962**
Lake Havasu City Herald (Lake Havasu
  City, AZ) **9958**
Lake Sun Leader (Camdenton, MO) **10005**
Lamar Daily News (Lamar, CO) **9969**
Lancaster Eagle-Gazette
  (Lancaster, OH) **10025**
Lancaster Intelligencer Journal
  (Lancaster, PA) **10034**
Lancaster New Era (Lancaster, PA) **10034**

Lansing State Journal (Lansing, MI) **10000**
La Porte Herald-Argus (La Porte, IN) **9984**
Laramie Daily Boomerang
 (Laramie, WY) **10055**
Laredo Morning Times (Laredo, TX) **10044**
Las Cruces Sun-News (Las Cruces, NM) **10013**
Las Vegas Daily Optic (Las Vegas, NM) **10013**
Las Vegas Review-Journal (Las
 Vegas, NV) **10010**
Las Vegas Sun (Las Vegas, NV) **10010**
Latrobe Bulletin (Latrobe, PA) **10034**
Laurel Leader-Call (Laurel, MS) **10004**
Laurinburg Exchange (Laurinburg, NC) **10020**
Lawrenceville Daily Record
 (Lawrenceville, IL) **9980**
Lawton Constitution (Lawton, OK) **10029**
† Lead Call (Lead, SD)
Leader-Herald, The (Gloversville, NY) **10015**
Leader-Telegram (Eau Claire, WI) **10054**
Leader, The (Corning, NY) **10014**
Leader Times (Kittanning, PA) **10034**
Leaf-Chronicle, The (Clarksville, TN) **10040**
Leavenworth Times (Leavenworth, KS) **9990**
Lebanon Daily News (Lebanon, PA) **10034**
Lebanon Daily Record (Lebanon, MO) **10007**
Lebanon Democrat, The (Lebanon, TN) **10041**
Ledger-Independent (Maysville, KY) **9993**
† Ledger-Star (Norfolk, VA)
Ledger Dispatch (Antioch, CA) **9961**
Ledger, The (Lakeland, FL) **9972**
Ledger Tribune, The (New Albany, IN) **9985**
Leesville Daily Leader (Leesville, LA) **9994**
Le Mars Daily Sentinel (Le Mars, IA) **9988**
Lenoir News-Topic (Lenoir, NC) **10020**
Lewisburg Daily Journal (Milton, PA) **10035**
Lewiston Morning Tribune (Lewiston, ID) **9977**
Lexington Dispatch (Lexington, NC) **10020**
Lexington Herald-Leader (Lexington, KY) **9992**
Liberal Southwest Daily Times
 (Liberal, KS) **9991**
Lima News (Lima, OH) **10025**
Lincoln Courier (Lincoln, IL) **9980**
Lincoln Journal Star (Lincoln, NE) **10009**
Linton Daily Citizen (Linton, IN) **9984**
Litchfield News-Herald (Litchfield, IL) **9980**
† Little Falls Transcript (Little Falls, MN)
Livingston Enterprise (Livingston, MT) **10009**
Lock Haven Express (Lock Haven, PA) **10034**
Lodi News-Sentinel (Lodi, CA) **9962**
Logan Banner (Logan, WV) **10052**
Logan Daily News (Logan, OH) **10025**
Log Cabin Democrat (Conway, AR) **9959**
Lompoc Record (Lompoc, CA) **9962**
Longview News Journal (Longview, TX) **10044**
Los Angeles Bulletin (Los Angeles, CA) **9963**

Los Angeles Daily Journal (Los
 Angeles, CA) **9963**
Los Angeles Times (Los Angeles, CA) **9963**
Loveland Daily Reporter-Herald
 (Loveland, CO) **9969**
Lovington Daily Leader (Lovington, NM) **10013**
Lowell Sun (Lowell, MA) **9997**
Lubbock Avalanche-Journal
 (Lubbock, TX) **10044**
Ludington Daily News (Ludington, MI) **10000**
Lufkin Daily News (Lufkin, TX) **10044**
Lyons Daily News (Lyons, KS) **9991**
Macomb Daily (Mt. Clemens, MI) **10001**
Macomb Journal (Macomb, IL) **9980**
Macon Chronicle-Herald (Macon, MO) **10007**
Macon Telegraph (Macon, GA) **9975**
Madera Tribune (Madera, CA) **9963**
Madison Courier (Madison, IN) **9984**
Madison Daily Leader (Madison, SD) **10039**
Madison Press, The (London, OH) **10025**
Mail Tribune (Medford, OR) **10031**
Malone Telegram (Malone, NY) **10015**
Malvern Daily Record (Malvern, AR) **9960**
Manhattan Mercury (Manhattan, KS) **9991**
Manistee News-Advocate (Manistee, MI) **10000**
Manitowoc Herald-Times Reporter
 (Manitowoc, WI) **10054**
Manteca Bulletin (Manteca, CA) **9963**
Marianas Variety News & Views
 (Saipan, MP) **10022**
Marietta Daily Journal (Marietta, GA) **9975**
Marietta Times (Marietta, OH) **10025**
† Marin County Daily Recording (San
 Rafael, CA)
Marin Independent Journal (Novato, CA) **9963**
Marion Chronicle-Tribune (Marion, IN) **9984**
Marion Daily Republican (Marion, IL) **9980**
Marion Star (Marion, OH) **10025**
Marquette Mining Journal
 (Marquette, MI) **10001**
Marshall Chronicle (Marshall, MI) **10001**
Marshall Democrat-News
 (Marshall, MO) **10007**
Marshall Independent (Marshall, MN) **10003**
Marshall News Messenger
 (Marshall, TX) **10045**
Marshalltown Times-Republican
 (Marshalltown, IA) **9988**
Marshfield News Herald
 (Marshfield, WI) **10054**
Martinsville Bulletin (Martinsville, VA) **10049**
Martinsville Daily Reporter
 (Martinsville, IN) **9984**
Marysville Journal-Tribune
 (Marysville, OH) **10025**
Maryville Daily Forum (Maryville, MO) **10007**

Mattoon Journal Gazette (Mattoon, IL) **9980**
Maui News (Wailuku, HI) **9976**
Mayfield Messenger (Mayfield, KY) **9993**
McAlester News-Capital
   (McAlester, OK) **10029**
McAllen Monitor (McAllen, TX) **10045**
McComb Enterprise-Journal
   (McComb, MS) **10004**
McCook Daily Gazette (McCook, NE) **10009**
McCurtain Daily Gazette (Idabel, OK) **10029**
McDowell News, The (Marion, NC) **10020**
McKeesport Daily News
   (McKeesport, PA) **10035**
McKinney Courier Gazette
   (McKinney, TX) **10045**
McPherson Sentinel (McPherson, KS) **9991**
Meadville Tribune, The (Meadville, PA) **10035**
Medina County Gazette (Medina, OH) **10025**
Merced Sun-Star (Merced, CA) **9963**
Mercury, The (Pottstown, PA) **10035**
Meridian Star (Meridian, MS) **10004**
Mesabi Daily News (Virginia, MN) **10003**
Mesa Tribune (Mesa, AZ) **9958**
Messenger, The (Troy, AL) **9956**
Messenger, The (Madisonville, KY) **9992**
Metropolitan, The (Los Angeles, CA) **9963**
Mexia Daily News (Mexia, TX) **10045**
Mexico Ledger (Mexico, MO) **10007**
Miami Herald (Miami, FL) **9972**
Miami News-Record (Miami, OK) **10029**
Michigan City News-Dispatch (Michigan
   City, IN) **9984**
Middlesboro Daily News
   (Middlesboro, KY) **9993**
Middlesex News (Framingham, MA) **9997**
Middletown Journal (Middletown, OH) **10025**
Middletown Press (Middletown, CT) **9970**
Midland Daily News (Midland, MI) **10001**
Midland Reporter-Telegram
   (Midland, TX) **10045**
Miles City Star (Miles City, MT) **10009**
† Milford Citizen (Milford, CT)
Milford Daily News (Milford, MA) **9998**
Milton Daily Standard (Milton, PA) **10035**
Milville News (Bridgeton, NJ) **10011**
Milwaukee Journal-Sentinel
   (Milwaukee, WI) **10054**
Minden Press-Herald (Minden, LA) **9994**
Mineral Daily Tribune (Keyser, WV) **10052**
Mineral Wells Index (Mineral Wells, TX) **10045**
Minot Daily News (Minot, ND) **10022**
Mississippi Press (Pascagoula, MS) **10005**
Missoulian, The (Missoula, MT) **10009**
Moberly Monitor Index (Moberly, MO) **10007**
Mobile Register, The (Mobile, AL) **9956**
Modesto Bee, The (Modesto, CA) **9963**

Mohave Valley Daily News (Bullhead
   City, AZ) **9957**
Monett Times (Monett, MO) **10007**
Monitor, The (Los Alamos, NM) **10013**
Monroe Evening News (Monroe, MI) **10001**
Monroe Times, The (Monroe, WI) **10054**
Montana Standard (Butte, MT) **10008**
Monterey County Herald, The
   (Monterey, CA) **9963**
Montgomery Advertiser
   (Montgomery, AL) **9956**
Montgomery Journal, The (Rockville, MD) **9996**
Montrose Daily Press (Montrose, CO) **9969**
▼Montrose Morning Sun (Montrose, CO) **9969**
Moorpark Star (Moorpark, CA) **9963**
Morning Call, The (Allentown, PA) **10032**
Morning Intelligencer, The
   (Wheeling, WV) **10053**
Morning Journal (Lisbon, OH) **10025**
Morning Journal (Lorain, OH) **10025**
Morning News of Northwest Arkansas
   (Springdale, AR) **9960**
Morning Sun (Mt. Pleasant, MI) **10001**
Morris Daily Herald (Morris, IL) **9980**
Moscow-Pullman Daily News
   (Moscow, ID) **9977**
Moundsville Daily Echo
   (Moundsville, WV) **10053**
Mountain Democrat (Placerville, CA) **9964**
Mountain Mail (Salida, CO) **9969**
Mountain Press, The (Sevierville, TN) **10041**
Mount Airy News (Mt. Airy, NC) **10020**
Mount Carmel Daily Republican-Register (Mt.
   Carmel, IL) **9980**
Mount Pleasant Daily Tribune (Mt.
   Pleasant, TX) **10045**
Mount Pleasant News (Mt. Pleasant, IA) **9988**
Mount Vernon News (Mt. Vernon, OH) **10025**
Mt. Vernon Daily Argus (Yonkers, NY) **10018**
Mt. Vernon Register News (Mt.
   Vernon, IL) **9980**
Murfreesboro Daily News Journal
   (Murfreesboro, TN) **10041**
Murray Ledger & Times (Murray, KY) **9993**
Muscatine Journal (Muscatine, IA) **9988**
Muskegon Chronicle, The
   (Muskegon, MI) **10001**
Muskogee Daily Phoenix & Times-Democrat
   (Muskogee, OK) **10029**
Napa Valley Register (Napa, CA) **9963**
Naples Daily News (Naples, FL) **9973**
Nashville Banner (Nashville, TN) **10041**
Natchez Democrat (Natchez, MS) **10005**
Natchitoches Times (Natchitoches, LA) **9994**
Naugatuck Daily News (Naugatuck, CT) **9970**

Nebraska City News-Press (Nebraska City, NE) **10009**
Neosho Daily News (Neosho, MO) **10007**
Nevada Appeal (Carson City, NV) **10010**
New Braunfels Herald & Zeitung (New Braunfels, TX) **10045**
† Newburgh Evening News (Newburgh, NY)
New Castle Courier-Times (New Castle, IN) **9985**
New Castle News (New Castle, PA) **10035**
New Haven Register (New Haven, CT) **9970**
New Jersey Herald (Newton, NJ) **10012**
Newport Daily Express (Newport, VT) **10048**
Newport Daily Independent (Newport, AR) **9960**
Newport Daily News, The (Newport, RI) **10037**
Newport News Daily Press (Newport News, VA) **10049**
News & Advance (Lynchburg, VA) **10049**
News & Observer (Raleigh, NC) **10020**
News & Record, The (Greensboro, NC) **10019**
News-Courier (Athens, AL) **9955**
News-Enterprise (Elizabethtown, KY) **9992**
News-Gazette, The (Winchester, IN) **9986**
News-Herald (Port Clinton, OH) **10026**
News-Herald (Willoughby, OH) **10027**
News-Herald (Oil City, PA) **10035**
News-Pilot, The (San Pedro, CA) **9965**
News-Press, The (Fort Myers, FL) **9972**
News-Record (Gillette, WY) **10055**
News-Review (Roseburg, OR) **10032**
News-Star, The (Monroe, LA) **9994**
News-Sun, The (Waukegan, IL) **9982**
News-Times (Danbury, CT) **9970**
News-Tribune (La Salle, IL) **9980**
News-Tribune (Framingham, MA) **9997**
News Chief (Winter Haven, FL) **9974**
Newsday (Melville, NY) **10016**
News Herald, The (Panama City, FL) **9973**
News Herald, The (Morganton, NC) **10020**
News Journal (Mansfield, OH) **10025**
News Journal, The (New Castle, DE) **9971**
New Smyrna Beach Observer (New Smyrna, FL) **9973**
† News of Paterson (Passaic, NJ)
† News Outlook (Aberdeen, NC)
News, The (Boca Raton, FL) **9971**
News, The (Southbridge, MA) **9998**
News, The (Frederick, MD) **9996**
News Tribune, The (Tacoma, WA) **10051**
Newton Daily News (Newton, IA) **9988**
Newton Kansan (Newton, KS) **9991**
† New York City Tribune (New York, NY)
New York Daily Challenge (Brooklyn, NY) **10014**

New York Daily News, The (New York, NY) **10016**
† New York Newsday (New York, NY)
New York Post (New York, NY) **10016**
New York Times, The (New York, NY) **10016**
Niagara Gazette (Niagara Falls, NY) **10016**
Niles Daily Star (Niles, MI) **10001**
Norfolk Daily News (Norfolk, NE) **10010**
Norman Transcript (Norman, OK) **10029**
North County Times (Escondido, CA) **9962**
Northeast Mississippi Daily Journal (Tupelo, MS) **10005**
Northern Virginia Daily (Strasburg, VA) **10050**
Northern Wyoming Daily News (Worland, WY) **10056**
North Hills News Record (Warrendale, PA) **10037**
North Jersey Herald & News, The (Passaic, NJ) **10012**
Northwest Colorado Daily Press (Craig, CO) **9968**
Northwest Florida Daily News (Fort Walton Beach, FL) **9972**
Northwest Herald (Crystal Lake, IL) **9978**
Northwest Signal (Napoleon, OH) **10026**
Norton Daily Telegram (Norton, KS) **9991**
Norwalk Reflector (Norwalk, OH) **10026**
Norwich Bulletin (Norwich, CT) **9970**
Oakland Press, The (Pontiac, MI) **10001**
Oak Ridger, The (Oak Ridge, TN) **10041**
Observer-Dispatch (Utica, NY) **10017**
Observer-Reporter (Waynesburg, PA) **10037**
Observer-Reporter, Washington County Edition (Washington, PA) **10037**
Observer News (Newton, NC) **10020**
Observer, The (New Smyrna, FL) **9973**
Observer, The (Moultrie, GA) **9975**
Observer, The (La Grande, OR) **10031**
Ocala Star Banner (Ocala, FL) **9973**
Ocean County's Observer (Toms River, NJ) **10012**
Odessa American (Odessa, TX) **10045**
Oelwein Daily Register (Oelwein, IA) **9988**
Ogdensburg Journal (Ogdensburg, NY) **10016**
Okmulgee Times (Okmulgee, OK) **10030**
Olathe Daily News (Olathe, KS) **9991**
Olean Times Herald (Olean, NY) **10016**
Olney Daily Mail (Olney, IL) **9981**
Olympian, The (Olympia, WA) **10051**
Omaha World-Herald (Omaha, NE) **10010**
Oneida Daily Dispatch (Oneida, NY) **10016**
Opelika-Auburn News (Opelika, AL) **9956**
Orange Coast Daily Pilot (Costa Mesa, CA) **9961**
Orange County Register (Santa Ana, CA) **9965**
Orange Leader (Orange, TX) **10045**

Oregonian, The (Portland, OR) 10032
Orlando Sentinel (Orlando, FL) 9973
Oroville Mercury-Register (Oroville, CA) 9963
Oshkosh Northwestern (Oshkosh, WI) 10054
Oskaloosa Herald (Oskaloosa, IA) 9988
Ottawa Herald (Ottawa, KS) 9991
Ottumwa Courier (Ottumwa, IA) 9988
Outlook, The (Santa Monica, CA) 9966
Owatonna People's Press
   (Owatonna, MN) 10003
Owensboro Messenger-Inquirer
   (Owensboro, KY) 9993
Oxford Eagle (Oxford, MS) 10005
† Oxnard Press-Courier (Oxnard, CA)
Pacific Daily News (Agana, GU) 9976
Paducah Sun (Paducah, KY) 9993
Palestine Herald-Press (Palestine, TX) 10045
Palladium-Times, The (Oswego, NY) 10016
Palm Beach Daily News (Palm Beach, FL) 9973
Palm Beach Post (West Palm Beach, FL) 9974
▼Palo Alto Daily News (Palo Alto, CA) 9964
Pampa News (Pampa, TX) 10045
Pantagraph, The (Bloomington, IL) 9978
Paragould Daily Press (Paragould, AR) 9960
Paris Beacon News (Paris, IL) 9981
Paris News (Paris, TX) 10045
Paris Post-Intelligencer, The (Paris, TN) 10041
Parkersburg Sentinel
   (Parkersburg, WV) 10053
Parsons Sun (Parsons, KS) 9991
Pasadena Citizen (Pasadena, TX) 10045
Pasadena Star-News, The
   (Pasadena, CA) 9964
Patriot-News (Harrisburg, PA) 10033
Patriot Ledger (Quincy, MA) 9998
Pauls Valley Daily Democrat (Pauls
   Valley, OK) 10030
Paxton Daily Record (Paxton, IL) 9981
† Peabody Times (Peabody, MA)
Pecos Enterprise (Pecos, TX) 10046
Peekskill Star (Yorktown Heights, NY) 10018
Pekin Daily Times (Pekin, IL) 9981
Peninsula Clarion (Kenai, AK) 9957
Peninsula Daily News (Port
   Angeles, WA) 10051
Pensacola News Journal (Pensacola, FL) 9973
Peoria Journal Star (Peoria, IL) 9981
Perry Daily Journal (Perry, OK) 10030
Peru Tribune (Peru, IN) 9985
Petoskey News-Review (Petoskey, MI) 10001
Pharos-Tribune (Logansport, IN) 9984
Philadelphia Daily News
   (Philadelphia, PA) 10035
Philadelphia Inquirer (Philadelphia, PA) 10035
Phoenix Gazette (Phoenix, AZ) 9958
Phoenix, The (Phoenixville, PA) 10035

Picayune Item (Picayune, MS) 10005
Pierre Capital Journal (Pierre, SD) 10039
Pilot-News (Plymouth, IN) 9985
Pine Bluff Commercial (Pine Bluff, AR) 9960
Pioneer, The (Bemidji, MN) 10002
Piqua Daily Call (Piqua, OH) 10026
Pittsburgh Post-Gazette
   (Pittsburgh, PA) 10035
† Pittsburgh Press (Pittsburgh, PA)
Pittsburg Morning Sun (Pittsburg, KS) 9991
Plainsman, The (Huron, SD) 10039
Plainview Daily Herald (Plainview, TX) 10046
Plano Star Courier (Plano, TX) 10046
Pocono Record (Stroudsburg, PA) 10036
Point Pleasant Register (Point
   Pleasant, WV) 10053
Ponca City News (Ponca City, OK) 10030
Pontiac Daily Leader (Pontiac, IL) 9981
Portales News-Tribune (Portales, NM) 10014
Port Arthur News (Port Arthur, TX) 10046
Porterville Recorder (Porterville, CA) 9964
Portland Commercial Review
   (Portland, IN) 9985
Portland Press Herald (Portland, ME) 9995
Portsmouth Daily Times
   (Portsmouth, OH) 10026
Portsmouth Herald (Portsmouth, NH) 10011
Post & Mail, The (Columbia City, IN) 9982
Post-Bulletin (Rochester, MN) 10003
Post-Crescent (Appleton, WI) 10053
Post-Journal, The (Jamestown, NY) 10015
Post-Standard (Syracuse, NY) 10017
Post-Star (Glen Falls, NY) 10015
Post-Tribune (Gary, IN) 9983
Post-Tribune (Jefferson City, MO) 10006
Poteau Daily News & Sun (Poteau, OK) 10030
Potomac News (Woodbridge, VA) 10050
Pottsville Republican (Pottsville, PA) 10035
Poughkeepsie Journal
   (Poughkeepsie, NY) 10017
Pratt Tribune (Pratt, KS) 9991
Press & Sun-Bulletin (Vestal, NY) 10017
Press-Enterprise, The (Riverside, CA) 9964
Press-Journal (Vero Beach, FL) 9974
Press-Republican (Plattsburgh, NY) 10016
Press-Telegram (Long Beach, CA) 9962
Press Enterprise, The (Bloomsburg, PA) 10032
Press Leader, The (Farmington, MO) 10006
Press of Atlantic City, The
   (Pleasantville, NJ) 10012
Prince Georges Journal (Lanham, MD) 9996
Princeton Daily Clarion (Princeton, IN) 9985
▼Prince William Journal
   (Manassas, VA) 10049
Progress-Index (Petersburg, VA) 10049
† Progress, The (Clearfield, PA)

Providence Journal-Bulletin
(Providence, RI) **10038**
Pryor Daily Times (Pryor, OK) **10030**
Public Opinion, The
(Chambersburg, PA) **10032**
Pueblo Chieftain (Pueblo, CO) **9969**
Punxsutawney Spirit
(Punxsutawney, PA) **10035**
Quad-City Times (Davenport, IA) **9987**
Quincy Herald-Whig (Quincy, IL) **9981**
Rapid City Journal (Rapid City, SD) **10039**
Ravalli Republic (Hamilton, MT) **10008**
Reading Eagle & Reading Times
(Reading, PA) **10036**
Record-Journal (Meriden, CT) **9970**
Recorder, The (Greenfield, MA) **9997**
Recorder, The (Amsterdam, NY) **10014**
Record Herald (Washington Court
House, OH) **10027**
Record Herald (Waynesboro, PA) **10037**
Record Searchlight (Redding, CA) **9964**
Record, The (Stockton, CA) **9966**
Record, The (Hackensack, NJ) **10012**
Record, The (Troy, NY) **10017**
Record, The (Horsham, PA) **10034**
Red Bluff Daily News (Red Bluff, CA) **9964**
Redlands Daily Facts (Redlands, CA) **9964**
Red Wing Republican Eagle (Red
Wing, MN) **10003**
Register-Guard (Eugene, OR) **10031**
Register-Mail (Galesburg, IL) **9979**
Register-Pajaronian (Watsonville, CA) **9967**
Register/Herald (Beckley, WV) **10052**
Register Citizen (Torrington, CT) **9971**
Register Star (Rockford, IL) **9981**
Register Star (Hudson, NY) **10015**
† Register, The (Shrewsbury, NJ)
Reidsville Review (Reidsville, NC) **10020**
Reno Gazette-Journal (Reno, NV) **10010**
Rensselaer Republican (Rensselaer, IN) **9985**
Reporter Dispatch, The (White
Plains, NY) **10018**
Reporter, The (Vacaville, CA) **9967**
Reporter, The (Lebanon, IN) **9984**
Reporter, The (Lansdale, PA) **10034**
Reporter, The (Fond Du Lac, WI) **10054**
Repository, The (Canton, OH) **10023**
Republic, The (Columbus, IN) **9982**
Review Times (Fostoria, OH) **10024**
Rhinelander Daily News
(Rhinelander, WI) **10055**
Richmond County Daily Journal
(Rockingham, NC) **10021**
Richmond Palladium-Item
(Richmond, IN) **9985**
Richmond Register (Richmond, KY) **9993**

Richmond Times-Dispatch
(Richmond, VA) **10050**
Ridgway Record (Ridgway, PA) **10036**
Riverton Ranger (Riverton, WY) **10056**
Roanoke Rapids Daily & Sunday Herald
(Roanoke Rapids, NC) **10020**
Roanoke Times, The (Roanoke, VA) **10050**
Robesonian, The (Lumberton, NC) **10020**
Robinson Daily News (Robinson, IL) **9981**
Rochester Democrat & Chronicle
(Rochester, NY) **10017**
Rochester Sentinel, The (Rochester, IN) **9985**
Rockdale Citizen (Conyers, GA) **9975**
Rock Island Argus Dispatch, The
(Moline, IL) **9980**
Rockland Journal-News (West
Nyack, NY) **10018**
Rock Springs Daily Rocket-Miner (Rock
Springs, WY) **10056**
Rocky Ford Daily Gazette (Rocky
Ford, CO) **9969**
Rocky Mountain News (Denver, CO) **9968**
Rocky Mount Telegram (Rocky
Mount, NC) **10021**
Rolla Daily News (Rolla, MO) **10007**
Rome News-Tribune (Rome, GA) **9975**
Roswell Daily Record (Roswell, NM) **10014**
Rushville Republican (Rushville, IN) **9985**
Russell Daily News (Russell, KS) **9991**
Ruston Daily Leader (Ruston, LA) **9995**
Rutland Herald (Rutland, VT) **10048**
Sacramento Bee (Sacramento, CA) **9965**
Saginaw News (Saginaw, MI) **10001**
Saipan Tribune (Saipan, MP) **10022**
Salamanca Press (Salamanca, NY) **10017**
Salem Evening News (Beverly, MA) **9996**
Salem News (Salem, OH) **10026**
Salina Journal (Salina, KS) **9991**
Salisbury Post (Salisbury, NC) **10021**
Salt Lake City Deseret News (Salt Lake
City, UT) **10047**
Salt Lake Tribune (Salt Lake City, UT) **10048**
Samoa News (Pago Pago, AS) **9957**
Sampson Independent, The
(Clinton, NC) **10018**
San Angelo Standard-Times (San
Angelo, TX) **10046**
San Antonio Express-News (San
Antonio, TX) **10046**
† San Antonio Light (San Antonio, TX)
San Bernardino County Sun (San
Bernardino, CA) **9965**
San Diego Transcript (San Diego, CA) **9965**
San Diego Union-Tribune (San
Diego, CA) **9965**
Sandusky Register (Sandusky, OH) **10026**

Sanford Herald (Sanford, FL) 9973
Sanford Herald, The (Sanford, NC) 10021
San Francisco Chronicle (San Francisco, CA) 9965
San Francisco Daily Journal (San Francisco, CA) 9965
San Francisco Examiner (San Francisco, CA) 9965
San Gabriel Valley Tribune (West Covina, CA) 9967
San Jose Mercury News (San Jose, CA) 9965
San Luis Obispo County Telegram-Tribune (San Luis Obisopo, CA) 9965
San Marcos Daily Record (San Marcos, TX) 10046
San Mateo Times (San Mateo, CA) 9965
San Ramon Valley Times, The (Danville, CA) 9961
Santa Barbara News Press (Santa Barbara, CA) 9965
Santa Cruz County Sentinel (Santa Cruz, CA) 9966
Santa Fe New Mexican (Santa Fe, NM) 10014
Santa Maria Times (Santa Maria, CA) 9966
Santa Rosa Press Democrat (Santa Rosa, CA) 9966
Sapulpa Daily Herald (Sapulpa, OK) 10030
Sarasota Herald Tribune (Sarasota, FL) 9973
Saratogian, The (Saratoga Springs, NY) 10017
Sault Ste. Marie Evening News (Sault Ste. Marie, MI) 10001
Savannah Morning News/Evening Press (Savannah, GA) 9976
Scottsdale Progress Tribune (Scottsdale, AZ) 9958
Scranton Times/Sunday Times (Scranton, PA) 10036
Seattle Daily Journal of Commerce (Seattle, WA) 10051
Seattle Post-Intelligencer (Seattle, WA) 10051
Seattle Times (Seattle, WA) 10051
Sedalia Democrat, The (Sedalia, MO) 10007
Seguin Gazette-Enterprise (Seguin, TX) 10046
Selma Times-Journal (Selma, AL) 9956
Seminole Daily Producer (Seminole, OK) 10030
Sentinel & Enterprise (Fitchburg, MA) 9997
Sentinel-Record, The (Hot Springs, AR) 9960
Sentinel-Tribune (Bowling Green, OH) 10023
Sentinel, The (Lewistown, PA) 10034
Shamokin News-Item (Shamokin, PA) 10036
Shawano Leader (Shawano, WI) 10055
Shawnee News-Star (Shawnee, OK) 10030
Sheboygan Press, The (Sheboygan, WI) 10055
Shelby Globe (Shelby, OH) 10026
Shelby Star (Shelby, NC) 10021

Shelbyville Daily Union (Shelbyville, IL) 9981
Shelbyville News (Shelbyville, IN) 9985
Shelbyville Times-Gazette (Shelbyville, TN) 10041
Sheridan Press (Sheridan, WY) 10056
Shoshone News-Press (Kellogg, ID) 9977
† Shreveport Journal (Shreveport, LA)
Sidney Daily News (Sidney, OH) 10026
Sidney Telegraph (Sidney, NE) 10010
Sierra Vista Herald (Sierra Vista, AZ) 9958
Signal, The (Valencia, CA) 9967
Sikeston Standard Democrat, The (Sikeston, MO) 10007
Silver City Daily Press & Independent (Silver City, NM) 10014
Simi Valley Star (Simi Valley, CA) 9966
Sioux City Journal (Sioux City, IA) 9988
Siskiyou Daily News (Yreka, CA) 9968
Skagit Valley Herald (Mt. Vernon, WA) 10051
Slidell Sentry-News (Slidell, LA) 9995
Snyder Daily News (Snyder, TX) 10046
South Bend Tribune (South Bend, IN) 9985
Southeast Missourian (Cape Girardeau, MO) 10005
Southern Illinoisan (Carbondale, IL) 9978
South Haven Daily Tribune (South Haven, MI) 10002
South Idaho Press (Burley, ID) 9977
Southwest Daily News (Sulphur, LA) 9995
Southwest Times, The (Pulaski, VA) 10050
Spectrum, The (St. George, UT) 10048
Spencer Daily Reporter (Spencer, IA) 9988
Spencer Evening World (Spencer, IN) 9986
Spokesman-Review, The (Spokane, WA) 10051
Springfield News-Leader, The (Springfield, MO) 10008
Springfield News-Sun (Springfield, OH) 10026
St. Albans Messenger (St. Albans, VT) 10048
Standard-Examiner (Ogden, UT) 10047
Standard-Observer (Greensburg, PA) 10033
Standard-Star (New Rochelle, NY) 10016
Standard-Times, The (New Bedford, MA) 9998
Star-Democrat, The (Easton, MD) 9996
Star-Gazette (Elmira, NY) 10015
Star-Herald (Scottsbluff, NE) 10010
Star-Ledger (Newark, NJ) 10012
Starkville Daily News (Starkville, MS) 10005
Star Press (Muncie, IN) 9985
Star Tribune (Minneapolis, MN) 10003
State Gazette (Dyersburg, TN) 10040
State Journal-Register (Springfield, IL) 9981
Staten Island Advance (Staten Island, NY) 10017
Statesboro Herald (Statesboro, GA) 9976
Statesman Journal (Salem, OR) 10032

Dailies Index

Statesville Record & Landmark
  (Statesville, NC) **10021**
State, The (Columbia, SC) **10038**
St. Augustine Record (St. Augustine, FL) **9973**
St. Cloud Times (St. Cloud, MN) **10003**
St. Croix Avis (St. Croix, VI) **10048**
Steamboat Today (Steamboat
  Springs, CO) **9969**
Stephenville Empire-Tribune
  (Stephenville, TX) **10046**
Sterling Journal-Advocate (Sterling, CO) **9969**
Stevens Point Journal (Stevens
  Point, WI) **10055**
Stillwater Gazette (Stillwater, MN) **10003**
Stillwater News-Press (Stillwater, OK) **10030**
St. Joseph News-Press (St.
  Joseph, MO) **10008**
St. Louis Post-Dispatch (St. Louis, MO) **10008**
St. Louis Watchman Advocate (St.
  Louis, MO) **10008**
Stoddard County News (Dexter, MO) **10006**
Storm Lake Pilot Tribune (Storm
  Lake, IA) **9988**
St. Paul Pioneer Press (St. Paul, MN) **10003**
St. Petersburg Times (St.
  Petersburg, FL) **9973**
Streator Times-Press (Streator, IL) **9981**
Stuart News (Stuart, FL) **9973**
Sturgis Journal (Sturgis, MI) **10002**
Stuttgart Daily Leader (Stuttgart, AR) **9960**
Suffolk News-Herald (Suffolk, VA) **10050**
Sullivan Daily Times (Sullivan, IN) **9986**
Sulphur Springs News-Telegram (Sulphur
  Springs, TX) **10046**
Summit Daily News (Frisco, CO) **9968**
Sun-Journal (Lewiston, ME) **9995**
Sun-Journal (New Bern, NC) **10020**
Sun-Sentinel (Fort Lauderdale, FL) **9972**
Sun Chronicle (Attleboro, MA) **9996**
Sun Herald, The (Gulfport, MS) **10004**
Sun News, The (Myrtle Beach, SC) **10038**
Sun, The (Bremerton, WA) **10050**
Superior Daily Telegram (Superior, WI) **10055**
Sweetwater Reporter (Sweetwater, TX) **10046**
Syracuse Herald-Journal/American
  (Syracuse, NY) **10017**
Tahlequah Daily Press (Tahlequah, OK) **10030**
Tahoe Daily Tribune (South Lake
  Tahoe, CA) **9966**
Tallahassee Democrat (Tallahassee, FL) **9974**
Tampa Tribune, The (Tampa, FL) **9974**
Tarrytown Daily News (White
  Plains, NY) **10018**
Taunton Daily Gazette (Taunton, MA) **9998**
Taylor Daily Press (Taylor, TX) **10046**
Taylorville Breeze-Courier (Taylorville, IL) **9981**

Telegram & Gazette (Worcester, MA) **9999**
Telegraph Herald (Dubuque, IA) **9987**
Telegraph, The (Alton, IL) **9977**
Telegraph, The (Dixon, IL) **9979**
Telegraph, The (North Platte, NE) **10010**
Telegraph, The (Hudson, NH) **10011**
Telluride Daily Planet (Telluride, CO) **9969**
Tempe Daily News Tribune (Tempe, AZ) **9958**
Temple Daily Telegram (Temple, TX) **10046**
Tennessean, The (Nashville, TN) **10041**
Terrell Tribune (Terrell, TX) **10047**
Texarkana Gazette (Texarkana, TX) **10047**
Texas City Sun (Texas City, TX) **10047**
The Dalles Daily Chronicle (The
  Dalles, OR) **10032**
Thomasville Times-Enterprise
  (Thomasville, GA) **9976**
Thousand Oaks Star (Thousand
  Oaks, CA) **9966**
Three Rivers Commercial-News (Three
  Rivers, MI) **10002**
Tifton Gazette (Tifton, GA) **9976**
Tiller & Toiler (Larned, KS) **9990**
Times & Democrat, The
  (Orangeburg, SC) **10038**
Times-Bulletin (Van Wert, OH) **10027**
Times-Georgian (Carrollton, GA) **9974**
Times-Journal, The (Fort Payne, AL) **9956**
Times-Mail (Bedford, IN) **9982**
Times-News, The (Burlington, NC) **10018**
Times-Picayune (New Orleans, LA) **9994**
Times-Record (Brunswick, ME) **9995**
Times-Reporter (New Philadelphia, OH) **10026**
Times-Standard (Eureka, CA) **9962**
Times-Union (Warsaw, IN) **9986**
Times-Union (Rochester, NY) **10017**
Times Argus (Barre, VT) **10048**
Times Daily (Florence, AL) **9956**
Times Herald (Port Huron, MI) **10001**
Times Herald-Record (Middletown, NY) **10016**
Times Herald, The (Norristown, PA) **10035**
Times Leader (Martins Ferry, OH) **10025**
Times Leader (Wilkes Barre, PA) **10037**
Times News (Lehighton, PA) **10034**
Times Recorder, The (Zanesville, OH) **10028**
Times Record News (Wichita Falls, TX) **10047**
Times, The (Gainesville, GA) **9975**
Times, The (Lansing, IL) **9980**
Times, The (Munster, IN) **9985**
Times, The (Shreveport, LA) **9995**
Times, The (Trenton, NJ) **10012**
Times, The (Pawtucket, RI) **10037**
† Times Tribune (Palo Alto, CA)
Times Union (Albany, NY) **10014**
Times West Virginian (Fairmont, WV) **10052**
Tipton Tribune (Tipton, IN) **9986**

Titusville Herald (Titusville, PA) **10036**

Today's Daily News-Herald (Lake Havasu City, AZ) **9958**

Today's Sunbeam (Salem, NJ) **10012**

Toledo Blade (Toledo, OH) **10027**

Tonawanda News (North Tonawanda, NY) **10016**

Tracy Press (Tracy, CA) **9966**

Transcript, The (North Adams, MA) **9998**

Traverse City Record-Eagle (Traverse City, MI) **10002**

Trentonian, The (Trenton, NJ) **10012**

Trenton Republican Times (Trenton, MO) **10008**

Tri-City Herald (Kennewick, WA) **10051**

Tri-Valley Herald (Pleasanton, CA) **9964**

Tribune-Review (Greensburg, PA) **10033**

Tribune-Star (Terre Haute, IN) **9986**

Tribune Chronicle, The (Warren, OH) **10027**

Tribune Democrat, The (Johnstown, PA) **10034**

Tribune, The (Oakland, CA) **9963**

Tribune, The (Fort Pierce, FL) **9972**

Tribune, The (Seymour, IN) **9985**

Tribune, The (Scranton, PA) **10036**

Troy Daily News (Troy, OH) **10027**

Tryon Daily Bulletin (Tryon, NC) **10021**

Tucson Citizen (Tucson, AZ) **9958**

Tulare Advance-Register (Tulare, CA) **9966**

Tulsa World (Tulsa, OK) **10030**

Turlock Journal (Turlock, CA) **9967**

Tuscaloosa News, The (Tuscaloosa, AL) **9957**

Twin Falls Times-News (Twin Falls, ID) **9977**

Tyler Morning Telegraph (Tyler, TX) **10047**

Ukiah Daily Journal (Ukiah, CA) **9967**

Union-News (Springfield, MA) **9998**

Union-Recorder (Milledgeville, GA) **9975**

Union-Sun & Journal (Lockport, NY) **10015**

Union City Daily Messenger (Union City, TN) **10041**

Union Daily Times (Union, SC) **10039**

Union Democrat, The (Sonora, CA) **9966**

Union Leader/New Hampshire Sunday News (Manchester, NH) **10011**

Union, The (Grass Valley, CA) **9962**

Upper Sandusky Daily Chief-Union (Upper Sandusky, OH) **10027**

Urbana Daily Citizen (Urbana, OH) **10027**

Vail Daily (Vail, CO) **9970**

Valdosta Daily Times (Valdosta, GA) **9976**

Vallejo Times-Herald (Vallejo, CA) **9967**

Valley City Times-Record (Valley City, ND) **10022**

Valley Courier (Alamosa, CO) **9968**

Valley Daily News (Kent, WA) **10051**

Valley Independent (Monessen, PA) **10035**

Valley Morning Star (Harlingen, TX) **10044**

Valley News (West Lebanon, NH) **10011**

Valley News Dispatch (Tarentum, PA) **10036**

Valley News Today-Daily Sentinel (Shenandoah, IA) **9988**

Valley Times (Pleasanton, CA) **9964**

Valley Times-News (Lanett, AL) **9956**

Valparaiso Vidette-Times (Valparaiso, IN) **9986**

Ventura County Star (Ventura, CA) **9967**

Vernon Daily Record (Vernon, TX) **10047**

Vicksburg Post (Vicksburg, MS) **10005**

Victoria Advocate (Victoria, TX) **10047**

Vincennes Sun-Commercial (Vincennes, IN) **9986**

Vindicator, The (Youngstown, OH) **10027**

Vinita Daily Journal (Vinita, OK) **10030**

Vinton Cedar Valley Daily Times (Vinton, IA) **9988**

Virginian-Pilot, The (Norfolk, VA) **10049**

Virginian Pilot (Kill Devil Hills, NC) **10020**

Virginian Review (Covington, VA) **10049**

Virgin Islands Daily News (St. Thomas, VI) **10048**

Visalia Times-Delta (Visalia, CA) **9967**

Wabash Plain Dealer (Wabash, IN) **9986**

Waco Tribune Herald (Waco, TX) **10047**

Wakefield Item (Wakefield, MA) **9998**

Walla Walla Union-Bulletin (Walla Walla, WA) **10052**

Wapakoneta Daily News (Wapakoneta, OH) **10027**

Warren Times Observer (Warren, PA) **10037**

Washington Daily News (Washington, NC) **10021**

Washington Evening Journal (Washington, IA) **9988**

Washington Post, The (Washington, DC) **9971**

Washington Times (Washington, DC) **9971**

Washington Times-Herald (Washington, IN) **9986**

Waterbury Republican-American (Waterbury, CT) **9971**

Waterloo Courier (Waterloo, IA) **9988**

Watertown Daily Times (Watertown, NY) **10017**

Watertown Daily Times (Watertown, WI) **10055**

Watertown Public Opinion (Watertown, SD) **10039**

Wausau Daily Herald (Wausau, WI) **10055**

Waxahachie Daily Light (Waxahachie, TX) **10047**

Waycross Journal Herald (Waycross, GA) **9976**

Wayne Independent, The (Honesdale, PA) **10033**

Waynesboro News-Virginian (Waynesboro, VA) **10050**

Weatherford Daily News
(Weatherford, OK) **10030**
Weatherford Democrat
(Weatherford, TX) **10047**
Weirton Daily Times (Weirton, WV) **10053**
Welch Daily News (Welch, WV) **10053**
Wellington Daily News (Wellington, KS) **9991**
Wellsville Daily Reporter (Wellsville, NY) **10017**
Wenatchee World (Wenatchee, WA) **10052**
West Central Tribune (Willmar, MN) **10003**
West County Times (Richmond, CA) **9964**
Westerly Sun (Westerly, RI) **10038**
Westfield Evening News (Westfield, MA) **9998**
West Hawaii Today (Kailua Kona, HI) **9976**
West Memphis Evening Times (West
Memphis, AR) **9961**
West Plains Daily Quill (West
Plains, MO) **10008**
West Virginia Daily News
(Lewisburg, WV) **10052**
Wheeling News-Register (Wheeling, WV) **10053**
Whittier Daily News (Whittier, CA) **9967**
Wichita Eagle (Wichita, KS) **9991**
Wilkes-Barre Citizens' Voice (Wilkes
Barre, PA) **10037**
Williamson Daily News (Williamson, WV) **10053**
Williamsport Sun-Gazette
(Williamsport, PA) **10037**
Williston Herald (Williston, ND) **10022**

Wilmington Morning Star
(Wilmington, NC) **10021**
Wilmington News-Journal
(Wilmington, OH) **10027**
Wilson Daily Times (Wilson, NC) **10021**
Winchester Star (Winchester, VA) **10050**
Winchester Sun (Winchester, KY) **9993**
Winfield Daily Courier (Winfield, KS) **9992**
Winona Daily News (Winona, MN) **10003**
Winston-Salem Journal
(Winston-Salem, NC) **10021**
Wisconsin State Journal (Madison, WI) **10054**
Woodward News (Woodward, OK) **10031**
Wooster Daily Record (Wooster, OH) **10027**
World, The (Coos Bay, OR) **10031**
Worthington Daily Globe
(Worthington, MN) **10004**
Wyoming Tribune-Eagle
(Cheyenne, WY) **10055**
Xenia Daily Gazette (Xenia, OH) **10027**
Yakima Herald-Republic (Yakima, WA) **10052**
Yankton Daily Press & Dakotan
(Yankton, SD) **10040**
Yonkers Herald Statesman
(Yonkers, NY) **10018**
York Daily Record (York, PA) **10037**
York Dispatch/York Sunday News
(York, PA) **10037**
York News-Times (York, NE) **10010**
Yuma Daily Sun (Yuma, AZ) **9959**

Weekly Newspapers Index

Abbeville Herald (Abbeville, AL) **10057**

Abbotsford Tribune-Phonograph
  (Abbotsford, WI) **10297**

Aberdeen Examiner (Aberdeen, MS) **10185**

Aberdeen Times (Aberdeen, ID) **10107**

Abernathy Weekly Review
  (Abernathy, TX) **10270**

Abingdon Argus (Abingdon, IL) **10109**

Abingdon Virginian (Abingdon, VA) **10284**

Abington Journal (Clarks Summit, PA) **10252**

Ace News, The (Heath, OH) **10239**

Acorn, The (Westlake Village, CA) **10084**

Action Advertiser (Fond Du Lac, WI) **10300**

Acworth Neighbor (Marietta, GA) **10104**

Ad-News (Greenfield, IN) **10132**

Ad-Visor (Beulah, MI) **10167**

Ad-Visor (Lansing, MI) **10172**

Ada/Cascade/Forest Hills Advance
  (Jenison, MI) **10171**

Adair County Free Press
  (Greenfield, IA) **10138**

Adair Progress, The (Columbia, KY) **10147**

Adair Russell Shopper, The
  (Columbia, KY) **10147**

† Adams County Leader (Council, ID)

Adams County Times (Adams, WI) **10297**

Ada Norman County Index (Ada, MN) **10176**

Addison County Independent
  (Middlebury, VT) **10284**

Addison Press (Elmhurst, IL) **10116**

† Adelanto Bulletin, The (Adelanto, CA)

Adel News-Tribune (Adel, GA) **10100**

Advance-Monticellonian
  (Monticello, AR) **10067**

Advance-Yeoman (Wickliffe, KY) **10152**

Advance Leader (Monroeville, PA) **10255**

Advance News (Lakehurst, NJ) **10203**

Advance of Bucks County
  (Newtown, PA) **10256**

Advance, The (Randolph, WI) **10304**

Advertiser-Gleam (Guntersville, AL) **10059**

Advertiser, The (Van Buren, AR) **10068**

Advertiser, The (Worden, IL) **10129**

Advertiser, The (Ligonier, IN) **10133**

Advertiser, The (Louisa, KY) **10149**

Advertiser, The (Mount Sterling, KY) **10150**

Advertiser, The (Paris, KY) **10150**

Advertiser, The (Iron Mountain, MI) **10171**

Advertiser, The (Bemidji, MN) **10176**

Advertiser, The (Chillicothe, OH) **10235**

Advertiser, The (McMurray, PA) **10254**

Advertizer-Herald, The (Bamberg, SC) **10261**

Advisor, The (Mt. Pleasant, PA) **10256**

Advocate (Winner, SD) **10265**

Advocate/South Advocate, The
  (Williamstown, MA) **10166**

Advocate Democrat (Madisonville, TN) **10268**

Advocate Penny Saver
  (Sweetwater, TN) **10270**

Advocate, The (Clifton, IL) **10114**

Advocate, The (Marion, MA) **10162**
Aegis, The (Bel Air, MD) **10158**
Afton Star-Enterprise (Afton, IA) **10136**
Aitkin Independent Age (Aitkin, MN) **10176**
Ajo Copper News (Ajo, AZ) **10063**
Akron News Reporter (Akron, CO) **10085**
Alabama Messenger (Birmingham, AL) **10057**
Alamance News (Graham, NC) **10228**
Albany Journal (Albany, GA) **10100**
Albany Ledger, The (Albany, MO) **10187**
Albia Union-Republican (Albia, IA) **10136**
Albion Advertiser (Albion, NY) **10209**
Albion News (Albion, NE) **10196**
Albion News, The (Albion, PA) **10251**
Albuquerque Street News
   (Albuquerque, NM) **10208**
Alexandria Gazette Packet
   (Alexandria, VA) **10284**
Alexandria News Weekly
   (Alexandria, LA) **10152**
Alexandria Times-Tribune
   (Alexandria, IN) **10129**
Algoma Record Herald (Algoma, WI) **10297**
† Algonac Courier Journal (Marine City, MI)
Algona Upper Des Moines (Algona, IA) **10136**
Algonquin Countryside (Barrington, IL) **10110**
Alhambra Post Advocate (Los
   Angeles, CA) **10075**
Aliso Viejo News (Lake Forest, CA) **10074**
Allegan County News (Allegan, MI) **10167**
Allen County Times (New Haven, IN) **10134**
Allied News (Grove City, PA) **10253**
Almanac, The (McMurray, PA) **10255**
Aloha Breeze (Hillsboro, OR) **10249**
† Alpena Journal (Wessington Springs, SD)
Alpena Star Advertiser (Alpena, MI) **10167**
Alpharetta Revue (Alpharetta, GA) **10100**
Alpine Avalanche (Alpine, TX) **10270**
Alsip Express (Midlothian, IL) **10123**
Altamont Enterprise, The
   (Altamont, NY) **10209**
Altamont News, The (Altamont, IL) **10109**
Altavista Journal (Altavista, VA) **10284**
Alternatives (Myrtle Beach, SC) **10263**
Altoona Herald, The (Altoona, IA) **10136**
Alvarado Post (Alvarado, TX) **10270**
Alvin Advertiser (Alvin, TX) **10270**
Alvin Sun (Alvin, TX) **10270**
† Alvin Tiller (Lamont, CA)
Ambler Gazette (Fort Washington, PA) **10253**
Amboy News, The (Amboy, IL) **10109**
Amelia Bulletin Monitor, The (Amelia Court
   House, VA) **10285**
American Journal (Westbrook, ME) **10157**
Amery Free Press (Amery, WI) **10297**
Amesbury News (Amesbury, MA) **10160**

Amherst Bee (Buffalo, NY) **10211**
Amherst New Era-Progress
   (Amherst, VA) **10285**
Amite Tangi Digest (Amite, LA) **10152**
Amityville Record (Amityville, NY) **10209**
Amory Advertiser, The (Amory, MS) **10185**
Anaconda Leader (Anaconda, MT) **10195**
Anacortes American (Anacortes, WA) **10290**
Anaheim Bulletin (Anaheim, CA) **10068**
Anaheim Hills News (Anaheim, CA) **10068**
Anamosa Journal-Eureka (Anamosa, IA) **10137**
† Anchor Bay Beacon (New Baltimore, MI)
† Anderson Countian (Garnett, KS)
Anderson News, The
   (Lawrenceburg, KY) **10149**
Andover Townsman (Andover, MA) **10160**
Andrews County News (Andrews, TX) **10270**
Angelina Free Press (Diboll, TX) **10274**
Angier Independent (Angier, NC) **10226**
Angleton Times (Angleton, TX) **10270**
Ankeny Press Citizen (Ankeny, IA) **10137**
Anoka County Union (Coon
   Rapids, MN) **10178**
Anson Record, The (Wadesboro, NC) **10231**
Anthony Republican, The (Anthony, KS) **10142**
Antigo Area Shoppers Guide
   (Antigo, WI) **10297**
Antioch News-Reporter (Grayslake, IL) **10118**
Apache Junction Independent (Apache
   Junction, AZ) **10063**
Apex Herald, The (Apex, NC) **10226**
Appalachian News-Express
   (Pikeville, KY) **10150**
Apple Valley/Rosemont Sun-Current
   (Burnsville, MN) **10177**
Apple Valley News (Hesperia, CA) **10073**
† Applewood/Wheat Ridge Transcript
   (Golden, CO)
Appomattox Times-Virginian
   (Appomattox, VA) **10285**
Arab Tribune (Arab, AL) **10057**
Arapahoe Public Mirror (Arapahoe, NE) **10196**
Arbutus Times (Baltimore, MD) **10157**
Arcadia News-Leader (Arcadia, WI) **10297**
Arcadian, The (Arcadia, FL) **10093**
† Arcadia Tribune (Arcadia, CA)
Archbold Buckeye (Archbold, OH) **10234**
Arco Advertiser (Arco, ID) **10107**
Arcola Record Herald (Arcola, IL) **10109**
Area News, The (Gillespie, IL) **10118**
Area Shopper (Springboro, PA) **10259**
Arenac County Independent
   (Standish, MI) **10175**
Argonaut, The (Los Angeles, CA) **10075**
Argus-Champion, The (Newport, NH) **10200**
Argyle Agenda (Argyle, WI) **10297**

Argyle Sun, The (Lake Dallas, TX) **10277**
Arizona City Independent (Arizona
   City, AZ) **10063**
Arizona Silver Belt (Globe, AZ) **10064**
Arkansas Valley Journal (La Junta, CO) **10087**
Ark, The (Bel Tiburon, CA) **10069**
Arlington Advocate (Arlington, MA) **10160**
Arlington Citizen (Blair, NE) **10196**
Arlington Courier, The (Arlington, VA) **10285**
Arlington Heights Journal & Topics (Des
   Plaines, IL) **10115**
▼Arrowhead Ranch Independent (Sun
   City, AZ) **10064**
Arrow, The (Glendale, AZ) **10064**
Arthur Enterprise, The (Arthur, NE) **10196**
Arthur Graphic Clarion (Arthur, IL) **10110**
Arvada Jefferson Sentinel
   (Lakewood, CO) **10087**
Ashley County Shoppers Guide
   (Crossett, AR) **10065**
Ashley News Observer (Crossett, AR) **10065**
Ashton Gazette (Ashton, IL) **10110**
Associated Newspaper (Stoughton, MA) **10166**
Astoria South Fulton Argus (Astoria, IL) **10110**
Atascadero News (Atascadero, CA) **10069**
Atchison County Mail, The (Rock
   Port, MO) **10192**
Athens News (Athens, OH) **10234**
Athens Observer, The (Athens, GA) **10100**
Atkins Chronicle, The (Atkins, AR) **10065**
Atkinson Graphic, The (Atkinson, NE) **10196**
Atlanta Bulletin (Atlanta, GA) **10100**
Atlanta Citizens Journal (Atlanta, TX) **10271**
Atlanta Daily World (Atlanta, GA) **10100**
Atlantic County Record
   (Hammonton, NJ) **10202**
Atmore Advance (Atmore, AL) **10057**
Atoka County Times (Atoka, OK) **10244**
Attica Hub (Attica, OH) **10234**
Atwater New Times (Winton, CA) **10085**
Atwood Herald (Atwood, IL) **10110**
Auburn Citizen (Auburn, IL) **10110**
Auburn News (Auburn, MA) **10160**
Auburn Press Tribune (Auburn, NE) **10196**
Auctioner, The (Pekin, IN) **10134**
Augusta Area Times (Augusta, WI) **10297**
Aurora Advertiser (Aurora, MO) **10188**
Aurora Advocate (Stow, OH) **10243**
Aurora News-Register (Aurora, NE) **10196**
Aurora Sentinel (Aurora, CO) **10085**
† Ausable Forks Adirondack Record Post
   (Elizabethtown, NY)
Austell Neighbor (Marietta, GA) **10104**
Austin Chronicle (Austin, TX) **10271**
† Austintown Leader (Niles, OH)
Austin Weekly News (Oak Park, IL) **10125**

Avalon Bay News, The (Avalon, CA) **10069**
Avenal Progress (Avenal, CA) **10069**
Aventura News (South Miami, FL) **10099**
Avenue News (Baltimore, MD) **10157**
Avon Lake Press (Avon Lake, OH) **10234**
Avon Sentinel (Abingdon, IL) **10109**
Avoyelles Journal (Marksville, LA) **10154**
† Azalea City News & Review (Bayou
   Labatre, AL)
Azle News (Azle, TX) **10271**
Azusa Herald (West Covina, CA) **10084**
Back of the Yards Journal (Chicago, IL) **10112**
Bainbridge Post-Searchlight
   (Bainbridge, GA) **10101**
Bainbridge Review (Bainbridge
   Island, WA) **10290**
Baker County Press, The
   (MacClenny, FL) **10096**
Baker Observer (Baker, LA) **10152**
Baker Record-Courier (Baker City, OR) **10247**
Baldwin Bulletin (Baldwin, WI) **10297**
Baldwin Citizen (Mineola, NY) **10218**
Baldwin Herald (Lawrence, NY) **10216**
Baldwinsville Messenger
   (Baldwinsville, NY) **10209**
Baldwin Times (Bay Minette, AL) **10057**
† Bal Harbor/Bay Harbour News (South
   Miami, FL)
Ballston Journal (Ballston Spa, NY) **10209**
Baltic Beacon (Dell Rapids, SD) **10264**
Baltimore Chronicle (Baltimore, MD) **10157**
Baltimore Messenger (Baltimore, MD) **10157**
Banner-Gazette (Pekin, IN) **10134**
Banner Journal (Black River Falls, WI) **10297**
Banner Press Newspaper, The
   (Columbus, TX) **10273**
Barberton Herald (Barberton, OH) **10234**
Barbour Democrat, The (Philippi, WV) **10295**
Barbourville Mountain Advocate
   (Barbourville, KY) **10146**
Bargain Express Newspaper
   (Milwaukee, WI) **10302**
Bar Harbor Times (Bar Harbor, ME) **10155**
Barnesboro Star, The (Barnesboro, PA) **10251**
Barnesville Enterprise (Barnesville, OH) **10234**
Barnstable Patriot, The (Hyannis, MA) **10162**
Barrington Courier Review
   (Barrington, IL) **10110**
Barrington Times (Warren, RI) **10261**
Barron County News Shield
   (Barron, WI) **10297**
Barry County Advertiser (Cassville, MO) **10189**
Bartow Neighbor, The (Cartersville, GA) **10101**
Batesville Herald-Tribune
   (Batesville, IN) **10129**

Bath County News-Outlook
  (Owingsville, KY) **10150**
Battle Creek Shopper (Hastings, MI) **10170**
Baudette Region, The (Baudette, MN) **10176**
Baxley News-Banner (Baxley, GA) **10101**
Baxter Springs Citizen (Baxter
  Springs, KS) **10142**
Bay Area Press (Oakland, CA) **10078**
Bay Beacon, The (Niceville, FL) **10097**
Bay Bulletin (Melbourne, FL) **10096**
Bay City Valley Farmer (Bay City, MI) **10167**
Baylor County Banner (Seymour, TX) **10280**
Bay News (Brooklyn, NY) **10210**
Bayonne Community News
  (Bayonne, NJ) **10200**
Bay Ridge Courier (Brooklyn, NY) **10210**
Bayshore Sun (La Porte, TX) **10277**
Bayside Times, The (Bayside, NY) **10210**
Bay State Banner (Boston, MA) **10160**
Bay St. Louis Sea Coast Echo (Bay St.
  Louis, MS) **10185**
Bay Times (Stevensville, MD) **10159**
Bay Viewer, The (Wauwatosa, WI) **10307**
Bay Voice (New Baltimore, MI) **10173**
Beach & Bay Press (San Diego, CA) **10080**
Beach Bulletin (Fort Myers Beach, FL) **10095**
Beachcomber, The (Surf City, NJ) **10207**
Beaches Leader (Jacksonville
  Beach, FL) **10095**
Beach Haven Times (Manahawkin, NJ) **10204**
Beach Reporter, The (Manhattan
  Beach, CA) **10077**
Beacon-Forum (Eldon, IA) **10138**
Beacon-Record (Hopewell, NJ) **10203**
Beacon Free Press (Wappingers
  Falls, NY) **10224**
Beacon Hill News, The/South District Journal
  (Seattle, WA) **10292**
Beacon Light (Mahopac, NY) **10217**
Beacon Newspaper (Babylon, NY) **10209**
Beacon Observer, The (Overton, NE) **10198**
Beacon, The (Concord, MA) **10161**
Beacon, The (Manahawkin, NJ) **10204**
Beacon, The (Port Clinton, OH) **10242**
Beardstown Illinoian-Star
  (Beardstown, IL) **10111**
Beaufort Shopper (Beaufort, SC) **10261**
Beaver Dam Ohio County Messenger (Beaver
  Dam, KY) **10146**
Beaverton Valley Times (Portland, OR) **10249**
Becker County Record (Detroit
  Lakes, MN) **10178**
Bedford Bulletin (Bedford, VA) **10285**
Bedford Minuteman (Concord, MA) **10161**
Bedford Sun Banner (Cleveland, OH) **10236**
Bedford Time Register (Bedford, OH) **10234**

Beebe News (Beebe, AR) **10065**
Beecher City Journal (Beecher City, IL) **10111**
Bee, The (Portland, OR) **10250**
Bee, The (Phillips, WI) **10304**
Beeville Bee-Picayune (Beeville, TX) **10271**
Belchertown Sentinel
  (Belchertown, MA) **10160**
Belevedere Citizen (Los Angeles, CA) **10075**
Belle Banner (Belle, MO) **10188**
Belle Fourche Post (Belle Fourche, SD) **10264**
Belle Plaine News, The (Belle
  Plaine, KS) **10143**
Belleview Voice of South Marion
  (Belleview, FL) **10093**
Belleville Enterprise (Wayne, MI) **10176**
Belleville Journal (Belleville, IL) **10111**
Belleville Post (Bloomfield, NJ) **10201**
Belleville Recorder (Belleville, WI) **10297**
Belleville Telescope (Belleville, KS) **10143**
Belleville Times News (Nutley, NJ) **10205**
Bellevue Leader (Bellevue, NE) **10196**
Bell Gardens Review (Los Angeles, CA) **10075**
Bell Maywood Cudahy Industrial Post (Los
  Angeles, CA) **10075**
Bellmore-Merrick Observer
  (Bellmore, NY) **10210**
Bellmore Life (Bellmore, NY) **10210**
Bellows Falls Town Crier (Bellows
  Falls, VT) **10283**
Bellville Times (Bellville, TX) **10271**
Belmont Banner (Belmont, NC) **10226**
Belmont Citizen-Herald (Needham, MA) **10164**
Benbrook News (Fort Worth, TX) **10275**
Bennetts Valley News (Weedville, PA) **10259**
Benning Leader, The (Columbus, GA) **10102**
Bensenville Press (Elmhurst, IL) **10116**
Benson County Farmers Press
  (Minnewaukan, ND) **10233**
Benson Swift County Monitor-News
  (Benson, MN) **10177**
Benton Bulletin (Philomath, OR) **10249**
Benton Review, The (Fowler, IN) **10131**
Bergen News, The (Palisades Park, NJ) **10205**
Berkeley Independent (Moncks
  Corner, SC) **10263**
Berkshire Courier (Great
  Barrington, MA) **10162**
Berkshire Penny Saver (Lee, MA) **10162**
Berkshire Record (Great
  Barrington, MA) **10162**
Berlin Buyers' Guide (Berlin, WI) **10297**
Berlin Journal (Berlin, WI) **10297**
Bernardsville News (Bernardsville, NJ) **10200**
Berne Tri-Weekly News (Berne, IN) **10130**
Berrien County Record (Buchanan, MI) **10168**
Berrien Press (Nashville, GA) **10105**

Berryessa Sun (Milpitas, CA) **10078**
Bertie Ledger-Advance (Windsor, NC) **10232**
Berwyn/Cicero Life (Berwyn, IL) **10111**
Bessemer City Record (Kings
   Mountain, NC) **10228**
Bethany Republican-Clipper
   (Bethany, MO) **10188**
▼Bethel Beacon (Bethel, CT) **10089**
Bethel Journal, The (Loveland, OH) **10240**
Bethesda/Chevy Chase Almanac
   (Potomac, MD) **10159**
Bettendorf News (Bettendorf, IA) **10137**
Beulah Beacon (Beulah, ND) **10232**
Beverly Hills Courier (Beverly Hills, CA) **10069**
Beverly Hills Independent (Santa
   Monica, CA) **10082**
Beverly News (Midlothian, IL) **10123**
Beverly Review (Chicago, IL) **10112**
Bexley News (Columbus, OH) **10237**
Biddeford-Saco-OOB Courier
   (Biddeford, ME) **10155**
Bienville Democrat & Ringgold Record
   (Arcadia, LA) **10152**
Big Bear Life (Big Bear Lake, CA) **10069**
Big Fork Eagle (Bigfork, MT) **10195**
Big Sandy News, The (Louisa, KY) **10149**
Billboard, The (Berlin, WI) **10297**
Billerica Minuteman (North
   Billerica, MA) **10164**
Biloxi-D'Iberville Press (D'Iberville, MS) **10185**
Bird City Times (Bird City, KS) **10143**
Bird Island Union (Bird Island, MN) **10177**
Birmingham Eccentric, The
   (Birmingham, MI) **10167**
† Birmingham Free Press (Birmingham, AL)
Birmingham World (Birmingham, AL) **10057**
▼Bisbee News, The (Bisbee, AZ) **10063**
▼Bisbee Now (Bisbee, AZ) **10063**
Bixby Bulletin (Tulsa, OK) **10247**
† Biz (Oxford, PA)
Black Forest News (Colorado
   Springs, CO) **10086**
Black Hills Press (Sturgis, SD) **10265**
Black Mountain News (Black
   Mountain, NC) **10226**
Blackstone Courier-Record
   (Blackstone, VA) **10285**
Blackstone Valley Tribune
   (Whitinsville, MA) **10166**
Blade Atlas (Blanchardville, WI) **10298**
Blade, The (Swainsboro, GA) **10106**
Blaine-Spring Lake Park Life (Coon
   Rapids, MN) **10178**
Blaine Banner (Blaine, MN) **10177**
Blair Enterprise (Blair, NE) **10196**
Blair Pilot-Tribune (Blair, NE) **10196**

Blair Press (Blair, WI) **10298**
Blairstown Press (Blairstown, NJ) **10201**
Blanco County News (Blanco, TX) **10271**
Bland Courier (Belle, MO) **10188**
Blandinsville Star Gazette
   (Abingdon, IL) **10109**
Bland Messenger (Wytheville, VA) **10290**
Blazer News (Jackson, MI) **10171**
Blissfield Advance (Blissfield, MI) **10167**
Bloomer Advance (Bloomer, WI) **10298**
Bloomfield Journal (Bristol, CT) **10090**
Bloomfield Life (Nutley, NJ) **10205**
Bloomingdale Press (Bloomingdale, IL) **10111**
Bloomington Sun-Current
   (Bloomington, MN) **10177**
Bloomville Gazette (Attica, OH) **10234**
Blount Countian, The (Oneonta, AL) **10061**
Blowing Rocket, The (Blowing
   Rock, NC) **10227**
Blue Mound Leader (Blue Mound, IL) **10111**
Blue Ridge Leader, The
   (Purcellville, VA) **10288**
Blue Water Voice (New Baltimore, MI) **10173**
Bluffton News, The (Bluffton, OH) **10234**
Blythe Advertiser (Palm Desert, CA) **10079**
Boardman News (Boardman, OH) **10235**
Boca Monday (Deerfield Beach, FL) **10094**
Boise City News, The (Boise City, OK) **10245**
Bolingbrook Metropolitan (Lemont IL) **10121**
Bolingbrook Sun (Bolingbrook, IL) **10111**
Bolivar Bulletin-Times (Bolivar, TN) **10265**
Bolivar Herald-Free Press (Bolivar, MC) **10188**
Bollinger County Banner-Press (Marble
   Hill, MO) **10191**
Bolton Common (Bolton, MA) **10160**
Bonita Banner (Bonita Springs, FL) **10093**
Bonners Ferry Herald (Bonners
   Ferry, ID) **10107**
Bonner Springs-Edwardsville Chieftain (Bonner
   Springs, KS) **10143**
Booker News, The (Booker, TX) **10271**
Boone County Journal (Ashland, MO) **10188**
Boone County Recorder (Florence, KY) **10148**
Booneville Banner-Independent
   (Booneville, MS) **10185**
Boone Watauga Democrat (Boone, NC) **10227**
Boonville Herald (Boonville, NY) **10210**
Boonville Standard (Boonville, IN) **10130**
Booster, The (Columbus, OH) **10237**
Boothbay Register (Boothbay
   Harbor, ME) **10155**
Boscobel Dial (Boscobel, WI) **10298**
Bosque County News (Meridian, TX) **10279**
Bossier Banner-Progress (Bossier
   City, LA) **10152**

Bossier Press-Tribune (Bossier City, LA) **10152**
Boston Phoenix (Boston, MA) **10160**
Boulder City News (Boulder City, NV) **10199**
Bound Brook Chronicle (Somerville, NJ) **10206**
Bourbon County Citizen (Paris, KY) **10150**
Bourne Courier (Yarmouthport, MA) **10167**
Boutique & Villager (Burlingame, CA) **10070**
Bowie Blade-News (Bowie, MD) **10158**
Bowie News (Bowie, TX) **10271**
Bowling Green Times (Bowling Green, MO) **10188**
Bowman Finder (Bowman, ND) **10232**
Box Elder News Journal (Brigham City, UT) **10282**
Boyertown Area Times (Boyertown, PA) **10251**
Boynton Beach Times (Deerfield Beach, FL) **10094**
Braceville Express (Wilmington, IL) **10129**
Brackett News The (Brackettville, TX) **10271**
Bradford County Telegraph (Starke, FL) **10099**
Bradford Journal/Miner (Bradford, PA) **10251**
Brady Standard (Brady, TX) **10271**
Braidwood Index (Wilmington, IL) **10129**
Braidwood Journal, The (Braidwood, IL) **10111**
Braintree Forum (Marshfield, MA) **10163**
Brandon News, The (Brandon, FL) **10093**
Brandon Valley Challenger (Dell Rapids, SD) **10264**
Brandywine Chronicle (Oxford, PA) **10256**
Branford Review (Branford, CT) **10090**
Brantley Enterprise (Nahunta, GA) **10105**
Brawley Advertiser (Palm Desert, CA) **10079**
Braxton Citizen's News (Sutton, WV) **10296**
Braxton Democrat-Central (Sutton, WV) **10296**
Brea Progress (Anaheim, CA) **10068**
Breckinridge County Herald-News (Hardinsburg, KY) **10148**
Brecksville Gazette (Cleveland, OH) **10236**
Breese Journal (Breese, IL) **10111**
† Breeze Herald (Conneut Lake Park, PA)
Breeze, The (Rockledge, PA) **10258**
Brentwood Journal (Brentwood, TN) **10266**
Brentwood Westwood Press (Santa Monica, CA) **10082**
Brevard Reporter, The (Cocoa, FL) **10094**
Brewery Gulch Gazette (Bisbee, AZ) **10063**
Brewster Times (Mahopac, NY) **10217**
Brewton Standard, The (Brewton, AL) **10058**
Brick Township Town News (Brick, NJ) **10201**
Bridgeport Index (Bridgeport, TX) **10272**
Bridgeport Leader (Bridgeport, IL) **10111**
Bridgeport News (Chicago, IL) **10112**
Bridger Valley Pioneer (Lyman, WY) **10309**
Bridgeview Independent (Midlothian, IL) **10123**
Bridgeville Area News (Monroeville, PA) **10255**

Bridgewater Independent (Middleboro, MA) **10163**
† Bridgewater Townsman (Bridgewater, MA)
Bridgton News (Bridgton, ME) **10155**
Brighton-Pittsford Post, The (Fishers, NY) **10214**
Brighton/Blade Market Place (Brighton, CO) **10085**
Brighton Argus (Brighton, MI) **10168**
Brighton Park-McKinley Park Life (Chicago, IL) **10112**
Brillion News (Brillion, WI) **10298**
Brinkley Argus (Brinkley, AR) **10065**
Bristol Phoenix (Bristol, RI) **10260**
Bristol Pilot (Bristol, PA) **10251**
Bristow News (Bristow, OK) **10245**
Britt News-Tribune (Britt, IA) **10137**
Broad Top Bulletin (Saxton, PA) **10259**
Brockport/Holley Suburban News (Spencerport, NY) **10223**
Brockport Post, The (Brockport, NY) **10210**
Broken Arrow Ledger & Scout (Broken Arrow, OK) **10245**
† Broken Arrow Scout (Broken Arrow, OK)
Bronx News (Bronx, NY) **10210**
Bronx Press-Review (Bronx, NY) **10210**
Brooke County Review (Wellsburg, WV) **10296**
Brookfield Journal (Brookfield, CT) **10090**
Brookfield News (Wauwatosa, WI) **10307**
Brookhaven Review (Smithtown, NY) **10223**
Brooklyn Center Sun Post (Minneapolis, MN) **10180**
Brooklyn Chronicle (Brooklyn, IA) **10137**
Brooklyn Graphic (Brooklyn, NY) **10210**
Brooklyn Heights Courier (Brooklyn, NY) **10210**
Brooklyn Heights Press (Brooklyn, NY) **10211**
Brooklyn Home Reporter & Sunset News (Brooklyn, NY) **10211**
Brooklyn Park Sun Post (Minneapolis, MN) **10180**
Brooklyn Record (Brooklyn, NY) **10211**
Brooklyn Spectator (Brooklyn, NY) **10211**
Brooklyn Sun Journal (Cleveland, OH) **10236**
† Brooklyn Times (Brooklyn, NY)
† Brooksville Sun Journal (Brooksville, FL)
† Brookville American (Brookville, PA)
Brookville American-Democrat (Brookville, IN) **10130**
Broomfield Enterprise (Broomfield, CO) **10086**
Broward News (Margate, FL) **10096**
Broward Times, The (Fort Lauderdale, FL) **10095**
Brown County Democrat (Nashville, IN) **10134**
Brown County Press (Mt. Orab, OH) **10241**
Brown Deer Herald (Wauwatosa, WI) **10307**

Brownfield News (Brownfield, TX) **10272**
Brownsville States-Graphic
   (Brownsville, TN) **10266**
Bruce Calhoun County Journal
   (Bruce, MS) **10185**
Brunswick Beacon, The (Shallotte, NC) **10230**
Brunswick Citizen (Brunswick, MD) **10158**
Brunswick Sun Times (Cleveland, OH) **10236**
Brunswick Times-Gazette
   (Lawrenceville, VA) **10287**
Brush News-Tribune (Brush, CO) **10086**
Bryan College Station Press (Bryan, TX) **10272**
Bryan County Star (Durant, OK) **10245**
Bryan County Times (Pembroke, GA) **10105**
Buckeye Review, The (Youngstown, OH) **10244**
Bucks County Tribune (Horsham, PA) **10253**
Budgeteer Press/Skyworld Duluth News
   (Duluth, MN) **10178**
Buffalo Bulletin (Buffalo, WY) **10308**
Buffalo County Journal (Cochrane, WI) **10298**
Buffalo Grove Countryside
   (Bannockburn, IL) **10110**
Buffalo Grove Journal & Topics (Des
   Plaines, IL) **10115**
Buffalo Reflex (Buffalo, MO) **10188**
Buffalo Ridge Gazette, The
   (Ruthton, MN) **10182**
Buffalo River Review (Linden, TN) **10268**
Buffalo Rocket (Buffalo, NY) **10211**
Bugle, The (Niles, IL) **10124**
Buhl Herald (Buhl, ID) **10107**
Bulletin, The (Crestview, FL) **10094**
Bulletin, The (Bedford, OH) **10234**
Bulletin, The (Santa Fe, TX) **10280**
Bulletin, The (Kenosha, WI) **10301**
Bunker Hill Gazette News (Bunker
   Hill, IL) **10112**
Burbank-Stickney Independent
   (Midlothian, IL) **10123**
Bureau County Republican
   (Princeton, IL) **10127**
Burke County Observer
   (Morganton, NC) **10229**
Burke Times, The (Reston, VA) **10288**
Burleson County Citizen Tribune
   (Caldwell, TX) **10272**
Burleson Star (Burleson, TX) **10272**
Burlington Standard Press
   (Burlington, WI) **10298**
Burlington Union (Lexington, MA) **10162**
Burnet Bulletin (Burnet, TX) **10272**
Burnett County Sentinel
   (Grantsburg, WI) **10300**
Burns Times-Herald (Burns, OR) **10248**
Burnsville Sun-Current (Burnsville, MN) **10177**
Burr Ridge Doings (Hinsdale, IL) **10120**

Burwell Tribune (Burwell, NE) **10196**
Business Examiner (Gig Harbor, WA) **10291**
Business Post, The (Alpharetta, GA) **10100**
Butler Choctaw Advocate (Butler, AL) **10058**
Butler County News (Georgiana, AL) **10059**
Butner-Creedmoor News, The
   (Creedmoor, NC) **10227**
Butte County Valley Irrigator
   (Newell, SD) **10265**
Butte Valley Star (Merrill, OR) **10249**
† Buyer's Guide (Napa, CA)
Buyer's Guide Cent Saver
   (Mauston, WI) **10302**
† Byron Center/Dorr Advance (Jenison, MI)
Cabell Record (Culloden, WV) **10294**
Cable Scene (Idaho Falls, ID) **10108**
Caddo Citizen (Vivian, LA) **10155**
Cadiz Record, The (Cadiz, KY) **10147**
Cadott Sentinel (Cadott, WI) **10298**
Cahokia Journal (Columbia, IL) **10114**
Cairo Citizen (Cairo, IL) **10112**
Cairo Messenger (Cairo, GA) **10101**
Calais Advertiser (Calais, ME) **10155**
Caldwell Burleson County Citizen-Tribune
   (Caldwell, TX) **10272**
Caledonia/Gaines Advance
   (Jenison, MI) **10171**
Calexico Advertiser (Palm Desert, CA) **10079**
Calhoun Chronicle (Grantsville, WV) **10294**
Calhoun News (Hardin, IL) **10119**
Calhoun Times (Calhoun, GA) **10101**
California Advocate, The (Fresno, CA) **10072**
California Courier (Glendale, CA) **10073**
California Democrat (California, MO) **10188**
▼Callaway Courier (Holts Summit, MO) **10190**
Call, The (Schuylkill Haven, PA) **10259**
Caloosa Belle (La Belle, FL) **10096**
Calumet Press, The (Highland, IN) **10132**
Calvert Independent (Prince
   Fredrick, MD) **10159**
Camas/Washougal Post Record
   (Camas, WA) **10290**
Cambridge Chronicle (Cambridge, IL) **10112**
Cambridge Chronicle (Somerville, MA) **10165**
Cambridge News (Cambridge, WI) **10298**
Camden Chronicle, The (Camden, TN) **10266**
Camden County Record (Camden, NJ) **10201**
Camden County Tribune (St.
   Marys, GA) **10106**
Camden Herald (Camden, ME) **10155**
Cameron Citizen Observer
   (Cameron, MO) **10188**
Cameron County Echo (Emporium, PA) **10252**
Cameron Herald (Cameron, TX) **10272**
Camilla Enterprise (Camilla, GA) **10101**
Camillus Advocate (Baldwinsville, NY) **10209**

Campbell County Recorder (Fort Thomas, KY) **10148**
Campbellsport News (Campbellsport, WI) **10298**
Canada News (Auburndale, FL) **10093**
Canarsie Courier (Brooklyn, NY) **10211**
Canarsie Digest (Brooklyn, NY) **10211**
Canastota Bee-Journal (Canastota, NY) **10211**
Canby Herald (Canby, OR) **10248**
Canby News (Canby, MN) **10177**
Candor Chronicle (Trumansburg, NY) **10224**
Canistota Clipper (Canistota, SD) **10264**
Canton Eagle (Wayne, MI) **10176**
Canton Independent-Sentinel (Canton, PA) **10251**
Canton Journal (Canton, MA) **10161**
Canton Observer (Plymouth, MI) **10174**
Canyon Courier (Evergreen, CO) **10087**
Canyon News (Canyon, TX) **10272**
Cape Codder (Orleans, MA) **10164**
† Cape Cod News (Yarmouth Port, MA)
Cape May County Gazette Leader (Wildwood, NJ) **10208**
Cape May Herald Dispatch (Rio Grande, NJ) **10206**
Cape May Star & Wave (Cape May, NJ) **10201**
Capeway News (Middleboro, MA) **10163**
Capistrano Valley News (Lake Forest, CA) **10074**
Capital City Weekly (Juneau, AK) **10062**
Capital Spotlight (Washington, DC) **10092**
▼Capital Weekly (Augusta, ME) **10155**
Capitol Hill Beacon (Oklahoma City, OK) **10246**
Capitol Hill Times (Seattle, WA) **10293**
Carbondale News (Carbondale, PA) **10251**
Carey Progressor-Times, The (Carey, OH) **10235**
Caribou Aroostook Republican & News (Caribou, ME) **10155**
Caribou County Sun (Soda Springs, ID) **10109**
Carlinville Democrat (Carlinville, IL) **10112**
Carlisle Mercury, The (Carlisle, KY) **10147**
Carlsbad Sun (Carlsbad, CA) **10070**
Carlyle Union Banner (Carlyle, IL) **10112**
Carmel News Tribune (Fishers, IN) **10131**
Carmel Pine Cone (Carmel, CA) **10070**
Carmel Times (Mahopac, NY) **10217**
Carmichael Times (Carmichael, CA) **10070**
Carol City/Opa-Locka News (Miami, FL) **10096**
Carolina Times (Durham, NC) **10227**
Caroline Progress, The (Bowling Green, VA) **10285**
Carolinian, The (Raleigh, NC) **10230**
Carol Stream Press (Bloomingdale, IL) **10111**
† Carpinteria Herald (Goleta, CA)

Carroll County Comet (Flora, IN) **10131**
Carroll County Independent (Center Ossipee, NH) **10199**
Carroll County News-Leader (Huntingdon, TN) **10267**
Carroll County Review (Thomson, IL) **10128**
Carroll Gardens/Cobble Hill Courier (Brooklyn, NY) **10211**
Carroll News, The (Hillsville, VA) **10286**
† Carrollton Chronicle (Carrollton, TX)
Carrollton Democrat (Carrollton, MO) **10188**
Carrollton Gazette Patriot (Carrollton, IL) **10112**
Carrollwood News (Tampa, FL) **10099**
Carson Press (Elgin, ND) **10232**
Carson Wave (Los Angeles, CA) **10075**
Carteret County News-Times (Morehead City, NC) **10229**
Carthage Courier (Carthage, TN) **10266**
Carthage Republican Tribune (Carthage, NY) **10212**
Carthaginian, The (Carthage, MS) **10185**
Carver Reporter (Plymouth, MA) **10164**
Cary-Grove Countryside (Barrington, IL) **10110**
Cary News (Cary, NC) **10227**
Casey County News (Liberty, KY) **10149**
Casey County Shopper, The (Columbia, KY) **10147**
Cashmere Valley Record (Cashmere, WA) **10291**
Cashton Record (Cashton, WI) **10298**
Cass City Chronicle (Cass City, MI) **10168**
Cass County Reporter (Casselton, ND) **10232**
Cassville Democrat (Cassville, MO) **10189**
Castleton Banner (Fishers, IN) **10131**
Caswell Messenger (Yanceyville, NC) **10232**
Catalina Islander, The (Avalon, CA) **10069**
† Cato Citizen (Red Creek, NY)
Catonsville Times (Baltimore, MD) **10157**
Catoosa County News (Ringgold, GA) **10105**
Catoosa Times Herald (Catoosa, OK) **10245**
Cavalier County Republican (Langdon, ND) **10232**
Cazenovia Republican (Cazenovia, NY) **10212**
Cedar County Republican (Stockton, MO) **10194**
Cedar Creek Pilot (Gun Barrel City, TX) **10276**
Cedar Hill Today (DeSoto, TX) **10273**
Cedar Key Beacon (Cedar, FL) **10094**
Cedar Lake Journal (Lowell, IN) **10133**
Cedartown Standard (Cedartown, GA) **10101**
Center Post Dispatch (Monte Vista, CO) **10088**
Center Republican (Washburn, ND) **10233**
Centerville-Bellbrook Times (Kettering, OH) **10240**
Centerville Crusader (Centerville, IN) **10130**

Central City Republican Nonpareil (Central City, NE) **10197**
Central City Times-Argus (Central City, KY) **10147**
Central Coast Sun-Bulletin (Morro Bay, CA) **10078**
† Central Coast Times (Paso Robles, CA)
Centralia Fireside Guard (Centralia, MO) **10189**
Central Kentucky News-Journal (Campbellsville, KY) **10147**
Central Missouri News (Sedalia, MO) **10192**
Central Oregonian, The (Prineville, OR) **10250**
Central Post (Dayton, NJ) **10202**
Central Record (Medford, NJ) **10204**
Central Saint Croix News (Hammond, WI) **10300**
Central Valley Times (Grants Pass, OR) **10248**
Central Virginian, The (Louisa, VA) **10287**
Central West End Journal (St. Louis, MO) **10193**
Centreville Press (Centreville, AL) **10058**
Centreville Times (Reston, VA) **10288**
Ceres Courier (Ceres, CA) **10070**
Chagrin Herald Sun (Cleveland, OH) **10236**
Chagrin Valley Times (Chagrin Falls, OH) **10235**
Challis Messenger (Challis, ID) **10107**
Chamblee-DeKalb Neighbor (Marietta, GA) **10104**
Chandler Independent (Chandler, AZ) **10063**
† Chandler Post (Boonville, IN)
Chanhassen Villager (Chanhassen, MN) **10177**
Chantilly Times (Reston, VA) **10288**
Chapel Hill News (Chapel Hill, NC) **10227**
Chariton Herald-Patriot (Chariton, IA) **10137**
Chariton Leader (Chariton, IA) **10137**
Charleston Chronicle, The (Charleston, SC) **10261**
Charleston Enterprise-Courier (Charleston, MO) **10189**
† Charlestown Citizen (Brookline, MA)
Charlevoix Courier (Charlevoix, MI) **10168**
Charlotte Gazette (Drakes Branch, VA) **10286**
Charlotte Shopping Guide (Charlotte, MI) **10168**
Charlottesville-Albemarle Tribune (Charlottesville, VA) **10285**
Charlton County Herald (Folkston, GA) **10103**
Chase County Leader-News (Cottonwood Falls, KS) **10143**
Chaska Herald (Chaska, MN) **10177**
† Chateaugay Record (Chateaugay, NY)
Chatham Clarion (Auburn, IL) **10110**
Chatham Courier (Madison, NJ) **10203**

Chatham Courier-Roughnotes (Chatham, NY) **10212**
Chatham Independent Press (New Providence, NJ) **10204**
Chatham News, The (Siler City, NC) **10230**
Chatsworth Times, The (Chatsworth, GA) **10101**
Chattooga Press (Summerville, GA) **10106**
Cheektowaga Bee (Williamsville, NY) **10225**
Cheektowaga Times (Cheektowaga, NY) **10212**
Chelmsford Independent (Chelmsford, MA) **10161**
Chelsea Clinton News (New York, NY) **10220**
Chelsea Record (Revere, MA) **10165**
Chelsea Standard, The (Chelsea, MI) **10168**
Chemung Valley Reporter (Horseheads, NY) **10216**
Chenango American (Greene, NY) **10215**
Cheney Free Press (Cheney, WA) **10291**
Cheraw Chronicle, The (Cheraw, SC) **10261**
Cherokee County Herald (Centre, AL) **10058**
Cherokee Messenger & Republican (Cherokee, OK) **10245**
Cherokee Scout (Murphy, NC) **10229**
Cherokee Tribune, The (Canton, GA) **10101**
† Cherry Hill News (Cherry Hill, NJ)
Cherryville Eagle (Cherryville, NC) **10227**
Chesapeake Post (Chesapeake, VA) **10285**
Cheshire Herald (Cheshire, CT) **10090**
Chester County Press (Oxford, PA) **10256**
Chesterfield Journal (St. Louis, MO) **10193**
Chesterland News (Chesterland, OH) **10235**
Chester News & Reporter (Chester, SC) **10261**
Chesterton Guide (Portage, IN) **10135**
Chesterton Town Crier (Valparaiso, IN) **10136**
Chestnut Hill Local (Philadelphia, PA) **10257**
Chetek Alert, The (Chetek, WI) **10298**
Cheyenne Mountain Journal (Manitou Springs, CO) **10088**
Chicago-Lawndale News (Chicago, IL) **10112**
Chicago's N.W. Side Press (Chicago, IL) **10113**
Chicago County Press (Lindstrom, MN) **10179**
Chicago Near North News (Chicago, IL) **10113**
Chicago Near West Gazette (Chicago, IL) **10113**
Chicago Post (Chicago, IL) **10113**
Chicago Reader (Chicago, IL) **10113**
Chicago Ridge Citizen (Midlothian, IL) **10123**
Chicago West Side Times (Chicago, IL) **10113**
Chicopee Herald Weekly, The (Chicopee, MA) **10161**
Chieftain & Toccoa Record (Toccoa, GA) **10106**
Childress Index (Childress, TX) **10272**
Chilkat Valley News (Haines, AK) **10062**
Chillicothe Bulletin (Chillicothe, IL) **10114**

Chilton Times-Journal (Chilton, WI) **10298**

Chisholm Free Press & Tribune Press
(Chisholm, MN) **10177**

Chittenango-Bridgeport Times
(Canastota, NY) **10212**

Chrisman Leader (Chrisman, IL) **10114**

Christian County Headliner News
(Ozark, MO) **10192**

Chronicle-Express (Penn Yan, NY) **10221**

Chronicle-Independent (Camden, SC) **10261**

Chronicle, The (Atwater, CA) **10069**

Chronicle, The (Milford, CT) **10091**

Chronicle, The (Milford, DE) **10092**

Chronicle, The (North Dartmouth, MA) **10164**

Chronicle, The (Somerville, NJ) **10206**

Chronicle, The (Carson City, NV) **10199**

Chronicle, The (Glens Falls, NY) **10214**

Chronicle, The (Creswell, OR) **10248**

Chronicle, The (Humboldt, TN) **10267**

Chula Vista Star-News (Chula
Vista, CA) **10070**

Church Point News (Church Point, LA) **10153**

Cibola County Beacon (Grants, NM) **10208**

Cisco Press (Cisco, TX) **10272**

Cissna Park News (Cissna Park, IL) **10114**

Citizen (American Fork, UT) **10282**

Citizen-Standard, The (Valley View, PA) **10259**

Citizen/Press Plus (Pulaski, TN) **10269**

Citizen Journal (St. Louis, MO) **10193**

Citizen of Morris County (Denville, NJ) **10202**

Citizen Outlet (Mexico, NY) **10218**

Citizens' Advocate Newspaper
(Coppell, TX) **10273**

Citizen Telegram, The (Rifle, CO) **10089**

Citizen, The (Mansfield, AR) **10066**

Citizen, The (Boyne City, MI) **10168**

Citizen, The (Houston, TX) **10276**

Citizen Voice & Times (Irvine, KY) **10149**

City News (Bronx, NY) **10210**

City Paper (Baltimore, MD) **10157**

City Terrace Comet (City of
Commerce, CA) **10070**

Civic Center NEWSource (Los
Angeles, CA) **10075**

Clackamas County Review
(Milwaukee, OR) **10249**

Claiborne Progress (Tazewell, TN) **10270**

Clanton Advertiser (Clanton, AL) **10058**

Claremont Courier (Claremont, CA) **10071**

Clarence Bee (Williamsville, NY) **10225**

Clarendon Hills Doings, The
(Hinsdale, IL) **10120**

Clarendon Hills Progress (Downers
Grove, IL) **10115**

Clare Sentinel (Clare, MI) **10168**

Clarinda Herald Journal (Clarinda, IA) **10137**

Clarion Journal, The (Columbia, IL) **10114**

Clarion News (Corydon, IN) **10130**

Clarion News (Clarion, PA) **10251**

Clark County Press (Neillsville, WI) **10303**

Clark Courier (Reston, VA) **10288**

Clark Eagle (Union, NJ) **10207**

Clarke County Democrat (Grove
Hill, AL) **10059**

Clarke County Tribune (Quitman, MS) **10187**

Clark Patriot (Rahway, NJ) **10206**

Clarkson Integrator (Potsdam, NY) **10221**

Clarkston News (Clarkston, MI) **10168**

Clarkstown Courier, The (Pearl
River, NY) **10221**

Clarksville Times, The (Clarksville, TX) **10272**

Classified Gazette (San Rafael, CA) **10082**

Clay City Times, The (Stanton, KY) **10151**

† Clay Countian (Orange Park, FL)

Clay County Crescent (Orange
Park, FL) **10098**

Clay County Free Press (Clay, WV) **10294**

Clay Dispatch-Tribune (Kansas
City, MO) **10190**

Clay Times Journal (Lineville, AL) **10060**

Clayton County Register (Elkader, IA) **10138**

Clayton Neighbor (Marietta, GA) **10104**

Clayton News-Star (Clayton, NC) **10227**

† Clayton Sun (Atlanta, GA)

Clayton Tribune (Clayton, GA) **10102**

Clear-Ridge Reporter (Chicago, IL) **10113**

Clear Creek Courant (Idaho
Springs, CO) **10087**

Clear Lake Observer-American
(Clearlake, CA) **10071**

Clearwater Tribune (Orofino, ID) **10108**

Cleburne News (Heflin, AL) **10060**

Clemmons Courier (Clemmons, NC) **10227**

† Clermont County Review (Cincinnati, OH)

† Clermont Courier (Cincinnati, OH)

Clermont Sun (Batavia, OH) **10234**

Cleveland Advocate (Cleveland, TX) **10272**

Cleveland Times (Shelby, NC) **10230**

Clewiston News (Clewiston, FL) **10094**

Clinch County News (Homerville, GA) **10103**

Clinch Valley News (Tazewell, VA) **10289**

Clinton Chronicle, The (Clinton, SC) **10262**

Clinton County News (Albany, KY) **10146**

Clinton County News (St. Johns, MI) **10175**

Clinton County Post (Mascoutah, IL) **10122**

Clinton County Shoppers Guide
(Wilmington, OH) **10244**

Clinton Courier (Clinton, NY) **10212**

Clinton Eye, The (Clinton, MO) **10189**

Clinton Recorder (Old Saybrook, CT) **10091**

Clinton Topper (Clinton, WI) **10298**

Clinton Van Buren County Democrat
  (Clinton, AR) **10065**
Clintonville Tribune-Gazette
  (Clintonville, WI) **10298**
Clipper-Herald (Lexington, NE) **10197**
Cloquet Billboard Shopper
  (Cloquet, MN) **10178**
Cloquet Pine Knot (Cloquet, MN) **10178**
Cloverdale Reveille (Cloverdale, CA) **10071**
Clover Herald (Clover, SC) **10262**
Clovis Independent (Clovis, CA) **10071**
Clyde Enterprise (Clyde, OH) **10237**
Coal City Courant (Coal City, IL) **10114**
Coal City Express (Wilmington, IL) **10129**
Coalfield Progress (Norton, VA) **10288**
Coalinga Record (Coalinga, CA) **10071**
Coal Valley News (Danville, WV) **10294**
Coastal Courier (Hinesville, GA) **10103**
Coastal Current, The (South Padre
  Island, TX) **10281**
Coastal Illustrated (St. Simons
  Island, GA) **10106**
Coastal Post (Bolinas, CA) **10070**
Coastal Times (Charleston, SC) **10261**
Coastland Times (Manteo, NC) **10229**
Coastside Chronicle (San Mateo, CA) **10082**
Cobleskill Times Journal
  (Cobleskill, NY) **10212**
Cody Enterprise (Cody, WY) **10308**
Coffey County Today (Burlington, KS) **10143**
Cohasset Mariner (Marshfield, MA) **10163**
Colbert County Reporter
  (Tuscumbia, AL) **10062**
Colchester Chronicle (Colchester, IL) **10114**
Coleman Chronicle & Democrat Voice
  (Coleman, TX) **10272**
Colfax Messenger (Colfax, WI) **10299**
Collierville Herald, The (Collierville, TN) **10266**
Collinsville Herald (Collinsville, IL) **10114**
Collinsville Journal (Collinsville, IL) **10114**
Collinsville News (Tulsa, OK) **10247**
Colonial, The (Fort Washington, PA) **10253**
Colonie Spotlight (Delmar, NY) **10213**
Colorado Statesman (Denver, CO) **10086**
Columbia Flier (Columbia, MD) **10158**
Columbia Heights-Findley Focus
  (Roseville, MN) **10182**
Columbian-Progress (Columbia, MS) **10185**
Columbia News, The (Columbia, KY) **10147**
Columbia News Times (Martinez, GA) **10104**
Columbus Alive! (Columbus, OH) **10237**
Columbus Journal (Columbus, WI) **10299**
Columbus Messenger (Columbus, OH) **10237**
Colusa County Sun-Herald (Colusa, CA) **10071**
Comanche Chief (Comanche, TX) **10273**
Commack News (Smithtown, NY) **10223**

Command Post, The (Mascoutah, IL) **10122**
Commerce Journal (Commerce, TX) **10273**
Commerce News (Commerce, GA) **10102**
Commercial-Express (Vicksburg, MI) **10175**
Commercial Record (Saugatuck, MI) **10175**
Commonwealth Progress (Scotland
  Neck, NC) **10230**
† Communicator Community News (Reno, NV)
Community Advertiser
  (Farmingdale, ME) **10156**
Community Adviser (Beaumont, CA) **10069**
Community Advisor (Marshall, MI) **10172**
Community Booster, The
  (Granville, OH) **10239**
Community Forum (Hackettstown, NJ) **10202**
Community Herald (Monona, WI) **10303**
Community Journal (Wading River, NY) **10224**
Community Journal, South
  (Loveland, OH) **10240**
Community Mirror (Gonzales, LA) **10153**
Community News (St. Louis, MO) **10193**
Community News (Clifton Park, NY) **10212**
Community News, The (Dora, AL) **10058**
Community Press, Mason
  (Loveland, OH) **10240**
† Community Press, West Chester
  (Loveland, OH)
Community Shopper (Birmingham, AL) **10058**
Community Times (Westminster, MD) **10160**
Compton Wave (Los Angeles, CA) **10075**
Concordia Sentinel (Ferriday, LA) **10153**
Concord Journal (Concord, MA) **10161**
Conejos County Citizen, The (Monte
  Vista, CO) **10088**
Conneautville Courier (Springboro, PA) **10259**
Connection, The (Grosse Point, MI) **10170**
Conservative, The (Carrollton, MS) **10185**
Contra Costa Sun (Lafayette, CA) **10074**
Conway County Petit Jean Country Headlight
  (Morrilton, AR) **10067**
† Conway Field & Herald (Conway, SC)
Coolidge Examiner (Coolidge, AZ) **10063**
Coon Rapids Herald (Coon Rapids, MN) **10178**
Coos County Democrat (Lancaster, NH) **10200**
Copiah County Courier
  (Hazlehurst, MS) **10186**
Coppell Gazette (Lewisville, TX) **10278**
Copperas Cove Leader Press (Copperas
  Cove, TX) **10273**
Copper Country News (Globe, AZ) **10064**
Copper Era (Clifton, AZ) **10063**
Coquille Valley Sentinel (Coquille, OR) **10248**
Coral Gables News (Miami, FL) **10097**
Cordell Beacon, The (Cordell, OK) **10245**
Cordova Times (Cordova, AK) **10062**

Cornell & Lake Holcombe Courier
  (Cornell, WI) **10299**
Corning Observer (Corning, CA) **10071**
Corona-Norco Independent
  (Corona, CA) **10071**
Coronado Journal (Coronado, CA) **10071**
Corridor News (San Diego, CA) **10080**
Corrigan Times, The (Corrigan, TX) **10273**
Cortez Montezuma Valley Journal
  (Cortez, CO) **10086**
Cortez Sentinel (Cortez, CO) **10086**
Cortland Democrat (Marathon, NY) **10218**
Corydon Democrat (Corydon, IN) **10130**
Corydon Times-Republican
  (Corydon, IA) **10137**
Cosmopolite-Herald (Girard, PA) **10253**
Cottage Grove Sentinel (Cottage
  Grove, OR) **10248**
Cottonwood Chronicle (Cottonwood, ID) **10107**
Cottonwood Journal Extra
  (Cottonwood, AZ) **10063**
Country Almanac (Menlo Park, CA) **10077**
Country Connection News (Eakly, OK) **10245**
Country Courier, The (Conklin, NY) **10212**
Country Shopper (Pound Ridge, NY) **10221**
Country Weekly (Grants Pass, OR) **10248**
County Courier (Enosburg Falls, VT) **10283**
County Edition, The (Jerseyville, IL) **10120**
County Journal (Belleville, IL) **10111**
County Journal (Percy, IL) **10126**
County Journal, The (Washburn, WI) **10306**
County Line Reminder (Ortonville, MI) **10173**
Countyline, The (Bryan, OH) **10235**
County Neighbors (Punxsutawney, PA) **10258**
County News Enterprise
  (Rutherfordton, NC) **10230**
County Observer (Yeagertown, PA) **10260**
County Press (Parma, MI) **10173**
County Press (Newtown Square, PA) **10256**
County Press, The (Lapeer, MI) **10172**
County Star (Stigler, OK) **10247**
County Star Journal East (St.
  Louis, MO) **10193**
County Star Journal West (St.
  Louis, MO) **10193**
County Transcript (Susquehanna, PA) **10259**
County Wide (Dover-Foxcroft, ME) **10156**
Courant, The (Bottineau, ND) **10232**
Courier-Gazette (Rockland, ME) **10157**
Courier-Journal (Palmyra, NY) **10220**
Courier-News (Clinton, TN) **10266**
Courier-Standard-Enterprise (Fort
  Plain, NY) **10214**
Courier-Times (Sutherland, NE) **10198**
Courier-Times, The (Roxboro, NC) **10230**
Courier-Wedge (Durand, WI) **10299**

Courier Gazette (Newark, NY) **10219**
Courier Hub (Stoughton, WI) **10305**
Courier Journal (Florence, AL) **10059**
Courier Press (Prairie du Chien, WI) **10304**
Courier, The (Plant City, FL) **10098**
† Courier, The (Thomasville, GA)
Courier, The (Rensselaer, IN) **10135**
Courier, The (Littleton, NH) **10200**
Courier, The (Conneaut, OH) **10239**
Courier, The (Reedsport, OR) **10250**
Courier, The (Savannah, TN) **10269**
Courier, The (Sun Prairie, WI) **10305**
Courtland Journal-Empire
  (Courtland, KS) **10143**
Coushatta Citizen (Coushatta, LA) **10153**
Cover Story, The (Murfreesboro, TN) **10268**
Covington Leader (Covington, TN) **10266**
Covington News (Covington, GA) **10102**
Covington Record (Covington, OK) **10245**
Covington St. Tammany Farmer
  (Covington, LA) **10153**
Coweta American (Coweta, OK) **10245**
Cranbury Press (Dayton, NJ) **10202**
Crane News (Crane, TX) **10273**
Cranford Chronicle (Cranford, NJ) **10202**
Cranston Herald (Cranston, RI) **10260**
Crawford County Independent-Kickapoo Scout
  (Gay Mills, WI) **10300**
Cresco Times-Plain Dealer (Cresco, IA) **10137**
Cresson-Gallitzin Mainliner, The
  (Cresson, PA) **10252**
Crestline Advocate (Crestline, OH) **10239**
Crestline Courier-News (Crestline, CA) **10071**
† Crestview Okaloosa-News Journal
  (Crestview, FL)
Crete News, The (Crete, NE) **10197**
Crewe-Burkeville Journal (Crewe, VA) **10286**
Crier Newspaper (Dunwoody, GA) **10102**
Crittenden Press (Marion, KY) **10149**
Crockett Times, The (Alamo, TN) **10265**
Crofton News-Crier (Bowie, MD) **10158**
Cromwell Chronicle (Cromwell, CT) **10090**
Crossville Chronicle (Crossville, TN) **10266**
Crothersville Times (Crothersville, IN) **10130**
Crowley Review (Burleson, TX) **10272**
Cuba Free Press (Cuba, MO) **10189**
† Cuba Journal (Cuba, IL)
Cudahy Reminder-Enterprise
  (Wauwatosa, WI) **10307**
Cuero Record (Cuero, TX) **10273**
Cullman Tribune (Cullman, AL) **10058**
Culpeper News (Culpeper, VA) **10286**
Culver Citizen (Culver, IN) **10130**
Culver City-Ladera Independent (Santa
  Monica, CA) **10082**
Culver City Star (Los Angeles, CA) **10076**

Cumberland Advocate
(Cumberland, WI) **10299**
Cumberland County News
(Burkesville, KY) **10147**
Cumberland Courier Weekly
(Lawrence, IN) **10133**
† Cumberland Times (Crossville, TN)
Cumberland Trading Post, The
(Middlesboro, KY) **10149**
Cupertino Courier (Cupertino, CA) **10071**
† Current (Potsdam, NY)
Curry Coastal Pilot (Brookings, OR) **10248**
Custer County Chief (Broken Bow, NE) **10196**
Cynthiana Democrat (Cynthiana, KY) **10147**
D/FW People (Euless, TX) **10274**
Dadeville Record (Alexander City, AL) **10057**
† Daily Milford Citizen (Milford, CT)
Daily News Press (Castle Rock, CO) **10086**
Dakatan, The (Wessington Springs, SD) **10265**
Dakota County Tribune (Burnsville, MN) **10177**
Dale News, The (Ferdinand, IN) **10131**
Dallas City Enterprise (Dallas City, IL) **10114**
Dallas New Era (Dallas, GA) **10102**
Dallas Park Cities News (Dallas, TX) **10273**
Dallas Polk County Itemizer-Observer
(Dallas, OR) **10248**
Dallas Post (Dallas, PA) **10252**
Dallas White Rocker News (Dallas, TX) **10273**
Dalton Gazette & Kidron News
(Dalton, OH) **10239**
Daly City Record (San Mateo, CA) **10082**
Damascus Gazette (Gatorsburg, MD) **10158**
Dan's Papers (Bridgehampton, NY) **10210**
Dana Point News (Lake Forest, CA) **10074**
Danbury Reporter (Walnut Cove, NC) **10231**
Dansville Genesee Country Express
(Dansville, NY) **10212**
Danvers Herald (Danvers, MA) **10161**
Darco News & Buyers Guide
(Hartsville, SC) **10262**
Darien Doings (Hinsdale, IL) **10120**
Darien Metropolitan (Lemont, IL) **10121**
Darien News (Darien, GA) **10102**
Darien News Review (Darien, CT) **10090**
Darien Progress (Downers Grove, IL) **10115**
Darke County Early Bird, The
(Arcanum, OH) **10234**
David City Banner-Press, The (David
City, NE) **10197**
Davie County Enterprise-Record
(Mocksville, NC) **10229**
Davis County Clipper (Bountiful, UT) **10282**
Davison Flagstaff (Swartz Creek, MI) **10175**
Davison Index, The (Davison, MI) **10169**
Dawson News, The (Dawson, GA) **10102**

Dawson Springs Progress (Dawson
Springs, KY) **10147**
Daytona Pennysaver (Ormond
Beach, FL) **10098**
Dayton Chronicle (Dayton, WA) **10291**
Dayton Tribune (Dayton, OR) **10248**
Dearborn County Register
(Lawrenceburg, IN) **10133**
Dearborn Press & Guide
(Dearborn, MI) **10169**
Dearborn Times-Herald (Dearborn, MI) **10169**
Decatur-DeKalb News/Era
(Decatur, GA) **10102**
Decatur Herald (Gentry, AR) **10066**
Decatur Tribune (Decatur, IL) **10114**
Declaration, The (Independence, VA) **10287**
Decorah Public Opinion & Journal
(Decorah, IA) **10137**
Deerfield Beach Observer (Deerfield
Beach, FL) **10094**
Deerfield Beach Thursday Times (Deerfield
Beach, FL) **10094**
Deerfield Review (Bannockburn, IL) **10110**
Deer Park Broadcaster, The (Deer
Park, TX) **10273**
Deer Park Progress, The (Deer
Park, TX) **10273**
Defensor Chieftain (Socorro, NM) **10209**
DeKalb County Advertiser (Auburn, IN) **10129**
† DeKalb News/Sun (Decatur, GA)
DeLand Beacon, The (DeLand, FL) **10094**
Delano Record (Delano, CA) **10071**
Delavan Enterprise (Delavan, WI) **10299**
Delavan Times, The (Delavan, IL) **10115**
Delaware Beachcomber (Rehoboth
Beach, DE) **10092**
Delaware Coast Press (Rehoboth
Beach, DE) **10092**
Delaware County Journal (Folsom, PA) **10253**
Delaware County Times (Delhi, NY) **10213**
Delaware Valley News (Frenchtown, NJ) **10202**
Delaware Wave (Bethany Beach, DE) **10092**
Delhi Express (Winton, CA) **10085**
Delhi Press (Cincinnati, OH) **10235**
Dell Rapids Tribune (Dell Rapids, SD) **10264**
Del Mar, Solana Beach, Carmel Valley, Rancho
Santa Fe Sun (Del Mar, CA) **10072**
Del Norte Prospector (Monte Vista, CO) **10088**
Delray Times (Deerfield Beach, FL) **10094**
Delta Atlas (Delta, OH) **10239**
Delta County Independent (Delta, CO) **10086**
Delta Waverly News Herald, The (Grand
Ledge, MI) **10170**
Democrat-Argus, The
(Caruthersville, MO) **10189**
Democrat-Leader (Fayette, MO) **10189**

Democrat-Message (Mt. Sterling, IL) **10124**
Democrat-Reporter, The (Linden, AL) **10060**
Democrat-Union (Lawrenceburg, TN) **10267**
Democrat, The (Senatobia, MS) **10187**
Democrat Tribune, The (Mineral Point, WI) **10302**
Demopolis Times (Demopolis, AL) **10058**
Denair Dispatch (Winton, CA) **10085**
Denbigh Gazette (Yorktown, VA) **10290**
Denham Springs-Livingston Parish News (Denham Springs, LA) **10153**
Denison Bulletin & Review (Denison, IA) **10137**
Denmark Press (Denmark, WI) **10299**
† Dennis Bulletin (South Yarmouth, MA)
Denton County Express (Lake Dallas, TX) **10277**
Denver Herald-Dispatch (Denver, CO) **10086**
De Pere Journal (De Pere, WI) **10299**
Depew Bee (Williamsville, NY) **10225**
Deposit Courier (Deposit, NY) **10213**
De Queen Bee (De Queen, AR) **10066**
De Quincy News (De Quincy, LA) **10153**
Derry News (Derry, NH) **10199**
Desert Mailer News (Lancaster, CA) **10075**
Desert Mobile Home News (Palm Desert, CA) **10079**
Desert Mountain Express (Hesperia, CA) **10073**
Desert Sentinel, The (Desert Hot Springs, CA) **10072**
Deshler Rustler, The (Deshler, NE) **10197**
Des Moines County News, The (West Burlington, IA) **10142**
Des Moines Lee Town News (Des Moines, IA) **10137**
Des Moines News (Seattle, WA) **10293**
De Soto Times (Southaven, MS) **10187**
DeSoto Today (DeSoto, TX) **10273**
Des Plaines Times (Park Ridge, IL) **10126**
Destin Log (Destin, FL) **10094**
Detroit Lakes Tribune (Detroit Lakes, MN) **10178**
Detroit Metro Times (Detroit, MI) **10169**
DeWitt Bath Review (St. Johns, MI) **10175**
DeWitt Observer (DeWitt, IA) **10137**
DeWitt Times (Fayetteville, NY) **10213**
Diamond Drill, The (Crystal Falls, MI) **10169**
Dickenson Star/Cumberland Times, The (Clintwood, VA) **10285**
Dickson Herald, The (Dickson, TN) **10266**
Digest, The (Hallandale, FL) **10095**
Digger Shopper & News, The (Oroville, CA) **10078**
Dillon Herald, The (Dillon, SC) **10262**
Dispatch-News, The (Lexington, SC) **10263**
Dispatch, The (New Providence, NJ) **10204**

† Dispatch, The (Cookeville, TN)
Divernon News (Auburn, IL) **10110**
Dixie News (Florence, KY) **10148**
Dixon Pilot (Dixon, MO) **10189**
Dodge County Independent-News (Juneau, WI) **10301**
Dodge County News, The (Eastman, GA) **10102**
Dodgeville Chronicle, Inc. (Dodgeville, WI) **10299**
Donaldsonville Chief (Donaldsonville, LA) **10153**
Donalsonville News (Donalsonville, GA) **10102**
Doon Press (Doon, IA) **10137**
Door County Advocate (Sturgeon Bay, WI) **10305**
Doraville-DeKalb Neighbor (Marietta, GA) **10104**
Dorchester Eagle Record (St. George, SC) **10264**
Dorchester Star (Cambridge, MD) **10158**
Douglas County Herald (Ava, MO) **10188**
Douglas County News Press (Castle Rock, CO) **10086**
Douglas County Post Gazette (Elkhorn, NE) **10197**
Douglas Enterprise (Douglas, GA) **10102**
Douglas Neighbor, The (Marietta, GA) **10104**
Dove Creek Press (Dove Creek, CO) **10086**
Dover-Sherborn Suburban Press (Needham, MA) **10164**
Downers Grove Reporter (Downers Grove, IL) **10115**
Downey Herald American (Los Angeles, CA) **10076**
Downriver Voice (New Baltimore, MI) **10173**
Downtown Express (New York, NY) **10220**
Downtown Gazette (Long Beach, CA) **10075**
Downtown News (South Miami, FL) **10099**
Dracut Dispatch, The (Dracut, MA) **10161**
Drain Enterprise (Drain, OR) **10248**
Dresden Enterprise (Dresden, TN) **10266**
Drexel Hill Press (Newtown Square, PA) **10256**
Dripping Springs Dispatch (Dripping Springs, TX) **10274**
Dublin Suburbia News (Columbus, OH) **10237**
Dublin Villager (Worthington, OH) **10244**
Dumas Clarion (Dumas, AR) **10066**
Duncannon Record (New Bloomfield, PA) **10256**
Duncanville Today (DeSoto, TX) **10274**
Dundalk Eagle (Baltimore, MD) **10157**
Dundee Observer (Dundee, NY) **10213**
Dunn County News (Menomonie, WI) **10302**

Dunwoody-DeKalb Neighbor, The (Marietta, GA)   **10104**

† DuPage Press Service (Wheaton, IL)

Durand-Dakota Volunteer (Durand, IL)   **10115**

Durand Express (Durand, MI)   **10169**

Durand Gazette (Love Park, IL)   **10122**

Duxbury Reporter (Plymouth, MA)   **10164**

Dyer County Tennessean (Newbern, TN)   **10268**

Dyersville Commercial (Dyersville, IA)   **10138**

Eagan Sun-Current (Burnsville, MN)   **10177**

Eagle Bulletin (Fayetteville, NY)   **10214**

Eagle Grove Eagle (Eagle Grove, IA)   **10138**

Eagle Lake Headlight (Eagle Lake, TX)   **10274**

Eagle Rock Sentinel (Los Angeles, CA)   **10076**

Eagle, The (Cambridge, NY)   **10211**

Eagle Valley Enterprise (Eagle, CO)   **10086**

Earlville Leader (Earlville, IL)   **10116**

Easley Progress (Easley, SC)   **10262**

East Aurora Advertiser (East Aurora, NY)   **10213**

East Aurora Bee (Williamsville, NY)   **10225**

East Baltimore Guide (Baltimore, MD)   **10157**

East Bay Breeze (Sun City Center, FL)   **10099**

East Bay Express (Berkeley, CA)   **10069**

East Bridgewater Star (Bridgewater, MA)   **10161**

Eastchester Record (Yonkers, NY)   **10225**

East County Chronicle (Kimberly, ID)   **10108**

Eastern Arizona Courier (Safford, AZ)   **10064**

Eastern Carolina Times-Inquirer (Goldsboro, NC)   **10228**

Eastern Colorado News (Strasburg, CO)   **10089**

Eastern Colorado Plainsman (Hugo, CO)   **10087**

Eastern Gazette, The (Dexter, ME)   **10155**

Eastern Hills Journal (Loveland, OH)   **10240**

Eastern Kentucky Shopper (Paintsville, KY)   **10150**

East Feliciana Watchman (Clinton, LA)   **10153**

East Fishkill Record (Mahopac, NY)   **10217**

East Grand Rapids Cadence (Jenison, MI)   **10171**

East Greenwich Pendulum (East Greenwich, RI)   **10260**

East Hampton Star (East Hampton, NY)   **10213**

East Hartford Gazette, The (East Hartford, CT)   **10090**

East Haven Advertiser (Milford, CT)   **10091**

East L.A./Commerce Tribune (Los Angeles, CA)   **10076**

Eastland Telegram (Eastland, TX)   **10274**

East Lauderdale News (Rogersville, AL)   **10061**

† East Los Angeles Gazette (South Gate, CA)

† East Los Angeles Tribune (South Gate, CA)

East Meadow Beacon (Hicksville, NY)   **10216**

East Mesa Independent (Apache Junction, AZ)   **10063**

Easton Bulletin (Stoughton, MA)   **10166**

East Orange Record (Orange, NJ)   **10205**

East Palestine Heritage, The (Columbiana, OH)   **10237**

East Penn Press (Allentown, PA)   **10251**

East Peoria Courier (Morton, IL)   **10124**

East Providence Post (East Providence, RI)   **10260**

East Riverside Advertiser (Palm Desert, CA)   **10079**

East Rochester Post-Herald (Fishers, NY)   **10214**

East Rockaway Observer (Mineola, NY)   **10218**

East Shelby Review (Somerville, TN)   **10269**

East Side Herald (Indianapolis, IN)   **10132**

Eastside Journal (Los Angeles, CA)   **10076**

Eastside Monthly (Providence, RI)   **10261**

East Side Review (North St. Paul, MN)   **10181**

Eastside Sun (City of Commerce, CA)   **10071**

† Eastside Times (Tulsa, OK)

East St. Louis Monitor (East St. Louis, IL)   **10116**

East St. Louis News Journal (Columbia, IL)   **10114**

East Troy News (East Troy, WI)   **10299**

Easy Reader (Hermosa Beach, CA)   **10073**

Eaton County News (Charlotte, MI)   **10168**

Ebbtide (Sausalito, CA)   **10083**

Ebensburg News Leader, The (Ebensburg, PA)   **10252**

Echoes-Sentinel (Stirling, NJ)   **10207**

Echo Press, The (Alexandria, MN)   **10176**

Echo, The (Berlin, NY)   **10210**

ECM Post-Review (North Branch, MN)   **10181**

Eddyville Tribune (Eddyville, IA)   **10138**

Eden Prairie Sun-Current (Bloomington, MN)   **10177**

Edgebrook Times Review (Park Ridge, IL)   **10126**

Edgerton Enterprise, The (Edgerton, MN)   **10178**

Edgerton Reporter (Edgerton, WI)   **10299**

Edgewood Enterprise (Edgewood, TX)   **10274**

Edgewood Reminder (Edgewood, IA)   **10138**

Edina Sun-Current (Minneapolis, MN)   **10180**

Edison-Norwood Times Review (Park Ridge, IL)   **10126**

Edwardsville Journal (Edwardsville, IL)   **10116**

Egg Harbor News (Hammonton, NJ)   **10203**

Elbert County News (Castle Rock, CO)   **10086**

Elberton Star (Elberton, GA)   **10103**

Elburn Herald (Elburn, IL)   **10116**

El Campo Leader-News (El Campo, TX)   **10274**

El Centro Advertiser (Palm Desert, CA)   **10079**

Eldon Advertiser (Eldon, MO) **10189**
Eldora Herald-Leader (Eldora, IA) **10138**
Elizabethtown Chronicle
  (Elizabethtown, PA) **10252**
Elk Grove Citizen (Elk Grove, CA) **10072**
Elkhorn Independent (Elkhorn, WI) **10299**
Elk Valley Times (Fayetteville, TN) **10266**
Ellenville Press (Ellenville, NY) **10213**
Ellsworth American, The
  (Ellsworth, ME) **10156**
Ellsworth Reporter, The (Ellsworth, KS) **10143**
Elma Review (East Aurora, NY) **10213**
Elmhurst Press (Elmhurst, IL) **10116**
Elm Leaves (Oak Park, IL) **10125**
Elm Leaves (Wauwatosa, WI) **10307**
Elmont Herald (Elmont, NY) **10213**
Elmwood Argus (Spring Valley, WI) **10305**
Elmwood Park-River Grove Times
  (Lincolnwood, IL) **10121**
Eloy Enterprise (Eloy, AZ) **10064**
El Paso Journal (El Paso, IL) **10116**
El Reno Tribune (El Reno, OK) **10245**
El Segundo Herald (El Segundo, CA) **10072**
El Sereno Star (Los Angeles, CA) **10076**
Elwood Express (Wilmington, IL) **10129**
Ely Echo (Ely, MN) **10178**
Emery County Progress (Castle
  Dale, UT) **10282**
Emmetsburg Democrat
  (Emmetsburg, IA) **10138**
Emmetsburg Reporter
  (Emmetsburg, IA) **10138**
Encinitas Sun (Encinitas, CA) **10072**
Enderlin Independent (Enderlin, ND) **10232**
Enfield Press (Enfield, CT) **10090**
England Democrat (England, AR) **10066**
Englewood Herald (Littleton, CO) **10088**
Enquirer-Gazette (Upper Marlboro, MD) **10160**
Enquirer Bulletin (Burlingame, CA) **10070**
Enterprise & Inner Harbor News
  (Baltimore, MD) **10157**
Enterprise Buyer's Catalogue
  (Wytheville, VA) **10290**
Enterprise Mountaineer, The
  (Fallbrook, CA) **10072**
Enterprise Mountaineer, The
  (Canton, NC) **10227**
† Enterprise News (Pixley, CA)
Enterprise, The (Plainfield, IL) **10126**
Enterprise, The (Ponchatoula, LA) **10154**
Enterprise, The (Falmouth, MA) **10162**
Enterprise, The (Lexington Park, MD) **10159**
Enterprise, The (Mason, MI) **10172**
Enterprise, The (Williamston, NC) **10231**
Enterprise, The
  (Hastings-on-Hudson, NY) **10215**

Enterprise, The (Stuart, VA) **10289**
Enterprise, The (Lynnwood, WA) **10292**
Enumclaw Courier-Herald
  (Enumclaw, WA) **10291**
Ephrata Review (Ephrata, PA) **10252**
† Erie County Reporter (Huron, OH)
Erskine Echo, The (Erskine, MN) **10178**
Erwin Record (Erwin, TN) **10266**
Escambia Sun Press (Pensacola, FL) **10098**
Escondido News-Reporter
  (Escondido, CA) **10072**
Essex Independent, The (Essex, IA) **10138**
Estancia Valley Citizen (Estancia, NM) **10208**
Estes Park Trail-Gazette (Estes
  Park, CO) **10087**
Estill County Tribune, The (Irvine, KY) **10149**
Euclid Sun Journal (Cleveland, OH) **10236**
Eufaula Tribune (Eufaula, AL) **10058**
Eunice News (Eunice, LA) **10153**
Eureka Herald (Eureka, KS) **10143**
Eureka Sentinel (Tonopah, NV) **10199**
Eureka Springs Times-Echo
  (Berryville, AR) **10065**
Eustis Lake Region News (Mount
  Dora, FL) **10097**
Evanston Review (Evanston, IL) **10117**
Evart Review, The (Big Rapids, MI) **10167**
Evergreen Courant, The
  (Evergreen, AL) **10058**
Evergreen Park Courier (Midlothian, IL) **10123**
Evergreen Shopping Guide
  (Spooner, MN) **10183**
Everman Times (Everman, TX) **10274**
Every Wednesday (Baltimore, MD) **10157**
Excelsior/Shorewood Sun-Sailor
  (Minnetonka, MN) **10180**
Exeter News-Letter (Stratham, NH) **10200**
Exponent, The (Brooklyn, MI) **10168**
Extra Merchandiser (St. Marys, OH) **10243**
Fairbury Journal-News, The
  (Fairbury, NE) **10197**
† Fairchild Strikehawk (Spokane, WA)
Fairfax Connection (McLean, VA) **10287**
Fairfax Station Times (Reston, VA) **10288**
Fairfax Times (Reston, VA) **10288**
Fairfield Chronicle, The (West
  Caldwell, NJ) **10207**
Fairfield Citizen News (Fairfield, CT) **10090**
Fairfield County Weekly (Stamford, CT) **10091**
Fairfield Echo (Fairfield, OH) **10239**
Fairfield Wayne County Press
  (Fairfield, IL) **10117**
† Fair Haven Register (Red Creek, NY)
Fairhope Courier, The (Fairhope, AL) **10059**
Fairmont Photo Press (Fairmont, MN) **10178**
† Fairport-Perinton Herald-Mail (Webster, NY)

Fairview Heights Journal (Belleville, IL) **10111**
Fairview Heights Tribune
   (Mascoutah, IL) **10122**
Fairview Republican (Fairview, OK) **10245**
Falfurrias Facts (Falfurrias, TX) **10274**
Falls Church News-Press (Falls
   Church, VA) **10286**
Falls City Journal (Falls City, NE) **10197**
Falls News-Press (Stow, OH) **10243**
Faribault County Register (Blue
   Earth, MN) **10177**
Farina News, The (Farina, IL) **10117**
Farmer & Miner (Frederick, CO) **10087**
Farmer's Weekly Review (Joliet, IL) **10121**
Farmer City Journal (Farmer City, IL) **10117**
Farmers' Advance (Camden, MI) **10168**
† Farmers Branch Times (Carrollton, TX)
Farmers Independent (Bagley, MN) **10176**
Farmingdale Observer (Mineola, NY) **10218**
Farmington Observer (Farmington, MI) **10169**
† Farmington Valley Herald (Simsbury, CT)
Farmland News (Archbold, OH) **10234**
Farmville Herald, The (Farmville, VA) **10286**
Farmweek (Knightstown, IN) **10133**
Fauquier Times-Democrat
   (Warrenton, VA) **10290**
Fayette Advertiser, The (Fayette, MO) **10189**
Fayette County News (Fayetteville, GA) **10103**
Fayette County Record, The (La
   Grange, TX) **10277**
Fayette County Review (Somerville, TN) **10269**
Fayette County Union (West Union, IA) **10142**
Fayette Falcon, The (Somerville, TN) **10269**
Fayette Neighbor, The (Fayetteville, GA) **10103**
Fayette Review, The (Fayette, OH) **10239**
† Fayette Sun (Fayetteville, GA)
Fayette Tribune (Oak Hill, WV) **10295**
Federal Way News (Federal Way, WA) **10291**
Fennimore Times (Fennimore, WI) **10300**
Fennville Herald (Allegan, MI) **10167**
Ferdinand News, The (Ferdinand, IN) **10131**
Fernley Leader-Dayton Courier
   (Yerington, NV) **10199**
Fillmore Herald (Fillmore, CA) **10072**
Fincastle Herald, The (Fincastle, VA) **10286**
Finder, The (Mandan, ND) **10233**
Firebaugh/Mendota Journal
   (Kerman, CA) **10074**
Fire Island Tide (Sayville, NY) **10222**
Fisher Reporter (Fisher, IL) **10117**
Fishers Sun-Herald (Fishers, IN) **10131**
Fishkill Standard (Mahopac, NY) **10217**
Fishtown Star (Philadelphia, PA) **10257**
Fitchburg Star (Fitchburg, WI) **10300**
Five Cities Times-Press-Recorder (Arroyo
   Grande, CA) **10069**

Five County/Buyer's Guide (Ripon, WI) **10304**
Flanagan Home Times (Flanagan, IL) **10117**
Flatbush Life (Brooklyn, NY) **10211**
† Flat River Lead Belt News (Flat River, MO)
Florala News, The (Florala, AL) **10059**
Floral Park Bulletin (Floral Park, NY) **10214**
Florence Citizen (Florence, CO) **10087**
Florence Mining News (Florence, WI) **10300**
Floresville Chronicle-Journal
   (Floresville, TX) **10274**
Florham Park Eagle (Madison, NJ) **10203**
Florida Keys Keynoter (Marathon, FL) **10096**
Florissant Valley Reporter
   (Florissant, MO) **10189**
Floyd County Hesperian-Beacon
   (Floydada, TX) **10274**
Floyd County Times (Prestonsburg, KY) **10150**
Floyd Press (Floyd, VA) **10286**
Flushing Times, The (Bayside, NY) **10210**
Folsom Telegraph (Folsom, CA) **10072**
Fontana Herald News (Fontana, CA) **10072**
Ford County Press (Melvin, IL) **10123**
Forest City Summit (Forest City, IA) **10138**
Forest Hill News (Everman, TX) **10274**
▼Forest Hills/Rego Park Times
   (Maspeth, NY) **10218**
Forest Hills Journal (Loveland, OH) **10241**
Forest Lake Press (St. Paul, MN) **10183**
Forest Leaves (Oak Park, IL) **10125**
Forest Press (Tionesta, PA) **10259**
Forest Republican, The (Crandon, WI) **10299**
Forest Times-Tribune (De Forest, WI) **10299**
Forreston Journal (Forreston, IL) **10117**
Forsyth County News (Cumming, GA) **10102**
Fort Bend Mirror (Rosenberg, TX) **10280**
Fort Bend Sun (Sugar Land, TX) **10281**
Fort Bragg Advocate-News (Fort
   Bragg, CA) **10072**
Fort Fairfield Review (Fort
   Fairfield, ME) **10156**
Fort Lupton Press (Fort Lupton, CO) **10087**
Fort Meade Leader, The (Fort
   Meade, FL) **10095**
Fort Mill Times (Fort Mill, SC) **10262**
Fort Myers Beach Observer (Fort Myers
   Beach, FL) **10095**
Fort Riley Post (Junction City, KS) **10144**
Fort Stockton Pioneer (Fort
   Stockton, TX) **10274**
Forum of Queens (Ozone Park, NY) **10220**
Fosston Thirteen Towns (Fosston, MN) **10178**
Foster City Progress (Burlingame, CA) **10070**
Foto News (Merrill, WI) **10302**
Fountain County Neighbor (Attica, IN) **10129**
Fountain Valley News & El Paso County News
   (Fountain, CO) **10087**

Four Oaks-Benson News in Review
(Benson, NC) **10226**
Fowler Tribune, The (Fowler, CO) **10087**
Fowlerville Review Shopping Guide
(Howell, MI) **10171**
Foxboro Reporter (Foxboro, MA) **10162**
Fox Lake Press (Grayslake, IL) **10118**
Fox Lake Representative (Berlin, WI) **10297**
Fox Point, Bayside, River Hills Herald
(Wauwatosa, WI) **10307**
Fox Valley Shopping News, The
(Plainfield, IL) **10126**
Fox Valley Sun (Naperville, IL) **10124**
Foxxy Shopper (Sparta, WI) **10305**
Frankenmuth News (Frankenmuth, MI) **10169**
Franklin-Hales Corner Hub
(Wauwatosa, WI) **10307**
Franklin Challenger (Greenwood, IN) **10132**
Franklin Chronicle (Franklin, OH) **10239**
Franklin County Citizen (Lavonia, GA) **10104**
Franklin County Graphic (Connell, WA) **10291**
Franklin County Plus (Russellville, AL) **10061**
Franklin County Times (Russellville, AL) **10061**
Franklin Favorite (Franklin, KY) **10148**
Franklin Journal & Farmington Chronicle
(Farmington, ME) **10156**
Franklin News-Post (Rocky Mount, VA) **10289**
Franklin News-Record (Princeton, NJ) **10206**
Franklin Park Herald-Journal (Oak
Park, IL) **10125**
Franklin Park Star-Sentinel (Melrose
Park, IL) **10123**
Franklin Pendleton Times
(Franklin, WV) **10294**
Franklin Press (Franklin, NC) **10228**
Franklin Square Bulletin (Floral
Park, NY) **10214**
Franklin Sun, The (Winnsboro, LA) **10155**
Franklin Times (Louisburg, NC) **10228**
Franklin Township Sentinel
(Franklinville, NJ) **10202**
Fredericksburg Standard/Radio Post
(Fredericksburg, TX) **10275**
Fredericktown Democrat-News
(Fredericktown, MO) **10189**
† Freeborn County Register (Albert Lea, MN)
Freeman's Journal (Cooperstown, NY) **10212**
Freemont Gazette (Fremont, IA) **10138**
Free News, The (Farmville, VA) **10286**
Freeport Advertiser Shopping News
(Freeport, IL) **10117**
Freeport Baldwin Leader, The
(Freeport, NY) **10214**
Free Press (Tampa, FL) **10099**
Free Press-Courier (Westfield, PA) **10260**
Free Press Standard (Carrollton, OH) **10235**

Free Press, The (Canton, OH) **10235**
Free Press, The (Braddock, PA) **10251**
Free Time (Wildwood, NJ) **10208**
Free Trader (Massena, NY) **10218**
Fremont County Herald-Chronicle (St.
Anthony, ID) **10109**
Fresh Meadows Times, The
(Flushing, NY) **10214**
Fridley Focus (Roseville, MN) **10182**
Friendswood & Pearland Reporter News
(Pearland, TX) **10279**
Frontier & Holt County Independent
(O'Neill, NE) **10197**
Frontiersman, The (Wasilla, AK) **10063**
Front Page (Lackawanna, NY) **10216**
Frostproof News (Frostproof, FL) **10095**
Fruita Times, The (Fruita, CO) **10087**
Fulton County Expositor (Wauseon, OH) **10244**
Fulton Journal (Fulton, IL) **10117**
Fulton Leader (Fulton, KY) **10148**
Fulton Patriot (Fulton, NY) **10214**
Fulton Shopper (Fulton, KY) **10148**
Gadsden County Times (Quincy, FL) **10098**
Gaffney Ledger, The (Gaffney, SC) **10262**
Gahanna Village Post (Gahanna, OH) **10239**
Gainesville Buyers Guide (Orange
Park, FL) **10098**
Gaithersburg Gazette
(Gaithersburg, MD) **10158**
Galax Gazette, The (Galax, VA) **10286**
Galena Gazette (Galena, IL) **10117**
Galesburg Post, The (Galesburg, IL) **10117**
Galesville Republican (Galesville, WI) **10300**
Galt Herald (Galt, CA) **10073**
Galva News (Galva, IL) **10117**
Gardena Valley News (Gardena, CA) **10073**
Garden City Observer (Livonia, MI) **10172**
Garden Island Extra (Lihue, HI) **10107**
Garden of the Gods Journal (Manitou
Springs, CO) **10088**
Gardner South Wilmington Post
(Wilmington, IL) **10129**
Garfield Maple-Sun (Cleveland, OH) **10236**
Garland News (Garland, TX) **10275**
Garner News (Garner, NC) **10228**
† Garnett Review (Garnett, KS)
Gary Crusader (Gary, IN) **10132**
Gary Info (Gary, IN) **10132**
Gasconade County Republican
(Owensville, MO) **10192**
Gates-Chili News (Rochester, NY) **10222**
Gates County Index (Gatesville, NC) **10228**
Gatesville Messenger (Gatesville, TX) **10275**
Gateway News, The (Streetsboro, OH) **10243**
Gateway Shopper, The (Clinton, IA) **10137**
Gateway, The (Floral Park, NY) **10214**

Gaylord Herald Times (Gaylord, MI) **10169**
Gazette-Advertiser (Rhinebeck, NY) **10222**
Gazette-Democrat (Anna, IL) **10109**
Gazette Shopper (Cleveland, OH) **10236**
Gazette, The (Elizabeth, IL) **10116**
Gazette, The (Mt. Holly, NJ) **10204**
Gazette, The (Port Jervis, NY) **10221**
Gazette, The (Jefferson, OH) **10240**
Geist Gazette (Fishers, IN) **10131**
Gem State Miner (Newport, WA) **10292**
Geneseo Republic (Geneseo, IL) **10117**
Geneseo Shopper (Geneseo, IL) **10117**
Geneva County Reaper (Geneva, AL) **10059**
Geneva Republican (Geneva, IL) **10117**
Genoa-Kingston-Kirkland News
   (Sycamore, IL) **10128**
Gentry Courier-Journal (Gentry, AR) **10066**
George County Times (Lucedale, MS) **10186**
Georgetown Current, The
   (Washington, DC) **10093**
Georgetowner, The (Washington, DC) **10093**
Georgetown News Graphic
   (Georgetown, KY) **10148**
Georgetown Record (Ipswich, MA) **10162**
Georgetown Times, The
   (Georgetown, SC) **10262**
Georgia South (Boston, GA) **10101**
Gering Courier (Gering, NE) **10197**
Germantown Banner-Press
   (Wauwatosa, WI) **10307**
Germantown Courier (Philadelphia, PA) **10257**
Germantown News, The
   (Germantown, TN) **10267**
Germantown Paper (Philadelphia, PA) **10257**
Gibson City Courier (Gibson City, IL) **10118**
Giddings Times & News (Giddings, TX) **10275**
Gilbert Independent (Scottsdale, AZ) **10064**
Gilman Star (Gilman, IL) **10118**
Gilmer Mirror (Gilmer, TX) **10275**
Girard Home News (Philadelphia, PA) **10257**
† Girard News (Niles, OH)
Girard Press (Girard, KS) **10143**
Giveaway, The (Scottsburg, IN) **10135**
Glades County Democrat
   (Clewiston, FL) **10094**
Gladewater Mirror (Gladewater, TX) **10275**
† Gladstone Delta Reporter (Escanaba, MI)
Gladwin County Record & Beaverton Clarion
   (Gladwin, MI) **10170**
Glasford Gazette, The (Glasford, IL) **10118**
Glasgow Courier, The (Glasgow, MT) **10195**
Glasgow Republican (Glasgow, KY) **10148**
Glastonbury Citizen (Glastonbury, CT) **10090**
Glencoe Enterprise (Glencoe, MN) **10178**
Glen Cove Record Pilot (Mineola, NY) **10219**
Glendale Heights Press (Elmhurst, IL) **10116**

Glendale Herald (Wauwatosa, WI) **10307**
Glendale Register (Maspeth, NY) **10218**
Glendale Star, The (Glendale, AZ) **10064**
Glendive Ranger-Review (Glendive, MT) **10195**
Glendora Press (West Covina, CA) **10084**
Glen Ellyn News (Glen Ellyn, IL) **10118**
Glen Ellyn Press (Bloomingdale, IL) **10111**
Glennville Sentinel (Glennville, GA) **10103**
Glen Oaks Ledger, The (Flushing, NY) **10214**
Glen Ridge Paper, The (Bloomfield, NJ) **10201**
Glen Rose Reporter (Glen Rose, TX) **10275**
Glenside News (Jenkintown, PA) **10254**
Glenview Announcements (Glenview, IL) **10118**
Glenville Democrat, The (Glenville, WV) **10294**
Glenville Pathfinder (Glenville, WV) **10294**
Glenwood Herald (Glenwood, AR) **10066**
Glenwood Opinion-Tribune
   (Glenwood, IA) **10138**
Glidden Enterprise (Glidden, WI) **10300**
Globe, The (Jenkintown, PA) **10254**
Gloucester-Mathews Gazette Journal
   (Gloucester, VA) **10286**
Gloucester City News (Gloucester
   City, NJ) **10202**
Glynco Observer (Brunswick, GA) **10101**
Gold Beach Curry County Reporter (Gold
   Beach, OR) **10248**
Goldendale Sentinel (Goldendale, WA) **10291**
Golden Prairie News (Assumption, IL) **10110**
Golden Times (Rochester, NY) **10222**
Golden Transcript (Golden, CO) **10087**
Golden Triangle Shopper
   (Columbus, MS) **10185**
Gold Leaf Farmer, The (Wendell, NC) **10231**
Gold River News (Sacramento, CA) **10080**
† Goleta Review (Goleta, CA)
† Goleta Sun (Santa Barbara, CA)
Golfmill Journal (Des Plaines, IL) **10115**
Gonzales Inquirer (Gonzales, TX) **10275**
Gonzales Tribune (Soledad, CA) **10083**
Gonzales Weekly (Gonzales, LA) **10153**
Goochland Gazette (Goochland, VA) **10286**
Gooding County Leader (Gooding, ID) **10107**
Good News Shopper (Coal City, IL) **10114**
Good Times (Santa Cruz, CA) **10082**
† Good Times News (Fayette, MO)
Goose Creek Gazette (Ladson, SC) **10262**
Gorman Progress, The (Gorman, TX) **10275**
Gouverneur Tribune Press
   (Gouverneur, NY) **10215**
Gowanda Pennysaver News
   (Gowanda, NY) **10215**
† Grace Citizen (Preston, ID)
Graceville News (Graceville, FL) **10095**
Grainger County News (Rutledge, TN) **10269**
Grand Gazette (St. Paul, MN) **10183**

Grand Island Pennysaver (Grand
Island, NY) **10215**
Grand Ledge Independent, The (Grand
Ledge, MI) **10170**
Grand Marais Pilot & Pictured Rocks Review
(Grand Marais, MI) **10170**
Grand Prairie News (Arlington, TX) **10270**
Grand Rapids Advance (Jenison, MI) **10171**
Grand Rapids Herald-Review (Grand
Rapids, MN) **10179**
Grand Saline Sun (Grand Saline, TX) **10275**
Grand Valley Advance (Jenison, MI) **10171**
Grandview Herald (Grandview, WA) **10291**
Granite City Press Journal (Granite
City, IL) **10118**
Granite Falls/Clerkfield Advocate Tribune
(Granite Falls, MN) **10179**
Granite State News (Wolfeboro, NH) **10200**
Grant County Herald Independent
(Lancaster, WI) **10301**
Grant County Journal (Ephrata, WA) **10291**
Grant County News (Williamstown, KY) **10152**
Grant County News (Elgin, ND) **10232**
Grant County Press (Petersburg, WV) **10295**
Grant County Review (Milbank, SD) **10265**
Granville Sentinel (Granville, NY) **10215**
Granville Sentinel, The (Granville, OH) **10239**
Gratiot County Herald (Ithaca, MI) **10171**
Gravette News Herald (Gravette, AR) **10066**
Grayslake Times (Grayslake, IL) **10118**
Grayson Advertiser (Leitchfield, KY) **10149**
Grayson County News-Gazette
(Leitchfield, KY) **10149**
Grayson County Shopper (Denison, TX) **10273**
Grayson Journal-Enquirer
(Grayson, KY) **10148**
Greater Baton Rouge Business Report (Baton
Rouge, LA) **10152**
Great Falls Times (Reston, VA) **10288**
Great Lakes Pilot (Grand Marais, MI) **10170**
Great Lander Bush Mailer
(Anchorage, AK) **10062**
Great Neck News (Great Neck, NY) **10215**
Great Neck Record (Mineola, NY) **10219**
Greece Post, The (Fishers, NY) **10214**
Greenbelt News Review
(Greenbelt, MD) **10159**
Greenbrier Gazette (Sherwood, AR) **10068**
Greenbrier Valley Ranger
(Lewisburg, WV) **10295**
Greendale Village Life (Wauwatosa, WI) **10307**
Greene County Independent
(Eutaw, AL) **10058**
Greene County Record
(Stanardsville, VA) **10289**
Greene Prairie Press (White Hall, IL) **10128**

Greene Recorder, The (Greene, IA) **10138**
Greenfield Observer (Wauwatosa, WI) **10307**
Green Forest Tribune (Berryville, AR) **10065**
Green Hills Weekly (Trenton, MO) **10194**
Greenhorn Valley News (Colorado
City, CO) **10086**
Green Lake County Reporter (Green
Lake, WI) **10300**
Greenpoint Gazette/Advertiser
(Brooklyn, NY) **10211**
† Green River Republican (Morgantown, KY)
Greensboro Watchman, The
(Greensboro, AL) **10059**
Green Sheet, The (Palm Desert, CA) **10079**
Green Tab (Moundsville, WV) **10295**
Greenup County News-Times
(Greenup, KY) **10148**
Greenup Press (Greenup, IL) **10119**
Green Valley News & Sun (Green
Valley, AZ) **10064**
Greenville Advocate, The
(Greenville, AL) **10059**
Greenville Advocate, The
(Greenville, IL) **10119**
Greenville Local (Ravena, NY) **10221**
Greenwich Journal & Salem Press
(Greenwich, NY) **10215**
† Greenwich News (Greenwich, CT)
▼Greenwich Post (Greenwich, CT) **10090**
Greenwood & Southside Challenger
(Greenwood, IN) **10132**
Greenwood Democrat (Greenwood, AR) **10066**
Greenwood Gazette, The (Fishers, IN) **10131**
Greenwood Lake & West Milford News
(Greenwood Lake, NY) **10215**
Greer Citizen, The (Greer, SC) **10262**
Gresham Outlook (Gresham, OR) **10248**
Gridley Herald, The (Gridley, CA) **10073**
Griffith Guide (Highland, IN) **10132**
Grinnell Herald-Register (Grinnell, IA) **10138**
Grizzly, The (Big Bear Lake, CA) **10069**
Groesbeck Journal (Groesbeck, TX) **10275**
Grosse Pointe News (Grosse Pointe
Farm, MI) **10170**
Groton Landmark (Ayer, MA) **10160**
Grove City Record (Columbus, OH) **10237**
Grove Sun (Grove, OK) **10245**
Grundy County Herald (Tracy City, TN) **10270**
Grundy Register (Grundy Center, IA) **10138**
Grunion Gazette (Long Beach, CA) **10075**
Grygla Eagle (Grygla, MN) **10179**
Guam Tribune (Agana, GU) **10106**
Guernsey Gazette/Lingle Guide
(Guernsey, WY) **10309**
Guilford American (Dover-Foxcroft, ME) **10156**

Gulf Coast Tribune, The (West Columbia, TX) **10281**
Gurnee Press (Grayslake, IL) **10118**
Guttenberg Press (Guttenberg, IA) **10139**
† Haddon Gazette (Cherry Hill, NJ)
Hagerstown Exponent, The (Hagerstown, IN) **10132**
† Haines City Herald (Haines City, FL)
Half Moon Bay Review (Half Moon Bay, CA) **10073**
Halifax Reporter (Plymouth, MA) **10165**
Hallettsville Tribune-Herald (Hallettsville, TX) **10276**
Halls Graphic (Ripley, TN) **10269**
Hamburg Item (Hamburg, PA) **10253**
Hamilton-Wenham Chronicle (Ipswich, MA) **10162**
† Hamilton County News (Elizabethtown, NY)
Hamilton County News (Speculator, NY) **10223**
Hamilton Herald-News (Hamilton, TX) **10276**
Hamilton Mid-York Weekly (Hamilton, NY) **10215**
Hamilton Tribune (Hamilton, NY) **10215**
Hammonton News (Hammonton, NJ) **10203**
Hampshire Register News (Sycamore, IL) **10128**
Hampshire Review (Romney, WV) **10296**
Hampton Chronicle & Times (Hampton, IA) **10139**
Hampton Chronicle-News (Westhampton Beach, NY) **10225**
Hampton Union (North Hampton, NH) **10200**
Hamtramck Citizen (Hamtramck, MI) **10170**
Hanahan News (North Charleston, SC) **10263**
Hanceville Herald (Hanceville, AL) **10059**
Hancock Clarion (Hawesville, KY) **10148**
Hancock County Journal-Pilot (Carthage, IL) **10112**
Hancock County Quill (La Harpe, IL) **10121**
Hancock News (Hancock, MD) **10159**
Hanover Eagle & Regional News (Madison, NJ) **10203**
Hanover Herald-Progress (Ashland, VA) **10285**
Hanover Mariner (Marshfield, MA) **10163**
† Hanover Park Township Times (Carol Stream, IL)
Hansford County Reporter-Statesman (Spearman, TX) **10281**
Haralson Gateway-Beacon, The (Bremen, GA) **10101**
Harbor Beach Times (Harbor Beach, MI) **10170**
Harbor Extra (Torrance, CA) **10084**
Harbor Sound (Brunswick, GA) **10101**
Harborwatch (Brooklyn, NY) **10211**
Hardin Calhoun Herald (Hardin, IL) **10119**

Hardin County Independent (Elizabethtown, IL) **10116**
Hardin County Index (Eldora, IA) **10138**
Hardwick Gazette (Hardwick, VT) **10283**
Harlan County Journal (Alma, NE) **10196**
Harlan News Advertiser (Harlan, IA) **10139**
Harlan Tribune (Harlan, IA) **10139**
Harlem-Foster-Norwood Park-Edison Park Times (Lincolnwood, IL) **10121**
Harlem-Irving Times (Lincolnwood, IL) **10121**
Harlem Valley Times (Amenia, NY) **10209**
† Harper Woods Herald (Birmingham, MI)
Harrah News, The (Harrah, OK) **10246**
Harriman Record (Kingston, TN) **10267**
Harrington Journal, The (Harrington, DE) **10092**
Harrison County Advisor (Bethany, MO) **10188**
Harrison Independent (Yonkers, NY) **10226**
Harrison News-Herald, The (Cadiz, OH) **10235**
Harrisonville Cass County Democrat Missourian (Harrisonville, MO) **10190**
Harrodsburg Herald (Harrodsburg, KY) **10148**
Hart County News-Herald (Munfordville, KY) **10150**
Harte-Hanks Pennysaver (Brea, CA) **10070**
Hartford Advocate (Hartford, CT) **10090**
Hartford Area News (Canistota, SD) **10264**
Hartland Herald Shopping Guide (Howell, MI) **10171**
Hartselle Enquirer (Hartselle, AL) **10059**
Hartsville Messenger, The (Hartsville, SC) **10262**
Hartsville Vidette, The (Hartsville, TN) **10267**
Hartville News (Hartville, OH) **10239**
Hartwell Sun, The (Hartwell, GA) **10103**
Harvard Spirit (Ayer, MA) **10160**
Harwich Oracle (Orleans, MA) **10164**
† Harwood Heights News (Park Ridge, IL)
Haskell Free Press (Haskell, TX) **10276**
Hastings Banner (Hastings, MI) **10170**
Hastings Reminder (Hastings, MI) **10170**
Hastings Star Gazette (Hastings, MN) **10179**
Havana Mason County Democrat (Havana, IL) **10119**
Haverford Press (Newtown Square, PA) **10256**
Hawley Herald (Hawley, MN) **10179**
Hawthorne Press (Hawthorne, NJ) **10203**
Haxtun-Fleming Herald, The (Haxtun, CO) **10087**
Hayden Valley Press (Craig, CO) **10086**
Hazard Herald-Voice (Hazard, KY) **10148**
Hazen Star (Hazen, ND) **10232**
Headland Observer (Headland, AL) **10060**
Headlight-Herald (Tillamook, OR) **10250**
Healdsburg Tribune (Healdsburg, CA) **10073**
Heights Herald (Fishers, IN) **10131**

Heights Times-Herald (Dearborn, MI) **10169**
Hempstead Beacon (Hicksville, NY) **10216**
Henderson County Quill
  (Stronghurst, IL) **10128**
† Hendersonville Free Press
  (Hendersonville, TN)
Hendersonville Star News
  (Hendersonville, TN) **10267**
Hendricks County Flyer (Plainfield, IN) **10135**
† Hendricks County Guide Gazette
  (Plainfield, IN)
† Henrico Gazette (Richmond, VA)
Henrietta Post (Fishers, NY) **10214**
Henry County Local (New Castle, KY) **10150**
Henry Herald, The (McDonough, GA) **10105**
Henry News Republican (Henry, IL) **10119**
Herald & Tribune (Jonesborough, TN) **10267**
Herald-Advocate (Wauchula, FL) **10100**
Herald-Chronicle, The (Winchester, TN) **10270**
Herald-Democrat (Leadville, CO) **10088**
Herald-Gazette, The (Barnesville, GA) **10101**
Herald-Independent, The
  (Winnsboro, SC) **10264**
Herald-Leader, The (Fitzgerald, GA) **10103**
Herald-News (Wolf Point, MT) **10196**
Herald-News (Dayton, TN) **10266**
Herald-Republican (Angola, IN) **10129**
Herald-Star, The (Edinburg, IL) **10116**
Herald-Tribune, The (Cartersville, GA) **10101**
Herald/Country Market, The
  (Bourbonnais, IL) **10111**
Herald/Leader (Siloam Springs, AR) **10068**
Herald Enterprise (Golconda, IL) **10118**
Herald Extra Express (Statesboro, GA) **10105**
Herald Gazette, The (Trenton, TN) **10270**
Herald Ledger (Eddyville, KY) **10147**
Herald News, The (Reed City, MI) **10174**
Herald of Randolph (Randolph, VT) **10284**
Herald Press (Harvey, ND) **10232**
Herald Record (West Union, WV) **10297**
† Herald, The (Tarpon Springs, FL)
Herald, The (Rincon, GA) **10105**
Herald, The (Truth or
  Consequences, NM) **10209**
Herald, The (Pittsburgh, PA) **10258**
Herald, The (Markesan, WI) **10302**
Hermann Advertiser-Courier
  (Hermann, MO) **10190**
Hermiston Herald (Hermiston, OR) **10249**
Hermitage Index (Hermitage, MO) **10190**
Herndon Times (Reston, VA) **10288**
Herrin Spokesman (Herrin, IL) **10119**
Herscher Pilot (Herscher, IL) **10119**
Hershey Chronicle, The (Hershey, PA) **10253**
Hesperia Resorter (Hesperia, CA) **10073**
Hi-Riser (Deerfield Beach, FL) **10094**

Hialeah/Opa-Lacka News (Miami, FL) **10097**
Hiawatha Valley Shopper (Red
  Wing, MN) **10182**
Hickory Hills Citizen (Midlothian, IL) **10123**
Hickory News/Extra, The (Hickory, NC) **10228**
Hicksville Illustrated News
  (Mineola, NY) **10219**
Highlander (West Covina, CA) **10084**
▼Highlander (Highlands Ranch, CO) **10087**
Highland Guide (Highland, IN) **10132**
Highland News Leader (Highland, IL) **10119**
Highland Park News (Bannockburn, IL) **10110**
Highland Park News/Herald/Journal (Los
  Angeles, CA) **10076**
Highlands Branch Herald (Littleton, CO) **10088**
† Highlands Press (Mulberry, FL)
Highline News (Burien, WA) **10290**
High Plains Journal (Dodge City, KS) **10143**
High Springs Herald, The (High
  Springs, FL) **10095**
High Timber Times (Pine, CO) **10089**
Hill City Times, The (Hill City, KS) **10143**
Hilliard Northwest News (Hilliard, OH) **10239**
Hillsboro Argus (Hillsboro, OR) **10249**
Hillsboro Journal (Hillsboro, IL) **10119**
Hillsboro Sentry-Enterprise
  (Hillsboro, WI) **10301**
Hillsboro Star-Journal (Hillsboro, KS) **10144**
Hillsborough Beacon (Somerville, NJ) **10206**
Hillside Leader (Union, NJ) **10207**
Hilltop News-Press (Cincinnati, OH) **10235**
Hilmar Times (Hilmar, CA) **10073**
Hingham Journal & Mariner
  (Quincy, MA) **10165**
Hinsdale Doings (Hinsdale, IL) **10120**
Hinton News (Hinton, WV) **10295**
Hobart Democrat-Chief (Hobart, OK) **10246**
Hobart Gazette (Merriville, IN) **10133**
Hobbs Flare (Hobbs, NM) **10208**
Hoboken Reporter (Hoboken, NJ) **10203**
Hocking Valley Advertiser (Logan, OH) **10240**
† Hodgkins Citizen (La Grange, IL)
Hoisington Dispatch (Hoisington, KS) **10144**
Holbrook Sun (Marshfield, MA) **10163**
Holbrook Times (Stoughton, MA) **10166**
Holbrook Tribune News & Snowflake Herald
  (Holbrook, AZ) **10064**
Holden Image-Progress, The
  (Holden, MO) **10190**
† Hollywood Citizen News (Los Angeles, CA)
Holmes County Advertiser (Bonifay, FL) **10093**
Holmes County Hub (Millersburg, OH) **10241**
Holt Community News (Holt, MI) **10171**
Holton Recorder (Holton, KS) **10144**
Holtville Tribune (Holtville, CA) **10073**
Home News, The (Marshville, NC) **10229**

Homer News (Homer, AK) **10062**
Homestead/Florida City News
  (Miami, FL) **10097**
Home Times Family Newspaper (West Palm
  Beach, FL) **10100**
Hometown News (Madison, WV) **10295**
Hominy News-Progress (Hominy, OK) **10246**
Hondo Anvil Herald (Hondo, TX) **10276**
Hood County News (Granbury, TX) **10275**
Hood River News (Hood River, OR) **10249**
Hoopeston Chronicle (Hoopeston, IL) **10120**
Hoosier Express (Washington, IN) **10136**
Hopkins Journal, The (Hopkins, MO) **10190**
Hopkins Sun-Sailor (Minnetonka, MN) **10180**
Horicon Reporter (Horicon, WI) **10301**
Horry Independent (Conway, SC) **10262**
Houghton Lake Resorter (Houghton
  Lake, MI) **10171**
Houlton Pioneer Times (Houlton, ME) **10156**
Housatonic Weekend (New Milford, CT) **10091**
Houston County Courier (Crockett, TX) **10273**
Houston Forward Times (Houston, TX) **10276**
Houston Herald & Republican
  (Houston, MO) **10190**
Houston Informer (Houston, TX) **10276**
Houston Times-Journal (Perry, GA) **10105**
▼Howard Beach Resident
  (Maspeth, NY) **10218**
Howard County Times (Columbia, MD) **10158**
Howe Enterprise (Howe, TX) **10276**
Hubbard City News (Mexia, TX) **10279**
† Hubbard News (Niles, OH)
Huber Heights Courier (Dayton, OH) **10239**
Hudson-Litchfield News (Hudson, NH) **10199**
Hudson Herald, The (Hudson, IA) **10139**
Hudson Hub-Times (Stow, OH) **10243**
Hudson Reporter (Hoboken, NJ) **10203**
Hudson Star-Observer (Hudson, WI) **10301**
Hughes County Times (Wetumka, OK) **10247**
Hughson Chronicle (Winton, CA) **10085**
Humble Sun (Humble, TX) **10276**
Humboldt Beacon (Fortuna, CA) **10072**
Humboldt Independent (Humboldt, IA) **10139**
† Humboldt Republican (Humboldt, IA)
Humbolt Journal (Canistota, SD) **10264**
Humeston New Era (Humeston, IA) **10139**
Hungry Horse News (Columbia
  Falls, MT) **10195**
Hunt County Shopper (Greenville, TX) **10275**
Hunterdon County Democrat
  (Flemington, NJ) **10202**
Hunterdon Review (Lebanon, NJ) **10203**
† Huntingdon Carroll Leader (Huntingdon, TN)
Huntington Beach/Fountain Valley Independent
  (Huntington Beach, CA) **10073**

Huntington Harbour Sun (Seal
  Beach, CA) **10083**
Huntington Park Bulletin (Los
  Angeles, CA) **10076**
Huntington Record (Huntington, NY) **10216**
Huntley Farmside, The (Huntley, IL) **10120**
Hurricane Breeze (Hurricane, WV) **10295**
Hustler, The (South Pittsburg, TN) **10269**
Hutchinson Herald (Menno, SD) **10265**
Hutchinson Leader (Hutchinson, MN) **10179**
Hyde Park Herald (Chicago, IL) **10113**
Hyde Park Townsman (Hyde Park, NY) **10216**
Idaho County Free Press
  (Grangeville, ID) **10107**
Idaho Enterprise (Malad City, ID) **10108**
Idaho Mountain Express (Ketchum, ID) **10108**
Idalou Beacon (Idalou, TX) **10276**
Ile Camera, The (Grosse Ile, MI) **10170**
Illinois Times (Springfield, IL) **10127**
Illiopolis Sentinel (Illiopolis, IL) **10120**
Impact of Laurel (Laurel, MS) **10186**
Improper Bostonian, The (Boston, MA) **10160**
Independence Bulletin-Journal
  (Independence, IA) **10139**
Independence News-Wave
  (Independence, WI) **10301**
Independence News, The
  (Independence, KS) **10144**
Independent (Collierville, TN) **10266**
Independent (Deerfield, WI) **10299**
Independent-Journal, The (Potosi, MO) **10192**
Independent-Messenger (Emporia, VA) **10286**
Independent-Register. The
  (Brodhead, WI) **10298**
Independent Appeal (Selmer, TN) **10269**
Independent Enterprise (Payette, ID) **10108**
Independent Herald, The (Pineville, WV) **10296**
Independent Mirror (Mexico, NY) **10218**
Independent News (Georgetown, IL) **10118**
Independent News Herald
  (Clarissa, MN) **10178**
Independent Observer, The
  (Scottdale, PA) **10259**
† Independent Press (Marine City, MI)
Independent Press (New
  Providence, NJ) **10205**
Independent Press of Bloomfield, The
  (Bloomfield, NJ) **10201**
Independent Republican (Goshen, NY) **10215**
Independent, The (Robertsdale, AL) **10061**
Independent, The (Livermore, CA) **10075**
Independent, The (Winamac, IN) **10136**
Independent, The (Flint, MI) **10169**
Independent, The (Durham, NC) **10227**
Independent, The (Morganville, NJ) **10204**
Independent, The (Collegeville, PA) **10252**

Independent, The (Montrose, PA) **10255**
Indianapolis East Side Herald
   (Indianapolis, IN) **10132**
Indianapolis Recorder (Indianapolis, IN) **10132**
Indianapolis Westside Enterprise
   (Indianapolis, IN) **10132**
Indianhead Advertiser (Frederic, WI) **10300**
Indian Head Park Citizen (Oak
   Brook, IL) **10125**
Indian Head Park Doings (Hinsdale, IL) **10120**
Indio Advertiser (Palm Desert, CA) **10079**
Indio Post (Indio, CA) **10073**
Indy Suburban Newspaper
   (Greenfield, IN) **10132**
Ingham County News (Mason, MI) **10172**
Inglewood/Hawthorne Wave (Los
   Angeles, CA) **10076**
Inkster Ledger-Star (Wayne, MI) **10176**
Inquirer & Mirror, The (Nantucket, MA) **10164**
Inside (Chicago, IL) **10113**
† Inside Ravenswood (Chicago, IL)
Inter-County Leader (Frederic, WI) **10300**
† Interboro News (Prospect Park, PA)
Interior Journal (Stanford, KY) **10151**
Interlaken Review (Trumansburg, NY) **10224**
Intermountain News (Burney, CA) **10070**
Iola Herald (Iola, WI) **10301**
Iosco County News Herald (East
   Tawas, MI) **10169**
Iowa Park Leader (Iowa Park, TX) **10276**
Ipswich Chronicle (Ipswich, MA) **10162**
Ipswich Tribune (Ipswich, SD) **10265**
Iron County Miner (Hurley, WI) **10301**
Irondequoit Press (Rochester, NY) **10222**
Iron River Reporter (Iron River, MI) **10171**
Irvine World News (Irvine, CA) **10073**
Irving News (Arlington, TX) **10271**
Irvington Viewpoint, The (Irvington, NY) **10216**
ISDA Unione (Pittsburgh, PA) **10258**
Island Ad-Vantages (Stonington, ME) **10157**
Island Connection (Portland, OR) **10250**
Island Dispatch (Grand Island, NY) **10215**
Islander, The (Gulf Shores, AL) **10059**
Islander, The (Pensacola Beach, FL) **10098**
Islander, The (St. Simons Island, GA) **10106**
Islander, The (South Hero, VT) **10284**
Island Reporter (Sanibel, FL) **10098**
Islesboro Island News (Islesboro, ME) **10156**
Islip Bulletin (Sayville, NY) **10222**
Islip News (Smithtown, NY) **10223**
Issaquah Press (Issaquah, WA) **10291**
Isthmus (Madison, WI) **10302**
Itawamba County Times, The
   (Fulton, MS) **10186**
Item (Clinton, MA) **10161**
Ithaca Times (Ithaca, NY) **10216**

Iuka Tishomingo County News
   (Iuka, MS) **10186**
Jackson-Vinton Journal-Herald
   (Jackson, OH) **10240**
Jackson Cash-Book Journal
   (Jackson, MO) **10190**
Jackson County Banner
   (Brownstown, IN) **10130**
Jackson County Herald/Tribune
   (Edna, TX) **10274**
Jackson County Livewire (Jackson, MN) **10179**
Jackson County Star (Walden, CO) **10089**
Jackson Heights News (Maspeth, NY) **10218**
Jackson Herald (Jefferson, GA) **10103**
Jackson Hole Guide (Jackson, WY) **10309**
Jackson Hole News (Jackson, WY) **10309**
Jackson Independent, The
   (Jonesboro, LA) **10153**
Jackson Progress-Argus (Jackson, GA) **10103**
Jackson Star News (Ravenswood, WV) **10296**
Jacksonville News (Jacksonville, AL) **10060**
Jacksonville Shopping Guide
   (Jacksonville, FL) **10095**
Jaffrey-Rindge Chronicle
   (Winchendon, MA) **10167**
▼Jamaica Times, The (Flushing, NY) **10214**
Jamestown Press, The (Jamestown, RI) **10260**
Jasper County News, The (Bay
   Springs, MS) **10185**
Jasper County Sun (Ridgeland, SC) **10263**
Jasper Journal (Jasper, MN) **10179**
Jasper Journal (Jasper, TN) **10267**
Jasper News (Jasper, FL) **10095**
Jasper News-Boy (Jasper, TX) **10276**
Jasper News-Boy Shopper (Jasper, TX) **10276**
Jeanerette Enterprise (Jeanerette, LA) **10153**
Jeannette Spirit (Jeannette, PA) **10254**
Jeff Davis Ledger (Hazlehurst, GA) **10103**
Jefferson Bee (Jefferson, IA) **10139**
Jefferson County Journal (Arnold, MO) **10188**
Jefferson County Journal (Adams, NY) **10209**
Jefferson County Transcript
   (Golden, CO) **10087**
Jefferson Herald (Jefferson, IA) **10139**
Jeffersonian Democrat (Brookville, PA) **10251**
Jeffersonian, The (Baltimore, MD) **10158**
Jeffersonian, The (Croswell, MI) **10169**
Jefferson Jimplecute (Jefferson, TX) **10276**
Jefferson Park-Portage Park-Bel Cragin Times
   (Lincolnwood, IL) **10121**
Jefferson Post (West Jefferson, NC) **10231**
† Jefferson Republic, The (De Soto, MO)
Jefferson Sentinel (Lakewood, CO) **10088**
Jefferson Star, The (Rigby, ID) **10109**
Jekyll's Golden Islander
   (Brunswick, GA) **10101**

Jellico Advance Sentinel (La Follette, TN) **10267**
Jena Times Olla-Tullos Signal (Jena, LA) **10153**
Jenks Journal (Tulsa, OK) **10247**
Jersey City Reporter (Hoboken, NJ) **10203**
Jessamine Journal (Nicholasville, KY) **10150**
† Jet Gazette (Austin, TX)
Jetmore Republican (Jetmore, KS) **10144**
† Jet Visitor (Cherokee, OK)
Johnsonburg Press (Johnsonburg, PA) **10254**
Johnson County Graphic (Clarksville, AR) **10065**
Johnson County Sun (Shawnee Mission, KS) **10145**
Johnson Pioneer (Johnson, KS) **10144**
Johnston County Capital-Democrat (Tishomingo, OK) **10247**
Johnstonian Sun (Selma, NC) **10230**
Johnstown Independent (Columbus, OH) **10237**
Jonesboro Review (Sherwood, AR) **10068**
Jones County Town Crier (Anamosa, IA) **10137**
Journal & Austin Chronicle (Scottsburg, IN) **10135**
Journal & Monitor Herald (Tomah, WI) **10306**
Journal & Republican (Lowville, NY) **10217**
Journal-Enterprise (Providence, KY) **10151**
Journal-Herald, The (White Haven, PA) **10260**
Journal-Leader (Caldwell, OH) **10235**
Journal-Patriot (North Wilkesboro, NC) **10229**
▼Journal/Valley Views (White Haven, PA) **10260**
Journal Courier (Moravia, NY) **10219**
Journal Herald, The (Shawnee, KS) **10145**
Journal News (Spencerville, OH) **10243**
Journal of the San Juan Islands (Friday Harbor, WA) **10291**
Journal Opinion (Bradford, VT) **10283**
Journal Press (Lawrenceburg, IN) **10133**
Journal Record (Hamilton, AL) **10059**
Journal Register (Palmer, MA) **10164**
Journal, The (Chicago, IL) **10113**
Journal, The (Ellettsville, IN) **10130**
Journal, The (Crosby, ND) **10232**
Journal, The (Berlin, NJ) **10200**
Journal, The (Struthers, OH) **10243**
Journal, The (Mt. Pleasant, SC) **10263**
Journal, The (Williamston, SC) **10264**
† Journal Transcript (Franklin, NH)
Journal Tribune (Williamsburg, IA) **10142**
Journal Tribune (Seneca, SC) **10264**
Julesburg Advocate (Julesburg, CO) **10087**
Junction Eagle, The (Junction, TX) **10277**

Juneau County Star-Times (Mauston, WI) **10302**
Juniata News (Philadelphia, PA) **10257**
Juniata Sentinel (Mifflintown, PA) **10255**
Jupiter Courier (Jupiter, FL) **10095**
Kalona News, The (Kalona, IA) **10139**
Kanabec County Times (Mora, MN) **10181**
† Kansas Business News (Augusta, KS)
Karnes Citation (Karnes City, TX) **10277**
Katahdin Times (Millinocket, ME) **10156**
Kaufman Herald, The (Kaufman, TX) **10277**
Kaukauna Times (Kaukauna, WI) **10301**
Kayo, The (Clinton, MO) **10189**
Keith County News (Ogallala, NE) **10198**
Keller Citizen, The (Keller, TX) **10277**
Kemmerer Gazette (Kemmerer, WY) **10309**
Kemper County Messenger (DeKalb, MS) **10185**
Ken-Ton Bee (Buffalo, NY) **10211**
Kenbridge-Victoria Dispatch (Victoria, VA) **10289**
Kendall County Record (Yorkville, IL) **10129**
Kendall News-Gazette (Miami, FL) **10097**
Kendrick-Gazette (Kendrick, ID) **10108**
Kenilworth Leader (Union, NJ) **10207**
Kenly News (Kenly, NC) **10228**
Kennedale News (Everman, TX) **10274**
Kennedy Advanced Times (Karnes City, TX) **10277**
Kennesaw Neighbor, The (Marietta, GA) **10104**
Kent County News (Chestertown, MD) **10158**
Kent Good Times Dispatch (Kent, CT) **10090**
Kenton County Recorder (Florence, KY) **10148**
Kentucky Standard (Bardstown, KY) **10146**
Kentwood Advance (Jenison, MI) **10171**
Kentwood News-Ledger (Kentwood, LA) **10153**
Kenyon Leader (Kenyon, MN) **10179**
Kerman News (Kerman, CA) **10074**
Kernersville News (Kernersville, NC) **10228**
Kern Valley Sun (Lake Isabella, CA) **10074**
Kettering-Oakwood Times (Kettering, OH) **10240**
Kettle Moraine Index (Hartland, WI) **10300**
Kewaskum Statesman (Kewaskum, WI) **10301**
Kewaunee Enterprise (Kewaunee, WI) **10301**
Keystone Tribune (Elroy, WI) **10300**
Kiel Tri-County Record (Kiel, WI) **10301**
King City Rustler (King City, CA) **10074**
Kingfisher Times & Free Press (Kingfisher, OK) **10246**
Kingman Journal/Leader Courier (Kingman, KS) **10144**
King of Prussia Courier (King of Prussia, PA) **10254**
Kingsburg Recorder (Kingsburg, CA) **10074**
Kings County News (Brooklyn, NY) **10211**

Kings Courier (Brooklyn, NY) **10211**
Kings Mountain Herald (Kings
    Mountain, NC) **10228**
Kingston Reporter (Plymouth, MA) **10165**
Kingsville Record, The (Kingsville, TX) **10277**
King Times News (King, NC) **10228**
Kingwood Sun (Humble, TX) **10276**
Kinmundy Express (Kinmundy, IL) **10121**
Kiowa County Press (Eads, CO) **10086**
† Kirtland Enterprise (Willoughby, OH)
Knoxville Journal/Express
    (Knoxville, IA) **10139**
Knoxville Journal, The (Galesburg, IL) **10117**
Konawa Leader (Konawa, OK) **10246**
† Kossuth County Advance (Algona, IA)
Kuna-Melba News (Kuna, ID) **10108**
L'Anse Sentinel (L'Anse, MI) **10172**
L'Observateur (La Place, LA) **10153**
Labor Herald (Baltimore, MD) **10158**
La Canada Valley Sun (La Canada, CA) **10074**
Lacon Home Journal (Lacon, IL) **10121**
La Crosse County Countryman (West
    Salem, WI) **10308**
Ladysmith News (Ladysmith, WI) **10301**
Lafayette Leader (Lafayette, IN) **10133**
Lafayette Sun, The (Lafayette, AL) **10060**
La Feria News (La Feria, TX) **10277**
La Follette Press (La Follette, TN) **10267**
La Grange Countryside Citizen (Oak
    Brook, IL) **10125**
La Grange Independent (Mahopac, NY) **10217**
La Grange Park Citizen (Oak Brook, IL) **10125**
La Grange Standard News (La
    Grange, IN) **10133**
Laguna Niguel News (Lake Forest, CA) **10074**
Laguna Post News (Lake Forest, CA) **10074**
La Habra Star (Anaheim, CA) **10068**
La Jolla Light (La Jolla, CA) **10074**
† Lake Alfred Press (Mulberry, FL)
Lake Area News (Land O' Lakes, FL) **10096**
Lake Cities Sun, The (Lake Dallas, TX) **10277**
Lake City Town Crier (La Follette, TN) **10267**
† Lake Country Chronicle (Buchanan, MI)
Lake Country Reporter (Hartland, WI) **10300**
Lake County Examiner (Lakeview, OR) **10249**
Lake County Leader (Ronan, MT) **10196**
Lake County News-Chronicle (Two
    Harbors, MN) **10184**
Lake County Star (Crown Point, IN) **10130**
Lake County Star (Big Rapids, MI) **10167**
Lake Edition, The (Lexington, SC) **10263**
Lake Elsinore Valley Sun-Tribune (Lake
    Elsinore, CA) **10074**
Lakefield Standard (Lakefield, MN) **10179**
Lake Forester (Bannockburn, IL) **10110**

Lake Geneva Regional News (Lake
    Geneva, WI) **10301**
Lake Havasu City Advertiser (Palm
    Desert, CA) **10079**
Lakeland Press (Grayslake, IL) **10118**
Lakeland Times (Minocqua, WI) **10303**
Lakeland Today (Butler, NJ) **10201**
Lake Michigan Examiner, The
    (Muskegon, MI) **10173**
Lake Mills Leader (Lake Mills, WI) **10301**
Lake News (Fruitland Park, FL) **10095**
Lake Oswego Review (Lake
    Oswego, OR) **10249**
Lake Placid Journal (Lake Placid, FL) **10096**
Lake Placid News (Lake Placid, NY) **10216**
Lake Powell Chronicle (Page, AZ) **10064**
Lakeshore Chronicle (Manitowoc, WI) **10302**
Lakeshore Weekly News (Wayzata, MN) **10184**
Lakeside Ledger, The (Woodstock, GA) **10106**
Lake Station Herald (Merrillville, IN) **10133**
Lake Tribune (Sherwood, AR) **10068**
Lakeview Enterprise (Big Rapids, MI) **10167**
Lake Villa Record (Grayslake, IL) **10119**
Lakeville Independent (Middleboro, MA) **10163**
Lakeville Journal, The (Lakeville, CT) **10090**
Lakeville Life & Times (Lakeville, MN) **10179**
Lakeville Sun-Current (Burnsville, MN) **10177**
† Lake Wales Highlander (Winter Haven, FL)
Lake Wales News (Lake Wales, FL) **10096**
Lakewood Sun Post (Cleveland, OH) **10236**
Lake Worth Herald Coastal Observer (Lake
    Worth, FL) **10096**
Lake Zurich Enterprise (Grayslake, IL) **10119**
Lakin Independent, The (Lakin, KS) **10144**
Lamar Democrat (Vernon, AL) **10062**
Lamar Democrat (Lamar, MO) **10191**
Lamar Leader (Sulligent, AL) **10061**
La Marque Times (La Marque, TX) **10277**
Lamb County Leader-News
    (Littlefield, TX) **10278**
Lamberton News (Lamberton, MN) **10179**
La Mesa Forum (Lemon Grove, CA) **10075**
Lamesa Press-Reporter (Lamesa, TX) **10277**
Lamont Reporter (Lamont, CA) **10074**
Lancaster Bee (Williamsville, NY) **10225**
Lancaster Fairfield Advertiser
    (Carroll, OH) **10235**
Lancaster News (Lancaster, SC) **10262**
Lancaster Today (DeSoto, TX) **10274**
Lander Wyoming State Journal
    (Lander, WY) **10309**
Larimore Pioneer (Northwood, ND) **10233**
LaRue County Herald-News
    (Hodgenville, KY) **10148**
Las Vegas Today (Las Vegas, NV) **10199**

Las Virgenes Enterprise (Woodland
Hills, CA) **10085**
Lauderdale County Enterprise
(Ripley, TN) **10269**
Laurel Leader (Laurel, MD) **10159**
Laurens County Advertiser
(Laurens, SC) **10263**
Laurens Sun, The (Laurens, IA) **10139**
La Vida News (Arlington, TX) **10271**
LaVilla News (Hot Springs Village, AR) **10066**
L.A. Weekly (Los Angeles, CA) **10076**
Lawrence County Centennial
(Deadwood, SD) **10264**
Lawrence County News
(Lawrenceville, IL) **10121**
Lawrence County Record (Mt.
Vernon, MO) **10191**
Lawrence Ledger (Pennington, NJ) **10206**
Lawrence Times (Fishers, IN) **10131**
Lawrence Township Journal
(Lawrence, IN) **10133**
Leader-Courier (Kingman, KS) **10144**
Leader-News (Central City, KY) **10147**
Leader-News (Washburn, ND) **10233**
Leader-Record (Gonvick, MN) **10179**
Leader-State Register, The
(Seaford, DE) **10092**
Leader-Tribune, The (Fort Valley, GA) **10103**
Leader-Vindicator, The (New
Bethlehem, PA) **10256**
Leader Enterprise (Montpelier, OH) **10241**
Leader Observer (Maspeth, NY) **10218**
Leader, The (Davenport, IA) **10137**
Leader, The (Solon, IA) **10141**
Leader, The (Charlestown, IN) **10130**
† Leader, The (Lansing, KS)
Leader, The (Northwood, ND) **10233**
Leader, The (Point Pleasant Beach, NJ) **10206**
Leader, The (Freeport, NY) **10214**
Leader, The (Cleveland, OH) **10236**
† Leader, The (East Palestine, OH)
Leader, The (Philadelphia, PA) **10257**
Leader, The (Tremonton, UT) **10283**
Leavenworth Echo (Leavenworth, WA) **10292**
Leawood Sun (Shawnee Mission, KS) **10145**
† Lebanon Connecticut Valley Reporter
(Lebanon, NH)
Lebanon Enterprise (Lebanon, KY) **10149**
Lebanon Express (Lebanon, OR) **10249**
▼Lebanon Herald (Mascoutah, IL) **10122**
Lebanon News (Lebanon, VA) **10287**
Lebanon Times, The (Lebanon, KS) **10144**
Le Center Leader (Le Center, MN) **10179**
Ledger, The (Moundridge, KS) **10145**
Lee's Summit Journal (Lee's
Summit, MO) **10191**

Lee County Eagle, The (Auburn, AL) **10057**
Lee County Observer (Bishopville, SC) **10261**
Leeds News (Leeds, AL) **10060**
Leelanau Enterprise (Leland, MI) **10172**
Leesburg Today (Leesburg, VA) **10287**
Lehi Free Press (American Fork, UT) **10282**
Lehigh Acres News-Star (Lehigh
Acres, FL) **10096**
Leisure World Golden Rain News (Seal
Beach, CA) **10083**
Leisure World News (Laguna Hills, CA) **10074**
Lemon Grove Review (Lemon
Grove, CA) **10075**
Lemont Metropolitan (Lemont, IL) **10121**
Lemont Reporter (Lemont, IL) **10121**
Lenexa Sun (Shawnee Mission, KS) **10146**
Leon Journal-Reporter (Leon, IA) **10139**
Leslie County News (Hyden, KY) **10148**
Leslie Local Independent (Leslie, MI) **10172**
Letcher County Community News-Press
(Cromona, KY) **10147**
Levelland Hockley County News-Press
(Levelland, TX) **10277**
Levittown Tribune (Mineola, NY) **10219**
Lewisboro Ledger, The (Ridgefield, CT) **10091**
Lewisburg Tribune (Lewisburg, TN) **10268**
Lewis County Herald (Nezperce, ID) **10108**
Lewiston-Porter Sentinel (Grand
Island, NY) **10215**
Lewiston Journal (Lewiston, MN) **10179**
Lewistown-Fulton Democrat
(Lewistown, IL) **10121**
Lewistown News-Argus (Lewistown, MT) **10195**
Lewisville Leader (Lewisville, TX) **10278**
Lexington Minuteman (Lexington, MA) **10162**
Lexington News (Lexington, MO) **10191**
Lexington Progress (Lexington, TN) **10268**
Liberty Gazette (Liberty, TX) **10278**
† Liberty News (Niles, OH)
Liberty Press, The (Liberty Center, OH) **10240**
Liberty Tribune (Kansas City, MO) **10190**
Libertyville News (Grayslake, IL) **10119**
Libertyville Review (Bannockburn, IL) **10110**
† Licking Countian (Newark, OH)
Licking Valley Courier (West
Liberty, KY) **10152**
Life at Ken-Caryl (Littleton, CO) **10088**
Light & Champion (Center, TX) **10272**
Ligonier Advance-Leader (Ligonier, IN) **10133**
Ligonier Echo (Ligonier, PA) **10254**
Ligonier Free Gazette, The
(Ligonier, PA) **10254**
Lillie Suburban Shopping Review (St.
Paul, MN) **10183**
Lime Springs Herald (Lime Springs, IA) **10139**

Limestone Independent News
(Bartonville, IL) 10111
† Lincoln-Belmont Booster (Chicago, IL)
Lincoln County Journal (Shoshone, ID) 10109
Lincoln County News (Newcastle, ME) 10156
Lincoln County News (Chandler, OK) 10245
Lincoln Heights Bulletin-News (Los
Angeles, CA) 10076
Lincoln Journal (Concord, MA) 10161
Lincoln Journal (Hamlin, WV) 10294
Lincoln Ledger (Star City, AR) 10068
Lincoln News (Lincoln, ME) 10156
Lincoln Times-News (Lincolnton, NC) 10228
Lincolnwood Life (Lincolnwood, IL) 10122
Lincolnwood Review (Evanston, IL) 10117
Linden Herald (Linden, CA) 10075
Lindenhurst News (Grayslake, IL) 10119
Linden Leader (Union, NJ) 10207
Lindsay Gazette (Lindsay, CA) 10075
† Linesville Herald (Conneaut Lake, PA)
Linn Unterrified Democrat (Linn, MO) 10191
Linton Emmons County Record
(Linton, ND) 10233
Lisbon Ransom County Gazette & Enterprise
(Lisbon, ND) 10233
Lisle Sun (Naperville, IL) 10124
Litchfield Enquirer (Litchfield, CT) 10090
Litchfield Independent Review
(Litchfield, MN) 10179
Lititz Record Express, The (Lititz, PA) 10254
Little Neck Ledger, The (Flushing, NY) 10214
Little Paper, The (Melbourne, FL) 10096
Littleton Independent (Littleton, CO) 10088
Littleton Independent (Concord, MA) 10161
Littleton Observer (Littleton, NC) 10228
† Littleton Times (Littleton, CO)
Livermore Falls Advertiser (Livermore
Falls, ME) 10156
Liverpool Review (Baldwinsville, NY) 10209
† Livingston East Texas Eye (Livingston, TX)
Livingston Enterprise (Livingston, TN) 10268
Livingston Leader (Denham
Springs, LA) 10153
Livonia Observer (Livonia, MI) 10172
Llano News (Llano, TX) 10278
Lockeford-Clements News
(Lockeford, CA) 10075
Lockhart Post Register (Lockhart, TX) 10278
Locust Valley Leader (Locust
Valley, NY) 10217
Loda Times (Paxton, IL) 10126
Lodi Enterprise (Lodi, WI) 10301
Logan Herald Observer (Logan, IA) 10139
Lombardian, The (Lombard, IL) 10122
Lombardian Villa Park Review
(Lombard, IL) 10122

Lombard Spectator (Elmhurst, IL) 10116
† London Mills Times (Roseville, IL)
Lone Tree Reporter, The (Lone
Tree, IA) 10140
Long Beach Chinook Observer (Long
Beach, WA) 10292
† Long Beach Community News (Long
Beach, CA)
Long Beach Herald (Long Beach, NY) 10217
Long Beach Independent Voice (Long
Beach, NY) 10217
Long Island Advance (Patchogue, NY) 10221
Long Island City/Astoria Journal
(Maspeth, NY) 10218
Long Island Graphic-Roosevelt Press
(Lawrence, NY) 10216
† Long Island Journal Newspaper Group (Long
Beach, NY)
Longmeadow News (Westfield, MA) 10166
Long Prairie Leader (Long Prairie, MN) 10179
Long Valley Advocate, The
(Cascade, ID) 10107
Lorain County Times, The (Rocky
River, OH) 10242
Lorenzo Examiner (Lorenzo, TX) 10278
Loris Times (Loris, SC) 10263
Los Altos Town Crier (Los Altos, CA) 10075
Los Angeles Independent (Los
Angeles, CA) 10076
Los Angeles Log (San Diego, CA) 10080
Los Banos Enterprise (Los Banos, CA) 10077
Los Gatos Weekly-Times (Los
Gatos, CA) 10077
Lost River Star (Merrill, OR) 10249
Loudenville Weekly (Delmar, NY) 10213
Loudonville Times, The
(Loudonville, OH) 10240
Loudoun Times-Mirror (Leesburg, VA) 10287
Louisiana Press-Journal
(Louisiana, MO) 10191
Louisville Defender Newspaper
(Louisville, KY) 10149
Louisville Herald, The (Louisville, OH) 10240
Louisville Winston County Journal
(Louisville, MS) 10186
Loveland Herald Press (Loveland, OH) 10241
Lovell Chronicle, The (Lovell, WY) 10309
Lovelock Review-Miner (Lovelock, NV) 10199
Lowell Ledger (Lowell, MI) 10172
Lowell Tribune (Lowell, IN) 10133
Lower Township Lantern (Rio
Grande, NJ) 10206
Loyal Tribune-Record-Gleaner
(Loyal, WI) 10302
Ludlow Register (Palmer, MA) 10164
Ludowici News (Ludowici, GA) 10104

Luling Newsboy & Signal (Luling, TX)   **10278**
Luray Page News & Courier (Luray, VA)   **10287**
Lusk Herald (Lusk, WY)   **10309**
Lutz Community News (Tampa, FL)   **10099**
Luverne Journal & News (Luverne, AL)   **10060**
Luxemburg News (Luxemburg, WI)   **10302**
Lynbrook Herald (Lawrence, NY)   **10216**
Lynbrook USA (Mineola, NY)   **10219**
Lynden Tribune (Lynden, WA)   **10292**
Lynwood Journal (Compton, CA)   **10071**
Lynwood Press (Los Angeles, CA)   **10076**
Lyon-Sioux Press (Rock Rapids, IA)   **10141**
Lyons Citizen (Oak Brook, IL)   **10125**
Lyons Mirror-Sun (Lyons, NE)   **10197**
M & M Journal (Hillsboro, IL)   **10120**
Mableton Neighbor, The (Marietta, GA)   **10104**
Machias Valley News Observer
   (Machias, ME)   **10156**
Macomb Voice, The (New
   Baltimore, MI)   **10173**
Macon Beacon, The (Macon, MS)   **10186**
Macon County Times (Lafayette, TN)   **10267**
Macoupin & Montgomery County Journal
   (Hillsboro, IL)   **10120**
Macoupin County Enquirer
   (Carlinville, IL)   **10112**
Macoupin County Shopper
   (Hillsboro, IL)   **10120**
Madawaska St. John Valley Times
   (Madawaska, ME)   **10156**
Madill Record (Madill, OK)   **10246**
Madison County Carrier (Madison, FL)   **10096**
Madison County Chronicle (Worden, IL)   **10129**
Madison County Eagle (Madison, VA)   **10287**
Madison County Herald (Canton, MS)   **10185**
Madison County Record (Madison, AL)   **10060**
Madison County Record
   (Huntsville, AR)   **10066**
Madison Eagle (Madison, NJ)   **10203**
Madison Enterprise Recorder
   (Madison, FL)   **10096**
Madisonian, The (Madison, GA)   **10104**
Madison Independent Press (New
   Providence, NJ)   **10205**
Madison Journal (Tallulah, LA)   **10155**
Madison News, The (Madison, KS)   **10144**
Madison Park Times (Seattle, WA)   **10293**
† Madison Tribune (Ontario, OH)
Madison Western Guard, The
   (Madison, MN)   **10180**
Madras Pioneer, The (Madras, OR)   **10249**
Magee Courier (Magee, MS)   **10186**
Magna Times (Magna, UT)   **10282**
Magnolia Gazette, The (Magnolia, MS)   **10186**
Mahnomen Pioneer, The
   (Mahnomen, MN)   **10180**

Mahopac Press (Mahopac, NY)   **10217**
Mail-Journal, The (Milford, IN)   **10134**
Maine Times (Portland, ME)   **10157**
Mainland Journal (Hammonton, NJ)   **10203**
† Main Line Chronicle (West Chester, PA)
Mainline Life (Ardmore, PA)   **10251**
Main Line Times (Ardmore, PA)   **10251**
Main Street Trilogy (Townsend, MA)   **10166**
Majic Valley Shopper's News
   (Camden, TN)   **10266**
† Malden Press-Merit (Malden, MO)
Malheur Enterprise (Vale, OR)   **10251**
Malibu Surfside News (Malibu, CA)   **10077**
Malibu Times (Malibu, CA)   **10077**
Malta Messenger (Ballston Spa, NY)   **10209**
Malvern Community News
   (Minerva, OH)   **10241**
Malverne Times (Mineola, NY)   **10219**
Malvern Leader, The (Malvern, IA)   **10140**
† Mammoth Lakes Review/Mono Herald
   (Mammoth Lakes, CA)
Mammoth Times (Mammoth Lakes, CA)   **10077**
Mamou Acadian Press (Mamou, LA)   **10154**
Manchester Enterprise
   (Manchester, KY)   **10149**
Manchester Journal (Manchester
   Center, VT)   **10284**
Manchester Press (Manchester, IA)   **10140**
Manchester Signal (Manchester, OH)   **10241**
Manchester Star-Mercury
   (Manchester, GA)   **10104**
Manchester Times (Manchester, TN)   **10268**
Mancos Times-Tribune (Mancos, CO)   **10088**
Mandan News (Mandan, ND)   **10233**
Manhasset Press (Mineola, NY)   **10219**
Manistee Observer (Manistee, MI)   **10172**
Manistique Pioneer-Tribune
   (Manistique, MI)   **10172**
Manitou Springs Pikes Peak Journal (Manitou
   Springs, CO)   **10088**
Mansfield Enterprise (Mansfield, LA)   **10154**
Mansfield News (Mansfield, MA)   **10162**
Mansfield News-Mirror (Mansfield, TX)   **10278**
Manville News (Somerville, NJ)   **10207**
Maple Heights Press (Bedford, OH)   **10234**
Maple Shade Progress (Maple
   Shade, NJ)   **10204**
Maple Valley News (Hastings, MI)   **10170**
Maplewood Review (St. Paul, MN)   **10183**
Maquoketa Sentinel-Press
   (Maquoketa, IA)   **10140**
† Marathon Independent Newspaper
   (Marathon, NY)
Marble Falls Highlander (Marble
   Falls, TX)   **10278**
Marblehead Reporter (Marblehead, MA)   **10162**

Marceline Press (Marceline, MO) **10191**
Marcellus Observer (Skaneateles, NY) **10223**
Marco Island Eagle, The (Marco
  Island, FL) **10096**
Marcus Hook Press (Drexel Hill, PA) **10252**
Marianas Review (Saipan, MP) **10233**
Marianna Courier Index (Marianna, AR) **10066**
Maries County Gazette (Vienna, MO) **10194**
Marina & Independent Voice
  (Marshfield, MA) **10163**
Marina News (Long Beach, CA) **10075**
Marin Scope (Sausalito, CA) **10083**
Marion Advertiser (Marion, WI) **10302**
Marion County Record (Marion, KS) **10144**
Marion Star & Mullins Enterprise
  (Marion, SC) **10263**
Marion Times-Standard (Marion, AL) **10060**
Mariposa Gazette (Mariposa, CA) **10077**
† Market Place (Vandergrift, PA)
Marketplace, The (Marianna, FL) **10096**
Market Shopper, The (Delano, CA) **10071**
Marlboro Herald-Advocate
  (Bennettsville, SC) **10261**
Marlboro Shopper (Bennettsville, SC) **10261**
Marquette County Tribune
  (Montello, WI) **10303**
† Marshall County Life (Culver, IN)
Marshall Gazette (Lewisburg, TN) **10268**
Marshall Mountain Wave (Marshall, AR) **10066**
Marshfield Mail (Marshfield, MO) **10191**
Marshfield Mariner (Marshfield, MA) **10163**
Marshfield Reporter (Plymouth, MA) **10165**
Marthasville Record, The
  (Marthasville, MO) **10191**
† Mart Herald (Mart, TX)
† Martin County News (Stuart, FL)
Martinez News Gazette (Martinez, CA) **10077**
Maryland Gazette (Glen Burnie, MD) **10159**
Maryland Independent (Waldorf, MD) **10160**
Maryland Times-Press (Ocean
  City, MD) **10159**
Marysville Advocate (Marysville, KS) **10144**
Mascoutah Herald (Mascoutah, IL) **10122**
Mashpee Messenger (Orleans, MA) **10164**
Mason County News (Mason, TX) **10278**
Mason Valley News (Yerington, NV) **10199**
Massapequan Observer (Mineola, NY) **10219**
Massapequa Post (Massapequa
  Park, NY) **10218**
Mathis News (Mathis, TX) **10278**
† Matthews News (Matthews, NC)
† Maumee Valley Herald (Toledo, OH)
Maynard Beacon (Concord, MA) **10161**
Mayville Monitor (Mayville, MI) **10172**
Mayville News (Mayville, WI) **10302**

Mayville Sentinel/Chautauqua News
  (Westfield, NY) **10225**
Maywood Herald (Oak Park, IL) **10125**
McConnellsburg Fulton County News
  (McConnellsburg, PA) **10254**
McCreary County Record (Whitley
  City, KY) **10152**
McDonough-Democrat (Bushnell, IL) **10112**
McDuffie Progress, The (Thomson, GA) **10106**
McFarland Community Life
  (Monona, WI) **10303**
McFarland Leader (Monona, WI) **10303**
McIntosh Times (McIntosh, MN) **10180**
McKenzie Banner (McKenzie, TN) **10268**
McLean County Independent
  (Garrison, ND) **10232**
McLean County Journal (Turtle
  Lake, ND) **10233**
McLean Providence Journal
  (Reston, VA) **10288**
McLeansboro Times-Leader
  (McLeansboro, IL) **10123**
Meade County Messenger
  (Brandenburg, KY) **10146**
Meade County Times-Tribune
  (Sturgis, SD) **10265**
Meadowbrook Times (Lawrence, NY) **10216**
Mebane Enterprise (Mebane, NC) **10229**
Mecklenburg Gazette (Davidson, NC) **10227**
Mecklenburg Sun (Clarksville, VA) **10285**
Medfield Suburban Press
  (Needham, MA) **10164**
▼Medina Sun, The (Cleveland, OH) **10236**
Meeker Herald, The (Meeker, CO) **10088**
Melrose Beacon (Melrose, MN) **10180**
Melrose Chronicle (Melrose, WI) **10302**
Melrose Free Press (Melrose, MA) **10163**
Melrose Park Herald (Oak Park, IL) **10125**
Melrose Park Star-Sentinel (Melrose
  Park, IL) **10123**
† Melrose Shoppers News (Stoneham, MA)
Menard County Review (Greenview, IL) **10119**
Menard News & Messenger, The
  (Menard, TX) **10279**
Mena Star (Mena, AR) **10067**
Mendocino Beacon, The
  (Mendocino, CA) **10077**
Mendota Reporter (Mendota, IL) **10123**
Menifee Valley News (Sun City, CA) **10084**
Menomonee Falls News
  (Wauwatosa, WI) **10307**
Mequon-Thiensville Courant
  (Wauwatosa, WI) **10307**
Merced County Times, The
  (Winton, CA) **10085**

Mercer County Chronicle
   (Coldwater, OH) **10237**
Mercer Island Reporter (Mercer
   Island, WA) **10292**
Meriwether Free Press (Greenville, GA) **10103**
Meriwether Vindicator
   (Manchester, GA) **10104**
Merrick Beacon (Hicksville, NY) **10216**
Merrick Life (Merrick, NY) **10218**
Merrillville Herald (Merrillville, IN) **10133**
Merrimac Valley Sunday
   (Amesbury, MA) **10160**
Mesa Tribune Wave (Los Angeles, CA) **10076**
Mesquite News (Mesquite, TX) **10279**
Message for the Week (Chester, VT) **10283**
Messenger-Press (Hightstown, NJ) **10203**
Messenger Index (Emmett, ID) **10107**
Messenger, The (Attica, IN) **10129**
Messenger, The (Madison, NC) **10229**
Messenger, The (Garfield, NJ) **10202**
Messenger, The (Clemson, SC) **10261**
Messenger, The (Madison, TN) **10268**
Metro (San Jose, CA) **10081**
Metrocrest News (Carrollton, TX) **10272**
Metropolis Planet (Metropolis, IL) **10123**
Metropolitan News (Brooklyn, NY) **10211**
Metro Press (Millbury, OH) **10241**
Metro Weekenders, The (Norfolk, VA) **10288**
Mexican-American Sun (City of
   Commerce, CA) **10071**
Miami Beach News (South Miami, FL) **10099**
Miami Beach Sun Post (Miami, FL) **10097**
Miami Chief, The (Miami, TX) **10279**
Miami County Republic (Paola, KS) **10145**
Miami Laker (Miami Lakes, FL) **10097**
Miamisburg News (Miamisburg, OH) **10241**
Miami Shores News (Miami, FL) **10097**
Miami Today (Miami, FL) **10097**
Michigan Chronicle (Detroit, MI) **10169**
Mid-Cities News (Arlington, TX) **10271**
Mid-County Journal (St. Louis, MO) **10193**
† Mid-County Times (Pardeeville, WI)
Mid-Island Times (Hicksville, NY) **10216**
Mid-South Horse Review
   (Somerville, TN) **10269**
Midcounty Chronicle (Nederland, TX) **10279**
Middleboro Gazette (Middleboro, MA) **10163**
Middleton Gazette (Middleton, ID) **10108**
Middleton Times-Tribune
   (Middleton, WI) **10302**
Middletown Courier (Middletown, NJ) **10204**
Middletown News, The (Middletown, IN) **10133**
Middletown Valley Citizen
   (Brunswick, MD) **10158**
Mid Hudson Times (Walden, NY) **10224**

Midlothian-Bremen Messenger
   (Midlothian, IL) **10123**
Midlothian Mirror (Midlothian, TX) **10279**
Midlothian Today (DeSoto, TX) **10274**
† MidMon Observer (Washington, PA)
Mid Valley News (El Monte, CA) **10072**
Mid Valley Town Crier (Weslaco, TX) **10281**
MidWeek (Kaneohe, HI) **10106**
Midweek Eagle (West Fargo, ND) **10233**
Midweek Plus (West Fargo, ND) **10233**
MidWeek, The (DeKalb, IL) **10114**
Mifflinburg Telegraph, The
   (Mifflinburg, PA) **10255**
Milan Area Leader (Milan, MI) **10172**
Milan Standard, The (Milan, MO) **10191**
Milford Advertiser (Loveland, OH) **10241**
Milford Cabinet & Wilton Journal
   (Milford, NH) **10200**
Milford Times (Milford, MI) **10173**
Milk Creek Sun (Erie, PA) **10252**
Millard County Gazette (Fillmore, UT) **10282**
Millbrae & San Bruno Sun
   (Burlingame, CA) **10070**
Millbrae Recorder-Progress (San
   Mateo, CA) **10082**
Millbrook Round Table (Millbrook, NY) **10218**
Millburn & Short Hills Item
   (Millburn, NJ) **10204**
Millburn-Short Hills Independent Press (New
   Providence, NJ) **10205**
Millbury/Sutton Chronicle
   (Millbury, MA) **10163**
Mille Lacs County Times (Milaca, MN) **10180**
Miller County Liberal (Colquitt, GA) **10102**
Millerton News, The (Millerton, NY) **10218**
Millington Star, The (Millington, TN) **10268**
Millstadt Enterprise (Columbia, IL) **10114**
Mill Valley Herald (Sausalito, CA) **10083**
Milpitas Post (Milpitas, CA) **10078**
Milton Courier (Milton, WI) **10302**
Milton Record-Transcript (Milton
   Village, MA) **10163**
Miltonvale Record (Miltonvale, KS) **10144**
Milwaukee Star (Milwaukee, WI) **10302**
Minden Courier (Minden, NE) **10197**
Mineola American (Mineola, NY) **10219**
Mineral County Independent-News
   (Hawthorne, NV) **10199**
Mineral County Miner (Monte
   Vista, CO) **10088**
Minerva Leader (Minerva, OH) **10241**
Minidoka County News (Rupert, ID) **10109**
Minifee County News (Morehead, KY) **10150**
Minnetonka Sun-Sailor
   (Minnetonka, MN) **10180**
Minonk News Dispatch (Minonk, IL) **10124**

Mira Mesa/Scripps Ranch Sentinel (San
   Diego, CA) **10081**
Mirror-Exchange (Milan, TN) **10268**
† Mirror-Recorder (Stamford, NY)
Mishawaka Enterprise (Mishawaka, IN) **10134**
Missouri Press News (Columbia, MO) **10189**
Missouri Valley Times-News (Missouri
   Valley, IA) **10140**
Mitchell County Press-News (Osage, IA) **10140**
Mitchell News Journal (Spruce
   Pine, NC) **10230**
Mobile Beacon (Mobile, AL) **10060**
Modern News (Harrisburg, AR) **10066**
Modoc County Record (Alturas, CA) **10068**
Mojave Desert News, The (California
   City, CA) **10070**
Monadnock Ledger (Peterborough, NH) **10200**
Monahans News (Monahans, TX) **10279**
Mondovi Herald News (Mondovi, WI) **10303**
Moneysaver, The (Ballston Spa, NY) **10209**
Monitor, The (Mabank, TX) **10278**
Monroe County Appeal (Paris, MO) **10192**
Monroe County Beacon
   (Woodsfield, OH) **10244**
Monroe County Clarion (Columbia, IL) **10114**
Monroe County Democrat (Sparta, WI) **10305**
Monroe County News (Albia, IA) **10136**
† Monroe County Sentinel (Woodsfield, OH)
Monroe Courier (Monroe, CT) **10091**
Monroe Journal (Monroeville, AL) **10060**
Monroe Watchman (Union, WV) **10296**
Montague County Shopper, The
   (Bowie, TX) **10271**
Montclair Times, The (Montclair, NJ) **10204**
Montclarion (Oakland, CA) **10078**
Montebello News (Los Angeles, CA) **10076**
† Montecito Life (Goleta, CA)
Monterey Park Progress (Los
   Angeles, CA) **10076**
Montevideo American-News
   (Montevideo, MN) **10180**
Monte Vista Journal (Monte Vista, CO) **10088**
Montezuma Republican, The
   (Montezuma, IA) **10140**
Montgomery County News, The
   (Hillsboro, IL) **10120**
Montgomery County Progress
   (Horsham, PA) **10253**
Montgomery County Sentinel
   (Gaithersburg, MD) **10158**
Montgomery Herald (Troy, NC) **10231**
Montgomery Herald (Montgomery, WV) **10295**
Montgomery Independent
   (Montgomery, AL) **10060**
Montgomery Post, The
   (Norristown, PA) **10256**

Montgomery Standard (Montgomery
   City, MO) **10191**
Montgomeryville Spirit (Fort
   Washington, PA) **10253**
Monticello Express (Monticello, IA) **10140**
Monticello News (Monticello, FL) **10097**
Montrose Herald (Canistota, SD) **10264**
Moody County Enterprise
   (Flandreau, SD) **10265**
Moody Courier, The (Moody, TX) **10279**
Moorcroft Leader (Moorcroft, WY) **10309**
Moore American (Moore, OK) **10246**
Moore County News-Press (Dumas, TX) **10274**
Moorefield Examiner (Moorefield, WV) **10295**
Mooresville Times, The
   (Mooresville, IN) **10134**
Mooresville Tribune (Mooresville, NC) **10229**
Moose Lake Star-Gazette (Moose
   Lake, MN) **10181**
Moravia Republican Register
   (Moravia, NY) **10219**
Morehead News (Morehead, KY) **10150**
Morenci Observer (Morenci, MI) **10173**
Morgan County Herald
   (McConnelsville, OH) **10241**
Morgan County News (Wartburg, TN) **10270**
Morgan Hill Times (Morgan Hill, CA) **10078**
Morgan Messenger, The (Berkeley
   Springs, WV) **10294**
Morongo Basin (Palm Desert, CA) **10079**
Morongo Basin Advertiser (Yucca
   Valley, CA) **10085**
Morris News Bee (Madison, NJ) **10204**
Morrisons Cove Herald
   (Martinsburg, PA) **10254**
Morris Sun (Morris, MN) **10181**
Morristown News, The (West
   Caldwell, NJ) **10207**
Morris Tribune (Morris, MN) **10181**
Morrow County Advertiser (Mt.
   Gilead, OH) **10241**
Morrow County Independent
   (Cardington, OH) **10235**
Morrow County Sentinel (Mt.
   Gilead, OH) **10241**
Morton Grove-Niles Life
   (Lincolnwood, IL) **10122**
Morton Grove Champion (Evanston, IL) **10117**
Mosinee Times, The (Mosinee, WI) **10303**
Motley County Tribune (Matador, TX) **10278**
Moulton Advertiser (Moulton, AL) **10060**
Moultrie News, The (Mt. Pleasant, SC) **10263**
Mound City News (Mound City, MO) **10191**
Mounds View-New Brighton-St. Anthony Focus
   (Roseville, MN) **10182**
Moundville Times (Moundville, AL) **10060**

Mountain Advisor (Richlands, VA) **10289**
Mountain Citizen, The (Inez, KY) **10148**
Mountain Eagle (Tannersville, NY) **10224**
Mountain Eagle, The (Whitesburg, KY) **10152**
Mountain Echo (Yellville, AR) **10068**
Mountain Echo (Ironton, MO) **10190**
Mountaineer-Herald, The
   (Ebensburg, PA) **10252**
Mountaineer, The (Big Sandy, MT) **10195**
† Mountaineer, The (Waynesville, NC)
Mountain Grove News-Journal (Mountain
   Grove, MO) **10191**
Mountain Home News (Mountain
   Home, ID) **10108**
Mountain Life (Mariposa, CA) **10077**
Mountain Messenger (Downieville, CA) **10072**
Mountain Messenger (Lewisburg, WV) **10295**
Mountain News, The (Lake
   Arrowhead, CA) **10074**
Mountain Press (Prather, CA) **10080**
Mountainside Echo (Union, NJ) **10207**
Mountain Statesman (Grafton, WV) **10294**
Mountain Sun, The (Kerrville, TX) **10277**
Mountain Times (Killington, VT) **10283**
Mountaintop Eagle (Mountain Top, PA) **10255**
† Mountain Visitor (Sevierville, TN)
Mountain Xpress (Asheville, NC) **10226**
Mount Ayr Record-News (Mt. Ayr, IA) **10140**
Mount Greenwood Express
   (Midlothian, IL) **10123**
Mount Holly News (Belmont, NC) **10226**
Mount Joy Merchandiser (Mt. Joy, PA) **10256**
Mount Olive Tribune (Mt. Olive, NC) **10229**
Mount Pleasant Journal (Mt.
   Pleasant, PA) **10256**
Mount Prospect Journal (Des
   Plaines, IL) **10115**
Mount Prospect Times (Glenview, IL) **10118**
Mount Shasta Herald (Mt. Shasta, CA) **10078**
Mount Vernon Democrat (Mt.
   Vernon, IN) **10134**
Mount Vernon Independent
   (Yonkers, NY) **10226**
Mt. Airy Times (Philadelphia, PA) **10257**
Mt. Laurel Progress Press (Maple
   Shade, NJ) **10204**
Mt. Olive Chronicle (Budd Lake, NJ) **10201**
Mt. Olive Herald, The (Mt. Olive, IL) **10124**
† Mt. Washington Press (Cincinnati, OH)
Mt. Washington Star Review (Los
   Angeles, CA) **10076**
Mt. Washington Valley Mountain Ear
   (Conway, NH) **10199**
Mukwonago Chief (Mukwonago, WI) **10303**
Mulberry Press (Mulberry, FL) **10097**
Mullens Advocate (Mullen, WV) **10295**

Munday Courier, The (Munday, TX) **10279**
Mundelein News (Grayslake, IL) **10119**
Mundelein Review (Bannockburn, IL) **10110**
Munising News (Munising, MI) **10173**
Munster Guide (Highland, IN) **10132**
Murfreesboro Diamond
   (Murfreesboro, AR) **10067**
Murray County Wheel Herald
   (Slayton, MN) **10183**
† Murray Eagle (Salt Lake City, UT)
Murrysville Area Star (Monroeville, PA) **10255**
Muskego Sun (Wauwatosa, WI) **10307**
N'West Iowa Review (Sheldon, IA) **10141**
Nantucket Beacon (Nantucket, MA) **10164**
Nanty Glo Journal, The (Nanty Glo, PA) **10256**
Napa County Record (Napa, CA) **10078**
Naperville Metropolitan (Lemont, IL) **10121**
Naperville Sun (Naperville, IL) **10124**
Naples Record, The (Naples, NY) **10219**
Narragansett Times (Wakefield, RI) **10261**
Nashua Reporter (Nashua, IA) **10140**
Nashville Graphic (Nashville, NC) **10229**
Nashville News (Nashville, AR) **10067**
Nashville News, The (Nashville, IL) **10124**
Nassau County Record (Callahan, FL) **10094**
Nassau Herald (Lawrence, NY) **10217**
Natick Bulletin (Needham, MA) **10164**
Nation's Center News (Buffalo, SD) **10264**
National Union (Eastern Caroline
   Islands, FM) **10093**
Navasota Examiner Review
   (Navasota, TX) **10279**
† Near South Herald (Chicago, IL)
Nebraska Signal (Geneva, NE) **10197**
Needles Desert Star (Needles, CA) **10078**
Nelson County Times (Lovingston, VA) **10287**
Nemaha County Herald (Auburn, NE) **10196**
Neodesha Derrick (Neodesha, KS) **10145**
Neshoba Democrat, The
   (Philadelphia, MS) **10187**
Ness County News, The (Ness City, KS) **10145**
Netcong News-Leader (Netcong, NJ) **10204**
Nevada County Picayune (Prescott, AR) **10067**
Nevada Journal (Nevada, IA) **10140**
† New Alaskan (Ketchikan, AK)
New Albany Gazette (New Albany, MS) **10186**
Newark/Licking Advertiser
   (Newark, OH) **10242**
Newark Post (Newark, DE) **10092**
Newberg Graphic (Newberg, OR) **10249**
New Berlin Citizen (Wauwatosa, WI) **10307**
Newberry Observer, The
   (Newberry, SC) **10263**
New Brighton-Mounds View Bulletin (North St.
   Paul, MN) **10181**
New Buffalo Times (New Buffalo, MI) **10173**

Newburgh-Chandler Register
   (Newburgh, IN) **10134**
New Canaan Advertiser (New
   Canaan, CT) **10091**
New Carlisle Sun (New Carlisle, OH) **10242**
Newcastle Pacer, The (Newcastle, OK) **10246**
New Castle Record (New Castle, VA) **10288**
New Center News (Detroit, MI) **10169**
New City (Chicago, IL) **10113**
Newcomerstown News
   (Newcomerstown, OH) **10242**
New Era, The (Sweet Home, OR) **10250**
Newfield News (Trumansburg, NY) **10224**
New Hampshire Week in Review
   (Hillsborough, NH) **10199**
New Hampton Economist (New
   Hampton, IA) **10140**
New Hampton Tribune (New
   Hampton, IA) **10140**
New Haven Advocate (New Haven, CT) **10091**
New Holstein Reporter (New
   Holstein, WI) **10303**
New Hope-Golden Valley Sun Post
   (Minneapolis, MN) **10180**
New Hope Gazette (New Hope, PA) **10256**
Newington Town Crier (Bristol, CT) **10090**
New Leader (Spencer, MA) **10165**
Newman News, The (Newman, CA) **10078**
New Milford Times (New Milford, CT) **10091**
Newnan Times-Herald (Newnan, GA) **10105**
Newport Mercury (Newport, RI) **10260**
Newport Miner (Newport, WA) **10292**
Newport This Week (Newport, RI) **10260**
New Prague Times (New Prague, MN) **10181**
New Prairie Town Crier (New
   Carlisle, IN) **10134**
New Richmond News (New
   Richmond, WI) **10303**
New River Record (Middle River, MN) **10180**
News & Press, The (Darlington, SC) **10262**
News & Sentinel, The (Colebrook, NH) **10199**
News-Banner, The (Covington, LA) **10153**
News-Democrat, The (Carrollton, KY) **10147**
News-Examiner (Montpelier, ID) **10108**
News-Examiner (Gallatin, TN) **10267**
News-Gazette (Lexington, VA) **10287**
News-Herald, The (Southgate, MI) **10175**
News-Herald, The (Ahoskie, NC) **10226**
News-Journal (North Manchester, IN) **10134**
News-Journal Shopper
   (Campbellsville, KY) **10147**
News-Ledger, The (West
   Sacramento, CA) **10085**
† News-Messenger, The (Rockingham, NC)
News-Progress (Sullivan, IL) **10128**
News-Progress, The (Chase City, VA) **10285**

News-Record of Maplewood & South Orange
   (Maplewood, NJ) **10204**
News-Record, The (Cerro Gordo, IL) **10112**
News-Register (McMinnville, OR) **10249**
News-Review, The (Mattituck, NY) **10218**
News-Sun (Fairmount, IN) **10131**
News-Sun, The (New Bloomfield, PA) **10256**
News-Times (Newport, OR) **10249**
News-X Press (Butler, MO) **10188**
News Beacon (Fair Lawn, NJ) **10202**
News Bulletin, The (Old Fort, NC) **10229**
News Buyer's Catalogue
   (Wytheville, VA) **10290**
News Buyers Catalog (Marion, VA) **10287**
News Democrat & Leader
   (Russellville, KY) **10151**
News Democrat Journal (Festus, MO) **10189**
News Eagle (Hawley, PA) **10253**
† NewsEAST (Columbus, OH)
News Enterprise, The (Los
   Alamitos, CA) **10075**
News Examiner, The (Lutcher, LA) **10153**
News Gazette, The (Love Park, IL) **10122**
News Gleaner Publications
   (Philadelphia, PA) **10257**
News Guard, The (Lincoln City, OR) **10249**
New Sharon Star (New Sharon, IA) **10140**
News Herald (Lenoir City, TN) **10268**
† News Herald, The (Mobile, AL)
News Leader (Fernandina, FL) **10095**
News Leader (Stow, OH) **10243**
News Leader (Richwood, WV) **10296**
News Leader, The (Royston, GA) **10105**
News Leader, The (Landrum, SC) **10263**
News Leader, The (Parsons, TN) **10269**
News Letter Journal (Newcastle, WY) **10309**
NewsMarketer, The (Chicago, IL) **10113**
News Messenger, The
   (Christiansburg, VA) **10285**
News of Delaware County
   (Havertown, PA) **10253**
News of Orange County, The
   (Hillsborough, NC) **10228**
News of Southern Berks, The
   (Boyertown, PA) **10251**
News of the Highlands (Highland
   Falls, NY) **10216**
News Pointer (Sausalito, CA) **10083**
News Report (Blackwood, NJ) **10201**
News Review (Ridgecrest, CA) **10080**
News Star (Lincolnwood, IL) **10122**
News Sun, The (Sebring, FL) **10099**
News Sun, The (Cleveland, OH) **10236**
News, The (Salem, AR) **10067**
News, The (Clay City, IN) **10130**
News, The (Belvidere, NJ) **10200**

News, The (Aliquippa, PA) **10251**
News, The (Kingstree, SC) **10262**
News Times (Amherst, OH) **10234**
News Times (Forest Grove, OR) **10248**
News Transcript (Morganville, NJ) **10204**
News Watchman, The (Waverly, OH) **10244**
Newsweekly (Sebewaing, MI) **10175**
News Weekly (Mt. Laurel, NJ) **10204**
New Times (Phoenix, AZ) **10064**
New Times (San Luis Obispo, CA) **10082**
New Times, The (Kansas City, MO) **10190**
Newton Graphic (Waltham, MA) **10166**
Newton Press-Mentor (Newton, IL) **10124**
Newton Record (Newton, MS) **10187**
Newtown Bee, The (Newtown, CT) **10091**
New Ulm Enterprise (New Ulm, TX) **10279**
New York Beacon (New York, NY) **10220**
New York Metropolitan News
  (Brooklyn, NY) **10211**
New York Observer (New York, NY) **10220**
New York Press (New York, NY) **10220**
Niagara/Wheatfield Tribune (Grand
  Island, NY) **10215**
Niantic-Harristown County Line Observer
  (Illiopolis, IL) **10120**
† Niantic News (East Lyme, CT)
Nicholas Chronicle (Summersville, WV) **10296**
Niles Herald Spectator (Park Ridge, IL) **10126**
Niles Journal (Des Plaines, IL) **10115**
Niles Life (Lincolnwood, IL) **10122**
Nishna Valley Tribune (Audubon, IA) **10137**
Nisqually Valley News (Yelm, WA) **10294**
Nokomis Free Press-Progress
  (Nokomis, IL) **10124**
Nome Nugget (Nome, AK) **10062**
Nora News Dispatch (Fisherspolis, IN) **10131**
▼Nordonia Hills Sun (Cleveland, OH) **10236**
Norridge-Harwood Heights News (Park
  Ridge, IL) **10126**
Norridge-Harwood Heights Times
  (Lincolnwood, IL) **10122**
North/South Beach Now (San
  Francisco, CA) **10081**
North Bartow News (Adairsville, GA) **10100**
North Bay Village News (South
  Miami, FL) **10099**
North Bergen/North Hudson Reporter
  (Hoboken, NJ) **10203**
Northbrook Star (Glenview, IL) **10118**
North Brunswick Post (Dayton, NJ) **10202**
North Castle News (Yonkers, NY) **10226**
North Center-Lincoln Belmont-Lake View Booster
  (Lincolnwood, IL) **10122**
North Central Outlook (Seattle, WA) **10293**
North Clermont Community Journal
  (Loveland, OH) **10241**

North Country Free Press
  (Granville, NY) **10215**
North Countryman, The
  (Elizabethtown, NY) **10213**
North Country Sun (Ironwood, MI) **10171**
North County Journal East (St.
  Louis, MO) **10193**
North County Journal West (St.
  Louis, MO) **10193**
North County News (Red Bud, IL) **10127**
North County News (Yorktown
  Heights, NY) **10226**
North County Shopping News
  (Atascadero, CA) **10069**
North East Breeze (North East, PA) **10256**
† Northeast Detroiter (Detroit, MI)
Northeast Georgian, The (Cornelia, GA) **10102**
Northeast Johnson County (Shawnee
  Mission, KS) **10146**
Northeast Reporter (Indianapolis, IN) **10132**
Northeast Reporter (Towson, MD) **10160**
Northeast Suburban Life Press
  (Cincinnati, OH) **10235**
Northeast Sun (City of Commerce, CA) **10071**
Northeast Times (Philadelphia, PA) **10257**
Northern Michigan News (Cadillac, MI) **10168**
Northern Ogle County Tempo
  (Byron, IL) **10112**
Northern Piedmont Express
  (Culpeper, VA) **10286**
Northern Star (Gaylord, MI) **10170**
Northern Star, The (Clinton, MN) **10178**
Northern Virginia Sun, The
  (Fairfax, VA) **10286**
Northern Watch (Thief River Falls, MN) **10184**
Northfield Advance (Jenison, MI) **10171**
Northfield News (Northfield, MN) **10181**
North Georgia News (Blairsville, GA) **10101**
Northglenn-Thornton Sentinel
  (Westminster, CO) **10089**
North Haven Wollington Post, The
  (Milford, CT) **10091**
North Jackson Progress
  (Stevenson, AL) **10061**
North Jefferson News (Gardendale, AL) **10059**
North Jersey Prospector (Clifton, NJ) **10202**
North Kitsap Herald (Poulsbo, WA) **10292**
North Knox News (Bicknell, IN) **10130**
Northlake Star-Sentinel (Melrose
  Park, IL) **10123**
North Lake Tahoe Bonanza (Incline
  Village, NV) **10199**
Northland News (Columbus, OH) **10237**
North Loop News (Chicago, IL) **10113**
North Macomb Voice (New
  Baltimore, MI) **10173**

North Meridian Observer (Fishers, IN) **10131**
North Miami Beach News (South Miami, FL) **10099**
North Miami News (Miami, FL) **10097**
North Minneapolis Sun Post (Minneapolis, MN) **10180**
North Missourian (Gallatin, MO) **10190**
North Myrtle Beach Times (North Myrtle Beach, SC) **10263**
Northome Record & Mizpah Message (Northome, MN) **10181**
North Riverside Citizen (Oak Brook, IL) **10125**
North Scott Press, The (Eldridge, IA) **10138**
† North Scottsdale Independent (Scottsdale, AZ)
Northshore Citizen (Bothell, WA) **10290**
North Shore Heralds (Wauwatosa, WI) **10307**
North Shore Shopper (Pacific Palisades, CA) **10078**
North Shore Sunday (Danvers, MA) **10161**
Northside Journal (St. Louis, MO) **10194**
Northside Neighbor, The (Atlanta, GA) **10100**
North Side News (Jerome, ID) **10108**
Northside Sun, The (Jackson, MS) **10186**
North Side Topics (Fishers, IN) **10131**
North Snohomish Weekly (Arlington, WA) **10290**
North Star (Philadelphia, PA) **10257**
North Star Journal (Presque Isle, WI) **10304**
North Suburban Herald (Love Park, IL) **10122**
North Syracuse Star-News (Syracuse, NY) **10223**
North Tahoe/Truckee Week (Carnelian Bay, CA) **10070**
Northumberland Echo (Heathsville, VA) **10286**
North Utah County Shopper (American Fork, UT) **10282**
North Vernon Plain Dealer (North Vernon, IN) **10134**
North Vernon Sun (North Vernon, IN) **10134**
Northville Record (Northville, MI) **10173**
Northwest Alabamian (Haleyville, AL) **10059**
Northwest Blade, The (Eureka, SD) **10264**
Northwest Columbus News (Columbus, OH) **10237**
Northwest Current, The (Washington, DC) **10093**
Northwestern Illinois Dispatch (Savanna, IL) **10127**
Northwestern Illinois Farmer (Lena, IL) **10121**
Northwest Iowa Shopper (Spencer, IA) **10141**
Northwest Journal & Topics (Des Plaines, IL) **10115**
Northwest Leader (Chicago, IL) **10113**
Northwest Press (Speedway, IN) **10135**
Northwest Press (Cincinnati, OH) **10235**

Northwest Side Press (Chicago, IL) **10113**
Northwest Star (Baltimore, MD) **10158**
Northwood Gleaner (Northwood, ND) **10233**
North Woods Call (Charlevoix, MI) **10168**
Norton Courier (Stoughton, MA) **10166**
Norwalk Herald American (Los Angeles, CA) **10076**
† Norwalk News (Westport, CT)
Norway Advertiser-Democrat (Norway, ME) **10156**
Norway Current (Norway, MI) **10173**
Norwell Mariner (Marshfield, MA) **10163**
Novato Advance (Novato, CA) **10078**
Novi News (Northville, MI) **10173**
Nowata Star (Nowata, OK) **10246**
Nueces County Record Star (Robstown, TX) **10280**
Nutley Journal (Bloomfield, NJ) **10201**
Nutley Sun (Nutley, NJ) **10205**
NUVO Newsweekly (Indianapolis, IN) **10132**
O-W Enterprise (Withee, WI) **10308**
O'Fallon Journal (O'Fallon, MO) **10191**
O'Fallon Progress (O'Fallon, IL) **10124**
Oak Brook Doings (Hinsdale, IL) **10120**
Oak Brook Press (Elmhurst, IL) **10116**
Oak Brook Terrace Doings (Hinsdale, IL) **10120**
Oak Cliff Tribune (Dallas, TX) **10273**
Oak Creek Pictorial (Wauwatosa, WI) **10307**
Oakdale-Lake Elmo Review (St. Paul, MN) **10183**
Oakdale Clarion (Oakdale, MN) **10181**
Oakdale Journal (Oakdale, LA) **10154**
Oakdale Leader (Oakdale, CA) **10078**
Oakland Indpendent (Oakland, NE) **10197**
Oak Lawn-Evergreen Park Reporter (Palos Heights, IL) **10125**
Oak Lawn Independent (Midlothian, IL) **10123**
Oak Leaves, The (Oak Park, IL) **10125**
Oakley Graphic (Oakley, KS) **10145**
Oakville-Mehville Journal (St. Louis, MO) **10194**
Oberlin Herald, The (Oberlin, KS) **10145**
† Observer-Patriot (Putnam, CT)
Observer-Tribune (Chester, NJ) **10202**
Observer, The (Royal Palm Beach, FL) **10098**
Observer, The (Belgrade, MN) **10176**
† Observer, The (Blackwood, NJ)
Observer, The (Kearny, NJ) **10203**
Observer, The (Rio Rancho, NM) **10208**
Observer, The (Northport, NY) **10220**
Observer, The (Greenville, RI) **10260**
Observer, The (Holly Hill, SC) **10262**
Oceana's Herald-Journal (Hart, MI) **10170**
Ocean County Reporter (Toms River, NJ) **10207**

Oceanside/Island Park Herald (Long Beach, NY) **10217**
Oceanside Centre Beacon (Mineola, NY) **10219**
Ocean Springs Record (Ocean Springs, MS) **10187**
Oconee Breeze (Madison, GA) **10104**
Oconomowoc Enterprise (Oconomowoc, WI) **10303**
Oconto County Times-Herald (Oconto Falls, WI) **10303**
▼OC Weekly (Los Angeles, CA) **10076**
Odem-Edroy Times (Sinton, TX) **10280**
Ogemaw County Herald (West Branch, MI) **10176**
Ogle County Life (Oregon, IL) **10125**
Ohio County News (Rising Sun, IN) **10135**
Ohio County Times News (Hartford, KY) **10148**
Ojai Valley News (Ojai, CA) **10078**
Oklahoma City Friday (Oklahoma City, OK) **10246**
Oklahoma Eagle (Tulsa, OK) **10247**
Oklee Herald (Oklee, MN) **10181**
Olathe Sun (Overland Park, KS) **10145**
Old Colony Memorial (Plymouth, MA) **10165**
Oldham Era, The (La Grange, KY) **10149**
Old Lyons Recorder, The (Lyons, CO) **10088**
Olive Hill Times (Olive Hill, KY) **10150**
Oliveville Times (Morehead, KY) **10150**
Olivia Times Journal (Olivia, MN) **10181**
Olney Enterprise, The (Olney, TX) **10279**
Olney Times (Philadelphia, PA) **10257**
Olympia Review (Minier, IL) **10124**
Omaha Star (Omaha, NE) **10198**
Omak-Okanogan County Chronicle (Omak, WA) **10292**
Omro Herald (Omro, WI) **10303**
Onawa Democrat (Onawa, IA) **10140**
Onawa Sentinel (Onawa, IA) **10140**
Onaway Outlook (Onaway, MI) **10173**
Onlooker, The (Foley, AL) **10059**
Onondaga Valley News (Syracuse, NY) **10223**
Ontario Advertiser (Palm Desert, CA) **10079**
Ontonagon Herald (Ontonagon, MI) **10173**
Oologah Lake Leader (Oologah, OK) **10246**
Opp News (Opp, AL) **10061**
Orange Bulletin (Milford, CT) **10091**
Orange Countian (Paoli, IN) **10134**
Orange County Log (San Diego, CA) **10081**
Orange County News (Garden Grove, CA) **10073**
Orange County Review (Orange, VA) **10288**
Orange Cove Mountain Times (Reedley, CA) **10080**
Orange Transcript (Orange, NJ) **10205**
Orangevale News (Folsom, CA) **10072**

Orchard Park Bee (Williamsville, NY) **10225**
Ord Quiz (Ord, NE) **10198**
Oregon Observer (Oregon, WI) **10303**
Orem-Geneva Times (Orem, UT) **10283**
Orion Gazette (Orion, IL) **10125**
† Orion Times (Orion, IL)
Orland Metropolitan (Lemont, IL) **10121**
Orlando Weekly, The (Winter Park, FL) **10100**
Orland Press-Register (Orland, CA) **10078**
Orland Township Messenger (Midlothian, IL) **10123**
† Orrville Courier-Crescent (Orrville, OH)
Ortonville Independent (Ortonville, MN) **10181**
Osage County Chronicle (Burlingame, KS) **10143**
Osakis Review, The (Osakis, MN) **10181**
Osawatomie Graphic (Osawatomie, KS) **10145**
Osborne County Farmer (Osborne, KS) **10145**
Osceola County Gazette-Tribune (Sibley, IA) **10141**
Osceola News-Gazette (Kissimmee, FL) **10095**
Osceola Sentinel-Tribune (Osceola, IA) **10140**
Osceola Sun (Osceola, WI) **10303**
Osceola Times (Osceola, AR) **10067**
Oscoda Press (Oscoda, MI) **10173**
Osgood Journal (Versailles, IN) **10136**
Oshkosh Buyers Guide (Oshkosh, WI) **10303**
Oskaloosa Independent (Oskaloosa, KS) **10145**
Ossian Bee, The (Ossian, IA) **10141**
Ossian Journal (Ossian, IN) **10134**
Othello Outlook, The (Othello, WA) **10292**
▼Other Side, The (Prairie Village, KS) **10145**
Ottawa Advance (Jenison, MI) **10171**
Ottawa County Exponent, The (Oak Harbor, OH) **10242**
Ottawa Times (Ottawa, KS) **10145**
Ottawa Times Shopper (Ottawa, KS) **10145**
Ouachita Citizen (West Monroe, LA) **10155**
Ouray County Plaindealer (Ouray, CO) **10089**
Our Home Town (Vanderbilt, MI) **10175**
Our Town (Maywood, NJ) **10204**
Our Town (New York, NY) **10220**
Our Town (Pearl River, NY) **10221**
Outlook Mail (Santa Monica, CA) **10082**
Overland Park Sun (Shawnee Mission, KS) **10146**
Over the Mountain Journal (Birmingham, AL) **10058**
Ovid Gazette (Trumansburg, NY) **10224**
Oviedo Voice, The (Oviedo, FL) **10098**
Owasso Reporter (Owasso, OK) **10246**
Owatonna Weekly Shopper (Owatonna, MN) **10181**
Owings Mills Times (Baltimore, MD) **10158**
Oxford Press (Oxford, OH) **10242**
Oxford Public Ledger (Oxford, NC) **10229**

Oxford Register, The (Belle Plaine, KS) **10143**
Oxford Review-Times (Greene, NY) **10215**
Oyster Bay-Syosset Guardian (Oyster Bay, NY) **10220**
Oyster Bay Enterprise Pilot (Mineola, NY) **10219**
Ozark County Times (Gainesville, MO) **10190**
Ozark Journal (Imboden, AR) **10066**
Ozaukee County News Graphic (Cedarburg, WI) **10298**
Ozaukee Guide (Cedarburg, WI) **10298**
Ozaukee Press (Port Washington, WI) **10304**
Pacifica Tribune (Pacifica, CA) **10078**
Pacific Sun (Mill Valley, CA) **10077**
Pageland Progressive-Journal, The (Pageland, SC) **10263**
Paintsville Herald, The (Paintsville, KY) **10150**
Palacios Beacon (Palacios, TX) **10279**
Palatine Countryside (Arlington Heights, IL) **10109**
Palatine Journal & Topics (Des Plaines, IL) **10115**
Palau Gazette (Koror, PW) **10251**
Palau Tribune (Saipan, MP) **10234**
Palisade Tribune (Palisade, CO) **10089**
Palisadian-Post (Pacific Palisades, CA) **10079**
Palm Desert (Indio, CA) **10073**
Palm Desert Advertiser (Palm Desert, CA) **10079**
Palm Spring Advertiser (Palm Desert, CA) **10079**
Palmyra Spectator (Palmyra, MO) **10192**
Palo Alto Weekly (Palo Alto, CA) **10079**
Palos Citizen (Midlothian, IL) **10123**
Palos Hills-Hickory Hills (Palos Heights, IL) **10126**
Palos Verdes Peninsula News (Palos Verdes Peninsula, CA) **10079**
Palouse Living (Moscow, ID) **10108**
Palo Verde Valley Times (Blythe, CA) **10069**
Pana News-Palladium (Pana, IL) **10126**
† Panhandle Press (Chester, WV)
Panola Watchman (Carthage, TX) **10272**
▼Panolian ADvantage, The (Batesville, MS) **10185**
Panolian, The (Batesville, MS) **10185**
Paoli News (Paoli, IN) **10134**
Paoli Republican (Paoli, IN) **10134**
Paper of Wabash County, The (Wabash, IN) **10136**
Paper, The (Barry, IL) **10110**
Paper, The (Elkhart, IN) **10130**
Paper, The (Goshen, IN) **10132**
Paper, The (Warsaw, IN) **10136**
† Paper, The (Spartanburg, SC)
Papillion Times (Papillion, NE) **10198**

Paradise Post (Paradise, CA) **10079**
Paradise Valley Independent (Scottsdale, AZ) **10064**
Paris Express (Paris, AR) **10067**
Parkchester News (Bronx, NY) **10210**
Parker Advertiser (Palm Desert, CA) **10079**
Parker Pioneer (Parker, AZ) **10064**
Park Falls Herald (Park Falls, WI) **10304**
Park LaBrea News/Beverly Press (Los Angeles, CA) **10076**
Park News (Library, PA) **10254**
Park Rapids Enterprise (Park Rapids, MN) **10181**
Park Record, The (Park City, UT) **10283**
Park Ridge Herald Advocate (Park Ridge, IL) **10126**
Park Ridge Journal (Des Plaines, IL) **10115**
Park Slope Courier (Brooklyn, NY) **10211**
Parkway Transcript (Dedham, MA) **10161**
Parlier Post (Sanger, CA) **10081**
Parma Sun Post (Cleveland, OH) **10236**
Parsippany Focus (Morris Plains, NJ) **10204**
Parsippany News, The (West Caldwell, NJ) **10208**
Parsons Advocate (Parsons, WV) **10295**
Parsons News (Parsons, KS) **10145**
Pasadena Weekly (Pasadena, CA) **10080**
Pascack Valley Community Life (Westwood, NJ) **10208**
Pasco News (Dade City, FL) **10094**
Passaic Citizen (Passaic, NJ) **10206**
Passaic Valley Today (Butler, NJ) **10201**
Pataskala Standard (Pataskala, OH) **10242**
Patent Trader (Cross River, NY) **10212**
Patriot & Free Press (Cuba, NY) **10212**
Patriot, The (Kutztown, PA) **10254**
Paulding Neighbor, The (Marietta, GA) **10104**
Paulding Progress (Paulding, OH) **10242**
Paullina Times (Paullina, IA) **10141**
Pawhuska Journal-Capital (Pawhuska, OK) **10246**
Pawling News Chronicle (Pawling, NY) **10221**
Pawnee Post (Auburn, IL) **10110**
Paw Paw Courier-Leader (Paw Paw, MI) **10173**
Paynesville Press, The (Paynesville, MN) **10182**
Payson Roundup (Payson, AZ) **10064**
Peekskill Herald (Peekskill, NY) **10221**
Pelham Journal (Pelham, GA) **10105**
Pelham Sun (Yonkers, NY) **10226**
Pelican Press (Sarasota, FL) **10098**
Pelican Rapids Press (Pelican Rapids, MN) **10182**
Pella Chronicle (Pella, IA) **10141**
Pembroke Mariner (Marshfield, MA) **10163**
Pembroke Reporter (Plymouth, MA) **10165**

Pender Chronicle (Burgaw, NC) 10227
Pender Post (Burgaw, NC) 10227
Pendleton Record, The (Pendleton, OR) 10249
Penfield Post Republican, The
  (Fishers, NY) 10214
Peninsula Beacon, The (San Diego, CA) 10081
Peninsula Gateway (Gig Harbor, WA) 10291
▼Peninsula Independent
  (Burlingame, CA) 10070
† Peninsula Review, The (Carmel, CA)
Pennington County Prevailer-News (Hill
  City, SD) 10265
Pennsboro News (Pennsboro, WV) 10295
Pennysaver (Vista, CA) 10084
Penny Saver (Tinley Park, IL) 10128
Penny Saver (Three Rivers, MI) 10175
Pennysaver (Elmsford, NY) 10213
Pennysaver (Yorktown Heights, NY) 10226
Penny Saver (Covington, OH) 10239
Pennysaver Press (Bennington, VT) 10283
Pennysaver, The (Sandwich, MA) 10165
Penobscot Times (Old Town, ME) 10157
Pensacola Voice (Pensacola, FL) 10098
People-Sentinel (Barnwell, SC) 10261
People's Defender, The (West
  Union, OH) 10244
People's Weekly World (New York, NY) 10220
Peoria Heights Herald (Peoria, IL) 10126
Peoria Observer (Peoria, IL) 10126
Peoria Times (Glendale, AZ) 10064
Perdido Pelican (Pensacola, FL) 10098
Perham Enterprise-Bulletin
  (Perham, MN) 10182
Perinton-Fairport Post, The
  (Pittsford, NY) 10221
Perkasie News-Herald (Perkasie, PA) 10257
Perquimans Weekly (Hertford, NC) 10228
Perry Chief (Perry, IA) 10141
Perry County News, The (Tell City, IN) 10136
Perry County Republic-Monitor, The
  (Perryville, MO) 10192
Perry County Times (New
  Bloomfield, PA) 10256
Perry County Tribune (New
  Lexington, OH) 10242
Perry News-Herald (Perry, FL) 10098
Perrysburg Messenger-Journal
  (Perrysburg, OH) 10242
Perry Taco Times (Perry, FL) 10098
Perry Township Weekly (Beech
  Grove, IN) 10129
Peshtigo Times (Peshtigo, WI) 10304
Petaluma Argus-Courier (Petaluma, CA) 10080
Peterborough Transcript
  (Peterborough, NH) 10200
Petersburg Observer (Petersburg, IL) 10126

Petersburg Pilot (Petersburg, AK) 10062
Phenix-Citizen (Phenix City, AL) 10061
Philadelphia City Paper
  (Philadelphia, PA) 10257
Philadelphia Guide Newspaper
  (Philadelphia, PA) 10257
Philadelphia Weekly (Philadelphia, PA) 10257
Philipsburg Mail, The (Philipsburg, MT) 10195
Phillipsburg Free Press
  (Phillipsburg, NJ) 10206
Phillips County Review
  (Phillipsburg, KS) 10145
Phoenix Newspaper, The (Brooklyn, NY) 10211
Phoenix Register (Phoenix, NY) 10221
Photo News (Monroe, NY) 10219
Photo Star (Willshire, OH) 10244
Piatt County Journal-Republican
  (Monticello, IL) 10124
Pickens County Herald (Carrollton, AL) 10058
Pickens Sentinel (Pickens, SC) 10263
Pickerington Times-Sun
  (Columbus, OH) 10237
Pickett County Press (Byrdstown, TN) 10266
Pico Rivera News (Los Angeles, CA) 10076
Pictorial Gazette (Old Saybrook, CT) 10091
† Pictorial Press (Tahlequah, OK)
Picture Post (Waupaca, WI) 10306
Piedmonter, The (Oakland, CA) 10078
Piedmont Herald (Piedmont, WV) 10296
Piedmont Journal-Independent
  (Piedmont, AL) 10061
Pierce City Leader-Journal (Pierce
  City, MO) 10192
Pierce County Herald (Ellsworth, WI) 10300
Pierce County Tribune (Rugby, ND) 10233
Pierre Times, The (Pierre, SD) 10265
Piggott Times, The (Piggott, AR) 10067
Pike County Dispatch (Milford, PA) 10255
Pike County News Watchman
  (Jackson, OH) 10240
Pike Register (Fishers, IN) 10131
Pikes Peak Journal (Manitou
  Springs, CO) 10088
Pinckney Post Shopping Guide
  (Pinckney, MI) 10174
† Pine Bluff News (Pine Bluff, AR)
Pine Bluff Shoppers News (Pine
  Bluff, AR) 10067
Pine Island Eagle (Bokeelia, FL) 10093
Pine Plains Register-Herald (Pine
  Plains, NY) 10221
Pine River Times (Bayfield, CO) 10085
Pineville Sun-Cumberland Courier
  (Pineville, KY) 10150
Pinnacle, The (Hollister, CA) 10073
Pioneer-News (Shepherdsville, KY) 10151

Pioneer Republican, The (Marengo, IA) **10140**
Pipestone County Star (Pipestone, MN) **10182**
Piscataquis Observer, The
  (Dover-Foxcroft, ME) **10156**
Pitch Weekly (Kansas City, MO) **10190**
Pittsburg Gazette (Pittsburg, TX) **10279**
Pittsburgh City Paper (Pittsburgh, PA) **10258**
Pittsburgh Renaissance News
  (Pittsburgh, PA) **10258**
Pittsfield Gazette, The (Pittsfield, MA) **10164**
Placentia News-Times (Anaheim, CA) **10069**
Placer Herald (Rocklin, CA) **10080**
Plain Dealer (Turnersville, NJ) **10207**
Plainsman Weekly News (Sedalia, MO) **10192**
Plain Talk (Newport, TN) **10269**
Plainview News (Plainview, MN) **10182**
Plainview News (Plainview, NE) **10198**
Plaquemines Gazette (Belle Chasse, LA) **10152**
Plaquemines Watchman (Belle
  Chasse, LA) **10152**
Platte County Gazette (Parkville, MO) **10192**
Platte County Record-Times
  (Wheatland, WY) **10309**
Platte Dispatch Tribune (Kansas
  City, MO) **10190**
Platteville Journal (Platteville, WI) **10304**
Plattsmouth Journal (Plattsmouth, NE) **10198**
Pleasant Grove Review (American
  Fork, UT) **10282**
Pleasanton Express (Pleasanton, TX) **10279**
Plymouth Observer (Plymouth, MI) **10174**
Plymouth Sun-Sailor (Minnetonka, MN) **10180**
Pocahontas Record-Democrat
  (Pocahontas, IA) **10141**
Pocahontas Star Herald
  (Pocahontas, AR) **10067**
Pocahontas Times (Marlinton, WV) **10295**
Pocono Shopper (East
  Stroudsburg, PA) **10252**
Point & Shoreland Journal (Toledo, OH) **10243**
Pointe Coupee Banner (New Roads, LA) **10154**
Point Reyes Light (Point Reyes
  Station, CA) **10080**
† Poland Leader (Niles, OH)
Polk City Press (Mulberry, FL) **10097**
Polk County Democrat, The
  (Bartow, FL) **10093**
Polk County Enterprise (Livingston, TX) **10278**
Pompano Ledger, The (Pompano
  Beach, FL) **10098**
Ponchatoula Times, The
  (Ponchatoula, LA) **10154**
Pontotoc Progress (Pontotoc, MS) **10187**
Pony Express Mail (Liberty, TX) **10278**
Pope County Tribune (Glenwood, MN) **10178**
Poquoson Post (Yorktown, VA) **10290**

Porcupine Press (Chatham, MI) **10168**
Portage Dispatch, The (Portage, PA) **10258**
Portage Journal-Press (Portage, IN) **10135**
Porter/New Caney Sun (Humble, TX) **10276**
Port Gibson Reveille (Port Gibson, MS) **10187**
Port Isabel-South Padre Press (Port
  Isabel, TX) **10279**
Portland News (Portland, TX) **10280**
Portland Review & Observer (Grand
  Ledge, MI) **10170**
Port Lavaca Wave (Port Lavaca, TX) **10280**
Port Orchard Independent (Port
  Orchard, WA) **10292**
Port Richmond Star (Philadelphia, PA) **10257**
Portsmouth Times (Chesapeake, VA) **10285**
Port Times-Record, The (Setauket, NY) **10222**
Port Townsend/Jefferson County Leader (Port
  Townsend, WA) **10292**
Port Washington News (Port
  Washington, NY) **10221**
Post-Herald (Red Creek, NY) **10222**
Post Falls Tribune (Post Falls, ID) **10108**
Post Report, The (Lewisburg, WV) **10295**
Post Review, The (Paramus, NJ) **10205**
Post South (Plaquemine, LA) **10154**
Post, The (Middleburg, PA) **10255**
Post, The (Big Stone Gap, VA) **10285**
Potomac Almanac (Potomac, MD) **10159**
Potter Leader-Enterprise
  (Coudersport, PA) **10252**
Pottsboro Press (Pottsboro, TX) **10280**
▼Poultney News, The (Rutland, VT) **10284**
Poway News Chieftain (San Diego, CA) **10081**
Powder Springs Neighbor, The
  (Marietta, GA) **10104**
Powell Valley News (Pennington
  Gap, VA) **10288**
Power County Press (American
  Falls, ID) **10107**
Prairie City News (Prairie City, IA) **10141**
Prairie Post (Jamestown, ND) **10232**
Prairie Shopper, The (La Fayette, IL) **10121**
Prairie Times, The (La Fayette, IL) **10121**
Prairie Village Sun (Shawnee
  Mission, KS) **10146**
Prattville Progress (Prattville, AL) **10061**
Prescott Journal (Prescott, WI) **10304**
Presque Isle Advance (Rogers City, MI) **10174**
Presque Isle Star (Gaylord, MI) **10170**
Press & Journal, The (Middletown, PA) **10255**
Press & Light (North Ridgeville, OH) **10242**
Press & Standard, The
  (Walterboro, SC) **10264**
Press-Dispatch (Petersburg, IN) **10134**
Press-News Journal (Canton, MO) **10188**
Press-News, The (Minerva, OH) **10241**

Press-Sentinel, The (Jesup, GA) **10103**
Press-Star (New London, WI) **10303**
Press Argus-Courier (Van Buren, AR) **10068**
Press Dispatch (Kansas City, MO) **10190**
Press Gazette, The (Hillsboro, OH) **10240**
Press Herald (Pine Grove, PA) **10258**
Press Journal (St. Louis, MO) **10194**
Press Journal, The (Palisades Park, NJ) **10205**
† Press, The (Alexandria, MN)
Preston Citizen (Preston, ID) **10108**
Preston County News (Kingwood, WV) **10295**
Price Hill Press (Cincinnati, OH) **10235**
Priest River Times (Priest River, ID) **10108**
PrimeTime (Lawrence, NY) **10217**
Prince Georges Sentinel
  (Seabrook, MD) **10159**
Princeton News Leader (Princeton, NC) **10229**
Princeton Packet, The (Princeton, NJ) **10206**
Princeton Times (Princeton, WV) **10296**
Princeton Times-Republic
  (Princeton, WI) **10304**
Princeton Union-Eagle (Princeton, MN) **10182**
Private Eye Weekly (Salt Lake City, UT) **10283**
Proctor Journal (Proctor, MN) **10182**
Progress, The (Cave City, KY) **10147**
Progress, The (Caldwell, NJ) **10201**
Progress, The (Monroeville, PA) **10255**
Progress, The (Anahuac, TX) **10270**
Prospect-News, The (Doniphan, MO) **10189**
Prospect Heights Journal (Des
  Plaines, IL) **10115**
Prospector, The (Doniphan, MO) **10189**
Provincetown Advocate
  (Provincetown, MA) **10165**
Proviso Star-Sentinel (Melrose Park, IL) **10123**
Pryor Jeffersonian (Pryor, OK) **10246**
Public Spirit (Ayer, MA) **10160**
Public Spirit (Hatboro, PA) **10253**
Pulaski Citizen (Pulaski, TN) **10269**
Pulaski County Journal (Winamac, IN) **10136**
Pulaski Enterprise (Mounds, IL) **10124**
Pulaski Giles Free Press (Pulaski, TN) **10269**
Pulse-Journal (Mason, OH) **10241**
Purcell Register (Purcell, OK) **10246**
Putnam County Record (Granville, IL) **10118**
Putnam County Sentinel (Ottawa, OH) **10242**
Putnam County Vidette (Columbus
  Grove, OH) **10239**
Putnam Courier-Trader, The
  (Carmel, NY) **10212**
Putnam Post-Cabell Bulletin
  (Culloden, WV) **10294**
Pymatuning Area News (Andover, OH) **10234**
Pyramid, The (Mt. Pleasant, UT) **10283**
Quad Community Press (White Bear
  Lake, MN) **10184**

Quad River News (Sheridan, MO) **10193**
Quakertown Free Press
  (Quakertown, PA) **10258**
Quay County Sun (Tucumcari, NM) **10209**
Queen Anne-Magnolia News
  (Seattle, WA) **10293**
Queen Anne's Record-Observer
  (Centreville, MD) **10158**
Queens Chronicle (Rego Park, NY) **10222**
Queens Ledger (Maspeth, NY) **10218**
Queens Tribune (Fresh Meadows, NY) **10214**
▼Queen Village Times, The
  (Flushing, NY) **10214**
Quik Quarter Want Ads (Hobbs, NM) **10208**
Quincy Sun (Quincy, MA) **10165**
Quoddy Tides (Eastport, ME) **10156**
Raeford News-Journal, The
  (Raeford, NC) **10230**
Rahway News-Record (Rahway, NJ) **10206**
Rahway Progress (Union, NJ) **10207**
Ramona Sentinel (Ramona, CA) **10080**
Ramsey-Mahwah Reporter (Palisades
  Park, NJ) **10205**
Ramsey County Review (St. Paul, MN) **10183**
Ramsey Home & Store News
  (Ramsey, NJ) **10206**
Rancho Bernardo Journal (San
  Diego, CA) **10081**
Rancho Santa Margarita News (Lake
  Forest, CA) **10074**
Randleman Reporter (Randleman, NC) **10230**
Randolph County Herald Tribune
  (Chester, IL) **10112**
† Randolph County Times-Herald (Moberly, MO)
Randolph Guide, The (Asheboro, NC) **10226**
Randolph Leader (Roanoke, AL) **10061**
Randolph Mariner (Marshfield, MA) **10163**
Randolph Reporter (Bernardsville, NJ) **10200**
Random Lengths News (San Pedro, CA) **10082**
Rankin County News, The
  (Brandon, MS) **10185**
Rankin Independent (Cissna Park, IL) **10114**
† Rantoul Pacesetter (Rantoul, IL)
Rantoul Press (Rantoul, IL) **10127**
Rappahannock News (Reston, VA) **10288**
Rappahannock Record
  (Kilmarnock, VA) **10287**
Raton Range, The (Raton, NM) **10208**
Ravena News Herald (Ravena, NY) **10221**
Rayne Acadian-Tribune (Rayne, LA) **10154**
Rayne Independent (Rayne, LA) **10154**
Raynham Journal (Stoughton, MA) **10166**
Raytown Dispatch Tribune
  (Raytown, MO) **10192**
Real American (Leakey, TX) **10277**
Reaper Extra (Richfield, UT) **10233**

Record-Advertiser (North Tonawanda, NY) **10220**
Record-Breeze (Blackwood, NJ) **10201**
Record-Citizen, The (Bristow, OK) **10245**
Record-Delta, The (Buckhannon, WV) **10294**
Record-Enterprise (McDonald, PA) **10254**
Record-Herald & Indianola Tribune (Indianola, IA) **10139**
Record-Review (Abbotsford, WI) **10297**
Record Enterprise (Plymouth, NH) **10200**
Recorder-Herald (Salmon, ID) **10109**
Recorder, The (Prince Frederick, MD) **10159**
Recorder, The (Conshohocken, PA) **10252**
Recorder, The (Monterey, VA) **10287**
Recorder Times, The (San Antonio, TX) **10280**
Record Ledger (San Fernando, CA) **10081**
Record, The (Gainesville, FL) **10095**
Record, The (Council, ID) **10107**
Record, The (Kansas City, KS) **10144**
Record, The (Havre De Grace, MD) **10159**
Record, The (Boonville, MO) **10188**
Record, The (Coraopolis, PA) **10252**
Record Times, The (Paxton, IL) **10126**
Red Bay News (Red Bay, AL) **10061**
Redding Pilot, The (Georgetown, CT) **10090**
Redfield Press (Redfield, SD) **10265**
Redford Observer (Livonia, MI) **10172**
Redlands Advertiser (Palm Desert, CA) **10079**
Redmond Sammamish Valley News (Redmond, WA) **10292**
Redmond Spokesman (Redmond, OR) **10250**
Red Oak Express (Red Oak, IA) **10141**
▼Redwood City Tribune (Redwood City, CA) **10080**
Redwood Gazette, The (Redwood Falls, MN) **10182**
Reedley Exponent (Reedley, CA) **10080**
Reedsburg Times-Press (Reedsburg, WI) **10304**
Reflector, The (Battle Ground, WA) **10290**
Regional News (Palos Heights, IL) **10126**
Regional News, The (La Crosse, IN) **10133**
Register-Herald (Eaton, OH) **10239**
Register-News (Bordentown, NJ) **10201**
Register Review (Bishop, CA) **10069**
Register, The (Yarmouth Port, MA) **10167**
Reminder, The (Vernon, CT) **10092**
Reminder, The (Pontiac, MI) **10174**
Remington Press (Rensselaer, IN) **10135**
Renville County Shopper (Olivia, MN) **10181**
Reporter of the Spring-Ford Area (Royersford, PA) **10258**
† Reporter, The (Tampa, FL)
Reporter, The (Casey, IL) **10112**
Reporter, The (Chicago, IL) **10113**
Reporter, The (Palos Heights, IL) **10126**

Reporter, The (Palisades Park, NJ) **10205**
Reporter, The (Walton, NY) **10224**
Republican-Journal (Darlington, WI) **10299**
Republican Journal (Belfast, ME) **10155**
Republican, The (Danville, IN) **10130**
Republican, The (Oakland, MD) **10159**
▼Resident Community News (New York, NY) **10220**
Reston Times (Reston, VA) **10288**
Retrospect, The (Collingswood, NJ) **10202**
Reveille/Between the Lakes (Seneca Falls, NY) **10222**
Revere Journal (Revere, MA) **10165**
† Review-Enterprise (Blackwood, NJ)
Review Herald, The (Mammoth Lakes, CA) **10077**
Review Press Reporter (Yonkers, NY) **10226**
Review, The (Erie, IL) **10116**
Review, The (Marion, IL) **10122**
Review, The (Richmond, MI) **10174**
Review, The (Paramus, NJ) **10205**
Review, The (Point Pleasant Beach, NJ) **10206**
Review, The (Plymouth, WI) **10304**
Reynolds County Courier (Ellington, MO) **10189**
RFD News, The (Bellevue, OH) **10234**
Rialto Record (San Bernardino, CA) **10080**
Rice Lake Chronotype (Rice Lake, WI) **10304**
Richardson News (Richardson, TX) **10280**
Richfield Reaper (Richfield, UT) **10283**
Richfield Sun-Current (Bloomington, MN) **10177**
Richland Beacon-News (Rayville, LA) **10154**
Richland Center Observer (Richland Center, WI) **10304**
Richlands-Beulaville Advertiser-News (Richlands, NC) **10230**
Richlands News Press (Richlands, VA) **10289**
Richton Dispatch, The (Richton, MS) **10187**
Ridgefield Press, The (Ridgefield, CT) **10091**
Ridgewood News (Paramus, NJ) **10205**
Ridgway Sun (Ouray, CO) **10089**
Ridley Press (Drexel Hill, PA) **10252**
Rio Grande Sun (Espanola, NM) **10208**
Ripley Jackson Herald (Ripley, WV) **10296**
Ripley Southern Sentinel (Ripley, MS) **10187**
Ripon Commonwealth Press (Ripon, WI) **10304**
Rising Star, The (Rising Star, TX) **10280**
Rising Sun Recorder (Rising Sun, IN) **10135**
Ritchie Gazette (Harrisville, WV) **10295**
Riverdale Press (Bronx, NY) **10210**
River East News Bulletin (Glastonbury, CT) **10090**
River Falls Journal (River Falls, WI) **10305**
River North News (Chicago, IL) **10113**

River Oaks News (Fort Worth, TX) **10275**
River Press (Rogue River, OR) **10250**
River Press, The (Fort Benton, MT) **10195**
River Reporter, The (Narrowsburg, NY) **10219**
Riverside Advertiser (Palm Desert, CA) **10079**
Riverside Bulletin, The (Los
   Angeles, CA) **10076**
Riverside Review (Buffalo, NY) **10211**
Riverton Register (Riverton, IL) **10127**
River Valley Shopper (Spring
   Valley, MN) **10183**
Roane County News, The
   (Kingston, TN) **10267**
Roane County Reporter (Spencer, WV) **10296**
Roanoke-Chowan News-Herald
   (Jackson, NC) **10228**
Roanoke Beacon (Plymouth, NC) **10229**
Roanoke Review (Roanoke, IL) **10127**
Robersonville Weekly Herald
   (Williamston, NC) **10231**
Robertson County Times
   (Springfield, TN) **10270**
Rochelle News Leader (Rochelle, IL) **10127**
Rochester Clarion (Rochester, MI) **10174**
† Rochester Courier (Rochester, NH)
Rochester Eccentric (Rochester
   Hills, MI) **10174**
Rochester Sun News, The (Tenino, WA) **10293**
Rochester Times (Auburn, IL) **10110**
Rochester Times, The (Rochester, NH) **10200**
Rockaway Journal (Lawrence, NY) **10217**
Rockbridge Weekly (Lexington, VA) **10287**
Rock County Star Herald (Luverne, MN) **10180**
Rockcreek Current, The
   (Washington, DC) **10093**
Rockdale Neighbor, The (Conyers, GA) **10102**
Rockdale Reporter (Rockdale, TX) **10280**
Rockford/Cedar Springs Advance
   (Jenison, MI) **10171**
Rockford Squire (Rockford, MI) **10174**
Rockland County Times
   (Haverstraw, NY) **10216**
Rockland Independent, The (Pearl
   River, NY) **10221**
Rockmart Journal (Rockmart, GA) **10105**
Rockrimmon Journal (Manitou
   Springs, CO) **10088**
Rockville Centre Herald (Lawrence, NY) **10217**
Rockville Centre Long Island News & Owl
   (Mineola, NY) **10219**
Rockville Parke County Sentinel
   (Rockville, IN) **10135**
Rockwood Times (Kingston, TN) **10267**
▼Rocky Fork Enterprise
   (Columbus, OH) **10237**

Rogers Park/Edgewater News/Uptown News
   Star (Lincolnwood, IL) **10122**
Rogersville Review (Rogersville, TN) **10269**
† Rohnert Park Cotati Clarion (Cotati, CA)
Rolling Meadows Journal & Topics (Des
   Plaines, IL) **10115**
Romeo Observer (Romeo, MI) **10174**
Romeoville Metropolitan (Lemont, IL) **10121**
Romeoville Sun (Bolingbrook, IL) **10111**
Romulus Roman (Wayne, MI) **10176**
Roosevelt Review (St. Paul, MN) **10183**
Rosamond News (Rosamond, CA) **10080**
Roscoe Hosmer Independent
   (Ipswich, SD) **10265**
Roscommon County Herald-News
   (Roscommon, MI) **10174**
Roseau Times-Region (Roseau, MN) **10182**
Roselle Park Leader (Union, NJ) **10207**
† Roselle Record (Carol Stream, IL)
Roselle Spectator (Union, NJ) **10207**
Rosemont Journal (Des Plaines, IL) **10115**
Rosemont Times (Park Ridge, IL) **10126**
Roseville-Falcon Heights-Arden Hills Focus
   (Roseville, MN) **10182**
Roseville Independent (Roseville, _) **10127**
Roseville Press-Tribune (Roseville, CA) **10080**
Roseville Review (St. Paul, MN) **10183**
Rossford Record-Journal
   (Perrysburg, OH) **10242**
Rossmoor News (Walnut Creek, CA) **10084**
Ross Valley Reporter (Sausalito, CA) **10083**
Roswell-Alpharetta Neighbor
   (Roswell, GA) **10105**
Roswell/Alpharetta Crier Newspaper
   (Dunwoody, GA) **10102**
Round Lake News (Grayslake, IL) **10119**
Round Rock Leader (Round Rock, TX) **10280**
Round Valley Paper, The (Eagar, AZ) **10063**
Roxborough Review (Philadelphia, PA) **10258**
Royal Review (Royal City, WA) **10292**
Ruidoso News, The (Ruidoso, NM) **10208**
Rumford Falls Times (Rumford, ME) **10157**
Rural-Urban Record (Columbia
   Station, OH) **10237**
Rural Virginian (Charlottesville, VA) **10285**
Rush County News (La Crosse, KS) **10144**
Rushville Times, The (Rushville, IL) **10127**
Russell County News (Russell
   Springs, KY) **10151**
Russell Record (Russell, KS) **10145**
Russell Springs Times Journal (Russell
   Springs, KY) **10151**
Rutherford Courier, The (Smyrna, TN) **10269**
Rutland Tribune, The (Rutland, VT) **10284**
Rye Chronicle (Yonkers, NY) **10226**
Sabina Advertiser (Sabina, OH) **10243**

Weeklies Index

Sabinal Sampler (Hondo, TX) **10276**
Sabine Banner (Many, LA) **10154**
Sabine County Reporter-Rambler
   (Hemphill, TX) **10276**
Sabine Index (Many, LA) **10154**
Sacramento Bulletin, The
   (Sacramento, CA) **10080**
† Sacramento Union (Sacramento, CA)
Saddleback Valley News (Lake
   Forest, CA) **10074**
Saginaw Press, The (Saginaw, MI) **10174**
Saint Elmo Banner (St. Elmo, IL) **10127**
Sakonnet Times (Portsmouth, RI) **10260**
Salem County Record (Salem, NJ) **10206**
Salem Democrat, The (Salem, IN) **10135**
Salem Leader (Salem, IN) **10135**
Salem News (Salem, MO) **10192**
Salem Observer (Salem, NH) **10200**
Salem Times-Commoner (Salem, IL) **10127**
Salem Times-Register (Salem, VA) **10289**
Saline Reporter (Saline, MI) **10174**
Salisbury News & Advertiser
   (Salisbury, MD) **10159**
Salmon River News (Pulaski, NY) **10221**
Saluda Standard Sentinel (Saluda, SC) **10263**
Salyersville Independent
   (Salyersville, KY) **10151**
Samford Crimson (Birmingham, AL) **10058**
Samson Ledger (Samson, AL) **10061**
San Augustine Tribune (San
   Augustine, TX) **10280**
San Benito News (San Benito, TX) **10280**
San Bernardino Advertiser (Palm
   Desert, CA) **10079**
San Bernardino Bulletin, The (Los
   Angeles, CA) **10076**
San Bruno Herald (San Mateo, CA) **10082**
† San Clemente News (San Clemente, CA)
Sandersville Progress
   (Sandersville, GA) **10105**
▼Sandhills Living (Southern Pines, NC) **10230**
† San Diego Bulletin (Los Angeles, CA)
San Diego Log (San Diego, CA) **10081**
San Diego Reader (San Diego, CA) **10081**
San Diego Review (San Diego, CA) **10081**
Sand Mountain Reporter
   (Albertville, AL) **10057**
† Sandpoint News-Bulletin (Sandpoint, ID)
Sand Springs Leader (Sand
   Springs, OK) **10247**
Sandwich Broadsider (Orleans, MA) **10164**
Sandy Post (Sandy, OR) **10250**
Sandy Springs Neighbor, The
   (Atlanta, GA) **10101**
San Fernando Valley Sun (San
   Fernando, CA) **10081**

Sanford News (Sanford, ME) **10157**
San Francisco Bay Guardian (San
   Francisco, CA) **10081**
San Francisco Independent (San
   Francisco, CA) **10081**
San Francisco Metro Reporter (San
   Francisco, CA) **10081**
San Francisco Sentinel (San
   Francisco, CA) **10081**
San Gabriel Progress (Los Angeles, CA) **10076**
Sanger Herald (Sanger, CA) **10081**
Sanibel-Captiva Islander (Sanibel, FL) **10098**
Sanilac County News (Sandusky, MI) **10175**
San Jacinto Valley Register (San
   Jacinto, CA) **10081**
San Marcos News Reporter (San
   Marcos, CA) **10082**
San Marino Tribune (San Marino, CA) **10082**
San Mateo Weekly (Burlingame, CA) **10070**
San Patricio County News (Sinton, TX) **10281**
San Rafael News Pointer
   (Sausalito, CA) **10083**
Santa Barbara Independent (Santa
   Barbara, CA) **10082**
Santa Fe Reporter, The (Santa Fe, NM) **10208**
Santa Fe Springs News (Los
   Angeles, CA) **10077**
† Santa Monica Life (Santa Monica, CA)
Santa Paula Times (Santa Paula, CA) **10082**
Santa Rosa Free Press (Milton, FL) **10097**
Santa Rosa Press Gazette (Milton, FL) **10097**
Saratoga News (Saratoga, CA) **10083**
Saratoga Sun (Saratoga, WY) **10309**
Sarcoxie Record, The (Sarcoxie, MO) **10192**
Sargent Leader (Burwell, NE) **10197**
Saturday Advantage, The (Monte
   Vista, CO) **10088**
Saturday Post-Star (Saugerties, NY) **10222**
Saugerties Post Star (Saugerties, NY) **10222**
Saugus Advertiser (Melrose, MA) **10163**
Sauk-Prairie Star (Sauk City, WI) **10305**
Sauk Centre Herald (Sauk Centre, MN) **10182**
Savannah Reporter & Andrew County Democrat
   (Savannah, MO) **10192**
Savanna Times Journal (Savanna, IL) **10127**
Sawyer County Gazette (Winter, WI) **10308**
Sawyer County Record (Hayward, WI) **10301**
Sayre Journal (Sayre, OK) **10247**
Scarsdale Inquirer, The (Scarsdale, NY) **10222**
Schaller Herald (Schaller, IA) **10141**
Schererville Guide (Highland, IN) **10132**
Schuyler Sun (Schuyler, NE) **10198**
Scioto Voice (Wheelersburg, OH) **10244**
Scotsman Press, The (Syracuse, NY) **10224**
Scott County Advertiser (Waldron, AR) **10068**
Scott County News (Oneida, TN) **10269**

Scott County Times (Forest, MS) **10186**
Scott Flier (Mascoutah, IL) **10122**
Scottsdale-Ashburn Independent
  (Midlothian, IL) **10124**
Scottsville Citizen-Times
  (Scottsville, KY) **10151**
Seaford-Wantagh Observer
  (Bellmore, NY) **10210**
Seal Beach Sun (Seal Beach, CA) **10083**
Sealy News (Sealy, TX) **10280**
Seaside Heights Ocean County Review (Point
  Pleasant Beach, NJ) **10206**
Seaside Signal (Seaside, OR) **10250**
Seattle Facts (Seattle, WA) **10293**
Seattle Skanner, The (Seattle, WA) **10293**
Seattle Weekly (Seattle, WA) **10293**
Sebastian Sun (Sebastian, FL) **10099**
Sebeka/Menahga Review Messenger
  (Sebeka, MN) **10182**
Secaucus Home News (Secaucus, NJ) **10206**
Sedona Red Rock News (Sedona, AZ) **10064**
Seekonk Star (East Providence, RI) **10260**
Selby Record (Selby, SD) **10265**
Selma Enterprise (Selma, CA) **10083**
† Seminole Outlook (Oviedo, FL)
Senior's Beacon, The (Lima, OH) **10240**
Senior Observer (Winter Park, FL) **10100**
Senior Times (Spokane, WA) **10293**
Sentinel (Cheyenne, WY) **10308**
Sentinel-Echo (London, KY) **10149**
Sentinel-Ledger, The (Ocean City, NJ) **10205**
† Sentinel/Altitudes (Frisco, CO)
Sentinel, The (Auburn, CA) **10069**
Sentinel, The (Gulf Breeze, FL) **10095**
Sentinel, The (Chicago, IL) **10113**
Sentinel, The (Radcliff, KY) **10151**
Sentinel, The (Marion, MA) **10162**
Sentinel, The (Havre, MT) **10195**
Sentinel, The (Jefferson, OH) **10240**
Sequim Gazette (Sequim, WA) **10293**
Sequoyah County Times (Sallisaw, OK) **10246**
Seward County Independent
  (Seward, NE) **10198**
Seward Phoenix Log (Seward, AK) **10062**
Sewickley Herald (Monroeville, PA) **10255**
SF Weekly (San Francisco, CA) **10081**
Shafter Press (Shafter, CA) **10083**
Shakopee Valley News (Shakopee, MN) **10183**
Sharon Advocate (Sharon, MA) **10165**
Sharon Reporter, The (Sharon, WI) **10305**
† Shawnee-Cridersville Press (Wapakoneta, OH)
Shawnee/Merriam Sun (Shawnee
  Mission, KS) **10146**
Sheboygan Falls News (Sheboygan
  Falls, WI) **10305**
Shelby County Herald (Shelbyville, MO) **10193**

Shelby County Reporter
  (Columbiana, AL) **10058**
Shelby Review (Wapakoneta, OH) **10244**
Shelby Sun Times (Germantown, TN) **10267**
Shelbyville Sentinel-News
  (Shelbyville, KY) **10151**
Sheldon Mail-Sun (Sheldon, IA) **10141**
Shelley Pioneer (Shelley, ID) **10109**
Shelter Island Reporter (Shelter Island
  Heights, NY) **10223**
Shelton-Mason County Journal
  (Shelton, WA) **10293**
Shenandoah Valley-Herald, The
  (Woodstock, VA) **10290**
Shepherdstown Chronicle
  (Shepherdstown, WV) **10296**
Sheridan Headlight (Sheridan, AR) **10067**
Sheridan News (Fishers, IN) **10131**
▼Sherman County Star, The
  (Goodland, KS) **10143**
Shiawassee County Journal (Perry, MI) **10174**
Shippensburg News-Chronicle
  (Shippensburg, PA) **10259**
Shopper/PLUS (Shelbyville, KY) **10151**
Shopper's Guide (Bardstown, KY) **10146**
Shopper's Guide, The (Louisville, MS) **10186**
Shopper Observer News (Ruskin, FL) **10098**
Shopper Spree (Burlington, IA) **10137**
Shopper Stopper (Merrimac, WI) **10302**
Shopper, The (Pensacola, FL) **10098**
Shopper, The (Grangeville, ID) **10107**
Shopper, The (South Holland, IL) **10127**
Shopper Zone I (Durant, OK) **10245**
Shopper Zone II (Denison, TX) **10273**
Shopping News (Fairport, NY) **10213**
Shopping News (Platteville, WI) **10304**
Shopping News, The (Newton, MS) **10187**
Shoreline Chronicle (Sheboygan, WI) **10305**
Shoreview-Arden Hills Bulletin (St
  Paul, MN) **10183**
Shoreview Press (St. Paul, MN) **10183**
Shorewood Herald (Wauwatosa, WI) **10307**
Sidney Herald-Leader (Sidney, MT) **10196**
Sierra County Sentinel (Truth or
  Consequences, NM) **10209**
Sierra Madre News (Sierra Madre, CA) **10083**
Sierra Sun (Truckee, CA) **10084**
Signal-Item (Monroeville, PA) **10255**
Signal, The (Atwater, CA) **10069**
Signal, The (Canal Fulton, OH) **10235**
Sigourney News-Review (Sigourney, IA) **10141**
Silsbee Bee (Silsbee, TX) **10280**
Silver Spring Gazette (Burtonsville, MD) **10158**
Silverton Appeal-Tribune/Mt. Angel News
  (Silverton, OR) **10250**

Silverton Standard & The Miner (Silverton, CO) **10089**
Sisseton Courier (Sisseton, SD) **10265**
Siuslaw News, The (Florence, OR) **10248**
Skaneateles Press (Skaneateles, NY) **10223**
Skiatook Journal (Skiatook, OK) **10247**
Skokie Life (Lincolnwood, IL) **10122**
Skokie Review (Evanston, IL) **10117**
Skyline (Lincolnwood, IL) **10122**
Slatebelt Hometown News, The (Bangor, PA) **10251**
Smith County Pioneer (Smith Center, KS) **10146**
Smith County Reformer (Raleigh, MS) **10187**
Smithfield Herald (Smithfield, NC) **10230**
Smith Mountain Eagle (Moneta, VA) **10287**
Smithtown Messenger (Smithtown, NY) **10223**
Smithtown News, The (Smithtown, NY) **10223**
Smithville Lake Democrat-Herald, The (Smithville, MO) **10193**
Smithville Review (Smithville, TN) **10269**
Smyth County News & Messenger (Marion, VA) **10287**
† Snake River Press (Craig, CO)
Snohomish County Tribune (Snohomish, WA) **10293**
Soledad Bee (Soledad, CA) **10083**
Solon Herald Sun (Beachwood, OH) **10234**
Solon Times, The (Chagrin Falls, OH) **10235**
Solvang Santa Ynez Valley News (Solvang, CA) **10083**
Somerset Herald (Princess Anne, MD) **10159**
Somerset Messenger Gazette (Somerville, NJ) **10207**
Somerset Spectator (Somerset, NJ) **10206**
Somerville Journal (West Somerville, MA) **10166**
Sonoma County Independent (Santa Rosa, CA) **10083**
Sonoma Index Tribune (Sonoma, CA) **10083**
Sonoma West (Sebastopal, CA) **10083**
Sorento News (Hillsboro, IL) **10120**
Souderton Independent (Souderton, PA) **10259**
Sounder, The (Random Lake, WI) **10304**
Sound View News (Yonkers, NY) **10226**
South-West Review (St. Paul, MN) **10184**
South Alabamian (Jackson, AL) **10060**
Southampton Press (Southampton, NY) **10223**
South Bay's Newspaper (Lindenhurst, NY) **10217**
South Bay's Shopper (Lindenhurst, NY) **10217**
South Bay Extra (Torrance, CA) **10084**
South Bend Tri-County News (South Bend, IN) **10135**
South Bergenite (Rutherford, NJ) **10206**

South Boston Gazette-Virginian (South Boston, VA) **10289**
South Boston News & Record (South Boston, VA) **10289**
South Boston Tribune (Boston, MA) **10160**
South Buffalo News (Lackawanna, NY) **10216**
South City Journal (St. Louis, MO) **10194**
South Coast Shoppers/Penny Savers (Laguna Hills, CA) **10074**
South County Advertiser (Webster, MA) **10166**
South County Express (Auburn, IL) **10110**
South County Journal (St. Louis, MO) **10194**
South County News & Advertiser (Fort Worth, TX) **10275**
South Dade News (South Miami, FL) **10099**
South Dade News Leader (Homestead, FL) **10095**
South Dekalb Neighbor, The (Marietta, GA) **10104**
South District Journal (Seattle, WA) **10293**
† South East Metro Shopper (Cottage Grove, MN)
Southern Cayuga Tribune (Moravia, NY) **10219**
Southern County News (Thornton, IA) **10142**
Southern Dutchess News (Wappingers Falls, NY) **10224**
Southern Herald, The (Liberty, MS) **10186**
Southern Oklahoma Leader (Durant, OK) **10245**
Southern Pines Pilot (Southern Pines, NC) **10230**
Southern Standard (McMinnville, TN) **10268**
Southern Star (Ozark, AL) **10061**
Southfield Eccentric (Birmingham, MI) **10167**
South Fork Times (Monte Vista, CO) **10088**
South Fulton Neighbor, The (Marietta, GA) **10104**
South Gate Press (Los Angeles, CA) **10077**
South Hill Enterprise (South Hill, VA) **10289**
South Hills Record (Pittsburgh, PA) **10258**
Southington Observer (Southington, CT) **10091**
South Jersey Advisor (Cologne, NJ) **10202**
South Lake Advertiser (Lowell, IN) **10133**
South Lyon Herald (South Lyon, MI) **10175**
South Miami News (Miami, FL) **10097**
South Milwaukee Voice Graphic (Wauwatosa, WI) **10307**
South Missourian News (Thayer, MO) **10194**
▼South Of The Boulevard (Woodland Hills, CA) **10085**
† South Pasadena Journal (Los Angeles, CA)
South Pasadena Review (South Pasadena, CA) **10084**
South Philadelphia Chronicle (Philadelphia, PA) **10258**

South Philadelphia Review (Philadelphia, PA) **10258**
South Pittsburgh Reporter (Pittsburgh, PA) **10258**
South Reporter, The (Holly Springs, MS) **10186**
South San Francisco Enterprise-Journal (San Mateo, CA) **10082**
South San Gabriel/Rosemead Progress (Los Angeles, CA) **10077**
South Shore News (Rockland, MA) **10165**
South Shore Record (Woodmere, NY) **10225**
Southside Journal (Los Angeles, CA) **10077**
Southside Journal (St. Louis, MO) **10194**
Southside Sentinel (Urbanna, VA) **10289**
† Southside Sun (East Point, GA)
South Sioux City Star (South Sioux City, NE) **10198**
South St. Paul/Inver Grove Heights Sun-Current (Burnsville, MN) **10177**
▼South Tampa News (Brandon, FL) **10093**
Southtowns Citizen (Orchard Park, NY) **10220**
† South Valley Eagle (Salt Lake City, UT)
Southwest Beacon (Chicago, IL) **10113**
Southwest City Journal (St. Louis, MO) **10194**
Southwest County Journal (St. Louis, MO) **10194**
Southwest Courier (Chicago, IL) **10113**
Southwestern Journal News (Brighton, IL) **10111**
Southwestern Pennsylvania Scene (Scottdale, PA) **10259**
Southwest Globe Times (Philadelphia, PA) **10258**
Southwest News (South Miami, FL) **10099**
Southwest News-Herald (Chicago, IL) **10113**
Southwest Newsweek, The (Louisville, KY) **10149**
Southwest Shopper (Chicago, IL) **10113**
Southwest Sun (Sugar Land, TX) **10281**
Southwest Town Crier (La Porte, IN) **10133**
Southwest Tulsa News (Tulsa, OK) **10247**
Southwest Virginia Enterprise (Wytheville, VA) **10290**
Southwest Wave/News (Los Angeles, CA) **10077**
Spackenkill Sentinel (Wappingers Falls, NY) **10224**
Sparta/Kent City Advance (Sparta, MI) **10175**
Sparta Expositor (Sparta, TN) **10269**
Sparta Herald (Sparta, WI) **10305**
Sparta Independent (Sparta, NJ) **10207**
Sparta Ishmaelite (Sparta, GA) **10105**
Sparta News Plaindealer (Sparta, IL) **10127**
Spectator (Raleigh, NC) **10230**
Spectator, The (Somerset, MA) **10165**

Speedway Town Press (Speedway, IN) **10135**
Spencer County Journal Democrat (Rockport, IN) **10135**
Spencer Magnet (Taylorsville, KY) **10151**
Spencer Random Harvest Weekly (Trumansburg, NY) **10224**
Spinal Column Newsweekly (Waterford, MI) **10176**
Spirit Lake Beacon (Spirit Lake, IA) **10141**
† Spirit of Bucks County (Hatboro, PA)
Spirit of Jefferson-Advocate (Charles Town, WV) **10294**
Spooner Advocate (Spooner, WI) **10305**
Spotlight, The (Washington, DC) **10093**
Spotlight, The (Indianapolis, IN) **10132**
Spotlight, The (Delmar, NY) **10213**
Sprague Advocate, The (Sprague, WA) **10293**
Springfield Advance-Press (Springfield, MN) **10183**
Springfield Advocate (Springfield, MA) **10165**
Springfield Leader (Union, NJ) **10207**
Springfield News, The (Springfield, OR) **10250**
Springfield Press (Springfield, PA) **10259**
Springfield Reporter, The (Springfield, VT) **10284**
Springfield Shopper (Springfield, IL) **10127**
Springfield Sun (Springfield, KY) **10151**
Springfield Sun (Fort Washington, PA) **10253**
Springfield Times Courier (Reston, VA) **10289**
Springhill Press (Springhill, LA) **10154**
Spring Hope Enterprise (Spring Hope, NC) **10230**
Springs Valley Herald (French Lick, IN) **10131**
Springtown Epigraph, The (Springtown, TX) **10281**
Spring Valley Bulletin (Lemon Grove, CA) **10075**
Spring Valley Sun (Spring Valley, WI) **10305**
Spring Valley Tribune (Spring Valley, MN) **10183**
Springview Herald (Springview, NE) **10198**
Springville Journal (Springville, NY) **10223**
† Squire, The (Prairie Village, KS)
Stamford American (Stamford, TX) **10281**
Standard & Times (Tuscumbia, AL) **10062**
Standard-Times (North Kingstown, RI) **10260**
Standard Banner (Jefferson, TN) **10267**
Standard Journal (Rexburg, ID) **10109**
Stanley Republican (Stanley, WI) **10305**
Stanly News & Press (Albemarle, NC) **10226**
St. Anthony Bulletin (North St. Paul, MN) **10181**
Staples World (Staples, MN) **10183**
Star-Advocate (Titusville, FL) **10099**
Star-Herald (Belton, MO) **10188**
Star-Herald, The (Presque Isle, ME) **10157**

Star-Herald, The (Kosciusko, MS) **10186**
Star-News, The (McCall, ID) **10108**
Star-News, The (North Syracuse, NY) **10220**
Star-Progress, The (Berryville, AR) **10065**
Star-Tribune (Chatham, VA) **10285**
Star Advertiser (Kalkaska, MI) **10172**
Star Buyers Guide (West Branch, MI) **10176**
Star Express (Covington, GA) **10102**
Star Gazette (Hackettstown, NJ) **10202**
Star Journal (Hope, IN) **10132**
Star News, The (Chula Vista, CA) **10070**
Star News, The (Medford, WI) **10302**
Star Press (Springboro, OH) **10243**
Star Republican (Wilmington, OH) **10244**
Star, The (Chicago Heights, IL) **10114**
Star, The (Sun Prairie, WI) **10306**
State Center Enterprise-Record (State
   Center, IA) **10141**
State Line Shopping Guide
   (Palmer, MA) **10164**
Staten Island Register (Staten
   Island, NY) **10223**
State Port Pilot, The (Southport, NC) **10230**
Statesman-Examiner (Colville, WA) **10291**
Staunton Star-Times (Staunton, IL) **10127**
Stayton Mail (Stayton, OR) **10250**
St. Bernard Voice (Arabi, LA) **10152**
St. Charles Journal (St. Charles, MO) **10193**
St. Charles Press (St. Charles, MN) **10183**
St. Clair Missourian (St. Clair, MO) **10193**
St. Clair News-Aegis (Pell City, AL) **10061**
St. Clair Shores Herald
   (Birmingham, MI) **10167**
St. Croix Valley Peach (Forest
   Lake, MN) **10178**
St. Croix Valley Press (St. Paul, MN) **10184**
Steamboat Pilot (Steamboat
   Springs, CO) **10089**
Steele Enterprise (Steel, MO) **10193**
Steelville Star/Crawford Mirror
   (Steelville, MO) **10193**
Ste. Genevieve Herald (Ste.
   Genevieve, MO) **10193**
Steuben Courier-Advocate (Bath, NY) **10210**
St. Francis Herald, The (St.
   Francis, KS) **10146**
St. Francis Reminder-Enterprise
   (Wauwatosa, WI) **10307**
St. Helena Star (St. Helena, CA) **10084**
St. Helens Chronicle (St. Helens, OR) **10250**
Stigler News-Sentinel (Stigler, OK) **10247**
St. Ignace News, The (St. Ignace, MI) **10175**
Stillwater Valley Advertiser
   (Covington, OH) **10239**
Stilwell Democrat-Journal (Stilwell, OK) **10247**

St. James Leader Journal (St.
   James, MO) **10193**
St. James Plaindealer (St. James, MN) **10183**
St. John News (St. John, KS) **10146**
St. Johns Reminder (St. Johns, MI) **10175**
St. Johns Review (Portland, OR) **10250**
St. Joseph Telegraph, The (St.
   Joseph, MO) **10193**
St. Lawrence Plaindealer (Canton, NY) **10212**
St. Louis American Newspaper (St.
   Louis, MO) **10194**
† St. Louis Naborhood Link News (St.
   Louis, MO)
St. Louis Park Sun-Sailor
   (Minnetonka, MN) **10180**
St. Louis Sentinel Newspaper (St.
   Louis, MO) **10194**
† St. Louis South St. Louis County News (St.
   Louis, MO)
St. Maries Gazette Record (St.
   Maries, ID) **10109**
St. Martinville Teche News (St.
   Martinville, LA) **10154**
St. Mary Journal (Morgan City, LA) **10154**
St. Marys Star (St. Marys, KS) **10146**
Stone County Citizen (Mountain
   View, AR) **10067**
Stone County Enterprise (Wiggins, MS) **10187**
Stone County Leader (Mountain
   View, AR) **10067**
† Stoneham Weekender News (Stoneham, MA)
Storm Lake Times (Storm Lake, IA) **10142**
Story City Herald (Story City, IA) **10142**
Stoughton Chronicle (Stoughton, MA) **10166**
Stowe Reporter (Stowe, VT) **10284**
Stow Sentry (Stow, OH) **10243**
St. Peter Herald (St. Peter, MN) **10184**
Straits Area Star (Cheboygan, MI) **10168**
Stratford Bard (Milford, CT) **10091**
Stratford Journal (Stratford, WI) **10305**
Stratford Star (Konawa, OK) **10246**
Sturgis News (Sturgis, KY) **10151**
Suburban & Wayne Times (Wayne, PA) **10259**
Suburban Advertiser (Wayne, PA) **10259**
Suburban Gazette (McKees Rocks, PA) **10254**
Suburbanite, The (Closter, NJ) **10202**
Suburbanite, The (Akron, OH) **10234**
Suburban Journal (Des Plaines, IL) **10115**
Suburban Leader (Chicago, IL) **10113**
Suburban Life (Butler, NJ) **10201**
Suburban Life (Loveland, OH) **10241**
Suburban Life Citizen (Oak Brook, IL) **10125**
Suburban Life Graphic (Oak Brook, IL) **10125**
Suburban News (Reading, MA) **10165**
Suburban News (Spencerport, NY) **10223**
Suburban News, The (Windham, ME) **10157**

Suburban Press (Millbury, OH) **10241**
Suburban Street News (White
   Plains, NY) **10225**
Suburban Town News (Paramus, NJ) **10205**
Suburban Trends (Butler, NJ) **10201**
Suburban Tribune (Balch Springs, TX) **10271**
Sudbury Town Crier (Waltham, MA) **10166**
Suffolk County News (Sayville, NY) **10222**
Suffolk Times (Mattituck, NY) **10218**
Sullivan County News (Blountville, TN) **10265**
Sullivan Independent News
   (Sullivan, MO) **10194**
Sullivan Review (Dushore, PA) **10252**
Summerville Journal Scene
   (Summerville, SC) **10264**
Summerville News (Summerville, GA) **10106**
Summit County Journal (Frisco, CO) **10087**
Summit Independent Press (New
   Providence, NJ) **10205**
Summit Observer (Union, NJ) **10207**
Sumner Gazette (Sumner, IA) **10142**
Sumner Press (Sumner, IL) **10128**
Sumter County Record-Journal, The
   (Livingston, AL) **10060**
Sumter County Times (Bushnell, FL) **10094**
Sun & Erie County Independent, The
   (Hamburg, NY) **10215**
Sun & News, The (Hastings, MI) **10171**
Sun-Bulletin, The (Palisades Park, NJ) **10205**
Sun-Reporter (San Francisco, CA) **10081**
Sun Advocate (Price, UT) **10283**
Sun Banner Pride (Cleveland, OH) **10236**
Sunbury News (Sunbury, OH) **10243**
Sun Cities Independent (Sun City, AZ) **10065**
Sun City/Youngtown (Sun City, AZ) **10065**
Sun City News (Sun City, CA) **10084**
Sun City West (Sun City, AZ) **10065**
Sun Coast News (New Port Richey, FL) **10097**
Sun Courier, The (Cleveland, OH) **10236**
Sunday Bucks County Telegraph
   (Horsham, PA) **10253**
Sunday Dispatch (Pittston, PA) **10258**
† Sunday Glades Trend (Clewiston, FL)
Sunday Independent, The (Owosso, MI) **10173**
Sunday Post (Lynn, MA) **10162**
† Sunday Sun (Scranton, PA)
Sunday Sun (Georgetown, TX) **10275**
Sun Herald (North Port, FL) **10097**
Sun Herald, The (Cleveland, OH) **10236**
Sun Journal, The (North Canton, OH) **10242**
Sun Messenger, The (Cleveland, OH) **10236**
Sun Post (Miami Beach, FL) **10097**
Sun Post News (San Clemente, CA) **10080**
Sun Press (Kaneohe, HI) **10107**
Sun Press (Cleveland, OH) **10236**
Sunriser News (Ossian, IN) **10134**

Sunrise Times (Coral Springs, FL) **10094**
Sun Scoop Journal (Cleveland, OH) **10236**
Sun Star, The (Cleveland, OH) **10236**
Sun, The (Exeter, CA) **10072**
Sun, The (Sun City Center, FL) **10099**
Sun, The (Mt. Vernon, IA) **10140**
Sun, The (Cleveland, OH) **10237**
Sun, The (Hummelstown, PA) **10253**
Sun Times (Heber Springs, AR) **10056**
Sun Times (Perryville, MO) **10192**
Superior Express, The (Superior, NE) **10198**
† Surfside News (South Miami, FL)
Surry Scene, The (Mount Airy, NC) **10229**
Susquehanna County Independent
   (Montrose, PA) **10255**
Sussex-Lannon-Lisbon News
   (Wauwatosa, WI) **10308**
Sussex-Surry Dispatch (Wakefield, VA) **10289**
Sussex Countian (Georgetown, DE) **10092**
Sussex County Chronicle (Byram, NJ) **10201**
Sussex Post, The (Lewes, DE) **10092**
Sussex Sun (Hartland, WI) **10300**
Swampscott Reporter
   (Marblehead, MA) **10162**
Swanton Enterprise (Swanton, OH) **10243**
Swap Sheet (Ridgecrest, CA) **10080**
† Sycamore Messenger (Cincinnati, OH)
Sycamore News (Sycamore, IL) **10128**
Sylva Herald & Ruralite (Sylva, NC) **10231**
Sylvania Herald (Toledo, OH) **10243**
Sylvester Local News (Sylvester, GA) **10106**
Syosset Jericho Tribune (Mineola, NY) **10219**
Syracuse Journal-Democrat
   (Syracuse, NE) **10198**
Syracuse New Times (Syracuse, NY) **10224**
T-Ville News Trader (Tompkinsville, KY) **10151**
Table Rock Gazette (Kimberling
   City, MO) **10191**
Tab, The (Needham, MA) **10164**
Taft Tribune (Taft, TX) **10281**
Tahoe World (Tahoe City, CA) **10084**
Tallahassean (Tallahassee, FL) **10099**
Tallassee Tribune (Tallassee, AL) **10062**
Tallmadge Express (Stow, OH) **10243**
Tama News-Herald (Tama, IA) **10142**
Tamarac Forum (Coral Springs, FL) **10094**
▼Taney County Times (Forsyth, MO) **10189**
Taos News (Taos, NM) **10209**
Tarkio Avalanche (Tarkio, MO) **10194**
Taunton Independent (Middleboro, MA) **10163**
Tavares Citizen (Mount Dora, FL) **10097**
Taylor Clarion (Burwell, NE) **10197**
Taylorsville Times, The
   (Taylorsville, NC) **10231**
Tazewell County Free Press
   (Richlands, VA) **10289**

Tazewell News (Morton, IL) **10124**

Tech Center News (Warren, MI) **10176**

Tecumseh Herald (Tecumseh, MI) **10175**

Tehachapi News (Tehachapi, CA) **10084**

Telegraph-County Edition
(Jerseyville, IL) **10120**

TeleGraphics (Lawrence, KS) **10144**

Telfair Enterprise (McRae, GA) **10105**

Telfair Times (Helena, GA) **10103**

Telluride Times-Journal (Telluride, CO) **10089**

Temple Terrace Beacon (Tampa, FL) **10099**

Temple Terrace News (Brandon, FL) **10093**

Tenino Independent (Tenino, WA) **10293**

Teton Valley News (Driggs, ID) **10107**

Texas Observer (Austin, TX) **10271**

Thief River Falls Times, The (Thief River
Falls, MN) **10184**

† This Week (Aledo, IL)

This Week (Cherry Hill, NJ) **10202**

This Week In Bexley (Columbus, OH) **10237**

This Week In Clintonville
(Columbus, OH) **10238**

This Week In Delaware (Columbus, OH) **10238**

This Week In Eastside (Columbus, OH) **10238**

This Week In Grandview
(Columbus, OH) **10238**

This Week In Hilliard (Columbus, OH) **10238**

This Week In New Albany
(Columbus, OH) **10238**

This Week In Northland
(Columbus, OH) **10238**

This Week In Peachtree City (Peachtree
City, GA) **10105**

This Week In Pickerington
(Columbus, OH) **10238**

This Week In Powell (Columbus, OH) **10238**

This Week In Reynoldsburg
(Columbus, OH) **10238**

This Week In Southside
(Columbus, OH) **10238**

This Week In Union County
(Columbus, OH) **10238**

This Week In Westerville
(Columbus, OH) **10238**

This Week In Westside (Columbus, OH) **10238**

This Week In Worthington
(Columbus, OH) **10238**

Thomaston Times (Thomaston, GA) **10106**

Thomasville Times (Thomasville, NC) **10231**

Thorp Courier (Thorp, WI) **10306**

Thousand Islands Sun (Alexandria
Bay, NY) **10209**

Thousandsticks (Hyden, KY) **10148**

Three Rivers Gazette (Helena, GA) **10103**

Three Star Edition (Philadelphia, PA) **10258**

Three Village Herald (East
Setauket, NY) **10213**

Three Village Times (Mineola, NY) **10219**

Thrif-T-Nikel Weekly Newspaper
(Ottawa, IL) **10125**

Thrifty Nickel (Birmingham, AL) **10058**

Thrifty Nickel (Champaign, IL) **10112**

Thrifty Nickel Want Ads (East
Moline, IL) **10116**

Tidewater Review (West Point, VA) **10290**

Tigard Times (Tigard, OR) **10250**

Times-Clarion, The (Harlowton, MT) **10195**

Times-Courier (Ellijay, GA) **10103**

Times-Express (Monroeville, PA) **10255**

Times-Herald (Timonium, MD) **10159**

Times-Indicator (Fremont, MI) **10169**

Times-Journal, The (Condon, OR) **10248**

Times-Leader (Union City, PA) **10259**

Times-Press (Hartford, WI) **10300**

Times-Press (Seymour, WI) **10305**

Times-Record, The (Denton, MD) **10158**

Times-Sentinel, The (Cheney, KS) **10143**

Times-Sun, The (West Newton, PA) **10260**

Times Chronicle (Jenkintown, PA) **10254**

Times Citizen (Iowa Falls, IA) **10139**

Times Dispatch (Walnut Ridge, AR) **10068**

Times Free Press (Ayer, MA) **10160**

Times Guthrian (Guthrie Center, IA) **10138**

Times Journal-Spotlight (Eastman, GA) **10103**

Times Leader, The (Princeton, KY) **10151**

Times Newsweekly (Ridgewood, NY) **10222**

Times of Nesconset, The
(Setauket, NY) **10222**

Times of Northeast Benton County (Pea
Ridge, AR) **10067**

Times of Smithtown (Setauket, NY) **10222**

Times of St. James (Setauket, NY) **10222**

Times of Ti (Elizabethtown, NY) **10213**

Times Post, The (Houston, MS) **10186**

Times Record (Fayette, AL) **10059**

Times Record (Aledo, IL) **10109**

Times Record (Spencer, WV) **10296**

Times, The (North Little Rock, AR) **10067**

Times, The (Melbourne, FL) **10096**

† Times, The (Augusta, KY)

Times, The (Webster, MA) **10166**

Times, The (Forest Lake, MN) **10178**

Times, The (Westfield, NJ) **10208**

Times, The (Columbus, OH) **10238**

Times, The (Port Royal, PA) **10258**

Times, The (Waitsburg, WA) **10294**

Times, The (Westby, WI) **10308**

Tioga County Gazette & Times
(Owego, NY) **10220**

Tipp City Herald (Tipp City, OH) **10243**

Tipton Conservative & Advertiser
(Tipton, IA) **10142**
† Tipton News Leader (Altus, OK)
Today (Orange Park, FL) **10098**
Todd County Standard (Elkton, KY) **10147**
Tomahawk Leader (Tomahawk, WI) **10306**
Tomahawk, The (Mountain City, TN) **10268**
Tomah Journal (Tomah, WI) **10306**
Tomah Monitor-Herald (Tomah, WI) **10306**
Tombstone Epitaph, The
(Tombstone, AZ) **10065**
Tomorrow (New Rochelle, NY) **10220**
Tompkinsville News (Tompkinsville, KY) **10151**
Tonkawa News, The (Tonkawa, OK) **10247**
Tonopah Times-Bonanza & Goldfield News
(Tonopah, NV) **10199**
Tooele Transcript-Bulletin (Tooele, UT) **10283**
Topics Sun Wave (Los Angeles, CA) **10077**
Toppenish Review (Toppenish, WA) **10293**
Torrington Telegram (Torrington, WY) **10309**
† Total, The (Heflin, AL)
† Town & Country (Bradford, PA)
Town & Country (Pennsburg, PA) **10257**
Town & Country Weekly (Ottawa, IL) **10125**
Town-Crier (West Palm Beach, FL) **10100**
Town 'n Country News (Tampa, FL) **10099**
Town Crier (Stockbridge, MI) **10175**
Town Crier, The (La Porte, IN) **10133**
Towne & Country Shopper
(Columbus, KS) **10143**
Towne Courier (East Lansing, MI) **10169**
Town of Paradise Valley Independent
(Scottsdale, AZ) **10064**
Township Times (Saginaw, MI) **10174**
Town Talk (Folsom, PA) **10253**
Town Talk (Media, PA) **10255**
Town Topics (Princeton, NJ) **10206**
Towson Times (Towson, MD) **10160**
Tracy Headlight-Herald (Tracy, MN) **10184**
Tradewinds (St. John, VI) **10284**
Traer Star-Clipper (Traer, IA) **10142**
† Transcript-Telegram (Holyoke, MA)
Transcript, The (Dover, NH) **10199**
Transcript, The (Morrisville, VT) **10284**
Transylvania Times, The (Brevard, NC) **10227**
Traveler/Watchman (Southold, NY) **10223**
Trenton Sun, The (Trenton, IL) **10128**
Trenton Tribune (Trenton, TX) **10281**
Tri-City Independent (Margate, FL) **10096**
Tri-City Ledger (Flomaton, AL) **10059**
Tri-City News (Cumberland, KY) **10147**
Tri-City Record, The (Watervliet, MI) **10176**
Tri-City Reporter (Dyer, TN) **10266**
† Tri-City Times (Geraldine, AL)
Tri-City Times (Imlay City, MI) **10171**
Tri-City Trib (Cozad, NE) **10197**

Tri-City Tribune (Marked Tree, AR) **10066**
Tri-County Advertiser (Brockport, NY) **10210**
Tri-County Banner (Knightstown, N) **10133**
Tri-County Citizen (Chesaning, MI) **10168**
Tri-County Journal (Pacific, MO) **10192**
Tri-County News (Elmwood, IL) **10116**
Tri-County News (Edinburgh, IN) **10130**
Tri-County News (Lockport, NY) **10217**
Tri-County News (Knoxville, TN) **10267**
Tri-County News (Osseo, WI) **10303**
Tri-County Press (Cincinnati, OH) **10236**
Tri-County Press (Cuba City, WI) **10299**
Tri-County Record (Rushford, MN) **10182**
Tri-County Times, The (Slater, IA) **10141**
Tri-County Trader (Waldron, AR) **10068**
Tri-State Advertiser (Palm Desert, CA) **10079**
Tri-Town News (Sidney, NY) **10223**
Tri-Town Transcript (Ipswich, MA) **10162**
Tri-Village News (Columbus, OH) **10238**
Tribune (Deer Park, WA) **10291**
Tribune-Courier (Ontario, OH) **10242**
Tribune-Times (Fountain Inn, SC) **10262**
Tribune Courier (Benton, KY) **10146**
Tribune Plus (Royal Oak, MI) **10174**
Tribune Press Reporter (Glenwood
City, WI) **10300**
Tribune Shopping News (New
Lexington, OH) **10242**
Tribune, The (Monument, CO) **10089**
Tribune, The (Melbourne, FL) **10096**
Tribune, The (Elkin, NC) **10227**
Tribune, The (Tabor City, NC) **10231**
Tribune, The (Bethany, OK) **10245**
Tri City Register (Riverton, IL) **10127**
Trinity Journal (Weaverville, CA) **10084**
Troy-Somerset Gazette (Troy, MI) **10175**
Troy Eccentric (Rochester Hills, MI) **10174**
Troy Free Press & Silex Index
(Troy, MO) **10194**
True Citizen, The (Waynesboro, GA) **10106**
Trumann Democrat (Trumann, AR) **10068**
Trumansburg Free Press
(Trumansburg, NY) **10224**
Trumbull Times (Monroe, CT) **10091**
Tucker-DeKalb Neighbor, The
(Atlanta, GA) **10101**
Tullahoma News (Tullahoma, TN) **10270**
Tundra Drums (Bethel, AK) **10062**
Tundra Times (Anchorage, AK) **10062**
Tunkhannock New Age-Examiner
(Tunkhannock, PA) **10259**
Tupper Lake Free Press & Herald (Tupper
Lake, NY) **10224**
Turtle Lake Times, The (Turtle
Lake, WI) **10306**
Turtle Mountain Star, The (Rolla, ND) **10233**

Tuscola County Advertiser (Caro, MI)　**10168**
Tuscola Review (Tuscola, IL)　**10128**
Tuskegee News (Tuskegee, AL)　**10062**
Tustin News (Santa Ana, CA)　**10082**
Twin-City News, The
　(Batesburg-Leesville, SC)　**10261**
Twin Cities Reader (Minneapolis, MN)　**10180**
Twin Cities Times (Corte Madera, CA)　**10071**
Twin City News, The
　(Chattahoochee, FL)　**10094**
▼Twinsburg Sun, The (Cleveland, OH)　**10237**
Tyler County Booster (Woodville, TX)　**10282**
Tyler Star News (Sistersville, WV)　**10296**
Tylertown Times (Tylertown, MS)　**10187**
Tyler Tribute (Tyler, MN)　**10184**
UA This Week (Columbus, OH)　**10238**
Uinta County Herald (Evanston, WY)　**10308**
Uintah Basin Standard (Roosevelt, UT)　**10283**
Ulster County Townsman
　(Woodstock, NY)　**10225**
Ulysses News (Ulysses, KS)　**10146**
Umpqua Free Press (Myrtle Creek, OR)　**10249**
Underwood News (Underwood, ND)　**10233**
Unida Latina (Oxford, PA)　**10257**
Union County Advocate
　(Morganfield, KY)　**10150**
Uniondale Beacon (Hicksville, NY)　**10216**
Union Enterprise (Plainwell, MI)　**10174**
Union Leader (Union, NJ)　**10207**
Union Press-Courier (Patton, PA)　**10257**
† Union Shopper, The (Arcata, CA)
Union Springs Herald (Union
　Springs, AL)　**10062**
† Union, The (Arcata, CA)
Unionville Republican, The
　(Unionville, MO)　**10194**
University Herald (Seattle, WA)　**10293**
Upper Arlington News (Columbus, OH)　**10238**
Upper Country News-Reporter
　(Cambridge, ID)　**10107**
Upper Darby Press (Drexel Hill, PA)　**10252**
Upper Dauphin Sentinel
　(Millersburg, PA)　**10255**
Upper Rogue Independent (Eagle
　Point, OR)　**10248**
Uptown San Diego Examiner (San
　Diego, CA)　**10081**
Utica Herald (Utica, OH)　**10243**
Uvalde Leader-News (Uvalde, TX)　**10281**
Vadnais Heights Press (St. Paul, MN)　**10184**
Vailsburg Leader (Maplewood, NJ)　**10204**
Vail Trail (Eagle-Vail, CO)　**10086**
Valders Journal (Valders, WI)　**10306**
Valdese News (Morganton, NC)　**10229**
Valdez Vanguard (Valdez, AK)　**10063**

Valencia County News-Bulletin
　(Belen, NM)　**10208**
Valentine Newspaper (Valentine, NE)　**10198**
Valley Advocate (Hatfield, MA)　**10162**
Valley Banner, The (Elkton, VA)　**10286**
Valley Falls Vindicator (Valley Falls, KS)　**10146**
Valley Farmer, The (Bay City, MI)　**10167**
Valley Gazette (Shelton, CT)　**10091**
Valley Gazette (Lansford, PA)　**10254**
Valley Herald, The (Spokane, WA)　**10293**
Valley Journal (Carbondale, CO)　**10086**
Valley Log, The (Orbisonia, PA)　**10256**
Valley News (Meridian, ID)　**10108**
Valley News (Elizabethtown, NY)　**10213**
Valley News (Fulton, NY)　**10214**
Valley News, The (Endwell, NY)　**10213**
Valley News, The (Jefferson, OH)　**10240**
Valley Post (Anderson, CA)　**10069**
Valley Reporter, The (Waitsfield, VT)　**10284**
Valley Roadrunner (Valley Center, CA)　**10084**
Valley Stream Courier (Freeport, NY)　**10214**
Valley Stream Herald (Lawrence, NY)　**10217**
Valley Stream Maileader (Mineola, NY)　**10219**
Valley Sun (Wasilla, AK)　**10063**
Valley Sun, The (Scottsboro, AL)　**10061**
Valley Times (Moreno Valley, CA)　**10078**
Valley Times-Star (Newville, PA)　**10256**
Valley Town Crier (McAllen, TX)　**10278**
Valley Trader (Lewisburg, PA)　**10254**
Valley Value Shopper (Spring
　Valley, WI)　**10305**
Valley Vantage (Sherman Oaks, CA)　**10083**
Valparaiso Guide (Portage, IN)　**10135**
Van Buren County Advertiser
　(Gobles, MI)　**10170**
Vandalia Leader-Union (Vandalia, IL)　**10128**
Vandergrift News (Vandergrift, PA)　**10259**
Van Horn Advocate (Van Horn, TX)　**10281**
Vashon-Maury Island Beachcomber
　(Vashon, WA)　**10293**
Vassar Pioneer Times (Vassar, MI)　**10175**
Vega Enterprise, The (Vega, TX)　**10281**
Venice-Marina News (Santa
　Monica, CA)　**10082**
Venice Gondolier (Venice, FL)　**10100**
† Ventura Bulletin, The (Los Angeles, CA)
Ventura County & Coast Reporter
　(Ventura, CA)　**10084**
Verde Independent (Cottonwood, AZ)　**10063**
Vermilion Photojournal (Vermilion, OH)　**10243**
Vermont News Guide (Manchester
　Center, VT)　**10284**
Vermont Times (Shelburne, VT)　**10284**
Vernal Express (Vernal, UT)　**10283**
Vernon County Broadcaster
　(Viroqua, WI)　**10306**

Vernon Hills News (Grayslake, IL) **10119**
Vernon Hills Review (Bannockburn, IL) **10110**
Verona-Cedar Grove Times
  (Verona, NJ) **10207**
Verona Press (Verona, WI) **10306**
Versailles Leader-Statesman
  (Versailles, MO) **10194**
Versailles Policy, The (Versailles, OH) **10243**
Versailles Republican (Versailles, IN) **10136**
Vestal Town Crier (Conklin, NY) **10212**
Vevay Reveille-Enterprise (Vevay, IN) **10136**
† Victor-Farmington Herald (Webster, NY)
Victor Echo (Victor, IA) **10142**
Victor Valley Advertiser (Palm
  Desert, CA) **10079**
† Victor Valley Living (Hesperia, CA)
Vidorian, The (Vidor, TX) **10281**
Vienna Times (Reston, VA) **10289**
Vienna Times, The (Vienna, IL) **10128**
Vilas County News-Review (Eagle
  River, WI) **10299**
Village Advocate (Chapel Hill, NC) **10227**
Village Beacon-Record, The
  (Setauket, NY) **10222**
† Village Journal (Osterville, MA)
Village News (Gaithersburg, MD) **10158**
Villager (St. Paul, MN) **10184**
Villager Newspaper (Austin, TX) **10271**
Villager, The (New York, NY) **10220**
Villager, The (Syracuse, NY) **10224**
Villager, The (Moscow, PA) **10255**
Village Times, The (Setauket, NY) **10222**
Village Voice, The (New York, NY) **10220**
Villa Park Argus (Elmhurst, IL) **10116**
Villa Rican (Villa Rica, GA) **10106**
Ville Platte Gazette (Ville Platte, LA) **10155**
† Vincennes Valley Advance (Vincennes, IN)
Vindicator, The (Liberty, TX) **10278**
Vineyard Gazette (Edgartown, MA) **10161**
† Vinton County Courier (McArthur, OH)
Vinton Messenger (Vinton, VA) **10289**
Virginia Beach Sun (Virginia Beach, VA) **10289**
Virginia Gazette (Beardstown, IL) **10111**
Virginia Gazette (Williamsburg, VA) **10290**
Virginia Mountaineer (Grundy, VA) **10286**
Virginian-Leader (Pearisburg, VA) **10288**
† Vista Press (Kansas City, MO)
Voice-Tribune, The (Louisville, KY) **10149**
Voice Ledger, The (Millbrook, NY) **10218**
Voice of the Valley (Maple Valley, WA) **10292**
Voices (Southbury, CT) **10091**
Voice, The (Phoenixville, PA) **10258**
Waco Citizen, The (Waco, TX) **10281**
Waconia Patriot (Waconia, MN) **10184**
Wadena Pioneer Journal (Wadena, MN) **10184**
Wagoner Tribune, The (Wagoner, OK) **10247**

Wahkiakum County Eagle, The
  (Cathlamet, WA) **10291**
Wahoo Newspaper (Wahoo, NE) **10198**
Wake Weekly, The (Wake Forest, NC) **10231**
Wakulla News (Crawfordville, FL) **10094**
Walker-Westside Advance (Jenison, MI) **10171**
Walker County Messenger (La
  Fayette, GA) **10104**
Wallace Enterprise (Wallace, NC) **10231**
† Wallace Miner (Kellogg, ID)
Waller County News-Citizen
  (Hempstead, TX) **10276**
Wallis News-Review (Wallis, TX) **10281**
Wallkill Valley Times, The (Walden, NY) **10224**
Walpole Times, The (Walpole, MA) **10166**
Walsh County Press (Park River, ND) **10233**
Walsh County Record, The
  (Grafton, ND) **10232**
Walton Tribune (Monroe, GA) **10105**
Walworth Times, The (Walworth, WI) **10306**
Wampum Saver (Show Low, AZ) **10064**
Wantagh-Seaford Citizen (Bellmore, NY) **10210**
Wapato Independent (Wapato, WA) **10294**
Wareham Courier (Marion, MA) **10163**
Ware River News (Ware, MA) **10166**
Warner Center News (Woodland
  Hills, CA) **10085**
Warren-Newport Press (Grayslake, IL) **10119**
Warren Record, The (Warrenton, NC) **10231**
Warrensburg-Lake George News
  (Elizabethtown, NY) **10213**
Warren Sheaf (Warren, MN) **10184**
Warren Times Gazette (Warren, RI) **10261**
† Warrenton Banner (Warrenton, MO)
Warrenton News-Journal
  (Warrenton, MO) **10194**
Warrenville Free Press (West
  Chicago, IL) **10128**
Warsaw-Faison News (Wallace, NC) **10231**
Warsaw Benton County Enterprise
  (Warsaw, MO) **10195**
Warwick Advertiser, The (Warwick, NY) **10224**
Warwick Beacon (Warwick, RI) **10261**
Warwick Valley Dispatch (Warwick, NY) **10224**
Wasco Tribune (Wasco, CA) **10084**
Waseca County News (Waseca, MN) **10184**
Washburn County Register (Shell
  Lake, WI) **10305**
Washburn Leader (Metamora, IL) **10123**
Washington City Paper
  (Washington, DC) **10093**
Washington County Edition (Salem, IN) **10135**
Washington County News (Chatom, AL) **10058**
Washington County News
  (Washington, KS) **10146**

Washington County News
(Abingdon, VA) **10284**
Washington Courier (Washington, IL) **10128**
Washington Missourian
(Washington, MO) **10195**
Washington News-Reporter
(Washington, GA) **10106**
Washington Reporter (Morton, IL) **10124**
Waterford News (Winton, CA) **10085**
Waterford Post (Waterford, WI) **10306**
Waterfront of Missaukee County (Lake
City, MI) **10172**
Waterloo Republic-Times (Waterloo, IL) **10128**
Watertown Press (Somerville, MA) **10165**
Watertown Sun (Needham, MA) **10164**
Watkins Review & Express (Watkins
Glen, NY) **10225**
Watonga Republican, The
(Watonga, OK) **10247**
Wauconda Leader (Grayslake, IL) **10119**
Waukon Standard (Waukon, IA) **10142**
Waunakee Tribune (Waunakee, WI) **10306**
Waupun Leader News (Waupun, WI) **10306**
Waushara Argus (Wautoma, WI) **10307**
Wauwatosa News-Times
(Wauwatosa, WI) **10308**
Waverly Bremer County Independent
(Waverly, IA) **10142**
Waverly Democrat (Waverly, IA) **10142**
Waverly Journal (Waverly, IL) **10128**
Wayland-Weston Town Crier
(Needham, MA) **10164**
Wayne County Journal-Banner
(Piedmont, MO) **10192**
Wayne County Mail (Webster, NY) **10225**
Wayne County News (Waynesboro, MS) **10187**
Wayne County News (Waynesboro, TN) **10270**
Wayne County News (Wayne, WV) **10296**
Wayne County Outlook (Monticello, KY) **10150**
Wayne County Star (Lyons, NY) **10217**
Wayne Eagle (Wayne, MI) **10176**
Wayne Herald (Wayne, NE) **10198**
Wayne Today (Butler, NJ) **10201**
Wayne Wilson News Leader
(Fremont, NC) **10228**
Wayzata/Orono/Long Lake Sun-Sailor
(Minnetonka, MN) **10180**
Weakley County Press (Martin, TN) **10268**
Webster County Citizen (Seymour, MO) **10193**
Webster Herald (Webster, NY) **10225**
Webster Post, The (Webster, NY) **10225**
Webster Progress-Times (Eupora, MS) **10186**
Webster Reporter & Farmer
(Webster, SD) **10265**
Webster Republican (Webster
Springs, WV) **10296**

Wednesday Journal of Oak Park & River Forest
(Oak Park, IL) **10125**
Wednesday Magazine (Kansas
City, MO) **10190**
Weed Press (Weed, CA) **10084**
Weehawken Reporter (Hoboken, NJ) **10203**
† Weekender Enquirer (Boonville, IN)
Weekender, The (Whitinsville, MA) **10166**
† Weekender, The (Bronx, NY)
Weekender, The (Lexington, VA) **10287**
Weekend Flyer, The (Plainfield, IN) **10135**
Weekend News (Montrose, PA) **10255**
Weekly Almanac, The (Honesdale, PA) **10253**
Weekly Calistogan (Calistoga, CA) **10070**
Weekly Challenger (St. Petersburg, FL) **10099**
Weekly News (Marksville, LA) **10154**
Weekly Observer, The (Hemingway, SC) **10262**
Weekly Packet (Blue Hill, ME) **10155**
Weekly Planet (Tampa, FL) **10099**
Weekly Post (Rainsville, AL) **10061**
Weekly Press (Baton Rouge, LA) **10152**
Weekly Recorder, The (Claysville, PA) **10252**
Weekly Reminder (Paulding, OH) **10242**
† Weekly Territorial (Tucson, AZ)
Weimar Mercury (Weimar, TX) **10281**
Weisbeck, The (Alden, NY) **10209**
Weiser Signal American (Weiser, ID) **10109**
Wellesley Townsman (Wellesley, MA) **10166**
Wellington Royal Palm Beach Forum
(Wellington, FL) **10100**
Wellsboro Gazette (Wellsboro, PA) **10260**
Wells Mirror, The (Wells, MN) **10184**
† Wellston Sentry (Wellston, OH)
Wellston Telegram, The (Wellston, OH) **10244**
Wenona Index (Henry, IL) **10119**
Wentzville Journal (Wentzville, MO) **10195**
West Alabama Gazette (Millport, AL) **10060**
West Allis Star (Wauwatosa, WI) **10308**
West Bloomfield Eccentric, The
(Birmingham, MI) **10167**
West Boca Times (Deerfield Beach, FL) **10094**
West Bridgewater Star
(Middleboro, MA) **10163**
Westbury Times (Mineola, NY) **10219**
West Carroll Gazette (Oak Grove, LA) **10154**
Westchester Herald (Oak Park, IL) **10125**
Westchester Observer (Santa
Monica, CA) **10082**
Westchester Star (Los Angeles, CA) **10077**
West Columbia Brazoria County News (West
Columbia, TX) **10281**
West Cook County Press (Elmhurst, IL) **10116**
West County Journal (St. Louis, MO) **10194**
Western Breeze (Cut Bank, MT) **10195**
▼Western Edition (San Francisco, CA) **10081**
Western Hills Press (Cincinnati, OH) **10236**

Western News (Libby, MT) **10195**
Western Springs Doings (Hinsdale, IL) **10120**
Western Star (Bessemer, AL) **10057**
Western Star (Lebanon, OH) **10240**
Western Wayne News (Cambridge
   City, IN) **10130**
Western World (Bandon, OR) **10248**
Westerville News & Public Opinion
   (Westerville, OH) **10244**
West Essex Tribune (Livingston, NJ) **10203**
West Fargo Pioneer (West Fargo, ND) **10233**
Westfield Enterprise (Fishers, IN) **10131**
Westfield Leader (Westfield, NJ) **10208**
Westfield Republican (Westfield, NY) **10225**
Westford Eagle (Chelmsford, MA) **10161**
▼West Geauga Sun (Cleveland, OH) **10237**
West Hartford News (West
   Hartford, CT) **10092**
West Haven News (Milford, CT) **10091**
West Hempstead Beacon
   (Hicksville, NY) **10216**
Westine Report (Union Grove, WI) **10306**
West Kentucky News (Paducah, KY) **10150**
Westlake Picayune (Austin, TX) **10271**
Westlaker Times, The (Rocky
   River, OH) **10242**
Westland Eagle (Wayne, MI) **10176**
Westland Observer (Livonia, MI) **10172**
West Liberty Index (West Liberty, IA) **10142**
West Life (Cleveland, OH) **10237**
West Linn Tidings (Lake Oswego, OR) **10249**
West Los Angeles Independent (Santa
   Monica, CA) **10082**
West Martin Weekly News
   (Sherburn, MN) **10183**
West Milton Record (West Milton, OH) **10244**
Westminster Window
   (Westminster, CO) **10089**
Westmont Progress (Downers
   Grove, IL) **10115**
Westmoreland News (Montross, VA) **10287**
Westmore News (Port Chester, NY) **10221**
West Morris Star-Journal
   (Ledgewood, NJ) **10203**
West News (West, TX) **10281**
Weston Democrat, The (Weston, WV) **10297**
Weston Forum, The (Weston, CT) **10092**
West Orange Chronicle (Orange, NJ) **10205**
West Orange Times (Winter
   Garden, FL) **10100**
Westosha Report (Twin Lakes, WI) **10306**
† West Plains Tribune (Spokane, WA)
West Point News (West Point, NE) **10199**
Westport News (Westport, CT) **10092**
West Proviso Herald (Oak Park, IL) **10125**

West Roxbury Transcript
   (Dedham, MA) **10161**
West Sacramento News-Ledger (West
   Sacramento, CA) **10085**
West San Bernardino Advertiser (Palm
   Desert, CA) **10079**
West Schuylkill Herald (Tower City, PA) **10259**
West Seattle Herald (Seattle, WA) **10293**
West Seneca Bee (Williamsville, NY) **10225**
West Side Advance (Kerman, CA) **10074**
Westside Enterprise (Greenfield, IN) **10132**
Westside Flyer (Indianapolis, IN) **10133**
West Side Journal (Port Allen, LA) **10154**
Westside Messenger (Speedway, IN) **10135**
Westside Record-Journal
   (Ferndale, WA) **10291**
Westsider, The (New York, NY) **10220**
West Side Sun News (Cleveland, OH) **10237**
West Side Times (Buffalo, NY) **10211**
West Springfield Record (West
   Springfield, MA) **10166**
West St. Paul/Mendota Heights Sun-Current
   (Burnsville, MN) **10177**
West Suburban Post (Chicago, IL) **10113**
West Toledo Herald (Toledo, OH) **10243**
West Valley Courier (Hillsboro, OR) **10249**
West Valley Eagle (Bountiful, UT) **10282**
West Valley News (Magna, UT) **10282**
West Valley News/Sunday Advance
   (Flint, MI) **10169**
West Valley View (Avondale, AZ) **10063**
Westville Indicator (Westville, IN) **10136**
West Virginia Hillbilly (Richwood, WV) **10296**
Westword (Denver, CO) **10086**
Wethersfield Post (West Hartford, CT) **10092**
Wet Mountain Tribune (Westcliffe, CO) **10089**
Wetumpka Herald (Wetumpka, AL) **10062**
Wetzel Chronicle (New
   Martinsville, WV) **10295**
Wewoka Times (Wewoka, OK) **10247**
Weymouth News (Marshfield, MA) **10163**
Weymouth News & Gazette
   (Braintree, MA) **10161**
Wharton Journal-Spectator
   (Wharton, TX) **10282**
Wheaton Leader (Glen Ellyn, IL) **10118**
Wheaton Press (Bloomingdale, IL) **10111**
Wheaton Sun (Naperville, IL) **10124**
† Wheat Ridge Sentinel (Lakewood, CO)
Wheeler County Independent
   (Burwell, NE) **10197**
Wheels 'N Deals (Columbia, MO) **10189**
Whidbey News-Times (Oak Harbor, WA) **10292**
Whitefish Bay Herald (Wauwatosa, WI) **10308**
Whitefish Pilot (Whitefish, MT) **10196**
White Hall Journal (Pine Bluff, AR) **10067**

Whitehall News (Columbus, OH) **10238**
Whitehall Times (Whitehall, NY) **10225**
Whitehall Times (Whitehall, WI) **10308**
White Lake Beacon (Whitehall, MI) **10176**
White Mountain Independent (Show Low, AZ) **10064**
White Oak Independent (White Oak, TX) **10282**
White River Current (Calico Rock, AR) **10065**
▼White River Gazette (Fishers, IN) **10131**
White River Journal (Des Arc, AR) **10066**
White Settlement News (Fort Worth, TX) **10275**
Whiteside Shopper (Fulton, IL) **10117**
Whitestone Times, The (Bayside, NY) **10210**
Whiteville News Reporter (Whiteville, NC) **10231**
Whitewright Sun, The (Whitewright, TX) **10282**
Whitley Republican News Journal (Williamsburg, KY) **10152**
Whitman County Gazette (Colfax, WA) **10291**
Whitman Times (Stoughton, MA) **10166**
Whitney Point Reporter (Greene, NY) **10215**
Wick-Qua-Boag Weekly (Spencer, MA) **10165**
Wickenburg Sun (Wickenburg, AZ) **10065**
Wiggins Courier, The (Wiggins, CO) **10089**
Wilcox Progressive Era (Camden, AL) **10058**
Wildwood Leader (Wildwood, NJ) **10208**
† Wilkes-Barre Sunday Independent (Wilkes Barre, PA)
Willamette Week (Portland, OR) **10250**
Willapa Harbor Herald (Raymond, WA) **10292**
Willard Times-Junction (Willard, OH) **10244**
Williams Grand Canyon News (Williams, AZ) **10065**
Williamson County Sun (Georgetown, TX) **10275**
Williamson Leader, The (Franklin, TN) **10266**
Williamston Enterprise (Williamston, NC) **10231**
Williamsville Sun (Riverton, IL) **10127**
Williston Plains Reporter (Williston, ND) **10233**
Willowbrook Doings (Hinsdale, IL) **10120**
Willow Grove Guide (Hatboro, PA) **10253**
Willows Journal (Willows, CA) **10085**
Wilmette Life (Glenview, IL) **10118**
Wilmington-Tewksbury Town Crier (Wilmington, MA) **10166**
Wilmington Advocate, The (Wilmington, IL) **10129**
Wilmington Defender (Wilmington, DE) **10092**
Wilmington Express (Wilmington, IL) **10129**
Wilmington Free Press (Wilmington, IL) **10129**
Wilmington Journal (Wilmington, NC) **10231**
Wilson County Citizen (Fredonia, KS) **10143**
Wilson World, The (Lebanon, TN) **10268**

Wilton Bulletin (Wilton, CT) **10092**
Wimberley Valley-News (Wimberley, TX) **10282**
Winchendon Courier (Winchendon, MA) **10167**
Winchester Star (Winchester, MA) **10167**
Winder News (Winder, GA) **10106**
Windham Journal (Windham, NY) **10225**
Windom Cottonwood County Citizen (Windom, MN) **10185**
Wind River News (Lander, WY) **10309**
Windsor Journal (West Hartford, CT) **10092**
Windsor Locks Journal (Bristol, CT) **10090**
Windsor Review (Windsor, MO) **10195**
Windsor Standard (Conklin, NY) **10212**
Winfield Estate (Glen Ellyn, IL) **10118**
Winfield Press (West Chicago, IL) **10128**
Winkler County News (Kermit, TX) **10277**
Winneconne News (Winneconne, WI) **10308**
Winnetka Talk (Glenview, IL) **10118**
Winnfield Winn Parish Enterprise (Winnfield, LA) **10155**
Winnsboro News (Winnsboro, TX) **10282**
Winona Times (Winona, MS) **10187**
Winslow Mail (Winslow, AZ) **10065**
Winter Park-Maitland Observer (Winter Park, FL) **10100**
Winter Park Manifest (Winter Park, CO) **10089**
Winterset Madisonian (Winterset, IA) **10142**
† Winter Visitor Independent (Mesa, AZ)
Winton Times (Winton, CA) **10085**
Wisconsin Dells Events (Wisconsin Dells, WI) **10308**
Wisconsin State Farmer (Waupaca, WI) **10306**
Wise County Messenger (Decatur, TX) **10273**
Wittenberg Enterprise News (Wittenberg, WI) **10308**
Woburn Advocate (Woburn, MA) **10167**
Wonewoc Reporter (Elroy, WI) **10300**
Woodbury-South Maplewood Review (St. Paul, MN) **10184**
Wood County Democrat (Quitman, TX) **10280**
Wood Dale Press (Elmhurst, IL) **10116**
Woodford County Journal (Eureka, IL) **10116**
Woodford Sun (Versailles, KY) **10152**
Woodland Lewis River News (Woodland, WA) **10294**
Woodridge Progress (Downers Grove, IL) **10115**
Wood River Journal (Hailey, ID) **10107**
Woodruff County Monitor Leader Advocate (McCrory, AR) **10066**
Woodside Herald (Sunnyside, NY) **10223**
Woodstock Independent, The (Woodstock, IL) **10129**
Worcester County Messenger (Pocomoke City, MD) **10159**
Worcester Magazine (Worcester, MA) **10167**

Worth-Palos Reporter (Palos Heights, IL) **10126**

Worth-Ridge Reporter (Palos Heights, IL) **10126**

Worth Citizen (Midlothian, IL) **10124**

Worthington Suburbia News (Columbus, OH) **10238**

Worthington Times, The (Worthington, IN) **10136**

Wrangell Sentinel (Wrangell, AK) **10063**

Wray Gazette (Wray, CO) **10089**

Wright County Journal-Press (Buffalo, MN) **10177**

Wrightsville Headlight, The (Wrightsville, GA) **10106**

† Wrova Reporter (Galva, IL)

Wyandotte West (Kansas City, KS) **10144**

Wylie News, The (Wylie, TX) **10282**

Wynne Progress (Wynne, AR) **10068**

Wyoming Advance (Jenison, MI) **10172**

Wyoming State Journal (Lander, WY) **10309**

Yadkin Ripple, The (Yadkinville, NC) **10232**

Yale News, The (Yale, OK) **10247**

Yancey Common Times Journal (Burnsville, NC) **10227**

Yankee Trader (Coram, NY) **10212**

Yardley News (Yardley, PA) **10260**

† Yarmouth Sun (Yarmouth Port, MA)

Yazoo Herald (Yazoo City, MS) **10187**

Yoakum Herald-Times & Four Star Reporter (Yoakum, TX) **10282**

Yonkers Home News & Times (Yonkers, NY) **10226**

York County Coast Star (Kennebunk, ME) **10156**

York Town Crier (Yorktown, VA) **10290**

Yorkville Enquirer (York, SC) **10264**

▼Your Paper (Spartanburg, SC) **10264**

Yucaipa & Calimesa News-Mirror (Yucaipa, CA) **10085**

Yucca Valley Hi-Desert Star (Yucca Valley, CA) **10085**

Yukon Review (Yukon, OK) **10247**

Yuma Pioneer (Yuma, CO) **10089**

Zachary Plainsman-News (Zachary, LA) **10155**

Zanesville Muskingum Advertiser (Zanesville, OH) **10244**

Zebulon Record, The (Zebulon, NC) **10232**

Zephyrhills News (Zephyrhills, FL) **10100**

Zion-Benton News (Zion, IL) **10129**

† Zionsville Eagle (Indianapolis, IN)

Zionsville Times Sentinel (Zionsville, IN) **10136**

1590 Broadcaster (Nashua, NH) **10200**

Geographic Index

ALABAMA

Abbeville Herald (Abbeville) **10057**
Advertiser-Gleam (Guntersville) **10059**
† Alabama Journal (Montgomery)
Alabama Messenger (Birmingham) **10057**
Alexander City Outlook (Alexander City) **9955**
Andalusia Star News (Andalusia) **9955**
Anniston Star (Anniston) **9955**
Arab Tribune (Arab) **10057**
Atmore Advance (Atmore) **10057**
† Azalea City News & Review (Bayou Labatre)
Baldwin Times (Bay Minette) **10057**
† Birmingham Free Press (Birmingham)
Birmingham News (Birmingham) **9955**
Birmingham Post-Herald (Birmingham) **9955**
Birmingham World (Birmingham) **10057**
Blount Countian, The (Oneonta) **10061**
Brewton Standard, The (Brewton) **10058**
Butler Choctaw Advocate (Butler) **10058**
Butler County News (Georgiana) **10059**
Centreville Press (Centreville) **10058**
Cherokee County Herald (Centre) **10058**
Clanton Advertiser (Clanton) **10058**
Clarke County Democrat (Grove Hill) **10059**
Clay Times Journal (Lineville) **10060**
Cleburne News (Heflin) **10060**
Colbert County Reporter (Tuscumbia) **10062**
Community News, The (Dora) **10058**
Community Shopper (Birmingham) **10058**
Courier Journal (Florence) **10059**

Cullman Times (Cullman) **9955**
Cullman Tribune (Cullman) **10058**
Dadeville Record (Alexander City) **10057**
Daily Home (Talladega) **9956**
Daily Sentinel, The (Scottsboro) **9956**
Decatur Daily (Decatur) **9955**
Democrat-Reporter, The (Linden) **10060**
Demopolis Times (Demopolis) **10058**
Dothan Eagle (Dothan) **9955**
East Lauderdale News (Rogersville) **10061**
Enterprise Ledger (Enterprise) **9956**
Eufaula Tribune (Eufaula) **10058**
Evergreen Courant, The (Evergreen) **10058**
Fairhope Courier, The (Fairhope) **10059**
Florala News, The (Florala) **10059**
Franklin County Plus (Russellville) **10061**
Franklin County Times (Russellville) **10061**
Gadsden Times (Gadsden) **9956**
Geneva County Reaper (Geneva) **10059**
Greene County Independent (Eutaw) **10058**
Greensboro Watchman, The (Greensboro) **10059**
Greenville Advocate, The (Greenville) **10059**
Hanceville Herald (Hanceville) **10059**
Hartselle Enquirer (Hartselle) **10059**
Headland Observer (Headland) **10060**
† Huntsville News (Huntsville)
Huntsville Times, The (Huntsville) **9956**
Independent, The (Robertsdale) **10061**

Islander, The (Gulf Shores) **10059**
Jacksonville News (Jacksonville) **10060**
Jasper Daily Mountain Eagle (Jasper) **9956**
Journal Record (Hamilton) **10059**
Lafayette Sun, The (Lafayette) **10060**
Lamar Democrat (Vernon) **10062**
Lamar Leader (Sulligent) **10061**
Lee County Eagle, The (Auburn) **10057**
Leeds News (Leeds) **10060**
Luverne Journal & News (Luverne) **10060**
Madison County Record (Madison) **10060**
Marion Times-Standard (Marion) **10060**
Messenger, The (Troy) **9956**
Mobile Beacon (Mobile) **10060**
Mobile Register, The (Mobile) **9956**
Monroe Journal (Monroeville) **10060**
Montgomery Advertiser (Montgomery) **9956**
Montgomery Independent
  (Montgomery) **10060**
Moulton Advertiser (Moulton) **10060**
Moundville Times (Moundville) **10060**
News-Courier (Athens) **9955**
† News Herald, The (Mobile)
North Jackson Progress (Stevenson) **10061**
North Jefferson News (Gardendale) **10059**
Northwest Alabamian (Haleyville) **10059**
Onlooker, The (Foley) **10059**
Opelika-Auburn News (Opelika) **9956**
Opp News (Opp) **10061**
Over the Mountain Journal
  (Birmingham) **10058**
Phenix-Citizen (Phenix City) **10061**
Pickens County Herald (Carrollton) **10058**
Piedmont Journal-Independent
  (Piedmont) **10061**
Prattville Progress (Prattville) **10061**
Randolph Leader (Roanoke) **10061**
Red Bay News (Red Bay) **10061**
Samford Crimson (Birmingham) **10058**
Samson Ledger (Samson) **10061**
Sand Mountain Reporter (Albertville) **10057**
Selma Times-Journal (Selma) **9956**
Shelby County Reporter (Columbiana) **10058**
South Alabamian (Jackson) **10060**
Southern Star (Ozark) **10061**
Standard & Times (Tuscumbia) **10062**
St. Clair News-Aegis (Pell City) **10061**
Sumter County Record-Journal, The
  (Livingston) **10060**
Tallassee Tribune (Tallassee) **10062**
Thrifty Nickel (Birmingham) **10058**
Times-Journal, The (Fort Payne) **9956**
Times Daily (Florence) **9956**
Times Record (Fayette) **10059**
† Total, The (Heflin)
Tri-City Ledger (Flomaton) **10059**

† Tri-City Times (Geraldine)
Tuscaloosa News, The (Tuscaloosa) **9957**
Tuskegee News (Tuskegee) **10062**
Union Springs Herald (Union Springs) **10062**
Valley Sun, The (Scottsboro) **10061**
Valley Times-News (Lanett) **9956**
Washington County News (Chatom) **10058**
Weekly Post (Rainsville) **10061**
West Alabama Gazette (Millport) **10060**
Western Star (Bessemer) **10057**
Wetumpka Herald (Wetumpka) **10062**
Wilcox Progressive Era (Camden) **10058**

ALASKA

Anchorage Daily News (Anchorage) **9957**
Capital City Weekly (Juneau) **10062**
Chilkat Valley News (Haines) **10062**
Cordova Times (Cordova) **10062**
Daily Sitka Sentinel (Sitka) **9957**
Fairbanks Daily News-Miner (Fairbanks) **9957**
Frontiersman, The (Wasilla) **10063**
Great Lander Bush Mailer (Anchorage) **10062**
Homer News (Homer) **10062**
Juneau Empire (Juneau) **9957**
Ketchikan Daily News (Ketchikan) **9957**
Kodiak Daily Mirror (Kodiak) **9957**
† New Alaskan (Ketchikan)
Nome Nugget (Nome) **10062**
Peninsula Clarion (Kenai) **9957**
Petersburg Pilot (Petersburg) **10062**
Seward Phoenix Log (Seward) **10062**
Tundra Drums (Bethel) **10062**
Tundra Times (Anchorage) **10062**
Valdez Vanguard (Valdez) **10063**
Valley Sun (Wasilla) **10063**
Wrangell Sentinel (Wrangell) **10063**

AMERICAN SAMOA

Samoa News (Pago Pago) **9957**

ARIZONA

Ajo Copper News (Ajo) **10063**
Apache Junction Independent (Apache
  Junction) **10063**
Arizona City Independent (Arizona City) **10063**
Arizona Daily Star (Tucson) **9958**
Arizona Daily Sun (Flagstaff) **9957**
Arizona Republic (Phoenix) **9958**
Arizona Silver Belt (Globe) **10064**
▼Arrowhead Ranch Independent (Sun
  City) **10064**
Arrow, The (Glendale) **10064**

Bisbee Daily Review (Bisbee) **9957**
▼Bisbee News, The (Bisbee) **10063**
▼Bisbee Now (Bisbee) **10063**
Brewery Gulch Gazette (Bisbee) **10063**
Casa Grande Dispatch (Casa Grande) **9957**
Chandler Arizonan Tribune (Chandler) **9957**
Chandler Independent (Chandler) **10063**
Coolidge Examiner (Coolidge) **10063**
Copper Country News (Globe) **10064**
Copper Era (Clifton) **10063**
Cottonwood Journal Extra
  (Cottonwood) **10063**
Daily Courier, The (Prescott) **9958**
Daily News-Sun (Sun City) **9958**
Douglas Dispatch (Douglas) **9957**
Eastern Arizona Courier (Safford) **10064**
East Mesa Independent (Apache
  Junction) **10063**
Eloy Enterprise (Eloy) **10064**
Gilbert Independent (Scottsdale) **10064**
Gilbert Tribune (Gilbert) **9958**
Glendale Star, The (Glendale) **10064**
Green Valley News & Sun (Green
  Valley) **10064**
Holbrook Tribune News & Snowflake Herald
  (Holbrook) **10064**
Kingman Daily Miner (Kingman) **9958**
Lake Havasu City Herald (Lake Havasu
  City) **9958**
Lake Powell Chronicle (Page) **10064**
Mesa Tribune (Mesa) **9958**
Mohave Valley Daily News (Bullhead
  City) **9957**
New Times (Phoenix) **10064**
† North Scottsdale Independent (Scottsdale)
Paradise Valley Independent
  (Scottsdale) **10064**
Parker Pioneer (Parker) **10064**
Payson Roundup (Payson) **10064**
Peoria Times (Glendale) **10064**
Phoenix Gazette (Phoenix) **9958**
Round Valley Paper, The (Eagar) **10063**
Scottsdale Progress Tribune (Scottsdale) **9958**
Sedona Red Rock News (Sedona) **10064**
Sierra Vista Herald (Sierra Vista) **9958**
Sun Cities Independent (Sun City) **10065**
Sun City/Youngtown (Sun City) **10065**
Sun City West (Sun City) **10065**
Tempe Daily News Tribune (Tempe) **9958**
Today's Daily News-Herald (Lake Havasu
  City) **9958**
Tombstone Epitaph, The (Tombstone) **10065**
Town of Paradise Valley Independent
  (Scottsdale) **10064**
Tucson Citizen (Tucson) **9958**
Verde Independent (Cottonwood) **10063**

Wampum Saver (Show Low) **10064**
† Weekly Territorial (Tucson)
West Valley View (Avondale) **10063**
White Mountain Independent (Show
  Low) **10064**
Wickenburg Sun (Wickenburg) **10065**
Williams Grand Canyon News (Williams) **10065**
Winslow Mail (Winslow) **10065**
† Winter Visitor Independent (Mesa)
Yuma Daily Sun (Yuma) **9959**

ARKANSAS

Advance-Monticellonian (Monticello) **10067**
Advertiser, The (Van Buren) **10068**
Arkadelphia Daily Siftings Herald
  (Arkadelphia) **9959**
Arkansas Democrat-Gazette (Little Rock) **9960**
Ashley County Shoppers Guide
  (Crossett) **10065**
Ashley News Observer (Crossett) **10065**
Atkins Chronicle, The (Atkins) **10065**
Banner-News (Magnolia) **9960**
Batesville Guard (Batesville) **9959**
Baxter Bulletin (Mountain Home) **9960**
Beebe News (Beebe) **10065**
Benton County Daily Record (Bentonville) **9959**
Benton Courier (Benton) **9959**
Brinkley Argus (Brinkley) **10065**
Camden News (Camden) **9959**
Citizen, The (Mansfield) **10066**
Clinton Van Buren County Democrat
  (Clinton) **10065**
Conway County Petit Jean Country Headlight
  (Morrilton) **10067**
Courier News (Blytheville) **9959**
Courier, The (Russellville) **9960**
Daily Citizen (Searcy) **9960**
Daily News (Mountain Home) **9960**
Decatur Herald (Gentry) **10066**
De Queen Bee (De Queen) **10066**
De Queen Daily Citizen (De Queen) **9959**
Dumas Clarion (Dumas) **10066**
El Dorado News-Times (El Dorado) **9959**
England Democrat (England) **10066**
Eureka Springs Times-Echo (Berryville) **10065**
Fayetteville Northwest Arkansas Times
  (Fayetteville) **9959**
Forrest City Times-Herald (Forrest City) **9959**
Fort Smith Southwest Times Record (Fort
  Smith) **9959**
Gentry Courier-Journal (Gentry) **10066**
Glenwood Herald (Glenwood) **10066**
Gravette News Herald (Gravette) **10066**
Greenbrier Gazette (Sherwood) **10068**
Green Forest Tribune (Berryville) **10065**

Greenwood Democrat (Greenwood) **10066**
Harrison Daily Times (Harrison) **9959**
Helena Daily World (Helena) **9959**
Herald/Leader (Siloam Springs) **10068**
Hope Star, The (Hope) **9959**
Jacksonville Patriot (Jacksonville) **9960**
Johnson County Graphic (Clarksville) **10065**
Jonesboro Review (Sherwood) **10068**
Jonesboro Sun (Jonesboro) **9960**
Lake Tribune (Sherwood) **10068**
LaVilla News (Hot Springs Village) **10066**
Lincoln Ledger (Star City) **10068**
Log Cabin Democrat (Conway) **9959**
Madison County Record (Huntsville) **10066**
Malvern Daily Record (Malvern) **9960**
Marianna Courier Index (Marianna) **10066**
Marshall Mountain Wave (Marshall) **10066**
Mena Star (Mena) **10067**
Modern News (Harrisburg) **10066**
Morning News of Northwest Arkansas
  (Springdale) **9960**
Mountain Echo (Yellville) **10068**
Murfreesboro Diamond (Murfreesboro) **10067**
Nashville News (Nashville) **10067**
Nevada County Picayune (Prescott) **10067**
Newport Daily Independent (Newport) **9960**
News, The (Salem) **10067**
Osceola Times (Osceola) **10067**
Ozark Journal (Imboden) **10066**
Paragould Daily Press (Paragould) **9960**
Paris Express (Paris) **10067**
Piggott Times, The (Piggott) **10067**
Pine Bluff Commercial (Pine Bluff) **9960**
† Pine Bluff News (Pine Bluff)
Pine Bluff Shoppers News (Pine Bluff) **10067**
Pocahontas Star Herald (Pocahontas) **10067**
Press Argus-Courier (Van Buren) **10068**
Scott County Advertiser (Waldron) **10068**
Sentinel-Record, The (Hot Springs) **9960**
Sheridan Headlight (Sheridan) **10067**
Star-Progress, The (Berryville) **10065**
Stone County Citizen (Mountain View) **10067**
Stone County Leader (Mountain View) **10067**
Stuttgart Daily Leader (Stuttgart) **9960**
Sun Times (Heber Springs) **10066**
Times Dispatch (Walnut Ridge) **10068**
Times of Northeast Benton County (Pea
  Ridge) **10067**
Times, The (North Little Rock) **10067**
Tri-City Tribune (Marked Tree) **10066**
Tri-County Trader (Waldron) **10068**
Trumann Democrat (Trumann) **10068**
West Memphis Evening Times (West
  Memphis) **9961**
White Hall Journal (Pine Bluff) **10067**
White River Current (Calico Rock) **10065**

White River Journal (Des Arc) **10066**
Woodruff County Monitor Leader Advocate
  (McCrory) **10066**
Wynne Progress (Wynne) **10068**

CALIFORNIA

Acorn, The (Westlake Village) **10084**
† Adelanto Bulletin, The (Adelanto)
Alameda Times Star (Alameda) **9961**
Alhambra Post Advocate (Los Angeles) **10075**
Aliso Viejo News (Lake Forest) **10074**
† Alvin Tiller (Lamont)
Amador Ledger Dispatch (Jackson) **9962**
Anaheim Bulletin (Anaheim) **10068**
Anaheim Hills News (Anaheim) **10068**
Antelope Valley Press (Palmdale) **9964**
Appeal-Democrat (Marysville) **9963**
Apple Valley News (Hesperia) **10073**
† Arcadia Tribune (Arcadia)
Argonaut, The (Los Angeles) **10075**
Argus, The (Fremont) **9962**
Ark, The (Bel Tiburon) **10069**
Atascadero News (Atascadero) **10069**
Atwater New Times (Winton) **10085**
Auburn Journal (Auburn) **9961**
Avalon Bay News, The (Avalon) **10069**
Avenal Progress (Avenal) **10069**
Azusa Herald (West Covina) **10084**
Bakersfield Californian (Bakersfield) **9961**
Banning Record Gazette (Banning) **9961**
Bay Area Press (Oakland) **10078**
Beach & Bay Press (San Diego) **10080**
Beach Reporter, The (Manhattan
  Beach) **10077**
Belevedere Citizen (Los Angeles) **10075**
Bell Gardens Review (Los Angeles) **10075**
Bell Maywood Cudahy Industrial Post (Los
  Angeles) **10075**
Benicia Herald (Benicia) **9961**
Berryessa Sun (Milpitas) **10078**
Beverly Hills Courier (Beverly Hills) **10069**
Beverly Hills Independent (Santa
  Monica) **10082**
Big Bear Life (Big Bear Lake) **10069**
Blythe Advertiser (Palm Desert) **10079**
Boutique & Villager (Burlingame) **10070**
Brawley Advertiser (Palm Desert) **10079**
Brea Progress (Anaheim) **10068**
Brentwood Westwood Press (Santa
  Monica) **10082**
† Buyer's Guide (Napa)
Calexico Advertiser (Palm Desert) **10079**
California Advocate, The (Fresno) **10072**
California Courier (Glendale) **10073**
Californian, The (Salinas) **9965**

Californian, The (Temecula) 9966
Camarillo Star (Simi Valley) 9966
Capistrano Valley News (Lake Forest) 10074
Carlsbad Sun (Carlsbad) 10070
Carmel Pine Cone (Carmel) 10070
Carmichael Times (Carmichael) 10070
† Carpinteria Herald (Goleta)
Carson Wave (Los Angeles) 10075
Catalina Islander, The (Avalon) 10069
Central Coast Sun-Bulletin (Morro Bay) 10078
† Central Coast Times (Paso Robles)
Ceres Courier (Ceres) 10070
Chico Enterprise-Record (Chico) 9961
Chronicle, The (Atwater) 10069
Chula Vista Star-News (Chula Vista) 10070
City Terrace Comet (City of Commerce) 10070
Civic Center NEWSource (Los Angeles) 10075
Claremont Courier (Claremont) 10071
Classified Gazette (San Rafael) 10082
Clear Lake Observer-American (Clearlake) 10071
Cloverdale Reveille (Cloverdale) 10071
Clovis Independent (Clovis) 10071
Coalinga Record (Coalinga) 10071
Coastal Post (Bolinas) 10070
Coastside Chronicle (San Mateo) 10082
Colusa County Sun-Herald (Colusa) 10071
Community Adviser (Beaumont) 10069
Compton Wave (Los Angeles) 10075
Contra Costa Sun (Lafayette) 10074
Contra Costa Times (Walnut Creek) 9967
Corning Observer (Corning) 10071
Corona-Norco Independent (Corona) 10071
Coronado Journal (Coronado) 10071
Corridor News (San Diego) 10080
Country Almanac (Menlo Park) 10077
Crestline Courier-News (Crestline) 10071
Culver City-Ladera Independent (Santa Monica) 10082
Culver City Star (Los Angeles) 10076
Cupertino Courier (Cupertino) 10071
Daily Breeze (Torrance) 9966
Daily Californian, The (El Cajon) 9961
Daily Democrat (Woodland) 9967
Daily Independent (Ridgecrest) 9964
Daily Midway Driller (Taft) 9966
Daily News (Woodland Hills) 9967
Daily Pilot, The (Costa Mesa) 9961
Daily Press (Victorville) 9967
Daily Press, The (Paso Robles) 9964
Daily Republic (Fairfield) 9962
Daily Review (Hayward) 9962
Daly City Record (San Mateo) 10082
Dana Point News (Lake Forest) 10074
Davis Enterprise (Davis) 9961
Delano Record (Delano) 10071

Delhi Express (Winton) 10085
Del Mar, Solana Beach, Carmel Valley, Rancho Santa Fe Sun (Del Mar) 10072
Del Norte Triplicate (Crescent City) 9961
Denair Dispatch (Winton) 10085
Desert Dispatch (Barstow) 9961
Desert Mailer News (Lancaster) 10075
Desert Mobile Home News (Palm Desert) 10079
Desert Mountain Express (Hesperia) 10073
Desert Sentinel, The (Desert Hot Springs) 10072
Desert Sun (Palm Springs) 9964
Digger Shopper & News, The (Orcville) 10078
Dispatch, The (Gilroy) 9962
Downey Herald American (Los Angeles) 10076
Downtown Gazette (Long Beach) 10075
Eagle Rock Sentinel (Los Angeles) 10076
East Bay Express (Berkeley) 10069
East L.A./Commerce Tribune (Los Angeles) 10076
† East Los Angeles Gazette (South Gate)
† East Los Angeles Tribune (South Gate)
East Riverside Advertiser (Palm Desert) 10079
Eastside Journal (Los Angeles) 10076
Eastside Sun (City of Commerce) 10071
Easy Reader (Hermosa Beach) 10073
Ebbtide (Sausalito) 10083
El Centro Advertiser (Palm Desert) 10079
Elk Grove Citizen (Elk Grove) 10072
El Segundo Herald (El Segundo) 10072
El Sereno Star (Los Angeles) 10076
Encinitas Sun (Encinitas) 10072
Enquirer Bulletin (Burlingame) 10070
Enterprise Mountaineer, The (Fallbrook) 10072
† Enterprise News (Pixley)
Escondido News-Reporter (Escondido) 10072
Fillmore Herald (Fillmore) 10072
Firebaugh/Mendota Journal (Kerman) 10074
Five Cities Times-Press-Recorder (Arroyo Grande) 10069
Folsom Telegraph (Folsom) 10072
Fontana Herald News (Fontana) 10072
Fort Bragg Advocate-News (Fort Bragg) 10072
Foster City Progress (Burlingame) 10070
Fresno Bee, The (Fresno) 9962
Galt Herald (Galt) 10073
Gardena Valley News (Gardena) 10073
Glendale News-Press (Glendale) 9962
Glendora Press (West Covina) 10084
Gold River News (Sacramento) 10080
† Goleta Review (Goleta)
† Goleta Sun (Santa Barbara)
Gonzales Tribune (Soledad) 10083
Good Times (Santa Cruz) 10082
Green Sheet, The (Palm Desert) 10079

Gridley Herald, The (Gridley) **10073**
Grizzly, The (Big Bear Lake) **10069**
Grunion Gazette (Long Beach) **10075**
Half Moon Bay Review (Half Moon Bay) **10073**
Hanford Sentinel (Hanford) **9962**
Harbor Extra (Torrance) **10084**
Harte-Hanks Pennysaver (Brea) **10070**
Healdsburg Tribune (Healdsburg) **10073**
Hemet News (San Jacinto) **9965**
Hesperia Resorter (Hesperia) **10073**
Highlander (West Covina) **10084**
Highland Park News/Herald/Journal (Los Angeles) **10076**
Hilmar Times (Hilmar) **10073**
Hollister Free Lance (Hollister) **9962**
† Hollywood Citizen News (Los Angeles)
Holtville Tribune (Holtville) **10073**
Hughson Chronicle (Winton) **10085**
Humboldt Beacon (Fortuna) **10072**
Huntington Beach/Fountain Valley Independent (Huntington Beach) **10073**
Huntington Harbour Sun (Seal Beach) **10083**
Huntington Park Bulletin (Los Angeles) **10076**
Imperial Valley Press (El Centro) **9961**
Independent, The (Livermore) **10075**
Indio Advertiser (Palm Desert) **10079**
Indio Post (Indio) **10073**
Inglewood/Hawthorne Wave (Los Angeles) **10076**
Inland Valley Daily Bulletin (Ontario) **9963**
Intermountain News (Burney) **10070**
Irvine World News (Irvine) **10073**
Kerman News (Kerman) **10074**
Kern Valley Sun (Lake Isabella) **10074**
King City Rustler (King City) **10074**
Kingsburg Recorder (Kingsburg) **10074**
La Canada Valley Sun (La Canada) **10074**
Laguna Niguel News (Lake Forest) **10074**
Laguna Post News (Lake Forest) **10074**
La Habra Star (Anaheim) **10068**
La Jolla Light (La Jolla) **10074**
Lake County Record-Bee (Lakeport) **9962**
Lake Elsinore Valley Sun-Tribune (Lake Elsinore) **10074**
Lake Havasu City Advertiser (Palm Desert) **10079**
La Mesa Forum (Lemon Grove) **10075**
Lamont Reporter (Lamont) **10074**
Las Virgenes Enterprise (Woodland Hills) **10085**
L.A. Weekly (Los Angeles) **10076**
Ledger Dispatch (Antioch) **9961**
Leisure World Golden Rain News (Seal Beach) **10083**
Leisure World News (Laguna Hills) **10074**
Lemon Grove Review (Lemon Grove) **10075**

Lincoln Heights Bulletin-News (Los Angeles) **10076**
Linden Herald (Linden) **10075**
Lindsay Gazette (Lindsay) **10075**
Lockeford-Clements News (Lockeford) **10075**
Lodi News-Sentinel (Lodi) **9962**
Lompoc Record (Lompoc) **9962**
† Long Beach Community News (Long Beach)
Los Altos Town Crier (Los Altos) **10075**
Los Angeles Bulletin (Los Angeles) **9963**
Los Angeles Daily Journal (Los Angeles) **9963**
Los Angeles Independent (Los Angeles) **10076**
Los Angeles Log (San Diego) **10080**
Los Angeles Times (Los Angeles) **9963**
Los Banos Enterprise (Los Banos) **10077**
Los Gatos Weekly-Times (Los Gatos) **10077**
Lynwood Journal (Compton) **10071**
Lynwood Press (Los Angeles) **10076**
Madera Tribune (Madera) **9963**
Malibu Surfside News (Malibu) **10077**
Malibu Times (Malibu) **10077**
† Mammoth Lakes Review/Mono Herald (Mammoth Lakes)
Mammoth Times (Mammoth Lakes) **10077**
Manteca Bulletin (Manteca) **9963**
Marina News (Long Beach) **10075**
† Marin County Daily Recording (San Rafael)
Marin Independent Journal (Novato) **9963**
Marin Scope (Sausalito) **10083**
Mariposa Gazette (Mariposa) **10077**
Market Shopper, The (Delano) **10071**
Martinez News Gazette (Martinez) **10077**
Mendocino Beacon, The (Mendocino) **10077**
Menifee Valley News (Sun City) **10084**
Merced County Times, The (Winton) **10085**
Merced Sun-Star (Merced) **9963**
Mesa Tribune Wave (Los Angeles) **10076**
Metro (San Jose) **10081**
Metropolitan, The (Los Angeles) **9963**
Mexican-American Sun (City of Commerce) **10071**
Mid Valley News (El Monte) **10072**
Millbrae & San Bruno Sun (Burlingame) **10070**
Millbrae Recorder-Progress (San Mateo) **10082**
Mill Valley Herald (Sausalito) **10083**
Milpitas Post (Milpitas) **10078**
Mira Mesa/Scripps Ranch Sentinel (San Diego) **10081**
Modesto Bee, The (Modesto) **9963**
Modoc County Record (Alturas) **10068**
Mojave Desert News, The (California City) **10070**
Montclarion (Oakland) **10078**
Montebello News (Los Angeles) **10076**
† Montecito Life (Goleta)

Monterey County Herald, The (Monterey) **9963**
Monterey Park Progress (Los Angeles) **10076**
Moorpark Star (Moorpark) **9963**
Morgan Hill Times (Morgan Hill) **10078**
Morongo Basin (Palm Desert) **10079**
Morongo Basin Advertiser (Yucca
  Valley) **10085**
Mountain Democrat (Placerville) **9964**
Mountain Life (Mariposa) **10077**
Mountain Messenger (Downieville) **10072**
Mountain News, The (Lake Arrowhead) **10074**
Mountain Press (Prather) **10080**
Mount Shasta Herald (Mt. Shasta) **10078**
Mt. Washington Star Review (Los
  Angeles) **10076**
Napa County Record (Napa) **10078**
Napa Valley Register (Napa) **9963**
Needles Desert Star (Needles) **10078**
Newman News, The (Newman) **10078**
News-Ledger, The (West Sacramento) **10085**
News-Pilot, The (San Pedro) **9965**
News Enterprise, The (Los Alamitos) **10075**
News Pointer (Sausalito) **10083**
News Review (Ridgecrest) **10080**
New Times (San Luis Obispo) **10082**
North/South Beach Now (San
  Francisco) **10081**
North County Shopping News
  (Atascadero) **10069**
North County Times (Escondido) **9962**
Northeast Sun (City of Commerce) **10071**
North Shore Shopper (Pacific
  Palisades) **10078**
North Tahoe/Truckee Week (Carnelian
  Bay) **10070**
Norwalk Herald American (Los Angeles) **10076**
Novato Advance (Novato) **10078**
Oakdale Leader (Oakdale) **10078**
▼OC Weekly (Los Angeles) **10076**
Ojai Valley News (Ojai) **10078**
Ontario Advertiser (Palm Desert) **10079**
Orange Coast Daily Pilot (Costa Mesa) **9961**
Orange County Log (San Diego) **10081**
Orange County News (Garden Grove) **10073**
Orange County Register (Santa Ana) **9965**
Orange Cove Mountain Times (Reedley) **10080**
Orangevale News (Folsom) **10072**
Orland Press-Register (Orland) **10078**
Oroville Mercury-Register (Oroville) **9963**
Outlook Mail (Santa Monica) **10082**
Outlook, The (Santa Monica) **9966**
† Oxnard Press-Courier (Oxnard)
Pacifica Tribune (Pacifica) **10078**
Pacific Sun (Mill Valley) **10077**
Palisadian-Post (Pacific Palisades) **10079**
Palm Desert (Indio) **10073**

Palm Desert Advertiser (Palm Desert) **10079**
Palm Spring Advertiser (Palm Desert) **10079**
▼Palo Alto Daily News (Palo Alto) **9964**
Palo Alto Weekly (Palo Alto) **10079**
Palos Verdes Peninsula News (Palos Verdes
  Peninsula) **10079**
Palo Verde Valley Times (Blythe) **10069**
Paradise Post (Paradise) **10079**
Parker Advertiser (Palm Desert) **10079**
Park LaBrea News/Beverly Press (Los
  Angeles) **10076**
Parlier Post (Sanger) **10081**
Pasadena Star-News, The (Pasadena) **9964**
Pasadena Weekly (Pasadena) **10080**
Peninsula Beacon, The (San Diego) **10081**
▼Peninsula Independent (Burlingame) **10070**
† Peninsula Review, The (Carmel)
Pennysaver (Vista) **10084**
Petaluma Argus-Courier (Petaluma) **10080**
Pico Rivera News (Los Angeles) **10076**
Piedmonter, The (Oakland) **10078**
Pinnacle, The (Hollister) **10073**
Placentia News-Times (Anaheim) **10069**
Placer Herald (Rocklin) **10080**
Point Reyes Light (Point Reyes Station) **10080**
Porterville Recorder (Porterville) **9964**
Poway News Chieftain (San Diego) **10081**
Press-Enterprise, The (Riverside) **9964**
Press-Telegram (Long Beach) **9962**
Ramona Sentinel (Ramona) **10080**
Rancho Bernardo Journal (San Diego) **10081**
Rancho Santa Margarita News (Lake
  Forest) **10074**
Random Lengths News (San Pedro) **10082**
Record Ledger (San Fernando) **10081**
Record Searchlight (Redding) **9964**
Record, The (Stockton) **9966**
Red Bluff Daily News (Red Bluff) **9964**
Redlands Advertiser (Palm Desert) **10079**
Redlands Daily Facts (Redlands) **9964**
▼Redwood City Tribune (Redwood
  City) **10080**
Reedley Exponent (Reedley) **10080**
Register-Pajaronian (Watsonville) **9967**
Register Review (Bishop) **10069**
Reporter, The (Vacaville) **9967**
Review Herald, The (Mammoth Lakes) **10077**
Rialto Record (San Bernardino) **10080**
Riverside Advertiser (Palm Desert) **10079**
Riverside Bulletin, The (Los Angeles) **10076**
† Rohnert Park Cotati Clarion (Cotati)
Rosamond News (Rosamond) **10080**
Roseville Press-Tribune (Roseville) **10080**
Rossmoor News (Walnut Creek) **10084**
Ross Valley Reporter (Sausalito) **10083**
Sacramento Bee (Sacramento) **9965**

Sacramento Bulletin, The (Sacramento) **10080**
† Sacramento Union (Sacramento)
Saddleback Valley News (Lake Forest) **10074**
San Bernardino Advertiser (Palm Desert) **10079**
San Bernardino Bulletin, The (Los Angeles) **10076**
San Bernardino County Sun (San Bernardino) **9965**
San Bruno Herald (San Mateo) **10082**
† San Clemente News (San Clemente)
† San Diego Bulletin (Los Angeles)
San Diego Log (San Diego) **10081**
San Diego Reader (San Diego) **10081**
San Diego Review (San Diego) **10081**
San Diego Transcript (San Diego) **9965**
San Diego Union-Tribune (San Diego) **9965**
San Fernando Valley Sun (San Fernando) **10081**
San Francisco Bay Guardian (San Francisco) **10081**
San Francisco Chronicle (San Francisco) **9965**
San Francisco Daily Journal (San Francisco) **9965**
San Francisco Examiner (San Francisco) **9965**
San Francisco Independent (San Francisco) **10081**
San Francisco Metro Reporter (San Francisco) **10081**
San Francisco Sentinel (San Francisco) **10081**
San Gabriel Progress (Los Angeles) **10076**
San Gabriel Valley Tribune (West Covina) **9967**
Sanger Herald (Sanger) **10081**
San Jacinto Valley Register (San Jacinto) **10081**
San Jose Mercury News (San Jose) **9965**
San Luis Obispo County Telegram-Tribune (San Luis Obisopo) **9965**
San Marcos News Reporter (San Marcos) **10082**
San Marino Tribune (San Marino) **10082**
San Mateo Times (San Mateo) **9965**
San Mateo Weekly (Burlingame) **10070**
San Rafael News Pointer (Sausalito) **10083**
San Ramon Valley Times, The (Danville) **9961**
Santa Barbara Independent (Santa Barbara) **10082**
Santa Barbara News Press (Santa Barbara) **9965**
Santa Cruz County Sentinel (Santa Cruz) **9966**
Santa Fe Springs News (Los Angeles) **10077**
Santa Maria Times (Santa Maria) **9966**
† Santa Monica Life (Santa Monica)
Santa Paula Times (Santa Paula) **10082**
Santa Rosa Press Democrat (Santa Rosa) **9966**

Saratoga News (Saratoga) **10083**
Seal Beach Sun (Seal Beach) **10083**
Selma Enterprise (Selma) **10083**
Sentinel, The (Auburn) **10069**
SF Weekly (San Francisco) **10081**
Shafter Press (Shafter) **10083**
Sierra Madre News (Sierra Madre) **10083**
Sierra Sun (Truckee) **10084**
Signal, The (Valencia) **9967**
Signal, The (Atwater) **10069**
Simi Valley Star (Simi Valley) **9966**
Siskiyou Daily News (Yreka) **9968**
Soledad Bee (Soledad) **10083**
Solvang Santa Ynez Valley News (Solvang) **10083**
Sonoma County Independent (Santa Rosa) **10083**
Sonoma Index Tribune (Sonoma) **10083**
Sonoma West (Sebastopal) **10083**
South Bay Extra (Torrance) **10084**
South Coast Shoppers/Penny Savers (Laguna Hills) **10074**
South Gate Press (Los Angeles) **10077**
▼South Of The Boulevard (Woodland Hills) **10085**
† South Pasadena Journal (Los Angeles)
South Pasadena Review (South Pasadena) **10084**
South San Francisco Enterprise-Journal (San Mateo) **10082**
South San Gabriel/Rosemead Progress (Los Angeles) **10077**
Southside Journal (Los Angeles) **10077**
Southwest Wave/News (Los Angeles) **10077**
Spring Valley Bulletin (Lemon Grove) **10075**
Star News, The (Chula Vista) **10070**
St. Helena Star (St. Helena) **10084**
Sun-Reporter (San Francisco) **10081**
Sun City News (Sun City) **10084**
Sun Post News (San Clemente) **10080**
Sun, The (Exeter) **10072**
Swap Sheet (Ridgecrest) **10080**
Tahoe Daily Tribune (South Lake Tahoe) **9966**
Tahoe World (Tahoe City) **10084**
Tehachapi News (Tehachapi) **10084**
Thousand Oaks Star (Thousand Oaks) **9966**
Times-Standard (Eureka) **9962**
† Times Tribune (Palo Alto)
Topics Sun Wave (Los Angeles) **10077**
Tracy Press (Tracy) **9966**
Tri-State Advertiser (Palm Desert) **10079**
Tri-Valley Herald (Pleasanton) **9964**
Tribune, The (Oakland) **9963**
Trinity Journal (Weaverville) **10084**
Tulare Advance-Register (Tulare) **9966**
Turlock Journal (Turlock) **9967**

Tustin News (Santa Ana) **10082**
Twin Cities Times (Corte Madera) **10071**
Ukiah Daily Journal (Ukiah) **9967**
Union Democrat, The (Sonora) **9966**
† Union Shopper, The (Arcata)
Union, The (Grass Valley) **9962**
† Union, The (Arcata)
Uptown San Diego Examiner (San Diego) **10081**
Vallejo Times-Herald (Vallejo) **9967**
Valley Post (Anderson) **10069**
Valley Roadrunner (Valley Center) **10084**
Valley Times (Pleasanton) **9964**
Valley Times (Moreno Valley) **10078**
Valley Vantage (Sherman Oaks) **10083**
Venice-Marina News (Santa Monica) **10082**
† Ventura Bulletin, The (Los Angeles)
Ventura County & Coast Reporter (Ventura) **10084**
Ventura County Star (Ventura) **9967**
Victor Valley Advertiser (Palm Desert) **10079**
† Victor Valley Living (Hesperia)
Visalia Times-Delta (Visalia) **9967**
Warner Center News (Woodland Hills) **10085**
Wasco Tribune (Wasco) **10084**
Waterford News (Winton) **10085**
Weed Press (Weed) **10084**
Weekly Calistogan (Calistoga) **10070**
Westchester Observer (Santa Monica) **10082**
Westchester Star (Los Angeles) **10077**
West County Times (Richmond) **9964**
▼Western Edition (San Francisco) **10081**
West Los Angeles Independent (Santa Monica) **10082**
West Sacramento News-Ledger (West Sacramento) **10085**
West San Bernardino Advertiser (Palm Desert) **10079**
West Side Advance (Kerman) **10074**
Whittier Daily News (Whittier) **9967**
Willows Journal (Willows) **10085**
Winton Times (Winton) **10085**
Yucaipa & Calimesa News-Mirror (Yucaipa) **10085**
Yucca Valley Hi-Desert Star (Yucca Valley) **10085**

COLORADO

Akron News Reporter (Akron) **10085**
† Applewood/Wheat Ridge Transcript (Golden)
Arkansas Valley Journal (La Junta) **10087**
Arvada Jefferson Sentinel (Lakewood) **10087**
Aspen Daily News (Aspen) **9968**
Aspen Times, The (Aspen) **9968**
Aurora Sentinel (Aurora) **10085**

Black Forest News (Colorado Springs) **10086**
Brighton/Blade Market Place (Brighton) **10085**
Broomfield Enterprise (Broomfield) **10086**
Brush News-Tribune (Brush) **10086**
Canyon Courier (Evergreen) **10087**
Center Post Dispatch (Monte Vista) **10088**
Cheyenne Mountain Journal (Manitou Springs) **10088**
Chronicle News, The (Trinidad) **9969**
Citizen Telegram, The (Rifle) **10089**
Clear Creek Courant (Idaho Springs) **10087**
Colorado Springs Gazette Telegraph (Colorado Springs) **9968**
Colorado Statesman (Denver) **10086**
Conejos County Citizen, The (Monte Vista) **10088**
Cortez Montezuma Valley Journal (Cortez) **10086**
Cortez Sentinel (Cortez) **10086**
Daily Camera (Boulder) **9968**
Daily News Press (Castle Rock) **10086**
Daily Record (Canon City) **9968**
Daily Sentinel, The (Grand Junction) **9969**
Daily Times-Call (Longmont) **9969**
Del Norte Prospector (Monte Vista) **10088**
Delta County Independent (Delta) **10086**
Denver Herald-Dispatch (Denver) **10086**
Denver Post (Denver) **9968**
Douglas County News Press (Castle Rock) **10086**
Dove Creek Press (Dove Creek) **10086**
Durango Herald (Durango) **9968**
Eagle Valley Enterprise (Eagle) **10086**
Eastern Colorado News (Strasburg) **10089**
Eastern Colorado Plainsman (Hugo) **10087**
Elbert County News (Castle Rock) **10086**
Englewood Herald (Littleton) **10088**
Estes Park Trail-Gazette (Estes Park) **10087**
Farmer & Miner (Frederick) **10087**
Florence Citizen (Florence) **10087**
Fort Collins Coloradoan (Fort Collins) **9968**
Fort Lupton Press (Fort Lupton) **10087**
Fort Morgan Times (Fort Morgan) **9968**
Fountain Valley News & El Paso County News (Fountain) **10087**
Fowler Tribune, The (Fowler) **10087**
Fruita Times, The (Fruita) **10087**
Garden of the Gods Journal (Manitou Springs) **10088**
Glenwood Post (Glenwood Springs) **9968**
Golden Transcript (Golden) **10087**
Greeley Tribune (Greeley) **9969**
Greenhorn Valley News (Colorado City) **10086**
Gunnison Country Times (Gunnison) **9969**
Haxtun-Fleming Herald, The (Haxtun) **10087**
Hayden Valley Press (Craig) **10086**

Herald-Democrat (Leadville) **10088**
▼Highlander (Highlands Ranch) **10087**
Highlands Branch Herald (Littleton) **10088**
High Timber Times (Pine) **10089**
Jackson County Star (Walden) **10089**
Jefferson County Transcript (Golden) **10087**
Jefferson Sentinel (Lakewood) **10088**
Julesburg Advocate (Julesburg) **10087**
Kiowa County Press (Eads) **10086**
La Junta Tribune-Democrat (La Junta) **9969**
Lamar Daily News (Lamar) **9969**
Life at Ken-Caryl (Littleton) **10088**
Littleton Independent (Littleton) **10088**
† Littleton Times (Littleton)
Loveland Daily Reporter-Herald
  (Loveland) **9969**
Mancos Times-Tribune (Mancos) **10088**
Manitou Springs Pikes Peak Journal (Manitou
  Springs) **10088**
Meeker Herald, The (Meeker) **10088**
Mineral County Miner (Monte Vista) **10088**
Monte Vista Journal (Monte Vista) **10088**
▼Montrose Morning Sun (Montrose) **9969**
Montrose Daily Press (Montrose) **9969**
Mountain Mail (Salida) **9969**
Northglenn-Thornton Sentinel
  (Westminster) **10089**
Northwest Colorado Daily Press (Craig) **9968**
Old Lyons Recorder, The (Lyons) **10088**
Ouray County Plaindealer (Ouray) **10089**
Palisade Tribune (Palisade) **10089**
Pikes Peak Journal (Manitou Springs) **10088**
Pine River Times (Bayfield) **10085**
Pueblo Chieftain (Pueblo) **9969**
Ridgway Sun (Ouray) **10089**
Rockrimmon Journal (Manitou Springs) **10088**
Rocky Ford Daily Gazette (Rocky Ford) **9969**
Rocky Mountain News (Denver) **9968**
Saturday Advantage, The (Monte Vista) **10088**
† Sentinel/Altitudes (Frisco)
Silverton Standard & The Miner
  (Silverton) **10089**
† Snake River Press (Craig)
South Fork Times (Monte Vista) **10088**
Steamboat Pilot (Steamboat Springs) **10089**
Steamboat Today (Steamboat Springs) **9969**
Sterling Journal-Advocate (Sterling) **9969**
Summit County Journal (Frisco) **10087**
Summit Daily News (Frisco) **9968**
Telluride Daily Planet (Telluride) **9969**
Telluride Times-Journal (Telluride) **10089**
Tribune, The (Monument) **10089**
Vail Daily (Vail) **9970**
Vail Trail (Eagle-Vail) **10086**
Valley Courier (Alamosa) **9968**
Valley Journal (Carbondale) **10086**

Westminster Window (Westminster) **10089**
Westword (Denver) **10086**
Wet Mountain Tribune (Westcliffe) **10089**
† Wheat Ridge Sentinel (Lakewood)
Wiggins Courier, The (Wiggins) **10089**
Winter Park Manifest (Winter Park) **10089**
Wray Gazette (Wray) **10089**
Yuma Pioneer (Yuma) **10089**

CONNECTICUT

Advocate, The (Stamford) **9971**
▼Bethel Beacon (Bethel) **10089**
Bloomfield Journal (Bristol) **10090**
Branford Review (Branford) **10090**
Bristol Press, The (Bristol) **9970**
Brookfield Journal (Brookfield) **10090**
Cheshire Herald (Cheshire) **10090**
Chronicle, The (Willimantic) **9971**
Chronicle, The (Milford) **10091**
Clinton Recorder (Old Saybrook) **10091**
Connecticut Post (Bridgeport) **9970**
Cromwell Chronicle (Cromwell) **10090**
† Daily Milford Citizen (Milford)
Darien News Review (Darien) **10090**
Day, The (New London) **9970**
East Hartford Gazette, The (East
  Hartford) **10090**
East Haven Advertiser (Milford) **10091**
Enfield Press (Enfield) **10090**
† Evening Sentinel (Ansonia)
Fairfield Citizen News (Fairfield) **10090**
Fairfield County Weekly (Stamford) **10091**
† Farmington Valley Herald (Simsbury)
Glastonbury Citizen (Glastonbury) **10090**
† Greenwich News (Greenwich)
▼Greenwich Post (Greenwich) **10090**
Greenwich Time (Greenwich) **9970**
Hartford Advocate (Hartford) **10090**
Hartford Courant (Hartford) **9970**
Herald, The (New Britain) **9970**
Hour, The (Norwalk) **9970**
Housatonic Weekend (New Milford) **10091**
Journal Inquirer (Manchester) **9970**
Kent Good Times Dispatch (Kent) **10090**
Lakeville Journal, The (Lakeville) **10090**
Lewisboro Ledger, The (Ridgefield) **10091**
Litchfield Enquirer (Litchfield) **10090**
Middletown Press (Middletown) **9970**
† Milford Citizen (Milford)
Monroe Courier (Monroe) **10091**
Naugatuck Daily News (Naugatuck) **9970**
New Canaan Advertiser (New Canaan) **10091**
New Haven Advocate (New Haven) **10091**
New Haven Register (New Haven) **9970**
Newington Town Crier (Bristol) **10090**

New Milford Times (New Milford) **10091**
News-Times (Danbury) **9970**
Newtown Bee, The (Newtown) **10091**
† Niantic News (East Lyme)
North Haven Wollington Post, The
  (Milford) **10091**
† Norwalk News (Westport)
Norwich Bulletin (Norwich) **9970**
† Observer-Patriot (Putnam)
Orange Bulletin (Milford) **10091**
Pictorial Gazette (Old Saybrook) **10091**
Record-Journal (Meriden) **9970**
Redding Pilot, The (Georgetown) **10090**
Register Citizen (Torrington) **9971**
Reminder, The (Vernon) **10092**
Ridgefield Press, The (Ridgefield) **10091**
River East News Bulletin (Glastonbury) **10090**
Southington Observer (Southington) **10091**
Stratford Bard (Milford) **10091**
Trumbull Times (Monroe) **10091**
Valley Gazette (Shelton) **10091**
Voices (Southbury) **10091**
Waterbury Republican-American
  (Waterbury) **9971**
West Hartford News (West Hartford) **10092**
West Haven News (Milford) **10091**
Weston Forum, The (Weston) **10092**
Westport News (Westport) **10092**
Wethersfield Post (West Hartford) **10092**
Wilton Bulletin (Wilton) **10092**
Windsor Journal (West Hartford) **10092**
Windsor Locks Journal (Bristol) **10090**

DELAWARE

Chronicle, The (Milford) **10092**
Daily Whale, The (Lewes) **9971**
Delaware Beachcomber (Rehoboth
  Beach) **10092**
Delaware Coast Press (Rehoboth
  Beach) **10092**
Delaware State News (Dover) **9971**
Delaware Wave (Bethany Beach) **10092**
Harrington Journal, The (Harrington) **10092**
Leader-State Register, The (Seaford) **10092**
Newark Post (Newark) **10092**
News Journal, The (New Castle) **9971**
Sussex Countian (Georgetown) **10092**
Sussex Post, The (Lewes) **10092**
Wilmington Defender (Wilmington) **10092**

DISTRICT OF COLUMBIA

Capital Spotlight (Washington) **10092**
Georgetown Current, The (Washington) **10093**

Georgetowner, The (Washington) **10093**
Northwest Current, The (Washington) **10093**
Rockcreek Current, The (Washington) **10093**
Spotlight, The (Washington) **10093**
Washington City Paper (Washington) **10093**
Washington Post, The (Washington) **9971**
Washington Times (Washington) **9971**

FEDERATED STATES OF MICRONESIA

National Union (Eastern Caroline
  Islands) **10093**

FLORIDA

Arcadian, The (Arcadia) **10093**
Aventura News (South Miami) **10099**
Baker County Press, The (MacClenny) **10096**
† Bal Harbor/Bay Harbour News (South Miami)
Bay Beacon, The (Niceville) **10097**
Bay Bulletin (Melbourne) **10096**
Beach Bulletin (Fort Myers Beach) **10095**
Beaches Leader (Jacksonville Beach) **10095**
Belleview Voice of South Marion
  (Belleview) **10093**
Boca Monday (Deerfield Beach) **10094**
Bonita Banner (Bonita Springs) **10093**
Boynton Beach Times (Deerfield Beach) **10094**
Bradenton Herald, The (Bradenton) **9971**
Bradford County Telegraph (Starke) **10099**
Brandon News, The (Brandon) **10093**
Brevard Reporter, The (Cocoa) **10094**
† Brooksville Sun Journal (Brooksville)
Broward News (Margate) **10096**
Broward Times, The (Fort Lauderdale) **10095**
Bulletin, The (Crestview) **10094**
Caloosa Belle (La Belle) **10096**
Canada News (Auburndale) **10093**
Carol City/Opa-Locka News (Miami) **10096**
Carrollwood News (Tampa) **10099**
Cedar Key Beacon (Cedar) **10094**
Charlotte Sun Herald (Charlotte Harbor) **9971**
Citrus County Chronicle (Crystal River) **9971**
† Clay Countian (Orange Park)
Clay County Crescent (Orange Park) **10098**
Clay Today (Orange Park) **9973**
Clewiston News (Clewiston) **10094**
Coral Gables News (Miami) **10097**
Courier, The (Plant City) **10098**
† Crestview Okaloosa-News Journal (Crestview)
Daily Breeze, The (Cape Coral) **9971**
Daily Commercial (Leesburg) **9972**
Daily News (Palatka) **9973**
Daily Okeechobee News, The
  (Okeechobee) **9973**

Daytona Beach News-Journal, The (Daytona Beach) **9972**
Daytona Pennysaver (Ormond Beach) **10098**
Deerfield Beach Observer (Deerfield Beach) **10094**
Deerfield Beach Thursday Times (Deerfield Beach) **10094**
DeLand Beacon, The (DeLand) **10094**
Delray Times (Deerfield Beach) **10094**
Destin Log (Destin) **10094**
Digest, The (Hallandale) **10095**
Downtown News (South Miami) **10099**
East Bay Breeze (Sun City Center) **10099**
Englewood Sun Herald (Englewood) **9972**
Escambia Sun Press (Pensacola) **10098**
Eustis Lake Region News (Mount Dora) **10097**
Florida Keys Keynoter (Marathon) **10096**
Florida Times-Union (Jacksonville) **9972**
Florida Today (Melbourne) **9972**
Fort Meade Leader, The (Fort Meade) **10095**
Fort Myers Beach Observer (Fort Myers Beach) **10095**
Free Press (Tampa) **10099**
Frostproof News (Frostproof) **10095**
Gadsden County Times (Quincy) **10098**
Gainesville Buyers Guide (Orange Park) **10098**
Gainesville Sun, The (Gainesville) **9972**
Glades County Democrat (Clewiston) **10094**
Graceville News (Graceville) **10095**
† Haines City Herald (Haines City)
Herald-Advocate (Wauchula) **10100**
† Herald, The (Tarpon Springs)
Hernando Today (Brooksville) **9971**
Hi-Riser (Deerfield Beach) **10094**
Hialeah/Opa-Lacka News (Miami) **10097**
† Highlands Press (Mulberry)
High Springs Herald, The (High Springs) **10095**
† Hollywood Sun (Hollywood)
Holmes County Advertiser (Bonifay) **10093**
Homestead/Florida City News (Miami) **10097**
Home Times Family Newspaper (West Palm Beach) **10100**
Islander, The (Pensacola Beach) **10098**
Island Reporter (Sanibel) **10098**
Jackson County Floridan (Marianna) **9972**
Jacksonville Shopping Guide (Jacksonville) **10095**
Jasper News (Jasper) **10095**
Jupiter Courier (Jupiter) **10095**
Kendall News-Gazette (Miami) **10097**
Key West Citizen (Key West) **9972**
† Lake Alfred Press (Mulberry)
Lake Area News (Land O' Lakes) **10096**
Lake City Reporter (Lake City) **9972**
Lake News (Fruitland Park) **10095**

Lake Placid Journal (Lake Placid) **10096**
† Lake Wales Highlander (Winter Haven)
Lake Wales News (Lake Wales) **10096**
Lake Worth Herald Coastal Observer (Lake Worth) **10096**
Ledger, The (Lakeland) **9972**
Lehigh Acres News-Star (Lehigh Acres) **10096**
Little Paper, The (Melbourne) **10096**
Lutz Community News (Tampa) **10099**
Madison County Carrier (Madison) **10096**
Madison Enterprise Recorder (Madison) **10096**
Marco Island Eagle, The (Marco Island) **10096**
Marketplace, The (Marianna) **10096**
† Martin County News (Stuart)
Miami Beach News (South Miami) **10099**
Miami Beach Sun Post (Miami) **10097**
Miami Herald (Miami) **9972**
Miami Laker (Miami Lakes) **10097**
Miami Shores News (Miami) **10097**
Miami Today (Miami) **10097**
Monticello News (Monticello) **10097**
Mulberry Press (Mulberry) **10097**
Naples Daily News (Naples) **9973**
Nassau County Record (Callahan) **10094**
News-Press, The (Fort Myers) **9972**
News Chief (Winter Haven) **9974**
News Herald, The (Panama City) **9973**
News Leader (Fernandina) **10095**
New Smyrna Beach Observer (New Smyrna) **9973**
News Sun, The (Sebring) **10099**
News, The (Boca Raton) **9971**
North Bay Village News (South Miami) **10099**
North Miami Beach News (South Miami) **10099**
North Miami News (Miami) **10097**
Northwest Florida Daily News (Fort Walton Beach) **9972**
Observer, The (New Smyrna) **9973**
Observer, The (Royal Palm Beach) **10098**
Ocala Star Banner (Ocala) **9973**
Orlando Sentinel (Orlando) **9973**
Orlando Weekly, The (Winter Park) **10100**
Osceola News-Gazette (Kissimmee) **10095**
Oviedo Voice, The (Oviedo) **10098**
Palm Beach Daily News (Palm Beach) **9973**
Palm Beach Post (West Palm Beach) **9974**
Pasco News (Dade City) **10094**
Pelican Press (Sarasota) **10098**
Pensacola News Journal (Pensacola) **9973**
Pensacola Voice (Pensacola) **10098**
Perdido Pelican (Pensacola) **10098**
Perry News-Herald (Perry) **10098**
Perry Taco Times (Perry) **10098**
Pine Island Eagle (Bokeelia) **10093**
Polk City Press (Mulberry) **10097**

Polk County Democrat, The (Bartow) **10093**
Pompano Ledger, The (Pompano
  Beach) **10098**
Press-Journal (Vero Beach) **9974**
Record, The (Gainesville) **10095**
† Reporter, The (Tampa)
Sanford Herald (Sanford) **9973**
Sanibel-Captiva Islander (Sanibel) **10098**
Santa Rosa Free Press (Milton) **10097**
Santa Rosa Press Gazette (Milton) **10097**
Sarasota Herald Tribune (Sarasota) **9973**
Sebastian Sun (Sebastian) **10099**
† Seminole Outlook (Oviedo)
Senior Observer (Winter Park) **10100**
Sentinel, The (Gulf Breeze) **10095**
Shopper Observer News (Ruskin) **10098**
Shopper, The (Pensacola) **10098**
South Dade News (South Miami) **10099**
South Dade News Leader (Homestead) **10095**
South Miami News (Miami) **10097**
▼South Tampa News (Brandon) **10093**
Southwest News (South Miami) **10099**
Star-Advocate (Titusville) **10099**
St. Augustine Record (St. Augustine) **9973**
St. Petersburg Times (St. Petersburg) **9973**
Stuart News (Stuart) **9973**
Sumter County Times (Bushnell) **10094**
Sun-Sentinel (Fort Lauderdale) **9972**
Sun Coast News (New Port Richey) **10097**
† Sunday Glades Trend (Clewiston)
Sun Herald (North Port) **10097**
Sun Post (Miami Beach) **10097**
Sunrise Times (Coral Springs) **10094**
Sun, The (Sun City Center) **10099**
† Surfside News (South Miami)
Tallahassean (Tallahassee) **10099**
Tallahassee Democrat (Tallahassee) **9974**
Tamarac Forum (Coral Springs) **10094**
Tampa Tribune, The (Tampa) **9974**
Tavares Citizen (Mount Dora) **10097**
Temple Terrace Beacon (Tampa) **10099**
Temple Terrace News (Brandon) **10093**
Times, The (Melbourne) **10096**
Today (Orange Park) **10098**
Town-Crier (West Palm Beach) **10100**
Town 'n Country News (Tampa) **10099**
Tri-City Independent (Margate) **10096**
Tribune, The (Fort Pierce) **9972**
Tribune, The (Melbourne) **10096**
Twin City News, The (Chattahoochee) **10094**
Venice Gondolier (Venice) **10100**
Wakulla News (Crawfordville) **10094**
Weekly Challenger (St. Petersburg) **10099**
Weekly Planet (Tampa) **10099**
Wellington Royal Palm Beach Forum
  (Wellington) **10100**

West Boca Times (Deerfield Beach) **10094**
West Orange Times (Winter Garden) **10100**
Winter Park-Maitland Observer (Winter
  Park) **10100**
Zephyrhills News (Zephyrhills) **10100**

GEORGIA

Acworth Neighbor (Marietta) **10104**
Adel News-Tribune (Adel) **10100**
Albany Herald, The (Albany) **9974**
Albany Journal (Albany) **10100**
Alpharetta Revue (Alpharetta) **10100**
Americus Times-Recorder (Americus) **9974**
Athens Banner Herald (Athens) **9974**
Athens Daily News (Athens) **9974**
Athens Observer, The (Athens) **10100**
Atlanta Bulletin (Atlanta) **10100**
Atlanta Daily World (Atlanta) **10100**
Atlanta Journal-Constitution (Atlanta) **9974**
Augusta Chronicle, The (Augusta) **9974**
† Augusta Herald (Augusta)
Austell Neighbor (Marietta) **10104**
Bainbridge Post-Searchlight
  (Bainbridge) **10101**
Bartow Neighbor, The (Cartersville) **10101**
Baxley News-Banner (Baxley) **10101**
Benning Leader, The (Columbus) **10102**
Berrien Press (Nashville) **10105**
Blade, The (Swainsboro) **10106**
Brantley Enterprise (Nahunta) **10105**
Brunswick News, The (Brunswick) **9974**
Bryan County Times (Pembroke) **10105**
Business Post, The (Alpharetta) **10100**
Cairo Messenger (Cairo) **10101**
Calhoun Times (Calhoun) **10101**
Camden County Tribune (St. Marys) **10106**
Camilla Enterprise (Camilla) **10101**
Cartersville Daily Tribune News
  (Cartersville) **9974**
Catoosa County News (Ringgold) **10105**
Cedartown Standard (Cedartown) **10101**
Chamblee-DeKalb Neighbor (Marietta) **10104**
Charlton County Herald (Folkston) **10103**
Chatsworth Times, The (Chatsworth) **10101**
Chattooga Press (Summerville) **10106**
Cherokee Tribune, The (Canton) **10101**
Chieftain & Toccoa Record (Toccoa) **10106**
Clayton Neighbor (Marietta) **10104**
Clayton News Daily (Jonesboro) **9975**
† Clayton Sun (Atlanta)
Clayton Tribune (Clayton) **10102**
Clinch County News (Homerville) **10103**
Coastal Courier (Hinesville) **10103**
Coastal Illustrated (St. Simons Island) **10106**
Columbia News Times (Martinez) **10104**

Columbus Ledger-Enquirer (Columbus) **9975**
Commerce News (Commerce) **10102**
Cordele Dispatch (Cordele) **9975**
Courier Herald, The (Dublin) **9975**
† Courier, The (Thomasville)
Covington News (Covington) **10102**
Crier Newspaper (Dunwoody) **10102**
Daily/Sunday Sun, The (Warner Robins) **9976**
Daily Citizen News (Dalton) **9975**
Daily Tribune News (Cartersville) **9975**
Dallas New Era (Dallas) **10102**
Darien News (Darien) **10102**
Dawson News, The (Dawson) **10102**
Decatur-DeKalb News/Era (Decatur) **10102**
† DeKalb News/Sun (Decatur)
Dodge County News, The (Eastman) **10102**
Donalsonville News (Donalsonville) **10102**
Doraville-DeKalb Neighbor (Marietta) **10104**
Douglas County Sentinel (Douglasville) **9975**
Douglas Enterprise (Douglas) **10102**
Douglas Neighbor, The (Marietta) **10104**
Dunwoody-DeKalb Neighbor, The
  (Marietta) **10104**
Elberton Star (Elberton) **10103**
Fayette County News (Fayetteville) **10103**
Fayette Neighbor, The (Fayetteville) **10103**
† Fayette Sun (Fayetteville)
Forsyth County News (Cumming) **10102**
Franklin County Citizen (Lavonia) **10104**
Georgia South (Boston) **10101**
Georgia Times-Union (Brunswick) **9974**
Glennville Sentinel (Glennville) **10103**
Glynco Observer (Brunswick) **10101**
Griffin Daily News (Griffin) **9975**
† Gwinnett Daily News (Lawrenceville)
Gwinnett Daily Post (Lawrenceville) **9975**
Haralson Gateway-Beacon, The
  (Bremen) **10101**
Harbor Sound (Brunswick) **10101**
Hartwell Sun, The (Hartwell) **10103**
Henry Herald, The (McDonough) **10105**
Herald-Gazette, The (Barnesville) **10101**
Herald-Leader, The (Fitzgerald) **10103**
Herald-Tribune, The (Cartersville) **10101**
Herald Extra Express (Statesboro) **10105**
Herald, The (Rincon) **10105**
Houston Times-Journal (Perry) **10105**
Islander, The (St. Simons Island) **10106**
Jackson Herald (Jefferson) **10103**
Jackson Progress-Argus (Jackson) **10103**
Jeff Davis Ledger (Hazlehurst) **10103**
Jekyll's Golden Islander (Brunswick) **10101**
Kennesaw Neighbor, The (Marietta) **10104**
La Grange Daily News (La Grange) **9975**
Lakeside Ledger, The (Woodstock) **10106**
Leader-Tribune, The (Fort Valley) **10103**

Ludowici News (Ludowici) **10104**
Mableton Neighbor, The (Marietta) **10104**
Macon Telegraph (Macon) **9975**
Madisonian, The (Madison) **10104**
Manchester Star-Mercury (Manchester) **10104**
Marietta Daily Journal (Marietta) **9975**
McDuffie Progress, The (Thomson) **10106**
Meriwether Free Press (Greenville) **10103**
Meriwether Vindicator (Manchester) **10104**
Miller County Liberal (Colquitt) **10102**
Newnan Times-Herald (Newnan) **10105**
News Leader, The (Royston) **10105**
North Bartow News (Adairsville) **10100**
Northeast Georgian, The (Cornelia) **10102**
North Georgia News (Blairsville) **10101**
Northside Neighbor, The (Atlanta) **10100**
Observer, The (Moultrie) **9975**
Oconee Breeze (Madison) **10104**
Paulding Neighbor, The (Marietta) **10104**
Pelham Journal (Pelham) **10105**
Powder Springs Neighbor, The
  (Marietta) **10104**
Press-Sentinel, The (Jesup) **10103**
Rockdale Citizen (Conyers) **9975**
Rockdale Neighbor, The (Conyers) **10102**
Rockmart Journal (Rockmart) **10105**
Rome News-Tribune (Rome) **9975**
Roswell-Alpharetta Neighbor (Roswell) **10105**
Roswell/Alpharetta Crier Newspaper
  (Dunwoody) **10102**
Sandersville Progress (Sandersville) **10105**
Sandy Springs Neighbor, The (Atlanta) **10101**
Savannah Morning News/Evening Press
  (Savannah) **9976**
South Dekalb Neighbor, The (Marietta) **10104**
South Fulton Neighbor, The (Marietta) **10104**
† Southside Sun (East Point)
Sparta Ishmaelite (Sparta) **10105**
Star Express (Covington) **10102**
Statesboro Herald (Statesboro) **9976**
Summerville News (Summerville) **10106**
Sylvester Local News (Sylvester) **10106**
Telfair Enterprise (McRae) **10105**
Telfair Times (Helena) **10103**
This Week In Peachtree City (Peachtree
  City) **10105**
Thomaston Times (Thomaston) **10106**
Thomasville Times-Enterprise
  (Thomasville) **9976**
Three Rivers Gazette (Helena) **10103**
Tifton Gazette (Tifton) **9976**
Times-Courier (Ellijay) **10103**
Times-Georgian (Carrollton) **9974**
Times Journal-Spotlight (Eastman) **10103**
Times, The (Gainesville) **9975**
True Citizen, The (Waynesboro) **10106**

Tucker-DeKalb Neighbor, The (Atlanta) **10101**
Union-Recorder (Milledgeville) **9975**
Valdosta Daily Times (Valdosta) **9976**
Villa Rican (Villa Rica) **10106**
Walker County Messenger (La Fayette) **10104**
Walton Tribune (Monroe) **10105**
Washington News-Reporter
  (Washington) **10106**
Waycross Journal Herald (Waycross) **9976**
Winder News (Winder) **10106**
Wrightsville Headlight, The
  (Wrightsville) **10106**

GUAM

Guam Tribune (Agana) **10106**
Pacific Daily News (Agana) **9976**

HAWAII

Garden Island Extra (Lihue) **10107**
Hawaii Tribune-Herald (Hilo) **9976**
Honolulu Advertiser (Honolulu) **9976**
Honolulu Star-Bulletin (Honolulu) **9976**
Island Times (Lihue) **9976**
Maui News (Wailuku) **9976**
MidWeek (Kaneohe) **10106**
Sun Press (Kaneohe) **10107**
West Hawaii Today (Kailua Kona) **9976**

IDAHO

Aberdeen Times (Aberdeen) **10107**
† Adams County Leader (Council)
Arco Advertiser (Arco) **10107**
Blackfoot Morning News (Blackfoot) **9976**
Bonner County Daily Bee (Sandpoint) **9977**
Bonners Ferry Herald (Bonners Ferry) **10107**
Buhl Herald (Buhl) **10107**
Cable Scene (Idaho Falls) **10108**
Caribou County Sun (Soda Springs) **10109**
Challis Messenger (Challis) **10107**
Clearwater Tribune (Orofino) **10108**
Coeur d'Alene Press (Coeur d'Alene) **9977**
Cottonwood Chronicle (Cottonwood) **10107**
East County Chronicle (Kimberly) **10108**
Fremont County Herald-Chronicle (St.
  Anthony) **10109**
Gooding County Leader (Gooding) **10107**
† Grace Citizen (Preston)
Idaho County Free Press (Grangeville) **10107**
Idaho Enterprise (Malad City) **10108**
Idaho Falls Post Register (Idaho Falls) **9977**
Idaho Mountain Express (Ketchum) **10108**
Idaho Press-Tribune (Nampa) **9977**

Idaho State Journal (Pocatello) **9977**
Idaho Statesman, The (Boise) **9976**
Independent Enterprise (Payette) **10108**
Jefferson Star, The (Rigby) **10109**
Kendrick-Gazette (Kendrick) **10108**
Kuna-Melba News (Kuna) **10108**
Lewis County Herald (Nezperce) **10108**
Lewiston Morning Tribune (Lewiston) **9977**
Lincoln County Journal (Shoshone) **10109**
Long Valley Advocate, The (Cascade) **10107**
Messenger Index (Emmett) **10107**
Middleton Gazette (Middleton) **10108**
Minidoka County News (Rupert) **10109**
Moscow-Pullman Daily News (Moscow) **9977**
Mountain Home News (Mountain
  Home) **10108**
News-Examiner (Montpelier) **10108**
North Side News (Jerome) **10108**
Palouse Living (Moscow) **10108**
Post Falls Tribune (Post Falls) **10108**
Power County Press (American Falls) **10107**
Preston Citizen (Preston) **10108**
Priest River Times (Priest River) **10108**
Recorder-Herald (Salmon) **10109**
Record, The (Council) **10107**
† Sandpoint News-Bulletin (Sandpoint)
Shelley Pioneer (Shelley) **10109**
Shopper, The (Grangeville) **10107**
Shoshone News-Press (Kellogg) **9977**
South Idaho Press (Burley) **9977**
Standard Journal (Rexburg) **10109**
Star-News, The (McCall) **10108**
St. Maries Gazette Record (St. Maries) **10109**
Teton Valley News (Driggs) **10107**
Twin Falls Times-News (Twin Falls) **9977**
Upper Country News-Reporter
  (Cambridge) **10107**
Valley News (Meridian) **10108**
† Wallace Miner (Kellogg)
Weiser Signal American (Weiser) **10109**
Wood River Journal (Hailey) **10107**

ILLINOIS

Abingdon Argus (Abingdon) **10109**
Addison Press (Elmhurst) **10116**
Advertiser, The (Worden) **10129**
Advocate, The (Clifton) **10114**
Algonquin Countryside (Barrington) **10110**
Alsip Express (Midlothian) **10123**
Altamont News, The (Altamont) **10109**
Amboy News, The (Amboy) **10109**
Antioch News-Reporter (Grayslake) **10118**
Arcola Record Herald (Arcola) **10109**
Area News, The (Gillespie) **10118**

Arlington Heights Journal & Topics (Des Plaines) **10115**
Arthur Graphic Clarion (Arthur) **10110**
Ashton Gazette (Ashton) **10110**
Astoria South Fulton Argus (Astoria) **10110**
Atwood Herald (Atwood) **10110**
Auburn Citizen (Auburn) **10110**
Austin Weekly News (Oak Park) **10125**
Avon Sentinel (Abingdon) **10109**
Back of the Yards Journal (Chicago) **10112**
Barrington Courier Review (Barrington) **10110**
Beacon News (Aurora) **9977**
Beardstown Illinoian-Star (Beardstown) **10111**
Beecher City Journal (Beecher City) **10111**
Belleville Journal (Belleville) **10111**
Belleville News-Democrat (Belleville) **9977**
Belvidere Daily Republican (Belvidere) **9978**
Bensenville Press (Elmhurst) **10116**
Berwyn/Cicero Life (Berwyn) **10111**
Beverly News (Midlothian) **10123**
Beverly Review (Chicago) **10112**
Blandinsville Star Gazette (Abingdon) **10109**
Bloomingdale Press (Bloomingdale) **10111**
Blue Mound Leader (Blue Mound) **10111**
Bolingbrook Metropolitan (Lemont) **10121**
Bolingbrook Sun (Bolingbrook) **10111**
Braceville Express (Wilmington) **10129**
Braidwood Index (Wilmington) **10129**
Braidwood Journal, The (Braidwood) **10111**
Breese Journal (Breese) **10111**
Bridgeport Leader (Bridgeport) **10111**
Bridgeport News (Chicago) **10112**
Bridgeview Independent (Midlothian) **10123**
Brighton Park-McKinley Park Life (Chicago) **10112**
Buffalo Grove Countryside (Bannockburn) **10110**
Buffalo Grove Journal & Topics (Des Plaines) **10115**
Bugle, The (Niles) **10124**
Bunker Hill Gazette News (Bunker Hill) **10112**
Burbank-Stickney Independent (Midlothian) **10123**
Bureau County Republican (Princeton) **10127**
Burr Ridge Doings (Hinsdale) **10120**
Cahokia Journal (Columbia) **10114**
Cairo Citizen (Cairo) **10112**
Calhoun News (Hardin) **10119**
Cambridge Chronicle (Cambridge) **10112**
Carlinville Democrat (Carlinville) **10112**
Carlyle Union Banner (Carlyle) **10112**
Carmi Times (Carmi) **9978**
Carol Stream Press (Bloomingdale) **10111**
Carroll County Review (Thomson) **10128**
Carrollton Gazette Patriot (Carrollton) **10112**
Cary-Grove Countryside (Barrington) **10110**

Centralia Sentinel (Centralia) **9978**
Champaign News Gazette (Champaign) **9978**
Charleston Times-Courier (Charleston) **9978**
Chatham Clarion (Auburn) **10110**
Chicago-Lawndale News (Chicago) **10112**
Chicago's N.W. Side Press (Chicago) **10113**
Chicago Defender (Chicago) **9978**
Chicago Near North News (Chicago) **10113**
Chicago Near West Gazette (Chicago) **10113**
Chicago Post (Chicago) **10113**
Chicago Reader (Chicago) **10113**
Chicago Ridge Citizen (Midlothian) **10123**
Chicago Sun Times (Chicago) **9978**
Chicago Tribune (Chicago) **9978**
Chicago West Side Times (Chicago) **10113**
Chillicothe Bulletin (Chillicothe) **10114**
Chrisman Leader (Chrisman) **10114**
Cissna Park News (Cissna Park) **10114**
Clarendon Hills Doings, The (Hinsdale) **10120**
Clarendon Hills Progress (Downers Grove) **10115**
Clarion Journal, The (Columbia) **10114**
Clear-Ridge Reporter (Chicago) **10113**
Clinton County Post (Mascoutah) **10122**
Clinton Daily Journal (Clinton) **9978**
Coal City Courant (Coal City) **10114**
Coal City Express (Wilmington) **10129**
Colchester Chronicle (Colchester) **10114**
Collinsville Herald (Collinsville) **10114**
Collinsville Journal (Collinsville) **10114**
Command Post, The (Mascoutah) **10122**
Commercial-News (Danville) **9978**
County Edition, The (Jerseyville) **10120**
County Journal (Belleville) **10111**
County Journal (Percy) **10126**
Courier-News, The (Elgin) **9979**
† Cuba Journal (Cuba)
Daily American (West Frankfort) **9982**
Daily Chronicle (De Kalb) **9979**
Daily Clay County Advocate-Press (Flora) **9979**
Daily Gazette (Sterling) **9981**
Daily Herald (Arlington Heights) **9977**
Daily Journal (Kankakee) **9980**
Daily Ledger (Canton) **9978**
Daily Review Atlas (Monmouth) **9980**
Daily Southtown (Chicago) **9978**
Daily Times (Ottawa) **9981**
Dallas City Enterprise (Dallas City) **10114**
Darien Doings (Hinsdale) **10120**
Darien Metropolitan (Lemont) **10121**
Darien Progress (Downers Grove) **10115**
Decatur Tribune (Decatur) **10114**
Deerfield Review (Bannockburn) **10110**
Delavan Times, The (Delavan) **10115**
Democrat-Message (Mt. Sterling) **10124**
Des Plaines Journal (Des Plaines) **9979**

Des Plaines Times (Park Ridge) **10126**
Divernon News (Auburn) **10110**

Downers Grove Reporter (Downers
   Grove) **10115**
† DuPage Press Service (Wheaton)
Du Quoin Evening Call (Du Quoin) **9979**
Durand-Dakota Volunteer (Durand) **10115**
Durand Gazette (Love Park) **10122**
Earlville Leader (Earlville) **10116**
East Peoria Courier (Morton) **10124**
East St. Louis Monitor (East St. Louis) **10116**
East St. Louis News Journal (Columbia) **10114**
Edgebrook Times Review (Park Ridge) **10126**
Edison-Norwood Times Review (Park
   Ridge) **10126**
Edwardsville Intelligencer (Edwardsville) **9979**
Edwardsville Journal (Edwardsville) **10116**
Effingham Daily News (Effingham) **9979**
Elburn Herald (Elburn) **10116**
Eldorado Daily Journal (Eldorado) **9979**
Elmhurst Press (Elmhurst) **10116**
Elm Leaves (Oak Park) **10125**
Elmwood Park-River Grove Times
   (Lincolnwood) **10121**
El Paso Journal (El Paso) **10116**
Elwood Express (Wilmington) **10129**
Enterprise, The (Plainfield) **10126**
Evanston Review (Evanston) **10117**
Evening News (Benton) **9978**
Evergreen Park Courier (Midlothian) **10123**
Fairfield Wayne County Press (Fairfield) **10117**
Fairview Heights Journal (Belleville) **10111**
Fairview Heights Tribune (Mascoutah) **10122**
Farina News, The (Farina) **10117**
Farmer's Weekly Review (Joliet) **10121**
Farmer City Journal (Farmer City) **10117**
Fisher Reporter (Fisher) **10117**
Flanagan Home Times (Flanagan) **10117**
Ford County Press (Melvin) **10123**
Forest Leaves (Oak Park) **10125**
Forreston Journal (Forreston) **10117**
Fox Lake Press (Grayslake) **10118**
Fox Valley Shopping News, The
   (Plainfield) **10126**
Fox Valley Sun (Naperville) **10124**
Franklin Park Herald-Journal (Oak
   Park) **10125**
Franklin Park Star-Sentinel (Melrose
   Park) **10123**
Freeport Advertiser Shopping News
   (Freeport) **10117**
Freeport Journal-Standard (Freeport) **9979**
Fulton Journal (Fulton) **10117**
Galena Gazette (Galena) **10117**
Galesburg Post, The (Galesburg) **10117**

Galva News (Galva) **10117**
Gardner South Wilmington Post
   (Wilmington) **10129**
Gazette-Democrat (Anna) **10109**
Gazette, The (Elizabeth) **10116**
Geneseo Republic (Geneseo) **10117**
Geneseo Shopper (Geneseo) **10117**
Geneva Republican (Geneva) **10117**
Genoa-Kingston-Kirkland News
   (Sycamore) **10128**
Gibson City Courier (Gibson City) **10118**
Gilman Star (Gilman) **10118**
Glasford Gazette, The (Glasford) **10118**
Glendale Heights Press (Elmhurst) **10116**
Glen Ellyn News (Glen Ellyn) **10118**
Glen Ellyn Press (Bloomingdale) **10111**
Glenview Announcements (Glenview) **10118**
Golden Prairie News (Assumption) **10110**
Golfmill Journal (Des Plaines) **10115**
Good News Shopper (Coal City) **10114**
Granite City Press Journal (Granite
   City) **10118**
Grayslake Times (Grayslake) **10118**
Greene Prairie Press (White Hall) **10128**
Greenup Press (Greenup) **10119**
Greenville Advocate, The (Greenville) **10119**
Gurnee Press (Grayslake) **10118**
Hampshire Register News (Sycamore) **10128**
Hancock County Journal-Pilot
   (Carthage) **10112**
Hancock County Quill (La Harpe) **10121**
† Hanover Park Township Times (Carol Stream)
Hardin Calhoun Herald (Hardin) **10119**
Hardin County Independent
   (Elizabethtown) **10116**
Harlem-Foster-Norwood Park-Edison Park Times
   (Lincolnwood) **10121**
Harlem-Irving Times (Lincolnwood) **10121**
Harrisburg Daily Register (Harrisburg) **9979**
† Harwood Heights News (Park Ridge)
Havana Mason County Democrat
   (Havana) **10119**
Henderson County Quill (Stronghurst) **10128**
Henry News Republican (Henry) **10119**
Herald-News, The (Joliet) **9980**
Herald-Review (Decatur) **9979**
Herald-Star, The (Edinburg) **10116**
Herald/Country Market, The
   (Bourbonnais) **10111**
Herald Enterprise (Golconda) **10118**
Herrin Spokesman (Herrin) **10119**
Herscher Pilot (Herscher) **10119**
Hickory Hills Citizen (Midlothian) **10123**
Highland News Leader (Highland) **10119**
Highland Park News (Bannockburn) **10110**
Hillsboro Journal (Hillsboro) **10119**

Geographic

Hinsdale Doings (Hinsdale) **10120**
† Hodgkins Citizen (La Grange)
Hoopeston Chronicle (Hoopeston) **10120**
Huntley Farmside, The (Huntley) **10120**
Hyde Park Herald (Chicago) **10113**
Illinois Times (Springfield) **10127**
Illiopolis Sentinel (Illiopolis) **10120**
Independent News (Georgetown) **10118**
Indian Head Park Citizen (Oak Brook) **10125**
Indian Head Park Doings (Hinsdale) **10120**
Inside (Chicago) **10113**
† Inside Ravenswood (Chicago)
Iroquois County Times Republic
  (Watseka) **9981**
Jacksonville Journal-Courier
  (Jacksonville) **9979**
Jefferson Park-Portage Park-Bel Cragin Times
  (Lincolnwood) **10121**
Journal, The (Chicago) **10113**
Kane County Chronicle (Geneva) **9979**
Kendall County Record (Yorkville) **10129**
Kewanee Star-Courier (Kewanee) **9980**
Kinmundy Express (Kinmundy) **10121**
Knoxville Journal, The (Galesburg) **10117**
Lacon Home Journal (Lacon) **10121**
La Grange Countryside Citizen (Oak
  Brook) **10125**
La Grange Park Citizen (Oak Brook) **10125**
Lake Forester (Bannockburn) **10110**
Lakeland Press (Grayslake) **10118**
Lake Villa Record (Grayslake) **10119**
Lake Zurich Enterprise (Grayslake) **10119**
Lawrence County News (Lawrenceville) **10121**
Lawrenceville Daily Record
  (Lawrenceville) **9980**
▼Lebanon Herald (Mascoutah) **10122**
Lemont Metropolitan (Lemont) **10121**
Lemont Reporter (Lemont) **10121**
Lewistown-Fulton Democrat (Lewistown) **10121**
Libertyville News (Grayslake) **10119**
Libertyville Review (Bannockburn) **10110**
Limestone Independent News
  (Bartonville) **10111**
† Lincoln-Belmont Booster (Chicago)
Lincoln Courier (Lincoln) **9980**
Lincolnwood Life (Lincolnwood) **10122**
Lincolnwood Review (Evanston) **10117**
Lindenhurst News (Grayslake) **10119**
Lisle Sun (Naperville) **10124**
Litchfield News-Herald (Litchfield) **9980**
Loda Times (Paxton) **10126**
Lombardian, The (Lombard) **10122**
Lombardian Villa Park Review
  (Lombard) **10122**
Lombard Spectator (Elmhurst) **10116**
† London Mills Times (Roseville)

Lyons Citizen (Oak Brook) **10125**
M & M Journal (Hillsboro) **10120**
Macomb Journal (Macomb) **9980**
Macoupin & Montgomery County Journal
  (Hillsboro) **10120**
Macoupin County Enquirer (Carlinville) **10112**
Macoupin County Shopper (Hillsboro) **10120**
Madison County Chronicle (Worden) **10129**
Marion Daily Republican (Marion) **9980**
Mascoutah Herald (Mascoutah) **10122**
Mattoon Journal Gazette (Mattoon) **9980**
Maywood Herald (Oak Park) **10125**
McDonough-Democrat (Bushnell) **10112**
McLeansboro Times-Leader
  (McLeansboro) **10123**
Melrose Park Herald (Oak Park) **10125**
Melrose Park Star-Sentinel (Melrose
  Park) **10123**
Menard County Review (Greenview) **10119**
Mendota Reporter (Mendota) **10123**
Metropolis Planet (Metropolis) **10123**
Midlothian-Bremen Messenger
  (Midlothian) **10123**
MidWeek, The (DeKalb) **10114**
Millstadt Enterprise (Columbia) **10114**
Minonk News Dispatch (Minonk) **10124**
Monroe County Clarion (Columbia) **10114**
Montgomery County News, The
  (Hillsboro) **10120**
Morris Daily Herald (Morris) **9980**
Morton Grove-Niles Life (Lincolnwood) **10122**
Morton Grove Champion (Evanston) **10117**
Mount Carmel Daily Republican-Register (Mt.
  Carmel) **9980**
Mount Greenwood Express (Midlothian) **10123**
Mount Prospect Journal (Des Plaines) **10115**
Mount Prospect Times (Glenview) **10118**
Mt. Olive Herald, The (Mt. Olive) **10124**
Mt. Vernon Register News (Mt. Vernon) **9980**
Mundelein News (Grayslake) **10119**
Mundelein Review (Bannockburn) **10110**
Naperville Metropolitan (Lemont) **10121**
Naperville Sun (Naperville) **10124**
Nashville News, The (Nashville) **10124**
† Near South Herald (Chicago)
New City (Chicago) **10113**
News-Progress (Sullivan) **10128**
News-Record, The (Cerro Gordo) **10112**
News-Sun, The (Waukegan) **9982**
News-Tribune (La Salle) **9980**
News Gazette, The (Love Park) **10122**
NewsMarketer, The (Chicago) **10113**
News Star (Lincolnwood) **10122**
Newton Press-Mentor (Newton) **10124**
Niantic-Harristown County Line Observer
  (Illiopolis) **10120**

Niles Herald Spectator (Park Ridge) 10126
Niles Journal (Des Plaines) 10115
Niles Life (Lincolnwood) 10122
Nokomis Free Press-Progress
    (Nokomis) 10124
Norridge-Harwood Heights News (Park
    Ridge) 10126
Norridge-Harwood Heights Times
    (Lincolnwood) 10122
Northbrook Star (Glenview) 10118
North Center-Lincoln Belmont-Lake View Booster
    (Lincolnwood) 10122
North County News (Red Bud) 10127
Northern Ogle County Tempo (Byron) 10112
Northlake Star-Sentinel (Melrose Park) 10123
North Loop News (Chicago) 10113
North Riverside Citizen (Oak Brook) 10125
North Suburban Herald (Love Park) 10122
Northwestern Illinois Dispatch
    (Savanna) 10127
Northwestern Illinois Farmer (Lena) 10121
Northwest Herald (Crystal Lake) 9978
Northwest Journal & Topics (Des
    Plaines) 10115
Northwest Leader (Chicago) 10113
Northwest Side Press (Chicago) 10113
O'Fallon Progress (O'Fallon) 10124
Oak Brook Doings (Hinsdale) 10120
Oak Brook Press (Elmhurst) 10116
Oak Brook Terrace Doings (Hinsdale) 10120
Oak Lawn-Evergreen Park Reporter (Palos
    Heights) 10125
Oak Lawn Independent (Midlothian) 10123
Oak Leaves, The (Oak Park) 10125
Ogle County Life (Oregon) 10125
Olney Daily Mail (Olney) 9981
Olympia Review (Minier) 10124
Orion Gazette (Orion) 10125
† Orion Times (Orion)
Orland Metropolitan (Lemont) 10121
Orland Township Messenger
    (Midlothian) 10123
Palatine Countryside (Arlington
    Heights) 10109
Palatine Journal & Topics (Des Plaines) 10115
Palos Citizen (Midlothian) 10123
Palos Hills-Hickory Hills (Palos Heights) 10126
Pana News-Palladium (Pana) 10126
Pantagraph, The (Bloomington) 9978
Paper, The (Barry) 10110
Paris Beacon News (Paris) 9981
Park Ridge Herald Advocate (Park
    Ridge) 10126
Park Ridge Journal (Des Plaines) 10115
Pawnee Post (Auburn) 10110
Paxton Daily Record (Paxton) 9981

Pekin Daily Times (Pekin) 9981
Penny Saver (Tinley Park) 10128
Peoria Heights Herald (Peoria) 10126
Peoria Journal Star (Peoria) 9981
Peoria Observer (Peoria) 10126
Petersburg Observer (Petersburg) 10126
Piatt County Journal-Republican
    (Monticello) 10124
Pontiac Daily Leader (Pontiac) 9981
Prairie Shopper, The (La Fayette) 10121
Prairie Times, The (La Fayette) 10121
Prospect Heights Journal (Des Plaines) 10115
Proviso Star-Sentinel (Melrose Park) 10123
Pulaski Enterprise (Mounds) 10124
Putnam County Record (Granville) 10118
Quincy Herald-Whig (Quincy) 9981
Randolph County Herald Tribune
    (Chester) 10112
Rankin Independent (Cissna Park) 10114
† Rantoul Pacesetter (Rantoul)
Rantoul Press (Rantoul) 10127
Record Times, The (Paxton) 10126
Regional News (Palos Heights) 10126
Register-Mail (Galesburg) 9979
Register Star (Rockford) 9981
Reporter, The (Casey) 10112
Reporter, The (Chicago) 10113
Reporter, The (Palos Heights) 10126
Review, The (Erie) 10116
Review, The (Marion) 10122
River North News (Chicago) 10113
Riverton Register (Riverton) 10127
Roanoke Review (Roanoke) 10127
Robinson Daily News (Robinson) 9981
Rochelle News Leader (Rochelle) 10127
Rochester Times (Auburn) 10110
Rock Island Argus Dispatch, The
    (Moline) 9980
Rogers Park/Edgewater News/Uptown News
    Star (Lincolnwood) 10122
Rolling Meadows Journal & Topics (Des
    Plaines) 10115
Romeoville Metropolitan (Lemont) 10121
Romeoville Sun (Bolingbrook) 10111
† Roselle Record (Carol Stream)
Rosemont Journal (Des Plaines) 10115
Rosemont Times (Park Ridge) 10126
Roseville Independent (Roseville) 10127
Round Lake News (Grayslake) 10119
Rushville Times, The (Rushville) 10127
Saint Elmo Banner (St. Elmo) 10127
Salem Times-Commoner (Salem) 10127
Savanna Times Journal (Savanna) 10127
Scott Flier (Mascoutah) 10122
Scottsdale-Ashburn Independent
    (Midlothian) 10124

Sentinel, The (Chicago)   10113
Shelbyville Daily Union (Shelbyville)   9981
Shopper, The (South Holland)   10127
Skokie Life (Lincolnwood)   10122
Skokie Review (Evanston)   10117
Skyline (Lincolnwood)   10122
Sorento News (Hillsboro)   10120
South County Express (Auburn)   10110
Southern Illinoisan (Carbondale)   9978
Southwest Beacon (Chicago)   10113
Southwest Courier (Chicago)   10113
Southwestern Journal News (Brighton)   10111
Southwest News-Herald (Chicago)   10113
Southwest Shopper (Chicago)   10113
Sparta News Plaindealer (Sparta)   10127
Springfield Shopper (Springfield)   10127
Star, The (Chicago Heights)   10114
State Journal-Register (Springfield)   9981
Staunton Star-Times (Staunton)   10127
Streator Times-Press (Streator)   9981
Suburban Journal (Des Plaines)   10115
Suburban Leader (Chicago)   10113
Suburban Life Citizen (Oak Brook)   10125
Suburban Life Graphic (Oak Brook)   10125
Sumner Press (Sumner)   10128
Sycamore News (Sycamore)   10128
Taylorville Breeze-Courier (Taylorville)   9981
Tazewell News (Morton)   10124
Telegraph-County Edition (Jerseyville)   10120
Telegraph, The (Alton)   9977
Telegraph, The (Dixon)   9979
† This Week (Aledo)
Thrif-T-Nikel Weekly Newspaper
  (Ottawa)   10125
Thrifty Nickel (Champaign)   10112
Thrifty Nickel Want Ads (East Moline)   10116
Times Record (Aledo)   10109
Times, The (Lansing)   9980
Town & Country Weekly (Ottawa)   10125
Trenton Sun, The (Trenton)   10128
Tri-County News (Elmwood)   10116
Tri City Register (Riverton)   10127
Tuscola Review (Tuscola)   10128
Vandalia Leader-Union (Vandalia)   10128
Vernon Hills News (Grayslake)   10119
Vernon Hills Review (Bannockburn)   10110
Vienna Times, The (Vienna)   10128
Villa Park Argus (Elmhurst)   10116
Virginia Gazette (Beardstown)   10111
Warren-Newport Press (Grayslake)   10119
Warrenville Free Press (West Chicago)   10128
Washburn Leader (Metamora)   10123
Washington Courier (Washington)   10128
Washington Reporter (Morton)   10124
Waterloo Republic-Times (Waterloo)   10128
Wauconda Leader (Grayslake)   10119

Waverly Journal (Waverly)   10128
Wednesday Journal of Oak Park & River Forest
  (Oak Park)   10125
Wenona Index (Henry)   10119
Westchester Herald (Oak Park)   10125
West Cook County Press (Elmhurst)   10116
Western Springs Doings (Hinsdale)   10120
Westmont Progress (Downers Grove)   10115
West Proviso Herald (Oak Park)   10125
West Suburban Post (Chicago)   10113
Wheaton Leader (Glen Ellyn)   10118
Wheaton Press (Bloomingdale)   10111
Wheaton Sun (Naperville)   10124
Whiteside Shopper (Fulton)   10117
Williamsville Sun (Riverton)   10127
Willowbrook Doings (Hinsdale)   10120
Wilmette Life (Glenview)   10118
Wilmington Advocate, The (Wilmington)   10129
Wilmington Express (Wilmington)   10129
Wilmington Free Press (Wilmington)   10129
Winfield Estate (Glen Ellyn)   10118
Winfield Press (West Chicago)   10128
Winnetka Talk (Glenview)   10118
Wood Dale Press (Elmhurst)   10116
Woodford County Journal (Eureka)   10116
Woodridge Progress (Downers Grove)   10115
Woodstock Independent, The
  (Woodstock)   10129
Worth-Palos Reporter (Palos Heights)   10126
Worth-Ridge Reporter (Palos Heights)   10126
Worth Citizen (Midlothian)   10124
† Wrova Reporter (Galva)
Zion-Benton News (Zion)   10129

INDIANA

Ad-News (Greenfield)   10132
Advertiser, The (Ligonier)   10133
Alexandria Times-Tribune (Alexandria)   10129
Allen County Times (New Haven)   10134
Auctioner, The (Pekin)   10134
Banner-Gazette (Pekin)   10134
Banner-Graphic (Greencastle)   9983
Batesville Herald-Tribune (Batesville)   10129
Benton Review, The (Fowler)   10131
Berne Tri-Weekly News (Berne)   10130
Bluffton News-Banner (Bluffton)   9982
Boonville Standard (Boonville)   10130
Brazil Times (Brazil)   9982
Brookville American-Democrat
  (Brookville)   10130
Brown County Democrat (Nashville)   10134
Call-Leader (Elwood)   9983
Calumet Press, The (Highland)   10132
Carmel News Tribune (Fishers)   10131
Carroll County Comet (Flora)   10131

Castleton Banner (Fishers) **10131**
Cedar Lake Journal (Lowell) **10133**
Centerville Crusader (Centerville) **10130**
† Chandler Post (Boonville)
Chesterton Guide (Portage) **10135**
Chesterton Town Crier (Valparaiso) **10136**
Chesterton Tribune (Chesterton) **9982**
Clarion News (Corydon) **10130**
Connersville News-Examiner
  (Connersville) **9982**
Corydon Democrat (Corydon) **10130**
Courier, The (Rensselaer) **10135**
Crawfordsville Journal Review
  (Crawfordsville) **9982**
Crothersville Times (Crothersville) **10130**
Culver Citizen (Culver) **10130**
Cumberland Courier Weekly (Lawrence) **10133**
Daily Clintonian (Clinton) **9982**
Daily Journal (Franklin) **9983**
Daily Ledger (Fisher) **9983**
Daily Reporter (Greenfield) **9983**
Dale News, The (Ferdinand) **10131**
Dearborn County Register
  (Lawrenceburg) **10133**
Decatur Daily Democrat (Decatur) **9983**
DeKalb County Advertiser (Auburn) **10129**
East Side Herald (Indianapolis) **10132**
Elkhart Truth, The (Elkhart) **9983**
Evansville Courier (Evansville) **9983**
Evansville Press (Evansville) **9983**
Evening Star (Auburn) **9982**
Evening World (Bloomfield) **9982**
Farmweek (Knightstown) **10133**
Ferdinand News, The (Ferdinand) **10131**
Fishers Sun-Herald (Fishers) **10131**
Fort Wayne News-Sentinel (Fort Wayne) **9983**
Fountain County Neighbor (Attica) **10129**
Frankfort Times (Frankfort) **9983**
Franklin Challenger (Greenwood) **10132**
Gary Crusader (Gary) **10132**
Gary Info (Gary) **10132**
Geist Gazette (Fishers) **10131**
Giveaway, The (Scottsburg) **10135**
Goshen News, The (Goshen) **9983**
Greensburg Daily News (Greensburg) **9983**
Greenwood & Southside Challenger
  (Greenwood) **10132**
Greenwood Gazette, The (Fishers) **10131**
Griffith Guide (Highland) **10132**
Hagerstown Exponent, The
  (Hagerstown) **10132**
Hartford City News-Times (Hartford City) **9983**
Heights Herald (Fishers) **10131**
Hendricks County Flyer (Plainfield) **10135**
† Hendricks County Guide Gazette (Plainfield)
Herald-Journal, The (Monticello) **9985**

Herald-Republican (Angola) **10129**
Herald-Times (Bloomington) **9982**
Herald Bulletin (Anderson) **9982**
Herald, The (Jasper) **9984**
Highland Guide (Highland) **10132**
Hobart Gazette (Merriville) **10133**
Hoosier Express (Washington) **10136**
Huntington Herald-Press (Huntington) **9983**
Independent, The (Winamac) **10136**
Indianapolis East Side Herald
  (Indianapolis) **10132**
Indianapolis News (Indianapolis) **9984**
Indianapolis Recorder (Indianapolis) **10132**
Indianapolis Star (Indianapolis) **9984**
Indianapolis Westside Enterprise
  (Indianapolis) **10132**
Indy Suburban Newspaper (Greenfield) **10132**
Jackson County Banner (Brownstown) **10130**
Jeffersonville Evening News
  (Jeffersonville) **9984**
Journal & Austin Chronicle
  (Scottsburg) **10135**
Journal & Courier (Lafayette) **9984**
Journal-Gazette, The (Fort Wayne) **9983**
Journal Press (Lawrenceburg) **10133**
Journal, The (Ellettsville) **10130**
Kendallville News-Sun (Kendallville) **9984**
Kokomo Tribune, The (Kokomo) **9984**
Lafayette Leader (Lafayette) **10133**
La Grange Standard News (La Grange) **10133**
Lake County Star (Crown Point) **10130**
Lake Station Herald (Merrillville) **10133**
La Porte Herald-Argus (La Porte) **9984**
Lawrence Times (Fishers) **10131**
Lawrence Township Journal (Lawrence) **10133**
Leader, The (Charlestown) **10130**
Ledger Tribune, The (New Albany) **9985**
Ligonier Advance-Leader (Ligonier) **10133**
Linton Daily Citizen (Linton) **9984**
Lowell Tribune (Lowell) **10133**
Madison Courier (Madison) **9984**
Mail-Journal, The (Milford) **10134**
Marion Chronicle-Tribune (Marion) **9984**
† Marshall County Life (Culver)
Martinsville Daily Reporter (Martinsville) **9984**
Merrillville Herald (Merrillville) **10133**
Messenger, The (Attica) **10129**
Michigan City News-Dispatch (Michigan
  City) **9984**
Middletown News, The (Middletown) **10133**
Mishawaka Enterprise (Mishawaka) **10134**
Mooresville Times, The (Mooresville) **10134**
Mount Vernon Democrat (Mt. Vernon) **10134**
Munster Guide (Highland) **10132**
Newburgh-Chandler Register
  (Newburgh) **10134**

New Castle Courier-Times (New Castle) **9985**
New Prairie Town Crier (New Carlisle) **10134**
News-Gazette, The (Winchester) **9986**
News-Journal (North Manchester) **10134**
News-Sun (Fairmount) **10131**
News, The (Clay City) **10130**
Nora News Dispatch (Fisherspolis) **10131**
Northeast Reporter (Indianapolis) **10132**
North Knox News (Bicknell) **10130**
North Meridian Observer (Fishers) **10131**
North Side Topics (Fishers) **10131**
North Vernon Plain Dealer (North
  Vernon) **10134**
North Vernon Sun (North Vernon) **10134**
Northwest Press (Speedway) **10135**
NUVO Newsweekly (Indianapolis) **10132**
Ohio County News (Rising Sun) **10135**
Orange Countian (Paoli) **10134**
Osgood Journal (Versailles) **10136**
Ossian Journal (Ossian) **10134**
Paoli News (Paoli) **10134**
Paoli Republican (Paoli) **10134**
Paper of Wabash County, The
  (Wabash) **10136**
Paper, The (Elkhart) **10130**
Paper, The (Goshen) **10132**
Paper, The (Warsaw) **10136**
Perry County News, The (Tell City) **10136**
Perry Township Weekly (Beech Grove) **10129**
Peru Tribune (Peru) **9985**
Pharos-Tribune (Logansport) **9984**
Pike Register (Fishers) **10131**
Pilot-News (Plymouth) **9985**
Portage Journal-Press (Portage) **10135**
Portland Commercial Review (Portland) **9985**
Post & Mail, The (Columbia City) **9982**
Post-Tribune (Gary) **9983**
Press-Dispatch (Petersburg) **10134**
Princeton Daily Clarion (Princeton) **9985**
Pulaski County Journal (Winamac) **10136**
Regional News, The (La Crosse) **10133**
Remington Press (Rensselaer) **10135**
Rensselaer Republican (Rensselaer) **9985**
Reporter, The (Lebanon) **9984**
Republican, The (Danville) **10130**
Republic, The (Columbus) **9982**
Richmond Palladium-Item (Richmond) **9985**
Rising Sun Recorder (Rising Sun) **10135**
Rochester Sentinel, The (Rochester) **9985**
Rockville Parke County Sentinel
  (Rockville) **10135**
Rushville Republican (Rushville) **9985**
Salem Democrat, The (Salem) **10135**
Salem Leader (Salem) **10135**
Schererville Guide (Highland) **10132**
Shelbyville News (Shelbyville) **9985**

Sheridan News (Fishers) **10131**
South Bend Tri-County News (South
  Bend) **10135**
South Bend Tribune (South Bend) **9985**
South Lake Advertiser (Lowell) **10133**
Southwest Town Crier (La Porte) **10133**
Speedway Town Press (Speedway) **10135**
Spencer County Journal Democrat
  (Rockport) **10135**
Spencer Evening World (Spencer) **9986**
Spotlight, The (Indianapolis) **10132**
Springs Valley Herald (French Lick) **10131**
Star Journal (Hope) **10132**
Star Press (Muncie) **9985**
Sullivan Daily Times (Sullivan) **9986**
Sunriser News (Ossian) **10134**
Times-Mail (Bedford) **9982**
Times-Union (Warsaw) **9986**
Times, The (Munster) **9985**
Tipton Tribune (Tipton) **9986**
Town Crier, The (La Porte) **10133**
Tri-County Banner (Knightstown) **10133**
Tri-County News (Edinburgh) **10130**
Tribune-Star (Terre Haute) **9986**
Tribune, The (Seymour) **9985**
Valparaiso Guide (Portage) **10135**
Valparaiso Vidette-Times (Valparaiso) **9986**
Versailles Republican (Versailles) **10136**
Vevay Reveille-Enterprise (Vevay) **10136**
Vincennes Sun-Commercial (Vincennes) **9986**
† Vincennes Valley Advance (Vincennes)
Wabash Plain Dealer (Wabash) **9986**
Washington County Edition (Salem) **10135**
Washington Times-Herald (Washington) **9986**
† Weekender Enquirer (Boonville)
Weekend Flyer, The (Plainfield) **10135**
Western Wayne News (Cambridge City) **10130**
Westfield Enterprise (Fishers) **10131**
Westside Enterprise (Greenfield) **10132**
Westside Flyer (Indianapolis) **10133**
Westside Messenger (Speedway) **10135**
Westville Indicator (Westville) **10136**
▼White River Gazette (Fishers) **10131**
Worthington Times, The (Worthington) **10136**
† Zionsville Eagle (Indianapolis)
Zionsville Times Sentinel (Zionsville) **10136**

IOWA

Adair County Free Press (Greenfield) **10138**
Ad Express & Daily Iowegian
  (Centerville) **9987**
Afton Star-Enterprise (Afton) **10136**
Albia Union-Republican (Albia) **10136**
Algona Upper Des Moines (Algona) **10136**
Altoona Herald, The (Altoona) **10136**

Anamosa Journal-Eureka (Anamosa) **10137**
Ankeny Press Citizen (Ankeny) **10137**
Atlantic News-Telegraph (Atlantic) **9986**
Beacon-Forum (Eldon) **10138**
Bettendorf News (Bettendorf) **10137**
Boone News-Republican (Boone) **9986**
Britt News-Tribune (Britt) **10137**
Brooklyn Chronicle (Brooklyn) **10137**
Carroll Times Herald (Carroll) **9987**
Cedar Rapids Gazette (Cedar Rapids) **9987**
Chariton Herald-Patriot (Chariton) **10137**
Chariton Leader (Chariton) **10137**
Charles City Press (Charles City) **9987**
Cherokee County's Daily Times
  (Cherokee) **9987**
Clarinda Herald Journal (Clarinda) **10137**
Clayton County Register (Elkader) **10138**
Clinton Herald (Clinton) **9987**
Corydon Times-Republican (Corydon) **10137**
Council Bluffs Daily Nonpareil (Council
  Bluffs) **9987**
Cresco Times-Plain Dealer (Cresco) **10137**
Creston News Advertiser (Creston) **9987**
Daily Freeman Journal (Webster City) **9989**
Daily Tribune, The (Ames) **9986**
Decorah Public Opinion & Journal
  (Decorah) **10137**
Denison Bulletin & Review (Denison) **10137**
Des Moines County News, The (West
  Burlington) **10142**
Des Moines Lee Town News (Des
  Moines) **10137**
Des Moines Register (Des Moines) **9987**
DeWitt Observer (DeWitt) **10137**
Doon Press (Doon) **10137**
Dyersville Commercial (Dyersville) **10138**
Eagle Grove Eagle (Eagle Grove) **10138**
Eddyville Tribune (Eddyville) **10138**
Edgewood Reminder (Edgewood) **10138**
Eldora Herald-Leader (Eldora) **10138**
Emmetsburg Democrat (Emmetsburg) **10138**
Emmetsburg Reporter (Emmetsburg) **10138**
Essex Independent, The (Essex) **10138**
Estherville Daily News (Estherville) **9987**
Fairfield Daily Ledger (Fairfield) **9987**
Fayette County Union (West Union) **10142**
Forest City Summit (Forest City) **10138**
Fort Dodge Messenger (Fort Dodge) **9987**
Fort Madison Daily Democrat (Fort
  Madison) **9987**
Freemont Gazette (Fremont) **10138**
Gateway Shopper, The (Clinton) **10137**
Glenwood Opinion-Tribune (Glenwood) **10138**
Globe-Gazette (Mason City) **9988**
Greene Recorder, The (Greene) **10138**
Grinnell Herald-Register (Grinnell) **10138**

Grundy Register (Grundy Center) **10138**
Guttenberg Press (Guttenberg) **10139**
Hampton Chronicle & Times (Hampton) **10139**
Hardin County Index (Eldora) **10138**
Harlan News Advertiser (Harlan) **10139**
Harlan Tribune (Harlan) **10139**
Hawk Eye, The (Burlington) **9985**
Hudson Herald, The (Hudson) **10139**
Humboldt Independent (Humboldt) **10139**
† Humboldt Republican (Humboldt)
Humeston New Era (Humeston) **10139**
Independence Bulletin-Journal
  (Independence) **10139**
Iowa City Press-Citizen (Iowa City) **9987**
Jefferson Bee (Jefferson) **10139**
Jefferson Herald (Jefferson) **10139**
Jones County Town Crier (Anamosa) **10137**
Journal Tribune (Williamsburg) **10142**
Kalona News, The (Kalona) **10139**
Keokuk Daily Gate City (Keokuk) **9987**
Knoxville Journal/Express (Knoxville) **10139**
† Kossuth County Advance (Algona)
Laurens Sun, The (Laurens) **10139**
Leader, The (Davenport) **10137**
Leader, The (Solon) **10141**
Le Mars Daily Sentinel (Le Mars) **9988**
Leon Journal-Reporter (Leon) **10139**
Lime Springs Herald (Lime Springs) **10139**
Logan Herald Observer (Logan) **10139**
Lone Tree Reporter, The (Lone Tree) **10140**
Lyon-Sioux Press (Rock Rapids) **10141**
Malvern Leader, The (Malvern) **10140**
Manchester Press (Manchester) **10140**
Maquoketa Sentinel-Press (Maquoketa) **10140**
Marshalltown Times-Republican
  (Marshalltown) **9988**
Missouri Valley Times-News (Missouri
  Valley) **10140**
Mitchell County Press-News (Osage) **10140**
Monroe County News (Albia) **10136**
Montezuma Republican, The
  (Montezuma) **10140**
Monticello Express (Monticello) **10140**
Mount Ayr Record-News (Mt. Ayr) **10140**
Mount Pleasant News (Mt. Pleasant) **9988**
Muscatine Journal (Muscatine) **9988**
N'West Iowa Review (Sheldon) **10141**
Nashua Reporter (Nashua) **10140**
Nevada Journal (Nevada) **10140**
New Hampton Economist (New
  Hampton) **10140**
New Hampton Tribune (New Hampton) **10140**
New Sharon Star (New Sharon) **10140**
Newton Daily News (Newton) **9988**
Nishna Valley Tribune (Audubon) **10137**
North Scott Press, The (Eldridge) **10138**

Northwest Iowa Shopper (Spencer) **10141**
Oelwein Daily Register (Oelwein) **9988**
Onawa Democrat (Onawa) **10140**
Onawa Sentinel (Onawa) **10140**
Osceola County Gazette-Tribune
  (Sibley) **10141**
Osceola Sentinel-Tribune (Osceola) **10140**
Oskaloosa Herald (Oskaloosa) **9988**
Ossian Bee, The (Ossian) **10141**
Ottumwa Courier (Ottumwa) **9988**
Paullina Times (Paullina) **10141**
Pella Chronicle (Pella) **10141**
Perry Chief (Perry) **10141**
Pioneer Republican, The (Marengo) **10140**
Pocahontas Record-Democrat
  (Pocahontas) **10141**
Prairie City News (Prairie City) **10141**
Quad-City Times (Davenport) **9987**
Record-Herald & Indianola Tribune
  (Indianola) **10139**
Red Oak Express (Red Oak) **10141**
Schaller Herald (Schaller) **10141**
Sheldon Mail-Sun (Sheldon) **10141**
Shopper Spree (Burlington) **10137**
Sigourney News-Review (Sigourney) **10141**
Sioux City Journal (Sioux City) **9988**
Southern County News (Thornton) **10142**
Spencer Daily Reporter (Spencer) **9988**
Spirit Lake Beacon (Spirit Lake) **10141**
State Center Enterprise-Record (State
  Center) **10141**
Storm Lake Pilot Tribune (Storm Lake) **9988**
Storm Lake Times (Storm Lake) **10142**
Story City Herald (Story City) **10142**
Sumner Gazette (Sumner) **10142**
Sun, The (Mt. Vernon) **10140**
Tama News-Herald (Tama) **10142**
Telegraph Herald (Dubuque) **9987**
Times Citizen (Iowa Falls) **10139**
Times Guthrian (Guthrie Center) **10138**
Tipton Conservative & Advertiser
  (Tipton) **10142**
Traer Star-Clipper (Traer) **10142**
Tri-County Times, The (Slater) **10141**
Valley News Today-Daily Sentinel
  (Shenandoah) **9988**
Victor Echo (Victor) **10142**
Vinton Cedar Valley Daily Times (Vinton) **9988**
Washington Evening Journal
  (Washington) **9988**
Waterloo Courier (Waterloo) **9988**
Waukon Standard (Waukon) **10142**
Waverly Bremer County Independent
  (Waverly) **10142**
Waverly Democrat (Waverly) **10142**
West Liberty Index (West Liberty) **10142**

Winterset Madisonian (Winterset) **10142**

KANSAS

Abilene Reflector-Chronicle (Abilene) **9989**
† Anderson Countian (Garnett)
Anthony Republican, The (Anthony) **10142**
Arkansas City Traveler (Arkansas City) **9989**
Atchison Daily Globe (Atchison) **9989**
Augusta Daily Gazette (Augusta) **9989**
Baxter Springs Citizen (Baxter Springs) **10142**
Belle Plaine News, The (Belle Plaine) **10143**
Belleville Telescope (Belleville) **10143**
Beloit Daily Call (Beloit) **9989**
Bird City Times (Bird City) **10143**
Bonner Springs-Edwardsville Chieftain (Bonner
  Springs) **10143**
Capital-Journal (Topeka) **9991**
Chanute Tribune (Chanute) **9989**
Chase County Leader-News (Cottonwood
  Falls) **10143**
Clay Center Dispatch (Clay Center) **9989**
Coffey County Today (Burlington) **10143**
Coffeyville Journal, The (Coffeyville) **9989**
Colby Free Press (Colby) **9989**
Columbus Daily Advocate (Columbus) **9989**
Concordia Blade-Empire (Concordia) **9989**
Council Grove Republican (Council
  Grove) **9989**
Courtland Journal-Empire (Courtland) **10143**
Daily Reporter, The (Derby) **9989**
Dodge City Daily Globe (Dodge City) **9989**
El Dorado Times (El Dorado) **9989**
Ellsworth Reporter, The (Ellsworth) **10143**
Emporia Gazette (Emporia) **9990**
Eureka Herald (Eureka) **10143**
Fort Riley Post (Junction City) **10144**
Fort Scott Tribune, The (Fort Scott) **9990**
Garden City Telegram (Garden City) **9990**
† Garnett Review (Garnett)
Girard Press (Girard) **10143**
Goodland Daily News (Goodland) **9990**
Great Bend Tribune (Great Bend) **9990**
Hays Daily News (Hays) **9990**
Hiawatha Daily World (Hiawatha) **9990**
High Plains Journal (Dodge City) **10143**
Hill City Times, The (Hill City) **10143**
Hillsboro Star-Journal (Hillsboro) **10144**
Hoisington Dispatch (Hoisington) **10144**
Holton Recorder (Holton) **10144**
Hutchinson News (Hutchinson) **9990**
Independence Daily Reporter
  (Independence) **9990**
Independence News, The
  (Independence) **10144**
Iola Register (Iola) **9990**

Jetmore Republican (Jetmore) **10144**
Johnson County Sun (Shawnee Mission) **10145**
Johnson Pioneer (Johnson) **10144**
Journal-World, The (Lawrence) **9990**
Journal Herald, The (Shawnee) **10145**
Junction City Daily Union (Junction City) **9990**
† Kansas Business News (Augusta)
† Kansas City Evening News (Shawnee Mission)
Kansas City Kansan (Kansas City) **9990**
Kingman Journal/Leader Courier
  (Kingman) **10144**
Lakin Independent, The (Lakin) **10144**
Leader-Courier (Kingman) **10144**
† Leader, The (Lansing)
Leavenworth Times (Leavenworth) **9990**
Leawood Sun (Shawnee Mission) **10145**
Lebanon Times, The (Lebanon) **10144**
Ledger, The (Moundridge) **10145**
Lenexa Sun (Shawnee Mission) **10146**
Liberal Southwest Daily Times (Liberal) **9991**
Lyons Daily News (Lyons) **9991**
Madison News, The (Madison) **10144**
Manhattan Mercury (Manhattan) **9991**
Marion County Record (Marion) **10144**
Marysville Advocate (Marysville) **10144**
McPherson Sentinel (McPherson) **9991**
Miami County Republic (Paola) **10145**
Miltonvale Record (Miltonvale) **10144**
Neodesha Derrick (Neodesha) **10145**
Ness County News, The (Ness City) **10145**
Newton Kansan (Newton) **9991**
Northeast Johnson County (Shawnee
  Mission) **10146**
Norton Daily Telegram (Norton) **9991**
Oakley Graphic (Oakley) **10145**
Oberlin Herald, The (Oberlin) **10145**
Olathe Daily News (Olathe) **9991**
Olathe Sun (Overland Park) **10145**
Osage County Chronicle (Burlingame) **10143**
Osawatomie Graphic (Osawatomie) **10145**
Osborne County Farmer (Osborne) **10145**
Oskaloosa Independent (Oskaloosa) **10145**
▼Other Side, The (Prairie Village) **10145**
Ottawa Herald (Ottawa) **9991**
Ottawa Times (Ottawa) **10145**
Ottawa Times Shopper (Ottawa) **10145**
Overland Park Sun (Shawnee Mission) **10146**
Oxford Register, The (Belle Plaine) **10143**
Parsons News (Parsons) **10145**
Parsons Sun (Parsons) **9991**
Phillips County Review (Phillipsburg) **10145**
Pittsburg Morning Sun (Pittsburg) **9991**
Prairie Village Sun (Shawnee Mission) **10146**
Pratt Tribune (Pratt) **9991**
Record, The (Kansas City) **10144**
Rush County News (La Crosse) **10144**

Russell Daily News (Russell) **9991**
Russell Record (Russell) **10145**
Salina Journal (Salina) **9991**
Shawnee/Merriam Sun (Shawnee
  Mission) **10146**
▼Sherman County Star, The
  (Goodland) **10143**
Smith County Pioneer (Smith Center) **10146**
† Squire, The (Prairie Village)
St. Francis Herald, The (St. Francis) **10146**
St. John News (St. John) **10146**
St. Marys Star (St. Marys) **10146**
TeleGraphics (Lawrence) **10144**
Tiller & Toiler (Larned) **9990**
Times-Sentinel, The (Cheney) **10143**
Towne & Country Shopper (Columbus) **10143**
Ulysses News (Ulysses) **10146**
Valley Falls Vindicator (Valley Falls) **10146**
Washington County News (Washington) **10146**
Wellington Daily News (Wellington) **9991**
Wichita Eagle (Wichita) **9991**
Wilson County Citizen (Fredonia) **10143**
Winfield Daily Courier (Winfield) **9992**
Wyandotte West (Kansas City) **10144**

KENTUCKY

Adair Progress, The (Columbia) **10147**
Adair Russell Shopper, The (Columbia) **10147**
Advance-Yeoman (Wickliffe) **10152**
Advertiser, The (Louisa) **10149**
Advertiser, The (Mount Sterling) **10150**
Advertiser, The (Paris) **10150**
Advocate-Messenger (Danville) **9992**
Anderson News, The (Lawrenceburg) **10149**
Appalachian News-Express (Pikeville) **10150**
Barbourville Mountain Advocate
  (Barbourville) **10146**
Bath County News-Outlook
  (Owingsville) **10150**
Beaver Dam Ohio County Messenger (Beaver
  Dam) **10146**
Big Sandy News, The (Louisa) **10149**
Boone County Recorder (Florence) **10148**
Bourbon County Citizen (Paris) **10150**
Breckinridge County Herald-News
  (Hardinsburg) **10148**
Cadiz Record, The (Cadiz) **10147**
Campbell County Recorder (Fort
  Thomas) **10148**
Carlisle Mercury, The (Carlisle) **10147**
Casey County News (Liberty) **10149**
Casey County Shopper, The (Columbia) **10147**
Central City Times-Argus (Central City) **10147**
Central Kentucky News-Journal
  (Campbellsville) **10147**

Citizen Voice & Times (Irvine) **10149**
Clay City Times, The (Stanton) **10151**
Clinton County News (Albany) **10146**
Columbia News, The (Columbia) **10147**
Commonwealth Journal (Somerset) **9993**
Corbin Times-Tribune (Corbin) **9992**
Courier-Journal, The (Louisville) **9992**
Crittenden Press (Marion) **10149**
Cumberland County News (Burkesville) **10147**
Cumberland Trading Post, The
  (Middlesboro) **10149**
Cynthiana Democrat (Cynthiana) **10147**
Daily Independent, The (Ashland) **9992**
Daily News (Bowling Green) **9992**
Dawson Springs Progress (Dawson
  Springs) **10147**
Dixie News (Florence) **10148**
Eastern Kentucky Shopper (Paintsville) **10150**
Estill County Tribune, The (Irvine) **10149**
Floyd County Times (Prestonsburg) **10150**
Frankfort State Journal (Frankfort) **9992**
Franklin Favorite (Franklin) **10148**
Fulton Leader (Fulton) **10148**
Fulton Shopper (Fulton) **10148**
Georgetown News Graphic
  (Georgetown) **10148**
Glasgow Daily Times (Glasgow) **9992**
Glasgow Republican (Glasgow) **10148**
Grant County News (Williamstown) **10152**
Grayson Advertiser (Leitchfield) **10149**
Grayson County News-Gazette
  (Leitchfield) **10149**
Grayson Journal-Enquirer (Grayson) **10148**
† Green River Republican (Morgantown)
Greenup County News-Times (Greenup) **10148**
Hancock Clarion (Hawesville) **10148**
Harlan Daily Enterprise (Harlan) **9992**
Harrodsburg Herald (Harrodsburg) **10148**
Hart County News-Herald
  (Munfordville) **10150**
Hazard Herald-Voice (Hazard) **10148**
Henderson Gleaner (Henderson) **9992**
Henry County Local (New Castle) **10150**
Herald Ledger (Eddyville) **10147**
Interior Journal (Stanford) **10151**
Jessamine Journal (Nicholasville) **10150**
Journal-Enterprise (Providence) **10151**
Kenton County Recorder (Florence) **10148**
Kentucky New Era (Hopkinsville) **9992**
Kentucky Post, The (Covington) **9992**
Kentucky Standard (Bardstown) **10146**
LaRue County Herald-News
  (Hodgenville) **10148**
Leader-News (Central City) **10147**
Lebanon Enterprise (Lebanon) **10149**
Ledger-Independent (Maysville) **9993**

Leslie County News (Hyden) **10148**
Letcher County Community News-Press
  (Cromona) **10147**
Lexington Herald-Leader (Lexington) **9992**
Licking Valley Courier (West Liberty) **10152**
Louisville Defender Newspaper
  (Louisville) **10149**
Manchester Enterprise (Manchester) **10149**
Mayfield Messenger (Mayfield) **9993**
McCreary County Record (Whitley City) **10152**
Meade County Messenger
  (Brandenburg) **10146**
Messenger, The (Madisonville) **9992**
Middlesboro Daily News (Middlesboro) **9993**
Minifee County News (Morehead) **10150**
Morehead News (Morehead) **10150**
Mountain Citizen, The (Inez) **10148**
Mountain Eagle, The (Whitesburg) **10152**
Murray Ledger & Times (Murray) **9993**
News-Democrat, The (Carrollton) **10147**
News-Enterprise (Elizabethtown) **9992**
News-Journal Shopper (Campbellsville) **10147**
News Democrat & Leader (Russellville) **10151**
Ohio County Times News (Hartford) **10148**
Oldham Era, The (La Grange) **10149**
Olive Hill Times (Olive Hill) **10150**
Oliveville Times (Morehead) **10150**
Owensboro Messenger-Inquirer
  (Owensboro) **9993**
Paducah Sun (Paducah) **9993**
Paintsville Herald, The (Paintsville) **10150**
Pineville Sun-Cumberland Courier
  (Pineville) **10150**
Pioneer-News (Shepherdsville) **10151**
Progress, The (Cave City) **10147**
Richmond Register (Richmond) **9993**
Russell County News (Russell Springs) **10151**
Russell Springs Times Journal (Russell
  Springs) **10151**
Salyersville Independent (Salyersville) **10151**
Scottsville Citizen-Times (Scottsville) **10151**
Sentinel-Echo (London) **10149**
Sentinel, The (Radcliff) **10151**
Shelbyville Sentinel-News (Shelbyville) **10151**
Shopper/PLUS (Shelbyville) **10151**
Shopper's Guide (Bardstown) **10146**
Southwest Newsweek, The (Louisville) **10149**
Spencer Magnet (Taylorsville) **10151**
Springfield Sun (Springfield) **10151**
Sturgis News (Sturgis) **10151**
T-Ville News Trader (Tompkinsville) **10151**
Thousandsticks (Hyden) **10148**
Times Leader, The (Princeton) **10151**
† Times, The (Augusta)
Todd County Standard (Elkton) **10147**
Tompkinsville News (Tompkinsville) **10151**

Tri-City News (Cumberland) **10147**
Tribune Courier (Benton) **10146**
Union County Advocate (Morganfield) **10150**
Voice-Tribune, The (Louisville) **10149**
Wayne County Outlook (Monticello) **10150**
West Kentucky News (Paducah) **10150**
Whitley Republican News Journal
   (Williamsburg) **10152**
Winchester Sun (Winchester) **9993**
Woodford Sun (Versailles) **10152**

LOUISIANA

Abbeville Meridional (Abbeville) **9993**
Advocate, The (Baton Rouge) **9993**
Alexandria Daily Town Talk (Alexandria) **9993**
Alexandria News Weekly (Alexandria) **10152**
Amite Tangi Digest (Amite) **10152**
Avoyelles Journal (Marksville) **10154**
Baker Observer (Baker) **10152**
Bastrop Daily Enterprise (Bastrop) **9993**
Beauregard Daily News (De Ridder) **9994**
Bienville Democrat & Ringgold Record
   (Arcadia) **10152**
Bogalusa Daily News & Sunday News
   (Bogalusa) **9993**
Bossier Banner-Progress (Bossier City) **10152**
Bossier Press-Tribune (Bossier City) **10152**
Caddo Citizen (Vivian) **10155**
Church Point News (Church Point) **10153**
Community Mirror (Gonzales) **10153**
Concordia Sentinel (Ferriday) **10153**
Courier, The (Houma) **9994**
Coushatta Citizen (Coushatta) **10153**
Covington St. Tammany Farmer
   (Covington) **10153**
Crowley Post-Signal (Crowley) **9993**
Daily Comet (Thibodaux) **9995**
Daily Iberian (New Iberia) **9994**
Daily Review, The (Morgan City) **9994**
Daily World (Opelousas) **9994**
Denham Springs-Livingston Parish News
   (Denham Springs) **10153**
De Quincy News (De Quincy) **10153**
Donaldsonville Chief (Donaldsonville) **10153**
East Feliciana Watchman (Clinton) **10153**
Enterprise, The (Ponchatoula) **10154**
Eunice News (Eunice) **10153**
Franklin Banner-Tribune (Franklin) **9994**
Franklin Sun, The (Winnsboro) **10155**
Gonzales Weekly (Gonzales) **10153**
Greater Baton Rouge Business Report (Baton
   Rouge) **10152**
Hammond Daily Star (Hammond) **9994**
Jackson Independent, The (Jonesboro) **10153**
Jeanerette Enterprise (Jeanerette) **10153**

Jena Times Olla-Tullos Signal (Jena) **10153**
Jennings Daily News (Jennings) **9994**
Kentwood News-Ledger (Kentwood) **10153**
L'Observateur (La Place) **10153**
Lafayette Advertiser (Lafayette) **9994**
Lake Charles American Press (Lake
   Charles) **9994**
Leesville Daily Leader (Leesville) **9994**
Livingston Leader (Denham Springs) **10153**
Madison Journal (Tallulah) **10155**
Mamou Acadian Press (Mamou) **10154**
Mansfield Enterprise (Mansfield) **10154**
Minden Press-Herald (Minden) **9994**
Natchitoches Times (Natchitoches) **9994**
News-Banner, The (Covington) **10153**
News-Star, The (Monroe) **9994**
News Examiner, The (Lutcher) **10153**
Oakdale Journal (Oakdale) **10154**
Ouachita Citizen (West Monroe) **10155**
Plaquemines Gazette (Belle Chasse) **10152**
Plaquemines Watchman (Belle Chasse) **10152**
Pointe Coupee Banner (New Roads) **10154**
Ponchatoula Times, The (Ponchatoula) **10154**
Post South (Plaquemine) **10154**
Rayne Acadian-Tribune (Rayne) **10154**
Rayne Independent (Rayne) **10154**
Richland Beacon-News (Rayville) **10154**
Ruston Daily Leader (Ruston) **9995**
Sabine Banner (Many) **10154**
Sabine Index (Many) **10154**
† Shreveport Journal (Shreveport)
Slidell Sentry-News (Slidell) **9995**
Southwest Daily News (Sulphur) **9995**
Springhill Press (Springhill) **10154**
St. Bernard Voice (Arabi) **10152**
St. Martinville Teche News (St.
   Martinville) **10154**
St. Mary Journal (Morgan City) **10154**
Times-Picayune (New Orleans) **9994**
Times, The (Shreveport) **9995**
Ville Platte Gazette (Ville Platte) **10155**
Weekly News (Marksville) **10154**
Weekly Press (Baton Rouge) **10152**
West Carroll Gazette (Oak Grove) **10154**
West Side Journal (Port Allen) **10154**
Winnfield Winn Parish Enterprise
   (Winnfield) **10155**
Zachary Plainsman-News (Zachary) **10155**

MAINE

American Journal (Westbrook) **10157**
Bangor Daily News (Bangor) **9995**
Bar Harbor Times (Bar Harbor) **10155**

Biddeford-Saco-OOB Courier
  (Biddeford) **10155**
Boothbay Register (Boothbay Harbor) **10155**
Bridgton News (Bridgton) **10155**
Calais Advertiser (Calais) **10155**
Camden Herald (Camden) **10155**
▼Capital Weekly (Augusta) **10155**
Caribou Aroostook Republican & News
  (Caribou) **10155**
Central Maine Morning Sentinel
  (Waterville) **9995**
Community Advertiser (Farmingdale) **10156**
County Wide (Dover-Foxcroft) **10156**
Courier-Gazette (Rockland) **10157**
Eastern Gazette, The (Dexter) **10155**
Ellsworth American, The (Ellsworth) **10156**
† Evening Express (Portland)
Fort Fairfield Review (Fort Fairfield) **10156**
Franklin Journal & Farmington Chronicle
  (Farmington) **10156**
Guilford American (Dover-Foxcroft) **10156**
Houlton Pioneer Times (Houlton) **10156**
Island Ad-Vantages (Stonington) **10157**
Islesboro Island News (Islesboro) **10156**
Journal Tribune (Biddeford) **9995**
Katahdin Times (Millinocket) **10156**
Kennebec Journal (Augusta) **9995**
Lincoln County News (Newcastle) **10156**
Lincoln News (Lincoln) **10156**
Livermore Falls Advertiser (Livermore
  Falls) **10156**
Machias Valley News Observer
  (Machias) **10156**
Madawaska St. John Valley Times
  (Madawaska) **10156**
Maine Times (Portland) **10157**
Norway Advertiser-Democrat (Norway) **10156**
Penobscot Times (Old Town) **10157**
Piscataquis Observer, The
  (Dover-Foxcroft) **10156**
Portland Press Herald (Portland) **9995**
Quoddy Tides (Eastport) **10156**
Republican Journal (Belfast) **10155**
Rumford Falls Times (Rumford) **10157**
Sanford News (Sanford) **10157**
Star-Herald, The (Presque Isle) **10157**
Suburban News, The (Windham) **10157**
Sun-Journal (Lewiston) **9995**
Times-Record (Brunswick) **9995**
Weekly Packet (Blue Hill) **10155**
York County Coast Star (Kennebunk) **10156**

MARYLAND

Aegis, The (Bel Air) **10158**
Arbutus Times (Baltimore) **10157**

Avenue News (Baltimore) **10157**
Baltimore Chronicle (Baltimore) **10157**
Baltimore Messenger (Baltimore) **10157**
Baltimore Sun (Baltimore) **9995**
Bay Times (Stevensville) **10159**
Bethesda/Chevy Chase Almanac
  (Potomac) **10159**
Bowie Blade-News (Bowie) **10158**
Brunswick Citizen (Brunswick) **10158**
Calvert Independent (Prince Fredrick) **10159**
Capital, The (Annapolis) **9995**
Carroll County Sun (Westminster) **9996**
Carroll County Times (Westminster) **9996**
Catonsville Times (Baltimore) **10157**
Cecil Whig (Elkton) **9996**
City Paper (Baltimore) **10157**
Columbia Flier (Columbia) **10158**
Community Times (Westminster) **10160**
† Countywide News (Westminster)
Crofton News-Crier (Bowie) **10158**
Cumberland Times-News (Cumberland) **9996**
Daily Banner (Cambridge) **9996**
Daily Mail, The (Hagerstown) **9996**
Daily Times (Salisbury) **9996**
Damascus Gazette (Gatorsburg) **10158**
Dorchester Star (Cambridge) **10158**
Dundalk Eagle (Baltimore) **10157**
East Baltimore Guide (Baltimore) **10157**
Enquirer-Gazette (Upper Marlboro) **10160**
Enterprise & Inner Harbor News
  (Baltimore) **10157**
Enterprise, The (Lexington Park) **10159**
Every Wednesday (Baltimore) **10157**
Frederick Post, The (Frederick) **9996**
Gaithersburg Gazette (Gaithersburg) **10158**
Greenbelt News Review (Greenbelt) **10159**
Hancock News (Hancock) **10159**
Herald, The (Hagerstown) **9996**
Howard County Times (Columbia) **10158**
Jeffersonian, The (Baltimore) **10158**
Kent County News (Chestertown) **10158**
Labor Herald (Baltimore) **10158**
Laurel Leader (Laurel) **10159**
Maryland Gazette (Glen Burnie) **10159**
Maryland Independent (Waldorf) **10160**
Maryland Times-Press (Ocean City) **10159**
Middletown Valley Citizen (Brunswick) **10158**
Montgomery County Sentinel
  (Gaithersburg) **10158**
Montgomery Journal, The (Rockville) **9996**
News, The (Frederick) **9996**
Northeast Reporter (Towson) **10160**
Northwest Star (Baltimore) **10158**
Owings Mills Times (Baltimore) **10158**
Potomac Almanac (Potomac) **10159**
Prince Georges Journal (Lanham) **9996**

Prince Georges Sentinel (Seabrook) **10159**
Queen Anne's Record-Observer
  (Centreville) **10158**
Recorder, The (Prince Frederick) **10159**
Record, The (Havre De Grace) **10159**
Republican, The (Oakland) **10159**
Salisbury News & Advertiser (Salisbury) **10159**
Silver Spring Gazette (Burtonsville) **10158**
Somerset Herald (Princess Anne) **10159**
Star-Democrat, The (Easton) **9996**
Times-Herald (Timonium) **10159**
Times-Record, The (Denton) **10158**
Towson Times (Towson) **10160**
Village News (Gaithersburg) **10158**
Worcester County Messenger (Pocomoke
  City) **10159**

MASSACHUSETTS

Advocate/South Advocate, The
  (Williamstown) **10166**
Advocate, The (Marion) **10162**
Amesbury News (Amesbury) **10160**
Andover Townsman (Andover) **10160**
Arlington Advocate (Arlington) **10160**
Associated Newspaper (Stoughton) **10166**
Athol Daily News (Athol) **9996**
Auburn News (Auburn) **10160**
Barnstable Patriot, The (Hyannis) **10162**
Bay State Banner (Boston) **10160**
Beacon, The (Concord) **10161**
Bedford Minuteman (Concord) **10161**
Belchertown Sentinel (Belchertown) **10160**
Belmont Citizen-Herald (Needham) **10164**
Berkshire Courier (Great Barrington) **10162**
Berkshire Eagle (Pittsfield) **9998**
Berkshire Penny Saver (Lee) **10162**
Berkshire Record (Great Barrington) **10162**
Billerica Minuteman (North Billerica) **10164**
Blackstone Valley Tribune (Whitinsville) **10166**
Bolton Common (Bolton) **10160**
Boston Globe (Boston) **9997**
Boston Herald (Boston) **9997**
Boston Phoenix (Boston) **10160**
Bourne Courier (Yarmouthport) **10167**
Braintree Forum (Marshfield) **10163**
Bridgewater Independent (Middleboro) **10163**
† Bridgewater Townsman (Bridgewater)
Brockton Enterprise, The (Brockton) **9997**
Burlington Union (Lexington) **10162**
Cambridge Chronicle (Somerville) **10165**
Canton Journal (Canton) **10161**
Cape Codder (Orleans) **10164**
† Cape Cod News (Yarmouth Port)
Cape Cod Times (Hyannis) **9997**
Capeway News (Middleboro) **10163**

Carver Reporter (Plymouth) **10164**
† Charlestown Citizen (Brookline)
Chelmsford Independent (Chelmsford) **10161**
Chelsea Record (Revere) **10165**
Chicopee Herald Weekly, The
  (Chicopee) **10161**
Chronicle, The (North Dartmouth) **10164**
Cohasset Mariner (Marshfield) **10163**
Concord Journal (Concord) **10161**
Daily Evening Item (Lynn) **9997**
Daily Hampshire Gazette (Northampton) **9998**
Daily News-Mercury, The (Malden) **9997**
Daily News of Newburyport, The
  (Newburyport) **9998**
Daily Times & Chronicle (Reading) **9998**
Daily Times Chronicle (Woburn) **9998**
Daily Transcript (Dedham) **9997**
Danvers Herald (Danvers) **10161**
† Dennis Bulletin (South Yarmouth)
Dover-Sherborn Suburban Press
  (Needham) **10164**
Dracut Dispatch, The (Dracut) **10161**
Duxbury Reporter (Plymouth) **10164**
Eagle Tribune, The (North Andover) **9998**
East Bridgewater Star (Bridgewater) **10161**
Easton Bulletin (Stoughton) **10166**
† Enterprise Sun (Marlborough)
Enterprise, The (Falmouth) **10162**
Foxboro Reporter (Foxboro) **10162**
Gardner News (Gardner) **9997**
Georgetown Record (Ipswich) **10162**
Gloucester Daily Times (Gloucester) **9997**
Groton Landmark (Ayer) **10160**
Halifax Reporter (Plymouth) **10165**
Hamilton-Wenham Chronicle (Ipswich) **10162**
Hanover Mariner (Marshfield) **10163**
Harvard Spirit (Ayer) **10160**
Harwich Oracle (Orleans) **10164**
Haverhill Gazette (Haverhill) **9997**
Herald News, The (Fall River) **9997**
Hingham Journal & Mariner (Quincy) **10165**
Holbrook Sun (Marshfield) **10163**
Holbrook Times (Stoughton) **10166**
Improper Bostonian, The (Boston) **10160**
Inquirer & Mirror, The (Nantucket) **10164**
Ipswich Chronicle (Ipswich) **10162**
Item (Clinton) **10161**
Jaffrey-Rindge Chronicle (Winchendon) **10167**
Journal Register (Palmer) **10164**
Kingston Reporter (Plymouth) **10165**
Lakeville Independent (Middleboro) **10163**
Lexington Minuteman (Lexington) **10162**
Lincoln Journal (Concord) **10161**
Littleton Independent (Concord) **10161**
Longmeadow News (Westfield) **10166**
Lowell Sun (Lowell) **9997**

Ludlow Register (Palmer) **10164**
Main Street Trilogy (Townsend) **10166**
Mansfield News (Mansfield) **10162**
Marblehead Reporter (Marblehead) **10162**
Marina & Independent Voice
  (Marshfield) **10163**
Marshfield Mariner (Marshfield) **10163**
Marshfield Reporter (Plymouth) **10165**
Mashpee Messenger (Orleans) **10164**
Maynard Beacon (Concord) **10161**
Medfield Suburban Press (Needham) **10164**
Melrose Free Press (Melrose) **10163**
† Melrose Shoppers News (Stoneham)
Merrimac Valley Sunday (Amesbury) **10160**
Middleboro Gazette (Middleboro) **10163**
Middlesex News (Framingham) **9997**
Milford Daily News (Milford) **9998**
Millbury/Sutton Chronicle (Millbury) **10163**
Milton Record-Transcript (Milton
  Village) **10163**
Nantucket Beacon (Nantucket) **10164**
Natick Bulletin (Needham) **10164**
New Leader (Spencer) **10165**
News-Tribune (Framingham) **9997**
News, The (Southbridge) **9998**
Newton Graphic (Waltham) **10166**
North Shore Sunday (Danvers) **10161**
Norton Courier (Stoughton) **10166**
Norwell Mariner (Marshfield) **10163**
Old Colony Memorial (Plymouth) **10165**
Parkway Transcript (Dedham) **10161**
Patriot Ledger (Quincy) **9998**
† Peabody Times (Peabody)
Pembroke Mariner (Marshfield) **10163**
Pembroke Reporter (Plymouth) **10165**
Pennysaver, The (Sandwich) **10165**
Pittsfield Gazette, The (Pittsfield) **10164**
Provincetown Advocate (Provincetown) **10165**
Public Spirit (Ayer) **10160**
Quincy Sun (Quincy) **10165**
Randolph Mariner (Marshfield) **10163**
Raynham Journal (Stoughton) **10166**
Recorder, The (Greenfield) **9997**
Register, The (Yarmouth Port) **10167**
Revere Journal (Revere) **10165**
Salem Evening News (Beverly) **9996**
Sandwich Broadsider (Orleans) **10164**
Saugus Advertiser (Melrose) **10163**
Sentinel & Enterprise (Fitchburg) **9997**
Sentinel, The (Marion) **10162**
Sharon Advocate (Sharon) **10165**
Somerville Journal (West Somerville) **10166**
South Boston Tribune (Boston) **10160**
South County Advertiser (Webster) **10166**
South Shore News (Rockland) **10165**
Spectator, The (Somerset) **10165**

Springfield Advocate (Springfield) **10165**
Standard-Times, The (New Bedford) **9998**
State Line Shopping Guide (Palmer) **10164**
† Stoneham Weekender News (Stoneham)
Stoughton Chronicle (Stoughton) **10166**
Suburban News (Reading) **10165**
Sudbury Town Crier (Waltham) **10166**
Sun Chronicle (Attleboro) **9996**
Sunday Post (Lynn) **10162**
Swampscott Reporter (Marblehead) **10162**
Tab, The (Needham) **10164**
Taunton Daily Gazette (Taunton) **9998**
Taunton Independent (Middleboro) **10163**
Telegram & Gazette (Worcester) **9999**
Times Free Press (Ayer) **10160**
Times, The (Webster) **10166**
† Transcript-Telegram (Holyoke)
Transcript, The (North Adams) **9998**
Tri-Town Transcript (Ipswich) **10162**
Union-News (Springfield) **9998**
Valley Advocate (Hatfield) **10162**
† Village Journal (Osterville)
Vineyard Gazette (Edgartown) **10161**
Wakefield Item (Wakefield) **9998**
Walpole Times, The (Walpole) **10166**
Wareham Courier (Marion) **10163**
Ware River News (Ware) **10166**
Watertown Press (Somerville) **10165**
Watertown Sun (Needham) **10164**
Wayland-Weston Town Crier (Needham) **10164**
Weekender, The (Whitinsville) **10166**
Wellesley Townsman (Wellesley) **10166**
West Bridgewater Star (Middleboro) **10163**
Westfield Evening News (Westfield) **9998**
Westford Eagle (Chelmsford) **10161**
West Roxbury Transcript (Dedham) **10161**
West Springfield Record (West
  Springfield) **10166**
Weymouth News (Marshfield) **10163**
Weymouth News & Gazette (Braintree) **10161**
Whitman Times (Stoughton) **10166**
Wick-Qua-Boag Weekly (Spencer) **10165**
Wilmington-Tewksbury Town Crier
  (Wilmington) **10166**
Winchendon Courier (Winchendon) **10167**
Winchester Star (Winchester) **10167**
Woburn Advocate (Woburn) **10167**
Worcester Magazine (Worcester) **10167**
† Yarmouth Sun (Yarmouth Port)

MICHIGAN

Ad-Visor (Beulah) **10167**
Ad-Visor (Lansing) **10172**
Ada/Cascade/Forest Hills Advance
  (Jenison) **10171**

Advertiser, The (Iron Mountain) **10171**
Advisor/Source (Utica) **10002**
Albion Recorder (Albion) **9999**
† Algonac Courier Journal (Marine City)
Allegan County News (Allegan) **10167**
Alpena News (Alpena) **9999**
Alpena Star Advertiser (Alpena) **10167**
† Anchor Bay Beacon (New Baltimore)
Ann Arbor News (Ann Arbor) **9999**
Arenac County Independent (Standish) **10175**
Argus-Press, The (Owosso) **10001**
Battle Creek Enquirer (Battle Creek) **9999**
Battle Creek Shopper (Hastings) **10170**
Bay City Times (Bay City) **9999**
Bay City Valley Farmer (Bay City) **10167**
Bay Voice (New Baltimore) **10173**
Belleville Enterprise (Wayne) **10176**
Berrien County Record (Buchanan) **10168**
Big Rapids Pioneer (Big Rapids) **9999**
Birmingham Eccentric, The
  (Birmingham) **10167**
Blazer News (Jackson) **10171**
Blissfield Advance (Blissfield) **10167**
Blue Water Voice (New Baltimore) **10173**
Brighton Argus (Brighton) **10168**
† Byron Center/Dorr Advance (Jenison)
Cadillac Evening News (Cadillac) **9999**
Caledonia/Gaines Advance (Jenison) **10171**
Canton Eagle (Wayne) **10176**
Canton Observer (Plymouth) **10174**
Cass City Chronicle (Cass City) **10168**
Charlevoix Courier (Charlevoix) **10168**
Charlotte Shopping Guide (Charlotte) **10168**
Cheboygan Daily Tribune (Cheboygan) **9999**
Chelsea Standard, The (Chelsea) **10168**
Citizen, The (Boyne City) **10168**
Clare Sentinel (Clare) **10168**
Clarkston News (Clarkston) **10168**
Clinton County News (St. Johns) **10175**
Commercial-Express (Vicksburg) **10175**
Commercial Record (Saugatuck) **10175**
Community Advisor (Marshall) **10172**
Connection, The (Grosse Point) **10170**
County Line Reminder (Ortonville) **10173**
County Press (Parma) **10173**
County Press, The (Lapeer) **10172**
Daily Mining Gazette (Houghton) **10000**
Daily News (Greenville) **10000**
Daily News (Iron Mountain) **10000**
Daily Press, The (Escanaba) **9999**
Daily Reporter, The (Coldwater) **9999**
Daily Telegram (Adrian) **9999**
Daily Tribune (Royal Oak) **10001**
Davison Flagstaff (Swartz Creek) **10175**
Davison Index, The (Davison) **10169**
Dearborn Press & Guide (Dearborn) **10169**

Dearborn Times-Herald (Dearborn) **10169**
Delta Waverly News Herald, The (Grand
  Ledge) **10170**
Detroit Free Press (Detroit) **9999**
Detroit Metro Times (Detroit) **10169**
Detroit News (Detroit) **9999**
DeWitt Bath Review (St. Johns) **10175**
Diamond Drill, The (Crystal Falls) **10169**
Dowagiac Daily News (Dowagiac) **9999**
Downriver Voice (New Baltimore) **10173**
Durand Express (Durand) **10169**
East Grand Rapids Cadence (Jenison) **10171**
Eaton County News (Charlotte) **10168**
Enterprise, The (Mason) **10172**
Evart Review, The (Big Rapids) **10167**
Exponent, The (Brooklyn) **10168**
Farmers' Advance (Camden) **10168**
Farmington Observer (Farmington) **10169**
Fennville Herald (Allegan) **10167**
Flint Journal (Flint) **10000**
Fowlerville Review Shopping Guide
  (Howell) **10171**
Frankenmuth News (Frankenmuth) **10169**
Garden City Observer (Livonia) **10172**
Gaylord Herald Times (Gaylord) **10169**
† Gladstone Delta Reporter (Escanaba)
Gladwin County Record & Beaverton Clarion
  (Gladwin) **10170**
Grand Haven Tribune (Grand Haven) **10000**
Grand Ledge Independent, The (Grand
  Ledge) **10170**
Grand Marais Pilot & Pictured Rocks Review
  (Grand Marais) **10170**
Grand Rapids Advance (Jenison) **10171**
Grand Rapids Press, The (Grand
  Rapids) **10000**
Grand Valley Advance (Jenison) **10171**
Gratiot County Herald (Ithaca) **10171**
Great Lakes Pilot (Grand Marais) **10170**
Grosse Pointe News (Grosse Pointe
  Farm) **10170**
Hamtramck Citizen (Hamtramck) **10170**
Harbor Beach Times (Harbor Beach) **10170**
† Harper Woods Herald (Birmingham)
Hartland Herald Shopping Guide
  (Howell) **10171**
Hastings Banner (Hastings) **10170**
Hastings Reminder (Hastings) **10170**
Heights Times-Herald (Dearborn) **10169**
Herald-Palladium (St. Joseph) **10002**
Herald News, The (Reed City) **10174**
Hillsdale Daily News (Hillsdale) **10000**
Holland Sentinel (Holland) **10000**
Holt Community News (Holt) **10171**
Houghton Lake Resorter (Houghton
  Lake) **10171**

Huron Daily Tribune (Bad Axe) **9999**
Ile Camera, The (Grosse Ile) **10170**
† Independent Press (Marine City)
Independent, The (Flint) **10169**
Ingham County News (Mason) **10172**
Inkster Ledger-Star (Wayne) **10176**
Ionia Sentinel-Standard (Ionia) **10000**
Iosco County News Herald (East
  Tawas) **10169**
Iron River Reporter (Iron River) **10171**
Ironwood Daily Globe (Ironwood) **10000**
Jackson Citizen Patriot (Jackson) **10000**
Jeffersonian, The (Croswell) **10169**
Kalamazoo Gazette (Kalamazoo) **10000**
Kentwood Advance (Jenison) **10171**
L'Anse Sentinel (L'Anse) **10172**
† Lake Country Chronicle (Buchanan)
Lake County Star (Big Rapids) **10167**
Lake Michigan Examiner, The
  (Muskegon) **10173**
Lakeview Enterprise (Big Rapids) **10167**
Lansing State Journal (Lansing) **10000**
Leelanau Enterprise (Leland) **10172**
Leslie Local Independent (Leslie) **10172**
Livonia Observer (Livonia) **10172**
Lowell Ledger (Lowell) **10172**
Ludington Daily News (Ludington) **10000**
Macomb Daily (Mt. Clemens) **10001**
Macomb Voice, The (New Baltimore) **10173**
Manistee News-Advocate (Manistee) **10000**
Manistee Observer (Manistee) **10172**
Manistique Pioneer-Tribune
  (Manistique) **10172**
Maple Valley News (Hastings) **10170**
Marquette Mining Journal (Marquette) **10001**
Marshall Chronicle (Marshall) **10001**
Mayville Monitor (Mayville) **10172**
Michigan Chronicle (Detroit) **10169**
Midland Daily News (Midland) **10001**
Milan Area Leader (Milan) **10172**
Milford Times (Milford) **10173**
Monroe Evening News (Monroe) **10001**
Morenci Observer (Morenci) **10173**
Morning Sun (Mt. Pleasant) **10001**
Munising News (Munising) **10173**
Muskegon Chronicle, The (Muskegon) **10001**
New Buffalo Times (New Buffalo) **10173**
New Center News (Detroit) **10169**
News-Herald, The (Southgate) **10175**
Newsweekly (Sebewaing) **10175**
Niles Daily Star (Niles) **10001**
North Country Sun (Ironwood) **10171**
† Northeast Detroiter (Detroit)
Northern Michigan News (Cadillac) **10168**
Northern Star (Gaylord) **10170**
Northfield Advance (Jenison) **10171**

North Macomb Voice (New Baltimore) **10173**
Northville Record (Northville) **10173**
North Woods Call (Charlevoix) **10168**
Norway Current (Norway) **10173**
Novi News (Northville) **10173**
Oakland Press, The (Pontiac) **10001**
Oceana's Herald-Journal (Hart) **10170**
Ogemaw County Herald (West Branch) **10176**
Onaway Outlook (Onaway) **10173**
Ontonagon Herald (Ontonagon) **10173**
Oscoda Press (Oscoda) **10173**
Ottawa Advance (Jenison) **10171**
Our Home Town (Vanderbilt) **10175**
Paw Paw Courier-Leader (Paw Paw) **10173**
Penny Saver (Three Rivers) **10175**
Petoskey News-Review (Petoskey) **10001**
Pinckney Post Shopping Guide
  (Pinckney) **10174**
Plymouth Observer (Plymouth) **10174**
Porcupine Press (Chatham) **10168**
Portland Review & Observer (Grand
  Ledge) **10170**
Presque Isle Advance (Rogers City) **10174**
Presque Isle Star (Gaylord) **10170**
Redford Observer (Livonia) **10172**
Reminder, The (Pontiac) **10174**
Review, The (Richmond) **10174**
Rochester Clarion (Rochester) **10174**
Rochester Eccentric (Rochester Hills) **10174**
Rockford/Cedar Springs Advance
  (Jenison) **10171**
Rockford Squire (Rockford) **10174**
Romeo Observer (Romeo) **10174**
Romulus Roman (Wayne) **10176**
Roscommon County Herald-News
  (Roscommon) **10174**
Saginaw News (Saginaw) **10001**
Saginaw Press, The (Saginaw) **10174**
Saline Reporter (Saline) **10174**
Sanilac County News (Sandusky) **10175**
Sault Ste. Marie Evening News (Sault Ste.
  Marie) **10001**
Shiawassee County Journal (Perry) **10174**
Southfield Eccentric (Birmingham) **10167**
South Haven Daily Tribune (South
  Haven) **10002**
South Lyon Herald (South Lyon) **10175**
Sparta/Kent City Advance (Sparta) **10175**
Spinal Column Newsweekly (Waterford) **10176**
Star Advertiser (Kalkaska) **10172**
Star Buyers Guide (West Branch) **10176**
St. Clair Shores Herald (Birmingham) **10167**
St. Ignace News, The (St. Ignace) **10175**
St. Johns Reminder (St. Johns) **10175**
Straits Area Star (Cheboygan) **10168**
Sturgis Journal (Sturgis) **10002**

Sun & News, The (Hastings) **10171**
Sunday Independent, The (Owosso) **10173**
Tech Center News (Warren) **10176**
Tecumseh Herald (Tecumseh) **10175**
Three Rivers Commercial-News (Three
  Rivers) **10002**
Times-Indicator (Fremont) **10169**
Times Herald (Port Huron) **10001**
Town Crier (Stockbridge) **10175**
Towne Courier (East Lansing) **10169**
Township Times (Saginaw) **10174**
Traverse City Record-Eagle (Traverse
  City) **10002**
Tri-City Record, The (Watervliet) **10176**
Tri-City Times (Imlay City) **10171**
Tri-County Citizen (Chesaning) **10168**
Tribune Plus (Royal Oak) **10174**
Troy-Somerset Gazette (Troy) **10175**
Troy Eccentric (Rochester Hills) **10174**
Tuscola County Advertiser (Caro) **10168**
Union Enterprise (Plainwell) **10174**
Valley Farmer, The (Bay City) **10167**
Van Buren County Advertiser (Gobles) **10170**
Vassar Pioneer Times (Vassar) **10175**
Walker-Westside Advance (Jenison) **10171**
Waterfront of Missaukee County (Lake
  City) **10172**
Wayne Eagle (Wayne) **10176**
West Bloomfield Eccentric, The
  (Birmingham) **10167**
Westland Eagle (Wayne) **10176**
Westland Observer (Livonia) **10172**
West Valley News/Sunday Advance
  (Flint) **10169**
White Lake Beacon (Whitehall) **10176**
Wyoming Advance (Jenison) **10172**

MINNESOTA

Ada Norman County Index (Ada) **10176**
Advertiser, The (Bemidji) **10176**
Aitkin Independent Age (Aitkin) **10176**
Albert Lea Tribune (Albert Lea) **10002**
Anoka County Union (Coon Rapids) **10178**
Apple Valley/Rosemont Sun-Current
  (Burnsville) **10177**
Austin Daily Herald (Austin) **10002**
Baudette Region, The (Baudette) **10176**
Becker County Record (Detroit Lakes) **10178**
Benson Swift County Monitor-News
  (Benson) **10177**
Bird Island Union (Bird Island) **10177**
Blaine-Spring Lake Park Life (Coon
  Rapids) **10178**
Blaine Banner (Blaine) **10177**

Bloomington Sun-Current
  (Bloomington) **10177**
Brainerd Daily Dispatch (Brainerd) **10002**
Brooklyn Center Sun Post (Minneapolis) **10180**
Brooklyn Park Sun Post (Minneapolis) **10180**
Budgeteer Press/Skyworld Duluth News
  (Duluth) **10178**
Buffalo Ridge Gazette, The (Ruthton) **10182**
Burnsville Sun-Current (Burnsville) **10177**
Canby News (Canby) **10177**
Chanhassen Villager (Chanhassen) **10177**
Chaska Herald (Chaska) **10177**
Chicago County Press (Lindstrom) **10179**
Chisholm Free Press & Tribune Press
  (Chisholm) **10177**
Cloquet Billboard Shopper (Cloquet) **10178**
Cloquet Pine Knot (Cloquet) **10178**
Columbia Heights-Findley Focus
  (Roseville) **10182**
Coon Rapids Herald (Coon Rapids) **10178**
Crookston Daily Times (Crookston) **10002**
Daily Journal, The (Fergus Falls) **10002**
Daily Journal, The (International Falls) **10003**
Dakota County Tribune (Burnsville) **10177**
Detroit Lakes Tribune (Detroit Lakes) **10178**
Duluth News-Tribune (Duluth) **10002**
Eagan Sun-Current (Burnsville) **10177**
East Side Review (North St. Paul) **10181**
Echo Press, The (Alexandria) **10176**
ECM Post-Review (North Branch) **10181**
Eden Prairie Sun-Current (Bloomington) **10177**
Edgerton Enterprise, The (Edgerton) **10178**
Edina Sun-Current (Minneapolis) **10180**
Ely Echo (Ely) **10178**
Erskine Echo, The (Erskine) **10178**
Evergreen Shopping Guide (Spooner) **10183**
Excelsior/Shorewood Sun-Sailor
  (Minnetonka) **10180**
Fairmont Photo Press (Fairmont) **10178**
Fairmont Sentinel (Fairmont) **10002**
Faribault County Register (Blue Earth) **10177**
Faribault Daily News (Faribault) **10002**
Farmers Independent (Bagley) **10176**
Forest Lake Press (St. Paul) **10183**
Fosston Thirteen Towns (Fosston) **10178**
† Freeborn County Register (Albert Lea)
Free Press (Mankato) **10003**
Fridley Focus (Roseville) **10182**
Glencoe Enterprise (Glencoe) **10178**
Grand Gazette (St. Paul) **10183**
Grand Rapids Herald-Review (Grand
  Rapids) **10179**
Granite Falls/Clerkfield Advocate Tribune
  (Granite Falls) **10179**
Grygla Eagle (Grygla) **10179**
Hastings Star Gazette (Hastings) **10179**

Hawley Herald (Hawley) **10179**
Hiawatha Valley Shopper (Red Wing) **10182**
Hibbing Daily Tribune (Hibbing) **10003**
Hopkins Sun-Sailor (Minnetonka) **10180**
Hutchinson Leader (Hutchinson) **10179**
Independent News Herald (Clarissa) **10178**
Jackson County Livewire (Jackson) **10179**
Jasper Journal (Jasper) **10179**
Journal, The (New Ulm) **10003**
Kanabec County Times (Mora) **10181**
Kenyon Leader (Kenyon) **10179**
Lake County News-Chronicle (Two
   Harbors) **10184**
Lakefield Standard (Lakefield) **10179**
Lakeshore Weekly News (Wayzata) **10184**
Lakeville Life & Times (Lakeville) **10179**
Lakeville Sun-Current (Burnsville) **10177**
Lamberton News (Lamberton) **10179**
Leader-Record (Gonvick) **10179**
Le Center Leader (Le Center) **10179**
Lewiston Journal (Lewiston) **10179**
Lillie Suburban Shopping Review (St.
   Paul) **10183**
Litchfield Independent Review
   (Litchfield) **10179**
† Little Falls Transcript (Little Falls)
Long Prairie Leader (Long Prairie) **10179**
Madison Western Guard, The (Madison) **10180**
Mahnomen Pioneer, The (Mahnomen) **10180**
Maplewood Review (St. Paul) **10183**
Marshall Independent (Marshall) **10003**
McIntosh Times (McIntosh) **10180**
Melrose Beacon (Melrose) **10180**
Mesabi Daily News (Virginia) **10003**
Mille Lacs County Times (Milaca) **10180**
Minnetonka Sun-Sailor (Minnetonka) **10180**
Montevideo American-News
   (Montevideo) **10180**
Moose Lake Star-Gazette (Moose Lake) **10181**
Morris Sun (Morris) **10181**
Morris Tribune (Morris) **10181**
Mounds View-New Brighton-St. Anthony Focus
   (Roseville) **10182**
Murray County Wheel Herald (Slayton) **10183**
New Brighton-Mounds View Bulletin (North St.
   Paul) **10181**
New Hope-Golden Valley Sun Post
   (Minneapolis) **10180**
New Prague Times (New Prague) **10181**
New River Record (Middle River) **10180**
Northern Star, The (Clinton) **10178**
Northern Watch (Thief River Falls) **10184**
Northfield News (Northfield) **10181**
North Minneapolis Sun Post
   (Minneapolis) **10180**

Northome Record & Mizpah Message
   (Northome) **10181**
Oakdale-Lake Elmo Review (St. Paul) **10183**
Oakdale Clarion (Oakdale) **10181**
Observer, The (Belgrade) **10176**
Oklee Herald (Oklee) **10181**
Olivia Times Journal (Olivia) **10181**
Ortonville Independent (Ortonville) **10181**
Osakis Review, The (Osakis) **10181**
Owatonna People's Press (Owatonna) **10003**
Owatonna Weekly Shopper (Owatonna) **10181**
Park Rapids Enterprise (Park Rapids) **10181**
Paynesville Press, The (Paynesville) **10182**
Pelican Rapids Press (Pelican Rapids) **10182**
Perham Enterprise-Bulletin (Perham) **10182**
Pioneer, The (Bemidji) **10002**
Pipestone County Star (Pipestone) **10182**
Plainview News (Plainview) **10182**
Plymouth Sun-Sailor (Minnetonka) **10180**
Pope County Tribune (Glenwood) **10178**
Post-Bulletin (Rochester) **10003**
† Press, The (Alexandria)
Princeton Union-Eagle (Princeton) **10182**
Proctor Journal (Proctor) **10182**
Quad Community Press (White Bear
   Lake) **10184**
Ramsey County Review (St. Paul) **10183**
Red Wing Republican Eagle (Red Wing) **10003**
Redwood Gazette, The (Redwood Falls) **10182**
Renville County Shopper (Olivia) **10181**
Richfield Sun-Current (Bloomington) **10177**
River Valley Shopper (Spring Valley) **10183**
Rock County Star Herald (Luverne) **10180**
Roosevelt Review (St. Paul) **10183**
Roseau Times-Region (Roseau) **10182**
Roseville-Falcon Heights-Arden Hills Focus
   (Roseville) **10182**
Roseville Review (St. Paul) **10183**
Sauk Centre Herald (Sauk Centre) **10182**
Sebeka/Menahga Review Messenger
   (Sebeka) **10182**
Shakopee Valley News (Shakopee) **10183**
Shoreview-Arden Hills Bulletin (St.
   Paul) **10183**
Shoreview Press (St. Paul) **10183**
South-West Review (St. Paul) **10184**
† South East Metro Shopper (Cottage Grove)
South St. Paul/Inver Grove Heights Sun-Current
   (Burnsville) **10177**
Springfield Advance-Press (Springfield) **10183**
Spring Valley Tribune (Spring Valley) **10183**
St. Anthony Bulletin (North St. Paul) **10181**
Staples World (Staples) **10183**
Star Tribune (Minneapolis) **10003**
St. Charles Press (St. Charles) **10183**
St. Cloud Times (St. Cloud) **10003**

St. Croix Valley Peach (Forest Lake) **10178**
St. Croix Valley Press (St. Paul) **10184**
Stillwater Gazette (Stillwater) **10003**
St. James Plaindealer (St. James) **10183**
St. Louis Park Sun-Sailor (Minnetonka) **10180**
St. Paul Pioneer Press (St. Paul) **10003**
St. Peter Herald (St. Peter) **10184**
Thief River Falls Times, The (Thief River
  Falls) **10184**
Times, The (Forest Lake) **10178**
Tracy Headlight-Herald (Tracy) **10184**
Tri-County Record (Rushford) **10182**
Twin Cities Reader (Minneapolis) **10180**
Tyler Tribute (Tyler) **10184**
Vadnais Heights Press (St. Paul) **10184**
Villager (St. Paul) **10184**
Waconia Patriot (Waconia) **10184**
Wadena Pioneer Journal (Wadena) **10184**
Warren Sheaf (Warren) **10184**
Waseca County News (Waseca) **10184**
Wayzata/Orono/Long Lake Sun-Sailor
  (Minnetonka) **10180**
Wells Mirror, The (Wells) **10184**
West Central Tribune (Willmar) **10003**
West Martin Weekly News (Sherburn) **10183**
West St. Paul/Mendota Heights Sun-Current
  (Burnsville) **10177**
Windom Cottonwood County Citizen
  (Windom) **10185**
Winona Daily News (Winona) **10003**
Woodbury-South Maplewood Review (St.
  Paul) **10184**
Worthington Daily Globe (Worthington) **10004**
Wright County Journal-Press (Buffalo) **10177**

MISSISSIPPI

Aberdeen Examiner (Aberdeen) **10185**
Amory Advertiser, The (Amory) **10185**
Bay St. Louis Sea Coast Echo (Bay St.
  Louis) **10185**
Biloxi-D'Iberville Press (D'Iberville) **10185**
Booneville Banner-Independent
  (Booneville) **10185**
Brookhaven Daily Leader (Brookhaven) **10004**
Bruce Calhoun County Journal (Bruce) **10185**
Carthaginian, The (Carthage) **10185**
Clarion-Ledger, The (Jackson) **10004**
Clarke County Tribune (Quitman) **10187**
Clarksdale Press Register (Clarksdale) **10004**
Cleveland Bolivar Commercial
  (Cleveland) **10004**
Columbian-Progress (Columbia) **10185**
Commercial Dispatch, The (Columbus) **10004**
Conservative, The (Carrollton) **10185**
Copiah County Courier (Hazlehurst) **10186**

Daily Corinthian (Corinth) **10004**
Daily Sentinel-Star, The (Grenada) **10004**
Daily Times Leader (West Point) **10005**
Delta Democrat-Times (Greenville) **10004**
Democrat, The (Senatobia) **10187**
De Soto Times (Southaven) **10187**
George County Times (Lucedale) **10186**
Golden Triangle Shopper (Columbus) **10185**
Greenwood Commonwealth
  (Greenwood) **10004**
Hattiesburg American (Hattiesburg) **10004**
Impact of Laurel (Laurel) **10186**
Itawamba County Times, The (Fulton) **10186**
Iuka Tishomingo County News (Iuka) **10186**
Jasper County News, The (Bay Springs) **10185**
Kemper County Messenger (DeKalb) **10185**
Laurel Leader-Call (Laurel) **10004**
Louisville Winston County Journal
  (Louisville) **10186**
Macon Beacon, The (Macon) **10186**
Madison County Herald (Canton) **10185**
Magee Courier (Magee) **10186**
Magnolia Gazette, The (Magnolia) **10186**
McComb Enterprise-Journal (McComb) **10004**
Meridian Star (Meridian) **10004**
Mississippi Press (Pascagoula) **10005**
Natchez Democrat (Natchez) **10005**
Neshoba Democrat, The (Philadelphia) **10187**
New Albany Gazette (New Albany) **10186**
Newton Record (Newton) **10187**
Northeast Mississippi Daily Journal
  (Tupelo) **10005**
Northside Sun, The (Jackson) **10186**
Ocean Springs Record (Ocean Springs) **10187**
Oxford Eagle (Oxford) **10005**
▼Panolian ADvantage, The (Batesville) **10185**
Panolian, The (Batesville) **10185**
Picayune Item (Picayune) **10005**
Pontotoc Progress (Pontotoc) **10187**
Port Gibson Reveille (Port Gibson) **10187**
Rankin County News, The (Brandon) **10185**
Richton Dispatch, The (Richton) **10187**
Ripley Southern Sentinel (Ripley) **10187**
Scott County Times (Forest) **10186**
Shopper's Guide, The (Louisville) **10186**
Shopping News, The (Newton) **10187**
Smith County Reformer (Raleigh) **10187**
Southern Herald, The (Liberty) **10186**
South Reporter, The (Holly Springs) **10186**
Star-Herald, The (Kosciusko) **10186**
Starkville Daily News (Starkville) **10005**
Stone County Enterprise (Wiggins) **10187**
Sun Herald, The (Gulfport) **10004**
Times Post, The (Houston) **10186**
Tylertown Times (Tylertown) **10187**
Vicksburg Post (Vicksburg) **10005**

Wayne County News (Waynesboro) **10187**
Webster Progress-Times (Eupora) **10186**
Winona Times (Winona) **10187**
Yazoo Herald (Yazoo City) **10187**

MISSOURI

Albany Ledger, The (Albany) **10187**
Atchison County Mail, The (Rock Port) **10192**
Aurora Advertiser (Aurora) **10188**
Barry County Advertiser (Cassville) **10189**
Belle Banner (Belle) **10188**
Bethany Republican-Clipper (Bethany) **10188**
Bland Courier (Belle) **10188**
Blue Springs Examiner (Blue Springs) **10005**
Bolivar Herald-Free Press (Bolivar) **10188**
Bollinger County Banner-Press (Marble
  Hill) **10191**
Boone County Journal (Ashland) **10188**
Boonville Daily News (Boonville) **10005**
Bowling Green Times (Bowling Green) **10188**
Branson Daily News (Hollister) **10006**
Buffalo Reflex (Buffalo) **10188**
California Democrat (California) **10188**
▼Callaway Courier (Holts Summit) **10190**
Cameron Citizen Observer (Cameron) **10188**
Carrollton Democrat (Carrollton) **10188**
Carthage Press (Carthage) **10005**
Cassville Democrat (Cassville) **10189**
Cedar County Republican (Stockton) **10194**
Centralia Fireside Guard (Centralia) **10189**
Central Missouri News (Sedalia) **10192**
Central West End Journal (St. Louis) **10193**
Charleston Enterprise-Courier
  (Charleston) **10189**
Chesterfield Journal (St. Louis) **10193**
Chillicothe Constitution-Tribune
  (Chillicothe) **10005**
Christian County Headliner News
  (Ozark) **10192**
Citizen Journal (St. Louis) **10193**
Clay Dispatch-Tribune (Kansas City) **10190**
Clinton Daily Democrat (Clinton) **10006**
Clinton Eye, The (Clinton) **10189**
Columbia Daily Tribune (Columbia) **10006**
Columbia Missourian (Columbia) **10006**
Community News (St. Louis) **10193**
County Star Journal East (St. Louis) **10193**
County Star Journal West (St. Louis) **10193**
Courier-Post, The (St. Charles) **10008**
Cuba Free Press (Cuba) **10189**
Daily American Republic (Poplar Bluff) **10007**
Daily Dunklin Democrat (Kennett) **10006**
Daily Guide (St. Robert) **10008**
Daily Journal (Park Hills) **10007**
Daily Mail & Sunday Herald (Nevada) **10007**

Daily News (Richmond) **10007**
Daily News-Bulletin, The (Brookfield) **10005**
Daily Standard (Excelsior Springs) **10006**
Daily Star-Journal, The (Warrensburg) **10008**
Democrat-Argus, The (Caruthersville) **10189**
Democrat-Leader (Fayette) **10189**
Dexter Daily Statesman (Dexter) **10006**
Dixon Pilot (Dixon) **10189**
Douglas County Herald (Ava) **10188**
Eldon Advertiser (Eldon) **10189**
Fayette Advertiser, The (Fayette) **10189**
† Flat River Lead Belt News (Flat River)
Florissant Valley Reporter (Florissant) **10189**
Fredericktown Democrat-News
  (Fredericktown) **10189**
Fulton Sun, The (Fulton) **10006**
Gasconade County Republican
  (Owensville) **10192**
† Good Times News (Fayette)
Green Hills Weekly (Trenton) **10194**
Hannibal Courier-Post (Hannibal) **10006**
Harrison County Advisor (Bethany) **10188**
Harrisonville Cass County Democrat Missourian
  (Harrisonville) **10190**
Hermann Advertiser-Courier (Hermann) **10190**
Hermitage Index (Hermitage) **10190**
Holden Image-Progress, The (Holden) **10190**
Hopkins Journal, The (Hopkins) **10190**
Houston Herald & Republican
  (Houston) **10190**
Independence Examiner, The
  (Independence) **10006**
Independent-Journal, The (Potosi) **10192**
Jackson Cash-Book Journal (Jackson) **10190**
Jefferson County Journal (Arnold) **10188**
† Jefferson Republic, The (De Soto)
Joplin Globe, The (Joplin) **10006**
Kansas City Star (Kansas City) **10006**
Kayo, The (Clinton) **10189**
Kirksville Daily Express (Kirksville) **10007**
Lake Sun Leader (Camdenton) **10005**
Lamar Democrat (Lamar) **10191**
Lawrence County Record (Mt. Vernon) **10191**
Lebanon Daily Record (Lebanon) **10007**
Lee's Summit Journal (Lee's Summit) **10191**
Lexington News (Lexington) **10191**
Liberty Tribune (Kansas City) **10190**
Linn Unterrified Democrat (Linn) **10191**
Louisiana Press-Journal (Louisiana) **10191**
Macon Chronicle-Herald (Macon) **10007**
† Malden Press-Merit (Malden)
Marceline Press (Marceline) **10191**
Maries County Gazette (Vienna) **10194**
Marshall Democrat-News (Marshall) **10007**
Marshfield Mail (Marshfield) **10191**
Marthasville Record, The (Marthasville) **10191**

Maryville Daily Forum (Maryville) **10007**
Mexico Ledger (Mexico) **10007**
Mid-County Journal (St. Louis) **10193**
Milan Standard, The (Milan) **10191**
Missouri Press News (Columbia) **10189**
Moberly Monitor Index (Moberly) **10007**
Monett Times (Monett) **10007**
Monroe County Appeal (Paris) **10192**
Montgomery Standard (Montgomery
  City) **10191**
Mound City News (Mound City) **10191**
Mountain Echo (Ironton) **10190**
Mountain Grove News-Journal (Mountain
  Grove) **10191**
Neosho Daily News (Neosho) **10007**
News-X Press (Butler) **10188**
News Democrat Journal (Festus) **10189**
New Times, The (Kansas City) **10190**
North County Journal East (St. Louis) **10193**
North County Journal West (St. Louis) **10193**
North Missourian (Gallatin) **10190**
Northside Journal (St. Louis) **10194**
O'Fallon Journal (O'Fallon) **10191**
Oakville-Mehville Journal (St. Louis) **10194**
Ozark County Times (Gainesville) **10190**
Palmyra Spectator (Palmyra) **10192**
Perry County Republic-Monitor, The
  (Perryville) **10192**
Pierce City Leader-Journal (Pierce City) **10192**
Pitch Weekly (Kansas City) **10190**
Plainsman Weekly News (Sedalia) **10192**
Platte County Gazette (Parkville) **10192**
Platte Dispatch Tribune (Kansas City) **10190**
Post-Tribune (Jefferson City) **10006**
Press-News Journal (Canton) **10188**
Press Dispatch (Kansas City) **10190**
Press Journal (St. Louis) **10194**
Press Leader, The (Farmington) **10006**
Prospect-News, The (Doniphan) **10189**
Prospector, The (Doniphan) **10189**
Quad River News (Sheridan) **10193**
† Randolph County Times-Herald (Moberly)
Raytown Dispatch Tribune (Raytown) **10192**
Record, The (Boonville) **10188**
Reynolds County Courier (Ellington) **10189**
Rolla Daily News (Rolla) **10007**
Salem News (Salem) **10192**
Sarcoxie Record, The (Sarcoxie) **10192**
Savannah Reporter & Andrew County Democrat
  (Savannah) **10192**
Sedalia Democrat, The (Sedalia) **10007**
Shelby County Herald (Shelbyville) **10193**
Sikeston Standard Democrat, The
  (Sikeston) **10007**
Smithville Lake Democrat-Herald, The
  (Smithville) **10193**

South City Journal (St. Louis) **10194**
South County Journal (St. Louis) **10194**
Southeast Missourian (Cape Girardeau) **10005**
South Missourian News (Thayer) **10194**
Southside Journal (St. Louis) **10194**
Southwest City Journal (St. Louis) **10194**
Southwest County Journal (St. Louis) **10194**
Springfield News-Leader, The
  (Springfield) **10008**
Star-Herald (Belton) **10188**
St. Charles Journal (St. Charles) **10193**
St. Clair Missourian (St. Clair) **10193**
Steele Enterprise (Steel) **10193**
Steelville Star/Crawford Mirror
  (Steelville) **10193**
Ste. Genevieve Herald (Ste. Genevieve) **10193**
St. James Leader Journal (St. James) **10193**
St. Joseph News-Press (St. Joseph) **10008**
St. Joseph Telegraph, The (St. Joseph) **10193**
St. Louis American Newspaper (St.
  Louis) **10194**
† St. Louis Naborhood Link News (St. Louis)
St. Louis Post-Dispatch (St. Louis) **10008**
St. Louis Sentinel Newspaper (St.
  Louis) **10194**
† St. Louis South St. Louis County News (St.
  Louis)
St. Louis Watchman Advocate (St.
  Louis) **10008**
Stoddard County News (Dexter) **10006**
Sullivan Independent News (Sullivan) **10194**
Sun Times (Perryville) **10192**
Table Rock Gazette (Kimberling City) **10191**
▼Taney County Times (Forsyth) **10189**
Tarkio Avalanche (Tarkio) **10194**
Trenton Republican Times (Trenton) **10008**
Tri-County Journal (Pacific) **10192**
Troy Free Press & Silex Index (Troy) **10194**
Unionville Republican, The (Unionville) **10194**
Versailles Leader-Statesman (Versailles) **10194**
† Vista Press (Kansas City)
† Warrenton Banner (Warrenton)
Warrenton News-Journal (Warrenton) **10194**
Warsaw Benton County Enterprise
  (Warsaw) **10195**
Washington Missourian (Washington) **10195**
Wayne County Journal-Banner
  (Piedmont) **10192**
Webster County Citizen (Seymour) **10193**
Wednesday Magazine (Kansas City) **10190**
Wentzville Journal (Wentzville) **10195**
West County Journal (St. Louis) **10194**
West Plains Daily Quill (West Plains) **10008**
Wheels 'N Deals (Columbia) **10189**

Windsor Review (Windsor) **10195**

MONTANA

Anaconda Leader (Anaconda) **10195**
Big Fork Eagle (Bigfork) **10195**
Billings Gazette (Billings) **10008**
Bozeman Daily Chronicle (Bozeman) **10008**
Daily Inter Lake, The (Kalispell) **10009**
Glasgow Courier, The (Glasgow) **10195**
Glendive Ranger-Review (Glendive) **10195**
Great Falls Tribune (Great Falls) **10008**
Havre Daily News (Havre) **10008**
Herald-News (Wolf Point) **10196**
Hungry Horse News (Columbia Falls) **10195**
Independent Record (Helena) **10008**
Lake County Leader (Ronan) **10196**
Lewistown News-Argus (Lewistown) **10195**
Livingston Enterprise (Livingston) **10009**
Miles City Star (Miles City) **10009**
Missoulian, The (Missoula) **10009**
Montana Standard (Butte) **10008**
Mountaineer, The (Big Sandy) **10195**
Philipsburg Mail, The (Philipsburg) **10195**
Ravalli Republic (Hamilton) **10008**
River Press, The (Fort Benton) **10195**
Sentinel, The (Havre) **10195**
Sidney Herald-Leader (Sidney) **10196**
Times-Clarion, The (Harlowton) **10195**
Western Breeze (Cut Bank) **10195**
Western News (Libby) **10195**
Whitefish Pilot (Whitefish) **10196**

NEBRASKA

Albion News (Albion) **10196**
Alliance Times-Herald (Alliance) **10009**
Arapahoe Public Mirror (Arapahoe) **10196**
Arlington Citizen (Blair) **10196**
Arthur Enterprise, The (Arthur) **10196**
Atkinson Graphic, The (Atkinson) **10196**
Auburn Press Tribune (Auburn) **10196**
Aurora News-Register (Aurora) **10196**
Beacon Observer, The (Overton) **10198**
Beatrice Daily Sun (Beatrice) **10009**
Bellevue Leader (Bellevue) **10196**
Blair Enterprise (Blair) **10196**
Blair Pilot-Tribune (Blair) **10196**
Burwell Tribune (Burwell) **10196**
Central City Republican Nonpareil (Central
  City) **10197**
Clipper-Herald (Lexington) **10197**
Columbus Telegram (Columbus) **10009**
Courier-Times (Sutherland) **10198**
Crete News, The (Crete) **10197**

Custer County Chief (Broken Bow) **10196**
David City Banner-Press, The (David
  City) **10197**
Deshler Rustler, The (Deshler) **10197**
Douglas County Post Gazette (Elkhorn) **10197**
Fairbury Journal-News, The (Fairbury) **10197**
Falls City Journal (Falls City) **10197**
Fremont Tribune (Fremont) **10009**
Frontier & Holt County Independent
  (O'Neill) **10197**
Gering Courier (Gering) **10197**
Grand Island Independent (Grand
  Island) **10009**
Harlan County Journal (Alma) **10196**
Hastings Daily Tribune (Hastings) **10009**
Holdrege Daily Citizen (Holdrege) **10009**
Kearney Hub (Kearney) **10009**
Keith County News (Ogallala) **10198**
Lincoln Journal Star (Lincoln) **10009**
Lyons Mirror-Sun (Lyons) **10197**
McCook Daily Gazette (McCook) **10009**
Minden Courier (Minden) **10197**
Nebraska City News-Press (Nebraska
  City) **10009**
Nebraska Signal (Geneva) **10197**
Nemaha County Herald (Auburn) **10196**
Norfolk Daily News (Norfolk) **10010**
Oakland Indpendent (Oakland) **10197**
Omaha Star (Omaha) **10198**
Omaha World-Herald (Omaha) **10010**
Ord Quiz (Ord) **10198**
Papillion Times (Papillion) **10198**
Plainview News (Plainview) **10198**
Plattsmouth Journal (Plattsmouth) **10198**
Sargent Leader (Burwell) **10197**
Schuyler Sun (Schuyler) **10198**
Seward County Independent (Seward) **10198**
Sidney Telegraph (Sidney) **10010**
South Sioux City Star (South Sioux
  City) **10198**
Springview Herald (Springview) **10198**

Star-Herald (Scottsbluff) **10010**
Superior Express, The (Superior) **10198**

Syracuse Journal-Democrat (Syracuse) **10198**
Taylor Clarion (Burwell) **10197**

Telegraph, The (North Platte) **10010**
Tri-City Trib (Cozad) **10197**

Valentine Newspaper (Valentine) **10198**
Wahoo Newspaper (Wahoo) **10198**

Wayne Herald (Wayne) **10198**
West Point News (West Point) **10199**

Wheeler County Independent (Burwell) **10197**
York News-Times (York) **10010**

NEVADA

Boulder City News (Boulder City) **10199**
Chronicle, The (Carson City) **10199**
† Communicator Community News (Reno)
Daily Sparks Tribune, The (Sparks) **10010**
Elko Daily Free Press (Elko) **10010**
Ely Daily Times (Ely) **10010**
Eureka Sentinel (Tonopah) **10199**
† Fallon Eagle Standard (Fallon)
Fernley Leader-Dayton Courier
   (Yerington) **10199**
Humboldt Sun (Winnemucca) **10011**
Lahontan Valley News (Fallon) **10010**
Las Vegas Review-Journal (Las Vegas) **10010**
Las Vegas Sun (Las Vegas) **10010**
Las Vegas Today (Las Vegas) **10199**
Lovelock Review-Miner (Lovelock) **10199**
Mason Valley News (Yerington) **10199**
Mineral County Independent-News
   (Hawthorne) **10199**
Nevada Appeal (Carson City) **10010**
North Lake Tahoe Bonanza (Incline
   Village) **10199**
Reno Gazette-Journal (Reno) **10010**
Tonopah Times-Bonanza & Goldfield News
   (Tonopah) **10199**

NEW HAMPSHIRE

Argus-Champion, The (Newport) **10200**
Berlin Daily Sun (Berlin) **10011**
Berlin Reporter, The (Berlin) **10011**
Carroll County Independent (Center
   Ossipee) **10199**
Citizen, The (Laconia) **10011**
Concord Monitor (Concord) **10011**
Conway Daily Sun, The (North Conway) **10011**
Coos County Democrat (Lancaster) **10200**
Courier, The (Littleton) **10200**
Derry News (Derry) **10199**
Eagle-Times (Claremont) **10011**
Exeter News-Letter (Stratham) **10200**
Foster's Daily Democrat (Dover) **10011**
Granite State News (Wolfeboro) **10200**
Hampton Union (North Hampton) **10200**
Hudson-Litchfield News (Hudson) **10199**
† Journal Transcript (Franklin)
Keene Sentinel (Keene) **10011**
† Lebanon Connecticut Valley Reporter
   (Lebanon)
Milford Cabinet & Wilton Journal
   (Milford) **10200**
Monadnock Ledger (Peterborough) **10200**
Mt. Washington Valley Mountain Ear
   (Conway) **10199**
New Hampshire Week in Review
   (Hillsborough) **10199**

News & Sentinel, The (Colebrook) **10199**
Peterborough Transcript
   (Peterborough) **10200**
Portsmouth Herald (Portsmouth) **10011**
Record Enterprise (Plymouth) **10200**
† Rochester Courier (Rochester)
Rochester Times, The (Rochester) **10200**
Salem Observer (Salem) **10200**
Telegraph, The (Hudson) **10011**
Transcript, The (Dover) **10199**
Union Leader/New Hampshire Sunday News
   (Manchester) **10011**
Valley News (West Lebanon) **10011**
1590 Broadcaster (Nashua) **10200**

NEW JERSEY

Advance News (Lakehurst) **10203**
Asbury Park Press (Neptune) **10012**
Atlantic County Record (Hammonton) **10202**
Bayonne Community News (Bayonne) **10200**
Beachcomber, The (Surf City) **10207**
Beach Haven Times (Manahawkin) **10204**
Beacon-Record (Hopewell) **10203**
Beacon, The (Manahawkin) **10204**
Belleville Post (Bloomfield) **10201**
Belleville Times News (Nutley) **10205**
Bergen News, The (Palisades Park) **10205**
Bernardsville News (Bernardsville) **10200**
Blairstown Press (Blairstown) **10201**
Bloomfield Life (Nutley) **10205**
Bound Brook Chronicle (Somerville) **10206**
Brick Township Town News (Brick) **10201**
Bridgeton Evening News (Bridgeton) **10011**
Burlington County Times (Willingboro) **10013**
Camden County Record (Camden) **10201**
Cape May County Gazette Leader
   (Wildwood) **10208**
Cape May Herald Dispatch (Rio
   Grande) **10206**
Cape May Star & Wave (Cape May) **10201**
Central Post (Dayton) **10202**
Central Record (Medford) **10204**
Chatham Courier (Madison) **10203**
Chatham Independent Press (New
   Providence) **10204**
† Cherry Hill News (Cherry Hill)
Chronicle, The (Somerville) **10206**
Citizen of Morris County (Denville) **10202**
Clark Eagle (Union) **10207**
Clark Patriot (Rahway) **10206**
Community Forum (Hackettstown) **10202**
Courier-News, The (Bridgewater) **10012**
Courier-Post, The (Cherry Hill) **10012**
Cranbury Press (Dayton) **10202**

Cranford Chronicle (Cranford) **10202**
Daily Journal (Vineland) **10013**
† Daily Journal (Elizabeth)
Daily Record, The (Parsippany) **10012**
Delaware Valley News (Frenchtown) **10202**
Dispatch, The (New Providence) **10204**
East Orange Record (Orange) **10205**
Echoes-Sentinel (Stirling) **10207**
Egg Harbor News (Hammonton) **10203**
Fairfield Chronicle, The (West Caldwell) **10207**
Florham Park Eagle (Madison) **10203**
Franklin News-Record (Princeton) **10206**
Franklin Township Sentinel
   (Franklinville) **10202**
Free Time (Wildwood) **10208**
Gazette, The (Mt. Holly) **10204**
Glen Ridge Paper, The (Bloomfield) **10201**
Gloucester City News (Gloucester City) **10202**
Gloucester County Times (Woodbury) **10013**
† Haddon Gazette (Cherry Hill)
Hammonton News (Hammonton) **10203**
Hanover Eagle & Regional News
   (Madison) **10203**
Hawthorne Press (Hawthorne) **10203**
Hillsborough Beacon (Somerville) **10206**
Hillside Leader (Union) **10207**
Hoboken Reporter (Hoboken) **10203**
Home News & Tribune, The (East
   Brunswick) **10012**
Hudson Reporter (Hoboken) **10203**
Hunterdon County Democrat
   (Flemington) **10202**
Hunterdon Review (Lebanon) **10203**
Independent Press (New Providence) **10205**
Independent Press of Bloomfield, The
   (Bloomfield) **10201**
Independent, The (Morganville) **10204**
Jersey City Reporter (Hoboken) **10203**
Jersey Journal, The (Jersey City) **10012**
Journal, The (Berlin) **10200**
Kenilworth Leader (Union) **10207**
Lakeland Today (Butler) **10201**
Lawrence Ledger (Pennington) **10206**
Leader, The (Point Pleasant Beach) **10206**
Linden Leader (Union) **10207**
Lower Township Lantern (Rio Grande) **10206**
Madison Eagle (Madison) **10203**
Madison Independent Press (New
   Providence) **10205**
Mainland Journal (Hammonton) **10203**
Manville News (Somerville) **10207**
Maple Shade Progress (Maple Shade) **10204**
Messenger-Press (Hightstown) **10203**
Messenger, The (Garfield) **10202**
Middletown Courier (Middletown) **10204**
Millburn & Short Hills Item (Millburn) **10204**

Millburn-Short Hills Independent Press (New
   Providence) **10205**
Milville News (Bridgeton) **10011**
Montclair Times, The (Montclair) **10204**
Morris News Bee (Madison) **10204**
Morristown News, The (West Caldwell) **10207**
Mountainside Echo (Union) **10207**
Mt. Laurel Progress Press (Maple
   Shade) **10204**
Mt. Olive Chronicle (Budd Lake) **10201**
Netcong News-Leader (Netcong) **10204**
New Jersey Herald (Newton) **10012**
News-Record of Maplewood & South Orange
   (Maplewood) **10204**
News Beacon (Fair Lawn) **10202**
† News of Paterson (Passaic)
News Report (Blackwood) **10201**
News, The (Belvidere) **10200**
News Transcript (Morganville) **10204**
News Weekly (Mt. Laurel) **10204**
North Bergen/North Hudson Reporter
   (Hoboken) **10203**
North Brunswick Post (Dayton) **10202**
North Jersey Herald & News, The
   (Passaic) **10012**
North Jersey Prospector (Clifton) **10202**
Nutley Journal (Bloomfield) **10201**
Nutley Sun (Nutley) **10205**
Observer-Tribune (Chester) **10202**
Observer, The (Kearny) **10203**
† Observer, The (Blackwood)
Ocean County's Observer (Toms River) **10012**
Ocean County Reporter (Toms River) **10207**
Orange Transcript (Orange) **10205**
Our Town (Maywood) **10204**
Parsippany Focus (Morris Plains) **10204**
Parsippany News, The (West Caldwell) **10208**
Pascack Valley Community Life
   (Westwood) **10208**
Passaic Citizen (Passaic) **10206**
Passaic Valley Today (Butler) **10201**
Phillipsburg Free Press (Phillipsburg) **10206**
Plain Dealer (Turnersville) **10207**
Post Review, The (Paramus) **10205**
Press Journal, The (Palisades Park) **10205**
Press of Atlantic City, The
   (Pleasantville) **10012**
Princeton Packet, The (Princeton) **10206**
Progress, The (Caldwell) **10201**
Rahway News-Record (Rahway) **10206**
Rahway Progress (Union) **10207**
Ramsey-Mahwah Reporter (Palisades
   Park) **10205**
Ramsey Home & Store News (Ramsey) **10206**
Randolph Reporter (Bernardsville) **10200**
Record-Breeze (Blackwood) **10201**

Record, The (Hackensack) **10012**
Register-News (Bordentown) **10201**
† Register, The (Shrewsbury)
Reporter, The (Palisades Park) **10205**
Retrospect, The (Collingswood) **10202**
† Review-Enterprise (Blackwood)
Review, The (Paramus) **10205**
Review, The (Point Pleasant Beach) **10206**
Ridgewood News (Paramus) **10205**
Roselle Park Leader (Union) **10207**
Roselle Spectator (Union) **10207**
Salem County Record (Salem) **10206**
Seaside Heights Ocean County Review (Point
  Pleasant Beach) **10206**
Secaucus Home News (Secaucus) **10206**
Sentinel-Ledger, The (Ocean City) **10205**
Somerset Messenger Gazette
  (Somerville) **10207**
Somerset Spectator (Somerset) **10206**
South Bergenite (Rutherford) **10206**
South Jersey Advisor (Cologne) **10202**
Sparta Independent (Sparta) **10207**
Springfield Leader (Union) **10207**
Star-Ledger (Newark) **10012**
Star Gazette (Hackettstown) **10202**
Suburbanite, The (Closter) **10202**
Suburban Life (Butler) **10201**
Suburban Town News (Paramus) **10205**
Suburban Trends (Butler) **10201**
Summit Independent Press (New
  Providence) **10205**
Summit Observer (Union) **10207**
Sun-Bulletin, The (Palisades Park) **10205**
Sussex County Chronicle (Byram) **10201**
This Week (Cherry Hill) **10202**
Times, The (Trenton) **10012**
Times, The (Westfield) **10208**
Today's Sunbeam (Salem) **10012**
Town Topics (Princeton) **10206**
Trentonian, The (Trenton) **10012**
Union Leader (Union) **10207**
Vailsburg Leader (Maplewood) **10204**
Verona-Cedar Grove Times (Verona) **10207**
Wayne Today (Butler) **10201**
Weehawken Reporter (Hoboken) **10203**
West Essex Tribune (Livingston) **10203**
Westfield Leader (Westfield) **10208**
West Morris Star-Journal (Ledgewood) **10203**
West Orange Chronicle (Orange) **10205**
Wildwood Leader (Wildwood) **10208**

NEW MEXICO

Alamogordo Daily News (Alamogordo) **10013**
Albuquerque Journal (Albuquerque) **10013**
Albuquerque Street News
  (Albuquerque) **10208**
Albuquerque Tribune (Albuquerque) **10013**
Artesia Daily Press (Artesia) **10013**
Cibola County Beacon (Grants) **10208**
Clovis News Journal (Clovis) **10013**
Current-Argus (Carlsbad) **10013**
Daily Times (Farmington) **10013**
Defensor Chieftain (Socorro) **10209**
Deming Headlight (Deming) **10013**
Estancia Valley Citizen (Estancia) **10208**
Herald, The (Truth or Consequences) **10209**
Hobbs Daily News-Sun (Hobbs) **10013**
Hobbs Flare (Hobbs) **10208**
Las Cruces Sun-News (Las Cruces) **10013**
Las Vegas Daily Optic (Las Vegas) **10013**
Lovington Daily Leader (Lovington) **10013**
Monitor, The (Los Alamos) **10013**
Observer, The (Rio Rancho) **10208**
Portales News-Tribune (Portales) **10014**
Quay County Sun (Tucumcari) **10209**
Quik Quarter Want Ads (Hobbs) **10208**
Raton Range, The (Raton) **10203**
Rio Grande Sun (Espanola) **10208**
Roswell Daily Record (Roswell) **10014**
Ruidoso News, The (Ruidoso) **10208**
Santa Fe New Mexican (Santa Fe) **10014**
Santa Fe Reporter, The (Santa Fe) **10208**
Sierra County Sentinel (Truth or
  Consequences) **10209**
Silver City Daily Press & Independent (Silver
  City) **10014**
Taos News (Taos) **10209**
Valencia County News-Bulletin (Belen) **10208**

NEW YORK

Adirondack Daily Enterprise (Saranac
  Lake) **10017**
Albion Advertiser (Albion) **10209**
Altamont Enterprise, The (Altamont) **10209**
Amherst Bee (Buffalo) **10211**
Amityville Record (Amityville) **10209**
Amsterdam Star, The (Albany) **10014**
† Ausable Forks Adirondack Record Fost
  (Elizabethtown)
Baldwin Citizen (Mineola) **10218**
Baldwin Herald (Lawrence) **10216**
Baldwinsville Messenger (Baldwinsville) **10209**
Ballston Journal (Ballston Spa) **10209**
Batavia Daily News (Batavia) **10014**
Bay News (Brooklyn) **10210**
Bay Ridge Courier (Brooklyn) **10210**
Bayside Times, The (Bayside) **10210**
Beacon Free Press (Wappingers Falls) **10224**
Beacon Light (Mahopac) **10217**

Beacon Newspaper (Babylon) **10209**
Bellmore-Merrick Observer (Bellmore) **10210**
Bellmore Life (Bellmore) **10210**
Boonville Herald (Boonville) **10210**
Brewster Times (Mahopac) **10217**
Brighton-Pittsford Post, The (Fishers) **10214**
Brockport/Holley Suburban News
  (Spencerport) **10223**
Brockport Post, The (Brockport) **10210**
Bronx News (Bronx) **10210**
Bronx Press-Review (Bronx) **10210**
Brookhaven Review (Smithtown) **10223**
Brooklyn Daily Bulletin (Brooklyn) **10014**
Brooklyn Graphic (Brooklyn) **10210**
Brooklyn Heights Courier (Brooklyn) **10210**
Brooklyn Heights Press (Brooklyn) **10211**
Brooklyn Home Reporter & Sunset News
  (Brooklyn) **10211**
Brooklyn Record (Brooklyn) **10211**
Brooklyn Spectator (Brooklyn) **10211**
† Brooklyn Times (Brooklyn)
Buffalo News, The (Buffalo) **10014**
Buffalo Rocket (Buffalo) **10211**
Camillus Advocate (Baldwinsville) **10209**
Canandaigua Daily Messenger
  (Canandaigua) **10014**
Canarsie Courier (Brooklyn) **10211**
Canarsie Digest (Brooklyn) **10211**
Canastota Bee-Journal (Canastota) **10211**
Candor Chronicle (Trumansburg) **10224**
Carmel Times (Mahopac) **10217**
Carroll Gardens/Cobble Hill Courier
  (Brooklyn) **10211**
Carthage Republican Tribune
  (Carthage) **10212**
† Cato Citizen (Red Creek)
Cazenovia Republican (Cazenovia) **10212**
† Chateaugay Record (Chateaugay)
Chatham Courier-Roughnotes
  (Chatham) **10212**
Cheektowaga Bee (Williamsville) **10225**
Cheektowaga Times (Cheektowaga) **10212**
Chelsea Clinton News (New York) **10220**
Chemung Valley Reporter (Horseheads) **10216**
Chenango American (Greene) **10215**
Chittenango-Bridgeport Times
  (Canastota) **10212**
Chronicle-Express (Penn Yan) **10221**
Chronicle, The (Glens Falls) **10214**
Citizen Outlet (Mexico) **10218**
Citizen Register (Yorktown Heights) **10018**
Citizen, The (Auburn) **10014**
City News (Bronx) **10210**
Clarence Bee (Williamsville) **10225**
Clarkson Integrator (Potsdam) **10221**
Clarkstown Courier, The (Pearl River) **10221**

Clinton Courier (Clinton) **10212**
Cobleskill Times Journal (Cobleskill) **10212**
Colonie Spotlight (Delmar) **10213**
Commack News (Smithtown) **10223**
Community Journal (Wading River) **10224**
Community News (Clifton Park) **10212**
Cortland Democrat (Marathon) **10218**
Cortland Standard (Cortland) **10014**
Country Courier, The (Conklin) **10212**
Country Shopper (Pound Ridge) **10221**
Courier-Journal (Palmyra) **10220**
Courier-Standard-Enterprise (Fort Plain) **10214**
Courier Gazette (Newark) **10219**
† Current (Potsdam)
Daily & Sunday Freeman (Kingston) **10015**
Daily & Sunday Sentinel (Rome) **10017**
Daily Courier Observer, The (Massena) **10015**
Daily Editor (Cobleskill) **10014**
Daily Gazette (Schenectady) **10017**
Daily Item, The (New Rochelle) **10016**
Daily Mail (Catskill) **10014**
Daily Star, The (Oneonta) **10016**
Daily Times, The (New Rochelle) **10016**
Dan's Papers (Bridgehampton) **10210**
Dansville Genesee Country Express
  (Dansville) **10212**
Delaware County Times (Delhi) **10213**
Depew Bee (Williamsville) **10225**
Deposit Courier (Deposit) **10213**
DeWitt Times (Fayetteville) **10213**
Downtown Express (New York) **10220**
Dundee Observer (Dundee) **10213**
Eagle Bulletin (Fayetteville) **10214**
Eagle, The (Cambridge) **10211**
East Aurora Advertiser (East Aurora) **10213**
East Aurora Bee (Williamsville) **10225**
Eastchester Record (Yonkers) **10225**
East Fishkill Record (Mahopac) **10217**
East Hampton Star (East Hampton) **10213**
East Meadow Beacon (Hicksville) **10216**
East Rochester Post-Herald (Fishers) **10214**
East Rockaway Observer (Mineola) **10218**
Echo, The (Berlin) **10210**
Ellenville Press (Ellenville) **10213**
Elma Review (East Aurora) **10213**
Elmont Herald (Elmont) **10213**
Enterprise, The (Hastings-on-Hudson) **10215**
Evening-Observer (Dunkirk) **10015**
Evening Sun, The (Norwich) **10016**
Evening Telegram (Herkimer) **10015**
Evening Times, The (Little Falls) **10015**
† Fair Haven Register (Red Creek)
† Fairport-Perinton Herald-Mail (Webster)
Farmingdale Observer (Mineola) **10218**
Finger Lakes Times, The (Geneva) **10015**
Fire Island Tide (Sayville) **10222**

Fishkill Standard (Mahopac) **10217**
Flatbush Life (Brooklyn) **10211**
Floral Park Bulletin (Floral Park) **10214**
Flushing Times, The (Bayside) **10210**
▼Forest Hills/Rego Park Times
   (Maspeth) **10218**
Forum of Queens (Ozone Park) **10220**
Franklin Square Bulletin (Floral Park) **10214**
Freeman's Journal (Cooperstown) **10212**
Freeport Baldwin Leader, The
   (Freeport) **10214**
Free Trader (Massena) **10218**
Fresh Meadows Times, The (Flushing) **10214**
Front Page (Lackawanna) **10216**
Fulton Patriot (Fulton) **10214**
Gates-Chili News (Rochester) **10222**
Gateway, The (Floral Park) **10214**
Gazette-Advertiser (Rhinebeck) **10222**
Gazette, The (Port Jervis) **10221**
Glen Cove Record Pilot (Mineola) **10219**
Glendale Register (Maspeth) **10218**
Glen Oaks Ledger, The (Flushing) **10214**
Golden Times (Rochester) **10222**
Gouverneur Tribune Press
   (Gouverneur) **10215**
Gowanda Pennysaver News (Gowanda) **10215**
Grand Island Pennysaver (Grand
   Island) **10215**
Granville Sentinel (Granville) **10215**
Great Neck News (Great Neck) **10215**
Great Neck Record (Mineola) **10219**
Greece Post, The (Fishers) **10214**
Greenpoint Gazette/Advertiser
   (Brooklyn) **10211**
Greenville Local (Ravena) **10221**
Greenwich Journal & Salem Press
   (Greenwich) **10215**
Greenwood Lake & West Milford News
   (Greenwood Lake) **10215**
Hamilton County News (Speculator) **10223**
† Hamilton County News (Elizabethtown)
Hamilton Mid-York Weekly (Hamilton) **10215**
Hamilton Tribune (Hamilton) **10215**
Hampton Chronicle-News (Westhampton
   Beach) **10225**
Harborwatch (Brooklyn) **10211**
Harlem Valley Times (Amenia) **10209**
Harrison Independent (Yonkers) **10226**
Hempstead Beacon (Hicksville) **10216**
Henrietta Post (Fishers) **10214**
Hicksville Illustrated News (Mineola) **10219**
Hornell Evening Tribune (Hornell) **10015**
▼Howard Beach Resident (Maspeth) **10218**
Huntington Record (Huntington) **10216**
Hyde Park Townsman (Hyde Park) **10216**
Independent Mirror (Mexico) **10218**

Independent Republican (Goshen) **10215**
Interlaken Review (Trumansburg) **10224**
Irondequoit Press (Rochester) **10222**
Irvington Viewpoint, The (Irvington) **10216**
Island Dispatch (Grand Island) **10215**
Islip Bulletin (Sayville) **10222**
Islip News (Smithtown) **10223**
Ithaca Journal, The (Ithaca) **10015**
Ithaca Times (Ithaca) **10216**
Jackson Heights News (Maspeth) **10218**
▼Jamaica Times, The (Flushing) **10214**
Jefferson County Journal (Adams) **10209**
Journal & Republican (Lowville) **10217**
Journal-Register (Medina) **10016**
Journal Courier (Moravia) **10219**
Ken-Ton Bee (Buffalo) **10211**
Kings County News (Brooklyn) **10211**
Kings Courier (Brooklyn) **10211**
La Grange Independent (Mahopac) **10217**
Lake Placid News (Lake Placid) **10216**
Lancaster Bee (Williamsville) **10225**
Leader-Herald, The (Gloversville) **10015**
Leader Observer (Maspeth) **10218**
Leader, The (Corning) **10014**
Leader, The (Freeport) **10214**
Levittown Tribune (Mineola) **10219**
Lewiston-Porter Sentinel (Grand Island) **10215**
Little Neck Ledger, The (Flushing) **10214**
Liverpool Review (Baldwinsville) **10209**
Locust Valley Leader (Locust Valley) **10217**
Long Beach Herald (Long Beach) **10217**
Long Beach Independent Voice (Long
   Beach) **10217**
Long Island Advance (Patchogue) **10221**
Long Island City/Astoria Journal
   (Maspeth) **10218**
Long Island Graphic-Roosevelt Press
   (Lawrence) **10216**
† Long Island Journal Newspaper Group (Long
   Beach)
Loudenville Weekly (Delmar) **10213**
Lynbrook Herald (Lawrence) **10216**
Lynbrook USA (Mineola) **10219**
Mahopac Press (Mahopac) **10217**
Malone Telegram (Malone) **10015**
Malta Messenger (Ballston Spa) **10209**
Malverne Times (Mineola) **10219**
Manhasset Press (Mineola) **10219**
† Marathon Independent Newspaper (Marathon)
Marcellus Observer (Skaneateles) **10223**
Massapequan Observer (Mineola) **10219**
Massapequa Post (Massapequa Park) **10218**
Mayville Sentinel/Chautauqua News
   (Westfield) **10225**
Meadowbrook Times (Lawrence) **10216**
Merrick Beacon (Hicksville) **10216**

Merrick Life (Merrick) **10218**
Metropolitan News (Brooklyn) **10211**
Mid-Island Times (Hicksville) **10216**
Mid Hudson Times (Walden) **10224**
Millbrook Round Table (Millbrook) **10218**
Millerton News, The (Millerton) **10218**
Mineola American (Mineola) **10219**
† Mirror-Recorder (Stamford)
Moneysaver, The (Ballston Spa) **10209**
Moravia Republican Register (Moravia) **10219**
Mountain Eagle (Tannersville) **10224**
Mount Vernon Independent (Yonkers) **10226**
Mt. Vernon Daily Argus (Yonkers) **10018**
Naples Record, The (Naples) **10219**
Nassau Herald (Lawrence) **10217**
† Newburgh Evening News (Newburgh)
Newfield News (Trumansburg) **10224**
News-Review, The (Mattituck) **10218**
Newsday (Melville) **10016**
News of the Highlands (Highland Falls) **10216**
New York Beacon (New York) **10220**
† New York City Tribune (New York)
New York Daily Challenge (Brooklyn) **10014**
New York Daily News, The (New York) **10016**
New York Metropolitan News
  (Brooklyn) **10211**
† New York Newsday (New York)
New York Observer (New York) **10220**
New York Post (New York) **10016**
New York Press (New York) **10220**
New York Times, The (New York) **10016**
Niagara/Wheatfield Tribune (Grand
  Island) **10215**
Niagara Gazette (Niagara Falls) **10016**
North Castle News (Yonkers) **10226**
North Country Free Press (Granville) **10215**
North Countryman, The (Elizabethtown) **10213**
North County News (Yorktown Heights) **10226**
North Syracuse Star-News (Syracuse) **10223**
Observer-Dispatch (Utica) **10017**
Observer, The (Northport) **10220**
Oceanside/Island Park Herald (Long
  Beach) **10217**
Oceanside Centre Beacon (Mineola) **10219**
Ogdensburg Journal (Ogdensburg) **10016**
Olean Times Herald (Olean) **10016**
Oneida Daily Dispatch (Oneida) **10016**
Onondaga Valley News (Syracuse) **10223**
Orchard Park Bee (Williamsville) **10225**
Our Town (New York) **10220**
Our Town (Pearl River) **10221**
Ovid Gazette (Trumansburg) **10224**
Oxford Review-Times (Greene) **10215**
Oyster Bay-Syosset Guardian (Oyster
  Bay) **10220**
Oyster Bay Enterprise Pilot (Mineola) **10219**

Palladium-Times, The (Oswego) **10016**
Parkchester News (Bronx) **10210**
Park Slope Courier (Brooklyn) **10211**
Patent Trader (Cross River) **10212**
Patriot & Free Press (Cuba) **10212**
Pawling News Chronicle (Pawling) **10221**
Peekskill Herald (Peekskill) **10221**
Peekskill Star (Yorktown Heights) **10018**
Pelham Sun (Yonkers) **10226**
Penfield Post Republican, The (Fishers) **10214**
Pennysaver (Elmsford) **10213**
Pennysaver (Yorktown Heights) **10226**
People's Weekly World (New York) **10220**
Perinton-Fairport Post, The (Pittsford) **10221**
Phoenix Newspaper, The (Brooklyn) **10211**
Phoenix Register (Phoenix) **10221**
Photo News (Monroe) **10219**
Pine Plains Register-Herald (Pine
  Plains) **10221**
Port Times-Record, The (Setauket) **10222**
Port Washington News (Port
  Washington) **10221**
Post-Herald (Red Creek) **10222**
Post-Journal, The (Jamestown) **10015**
Post-Standard (Syracuse) **10017**
Post-Star (Glen Falls) **10015**
Poughkeepsie Journal (Poughkeepsie) **10017**
Press & Sun-Bulletin (Vestal) **10017**
Press-Republican (Plattsburgh) **10016**
PrimeTime (Lawrence) **10217**
Putnam Courier-Trader, The (Carmel) **10212**
Queens Chronicle (Rego Park) **10222**
Queens Ledger (Maspeth) **10218**
Queens Tribune (Fresh Meadows) **10214**
▼Queen Village Times, The (Flushing) **10214**
Ravena News Herald (Ravena) **10221**
Record-Advertiser (North Tonawanda) **10220**
Recorder, The (Amsterdam) **10014**
Record, The (Troy) **10017**
Register Star (Hudson) **10015**
Reporter Dispatch, The (White Plains) **10018**
Reporter, The (Walton) **10224**
▼Resident Community News (New
  York) **10220**
Reveille/Between the Lakes (Seneca
  Falls) **10222**
Review Press Reporter (Yonkers) **10226**
Riverdale Press (Bronx) **10210**
River Reporter, The (Narrowsburg) **10219**
Riverside Review (Buffalo) **10211**
Rochester Democrat & Chronicle
  (Rochester) **10017**
Rockaway Journal (Lawrence) **10217**
Rockland County Times (Haverstraw) **10216**
Rockland Independent, The (Pearl
  River) **10221**

Rockland Journal-News (West Nyack) **10018**
Rockville Centre Herald (Lawrence) **10217**
Rockville Centre Long Island News & Owl
  (Mineola) **10219**
Rye Chronicle (Yonkers) **10226**
Salamanca Press (Salamanca) **10017**
Salmon River News (Pulaski) **10221**
Saratogian, The (Saratoga Springs) **10017**
Saturday Post-Star (Saugerties) **10222**
Saugerties Post Star (Saugerties) **10222**
Scarsdale Inquirer, The (Scarsdale) **10222**
Scotsman Press, The (Syracuse) **10224**
Seaford-Wantagh Observer (Bellmore) **10210**
Shelter Island Reporter (Shelter Island
  Heights) **10223**
Shopping News (Fairport) **10213**
Skaneateles Press (Skaneateles) **10223**
Smithtown Messenger (Smithtown) **10223**
Smithtown News, The (Smithtown) **10223**
Sound View News (Yonkers) **10226**
Southampton Press (Southampton) **10223**
South Bay's Newspaper (Lindenhurst) **10217**
South Bay's Shopper (Lindenhurst) **10217**
South Buffalo News (Lackawanna) **10216**
Southern Cayuga Tribune (Moravia) **10219**
Southern Dutchess News (Wappingers
  Falls) **10224**
South Shore Record (Woodmere) **10225**
Southtowns Citizen (Orchard Park) **10220**
Spackenkill Sentinel (Wappingers Falls) **10224**
Spencer Random Harvest Weekly
  (Trumansburg) **10224**
Spotlight, The (Delmar) **10213**
Springville Journal (Springville) **10223**
Standard-Star (New Rochelle) **10016**
Star-Gazette (Elmira) **10015**
Star-News, The (North Syracuse) **10220**
Staten Island Advance (Staten Island) **10017**
Staten Island Register (Staten Island) **10223**
Steuben Courier-Advocate (Bath) **10210**
St. Lawrence Plaindealer (Canton) **10212**
Suburban News (Spencerport) **10223**
Suburban Street News (White Plains) **10225**
Suffolk County News (Sayville) **10222**
Suffolk Times (Mattituck) **10218**
Sun & Erie County Independent, The
  (Hamburg) **10215**
Syosset Jericho Tribune (Mineola) **10219**
Syracuse Herald-Journal/American
  (Syracuse) **10017**
Syracuse New Times (Syracuse) **10224**
Tarrytown Daily News (White Plains) **10018**
Thousand Islands Sun (Alexandria Bay) **10209**
Three Village Herald (East Setauket) **10213**
Three Village Times (Mineola) **10219**
Times-Union (Rochester) **10017**

Times Herald-Record (Middletown) **10016**
Times Newsweekly (Ridgewood) **10222**
Times of Nesconset, The (Setauket) **10222**
Times of Smithtown (Setauket) **10222**
Times of St. James (Setauket) **10222**
Times of Ti (Elizabethtown) **10213**
Times Union (Albany) **10014**
Tioga County Gazette & Times (Owego) **10220**
Tomorrow (New Rochelle) **10220**
Tonawanda News (North Tonawanda) **10016**
Traveler/Watchman (Southold) **10223**
Tri-County Advertiser (Brockport) **10210**
Tri-County News (Lockport) **10217**
Tri-Town News (Sidney) **10223**
Trumansburg Free Press
  (Trumansburg) **10224**
Tupper Lake Free Press & Herald (Tupper
  Lake) **10224**
Ulster County Townsman (Woodstock) **10225**
Union-Sun & Journal (Lockport) **10015**
Uniondale Beacon (Hicksville) **10216**
Valley News (Elizabethtown) **10213**
Valley News (Fulton) **10214**
Valley News, The (Endwell) **10213**
Valley Stream Courier (Freeport) **10214**
Valley Stream Herald (Lawrence) **10217**
Valley Stream Maileader (Mineola) **10219**
Vestal Town Crier (Conklin) **10212**
† Victor-Farmington Herald (Webster)
Village Beacon-Record, The (Setauket) **10222**
Villager, The (New York) **10220**
Villager, The (Syracuse) **10224**
Village Times, The (Setauket) **10222**
Village Voice, The (New York) **10220**
Voice Ledger, The (Millbrook) **10218**
Wallkill Valley Times, The (Walden) **10224**
Wantagh-Seaford Citizen (Bellmore) **10210**
Warrensburg-Lake George News
  (Elizabethtown) **10213**
Warwick Advertiser, The (Warwick) **10224**
Warwick Valley Dispatch (Warwick) **10224**
Watertown Daily Times (Watertown) **10017**
Watkins Review & Express (Watkins
  Glen) **10225**
Wayne County Mail (Webster) **10225**
Wayne County Star (Lyons) **10217**
Webster Herald (Webster) **10225**
Webster Post, The (Webster) **10225**
† Weekender, The (Bronx)
Weisbeck, The (Alden) **10209**
Wellsville Daily Reporter (Wellsville) **10017**
Westbury Times (Mineola) **10219**
Westfield Republican (Westfield) **10225**
West Hempstead Beacon (Hicksville) **10216**
Westmore News (Port Chester) **10221**
West Seneca Bee (Williamsville) **10225**

Westsider, The (New York) **10220**
West Side Times (Buffalo) **10211**
Whitehall Times (Whitehall) **10225**
Whitestone Times, The (Bayside) **10210**
Whitney Point Reporter (Greene) **10215**
Windham Journal (Windham) **10225**
Windsor Standard (Conklin) **10212**
Woodside Herald (Sunnyside) **10223**
Yankee Trader (Coram) **10212**
Yonkers Herald Statesman (Yonkers) **10018**
Yonkers Home News & Times
  (Yonkers) **10226**

NORTH CAROLINA

Alamance News (Graham) **10228**
Angier Independent (Angier) **10226**
Anson Record, The (Wadesboro) **10231**
Apex Herald, The (Apex) **10226**
Asheboro Courier-Tribune (Asheboro) **10018**
Asheville Citizen-Times (Asheville) **10018**
Belmont Banner (Belmont) **10226**
Bertie Ledger-Advance (Windsor) **10232**
Bessemer City Record (Kings Mountain) **10228**
Black Mountain News (Black Mountain) **10226**
Bladen Daily Journal (Elizabethtown) **10019**
Blowing Rocket, The (Blowing Rock) **10227**
Boone Watauga Democrat (Boone) **10227**
Brunswick Beacon, The (Shallotte) **10230**
Burke County Observer (Morganton) **10229**
Butner-Creedmoor News, The
  (Creedmoor) **10227**
Carolina Times (Durham) **10227**
Carolinian, The (Raleigh) **10230**
Carteret County News-Times (Morehead
  City) **10229**
Cary News (Cary) **10227**
Caswell Messenger (Yanceyville) **10232**
Chapel Hill Herald (Chapel Hill) **10018**
Chapel Hill News (Chapel Hill) **10227**
Charlotte Observer (Charlotte) **10018**
Chatham News, The (Siler City) **10230**
Cherokee Scout (Murphy) **10229**
Cherryville Eagle (Cherryville) **10227**
Clayton News-Star (Clayton) **10227**
Clemmons Courier (Clemmons) **10227**
Cleveland Times (Shelby) **10230**
Coastland Times (Manteo) **10229**
Commonwealth Progress (Scotland
  Neck) **10230**
Concord Tribune (Concord) **10018**
County News Enterprise
  (Rutherfordton) **10230**
Courier-Times, The (Roxboro) **10230**
Daily Advance (Elizabeth City) **10019**
Daily Courier (Forest City) **10019**

Daily Dispatch, The (Henderson) **10019**
Daily News, The (Eden) **10019**
Daily Southerner, The (Tarboro) **10021**
Danbury Reporter (Walnut Cove) **10231**
Davie County Enterprise-Record
  (Mocksville) **10229**
Dunn Daily Record (Dunn) **10018**
Eastern Carolina Times-Inquirer
  (Goldsboro) **10228**
Enquirer-Journal, The (Monroe) **10020**
Enterprise Mountaineer, The (Canton) **10227**
Enterprise, The (Williamston) **10231**
Fayetteville Observer-Times
  (Fayetteville) **10019**
Four Oaks-Benson News in Review
  (Benson) **10226**
Franklin Press (Franklin) **10228**
Franklin Times (Louisburg) **10228**
Garner News (Garner) **10228**
Gaston Gazette (Gastonia) **10019**
Gates County Index (Gatesville) **10228**
Gold Leaf Farmer, The (Wendell) **10231**
Goldsboro News-Argus (Goldsboro) **10019**
Greenville Daily Reflector (Greenville) **10019**
Hendersonville Times-News
  (Hendersonville) **10019**
Herald-Sun, The (Durham) **10019**
Hickory Daily Record (Hickory) **10019**
Hickory News/Extra, The (Hickory) **10228**
High Point Enterprise (High Point) **10019**
Home News, The (Marshville) **10229**
Independent, The (Durham) **10227**
Jacksonville Daily News (Jacksonville) **10019**
Jefferson Post (West Jefferson) **10231**
Johnstonian Sun (Selma) **10230**
Journal-Patriot (North Wilkesboro) **10229**
Kannapolis Daily Independent
  (Kannapolis) **10020**
Kenly News (Kenly) **10228**
Kernersville News (Kernersville) **10228**
Kings Mountain Herald (Kings
  Mountain) **10228**
King Times News (King) **10228**
Kinston Daily Free Press (Kinston) **10020**
Laurinburg Exchange (Laurinburg) **10020**
Lenoir News-Topic (Lenoir) **10020**
Lexington Dispatch (Lexington) **10020**
Lincoln Times-News (Lincolnton) **10228**
Littleton Observer (Littleton) **10228**
† Matthews News (Matthews)
McDowell News, The (Marion) **10020**
Mebane Enterprise (Mebane) **10229**
Mecklenburg Gazette (Davidson) **10227**
Messenger, The (Madison) **10229**
Mitchell News Journal (Spruce Pine) **10230**
Montgomery Herald (Troy) **10231**

Mooresville Tribune (Mooresville) **10229**
† Mountaineer, The (Waynesville)
Mountain Xpress (Asheville) **10226**
Mount Airy News (Mt. Airy) **10020**
Mount Holly News (Belmont) **10226**
Mount Olive Tribune (Mt. Olive) **10229**
Nashville Graphic (Nashville) **10229**
News & Observer (Raleigh) **10020**
News & Record, The (Greensboro) **10019**
News-Herald, The (Ahoskie) **10226**
† News-Messenger, The (Rockingham)
News Bulletin, The (Old Fort) **10229**
News Herald, The (Morganton) **10020**
News of Orange County, The
   (Hillsborough) **10228**
† News Outlook (Aberdeen)
Observer News (Newton) **10020**
Oxford Public Ledger (Oxford) **10229**
Pender Chronicle (Burgaw) **10227**
Pender Post (Burgaw) **10227**
Perquimans Weekly (Hertford) **10228**
Princeton News Leader (Princeton) **10229**
Raeford News-Journal, The (Raeford) **10230**
Randleman Reporter (Randleman) **10230**
Randolph Guide, The (Asheboro) **10226**
Reidsville Review (Reidsville) **10020**
Richlands-Beulaville Advertiser-News
   (Richlands) **10230**
Richmond County Daily Journal
   (Rockingham) **10021**
Roanoke-Chowan News-Herald
   (Jackson) **10228**
Roanoke Beacon (Plymouth) **10229**
Roanoke Rapids Daily & Sunday Herald
   (Roanoke Rapids) **10020**
Robersonville Weekly Herald
   (Williamston) **10231**
Robesonian, The (Lumberton) **10020**
Rocky Mount Telegram (Rocky Mount) **10021**
Salisbury Post (Salisbury) **10021**
Sampson Independent, The (Clinton) **10018**
▼Sandhills Living (Southern Pines) **10230**
Sanford Herald, The (Sanford) **10021**
Shelby Star (Shelby) **10021**
Smithfield Herald (Smithfield) **10230**
Southern Pines Pilot (Southern Pines) **10230**
Spectator (Raleigh) **10230**
Spring Hope Enterprise (Spring Hope) **10230**
Stanly News & Press (Albemarle) **10226**
State Port Pilot, The (Southport) **10230**
Statesville Record & Landmark
   (Statesville) **10021**
Sun-Journal (New Bern) **10020**
Surry Scene, The (Mount Airy) **10229**
Sylva Herald & Ruralite (Sylva) **10231**
Taylorsville Times, The (Taylorsville) **10231**

Thomasville Times (Thomasville) **10231**
Times-News, The (Burlington) **10018**
Transylvania Times, The (Brevard) **10227**
Tribune, The (Elkin) **10227**
Tribune, The (Tabor City) **10231**
Tryon Daily Bulletin (Tryon) **10021**
Valdese News (Morganton) **10229**
Village Advocate (Chapel Hill) **10227**
Virginian Pilot (Kill Devil Hills) **10020**
Wake Weekly, The (Wake Forest) **10231**
Wallace Enterprise (Wallace) **10231**
Warren Record, The (Warrenton) **10231**
Warsaw-Faison News (Wallace) **10231**
Washington Daily News (Washington) **10021**
Wayne Wilson News Leader (Fremont) **10228**
Whiteville News Reporter (Whiteville) **10231**
Williamston Enterprise (Williamston) **10231**
Wilmington Journal (Wilmington) **10231**
Wilmington Morning Star (Wilmington) **10021**
Wilson Daily Times (Wilson) **10021**
Winston-Salem Journal (Winston-Salem) **10021**
Yadkin Ripple, The (Yadkinville) **10232**
Yancey Common Times Journal
   (Burnsville) **10227**
Zebulon Record, The (Zebulon) **10232**

NORTH DAKOTA

Benson County Farmers Press
   (Minnewaukan) **10233**
Beulah Beacon (Beulah) **10232**
Bismarck Tribune (Bismarck) **10021**
Bowman Finder (Bowman) **10232**
Carson Press (Elgin) **10232**
Cass County Reporter (Casselton) **10232**
Cavalier County Republican (Langdon) **10232**
Center Republican (Washburn) **10233**
Courant, The (Bottineau) **10232**
Daily News (Wahpeton) **10022**
Devils Lake Journal (Devils Lake) **10021**
Dickinson Press, The (Dickinson) **10021**
Enderlin Independent (Enderlin) **10232**
Finder, The (Mandan) **10233**
Forum, The (Fargo) **10022**
Grand Forks Herald (Grand Forks) **10022**
Grant County News (Elgin) **10232**
Hazen Star (Hazen) **10232**
Herald Press (Harvey) **10232**
Jamestown Sun, The (Jamestown) **10022**
Journal, The (Crosby) **10232**
Larimore Pioneer (Northwood) **10233**
Leader-News (Washburn) **10233**
Leader, The (Northwood) **10233**
Linton Emmons County Record (Linton) **10233**
Lisbon Ransom County Gazette & Enterprise
   (Lisbon) **10233**

Mandan News (Mandan) **10233**
McLean County Independent (Garrison) **10232**
McLean County Journal (Turtle Lake) **10233**
Midweek Eagle (West Fargo) **10233**
Midweek Plus (West Fargo) **10233**
Minot Daily News (Minot) **10022**
Northwood Gleaner (Northwood) **10233**
Pierce County Tribune (Rugby) **10233**
Prairie Post (Jamestown) **10232**
Turtle Mountain Star, The (Rolla) **10233**
Underwood News (Underwood) **10233**
Valley City Times-Record (Valley City) **10022**
Walsh County Press (Park River) **10233**
Walsh County Record, The (Grafton) **10232**
West Fargo Pioneer (West Fargo) **10233**
Williston Herald (Williston) **10022**
Williston Plains Reporter (Williston) **10233**

NORTHERN MARIANA ISLANDS

Marianas Review (Saipan) **10233**
Marianas Variety News & Views
  (Saipan) **10022**
Palau Tribune (Saipan) **10234**
Saipan Tribune (Saipan) **10022**

OHIO

Ace News, The (Heath) **10239**
Advertiser-Tribune (Tiffin) **10027**
Advertiser, The (Chillicothe) **10235**
Advocate, The (Newark) **10026**
Akron Beacon Journal (Akron) **10022**
Alliance Review (Alliance) **10022**
Archbold Buckeye (Archbold) **10234**
Ashland Times-Gazette (Ashland) **10022**
Ashtabula Star-Beacon (Ashtabula) **10022**
Athens Messenger (Athens) **10022**
Athens News (Athens) **10234**
Attica Hub (Attica) **10234**
Aurora Advocate (Stow) **10243**
† Austintown Leader (Niles)
Avon Lake Press (Avon Lake) **10234**
Barberton Herald (Barberton) **10234**
Barnesville Enterprise (Barnesville) **10234**
Beacon, The (Port Clinton) **10242**
Beavercreek News-Current (Dayton) **10023**
Bedford Sun Banner (Cleveland) **10236**
Bedford Time Register (Bedford) **10234**
Bellefontaine Examiner (Bellefontaine) **10022**
Bellevue Gazette (Bellevue) **10023**
Bethel Journal, The (Loveland) **10240**
Bexley News (Columbus) **10237**
Bloomville Gazette (Attica) **10234**
Bluffton News, The (Bluffton) **10234**

Boardman News (Boardman) **10235**
Booster, The (Columbus) **10237**
Brecksville Gazette (Cleveland) **10236**
Brooklyn Sun Journal (Cleveland) **10236**
Brown County Press (Mt. Orab) **10241**
Brunswick Sun Times (Cleveland) **10236**
Bryan Times (Bryan) **10023**
Buckeye Review, The (Youngstown) **10244**
Bucyrus Telegraph-Forum (Bucyrus) **10023**
Bulletin, The (Bedford) **10234**
Carey Progressor-Times, The (Carey) **10235**
Celina Daily Standard (Celina) **10023**
Centerville-Bellbrook Times (Kettering) **10240**
Chagrin Herald Sun (Cleveland) **10236**
Chagrin Valley Times (Chagrin Falls) **10235**
Chesterland News (Chesterland) **10235**
Chillicothe Gazette (Chillicothe) **10023**
Cincinnati Enquirer (Cincinnati) **10023**
Cincinnati Post (Cincinnati) **10023**
Circleville Herald (Circleville) **10023**
† Clermont County Review (Cincinnati)
† Clermont Courier (Cincinnati)
Clermont Sun (Batavia) **10234**
Cleveland Plain Dealer (Cleveland) **10023**
Clinton County Shoppers Guide
  (Wilmington) **10244**
Clyde Enterprise (Clyde) **10237**
Columbus Alive! (Columbus) **10237**
Columbus Dispatch (Columbus) **10023**
Columbus Messenger (Columbus) **10237**
Community Booster, The (Granville) **10239**
Community Journal, South (Loveland) **10240**
Community Press, Mason (Loveland) **10240**
† Community Press, West Chester (Loveland)
† Conneaut News-Herald (Conneaut)
Coshocton Tribune (Coshocton) **10023**
Countyline, The (Bryan) **10235**
Courier, The (Findlay) **10024**
Courier, The (Conneaut) **10239**
Crescent-News (Defiance) **10024**
Crestline Advocate (Crestline) **10239**
Daily Advocate (Greenville) **10024**
Daily Herald (Delphos) **10024**
Daily Jeffersonian, The (Cambridge) **10023**
Daily Reporter (Columbus) **10023**
Daily Sentinel, The (Pomeroy) **10026**
Dalton Gazette & Kidron News (Dalton) **10239**
Darke County Early Bird, The
  (Arcanum) **10234**
Dayton Daily News (Dayton) **10023**
Delaware Gazette (Delaware) **10024**
Delhi Press (Cincinnati) **10235**
Delta Atlas (Delta) **10239**
Dublin Suburbia News (Columbus) **10237**
Dublin Villager (Worthington) **10244**
Eastern Hills Journal (Loveland) **10240**

East Palestine Heritage, The
  (Columbiana) **10237**
Elyria Chronicle-Telegram (Elyria) **10024**
† Erie County Reporter (Huron)
Euclid Sun Journal (Cleveland) **10236**
Evening Leader, The (St. Marys) **10027**
Evening Review, The (East Liverpool) **10024**
Extra Merchandiser (St. Marys) **10243**
Fairborn Daily Herald (Fairborn) **10024**
Fairfield Echo (Fairfield) **10239**
Falls News-Press (Stow) **10243**
Farmland News (Archbold) **10234**
Fayette Review, The (Fayette) **10239**
Forest Hills Journal (Loveland) **10241**
Franklin Chronicle (Franklin) **10239**
Free Press Standard (Carrollton) **10235**
Free Press, The (Canton) **10235**
Fremont News-Messenger (Fremont) **10024**
Fulton County Expositor (Wauseon) **10244**
Gahanna Village Post (Gahanna) **10239**
Galion Inquirer (Galion) **10024**
Gallipolis Daily Tribune (Gallipolis) **10024**
Garfield Maple-Sun (Cleveland) **10236**
Gateway News, The (Streetsboro) **10243**
Gazette Shopper (Cleveland) **10236**
Gazette, The (Jefferson) **10240**
† Geauga Times-Leader (Chardon)
† Girard News (Niles)
Granville Sentinel, The (Granville) **10239**
Greenfield Daily Times (Greenfield) **10024**
Grove City Record (Columbus) **10237**
Harrison News-Herald, The (Cadiz) **10235**
Hartville News (Hartville) **10239**
Herald-Star (Steubenville) **10026**
Hilliard Northwest News (Hilliard) **10239**
Hilltop News-Press (Cincinnati) **10235**
Hocking Valley Advertiser (Logan) **10240**
Holmes County Hub (Millersburg) **10241**
† Hubbard News (Niles)
Huber Heights Courier (Dayton) **10239**
Hudson Hub-Times (Stow) **10243**
Independent, The (Massillon) **10025**
Ironton Tribune (Ironton) **10024**
Jackson-Vinton Journal-Herald
  (Jackson) **10240**
Johnstown Independent (Columbus) **10237**
Journal-Leader (Caldwell) **10235**
Journal News (Hamilton) **10024**
Journal News (Spencerville) **10243**
Journal, The (Struthers) **10243**
Kent-Ravenna Record-Courier
  (Ravenna) **10026**
Kenton Times (Kenton) **10024**
Kettering-Oakwood Times (Kettering) **10240**
† Kirtland Enterprise (Willoughby)
Lakewood Sun Post (Cleveland) **10236**

Lancaster Eagle-Gazette (Lancaster) **10025**
Lancaster Fairfield Advertiser (Carroll) **10235**
Leader Enterprise (Montpelier) **10241**
Leader, The (Cleveland) **10236**
† Leader, The (East Palestine)
† Liberty News (Niles)
Liberty Press, The (Liberty Center) **10240**
† Licking Countian (Newark)
Lima News (Lima) **10025**
Logan Daily News (Logan) **10025**
Lorain County Times, The (Rocky River) **10242**
Loudonville Times, The (Loudonville) **10240**
Louisville Herald, The (Louisville) **10240**
Loveland Herald Press (Loveland) **10241**
Madison Press, The (London) **10025**
† Madison Tribune (Ontario)
Malvern Community News (Minerva) **10241**
Manchester Signal (Manchester) **10241**
Maple Heights Press (Bedford) **10234**
Marietta Times (Marietta) **10025**
Marion Star (Marion) **10025**
Marysville Journal-Tribune (Marysville) **10025**
† Maumee Valley Herald (Toledo)
Medina County Gazette (Medina) **10025**
▼Medina Sun, The (Cleveland) **10236**
Mercer County Chronicle (Coldwater) **10237**
Metro Press (Millbury) **10241**
Miamisburg News (Miamisburg) **10241**
Middletown Journal (Middletown) **10025**
Milford Advertiser (Loveland) **10241**
Minerva Leader (Minerva) **10241**
Monroe County Beacon (Woodsfield) **10244**
† Monroe County Sentinel (Woodsfield)
Morgan County Herald (McConnelsville) **10241**
Morning Journal (Lisbon) **10025**
Morning Journal (Lorain) **10025**
Morrow County Advertiser (Mt. Gilead) **10241**
Morrow County Independent
  (Cardington) **10235**
Morrow County Sentinel (Mt. Gilead) **10241**
Mount Vernon News (Mt. Vernon) **10025**
† Mt. Washington Press (Cincinnati)
Newark/Licking Advertiser (Newark) **10242**
New Carlisle Sun (New Carlisle) **10242**
Newcomerstown News
  (Newcomerstown) **10242**
News-Herald (Port Clinton) **10025**
News-Herald (Willoughby) **10027**
† NewsEAST (Columbus)
News Journal (Mansfield) **10025**
News Leader (Stow) **10243**
News Sun, The (Cleveland) **10235**
News Times (Amherst) **10234**
News Watchman, The (Waverly) **10244**
▼Nordonia Hills Sun (Cleveland) **10236**

North Clermont Community Journal (Loveland) **10241**
Northeast Suburban Life Press (Cincinnati) **10235**
Northland News (Columbus) **10237**
Northwest Columbus News (Columbus) **10237**
Northwest Press (Cincinnati) **10235**
Northwest Signal (Napoleon) **10026**
Norwalk Reflector (Norwalk) **10026**
† Orrville Courier-Crescent (Orrville)
Ottawa County Exponent, The (Oak Harbor) **10242**
Oxford Press (Oxford) **10242**
Parma Sun Post (Cleveland) **10236**
Pataskala Standard (Pataskala) **10242**
Paulding Progress (Paulding) **10242**
Penny Saver (Covington) **10239**
People's Defender, The (West Union) **10244**
Perry County Tribune (New Lexington) **10242**
Perrysburg Messenger-Journal (Perrysburg) **10242**
Photo Star (Willshire) **10244**
Pickerington Times-Sun (Columbus) **10237**
Pike County News Watchman (Jackson) **10240**
Piqua Daily Call (Piqua) **10026**
Point & Shoreland Journal (Toledo) **10243**
† Poland Leader (Niles)
Portsmouth Daily Times (Portsmouth) **10026**
Press & Light (North Ridgeville) **10242**
Press-News, The (Minerva) **10241**
Press Gazette, The (Hillsboro) **10240**
Price Hill Press (Cincinnati) **10235**
Pulse-Journal (Mason) **10241**
Putnam County Sentinel (Ottawa) **10242**
Putnam County Vidette (Columbus Grove) **10239**
Pymatuning Area News (Andover) **10234**
Record Herald (Washington Court House) **10027**
Register-Herald (Eaton) **10239**
Repository, The (Canton) **10023**
Review Times (Fostoria) **10024**
RFD News, The (Bellevue) **10234**
▼Rocky Fork Enterprise (Columbus) **10237**
Rossford Record-Journal (Perrysburg) **10242**
Rural-Urban Record (Columbia Station) **10237**
Sabina Advertiser (Sabina) **10243**
Salem News (Salem) **10026**
Sandusky Register (Sandusky) **10026**
Scioto Voice (Wheelersburg) **10244**
Senior's Beacon, The (Lima) **10240**
Sentinel-Tribune (Bowling Green) **10023**
Sentinel, The (Jefferson) **10240**
† Shawnee-Cridersville Press (Wapakoneta)
Shelby Globe (Shelby) **10026**
Shelby Review (Wapakoneta) **10244**

Sidney Daily News (Sidney) **10026**
Signal, The (Canal Fulton) **10235**
Solon Herald Sun (Beachwood) **10234**
Solon Times, The (Chagrin Falls) **10235**
Springfield News-Sun (Springfield) **10026**
Star Press (Springboro) **10243**
Star Republican (Wilmington) **10244**
Stillwater Valley Advertiser (Covington) **10239**
Stow Sentry (Stow) **10243**
Suburbanite, The (Akron) **10234**
Suburban Life (Loveland) **10241**
Suburban Press (Millbury) **10241**
Sun Banner Pride (Cleveland) **10236**
Sunbury News (Sunbury) **10243**
Sun Courier, The (Cleveland) **10236**
Sun Herald, The (Cleveland) **10236**
Sun Journal, The (North Canton) **10242**
Sun Messenger, The (Cleveland) **10236**
Sun Press (Cleveland) **10236**
Sun Scoop Journal (Cleveland) **10236**
Sun Star, The (Cleveland) **10236**
Sun, The (Cleveland) **10237**
Swanton Enterprise (Swanton) **10243**
† Sycamore Messenger (Cincinnati)
Sylvania Herald (Toledo) **10243**
Tallmadge Express (Stow) **10243**
This Week In Bexley (Columbus) **10237**
This Week In Clintonville (Columbus) **10238**
This Week In Delaware (Columbus) **10238**
This Week In Eastside (Columbus) **10238**
This Week In Grandview (Columbus) **10238**
This Week In Hilliard (Columbus) **10238**
This Week In New Albany (Columbus) **10238**
This Week In Northland (Columbus) **10238**
This Week In Pickerington (Columbus) **10238**
This Week In Powell (Columbus) **10238**
This Week In Reynoldsburg (Columbus) **10238**
This Week In Southside (Columbus) **10238**
This Week In Union County (Columbus) **10238**
This Week In Westerville (Columbus) **10238**
This Week In Westside (Columbus) **10238**
This Week In Worthington (Columbus) **10238**
Times-Bulletin (Van Wert) **10027**
Times-Reporter (New Philadelphia) **10026**
Times Leader (Martins Ferry) **10025**
Times Recorder, The (Zanesville) **10028**
Times, The (Columbus) **10238**
Tipp City Herald (Tipp City) **10243**
Toledo Blade (Toledo) **10027**
Tri-County Press (Cincinnati) **10236**
Tri-Village News (Columbus) **10238**
Tribune-Courier (Ontario) **10242**
Tribune Chronicle, The (Warren) **10027**
Tribune Shopping News (New Lexington) **10242**
Troy Daily News (Troy) **10027**

▼Twinsburg Sun, The (Cleveland) **10237**
UA This Week (Columbus) **10238**
Upper Arlington News (Columbus) **10238**
Upper Sandusky Daily Chief-Union (Upper
  Sandusky) **10027**
Urbana Daily Citizen (Urbana) **10027**
Utica Herald (Utica) **10243**
Valley News, The (Jefferson) **10240**
Vermilion Photojournal (Vermilion) **10243**
Versailles Policy, The (Versailles) **10243**
Vindicator, The (Youngstown) **10027**
† Vinton County Courier (McArthur)
Wapakoneta Daily News (Wapakoneta) **10027**
Weekly Reminder (Paulding) **10242**
† Wellston Sentry (Wellston)
Wellston Telegram, The (Wellston) **10244**
Western Hills Press (Cincinnati) **10236**
Western Star (Lebanon) **10240**
Westerville News & Public Opinion
  (Westerville) **10244**
▼West Geauga Sun (Cleveland) **10237**
Westlaker Times, The (Rocky River) **10242**
West Life (Cleveland) **10237**
West Milton Record (West Milton) **10244**
West Side Sun News (Cleveland) **10237**
West Toledo Herald (Toledo) **10243**
Whitehall News (Columbus) **10238**
Willard Times-Junction (Willard) **10244**
Wilmington News-Journal (Wilmington) **10027**
Wooster Daily Record (Wooster) **10027**
Worthington Suburbia News
  (Columbus) **10238**
Xenia Daily Gazette (Xenia) **10027**
Zanesville Muskingum Advertiser
  (Zanesville) **10244**

OKLAHOMA

Ada Evening News (Ada) **10028**
Altus Times (Altus) **10028**
Alva Review-Courier (Alva) **10028**
Anadarko Daily News (Anadarko) **10028**
Atoka County Times (Atoka) **10244**
Bartlesville Examiner-Enterprise
  (Bartlesville) **10028**
Bixby Bulletin (Tulsa) **10247**
Blackwell Journal-Tribune (Blackwell) **10028**
Boise City News, The (Boise City) **10245**
Bristow News (Bristow) **10245**
Broken Arrow Ledger & Scout (Broken
  Arrow) **10245**
† Broken Arrow Scout (Broken Arrow)
Bryan County Star (Durant) **10245**
Capitol Hill Beacon (Oklahoma City) **10246**
Catoosa Times Herald (Catoosa) **10245**

Cherokee Messenger & Republican
  (Cherokee) **10245**
Chickasha Daily Express (Chickasha) **10028**
Claremore Progress (Claremore) **10028**
Clinton Daily News (Clinton) **10028**
Collinsville News (Tulsa) **10247**
Cordell Beacon, The (Cordell) **10245**
Country Connection News (Eakly) **10245**
County Star (Stigler) **10247**
Covington Record (Covington) **10245**
Coweta American (Coweta) **10245**
Cushing Daily Citizen (Cushing) **10028**
Daily Ardmoreite (Ardmore) **10028**
Daily Oklahoman (Oklahoma City) **10030**
Duncan Banner (Duncan) **10028**
Durant Daily Democrat (Durant) **10028**
† Eastside Times (Tulsa)
Edmond Evening Sun (Edmond) **10028**
Elk City Daily News (Elk City) **10029**
El Reno Tribune (El Reno) **10245**
Enid News & Eagle (Enid) **10029**
Fairview Republican (Fairview) **10245**
Frederick Leader (Frederick) **10029**
▼Grove Daily News (Grove) **10029**
Grove Sun (Grove) **10245**
Guthrie Daily Leader (Guthrie) **10029**
Guymon Daily Herald (Guymon) **10029**
Harrah News, The (Harrah) **10246**
Henryetta Daily Free-Lance (Henryetta) **10029**
Hobart Democrat-Chief (Hobart) **10246**
Holdenville Daily News (Holdenville) **10029**
Hominy News-Progress (Hominy) **10246**
Hughes County Times (Wetumka) **10247**
Hugo Daily News (Hugo) **10029**
Jenks Journal (Tulsa) **10247**
† Jet Visitor (Cherokee)
Johnston County Capital-Democrat
  (Tishomingo) **10247**
Kingfisher Times & Free Press
  (Kingfisher) **10246**
Konawa Leader (Konawa) **10246**
Lawton Constitution (Lawton) **10029**
Lincoln County News (Chandler) **10245**
Madill Record (Madill) **10246**
McAlester News-Capital (McAlester) **10029**
McCurtain Daily Gazette (Idabel) **10029**
Miami News-Record (Miami) **10029**
Moore American (Moore) **10246**
Muskogee Daily Phoenix & Times-Democrat
  (Muskogee) **10029**
Newcastle Pacer, The (Newcastle) **10246**
Norman Transcript (Norman) **10029**
Nowata Star (Nowata) **10246**
Oklahoma City Friday (Oklahoma City) **10246**
Oklahoma Eagle (Tulsa) **10247**
Okmulgee Times (Okmulgee) **10030**

Oologah Lake Leader (Oologah) **10246**
Owasso Reporter (Owasso) **10246**
Pauls Valley Daily Democrat (Pauls Valley) **10030**
Pawhuska Journal-Capital (Pawhuska) **10246**
Perry Daily Journal (Perry) **10030**
† Pictorial Press (Tahlequah)
Ponca City News (Ponca City) **10030**
Poteau Daily News & Sun (Poteau) **10030**
Pryor Daily Times (Pryor) **10030**
Pryor Jeffersonian (Pryor) **10246**
Purcell Register (Purcell) **10246**
Record-Citizen, The (Bristow) **10245**
Sand Springs Leader (Sand Springs) **10247**
Sapulpa Daily Herald (Sapulpa) **10030**
Sayre Journal (Sayre) **10247**
Seminole Daily Producer (Seminole) **10030**
Sequoyah County Times (Sallisaw) **10246**
Shawnee News-Star (Shawnee) **10030**
Shopper Zone I (Durant) **10245**
Skiatook Journal (Skiatook) **10247**
Southern Oklahoma Leader (Durant) **10245**
Southwest Tulsa News (Tulsa) **10247**
Stigler News-Sentinel (Stigler) **10247**
Stillwater News-Press (Stillwater) **10030**
Stilwell Democrat-Journal (Stilwell) **10247**
Stratford Star (Konawa) **10246**
Tahlequah Daily Press (Tahlequah) **10030**
† Tipton News Leader (Altus)
Tonkawa News, The (Tonkawa) **10247**
Tribune, The (Bethany) **10245**
Tulsa World (Tulsa) **10030**
Vinita Daily Journal (Vinita) **10030**
Wagoner Tribune, The (Wagoner) **10247**
Watonga Republican, The (Watonga) **10247**
Weatherford Daily News (Weatherford) **10030**
Wewoka Times (Wewoka) **10247**
Woodward News (Woodward) **10031**
Yale News, The (Yale) **10247**
Yukon Review (Yukon) **10247**

OREGON

Albany Democrat-Herald (Albany) **10031**
Aloha Breeze (Hillsboro) **10249**
Argus Observer (Ontario) **10031**
Ashland Daily Tidings (Ashland) **10031**
Baker City Herald (Baker City) **10031**
Baker Record-Courier (Baker City) **10247**
Beaverton Valley Times (Portland) **10249**
Bee, The (Portland) **10250**
Benton Bulletin (Philomath) **10249**
Bulletin, The (Bend) **10031**
Burns Times-Herald (Burns) **10248**
Butte Valley Star (Merrill) **10249**
Canby Herald (Canby) **10248**

Central Oregonian, The (Prineville) **10250**
Central Valley Times (Grants Pass) **10248**
Chronicle, The (Creswell) **10248**
Clackamas County Review (Milwaukee) **10249**
Coquille Valley Sentinel (Coquille) **10248**
Corvallis Gazette-Times (Corvallis) **10031**
Cottage Grove Sentinel (Cottage Grove) **10248**
Country Weekly (Grants Pass) **10248**
Courier, The (Reedsport) **10250**
Curry Coastal Pilot (Brookings) **10248**
Daily Astorian (Astoria) **10031**
Dallas Polk County Itemizer-Observer (Dallas) **10248**
Dayton Tribune (Dayton) **10248**
Drain Enterprise (Drain) **10248**
East Oregonian, The (Pendleton) **10031**
Gold Beach Curry County Reporter (Gold Beach) **10248**
Grants Pass Daily Courier (Grants Pass) **10031**
Gresham Outlook (Gresham) **10248**
Headlight-Herald (Tillamook) **10250**
Herald & News (Klamath Falls) **10031**
Hermiston Herald (Hermiston) **10249**
Hillsboro Argus (Hillsboro) **10249**
Hood River News (Hood River) **10249**
Island Connection (Portland) **10250**
Lake County Examiner (Lakeview) **10249**
Lake Oswego Review (Lake Oswego) **10249**
Lebanon Express (Lebanon) **10249**
Lost River Star (Merrill) **10249**
Madras Pioneer, The (Madras) **10249**
Mail Tribune (Medford) **10031**
Malheur Enterprise (Vale) **10251**
Newberg Graphic (Newberg) **10249**
New Era, The (Sweet Home) **10250**
News-Register (McMinnville) **10249**
News-Review (Roseburg) **10032**
News-Times (Newport) **10249**
News Guard, The (Lincoln City) **10249**
News Times (Forest Grove) **10248**
Observer, The (La Grande) **10031**
Oregonian, The (Portland) **10032**
Pendleton Record, The (Pendleton) **10249**
Redmond Spokesman (Redmond) **10250**
Register-Guard (Eugene) **10031**
River Press (Rogue River) **10250**
Sandy Post (Sandy) **10250**
Seaside Signal (Seaside) **10250**
Silverton Appeal-Tribune/Mt. Angel News (Silverton) **10250**
Siuslaw News, The (Florence) **10248**
Springfield News, The (Springfield) **10250**
Statesman Journal (Salem) **10032**
Stayton Mail (Stayton) **10250**
St. Helens Chronicle (St. Helens) **10250**

St. Johns Review (Portland) **10250**
The Dalles Daily Chronicle (The Dalles) **10032**
Tigard Times (Tigard) **10250**
Times-Journal, The (Condon) **10248**
Umpqua Free Press (Myrtle Creek) **10249**
Upper Rogue Independent (Eagle Point) **10248**
Western World (Bandon) **10248**
West Linn Tidings (Lake Oswego) **10249**
West Valley Courier (Hillsboro) **10249**
Willamette Week (Portland) **10250**
World, The (Coos Bay) **10031**

PALAU

Palau Gazette (Koror) **10251**

PENNSYLVANIA

Abington Journal (Clarks Summit) **10252**
Advance Leader (Monroeville) **10255**
Advance of Bucks County (Newtown) **10256**
Advertiser, The (McMurray) **10254**
Advisor, The (Mt. Pleasant) **10256**
Albion News, The (Albion) **10251**
Allegheny Times (Moon Township) **10035**
Allied News (Grove City) **10253**
Almanac, The (McMurray) **10255**
Altoona Mirror (Altoona) **10032**
Ambler Gazette (Fort Washington) **10253**
Area Shopper (Springboro) **10259**
Barnesboro Star, The (Barnesboro) **10251**
Beaver County Times (Beaver) **10032**
Bedford Gazette/Gazette Sunday
  (Bedford) **10032**
Bennetts Valley News (Weedville) **10259**
† Biz (Oxford)
Boyertown Area Times (Boyertown) **10251**
Bradford Era, The (Bradford) **10032**
Bradford Journal/Miner (Bradford) **10251**
Brandywine Chronicle (Oxford) **10256**
† Breeze Herald (Conneut Lake Park)
Breeze, The (Rockledge) **10258**
Bridgeville Area News (Monroeville) **10255**
Bristol Pilot (Bristol) **10251**
Broad Top Bulletin (Saxton) **10259**
† Brookville American (Brookville)
Bucks County Courier Times
  (Levittown) **10034**
Bucks County Tribune (Horsham) **10253**
Butler Eagle (Butler) **10032**
Call, The (Schuylkill Haven) **10259**
Cameron County Echo (Emporium) **10252**
Canton Independent-Sentinel (Canton) **10251**
Carbondale News (Carbondale) **10251**
Carlisle Sentinel (Carlisle) **10032**

Centre Daily Times (State College) **10036**
Chester County Press (Oxford) **10256**
Chestnut Hill Local (Philadelphia) **10257**
Citizen-Standard, The (Valley View) **10259**
Clarion News (Clarion) **10251**
Colonial, The (Fort Washington) **10253**
Conneautville Courier (Springboro) **10259**
Corry Journal (Corry) **10033**
Cosmopolite-Herald (Girard) **10253**
County Neighbors (Punxsutawney) **10258**
County Observer (Yeagertown) **10260**
County Press (Newtown Square) **10256**
County Transcript (Susquehanna) **10259**
Courier-Express (Du Bois) **10033**
Cresson-Gallitzin Mainliner, The
  (Cresson) **10252**
Daily American (Somerset) **10036**
Daily Courier, The (Connellsville) **10032**
Daily Herald, The (Tyrone) **10037**
Daily Item, The (Sunbury) **10036**
Daily Local News (West Chester) **10037**
Daily News (Huntingdon) **10034**
Daily Press, The (St. Marys) **10036**
Daily Record, The (Westchester) **10037**
Daily Review & Sunday Review
  (Towanda) **10036**
Dallas Post (Dallas) **10252**
Danville News (Danville) **10033**
Delaware County Daily-Sunday Times (Clifton
  Heights) **10032**
Delaware County Journal (Folsom) **10253**
Derrick, The (Oil City) **10035**
Drexel Hill Press (Newtown Square) **10256**
Duncannon Record (New Bloomfield) **10256**
East Penn Press (Allentown) **10251**
Ebensburg News Leader, The
  (Ebensburg) **10252**
Elizabethtown Chronicle (Elizabethtown) **10252**
Ellwood City Ledger (Ellwood City) **10033**
Ephrata Review (Ephrata) **10252**
Erie Daily Times/Sunday Times News
  (Erie) **10033**
Erie Morning News (Erie) **10033**
Evening Sun (Hanover) **10033**
Evening Times (Sayre) **10036**
Express-Times, The (Easton) **10033**
Fishtown Star (Philadelphia) **10257**
Forest Press (Tionesta) **10259**
Free Press-Courier (Westfield) **10260**
Free Press, The (Braddock) **10251**
Germantown Courier (Philadelphia) **10257**
Germantown Paper (Philadelphia) **10257**
Gettysburg Times (Gettysburg) **10033**
Girard Home News (Philadelphia) **10257**
Glenside News (Jenkintown) **10254**
Globe, The (Jenkintown) **10254**

Greenville Record-Argus (Greenville)   **10033**
Hamburg Item (Hamburg)   **10253**
Haverford Press (Newtown Square)   **10256**
Hazleton Standard Speaker (Hazleton)   **10033**
Herald Standard (Uniontown)   **10037**
Herald, The (Sharon)   **10036**
Herald, The (Pittsburgh)   **10258**
Hershey Chronicle, The (Hershey)   **10253**
Independent Observer, The (Scottdale)   **10259**
Independent, The (Collegeville)   **10252**
Independent, The (Montrose)   **10255**
Indiana Gazette (Indiana)   **10034**
Intelligencer Record, The (Doylestown)   **10033**
† Interboro News (Prospect Park)
ISDA Unione (Pittsburgh)   **10258**
Jeannette Spirit (Jeannette)   **10254**
Jeffersonian Democrat (Brookville)   **10251**
Johnsonburg Press (Johnsonburg)   **10254**
Journal-Herald, The (White Haven)   **10260**
▼Journal/Valley Views (White Haven)   **10260**
Juniata News (Philadelphia)   **10257**
Juniata Sentinel (Mifflintown)   **10255**
Kane Republican (Kane)   **10034**
King of Prussia Courier (King of
   Prussia)   **10254**
Lancaster Intelligencer Journal
   (Lancaster)   **10034**
Lancaster New Era (Lancaster)   **10034**
Latrobe Bulletin (Latrobe)   **10034**
Leader-Vindicator, The (New
   Bethlehem)   **10256**
Leader, The (Philadelphia)   **10257**
Leader Times (Kittanning)   **10034**
Lebanon Daily News (Lebanon)   **10034**
Lewisburg Daily Journal (Milton)   **10035**
Ligonier Echo (Ligonier)   **10254**
Ligonier Free Gazette, The (Ligonier)   **10254**
† Linesville Herald (Conneaut Lake)
Lititz Record Express, The (Lititz)   **10254**
Lock Haven Express (Lock Haven)   **10034**
† Main Line Chronicle (West Chester)
Mainline Life (Ardmore)   **10251**
Main Line Times (Ardmore)   **10251**
Marcus Hook Press (Drexel Hill)   **10252**
† Market Place (Vandergrift)
McConnellsburg Fulton County News
   (McConnellsburg)   **10254**
McKeesport Daily News (McKeesport)   **10035**
Meadville Tribune, The (Meadville)   **10035**
Mercury, The (Pottstown)   **10035**
† MidMon Observer (Washington)
Mifflinburg Telegraph, The (Mifflinburg)   **10255**
Milk Creek Sun (Erie)   **10252**
Milton Daily Standard (Milton)   **10035**
Montgomery County Progress
   (Horsham)   **10253**

Montgomery Post, The (Norristown)   **10256**
Montgomeryville Spirit (Fort
   Washington)   **10253**
Morning Call, The (Allentown)   **10032**
Morrisons Cove Herald (Martinsburg)   **10254**
Mountaineer-Herald, The (Ebensburg)   **10252**
Mountaintop Eagle (Mountain Top)   **10255**
Mount Joy Merchandiser (Mt. Joy)   **10256**
Mount Pleasant Journal (Mt. Pleasant)   **10256**
Mt. Airy Times (Philadelphia)   **10257**
Murrysville Area Star (Monroeville)   **10255**
Nanty Glo Journal, The (Nanty Glo)   **10256**
New Castle News (New Castle)   **10035**
New Hope Gazette (New Hope)   **10256**
News-Herald (Oil City)   **10035**
News-Sun, The (New Bloomfield)   **10256**
News Eagle (Hawley)   **10253**
News Gleaner Publications
   (Philadelphia)   **10257**
News of Delaware County (Havertown)   **10253**
News of Southern Berks, The
   (Boyertown)   **10251**
News, The (Aliquippa)   **10251**
North East Breeze (North East)   **10256**
Northeast Times (Philadelphia)   **10257**
North Hills News Record (Warrendale)   **10037**
North Star (Philadelphia)   **10257**
Observer-Reporter (Waynesburg)   **10037**
Observer-Reporter, Washington County Edition
   (Washington)   **10037**
Olney Times (Philadelphia)   **10257**
Park News (Library)   **10254**
Patriot-News (Harrisburg)   **10033**
Patriot, The (Kutztown)   **10254**
Perkasie News-Herald (Perkasie)   **10257**
Perry County Times (New Bloomfield)   **10256**
Philadelphia City Paper (Philadelphia)   **10257**
Philadelphia Daily News (Philadelphia)   **10035**
Philadelphia Guide Newspaper
   (Philadelphia)   **10257**
Philadelphia Inquirer (Philadelphia)   **10035**
Philadelphia Weekly (Philadelphia)   **10257**
Phoenix, The (Phoenixville)   **10035**
Pike County Dispatch (Milford)   **10255**
Pittsburgh City Paper (Pittsburgh)   **10258**
Pittsburgh Post-Gazette (Pittsburgh)   **10035**
† Pittsburgh Press (Pittsburgh)
Pittsburgh Renaissance News
   (Pittsburgh)   **10258**
Pocono Record (Stroudsburg)   **10036**
Pocono Shopper (East Stroudsburg)   **10252**
Portage Dispatch, The (Portage)   **10258**
Port Richmond Star (Philadelphia)   **10257**
Post, The (Middleburg)   **10255**
Potter Leader-Enterprise (Coudersport)   **10252**
Pottsville Republican (Pottsville)   **10035**

Press & Journal, The (Middletown) **10255**
Press Enterprise, The (Bloomsburg) **10032**
Press Herald (Pine Grove) **10258**
Progress, The (Monroeville) **10255**
† Progress, The (Clearfield)
Public Opinion, The (Chambersburg) **10032**
Public Spirit (Hatboro) **10253**
Punxsutawney Spirit (Punxsutawney) **10035**
Quakertown Free Press (Quakertown) **10258**
Reading Eagle & Reading Times
   (Reading) **10036**
Record-Enterprise (McDonald) **10254**
Recorder, The (Conshohocken) **10252**
Record Herald (Waynesboro) **10037**
Record, The (Horsham) **10034**
Record, The (Coraopolis) **10252**
Reporter of the Spring-Ford Area
   (Royersford) **10258**
Reporter, The (Lansdale) **10034**
Ridgway Record (Ridgway) **10036**
Ridley Press (Drexel Hill) **10252**
Roxborough Review (Philadelphia) **10258**
Scranton Times/Sunday Times
   (Scranton) **10036**
Sentinel, The (Lewistown) **10034**
Sewickley Herald (Monroeville) **10255**
Shamokin News-Item (Shamokin) **10036**
Shippensburg News-Chronicle
   (Shippensburg) **10259**
Signal-Item (Monroeville) **10255**
Slatebelt Hometown News, The
   (Bangor) **10251**
Souderton Independent (Souderton) **10259**
South Hills Record (Pittsburgh) **10258**
South Philadelphia Chronicle
   (Philadelphia) **10258**
South Philadelphia Review
   (Philadelphia) **10258**
South Pittsburgh Reporter (Pittsburgh) **10258**
Southwestern Pennsylvania Scene
   (Scottdale) **10259**
Southwest Globe Times (Philadelphia) **10258**
† Spirit of Bucks County (Hatboro)
Springfield Press (Springfield) **10259**
Springfield Sun (Fort Washington) **10253**
Standard-Observer (Greensburg) **10033**
Suburban & Wayne Times (Wayne) **10259**
Suburban Advertiser (Wayne) **10259**
Suburban Gazette (McKees Rocks) **10254**
Sullivan Review (Dushore) **10252**
Sunday Bucks County Telegraph
   (Horsham) **10253**
Sunday Dispatch (Pittston) **10258**
† Sunday Sun (Scranton)
Sun, The (Hummelstown) **10253**

Susquehanna County Independent
   (Montrose) **10255**
Three Star Edition (Philadelphia) **10258**
Times-Express (Monroeville) **10255**
Times-Leader (Union City) **10259**
Times-Sun, The (West Newton) **10260**
Times Chronicle (Jenkintown) **10254**
Times Herald, The (Norristown) **10035**
Times Leader (Wilkes Barre) **10037**
Times News (Lehighton) **10034**
Times, The (Port Royal) **10258**
Titusville Herald (Titusville) **10036**
Town & Country (Pennsburg) **10257**
† Town & Country (Bradford)
Town Talk (Folsom) **10253**
Town Talk (Media) **10255**
Tribune-Review (Greensburg) **10033**
Tribune Democrat, The (Johnstown) **10034**
Tribune, The (Scranton) **10036**
Tunkhannock New Age-Examiner
   (Tunkhannock) **10259**
Unida Latina (Oxford) **10257**
Union Press-Courier (Patton) **10257**
Upper Darby Press (Drexel Hill) **10252**
Upper Dauphin Sentinel (Millersburg) **10255**
Valley Gazette (Lansford) **10254**
Valley Independent (Monessen) **10035**
Valley Log, The (Orbisonia) **10256**
Valley News Dispatch (Tarentum) **10036**
Valley Times-Star (Newville) **10256**
Valley Trader (Lewisburg) **10254**
Vandergrift News (Vandergrift) **10259**
Villager, The (Moscow) **10255**
Voice, The (Phoenixville) **10258**
Warren Times Observer (Warren) **10037**
Wayne Independent, The (Honesdale) **10033**
Weekend News (Montrose) **10255**
Weekly Almanac, The (Honesdale) **10253**
Weekly Recorder, The (Claysville) **10252**
Wellsboro Gazette (Wellsboro) **10260**
West Schuylkill Herald (Tower City) **10259**
Wilkes-Barre Citizens' Voice (Wilkes
   Barre) **10037**
† Wilkes-Barre Sunday Independent (Wilkes
   Barre)
Williamsport Sun-Gazette (Williamsport) **10037**
Willow Grove Guide (Hatboro) **10253**
Yardley News (Yardley) **10260**
York Daily Record (York) **10037**
York Dispatch/York Sunday News
   (York) **10037**

RHODE ISLAND

Barrington Times (Warren) **10251**
Bristol Phoenix (Bristol) **10260**

Call, The (Woonsocket) **10038**
Cranston Herald (Cranston) **10260**
East Greenwich Pendulum (East
  Greenwich) **10260**
East Providence Post (East Providence) **10260**
Eastside Monthly (Providence) **10261**
Jamestown Press, The (Jamestown) **10260**
Kent County Daily Times (West
  Warwick) **10038**
Narragansett Times (Wakefield) **10261**
Newport Daily News, The (Newport) **10037**
Newport Mercury (Newport) **10260**
Newport This Week (Newport) **10260**
Observer, The (Greenville) **10260**
Providence Journal-Bulletin
  (Providence) **10038**
Sakonnet Times (Portsmouth) **10260**
Seekonk Star (East Providence) **10260**
Standard-Times (North Kingstown) **10260**
Times, The (Pawtucket) **10037**
Warren Times Gazette (Warren) **10261**
Warwick Beacon (Warwick) **10261**
Westerly Sun (Westerly) **10038**

SOUTH CAROLINA

Advertizer-Herald, The (Bamberg) **10261**
Aiken Standard (Aiken) **10038**
Alternatives (Myrtle Beach) **10263**
Anderson Independent-Mail (Anderson) **10038**
Beaufort Gazette (Beaufort) **10038**
Beaufort Shopper (Beaufort) **10261**
Berkeley Independent (Moncks Corner) **10263**
Charleston Chronicle, The (Charleston) **10261**
Charleston Post & Courier (Charleston) **10038**
Cheraw Chronicle, The (Cheraw) **10261**
Chester News & Reporter (Chester) **10261**
Chronicle-Independent (Camden) **10261**
Clinton Chronicle, The (Clinton) **10262**
Clover Herald (Clover) **10262**
Coastal Times (Charleston) **10261**
† Conway Field & Herald (Conway)
Darco News & Buyers Guide
  (Hartsville) **10262**
Dillon Herald, The (Dillon) **10262**
Dispatch-News, The (Lexington) **10263**
Dorchester Eagle Record (St. George) **10264**
Easley Progress (Easley) **10262**
Florence Morning News (Florence) **10038**
Fort Mill Times (Fort Mill) **10262**
Gaffney Ledger, The (Gaffney) **10262**
Georgetown Times, The (Georgetown) **10262**
Goose Creek Gazette (Ladson) **10262**
Greenville News (Greenville) **10038**
† Greenville Piedmont (Greenville)
Greer Citizen, The (Greer) **10262**

Hanahan News (North Charleston) **10263**
Hartsville Messenger, The (Hartsville) **10262**
Herald-Independent, The (Winnsboro) **10264**
Herald-Journal (Spartanburg) **10039**
Herald, The (Rock Hill) **10039**
Hilton Head Island Packet (Hilton
  Head) **10038**
Horry Independent (Conway) **10262**
Index-Journal (Greenwood) **10038**
Item, The (Sumter) **10039**
Jasper County Sun (Ridgeland) **10263**
Journal, The (Mt. Pleasant) **10263**
Journal, The (Williamston) **10264**
Journal Tribune (Seneca) **10264**
Lake Edition, The (Lexington) **10263**
Lancaster News (Lancaster) **10262**
Laurens County Advertiser (Laurens) **10263**
Lee County Observer (Bishopville) **10261**
Loris Times (Loris) **10263**
Marion Star & Mullins Enterprise
  (Marion) **10263**
Marlboro Herald-Advocate
  (Bennettsville) **10261**
Marlboro Shopper (Bennettsville) **10261**
Messenger, The (Clemson) **10261**
Moultrie News, The (Mt. Pleasant) **10263**
Newberry Observer, The (Newberry) **10263**
News & Press, The (Darlington) **10262**
News Leader, The (Landrum) **10263**
News, The (Kingstree) **10262**

North Myrtle Beach Times (North Myrtle
  Beach) **10263**
Observer, The (Holly Hill) **10262**

Pageland Progressive-Journal, The
  (Pageland) **10263**
† Paper, The (Spartanburg)

People-Sentinel (Barnwell) **10261**
Pickens Sentinel (Pickens) **10263**

Press & Standard, The (Walterboro) **10264**
Saluda Standard Sentinel (Saluda) **10263**

State, The (Columbia) **10038**
Summerville Journal Scene
  (Summerville) **10264**

Sun News, The (Myrtle Beach) **10038**
Times & Democrat, The (Orangeburg) **10038**

Tribune-Times (Fountain Inn) **10262**
Twin-City News, The
  (Batesburg-Leesville) **10261**
Union Daily Times (Union) **10039**

Weekly Observer, The (Hemingway) **10262**
Yorkville Enquirer (York) **10264**
▼Your Paper (Spartanburg) **10264**

SOUTH DAKOTA

Aberdeen American News (Aberdeen) **10039**
Advocate (Winner) **10265**
† Alpena Journal (Wessington Springs)
Argus Leader (Sioux Falls) **10039**
Baltic Beacon (Dell Rapids) **10264**
Belle Fourche Post (Belle Fourche) **10264**
Black Hills Pioneer (Spearfish) **10039**
Black Hills Press (Sturgis) **10265**
Brandon Valley Challenger (Dell Rapids) **10264**
Brookings Register (Brookings) **10039**
Butte County Valley Irrigator (Newell) **10265**
Canistota Clipper (Canistota) **10264**
Daily Republic (Mitchell) **10039**
Dakatan, The (Wessington Springs) **10265**
Dell Rapids Tribune (Dell Rapids) **10264**
Grant County Review (Milbank) **10265**
Hartford Area News (Canistota) **10264**
Humbolt Journal (Canistota) **10264**
Hutchinson Herald (Menno) **10265**
Ipswich Tribune (Ipswich) **10265**
Lawrence County Centennial
   (Deadwood) **10264**
† Lead Call (Lead)
Madison Daily Leader (Madison) **10039**
Meade County Times-Tribune (Sturgis) **10265**
Montrose Herald (Canistota) **10264**
Moody County Enterprise (Flandreau) **10265**
Nation's Center News (Buffalo) **10264**
Northwest Blade, The (Eureka) **10264**
Pennington County Prevailer-News (Hill
   City) **10265**
Pierre Capital Journal (Pierre) **10039**
Pierre Times, The (Pierre) **10265**
Plainsman, The (Huron) **10039**
Rapid City Journal (Rapid City) **10039**
Redfield Press (Redfield) **10265**
Roscoe Hosmer Independent (Ipswich) **10265**
Selby Record (Selby) **10265**
Sisseton Courier (Sisseton) **10265**
Watertown Public Opinion (Watertown) **10039**
Webster Reporter & Farmer (Webster) **10265**
Yankton Daily Press & Dakotan
   (Yankton) **10040**

TENNESSEE

Advocate Democrat (Madisonville) **10268**
Advocate Penny Saver (Sweetwater) **10270**
Athens Daily Post (Athens) **10040**
Bolivar Bulletin-Times (Bolivar) **10265**
Brentwood Journal (Brentwood) **10266**
Brownsville States-Graphic
   (Brownsville) **10266**
Buffalo River Review (Linden) **10268**
Camden Chronicle, The (Camden) **10266**

Carroll County News-Leader
   (Huntingdon) **10267**
Carthage Courier (Carthage) **10266**
Chattanooga Free Press (Chattanooga) **10040**
Chattanooga Times (Chattanooga) **10040**
Chronicle, The (Humboldt) **10257**
Citizen/Press Plus (Pulaski) **10269**
Citizen Tribune (Morristown) **10041**
Claiborne Progress (Tazewell) **10270**
Cleveland Daily Banner (Cleveland) **10040**
Collierville Herald, The (Collierville) **10266**
Commercial Appeal, The (Memphis) **10041**
Courier-News (Clinton) **10266**
Courier, The (Savannah) **10269**
Cover Story, The (Murfreesboro) **10268**
Covington Leader (Covington) **10266**
Crockett Times, The (Alamo) **10265**
Crossville Chronicle (Crossville) **10266**
† Cumberland Times (Crossville)
Daily Herald (Columbia) **10040**
Daily Times (Maryville) **10041**
Democrat-Union (Lawrenceburg) **10267**
Dickson Herald, The (Dickson) **10266**
† Dispatch, The (Cookeville)
Dresden Enterprise (Dresden) **10266**
Dyer County Tennessean (Newbern) **10268**
East Shelby Review (Somerville) **10269**
Elizabethton Star (Elizabethton) **10040**
Elk Valley Times (Fayetteville) **10266**
Erwin Record (Erwin) **10266**
Fayette County Review (Somerville) **10269**
Fayette Falcon, The (Somerville) **10269**
Germantown News, The (Germantown) **10267**
Grainger County News (Rutledge) **10269**
Greeneville Sun (Greeneville) **10040**
Grundy County Herald (Tracy City) **10270**
Halls Graphic (Ripley) **10269**
Harriman Record (Kingston) **10267**
Hartsville Vidette, The (Hartsville) **10267**
† Hendersonville Free Press (Hendersonville)
Hendersonville Star News
   (Hendersonville) **10267**
Herald & Tribune (Jonesborough) **10267**
Herald-Chronicle, The (Winchester) **10270**
Herald-Citizen (Cookeville) **10040**
Herald-News (Dayton) **10266**
Herald Gazette, The (Trenton) **10270**
† Huntingdon Carroll Leader (Huntingdon)
Hustler, The (South Pittsburg) **10269**
Independent (Collierville) **10266**
Independent Appeal (Selmer) **10269**
Jackson Sun (Jackson) **10040**
Jasper Journal (Jasper) **10267**
Jellico Advance Sentinel (La Follette) **10267**
Johnson City Press (Johnson City) **10040**
Kingsport Daily News (Kingsport) **10040**

Kingsport Times-News (Kingsport) **10040**
Knoxville News-Sentinel (Knoxville) **10041**
La Follette Press (La Follette) **10267**
Lake City Town Crier (La Follette) **10267**
Lauderdale County Enterprise (Ripley) **10269**
Leaf-Chronicle, The (Clarksville) **10040**
Lebanon Democrat, The (Lebanon) **10041**
Lewisburg Tribune (Lewisburg) **10268**
Lexington Progress (Lexington) **10268**
Livingston Enterprise (Livingston) **10268**
Macon County Times (Lafayette) **10267**
Majic Valley Shopper's News (Camden) **10266**
Manchester Times (Manchester) **10268**
Marshall Gazette (Lewisburg) **10268**
McKenzie Banner (McKenzie) **10268**
Messenger, The (Madison) **10268**
Mid-South Horse Review (Somerville) **10269**
Millington Star, The (Millington) **10268**
Mirror-Exchange (Milan) **10268**
Morgan County News (Wartburg) **10270**
Mountain Press, The (Sevierville) **10041**
† Mountain Visitor (Sevierville)
Murfreesboro Daily News Journal
    (Murfreesboro) **10041**
Nashville Banner (Nashville) **10041**
News-Examiner (Gallatin) **10267**
News Herald (Lenoir City) **10268**
News Leader, The (Parsons) **10269**
Oak Ridger, The (Oak Ridge) **10041**
Paris Post-Intelligencer, The (Paris) **10041**
Pickett County Press (Byrdstown) **10266**
Plain Talk (Newport) **10269**
Pulaski Citizen (Pulaski) **10269**
Pulaski Giles Free Press (Pulaski) **10269**
Roane County News, The (Kingston) **10267**
Robertson County Times (Springfield) **10270**
Rockwood Times (Kingston) **10267**
Rogersville Review (Rogersville) **10269**
Rutherford Courier, The (Smyrna) **10269**
Scott County News (Oneida) **10269**
Shelby Sun Times (Germantown) **10267**
Shelbyville Times-Gazette (Shelbyville) **10041**
Smithville Review (Smithville) **10269**
Southern Standard (McMinnville) **10268**
Sparta Expositor (Sparta) **10269**
Standard Banner (Jefferson) **10267**
State Gazette (Dyersburg) **10040**
Sullivan County News (Blountville) **10265**
Tennessean, The (Nashville) **10041**
Tomahawk, The (Mountain City) **10268**
Tri-City Reporter (Dyer) **10266**
Tri-County News (Knoxville) **10267**
Tullahoma News (Tullahoma) **10270**
Union City Daily Messenger (Union
    City) **10041**
Wayne County News (Waynesboro) **10270**

Weakley County Press (Martin) **10268**
Williamson Leader, The (Franklin) **10266**
Wilson World, The (Lebanon) **10268**

TEXAS

Abernathy Weekly Review (Abernathy) **10270**
Abilene Reporter-News (Abilene) **10041**
Alice Echo-News (Alice) **10041**
Alpine Avalanche (Alpine) **10270**
Alvarado Post (Alvarado) **10270**
Alvin Advertiser (Alvin) **10270**
Alvin Sun (Alvin) **10270**
Amarillo Daily News/Sunday News Globe
    (Amarillo) **10041**
Amarillo Globe Times (Amarillo) **10042**
Andrews County News (Andrews) **10270**
Angelina Free Press (Diboll) **10274**
Angleton Times (Angleton) **10270**
Argyle Sun, The (Lake Dallas) **10277**
▼Arlington Morning News (Arlington) **10042**
Arlington Star Telegram (Fort Worth) **10043**
Athens Daily Review (Athens) **10042**
Atlanta Citizens Journal (Atlanta) **10271**
Austin American-Statesman (Austin) **10042**
Austin Chronicle (Austin) **10271**
Azle News (Azle) **10271**
Banner Press Newspaper, The
    (Columbus) **10273**
Baylor County Banner (Seymour) **10280**
Bayshore Sun (La Porte) **10277**
Baytown Sun (Baytown) **10042**
Beaumont Enterprise (Beaumont) **10042**
Beeville Bee-Picayune (Beeville) **10271**
Bellville Times (Bellville) **10271**
Benbrook News (Fort Worth) **10275**
Big Spring Herald (Big Spring) **10042**
Blanco County News (Blanco) **10271**
Bonham Daily Favorite (Bonham) **10042**
Booker News, The (Booker) **10271**
Borger News-Herald (Borger) **10042**
Bosque County News (Meridian) **10279**
Bowie News (Bowie) **10271**
Brackett News The (Brackettville) **10271**
Brady Standard (Brady) **10271**
Brazosport Facts, The (Clute) **10042**
Brenham Banner-Press (Brenham) **10042**
Bridgeport Index (Bridgeport) **10272**
Brownfield News (Brownfield) **10272**
Brownsville Herald (Brownsville) **10042**
Brownwood Bulletin (Brownwood) **10042**
Bryan College Station Eagle (Bryan) **10042**
Bryan College Station Press (Bryan) **10272**
Bulletin, The (Santa Fe) **10280**
Burleson County Citizen Tribune
    (Caldwell) **10272**

Burleson Star (Burleson) **10272**
Burnet Bulletin (Burnet) **10272**
Caldwell Burleson County Citizen-Tribune
  (Caldwell) **10272**
Cameron Herald (Cameron) **10272**
Canyon News (Canyon) **10272**
† Carrollton Chronicle (Carrollton)
Cedar Creek Pilot (Gun Barrel City) **10276**
Cedar Hill Today (DeSoto) **10273**
Childress Index (Childress) **10272**
Cisco Press (Cisco) **10272**
Citizens' Advocate Newspaper (Coppell) **10273**
Citizen, The (Houston) **10276**
Clarksville Times, The (Clarksville) **10272**
Cleburne Times-Review (Cleburne) **10042**
Cleveland Advocate (Cleveland) **10272**
Coastal Current, The (South Padre
  Island) **10281**
Coleman Chronicle & Democrat Voice
  (Coleman) **10272**
Comanche Chief (Comanche) **10273**
Commerce Journal (Commerce) **10273**
Conroe Courier, The (Conroe) **10043**
Coppell Gazette (Lewisville) **10278**
Copperas Cove Leader Press (Copperas
  Cove) **10273**
Corpus Christi Caller-Times (Corpus
  Christi) **10043**
Corrigan Times, The (Corrigan) **10273**
Corsicana Daily Sun (Corsicana) **10043**
Crane News (Crane) **10273**
Crowley Review (Burleson) **10272**
Cuero Record (Cuero) **10273**
D/FW People (Euless) **10274**
Daily Sentinel, The (Nacogdoches) **10045**
Daily Tribune, The (Bay City) **10042**
Dalhart Daily Texan (Dalhart) **10043**
Dallas Morning News, The (Dallas) **10043**
Dallas Park Cities News (Dallas) **10273**
Dallas White Rocker News (Dallas) **10273**
Deer Park Broadcaster, The (Deer
  Park) **10273**
Deer Park Progress, The (Deer Park) **10273**
Del Rio News-Herald (Del Rio) **10043**
Denton County Express (Lake Dallas) **10277**
Denton Record-Chronicle (Denton) **10043**
DeSoto Today (DeSoto) **10273**
Dripping Springs Dispatch (Dripping
  Springs) **10274**
Duncanville Today (DeSoto) **10274**
Eagle Lake Headlight (Eagle Lake) **10274**
Eagle Pass News Guide/Brief (Eagle
  Pass) **10043**
Eastland Telegram (Eastland) **10274**
Edgewood Enterprise (Edgewood) **10274**
Edinburg Daily Review (Edinburg) **10043**

El Campo Leader-News (El Campo) **10274**
El Paso Herald-Post (El Paso) **10043**
El Paso Times (El Paso) **10043**
Ennis Daily News (Ennis) **10043**
Everman Times (Everman) **10274**
Falfurrias Facts (Falfurrias) **10274**
† Farmers Branch Times (Carrollton)
Fayette County Record, The (La
  Grange) **10277**
Floresville Chronicle-Journal
  (Floresville) **10274**
Floyd County Hesperian-Beacon
  (Floydada) **10274**
Forest Hill News (Everman) **10274**
Fort Bend Mirror (Rosenberg) **10280**
Fort Bend Sun (Sugar Land) **10281**
Fort Stockton Pioneer (Fort Stockton) **10274**
Fort Worth Star-Telegram (Fort Worth) **10043**
Fredericksburg Standard/Radio Post
  (Fredericksburg) **10275**
Friendswood & Pearland Reporter News
  (Pearland) **10279**
Gainesville Daily Register (Gainesville) **10043**
Galveston County Daily News, The
  (Galveston) **10044**
Garland News (Garland) **10275**
Gatesville Messenger (Gatesville) **10275**
Giddings Times & News (Giddings) **10275**
Gilmer Mirror (Gilmer) **10275**
Gladewater Mirror (Gladewater) **10275**
Glen Rose Reporter (Glen Rose) **10275**
Gonzales Inquirer (Gonzales) **10275**
Gorman Progress, The (Gorman) **10275**
Grand Prairie News (Arlington) **10270**
Grand Saline Sun (Grand Saline) **10275**
Grayson County Shopper (Denison) **10273**
Greenville Herald Banner (Greenville) **10044**
Groesbeck Journal (Groesbeck) **10275**
Gulf Coast Tribune, The (West
  Columbia) **10281**
Hallettsville Tribune-Herald
  (Hallettsville) **10276**
Hamilton Herald-News (Hamilton) **10276**
Hansford County Reporter-Statesman
  (Spearman) **10281**
Haskell Free Press (Haskell) **10276**
Henderson Daily News (Henderson) **10044**
Herald-Democrat (Denison) **10043**
Herald Coaster (Rosenberg) **10046**
Hereford Brand (Hereford) **10044**
Hondo Anvil Herald (Hondo) **10276**
Hood County News (Granbury) **10275**
Houston Chronicle (Houston) **10044**
Houston County Courier (Crockett) **10273**
Houston Forward Times (Houston) **10276**
Houston Informer (Houston) **10276**

† Houston Post (Houston)
Howe Enterprise (Howe) **10276**
Hubbard City News (Mexia) **10279**
Humble Sun (Humble) **10276**
Hunt County Shopper (Greenville) **10275**
Huntsville Item (Huntsville) **10044**
Idalou Beacon (Idalou) **10276**
Iowa Park Leader (Iowa Park) **10276**
Irving News (Arlington) **10271**
Jackson County Herald/Tribune (Edna) **10274**
Jacksonville Daily Progress
   (Jacksonville) **10044**
Jasper News-Boy (Jasper) **10276**
Jasper News-Boy Shopper (Jasper) **10276**
Jefferson Jimplecute (Jefferson) **10276**
† Jet Gazette (Austin)
Junction Eagle, The (Junction) **10277**
Karnes Citation (Karnes City) **10277**
Kaufman Herald, The (Kaufman) **10277**
Keller Citizen, The (Keller) **10277**
Kennedale News (Everman) **10274**
Kennedy Advanced Times (Karnes City) **10277**
Kerrville Daily Times (Kerrville) **10044**
Kilgore News Herald (Kilgore) **10044**
Killeen Daily Herald (Killeen) **10044**
Kingsville Record, The (Kingsville) **10277**
Kingwood Sun (Humble) **10276**
La Feria News (La Feria) **10277**
Lake Cities Sun, The (Lake Dallas) **10277**
La Marque Times (La Marque) **10277**
Lamb County Leader-News (Littlefield) **10278**
Lamesa Press-Reporter (Lamesa) **10277**
Lancaster Today (DeSoto) **10274**
Laredo Morning Times (Laredo) **10044**
La Vida News (Arlington) **10271**
Levelland Hockley County News-Press
   (Levelland) **10277**
Lewisville Leader (Lewisville) **10278**
Liberty Gazette (Liberty) **10278**
Light & Champion (Center) **10272**
† Livingston East Texas Eye (Livingston)
Llano News (Llano) **10278**
Lockhart Post Register (Lockhart) **10278**
Longview News Journal (Longview) **10044**
Lorenzo Examiner (Lorenzo) **10278**
Lubbock Avalanche-Journal (Lubbock) **10044**
Lufkin Daily News (Lufkin) **10044**
Luling Newsboy & Signal (Luling) **10278**
Mansfield News-Mirror (Mansfield) **10278**
Marble Falls Highlander (Marble Falls) **10278**
Marshall News Messenger (Marshall) **10045**
† Mart Herald (Mart)
Mason County News (Mason) **10278**
Mathis News (Mathis) **10278**
McAllen Monitor (McAllen) **10045**
McKinney Courier Gazette (McKinney) **10045**

Menard News & Messenger, The
   (Menard) **10279**
Mesquite News (Mesquite) **10279**
Metrocrest News (Carrollton) **10272**
Mexia Daily News (Mexia) **10045**
Miami Chief, The (Miami) **10279**
Mid-Cities News (Arlington) **10271**
Midcounty Chronicle (Nederland) **10279**
Midland Reporter-Telegram (Midland) **10045**
Midlothian Mirror (Midlothian) **10279**
Midlothian Today (DeSoto) **10274**
Mid Valley Town Crier (Weslaco) **10281**
Mineral Wells Index (Mineral Wells) **10045**
Monahans News (Monahans) **10279**
Monitor, The (Mabank) **10278**
Montague County Shopper, The (Bowie) **10271**
Moody Courier, The (Moody) **10279**
Moore County News-Press (Dumas) **10274**
Motley County Tribune (Matador) **10278**
Mountain Sun, The (Kerrville) **10277**
Mount Pleasant Daily Tribune (Mt.
   Pleasant) **10045**
Munday Courier, The (Munday) **10279**
Navasota Examiner Review (Navasota) **10279**
New Braunfels Herald & Zeitung (New
   Braunfels) **10045**
New Ulm Enterprise (New Ulm) **10279**
Nueces County Record Star (Robstown) **10280**
Oak Cliff Tribune (Dallas) **10273**
Odem-Edroy Times (Sinton) **10280**
Odessa American (Odessa) **10045**
Olney Enterprise, The (Olney) **10279**
Orange Leader (Orange) **10045**
Palacios Beacon (Palacios) **10279**
Palestine Herald-Press (Palestine) **10045**
Pampa News (Pampa) **10045**
Panola Watchman (Carthage) **10272**
Paris News (Paris) **10045**
Pasadena Citizen (Pasadena) **10045**
Pecos Enterprise (Pecos) **10046**
Pittsburg Gazette (Pittsburg) **10279**
Plainview Daily Herald (Plainview) **10046**
Plano Star Courier (Plano) **10046**
Pleasanton Express (Pleasanton) **10279**
Polk County Enterprise (Livingston) **10278**
Pony Express Mail (Liberty) **10278**
Port Arthur News (Port Arthur) **10046**
Porter/New Caney Sun (Humble) **10276**
Port Isabel-South Padre Press (Port
   Isabel) **10279**
Portland News (Portland) **10280**
Port Lavaca Wave (Port Lavaca) **10280**
Pottsboro Press (Pottsboro) **10280**
Progress, The (Anahuac) **10270**
Real American (Leakey) **10277**
Recorder Times, The (San Antonio) **10280**

Richardson News (Richardson) **10280**
Rising Star, The (Rising Star) **10280**
River Oaks News (Fort Worth) **10275**
Rockdale Reporter (Rockdale) **10280**
Round Rock Leader (Round Rock) **10280**
Sabinal Sampler (Hondo) **10276**
Sabine County Reporter-Rambler
   (Hemphill) **10276**
San Angelo Standard-Times (San
   Angelo) **10046**
San Antonio Express-News (San
   Antonio) **10046**
† San Antonio Light (San Antonio)
San Augustine Tribune (San Augustine) **10280**
San Benito News (San Benito) **10280**
San Marcos Daily Record (San Marcos) **10046**
San Patricio County News (Sinton) **10281**
Sealy News (Sealy) **10280**
Seguin Gazette-Enterprise (Seguin) **10046**
Shopper Zone II (Denison) **10273**
Silsbee Bee (Silsbee) **10280**
Snyder Daily News (Snyder) **10046**
South County News & Advertiser (Fort
   Worth) **10275**
Southwest Sun (Sugar Land) **10281**
Springtown Epigraph, The (Springtown) **10281**
Stamford American (Stamford) **10281**
Stephenville Empire-Tribune
   (Stephenville) **10046**
Suburban Tribune (Balch Springs) **10271**
Sulphur Springs News-Telegram (Sulphur
   Springs) **10046**
Sunday Sun (Georgetown) **10275**
Sweetwater Reporter (Sweetwater) **10046**
Taft Tribune (Taft) **10281**
Taylor Daily Press (Taylor) **10046**
Temple Daily Telegram (Temple) **10046**
Terrell Tribune (Terrell) **10047**
Texarkana Gazette (Texarkana) **10047**
Texas City Sun (Texas City) **10047**
Texas Observer (Austin) **10271**
Times Record News (Wichita Falls) **10047**
Trenton Tribune (Trenton) **10281**
Tyler County Booster (Woodville) **10282**
Tyler Morning Telegraph (Tyler) **10047**
Uvalde Leader-News (Uvalde) **10281**
Valley Morning Star (Harlingen) **10044**
Valley Town Crier (McAllen) **10278**
Van Horn Advocate (Van Horn) **10281**
Vega Enterprise, The (Vega) **10281**
Vernon Daily Record (Vernon) **10047**
Victoria Advocate (Victoria) **10047**
Vidorian, The (Vidor) **10281**
Villager Newspaper (Austin) **10271**
Vindicator, The (Liberty) **10278**
Waco Citizen, The (Waco) **10281**

Waco Tribune Herald (Waco) **10047**
Waller County News-Citizen
   (Hempstead) **10276**
Wallis News-Review (Wallis) **10281**
Waxahachie Daily Light (Waxahachie) **10047**
Weatherford Democrat (Weatherford) **10047**
Weimar Mercury (Weimar) **10281**
West Columbia Brazoria County News (West
   Columbia) **10281**
Westlake Picayune (Austin) **10271**
West News (West) **10281**
Wharton Journal-Spectator (Wharton) **10282**
White Oak Independent (White Oak) **10282**
White Settlement News (Fort Worth) **10275**
Whitewright Sun, The (Whitewright) **10282**
Williamson County Sun (Georgetown) **10275**
Wimberley Valley-News (Wimberley) **10282**
Winkler County News (Kermit) **10277**
Winnsboro News (Winnsboro) **10282**
Wise County Messenger (Decatur) **10273**
Wood County Democrat (Quitman) **10280**
Wylie News, The (Wylie) **10282**
Yoakum Herald-Times & Four Star Reporter
   (Yoakum) **10282**

UTAH

Box Elder News Journal (Brigham City) **10282**
Citizen (American Fork) **10282**
Daily Herald, The (Provo) **10047**
Davis County Clipper (Bountiful) **10282**
Emery County Progress (Castle Dale) **10282**
Herald Journal, The (Logan) **10047**
Leader, The (Tremonton) **10283**
Lehi Free Press (American Fork) **10282**
Magna Times (Magna) **10282**
Millard County Gazette (Fillmore) **10282**
† Murray Eagle (Salt Lake City)
North Utah County Shopper (American
   Fork) **10282**
Orem-Geneva Times (Orem) **10283**
Park Record, The (Park City) **10283**
Pleasant Grove Review (American Fork) **10282**
Private Eye Weekly (Salt Lake City) **10283**
Pyramid, The (Mt. Pleasant) **10283**
Reaper Extra (Richfield) **10283**
Richfield Reaper (Richfield) **10283**
Salt Lake City Deseret News (Salt Lake
   City) **10047**
Salt Lake Tribune (Salt Lake City) **10048**
† South Valley Eagle (Salt Lake City)
Spectrum, The (St. George) **10048**
Standard-Examiner (Ogden) **10047**
Sun Advocate (Price) **10283**
Tooele Transcript-Bulletin (Tooele) **10283**
Uintah Basin Standard (Roosevelt) **10283**

Vernal Express (Vernal) **10283**
West Valley Eagle (Bountiful) **10282**
West Valley News (Magna) **10282**

VERMONT

Addison County Independent
  (Middlebury) **10284**
Bellows Falls Town Crier (Bellows Falls) **10283**
Bennington Banner (Bennington) **10048**
Brattleboro Reformer (Brattleboro) **10048**
Burlington Free Press (Burlington) **10048**
Caledonian-Record, The (St. Johnsbury) **10048**
County Courier (Enosburg Falls) **10283**
Hardwick Gazette (Hardwick) **10283**
Herald of Randolph (Randolph) **10284**
Islander, The (South Hero) **10284**
Journal Opinion (Bradford) **10283**
Manchester Journal (Manchester
  Center) **10284**
Message for the Week (Chester) **10283**
Mountain Times (Killington) **10283**
Newport Daily Express (Newport) **10048**
Pennysaver Press (Bennington) **10283**
▼Poultney News, The (Rutland) **10284**
Rutland Herald (Rutland) **10048**
Rutland Tribune, The (Rutland) **10284**
Springfield Reporter, The (Springfield) **10284**
St. Albans Messenger (St. Albans) **10048**
Stowe Reporter (Stowe) **10284**
Times Argus (Barre) **10048**
Transcript, The (Morrisville) **10284**
Valley Reporter, The (Waitsfield) **10284**
Vermont News Guide (Manchester
  Center) **10284**
Vermont Times (Shelburne) **10284**

VIRGIN ISLANDS

St. Croix Avis (St. Croix) **10048**
Tradewinds (St. John) **10284**
Virgin Islands Daily News (St. Thomas) **10048**

VIRGINIA

Abingdon Virginian (Abingdon) **10284**
Alexandria Gazette Packet (Alexandria) **10284**
Alexandria Journal (Fairfax) **10049**
Altavista Journal (Altavista) **10284**
Amelia Bulletin Monitor, The (Amelia Court
  House) **10285**
Amherst New Era-Progress (Amherst) **10285**
Appomattox Times-Virginian
  (Appomattox) **10285**
Arlington Courier, The (Arlington) **10285**

Arlington Journal (Fairfax) **10049**
Bedford Bulletin (Bedford) **10285**
Blackstone Courier-Record (Blackstone) **10285**
Bland Messenger (Wytheville) **10290**
Blue Ridge Leader, The (Purcellville) **10288**
Bristol Herald-Courier, The (Bristol) **10048**
Brunswick Times-Gazette
  (Lawrenceville) **10287**
Burke Times, The (Reston) **10288**
Caroline Progress, The (Bowling Green) **10285**
Carroll News, The (Hillsville) **10286**
Central Virginian, The (Louisa) **10287**
Centreville Times (Reston) **10288**
Chantilly Times (Reston) **10288**
Charlotte Gazette (Drakes Branch) **10286**
Charlottesville-Albemarle Tribune
  (Charlottesville) **10285**
Chesapeake Post (Chesapeake) **10285**
Clark Courier (Reston) **10288**
Clinch Valley News (Tazewell) **10289**
Coalfield Progress (Norton) **10288**
Crewe-Burkeville Journal (Crewe) **10286**
Culpeper News (Culpeper) **10286**
Culpeper Star Exponent (Culpeper) **10049**
Daily News-Record (Harrisonburg) **10049**
Daily News Leader, The (Staunton) **10050**
Daily Progress (Charlottesville) **10049**
Danville Register & Bee (Danville) **10049**
Declaration, The (Independence) **10287**
Denbigh Gazette (Yorktown) **10290**
Dickenson Star/Cumberland Times, The
  (Clintwood) **10285**
Enterprise Buyer's Catalogue
  (Wytheville) **10290**
Enterprise, The (Stuart) **10289**
Fairfax Connection (McLean) **10287**
Fairfax Journal (Fairfax) **10049**
Fairfax Station Times (Reston) **10288**
Fairfax Times (Reston) **10288**
Falls Church News-Press (Falls Church) **10286**
Farmville Herald, The (Farmville) **10286**
Fauquier Times-Democrat (Warrenton) **10290**
Fincastle Herald, The (Fincastle) **10286**
Floyd Press (Floyd) **10286**
Franklin News-Post (Rocky Mount) **10289**
Fredericksburg Free Lance-Star
  (Fredericksburg) **10049**
Free News, The (Farmville) **10286**
Galax Gazette, The (Galax) **10286**
Gloucester-Mathews Gazette Journal
  (Gloucester) **10286**
Goochland Gazette (Goochland) **10286**
Great Falls Times (Reston) **10288**
Greene County Record (Stanardsville) **10289**
Hanover Herald-Progress (Ashland) **10285**
† Henrico Gazette (Richmond)

Herndon Times (Reston) **10288**
Hopewell News (Hopewell) **10049**
Independent-Messenger (Emporia) **10286**
Journal Messenger (Manassas) **10049**
Kenbridge-Victoria Dispatch (Victoria) **10289**
Lebanon News (Lebanon) **10287**
† Ledger-Star (Norfolk)
Leesburg Today (Leesburg) **10287**
Loudoun Times-Mirror (Leesburg) **10287**
Luray Page News & Courier (Luray) **10287**
Madison County Eagle (Madison) **10287**
Martinsville Bulletin (Martinsville) **10049**
McLean Providence Journal (Reston) **10288**
Mecklenburg Sun (Clarksville) **10285**
Metro Weekenders, The (Norfolk) **10288**
Mountain Advisor (Richlands) **10289**
Nelson County Times (Lovingston) **10287**
New Castle Record (New Castle) **10288**
Newport News Daily Press (Newport
   News) **10049**
News & Advance (Lynchburg) **10049**
News-Gazette (Lexington) **10287**
News-Progress, The (Chase City) **10285**
News Buyer's Catalogue (Wytheville) **10290**
News Buyers Catalog (Marion) **10287**
News Messenger, The (Christiansburg) **10285**
Northern Piedmont Express (Culpeper) **10286**
Northern Virginia Daily (Strasburg) **10050**
Northern Virginia Sun, The (Fairfax) **10286**
Northumberland Echo (Heathsville) **10286**
Orange County Review (Orange) **10288**
Poquoson Post (Yorktown) **10290**
Portsmouth Times (Chesapeake) **10285**
Post, The (Big Stone Gap) **10285**
Potomac News (Woodbridge) **10050**
Powell Valley News (Pennington Gap) **10288**
▼Prince William Journal (Manassas) **10049**
Progress-Index (Petersburg) **10049**
Rappahannock News (Reston) **10288**
Rappahannock Record (Kilmarnock) **10287**
Recorder, The (Monterey) **10287**
Reston Times (Reston) **10288**
Richlands News Press (Richlands) **10289**
Richmond Times-Dispatch (Richmond) **10050**
Roanoke Times, The (Roanoke) **10050**
Rockbridge Weekly (Lexington) **10287**
Rural Virginian (Charlottesville) **10285**
Salem Times-Register (Salem) **10289**
Shenandoah Valley-Herald, The
   (Woodstock) **10290**
Smith Mountain Eagle (Moneta) **10287**
Smyth County News & Messenger
   (Marion) **10287**
South Boston Gazette-Virginian (South
   Boston) **10289**

South Boston News & Record (South
   Boston) **10289**
South Hill Enterprise (South Hill) **10289**
Southside Sentinel (Urbanna) **10289**
Southwest Times, The (Pulaski) **10050**
Southwest Virginia Enterprise
   (Wytheville) **10290**
Springfield Times Courier (Reston) **10289**
Star-Tribune (Chatham) **10285**
Suffolk News-Herald (Suffolk) **10050**
Sussex-Surry Dispatch (Wakefield) **10289**
Tazewell County Free Press (Richlands) **10289**
Tidewater Review (West Point) **10290**
Valley Banner, The (Elkton) **10286**
Vienna Times (Reston) **10289**
Vinton Messenger (Vinton) **10289**
Virginia Beach Sun (Virginia Beach) **10289**
Virginia Gazette (Williamsburg) **10290**
Virginia Mountaineer (Grundy) **10286**
Virginian-Leader (Pearisburg) **10288**
Virginian-Pilot, The (Norfolk) **10049**
Virginian Review (Covington) **10049**
Washington County News (Abingdon) **10284**
Waynesboro News-Virginian
   (Waynesboro) **10050**
Weekender, The (Lexington) **10287**
Westmoreland News (Montross) **10287**
Winchester Star (Winchester) **10050**
York Town Crier (Yorktown) **10290**

WASHINGTON

Anacortes American (Anacortes) **10290**
Bainbridge Review (Bainbridge Island) **10290**
Beacon Hill News, The/South District Journal
   (Seattle) **10292**
Bellingham Herald (Bellingham) **10050**
Business Examiner (Gig Harbor) **10291**
Camas/Washougal Post Record
   (Camas) **10290**
Capitol Hill Times (Seattle) **10293**
Cashmere Valley Record (Cashmere) **10291**
Cheney Free Press (Cheney) **10291**
Chronicle, The (Centralia) **10050**
Columbia Basin Herald (Moses Lake) **10051**
Columbian, The (Vancouver) **10051**
Daily News (Longview) **10051**
Daily Record (Ellensburg) **10050**
Daily Sun-News (Sunnyside) **10051**
Daily World, The (Aberdeen) **10050**
Dayton Chronicle (Dayton) **10291**
Des Moines News (Seattle) **10293**
Enterprise, The (Lynnwood) **10292**
Enumclaw Courier-Herald (Enumclaw) **10291**
† Fairchild Strikehawk (Spokane)
Federal Way News (Federal Way) **10291**

Franklin County Graphic (Connell) **10291**
Gem State Miner (Newport) **10292**
Goldendale Sentinel (Goldendale) **10291**
Grandview Herald (Grandview) **10291**
Grant County Journal (Ephrata) **10291**
Herald, The (Everett) **10051**
Highline News (Burien) **10290**
Issaquah Press (Issaquah) **10291**
Journal American (Bellevue) **10050**
Journal of the San Juan Islands (Friday
   Harbor) **10291**
Leavenworth Echo (Leavenworth) **10292**
Long Beach Chinook Observer (Long
   Beach) **10292**
Lynden Tribune (Lynden) **10292**
Madison Park Times (Seattle) **10293**
Mercer Island Reporter (Mercer Island) **10292**
Newport Miner (Newport) **10292**
News Tribune, The (Tacoma) **10051**
Nisqually Valley News (Yelm) **10294**
North Central Outlook (Seattle) **10293**
North Kitsap Herald (Poulsbo) **10292**
Northshore Citizen (Bothell) **10290**
North Snohomish Weekly (Arlington) **10290**
Olympian, The (Olympia) **10051**
Omak-Okanogan County Chronicle
   (Omak) **10292**
Othello Outlook, The (Othello) **10292**
Peninsula Daily News (Port Angeles) **10051**
Peninsula Gateway (Gig Harbor) **10291**
Port Orchard Independent (Port
   Orchard) **10292**
Port Townsend/Jefferson County Leader (Port
   Townsend) **10292**
Queen Anne-Magnolia News (Seattle) **10293**
Redmond Sammamish Valley News
   (Redmond) **10292**
Reflector, The (Battle Ground) **10290**
Rochester Sun News, The (Tenino) **10293**
Royal Review (Royal City) **10292**
Seattle Daily Journal of Commerce
   (Seattle) **10051**
Seattle Facts (Seattle) **10293**
Seattle Post-Intelligencer (Seattle) **10051**
Seattle Skanner, The (Seattle) **10293**
Seattle Times (Seattle) **10051**
Seattle Weekly (Seattle) **10293**
Senior Times (Spokane) **10293**
Sequim Gazette (Sequim) **10293**
Shelton-Mason County Journal
   (Shelton) **10293**
Skagit Valley Herald (Mt. Vernon) **10051**
Snohomish County Tribune
   (Snohomish) **10293**
South District Journal (Seattle) **10293**
Spokesman-Review, The (Spokane) **10051**

Sprague Advocate, The (Sprague) **10293**
Statesman-Examiner (Colville) **10291**
Sun, The (Bremerton) **10050**
Tenino Independent (Tenino) **10293**
Times, The (Waitsburg) **10294**
Toppenish Review (Toppenish) **10293**
Tri-City Herald (Kennewick) **10051**
Tribune (Deer Park) **10291**
University Herald (Seattle) **10293**
Valley Daily News (Kent) **10051**
Valley Herald, The (Spokane) **10293**
Vashon-Maury Island Beachcomber
   (Vashon) **10293**
Voice of the Valley (Maple Valley) **10292**
Wahkiakum County Eagle, The
   (Cathlamet) **10291**
Walla Walla Union-Bulletin (Walla Walla) **10052**
Wapato Independent (Wapato) **10294**
Wenatchee World (Wenatchee) **10052**
† West Plains Tribune (Spokane)
West Seattle Herald (Seattle) **10293**
Westside Record-Journal (Ferndale) **10291**
Whidbey News-Times (Oak Harbor) **10292**
Whitman County Gazette (Colfax) **10291**
Willapa Harbor Herald (Raymond) **10292**
Woodland Lewis River News
   (Woodland) **10294**
Yakima Herald-Republic (Yakima) **10052**

WEST VIRGINIA

Barbour Democrat, The (Philippi) **10295**
Bluefield Daily Telegraph (Bluefield) **10052**
Braxton Citizen's News (Sutton) **10296**
Braxton Democrat-Central (Sutton) **10296**
Brooke County Review (Wellsburg) **10296**
Cabell Record (Culloden) **10294**
Calhoun Chronicle (Grantsville) **10294**
Charleston Daily Mail (Charleston) **10052**
Charleston Gazette, The (Charleston) **10052**
Clarksburg Exponent (Clarksburg) **10052**
Clarksburg Telegram (Clarksburg) **10052**
Clay County Free Press (Clay) **10294**
Coal Valley News (Danville) **10294**
Dominion Post, The (Morgantown) **10053**
Fayette Tribune (Oak Hill) **10295**
Franklin Pendleton Times (Franklin) **10294**
Glenville Democrat, The (Glenville) **10294**
Glenville Pathfinder (Glenville) **10294**
Grant County Press (Petersburg) **10295**
Greenbrier Valley Ranger (Lewisburg) **10295**
Green Tab (Moundsville) **10295**
Hampshire Review (Romney) **10296**
Herald Record (West Union) **10297**
Hinton News (Hinton) **10295**
Hometown News (Madison) **10295**

Huntington Herald-Dispatch
   (Huntington) **10052**
Hurricane Breeze (Hurricane) **10295**
Independent Herald, The (Pineville) **10296**
Inter-Mountain, The (Elkins) **10052**
Jackson Star News (Ravenswood) **10296**
Journal, The (Martinsburg) **10052**
Lincoln Journal (Hamlin) **10294**
Logan Banner (Logan) **10052**
Mineral Daily Tribune (Keyser) **10052**
Monroe Watchman (Union) **10296**
Montgomery Herald (Montgomery) **10295**
Moorefield Examiner (Moorefield) **10295**
Morgan Messenger, The (Berkeley
   Springs) **10294**
Morning Intelligencer, The (Wheeling) **10053**
Moundsville Daily Echo (Moundsville) **10053**
Mountain Messenger (Lewisburg) **10295**
Mountain Statesman (Grafton) **10294**
Mullens Advocate (Mullen) **10295**
News Leader (Richwood) **10296**
Nicholas Chronicle (Summersville) **10296**
† Panhandle Press (Chester)
Parkersburg Sentinel (Parkersburg) **10053**
Parsons Advocate (Parsons) **10295**
Pennsboro News (Pennsboro) **10295**
Piedmont Herald (Piedmont) **10296**
Pocahontas Times (Marlinton) **10295**
Point Pleasant Register (Point Pleasant) **10053**
Post Report, The (Lewisburg) **10295**
Preston County News (Kingwood) **10295**
Princeton Times (Princeton) **10296**
Putnam Post-Cabell Bulletin (Culloden) **10294**
Record-Delta, The (Buckhannon) **10294**
Register/Herald (Beckley) **10052**
Ripley Jackson Herald (Ripley) **10296**
Ritchie Gazette (Harrisville) **10295**
Roane County Reporter (Spencer) **10296**
Shepherdstown Chronicle
   (Shepherdstown) **10296**
Spirit of Jefferson-Advocate (Charles
   Town) **10294**
Times Record (Spencer) **10296**
Times West Virginian (Fairmont) **10052**
Tyler Star News (Sistersville) **10296**
Wayne County News (Wayne) **10296**
Webster Republican (Webster Springs) **10296**
Weirton Daily Times (Weirton) **10053**
Welch Daily News (Welch) **10053**
Weston Democrat, The (Weston) **10297**
West Virginia Daily News (Lewisburg) **10052**
West Virginia Hillbilly (Richwood) **10296**
Wetzel Chronicle (New Martinsville) **10295**
Wheeling News-Register (Wheeling) **10053**

Williamson Daily News (Williamson) **10053**

WISCONSIN

Abbotsford Tribune-Phonograph
   (Abbotsford) **10297**
Action Advertiser (Fond Du Lac) **10300**
Adams County Times (Adams) **10297**
Advance, The (Randolph) **10304**
Algoma Record Herald (Algoma) **10297**
Amery Free Press (Amery) **10297**
Antigo Area Shoppers Guide (Antigo) **10297**
Antigo Daily Journal (Antigo) **10053**
Arcadia News-Leader (Arcadia) **10297**
Argyle Agenda (Argyle) **10297**
Augusta Area Times (Augusta) **10297**
Baldwin Bulletin (Baldwin) **10297**
Banner Journal (Black River Falls) **10297**
Baraboo News-Republic (Baraboo) **10053**
Bargain Express Newspaper
   (Milwaukee) **10302**
Barron County News Shield (Barron) **10297**
Bay Viewer, The (Wauwatosa) **10307**
Beaver Dam Daily Citizen (Beaver Dam) **10053**
Bee, The (Phillips) **10304**
Belleville Recorder (Belleville) **10297**
Beloit Daily News (Beloit) **10053**
Berlin Buyers' Guide (Berlin) **10297**
Berlin Journal (Berlin) **10297**
Billboard, The (Berlin) **10297**
Blade Atlas (Blanchardville) **10298**
Blair Press (Blair) **10298**
Bloomer Advance (Bloomer) **10298**
Boscobel Dial (Boscobel) **10298**
Brillion News (Brillion) **10298**
Brookfield News (Wauwatosa) **10307**
Brown Deer Herald (Wauwatosa) **10307**
Buffalo County Journal (Cochrane) **10298**
Bulletin, The (Kenosha) **10301**
Burlington Standard Press (Burlington) **10298**
Burnett County Sentinel (Grantsburg) **10300**
Buyer's Guide Cent Saver (Mauston) **10302**
Cadott Sentinel (Cadott) **10298**
Cambridge News (Cambridge) **10298**
Campbellsport News (Campbellsport) **10298**
Capital Times, The (Madison) **10054**
Cashton Record (Cashton) **10298**
Central Saint Croix News (Hammond) **10300**
Chetek Alert, The (Chetek) **10298**
Chilton Times-Journal (Chilton) **10298**
Chippewa Herald-Telegram (Chippewa
   Falls) **10053**
Clark County Press (Neillsville) **10303**
Clinton Topper (Clinton) **10298**
Clintonville Tribune-Gazette
   (Clintonville) **10298**

Colfax Messenger (Colfax) **10299**
Columbus Journal (Columbus) **10299**
Community Herald (Monona) **10303**
Cornell & Lake Holcombe Courier
    (Cornell) **10299**
County Journal, The (Washburn) **10306**
Courier-Wedge (Durand) **10299**
Courier Hub (Stoughton) **10305**
Courier Press (Prairie du Chien) **10304**
Courier, The (Sun Prairie) **10305**
Crawford County Independent-Kickapoo Scout
    (Gay Mills) **10300**
Cudahy Reminder-Enterprise
    (Wauwatosa) **10307**
Cumberland Advocate (Cumberland) **10299**
Daily Jefferson County Union (Fort
    Atkinson) **10054**
Daily News (West Bend) **10055**
Daily Press, The (Ashland) **10053**
Daily Register, The (Portage) **10054**
Daily Tribune, The (Wisconsin Rapids) **10055**
Delavan Enterprise (Delavan) **10299**
Democrat Tribune, The (Mineral Point) **10302**
Denmark Press (Denmark) **10299**
De Pere Journal (De Pere) **10299**
Dodge County Independent-News
    (Juneau) **10301**
Dodgeville Chronicle, Inc. (Dodgeville) **10299**
Door County Advocate (Sturgeon Bay) **10305**
Dunn County News (Menomonie) **10302**
Eagle-Herald (Marinette) **10054**
East Troy News (East Troy) **10299**
Edgerton Reporter (Edgerton) **10299**
Elkhorn Independent (Elkhorn) **10299**
Elm Leaves (Wauwatosa) **10307**
Elmwood Argus (Spring Valley) **10305**
Fennimore Times (Fennimore) **10300**
Fitchburg Star (Fitchburg) **10300**
Five County/Buyer's Guide (Ripon) **10304**
Florence Mining News (Florence) **10300**
Forest Republican, The (Crandon) **10299**
Forest Times-Tribune (De Forest) **10299**
Foto News (Merrill) **10302**
Fox Lake Representative (Berlin) **10297**
Fox Point, Bayside, River Hills Herald
    (Wauwatosa) **10307**
Foxxy Shopper (Sparta) **10305**
Franklin-Hales Corner Hub
    (Wauwatosa) **10307**
Freeman, The (Waukesha) **10055**
Galesville Republican (Galesville) **10300**
Germantown Banner-Press
    (Wauwatosa) **10307**
Glendale Herald (Wauwatosa) **10307**
Glidden Enterprise (Glidden) **10300**

Grant County Herald Independent
    (Lancaster) **10301**
Green Bay News-Chronicle (Green Bay) **10054**
Green Bay Press-Gazette (Green Bay) **10054**
Greendale Village Life (Wauwatosa) **10307**
Greenfield Observer (Wauwatosa) **10307**
Green Lake County Reporter (Green
    Lake) **10300**
Herald, The (Markesan) **10302**
Hillsboro Sentry-Enterprise (Hillsboro) **10301**
Horicon Reporter (Horicon) **10301**
Hudson Star-Observer (Hudson) **10301**
Independence News-Wave
    (Independence) **10301**
Independent (Deerfield) **10299**
Independent-Register, The (Brodhead) **10298**
Indianhead Advertiser (Frederic) **10300**
Inter-County Leader (Frederic) **10300**
Iola Herald (Iola) **10301**
Iron County Miner (Hurley) **10301**
Isthmus (Madison) **10302**
Janesville Gazette (Janesville) **10054**
Journal & Monitor Herald (Tomah) **10306**
Journal Times (Racine) **10055**
Juneau County Star-Times (Mauston) **10302**
Kaukauna Times (Kaukauna) **10301**
Kenosha News (Kenosha) **10054**
Kettle Moraine Index (Hartland) **10300**
Kewaskum Statesman (Kewaskum) **10301**
Kewaunee Enterprise (Kewaunee) **10301**
Keystone Tribune (Elroy) **10300**
Kiel Tri-County Record (Kiel) **10301**
La Crosse County Countryman (West
    Salem) **10308**
La Crosse Tribune (La Crosse) **10054**
Ladysmith News (Ladysmith) **10301**
Lake Country Reporter (Hartland) **10300**
Lake Geneva Regional News (Lake
    Geneva) **10301**
Lakeland Times (Minocqua) **10303**
Lake Mills Leader (Lake Mills) **10301**
Lakeshore Chronicle (Manitowoc) **10302**
Leader-Telegram (Eau Claire) **10054**
Lodi Enterprise (Lodi) **10301**
Loyal Tribune-Record-Gleaner (Loyal) **10302**
Luxemburg News (Luxemburg) **10302**
Manitowoc Herald-Times Reporter
    (Manitowoc) **10054**
Marion Advertiser (Marion) **10302**
Marquette County Tribune (Montello) **10303**
Marshfield News Herald (Marshfield) **10054**
Mayville News (Mayville) **10302**
McFarland Community Life (Monona) **10303**
McFarland Leader (Monona) **10303**
Melrose Chronicle (Melrose) **10302**
Menomonee Falls News (Wauwatosa) **10307**

Mequon-Thiensville Courant
(Wauwatosa) **10307**
† Mid-County Times (Pardeeville)
Middleton Times-Tribune (Middleton) **10302**
Milton Courier (Milton) **10302**
Milwaukee Journal-Sentinel (Milwaukee) **10054**
Milwaukee Star (Milwaukee) **10302**
Mondovi Herald News (Mondovi) **10303**
Monroe County Democrat (Sparta) **10305**
Monroe Times, The (Monroe) **10054**
Mosinee Times, The (Mosinee) **10303**
Mukwonago Chief (Mukwonago) **10303**
Muskego Sun (Wauwatosa) **10307**
New Berlin Citizen (Wauwatosa) **10307**
New Holstein Reporter (New Holstein) **10303**
New Richmond News (New Richmond) **10303**
North Shore Heralds (Wauwatosa) **10307**
North Star Journal (Presque Isle) **10304**
O-W Enterprise (Withee) **10308**
Oak Creek Pictorial (Wauwatosa) **10307**
Oconomowoc Enterprise (Oconomowoc) **10303**
Oconto County Times-Herald (Oconto
Falls) **10303**
Omro Herald (Omro) **10303**
Oregon Observer (Oregon) **10303**
Osceola Sun (Osceola) **10303**
Oshkosh Buyers Guide (Oshkosh) **10303**
Oshkosh Northwestern (Oshkosh) **10054**
Ozaukee County News Graphic
(Cedarburg) **10298**
Ozaukee Guide (Cedarburg) **10298**
Ozaukee Press (Port Washington) **10304**
Park Falls Herald (Park Falls) **10304**
Peshtigo Times (Peshtigo) **10304**
Picture Post (Waupaca) **10306**
Pierce County Herald (Ellsworth) **10300**
Platteville Journal (Platteville) **10304**
Post-Crescent (Appleton) **10053**
Prescott Journal (Prescott) **10304**
Press-Star (New London) **10303**
Princeton Times-Republic (Princeton) **10304**
Record-Review (Abbotsford) **10297**
Reedsburg Times-Press (Reedsburg) **10304**
Reporter, The (Fond Du Lac) **10054**
Republican-Journal (Darlington) **10299**
Review, The (Plymouth) **10304**
Rhinelander Daily News (Rhinelander) **10055**
Rice Lake Chronotype (Rice Lake) **10304**
Richland Center Observer (Richland
Center) **10304**
Ripon Commonwealth Press (Ripon) **10304**
River Falls Journal (River Falls) **10305**
Sauk-Prairie Star (Sauk City) **10305**
Sawyer County Gazette (Winter) **10308**
Sawyer County Record (Hayward) **10301**
Sharon Reporter, The (Sharon) **10305**

Shawano Leader (Shawano) **10055**
Sheboygan Falls News (Sheboygan
Falls) **10305**
Sheboygan Press, The (Sheboygan) **10055**
Shopper Stopper (Merrimac) **10302**
Shopping News (Platteville) **10304**
Shoreline Chronicle (Sheboygan) **10305**
Shorewood Herald (Wauwatosa) **10307**
Sounder, The (Random Lake) **10304**
South Milwaukee Voice Graphic
(Wauwatosa) **10307**
Sparta Herald (Sparta) **10305**
Spooner Advocate (Spooner) **10305**
Spring Valley Sun (Spring Valley) **10305**
Stanley Republican (Stanley) **10305**
Star News, The (Medford) **10302**
Star, The (Sun Prairie) **10306**
Stevens Point Journal (Stevens Point) **10055**
St. Francis Reminder-Enterprise
(Wauwatosa) **10307**
Stratford Journal (Stratford) **10305**
Superior Daily Telegram (Superior) **10055**
Sussex-Lannon-Lisbon News
(Wauwatosa) **10308**
Sussex Sun (Hartland) **10300**
Thorp Courier (Thorp) **10306**
Times-Press (Hartford) **10300**
Times-Press (Seymour) **10305**
Times, The (Westby) **10308**
Tomahawk Leader (Tomahawk) **10306**
Tomah Journal (Tomah) **10306**
Tomah Monitor-Herald (Tomah) **10306**
Tri-County News (Osseo) **10303**
Tri-County Press (Cuba City) **10299**
Tribune Press Reporter (Glenwood
City) **10300**
Turtle Lake Times, The (Turtle Lake) **10306**
Valders Journal (Valders) **10306**
Valley Value Shopper (Spring Valley) **10305**
Vernon County Broadcaster (Viroqua) **10306**
Verona Press (Verona) **10306**
Vilas County News-Review (Eagle River) **10299**
Walworth Times, The (Walworth) **10306**
Washburn County Register (Shell Lake) **10305**
Waterford Post (Waterford) **10306**
Watertown Daily Times (Watertown) **10055**
Waunakee Tribune (Waunakee) **10306**
Waupun Leader News (Waupun) **10306**
Wausau Daily Herald (Wausau) **10055**
Waushara Argus (Wautoma) **10307**
Wauwatosa News-Times (Wauwatosa) **10308**
West Allis Star (Wauwatosa) **10308**
Westine Report (Union Grove) **10306**
Westosha Report (Twin Lakes) **10306**
Whitefish Bay Herald (Wauwatosa) **10308**
Whitehall Times (Whitehall) **10308**

Winneconne News (Winneconne) **10308**
Wisconsin Dells Events (Wisconsin
  Dells) **10308**
Wisconsin State Farmer (Waupaca) **10306**
Wisconsin State Journal (Madison) **10054**
Wittenberg Enterprise News
  (Wittenberg) **10308**
Wonewoc Reporter (Elroy) **10300**

WYOMING

Bridger Valley Pioneer (Lyman) **10309**
Buffalo Bulletin (Buffalo) **10308**
Casper Star Tribune (Casper) **10055**
Cody Enterprise (Cody) **10308**
Daily Times, The (Rawlins) **10056**
Guernsey Gazette/Lingle Guide
  (Guernsey) **10309**
Jackson Hole Guide (Jackson) **10309**
Jackson Hole News (Jackson) **10309**
Kemmerer Gazette (Kemmerer) **10309**

Lander Wyoming State Journal (Lander) **10309**
Laramie Daily Boomerang (Laramie) **10055**
Lovell Chronicle, The (Lovell) **10309**
Lusk Herald (Lusk) **10309**
Moorcroft Leader (Moorcroft) **10309**
News-Record (Gillette) **10055**
News Letter Journal (Newcastle) **10309**
Northern Wyoming Daily News
  (Worland) **10056**
Platte County Record-Times
  (Wheatland) **10309**
Riverton Ranger (Riverton) **10056**
Rock Springs Daily Rocket-Miner (Rock
  Springs) **10056**
Saratoga Sun (Saratoga) **10309**
Sentinel (Cheyenne) **10308**
Sheridan Press (Sheridan) **10056**
Torrington Telegram (Torrington) **10309**
Uinta County Herald (Evanston) **10308**
Wind River News (Lander) **10309**
Wyoming State Journal (Lander) **10309**
Wyoming Tribune-Eagle (Cheyenne) **10055**

Cessations

Adams County Leader (Council, ID).
Adelanto Bulletin, The (Adelanto, CA).
Alabama Journal (Montgomery, AL).
Algonac Courier Journal (Marine City, MI).
Alpena Journal (Wessington Springs, SD).
Alvin Tiller (Lamont, CA).
Anchor Bay Beacon (New Baltimore, MI).
Anderson Countian (Garnett, KS).
Applewood/Wheat Ridge Transcript
  (Golden, CO).
Arcadia Tribune (Arcadia, CA).
Augusta Herald (Augusta, GA).
Ausable Forks Adirondack Record Post
  (Elizabethtown, NY).
Austintown Leader (Niles, OH).
Azalea City News & Review (Bayou Labatre, AL).
Bal Harbor/Bay Harbour News (South
  Miami, FL).
Birmingham Free Press (Birmingham, AL).
Biz (Oxford, PA).
Breeze Herald (Conneut Lake Park, PA).
Bridgewater Townsman (Bridgewater, MA).
Broken Arrow Scout (Broken Arrow, OK).
Brooklyn Times (Brooklyn, NY).
Brooksville Sun Journal (Brooksville, FL).
Brookville American (Brookville, PA).
Buyer's Guide (Napa, CA).
Byron Center/Dorr Advance (Jenison, MI).
Cape Cod News (Yarmouth Port, MA).
Carpinteria Herald (Goleta, CA).

Carrollton Chronicle (Carrollton, TX).
Cato Citizen (Red Creek, NY).
Central Coast Times (Paso Robles, CA).
Chandler Post (Boonville, IN).
Charlestown Citizen (Brookline, MA).
Chateaugay Record (Chateaugay NY).
Cherry Hill News (Cherry Hill, NJ).
Clay Countian (Orange Park, FL)
Clayton Sun (Atlanta, GA).
Clermont County Review (Cincinnati, OH).
Clermont Courier (Cincinnati, OH).
Communicator Community News (Reno, NV).
Community Press, West Chester (Loveland, OH).
Conneaut News-Herald (Conneaut, OH).
Conway Field & Herald (Conway, SC).
Countywide News (Westminster, MD).
Courier, The (Thomasville, GA).
Crestview Okaloosa-News Journal
  (Crestview, FL).
Cuba Journal (Cuba, IL).
Cumberland Times (Crossville, TN).
Current (Potsdam, NY).
Daily Journal (Elizabeth, NJ).
Daily Milford Citizen (Milford, CT).
DeKalb News/Sun (Decatur, GA).
Dennis Bulletin (South Yarmouth MA).
Dispatch, The (Cookeville, TN).
DuPage Press Service (Wheaton, IL).
East Los Angeles Gazette (South Gate, CA).
East Los Angeles Tribune (South Gate, CA).

Eastside Times (Tulsa, OK).
Enterprise News (Pixley, CA).
Enterprise Sun (Marlborough, MA).
Erie County Reporter (Huron, OH).
Evening Express (Portland, ME).
Evening Sentinel (Ansonia, CT).
Fairchild Strikehawk (Spokane, WA).
Fair Haven Register (Red Creek, NY).
Fairport-Perinton Herald-Mail (Webster, NY).
Fallon Eagle Standard (Fallon, NV).
Farmers Branch Times (Carrollton, TX).
Farmington Valley Herald (Simsbury, CT).
Fayette Sun (Fayetteville, GA).
Flat River Lead Belt News (Flat River, MO).
Freeborn County Register (Albert Lea, MN).
Garnett Review (Garnett, KS).
Geauga Times-Leader (Chardon, OH).
Girard News (Niles, OH).
Gladstone Delta Reporter (Escanaba, MI).
Goleta Review (Goleta, CA).
Goleta Sun (Santa Barbara, CA).
Good Times News (Fayette, MO).
Grace Citizen (Preston, ID).
Green River Republican (Morgantown, KY).
Greenville Piedmont (Greenville, SC).
Greenwich News (Greenwich, CT).
Gwinnett Daily News (Lawrenceville, GA).
Haddon Gazette (Cherry Hill, NJ).
Haines City Herald (Haines City, FL).
Hamilton County News (Elizabethtown, NY).
Hanover Park Township Times (Carol Stream, IL).
Harper Woods Herald (Birmingham, MI).
Harwood Heights News (Park Ridge, IL).
Hendersonville Free Press (Hendersonville, TN).
Hendricks County Guide Gazette (Plainfield, IN).
Henrico Gazette (Richmond, VA).
Herald, The (Tarpon Springs, FL).
Highlands Press (Mulberry, FL).
Hodgkins Citizen (La Grange, IL).
Hollywood Citizen News (Los Angeles, CA).
Hollywood Sun (Hollywood, FL).
Houston Post (Houston, TX).
Hubbard News (Niles, OH).
Humboldt Republican (Humboldt, IA).
Huntingdon Carroll Leader (Huntingdon, TN).
Huntsville News (Huntsville, AL).
Independent Press (Marine City, MI).
Inside Ravenswood (Chicago, IL).
Interboro News (Prospect Park, PA).
Jefferson Republic, The (De Soto, MO).
Jet Gazette (Austin, TX).
Jet Visitor (Cherokee, OK).
Journal Transcript (Franklin, NH).
Kansas Business News (Augusta, KS).

Kansas City Evening News (Shawnee Mission, KS).
Kirtland Enterprise (Willoughby, OH).
Kossuth County Advance (Algona, IA).
Lake Alfred Press (Mulberry, FL).
Lake Country Chronicle (Buchanan, MI).
Lake Wales Highlander (Winter Haven, FL).
Lead Call (Lead, SD).
Leader, The (Lansing, KS).
Leader, The (East Palestine, OH).
Lebanon Connecticut Valley Reporter (Lebanon, NH).
Ledger-Star (Norfolk, VA).
Liberty News (Niles, OH).
Licking Countian (Newark, OH).
Lincoln-Belmont Booster (Chicago, IL).
Linesville Herald (Conneaut Lake, PA).
Little Falls Transcript (Little Falls, MN).
Littleton Times (Littleton, CO).
Livingston East Texas Eye (Livingston, TX).
London Mills Times (Roseville, IL).
Long Beach Community News (Long Beach, CA).
Long Island Journal Newspaper Group (Long Beach, NY).
Madison Tribune (Ontario, OH).
Main Line Chronicle (West Chester, PA).
Malden Press-Merit (Malden, MO).
Mammoth Lakes Review/Mono Herald (Mammoth Lakes, CA).
Marathon Independent Newspaper (Marathon, NY).
Marin County Daily Recording (San Rafael, CA).
Market Place (Vandergrift, PA).
Marshall County Life (Culver, IN).
Mart Herald (Mart, TX).
Martin County News (Stuart, FL).
Matthews News (Matthews, NC).
Maumee Valley Herald (Toledo, OH).
Melrose Shoppers News (Stoneham, MA).
Mid-County Times (Pardeeville, WI).
MidMon Observer (Washington, PA).
Milford Citizen (Milford, CT).
Mirror-Recorder (Stamford, NY).
Monroe County Sentinel (Woodsfield, OH).
Montecito Life (Goleta, CA).
Mountaineer, The (Waynesville, NC).
Mountain Visitor (Sevierville, TN).
Mt. Washington Press (Cincinnati, OH).
Murray Eagle (Salt Lake City, UT).
Near South Herald (Chicago, IL).
New Alaskan (Ketchikan, AK).
Newburgh Evening News (Newburgh, NY).
News-Messenger, The (Rockingham, NC).
NewsEAST (Columbus, OH).
News Herald, The (Mobile, AL).
News of Paterson (Passaic, NJ).

News Outlook (Aberdeen, NC).
New York City Tribune (New York, NY).
New York Newsday (New York, NY).
Niantic News (East Lyme, CT).
Northeast Detroiter (Detroit, MI).
North Scottsdale Independent (Scottsdale, AZ).
Norwalk News (Westport, CT).
Observer-Patriot (Putnam, CT).
Observer, The (Blackwood, NJ).
Orion Times (Orion, IL).
Orrville Courier-Crescent (Orrville, OH).
Oxnard Press-Courier (Oxnard, CA).
Panhandle Press (Chester, WV).
Paper, The (Spartanburg, SC).
Peabody Times (Peabody, MA).
Peninsula Review, The (Carmel, CA).
Pictorial Press (Tahlequah, OK).
Pine Bluff News (Pine Bluff, AR).
Pittsburgh Press (Pittsburgh, PA).
Poland Leader (Niles, OH).
Press, The (Alexandria, MN).
Progress, The (Clearfield, PA).
Randolph County Times-Herald (Moberly, MO)
Rantoul Pacesetter (Rantoul, IL).
Register, The (Shrewsbury, NJ).
Reporter, The (Tampa, FL).
Review-Enterprise (Blackwood, NJ).
Rochester Courier (Rochester, NH).
Rohnert Park Cotati Clarion (Cotati, CA).
Roselle Record (Carol Stream, IL).
Sacramento Union (Sacramento, CA).
San Antonio Light (San Antonio, TX).
San Clemente News (San Clemente, CA).
San Diego Bulletin (Los Angeles, CA).
Sandpoint News-Bulletin (Sandpoint, ID).
Santa Monica Life (Santa Monica, CA).
Seminole Outlook (Oviedo, FL).
Sentinel/Altitudes (Frisco, CO).
Shawnee-Cridersville Press (Wapakoneta, OH).
Shreveport Journal (Shreveport, LA).
Snake River Press (Craig, CO).
South East Metro Shopper (Cottage Grove, MN).
South Pasadena Journal (Los Angeles, CA).

Southside Sun (East Point, GA).
South Valley Eagle (Salt Lake City, UT).
Spirit of Bucks County (Hatboro, PA).
Squire, The (Prairie Village, KS).
St. Louis Naborhood Link News (St. Louis, MO).
St. Louis South St. Louis County News (St. Louis, MO).
Stoneham Weekender News (Stoneham, MA).
Sunday Glades Trend (Clewiston, FL).
Sunday Sun (Scranton, PA).
Surfside News (South Miami, FL).
Sycamore Messenger (Cincinnati, OH).
This Week (Aledo, IL).
Times, The (Augusta, KY).
Times Tribune (Palo Alto, CA).
Tipton News Leader (Altus, OK).
Total, The (Heflin, AL).
Town & Country (Bradford, PA).
Transcript-Telegram (Holyoke, MA).
Tri-City Times (Geraldine, AL).
Union Shopper, The (Arcata, CA).
Union, The (Arcata, CA).
Ventura Bulletin, The (Los Angeles, CA).
Victor-Farmington Herald (Webster, NY).
Victor Valley Living (Hesperia, CA).
Village Journal (Osterville, MA).
Vincennes Valley Advance (Vincennes, IN).
Vinton County Courier (McArthur, OH).
Vista Press (Kansas City, MO).
Wallace Miner (Kellogg, ID).
Warrenton Banner (Warrenton, MO).
Weekender Enquirer (Boonville, IN).
Weekender, The (Bronx, NY).
Weekly Territorial (Tucson, AZ).
Wellston Sentry (Wellston, OH).
West Plains Tribune (Spokane, WA).
Wheat Ridge Sentinel (Lakewood, CO).
Wilkes-Barre Sunday Independent (Wilkes Barre, PA).
Winter Visitor Independent (Mesa, AZ).
Wrova Reporter (Galva, IL).
Yarmouth Sun (Yarmouth Port, MA).
Zionsville Eagle (Indianapolis, IN).